C000281185

SKY SP

FOOTBALL YEARBOOK 2007-2008

EDITORS: GLENDA ROLLIN AND JACK ROLLIN

headline

Copyright © 2007 HEADLINE PUBLISHING GROUP

First published in 2007
by HEADLINE PUBLISHING GROUP

1

Apart from any use permitted under UK copyright law, this publication may only be reproduced, stored, or transmitted, in any form, or by any means, with prior permission in writing of the publishers or, in the case of reprographic production, in accordance with the terms of licences issued by the Copyright Licensing Agency.

This publication contains material that is the copyright and database right of the FA Premiership, the Football League Limited and PA Sport.
PA Sport is a division of PA News Limited.

Front cover photographs: (left) Dimitar Berbatov (Tottenham Hotspur) – *Action Images/Henry Browne*; (centre and background) Cristiano Ronaldo (Manchester United) – *Neil Simpson/Empics Sport/PA Photos*; (right) Michael Essien (Chelsea) – *Kieran Galvin/Colorsport*.

Spine photograph: Andrea Pirlo (AC Milan) and Javier Mascherano (Liverpool) – *Phil Noble/Reuters/Action Images*.

Back cover photographs: (above) Shunsuke Nakamura (Celtic) and Steven Smith (Glasgow Rangers) – *Lynne Cameron/Rangers FC/PA Photos*; (below) Carlos Edwards (Sunderland) and Matthew Sadler (Birmingham City) – *Action Images/Paul Harding*.

Cataloguing in Publication Data is available from the British Library

ISBN 978 0 7553 1663 2 (Hardback)
ISBN 978 0 7553 1664 9 (Trade paperback)

Typeset by Wearset Ltd, Boldon, Tyne and Wear

Printed and bound in Great Britain by
Mackays of Chatham PLC,
Chatham, Kent

Headline's policy is to use papers that are natural, renewable and recyclable products and made from wood grown in sustainable forests. The logging and manufacturing processes are expected to conform to the environmental regulations of the country of origin.

HEADLINE PUBLISHING GROUP
An Hachette Livre UK Company
338 Euston Road
London NW1 3BH

www.headline.co.uk
www.hodderheadline.com

CONTENTS

Foreword by Richard Keys 5
Introduction and Acknowledgements 6
Editorial 7
Sky Sports Football Yearbook Honours 10
Daily Round-Up 2006–07 25
Review of the Season 51

THE FA PREMIER LEAGUE AND FOOTBALL LEAGUE: THE CLUBS
The Clubs 56
English League Players Directory 428
English League Players – Index 563

ENGLISH CLUBS STATISTICS
English League Tables 2006–07 46
Football League Play-Offs 2006–07 48
Leading Goalscorers 2006–07 50
The FA Charity Shield Winners 1908–2006 55
The FA Community Shield 2006 55
Transfers 2006–07 570
The New Foreign Legion 2006–07 580
English League Honours 1888 to 2007 586
League Attendances since 1946–47 595
English League Attendances 2006–07 596

THE LEAGUE CUP AND OTHER FOOTBALL LEAGUE COMPETITIONS
Football League Competition Attendances 594
League Cup Finalists 1961–2007 598
Carling Cup 2006–07 599
Johnstone's Paint Trophy 2006–07 605

THE FA CUP
FA Cup Finals 1872–2007 609
FA Cup Attendances 1969–2007 611
FA Cup 2006–07 (*preliminary and qualifying rounds*) 612
The E.ON FA Cup 2006–07 (*competition proper*) 616

SCOTTISH FOOTBALL
Review of the Scottish Season 2006–07 680
Scottish League Tables 2006–07 681
The Scottish Football League Clubs 682
Scottish League Play-Offs 2006–07 766
Scottish League Honours 1890 to 2007 767
Scottish League Cup Finals 1946–2007 772
CIS Scottish League Cup 2006–07 773
Scottish League Attendances 2006–07 775
League Challenge Cup 2006–07 776
Scottish Cup Finals 1874–2007 778
League Challenge Finals 1991–2007 779
Tennent's Scottish Cup 2006–07 780

WELSH AND NORTHERN IRISH FOOTBALL
Welsh Football 2006–07 784
Northern Irish Football 2006–07 789

EUROPEAN FOOTBALL
Champions League Review 2006–07 793
European Cup Finals 1956–1992 and UEFA Champions League Finals 1993–2007 794
UEFA Champions League 2006–07 795
European Cup-Winners' Cup Finals 1961–99 809
Inter-Cities Fairs Cup Finals 1958–71 809
UEFA Cup Finals 1972–97 810
UEFA Cup Finals 1998–2007 810
UEFA Cup 2006–07 811
UEFA Champions League 2007–08 – participating clubs 826
UEFA Cup 2007–08 – participating clubs 826
Summary of Appearances (*British and Irish Clubs*) 827
Intertoto Cup 2006 828
World Club Championship 828
European Super Cup 829
FIFA Club World Cup 2006 829

INTERNATIONAL FOOTBALL

International Directory 830
The World Cup 1930–2006 853
European Football Championship (*formerly European Nations' Cup*) 853
Euro 2008 Qualifying Competition 854
Euro 2008 Qualifying Competition – remaining fixtures 867
British and Irish International Results 1872–2007 868
Other British and Irish International Matches 2006–07 888
B Internationals 889
British & Irish International Managers 889
International Appearances 1872–2007 890
British and Irish International Goalscorers since 1872 943
South America 948
North America 949
UEFA Under-21 Championship 2006–07 950
UEFA Under-19 Championship 2007 951
UEFA Under-17 Championship 2007 951
England Under-21 Results 1976–2007 952
British and Irish Under-21 Teams 2006–07 954
British Under-21 Appearances 1976–2007 956
England National Game XI 2006–07 972
Four Nations Tournament 2007 972

NON-LEAGUE FOOTBALL

Nationwide Conference 2006–07 626
Nationwide Conference Second Division 2006–07 629
Schools Football 2006–07 972
FA Schools & Youth Games 2006–07 973
Women's Football 2006–07 976
Unibond League 2006–07 982
Southern League 2006–07 984
Ryman League 2006–07 986
The FA Trophy 2006–07 988
The FA Vase 2006–07 990
The FA County Youth Cup 2006–07 993
The FA Youth Cup 2006–07 993
The FA Sunday Cup 2006–07 997
FA Premier Reserve Leagues 2006–07 998
Pontin's Reserve Leagues 2006–07 999
FA Academy Under-18 League 2006–07 999
Puma Youth Alliance 2006–07 1000
Non-League Tables 2006–07 1001
Amateur Football Alliance 2006–07 1005
University Football 2006–07 1010

INFORMATION AND RECORDS

Football Awards 2007 10
We are the Champions! 12
Refereeing and the Laws of the Game 581
National List of Referees for Season 2007–08 582
The Things They Said 584
Important Addresses 1011
Football Club Chaplaincy 1012
Obituaries 1013
The Football Records 1023
International Records 1032
The FA Barclays Premiership and Coca-Cola Football League Fixtures 2007–08 1033
Blue Square Premier Fixtures 2007–08 1044
The Scottish Premier League and Football League Fixtures 2007–08 1047
Other Fixtures 2007–08 1052
Stop Press 1054

FOREWORD

We recently screened our 1000th live game from the Premier League, which prompted a bit of minor nostalgia here at Sky Sports. In fact, a promo you may have seen during the close season reminds us of just some of the more memorable moments. Teddy Sheringham scoring the first televised Premier League goal on Sky Sports – for Nottingham Forest against Liverpool – back in August 1992. There was the sheer unbridled emotion of Kevin Keegan's 'I would love it' tirade, Delia addressing her supporters on the pitch at Norwich, plus shots of the superstars who've enlightened football since we kicked off in earnest back in August 1992. They're classic moments from the expanding archive we have at our disposal here at Sky Sports.

There's a common thread running through all those moments: passion. If you're picking up this book you share the same passion for the game. It remains the only choice for serious football fans, who want the ultimate resource at their disposal. It's a classic and an annual must-have for all of us here at Sky Sports, as it is across the desks of the football media everywhere.

The sight of the 'big blue book' heralds the beginning of every season, a sure sign that we're nearly underway. It's as reliable as a trusted friend and I have had it by my side throughout my working life as a journalist and it'll remain by my side for the 2007–2008 season.

Richard Keys, presenter, Sky Sports

Richard Keys with Sky Sports colleagues Jamie Redknapp and Andy Gray.

INTRODUCTION

The 38th edition of the Yearbook, our fifth with sponsors Sky Sports, has maintained its expansion of recent years to 1,056 pages. One important innnovation is a We are the Champions section, detailing the players, appearances and goals of each championship-winning team from 1888–89 to 2006–07 from the fledgling Football League days to the present Premier League. There has been extensive revision of figures in this section with recent research highlighting different historical information from statistics which had been previously accepted as factual.

At the same time in conjunction with the Sky Sports Football Yearbook Honours, the Editorial panel of the yearbook has produced a similar team of the season covering the Championship, to reflect its continually growing stature.

Once again, there is an A to Z index of names with a cross reference to the Players Directory, enabling readers to check on the whereabouts of any specific player during the 2006–07 season. The who's who style directory again provides a season-by-season account of individual player's appearances and goals. The fullest possible available details have been provided for players in this section, including all players who appeared in first-class matches.

Throughout the book players sent off are designated thus ■, substitutes in the club pages are 12, 13 and 14 with 15 for the substitute goalkeeper. Squad numbers are not used.

Because of the recent changes in designation of divisions in the Football League and references to levels, steps and pyramids, attempting to place in a historical sense just where to place any given club in any given season's finishing has become almost impossible. Therefore in any particular section of the Records Section, the top club in the Football League is mentioned regardless of its actual status at the time. Individual records of players on the other hand have been retained.

With the continual increase in interest in non-League football, all Conference clubs have again been given the same style of recognition as the FA Premier League and Football League teams. For the coming season this competition has a new sponsor in Blue Square with the second second echelon to be known as Blue Square North and South..

As far as the club pages are concerned, a more uniform approach has been retained in respect of individual entries, without losing any of the essential information, including records over the previous ten seasons, latest sequences and runs of scoring and non-scoring.

Once more, our unrivalled coverage reveals every match played in the Champions League, including the qualifying competition, has full teams and line-ups. Also, with the expansion of the UEFA Cup with its group stage, there are full line-ups from that point onwards.

The usual detailed and varied coverage involves Scottish, Welsh and Irish football, amateur, schools, university, reserve team, extensive non-League information, awards, records and an international directory. Women's football, referees and the work of chaplains are also featured.

Transfer fees quoted in the Daily Round-up are invariably those initially mentioned when a deal is imminent. They may not reflect the figures which appear elsewhere in the edition. Moves during the summer months, together with any specific changes affecting the book appear in the Stop Press section.

The Editors would like to express their appreciation of the response from FA Premier League and Football League clubs when requesting information. Thanks are also due to Alan Elliott for the Scottish section, Tony Brown for sequences and instances of match results in the records section, Richard Beal for research into international anomalies, Ian Nannestad for the obituaries and Andrew Howe on foreign players. Thanks are also due to John English, who provided invaluable and conscientious reading of the proofs.

ACKNOWLEDGEMENTS

The Editors would like to express appreciation of the following individuals and organisations for their co-operation: David Barber, Dawn Keleher and Jill Roberts (Football Association), David C. Thomson (Scottish League), Heather Elliott, Dr Malcolm Brodie, Wally Goss (AFA), Rev. Nigel Sands, Ken Goldman, Grahame Lloyd, Marshall Gillespie, Sean Creedon, Valery Karpoushkin, Mike Kelleher and Alan Platt. Special mention, too, of Philippa Hobbs and Rhea Halford (Headline Book Publishing). The highest praise is due to the indefatigable, ebullient and loquacious Lorraine Jerram, Headline's Managing Editor for her generosity, expertise, constant support, determined resilience, patience, sincerity, perspicacity and appreciation, not to mention her unfailing humour, stoicism, quick-wittedness, courtesy, consideration and understated authority.

Finally sincere thanks to John Anderson, Simon Dunnington, Geoff Turner, Brian Tait and the staff at Wearset for their efforts in the production of this book, which was much appreciated throughout the year.

EDITORIAL

Just as the literary student who had failed to satisfy the examiners with his thesis and in desperation decided to scan it instead, thus merely going from bad to verse, there seems no rhyme or reason why our beautiful game beset as ever with ugly people finds itself in such a mess.

Bungs are scarcely fitting for football. There is more than enough legitimate money available. The begging bowl has yet to be passed around. Alas, the problem is that too much of the finance drains away unnecessarily without benefit to those in need. It has to stop but the will so to do is missing.

Investigations and undercurrent hints of wrongdoing in high places must be eradicated, once and for all. Once again, freedom of information has yet to reach every area of the game. Such a pity. Its image continues to suffer serious wounding but who seems to care? Some wringing of the hands, more ringing of the tills.

Unfortunately the problems begin at the top where far too many in authority have no genuine feeling for football. We might get the governments we deserve, but there is no choice in the game.

As to the sport itself, what used to be a pastime easy on the eye and understanding, simple and uncertain in outcome, has become complicated for the spectator to understand because of continued tinkering.

There also seems to be a gradual drift towards it becoming a non-contact sport. The free flowing spectacle of yesteryear is gradually disappearing. You can still have tackling without the recourse to kick seven kinds of muck out of the opposition.

The offside rule was never straightforward. Now it is twisted to a degree which defies even those responsible for implementing it. The game is faster than ever and even the electronic eye can be confused. What chance for a human.

Technology at least to signify a goal has had experimentation. We hear Hawk-Eye is the latest to be tried out. Not your James Fenimore Cooper version, more of his mate Trapper in *M*A*S*H*, designed to stop making a hash of goal-line decisions. This will only benefit the elite of course.

Then again the referee takes the flak and there is no point in criticising him or her for incompetence over any interpretation of the rules. The abuse heaped on the unfortunate officials by players, managers and spectators is unacceptable.

It is often far worse for the wretched assistant referee who can only carry out his offside duties efficiently if he has a large cranium and wide eyes spanning the half-way line. It is almost impossible to guarantee being able to follow the flight of the ball and watch the movement of players at the same time.

If you want better referees, treat those we have now properly. Then there will be more candidates for the worst job in football and the standard will inevitably rise. No good blaming society as it is today, football must take the lead in respect of authority. The alternative is anarchy on the pitch.

What we have at present has been said to be the good, the bad and the smugly. But when Graham Poll exits long before his term of office sell-by date with the Thing from Tring jibe ringing in his ears, is it any wonder he has had enough. There is no record of Pier Luigi Collina being called the Comb from Rome or the Baldie from Bari. Anyway he was born in Bologna or is that just splitting non-existent hairs.

If you want more ego-friendly officials only better behaviour towards them will answer the problem. Rhino-skinned politicians have rarely helped solve the country's needs and blinkered football officials are no exception.

Confrontation has escalated on the touchline and chiefly since managers and coaches have been allowed to scowl and prowl. Jobs for the boys of course with a fourth official acting as peacemaker. Odd that when spectators are supposed to be sitting still while watching, those in charge of teams are considered to be above such restrictions.

The increase in matches is not in the domestic area, but lies in the proliferation of those competitions involving those outside the country. No wonder the players are suffering fatigue. There is a virtual twelve-month season.

The clogged calendar means no room for replays. Only the FA Cup has managed to hold on to that blast from the past. Yet it, too, has succumbed to the penalty shoot-out after the second attempt. Yet sixty years ago when European cup competitions were still in the planning stage, aggregate scores were allowed in the 1945–46 season when ties were played over two legs. Where is the consistency?

Some competitions allow no extra time, the golden goal has been discarded because of the obsession with penalty kicks. Originally introduced as a punishment for offending teams it is now an artificial lottery to success. Precious little point in appealing to the spirit of the game, it still infringes its laws.

The Football League introduced penalties after 90 minutes and even toyed with the idea to decide all their drawn fixtures in this manner. Asylum, inmates? Is there a belief that the only excitement produced by the game lies in the penalty shoot-out?

Espanyol's Marc Torrejon misses his penalty during the shoot out in the UEFA Cup Final at Hampden Park. (Action Images/Lee Smith)

While players are fitter and faster than ever everything else is arguable. But one sure way of proving stamina would be to carry on playing until the decisive goal is scored, because penalty shoot-outs can take even longer. A few more 32-shot England Under-21s v Holland and you can be sure a different solution would be found. Bring back the sudden death penalty.

Why not an experiment in a cup competition? Scrap extra time saving the legs of the players for thirty minutes while they go through the motions content to move into the comfort zone of penalties offering excuses when they lose.

Somehow the fear has to be taken out of the game. Goals are becoming rarer, but a solution other than penalties has to be found. And talking of that 32-kick marathon, if either goalkeeper had stood still on his line at least six more shots would have been saved. But they go into hypo-drive and forget the basics of facing a normal penalty. Anyway, it is not a shoot-out, just a cop-out.

Time-wasting can be firmly planted at the door of the game's hierarchy. Goalkeepers allowed to take goal-kicks on either side, continual stoppages in play for minor infringements. Then the farce of instructing players exactly where to kick the ball and lengthy pantomime situations when substitutions are made with the fourth official making a nursery school attempt at the numbers game. And the best said about him or her trying to bowl the ball onto the pitch when necessary is really to say nothing.

Of less importance but still a niggling concern is the use of football-speak when it comes to the game's statistics. Why the need to emphasise players making starts and full debuts. A debut is an appearance however brief. But then substitutes have never really been taken seriously. A player who goes off injured after twenty minutes has a larger profile than the replacement who lasted seventy.

Get a grip, chaps. This is statistical rubbish. Bin it. No point in suffering irritable vowel syndrome and becoming in-consonant at the same time. No more fits and starts, please. There were fewer than 20 players ever present in the Premier League last season. Squad system rules. It is a 14 man operation in the domestic arena these days, double that in friendly internationals – at least ever since Sven's last stand of complete team replacements at half-time called a halt to it.

This multi-media masonic-mafiosa, mumbo-jumbo of the meaningless will only be squashed by the chip paper hacks, the real men of the reporting game deciding to restore some sanity to stats.

Anyone scoring a goal in the 90th minute – the longest in the game naturally going on for minutes on end – can often find at least one other player doing the same, though it is difficult to work out which one scored first.

If the fourth official controlled the watch, there would be no need for injury time at all. The referee has enough on his hands without looking at it. Injury time could be eradicated and we might even get more actual playing time. Might also stop the fourth man staring at the TV screen in World Cup games. Little bit of controversy there!

In Europe at club and country level we are still hanging in there. Liverpool reached the final of the Champions League again but were unable to repeat their previous success against AC Milan. Chelsea and Manchester United both missed each other in the semi-finals and lost out there, too. Tottenham Hotspur were in the last four of the UEFA Cup. Not too many complaints about foreign players when our own country's teams are chasing the prizes.

Over the lifetime of the Premier League the top placings have been dominated by four teams – Manchester United, Arsenal, Liverpool and Chelsea. In Scotland it is half that number with Celtic and Rangers dividing it between them.

As far as Euro 2008 is concerned, Big Mac's – still known in the trade as first choice – boys can and must do better. They have the advantage of more home games in the second half of the qualifying programme, so in theory results should improve. However, a note of caution: eastern European teams have had a history of getting a result under the old Twin Towers, but perhaps the New Wembley will be different. It might have been a long wait for the re-opening at horrendous cost, but already half a million fans have watched games there.

Russia have to come here, but we are also due out there and with diplomatic relationships between the two countries in poor state at present, there will be double the spice surrounding the matches. Irresistible headline material for the red masts.

Mention, too, of the performances of the other England teams. The Under-21s as referred to above went through the season without losing – apart from the Dutch penalty affair. But then we rarely do penalties. The Under-17s did well to reach the European Championship at that level and at least narrowly lost in open play to Spain. Yet we seem still unhappy about the flow of home-grown talent.

We have always had non-English players in our teams and welcomed them. They used to be Welsh, Scots and Irish. Now they come from further afield. None past or present have been qualified for England. But that is not the issue. We have outlined the real problem areas. And surely the bottom line must be – may we have our game back, please?

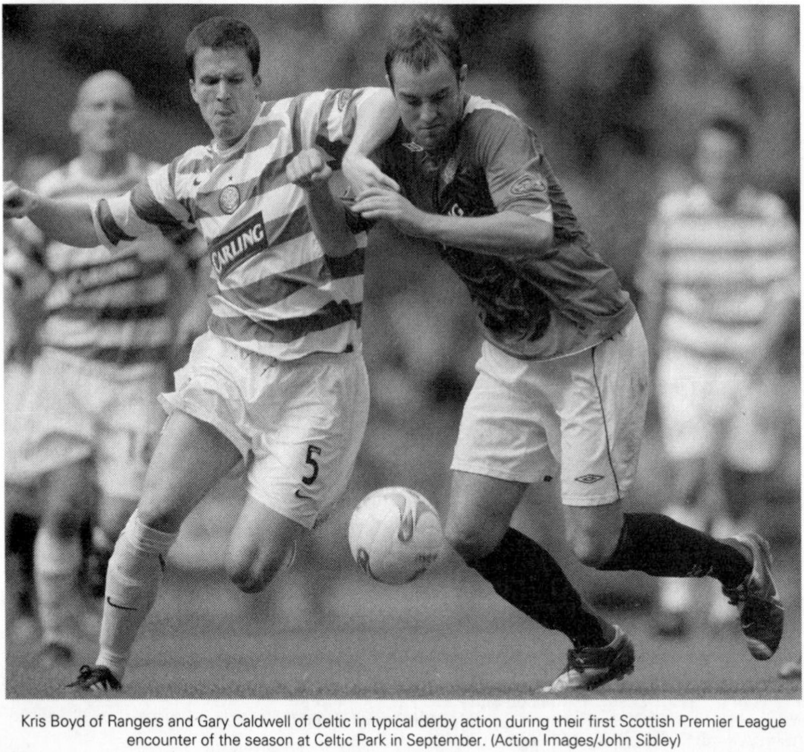

Kris Boyd of Rangers and Gary Caldwell of Celtic in typical derby action during their first Scottish Premier League encounter of the season at Celtic Park in September. (Action Images/John Sibley)

SKY SPORTS FOOTBALL YEARBOOK HONOURS

The Football Writers' Association members chose the following team for the season.

Sky Sports Football Yearbook Team of the Season 2006–07

David James
(Portsmouth)

Michael Essien *(Chelsea)*
Nemanja Vidic *(Manchester U)*
Ricardo Carvalho *(Chelsea)*
Jamie Carragher *(Liverpool)*

Cristiano Ronaldo *(Manchester U)*
Paul Scholes *(Manchester U)*
Steven Gerrard *(Liverpool)*
Ryan Giggs *(Manchester U)*

Didier Drogba *(Chelsea)*
Wayne Rooney *(Manchester U)*

Manager:
Sir Alex Ferguson CBE
(Manchester U)

Substitutes:
John Terry (Chelsea), Frank Lampard (Chelsea), Dimitar Berbatov (Tottenham H)

FOOTBALL AWARDS 2007

FOOTBALLER OF THE YEAR

The Football Writers' Association Sir Stanley Matthews Trophy for the Footballer of the Year was awarded to Cristiano Ronaldo of Manchester United and Portugal. Didier Drogba was runner-up, Ryan Giggs third and Paul Scholes fourth.

Past Winners
1947–48 Stanley Matthews (Blackpool), 1948–49 Johnny Carey (Manchester U), 1949–50 Joe Mercer (Arsenal), 1950–51 Harry Johnston (Blackpool), 1951–52 Billy Wright (Wolverhampton W), 1952–53 Nat Lofthouse (Bolton W), 1953–54 Tom Finney (Preston NE), 1954–55 Don Revie (Manchester C), 1955–56 Bert Trautmann (Manchester C), 1956–57 Tom Finney (Preston NE), 1957–58 Danny Blanchflower (Tottenham H), 1958–59 Syd Owen (Luton T), 1959–60 Bill Slater (Wolverhampton W), 1960–61 Danny Blanchflower (Tottenham H), 1961–62 Jimmy Adamson (Burnley), 1962–63 Stanley Matthews (Stoke C), 1963–64 Bobby Moore (West Ham U), 1964–65 Bobby Collins (Leeds U), 1965–66 Bobby Charlton (Manchester U), 1966–67 Jackie Charlton (Leeds U), 1967–68 George Best (Manchester U), 1968–69 Dave Mackay (Derby Co) shared with Tony Book (Manchester C), 1969–70 Billy Bremner (Leeds U), 1970–71 Frank McLintock (Arsenal), 1971–72 Gordon Banks (Stoke C), 1972–73 Pat Jennings (Tottenham H), 1973–74 Ian Callaghan (Liverpool), 1974–75 Alan Mullery (Fulham), 1975–76 Kevin Keegan (Liverpool), 1976–77 Emlyn Hughes (Liverpool), 1977–78 Kenny Burns (Nottingham F), 1978–79 Kenny Dalglish (Liverpool), 1979–80 Terry McDermott (Liverpool), 1980–81 Frans Thijssen (Ipswich T), 1981–82 Steve Perryman (Tottenham H), 1982–83 Kenny Dalglish (Liverpool), 1983–84 Ian Rush (Liverpool), 1984–85 Neville Southall (Everton), 1985–86 Gary Lineker (Everton), 1986–87 Clive Allen (Tottenham H), 1987–88 John Barnes (Liverpool), 1988–89 Steve Nicol (Liverpool), 1989–90 John Barnes (Liverpool), 1990–91 Gordon Strachan (Leeds U), 1991–92 Gary Lineker (Tottenham H), 1992–93 Chris Waddle (Sheffield W), 1993–94 Alan Shearer (Blackburn R), 1994–95 Jurgen Klinsmann (Tottenham H), 1995–96 Eric Cantona (Manchester U), 1996–97 Gianfranco Zola (Chelsea), 1997–98 Dennis Bergkamp (Arsenal), 1998–99 David Ginola (Tottenham H), 1999–2000 Roy Keane (Manchester U), 2000–01 Teddy Sheringham (Manchester U), 2001–02 Robert Pires (Arsenal), 2002–03 Thierry Henry (Arsenal), 2003–04 Thierry Henry (Arsenal), 2004–05 Frank Lampard (Chelsea), 2005–06 Thierry Henry (Arsenal).

THE PFA AWARDS 2007

Player of the Year: Cristiano Ronaldo Manchester U and Portugal.
Young Player of the Year: Cristiano Ronaldo Manchester U and Portugal.
Merit Award: Sir Alex Ferguson CBE.

Cristiano Ronaldo swept the board for individual honours in 2006-07. His Football Writers' Association award followed the double of PFA Player and Young Player of the Year. (Mike Egerton/EMPICS Sport/PA Photos)

The Football Yearbook Championship Team of the Season 2006–07

Stephen Bywater
(Derby Co)

Carl Hoefkens *(Stoke C)*
Alex Bruce *(Ipswich T)*
Patrick Kisnorbo *(Leicester C)*
Gareth Bale *(Southampton)*

Carlos Edwards *(Sunderland)*
Steve McPhail *(Cardiff C)*
Jason Koumas *(WBA)*
Gary McSheffrey *(Birmingham C)*

Jamie Cureton *(Colchester U)*
David Nugent *(Preston NE)*

Manager:
Roy Keane *(Sunderland)*

Substitutes:
Sam Ricketts (Hull C), Chris Brunt (Sheffield W), David Healy (Leeds U)

OTHER AWARDS

SCOTTISH FOOTBALL WRITERS' ASSOCIATION 2007

Player of the Year: Shunsuke Nakamura (Celtic).
Young Player of the Year: Scott Brown (Hibernian).
Manager of the Year: Gordon Strachan (Celtic).

SCOTTISH PFA 'PLAYER OF THE YEAR' AWARDS 2007

Player of the Year: Shunsuke Nakamura (Celtic).
First Division: Colin McMenamin (Gretna)
Second Division: Iain Russell (Brechin City)
Third Division: Scott Chaplain (Albion Rovers)
Young Player of the Year: Steven Naismith (Kilmarnock).

EUROPEAN FOOTBALLER OF THE YEAR 2006

Fabio Cannavaro, Real Madrid and Italy

WORLD PLAYER OF THE YEAR 2006

Fabio Cannavaro, Real Madrid and Italy

WOMEN'S PLAYER OF THE YEAR 2006

Marta, Umea and Brazil

WE ARE THE CHAMPIONS!

CHAMPIONSHIP WINNING TEAMS 1888–89 to 2006–07

PRESTON NORTH END 1888–89

Dewhurst, F 16
Drummond, G 12
Edwards, J 4
Goodall, A L 2
Goodall, J 21
Gordon, J B 20
Graham, J 22
Graham, W 5
Holmes, R 22
Howarth, R H 18
Inglis, J 1
Mills-Roberts, R H 2
Robertson, T 21
Ross, J D 21
Russell, D 18
Thomson, S 16
Trainer, J 20
Whittle, R 1

Goalscorers (74): Goodall J 20, Ross J 19, Dewhurst 12, Gordon 10, Thomson 3, Edwards 3, Robertson 3, Drummond 1, Goodall A 1, Inglis 1, Whittle 1.

PRESTON NORTH END 1889–90

Dewhurst, F 6
Drummond, G 18
Gordon, J B 22
Graham, J 17
Gray, F J S 1
Heaton, C 2
Hendry, W H 1
Holmes, R 18
Howarth, R H 21
Inglis, J 2
Johnstone, W 2
Kelso, R 20
Pauls, C A 3
Robertson, T 7
Ross, J D 21
Ross, N J 20
Russell, D 21
Thomson, S 18
Trainer, J 22

Goalscorers (71): Ross J 21, Ross N 20, Drummond 10, Thomson 7, Gordon 5, Russell 4, Inglis 1, Gray 1, Heaton 1, own goal 1.

EVERTON 1890–91

Angus, J A 11
Brady, A 21
Campbell, W C 13
Chadwick, E W 22
Doyle, D 20
Elliott, J 1
Geary, F 22
Gordon, P 3
Hannah, A B 20
Holt, J 21
Jardine, D 10
Kirkwood, D 19
Latta, A 10
Lochhead, A 1
McLean, D 5
Milward, A 22
Parry, C F 13
Robertson, H 3
Smalley, R E 1
Wylie, T G 4

Goalscorers (63): Geary 20, Milward 11, Chadwick 10, Brady 9, Latta 4, Wylie 4, Campbell 1, Kirkwood 1, Robertson 1, Holt 1, own goal 1.

SUNDERLAND 1891–92

Auld, J R 24
Campbell, J M 24
Doig, J E 26
Gibson, W 20
Gow, D R 16
Hannah, D 18
Hannah, J 22
Logan, J 2
Millar, J 24
Murray, J W 22
Oliver, J 3
Porteous, T S 25
Scott, J 24
Smith, J 14
Wilson, H 22

Goalscorers (93): Campbell 32, Hannah J 17, Millar 15, Scott 10, Wilson 9, Auld 4, Hannah D 3, Smith 1, own goals 2.

SUNDERLAND 1892–93

Auld, J R 27
Campbell, J M 27
Doig, J E 30
Dunlop, W 5
Gibson, W 30
Gillespie, James 23
Gillespie, John 5
Hannah, D 20
Hannah, J 28
Harvie, J 21
Millar, J 22
Porteous, T S 30
Scott, J 10
Smellie, R J 23
Wilson, H 29

Goalscorers (100): Campbell 30, Hannah J 19, Miller 13, James Gillespie 12, Wilson 8, Harvie 5, Scott 5, Hannah D 4, Gibson 3, own goal 1.

ASTON VILLA 1893–94

Athersmith, W C 25
Baird, J 29
Benwell, L A 1
Brown, A 6
Burton, G F 4
Chatt, R 13
Coulton, F 1
Cowan, James 30
Devey, J H G 29
Devey, W 4
Dunning, W 28
Elliott, J E 12
Gillan, J 3
Groves, W 22
Hare, C B 10
Hodgetts, D 29
Logan, J 4
Randle, W 1
Reynolds, J 26
Russell, G 5
Smith, S 15
Welford, J W 19
Woolley, A 14

Goalscorers (84): Devey J 20, Hodgetts 12, Athersmith 10, Woolley 8, Hare 7, Reynolds 7, Chatt 5, James Cowan 3, Groves 3, Brown 2, Smith 2, Logan 1, own goals 4.

SUNDERLAND 1894–95

Auld, J R 4
Campbell, J M 30
Doig, J E 30
Dunlop, W 17
Gillespie, James 26
Goodchild, G 1
Gow, D R 7
Hannah, D 1
Hannah, J 28
Harvie, J 6
Hyslop, T 12
Johnston, H 29
McCreadie, A 27
McNeil, R 22
Meechan, P 19
Millar, J 29
Scott, J 16
Wilson, H 25

Goalscorers (80): Campbell 19, James Gillespie 12, Millar 12, Hannah J 12, McCreadie 8, Hyslop 7, Wilson 4, Johnston 2, Dunlop 1, Meechan 1, Scott 1, own goal 1.

ASTON VILLA 1895–96

Athersmith, W C 29
Burton, G F 14
Campbell, J 26
Chatt, R 17
Cowan, James 23
Cowan, John 22
Crabtree, J W 28
Devey, J H G 30
Dorrell, W 2
Elliott, J E 1
Griffiths, A 1
Harris, E J 1
Hodgetts, D 21
Reynolds, J 22
Smith, S 11
Spencer, H 29
Welford, J W 24
Wilkes, T H 29

Goalscorers (78): Campbell 26, Devey J 16, John Cowan 9, Athersmith 8, Chatt 3, Crabtree 3, Hodgetts 3, James Cowan 2, Reynolds 2, Smith 2, Dorrell 1, Spencer 1, Welford 1, own goal 1.

ASTON VILLA 1896–97

Athersmith, W C 30	Cowan, John 15	Reynolds, J 24	Whitehouse, J 22
Burton, G F 8	Crabtree, J W 25	Smith, S 15	Wilkes, T H 8
Campbell, J 29	Devey, J H G 29	Spencer, H 28	
Chatt, R 11	Evans, A J 15	Welford, J W 10	
Cowan, James 30	Griffiths, A 1	Wheldon, G F 30	

Goalscorers (73): Wheldon 18, Devey J 17, Campbell 13, Athersmith 8, John Cowan 7, Smith 3, Reynolds 2, Burton 1, Chatt 1, James Cowan 1, own goals 2.

SHEFFIELD UNITED 1897–98

Almond, J 20	Foulke, W J 29	Jenkinson, T J 2	Needham, E 29
Bennett, W 26	French, A 1	Johnson, W H 10	Priest, A E 28
Blair, J 1	Gaudie, R 6	Logan, N 5	Thickett, H 29
Bradshaw, A E 1	Hedley, G A 2	McKay, K 25	White, H 6
Cain, R 30	Howard, H 3	Morren, T 26	Whitham, M 1
Cunningham, J 24	Howell, R 24	Morton, D 2	

Goalscorers (56): Bennett 12, Needham 8, Almond 8, Cunningham 7, McKay 5, Logan 4, Priest 4, Gaudie 2, Johnson 2, Morren 2, own goal 1, 1 untraced.

ASTON VILLA 1898–99

Aston, C L 13	Crabtree, J W 31	Haggart, W 1	Spencer, H 10
Athersmith, W C 28	Devey, J H G 30	Johnson, G 24	Templeton, R 1
Bedingfield, F 1	Evans, A J 29	Leigh, W 1	Wheldon, G F 33
Bowman, T 34	Garraty, W 10*	Sharp, B 4	Wilkes, A 11
Cowan, James 33	Gaudie, R 5	Sharp, J 8	Wilkes, T H 4
Cowan, John 7	George, W 30	Smith, S 27	

Goalscorers (76): Devey J 21, Wheldon 16, Johnson 9, Garraty 6, Athersmith 4, Sharp J 4, John Cowan 4, James Cowan 2, Bowman 2, Crabtree 2, Smith 2, Bedingfield 1, Gaudie 1, Wilkes A 1, own goal 1.

* Match abandoned v Sheffield Wednesday who were leading 3-1 after 79 and a half minutes. Football League insisted remaining ten and a half minutes be played later in the season. Bedingfield who had scored in the first game did not play, Garraty taking his place, hence the extra appearance. Final result 4-1.

ASTON VILLA 1899–1900

Aston, C L 3	Evans, A J 26	Mann, J 7	Watkins, A E 1
Athersmith, W C 24	Garfield, J 1	McEleny, C 1	Wheldon, G F 34
Bowman, T 27	Garraty, W 33	Noon, M 15	Wilkes, A 21
Cowan, James 25	George, W 34	Smith, S 31	
Crabtree, J W 17	Haggart, W 1	Spencer, H 28	
Devey, J H G 25	Johnson, G 9	Templeton, R 11	

Goalscorers (77): Garraty 27, Devey J 13, Wheldon 11, Smith 7, Johnson 5, Athersmith 4, Templeton 4, James Cowan 1, Garfield 1, Wilkes A 1, own goals 3.

LIVERPOOL 1900–01

Cox, J 32	Howell, R 2	Perkins, W H 34	Satterthwaite, S 22
Davies, J 1	Hunter, S 8	Raisbeck, A G 31	Walker J, 29
Dunlop, W 32	Hunter, T 2	Raybould, S F 31	Wilson, C 25
Glover, J 11	McGuigan, A 13	Robertson, J T 25	
Goldie, W 34	Parry, M 8	Robertson, T 34	

Goalscorers (59): Raybould 16, Cox 10, Robertson T 9, Walker 7, McGuigan 5, Satterthwaite 5, Hunter S 3, Goldie 2, Raisbeck 1, Wilson 1.

SUNDERLAND 1901–02

Common, A 4	Gemmell, J 31	Jackson, R W 32	Millar, J 32
Craggs, J 6	Gibson, W K 1	McAllister, A 34	Murray, B W 7
Doig, J E 32	Hewitt, J 5	McCombie, A 26	Prior, J 5
Farquhar, W 13	Hogg, R 29	McLatchie, C 25	Watson, J 33
Ferguson, M 29	Hogg, W 28	Mearns, F 2	

Goalscorers (50): Gemmell 10, Hogg W 10, Millar 9, Hogg R 5, McLatchie 4, Jackson 3, Craggs 2, Murray 2, Common 2, Hewitt 1, McAllister 1, McCombie 1.

SHEFFIELD WEDNESDAY 1902–03

Barron, G 1	Ferrier, R 33	Marrison, T 1	Spiksley, F 32
Beech, G C 3	Hounsfield, R E 2	Moralee, M 1	Stewart, J 1
Chapman, H 32	Langley, A 34	Ruddlesdin, H 34	Stubbs, F L 1
Crawshaw, P 1	Layton, W 29	Ryalls, J 1	Thackeray, F 5
Crawshaw, T H 33	Lyall, J 33	Simpson, G 1	Wilson, A 34
Davis, H 26	Malloch, J N 33	Simpson, V S 3	

Goalscorers (54): Davis 13, Chapman 12, Wilson 12, Spiksley 8, Langley 5, Ruddlesdin 2, Malloch 1, Marrison 1.

SHEFFIELD WEDNESDAY 1903–04

Bartlett, W J 4	Eyre, J 1	Layton, W 34	Simpson, G 24
Bolsover, W 4	Ferrier, R 31	Lyall, J 33	Simpson, V S 7
Burton, H A 26	Hemmingfield, W 6	Malloch, J N 25	Stewart, J 10
Chapman, H 34	Hoyland, G F 1	Moralee, M 1	Wilson, A 29
Crawshaw, T H 32	Jarvis, R T 1	Ruddlesdin, H 30	
Davis, H 32	Langley, A 8	Ryalls, J 1	

Goalscorers (48): Chapman 16, Wilson 10, Simpson G 7, Davis 5, Crawshaw T 2, Malloch 2, Simpson V 2, Hemmingfield 1, Langley 1, Stewart 1, own goal 1.

NEWCASTLE UNITED 1904–05

Aitken, A 28
Appleyard, G W 28
Carr, J 27
Crumley, J 1
Gardner, A 32
Gosnell, A A 25
Graham, S 3
Howie, J 31
Innerd, W 1
Lawrence, J 29
McClarence, J P 6
McCombie, A 31
McCracken, W 13
McIntyre, E 2
McWilliam, P 26
Orr, R 20
Rutherford, J 31
Templeton, R 10
Veitch, C C M 24
Watts, C 4
Wills, T 2

Goalscorers (72): Howie 14, Appleyard 13, Rutherford 10, Veitch 10, Orr 9, Gosnell 4, McClarence 4, McWilliam 4, Aitken 2, Gardner 1, own goal 1.

LIVERPOOL 1905–06

Bradley, J 31
Carlin, J 14
Chorlton, T 6
Cox, J 28
Doig, J E 8
Dunlop, W 31
Fleming, G 4
Garside, J 4
Goddard, A M 38
Gorman, J 1
Griffiths, H 1
Hardy, S 30
Hewitt, J 37
Latham, G 5
Murray, D B 3
Parkinson, J 9
Parry, M 36
Raisbeck, A G 36
Raybould, S F 25
Robinson, R S 34
West, A 37

Goalscorers (79): Hewitt 23, Robinson 11, Raybould 10, Cox 8, Goddard 7, Parkinson 7, Carlin 6, West 3, Chorlton 1, Parry 1, Raisbeck 1, own goal 1.

NEWCASTLE UNITED 1906–07

Aitken, A 3
Appleyard, G W 23
Blackburn, R 3
Brown, H 22
Carr, J 26
Dodds, J T 4
Duffy, C F 7
Gardner, A 33
Gosnell, A A 26
Higgins, A 1
Howie, J 31
Jobey, G 1
Kelsey, W J 2
Kirkcaldy, J 3
Lawrence, J 33
Liddell, R 1
McClarence, J P 5
McCombie, A 26
McCracken, W 22
McWilliam, P 32
Nicholson, B 1
Orr, R 19
Rutherford, J 34
Sinclair, T S 3
Soye, J 1
Speedie, F 27
Veitch, C C M 29

Goalscorers (74): Appleyard 17, Rutherford 10, Speedie 10, Brown 8, Howie 7, Veitch 7, Orr 4, Gosnell 3, McClarence 2, McWilliam 2, Duffy 1, Gardner 1, Kirkaldy 1, McCracken 1.

MANCHESTER UNITED 1907–08

Bannister, J 36
Bell, A 35
Berry, W 3
Bloomfield, H 9
Burgess, H 27
Dalton, E 1
Downie, A L B 10
Duckworth, R 35
Halse, H J 6
Holden, R 26
Hulme, A 1
McGillivray, J 1
Menzies, A 6
Meredith, W H 37
Moger, H H 29
Picken, J 8
Roberts, C 32
Stacey, G 18
Thomson, E 3
Turnbull, A 30
Turnbull, J M 26
Wall, G 36
Whiteside, K D 1
Williams, H 1
Wilson, T 1

Goalscorers (81): Turnbull A 25, Wall 19, Meredith 10, Turnbull J 10, Bannister 5, Halse 4, Roberts 2, Bell 1, Berry 1, Picken 1, Stacey 1, own goals 2.

NEWCASTLE UNITED 1908–09

Allan, J S 9
Anderson, A I 19
Branslie, R 1
Carr, J 11
Duncan, A S M 14
Gardner, A 12
Gosnell, A A 5
Higgins, A 26
Howie, J 26
Jobey, G 10
Lawrence, J 38
Liddell, R 5
McCombie, A 1
McCracken, W 30
McWilliam, P 27
Pudan, A E 3
Randall, C E 1
Ridley, J 5
Rutherford, J 24
Shepherd, A 14
Stewart, J 25
Veitch, C C M 34
Whitson, T T 30
Willis, D 20
Wilson, G W 28

Goalscorers (65): Shepherd 11, Veitch 9, Stewart 8, Howie 6, Allan 5, Higgins 5, Rutherford 5, Wilson 5, Anderson 3, Duncan 2, Jobey 1, Liddell 1, McCracken 1, Ridley 1, Willis 1, own goal 1.

ASTON VILLA 1909–10

Bache, J W 32
Buckley, C S 37
Cartlidge, A 35
Eyre, E 13
George, W 3
Gerrish, W W 36
Hall, A E 25
Hampton, H 32
Hunter, G H 32
Kearns, J 10
Layton, A E 4
Logan, J L 16
Lyons, A T 35
Miles, A 27
Moss, A J 1
Tranter, G H 28
Wallace, C W 38
Walters, J 14

Goalscorers (84): Hampton 26, Bache 20, Gerrish 14, Wallace 7, Hall 6, Walters 6, Eyre 2, Buckley 1, Hunter 1, own goal 1.

MANCHESTER UNITED 1910–11

Bell, A 27
Blott, S P 1
Connor, E 7
Curry, J 5
Donnelly, A 15
Duckworth, R 22
Edmonds, H 13
Halse, H J 23
Hayes, J V 1
Hodge, J 2
Hofton, L 9
Holden, R 8
Homer, T P 7
Hooper, A 2
Linkson, O H S 7
Livingstone, G T 10
Meredith, W H 35
Moger, H H 25
Picken, J 14
Roberts, C 33
Sheldon, J 5
Stacey, G 36
Turnbull, A 35
Wall, G 26
West, E J 35
Whalley, A 15

Goalscorers (72): West 19, Turnbull A 18, Halse 9, Homer 6, Meredith 5, Wall 5, Picken 4, Duckworth 2, Connor 1, Roberts 1, own goals 2.

BLACKBURN ROVERS 1911–12

Aitkenhead, W A C 29
Anthony, W 27
Ashcroft, J 8
Bradshaw, W 36
Cameron, W S 13
Chapman, G R 23
Clennell, J 18
Cowell, A 31
Crompton, R 33
Davies, W 11
Dennison, R 1
Garbutt, W 1
Johnston, J 5
Latheron, E G 22
Orr, J 19
Proctor, J 1
Robinson, A 30
Simpson, J 35
Smith, P J 31
Suttie, T 7
Walmsley, A 37

Goalscorers (60): Aitkenhead 15, Chapman 9, Clennell 9, Orr 9, Latheron 7, Bradshaw 3, Davies 2, Simpson 2, Anthony 1, Cameron 1, Smith 1, own goal 1.

SUNDERLAND 1912–13

Anderson, G A 2	Cuggy, F 32	Martin, H 38	Small, J 1
Best, R 3	Gladwin, C E 27	Milton, A 27	Thomson, C 35
Buchan, C M 36	Hall, T 20	Mordue, J 35	Tinsley, W 7
Butler, J H 32	Hobson, B 3	Ness, H M 13	Troughear, W B 6
Conner, J 2	Holley, G H 30	Richardson, J 18	
Cringan, W 10	Low, H F 37	Scott, W 4	

Goalscorers (86): Buchan 27, Mordue 15, Holley 12, Richardson 11, Hall 7, Martin 5, Low 4, Tinsley 3, Cuggy 1, Thomson 1.

BLACKBURN ROVERS 1913–14

Aitkenhead, W A C 17	Cowell, A 38	Latheron, E G 35	Simpson, J 34
Anthony, W 1	Crabtree, J 10	McGhie, A 9	Smith, P J 33
Bell, A 8	Crompton, R 33	Orr, J 5	Walmsley, A 37
Bradshaw, W 27	Dawson, P 8	Porteous, G 1	
Chapman, G R 19	Hodkinson, J 33	Robinson, A 28	
Clennell, J 4	Johnston, J 2	Shea, D 36	

Goalscorers (78): Shea 27, Latheron 13, Chapman 9, Aitkenhead 7, Bradshaw 3, Dawson 3, McGhie 3, Smith 3, Hodkinson 2, Orr 2, Simpson 2, Clennell 1, Warmsley 1, own goals 2.

EVERTON 1914–15

Brown, W 4	Grenyer, A 14	Maconnachie, J S 28	Roberts, J 1
Chedgzoy, S 30	Harrison, G 26	Makepeace, H 23	Simpson, R H 9
Clennell, J 36	Houston, J 1	Mitchell, F W 2	Thompson, R 33
Fern, T E 36	Howarth, H B 1	Nuttall, T A 5	Wareing, W 8
Fleetwood, T 35	Jefferis, F 18	Palmer, W 17	Weller, L C 6
Galt, J H 32	Kirsopp, W H J 16	Parker, R N 35	Wright, W P 2

Goalscorers (76): Parker 36, Clennell 14, Kirsopp 9, Harrison 4, Jefferis 4, Chedgzoy 2, Fleetwood 2, Galt 2, Grenyer 1, Makepeace 1, Palmer 1.

WEST BROMWICH ALBION 1919–20

Bentley, A 24	Hatton, S 1	Morris, F 39	Smith, A W 29
Bowser, S 41	Jephcott, A C 21	Pearson, H P 39	Smith, J 40
Cook, A F 7	Magee, T P 24	Pennington, J 37	Waterhouse, F 2
Crisp, J 38	McNeal, R 42	Reed, F W M 1	
Gregory, H 34	Moorwood, L 3	Richardson, S 40	

Goalscorers (104): Morris 37, Bentley 15, Gregory 12, Bowser 10, Crisp 8, Magee 7, Smith A 7, Jephcott 5, McNeal 2, own goal 1.

BURNLEY 1920–21

Anderson, J 41	Dawson, J 39	Lane, J W 1	Smelt, L 8
Basnett, A 15	Douglas, G H 2	Lindsay, J 8	Taylor, D 11
Birchenough, F 2	Freeman, B C 3	McGrory, R 34	Taylor, W 2
Boyle, T W 38	Halley, G 26	Moorwood, L 1	Watson, W 42
Brophy, T 3	Jones, C 31	Mosscrop, E 14	Weaver, W 27
Cross, B 37	Kelly, R F 37	Nesbitt, W 40	

Goalscorers (79): Anderson 25, Kelly 20, Cross 14, Boyle 7, Nesbitt 5, Lindsay 2, Watson 2, Weaver 2, Mosscrop 1, own goal 1.

LIVERPOOL 1921–22

Bamber, J 8	Forshaw, R 42	Lucas, T 27	Scott, E 39
Beadles, G H 11	Gilhespy, C 2	Matthews, R W 7	Shone, D 15
Bromilow, T G 40	Hopkin, F 42	McKinlay, D 29	Wadsworth, H 1
Chambers, H 32	Lacy, W 39	McNab, J S 29	Wadsworth, W 38
Checkland, F 5	Lewis, H 19	Mitchell, F 3	
Cunningham, W 1	Longworth, E 26	Parry, F 7	

Goalscorers (63): Chambers 19, Forshaw 17, Beadles 6, Shone 6, Matthews 4, Bromilow 2, Lucas 2, McNab 2, Gilhespy 1, Lacy 1, Lewis 1, McKinlay 1, own goal 1.

LIVERPOOL 1922–23

Bamber, J 4	Gilhespy, C 10	Lucas, T 1	Scott, E 42
Beadles, G H 4	Hopkin, F 40	McKinlay, D 42	Shone, D 1
Bromilow, T G 41	Johnson, R K 37	McNab, J S 39	Wadsworth, H 3
Chambers, H 39	Lacy, W 30	Pratt, D 7	Wadsworth, W 37
Forshaw, R 42	Longworth, E 41	Sambrooke, J H 2	

Goalscorers (70): Chambers 22, Forshaw 19, Johnson 14, McKinlay 5, Bromilow 3, Gilhespy 2, Wadsworth W 2, Hopkin 1, Lacy 1, McNab 1.

HUDDERSFIELD TOWN 1923–24

Barkas, E 21	Goodall, F R 14	Smith, A W 8	Walter, J D 26
Boot, L G W 5	Islip, E 3	Smith, W H 39	Watson, W 42
Brown, G 22	Johnston, W G 8	Steele, D M 31	Wilson, C 31
Cawthorne, H 16	Richardson, E 5	Stephenson, C 40	Wilson, T 41
Cook, G W 25	Richardson, G E 2	Taylor, E H 35	
Cowell, W 2	Shaw, G E 9	Wadworth, S J 37	

Goalscorers (60): Wilson C 18, Smith W 13, Stephenson 11, Cook 9, Brown 8, own goal 1.

HUDDERSFIELD TOWN 1924–25

Barkas, E 1	Goodall, F R 38	Spence, M B 4	Watson, W 41
Binks, S 2	Mercer, W 27	Steele, D M 39	Williams, J J 35
Boot, L G W 5	Richardson, E 1	Stephenson, C 29	Wilson T 40
Brown, G 32	Shaw, G E 11	Taylor, E H 10	Wilson, C 38
Cawthorne, H 2	Smith, N 1	Wadsworth, S J 33	
Cook, G W 25	Smith, W H 41	Walter, J D 7	

Goalscorers (69): Wilson C 24, Brown 20, Cook 9, Smith W 9, Stephenson 5, Cawthorne 1, Walter 1.

HUDDERSFIELD TOWN 1925–26

Barkas, E 13	Devlin, W 4	Shaw, G E 4	Taylor, E H 29
Binks, S 2	Goodall, F R 29	Smith, A W 1	Wadsworth, S J 38
Brown, G 41	Hobson, R G 2	Smith, W H 28	Watson, W 40
Cawthorne, H 24	Jackson, A 39	Spence, M B 1	Williams, J J 23
Cook, G W 29	Mercer, W 13	Steele, D M 18	Wilson, C 4
Dennis, H 1	Raw, H 2	Stephenson, C 36	Wilson, T 41

Goalscorers (92): Brown 35, Jackson 16, Cook 14, Smith W 6, Williams 6, Devlin 4, Stephenson 4, Goodall 2, Wilson C 2, Binks 1, Smith A 1, own goal 1.

NEWCASTLE UNITED 1926–27

Boyd, J M 2	Hampson, W 2	McDonald, T H 41	Spencer, C W 34
Chandler, A 4	Harris, J 9	McKay, R 25	Urwin, T 39
Clark, J R 17	Hudspeth, F C 42	McKenzie, R R 38	Wilson, W 42
Curry, T 5	Loughlin, J 4	Mooney, E 3	
Gallacher, H K 38	Low, J 2	Park, O 5	
Gibson, W M 32	Maitland, A E 36	Seymour, G S 42	

Goalscorers (96): Gallacher 36, Seymour 18, McDonald 17, McKay 10, Clark 4, Urwin 4, Hudspeth 3, McKenzie 2, Low 1, own goal 1.

EVERTON 1927–28

Bain, D 2	Dominy, A A 1	Irvine, R W 9	Rooney, W F 4
Brown, W 2	Easton, W C 3	Kelly, J 40	Taylor, E H 26
Cresswell, W 36	Forshaw, R 23	Martin, G S 10	Troup, A 42
Critchley, E 40	Hardy, H 6	Meston, S W 1	Virr, A E 39
Davies, A L 10	Hart, H 41	O'Donnell, J 42	Weldon, A 38
Dean, W R 39	Houghton, H 1	Raitt, D 6	White, T A 1

Goalscorers (102): Dean 60, Troup 10, Weldon 7, Critchley 6, Forshaw 5, Irvine 3, Martin 3, White 2, Easton 1, Hart 1, Kelly 1, O'Donnell 1, Virr 1, own goal 1.

SHEFFIELD WEDNESDAY 1928–29

Allen, J W A 35	Hargreaves, L 2	Leach, T J 36	Walker, T 41
Blenkinsop, E 39	Harper, E C 6	Marsden, W 42	Whitehouse, J C 6
Brown, J H 42	Hatfield, E 1	Rimmer, E J 34	Wilkinson, J 6
Burridge, B J H 2	Hill, H 1	Seed, J M 39	Wilson, C 3
Felton, W 3	Hooper, M 42	Strange, A H 42	
Gregg, R E 30	Kean, F W 4	Trotter, J W 6	

Goalscorers (86): Allen 33, Hooper 15, Seed 8, Gregg 7, Rimmer 7, Harper 5, Strange 5, Blenkinsop 1, Hargreaves 1, Marsden 1, Trotter 1, Whitehouse 1, Wilson 1.

SHEFFIELD WEDNESDAY 1929–30

Allen, J W A 41	Gregg, R E 5	Mellors, R D 1	Walker, T 34
Beeson, G W 2	Hooper, M 42	Millership, W 6	Whitehouse, J C 4
Blenkinsop, E 39	Jones, T J 1	Rimmer, E J 40	Wilkinson, J 1
Brown, J H 41	Leach, T J 40	Seed, J M 32	Wilson, C 9
Burgess, H 39	Mackey, T S 1	Smith, W S 4	
Burridge, B J H 2	Marsden, W 37	Strange, A H 41	

Goalscorers (105): Allen 33, Burgess 19, Hooper 18, Rimmer 15, Seed 9, Marsden 3, Strange 3, Leach 2, Millership 1, own goals 2.

ARSENAL 1930–31

Baker, A 1	Haynes, A E 2	Jones, C 24	Roberts, H 40
Bastin, C S 42	Hulme, J H A 32	Keizer, G P 12	Seddon, W C 18
Brain, J 16	Jack, D B N 35	Lambert, J 34	Thompson, L 2
Cope, H W 1	James, A W 40	Male, C G 3	Williams, J J 9
Hapgood, E A 38	John, R F 40	Parker, T R 41	
Harper, W 19	Johnstone, W 2	Preedy, C J F 11	

Goalscorers (127): Lambert 38, Jack 31, Bastin 28, Hulme 14, James 5, Brain 4, John 2, Williams 2, Johnstone 1, Jones 1, Roberts 1.

EVERTON 1931–32

Bocking, W 10	Dean, W R 38	Lowe, H 1	Sagar, E 41
Clark, A 39	Dunn, J 22	Martin, G S 2	Stein, J 37
Coggins, W H 1	Gee, C W 38	McClure, J H 7	Thomson, J R 39
Cresswell, W 40	Griffiths, P H 7	McPherson, L 3	White, T A 23
Critchley, E 37	Johnson, T C F 41	Rigby, A 3	Williams, B D 33

Goalscorers (116): Dean 45, Johnson 22, White 18, Dunn 10, Stein 9, Critchley 8, Griffiths 3, Clark 1.

ARSENAL 1932–33

Bastin, C S 42	Haynes, A E 6	Jones, C 16	Preedy, C J F 1
Bowden, E R 7	Hill, F R 26	Lambert, J 12	Roberts, H 36
Coleman, E 27	Hulme, J H A 40	Male, C G 35	Sidey, N W 2
Compton, L H 4	Jack, D B N 34	Moss, F 41	Stockill, R R 4
Cope, H W 4	James, A W 40	Parker, T R 5	
Hapgood, E A 38	John, R F 37	Parkin, R 5	

Goalscorers (118): Bastin 33, Coleman 24, Hulme 20, Jack 18, Lambert 14, James 3, Stockill 3, Bowden 2, Hill 1.

ARSENAL 1933–34

Bastin, C S 38	Dougall, P 5	Hulme, J H A 8	Male, C G 42
Beasley, A 23	Drake, E J 10	Jack, D B N 14	Moss, F 37
Birkett, R J E 15	Dunne, J 21	James, A W 22	Parkin, R 5
Bowden, E R 32	Hapgood, E A 40	John, R F 31	Roberts, H 30
Coleman, E 12	Haynes, A E 1	Jones, C 29	Sidey, N W 12
Cox, G 2	Hill, R F 25	Lambert, J 3	Wilson, A 5

Goalscorers (75): Bastin 13, Bowden 13, Beasley 10, Dunne 9, Drake 7, Birkett 5, Hulme 5, Jack 5, James 3, Coleman 1, John 1, Lambert 1, Roberts 1, own goal 1.

ARSENAL 1934–35

Bastin, C S 36	Davidson, R T 11	James, A W 30	Rogers, E 5
Beasley, A 20	Dougall, P 8	John, R F 9	Sidey, N W 6
Birkett, R J E 4	Drake, E J 41	Kirchen, A J 7	Trim, R F 1
Bowden, E R 24	Dunne, J 1	Male, C G 39	Wilson, A 9
Compton, L H 5	Hapgood, E A 34	Marshall, J 4	
Copping, W 31	Hill, F R 15	Moss, F 33	
Crayston, W J 37	Hulme, J H A 16	Roberts, H 36	

Goalscorers (115): Drake 42, Bastin 20, Bowden 14, Hulme 8, Beasley 6, James 4, Crayston 3, Hill 3, Birkett 2, Davidson 2, Kirchen 2, Rogers 2, Compton 1, Dougall 1, Hapgood 1, Moss 1, own goals 3.

SUNDERLAND 1935–36

Carter, H S 39	Goddard, G 3	Mapson, J D 7	Rodgerson, R 3
Clarke, J M C 28	Gurney, R 39	McDowall, L J 1	Russell, J 1
Connor, J 42	Hall, A W 38	McNab, A 13	Shaw, H B 1
Davis, H 25	Hastings, A C 31	Middleton, M Y 9	Thomson, C 42
Duns, L 17	Hornby, C F 8	Morrison, T 21	Thorpe, J 26
Gallacher, P 37	Johnston, R 10	Murray, W 21	

Goalscorers (109): Carter 31, Gurney 31, Gallacher 19, Davis 10 Connor 7, Duns 5, Hornby 2, Goddard 1, McNab 1, Thomson 1, own goal 1.

MANCHESTER CITY 1936–37

Barkas, S 30	Doherty, P D 41	McCullough, K 2	Rogers, J 2
Bray, J 40	Donnelly, R 7	McLeod, J S 3	Swift, F V 42
Brook, E F G 42	Freeman, R A 1	Neilson, R 2	Tilson, S F 23
Cassidy, J A 1	Heale, J A 10	Percival, J 42	Toseland, E 42
Clark, G V 13	Herd, A 32	Regan, R 4	
Dale, W 36	Marshall, R S 38	Rodger, C 9	

Goalscorers (107): Doherty 30, Brook 20, Herd 15, Tilson 15, Rodger 7, Toseland 7, Heale 6, Bray 2, McLeod 2, Donnelly 1, Neilson 1, Percival 1.

ARSENAL 1937–38

Bastin, C S 38	Compton, D C S 7	Hapgood, E A 41	Milne, J V 16
Biggs, A G 2	Compton, L H 9	Hulme, J H A 7	Roberts, H 13
Boulton, F P 15	Copping, W 38	Hunt, G S 18	Sidey, N W 3
Bowden, E R 10	Crayston, W J 31	Jones, L J 28	Swindin, G H 17
Bremner, G H 2	Davidson, R T 5	Joy, B 26	Wilson, A 10
Carr, E M 11	Drake, E J 27	Kirchen, A J 19	
Cartwright, S 6	Drury, G B 11	Lewis, R J 4	
Collett, E 5	Griffiths, M W 9	Male, C G 34	

Goalscorers (77): Drake 17, Bastin 15, Carr 7, Kirchen 6, Griffiths 5, Crayston 4, Milne 4, Hunt 3, Jones 3, Cartwright 2, Davidson 2, Hulme 2, Lewis 2, Bowden 1, Bremner 1, Compton D 1, Compton L 1, own goal 1.

EVERTON 1938–39

Barber, A W 2	Cook, W 40	Jones, T G 39	Stevenson, A E 36
Bell, R J 4	Cunliffe, J N 7	Lawton, T 38	Thomson, J R 26
Bentham, S J 41	Gee, C W 2	Mercer, J 41	Trentham, D H 1
Boyes, W E 36	Gillick, T 40	Milligan, G H 1	Watson, T G 16
Britton, C S 1	Greenhalgh, N H 42	Morton, H 1	
Caskie, J 5	Jackson, G 2	Sagar, E 41	

Goalscorers (88): Lawton 34, Gillick 14, Stevenson 11, Bentham 9, Cook 5, Boyes 4, Bell 3, Cunliffe 3, Caskey 1, Greenhalgh 1, Trentham 1, own goals 2.

LIVERPOOL 1946–47

Ashcroft, C T 2	Fagan, W 18	McLeod, T 3	Sidlow, C 34
Balmer, J 39	Harley, J 17	Minshull, R 6	Spicer, E W 10
Bush, T W 3	Hughes, L 30	Nieuwenhuys, B 15	Stubbins, A 36
Carney, L F 2	Jones, W H 26	Paisley, R 33	Taylor, P H 35
Done, C C 17	Kaye, G H 1	Polk, S 6	Watkinson, W W 6
Easdale, J 2	Lambert, R 36	Priday, R H 8	
Eastham, H 19	Liddell, W B 35	Ramsden, B 23	

Goalscorers (84): Balmer 24, Stubbins 24, Done 10, Fagan 7, Liddell 7, Nieuwenhuys 5, Jones 2, Priday 2, Carney 1, Taylor 1, Watkinson 1.

ARSENAL 1947–48

Barnes, W 35
Compton, D C S 14
Compton, L H 35
Fields, A G 6
Forbes, A R 11
Jones, B 7
Lewis, R J 28
Logie, J T 39
Macaulay, A R 40
Male, C G 8
McPherson, I B 29
Mercer, J 40
Rooke, R L 42
Roper, D G B 40
Scott, L 39
Sloan, J W 3
Smith, L 1
Swindin, G H 42
Wade, S J 3

Goalscorers (81): Rooke 33, Lewis 14, Roper 10, Logie 8, Compton D 6, McPherson 5, Forbes 2, Jones 1, own goals 2.

PORTSMOUTH 1948–49

Barlow, H 29
Bowler, G C 2
Butler, E A E 42
Clarke, I 24
Delapenha, L L 2
Dickinson, J W 41
Ferrier, H 40
Flewin, R 39
Froggatt, J 41
Harris, P P 40
Hindmarsh, W J 10
Parker, C H 5
Phillips, L H 40
Reid, J D J 29
Rookes, P W 25
Scoular, J 42
Thompson, W G 3
Yeuell, J H 8

Goalscorers (84): Harris 17, Reid 17, Froggatt 15, Clarke 14, Phillips 11, Barlow 8, own goals 2.

PORTSMOUTH 1949–50

Barlow, H 2
Bennett, R 2
Butler, E A E 42
Clarke, I 37
Dawson, J E L B 1
Delapenha, L L 5
Dickinson, J W 40
Ekner, D H 5
Elder, J 1
Ferrier, H 42
Flewin, R 24
Froggatt, J 39
Harris, P P 40
Higham, P 1
Hindmarsh, W J 34
Parker, C H 3
Phillips, L H 34
Pickett, R A 14
Reid, J D J 27
Rookes, P W 3
Scoular, J 36
Spence, W J 16
Stephen, J W 1
Thompson, W G 9
Yeuell, J H 4

Goalscorers (74): Clarke 17, Harris 16, Reid 16, Froggatt 15, Phillips 5, Thompson 2, Barlow 1, Bennett 1, Pickett 1.

TOTTENHAM HOTSPUR 1950–51

Baily, E F 40
Bennett, L D 25
Brittan, C 8
Burgess, R W A 35
Clarke, H A 42
Ditchburn, E G 42
Duquemin, L S 33
McClellan, S B 7
Medley, L D 35
Murphy, P 25
Nicholson, W E 41
Ramsey, A E 40
Scarth, J W 1
Tickridge, S 1
Uphill, D E 2
Walters, W E 40
Willis, A 39
Withers, C F 4
Wright, A M 2

Goalscorers (82): Walters 15, Duquemin 14, Baily 12, Medley 11, Murphy 9, Bennett 7, Ramsey 4, McClellan 3, Burgess 2, Nicholson 1, Uphill 1, Wright 1, own goals 2.

MANCHESTER UNITED 1951–52

Allen, R A 33
Aston, J 18
Berry, J J 36
Birch, B 2
Blanchflower, J 1
Bond, J E 19
Byrne, R W 24
Carey, J J 38
Cassidy, L 1
Chilton, A 42
Clempson, F 8
Cockburn, H 38
Crompton, J 9
Downie, J D 31
Gibson, T R D 17
Jones, M 3
McGlen W 2
McNulty, T 24
McShane, H 12
Pearson, S C 41
Redman, W 18
Rowley, J F 40
Walton, J A 2
Whitefoot, J 3

Goalscorers (95): Rowley 30, Pearson 22, Downie 11, Byrne 7, Berry 6, Aston 4, Bond 4, Carey 3, Clempson 2, Cockburn 2, McShane 1, own goals 3.

ARSENAL 1952–53

Bowen, D L 2
Chenhall, J C 13
Cox, F J A 9
Daniel, R W 41
Dodgin, W 1
Forbes, A R 33
Goring, H 29
Holton, C C 21
Kelsey, A J 25
Lishman, D J 39
Logie, J T 32
Marden, R J 8
Mercer, J 28
Milton, C A 25
Oakes, D J 2
Platt, E H 3
Roper, D G B 41
Shaw, A 25
Smith, L 31
Swindin, G H 14
Wade, S J 40

Goalscorers (97): Lishman 22, Holton 19, Roper 14, Goring 10, Logie 10, Milton 7, Daniel 5, Marden 4, Mercer 2, Cox 1, Forbes 1, Oakes 1, own goal 1.

WOLVERHAMPTON WANDERERS 1953–54

Baxter, W A 5
Broadbent, P F 36
Chatham, R H 1
Clamp, E 2
Deeley, N V 6
Flowers, R 15
Gibbons, L 1
Guttridge, W H 2
Hancocks, J 42
Mullen, J 38
Pritchard, R T 27
Short, J 26
Shorthouse, W H 40
Sims, N D 8
Slater, W J 39
Smith, L J 4
Stockin, R 6
Stuart, E A 12
Swinbourne, R H 40
Williams, B F 34
Wilshaw, D J 39
Wright, W A 39

Goalscorers (96): Hancocks 25, Wilshaw 25, Swinbourne 24, Broadbent 12, Mullen 7, Slater 2, Smith 1.

CHELSEA 1954–55

Armstrong, K 39
Bentley, R T F 41
Blunstone, F 23
Brabrook, P 3
Dicks, A V 1
Edwards, R H 1
Greenwood, R 21
Harris, J 31
Lewis, J L 17
McNichol, J 40
O'Connell, S C P 10
Parsons, E G 42
Robertson, W G 26
Saunders, D W 42
Sillett, R P 21
Smith, R A 4
Stubbs, L L 27
Thomson, C R 16
Wicks, M S 21
Willemse, S B 36

Goalscorers (81): Bentley 22, McNichol 14, Parsons 11, O'Connell 7, Lewis 6, Sillett 6, Stubbs 5, Blunstone 3, Armstrong 1, Saunders 1, Wicks 1, Willemse 1, own goals 3.

MANCHESTER UNITED 1955–56

Bent, G 4
Berry, J J 34
Blanchflower, J 18
Byrne, R W 39
Colman, E 25
Crompton, J 1
Doherty, J 16
Edwards, D 33
Foulkes, W A 26
Goodwin, F 8
Greaves, I D 15
Jones, M 42
Lewis, E 4
McGuinness, W 3
Pegg, D 35
Scanlon, A J 6
Scott, J 1
Taylor, T 33
Viollet, D S 34
Webster, C 15
Whelan, W 13
Whitefoot, J 15
Whitehurst, W 1
Wood, R E 41

Goalscorers (83): Taylor 25, Viollet 20, Pegg 9, Berry 4, Doherty 4, Webster 4, Whelan 4, Blanchflower 3, Byrne 3, Edwards 3, Jones 1, Lewis 1, McGuinness 1, Scanlon 1.

MANCHESTER UNITED 1956–57

Bent, G 6	Colman, E 36	Goodwin, F 6	Scanlon, A J 5
Berry, J J 40	Cope, R 2	Greaves, I D 3	Taylor, T 32
Blanchflower, J 11	Dawson, A D 3	Hawksworth, A 1	Viollet, D S 27
Byrne, R W 36	Doherty, J 3	Jones, M 29	Webster, C 5
Charlton, R 14	Edwards, D 34	McGuinness, W 13	Whelan, W 39
Clayton, G 2	Foulkes, W A 39	Pegg, D 37	Wood, R E 39

Goalscorers (103): Whelan 26, Taylor 22, Viollet 16, Charlton 10, Berry 8, Pegg 6, Edwards 5, Dawson 3, Webster 3, Scanlon 2, Colman 1, own goal 1.

WOLVERHAMPTON WANDERERS 1957–58

Booth, C 13	Flowers, R 28	Lill, M J 1	Stuart, E A 40
Broadbent, P F 40	Harris, G W 39	Mason, R H 20	Wilshaw, D J 12
Clamp, E 41	Henderson, J G 1	Mullen, J 38	Wright, W A 38
Deeley, N V 41	Howells, R 2	Murray, J R 41	
Dwyer, N M 5	Jackson, A 2	Showell, G W 7	
Finlayson, M J 37	Jones, G 2	Slater, W J 14	

Goalscorers (103): Murray 29, Deeley 23, Broadbent 17, Clamp 10, Mason 7, Mullen 4, Wilshaw 4, Flowers 3, Booth 2, Lill 1, Showell 1, own goals 2.

WOLVERHAMPTON WANDERERS 1958–59

Booth, C 13	Flowers, R 31	Kelly, J P V 1	Sidebottom, G 3
Broadbent, P F 40	Harris, G W 40	Lill, M J 18	Slater, W J 27
Clamp, E 26	Henderson, J G 8	Mason, R H 34	Stuart, E A 38
Deeley, N V 38	Horne, D T 8	Mullen, J 16	Wright, W A 39
Durandt, C M 1	Jackson, A 2	Murray, J R 28	
Finlayson, M J 39	Jones, G 4	Showell, G W 8	

Goalscorers (110): Murray 21, Broadbent 20, Deeley 17, Mason 13, Lill 12, Booth 7, Mullen 4, Clamp 3, Henderson 3, Horne 3, Showell 2, Harris 1, Jackson 1, Slater 1, own goals 2.

BURNLEY 1959–60

Adamson, J 42	Elder, A R 34	McIlroy, J 32	Robson, J 38
Angus, J 41	Furnell, J 1	Meredith, T G 7	Seith, R 27
Blacklaw, A S 41	Harris, G 2	Miller, B G 42	White, W H 6
Connelly, J M 34	Lawson, F I A 8	Pilkington, B 41	
Cummings, T S 23	Marshall, W 1	Pointer, R 42	

Goalscorers (85): Connelly 20, Pointer 19, Robson 18, Pilkington 9, McIlroy 6, Lawson 3, Meredith 3, Miller 3, White 2, Adamson 1, own goal 1.

TOTTENHAM HOTSPUR 1960–61

Allen, L W 42	Dyson, T K 40	Marchi, A V 6	Smith, R A 36
Baker, P R B 41	Henry, R P 42	Medwin, T C 14	White, J A 42
Barton, K R 1	Hollowbread, J F 1	Norman, M 41	
Blanchflower, R D 42	Jones, C W 29	Saul, F L 6	
Brown, W D F 41	Mackay, D C 37	Smith, J 1	

Goalscorers (115): Smith R 28, Allen 23, Jones 15, White 13, Dyson 12, Blanchflower 6, Medwin 5, Mackay 4, Norman 4, Saul 3, Baker 1, own goal 1.

IPSWICH TOWN 1961–62

Bailey, R M 37	Crawford, R 41	Leadbetter, J 41	Owen, A W 1
Baxter, W A 40	Curtis, D P 4	Malcolm, K C 3	Phillips, E J 40
Carberry, L J 42	Elsworthy, J T 41	Moran, D W 42	Pickett, R A 3
Compton, J F 39	Hall, W 5	Nelson, A N 42	Stephenson, R 41

Goalscorers (93): Crawford 33, Phillips 28, Moran 14, Leadbetter 8, Stephenson 7, Elsworthy 2, own goal 1.

EVERTON 1962–63

Bingham, W L 23	Kay, A H 19	Scott, A S 17	Veall, R 11
Dunlop, A 4	Labone, B L 40	Sharples, G F V 2	Vernon, T R 41
Gabriel, J 40	Meagan, M K 32	Stevens, D 42	West, G 38
Harris, B 24	Morrissey, J J 28	Temple, D W 5	Wignall, F 1
Heslop, G W 1	Parker, A H 33	Thomson, G M 19	Young, A 42

Goalscorers (84): Vernon 24, Young 22, Morrissey 7, Stevens 7, Bingham 5, Gabriel 5, Scott 4, Parker 2, Harris 1, Kay 1, Temple 1, Veall 1, Wignall 1, own goals 3.

LIVERPOOL 1963–64

Arrowsmith, A W 20	Hunt, R 41	Moran, R 35	Wallace, G H 1
Byrne, G 33	Lawler, C 6	St John, I 40	Yeats, R 36
Callaghan, I R 42	Lawrence, T 40	Stevenson, W 38	
Ferns, P 18	Melia, J 24	Thompson, P 42	
Furnell, J 2	Milne, G 42	Thomson, R 2	

Goalscorers (92): Hunt 31, St John 21, Arrowsmith 15, Callaghan 8, Thompson 6, Melia 4, Milne 3, Moran 1, Stevenson 1, Yeats 1, own goal 1.

MANCHESTER UNITED 1964–65

Aston, J 1	Connelly, J 42	Foulkes, W A 42	Sadler, D 6
Best, G 41	Crerand, P T 39	Gaskell, J D 5	Setters, M E 5
Brennan, S A 42	Dunne, A P 42	Herd, D G 37	Stiles, N P 41
Cantwell, N 2	Dunne, P A J 37	Law, D 36	
Charlton, R 41	Fitzpatrick, J 2	Moir, I 1	

Goalscorers (89): Law 28, Herd 20, Connelly 15, Best 10, Charlton 10, Crerand 3, Cantwell 1, Sadler 1, own goal 1.

LIVERPOOL 1965–66

Arrowsmith, A W 3+2
Byrne, G 42
Callaghan, I R 42
Graham, R 1
Hunt, R 37
Lawler, C 40
Lawrence, T 42
Milne, G 28
Smith, T 42
St John, I 41
Stevenson, W 41
Strong, G 21+1
Thompson, P 40
Yeats, R 42

Goalscorers (79): Hunt 30, St John 10, Milne 7, Callaghan 5, Lawler 5, Stevenson 5, Strong 5, Thompson 5, Smith 3, Yeats 2, Arrowsmith 1, Byrne 1.

MANCHESTER UNITED 1966–67

Anderson, W J +1
Aston, J 26+4
Best, G 42
Brennan, S A 16
Cantwell, N 4
Charlton, R 42
Connelly, J 6
Crerand, P T 39
Dunne, A P 40
Fitzpatrick, J H N 3
Foulkes, W A 33
Gaskell, J D 5
Gregg, H 2
Herd, D G 28
Law, D 36
Noble, R 29
Ryan, J 4+1
Sadler, D 35+1
Stepney, A C 35
Stiles, N P 37

Goalscorers (84): Law 23, Herd 16, Charlton 12, Best 10, Aston 5, Sadler 5, Foulkes 4, Crerand 3, Stiles 3, Connelly 2, own goal 1.

MANCHESTER CITY 1967–68

Bell, C 35
Book, A K 42
Bowles, S 4
Cheetham, R A 2+1
Clay, J H 1+1
Coleman, A G 38
Connor, D R 10+3
Dowd, H W 7
Doyle, M 37+1
Heslop, G W 41
Hince, P F 6
Horne, S F 4+1
Jones, C M N 2
Kennedy, R 4+2
Lee, F H 31
Mulhearn, K J 33
Oakes, A A 41
Ogley, A 2
Pardoe, G 41
Summerbee, M G 41
Young, N J 40

Goalscorers (86): Young 19, Lee 16, Bell 14, Summerbee 14, Coleman 8, Doyle 5, Bowles 2, Hince 2, Oakes 2, Book 1, Connor 1, Heslop 1, own goal 1.

LEEDS UNITED 1968–69

Bates, M J 3+1
Belfitt, R M 6+2
Bremner, W J 42
Charlton, J 41
Cooper, T 34+1
Giles, M J 32
Gray, E 32+1
Greenhough, J 3
Hibbitt, T A 9+3
Hunter, N 42
Johanneson, A +1
Jones, M D 40
Lorimer, P P 25+4
Madeley, P E 31
O'Grady, M 38
Reaney, P 42
Sprake, G 42

Goalscorers (66): Jones 14, Lorimer 9, Giles 8, O'Grady 8, Bremner 6, Gray 5, Belfitt 3, Charlton 3, Hibbitt 3, Madeley 3, Cooper 1, Johanneson 1, Reaney 1, own goal 1.

EVERTON 1969–70

Ball, A J 37
Brown, A D 31+5
Darcy, F A +5
Harvey, J C 35
Humphreys, A 1
Hurst, J 42
Husband, J 30
Jackson, T 14+1
Kendall, H 36
Kenyon, R N 8+1
Lebone, B L 34
Morrissey, J J 41
Newton, K R 12
Royle, J 42
West, G 42
Whittle, A 15
Wright, T J 42

Goalscorers (72): Royle 23, Whittle 11, Ball 10, Morrissey 9, Husband 6, Hurst 5, Kendall 4, Harvey 3, Wright 1.

ARSENAL 1970–71

Armstrong, G 42
George, F C 17
Graham, G 36+2
Kelly, E P 21+2
Kennedy, R 41
Marinello, P 1+2
McLintock, F 42
McNab, R 40
Nelson, S 2+2
Radford, J 41
Rice, P J 41
Roberts, J G 18
Sammels, J C 13+2
Simpson, P F 25
Storey, P E 40
Wilson, R P 42

Goalscorers (71): Kennedy 19, Radford 15, Graham 11, Armstrong 7, George 5, McLintock 5, Kelly 4, Storey 2, Sammels 1, own goals 2.

DERBY COUNTY 1971–72

Bailey, A 1
Boulton, C D 42
Durban, W A 31
Gemmill, A 40
Hector, K J 42
Hennessey, W T 17+1
Hinton, A T 38
McFarland, R L 38
McGovern, J P 39+1
O'Hare, J 40
Powell, S 2+1
Robson, J D 41
Todd, C 40
Walker, J M 3+3
Webster, R 38
Wignall, F 10+1

Goalscorers (69): Hinton 15, O'Hare 13, Hector 12, Durban 6, Wignall 5, McFarland 4, Gemmill 3, McGovern 3, Robson 2, Todd 2, Walker 1, Webster 1, own goals 2.

LIVERPOOL 1972–73

Boersma, P 19
Callaghan, I R 42
Clemence, R N 41
Cormack, P B 30
Hall, B W 17+4
Heighway, S D 38
Hughes, E W 41
Keegan, J K 41
Lane, F 1
Lawler, C 42
Lindsay, A 37
Lloyd, L B 42
Smith, T 33
Storton, T G 4
Thompson, P B 12+2
Toshack, J B 22

Goalscorers (72): Keegan 13, Toshack 13, Cormack 8, Boersma 7, Hughes 7, Heighway 6, Lindsay 4, Callaghan 3, Lawler 3, Hall 2, Lloyd 2, Smith 2, own goals 2.

LEEDS UNITED 1973–74

Bates, M J 9+1
Bremner, W J 42
Cherry, T J 37+1
Clarke, A J 34
Cooper, T 1+1
Ellam, R 3+1
Giles, M J 17
Gray, E 8
Gray, F T 3+3
Harvey, D 39
Hunter, N 42
Jones, M D 28+3
Jordan, J 25+8
Liddell, G +1
Lorimer, P P 37
Madeley, P E 39
McQueen, G 36
Reaney, P 36
Stewart, D 3
Yorath, T C 23+5

Goalscorers (66): Jones 14, Clarke 13, Lorimer 12, Bremner 10, Jordan 7, Bates 2, Giles 2, Madeley 2, Yorath 2, Cherry 1, own goal 1.

DERBY COUNTY 1974–75

Boulton, C D 42	Gemmill, A 41	McFarland, R L 4	Rioch, B D 42
Bourne, J A 7+10	Hector, K J 38	Newton, H A 35+1	Thomas, R J 22
Daniel, P A 37	Hinton, A T 8+5	Nish, D J 38	Todd, C 39
Davies, R 39+1	Lee, F H 34	Powell, S 12+3	Webster, R 24

Goalscorers (67): Rioch 15, Hector 13, Davies 12, Lee 12, Daniel 3, Newton 3, Bourne 2, Hinton 2, Nish 2, Powell 2, Webster 1.

LIVERPOOL 1975–76

Boersma, P 1+2	Fairclough, D 5+9	Keegan, J K 41	Neal, P G 42
Callaghan, I R 40	Hall, B W 12+1	Kennedy, R 29+1	Smith, T 24
Case, J R 27	Heighway, S D 39	Kettle, B 1	Thompson, P B 41
Clemence, R N 42	Hughes, E W 41	Lindsay, A 6	Toshack, J B 35
Cormack, P B 16+1	Jones, J P 13	McDermott, T 7+2	

Goalscorers (66): Toshack 16, Keegan 12, Fairclough 7, Case 6, Kennedy 6, Neal 6, Heighway 4, Callaghan 3, Hall 2, Hughes 2, Cormack 1, McDermott 1.

LIVERPOOL 1976–77

Callaghan, I R 32+1	Hughes, E W 42	Kettle, B 2	Thompson, P B 26
Case, J R 24+3	Johnson, D E 19+7	Lindsay, A 1	Toshack, J B 22
Clemence, R N 42	Jones, J P 39	McDermott, T 25+1	
Fairclough, D 12+8	Keegan, J K 38	Neal, P G 42	
Heighway, S D 39	Kennedy, R 41	Smith, T 16	

Goalscorers (62): Keegan 12, Toshack 10, Heighway 8, Kennedy 7, Neal 7, Johnson 5, Fairclough 3, Jones 3, Thompson 2, Callaghan 1, Case 1, Hughes 1, McDermott 1, own goal 1.

NOTTINGHAM FOREST 1977–78

Anderson, V A 37	Clark, F A 12+1	Middleton, J 5	Robertson, J N 42
Barrett, C 33+2	Gemmill, A 32+2	Needham, D W 16	Shilton, P L 37
Bowyer, I 26+3	Lloyd, L V 26	O'Hare, J 10	Withe, P 40
Burns, K 41	McGovern, J P 31	O'Neill, M H M 38+2	Woodcock, A S 36

Goalscorers (69): Robertson 12, Withe 12, Woodcock 11, O'Neill 8, Bowyer 4, Burns 4, McGovern 4, Needham 4, Anderson 3, Gemmill 3, Barrett 1, Clark 1, own goals 2.

LIVERPOOL 1978–79

Case, J R 37	Hansen, A D 34	Kennedy, A P 37	Neill, P G 42
Clemence, R N 42	Heighway, S D 26+2	Kennedy, R 42	Souness, G J 41
Dalglish, K M 42	Hughes, E W 16	Lee, S 1+1	Thompson, P B 39
Fairclough, D 3+1	Johnson, D E 26+4	McDermott, T 34+3	

Goalscorers (85): Dalglish 21, Johnson 16, Kennedy R 10, McDermott 8, Souness 8, Case 7, Neill 5, Heighway 4, Kennedy A 3, Fairclough 2, Hansen 1.

LIVERPOOL 1979–80

Case, J R 37	Hansen, A D 38	Kennedy, R 40	Souness, G J 41
Clemence, R N 41	Heighway, S D 2+7	Lee, S 6+1	Thompson, P B 42
Cohen, A 3+1	Irwin, C T 7+1	McDermott, T 37	
Dalglish, K M 42	Johnson, D E 37	Neal, P G 42	
Fairclough, D 9+5	Kennedy, A P 37	Ogrizovic, S 1	

Goalscorers (81): Johnson 21, Dalglish 16, McDermott 11, Kennedy R 9, Fairclough 5, Hansen 4, Case 3, Irwin 2, Cohen 1, Kennedy A 1, Neal 1, Souness 1, own goals 6.

ASTON VILLA 1980–81

Bremner, D G 42	Geddis, D 8+1	Mortimer, D G 42	Williams, G 21+1
Cowans, G S 42	Gibson, C J 19+2	Rimmer, J J 42	Withe, P 36
Deacy, E 5+4	McNaught, K 42	Shaw, G R 40	
Evans, A 39	Morley, A W 42	Swain, K 42	

Goalscorers (72): Withe 20, Shaw 18, Morley 10, Evans 7, Cowans 5, Geddis 4, Mortimer 4, Bremner 2, own goals 2.

LIVERPOOL 1981–82

Dalglish, K M 42	Johnston, C P 13+5	Lee, S 35	Sheedy, K M +2
Grobbelaar, B D 42	Kennedy, A P 32+2	McDermott, T 28+1	Souness, G J 34+1
Hansen, A D 35	Kennedy, R 15	Neal, P G 42	Thompson, P B 34
Johnson, D E 10+5	Lawrenson, M T 37+2	Rush, I J 32	Whelan, R A 31+1

Goalscorers (80): Rush 17, McDermott 14, Dalglish 13, Whelan 10, Johnston 6, Souness 5, Kennedy A 3, Lee 3, Johnson 2, Kennedy R 2, Lawrenson 2, Neal 2, own goal 1.

LIVERPOOL 1982–83

Dalglish K M 42	Hodgson, D J 20+3	Lee, S 40	Rush, I J 34
Fairclough, D 3+5	Johnston, C P 30+3	McDermott, T +2	Souness, G J 41
Grobbelaar, B D 42	Kennedy, A P 42	Neal, P G 42	Thompson, P B 24
Hansen, A D 34	Lawrenson, M T 40	Nicol, S 2+2	Whelan, R A 26+2

Goalscorers (87): Rush 24, Dalglish 18, Souness 9, Neal 8, Johnston 7, Lawrenson 5, Hodgson 4, Fairclough 3, Kennedy 3, Lee 3, Whelan 2, own goal 1.

LIVERPOOL 1983–84

Dalglish, K M 33	Johnston, C P 28+1	Neal, P G 41	Souness, G J 37
Grobbelaar, B D 42	Kennedy, A P 42	Nicol, S 19+4	Wark, J 9
Hansen, A D 42	Lawrenson, M T 42	Robinson, M J 23+1	Whelan, R A 20+3
Hodgson, D J 1+4	Lee, S 42	Rush, I J 41	

Goalscorers (73): Rush 32, Dalglish 7, Souness 7, Nicol 6, Robinson 6, Whelan 3, Johnston 2, Kennedy 2, Lee 2, Wark 2, Hansen 1, Neal 1, own goals 2.

EVERTON 1984–85

Atkins, I 6
Bailey, J A 15
Bracewell, P W 37
Curran, E 4+5
Danskin, J 1
Gray, A M 21+5
Harper, A 10+3
Heath, A P 17
Hughes, D J 2
Morrissey, J 1
Mountfield, D N 37
Oldroyd, D R +1
Ratcliffe, K 40
Reid, P 36
Richardson, K 14+1
Rimmer, N +1
Sharp, G M 36
Sheedy, K M 29
Southall, M 42
Steven, T M 40
Stevens, M G 37
Van Den Hauwe, P W R 31
Wakenshaw, R A 1+1
Walsh, D 1
Wilkinson, P 4+1

Goalscorers (88): Sharp 21, Steven 12, Heath 11, Sheedy 11, Mountfield 10, Gray 9, Richardson 4, Stevens 3, Bracewell 2, Reid 2, Wilkinson 2, Atkins 1.

LIVERPOOL 1985–86

Beglin, J M 34
Dalglish, K M 17+4
Gillespie, G T 14
Grobbelaar, B D 42
Hansen, A D 41
Johnston, C P 38+3
Kennedy, A P 8
Lawrenson, M T 36+2
Lee, S 13+2
MacDonald, K D 10+7
McMahon, S 23
Molby, J 39
Neal, P G 11+2
Nicol, S 33+1
Rush, I J 40
Walsh, P A 17+3
Wark, J 7+2
Whelan, R A 39

Goalscorers (89): Rush 22, Molby 14, Walsh 11, Whelan 10, Johnston 7, McMahon 6, Nicol 4, Dalglish 3, Gillespie 3, Lawrenson 3, Wark 3, Beglin 1, MacDonald 1, Neal 1.

EVERTON 1986–87

Adams, N J 10+2
Aspinall, W +6
Clarke, W 10
Harper, A 29+7
Heath, A P 41
Langley, K J 16
Marshall, I P +2
Mimms, R A 11
Mountfield, D N 12+1
Pointon, N G 10+2
Power, P C 40
Ratcliffe, K 42
Reid, P 15+1
Richardson, K 1
Sharp, G M 27
Sheedy, K M 28
Snodin, I 15+1
Southall, N 31
Steven, T M 41
Stevens, N G 25
Van Den Hauwe, P W R 11
Watson, D 35
Wilkinson, P 12+10

Goalscorers (76): Steven 14, Sheedy 13, Heath 11, Clarke 5, Sharp 5, Power 4, Harper 3, Mountfield 3, Stevens 3, Watson 3, Wilkinson 3, Langley 2, Marshall 1, Pointon 1, Reid 1, Van Den Hauwe 1, own goals 3.

LIVERPOOL 1987–88

Ablett, G I 15+2
Aldridge, J W 36
Barnes, J C B 38
Beardsley, P A 36+2
Dalglish, K M +2
Gillespie, G T 35
Grobbelaar, B D 38
Hansen, A D 39
Hooper, M D 2
Houghton, R J 26+2
Johnston, C P 18+12
Lawrenson, M T 10+4
MacDonald, K D +1
McMahon, S 40
Molby, J 1+6
Nicol, S 40
Spackman, N J 19+8
Venison, B 18
Walsh, P A 1+7
Wark, J +1
Watson, A F 2
Whelan, R A 26+2

Goalscorers (87): Aldridge 26, Barnes 15, Beardsley 15, McMahon 9, Nicol 6, Houghton 5, Johnston 5, Gillespie 4, Hansen 1, Whelan 1.

ARSENAL 1988–89

Adams, T A 36
Bould, S A 26+4
Caesar, G C 2
Davis, P V 11+1
Dixon, L M 31+2
Groves, P 6+15
Hayes, M 3+14
Lukic, J 38
Marwood, B 31
Merson, P C 29+8
O'Leary, D A 26
Quinn, N J 2+1
Richardson, K 32+2
Rocastle, D 38
Smith, A M 36
Thomas, M L 33+4
Winterburn, N 38

Goalscorers (73): Smith 23, Merson 10, Marwood 9, Thomas 7, Rocastle 6, Adams 4, Groves 4, Winterburn 3, Bould 2, Davis 1, Dixon 1, Hayes 1, Quinn 1, Richardson 1.

LIVERPOOL 1989–90

Ablett, G I 13+2
Aldridge, J W +2
Barnes, J C B 34
Beardsley, P A 27+2
Burrows, D 23+3
Dalglish, K M +1
Gillespie, G T 11+2
Grobbelaar, B D 38
Hansen, A D 31
Houghton, R J 16+3
Hysen, G I 35
Marsh, M A +2
McMahon, S 37+1
Molby, J 12+5
Nicol, S 21+2
Rosenthal, R 5+3
Rush, I J 36
Staunton, S 18+2
Tanner, N 2+2
Venison, B 25
Whelan, R A 34

Goalscorers (78): Barnes 22, Rush 18, Beardsley 10, Rosenthal 7, Nicol 6, McMahon 5, Gillespie 4, Aldridge 1, Houghton 1, Hysen 1, Molby 1, Whelan 1, own goal 1.

ARSENAL 1990–91

Adams, T A 30
Bould, S A 38
Campbell, K J 15+7
Cole, A A +1
Davis, P V 36+1
Dixon, L M 38
Groves, P 13+19
Hillier, D 9+7
Jonsson, S 2
Limpar, A 32+2
Linighan, A 7+3
Merson, P C 36+1
O'Leary, D A 11+10
Pates, C G +1
Rocastle, D 13+3
Seaman, D A 38
Smith, A M 35+2
Thomas, M L 27+4
Winterburn, N 38

Goalscorers (74): Smith 22, Merson 13, Limpar 11, Campbell 9, Dixon 5, Davis 3, Groves 3, Rocastle 2, Thomas 2, Adams 1, O'Leary 1, own goals 2.

LEEDS UNITED 1991–92

Agana, P A O 1+1
Batty, D 40
Cantona, E 6+9
Chapman, L R 38
Davison, R +2
Dorigo, A R 38
Fairclough, C H 30+1
Hodge, S B 12+11
Kamara, C +2
Kelly, G +2
Lukic, J 42
McAllister, G 41+1
McClelland, J 16+2
Newsome, J 7+3
Shutt, C S 6+8
Speed, G A 41
Sterland, M 29+2
Strachan, G D 35+1
Varadi, I 2+1
Wallace, R S 34
Wetherall, D +1
Whitlow, M 3+7
Whyte, C A 41

Goalscorers (74): Chapman 16, Wallace 11, Hodge 7, Speed 7, Sterland 6, McAllister 5, Strachan 4, Cantona 3, Dorigo 3, Batty 2, Fairclough 2, Newsome 2, Shutt 2, Whitlow 1, Whyte 1, own goals 2.

MANCHESTER UNITED 1992–93

Blackmore, C 12+2	Ferguson, D 15	Kanchelskis, A 14+13	Robson, B 5+9
Bruce, S R 42	Giggs, R J 40+1	McClair, B J 41+1	Schmeichel, P B 42
Butt, N +1	Hughes, L M 41	Pallister, G A 42	Sharpe, L S 27
Cantona, E 21+1	Ince, P E 41	Parker, P A 31	Wallace, D L +2
Dublin, D 3+4	Irwin, D J 40	Phelan, M C 5+6	Webb, N J +1

Goalscorers (67): Hughes 15, Cantona 9, Giggs 9, McClair 9, Ince 6, Bruce 5, Irwin 5, Kanchelskis 3, Dublin 1, Pallister 1, Parker 1, Robson 1, Sharpe 1, own goal 1.

MANCHESTER UNITED 1993–94

Bruce, S R 41	Hughes, L M 36	McClair, B J 12+14	Robson, B 10+5
Butt, N +1	Ince, P E 39	McKee, C 1	Schmeichel, P B 40
Cantona, E 34	Irwin, J D 42	Neville, G A 1	Sharpe, L S 26+4
Dublin, D 1+4	Kanchelskis, A 28+3	Pallister, G A 41	Thornley, B +1
Ferguson, D 1+2	Keane, R M 34+3	Parker, P A 39+1	Walsh, G 2+1
Giggs, R J 32+6	Martin, L A 1	Phelan, M C 1+1	

Goalscorers (80): Cantona 18, Giggs 13, Hughes 11, Sharpe 9, Ince 8, Kanchelskis 6, Keane 5, Bruce 3, Irwin 2, Dublin 1, McClair 1, Pallister 1, Robson 1, own goal 1.

BLACKBURN ROVERS 1994–95

Atkins, M N 30+4	Hendry, E C J 38	Ripley, S E 36+1	Wilcox, J M 27
Batty, D 4+1	Kenna, J J 9	Shearer, A 42	Witschge, R 1
Berg, H 40	Le Saux, G P 39	Sherwood, T M 38	Wright, A 4+1
Flowers, T D 39	Mimms, R A 3+1	Slater, R 12+6	
Gale, A P 15	Newell, M C 2+10	Sutton, C R 40	
Gallacher, K W 1	Pearce, I A 22+6	Warhurst, P 20+7	

Goalscorers (80): Shearer 34, Sutton 15, Atkins 6, Sherwood 6, Wilcox 5, Hendry 4, Le Saux 3, Warhurst 2, Berg 1, Gallacher 1, Kenna 1, own goals 2.

MANCHESTER UNITED 1995–96

Beckham, D R J 26+7	Davies, S I 1+5	Neville, G A 30+1	Prunier, W 2
Bruce, S R 30	Giggs, R J 30+3	Neville, P J 21+3	Schmeichel, P B 36
Butt, N 31+1	Irwin, J D 31	O'Kane, J A +1	Scholes, P 16+10
Cantona, E 30	Keane, R M 29	Pallister, G A 21	Sharpe, L S 21+10
Cole, A 32+2	May, D 11+5	Parker, P A 5+1	Thornley, B L +1
Cooke, T J 1+3	McClair, B J 12+10	Pilkington, K W 2+1	

Goalscorers (73): Cantona 14, Cole 11, Giggs 11, Scholes 10, Beckham 7, Keane 6, Sharpe 4, McClair 3, Butt 2, Bruce 1, Irwin 1, May 1, Pallister 1, own goal 1.

MANCHESTER UNITED 1996–97

Beckham, D R J 33+3	Cruyff, J 11+5	McClair, B J 4+15	Schmeichel, P B 36
Butt, N 24+2	Giggs, R J 25+1	Neville, G A 30+1	Scholes, P 16+8
Cantona, E 36	Irwin, J D 29+2	Neville, P J 15+3	Solskjaer, O G 25+8
Casper, C M +2	Johnsen, J R 26+5	O'Kane, J A 1	Thornley, B L 1+1
Clegg, M J 3+1	Keane, R M 21	Pallister, G A 27	Van der Gouw, R 2
Cole, A 10+10	May, D 28+1	Poborsky, P 15+7	

Goalscorers (76): Solskjaer 18, Cantona 11, Beckham 8, Cole 6, Butt 5, Cruyff 3, Giggs 3, May 3, Pallister 3, Poborsky 3, Scholes 3, Keane 2, Irwin 1, Neville G 1, own goals 6.

ARSENAL 1997–98

Adams, T A 26	Grimandi, G 16+6	Overmars, M 32	Vernazza, P A P 1
Anelka, N 16+10	Hughes, S J 7+10	Parlour, R 34	Vieira, P 31+2
Bergkamp, D N 28	Keown, M R 18	Petit, E 32	Winterburn, N 35+1
Boa Morte, L 4+11	Manninger, A 7	Platt, D A 11+20	Wreh, C 7+9
Bould, S A 21+3	Marshall, S R 1+2	Rankin, I +1	Wright, I E 22+2
Dixon, L M 26+2	McGowan, G G +1	Seaman, D A 31	
Garde, R 6+4	Mendez, A 1+2	Upson, M J 5	

Goalscorers (68): Bergkamp 16, Overmars 12, Wright 10, Anelka 6, Parlour 5, Adams 3, Platt 3, Wreh 3, Hughes 2, Petit 2, Vieira 2, Grimandi 1, Winterburn 1, own goals 2.

MANCHESTER UNITED 1998–99

Beckham, D R J 33 + 1	Cruyff, J — + 5	Keane, R M 33 + 2	Sheringham, E P 7 + 10
Berg, H 10 + 6	Curtis, J C K 1 + 3	May, D 4 + 2	Solskjaer, O G 9 + 10
Blomqvist, L J 20 + 5	Giggs, R J 20 + 4	Neville, G A 34	Stam, J 30
Brown, W M 11 + 3	Greening, J — + 3	Neville, P J 19 + 9	Van der Gouw, R 4 + 1
Butt, N 22 + 9	Irwin, J D 26 + 3	Schmeichel, P B 34	Yorke, D 32
Cole, A A 26 + 6	Johnsen, J R 19 + 3	Scholes, P 24 + 7	

Goalscorers (80): Yorke 18, Cole 17, Solskjaer 12, Beckham 6, Scholes 6, Giggs 3, Johnsen 3, Butt 2, Cruyff 2, Irwin 2 (2 pens), Keane 2, Sheringham 2, Blomqvist 1, Neville G 1, Stam 1, own goals 2.

MANCHESTER UNITED 1999–2000

Beckham, D R J 30 + 1	Curtis, J C K — + 1	May, D — + 1	Taibi, M 4
Berg, H 16 + 6	Fortune, Q 4 + 2	Neville, G A 22	Van der Gouw, R 11 + 3
Bosnich, M J 23	Giggs, R J 30	Neville, P J 25 + 4	Wallwork, R — + 5
Butt, N 21 + 11	Greening, J 1 + 3	Scholes, P 27 + 4	Wilson, M A 1 + 2
Clegg, M J — + 2	Higginbotham, D J 2 + 1	Sheringham, E P 15 + 12	Yorke, D 29 + 3
Cole, A A 23 + 5	Irwin, J D 25	Silvestre, M S 30 + 1	
Cruyff, J 1 + 7	Johnsen, J R 2 + 1	Solskjaer, O G 15 + 13	
Culkin, N J — + 1	Keane, R M 28 + 1	Stam, J 33	

Goalscorers (97): Yorke 20, Cole 19, Solskjaer 12, Scholes 9 (1 pen), Beckham 6, Giggs 6, Keane 5, Sheringham 5, Butt 3, Cruyff 3, Irwin 3 (3 pens), Fortune 2, Berg 1, own goals 3.

MANCHESTER UNITED 2000–01

Barthez, F A 30
Beckham, D R J 29 + 2
Berg, H — + 1
Brown, W M 25 + 3
Butt, N 24 + 4
Chadwick, L H 6 + 10
Cole, A A 15 + 4
Djordjic, B — + 1
Fortune, Q 6 + 1
Giggs, R J 24 + 7
Goram, A L 2
Greening, J 3 + 4
Healy, D J — + 1
Irwin, J D 20 + 1
Johnsen, J R 11
Keane, R M 28
May, D 1 + 1
Neville, G A 32
Neville, P J 24 + 5
Rachubka, P S 1
Scholes, P 28 + 4
Sheringham, E P 23 + 6
Silvestre, M S 25 + 5
Solskjaer, O G 19 + 12
Stam, J 15
Stewart, M J 3
Van der Gouw, R 5 + 5
Wallwork, R 4 + 8
Yorke, D 15 + 7

Goalscorers (79): Sheringham 15 (1 pen), Solskjaer 10, Beckham 9 (1 pen), Cole 9, Yorke 9, Scholes 6, Giggs 5, Butt 3, Chadwick 2, Fortune 2, Keane 2, Johnsen 1, Neville G 1, Neville P 1, Silvestre 1, own goals 3.

ARSENAL 2001–02

Adams, T A 10
Aliadiere, J — + 1
Bergkamp, D N 22 + 11
Campbell, S J 29 + 2
Cole, A 29
Dixon, L M 3 + 10
Edu 8 + 6
Grimandi, G 11 + 15
Henry, T 31 + 2
Jeffers, F 2 + 4
Kanu, N 9 + 14
Keown, M R 21 + 1
Lauren, E 27
Ljungberg, K F 24 + 1
Luzhny, O 15 + 3
Parlour, R 25 + 2
Pires, R 27 + 1
Seaman, D A 17
Stepanovs, I 6
Taylor, S J 9 + 1
Upson, M J 10 + 4
Van Bronckhorst, G C 13 + 8
Vieira, P 35 + 1
Wiltord, S 23 + 10
Wright, R I 12

Goalscorers (79): Henry 24 (4 pens), Ljungberg 12, Wiltord 10, Bergkamp 9, Pires 9 (1 pen), Kanu 3, Campbell 2, Cole 2, Jeffers 2, Lauren 2 (1 pen), Vieira 2, Edu 1, Van Bronckhorst 1.

MANCHESTER UNITED 2002–03

Barthez, F A 30
Beckham, D R J 27 + 4
Blanc, L R 15 + 4
Brown, W M 22
Butt, N 14 + 4
Carroll, R E 8 + 2
Chadwick, L H — + 1
Ferdinand, R G 27 + 1
Forlan, D 7 + 18
Fortune, Q 5 + 4
Giggs, R J 32 + 4
Keane, R M 19 + 2
May, D — + 1
Neville, G A 19 + 7
Neville, P J 19 + 6
O'Shea, J F 26 + 6
Pugh, D A — + 1
Ricardo — + 1
Richardson, K E — + 2
Roche, L P — + 1
Scholes, P 31 + 2
Silvestre, M S 34
Solskjaer, O G 29 + 8
Stewart, M J — + 1
Van Nistelrooy, R J M 33 + 1
Veron, J S 21 + 4

Goalscorers (74): Van Nistelrooy 25 (8 pens), Scholes 14, Solskjaer 9, Giggs 8, Beckham 6, Forlan 6, Veron 2, Neville P 1, Silvestre 1, own goals 2.

ARSENAL 2003–04

Aliadiere, J 3 + 7
Bentley, D M 1
Bergkamp, D N 21 + 7
Campbell, S J 35
Clichy, G 7 + 5
Cole, A 32
Cygan, P 10 + 8
Edu 13 + 17
Henry, T 37
Hoyte, J R — + 1
Kanu, N 3 + 7
Keown, M R 3 + 7
Lauren, E 30 + 2
Lehmann, J 38
Ljungberg, K F 27 + 3
Parlour, R 16 + 9
Pires, R 33 + 3
Reyes, J A 7 + 6
Silva, G 29 + 3
Toure, H K 36 + 1
Vieira, P 29
Wiltord, S 8 + 4

Goalscorers (73): Henry 30 (7 pens), Pires 14, Bergkamp 4, Ljungberg 4, Silva 4, Vieira 3, Wiltord 3, Edu 2, Reyes 2, Campbell 1, Kanu 1, Toure 1, own goals 4.

CHELSEA 2004–05

Babayaro, C 3 + 1
Bridge, W M 12 + 3
Cech, P 35
Cole, J J 19 + 9
Cudicini, C 3
Drogba, D Y T 18 + 8
Duff, D A 28 + 2
Forssell, M K — + 1
Gallas, W 28
Geremi 6 + 7
Grant, A P S A — + 1
Gudjohnsen, E S 30 + 7
Huth, R 6 + 4
Jarosik, J 3 + 11
Johnson, G M C 13 + 4
Kezman, M 6 + 19
Lampard, F J 38
Makelele, C 36
Mutu, A — + 2
Nuno Morais — + 2
Oliveira, F V — + 1
Parker, S M 1 + 3
Paulo Ferreira 29
Pidgeley, L J — + 1
Ricardo Carvalho 22 + 3
Robben, A 14 + 4
Smertin, A 11 + 5
Terry, J G 36
Tiago 21 + 13
Watt, S M — + 1

Goalscorers (72): Lampard 13 (3 pens), Gudjohnsen 12 (1 pen), Drogba 10, Cole 8, Robben 7, Duff 6, Kezman 4 (1 pen), Tiago 4, Terry 3, Gallas 2, Makelele 1, Ricardo Carvalho 1, own goal 1.

CHELSEA 2005–06

Cech, P 34
Cole, C M — + 9
Cole, J J 26 + 8
Crespo, H J 20 + 10
Cudicini, C 3 + 1
Del Horno, A 25
Diarra, L 2 + 1
Drogba, D Y T 20 + 9
Duff, D A 18 + 10
Essien, M 27 + 4
Gallas, W 33 + 1
Geremi 8 + 7
Gudjohnsen, E S 16 + 10
Huth, R 7 + 6
Johnson, G M C 4
Lampard, F J 35
Makelele, C 29 + 2
Maniche 3 + 5
Paulo Ferreira 18 + 3
Pidgeley, L J 1
Ricardo Carvalho 22 + 2
Robben, A 21 + 7
Smith, J D — + 1
Terry, J G 36
Wright-Phillips, S C 10 + 17

Goalscorers (72): Lampard 16 (4 pens), Drogba 12, Crespo 10, Cole J 7, Robben 6, Gallas 5, Terry 4, Duff 3, Essien 2, Geremi 2, Gudjohnsen 2, Del Horno 1, Ricardo Carvalho 1, own goal 1.

MANCHESTER UNITED 2006–07

Brown, W M 17 + 5
Carrick, M 29 + 4
Dong Fangzhou 1
Eagles, C M 1 + 1
Evra, P L 22 + 2
Ferdinand, R G 33
Fletcher, D B 16 + 8
Giggs, R J 25 + 5
Heinze, G I 17 + 5
Kuszczak, T 6
Larsson, H 5 + 2
Lee, K C 1
Neville, G A 24
O'Shea, J F 16 + 16
Park, J-S 8 + 6
Richardson, K E 8 + 7
Ronaldo, C 31 + 3
Rooney, W M 33 + 2
Saha, L L 18 + 6
Scholes, P 29 + 1
Silvestre, M S 6 + 8
Smith, A 6 + 3
Solskjaer, O G 9 + 10
Van der Sar, E 32
Vidic, N 25

Goalscorers (83): Ronaldo 17 (3 pens), Rooney 14, Saha 8 (2 pens), Solskjaer 7, Scholes 6, Park 5, Giggs 4, O'Shea 4, Carrick 3, Fletcher 3, Vidic 3, Eagles 1, Evra 1, Ferdinand 1, Larsson 1, Richardson 1, Silvestre 1, own goals 3.

DAILY ROUND-UP 2006–07

JULY 2006

Italian clubs savaged in bribery scandal ... Rooney and Ronaldo to make up ... Zidane gets community service, Materazzi a ban.

10 Materazzi's role in Zidane dismissal being aired.

11 Juve to sell off stars if demoted. Materazzi admits insults. Xavier ban reduced to one year. Reading secure Seol £1m. Oh yes, Ch Lge starts with no noticeable coverage; Linfield lose to Gorica among other results.

12 Lippi quits Italy, Klinsmann Germany. Zidane blames Materazzi. FIFA lift Greece suspension. More Ch Lge and Cork beat Apollon, The New Saints (ex-TNS) beaten by MyPa.

13 Hamann already signed for Bolton leaves for Man City in £400,000 deal without kicking a ball for them! Rumours of strife within FA. UEFA Cup opening shocks: Derry win in Gothenburg, Llanelli in Gefle, Drogheda draw in Helsinki; Rhyl get a home draw against Suduva, but home defeats for Portadown and Glentoran.

14 Juve relegated to Serie B, minus 30 pts and loss of last two titles; Fiorentina also down lose 12 pts; Lazio, too, with seven deducted, but AC Milan stay with 15 pt penalty. Van Nistelrooy can go for £15m. Big Phil signs new Portugal contract. WC stars come here: Abdoulaye Meite, Marseille to Bolton; Denny Landzaat, AZ to Wigan; Pascal Zuberbuhler, Basle to WBA. Villa in turmoil.

15 Intertoto: Newcastle held by Lillestrom. Born-again Solskjaer hits two in Man Utd SA win over Orlando Pirates. Roo and Ron to make-up at Old Trafford?

16 Venables not interested in McClaren's job.

17 Ron to stay says Sir Alex. Gretna money man Brooks Mileson has surgery. Juve team manager Gianluca Pessotto recovering after suicide attempt last month.

18 Ch Lge tick off four more games. Chinese Dong – banned from PL with no permit – helps Man Utd beat Kaizer Chiefs. They also announce £660m refinancing package. New Serbia coach: Javier Clemente.

19 Mutual Villa departure for David O'Leary. Graham Poll gets a Euro 2008 qualifier! Hammers Newton banned for seven months after drug test failure. Ch Lge: Cork hold out in Limassol, but draw not enough for Linfield and Saints lose again.

20 Zidane three days community service, Materazzi two-match ban and both fined. Crowd of 20,000 watch Arsenal train at Emirates Stadium! Man City add Bernardo Corradi £2m from Valencia. Chelsea to start unloading. Death of Hereford FA Cup hero Roger Griffiths at 61.

21 Mick McCarthy gets Wolves job. Newcastle sign Duff from Chelsea – knockdown price £5m. Ivica Osim is new Japan coach.

22 Bergkamp farewell at Emirates after 423 games, 120 goals, 54,000 present. Newcastle ease in 3-0 in Norway. Juve plead to keep titles.

23 Man Utd lose to the Chiefs in penalty shoot-out as doubts exist over current squad.

24 Only 25 pre-named players can figure in the Champions League with minimum of two English players. Gerrard wants England armband. Man Utd withdraw financial support for Ladies team. Dunga replaces Carlos Alberto Parreira as Brazil No. 1. Hulse to Sheff Utd for £2.2m. Van the man in Old Trafford limbo.

25 Italian clubs appeal: Juve demotion stays, only 17 pt penalty; Fiorentina can remain with 19 pts taken off; Lazio stay minus 11 pts; AC Milan deduction cut to eight pts and can play in Ch Lge. Denizli (Turkey) face match-fixing probe, too. Price of Cole upped to £30m by Arsenal. Villa interest US money. Niall Quinn makes himself Sunderland manager. Barton to stay at Man City. Real Madrid unveil Fabio Cannavaro from Juve. New coaches: Slaven Bilic (Croatia), Roberto Donadoni (Italy) with Joachim Loew already installed for Germany.

26 Ch Lge: Hearts attract 28,486 to Murrayfield and beat Siroki 3-0, but Cork pipped by own goal against Red Star. Euro U-19 semis: Scotland edge Czechs 1-0, Spain whack Austria 5-0. Inter (3rd) get Juve's last title! Pennant £6.7m move from Brum to Liverpool. Young Man Utd team wins 3-0 at Celtic.

27 Ruud Van costs £10.3m in Real terms. Blackburn Pedersen to be known as Gamst – his mother's surname. Villa bidder problems. UEFA Cup: Derry do it again, Drogheda march on, too, Llanelli are held but still go through, but curtains for Glentoran, Portadown and Rhyl.

28 Ch Lge: Benitez unhappy over Maccabi Haifa tie. Arsenal likely to play Dynamo Zagreb, Hearts if successful, AEK Athens likewise Cork against Red Star. UEFA Cup draw: Newcastle to meet Ventspils (Latvia), Gretna get Derry, Llanelli play Odense and Drogheda face Start (Norway). Villa suitors gathering. Blackburn sign Benni McCarthy, Porto's South African for £2.5m. Colchester appoint caretaker Geraint Williams as manager.

29 Minder for Ronaldo at Old Trafford. UEFA U-19 final: Spain 2 Scotland 1. SPL: Celtic, Hearts off to winning start. Shearer for BBC role. Wembley fiasco heading for the courts.

30 Le Guen off to a winner, too, for Rangers at Motherwell.

31 Carrick in at Old Trafford in £18.6m deal. Rooney is Utd captain; 6000 watch training. Wolves chairman Rick Hayward steps down. Lord Mawhinney hits out at Trevor Brooking over coaching problems.

AUGUST 2006

Martin O'Neill is Villa boss ... then they go American ... Reading's promising PL start ... Owen may miss entire season ... Roy Keane is Sunderland manager ... Ashley Cole finally goes to Chelsea.

1 Steve (first choice) McClaren takes over England. Gallas no show for Chelsea. Juventus to lodge second appeal. Brazil v Argentina at the Emirates!

2 Wembley costs soar to £1b! Ballack gets Gallas No. 13 shirt.

3 Martin O'Neill nears Villa post. Ken Bates wants Chelsea docked for luring two Leeds youths. Wrexham out of administration. Absentee Gallas to leave Chelsea.

4 Rooney and Scholes sent off for Man Utd against Porto in Amsterdam. O'Neill unveiled at Villa. Keith Curle gets compensation from Mansfield sacking.

5 FL kicks-off: 200 club Hartson debut double delights Baggies; Bendtner bow, too, aids Birmingham; Eastwood penalty brings Southend joy but Stoke's Chadwick carted off with heat stroke; Palace recover to win at Ipswich where Sir Bobby Robson is taken ill; birthday boy Healy on the spot for Leeds; Jones brace in Burnley debut; In Lge 1 promoted Cheltenham win at Swansea; Port Vale hit Orient for three and Chesterfield have similar result at Bournemouth. Lge 2: Conlon hat-trick as Darlo hit Macclesfield 4-0 and Posh turn over Bristol Rovers 4-1; Swindon's Czech goalie Brezovan saves two penalties at Hartlepool; sub Peter Bore, is Grimsby teenage marksman, new boys Hereford success at Stockport, but Accrington go down at Chester. Goals scarce at 75. but seven red cards – two for Oldham. SPL: Rangers scramble for a draw after Dundee Utd go two up. SL; Gretna hit Accies for six! Partick win at Dundee. Cowden in 6-1 romp against Alloa. Even East Stirling make winning start.

6 Sunderland start with loss at Coventry; Derby snatch equaliser with Saints. SPL: Lennon gaffe costs Celtic in Hearts defeat. Carrick out for a month. Alan Curbishley "bung" claim to be investigated.

7 Crespo two-year loan at Inter. Van der Meyde ill after drink spiking. Sir Bobby out of hospital. Liverpool not to play in Israel. Reggina match-fixing investigation.

8 Ch Lge: Arsenal coast it in Zagreb amid hostile Dynamo environment. Gary Taylor-Fletcher creates English League history scoring the 500,000th goal since 1888 in the 79th minute for Huddersfield against Rotherham. Barnsley two-down at Hull win 3-2. Accrington suffer second defeat. CIS Cup: Partick again dump Dundee. Rooney and Scholes likely to escape ban.

9 Ch Lge: Liverpool need born again Gonzalez to edge out Maccabi Haifa; Hearts fade away in last minutes to AEK; Inzaghi's 33rd birthday goal eases AC Milan worries. Teen starlet Bale again on Saints mark; Sunderland lose again.

10 Terry J is new England skipper, Terry V is new assistant and Becks is not in the squad for the friendly with the Greeks. UEFA Cup; Gretna green in Europe – lose 5-1 to Derry; Newcastle one up in Latvia; Llanelli one down in Odense. Rooney biog (to date) is out. Crawley reprieve.

11 James to Pompey from Man City. David Pleat is football consultant at Forest. Chelsea bid £23m for Ashley Cole. Wolves bitten by North End Nugent. Leacock to Derby for £375,000 – the fee for which he was due to go to Swansea.

12 Luton blow two-goal lead at Norwich who score three in 14 mins; Simonsen saves Forssell penalty to thwart Brum; Sunderland, Colchester, Hull and Ipswich still search for a point. O'Connor goal for Brentford in 200th game; Chesterfield hit five; Hartlepool miss another penalty – Abbey saves one for Torquay but Lincoln strike twice late to win. SPL: Hearts still top despite draw; Celtic beat St Mirren 2-0. SL: Stenhousemuir hit five.

13 Liverpool hex on Chelsea again as they take the Community Shield; gate 56,275. Horsfield 15th min red card and Leeds suffer injury time defeat to sub Morrison as Palace go top. SPL: Rangers draw at Dunfermline leaves them 6th. SL: Gretna return to winning ways.

14 Villa takeover complete by Randy Lerner, American billionaire. Gareth Southgate reveals past problems at Boro with Steve McClaren. Wigan supremo Dave Whelan is 317th richest man in the country.

15 Ashton fractures ankle in England training. Wales hold Bulgaria in Swansea. England U21 goal for Walcott but Moldova get a draw. Steve Staunton shrugs off Monday evening's gun-toting loony. Conf: Only Oxford and Weymouth have maximum points after two games; Crawley would have same but for ten point deduction! Rooney, Scholes bans to stay.

16 Born-again England hammer Euro champs Greece with four first half goals, captain Terry leading the Big (first choice) Mac revolution. Northern Ireland win in Finland, Dutch deliver Dublin drubbing on Republic. Euro 2008 qualifiers start and Georgia score six in the Faeroes. U21s: defeats for Wales, Northern Ireland and Scotland away, but Republic win in Greece. Spurs Reid goes to Charlton for £3m, Birmingham get McSheffrey from Coventry for £4m. Owen may miss season.

17 Hargreaves for Man Utd, Kuyt for Liverpool? Chelsea complain about Bates alleged racist remarks.

18 Cole comfort for Ashley at Arsenal. Coventry and Leicester scoreless, but Oxford make Conf presence felt at Burton. Juve fail in appeal bid. Plymouth axe Zebroski for misconduct in Austria.

19 Right regal response by Reading Royals – give Boro two goals and beat them! Super baby sub Walcott helps scramble a point for Arsenal against O'Neill's Villa; Liverpool need disputed penalty to avoid defeat at Sheff Utd; Pompey put nine-man Rovers to the sword with sub Kanu; Zamora helps Hammers harass ten-man Charlton; early Bolton strikes flatten Spurs; Watford, Wigan edged out at Everton and Newcastle, but Hornets hit by spot kick error and Latics robbed by Bramble hand. Buoyant gates average 35,000. Championship: No 100% teams, Colchester beaten by Baggies, Sunderland by Southend (Prior's 500th League game) both pointless. Lge 1: Port Vale, Forest maximum points. Lge 2: Swindon 2-1 at Darlo alone with 12 pts, Rochdale, Bury still looking – after early Easter hat-trick for Wycombe. Shrewsbury hit five against Boston. Conf: new boys Weymouth maximum points, Shots win 5-3 at St Albans. SPL: Boyd brace beats Hearts for Rangers. SL: only Gretna are 100%! Rooney threatens FA over ban.

20 Man Utd high five against Fulham, Roo brace, one for Ron, too, plus PL record 75,115. Chelsea ease 3-0 over ten-finishing Man City. Average PL gate soars to 40,000! SPL: Celtic have to settle for draw at Caley.

21 C Cup: Accrington hew the Forest. Chelsea sign "Canabal" Boulharouz from Hamburg.

22 Ch Lge: Liverpool draw in Kiev against Maccabi enough. PL: Berbatov the Spur against Sheff Utd; West Ham draw at Watford, Zamora again the marksman. C Cup: Ten-man Sunderland even lose to Bury now. Fleetwood hat-trick for Hereford sinks Coventry; Barnet shake Cardiff, Walsall edge Plymouth, Ipswich go down on penalties to Posh. Notts win away to Palace. Newcastle transfer Boumsong to Juve, may sign Obafemi Martins from Inter. Phillips switches from Villa to WBA. Todd wins his red card appeal for Blackburn, who sign Andre Ooijer from PSV for £2.1m.

23 Shevchenko scores but it's crisis club Chelsea as Boro nick it again! No Roo but Man Utd hit Charlton 3-0; Cahill rescues point for Everton at Blackburn; Bullard penalty at the death saves Fulham against Bolton; Harry R rages over Thatcher one-arm strike as Pompey draw with Man City; Reading edged out at Villa. Ch Lge: Arsenal in with 2-1 over Dynamo, Hearts out after 3-0 in Athens. C Cup: Saints give

Glovers a nap hand defeat, 20,653 present; Wolves lose on penalties to Chesterfield; Wrexham dump Sheff Wed. Roy Keane may be Black Cats boss.

24 UEFA Cup: Newcastle held but Ventspils out; Start taken to 11-10 penalty win at Drogheda; Gretna save face not tie in Derry; Llanelli cave in to Odense. Ch Lge draw: Chelsea get Barca again; Liverpool, Arsenal miss each other but Celtic in Man Utd group. C Cup: Baggies threesome at Orient. Thatcher could face assault charge.

25 Man City suspend Thatcher. FIFA fine Togo FA for WC mutiny threat. Super Cup: Sevilla whack Barca 3-0.

26 Barton on the spot as Man City beat Arsenal; Bullard celebrates Johnny Haynes day as Fulham beat Sheff Utd; Heskey goal enough for Wigan over Reading; Bent D double strike for Charlton against Bolton; Spurs go down to Everton who play with ten for an hour; veteran Giggs on hand as Man Utd win at Watford; 100 years at the Kop and Anfield celebrate with 2-1 over Hammers and staggering Agger strike. FL: Cureton hat-trick lifts Colchester to victory; Cardiff displace Brummie at the top in 2-0 win; Forrester hits four for Lincoln at Mansfield. Five wins in a row for Swindon. Rotherham still minus three points. SPL: Hearts keeping pace with Celtic as both win. SL: East Stirling hit Stenhousemuir for five! Conf: Oxford five, too, against Northwich with 5364 present.

27 Villa go second with Mags beaten; Chelsea at the double over Rovers. Healy penalty sees Leeds through at Sheff Wed derby. Crewe 4-1 at Brighton. SPL: Rangers draw at Killie leaves them trailing by a point alongside Aberdeen.

28 Roy Keane new ray of hope at Stadium of Light as Black Cats claw first win. Makelele at odds with JM over "slave" remark re-French international career. Pompey Hughes warned over "inside trading" bet on Harry R move from Saints and Kanu double rocks rocky Boro in 4-0 trouncing. FIFA cool on England hosting 2018 WC.

29 Bristol City's Orr sent off for butting team-mate but they still win at Northampton. Mido back at Spurs for £3.8m. Iran WC star Andranik Teimourian joins Bolton from Abu Moslem. Cole move to Chelsea in ashes.

30 Inquiry pending into Chelsea–Leeds row. Anelka returns this time to Bolton. Charlton sign Senegal defender Souleymane Diawara from Sochaux for £3.7m. Man City ban Thatcher for six weeks. Lita on alleged GBH attack. Doncaster dispense with Dave Penney, Kevin Keegan may be in frame. Crawley saved for now.

31 Cole shifted to Bridge in late, late move with Gallas taking opposite route to Gunners; Hammers double dealing as two WC Argies – Carlos Tevez and Javier Mascherano arrive. Spurs sign Chimbonda (Wigan), Malbranque (Fulham). Wigan get Kilbane (Everton), Cotterill (Bristol C); Andy Cole moves to Pompey who also secure Nico Kranjcar from Hajduk Split. Ipswich sign Legwinski from Fulham, Sunderland add Kavanagh (Wigan) and Dwight Yorke from Sydney. Newcastle sign Sibierski from Man City, Boro get Euell (Charlton), Woodgate on loan from Real and Huth (Chelsea) while Martin O'Neill obtains Stilian Petrov from old club Celtic as window shopping ends. Chelsea fined £40,000 for drug test on Mutu. Curtis Davies out with metatarsal injury. England Ladies beat Dutch 4-0 in WC qualifier.

SEPTEMBER 2006

Sir Alex wants a winter break ... England's useful Euro 2008 start ... Thatcher gets eight match ban ... Bung allegations revealed ... Wenger celebrates tenth anniversary at Arsenal ... Chelsea not on song.

1 Chelsea to scan new Ashley Cole book proofs; David Moyes to take over over Rooney's latest. U21s: trio of home defeats for both Irish and Scots – Belgium, Germany and France respective winners. Oxford win again and boost average Conf gates, but Rob Newman sacked at Cambridge.

2 Euro 2008: England's 76th different opponents Andorra beaten 5-0, doubles for Defoe and Crouch; joy of six for Scots over Faeroes; Czechs bounce back late to floor Wales; Republic just edged out in Germany; Iceland surprise for Northern Ireland; Lithuania hold the Italians. Lge 1: Forest three points clear after 4-0 v Chesterfield. Lge 2: MK Dons go second after 3-2 over Notts. Conf: Morecambe inflict first defeat on Weymouth.

3 New-look Brazil down the Argies 3-0 at the Emirates. French coach Raymond Domenech "staggered" by Mourinho "slave" remark over Makelele. Conf: Daggers five at Altrincham.

4 Sir Alex calls for winter break. Wigan get clearance for ex-Hearts Webster. Giacinto Facchetti, Inter and Italy left-back dies at 64.

5 Brazil late showing over Wales at White Hart Lane of course! Materazzi admits he insulted Zidane's sister.

6 Euro 2008: Crouch goal enough for England in Macedonia; Healy treble has Spain reeling in Belfast; Scots edge home in Lithuania; England U21s qualify after 3-2 win in Lucerne; Germany's competition record 13-0 win in San Marino; revenge as France beat Italy. Gibraltar aim for UEFA status.

7 PL and FIFA will sort out differences over number of clubs. Second knee op for Owen. Mido reveals shedding of 22 lbs!

8 Steve Staunton one month ban over ref protest. England U21 to face Germany. New Liverpool venue Stanley Park gets green light. Henchoz back at Blackburn. Didier Agathe in at Villa. Brighton axe boss man Mark McGhee. Gravesen unveiled at Celtic.

9 Everton win 204th Merseyside derby and Johnson double helps end Liverpool's 17-match unbeaten run 3-0; Man Utd maximum points from Gibbs strike; Friedel saves two Sheff Utd penalties, Kenny one from Blackburn in goalless draw; Jimmy Floyd hits old Chelsea mates but Blues prevail over Addicks; veteran Speed spot on for Trotters; Pompey still displaying winning chime; Toon defence gifts it to Fulham, who lose Bullard with serious knee injury; Henry penalty saves point for under par Gunners. FL: Cardiff cling to top despite losing ten-a-side to Preston; Sunderland two-in-a row revival. Forest maintain three point lead in Lge 1, Bournemouth boss Sean O'Driscoll to join Doncaster. Swindon slender advantage despite first defeat at Wrexham in Lge 2. Hartlepool's fourth penalty miss of season. SPL: Hearts slip to third after St Mirren win. SL: Gretna humbled by visiting Dundee. Hamilton sub McCabe suffers serious neck

injury, Clyde game abandoned at 3-3. St Johnstone hit five at Partick. Conf: Stevenage crack six against ten-man Stafford. Matt Gadsby (Hinckley) dies at 27 during Harrogate match.

10 Hammers fight back earns Villa draw. Leeds lowest gate (16,268) since 1989 as Wolves steal the points. Ruud hat-trick for Real, Rimini's ten hold once-mightly Juve in Serie B. Chile sub striker Nicolas Millan, 14 years, nine months, debuts for Colo Colo at Santiago Wanderers.

11 Reading edge Man City for second PL win. Eriksson unhappy about the flak. Brian Kidd is Sheff Utd coach No. 2. Sean O'Driscoll takes over at Doncaster, Richard O'Kelly as coach.

12 Ch Lge: Liverpool goalless in Eindhoven, Chelsea ease 2-0 over Werder; Morientes hat-trick for Valencia at Olympiakos; goals, too, for Barca (five), Bayern and Roma four apiece. Fabregas signs eight year deal at Arsenal. FL: Cardiff share six goals at Plymouth, but Birmingham go ahead after 2-0 at QPR. Six goals as Shrimpers and Canaries level it, too. Forest suffer first defeat at home to Oldham but stay in front as Tranmere, Port Vale lose. Rotherham wipe out ten point deficit. Walsall whack Posh 5-0. Conf: Oxford have five point lead; Jackson hat-trick for Rushden. SC Cup: another Gretna reverse! Thatcher eight-match ban.

13 Ch Lge: Gunners take out ten-man Hamburg; gritty Celtic restrict Man Utd to 3-2 win; shock for Dynamo Kiev supplied by Steaua; Lyon "two" good for Real. Buoyant Sunderland make it three at sad Leeds. Stanley take five off Wrexham. Puskas in intensive care. Forest's David Johnson forced to retire. Charlton's Traore has a broken leg.

14 UEFA Cup: mixed results: Newcastle in Tallinn, Spurs in Prague both win; Hearts slump at home to Sparta as do West Ham against Palermo, while Rangers, Blackburn draw at Molde and Salzburg respectively and Derry at home to PSG. Riquelme retires from Argentine internationals.

15 Seb Coe to clean up football! Trinidad supremo Jack Warner in alleged WC ticket scam. Wenger prefers English owners. Hull off the foot after win over Sheff Wed. Eriksson in line for USA job.

16 Chiming days for Pompey, Premier leaders after Lua Lua goal at Charlton; Doyle on the boil for Reading after 16 seconds, PL's 8th quickest hit as Sheff Utd lose. three drawn affairs: Boro at Bolton, villa at Watford both goalless, while Everton and Wigan share four goals. FL: Cardiff cap ten-man Hatters; Sunderland held, Leeds go down again. Forest miss fourth penalty of season in goalless with Carlisle. Chairboys in driving seat after 2-1 at Rochdale. Posh surprise Swindon. Conf: Oxford held by Grays.

17 Super Sunday: Ballack "stamping" leaves Chelsea to beat Liverpool with ten men courtesy of classical Drogba hit; Arsenal snatch it at the Old Trafford death; Newcastle survive Given injury blow to win at Hammers; Blackburn overcome Man City 4-2 while Spurs – 343 goalless minutes – and Fulham join the scoreless ranks. SPL: Hibs edge Rangers, Hearts win at Motherwell on Edinburgh's day. Harry Redknapp dismisses "bung" allegations. German football hit by racist abuse. sub Becks on target for Real.

18 WBA axe Bryan Robson. Sam Allardyce gets his "bung" retaliation in first ahead of Panorama programme. Conf: Oxford late win at Crawley. Death of George Heslop, Man City defender at 66.

19 BBC Panorama "bung" allegations centre around Sam Allardyce, son Craig, Kevin Bond at Newcastle plus Frank Arnesen at Chelsea for poaching Porritt from Boro. Randy Lerner takeover at Villa nears conclusion. C Cup: Stanley force Watford to penalties, as do Darlington at Reading's equally reserve team. Crewe oust Wigan. Managerial casualties: Gary Waddock (QPR), Kevin Blackwell (Leeds). CIS Cup: Celtic through and St Johnstone beat Dundee Utd. Conf: Grays, Dagenham, Weymouth all lose out.

20 Xabi Alonso's 60 yard wonder strike seals Liverpool 2-0 win over Newcastle. C Cup: senior casualties as Chesterfield, Wycombe and Notts dispose of Man City, Fulham and Boro. CIS Cup: Hibs tonk Gretna 6-0. Kevin Blackwell axed at Leeds, John Gregory in at QPR. Arsenal have £262m debt.

21 Pressure on BBC to hand over evidence. John Carver appointed Leeds caretaker. Reading want ground extension. France beat England U-18s 2-0.

22 Clubs fury rises over BBC allegations. Preston move up with lucky Agyemang rebound against Barnsley.

23 New Lamps for old – penalty nightmare over and stunning strike puts Chelsea top again; Ronaldo rocks Royals in rescue point for Man Utd at Reading; Arsenal mark Arsene Wenger's 10th anniversary week with Henry shining in 3-0 over winless Sheff Utd on Neil Warnock's 1000th managerial match; Nonda stars as Rovers return from Boro with points; Samaras double for Man City against West Ham; Jenas miss costly as Spurs crash at Liverpool; away misery continues for Charlton with Villa claiming victory; Watford earn draw at Wigan. FL: John Carver cuts a caretaker dash as Leeds clip ten-man Brummies; Rasiak in Pole position as Saints edge ten-man Burnley; first defeat for Sunderland under Keane after Lee's double for Ipswich; joy for new boss Gregory as QPR shove Hull bottom. Lge 1: vet Anderton scores on Bournemouth bow. Lge 2: Hartlepool win 5-3 at Posh and end penalty jinx. Conf: Oxford still unbeaten stay six points clear of high-scoring Daggers. SPL: Celtic win first Old Firm clash of season 2-0. SL; Gretna back on song and top – 6-0 at Partick. Becks sub for Real, but later reports sick.

24 All square at Newcastle with Everton. Successful Cardiff day out at the Southend seaside. SPL: Hearts away winners at Aberdeen keep in touch with leaders Celtic. Barca top in Spain despite Valencia draw, Inter lead in Italy.

25 Pompey suffer first reverse to Bolton as Sam the Man threatens to sue the BBC. Dario Silva has right leg amputated after Uruguay car crash. Liverpool financial thoughts over new ground. Nigel Spackman leaves Millwall mutually after dozen games.

26 Ch Lge: Henry uses his head again for two-goal Arsenal against Porto; Saha strike enough for Man Utd at Benfica; Miller penalty edges Celtic home against FC Copenhagen; Becks quiet second half outing but Real hit five against Kiev. Lge 1: As Forest, Tranmere are both held, winners Bristol City, Carlisle and Yeovil progress. Defender Lockwood saves Orient point with hat-trick. Lge 2: MK Dons the only pacemaking winners after going two down to ten-man Torquay, but Walsall's draw keeps them top. Jonathan Barnett, Ashley Cole agent fined £100,000 and suspended for 18 months. Newcastle sack Kevin Bond.

27 Ch Lge: Drogba treble tonic for Chelsea at Levski; Liverpool go three up, lose two goals to Galatasaray; Inter have two dismissed by ref Bennett and go down 2-0 at home to Bayern; Barca scrape a draw in Bremen. Shock, horror – Blatter wants end to shoot-outs, but only in WC finals. Barclays to extend PL sponsorship until 2010 for £65.8m. Steve McClaren agent Colin Gordon hits out at bung culture.

28 UEFA Cup: Blackburn, Newcastle, Rangers and Tottenham all safely through, but West Ham crash in Palermo and out go Derry and Hearts, too. FA dismiss Ken Bates case against Chelsea. Barca to lose Eto'o with long term injury. Liverpool stadium moves forward, Watford to expand Vicarage Road. Job for life at Arsenal offered to Wenger.
29 Boost for Colchester beating Ipswich. Silvestre out with injury. Police not to charge Thatcher. Dean Wilkins confirmed as Brighton boss. Raymond Domenech extends France contract to 2010.
30 Villa frustrate Chelsea at the Bridge; Van Persie screamer lifts Arsenal at Charlton; Jagielka breaks Sheff Utd duck against Boro; tinkerman Benitez sees Liverpool go down at Bolton with Speed marking 750th club game from free-kick wrongly awarded against Reina; Man City grab late draw at Everton but Barton in bother. Championship: Cardiff hit ten-man Wolves 4-0 and go five points clear, Soton shocked by QPR. Lge 1: Millwall first away win, Crewe strike five against Carlisle. Lge 2: Walsall take four off Mansfield, improving Accrington beat Wycombe. SPL: Motherwell hit Killie for five. SL; topsy-turvy Gretna lose to Airdrie. Peterhead crash eight past Forfar. Stenhousemuir get five at Albion. Conf: Oxford still on course eight points ahead.

OCTOBER 2006

Manchester United in driving seat ... England wilt in Croatia ... Chelsea fury over goalkeeper injury ... Wembley to reopen in 2007 ... Villa still unbeaten ... Scholes, Rooney milestones ... Hammer horror: worst run for years ... Tinkerman Benitez at Liverpool.

1 Man Utd back on top after Solskjaer double over Newcastle; Pompey rage over Zokora dive leads to penalty and defeat at Spurs; Reading victory at West Ham puts pressure on ex-Royal Alan Pardew; Blackburn edge Wigan in Lancs derby. Norwich beaten 4-1 at Carrow Road by Burnley sack Nigel Worthington; Brian Horton axed by Macclesfield. SPL: Big three all win, Hearts getting four against Dundee Utd.
2 Bung boss Lord Stevens still investigating eight clubs. PL: see-saw at Vicarage Road ends with Watford and Fulham sharing six goals. Mark Bowen mentioned for Norwich job. Soton announce £3.3m loss.
3 FA to get tough over corruption. Owen off crutches. Villa sign Chris Sutton to replace injured Moore. Bellamy to captain Wales. British survivors avoid each other in UEFA Cup group stages. Conf: Narrow squeak for Oxford levelling in injury-time against visiting Southport. Shots and Lambs share six goals.
4 Kevin MacDonald to stand in for suspended boss Steve Staunton for Republic in Cyprus. Becks denies retirement story. Ince leaves Swindon. Darlo part with manager David Hodgson.
5 Newcastle chasing Owen compensation. Barthez to retire. Eriksson link with Benfica dismissed. David Dein is new chairman of G14 clubs. Man City Barton charged over "shorts fall", but police to take no action.
6 U21: Baines gives England slender advantage over Germany in play-off. Lge 1: Cheltenham surprise Yeovil. Lge 2: ten-man Darlo ship five to visiting Rochdale. Conf: Oxford five at Forest Green.
7 Euro 2008: Scots on a reel as they turnover France, but England fail to beat Macedonia, the Republic is humiliated in Cyprus – plus Dunne dismissed – as are Wales in Cardiff by Slovakia both by high fives, yet Northern Ireland earn draw in Denmark. Warning for England as Croatia beat Andorra 7-0. Lge 1: Forest chopped up by Scunthorpe four-play, Crewe edge Gillingham 4-3. Lge 2: Swindon held at Accrington. Conf: Daggers strike five against Northwich.
8 Grimsby beat Hereford with Jones double on day of international reflection!
9 Liverpool unhappy over Kuyt injury with Holland. Norwich refused permission to talk to Steve Tilson (Southend), Millwall interested in Peter Jackson (Huddersfield).
10 U-21s: Walcott plays and scores in Germany as England qualify for finals! Barton escapes ban. BBC get PL radio package. Simon Jordan buys Selhurst Park freehold from Ron Noades, Icelandic business interest in West Ham. Conf: Oxford held at Kidderminster.
11 Euro 2008: England's 3-5-2 leaves them at 6s and 7s plus a 2-0 defeat in Croatia with Robinson own goal howler to boot; even Scots lose in Ukraine; Republic manage a draw with Czechs; Wales beat Cyprus and Northern Ireland edge Latvia. U-21s: surprise elimination for France in Israel. Joe Cole comes through reserve friendly ok.
12 Big Mac under pressure, Roo admits to V-sign at fans, Walcott may come into contention, Becks return hint. German U-21s may face racist charge. Leicester's £1.6m profit. Villa's Petrov quits Bulgarian internationals. Kevin Bond is new Bournemouth manager. Tony Mowbray in WBA frame.
13 Norwich appoint Peter Grant, No. 2 at West Ham as manager; Mowbray to move in as a Throstle. Coventry edge Southend at Roots Hall. Port Vale win at Tranmere, Cobblers and Bradford scoreless. SL: Accies win at Livingston.
14 Cech then Cudicini taken to hospital with injuries, Terry finishes in goal as Chelsea win ten-a-side game at Reading; Angel has a devil of a game: misses penalty, concedes og as Villa held by Spurs; Pompey make it six defeats on trot for Hammers; Boro end Everton unbeaten record; Roo looks livelier as Man Utd come back after Wigan lose the lead again; Bellamy saves point for Liverpool against Rovers; no goals for Man City and Sheff Utd; Arsenal march on 3-0 over Watford. Championship: top four all win – Albion hit five at Ipswich as caretaker Nigel Pearson packs his bags; QPR and Norwich share six goals; Saints go down at Leicester; Stoke stun Leeds on Duberry's birthday against his old team. Another Forrester hat-trick for Lincoln. SPL: Rangers slump to Caley home defeat and Nakamura treble as Celtic win 4-1 at Dundee Utd. SL: Gretna share six goals with St Johnstone and Elgin celebrate first points in style – whacking East Stirling 5-0!
15 Diouf double does it for Bolton at Newcastle. Wotton two pens help Plymouth to Sunday best over Derby.
16 Chelsea ref Mike Riley defends action taken over Cech injury and Hunt denies intent. Charlton downed at Fulham leaves Iain Dowie in the dumps.
17 Ch Lge: Arsenal denied Henry equaliser in Moscow for "hands" as CSKA win 1-0; Celtic superior three times against Benfica, Man Utd similarly against FC Copenhagen. Championship: Baggies continue winning ways at Palace; Brum glum as Norwich win; ten-man Leeds lose again, but Cardiff edge the Saints and Preston give Ipswich two goals start and beat them. Paint Trophy: with no extra time five ties

go to penalties. Darlington sack David Hodgson. McClaren to step up scouting missions and fit-again Sir Bobby to resume Republic duties. Bolton hope to enlist 6ft 9in striker Yan Changpeng from Chinese nursery team Wuham.

18 Ch Lge: Drogba strike edges Chelsea home over Barca; Crouch does it for Liverpool in Bordeaux; Schweinsteiger scores then sent off as ten-man Bayern owe it to goalie Kahn in win at Sporting. Colchester stun Sheff Wed 4-0. Dudek sent off in last week's 2-1 reserve derby defeat at Everton (5556) may face further charges.

19 UEFA Cup: away day joy for winners Tottenham, Blackburn and Rangers; even Newcastle win at home against Fenerbahce. Wembley to open next year! Chelsea fail in bid to have Hunt charged over Cech injury. Sheff Wed sack Paul Sturrock five weeks after new three-year deal. Ossie Ardiles axed by Beitar Jerusalem.

20 Planet Hollywood man gets 23 percent of Everton. Hammers interested in taking over Olympic stadium after 2010. Conf: Oxford beat Cambridge. Sky Sports Victory Shield: England U16 draw in Wales. Platini aiming for UEFA post wants to cut Ch Lge entry to three maximum per country. Blackburn's McCarthy cites racism over Wisla tie.

21 The Shevy and Ball show reaps scoring dividends at last for Chelsea over Portsmouth; Wigan four play hits sad Man City; Neil Warnock unhappy over dismissal and Everton penalty in Sheff Utd defeat; Villa keep lone unbeaten record but Fulham hold them; strugglers Charlton and Watford settle for no goals. Championship: as Sam Hammam prepares to hand over to Peter Ridsdale, Cardiff lose at Norwich and Preston's win over Hull reduces their lead to three points; Luton high five against poor Leeds; managerless Sheff Wed edge QPR. Lge 1: Rotherham's seventh win of the season at Bournemouth, but with deduction are level bottom with Leyton Orient who win for first time in 12 attempts. Lge 2: Forrester's third hat-trick of the season helps Imps blast Rochdale 7-1 in biggest win in 24 years; still without a win ten-man Macclesfield manage a point at Bristol R. SPL: Hearts stopped by Killie and Celtic extend lead to eight points. SL: Gretna share six goals with Clyde, St Johnstone hit Q of S for five.

22 Scholes opens the scoring against Liverpool in his 500th game, the eighth to reach the figure for Man Utd, Rooney posts his 100th and Gerrard reaches 350 on milestone day all round; Defoe nibbles Mascherano's arm in bite-size incident during Spurs win over Hammers; Arsenal four play in top gear at Reading; Boro late win over Newcastle; Bolton derby win at Blackburn but only after Jaaskelainen saves two late penalties and surviving late dismissal of Nolan. Championship: West Bromwich win the 150th Black Country derby beating Wolves 3-0 to give new boss Tony Mowbray the perfect day. Swansea move into fifth place in Lge 1 after success over Millwall. SPL: Novo canes St Mirren late on as Rangers close gap behind second place Hearts.

23 Catholic boy Defoe relaxed over incident, but Mascharano outraged by biting. Becks want to heal Man Utd wounds. Man City board unhappy about team. FA receive Cech letter from Chelsea. Paul Ince takes Macclesfield hot seat, Dennis Wise to move into Leeds. Hearts boss Valdas Ivanauskas on sick leave. Coventry edge Colchester. Hibs hit four at Dunfermline.

24 C Cup: Alan Pardew under more pressure as Chesterfield dump the Hammers suffering worst run for 74 years; Notts dispose of the Saints; Southend add to Leeds' misery; Villa need extra time at Leicester; Norwich pay penalty at Port Vale. FA charged over Croatia crowd trouble! South Africa concerns over violent crime ahead of 2010 WC. Dave Tuttle declines Swindon job.

25 C Cup: teenager Lee saves Man Utd (reserves) blushes in extra time at Crewe; Liverpool beat Reading by odd goal in seven; Defoe helps putting the bite on MK Dons with a brace in 5-0 romp; Bent M relieves pressure on Charlton boss in win over Bolton as do two-goal Solano and loanee Rossi for Newcastle over Pompey; Chelsea winning in the rain at Blackburn. England ladies lose 5-1 in Germany whose Birgit Prinz scores her 100th international goal.

26 Eriksson still getting £13,000 a day from the FA could be a manager somewhere by January. Shearer donates £1.64m to various charities from his testimonial year and pleads for return of apprentice scheme. Another crisis at the FA. Iain Dowie takes a break at Charlton. Dennis Wise installed as Leeds manager, plans to turn the clock back to guts and glory days at Elland Road. UEFA ban Wisla's racist Nikola Mijailovic for five matches. Jim Leishman quits as Dunfermline manager.

27 FA agree to change. Romanov threat to axe all Hearts stars. Newcastle announce £12m loss. Last gasp Gray lifts Burnley against PNE.

28 Treble-shooter Rooney ignites Man Utd to four-goal win at Bolton; No Shevy and Drogba injured by half-time but Chelsea 2-0 success at Sheff Utd; Liverpool with 99th starting changes respond with 3-1 win over Villa; Everton unhappy over free-kick award as Van Persie special saves Henry-weary Arsenal a point; Wigan win at Fulham, Charlton get a point at Newcastle, Spurs in similar scoreless affair at Watford; PL top scorer Kanu helps Pompey to win over Reading. Championship: Relief for Wise as Leeds win for first time in six games; Burley unhappy with Saints at Colchester; Norwich let in five at Stoke; super-sub Andrews gets winner for Coventry but fans booed his entry! Brummie joy at win over WBA but controversy over Johnson injury. Lge 1: Robinson trio in Huddersfield lifts Brighton. Boss Ince attracts best Macc gate (2599) but let lead slip; Shrewsbury go 585 scoreless minutes. SPL: Rangers held by Motherwell, Hearts by Dunfermline, Falkirk hit five. SL: five for Ayr, another Elgin win! FA Cup: Conf giant-killing casualties: Gravesend at Chelmsford, Crawley at home to Lewes, Southport to Kettering, St Albans at Yeading and Grays to Bromley and sack boss Frank Gray.

29 Sheri helps to tipple Rovers return for Hammers. SPL: below par Celtic still win and lead by ten points! Dundee Utd sack Craig Brewster. Inter beat AC Milan in derby 4-3 after 3-0 lead. Barca 3-0 win "unimpressive". Thatcher back in Man City favour. Chelsea pay Leeds £5m for youth grab.

30 Dunne goal relieves pressure at Man City as Boro are beaten. Darlington appoint Dave Penney as manager, Craig Levein is in at Dundee United. Micky Adams threatens to quit Coventry and John Hollins sacked by Crawley. Stroke victim Davis improves. JM already winding up Barca ahead of Ch Lge clash.

31 Ch Lge: Chelsea twice level in Barca, Drogba in the dying moments; Benitez stops tinkering first time in 100 games as Liverpool hit Bordeaux direct, but Noel White resigns as director over criticism towards manager. Championship: ten-man Hull swap places with Southend after win there; QPR snatch point in six goal share with Baggies; Leeds in the toils again at PNE and Chopra hews out a couple at Sunderland

for Cardiff; MacLean nips injury-time winner for Sheff Wed over Palace. Paint: Accrington 4-4 with Blackpool, beat them on penalties. Hibs appoint old boy John Collins as manager. Bungs enquiry continues.

NOVEMBER 2006

Danish shock for Manchester United . . . Southend dump them in the Carling Cup . . . Mighty Magyar Puskas dies . . . England toil in Euro group . . . Iceman takes West Ham control . . . Chelsea hold United at Old Trafford.

1 Ch Lge: Not wonderful, wonderful for Man Utd in Copenhagen, Arsenal leave shooting boots in the locker and Celtic ship three to Benfica on no Brit awards night. UEFA to get tough over intimidation of referees in light of Barca–Chelsea game. Barwick rejects anti-foreign stance. Soton relief at win over Wolves, Derby edge Barnsley. Paint: Brighton in the picture with Bristol City and Chesterfield. PL relaxed about poor crowds.

2 UEFA Cup: Teens help Toon in Palermo with Krul, 18, keeping clean sheet; Berbatov Bulgar brace for Spurs; Rangers hit Maccabi early and late; Blackburn take three off Basle – and all four Brits top their groups! Livorno goalkeeper Amelia "heads" equaliser against Partizan!

3 FIFA and FIFPRO the international players union are ganging up together to legislate for at least six home grown players in a team. Prodigal son Xavier likely to sign for Middlesbrough again after two reserve outings. Swansea, Tranmere winners in Lge 1, Darlington in Lge 2 and Burton in the Conf. Boston manager Steve Evans gets one-year suspended sentence for tax fraud.

4 Man Utd see off Pompey as Sir Alex prepares to celebrate his 20 years at Old Trafford; Kuyt double inspires Liverpool; Watford win first PL game 2-0 against Boro; one goal enough for Wigan, Charlton, Fulham and Sheff Utd to record victories. Fulham's Jensen hit by coin. Championship: Colchester's late show shakes Cardiff and Preston's treble closes gap to one point. Lge 1: Forest keep that seven point advantage. Lge 2: Walsall stretch lead to six points beating Torquay. Conf: Oxford down the Shots 2-0 watched bg 8185. SPL: Celtic leave it late to edge Hearts. SL: Stirling five over Alloa.

5 Topsy-turvy Sunday as Spurs end their 32 League game, 17-year Chelsea nightmare as Terry is red-carded and Jose M complains about Poll findings; Harewood hammers late nail in Arsenal coffin as Pardew and Wenger "face" each other; Villa go sixth after 2-0 against Blackburn but Mark Hughes riles over penalties. SPL: Craig Levein has great start for Dundee Utd in win over Rangers. Sub Becks tries but Real slip to Celta defeat. Pietro Rava last surviving 1938 World Cup winner with Italy dies at 90.

6 Ashley Cole enters ref anti-Chelsea debate. Managerial changes: Brian Laws ex-Scunthorpe in at Sheff Wed, Graham Rodger out at Grimsby. Becks wanted by LA Galaxy.

7 C Cup: Southend beach boys leave Man Utd – Ron and Roo, too – all at sea as Eastwood free-kick tides them over; Chesterfield force Charlton to penalty win as do Watford against Newcastle; Easter comes early for Wycombe at Notts. CIS Cup: Falkirk put Celtic out on spot kicks, Killie edge Motherwell 3-2. Swindon appoint Paul Sturrock. JM calls for peace summit with ref supremo.

8 C Cup: Chelsea four-play dumps Villa; Vale push Spurs to overtime; Liverpool at the interval, Arsenal near the end win respectively at Birmingham and Everton where Poll sends off McFadden for "cheat" remark in David Moyes' 200th. CIS Cup: St Johnstone overturn Rangers at Ibrox, Hibs edge Hearts. FA to charge Hammers and Arsenal bosses. US teenager Freddy Adu to train with Man Utd.

9 Roy Keane is on refs side as elsewhere Everton prepare to fine McFadden over Poll. PL not to announce cleared bung clubs. Sissoko out for three months with injury. Becks starts and scores Real cup goal. Alan Buckley back for third time at Grimsby. UEFA fine FA for Zagreb "violence".

10 FA Cup: quiet start with Cheltenham and Scunthorpe goalless. Havant fear £35,000 policing costs at Portsmouth move.

11 Drogba treble in Chelsea four-play over Watford, but Man Utd's Saha keeps them ahead of the pack at Blackburn; Charlton lose 3-2 at Wigan to leave Iain Dowie in more trouble; Sutton goal gives Villa win at Everton as does Maccarone for Boro at home to West Ham; Cole rescues point for Pompey after Fulham lead; Sheff Utd and Bolton share four goals; Man City and Newcastle settle goalless. Championship: Cardiff increase lead after 1-0 over Burnley as Preston draw at Southend and Birmingham make ground after win against Barnsley who fall back to 23rd after Hull and Leeds both win. FA Cup: Carling giant-killers Chesterfield felled by Conf South cellar-dwellers Basingstoke; Rushden take care of Yeovil; first season defeat for Oxford at Wycombe, whose one-time cup hero Essandoh scores for Bishop's Stortford but they lose 5-3 to King's Lynn; Robinson treble as Brighton whack Northwich 8-0; nine-man Maidenhead draw at Stafford. SL: another five for Gretna; East Stirling win away.

12 North London turnaround: Arsenal impressively beat Liverpool, Spurs slump at Reading. FA Cup: MK Dons held at Farsley, Bury at Weymouth.

13 Charlton sack Iain Dowie after 15 games (Curbishley had 15 years). Mike Newell in strife after sexist comments over assistant referee Amy Rayner. FA Cup: Millwall end Havant run; Macclesfield draw with ten-man Walsall. Stand-in U-21 boss Sammy Lee calls for full-time appointment and injuries plague full international team.

14 Koumas brace as Wales beat Liechtenstein 4-0; Aussies draw 1-1 with Ghana – at QPR of course! Republic and Scotland scoreless B game; Hoyte goal enough for England U-21s in Holland, Germans beat N. Ireland 2-1. Assistant Les Reed gets Charlton job. England call up Micah Richards (Man City) for Holland friendly. Chelsea sign veteran Hedman as goalie cover.

15 Euro 2008: Robbie Keane hits three as Republic beat San Marino 5-0 taking him to 29 goals in 70 appearances in Lansdowne Road finale; Croatia's Eduardo da Silva hat-trick and Russian win leaves England third in Group E. Meanwhile Rooney scores for England but only draw in Holland. Egypt beat South Africa at Brentford – naturally! On the carpet Mike Newell keeps Luton job despite outburst over "lino" Amy Rayner on Saturday.

16 Wembley costs and delays almost brought crisis to FA. Hargreaves fee might be too high for Man Utd.

17 Ferenc Puskas, the mighty Magyar of Hungary, dies at 79. FA dismiss Wembley financial concerns. QPR inflict late defeat on Cardiff. Levski fined for Chelsea crowd trouble. Lord Mawhinney feels wrath of Managers Association over remarks. Reading players death threats.

18 Rooney double keeps Man Utd ahead at Sheff Utd, Geremi free-kick and it's enough for Chelsea over West Ham to stay three points behind; late controversial penalty gives Pompey a win v Watford lifting them to third; sub Henry rescues a point for Gunners against Toon; Arteta the Everton winner; Corradi brace in Man City victory; Liverpool held scoreless at Boro; Reading wrap up the points over Charlton. Championship: Preston catch Cardiff on points, but one goal fewer leaves them second; Rasiak double for Saints hits Leeds. Lge 1: Forest held at Rotherham, so Scunthorpe make ground; free-fall Brentford ship four at home to Crewe and manager Leroy Rosenior chucks it in; Swans first win at Vale since 1957. Lge 2: Walsall increase lead to six points as Lincoln lose to Darlington. SPL: Hibees hit six at Motherwell. S Cup: giant-killing: Deveronvale over Montrose, Preston Ath over Stenhousemuir. Conf: Oxford's 18 match unbeaten run ends at Gravesend.

19 Rovers and Spurs draw but unite against ref Dowd; Wigan's 50th PL ends in first goalless effort with Villa. Gudjohnsen double in Barca win; Den Haag fans get came abandoned against Vitesse. Championship: super-sub Haynes doubles it for Ipswich over Norwich. SPL: Novo goal for Rangers piles more agony on Hearts.

20 Crumbs! Icelandic biscuit magnate Eggert Magnusson takes over West Ham and it could cost him £150m. Palace chairman Simon Jordan to sue Charlton. Drug cheats face two-year bans. FA Cup: Hartlepool beat Rochdale on penalties.

21 Ch Lge: Saha has "lucky" penalty kick saved by Boruc, Nakamura strikes and Celtic put query over Man Utd qualification; Arsenal go one down again but fight back to dismiss Hamburg 3-1; Coupet penalty save for Lyon against Real puts both in last 16; AC Milan lose in Athens but go through, too. FIFA to test goal-line technology again in World Club Championship. FA Cup: Weymouth lead Bury but are finally edged out 4-3; Macclesfield surprise Walsall. Tugay and Ghaly have red-card appeals turned down. Barnsley sack manager Andy Ritchie. Torquay to discipline "divers". Doncaster's new ground £32 Keepmoat Stadium 15,000 all-seater opens 1 January and shares Doncaster Belles (ladies), Lakers (rugby league) and athletics club.

22 Ch Lge: Chelsea lose to Werder, have Ballack and Drogba injured, but qualify but Barca have to face the Germans next; Liverpool see off PSV but both go through; Bayern draw and Inter win puts them in the frame, too; Valencia make it in Group D.

23 UEFA Cup: Brits joy as Blackburn and Rangers draw away, Spurs win in Leverkusen and Newcastle edge Celta Vigo and all four top their groups.

24 Sir Alex dismisses Chelsea claim to become world's biggest club. McCarthy–Keane share hand shake after Wolves and Sunderland share points. Euro U-21 draw gives England toughie group with Italy and Czechs.

25 Old boy Anelka hits double for Trotters against Gunners to end his ten-game goal drought; respite for Hammers beating Sheff Utd; one goal enough for Liverpool over Man City – Gerrard's first PL goal in seven months, Reading at Fulham. Villa, Boro plus Charlton, Everton share two goals each. Championship: Cardiff held at Sheff Wed still have same points, goal difference as Preston held by Palace. Birmingham 2-1 winners at Burnley level with both; fiery Essex derby leaves Southend with nine men, winners Colchester ten. Lge 1: Forest keep six lead, Scunthorpe leapfrog Tranmere. Lge 2: Walsall, Swindon both win Lincoln lose; All the fives for Posh – goals, win run and placing. SL: Gretna beat nearest rivals Partick 4-0. Conf: Woking hit Weymouth 4-0. Ronaldinho mid-air overhead stunner for Barca in 4-0 over Villarreal.

26 Crucial draw for Chelsea at Old Trafford; Newcastle stop Pompey, Spurs 3-1 over Wigan. Oddity: both Bristol teams on Sunday best form: Rovers beating Barnet, City drawing at Swansea. SPL: Rangers close the gap; they win, Celtic held at Hibs.

27 Fabio Cannavaro named as European F of Y. Lubos Kubik ex-Czech international named as Torquay manager, as Ian Atkins departs! Bayern may pull out of achieving nothing G14. Conf: Burton go fourth.

28 Webber strike against old mates lifts Sheff Utd at Watford. Championship: Three in five minute Stoke blast ends Cardiff resistance; Iwelumo foursome has Hull reeling at Colchester; Preston held but sneak top spot. UEFA reforms rile PL.

29 UEFA Cup: farce of group system underlined as with most teams still needing one more game – only Group D has a vacancy for qualification, any one from the remaining four. PL: Ballack strikes for Chelsea at Bolton; Arsenal go down at Fulham who record first such Gunners win for 40 years; Man Utd take three off Everton; Man City relief for better performance at Villa; Liverpool find no way round stoic Pompey. Saints go three up then finish just one goal in seven better off than Brummies; Derby edge into fourth place with late strike. Paint boys: Chesterfield, Crewe and both Bristol teams in regional semis. Bellamy cleared of assault. Sports Minister Caborn may not be PL friend.

30 UEFA Cup: Newcastle make a point in Frankfurt and qualify while Toon takeover talks carry on. FA charge Terry over Poll. Shevy not leaving Chelsea. Arsene Wenger unhappy with fixture pile up.

DECEMBER 2006

Return of Larsson ... Brits progess in Europe ... Speed marks PL 500 ... Celtic walking away with title ... Curbishley at West Ham – Pardew at Charlton ... Ronaldo simply outstanding for Manchester United ... Gerrard gets the MBE ... Sir Alex qualifies as OAP.

1 FA Cup: first minnow casualty: King's Lynn to Oldham. Sir Alex coup: Larsson on loan from January. Veron faces jail term for passport fraud.

2 Ronaldo "dive" helps Man Utd win at Boro; Liverpool four-play floors Wigan; Pompey and Villa share four of their own; Gillespie belter lifts Sheff Utd; Arsenal win 152nd north London derby with Spurs, but Poll under fire again; Bolton are Reading – up to sixth – latest victims; Rovers hit two against Fulham as Chris Coleman blames himself. Championship: Luton end worst run since 1899–1900 and beat Preston letting Birmingham, 3-0 winners over Plymouth go top; Saints hit another four. FA Cup: no major upsets but giant-killers Basingstoke hold the Shots at the Rec and Swindon need last minute penalty to beat Morecambe. SPL: Hearts drop to sixth after draw at St Mirren; Boruc wonder save helps Celtic beat the Dons. Killie hit five. Conf: nine-man Stevenage hold Oxford.

3 Patched-up Everton nail the unlucky Hammers. FA Cup: Salisbury deserve another walk in the Forest. Jevons hat-trick gives Bristol C odd goal in seven edge over Gills. SPL: Don't mention Twaddle to Rangers, he scores for Falkirk, leaving Celtic 16 pts ahead!

4 Watford secure point in goalless visit to Man City. The barking Blatter wants summer football. Hull axe manager Phil Parkinson. Phil Brown the coach in charge now. Liverpool latest takeover target – and by Dubai group.

5 Ch Lge: A Shevy goal for Chelsea his 57th in Europe making him second only to Gerd Muller; Barca beat Werder to qualify, too; Bayern and Inter draw but make it; Liverpool lose to Galatasaray, so do PSV at home to Bordeaux but it's academic; Roma beat Valencia to clinch a place with their victims. PL: relief for Charlton in last gasp win over Blackburn; Spurs win ten-a-side game with Boro. Lge 1: Forest chopped down at Bournemouth, other contenders make ground; three London clubs in bottom four! Lge 2: Macclesfield win with ten. Twenty-one players in Italy identified in illegal betting ring. Newcastle answer Sir Alex complaint over loanee Rossi's lack of games.

6 Ch Lge: Man Utd recover to beat Benfica and go through along with Celtic beaten in Copenhagen; point for Arsenal enough for both teams at Porto; Lyon, Real, AC Milan and Lille also qualify. PL: Wigan pile misery on West Ham; manager Steve Coppell blames ref Styles for penalty decision as Reading lose 3-2 at Newcastle. Luton boss Mike Newell charged with improper conduct. Spurs and Boro charged for Tuesday brawl; Jack Warner WC ticket man let off by FIFA with caution.

7 G14 chairman Dein warns FIFA over cutting foreigners. Three Sunderland players in sex film inquiry. Scunthorpe appoint caretaker Nigel Adkins as boss.

8 Spurs chairman Daniel Levy hits out at Caborn gambling probe. Sven on the way back? Wenger ridicules Mourinho plan for Chelsea stiffs in FL. UEFA plan 24 team Euro. England win Sky Sports Victory Shield after beating Scots 2-1 at York.

9 Goal glut: Lennon inspired Spurs hit Addicks for five; four each for Bolton – on Speed's 500th PL game, Liverpool respectively against Hammers and Fulham. Mancunian derby Utd way 3-1 – Rooney's 50th PL goal, too, giving them a 9pt lead over Chelsea who have two in hand; improving Newcastle win at Blackburn, Pompey at home to Everton, helped by Taylor's 45-yard screamer; draws for Boro and Wigan (Kirkland head injury), Watford and Reading. Championship: McSheffrey treble boosts Brummies; Southend end 17 match run without a win to beat Saints; Plymouth's Wotton out for rest of season. Lge 1: Tyson eight-minute trio for Forest; Claridge's unmemorable 1000th as Bournemouth crash to Port Vale; Scunthorpe's Keogh also hits one from 45 yards. Lge 2: more goal flurries: Stockport hit five, Boston, Chester four each and MK Dons win best of seven at Accrington. SPL: Rangers beat Hibs 3-0, Hearts 4-1 over Motherwell on day Steven Pressley leaves Tynecastle. SL: Airdrie off the bottom beating Gretna! S Cup: Cowden give Edinburgh Uni a five goal lesson. Conf: Rushden stun Oxford. Recalled Becks scores, Real lose.

10 PL title over? Chelsea only scrape draw with Arsenal but twice hit the woodwork late on. SPL: Celtic win gives them 16pt lead over Rangers.

11 Alan Pardew axed at West Ham, Curbs the favourite, but sackings incite LMA. Sheff Utd share four goals after Villa goalie Taylor holds them up. Sir Alex takes verbal swipe at JM and Joe Cole is out with foot injury. Man charged with stabbing Wallwork.

12 Alan Curbishley gets £2m West Ham job. FA Cup replays: Salisbury go down at the Forest, Shots avoid Basingstoke banana-skin. Wenger against foreign owners, Henry out with injury.

13 Drogba is Chelsea saviour in minimum win over Toon, Arsenal leave it late at Wigan. UEFA Cup: Blackburn secure top billing after 1-0 against Nancy; no-play Newcastle five points clear in their group. Sir Alex leaves Becks off his World Class list.

14 UEFA Cup: Spurs complete 100% quartet beating Dinamo Bucharest 3-1, Rangers edge Partizan to top their group, too. FA fine Wenger £10,000 for West Ham touchline row.

15 Ch Lge draw: Chelsea at Porto, Arsenal at PSV, Man Utd at Lille, Liverpool at Barca, Celtic at home to AC Milan. UEFA Cup: Spurs to meet Feyenoord, Blackburn face Leverkusen, Newcastle paired with Waregem and Rangers against Hapoel Tel Aviv. Eastwood hits post as Southend draw at Luton. After defeat at Hartlepool, Rochdale manager Steve Parkin leaves the club with assistant Tony Ford, Keith Hill is caretaker. Dong Fangzhou, 21, China cap gets work permit at Man Utd after three years trying.

16 Wenger unhappy again as Pompey hold on for a draw at the Emirates; spot on Speed merchant delivers another Bolton win; Martins double brings another Toon success; Liverpool latest to put skids under Charlton; Blackburn recover to win at Reading despite McCarthy having three goals disallowed; ref Walton changes mind over penalty but Wigan still lose to Sheff Utd; Birmingham "lucky" 3-0 winners at Sheff Wed; Derby, Preston and the Saints all win, too, but Cardiff crash 4-1 at Hull; Colchester climb to sixth; WBA take five off Coventry; ten-man Leeds in the toils again. Lge 1: another Forest slump as Orient surprise; Swansea hit Carlisle for five. Lge 2: Macc and Stanley share six goals. Steve Parkin leaves Rochdale. SPL: Hearts lose at home again to Dons. SL: Queens Park have three sent off and lose 3-1 to East Stirling. Trophy: FA Cup surprises Salisbury take out Woking, while other Conf casualties include Aldershot and Stafford, while Cambridge are hit for six by Histon and Oxford are held at Lewes.

17 Curbishley fashions a Hammer blow against Man Utd and Chelsea close the gap to two points after Drogba rifles another winner at Everton; Man City edged out by Spurs. SPL: Auld Firm draw enough for Celtic at Rangers. Brazil's Internacional beat Barca in the WCC final in Yokohama. Italy's Inter set club record ninth win on the trot beating Messina 2-0. Bury may be booted out of the FA Cup for fielding an ineligible player.

18 Fulham looking to pass 11-plus stage after beating Boro 2-1. Wenger facing another FA charge, but intends to dispute it. Cannavaro is World Player of the Year, surprise, surprise. Wigan's McCulloch charged with violent conduct. Gary Charles ex-Forest gets 12-month jail sentence for threatening behaviour. Everton unhappy over Mourinho view of Johnson "diving". Becks interests Bolton.

19 C Cup: Easter gives Wycombe early Christmas present at Charlton. Germany to play England at Wembley in August. Liverpool–Arsenal fogged off. Orient win again – at Northampton. Peter Shirtliff sacked at Mansfield. Everton to sign Anderson da Silva, a Brazilian from Nacional (Uruguay). Wigan's McCulloch has a three match ban, Leeds fined £2000 for six loan players in one game.

20 C Cup: Drogba, naturally, is Chelsea scorer at Newcastle, Southend push Spurs all the way to extra time before Defoe strikes. Agents likely to bear brunt of bung result. John Gorman resigns as Northampton manager. Bury appeal against FA Cup ousting. *Daily Telegraph* reports PL gates up – 34,164 (33,560 last season) – entirely down to Arsenal's increase!

21 Police conducting own bung enquiry. Owen out for season. Becks and Real at loggerheads. Donny prepare farewell to Belle Vue.

22 Palace lift spirits with win over Sunderland. Crucial win for Scunny at Millwall. More misery for Torquay.

23 On fire Ronaldo's twosome and Scholes screamer equals Man Utd win at Villa, while struggling Chelsea are reliant on Robben to grab late win at Wigan; vintage Arsenal in 6-2 Blackburn burying; Hammers get at point at Fulham; Spurs with Robinson nightmare show in goal well beaten at Newcastle as are Sheff Utd at Portsmouth; Everton (Johnson first goal in 12 games) and Bolton have 2-0 wins at Reading and Man City respectively, Liverpool and Boro achieve similar results at home to Watford and Charlton. However, Steve Coppell unhappy with rookie ref Tanner no penalty decision for Reading and Alan Curbishley cross over Konchesky red card. Championship: Birmingham four play crushes Southend Shrimpers; veteran goalie Crossley heads Sheff Wed equaliser against Saints!; Stoke move to fourth. Lge 1: Donny down the Forest on Belle Vue departure day; Oldham give best gate of the season a comfortable win; Lge 2: Paul Ince delight as Macc beat old club Swindon; sixth successive win for Hartlepool. SPL: Lennon sent off late but Celtic win as do Rangers at Aberdeen; five for Hibs against St Mirren. SL; Forfar, Cowdenbeath five goals in victories.

24 Christmas eve waltz of the entrenadors: Pardew in at Charlton vice Reed.

26 Yet another two-Ronnie strike for Man Utd as Wigan are beaten, but Chelsea held by Reading thanks to bizarre Cole–Essien own goal; north London joy as Arsenal just win at Watford and Spurs (Defoe's 50th, goal, too) edge Villa at home; veteran Sheri for Hammers but Primus pair Pompey take the points; Man City success in rough affair at Sheff Utd; Bolton's Anelka (sixth in last seven) again the winner over Newcastle; Blackburn look to McCarthy – and Friedel – to beat Liverpool; Everton and Boro goalless. Crowds: 334,355. Championship: Baggies do Birmingham a favour beating Preston 4-2, as the Blues beat Rangers 2-1; Colchester impress in 4-1 over Luton; Saints have full house and their ten hold Palace. Lge 1: Forest, Scunthorpe and Oldham keep winning ways, Millwall heap more gloom at Brentford. Lge 2: Macc win again as do the top five. FL gates: 451,135. SPL: Celtic held by Dundee Utd, Hearts win Edinburgh derby but Shiels sent off for Hibs. First five-figure Conf gate 11,065 see Oxford draw again

27 Wrong team hands by "lino" and Fulham get a draw at Charlton. Elland Road sold again. SPL: now Rangers lose to Caley.

28 Terry back op causes Chelsea consternation. Hammers Ashton no nearer comeback. FA dismiss Bury cup appeal. Billy Dearden is new Mansfield boss.

29 Gerrard gets MBE – presumably not for his PL goals this season! Birmingham drop two points to visiting Luton and sub Danns saves them. Pardew's Chinese takeaway – Zheng Zhi, on loan from Shandong Luneng. Pressley joins Celtic from Hearts. Stuart Pearce hails Hammers – their best since the 1960s!

30 Ten-man Reading make Ron inspired Man Utd fight for the points but Chelsea defence caught out by Fulham whose Volz hits the PL's 15,000th goal and the top gap widens to six; north London gloom as Arsenal lose at battling Sheff Utd who have makeshift deputy goalie in Jagielka, Spurs slip at home to Liverpool; Charlton snatch it late against ten Villans; Rovers edge out Boro; early and late goals not enough for Pompey at Bolton; Anichebe double aids Everton over Newcastle; Man City latest to beat the Hammers; monsoon conditions call a halt to Watford v Wigan. Championship: Preston, Derby, Soton, Baggies, Colchester and Stoke take advantage of Birmingham inactivity to notch victories. Lge 1: Scunny clip top spot after beating Bournemouth while Forest are held by Tranmere; Brentford end 22 match hell with welcome win. Lge 2: Walsall suffer as Bristol Rovers equalise in injury time and MK Dons reduce deficit to two points; Macclesfield off the bottom swapping places with victims Torquay. Conf: Daggers slide over Oxford on goal difference by beating Halifax while United are held by Crawley; Shots v Grays lasts nine minutes in the rain. SPL: Dons lose, Celtic, Rangers and Hearts all draw; third hat-trick for Falkirk's Arsenal loanee Stokes, now 14 goals in 16 games. SL: Raith hit five goals.

31 Sir Alex celebrates becoming an OAP at 65 with Man Utd at the front of the queue. Petrov urges Villa to buy to avoid drop.

JANUARY 2007

FA Cup magic returns ... Liverpool crash at Anfield ... Jose Mourinho under fire ... Inter's serie A record ... Arsenal upset Man Utd ... Michel Platini elected.

1 Rookie Edgar salvages point for Toon after Scholes double for Man Utd, now seven clear of Chelsea who play tomorrow; Reading roast the Hammers in 6-0 sensation; Liverpool's second half flurry floors Bolton; Spurs divide spoils at Pompey; tired Sheff Utd lose at Boro; fifth reverse in a row for Wigan as Rovers return with the points; Niemi hurt in Fulham's goalless with Watford; supersub Samaras ensures Man City win over Everton; Championship: Ipswich leave it late to upset Birmingham. while Derby edge out rivals Preston at Deepdale; cellar-dwellers Southend crucial win over Baggies, while Leeds and Hull also win. Barnsley confirm Simon Davey as manager. Lge 1: Nine Foresters hit for five at Oldham, the Huddersfield nine go down at Donny; Byfield hat-trick lifts Millwall. Lge 2: Walsall extend lead as Swindon win at MK Dons; Cooke treble helps Shrewsbury.

2 Chelsea three-in-a row draw at Villa leaves Man Utd with the joy of six point lead; Arsenal four play with Henry on his 250th League outing finishes ten-man Charlton. SPL: Celtic, Rangers, Hearts all win, Aberdeen draw at Hibs. Rangers axe skipper Ferguson. Northampton appoint Stuart Gray as manager. Signings: Alnwick, Sunderland–Spurs £1.3m, Edwards, Luton–Sunderland £1.4m. Bowyer out six weeks with injury.

3 Becks unsure of Real future. West Ham owner Magnusson offers free travel to Villa game. Rochdale give caretaker Keith Hill the manager's job.

4 Rangers sack manager Paul Le Guen – Walter Smith and Ally McCoist come in. Hammers go for Boa Morte as ex-boss Alan Pardew cleared of Arsenal flare-up. Fulham sign Vicenzo Montella on loan from

Roma. Forest players accused of rowdyism. Yanks pull out of Newcastle idea. Phil Brown gets Hull role until season's end.

5 FA Cup: Stoke, Bristol Rovers both win. Lge 1: Yeovil improve their position with Huddersfield win.

6 FA Cup: Swansea lead in the shock stakes with 3-0 win at Sheff Utd, close second are Forest victors over sad Charlton; holders Liverpool taken out by Arsenal at Anfield; Newcastle, Middlesbrough and Fulham to replay; Chelsea's six shot sees off Macc and Bolton get four at Donny. S Cup: Second Division Morton kill off Killie, Caley get six at Stirling, Hearts four at Stranraer, but non-league Deveronvale win nine-goal thriller with Elgin.

7 FA Cup: Larsson scores on Man Utd bow but Solskjaer has to save the day against Villa; Sheff Wed hold Man City, Cardiff draw with Spurs but Blackburn have easy 4-1 win at Everton. S Cup: misery for caretaker Iain Durrant as Rangers sink to defeat at lowly Dunfermline. Sunderland pull off coup by getting Stokes from Arsenal for £2m.

8 FA claim the cup magic still exists with 3rd rd average gate 17,664 highest for 25 years and 97 goals best for 41 years. Plea for bung clubs to be named. Terry admits improper conduct. Quashie, WBA to Hammers for £1.5m, similarly Kilgallon, Leeds to Sheff Utd. Walter Smith quits Scotland job to take Rangers.

9 C Cup: Gunners fire six salvo to double Liverpool score with Julio Baptista getting four – equalling Denis Westcott's tally for Wolves at Anfield in 1946 and Liverpool's heaviest home leaking since Sunderland in 1930. FA Cup: Barnet surprise Colchester, Reading edge Burnley. Paint: Donny do for Darlo in Northern semi, Southern ties off. Souness fails to get Wolves.

10 C Cup: another draw for Chelsea at Wycombe as speculation over JM continues. Paint: Crewe win at Chesterfield. S Cup: Dons and Hibees to replay. Big bucks Becks future lies in LA Galaxy. SFA to sue Smith.

11 Barrow's Cotterill jailed for FA Cup punch. Watford refused £7m for Young. Birmingham to sign Vine, Luton for £2.5m, Stead to Sheff Utd from Sunderland. Denis Smith axed at Wrexham, Brian Carey in as caretaker.

12 Baggies leave it late with two goals overturning Luton.

13 Order restored as top PL four all win, but Arsenal unhappy over Silva red in brush with Rovers Savage; JM professes love for Chelsea, four goals better than Wigan; Man Utd sew it up in first half against Villa; sad Watford slumping against Liverpool; Barton credited with miss of the day for Man City in goalless draw at Bolton; Hammers and Fulham share joy of six; Pompey get draw at Sheff Utd as Harry Redknapp celebrates 1000 games or is it 1039?; Charlton crash to Boro and still miss injured Bent D. Championship: Derby level with inactive Birmingham after 1-0 stoppage time v Sheff Wed; Southend stun Cardiff. Lge 1: nine-man Scunny frustrated by Oldham's injury-time leveller. Lge 2: Torquay can only draw with ten-man Bury; Barnet make it five wins in a row; Easter hero scorer against Chelsea gets winner for Wycombe. Wrexham confirm Brian Carey as boss to end of season. SPL: Rangers under Smith hit five against Dundee Utd. Trophy: Conf leaders Dagenham go out at Redditch, AFC Wimbledon win at Gravesend and another top casualty sees Worcester beat Burton. Inter create Serie A record with 12th straight win 3-1 at Torino, but Barca suffer worst defeat this season 3-1 at Espanyol.

14 Everton scrape a draw with Reading, Newcastle recover to win at Spurs. SPL: Celtic fight back to beat Hearts.

15 Cech will wear protective helmet on return. Alex McLeish likely new Scotland manager, Posh dispense with Keith Alexander, Taylor is caretaker. Eto'o back in training. Young turns down the Hammers offer. Lge 2: Butler double keeps Walsall in the saddle.

16 FA Cup: no replay shocks, Boro top scorers in 4-2 win over Hull. Lge 1: Scunny draw at Cheltenham. S Cup: Dundee Utd beat St Mirren, Q of S need penalties to oust Dundee. Injured players may be treated on the pitch! Claridge joins club No. 20 – Worthing.

17 FA Cup: shocks aplenty: ten-man Newcastle's defence collapses as Birmingham score five, Fulham win odd goal in seven win over Leicester and Spurs four play sinks Cardiff. Micky Adams sacked at Coventry.

18 JM and Chelsea, the intrigue deepens. PL TV windfall nets £2.7m. Young likely to go to Villa.

19 Man Utd to go for Hargreaves, Newcastle takeover dies away. Feyenoord awaiting axe from UEFA Cup because of rioting in Nancy match, Spurs watch with interest. FL to ban smoking next season at grounds.

20 Wheels finally come off for Chelsea, beaten at Liverpool; Gillespie 10-second equalling record PL red as Sheff Utd lose brawl at Reading; Addicks respite in win at Pompey; Boro whack five past Bolton as Diouf dismissed; Pedersen inspired Rovers hit Man City for three; Newcastle recover to draw with Hammers though ref Rennie gaffes over Toon offside goal; Fulham and Spurs also draw; Villa 2-0 over a Watford on verge of selling £9.65m Young to them!. Championship: Derby top as Birmingham game at Leicester called off for ground safety reasons after storm; Sunderland win 4-2 at injury-hit Sheff Wed, but Roy Keane unhappy!; new players fail to lift Leeds, though Cardiff conversely benefit at Wolves; Saints helped by ref decisions at QPR. Lge 1: Forest drop to third despite point at Swansea; prodigal son Harris sparks Millwall foursome; Brighton win ends six reverses. Lge 2: Macc make it seven wins in nine; Barnet nine lose at MK Dons; Torquay club record 19 without a win; new Posh boss Darren Ferguson watches them crash. SPL: big Jan – Vennegoor of Hesselink hat-trick in Celtic five. SL: Peterhead, Queen's five, Albion six. Conf: Daggers, Oxford both held.

21 Not all over yet as Henry stoppage time header gives Arsenal the edge over Man Utd; Arteta brace for Everton leaves Wigan teetering on the relegation zone. SPL: Rangers close gap (!) on Celtic to only 17 pts after 1-0 at Dunfermline.

22 Odds favour Man Utd in title race; only four PL titles gone against leaders after 24 matches. Villa get John Carew in Lyon swap with Baros.

23 C Cup: Shevy lives! two goals in Chelsea's four over Wycombe. Watford rare win as Rovers Savage suffers broken leg as Neill moves to West Ham. FA Cup: own goal luck puts Luton through, Rangers out. Stoke go sixth after win at Burnley. Swansea sixth, too, after beating Gills. Bristol C win Southern Paint semi. Conf: slumping Oxford lose at Woking, Daggers go six points clear.

24 C Cup: Arsenal give Spurs two goals starts then draw on atonement for one own goal as Baptista equalises. Davies, Everton to Fulham. England to play Andorra in Barcelona. Southend green light for

Fossetts Way ground. Derby boss Billy Davies charged with verbal abuse, Sheff Utd and Reading for not controlling players.

25 Spurs get a bye in the UEFA Cup as Feyenoord booted out. Blatter barks out support for Platini in UEFA controversy. Drogba reveals JM–Roman problem. Emre refutes FA racist slant. Stuart Pearce U-21 candidate as Peter Taylor steps down. Torquay doggedly raid vets ranks for recruits.

26 Platini gets UEFA job by four votes. Thorpe trio revives Torquay in first win for four months.

27 FA Cup: no earth-shattering shocks, but Watford's bicycle-kicking McNamee helps the wheels fall off for West Ham; Bristol City fight back against Boro earns draw from Murray 25 yard volley; Reading win at Birmingham, easing up; Man Utd have two disallowed and sub Rooney double helping with a chip thrown in against Pompey; Preston steal from the Palace; Bristol Rovers boss Paul Trollope unhappy with ref D'Urso over disallowed goal and sending-off in Derby defeat; Plymouth's Chelsea loanee Sinclair sparks win at Barnet; Blackpool earn Norwich draw; Montella – the Little Aeroplane – leaves Stoke grounded for Fulham; one Lee pen enough for Ipswich over Swansea; Blackburn foursome at Luton; Southend not disgraced in Spurs defeat. Championship loner sees Chopra treble downing Leicester. Scunny take six point lead in Lge 1 after 3-0 v Millwall. Lge 2: Rochdale hit five, Walsall held by Boston. SPL: Rangers held by Hearts. Conf: Benson hat-trick keeps Daggers on course. Ron Atkinson sees Kettering win with 2300 watching.

28 FA Cup: Shevy still lives – and scores as Chelsea hit Forest for three; Arsenal force a replay with Bolton; Saints lead then lose to Man City; Albion bag the Black Country derby with Wolves. Lge 1: Oldham win at Northampton puts them three points behind Scunthorpe. SPL: Vennegoor of Hesselink scores Celtic winner and gets a red for celebrating. Inter now unbeaten in 14.

29 Newcastle line up Yank cap Oguchi Onyewu from Standard. McLeish as Scotland boss. Hammers Ashton still out injured. Conf: Oxford lose home record to Rushden.

30 Liverpool – with Yanks likely to outbid Dubai buyers after all – win at West Ham; Sheff Utd take points off Fulham; Reading edge eight-in-a-row sufferers Wigan and Pompey and Boro share no goals. Championship: battling Southend stun Brummies on their patch; nine-man Wolves win at Norwich; Barnsley plus new cellar dwellers Leeds get danger zone points; Colchester sell Halford to Reading for £2.5m but beat Preston. Lge 2: Gritton (Mansfield) hits his old loan side Torquay for three goals. Paint: Crewe and Donny share six goals in first Northern final; Bristol Rovers win Southern semi at Shrewsbury. CIS Cup: Naismith hat-trick puts Killie in final after Falkirk win.

31 C Cup: Arsenal go the extra time to defeat Spurs. PL: Man Utd four play too much for Watford; another win and clean sheet for Chelsea; Newcastle go 9th after downing Villa; Charlton crucial point at Bolton. Championship: Jones double lifts Soton over Sheff Wed; Kamara brace does same for WBA against Plymouth. Window closes on shopping with Upson Birmingham to West Ham £6m, Watford getting four: Williams (Leicester), Rinaldi a Brazilian, Cedric Avinel (Creteil) and Johan Cavalli (Istres) and Michael Ball bouncing back from PSV to Man City.

FEBRUARY 2007

Liverpool go Yank . . . Northern Ireland's 200th international . . . Spanish lesson for England . . . Italian ban on matches . . . Platini wants five referees . . . Becks for the USA.

1 Dual role for Pearce likely to continue in short term. A Yank at Liverpool? Ashley Cole ligament damage confirmed and Sonko out for similar reasons at Reading. Leicester chairman Andrew Taylor resigns.

2 Italian football suspended after policeman killed at Catania v Palermo match. Spurs King out for two months with injury. Liverpool expect Thomas Hicks to takeover in £170m deal. Cardiff consolidate play-off zone place after Barnsley victory.

3 Chelsea, a game more played, go three points behind idle Man Utd after Lamps goal in off-colour win at Charlton; Liverpool frustrated in Merseyside derby as Rafael Benitez hits out at Everton; double Lita for Reading at Man City; Boro controversial penalty and Senderos red card in draw with Gunners; welcome win for Wigan courtesy of wonder strike from McCulloch over Pompey; Fulham edge out poor Toon; Pedersen brace – one a stunner – for Blackburn finishes Sheff Utd; Carew goal nails Hammers who lose injured Upson after half-an-hour; Bolton put Watford in more strife. Championship: Derby mug Saints at St Mary's; Peter Taylor relief as Palace continue eight game unbeaten run; Rangers first win since 1 Jan; Nugent brace for Preston. Lge 1: Hall's late strike puts Oldham top; Brentford surprise Blackpool. Lge 2: Batista boots ball into crowd for his red card but Wycombe still beat Wrexham; five-in-a-row Stockport wins; Monkhouse the Hartlepool talisman 12 games unbeaten. Grimsby's joy of six at Boston; S Cup: plucky Deveronvale are Jagged by Thistle; Saints stun the Bairns; Dunfermline surprise Hearts. Conf: another Oxford draw. Trophy: Salisbury march on at Kettering; holders Grays beat Yeading.

4 Spurs no match for four-play Man Utd, but Rooney is injured. S Cup: Celtic 4-1 at Livi. Caborn salary-cap idea unlikely to be welcomed.

5 England have injury concerns before Spanish game. Stuart Pearce wants long-term U-21 role. Sharp move puts Scunny ahead against Bristol C. John McBeth gets FIFA vice-president job ahead of Geoff Thompson. Torquay to appoint Colin Lee as boss again.

6 Northern Ireland's 200th international at Windsor Park ends goalless with Wales. Portugal beat Brazil at the Emirates! U-21: Spain hold England, Wales four against Northern Ireland; Scots lose to Germany. Goalie Foster to get England debut.

7 England, lacking several certs, given all-round Spanish lesson in 1-0 defeat; Republic escape red faces with last gasp San Marino victory; Ballack injured playing for Germany. Pearce and Man City hit another snag. Italy may resume – but without crowds. Marlon King gets two-year Jamaica international ban over last summer's tour. Colin Lee is Torquay D of F, replacing Lubos Kubik. AFC Wimbledon deducted 18 pts for unregistered player. QPR XI v China Olympic team abandoned after brawl. West Ham unlikely to get Olympic Stadium. Spain's Real Madrid and Barcelona world's biggest earners.

8 Big Mac defends his England stance. Torquay appoint Keith Curle as head coach. Terry Butcher sacked by Sydney.

9 Texas takeover man Tom Hicks £100m Liverpool owner eyes improving new ground. Becks back in Real favour. Southend's best – high five over QPR. David Taylor is new UEFA general-secretary. Partial return to normality in Italy this weekend.

10 Chelsea relieve London gloom with Drogba double against Boro as Hammers lose crucially to fellow-strugglers Watford, Charlton go down at Man Utd and Spurs are edged out at Sheff Utd; Newcastle clip Liverpool; Kanu late delivery for Pompey; Sidwell double for Reading as Villa lose out; Johnson celebrates 26th birthday with Everton winner. Championship: Derby held by Hull; Albion by the Saints, Preston lose to Wolves but Sunderland move closer to play-off zone; welcome win for Leeds. Lge 1: With Scunny game frozen off at Crewe, Oldham take opportunity of going top on goal difference; vet Anderton hits three for Bournemouth. Lge 2: Hartlepool win table-topper with Walsall to cut Saddlers lead to three points. Conf: Daggers lose at home, but Oxford still fail to win.

11 Wigan edged out at Arsenal unhappy with ref Phil Dowd; Bolton similarly clip Fulham 2-1. Birmingham's crucial 1-0 win over Stoke pushes them second. Italy resumes with some closed door matches. Riots in eastern Germany at a cup game. Becks on form for Real as 800 tryout for LA Galaxy. SPL; Boyd hat-trick sparks Rangers at Killie.

12 Managers want end to international friendlies. Colin Todd sacked by Bradford, skipper Wetherall is caretaker. Paint: Doncaster give Crewe two goals start and beat them in Northern finale.

13 FA Cup: Boro need shoot-out to overcome Bristol C, Norwich require extra time to dispose of Blackpool. Luton manager Mike Newell fined £6500 for outburst against Amy Rayner. Albion puncture Colchester home run. Brighton rattled the Orient four times. Owen may return in April.

14 UEFA Cup: Blackburn claw a late goal back at Leverkusen but lose 3-2; Rangers lose in Tel Aviv. FA Cup: Arsenal triumph in extra time at Bolton. Big Mac sends England players DVD "nasty" of their Spanish defeat. Platini favours five referees for matches!

15 UEFA Cup: Newcastle take encouraging 3-1 lead away to Waregem. Vladimir Romanov the Hearts owner in hot water over alleged Auld Firm bribe accusation. Gary Neville promotes PFA agents idea. England fans boycotting matches in Tel Aviv and Barca. Kenny Jackett off at Swansea by mutual agreement.

16 Becks back in Real favour. Walsall beaten at home by Lincoln.

17 FA Cup: Chelsea see off Norwich four times, but Arsenal frustrated by Blackburn and Man Utd by Reading have to replay; Baggies, too, must travel to Boro after 2-2, but Plymouth beat Derby and late on Watford account for Ipswich. Championship: Sunderland's season best four over Southend; Saints Surman lets treble do the talking after Barnsley shocks; caretaker Heath at Coventry about to depart for Iain Dowie in wake of Leicester defeat. Lge 1: reeling Forest drop to fourth after Brighton win; Oldham surprised by Millwall. Lge 2: Wycombe hit four at Bury. SPL: Celtic maximum points at Aberdeen. SL: Clyde, Gretna, St Johnstone – all it four. Conf: Oxford misery ends at last, but Daggers still lead.

18 FA Cup: Keane and Berbatov Spurs doubles as Fulham double up with defeat; Man City recover to beat Preston. SPL: Rangers still 19 behind Celtic after unconvincing 2-1 against Falkirk.

19 Chelsea "happy" with £80m loss. FA insist on keeping cup replays. Coventry appoint Iain Dowie as manager.

20 Ch Lge: Fans crush at Lens as quick-thinking Giggs puts Man Utd ahead at Lille; Milan hold Celtic at Parkhead; PSV edge out Arsenal; Becks in form influences Real's threesome reel in 3-2 against Bayern. Rick Parry in the chips before Liverpool takeover deal. Championship: Brummies scrape a draw against Sunderland, but Baggies clip Cardiff and go a point behind Derby; Saints lose at Coventry as Iain Dowie has winning start. Lge 1: Scunny open six point lead at top. Lge 2: late Pools produce dividend as they overhaul Walsall beaten at Stockport. Conf: Daggers take ten point lead after 4-1 at Kidderminster. FA ignore legal row and insist Wembley on course.

21 Ch Lge: Late striking Liverpool lower Barca colours; Terry injury mars Chelsea draw in Porto with Shevy the scorer; Valencia snatch draw at Inter as do Lyon in goalless at Roma. PL: Spurs Jenas seals win at unhappy Everton; ref Styles upsets Wigan as Hall is dismissed in Watford draw. Championship: Derby stunned by Stoke but stay top. Paint: Bristol derby ends goalless at Ashton Gate. Born again Becks may get England recall. Mendham, ex-Norwich jailed for stabbing girlfriend.

22 UEFA Cup: Newcastle, Rangers safely through but goalless Blackburn lose out; AZ preserve 30 year unbeaten Euro home record after going two down to Fenerbahce; Spain have four still in: Sevilla, Celta, Osasuna and Espanyol! Had Sir Alex quit Man Utd in 2002 Eriksson would have been boss!

23 UEFA uphold Man Utd result over Lille. Cardiff hit pan Preston four times. Swansea offer Roberto Martinez the Chester midfield player the manager's job!

24 Man Utd win again at Fulham courtesy of Ronaldo, but Cottagers denied penalty; four goal Charlton dump the Hammers; Sheff Utd unhappy about Gerrard "dive" and go on to lose four goals to Liverpool who have Crouch with a facial injury; Watford in the toils again facing Everton; Reading's nine unbeaten run goes at Boro. Championship: Saints 54 second "Saga" strike enough to down Ipswich; Black Cats late but still beat Derby; Wolves fourth win in a row; Southend hit by crucial last gasp Owls penalty; Hull vet Windass ko's Brummies. Lge 1: Glennon saves three spot kicks, one retaken, but Huddersfield still lose to Crewe; Oldham lose third in a week; loanee Jarvis again the Orient saviour. Swansea appoint Roberto Martinez, Chester midfield player as manager. Lge 2: Bury 12 without a win as Mackail-Smith scores for Posh on 23rd birthday eve; Darlo ten unbeaten. Conf: Daggers still point to promotion, but boss Graham Westley axed by Rushden despite recovering to draw at Aldershot. Trophy: Salisbury beaten at Stevenage. S Cup: Hibs and Fifers beat off Div 1 opposition. SL: respective leaders Gretna, Morton and Berwick all lose.

25 C Cup final: Terry head injury, two Arsenal one Chelsea sent off in mass brawl, Walcott scores, but so does Drogba – twice. PL: Keane gets two of Spurs four but Poll sends him off for hands; Wigan win puts pressure on bottom trio as Filan saves Toon penalty and Taylor hits cracking free kick; Nonda double sparks Rovers as Pompey slump. S Cup: Celtic leave it so late to tip over unlucky Caley.

26 Arsenal and Chelsea to appeal dismissals and fans seek redress over train delays. Terry likely to return soon. Lille to appeal, QPR face Chinese aftermath. Saints chairman quits. Spurs to appeal over Keane red. PL clubs unhappy over UEFA stance. Barnsley shake Stoke

27 FA Cup: Man Utd three in six minutes then face Reading two-goal comeback; Boro need penalties to back the Baggies off. Championship: Leeds misery continues with goal disallowed and narrow defeat at Birmingham; Norwich late, late win at Luton. Lge 1: Scunny go 11 ahead, Oldham decline continues. Paint: Rovers return ends Bristol City hopes. Wenger to apologise for fracas.

28 FA Cup: McCarthy stuns the Gunners with Rovers winner. S Cup: Saints (Johnstone) go marching in at Motherwell.

MARCH 2007

Giggs on edge of 700th ... Arsene Wenger milestone at Arsenal ... record Youth Cup crowd ... Football League want shoot-out for drawn games! ... England held in Tel Aviv ... Wembley reopens!

1 Terry to have routine brain scan. Assistant referees (ex-linesmen) face managerial wrath now. Giggs on brink of 700th Man Utd outing heads for Sir Bobby record. Wembley for play-offs? Newcastle to back Emre in racism charge. Rotherham sack boss Alan Knill, Mark Robins in as caretaker.

2 Chelsea hold hands up for brawl, Wenger unfazed by FA charge, West Ham in strife over Argies, Sir Alex tells JM to shut up – just another happy PL day! Derby back on form with five over Colchester. Yanks buy into Millwall. UEFA refuse Lille appeal.

3 Man Utd luck continues with O'Shea scoring so late with their only shot at Anfield, but Scholes sent off; Chelsea take lead from Drogba again; Arsenal mix and match team beat Reading; Wigan put Man City under more pressure; Fulham and Villa share two goals as do Sheff Utd and Everton; strugglers Watford and Charlton double it up similarly while Newcastle and Boro go halves on none. Championship: Sunderland significant win at WBA as major partners inactive; Leeds now lose to ten-man Sheff Wed; five wins in a row for Wolves. Lge 1: All smiles at Scunny win at Brentford; Forest revive with 5-1 over Huddersfield; even Rotherham score four. Lge 2: with Walsall held at Darlo, Hartlepool extend lead to five points with 3-2 over Hereford; near the foot Wrexham jump over Boston, beaten at MK Dons. Stockport all-time Football League record 9 wins in a row without conceding a goal. Conf: Daggers maintain ten point lead over Oxford. SL: Gretna bow at home to Queens; Thistle slump carries on. Five for Queens Park.

4 Suicidal Hammers lose two goals in injury time as Spurs win odd goal in seven; McCarthy penalty brace helps Rovers overcome Trotters. Championship: Birmingham back on top after clipping Cardiff. SPL: Rangers win at Hibs but still 19 points behind Celtic.

5 JM blaze about his vulnerability at the Bridge. Becks out with knee injury. Championship: Saints lose ground at Preston. SPL: Hearts win at Motherwell levels points with Aberdeen. Owners promise West Ham clear-out but manager safe. Minor scuffle at Aldershot involving Chelsea and Arsenal reserves is upgraded by the media!

6 Ch Lge: Liverpool hang on despite Barca goal to ko the champions; Ballack hits Chelsea winner against Porto; mass brawl as Valencia beat Inter on away goals; away day success for Roma at Lyon. Lille accuse Man Utd fans. Championship: Derby continue winning ways at Norwich while Ipswich trounce Hull 5-2. Lge 1: Forest slump again to Donny. Conf: as Daggers held, Oxford cut their lead to eight points. Mikel under Norwegian police probe. FA want more home grown. Peter Jackson quits Huddersfield post by mutual consent.

7 Ch Lge: Larsson bows out with a winner over Lille to put Man Utd through, but an Alex double – one at each end in a draw – sends Arsenal crashing out to PSV; extra time heartache for Celtic in Milan; ten second record goal for Makaay shoots Bayern on to victory over Real. Bung findings likely to produce charges for 16 clubs. Foreign buyers target Championship clubs. Lge 1: Bristol C leapfrog to second with Chesterfield win.

8 UEFA Cup: Newcastle at home, Spurs away both take significant leads over AZ and Braga respectively, but Rangers held by Osasuna. Joy of six for England Ladies over Russia. Man Utd to break bank to keep Ronaldo. Mike Bateson back as Torquay chairman.

9 Henry out for the season. Eriksson on way back to PL says Nancy. Terry contract stall has Chelsea worried. Birmingham nudge Derby to grab top spot. Hartlepool frustrated by Lincoln, nine-man Wrexham held in injury time by Bury.

10 FA Cup: debatable Boateng hands Man Utd penalty to earn Boro draw. Championship: Roy Keane delight with win over Barnsley but axes Hysen, Stokes and Fulop for missing bus; Saints throw lead at Stoke; Luton see late penalty saved by Ankergren and Leeds get rare win; first win in 57 years at Ipswich for Southend; vet Windass boosts Hull, too. Lge 1: Bradford nine without a win lose at Huddersfield in caretakers game; Sodje foursome for Port Vale at Rotherham; Scunny equal club unbeaten 15 and draw Forest in front of record Glanford Park. Lge 2: ten-man Posh whack MK Dons 4-0; Torquay revive with 3-0 over Wycombe; Barnet end Stockport run. SPL: Dons leapfrog Hearts for third place. SL; Elgin off the bottom at last, vice East Stirling. Conf: Oxford lose at home to Forest Green. Trophy: Stevenage at Grays, Kidderminster against Northwich take useful leads. Messi hat-trick for Barca in 3-3 draw with Real.

11 FA Cup: Spurs chuck 3-1 lead and Chelsea force replay; more Man City misery as Rovers beat them; Watford in semis, too, after Plymouth victory. Championship: Wolves win black country derby to pinch fourth spot over Albion. Lge 1: Oldham foursome against Donny. SPL: rare success for Rangers at Celtic courtesy of Ehiogu, reducing leeway to 16 points.

12 Surprise, surprise – Chelsea, Man Utd avoid each other in FA Cup semi draw – if they get through replays. Wembley ticket rush ko's FA website. JM escapes abusive language comment to ref Riley. Roy McFarland sacked by Chesterfield. Conf: Burton fourth after beating Forest Green.

13 Championship: tough at the top: Brummies lose at Norwich, Derby held by QPR, Sunderland by Stoke, Wolves slip up at Coventry, Cardiff fight back to share it with the Saints; Preston make ground however beating Ipswich; easier at the bottom as Southend make it 17 without a win for Burnley, Hull win at Luton and Leeds manage a point away to Leicester. Lge 1: Bristol C caught by Bradford. Lge 2: MK Dons hit three against Macc. Conf: another home defeat for Oxford as Daggers go 11 pts ahead of them. SPL: Dons make third place more secure after 2-0 at Motherwell. SL: Ross off the foot 4-1 v Accies. Crowd of 74,343 see Man Utd beat Europe XI 4-3 watched by injured Becks. Police arrest Barton. Reports link JM with Real.

Chelsea's John Terry bravely attacks the ball during the Carling Cup Final against Arsenal at the Millennium Stadium. (Action Images/Michael Regan)

14 UEFA Cup: Berbatov treble edges Spurs into quarter-finals, but Rangers slip out in Pamplona. PL: Lamps on the spot to make it dim for Man City as Chelsea reduce Utd lead to six points; Arsenal celebrate Arsene Wenger's 400th PL game with a Diaby goal at Villa. Championship: crucial 4-2 victory for Barnsley at Plymouth; Palace grab win at Albion with last kick – from Grabban. Record FA Youth Cup crowd 38,187 at the Emirates sees Arsenal take 1-0 lead over Man Utd in semi. Platini repeats threat to European places. David Navarro (Valencia) seven month Euro ban for punching Inter player. FL to discuss scrapping draws in favour of shoot-outs as inmates threaten to take over asylum.

15 UEFA Cup: Newcastle slump out after 2-0 defeat to AZ. Wenger charged with "liar" remark to assistant ref and Walcott out injured for rest of season. Mike Newell sacked at Luton.

16 Goalie Carson only uncapped England party member, Gary Neville with 85 the most experienced. Spurs get holders Sevilla in UEFA Cup draw. Saints lose at home again, this time to Colchester. Swans soar into play-off zone. Roy Keane riled by Republic ignoring two of his players.

17 Unplayable Rooney roasts Trotters as Shevy shines for Drogba-rested Chelsea; dodgy penalty and Tevez evens stops the "winner" on the line as Hammers win; goalie Robinson's 95 yard free-kick goal as Spurs climb to sixth; Man City relief at Boro success; Wigan, Pompey and Wigan, Fulham settle for no goals at all. Championship: Derby follow Howard's way back to top; loanee Evans keeps Black Cats purring; Rangers surprise Leicester; Shrimpers fail to trawl in fellow sufferers Leeds. Lge 1: Scunthorpe club record 16 undefeated in Brighton draw; Academy pupil McGugan passes free-kick test for Forest; ten man Orient throw two goal lead as Oldham make a point; first win in six for Cheltenham. Lge 2: Hartlepool three down grab a point at Stockport for club record 21 games without losing. Darlo themselves make it 13 without defeat. SPL: Boyd hat-trick for Rangers. Conf: Oxford cut Daggers lead to nine points, though the Essex men have a game in hand. Trophy: Stevenage and Kidderminster for final after holders Grays bow out and Vics win is not enough. Varsity match goes to penalty kicks, Cambridge winning after 1-1 draw with Oxford.

18 Opportunist Johnson sticks it for Toffees at Arsenal expense; Chinese take away for Charlton as Zheng Zhi floors Newcastle; Villa and Liverpool finish goalless. SPL: crisis club Celtic lose third in a row to Falkirk as lead shrinks to 13 pts. CIS final: Hibees hammer Killie 5-1.

19 FA Cup: another Shevy special as Chelsea clip Spurs but fan tries to punch lights out of Lamps; Ronaldo penalty sees off Boro as dream final still on. England shovel in Nugent and Barry. Bournemouth takeover. Youth Cup: Liverpool beat Newcastle 3-1 for final spot. Emre cleared of racial slur.

20 PL minnows want share of TV dosh. Big Mac battle cry. Neville and Neville about to topple Charlton and Charlton cap record. Chelsea–Man Utd switch to 9 May. FL dismiss Benitez idea for reserves. SFL to hold emergency talks re-breakaway. Conf: Daggers win over Stevenage puts them 12 pts ahead.

21 England players train at Wembley ahead of crucial Israel game in Tel Aviv. Drogba cleared of involvement in Spurs fan fracas. PM Blair backs AFC Wimbledon pts deduction plea.

22 Zahavi, Sven's agent hits out at the Becks factor which he says cost England dearly in the WC. FA Chase new TV deal. Scots look to Boyd, Irish don't want to croak to Wales at Croke, Northern Ireland worry over yellow (card) peril. UEFA fine Lille and Man Utd, FA fine Paul Jewell. Benitez to stay at Anfield. Doubts raised re-WC and South Africa. Ashton no play for Hammers this season. Sevilla must play Spurs on religious festival. Wembley awaits after £757m spent.

23 Blatter claims football is ill because of brawling players. Unnamed Barnsley players in alleged racist attack. Macc win at Mansfield lifts them two places. Boston takeover hits financial buffer.

24 Euro 2008: England running on empty again in Israel draw leaving Big Mac still hungry for goals; Scots squeak in with late winner over Georgia; Dublin Irish just send Wales packing and Healy hat-trick for Northern Ireland in Liechtenstein. Other PL Euro marksmen: Ronaldo (2) for Portugal, Anelka spares French blushes, Carew penalty fails to save Norway. Historic notes: U21s open Wembley with six goals England v Italy, but Pazzini 29nd second goal of a hat-trick and only 55,700 present; Montenegro beat Hungary 2-1 in first international. In truncated FL programme Gary Holt's first goal in three years helps Forest fire and Rochdale shake Stockport with seven at Edgeley Park.

25 Rumours of bust-up between Big Mac and Rooney. Togo axe Adebayor from national team. Sydney not interested in Hammers vintage Sheri. FL fare: Hartlepool make it 22 unbeaten after Darlo derby win; late Clarke strikes save point for Oldham at Brentford SL; Stranraer clobbered 6-1 at home by Cowden.

26 Big Mac has to go before the FA. Becks first game for LA to be v Chelsea. Reading extend Steve Coppell's contract. AFC Wimbledon penalty reduced to three pts. Conf: Daggers fight back to steal point at Oxford on march to FL.

27 Arsenal, Chelsea fined £100,000 each for fracas. Spurs pitch invader banned for three years. Mystery over Arsenal "sale". Wembley FA Cup final ok. U-21: Republic lose in Holland. U-18: England beat Dutch 4-1. Luton appoint Kevin Blackwell as manager. Pat Terry, Millwall, Charlton etc., dies at 73.

28 Euro 2008: Gerrard twice and new boy Nugent barely save face for England against Andorra as Big Mac's men slip to fourth as Israel hit Estonia for four goals; Healy, the Leeds sub, gets another brace for Northern Ireland to head group; Wales take three off San Marino; another vast Croke Park crowd sees Republic edge out Slovakia. Liverpool urged to ground share with Everton at new HQ!

29 Barwick factor helps ITV and Setanta to get FA Cup over BBC and Sky. Big Mac's High Noon will be in High Summer. Maradona treated for alcoholism.

30 In form Healy snatches crucial Leeds win at the death. Hartlepool continue run. Man Utd top world's most valuable teams, ten Pl clubs in leading 25, but Utd no longer largest annual revenue outfit. Wembley to host FL play-off finals. Claims that Lineker–Hansen alleged anti-England campaign influenced TV deal.

31 Man Utd leave it late before destroying Blackburn, but Vidic injury mars the occasion, Chelsea even later grabbing Watford win; Hammers, Addicks crucial successes; Oh! calamity, Fulham just stop Pompey's James creating record number of PL clean sheets, 141 held by Seaman; born-again Crouch hat-trick floors Gunners at Anfield; Bolton put Sheff Utd towards danger zone; Man City get another minimum win. Championship: Saints alive! hit Wolves for six at Molineux, their worst home defeat for 39 years; veteran Windass on eve of 38th birthday has three in Hull win over Southend; Burnley draw but it's 19 without a win; away day wins for Derby, Sunderland keep them in front. Lge 1: while Forest and Bristol City share two goals, Scunny move four points clear at the top after beating Bradford. Lge 2: wins for Walsall, Swindon while MK Dons are held. SPL: Celtic draw at Dundee Utd, Rangers at home to Caley. SL: with St Johnstone losing, Gretna go seven pts ahead. Conf: Daggers win at Tamworth leaves them three points away from FL status! Vase semis: Truro on aggregate, Totton on penalties make the final.

APRIL 2007

Liverpool records in Europe ... Man Utd in seventh heaven ... James clean sheet record ... Ronaldo sweeps the board ... death of Alan Ball ... Sam Allardyce leaves Bolton.

1 Keane on the spot for Spurs who leapfrog Everton after Reading win. Championship: DJ Campbell spins Brummies with two in 3-0 success over Coventry to overtake Sunderland. Paint final: Donny win in extra time against Bristol R with 59,024 present at Cardiff's Millennium – an Associate Members record. Lineker still unhappy over TV outcome.

2 Agbonlahor rescues point for Villa against Everton. FA Youth Cup: 114th minute winner edges Man Utd over Arsenal Sir Bobby Charlton springs to Big Mac's defence. Liverpool to get £40m more for players and new ground to be expanded. Man Utd fans warned over Rome "Ultras." JM and Roman in Chelsea freeze zone. Rupert Lowe criticises Saints board. Blatter to go on till 2011. Virgin trains may not go all the way for fans.

3 Ch Lge: Liverpool records as Gerrard hits 15th goal (beating Rush) and Carragher makes 58th appearance (beating Neal) in demolition of PSV; injury time saviour for Bayern away to AC Milan. Championship: Burnley hit Plymouth for four after 19 misery; QPR take out Preston. SL: Stranraer throw three goal lead and lose to Alloa. Becks back in training. Spurs cleared of pitch man. Maradona's health improves.

4 Ch Lge: No Roman holiday for Man Utd: Scholes sent off, crowd trouble and 2-1 down; Chelsea need another dose of Drog to draw with Valencia. Phil Parkinson turns down Huddersfield job at 11th hour. Juande Ramos, Sevilla coach, rumoured to be next Chelsea boss.

5 UEFA Cup: now Spurs fans hit by Spanish police in more riots as Sevilla take 2-1 lead; Benfica claw back two goals after Espanyol get three; Osasuna stun Leverkusen with three of their own; Werder scoreless draw away to AZ. Platini worried over violence. Yank Stan Kroenke joins the buy into PL with stake in Arsenal.

6 Good Friday but not for Fulham at Everton; Charlton get a draw at Man City. Hull lose at home to Norwich, Southend to Colchester and Derby held at Leicester. Sunny for Scunny as they increase lead to seven pts. Darlo draw at Chester. UEFA plan sports "police." Mark Robins appointed Rotherham manager.

7 Crisis club Man Utd as Ferdinand og puts them down at Pompey while Chelsea through action man Ricardo Carvalho snatch another single goal win over Spurs and close the gap to three points; Arsenal foiled by Hammers 16 stop-goalie Green as Zamora scores at the Emirates; Liverpool 2-1 at Reading, Villa similarly at Blackburn and Newcastle at Sheff Utd, but Bolton go 3-1 at Wigan; Middlesbrough make life harder for Watford in 4-1 victory. Championship: Sunderland go 15 without defeat to trap the Wolves; Burnley shake Birmingham, Stoke do the same for WBA and Sheff Wed for Cardiff on away-day wins; Leeds creep out of the relegation zone, too. Lge 1: Harris sinks old mates Forest for Millwall; Tranmere have two sent off in Blackpool defeat. Lge 2: Barnet stop Hartlepool's 23 match unbeaten run.

Conf: Dagenham clinch FL place after beating Shots 2-1. SL: St Johnstone cut Gretna lead to five pts. Morton trounce Forfar 9-1.

8 Rangers win at St Mirren postpones the inevitable Celtic triumph a little longer. Andy Ritchie agrees to take on Huddersfield job. Real – minus Becks – close in on Barca and LA Galaxy in goalless opener against ten man Houston.

9 Watford dismiss Pompey, Man City put Fulham in danger, Arsenal manage a point at Newcastle – the rest also settle for a point apiece – Villa with Wigan, Bolton and Everton, Charlton against Reading, where Addicks boss Alan Pardew praises ref Poll for warning over Song's likely dismissal. Championship: the seemingly doomed fight back! – Southend win at Preston, Barnsley and Burnley at home to Birmingham and Cardiff respectively (with the Tykes and Blues in 20 man brawl); Colchester down Leeds and Wolves take out Hull; Sunderland come back at Southampton to take pole position. Lge 1: Cobblers nail Scunthorpe's first defeat in 20 games, relegation confirmed Rotherham draw at Forest and Bristol City edged out at Gillingham; Brentford demoted after losing at Crewe. Lge 2: Walsall leave it late, so do penalty failing Swindon – both against ten men – and Hartlepool are spot on/ Conf: plenty of four play as Cambridge beat promoted Daggers 4-2, while others with a quartet are Forest Green and Stevenage against each other, Aldershot, Morecambe and Oxford, but St Albans draw at Tamworth is not enough to stave off the drop.

10 Ch Lge: Man Utd on cloud seven as Roma brought down to earth, but there are crowd scuffles; Chelsea snatch injury-time win in Valencia. Fulham sack manager Chris Coleman and assistant Steve Kean; Lawrie Sanchez takes over for rest of season. Scott Fitzgerald replaced as Brentford manager by caretaker Barry Quinn. Owen plays in a Newcastle friendly v Gretna.

11 Ch Lge: Liverpool take one goal off PSV; AC Milan stun Bayern. Brazil to get Wembley game in June. South Africa want to farm out teams in other countries. Lita charged with violent conduct. Luton have agent problems. Leicester sack Rob Kelly and install Nigel Worthington as caretaker. Andy Ritchie gets Huddersfield job.

12 UEFA Cup: Spurs let in two in eight minutes – an og and an ob (old boy, Kanoute) and draw level too late; Espanyol hold Benfica, Werder take out AZ and Osasuna ease against Leverkusen. JM hints at more HQ trouble. Bayern to sell Hargreaves for £17m. FA Cup semis a no-no for many cash-strapped fans.

13 WBA finish with nine men and a loss to Sheff Wed. Ronaldo deal at Man Utd to 2010. World Cup 2014 for Brazil. Steve Bennett to referee FA Cup final. Lita banned for three games.

14 FA Cup semi: the Ronny–Roo show sends Watford packing and sets up Man Utd for final. PL: Hammers suffer three-goal defeat at Sheff Utd; Fabregas first League goal of the season puts Arsenal nearer Ch Lge qualification in scuppering Bolton; Portsmouth edge out Mags; Man City settle for scoreless with Liverpool; new look Fulham old problem defeat at Reading. Championship: Derby boss Billy Davies gets third red card of season as the Rams hit the skids at Ipswich; Black Cats purr late on against QPR; ten man Wolves hold Palace; hot-shot Cureton keeps Colchester going, but Luton suffer ninth loss in ten. Lge 1: Scunny back on track against Huddersfield; Forest recover to hit Brentford. Lge 2: Hartlepool's promotion clinching win at Wycombe makes it eight without a win for the Chairboys; Walsall join the party with late win at Notts; Torquay draw with Posh but lose League status after 80 years. S Cup semi: Celtic 2-1 v St Johnstone, courtesy of Dutchman V of H.

15 FA Cup semi: even Roman is pleased with JM as Chelsea need extra time to beat Blackburn. S Cup semi: Hibs and Fifers to play it again.

16 Fans unhappy about cup prices at Wembley. Ronaldo a cert for PFA award. FA Youth Cup: Man Utd win first leg in Liverpool with 19,518 present.

17 Man Utd put more pressure on Chelsea after beating Sheff Utd, though losers denied penalty; Arsenal climb into third place after axing Man City. Championship: Brummies second with win at Leicester, Burnley can't stop winning. SL: St Johnstone success at Clyde cuts Gretna lead to three points! Rafael Benitez admits turning down Real offer. Arsene Wenger fined £2500 for abusing officials. Villa's Angel is New York bound. Bobby Cram, Colchester 1971 cup hero dies at 68.

18 Chelsea close gap once more taking four off the Hammers; Liverpool back to third after Gerrard double; Watford nearer the drop following loss at Blackburn. Arsenal vice-chairman David Dein removed from board. Euro 2012 goes to Poland–Ukraine as Italy's violence proves costly.

19 Will Wenger want away, too, at Arsenal? Reading and Sheff Utd fined for touchline fracas.

20 Luton lose at Derby and are relegated. Stan Kroenke moves closer to Arsenal bid. Thaw at Chelsea?

21 Man Utd held by penalty-denied Boro; Zamora again the Hammers hero; Jenas rescues point for Spurs in north London derby at Arsenal; Watford get a draw but are relegated; Charlton and Sheff Utd share the points as do Fulham and Blackburn; Reading hit three in last six minutes to floor Bolton after being a goal adrift; Liverpool firm up on third place. Championship: Colchester end Sunderland's 17 game unbeaten run; three points separate seven teams chasing play-off places in it; crucial late defeats for Southend, ten-man Leeds while Hull get a draw and QPR move out of danger zone. Lge 1: away day joy for promoted Scunny and Bristol City also aiming for an automatic ascendancy. Lge 2: high fives for Rochdale, Grimsby; Boston, Wrexham wins put pressure on Accrington and Macclesfield. SPL: Rangers recover to beat Hearts and hold up Celtic. SL; Gretna held and St Johnstone close gap to one point! Berwick promoted as champions in Division Three. Conf: Oxford ensure play-off place watched by 7007.

22 Status quo as Chelsea only draw at Newcastle, claiming a non-awarded penalty; James clean sheet makes it record 142 for Pompey last line. Championship: Birmingham top after derby win at Wolves. SPL: Celtic title with late Nakamura free-kick. Another Ronaldo double – PFA Player and Young Player of the Year.

23 Burnley make it five wins from six as Baggies are downed. Ex-Thai PM covets Man City. SPL: crucial win for St Mirren at Falkirk to ease relegation fears.

24 Ch Lge semi: Man Utd owe it to the Ronny–Roo duo to sneak a 3-2 lead. Wrexham move out of the danger area, but Macc slip back after losing to Bristol Rovers. S Cup replay: Dunfermline's one goal enough to finish Hibs. Conf: Grays and Halifax ease fears. Terry Butcher is new Brentford boss. Alan Ball 1966 WC winner dies at 61.

25 Ch Lge semi: Cole J humps Chelsea over Liverpool, but JM boobs over penalty claim. Roma fined £34,000, Man Utd £14,500 for fans fracas. Pompey aim for 2011 new ground. Arthur Milton, last of dual England soccer-cricketers, dies at 79.

26 UEFA Cup semis: Espanyol hit Werder for three; Osasuna take slender lead over Sevilla. JM has a verbal go at Ronaldo. FA Youth Cup final: Liverpool turn tables on Man Utd and win on penalties. Woodgate to stay at Boro. Chesterfield appoint Lee Richardson as manager.

27 West Ham fined record £5.5m – but no points deduction for Argy signings. Sir Alex hits back at JM. Sunderland go step nearer PL after odd goal in five win over Burnley.

28 Man Utd on the brink of the title after 4-2 at Everton, but Chelsea on the edge of losing it after draw with Bolton; Hammers threaten Wigan after beating them; own goal win for Sheff Utd over Watford, but Charlton crash ominously at Blackburn; Villa ease to Man City win after Barton fluffs penalty; Spurs, Pompey improve positions following respective wins at Boro and home to stars-resting Liverpool. Championship: title-chasing Birmingham end Sheff Wed play-off hopes, Baggies, Wolves and Saints on win bonuses as do Stoke who finish off Colchester; Preston defeat does them no favours; already doomed Luton relegate Southend; Leeds on the verge, too, and pitch invasion is no help. Lge 1: Scunthorpe lose but get the title; Bristol C automatic sweat in losing at Millwall; only Swansea can break into play-offs at Oldham's expense with Forest, Blackpool and Yeovil assured; Cheltenham two down recover to win at Rotherham and relegate both Chesterfield and their victims Bradford. Lge 2: Swindon dip at Bristol R leaves them automatically concerned; Stockport still chasing a play-off with MK Dons safe there, Lincoln, Shrewsbury in the frame with Rovers. Drop spot to be decided by Wrexham v Boston and Macclesfield v Notts. Rochdale ten beat Hartlepool nine. Conf: Exeter (6670) confirm play-off place with Oxford beaten 1-0 at happy York and reliable Morecambe; Altrincham relegated after failing to beat Aldershot. SL: dramatic finale as Gretna's Grady injury-time winner at Ross thwarts St Johnstone and shoots them into the PL, via Motherwell groundshare.

29 Fulham in peril after late collapse at Arsenal; Sam Allardyce quits Bolton. Championship: Palace win over Derby lifts Brummies and Sunderland to promotion. UEFA Women's Cup joy for Arsenal over Sweden's Umea.

30 Reading spoil Owen comeback for Newcastle. Sammy Lee appointed as Bolton boss. Chester axe boss Mark Wright. SPL: Fifers drum up a must-win at St Mirren. WC for South Africa ok, unless . . .

MAY 2007

Man Utd claim title as Chelsea only draw . . . Lawrie Sanchez quits Northern Ireland for Fulham . . . Whistler Poll to blow his last . . . Briggs youngest PL player . . . Top managerial heads roll . . . Liverpool come a cropper in Athens final . . . Becks back for England.

1 Ch Lge semi: Reina is penalty hero after extra time as Liverpool pile more misery on JM. Man City suspend Barton after training ground incident. Speed to carry on playing as Lee assistant. SL Div 2 play-off: Queens Park take two goal lead over Arbroath.

2 Ch Lge semi: AC Milan set up re-match with Liverpool after destroying Man Utd. Dabo may sue Barton for injuries. SL play-offs: Airdrie significantly, Stirling cautiously take first leg advantage, East Fife crucially.

3 UEFA Cup: all-Spanish final looms as Sevilla overturn Osasuna and Espanyol win in Bremen. Wigan lead clubs in revolt against no-points deduction for Hammers. Alan Ball send off is remarkable. Arsene Wenger fined £2500. Paul Ince to take charge of Leicester? Administration threatens Leeds.

4 Ronaldo is FWA Footballer of the Year; Drogba runner-up, Giggs third, Scholes fourth. Leeds deducted ten points for administration and are relegated, rescue package already in place! Conf play-offs: Oxford lead at Exeter, Morecambe draw at York.

5 Man Utd nearly there: Ronaldo spot on, Vassell's saved, Ball escapes despite early delivery from first class stamp on Ron; Tevez double as Hammers overtake Wigan beaten by Boro; Fulham beat disinterested Liverpool; Watford surprise Reading; Blackburn pile misery on Newcastle where Glenn comes to the end of the Roeder with his resignation there; triple scoring wins for Villa, Everton. Lge 1: Bristol City promoted; Swansea miss out after crashing to a 6-3 home defeat by a Morrell foursome inspired Blackpool, giving Oldham last play-off place after win against Chesterfield. Crewe's Dario Gradi bows out in 1296th game – a draw at Forest. Lge 2: Walsall champions despite being held by promoted Swindon; MK Dons forced to settle for play-offs; Bristol Rovers win at promoted Hartlepool enough to secure a berth, too; Lincoln make it five times in the frame as well, but drawing Shrewsbury pip going-for goals high five – best away for 40-odd years – Stockport on goal difference! Wrexham's highest League gate for 25 years (12,374) sees salvation in a 3-1 win over Boston, relegated in administration with ten points deducted. SPL: Rangers confirm Ch Lge place beating Celtic with Boyd's 100th PL goal; St Mirren take another step towards safety with win at Dundee Utd. SL play-offs: Airdrie, Stirling through in Div 1; Queens Park and East Fife in Div 2.

6 Man Utd champions as depleted and ten-man Chelsea can only draw at Arsenal, giving Sir Alex his ninth title. Championship goal-glut day with 44 scored. Sunderland win title with five-star performance at Luton, Preston plagued by off-field woes miss out on play-offs despite depriving promoted Birmingham of the prize; Wolves, Saints each with four play join with seven goal WBA in the frame, too. Leeds take opportunity to go into administration and lose ten points once they see themselves relegated at Derby! Star man Kaka hits a post for Milan with a penalty and they must wait for Ch Lge place.

7 Charlton relegated as Spurs win at The Valley; Fulham safe as a result. Conf play-off: Morecambe in final after 2-1 v York. Women's FA Cup final: Arsenal beat Charlton 4-1 for their fourth trophy of season with record 24,529 at Forest's ground. Ball and Brown (Fulham) face possible bans. Conf: Morecambe beat York for final place. Dunfermline move within a point of St Mirren.

8 Ball sorry for his stamping. Adrian Boothroyd job safe at Watford to 2010. Conf: Exeter overturn Oxford on penalties to reach Wembley.

9 Man Utd reserve judgement on Chelsea in goalless meeting. SL play-offs: Airdrie draw at Stirling, Queens Park take useful lead over East Fife. New Wembley seats colour failing.

Sir Alex Ferguson 18 major trophies in 16 seasons of which 9 were Premier League titles. (Action Images/Michael Regan)

10 Spurs draw with Blackburn good enough for Europe. PL adamant over West Ham decision despite "Gang of Four" opposition, but unhappy over Howard exclusion clause playing v Man Utd. Fulham's Brown three-game ban along with Man City's Ball. Ballack op furore at Chelsea. England beat France in Euro U-17 semi and face Spain.

11 Controversy before the final PL games surrounding West Ham's escape from points deduction. Lawrie Sanchez quits Irish for Fulham job. Bobby Williamson is Chester manager replacing Mark Wright. Refs Graham Poll and Dermot Gallagher to blow whistle on careers. Play-offs: Forest two pens put paid to Yeovil. Black market prices for cup final tickets soar.

12 Championship play-off: Derby do it Howard's way at Soton. Div 2: Bristol Rovers take slender lead over Lincoln. SP: Dunfermline relegated in losing at Caley; Rangers unbeaten run under Walter Smith hits the buffers against Killie. SL play-offs: Stirling surprise Airdrie, Queen's ease over East Fife. Trophy final: Child's play for Stevenage who give Kiddy two goals start and beat them, leaving boss Mark Stimson with three year hat-trick – two with Grays; Wembley gate 53,262. Kai Johansen, Rangers Danish defender, dies at 67.

13 Escape for Wigan as ex-Blade Unsworth puts the knife in downing Sheff Utd; West Ham survive – Tevez of course the winner at Old Trafford; draw experts Chelsea held by Everton, Drogba naturally their saviour. Spurs beat Man City to get into Europe as do Bolton despite a draw with Villa; exit-man Poll denies Pompey a valid goal as they are held by Arsenal; Reading share six goals with Blackburn but miss Europe; Owen injured again as Newcastle draw at Watford; Fowler farewell to Anfield in Liverpool draw with Charlton; wanting away Viduka brace as Boro beat Fulham, whose sub Matthew Briggs at 16 years 65 days is their youngest in the League and also in Premier League history. Championship play-off: Baggies on top at Wolves. Lge 1: away-day specialists Blackpool do it at Oldham. Vase: Truro treble triumph – Vase, League and County Cup – in beating Totton. Spain beat England U-17s 1-0 in Euro final.

14 Managerial shocks: Stuart Pearce axed at Man City, Paul Jewell quits Wigan and is replaced by Chris Hutchings. Play-off: Shrews end Gay Meadow days with MK Dons draw.

15 Sam Allardyce takes charge of Newcastle; Neil Warnock may be leaving Sheff Utd. Blatter to look at Tevez case. Play-off: Saints lose on penalties to Derby – whatever happened to away goals? England U-19s lose to Russia 2-0.

16 UEFA Cup final: Sevilla need penalties to dispose of ten-man Espanyol. Neil Warnock and Sheff Utd part company, but the Blades stick in legal challenge to Tevez affair. Play-off: Albion bag place in final after Phillips goal v Wolves. G14 clubs (actually 18 now) plan increase to 34 – is it the start of the European League breakaway?

17 Wigan chairman David Whelan still intent on nailing PL over Tevez, but Latics ditch penalty hero Unsworth. Play-off: Rovers return from Lincoln with high five smiles. FL announce gates boost: 16.4m

with Championship average 18,221, Lge 1: 7492 and Lge 2: 4131. Claudio Ranieri mentioned for Man City job. England U-19s lose to Holland, but the Ladies beat Iceland.

18 Championship play-off: extra-time Yeovil turn tables on ten-man Forest with five-star display on Poll's last spin. Lge 2: Shrews shrewd enough to beat MK Dons in last at the Hockey Stadium.

19 FA Cup final: Drogba 116th minute goal gives Chelsea the cup, but Man Utd rile over no penalty or Giggs over-the-line goal. Play-off: Blackpool see off Oldham.

20 Conf final: Morecambe in the FL as they give Exeter a goal start and win 2-1. Aberdeen clinch UEFA Cup place after downing Rangers. Man Utd line up Hargreaves signing.

21 Rafa gets transfer fund promise ahead of Ch Lge final, while Steve Morgan one-time Anfield chaser hopes to buy Wolves. Pompey sign Sulley Muntari, £7m from Udinese; Charlton add Varney (Crewe), Iwelumo (Colchester). Bulk of Leeds players agree wage freeze.

22 Bryan Robson is Sheff Utd manager but the club is unhappy about the terms of a "Tevez arbitration." Ex-United favourite Stuart McCall takes the Bradford post. Reading's Sidwell to join Chelsea.

23 Ch Lge final: Acropperlis for Reds: In-zaghi 2 out-Liverpool 1; one deflected goal, one well taken and goodbye Athens. Takeover planned for Newcastle. Free man Distin for Pompey.

24 Big Mac may recall Becks, Owen for the B men. UEFA blame Liverpool fans for ticket and trouble and Rafa wants to ditch and spend. Martin Allen likely to become Leicester boss. Republic blood 11 new caps in New York draw v Ecuador.

25 Owen back as England Bs beat Albania 3-1 and the buzz is that in-form Becks might be back for Brazil game. Eriksson in line for Man City job, Allen confirmed at Leicester. Bale to Spurs, Hreidarsson to Pompey.

26 Becks back in favour. Wales draw with NZ, Republic with Bolivia. Play-off: Bristol Rovers on the Gas pedal overtake Shrews to promotion. S Cup: Celtic leave it late to down Fifers for the double.

27 Play-off: Blackpool power above Yeovil. Boston manager Steve Evans resigns. Arsenal sign goalie Lukasz Fabianski (Legia) and Poom goes to Watford. England semi-pros wrap up title with 3-0 win over Wales, following 5-0 v Republic, 3-0 v Scots.

28 Play-off: Ram raid nets £60m as Derby beat the Baggies and head for the heights. Ferdinand out with injury for England. Gazza has stomach surgery. Platini wants G14 scrapped.

29 FA to appoint independent head man, but row over allegations concerning Scots John McBeth and racism could cost UK its FIFA privileges. Liverpool fans to sue UEFA. Poll early doors hints at FA over Chelsea–Terry incident.

30 English football clubs £2 billion in debt but healthier than ever! Man Utd spend £34m on two Latinos one Brazilian Anderson and a Portuguese Nani. Giggs to retire for Wales. Lee Hughes out of jail signs for Oldham. McBeth off stage as Geoff Thompson gets FIFA role. Scotland beat Austria in Vienna.

31 Blatter re-elected unopposed at FIFA and pours cold water on England WC bid. Ranieri quits Parma and speculation grows over Man City job.

JUNE 2007

Bung inquiry names names ... Becks wins Real medal ... England Under-21s lose marathon shoot-out.

1 Becks free gives Terry and England lead but Brazil snatch late leveller at Wembley. Northern Ireland appoint Nigel Worthington as manager. Ken Bates bid for Leeds going ahead. Chelsea get Peru's Claudio Pizzaro, free from Bayern. Managers association has a go at Poll over his comments on their members.

2 Euro 2008: England's group danger teams all win: Croatia narrowly in Estonia, Israel in Macedonia and Russia easily over Andorra; Germany only hit ten-man San Marino for six; Giggs bows out for Wales in goalless game with Czech Republic in Cardiff; ref abandons Denmark–Sweden when drunken fan hits him following red card and penalty award to the Swedes in the 3-3 match. Twelve killed in stampede after Zambia beat Congo 3-0. Poll verbal swipe at The Special One.

3 UEFA preparing document against Liverpool fans. Sheff Utd chairman confident of reinstatement in Premier League.

4 Impatient Ranieri opts for Juve rather than Man City delay. AC Milan covet Henry. Wigan sign Toon double Bramble and Sibierski. Bates gets confirmation.

5 Big Mac awaits another day of destiny in Estonia. U-21s beat Slovakia 5-0 and also win a penalty shoot-out! Platini admits stadium faults in Ch Lge final, appeasing irate Liverpool fans.

6 D-Day and Becks inspired victory for Group E England in Estonia with Owen scoring a record 23rd competitive goal, but Croatia and Russia 0-0 and Israel win leaving Big Mac's men fourth and two Russian games to go; Scots win in Faroes and go third in Group B; Finland surprise top of Group A; Greece lead Group C; Germans in Group D, Sweden Group F, Romania in Group G as one of three unbeaten teams. Freddy Shepherd sells shares to Mike Ashley but keeps his Newcastle job. Liverpool legend Tommy Smith suffers heart attack.

7 Alan Sugar sacks himself as Spurs shareholder. Franck Ribery, Marseille to Bayern £17m.

8 Becks surely heading for Knighthood, to boost WC 2018 bid. Northern Ireland unhappy over UEFA awarding Sweden game v Denmark. FL to close Leeds ten-point loophole in future. Fatigued Bentley quits U-21 squad.

9 Spanish inquisition: Real trailing draw, Barca winning draw, level on pts with game each to go. Boston dumped in Blue Square Premier, Altrincham reprieved.

10 Real want to keep Becks. Agbonlahor may play for Scotland. Euro U-21s: Dutch beat Israel 1-0, Portugal and Belgium scoreless.

11 England U-21s held by Czechs, Lita fires spot kick wide; Italy shaken by Serbs. Man City takeover in disarray. FIFA part company with secretary Urs Linsi over row. Plymouth capacity cut by 4500 over terracing.

12 Ex-Chelsea Zola (Italian) wants curb on foreigners. Trevor Birch is Derby chief executive. Sheff Utd to appeal to PM over points issue. Warren Bradley, ex-Man Utd, England amateur and full international, dies at 73.

13 Nani stars for Portugal U-21s. Boston in danger of folding.
14 Five bung clubs to be named. Simon Jordan wins Iain Dowie case. Lita fluffs two chances, England U-21s chuck away 2-0 lead in Italian draw. Barton finally signs for Newcastle.
15 Bung verdict: five clubs – Bolton, Chelsea, Middlesbrough, Newcastle, Portsmouth; three managers – Sam Allardyce, Harry Redknapp and Graeme Souness; 17 transfers and 15 agents implicated, but no actual wrongdoing!
16 UEFA U-21s: Belgium and Holland go through after 2-2 draw, Portugal 4-0 winners over Israel do not. PM elect Gordon Brown promises bung action.
17 U-21s suffer racist abuse from Serb fans, Huddlestone sent off but they still win to reach semis. Lord Stevens firm over Quest verdict. Becks gets Real medal in La Liga.
18 Agents reject FA reform proposals. UEFA urged to take action over Serbia. GB team in Olympics a non-runner. Motherwell appoint Mark McGhee as manager. Barnet coach John Harding, 54, dies after heart attack. Eriksson back in Man City frame.
19 Ten-day wait for Sheff Utd decision. Pini Zahavi demands bung apology.
20 Not even Arnhem but a penalty too far for England U-21s, beaten 13-12 in a 32 shoot-out marathon by the Dutch in Heerenveen; Serbs reach final 2-0 v Belgium. Scarborough wound up.
21 Thai Thaksin tempts Sven to £3m Man City job as ex-boss Stuart Pearce covets U-21 role full-time. FIFA pay MasterCard £45m compensation. Boca win Copa Libertadores.
22 Barca bagging Henry for £16m. Iain Dowie facing bill.
23 Holland beat ten-man Serbs 4-1 to win Euro U-21 final. UEFA relax ban on Israel home games. Intertoto starts! Cliftonville held by Dinaburg.
24 Intertoto: Llanelli go down in Lithuania, but Cork pop up with win in Iceland. Derek Dougan ex-Wolves and Irish international dies at 69.
25 Paul Ince gets MK Dons job. Henry watched by 25,000 Barca fans on first visit. UEFA to improve security arrangements.
26 Thai man confident of his bid and Sven involvement. Tax man looketh at Ken Bates deal. Mike Ashley completes takeover on the Tyne.
27 Lampard latest in Barca sights. Jupp Derwall, ex-Germany coach, dies at 80.
28 FA to launch skills scheme for youngsters. Real (Madrid) sack Fabio Capello after title win! Chris Coleman interests Real (Sociedad).
29 In overall record transaction Spurs snap up Darren Bent from Charlton for £16.5m as Derby tweak club transfer record by paying £3.5m for Canary Robert Earnshaw. Graham Roberts gets £32,000 compensation for wrongful dismissal at Clyde. Macclesfield appoint Ian Brightwell as manager, Asa Hartford as assistant.
30 Liverpool labour over Torres signing. Cork lose second leg but go through.

LANDMARKS

Gary Taylor-Fletcher (Huddersfield T) scores the 500,000th League goal since 1888.
Andriy Shevchenko (Chelsea) scores his 57th goal in European games.
Gary Speed (Bolton W) completes his 500th Premier League match.
Teddy Sheringham becomes the oldest Premier League goalscorer at 40 years 268 days.
Internazionale create Serie A record with their 12th straight win.
Moritz Volz (Fulham) scores the Premier League's 15,000th goal.
Thierry Henry makes his 250th League appearance for Arsenal.
Northern Ireland play their 200th international at Windsor Park.
Stockport County create Football League record: 9 wins in succession without conceding a goal.
Roy Makaay scores Champions League record goal in 10.2 seconds for Bayern Munich against Real Madrid.
David James (Portsmouth) completes 143 matches without conceding a goal in the Premier League.
Matthew Briggs (Fulham) becomes the youngest player in the Premier League at 16 years 65 days.
Michael Owen scores against Estonia, his 23rd competitive goal is an England record.
England Under-21s lose 13-12 in a 32 shoot-out against Holland; the most penalties involving an England team.
Record Premier League attendance 76,098 Manchester U v Blackburn R 31 March 2007.

ENGLISH LEAGUE TABLES 2006–07

FA BARCLAYCARD PREMIERSHIP

			Home					Away					Total						
		P	W	D	L	F	A	W	D	L	F	A	W	D	L	F	A	GD	Pts
1	Manchester U	38	15	2	2	46	12	13	3	3	37	15	28	5	5	83	27	56	89
2	Chelsea	38	12	7	0	37	11	12	4	3	27	13	24	11	3	64	24	40	83
3	Liverpool	38	14	4	1	39	7	6	4	9	18	20	20	8	10	57	27	30	68
4	Arsenal	38	12	6	1	43	16	7	5	7	20	19	19	11	8	63	35	28	68
5	Tottenham H	38	12	3	4	34	22	5	6	8	23	32	17	9	12	57	54	3	60
6	Everton	38	11	4	4	33	17	4	9	6	19	19	15	13	10	52	36	16	58
7	Bolton W	38	9	5	5	26	20	7	3	9	21	32	16	8	14	47	52	–5	56
8	Reading	38	11	2	6	29	20	5	5	9	23	27	16	7	15	52	47	5	55
9	Portsmouth	38	11	5	3	28	15	3	7	9	17	27	14	12	12	45	42	3	54
10	Blackburn R	38	9	3	7	31	25	6	4	9	21	29	15	7	16	52	54	–2	52
11	Aston Villa	38	7	8	4	20	14	4	9	6	23	27	11	17	10	43	41	2	50
12	Middlesbrough	38	10	3	6	31	24	2	7	10	13	25	12	10	16	44	49	–5	46
13	Newcastle U	38	7	7	5	23	20	4	3	12	15	27	11	10	17	38	47	–9	43
14	Manchester C	38	5	6	8	10	16	6	3	10	19	28	11	9	18	29	44	–15	42
15	West Ham U	38	8	2	9	24	26	4	3	12	11	33	12	5	21	35	59	–24	41
16	Fulham	38	7	7	5	18	18	1	8	10	20	42	8	15	15	38	60	–22	39
17	Wigan Ath	38	5	4	10	18	30	5	4	10	19	29	10	8	20	37	59	–22	38
18	Sheffield U	38	7	6	6	24	21	3	2	14	8	34	10	8	20	32	55	–23	38
19	Charlton Ath	38	7	5	7	19	20	1	5	13	15	40	8	10	20	34	60	–26	34
20	Watford	38	3	9	7	19	25	2	4	13	10	34	5	13	20	29	59	–30	28

COCA-COLA FOOTBALL LEAGUE CHAMPIONSHIP

			Home					Away					Total						
		P	W	D	L	F	A	W	D	L	F	A	W	D	L	F	A	GD	Pts
1	Sunderland	46	15	4	4	38	18	12	3	8	38	29	27	7	12	76	47	29	88
2	Birmingham C	46	15	5	3	37	18	11	3	9	30	24	26	8	12	67	42	25	86
3	Derby Co	46	13	6	4	33	19	12	3	8	29	27	25	9	12	62	46	16	84
4	WBA	46	14	4	5	51	24	8	6	9	30	31	22	10	14	81	55	26	76
5	Wolverhampton W	46	12	5	6	33	28	10	5	8	26	28	22	10	14	59	56	3	76
6	Southampton	46	13	6	4	36	20	8	6	9	41	33	21	12	13	77	53	24	75
7	Preston NE	46	15	4	4	38	17	7	4	12	26	36	22	8	16	64	53	11	74
8	Stoke C	46	12	8	3	35	16	7	8	8	27	25	19	16	11	62	41	21	73
9	Sheffield W	46	10	6	7	38	36	10	5	8	32	30	20	11	15	70	66	4	71
10	Colchester U	46	15	4	4	46	19	5	5	13	24	37	20	9	17	70	56	14	69
11	Plymouth Arg	46	10	8	5	36	26	7	8	8	27	36	17	16	13	63	62	1	67
12	Crystal Palace	46	12	3	8	33	22	6	8	9	26	29	18	11	17	59	51	8	65
13	Cardiff C	46	11	7	5	33	18	6	6	11	24	35	17	13	16	57	53	4	64
14	Ipswich T	46	13	2	8	40	29	5	6	12	24	30	18	8	20	64	59	5	62
15	Burnley	46	10	6	7	35	23	5	6	12	17	26	15	12	19	52	49	3	57
16	Norwich C	46	10	5	8	29	25	6	4	13	27	46	16	9	21	56	71	–15	57
17	Coventry C	46	11	4	8	30	25	5	4	14	17	37	16	8	22	47	62	–15	56
18	QPR	46	9	6	8	31	29	5	5	13	23	39	14	11	21	54	68	–14	53
19	Leicester C	46	6	8	9	26	31	7	6	10	23	33	13	14	19	49	64	–15	53
20	Barnsley	46	9	4	10	27	29	6	1	16	26	56	15	5	26	53	85	–32	50
21	Hull C	46	8	3	12	33	32	5	7	11	18	35	13	10	23	51	67	–16	49
22	Southend U	46	6	6	11	29	38	4	6	13	18	42	10	12	24	47	80	–33	42
23	Luton T	46	7	5	11	33	40	3	5	15	20	41	10	10	26	53	81	–28	40
24	Leeds U*	46	10	4	9	27	30	3	3	17	19	42	13	7	26	46	72	–26	36

**Deducted 10 points for breach of rule.*

COCA–COLA FOOTBALL LEAGUE DIVISION 1

			Home					Away					Total						
		P	W	D	L	F	A	W	D	L	F	A	W	D	L	F	A	GD	Pts
1	Scunthorpe U	46	15	6	2	40	17	11	7	5	33	18	26	13	7	73	35	38	91
2	Bristol C	46	15	5	3	35	20	10	5	8	28	19	25	10	11	63	39	24	85
3	Blackpool	46	12	6	5	40	25	12	5	6	36	24	24	11	11	76	49	27	83
4	Nottingham F	46	14	5	4	37	17	9	8	6	28	24	23	13	10	65	41	24	82
5	Yeovil T	46	14	3	6	22	12	9	7	7	33	27	23	10	13	55	39	16	79
6	Oldham Ath	46	13	4	6	36	18	8	8	7	33	29	21	12	13	69	47	22	75
7	Swansea C	46	12	6	5	36	20	8	6	9	33	33	20	12	14	69	53	16	72
8	Carlisle U	46	12	5	6	35	24	7	6	10	19	31	19	11	16	54	55	–1	68
9	Tranmere R	46	13	5	5	33	22	5	8	10	25	31	18	13	15	58	53	5	67
10	Millwall	46	11	8	4	33	19	8	1	14	26	43	19	9	18	59	62	–3	66
11	Doncaster R	46	8	10	5	30	23	8	5	10	22	24	16	15	15	52	47	5	63
12	Port Vale	46	12	3	8	35	26	6	3	14	29	39	18	6	22	64	65	–1	60
13	Crewe Alex	46	11	4	8	39	38	6	5	12	27	34	17	9	20	66	72	–6	60
14	Northampton T	46	8	5	10	27	28	7	9	7	21	23	15	14	17	48	51	–3	59
15	Huddersfield T	46	9	8	6	37	33	5	9	9	23	36	14	17	15	60	69	–9	59
16	Gillingham	46	14	2	7	29	24	3	6	14	27	53	17	8	21	56	77	–21	59
17	Cheltenham T	46	8	6	9	25	27	7	3	13	24	34	15	9	22	49	61	–12	54
18	Brighton & HA	46	5	7	11	23	34	9	4	10	26	24	14	11	21	49	58	–9	53
19	Bournemouth	46	10	5	8	28	27	3	8	12	22	37	13	13	20	50	64	–14	52
20	Leyton Orient	46	6	10	7	30	32	6	5	12	31	45	12	15	19	61	77	–16	51
21	Chesterfield	46	9	5	9	29	22	3	6	14	16	31	12	11	23	45	53	–8	47
22	Bradford C	46	5	9	9	27	31	6	5	12	20	34	11	14	21	47	65	–18	47
23	Rotherham U	46	8	4	11	37	39	5	5	13	21	36	13	9	24	58	75	–17	38
24	Brentford	46	5	8	10	24	41	3	5	15	16	38	8	13	25	40	79	–39	37

COCA–COLA FOOTBALL LEAGUE DIVISION 2

			Home					Away					Total						
		P	W	D	L	F	A	W	D	L	F	A	W	D	L	F	A	GD	Pts
1	Walsall	46	16	4	3	39	13	9	10	4	27	21	25	14	7	66	34	32	89
2	Hartlepool U	46	14	5	4	34	17	12	5	6	31	23	26	10	10	65	40	25	88
3	Swindon T	46	15	4	4	34	17	10	6	7	24	21	25	10	11	58	38	20	85
4	Milton Keynes D	46	14	4	5	41	26	11	5	7	35	32	25	9	12	76	58	18	84
5	Lincoln C	46	12	4	7	36	28	9	7	7	34	31	21	11	14	70	59	11	74
6	Bristol R	46	13	5	5	27	14	7	7	9	22	28	20	12	14	49	42	7	72
7	Shrewsbury T	46	11	7	5	38	23	7	10	6	30	23	18	17	11	68	46	22	71
8	Stockport Co	46	14	4	5	41	25	7	4	12	24	29	21	8	17	65	54	11	71
9	Rochdale	46	9	6	8	33	20	9	6	8	37	30	18	12	16	70	50	20	66
10	Peterborough U	46	10	6	7	48	36	8	5	10	22	25	18	11	17	70	61	9	65
11	Darlington	46	10	6	7	28	30	7	8	8	24	26	17	14	15	52	56	–4	65
12	Wycombe W	46	8	11	4	23	14	8	3	12	29	33	16	14	16	52	47	5	62
13	Notts Co	46	8	6	9	29	25	8	8	7	26	28	16	14	16	55	53	2	62
14	Barnet	46	12	5	6	35	30	4	6	13	20	40	16	11	19	55	70	–15	59
15	Grimsby T	46	11	4	8	33	32	6	4	13	24	41	17	8	21	57	73	–16	59
16	Hereford U	46	9	7	7	23	17	5	6	12	22	36	14	13	19	45	53	–8	55
17	Mansfield T	46	10	4	9	38	31	4	8	11	20	32	14	12	20	58	63	–5	54
18	Chester C	46	7	9	7	23	23	6	5	12	17	25	13	14	19	40	48	–8	53
19	Wrexham	46	8	8	7	23	21	5	4	14	20	44	13	12	21	43	65	–22	51
20	Accrington S	46	10	6	7	42	33	3	5	15	28	48	13	11	22	70	81	–11	50
21	Bury	46	4	7	12	22	35	9	4	10	24	26	13	11	22	46	61	–15	50
22	Macclesfield T	46	8	7	8	36	34	4	5	14	19	43	12	12	22	55	77	–22	48
23	Boston U*	46	9	5	9	29	32	3	5	15	22	48	12	10	24	51	80	–29	36
24	Torquay U	46	5	8	10	19	22	2	6	15	17	41	7	14	25	36	63	–27	35

**Deducted 10 points for breach of rule.*

FOOTBALL LEAGUE PLAY-OFFS 2006–07

CHAMPIONSHIP SEMI-FINALS FIRST LEG

Saturday, 12 May 2007

Southampton (1) 1 *(Surman 7)*

Derby Co (1) 2 *(Howard 36, 58 (pen))* 30,602

Southampton: Bialkowski; Ostlund, Bale (Skacel), Viafara, Baird, Pele, Belmadi, Guthrie, Saganowski (Rasiak), Jones (Best), Surman.
Derby Co: Bywater; Mears, McEveley, Oakley, Moore, Leacock, Macken (Teale), Pearson, Howard, Johnson S (Nyatanga), Fagan.

Sunday, 13 May 2007

Wolverhampton W (1) 2 *(Craddock 44, Olofinjana 52)*

WBA (1) 3 *(Phillips 25, 54, Kamara 73)* 27,750

Wolverhampton W: Hennessey; Collins, McNamara (Little), Olofinjana, Breen, Craddock, Kightley, Potter, Keogh, Bothroyd (Ward), McIndoe.
WBA: Kiely; McShane, Robinson, Chaplow (Carter), Sodje, Perry, Koumas, Koren (Gera), Phillips (Ellington), Kamara, Greening.

CHAMPIONSHIP SEMI-FINALS SECOND LEG

Tuesday, 15 May 2007

Derby Co (1) 2 *(Moore 3, Best 66 (og))*

Southampton (1) 3 *(Viafara 4, 54, Rasiak 89)* 31,569

Derby Co: Bywater; Mears, McEveley, Oakley, Moore, Leacock, Macken (Barnes), Pearson, Howard, Johnson S (Jones), Fagan (Currie).
Southampton: Davis; Makin (Belmadi), Cranie, Viafara, Baird, Pele, Skacel, Guthrie (Idiakez), Saganowski (Rasiak), Best, Surman.
aet; Derby Co won 4-3 on penalties.

Wednesday, 16 May 2007

WBA (0) 1 *(Phillips 65)*

Wolverhampton W (0) 0 27,415

WBA: Kiely; McShane, Robinson, Koumas, Sodje, Perry, Gera, Koren, Phillips (Ellington), Kamara (MacDonald), Greening.
Wolverhampton W: Hennessey; Collins, McNamara (Mulgrew), Olofinjana, Breen, Craddock, Kightley (Ward), Potter, Keogh, Bothroyd, McIndoe (Gleeson).

CHAMPIONSHIP FINAL (AT WEMBLEY)

Monday, 28 May 2007

Derby Co (0) 1 *(Pearson 61)*

WBA (0) 0 74,993

Derby Co: Bywater; Mears, McEveley, Oakley, Moore, Leacock, Fagan (Edworthy), Pearson, Howard, Peschisolido (Barnes), Johnson S (Jones).
WBA: Kiely; McShane (Ellington), Robinson, Koumas, Sodje (Clement), Perry, Gera (Carter), Koren, Phillips, Kamara, Greening.
Referee: G. Poll (Hertfordshire).

LEAGUE 1 SEMI-FINALS FIRST LEG

Saturday, 12 May 2007

Yeovil T (0) 0

Nottingham F (1) 2 *(Commons 23 (pen), Perch 90 (pen))* 8935

Yeovil T: Mildenhall; Lindegaard, Jones, Cohen, Guyet, Forbes, Barry, Davies, Gray, Stewart, Morris.
Nottingham F: Smith; Gary Holt, Wright, Curtis, Breckin, Chambers, McGugan (Bennett), Perch, Lester, Dobie (Morgan), Commons (Weir-Daley).

Sunday, 13 May 2007

Oldham Ath (0) 1 *(Liddell 75 (pen))*

Blackpool (0) 2 *(Barker 52, Hoolahan 87)* 12,154

Oldham Ath: Pogliacomi (Blayney); Wellens, Taylor, Eardley, Gregan, Haining, Charlton (Edwards), McDonald, Porter, Warne (Glombard), Liddell.
Blackpool: Rachubka; Evatt, Williams, Forbes, Jackson, Barker, Jorgensen, Southern, Morrell, Parker, Hoolahan.

LEAGUE 1 SEMI-FINALS SECOND LEG

Friday, 18 May 2007

Nottingham F (0) 2 *(Dobie 47, Grant Holt 93)*

Yeovil T (1) 5 *(Davies 22, 109, Wright 82 (og), Stewart 87, Morris 92)* 27,819

Nottingham F: Smith; Gary Holt, Wright, Curtis, Breckin, Chambers, McGugan (Prutton■), Perch, Lester (Morgan), Dobie (Grant Holt), Commons.
Yeovil T: Mildenhall; Lindegaard, Jones, Cohen (Kamudimba Kalala), Guyett, Forbes, Barry, Davies, Gray, Stewart, Morris.
aet.

Adrian Forbes of Blackpool scores a free kick during the League One Play-off final against Yeovil at Wembley. (Getty Images/Julian Finney)

Bristol Rovers' Sammy Igoe runs through to score his side's third goal in the League Two play-off final at Wembley. (Adam Davy/EMPICS Sport/PA Photos)

Saturday, 19 May 2007
Blackpool (1) 3 *(Southern 28, Morrell 75, Parker 90)*
Oldham Ath (0) 1 *(Wolfenden 83)* 9453
Blackpool: Rachubka; Evatt, Williams, Forbes (Gillett), Jackson, Barker, Jorgensen, Southern (Fox), Morrell, Parker, Hoolahan (Burgess).
Oldham Ath: Blayney; Wellens, Taylor, Lomax, Gregan, Haining, Edwards, Rocastle (McDonald), Porter, Warne (Glombard), Liddell (Wolfenden).

LEAGUE 1 FINAL (AT WEMBLEY)

Sunday, 27 May 2007
Yeovil T (0) 0
Blackpool (1) 2 *(Williams 43, Parker 52)* 59,313
Yeovil T: Mildenhall; Lindegaard (Lynch), Gray, Cohen (Kamudimba Kalala), Guyett, Forbes, Barry, Davies, Gray, Stewart, Morris (Knights).
Blackpool: Rachubka; Evatt, Williams, Jorgensen, Jackson, Barker, Forbes (Fox), Southern, Morrell, Parker (Gillett), Hoolahan (Vernon).
Referee: A. D'Urso (Essex).

LEAGUE 2 SEMI-FINALS FIRST LEG

Saturday, 12 May 2007
Bristol R (1) 2 *(Disley 10, Walker 54)*
Lincoln C (1) 1 *(Hughes 31)* 10,654
Bristol R: Phillips; Green, Carruthers, Campbell, Anthony, Elliott, Haldane (Igoe), Disley, Walker R, Lambert (Rigg), Jacobson.
Lincoln C: Marriott; Eaden, Green, Brown, Morgan, Kerr, Frecklington, Beevers, Stallard (Gritton), Forrester (Mendes), Hughes.

Monday, 14 May 2007
Shrewsbury T (0) 0
Milton Keynes D (0) 0 7126
Shrewsbury T: Shearer; Jones L, Tierney, Drummond, Hope, Langmead, Davies, Humphrey (Symes), Fortune-West (Cooke), Asamoah, Ashton.
Milton Keynes D: Bankole; Edds, Lewington, Andrews, O'Hanlon, Diallo, McGovern (Dyer), Blizzard, Hayes, McLeod (Knight), Stirling.

LEAGUE 2 SEMI-FINALS SECOND LEG

Thursday, 17 May 2007
Lincoln C (2) 3 *(Hughes 25, 90, Stallard 43)*
Bristol R (3) 5 *(Campbell 3, Lambert 11, Walker R 36, Igoe 82, Rigg 89)* 7694
Lincoln C: Marriott; Eaden (Mayo), Green (Brown), Beevers, Morgan, Kerr, Frecklington, Amoo, Stallard (Gritton), Forrester, Hughes.
Bristol R: Phillips; Green, Carruthers, Campbell, Anthony, Elliott, Haldane (Lines), Disley, Walker R (Rigg), Lambert, Jacobson (Igoe).

Friday, 18 May 2007
Milton Keynes D (0) 1 *(Andrews 74)*
Shrewsbury T (0) 2 *(Cooke 58, 76)* 8212
Milton Keynes D: Bankole; Edds, Lewington (Knight), Andrews, O'Hanlon, Diallo, Hayes (Dyer), Blizzard (Taylor), Platt, McLeod, Stirling.
Shrewsbury T: Shearer; Hall, Tierney, Drummond, Hope, Langmead, Jones L, Davies, Fortune-West (Cooke), Symes (Burton), Ashton.

LEAGUE 2 FINAL (AT WEMBLEY)

Saturday, 26 May 2007
Bristol R (2) 3 *(Walker R 21, 35, Igoe 90)*
Shrewsbury T (1) 1 *(Drummond 3)* 61,589
Bristol R: Phillips; Green, Carruthers, Campbell, Anthony, Elliott, Igoe, Disley, Walker R, Lambert, Haldane (Rigg).
Shrewsbury T: MacKenzie; Herd (Burton), Tierney■, Drummond, Hope, Langmead, Hall, Cooke (Humphrey), Symes (Fortune-West), Asamoah, Ashton.
Referee: M. Jones (Cheshire).

LEADING GOALSCORERS 2006–07

	League	*Carling Cup*	*FA Cup*	*Other*	*Total*
BARCLAYS PREMIERSHIP					
Players in this competition scoring eleven or more League goals are listed. Other leading scorers classified by total number of goals in all competitions.					
Didier Drogba *(Chelsea)*	20	4	3	6	33
Benny McCarthy *(Blackburn R)*	18	0	3	3	24
Cristiano Ronaldo *(Manchester U)*	17	0	3	3	23
Wayne Rooney *(Manchester U)*	14	0	5	4	23
Mark Viduka *(Middlesbrough)*	14	0	5	0	19
Kevin Doyle *(Reading)*	13	0	0	0	13
Dimitar Berbatov *(Tottenham H)*	12	1	3	7	23
Ayegbeni Yakubu *(Middlesbrough)*	12	0	4	0	16
Dirk Kuyt *(Liverpool)*	12	0	1	1	14
Robbie Keane *(Tottenham H)*	11	1	5	5	22
Frank Lampard *(Chelsea)*	11	3	6	1	21
Obi Martins *(Newcastle U)*	11	0	0	6	17
Robin Van Persie *(Arsenal)*	11	0	0	2	13
Nicolas Anelka *(Bolton W)*	11	1	0	0	12
Andrew Johnson *(Everton)*	11	0	1	0	12
Bobby Zamora *(West Ham U)*	11	0	0	0	11
In order of total goals:					
Peter Crouch *(Liverpool)*	9	1	0	8	18
Andriy Shevchenko *(Chelsea)*	4	3	3	4	14
COCA-COLA CHAMPIONSHIP					
Players in this competition scoring 13 or more League goals are listed.					
Jamie Cureton *(Colchester U)*	23	0	1	0	24
Michael Chopra *(Cardiff C)*	22	0	0	0	22
Diomansy Kamara *(WBA)*	20	0	2	1	23
Robert Earnshaw *(Norwich C)*	19	0	0	0	19
Grzegorz Rasiak *(Southampton)*	18	0	2	1	21
Chris Iwelumo *(Colchester U)*	18	0	0	0	18
Alan Lee *(Ipswich T)*	16	0	1	0	17
Kevin Phillips *(WBA)*	16	0	3	3	22
Steve Howard *(Derby Co)*	16	1	0	2	19
Dave Nugent *(Preston NE)*	15	0	2	0	17
Gary McSheffrey *(Birmingham C)*	14	2	1	0	17
(Includes 1 League goal for Coventry C).					
Kenwyne Jones *(Southampton)*	14	1	1	0	16
Andy Gray *(Burnley)*	14	0	0	0	14
Iain Hume *(Leicester C)*	13	1	0	0	14
Dexter Blackstock *(QPR)*	13	0	1	0	14
Barry Hayles *(Plymouth Arg)*	13	0	1	0	14
David Connolly *(Sunderland)*	13	0	0	0	13
COCA-COLA LEAGUE 1					
Billy Sharp *(Scunthorpe U)*	30	1	1	0	32
Leon Constantine *(Port Vale)*	22	2	0	2	26
Chris Porter *(Oldham Ath)*	21	0	1	0	22
Lee Trundle *(Swansea C)*	19	0	1	0	20
Luke Varney *(Crewe Alex)*	17	1	0	7	25
Chris Greenacre *(Tranmere R)*	17	0	2	0	19
Andy Morrell *(Blackpool)*	16	0	3	1	20
Nicky Maynard *(Crewe Alex)*	16	2	0	1	19
Darren Byfield *(Millwall)*	16	0	0	0	16
Will Hoskins *(Rotherham U)*	15	1	0	0	16
(now Watford).					
Luke Beckett *(Huddersfield T)*	15	0	0	0	15
Grant Holt *(Nottingham F)*	14	0	1	4	19
Akpo Sodje *(Port Vale)*	14	1	1	0	16
Keigan Parker *(Blackpool)*	13	0	1	2	16
COCA-COLA LEAGUE 2					
Richard Barker *(Hartlepool U)*	21	1	2	0	24
(Includes 12 League goals, 1 Carling Cup and 2 FA Cup matches for Mansfield T).					
Izale McLeod *(Milton Keynes D)*	21	1	2	0	24
Glenn Murray *(Rochdale)*	19	0	0	0	19
(Includes 3 League goals on loan to Stockport Co).					
Jamie Forrester *(Lincoln C)*	18	0	0	0	18
Clive Platt *(Milton Keynes D)*	18	0	0	0	18
Jermaine Easter *(Wycombe W)*	17	6	1	0	24
Chris Dagnall *(Rochdale)*	17	0	0	1	18
Anthony Elding *(Stockport Co)*	16	0	0	0	16
(Includes 5 League goals for Boston U).					
Andy Bishop *(Bury)*	15	1	5	0	21
Mark Stallard *(Lincoln C)*	15	1	0	1	17
Jason Lee *(Notts Co)*	15	1	0	0	16
Paul Mullin *(Accrington S)*	14	1	0	1	16
Dean Keates *(Walsall)*	13	0	0	0	13

Other matches consist of European games, J Paint Trophy, Community Shield and Football League play-offs. Players listed in order of League goals total.

REVIEW OF THE SEASON

League tables rarely represent an accurate account of the proceedings in a given season. The 2006–07 Premier League was no exception to this fact, the bare statistics of which saw Manchester United wrest the championship away from Chelsea with a six-point finishing margin between the two teams.

The reality was that the gap could have been nine points, as the resting place of the trophy had been decided beforehand.

Just how you evaluate the merits of whether United won or Chelsea lost it depends on a particular viewpoint. Factually there were some indications early on for Chelsea, that their quest for a third successive title was under threat.

Again it was the Riverside hoodoo which engulfed them. This time it was in the second game of the season at Middlesbrough. Yet if there had to be a more general reason for their failure it was obvious even from the final table: they drew eleven matches, not recommended with three points for a win.

Though United lost more games – five to Chelsea's three, they also had the advantage of a superior goal difference which meant the Blues always needed that extra point.

Both suffered from injuries, though Chelsea's in defence proved more crucial. They also failed to capitalise on the errors made by United. This was particularly significant on 21 April when Middlesbrough – once again – drew at Old Trafford. The following day Chelsea were at Newcastle but could only draw themselves.

Having a game in hand for much of the time was no help either to Chelsea, in the wake of Manchester United's lead. Also Sir Alex Ferguson's front line was a much more potent force with Cristiano Ronaldo and Wayne Rooney at times seemingly irresistible.

For Chelsea there was always the threat posed by Didier Drogba who time and again rescued them with a goal. He finished the season as the Premier League's leading scorer on 20 goals. Consolation for Jose Mourinho came through the Carling Cup at the expense of Arsenal and the FA Cup giving more satisfaction one imagines against United themselves. The two teams shared Champions League semi-final places, too.

Since first team squads became the vogue, ever-present numbers of players have virtually disappeared. Only 18 were mustered in the Premier League including appearances as substitute, none from Manchester United's twenty-five different players. Wayne Rooney came nearest with 35 outings including two off the bench. Ronaldo made one less, three of his as substitute.

Henrik Larsson in something of a cameo role between Swedish seasons had seven appearances and the Chinese international Dong Fangzhou – at last granted permission to play – made a solitary outing. The evergreen Ryan Giggs played 30 times.

Goalscoring was chiefly shared by Ronaldo and Rooney with 17 and 14 respectively. Fifteen other players shared the scoring. Defensively despite missing much of the season, Nemanja Vidic was outstanding.

The Premier League being what it is, a succession of small groups of teams who only occasionally move out of their own status, the next pairing saw Liverpool and Arsenal in third and fourth place respectively, the separation being one of just two goals difference.

Liverpool, beaten in mid-October at Manchester United were as low as eleventh, but for them it was a race for third place with the Gunners, capable of producing the most attractive, flowing football, but prone to inconsistency. Four draws out of the last seven games proved costly.

Fast-finishing Tottenham Hotspur hauled themselves up from eleventh place in mid-February for a best term fifth position and added an enthusiastic UEFA Cup run which shadowed even the final at one time.

Despite stringing only two wins in succession on one occasion, Everton finished in the top six and the defence was often hard to breach. Bolton Wanderers after a slow start and a dreadful run-in with just two victories in eleven games probably looked upon seventh as disappointing. Manager Sam Allardyce must have agreed before moving on to Newcastle United.

Wayne Rooney puts Manchester United in front against Everton at Goodison Park. United had trailed 2-0 after an hour but came back to win the match 4-2. (Peter Byrne/PA wire/PA Photos)

Yet eighth spot was an outstanding achievement for newcomers Reading, tipped as non-survivors. Two spells of four consecutive wins showed their mettle and Europe only just eluded them.

Having led the table in September and still third in early December, the second half of the season petered away for Portsmouth. Two wins in eleven for Blackburn Rovers from early October proved a handicap though newcomer Benni McCarthy was a useful marksman with 18 goals.

Aston Villa were the longest without defeat, lasting until their tenth, though six of these had been drawn, a trend which punctured their season as they finished with seventeen such. Despite the quick scalp of the reigning champions, Middlesbrough were unable to put together a run of any consequence.

Newcastle United were sadly lacking in the goalscoring department failing to score in 17 matches and won only one of their last eleven. They did enjoy some success in the UEFA Cup via the Intertoto.

Manchester City were even more goal-shy, with nineteen blanks and the eventual departure of manager Stuart Pearce. However, there was more drama for West Ham United rock-bottom in early March with a new manager in Alan Curbishley.

Reprieved with a fine when expecting a points deduction for the registrations of their two Argentines, the remaining one Carlos Tevez scored seven crucial goals, none more so than in the last at Old Trafford.

Managerial change, too, at Fulham with Chris Coleman giving way to Lawrie Sanchez of Northern Ireland fame. They managed one win bonus in their last twelve. Wigan Athletic as elevated as eighth in November fell slowly away and had to rely on beating Sheffield United in their last game.

United were less fortunate of course. A wretched start with one win in ten led to ultimate relegation along with Charlton Athletic who took on manager Alan Pardew from West Ham. Only once out of the bottom three, no wins in the last seven. Finally newly-promoted Watford were light up front; only a dozen goals for their first half of the season and in the bottom two in the last of it. They did, however, merit their FA Cup semi-final berth.

Naturally with the prize of a Premiership place at the end of it, the fortunate Championship trio were Sunderland, Birmingham City and via the play-offs – and a final at the new Wembley – Derby County.

Sunderland who won the title were transformed from the trauma of four opening defeats into a formidable outfit once Roy Keane became manager. Despite his fledgling status in the role, he acquitted himself with distinction. From the turn of the year, they lost only once in 20 outings.

Runners-up Birmingham were none too carefree in the early weeks and even eighth in mid-October. But December proved a fine month and heading the pack had expectations of finishing in front, though always looking north-eastwards over their shoulders.

Again Derby were indifferent openers with just two wins in the first eight. However, from early December they were never out of the top three. In the play-offs they won at Southampton and had away goals counted double would have exited at Pride Park. Penalties changed all that.

In the final at Wembley watched by 74,993, they edged West Bromwich Albion out without the aid of the lottery. Albion had some spectacular wins, not the least 7-0 against Barnsley on the last day. They also hit two 5s and two 4s.

The Baggies had proved Black Country champions having beaten Wolverhampton Wanderers home and away in the semi-final play-offs. Wolves best spell had been six wins in a row into March.

For the Saints, third in late September, a late rally into the frame with three crucial wins ended in the disappointment in the semi-final.

A point off the zone were Preston North End courtesy of a collapse in the last quarter of the season which yielded just four wins out of eleven. A further point adrift came Stoke City. Fourth prior to Christmas was their highest placing.

Sheffield Wednesday would surely have figured in the play-offs but for taking just one point from a possible 21 from New Year's Day. Yet Colchester United must have been satisfied with tenth. They also lowered the colours of high-flying Sunderland.

Plymouth Argyle had five successive wins at the death, but it moved them only fractionally in mid-table. Crystal Palace suffered from scraping just two points from 24 into November and Cardiff City stopped free scoring in 2007 when they managed just five goals in eleven games.

Gilberto Silva of Arsenal scores a tenth-minute equaliser, setting the Gunners on their way to a 6-2 victory over Blackburn Rovers at the Emirates Stadium in December. (Phil Cole/Getty Images)

Jason Koumas of West Bromwich Albion attempts to evade Derby County's Tyrone Mears during the Championship Play-off final at Wembley. (Adam Davy/EMPICS Sport/PA Photos)

Ipswich Town captured the scalp of Sunderland in September which put them eighth, their highest all season but a string of victories never materialised. Burnley's attack was often non-existent with 18 non-scoring games. A pity as mid-October they had been lying second.

Norwich City, second, too, in late August then fell 17 places in half a dozen matches and never more than two consecutive wins. Coventry City were in a similar double-win rut and one point from 21 into January.

A 1-1 draw at Derby in early March was a turning point for Queens Park Rangers who had five wins in the last nine and safety. But it was just as well Leicester City had contrived as many points as they had by late February. They won only two of the last thirteen.

Barnsley had looked vulnerable until a best of season run of three wins from 7 April. Hull City for their part were still rock bottom in October and hovered around the danger zone.

Yet, the unsuccessful trio proved to be Southend United, Luton Town and Leeds United. Southend, despite some notable triumphs, not the least beating Manchester United in the Carling Cup, succumbed having started with two victories in the opening 21 fixtures. Luton having beaten Leeds 5-1 in October to be fifth were in freefall at the close after one win in the last 13.

For Leeds who surrendered ten points when salvation was lost were only once out of the bottom three in the second half of the season.

Scunthorpe United had in striker Billy Sharp, the most potent League marksman in the country, collecting 30 of the 73 which ensured the League 1 title. Not bad after being third from bottom from the opening five games. They also eroded Nottingham Forest's advantage.

Bristol City accompanied United automatically. Their final run-in was well-timed from 17 February when they won crucially 1-0 at Blackpool, the first of five consecutive wins; the basis for subsequent success.

That result did nothing for the losers and arguably cost them second spot. But they did emerge with success from the play-offs beating Oldham Athletic and then Yeovil Town in the final at Wembley. Oddly enough a draw with Yeovil in October had Blackpool as low as 20th.

However the fall from grace by Nottingham Forest was almost inexplicable. Boxing Day and they were still holding onto top billing, recaptured it against Yeovil of all teams on 13 January then failed. They did win at Yeovil in the play-off first leg but were crushed at the City Ground.

Oldham had their moments, too, topping affairs in February only to lose the next four. Out of the frame were Swansea City never higher than fifth all term and losing 6-3 at home to Blackpool on the last day of the season when a place was still a possibility.

Losing their last three games cost Carlisle United, especially following a season's best five consecutive victories. Second in late September was a false image as it turned out for Tranmere Rovers with two spells of four wins in a row their best.

Millwall had a season of distinctly two halves, the first dreadful, the second most encouraging with a more settled team. For Doncaster it was their middle third of the season which saved them. They also took the Johnstone's Paint Trophy.

Port Vale need to look at the flying start of four wins to ponder on why they finished only twelfth and Crewe Alexandra's four wins in February proved unsustainable.

Northampton Town struggled for goals at times, Fifteen times they were unable to score at all. Improvement in the last six outings with only one defeat. The draw champions were Huddersfield Town with 17 such results; sixth place in October just a false dawn.

An unhelpful start followed by three consecutive wins and three again near the end left Gillingham 16th. Cheltenham Town waited until the penultimate game. Two down at Rotherham they recovered to win 4-2 and escape from the congested lower reaches.

Brighton & Hove Albion had accumulated sufficient points before plunging into just one win in the last twelve and Bournemouth, one from bottom at the turn of the year collected only three points from their last six matches.

Leyton Orient, bottom early in November survived despite managing just one win in the last nine, but for Chesterfield, Bradford City, Rotherham United and Brentford there was no way out.

Chesterfield beat Millwall 5-1 in August but later found goals scarce with 21 non-scoring occasions. Consolation for them came from some splendid cup performances. Bradford with 18 of their own scoreless days were leakier at the back though as high as eighth in October.

Rotherham went fourteen games for a miserable four points to the end of February and four subsequent successes proved too little, too late. Cellar-dwellers Brentford fourth in September lost it, scoring fewer and conceding more than any others. One win in the last thirteen, too.

In contrast, Walsall, the winners of League 2, were miserly in defence recording 21 clean sheets. Never lower than fifth, they were most consistent, the one blip coming with three straight defeats in February.

Hartlepool United cracked it spectacularly with an astonishing 23 games without defeat and just four points dropped until April. This included nine wins in one sequence. They were joined in automatic promotion by Swindon Town. Pretty consistent most of the season with just two successive defeats causing a frown they had the second best defensive record, too.

Milton Keynes Dons came again with a final flourish of four wins, just failing to make the cut. In December with second place in tow they looked likely candidates. In the play-offs they lost at home to Shrewsbury Town.

Strangely enough Shrewsbury had as good a goal difference as any team despite drawing as many as 17 matches. In the play-off final they were edged out by Bristol Rovers, who beat Lincoln City 8-4 on aggregate in the semi-final.

Rovers had galloped through at the death undefeated in the last eight to their best position all season. Lincoln, serial play-off losers, had gone into them in poor shape: three goals in seven matches.

Goal difference was costly for Stockport County despite their record nine wins without conceding a goal. They later shipped seven goals at home to Rochdale! On the last day their 5-0 win at Darlington still fell short.

As witness their seven, Rochdale were capable of scoring. They also had three 5s and three 4s. Peterborough United's problems began in December: ten games, one point and five goals.

Six consecutive reverses to the end of the year threatened Darlington, but they responded with 13 without defeat. Wycombe Wanderers, flattered only to flutter away finishing with eleven games without a win bonus.

Notts County looked capable in mid-October but inconsistency – seven games without a win followed by four wins on the trot – consigned them to mid-table. Yet Barnet improved after just two wins in the first 15 to a respectable fourteenth.

Any Grimsby Town revival was damaged by seven successive defeats (and one goal) by the end of January. Back in the fold Hereford United foundered late on, too, with one win in the last thirteen and just five goals.

Mansfield Town were another team who petered out in the scoring stakes collecting one win from the last ten and scoring just six times, while Chester City with the second worst attack in the division, 22 no scoring games, yet 13 clean sheets.

Neighbours Wrexham similar in attack, far worse at the back, made a concerted effort towards the end with four wins out of the last five. Of the others Accrington Stanley avoided relegation with five wins in the last nine fixtures.

Bury had an unsettling time of it after mid-December; 16 games without a win before arresting the problem and Macclesfield Town, looking all but buried themselves following a 19-game no-win opening pulled out of danger with an eight game no defeat run into January.

Boston United not only succumbed to relegation, but with a ten point penalty and further demotion, had a tough season indeed, including nine games without a win into March.

Torquay United lost their League status, too, even seventh in September but fixed on the bottom virtually after Christmas. At one stage 19 games without a win.

Up from the Conference, new boys Dagenham & Redbridge and Morecambe.

England collegues Steven Gerrard of Liverpool in action with Tottenham's Jermain Defoe.
(Action Images/Keith Williams)

THE FA CHARITY SHIELD WINNERS 1908–2006

1908	Manchester U v QPR	4-0 after 1-1 draw
1909	Newcastle U v Northampton T	2-0
1910	Brighton v Aston Villa	1-0
1911	Manchester U v Swindon T	8-4
1912	Blackburn R v QPR	2-1
1913	Professionals v Amateurs	7-2
1920	WBA v Tottenham H	2-0
1921	Tottenham H v Burnley	2-0
1922	Huddersfield T v Liverpool	1-0
1923	Professionals v Amateurs	2-0
1924	Professionals v Amateurs	3-1
1925	Amateurs v Professionals	6-1
1926	Amateurs v Professionals	6-3
1927	Cardiff C v Corinthians	2-1
1928	Everton v Blackburn R	2-1
1929	Professionals v Amateurs	3-0
1930	Arsenal v Sheffield W	2-1
1931	Arsenal v WBA	1-0
1932	Everton v Newcastle U	5-3
1933	Arsenal v Everton	3-0
1934	Arsenal v Manchester C	4-0
1935	Sheffield W v Arsenal	1-0
1936	Sunderland v Arsenal	2-1
1937	Manchester C v Sunderland	2-0
1938	Arsenal v Preston NE	2-1
1948	Arsenal v Manchester U	4-3
1949	Portsmouth v Wolverhampton W	1-1*
1950	World Cup Team v Canadian Touring Team	4-2
1951	Tottenham H v Newcastle U	2-1
1952	Manchester U v Newcastle U	4-2
1953	Arsenal v Blackpool	3-1
1954	Wolverhampton W v WBA	4-4*
1955	Chelsea v Newcastle U	3-0
1956	Manchester U v Manchester C	1-0
1957	Manchester U v Aston Villa	4-0
1958	Bolton W v Wolverhampton W	4-1
1959	Wolverhampton W v Nottingham F	3-1
1960	Burnley v Wolverhampton W	2-2*
1961	Tottenham H v FA XI	3-2
1962	Tottenham H v Ipswich T	5-1
1963	Everton v Manchester U	4-0
1964	Liverpool v West Ham U	2-2*
1965	Manchester U v Liverpool	2-2*
1966	Liverpool v Everton	1-0
1967	Manchester U v Tottenham H	3-3*
1968	Manchester C v WBA	6-1
1969	Leeds U v Manchester C	2-1
1970	Everton v Chelsea	2-1
1971	Leicester C v Liverpool	1-0
1972	Manchester C v Aston Villa	1-0
1973	Burnley v Manchester C	1-0
1974	Liverpool† v Leeds U	1-1
1975	Derby Co v West Ham U	2-0
1976	Liverpool v Southampton	1-0
1977	Liverpool v Manchester U	0-0*
1978	Nottingham F v Ipswich T	5-0
1979	Liverpool v Arsenal	3-1
1980	Liverpool v West Ham U	1-0
1981	Aston Villa v Tottenham H	2-2*
1982	Liverpool v Tottenham H	1-0
1983	Manchester U v Liverpool	2-0
1984	Everton v Liverpool	1-0
1985	Everton v Manchester U	2-0
1986	Everton v Liverpool	1-1*
1987	Everton v Coventry C	1-0
1988	Liverpool v Wimbledon	2-1
1989	Liverpool v Arsenal	1-0
1990	Liverpool v Manchester U	1-1*
1991	Arsenal v Tottenham H	0-0*
1992	Leeds U v Liverpool	4-3
1993	Manchester U† v Arsenal	1-1
1994	Manchester U v Blackburn R	2-0
1995	Everton v Blackburn R	1-0
1996	Manchester U v Newcastle U	4-0
1997	Manchester U† v Chelsea	1-1
1998	Arsenal v Manchester U	3-0
1999	Arsenal v Manchester U	2-1
2000	Chelsea v Manchester U	2-0
2001	Liverpool v Manchester U	2-1
2002	Arsenal v Liverpool	1-0
2003	Manchester U† v Arsenal	1-1
2004	Arsenal v Manchester U	3-1
2005	Chelsea v Arsenal	2-1
2006	Liverpool v Chelsea	2-1

* *Each club retained shield for six months.* † *Won on penalties.*

THE FA COMMUNITY SHIELD 2006

Chelsea (1) 1, Liverpool (1) 2

At Millennium Stadium, 13 August 2006, attendance 56,275

Chelsea: Cudicini; Geremi (Bridge), Paulo Ferreira (Mikel), Essien, Terry, Ricardo Carvalho, Ballack (Kalou), Lampard, Drogba (Wright-Phillips), Shevchenko, Robben (Diarra).

Scorer: Shevchenko 43.

Liverpool: Reina; Finnan, Riise, Sissoko, Carragher, Agger, Pennant (Gerrard), Luis Garcia (Bellamy), Crouch (Sinama-Pongolle), Gonzalez (Aurelio), Zenden (Xabi Alonso).

Scorers: Riise 9, Crouch 80.

Referee: M. Atkinson (West Yorkshire).

ACCRINGTON STANLEY FL Championship 2

FOUNDATION

Accrington Football Club founder members of the Football League in 1888, were not connected with Accrington Stanley. In fact both clubs ran concurrently between 1891 when Stanley were formed and 1895 when Accington FC folded. Actually Stanley Villa was the original name, those responsible for forming the club living in Stanley Street and using the Stanley Arms as their meeting place. They became Accrington Stanley in 1893. In 1894–95 they joined the Accrington & District League, playing at Moorhead Park. Subsequently in the North-East Lancashire Combination and the Lancashire Combination before becoming founder members of the Third Division (North) in 1921, two years after moving to Peel Park. In 1962 they resigned from the Football League, were wound-up, reformed 1963, disbanded in 1966 only to restart as Accrington Stanley (1968), returning to the Lancashire Combination in 1970.

The Fraser Eagle Stadium, Livingstone Road, Accrington, Lancashire BB5, 5BX.

Telephone: (01254) 356 950.

Ticket Office: (01254) 356 950/336 954.

Fax: (01254) 356 951.

Website: www.accringtonstanley.co.uk

Email: info@accringtonstanley.co.uk

Ground Capacity: 5,057.

Record Attendance: 4,368 v Colchester U, FA Cup 1st rd, 3 January 2004.

Pitch Measurements: 111yds × 72yds.

Chairman: Eric Whalley.

Vice-chairman: Frank Martindale.

Chief Executive: Robert Heys.

Secretary: Hannah Bailey.

Manager: John Coleman.

Assistant Manager: Jimmy Bell.

Physio: Ian Liversedge.

Club Nickname: 'Reds'.

Colours: Red shirts, white shorts, red stockings.

Change Colours: Blue shirts, blue shorts, blue stockings.

Year Formed: 1891, re-formed 1968.

Turned Professional: 1919.

Grounds: 1891, Moorhead Park; 1897, Bell's Ground; 1919, Peel Park; 1970, Crown Inn.

HONOURS

Football League: Division 3 (N) – Runners-up 1954–55, 1957–58.

Conference: Champions 2005–06.

FA Cup: 4th rd 1927, 1937, 1959.

Football League Cup: never past 2nd rd.

Northern Premier League: Champions 2002–03.

Northern League: Division 1 – Champions 1999–2000.

North West Counties: Runners-up 1986–87.

Cheshire County League: Division 2 – Champions 1980–81; Runners-up 1979–80.

Lancashire Combination: Champions 1973–74, 1977–78; Runners-up 1971–72, 1975–76.

Lancashire Combination Cup: Winners 1971–72, 1972–73, 1973–74, 1976–77.

SKY SPORTS FACT FILE

On 26 November 1932 Accrington Stanley beat Hereford United 2–1 in a first round FA Cup tie. It was the first time the teams had met each other. At the end of the 2005–06 season both were able to regain their Football League status.

First Football League Game: 27 August 1921, Division 3 (N), v Rochdale (a) L 3-6 – Tattersall; Newton, Baines, Crawshaw, Popplewell, Burkinshaw, Oxley, Makin, Green (1), Hosker (2), Hartles.

Record League Victory: 8-0 v New Brighton, Division 3 (N), 17 March 1934 – Maidment; Armstrong (pen), Price, Dodds, Crawshaw, McCulloch, Wyper, Lennox (2), Cheetham (4), Leedham (1), Watson.

Record Cup Victory: 7-0 v Spennymoor U, FA Cup 2nd rd, 8 December 1938 – Tootill; Armstrong, Whittaker, Latham, Curran, Lee, Parry (2), Chadwick, Jepson (3), McLoughlin (2), Barclay.

Record Defeat: 9-1 v Lincoln C, Division 3 (N), 3 March 1951.

Most League Points (2 for a win): 61, Division 3 (N), 1954–55.

Most League Points (3 for a win): 50, FL 2, 2006–07.

Most League Goals: 96, Division 3 (N) 1954–55.

Highest League Scorer in Season: George Stewart, 35, 1955–56 Division 3 (N); George Hudson, 35, 1960–61, Division 4.

Most League Goals in Total Aggregate: George Stewart, 136, 1954–58.

Most League Goals in One Match: 5, Billy Harker v Gateshead, Division 3 (N), 16 November 1935; George Stewart v Gateshead, Division 3 (N), 27 November 1954.

Most Capped Player: Romuald Boco, (17), Benin.

Most League Appearances: Jim Armstrong, 260, 1927–34.

Record Transfer Fee Received: £180,000 from Ipswich T for Gary Roberts, January 2007.

Record Transfer Fee Paid: £17,500 to Altrincham FC for Ian Craney, July 2004.

Football League Record: Original members of Division 3 (N) 1921–58; Division 3 1958–60; Division 4 1960–62; FL 2 2006–.

MANAGERS

William Cronshaw c.1894
John Haworth 1897–1910
Johnson Haworth c.1916
Sam Pilkingson 1919–24
(Tommy Booth p-m 1923–24)
Ernie Blackburn 1924–32
Amos Wade 1932–35
John Hacking 1935–49
Jimmy Porter 1949–51
Walter Crook 1951–53
Walter Galbraith 1953–58
George Eastham snr 1958–59
Harold Bodle 1959–60
James Harrower 1960–61
Harold Mather 1962–63
Jimmy Hinksman 1963–64
Terry Neville 1964–65
Ian Bryson 1965
Danny Parker 1965–66
John Coleman May 1999–

LATEST SEQUENCES

Longest Sequence of League Wins: 7, 27.12.1954 – 5.2.1955.

Longest Sequence of League Defeats: 9, 8.3.1030 – 21.4.1930.

Longest Sequence of League Draws: 4, 10.9.1927 – 27.9.1927.

Longest Sequence of Unbeaten League Matches: 11, 27.11.1954 – 5.2.1955.

Longest Sequence Without a League Win: 18, 17.9.1938 – 31.12.1938.

Successive Scoring Runs: 22 from 14.11.1936.

Successive Non-scoring Runs: 5 from 15.3.1930.

TEN YEAR LEAGUE RECORD

		P	*W*	*D*	*L*	*F*	*A*	*Pts*	*Pos*
1997-98	U Pr	42	8	14	20	49	68	38	20
1998-99	U Pr	42	9	9	24	47	77	36	22
1999-2000	U D I	42	25	9	8	96	43	84	1
2000-01	U Pr	44	18	10	16	72	67	64	9
2001-02	U Pr	44	21	9	14	89	64	72	6
2002-03	U Pr	44	30	10	4	97	44	100	1
2003-04	Conf	42	15	13	14	68	61	58	10
2004-05	Conf	42	18	11	13	72	58	65	10
2005-06	Conf	42	28	7	7	76	45	91	1
2006-07	FL 2	46	13	11	22	70	81	50	20

DID YOU KNOW ?

Goalscoring hero for Accrington Stanley in the two third round FA Cup ties with Blackburn Rovers in January 1937 was Bob Mortimer with two goals in each match, the original 2–2 draw and the subsequent 3–1 win. Suitably impressed Blackburn signed him!

ACCRINGTON STANLEY 2006–07 LEAGUE RECORD

Match No.	Date	Venue	Opponents	Result		H/T Score	Lg. Pos.	Goalscorers	Attendance
1	Aug 5	A	Chester C	L	0-2	0-1	—		3779
2	8	H	Darlington	L	0-2	0-2	—		2667
3	12	H	Barnet	W	2-1	1-0	18	Boco 2 [35, 53]	1639
4	18	A	Stockport Co	D	1-1	0-1	—	Welch [78]	5291
5	26	H	Rochdale	D	1-1	0-1	16	Roberts (pen) [76]	3045
6	Sept 1	A	Lincoln C	L	1-3	0-2	—	Roberts [82]	4999
7	9	A	Notts Co	L	2-3	0-3	21	Roberts (pen) [89], Mullin [90]	4677
8	13	H	Wrexham	W	5-0	1-0	—	Mullin [41], Craney [49], Roberts 2 [52, 67], Cavanagh [55]	2689
9	16	H	Boston U	W	2-1	1-0	13	Roberts [11], Todd [90]	1916
10	23	A	Mansfield T	D	2-2	1-0	13	Mullin 2 [16, 85]	3088
11	26	A	Bury	D	2-2	2-2	—	Roberts [12], Boco [37]	2912
12	30	H	Wycombe W	W	2-1	1-0	12	Craney [27], Mangan [90]	2243
13	Oct 7	H	Swindon T	D	1-1	1-0	10	Todd [33]	3083
14	14	A	Torquay U	W	2-0	0-0	9	Welch [47], Roberts [73]	2743
15	21	H	Walsall	L	1-2	0-1	9	Craney [78]	3142
16	28	A	Hereford U	L	0-1	0-0	13		3391
17	Nov 4	A	Peterborough U	L	2-4	1-0	15	Craney 2 [23, 79]	3990
18	18	H	Hartlepool U	L	1-2	1-0	18	Todd [38]	1787
19	25	A	Grimsby T	L	0-2	0-1	19		4511
20	Dec 2	H	Shrewsbury T	D	3-3	1-2	—	Todd (pen) [19], Edwards [55], Williams [89]	1602
21	9	H	Milton Keynes D	L	3-4	2-1	20	Mullin 2 [39, 43], Mangan [83]	1384
22	16	A	Macclesfield T	D	3-3	1-0	21	McGivern [27], Jacobson [75], Mangan [90]	2242
23	23	A	Bristol R	L	0-4	0-3	21		5205
24	26	H	Bury	D	1-1	1-0	21	Todd (pen) [5]	3225
25	Jan 1	A	Wrexham	W	3-1	1-1	22	Mullin [17], Brown 2 [83, 86]	3805
26	6	A	Boston U	L	0-1	0-0	22		1664
27	13	H	Notts Co	L	1-2	1-2	22	Brown [14]	1702
28	16	H	Mansfield T	W	3-2	1-2	—	Mullin [1], Welch [60], Whalley [83]	1234
29	20	A	Wycombe W	D	1-1	0-0	18	Harris [63]	5884
30	Feb 3	H	Chester C	L	0-1	0-1	21		1900
31	10	A	Barnet	W	2-1	1-1	19	Todd (pen) [40], Proctor [84]	2041
32	17	H	Stockport Co	L	0-1	0-1	20		3004
33	20	A	Darlington	L	1-2	0-2	—	Mullin [50]	2790
34	24	H	Lincoln C	D	2-2	1-1	21	Todd [23], Mullin [73]	1930
35	Mar 3	A	Rochdale	L	2-4	0-3	21	Mullin [70], Mangan [90]	3433
36	6	H	Bristol R	D	1-1	0-0	—	Whalley [90]	1302
37	10	A	Swindon T	L	0-2	0-1	21		6197
38	17	H	Torquay U	W	1-0	0-0	20	Cavanagh [90]	4004
39	24	H	Hereford U	W	2-0	1-0	19	Brown [26], Cavanagh [54]	1848
40	31	A	Walsall	L	2-3	1-1	20	Mullin [25], Williams [65]	6062
41	Apr 7	H	Peterborough U	W	3-2	2-1	20	Todd 2 [2, 90], Harris [45]	1808
42	9	A	Hartlepool U	L	0-1	0-0	20		5867
43	14	H	Grimsby T	W	4-1	2-1	19	Mullin [32], Todd (pen) [44], Doherty [55], Cavanagh [88]	1818
44	21	A	Shrewsbury T	L	1-2	1-1	20	Mullin [10]	5438
45	28	H	Macclesfield T	W	3-2	2-2	19	Williams [11], Proctor 2 [45, 48]	3012
46	May 5	A	Milton Keynes D	L	1-3	1-0	20	Brown [14]	8102

Final League Position: 20

GOALSCORERS

League (70): Mullin 14, Todd 10 (4 pens), Roberts 8 (2 pens), Brown 5, Craney 5, Cavanagh 4, Mangan 4, Boco 3, Proctor 3, Welch 3, Williams 3, Harris 2, Whalley 2, Doherty 1, Edwards 1, Jacobson 1, McGivern 1.
Carling Cup (1): Mullin 1.
FA Cup (0).
J Paint Trophy (5): Craney 1, Mullin 1, Todd 1, Williams 1, own goal 1.

Dunbavin I 22+1	Cavanagh P 26	Richardson L 34+4	Proctor A 38+5	Williams R 43	Welch M 25+6	Doherty S 14+6	Craney I 18	Boco R 28+4	Mullin P 46	Roberts G 14	Harris J 26+6	Todd A 44+2	Mangan A 6+28	Brown D 8+9	Edwards P 29+4	N'Da J —+3	Ventre D 4+2	Whalley S 13+7	Jacobson J 6	Dugdale A 2	McGivern L 3+4	Mannix D 1	Byrom J —+1	Elliot R 7	Bains R 2+1	Rogers A 6	McGrail C —+2	Kazimierczak P 7+1	Grant T 6	Fleetwood S 3	Almeida M 5	Martin D 10	Antwi-Birago G 9	Grant R 1	*Match No.*
1	2	3	4^{1}	5	6	7^{2}	8	9	10^{3}	11	12	13	14																						1
1	2	3	4■	5	6		8	9^{2}	10	11		7^{1}	13	12																					2
1	2	3		5	6		8	9^{2}	10	11	4	7^{1}			12	13																			3
1	2	3		5	6	12	8	9	10	11	4^{2}	7^{1}	13																						4
1	2	3		5	6	12	8	9	10	11	4^{2}	7^{1}	13																						5
1	2■	3	9	5	6■		8^{2}		10	11	4^{1}	7	12			13																			6
1		3	4	5^{3}		12	8	9^{2}	10	11		7	13		6	14	2^{1}																		7
1	2	3	4	5		7^{2}	8	12	10^{3}	9		11^{1}	13	14	6																				8
1	2^{1}	3	4^{2}	5	12	7^{3}	8	13	10	9		11	14		6																				9
1	2^{2}	3	4^{3}	5		11^{1}	8	12	10	9	14	7	13		6																				10
1	2	3	4^{2}	5	12		8	9	10	11	13	7			6^{1}																				11
1	2	3	4^{2}	5	6	14	8	9	10	11^{1}	13	7^{3}	12																						12
1	2	3	4	5	6	11^{1}	8		10	9		7	12																						13
1	2	3	4	5	6		8	9	10	11		7																							14
1		3	4^{3}	5	6	11^{1}	8	9	10		14	7	12	13	2^{2}																				15
1	2		4	5	6	11^{1}	8	12	10			7	13	9^{2}	3																				16
1	2	3	4	5^{1}	6	7^{2}	8		10		11	9	13		12																				17
1	2^{2}	3^{1}	4	5	6	7^{3}	8		10		11■	9	12		13			14																	18
1		12	4	5	6				10			7	13		14			11	3^{3}	2^{1}	9^{2}	8													19
1		3	4	8	6				10			7	9^{1}		5		2		11^{2}		12		13												20
1		3	4	5■					10		8	7	12		2^{1}		13		11	6	9^{2}														21
		3	4		6				10		8	7	12		5		2		11		9^{1}			1											22
		2	4	5					10		8	7	9■		6			11	3					1											23
1		3	4	5					10		8	7		9^{1}	6		2^{2}	12	11						13										24
		3	4	5	6				10		8	7		9				11						1	2										25
		3	4	5	6				10			7	12	9^{1}	8			11						1	2										26
		2	4	5	6			8	10			7^{1}	12	9				11						1		3■									27
		3	12	5	6			8	10		4^{1}	7		9^{2}	2			11						1			13								28
		3	4	5	6^{1}			9	10		8	7			2			11						1			12								29
		3^{2}	12	5	6			11	10		4	7	14	13	2													1	8^{1}	9^{3}					30
			12	5				8^{3}	10		4^{1}	7	13		3			14								2		1	11	9^{2}	6				31
		2^{3}	12	5				8	10		4	13			6			14								7		1	11^{1}	9^{2}	3				32
			12	5				9^{2}	10		4^{1}	7	13		2			11								3		1	8		6				33
			4	5	6			9^{1}	10			7	12		2			11								3		15	8			1^{6}			34
	2	12	4		6			9^{2}	10		13	7	14		5			11								3^{1}		1	8^{3}						35
		2	4	5				11^{2}	10		8	7	9	12	6			13										1			3^{1}				36
		2	4	5	12			11^{3}	10		8	7^{2}	9	13	6			14										1			3^{1}				37
	2	3	4	5					10		8	7	9					11														1	6		38
	2	3	4	5		12		8^{2}	10			7	13	9■				11^{1}														1	6		39
	2		4	5	12	13		8	10			7	9^{2}		3^{1}			11														1	6		40
	2		4	5	12	11^{2}		9	10		8	7	13		3																	1	6^{1}		41
	2	12	4	5		11^{1}		9	10		8^{2}	7	13■		3																	1	6		42
	2		4	5		11		9	10^{2}		8^{1}	7		12	3						13											1	6		43
	2	12	4	5		11^{2}		9	10		8^{3}	7		13	3^{1}						14											1	6		44
	2		4	5^{1}	12	11^{3}		9^{2}	10		8	7		13	3			14														1	6		45
15	2	3	4		6				10^{2}		8	7		9			12				13											1^{6}	5^{1}	11	46

FA Cup

First Round	Mansfield T	(a)	0-1

Carling Cup

First Round	Nottingham F	(h)	1-0
Second Round	Watford	(a)	0-0

J Paint Trophy

First Round	Carlisle U	(h)	1-1
Second Round	Blackpool	(h)	4-4
Quarter-Final	Doncaster R	(a)	0-2

ARSENAL — FA Premiership

FOUNDATION

Formed by workers at the Royal Arsenal, Woolwich in 1886, they began as Dial Square (name of one of the workshops), and included two former Nottingham Forest players, Fred Beardsley and Morris Bates. Beardsley wrote to his old club seeking help and they provided the new club with a full set of red jerseys and a ball. The club became known as the 'Woolwich Reds' although their official title soon after formation was Woolwich Arsenal.

Emirates Stadium, Drayton Park, London N5 1BU.

Telephone: (020) 7704 4000.

Fax: (020) 7704 4001.

Ticket Office: (020) 7704 4040.

Website: www.arsenal.com

Email: info@arsenal.co.uk

Ground Capacity: 60,432.

Record Attendance: 73,295 v Sunderland, Div 1, 9 March 1935.

At Wembley: 73,707 v RC Lens, UEFA Champions League, 25 November 1998.

Pitch Measurements: 105m × 68m.

Chairman: Peter Hill-Wood.

Managing Director: Keith Edelman.

Secretary: David Miles.

Manager: Arsène Wenger.

Assistant Manager: Pat Rice.

Physio: Gary Lewin.

Colours: Red shirts with white sleeves, white shorts, white stockings.

Change Colours: All yellow.

Year Formed: 1886.

Turned Professional: 1891.

Ltd Co: 1893.

Previous Names: 1886, Dial Square; 1886, Royal Arsenal; 1891, Woolwich Arsenal; 1914 Arsenal.

Club Nickname: 'Gunners'.

Grounds: 1886, Plumstead Common; 1887, Sportsman Ground; 1888, Manor Ground; 1890, Invicta Ground; 1893, Manor Ground; 1913, Highbury; 2006, Emirates Stadium.

HONOURS

FA Premier League: Champions 1997–98, 2001–02, 2003–04. Runners-up 1998–99, 1999–2000, 2000–01, 2002–03, 2004–05.

Football League: Division 1 – Champions 1930–31, 1932–33, 1933–34, 1934–35, 1937–38, 1947–48, 1952–53, 1970–71, 1988–89, 1990–91; Runners-up 1925–26, 1931–32, 1972–73; Division 2 – Runners-up 1903–04.

FA Cup: Winners 1930, 1936, 1950, 1971, 1979, 1993, 1998, 2002, 2003, 2005; Runners-up 1927, 1932, 1952, 1972, 1978, 1980, 2001.

Double performed: 1970–71, 1997–98, 2001–02.

Football League Cup: Winners 1987, 1993; Runners-up 1968, 1969, 1988, 2007.

European Competitions: *Fairs Cup:* 1963–64, 1969–70 (winners), 1970–71. *European Cup:* 1971–72, 1991–92. *UEFA Champions League:* 1998–99, 1999–2000, 2000–01, 2001–02, 2002–03, 2003–04, 2004–05, 2005–06 (runners-up), 2006–07. *UEFA Cup:* 1978–79, 1981–82, 1982–83, 1996–97, 1997–98, 1999–2000 (runners-up). *European Cup-Winners' Cup:* 1979–80 (runners-up), 1993–94 (winners), 1994–95 (runners-up).

SKY SPORTS FACT FILE

On 13 September 2006 Arsenal set a Champions League record fielding for 41 minutes at Hamburg 11 players from 11 different countries: Germany, Ivory Coast, Switzerland, England, France, Czech Republic, Brazil, Spain, Belarus, Togo and Holland.

First Football League Game: 2 September 1893, Division 2, v Newcastle U (h) D 2–2 – Williams; Powell, Jeffrey; Devine, Buist, Howat; Gemmell, Henderson, Shaw (1), Elliott (1), Booth.

Record League Victory: 12–0 v Loughborough T, Division 2, 12 March 1900 – Orr; McNichol, Jackson; Moir, Dick (2), Anderson (1); Hunt, Cottrell (2), Main (2), Gaudie (3), Tennant (2).

Record Cup Victory: 11–1 v Darwen, FA Cup 3rd rd, 9 January 1932 – Moss; Parker, Hapgood; Jones, Roberts, John; Hulme (2), Jack (3), Lambert (2), James, Bastin (4).

Record Defeat: 0–8 v Loughborough T, Division 2, 12 December 1896.

Most League Points (2 for a win): 66, Division 1, 1930–31.

Most League Points (3 for a win): 90, Premier League 2003–04.

Most League Goals: 127, Division 1, 1930–31.

Highest League Scorer in Season: Ted Drake, 42, 1934–35.

Most League Goals in Total Aggregate: Thierry Henry, 174, 1999–2007.

Most League Goals in One Match: 7, Ted Drake v Aston Villa, Division 1, 14 December 1935.

Most Capped Player: Thierry Henry, 81 (92), France.

Most League Appearances: David O'Leary, 558, 1975–93.

Youngest League Player: Gerry Ward, 16 years 321 days v Huddersfield T, 22 August 1953 (Jermaine Pennant, 16 years 319 days v Middlesbrough, League Cup, 30 November 1999).

Record Transfer Fee Received: A reported £22,900,000 from Real Madrid for Nicolas Anelka, August 1999.

Record Transfer Fee Paid: A reported £11,000,000 to Bordeaux for Sylvain Wiltord, August 2000.

Football League Record: 1893 Elected to Division 2; 1904–13 Division 1; 1913–19 Division 2; 1919–92 Division 1; 1992– FA Premier League.

MANAGERS

Sam Hollis 1894–97
Tom Mitchell 1897–98
George Elcoat 1898–99
Harry Bradshaw 1899–1904
Phil Kelso 1904–08
George Morrell 1908–15
Leslie Knighton 1919–25
Herbert Chapman 1925–34
George Allison 1934–47
Tom Whittaker 1947–56
Jack Crayston 1956–58
George Swindin 1958–62
Billy Wright 1962–66
Bertie Mee 1966–76
Terry Neill 1976–83
Don Howe 1984–86
George Graham 1986–95
Bruce Rioch 1995–96
Arsène Wenger September 1996–

LATEST SEQUENCES

Longest Sequence of League Wins: 14, 10.2.2002 – 18.8.2002.

Longest Sequence of League Defeats: 7, 12.2.1977 – 12.3.1977.

Longest Sequence of League Draws: 6, 4.3.1961 – 1.4.1961.

Longest Sequence of Unbeaten League Matches: 49, 7.5.2003 – 24.10.2004.

Longest Sequence Without a League Win: 23, 28.9.1912 – 1.3.1913.

Successive Scoring Runs: 55 from 19.5.2001.

Successive Non-scoring Runs: 6 from 25.2.1987.

TEN YEAR LEAGUE RECORD

		P	W	D	L	F	A	Pts	Pos
1997-98	PR Lge	38	23	9	6	68	33	78	1
1998-99	PR Lge	38	22	12	4	59	17	78	2
1999-2000	PR Lge	38	22	7	9	73	43	73	2
2000-01	PR Lge	38	20	10	8	63	38	70	2
2001-02	PR Lge	38	26	9	3	79	36	87	1
2002-03	PR Lge	38	23	9	6	85	42	78	2
2003-04	PR Lge	38	26	12	0	73	26	90	1
2004-05	PR Lge	38	25	8	5	87	36	83	2
2005-06	PR Lge	38	20	7	11	68	31	67	4
2006-07	PR Lge	38	19	11	8	63	35	68	4

DID YOU KNOW ?

The average attendance in the Premier League for Arsenal during their 2006–07 inaugural season at the Emirates Stadium yielded the highest figure (60,045) in the club's history. The previous best was 54,892 in 1947–48 when they won the First Division title.

ARSENAL 2006–07 LEAGUE RECORD

Match No.	Date	Venue	Opponents	Result		H/T Score	Lg. Pos.	Goalscorers	Atten-dance
1	Aug 19	H	Aston Villa	D	1-1	0-0	—	Silva [84]	60,023
2	26	A	Manchester C	L	0-1	0-1	17		40,699
3	Sept 9	H	Middlesbrough	D	1-1	0-1	17	Henry (pen) [67]	60,007
4	17	A	Manchester U	W	1-0	0-0	10	Adebayor [86]	75,595
5	23	H	Sheffield U	W	3-0	0-0	8	Gallas [65], Jagielka (og) [69], Henry [80]	59,912
6	30	A	Charlton Ath	W	2-1	1-1	8	Van Persie 2 [32, 49]	26,770
7	Oct 14	H	Watford	W	3-0	2-0	5	Stewart (og) [33], Henry [43], Adebayor [67]	60,018
8	22	A	Reading	W	4-0	2-0	4	Henry 2 (1 pen) [1, 70 (p)], Hleb [39], Van Persie [50]	24,004
9	28	H	Everton	D	1-1	0-1	5	Van Persie [71]	60,047
10	Nov 5	A	West Ham U	L	0-1	0-0	5		34,969
11	12	H	Liverpool	W	3-0	1-0	3	Flamini [41], Toure [56], Gallas [80]	60,110
12	18	H	Newcastle U	D	1-1	0-1	4	Henry [70]	60,058
13	25	A	Bolton W	L	1-3	1-2	6	Silva [45]	24,409
14	29	A	Fulham	L	1-2	1-2	—	Van Persie [36]	24,510
15	Dec 2	H	Tottenham H	W	3-0	2-0	3	Adebayor [20], Silva 2 (2 pens) [42, 72]	60,115
16	10	A	Chelsea	D	1-1	0-0	6	Flamini [78]	41,917
17	13	A	Wigan Ath	W	1-0	0-0	—	Adebayor [88]	15,311
18	16	H	Portsmouth	D	2-2	0-1	4	Adebayor [58], Silva [60]	60,037
19	23	H	Blackburn R	W	6-2	3-1	4	Silva [10], Hleb [23], Adebayor (pen) [27], Van Persie 2 [85, 88], Flamini [90]	59,913
20	26	A	Watford	W	2-1	1-1	3	Silva [19], Van Persie [83]	19,750
21	30	A	Sheffield U	L	0-1	0-1	5		32,086
22	Jan 2	H	Charlton Ath	W	4-0	2-0	—	Henry (pen) [30], Hoyte [45], Van Persie 2 (1 pen) [76 (p), 90]	60,057
23	13	A	Blackburn R	W	2-0	1-0	4	Toure [37], Henry [71]	21,852
24	21	H	Manchester U	W	2-1	0-0	4	Van Persie [83], Henry [90]	60,128
25	Feb 3	A	Middlesbrough	D	1-1	0-0	4	Henry [77]	31,122
26	11	H	Wigan Ath	W	2-1	0-1	4	Hall (og) [81], Rosicky [85]	60,049
27	Mar 3	H	Reading	W	2-1	0-0	4	Silva (pen) [51], Baptista [62]	60,132
28	14	A	Aston Villa	W	1-0	1-0	—	Diaby [10]	39,968
29	18	A	Everton	L	0-1	0-0	3		37,162
30	31	A	Liverpool	L	1-4	0-2	4	Gallas [73]	43,958
31	Apr 7	H	West Ham U	L	0-1	0-1	4		60,098
32	9	A	Newcastle U	D	0-0	0-0	4		52,293
33	14	H	Bolton W	W	2-1	1-1	4	Rosicky [31], Fabregas [46]	60,101
34	17	H	Manchester C	W	3-1	1-1	—	Rosicky [12], Fabregas [73], Baptista [80]	59,913
35	21	A	Tottenham H	D	2-2	0-1	4	Toure [64], Adebayor [78]	36,050
36	29	H	Fulham	W	3-1	1-0	4	Baptista [4], Adebayor [84], Silva (pen) [87]	60,043
37	May 6	H	Chelsea	D	1-1	1-0	4	Silva (pen) [43]	60,102
38	13	A	Portsmouth	D	0-0	0-0	4		20,188

Final League Position: 4

GOALSCORERS

League (63): Van Persie 11 (1 pen), Henry 10 (3 pens), Silva 10 (5 pens), Adebayor 8 (1 pen), Baptista 3, Flamini 3, Gallas 3, Rosicky 3, Toure 3, Fabregas 2, Hleb 2, Diaby 1, Hoyte 1, own goals 3.
Carling Cup (15): Julio Baptista 6, Aliadiere 4 (1 pen), Adebayor 2, Song Billong 1, Walcott 1, own goal 1.
FA Cup (7): Adebayor 2, Rosicky 2, Henry 1, Ljungberg 1, Toure 1.
Champions League (13): Fabregas 2, Van Persie 2, Eboue 1, Flamini 1, Henry 1, Hleb 1, Julio Baptista 1, Ljungberg 1, Rosicky 1, Silva 1 (pen), own goal 1.

Lehmann J 36	Eboue E 23 + 1	Hoyte J 18 + 4	Silva G 34	Toure K 35	Djourou J 18 + 3	Hleb A 27 + 6	Fabregas F 34 + 4	Adebayor E 21 + 8	Henry T 16 + 1	Ljungberg F 16 + 2	Flamini M 9 + 11	Van Persie R 17 + 5	Walcott T 5 + 11	Rosicky T 22 + 4	Gallas W 21	Baptista J 11 + 13	Clichy G 26 + 1	Song Billong A 1 + 1	Aliadiere J 4 + 7	Almunia M 1	Senderos P 9 + 5	Denilson 4 + 6	Diaby V 9 + 3	Poom M 1	*Match No.*
1	2	3^1	4	5	6	7	8	9^2	10	11^3	12	13	14												1
1	2^2	3	4	5	6	7^1	8	12	10		13	9	14	11^3											2
1	2		4^1	5	6	7	8	13	10	11^3		9^2		12	3	14									3
1	2		4	5	6	7^2	8	9^1		11	12			10	3	13									4
1	2		4	5	6	12	8	9^2	10	7^3		13		11^1	3	14									5
1	2	3	4	5	12	7^1	8		10	11		9^2		13	6										6
1		3	4	5	2	12	8	9	10			13	7^1	11^2	6^3		14								7
1		2	4	5	6	7^1	8	12	10			9^2	13	11^3	3			14							8
1		2^1	4	5	6^2	7^3	8		10		12	9	13	11	3				14						9
1	12	2^3	4	5		7^1	8	13	10		14	9^2		11	6		3								10
	2		4	5		7	8	12	10		11	9^1			6		3			1					11
1	2			5		7	8	9	12		4	10^1	13		6	11^2	3								12
1	2		4	5		12	8	9		11^1	7^2		10			13	3				6				13
1		2	4	5	12	7^1	13		10		3	9	14	11^3				8^2			6■				14
1	2		4	5	6	12	8	9^2		7		10^3	13	11^1		14	3								15
1	2		4		5	7	8	9		12	11	10^1					3				6				16
1	2	12	4	5	6		13	9		11	8^2	14	7^1			10^3	3								17
1	2^1		4	5	6	7	8	13		11^3	12	10	14				3		9^2						18
1		2	4	5	6	7^2	8	9^3			12	10	13	11^1		14	3								19
1		2	4	5	6^3	7^1	8	9				10	12	11^2		13	3				14				20
1		2^1	4	5			12				11	10		8^2		7	3		9		6	13			21
1		2	4^1	5		7	8^3		10		12	9		11^2			3		13		6	14			22
1		2	4■	5	12	7	8^1	13	10^2		14	9^3		11			3				6				23
1	2^1	12		5		7^2	8	9	10		4^3	13		11		14	3				6				24
1		2^2	4	5			8	9^1	10		7			11			3		12		6■	13			25
1		2^3	4	5	6^1		8	12	10		13		7^2	11		9	3		14						26
1			4		2	7^1	8			11^3			9^2		5	10	3		13		12	6	14		27
1		2	4		5		8			7	12			13	3	10^1			9^3		14	6	11^2		28
1		3	4	2		12	8			7			13	11^1	5	10^3			9^2			14	6		29
1	2^1	12		5		7	8	9		13				14	6	10^2	3					4	11^3		30
1	2		4^3	5		7^1	8	9		11^2				10	6	13	3		12				14		31
1	2		4	5		7^1	8	9^2		10					6	12	3		13				11		32
1	2		4	5		7^1	8	9		10^2				11	6	12	3						13		33
1	2		4	5		7	8^2	9						11^3	6	12	3				14	13	10^1		34
1	2		4	5		7^3	12	9		10^1				11^2	6	13	3				14		8		35
1	2		4	5		7	8	9							6	10^1	3					12	11		36
1	2	13	4	5		12	8	9							6	10	3					11^1	7^2		37
	7	2		5	4	11	8									10	3				6		9	1	38

FA Cup

Third Round	Liverpool	(a)	3-1
Fourth Round	Bolton W	(h)	1-1
		(a)	3-1
Fifth Round	Blackburn R	(h)	0-0
		(a)	0-1

Champions League

Third Qualifying Round			
	Dynamo Zagreb	(a)	3-0
		(h)	2-1
Group G	Hamburg	(a)	2-1
	Porto	(h)	2-0
	CSKA Moscow	(a)	0-1
		(h)	0-0
	Hamburg	(h)	3-1
	Porto	(a)	0-0
Knock-Out Round	PSV Eindhoven	(a)	0-1
		(h)	1-1

Carling Cup

Third Round	WBA	(a)	2-0
Fourth Round	Everton	(a)	1-0
Quarter-Final	Liverpool	(a)	6-3
Semi-Final	Tottenham H	(a)	2-2
		(h)	3-1
Final *(at Millennium Stadium)*	Chelsea		1-2

ASTON VILLA — FA Premiership

FOUNDATION

Cricketing enthusiasts of Villa Cross Wesleyan Chapel, Aston, Birmingham decided to form a football club during the winter of 1874–75. Football clubs were few and far between in the Birmingham area and in their first game against Aston Brook St Mary's Rugby team they played one half rugby and the other soccer. In 1876 they were joined by a Scottish soccer enthusiast George Ramsay who was immediately appointed captain and went on to lead Aston Villa from obscurity to one of the country's top clubs in a period of less than 10 years.

Villa Park, Birmingham B6 6HE.
Telephone: (0871) 423 8100.
Fax: (0871) 423 8102.
Ticket Office/Consumer Sales: (0871) 423 8101.
Website: www.avfc.co.uk
Email: postmaster@avfc.co.uk
Ground Capacity: 42,551.
Record Attendance: 76,588 v Derby Co, FA Cup 6th rd, 2 March 1946.
Pitch Measurements: 115yd × 75yd.
Chairman: R. Lerner.
Chief Executive: R. Fitzgerald.
Club Secretary: Sharon Barnhurst.
Manager: Martin O'Neill.
Assistant Manager: John Robertson.
Physio: Alan Smith.
Sports Science Manager: Dr Stephen McGregor.
Colours: Claret body, blue sleeve shirts, white shorts, sky blue stockings with claret turnover.
Change Colours: White body and sleeves with thin sky blue pinstripe shirts, sky blue shorts, white stockings with sky blue trim to turnover.
Year Formed: 1874.
Turned Professional: 1885.
Ltd Co.: 1896.
Public Ltd Company: 1969.
Club Nickname: 'The Villans'.
Grounds: 1874, Wilson Road and Aston Park (also used Aston Lower Grounds for some matches); 1876, Wellington Road, Perry Barr; 1897, Villa Park.
First Football League Game: 8 September 1888, Football League, v Wolverhampton W (a) D 1–1 – Warner; Cox, Coulton; Yates, H. Devey, Dawson; A. Brown, Green (1), Allen, Garvey, Hodgetts.

HONOURS

FA Premier League: Runners-up 1992–93.

Football League: Division 1 – Champions 1893–94, 1895–96, 1896–97, 1898–99, 1899–1900, 1909–10, 1980–81; Runners-up 1888–89, 1902–03, 1907–08, 1910–11, 1912–13, 1913–14, 1930–31, 1932–33, 1989–90; Division 2 – Champions 1937–38, 1959–60; Runners-up 1974–75, 1987–88; Division 3 – Champions 1971–72.

FA Cup: Winners 1887, 1895, 1897, 1905, 1913, 1920, 1957; Runners-up 1892, 1924, 2000.

Double Performed: 1896–97.

Football League Cup: Winners 1961, 1975, 1977, 1994, 1996; Runners-up 1963, 1971.

European Competitions: *European Cup:* 1981–82 (winners), 1982–83. *UEFA Cup:* 1975–76, 1977–78, 1983–84, 1990–91, 1993–94, 1994–95, 1996–97, 1997–98, 1998–99, 2001–02. *World Club Championship:* 1982. *European Super Cup:* 1982–83 (winners). *Intertoto Cup:* 2000, 2001 (winners), 2002.

SKY SPORTS FACT FILE

On 25 January 1930 Aston Villa beat Walsall 3–1 in a fourth round FA Cup tie at Villa Park. Impressed by the outstanding performance of Saddlers goalkeeper Fred Biddlestone they signed him and he completed over 150 League games for the club.

Record League Victory: 12–2 v Accrington S, Division 1, 12 March 1892 – Warner; Evans, Cox; Harry Devey, Jimmy Cowan, Baird; Athersmith (1), Dickson (2), John Devey (4), L. Campbell (4), Hodgetts (1).

Record Cup Victory: 13–0 v Wednesbury Old Ath, FA Cup 1st rd, 30 October 1886 – Warner; Coulton, Simmonds; Yates, Robertson, Burton (2); R. Davis (1), A. Brown (3), Hunter (3), Loach (2), Hodgetts (2).

Record Defeat: 1–8 v Blackburn R, FA Cup 3rd rd, 16 February 1889.

Most League Points (2 for a win): 70, Division 3, 1971–72.

Most League Points (3 for a win): 78, Division 2, 1987–88.

Most League Goals: 128, Division 1, 1930–31.

Highest League Scorer in Season: 'Pongo' Waring, 49, Division 1, 1930–31.

Most League Goals in Total Aggregate: Harry Hampton, 215, 1904–15.

Most League Goals in One Match: 5, Harry Hampton v Sheffield W, Division 1, 5 October 1912; 5, Harold Halse v Derby Co, Division 1, 19 October 1912; 5, Len Capewell v Burnley, Division 1, 29 August 1925; 5, George Brown v Leicester C, Division 1, 2 January 1932; 5, Gerry Hitchens v Charlton Ath, Division 2, 18 November 1959.

Most Capped Player: Steve Staunton 64 (102), Republic of Ireland.

Most League Appearances: Charlie Aitken, 561, 1961–76.

Youngest League Player: Jimmy Brown, 15 years 349 days v Bolton W, 17 September 1969.

MANAGERS

George Ramsay 1884–1926
(Secretary-Manager)
W. J. Smith 1926–34
(Secretary-Manager)
Jimmy McMullan 1934–35
Jimmy Hogan 1936–44
Alex Massie 1945–50
George Martin 1950–53
Eric Houghton 1953–58
Joe Mercer 1958–64
Dick Taylor 1964–67
Tommy Cummings 1967–68
Tommy Docherty 1968–70
Vic Crowe 1970–74
Ron Saunders 1974–82
Tony Barton 1982–84
Graham Turner 1984–86
Billy McNeill 1986–87
Graham Taylor 1987–90
Dr Jozef Venglos 1990–91
Ron Atkinson 1991–94
Brian Little 1994–98
John Gregory 1998–2002
Graham Taylor OBE 2002–03
David O'Leary 2003–2006
Martin O'Neill August 2006–

Record Transfer Fee Received: £12,600,000 from Manchester U for Dwight Yorke, August 1998.

Record Transfer Fee Paid: £9,600,000 to Watford for Ashley Young, January 2007.

Football League Record: 1888 Founder Member of the League; 1936–38 Division 2; 1938–59 Division 1; 1959–60 Division 2; 1960–67 Division 1; 1967–70 Division 2; 1970–72 Division 3; 1972–75 Division 2; 1975–87 Division 1; 1987–88 Division 2; 1988–92 Division 1; 1992– FA Premier League.

LATEST SEQUENCES

Longest Sequence of League Wins: 9, 15.10.1910 – 10.12.1910.

Longest Sequence of League Defeats: 11, 23.3.1963 – 4.5.1963.

Longest Sequence of League Draws: 6, 12.9.1981 – 10.10.1981.

Longest Sequence of Unbeaten League Matches: 15, 12.3.1949 – 27.8.1949.

Longest Sequence Without a League Win: 12, 27.12.1986 – 25.3.1987.

Successive Scoring Runs: 35 from 10.11.1895.

Successive Non-scoring Runs: 5 from 29.2.1992.

TEN YEAR LEAGUE RECORD

		P	W	D	L	F	A	Pts	Pos
1997-98	PR Lge	38	17	6	15	49	48	57	7
1998-99	PR Lge	38	15	10	13	51	46	55	6
1999-2000	PR Lge	38	15	13	10	46	35	58	6
2000-01	PR Lge	38	13	15	10	46	43	54	8
2001-02	PR Lge	38	12	14	12	46	47	50	8
2002-03	PR Lge	38	12	9	17	42	47	45	16
2003-04	PR Lge	38	15	11	12	48	44	56	6
2004-05	PR Lge	38	12	11	15	45	52	47	10
2005-06	PR Lge	38	10	12	16	42	55	42	16
2006-07	PR Lge	38	11	17	10	43	41	50	11

DID YOU KNOW?

Tommy Dodds made his League debut for Aston Villa at inside-left on 31 August 1946 after wartime service in the Royal Navy. He had played in Villa's Midweek League side from January 1939. He was transferred to Swansea Town in the Trevor Ford deal in January 1947.

ASTON VILLA 2006–07 LEAGUE RECORD

Match No.	Date	Venue	Opponents	Result		H/T Score	Lg. Pos.	Goalscorers	Attendance
1	Aug 19	A	Arsenal	D	1-1	0-0	—	Mellberg [53]	60,023
2	23	H	Reading	W	2-1	1-1	—	Angel (pen) [34], Barry [61]	37,329
3	27	H	Newcastle U	W	2-0	2-0	2	Moore [3], Angel [38]	35,141
4	Sept 10	A	West Ham U	D	1-1	1-0	5	Ridgewell [4]	34,576
5	16	A	Watford	D	0-0	0-0	5		18,620
6	23	H	Charlton Ath	W	2-0	1-0	5	Agbonlahor [35], Moore [62]	35,513
7	30	A	Chelsea	D	1-1	1-1	6	Agbonlahor [45]	41,951
8	Oct 14	H	Tottenham H	D	1-1	0-0	6	Barry [81]	42,551
9	21	H	Fulham	D	1-1	1-1	7	Barry (pen) [26]	30,919
10	28	A	Liverpool	L	1-3	0-3	7	Agbonlahor [56]	44,117
11	Nov 5	H	Blackburn R	W	2-0	1-0	6	Barry (pen) [41], Angel [50]	30,089
12	11	A	Everton	W	1-0	1-0	4	Sutton [42]	36,376
13	19	A	Wigan Ath	D	0-0	0-0	5		18,455
14	25	H	Middlesbrough	D	1-1	1-1	5	Barry (pen) [45]	33,162
15	29	H	Manchester C	L	1-3	0-2	—	McCann [66]	30,124
16	Dec 2	A	Portsmouth	D	2-2	1-0	8	Barry (pen) [37], Angel [82]	20,042
17	11	A	Sheffield U	D	2-2	1-0	—	Petrov [2], Baros [64]	30,957
18	16	H	Bolton W	L	0-1	0-0	9		27,450
19	23	H	Manchester U	L	0-3	0-0	10		42,551
20	26	A	Tottenham H	L	1-2	0-0	10	Barry [81]	35,293
21	30	A	Charlton Ath	L	1-2	1-0	12	Barry (pen) [40]	26,699
22	Jan 2	H	Chelsea	D	0-0	0-0	—		41,006
23	13	A	Manchester U	L	1-3	0-3	15	Agbonlahor [52]	76,073
24	20	H	Watford	W	2-0	0-0	14	Mahon (og) [86], Agbonlahor [90]	35,892
25	31	A	Newcastle U	L	1-3	1-2	—	Young [25]	49,201
26	Feb 3	H	West Ham U	W	1-0	1-0	13	Carew [36]	41,202
27	10	A	Reading	L	0-2	0-1	13		24,122
28	Mar 3	A	Fulham	D	1-1	1-1	13	Carew [21]	24,552
29	14	H	Arsenal	L	0-1	0-1	—		39,968
30	18	H	Liverpool	D	0-0	0-0	13		42,551
31	Apr 2	H	Everton	D	1-1	0-1	—	Agbonlahor [83]	36,407
32	7	A	Blackburn R	W	2-1	1-1	13	Berger [34], Agbonlahor [73]	24,211
33	9	H	Wigan Ath	D	1-1	0-1	14	Agbonlahor [50]	31,920
34	14	A	Middlesbrough	W	3-1	1-1	10	Gardner [45], Moore [70], Petrov [77]	26,959
35	22	H	Portsmouth	D	0-0	0-0	11		31,745
36	28	A	Manchester C	W	2-0	1-0	11	Carew [24], Maloney [75]	40,799
37	May 5	H	Sheffield U	W	3-0	2-0	11	Agbonlahor [25], Young [42], Berger [59]	42,551
38	13	A	Bolton W	D	2-2	1-1	11	Gardner [37], Moore [81]	26,255

Final League Position: 11

GOALSCORERS

League (43): Agbonlahor 9, Barry 8 (5 pens), Angel 4 (1 pen), Moore 4, Carew 3, Berger 2, Gardner 2, Petrov 2, Young 2, Baros 1, Maloney 1, McCann 1, Mellberg 1, Ridgewell 1, Sutton 1, own goal 1.
Carling Cup (5): Angel 3, Agbonlahor 1, Barry 1 (pen).
FA Cup (1): Baros 1.

Sorensen T 29	Hughes A 15 + 4	Samuel J 2 + 2	Davis S 17 + 11	Mellberg O 38	Ridgewell L 19 + 2	Agbonlahor G 37 + 1	McCann G 28 + 2	Angel J 18 + 5	Moore L 7 + 6	Barry G 35	Hendrie L — + 1	Laursen M 12 + 2	Djemba-Djemba E — + 1	Whittingham P 2 + 1	Petrov S 30	Baros M 10 + 7	Gardner C 11 + 2	Taylor S 4 + 2	Berger P 5 + 8	Agathe D — + 5	Osbourne I 6 + 5	Sutton C 6 + 2	Bouma W 23 + 2	Cahill G 19 + 1	Kiraly G 5	Bardsley P 13	Carew J 11	Young A 11 + 2	Maloney S 5 + 3	*Match No.*
1	2	3	4^{1}	5	6	7	8	9^{2}	10^{3}	11	12	13	14																	1
1	2	3^{1}	4	5	6	7	8	9	10	11				12																2
1	2		4	5	6	7	8	9	10	11				3																3
1			4	5	6	7	8	9^{1}	10	3		2			11	12														4
1			4^{2}	2	6	7	8	9	10^{1}	3		5			11	12	13													5
1	2		4	5	6	7	8	9	10^{1}	3					11	12														6
1	2		4^{1}	5	6	7	8	9	10^{2}	3		12			11	13														7
	2		4^{1}	5	6	7	8	9		3					11	10^{2}		1	12	13										8
1	2		4^{1}	5	3	7		9^{2}		11		6			8	10^{3}				14	12	13								9
1	2		12	5	6	7		9^{2}		11					8	10^{3}				14	4^{1}	13	3							10
1	2			5		7	4	9		11		6			8	12						10^{1}	3							11
1			12	2	6	7	8	9^{2}							11					13	4	10^{1}	3	5						12
1			12	2	6	7		9^{1}		11				8^{2}						13	4	10	3	5						13
1^{G}			12	2	6	7	8	9^{2}		11					10	13		15			4^{1}		3	5						14
			12	2	6	7	4	9		11					8	10		1					3^{1}	5						15
	12		4^{1}	2	6	9	8	13		3					11	10^{2}		1			7			5						16
	12		4^{3}	2	6	7	8	13							11	10		1			14	9^{2}	3^{1}	5						17
			4	2	6	7	8^{2}	12		3					11	10^{1}	13					9		5	1					18
	2		4	5		10	8^{1}	12		3					11		7					9		6	1					19
	2^{1}		4	5^{2}	12	9	8			3					11^{3}	10	7				13		14	6	1					20
	2		4	5		10	8	9^{2}		3■					11^{1}		7				12		13	6	1					21
			4^{1}	2	6	10	8	9							11	12	7^{2}				13		3	5	1					22
1	4^{1}	13	12	2	6	9	8			11						10					7		3^{2}	5						23
1		12	4	5		7	8	9^{2}		11						10^{1}			13				3	6		2				24
1				5		7	4	12		11					8				13				3^{1}	6		2	9^{2}	10		25
1				5	12	7	4			11					8				13				3	6		2	9^{2}	10^{1}		26
1			12	5		7^{2}	8			3					11				13					6		2	9	10^{1}	4	27
1				5		12	8			11		6^{2}			7								3	13		2	9	10	4^{1}	28
1				5		7	4^{1}			11					8				12				3	6		2	9	10		29
1				5		7	4			11					8				12				3	6		2	9	10^{1}		30
1				5		7	4^{1}			11					8				12				3	6		2	9	10^{2}	13	31
1	12		13	5		9	14			11		6			8		7		10^{2}				3			2^{1}			4^{3}	32
1				5		9			12	11		6			8		4		10				3^{2}			2		13	7^{1}	33
1	12		13	5		9			14	11		6			8		4^{1}						3			2		10^{2}	7^{3}	34
1				5		10			12	11		6			7		4		8^{3}				3			2^{2}	9^{1}	13	14	35
1				5		7^{1}			12	11		6			8		4						3			2	9^{2}	10	13	36
1	2		12	5		7^{2}	13		14	11		6					4		8^{1}				3				9^{3}	10		37
1^{G}	2		12	5		7			13	11		6					4	15	8^{2}				3^{1}				9	10		38

FA Cup

Third Round	Manchester U	(a)	1-2

Carling Cup

Second Round	Scunthorpe U	(a)	2-1
Third Round	Leicester C	(a)	3-2
Fourth Round	Chelsea	(a)	0-4

BARNET FL Championship 2

FOUNDATION

Barnet Football Club was formed in 1888 as an amateur organisation and they played at a ground in Queen's Road until they disbanded in 1901. A club known as Alston Works FC was then formed and they played at Totteridge Lane until changing to Barnet Alston FC in 1906. They moved to their present ground a year later, combining with The Avenue to form Barnet and Alston in 1912. The club progressed to senior amateur football by way of the Athenian and Isthmian Leagues, turning professional in 1965. It was as a Southern League and Conference club that they made their name.

Underhill Stadium, Barnet Lane, Barnet, Herts EN5 2DN.

Telephone: 0208 441 6932.

Fax: 0208 447 0655.

Ticket Office: 0208 449 6325.

Website: www.barnetfc.com

Email: info@barnetfc.com

Ground Capacity: 5,300.

Record Attendance: 11,026 v Wycombe Wanderers, FA Amateur Cup 4th Round 1951–52.

Record Receipts: £31,202 v Portsmouth, FA Cup 3rd Round, 5 January 1991.

Pitch Measurements: 100m × 64m.

Chairman: Anthony Kleanthous.

Secretary: Andrew Adie.

Manager: Paul Fairclough.

Assistant Manager: Ian Hendon.

Physio: Mark Stein.

Colours: Old gold and black striped shirts, black shorts, Old gold and black stockings.

Change Colours: Blue and white striped shirts, white shorts, white stockings.

Year Formed: 1888.

Turned Professional: 1965.

Previous Names: 1906, Barnet Alston FC; 1919, Barnet.

Club Nickname: The Bees.

Grounds: 1888, Queens Road; 1901, Totteridge Lane; 1907, Barnet Lane.

First Football League Game: 17 August 1991, Division 4, v Crewe Alex (h) L 4–7 – Phillips; Blackford, Cooper (Murphy), Horton, Bodley (Stein), Johnson, Showler, Carter (2), Bull (2), Lowe, Evans.

HONOURS

Football League: Division 2 best season: 24th, 1993–94.

FA Amateur Cup: Winners 1946.

FA Trophy: Finalists 1972.

GM Vauxhall Conference: Winners 1990–91. *Conference:* Winners 2004–05

FA Cup: 4th rd, 2007.

League Cup: best season: 3rd rd, 2006.

SKY SPORTS FACT FILE

Former Chelsea, AC Milan, Tottenham Hotspur, West Ham United and England forward Jimmy Greaves joined Barnet in 1977 after a season with Chelmsford City. From midfield he still finished top scorer and was elected Player of the Year at the club.

Record League Victory: 7–0 v Blackpool, Division 3, 11 November 2000 – Naisbitt; Stockley, Sawyers, Niven (Brown), Heald, Arber (1), Currie (3), Doolan, Richards (2) (McGleish), Cottee (1) (Riza), Toms.

Record Cup Victory: 6–1 v Newport Co, FA Cup 1st rd, 21 November 1970 – McClelland; Lye, Jenkins, Ward, Embery, King, Powell (1), Ferry, Adams (1), Gray, George (3), (1 og).

Record Defeat: 1–9 v Peterborough U, Division 3, 5 September 1998.

Most League Points (3 for a win): 79, Division 3, 1992–93.

Most League Goals: 81, Division 4, 1991–92.

Highest League Scorer in Season: Dougie Freedman, 24, Division 3, 1994–95.

Most League Goals in Total Aggregate: Sean Devine, 47, 1995–99.

Most League Goals in One Match: 4, Dougie Freedman v Rochdale, Division 3, 13 September 1994; 4, Lee Hodges v Rochdale, Division 3, 8 April 1996.

Most Capped Player: Ken Charlery, 4, St Lucia.

Most League Appearances: Paul Wilson, 263, 1991–2000.

Youngest League Player: Kieran Adams, 17 years 71 days v Mansfield T, 31 December 1994.

Record Transfer Fee Received: £800,000 from Crystal Palace for Dougie Freedman, September 1995.

Record Transfer Fee Paid: £130,000 to Peterborough U for Greg Heald, August 1997.

Football League Record: Promoted to Division 4 from GMVC 1991; 1991–92 Division 4; 1992–93 Division 3; 1993–94 Division 2; 1994–2001 Division 3; 2001–05 Conference; 2005– FL 2.

MANAGERS

Lester Finch
George Wheeler
Dexter Adams
Tommy Coleman
Gerry Ward
Gordon Ferry
Brian Kelly
Bill Meadows 1976–79
Barry Fry 1979–85
Roger Thompson 1985
Don McAllister 1985–86
Barry Fry 1986–93
Edwin Stein 1993
Gary Phillips (Player–Manager) 1993–94
Ray Clemence 1994–96
Alan Mullery (Director of Football) 1996–97
Terry Bullivant 1997
John Still 1997–2000
Tony Cottee 2000–01
John Still 2001–02
Peter Shreeves 2002–03
Martin Allen 2003–04
Paul Fairclough March 2004–

LATEST SEQUENCES

Longest Sequence of League Wins: 6, 28.8.1993 – 25.9.1999.

Longest Sequence of League Defeats: 11, 8.5.1993 – 2.10.1993.

Longest Sequence of League Draws: 4, 22.1.1994 – 12.2.1994.

Longest Sequence of Unbeaten League Matches: 12, 5.12.1992 – 2.3.1993.

Longest Sequence Without a League Win: 14, 24.4.1993 – 10.10.1993.

Successive Scoring Runs: 12 from 19.3.1995.

Successive Non-scoring Runs: 5 from 12.2.2000.

TEN YEAR LEAGUE RECORD

		P	W	D	L	F	A	Pts	Pos
1997-98	Div 3	46	19	13	14	61	51	70	7
1998-99	Div 3	46	14	13	19	54	71	55	16
1999-2000	Div 3	46	21	12	13	59	53	75	6
2000–01	Div 3	46	12	9	25	67	81	45	24
2001–02	Conf	42	19	10	13	64	48	67	5
2002–03	Conf	42	13	14	15	65	68	53	11
2003–04	Conf	42	19	14	9	60	48	71	4
2004–05	Conf	42	26	8	8	90	44	86	1
2005–06	FL 2	46	12	18	16	44	57	54	18
2006–07	FL 2	46	16	11	19	55	70	59	14

DID YOU KNOW ?

On 25 September 1966 the Benefit Match for long-serving left-winger Reg Finch saw Barnet beat a Dexter Adams XI 4–2, the visitors including such illustrious names in their line-up as Danny Blanchflower, Mel Hopkins and Arsenal goalkeeper Bob Wilson.

BARNET 2006–07 LEAGUE RECORD

Match No.	Date	Venue	Opponents	Result		H/T Score	Lg. Pos.	Goalscorers	Attendance
1	Aug 5	H	Torquay U	L	0-1	0-0	—		2827
2	8	A	Swindon T	L	1-2	1-0	—	Bailey 18	7475
3	12	A	Accrington S	L	1-2	0-1	22	King 89	1639
4	19	H	Hereford U	W	3-0	1-0	17	Grazioli 28, Bailey 62, Puncheon 90	1945
5	26	A	Wrexham	D	1-1	0-1	17	Kandol 62	4304
6	Sept 2	H	Walsall	D	1-1	1-0	17	Sinclair 16	2356
7	9	A	Macclesfield T	W	3-2	0-0	14	Hendon (pen) 60, Cogan 64, Bailey 74	1770
8	12	H	Boston U	D	3-3	1-2	—	Vieira 2 29, 62, Grazioli 90	1461
9	16	H	Notts Co	L	2-3	2-2	15	Hendon (pen) 25, Puncheon 30	2317
10	23	A	Bury	D	2-2	1-1	18	Kandol 21, Hendon (pen) 81	1901
11	26	A	Peterborough U	D	1-1	0-1	—	Hessenthaler 46	3193
12	30	H	Milton Keynes D	D	3-3	1-1	18	Hendon (pen) 38, Kandol 52, Graham 57	2819
13	Oct 7	A	Stockport Co	L	0-2	0-1	21		4133
14	14	H	Lincoln C	L	0-5	0-3	22		2409
15	21	A	Darlington	L	0-2	0-0	22		3268
16	28	H	Chester C	W	1-0	1-0	22	Sinclair (pen) 29	2301
17	Nov 4	A	Hartlepool U	W	1-0	0-0	20	Cogan 83	3778
18	18	H	Rochdale	W	3-2	1-1	17	Kandol 3 39, 49, 90	1972
19	26	A	Bristol R	L	0-2	0-0	18		5351
20	Dec 5	H	Grimsby T	L	0-1	0-1	—		1588
21	9	A	Wycombe W	D	1-1	0-0	19	Hatch 60	4711
22	16	H	Mansfield T	W	2-1	1-0	17	Yakubu 45, Gross 54	1790
23	22	A	Shrewsbury T	W	1-0	0-0	—	Puncheon 82	3620
24	26	H	Peterborough U	W	1-0	1-0	13	Birchall 13	2958
25	30	H	Bury	W	2-1	2-1	11	Bailey 7, Birchall 18	1959
26	Jan 1	A	Boston U	L	1-2	1-1	13	Graham 12	1780
27	13	H	Macclesfield T	W	1-0	1-0	13	Birchall 40	2018
28	20	A	Milton Keynes D	L	1-3	1-1	15	King 27	6447
29	30	A	Notts Co	D	1-1	0-1	—	Bailey 74	3010
30	Feb 3	A	Torquay U	D	1-1	0-1	13	Nicolau 89	1942
31	10	H	Accrington S	L	1-2	1-1	14	Birchall 45	2041
32	17	A	Hereford U	L	0-2	0-0	15		2608
33	20	H	Swindon T	W	1-0	1-0	—	Allen 6	2639
34	24	A	Walsall	L	1-4	1-1	16	Allen 22	4635
35	Mar 3	H	Wrexham	L	1-2	1-0	18	Allen 27	2180
36	10	H	Stockport Co	W	3-1	1-1	17	Allen 44, Sinclair 47, Hatch 82	2647
37	17	A	Lincoln C	L	0-1	0-0	18		4339
38	20	H	Shrewsbury T	D	0-0	0-0	—		1672
39	24	A	Chester C	L	0-2	0-1	18		1591
40	31	H	Darlington	W	2-1	1-1	18	Sinclair 4, Hatch 52	2364
41	Apr 7	H	Hartlepool U	W	2-1	1-0	15	Birchall 4, Puncheon 81	2906
42	9	A	Rochdale	W	2-0	2-0	14	Cogan 24, Sinclair 33	2525
43	14	H	Bristol R	D	1-1	1-1	14	Puncheon 45	2541
44	21	A	Grimsby T	L	0-5	0-2	15		3675
45	28	A	Mansfield T	L	1-2	0-1	15	Birchall 68	2446
46	May 5	H	Wycombe W	W	2-1	0-1	14	Sinclair 53, Vieira 89	2707

Final League Position: 14

GOALSCORERS

League (55): Birchall 6, Kandol 6, Sinclair 6 (1 pen), Bailey 5, Puncheon 5, Allen 4, Hendon 4 (4 pens), Cogan 3, Hatch 3, Vieira 3, Graham 2, Grazioli 2, King 2, Gross 1, Hessenthaler 1, Nicolau 1, Yakubu 1.
Carling Cup (3): Kandol 2, Vieira 1.
FA Cup (9): Kandol 2 (1 pen), Sinclair 2, Birchall 1, Hendon 1 (pen), Puncheon 1, Vieira 1, Yakubu 1.
J Paint Trophy (3): Kandol 3.

Harrison L 28	Hendon I 25 + 1	King S 43	Hessenthaler A 19 + 5	Gross A 27	Warhurst P 11 + 8	Bailey N 43 + 1	Sinclair D 42	Grazioli G 7 + 10	Hatch L 18 + 13	Graham R 22 + 12	Vieira M 8 + 13	Kandol T 14 + 2	Puncheon J 34 + 3	Charles A 13 + 4	Nicolau N 17 + 5	Cogan B 33 + 6	Norville J 1 + 2	Yakubu I 28 + 1	Devera J 23 + 3	Flitney R 12 + 3	Birchall A 22 + 1	Burch R 6	Allen O 7 + 7	Lewis S 2 + 2	Ioannou N 1 + 1	Match No.
1	2	3	4	5	6	7	8	9¹	10²	11³	12	13	14													1
1	2	3	4	5	6	7	8	14	10²	11¹	9³	13	12													2
1	2³	5	4		6	7	8		10²	12	13	9		14	3	11¹										3
1	2	5				7	8	9¹	12	13		10	11	6	3	4²										4
1	2¹	3		5	12	7	8	9²				10	11	6		4	13									5
1	2	5				7	8	9¹			13	10	11	6	3	4²	12									6
1	2	3		5		7	8			12	13	10	11¹	6		4	9²									7
1	2	3		5		7	8	12		13	9¹	10	11	6		4²										8
1	2	3	12	5¹		7	8	13		14	9²	10	11	6		4³										9
1	2	3	4	5		7	8		12	13	9²	10¹	11▪	14				6³								10
1		3	4	5		7	8		9	11¹		10		6	12				2							11
1	2	3	4	5		7	8		9	11²	12	10¹		6		13										12
1⁶	2		4		5	7	8		9¹	11²	12	10		6	3	13				15						13
	2³				5²	7	8		10	12	9		11	6	3	4¹		13	14	1						14
			4			7	8	12		11	9¹	10		6	3			5	2	1						15
		6	4		12	7	8			13	9¹	10	11²		3			5	2	1						16
1		6	8		9	7	10						11		3	4		5	2							17
1	2	6	8		12	7	9		13			10	11¹		3	4²		5								18
1	2	6	8			7	10		9				11		3	4¹		5			12					19
1		3		6²	12	7	8		9¹	14	13		11			4³		5	2		10					20
1	2	3		6	12	7	8		9¹	4²			11			13		5			10					21
1	2	3		6	4	7	8			10	9¹		11			12		5								22
1⁶		3		6	12	7	8			10²			11¹	13		4		5	2	15	9					23
		3		6²		7	8		12	10			11¹	13		4		5	2	1	9					24
		3	12			7	8▪		13	10			11²	6		4		5	2	1	9¹					25
		3	8			7			12	10	13		11	6		4²		5	2¹	1	9					26
1	2	6				7	8	12	13	10			11²		3	4		5			9¹					27
1⁶	2▪	6	12			7²	8▪		13	10¹			11		3	4		5		15	9					28
		3	8	6		7				10			11¹			4		5	2		9	1	12			29
		3	8	6³	10¹					11²	12				13	4		5	2		9	1	14	7		30
	2	3	8³	6²		7			12▪	10			11¹			4▪		5			9	1	13	14		31
		3		6¹	13	7	8	9		10			11³		12			5	2			1	14	4²		32
	2	3		6		7	8	9		11			12			4		5²	13			1	10¹			33
	2	3	12	6		7	8	9		11	13					4¹			5			1	10²			34
	2³	3	12	6		7	8		9	4¹	13		11			14		5		1			10²			35
		3	7	6			8		12				11			4²		5	2	1	9¹		10	13		36
		3	7	6²		12	8		14	13			11			4¹		5	2	1	9		10³			37
		3	4¹	6		7	8		10				11			12		5	2	1	9²		13			38
	2	3³		6		7	8	12	13	11						4²		5	14	1	9		10¹			39
1	12	3²		6¹	13	7	8	14	10						11	4		5	2		9³					40
1		3			6²	7	8	12	10				11		13	4		5	2		9¹					41
1		6				7	8	12	10¹	13			11²		3	4		5	2		9					42
		6				7	8		10				11		3	4			2	1	9		12		5¹	43
1		6			5	7	8		10¹		12		11		3	4			2²		9				13	44
1		6			5	7	8	12	10³	13			11		3²	4			2		9¹		14			45
1	2	3		6▪		7	8		12		13		11		14	4³			5		9¹		10²			46

Carling Cup

First Round	Cardiff C	(a)	2-0
Second Round	Leeds U	(a)	1-3

J Paint Trophy

First Round	Notts Co	(a)	1-0
Second Round	Cheltenham T	(a)	2-3

FA Cup

First Round	Gainsborough T	(a)	3-1
Second Round	Northampton T	(h)	4-1
Third Round	Colchester U	(h)	2-1
Fourth Round	Plymouth Arg	(h)	0-2

BARNSLEY FL Championship

FOUNDATION

Many clubs owe their inception to the church and Barnsley are among them, for they were formed in 1887 by the Rev. T. T. Preedy, curate of Barnsley St Peter's and went under that name until it was dropped in 1897 a year before being admitted to the Second Division of the Football League.

Oakwell Stadium, Grove Street, Barnsley, South Yorkshire S71 1ET.

Telephone: (01226) 211 211.

Fax: (01226) 211 444.

Ticket Office: (0871) 22 66 777.

Website: www.barnsleyfc.co.uk

Email: thereds@barnsleyfc.co.uk

Ground Capacity: 23,186.

Record Attendance: 40,255 v Stoke C, FA Cup 5th rd, 15 February 1936.

Pitch Measurements: 100m × 67m.

Chairman: Gordon Shepherd.

Secretary: A. D. Rowing.

Manager: Simon Davey.

Assistant Manager: Ryan Kidd.

Physio: Richard Kay.

Colours: Red shirts, white shorts, red stockings.

Change Colours: Yellow shirts with black trim, black shorts, black stockings.

Year Formed: 1887.

Turned Professional: 1888.

Ltd Co.: 1899.

Previous Name: 1887, Barnsley St Peter's; 1897, Barnsley.

Club Nickname: 'The Tykes', 'Reds' or 'Colliers'.

Ground: 1887, Oakwell.

First Football League Game: 1 September 1898, Division 2, v Lincoln C (a) L 0–1 – Fawcett; McArtney, Nixon; King, Burleigh, Porteous; Davis, Lees, Murray, McCullough, McGee.

Record League Victory: 9–0 v Loughborough T, Division 2, 28 January 1899 – Greaves; McArtney, Nixon; Porteous, Burleigh, Howard; Davis (4), Hepworth (1), Lees (1), McCullough (1), Jones (2). 9–0 v Accrington S, Division 3 (N), 3 February 1934 – Ellis; Cookson, Shotton; Harper, Henderson, Whitworth; Spence (2), Smith (1), Blight (4), Andrews (1), Ashton (1).

Record Cup Victory: 6–0 v Blackpool, FA Cup 1st rd replay, 20 January 1910 – Mearns; Downs, Ness; Glendinning, Boyle (1), Utley; Bartrop, Gadsby (1), Lillycrop (2), Tufnell (2), Forman. 6–0 v Peterborough U, League Cup 1st rd 2nd leg, 15 September 1981 – Horn; Joyce, Chambers, Glavin (2), Banks, McCarthy, Evans, Parker (2), Aylott (1), McHale, Barrowclough (1).

HONOURS

Football League: Division 1 – Runners-up 1996–97; Promoted from FL 1 (play-offs) 2005–06; Division 3 (N) – Champions 1933–34, 1938–39, 1954–55; Runners-up 1953–54; Division 3 – Runners-up 1980–81; Division 4 – Runners-up 1967–68; Promoted 1978–79.

FA Cup: Winners 1912; Runners-up 1910.

Football League Cup: best season: 5th rd, 1982.

SKY SPORTS FACT FILE

George Utley, left-half in their 1912 FA Cup winning team became the first England international player for Barnsley when he was capped the following year. He reprised his cup-winning performance with Sheffield United in the famous 1915 Khaki Cup Final.

Record Defeat: 0–9 v Notts Co, Division 2, 19 November 1927.

Most League Points (2 for a win): 67, Division 3 (N), 1938–39.

Most League Points (3 for a win): 82, Division 1, 1999–2000.

Most League Goals: 118, Division 3 (N), 1933–34.

Highest League Scorer in Season: Cecil McCormack, 33, Division 2, 1950–51.

Most League Goals in Total Aggregate: Ernest Hine, 123, 1921–26 and 1934–38.

Most League Goals in One Match: 5, Frank Eaton v South Shields, Division 3N, 9 April 1927; 5, Peter Cunningham v Darlington, Division 3N, 4 February 1933; 5, Beau Asquith v Darlington, Division 3N, 12 November 1938; 5, Cecil McCormack v Luton T, Division 2, 9 September 1950.

Most Capped Player: Gerry Taggart, 35 (50), Northern Ireland.

Most League Appearances: Barry Murphy, 514, 1962–78.

Youngest League Player: Alan Ogley, 16 years 226 days v Bristol R, 18 September 1962.

Record Transfer Fee Received: £4,500,000 from Blackburn R for Ashley Ward, December 1998.

Record Transfer Fee Paid: £1,500,000 to Partizan Belgrade for Georgi Hristov, July 1997.

Football League Record: 1898 Elected to Division 2; 1932–34 Division 3 (N); 1934–38 Division 2; 1938–39 Division 3 (N); 1946–53 Division 2; 1953–55 Division 3 (N); 1955–59 Division 2; 1959–65 Division 3; 1965–68 Division 4; 1968–72 Division 3; 1972–79 Division 4; 1979–81 Division 3; 1981–92 Division 2; 1992–97 Division 1; 1997–98 FA Premier League; 1998–2002 Division 1; 2002–04 Division 2; 2004–06 FL 1; 2006– FL C.

MANAGERS

Arthur Fairclough 1898–1901
(Secretary-Manager)
John McCartney 1901–04
(Secretary-Manager)
Arthur Fairclough 1904–12
John Hastie 1912–14
Percy Lewis 1914–19
Peter Sant 1919–26
John Commins 1926–29
Arthur Fairclough 1929–30
Brough Fletcher 1930–37
Angus Seed 1937–53
Tim Ward 1953–60
Johnny Steele 1960–71
(continued as General Manager)
John McSeveney 1971–72
Johnny Steele *(General Manager)* 1972–73
Jim Iley 1973–78
Allan Clarke 1978–80
Norman Hunter 1980–84
Bobby Collins 1984–85
Allan Clarke 1985–89
Mel Machin 1989–93
Viv Anderson 1993–94
Danny Wilson 1994–98
John Hendrie 1998–99
Dave Bassett 1999–2000
Nigel Spackman 2001
Steve Parkin 2001–02
Glyn Hodges 2002–03
Gudjon Thordarson 2003–04
Paul Hart 2004–05
Andy Ritchie 2005–06
Simon Davey January 2007–

LATEST SEQUENCES

Longest Sequence of League Wins: 10, 5.3.1955 – 23.4.1955.

Longest Sequence of League Defeats: 9, 14.3.1953 – 25.4.1953.

Longest Sequence of League Draws: 7, 28.3.1911 – 22.4.1911.

Longest Sequence of Unbeaten League Matches: 21, 1.1.1934 – 5.5.1934.

Longest Sequence Without a League Win: 26, 13.12.1952 – 26.8.1953.

Successive Scoring Runs: 44 from 2.10.1926.

Successive Non-scoring Runs: 6 from 7.10.1899.

TEN YEAR LEAGUE RECORD

		P	*W*	*D*	*L*	*F*	*A*	*Pts*	*Pos*
1997-98	PR Lge	38	10	5	23	37	82	35	19
1998-99	Div 1	46	14	17	15	59	56	59	13
1999-2000	Div 1	46	24	10	12	88	67	82	4
2000-01	Div 1	46	15	9	22	49	62	54	16
2001-02	Div 1	46	11	15	20	59	86	48	23
2002-03	Div 2	46	13	13	20	51	64	52	19
2003-04	Div 2	46	15	17	14	54	58	62	12
2004-05	FL 1	46	14	19	13	69	64	61	13
2005-06	FL 1	46	18	18	10	62	44	72	5
2006-07	FL C	46	15	5	26	53	85	50	20

DID YOU KNOW?

The void left when Ernie Hine moved on for several seasons before returning to Barnsley was well filled by Frank Eaton. Signed in 1925 from New Mills his 5ft 9in stature allied to a lengthy stride helped to contribute 59 goals in 151 League games.

BARNSLEY 2006–07 LEAGUE RECORD

Match No.	Date	Venue	Opponents	Result		H/T Score	Lg. Pos.	Goalscorers	Attendance
1	Aug 5	H	Cardiff C	L	1-2	1-2	—	Howard [31]	12,082
2	8	A	Hull C	W	3-2	1-2	—	McIndoe [45], Richards [49], Hayes [73]	18,207
3	12	A	Colchester U	W	2-1	0-1	8	Richards [57], Howard [78]	4249
4	19	H	Southampton	D	2-2	1-0	8	Richards [45], Hayes (pen) [71]	11,306
5	26	A	Norwich C	L	1-5	1-2	14	Hayes [38]	24,876
6	Sept 9	H	Stoke C	D	2-2	0-2	12	Wright [73], Hayes [76]	10,464
7	12	A	Burnley	L	2-4	2-1	—	McIndoe 2 [21, 32]	10,304
8	16	H	Wolverhampton W	W	1-0	1-0	13	Richards [10]	11,350
9	22	A	Preston NE	L	0-1	0-1	—		11,728
10	30	H	Luton T	L	1-2	0-0	18	Howard [48]	10,175
11	Oct 14	A	Sheffield W	L	1-2	0-1	20	Howard [56]	28,687
12	17	H	Plymouth Arg	D	2-2	1-2	—	Kay [2], Richards [50]	9479
13	21	A	Sunderland	L	0-2	0-0	21		27,918
14	28	H	Coventry C	L	0-1	0-0	22		10,470
15	Nov 1	A	Derby Co	L	1-2	1-0	—	Hassell [13]	21,295
16	4	H	Leeds U	W	3-2	1-2	21	Devaney [30], McIndoe [62], Howard [76]	16,943
17	11	A	Birmingham C	L	0-2	0-1	23		19,344
18	18	A	Crystal Palace	L	0-2	0-2	23		20,159
19	25	H	Ipswich T	W	1-0	0-0	22	McCann [90]	10,556
20	28	H	Southend U	W	2-0	1-0	—	Howard [24], Reid K [87]	9588
21	Dec 2	A	Leeds U	D	2-2	2-2	21	Nardiello 2 [3, 36]	21,378
22	10	H	WBA	D	1-1	1-1	21	Hayes [35]	9512
23	16	A	Leicester C	L	0-2	0-1	21		30,457
24	23	A	QPR	L	0-1	0-1	21		11,307
25	26	H	Burnley	W	1-0	1-0	21	Devaney [30]	12,842
26	30	H	Sheffield W	L	0-3	0-1	21		21,253
27	Jan 1	A	Wolverhampton W	L	0-2	0-0	22		20,064
28	13	H	Preston NE	L	0-1	0-0	22		10,810
29	20	A	Luton T	W	2-0	1-0	22	Howard [7], Devaney [90]	7441
30	30	H	QPR	W	2-0	1-0	—	Richards [45], Howard [90]	9890
31	Feb 2	A	Cardiff C	L	0-2	0-2	—		11,549
32	10	H	Colchester U	L	0-3	0-2	22		11,192
33	17	A	Southampton	L	2-5	1-1	22	Nardiello [2], Ferenczi [68]	22,460
34	20	H	Hull C	W	3-0	1-0	—	Ferenczi 2 [16, 76], Rajczi [46]	12,526
35	26	A	Stoke C	W	1-0	1-0	—	Ferenczi [43]	13,114
36	Mar 3	H	Norwich C	L	1-3	1-3	19	Rajczi [45]	11,010
37	10	H	Sunderland	L	0-2	0-0	20		18,207
38	14	A	Plymouth Arg	W	4-2	2-2	—	Nyatanga [20], Devaney 2 [31, 61], Ferenczi [90]	10,265
39	17	A	Coventry C	L	1-4	0-3	20	Hassell [79]	21,609
40	31	H	Derby Co	L	1-2	0-1	20	Togwell [90]	17,059
41	Apr 7	A	Ipswich T	L	1-5	0-2	22	Nardiello [79]	20,585
42	9	H	Birmingham C	W	1-0	0-0	21	Nardiello [52]	15,857
43	14	A	Southend U	W	3-1	2-0	20	Nardiello 2 [15, 51], Reid K [29]	10,089
44	21	H	Crystal Palace	W	2-0	1-0	20	Nardiello 2 (1 pen) [15, 68 (p)]	10,277
45	28	H	Leicester C	L	0-1	0-0	20		20,012
46	May 6	A	WBA	L	0-7	0-4	20		23,568

Final League Position: 20

GOALSCORERS

League (53): Nardiello 9 (1 pen), Howard 8, Richards 6, Devaney 5, Ferenczi 5, Hayes 5 (1 pen), McIndoe 4, Hassell 2, Rajczi 2, Reid K 2, Kay 1, McCann 1, Nyatanga 1, Togwell 1, Wright 1.
Carling Cup (3): Devaney 1, McIndoe 1, Williams 1 (pen).
FA Cup (1): Coulson 1.

Colgan N 43 + 1	Hassell B 37 + 2	Heckingbottom P 28 + 3	Reid P 36 + 1	Kay A 31 + 1	Howard B 42	Devaney M 37 + 4	Togwell S 44	Hayes P 25 + 5	Richards M 22 + 9	McIndoe M 18	Williams R 8 + 7	Wright T 4 + 13	Tonge D 2 + 4	Wroe N — + 3	Healy C — + 8	Austin N 21 + 3	Mannone V 1 + 1	Nardiello D 19 + 11	McCann G 17 + 5	Reid K 12 + 14	Wallwork R 2	Knight L 6 + 3	Atkinson R 6	Eckersley A 6	Mattis D 3	Coulson M — + 2	Ferenczi I 14 + 2	Rajczi P 8 + 7	Nyatanga L 10	Jones R 1 + 3	Lucas D 2 + 1	Potter L 1	Heslop S — + 1	*Match No.*
1	2	3^{1}	4	5	6	7^{2}	8	9	10	11	12	13																						1
1	2	3	4	5	6^{3}	7	8	9	10^{1}	11^{2}	13	12	14																					2
1	2	3	4	5	6	7	8^{1}	9^{3}	10^{2}	11		14		12	13																			3
1	2		4	5	6^{3}	7	8^{1}	9	10^{2}	11	3	13	12		14																			4
1	2		4	5■	6	7^{2}	8	9	10^{1}	11	3^{3}	12	14		13																			5
1	5		4		6^{2}	7	8	9	10^{1}	11	3	12	2		13																			6
1	2		4	5	6	7	8	9	10^{1}	11	3	12																						7
1	4	3		5	6	7^{1}	8	9^{2}	10^{3}	11	14	13	2		12																			8
1■	2^{1}	3		5	6	7	8	9	10^{G}	11	12	13				4^{2}	15																	9
	2	3		5	6	7^{1}	8	9	10	11	13	12				4^{2}	1																	10
1	2	3■		5	6	7^{2}	8	9^{1}	10^{3}	11	12				13	4		14																11
1	4		12	5	6	7	8	9^{2}	10^{3}	11	3	13				2^{1}		14																12
1	2		4	5	6^{2}	7	8	9^{3}	10^{1}	11	3	12			13			14																13
1	2		4	5	6	7^{2}	8	9^{3}	10^{1}	11	3	12			13			14																14
1	2^{2}	3	4	5	6	7	8	12	10^{3}	11		9^{1}				13		14																15
1		3	4	5	6^{2}	7	8	12	10^{3}	11		9^{1}		13		2		14																16
1	12	3	4	5	6	7^{2}	8	13	10^{3}	11		9^{1}				2		14																17
1	2	3	4	5	6	7^{2}	8	12		11		9^{1}		13				10																18
1	2^{2}	3	4	5			8	9^{3}	12							13		10^{1}	6	14	7	11												19
1	2	3		5	6	13	8^{2}	7^{1}	10^{3}							4		14		12■	11	9												20
1	2	3	4		6		8	7	12							5		10^{1}	11			9												21
1	2	3	4		6	12	8	7	13							5		10		11^{1}		9^{2}												22
1	2	3	4^{2}		6	12	8^{3}	7			13					5		10	14	11		9^{1}												23
1	2		4	5	6^{3}	12	8	7^{1}	13							3		10	11	14		9^{2}												24
1	2	12		5		7	8	9^{3}	13							3^{1}		10^{2}	6	11		14	4											25
1	2			5		7		9^{1}	12		3^{2}		13			6		10	8	11^{3}		14	4											26
1	2	12	4^{1}	5		7	8	9^{2}								3		10	11^{3}	14		13	6											27
1	2		4		6		8^{1}	9^{2}										10	12	11			5	3	7	13								28
1	2		4	5	6	7	8		9^{1}									10^{2}	11	12				3		13								29
1	2		4	5	6	7	8		9									10^{1}	11	12				3										30
1	2		4	5	6	7	8^{1}		9									10^{3}	11	12				3^{2}			13	14						31
1	2		4		6	7			9^{2}										11	12			5	3	8^{1}		13	10						32
1	2	3	4		6	7^{3}	8		12									10■		13					11^{2}		9^{1}		5	14				33
1^{G}	2	3	4		6	7	8		12										11	13							9^{1}	10^{2}	5		15			34
1		3	4		6	7	8									2			11	12							9	10^{1}	5					35
1	2	3	4		6	7^{2}	8		12										11^{3}	13							9	10^{1}	5	14				36
1		3	4		6	7^{2}	8									2		12	11	13							9	10^{1}	5					37
1		3	4		6	7	8									2			11								9	10	5					38
1	12	3	4		6^{2}	7^{3}	8									2^{1}		13	11	14							9	10	5					39
15	2	3	4^{1}	5	6		8	13								12			11^{2}	7							9	10			1^{G}			40
1	2	3^{3}	4^{1}	12	6		8	9^{2}										13		11							10	14	5	7				41
1	2	12		4	6	7^{2}	8											10^{3}	13	11				3^{1}			9	14	5					42
1		3	4	2	6^{1}	7	8											10^{2}	12	11							9	13	5					43
1		3	4	5	6	7^{2}	8									2		10^{1}		11							9	12		13				44
1		3	4	5	6	7	8									2		10		11^{1}							9	12						45
	2				6	7^{1}	8^{3}									3		10	12	11			5				9^{2}	13			1	4	14	46

FA Cup			
Third Round	Southend U	(a)	1-1
		(h)	0-2

Carling Cup			
First Round	Blackpool	(a)	2-2
Second Round	Milton Keynes D	(h)	1-2

BIRMINGHAM CITY — FA Premiership

FOUNDATION

In 1875, cricketing enthusiasts who were largely members of Trinity Church, Bordesley, determined to continue their sporting relationships throughout the year by forming a football club which they called Small Heath Alliance. For their earliest games played on waste land in Arthur Street, the team included three Edden brothers and two James brothers.

St Andrews Stadium, Birmingham B9 4NH.
Telephone: 0871 226 1875.
Fax: 0871 226 1975.
Ticket Office: (0871) 226 1875 (option 2).
Website: www.bcfc.com
Email: reception@bcfc.com
Ground Capacity: 30,079 (all seated).
Record Attendance: 66,844 v Everton, FA Cup 5th rd, 11 February 1939.
Pitch Measurements: 101m × 68m.
Chairman: David Sullivan (PLC), David Gold (FC).
Vice-chairman: Jack Wiseman.
Managing Director: Karren Brady.
Secretary: Julia Shelton.
Manager: Steve Bruce.
Assistant Manager: Eric Black.
Physio: Neil McDiarmid.
Colours: Royal blue shirts, white shorts white stockings.
Change Colours: Black shirts with yellow trim, black shorts with yellow trim, black stockings with yellow trim.
Year Formed: 1875.
Turned Professional: 1885.
Ltd Co.: 1888.
Previous Names: 1875, Small Heath Alliance; 1888, dropped 'Alliance'; 1905, Birmingham; 1945, Birmingham City.
Club Nickname: 'Blues'.
Grounds: 1875, waste ground near Arthur St; 1877, Muntz St, Small Heath; 1906, St Andrews.
First Football League game: 3 September 1892, Division 2, v Burslem Port Vale (h) W 5–1 – Charsley; Bayley, Speller; Ollis, Jenkyns, Devey; Hallam (1), Edwards (1), Short (1), Wheldon (2), Hands.
Record League Victory: 12–0 v Walsall T Swifts, Division 2, 17 December 1892 – Charsley; Bayley, Jones; Ollis, Jenkyns, Devey; Hallam (2), Walton (3), Mobley (3), Wheldon (2), Hands (2). 12–0 v Doncaster R, Division 2, 11 April 1903 – Dorrington; Goldie, Wassell; Beer, Dougherty (1), Howard; Athersmith (1), Leonard (3), McRoberts (1), Wilcox (4), Field (1). Aston, (1 og).

HONOURS

Football League: Promoted from FL C – Runners-up 2006–07; Division 1 (play-offs) 2001–02; Division 2 – Champions 1892–93, 1920–21, 1947–48, 1954–55, 1994–95; Runners-up 1893–94, 1900–01, 1902–03, 1971–72, 1984–85; Division 3 Runners-up 1991–92.

FA Cup: Runners-up 1931, 1956.

Football League Cup: Winners 1963; Runners-up 2001.

Leyland Daf Cup: Winners 1991.

Auto Windscreens Shield: Winners 1995.

European Competitions: *European Fairs Cup:* 1955–58, 1958–60 (runners-up), 1960–61 (runners-up), 1961–62.

SKY SPORTS FACT FILE

Because the Premier and Football League lists of retained and open to transfer players are released at different times in May each year, Cameron Jerome appeared under both Cardiff City and Birmingham City. He was transferred to Birmingham on 31 May 2006.

Record Cup Victory: 9–2 v Burton W, FA Cup 1st rd, 31 October 1885 – Hedges; Jones, Evetts (1); F. James, Felton, A. James (1); Davenport (2), Stanley (4), Simms, Figures, Morris (1).

Record Defeat: 1–9 v Sheffield W, Division 1, 13 December 1930. 1–9 v Blackburn R, Division 1, 5 January 1895.

Most League Points (2 for a win): 59, Division 2, 1947–48.

Most League Points (3 for a win): 89, Division 2, 1994–95.

Most League Goals: 103, Division 2, 1893–94 (only 28 games).

Highest League Scorer in Season: Joe Bradford, 29, Division 1, 1927–28.

Most League Goals in Total Aggregate: Joe Bradford, 249, 1920–35.

Most League Goals in One Match: 5, Walter Abbott v Darwen, Division 2, 26 November, 1898; 5, John McMillan v Blackpool, Division 2, 2 March 1901; 5, James Windridge v Glossop, Division 2, 23 January 1915.

Most Capped Player: Kenny Cunningham, 32 (72), Republic of Ireland.

Most League Appearances: Frank Womack, 491, 1908–28.

Youngest League Player: Trevor Francis, 16 years 7 months v Cardiff C, 5 September 1970.

Record Transfer Fee Received: £6,800,000 from Liverpool for Jermaine Pennant, July 2006.

Record Transfer Fee Paid: £5,875,000 to Liverpool for Emile Heskey, July 2004.

Football League Record: 1892 elected to Division 2; 1894–96 Division 1; 1896–1901 Division 2; 1901–02 Division 1; 1902–03 Division 2; 1903–08 Division 1; 1908–21 Division 2; 1921–39 Division 1; 1946–48 Division 2; 1948–50 Division 1; 1950–55 Division 2; 1955–65 Division 1; 1965–72 Division 2; 1972–79 Division 1; 1979–80 Division 2; 1980–84 Division 1; 1984–85 Division 2; 1985–86 Division 1; 1986–89 Division 2; 1989–92 Division 3; 1992–94 Division 1; 1994–95 Division 2; 1995–2002 Division 1; 2002–06 FA Premier League; 2006–07 FL C; 2007– FA Premier League.

MANAGERS

Alfred Jones 1892–1908
(Secretary-Manager)
Alec Watson 1908–10
Bob McRoberts 1910–15
Frank Richards 1915–23
Billy Beer 1923–27
William Harvey 1927–28
Leslie Knighton 1928–33
George Liddell 1933–39
Harry Storer 1945–48
Bob Brocklebank 1949–54
Arthur Turner 1954–58
Pat Beasley 1959–60
Gil Merrick 1960–64
Joe Mallett 1965
Stan Cullis 1965–70
Fred Goodwin 1970–75
Willie Bell 1975–77
Sir Alf Ramsay 1977–78
Jim Smith 1978–82
Ron Saunders 1982–86
John Bond 1986–87
Garry Pendrey 1987–89
Dave Mackay 1989–91
Lou Macari 1991
Terry Cooper 1991–93
Barry Fry 1993–96
Trevor Francis 1996–2001
Steve Bruce December 2001–

LATEST SEQUENCES

Longest Sequence of League Wins: 13, 17.12.1892 – 16.9.1893.

Longest Sequence of League Defeats: 8, 28.9.1985 – 23.11.1985.

Longest Sequence of League Draws: 8, 18.9.1990 – 23.10.1990.

Longest Sequence of Unbeaten League Matches: 20, 3.9.1994 – 2.1.1995.

Longest Sequence Without a League Win: 17, 28.9.1985 – 18.1.1986.

Successive Scoring Runs: 24 from 24.9.1892.

Successive Non-scoring Runs: 6 from 1.10.1949.

TEN YEAR LEAGUE RECORD

		P	W	D	L	F	A	Pts	Pos
1997-98	Div 1	46	19	17	10	60	35	74	7
1998-99	Div 1	46	23	12	11	66	37	81	4
1999-2000	Div 1	46	22	11	13	65	44	77	5
2000-01	Div 1	46	23	9	14	59	48	78	5
2001-02	Div 1	46	21	13	12	70	49	76	5
2002-03	PR Lge	38	13	9	16	41	49	48	13
2003-04	PR Lge	38	12	14	12	43	48	50	10
2004-05	PR Lge	38	11	12	15	40	46	45	12
2005-06	PR Lge	38	8	10	20	28	50	34	18
2006-07	FL C	46	26	8	12	67	42	86	2

DID YOU KNOW ?

In 1954–55 Birmingham City were declared Second Division champions on the only occasion the top three clubs finished level on points. City led on goal average from Luton Town and Rotherham United.

BIRMINGHAM CITY 2006–07 LEAGUE RECORD

Match No.	Date	Venue	Opponents	Result	H/T Score	Lg. Pos.	Goalscorers	Attendance
1	Aug 5	H	Colchester U	W 2-1	1-0	—	Campbell [30], Bendtner [79]	24,238
2	9	A	Sunderland	W 1-0	1-0	—	Forssell (pen) [40]	26,668
3	12	A	Stoke C	D 0-0	0-0	5		12,347
4	19	H	Crystal Palace	W 2-1	1-1	1	Bendtner [23], Larsson [90]	20,223
5	26	A	Cardiff C	L 0-2	0-1	4		20,109
6	Sept 9	H	Hull C	W 2-1	1-0	2	Campbell [16], Bendtner [53]	19,228
7	12	A	QPR	W 2-0	1-0	—	N'Gotty [23], Jerome [90]	10,936
8	16	H	Ipswich T	D 2-2	0-0	2	Campbell [74], Dunn [86]	20,841
9	23	A	Leeds U	L 2-3	1-2	2	Warner (og) [13], Bendtner [74]	18,898
10	30	H	Leicester C	D 1-1	0-0	2	McSheffrey [58]	18,002
11	Oct 14	A	Luton T	L 2-3	1-2	7	Campbell [14], Danns [66]	9275
12	17	H	Norwich C	L 0-1	0-0	—		20,537
13	21	A	Derby Co	W 1-0	0-0	8	Clemence [84]	25,673
14	28	H	WBA	W 2-0	1-0	6	McSheffrey 2 [19, 90]	21,009
15	31	A	Coventry C	W 1-0	1-0	—	Bendtner [26]	27,212
16	Nov 4	A	Plymouth Arg	W 1-0	0-0	4	Jaidi [75]	17,008
17	11	H	Barnsley	W 2-0	1-0	3	McSheffrey [35], Danns [90]	19,344
18	18	H	Wolverhampton W	D 1-1	1-0	3	McSheffrey [30]	22,256
19	25	A	Burnley	W 2-1	1-1	3	Bendtner [15], Campbell [83]	12,889
20	29	A	Southampton	L 3-4	0-3	—	Jerome [68], Bendtner [72], Jaidi [90]	21,889
21	Dec 2	H	Plymouth Arg	W 3-0	3-0	1	Bendtner [21], Upson [30], McSheffrey [41]	22,592
22	9	H	Preston NE	W 3-1	2-1	1	McSheffrey 3 (1 pen) [32, 40, 89 (p)]	23,159
23	16	A	Sheffield W	W 3-0	1-0	1	Clemence [42], McSheffrey [65], Jerome [90]	26,083
24	23	A	Southend U	W 4-0	2-0	1	Campbell [8], Clemence [38], McSheffrey [54], Jaidi [84]	9781
25	26	H	QPR	W 2-1	1-1	1	Upson [22], Jerome [62]	29,431
26	29	H	Luton T	D 2-2	1-1	—	McSheffrey [31], Danns [90]	24,642
27	Jan 1	A	Ipswich T	L 0-1	0-0	1		22,436
28	30	H	Southend U	L 1-3	1-1	—	Clarke (og) [9]	19,177
29	Feb 3	A	Colchester U	D 1-1	0-0	4	Clemence [66]	5918
30	11	H	Stoke C	W 1-0	0-0	2	McSheffrey [71]	15,854
31	17	A	Crystal Palace	W 1-0	1-0	2	Jerome [34]	17,233
32	20	H	Sunderland	D 1-1	0-1	—	Campbell [90]	20,941
33	24	A	Hull C	L 0-2	0-1	3		18,811
34	27	H	Leeds U	W 1-0	1-0	—	Bendtner [15]	18,363
35	Mar 4	H	Cardiff C	W 1-0	0-0	1	Larsson [56]	28,223
36	9	H	Derby Co	W 1-0	1-0	—	Vine [45]	20,962
37	13	A	Norwich C	L 0-1	0-0	—		23,504
38	18	A	WBA	D 1-1	0-0	2	Johnson [86]	21,434
39	Apr 1	H	Coventry C	W 3-0	1-0	2	Jaidi [13], Campbell 2 [65, 78]	25,424
40	7	H	Burnley	L 0-1	0-0	3		28,777
41	9	A	Barnsley	L 0-1	0-0	3		15,857
42	14	H	Southampton	W 2-1	1-0	3	Jaidi [32], Bendtner [79]	19,754
43	17	A	Leicester C	W 2-1	2-0	—	Jaidi [16], Larsson [19]	24,290
44	22	A	Wolverhampton W	W 3-2	0-0	1	Cole [54], Bendtner [77], Jerome [88]	22,754
45	28	H	Sheffield W	W 2-0	0-0	1	Jerome [74], Larsson [84]	29,317
46	May 6	A	Preston NE	L 0-1	0-0	2		16,837

Final League Position: 2

GOALSCORERS

League (67): McSheffrey 13 (1 pen), Bendtner 11, Campbell 9, Jerome 7, Jaidi 6, Clemence 4, Larsson 4, Danns 3, Upson 2, Cole 1, Dunn 1, Forssell 1 (pen), Johnson 1, N'Gotty 1, Vine 1, own goals 2.
Carling Cup (9): Bendtner 2, Jerome 2, Larsson 2, McSheffrey 2, Campbell 1.
FA Cup (9): Larsson 3, Campbell 2, McSheffrey 1, N'Gotty 1, Martin Taylor 1, own goal 1.

Taylor Maik 27	Kelly S 35 + 1	Sadler M 36	Tebily O 5 + 1	N'Gotty B 25	Clemence S 31 + 3	Johnson D 24 + 2	Danns N 11 + 18	Forssell M 3 + 5	Campbell D 15 + 17	Dunn D 9 + 2	Bendtner N 38 + 4	Jerome C 20 + 18	Larsson S 27 + 16	Nafti M 18 + 14	Muamba F 30 + 4	Jaidi R 38	McSheffrey G 40	Doyle C 19	Gray J 2 + 5	Kilkenny N — + 8	Taylor Martin 29 + 2	Painter M 1	Upson M 8 + 1	Vine R 10 + 7	Cole A 5	Match No.
1	2	3	4	5	6^{1}	7	8	9^{2}	10^{3}	11	12	13■	14													1
1	2	3	4	5	13	7	12	9^{3}		14	10		11	6^{1}	8^{2}											2
1	2	3	4	5	12	7	13	9^{1}		14	10		11^{3}	6	8^{2}											3
1	2	3		5		7^{1}	13	12	10	8	9^{2}		14	4^{3}		6	11									4
	2^{2}	3		5		7			10^{1}	8	9	12	13	4		6	11	1								5
1				5		7	12		10	8^{1}	9		2	4^{2}		6	11		3	13						6
1				5		2	8		10^{1}	7^{2}	9■	12	3		4^{3}	6	11			13	14					7
1				5■		2	8	12	10	7		9^{1}	3	4^{2}		6^{3}	11			13	14					8
1			12			2■	8		10^{2}	7	9	13	14	4^{3}		6	11				5^{1}	3				9
1	2	3	5				12	13	10^{3}		9^{2}	14	7	4^{1}	8	6	11									10
1	2	3		5			8	12	10			9^{1}	13	4^{2}	7^{3}	6	11			14						11
1		3	2	5			8		10	7^{3}		9^{2}	12		4^{1}	6	11		13	14						12
1	2	3			6	7	12			10^{2}	9	13	14	8^{3}		4	11^{1}				5					13
1	2	3			6^{3}	7	12				10	9^{2}	13	14	8^{1}	4	11				5					14
1	2	3			6		8		12		10	9^{2}	13		7	4	11^{1}				5					15
1	2	3			6^{3}		8^{1}				10	9^{2}	12	14	7	4	11		13		5					16
1	2	3			6^{3}		12		13		10	9^{1}	7	14	8	4	11^{2}				5					17
1	2	3			6		12				10	9^{1}	7	13	8^{2}	4	11				5					18
1	2	3			11		8		12		10		7^{1}	13	4^{2}	6	9^{3}				5		14			19
1	2	3			6		8^{2}		12		10	13	11^{1}	14	7^{3}	4	9				5					20
1	2	3			6^{1}		12		13		10^{2}	9	7	8		4	11						5			21
1	2	3			6				12		10	9^{2}	7	13	8	4	11^{1}						5			22
1	2	3			6		12		13		10^{2}	9	7^{1}	8		4	11^{3}			14			5			23
1	2	3			6^{2}	7	12		10		9^{3}			8	13	4	11^{1}			14			5			24
1	2	3			6	7			10^{1}		9	12^{2}	14	8	13	4	11						5^{3}			25
1	2	3					12		13		10	9^{2}	7^{3}	4^{1}	8	6	11			14			5			26
1	2	3			6	7	12		10^{1}		9		13		8^{2}		11				4		5			27
1		3		2^{2}	12	8			14			9	7^{3}	4^{1}	13		11				6		5	10		28
		3		2	6	7			12		13	9^{1}	14		8^{3}	4	11	1			5			10^{2}		29
		3		2	6^{1}	7					10	9^{2}	12		8	4	11	1			5			13		30
		3		2	6	7	12				10^{3}	9^{1}	13		8^{2}	4	11	1			5			14		31
		3		2^{2}	6		12		13		10^{3}	9	7		8^{1}	4	11	1			5			14		32
	12	3		2	6		8		10^{1}		13	9^{3}	7^{2}			4■	11	1			5			14		33
	2	3		4	6						10	12	7^{2}	14	8^{3}		11	1	13		5			9^{1}		34
	2	3		4	6						10	12	7	13	8^{2}		11	1			5			9^{1}		35
	2	3		4	6	12					10^{2}	13	7^{1}		8		11■	1			5			9		36
	2	3			6	7		12			10^{3}	13	11		8^{1}	4		1	14		5			9^{2}		37
	2	3			6	7			12		10	13	14		8^{3}	4		1	11■		5^{2}			9^{1}		38
	2	3			6^{3}	8			12		10^{2}	9^{1}	7	14	13	4		1			5			11		39
	2	3^{1}				8	12		13		10^{3}	14	7	4^{2}		6	11	1			5			9		40
	2			5^{3}		8^{1}	12		10		13	9			4	6	11	1	14		3			7^{2}		41
	2			5	6^{2}	7^{3}			12		10			13	8	4	11	1			3			14	9^{1}	42
	3			2	6				12		10^{2}	13	7^{3}	14	8	4	11	1			5				9^{1}	43
	3			2	6						10	12	7^{2}	13	8	4	11^{3}	1			5			14	9^{1}	44
	3			2	6						10^{1}	12	7	13	8■	4	11^{2}	1			5			14	9^{3}	45
	3			2^{1}	6	12			13		10	14	7	8^{2}		4	11	1			5				9^{3}	46

FA Cup

Third Round	Newcastle U	(h)	2-2
		(a)	5-1
Fourth Round	Reading	(h)	2-3

Carling Cup

First Round	Shrewsbury T	(h)	1-0
Second Round	Wrexham	(h)	4-1
Third Round	Sheffield U	(a)	4-2
Fourth Round	Liverpool	(h)	0-1

BLACKBURN ROVERS FA Premiership

FOUNDATION

It was in 1875 that some Public School old boys called a meeting at which the Blackburn Rovers club was formed and the colours blue and white adopted. The leading light was John Lewis, later to become a founder of the Lancashire FA, a famous referee who was in charge of two FA Cup Finals, and a vice-president of both the FA and the Football League.

Ewood Park, Blackburn BB2 4JF.

Telephone: 0870 111 3232.

Fax: (01254) 671 042.

Ticket Office: 0870 112 3456.

Website: www.rovers.co.uk

Email: enquiries@rovers.co.uk

Ground Capacity: 31,154.

Record Attendance: 62,522 v Bolton W, FA Cup 6th rd, 2 March 1929.

Pitch Measurements: 105m × 65.8m.

Chairman: John Williams.

Vice-chairman: David Brown.

Managing Director: Tom Finn.

Secretary: Andrew Pincher.

Manager: Mark Hughes.

Assistant Manager: Mark Bowen.

Physio: Dave Fevre.

Colours: Blue and white halved shirts.

Change Colours: Red and black halved shirts.

Year Formed: 1875.

Turned Professional: 1880.

Ltd Co.: 1897.

Club Nickname: Rovers.

Grounds: 1875, all matches played away; 1876, Oozehead Ground; 1877, Pleasington Cricket Ground; 1878, Alexandra Meadows; 1881, Leamington Road; 1890, Ewood Park.

First Football League Game: 15 September 1888, Football League, v Accrington (h) D 5–5 – Arthur; Beverley, James Southworth; Douglas, Almond, Forrest; Beresford (1), Walton, John Southworth (1), Fecitt (1), Townley (2).

Record League Victory: 9–0 v Middlesbrough, Division 2, 6 November 1954 – Elvy; Suart, Eckersley; Clayton, Kelly, Bell; Mooney (3), Crossan (2), Briggs, Quigley (3), Langton (1).

HONOURS

FA Premier League: Champions 1994–95; Runners-up 1993–94.

Football League: Division 1 – Champions 1911–12, 1913–14; 1991–92 (play-offs); Runners-up 2000–01; Division 2 – Champions 1938–39; Runners-up 1957–58; Division 3 – Champions 1974–75; Runners-up 1979–80.

FA Cup: Winners 1884, 1885, 1886, 1890, 1891, 1928; Runners-up 1882, 1960.

Football League Cup: Winners 2002.

Full Members' Cup: Winners 1987.

European Competitions: *European Cup:* 1995–96. *UEFA Cup:* 1994–95, 1998–99, 2002–03, 2003–04, 2006–07.

SKY SPORTS FACT FILE

Eamonn Rogers twice played for the Eire boys team which suffered 8–0 and 6–0 defeats against England. Yet he did enough to impress visiting Blackburn Rovers manager Jack Marshall that he signed the wing-half at 15 in 1962 and saw him win full caps.

Record Cup Victory: 11–0 v Rossendale, FA Cup 1st rd, 13 October 1884 – Arthur; Hopwood, McIntyre; Forrest, Blenkhorn, Lofthouse; Sowerbutts (2), J. Brown (1), Fecitt (4), Barton (3), Birtwistle (1).

Record Defeat: 0–8 v Arsenal, Division 1, 25 February 1933.

Most League Points (2 for a win): 60, Division 3, 1974–75.

Most League Points (3 for a win): 91, Division 1, 2000–01.

Most League Goals: 114, Division 2, 1954–55.

Highest League Scorer in Season: Ted Harper, 43, Division 1, 1925–26.

Most League Goals in Total Aggregate: Simon Garner, 168, 1978–92.

Most League Goals in One Match: 7, Tommy Briggs v Bristol R, Division 2, 5 February 1955.

Most Capped Player: Henning Berg, 58 (100), Norway.

Most League Appearances: Derek Fazackerley, 596, 1970–86.

Youngest League Player: Harry Dennison, 16 years 155 days v Bristol C, 8 April 1911.

Record Transfer Fee Received: £16,000,000 from Chelsea for Damian Duff, July 2003.

Record Transfer Fee Paid: £7,500,000 to Manchester U for Andy Cole, December 2001.

Football League Record: 1888 Founder Member of the League; 1936–39 Division 2; 1946–48 Division 1; 1948–58 Division 2; 1958–66 Division 1; 1966–71 Division 2; 1971–75 Division 3; 1975–79 Division 2; 1979–80 Division 3; 1980–92 Division 2; 1992–99 FA Premier League; 1999–2001 Division 1; 2001– FA Premier League.

MANAGERS

Thomas Mitchell 1884–96
(Secretary-Manager)
J. Walmsley 1896–1903
(Secretary-Manager)
R. B. Middleton 1903–25
Jack Carr 1922–26
(Team Manager under Middleton to 1925)
Bob Crompton 1926–30
(Hon. Team Manager)
Arthur Barritt 1931–36
(had been Secretary from 1927)
Reg Taylor 1936–38
Bob Crompton 1938–41
Eddie Hapgood 1944–47
Will Scott 1947
Jack Bruton 1947–49
Jackie Bestall 1949–53
Johnny Carey 1953–58
Dally Duncan 1958–60
Jack Marshall 1960–67
Eddie Quigley 1967–70
Johnny Carey 1970–71
Ken Furphy 1971–73
Gordon Lee 1974–75
Jim Smith 1975–78
Jim Iley 1978
John Pickering 1978–79
Howard Kendall 1979–81
Bobby Saxton 1981–86
Don Mackay 1987–91
Kenny Dalglish 1991–95
Ray Harford 1995–97
Roy Hodgson 1997–98
Brian Kidd 1998–99
Tony Parkes 1999–2000
Graeme Souness 2000–04
Mark Hughes September 2004–

LATEST SEQUENCES

Longest Sequence of League Wins: 8, 1.3.1980 – 7.4.1980.

Longest Sequence of League Defeats: 7, 12.3.1966 – 16.4.1966.

Longest Sequence of League Draws: 5, 11.10.1975 – 1.11.1975.

Longest Sequence of Unbeaten League Matches: 23, 30.9.1987 – 27.3.1988.

Longest Sequence Without a League Win: 16, 11.11.1978 – 24.3.1979.

Successive Scoring Runs: 32 from 24.4.1954.

Successive Non-scoring Runs: 4 from 12.12.1908.

TEN YEAR LEAGUE RECORD

		P	W	D	L	F	A	Pts	Pos
1997-98	PR Lge	38	16	10	12	57	52	58	6
1998-99	PR Lge	38	7	14	17	38	52	35	19
1999-2000	Div 1	46	15	17	14	55	51	62	11
2000-01	Div 1	46	26	13	7	76	39	91	2
2001-02	PR Lge	38	12	10	16	55	51	46	10
2002-03	PR Lge	38	16	12	10	52	43	60	6
2003-04	PR Lge	38	12	8	18	51	59	44	15
2004-05	PR Lge	38	9	15	14	32	43	42	15
2005-06	PR Lge	38	19	6	13	51	42	63	6
2006-07	PR Lge	38	15	7	16	52	54	52	10

DID YOU KNOW?

On 5 September 1896 Blackburn Rovers defeated Liverpool 1–0 at Ewood Park, but they had six goals disallowed – five for offside, the sixth when the referee blew for half-time to frustrate Harry Chippendale. Late in the game Jim Stuart's effort was approved!

BLACKBURN ROVERS 2006–07 LEAGUE RECORD

Match No.	Date	Venue	Opponents	Result		H/T Score	Lg. Pos.	Goalscorers	Attendance
1	Aug 19	A	Portsmouth	L	0-3	0-1	—		19,523
2	23	H	Everton	D	1-1	0-0	—	McCarthy[50]	22,015
3	27	H	Chelsea	L	0-2	0-0	20		19,398
4	Sept 9	A	Sheffield U	D	0-0	0-0	19		29,876
5	17	H	Manchester C	W	4-2	2-2	12	Sinclair (og)[18], Pedersen[44], McCarthy[66], Gallagher[89]	18,403
6	23	A	Middlesbrough	W	1-0	1-0	10	Nonda[27]	24,959
7	Oct 1	H	Wigan Ath	W	2-1	1-1	9	Bentley[45], McCarthy[81]	17,859
8	14	A	Liverpool	D	1-1	1-0	9	McCarthy[17]	44,206
9	22	H	Bolton W	L	0-1	0-0	10		27,662
10	29	A	West Ham U	L	1-2	0-1	11	Bentley[90]	33,833
11	Nov 5	A	Aston Villa	L	0-2	0-1	13		30,089
12	11	H	Manchester U	L	0-1	0-0	15		26,162
13	19	H	Tottenham H	D	1-1	1-0	15	Tugay[23]	18,083
14	Dec 2	H	Fulham	W	2-0	2-0	14	Nonda[6], McCarthy[24]	16,799
15	5	A	Charlton Ath	L	0-1	0-0	—		23,423
16	9	H	Newcastle U	L	1-3	0-2	16	Pedersen[47]	19,225
17	16	A	Reading	W	2-1	0-1	16	McCarthy[64], Bentley[84]	23,074
18	23	A	Arsenal	L	2-6	1-3	17	Nonda 2 (1 pen)[3 (p), 69]	59,913
19	26	H	Liverpool	W	1-0	0-0	15	McCarthy[49]	29,342
20	30	H	Middlesbrough	W	2-1	1-0	14	Nonda[9], McCarthy[74]	22,653
21	Jan 1	A	Wigan Ath	W	3-0	1-0	11	Heskey (og)[37], Derbyshire[58], McCarthy (pen)[76]	14,864
22	13	H	Arsenal	L	0-2	0-1	12		21,852
23	20	A	Manchester C	W	3-0	1-0	10	Pedersen 2[44, 62], Derbyshire[90]	36,590
24	23	A	Watford	L	1-2	1-1	—	McCarthy[45]	13,760
25	31	A	Chelsea	L	0-3	0-1	—		38,000
26	Feb 3	H	Sheffield U	W	2-1	1-1	9	Pedersen 2[22, 90]	20,917
27	10	A	Everton	L	0-1	0-1	10		35,593
28	25	H	Portsmouth	W	3-0	2-0	10	Nonda 2[1, 25], Warnock[50]	17,434
29	Mar 4	A	Bolton W	W	2-1	0-0	10	McCarthy 2 (2 pens)[58, 68]	21,743
30	17	H	West Ham U	L	1-2	0-0	10	Samba[47]	18,591
31	31	A	Manchester U	L	1-4	1-0	10	Derbyshire[29]	76,098
32	Apr 7	H	Aston Villa	L	1-2	1-1	11	McCarthy (pen)[24]	24,211
33	18	H	Watford	W	3-1	3-1	—	Samba[7], Roberts[10], McCarthy[32]	16,035
34	21	A	Fulham	D	1-1	0-1	10	McCarthy[61]	23,652
35	28	H	Charlton Ath	W	4-1	0-0	10	Roberts 2[60, 80], Hreidarsson (og)[77], Derbyshire[83]	24,921
36	May 5	A	Newcastle U	W	2-0	1-0	10	McCarthy[14], Roberts[73]	51,226
37	10	A	Tottenham H	D	1-1	1-0	—	McCarthy[32]	35,974
38	13	H	Reading	D	3-3	1-1	10	McCarthy[21], Bentley[56], Derbyshire[67]	22,671

Final League Position: 10

GOALSCORERS

League (52): McCarthy 18 (4 pens), Nonda 7 (1 pen), Pedersen 6, Derbyshire 5, Bentley 4, Roberts 4, Samba 2, Gallagher 1, Tugay 1, Warnock 1, own goals 3.
Carling Cup (0).
FA Cup (12): Derbyshire 4, McCarthy 3, Pedersen 2, Gallagher 1, Mokoena 1, Roberts 1.
UEFA Cup (12): Bentley 3, McCarthy 3, Savage 2, Jeffers 1 (pen), Neill 1, Nonda 1, Tugay 1.

Friedel B 38	Mokoena A 18 + 9	Gray M 10 + 1	Savage R 21	Neill L 20	Todd A 6 + 3	Reid S 3	Bentley D 36	Roberts J 9 + 9	McCarthy B 36	Pedersen M 36	Emerton B 32 + 2	Kuqi S — + 1	Khizanishvili Z 17 + 1	Ooijer A 20	Gallagher P 2 + 14	Jeffers F 3 + 7	Tugay K 26 + 4	Nonda S 17 + 9	Brown J — + 1	Peter S 1 + 8	McEveley J 3 + 1	Henchoz S 10 + 2	Derbyshire M 8 + 14	Warnock S 13	Nelsen R 12	Samba C 13 + 1	Dunn D 7 + 4	Berner B 1	Match No.
1	2	3	4	$5^{\blacksquare}$	$6^{\blacksquare}$	7	8^{1}	9	10^{2}	11	12	13																	1
1		3	4		6	7	8^{1}	9^{2}	10	11	2		5		12	13													2
1			4	3		7	8	9	10	11^{1}	2		5	6	12														3
1			8	3			7		10^{1}	11	2		5	6		9	4	12											4
1	12		8	3			7		10^{2}	11	2		5	6	13	9^{3}	4^{1}	14											5
1	12	13	8	3			7		10^{3}	11^{2}	2		5	6	14		4^{1}	9											6
1^{6}	12		8	3			7	13	10	11	2		5	6		9^{2}	4^{1}		15										7
1	12		8	3			7	13	10^{2}	11^{3}	2		5	6	14		4^{1}	9											8
1	12		8^{1}	3			7	13	10	11^{2}	2		5	6			4^{3}	9		14									9
1	8^{2}	3^{3}		2			7	9^{1}	10				5	6	13	12	4			11	14								10
1	8	3		2^{3}			7		10^{1}	11			5	6		12	4^{2}	9		13		14							11
1	8			3			7^{2}		10	11	2		5	6		12	4	9^{1}		13									12
1	12	3	8				7^{3}		10^{2}	11	2			6		13	$4^{\blacksquare}$	9^{1}		14		5							13
1	12	3	4	2			8^{1}		10^{3}	11	7			6				9^{2}		13		5	14						14
1		3	4	2			8^{1}		10	11^{2}	7^{3}			6	13		12	9		14		5							15
1		3	8	2	12		7^{1}		10	11				6			4	9^{2}				$5^{\blacksquare}$	13						16
1		3	8	2	5		7		10^{2}	11				6			4	12			9^{1}		13						17
1		3^{1}	8	2	5		10			11	7			6			4	9					12						18
1	12		8	3	5		7^{1}		10	11	2			6			4^{2}	9^{3}				13	14						19
1	12		8	3	5		7		10	11	2			6			4^{1}	9^{2}					13						20
1	4		8	3	12		7		10^{2}	11	2		5		13			9^{3}				6^{1}	14						21
1	4^{1}		8	3					10	11	7		5	2^{2}			12	13				6	9						22
1			8				7		10	11	12		5	2^{1}	13		4^{2}	9^{3}			3	6	14						23
1	4		8^{1}				7		10^{2}	11	2		5		12			9			3	6	13						24
1							8		10	11	2				7^{1}	13	4	12				6^{3}	9^{2}	3	5	14			25
1	8^{3}						7	12	10	11	2						4^{2}	13					9^{1}	$3^{\blacksquare}$	5	6	14		26
1					12		11	13	10		7		2^{1}		9^{3}	14	4								5	6	8^{2}	3	27
1	8						7	12		11^{3}	2		13				4	9				6	10^{1}	3		5^{2}	14		28
1	4						7^{2}	12	10	11	2				13								9^{1}	3	5	6	8		29
1							$7^{\blacksquare}$	12	10	11	2		5				4^{2}			13			9^{1}	3		6	8		30
1	8							12	10^{1}	11	2						4^{2}			13			9	3	5	6	7		31
1	8						7		10	11	2						4^{2}	12					9^{1}	3	5	6	13		32
1	4						7	9	10^{2}	11^{3}	2				14		12						13	3	5	6	8^{1}		33
1	4						7	9	10	11	2													3	5	6	8		34
1	4						7^{1}	9	10^{3}	11	2						13	12					14	3	5	6	8^{2}		35
1	8						7	9^{1}	10^{2}	11	2				14		4^{3}	12					13	3	5	6			36
1	8^{2}						7	$9^{\blacksquare}$	10	11	2				12		4^{1}						13	3	5	6			37
1	8						7		10	11	2						4^{2}	9^{1}					12	3	5	6	13		38

FA Cup

Third Round	Everton	(a)	4-1
Fourth Round	Luton T	(a)	4-0
Fifth Round	Arsenal	(a)	0-0
		(h)	1-0
Sixth Round	Manchester C	(h)	2-0
Semi-Final	Chelsea		1-2
(at Old Trafford)			

Carling Cup

Third Round	Chelsea	(h)	0-2

UEFA Cup

First Round	Salzburg	(a)	2-2
		(h)	2-0
Group E	Wisla	(a)	2-1
	Basle	(h)	3-0
	Feyenoord	(a)	0-0
	Nancy	(h)	1-0
Third Round	Leverkusen	(a)	2-3
		(h)	0-0

BLACKPOOL FL Championship

FOUNDATION

Old boys of St John's School who had formed themselves into a football club decided to establish a club bearing the name of their town and Blackpool FC came into being at a meeting at the Stanley Arms Hotel in the summer of 1887. In their first season playing at Raikes Hall Gardens, the club won both the Lancashire Junior Cup and the Fylde Cup.

Bloomfield Road, Seasiders Way, Blackpool FY1 6JJ.

Telephone: 0870 443 1953.

Fax: (01253) 405 011.

Ticket Office: 0870 443 1953 (option 1).

Website: www.blackpoolfc.co.uk

Email: info@blackpoolfc.co.uk

Ground Capacity: 9,491.

Record Attendance: 38,098 v Wolverhampton W, Division 1, 17 September 1955.

Pitch Measurements: 110yd × 74yd.

Chairman: Karl Oyston.

President: Valery Belokon.

Secretary: Matt Williams.

Manager: Simon Grayson.

Assistant Manager: Tony Parkes.

Physio: Phil Horner.

Colours: Tangerine shirts, white shorts, tangerine stockings.

Change Colours: White shirts, tangerine shorts, white stockings.

Year Formed: 1887.

Turned Professional: 1887.

Ltd Co.: 1896.

Previous Name: 'South Shore' combined with Blackpool in 1899, twelve years after the latter had been formed on the breaking up of the old 'Blackpool St John's' club.

Club Nickname: 'The Seasiders'.

Grounds: 1887, Raikes Hall Gardens; 1897, Athletic Grounds; 1899, Raikes Hall Gardens; 1899, Bloomfield Road.

First Football League game: 5 September 1896, Division 2, v Lincoln C (a) L 1–3 – Douglas; Parr, Bowman; Stuart, Stirzaker, Norris; Clarkin, Donnelly, R. Parkinson, Mount (1), J. Parkinson.

Record League Victory: 7–0 v Reading, Division 2, 10 November 1928 – Mercer; Gibson, Hamilton, Watson, Wilson, Grant, Ritchie, Oxberry (2), Hampson (5), Tufnell, Neal. 7–0 v Preston NE (away), Division 1, 1 May 1948 – Robinson; Shimwell, Crosland; Buchan, Hayward, Kelly; Hobson, Munro (1), McIntosh (5), McCall, Rickett (1). 7–0 v Sunderland, Division 1, 5 October 1957 – Farm; Armfield, Garrett, Kelly (J), Gratrix, Kelly (H), Matthews, Taylor (2), Charnley (2), Durie (2), Perry (1).

HONOURS

Football League: Division 1 – Runners-up 1955–56; Promoted from FL 1 – 2006–07 (play-offs); Division 2 – Champions 1929–30; Runners-up 1936–37, 1969–70; Promoted from Division 3 – 2000–01 (play-offs); Division 4 – Runners-up 1984–85.

FA Cup: Winners 1953; Runners-up 1948, 1951.

Football League Cup: Semi-final 1962.

Anglo-Italian Cup: Winners 1971; Runners-up 1972.

LDV Vans Trophy: Winners 2002, 2004.

SKY SPORTS FACT FILE

Harry Johnston and Jimmy McIntosh were signed by Blackpool from Droylsden Athletic in 1935. Johnston made his League debut on 20 November 1937 against Preston North End. McIntosh, a week after missing the FA Cup final, hit five in the League at Preston.

Record Cup Victory: 7–1 v Charlton Ath, League Cup 2nd rd, 25 September 1963 – Harvey; Armfield, Martin; Crawford, Gratrix, Cranston; Lea, Ball (1), Charnley (4), Durie (1), Oates (1).

Record Defeat: 1–10 v Small Heath, Division 2, 2 March 1901 and v Huddersfield T, Division 1, 13 December 1930.

Most League Points (2 for a win): 58, Division 2, 1929–30 and Division 2, 1967–68.

Most League Points (3 for a win): 86, Division 4, 1984–85.

Most League Goals: 98, Division 2, 1929–30.

Highest League Scorer in Season: Jimmy Hampson, 45, Division 2, 1929–30.

Most League Goals in Total Aggregate: Jimmy Hampson, 246, 1927–38.

Most League Goals in One Match: 5, Jimmy Hampson v Reading, Division 2, 10 November 1928; 5, Jimmy McIntosh v Preston NE, Division 1, 1 May 1948.

Most Capped Player: Jimmy Armfield, 43, England.

Most League Appearances: Jimmy Armfield, 568, 1952–71.

Youngest League Player: Matty Kay, 16 years 32 days v Scunthorpe U, 13 November 2005.

Record Transfer Fee Received: £1,750,000 from Southampton for Brett Ormerod, December 2001.

Record Transfer Fee Paid: £275,000 to Millwall for Chris Malkin, October 1996.

Football League Record: 1896 Elected to Division 2; 1899 Failed re-election; 1900 Re-elected; 1900–30 Division 2; 1930–33 Division 1; 1933–37 Division 2; 1937–67 Division 1; 1967–70 Division 2; 1970–71 Division 1; 1971–78 Division 2; 1978–81 Division 3; 1981–85 Division 4; 1985–90 Division 3; 1990–92 Division 4; 1992–2000 Division 2; 2000–01 Division 3; 2001–04 Division 2; 2004–07 FL 1; 2007– FL C.

MANAGERS

Tom Barcroft 1903–33
(Secretary-Manager)
John Cox 1909–11
Bill Norman 1919–23
Maj. Frank Buckley 1923–27
Sid Beaumont 1927–28
Harry Evans 1928–33
(Hon. Team Manager)
Alex 'Sandy' Macfarlane 1933–35
Joe Smith 1935–58
Ronnie Suart 1958–67
Stan Mortensen 1967–69
Les Shannon 1969–70
Bob Stokoe 1970–72
Harry Potts 1972–76
Allan Brown 1976–78
Bob Stokoe 1978–79
Stan Ternent 1979–80
Alan Ball 1980–81
Allan Brown 1981–82
Sam Ellis 1982–89
Jimmy Mullen 1989–90
Graham Carr 1990
Bill Ayre 1990–94
Sam Allardyce 1994–96
Gary Megson 1996–97
Nigel Worthington 1997–99
Steve McMahon 2000–04
Colin Hendry 2004–06
Simon Grayson June 2006–

LATEST SEQUENCES

Longest Sequence of League Wins: 9, 21.11.1936 – 1.1.1937.

Longest Sequence of League Defeats: 8, 26.11.1898 – 7.1.1899.

Longest Sequence of League Draws: 5, 4.12.1976 – 1.1.1977.

Longest Sequence of Unbeaten League Matches: 17, 6.4.1968 – 21.9.1968.

Longest Sequence Without a League Win: 19, 19.12.1970 – 24.4.1971.

Successive Scoring Runs: 33 from 23.2.1929.

Successive Non-scoring Runs: 5 from 12.4.1975.

TEN YEAR LEAGUE RECORD

		P	W	D	L	F	A	Pts	Pos
1997-98	Div 2	46	17	11	18	59	67	62	12
1998-99	Div 2	46	14	14	18	44	54	56	14
1999-2000	Div 2	46	8	17	21	49	77	41	22
2000-01	Div 2	46	22	6	18	74	58	72	7
2001-02	Div 2	46	14	14	18	66	69	56	16
2002-03	Div 2	46	15	13	18	56	64	58	13
2003-04	Div 2	46	16	11	19	58	65	59	14
2004-05	FL 1	46	15	12	19	54	59	57	16
2005-06	FL 1	46	12	17	17	56	64	53	19
2006-07	FL 1	46	24	11	11	76	49	83	3

DID YOU KNOW ?

Versatile forward Gerry Ingram was snapped up by Blackpool from little known Hull Brunswick in March 1967 and went on to make over 300 League appearances in a career which carried on with Preston North End and Bradford City.

BLACKPOOL 2006–07 LEAGUE RECORD

Match No.	Date	Venue	Opponents	Result		H/T Score	Lg. Pos.	Goalscorers	Attendance
1	Aug 5	A	Brentford	L	0-1	0-0	—		6048
2	8	H	Nottingham F	L	0-2	0-1	—		7635
3	12	H	Rotherham U	L	0-1	0-0	23		5677
4	19	A	Bristol C	W	4-2	1-1	18	Vernon [27], Jackson [50], Parker [77], Graham [89]	10,630
5	26	H	Gillingham	D	1-1	1-1	18	Vernon [35]	5056
6	Sept 2	A	Millwall	D	0-0	0-0	20		7692
7	9	A	Port Vale	L	1-2	0-1	22	Southern [90]	5171
8	12	H	Chesterfield	D	1-1	1-0	—	Gillett [33]	4600
9	16	H	Oldham Ath	D	2-2	1-0	21	Vernon [41], Morrell [90]	6794
10	23	A	Doncaster R	D	0-0	0-0	21		5424
11	26	A	Carlisle U	L	0-2	0-1	—		8401
12	30	H	Leyton Orient	W	3-0	1-0	21	Morrell [21], Hoolahan (pen) [82], Parker [86]	5298
13	Oct 8	A	Brighton & HA	W	3-0	1-0	19	Southern [17], Vernon 2 [61, 87]	5146
14	14	H	Yeovil T	D	1-1	0-0	20	Vernon [56]	6812
15	21	A	Crewe Alex	W	2-1	1-0	14	Morrell [3], Barker [90]	5785
16	28	H	Bradford C	W	4-1	2-0	12	Fox [39], Hoolahan (pen) [45], Parker 2 [64, 70]	7937
17	Nov 4	A	Northampton T	D	1-1	1-0	14	Morrell [20]	5762
18	18	H	Huddersfield T	W	3-1	2-1	10	Parker [26], Southern [30], Morrell [60]	7414
19	24	A	Tranmere R	L	0-2	0-1	—		8247
20	Dec 5	H	Cheltenham T	W	2-1	1-1	—	Morrell [29], Hoolahan [80]	4851
21	9	H	Swansea C	D	1-1	0-1	11	Vernon [83]	6216
22	15	A	Scunthorpe U	W	3-1	1-0	—	Morrell [27], Hoolahan (pen) [58], Parker [88]	4527
23	23	A	Bournemouth	W	3-1	0-0	7	Parker 2 [47, 52], Fox [88]	5758
24	26	H	Carlisle U	W	2-1	2-0	6	Murphy (og) [5], Parker [29]	9473
25	30	H	Doncaster R	W	3-1	0-0	5	Vernon 2 [77, 83], Barker [81]	7952
26	Jan 1	A	Chesterfield	L	0-2	0-2	7		4351
27	13	H	Port Vale	W	2-1	0-0	6	Morrell [72], Fox [76]	6661
28	20	A	Leyton Orient	W	1-0	0-0	6	Southern [85]	5217
29	Feb 3	H	Brentford	L	1-3	0-3	7	Vernon [90]	6086
30	17	H	Bristol C	L	0-1	0-0	8		6696
31	20	A	Nottingham F	D	1-1	0-1	—	Hoolahan (pen) [90]	16,849
32	24	H	Millwall	L	0-1	0-1	10		6547
33	27	A	Oldham Ath	W	1-0	0-0	—	Morrell [67]	6956
34	Mar 3	A	Gillingham	D	2-2	1-2	8	Burgess [12], Fox [64]	5949
35	6	H	Bournemouth	W	2-0	1-0	—	Forbes [36], Burgess [54]	6184
36	10	H	Brighton & HA	D	0-0	0-0	6		8164
37	17	A	Yeovil T	W	1-0	0-0	6	Morrell [57]	6012
38	24	A	Bradford C	W	3-1	1-0	6	Williams [6], Morrell [77], Vernon [90]	8984
39	27	A	Rotherham U	L	0-1	0-0	—		4025
40	31	H	Crewe Alex	W	2-1	1-0	6	Hoolahan [15], Williams [57]	7203
41	Apr 7	H	Tranmere R	W	3-2	2-1	5	Parker [9], Hoolahan [36], Morrell [73]	8091
42	9	A	Huddersfield T	W	2-0	1-0	4	Jorgensen [29], Williams [59]	11,432
43	14	H	Northampton T	W	4-1	0-1	4	Brandon 2 [49, 62], Hoolahan (pen) [55], Dyche (og) [84]	7334
44	21	A	Cheltenham T	W	2-1	1-0	4	Williams [39], Southern [85]	5093
45	28	H	Scunthorpe U	W	3-1	2-1	4	Jorgensen [8], Parker [25], Barker [56]	9482
46	May 5	A	Swansea C	W	6-3	2-1	3	Morrell 4 [25, 57, 61, 79], Parker 2 [32, 89]	18,903

Final League Position: 3

GOALSCORERS

League (76): Morrell 16, Parker 13, Vernon 11, Hoolahan 8 (5 pens), Southern 5, Fox 4, Williams 4, Barker 3, Brandon 2, Burgess 2, Jorgensen 2, Forbes 1, Gillett 1, Graham 1, Jackson 1, own goals 2.
Carling Cup (2): Vernon 2.
FA Cup (10): Morrell 3, Barker 1, Burgess 1 (pen), Evatt 1, Hoolahan 1 (pen), Jackson 1, Parker 1, Vernon 1.
J Paint Trophy (4): Burgess 2 (1 pen), Barker 1, Gillett 1.
Play-Offs (7): Parker 2, Barker 1, Hoolahan 1, Morrell 1, Southern 1, Williams 1.

Evans R 32	Joseph M 3 + 5	Tierney P 8 + 2	Fox D 33 + 4	Jackson M 42 + 1	Barker S 45	Forbes A 26 + 8	Southern K 37 + 2	Vernon S 21 + 17	Parker K 24 + 21	Prendergast R 3 + 2	Coid D 15 + 3	Graham D 1 + 3	Hoolahan W 37 + 5	Evatt I 42 + 2	Gillett S 20 + 11	Morrell A 34 + 6	Bean M 2 + 4	Burgess B 13 + 14	Jorgensen C 21 + 10	Dickinson C 7	Blinkhorn M — + 2	Wilkinson A 5 + 2	Farrelly G — + 1	Fernandez V — + 1	Gorkss K 8 + 2	Rachubka P 8	Williams R 9	Brandon C 4 + 1	Edge L 1	Hart J 5	Match No.
1	2	3^1	4	5	6	7	8	9^2	10	11^3	12	13	14																		1
1	2	3^2	4	5^1	6	7	8	9	10^3	11		14	13	12																	2
1		3^3		5	6	7	8	9^1	13	11^2	2	10	12	14	4																3
1	12	3^1	4	5	6	7^2	8	9	13			14		2	11	10^3															4
1	12			5^3	6	7	8	9	13		3		11^1	2	4	10^2	14														5
1	12	3		5^1	6		8	9^2	11					2	4	10	7	13													6
1	2	3^2			6		8	9^1	12		13		11	5	4	10		14	7^3												7
1				5	6		8	9^3	12	13	3		11^2	2	4^1	14		10	7												8
1			12	5	6		8^1	9^2	13		3		11	2	4^3	14		10	7												9
1			12	5	6		8	9	13		3		11^1	2	4			10^2	7												10
1			7^1	5	6		8	9^2	12		3		11	2	4	13		10													11
1	12		7^3	5	6		8		13		3		11	2^1	4^2	9		10	14												12
1			7	5	6		8	12	13		3		11	2	4^3	9^2		10^1	14												13
1	12		7	5	6		8	9	13		3^1		11	2	4^3	10^2			14												14
1			7^2	5	6		8	9^3	12				11	2	4▮	10^1			13	3	14										15
1			4	5	6	7^2	8		10^3	12			11^1	2		9			13	3	14										16
1			4	5	6	7^2	8		10				11	2	13	9^1		12		3											17
1			4^3	5	6	7^2	8	12	10^1				11	2		9		13	14	3											18
1			4^1	5	6	7	8	12	10^2				11	2^3		9		13		3		14									19
1			4	5	6	7^2	8	12	10^3				11	2		9^1		13		3		14									20
1			4	5^1	6	7	8	12	10				11	2		9^2		13		3											21
1			4^3	5	6	7^1	8	12	10				11▮	2		9^2			13			3	14								22
1		12	4	5	6	7^1		13	10^2					2		9	8	14	11^3			3									23
1			4	5	6	7^2	8		10				11	2		9^1		12	13			3^3		14							24
1			4^2	5	6		8	12	10^3				11	2		9^1	13	14	7			3									25
1		12	4	5	6	13	8	9					11	2		14		10^3	7^2			3^1									26
1		2	4	5	6	7	8	10^2	12							9		13	11^1						3						27
1			4	5	6	7	8	10^1	12				11^3	2		9^2		13	14						3						28
1			4	5^2	6	7^3		12	10				11	2	14	13		9	8^1						3						29
1		3^3	4^1	5	6	7^2	8	9	10				11	2	12			13	14												30
1			7	5	6	12	8^1	9^2	10				11	2	4			13							3						31
1			7	5	6	12	8^1	13	10^3				11	2	4	14		9							3^2						32
			7	5	6	12	8		13		3		11^1	2	4	9^2		10								1					33
			7	5	6	12	8^2	13	14		3		11^3	2	4^1	9		10								1					34
			4		6	7^3		12	13		3		14	2	8^2	9		10^1	11						5	1					35
			4		6	7^3		12	13		3		14	2	8	9^2		10^1	11						5	1					36
			4	14	6▮	7^2		10^1	12		3		11^3	2	13	9			8						5	1					37
			4^2	5		7^1		10	12		6		11^3	2	13	9	14		8							1	3				38
				5	6	7^2		10^1	12				11	2	4	9	13		8							1	3				39
			4^1	5	6		12	13	10				11	2	14	9^2			8							1	3	7^3			40
			4^2	5^1	6	12	13	14	10				11	2		9			8								3	7^3	1		41
				5	6	4^2	8	12	10				11^3	2	13	9^1			7						14		3			1	42
				5	6	7^3	8		10		12		11^2	2	13	9			4								3^1	14		1	43
				5	6	12	8		10^1				11^3	2	13	9			4						14		3	7^2		1	44
			12	5	6	13	8		10^2				11	2	14	9^3			4^1								3	7▮		1	45
			12	5	6	7^1	8	13	10				11^3	2	14	9^2			4								3			1	46

FA Cup

First Round	Huddersfield T	(a)	1-0
Second Round	Milton Keynes D	(a)	2-0
Third Round	Aldershot T	(h)	4-2
Fourth Round	Norwich C	(h)	1-1
		(a)	2-3

Carling Cup

First Round	Barnsley	(h)	2-2

J Paint Trophy

Second Round	Accrington S	(a)	4-4

Play-Offs

Semi-Final	Oldham	(a)	2-1
		(h)	3-1
Final *(at Wembley)*	Yeovil T		2-0

BOLTON WANDERERS FA Premiership

FOUNDATION

In 1874 boys of Christ Church Sunday School, Blackburn Street, led by their master Thomas Ogden, established a football club which went under the name of the school and whose president was Vicar of Christ Church. Membership was 6d (two and a half pence). When their president began to lay down too many rules about the use of church premises, the club broke away and formed Bolton Wanderers in 1877, holding their earliest meetings at the Gladstone Hotel.

Reebok Stadium, Burnden Way, Lostock, Bolton BL6 6JW.

Telephone: (01204) 673 673. ***Fax:*** (01204) 673 773.

Ticket Office: 0871 871 2932.

Website: www.bwfc.co.uk

Email: reception@bwfc.co.uk

Ground Capacity: 28,500.

Record Attendance: 69,912 v Manchester C, FA Cup 5th rd, 18 February 1933.

Pitch Measurements: 105m × 68m.

Chairman: Phil A. Gartside.

Chief Executive: Allan Duckworth.

Vice-chairman: Brett Warburton.

Secretary: Simon Marland.

Manager: Sammy Lee.

First Team Coaches: Ricky Sbragia, Jimmy Phillips, Gary Speed.

Head of Sport Science & Medicine: Mark Taylor.

Colours: White shirts, white shorts, white stockings.

Change Colours: Maroon shirts, maroon shorts, maroon stockings.

Year Formed: 1874. ***Turned Professional:*** 1880. ***Ltd Co.:*** 1895.

Previous Name: 1874, Christ Church FC; 1877, Bolton Wanderers.

Club Nickname: 'The Trotters'.

Grounds: Park Recreation Ground and Cockle's Field before moving to Pike's Lane ground 1881; 1895, Burnden Park; 1997, Reebok Stadium.

First Football League Game: 8 September 1888, Football League, v Derby Co (h) L 3–6 – Harrison; Robinson, Mitchell; Roberts, Weir, Bullough, Davenport (2), Milne, Coupar, Barbour, Brogan (1).

Record League Victory: 8–0 v Barnsley, Division 2, 6 October 1934 – Jones; Smith, Finney; Goslin, Atkinson, George Taylor; George T. Taylor (2), Eastham, Milsom (1), Westwood (4), Cook, (1 og).

HONOURS

Football League: Division 1 – Champions 1996–97; Promoted from Division 1 (play-offs) 2000–01. Division 2 – Champions 1908–09, 1977–78; Runners-up 1899–1900, 1904–05, 1910–11, 1934–35, 1992–93; Division 3 – Champions 1972–73; Promoted from Division 4 (3rd) 1987–88.

FA Cup: Winners 1923, 1926, 1929, 1958; Runners-up 1894, 1904, 1953.

Football League Cup: Runners-up 1995, 2004.

Freight Rover Trophy: Runners-up 1986.

Sherpa Van Trophy: Winners 1989.

European Competitions: *UEFA Cup:* 2005–06.

SKY SPORTS FACT FILE

Gary Speed celebrated his 750th overall club appearance by scoring the first goal for Bolton Wanderers against Liverpool on 30 September 2006 in a 2–0 win. He is one of only three players who featured on the FA Premier League's bow in 1992.

Record Cup Victory: 13–0 v Sheffield U, FA Cup 2nd rd, 1 February 1890 – Parkinson; Robinson (1), Jones; Bullough, Davenport, Roberts; Rushton, Brogan (3), Cassidy (5), McNee, Weir (4).

Record Defeat: 1–9 v Preston NE, FA Cup 2nd rd, 10 December 1887.

Most League Points (2 for a win): 61, Division 3, 1972–73.

Most League Points (3 for a win): 98, Division 1, 1996–97.

Most League Goals: 100, Division 1, 1996–97.

Highest League Scorer in Season: Joe Smith, 38, Division 1, 1920–21.

Most League Goals in Total Aggregate: Nat Lofthouse, 255, 1946–61.

Most League Goals in One Match: 5, Tony Caldwell v Walsall, Division 3, 10 September 1983.

Most Capped Player: Mark Fish, 34 (62), South Africa.

Most League Appearances: Eddie Hopkinson, 519, 1956–70.

Youngest League Player: Ray Parry, 15 years 267 days v Wolverhampton W, 13 October 1951.

Record Transfer Fee Received: £4,500,000 from Liverpool for Jason McAteer, September 1995.

Record Transfer Fee Paid: £8,000,000 to Fenerbahce for Nicolas Anelka, August 2006.

Football League Record: 1888 Founder Member of the League; 1899–1900 Division 2; 1900–03 Division 1; 1903–05 Division 2; 1905–08 Division 1; 1908–09 Division 2; 1909–10 Division 1; 1910–11 Division 2; 1911–33 Division 1; 1933–35 Division 2; 1935–64 Division 1; 1964–71 Division 2; 1971–73 Division 3; 1973–78 Division 2; 1978–80 Division 1; 1980–83 Division 2; 1983–87 Division 3; 1987–88 Division 4; 1988–92 Division 3; 1992–93 Division 2; 1993–95 Division 1; 1995–96 FA Premier League; 1996–97 Division 1; 1997–98 FA Premier League; 1998–2001 Division 1; 2001– FA Premier League.

MANAGERS

Tom Rawthorne 1874–85
(Secretary)
J. J. Bentley 1885–86
(Secretary)
W. G. Struthers 1886–87
(Secretary)
Fitzroy Norris 1887
(Secretary)
J. J. Bentley 1887–95
(Secretary)
Harry Downs 1895–96
(Secretary)
Frank Brettell 1896–98
(Secretary)
John Somerville 1898–1910
Will Settle 1910–15
Tom Mather 1915–19
Charles Foweraker 1919–44
Walter Rowley 1944–50
Bill Ridding 1951–68
Nat Lofthouse 1968–70
Jimmy McIlroy 1970
Jimmy Meadows 1971
Nat Lofthouse 1971
(then Admin. Manager to 1972)
Jimmy Armfield 1971–74
Ian Greaves 1974–80
Stan Anderson 1980–81
George Mulhall 1981–82
John McGovern 1982–85
Charlie Wright 1985
Phil Neal 1985–92
Bruce Rioch 1992–95
Roy McFarland 1995–96
Colin Todd 1996–99
Sam Allardyce 1999–2007
Sammy Lee May 2007–

LATEST SEQUENCES

Longest Sequence of League Wins: 11, 5.11.1904 – 2.1.1905.

Longest Sequence of League Defeats: 11, 7.4.1902 – 18.10.1902.

Longest Sequence of League Draws: 6, 25.1.1913 – 8.3.1913.

Longest Sequence of Unbeaten League Matches: 23, 13.10.1990 – 9.3.1991.

Longest Sequence Without a League Win: 26, 7.4.1902 – 10.1.1903.

Successive Scoring Runs: 24 from 22.11.1996.

Successive Non-scoring Runs: 5 from 3.1.1898.

TEN YEAR LEAGUE RECORD

		P	W	D	L	F	A	Pts	Pos
1997-98	PR Lge	38	9	13	16	41	61	40	18
1998-99	Div 1	46	20	16	10	78	59	76	6
1999-2000	Div 1	46	21	13	12	69	50	76	6
2000-01	Div 1	46	24	15	7	76	45	87	3
2001-02	PR Lge	38	9	13	16	44	62	40	16
2002-03	PR Lge	38	10	14	14	41	51	44	17
2003-04	PR Lge	38	14	11	13	48	56	53	8
2004-05	PR Lge	38	16	10	12	49	44	58	6
2005-06	PR Lge	38	15	11	12	49	41	56	8
2006-07	PR Lge	38	16	8	14	47	52	56	7

DID YOU KNOW ?

On 21 October 2006 Bolton Wanderers' Finland international goalkeeper Jussi Jaaskelainen saved two penalties in the dying moments of a dramatic 1–0 win at Blackburn Rovers. There was still time for Bolton to finish the match with ten players!

BOLTON WANDERERS 2006–07 LEAGUE RECORD

Match No.	Date	Venue	Opponents	Result	H/T Score	Lg. Pos.	Goalscorers	Attendance
1	Aug 19	H	Tottenham H	W 2-0	2-0	—	Davies [9], Campo [13]	22,899
2	23	A	Fulham	D 1-1	0-0	—	Diouf (pen) [73]	18,559
3	26	A	Charlton Ath	L 0-2	0-0	8		23,638
4	Sept 9	H	Watford	W 1-0	0-0	6	Speed (pen) [90]	21,140
5	16	H	Middlesbrough	D 0-0	0-0	7		21,164
6	25	A	Portsmouth	W 1-0	1-0	—	Nolan [22]	19,105
7	30	H	Liverpool	W 2-0	1-0	3	Speed [30], Campo [51]	25,061
8	Oct 15	A	Newcastle U	W 2-1	0-1	3	Diouf 2 [55, 57]	48,145
9	22	A	Blackburn R	W 1-0	0-0	3	Campo [62]	27,662
10	28	H	Manchester U	L 0-4	0-2	3		27,229
11	Nov 4	H	Wigan Ath	L 0-1	0-0	3		21,255
12	11	A	Sheffield U	D 2-2	1-0	5	Diouf [34], Davies [59]	28,294
13	18	A	Everton	L 0-1	0-0	6		34,417
14	25	H	Arsenal	W 3-1	2-1	3	Diagne-Faye [9], Anelka 2 [45, 76]	24,409
15	29	H	Chelsea	L 0-1	0-1	—		23,559
16	Dec 2	A	Reading	L 0-1	0-1	9		23,556
17	9	H	West Ham U	W 4-0	1-0	5	Davies 2 [17, 52], Diouf [77], Anelka [78]	22,283
18	16	A	Aston Villa	W 1-0	0-0	5	Speed (pen) [75]	27,450
19	23	A	Manchester C	W 2-0	2-0	5	Anelka 2 [8, 25]	40,157
20	26	H	Newcastle U	W 2-1	1-1	4	Ramage (og) [32], Anelka [57]	26,437
21	30	H	Portsmouth	W 3-2	2-1	3	Diagne-Faye [30], Campo [50], Anelka [62]	22,447
22	Jan 1	A	Liverpool	L 0-3	0-0	4		41,370
23	13	H	Manchester C	D 0-0	0-0	5		22,334
24	20	A	Middlesbrough	L 1-5	1-4	5	Nolan [25]	24,614
25	31	H	Charlton Ath	D 1-1	1-1	—	Pedersen [6]	22,357
26	Feb 3	A	Watford	W 1-0	0-0	5	Anelka [63]	18,722
27	11	H	Fulham	W 2-1	1-0	5	Speed (pen) [23], Nolan [51]	24,919
28	25	A	Tottenham H	L 1-4	1-3	5	Speed (pen) [37]	35,747
29	Mar 4	H	Blackburn R	L 1-2	0-0	5	Anelka [87]	21,743
30	17	A	Manchester U	L 1-4	0-3	5	Speed (pen) [87]	76,058
31	31	H	Sheffield U	W 1-0	0-0	5	Davies [80]	24,312
32	Apr 7	A	Wigan Ath	W 3-1	1-1	5	Anelka [44], Teimourian 2 [68, 73]	18,610
33	9	H	Everton	D 1-1	1-1	5	Davies [18]	25,179
34	14	A	Arsenal	L 1-2	1-1	6	Anelka [11]	60,101
35	21	H	Reading	L 1-3	0-0	6	Shorey (og) [64]	23,533
36	28	A	Chelsea	D 2-2	1-2	5	Michalik [19], Davies [54]	41,105
37	May 5	A	West Ham U	L 1-3	0-3	6	Speed [67]	34,404
38	13	H	Aston Villa	D 2-2	1-1	7	Speed [32], Davies [58]	26,255

Final League Position: 7

GOALSCORERS

League (47): Anelka 11, Davies 8, Speed 8 (5 pens), Diouf 5 (1 pen), Campo 4, Nolan 3, Diagne-Faye 2, Teimourian 2, Michalik 1, Pedersen 1, own goals 2.
Carling Cup (3): Anelka 1, Campo 1, Nolan 1.
FA Cup (6): Teimourian 2, Davies 1, Meite 1, Nolan 1, Tal 1.

Jaaskelainen J 38	Hunt N 32 + 1	Fortune Q 5 + 1	Campo I 31 + 3	Ben Haim T 30 + 2	Meite A 35	Nolan K 31	Speed G 38	Vaz Te R 2 + 23	Davies K 30	Diouf E 32 + 1	Giannakopoulos S 11 + 12	Tal I 4 + 12	Pedersen H 10 + 8	Diagne-Faye A 29 + 3	Teimourian A 6 + 11	Anelka N 35	Smith J — + 1	Gardner R 13 + 5	Thompson D 3 + 5	Michalik L 3 + 1	Martin C — + 1	Sinclair J — + 2	*Match No.*
1	2	3	4	5	6	7	8	9^{1}	10	11	12												1
1	2	3^{1}	4	5	6	7	8	9	10^{2}	11			12	13									2
1	2^{3}		4	5	6	7	8	12	10▪	9	11^{1}	14	3^{2}	13									3
1	2^{1}	3	4	5	6	7	11	12		9^{3}		13		8	14	10^{2}							4
1		3	4	2	6	7^{2}	8	12		10	11^{1}	13		5		9							5
1	2		4^{3}	3	6	7	8	12	10	11^{2}	13	14		5		9^{1}							6
1	2		4	3	6	7	8	12	10	11^{2}	13			5		9^{1}							7
1	2		4	3	6	7	8		10	11^{1}	12			5		9							8
1	2	12	4	3	6	7▪	8	13	10	11^{2}	14			5^{1}		9^{3}							9
1	2^{1}		4	3	6		8		10^{3}	11	7^{2}	13	12	5		9	14						10
1	12		4	2	6		8^{3}	13	10^{2}	11	7	14	3^{1}	5		9							11
1			12	2	6	7	8		10	11		4^{1}	3	5		9							12
1	2		4^{2}	5	6		8^{1}	14	10^{3}	11	13	7	3	12		9							13
1	2^{2}	3^{1}	12	5	6	7	8	14	10	11^{3}	13			4		9							14
1	2		4	3	6	7	8	12	10^{1}	11				5		9							15
1	2		12	3^{2}	6	7	4^{1}	14	10	8^{3}	11		13	5		9							16
1	2		4		6	7	8^{3}	12	10^{1}	11^{2}		13	3	5		9		14					17
1	2		4	12	6^{1}	7	8		10		11^{2}	13^{3}	3	5		9		14					18
1	2		4	3	6	7	8	12		10^{1}			11^{2}	5		9		13					19
1	2		4	3	6	7	8		10	11^{1}			12	5		9							20
1	2		4	3	6	7	8		10	11^{1}			12	5		9							21
1	2		4	5		7^{3}	8^{2}	12	10	11^{1}		13		6	14	9		3					22
1	2		4	5	6		8	12	10^{2}	11^{1}	13	7^{3}			14	9		3					23
1	2^{3}		4	3	6	7	8^{2}	12	10^{1}	11▪				5	13	9		14					24
1	2		4	12	6	7	8	13			10^{2}		11	5^{1}	14	9^{3}		3					25
1	2		4	3	6	7	8			11^{1}	10^{2}		12	5	13	9							26
1	2			5	6	7	8^{3}			11^{2}	10	12	13		4^{1}	9		3	14				27
1	2		4		6	7^{1}	8	12		10	11		13	5^{3}	14	9		3^{2}					28
1	2		4	6		7	8^{2}	12		10	11^{1}		3	5	13	9							29
1	2		4^{2}	6		7	8		10^{3}	12			11^{1}	5	14	9		3	13				30
1	2			4	6	7	8		10	11^{1}				5	12	9		3					31
1	2			3^{3}	6		8		10	11	12	13		5	4	9^{1}		14	7^{2}				32
1	2		4		6		8		10	11^{1}	12			5	7^{2}	9		3	13				33
1	2		4▪		6	7^{3}	8	12	10	11^{1}				5	13	9		3^{2}	14				34
1	2^{3}			5	6	7^{1}	8		10	11^{2}	12				4	9		3	13	14			35
1			2		6		8	12	10			11^{2}			4	9^{3}		3	7^{1}	5	14	13	36
1			2		6	7	8	12	10		13				4^{1}	9		3^{2}	11^{3}	5		14	37
1			4	2	6	7	8^{1}	12	10			13		11		9^{2}		3		5			38

FA Cup

Third Round	Doncaster R	(a)	4-0
Fourth Round	Arsenal	(a)	1-1
		(h)	1-3

Carling Cup

Second Round	Walsall	(a)	3-1
Third Round	Charlton Ath	(a)	0-1

BOSTON UNITED — Blue Square North

FOUNDATION

Although it was 1934 before the name Boston United first appeared, football had been played in the town since the late 1800s and indeed, always on the same site as the present York Street stadium. In fact Boston Football Club was established in March 1870 playing their first match against Louth the following month. Before the First World War, there were two clubs, Boston Town, whose headquarters were The Coach and Horses, and Boston Swifts, who used The Indian Queen. In fact, as both public houses were situated on Main Ridge and the pitch was virtually just opposite, it was not surprising that for the first forty years or so, that was what the ground was called. Swifts never reappeared after the First World War and it was left to the club called simply Boston to achieve the first giant-killing in the FA Cup by beating Bradford Park Avenue 1-0 on 12 December 1925. The club was now competing in the Midland League and subsequently reformed under the new title of Boston United.

York Street Ground, York Street, Boston, Lincolnshire, PE21 6HJ.

Telephone: (01205) 364 406.

Fax: (01205) 354 063.

Ticket Office: (01205) 364 406, (01205) 365 525.

Website: www.bufc.co.uk

Email: admin@bufc.co.uk

Ground Capacity: 6,300.

Record Attendance: 10,086 v Corby Town, Friendly, 1955.

Pitch Measurements: 110yd × 70yd.

Chairman: James Rodwell.

Secretary: John Blackwell.

Manager: Tommy Taylor.

Colours: Amber and black shirts, black shorts, black stockings.

Change Colours: All red.

Year formed: 1934.

HONOURS

FA Cup: best season: 3rd rd, 1926, 1956, 1972, 1974.
Football League Cup: never past 1st rd.
Conference: Champions 2001–02.
Dr. Martens: Champions 1999–2000. Runners-up: 1998–99.
Unibond League: Runners-up 1995–96, 1997–98.
Unibond Challenge Cup: Runners-up 1996–97.
FA Trophy: Runners-up 1984–85.
Northern Premier League: Champions 1972–73, 1973–74, 1976–77, 1977–78.
Northern Premier League Cup: Winners 1974, 1976.
Northern Premier League Challenge Shield: Winners 1974, 1975, 1977, 1978.
Lincolnshire Senior Cup: Winners 1935, 1937, 1938, 1946, 1950, 1955, 1956, 1960, 1977, 1979, 1986, 1988, 1989.
Non-League Champions of Champions Cup: Winners 1973, 1977.
East Anglian Cup: Winners 1961.
Central Alliance League: Champions 1961–62.
United Counties League: Champions 1965–66.
West Midlands League: Champions 1966–67, 1967–68.
Eastern Professional Floodlit Cup: Winners 1972.

SKY SPORTS FACT FILE

In the qualifying rounds of the FA Cup, Boston United recorded a 10–0 win over Bilsthorpe in 1937–38. Moreover when known as Boston Town they inflicted a 10–2 defeat on Selby in 1928–29 and an 11–1 success against East Riding Amateurs in 1931–32.

Club Nickname: 'The Pilgrims'.

First Football League Game: 10 August 2002, Division 3, v Bournemouth (h), D 2–2 – Bastock; Hocking, Chapman, Morley (Rodwell), Warburton, Ellender, Gould (1), Bennett, Clare, Elding (Cook), Weatherstone S. (1 og).

Record League Victory: 6–0 v Shrewsbury T, Division 3, 21 December 2002 – Bastock; Costello, Chapman, Redfearn (1), Balmer, Hocking (McCarthy), Weatherstone S, Higgins, Douglas (1), Logan (2) (Thompson L), Angel (Gould (1)). (1 og).

Most League Points (3 for a win): 61, League 2, 2005–06.

Most League Goals: 62, FL 2, 2004–05.

Highest League Scorer in Season: Andy Kirk, 19, 2004–05.

Most Capped Player: Andy Kirk, 1(8), Northern Ireland.

Most League Appearances: Paul Ellender, 174, 2002–.

Youngest League Player: Rob Norris, 17 years 18 days v Bristol R, 30 October 2004.

Record Transfer Fee Received: £100,000 from Darlington for Julian Joachim, August 2006.

Record Transfer Fee Paid: £30,000 to Scarborough for Paul Ellender, August 2001.

Football League Record: 2002 Promoted to Division 3; 2004–07 FL 2; 2007– Blue Square North.

MANAGERS

Jimmy Cringan 1934–35
Willie Vaughton 1935–36
Arthur Greaves 1936–37
Freddy Tunstall 1937–48
Jimmy McGraham 1948–49
Jimmy Ithell 1950–52
Freddy Tunstall 1952–54
Ray Middleton 1954–57
Ray King 1957–60
Ray Middleton 1960–61
Paul Todd 1961–64
Freddy Tunstall 1964–65
Don Donovan 1965–69
Jim Smith 1969–72
Keith Jobling 1972–75
Howard Wilkinson 1975–76
Gordon Bolland/Freddie Taylor 1976–77
Mick Walker 1977–79
Albert Phelan 1979–81
John Froggatt 1981–84
Arthur Mann 1984–86
Ray O'Brien 1986–87
George Kerr 1987–90
Dave Cusack 1990–92
Peter Morris 1992–94
Mel Sterland 1994–96
Greg Fee 1996–98
Steve Evans 1998–2002
Neil Thompson 2002–04
Steve Evans 2004–07
Tommy Taylor 2007–

LATEST SEQUENCES

Longest Sequence of League Wins: 4, 19.4.2003 – 3.5.2003.

Longest Sequence of League Defeats: 6, 29.10.2002 – 14.12.2002.

Longest Sequence of League Draws: 4, 6.12.2005 – 26.12.2005.

Longest Sequence of Unbeaten League Matches: 10, 4.9.2005 – 29.10.2005 .

Longest Sequence Without a League Win: 9, 30.4.2005 – 4.9.2005.

Successive Scoring Runs: 8 from 26.3.2005.

Successive Non-scoring Runs: 5 from 29.10.2002.

TEN YEAR LEAGUE RECORD

		P	W	D	L	F	A	Pts	Pos
1997-98	NP pr	42	22	12	8	55	40	78	2
1998-99	SL pr	42	17	16	9	69	51	67	2
1999-2000	SL pr	42	27	11	4	102	39	92	1
2000-01	Conf.	42	13	17	12	74	63	56	12
2001-02	Conf.	42	25	9	8	84	42	84	1
2002-03	Div 3	46	15	13	18	55	56	54*	15
2003-04	Div 3	46	16	11	19	50	54	59	11
2004-05	FL 2	46	14	16	16	62	58	58	16
2005-06	FL 2	46	15	16	15	50	60	61	11
2006-07	FL 2	46	12	10	24	51	80	36†	23

**4 pts deducted at start of season.*
†10 pts deducted for entering administration.

DID YOU KNOW ?

On 16 November 1957 Boston United defeated Billingham Synthonia 5–2 in an FA Cup first round tie, with four of the goals from Andy Graver whose marksmanship with Lincoln City (three spells), Leicester City and Stoke City had yielded 158 League goals.

BOSTON UNITED 2006–07 LEAGUE RECORD

Match No.	Date	Venue	Opponents	Result		H/T Score	Lg. Pos.	Goalscorers	Attendance
1	Aug 5	A	Grimsby T	L	2-3	1-0	—	Green 16, Joachim 54	5012
2	9	H	Peterborough U	L	0-1	0-0	—		3528
3	12	H	Darlington	W	4-1	1-1	15	Tait 13, Ryan T (pen) 68, Joachim 2 76, 90	1934
4	19	A	Shrewsbury T	L	0-5	0-2	18		3502
5	26	H	Milton Keynes D	L	0-1	0-0	20		2032
6	Sept 1	A	Hartlepool U	L	1-2	0-1	—	N'Guessan 83	4054
7	9	H	Stockport Co	W	2-1	2-1	20	Ryan T (pen) 25, Elding 39	1796
8	12	A	Barnet	D	3-3	2-1	—	Galbraith 23, Ryan T 2 (2 pens) 44, 84	1461
9	16	A	Accrington S	L	1-2	0-1	21	Farrell 49	1916
10	23	H	Rochdale	L	0-3	0-2	23		1709
11	27	H	Lincoln C	W	1-0	0-0	—	Green 59	4327
12	30	A	Swindon T	D	1-1	0-1	23	N'Guessan 88	6074
13	Oct 7	A	Bristol R	L	0-1	0-0	23		4327
14	14	H	Mansfield T	D	1-1	1-0	23	N'Guessan 25	2314
15	21	A	Bury	L	1-2	0-0	23	Tait 78	2246
16	28	H	Wycombe W	L	0-1	0-0	23		1762
17	Nov 4	H	Notts Co	D	3-3	1-1	23	Stevens 24, Elding 75, Green 86	2539
18	18	A	Macclesfield T	W	3-2	3-1	23	Ellender 3, Broughton 18, Greaves 40	1895
19	25	H	Hereford U	D	1-1	0-0	23	Clarke 74	1731
20	Dec 5	A	Chester C	L	1-3	0-0	—	N'Guessan 88	1527
21	9	H	Wrexham	W	4-0	1-0	22	Elding 2 22, 83, Broughton 2 48, 69	1706
22	16	A	Torquay U	W	1-0	1-0	20	Elding 41	2107
23	23	H	Walsall	D	1-1	0-0	19	N'Guessan 55	2083
24	26	A	Lincoln C	L	1-2	1-1	20	Kennedy 38	6820
25	30	A	Rochdale	L	0-4	0-1	21		2159
26	Jan 1	H	Barnet	W	2-1	1-1	21	Greaves 8, Yakubu (og) 46	1780
27	6	H	Accrington S	W	1-0	0-0	17	Broughton 72	1664
28	13	A	Stockport Co	L	0-2	0-1	18		4568
29	20	H	Swindon T	L	1-3	1-1	19	Thomas 17	2101
30	27	A	Walsall	D	1-1	1-1	19	Dann (og) 25	5058
31	Feb 3	H	Grimsby T	L	0-6	0-4	20		2915
32	10	A	Darlington	L	0-2	0-0	21		2764
33	17	H	Shrewsbury T	L	0-3	0-2	23		1571
34	20	A	Peterborough U	D	1-1	0-0	—	Joynes 61	4882
35	24	H	Hartlepool U	L	0-1	0-0	22		2120
36	Mar 3	A	Milton Keynes D	L	2-3	2-1	23	Thomas 20, Broughton 32	6605
37	10	H	Bristol R	W	2-1	2-0	23	Jarrett 2 (1 pen) 3 (p), 9	1697
38	17	A	Mansfield T	W	2-1	2-1	22	Talbot 18, Broughton 40	2790
39	23	A	Wycombe W	D	0-0	0-0	—		4417
40	31	H	Bury	L	0-1	0-0	23		1946
41	Apr 7	A	Notts Co	L	0-2	0-1	23		4170
42	9	H	Macclesfield T	W	4-1	2-0	22	Galbraith 22, Broughton 44, Greaves 65, Clarke (pen) 80	1816
43	14	A	Hereford U	L	0-3	0-0	23		2176
44	21	H	Chester C	W	1-0	0-0	23	Stevens 83	1752
45	28	H	Torquay U	D	1-1	0-0	23	Broughton 83	2664
46	May 5	A	Wrexham	L	1-3	1-0	23	Green 39	12,374

Final League Position: 23

GOALSCORERS

League (51): Broughton 8, Elding 5, N'Guessan 5, Green 4, Ryan T 4 (4 pens), Greaves 3, Joachim 3, Clarke 2 (1 pen), Galbraith 2, Jarrett 2 (1 pen), Stevens 2, Tait 2, Thomas 2, Ellender 1, Farrell 1, Joynes 1, Kennedy 1, Talbot 1, own goals 2.
Carling Cup (0).
FA Cup (0).
J Paint Trophy (0).

Marriott A 46	Canoville L 15+1	Ryan T 23	Ellender P 40+2	Greaves M 38+1	Albrighton M 12	Clarke J 30+7	Green F 35+4	Joachim J 3	Tait P 9+5	Galbraith D 21+9	Farrell D 23+16	Holland C 12+2	Talbot S 16+2	Forbes L —+1	N'Guessan D 13+10	Davidson R 3+6	Maylett B 4+17	Ryan R 9+4	Elding A 18+1	Cotton D —+2	Rusk S 2+1	Broughton D 25	Stevens J 11+1	Miller I 12	Kennedy J 13	Rowson D 6	Thomas B 11	Richards J 3	Nicholson S 5+1	Vaughan S 6+1	Joynes N 9+1	Cooksey E 11+5	Cryan C 15	Benjamin T 2+1	Jarrett A 5	Rowntree A —+3	Nunn B —+1	*Match No.*
1	2	3	4	5	6	7	8	9	10	11^1	12																											1
1	2	3	4	5^1	6	7	8	9	10	11^2	13	12																										2
1	2	3	4	5	6	7^3	8^1	9^2	10	12		11	14	13																								3
1	2	3	4	5	6	7^2			10		13	11			8^1	9	12																					4
1	2	3	4	5			8		9^1	10^2	13	6	7^3		11	12		14																				5
1	2	3	4■			7	8^2		9	11^1	12	6	5		13	10^3			14																			6
1	2^3	3			6	7	8		9^2	12	11	4^1	5		13			14	10																			7
1		3	4		6	2	8^3		12	11	7		5		14	13		10^1	9^2																			8
1		3	4	5	6^1	2	8		12	11	9		7		13				10^2																			9
1		3	4	5		2^3	8		9	11	7^1		6		12	13		14	10^2																			10
1		3	4		6		8^2			2	12	7^1	5		9	13		11	10																			11
1		3	4	5	6^3		8■		12	9^2	13		2		7	14		11	10^1																			12
1		3■	4	5	6				12		13	8^3	2^2		7	10		11	9^1	14																		13
1			4	5	6	2^3			10	8	12	7^2	3		11	13			9^1		14																	14
1		3	4	5		12	8		14	10	13	6^2			7			11^3	9		2^1																	15
1		3	4	5	6		8^2			10	11				7		14	12		13^3	2^1	9■																16
1		3	4^1			2	8				9				7			11	10				12	5	6													17
1		3	4	5		2	8											11	10			9		6	7													18
1		3	4	5		2	8				12				13			11	10^1			9^2		6	7													19
1	12	3	4	5		2	8								7			11^1	9					6	10													20
1	2^3	3	4	5		14	10^1				12						13		11			9^2		6	8	7												21
1		3	4	5		2	11^3			12■					14		13		10^2			9■		6^1	8	7												22
1	2	3	4	5		13	10								11^1		12		9					6	8^2	7												23
1	2	3	4				10			5^1	12				11^2		13		9					6	8	7												24
1	3		4^2	5		2				12		13			11^3		14		10			9		6	8^1	7												25
1	2		4	5		12	10^2			3	14	8^3			13		11^1					9		6		7												26
1	2			5			10			3	12	11^1			13		7^2					9		6	8		4											27
1	2		12	5			11^3			3	13	7^2			14							9		6	8		4^1	10										28
1	2^1		4	5^2		12	7				11						13					9^3			8		6	10	3	14								29
1			4	5		2	12				7											9			8		6	10^1	3	11								30
1			4	5		2	8				11											9					6		3	7	10^1	12						31
1			12	5		2	13				9^2						7^1										4■		3	11		8	6	10				32
1			4	5		2^1											12					9							3	7		8	6	10	11			33
1			4^1			13					11		12^2				14					9	5^3				2			7	10	8	3		6			34
1			4	12							11						13					9^3	2				6			3^2	10	8^1	5	14	7			35
1			4	5		14	12			13	11											9	2^1				7^3				10	8	6		3^2			36
1			4	5^3		2	12				11		7^2									9					3		14		10	13	6		8^1			37
1			4	5		2	8			12	7		11^2									9					3■				10^1	13	6					38
1			4	5		2	8^1			12	11		7^2									9	3								10^3	13	6			14		39
1				5		2	8			12	7		4				13					9	3								10^2	11^1	6					40
1				5		2	8			12	11		4^3				13					9	3								10^1	7^2	6			14		41
1			4	5^3		2	10			8^2	11		7^1				13					9	3								14	12	6					42
1			4	5		2	10			8^2	11						12					9	3^3									7^1	6			13	14	43
1			4	5		2	8			9	11						10						3									7	6					44
1			4	5		2	10			11^1	7						12					9	3									8	6					45
1			4	5		2	10			7^1	11						12					9	3									8	6					46

FA Cup
First Round Bournemouth (a) 0-4

Carling Cup
First Round Brighton & HA (a) 0-1

J Paint Trophy
First Round Brighton & HA (a) 0-2

AFC BOURNEMOUTH FL Championship 1

FOUNDATION

There was a Bournemouth FC as early as 1875, but the present club arose out of the remnants of the Boscombe St John's club (formed 1890). The meeting at which Boscombe FC came into being was held at a house in Gladstone Road in 1899. They began by playing in the Boscombe and District Junior League.

The Fitness First Stadium at Dean Court, Bournemouth, Dorset BH7 7AF.

Telephone: (01202) 726 300.

Fax: (01202) 726 301.

Ticket Office: 08700 340 380.

Website: www.afcb.co.uk

Email: admin@afcb.co.uk

Ground Capacity: 10,375.

Record Attendance: 28,799 v Manchester U, FA Cup 6th rd, 2 March 1957.

Pitch Measurements: 115yd × 74yd.

Chairman: J. A. Mostyn.

Vice-chairman: S. M. Sly.

Chief Executive: L. C. Jones.

Secretary: K. R. J. MacAlister.

Manager: Kevin Bond.

Assistant Manager: Rob Newman.

Physio: Steve Hard.

Colours: Red shirts with three black stripes front and back, black shorts, black stockings.

Change Colours: White with red trim shirts, red with white trim shorts, white with red trim stockings.

Year Formed: 1899.

Turned Professional: 1912.

Ltd Co.: 1914.

Previous Names: 1890, Boscombe St Johns; 1899, Boscombe FC; 1923, Bournemouth & Boscombe Ath FC; 1971, AFC Bournemouth.

Club Nickname: 'Cherries'.

Grounds: 1899, Castlemain Road, Pokesdown; 1910, Dean Court.

First Football League Game: 25 August 1923, Division 3 (S), v Swindon T (a) L 1–3 – Heron; Wingham, Lamb; Butt, C. Smith, Voisey; Miller, Lister (1), Davey, Simpson, Robinson.

Record League Victory: 7–0 v Swindon T, Division 3 (S), 22 September 1956 – Godwin; Cunningham, Keetley; Clayton, Crosland, Rushworth; Siddall (1), Norris (2), Arnott (1), Newsham (2), Cutler (1). 10–0 win v Northampton T at start of 1939–40 expunged from the records on outbreak of war.

HONOURS

Football League: Division 3 – Champions 1986–87; Promoted from Division 3, 2002–03 (play-offs); Division 3 (S) – Runners-up 1947–48; Division 4 – Runners-up 1970–71; Promotion from Division 4 1981–82 (4th).

FA Cup: best season: 6th rd, 1957.

Football League Cup: best season: 4th rd, 1962, 1964.

Associate Members' Cup: Winners 1984.

Auto Windscreens Shield: Runners-up 1998.

SKY SPORTS FACT FILE

On 15 February 1930 Sammy Beswick won his first England amateur international cap in a 2–1 win over Wales at Aberystwyth, the first such honour for a Bournemouth player. That season he made 38 League and Cup appearances and scored 12 goals.

Record Cup Victory: 11–0 v Margate, FA Cup 1st rd, 20 November 1971 – Davies; Machin (1), Kitchener, Benson, Jones, Powell, Cave (1), Boyer, MacDougall (9 incl. 1p), Miller, Scott (De Garis).

Record Defeat: 0–9 v Lincoln C, Division 3, 18 December 1982.

Most League Points (2 for a win): 62, Division 3, 1971–72.

Most League Points (3 for a win): 97, Division 3, 1986–87.

Most League Goals: 88, Division 3 (S), 1956–57.

Highest League Scorer in Season: Ted MacDougall, 42, 1970–71.

Most League Goals in Total Aggregate: Ron Eyre, 202, 1924–33.

Most League Goals in One Match: 4, Jack Russell v Clapton Orient, Division 3S, 7 January 1933; 4, Jack Russell v Bristol C, Division 3S, 28 January 1933; 4, Harry Mardon v Southend U, Division 3S, 1 January 1938; 4, Jack McDonald v Torquay U, Division 3S, 8 November 1947; 4, Ted MacDougall v Colchester U, 18 September 1970; 4, Brian Clark v Rotherham U, 10 October 1972, 4, Luther Blissett v Hull C, 29 November 1988; 4, James Hayter v Bury, Division 2, 21 October 2000.

Most Capped Player: Gerry Peyton, 7 (33), Republic of Ireland.

Most League Appearances: Steve Fletcher, 466, 1992–2007.

Youngest League Player: Jimmy White, 15 years 321 days v Brentford, 30 April 1958.

Record Transfer Fee Received: £800,000 from Everton for Joe Parkinson, March 1994 and £800,000 from Ipswich T for Matt Holland, July 1997.

Record Transfer Fee Paid: £210,000 to Gillingham for Gavin Peacock, August 1989.

Football League Record: 1923 Elected to Division 3 (S) and remained a Third Division club for record number of years until 1970; 1970–71 Division 4; 1971–75 Division 3; 1975–82 Division 4; 1982–87 Division 3; 1987–90 Division 2; 1990–92 Division 3; 1992–2002 Division 2; 2002–03 Division 3; 2003–04 Division 2; 2004– FL 1.

MANAGERS

Vincent Kitcher 1914–23
(Secretary-Manager)
Harry Kinghorn 1923–25
Leslie Knighton 1925–28
Frank Richards 1928–30
Billy Birrell 1930–35
Bob Crompton 1935–36
Charlie Bell 1936–39
Harry Kinghorn 1939–47
Harry Lowe 1947–50
Jack Bruton 1950–56
Fred Cox 1956–58
Don Welsh 1958–61
Bill McGarry 1961–63
Reg Flewin 1963–65
Fred Cox 1965–70
John Bond 1970–73
Trevor Hartley 1974–75
John Benson 1975–78
Alec Stock 1979–80
David Webb 1980–82
Don Megson 1983
Harry Redknapp 1983–92
Tony Pulis 1992–94
Mel Machin 1994–2000
Sean O'Driscoll 2000–2006
Kevin Bond October 2006–

LATEST SEQUENCES

Longest Sequence of League Wins: 7, 22.8.1970 – 23.9.1970.

Longest Sequence of League Defeats: 7, 13.8.1994 – 13.9.1994.

Longest Sequence of League Draws: 5, 25.4.2000 – 12.8.2000.

Longest Sequence of Unbeaten League Matches: 18, 6.3.1982 – 28.8.1982.

Longest Sequence Without a League Win: 14, 6.3.1974 – 27.4.1974.

Successive Scoring Runs: 31 from 28.10.2000.

Successive Non-scoring Runs: 6 from 1.2.1975.

TEN YEAR LEAGUE RECORD

		P	*W*	*D*	*L*	*F*	*A*	*Pts*	*Pos*
1997-98	Div 2	46	18	12	16	57	52	66	9
1998-99	Div 2	46	21	13	12	63	41	76	7
1999-2000	Div 2	46	16	9	21	59	62	57	16
2000-01	Div 2	46	20	13	13	79	55	73	7
2001-02	Div 2	46	10	14	22	56	71	44	21
2002-03	Div 3	46	20	14	12	60	48	74	4
2003-04	Div 2	46	17	15	14	56	51	66	9
2004-05	FL 1	46	20	10	16	77	64	70	8
2005-06	FL 1	46	12	19	15	49	53	55	17
2006-07	FL 1	46	13	13	20	50	64	52	19

DID YOU KNOW ?

Centre-forward Frank Fidler with Manchester United at 17, wartime in the Irish Guards, scored 179 goals for Witton Albion in three seasons, then Wrexham and Leeds United before hitting 31 League goals in 61 League games for Bournemouth from December 1952.

AFC BOURNEMOUTH 2006–07 LEAGUE RECORD

Match No.	Date	Venue	Opponents	Result		H/T Score	Lg. Pos.	Goalscorers	Attendance
1	Aug 5	H	Chesterfield	L	0-3	0-0	—		5499
2	8	A	Yeovil T	D	0-0	0-0	—		6451
3	12	A	Leyton Orient	L	2-3	0-1	21	Hayter [57], Cooke [62]	4474
4	19	H	Cheltenham T	W	2-1	1-1	16	Fletcher [2], Best [55]	5378
5	26	A	Doncaster R	D	1-1	0-0	16	Hayter (pen) [90]	5190
6	Sept 2	H	Oldham Ath	W	3-2	2-0	14	Hayter 2 [28, 43], Browning [90]	4838
7	9	H	Crewe Alex	W	1-0	1-0	8	Best [22]	5627
8	12	A	Brighton & HA	D	2-2	0-1	—	Foley-Sheridan [35], Howe [74]	5958
9	16	A	Brentford	D	0-0	0-0	13		6272
10	23	H	Scunthorpe U	D	1-1	1-1	13	Anderton [22]	5256
11	26	H	Bristol C	L	0-1	0-0	—		6484
12	30	A	Huddersfield T	D	2-2	1-1	14	Hayter [10], Best [48]	11,350
13	Oct 6	H	Northampton T	D	0-0	0-0	—		5746
14	14	A	Millwall	L	0-1	0-1	18		9838
15	21	H	Rotherham U	L	1-3	1-3	20	Gowling [31]	5544
16	28	A	Tranmere R	L	0-1	0-1	21		6076
17	Nov 3	A	Swansea C	L	2-4	0-1	—	Hollands [79], Pitman [85]	11,795
18	18	H	Carlisle U	L	0-1	0-1	22		5682
19	25	A	Bradford C	D	0-0	0-0	21		10,347
20	Dec 5	H	Nottingham F	W	2-0	0-0	—	Connolly [51], Pitman (pen) [89]	7067
21	9	H	Port Vale	L	0-4	0-2	21		4538
22	16	A	Gillingham	D	1-1	1-0	20	Vokes [38]	6296
23	23	H	Blackpool	L	1-3	0-0	22	Gillett [82]	5758
24	26	A	Bristol C	D	2-2	1-0	22	Pitman [16], Browning [47]	13,848
25	30	A	Scunthorpe U	L	2-3	0-3	23	Vokes 2 [46, 74]	4794
26	Jan 1	H	Brighton & HA	W	1-0	0-0	21	Pitman [90]	6686
27	6	H	Brentford	W	1-0	1-0	19	Anderton [42]	5782
28	13	A	Crewe Alex	L	0-2	0-1	21		4739
29	20	H	Huddersfield T	L	1-2	1-1	21	Purches [43]	5263
30	Feb 3	A	Chesterfield	W	1-0	0-0	22	Hayter [52]	3854
31	10	H	Leyton Orient	W	5-0	2-0	20	Wilson [10], Anderton 3 [16, 47, 83], Hayter [68]	5985
32	17	A	Cheltenham T	L	0-1	0-0	22		4530
33	20	H	Yeovil T	L	0-2	0-1	—		7285
34	24	A	Oldham Ath	W	2-1	2-1	21	McGoldrick [29], Vidarsson [31]	5429
35	Mar 3	H	Doncaster R	W	2-0	1-0	19	Pitman [45], McGoldrick [47]	6166
36	6	A	Blackpool	L	0-2	0-1	—		6184
37	10	A	Northampton T	L	1-3	0-1	19	Wilson [55]	5921
38	17	H	Millwall	W	1-0	1-0	19	Anderton [19]	7194
39	24	H	Tranmere R	W	2-0	1-0	18	McGoldrick [13], Hayter (pen) [57]	5640
40	31	A	Rotherham U	W	2-0	2-0	16	McGoldrick [12], Hayter [28]	3657
41	Apr 7	H	Bradford C	D	1-1	0-0	17	McGoldrick [61]	6440
42	9	A	Carlisle U	L	1-3	0-2	18	Vokes [62]	8989
43	14	H	Swansea C	D	2-2	1-0	18	Wilson [22], McGoldrick [60]	6786
44	21	A	Nottingham F	L	0-3	0-1	19		19,898
45	28	H	Gillingham	D	1-1	1-1	19	Hayter [45]	8001
46	May 5	A	Port Vale	L	1-2	0-0	19	Summerfield [80]	5080

Final League Position: 19

GOALSCORERS

League (50): Hayter 10 (2 pens), Anderton 6, McGoldrick 6, Pitman 5 (1 pen), Vokes 4, Best 3, Wilson 3, Browning 2, Connolly 1, Cooke 1, Fletcher 1, Foley-Sheridan 1, Gillett 1, Gowling 1, Hollands 1, Howe 1, Purches 1, Summerfield 1, Vidarsson 1.
Carling Cup (1): Fletcher 1.
FA Cup (5): Fletcher 2, Hayter 2, Hollands 1.
J Paint Trophy (0).

Stewart G 20	Purches J 38 + 5	Hart C 8	Browning M 17 + 4	Broadhurst K 25 + 2	Howe E 14 + 1	Ainsworth L 2 + 5	Cooper S 29 + 4	Hayter J 41 + 1	Best L 12 + 3	Foley-Sheridan S 15 + 3	Cummings W 26 + 5	Fletcher S 32 + 9	Cooke S 6 + 4	Hollands D 14 + 19	Maher S 5 + 2	Gowling J 25 + 8	Pitman B 8 + 21	Young N 34	Anderton D 28	Songo'o F 3 + 1	Bertrand R 5	Cork J 7	Moss N 26	Gillett S 7	Connolly M 3 + 2	Vokes S 8 + 5	Claridge S 1	Wilson M 19	Lawson J 2 + 2	Vidarsson B 4 + 2	McGoldrick D 12	McQuoid J — + 2	Walker J 5 + 1	Standing M — + 1	Summerfield L 5 + 3	*Match No.*
1	2	3^{1}	4^{3}	5	6^{2}	7	8	9	10	11	12	13	14																							1
1	2			5	6	12	3	9	10^{1}	11		8	7	4																						2
1	2			5	6	12	3^{3}	9	10	11	14	8^{1}	7^{2}	4	13																					3
1	2	3^{1}		5	6		4^{2}	9	10	11	12	8	7^{3}	13		14																				4
1	2	3^{1}	13	5	6^{3}		4	9	10	11		8^{2}	7	12		14																				5
1	2		12	5	6^{3}		4	9	10^{1}	11	3	8	7^{2}		13		14																			6
1	7		4	5	2^{3}		8	9	10^{1}	11^{2}	3	12		13		14		6																		7
1	2		4■	5	6^{2}		7	9	10^{1}	11^{3}	8	12		14		13		3																		8
1	2			5	6		4^{2}	9	10^{1}	11	7	8	12	13				3																		9
1	7			5		14	12	9	13	11	3	10^{2}	8^{3}			6		2	4^{1}																	10
1	7			5		12	4	9	13	11^{1}	3	10^{2}		14		6		2	8^{3}																	11
1	7		12	5			4	9	10	11^{2}	3	13				6		2	8^{1}																	12
1	7	2	4	5			11^{3}	9	10^{1}		3	12	13	14				6	8^{2}																	13
1	7							9	10	12	3	11^{2}		4^{1}	5	6	13	2	8																	14
1	7		4^{2}					9		12	3	10		13	5	6	14	2^{1}	8	11^{3}																15
1	2					12		9	13	11^{2}	3	10	14	4^{1}	5	6			8	7^{3}																16
1	4							9^{1}		11		10		13	5		12	2	8	7^{2}	3	6														17
	2							9		11^{2}		10		4	5		12	6	8^{1}	13	3	7	1													18
	2			5			12	9^{2}				10		4			13	6			3	7^{1}	1	8	11											19
	12			5	6		8^{2}							13		14	10	2^{1}			3	7	1	11	4	9^{3}										20
				5	6	7^{1}	8			12				13			10	2	4^{2}				1	11	3	14	9^{3}									21
	2^{3}	3		5				9^{2}				10		4		13	12	6	8				1	7	14	11^{1}										22
	2	3^{1}		5			13	9				10		4^{2}			12	6	8■				1	7		11										23
	2	3	4	5^{1}			8	9						11		12	10^{3}	6					1	7^{2}	13	14										24
	2	3	4		12		8	9				10^{1}		11^{3}		6^{2}	13	5	7				1			14										25
	2		4		6		3	9									10	5	8				1	7		11										26
	2		4		6			7				11		12		13	10	5	8^{1}				1					3	9^{2}							27
	2		4		6			7				10^{1}		13			12	5	8				1			11		3	9^{2}							28
	2		4					9				12		13		6	10	5	8^{2}		3		1			11^{1}		7^{3}	14							29
			4				2	9			3	12				6		5	8^{2}			7	1			10^{1}		11	13							30
			4				2	9			3	10^{1}				6	12	5	8			7	1					11^{2}		13						31
	12						2	9			3	10		4		6		5				7^{1}	1					8		11						32
	12						2	9			3	13		4^{2}		6	14	5	8^{1}				1					7		11^{3}	10					33
	12		4	5			7				11	10^{1}		13		6	14	2^{2}					1					3		8^{3}	9					34
	12		4	5			2				3	10^{1}		13		6	9^{3}						1					8		11	7^{2}	14				35
	2		4^{2}	5			7	12			3	10^{3}		13		6	9^{1}						1					8		14	11					36
	7^{1}			5			8^{2}	9			3	12		4		6		2					1					11			10^{3}		13	14		37
	2						7^{1}	9			12	10				6		5	8				1					3			11		4			38
	2						3^{1}	9^{3}			12	10				6	13	5	8				1					7			11^{2}		4		14	39
	2						7^{1}	9			3	10		12		6	13		8^{3}				1					4			11^{2}		5		14	40
	2							9			3	10^{2}				6	12	5	8				1					7			11		4^{1}		13	41
	2							9			3					6	12	5	8				1			13		4			10		11^{1}		7^{2}	42
	2			12				9			3	10		13		6	14	5	8^{2}				1					4			11^{3}				7^{1}	43
1	2			12			13	9			3	10^{1}				6	14	5■								8^{3}		4			11				7^{2}	44
1	2		12	5			11^{1}	9			3	10^{3}				6	13		8							14		4^{2}							7	45
1	2		4	5				9			3	10^{1}		11		6	12		8													13			7^{2}	46

FA Cup

First Round	Boston U	(h)	4-0
Second Round	Bristol R	(a)	1-1
		(h)	0-1

Carling Cup

First Round	Southend U	(h)	1-3

J Paint Trophy

Second Round	Millwall	(a)	0-2

BRADFORD CITY FL Championship 2

FOUNDATION

Bradford was a rugby stronghold around the turn of the century but after Manningham RFC held an archery contest to help them out of financial difficulties in 1903, they were persuaded to give up the handling code and turn to soccer. So they formed Bradford City and continued at Valley Parade. Recognising this as an opportunity of spreading the dribbling code in this part of Yorkshire, the Football League immediately accepted the new club's first application for membership of the Second Division.

Intersonic Stadium, Valley Parade, Bradford, West Yorkshire BD8 7DY.

Telephone: 0870 822 0000.

Fax: (01274) 773 356.

Ticket Office: 0870 822 1911.

Website: www.bradfordcityfc.co.uk

Email: bradfordcityfc@compuserve.com

Ground Capacity: 25,136.

Record Attendance: 39,146 v Burnley, FA Cup 4th rd, 11 March 1911.

Pitch Measurements: 113yd × 70yd.

Chairman: Julian Rhodes.

Vice-chairman: Jim Brown.

Secretary: Jon Pollard.

Manager: Stuart McCall.

Assistant Manager: Wayne Jacobs.

Physio: Steve Redmond.

Colours: Claret and amber.

Change Colours: Black and blue.

Year Formed: 1903.

Turned Professional: 1903.

Ltd Co.: 1908.

Club Nickname: 'The Bantams'.

Ground: 1903, Valley Parade.

First Football League Game: 1 September 1903, Division 2, v Grimsby T (a) L 0–2 – Seymour; Wilson, Halliday; Robinson, Millar, Farnall; Guy, Beckram, Forrest, McMillan, Graham.

Record League Victory: 11–1 v Rotherham U, Division 3 (N), 25 August 1928 – Sherlaw; Russell, Watson; Burkinshaw (1), Summers, Bauld; Harvey (2), Edmunds (3), White (3), Cairns, Scriven (2).

Record Cup Victory: 11–3 v Walker Celtic, FA Cup 1st rd (replay), 1 December 1937 – Parker; Rookes, McDermott; Murphy, Mackie, Moore; Bagley (1), Whittingham (1), Deakin (4 incl. 1p), Cooke (1), Bartholomew (4).

HONOURS

Football League: Division 1 – Runners-up 1998–99; Division 2 – Champions 1907–08; Promoted from Division 2 1995–96 (play-offs); Division 3 – Champions 1984–85; Division 3 (N) – Champions 1928–29; Division 4 – Runners-up 1981–82.

FA Cup: Winners 1911.

Football League Cup: best season: 5th rd, 1965, 1989.

European Competitions: *Intertoto Cup:* 2000.

SKY SPORTS FACT FILE

On 19 August 2006 Eddie Johnson came on as a substitute for Bradford City in the 43rd minute and scored within a minute against Crewe Alexandra where he had once been on loan. He added a second goal in the 57th during the 3–0 victory.

Record Defeat: 1–9 v Colchester U, Division 4, 30 December 1961.

Most League Points (2 for a win): 63, Division 3 (N), 1928–29.

Most League Points (3 for a win): 94, Division 3, 1984–85.

Most League Goals: 128, Division 3 (N), 1928–29.

Highest League Scorer in Season: David Layne, 34, Division 4, 1961–62.

Most League Goals in Total Aggregate: Bobby Campbell, 121, 1981–84, 1984–86.

Most League Goals in One Match: 7, Albert Whitehurst v Tranmere R, Division 3N, 6 March 1929.

Most Capped Player: Jamie Lawrence (42), Jamaica.

Most League Appearances: Cec Podd, 502, 1970–84.

Youngest League Player: Robert Cullingford, 16 years 141 days v Mansfield T, 22 April 1970.

Record Transfer Fee Received: £2,000,000 from Newcastle U for Des Hamilton, March 1997 and £2,000,000 from Newcastle U for Andrew O'Brien, March 2001.

Record Transfer Fee Paid: £2,500,000 to Leeds U for David Hopkins, July 2000.

Football League Record: 1903 Elected to Division 2; 1908–22 Division 1; 1922–27 Division 2; 1927–29 Division 3 (N); 1929–37 Division 2; 1937–61 Division 3; 1961–69 Division 4; 1969–72 Division 3; 1972–77 Division 4; 1977–78 Division 3; 1978–82 Division 4; 1982–85 Division 3; 1985–90 Division 2; 1990–92 Division 3; 1992–96 Division 2; 1996–99 Division 1; 1999–2001 FA Premier League; 2001–04 Division 1; 2004–07 FL 1; 2007– FL 2.

LATEST SEQUENCES

Longest Sequence of League Wins: 10, 26.11.1983 – 3.2.1984.

Longest Sequence of League Defeats: 8, 21.1.1933 – 11.3.1933.

Longest Sequence of League Draws: 6, 30.1.1976 – 13.3.1976.

Longest Sequence of Unbeaten League Matches: 21, 11.1.1969 – 2.5.1969.

Longest Sequence Without a League Win: 16, 28.8.1948 – 20.11.1948.

Successive Scoring Runs: 30 from 26.12.1961.

Successive Non-scoring Runs: 7 from 18.4.1925.

MANAGERS

Robert Campbell 1903–05
Peter O'Rourke 1905–21
David Menzies 1921–26
Colin Veitch 1926–28
Peter O'Rourke 1928–30
Jack Peart 1930–35
Dick Ray 1935–37
Fred Westgarth 1938–43
Bob Sharp 1943–46
Jack Barker 1946–47
John Milburn 1947–48
David Steele 1948–52
Albert Harris 1952
Ivor Powell 1952–55
Peter Jackson 1955–61
Bob Brocklebank 1961–64
Bill Harris 1965–66
Willie Watson 1966–69
Grenville Hair 1967–68
Jimmy Wheeler 1968–71
Bryan Edwards 1971–75
Bobby Kennedy 1975–78
John Napier 1978
George Mulhall 1978–81
Roy McFarland 1981–82
Trevor Cherry 1982–87
Terry Dolan 1987–89
Terry Yorath 1989–90
John Docherty 1990–91
Frank Stapleton 1991–94
Lennie Lawrence 1994–95
Chris Kamara 1995–98
Paul Jewell 1998–2000
Chris Hutchings 2000
Jim Jefferies 2000–01
Nicky Law 2002–03
Bryan Robson 2003–04
Colin Todd 2004–07
Stuart McCall May 2007–

TEN YEAR LEAGUE RECORD

		P	W	D	L	F	A	Pts	Pos
1997-98	Div 1	46	14	15	17	46	59	57	13
1998-99	Div 1	46	26	9	11	82	47	87	2
1999-2000	PR Lge	38	9	9	20	38	68	36	17
2000-01	PR Lge	38	5	11	22	30	70	26	20
2001-02	Div 1	46	15	10	21	69	76	55	15
2002-03	Div 1	46	14	10	22	51	73	52	19
2003-04	Div 1	46	10	6	30	38	69	36	23
2004-05	FL 1	46	17	14	15	64	62	65	11
2005-06	FL 1	46	14	19	13	51	49	61	11
2006-07	FL 1	46	11	14	21	47	65	47	22

DID YOU KNOW ?

In successive seasons 1958–59 and 1959–60 the leading goalscorers for Bradford City were respectively John McCole and Derek Stokes with 25 goals. However this club record total merely lasted two years. But both players signed for the club again later.

BRADFORD CITY 2006–07 LEAGUE RECORD

Match No.	*Date*	*Venue*	*Opponents*	*Result*		*H/T Score*	*Lg. Pos.*	*Goalscorers*	*Attendance*
1	Aug 5	A	Nottingham F	L	0-1	0-1	—		19,665
2	8	H	Bristol C	W	2-1	2-1	—	Windass [42], Graham [43]	7356
3	12	H	Gillingham	W	4-2	1-2	7	Bower [43], Windass 2 [61, 82], Johnson J [90]	7807
4	19	A	Crewe Alex	W	3-0	1-0	3	Johnson E 2 [44, 57], Bridge-Wilkinson [52]	5274
5	26	H	Rotherham U	D	1-1	0-1	3	Windass [76]	8669
6	Sept 2	A	Brentford	L	1-2	1-0	6	Bower [14]	5471
7	9	A	Swansea C	L	0-1	0-0	9		11,481
8	12	H	Carlisle U	D	1-1	1-0	—	Windass [21]	7966
9	16	H	Port Vale	W	2-0	0-0	5	Bridge-Wilkinson [60], Graham [64]	7829
10	23	A	Cheltenham T	W	2-1	0-1	4	Graham [52], Johnson J [69]	3830
11	26	A	Doncaster R	D	3-3	2-1	—	Windass 2 [1, 23], Bridge-Wilkinson [83]	6304
12	30	H	Tranmere R	W	2-0	0-0	4	Bower [54], Schumacher [71]	8877
13	Oct 7	H	Huddersfield T	L	0-1	0-1	6		14,925
14	13	A	Northampton T	D	0-0	0-0	—		5625
15	21	H	Scunthorpe U	L	0-1	0-0	8		8723
16	28	A	Blackpool	L	1-4	0-2	11	Johnson J [84]	7937
17	Nov 4	H	Brighton & HA	L	2-3	0-1	15	Windass (pen) [56], Schumacher [80]	7610
18	18	A	Oldham Ath	L	0-2	0-0	15		6001
19	25	H	Bournemouth	D	0-0	0-0	15		10,347
20	Dec 5	A	Leyton Orient	W	2-1	2-1	—	Johnson E [4], Bridge-Wilkinson [34]	3529
21	9	A	Millwall	L	0-2	0-2	16		7588
22	16	H	Chesterfield	W	1-0	0-0	13	Windass [57]	7228
23	23	A	Yeovil T	D	0-0	0-0	14		6208
24	26	H	Doncaster R	L	0-1	0-1	14		10,069
25	30	H	Cheltenham T	D	2-2	1-0	13	Wetherall [15], Johnson J [65]	7264
26	Jan 1	A	Carlisle U	L	0-1	0-1	14		7548
27	6	A	Port Vale	W	1-0	0-0	12	Schumacher [54]	4146
28	13	H	Swansea C	D	2-2	1-1	12	Windass 2 (1 pen) [23, 88 (p)]	7347
29	19	A	Tranmere R	D	1-1	1-1	—	Schumacher [34]	6567
30	27	H	Yeovil T	L	0-2	0-1	14		7474
31	Feb 3	H	Nottingham F	D	2-2	1-2	14	Dyer [8], Paynter [89]	10,160
32	10	A	Gillingham	L	0-1	0-1	16		5513
33	17	H	Crewe Alex	L	0-1	0-0	18		7778
34	24	H	Brentford	D	1-1	0-0	20	Schumacher (pen) [88]	7627
35	Mar 3	A	Rotherham U	L	1-4	0-1	21	Daley [54]	4568
36	10	A	Huddersfield T	L	0-2	0-1	21		14,772
37	13	A	Bristol C	W	3-2	1-1	—	Paynter [44], Ashikodi [49], Schumacher [55]	13,201
38	17	H	Northampton T	L	1-2	0-0	20	Paynter [62]	8190
39	24	H	Blackpool	L	1-3	0-1	20	Daley [61]	8984
40	31	A	Scunthorpe U	L	0-2	0-0	21		6437
41	Apr 7	A	Bournemouth	D	1-1	0-0	22	Weir-Daley [90]	6440
42	9	H	Oldham Ath	D	1-1	0-0	22	Ashikodi [65]	9940
43	14	A	Brighton & HA	W	1-0	1-0	21	Paynter [35]	5757
44	21	H	Leyton Orient	L	0-2	0-0	21		10,665
45	28	A	Chesterfield	L	0-3	0-2	22		5207
46	May 5	H	Millwall	D	2-2	1-0	22	Barrau 2 [45, 67]	7134

Final League Position: 22

GOALSCORERS

League (47): Windass 11 (2 pens), Schumacher 6 (1 pen), Bridge-Wilkinson 4, Johnson J 4, Paynter 4, Bower 3, Graham 3, Johnson E 3, Ashikodi 2, Barrau 2, Daley 2, Dyer 1, Weir-Daley 1, Wetherall 1.
Carling Cup (1): Johnson E 1.
FA Cup (4): Bridge-Wilkinson 1, Schumacher 1, Windass 1, own goal 1.
J Paint Trophy (1): Brown 1.

Ricketts D 46	Edghill R 20 + 4	Parker B 35 + 4	Schumacher S 44	Wetherall D 41	Bower M 46	Johnson J 26 + 1	Bridge-Wilkinson M 39	Graham D 17 + 5	Windass D 25	Holmes L 16	Doyle N 25 + 3	Johnson E 17 + 15	Colbeck J 14 + 18	Rogers A 4 + 4	Brown J 1 + 5	Ainge S 5 + 4	Healy C 2	Black T 4	Clarke M 5 + 3	Muirhead B 1 + 3	Bentham C 12 + 6	Penford T 1 + 2	Swift J 1 + 1	Hibbert D 4 + 4	Logan C 3 + 1	Daley O 13 + 1	Youga K 11	Paynter B 15	Dyer B 2 + 3	Ashikodi M 8	Barrau X 1 + 2	Weir-Daley S 2 + 3	Osborne L — + 1	*Match No.*
1	2	3	4	5	6	7	8^{1}	9^{2}	10	11^{3}	12	13	14																					1
1	2	3	4	5^{1}	6	7	8	9	10	11	12																							2
1	2^{2}	3	4	5	6	7	8	9^{1}	10	11^{3}	13	12		14																				3
1	12	3	4	5	6	7^{1}	8	9^{2}	10^{3}	11	2	13		14																				4
1		3^{2}	4	5	6	7^{3}	8	12	10	11	2	9^{1}	13	14																				5
1			4	5	6	7^{2}	8	9^{1}	10	11	2	12	13	3																				6
1		12	4	5	6	7	8	13	10^{2}	11^{3}	2	9^{1}	14	3																				7
1		3^{2}	4	5	6	7	8	12	10		2	9^{1}	13	11																				8
1	12		4	5	6	7	8	9	10	11^{2}	2		13	3^{1}																				9
1	3		4	5	6	7	8	9^{1}	10	11	2		12																					10
1	3^{1}	12	4	5	6	7	8	9^{2}	10	11^{3}	2	13	14																					11
1		3	4	5	6	7^{1}	8	9	10	11	2		12																					12
1		3^{1}	4	5	6		8	9	10	11	2	12	7^{2}	13																				13
1	12	3	4	5	6		8	9^{2}	10	11	2	13	7^{1}																					14
1		3	4	5	6	7	8		10	11	2	9^{1}			12																			15
1	12	3^{1}	4	5	6	7	8^{2}		10	11	2		13		9■																			16
1	2^{2}	3	4	5	6	7			10	11	8	9^{1}	12			13																		17
1			4	5	6	12	8	13	10		2	9^{2}				3	7	11^{1}																18
1		12	4	5	6	7^{3}	8^{1}	9^{2}	10■		2		14		13	3	11																	19
1	2	3	4	5^{1}	6	7	8	10				9						11^{2}	12	13														20
1	2	3	4	5	6	7	8	10				9						11																21
1				5	6	7^{3}	8	12	10		2	9^{1}						11^{2}	3	13	4	14												22
1		11^{2}	4	5	6	7	8	9^{1}	10		2				12				3		13													23
1			4	5	6	7	8	9^{1}	10		2^{2}				12				3		11		13											24
1		3	4	5■	6	7	8	9^{1}	10		2		12								11													25
1	2^{2}	3	4		6	9	8		10		5		12			13				7^{1}	11													26
1		3	4	5	6	9^{1}	8				2		7		12						11			10										27
1		3	4	5	6		8		10		2		7								11^{1}			9	12									28
1		3	4	5	6	9	8				2	12									11			10^{1}	7									29
1		3^{2}	4	5	6	7■	8				2	12	13								14			10^{1}	9^{3}	11								30
1	2	13	4	5	6		8					12									11^{1}					7	3^{2}	9	10					31
1	2		4	5	6		8					12							13					14	11^{2}	7^{3}	3■	9^{1}	10					32
1	2	3	4		6		8					10^{3}	7^{2}			5					12			13		11^{1}		9	14					33
1	2^{2}	3	4		6		8					10^{1}	7			5								13		11		9	12					34
1		3	4		6		8					10	7			5							2^{1}			11		9	12					35
1	2^{1}	11	4	5	6		8					12	13													7^{2}	3	9		10				36
1		3	4	5	6		8					12	7			13					11						2	9^{2}		10^{1}				37
1		3	4	5	6		8						7								11^{1}						2	9		10	12			38
1		3	4■	5^{1}	6		8					12	7													11	2	9		10				39
1		3		5	6		8^{1}					12	7								4			13		11^{3}	2	9^{2}		10	14			40
1	2	11^{1}	4	5	6							8	7													12	3	9		10^{2}		13		41
1	2	3	4	5	6							8	7■								12						11	9^{1}		10^{2}		13		42
1	2	3	4	5	6							8							13		12					7^{1}	11	9^{2}		10^{3}		14		43
1	2	3	4	5	6							8	12													7	11^{1}	9				10		44
1	2^{3}	3^{1}	4	5	6							8	12						7		13	14				11		9^{2}				10		45
1	2	3	4^{2}		6								7^{1}			13			5	12	8	10				11^{3}					9		14	46

FA Cup

First Round	Crewe Alex	(h)	4-0
Second Round	Millwall	(h)	0-0
		(a)	0-1

Carling Cup

First Round	Carlisle U	(a)	1-1

J Paint Trophy

First Round	Scunthorpe U	(h)	1-2

BRENTFORD — FL Championship 2

FOUNDATION

Formed as a small amateur concern in 1889 they were very successful in local circles. They won the championship of the West London Alliance in 1893 and a year later the West Middlesex Junior Cup before carrying off the Senior Cup in 1895. After winning both the London Senior Amateur Cup and the Middlesex Senior Cup in 1898 they were admitted to the Second Division of the Southern League.

Griffin Park, Braemar Road, Brentford, Middlesex, TW8 0NT.

Telephone: 0845 3456 442.

Fax: (0208) 568 9947.

Ticket Office: 0845 3456 442.

Website: www.brentfordfc.co.uk

E-mail: enquiries@brentfordfc.co.uk

Ground Capacity: 12,500.

Record Attendance: 38,678 v Leicester C, FA Cup 6th rd, 26 February 1949.

Pitch Measurements: 111yd × 74yd.

Chairman: Greg Dyke.

Managing Director: Keith Dickens.

Secretary: Lisa Hall.

Manager: Terry Butcher.

Assistant Manager: Andy Scott.

Physio: Brett Hutchinson.

Colours: Red and white striped shirts, black shorts, red and black stockings.

Change Colours: Light and dark blue shirts.

Year Formed: 1889.

Turned Professional: 1899.

Ltd Co.: 1901.

Club Nickname: 'The Bees'.

Grounds: 1889, Clifden Road; 1891, Benns Fields, Little Ealing; 1895, Shotters Field; 1898, Cross Road, S. Ealing; 1900, Boston Park; 1904, Griffin Park.

First Football League Game: 28 August 1920, Division 3, v Exeter C (a) L 0–3 – Young; Hodson, Rosier, Elliott J, Levitt, Amos, Smith, Thompson, Spreadbury, Morley, Henery.

Record League Victory: 9–0 v Wrexham, Division 3, 15 October 1963 – Cakebread; Coote, Jones; Slater, Scott, Higginson; Summers (1), Brooks (2), McAdams (2), Ward (2), Hales (1), (1 og).

Record Cup Victory: 7–0 v Windsor & Eton (away), FA Cup 1st rd, 20 November 1982 – Roche; Rowe, Harris (Booker), McNichol (1), Whitehead, Hurlock (2), Kamara, Joseph (1), Mahoney (3), Bowles, Roberts. *N.B.* 8–0 v Uxbridge, FA Cup, 3rd Qual rd, 31 October 1903.

HONOURS

Football League: Division 1 best season: 5th, 1935–36; Division 2 – Champions 1934–35; Division 3 – Champions 1991–92, 1998–99; Division 3 (S) – Champions 1932–33, Runners-up 1929–30, 1957–58; Division 4 – Champions 1962–63.

FA Cup: best season: 6th rd, 1938, 1946, 1949, 1989.

Football League Cup: best season: 4th rd, 1983.

Freight Rover Trophy: Runners-up 1985.

LDV Vans Trophy: Runners-up 2001.

SKY SPORTS FACT FILE

In the 1967–68 season of the 18 outfield players used by Brentford in the Fourth Division, only two failed to figure among their goalscorers. The other oddity for the club that season was in recording just seven draws, the fewest in the division.

Record Defeat: 0–7 v Swansea T, Division 3 (S), 8 November 1924 and v Walsall, Division 3 (S), 19 January 1957.

Most League Points (2 for a win): 62, Division 3 (S), 1932–33 and Division 4, 1962–63.

Most League Points (3 for a win): 85, Division 2, 1994–95 and Division 3, 1998–99.

Most League Goals: 98, Division 4, 1962–63.

Highest League Scorer in Season: Jack Holliday, 38, Division 3 (S), 1932–33.

Most League Goals in Total Aggregate: Jim Towers, 153, 1954–61.

Most League Goals in One Match: 5, Jack Holliday v Luton T, Division 3S, 28 January 1933; Billy Scott v Barnsley, Division 2, 15 December 1934; Peter McKennan v Bury, Division 2, 18 February 1949.

Most Capped Player: John Buttigieg, 22 (98), Malta.

Most League Appearances: Ken Coote, 514, 1949–64.

Youngest League Player: Danis Salman, 15 years 243 days v Watford, 15 November 1975.

Record Transfer Fee Received: £2,500,000 from Wimbledon for Hermann Hreidarsson, October 1999.

Record Transfer Fee Paid: £750,000 to Crystal Palace for Hermann Hreidarsson, September 1998.

Football League Record: 1920 Original Member of Division 3; 1921–33 Division 3 (S); 1933–35 Division 2; 1935–47 Division 1; 1947–54 Division 2; 1954–62 Division 3 (S); 1962–63 Division 4; 1963–66 Division 3; 1966–72 Division 4; 1972–73 Division 3; 1973–78 Division 4; 1978–92 Division 3; 1992–93 Division 1; 1993–98 Division 2; 1998–99 Division 3; 1999–04 Division 2; 2004–07 FL 1; 2007– FL 2.

MANAGERS

Will Lewis 1900–03
(*Secretary-Manager*)
Dick Molyneux 1902–06
W. G. Brown 1906–08
Fred Halliday 1908–12, 1915–21, 1924–26
(*only Secretary to 1922*)
Ephraim Rhodes 1912–15
Archie Mitchell 1921–24
Harry Curtis 1926–49
Jackie Gibbons 1949–52
Jimmy Bain 1952–53
Tommy Lawton 1953
Bill Dodgin Snr 1953–57
Malcolm Macdonald 1957–65
Tommy Cavanagh 1965–66
Billy Gray 1966–67
Jimmy Sirrel 1967–69
Frank Blunstone 1969–73
Mike Everitt 1973–75
John Docherty 1975–76
Bill Dodgin Jnr 1976–80
Fred Callaghan 1980–84
Frank McLintock 1984–87
Steve Perryman 1987–90
Phil Holder 1990–93
David Webb 1993–97
Eddie May 1997
Micky Adams 1997–98
Ron Noades 1998–2000
Ray Lewington 2001
Steve Coppell 2001–02
Wally Downes 2002–04
Martin Allen 2004–2006
Leroy Rosenior 2006
Scott Fitzgerald 2006–07
Terry Butcher April 2007–

LATEST SEQUENCES

Longest Sequence of League Wins: 9, 30.4.1932 – 24.9.1932.

Longest Sequence of League Defeats: 9, 20.10.1928 – 25.12.1928.

Longest Sequence of League Draws: 5, 16.3.1957 – 6.4.1957.

Longest Sequence of Unbeaten League Matches: 26, 20.2.1999 – 16.10.1999.

Longest Sequence Without a League Win: 18, 9.9.2006 – 26.12.2006.

Successive Scoring Runs: 26 from 4.3.1963.

Successive Non-scoring Runs: 7 from 7.3.2000.

TEN YEAR LEAGUE RECORD

		P	*W*	*D*	*L*	*F*	*A*	*Pts*	*Pos*
1997-98	Div 2	46	11	17	18	50	71	50	21
1998-99	Div 3	46	26	7	13	79	56	85	1
1999-2000	Div 2	46	13	13	20	47	61	52	17
2000-01	Div 2	46	14	17	15	56	70	59	14
2001-02	Div 2	46	24	11	11	77	43	83	3
2002-03	Div 2	46	14	12	20	47	56	54	16
2003-04	Div 2	46	14	11	21	52	69	53	17
2004-05	FL 1	46	22	9	15	57	60	75	4
2005-06	FL 1	46	20	16	10	72	52	76	3
2006-07	FL 1	46	8	13	25	40	79	37	24

DID YOU KNOW ?

The goalscoring partnership of the unrelated Jack and Bill Lane for Brentford in the 1920s was particularly potent in FA Cup ties. Jack, an inside-forward scored 12 goals in 19 such ties, while centre-forward Bill contributed ten in only 11 cup games.

BRENTFORD 2006–07 LEAGUE RECORD

Match No.	Date	Venue	Opponents	Result		H/T Score	Lg. Pos.	Goalscorers	Attendance
1	Aug 5	H	Blackpool	W	1-0	0-0	—	Skulason [74]	6048
2	8	A	Northampton T	W	1-0	0-0	—	Moore [71]	5707
3	12	A	Brighton & HA	D	2-2	1-2	4	O'Connor [38], Moore [90]	6745
4	19	H	Huddersfield T	D	2-2	0-0	4	Osei-Kuffour 2 [70, 89]	5709
5	26	A	Scunthorpe U	D	1-1	1-0	5	Osei-Kuffour [39]	3942
6	Sept 2	H	Bradford C	W	2-1	0-1	4	O'Connor [74], Osei-Kuffour [81]	5471
7	9	A	Leyton Orient	D	1-1	0-1	4	Tillen [88]	5420
8	12	H	Swansea C	L	0-2	0-1	—		5392
9	16	H	Bournemouth	D	0-0	0-0	10		6272
10	23	A	Chesterfield	L	1-3	1-3	14	Griffiths [45]	3877
11	26	A	Millwall	D	1-1	1-1	—	Willock [13]	7618
12	30	H	Yeovil T	L	1-2	0-0	15	Osei-Kuffour [80]	5770
13	Oct 7	H	Bristol C	D	1-1	0-1	16	O'Connor (pen) [68]	6740
14	14	A	Rotherham U	L	0-2	0-0	19		4722
15	21	H	Gillingham	D	2-2	2-1	19	Heywood [36], Willock [45]	5759
16	28	A	Oldham Ath	L	0-3	0-1	19		4708
17	Nov 4	A	Nottingham F	L	0-2	0-2	20		18,003
18	18	H	Crewe Alex	L	0-4	0-1	21		4771
19	24	A	Cheltenham T	L	0-2	0-1	—		3646
20	Dec 5	H	Doncaster R	L	0-4	0-1	—		4296
21	9	H	Tranmere R	D	1-1	1-1	24	Ide [38]	4878
22	16	A	Port Vale	L	0-1	0-0	24		4166
23	23	A	Carlisle U	L	0-2	0-0	24		6805
24	26	H	Millwall	L	1-4	0-1	24	O'Connor (pen) [78]	6925
25	30	H	Chesterfield	W	2-1	1-0	24	Osei-Kuffour 2 [2, 67]	4540
26	Jan 1	A	Swansea C	L	0-2	0-2	24		12,554
27	6	A	Bournemouth	L	0-1	0-1	24		5782
28	13	H	Leyton Orient	D	2-2	0-1	24	Ide 2 [66, 90]	6765
29	20	A	Yeovil T	L	0-1	0-0	24		5373
30	27	H	Carlisle U	D	0-0	0-0	24		5381
31	Feb 3	A	Blackpool	W	3-1	3-0	23	Frampton [13], Osei-Kuffour 2 [29, 30]	6086
32	10	H	Brighton & HA	W	1-0	1-0	23	Osei-Kuffour [31]	7023
33	17	A	Huddersfield T	W	2-0	0-0	23	Ide [49], Osei-Kuffour [58]	10,520
34	19	H	Northampton T	L	0-1	0-1	—		5164
35	24	A	Bradford C	D	1-1	0-0	23	O'Connor (pen) [48]	7627
36	Mar 3	H	Scunthorpe U	L	0-2	0-1	23		5645
37	10	A	Bristol C	L	0-1	0-1	23		11,826
38	17	H	Rotherham U	L	0-1	0-1	23		4937
39	25	H	Oldham Ath	D	2-2	0-0	23	Richards [59], Keith [85]	4720
40	31	A	Gillingham	L	1-2	1-1	24	Osei-Kuffour [7]	6113
41	Apr 7	H	Cheltenham T	L	0-2	0-1	24		4831
42	9	A	Crewe Alex	L	1-3	0-2	24	O'Connor (pen) [69]	4667
43	14	H	Nottingham F	L	2-4	1-0	24	Pinault [16], Ide [47]	6637
44	21	A	Doncaster R	L	0-3	0-1	24		8713
45	28	H	Port Vale	W	4-3	2-0	24	Ide 2 [2, 39], Keith (pen) [68], Charles [89]	5125
46	May 5	A	Tranmere R	L	1-3	1-3	24	Willock [35]	6529

Final League Position: 24

GOALSCORERS

League (40): Osei-Kuffour 12, Ide 7, O'Connor 6 (4 pens), Willock 3, Keith 2 (1 pen), Moore 2, Charles 1, Frampton 1, Griffiths 1, Heywood 1, Pinault 1, Richards 1, Skulason 1, Tillen 1.
Carling Cup (2): O'Connor 1, Osei-Kuffour 1.
FA Cup (0).
J Paint Trophy (1): Osei-Kuffour 1.

Masters C 11	O'Connor K 38 + 1	Frampton A 32	Pinault T 24 + 3	Heywood M 25 + 3	Charles D 9 + 8	Brooker P 24 + 10	Skulason O 10	Willock C 18 + 10	Osei-Kuffour J 38 + 1	Rhodes A 8 + 7	Tillen S 28 + 6	Tomlin G 6 + 6	Nelson S 19	Griffiths A 32 + 5	Moore C 8 + 8	Ide C 24 + 2	Mousinho J 29 + 5	Osborne K 17 + 4	Carder-Andrews K 2 + 3	Cox S 11 + 2	Peters R — + 13	Wijnhard C 7 + 2	Onibuje F — + 2	Abbey N 16	Leary M 17	Partridge D 3	Keith J 17 + 1	Wilson C 3	Shipperley N 11	Richards G 10	Taylor S 3 + 3	Owusu L 4 + 3	Montague R — + 4	Dark L 2 + 1	*Match No.*
1	2	3	4	5	6	7^1	8	9	10^2	11	12	13																							1
	2	3	4^1	5	6		8		10^2	14	11	7	1	12	9^3	13																			2
	2	3	4^1	5		12	8	13	10	14	11^3	7^2	1	6	9																				3
	2		4	5		7^1	8^2	9^3	10	14	3		1	6	11		12	13																	4
	2		4	5	12	7			10	11^2	3	13	1	6	9^1		8																		5
	2		4	5	3^1	7		9^3	10	12	11		1	6	14		8^2	13																	6
	8		4	5	12	7		9^2	10	11^1	3		1	6	13			2^3	14																7
	2		4	5		7		12	10	11^3	3^2	14	1	6	9			13		8^1															8
	2		4	5		7			10	11^1	3	9	1	6^2	12			13		8															9
			4^3	5	12	7^2		9	10		3	11^1	1	6			14	2		8	13														10
				5	12	7		11	10		3	13	1	6^1			4	2		8^2	14	9^3													11
	2		4	5		7		11	10^3	12	3^1	13	1	6			8				14	9^2													12
	2	3	4	5		7^3	8		10	11^1	12		1	6	13						14	9^2													13
	2	3	4	5		7^1	8		10^3		11^2		1	6	12		14				13	9													14
1■	2	3	12	5			8	13	10			11^1		4			15	6	7^G			9^2													15
1	2	3	14	5			8	9^2	10		12	11		6^1				4	7			13^3													16
1	2	3		5		7	8		10		11^2			6	12	9	4^1					13													17
1	2	3	4		5	7			12		11^1	13		6	9^3		8					10^2	14												18
1	2		4	5	3	12	8^2		10	11^1				6			7			13		9^3	14												19
1	2	6	4^2	5	12				10	11^1	3				9	13	8			7															20
1	2	3		5		12		13	10					6	9^2	11^1	8	4		7															21
1	4	3		5		12		9	10	13				6		11^1	8	2		7^2															22
1	4	3		5				9	10					6	12	11^2	8	2		7^1	13														23
1	2	3		5				9	10					6	12	11■	8	4		7^1															24
	2	3		5	12	7^1		9	10		13			6			8	4		11^2				1											25
	5	3	12		8	7^2		9	10		14			6			2	4^1		11^3	13			1											26
	2	3	4^2			12		9	10					6		7^1				13				1	8	5	11								27
	2	3				12		9^1	10					6		7	8				13			1	4	5	11^2								28
		3				7^1		12	10					6		9^2	8				13			1	4	5■	11	2■							29
		3				12		13	10		5			6		7	8	2						1	4		11^1		9^2						30
		5	4^2						10^1		3			12		7	8	6	13					1			11	2	9						31
	12	3							10		6					7	8							1	4^1		11	2	9	5					32
	2	5				12		13	10^2		3^1			14		7^3		6						1	4		11		9	8					33
	2	5				12		13	10		3^3			14		7^2	8	4^1						1			11		9	6					34
	2								10■		3					7	8	5						1	4		11		9	6					35
	2	5				7		10^1			3					11	8				12			1	4				9	6					36
	2	5		12							11			6^2		7	8							1	4^1		13		9	3	10				37
	2	5		12		7^2					13					11	8							1	4		3		9	6^1	10^3	14			38
	2	5							10^1		3		1	12		7^2	8								4		11		9^3	6	13	14			39
	2	5							10		3		1			7	8								4		11^1		9^2	6	12	13			40
	2	5	4	12		13			10		3^1		1			7^3									8		11			6^2	14	9			41
	2	5	4	6	13	7		12	10^1				1				14								11^3		3^2				8	9			42
	2	5	4		12	7		13					1	6		10^3	8^2								11^1		3					9	14		43
	2^1		4		3	7					11		1	6		10^3		5■			12				8							9^2	13	14	44
			4		5	7^2		10			3			6		9^3	8		13		12			1			11						14	2^1	45
			4		5	7^1		9		13				6		10^3	8				12			1	11^2		3						14	2	46

FA Cup

First Round	Doncaster R	(h)	0-1

Carling Cup

First Round	Swindon T	(a)	2-2
Second Round	Luton T	(h)	0-3

J Paint Trophy

First Round	Northampton T	(a)	0-0
Second Round	Nottingham F	(a)	1-2

BRIGHTON & HOVE ALBION FL Championship 1

FOUNDATION

A professional club Brighton United was formed in November 1897 at the Imperial Hotel, Queen's Road, but folded in March 1900 after less than two seasons in the Southern League at the County Ground. An amateur team, Brighton & Hove Rangers was then formed by some prominent United supporters and after one season at Withdean, decided to turn semi-professional and play at the County Ground. Rangers were accepted into the Southern League but then also folded June 1901. John Jackson the former United manager organised a meeting at the Seven Stars public house, Ship Street on 24 June 1901 at which a new third club Brighton & Hove United was formed. They took over Rangers' place in the Southern League and pitch at County Ground. The name was changed to Brighton & Hove Albion before a match was played because of objections by Hove FC.

Withdean Stadium, Tongdean Lane, Brighton, East Sussex BN1 5JD.

Telephone: (01273) 695 400 (admin office 44 North Road, Brighton).

Fax: (01273) 648 179 (admin office 44 North Road, Brighton).

Ticket Office: (01273) 776 992.

Website: www.seagulls.co.uk

Email: seagulls@bhafc.co.uk

Ground Capacity: 8,850.

Record Attendance: 36,747 v Fulham, Division 2, 27 December 1958 (at Goldstone Ground).

Pitch Measurements: 110yd × 70yd.

Chairman: Dick Knight.

Chief Executive: Martin Perry.

Secretary: Derek J. Allan.

Manager: Dean Wilkins.

Assistant to Manager: Dean White.

Physio: Malcolm Stuart.

Colours: Blue and white striped shirts, white shorts, white stockings.

Change Colours: White shirts, blue shorts, blue stockings.

Year Formed: 1901.

Turned Professional: 1901.

Ltd Co.: 1904.

Grounds: 1901, County Ground; 1902, Goldstone Ground.

Club Nickname: 'The Seagulls'.

First Football League Game: 28 August 1920, Division 3, v Southend U (a) L 0–2 – Hayes; Woodhouse, Little; Hall, Comber, Bentley; Longstaff, Ritchie, Doran, Rodgerson, March.

HONOURS

Football League: Division 1 best season: 13th, 1981–82; Division 2 – Champions 2001–02; Runners-up 1978–79; Promoted from Division 2 2003–04 (play-offs); Division 3 (S) – Champions 1957–58; Runners-up 1953–54, 1955–56; Division 3 – Champions 2000–01; Runners-up 1971–72, 1976–77, 1987–88; Division 4 – Champions 1964–65.

FA Cup: Runners-up 1983.

Football League Cup: best season: 5th rd, 1979.

SKY SPORTS FACT FILE

Failing to gain exemption from the earlier rounds did Brighton & Hove Albion no harm in 1932–33 as they reached the fifth round and forced a replay with West Ham United in game eleven. The highlight was beating First Division Chelsea 2–1 on 14 January.

Record League Victory: 9–1 v Newport Co, Division 3 (S), 18 April 1951 – Ball; Tennant (1p), Mansell (1p); Willard, McCoy, Wilson; Reed, McNichol (4), Garbutt, Bennett (2), Keene (1). 9–1 v Southend U, Division 3, 27 November 1965 – Powney; Magill, Baxter; Leck, Gall, Turner; Gould (1), Collins (1), Livesey (2), Smith (3), Goodchild (2).

Record Cup Victory: 10–1 v Wisbech, FA Cup 1st rd, 13 November 1965 – Powney; Magill, Baxter; Collins (1), Gall, Turner; Gould, Smith (2), Livesey (3), Cassidy (2), Goodchild (1), (1 og).

Record Defeat: 0–9 v Middlesbrough, Division 2, 23 August 1958.

Most League Points (2 for a win): 65, Division 3 (S), 1955–56 and Division 3, 1971–72.

Most League Points (3 for a win): 92, Division 3, 2000–01.

Most League Goals: 112, Division 3 (S), 1955–56.

Highest League Scorer in Season: Peter Ward, 32, Division 3, 1976–77.

Most League Goals in Total Aggregate: Tommy Cook, 114, 1922–29.

Most League Goals in One Match: 5, Jack Doran v Northampton T, Division 3S, 5 November 1921; 5, Adrian Thorne v Watford, Division 3S, 30 April 1958.

Most Capped Player: Steve Penney, 17, Northern Ireland.

Most League Appearances: 'Tug' Wilson, 509, 1922–36.

Youngest League Player: Ian Chapman, 16 years 259 days v Birmingham C, 14 February 1987.

Record Transfer Fee Received: £1,500,000 from Tottenham H for Bobby Zamora, July 2003 and £1,500,000 from Celtic for Adam Virgo, July 2005.

Record Transfer Fee Paid: £500,000 to Manchester U for Andy Ritchie, October 1980.

Football League Record: 1920 Original Member of Division 3; 1921–58 Division 3 (S); 1958–62 Division 2; 1962–63 Division 3; 1963–65 Division 4; 1965–72 Division 3; 1972–73 Division 2; 1973–77 Division 3; 1977–79 Division 2; 1979–83 Division 1; 1983–87 Division 2; 1987–88 Division 3; 1988–96 Division 2; 1996–2001 Division 3; 2001–02 Division 2; 2002–03 Division 1; 2003–04 Division 2; 2004–06 FL C; 2006– FL 1.

MANAGERS

John Jackson 1901–05
Frank Scott-Walford 1905–08
John Robson 1908–14
Charles Webb 1919–47
Tommy Cook 1947
Don Welsh 1947–51
Billy Lane 1951–61
George Curtis 1961–63
Archie Macaulay 1963–68
Fred Goodwin 1968–70
Pat Saward 1970–73
Brian Clough 1973–74
Peter Taylor 1974–76
Alan Mullery 1976–81
Mike Bailey 1981–82
Jimmy Melia 1982–83
Chris Cattlin 1983–86
Alan Mullery 1986–87
Barry Lloyd 1987–93
Liam Brady 1993–95
Jimmy Case 1995–96
Steve Gritt 1996–98
Brian Horton 1998–99
Jeff Wood 1999
Micky Adams 1999–2001
Peter Taylor 2001–02
Martin Hinshelwood 2002
Steve Coppell 2002–03
Mark McGhee 2003–06
Dean Wilkins September 2006–

LATEST SEQUENCES

Longest Sequence of League Wins: 9, 2.10.1926 – 20.11.1926.

Longest Sequence of League Defeats: 12, 17.8.2002 – 26.10.2002.

Longest Sequence of League Draws: 6, 16.2.1980 – 15.3.1980.

Longest Sequence of Unbeaten League Matches: 16, 8.10.1930 – 28.1.1931.

Longest Sequence Without a League Win: 15, 21.10.1972 – 27.1.1973

Successive Scoring Runs: 31 from 4.2.1956.

Successive Non-scoring Runs: 6 from 8.11.1924.

TEN YEAR LEAGUE RECORD

		P	W	D	L	F	A	Pts	Pos
1997-98	Div 3	46	6	17	23	38	66	35	23
1998-99	Div 3	46	16	7	23	49	66	55	17
1999-2000	Div 3	46	17	16	13	64	46	67	11
2000-01	Div 3	46	28	8	10	73	35	92	1
2001-02	Div 2	46	25	15	6	66	42	90	1
2002-03	Div 1	46	11	12	23	49	67	45	23
2003-04	Div 2	46	22	11	13	64	43	77	4
2004-05	FL C	46	13	12	21	40	65	51	20
2005-06	FL C	46	7	17	22	39	71	38	24
2006-07	FL 1	46	14	11	21	49	58	53	18

DID YOU KNOW ?

In four successive seasons from 1924–25 Brighton & Hove Albion were paired with Watford in the FA Cup. Including replays the teams met six times, Albion coming out on top with three wins and two draws to a single reverse in the 1925–26 replay.

BRIGHTON & HOVE ALBION 2006–07 LEAGUE RECORD

Match No.	Date		Venue	Opponents	Result		H/T Score	Lg. Pos.	Goalscorers	Atten-dance
1	Aug	5	A	Rotherham U	W	1-0	1-0	—	Revell 43	4998
2		8	H	Gillingham	W	1-0	0-0	—	Robinson 67	6643
3		12	H	Brentford	D	2-2	2-1	5	Hammond (pen) 10, Hart 13	6745
4		19	A	Nottingham F	L	1-2	1-0	8	Robinson 39	18,586
5		27	H	Crewe Alex	L	1-4	1-2	12	Cox 40	5848
6	Sept	2	A	Bristol C	L	0-1	0-1	17		10,552
7		9	A	Millwall	W	1-0	0-0	11	Elliott (og) 88	9372
8		12	H	Bournemouth	D	2-2	1-0	—	Hammond 53, Revell 60	5958
9		16	H	Leyton Orient	W	4-1	3-0	9	Reid 16, El-Abd 31, Cox 45, Loft 90	6003
10		23	A	Carlisle U	L	1-3	0-2	12	Revell 87	7704
11		26	A	Yeovil T	L	0-2	0-1	—		5243
12		30	H	Chesterfield	L	1-2	0-1	18	Williams 54	5499
13	Oct	8	H	Blackpool	L	0-3	0-1	20		5146
14		14	A	Scunthorpe U	W	2-1	1-1	16	Cox 23, Hart 52	5607
15		21	H	Northampton T	D	1-1	1-0	18	Robinson 39	5862
16		28	A	Huddersfield T	W	3-0	2-0	15	Robinson 3 23, 30, 50	10,616
17	Nov	4	A	Bradford C	W	3-2	1-0	11	Revell 13, Hammond (pen) 48, Bowditch 89	7610
18		18	H	Tranmere R	L	0-1	0-1	12		6069
19		25	A	Doncaster R	L	0-1	0-1	13		5804
20	Dec	5	H	Swansea C	W	3-2	1-0	—	Cox 13, Revell 2 66, 81	5209
21		9	H	Cheltenham T	W	2-1	0-0	10	Hammond 2 (1 pen) 56, 89 (p)	5386
22		16	A	Oldham Ath	D	1-1	0-1	10	Hammond 61	9321
23		23	A	Port Vale	L	1-2	0-2	12	Fraser 84	4349
24		26	H	Yeovil T	L	1-3	0-1	13	Gatting 72	6554
25		30	H	Carlisle U	L	1-2	1-0	15	Gatting 37	5436
26	Jan	1	A	Bournemouth	L	0-1	0-0	15		6686
27		13	H	Millwall	L	0-1	0-1	18		6226
28		20	A	Chesterfield	W	1-0	0-0	17	Gatting 50	3984
29		27	H	Port Vale	D	0-0	0-0	18		5177
30	Feb	3	H	Rotherham U	D	0-0	0-0	16		5444
31		10	A	Brentford	L	0-1	0-1	17		7023
32		13	A	Leyton Orient	W	4-1	1-0	—	Hammond 39, Savage 57, Gatting 67, Cox 89	4670
33		17	H	Nottingham F	W	2-1	0-0	11	Hammond 72, Ward 73	7749
34		20	A	Gillingham	W	1-0	1-0	—	Savage 18	6609
35		24	H	Bristol C	L	0-2	0-1	12		6280
36	Mar	3	A	Crewe Alex	D	1-1	1-1	14	Savage 31	5202
37		10	A	Blackpool	D	0-0	0-0	15		8164
38		17	H	Scunthorpe U	D	1-1	0-0	16	Savage 72	6276
39		24	H	Huddersfield T	D	0-0	0-0	15		5974
40		31	A	Northampton T	W	2-0	0-0	13	Savage 2 60, 66	6613
41	Apr	7	H	Doncaster R	L	0-2	0-1	13		6267
42		9	A	Tranmere R	L	1-2	1-0	15	Goodison (og) 11	5528
43		14	H	Bradford C	L	0-1	0-1	16		5757
44		21	A	Swansea C	L	1-2	1-2	17	Revell 14	11,972
45		28	H	Oldham Ath	L	1-2	0-2	18	Cox 85	7588
46	May	5	A	Cheltenham T	D	1-1	1-0	18	Elder 23	6232

Final League Position: 18

GOALSCORERS

League (49): Hammond 8 (3 pens), Revell 7, Cox 6, Robinson 6, Savage 6, Gatting 4, Hart 2, Bowditch 1, El-Abd 1, Elder 1, Fraser 1, Loft 1, Reid 1, Ward 1, Williams 1, own goals 2.
Carling Cup (3): Cox 1, El-Abd 1, Reid 1.
FA Cup (11): Robinson 4, Cox 2, Revell 2, Gatting 1, Hammond 1, Rents 1.
J Paint Trophy (7): Hammond 2, Revell 2, Robinson 2, Cox 1.

Henderson W 20	Reid P 10	Mayo K 28 + 2	Carpenter R 13 + 2	Lynch J 34 + 5	El-Abd A 39 + 3	Cox D 40 + 2	Hammond D 37	Hart G 18 + 7	Revell A 34 + 4	Stokes T 5 + 1	Kazim-Richards C — + 1	Robinson J 28 + 10	Frutos A 5 + 5	Gatting J 10 + 13	Loft D 5 + 6	Santos G 7 + 4	Kuipers M 14	Rents S 19 + 6	Fraser T 18 + 10	Molango M — + 1	Williams S 3	Whing A 12	Butters G 31	Hinshelwood A 10 + 1	Bowditch D 1 + 2	John A 1 + 3	O'Cearuill J 6 + 2	Elder N 1 + 12	Bertin A 15 + 1	Savage B 14 + 1	Ward N 6 + 2	Flinders S 12	Rehman Z 8	Elphick T 2 + 1	*Match No.*
1	2	3	4	5	6	7■	8	9	10^{1}	11	12^{2}	13																							1
1	2	3	4	5	6		8	9^{1}	10^{2}	11		7^{3}	12	13	14																				2
1	2	3	4	5	6	12	8	9^{1}	10	7		11^{2}			13																				3
1	2^{3}	3	4	5	6■	12	8	9	10	7^{2}		11^{1}	13			14																			4
1	2	3■	4	5	12	7	8^{3}	9	10^{1}	11^{2}		13			14	6																			5
	2		4	5^{3}	3	7	8		10	12		13	11^{2}		9^{1}	6	1	14																	6
	2^{2}	12	4■	5	3	7	8	9	10							6	1	11^{1}	13																7
	2^{2}	3		5	13	7	8	9^{1}	10			12	11		14	6	1		4^{3}																8
	4	3		5	2	7	8	9^{1}	10			12	11^{2}		13	6^{3}	1		14																9
	4^{2}	3		5	2	7	8	9	10				11^{1}			6^{3}	1	12	13	14															10
1		3	4	5	2	7	8	9^{1}	10			12		13		6			11^{2}																11
1			4^{2}	5	6	7	8	2	10			12		14	11^{1}	13		3			9^{3}														12
		11	4^{3}	3^{2}	6	7	8	12	10				13■				1				9	2	5^{1}	14											13
1		3^{2}		13		7	8	4	10			12						14	11^{3}		9^{1}	2	5	6											14
1		3		12	6	7^{3}	8^{1}					9		10^{2}		13		14	11			2	5	4											15
1		3		13	6	7	8	12^{2}	10			9^{3}						14	11^{1}			2	5	4											16
		3^{1}		12	6	7	8		10			9^{2}					1		11			2	5	4	13										17
1				3	6	7	8		10			9							11^{1}			2	5	4	12										18
1				3	6	7	8		10			9^{1}		12					11^{2}			2	5	4		13									19
1		3	12	5		7^{2}	8		10			9^{3}		14		13		6	11^{1}			2		4											20
1		11		5		7	8	12	10			9						3	6^{2}			2		4^{1}		13									21
1		11	12	6^{1}			8		10			9		13				3	4			2	5		7^{2}										22
1			4^{1}		12		8		10			9	13	14				3	11^{3}			2	5	6		7^{2}									23
1			4	12	6^{3}	7			10			9		13				3	11^{2}			2	5	8^{1}		14									24
1		3^{1}		4	6	7	8	12	10			9		11				2					5												25
1		12			6	7	4	2	10			9		8^{1}				3	11				5												26
1			4^{2}	6	8	7		11^{1}				9	12	10^{3}				3	13				5				2	14							27
				4	6	7	8	11				9		10^{1}			1	3	2				5					12							28
		3		4	6	7	8	12				9		10^{2}			1		11^{1}				5				2	13							29
		3		4	6^{1}	7	8					9					1						5				2		12	10	11				30
		3■		4	6	7	8					9		12			1	13					5^{1}				2^{2}		11	14	10^{3}				31
				2	6	7	8							9^{1}			1	3					5					12	11	10	4				32
				2	6	7	8		12					9^{1}			1	3^{3}	13				5					14	11	10	4^{2}				33
				2^{3}	6	7	8		12					9				3	13				5				14		11	10^{1}	4^{2}	1			34
		3			6	7	8		12					9^{1}					13■				5^{3}				2	14	11	10	4^{2}	1			35
		3		2	6	7	4	12	10^{1}			9											5						11	8		1			36
		3		2	6	7	4		10^{2}			9											5				13	12	11	8^{1}		1			37
				2	6	7	4		10^{1}			9		12									5				3		11	8		1			38
				2	6^{1}	7^{2}	4		10			9		12	13								5					14	11	8^{3}		1	3		39
		3		2	6	7^{2}			10^{1}			9		12					13				5						11	8		1	4		40
		3		2	6^{2}				10^{1}			12	7		9				13									14	11^{3}	8		1	4	5	41
				2	6	7		12				9			11^{3}			3	8^{1}				5^{2}					13		10	14	1	4		42
					6	7			12			9		13	8			3	2^{1}				5^{2}						11	10		1	4		43
		3			6^{3}	7		9^{2}	10			12						2					5					13	11	8^{1}	14	1	4		44
		3^{2}			6	7		8^{1}	10			9						2					5					12	11			1	4	13	45
					6	7^{1}		9	10								1	3	12				5					8	11				2	4	46

FA Cup

First Round	Northwich Vic	(h)	8-0
Second Round	Stafford R	(h)	3-0
Third Round	West Ham U	(a)	0-3

Carling Cup

First Round	Boston U	(h)	1-0
Second Round	Southend U	(a)	2-3

J Paint Trophy

First Round	Boston U	(h)	2-0
Second Round	Milton Keynes D	(h)	4-1
Quarter-Final	Millwall	(a)	1-1
Semi-Final	Bristol C	(a)	0-2

BRISTOL CITY — FL Championship

FOUNDATION

The name Bristol City came into being in 1897 when the Bristol South End club, formed three years earlier, decided to adopt professionalism and apply for admission to the Southern League after competing in the Western League. The historic meeting was held at The Albert Hall, Bedminster. Bristol City employed Sam Hollis from Woolwich Arsenal as manager and gave him £40 to buy players. In 1900 they merged with Bedminster, another leading Bristol club.

Ashton Gate Stadium, Bristol BS3 2EJ.

Telephone: (0117) 9630 630.

Fax: (0117) 9630 700.

Ticket Office: 0870 112 1897.

Website: www.bcfc.co.uk

E-mail: commercial@bcfc.co.uk

Ground Capacity: 21,497.

Record Attendance: 43,335 v Preston NE, FA Cup 5th rd, 16 February 1935.

Pitch Measurements: 115yd × 75yd.

Chairman: Stephen Lansdown.

Vice-chairman: Keith Dawe.

Chief Executive: Colin Sexstone.

Secretary: Michelle McDonald.

Manager: Gary Johnson.

Assistant Manager: Keith Millen.

Physio: John Wiley.

Colours: Red shirts, white shorts, white and red stockings.

Change Colours: Black shirts, black shorts, black and white stockings.

Year Formed: 1894.

Turned Professional: 1897.

Ltd Co.: 1897. Bristol City Football Club Ltd.

Previous Name: 1894, Bristol South End; 1897, Bristol City.

Club Nickname: 'Robins'.

Grounds: 1894, St John's Lane; 1904, Ashton Gate.

First Football League Game: 7 September 1901, Division 2, v Blackpool (a) W 2–0 – Moles; Tuft, Davies; Jones, McLean, Chambers; Bradbury, Connor, Boucher, O'Brien (2), Flynn.

Record League Victory: 9–0 v Aldershot, Division 3 (S), 28 December 1946 – Eddols; Morgan, Fox; Peacock, Roberts, Jones (1); Chilcott, Thomas, Clark (4 incl. 1p), Cyril Williams (1), Hargreaves (3).

HONOURS

Football League: Division 1 – Runners-up 1906–07; Division 2 – Champions 1905–06; Runners-up 1975–76, 1997–98; FL 1 – Runners-up 2006–07; Division 3 (S) – Champions 1922–23, 1926–27, 1954–55; Runners-up 1937–38; Division 3 – Runners-up 1964–65, 1989–90.

FA Cup: Runners-up 1909.

Football League Cup: Semi-final 1971, 1989.

Welsh Cup: Winners 1934.

Anglo-Scottish Cup: Winners 1978.

Freight Rover Trophy: Winners 1986; Runners-up 1987.

Auto Windscreens Shield: Runners-up 2000.

LDV Vans Trophy: Winners 2003.

SKY SPORTS FACT FILE

In these days of numbered and named shirts it could not happen, but in 1967–68 Jantzen Derrick appeared in all five forward positions for Bristol City wearing, of course, the numbers 7, 8, 9, 10 and 11. He even managed a substitute outing as No. 12!

Record Cup Victory: 11–0 v Chichester C, FA Cup 1st rd, 5 November 1960 – Cook; Collinson, Thresher; Connor, Alan Williams, Etheridge; Tait (1), Bobby Williams (1), Atyeo (5), Adrian Williams (3), Derrick, (1 og).

Record Defeat: 0–9 v Coventry C, Division 3 (S), 28 April 1934.

Most League Points (2 for a win): 70, Division 3 (S), 1954–55.

Most League Points (3 for a win): 91, Division 3, 1989–90.

Most League Goals: 104, Division 3 (S), 1926–27.

Highest League Scorer in Season: Don Clark, 36, Division 3 (S), 1946–47.

Most League Goals in Total Aggregate: John Atyeo, 314, 1951–66.

Most League Goals in One Match: 6, Tommy 'Tot' Walsh v Gillingham, Division 3S, 15 January 1927.

Most Capped Player: Billy Wedlock, 26, England.

Most League Appearances: John Atyeo, 597, 1951–66.

Youngest League Player: Marvin Brown, 16 years 105 days v Bristol R, 17 October 1999.

Record Transfer Fee Received: £3,000,000 from Wolverhampton W for Ade Akinbiyi, September 1999.

Record Transfer Fee Paid: £1,200,000 to Gillingham for Ade Akinbiyi, May 1998.

Football League Record: 1901 Elected to Division 2; 1906–11 Division 1; 1911–22 Division 2; 1922–23 Division 3 (S); 1923–24 Division 2; 1924–27 Division 3 (S); 1927–32 Division 2; 1932–55 Division 3 (S); 1955–60 Division 2; 1960–65 Division 3; 1965–76 Division 2; 1976–80 Division 1; 1980–81 Division 2; 1981–82 Division 3; 1982–84 Division 4; 1984–90 Division 3; 1990–92 Division 2; 1992–95 Division 1; 1995–98 Division 2; 1998–99 Division 1; 1999–04 Division 2; 2004–07 FL 1; 2007 – FL C.

MANAGERS

Sam Hollis 1897–99
Bob Campbell 1899–1901
Sam Hollis 1901–05
Harry Thickett 1905–10
Frank Bacon 1910–11
Sam Hollis 1911–13
George Hedley 1913–17
Jack Hamilton 1917–19
Joe Palmer 1919–21
Alex Raisbeck 1921–29
Joe Bradshaw 1929–32
Bob Hewison 1932–49
(under suspension 1938–39)
Bob Wright 1949–50
Pat Beasley 1950–58
Peter Doherty 1958–60
Fred Ford 1960–67
Alan Dicks 1967–80
Bobby Houghton 1980–82
Roy Hodgson 1982
Terry Cooper 1982–88
(Director from 1983)
Joe Jordan 1988–90
Jimmy Lumsden 1990–92
Denis Smith 1992–93
Russell Osman 1993–94
Joe Jordan 1994–97
John Ward 1997–98
Benny Lennartsson 1998–99
Tony Pulis 1999
Tony Fawthrop 2000
Danny Wilson 2000–04
Brian Tinnion 2004–05
Gary Johnson September 2005–

LATEST SEQUENCES

Longest Sequence of League Wins: 14, 9.9.1905 – 2.12.1905.

Longest Sequence of League Defeats: 7, 3.10.1970 – 7.11.1970.

Longest Sequence of League Draws: 4, 6.11.1999 – 27.11.1999.

Longest Sequence of Unbeaten League Matches: 24, 9.9.1905 – 10.2.1906.

Longest Sequence Without a League Win: 15, 29.4.1933 – 4.11.1933.

Successive Scoring Runs: 25 from 26.12.1905.

Successive Non-scoring Runs: 6 from 10.9.1910.

TEN YEAR LEAGUE RECORD

		P	*W*	*D*	*L*	*F*	*A*	*Pts*	*Pos*
1997-98	Div 2	46	25	10	11	69	39	85	2
1998-99	Div 1	46	9	15	22	57	80	42	24
1999-2000	Div 2	46	15	19	12	59	57	64	9
2000-01	Div 2	46	18	14	14	70	56	68	9
2001-02	Div 2	46	21	10	15	68	53	73	7
2002-03	Div 2	46	24	11	11	79	48	83	3
2003-04	Div 2	46	23	13	10	58	37	82	3
2004-05	FL 1	46	18	16	12	74	57	70	7
2005-06	FL 1	46	18	11	17	66	62	65	9
2006-07	FL 1	46	25	10	11	63	39	85	2

DID YOU KNOW ?

In 1922–23 when Bristol City won Division Three (South) the reserves took the English Section of the Southern League, finishing two points ahead of Boscombe who then became Bournemouth and were then elected to the Football League!

BRISTOL CITY 2006–07 LEAGUE RECORD

Match No.	Date	Venue	Opponents	Result	H/T Score	Lg. Pos.	Goalscorers	Attendance
1	Aug 5	H	Scunthorpe U	W 1-0	0-0	—	Showunmi [69]	13,268
2	8	A	Bradford C	L 1-2	1-2	—	Murray [2]	7356
3	12	A	Huddersfield T	L 1-2	0-0	14	Jevons [49]	10,492
4	19	H	Blackpool	L 2-4	1-1	20	Showunmi 2 (1 pen) [43, 64 (p)]	10,630
5	29	A	Northampton T	W 3-1	1-1	—	Jevons (pen) [32], Brooker [71], Cotterill (pen) [90]	4919
6	Sept 2	H	Brighton & HA	W 1-0	1-0	8	Brown [21]	10,552
7	8	A	Tranmere R	L 0-1	0-0	—		8111
8	12	H	Leyton Orient	W 2-1	2-0	—	Jevons [19], Showunmi [44]	9726
9	16	H	Chesterfield	W 3-1	2-1	3	Carey [4], Brown [40], Myrie-Williams [51]	10,398
10	23	A	Port Vale	W 2-0	1-0	3	Brown [45], Jevons [76]	5295
11	26	A	Bournemouth	W 1-0	0-0	—	Jevons [70]	6484
12	30	H	Oldham Ath	D 0-0	0-0	3		11,656
13	Oct 7	A	Brentford	D 1-1	1-0	2	McCombe [41]	6740
14	14	H	Crewe Alex	W 2-1	2-0	2	Murray [26], Brown [32]	11,899
15	21	A	Nottingham F	L 0-1	0-1	3		23,456
16	28	H	Doncaster R	W 1-0	1-0	2	Carey [37]	11,909
17	Nov 4	A	Yeovil T	L 1-2	0-0	4	Jevons (pen) [90]	9009
18	18	H	Gillingham	W 3-1	1-1	3	Keogh [29], Showunmi [77], Murray [90]	11,823
19	26	A	Swansea C	D 0-0	0-0	4		15,531
20	Dec 5	H	Carlisle U	W 1-0	0-0	—	Showunmi [85]	10,792
21	9	A	Rotherham U	D 1-1	0-0	3	Murray [72]	4862
22	16	H	Millwall	W 1-0	1-0	2	Murray [1]	12,067
23	23	A	Cheltenham T	D 2-2	0-2	3	Orr [53], McCombe [90]	5863
24	26	H	Bournemouth	D 2-2	0-1	4	Murray [74], Johnson [80]	13,848
25	30	H	Port Vale	W 2-1	0-0	4	Brooker [69], Murray [76]	12,776
26	Jan 1	A	Leyton Orient	D 1-1	0-0	4	Johnson [68]	4814
27	13	H	Tranmere R	W 3-2	0-2	4	Showunmi [48], Jevons [59], Myrie-Williams [68]	10,822
28	20	A	Oldham Ath	W 3-0	2-0	2	Showunmi [9], McAllister [37], Andrews [65]	6924
29	31	H	Cheltenham T	L 0-1	0-1	—		12,227
30	Feb 5	A	Scunthorpe U	L 0-1	0-1	—		5108
31	10	H	Huddersfield T	D 1-1	0-0	5	Johnson [88]	11,636
32	17	A	Blackpool	W 1-0	0-0	3	Andrews [53]	6696
33	24	A	Brighton & HA	W 2-0	1-0	4	Jevons 2 (1 pen) [43, 84 (p)]	6280
34	Mar 3	H	Northampton T	W 1-0	1-0	3	Betsy [19]	11,965
35	7	A	Chesterfield	W 3-1	3-0	—	Keogh [8], Johnson [36], Noble [45]	3471
36	10	H	Brentford	W 1-0	1-0	2	Jevons (pen) [5]	11,826
37	13	H	Bradford C	L 2-3	1-1	—	Jevons [13], Russell [90]	13,201
38	17	A	Crewe Alex	W 1-0	0-0	2	Showunmi [85]	5731
39	24	A	Doncaster R	W 1-0	0-0	2	McCombe [88]	7945
40	31	H	Nottingham F	D 1-1	1-1	2	Orr [38]	19,249
41	Apr 7	H	Swansea C	D 0-0	0-0	2		14,025
42	9	A	Gillingham	L 0-1	0-0	2		6292
43	14	H	Yeovil T	W 2-0	1-0	2	Johnson [4], Orr (pen) [71]	19,002
44	21	A	Carlisle U	W 3-1	1-1	2	McCombe [45], Showunmi [65], Orr [84]	10,232
45	28	A	Millwall	L 0-1	0-0	2		12,547
46	May 5	H	Rotherham U	W 3-1	2-0	2	Noble 2 [8, 44], Russell [55]	19,517

Final League Position: 2

GOALSCORERS

League (63): Jevons 11 (4 pens), Showunmi 10 (1 pen), Murray 7, Johnson 5, Brown 4, McCombe 4, Orr 4 (1 pen), Noble 3, Andrews 2, Brooker 2, Carey 2, Keogh 2, Myrie-Williams 2, Russell 2, Betsy 1, Cotterill 1 (pen), McAllister 1.
Carling Cup (1): Cotterill 1.
FA Cup (14): Jevons 4, Showunmi 3, McCombe 2, Murray 2, Brooker 1, Keogh 1, Noble 1.
J Paint Trophy (7): Jevons 2, Showunmi 2, Andrews 1, Corr 1, Keogh 1.

Basso A 45	Orr B 29 + 6	Woodman C 5 + 6	Fontaine L 23 + 7	Carey L 36 + 2	Skuse C 31 + 11	Cotterill D 3 + 2	Noble D 18 + 8	Brooker S 19 + 4	Jevons P 31 + 10	Murray S 21 + 7	Brown S 12 + 3	McCombe J 38 + 3	Showunmi E 28 + 5	Russell A 20 + 8	McAllister J 29 + 2	Johnson L 41 + 1	Keogh R 20 + 11	Myrie-Williams J 15 + 10	Wright N 1 + 3	Corr B 1 + 2	Wilson B 17 + 2	Andrews W 3 + 4	Betsy K 16 + 1	Weale C — + 1	Smith A 3 + 7	Ruddy J 1	*Match No.*
1	2	3	4	5	6	7^1	8	9	10^2	11^3	12	13	14														1
1	2	3	4	5	6^2	7^1	8	9	12	11^3		14	10	13													2
1	2	3	4	5	6	12	8	9	10^3	7^1			13		11^2	14											3
1	2^2	3	4	5	6^1	12	8	9	10^3				11			7	13	14									4
1	2■		4	5		7	8	9^2	10^1		13		11^3		3	6	14	12									5
1		12	4	5	13		8^1		10^2	7	11			14	3	6^3	2	9									6
1		12	4	5	13		8		10	7^2	11	14			3^3	6	2^1	9									7
1			12	5	13		8^3		10^1		7	6	11^2	14	3	4	2	9									8
1		12		5				9^1	10	13	7^2	6		8	3	4	2	11									9
1			13	5	12			9^3	10^2	14	7^1	6		8	3	4	2	11									10
1	12			5	13^3		14		10	7	11^1	6		4	3	8	2	9^2									11
1				5	12				10	7	11	6	9^2	4^1	3	8	2	13									12
1	2				12		13		10	14	7	6	9	4^1	3	8^3	5	11^2									13
1	2		12	5	6				10	7^1	11^2	4			3	8		9	13								14
1	2^2	3	12	5	6				10^1	7	11^3	4				8	13	9	14								15
1				5	6^1				10^3	7	11^2	4		12	3	8	2	9	13	14							16
1				5■	6		12		10			4			3	8	2	11	7^1	9							17
1	12		4		6				10^1	13		5	9^3	7	3	8	2	11^2		14							18
1		12	4		6			9^1	10^3	13		5	7	11^2	3	8	2	14									19
1	12		4	5	6			13	9	14		3	10	7		8^3	2^1	11^2									20
1			4		6			12	9	7	11^1	5	10	8	3		2										21
1	12		4		6			13	9^1	7^2		5	10	11	3	8	2										22
1	2		4^1	12	6^2			13	9	7		5	10	11	3^3	8		14									23
1	2			5	6^1			9	10	11		4		7	3	8		12									24
1	2^2			5	12			9^3	13	7		4	10	6^1	3	8	14	11									25
1	2			5^2	6		12		9	7	14	4	10		3	8^1	13	11^3									26
1	2^2			5	6			9	10^3	7		4	11		3	8^1	12	13			14						27
1	2			5	6^1		12	9^3		7		4	10		3	8^2	13				11	14					28
1	2			5	6		12			7		4	10	13	3^1	8^2					11	9^3	14				29
1	2^3			5	6^1		12			7		4	10		3	8	13				11^2	14	9				30
1■	2			5	6				9^1	7		4	10^2		3^G	8					12	13	11	15			31
1	12	13	2				7	9		14		4^2		6^3		8^1	5				11	10	3				32
1	2	12	3	5	6		7^1	9^3	13								4				8	10^2	11		14		33
1			12	5	6		7	9^3	13			4				8^1	2				3	14	11		10^2		34
1	12			2	6		7^1	9^2	13			4	14			8	5				3		11		10^3		35
1	2		4		6^2		7^1		10^3			5	9	12	13	8					3		11		14		36
1	2		4^1	12	6		7^3		9			5	10	13		8^2					3		11		14		37
1	2		12	5	6				13			4	9^2	7^3	11	8		14			3				10^1		38
1	2		4	5	6		12	9^3	13			3	10^2	7^1		8							11		14		39
1	2		4	5	7			9^1	10			6	12			8					3		11				40
1	2		3^2	5	6			9^1	10^3			4	12			8	13				7		11		14		41
1	2			5	6^1				10^3			4	9	12		8	3^2	13			7		11		14		42
1	2		3	5			7^2		12			4	9^1	6		8	13	14			10^3		11				43
	2		3	5	12		7^1					4	9	6^3	13	8	14				10^2		11			1	44
1	2		4		12		7		13			5	9	8^1	3	6					10^2		11^3		14		45
1	2		12	5	13		10^3		14			4	9	6	3^1	8^2					7		11				46

FA Cup

First Round	York C	(a)	1-0
Second Round	Gillingham	(h)	4-3
Third Round	Coventry C	(h)	3-3
		(a)	2-0
Fourth Round	Middlesbrough	(h)	2-2
		(a)	2-2

Carling Cup

First Round	Cheltenham T	(a)	1-2

J Paint Trophy

Second Round	Leyton Orient	(a)	3-1
Quarter-Final	Nottingham F	(a)	2-2
Semi-Final	Brighton & HA	(h)	2-0
Southern Final	Bristol R	(h)	0-0
		(a)	0-1

BRISTOL ROVERS FL Championship 1

FOUNDATION

Bristol Rovers were formed at a meeting in Stapleton Road, Eastville, in 1883. However, they first went under the name of the Black Arabs (wearing black shirts). Changing their name to Eastville Rovers in their second season, they won the Gloucestershire Senior Cup in 1888–89. Original members of the Bristol & District League in 1892, this eventually became the Western League and Eastville Rovers adopted professionalism in 1897.

The Memorial Stadium, Filton Avenue, Horfield, Bristol BS7 0BF.

Telephone: (0117) 909 6648.

Fax: (0117) 907 4312.

Ticket Office: (0117) 909 6648.

Website: www.bristolrovers.co.uk

Email: admin@bristolrovers.co.uk

Ground Capacity: 11,626.

Record Attendance: 11,433 v Sunderland, Worthington Cup 3rd rd, 31 October 2000 (Memorial Stadium). 9464 v Liverpool, FA Cup 4th rd, 8 February 1992 (Twerton Park). 38,472 v Preston NE, FA Cup 4th rd, 30 January 1960 (Eastville).

Pitch Measurements: 110yd × 73yd 6in.

Chairman: Ron Craig.

Vice-chairman: Nick Higgs.

Chief Executive: Bill Smith.

Secretary: Rod Wesson.

Manager: Paul Trollope.

Physio: Phil Kite.

Colours: Blue and white quarters.

Change Colours: All green.

HONOURS

Football League: Division 2 best season: 4th, 1994–95; Promoted from FL 2 – 2006–07 (play-offs); Division 3 (S) – Champions 1952–53; Division 3 – Champions 1989–90; Runners-up 1973–74.

FA Cup: best season: 6th rd, 1951, 1958.

Football League Cup: best season: 5th rd, 1971, 1972.

J Paint Trophy: Runners-up 2007.

Year Formed: 1883. ***Turned Professional:*** 1897. ***Ltd Co.:*** 1896.

Previous Names: 1883, Black Arabs; 1884, Eastville Rovers; 1897, Bristol Eastville Rovers; 1898, Bristol Rovers. ***Club Nickname:*** 'Pirates'.

Grounds: 1883, Purdown; Three Acres, Ashley Hill; Rudgeway, Fishponds; 1897, Eastville; 1986, Twerton Park; 1996, The Memorial Stadium.

First Football League Game: 28 August 1920, Division 3, v Millwall (a) L 0–2 – Stansfield; Bethune, Panes; Boxley, Kenny, Steele; Chance, Bird, Sims, Bell, Palmer.

Record League Victory: 7–0 v Brighton & HA, Division 3 (S), 29 November 1952 – Hoyle; Bamford, Fox; Pitt, Warren, Sampson; McIlvenny, Roost (2), Lambden (1), Bradford (1), Petherbridge (2), (1 og). 7–0 v Swansea T, Division 2, 2 October 1954 – Radford; Bamford, Watkins; Pitt, Muir, Anderson; Petherbridge, Bradford (2), Meyer, Roost (1), Hooper (2), (2 og). 7–0 v Shrewsbury T, Division 3, 21 March 1964 – Hall; Hillard, Gwyn Jones; Oldfield, Stone (1), Mabbutt; Jarman (2), Brown (1), Biggs (1p), Hamilton, Bobby Jones (2).

SKY SPORTS FACT FILE

The club records at Bristol Rovers may have tumbled in 1952–53 but they were hard pressed at the finale to secure the championship of Division Three (South) by two points despite an unbeaten run of 27 League matches from September to March.

Record Cup Victory: 6–0 v Merthyr Tydfil, FA Cup 1st rd, 14 November 1987 – Martyn; Alexander (Dryden), Tanner, Hibbitt, Twentyman, Jones, Holloway, Meacham (1), White (2), Penrice (3) (Reece), Purnell.

Most League Points (2 for a win): 64, Division 3 (S), 1952–53.

Most League Points (3 for a win): 93, Division 3, 1989–90.

Most League Goals: 92, Division 3 (S), 1952–53.

Highest League Scorer in Season: Geoff Bradford, 33, Division 3 (S), 1952–53.

Most League Goals in Total Aggregate: Geoff Bradford, 242, 1949–64.

Most League Goals in One Match: 4, Sidney Leigh v Exeter C, Division 3S, 2 May 1921; 4, Jonah Wilcox v Bournemouth, Division 3S, 12 December 1925; 4, Bill Culley v QPR, Division 3S, 5 March 1927; Frank Curran v Swindon T, Division 3S, 25 March 1939; Vic Lambden v Aldershot, Division 3S, 29 March 1947; George Petherbridge v Torquay U, Division 3S, 1 December 1951; Vic Lambden v Colchester U, Division 3S, 14 May 1952; Geoff Bradford v Rotherham U, Division 2, 14 March 1959; Robin Stubbs v Gillingham, Division 2, 10 October 1970; Alan Warboys v Brighton & HA, Division 3, 1 December 1973; Jamie Cureton v Reading, Division 2, 16 January 1999.

Most Capped Player: Vitalijs Astafjevs, 31 (133), Latvia.

Most League Appearances: Stuart Taylor, 546, 1966–80.

Youngest League Player: Ronnie Dix, 15 years 173 days v Charlton Ath, 25 February 1928.

Record Transfer Fee Received: £2,100,000 from Fulham for Barry Hayles, November 1998 and £2,100,000 from WBA for Jason Roberts, July 2000.

Record Transfer Fee Paid: £375,000 to QPR for Andy Tillson, November 1992.

Football League Record: 1920 Original Member of Division 3; 1921–53 Division 3 (S); 1953–62 Division 2; 1962–74 Division 3; 1974–81 Division 2; 1981–90 Division 3; 1990–92 Division 2. 1992–93 Division 1; 1993–2001 Division 2; 2001–04 Division 3; 2004–07 FL 2; 2007– FL 1.

MANAGERS

Alfred Homer 1899–1920 *(continued as Secretary to 1928)*
Ben Hall 1920–21
Andy Wilson 1921–26
Joe Palmer 1926–29
Dave McLean 1929–30
Albert Prince-Cox 1930–36
Percy Smith 1936–37
Brough Fletcher 1938–49
Bert Tann 1950–68 *(continued as General Manager to 1972)*
Fred Ford 1968–69
Bill Dodgin Snr 1969–72
Don Megson 1972–77
Bobby Campbell 1978–79
Harold Jarman 1979–80
Terry Cooper 1980–81
Bobby Gould 1981–83
David Williams 1983–85
Bobby Gould 1985–87
Gerry Francis 1987–91
Martin Dobson 1991
Dennis Rofe 1992
Malcolm Allison 1992–93
John Ward 1993–96
Ian Holloway 1996–2001
Garry Thompson 2001
Gerry Francis 2001
Garry Thompson 2001–02
Ray Graydon 2002–04
Ian Atkins 2004–05
Lennie Lawrence 2005
Paul Trollope September 2005–

LATEST SEQUENCES

Longest Sequence of League Wins: 12, 18.10.1952 – 17.1.1953.

Longest Sequence of League Defeats: 8, 26.10.2002 – 21.12.2002.

Longest Sequence of League Draws: 5, 1.11.1975 – 22.11.1975.

Longest Sequence of Unbeaten League Matches: 32, 7.4.1973 – 27.1.1974.

Longest Sequence Without a League Win: 20, 5.4.1980 – 1.11.1980.

Successive Scoring Runs: 26 from 26.3.1927.

Successive Non-scoring Runs: 6 from 14.10.1922.

TEN YEAR LEAGUE RECORD

		P	W	D	L	F	A	Pts	Pos
1997-98	Div 2	46	20	10	16	70	64	70	5
1998-99	Div 2	46	13	17	16	65	56	56	13
1999-2000	Div 2	46	23	11	12	69	45	80	7
2000-01	Div 2	46	12	15	19	53	57	51	21
2001-02	Div 3	46	11	12	23	40	60	45	23
2002-03	Div 3	46	12	15	19	50	57	51	20
2003-04	Div 3	46	14	13	19	50	61	55	15
2004-05	FL 2	46	13	21	12	60	57	60	12
2005-06	FL 2	46	17	9	20	59	67	60	12
2006-07	FL 2	46	20	12	14	49	42	72	6

DID YOU KNOW ?

Bristol Rovers were involved in one of the first two League Cup matches on 26 September 1960 when their opponents were Fulham. Goals by locally born favourites Harold Jarman and Geoff Bradford helped to force a 2–1 win at Eastville.

BRISTOL ROVERS 2006–07 LEAGUE RECORD

Match No.	Date	Venue	Opponents	Result		H/T Score	Lg. Pos.	Goalscorers	Attendance
1	Aug 5	A	Peterborough U	L	1-4	0-3	—	Igoe [52]	4890
2	8	H	Wycombe W	L	1-2	0-0	—	Hunt [72]	5349
3	12	H	Grimsby T	W	1-0	0-0	16	Sandell [50]	4596
4	19	A	Milton Keynes D	L	0-2	0-1	19		5125
5	26	H	Shrewsbury T	W	1-0	1-0	15	Haldane [21]	4774
6	Sept 3	A	Stockport Co	L	1-2	0-1	16	Walker R [83]	4846
7	9	H	Rochdale	D	0-0	0-0	17		4689
8	13	A	Torquay U	D	0-0	0-0	—		3145
9	16	A	Darlington	D	1-1	0-0	17	Haldane [55]	3654
10	23	H	Walsall	L	1-2	0-2	21	Sandell [90]	5260
11	27	H	Hereford U	W	2-1	0-1	—	Walker R 2 [67, 68]	4975
12	30	A	Chester C	L	0-2	0-2	19		2151
13	Oct 7	H	Boston U	W	1-0	0-0	17	Walker J [52]	4327
14	14	A	Notts Co	W	2-1	0-0	11	Walker R [54], Haldane [67]	5797
15	21	H	Macclesfield T	D	0-0	0-0	14		5130
16	28	A	Wrexham	L	0-2	0-1	17		3803
17	Nov 4	H	Mansfield T	W	1-0	0-0	13	Disley [87]	5044
18	18	A	Bury	W	2-0	0-0	12	Haldane [74], Walker R [86]	2635
19	26	H	Barnet	W	2-0	0-0	9	Nicholson [60], Lambert [90]	5351
20	Dec 5	A	Lincoln C	L	0-1	0-1	—		3913
21	9	H	Hartlepool U	L	0-2	0-0	13		4906
22	16	A	Swindon T	L	1-2	1-2	15	Walker R [12]	10,010
23	23	H	Accrington S	W	4-0	3-0	11	Walker R 2 (1 pen) [6, 26 (p)], Elliott [22], Nicholson [88]	5205
24	26	A	Hereford U	D	0-0	0-0	12		5201
25	30	A	Walsall	D	2-2	0-0	13	Elliott 2 [65, 90]	5941
26	Jan 1	H	Torquay U	W	1-0	0-0	9	Sandell [84]	6475
27	13	A	Rochdale	W	1-0	0-0	7	Lambert [54]	2547
28	20	H	Chester C	D	0-0	0-0	9		5694
29	Feb 3	H	Peterborough U	W	3-2	1-0	9	Lambert [1], Walker R [52], Campbell [90]	5700
30	6	H	Darlington	L	1-2	0-1	—	Disley [89]	5511
31	10	A	Grimsby T	L	3-4	2-1	10	Disley 2 [14, 90], Haldane [20]	5883
32	17	H	Milton Keynes D	D	1-1	0-0	10	Nicholson [80]	5489
33	Mar 2	A	Shrewsbury T	D	0-0	0-0	—		4227
34	6	A	Accrington S	D	1-1	0-0	—	Walker R [58]	1302
35	10	A	Boston U	L	1-2	0-2	16	Haldane [68]	1697
36	17	H	Notts Co	W	2-0	0-0	13	Nicholson 2 [53, 72]	4642
37	20	H	Stockport Co	W	2-1	1-0	—	Lambert (pen) [15], Nicholson [61]	4725
38	24	H	Wrexham	L	0-1	0-0	11		5209
39	27	A	Wycombe W	W	1-0	1-0	—	Elliott [16]	4299
40	Apr 7	A	Mansfield T	W	1-0	1-0	9	Elliott [35]	2392
41	9	H	Bury	W	2-0	1-0	9	Lambert 2 [30, 61]	6266
42	14	A	Barnet	D	1-1	1-1	9	Walker R [12]	2541
43	21	H	Lincoln C	D	0-0	0-0	9		6828
44	24	A	Macclesfield T	W	1-0	0-0	—	Rigg [76]	1940
45	28	H	Swindon T	W	1-0	1-0	7	Lambert [27]	9902
46	May 5	A	Hartlepool U	W	2-1	0-1	6	Walker R (pen) [54], Lambert [86]	7629

Final League Position: 6

GOALSCORERS

League (49): Walker R 12 (2 pens), Lambert 8 (1 pen), Haldane 6, Nicholson 6, Elliott 5, Disley 4, Sandell 3, Campbell 1, Hunt 1, Igoe 1, Rigg 1, Walker J 1.
Carling Cup (1): Walker R 1.
FA Cup (6): Walker R 4 (2 pens), Anthony 1, Disley 1.
J Paint Trophy (8): Igoe 2, Walker R 2 (1 pen), Anthony 1, Easter 1, Lambert 1, Nicholson 1.
Play-Offs (10): Walker R 4, Igoe 2, Campbell 1, Disley 1, Lambert 1, Rigg 1.

Phillips S 44	Lescott A 30 + 4	Carruthers C 33 + 5	Hunt J 12 + 2	Hinton C 28 + 2	Elliott S 39	Igoe S 35 + 5	Disley C 42 + 3	Walker R 39 + 7	Agogo J 3	Campbell S 35 + 6	Green R 29 + 4	Haldane L 32 + 13	Sandell A 20 + 16	Anthony B 20 + 3	Rigg S 1 + 17	Lambert R 28 + 8	Lines C 4 + 3	Walker J 3 + 1	Shearer S 2	Easter J 1 + 2	Nicholson S 12 + 10	Oji S 5	Jacobson J 9 + 2	*Match No.*
1	2	3^{1}	4	5	6	7	8	9	10^{2}	11^{3}	12	13	14											1
1	2^{1}	3	4	5	6	11^{3}	8^{2}	9	10	13	12	7	14											2
1	3		4	5		11	8^{1}	9	10^{2}	12	2	13	7	6										3
1	3		4	5		11	8^{1}	9		12	2	10^{2}	7	6	13									4
1	3	12	4	5		11	8^{2}	9		13	2	10^{3}	7^{1}	6	14									5
1	3^{1}	12	4	5		11	8^{2}	9		13	2	10^{3}	7	6		14								6
1	3		4	5	6	11	8	9			2	10^{1}	7		12									7
1	3		4■	5	6	11	8	9^{1}		12	2	13	7^{2}			10								8
1	3	12		5	6		8	9^{2}		4	2	11^{1}	7^{3}		13	10	14							9
1	2^{1}	12	13	5	6	11	8^{3}	14		4^{2}	3	10	7			9								10
1	3	12	4	5	6	11^{2}	13	9		7	2	8^{3}				10^{1}		14						11
1	3		4	5^{2}	6	11^{3}	12	9		7^{1}	2	14		13		10		8						12
1	3		8		6	11		9^{2}		4	2	12	7^{1}	5		13		10						13
	2	3		12	6	11	8	9		4		13	7^{2}	5				10^{1}	1					14
	3		12		6	11	8^{1}	9		4	2	10	7^{2}	5	13				1					15
1	3		8		6	7^{1}	12	9		4	2	11^{2}	13	5	10^{3}					14				16
1		3			6	11	8	9		4	2	12	7^{1}	5	13					10^{2}				17
1	12	3			6	11	8	9		4	2^{1}	7^{2}	13	5		14					10^{3}			18
1		3			6	7	8	9		4	2	11^{1}	12	5		13					10^{2}			19
1	12	3			6	7	8^{1}	13		4	2	11^{3}	14	5		9					10^{2}			20
1		3			6	7	8	12		4	2	11^{2}	13	5		9^{1}				14	10^{3}			21
1	2^{1}	3		5	6	7	8^{2}	9		4	12	11^{3}	14			13					10			22
1	12	3			6	11^{3}	8^{1}	9^{2}		4	2		7	5		13	14				10			23
1		3			6	11	8	9		4	2	12	7^{1}	5		13					10^{2}			24
1		3		12	6	11	8	9		4	2	13	7^{2}	5^{1}		14					10^{3}			25
1		3		5	6	7	8	9		4	2	11^{1}	12			10^{2}					13			26
1	2	3		5	6	11■	8	9^{3}		4	12	13	7^{2}			10^{1}					14			27
1	2	3		5	6		8	9				11	7		12	10^{1}	4							28
1		3		5	6	11	8	9		4	2	12	7^{1}			10^{2}					13			29
1		3		5	6	11^{2}	8	9		4	2	12	7^{1}		13	10^{3}					14			30
1	12	3		5	6	7	8	9^{3}		4	2^{1}	11^{2}	13			10					14			31
1	2	3		5	6	11^{1}	8	9^{2}		4		7	12			10					13			32
1	2	3		5■	6	7	8	12		4		11	13			9^{1}					10^{2}			33
1	2	3			6	7	8	9^{1}		4■		11				10					12	5		34
1	2	11			6	7	8	9^{1}				12	13		14	10	4^{3}					5	3^{2}	35
1	2	3		5			8	12				7			13	9^{1}	4				10^{2}	6	11	36
1	2	3		5		12	8	13				7			14	9^{2}	4				10^{3}	6	11^{1}	37
1	2	3		5		7^{2}	8	12		4		11			13	9^{1}					10	6		38
1	2	3		5	6	7	8	9^{3}		4		11^{2}	12		13	10^{1}							14	39
1	2	3		5	6		8	9		4		7^{3}	12	14		10^{2}					13		11^{1}	40
1	2	3		5	6		8	9^{1}		4		11	7^{2}			10					12		13	41
1	2■	3		5^{1}	6	12	8	9^{3}		4		7^{2}		13		10					14		11	42
1		3			6	12	8	9		4	2	7		5	13	10^{1}							11^{2}	43
1		3			6		8	9		4	2	7^{1}		5	12	10							11	44
1		3			6	12	8	9^{3}		4	2	7^{1}	13	5	14	10							11^{2}	45
1		3^{1}			6	12	8	9^{3}		4	2	7^{2}		5	13	10	14						11	46

FA Cup

First Round	Barrow	(a)	3-2
Second Round	Bournemouth	(h)	1-1
		(a)	1-0
Third Round	Hereford U	(h)	1-0
Fourth Round	Derby Co	(a)	0-1

Carling Cup

First Round	Luton T	(h)	1-1

J Paint Trophy

First Round	Torquay U	(h)	1-0
Second Round	Wycombe W	(a)	2-0
Quarter-Final	Peterborough U	(h)	1-0
Semi-Final	Shrewsbury T	(a)	1-0
Southern Final	Bristol C	(a)	0-0
		(h)	1-0
Final (*at Millennium Stadium*)	Doncaster R		2-3

Play-Offs

Semi-Final	Lincoln C	(h)	2-1
		(a)	5-3
Final (*at Wembley*)	Shrewsbury T		3-1

BURNLEY FL Championship

FOUNDATION

The majority of those responsible for the formation of the Burnley club in 1881 were from the defunct rugby club Burnley Rovers. Indeed, they continued to play rugby for a year before changing to soccer and dropping 'Rovers' from their name. The changes were decided at a meeting held in May 1882 at the Bull Hotel.

Turf Moor, Harry Potts Way, Burnley, Lancashire BB10 4BX.

Telephone: 0870 443 1882.

Fax: (01282) 700 014.

Ticket Office: 0870 443 1914.

Website: www.burnleyfc.com

Email: info@burnleyfootballclub.net

Ground Capacity: 22,619.

Record Attendance: 54,775 v Huddersfield T, FA Cup 3rd rd, 23 February 1924.

Pitch Measurements: 112yd × 72yd.

Chairman: Barry Kilby.

Vice-chairman: Ray Ingleby.

Secretary: Cathy Pickup.

Manager: Steve Cotterill.

Assistant Manager: Dave Kevan.

Physio: Andy Mitchell.

Colours: Claret shirts, white shorts, white stockings.

Change Colours: White shirts, claret shorts, claret stockings.

Year Formed: 1882.

Turned Professional: 1883. ***Ltd Co.:*** 1897.

Previous Name: 1881, Burnley Rovers; 1882, Burnley.

Club Nickname: 'The Clarets'.

Grounds: 1881, Calder Vale; 1882, Turf Moor.

First Football League Game: 8 September 1888, Football League, v Preston NE (a) L 2–5 – Smith; Lang, Bury, Abrams, Friel, Keenan, Brady, Tait, Poland (1), Gallocher (1), Yates.

Record League Victory: 9–0 v Darwen, Division 1, 9 January 1892 – Hillman; Walker, McFettridge, Lang, Matthews, Keenan, Nicol (3), Bowes, Espie (1), McLardie (3), Hill (2).

Record Cup Victory: 9–0 v Crystal Palace, FA Cup 2nd rd (replay), 10 February 1909 – Dawson; Barron, McLean; Cretney (2), Leake, Moffat; Morley, Ogden, Smith (3), Abbott (2), Smethams (1). 9–0 v New Brighton, FA Cup 4th rd, 26 January 1957 – Blacklaw; Angus, Winton; Seith, Adamson, Miller; Newlands (1), McIlroy (3), Lawson (3), Cheesebrough (1), Pilkington (1). 9–0 v Penrith, FA Cup 1st rd, 17 November 1984 – Hansbury; Miller, Hampton, Phelan, Overson (Kennedy), Hird (3 incl. 1p), Grewcock (1), Powell (2), Taylor (3), Biggins, Hutchison.

HONOURS

Football League: Division 1 – Champions 1920–21, 1959–60; Runners-up 1919–20, 1961–62; Division 2 – Champions 1897–98, 1972–73; Runners-up 1912–13, 1946–47, 1999–2000; Promoted from Division 2, 1993–94 (play-offs); Division 3 – Champions 1981–82; Division 4 – Champions 1991–92. Record 30 consecutive Division 1 games without defeat 1920–21.

FA Cup: Winners 1914; Runners-up 1947, 1962.

Football League Cup: Semi-final 1961, 1969, 1983.

Anglo–Scottish Cup: Winners 1979.

Sherpa Van Trophy: Runners-up 1988.

European Competitions: *European Cup:* 1960–61. *European Fairs Cup:* 1966–67.

SKY SPORTS FACT FILE

In 1961–62 Burnley, runners-up in the First Division and FA Cup, had ten players with various international level honours including John Angus, John Connelly, Ray Pointer and Brian Miller (all England), Jimmy McIlroy and Alex Elder (Northern Ireland).

Record Defeat: 0–10 v Aston Villa, Division 1, 29 August 1925 and v Sheffield U, Division 1, 19 January 1929.

Most League Points (2 for a win): 62, Division 2, 1972–73.

Most League Points (3 for a win): 88, Division 2, 1999–2000.

Most League Goals: 102, Division 1, 1960–61.

Highest League Scorer in Season: George Beel, 35, Division 1, 1927–28.

Most League Goals in Total Aggregate: George Beel, 178, 1923–32.

Most League Goals in One Match: 6, Louis Page v Birmingham C, Division 1, 10 April 1926.

Most Capped Player: Jimmy McIlroy, 51 (55), Northern Ireland.

Most League Appearances: Jerry Dawson, 522, 1907–28.

Youngest League Player: Tommy Lawton, 16 years 174 days v Doncaster R, 28 March 1936.

Record Transfer Fee Received: £1,750,000 from Sheffield United for Ade Akinbiyi, January 2006.

Record Transfer Fee Paid: £1,000,000 to Stockport Co for Ian Moore, November 2000 and £1,000,000 to Bradford C for Robbie Blake, January 2002.

Football League Record: 1888 Original Member of the Football League; 1897–98 Division 2; 1898–1900 Division 1; 1900–13 Division 2; 1913–30 Division 1; 1930–47 Division 2; 1947–71 Division 1; 1971–73 Division 2; 1973–76 Division 1; 1976–80 Division 2; 1980–82 Division 3; 1982–83 Division 2; 1983–85 Division 3; 1985–92 Division 4; 1992–94 Division 2; 1994–95 Division 1; 1995–2000 Division 2; 2000–04 Division 1; 2004– FL C.

MANAGERS

Arthur F. Sutcliffe 1893–96
(Secretary-Manager)
Harry Bradshaw 1896–99
(Secretary-Manager)
Ernest Magnall 1899–1903
(Secretary-Manager)
Spen Whittaker 1903–10
R. H. Wadge 1910–11
(Secretary-Manager)
John Haworth 1911–25
Albert Pickles 1925–32
Tom Bromilow 1932–35
Alf Boland 1935–39
(Secretary-Manager)
Cliff Britton 1945–48
Frank Hill 1948–54
Alan Brown 1954–57
Billy Dougall 1957–58
Harry Potts 1958–70
(General Manager to 1972)
Jimmy Adamson 1970–76
Joe Brown 1976–77
Harry Potts 1977–79
Brian Miller 1979–83
John Bond 1983–84
John Benson 1984–85
Martin Buchan 1985
Tommy Cavanagh 1985–86
Brian Miller 1986–89
Frank Casper 1989–91
Jimmy Mullen 1991–96
Adrian Heath 1996–97
Chris Waddle 1997–98
Stan Ternent 1998–2004
Steve Cotterill June 2004–

LATEST SEQUENCES

Longest Sequence of League Wins: 10, 16.11.1912 – 18.1.1913.

Longest Sequence of League Defeats: 8, 2.1.1995 – 25.2.1995.

Longest Sequence of League Draws: 6, 21.2.1931 – 28.3.1931.

Longest Sequence of Unbeaten League Matches: 30, 6.9.1920 – 25.3.1921.

Longest Sequence Without a League Win: 24, 16.4.1979 – 17.11.1979.

Successive Scoring Runs: 27 from 13.2.1926.

Successive Non-scoring Runs: 6 from 9.8.1997.

TEN YEAR LEAGUE RECORD

		P	*W*	*D*	*L*	*F*	*A*	*Pts*	*Pos*
1997-98	Div 2	46	13	13	20	55	65	52	20
1998-99	Div 2	46	13	16	17	54	73	55	15
1999-2000	Div 2	46	25	13	8	69	47	88	2
2000-01	Div 2	46	21	9	16	50	54	72	7
2001-02	Div 1	46	21	12	13	70	62	75	7
2002-03	Div 1	46	15	10	21	65	89	55	16
2003-04	Div 1	46	13	14	19	60	77	53	19
2004-05	FL C	46	15	15	16	38	39	60	13
2005-06	FL C	46	14	12	20	46	54	54	17
2006-07	FL C	46	15	12	19	52	49	57	15

DID YOU KNOW ?

Colin Waldron was signed by Burnley from Chelsea for £30,000 at the age of 19 in October 1967. He thus became the youngest player at the time to have been transferred twice for such an amount having gone to Stamford Bridge from Bury four months earlier.

BURNLEY 2006–07 LEAGUE RECORD

Match No.	Date	Venue	Opponents	Result	H/T Score	Lg. Pos.	Goalscorers	Attendance
1	Aug 5	H	QPR	W 2-0	0-0	—	Jones 2 $^{59, 69}$	12,190
2	8	A	Leicester C	W 1-0	1-0	—	Gray ^{45}	19,035
3	12	A	Sheffield W	D 1-1	0-0	2	O'Connor J ^{82}	22,425
4	19	H	Wolverhampton W	L 0-1	0-1	7		12,245
5	26	A	Crystal Palace	D 2-2	1-0	7	Mahon ^{23}, Lafferty ^{52}	16,396
6	Sept 9	H	Colchester U	L 1-2	0-1	11	Gray ^{88}	10,039
7	12	H	Barnsley	W 4-2	1-2	—	Harley ^{42}, Noel-Williams 3 $^{57, 83, 90}$	10,304
8	16	A	Stoke C	W 1-0	1-0	3	Gray ^{1}	12,247
9	23	H	Southampton	L 2-3	2-1	7	Jones ^{4}, Gray ^{33}	13,051
10	Oct 1	A	Norwich C	W 4-1	2-0	3	O'Connor J ^{32}, Gray 2 $^{45, 64}$, Mahon ^{89}	24,717
11	14	H	Hull C	W 2-0	2-0	2	Duff ^{10}, Noel-Williams ^{13}	11,530
12	17	H	Southend U	D 0-0	0-0	—		10,461
13	21	A	Plymouth Arg	D 0-0	0-0	4		12,817
14	27	H	Preston NE	W 3-2	1-0	—	O'Connor J ^{44}, St Ledger-Hall (og) ^{82}, Gray ^{89}	14,871
15	31	A	Luton T	W 2-0	2-0	—	Gray 2 $^{31, 36}$	7664
16	Nov 4	H	Ipswich T	W 1-0	0-0	3	McCann ^{90}	11,709
17	11	A	Cardiff C	L 0-1	0-1	4		15,744
18	18	A	WBA	L 0-3	0-3	4		18,707
19	25	H	Birmingham C	L 1-2	1-1	5	McCann ^{4}	12,889
20	28	H	Leeds U	W 2-1	0-0	—	Noel-Williams ^{67}, Gray ^{69}	15,061
21	Dec 2	A	Ipswich T	D 1-1	0-0	6	Lafferty ^{86}	20,254
22	9	A	Coventry C	L 0-1	0-1	7		18,362
23	16	H	Sunderland	D 2-2	1-0	9	Lafferty 2 $^{9, 52}$	14,798
24	23	H	Derby Co	D 0-0	0-0	9		12,825
25	26	A	Barnsley	L 0-1	0-1	10		12,842
26	30	A	Hull C	L 0-2	0-2	11		17,731
27	Jan 13	A	Southampton	D 0-0	0-0	13		20,486
28	23	H	Stoke C	L 0-1	0-1	—		12,109
29	30	A	Derby Co	L 0-1	0-1	—		23,122
30	Feb 3	A	QPR	L 1-3	1-1	15	McCann ^{18}	10,811
31	10	H	Sheffield W	D 1-1	0-0	14	Elliott ^{55}	12,745
32	17	A	Wolverhampton W	L 1-2	0-2	15	McCann ^{53}	19,521
33	20	H	Leicester C	L 0-1	0-0	—		10,274
34	24	A	Colchester U	D 0-0	0-0	16		4934
35	Mar 3	H	Crystal Palace	D 1-1	1-1	18	Akinbiyi ^{38}	10,659
36	13	A	Southend U	L 0-1	0-0	—		8855
37	17	A	Preston NE	L 0-2	0-1	18		17,666
38	31	H	Luton T	D 0-0	0-0	19		11,088
39	Apr 3	H	Plymouth Arg	W 4-0	3-0	—	Duff ^{13}, McVeigh ^{20}, Jones ^{38}, Elliott ^{61}	9793
40	7	A	Birmingham C	W 1-0	0-0	17	Spicer ^{80}	28,777
41	9	H	Cardiff C	W 2-0	1-0	17	Jones ^{4}, McVeigh ^{48}	11,347
42	14	A	Leeds U	L 0-1	0-1	17		23,528
43	17	H	Norwich C	W 3-0	1-0	—	Akinbiyi ^{30}, Gray ^{86}, Elliott ^{89}	9681
44	23	H	WBA	W 3-2	1-2	—	Gray 2 $^{15, 48}$, McCann ^{87}	12,500
45	27	A	Sunderland	L 2-3	1-1	—	Gray (pen) ^{39}, Elliott ^{50}	44,448
46	May 6	H	Coventry C	L 1-2	0-1	15	McVeigh ^{62}	12,830

Final League Position: 15

GOALSCORERS

League (52): Gray 14 (1 pen), Jones 5, McCann 5, Noel-Williams 5, Elliott 4, Lafferty 4, McVeigh 3, O'Connor J 3, Akinbiyi 2, Duff 2, Mahon 2, Harley 1, Spicer 1, own goal 1.
Carling Cup (0).
FA Cup (2): Akinbiyi 1, O'Connor G 1.

Jensen B 30 + 1	Sinclair F 16 + 3	Harley J 44 + 1	McCann C 24 + 14	Thomas M 33	Duff M 42 + 2	O'Connor J 39 + 4	Mahon A 10 + 15	Lafferty K 15 + 20	Gray A 34 + 1	Jones S 37 + 4	Elliott W 40 + 2	O'Connor G — + 8	Hyde M 19 + 4	Foster S 7 + 10	Noel-Williams G 19 + 4	McGreal J 21 + 1	Branch G — + 5	Spicer J — + 11	Coyne D 12	Pollitt M 4	Akinbiyi A 15 + 5	Djemba-Djemba E 13 + 2	Gudjonsson J 9 + 2	Caldwell S 16 + 1	Coughlan G 1 + 1	McVeigh P 6 + 2	Match No.
1	2	3	4	5	6	7^1	8^2	9^3	10	11	12	13	14														1
1	2	3	4	5	6	12	8^2	13	10^3	9	7^1		11	14													2
1	2	3	4	5	6	12	8^2	13	10■	9^3	7^1		11	14													3
1	2	3	4	5	6	12	8^2	9		10	7^3		11^1	13	14												4
1	2	3			6	7	8	9^2	10	11^3			4	12	13	5^1	14										5
1	2^1	3		5	12	7	8	9^2	10	11^3	13		4		14	6											6
1		3	12	5	2	7	8^2	14	10	9^1	11		4		13^3	6											7
1	12	3	13	5	2	7		14	10	8^3	11^1		4		9^2	6											8
1	12	3	13	5■	2	7	14		10	8^2	11^1		4^3		9	6											9
1	5	3	12		2	7	13	14	10	8^1	11^2		4		9^3	6											10
1	2	3	12		6	7	13		10	8^3	11^2	14	4^1		9	5											11
1	2	3			6	7	12		10	8^1	11^2	13	4	14	9	5^3											12
1	2	3			6	7	12	13	10	8	11^1		4	5	9^2												13
1	2	3		5^3	6	7	12	13	10	8	11^1		4	14	9^2												14
1	2	3	12		6	7		9	10	8^1	11		4	5■													15
1	2	3	5		6	7	12	13	10	8^3	11^1		4■		9^2			14									16
1	5	3	4	2	6	7	12	13	10	8	11^1				9^2												17
1	2■	3^1	4	5	6	7	13	14	10	8	11^2		12		9^3												18
1		3	4^1	5	6	7	12	13	10	11			8	2	9^2												19
		3	12	5	2	7	13	14	10^3	8	11^2		4^1		9	6			1								20
	12	3	4	5	2	7		10		8^1	11^2		13		9	6			1								21
		3	4	2	5	7^1	12	9		8^3	11^2			14	10	6	13		1								22
			3	2	5		8	9		7	11^2		4		10^1	6	12	13	1								23
15		3	4	2	6	7		9		8	11			5	10				1^G								24
1		3^3	4	2	6	7	12	9^1		8^2	11	13	14	5	10												25
1		3	4^1	2	6	7^2	12	13		9	11		8	5^3	10	14											26
		3	4	2	5	7		9			11					6				1	10	8					27
	2	3	4^1	5	6	7		12			11^2	13			10					1	9	8^3	14				28
		3^1	12	2^3	5	7	13	9			11^2			14		6				1	10	8■	4				29
		3	11		5	7	8^2	9	12	13				2^3		6				1	10		4^1	14			30
		3	12		2	7		13	10^2	8^1	11					6			1		9	14	4^3	5			31
		3	12		5^3	7		13	10	8^2	11			14		6			1		9		4^1	2			32
		3^1	4	2		7		12	10	13	11^2					6			1		9	14	8^3	5			33
		12	3^1	2^2	13	7		8	10		11^3					6	14		1		9		4	5			34
		3	4^1		2	7			10^2	12	11	13				6			1		9		8	5			35
		3	4		2	7		12	10		11			13^3		6^2		14	1		9		8^1	5			36
		3	4		2	7^2		10		8	11						12	13	1		9	6		5^1			37
1		3	4	2		12		13	10	11^1		14									9^2	8		5	6	7^3	38
1		3	12	2	6	7^1			10^3	8	11^2	13									14	4		5		9	39
1		3		2	6	7			10^1	8^3	11							13			12	4		5	14	9^2	40
1		3	12	6	2	7			10^3	8	11^2							14			13	4		5		9^1	41
1		3		6	2	7^2			10	8	11^1							13			12	4		5		9	42
1		3	12	6	2	7		13	10^3	8^1	11							14			9^2	4		5			43
1		3	12	6	2	7^1			10	8	11^2							13			9^3	4		5		14	44
1		3	4^3	6	2				10	11^1	7^2							13			12	8	14	5		9	45
1		3		6	2		8^1		10	12	11							13			9^3	4	7^2	5		14	46

FA Cup
Third Round — Reading — (a) — 2-3

Carling Cup
First Round — Hartlepool U — (h) — 0-1

BURY

FL Championship 2

FOUNDATION

A meeting at the Waggon & Horses Hotel, attended largely by members of Bury Wesleyans and Bury Unitarians football clubs, decided to form a new Bury club. This was officially formed at a subsequent gathering at the Old White Horse Hotel, Fleet Street, Bury on 24 April 1885.

Gigg Lane, Bury BL9 9HR.

Telephone: (0161) 764 4881.

Fax: (0161) 764 5521.

Ticket Office: (0161) 764 4881.

Website: www.buryfc.co.uk

Email: info@buryfc.co.uk

Ground Capacity: 11,669.

Record Attendance: 35,000 v Bolton W, FA Cup 3rd rd, 9 January 1960.

Pitch Measurements: 112yd × 70yd.

Secretary: Mrs Jill Neville.

Director of Football: Keith Alexander.

Manager: Chris Casper.

Director of Football: Keith Alexander.

Physio: Alan Bent.

Colours: White shirts, royal blue shorts.

Change Colours: Chocolate and sky blue.

Year Formed: 1885.

Turned Professional: 1885.

Ltd Co.: 1897.

Club Nickname: 'Shakers'.

Ground: 1885, Gigg Lane.

First Football League Game: 1 September 1894, Division 2, v Manchester C (h) W 4–2 – Lowe; Gillespie, Davies; White, Clegg, Ross; Wylie, Barbour (2), Millar (1), Ostler (1), Plant.

Record League Victory: 8–0 v Tranmere R, Division 3, 10 January 1970 – Forrest; Tinney, Saile; Anderson, Turner, McDermott; Hince (1), Arrowsmith (1), Jones (4), Kerr (1), Grundy, (1 og).

Record Cup Victory: 12–1 v Stockton, FA Cup 1st rd (replay), 2 February 1897 – Montgomery; Darroch, Barbour; Hendry (1), Clegg, Ross (1); Wylie (3), Pangbourn, Millar (4), Henderson (2), Plant, (1 og).

Record Defeat: 0–10 v Blackburn R, FA Cup pr rd, 1 October 1887. 0–10 v West Ham U, Milk Cup 2nd rd 2nd leg, 25 October 1983.

HONOURS

Football League: Division 1 best season: 4th, 1925–26; Division 2 – Champions 1894–95, 1996–97; Runners-up 1923–24; Division 3 – Champions 1960–61; Runners-up 1967–68; Promoted from Division 3 (3rd) 1995–96.

FA Cup: Winners 1900, 1903.

Football League Cup: Semi-final 1963.

SKY SPORTS FACT FILE

In 1902–03 when Bury won the FA Cup they did so without conceding a goal. Their victims were Wolverhampton Wanderers 1–0, Sheffield United 1–0, Notts County 1–0, Aston Villa 3–0 and finally Derby County 6–0. Seven players and an opponent shared the goals.

Most League Points (2 for a win): 68, Division 3, 1960–61.

Most League Points (3 for a win): 84, Division 4, 1984–85 and Division 2, 1996–97.

Most League Goals: 108, Division 3, 1960–61.

Highest League Scorer in Season: Craig Madden, 35, Division 4, 1981–82.

Most League Goals in Total Aggregate: Craig Madden, 129, 1978–86.

Most League Goals in One Match: 5, Eddie Quigley v Millwall, Division 2, 15 February 1947; 5, Ray Pointer v Rotherham U, Division 2, 2 October 1965.

Most Capped Player: Bill Gorman, 11 (13), Republic of Ireland and (4), Northern Ireland.

Most League Appearances: Norman Bullock, 506, 1920–35.

Youngest League Player: Brian Williams, 16 years 133 days v Stockport Co, 18 March 1972.

Record Transfer Fee Received: £1,000,000 from Ipswich T for David Johnson, November 1997.

Record Transfer Fee Paid: £200,000 to Ipswich T for Chris Swailes, November 1997 and £200,000 to Swindon T for Darren Bullock, February 1999.

Football League Record: 1894 Elected to Division 2; 1895–1912 Division 1; 1912–24 Division 2; 1924–29 Division 1; 1929–57 Division 2; 1957–61 Division 3; 1961–67 Division 2; 1967–68 Division 3; 1968–69 Division 2; 1969–71 Division 3; 1971–74 Division 4; 1974–80 Division 3; 1980–85 Division 4; 1985–96 Division 3; 1996–97 Division 2; 1997–99 Division 1; 1999–2002 Division 2; 2002–04 Division 3; 2004– FL 2.

MANAGERS

T. Hargreaves 1887
(Secretary-Manager)
H. S. Hamer 1887–1907
(Secretary-Manager)
Archie Montgomery 1907–15
William Cameron 1919–23
James Hunter Thompson 1923–27
Percy Smith 1927–30
Arthur Paine 1930–34
Norman Bullock 1934–38
Jim Porter 1944–45
Norman Bullock 1945–49
John McNeil 1950–53
Dave Russell 1953–61
Bob Stokoe 1961–65
Bert Head 1965–66
Les Shannon 1966–69
Jack Marshall 1969
Colin McDonald 1970
Les Hart 1970
Tommy McAnearney 1970–72
Alan Brown 1972–73
Bobby Smith 1973–77
Bob Stokoe 1977–78
David Hatton 1978–79
Dave Connor 1979–80
Jim Iley 1980–84
Martin Dobson 1984–89
Sam Ellis 1989–90
Mike Walsh 1990–95
Stan Ternent 1995–98
Neil Warnock 1998–99
Andy Preece 2000–04
Graham Barrow 2004–05
Chris Casper October 2005–

LATEST SEQUENCES

Longest Sequence of League Wins: 9, 26.9.1960 – 19.11.1960.

Longest Sequence of League Defeats: 8, 18.8.2001 – 25.9.2001.

Longest Sequence of League Draws: 6, 6.3.1999 – 3.4.1999.

Longest Sequence of Unbeaten League Matches: 18, 4.2.1961 – 29.4.1961.

Longest Sequence Without a League Win: 19, 1.4.1911 – 2.12.1911.

Successive Scoring Runs: 24 from 1.9.1894.

Successive Non-scoring Runs: 6 from 11.1.1969.

TEN YEAR LEAGUE RECORD

		P	*W*	*D*	*L*	*F*	*A*	*Pts*	*Pos*
1997-98	Div 1	46	11	19	16	42	58	52	17
1998-99	Div 1	46	10	17	19	35	60	47	22
1999-2000	Div 2	46	13	18	15	61	64	57	15
2000-01	Div 2	46	16	10	20	45	59	58	16
2001-02	Div 2	46	11	11	24	43	75	44	22
2002-03	Div 3	46	18	16	12	57	56	70	7
2003-04	Div 3	46	15	11	20	54	64	56	12
2004-05	FL 2	46	14	16	16	54	54	58	17
2005-06	FL 2	46	12	17	17	45	57	52*	19
2006-07	FL 2	46	13	11	22	46	61	50	21

**1 pt deducted.*

DID YOU KNOW ?

Versatile forward Derek Spence was signed by Bury from Oldham Athletic in February 1973 and became the club's first international player for 37 years when selected to play for Northern Ireland against Yugoslavia on 16 March 1975.

BURY 2006–07 LEAGUE RECORD

Match No.	Date	Venue	Opponents	Result	H/T Score	Lg. Pos.	Goalscorers	Attendance
1	Aug 5	A	Milton Keynes D	L 1-2	0-0	—	Bishop (pen) [81]	5329
2	8	H	Chester C	L 1-3	1-1	—	Pittman [45]	2719
3	12	H	Shrewsbury T	L 1-2	1-0	24	Fitzgerald [34]	2329
4	19	A	Wycombe W	L 0-3	0-0	24		4184
5	26	H	Grimsby T	W 3-0	3-0	19	Youngs 2 [6, 20], Adams [45]	2118
6	Sept 3	A	Peterborough U	W 1-0	0-0	15	Bishop (pen) [90]	5561
7	9	H	Torquay U	L 0-1	0-1	18		2317
8	12	A	Darlington	L 0-1	0-0	—		3335
9	16	A	Hereford U	L 0-1	0-0	23		2885
10	23	H	Barnet	D 2-2	1-1	22	Hurst 2 [15, 74]	1901
11	26	H	Accrington S	D 2-2	2-2	—	Bishop 2 [7, 36]	2912
12	30	A	Lincoln C	W 2-0	1-0	21	Baker [43], Hurst [54]	4748
13	Oct 14	A	Macclesfield T	W 3-2	1-1	21	Baker 2 [33, 49], Hurst [59]	2512
14	21	H	Boston U	W 2-1	0-0	17	Hurst [70], Pugh [73]	2246
15	28	A	Notts Co	W 1-0	1-0	15	Bishop [31]	4770
16	Nov 4	A	Rochdale	W 3-1	2-1	11	Fitzgerald [15], Bishop 2 (2 pens) [29, 90]	4499
17	7	H	Wrexham	W 1-0	1-0	—	Mattis [7]	2506
18	18	H	Bristol R	L 0-2	0-0	9		2635
19	25	A	Swindon T	L 1-2	1-1	13	Scott [21]	5628
20	Dec 5	H	Walsall	L 1-2	0-0	—	Scott [52]	2148
21	9	A	Mansfield T	W 2-0	1-0	11	Pugh [18], Hurst [51]	2197
22	16	H	Stockport Co	W 2-0	1-0	9	Hurst [2], Bishop [66]	4466
23	23	H	Hartlepool U	L 0-1	0-0	9		2839
24	26	A	Accrington S	D 1-1	0-1	9	Bishop [77]	3225
25	30	A	Barnet	L 1-2	1-2	12	Baker (pen) [3]	1959
26	Jan 13	A	Torquay U	D 2-2	0-1	15	Pugh [79], Bishop (pen) [90]	2063
27	16	H	Darlington	D 1-1	1-0	—	Bishop (pen) [42]	1870
28	20	H	Lincoln C	D 2-2	1-1	16	Bishop [5], Fitzgerald [79]	2476
29	27	A	Hartlepool U	L 0-2	0-1	16		4901
30	30	H	Hereford U	D 2-2	1-0	—	Baker [29], Hurst [58]	1775
31	Feb 3	H	Milton Keynes D	L 0-2	0-1	17		2325
32	17	H	Wycombe W	L 0-4	0-2	18		1988
33	21	A	Chester C	L 0-1	0-0	—		1642
34	24	H	Peterborough U	L 0-3	0-0	19		2085
35	Mar 3	A	Grimsby T	L 0-2	0-2	19		4733
36	9	A	Wrexham	D 1-1	0-1	—	Hurst [90]	7030
37	17	H	Macclesfield T	D 1-1	0-0	19	Hurst [75]	2561
38	24	H	Notts Co	L 0-1	0-1	21		2310
39	31	A	Boston U	W 1-0	0-0	19	Bishop [66]	1946
40	Apr 3	A	Shrewsbury T	W 3-1	1-1	—	Bishop 2 [1, 51], Hurst [65]	4419
41	7	H	Rochdale	L 0-1	0-0	19		5075
42	9	A	Bristol R	L 0-2	0-1	19		6266
43	14	H	Swindon T	L 0-1	0-0	21		2401
44	21	A	Walsall	W 1-0	1-0	19	Youngs [42]	6568
45	28	A	Stockport Co	D 0-0	0-0	20		7246
46	May 5	H	Mansfield T	D 1-1	0-1	21	Youngs [50]	3532

Final League Position: 21

GOALSCORERS

League (46): Bishop 15 (6 pens), Hurst 11, Baker 5 (1 pen), Youngs 4, Fitzgerald 3, Pugh 3, Scott 2, Adams 1, Mattis 1, Pittman 1.
Carling Cup (2): Bishop 1, Fitzgerald 1.
FA Cup (11): Bishop 5, Mattis 3, Baker 1, Hurst 1, Pugh 1.
J Paint Trophy (0).

Fettis A 9	Scott P 45 + 1	Woodthorpe C 12 + 4	Fitzgerald J 20 + 3	Challinor D 43	Flitcroft D 3 + 1	Goodfellow M 2 + 2	Mattis D 22	Pittman J 5 + 4	Bishop A 43	Barry-Murphy B 8 + 6	Kennedy T 35 + 2	Adams N 11 + 8	Speight J — + 13	Pugh M 27 + 8	Buchanan D 36 + 5	Youngs T 9 + 10	Brass C 20 + 2	Baker R 34 + 5	Schmeichel K 14	Taylor D 1 + 3	Hurst G 32 + 3	Edge L 1	Worrall D — + 1	Blinkhorn M 1 + 9	Warrington A 20	Jones L 2	Parrish A 6 + 3	Turnbull S 4 + 1	Grundy A — + 1	Wroe N 4 + 1	Rouse D — + 2	Kempson D 12	Stephens D 2 + 1	Bedeau A 2 + 2	Kennedy J 12	Mocquet W 9	*Match No.*
1	2	3^1	4	5	6^2	7	8	9^3	10	11	12	13	14																								1
1	2	3	4	5	13	7^1	8	9	10	11^2		6^3		14	12																						2
1	2^2		4	5	6		8	9	10	11^1	3			7	12	13																					3
1	2	5	4		6			9^1	10	11^3	3^2	8			7	12	13	14																			4
	4			5			8	12	10		3	6			11	9^1	2	7	1																		5
	4			5			8	12	10		3	6			11	9^1	2	7	1																		6
	2	12		5			8	13	10^2		3	4			11^3	9	6^1	7	1	14																	7
	2			5		12	8	10^2			3	4			11^1	9	6	7	1	13																	8
	2			5		12	8	13	10		3	4^3			11^1	9^2	6	7	1	14																	9
	2		4	5			8		10		3	12		11				7	1	6^1	9																10
	2		4	5			8		10	12	3	6^2		11	13			7^1	1		9																11
	2		4	5			8		10	12	3			6	11			7	1		9^1																12
	2		4	5			8		10^1	12	3		13	6	11			7			9^2	1															13
	2		4	5			8		10		3	12	13	6	11^1			7	1		9^2																14
	2		4	5			8		10		3	12		6^1	11	13		7	1		9^2																15
	5		4				8		10	12	3	13		6^2	11		2	7	1		9^1																16
	5	12	4				8		10		3			6	11	13	2^1	7	1		9^2																17
	2		4	5			8		10		3		12^2	6	11	9^1		7	1				13														18
	2^1	12	4	5			8		10^3		3		13	6	11			7	1		9^2			14													19
	2		4^1	5			8		10		3		15	6	11		12	7			9^2			13	1^G												20
	2			5					10	11	3			8	6		4^3	7^2			9^1			12		1	14	13									21
	4			5			8		10	12	3			6	11^2		2	13			9^3			14		1		7^1									22
1	4			5					10	8	3^1			6	11		2	7			9			12													23
1	4			5			8		10		3^1			6	11		2				9			12				7									24
1	4	3^2		5			8^1			12	13			6	11^3	14	2	7			9			10													25
1■	4			5					10		3			6	11^1		2	7			9^G			12				8	15								26
	4			5					10		3			6	11		2	7			9^1			12	1			8									27
1	4		12	5					10	8	3	13		6	11^2		2^1	7			9																28
	4		12	5					10	8^3	3		13	6	11^1		2	7			9^2			14	1												29
	2		4	5					10		11	8	12	6^2	13		3	7			9^1				1												30
	6		4	5					10		3	8^1	12	13	11^2		2^3	7			9				1		14										31
	6	12	4	5					10		3		13	11^3			2^1	7			9^2				1					8	14						32
	6		4	5					10		3			9^1	11			7			12				1		2			8							33
	6			5					10		3		12	11^2							9^1				1		2			8		4	13	7			34
	2			5					10		3			12	11			7^1			13				1					8		6		9^2	4		35
	2			5					10		3		12	6	11^2			7^1			9				1							4		13	8		36
	2			5					10		3		12	6^2	11			7			9^1				1							4		13	8		37
	2			5					10^1		3			13		12		7^3			9				1					14		4	6^2		8	11	38
	2	3		5					10					12	11	13	4^2	14			9^3				1							6			8	7^1	39
	2	3	12	5					10^1					13	4	14		7			9^3				1							6			8	11^2	40
	2	3		5					10					12	6			7			9				1							4■			8	11^1	41
	2	3	4^2	5					10					12	6	14		7			9^3				1		13								8	11^1	42
	2	3		5					10						11	12					9^1				1		6					4			8	7	43
	2	3		5					10			12			11	9^2		13							1		6					4			8	7^1	44
	2	3		5					10^3			12			11	9^2		13			14				1		4					6			8	7^1	45
	12	3		5								6			13	10					9^3				1		2				14	4	11^2		8	7^1	46

FA Cup

First Round	Weymouth	(a)	2-2
		(h)	4-3
Second Round	Chester C	(h)	2-2
		(a)	3-1
Third Round	Tie awarded to Chester C		

Carling Cup

First Round	Sunderland	(h)	2-0
Second Round	Sheffield U	(a)	0-1

J Paint Trophy

First Round	Tranmere R	(h)	0-2

CARDIFF CITY — FL Championship

FOUNDATION

Credit for the establishment of a first class professional football club in such a rugby stronghold as Cardiff, is due to members of the Riverside club formed in 1899 out of a cricket club of that name. Cardiff became a city in 1905 and in 1908 the South Wales and Monmouthshire FA granted Riverside permission to call themselves Cardiff City. The club turned professional under that name in 1910.

Ninian Park, Sloper Road, Cardiff CF11 8SX.

Telephone: (029) 2022 1001.

Fax: (029) 2034 1148.

Ticket Office: 0845 345 1400.

Website: www.cardiffcityfc.co.uk

Email: club@cardiffcityfc.co.uk

Ground Capacity: 20,340.

Record Attendance: 62,634, Wales v England, 17 October 1959.

Club Record Attendance: 57,893 v Arsenal, Division 1, 22 April 1953.

Pitch Measurements: 110yd × 75yd.

Chairman: Peter Ridsdale.

Secretary: Jason Turner.

Manager: Dave Jones.

Assistant Manager: Terry Burton.

Physio: Sean Connelly BHSc MCSP, SRP.

Colours: Royal blue shirts, white shorts, royal blue stockings.

Change Colours: All black.

Year Formed: 1899.

Turned Professional: 1910.

Ltd Co.: 1910.

Previous Names: 1899, Riverside; 1902, Riverside Albion; 1908, Cardiff City.

Club Nickname: 'Bluebirds'.

Grounds: Riverside, Sophia Gardens, Old Park and Fir Gardens. Moved to Ninian Park, 1910.

First Football League Game: 28 August 1920, Division 2, v Stockport Co (a) W 5–2 – Kneeshaw; Brittan, Leyton; Keenor (1), Smith, Hardy; Grimshaw (1), Gill (2), Cashmore, West, Evans (1).

Record League Victory: 9–2 v Thames, Division 3 (S), 6 February 1932 – Farquharson; E. L. Morris, Roberts; Galbraith, Harris, Ronan; Emmerson (1), Keating (1), Jones (1), McCambridge (1), Robbins (5).

HONOURS

Football League: Division 1 – Runners-up 1923–24; Division 2 – Runners-up 1920–21, 1951–52, 1959–60; Division 2 – 2002–03 (play-offs); Division 3 (S) – Champions 1946–47; Division 3 – Champions 1992–93. Runners-up 1975–76, 1982–83, 2000–01; Division 4 – Runners-up 1987–88.

FA Cup: Winners 1927 (only occasion the Cup has been won by a club outside England); Runners-up 1925.

Football League Cup: Semi-final 1966.

Welsh Cup: Winners 22 times (joint record).

Charity Shield: Winners 1927.

European Competitions: *European Cup-Winners' Cup:* 1964–65, 1965–66, 1967–68 (semi-finalists), 1968–69, 1969–70, 1970–71, 1971–72, 1973–74, 1974–75, 1976–77, 1977–78, 1988–89, 1992–93, 1993–94.

SKY SPORTS FACT FILE

The 1931–32 season was a curious one for Cardiff City. They could finish no higher than ninth in Division Three (South), but apart from their record 9–2 League victory, hit one 6 and five 5s plus two 4s during other successes in the campaign.

Record Cup Victory: 8–0 v Enfield, FA Cup 1st rd, 28 November 1931 – Farquharson; Smith, Roberts; Harris (1), Galbraith, Ronan; Emmerson (2), Keating (3); O'Neill (2), Robbins, McCambridge.

Record Defeat: 2–11 v Sheffield U, Division 1, 1 January 1926.

Most League Points (2 for a win): 66, Division 3 (S), 1946–47.

Most League Points (3 for a win): 86, Division 3, 1982–83.

Most League Goals: 95, Division 3, 2000–01.

Highest League Scorer in Season: Robert Earnshaw, 31, Division 2, 2002–03.

Most League Goals in Total Aggregate: Len Davies, 128, 1920–31.

Most League Goals in One Match: 5, Hugh Ferguson v Burnley, Division 1, 1 September 1928; 5, Walter Robbins v Thames, Division 3S, 6 February 1932; 5, William Henderson v Northampton T, Division 3S, 22 April 1933.

Most Capped Player: Alf Sherwood, 39 (41), Wales.

Most League Appearances: Phil Dwyer, 471, 1972–85.

Youngest League Player: John Toshack, 16 years 236 days v Leyton Orient, 13 November 1965.

Record Transfer Fee Received: Undisclosed from Birmingham C for Cameron Jerome, May 2006.

Record Transfer Fee Paid: £1,700,000 to Stoke C for Peter Thorne, September 2001.

Football League Record: 1920 Elected to Division 2; 1921–29 Division 1; 1929–31 Division 2; 1931–47 Division 3 (S); 1947–52 Division 2; 1952–57 Division 1; 1957–60 Division 2; 1960–62 Division 1; 1962–75 Division 2; 1975–76 Division 3; 1976–82 Division 2; 1982–83 Division 3; 1983–85 Division 2; 1985–86 Division 3; 1986–88 Division 4; 1988–90 Division 3; 1990–92 Division 4; 1992–93 Division 3; 1993–95 Division 2; 1995–99 Division 3; 1999–2000 Division 2; 2000–01 Division 3; 2001–03 Division 2; 2003–04 Division 1; 2004– FL C.

MANAGERS

Davy McDougall 1910–11
Fred Stewart 1911–33
Bartley Wilson 1933–34
B. Watts-Jones 1934–37
Bill Jennings 1937–39
Cyril Spiers 1939–46
Billy McCandless 1946–48
Cyril Spiers 1948–54
Trevor Morris 1954–58
Bill Jones 1958–62
George Swindin 1962–64
Jimmy Scoular 1964–73
Frank O'Farrell 1973–74
Jimmy Andrews 1974–78
Richie Morgan 1978–82
Len Ashurst 1982–84
Jimmy Goodfellow 1984
Alan Durban 1984–86
Frank Burrows 1986–89
Len Ashurst 1989–91
Eddie May 1991–94
Terry Yorath 1994–95
Eddie May 1995
Kenny Hibbitt *(Chief Coach)* 1995
Phil Neal 1996
Russell Osman 1996–97
Kenny Hibbitt 1996–98
Frank Burrows 1998–99
Billy Ayre 1999–2000
Bobby Gould 2000
Alan Cork 2000–02
Lennie Lawrence 2002–05
Dave Jones May 2005–

LATEST SEQUENCES

Longest Sequence of League Wins: 9, 26.10.1946 – 28.12.1946.

Longest Sequence of League Defeats: 7, 4.11.1933 – 25.12.1933.

Longest Sequence of League Draws: 6, 29.11.1980 – 17.1.1981.

Longest Sequence of Unbeaten League Matches: 21, 21.9.1946 – 1.3.1947.

Longest Sequence Without a League Win: 15, 21.11.1936 – 6.3.1937.

Successive Scoring Runs: 23 from 24.10.1992.

Successive Non-scoring Runs: 8 from 20.12.1952.

TEN YEAR LEAGUE RECORD

		P	*W*	*D*	*L*	*F*	*A*	*Pts*	*Pos*
1997-98	Div 3	46	9	23	14	48	52	50	21
1998-99	Div 3	46	22	14	10	60	39	80	3
1999-2000	Div 2	46	9	17	20	45	67	44	21
2000-01	Div 3	46	23	13	10	95	58	82	2
2001-02	Div 2	46	23	14	9	75	50	83	4
2002-03	Div 2	46	23	12	11	68	43	81	6
2003-04	Div 1	46	17	14	15	68	58	65	13
2004-05	FL C	46	13	15	18	48	51	54	16
2005-06	FL C	46	16	12	18	58	59	60	11
2006-07	FL C	46	17	13	16	57	53	64	13

DID YOU KNOW?

Promotion as runners-up in the Second Division in 1959–60 just a point behind the champions Aston Villa saw Cardiff City in goalscoring highlight. They failed to score in just three matches and victories included one 6, two 5s and five games with four.

CARDIFF CITY 2006–07 LEAGUE RECORD

Match No.	Date	Venue	Opponents	Result	H/T Score	Lg. Pos.	Goalscorers	Attendance
1	Aug 5	A	Barnsley	W 2-1	2-1	—	Ledley [19], Thompson [22]	12,082
2	8	H	WBA	D 1-1	1-1	—	Scimeca [33]	18,506
3	12	H	Coventry C	W 1-0	0-0	4	Chopra [79]	13,965
4	19	A	Leeds U	W 1-0	0-0	2	Flood [83]	18,246
5	26	H	Birmingham C	W 2-0	1-0	1	Ledley [12], Parry [75]	20,109
6	Sept 9	A	Preston NE	L 1-2	0-0	1	Chopra [51]	12,435
7	12	A	Plymouth Arg	D 3-3	2-0	—	Thompson [8], Chopra 2 [29, 49]	11,655
8	16	H	Luton T	W 4-1	2-1	1	Purse (pen) [10], Parry [30], Chopra 2 [58, 77]	14,108
9	24	A	Southend U	W 3-0	2-0	1	Purse [11], Scimeca [45], Francis (og) [65]	7901
10	30	H	Wolverhampton W	W 4-0	1-0	1	Scimeca [40], Craddock (og) [50], Kamara [70], Parry [78]	19,915
11	Oct 14	A	Crystal Palace	W 2-1	1-1	1	Chopra [2], Scimeca [84]	18,876
12	17	H	Southampton	W 1-0	0-0	—	Thompson [84]	19,345
13	21	A	Norwich C	L 0-1	0-1	1		25,014
14	28	H	Derby Co	D 2-2	0-0	1	Loovens [52], Chopra [74]	17,371
15	31	A	Sunderland	W 2-1	2-1	—	Chopra 2 [4, 37]	26,528
16	Nov 4	A	Colchester U	L 1-3	0-0	1	Chopra [66]	5393
17	11	H	Burnley	W 1-0	1-0	1	Scimeca [24]	15,744
18	17	H	QPR	L 0-1	0-0	—		13,250
19	25	A	Sheffield W	D 0-0	0-0	1		23,935
20	28	A	Stoke C	L 0-3	0-0	—		15,039
21	Dec 2	H	Colchester U	D 0-0	0-0	3		13,512
22	9	H	Ipswich T	D 2-2	1-0	3	Purse 2 (1 pen) [3, 66 (p)]	16,015
23	16	A	Hull C	L 1-4	0-3	5	Chopra [55]	23,089
24	23	A	Leicester C	D 0-0	0-0	6		22,274
25	26	H	Plymouth Arg	D 2-2	0-1	5	Thompson 2 [47, 52]	17,299
26	30	H	Crystal Palace	D 0-0	0-0	8		13,704
27	Jan 1	A	Luton T	D 0-0	0-0	8		8004
28	13	H	Southend U	L 0-1	0-1	8		13,822
29	20	A	Wolverhampton W	W 2-1	1-0	6	Chopra [27], Byrne [88]	16,772
30	27	H	Leicester C	W 3-2	1-0	—	Chopra 3 [21, 57, 69]	12,057
31	Feb 2	H	Barnsley	W 2-0	2-0	—	Whittingham [11], Chopra [44]	11,549
32	10	A	Coventry C	D 2-2	1-1	6	Chopra (pen) [45], Whittingham [58]	17,107
33	17	H	Leeds U	W 1-0	1-0	7	Chopra [45]	16,544
34	20	A	WBA	L 0-1	0-0	—		18,802
35	23	H	Preston NE	W 4-1	1-0	—	Whittingham [44], Chopra 2 (1 pen) [52 (p), 67], Johnson [54]	12,889
36	Mar 4	A	Birmingham C	L 0-1	0-0	7		28,223
37	10	H	Norwich C	W 1-0	1-0	6	Parry [3]	13,276
38	13	A	Southampton	D 2-2	0-2	—	Thompson [61], Whittingham [85]	20,383
39	17	A	Derby Co	L 1-3	1-1	7	Parry [32]	27,689
40	31	H	Sunderland	L 0-1	0-0	8		19,353
41	Apr 7	H	Sheffield W	L 1-2	1-1	9	Johnson [45]	13,621
42	9	A	Burnley	L 0-2	0-1	10		11,347
43	14	H	Stoke C	D 1-1	0-1	11	Chopra [90]	11,664
44	21	A	QPR	L 0-1	0-1	11		12,710
45	28	H	Hull C	L 0-1	0-0	11		12,421
46	May 6	A	Ipswich T	L 1-3	1-1	13	Parry [37]	26,488

Final League Position: 13

GOALSCORERS

League (57): Chopra 22 (2 pens), Parry 6, Thompson 6, Scimeca 5, Purse 4 (2 pens), Whittingham 4, Johnson 2, Ledley 2, Byrne 1, Flood 1, Kamara 1, Loovens 1, own goals 2.
Carling Cup (0).
FA Cup (0).

Alexander N 39	Gilbert K 21 + 3	McNaughton K 39 + 3	Scimeca R 35	Purse D 31	Loovens G 30	Parry P 41 + 1	McPhail S 43	Thompson S 39 + 4	Chopra M 42	Ledley J 46	Johnson R 26 + 6	Campbell K 4 + 15	Flood W 5 + 20	Glombard L 1 + 5	Kamara M 3 + 12	Blake D 3 + 7	Chambers J 7	Gunter C 9 + 6	Wright A 6 + 1	Cooper K — + 4	Whittingham P 18 + 1	Ferretti A — + 1	Byrne J 2 + 8	Walton S 5 + 1	Redan I — + 2	Forde D 7	Green M — + 6	Feeney W 4 + 2	Ramsey A — + 1	Match No.
1	2	3	4	5^{1}	6	7	8	9^{2}	10^{3}	11	12	13	14																	1
1	2	3	4		6	7^{1}	8	9^{2}	10	11	5	13	12																	2
1	2^{1}	3	4	5	6	7	8	9^{3}	10^{2}	11		14	12	13																3
1		2^{1}	4	5■	6	11	8	9	10^{3}	3	12		13		7^{2}	14														4
1	2	3	4		6	7	8	9^{1}	10	11	5	12																		5
1	2	3	4		6■	7^{2}	8^{1}	9	10	11	5		12		13															6
1	2	3	4	5		7^{1}	8	9^{2}	10	11	6	13	12																	7
1	2	3^{3}	4	5	6	7^{1}	8	9^{2}	10	11			12	13	14															8
1	2	3	4	5	6	7^{3}	8	9	10^{1}	11^{2}		12	13		14															9
1	2	3^{3}	4	5	6	7^{2}	8	9^{1}	10	11		12	13		14															10
1	2		4	5	6	7	8	9^{1}	10	11^{2}		12			13		3													11
1	2		4	5	6	7	8	9	10	11							3													12
1	2■		4	5	6	7	8	9^{1}		11^{2}		12	13	10^{3}	14		3													13
1		2	4	5	6^{1}	7	8	9	10	11	12						3													14
1		2^{2}	4	5	6	7	8	9^{1}	10	11		12			13		3													15
1		2	4	5	6^{3}	7^{2}	8■		10	11^{1}	14	9	12		13		3													16
1		2	4	5	6	7^{1}	8		10	11	13	9^{2}	12				3													17
1		3	4	5	6	7^{1}	8	9	10	11					12			2												18
1		3	4	5		7^{1}	8	9^{2}	10	11	6	13			12				2											19
1		2	4	5		7	8■	9^{1}	10	11^{2}	6	12			13				3											20
1		3	4	5		7		9^{1}	10	11	6	12			8^{2}				2	13										21
1		2	4	5				12	10	11	6	9^{1}		13	8^{2}			3	7^{3}	14										22
1		2	4	5	6	7		9	10	11			8^{1}	13	12^{2}			3												23
1	2^{2}	3	4^{1}	5	6	7	8	9	10	11						12			13											24
1		2	4	5		7^{2}	8	9	10	11	6		12			13			3^{1}											25
1	2	3^{3}	4	5	6		8	9^{1}	10	11		12	7^{2}			13				14										26
1	2^{3}		4	5	6		8	9	10	11^{1}			7^{2}			13		14	3	12										27
1	2	3^{2}	4	5	6		8		10	11		9^{3}	7^{1}	12							13	14								28
1		2	4	5^{2}	6	7	8	9^{3}	10	11	13		12								3^{1}		14							29
1	2	12	4^{1}		6	7	8	9^{3}	10	11	5		13								3^{2}		14							30
1	2	12^{2}			6	7	8	9^{3}	10	11^{1}	5		13								3		14	4						31
1	2^{2}	12			6■	7	8	9^{3}	10	11	5		13								3^{1}			4	14					32
1	2^{1}	3				7	8	9^{2}	10■	11	5							12			6		13	4■						33
1		3				7^{1}	8	9^{2}		11	5	13	12			4		2			6		10^{3}		14					34
		2	4		6	7	8	9^{1}	10^{2}	11	5										3		12			1	13			35
1	12	2^{1}	4		6	7	8	9^{2}	10	11	5										3						13			36
1		2	4		6	7^{1}	8	9^{2}	10	11	5							12			3		13							37
1		2	4		6^{1}	7	8	13	10	11	5							12			3		9^{2}							38
1		3				7	8	9	10^{1}	11	5							2			6		12^{2}	4			13			39
1		3	4^{1}			7^{3}	8	9	10^{2}	11	5							2			6		12	13				14		40
		2		5		7	8	12	10	11	6										3^{1}			4■		1	13	9^{2}		41
		3		5		7^{2}	8	12	10	11	6					13		2			4^{1}					1	14	9^{3}		42
	12	3		5^{1}		7^{2}	8	9	10	11	6		13					2			4					1				43
	2^{1}	3				12	8	9^{3}	10	11	6		7^{2}			13		5			4					1		14		44
		3^{2}		5		7^{3}	8	9		11	6		12			2		13			4^{1}					1		10	14	45
	12	2		5		7^{1}	8^{2}	9		11	6					4		13			3					1	14	10^{3}		46

FA Cup
Third Round Tottenham H (h) 0-0
(a) 0-4

Carling Cup
First Round Barnet (h) 0-2

CARLISLE UNITED FL Championship 1

FOUNDATION

Carlisle United came into being in 1903 through the amalgamation of Shaddongate United and Carlisle Red Rose. The new club was admitted to the Second Division of the Lancashire Combination in 1905–06, winning promotion the following season. Devonshire Park was officially opened on 2 September 1905, when St Helens Town were the visitors. Despite defeat in a disappointing 3-2 start, a respectable mid-table position was achieved.

Brunton Park, Warwick Road, Carlisle CA1 1LL.

Telephone: (01228) 526 237.

Fax: (01228) 554 141.

Ticket Office: (01228) 526 237 (option 1).

Website: www.carlisleunited.co.uk

Email: enquiries@carlisleunited.co.uk

Ground Capacity: 16,982.

Record Attendance: 27,500 v Birmingham C, FA Cup 3rd rd, 5 January 1957 and v Middlesbrough, FA Cup 5th rd, 7 February 1970.

Pitch Measurements: 114yd × 74yd.

Chairman: Andrew Jenkins.

Chief Executive: John Nixon.

Secretary: Sarah McKnight.

Manager: Neil McDonald.

Assistant Manager: Greg Abbott.

Physio: Neil Dalton.

Colours: Blue shirts, white shorts, blue stockings.

Change Colours: Red shirts, red shorts, red stockings.

Year Formed: 1903.

Ltd Co.: 1921.

Previous Name: 1903, Shaddongate United; 1904, Carlisle United.

Club Nicknames: 'Cumbrians' or 'The Blues'.

Grounds: 1903, Milholme Bank; 1905, Devonshire Park; 1909, Brunton Park.

First Football League Game: 25 August 1928, Division 3 (N), v Accrington S (a) W 3–2 – Prout; Coulthard, Cook; Harrison, Ross, Pigg; Agar (1), Hutchison, McConnell (1), Ward (1), Watson.

Record League Victory: 8–0 v Hartlepool U, Division 3 (N), 1 September 1928 – Prout; Smiles, Cook; Robinson (1) Ross, Pigg; Agar (1), Hutchison (1), McConnell (4), Ward (1), Watson. 8–0 v Scunthorpe U, Division 3 (N), 25 December 1952 – MacLaren; Hill, Scott; Stokoe, Twentyman, Waters; Harrison (1), Whitehouse (5), Ashman (2), Duffett, Bond.

Record Cup Victory: 6–0 v Shepshed Dynamo, FA Cup 1st rd, 16 November 1996 – Caig; Hopper, Archdeacon (pen), Walling, Robinson, Pounewatchy, Peacock (1), Conway (1) (Jansen), Smart (McAlindon (1)), Hayward, Aspinall (Thorpe), (2 og).

HONOURS

Football League: Division 1 best season: 22nd, 1974–75; Promoted from Division 2 (3rd) 1973–74; Division 3 – Champions 1964–65, 1994–95; Runners-up 1981–82; Promoted from Division 3 1996–97; Division 4 – Runners-up 1963–64; FL 2 – Champions 2005–06. Promoted from Conference (play-offs) 2004–05.

FA Cup: best season: 6th rd 1975.

Football League Cup: Semi-final 1970.

Auto Windscreens Shield: Winners 1997; Runners-up 1995.

LDV Vans Trophy: Runners-up 2003, 2006.

SKY SPORTS FACT FILE

Hugh McIlmoyle achieved the rare feat of scoring two headed hat-tricks in the space of two months during 1963 for Carlisle United: on 1 October in a 7–1 win over Hartlepools United (scored four goals) and 21 December v Tranmere Rovers in a 5–2 victory.

Record Defeat: 1–11 v Hull C, Division 3 (N), 14 January 1939.

Most League Points (2 for a win): 62, Division 3 (N), 1950–51.

Most League Points (3 for a win): 91, Division 3, 1994–95.

Most League Goals: 113, Division 4, 1963–64.

Highest League Scorer in Season: Jimmy McConnell, 42, Division 3 (N), 1928–29.

Most League Goals in Total Aggregate: Jimmy McConnell, 126, 1928–32.

Most League Goals in One Match: 5, Hugh Mills v Halifax T, Division 3N, 11 September 1937; 5, Jim Whitehouse v Scunthorpe U, Division 3N, 25 December 1952.

Most Capped Player: Eric Welsh, 4, Northern Ireland.

Most League Appearances: Allan Ross, 466, 1963–79.

Youngest League Player: John Slaven, 16 years 162 days v Scunthorpe U, 16 March 2002.

Record Transfer Fee Received: £1,500,000 from Crystal Palace for Matt Jansen, February 1998.

Record Transfer Fee Paid: £121,000 to Notts Co for David Reeves, December 1993.

Football League Record: 1928 Elected to Division 3 (N); 1958–62 Division 4; 1962–63 Division 3; 1963–64 Division 4; 1964–65 Division 3; 1965–74 Division 2; 1974–75 Division 1; 1975–77 Division 2; 1977–82 Division 3; 1982–86 Division 2; 1986–87 Division 3; 1987–92 Division 4; 1992–95 Division 3; 1995–96 Division 2; 1996–97 Division 3; 1997–98 Division 2; 1998–04 Division 3; 2004–05 Conference; 2005–06 FL 2; 2006– FL 1.

LATEST SEQUENCES

Longest Sequence of League Wins: 7, 18.2.06 – 8.4.06.

Longest Sequence of League Defeats: 12, 27.9.2003 – 13.12.2003.

Longest Sequence of League Draws: 6, 11.2.1978 – 11.3.1978.

Longest Sequence of Unbeaten League Matches: 19, 1.10.1994 – 11.2.1995.

Longest Sequence Without a League Win: 14, 19.1.1935 – 19.4.1935.

Successive Scoring Runs: 26 from 23.8.1947.

Successive Non-scoring Runs: 5 from 24.8.1968.

MANAGERS

Harry Kirkbride 1904–05 *(Secretary-Manager)*
McCumiskey 1905–06 *(Secretary-Manager)*
Jack Houston 1906–08 *(Secretary-Manager)*
Bert Stansfield 1908–10
Jack Houston 1910–12
Davie Graham 1912–13
George Bristow 1913–30
Billy Hampson 1930–33
Bill Clarke 1933–35
Robert Kelly 1935–36
Fred Westgarth 1936–38
David Taylor 1938–40
Howard Harkness 1940–45
Bill Clark 1945–46 *(Secretary-Manager)*
Ivor Broadis 1946–49
Bill Shankly 1949–51
Fred Emery 1951–58
Andy Beattie 1958–60
Ivor Powell 1960–63
Alan Ashman 1963–67
Tim Ward 1967–68
Bob Stokoe 1968–70
Ian MacFarlane 1970–72
Alan Ashman 1972–75
Dick Young 1975–76
Bobby Moncur 1976–80
Martin Harvey 1980
Bob Stokoe 1980–85
Bryan 'Pop' Robson 1985
Bob Stokoe 1985–86
Harry Gregg 1986–87
Cliff Middlemass 1987–91
Aidan McCaffery 1991–92
David McCreery 1992–93
Mick Wadsworth *(Director of Coaching)* 1993–96
Mervyn Day 1996–97
David Wilkes and John Halpin *(Directors of Coaching)*, and Michael Knighton 1997–99
Nigel Pearson 1998–99
Keith Mincher 1999
Martin Wilkinson 1999–2000
Ian Atkins 2000–01
Roddy Collins 2001–02; 2002–03
Paul Simpson 2003–06
Neil McDonald June 2006–

TEN YEAR LEAGUE RECORD

		P	W	D	L	F	A	Pts	Pos
1997-98	Div 2	46	12	8	26	57	73	44	23
1998-99	Div 3	46	11	16	19	43	53	49	23
1999-2000	Div 3	46	9	12	25	42	75	39	23
2000-01	Div 3	46	11	15	20	42	65	48	22
2001-02	Div 3	46	12	16	18	49	56	52	17
2002-03	Div 3	46	13	10	23	52	78	49	22
2003-04	Div 3	46	12	9	25	46	69	45	23
2004-05	Conf	42	20	13	9	74	37	73	3
2005-06	FL 2	46	25	11	10	84	42	86	1
2006-07	FL 1	46	19	11	16	54	55	68	8

DID YOU KNOW ?

From 1950–51 to 1959–60 the tenacity shown by Carlisle United in the FA Cup was such that they were involved in seven replays including famously one with Arsenal after a goalless draw at Highbury in January 1951 as well as a threesome with Darlington.

CARLISLE UNITED 2006–07 LEAGUE RECORD

Match No.	Date	Venue	Opponents	Result		H/T Score	Lg. Pos.	Goalscorers	Attendance
1	Aug 5	H	Doncaster R	W	1-0	1-0	—	Murray P[4]	12,031
2	9	A	Chesterfield	D	0-0	0-0	—		4525
3	12	A	Yeovil T	L	1-2	1-2	12	Gall[23]	4709
4	19	H	Leyton Orient	W	3-1	1-0	7	Gall 2[24, 59], Hawley[49]	7160
5	27	A	Oldham Ath	D	0-0	0-0	8		6080
6	Sept 3	H	Cheltenham T	W	2-0	2-0	5	Gall[27], Hawley[45]	7248
7	9	H	Northampton T	D	1-1	0-0	5	Hawley[56]	7602
8	12	A	Bradford C	D	1-1	0-1	—	Lumsdon[50]	7966
9	16	A	Nottingham F	D	0-0	0-0	6		19,535
10	23	H	Brighton & HA	W	3-1	2-0	5	Hawley[6], Gray[31], Hackney[82]	7704
11	26	H	Blackpool	W	2-0	1-0	—	Lumsdon[18], Hawley[88]	8401
12	30	A	Crewe Alex	L	1-5	1-2	6	Hawley[24]	5989
13	Oct 7	H	Millwall	L	1-2	1-2	8	Beckford[33]	8413
14	14	A	Huddersfield T	L	1-2	1-2	12	Hackney[43]	10,830
15	21	H	Tranmere R	W	1-0	1-0	7	Gall[35]	7328
16	28	A	Gillingham	L	0-2	0-1	8		5973
17	Nov 4	H	Rotherham U	D	1-1	0-1	8	Gray[64]	7247
18	18	A	Bournemouth	W	1-0	1-0	8	Hawley (pen)[5]	5682
19	25	H	Port Vale	W	3-2	0-2	8	Holmes[66], Hawley[77], Murphy[81]	7543
20	Dec 5	A	Bristol C	L	0-1	0-0	—		10,792
21	9	H	Scunthorpe U	L	0-2	0-0	9		6954
22	16	A	Swansea C	L	0-5	0-3	12		12,550
23	23	H	Brentford	W	2-0	0-0	11	Holmes[69], McDermott[74]	6805
24	26	A	Blackpool	L	1-2	0-2	12	Hawley[73]	9473
25	30	A	Brighton & HA	W	2-1	0-1	10	Aranalde[56], McDermott[82]	5436
26	Jan 1	H	Bradford C	W	1-0	1-0	10	Hawley[26]	7548
27	13	A	Northampton T	L	2-3	0-1	10	Graham[82], Gall[86]	5549
28	20	H	Crewe Alex	L	0-2	0-0	10		7075
29	27	A	Brentford	D	0-0	0-0	10		5381
30	31	H	Nottingham F	W	1-0	1-0	—	Hawley[45]	9022
31	Feb 3	A	Doncaster R	W	2-1	0-1	10	Jeff Smith[56], Hawley[78]	9036
32	10	H	Yeovil T	L	1-4	1-0	10	Garner[43]	7112
33	17	A	Leyton Orient	D	1-1	1-0	10	Garner[15]	4449
34	20	H	Chesterfield	D	0-0	0-0	—		6196
35	24	A	Cheltenham T	W	1-0	1-0	7	Garner[15]	3831
36	Mar 3	H	Oldham Ath	D	1-1	0-1	9	Holmes[87]	7951
37	10	A	Millwall	L	0-2	0-0	10		10,415
38	17	H	Huddersfield T	D	1-1	1-1	10	Garner[45]	6629
39	24	H	Gillingham	W	5-0	1-0	9	Murphy[14], Joyce[81], Gall[83], Graham 2 (1 pen)[89 (p), 90]	6087
40	30	A	Tranmere R	W	2-0	1-0	—	Graham[10], Gall[67]	7289
41	Apr 7	A	Port Vale	W	2-0	1-0	8	Graham[27], Garner[90]	4882
42	9	H	Bournemouth	W	3-1	2-0	8	Graham (pen)[3], Livesey[29], McDermott[85]	8989
43	14	A	Rotherham U	W	1-0	0-0	7	Gray[68]	4428
44	21	H	Bristol C	L	1-3	1-1	8	Graham[5]	10,232
45	28	H	Swansea C	L	1-2	0-1	8	Johann Smith[49]	10,578
46	May 5	A	Scunthorpe U	L	0-3	0-1	8		8720

Final League Position: 8

GOALSCORERS

League (54): Hawley 12 (1 pen), Gall 8, Graham 7 (2 pens), Garner 5, Gray 3, Holmes 3, McDermott 3, Hackney 2, Lumsdon 2, Murphy 2, Aranalde 1, Beckford 1, Joyce 1, Livesey 1, Murray P 1, Jeff Smith 1, Johann Smith 1.
Carling Cup (1): Holmes 1.
FA Cup (1): Gray 1.
J Paint Trophy (1): Holmes 1.

Westwood K 46	Raven D 36	Aranalde Z 43	Billy C 16 + 4	Gray K 27 + 4	Murphy P 40	Murray P 14	Gall K 44 + 1	Bridges M 5	Hawley K 30 + 2	Lumsdon C 36 + 3	Arnison P 6 + 5	Holmes D 8 + 28	Hackney S 14 + 4	McDermott N 6 + 9	Joyce L 7 + 9	Hindmarch S — + 7	Thirlwell P 29 + 1	Livesey D 29 + 2	Beckford J 4	Harper K 7	Grand S 1 + 3	Krause J 3	Graham D 11	Murray G — + 1	Garner J 17 + 1	Smith Jeff 17	Smith Johann 9 + 5	Vipond S 1 + 3	Match No.
1	2^1	3	4	5	6	7	8^2	9	10	11	12	13																	1
1	2	3	4	5^1	6	7^2	8^3	9	10	11	12	14	13																2
1	2	3	4^2	5	6	7^1	8	9	10	11		12	13																3
1	2	3	4	5^1	6	7	8	9^2	10	11^3	12	13		14															4
1	2	3		5	6	7	8	9	10	11			4																5
1	2	3		5	6	7	8		10	11		9	4^1		12														6
1	2	3		5	6	7	8		10	11		9^2	4^1			12	13												7
1	2	3			6	7	8		10	11		9^1				12	4	5											8
1	2^3	3	12	5	6	7^1	8		10	11	14	13	9^2				4												9
1	2^1	3	4	5	6		8		10	11	12		9				7												10
1		3	4	5	6		8		10	11	2		9				7												11
1		3	4^2		6		8^1		10^3	11	2	12	9	14		13	7	5											12
1		3	4^1	5			8			11	2	12	9				7	6	10										13
1		3	4	5	6		8			11^1	2	13	9				7		10^2					12					14
1		3	12	5	6		8			11	2^3	13	9^1				4	14	10	7^2									15
1	2	3^3	12	5	6		8			11		13	9				4^1		10^2	7	14								16
1	2	3	4	5	6		8		10	11^1		12	9							7									17
1		3	4^2	5	6		8^3		10	11		12	13				7	2		9^1	14								18
1		3		5	6		8		10	11^1		12	9	13			4	2		7^2									19
1		3	4	5^3	6		9		10	8^1		12	13				7	2		11^2	14								20
1		3		5	6		8^1		10	7^2		12	9	13			4	2		11									21
1	2		4	5			8		10	11		9		7							6	3							22
1	2	3	4^1	5	6		8		10	11		9		7	12														23
1	2	3	4^1	5^3	6		8		10	11		9		7^2	12	13		14											24
1	2	11	12	5			8		10	7		9^3		4^2	13	14		6				3^1							25
1	2	3	4	5			8		10	11^1				7	12	13		6					9^2						26
1		3		5			8		10	11	2	12		7^1			4	6					9						27
1	2	3		5		7^1	8		10	11		12					4	6							9				28
1	2	3			6	7^3	8		10	9^2		12		13			4	5							14	11^1			29
1	2	3			6	7^2	8		10			12		13			4	5							9^1	11			30
1	2	3		12	6	7^2	8^3		10					13			4	5^1							9	11	14		31
1	2	3			6	7^1	8^2		10			12			4			5							9	11	13		32
1	2	3		12	6		8^2		10			13			14		4	5^1							9	11	7^3		33
1	2	3			6		8^1		10^2			12			13		4	5							9	11	7		34
1	2	3			6		8										4	5					10		9	11	7		35
1	2	3			6		8			11		12			13		4	5					10^1		9		7^2		36
1	2	3			6					8^1					10^2	12	4	5							9	11	7	13	37
1	2	3			6		12			13		14			8^2		4	5					10^3		9▪	11	7^1		38
1	2	3			6		8			12		9^2			7^3		4^1	5					10			11	13	14	39
1	2	3			6		8			12		13			7		4▪	5					10^2		9^1	11			40
1	2			12	6		8^2			7					4▪			5				3^1	10		9	11		13	41
1	2			5	3		8			4		12		13				6					10		9^1	11	7^2		42
1	2	3		12	6^1		8			4				13	7^2			5					10		9^3	11	14		43
1	2^2	3			6		8^3		12	7		13					4	5					10^1		9	11	14		44
1	2	3			6		8^2		12	7		13					4	5							9^1	11	10		45
1	2	3			6		8								12		4	5							9	11	10	7^1	46

FA Cup
First Round Swindon T (a) 1-3

Carling Cup
First Round Bradford C (h) 1-1
Second Round Charlton Ath (a) 0-1

J Paint Trophy
First Round Accrington S (a) 1-1

CHARLTON ATHLETIC FL Championship

FOUNDATION

The club was formed on 9 June 1905, by a group of 14- and 15-year-old youths living in streets by the Thames in the area which now borders the Thames Barrier. The club's progress through local leagues was so rapid that after the First World War they joined the Kent League where they spent a season before turning professional and joining the Southern League in 1920. A year later they were elected to the Football League's Division 3 (South).

The Valley, Floyd Road, Charlton, London SE7 8BL.

Telephone: (020) 8333 4000.

Fax: (020) 8333 4001.

Ticket Office: (0871) 226 1905.

Website: www.cafc.co.uk

Email: info@cafc.co.uk

Ground Capacity: 27,113.

Record Attendance: 75,031 v Aston Villa, FA Cup 5th rd, 12 February 1938 (at The Valley).

Pitch Measurements: 101.5m × 65.8m.

Chairman: Martin Simons.

Vice-chairman: Richard Murray.

Chief Executive: Peter Varney.

Secretary: Chris Parkes.

Manager: Alan Pardew.

Assistant Manager: Phil Parkinson.

Physio: George Cooper.

Colours: Red shirts, white shorts, red stockings.

Change Colours: Black shirts, black shorts, black stockings.

Year Formed: 1905.

Turned Professional: 1920.

Ltd Co.: 1919.

Club Nickname: 'Addicks'.

Grounds: 1906, Siemen's Meadow; 1907, Woolwich Common; 1909, Pound Park; 1913, Horn Lane; 1920, The Valley; 1923, Catford (The Mount); 1924, The Valley; 1985, Selhurst Park; 1991, Upton Park; 1992, The Valley.

First Football League Game: 27 August 1921, Division 3 (S), v Exeter C (h) W 1–0 – Hughes; Mitchell, Goodman; Dowling (1), Hampson, Dunn; Castle, Bailey, Halse, Green, Wilson.

HONOURS

Football League: Division 1 – Champions 1999–2000; Runners-up 1936–37; Promoted from Division 1, 1997–98 (play-offs); Division 2 – Runners-up 1935–36, 1985–86; Division 3 (S) – Champions 1928–29, 1934–35; Promoted from Division 3 (3rd) 1974–75, 1980–81.

FA Cup: Winners 1947; Runners-up 1946.

Football League Cup: Quarter-final 2007.

Full Members' Cup: Runners-up 1987.

SKY SPORTS FACT FILE

Though Ralph Allen still holds the individual scoring record for Charlton Athletic during one season, who knows what might have happened previously in 1933–34 had Cyril Pearce not broken his leg against Norwich City on 31 March when he had scored 26.

Record League Victory: 8–1 v Middlesbrough, Division 1, 12 September 1953 – Bartram; Campbell, Ellis; Fenton, Ufton, Hammond; Hurst (2), O'Linn (2), Leary (1), Firmani (3), Kiernan.

Record Cup Victory: 7–0 v Burton A, FA Cup 3rd rd, 7 January 1956 – Bartram; Campbell, Townsend; Hewie, Ufton, Hammond; Hurst (1), Gauld (1), Leary (3), White, Kiernan (2).

Record Defeat: 1–11 v Aston Villa, Division 2, 14 November 1959.

Most League Points (2 for a win): 61, Division 3 (S), 1934–35.

Most League Points (3 for a win): 91, Division 1, 1999–2000.

Most League Goals: 107, Division 2, 1957–58.

Highest League Scorer in Season: Ralph Allen, 32, Division 3 (S), 1934–35.

Most League Goals in Total Aggregate: Stuart Leary, 153, 1953–62.

Most League Goals in One Match: 5, Wilson Lennox v Exeter C, Division 3S, 2 February 1929; 5, Eddie Firmani v Aston Villa, Division 1, 5 February 1955; 5, John Summers v Huddersfield T, Division 2, 21 December 1957; 5, John Summers v Portsmouth, Division 2, 1 October 1960.

MANAGERS

Walter Rayner 1920–25
Alex Macfarlane 1925–27
Albert Lindon 1928
Alex Macfarlane 1928–32
Albert Lindon 1932–33
Jimmy Seed 1933–56
Jimmy Trotter 1956–61
Frank Hill 1961–65
Bob Stokoe 1965–67
Eddie Firmani 1967–70
Theo Foley 1970–74
Andy Nelson 1974–79
Mike Bailey 1979–81
Alan Mullery 1981–82
Ken Craggs 1982
Lennie Lawrence 1982–91
Steve Gritt/Alan Curbishley 1991–95
Alan Curbishley 1995–2006
Iain Dowie 2006
Les Reed 2006
Alan Pardew December 2006–

Most Capped Player: Jonatan Johansson, 41 (70), Finland.

Most League Appearances: Sam Bartram, 583, 1934–56.

Youngest League Player: Paul Konchesky, 16 years 93 days v Oxford U, 16 August 1997.

Record Transfer Fee Received: £16,500,000 from Tottenham H for Darren Bent, May 2007

Record Transfer Fee Paid: £4,750,000 to Wimbledon for Jason Euell, July 2001.

Football League Record: 1921 Elected to Division 3 (S); 1929–33 Division 2; 1933–35 Division 3 (S); 1935–36 Division 2; 1936–57 Division 1; 1957–72 Division 2; 1972–75 Division 3; 1975–80 Division 2; 1980–81 Division 3; 1981–86 Division 2; 1986–90 Division 1; 1990–92 Division 2; 1992–98 Division 1; 1998–99 FA Premier League; 1999–2000 Division 1; 2000–07 FA Premier League; 2007– FL C.

LATEST SEQUENCES

Longest Sequence of League Wins: 12, 26.12.1999 – 7.3.2000.

Longest Sequence of League Defeats: 10, 11.4.1990 – 15.9.1990.

Longest Sequence of League Draws: 6, 13.12.1992 – 16.1.1993.

Longest Sequence of Unbeaten League Matches: 15, 4.10.1980 – 20.12.1980.

Longest Sequence Without a League Win: 16, 26.2.1955 – 22.8.1955.

Successive Scoring Runs: 25 from 26.12.1935.

Successive Non-scoring Runs: 5 from 6.9.1922.

TEN YEAR LEAGUE RECORD

		P	W	D	L	F	A	Pts	Pos
1997-98	Div 1	46	26	10	10	80	49	88	4
1998-99	PR Lge	38	8	12	18	41	56	36	18
1999-2000	Div 1	46	27	10	9	79	45	91	1
2000-01	PR Lge	38	14	10	14	50	57	52	9
2001-02	PR Lge	38	10	14	14	38	49	44	14
2002-03	PR Lge	38	14	7	17	45	56	49	12
2003-04	PR Lge	38	14	11	13	51	51	53	7
2004-05	PR Lge	38	12	10	16	42	58	46	11
2005-06	PR Lge	38	13	8	17	41	55	47	13
2006-07	PR Lge	38	8	10	20	34	60	34	19

DID YOU KNOW ?

John Hewie, South African born Scottish international defender played 530 League and Cup games for Charlton Athletic from 1951 to 1966. He played in every position on the field for the club including four times as emergency goalkeeper, with two wins and two draws.

CHARLTON ATHLETIC 2006–07 LEAGUE RECORD

Match No.	Date	Venue	Opponents	Result		H/T Score	Lg. Pos.	Goalscorers	Attendance
1	Aug 19	A	West Ham U	L	1-3	1-0	—	Bent D (pen) [15]	34,937
2	23	H	Manchester U	L	0-3	0-0	—		25,422
3	26	H	Bolton W	W	2-0	0-0	16	Bent D 2 (1 pen) [65 (p), 85]	23,638
4	Sept 9	A	Chelsea	L	1-2	0-1	16	Hasselbaink [54]	41,194
5	16	H	Portsmouth	L	0-1	0-0	18		26,130
6	23	A	Aston Villa	L	0-2	0-1	19		35,513
7	30	H	Arsenal	L	1-2	1-1	20	Bent D [21]	26,770
8	Oct 16	A	Fulham	L	1-2	0-0	—	Bent D [78]	19,179
9	21	H	Watford	D	0-0	0-0	20		27,011
10	28	A	Newcastle U	D	0-0	0-0	20		48,642
11	Nov 4	H	Manchester C	W	1-0	1-0	20	Bent D [28]	26,011
12	11	A	Wigan Ath	L	2-3	0-2	20	De Zeeuw (og) [52], Bent M [90]	16,572
13	18	A	Reading	L	0-2	0-1	20		24,093
14	25	H	Everton	D	1-1	0-0	20	Reid [68]	26,435
15	Dec 2	A	Sheffield U	L	1-2	1-0	20	Reid [17]	27,368
16	5	H	Blackburn R	W	1-0	0-0	—	El Karkouri [90]	23,423
17	9	A	Tottenham H	L	1-5	1-2	19	Dawson (og) [43]	35,565
18	16	H	Liverpool	L	0-3	0-1	19		27,111
19	23	A	Middlesbrough	L	0-2	0-1	19		32,013
20	27	H	Fulham	D	2-2	2-1	—	Ambrose [19], Bent D [45]	25,203
21	30	H	Aston Villa	W	2-1	0-1	19	Bent D [57], Hughes [90]	26,699
22	Jan 2	A	Arsenal	L	0-4	0-2	—		60,057
23	13	H	Middlesbrough	L	1-3	1-1	19	Hasselbaink [27]	26,384
24	20	A	Portsmouth	W	1-0	0-0	19	Faye [79]	19,567
25	31	A	Bolton W	D	1-1	1-1	—	El Karkouri [12]	22,357
26	Feb 3	H	Chelsea	L	0-1	0-1	19		27,111
27	10	A	Manchester U	L	0-2	0-1	19		75,883
28	24	H	West Ham U	W	4-0	3-0	18	Ambrose [24], Thomas 2 [34, 80], Bent D [41]	27,111
29	Mar 3	A	Watford	D	2-2	0-2	18	Young [67], Ambrose [89]	19,782
30	18	H	Newcastle U	W	2-0	0-0	18	Zheng-Zhi [53], Thomas (pen) [88]	27,028
31	31	H	Wigan Ath	W	1-0	0-0	18	Bent D (pen) [86]	26,500
32	Apr 6	A	Manchester C	D	0-0	0-0	—		41,424
33	9	H	Reading	D	0-0	0-0	17		26,271
34	15	A	Everton	L	1-2	0-0	18	Bent D [89]	34,028
35	21	H	Sheffield U	D	1-1	0-0	18	El Karkouri [59]	27,111
36	28	A	Blackburn R	L	1-4	0-0	19	Bent D [71]	24,921
37	May 7	H	Tottenham H	L	0-2	0-1	—		26,339
38	13	A	Liverpool	D	2-2	1-0	19	Holland [2], Bent D [72]	43,134

Final League Position: 19

GOALSCORERS

League (34): Bent D 13 (3 pens), Ambrose 3, El Karkouri 3, Thomas 3 (1 pen), Hasselbaink 2, Reid 2, Bent M 1, Faye 1, Holland 1, Hughes 1, Young 1, Zheng-Zhi 1, own goals 2.
Carling Cup (5): Bent D 2, Hasselbaink 2, Bent M 1.
FA Cup (0).

Carson S 36	Young L 29	Traore D 11	Holland M 27 + 6	El Karkouri T 36	Hreidarsson H 30 + 1	Ambrose D 21 + 5	Faye A 25 + 3	Hasselbaink J 11 + 14	Bent D 32	Hughes B 15 + 9	Sorondo G — + 1	Bent M 17 + 13	Reid A 15 + 1	Kishishev R 6 + 8	Fortune J 6 + 2	Rommedahl D 19 + 9	Diawara S 18 + 5	Lisbie K 1 + 7	Pouso O 1	Thomas J 16 + 4	Sam L 3 + 4	Myhre T 1	Sankofa O 9	Thatcher B 10 + 1	Bougherra M 2 + 3	Song Billong A 12	Zheng-Zhi 8 + 4	Randolph D 1	*Match No.*
1	2	3▪	4	5	6	7^{1}	8	9^{2}	10	11^{3}	12	13	14																1
1	2		4	5	3	7	8^{2}	9^{1}	10	11		12			6	13													2
1	2	3	12	5	6▪	7^{2}	4	9^{1}	10	8		14	11^{3}	13															3
1	2	3^{2}		5		7	8	9	10	4		12	11^{3}	13		14	6^{1}												4
1	3		12	5		7	6	9	10			8^{2}		2^{3}	13	11		14	4^{1}										5
1	2		4^{2}	5	3	12	8	9^{1}	10	11		13			6	7													6
1	2			5	3	12	4^{2}	9	10	8			11^{1}	13	6			7											7
1	2		12	5	3		4	9^{3}	10	8^{2}		13	7			11	6^{1}			14									8
1	2		4	5	3		8	12	10				11			7	6			9^{1}									9
1	2		4	5	3		8		10	12		9^{1}	11^{2}	13		7	6												10
1	2		4	5	3		8	12	10	13			11^{1}			7^{2}	6			9									11
1	2		4^{1}	5	3	7^{2}	8	12	10			13	11	14			6^{3}			9									12
1	2		4	5	3	12			10			9^{2}	11		6	7				8^{1}	13								13
1	2	3	4	5	6	9^{1}	8		10			12	11			7													14
1	2	3	4	5	6	9^{2}	8^{3}		10			12	11	13		7^{1}					14								15
1	2	3^{3}	12	5	6		8		10	4		13	11	7^{1}			14				9^{2}								16
1	2			5	3		8	12	10	4			11^{1}	7^{2}		13	6				9								17
	2^{3}	3	4	5	6	12	8^{2}	9	10	13			11^{1}			7	14					1							18
1		3^{2}	4	5	11		8^{1}		10	9		12		7	6	13							2						19
1		3	4	5	6	8^{2}		12	10	13		9^{1}		7		14				11^{3}			2						20
1		3	4	5	6	8		12	10	13		9^{1}		7^{2}		11^{3}				14			2						21
1		3	4	5		10^{3}	8^{1}			11^{2}		9		12	13	7	6			14			2▪						22
1			4	2	6	8^{1}		9		12		10^{3}	11			7^{2}	5			13	14			3					23
1			4	5	6		8^{3}	12		11		9		13		7^{2}	14			10^{1}			2	3					24
1			4	5	6		8	12		11^{3}		9^{1}				7^{2}	14	13		10			2	3					25
1			4^{2}	5	6		8	12		11		9				7^{1}	14	13		10^{3}			2	3					26
1			4^{1}			10^{2}	8^{3}			12		9				7	6	13					2	3	5	11	14		27
1	2		4	5		7	12	13	10^{3}			9^{2}					6			11				3		8^{1}	14		28
1	3		4^{2}	5		7		9^{3}	10						6	12		13		11^{1}			2			8	14		29
1	2		4	5	3		12		10^{2}			9^{3}				14	6	13		11						8^{1}	7		30
1	2		4^{1}	5	3	12^{2}	13		10			14				7^{3}	6			11						8	9		31
1	2			5	3		8		10			9				12	6			11^{1}						4	7		32
1	2		12	5	3^{3}	7			10			9^{1}					6	13		11				14		4^{2}	8		33
1	2		12	5		7	8^{1}	13	10	11^{2}							6							3^{3}	14	4	9		34
1	2			5	12	7		13	10							8	6^{3}			11^{2}				3^{1}	14	4	9		35
1	2		4	5	6	7^{1}			10			9^{3}				12				11^{2}				3▪	14	8	13		36
1	2		4	5	3	7		12	10	13		9^{1}					6				14					8^{3}	11^{2}		37
	2		4		6	7^{2}		12	10	13		14									9^{1}			3	5	8	11^{3}	1	38

FA Cup

Third Round	Nottingham F	(a)	0-2

Carling Cup

Second Round	Carlisle U	(h)	1-0
Third Round	Bolton W	(h)	1-0
Fourth Round	Chesterfield	(a)	3-3
Quarter-Final	Wycombe W	(h)	0-1

CHELSEA FA Premiership

FOUNDATION

Chelsea may never have existed but for the fact that Fulham rejected an offer to rent the Stamford Bridge ground from Mr H. A. Mears who had owned it since 1904. Fortunately he was determined to develop it as a football stadium rather than sell it to the Great Western Railway and got together with Frederick Parker, who persuaded Mears of the financial advantages of developing a major sporting venue. Chelsea FC was formed in 1905, and when admission to the Southern League was denied, they immediately gained admission to the Second Division of the Football League.

Stamford Bridge, Fulham Road, London SW6 1HS.

Telephone: 0870 300 1212 (UK). 0044 207 386 9373 (INTL).

Fax: (020) 7381 4831.

Ticket Office: 0870 300 2322 (UK). 0044 207 915 2900 (INTL).

Website: www.chelseafc.com

Ground Capacity: 42,055.

Record Attendance: 82,905 v Arsenal, Division 1, 12 October 1935.

Pitch Measurements: 103m × 67m.

Chairman: Bruce Buck.

Director: Eugene Tenenbaum.

Chief Executive: Peter Kenyon.

Secretary: David Barnard.

Manager: José Mourinho.

Assistant Managers: Steve Clarke and Baltemar Brito.

Doctor: Brian English.

Physio: Dave Hancock.

Colours: Blue.

Change Colours: White.

Year Formed: 1905.

Turned Professional: 1905.

Ltd Co.: 1905.

Club Nickname: 'The Blues'.

Ground: 1905, Stamford Bridge.

First Football League Game: 2 September 1905, Division 2, v Stockport Co (a) L 0–1 – Foulke; Mackie, McEwan; Key, Harris, Miller; Moran, J. T. Robertson, Copeland, Windridge, Kirwan.

Record League Victory: 9–2 v Glossop N E, Division 2, 1 September 1906 – Byrne; Walton, Miller; Key (1), McRoberts, Henderson; Moran, McDermott (1), Hilsdon (5), Copeland (1), Kirwan (1).

HONOURS

FA Premier League: Champions 2004–05, 2005–06. Runners-up 2003–04, 2006–07.

Football League: Division 1 – Champions 1954–55; Division 2 – Champions 1983–84, 1988–89; Runners-up 1906–07, 1911–12, 1929–30, 1962–63, 1976–77.

FA Cup: Winners 1970, 1997, 2000, 2007. Runners-up 1915, 1967, 1994, 2002.

Football League Cup: Winners 1965, 1998, 2005, 2007; Runners-up 1972.

Full Members' Cup: Winners 1986.

Zenith Data Systems Cup: Winners 1990.

European Competitions: *Champions League:* 1999–2000, 2003–04 (semi-finals), 2004–05 (semi-finals), 2005–06, 2006–07 (semi-finals). *European Fairs Cup:* 1958–60, 1965–66, 1968–69. *European Cup-Winners' Cup:* 1970–71 (winners), 1971–72, 1994–95, 1997–98 (winners), 1998–99 (semi-finals). *UEFA Cup:* 2000–01, 2001–02, 2002–03. *Super Cup:* 1998–99 (winners).

SKY SPORTS FACT FILE

In 1905–06 Chelsea goalkeeper Willie "Fatty" Foulke managed to keep a clean sheet on nine consecutive Football League occasions from 4 November at home to Barnsley to Christmas Day away to Manchester United in a goalless draw.

Record Cup Victory: 13–0 v Jeunesse Hautcharage, ECWC, 1st rd 2nd leg, 29 September 1971 – Bonetti; Boyle, Harris (1), Hollins (1p), Webb (1), Hinton, Cooke, Baldwin (3), Osgood (5), Hudson (1), Houseman (1).

Record Defeat: 1–8 v Wolverhampton W, Division 1, 26 September 1953.

Most League Points (2 for a win): 57, Division 2, 1906–07.

Most League Points (3 for a win): 99, Division 2, 1988–89.

Most League Goals: 98, Division 1, 1960–61.

Highest League Scorer in Season: Jimmy Greaves, 41, 1960–61.

Most League Goals in Total Aggregate: Bobby Tambling, 164, 1958–70.

Most League Goals in One Match: 5, George Hilsdon v Glossop, Division 2, 1 September 1906; 5, Jimmy Greaves v Wolverhampton W, Division 1, 30 August 1958; 5, Jimmy Greaves v Preston NE, Division 1, 19 December 1959; 5, Jimmy Greaves v WBA, Division 1, 3 December 1960; 5, Bobby Tambling v Aston Villa, Division 1, 17 September 1966; 5, Gordon Durie v Walsall, Division 2, 4 February 1989.

Most Capped Player: Marcel Desailly, 67 (116), France.

Most League Appearances: Ron Harris, 655, 1962–80.

Youngest League Player: Ian Hamilton, 16 years 138 days v Tottenham H, 18 March 1967.

MANAGERS

John Tait Robertson 1905–07
David Calderhead 1907–33
Leslie Knighton 1933–39
Billy Birrell 1939–52
Ted Drake 1952–61
Tommy Docherty 1962–67
Dave Sexton 1967–74
Ron Suart 1974–75
Eddie McCreadie 1975–77
Ken Shellito 1977–78
Danny Blanchflower 1978–79
Geoff Hurst 1979–81
John Neal 1981–85 *(Director to 1986)*
John Hollins 1985–88
Bobby Campbell 1988–91
Ian Porterfield 1991–93
David Webb 1993
Glenn Hoddle 1993–96
Ruud Gullit 1996–98
Gianluca Vialli 1998–2000
Claudio Ranieri 2000–04
Jose Mourinho June 2004–

Record Transfer Fee Received: £12,000,000 from Rangers for Tore Andre Flo, November 2000.

Record Transfer Fee Paid: £29,500,000 to AC Milan for Andriy Shevchenko, June 2006.

Football League Record: 1905 Elected to Division 2; 1907–10 Division 1; 1910–12 Division 2; 1912–24 Division 1; 1924–30 Division 2; 1930–62 Division 1; 1962–63 Division 2; 1963–75 Division 1; 1975–77 Division 2; 1977–79 Division 1; 1979–84 Division 2; 1984–88 Division 1; 1988–89 Division 2; 1989–92 Division 1; 1992– FA Premier League.

LATEST SEQUENCES

Longest Sequence of League Wins: 10, 19.11.2005 – 15.1.2006.

Longest Sequence of League Defeats: 7, 1.11.1952 – 20.12.1952.

Longest Sequence of League Draws: 6, 20.8.1969 – 13.9.1969.

Longest Sequence of Unbeaten League Matches: 40, 23.10.2004 – 29.10.2005.

Longest Sequence Without a League Win: 21, 3.11.1987 – 2.4.1988.

Successive Scoring Runs: 27 from 29.10.1988.

Successive Non-scoring Runs: 9 from 14.3.1981.

TEN YEAR LEAGUE RECORD

		P	*W*	*D*	*L*	*F*	*A*	*Pts*	*Pos*
1997-98	PR Lge	38	20	3	15	71	43	63	4
1998-99	PR Lge	38	20	15	3	57	30	75	3
1999-2000	PR Lge	38	18	11	9	53	34	65	5
2000-01	PR Lge	38	17	10	11	68	45	61	6
2001-02	PR Lge	38	17	13	8	66	38	64	6
2002-03	PR Lge	38	19	10	9	68	38	67	4
2003-04	PR Lge	38	24	7	7	67	30	79	2
2004-05	PR Lge	38	29	8	1	72	15	95	1
2005-06	PR Lge	38	29	4	5	72	22	91	1
2006-07	PR Lge	38	24	11	3	64	24	83	2

DID YOU KNOW?

Chelsea had their great escape tale in 1950–51. With four matches remaining and a run of 14 without a win behind them they needed maximum points. But they beat Liverpool, Wolverhampton Wanderers, Fulham and Bolton Wanderers to survive by 0.044 of a goal!

CHELSEA 2006–07 LEAGUE RECORD

Match No.	Date	Venue	Opponents	Result		H/T Score	Lg. Pos.	Goalscorers	Attendance
1	Aug 20	H	Manchester C	W	3-0	2-0	—	Terry [11], Lampard [26], Drogba [78]	41,953
2	23	A	Middlesbrough	L	1-2	1-0	—	Shevchenko [16]	29,198
3	27	A	Blackburn R	W	2-0	0-0	4	Lampard (pen) [50], Drogba [81]	19,398
4	Sept 9	H	Charlton Ath	W	2-1	1-0	4	Drogba [6], Ricardo Carvalho [63]	41,194
5	17	H	Liverpool	W	1-0	1-0	3	Drogba [42]	41,882
6	23	A	Fulham	W	2-0	0-0	1	Lampard 2 (1 pen) [73 (p), 80]	24,290
7	30	H	Aston Villa	D	1-1	1-1	2	Drogba [3]	41,951
8	Oct 14	A	Reading	W	1-0	1-0	2	Ingimarsson (og) [45]	24,025
9	21	H	Portsmouth	W	2-1	0-0	2	Shevchenko [55], Ballack [57]	41,838
10	28	A	Sheffield U	W	2-0	1-0	2	Lampard [43], Ballack [49]	32,321
11	Nov 5	A	Tottenham H	L	1-2	1-1	2	Makelele [15]	36,070
12	11	H	Watford	W	4-0	2-0	2	Drogba 3 [27, 36, 69], Shevchenko [52]	41,936
13	18	H	West Ham U	W	1-0	1-0	2	Geremi [22]	41,916
14	26	A	Manchester U	D	1-1	0-1	2	Ricardo Carvalho [69]	75,948
15	29	A	Bolton W	W	1-0	1-0	—	Ballack [45]	23,559
16	Dec 10	H	Arsenal	D	1-1	0-0	2	Essien [84]	41,917
17	13	H	Newcastle U	W	1-0	0-0	—	Drogba [74]	41,945
18	17	A	Everton	W	3-2	0-1	2	Ballack [49], Lampard [81], Drogba [87]	33,970
19	23	A	Wigan Ath	W	3-2	2-1	2	Lampard [13], Kalou [31], Robben [90]	22,077
20	26	H	Reading	D	2-2	1-0	2	Drogba 2 [38, 72]	41,885
21	30	H	Fulham	D	2-2	1-1	2	Rosenior (og) [35], Drogba [62]	41,926
22	Jan 2	A	Aston Villa	D	0-0	0-0	—		41,006
23	13	H	Wigan Ath	W	4-0	1-0	2	Lampard [13], Robben [63], Kirkland (og) [70], Drogba [90]	40,846
24	20	A	Liverpool	L	0-2	0-2	2		44,245
25	31	H	Blackburn R	W	3-0	1-0	—	Drogba [6], Lampard [67], Kalou [90]	38,000
26	Feb 3	A	Charlton Ath	W	1-0	1-0	2	Lampard [18]	27,111
27	10	H	Middlesbrough	W	3-0	1-0	2	Drogba 2 [45, 83], Xavier (og) [66]	41,699
28	Mar 3	A	Portsmouth	W	2-0	1-0	2	Drogba [33], Kalou [82]	20,219
29	14	A	Manchester C	W	1-0	1-0	—	Lampard (pen) [28]	39,429
30	17	H	Sheffield U	W	3-0	2-0	2	Shevchenko [4], Kalou [17], Ballack [58]	41,897
31	31	A	Watford	W	1-0	0-0	2	Kalou [90]	19,793
32	Apr 7	H	Tottenham H	W	1-0	0-0	2	Ricardo Carvalho [52]	41,864
33	18	A	West Ham U	W	4-1	2-1	—	Wright-Phillips 2 [31, 36], Kalou [52], Drogba [62]	34,966
34	22	A	Newcastle U	D	0-0	0-0	2		52,056
35	28	H	Bolton W	D	2-2	2-1	2	Kalou [22], Jaaskelainen (og) [34]	41,105
36	May 6	A	Arsenal	D	1-1	0-1	2	Essien [70]	60,102
37	9	H	Manchester U	D	0-0	0-0	—		41,794
38	13	H	Everton	D	1-1	0-0	2	Drogba [57]	41,746

Final League Position: 2

GOALSCORERS

League (64): Drogba 20, Lampard 11 (3 pens), Kalou 7, Ballack 5, Shevchenko 4, Ricardo Carvalho 3, Essien 2, Robben 2, Wright-Phillips 2, Geremi 1, Makelele 1, Terry 1, own goals 5.
Carling Cup (14): Drogba 4, Lampard 3, Shevchenko 3, Bridge 1, Cole J 1, Essien 1, Kalou 1.
FA Cup (21): Lampard 6 (1 pen), Drogba 3, Shevchenko 3, Wright-Phillips 3, Mikel 2, Ballack 1, Essien 1, Kalou 1, Ricardo Carvalho 1.
Champions League (17): Drogba 6, Shevchenko 3, Ballack 2 (1 pen), Essien 2, Cole J 1, Lampard 1, Robben 1, Wright-Phillips 1.
Community Shield (1): Shevchenko 1.

Cudicini C 7 + 1	Paulo Ferreira 18 + 6	Bridge W 17 + 5	Essien M 33	Terry J 27 + 1	Ricardo Carvalho 31	Wright-Phillips S 13 + 14	Lampard F 36 + 1	Drogba D 32 + 4	Shevchenko A 22 + 8	Robben A 16 + 5	Kalou S 19 + 14	Mikel J 10 + 12	Diarra L 7 + 3	Cech P 20	Boulahrouz K 10 + 3	Makelele C 26 + 3	Ballack M 23 + 3	Cole A 21 + 2	Geremi 15 + 4	Cole J 3 + 10	Hilario 11	Sahar B — + 3	Sinclair S 1 + 1	Nuno Morais — + 2	Hutchinson S — + 1	*Match No.*
1	2	3	4	5	6	7^1	8	9^2	10	11^3	12	13	14													1
1	2	3	7	5	6	12	8	9	10		11					4^1										2
		3	7	5	6	12	8	13	10^1		9^2	14		1	2	4^3	11									3
		3^3	4	5	6	7^1	8	9	10^2		12	13		1	2		11	14								4
	12		7	5	6		8	9^2	10^3	14	13			1	2^1	4	11■	3								5
	5	12	7		6		8^1	9	10^3	11^2	13	14		1		4		3	2							6
			7	5	6	12	8	9	10	11^1	13			1		4		3	2^2							7
15	2	3	4	5			8	9	10^2	11^1	12	7■		1^G	6					13						8
	2		4	5	6		8	9	10^2	11^3					12	13	7^1	3		14	1					9
	2	3	4	5	6	12	8	9^2		11^3	13					14	7			10^1	1					10
	2^1		7	5■	6	14	8	9		11	13				12^2	4^3	10	3			1					11
1			7	5	6	12	8	9	10^2	13						4^1	11^3	3	2	14						12
1			7	5	6^2		8	9	10^3	11^1		12			14	4		3	2	13						13
1	12		7	5	6		8	9	10^3	13						4	11^1	3	2^2	14						14
1			7	5	6		8	9^2	10^1		12	13				4	11	3	2							15
			7	5	6	12	8	9	10^2	13						4	11	3	2^1		1					16
			4	5	6^3	7^1	8	12	13	10	9					14	11	3	2^2		1					17
		12	7		6		8	9	13	10^2	14				5^1	4	11	3	2^3		1					18
			2		6		8	9	12	11^3	10	13			5^1	4^2	7	3	14		1					19
	5	3^3	4		6	12	8	9	10^1		7	13					11	14	2^2		1					20
	5	12	7		6	13	8	9	14		10^1					4^2	11	3	2^3		1					21
	2		7		6	11^1	8	9	12		10^2	13			5^3	4		3	14		1					22
	2^1	3	5		6		8	9		11^3	10^2	13				4	7		12		1	14				23
	5		6			12	8	9	13	11^1	10	4^2		1			7	3	2							24
	12	13	5		6		8	9	10^3		14	7^1	2	1		4	11	3^2								25
		3	5	12	6	13	8	9	10^3		14	7^2	2	1		4^1	11									26
	6	3	7	5		12	8	9	10^3	13	11^1		2^2	1		4			14							27
		12	5		6	13	8	9^1	10^3	11^2	14		2	1		4	7	3								28
				5	6	12	8	9		11^1	10		13	1		4^2	7	3	2							29
	12			5	6	7	8^3	13	10^2	11	9			1	2	4	14	3^1								30
	12			5	6	7	8	9	10		13	14		1		4^2	11	3^3	2^1							31
	2	3		5	6	7^2	8	9	12		10^1	11^3		1		4	13			14						32
	12	3	7	5	6	11	8^2	9^3			10	4	2^1	1			13			14						33
	2	3	6	5		7^2	8	9	12		10	14		1		4^1	11^3			13						34
		3	7	5	6^1	11	12	13	10^2		9	8	4^3	1					2	14						35
	2	3	4	5		11^2	8				9	7^1	12	1	6■					10			13			36
1	6	3	8	5		7					9	10^1	2^3			4				12		13	11^2	14		37
	2	3^3		5		7	8	9			10	4^2		1	6					11^1		12		13	14	38

FA Cup

Third Round	Macclesfield T	(h)	6-1
Fourth Round	Nottingham F	(h)	3-0
Fifth Round	Norwich C	(h)	4-0
Sixth Round	Tottenham H	(h)	3-3
		(a)	2-1
Semi-Final *(at Old Trafford)*	Blackburn R		2-1
Final *(at Wembley)*	Manchester U		1-0

Carling Cup

Third Round	Blackburn R	(a)	2-0
Fourth Round	Aston Villa	(h)	4-0
Quarter-Final	Newcastle U	(a)	1-0
Semi-Final	Wycombe W	(a)	1-1
		(h)	4-0
Final *(at Millennium Stadium)*	Arsenal		2-1

Champions League

Group A	Werder Bremen	(h)	2-0
	Levski	(a)	3-1
	Barcelona	(h)	1-0
		(a)	2-2
	Werder Bremen	(a)	0-1
	Levski	(h)	2-0
Knock-Out Round	Porto	(a)	1-1
		(h)	2-1
Quarter-Final	Valencia	(h)	1-1
		(a)	2-1
Semi-Final	Liverpool	(h)	1-0
		(a)	0-1

Community Shield

Final *(at Millennium Stadium)*	Liverpool		1-2

CHELTENHAM TOWN FL Championship 1

FOUNDATION

Although a scratch team representing Cheltenham played a match against Gloucester in 1884, the earliest recorded match for Cheltenham Town FC was a friendly against Dean Close School on 12 March 1892. The School won 4–3 and the match was played at Prestbury (half a mile from Whaddon Road). Cheltenham Town played Wednesday afternoon friendlies at a local cricket ground until entering the Mid Gloucester League. In those days the club played in deep red coloured shirts and were nicknamed 'the Rubies'. The club moved to Whaddon Lane for season 1901–02 and changed to red and white colours two years later.

Whaddon Road, Cheltenham, Gloucester, GL52 5NA.

Telephone: (01242) 573 558.

Fax: (01242) 224 675.

Ticket Office: (01242) 573 558.

Website: www.ctfc.com

Email: info@ctfc.com

Ground Capacity: 7,013.

Record Attendance: at Whaddon Road: 8,326 v Reading, FA Cup 1st rd, 17 November 1956; at Cheltenham Athletic Ground: 10,389 v Blackpool, FA Cup 3rd rd, 13 January 1934.

Pitch Measurements: 101m × 66m.

Chairman: Paul Baker.

Vice-chairman: Colin Farmer.

Chief Executive: Nick Hale.

Secretary: Paul Godfrey.

Manager: John Ward.

Assistant Manager: Keith Downing.

Physio: Ian Weston.

Colours: Red and white striped shirts, white shorts, red stockings.

Change Colours: All blue with white trim.

Year Formed: 1892.

Turned Professional: 1932.

Ltd Co.: 1937.

Club Nickname: 'The Robins'.

Grounds: Grafton Cricket Ground, Whaddon Lane, Carter's Field (pre 1932).

HONOURS

Football League: Promoted from Division 3 (play-offs) 2001–02; Promoted from FL 2 (play-offs) 2005–06.

FA Cup: best season: 5th rd 2002.

Football League Cup: never past 2nd rd.

Football Conference: Champions 1998–99, runners-up 1997–98.

Trophy: Winners 1997–98.

Southern League: Champions 1984–85; *Southern League Cup:* Winners 1957–58, runners-up 1968–69, 1984–85; *Southern League Merit Cup:* Winners 1984–85; *Southern League Championship Shield:* Winners 1985.

Gloucestershire Senior Cup: Winners 1998–99; *Gloucestershire Northern Senior Professional Cup:* Winners 30 times; *Midland Floodlit Cup:* Winners 1985–86, 1986–87, 1987–88; *Mid Gloucester League:* Champions 1896–97; *Gloucester and District League:* Champions 1902–03, 1905–06; *Cheltenham League:* Champions 1910–11, 1913–14; *North Gloucestershire League:* Champions 1913–14; *Gloucestershire Northern Senior League:* Champions 1928–29, 1932–33; *Gloucestershire Northern Senior Amateur Cup:* Winners 1929–30, 1930–31, 1932–33, 1933–34, 1934–35; *Leamington Hospital Cup:* Winners 1934–35.

SKY SPORTS FACT FILE

Before his memorable FA Cup goal for Hereford United on 5 February 1972 against Newcastle United, Ronnie Radford had played for Sheffield Wednesday and Leeds United. Moreover it was from Cheltenham Town that his career was relaunched at Newport County.

Record League Victory: 11–0 v Bourneville Ath, Birmingham Combination, 29 April 1933 – Davis; Jones, Williams; Lang (1), Blackburn, Draper; Evans, Hazard (4), Haycox (4), Goodger (1), Hill (1).

Record Cup Victory: 12–0 v Chippenham R, FA Cup 3rd qual. rd, 2 November 1935 – Bowles; Whitehouse, Williams; Lang, Devonport (1), Partridge (2); Perkins, Hackett, Jones (4), Black (4), Griffiths (1).

Record Defeat: 0–7 v Crystal Palace, League Cup 2nd rd, 2 October 2002.
N.B. 1–10 v Merthyr T, Southern League, 8 March 1952.

Most League Points (2 for a win): 60, Southern League Division 1, 1963–64.

Most League Points (3 for a win): 78, Division 3, 2001–02.

Most League Goals: 66, Division 3, 2001–02.

Highest League Scorer in Season: Julian Alsop, 20, Division 3, 2001–02.

Most League Goals in Total Aggregate: Martin Devaney, 38, 1999–2005.

Most Capped Player: Grant McCann, 7 (15), Northern Ireland.

Most League Appearances: Jamie Victory, 258, 1999–.

Record Transfer Fee Received: £100,000 from Barnsley for Grant McCann, January 2007.

Record Transfer Fee Paid: £50,000 to West Ham U for Grant McCann, January 2003 and £50,000 to Stoke C for Brian Wilson, March 2004.

Football League Record: 1999 Promoted to Division 3; 2002 Division 2; 2003–04 Division 3; 2004–06 FL 2; 2006– FL 1.

MANAGERS

George Blackburn 1932–34
George Carr 1934–37
Jimmy Brain 1937–48
Cyril Dean 1948–50
George Summerbee 1950–52
William Raeside 1952–53
Arch Anderson 1953–58
Ron Lewin 1958–60
Peter Donnelly 1960–61
Tommy Cavanagh 1961
Arch Anderson 1961–65
Harold Fletcher 1965–66
Bob Etheridge 1966–73
Willie Penman 1973–74
Dennis Allen 1974–79
Terry Paine 1979
Alan Grundy 1979–82
Alan Wood 1982–83
John Murphy 1983–88
Jim Barron 1988–90
John Murphy 1990
Dave Lewis 1990–91
Ally Robertson 1991–92
Lindsay Parsons 1992–95
Chris Robinson 1995–97
Steve Cotterill 1997–2002
Graham Allner 2002–03
Bobby Gould 2003
John Ward November 2003–

LATEST SEQUENCES

Longest Sequence of League Wins: 4, 29.4.2006 – 8.8.2006.

Longest Sequence of League Defeats: 5, 13.1.2001 – 13.2.2001.

Longest Sequence of League Draws: 5, 5.4.2003 – 21.4.2003.

Longest Sequence of Unbeaten League Matches: 16, 1.12.2001 – 12.3.2002.

Longest Sequence Without a League Win: 10, 16.4.2002 – 14.9.2002.

Successive Scoring Runs: 15 from 15.2.2003.

Successive Non-scoring Runs: 4 from 12.9.1999.

TEN YEAR LEAGUE RECORD

		P	*W*	*D*	*L*	*F*	*A*	*Pts*	*Pos*
1997–98	Conf.	42	23	9	10	63	43	78	2
1998-99	Conf.	42	22	14	6	71	36	80	1
1999-2000	Div 3	46	20	10	16	50	42	70	8
2000-01	Div 3	46	18	14	14	59	52	68	9
2001-02	Div 3	46	21	15	10	66	49	78	4
2002-03	Div 2	46	10	18	18	53	68	48	21
2003-04	Div 3	46	14	14	18	57	71	56	14
2004-05	FL 2	46	16	12	18	51	54	60	14
2005-06	FL 2	46	19	15	12	65	53	72	5
2006-07	FL 1	46	15	9	22	49	61	54	17

DID YOU KNOW ?

With points needed to ensure escape from relegation on 28 April 2007, Cheltenham Town were away to Rotherham United. Trailing 2–0 after 22 minutes they retrieved one goal before the interval and proceeded to banish all fears with a final score of 4–2.

CHELTENHAM TOWN 2006–07 LEAGUE RECORD

Match No.	Date	Venue	Opponents	Result	H/T Score	Lg. Pos.	Goalscorers	Attendance
1	Aug 5	A	Swansea C	W 2-1	0-0	—	Odejayi [48], McCann [54]	15,199
2	8	H	Tranmere R	W 1-0	1-0	—	Odejayi [8]	3875
3	12	H	Port Vale	L 0-1	0-0	8		4309
4	19	A	Bournemouth	L 1-2	1-1	10	McCann [15]	5378
5	26	H	Millwall	W 3-2	1-2	6	McCann (pen) [14], Odejayi [67], Melligan [82]	4386
6	Sept 3	A	Carlisle U	L 0-2	0-2	9		7248
7	9	H	Huddersfield T	W 2-1	1-0	6	McCann [10], Melligan [71]	3720
8	12	A	Crewe Alex	L 1-3	1-1	—	Wilson [39]	4062
9	16	A	Scunthorpe U	L 0-1	0-0	15		4288
10	23	H	Bradford C	L 1-2	1-0	19	Odejayi [4]	3830
11	26	H	Northampton T	L 0-2	0-0	—		3224
12	30	A	Gillingham	L 1-2	1-2	20	McCann [28]	5688
13	Oct 6	A	Yeovil T	W 1-0	0-0	—	Melligan [88]	6220
14	14	H	Doncaster R	L 0-2	0-1	22		3872
15	21	A	Leyton Orient	L 0-2	0-1	22		4500
16	28	H	Nottingham F	L 0-2	0-2	23		6554
17	Nov 4	H	Oldham Ath	L 1-2	0-2	23	Odejayi [90]	4054
18	18	A	Chesterfield	L 0-1	0-0	24		3488
19	24	H	Brentford	W 2-0	1-0	—	Odejayi 2 [5, 75]	3646
20	Dec 5	A	Blackpool	L 1-2	1-1	—	Spencer [14]	4851
21	9	A	Brighton & HA	L 1-2	0-0	23	Victory [74]	5386
22	16	H	Rotherham U	W 2-0	0-0	22	Wilson [64], Bird [90]	3525
23	23	H	Bristol C	D 2-2	2-0	21	O'Leary [36], Bird [38]	5863
24	26	A	Northampton T	L 0-2	0-1	23		5239
25	30	A	Bradford C	D 2-2	0-1	22	Finnigan (pen) [57], Odejayi [60]	7264
26	Jan 2	H	Crewe Alex	D 1-1	1-1	—	Finnigan [31]	3154
27	13	A	Huddersfield T	L 0-2	0-2	23		9813
28	16	H	Scunthorpe U	D 1-1	1-0	—	Gillespie [17]	3036
29	20	H	Gillingham	D 1-1	1-1	22	Melligan [17]	3598
30	31	A	Bristol C	W 1-0	1-0	—	Spencer [44]	12,227
31	Feb 3	H	Swansea C	W 2-1	1-1	21	Odejayi [40], Connor [67]	5221
32	17	H	Bournemouth	W 1-0	0-0	20	Spencer [90]	4530
33	20	A	Tranmere R	D 2-2	2-0	—	Lowe [18], Odejayi [26]	5576
34	24	H	Carlisle U	L 0-1	0-1	22		3831
35	Mar 3	A	Millwall	L 0-2	0-2	22		10,261
36	6	A	Port Vale	D 1-1	0-1	—	Townsend [70]	3340
37	10	H	Yeovil T	L 1-2	0-1	22	Finnigan [90]	5314
38	17	A	Doncaster R	W 2-0	1-0	21	Gillespie [34], Odejayi [71]	6777
39	24	A	Nottingham F	L 0-3	0-1	22		22,640
40	31	H	Leyton Orient	W 2-1	1-0	20	Finnigan [13], Melligan [61]	4300
41	Apr 7	A	Brentford	W 2-0	1-0	20	Gillespie [8], Melligan [47]	4831
42	9	H	Chesterfield	D 0-0	0-0	20		5089
43	14	A	Oldham Ath	W 2-0	2-0	19	Odejayi [22], Finnigan [31]	5426
44	21	H	Blackpool	L 1-2	0-1	20	Finnigan (pen) [51]	5093
45	28	A	Rotherham U	W 4-2	1-2	17	Odejayi [44], Gillespie 2 [46, 56], Melligan [88]	3876
46	May 5	H	Brighton & HA	D 1-1	0-1	17	Finnigan (pen) [87]	6232

Final League Position: 17

GOALSCORERS

League (49): Odejayi 13, Finnigan 7 (3 pens), Melligan 7, Gillespie 5, McCann 5 (1 pen), Spencer 3, Bird 2, Wilson 2, Connor 1, Lowe 1, O'Leary 1, Townsend 1, Victory 1.
Carling Cup (3): Guinan 1, Odejayi 1, Wilson 1.
FA Cup (0).
J Paint Trophy (5): McCann 2 (1 pen), Finnigan 1, Mulligan 1, Odejayi 1.

Higgs S 36	Gill J 38 + 1	Victory J 7 + 3	Duff S 34	Caines G 26 + 13	McCann G 15	Melligan J 38 + 5	Finnigan J 40	Guinan S 17 + 2	Odejayi K 38 + 7	Armstrong C 42	Wilson B 22 + 3	Gillespie S 13 + 10	Vincent A — + 5	Wylde M 4 + 3	Yao S 2 + 13	Bell M 5 + 2	Connolly A 6 + 2	Lowe K 14 + 2	Elvins R — + 5	Spencer D 23 + 4	Brown S 10 + 1	Bird D 26 + 5	Townsend M 27 + 3	Smith A 2	O'Leary K 5	Reid C — + 6	Brown S 4	Connor P 9 + 6	Gallinagh A — + 1	Rosa D 3 + 1	*Match No.*
1	2	3	4[1]	5	6	7	8	9[2]	10[3]	11	12	13	14																		1
1	2	3	4	5	6	7[1]	8	9[3]	10[2]	11	13	14	12																		2
1	2[1]	3		5	6	7	8	9	10[2]	11	4	13	12																		3
1	2	4		5	6	7[1]	8	9[3]	10	3	11[2]		12	13	14																4
1	2[1]	4		5	6	7	8	9[2]	10	3	11	13[3]	12			14															5
1	2	4		5		7	8	9	10	11				12	13	3[2]	6[1]														6
1	2	12		5	6	7	8	9[2]	10	3	11[1]							4	13												7
1	2	12		5	6	7[1]	8	9	10[3]	3[2]	11				13			4	14												8
1	2			5	6		8	9[2]	10	3	11				7[1]			4	12	13											9
	2[2]			5	6	7[1]	8■	9[3]	10	3	11				12			4	13		1	14									10
	2			5	6	7[1]		9	10	3	11								12		1	8	4								11
	2			5	6	12		9[3]	10	3[1]	7			13		11		14			1	8	4[2]								12
	2			5		7[1]		9	10	6	11				12	3		4			1	8									13
	2[2]		4	5	6	7	8[3]	9[1]	10	3	11					13					1	12	14								14
1	2		4	5	6[1]	13	8	12	10[3]	3	11									9[2]		7	14								15
1	2		4[2]	5	6	12	8		13	11	14					3[3]		10		9		7[1]									16
1	2		5	12	6	7[2]			13	3	11							4[1]		9		8		10							17
1	2[1]		4	5		7		12	13	6	11			3						9		8		10[2]							18
1	2		4	5		7[1]			10	3	11				12					9		8			6						19
1	2[2]		4	5		12	8		10[1]	3	11									9		7	13		6						20
1		12	4	5		7	8[1]		10	3	2				13					9		11[2]			6						21
1		3[3]	4			7[1]	8	9[2]	10	11	2	13								14		12	5		6						22
1	12		4	13			8	9[3]	10	3[1]	2[2]	14								11		7	5		6						23
1			4	12		7[2]	8	9[3]	10		2	13			14	3[1]				11		6	5								24
1	2		4	5		7	8[1]		10		3				12		11			9■			6								25
1	2		4	5		7	8[1]		10		3				12		11			9			6								26
1			4	5		12	8		10	3		7[2]						2[1]				6	9			13	11				27
1	2		4	12		7[3]	8		13	3		9■										6	5			14	11[1]	10[2]			28
1	2		6	12		7	8		10					3[1]			4						5				11	9			29
1	2		5	12		7[2]	8		13	3					14					9[1]		4	6				11[3]	10			30
1	2		5	12		7[1]	8		9	3								13		11		4[2]	6					10			31
1				5		7[1]	8			4		9[2]		3[3]	12			2		11			6			13		10	14		32
1	2		5	12		7	8		9	3							10	4		11[1]			6								33
1	2		5			7[2]	8		9	3		12			13		14	4[3]		11			6					10[1]			34
1	2[1]		5				8		9	11		13			7[2]		6	4		10[3]		12	3					14			35
1			5	12		7	8[1]		9	3		13						2		11		4	6					10[2]			36
1			5	12		7	8		9[3]	3		10						2[1]		13		4	6					14		11[2]	37
1	2		5[1]	12		7	8		13	3		9										4	6					10[2]		11	38
1	2[1]		5	12		7	8		13	3		9								14		4	6					10[2]		11[3]	39
1	2		5			7	8		9	4		10[2]		3						11[1]		12	6					13			40
1[6]	2		5	12		7[1]	8		9	3		10[2]								11	15	4	6			13					41
	2		5			7[2]	8		9[1]	3		10[3]								11	1	4	6			14		12		13	42
	2		5			7	8		9	3		10[1]					12			11	1	4	6								43
	2		5			7	8		9	3		10								11[1]	1	4	6					12			44
	2		5	4		7	8		9	3		10									1	11	6								45
	2		5	4[2]		7	8		9[1]	3		10									1	11	6			13		12			46

FA Cup

First Round	Scunthorpe U	(h)	0-0
		(a)	0-2

J Paint Trophy

Second Round	Barnet	(h)	3-2
Quarter-Final	Shrewsbury T	(h)	2-3

Carling Cup

First Round	Bristol C	(h)	2-1
Second Round	WBA	(a)	1-3

CHESTER CITY FL Championship 2

FOUNDATION

All students of soccer history have read about the medieval games of football in Chester, but the present club was not formed until 1884 through the amalgamation of King's School Old Boys with Chester Rovers. For many years Chester were overshadowed in Cheshire by Northwich Victoria and Crewe Alexandra who had both won the Senior Cup several times before Chester's first success in 1894–95. The final against Macclesfield saw Chester face the team that had not only beaten them in the previous year's final, but also knocked them out of the FA Cup two seasons in succession. The final was held at the Drill Field, Northwich and Chester had the support of more than 1000 fans. Chester won 2-1.

Saunders Honda Stadium, Bumpers Lane, Chester CH1 4LT.

Telephone: (01244) 371 376.

Fax: (01244) 390 265.

Ticket Offfice: (01244) 371 376.

Website: www.chestercityfc.net

Email: info@chestercityfc.net

Ground Capacity: 6,012.

Record Attendance: 20,500 v Chelsea, FA Cup 3rd rd (replay), 16 January 1952 (at Sealand Road).

Pitch Measurements: 115yd × 75yd.

Chairman: Stephen Vaughan.

Secretary: Tony Allen.

Manager: Bobby Williamson.

Physio: Mark Leather and Ben Holt.

Colours: Blue and white striped shirts, blue shorts, blue stockings.

Change Colours: Yellow shirts, yellow shorts, yellow stockings.

Year Formed: 1885.

Turned Professional: 1902.

Ltd Co.: 1909.

Previous Name: Chester until 1983.

Club Nickname: 'Blues' and 'City'.

Grounds: 1885, Faulkner Street; 1898, The Old Showground; 1901, Whipcord Lane; 1906, Sealand Road; 1990, Moss Rose Ground, Macclesfield; 1992, Deva Stadium, Bumpers Lane.

First Football League Game: 2 September 1931, Division 3 (N), v Wrexham (a) D 1–1 – Johnson; Herod, Jones; Keeley, Skitt, Reilly; Thompson, Ranson, Jennings (1), Cresswell, Hedley.

HONOURS

Football League: Division 3 – Runners-up 1993–94; Division 3 (N) – Runners-up 1935–36; Division 4 – Runners-up 1985–86.

Conference: Champions 2003–04.

FA Cup: best season: 5th rd, 1977, 1980.

Football League Cup: Semi-final 1975.

Welsh Cup: Winners 1908, 1933, 1947.

Debenhams Cup: Winners 1977.

SKY SPORTS FACT FILE

When centre-forward Paddy Wrightson settled at Chester in 1935 for the next four seasons he doubled the time he had spent playing successfully for Darlington, Manchester City, Fulham and Exeter City in the previous seven seasons.

Record League Victory: 12–0 v York C, Division 3 (N), 1 February 1936 – Middleton; Common, Hall; Wharton, Wilson, Howarth; Horsman (2), Hughes, Wrightson (4), Cresswell (2), Sargeant (4).

Record Cup Victory: 6–1 v Darlington, FA Cup 1st rd, 25 November 1933 – Burke; Bennett, Little; Pitcairn, Skitt, Duckworth; Armes (3), Whittam, Mantle (2), Cresswell (1), McLachlan.

Record Defeat: 2–11 v Oldham Ath, Division 3 (N), 19 January 1952.

Most League Points (2 for a win): 56, Division 3 (N), 1946–47 and Division 4, 1964–65.

Most League Points (3 for a win): 84, Division 4, 1985–86.

Most League Goals: 119, Division 4, 1964–65.

Highest League Scorer in Season: Dick Yates, 36, Division 3 (N), 1946–47.

Most League Goals in Total Aggregate: Stuart Rimmer, 135, 1985–88, 1991–98.

Most League Goals in One Match: 5, Tom Jennings v Walsall, Division 3N, 30 January 1932; 5, Barry Jepson v York C, Division 4, 8 February 1958.

Most Capped Player: Angus Eve, 35 (117), Trinidad & Tobago.

Most League Appearances: Ray Gill, 406, 1951–62.

Youngest League Player: Aidan Newhouse, 15 years 350 days v Bury, 7 May 1988.

Record Transfer Fee Received: £300,000 from Liverpool for Ian Rush, May 1980.

Record Transfer Fee Paid: £100,000 to Doncaster R for Gregg Blundell, August 2005.

Football League Record: 1931 Elected Division 3 (N); 1958–75 Division 4; 1975–82 Division 3; 1982–86 Division 4; 1986–92 Division 3; 1992–93 Division 2; 1993–94 Division 3; 1994–95 Division 2; 1995–2000 Division 3; 2000–04 Conference; 2004– FL 2.

MANAGERS

Charlie Hewitt 1930–36
Alex Raisbeck 1936–38
Frank Brown 1938–53
Louis Page 1953–56
John Harris 1956–59
Stan Pearson 1959–61
Bill Lambton 1962–63
Peter Hauser 1963–68
Ken Roberts 1968–76
Alan Oakes 1976–82
Cliff Sear 1982
John Sainty 1982–83
John McGrath 1984
Mick Speight 1985
Harry McNally 1985–92
Graham Barrow 1992–94
Mike Pejic 1994–95
Derek Mann 1995
Kevin Ratcliffe 1995–99
Terry Smith 1999
Ian Atkins 2000
Graham Barrow 2000–01
Gordon Hill 2001
Steve Mungall 2001
Mark Wright 2002–04
Ian Rush 2004–05
Keith Curle 2005–06.
Mark Wright 2006–07
Bobby Williamson May 2007–

LATEST SEQUENCES

Longest Sequence of League Wins: 8, 12.4.1978 – 26.8.1978.

Longest Sequence of League Defeats: 9, 30.4.1994 – 13.9.1994.

Longest Sequence of League Draws: 6, 11.10.1986 – 1.11.1986.

Longest Sequence of Unbeaten League Matches: 18, 27.10.1934 – 16.2.1935.

Longest Sequence Without a League Win: 25, 19.9.1961 – 3.3.1962.

Successive Scoring Runs: 24 from 31.8.1932.

Successive Non-scoring Runs: 5, 17.11.1951.

TEN YEAR LEAGUE RECORD

		P	W	D	L	F	A	Pts	Pos
1997-98	Div 3	46	17	10	19	60	61	61	14
1998-99	Div 3	46	13	18	15	57	66	57	14
1999-2000	Div 3	46	10	9	27	44	79	39	24
2000-01	Conf.	42	16	14	12	49	43	62	8
2001-02	Conf.	42	15	9	18	54	51	54	14
2002-03	Conf.	42	21	12	9	59	31	75	4
2003-04	Conf.	42	27	11	4	85	34	92	1
2004-05	FL 2	46	12	16	18	43	69	52	20
2005-06	FL 2	46	14	12	20	53	59	54	15
2006-07	FL 2	46	13	14	19	40	48	53	18

DID YOU KNOW ?

On 14 January 1933, left-winger Foster Hedley scored four of the five Chester goals against Fulham in an FA Cup third round tie. A week later he hit a hat-trick in the 4–2 victory against Accrington Stanley in Division Three (North).

CHESTER CITY 2006–07 LEAGUE RECORD

Match No.	Date	Venue	Opponents	Result	H/T Score	Lg. Pos.	Goalscorers	Attendance
1	Aug 5	H	Accrington S	W 2-0	1-0	—	Broughton [15], Blundell (pen) [86]	3779
2	8	A	Bury	W 3-1	1-1	—	Woodthorpe (og) [36], Walters 2 [49, 90]	2719
3	12	A	Hereford U	L 0-2	0-0	7		3834
4	20	H	Wrexham	L 1-2	0-1	12	Hand [81]	4206
5	26	A	Torquay U	D 2-2	0-1	12	Broughton [55], Martinez [90]	2541
6	Sept 1	H	Swindon T	L 0-2	0-0	—		3382
7	9	A	Wycombe W	L 0-1	0-1	16		4277
8	12	H	Notts Co	D 0-0	0-0	—		1818
9	16	H	Grimsby T	L 0-2	0-0	19		1957
10	23	A	Milton Keynes D	W 2-1	0-1	15	Westwood [57], Walters [88]	5476
11	26	A	Macclesfield T	D 1-1	0-1	—	Sandwith [61]	2022
12	30	H	Bristol R	W 2-0	2-0	14	Sandwith [18], Martinez [37]	2151
13	Oct 6	H	Walsall	D 0-0	0-0	—		3241
14	14	A	Rochdale	D 0-0	0-0	13		3149
15	20	H	Hartlepool U	W 2-1	1-1	—	Westwood [45], Walters [52]	2580
16	28	A	Barnet	L 0-1	0-1	16		2301
17	Nov 3	A	Darlington	L 0-1	0-1	—		3630
18	17	H	Stockport Co	D 1-1	0-1	—	Walters [59]	3624
19	25	A	Shrewsbury T	L 1-2	1-0	16	Blundell [8]	4464
20	Dec 5	H	Boston U	W 3-1	0-0	—	Blundell 2 (1 pen) [50, 65 (p)], Walters [72]	1527
21	9	H	Lincoln C	W 4-1	1-0	14	Martinez [20], Walters [54], Blundell [76], Wilson [82]	2142
22	16	A	Peterborough U	W 2-0	2-0	10	Walters [9], Arber (og) [40]	4491
23	26	H	Macclesfield T	L 0-3	0-1	14		3365
24	30	H	Milton Keynes D	L 0-3	0-0	15		2271
25	Jan 1	A	Notts Co	W 2-1	1-1	15	Walters [34], Westwood [79]	4019
26	9	A	Grimsby T	W 2-0	0-0	—	Artell [53], Blundell [72]	3012
27	13	H	Wycombe W	L 0-1	0-0	14		2336
28	20	A	Bristol R	D 0-0	0-0	12		5694
29	27	H	Mansfield T	D 1-1	0-1	11	Steele [62]	2129
30	Feb 3	A	Accrington S	W 1-0	1-0	10	Linwood [23]	1900
31	18	A	Wrexham	D 0-0	0-0	12		6801
32	21	H	Bury	W 1-0	0-0	—	Yeo (pen) [90]	1642
33	24	A	Swindon T	L 0-1	0-1	13		5462
34	27	H	Hereford U	D 1-1	0-0	—	Yeo [71]	1842
35	Mar 2	H	Torquay U	D 1-1	0-0	—	Bennett [53]	1996
36	6	A	Mansfield T	L 1-2	1-1	—	Maylett [9]	2366
37	10	A	Walsall	L 0-1	0-0	14		5282
38	16	H	Rochdale	L 0-1	0-1	—		2197
39	24	H	Barnet	W 2-0	1-0	13	Bolland [45], Hand [58]	1591
40	30	A	Hartlepool U	L 0-3	0-2	—		6059
41	Apr 6	H	Darlington	D 1-1	0-0	—	Yeo [51]	1942
42	9	A	Stockport Co	L 0-2	0-1	16		5719
43	15	H	Shrewsbury T	D 0-0	0-0	17		3266
44	21	A	Boston U	L 0-1	0-0	17		1752
45	28	H	Peterborough U	D 1-1	1-0	18	Yeo [13]	1905
46	May 5	A	Lincoln C	L 0-2	0-0	18		5267

Final League Position: 18

GOALSCORERS

League (40): Walters 9, Blundell 6 (2 pens), Yeo 4 (1 pen), Martinez 3, Westwood 3, Broughton 2, Hand 2, Sandwith 2, Artell 1, Bennett 1, Bolland 1, Linwood 1, Maylett 1, Steele 1, Wilson 1, own goals 2.
Carling Cup (0).
FA Cup (7): Steele 2, Wilson 2, Blundell 1, Hand 1, Walters 1.
J Paint Trophy (7): Blundell 2, Wilson 2, Bolland 1, Hand 1, Linwood 1.

Danby J 46	Vaughan S 20	Wilson L 34 + 7	Linwood P 33 + 4	Westwood A 21	Artell D 42 + 1	Bennett D 27 + 5	Martinez R 31	Broughton D 9 + 5	Walters J 24 + 2	Hand J 43	Marples S 24 + 6	McSporran J — + 1	Blundell G 21 + 6	Ravenhill R 1 + 2	Holroyd C 7 + 15	Hessey S 22 + 4	Sandwith K 27 + 5	Allen G 2 + 1	Bolland P 23 + 3	Steele L 11 + 9	Semple R — + 3	Rutherford P 6 + 3	Meechan A 2 + 6	Yeo S 14 + 1	Kearney A 4 + 2	Brownlie R 3 + 1	Maylett B 3 + 2	Cronin G 1 + 3	Vaughan J 5 + 1	Kelly S — + 2	*Match No.*
1	2^1	3	4	5	6	7	8^2	9^3	10	11	12	13	14																		1
1	2^1	3	4	5	6	7	8^2	9	10	11	12			13																	2
1	2^1	3	4	5	6	7^3	8	9^2	10	11	12		13	14																	3
1	2	3	4	5^2	6		8	12	10^1	11	13		9^3	7■	14																4
1	2	3^2	4		6	7^1	8	12	10	11			9		13	5															5
1	2	3	4		6		8	9^1	10	11			12		13	5	7^2														6
1	2	3	4	5	6^2		8	9^1	10^3	11	14		12		13		7														7
1	2	3	4	5	6		8	9		11	7		10^1		12																8
1	2	3	4	5	6		8	9^1		11	7^2		10		12		13														9
1	2^3	3	4	5	6	12	8	9	13	11	14		10^2				7^1														10
1	2	3		5	6		8	9^1	12	11	4		10				7														11
1	2	3		5^2	6		8	12	9^1	11	4		10				7	13													12
1	2^1	3			6	10	8	12	9	11	4						7	5													13
1		3^2		5^3	6	7	8	12	9	11	2		10^1			13	4		14												14
1		3^1	12	5	6	7	8		9	11	2		10				4														15
1	2^3	3	12	5	6^1	7	8■		9		4		10		13		11^2		14												16
1		3		5■	6	7^2	8		9^1	11	2		12				13		4	10											17
1	2^1	3			6	12	8		9	11	4		13				7		5	10^2											18
1	2	12	4		6	3			9	11	8^2		10^3			13	7^1		5		14										19
1	2^2	3		5	6	12	8		9	11	4		10^1				7				13										20
1	2	3	12		6		8		9	11	4^1		10				7		5												21
1	2	3	4	5^1	12		8		9	11			10^3			7^2	13		6	14											22
1	2	3■	4	5			8		9	11			10^1			7^2			6	12	13										23
1			4■	5^1	6	7^2	8		9	11	2		10			3			12	13											24
1		3		5^1	6	12	8		9	11	2		10^2			7			4	13											25
1		3	4	5	6	7^1	8		9^2	11	2		10			12				13											26
1		3	12	5^1	6	7^2	8		9	11	2		10^3				13		4	14											27
1		2	4		6		8		9	11			10			3	7		5												28
1		3^1				7^2	8			11	2		10		13	6	12	4	5	9^3		14									29
1			4		6	7	8			11					12	2	3		5	9^2			13	10^1							30
1			4		6	3	8				2				12	7^3	11		5	9^2			13	10^1	14						31
1		12	4		6	3^1	8				2						11		5	9^2			13	10	7						32
1		12	4		6	3^1				11	2^2				14	13	7		5				9^3	10	8						33
1		12	4		6					11					13	2	3		5	9^2			8^1	10	7						34
1		12	4		6^1	3				11						2	7		5					10^2	8	9	13				35
1		3	4			8				11	2					6	7		5	12			13			9^1	10^2				36
1		3	4		6	7^3				11	2				10				5	9^2					12	13	8^1	14			37
1		3	4		6					11	2				12	7			5	13				10		9^2	8^1				38
1		3	4		6	12				11					9	7			5			8^2		10			13		2^1		39
1		2	4		6	3				11					9	8	7		5■			12		10^1							40
1		12	4		6	2				11					9^2	5	7			13		8		10^1					3		41
1		3^3	4		6	8				11					12	2^2	7		5	9^1		14		10					13		42
1			4^2		6	3				11					9	5	7					8	12	10^1					2	13	43
1		12	4		6	3				11					9^1	5	7■					8^3		10				14	2^2	13	44
1		3	4		6					11					12	2			5	9^1		8^2	13	10				7			45
1			4		6	2^2				11					9^1	3	7			10		8		12				13	5		46

FA Cup

First Round	Clevedon T	(a)	4-1
Second Round	Bury	(a)	2-2
		(h)	1-3
Third Round	Ipswich T	(h)	0-0
		(a)	0-1

Carling Cup

First Round	Leeds U	(a)	0-1

J Paint Trophy

Second Round	Stockport Co	(h)	3-0
Quarter-Final	Chesterfield	(a)	4-4

CHESTERFIELD FL Championship 2

FOUNDATION

Chesterfield are fourth only to Stoke, Notts County and Nottingham Forest in age for they can trace their existence as far back as 1866, although it is fair to say that they were somewhat casual in the first few years of their history playing only a few friendlies a year. However, their rules of 1871 are still in existence showing an annual membership of 2s (10p), but it was not until 1891 that they won a trophy (the Barnes Cup) and followed this a year later by winning the Sheffield Cup, Barnes Cup and the Derbyshire Junior Cup.

The Recreation Ground, Saltergate, Chesterfield, Derbyshire S40 4SX.

Telephone: (01246) 209 765.

Fax: (01246) 556 799.

Ticket Office: (01246) 209 765.

Website: www.chesterfield-fc.co.uk

Email: reception@chesterfield-fc.co.uk

Ground Capacity: 8,502.

Record Attendance: 30,968 v Newcastle U, Division 2, 7 April 1939.

Pitch Measurements: 111yd × 71yd.

Chairman: Barrie Hubbard.

Vice-chairman: Jason Elliott.

Chief Executive/Managing Director: Mike Warner.

Secretary: Alan Walters.

Manager: Lee Richardson.

Assistant Manager: Alan Knill.

Physio: Jamie Hewitt.

Colours: Royal blue shirts, white shorts, royal blue stockings.

Change Colours: Sky blue and white shirts, black shorts, black stockings.

Year Formed: 1866.

Turned Professional: 1891.

Ltd Co: 1871.

Previous Name: Chesterfield Town.

Club Nicknames: 'Blues' or 'Spireites'.

Grounds: 1867, Drill Field; 1871, Recreation Ground.

First Football League Game: 2 September 1899, Division 2, v Sheffield W (a) L 1–5 – Hancock; Pilgrim, Fletcher; Ballantyne, Bell, Downie; Morley, Thacker, Gooing, Munday (1), Geary.

Record League Victory: 10–0 v Glossop NE, Division 2, 17 January 1903 – Clutterbuck; Thorpe, Lerper; Haig, Banner, Thacker; Tomlinson (2), Newton (1), Milward (3), Munday (2), Steel (2).

Record Cup Victory: 5–0 v Wath Ath (a), FA Cup 1st rd, 28 November 1925 – Birch; Saxby, Dennis; Wass, Abbott, Thompson; Fisher (1), Roseboom (1), Cookson (2), Whitfield (1), Hopkinson.

HONOURS

Football League: Division 2 best season: 4th, 1946–47; Division 3 (N) – Champions 1930–31, 1935–36; Runners-up 1933–34; Promoted to Division 2 (3rd) – 2000–01; Division 4 – Champions 1969–70, 1984–85.

FA Cup: Semi-final 1997.

Football League Cup: best season: 4th rd, 1965, 2007.

Anglo-Scottish Cup: Winners 1981.

SKY SPORTS FACT FILE

Johannesburg born of Irish parents, centre-forward Dudley Milligan was the second fully capped Chesterfield player. He made a scoring debut for Northern Ireland against Wales on 15 March 1939, but had previously played three times for South Africa.

Record Defeat: 0–10 v Gillingham, Division 3, 5 September 1987.

Most League Points (2 for a win): 64, Division 4, 1969–70.

Most League Points (3 for a win): 91, Division 4, 1984–85.

Most League Goals: 102, Division 3 (N), 1930–31.

Highest League Scorer in Season: Jimmy Cookson, 44, Division 3 (N), 1925–26.

Most League Goals in Total Aggregate: Ernie Moss, 161, 1969–76, 1979–81 and 1984–86.

Most League Goals in One Match: 4, Jimmy Cookson v Accrington S, Division 3N, 16 January 1926; 4, Jimmy Cookson v Ashington, Division 3N, 1 May 1926; 4, Jimmy Cookson v Wigan Borough, Division 3N, 4 September 1926; 4, Tommy Lyon v Southampton, Division 2, 3 December 1938.

Most Capped Player: Walter McMillen, 4 (7), Northern Ireland; Mark Williams, 4 (30), Northern Ireland.

Most League Appearances: Dave Blakey, 613, 1948–67.

Youngest League Player: Dennis Thompson, 16 years 160 days v Notts Co, 26 December 1950.

Record Transfer Fee Received: £750,000 from Southampton for Kevin Davies, May 1997.

Record Transfer Fee Paid: £250,000 to Watford for Jason Lee, August 1998.

Football League Record: 1899 Elected to Division 2; 1909 failed re-election; 1921–31 Division 3 (N); 1931–33 Division 2; 1933–36 Division 3 (N); 1936–51 Division 2; 1951–58 Division 3 (N); 1958–61 Division 3; 1961–70 Division 4; 1970–83 Division 3; 1983–85 Division 4; 1985–89 Division 3; 1989–92 Division 4; 1992–95 Division 3; 1995–2000 Division 2; 2000–01 Division 3; 2001–04 Division 2; 2004–07 FL 1; 2007– FL 2.

MANAGERS

E. Russell Timmeus 1891–95
(Secretary-Manager)
Gilbert Gillies 1895–1901
E. F. Hind 1901–02
Jack Hoskin 1902–06
W. Furness 1906–07
George Swift 1907–10
G. H. Jones 1911–13
R. L. Weston 1913–17
T. Callaghan 1919
J. J. Caffrey 1920–22
Harry Hadley 1922
Harry Parkes 1922–27
Alec Campbell 1927
Ted Davison 1927–32
Bill Harvey 1932–38
Norman Bullock 1938–45
Bob Brocklebank 1945–48
Bobby Marshall 1948–52
Ted Davison 1952–58
Duggie Livingstone 1958–62
Tony McShane 1962–67
Jimmy McGuigan 1967–73
Joe Shaw 1973–76
Arthur Cox 1976–80
Frank Barlow 1980–83
John Duncan 1983–87
Kevin Randall 1987–88
Paul Hart 1988–91
Chris McMenemy 1991–93
John Duncan 1993–2000
Nicky Law 2000–02
Dave Rushbury 2002–03
Roy McFarland 2003–07
Lee Richardson April 2007–

LATEST SEQUENCES

Longest Sequence of League Wins: 10, 6.9.1933 – 4.11.1933.

Longest Sequence of League Defeats: 9, 22.10.1960 – 27.12.1960.

Longest Sequence of League Draws: 8, 26.11.2005 – 2.1.2006.

Longest Sequence of Unbeaten League Matches: 21, 26.12.1994 – 29.4.1995.

Longest Sequence Without a League Win: 18, 11.9.1999 – 3.1.2000.

Successive Scoring Runs: 46 from 25.12.1929.

Successive Non-scoring Runs: 7 from 23.9.1977.

TEN YEAR LEAGUE RECORD

		P	W	D	L	F	A	Pts	Pos
1997-98	Div 2	46	16	17	13	46	44	65	10
1998-99	Div 2	46	17	13	16	46	44	64	9
1999-2000	Div 2	46	7	15	24	34	63	36	24
2000-01	Div 3	46	25	14	7	79	42	80*	3
2001-02	Div 2	46	13	13	20	53	65	52	18
2002-03	Div 2	46	14	8	24	43	73	50	20
2003-04	Div 2	46	12	15	19	49	71	51	20
2004-05	FL 1	46	14	15	17	55	62	57	17
2005-06	FL 1	46	14	14	18	63	73	56	16
2006-07	FL 1	46	12	11	23	45	53	47	21

**9 pts deducted.*

DID YOU KNOW ?

Having disposed of Championship team Wolverhampton Wanderers and Premier League Manchester City, Chesterfield complete a Carling Cup hat-trick of giant-killing acts by beating Premier side West Ham United 2–1 in the third round on 24 October 2006.

CHESTERFIELD 2006–07 LEAGUE RECORD

Match No.	*Date*	*Venue*	*Opponents*	*Result*		*H/T Score*	*Lg. Pos.*	*Goalscorers*	*Atten-dance*
1	Aug 5	A	Bournemouth	W	3-0	0-0	—	Niven [47], Larkin [62], Shaw [90]	5499
2	9	H	Carlisle U	D	0-0	0-0	—		4525
3	12	H	Millwall	W	5-1	3-0	3	Hall 2 [13, 51], Allison 2 [24, 65], Folan [32]	4136
4	19	A	Port Vale	L	2-3	1-1	5	Downes [23], Folan [85]	5622
5	26	H	Tranmere R	L	0-2	0-1	10		4163
6	Sept 2	A	Nottingham F	L	0-4	0-2	15		19,480
7	9	H	Rotherham U	W	2-1	2-1	10	Folan [8], Shaw [28]	4803
8	12	A	Blackpool	D	1-1	0-1	—	Hurst [60]	4600
9	16	A	Bristol C	L	1-3	1-2	17	Larkin [21]	10,398
10	23	H	Brentford	W	3-1	3-1	9	Folan 2 [30, 40], Shaw [37]	3877
11	27	H	Scunthorpe U	L	0-1	0-1	—		4849
12	30	A	Brighton & HA	W	2-1	1-0	11	Folan [20], Niven [74]	5499
13	Oct 7	A	Leyton Orient	D	0-0	0-0	11		4309
14	14	H	Swansea C	L	2-3	0-2	13	Hall [47], Hazell [77]	3915
15	21	A	Doncaster R	L	0-1	0-1	15		6280
16	28	H	Yeovil T	D	1-1	0-0	17	O'Hare [50]	5413
17	Nov 4	A	Gillingham	L	1-2	1-0	18	Hughes [39]	5856
18	18	H	Cheltenham T	W	1-0	0-0	16	O'Hare [48]	3488
19	25	A	Crewe Alex	D	2-2	0-0	16	Niven [85], Hurst [90]	5078
20	Dec 6	H	Northampton T	D	0-0	0-0	—		3341
21	9	H	Oldham Ath	W	2-1	2-1	13	Larkin 2 [14, 33]	4059
22	16	A	Bradford C	L	0-1	0-0	16		7228
23	23	H	Huddersfield T	D	0-0	0-0	16		4472
24	26	A	Scunthorpe U	L	0-1	0-0	15		6123
25	30	A	Brentford	L	1-2	0-1	16	Hazell [79]	4540
26	Jan 1	H	Blackpool	W	2-0	2-0	13	Hurst [13], Folan [42]	4351
27	13	A	Rotherham U	W	1-0	1-0	13	Folan [33]	5188
28	20	H	Brighton & HA	L	0-1	0-0	16		3984
29	27	A	Huddersfield T	D	1-1	1-0	15	Holmes [23]	9872
30	Feb 3	H	Bournemouth	L	0-1	0-0	18		3854
31	10	A	Millwall	L	1-2	0-1	18	Hall [58]	9711
32	17	H	Port Vale	W	3-0	1-0	17	Picken [38], Ward [79], Allison [90]	3752
33	20	A	Carlisle U	D	0-0	0-0	—		6196
34	24	H	Nottingham F	L	1-2	0-0	19	Downes [67]	6641
35	Mar 2	A	Tranmere R	L	0-2	0-1	—		6254
36	7	H	Bristol C	L	1-3	0-3	—	Allison [59]	3471
37	10	H	Leyton Orient	L	0-1	0-0	20		3665
38	16	A	Swansea C	L	0-2	0-0	—		11,384
39	21	H	Doncaster R	D	1-1	1-1	—	Hall (pen) [41]	3868
40	24	A	Yeovil T	L	0-1	0-0	21		4735
41	Apr 7	H	Crewe Alex	W	2-1	1-1	21	Downes [29], Shaw [67]	3698
42	9	A	Cheltenham T	D	0-0	0-0	21		5089
43	14	H	Gillingham	L	0-1	0-0	22		3867
44	21	A	Northampton T	L	0-1	0-0	22		5730
45	28	H	Bradford C	W	3-0	2-0	21	Ward 2 [15, 28], Bower (og) [60]	5207
46	May 5	A	Oldham Ath	L	0-1	0-0	21		8148

Final League Position: 21

GOALSCORERS

League (45): Folan 8, Hall 5 (1 pen), Allison 4, Larkin 4, Shaw 4, Downes 3, Hurst 3, Niven 3, Ward 3, Hazell 2, O'Hare 2, Holmes 1, Hughes 1, Picken 1, own goal 1.
Carling Cup (7): Folan 3, Larkin 2, Allison 1, Niven 1.
FA Cup (0).
J Paint Trophy (7): Downes 2, Folan 1, Hall 1, Niven 1, Shaw 1, Smith 1.

Roche B 40	Picken P 38 + 1	O'Hare A 16 + 1	Hazell R 39	Downes A 45	Niven D 45	Hall P 40 + 6	Allott M 39	Shaw P 23 + 7	Larkin C 27 + 12	Hurst K 25	Folan C 19 + 4	Allison W 13 + 23	Bailey A 25 + 5	Jackson J 1 + 13	Smith A 5 + 8	Nicholson S — + 2	Kovacs J 5 + 2	Lowry J 6 + 2	Hughes M 2	Davies G 6 + 8	Jordan M 6	Holmes P 10	Critchell K 6 + 4	Grimaldi S 8	Ward J 8 + 1	Meredith J 1	Daniels C 2	Boertien P 4	Rizzo N 2 + 2	*Match No.*
1	2	3	4	5	6	7	8	9	10^{1}	11	12																			1
1	2	3	4	5	6	7	8	9^{2}	10	11^{1}	12	13																		2
1	2	3	4	5	6	7	8			11^{1}	9	10^{2}	13	12																3
1	2	3	4	5	6	7	8		12	11	9	10^{1}																		4
1	2	3	4	5	6	7^{3}	8	9^{1}	10^{2}	11	12	13	14																	5
1	2	3	4	5	6	7	8		10	11^{1}	9				12															6
1	2	3	4	5	6	7	8	9^{1}	13	11^{3}	10^{2}	12			14															7
1	2	3^{2}	4	5	6	7	8	9^{1}	12	11	10					13														8
1	2		4	5	6	7	8		9^{2}	11	12	10^{1}	3		13															9
1	2		4	5	6	7	8	9^{2}	13^{3}	11	10^{1}	12	3				14													10
1	2		4	5	6	7^{2}	8		10^{1}	11	9	12	3	13																11
1	2	12	4	5	6	7	8			11^{2}	9■	10^{1}	3		13															12
1		3	4	5	6	7	8		9	11^{1}		10	2		12															13
1	2		4	5	6	7	8		9^{1}	11^{2}		10	3	13	12															14
1	2	3	4	5	6	7^{1}	8		12		9	13	11^{2}	14	10^{3}															15
1		2	4	5	6	7	8		10^{1}	11	9	12						3												16
1		3	4	5	6	7			10^{2}	11	9^{1}	12				13		2	8											17
1	12	3	4	5	6	7	8	10^{1}		11	9		2																	18
1		3	4	5	6	7	8	9^{2}	10^{1}	11		12	2	13																19
1	3		4	5	6	7	8	10^{2}	12	11	9^{1}	13	2																	20
1	3		4	5	6	7	8	9	10	11			2																	21
1	3		4	5	6	7		9^{3}	10^{2}	11		12	2	13			14		8^{1}											22
1	3		4	5	6	7	8	9^{1}		11	10	12	2																	23
1	3			5	6	7	8	12	10^{1}	11^{2}	9	13	2				4													24
1	3		4	5	6	7^{3}	8	10^{1}		11	9	12	2^{2}		13					14										25
1	2		4	5	6	12	8			11	9	10			7^{1}					3										26
	2		4	5	6	12	8	10			9				7^{1}					3	1	11								27
	2		4	5	6^{3}	12	8	10^{2}	13		9				11					3^{1}	1	7	14							28
	3		4	5	6	7^{3}	8■	10^{2}	12			13			11^{1}					14	1	9	2							29
	2			5	6	7		9^{1}	10^{2}			12			13		4				1	11	8	3^{3}	14					30
	2		4		6	12	8	9^{2}	10^{1}			13								14	1	7	3^{3}	5	11					31
1	3			5	6	7	8		12			10	2							13		11^{2}		4	9^{1}					32
1	3			5	6	7	8		9^{2}			10	2							12		11^{1}	13	4						33
1	3^{1}			5	6	7	8	12	9			10	2	13								11^{2}		4						34
1	3			5		7	8	9	10^{1}			12	2	13								6^{2}		4		11				35
1	2^{1}			5	6	7	8		9^{3}			10	12	14						13		11^{2}	3	4						36
1			4	5	6	12	8	13	14			10^{1}	2^{2}	9						7				3^{3}			11			37
1	2		4	5	6	7	8	13	9				3	14						12^{2}			11^{3}				10^{1}			38
1	3		4	5	6	7	8	9^{1}	10			12	11^{3}	14				2^{2}					13							39
1	3		4	5	6	7	8^{3}	9^{1}	10			12	13					14					2					11^{2}		40
1			4	5	6	7		12	9^{1}				2					13		8^{3}			14		10			11	3^{2}	41
1			4	5	6	7^{3}		9^{2}	12			13	11				2			8					10^{1}			3	14	42
	2^{1}		4	5	6	7		12	9^{2}			13	14				8				1				10			3	11^{3}	43
1	2		4	5	6	12		9^{1}	10			13	3				11^{2}	7							8^{3}				14	44
1	2	3^{2}	4	5	6	7	8		12			10		13				11							9^{1}					45
1	2	3	4	5	6^{2}	7^{1}	8	12	9^{3}					14				11		13					10					46

FA Cup

First Round	Basingstoke T	(h)	0-1

Carling Cup

First Round	Wolverhampton W	(h)	0-0
Second Round	Manchester C	(h)	2-1
Third Round	West Ham U	(h)	2-1
Fourth Round	Charlton Ath	(h)	3-3

J Paint Trophy

Second Round	Oldham Ath	(a)	1-0
Quarter-Final	Chester C	(h)	4-4
Semi-Final	Crewe Alex	(h)	2-4

COLCHESTER UNITED FL Championship

FOUNDATION

Colchester United was formed in 1937 when a number of enthusiasts of the much older Colchester Town club decided to establish a professional concern as a limited liability company. The new club continued at Layer Road which had been the amateur club's home since 1909.

Layer Road, Colchester, Essex CO2 7JJ.

Telephone: 0871 226 2161.

Fax: (01206) 715 327.

Ticket Office: 0871 226 2161.

Website: www.cu-fc.com

Email: caroline@colchesterunited.net

Ground Capacity: 6,300.

Record Attendance: 19,072 v Reading, FA Cup 1st rd, 27 November 1948.

Pitch Measurements: 111yd × 71yd.

Chief Executive: Mrs Marie Partner.

Secretary: Miss Caroline Pugh.

Manager: Geraint Williams.

Assistant Manager: Micky Adams.

Physio: Tony Flynn.

Colours: Blue and white striped shirts, royal blue shorts, white with blue hoop stockings.

Change Colours: White with navy trim shirts, navy with white trim shorts, navy stockings.

Year Formed: 1937.

Turned Professional: 1937.

Ltd Co.: 1937.

Club Nickname: 'The U's'.

Grounds: 1937, Layer Road.

First Football League Game: 19 August 1950, Division 3 (S), v Gillingham (a) D 0–0 – Wright; Kettle, Allen; Bearryman, Stewart, Elder; Jones, Curry, Turner, McKim, Church.

Record League Victory: 9–1 v Bradford C, Division 4, 30 December 1961 – Ames; Millar, Fowler; Harris, Abrey, Ron Hunt; Foster, Bobby Hunt (4), King (4), Hill (1), Wright.

Record Cup Victory: 9-1 v Leamington, FA Cup 1st rd, 5 November 2005 – Davison; Stockley (Garcia), Duguid, Brown (1), Chilvers, Watson (1), Halford (1), Izzet (Danns) (2), Iwelumo (1) (Williams), Cureton (2), Yeates (1).

HONOURS

Football League: Promoted from Division 3 – 1997–98 (play-offs); Division 4 – Runners-up 1961–62; FL 1 – Runners-up 2005–06.

FA Cup: best season: 6th rd, 1971.

Football League Cup: best season: 5th rd, 1975.

Auto Windscreens Shield: Runners-up 1997.

GM Vauxhall Conference: Winners 1991–92.

FA Trophy: Winners 1992.

SKY SPORTS FACT FILE

In 1956–57 Colchester United full-back George Fisher was a busy man. Weekdays he caught the 8.17 am train from Ilford to Colchester for training. Evenings he coached under the LCC in the Stepney area. And he missed only three first team games.

Record Defeat: 0–8 v Leyton Orient, Division 4, 15 October 1989.

Most League Points (2 for a win): 60, Division 4, 1973–74.

Most League Points (3 for a win): 81, Division 4, 1982–83.

Most League Goals: 104, Division 4, 1961–62.

Highest League Scorer in Season: Bobby Hunt, 38, Division 4, 1961–62.

Most League Goals in Total Aggregate: Martyn King, 130, 1956–64.

Most League Goals in One Match: 4, Bobby Hunt v Bradford C, Division 4, 30 December 1961; 4, Martyn King v Bradford C, Division 4, 30 December 1961; 4, Bobby Hunt v Doncaster R, Division 4, 30 April 1962.

Most Capped Player: None.

Most League Appearances: Micky Cook, 613, 1969–84.

Youngest League Player: Lindsay Smith, 16 years 218 days v Grimsby T, 24 April 1971.

Record Transfer Fee Received: £2,250,000 from Newcastle U for Lomano Tresor Lua-Lua, September 2000.

Record Transfer Fee Paid: £300,000 to Milton Keynes Dons for Clive Platt, July 2007.

MANAGERS

Ted Fenton 1946–48
Jimmy Allen 1948–53
Jack Butler 1953–55
Benny Fenton 1955–63
Neil Franklin 1963–68
Dick Graham 1968–72
Jim Smith 1972–75
Bobby Roberts 1975–82
Allan Hunter 1982–83
Cyril Lea 1983–86
Mike Walker 1986–87
Roger Brown 1987–88
Jock Wallace 1989
Mick Mills 1990
Ian Atkins 1990–91
Roy McDonough 1991–94
George Burley 1994
Steve Wignall 1995–99
Mick Wadsworth 1999
Steve Whitton 1999–2003
Phil Parkinson 2003–06
Geraint Williams July 2006–

Football League Record: 1950 Elected to Division 3 (S); 1958–61 Division 3; 1961–62 Division 4; 1962–65 Division 3; 1965–66 Division 4; 1966–68 Division 3; 1968–74 Division 4; 1974–76 Division 3, 1976–77 Division 4; 1977–81 Division 3; 1981–90 Division 4; 1990–92 GM Vauxhall Conference; 1992–98 Division 3; 1998–04 Division 2; 2004–06 FL 1; 2006– FL C.

LATEST SEQUENCES

Longest Sequence of League Wins: 7, 29.11.1968 – 1.2.1969.

Longest Sequence of League Defeats: 8, 9.10.1954 – 4.12.1954.

Longest Sequence of League Draws: 6, 21.3.1977 – 11.4.1977.

Longest Sequence of Unbeaten League Matches: 20, 22.12.1956 – 19.4.1957.

Longest Sequence Without a League Win: 20, 2.3.1968 – 31.8.1968.

Successive Scoring Runs: 24 from 15.9.1962.

Successive Non-scoring Runs: 5 from 7.4.1981.

TEN YEAR LEAGUE RECORD

		P	*W*	*D*	*L*	*F*	*A*	*Pts*	*Pos*
1997-98	Div 3	46	21	11	14	72	60	74	4
1998-99	Div 2	46	12	16	18	52	70	52	18
1999-2000	Div 2	46	14	10	22	59	82	52	18
2000-01	Div 2	46	15	12	19	55	59	57	17
2001-02	Div 2	46	15	12	19	65	76	57	15
2002-03	Div 2	46	14	16	16	52	56	58	12
2003-04	Div 2	46	17	13	16	52	56	64	11
2004-05	FL 1	46	14	17	15	60	50	59	15
2005-06	FL 1	46	22	13	11	58	40	79	2
2006-07	FL C	46	20	9	17	70	56	69	10

DID YOU KNOW ?

On 21 April 2007, Colchester United entertained Sunderland at Layer Road, the visitors having had a run of 17 League games undefeated. United won 3–1 to reverse the scoreline sustained in their loss at the Stadium of Light earlier in the term.

COLCHESTER UNITED 2006–07 LEAGUE RECORD

Match No.	*Date*	*Venue*	*Opponents*	*Result*		*H/T Score*	*Lg. Pos.*	*Goalscorers*	*Atten-dance*
1	Aug 5	A	Birmingham C	L	1-2	0-1	—	Garcia [51]	24,238
2	8	H	Plymouth Arg	L	0-1	0-1	—		4627
3	12	H	Barnsley	L	1-2	1-0	22	Halford [42]	4249
4	19	A	WBA	L	1-2	0-2	23	Guy [83]	17,509
5	26	H	Derby Co	W	4-3	2-1	22	Cureton 3 [28, 30, 67], Iwelumo (pen) [49]	4574
6	Sept 9	A	Burnley	W	2-1	1-0	20	Watson [26], Iwelumo (pen) [54]	10,039
7	12	A	Luton T	D	1-1	1-1	—	Cureton [40]	7609
8	16	H	QPR	W	2-1	2-0	16	Iwelumo [9], Garcia [18]	5246
9	23	A	Leicester C	D	0-0	0-0	15		22,449
10	29	H	Ipswich T	W	1-0	1-0	—	Duguid [9]	6065
11	Oct 14	A	Wolverhampton W	L	0-1	0-0	13		19,318
12	18	H	Sheffield W	W	4-0	1-0	—	Cureton [28], Halford [56], Iwelumo [61], Duguid [83]	5097
13	23	A	Coventry C	L	1-2	0-1	—	Guy [85]	16,178
14	28	H	Southampton	W	2-0	1-0	10	McLeod [3], Cureton [90]	5893
15	31	A	Norwich C	D	1-1	0-0	—	Cureton [53]	25,065
16	Nov 4	H	Cardiff C	W	3-1	0-0	9	McLeod [49], Guy [84], Cureton (pen) [90]	5393
17	11	A	Leeds U	L	0-3	0-1	11		17,678
18	18	A	Sunderland	L	1-3	0-1	14	Iwelumo [79]	25,197
19	25	H	Southend U	W	3-0	0-0	11	Halford [68], Baldwin [74], Cureton [85]	5954
20	28	H	Hull C	W	5-1	1-1	—	Iwelumo 4 (1 pen) [19, 54 (p), 66, 79], Cureton [57]	5373
21	Dec 2	A	Cardiff C	D	0-0	0-0	10		13,512
22	9	A	Crystal Palace	W	3-1	0-0	8	Duguid [63], Garcia [70], Iwelumo (pen) [90]	16,762
23	16	H	Stoke C	W	3-0	2-0	6	Cureton 2 [2, 17], Garcia [63]	5345
24	23	A	Preston NE	L	0-1	0-1	8		14,225
25	26	H	Luton T	W	4-1	2-0	7	McLeod [23], Iwelumo 2 [41, 65], Garcia [59]	5427
26	30	H	Wolverhampton W	W	2-1	2-0	6	Cureton [4], Iwelumo [45]	5893
27	Jan 1	A	QPR	L	0-1	0-1	6		11,319
28	13	H	Leicester C	D	1-1	0-1	6	Iwelumo (pen) [48]	5915
29	20	A	Ipswich T	L	2-3	1-1	8	Duguid [15], Iwelumo (pen) [90]	28,355
30	30	H	Preston NE	W	1-0	0-0	—	Richards [67]	5085
31	Feb 3	H	Birmingham C	D	1-1	0-0	9	Izzet [55]	5918
32	10	A	Barnsley	W	3-0	2-0	8	Duguid [3], Cureton [10], Ephraim [83]	11,192
33	13	H	WBA	L	1-2	0-0	—	Jackson [55]	5611
34	20	A	Plymouth Arg	L	0-3	0-1	—		12,895
35	24	H	Burnley	D	0-0	0-0	10		4934
36	Mar 2	A	Derby Co	L	1-5	0-3	—	Jackson [56]	26,704
37	10	H	Coventry C	D	0-0	0-0	10		5453
38	13	A	Sheffield W	L	0-2	0-2	—		18,752
39	16	A	Southampton	W	2-1	2-1	—	Cureton 2 [4, 27]	18,736
40	31	H	Norwich C	W	3-0	0-0	10	Cureton [52], Garcia [64], Iwelumo [73]	5851
41	Apr 6	A	Southend U	W	3-0	1-0	—	Cureton 3 [1, 63, 79]	10,552
42	9	H	Leeds U	W	2-1	0-0	9	Iwelumo [82], Cureton [90]	5916
43	14	A	Hull C	D	1-1	0-1	9	Cureton [63]	20,887
44	21	H	Sunderland	W	3-1	1-0	9	Brown [45], Garcia [82], Cureton (pen) [89]	6042
45	28	A	Stoke C	L	1-3	1-0	9	Iwelumo (pen) [38]	20,108
46	May 6	H	Crystal Palace	L	0-2	0-1	10		5857

Final League Position: 10

GOALSCORERS

League (70): Cureton 23 (2 pens), Iwelumo 18 (7 pens), Garcia 7, Duguid 5, Guy 3, Halford 3, McLeod 3, Jackson 2, Baldwin 1, Brown 1, Ephraim 1, Izzet 1, Richards 1, Watson 1.
Carling Cup (0).
FA Cup (1): Cureton 1.

Davison A 19	Halford G 28	Elokobi G 8 + 2	Baldwin P 35 + 3	Brown W 46	Watson K 38 + 2	Izzet K 45	Jackson J 24 + 8	Garcia R 33 + 3	Cureton J 44	Duguid K 42 + 1	White J 8 + 8	Iwelumo C 41 + 5	Guy J 1 + 31	Richards G 3 + 2	Barker C 38	McLeod K 13 + 11	Gerken D 27	Jones R — + 6	Ephraim H 5 + 16	Mills M 8 + 1	Match No.
1	2	3	4	5	6	7^{1}	8	9^{2}	10^{3}	11	12	13	14								1
1	2	3	4^{2}	5	6	7^{1}	8	9	10	11		12		13							2
1	2	3		5	6	7	8^{1}	9	10^{2}	11		12	13	4							3
1	2		12	5	6	7^{2}		9	10	11		8	13	4^{1}	3						4
1	2		4	5	6	7		8	10^{1}	11	12	9^{2}	13		3						5
1	2	13	4	5	6	7^{1}		8	10^{3}	11	12^{2}	9			3	14					6
1	2		4	5	6	7		8^{2}	10	11		9^{1}	12		3	13					7
	2		4	5	6	7		8^{1}	10	11		9			3	12	1				8
1	2		4	5	6	7		8	10	11	12	9			3^{1}						9
1	2		4	5	6	7		8	10	11		9			3						10
1	2		4	5	6^{1}	7	12	8	10^{2}	11		9^{3}	13		3	14					11
1	2^{1}		4	5	6	7		8^{3}	10^{2}	11	12	9	13		3	14					12
1	2		4	5	6^{1}	7	12	8^{3}	10	11		9^{2}	13		3	14					13
1	2		4	5		7	8		10	11		9			3	6^{1}		12			14
1	2		4	5		7	8		10^{1}	11		9	12		3	6^{2}		13			15
1	2	3	4	5		7	8		10	11		9^{1}	12			6^{2}		13			16
1			4	5		7	8		10	11	2^{2}	9^{1}	12		3	6		13			17
1	2		4	5		7	8		10	11		12	9^{1}		3	6^{2}		13			18
1	2		4	5	12	7^{3}	8		10	11		9^{2}	13		3■	6^{1}		14			19
1	2	3	4	5	12	7	8		10^{3}	11		9^{2}	13			6^{1}			14		20
	2	3	4	5	6	7	8		10	11		9^{1}	12				1				21
	2		4	5	6	7	8^{1}	12	10	11		9			3		1				22
	2		4	5	6^{1}	7	12	8^{3}	10	11		9^{2}	13		3		1		14		23
	2		4	5	6	7^{3}	12	8	10	11^{1}		9^{2}	13		3		1		14		24
	2		4	5	6	7	12	8	10^{3}			9^{2}	13		3	11^{1}	1		14		25
	2		4	5	6	7		8	10	12		9^{2}	13		3	11^{1}	1				26
	2		4^{2}	5	6	7^{3}	12	8	10			9	13		3	11^{1}	1		14		27
	2		4	5	6	7		8	10^{1}	11		9			3		1		12		28
	2			5	6	7^{1}	12	8		11	13	9	14	4^{2}	3		1		10^{3}		29
				5	6	7	8		10^{1}	11	2	9	12	13	3		1			4^{2}	30
				5	6	7^{1}	8		10	11	2	9			3		1		12	4	31
				5	6	7	8	12	10^{2}	11	2	9^{1}			3		1		13	4	32
				5	6	7^{2}	8	12	10	11	2^{1}	9			3	13	1			4	33
				5	6		8	7^{2}	10	11	2^{3}	9^{1}	12		3	13	1		14	4	34
				5	6	7		11	10	2		9^{1}	12		3	8^{2}	1		13	4	35
			12	5	6^{3}	7	8	9	10^{2}	11	2^{1}	13			3		1		14	4	36
			4	5	6	7		8	10	2		9			3	11^{1}	1		12		37
		3	12	5	6^{3}	7	13	10		2^{1}		9	14			8^{2}	1		11	4	38
			4	5	6	7	8	11	10^{1}		2^{2}	9	12		3		1			13	39
			4	5	6	7	8	11	10^{2}	2		9^{1}	12		3		1		13		40
			4	5	6	7	8	11^{2}	10^{3}	2	13	9^{1}	12		3		1		14		41
			4	5	6^{2}	7	8	11^{1}	10	2		9	12		3		1		13		42
			4	5		7	8	11	10^{1}	2		9	12		3	13	1		6^{2}		43
			4	5	6	7	8^{2}	11	10	2		9^{1}	12		3		1		13		44
		12	4	5	6	7		11^{3}	10^{1}	2		9	13		3■	14	1		8^{2}		45
		3^{2}	4^{1}	5	6	7		8	10	2	12	9				13	1		11		46

FA Cup
Third Round Barnet (a) 1-2

Carling Cup
First Round Milton Keynes D (a) 0-1

COVENTRY CITY FL Championship

FOUNDATION

Workers at Singers' cycle factory formed a club in 1883. The first success of Singers' FC was to win the Birmingham Junior Cup in 1891 and this led in 1894 to their election to the Birmingham and District League. Four years later they changed their name to Coventry City and joined the Southern League in 1908 at which time they were playing in blue and white quarters.

Ricoh Arena, Phoenix Way, Foleshill, Coventry CV6 6GE.

Telephone: 0870 421 1987.

Fax: 0870 421 1988.

Ticket Office: 0870 421 1987.

Website: www.ccfc.co.uk

Email: info@ccfc.co.uk

Ground Capacity: 32,609.

Record Attendance: 51,455 v Wolverhampton W, Division 2, 29 April 1967 (at Highfield Road). 27,212 v Birmingham C, FL Championship, 31 October (at Ricoh Arena).

Pitch Measurements: 110yd × 75yd.

Chairman: Geoffrey Robinson (acting chairman).

Chief Executive: Paul Fletcher

Secretary: Roger Brinsford.

Manager: Iain Dowie.

Assistant Manager: Tim Flowers.

Physio: Michael McBride.

Colours: Sky blue.

Change Colours: Red.

Year Formed: 1883. ***Turned Professional:*** 1893.

Ltd Co.: 1907.

Previous Names: 1883, Singers FC; 1898, Coventry City FC.

Club Nickname: 'Sky Blues'.

Grounds: 1883, Binley Road; 1887, Stoke Road; 1899, Highfield Road; 2005, Ricoh Arena.

First Football League Game: 30 August 1919, Division 2, v Tottenham H (h) L 0–5 – Lindon; Roberts, Chaplin, Allan, Hawley, Clarke, Sheldon, Mercer, Sambrooke, Lowes, Gibson.

Record League Victory: 9–0 v Bristol C, Division 3 (S), 28 April 1934 – Pearson; Brown, Bisby; Perry, Davidson, Frith; White (2), Lauderdale, Bourton (5), Jones (2), Lake.

Record Cup Victory: 8–0 v Rushden & D, League Cup 2nd rd, 2 October 2002 – Debec; Caldwell, Quinn, Betts (1p), Konjic (Shaw), Davenport, Pipe, Safri (Stanford), Mills (2) (Bothroyd (2)), McSheffery (3), Partridge.

HONOURS

Football League: Division 1 best season: 6th, 1969–70; Division 2 – Champions 1966–67; Division 3 – Champions 1963–64; Division 3 (S) – Champions 1935–36; Runners-up 1933–34; Division 4 – Runners-up 1958–59.

FA Cup: Winners 1987.

Football League Cup: Semi-final 1981, 1990.

European Competitions: *European Fairs Cup:* 1970–71.

SKY SPORTS FACT FILE

Coventry City have played in more divisions than any other League club: Premier, Championship, all four in the pre-1992 Football League and both regional sections of Division Three. They are also the only club with letters making the word "victory".

Record Defeat: 2–10 v Norwich C, Division 3 (S), 15 March 1930.

Most League Points (2 for a win): 60, Division 4, 1958–59 and Division 3, 1963–64.

Most League Points (3 for a win): 66, Division 1, 2001–02.

Most League Goals: 108, Division 3 (S), 1931–32.

Highest League Scorer in Season: Clarrie Bourton, 49, Division 3 (S), 1931–32.

Most League Goals in Total Aggregate: Clarrie Bourton, 171, 1931–37.

Most League Goals in One Match: 5, Clarrie Bourton v Bournemouth, Division 3S, 17 October 1931; 5, Arthur Bacon v Gillingham, Division 3S, 30 December 1933.

Most Capped Player: Magnus Hedman 44 (58), Sweden.

Most League Appearances: Steve Ogrizovic, 507, 1984–2000.

Youngest League Player: Ben Mackey, 16 years 167 days v Ipswich T, 12 April 2003.

Record Transfer Fee Received: £13,000,000 from Internazionale for Robbie Keane, July 2000.

Record Transfer Fee Paid: £6,500,000 to Wolverhampton W for Robbie Keane, August 1999.

Football League Record: 1919 Elected to Division 2; 1925–26 Division 3 (N); 1926–36 Division 3 (S); 1936–52 Division 2; 1952–58 Division 3 (S); 1958–59 Division 4; 1959–64 Division 3; 1964–67 Division 2; 1967–92 Division 1; 1992–2001 FA Premier League; 2001–04 Division 1; 2004– FL C.

LATEST SEQUENCES

Longest Sequence of League Wins: 6, 25.4.1964 – 5.9.1964.

Longest Sequence of League Defeats: 9, 30.8.1919 – 11.10.1919.

Longest Sequence of League Draws: 6, 1.11.2003 – 29.11.2003.

Longest Sequence of Unbeaten League Matches: 25, 26.11.1966 – 13.5.1967.

Longest Sequence Without a League Win: 19, 30.8.1919 – 20.12.1919.

Successive Scoring Runs: 25 from 10.9.1966.

Successive Non-scoring Runs: 11 from 11.10.1919.

MANAGERS

H. R. Buckle 1909–10
Robert Wallace 1910–13
(Secretary-Manager)
Frank Scott-Walford 1913–15
William Clayton 1917–19
H. Pollitt 1919–20
Albert Evans 1920–24
Jimmy Kerr 1924–28
James McIntyre 1928–31
Harry Storer 1931–45
Dick Bayliss 1945–47
Billy Frith 1947–48
Harry Storer 1948–53
Jack Fairbrother 1953–54
Charlie Elliott 1954–55
Jesse Carver 1955–56
Harry Warren 1956–57
Billy Frith 1957–61
Jimmy Hill 1961–67
Noel Cantwell 1967–72
Bob Dennison 1972
Joe Mercer 1972–75
Gordon Milne 1972–81
Dave Sexton 1981–83
Bobby Gould 1983–84
Don Mackay 1985–86
George Curtis 1986–87
(became Managing Director)
John Sillett 1987–90
Terry Butcher 1990–92
Don Howe 1992
Bobby Gould 1992–93
Phil Neal 1993–95
Ron Atkinson 1995–96
(became Director of Football)
Gordon Strachan 1996–2001
Roland Nilsson 2001–02
Gary McAllister 2002–04
Eric Black 2004
Peter Reid 2004–05
Micky Adams 2005–07
Iain Dowie February 2007–

TEN YEAR LEAGUE RECORD

		P	W	D	L	F	A	Pts	Pos
1997-98	PR Lge	38	12	16	10	46	44	52	11
1998-99	PR Lge	38	11	9	18	39	51	42	15
1999-2000	PR Lge	38	12	8	18	47	54	44	14
2000-01	PR Lge	38	8	10	20	36	63	34	19
2001-02	Div 1	46	20	6	20	59	53	66	11
2002-03	Div 1	46	12	14	20	46	62	50	20
2003-04	Div 1	46	17	14	15	67	54	65	12
2004-05	FL C	46	13	13	20	61	73	52	19
2005-06	FL C	46	16	15	15	62	65	63	8
2006-07	FL C	46	16	8	22	47	62	56	17

DID YOU KNOW ?

On 28 October 2006 substitute Wayne Andrews, making his debut for the club after breaking his ankle in pre-season, scored within 25 seconds of coming off the bench to clinch an 83rd minute winning goal for Coventry City away to Barnsley.

COVENTRY CITY 2006–07 LEAGUE RECORD

Match No.	*Date*	*Venue*	*Opponents*	*Result*		*H/T Score*	*Lg. Pos.*	*Goalscorers*	*Attendance*
1	Aug 6	H	Sunderland	W	2-1	0-0	—	John [71], McSheffrey [78]	22,366
2	9	A	Southampton	L	0-2	0-0	—		21,088
3	12	A	Cardiff C	L	0-1	0-0	18		13,965
4	18	H	Leicester C	D	0-0	0-0	—		20,261
5	26	A	Hull C	W	1-0	0-0	13	Thornton [85]	16,145
6	Sept 9	H	Norwich C	W	3-0	1-0	8	Kyle [63], Birchall [12], John [67]	20,006
7	12	A	Ipswich T	L	1-2	0-0	—	Ward [72]	19,465
8	16	H	Leeds U	W	1-0	1-0	6	John [26]	22,146
9	23	A	Crystal Palace	L	0-1	0-0	11		16,093
10	30	H	Plymouth Arg	L	0-1	0-0	15		19,545
11	Oct 13	A	Southend U	W	3-2	1-1	—	Hughes [42], Cameron (pen) [47], Adebola [80]	9821
12	17	A	Wolverhampton W	L	0-1	0-1	—		19,823
13	23	H	Colchester U	W	2-1	1-0	—	John [45], Doyle [69]	16,178
14	28	A	Barnsley	W	1-0	0-0	8	Andrews [84]	10,470
15	31	H	Birmingham C	L	0-1	0-1	—		27,212
16	Nov 6	A	Stoke C	L	0-1	0-0	—		19,055
17	11	H	Derby Co	L	1-2	1-1	15	John [22]	19,701
18	18	H	Sheffield W	W	3-1	1-1	11	Bougherra (og) [25], McKenzie 2 [51, 55]	19,489
19	25	A	QPR	W	1-0	0-0	9	Adebola [48]	12,840
20	28	A	Preston NE	D	1-1	0-1	—	Adebola [80]	13,104
21	Dec 2	H	Stoke C	D	0-0	0-0	12		19,073
22	9	H	Burnley	W	1-0	1-0	11	Cameron (pen) [31]	18,362
23	16	A	WBA	L	0-5	0-3	14		20,370
24	23	A	Luton T	L	1-3	0-1	14	Brkovic (og) [59]	8299
25	26	H	Ipswich T	L	1-2	0-0	14	Doyle [90]	22,154
26	30	H	Southend U	D	1-1	1-0	14	Ward [12]	16,623
27	Jan 1	A	Leeds U	L	1-2	1-1	16	Virgo [43]	18,158
28	13	H	Crystal Palace	L	2-4	1-4	16	McKenzie [45], Kyle [57]	16,582
29	22	A	Plymouth Arg	L	2-3	1-2	—	Birchall [22], Mifsud [70]	9841
30	30	H	Luton T	W	1-0	0-0	—	McKenzie [76]	18,781
31	Feb 3	A	Sunderland	L	0-2	0-1	17		33,591
32	10	H	Cardiff C	D	2-2	1-1	16	McKenzie [8], Adebola [71]	17,107
33	17	A	Leicester C	L	0-3	0-3	17		25,816
34	20	H	Southampton	W	2-1	2-1	—	Adebola [5], Kyle [30]	17,194
35	24	A	Norwich C	D	1-1	1-0	15	Tabb [42]	24,220
36	Mar 3	H	Hull C	W	2-0	2-0	15	Doyle (pen) [21], McKenzie [34]	21,079
37	10	A	Colchester U	D	0-0	0-0	14		5453
38	13	H	Wolverhampton W	W	2-1	1-1	—	Adebola [26], Ward [71]	22,099
39	17	H	Barnsley	W	4-1	3-0	14	Tabb [27], Mifsud [32], Adebola 2 [38, 50]	21,609
40	Apr 1	A	Birmingham C	L	0-3	0-1	14		25,424
41	7	H	QPR	L	0-1	0-0	16		22,850
42	9	A	Derby Co	D	1-1	0-0	15	McKenzie [73]	29,940
43	14	H	Preston NE	L	0-4	0-2	16		21,117
44	21	A	Sheffield W	L	1-2	1-1	17	Mifsud [37]	23,632
45	28	H	WBA	L	0-1	0-1	18		26,343
46	May 6	A	Burnley	W	2-1	1-0	17	Mifsud [40], Tabb [55]	12,830

Final League Position: 17

GOALSCORERS

League (47): Adebola 8, McKenzie 7, John 5, Mifsud 4, Doyle 3 (1 pen), Kyle 3, Tabb 3, Ward 3, Birchall 2, Cameron 2 (2 pens), Andrews 1, Hughes 1, McSheffrey 1, Thornton 1, Virgo 1, own goals 2.
Carling Cup (1): Adebola 1.
FA Cup (3): Cameron 1, John 1, McKenzie 1.

Marshall A 41	McNamee D 16	Hall M 38 + 2	Doyle M 40	Heath M 7	Ward E 39	Hughes S 36 + 1	Birchall C 17 + 11	Adebola D 28 + 12	John S 19 + 4	McSheffrey G 3	Thornton K 5 + 6	Hutchison D 3 + 11	Whing A 15 + 1	Cameron C 16 + 8	Virgo A 10 + 5	Tabb J 22 + 9	El Idrissi F — + 1	Page R 28 + 1	Kyle K 18 + 13	Osbourne I 16 + 3	McKenzie L 23 + 8	Duffy R 13	Clarke C 12	Andrews W — + 3	Currie D 6 + 2	Bischoff M 2 + 1	Steele L 5	Mifsud M 12 + 7	Hawkins C 13	Giddings S — + 1	Fadiga K 1 + 5	Davis L 1 + 2	Turner B 1	Hildreth L — + 1	*Match No.*
1	2	3	4	5	6	7	8^{1}	9^{2}	10	11^{3}	12	13	14																						1
1	2	3	4	5	6	7	8^{1}	9^{3}	10	11^{2}		13		12	14																				2
1	2^{1}	3	4	5	6	7	8	9^{3}	10	11		14			12^{2}	13																			3
1		3	4^{2}	5	6	7	8^{3}	12	10		13	9^{1}	2	11			14																		4
1		3	4^{2}	2	6	7	8	12	10^{3}		14	13		11^{1}				5	9																5
1		3	4		6	7	8		10^{3}		11^{1}	13	2	12				5	9^{2}	14															6
1		3	4^{1}		6	7	8		10		11^{2}	13	2^{3}	12				5	9		14														7
1	2	3	4		6	7	8		10^{3}			13		12		11^{1}		5	9^{2}		14														8
1	2■	3	4^{2}		6	7	8	13	12					14		11		5	9^{3}		10^{1}														9
1		3			6	7	8^{1}	12	10			13	2	4		11^{2}		5	9																10
1	2	3	4	5	6	7		9						11				8			10														11
1	2^{2}		4^{3}	3^{1}	6	7	8	9	12					11		13		5	14		10														12
1			4		6	7	12		10^{2}			13		11^{1}		14		5	9		8^{3}	2	3												13
1		12	4		6	7		9						11^{2}		13		5	10		8^{3}	2	3^{1}	14											14
1		3	4		6	7^{2}		12	10			13		11^{3}				5	9^{1}		8	2		14											15
1		3^{2}	4^{1}		6	7	8^{3}	12	10			13				14		5			9	2	11												16
1		3	4		6			12	10			8^{2}		13		7^{1}		5			9	2	11												17
1		6	4				8^{3}	9^{2}				7^{1}		12		11		5	13		10	2	3	14											18
1		3	4		6			9						8				5	12		10	2	11		7^{1}										19
1		3	4		6			9	12					8^{2}		13		5	14		10^{1}	2^{3}	11		7										20
1		3	4		6		12	9	13					8^{2}				5			10^{1}	2	11		7										21
1			4		6	12		9	10					8				5	13		11^{2}	2	3		7^{1}										22
1		3	4		6^{3}		12	9	10					8				5	13			2	11^{1}		7^{2}	14									23
			4		6	7		9^{1}	10^{2}					8^{3}	12				13		11	2	3		14	5	1								24
1		12	4		6	7	13	9^{3}	10					8^{2}					14		11	2	3^{1}			5									25
1		3	4		6	7^{3}	8^{1}	12					2			13		5	9	14	10^{2}				11										26
1		3	4		6		8^{3}	12					2^{2}		10	11^{1}		5	9	7	14				13										27
		3				8	12		10				2		6^{1}	7		5	9	4	11^{2}						1	13							28
	3	6	4			7	8^{1}	9	10		12		2			11^{2}		5									1	13							29
	3	5				7	8^{3}	9^{1}			13		2			11			12	4^{2}	14						1	10	6						30
	3	5^{1}	4			7		13			8^{3}		2		12	14			9		11						1	10^{2}	6						31
1	3		4					9					2^{1}			11		5		7	8							10	6	12					32
1	3					7^{1}	12	9^{2}					2		13	11		5	14	4	8							10^{3}	6						33
1	3^{1}	5	8		6	7		9					2			11^{2}			10^{3}	12	13							14	4						34
1		3	4		6	7	12	9^{2}					2			11^{3}			10	5^{1}								13	8		14				35
1		3	8		6	4	12	9							2	11^{1}				7^{2}	10^{3}							14	5		13				36
1		3	4		6	8		9							2	11				7	10^{1}							12	5						37
1		3	4		6	7	12	9							2	11^{2}				8^{1}								10	5		13				38
1		3	4		6	7	12	9						13	2	11^{3}				8^{1}	14							10^{2}	5						39
1		3	4		6	8		9							2	11^{1}			12	7^{2}								10	5		13				40
1		3	4		6	8		9					7^{3}		2			12	13		14							10^{2}	5^{1}		11				41
1		3	4		6	8		12							2	11		5	9^{1}	7	10^{2}							13							42
1		3			6	4		12						8	2	11^{2}		5	9	7	13^{3}							10^{1}			14				43
1	2	3			6	8		9			12					11^{2}		5	13	7								10				4^{1}			44
1	2	3^{1}	4		6	8^{3}	12	9			11^{2}					13				7								10				14	5■		45
1	2	3	4		6						8^{1}					11^{2}			9	7								10	5			12		13	46

FA Cup

Third Round	Bristol C	(a)	3-3
		(h)	0-2

Carling Cup

First Round	Hereford U	(a)	1-3

CREWE ALEXANDRA FL Championship 1

FOUNDATION

The first match played at Crewe was on 1 December 1877 against Basford, the leading North Staffordshire team of that time. During the club's history they have also played in a number of other leagues including the Football Alliance, Football Combination, Lancashire League, Manchester League, Central League and Lancashire Combination. Two former players, Aaron Scragg in 1899 and Jackie Pearson in 1911, had the distinction of refereeing FA Cup finals. Pearson was also capped for England against Ireland in 1892.

The Alexandra Stadium, Gresty Road, Crewe, Cheshire CW2 6EB.

Telephone: (01270) 213 014.

Fax: (01270) 216 320.

Ticket Office: (01270) 252 610.

Website: www.crewealex.net

Email: info@crewealex.net

Ground Capacity: 10,109.

Record Attendance: 20,000 v Tottenham H, FA Cup 4th rd, 30 January 1960.

Pitch Measurements: 110m × 73.1m.

Chairman: John Bowler.

Vice-chairman: Norman Hassall.

Secretary: Alison Bowler.

Technical Director: Dario Gradi MBE.

First Team Coach: Steve Holland.

Assistant Manager: Neil Baker.

Physio: Matt Radcliffe.

Colours: Red shirts, white shorts, red stockings.

Change Colours: White shirts, navy shorts, navy stockings.

Year Formed: 1877.

Turned Professional: 1893.

Ltd Co.: 1892.

Club Nickname: 'Railwaymen'.

Ground: 1898, Gresty Road.

First Football League Game: 3 September 1892, Division 2, v Burton Swifts (a) L 1–7 – Hickton; Moore, Cope; Linnell, Johnson, Osborne; Bennett, Pearson (1), Bailey, Barnett, Roberts.

Record League Victory: 8–0 v Rotherham U, Division 3 (N), 1 October 1932 – Foster; Pringle, Dawson; Ward, Keenor (1), Turner (1); Gillespie, Swindells (1), McConnell (2), Deacon (2), Weale (1).

HONOURS

Football League: Division 2 – Runners-up 2002–03; Promoted from Division 2 1996–97 (play-offs).

FA Cup: Semi-final 1888.

Football League Cup: best season: 3rd rd, 1975, 1976, 1979, 1993, 1999, 2000, 2002, 2007.

Welsh Cup: Winners 1936, 1937.

SKY SPORTS FACT FILE

When Ernie Tagg took over as manager of Crewe Alexandra in November 1964, he was returning to his home town club and the one where he made his debut as a player on 15 January 1938 at inside-left against Oldham Athletic.

Record Cup Victory: 8–0 v Hartlepool U, Auto Windscreens Shield 1st rd, 17 October 1995 – Gayle; Collins (1), Booty, Westwood (Unsworth), Macauley (1), Whalley (1), Garvey (1), Murphy (1), Savage (1) (Rivers (1p)), Lennon, Edwards, (1 og). 8–0 v Doncaster R, LDV Vans Trophy 3rd rd, 10 November 2002 – Bankole; Wright, Walker, Foster, Tierney; Lunt (1), Brammer, Sorvel, Vaughan (1) (Bell); Ashton (3) (Miles), Jack (2) (Jones (1)).

Record Defeat: 2–13 v Tottenham H, FA Cup 4th rd replay, 3 February 1960.

Most League Points (2 for a win): 59, Division 4, 1962–63.

Most League Points (3 for a win): 86, Division 2, 2002–03.

Most League Goals: 95, Division 3 (N), 1931–32.

Highest League Scorer in Season: Terry Harkin, 35, Division 4, 1964–65.

Most League Goals in Total Aggregate: Bert Swindells, 126, 1928–37.

Most League Goals in One Match: 5, Tony Naylor v Colchester U, Division 3, 24 April 1993.

Most Capped Player: Clayton Ince, 38 (63), Trinidad & Tobago.

Most League Appearances: Tommy Lowry, 436, 1966–78.

Youngest League Player: Steve Walters, 16 years 119 days v Peterborough U, 6 May 1988.

Record Transfer Fee Received: £3,400,000 from Norwich C for Dean Ashton, January 2005.

Record Transfer Fee Paid: £650,000 to Torquay U for Rodney Jack, June 1998.

Football League Record: 1892 Original Member of Division 2; 1896 Failed re-election; 1921 Re-entered Division (N); 1958–63 Division 4; 1963–64 Division 3; 1964–68 Division 4; 1968–69 Division 3; 1969–89 Division 4; 1989–91 Division 3; 1991–92 Division 4; 1992–94 Division 3; 1994–97 Division 2; 1997–2002 Division 1; 2002–03 Division 2; 2003–04 Division 1; 2004–06 FL C; 2006– FL 1.

MANAGERS

W. C. McNeill 1892–94 *(Secretary-Manager)*
J. G. Hall 1895–96 *(Secretary-Manager)*
R. Roberts *(1st team Secretary-Manager)* 1897
J. B. Blomerley 1898–1911 *(Secretary-Manager, continued as Hon. Secretary to 1925)*
Tom Bailey *(Secretary only)* 1925–38
George Lillycrop *(Trainer)* 1938–44
Frank Hill 1944–48
Arthur Turner 1948–51
Harry Catterick 1951–53
Ralph Ward 1953–55
Maurice Lindley 1956–57
Willie Cook 1957–58
Harry Ware 1958–60
Jimmy McGuigan 1960–64
Ernie Tagg 1964–71 *(continued as Secretary to 1972)*
Dennis Viollet 1971
Jimmy Melia 1972–74
Ernie Tagg 1974
Harry Gregg 1975–78
Warwick Rimmer 1978–79
Tony Waddington 1979–81
Arfon Griffiths 1981–82
Peter Morris 1982–83
Dario Gradi 1983–2007
Steve Holland May 2007–

LATEST SEQUENCES

Longest Sequence of League Wins: 7, 30.4.1994 – 3.9.1994.

Longest Sequence of League Defeats: 10, 16.4.1979 – 22.8.1979.

Longest Sequence of League Draws: 5, 31.8.1987 – 18.9.1987.

Longest Sequence of Unbeaten League Matches: 17, 25.3.1995 – 16.9.1995.

Longest Sequence Without a League Win: 30, 22.9.1956 – 6.4.1957.

Successive Scoring Runs: 26 from 7.4.1934.

Successive Non-scoring Runs: 9 from 6.11.1974.

TEN YEAR LEAGUE RECORD

		P	W	D	L	F	A	Pts	Pos
1997-98	Div 1	46	18	5	23	58	65	59	11
1998-99	Div 1	46	12	12	22	54	78	48	18
1999-2000	Div 1	46	14	9	23	46	67	51	19
2000-01	Div 1	46	15	10	21	47	62	55	14
2001-02	Div 1	46	12	13	21	47	76	49	22
2002-03	Div 2	46	25	11	10	76	40	86	2
2003-04	Div 1	46	14	11	21	57	66	53	18
2004-05	FL C	46	12	14	20	66	86	50	21
2005-06	FL C	46	9	15	22	57	86	42	22
2006-07	FL 1	46	17	9	20	66	72	60	13

DID YOU KNOW?

John Hargreaves Pearson, the first Crewe Alexandra player capped for England on 5 March 1892 v Northern Ireland, was a reserve debutant at just over 13. Retired early with injury, he became a Cup Final referee and appropriately worked on the railway!

CREWE ALEXANDRA 2006–07 LEAGUE RECORD

Match No.	Date	Venue	Opponents	Result		H/T Score	Lg. Pos.	Goalscorers	Attendance
1	Aug 5	H	Northampton T	D	2-2	2-2	—	Lowe [7], Vaughan [19]	5553
2	8	A	Doncaster R	L	1-3	1-1	—	Maynard [11]	6081
3	12	A	Scunthorpe U	D	2-2	1-1	18	Rodgers (pen) [30], Vaughan [49]	4329
4	19	H	Bradford C	L	0-3	0-1	23		5274
5	27	A	Brighton & HA	W	4-1	2-1	15	Jones [44], Lowe (pen) [45], Maynard 2 [56, 85]	5848
6	Sept 2	H	Huddersfield T	W	2-0	1-0	12	Maynard 2 [41, 53]	4868
7	9	A	Bournemouth	L	0-1	0-1	15		5627
8	12	H	Cheltenham T	W	3-1	1-1	—	Maynard [23], Cox [70], Varney [81]	4062
9	16	H	Millwall	W	1-0	0-0	7	Varney [65]	4875
10	23	A	Yeovil T	L	0-2	0-1	11		5333
11	26	A	Swansea C	L	1-2	1-1	—	Roberts (pen) [32]	10,031
12	30	H	Carlisle U	W	5-1	2-1	10	Varney 2 [42, 73], Lowe 3 [45, 63, 90]	5989
13	Oct 7	H	Gillingham	W	4-3	1-3	7	Maynard [36], Jack [68], O'Donnell [88], Varney [90]	5022
14	14	A	Bristol C	L	1-2	0-2	10	Varney [60]	11,899
15	21	H	Blackpool	L	1-2	0-1	12	Maynard [67]	5785
16	28	A	Rotherham U	L	1-5	1-3	16	Varney [10]	5407
17	Nov 4	H	Port Vale	W	2-1	1-1	12	Maynard [32], Rodgers (pen) [90]	7632
18	18	A	Brentford	W	4-0	1-0	9	Varney 2 [5, 63], Rix [58], Vaughan [67]	4771
19	25	H	Chesterfield	D	2-2	0-0	9	Varney [64], Rodgers [89]	5078
20	Dec 5	A	Oldham Ath	L	0-1	0-1	—		4798
21	9	H	Nottingham F	L	1-4	1-4	14	Roberts (pen) [36]	7253
22	23	A	Leyton Orient	D	1-1	1-0	15	Maynard [30]	4371
23	26	H	Swansea C	L	1-3	0-2	16	Varney [59]	6083
24	30	H	Yeovil T	L	2-3	0-2	17	Maynard [77], Roberts [80]	5450
25	Jan 2	A	Cheltenham T	D	1-1	1-1	—	Varney [15]	3154
26	13	H	Bournemouth	W	2-0	1-0	16	Varney [9], Maynard [62]	4739
27	16	A	Tranmere R	L	0-1	0-1	—		5708
28	20	A	Carlisle U	W	2-0	0-0	14	Baudet [53], Maynard [90]	7075
29	27	H	Leyton Orient	L	0-4	0-1	17		5280
30	Feb 3	A	Northampton T	W	2-1	1-0	12	Varney 2 [26, 57]	5262
31	17	A	Bradford C	W	1-0	0-0	15	Lowe [89]	7778
32	20	H	Doncaster R	W	2-1	0-0	—	Rix [50], Higdon [90]	4483
33	24	A	Huddersfield T	W	2-1	1-1	11	Higdon [45], Lowe [69]	10,052
34	27	H	Scunthorpe U	L	1-3	1-2	—	Varney [26]	4842
35	Mar 3	H	Brighton & HA	D	1-1	1-1	11	Varney [18]	5202
36	10	A	Gillingham	L	0-1	0-0	13		6373
37	13	A	Millwall	D	2-2	1-1	—	Higdon [30], Moss [84]	8867
38	17	H	Bristol C	L	0-1	0-0	13		5731
39	24	H	Rotherham U	W	1-0	1-0	12	Moss [16]	5675
40	31	A	Blackpool	L	1-2	0-1	14	Miller [90]	7203
41	Apr 7	A	Chesterfield	L	1-2	1-1	14	Miller [8]	3698
42	9	H	Brentford	W	3-1	2-0	12	Vaughan [18], Lowe [23], Maynard [70]	4667
43	14	A	Port Vale	L	0-3	0-1	13		5740
44	21	H	Oldham Ath	W	2-1	1-0	12	Maynard 2 [25, 71]	6304
45	28	H	Tranmere R	D	1-1	0-0	12	Miller [90]	5777
46	May 5	A	Nottingham F	D	0-0	0-0	13		27,472

Final League Position: 13

GOALSCORERS

League (66): Varney 17, Maynard 16, Lowe 8 (1 pen), Vaughan 4, Higdon 3, Miller 3, Roberts 3 (2 pens), Rodgers 3 (2 pens), Moss 2, Rix 2, Baudet 1, Cox 1, Jack 1, Jones 1, O'Donnell 1.
Carling Cup (6): Maynard 2, Jack 1, Lowe 1 (pen), O'Connor 1, Varney 1.
FA Cup (0).
J Paint Trophy (13): Varney 7, Lowe 3 (1 pen), Jack 1, Maynard 1, Moss 1.

Williams B 39	Otsemobor J 27	Jones B 41	Roberts G 41 + 2	Baudet J 42	Kempson D 6 + 1	Lowe R 31 + 6	Grant T 3 + 1	Rodgers L 5 + 7	Higdon M 13 + 12	Vaughan D 26 + 3	O'Connor M 25 + 4	Maynard N 27 + 4	Varney L 31 + 3	O'Donnell D 21 + 4	Cox N 29 + 2	Rix B 24 + 7	Jack R 19 + 11	Matthews L — + 10	Moss D 18 + 4	Osbourne I 2	Taylor A 4	Flynn C — + 1	Suhaj P — + 2	Tomlinson S 7	Bignot P 9 + 2	Woodards D 9 + 2	Pope T — + 4	Miller S 2 + 5	McNamee A 5	Coo C — + 1	Carrington M — + 3	*Match No.*
1	2	3	4	5	6	7	8^1	9^2	10	11	12	13																				1
1	2	3	4	5	6	7	8^1		10	11	12	9^2	13																			2
1	2	3	4	5	6^2	7		9^1	10	11	8	12		13																		3
1	2	3	4	5		7^2		9^1	10	11	8	12	13	6																		4
1	2	3	4	5	12	7				11	8^2	9^3	10		6^1	13	14															5
1	2	3	4	5		12		13			8	9^2	10	7	6		11^1															6
1	2	3	4	5		12				11	7		10	8^1	6		9^2	13														7
1	2	3	4	5						11^1	7	9^2	10	8	6		12	13														8
1	2	3	4	5		12				11	7^1	9^2	10	8	6		13															9
1	2	3	4	5					12	11	7^2	9	10		6	13	8^1															10
1		3	4	5		12		13		11		9	10	2^1	6^2	7			8													11
1	2	3	4	5^2		7		12		11	8^3	9^1	10		6	14			13													12
1	2	3^1	4	5	6	7^2					8	9^3	10	12	11		13	14														13
1	2		4 ■	5		7				11	8^2	9	10	3^1	6	13	12															14
1	2			5					12	11		9	10		6	7	8^1			4	3											15
1	2	3^1			6	7		13	11^2			9	10^3	5		8				4		12	14									16
	2		4		6		8	9				11^1		5		7	10				3		12	1								17
	2	6	4			12		9^1	13	11			10^2	5		7	8				3			1								18
	2	6	4			8		12	13	11			10^1	5		7	9^2				3			1								19
	2	3	4	5		8^2		13	12	11			10		6	7	9^1							1								20
	2	3	4	5					12	13	8^2	9^1	10		6	7	11							1								21
	2	3	4	5				12		11	8	9^1	10		6	7^2		13						1								22
	2	3	4	5		7^2				11	8^1	9	10		6	12		13						1								23
1	2	3	4	5		8^3				11	12^2	9	10		6^1	7	13	14														24
1	2	6	4	5						11	8^1	9	10			7		12							3							25
1		6	4	5						11	8	9	10			7			2						3							26
1		6	4	5		12				11	8	9^2	10			7^1	13		2						3							27
1		6	4	5					12	11	8	9^1				7	10^2	13	2						3							28
1		6	4	5		7	12		13	11^3	8^1		10				9^2	14	2						3							29
1	2	6^2	4	5		7^1			12	11	9		10	13	3				8													30
1	2^2	6	4	5		8			12				10		11	7	9^1		3							13						31
1	2^3	6	4^2	5		8^1			12		13		10		11	7	9		3							14						32
1			4	5		8^1			9				10	6	11	7	12		3							2						33
1			4	5		8			9				10	6	11	7^1	12		3							2						34
1		6		5		8			12	13	11^3	9^1	10	14	4	7^2			3							2						35
1		6	4^1	5		7			9					8	11		10^2		3							2	12	13				36
1		6	4	5		7			9					8	11		10^1	12	3						13	2^2						37
1		6	4	5^1		7			9^3					8	11	12	10^2								3	2	14	13				38
1		6	4	5		8			9						7	12	10		3						13	2^2			11^1			39
1		6	4	5		7^2			9^1						8		12		3						2^3		13	10	11	14		40
1		3	4	5		7			9^2	12		14			6		13		8						2			10^3	11^1			41
1		3	12	5		8				11^2	2	9^3		6	13	7	10^1		4									14				42
1		3	4	5		8					11	9^2		6		7^3	10^1		2								13	12			14	43
1		3	4	5		8					10^3	9^1	12	6		7			13							2^2			11		14	44
1		3	4^3	5		8						9	10	6	12	7			13							2^2		14	11^1			45
1		3^2	12	5		8					4^1	9	10	6	11	7^3			13						2						14	46

FA Cup

First Round	Bradford C	(a)	0-4

Carling Cup

First Round	Grimsby T	(a)	3-0
Second Round	Wigan Ath	(h)	2-0
Third Round	Manchester U	(h)	1-2

J Paint Trophy

Second Round	Rochdale	(a)	1-1
Quarter-Final	Port Vale	(a)	3-2
Semi-Final	Chesterfield	(a)	4-2
Northern Final	Doncaster R	(h)	3-3
		(a)	2-3

CRYSTAL PALACE FL Championship

FOUNDATION

There was a Crystal Palace club as early as 1861 but the present organisation was born in 1905 after the formation of a club by the company that controlled the Crystal Palace (building), had been rejected by the FA who did not like the idea of the Cup Final hosts running their own club. A separate company had to be formed and they had their home on the old Cup Final ground until 1915.

Selhurst Park Stadium, Whitehorse Lane, London SE25 6PU.

Telephone: (020) 8768 6000.

Fax: (020) 8771 5311.

Ticket Office: 0871 200 0071.

Website: www.cpfc.co.uk

Email: info@cpfc.co.uk

Ground Capacity: 26,225.

Record Attendance: 51,482 v Burnley, Division 2, 11 May 1979.

Pitch Measurements: 110yd × 74yd.

Chairman: Simon Jordan.

Vice-chairman: Dominic Jordan.

Chief Executive: Phil Alexander.

Secretary: Christine Dowdeswell.

Manager: Peter Taylor.

First Team Coach: Kit Symons.

Physio: Paul Caton.

Colours: Red and royal blue striped shirts, red shorts, red stockings.

Change Colours: White shirts, white shorts, white stockings.

Year Formed: 1905.

Turned Professional: 1905.

Ltd Co.: 1905.

Club Nickname: 'The Eagles'.

Grounds: 1905, Crystal Palace; 1915, Herne Hill; 1918, The Nest; 1924, Selhurst Park.

First Football League Game: 28 August 1920, Division 3, v Merthyr T (a) L 1–2 – Alderson; Little, Rhodes; McCracken, Jones, Feebury; Bateman, Conner, Smith, Milligan (1), Whibley.

Record League Victory: 9–0 v Barrow, Division 4, 10 October 1959 – Rouse; Long, Noakes; Truett, Evans, McNichol; Gavin (1), Summersby (4 incl. 1p), Sexton, Byrne (2), Colfar (2).

Record Cup Victory: 8–0 v Southend U, Rumbelows League Cup 2nd rd (1st leg), 25 September 1989 – Martyn; Humphrey (Thompson (1)), Shaw, Pardew, Young, Thorn, McGoldrick, Thomas, Bright (3), Wright (3), Barber (Hodges (1)).

HONOURS

Football League: Division 1 – Champions 1993–94; Promoted from Division 1, 1996–97 (play-offs), 2003–04 (play-offs); Division 2 – Champions 1978–79; Runners-up 1968–69; Division 3 – Runners-up 1963–64; Division 3 (S) – Champions 1920–21; Runners-up 1928–29, 1930–31, 1938–39; Division 4 – Runners-up 1960–61.

FA Cup: Runners-up 1990.

Football League Cup: Semi-final 1993, 1995, 2001.

Zenith Data Systems Cup: Winners 1991.

European Competition: *Intertoto Cup:* 1998.

SKY SPORTS FACT FILE

The longest period before a goal was scored in an FA Cup tie was six hours 14 minutes in February 1924 in the third replay second round tie between Crystal Palace and Notts County. Notts led but first Frank Hoddinott equalised then Bill Hand hit the winner.

Record Defeat: 0–9 v Burnley, FA Cup 2nd rd replay, 10 February 1909. 0–9 v Liverpool, Division 1, 12 September 1990.

Most League Points (2 for a win): 64, Division 4, 1960–61.

Most League Points (3 for a win): 90, Division 1, 1993–94.

Most League Goals: 110, Division 4, 1960–61.

Highest League Scorer in Season: Peter Simpson, 46, Division 3 (S), 1930–31.

Most League Goals in Total Aggregate: Peter Simpson, 153, 1930–36.

Most League Goals in One Match: 6, Peter Simpson v Exeter C, Division 3S, 4 October 1930.

Most Capped Player: Aleksandrs Kolinko 23 (76), Latvia.

Most League Appearances: Jim Cannon, 571, 1973–88.

Youngest League Player: Phil Hoadley, 16 years 112 days v Bolton W, 27 April 1968.

Record Transfer Fee Received: £8,500,000 from Everton for Andy Johnson, May 2006.

Record Transfer Fee Paid: £2,750,000 to RC Strasbourg for Valerien Ismael, January 1998.

Football League Record: 1920 Original Members of Division 3; 1921–25 Division 2; 1925–58 Division 3 (S); 1958–61 Division 4; 1961–64 Division 3; 1964–69 Division 2; 1969–73 Division 1; 1973–74 Division 2; 1974–77 Division 3; 1977–79 Division 2; 1979–81 Division 1; 1981–89 Division 2; 1989–92 Division 1; 1992–93 FA Premier League; 1993–94 Division 1; 1994–95 FA Premier League; 1995–97 Division 1; 1997–98 FA Premier League; 1998–2004 Division 1; 2004–05 FA Premier League; 2005– FL C.

LATEST SEQUENCES

Longest Sequence of League Wins: 8, 9.2.1921 – 26.3.1921.

Longest Sequence of League Defeats: 8, 10.1.1998 – 14.3.1998.

Longest Sequence of League Draws: 5, 21.9.2002 – 19.10.2002.

Longest Sequence of Unbeaten League Matches: 18, 22.2.1969 – 13.8.1969.

Longest Sequence Without a League Win: 20, 3.3.1962 – 8.9.1962.

Successive Scoring Runs: 24 from 27.4.1929.

Successive Non-scoring Runs: 9 from 19.11.1994.

MANAGERS

John T. Robson 1905–07
Edmund Goodman 1907–25 *(had been Secretary since 1905 and afterwards continued in this position to 1933)*
Alec Maley 1925–27
Fred Mavin 1927–30
Jack Tresadern 1930–35
Tom Bromilow 1935–36
R. S. Moyes 1936
Tom Bromilow 1936–39
George Irwin 1939–47
Jack Butler 1947–49
Ronnie Rooke 1949–50
Charlie Slade and Fred Dawes *(Joint Managers)* 1950–51
Laurie Scott 1951–54
Cyril Spiers 1954–58
George Smith 1958–60
Arthur Rowe 1960–62
Dick Graham 1962–66
Bert Head 1966–72 *(continued as General Manager to 1973)*
Malcolm Allison 1973–76
Terry Venables 1976–80
Ernie Walley 1980
Malcolm Allison 1980–81
Dario Gradi 1981
Steve Kember 1981–82
Alan Mullery 1982–84
Steve Coppell 1984–93
Alan Smith 1993–95
Steve Coppell *(Technical Director)* 1995–96
Dave Bassett 1996–97
Steve Coppell 1997–98
Attilio Lombardo 1998
Terry Venables *(Head Coach)* 1998–99
Steve Coppell 1999–2000
Alan Smith 2000–01
Steve Bruce 2001
Trevor Francis 2001–03
Steve Kember 2003
Iain Dowie 2003–06
Peter Taylor June 2006–

TEN YEAR LEAGUE RECORD

		P	W	D	L	F	A	Pts	Pos
1997-98	PR Lge	38	8	9	21	37	71	33	20
1998-99	Div 1	46	14	16	16	58	71	58	14
1999-2000	Div 1	46	13	15	18	57	67	54	15
2000-01	Div 1	46	12	13	21	57	70	49	21
2001-02	Div 1	46	20	6	20	70	62	66	10
2002-03	Div 1	46	14	17	15	59	52	59	14
2003-04	Div 1	46	21	10	15	72	61	73	6
2004-05	PR Lge	38	7	12	19	41	62	33	18
2005-06	FL C	46	21	12	13	67	48	75	6
2006-07	FL C	46	18	11	17	59	51	65	12

DID YOU KNOW ?

Harold Colclough was the first Crystal Palace player capped for England. He appeared at left-back against Wales on 6 March 1914. A former Crewe Alexandra discovery he represented the Southern League three times while with the London club.

CRYSTAL PALACE 2006–07 LEAGUE RECORD

Match No.	Date	Venue	Opponents	Result		H/T Score	Lg. Pos.	Goalscorers	Attendance
1	Aug 5	A	Ipswich T	W	2-1	0-1	—	McAnuff [58], Scowcroft [61]	25,413
2	8	H	Southend U	W	3-1	0-1	—	Cort [52], Freedman [55], Hudson [61]	18,072
3	13	H	Leeds U	W	1-0	0-0	1	Morrison [90]	17,218
4	19	A	Birmingham C	L	1-2	1-1	3	McAnuff [11]	20,223
5	26	H	Burnley	D	2-2	0-1	3	Cort [48], Scowcroft [74]	16,396
6	Sept 9	A	Luton T	L	1-2	0-1	6	Scowcroft [90]	9187
7	12	H	Southampton	L	0-2	0-1	—		17,084
8	16	A	Norwich C	W	1-0	0-0	7	Kuqi [90]	24,618
9	23	H	Coventry C	W	1-0	0-0	5	Morrison [55]	16,093
10	30	A	Hull C	D	1-1	0-0	5	Cort [57]	18,099
11	Oct 14	H	Cardiff C	L	1-2	1-1	9	Green [40]	18,876
12	17	H	WBA	L	0-2	0-1	—		16,105
13	21	A	Leicester C	D	1-1	1-1	12	Soares [16]	28,762
14	28	H	Plymouth Arg	L	0-1	0-1	17		17,084
15	31	A	Sheffield W	L	2-3	1-1	—	Kuqi [21], Soares [64]	19,034
16	Nov 4	A	QPR	L	2-4	2-1	20	Soares [30], Morrison [43]	13,989
17	11	H	Stoke C	L	0-1	0-1	20		18,868
18	18	H	Barnsley	W	2-0	2-0	20	Scowcroft [16], Morrison [32]	20,159
19	25	A	Preston NE	D	0-0	0-0	19		14,202
20	28	A	Wolverhampton W	D	1-1	0-0	—	Freedman [84]	17,806
21	Dec 2	H	QPR	W	3-0	2-0	16	Freedman [13], Kuqi [32], Morrison [86]	17,017
22	9	H	Colchester U	L	1-3	0-0	17	Morrison [87]	16,762
23	16	A	Derby Co	L	0-1	0-1	18		23,875
24	22	H	Sunderland	W	1-0	1-0	—	Hudson [41]	17,439
25	26	A	Southampton	D	1-1	0-0	18	McAnuff [54]	30,548
26	30	A	Cardiff C	D	0-0	0-0	18		13,704
27	Jan 1	H	Norwich C	W	3-1	3-1	15	Hudson [26], Kuqi [29], Green [45]	16,765
28	13	A	Coventry C	W	4-2	4-1	14	Fletcher [19], Kuqi [27], Cort [28], McAnuff [39]	16,582
29	20	H	Hull C	D	1-1	0-0	14	Fletcher [51]	17,012
30	30	A	Sunderland	D	0-0	0-0	—		26,958
31	Feb 3	H	Ipswich T	W	2-0	1-0	12	Cort [33], Ifill [51]	17,090
32	10	A	Leeds U	L	1-2	0-1	12	Cort [83]	19,228
33	17	H	Birmingham C	L	0-1	0-1	12		17,233
34	20	A	Southend U	W	1-0	0-0	—	Ifill [65]	10,419
35	24	H	Luton T	W	2-1	1-0	11	Morrison 2 [45, 68]	16,177
36	Mar 3	A	Burnley	D	1-1	1-1	11	Morrison [15]	10,659
37	10	H	Leicester C	W	2-0	1-0	11	Fletcher [14], Watson (pen) [90]	16,969
38	14	A	WBA	W	3-2	2-1	—	Morrison [35], Watson (pen) [42], Grabban [90]	17,960
39	17	A	Plymouth Arg	L	0-1	0-0	11		11,239
40	31	H	Sheffield W	L	1-2	0-0	12	Morrison [80]	21,523
41	Apr 7	H	Preston NE	W	3-0	2-0	12	Kuqi 2 [16, 21], Cort [68]	15,985
42	9	A	Stoke C	L	1-2	1-2	12	Zakuani (og) [30]	13,616
43	14	H	Wolverhampton W	D	2-2	2-2	12	Hudson [12], McAnuff [37]	17,981
44	21	A	Barnsley	L	0-2	0-1	13		10,277
45	29	H	Derby Co	W	2-0	1-0	13	Morrison [29], Kennedy [67]	19,545
46	May 6	A	Colchester U	W	2-0	1-0	12	Scowcroft [11], Watson [69]	5857

Final League Position: 12

GOALSCORERS

League (59): Morrison 12, Cort 7, Kuqi 7, McAnuff 5, Scowcroft 5, Hudson 4, Fletcher 3, Freedman 3, Soares 3, Watson 3 (2 pens), Green 2, Ifill 2, Grabban 1, Kennedy 1, own goal 1.
Carling Cup (1): Hughes 1.
FA Cup (2): Kuqi 1, McAnuff 1.

Kiraly G 29	Butterfield D 25 + 3	Granville D 15	Fletcher C 33 + 4	Hudson M 38 + 1	Cort L 37	McAnuff J 31 + 3	Soares T 32 + 5	Scowcroft J 26 + 9	Morrison C 31 + 10	Kennedy M 34 + 4	Freedman D 11 + 23	Watson B 19 + 6	Macken J 1	Lawrence M 31 + 3	Hughes M 12 + 4	Kuqi S 24 + 11	Borrowdale G 24 + 1	Green S 5 + 9	Ward D 20	Reich M 4 + 2	Flinders S 7 + 1	Turner I 5	Speroni J 5	Ifill P 6 + 7	Spence L 1 + 1	Martin D — + 5	Grabban L — + 8	Match No.
1	2	3	4	5	6	7	8	9	10^{1}	11^{2}	12	13																1
1	2	3	4	5	6	7	8	9		11^{2}	12	13	10^{1}															2
1	2	3	4	5	6	7	8^{2}	9	13	11	12	10^{1}																3
1	2^{3}	3	4	5	6	7	8	9^{2}	13	11	12	10^{1}		14														4
1	2	3	4^{2}	5	6	7	8	9	12	11	10^{1}				13													5
1	2^{2}	3	4^{3}	5	6	7	8	9	12	11	13				14	10^{1}												6
1				5	6	7^{2}	8^{3}	9	12	11	13			2	4	10^{1}	3	14										7
1	4				6	7		9	10^{1}	11				2	8^{2}	12	3	13	5									8
1	2^{1}				6	7		9	10^{2}	11	13	12		4	8^{3}	14	3		5									9
1					6	7		9	10^{2}	11	12	4		2		8^{1}	3	13	5									10
1				12	6	7^{3}	13	9		11	14	4		2^{1}		10	3	8^{2}	5									11
1			4^{3}	5^{2}	6		8	9	12	11	13	7				10^{1}	3	14	2									12
1			4		6		8^{2}		9	11	12	13		2		10^{1}	3	14	5	7^{3}								13
1	12		4^{1}		6		8		9	11	10			2		13	3	14	5^{3}	7^{2}								14
	2		4		6	12	8		9	13	14	7^{1}		5		10^{3}	3			11^{2}	1							15
	2^{2}	3			6	7^{1}	8		9	11	13			4	12	10			5		1							16
1	2	3		5	6	7	8^{2}	9^{1}	10	11	13				4	12												17
	2	3	12	5		7	8	9^{3}	10^{2}	11^{1}	13				6	14			4			1						18
	2	3	12	5		7	8	9^{2}	10^{3}	11^{1}	14				6	13			4			1						19
	2	3	12	5		7	8	9^{2}	10^{3}	11	14				6^{1}	13			4			1						20
	2^{2}	3		5		7	8		12		9^{1}	6		13	11^{3}	10		14	4			1						21
		3		5		7	11	12	9			6^{2}		2	8	10^{1}		13	4		15	1^{G}						22
		3	12	5		7^{2}	8	13	9	11		6^{1}		2		10^{3}		14	4				1					23
	2		4	5		7	8	12	9^{2}	11^{3}	13			14		10^{1}	3		6				1					24
	2	3	4^{2}	5		7	8		9^{1}	11	12					10			6	13	1							25
	3		4	5		7		9	10^{1}	11		8^{2}		2		12			6	13	1							26
			4	5	6	12			13		9^{2}			2	8	10		11	3	7^{1}	1							27
			4	5	6	7	12			11	9^{2}			2		10		8^{1}	3		1			13				28
			4	5	6	7	12		13	11^{2}	9^{1}			2		10		8^{3}	3		1			14				29
1	2		4	5	6	7	12			11	13			3		10		8^{2}						9^{1}				30
1	2		4	5	6		8■	12		11^{2}	9^{3}	13		3		10^{1}	14							7				31
1	2^{3}		4	5	6			9^{1}	10	11	13			8		12	3							7^{2}	14			32
1	2		4	5	6	12		13	14	11^{1}	9^{2}			8		10^{3}	3							7				33
1	2^{1}		4	5	6			9	10^{3}	11	12			8			3							7^{2}		13	14	34
1	12		4	5	6		8	9	10	11^{1}	7			2^{2}			3									13		35
1	2		4	5	6		8	9	10		11^{2}	12		3											7^{1}		13	36
1			4	5	6		8	9	10^{2}		11^{1}	7		2	12		3										13	37
1	12		4	5	6		7	9	10^{2}			8		2	11^{3}		3^{1}									13	14	38
1	2		4	5	6		8^{2}	9	10^{3}		12	7			11^{1}	13	3										14	39
1			4	5	6	7^{1}	8	9^{2}	10	13		11^{3}		2		12	3							14				40
1			4^{1}	5	6	7^{2}	8		9	12		11^{3}		2		10	3							13			14	41
1			4	5	6		8^{2}	12	9	11^{1}				2		10	3							7^{3}		13	14	42
1			4	5	6	7^{2}	8^{3}	12	9	13		11		2		10^{1}	3							14				43
			4	5	6	7	8	12	9^{3}			11^{2}		2		10^{1}	3						1			13	14	44
			4	5	6	7		12	9^{2}	11		8		2		10^{1}	3						1	13				45
			4^{1}	5	6	7	12	9	10^{2}	11		8		2			3						1	13				46

FA Cup

Third Round	Swindon T	(h)	2-1
Fourth Round	Preston NE	(h)	0-2

Carling Cup

First Round	Notts Co	(h)	1-2

DAGENHAM & REDBRIDGE FL Championship 2

FOUNDATION

The roots of Dagenham & Redbridge live firmly in the Essex side of the Greater London area. Though only formed in 1992 their complex origins date back to the 19th century involving Ilford (founded 1881) and Leytonstone (1886) who merged in 1979 to form Leytonstone-Ilford. They and Walthamstow Avenue (1900) joined together in 1988 to becom Redbridge Forest who in turn merged with Dagenham FC (1949) in 1992. Victoria Road has existed as a football ground since 1917. Initially used by Sterling Works, in the summer of 1955 Briggs Sports vacated the premises and Dagenham FC moved in and the pitch was enclosed.

The London Borough of Barking and Dagenham Stadium, Victoria Road, Dagenham, Essex RM10 7XL.

Telephone: (0208) 592 1549.

Fax: (0208) 593 7227.

Ticket Office: (0208) 592 7194.

Website: www.daggers.co.uk

Email: info@daggers.co.uk

Ground Capacity: 6,087.

Record Attendance: 5,949 v Ipswich T, FA Cup 3rd rd, 5 January 2002.

Pitch Measurements: 100m × 64.5m.

Chairman: David J. Andrews.

Vice-chairman: David E. Ward.

Managing Director: Stephen R. Thompson.

Secretary: Derek P. Almond.

Manager: John L. Still.

Assistant Manager: Terry W. Harris.

Physio: John Gowens.

Colours: Red and blue striped shirts, white shorts, blue stockings.

Change Colours: Light blue shirts, dark blue shorts, dark blue stockings.

Year Formed: 1992.

SKY SPORTS FACT FILE

Between 31 January and 5 April 1998 Dagenham & Redbridge produced an outstanding Isthmian League record of completing 1144 minutes without conceding a goal. They finished fourth having let in just 50 goals in 42 League games in the Premier Division.

Grounds: Victoria Road 1992.

Club Nickname: Daggers.

Record League Victory: 8-1 v Woking (a), Conference 19 April 1994.

Record Defeat: 0-9 v Hereford U, Conference 27 February 2004.

Most League Points (3 for a win): 101, 1999–2000 Ryman Premier.

Most League Goals: 97, Ryman Premier, 1999–2000.

Highest League Scorer in Season: Paul Benson, 28 Conference, 2006–07.

Most League Goals in Total Aggregate: 105, Danny Shipp, 1997–2004.

Most League Appearances: Jason Broom, 462, 1992–2003.

Record Transfer Fee Received: Reported figure of £250,000 from Peterborough U for Craig Mackail-Smith and Shane Blackett, January 2007.

Record Transfer Fee Paid: £16,000 to Purfleet for Paul Cobb, 1998.

Football League Record: Promoted from Conference 2006–07; FL 2 2007–.

LATEST SEQUENCES

Longest Sequence of Wins: 11, 13.2.2001 – 27.3.2001.

Longest Sequence of Defeats: 7, 5.11.2005 – 7.12.2005.

Longest Sequence of Draws: 4, 26.11.94 – 17.12.94.

Longest Sequence of Unbeaten Matches: 14, 23.1.99 – 3.4.99.

Longest Sequence Without a Win: 9, 11.12.95 – 10.1.96.

HONOURS

Conference: Champions – 2006–07. Runners-up – 2001–02.
Isthmian League (Premier): Champions 1999–2000.
Essex Senior Cup: Winners – 1997–98, 2000–01. Runners-up 2001–02.

AS DAGENHAM FC
FA Trophy: Winners 1979–80; Runners-up 1976–77. *Amateur Cup:* Runners-up 1969–70, 1970–71.

AS ILFORD
FA Amateur Cup: Winners 1929, 1930. *Isthmian League:* Champions 1906–07, 1920–21, 1921–22.

AS LEYTONSTONE
FA Amateur Cup: Winners 1947, 1948, 1968. *Isthmian League:* Champions 1918–19, 1937–38, 1938–39, 1946–47, 1947–48, 1949–50, 1950–51, 1951–52, 1965–66.

AS LEYTONSTONE/ILFORD
Isthmian League: Champions 1981–82, 1988–89.

AS WALTHAMSTOW AVENUE
FA Amateur Cup: Winners 1952, 1961. *Isthmian League:* Champions 1945–46, 1948–49, 1952–53, 1954–55. *Athenian League:* Champions 1929–30, 1932–33, 1933–34, 1937–38, 1938–39.

AS REDBRIDGE FOREST
Isthmian League: Winners 1990–91.

TEN YEAR LEAGUE RECORD

		P	*W*	*D*	*L*	*F*	*A*	*Pts*	*Pos*
1997–98	IPL	42	21	10	11	73	50	73	4
1998–99	IPL	42	20	13	9	71	44	73	3
1999–00	IPL	42	32	5	5	97	35	101	1
2000–01	Conf	42	23	8	11	71	54	77	3
2001–02	Conf	42	24	12	8	70	47	84	3
2002–03	Conf	42	21	9	12	71	59	72	5
2003–04	Conf	42	15	9	18	59	64	54	13
2004–05	Conf	42	19	8	15	68	60	65	11
2005–06	Conf	42	16	19	16	63	59	58	10
2006–07	Conf	46	28	11	7	93	48	95	1

DID YOU KNOW ?

Dagenham & Redbridge's Victoria Road ground has hosted a number of important representative matches in recent years, including England Ladies v Swindon, several UEFA Youth Internationals and an FA XI against the Ryman League team.

DARLINGTON FL Championship 2

FOUNDATION

A football club was formed in Darlington as early as 1861 but the present club began in 1883 and reached the final of the Durham Senior Cup in their first season, losing to Sunderland in a replay after complaining that they had suffered from intimidation in the first. On 5 April 1884, Sunderland had defeated Darlington 4-3. Darlington's objection was upheld by the referee and the replay took place on 3 May. The new referee for the match was Major Marindin, appointed by the Football Association to ensure fair play. Sunderland won 2-0. The following season Darlington won this trophy and for many years were one of the leading amateur clubs in their area.

96.6 TFM Darlington Arena, Neasham Road, Darlington DL2 1DL.

Telephone: (01325) 387 000.

Fax: (01325) 387 050.

Ticket Office: 0870 0272 949.

Website: www.darlington-fc.net

Email: enquiries@darlington-fc.net

Ground Capacity: 25,000.

Record Attendance: 21,023 v Bolton W, League Cup 3rd rd, 14 November 1960.

Pitch Measurements: 105m × 68m.

Chairman: George Houghton.

Directors: George Luke, David Jones.

Chief Executive: Jon Sotnick.

Secretary: Lisa Charlton.

Manager: Dave Penney.

Assistant Manager: Martin Gray.

Physio: Paul Gough.

Colours: Black and white.

Change Colours: Red.

Year Formed: 1883. ***Turned Professional:*** 1908. ***Ltd Co.:*** 1891.

Grounds: 1918, Feethams Ground; 2003, Reynolds Arena, Hurworth Moor.

Club Nickname: 'The Quakers'.

First Football League Game: 27 August 1921, Division 3 (N), v Halifax T (h) W 2–0 – Ward; Greaves, Barbour; Dickson (1), Sutcliffe, Malcolm; Dolphin, Hooper (1), Edmunds, Wolstenholme, Winship.

Record League Victory: 9–2 v Lincoln C, Division 3 (N), 7 January 1928 – Archibald; Brooks, Mellen; Kelly, Waugh, McKinnell; Cochrane (1), Gregg (1), Ruddy (3), Lees (3), McGiffen (1).

HONOURS

Football League: Division 2 best season: 15th, 1925–26; Division 3 (N) – Champions 1924–25; Runners-up 1921–22; Division 4 – Champions 1990–91; Runners-up 1965–66.

FA Cup: best season: 5th rd, 1958.

Football League Cup: best season: 5th rd, 1968.

GM Vauxhall Conference: Champions 1989–90.

SKY SPORTS FACT FILE

Both Dick Healey and George Stevens, goalscorers when non-league Darlington accounted for Sheffield Wednesday in their memorable first round FA Cup replay at Hillsborough on 19 January 1920, made it into the Football League with the club a year later.

Record Cup Victory: 7–2 v Evenwood T, FA Cup 1st rd, 17 November 1956 – Ward; Devlin, Henderson; Bell (1p), Greener, Furphy; Forster (1), Morton (3), Tulip (2), Davis, Moran.

Record Defeat: 0–10 v Doncaster R, Division 4, 25 January 1964.

Most League Points (2 for a win): 59, Division 4, 1965–66.

Most League Points (3 for a win): 85, Division 4, 1984–85.

Most League Goals: 108, Division 3 (N), 1929–30.

Highest League Scorer in Season: David Brown, 39, Division 3 (N), 1924–25.

Most League Goals in Total Aggregate: Alan Walsh, 90, 1978–84.

Most League Goals in One Match: 5, Tom Ruddy v South Shields, Division 2, 23 April 1927; 5, Maurice Wellock v Rotherham U, Division 3N, 15 February 1930.

Most Capped Player: Jason Devos, 3 (46), Canada; Adrian Webster, 3, New Zealand.

Most League Appearances: Ron Greener, 442, 1955–68.

Youngest League Player: Dale Anderson, 16 years 254 days v Chesterfield, 4 May 1987.

Record Transfer Fee Received: £400,000 from Dundee U for Jason De Vos, October 1998.

Record Transfer Fee Paid: £100,000 to Boston U for Julian Joachim, August 2006.

Football League Record: 1921 Original Member Division 3 (N); 1925–27 Division 2; 1927–58 Division 3 (N); 1958–66 Division 4; 1966–67 Division 3; 1967–85 Division 4; 1985–87 Division 3; 1987–89 Division 4; 1989–90 GM Vauxhall Conference; 1990–91 Division 4; 1991–2004 Division 3; 2004– FL 2.

LATEST SEQUENCES

Longest Sequence of League Wins: 6, 6.2.2000 – 7.3.2000.

Longest Sequence of League Defeats: 8, 31.8.1985 – 19.10.1985.

Longest Sequence of League Draws: 5, 31.12.1988 – 28.1.1989.

Longest Sequence of Unbeaten League Matches: 17, 27.4.1968 – 19.10.1968.

Longest Sequence Without a League Win: 19, 27.4.1988 – 8.11.1988.

Successive Scoring Runs: 22 from 3.12.1932.

Successive Non-scoring Runs: 7 from 5.9.1975.

MANAGERS

Tom McIntosh 1902–11
W. L. Lane 1911–12
(Secretary-Manager)
Dick Jackson 1912–19
Jack English 1919–28
Jack Fairless 1928–33
George Collins 1933–36
George Brown 1936–38
Jackie Carr 1938–42
Jack Surtees 1942
Jack English 1945–46
Bill Forrest 1946–50
George Irwin 1950–52
Bob Gurney 1952–57
Dick Duckworth 1957–60
Eddie Carr 1960–64
Lol Morgan 1964–66
Jimmy Greenhalgh 1966–68
Ray Yeoman 1968–70
Len Richley 1970–71
Frank Brennan 1971
Ken Hale 1971–72
Allan Jones 1972
Ralph Brand 1972–73
Dick Conner 1973–74
Billy Horner 1974–76
Peter Madden 1976–78
Len Walker 1978–79
Billy Elliott 1979–83
Cyril Knowles 1983–87
Dave Booth 1987–89
Brian Little 1989–91
Frank Gray 1991–92
Ray Hankin 1992
Billy McEwan 1992–93
Alan Murray 1993–95
Paul Futcher 1995
David Hodgson/Jim Platt
(Director of Coaching) 1995
Jim Platt 1995–96
David Hodgson 1996–2000
Gary Bennett 2000–01
Tommy Taylor 2001–02
Mick Tait 2003
David Hodgson 2003–06
Dave Penney October 2006–

TEN YEAR LEAGUE RECORD

		P	*W*	*D*	*L*	*F*	*A*	*Pts*	*Pos*
1997-98	Div 3	46	14	12	20	56	72	54	19
1998-99	Div 3	46	18	11	17	69	58	65	11
1999-2000	Div 3	46	21	16	9	66	36	79	4
2000-01	Div 3	46	12	13	21	44	56	49	20
2001-02	Div 3	46	15	11	20	60	71	56	15
2002-03	Div 3	46	12	18	16	58	59	54	14
2003-04	Div 3	46	14	11	21	53	61	53	18
2004-05	FL 2	46	20	12	14	57	49	72	8
2005-06	FL 2	46	16	15	15	58	52	63	8
2006-07	FL 2	46	17	14	15	52	56	65	11

DID YOU KNOW ?

On 22 September 1965 Jimmy Lawton and Bryan Conlon were Darlington scorers in the 2–1 League Cup win over Swindon Town. Lawton was transferred to Swindon. On 31 October 1967 Conlon was a scorer in the 2–0 win over Millwall and then joined the Lions.

DARLINGTON 2006–07 LEAGUE RECORD

Match No.	Date	Venue	Opponents	Result	H/T Score	Lg. Pos.	Goalscorers	Attendance
1	Aug 5	H	Macclesfield T	W 4-0	3-0	—	Giallanza [12], Conlon 3 [32, 41, 73]	4095
2	8	A	Accrington S	W 2-0	2-0	—	Cummins [33], Smith [43]	2667
3	12	A	Boston U	L 1-4	1-1	5	Conlon [30]	1934
4	19	H	Swindon T	L 1-2	1-2	11	Giallanza [45]	4571
5	26	A	Walsall	L 0-1	0-1	13		4651
6	Sept 1	H	Torquay U	D 1-1	1-1	—	Ngoma [45]	4007
7	9	A	Peterborough U	W 3-1	3-0	10	Conlon (pen) [3], Joachim 2 [21, 24]	3848
8	12	H	Bury	W 1-0	0-0	—	Conlon (pen) [67]	3335
9	16	H	Bristol R	D 1-1	0-0	9	Smith [90]	3654
10	23	A	Shrewsbury T	D 2-2	1-0	9	Giallanza [29], Wainwright [67]	3931
11	26	A	Mansfield T	L 0-1	0-0	—		2794
12	29	H	Grimsby T	D 2-2	2-0	—	Armstrong [8], Smith [25]	3636
13	Oct 6	H	Rochdale	L 0-5	0-4	—		3752
14	14	A	Hereford U	D 1-1	1-0	14	Armstrong [37]	2838
15	21	H	Barnet	W 2-0	0-0	10	Johnson [75], Devera (og) [78]	3268
16	28	A	Hartlepool U	D 0-0	0-0	10		7458
17	Nov 3	H	Chester C	W 1-0	1-0	—	Cummins [18]	3630
18	18	A	Lincoln C	W 3-1	1-0	8	Holloway [43], Cummins [55], Johnson [73]	5292
19	25	H	Milton Keynes D	W 1-0	1-0	8	Wainwright [38]	4017
20	Dec 5	A	Wycombe W	L 0-1	0-1	—		3885
21	9	A	Stockport Co	L 2-5	2-4	9	Smith [7], Keltie (pen) [40]	4564
22	16	H	Notts Co	L 0-1	0-0	11		3253
23	23	A	Wrexham	L 0-1	0-1	13		3401
24	26	H	Mansfield T	L 0-2	0-1	15		3808
25	30	H	Shrewsbury T	L 1-2	0-1	16	Joachim [48]	2825
26	Jan 13	H	Peterborough U	W 3-1	1-1	16	Wheater [41], Joachim 2 [51, 61]	2321
27	16	A	Bury	D 1-1	0-1	—	Wright T [87]	1870
28	20	A	Grimsby T	W 1-0	0-0	13	Ryan [83]	3282
29	27	H	Wrexham	D 1-1	1-1	12	Wright T (pen) [45]	3301
30	Feb 3	A	Macclesfield T	D 1-1	1-0	12	Ravenhill [34]	2173
31	6	A	Bristol R	W 2-1	1-0	—	Blundell [7], Cummins [70]	5511
32	10	H	Boston U	W 2-0	0-0	9	Miller [59], Wainwright [64]	2764
33	17	A	Swindon T	D 1-1	0-1	9	Smith [71]	5570
34	20	H	Accrington S	W 2-1	2-0	—	Wright T [21], Blundell [29]	2790
35	24	A	Torquay U	W 1-0	0-0	8	Joachim [87]	2109
36	Mar 3	H	Walsall	D 0-0	0-0	8		3745
37	10	A	Rochdale	D 0-0	0-0	8		3256
38	17	H	Hereford U	W 1-0	0-0	8	Wright T [67]	3165
39	25	H	Hartlepool U	L 0-3	0-1	8		9987
40	31	A	Barnet	L 1-2	1-1	9	Wheater [22]	2364
41	Apr 6	A	Chester C	D 1-1	0-0	—	Blundell (pen) [89]	1942
42	9	H	Lincoln C	D 1-1	1-0	12	Joachim [39]	3878
43	14	A	Milton Keynes D	L 0-1	0-0	13		5730
44	21	H	Wycombe W	W 3-2	1-1	12	Wainwright 2 [26, 47], Rowson [70]	2727
45	28	A	Notts Co	W 1-0	0-0	10	Rowson [82]	5264
46	May 5	H	Stockport Co	L 0-5	0-1	11		5184

Final League Position: 11

GOALSCORERS

League (52): Joachim 7, Conlon 6 (2 pens), Smith 5, Wainwright 5, Cummins 4, Wright T 4 (1 pen), Blundell 3 (1 pen), Giallanza 3, Armstrong 2, Johnson 2, Rowson 2, Wheater 2, Holloway 1, Keltie 1 (pen), Miller 1, Ngoma 1, Ravenhill 1, Ryan 1, own goal 1.
Carling Cup (5): Joachim 3, Johnson 1 (pen), Logan 1.
FA Cup (5): Smith 3, Collins 1, Ngoma 1.
J Paint Trophy (2): Giallanza 1 (pen), Smith 1.

Russell S 31	Collins P 28+3	James C 22+1	Martis S 2	Hutchinson J 13	Ngoma K 15+3	Keltie C 25+2	Conlon B 12+7	Giallanza G 12+2	Smith M 30+4	Cummins M 38+1	Holloway D 14+7	Duke D 4+9	Johnson S 8+16	Logan C —+9	Wainwright N 30+11	Close B 26+1	Joachim J 26+10	Rowson D 20+4	Vaisanen V 5	Armstrong A 16+13	McLeod M 2	Horwood E 20	Clarke M 2	Albrighton M 3 / Prendergast R 5+3	Griffith A 2+2	Stockdale D 6 / Burgess K —+1	Reay S 1+2	Wright J —+1 / Hardman L —+1	Jones L 9	Ryan T 4+1	Wheater D 15	Ravenhill R 13+2	Wright T 9+4	Blundell G 14+1	Miller I 7	Wiseman S 10	Phillips M 7+1	*Match No.*
1	2	3	4^{1}	5	6^{2}	7	8	9	10^{3}	11	12	13	14																									1
1	2	3	4	5	6^{1}	7	8	9^{3}	10^{2}	11		12	14	13																								2
1	4	3		5	6^{1}	7	8	9	10^{2}	11^{3}	2	12	13		14																							3
1	4	3		5	6		8	9^{1}	10^{3}	11	2^{2}	7			12	13	14																					4
1	4			5	6		8^{2}	9		11	2^{3}	3	14	13	12	7	10^{1}																					5
1	4^{1}			5	6		8	9		11	12	3		13	14	2	10^{3}	7^{2}																				6
1	4			5	6^{1}		8^{2}	9■	12	11						2	10	7	3	13																		7
1	4	3		5	6		8^{3}		9^{2}	11^{1}		12	13			2	10	7		14																		8
1	4^{1}	3		5	6^{3}		8^{2}		9	11	12				13	2	10	7		14																		9
1		3			6			9^{2}		11	5		8^{1}	13	12		10	2	4	14	7^{3}																	10
1		3			6^{1}			9		11	5	12	8		13		10^{3}	2^{2}	4	14	7																	11
1		3			6	7	12	10^{2}	9	11	5■	2	13^{3}		14				4	8^{1}																		12
1	4	3■		5			8^{2}		10^{3}	6		12	13	14	7^{1}			11	2	9																		13
1				5	6^{3}	8	12		10	11^{2}	4			14	7	2		13		9^{1}		3																14
1	12			5	6^{2}	8		13	10	11	4		14		7	2				9^{3}		3^{1}																15
1	2			5		6	12		10	11			13		7	3	8^{2}			9^{1}			4															16
1	5	3				6	8^{2}		10	11	12		9^{1}		7	2				13			4															17
1	2	3			12	6	13		10	11	5^{1}		8^{2}		7	4	14			9^{3}																		18
1	5	3				6■			10	11			8^{2}		7	2	12			9^{1}				4	13													19
	5	3				6	12		8	11			14		7	2	10			9^{1}				4^{2}	13^{3}	1												20
	5	3				6	12		8^{1}	11		13	14		7	2	10			9^{3}					4^{2}	1												21
	5	3^{2}				6	12		8	11	4		13		7	2	10			9^{1}						1												22
	4	3				6			8	11	5^{1}	12	9^{2}	13	7^{3}	2	10			14						1												23
	5	3			6				8	11		12	9^{3}	13		2								4^{1}	7^{2}	1	10	14										24
	5	3				6	8^{2}		9^{1}	11	4			12	7	2	10									1	13											25
		12			13	6							8^{1}		11	2	10	7		9^{2}		3							1	4	5							26
		11^{1}				6					13		12^{2}		8	2	10	7^{3}				3■							1	4	5	14	9					27
	12					6			8^{3}	13	3		14		11	2	10	7^{2}											1	4	5		9^{1}					28
1	12	3							8^{3}	11	6^{1}				7^{2}	2	10	14		13											5	4	9					29
	5	3				7				11	12				13	2	10^{1}												1		6	4	8^{2}	9				30
	5					8				11^{2}	12				7^{1}	2	14	13		9^{3}		3							1		6	4		10				31
						8				11			12		7	2				9^{2}		3					13		1		6	4^{1}		10	5			32
									12	11					8^{2}	2	13	7		9^{1}		3							1		6	4^{3}	14	10	5			33
						12			8^{2}	11					13	2^{1}	4	7		14		3							1		6		9^{3}	10	5			34
						12			8^{2}	11					7		13	2		14		3							1		6	4^{1}	9^{3}	10	5			35
1						4			8^{1}	11					7		10	2				3									6		12	9	5			36
1						4			8^{2}	11^{1}					7		10^{3}	13				3									6	12	14	9	5	2		37
1						11			8^{2}						7^{1}		12					3								13	6	4	9	10	5	2		38
1						11			8^{3}						7^{1}		12					3		14						5^{2}	6	4	9	10		2	13	39
1									8^{3}						7		12	11		13		3^{1}		14							5	4	9■	10^{2}		2	6	40
1	5								8^{3}	11					12		13	7		9^{2}		3		14								4^{1}		10		2	6	41
1	5								12^{2}	8					7		10			13		3		11^{1}								4		9		2	6	42
1	5				12					4			13		7^{2}		10	8^{3}		14		3^{1}		11										9		2	6	43
1	5							12		4					7		10	8		9^{1}		3		11												2	6	44
1	5							9^{2}	12						7		10	8				3		11^{1}								4	13			2	6	45
1	5							9							7		10^{1}	8				3■		11		1		1				4		12		2	6^{2}	46

FA Cup

First Round	Lewes	(a)	4-1
Second Round	Swansea C	(h)	1-3

Carling Cup

First Round	Stoke C	(a)	2-1
Second Round	Reading	(a)	3-3

J Paint Trophy

Second Round	Tranmere R	(a)	1-0
Quarter-Final	Mansfield T	(h)	1-0
Semi-Final	Doncaster R	(a)	0-2

DERBY COUNTY FA Premiership

FOUNDATION

Derby County was formed by members of the Derbyshire County Cricket Club in 1884, when football was booming in the area and the cricketers thought that a football club would help boost finances for the summer game. To begin with, they sported the cricket club's colours of amber, chocolate and pale blue, and went into the game at the top immediately entering the FA Cup.

Pride Park Stadium, Pride Park, Derby DE24 8XL.

Telephone: 0870 444 1884.

Fax: (01332) 667 519.

Ticket Office: 0870 444 1884.

Website: www.dcfc.co.uk

Email: derby-county@dcfc.co.uk

Ground Capacity: 33,597.

Record Attendance: Baseball ground: 41,826 v Tottenham H, Division 1, 20 September 1969. Pride Park: 33,475 Derby Co Legends v Rangers 9 in a row Legends, 1 May 2006 (Ted McMinn Benefit).

Pitch Measurements: 110yd × 74yd.

Chairman: Peter Gadsby.

Vice-chairman: Mike Horton.

Secretary: Marian McMinn.

Manager: Billy Davies.

Assistant Manager: David Kelly.

Physio: Andy Balderston.

Colours: White shirts, black shorts, white stockings.

Change Colours: Navy shirts, navy shorts, yellow stockings.

Year Formed: 1884.

Turned Professional: 1884.

Ltd Co.: 1896.

Club Nickname: 'The Rams'.

Grounds: 1884, Racecourse Ground; 1895, Baseball Ground; 1997, Pride Park.

First Football League Game: 8 September 1888, Football League, v Bolton W (a) W 6–3 – Marshall; Latham, Ferguson, Williamson; Monks, W. Roulstone; Bakewell (2), Cooper (2), Higgins, H. Plackett, L. Plackett (2).

Record League Victory: 9–0 v Wolverhampton W, Division 1, 10 January 1891 – Bunyan; Archie Goodall, Roberts; Walker, Chalmers, Roulstone (1); Bakewell, McLachlan, Johnny Goodall (1), Holmes (2), McMillan (5). 9–0 v Sheffield W, Division 1, 21 January 1899 – Fryer; Methven, Staley; Cox, Archie Goodall, May; Oakden (1), Bloomer (6), Boag, McDonald (1), Allen, (1 og).

HONOURS

Football League: Division 1 – Champions 1971–72, 1974–75; Runners-up 1895–96, 1929–30, 1935–36, 1995–96; Promoted from FL C – 2006–07 (play-offs); Division 2 – Champions 1911–12, 1914–15, 1968–69, 1986–87; Runners-up 1925–26; Division 3 (N) Champions 1956–57; Runners-up 1955–56.

FA Cup: Winners 1946; Runners-up 1898, 1899, 1903.

Football League Cup: Semi-final 1968.

Texaco Cup: Winners 1972.

European Competitions: *European Cup:* 1972–73, 1975–76. *UEFA Cup:* 1974–75, 1976–77. *Anglo-Italian Cup:* Runners-up 1993.

SKY SPORTS FACT FILE

On 16 December 1950 Derby County beat Sunderland 6–5 with Jack Lee scoring four for them. They had edged the first half 3–2. The referee on the day was Arthur Ellis who subsequently described it as one of the most exciting matches he had ever controlled.

Record Cup Victory: 12–0 v Finn Harps, UEFA Cup 1st rd 1st leg, 15 September 1976 – Moseley; Thomas, Nish, Rioch (1), McFarland, Todd (King), Macken, Gemmill, Hector (5), George (3), James (3).

Record Defeat: 2–11 v Everton, FA Cup 1st rd, 1889–90.

Most League Points (2 for a win): 63, Division 2, 1968–69 and Division 3 (N), 1955–56 and 1956–57.

Most League Points (3 for a win): 84, Division 3, 1985–86, Division 3, 1986–87 and FL C, 2006–07.

Most League Goals: 111, Division 3 (N), 1956–57.

Highest League Scorer in Season: Jack Bowers, 37, Division 1, 1930–31; Ray Straw, 37 Division 3 (N), 1956–57.

Most League Goals in Total Aggregate: Steve Bloomer, 292, 1892–1906 and 1910–14.

Most League Goals in One Match: 6, Steve Bloomer v Sheffield W, Division 1, 2 January 1899.

Most Capped Players: Deon Burton, 41 (49), Jamaica and Mart Poom, 41 (104), Estonia.

Most League Appearances: Kevin Hector, 486, 1966–78 and 1980–82.

Youngest League Player: Lee Holmes, 15 years 268 days v Grimsby T, 26 December 2002.

Record Transfer Fee Received: £7,000,000 rising to £9,000,000 for Seth Johnson from Leeds U, October 2001.

Record Transfer Fee Paid: £3,500,000 to Norwich C for Robert Earnshaw, June 2007.

Football League Record: 1888 Founder Member of the Football League; 1907–12 Division 2; 1912–14 Division 1; 1914–15 Division 2; 1915–21 Division 1; 1921–26 Division 2; 1926–53 Division 1; 1953–55 Division 2; 1955–57 Division 3 (N); 1957–69 Division 2; 1969–80 Division 1; 1980–84 Division 2; 1984–86 Division 3; 1986–87 Division 2; 1987–91 Division 1; 1991–92 Division 2; 1992–96 Division 1; 1996–2002 FA Premier League; 2002–04 Division 1; 2004–07 FL C; 2007– FA Premier League.

MANAGERS

W. D. Clark 1896–1900
Harry Newbould 1900–06
Jimmy Methven 1906–22
Cecil Potter 1922–25
George Jobey 1925–41
Ted Magner 1944–46
Stuart McMillan 1946–53
Jack Barker 1953–55
Harry Storer 1955–62
Tim Ward 1962–67
Brian Clough 1967–73
Dave Mackay 1973–76
Colin Murphy 1977
Tommy Docherty 1977–79
Colin Addison 1979–82
Johnny Newman 1982
Peter Taylor 1982–84
Roy McFarland 1984
Arthur Cox 1984–93
Roy McFarland 1993–95
Jim Smith 1995–2001
Colin Todd 2001–02
John Gregory 2002–03
George Burley 2003–05
Phil Brown 2005–06
Billy Davies June 2006–

LATEST SEQUENCES

Longest Sequence of League Wins: 9, 15.3.1969 – 19.4.1969.

Longest Sequence of League Defeats: 8, 12.12.1987 – 10.2.1988.

Longest Sequence of League Draws: 6, 26.3.1927 – 18.4.1927.

Longest Sequence of Unbeaten League Matches: 22, 8.3.1969 – 20.9.1969.

Longest Sequence Without a League Win: 20, 15.12.1990 – 23.4.1991.

Successive Scoring Runs: 29 from 3.12.1960.

Successive Non-scoring Runs: 8 from 30.10.1920.

TEN YEAR LEAGUE RECORD

		P	W	D	L	F	A	Pts	Pos
1997-98	PR Lge	38	16	7	15	52	49	55	9
1998-99	PR Lge	38	13	13	12	40	45	52	8
1999-2000	PR Lge	38	9	11	18	44	57	38	16
2000-01	PR Lge	38	10	12	16	37	59	42	17
2001-02	PR Lge	38	8	6	24	33	63	30	19
2002-03	Div 1	46	15	7	24	55	74	52	18
2003-04	Div 1	46	13	13	20	53	67	52	20
2004-05	FL C	46	22	10	14	71	60	76	4
2005-06	FL C	46	10	20	16	53	67	50	20
2006-07	FL C	46	25	9	12	62	46	84	3

DID YOU KNOW ?

Full-back Jack Nicholas who skippered Derby County to their 1946 FA Cup success was a remarkably consistent player. Pre-war he missed just three matches in seven seasons. Derby born but raised in Swansea he won Welsh schoolboy international honours.

DERBY COUNTY 2006–07 LEAGUE RECORD

Match No.	Date	Venue	Opponents	Result		H/T Score	Lg. Pos.	Goalscorers	Attendance
1	Aug 6	H	Southampton	D	2-2	1-0	—	Johnson S 35, Peschisolido 90	21,939
2	8	A	Stoke C	L	0-2	0-1	—		20,013
3	12	A	Hull C	W	2-1	1-1	15	Oakley 7, Smith T (pen) 74	15,621
4	19	H	Norwich C	D	0-0	0-0	17		22,196
5	26	A	Colchester U	L	3-4	1-2	19	Lupoli 2 42, 80, Peschisolido 89	4574
6	Sept 9	H	Sunderland	L	1-2	1-0	23	Oakley 45	26,502
7	12	A	Wolverhampton W	W	1-0	1-0	—	Howard 34	21,546
8	16	H	Preston NE	D	1-1	1-1	17	Howard (pen) 44	22,220
9	23	A	Sheffield W	W	2-1	0-0	13	Peschisolido 79, Howard 90	23,659
10	30	H	Southend U	W	3-0	1-0	10	Lupoli 2 40, 63, Johnson M 48	22,395
11	Oct 15	A	Plymouth Arg	L	1-3	1-1	12	Lupoli 45	13,622
12	17	A	QPR	W	2-1	2-1	—	Bisgaard 4, Howard 33	10,882
13	21	H	Birmingham C	L	0-1	0-0	10		25,673
14	28	A	Cardiff C	D	2-2	0-0	13	Howard 66, Barnes 90	17,371
15	Nov 1	H	Barnsley	W	2-1	0-1	—	Barnes 2 72, 76	21,295
16	4	H	WBA	W	2-1	0-1	8	Oakley 69, Barnes 72	25,342
17	11	A	Coventry C	W	2-1	1-1	5	Stead 11, Howard 76	19,701
18	18	A	Luton T	W	2-0	0-0	5	Stead 72, Howard 75	9708
19	25	H	Leicester C	W	1-0	0-0	4	Stead 53	28,315
20	29	H	Ipswich T	W	2-1	0-1	—	Howard 54, Lupoli 90	22,606
21	Dec 2	A	WBA	L	0-1	0-0	4		20,494
22	9	A	Leeds U	W	1-0	1-0	2	Barnes 9	20,087
23	16	H	Crystal Palace	W	1-0	1-0	2	Jones 22	23,875
24	23	A	Burnley	D	0-0	0-0	3		12,825
25	26	H	Wolverhampton W	L	0-2	0-0	3		31,920
26	30	H	Plymouth Arg	W	1-0	0-0	3	Bisgaard 81	25,775
27	Jan 1	A	Preston NE	W	2-1	0-0	2	Howard 2 (1 pen) 48, 51 (p)	19,204
28	13	H	Sheffield W	W	1-0	0-0	2	Jones 90	28,936
29	20	A	Southend U	W	1-0	1-0	1	Howard 33	10,745
30	30	H	Burnley	W	1-0	1-0	—	Howard 4	23,122
31	Feb 3	A	Southampton	W	1-0	0-0	1	Howard 83	27,656
32	10	H	Hull C	D	2-2	2-1	1	Teale 29, Moore 45	28,140
33	21	H	Stoke C	L	0-2	0-2	—		24,897
34	24	A	Sunderland	L	1-2	0-1	2	Barnes 59	36,049
35	Mar 2	H	Colchester U	W	5-1	3-0	—	Jones 2, Lupoli 20, Barnes 30, Howard (pen) 62, Barker (og) 69	26,704
36	6	A	Norwich C	W	2-1	0-0	—	Jones 2 62, 72	23,462
37	9	A	Birmingham C	L	0-1	0-1	—		20,962
38	13	H	QPR	D	1-1	0-1	—	Moore 87	27,567
39	17	H	Cardiff C	W	3-1	1-1	1	Howard 2 (1 pen) 28 (p), 60, Barnes 49	27,689
40	31	A	Barnsley	W	2-1	1-0	1	Jones 11, Oakley 48	17,059
41	Apr 6	A	Leicester C	D	1-1	1-0	—	Fagan 23	24,704
42	9	H	Coventry C	D	1-1	0-0	2	Oakley 79	29,940
43	14	A	Ipswich T	L	1-2	1-0	2	Oakley 9	24,319
44	20	H	Luton T	W	1-0	1-0	—	Nyatanga 37	28,499
45	29	A	Crystal Palace	L	0-2	0-1	3		19,545
46	May 6	H	Leeds U	W	2-0	1-0	3	Currie 45, Mears 86	31,183

Final League Position: 3

GOALSCORERS

League (62): Howard 16 (4 pens), Barnes 8, Lupoli 7, Jones 6, Oakley 6, Peschisolido 3, Stead 3, Bisgaard 2, Moore 2, Currie 1, Fagan 1, Johnson M 1, Johnson S 1, Mears 1, Nyatanga 1, Smith T 1 (pen), Teale 1, own goal 1.
Carling Cup (4): Howard 1, Johnson M 1, Lupoli 1, Moore 1.
FA Cup (4): Lupoli 3, Peschisolido 1.
Play-Offs (5): Howard 2 (1 pen), Moore 1, Pearson 1, own goal 1.

Camp L 3	Edworthy M 38	Jackson R 3 + 2	Barnes G 31 + 8	Moore D 28 + 7	Johnson M 22 + 7	Johnson S 21 + 6	Idiakez I 4 + 1	Howard S 43	Smith T 4 + 1	Smith R 5 + 10	Peschisolido P 3 + 11	Bolder A 9 + 4	Bisgaard M 17 + 15	Grant L 6 + 1	Nyatanga L 5 + 2	Oakley M 36 + 1	Bywater S 37	Leacock D 36 + 2	Boertien P 10 + 1	Camara M 19	Lupoli A 18 + 17	Malcolm B 6 + 3	Stead J 15 + 2	Jones D 27 + 1	Fagan C 12 + 5	Teale G 11 + 5	Pearson S 6 + 3	Mears T 8 + 5	McEveley J 15	Macken J 4 + 4	Currie D 4 + 3	*Match No.*
1	2	3	4	5	6	7^1	8^2	9	10	11^3	12	13	14																			1
	2		4	5	3	7^2	14	9	10	11^1	13		12	1	6	8^3																2
		3^1	4^3	5	2	7^2	11	9	10	13		14				8	1	12	6													3
	3		4	5^2	6		11^1	9	10		8^3	12	7		13		1			2	14											4
1			4		5	12	8^2	9	13	11^3	14		7^1		6			2		3	10											5
	2^2		4		6	12		9		11	8^1	13				7	1	5		3	10											6
	2		12		6			9		13		11^3	7^1		14	8	1	5		3	10^2	4										7
	2^1		12		6			9			13	11	7^2			8	1	5		3	10	4										8
	2		12■		6	10^2		9		11^1	13	4^3	7	1		8		5		3		14										9
	2			5	6	12		9		13		4	7^2	1		8^1				3	10	11										10
	2			5^3	6	12		9		13		4	7^2	1		8^1		14		3	10		11									11
	2			12	6	11		9				4	7^1	1		8		5^2	13	3	10^3		14									12
	2		12	5	6	11		9				4	7	1						3	10^1		8									13
	2	12	13		6^1	8		9		14			7^2			4	1	5		3	10		11^3									14
	2^1	12	4	5		11		9		13		7^3	14				1	6		3	10		8^2									15
	2		4	12	6	11^2		9		13			7^1			8	1	5		3	10^3		14									16
	2		4	12	6^1	11		9		13			7^2			8	1	5	3		14		10^3									17
	2		4	5		11^3		9		12			7^1			8	1	6	3		13		10^2	14								18
	2		4	12	6	7^2		9					13			8^1	1	5	3		14		10^3	11								19
	2		4	12	6	8^2		9					7				1	5	3		13		10^1	11								20
	2		4	12	6^1			9			13	7	14				1	5	3		8^2		10^3	11								21
	2		4^1	5	12	7^2		9					13			8	1	6	3		14		10^3	11								22
	2		4	5	12	7^1				13						8^3	1	6	3		10^2	14	9	11								23
		2	4^1	5	12	7		9					13			8^2	1	6	3		14		10^3	11								24
	2		4	5	12	7^3		9			13					8^2	1	6	3^1		14		10	11								25
	2		12	5	13			9					7			4	1	6		3	14	8^3	10^2	11^1								26
	2		4^3	12	6			9					7^2			8	1	5		3	13	14	10^1	11								27
	2		4^2	5		8^3		9					12				1	6		3	10			11	13	7^1	14					28
	2			5	12			9					13			14	1	6		3		8^3		11	10^1	7^2	4					29
	2			5				9					12			4	1	6		3				11	7	10^1	8					30
	2		12	5				9								4^3	1	6		3		8^2		11	10^1	13	7	14				31
	2		4^2	5				9					12			7^1	1	6			13			11		10^3	8		3	14		32
	2				6			9								4	1	5^2			12			11^3	8	7	14	13	3	10^1		33
	2		12	5	13			9			14					4	1							11	10^3	7^1	8^2	6	3			34
	2		4	5	6^1			9								8^3	1				10^2			11	13	7		12	3	14		35
	2^3		4	5				9								8	1	6			10^2			11	7^1	12		14	3	13		36
			4	5				9			12		13			8^3	1	6			14			11		7		2	3^1	10^2		37
	2		4	5				9			12					8	1	6			10			11^1	13	7^2			3			38
			4	5		7^1		9								8	1	6						11	10			2	3		12	39
			4	5		12					13					8	1	6						11^1	9^2	14		2	3	10	7^3	40
			4	5									12			8	1	6			13			11^1	9	14		2	3	10^3	7^2	41
	6		4	5		12		9					13			8^1	1				10^3			11	7^2			2	3		14	42
	5		4^2			7^1		9					12	15		8	1■	6						11	10^G	13		2	3			43
	2		4^2					9							5	8	1	6			12			11	13	10^3	14		3		7^1	44
1	2^3		4^1					9							5	8		6			12			11	13	7		14	3		10^2	45
						11		9^2			10^1		7^3		5		1	6			12				8		4	2	3	13	14	46

FA Cup

Third Round	Wrexham	(h)	3-1
Fourth Round	Bristol R	(h)	1-0
Fifth Round	Plymouth Arg	(a)	0-2

Carling Cup

First Round	Stockport Co	(a)	1-0
Second Round	Doncaster R	(a)	3-3

Play-Offs

Semi-Final	Southampton	(a)	2-1
		(h)	2-3
Final *(at Wembley)*	WBA		1-0

DONCASTER ROVERS FL Championship 1

FOUNDATION

In 1879, Mr Albert Jenkins assembled a team to play a match against the Yorkshire Institution for the Deaf. The players remained together as Doncaster Rovers, joining the Midland Alliance in 1889 and the Midland Counties League in 1891.

Keepmoat Stadium, Stadium Way, Lakeside, Doncaster DN4 5JW.

Telephone: (01302) 764 664.

Fax: (01302) 363 525.

Ticket Office: (01302) 762 576.

Website: www.doncasterroversfc.co.uk

Email: info@doncasterroversfc.co.uk

Ground Capacity: 15,269.

Record Attendance: 3,714 v Hull C, Division 3 (N), 2 October 1948.

Pitch Measurements: 100m × 70m.

Chairman: John Ryan.

Vice-chairman: Jim Beresford.

Chief Executive: David Morris.

Secretary: Jenny Short.

Manager: Sean O'Driscoll.

Assistant Manager: Richard O'Kelly.

Physio: John Dickens.

Colours: Red and white hooped shirts, black shorts, black stockings.

Change Colours: Chelsea blue and white hooped shirts, blue shorts, blue stockings.

Year Formed: 1879.

Turned Professional: 1885.

Ltd Co.: 1905 & 1920.

Club Nickname: 'Rovers'.

Grounds: 1880–1916, Intake Ground; 1920, Benetthorpe Ground; 1922, Low Pasture, Belle Vue; 2007, Keepmoat Stadium.

Record League Victory: 10–0 v Darlington, Division 4, 25 January 1964: Potter; Raine, Meadows, Windross (1), White, Ripley (2), Robinson, Book (2), Hale (4), Jeffrey, Broadbent (1).

Record Cup Victory: 7–0 v Blyth Spartans, FA Cup 1st rd, 27 November 1937: Imrie; Shaw, Rodgers, McFarlane, Bycroft, Cyril Smith, Burton (1), Killourhy (4), Morgan (2), Malam, Dutton.

HONOURS

Football League: Division 2 best season: 7th, 1901–02; Division 3 Champions 2003–04; Division 3 (N) Champions – 1934–35, 1946–47, 1949–50; Runners-up: 1937–38, 1938–39; Division 4 Champions 1965–66, 1968–69; Runners-up: 1983–84. Promoted 1980–81 (3rd).

FA Cup: best season 5th rd, 1952, 1954, 1955, 1956.

Football League Cup: best season: 5th rd, 1976.

J Paint Trophy: Winners 2007.

Football Conference: Champions 2002–03

Sheffield County Cup: Winners 1891, 1912, 1936, 1938, 1956, 1968, 1976, 1986.

Midland Counties League: Champions 1897, 1899.

Conference Trophy: Winners 1999, 2000.

Sheffield & Hallamshire Senior Cup: Winners 2001, 2002.

SKY SPORTS FACT FILE

Though Tom Keetley's outstanding individual performance is well documented for Doncaster Rovers, left-winger Bert Turner scored five of the goals in the 7–1 victory over New Brighton on 16 February 1935, when he was their top goalscorer with 25.

Record Defeat: 0–12 v Small Heath, Division 2, 11 April 1903.

Most League Points (2 for a win): 72, Division 3 (N), 1946–47.

Most League Points (3 for a win): 92, Division 3, 2003–04.

Most League Goals: 123, Division 3 (N), 1946–47.

Highest League Scorer in Season: Clarrie Jordan, 42, Division 3 (N), 1946–47.

Most League Goals in Total Aggregate: Tom Keetley, 180, 1923–29.

Most League Goals in One Match: 6, Tom Keetley v Ashington, Division 3 (N), 16 February 1929.

Most Capped Player: Len Graham, 14, Northern Ireland.

Most League Appearances: Fred Emery, 417, 1925–36.

Youngest League Player: Alick Jeffrey, 15 years 229 days v Fulham, 15 September 1954.

Record Transfer Fee Received: £275,000 from QPR for Rufus Brevett, February 1991.

Record Transfer Fee Paid: £175,000 to Sunderland for Sean Thornton, July 2005.

Football League Record: 1901 Elected to Division 2; 1903 Failed re-election; 1904 Re-elected; 1905 Failed re-election; 1923 Re-elected to Division 3 (N); 1935–37 Division 2; 1937–47 Division 3 (N); 1947–48 Division 2; 1948–50 Division 3 (N); 1950–58 Division 2; 1958–59 Division 3; 1959–66 Division 4; 1966–67 Division 3; 1967–69 Division 4; 1969–71 Division 3; 1971–81 Division 4; 1981–83 Division 3; 1983–84 Division 4; 1984–88 Division 3; 1988–92 Division 4; 1992–98 Division 3; 1998–2003 Conference; 2003–04 Division 3; 2004– FL 1.

MANAGERS

Arthur Porter 1920–21
Harry Tufnell 1921–22
Arthur Porter 1922–23
Dick Ray 1923–27
David Menzies 1928–36
Fred Emery 1936–40
Bill Marsden 1944–46
Jackie Bestall 1946–49
Peter Doherty 1949–58
Jack Hodgson & Sid Bycroft (*Joint Managers*) 1958
Jack Crayston 1958–59 (*continued as Secretary-Manager to 1961*)
Jackie Bestall (TM) 1959–60
Norman Curtis 1960–61
Danny Malloy 1961–62
Oscar Hold 1962–64
Bill Leivers 1964–66
Keith Kettleborough 1966–67
George Raynor 1967–68
Lawrie McMenemy 1968–71
Morris Setters 1971–74
Stan Anderson 1975–78
Billy Bremner 1978–85
Dave Cusack 1985–87
Dave Mackay 1987–89
Billy Bremner 1989–91
Steve Beaglehole 1991–93
Ian Atkins 1994
Sammy Chung 1994–96
Kerry Dixon (*Player–Manager*) 1996–97
Dave Cowling 1997
Mark Weaver 1997–98
Ian Snodin 1998–99
Steve Wignall 1999–2001
Dave Penney 2002–06
Sean O'Driscoll September 2006–

LATEST SEQUENCES

Longest Sequence of League Wins: 10, 22.1.1947 – 4.4.1947.

Longest Sequence of League Defeats: 9, 14.1.1905 – 1.4.1905.

Longest Sequence of League Draws: 4, 29.10.1932 – 19.11.1932.

Longest Sequence of Unbeaten League Matches: 20, 26.12.1968 – 12.4.1969.

Longest Sequence Without a League Win: 20, 9.8.1997 – 29.11.1997.

Successive Scoring Runs: 27 from 10.11.1934.

Successive Non-scoring Runs: 7 from 27.9.1947.

TEN YEAR LEAGUE RECORD

		P	W	D	L	F	A	Pts	Pos
1997-98	Div 3	46	4	8	34	30	113	20	24
1998-99	Conf.	42	12	12	18	51	55	48	16
1999-2000	Conf.	42	15	9	18	46	48	54	12
2000-01	Conf.	42	15	13	14	47	43	58	9
2001-02	Conf.	42	18	13	11	68	46	67	4
2002-03	Conf.	42	22	12	8	73	47	78	3
2003-04	Div 3	46	27	11	8	79	37	92	1
2004-05	FL 1	46	16	18	12	65	60	66	10
2005-06	FL 1	46	20	9	17	55	51	69	8
2006-07	FL 1	46	16	15	15	52	47	63	11

DID YOU KNOW?

Northern Ireland amateur international forward Tommy Aiken signed from Ballymena United scored on his debut in the Football League for Doncaster Rovers with one of the quickest in the competition: six and a half seconds at Halifax Town on 2 December 1967.

DONCASTER ROVERS 2006–07 LEAGUE RECORD

Match No.	*Date*	*Venue*	*Opponents*	*Result*	*H/T Score*	*Lg. Pos.*	*Goalscorers*	*Attendance*
1	Aug 5	A	Carlisle U	L 0-1	0-1	—		12,031
2	8	H	Crewe Alex	W 3-1	1-1	—	Dyer [19], Horlock [63], Coppinger [71]	6081
3	12	H	Tranmere R	D 0-0	0-0	11		6014
4	19	A	Swansea C	L 0-2	0-0	14		12,218
5	26	H	Bournemouth	D 1-1	0-0	14	Guy [60]	5190
6	Sept 3	A	Port Vale	W 2-1	0-1	13	Heffernan 2 (1 pen) [88 (p), 90]	4862
7	9	H	Gillingham	L 1-2	0-2	16	Clohessy (og) [78]	5772
8	12	A	Huddersfield T	D 0-0	0-0	—		10,151
9	16	A	Rotherham U	D 0-0	0-0	18		6348
10	23	H	Blackpool	D 0-0	0-0	20		5424
11	26	H	Bradford C	D 3-3	1-2	—	Green P 2 [43, 51], Coppinger [53]	6304
12	30	A	Scunthorpe U	L 0-2	0-0	19		6441
13	Oct 6	H	Oldham Ath	D 1-1	1-1	—	Lee [23]	6241
14	14	A	Cheltenham T	W 2-0	1-0	17	Guy [45], Forte [82]	3872
15	21	H	Chesterfield	W 1-0	1-0	13	Forte [24]	6280
16	28	A	Bristol C	L 0-1	0-1	18		11,909
17	Nov 4	H	Leyton Orient	D 0-0	0-0	17		5447
18	18	A	Millwall	D 2-2	1-1	18	Forte [16], Price [53]	8670
19	25	H	Brighton & HA	W 1-0	1-0	12	McCammon [25]	5804
20	Dec 5	A	Brentford	W 4-0	1-0	—	Price [25], Forte [53], O'Connor [64], Heffernan [73]	4296
21	9	A	Northampton T	W 2-0	0-0	8	Heffernan [75], Guy [86]	5131
22	23	H	Nottingham F	W 1-0	0-0	10	Streete [60]	8923
23	26	A	Bradford C	W 1-0	1-0	9	Heffernan [14]	10,069
24	30	A	Blackpool	L 1-3	0-0	9	Heffernan [90]	7952
25	Jan 1	H	Huddersfield T	W 3-0	1-0	9	McCammon [9], Heffernan [47], Forte [51]	14,470
26	13	A	Gillingham	W 2-0	0-0	8	Price [81], Stock [88]	6202
27	20	H	Scunthorpe U	D 2-2	0-2	9	Lee [57], Price [59]	12,414
28	27	H	Rotherham U	W 3-2	1-1	8	Heffernan 2 [12, 59], Lee [47]	12,126
29	Feb 3	H	Carlisle U	L 1-2	1-0	8	Coppinger [3]	9036
30	10	A	Tranmere R	L 0-1	0-1	9		5965
31	17	H	Swansea C	D 2-2	1-2	9	Price [32], Heffernan [59]	7900
32	20	A	Crewe Alex	L 1-2	0-0	—	Heffernan (pen) [58]	4483
33	24	H	Port Vale	W 1-0	0-0	8	Price [49]	7848
34	27	H	Yeovil T	D 0-0	0-0	—		8046
35	Mar 3	A	Bournemouth	L 0-2	0-1	10		6166
36	6	A	Nottingham F	W 1-0	1-0	—	Stock [44]	16,785
37	11	A	Oldham Ath	L 0-4	0-1	9		6619
38	17	H	Cheltenham T	L 0-2	0-1	9		6777
39	21	A	Chesterfield	D 1-1	1-1	—	Stock [25]	3868
40	24	H	Bristol C	L 0-1	0-0	10		7945
41	Apr 7	A	Brighton & HA	W 2-0	1-0	10	Lee [28], Cadamarteri [47]	6267
42	9	H	Millwall	L 1-2	1-1	11	Coppinger [13]	7870
43	14	A	Leyton Orient	D 1-1	0-1	11	Lockwood [54]	4697
44	21	H	Brentford	W 3-0	1-0	10	Lockwood [45], Wilson [67], Guy (pen) [76]	8713
45	28	A	Yeovil T	L 0-1	0-0	11		6253
46	May 5	H	Northampton T	D 2-2	1-1	11	Nelthorpe [13], Roberts G [59]	7534

Final League Position: 11

GOALSCORERS

League (52): Heffernan 11 (2 pens), Price 6, Forte 5, Coppinger 4, Guy 4 (1 pen), Lee 4, Stock 3, Green P 2, Lockwood 2, McCammon 2, Cadamarteri 1, Dyer 1, Horlock 1, Nelthorpe 1, O'Connor 1, Roberts G 1, Streete 1, Wilson 1, own goal 1.
Carling Cup (8): Forte 3, McCammon 2, Coppinger 1, Stock 1, own goal 1.
FA Cup (4): Guy 1, Heffernan 1, McCammon 1, Stock 1.
J Paint Trophy (18): Heffernan 9 (2 pens), Price 4, Forte 1, Guy 1, Lee 1, Stock 1, Thornton 1.

Blayney A 8	Lockwood A 42 + 2	Roberts G 28 + 2	Roberts S 15 + 6	Lee G 36 + 3	Horlock K 2	Coppinger J 34 + 5	Green P 36 + 5	Heffernan P 23 + 6	Dyer B 9 + 6	Forte J 31 + 10	McCammon M 14 + 8	Price J 19 + 12	Thornton S 15 + 15	Griffith A 2	McDaid S 16 + 4	O'Connor J 39 + 1	Guy L 19 + 17	Di Piedi M 1 + 2	Budtz J 6 + 1	Stock B 35 + 1	Streete T 2 + 4	Filan J 3	Smith B 13	Sullivan N 16	Wilson M 17 + 5	Gilbert P 4	Wright A 3	Nelthorpe C 2 + 4	Worley H 10	Hird S — + 5	Cadamarteri D 6	Green L — + 2	*Match No.*
1	2^{1}	3	4	5	6	7^{2}	8^{3}	9	10	11	12	13	14																				1
1	2	3	4	5	6	7		9	10	11^{1}		12	8																				2
1	2	3	4	5		7	12	9	10^{3}	11^{2}	14	13	8	6^{1}																			3
1	2		4	5		9	13		12^{2}	14	8	10^{3}	11	6^{1}	3	7																	4
1	12	3	4	5		7	8			13	10^{3}		6^{1}		11	2	9^{2}	14															5
1	2	3	4^{2}	5		7	8	12		11	10^{1}	13				6	14	9^{3}															6
1	2	3^{2}	4			7	8	9		10^{3}	12	11	6^{1}		13	5		14															7
1^{6}	12	3	4^{1}	5		7	8	9		13		11^{2}				2	10		15	6													8
	6	3		5		7	8	9^{1}		13	12				11	2	10^{2}		1	4													9
	2	3^{3}		5		7	8	9^{2}		12		14	13		11	4	10^{1}		1	6													10
	2	3	12	5■		7^{2}	8	9^{1}		14		13			11	4	10^{3}		1	6													11
	2		4			7	8	9^{2}		12	14	13			3	11	10^{3}		1	6	5^{1}												12
	2		4	5			8	9^{2}	12	7		13			11	3	10^{1}			6		1											13
	2		4^{3}	5			8		9^{1}	7		12	13		11	3	10^{2}			6	14	1											14
	2	12	4	5			8		10^{2}	7		13			11^{1}	3	9^{3}			6	14	1											15
	2	3	4	5^{1}		13	8	12		9		14			11^{3}	7	10^{2}			6			1										16
	2	3	4	5^{3}		12	8^{1}	13		9		11	14			7	10^{2}			6			1										17
	2	3	4^{1}	12			8	13		11	9^{2}	7			14	5	10^{3}			6			1										18
	2	3		5		12	8^{2}			11	9^{1}	7			13	4	10^{3}			6	14			1									19
	4^{3}	3		5^{2}		7	8	12		9	10	11^{1}	13			2				6	14			1									20
	2	3		5		7^{3}	8	12		9^{2}	10	11^{1}				4	13			6				1	14								21
	2	3		5		7^{1}	8	9^{2}		11	10		13				12			6	4^{3}		1		14								22
	2	3		5		7^{1}	8	9		11^{2}	10		12			4	13						1		6								23
	2^{2}	3		5		7	8	9		11^{3}	10^{1}	12	13			4	14						1		6								24
	2^{2}	3■		5		7^{1}	8	9^{3}	14	11	10		13			4	12						1		6								25
	2		12	5		7^{3}	8	9^{2}		11^{1}		10				4	13			6			1		14	3							26
	2	12		5		7	8^{3}	9		11		10^{2}	14			4	13			6			1			3^{1}							27
	2		12	5		7^{3}	8	9		11^{2}		10^{1}				4	13			6			1		14	3							28
	2		12	5		7	8^{1}	9		11^{2}	13	10^{3}				4	14			6			1			3							29
	2	3	12	5		7	8^{2}			10^{1}		9	11			4	13			6			1										30
	2			5		7^{1}	12	9		10^{3}	13	11^{2}				4	14			6			1		8		3						31
	3		12	5		13		9			10	7^{2}	14			4	11^{1}			6				1	8^{3}		2						32
	2			5		7^{2}	8^{3}	9^{1}			12	10	14			4	13			6				1	11		3						33
	2			5			8			11^{2}		9	12		3	4	10^{1}			6				1	7			13					34
	2			5		7	12			11	10^{2}		13		3^{3}	4	9			6				1	8^{1}			14					35
	2			12		7^{3}	8		13		10^{2}	9	11		3					6				1	4				5^{1}	14			36
				5		7	2		10^{2}	12		9^{3}	8^{1}		3		13			6				1	11				4	14			37
	2			5		9^{2}	8			10			14		3	12	13			6				1	7^{3}				4^{1}		11		38
	2	3				7				9			8			4	12			6				1	11^{1}				5		10		39
	2			5			8^{1}		10	9^{2}			7		3	4				6				1	12			13			11		40
		3		5		12	13	9^{2}	14				11			2	7^{1}			6				1	8				4		10^{3}		41
	2	3		12		7	8^{3}	9^{2}		13			11			4				14				1	6				5^{1}		10		42
	2	3^{3}				7	8		9^{1}	12			11^{2}			4	13			6				1				14	5		10		43
	2^{2}	3				7^{1}			12	9						4	10			6				1	8^{3}			11	5	13		14	44
	2	3					8^{2}			9^{1}			11			4	10		1	6					7				5	12		13	45
	2	3				9			10^{2}				8		12	4			1	6					7^{1}			11	5	13			46

FA Cup

First Round	Brentford	(a)	1-0
Second Round	Mansfield T	(a)	1-1
		(h)	2-0
Third Round	Bolton W	(h)	0-4

Carling Cup

First Round	Rochdale	(h)	3-2
Second Round	Derby Co	(h)	3-3
Third Round	Wycombe W	(a)	2-2

J Paint Trophy

First Round	Huddersfield T	(a)	2-1
Second Round	Hartlepool U	(a)	3-1
Quarter-Final	Accrington S	(h)	2-0
Semi-Final	Darlington	(h)	2-0
Northern Final	Crewe Alex	(a)	3-3
		(h)	3-2
Final *(at Millennium Stadium)*	Bristol R		3-2

EVERTON

FA Premiership

FOUNDATION

St Domingo Church Sunday School formed a football club in 1878 which played at Stanley Park. Enthusiasm was so great that in November 1879 they decided to expand membership and changed the name to Everton playing in black shirts with a scarlet sash and nicknamed the 'Black Watch'. After wearing several other colours, royal blue was adopted in 1901.

Goodison Park, Goodison Road, Liverpool L4 4EL.

Telephone: (0870) 442 1878.

Fax: (0151) 286 9112.

Ticket Office: 0870 442 1878.

Website: www.evertonfc.com

Email: everton@evertonfc.com

Ground Capacity: 40,394.

Record Attendance: 78,299 v Liverpool, Division 1, 18 September 1948.

Pitch Measurements: 100.48m × 68m.

Chairman: Bill Kenwright CBE.

Vice chairman: Jon Woods.

Chief Executive: Keith Wyness.

Secretary: David Harrison.

Manager: David Moyes.

Assistant Manager: Alan Irvine.

Head of Physiotherapy: Mick Rathbone Bsc (Hons), MCSP.

Colours: Blue shirts, white shorts, white stockings.

Change Colours: White shirts, black shorts, black stockings.

Year Formed: 1878.

Turned Professional: 1885.

Ltd Co.: 1892.

Previous Name: 1878, St Domingo FC; 1879, Everton.

Club Nickname: 'The Toffees'.

Grounds: 1878, Stanley Park; 1882, Priory Road; 1884, Anfield Road; 1892, Goodison Park.

First Football League Game: 8 September 1888, Football League, v Accrington (h) W 2–1 – Smalley; Dick, Ross; Holt, Jones, Dobson; Fleming (2), Waugh, Lewis, E. Chadwick, Farmer.

HONOURS

Football League: Division 1 – Champions 1890–91, 1914–15, 1927–28, 1931–32, 1938–39, 1962–63, 1969–70, 1984–85, 1986–87; Runners-up 1889–90, 1894–95, 1901–02, 1904–05, 1908–09, 1911–12, 1985–86; Division 2 – Champions 1930–31; Runners-up 1953–54.

FA Cup: Winners 1906, 1933, 1966, 1984, 1995; Runners-up 1893, 1897, 1907, 1968, 1985, 1986, 1989.

Football League Cup: Runners-up 1977, 1984.

League Super Cup: Runners-up 1986.

Simod Cup: Runners-up 1989.

Zenith Data Systems Cup: Runners-up 1991.

European Competitions: *European Cup:* 1963–64, 1970–71. *European Cup-Winners' Cup:* 1966–67, 1984–85 (winners), 1995–96. *European Fairs Cup:* 1962–63, 1964–65, 1965–66. *Champions League:* 2005–06. *UEFA Cup:* 1975–76, 1978–79, 1979–80, 2005–06.

SKY SPORTS FACT FILE

On 9 September 2006 Everton beat Liverpool 3–0. It was their first such margin of a derby win at Goodison Park since 5–0 on 9 April 1909 and the biggest such after 4–0 at Anfield on 19 September 1964 as well as the first three v the Reds in 40 years.

Record League Victory: 9–1 v Manchester C, Division 1, 3 September 1906 – Scott; Balmer, Crelley; Booth, Taylor (1), Abbott (1); Sharp, Bolton (1), Young (4), Settle (2), George Wilson. 9–1 v Plymouth Arg, Division 2, 27 December 1930 – Coggins; Williams, Cresswell; McPherson, Griffiths, Thomson; Critchley, Dunn, Dean (4), Johnson (1), Stein (4).

Record Cup Victory: 11–2 v Derby Co, FA Cup 1st rd, 18 January 1890 – Smalley; Hannah, Doyle (1); Kirkwood, Holt (1), Parry; Latta, Brady (3), Geary (3), Chadwick, Millward (3).

Record Defeat: 4–10 v Tottenham H, Division 1, 11 October 1958.

Most League Points (2 for a win): 66, Division 1, 1969–70.

Most League Points (3 for a win): 90, Division 1, 1984–85.

Most League Goals: 121, Division 2, 1930–31.

Highest League Scorer in Season: William Ralph 'Dixie' Dean, 60, Division 1, 1927–28 (All-time League record).

Most League Goals in Total Aggregate: William Ralph 'Dixie' Dean, 349, 1925–37.

Most League Goals in One Match: 6, Jack Southworth v WBA, Division 1, 30 December 1893.

Most Capped Player: Neville Southall, 92, Wales.

Most League Appearances: Neville Southall, 578, 1981–98.

Youngest League Player: James Vaughan, 16 years 271 days v Crystal Palace, 10 April 2005.

MANAGERS

W. E. Barclay 1888–89
(Secretary-Manager)
Dick Molyneux 1889–1901
(Secretary-Manager)
William C. Cuff 1901–18
(Secretary-Manager)
W. J. Sawyer 1918–19
(Secretary-Manager)
Thomas H. McIntosh 1919–35
(Secretary-Manager)
Theo Kelly 1936–48
Cliff Britton 1948–56
Ian Buchan 1956–58
Johnny Carey 1958–61
Harry Catterick 1961–73
Billy Bingham 1973–77
Gordon Lee 1977–81
Howard Kendall 1981–87
Colin Harvey 1987–90
Howard Kendall 1990–93
Mike Walker 1994
Joe Royle 1994–97
Howard Kendall 1997–98
Walter Smith 1998–2002
David Moyes March 2002–

Record Transfer Fee Received: £23,000,000 from Manchester U for Wayne Rooney, August 2004.

Record Transfer Fee Paid: £8,500,000 to Crystal Palace for Andy Johnson, June 2006.

Football League Record: 1888 Founder Member of the Football League; 1930–31 Division 2; 1931–51 Division 1; 1951–54 Division 2; 1954–92 Division 1; 1992– FA Premier League.

LATEST SEQUENCES

Longest Sequence of League Wins: 12, 24.3.1894 – 13.10.1894.

Longest Sequence of League Defeats: 6, 26.12.1996 – 29.1.1997.

Longest Sequence of League Draws: 5, 4.5.1977 – 16.5.1977.

Longest Sequence of Unbeaten League Matches: 20, 29.4.1978 – 16.12.1978.

Longest Sequence Without a League Win: 14, 6.3.1937 – 4.9.1937.

Successive Scoring Runs: 40 from 15.3.1930.

Successive Non-scoring Runs: 6 from 3.3.1951.

TEN YEAR LEAGUE RECORD

		P	*W*	*D*	*L*	*F*	*A*	*Pts*	*Pos*
1997-98	PR Lge	38	9	13	16	41	56	40	17
1998-99	PR Lge	38	11	10	17	42	47	43	14
1999-2000	PR Lge	38	12	14	12	59	49	50	13
2000-01	PR Lge	38	11	9	18	45	59	42	16
2001-02	PR Lge	38	11	10	17	45	57	43	15
2002-03	PR Lge	38	17	8	13	48	49	59	7
2003-04	PR Lge	38	9	12	17	45	57	39	17
2004-05	PR Lge	38	18	7	13	45	46	61	4
2005-06	PR Lge	38	14	8	16	34	49	50	11
2006-07	PR Lge	38	15	13	10	52	36	58	6

DID YOU KNOW?

David Johnson scored for Everton after just 20 seconds against Watford after coming on as a substitute on 15 January 1983. Yet his quickest scoring performance for the club had been in the FA Youth Cup when he registered after just five seconds.

EVERTON 2006–07 LEAGUE RECORD

Match No.	*Date*	*Venue*	*Opponents*	*Result*		*H/T Score*	*Lg. Pos.*	*Goalscorers*	*Attendance*
1	Aug 19	H	Watford	W	2-1	1-0	—	Johnson [15], Arteta (pen) [82]	39,691
2	23	A	Blackburn R	D	1-1	0-0	—	Cahill [84]	22,015
3	26	A	Tottenham H	W	2-0	0-0	3	Davenport (og) [53], Johnson [66]	35,540
4	Sept 9	H	Liverpool	W	3-0	2-0	3	Cahill [24], Johnson 2 [36, 90]	40,004
5	16	H	Wigan Ath	D	2-2	0-0	4	Johnson [49], Beattie (pen) [66]	37,117
6	24	A	Newcastle U	D	1-1	1-1	4	Cahill [41]	50,107
7	30	H	Manchester C	D	1-1	1-0	5	Johnson [44]	38,250
8	Oct 14	A	Middlesbrough	L	1-2	0-1	7	Cahill [77]	27,156
9	21	H	Sheffield U	W	2-0	2-0	6	Arteta [13], Beattie (pen) [33]	37,900
10	28	A	Arsenal	D	1-1	1-0	6	Cahill [11]	60,047
11	Nov 4	A	Fulham	L	0-1	0-0	7		23,327
12	11	H	Aston Villa	L	0-1	0-1	7		36,376
13	18	H	Bolton W	W	1-0	0-0	7	Arteta [60]	34,417
14	25	A	Charlton Ath	D	1-1	0-0	8	Hreidarsson (og) [52]	26,435
15	29	A	Manchester U	L	0-3	0-1	—		75,723
16	Dec 3	H	West Ham U	W	2-0	0-0	7	Osman [51], Vaughan [90]	32,968
17	9	A	Portsmouth	L	0-2	0-2	10		19,528
18	17	H	Chelsea	L	2-3	1-0	10	Arteta (pen) [38], Yobo [64]	33,970
19	23	A	Reading	W	2-0	1-0	8	Johnson [14], McFadden [47]	24,053
20	26	H	Middlesbrough	D	0-0	0-0	8		38,126
21	30	H	Newcastle U	W	3-0	1-0	7	Anichebe 2 [9, 58], Neville [62]	38,682
22	Jan 1	A	Manchester C	L	1-2	0-0	8	Osman [84]	39,836
23	14	H	Reading	D	1-1	0-1	7	Johnson [81]	34,722
24	21	A	Wigan Ath	W	2-0	0-0	7	Arteta 2 (1 pen) [65 (p), 90]	18,149
25	Feb 3	A	Liverpool	D	0-0	0-0	8		44,234
26	10	H	Blackburn R	W	1-0	1-0	8	Johnson [10]	35,593
27	21	H	Tottenham H	L	1-2	1-1	—	Arteta [42]	34,121
28	24	A	Watford	W	3-0	2-0	7	Fernandes [23], Johnson (pen) [25], Osman [90]	18,761
29	Mar 3	A	Sheffield U	D	1-1	0-0	6	Arteta (pen) [75]	32,019
30	18	H	Arsenal	W	1-0	0-0	6	Johnson [90]	37,162
31	Apr 2	A	Aston Villa	D	1-1	1-0	—	Lescott [15]	36,407
32	6	H	Fulham	W	4-1	3-1	—	Carsley [25], Stubbs [34], Vaughan [45], Anichebe [80]	35,612
33	9	A	Bolton W	D	1-1	1-1	6	Vaughan [33]	25,179
34	15	H	Charlton Ath	W	2-1	0-0	5	Lescott [81], McFadden [90]	34,028
35	21	A	West Ham U	L	0-1	0-1	5		34,945
36	28	H	Manchester U	L	2-4	1-0	6	Stubbs [12], Fernandes [50]	39,682
37	May 5	H	Portsmouth	W	3-0	0-0	5	Arteta (pen) [59], Yobo [62], Naysmith [90]	39,619
38	13	A	Chelsea	D	1-1	0-0	6	Vaughan [50]	41,746

Final League Position: 6

GOALSCORERS

League (52): Johnson 11 (1 pen), Arteta 9 (5 pens), Cahill 5, Vaughan 4, Anichebe 3, Osman 3, Beattie 2 (2 pens), Fernandes 2, Lescott 2, McFadden 2, Stubbs 2, Yobo 2, Carsley 1, Naysmith 1, Neville 1, own goals 2.
Carling Cup (6): Cahill 2, Anichebe 1, McFadden 1, own goals 2.
FA Cup (1): Johnson 1 (pen).

Howard T 36	Neville P 35	Nuno Valente 10 + 4	Yobo J 38	Stubbs A 23	Carsley L 38	Davies S 13 + 2	Cahill T 17 + 1	Beattie J 15 + 18	Johnson A 32	Arteta M 35	Lescott J 36 + 2	McFadden J 6 + 13	Anichebe V 5 + 14	Naysmith G 10 + 5	Weir D 2 + 3	Osman L 31 + 3	Kilbane K 2	Hibbert T 12 + 1	Van der Meyde A 5 + 3	Vaughan J 7 + 7	Wright R 1	Hughes M — + 1	Fernandes M 8 + 1	Anderson — + 1	Turner I 1	*Match No.*
1	2	3^{1}	4	5	6	7^{2}	8	9^{3}	10	11	12	13	14													1
1	2		4	5^{2}	6		12	9^{3}	10	8	13	14		3		7	11^{1}									2
1	2		4		6		10		9	8	5^{1}			3	12	7	11▪									3
1	8	12	4		6		10	13	9	11^{1}	5			3		7^{2}		2								4
1	8	12	4		6^{2}		10	13	9	11	5			3^{1}		7		2								5
1	8	12	4		6		10	13	9	11^{2}	5			3^{1}		7		2▪								6
1	2	3	4		6	12	8	9^{3}	10^{2}	11^{1}	5		14		13	7										7
1	8	3^{3}	4		6	7^{2}	10	12	9	11	5	13						2^{1}	14							8
1	2^{2}		4		6	7	8^{3}	9^{1}	10	11	3	12	13		5	14										9
1	2		4	5	6	7	10		9	11	3					8										10
1	2		3	5	6^{2}	7^{1}	10	12	9	11	4		13			8										11
1	2		4	5	6	7	10^{1}	12	9	11	3		13			8^{2}										12
1	8	3	2	5	6			9^{1}	10	11	4		12			7										13
1	2	3	4		6	7		9^{2}		11	5	10^{1}	12			8				13						14
	8	3	2	4	6			9		11	5	10				7^{1}				12	1					15
1		3	2	4	6			9^{3}	10		5	11			12	8^{1}			7^{2}	13		14				16
1		11	2	5	6	7		9^{2}	10		3	12	13		4^{1}				8^{3}	14						17
1	2		4	5	6^{1}	7		12	10	11	3	13	9^{2}			8										18
1	2		4		6	7		12	10	11	5	9^{1}		3		8										19
1		12	4		6	2		13	10	11	5	8^{3}	9^{2}	3^{1}		7			14							20
1	2	3	4		6	12		13	10^{2}	11	5	14	9^{3}			7			8^{1}							21
1	2	3^{2}	4		6	7^{1}		9^{3}	10	11	5	12	14	13		8										22
1	2		4		6		11	12	10		5	9^{2}	13	3		7			8^{1}							23
1	2		4	5	6	7	10^{1}	12	9^{2}	11	3		13			8										24
1	8		4	5	6		10		9^{1}	11	3		12			7		2								25
1	2		4	5	6		10	12	9	11	3								7^{1}				8			26
1	2		4	5	6			9		11	3		10^{1}	12^{2}		7		14		13			8^{3}			27
1	2		4		6		7	9	10^{2}	11	5			3		12				13			8^{1}			28
1	2		4		6		7^{1}	9^{2}	10	11	5			3		12				13			8			29
1	2		4	5	6				9	11	3		12			7				10^{1}			8			30
1	8		4	5	6				9	11	3					7		2		10						31
1	8		4	5	6			12	9^{1}	11^{2}	3		14	13		7		2		10^{3}						32
1	8		4	5	6			12	9	11	3					7		2		10^{1}						33
1	8		4	5^{2}	6			9^{1}	10	11^{3}	3	12		13		7		2						14		34
1	8^{2}		4	5	6			9	10^{1}	11	3	12				7		2					13			35
	8		4	5	6^{3}			12		11	3	13				7^{2}		2	14	9^{1}			10		1	36
1	2		4	5	6			12		11	3	13	10^{2}	14		7				9^{1}			8^{3}			37
1	10		4	5	6			12		11	3	13				7		2		9^{1}			8^{2}			38

FA Cup

Third Round	Blackburn R	(h)	1-4

Carling Cup

Second Round	Peterborough U	(a)	2-1
Third Round	Luton T	(h)	4-0
Fourth Round	Arsenal	(h)	0-1

FULHAM

FA Premiership

FOUNDATION

Churchgoers were responsible for the foundation of Fulham, which first saw the light of day as Fulham St Andrew's Church Sunday School FC in 1879. They won the West London Amateur Cup in 1887 and the championship of the West London League in its initial season of 1892–93. The name Fulham had been adopted in 1888.

Craven Cottage, Stevenage Road, London SW6 6HH
Telephone: 0870 442 1222.
Fax: 0870 442 0236.
Ticket Office: 0870 442 1234.
Website: www.fulhamfc.co.uk
Email: enquiries@fulhamfc.com
Ground Capacity: 24,590.
Record Attendance: 49,335 v Millwall, Division 2, 8 October 1938.
Pitch Measurements: 100m × 67m.
Chairman: Mohamed Al Fayed.
Managing Director: David McNally.
Secretary: Darren Preston.
Manager: Lawrie Sanchez.
Assistant Manager: Les Reed.
Physio: Jason Palmer.
Colours: White shirts, black shorts, white stockings.
Change Colours: Red and black striped shirts, white shorts, white stockings.
Year Formed: 1879.
Turned Professional: 1898.
Ltd Co.: 1903.
Reformed: 1987.
Previous Name: 1879, Fulham St Andrew's; 1888, Fulham.
Club Nickname: 'Cottagers'.
Grounds: 1879, Star Road, Fulham; c.1883, Eel Brook Common, 1884, Lillie Road; 1885, Putney Lower Common; 1886, Ranelagh House, Fulham; 1888, Barn Elms, Castelnau; 1889, Purser's Cross (Roskell's Field), Parsons Green Lane; 1891, Eel Brook Common; 1891, Half Moon, Putney; 1895, Captain James Field, West Brompton; 1896, Craven Cottage.
First Football League Game: 3 September 1907, Division 2, v Hull C (h) L 0–1 – Skene; Ross, Lindsay; Collins, Morrison, Goldie; Dalrymple, Freeman, Bevan, Hubbard, Threlfall.
Record League Victory: 10–1 v Ipswich T, Division 1, 26 December 1963 – Macedo; Cohen, Langley; Mullery (1), Keetch, Robson (1); Key, Cook (1), Leggat (4), Haynes, Howfield (3).
Record Cup Victory: 7–0 v Swansea C, FA Cup 1st rd, 11 November 1995 – Lange; Jupp (1), Herrera, Barkus (Brooker (1)), Moore, Angus, Thomas (1), Morgan, Brazil (Hamill), Conroy (3) (Bolt), Cusack (1).

HONOURS

Football League: Division 1 – Champions 2000–01; Division 2 – Champions 1948–49, 1998–99; Runners-up 1958–59; Division 3 (S) – Champions 1931–32; Division 3 – Runners-up 1970–71, 1996–97.

FA Cup: Runners-up 1975.

Football League Cup: best season: 5th rd, 1968, 1971, 2000.

European Competitions: *UEFA Cup:* 2002–03. *Intertoto Cup:* 2002 (winners)

SKY SPORTS FACT FILE

On 26 August 2006 Fulham celebrated Johnny Haynes day with a 1–0 win over Sheffield United, courtesy of Jimmy Bullard's 40th minute goal. It was the first time since 3 September 1966 that the two teams had met in the top flight at Craven Cottage.

Record Defeat: 0–10 v Liverpool, League Cup 2nd rd 1st leg, 23 September 1986.

Most League Points (2 for a win): 60, Division 2, 1958–59 and Division 3, 1970–71.

Most League Points (3 for a win): 101, Division 2, 1998–99. 101, Division 1, 2000–01.

Most League Goals: 111, Division 3 (S), 1931–32.

Highest League Scorer in Season: Frank Newton, 43, Division 3 (S), 1931–32.

Most League Goals in Total Aggregate: Gordon Davies, 159, 1978–84, 1986–91.

Most League Goals in One Match: 5, Fred Harrison v Stockport Co, Division 2, 5 September 1908; 5, Bedford Jezzard v Hull C, Division 2, 8 October 1955; 5, Jimmy Hill v Doncaster R, Division 2, 15 March 1958; 5, Steve Earle v Halifax T, Division 3, 16 September 1969.

Most Capped Player: Johnny Haynes, 56, England.

Most League Appearances: Johnny Haynes, 594, 1952–70.

Youngest League Player: Matthew Briggs, 16 years 65 days v Middlesbrough, 13 May 2007.

Record Transfer Fee Received: £11,500,000 from Manchester U for Louis Saha, January 2004.

Record Transfer Fee Paid: £11,500,000 to Lyon for Steve Marlet, August 2001.

Football League Record: 1907 Elected to Division 2; 1928–32 Division 3 (S); 1932–49 Division 2; 1949–52 Division 1; 1952–59 Division 2; 1959–68 Division 1; 1968–69 Division 2; 1969–71 Division 3; 1971–80 Division 2; 1980–82 Division 3; 1982–86 Division 2; 1986–92 Division 3; 1992–94 Division 2; 1994–97 Division 3; 1997–99 Division 2; 1999–2001 Division 1; 2001– FA Premier League.

MANAGERS

Harry Bradshaw 1904–09
Phil Kelso 1909–24
Andy Ducat 1924–26
Joe Bradshaw 1926–29
Ned Liddell 1929–31
Jim MacIntyre 1931–34
Jimmy Hogan 1934–35
Jack Peart 1935–48
Frank Osborne 1948–64
(was Secretary-Manager or General Manager for most of this period and Team Manager 1953–56)
Bill Dodgin Snr 1949–53
Duggie Livingstone 1956–58
Bedford Jezzard 1958–64
(General Manager for last two months)
Vic Buckingham 1965–68
Bobby Robson 1968
Bill Dodgin Jnr 1969–72
Alec Stock 1972–76
Bobby Campbell 1976–80
Malcolm Macdonald 1980–84
Ray Harford 1984–96
Ray Lewington 1986–90
Alan Dicks 1990–91
Don Mackay 1991–94
Ian Branfoot 1994–96
(continued as General Manager)
Micky Adams 1996–97
Ray Wilkins 1997–98
Kevin Keegan 1998–99
(Chief Operating Officer)
Paul Bracewell 1999–2000
Jean Tigana 2000–03
Chris Coleman 2003–07
Lawrie Sanchez May 2007–

LATEST SEQUENCES

Longest Sequence of League Wins: 12, 7.5.2000 – 18.10.2000.

Longest Sequence of League Defeats: 11, 2.12.1961 – 24.2.1962.

Longest Sequence of League Draws: 6, 14.10.1995 – 18.11.1995.

Longest Sequence of Unbeaten League Matches: 15, 26.1.1999 – 13.4.1999.

Longest Sequence Without a League Win: 15, 25.2.1950 – 23.8.1950.

Successive Scoring Runs: 26 from 28.3.1931.

Successive Non-scoring Runs: 6 from 21.8.1971.

TEN YEAR LEAGUE RECORD

		P	W	D	L	F	A	Pts	Pos
1997-98	Div 2	46	20	10	16	60	43	70	6
1998-99	Div 2	46	31	8	7	79	32	101	1
1999-2000	Div 1	46	17	16	13	49	41	67	9
2000-01	Div 1	46	30	11	5	90	32	101	1
2001-02	PR Lge	38	10	14	14	36	44	44	13
2002-03	PR Lge	38	13	9	16	41	50	48	14
2003-04	PR Lge	38	14	10	14	52	46	52	9
2004-05	PR Lge	38	12	8	18	52	60	44	13
2005-06	PR Lge	38	14	6	18	48	58	48	12
2006-07	PR Lge	38	8	15	15	38	60	39	16

DID YOU KNOW ?

England schoolboy cap Albert Barrett assisted West Ham United, Leytonstone and Southampton as an amateur while an accountant. Moved to Fulham June 1925 and cleared over 400 League games as left-half. Also won four England amateur and one full cap.

FULHAM 2006–07 LEAGUE RECORD

Match No.	*Date*	*Venue*	*Opponents*	*Result*	*H/T Score*	*Lg. Pos.*	*Goalscorers*	*Attendance*
1	Aug 20	A	Manchester U	L 1-5	1-4	—	Helguson [40]	75,115
2	23	H	Bolton W	D 1-1	0-0	—	Bullard (pen) [90]	18,559
3	26	H	Sheffield U	W 1-0	1-0	10	Bullard [40]	18,362
4	Sept 9	A	Newcastle U	W 2-1	0-0	7	McBride [82], Bocanegra [89]	50,365
5	17	A	Tottenham H	D 0-0	0-0	8		36,131
6	23	H	Chelsea	L 0-2	0-0	11		24,290
7	Oct 2	A	Watford	D 3-3	0-1	—	McBride [71], Helguson [83], Francis (og) [87]	17,982
8	16	H	Charlton Ath	W 2-1	0-0	—	McBride [65], Jensen [67]	19,179
9	21	A	Aston Villa	D 1-1	1-1	8	Volz [45]	30,919
10	28	H	Wigan Ath	L 0-1	0-0	9		22,882
11	Nov 4	H	Everton	W 1-0	0-0	9	Jensen [66]	23,327
12	11	A	Portsmouth	D 1-1	0-0	10	Knight [57]	19,563
13	18	A	Manchester C	L 1-3	0-3	11	John [62]	35,776
14	25	H	Reading	L 0-1	0-1	12		22,673
15	29	H	Arsenal	W 2-1	2-1	—	McBride [6], Radzinski [19]	24,510
16	Dec 2	A	Blackburn R	L 0-2	0-2	10		16,799
17	9	A	Liverpool	L 0-4	0-0	13		43,189
18	18	H	Middlesbrough	W 2-1	2-0	—	Helguson (pen) [12], McBride [35]	17,000
19	23	H	West Ham U	D 0-0	0-0	12		22,452
20	27	A	Charlton Ath	D 2-2	1-2	—	McBride [13], Queudrue [90]	25,203
21	30	A	Chelsea	D 2-2	1-1	11	Volz [16], Bocanegra [84]	41,926
22	Jan 1	H	Watford	D 0-0	0-0	12		19,698
23	13	A	West Ham U	D 3-3	1-1	13	Radzinski [16], McBride [59], Christanval [90]	34,977
24	20	H	Tottenham H	D 1-1	0-0	15	Montella (pen) [84]	23,580
25	30	A	Sheffield U	L 0-2	0-2	—		27,540
26	Feb 3	H	Newcastle U	W 2-1	0-0	14	Helguson [49], McBride [73]	24,340
27	11	A	Bolton W	L 1-2	0-1	14	Knight [66]	24,919
28	24	H	Manchester U	L 1-2	1-1	14	McBride [17]	24,459
29	Mar 3	H	Aston Villa	D 1-1	1-1	14	Bocanegra [23]	24,552
30	17	A	Wigan Ath	D 0-0	0-0	14		16,001
31	31	H	Portsmouth	D 1-1	0-1	14	Pearce [90]	22,806
32	Apr 6	A	Everton	L 1-4	1-3	—	Bocanegra [22]	35,612
33	9	H	Manchester C	L 1-3	0-2	15	Bocanegra [76]	22,435
34	14	A	Reading	L 0-1	0-1	16		24,082
35	21	H	Blackburn R	D 1-1	1-0	15	Montella [10]	23,652
36	29	A	Arsenal	L 1-3	0-1	16	Davies [78]	60,043
37	May 5	H	Liverpool	W 1-0	0-0	15	Dempsey [69]	24,554
38	13	A	Middlesbrough	L 1-3	1-2	16	Davies [42]	29,556

Final League Position: 16

GOALSCORERS

League (38): McBride 9, Bocanegra 5, Helguson 4 (1 pen), Bullard 2 (1 pen), Davies 2, Jensen 2, Knight 2, Montella 2 (1 pen), Radzinski 2, Volz 2, Christanval 1, Dempsey 1, John 1, Pearce 1, Queudrue 1, own goal 1.
Carling Cup (1): Helguson 1.
FA Cup (9): McBride 3, Montella 3, Radzinski 1, Routledge 1, Volz 1.

Niemi A 31	Rosenior L 38	Queudrue F 28 + 1	Diop P 20 + 3	Pearce I 22	Christanval P 19 + 1	Brown M 34	Bullard J 4	Helguson H 16 + 14	John C 9 + 14	Boa Morte L 12 + 3	Radzinski T 25 + 10	McBride B 34 + 4	Knight Z 22 + 1	Bocanegra C 26 + 4	Routledge W 13 + 11	Volz M 24 + 5	Runstrom B — + 1	Jensen C 10 + 2	Lastuvka J 7 + 1	Montella V 3 + 7	Dempsey C 1 + 9	Davies S 14	Smertin A 6 + 1	Briggs M — + 1	*Match No.*
1	2	3	4	5	6	7^1	8	9	10^2	11	12	13													1
1	2	3	4	5	6	7^2	8	10^1	12	11	13	9													2
1	2	3	4	5	6	7^2	8	12	10^1	11	13	9													3
1	2	3	4^1	5		7	8^3		10	11	12	9	6^2	13	14										4
1	2	3		5		7		12	10^3	11^2	13	9^1	6	4		8	14								5
1	2	3	8	5		11		12	10^2			13	6	4^1	9	7									6
1	2	3	4	5		8		9	10^2		12	13	6	11^3	14	7^1									7
1	2	3	4^1	5		11		10^3			8	9	6	12	7^2	13		14							8
1	2	3		5		11			12		10	9^1	6	4		7		8							9
1	2	3		5		11^1				12	8	9	6	4	13	7^2		10							10
1	2	3		5				12	13	11^3	10	9^1	6	4	7^2	14		8							11
1	2	3	12	5					13	11	10	9^2	6	4	14	7^3		8^1							12
1	2	3	8	5				12	14	11	13	9^1	6	4^3		7^2		10							13
1	2	3^2	12	5■		7^1			10	11	4^3	9	6	13	14			8							14
1	3		4		6	7		12		11	8^2	9^1	5		13	2		10							15
	3		4	5		7		9^1	10^3	11^2	13	12	6		14	2		8	1						16
	3		4^2	5^1	13	7		12	14	11	8	9^3	6			2		10	1						17
1	2	3			6	11		10			8^1	9	5	12	7	4									18
1	2	3			6	11		10			8	9		5	7	4									19
1	2	3			6	11		10^1	12		8	9		5	7	4^2		13							20
1	2	3			6	11			10^1	12	8	9		5	7	4									21
1^6	2	3			6	11		10	12	13	8	9^1		5	7^2	4			15						22
	2	3			6	11		10^1			8	9		5	7	4			1	12					23
	2	3		4	6	11		10■			8^1	9		5		7^2			1	12	13				24
1	2	3		5		11		12			8^2	9	6		13	4^3				10^1	14	7			25
	2	3	12		6	11		10				9^2		5	7^3	4^1			1	13	14	8			26
	2	3	4		6	11^3		10^2			12	9	5			7^1			1	13		8	14		27
	3		4^3		6	11		12	13		10^2	9^1		5		2			1		14	8	7		28
1	2	3	4^3	6		11		12	13		10^1	9^2		5	14							8	7		29
1	2	3	4	6		11		12	13		10^2	9^1		5								8	7		30
1	2	3	4^2	6		11			12		10^3	9^1		5	13					14		8	7		31
1	3					4		13	12^2		10^1	9	6	5	11	2						8	7		32
1	3				6	4		10^2			12	9		5	11^3	2				13	14	8	7^1		33
1	2	3	4	6^1		11		10^2				9	12	5	7					13	14	8^3			34
1	2		4		6^2	11					8^3	9	5	3	12	13				10^1	14	7			35
1	2^2		4		6	11		12			10	9^1	5	3		13		8^3			14	7			36
1	2		4■		6	11		12			8^2	9^1	5	3		13				10^3	14	7			37
1	2	12			6^1			10^2	13		8	9	5	3		4^3					11	7		14	38

FA Cup

Third Round	Leicester C	(a)	2-2
		(h)	4-3
Fourth Round	Stoke C	(h)	3-0
Fifth Round	Tottenham H	(h)	0-4

Carling Cup

Second Round	Wycombe W	(h)	1-2

GILLINGHAM FL Championship 1

FOUNDATION

The success of the pioneering Royal Engineers of Chatham excited the interest of the residents of the Medway Towns and led to the formation of many clubs including Excelsior. After winning the Kent Junior Cup and the Chatham District League in 1893, Excelsior decided to go for bigger things and it was at a meeting in the Napier Arms, Brompton, in 1893 that New Brompton FC came into being, buying and developing the ground which is now Priestfield Stadium. Changed name to Gillingham in 1913, when they also changed their strip from black and white stripes to predominantly blue.

Priestfield Stadium, Redfern Avenue, Gillingham, Kent ME7 4DD.

Telephone: (01634) 300 000.

Fax: (01634) 850 986.

Ticket Office: (01634) 300 000 (option 3).

Website: www.gillinghamfootballclub.com

Email: info@gillinghamfootballclub.com

Ground Capacity: 11,400.

Record Attendance: 23,002 v QPR, FA Cup 3rd rd, 10 January 1948.

Pitch Measurements: 110yd × 70yd.

Chairman/Chief Executive: Paul D. P. Scally.

Vice-chairman: Peter A. Spokes.

Secretary: Gwen E. Poynter.

Manager: Ronnie Jepson.

Assistant Manager: Mick Docherty.

Physio: Colin Clifford.

Colours: Blue with white insert.

Change Colours: Yellow with blue insert.

Year Formed: 1893.

Turned Professional: 1894.

Ltd Co.: 1893.

Previous Name: 1893, New Brompton; 1913, Gillingham.

Club Nickname: 'The Gills'.

Ground: 1893, Priestfield Stadium.

First Football League Game: 28 August 1920, Division 3, v Southampton (h) D 1–1 – Branfield; Robertson, Sissons; Battiste, Baxter, Wigmore; Holt, Hall, Gilbey (1), Roe, Gore.

HONOURS

Football League: Promoted from Division 2 1999–2000 (play-offs); Division 3 – Runners-up 1995-96; Division 4 – Champions 1963–64; Runners-up 1973–74.

FA Cup: best season: 6th rd, 2000.

Football League Cup: best season: 4th rd, 1964, 1997.

SKY SPORTS FACT FILE

Billy Hales, an amateur centre-forward and local butcher signed from Sittingbourne, made an outstanding debut for Gillingham against Port Vale on 31 March 1951, scoring a hat-trick and finished the season with nine goals in 15 League appearances.

Record League Victory: 10–0 v Chesterfield, Division 3, 5 September 1987 – Kite; Haylock, Pearce, Shipley (2) (Lillis), West, Greenall (1), Pritchard (2), Shearer (2), Lovell, Elsey (2), David Smith (1).

Record Cup Victory: 10–1 v Gorleston, FA Cup 1st rd, 16 November 1957 – Brodie; Parry, Hannaway; Riggs, Boswell, Laing; Payne, Fletcher (2), Saunders (5), Morgan (1), Clark (2).

Record Defeat: 2–9 v Nottingham F, Division 3 (S), 18 November 1950.

Most League Points (2 for a win): 62, Division 4, 1973–74.

Most League Points (3 for a win): 85, Division 2, 1999–2000.

Most League Goals: 90, Division 4, 1973–74.

Highest League Scorer in Season: Ernie Morgan, 31, Division 3 (S), 1954–55; Brian Yeo, 31, Division 4, 1973–74.

Most League Goals in Total Aggregate: Brian Yeo, 135, 1963–75.

Most League Goals in One Match: 6, Fred Cheesmur v Merthyr T, Division 3S, 26 April 1930.

Most Capped Player: Mamady Sidibe, 7, Mali.

Most League Appearances: John Simpson, 571, 1957–72.

Youngest League Player: Billy Hughes, 15 years 275 days v Southend U, 13 April 1976.

Record Transfer Fee Received: £1,500,000 from Manchester C for Robert Taylor, November 1999.

Record Transfer Fee Paid: £600,000 to Reading for Carl Asaba, August 1998.

Football League Record: 1920 Original Member of Division 3; 1921 Division 3 (S); 1938 Failed re-election; Southern League 1938–44; Kent League 1944–46; Southern League 1946–50; 1950 Re-elected to Division 3 (S); 1958–64 Division 4; 1964–71 Division 3; 1971–74 Division 4; 1974–89 Division 3; 1989–92 Division 4; 1992–96; Division 3; 1996–2000 Division 2; 2000–04 Division 1; 2004–05 FL C; 2005– FL 1.

MANAGERS

W. Ironside Groombridge 1896–1906 *(Secretary-Manager)* *(previously Financial Secretary)*
Steve Smith 1906–08
W. I. Groombridge 1908–19 *(Secretary-Manager)*
George Collins 1919–20
John McMillan 1920–23
Harry Curtis 1923–26
Albert Hoskins 1926–29
Dick Hendrie 1929–31
Fred Mavin 1932–37
Alan Ure 1937–38
Bill Harvey 1938–39
Archie Clark 1939–58
Harry Barratt 1958–62
Freddie Cox 1962–65
Basil Hayward 1966–71
Andy Nelson 1971–74
Len Ashurst 1974–75
Gerry Summers 1975–81
Keith Peacock 1981–87
Paul Taylor 1988
Keith Burkinshaw 1988–89
Damien Richardson 1989–92
Glenn Roeder 1992–93
Mike Flanagan 1993–95
Neil Smillie 1995
Tony Pulis 1995–99
Peter Taylor 1999–2000
Andy Hessenthaler 2000–04
Stan Ternent 2004–05
Neale Cooper 2005
Ronnie Jepson November 2005–

LATEST SEQUENCES

Longest Sequence of League Wins: 7, 18.12.1954 – 29.1.1955.

Longest Sequence of League Defeats: 10, 20.9.1988 – 5.11.1988.

Longest Sequence of League Draws: 5, 28.8.1993 – 18.9.1993.

Longest Sequence of Unbeaten League Matches: 20, 13.10.1973 – 10.2.1974.

Longest Sequence Without a League Win: 15, 1.4.1972 – 2.9.1972.

Successive Scoring Runs: 20 from 31.10.1959.

Successive Non-scoring Runs: 6 from 11.2.1961.

TEN YEAR LEAGUE RECORD

		P	*W*	*D*	*L*	*F*	*A*	*Pts*	*Pos*
1997-98	Div 2	46	19	13	14	52	47	70	8
1998-99	Div 2	46	22	14	10	75	44	80	4
1999-2000	Div 2	46	25	10	11	79	48	85	3
2000-01	Div 1	46	13	16	17	61	66	55	13
2001-02	Div 1	46	18	10	18	64	67	64	12
2002-03	Div 1	46	16	14	16	56	65	62	11
2003-04	Div 1	46	14	9	23	48	67	51	21
2004-05	FL C	46	12	14	20	45	66	50	22
2005-06	FL 1	46	16	12	18	50	64	60	14
2006-07	FL 1	46	17	8	21	56	77	59	16

DID YOU KNOW?

In the late 1960s when Basil Hayward was manager of Gillingham, he managed to attract no fewer than eight players who had been previously with Bedford Town, initially taking four: Ray Bailey, Billy Brown, Derek Bellotti and Dave Quirke.

GILLINGHAM 2006–07 LEAGUE RECORD

Match No.	Date	Venue	Opponents	Result	H/T Score	Lg. Pos.	Goalscorers	Attendance
1	Aug 5	H	Huddersfield T	W 2-1	0-0	—	Jarvis [57], McDonald [67]	6075
2	8	A	Brighton & HA	L 0-1	0-0	—		6643
3	12	A	Bradford C	L 2-4	2-1	16	Bentley [6], Flynn [14]	7807
4	19	H	Northampton T	L 0-1	0-1	21		5654
5	26	A	Blackpool	D 1-1	1-1	20	N'Dumbu Nsungu [3]	5056
6	Sept 1	H	Scunthorpe U	L 0-2	0-2	—		5749
7	9	A	Doncaster R	W 2-1	2-0	19	Crofts [9], Flynn (pen) [39]	5772
8	12	H	Millwall	W 2-1	1-0	—	Easton [14], Jarvis [64]	7934
9	16	H	Swansea C	W 3-1	2-0	12	Cox 2 [14, 79], Jarvis [30]	5500
10	23	A	Oldham Ath	L 1-4	0-2	16	Flynn (pen) [51]	4652
11	26	A	Leyton Orient	D 3-3	2-0	—	Bentley [43], N'Dumbu Nsungu [45], Jarvis [57]	4648
12	30	H	Cheltenham T	W 2-1	2-1	13	Jarvis [13], Bentley [45]	5688
13	Oct 7	A	Crewe Alex	L 3-4	3-1	14	Pouton [21], Flynn [28], McDonald [45]	5022
14	14	H	Nottingham F	L 0-1	0-0	15		7800
15	21	A	Brentford	D 2-2	1-2	17	Flynn 2 (1 pen) [26 (p), 74]	5759
16	28	H	Carlisle U	W 2-0	1-0	14	Bentley [8], Mulligan [89]	5973
17	Nov 4	H	Chesterfield	W 2-1	0-1	10	Mulligan [89], McDonald [90]	5856
18	18	A	Bristol C	L 1-3	1-1	13	Flynn [15]	11,823
19	25	H	Rotherham U	W 1-0	1-0	10	Mulligan [23]	5103
20	Dec 5	A	Port Vale	L 0-2	0-1	—		3077
21	9	A	Yeovil T	L 0-2	0-1	15		4933
22	16	H	Bournemouth	D 1-1	0-1	14	Crofts [90]	6296
23	23	A	Tranmere R	W 3-2	3-2	13	Mulligan 2 [11, 19], Chorley [42]	6407
24	26	H	Leyton Orient	W 2-1	0-1	11	Saah (og) [81], N'Dumbu Nsungu (pen) [88]	8216
25	30	H	Oldham Ath	L 0-3	0-2	12		6790
26	Jan 1	A	Millwall	L 1-4	1-1	12	Mulligan [10]	10,055
27	13	H	Doncaster R	L 0-2	0-0	15		6202
28	20	A	Cheltenham T	D 1-1	1-1	15	Savage [6]	3598
29	23	A	Swansea C	L 0-2	0-1	—		9675
30	26	H	Tranmere R	W 2-0	2-0	—	McCready (og) [22], Crofts [29]	5378
31	Feb 3	A	Huddersfield T	L 1-3	0-2	13	Mulligan [70]	9167
32	10	H	Bradford C	W 1-0	1-0	12	Johnson [45]	5513
33	16	A	Northampton T	D 1-1	0-0	—	McDonald [61]	5618
34	20	H	Brighton & HA	L 0-1	0-1	—		6609
35	24	A	Scunthorpe U	L 1-3	0-1	17	Jarvis [54]	5312
36	Mar 3	H	Blackpool	D 2-2	2-1	16	McDonald [9], Crofts [34]	5949
37	10	H	Crewe Alex	W 1-0	0-0	16	Flynn [71]	6373
38	17	A	Nottingham F	L 0-1	0-0	18		17,950
39	24	A	Carlisle U	L 0-5	0-1	19		6087
40	31	H	Brentford	W 2-1	1-1	17	Crofts [29], Jackman [88]	6113
41	Apr 7	A	Rotherham U	L 2-3	2-1	18	Bastians [21], Crofts [24]	3223
42	9	H	Bristol C	W 1-0	0-0	17	McDonald [55]	6292
43	14	A	Chesterfield	W 1-0	0-0	14	Crofts [90]	3867
44	21	H	Port Vale	W 3-2	1-0	13	Cox [37], Flynn 2 [49, 53]	5928
45	28	A	Bournemouth	D 1-1	1-1	13	Crofts [24]	8001
46	May 5	H	Yeovil T	L 0-2	0-0	16		7484

Final League Position: 16

GOALSCORERS

League (56): Flynn 10 (3 pens), Crofts 8, Mulligan 7, Jarvis 6, McDonald 6, Bentley 4, Cox 3, N'Dumbu Nsungu 3 (1 pen), Bastians 1, Chorley 1, Easton 1, Jackman 1, Johnson 1, Pouton 1, Savage 1, own goals 2.
Carling Cup (1): Crofts 1.
FA Cup (7): Bentley 2, Flynn 2 (1 pen), Ndumbu-Nsungu 2, Mulligan 1.
J Paint Trophy (1): Mulligan 1.

Jack K 9	Jupp D 26 + 1	Jackman D 30 + 1	Flynn M 44 + 1	Cox I 33	Sancho B 19 + 7	Crofts A 43	Bentley M 41	Mulligan G 37 + 1	McDonald D 16 + 10	Jarvis M 34 + 1	N'Dumbu Nsungu G 14 + 18	Spiller D 11 + 14	Pouton A 3 + 5	Randolph D 3	Johnson L 23 + 1	Easton C 26 + 6	Flinders S 9	Clohessy S 3 + 3	Savage B 8 + 6	Howell L — + 1	Chorley B 24 + 3	Brill D 8	Larrieu R 14	Collin F — + 3	Southall N 15	Pugh A — + 3	Stone C 2 + 1	Tonge D 3	Bastians F 5	Royce S 3	Cumbers L — + 1	Match No.
1	2	3	4	5	6	7	8	9	10¹	11²	12	13																				1
1	2	3	4	5	6	7¹	8	9	10	11	12																					2
1	2	3	4	5	6	7³	8	9²	10¹	11	12	13	14																			3
	2	3	4	5	6	7²	8	9¹	10	11	12	13		1																		4
	2	3	4	5	6	7		12		11	9¹	13	10²	1	8																	5
	2	3	4	5	6			9¹	13	11	10	12	8²	1		7																6
	2	3■	4	5	6³	7	8¹			11	9²		12		10	13	1	14														7
	2		4	5		7	8	9¹	13	11	10²	12			6	3	1															8
	2	3	4	5		7	8	9¹		11	12				6	10	1															9
	2	3	4	5		7²	8	9		11	12	13			6	10¹	1															10
	2	3	4	5		7	8			11	9				6	10	1															11
	2	3	4	5		7	8		12	11	9¹				6	10²	1		13													12
	2		4	5			8		10¹	11	9	12	7²		6	3	1	13														13
	2		4²	5³		7	8	9¹	12	11	10				6	3	1		13	14												14
	2	3	4	5		7		9	12		10	8¹			6	11	1															15
1	2	12	4	5		7³	8	9²		11	10¹				6	3			13		14											16
1	2		4³	5		7¹	8	9	13	11	10²		12		6	3					14											17
1	2		4	5	6¹	7	8	9		11	12					10²			13		3											18
1	2		4	5		7	8	9	10¹	11						3			12		6											19
1	2		4²		6	7	8	9	12	11	10¹					3			13		5											20
	2		4¹	5	6	7	8²	9		11	12	14	13			3					10³	1										21
	2	3	4	5	6	7	8	9		11	10¹	12										1										22
	2		4	5	12	7	8	9		11						3			10¹		6	1										23
	2²		4³	5	12	7	8	9		11	13		14			3			10¹		6	1										24
	2		4	5■	12	7	8³	9²		11	13	14				3			10¹		6	1										25
	2¹		4		6	7	8²	9		11	12	13				3			10		5	1										26
			4	5	6	7	8²	9		11	12	13				2			10¹		3	1										27
			4	5■		7	8	9		11					12	3		2	10¹		6	1										28
	12		4			7	8²	9		11³	13				6	3		2	10¹		5		1	14								29
		3	4		2	7	8	9		11					6				10		5		1									30
		3	4		2	7		9	10¹	11	12				6						5		1		8							31
		3	4			7	8	9¹	13	11	12				6	10²					5		1		2							32
		3	4		12	7	8	9	10¹	11					6						5		1		2							33
		3	4		12	7	8	9	10²	11					6¹						5		1		2	13						34
		3	4		12	7	8	9	10¹	11²		13			6						5■		1		2							35
		3	4		6	7	8	9	10			11			5								1		2							36
		3	4		6	7	8	9	10¹		12	11²			5						13		1		2							37
		3	4¹		6	7	8	9	10			11			5	12		2					1									38
		3	12		6		8■	9	10²		13				5								1		2		4¹	7	11			39
		3		5		7		9	10²			8				12					4		1		2	13		6	11¹			40
1		3	4³	5		7	8	9¹			12	10				13					6				2	14			11²			41
		3	4	5		7	8		12²		10¹	9				14					6		1	13	2				11³			42
		3	4	5	12	7	8					9				13					6		1		2			10¹	11²			43
		3	4	5		7	8	9¹	12			10				11					6				2					1		44
		3	4	5		7	8			12		9²				10¹					6			13	2		11			1		45
		3	4²	5		7	8		10¹			9				11³		12			6				2		13			1	14	46

FA Cup
First Round Bromley (h) 4-1
Second Round Bristol C (a) 3-4

Carling Cup
First Round Millwall (a) 1-2

J Paint Trophy
First Round Nottingham F (h) 1-2

GRIMSBY TOWN FL Championship 2

FOUNDATION

Grimsby Pelham FC, as they were first known, came into being at a meeting held at the Wellington Arms in September 1878. Pelham is the family name of big landowners in the area, the Earls of Yarborough. The receipts for their first game amounted to 6s. 9d. (approx. 39p). After a year, the club name was changed to Grimsby Town.

Blundell Park, Cleethorpes, North East Lincolnshire DN35 7PY.

Telephone: (01472) 605 050.

Fax: (01472) 693 665.

Ticket Office: (01472) 608 026.

Website: www.gtfc.co.uk.

Email: enquiries@gtfc.co.uk.

Ground Capacity: 10,033.

Record Attendance: 31,657 v Wolverhampton W, FA Cup 5th rd, 20 February 1937.

Pitch Measurements: 110yd × 74yd.

Chairman: John Fenty.

Chief Executive: Ian Fleming.

Manager: Alan Buckley.

Assistant Manager: Stuart Watkiss.

Physio: David Moore.

Colours: Black and white shirts, black shorts, black stockings with white trim.

Change Colours: All blue.

Year Formed. 1878.

Turned Professional: 1890. ***Ltd Co.:*** 1890.

Previous Name: 1878, Grimsby Pelham; 1879, Grimsby Town.

Club Nickname: 'The Mariners'.

Grounds: 1880, Clee Park; 1889, Abbey Park; 1899, Blundell Park.

First Football League Game: 3 September 1892, Division 2, v Northwich Victoria (h) W 2–1 – Whitehouse; Lundie, T. Frith; C. Frith, Walker, Murrell; Higgins, Henderson, Brayshaw, Riddoch (2), Ackroyd.

Record League Victory: 9–2 v Darwen, Division 2, 15 April 1899 – Bagshaw; Lockie, Nidd; Griffiths, Bell (1), Nelmes; Jenkinson (3), Richards (1), Cockshutt (3), Robinson, Chadburn (1).

Record Cup Victory: 8–0 v Darlington, FA Cup 2nd rd, 21 November 1885 – G. Atkinson; J. H. Taylor, H. Taylor; Hall, Kimpson, Hopewell; H. Atkinson (1), Garnham, Seal (3), Sharman, Monument (4).

HONOURS

Football League: Division 1 best season: 5th, 1934–35; Division 2 – Champions 1900–01, 1933–34; Runners-up 1928–29; Promoted from Division 2 1997–98 (play-offs); Division 3 (N) – Champions 1925–26, 1955–56; Runners-up 1951–52; Division 3 – Champions 1979–80; Runners-up 1961–62; Division 4 – Champions 1971–72; Runners-up 1978–79; 1989–90.

FA Cup: Semi-finals, 1936, 1939.

Football League Cup: best season: 5th rd, 1980, 1985.

League Group Cup: Winners 1982.

Auto Windscreen Shield: Winners 1998.

SKY SPORTS FACT FILE

On 14 January 1911 Grimsby Town beat Croydon Common 3–0 in a first round FA Cup tie. After a protest lodged because Grimsby players had extended the half-time interval by ten minutes to restud their boots, a replay was ordered. Grimsby won it 8–1!

Record Defeat: 1–9 v Arsenal, Division 1, 28 January 1931.

Most League Points (2 for a win): 68, Division 3 (N), 1955–56.

Most League Points (3 for a win): 83, Division 3, 1990–91.

Most League Goals: 103, Division 2, 1933–34.

Highest League Scorer in Season: Pat Glover, 42, Division 2, 1933–34.

Most League Goals in Total Aggregate: Pat Glover, 180, 1930–39.

Most League Goals in One Match: 6, Tommy McCairns v Leicester Fosse, Division 2, 11 April 1896.

Most Capped Player: Pat Glover, 7, Wales.

Most League Appearances: John McDermott, 647, 1987– 2007.

Youngest League Player: Tony Ford, 16 years 143 days v Walsall, 4 October 1975.

Record Transfer Fee Received: £1,500,000 from Everton for John Oster, July 1997.

Record Transfer Fee Paid: £500,000 to Preston NE for Lee Ashcroft, August 1998.

Football League Record: 1892 Original Member Division 2; 1901–03 Division 1; 1903 Division 2; 1910 Failed re-election; 1911 re-elected Division 2; 1920–21 Division 3; 1921–26 Division 3 (N); 1926–29 Division 2; 1929–32 Division 1; 1932–34 Division 2; 1934–48 Division 1; 1948–51 Division 2; 1951–56 Division 3 (N); 1956–59 Division 2; 1959–62 Division 3; 1962–64 Division 2; 1964–68 Division 3; 1968–72 Division 4; 1972–77 Division 3; 1977–79 Division 4; 1979–80 Division 3; 1980–87 Division 2; 1987–88 Division 3; 1988–90 Division 4; 1990–91 Division 3; 1991–92 Division 2; 1992–97 Division 1; 1997–98 Division 2; 1998–2003 Division 1; 2003–04 Division 2; 2004– FL 2.

MANAGERS

H. N. Hickson 1902–20
(Secretary-Manager)
Haydn Price 1920
George Fraser 1921–24
Wilf Gillow 1924–32
Frank Womack 1932–36
Charles Spencer 1937–51
Bill Shankly 1951–53
Billy Walsh 1954–55
Allenby Chilton 1955–59
Tim Ward 1960–62
Tom Johnston 1962–64
Jimmy McGuigan 1964–67
Don McEvoy 1967–68
Bill Harvey 1968–69
Bobby Kennedy 1969–71
Lawrie McMenemy 1971–73
Ron Ashman 1973–75
Tom Casey 1975–76
Johnny Newman 1976–79
George Kerr 1979–82
David Booth 1982–85
Mike Lyons 1985–87
Bobby Roberts 1987–88
Alan Buckley 1988–94
Brian Laws 1994–96
Kenny Swain 1997
Alan Buckley 1997–2000
Lennie Lawrence 2000–01
Paul Groves 2001–04
Nicky Law 2004
Russell Slade 2004–06
Graham Rodger 2006
Alan Buckley November 2006–

LATEST SEQUENCES

Longest Sequence of League Wins: 11, 19.1.1952 – 29.3.1952.

Longest Sequence of League Defeats: 9, 30.11.1907 – 18.1.1908.

Longest Sequence of League Draws: 5, 6.2.1965 – 6.3.1965.

Longest Sequence of Unbeaten League Matches: 19, 16.2.1980 – 30.8.1980.

Longest Sequence Without a League Win: 18, 10.10.1981 – 16.3.1982.

Successive Scoring Runs: 33 from 6.10.1928.

Successive Non-scoring Runs: 6 from 11.3.2000.

TEN YEAR LEAGUE RECORD

		P	W	D	L	F	A	Pts	Pos
1997-98	Div 2	46	19	15	12	55	37	72	3
1998-99	Div 1	46	17	10	19	40	52	61	11
1999-2000	Div 1	46	13	12	21	41	67	51	20
2000-01	Div 1	46	14	10	22	43	62	52	18
2001-02	Div 1	46	12	14	20	50	72	50	19
2002-03	Div 1	46	9	12	25	48	85	39	24
2003-04	Div 2	46	13	11	22	55	81	50	21
2004-05	FL 2	46	14	16	16	51	52	58	18
2005-06	FL 2	46	22	12	12	64	44	78	4
2006-07	FL 2	46	17	8	21	57	73	59	15

DID YOU KNOW ?

Full-back Jimmy "Ned" Kelly joined Grimsby Town for £1000 on transfer deadline day 1933 from Barrow, helped them avoid relegation then promotion the following season. After a lengthy career he even returned to Barrow after the Second World War.

GRIMSBY TOWN 2006–07 LEAGUE RECORD

Match No.	Date	Venue	Opponents	Result		H/T Score	Lg. Pos.	Goalscorers	Attendance
1	Aug 5	H	Boston U	W	3-2	0-1	—	Bore 2 [68, 79], Rankin [73]	5012
2	8	A	Wrexham	L	0-3	0-2	—		5180
3	12	A	Bristol R	L	0-1	0-0	17		4596
4	18	H	Mansfield T	D	1-1	0-0	—	Bore [73]	4604
5	26	A	Bury	L	0-3	0-3	18		2118
6	Sept 1	H	Macclesfield T	D	1-1	1-0	—	Toner (pen) [18]	3638
7	9	H	Walsall	W	2-1	1-1	15	Bolland [38], Bore [73]	3669
8	12	A	Rochdale	L	0-1	0-0	—		1997
9	16	A	Chester C	W	2-0	0-0	14	Jones [89], Taylor [90]	1957
10	23	H	Stockport Co	L	0-1	0-1	17		4708
11	26	H	Hartlepool U	L	1-4	1-1	—	Fenton [16]	3486
12	29	A	Darlington	D	2-2	0-2	—	Toner (pen) [66], Ravenhill [82]	3636
13	Oct 8	H	Hereford U	W	2-1	1-1	18	Jones 2 [9, 61]	4147
14	14	A	Swindon T	L	0-3	0-2	20		5719
15	21	H	Notts Co	L	0-2	0-0	21		4029
16	28	A	Peterborough U	D	2-2	0-0	21	Toner [52], Bore [73]	4203
17	Nov 4	H	Milton Keynes D	L	1-3	0-0	22	Ravenhill [90]	3268
18	18	A	Wycombe W	D	1-1	0-0	22	Jones [71]	5037
19	25	H	Accrington S	W	2-0	1-0	21	Paterson [12], Jones [56]	4511
20	Dec 5	A	Barnet	W	1-0	1-0	—	Paterson [28]	1588
21	9	H	Shrewsbury T	W	2-1	1-0	16	Paterson 2 [38, 72]	4076
22	16	A	Lincoln C	L	0-2	0-1	16		5919
23	22	H	Torquay U	W	2-0	1-0	—	Rankin [18], Fenton [78]	4666
24	26	A	Hartlepool U	L	0-2	0-0	17		5290
25	30	A	Stockport Co	L	0-3	0-2	17		5032
26	Jan 1	H	Rochdale	L	0-4	0-2	17		4302
27	9	H	Chester C	L	0-2	0-0	—		3012
28	15	A	Walsall	L	0-2	0-1	—		4889
29	20	H	Darlington	L	0-1	0-0	22		3282
30	26	A	Torquay U	L	1-4	0-2	—	Paterson [88]	2095
31	Feb 3	A	Boston U	W	6-0	4-0	19	Bore 3 [4, 42, 78], Hunt [7], Toner [20], Paterson [63]	2915
32	10	H	Bristol R	W	4-3	1-2	18	North [33], Whittle [48], Boshell [53], Toner [66]	5883
33	17	A	Mansfield T	W	2-1	1-1	17	Bolland [42], North [83]	4033
34	20	H	Wrexham	W	2-1	1-1	—	Bolland [45], Toner [90]	5850
35	24	A	Macclesfield T	L	1-2	0-2	17	Jones [73]	2598
36	Mar 3	H	Bury	W	2-0	2-0	16	North [10], Toner [24]	4733
37	10	A	Hereford U	W	1-0	0-0	15	Bolland [76]	2914
38	17	H	Swindon T	W	1-0	0-0	11	Toner [73]	4595
39	24	H	Peterborough U	L	0-2	0-0	14		5164
40	31	A	Notts Co	L	0-2	0-0	17		4724
41	Apr 7	A	Milton Keynes D	W	2-1	1-0	14	Boshell [32], Hunt [53]	6101
42	9	H	Wycombe W	D	2-2	0-2	15	Jones [71], Bolland [83]	4271
43	14	A	Accrington S	L	1-4	1-2	16	Newey [41]	1818
44	21	H	Barnet	W	5-0	2-0	14	Jones [26], North 3 (1 pen) [39, 72, 90 (p)], Fenton [80]	3675
45	28	H	Lincoln C	D	0-0	0-0	14		6137
46	May 5	A	Shrewsbury T	D	2-2	1-0	15	Taylor [29], Fenton [90]	7782

Final League Position: 15

GOALSCORERS

League (57): Bore 8, Jones 8, Toner 8 (2 pens), North 6 (1 pen), Paterson 6, Bolland 5, Fenton 4, Boshell 2, Hunt 2, Rankin 2, Ravenhill 2, Taylor 2, Newey 1, Whittle 1.
Carling Cup (0).
FA Cup (0).
J Paint Trophy (0).

Barnes P 46	McDermott J 20 + 3	Newey T 42 + 1	Harkins G 11 + 6	Futcher B 3 + 1	Whittle J 33 + 4	Rankin I 15 + 5	Bolland P 37 + 2	Reddy M 4 + 6	Jones G 29 + 10	Beagrie P 6 + 3	Bore P 21 + 11	Toner C 31 + 2	McIntosh M 4	Croft G 26 + 2	Fenton N 37 + 1	Boshell D 23 + 6	Taylor A 2 + 9	Ravenhill R 15 + 2	Lawson J — + 1	Thorpe T 5 + 1	Butler A 4	North D 12 + 8	Hegarty N 9 + 6	James K 2	Pulis A 9	Till P 17 + 5	Paterson M 15	Grand S 4 + 3	Rizzo N 1	Hunt J 15	Bloomer M 5 + 4	Bennett R 3 + 2	*Match No.*
1	2	3	4	5	6	7	8	9^{1}	10	11	12																						1
1	2	3	4	5	6	7	8	9^{2}	10	11^{1}	13	12																					2
1	2	3	4^{1}	5	6	7^{2}	8	9	10	12	13	11																					3
1	2^{3}	3	12	13	6	9	8		10^{2}	11	7^{1}	4	5	14																			4
1		3	4^{3}		12	9	8	13	10^{2}	14	7	11	5^{1}	2	6																		5
1		3				10^{3}	8	9^{1}	12	11^{2}	13	7	5	2	4	6	14																6
1		3			12	9^{3}	8		10	11^{2}	13	7	5^{1}	2	4		14	6															7
1		3			6	9	8		10		7^{2}	11^{1}		2	5	12	13	4															8
1		3			6	9^{1}	8		10		7			2	5	11	12	4															9
1		3			6		8		10	12	7			2	5	11^{1}	9^{2}	4	13														10
1	2				6		8		10	11^{1}	12	7		3	5		13	4		9^{2}													11
1	2^{1}	12			6		8		10		7	11		3	5			4		9													12
1	2						8		10		7	11		3	5			4		9	6												13
1	2						8		10		7	11		3	5			4		9^{1}	6	12											14
1	12	3^{1}	13				8^{2}		10		7	11		2	5	4				9^{3}	6		14										15
1		3^{1}			12				10▪		7	11		2	6	8		4			5			9									16
1		3			6	9	8				10^{2}	11		2	5			4				13	12	7^{1}									17
1	12	3▪	4^{3}		6		8		10		13			2	5	11^{1}		14				9^{2}	7										18
1		3			6	12	8^{2}		10					2	5	13							7		4	11	9^{1}						19
1		3			6				10					2	5			4					11		8	7	9						20
1		3	12		6	13			10					2	5			4					11^{1}		8	7^{2}	9						21
1		3	12		6	9^{3}		13	5▪		7^{1}			2		14		4					11^{2}		8		10						22
1		3	4^{3}			10^{1}		12				13		2	5	6		14					11^{2}		8	7	9						23
1		3	4		6	10	8^{2}	12						2	5								13		11	7^{1}	9						24
1		3			6	10	12	13						2^{1}	5▪	14		4^{2}					11^{3}		8	7	9						25
1	2	3	4			10^{2}	12	13							5	6						14	11^{3}		8^{1}	7	9						26
1	2	3	12		6				10							13		4				14			8^{2}	7^{3}	9	5	11^{1}				27
1		3			6		8		10^{1}			11		2								13	12			7	9^{2}	5		4			28
1		3	12		6^{1}	13	8		10			11		2												7^{2}	9	5		4			29
1		3^{1}	4				8		10^{3}		13			2	12	6				14			11^{2}				9	5		7			30
1		3^{2}			6		8		12		10^{1}	11		13	5	7										14	9^{3}			4	2		31
1		3	4^{2}		6	12	8		13		10	11			5	7						9^{1}									2		32
1		3			6		8				10	11			5	7						12					9^{1}			4	2		33
1		3			6		8		12		10^{2}	11			5	7						13					9			4^{1}	2		34
1	12	3			6		8		13		10	11		7^{2}	5							9								4	2^{1}		35
1	2	3			6	12	8		10		7^{3}	11			5	13						9^{1}				14				4^{2}			36
1	2	3			6		8		12		10^{2}	11			5^{3}	7						9^{1}				13		14		4			37
1	2	3			6		8		12		10^{2}	11			5	7^{1}						9				13				4			38
1	2	3			6		8		12			11			5^{3}	4^{1}	13					9				7^{2}		14		10			39
1	2	3			6		8		10			11^{1}			5^{3}	4	12					13				7^{2}				9	14		40
1	2	3			6		8				10^{1}	11			5^{2}	4^{3}						9				12		13		7		14	41
1	2^{3}	3			6		8		12		13	11			5	4^{2}						9				7				10^{1}		14	42
1		3			6		8		12		13	11		2▪	5	4^{3}						9^{1}				7^{2}				10	14		43
1	2^{3}	3					8		10			11^{2}			5	6	12					9	13			7^{1}					14	4	44
1	2^{3}	3	4^{1}						10^{2}			11			5	8	12					9	13			7					14	6	45
1	2^{1}	3			12		8		10		13	11			5	6	9^{2}									7						4	46

FA Cup
First Round — Northampton T — (a) 0-0; (h) 0-2

Carling Cup
First Round — Crewe Alex — (h) 0-3

J Paint Trophy
First Round — Lincoln C — (a) 0-0
Second Round — Mansfield T — (a) 0-3

HARTLEPOOL UNITED FL Championship 1

FOUNDATION

The inspiration for the launching of Hartlepool United was the West Hartlepool club which won the FA Amateur Cup in 1904–05. They had been in existence since 1881 and their Cup success led in 1908 to the formation of the new professional concern which first joined the North-Eastern League. In those days they were Hartlepools United and won the Durham Senior Cup in their first two seasons.

Victoria Park, Clarence Road, Hartlepool TS24 8BZ.

Telephone: (01429) 272 584.

Fax: (01429) 863 007.

Ticket Office: (01429) 272 584 (ext 2).

Website: www.hartlepoolunited.co.uk

Email: enquires@hartlepoolunited.co.uk

Ground Capacity: 7,629.

Record Attendance: 17,426 v Manchester U, FA Cup 3rd rd, 5 January 1957.

Pitch Measurements: 100m × 68m.

Chairman: Ken Hodcroft.

Chief Executive: Russ Green.

Secretary: Maureen Smith.

Manager: Danny Wilson.

Reserve Team Manager: Ian Butterworth.

Physio: James Haycock.

Colours: Blue and white striped shirts, blue shorts, white stockings.

Change Colours: Red and black striped shirts, black shorts, black stockings.

Year Formed: 1908.

Turned Professional: 1908.

Ltd Co.: 1908.

Previous Names: 1908, Hartlepools United; 1968, Hartlepool; 1977, Hartlepool United.

Club Nickname: 'The Pool'.

Ground: 1908, Victoria Park.

First Football League Game: 27 August 1921, Division 3 (N), v Wrexham (a) W 2–0 – Gill; Thomas, Crilly; Dougherty, Hopkins, Short; Kessler, Mulholland (1), Lister (1), Robertson, Donald.

Record League Victory: 10–1 v Barrow, Division 4, 4 April 1959 – Oakley; Cameron, Waugh; Johnson, Moore, Anderson; Scott (1), Langland (1), Smith (3), Clark (2), Luke (2), (1 og).

Record Cup Victory: 6–0 v North Shields, FA Cup 1st rd, 30 November 1946 – Heywood; Brown, Gregory; Spelman, Lambert, Jones; Price, Scott (2), Sloan (4), Moses, McMahon.

HONOURS

Football League: FL 2 – Runners-up 2006–07; Division 3 – Runners-up 2002–03; Division 3 (N) – Runners-up 1956–57.

FA Cup: best season: 4th rd, 1955, 1978, 1989, 1993, 2005.

Football League Cup, best season: 4th rd, 1975.

SKY SPORTS FACT FILE

Fred Westgarth had a lengthy association with Hartlepools United as manager. During his service at the Victoria Ground he formed a useful association with Arsenal and led to the club having a reasonable supply of used red and white strip for the reserves!

Record Defeat: 1–10 v Wrexham, Division 4, 3 March 1962.

Most League Points (2 for a win): 60, Division 4, 1967–68.

Most League Points (3 for a win): 88, FL 2, 2006–07.

Most League Goals: 90, Division 3 (N), 1956–57.

Highest League Scorer in Season: William Robinson, 28, Division 3 (N), 1927–28; Joe Allon, 28, Division 4, 1990–91.

Most League Goals in Total Aggregate: Ken Johnson, 98, 1949–64.

Most League Goals in One Match: 5, Harry Simmons v Wigan Borough, Division 3N, 1 January 1931; 5, Bobby Folland v Oldham Ath, Division 3N, 15 April 1961.

Most Capped Player: Ambrose Fogarty, 1 (11), Republic of Ireland.

Most League Appearances: Wattie Moore, 447, 1948–64.

Youngest League Player: David Foley, 16 years 105 days v Port Vale, 25 August 2003.

Record Transfer Fee Received: £750,000 from Ipswich T for Tommy Miller, July 2001.

Record Transfer Fee Paid: £75,000 to Northampton for Chris Freestone, March 1993; £75,000 to Notts Co for Gary Jones, March 1999; £75,000 to Mansfield T for Darrell Clarke, July 2001.

Football League Record: 1921 Original Member of Division 3 (N); 1958–68 Division 4; 1968–69 Division 3; 1969–91 Division 4; 1991–92 Division 3; 1992–94 Division 2; 1994–2003 Division 3; 2003–04 Division 2; 2004–06 FL 1; 2006–07 FL 2; 2007– FL 1.

LATEST SEQUENCES

Longest Sequence of League Wins: 9, 18.11.2006 – 1.1.2007.

Longest Sequence of League Defeats: 8, 27.1.1993 – 27.2.1993.

Longest Sequence of League Draws: 5, 24.2.2001 – 17.3.2001.

Longest Sequence of Unbeaten League Matches: 23, 18.11.2006 – 30.3.2007.

Longest Sequence Without a League Win: 18, 9.1.1993 – 3.4.1993.

Successive Scoring Runs: 27 from 18.11.2006.

Successive Non-scoring Runs: 11 from 9.1.1993.

MANAGERS

Alfred Priest 1908–12
Percy Humphreys 1912–13
Jack Manners 1913–20
Cecil Potter 1920–22
David Gordon 1922–24
Jack Manners 1924–27
Bill Norman 1927–31
Jack Carr 1932–35
(had been Player-Coach since 1931)
Jimmy Hamilton 1935–43
Fred Westgarth 1943–57
Ray Middleton 1957–59
Bill Robinson 1959–62
Allenby Chilton 1962–63
Bob Gurney 1963–64
Alvan Williams 1964–65
Geoff Twentyman 1965
Brian Clough 1965–67
Angus McLean 1967–70
John Simpson 1970–71
Len Ashurst 1971–74
Ken Hale 1974–76
Billy Horner 1976–83
Johnny Duncan 1983
Mike Docherty 1983
Billy Horner 1984–86
John Bird 1986–88
Bobby Moncur 1988–89
Cyril Knowles 1989–91
Alan Murray 1991–93
Viv Busby 1993
John MacPhail 1993–94
David McCreery 1994–95
Keith Houchen 1995–96
Mick Tait 1996–99
Chris Turner 1999–2002
Mike Newell 2002–03
Neale Cooper 2003–05
Martin Scott 2005–06
Danny Wilson June 2006–

TEN YEAR LEAGUE RECORD

		P	W	D	L	F	A	Pts	Pos
1997-98	Div 3	46	12	23	11	61	53	59	17
1998-99	Div 3	46	13	12	21	52	65	51	22
1999-2000	Div 3	46	21	9	16	60	49	72	7
2000-01	Div 3	46	21	14	11	71	54	77	4
2001-02	Div 3	46	20	11	15	74	48	71	7
2002-03	Div 3	46	24	13	9	71	51	85	2
2003-04	Div 2	46	20	13	13	76	61	73	6
2004-05	FL 1	46	21	8	17	76	66	71	6
2005-06	FL 1	46	11	17	18	44	59	50	21
2006-07	FL 2	46	26	10	10	65	40	88	2

DID YOU KNOW ?

Harry Procter began with Ushaw Moor and after Portsmouth trials joined Hartlepools United at 19 as an inside-forward, made 61 League appearances and was transferred to Norwich City in May 1934. Skippered the Eastern Command team while serving in the Army.

HARTLEPOOL UNITED 2006–07 LEAGUE RECORD

Match No.	Date	Venue	Opponents	Result	H/T Score	Lg. Pos.	Goalscorers	Attendance
1	Aug 5	H	Swindon T	L 0-1	0-1	—		4690
2	8	A	Macclesfield T	D 0-0	0-0	—		1843
3	12	A	Walsall	L 0-2	0-2	19		5637
4	19	H	Torquay U	D 1-1	0-1	20	Bullock [81]	3688
5	26	A	Hereford U	L 1-3	0-1	21	Brown [53]	3156
6	Sept 1	H	Boston U	W 2-1	1-0	—	Sweeney [29], Daly [71]	4054
7	9	A	Milton Keynes D	D 0-0	0-0	19		5630
8	12	H	Mansfield T	W 2-0	0-0	—	Porter 2 [77, 90]	3899
9	16	H	Shrewsbury T	L 0-3	0-1	18		4291
10	23	A	Peterborough U	W 5-3	3-0	14	Liddle 2 [30, 53], Daly 2 (1 pen) [32 (p), 45], Robson [84]	3916
11	26	A	Grimsby T	W 4-1	1-1	—	Daly 2 (1 pen) [45 (p), 85], Liddle [52], Porter [90]	3486
12	30	H	Wrexham	W 3-0	2-0	7	Daly 3 [20, 22, 68]	4452
13	Oct 6	A	Lincoln C	L 0-2	0-1	—		5332
14	14	H	Stockport Co	D 1-1	1-1	10	Robson [43]	4372
15	20	A	Chester C	L 1-2	1-1	—	Porter [9]	2580
16	28	H	Darlington	D 0-0	0-0	14		7458
17	Nov 4	H	Barnet	L 0-1	0-0	16		3778
18	18	A	Accrington S	W 2-1	0-1	13	Williams E [75], Humphreys [90]	1787
19	25	H	Wycombe W	W 2-0	1-0	11	Duffy 2 [24, 59]	3711
20	Dec 5	A	Notts Co	W 1-0	1-0	—	Monkhouse [8]	3546
21	9	A	Bristol R	W 2-0	0-0	7	Clark [79], Duffy [90]	4906
22	15	H	Rochdale	W 1-0	1-0	—	Duffy [17]	3659
23	23	A	Bury	W 1-0	0-0	6	Sweeney [46]	2839
24	26	H	Grimsby T	W 2-0	0-0	5	Daly [52], Monkhouse [82]	5290
25	30	H	Peterborough U	W 1-0	0-0	5	Duffy [90]	4854
26	Jan 1	A	Mansfield T	W 1-0	0-0	5	Monkhouse [77]	3531
27	6	A	Shrewsbury T	D 1-1	1-0	5	Brown [35]	4334
28	13	H	Milton Keynes D	W 1-0	0-0	5	Sweeney [55]	4851
29	20	A	Wrexham	D 1-1	1-0	5	Barker [9]	3828
30	27	H	Bury	W 2-0	1-0	4	Brown [33], Sweeney [57]	4901
31	Feb 3	A	Swindon T	W 1-0	0-0	3	Monkhouse [49]	6841
32	10	H	Walsall	W 3-1	0-1	2	Nelson [52], Humphreys [88], Barker [90]	5847
33	17	A	Torquay U	W 1-0	1-0	2	Williams E [7]	2194
34	20	H	Macclesfield T	W 3-2	1-0	—	Brown [26], Barker [60], Morley (og) [88]	5242
35	24	A	Boston U	W 1-0	0-0	1	Humphreys [64]	2120
36	Mar 3	H	Hereford U	W 3-2	1-0	1	Clark [32], Brown [54], Williams E [68]	5535
37	9	H	Lincoln C	D 1-1	0-1	—	Barker (pen) [90]	6903
38	17	A	Stockport Co	D 3-3	1-3	1	Monkhouse [38], Barker 2 (1 pen) [47 (p), 65]	7860
39	25	A	Darlington	W 3-0	1-0	1	Williams E 2 [39, 51], Monkhouse [80]	9987
40	30	H	Chester C	W 3-0	2-0	—	Barker [3], Monkhouse [26], Clark [71]	6059
41	Apr 7	A	Barnet	L 1-2	0-1	1	Williams E [77]	2906
42	9	H	Accrington S	W 1-0	0-0	1	Barker (pen) [65]	5867
43	14	A	Wycombe W	W 1-0	0-0	1	Barker [81]	5540
44	20	H	Notts Co	D 1-1	1-1	—	Brown [3]	6174
45	28	A	Rochdale	L 0-2	0-1	2		5846
46	May 5	H	Bristol R	L 1-2	1-0	2	Porter [32]	7629

Final League Position: 2

GOALSCORERS

League (65): Barker 9 (3 pens), Daly 9 (2 pens), Monkhouse 7, Brown 6, Williams E 6, Duffy 5, Porter 5, Sweeney 4, Clark 3, Humphreys 3, Liddle 3, Robson 2, Bullock 1, Nelson 1, own goal 1.
Carling Cup (1): Porter 1 (pen).
FA Cup (2): Brown 1, own goal 1.
J Paint Trophy (4): Bullock 1, Foley 1, Humphreys 1, Liddle 1.

Konstantopoulos D 46	Williams D 19 + 7	Robson M 18 + 2	Tinkler M 4 + 2	Nelson M 42	Clark B 40	Bullock L 8 + 17	Brown J 29 + 7	Porter J 14 + 8	Daly J 14 + 5	Humphreys R 37 + 1	Sweeney A 31 + 4	Foley D 4 + 21	Williams E 32 + 8	Strachan G 2 + 2	Proctor M 1 + 1	Brackstone J 6 + 2	Maidens M — + 4	Liddle G 42	Boland W 25 + 2	Gibb A 12 + 13	Barron M 26 + 3	Duffy D 10	Monkhouse A 26	Barker R 18	Hignett C — + 2	MacKay M — + 1	Match No.
1	2	3	4^{1}	5	6	7	8^{2}	9	10^{3}	11	12	13	14														1
1	2	3		5	6		8^{1}	9		11	7		10	4	12												2
1	2	3	4^{2}	5	6		12	9		11	7^{3}		10^{1}	8		13	14										3
1	2	3	4^{3}	5	6	13	8	9^{1}		11^{2}	7	12	10	14													4
1	2	6		5		7	12	9			8		11		10^{1}	3		4									5
1	2	11		5			10^{2}	9^{1}	12	13	8		7^{3}			3■	14	6	4								6
1	2	3		5	6	12	9^{3}	14	10^{1}		7		13					4	8	11^{2}							7
1	2	11		5	6		9	12	10^{1}		8		13	14				3	4^{3}	7^{2}							8
1	2	11		5	6^{1}		9	12	10^{2}		8		13					3	4	7							9
1	2	11		5	6			9^{2}	10		8^{3}	13				3		4	12	7^{1}	14						10
1	2	11		5	6			9	10		8^{2}		12			3		4	13	7^{1}							11
1	2	11		5	6	12	13	9^{2}	10^{3}				14			3		4^{1}	8	7							12
1	2^{3}	11		5	6	12		9^{2}	10			13				3		4	8^{1}	7	14						13
1		11		5	6	12		9^{1}	10	3		13					14	4	8^{2}	7^{3}	2						14
1		11^{3}		5	6	7	12	9^{1}	10■	3		8^{2}				14	13	4			2						15
1		11		5	6	12	13	9^{2}	10	3		7^{1}						4	8		2						16
1		11		5	6	12			10^{1}	3		7^{2}	13					4	8	14	2	9^{3}					17
1	2^{3}	11^{1}		5	6		13		10	3			12					4	8	7^{2}	14	9					18
1				5	6	12			10^{1}	3	13	14	7^{2}					4	8		2	9^{3}	11				19
1	12			5	6	13				3		14	9^{3}					4	8	7	2^{1}	10^{2}	11				20
1	12			5	6	13				3	10							4	8	7^{2}	2^{1}	9	11				21
1				5	6				12	3	7		9					4	8		2	10	11^{1}				22
1		12		5	6				13	3	7		9^{2}					4	8		2	10	11^{1}				23
1				5^{2}	6		12		13	3	7		9^{1}					4	8	14	2	10^{3}	11				24
1					6	12	8^{1}			3	7	13	9^{2}					5	4		2	10	11				25
1	13				6		8		12	3	7		9^{1}					5	4		2	10	11^{2}				26
1				5	6		11			3	7	12	9^{1}					4	8		2			10			27
1				5		7	8			3	4	12	9^{1}					6			2		11	10			28
1	12	13			6	7	8			3	4		9^{2}					5		14	2^{1}		11^{3}	10			29
1				5	6		8^{1}			3	7	12	9^{2}					4		13	2		11	10			30
1	12			5	6	7	10			3	8		9^{2}					4		13	2^{1}		11				31
1				5	6		8^{2}			3	7	12	9^{1}					4		13	2		11	10			32
1				5		7	8^{2}			3	6	12	9^{1}					4		13	2		11	10			33
1				5	6		8^{2}			3	7	12	9					4		13	2		11^{1}	10			34
1				5	6	12	8^{2}			3	7		9^{1}					4		13	2		11	10			35
1	12			5	6		8^{2}			3	7	13	9					4			2^{1}		11	10			36
1				5	6	12	8			3	7^{1}	13	9^{2}					4		14	2		11^{3}	10			37
1			12	5	6	13	8^{3}			3	7^{1}	14	9					4			2^{2}		11	10			38
1				5	6	12	8^{3}			3	7	13	9^{2}					4		14	2^{1}		11	10			39
1				5	6	12	8^{3}			3	7^{1}		9					4		13	2^{2}		11	10	14		40
1	12			5		7	8^{1}	13		3			9^{2}					4	6	2^{3}			11	10	14		41
1	2			5	6		7^{2}	13		3		12	9^{1}					4	8				11	10			42
1	2			5	6		7^{2}	12		3		13	9^{1}					4	8				11	10			43
1	2		12	5	6■		7^{3}	13		3	14		9^{2}					4	8^{1}				11	10			44
1	2		6	5^{1}			7	13		3	12	14	9^{3}					4	8^{2}				11■	10■			45
1	2				6	12	8^{3}	10^{1}		3	7	11	9^{2}					5	4	13						14	46

FA Cup

First Round	Rochdale	(a)	1-1
		(h)	0-0
Second Round	Macclesfield T	(a)	1-2

Carling Cup

First Round	Burnley	(a)	1-0
Second Round	Hull C	(a)	0-0

J Paint Trophy

First Round	Rotherham U	(h)	3-1
Second Round	Doncaster R	(h)	1-3

HEREFORD UNITED FL Championship 2

FOUNDATION

Two local teams RAOC and St Martins amalgamated in 1924 under the chairmanship of Dr. E.W. Maples to form Hereford United and joined the Birmingham Combination. The first game at Edgar Street was against Atherstone Town on 24 August 1924, the visitors winnning 3-2. The players used the Wellington Hotel as a changing room. They graduated to the Birmingham League four years later and the Southern League in 1939.

Edgar Street, Hereford HR4 9JU.

Telephone: (01432) 276 666.

Fax: (01432) 341 359.

Ticket Office: (01432) 276 666.

Website: www.herefordunited.co.uk

Email: hufc1939@hotmail.com

Ground capacity: 7,873.

Record Attendance: 18,114 v Sheffield W, FA Cup 3rd rd, 4 January 1958.

Pitch measurements: 100m × 72m.

Chairman: Graham Turner.

Secretary: Mrs Joan Fennessy.

Manager: Graham Turner.

First Team Coach: John Trewick.

Physio: Wayne Jones.

Colours: White shirts, black shorts, white stockings.

Change colours: Yellow shirts, blue shorts, blue stockings.

Year Formed: 1924.

Turned Professional: 1924.

Ltd Co.: 1939.

Club Nickname: 'United'.

Ground: 1924, Edgar Street.

First Football League game: 12 August 1972, Division 4, v Colchester U (a) L 0-1 – Potter; Mallender, Naylor; Jones, McLaughlin, Tucker; Slattery, Hollett, Owen, Radford, Wallace.

HONOURS

Football League: Division 2 best season: 22nd, 1976–77; Division 3 – Champions 1975–76; Division 4 – Runners-up 1972–73.

FA Cup: best season: 4th rd, 1972, 1974, 1977, 1982, 1990, 1992.

Football League Cup: best season: 3rd rd, 1975.

Welsh Cup: Winners 1990.

Conference (runners-up): 2003–04, 2004–05. Promoted from Conference 2005–06 (Play-offs).

SKY SPORTS FACT FILE

On 7 December 1957 Hereford United beat Queens Park Rangers 6–1 in a second round FA Cup tie at Edgar Street. At the time it was the highest victory by a non-league team against one from the Football League. Five players shared the goals.

Record League Victory: 6–0 v Burnley (away), Division 4, 24 January 1987 – Rose; Rodgerson, Devine, Halliday, Pejic, Dalziel, Harvey (1p), Wells, Phillips (3), Kearns (2), Spooner.

Record Cup Victory: 6–1 v QPR, FA Cup 2nd rd, 7 December 1957 – Sewell; Tomkins, Wade; Masters, Niblett, Horton (2p); Reg Bowen (1), Clayton (1), Fidler, Williams (1), Cyril Beech (1).

Record Defeat: 0–7 v Middlesbrough, Coca-Cola Cup 2nd rd, 1st leg, 18 September 1996.

Most League Points (2 for a win): 63, Division 3, 1975–76.

Most League Points (3 for a win): 77, Division 4, 1984–85.

Most League Goals: 86, Division 3, 1975–76.

Highest League Scorer in Season: Dixie McNeil, 35, 1975–76.

Most League Goals in Total Aggregate: Stewart Phillips, 93, 1980–88, 1990–91.

Most Capped Player: Brian Evans, 1 (7), Wales.

Most League Appearances: Mel Pejic, 412, 1980–92.

Record Transfer Fee Received: £440,000 from QPR for Darren Peacock, December 1990.

Record Transfer Fee Paid: £80,000 to Walsall for Dean Smith, June 1994.

Football League Record: 1972 Elected to Division 4; 1973–76 Division 3; 1976–77 Division 2; 1977–78 Division 3; 1978–92 Division 4; 1992–97 Division 3; 1997–2006 Vauxhall Conference; 2006– FL 2.

MANAGERS

Eric Keen 1939
George Tranter 1948–49
Alex Massie 1952
George Tranter 1953–55
Joe Wade 1956–62
Ray Daniels 1962–63
Bob Dennison 1963–67
John Charles 1967–71
Colin Addison 1971–74
John Sillett 1974–78
Mike Bailey 1978–79
Frank Lord 1979–82
Tommy Hughes 1982–83
Johnny Newman 1983–87
Ian Bowyer 1987–90
Colin Addison 1990–91
John Sillett 1991–92
Greg Downs 1992–94
John Layton 1994–95
Graham Turner 1995–

LATEST SEQUENCES

Longest Sequence of League Wins: 6, 2.4.1996 – 20.4.1996.

Longest Sequence of League Defeats: 8, 7.2.1987 – 18.3.1987.

Longest Sequence of League Draws: 6, 12.4.1975 – 23.8.1975.

Longest Sequence of Unbeaten League Matches: 14, 21.10.1972 – 17.1.1973.

Longest Sequence Without a League Win: 13, 19.11.1977 – 25.2.1978.

Successive Scoring Runs: 23 from 20.9.1975.

Successive Non-scoring Runs: 6 from 10.3.2007.

TEN YEAR LEAGUE RECORD

		P	W	D	L	F	A	Pts	Pos
1997-98	Conf	42	18	13	11	56	49	67	6
1998-99	Conf	42	15	10	17	49	46	55	13
1999-2000	Conf	42	15	14	13	61	52	59	8
2000-01	Conf	42	14	15	13	60	46	57	11
2001-02	Conf	42	14	10	18	50	53	52	17
2002-03	Conf	42	19	7	16	64	51	64	6
2003-04	Conf	42	28	7	7	103	44	91	2
2004-05	Conf	42	21	11	10	68	41	74	2
2005-06	Conf	42	22	14	6	59	33	80	2
2006-07	FL 2	46	14	13	19	45	53	55	16

DID YOU KNOW?

One of the earliest FA Cup ties televised was on 27 November 1952 when Hereford United, then of the Southern League, met Athenian League team Leyton in a replay at Edgar Street. Hereford, who had drawn the first game scoreless, won 3–2.

HEREFORD UNITED 2006–07 LEAGUE RECORD

Match No.	Date	Venue	Opponents	Result		H/T Score	Lg. Pos.	Goalscorers	Attendance
1	Aug 5	A	Stockport Co	W	2-0	1-0	—	Fleetwood 36, Mkandawire 59	5297
2	8	H	Lincoln C	L	1-2	0-2	—	Purdie (pen) 77	4405
3	12	H	Chester C	W	2-0	0-0	6	Fleetwood 71, Rose 73	3834
4	19	A	Barnet	L	0-3	0-1	14		1945
5	26	H	Hartlepool U	W	3-1	1-0	8	Sills 33, Purdie (pen) 51, Williams 73	3156
6	Sept 2	A	Rochdale	D	1-1	0-0	7	Purdie (pen) 89	2146
7	9	A	Mansfield T	L	1-4	0-2	11	Connell 68	3242
8	12	H	Wycombe W	L	1-2	0-1	—	Williams 51	2585
9	16	H	Bury	W	1-0	0-0	11	Williams 80	2885
10	24	A	Wrexham	L	0-1	0-1	12		4705
11	27	A	Bristol R	L	1-2	1-0	—	Purdie (pen) 18	4975
12	30	H	Macclesfield T	W	1-0	0-0	13	Connell 80	2705
13	Oct 8	A	Grimsby T	L	1-2	1-1	15	Purdie (pen) 26	4147
14	14	H	Darlington	D	1-1	0-1	15	Mkandawire 71	2838
15	21	A	Milton Keynes D	W	3-1	2-0	12	Connell 8, Purdie (pen) 22, Fleetwood 90	5609
16	28	H	Accrington S	W	1-0	0-0	8	Connell 85	3391
17	Nov 4	A	Swindon T	W	2-1	1-1	8	Williams 2 36, 81	6910
18	18	H	Walsall	L	0-1	0-0	10		4462
19	25	A	Boston U	D	1-1	0-0	10	Williams 68	1731
20	Dec 5	H	Peterborough U	D	0-0	0-0	—		2309
21	9	H	Torquay U	D	1-1	1-1	12	Jeannin 33	3078
22	16	A	Shrewsbury T	L	0-3	0-1	14		4177
23	22	A	Notts Co	W	1-0	0-0	—	Sills 81	4106
24	26	H	Bristol R	D	0-0	0-0	10		5201
25	30	H	Wrexham	W	2-0	1-0	8	Connell 2 37, 88	3444
26	Jan 1	A	Wycombe W	D	0-0	0-0	8		4851
27	13	H	Mansfield T	L	1-3	0-1	12	Sheldon 89	3048
28	20	A	Macclesfield T	L	0-3	0-1	14		2494
29	27	H	Notts Co	W	3-2	2-1	10	McClenahan 9, Guinan 2 27, 68	3280
30	30	A	Bury	D	2-2	0-1	—	Adams (og) 63, Williams 78	1775
31	Feb 3	H	Stockport Co	L	0-2	0-2	11		3310
32	17	H	Barnet	W	2-0	0-0	11	Smith 48, Thomas 90	2608
33	20	A	Lincoln C	W	4-1	2-0	—	Connell 3, Guinan 3 36, 46, 54	4695
34	24	H	Rochdale	D	0-0	0-0	9		3090
35	27	A	Chester C	D	1-1	0-0	—	Connell 82	1842
36	Mar 3	A	Hartlepool U	L	2-3	0-1	10	Thomas 46, Guinan 56	5535
37	10	H	Grimsby T	L	0-1	0-0	12		2914
38	17	A	Darlington	L	0-1	0-0	14		3165
39	24	A	Accrington S	L	0-2	0-1	17		1848
40	31	H	Milton Keynes D	D	0-0	0-0	16		2715
41	Apr 7	H	Swindon T	D	0-0	0-0	17		4740
42	9	A	Walsall	L	0-1	0-0	17		5658
43	14	H	Boston U	W	3-0	0-0	15	Guinan 56, Williams 71, Connell 90	2176
44	21	A	Peterborough U	L	0-3	0-2	16		3759
45	28	H	Shrewsbury T	L	0-1	0-1	16		4359
46	May 5	A	Torquay U	D	0-0	0-0	16		2942

Final League Position: 16

GOALSCORERS

League (45): Connell 9, Williams 8, Guinan 7, Purdie 6 (6 pens), Fleetwood 3, Mkandawire 2, Sills 2, Thomas 2, Jeannin 1, McClenahan 1, Rose 1, Sheldon 1, Smith 1, own goal 1.
Carling Cup (4): Fleetwood 3, Purdie 1 (pen).
FA Cup (6): Purdie 2 (1 pen), Webb 2, Connell 1, Ferrell 1.
J Paint Trophy (1): Williams 1.

Brown W 39	Travis S 34+2	Rose R 29+4	Purdie R 43+1	Mkandawire T 39	Beckwith D 32	Williams A 30+11	Ferrell A 15+6	Fleetwood S 21+6	Sills T 22+14	Sheldon G 3+5	Harrison P —+1	Gulliver P 24+2	Giles M 11+2	Tynan S 7	Connell A 33+11	McClenahan T 24+2	Osborn S —+1	Wallis J —+2	Jeannin A 11+1	Webb L 13+8	Eustace J 8	MacKenzie N 7	Jennings S 11	Smith B 18	Guinan S 16	Thomas D 15	Palmer M 1+2	Fitzpatrick J —+1	*Match No.*
1^{G}	2	3	4	5	6^{1}	7	8	9	10	11^{2}	15	12	13																1
	2	3	4	5		7	8	9	10	11^{2}		6^{1}	13	1	12														2
	2	3	4		6	7	8	9	10			5	11	1															3
	2	3^{2}	4		6	7	8^{3}	9	10			5^{1}	11	1	12	13	14												4
	2	3	4^{3}	5	6	12	8	9^{2}	10^{1}				11	1	13	7		14											5
	2	3	4	5	6	9	8		10				11	1	12	7^{1}													6
	2	3	4^{1}	5	6	13	8	9	10^{2}				11	1	12	7													7
	12			5		7	8^{2}	9	10	11		6		1	4^{1}	2		13	3										8
1	2	3	4^{1}	5	6	7		9	10^{2}	12			11		13	8													9
1	2	11^{1}	4	5	6		13	9	10				7		8^{2}				3	12									10
1	2	3	4^{2}	5	6		12	9	10				11		8^{1}	7				13									11
1	2	3	4	5	6	10^{1}		9	12				11		8	7													12
1	2	3	4^{2}	5	6^{1}	10		9	12				11		8	7				13									13
1	2	3	4^{1}	5	6	10		9				13	11^{2}		12	7					8								14
1		11	12	5	6	7		9				2			10	4^{1}			3		8								15
1			4	5	6	10^{1}		9	12			2			11				3		7	8							16
1			4	5	6	7		9^{1}	12			2			10				3		11	8							17
1			4	5	6	9			10^{1}	12		2			11				3		7	8							18
1			4	5	6	9^{1}			10	12		2			11^{2}				3	13	7	8							19
1			4	5	6	12		9^{1}	10			2			11^{2}				3	13	7	8							20
1			4	5	6	12		9^{1}	10			2			11^{2}				3	13	7	8							21
1	12		4	5	6■		13	9^{2}	10			2			11				3^{1}	7		8							22
1	2	3	4	5			8	12	10			6			9^{1}	7				11									23
1	2	3	4	5			8	12	10			6			9^{1}	7				11									24
1	2	3		5		12	8	9^{1}	10^{2}	13		6			11	7				4									25
1	2	3	4	5^{3}		12	8	13	10^{1}			9			11^{2}	7			14	6									26
1	2	3	4		6^{2}	9	8	12	10	13		5			11^{1}					7									27
1	2	3^{1}	4		6	10	7■	9^{2}	12			5			13				11				8						28
1	2	3	4	5		12						6			9^{1}	7				13			11^{2}	8	10				29
1	2	3	4	5		12						6			9	7							11^{1}	8	10				30
1	2	3	4	5		12			13			6			9^{2}	7							11^{1}	8	10				31
1	2^{1}	3	4		6	12	13		14						9^{3}	5							11^{2}	7	10	8			32
1		3	4		6	7			12						9^{1}	5							11	8	10	2			33
1		3	4		6	7			12						9^{1}	5							11	8	10	2			34
1	2	12	4	5	6^{1}	7									9								11	8	10	3			35
1	2	3	4	5		7	12								9								11^{1}	8	10	6			36
1	2^{2}	3	4	5		7	8^{1}		12						9	13								6	10	11			37
1	2	3	4	5		7	12		13						9^{2}					6^{1}				8	10	11			38
1	2		4	5	6	7^{2}		12				9^{1}			13					11				8	10	3			39
1	2		4	5	6	7									9					8				3	10	11			40
1	2		4	5	6	7			12■						9^{2}					8				11	10^{1}	3	13		41
1	2	12	4	5	6■	7^{2}		13							9^{1}					11				8	10	3			42
1	2	12	4^{1}	5		9^{2}			13			6			14	7							11	8	10^{3}	3			43
1		12	4	5		7						6			9^{3}	2				13			11^{2}	8	10	3^{1}	14		44
1	2		4	5	6	12			10^{2}						13	7				11				8		3	9^{1}		45
1	2		4	5	6	9			12						10^{2}	7				11				8^{1}		3		13	46

FA Cup

First Round	Shrewsbury T	(a)	0-0
		(h)	2-0
Second Round	Port Vale	(h)	4-0
Third Round	Bristol R	(a)	0-1

Carling Cup

First Round	Coventry C	(h)	3-1
Second Round	Leicester C	(h)	1-3

J Paint Trophy

First Round	Shrewsbury T	(h)	1-2

HUDDERSFIELD TOWN FL Championship 1

FOUNDATION

A meeting, attended largely by members of the Huddersfield & District FA, was held at the Imperial Hotel in 1906 to discuss the feasibility of establishing a football club in this rugby stronghold. However, it was not until a man with both the enthusiasm and the money to back the scheme came on the scene, that real progress was made. This benefactor was Mr Hilton Crowther and it was at a meeting at the Albert Hotel in 1908, that the club formally came into existence with a capital of £2,000 and joined the North-Eastern League.

The Galpharm Stadium, Stadium Way, Leeds Road, Huddersfield HD1 6PX.

Telephone: 0870 4444 677.

Fax: (01484) 484 101.

Ticket Office: 0870 4444 552.

Website: www.htafc.com

Email: info@htafc.com

Ground Capacity: 24,500.

Record Attendance: 67,037 v Arsenal, FA Cup 6th rd, 27 February 1932 (at Leeds Road); 23,678 v Liverpool, FA Cup 3rd rd, 12 December 1999 (at Alfred McAlpine Stadium).

Pitch Measurements: 105m × 68m.

Chairman: Ken Davy.

Vice-chairman: Andrew Watson.

Secretary: J. Ann Hough.

Manager: Andy Ritchie.

Assistant Manager: John Dungworth.

Physio: Lee Martin.

Colours: Blue and white striped shirts, white shorts, white stockings.

Change Colours: Red shirts with black trim, red shorts, red stockings.

Year Formed: 1908. ***Turned Professional:*** 1908. ***Ltd Co.:*** 1908.

Club Nickname: 'The Terriers'.

Grounds: 1908, Leeds Road; 1994, The Alfred McAlpine Stadium.

First Football League Game: 3 September 1910, Division 2, v Bradford PA (a) W 1–0 – Mutch; Taylor, Morris; Beaton, Hall, Bartlett; Blackburn, Wood, Hamilton (1), McCubbin, Jee.

Record League Victory: 10–1 v Blackpool, Division 1, 13 December 1930 – Turner; Goodall, Spencer; Redfern, Wilson, Campbell; Bob Kelly (1), McLean (4), Robson (3), Davies (1), Smailes (1).

Record Cup Victory: 7–0 v Lincoln U, FA Cup 1st rd, 16 November 1991 – Clarke; Trevitt, Charlton, Donovan (2), Mitchell, Doherty, O'Regan (1), Stapleton (1) (Wright), Roberts (2), Onuora (1), Barnett (Ireland). *N.B.* 11-0 v Heckmondwike (a), FA Cup pr rd, 18 September 1909 – Doggart; Roberts, Ewing; Hooton, Stevenson, Randall; Kenworthy (2), McCreadie (1), Foster (4), Stacey (4), Jee.

HONOURS

Football League: Division 1 – Champions 1923–24, 1924–25, 1925–26; Runners-up 1926–27, 1927–28, 1933–34; Division 2 – Champions 1969–70; Runners-up 1919–20, 1952–53; Promoted from Division 2 1994–95 (play-offs); Promoted from Division 3 2003–04 (play-offs); Division 4 – Champions 1979–80.

FA Cup: Winners 1922; Runners-up 1920, 1928, 1930, 1938.

Football League Cup: Semi-final 1968.

Autoglass Trophy: Runners-up 1994.

SKY SPORTS FACT FILE

On 8 August 2006 the 79th minute goal scored by Gary Taylor-Fletcher for Huddersfield Town against Rotherham United was the 500,000th in English League football since 1888. The club's first marksman in the competition had been Henry Gilhespy Hamilton.

Record Defeat: 1–10 v Manchester C, Division 2, 7 November 1987.

Most League Points (2 for a win): 66, Division 4, 1979–80.

Most League Points (3 for a win): 82, Division 3, 1982–83.

Most League Goals: 101, Division 4, 1979–80.

Highest League Scorer in Season: Sam Taylor, 35, Division 2, 1919–20; George Brown, 35, Division 1, 1925–26.

Most League Goals in Total Aggregate: George Brown, 142, 1921–29; Jimmy Glazzard, 142, 1946–56.

Most League Goals in One Match: 5, Dave Mangnall v Derby Co, Division 1, 21 November 1931; 5, Alf Lythgoe v Blackburn R, Division 1, 13 April 1935.

Most Capped Player: Jimmy Nicholson, 31 (41), Northern Ireland.

Most League Appearances: Billy Smith, 520, 1914–34.

Youngest League Player: Denis Law, 16 years 303 days v Notts Co, 24 December 1956.

Record Transfer Fee Received: £2,750,000 from Ipswich T for Marcus Stewart, February 2000.

Record Transfer Fee Paid: £1,200,000 to Bristol R for Marcus Stewart, July 1996.

Football League Record: 1910 Elected to Division 2; 1920–52 Division 1; 1952–53 Division 2; 1953–56 Division 1; 1956–70 Division 2; 1970–72 Division 1; 1972–73 Division 2; 1973–75 Division 3; 1975–80 Division 4; 1980–83 Division 3; 1983–88 Division 2; 1988–92 Division 3; 1992–95 Division 2; 1995–2001 Division 1; 2001–03 Division 2; 2003–04 Division 3; 2004– FL 1.

MANAGERS

Fred Walker 1908–10
Richard Pudan 1910–12
Arthur Fairclough 1912–19
Ambrose Langley 1919–21
Herbert Chapman 1921–25
Cecil Potter 1925–26
Jack Chaplin 1926–29
Clem Stephenson 1929–42
David Steele 1943–47
George Stephenson 1947–52
Andy Beattie 1952–56
Bill Shankly 1956–59
Eddie Boot 1960–64
Tom Johnston 1964–68
Ian Greaves 1968–74
Bobby Collins 1974
Tom Johnston 1975–78
(had been General Manager since 1975)
Mike Buxton 1978–86
Steve Smith 1986–87
Malcolm Macdonald 1987–88
Eoin Hand 1988–92
Ian Ross 1992–93
Neil Warnock 1993–95
Brian Horton 1995–97
Peter Jackson 1997–99
Steve Bruce 1999–2000
Lou Macari 2000–02
Mick Wadsworth 2002–03
Peter Jackson 2003–07
Andy Ritchie April 2007–

LATEST SEQUENCES

Longest Sequence of League Wins: 11, 5.4.1920 – 4.9.1920.

Longest Sequence of League Defeats: 7, 8.10.1955 – 19.11.1955.

Longest Sequence of League Draws: 6, 3.3.1987 – 3.4.1987.

Longest Sequence of Unbeaten League Matches: 27, 24.1.1925 – 17.10.1925.

Longest Sequence Without a League Win: 22, 4.12.1971 – 29.4.1972.

Successive Scoring Runs: 27 from 12.3.2005.

Successive Non-scoring Runs: 7 from 22.1.1972.

TEN YEAR LEAGUE RECORD

		P	W	D	L	F	A	Pts	Pos
1997-98	Div 1	46	14	11	21	50	72	53	16
1998-99	Div 1	46	15	16	15	62	71	61	10
1999-2000	Div 1	46	21	11	14	62	49	74	8
2000-01	Div 1	46	11	15	20	48	57	48	22
2001-02	Div 2	46	21	15	10	65	47	78	6
2002-03	Div 2	46	11	12	23	39	61	45	22
2003-04	Div 3	46	23	12	11	68	52	81	4
2004-05	FL 1	46	20	10	16	74	65	70	9
2005-06	FL 1	46	19	16	11	72	59	73	4
2006-07	FL 1	46	14	17	15	60	69	59	15

DID YOU KNOW ?

Goalscoring winger Alex Jackson hit 18 FA Cup goals for Huddersfield Town including 11 in a brilliant run of seven games in which the club scored between 1928–29 and 1929–30. Formerly with Aberdeen, he was capped 17 times by Scotland in his career.

HUDDERSFIELD TOWN 2006–07 LEAGUE RECORD

Match No.	Date	Venue	Opponents	Result	H/T Score	Lg. Pos.	Goalscorers	Attendance
1	Aug 5	A	Gillingham	L 1-2	0-0	—	Taylor-Fletcher [81]	6075
2	8	H	Rotherham U	W 3-0	2-0	—	Beckett (pen) [36], Abbott [45], Taylor-Fletcher [79]	10,161
3	12	H	Bristol C	W 2-1	0-0	6	Beckett [64], Abbott [90]	10,492
4	19	A	Brentford	D 2-2	0-0	6	Schofield [72], Beckett [90]	5709
5	26	H	Nottingham F	D 1-1	0-1	7	Taylor-Fletcher [72]	11,720
6	Sept 2	A	Crewe Alex	L 0-2	0-1	10		4868
7	9	A	Cheltenham T	L 1-2	0-1	14	Abbott [86]	3720
8	12	H	Doncaster R	D 0-0	0-0	—		10,151
9	16	H	Yeovil T	L 2-3	1-1	19	Hudson [27], Taylor-Fletcher [63]	9573
10	23	A	Swansea C	W 2-1	0-0	17	Taylor-Fletcher 2 [50, 60]	12,202
11	26	A	Tranmere R	D 2-2	0-2	—	Booth [55], Taylor-Fletcher [78]	6702
12	30	H	Bournemouth	D 2-2	1-1	17	Taylor-Fletcher [27], Beckett [69]	11,350
13	Oct 7	A	Bradford C	W 1-0	1-0	13	Hudson [25]	14,925
14	14	H	Carlisle U	W 2-1	2-1	11	Beckett 2 (1 pen) [21, 32 (p)]	10,830
15	21	A	Port Vale	W 2-1	0-1	6	Booth [77], Collins [79]	5225
16	28	H	Brighton & HA	L 0-3	0-2	9		10,616
17	Nov 4	H	Scunthorpe U	D 1-1	0-0	9	Booth [86]	10,456
18	18	A	Blackpool	L 1-3	1-2	11	Taylor-Fletcher [45]	7414
19	25	H	Oldham Ath	L 0-3	0-1	14		13,280
20	Dec 5	A	Millwall	D 0-0	0-0	—		6251
21	9	A	Leyton Orient	L 0-1	0-1	17		4300
22	16	H	Northampton T	D 1-1	0-1	17	Schofield [65]	8723
23	23	A	Chesterfield	D 0-0	0-0	17		4472
24	26	H	Tranmere R	D 2-2	1-1	17	Booth [9], Schofield (pen) [63]	10,228
25	30	H	Swansea C	W 3-2	0-2	14	Worthington [67], Abbott 2 (1 pen) [75, 90 (p)]	9399
26	Jan 1	A	Doncaster R	L 0-3	0-1	16		14,470
27	5	A	Yeovil T	L 1-3	0-3	—	Taylor-Fletcher [50]	5554
28	13	H	Cheltenham T	W 2-0	2-0	14	Beckett [31], Booth [43]	9813
29	20	A	Bournemouth	W 2-1	1-1	11	Worthington [12], Schofield [85]	5263
30	27	H	Chesterfield	D 1-1	0-1	11	Young [53]	9872
31	Feb 3	H	Gillingham	W 3-1	2-0	11	Beckett [3], Booth 2 [8, 83]	9167
32	10	A	Bristol C	D 1-1	0-0	11	Taylor-Fletcher [52]	11,636
33	17	H	Brentford	L 0-2	0-0	13		10,520
34	20	A	Rotherham U	W 3-2	1-1	—	Beckett 2 [3, 46], Collins [59]	4448
35	24	H	Crewe Alex	L 1-2	1-1	13	Brandon [22]	10,052
36	Mar 3	A	Nottingham F	L 1-5	0-4	15	Young [82]	19,070
37	10	H	Bradford C	W 2-0	1-0	14	Hayes [3], Schofield [75]	14,772
38	17	A	Carlisle U	D 1-1	1-1	14	Beckett [26]	6629
39	24	A	Brighton & HA	D 0-0	0-0	14		5974
40	31	H	Port Vale	D 2-2	1-1	15	Beckett [4], McAliskey [46]	10,313
41	Apr 7	A	Oldham Ath	D 1-1	0-1	15	Beckett [78]	7096
42	9	H	Blackpool	L 0-2	0-1	16		11,432
43	14	A	Scunthorpe U	L 0-2	0-0	17		7518
44	21	H	Millwall	W 4-2	1-1	16	Collins [20], Hudson [59], Beckett 2 (1 pen) [73 (p), 79]	9406
45	27	A	Northampton T	D 1-1	0-0	—	Mirfin [75]	5842
46	May 5	H	Leyton Orient	W 3-1	3-0	15	Collins [11], Holdsworth 2 [26, 45]	10,842

Final League Position: 15

GOALSCORERS

League (60): Beckett 15 (3 pens), Taylor-Fletcher 11, Booth 7, Abbott 5 (1 pen), Schofield 5 (1 pen), Collins 4, Hudson 3, Holdsworth 2, Worthington 2, Young 2, Brandon 1, Hayes 1, McAliskey 1, Mirfin 1.
Carling Cup (0).
FA Cup (0).
J Paint Trophy (1): Booth 1.

Glennon M 46	Holdsworth A 35	Adams D 23	Hudson M 30 + 2	McIntosh M 24 + 2	Clarke N 16	Taylor-Fletcher G 39	Worthington J 27 + 1	Booth A 29 + 5	Beckett L 32 + 9	Schofield D 25 + 10	Collins M 39 + 4	Abbott P 8 + 10	Brandon C 17 + 6	Mirfin D 38	McAliskey J 3 + 5	Young M 16 + 13	Clarke T 6 + 3	Hardy A 5 + 4	McCombe J 5 + 2	Skarz J 15 + 2	Ahmed A 4 + 5	Taylor A 7 + 1	Sinclair F 13	Hayes P 4	Racchi D — + 3	Berrett J — + 2	Hand J — + 1	Akins L — + 2	*Match No.*
1	2	3	4^1	5	6	7	8	9^2	10	11^3	12	13	14																1
1	2	3	4		6	7^2	8^1		10	13	12	9	11	5															2
1	2	3	4		6	7^2	8		10^3	12	13	9	11^1	5	14														3
1	2	3	4		6	7^1	8	12	10	11		9^2		5		13													4
1	2	3	4		6	7^2		9	10^1	11	8	12		5		13													5
1	2	3^3	4		6	7^2		9	10	11^1	8	12		5		13	14												6
1		3	4		6	7		9	10^2	12	8	13		5		11^1	2												7
1		3	4		6	7		9^1	12	11	8	10		5			2												8
1		3	4		6	7		9^1	12	11	8	10		5			2												9
1	2	3	4	6		10^1		9		11	8			5		12	7												10
1	2	3	4	6		10		9^2	13	11^3	8	12		5		14	7^1												11
1	2	3	4^1	5	6	7	12		10		8	9^2	13			11^3	14												12
1	2	3▮	4	5	6	9^2	7		10^1	13	8^3	12				11	14												13
1	2		4	5	6		7	12	10^1	11	8		13			9	3^2												14
1		3	4^2	5			7	12	10^1	11	8	13	14			9^3		2	6										15
1		3▮		5			7	12	10	11^1	8	9	13			4^2		2	6										16
1	2		4	5	6	10	7^2	9	12	11	8^1					13				3									17
1			4		6	7		9	12	11^1	8					10		2	5	3									18
1	2		4^3	12	6^1	11^2	7	9	10	13	14		8	5						3									19
1	2	3	4	6		11^1	7	9		12	8		10^2	5		13													20
1	2	3	4	6▮		11^2	7^1	9	12	13	8		10^3	5					14										21
1	2	3	4			10		9	12	11	8			5		7^1			6										22
1	2	3	4^2	6		10		9		11	8	12	7^1	5		13													23
1	2	3	12	6		10^2	7	9		11	4	13	8^1	5															24
1	2^1	3		6		10	7	9			4	12	8	5		11													25
1		3		6		7^3		9^1	12		4	10▮	8^2	5		13		2		14	11▮								26
1	2	3	4			10		9^1	12		7		8	5		11		13	6^2										27
1	2			6		11	7^2	9	10	12			8^1	5		4		13		3									28
1	2			6		11^1	7^2	9	10^3	12	4		8	5	14	13				3									29
1	2			6		11	7^2	9	10	12	4		8^1	5		13				3									30
1	2				6^1	7		9	10	11	4		8^2	5		13			12	3									31
1	2					8		9	10	11	4			5		7^1					12	3	6						32
1	2					7		9	10	11	4		12	5		8^1						3	6						33
1	2▮					9			10	11	4		7^1	5		8		12				3	6						34
1						11			10		4		7	5		8		2				3	6	9					35
1	2								10	11	4		7^1	5		8		12		13		3^2	6	9					36
1	2					8	7^1		10	11	4			5		12						3	6	9					37
1	2					8	7	12	10	11	4			5								3	6	9^1					38
1	2^2		12	13		8^3	7	9	10	11^1	4			5						3	14		6▮						39
1			2	6		7	8		10	11^2	4			5	9^3					3^1	12	13			14				40
1			2	6		11^3	8	9	10^1		4			5	12					3	7^2					13	14		41
1	2^3		8	6^1			7^2	9	10		11			5	13					3	12		4			14			42
1			2				8	9	10		4			5	11^1					3	7		6		12				43
1	2		8	6		9^1	7		10		11▮			5	12					3			4						44
1	2		8	6			7		10^2					5	9					3	11^1		4		12			13	45
1	2		8	6		9^2	7^1		10		11			5						3	12		4					13	46

FA Cup
First Round Blackpool (h) 0-1

Carling Cup
First Round Mansfield T (h) 0-2

J Paint Trophy
First Round Doncaster R (h) 1-2

HULL CITY — FL Championship

FOUNDATION

The enthusiasts who formed Hull City in 1904 were brave men indeed. More than that they were audacious for they immediately put the club on the map in this Rugby League fortress by obtaining a three-year agreement with the Hull Rugby League club to rent their ground! They had obtained quite a number of conversions to the dribbling code, before the Rugby League forbade the use of any of their club grounds by Association Football clubs. By that time, Hull City were well away having entered the FA Cup in their initial season and the Football League, Second Division after only a year.

KC Stadium, The Circle, Walton Street, Anlaby Road, Hull HU3 6HU.

Telephone: 0870 837 0003.

Fax: (01482) 304 882.

Ticket Office: 0870 837 0004.

Website: www.hullcityafc.net

Ground Capacity: 25,104.

Record Attendance: KC Stadium: 25,512 v Sunderland, FL C, 28 October 2007. Boothferry Park: 55,019 v Manchester U, FA Cup 6th rd, 26 February 1949.

Pitch Measurements: 115yd × 75yd.

Chairman/Chief Executive: Adam Pearson.

Secretary: Phil Hough.

Manager: Phil Brown.

Assistant Manager: Brian Horton.

Physio: Simon Maltby.

Colours: Amber shirts, black shorts, black stockings.

Change Colours: All white.

Year Formed: 1904. ***Turned Professional:*** 1905.

Ltd Co.: 1905.

Club Nickname: 'The Tigers'.

Grounds: 1904, Boulevard Ground (Hull RFC); 1905, Anlaby Road (Hull CC); 1944, Boulevard Ground; 1946, Boothferry Park; 2002, Kingston Communications Stadium.

First Football League Game: 2 September 1905, Division 2, v Barnsley (h) W 4–1 – Spendiff; Langley, Jones; Martin, Robinson, Gordon (2); Rushton, Spence (1), Wilson (1), Howe, Raisbeck.

Record League Victory: 11–1 v Carlisle U, Division 3 (N), 14 January 1939 – Ellis; Woodhead, Dowen; Robinson (1), Blyth, Hardy; Hubbard (2), Richardson (2), Dickinson (2), Davies (2), Cunliffe (2).

HONOURS

Football League: Championship 1 runners-up 2004–05; Division 2 best season: 3rd, 1909–10; Division 3 (N) – Champions 1932–33, 1948–49; Division 3 – Champions 1965–66; Runners-up 1958–59, 2003–04; Division 4 – Runners-up 1982–83.

FA Cup: Semi-final 1930.

Football League Cup: best season: 4th, 1974, 1976, 1978.

Associate Members' Cup: Runners-up 1984.

SKY SPORTS FACT FILE

Inside-forward Andy Conway was outstanding on the 1948 close season Scandinavian tour by Hull City. Signed in June 1947 from North Shields after 28 goals in 1946–47, first team chances were limited to six League games – but he still scored five.

Record Cup Victory: 8–2 v Stalybridge Celtic (a), FA Cup 1st rd, 26 November 1932 – Maddison; Goldsmith, Woodhead; Gardner, Hill (1), Denby; Forward (1), Duncan, McNaughton (1), Wainscoat (4), Sargeant (1).

Record Defeat: 0–8 v Wolverhampton W, Division 2, 4 November 1911.

Most League Points (2 for a win): 69, Division 3, 1965–66.

Most League Points (3 for a win): 90, Division 4, 1982–83.

Most League Goals: 109, Division 3, 1965–66.

Highest League Scorer in Season: Bill McNaughton, 39, Division 3 (N), 1932–33.

Most League Goals in Total Aggregate: Chris Chilton, 195, 1960–71.

Most League Goals in One Match: 5, Ken McDonald v Bristol C, Division 2, 17 November 1928; 5, Simon 'Slim' Raleigh v Halifax T, Division 3N, 26 December 1930.

Most Capped Player: Theo Whitmore, Jamaica.

Most League Appearances: Andy Davidson, 520, 1952–67.

Youngest League Player: Matthew Edeson, 16 years 63 days v Fulham, 10 October 1992.

Record Transfer Fee Received: £750,000 from Middlesbrough for Andy Payton, November 1991.

Record Transfer Fee Paid: £250,000 to Falkirk for Darryl Duffy, January 2006.

Football League Record: 1905 Elected to Division 2; 1930–33 Division 3 (N); 1933–36 Division 2; 1936–49 Division 3 (N); 1949–56 Division 2; 1956–58 Division 3 (N); 1958–59 Division 3; 1959–60 Division 2; 1960–66 Division 3; 1966–78 Division 2; 1978–81 Division 3; 1981–83 Division 4; 1983–85 Division 3; 1985–91 Division 2; 1991–92 Division 3; 1992–96 Division 2; 1996–2004 Division 3; 2004–05 FL 1; 2005– FL C.

MANAGERS

James Ramster 1904–05 *(Secretary-Manager)*
Ambrose Langley 1905–13
Harry Chapman 1913–14
Fred Stringer 1914–16
David Menzies 1916–21
Percy Lewis 1921–23
Bill McCracken 1923–31
Haydn Green 1931–34
John Hill 1934–36
David Menzies 1936
Ernest Blackburn 1936–46
Major Frank Buckley 1946–48
Raich Carter 1948–51
Bob Jackson 1952–55
Bob Brocklebank 1955–61
Cliff Britton 1961–70 *(continued as General Manager to 1971)*
Terry Neill 1970–74
John Kaye 1974–77
Bobby Collins 1977–78
Ken Houghton 1978–79
Mike Smith 1979–82
Bobby Brown 1982
Colin Appleton 1982–84
Brian Horton 1984–88
Eddie Gray 1988–89
Colin Appleton 1989
Stan Ternent 1989–91
Terry Dolan 1991–97
Mark Hateley 1997–98
Warren Joyce 1998–2000
Brian Little 2000–02
Jan Molby 2002
Peter Taylor 2002–06
Phil Parkinson 2006
Phil Brown January 2007–

LATEST SEQUENCES

Longest Sequence of League Wins: 10, 23.2.1966 – 20.4.1966.

Longest Sequence of League Defeats: 8, 7.4.1934 – 8.9.1934.

Longest Sequence of League Draws: 5, 30.3.1929 – 15.4.1929.

Longest Sequence of Unbeaten League Matches: 19, 13.3.2001 – 22.9.2001.

Longest Sequence Without a League Win: 27, 27.3.1989 – 4.11.1989.

Successive Scoring Runs: 26 from 10.4.1990.

Successive Non-scoring Runs: 6 from 13.11.1920.

TEN YEAR LEAGUE RECORD

		P	W	D	L	F	A	Pts	Pos
1997-98	Div 3	46	11	8	27	56	83	41	22
1998-99	Div 3	46	14	11	21	44	62	53	21
1999-2000	Div 3	46	15	14	17	43	43	59	14
2000-01	Div 3	46	19	17	10	47	39	74	6
2001-02	Div 3	46	16	13	17	57	51	61	11
2002-03	Div 3	46	14	17	15	58	53	59	13
2003-04	Div 3	46	25	13	8	82	44	88	2
2004-05	FL 1	46	26	8	12	80	53	86	2
2005-06	FL C	46	12	16	18	49	55	52	18
2006-07	FL C	46	13	10	23	51	67	49	21

DID YOU KNOW ?

When Burnley were enjoying a record run of 30 League games without defeat in 1920–21, Hull City achieved the notable feat of beating them 3–0 in an FA Cup tie on 19 February 1921. Two goals from Tom Brandon, one from Henry Wilson settled the game.

HULL CITY 2006–07 LEAGUE RECORD

Match No.	Date	Venue	Opponents	Result		H/T Score	Lg. Pos.	Goalscorers	Atten-dance
1	Aug 5	A	WBA	L	0-2	0-0	—		20,682
2	8	H	Barnsley	L	2-3	2-1	—	Parkin 2 [6, 9]	18,207
3	12	H	Derby Co	L	1-2	1-1	23	Parkin (pen) [45]	15,621
4	19	A	Ipswich T	D	0-0	0-0	21		19,790
5	26	H	Coventry C	L	0-1	0-0	23		16,145
6	Sept 9	A	Birmingham C	L	1-2	0-1	24	Livermore [67]	19,228
7	12	A	Leicester C	W	1-0	0-0	—	Bridges [58]	18,677
8	15	H	Sheffield W	W	2-1	2-1	—	Parkin 2 [11, 17]	17,685
9	23	A	QPR	L	0-2	0-0	24		11,381
10	30	H	Crystal Palace	D	1-1	0-0	23	Turner [90]	18,099
11	Oct 14	A	Burnley	L	0-2	0-2	24		11,530
12	17	H	Luton T	D	0-0	0-0	—		14,895
13	21	A	Preston NE	L	1-2	0-2	24	Welsh [58]	13,728
14	28	H	Sunderland	L	0-1	0-0	24		25,512
15	31	A	Southend U	W	3-2	1-1	—	Parkin [35], Elliott [56], Fagan [65]	10,234
16	Nov 4	A	Southampton	D	0-0	0-0	22		20,560
17	11	H	Wolverhampton W	W	2-0	1-0	21	Fagan [13], Elliott [75]	16,962
18	18	H	Stoke C	L	0-2	0-1	21		16,940
19	25	A	Norwich C	D	1-1	0-0	23	Turner [90]	24,129
20	28	A	Colchester U	L	1-5	1-1	—	Forster [16]	5373
21	Dec 2	H	Southampton	L	2-4	2-2	23	Barmby [44], Fagan [45]	15,697
22	9	A	Plymouth Arg	L	0-1	0-0	23		12,101
23	16	H	Cardiff C	W	4-1	3-0	22	Delaney [6], Marney [9], Fagan [36], Bridges [71]	23,089
24	23	A	Leeds U	D	0-0	0-0	22		22,578
25	26	H	Leicester C	L	1-2	1-0	22	Fagan [45]	18,523
26	30	H	Burnley	W	2-0	2-0	22	Marney [6], Fagan (pen) [23]	17,731
27	Jan 1	A	Sheffield W	W	2-1	1-0	21	Barmby 2 [9, 65]	28,600
28	13	H	QPR	W	2-1	0-1	21	Elliott 2 [85, 90]	19,791
29	20	A	Crystal Palace	D	1-1	0-0	19	Ashbee [72]	17,012
30	30	H	Leeds U	L	1-2	1-1	—	Forster [45]	24,311
31	Feb 3	H	WBA	L	0-1	0-0	22		18,005
32	10	A	Derby Co	D	2-2	1-2	20	Dawson [33], Livermore [88]	28,140
33	20	A	Barnsley	L	0-3	0-1	—		12,526
34	24	H	Birmingham C	W	2-0	1-0	20	Windass 2 (1 pen) [10, 57 (p)]	18,811
35	Mar 3	A	Coventry C	L	0-2	0-2	21		21,079
36	6	H	Ipswich T	L	2-5	1-2	—	Windass 2 (1 pen) [22, 83 (p)]	18,056
37	10	H	Preston NE	W	2-0	1-0	19	Forster [29], Livermore [70]	17,118
38	13	A	Luton T	W	2-1	1-0	—	Livermore [22], Turner [62]	7777
39	17	A	Sunderland	L	0-2	0-1	19		38,448
40	31	H	Southend U	W	4-0	1-0	18	Windass 3 [43, 73, 79], Ricketts [81]	19,629
41	Apr 6	H	Norwich C	L	1-2	0-1	—	Dawson [88]	19,053
42	9	A	Wolverhampton W	L	1-3	0-2	20	Forster [61]	20,772
43	14	H	Colchester U	D	1-1	1-0	21	Forster [24]	20,887
44	21	A	Stoke C	D	1-1	0-1	21	Barmby [90]	17,109
45	28	A	Cardiff C	W	1-0	0-0	21	Windass [52]	12,421
46	May 6	H	Plymouth Arg	L	1-2	0-1	21	Elliott [61]	20,661

Final League Position: 21

GOALSCORERS

League (51): Windass 8 (2 pens), Fagan 6 (1 pen), Parkin 6 (1 pen), Elliott 5, Forster 5, Barmby 4, Livermore 4, Turner 3, Bridges 2, Dawson 2, Marney 2, Ashbee 1, Delaney 1, Ricketts 1, Welsh 1.
Carling Cup (3): Barmby 1, Burgess 1, Duffy 1.
FA Cup (4): Dawson 2, Forster 1, Parkin 1 (pen).

Myhill B 46	Dawson A 38	Ricketts S 40	Marney D 26+11	Delaney D 36+1	Turner M 42+1	Elliott S 20+12	Welsh J 9+9	Duffy D 4+5	Fagan C 27	Parkin J 22+7	France R 13+11	Andrews K —+3	Burgess B —+3	Collins S 6	Livermore D 24+1	Barmby N 7+13	Ashbee I 35	Bridges M 8+7	Forster N 26+9	Mills D 9	Yeates M 2+3	Thelwell A 2	Coles D 16+5	Jarrett J 3	McPhee S 9+3	Featherstone N —+2	Duke M —+1	Windass D 15+3	Parlour R 14+1	Vaz Te R 1+5	Peltier L 5+2	Doyle N 1	Match No.
1	2	3	4	5	6	7^{1}	8	9^{2}	10	11^{3}	12	13	14																				1
1	2	3	4^{2}	5	6	12	8^{1}	9	10	11^{3}	7	13	14																				2
1	2	3	4		6	13		9^{3}	10	11	7^{2}	12		5	8^{1}	14																	3
1	2	3	4^{1}		6		12	13	10	9	7			5	11	8^{2}																	4
1	2	3	4		6			9^{1}	10	11^{2}	7		13	5	8	12																	5
1	2	3	4^{2}		6		12		11	13■	14			5	8		7^{3}	9^{1}	10														6
1	2	3	12		6				11		7			5	8		4	9	10^{1}														7
1	2	3			6				11	10	7				8	12	4	9^{1}		5													8
1	2		12		6				11	10	7^{3}			5	8^{1}		4	9^{2}	13	3	14												9
1	3		4		6				11	10	12						8	9^{2}	13	5	7	2^{1}											10
1	3		4^{1}		6		12		11	10^{2}							8	9	13	5	7	2^{3}	14										11
1		3		12	6	11^{1}	8		7	10^{2}	13						4	14	9^{3}	2			5										12
1		3		7	6	11	8		9^{1}	13	12						4		10	2			5^{2}										13
1	2	3		4	6		11^{1}		7^{3}	10	13					12	8	14	9^{2}	5													14
1	2	3	4	11	6	9			7	10							8■			5													15
1	2	3	4^{1}	8	6	9	12		7	10													5	11									16
1		3	4	8	6	9^{2}	13		11	10^{1}									12	2			5	7									17
1	2^{1}	3	4	11	6	9^{3}			7							12		13	10^{2}		14		5	8									18
1		3	4	5	6	7			9		12				11^{1}	13	8		10^{2}				2										19
1		2	4	3	6	10	8^{1}		7		12				11	13			9^{2}				5										20
1		2^{1}	4^{2}	3	6	9	14		7		13				11^{3}	10	8		12				5										21
1	2	3^{3}	12	6		9^{2}	8		7		13				11^{1}	10	4						5		14								22
1	2	3	4	6		12			7						11	10^{2}	8	13					5		9^{1}								23
1	2	3	4	8	6				11		7							10^{2}	12		13		5		9^{1}								24
1	2^{1}	3	4	6		12			9	13	7^{3}				11		8	10^{2}	14				5■										25
1	3		4	5	6	12			7	10^{1}	2^{3}				11	9^{2}	8		13							14							26
1^{6}	3		4	5	6				7	10^{1}	2				11	9^{2}	8						12		13		15						27
1	2	3	4	5	6	12		13		10					11^{1}	9^{3}	8		14						7^{2}								28
1	2	3	4	5	6	12				10	7^{1}						8		9						11^{2}			13					29
1	2	3	4	5	6	12		13		10^{2}	7^{3}						8	14	9									11^{1}					30
1	2	3	4^{2}	5	6	12				10^{3}	13				11		7	14	9									8^{1}					31
1	2	3		5	6	12	8^{3}			10^{2}					11				9				4		7^{1}			13	14				32
1	2^{2}	3		5	6			12		10^{3}					11		4		9				13		7^{1}			14	8				33
1		3	12	5	6	7	13			14					11^{1}		4		9				2					10^{3}	8^{2}				34
1		3	12	2	6	7	13			14					11^{1}		4^{2}		9				5					10	8^{3}				35
1	2	3	4	5	12	11^{3}	13	14									7		9				6^{1}					10	8^{2}				36
1	2	3		5	6	11	7^{1}								12	13	4		9^{3}									10^{2}	8	14			37
1	2	3		5	6	11									7	12	4		9^{3}				13					10^{1}	8^{2}	14			38
1	2	3	12	5	6	11^{3}									7^{2}	13	4		9^{1}									10	8	14			39
1	2	3	12	5	6	11											4		9				13					10^{3}	8^{2}	14	7^{1}		40
1	2	3	12	5	6	11^{2}										13	4		9^{3}									10	8	14	7^{1}		41
1	2	3	12	5	6	13											4	14	9									10	8^{3}	11^{1}	7^{2}		42
1	2	3		5	6	11^{1}				12					7^{3}		4		9						13			10^{2}	8		14		43
1	2	3	12	5	6					14						13	4		9						11^{2}			10	8^{3}		7^{1}		44
1	2	3	12	5	6											13	4		9						11^{2}			10	8^{1}		7		45
1	2		4^{2}	5	6	12											7		9						11^{1}	13		10	8^{3}		14	3	46

FA Cup

Third Round	Middlesbrough	(h)	1-1
		(a)	3-4

Carling Cup

First Round	Tranmere R	(h)	2-1
Second Round	Hartlepool U	(h)	0-0
Third Round	Watford	(a)	1-2

IPSWICH TOWN — FL Championship

FOUNDATION

Considering that Ipswich Town only reached the Football League in 1938, many people outside of East Anglia may be surprised to learn that this club was formed at a meeting held in the Town Hall as far back as 1878 when Mr T. C. Cobbold, MP, was voted president. Originally it was the Ipswich Association FC to distinguish it from the older Ipswich Football Club which played rugby. These two amalgamated in 1888 and the handling game was dropped in 1893.

Portman Road, Ipswich, Suffolk IP1 2DA.

Telephone: (01473) 400 500.

Fax: (01473) 400 042.

Ticket Office: 0870 1110 555.

Website: www.itfc.co.uk

Email: enquiries@itfc.co.uk

Ground Capacity: 30,311.

Record Attendance: 38,010 v Leeds U, FA Cup 6th rd, 8 March 1975.

Pitch Measurements: 102.46m × 66m.

Chairman: David Sheepshanks.

Chief Executive: Derek Bowden.

Secretary: Sally Webb.

Manager: Jim Magilton.

Assistant Manager: Bryan Klug.

Physio: Matt Byard.

Colours: Blue shirts, white shorts, blue stockings

Change Colours: White shirts, navy shorts, white stockings.

Year Formed: 1878.

Turned Professional: 1936.

Ltd Co.: 1936.

Club Nicknames: 'Blues' or 'Town' or 'Tractor Boys'.

Grounds: 1878, Broom Hill and Brook's Hall; 1884, Portman Road.

Record League Victory: 7–0 v Portsmouth, Division 2, 7 November 1964 – Thorburn; Smith, McNeil; Baxter, Bolton, Thompson; Broadfoot (1), Hegan (2), Baker (1), Leadbetter, Brogan (3). 7–0 v Southampton, Division 1, 2 February 1974 – Sivell; Burley, Mills (1), Morris, Hunter, Beattie (1), Hamilton (2), Viljoen, Johnson, Whymark (2), Lambert (1) (Woods). 7–0 v WBA, Division 1, 6 November 1976 – Sivell; Burley, Mills, Talbot, Hunter, Beattie (1), Osborne, Wark (1), Mariner (1) (Bertschin), Whymark (4), Woods.

HONOURS

Football League: Division 1 – Champions 1961–62; Runners-up 1980–81, 1981–82; Promoted from Division 1 1999–2000 (play-offs); Division 2 – Champions 1960–61, 1967–68, 1991–92; Division 3 (S) – Champions 1953–54, 1956–57.

FA Cup: Winners 1978.

Football League Cup: Semi-final 1982, 1985.

Texaco Cup: Winners 1973.

European Competitions: *European Cup:* 1962–63. *European Cup-Winners' Cup:* 1978–79. *UEFA Cup:* 1973–74, 1974–75, 1975–76, 1977–78, 1979–80, 1980–81 (winners), 1981–82, 1982–83, 2001–02, 2002–03.

SKY SPORTS FACT FILE

Ipswich Town signed ex-Chelsea's John "Jock" Hutcheson in 1938. Absent with injury for two years and compensated, he was refused Football League permission to play, but did so in the Southern League side and even scored in the FA Cup against Aston Villa!

First Football League Game: 27 August 1938, Division 3 (S), v Southend U (h) W 4–2 – Burns; Dale, Parry; Perrett, Fillingham, McLuckie; Williams, Davies (1), Jones (2), Alsop (1), Little.

Record Cup Victory: 10–0 v Floriana, European Cup prel. rd, 25 September 1962 – Bailey; Malcolm, Compton; Baxter, Laurel, Elsworthy (1); Stephenson, Moran (2), Crawford (5), Phillips (2), Blackwood.

Record Defeat: 1–10 v Fulham, Division 1, 26 December 1963.

Most League Points (2 for a win): 64, Division 3 (S), 1953–54 and 1955–56.

Most League Points (3 for a win): 87, Division 1, 1999–2000.

Most League Goals: 106, Division 3 (S), 1955–56.

Highest League Scorer in Season: Ted Phillips, 41, Division 3 (S), 1956–57.

Most League Goals in Total Aggregate: Ray Crawford, 203, 1958–63 and 1966–69.

Most League Goals in One Match: 5, Alan Brazil v Southampton, Division 1, 16 February 1981.

Most Capped Player: Allan Hunter, 47 (53), Northern Ireland.

Most League Appearances: Mick Mills, 591, 1966–82.

Youngest League Player: Jason Dozzell, 16 years 56 days v Coventry C, 4 February 1984.

Record Transfer Fee Received: £6,000,000 from Newcastle U for Kieron Dyer, July 1999 and £6,000,000 from Arsenal for Richard Wright, July 2001.

Record Transfer Fee Paid: £4,750,000 to Sampdoria for Matteo Sereni, July 2001.

Football League Record: 1938 Elected to Division 3 (S); 1954–55 Division 2; 1955–57 Division 3 (S); 1957–61 Division 2; 1961–64 Division 1; 1964–68 Division 2; 1968–86 Division 1; 1986–92 Division 2; 1992–95 FA Premier League; 1995–2000 Division 1; 2000–02 FA Premier League; 2002–04 Division 1; 2004– FL C.

MANAGERS

Mick O'Brien 1936–37
Scott Duncan 1937–55
(continued as Secretary)
Alf Ramsey 1955–63
Jackie Milburn 1963–64
Bill McGarry 1964–68
Bobby Robson 1969–82
Bobby Ferguson 1982–87
Johnny Duncan 1987–90
John Lyall 1990–94
George Burley 1994–2002
Joe Royle 2002–06
Jim Magilton June 2006–

LATEST SEQUENCES

Longest Sequence of League Wins: 8, 23.9.1953 – 31.10.1953.

Longest Sequence of League Defeats: 10, 4.9.1954 – 16.10.1954.

Longest Sequence of League Draws: 7, 10.11.1990 – 21.12.1990.

Longest Sequence of Unbeaten League Matches: 23, 8.12.1979 – 26.4.1980.

Longest Sequence Without a League Win: 21, 28.8.1963 – 14.12.1963.

Successive Scoring Runs: 31 from 7.3.2004.

Successive Non-scoring Runs: 7 from 28.2.1995.

TEN YEAR LEAGUE RECORD

		P	W	D	L	F	A	Pts	Pos
1997-98	Div 1	46	23	14	9	77	43	83	5
1998-99	Div 1	46	26	8	12	69	32	86	3
1999-2000	Div 1	46	25	12	9	71	42	87	3
2000-01	PR Lge	38	20	6	12	57	42	66	5
2001-02	PR Lge	38	9	9	20	41	64	36	18
2002-03	Div 1	46	19	13	14	80	64	70	7
2003-04	Div 1	46	21	10	15	84	72	73	5
2004-05	FL C	46	24	13	9	85	56	85	3
2005-06	FL C	46	14	14	18	53	66	56	15
2006-07	FL C	46	18	8	20	64	59	62	14

DID YOU KNOW ?

Centre-forward Tom Garneys had been with amateurs Leytonstone, Notts County, Southern League Chingford Town and Brentford where he made his League debut before signing for Ipswich Town in May 1951 at 28 and scoring 123 goals in 248 League games.

IPSWICH TOWN 2006–07 LEAGUE RECORD

Match No.	*Date*	*Venue*	*Opponents*	*Result*		*H/T Score*	*Lg. Pos.*	*Goalscorers*	*Attendance*
1	Aug 5	H	Crystal Palace	L	1-2	1-0	—	Forster [30]	25,413
2	8	A	Wolverhampton W	L	0-1	0-1	—		19,199
3	12	A	Leicester C	L	1-3	0-1	24	Richards [85]	18,820
4	19	H	Hull C	D	0-0	0-0	22		19,790
5	25	A	QPR	W	3-1	0-0	—	Walton (pen) [62], De Vos [68], Bowditch [86]	10,918
6	Sept 9	H	Southampton	W	2-1	0-1	15	Walton (pen) [67], Clarke [78]	21,422
7	12	H	Coventry C	W	2-1	0-0	—	Noble [52], Clarke [85]	19,465
8	16	A	Birmingham C	D	2-2	0-0	11	Lee [48], Walton [78]	20,841
9	23	H	Sunderland	W	3-1	1-1	8	Currie [32], Lee 2 [63, 66]	23,311
10	29	A	Colchester U	L	0-1	0-1	—		6065
11	Oct 14	H	WBA	L	1-5	1-2	14	Perry (og) [36]	22,581
12	17	H	Preston NE	L	2-3	2-0	—	Macken (pen) [10], Lee [37]	19,337
13	21	A	Southend U	W	3-1	1-0	15	Clarke [30], Legwinski [47], Lee [50]	11,415
14	29	H	Luton T	W	5-0	1-0	11	Legwinski [20], Peters [54], Lee 3 (1 pen) [66, 76, 90 (p)]	20,975
15	31	A	Plymouth Arg	D	1-1	1-1	—	Legwinski [1]	12,210
16	Nov 4	A	Burnley	L	0-1	0-0	14		11,709
17	11	H	Sheffield W	L	0-2	0-1	17		21,830
18	19	H	Norwich C	W	3-1	1-1	13	Legwinski [40], Haynes 2 [77, 90]	27,276
19	25	A	Barnsley	L	0-1	0-0	14		10,556
20	29	A	Derby Co	L	1-2	1-0	—	Roberts [39]	22,606
21	Dec 2	H	Burnley	D	1-1	0-0	17	Lee (pen) [90]	20,254
22	9	A	Cardiff C	D	2-2	0-1	16	Macken 2 (1 pen) [48, 73 (p)]	16,015
23	16	H	Leeds U	W	1-0	1-0	15	Williams [45]	23,661
24	23	H	Stoke C	L	0-1	0-0	16		20,369
25	26	A	Coventry C	W	2-1	0-0	15	Macken [62], Lee [85]	22,154
26	30	A	WBA	L	0-2	0-0	16		20,328
27	Jan 1	H	Birmingham C	W	1-0	0-0	14	Williams [90]	22,436
28	13	A	Sunderland	L	0-1	0-1	15		27,604
29	20	H	Colchester U	W	3-2	1-1	15	Lee (pen) [30], Legwinski [56], Haynes [82]	28,355
30	30	A	Stoke C	D	0-0	0-0	—		11,812
31	Feb 3	A	Crystal Palace	L	0-2	0-1	14		17,090
32	10	H	Leicester C	L	0-2	0-1	15		21,221
33	20	H	Wolverhampton W	L	0-1	0-1	—		20,602
34	24	A	Southampton	L	0-1	0-1	17		27,974
35	Mar 3	H	QPR	W	2-1	1-0	17	Lee [26], Walters [54]	21,412
36	6	A	Hull C	W	5-2	2-1	—	Jeffers [24], Peters [41], Lee [49], De Vos [62], Haynes [81]	18,056
37	10	H	Southend U	L	0-2	0-2	15		24,051
38	13	A	Preston NE	L	0-1	0-1	—		13,100
39	17	A	Luton T	W	2-0	1-0	16	Lee [39], Richards [62]	8880
40	31	H	Plymouth Arg	W	3-0	2-0	15	Garvan [9], Lee [15], Haynes [90]	21,078
41	Apr 7	H	Barnsley	W	5-1	2-0	13	Roberts [2], O'Callaghan [43], Haynes [82], Jeffers [86], Walters [90]	20,585
42	9	A	Sheffield W	L	0-2	0-0	14		23,232
43	14	H	Derby Co	W	2-1	0-1	14	Jeffers [69], Haynes (pen) [89]	24,319
44	22	A	Norwich C	D	1-1	0-1	14	Wright [62]	25,476
45	28	A	Leeds U	D	1-1	0-1	14	Lee [88]	31,269
46	May 6	H	Cardiff C	W	3-1	1-1	14	Jeffers [4], Walters 2 [68, 79]	26,488

Final League Position: 14

GOALSCORERS

League (64): Lee 16 (3 pens), Haynes 7 (1 pen), Legwinski 5, Jeffers 4, Macken 4 (2 pens), Walters 4, Clarke 3, Walton 3 (2 pens), De Vos 2, Peters 2, Richards 2, Roberts 2, Williams 2, Bowditch 1, Currie 1, Forster 1, Garvan 1, Noble 1, O'Callaghan 1, Wright 1, own goal 1.
Carling Cup (2): Clarke 1, De Vos 1.
FA Cup (2): Lee 1 (pen), Richards 1.

Supple S 11 + 1	Wilnis F 19 + 2	Harding D 40 + 2	Bruce A 40 + 1	De Vos J 39	Naylor R 21 + 4	Peters J 20 + 3	Williams G 25 + 4	Bowditch D 3 + 6	Forster N 4	Currie D 6 + 7	Haynes D 4 + 27	Richards M 20 + 8	Lee A 38 + 3	Sito 6 + 2	Parkin S — + 2	Clarke B 10 + 17	Price L 34	Noble M 12 + 1	Walton S 13 + 6	Macken J 13 + 1	Legwinski S 31 + 1	Moore S — + 1	Roberts G 30 + 3	Pollitt M 1	Bates M 2	Garvan O 24 + 3	Wright D 19	O'Callaghan G 3 + 8	Walters J 11 + 5	Jeffers F 7 + 2	Miller I — + 1	*Match No.*
1	2	3	4	5	6	7^1	8^2	9^3	10	11	12	13	14																			1
1		3	4	5	6	7^2	8	9^3	10	12		11^1	14	2	13																	2
1		3	4	5	6		8	9	10^3	7^1		12	11^2	2	14	13																3
	12	3	2^1	5	6	7^2	8		10	13	14		9^3				1	11	4													4
	2	3	4	5			8^1	13		12	14	11	9^3			10^2	1	7	6													5
		3	2	5	6		8	12				11^3	9^1			13	1	7	4	10^2	14											6
	2^1	3	4	5	12		8			13			9			14	1	11^2	6	10^3	7											7
		3		5	6		8^1	13		12			9	2		14	1	7	4^2	10^3	11											8
		3		5	6		8^1	12		11		2^3	9	4		13	1	7		10^2		14										9
		3		5	6			12		11			9	2		13	1	7	4^1	10^2	8											10
		3	2	5	6			12		7^1		13	10			9	1	4	11^2		8											11
	2	3	4	5		7						11^2	9			12	1	6		10^1	8		13									12
15	2	3	4	5		7						11	9			12	1^G	6^2	13	10^1	8											13
1	2	3	4	5^1	12	7^2					13	11	9			10^3			6		8		14									14
1	2■	3^3	4	5	12	7^2						11	10			9^1		14	6		8		13									15
1		3	2^1	5	6							11	10	12				7	4		8		9									16
1	2	3^1	4	5	12					13	9^3	11	10					6^2		14	8		7									17
		3	4	5							12	11	10			9^1			6		8		7	1	2							18
		3	4	5			12				13	11	9				1		6	10^2	8		7^1		2^3	14						19
		3	2	5	6		12					11	9	13		10^1	1		8■				7^2			4						20
			2	5	6	12	7^2				13	3	9			10^1	1				8		11			4						21
		3	2	5	6		11				9^2	12				13	1			10	8		7^1			4						22
		3	2	5	6		7^1				12		9^2				1		13	10	8		11			4						23
		3	2^1	5	6	12	7				13		9^2				1		14	10	8		11^3			4						24
		3^1	2	5	6		7^3					12	9			13	1		14	10^2	8		11			4						25
		3	2^3	5	6		7				12		9			13	1		14	10^2	8		11^1			4						26
		3	2	5	6		12				13	11^2	9			10^1	1		14		8		7			4^3						27
		3		5	6		10			12	13	11^3	9			14	1				8		7^2			4^1	2					28
		3	5		6	7	4				12	13	9^3			10^1	1				8		11^2				2■	14				29
	5	3				7^1	10^2				12			2			1				8		11			4	6	13	9			30
	5^1	3	12		6	7^2					13		10				1				8		11^3			4	2	14	9			31
	5	3	6			7				11	12					10^1	1				8^2					4■	2	13	9			32
		3	4	5		7					12	6	10^1			13	1				8^2		11^3			14	2		9			33
		3	6	5		12					13	11^1	9^2				1				8		7			4	2	10^3	14			34
		3	6	5		7^1					12		10				1				8		11			4	2		9^2	13		35
		3	6	5		7^1					12	13	9^2				1				8		11			4	2		14	10^3		36
		3	6	5		7					12		9■			13	1				8^3		11^2			4	2	14		10^1		37
	12	3^1	4	5			13				9	11^2					1				8		7			14	2	6^3	10			38
	2		6	5			11				12	13	9^1			14	1				8^2		7			4	3		10^3			39
	2^3		6	5			8				12	11^1	9			14	1						7			4	3		10^2		13	40
	2		6	5		7					12		9^2				1						11^1			4	3	8	10	13		41
	2	12	6	5			7				9^2		10				1						11^1			4	3		13	8		42
1	2	12	6■	5		7	8				13												11^1			4^3	3	14	10	9^2		43
1	2	5	6			7^2	8				13		12										11			4	3		10^1	9		44
1	5	3	6			7^1	8^2						10			12							11			4	2	13	14	9^3		45
1	5	3	6			7	8				12		10^2										11^1			4	2	14	13	9^3		46

FA Cup

Third Round	Chester C	(a)	0-0
		(h)	1-0
Fourth Round	Swansea C	(h)	1-0
Fifth Round	Watford	(a)	0-1

Carling Cup

First Round	Peterborough U	(a)	2-2

LEEDS UNITED FL Championship 1

FOUNDATION

Immediately the Leeds City club (founded in 1904) was wound up by the FA in October 1919, following allegations of illegal payments to players, a meeting was called by a Leeds solicitor, Mr Alf Masser, at which Leeds United was formed. They joined the Midland League playing their first game in that competition in November 1919. It was in this same month that the new club had discussions with the directors of a virtually bankrupt Huddersfield Town who wanted to move to Leeds in an amalgamation. But Huddersfield survived even that crisis.

Elland Road, Leeds, West Yorkshire LS11 0ES.

Telephone: (0113) 367 6000.

Fax: (0113) 367 6050.

Ticket Office: 0871 334 1992.

Website: www.leedsunited.com

Email: tickets@leedsunited.com

Ground Capacity: 39,419.

Record Attendance: 57,892 v Sunderland, FA Cup 5th rd (replay), 15 March 1967.

Pitch Measurements: 105m × 68m.

Chairman: Ken Bates.

Chief Executive: Shaun Harvey.

Head of Football Administration: Alison Royston.

Manager: Dennis Wise.

Assistant Manager: Gus Poyet.

Physio: Harvey Sharman.

Colours: White shirts, white shorts, white stockings all with royal blue trim and yellow piping.

Change Colours: Yellow shirts, yellow shorts, yellow stockings all with royal blue trim.

Year Formed: 1919, as Leeds United after disbandment (by FA order) of Leeds City (formed in 1904).

Turned Professional: 1920.

Ltd Co.: 1920.

Club Nickname: 'The Whites'.

Ground: 1919, Elland Road.

First Football League Game: 28 August 1920, Division 2, v Port Vale (a) L 0–2 – Down; Duffield, Tillotson; Musgrove, Baker, Walton; Mason, Goldthorpe, Thompson, Lyon, Best.

HONOURS

Football League: Division 1 – Champions 1968–69, 1973–74, 1991–92; Runners-up 1964–65, 1965–66, 1969–70, 1970–71, 1971–72; Division 2 – Champions 1923–24, 1963–64, 1989–90; Runners-up 1927–28, 1931–32, 1955–56.

FA Cup: Winners 1972; Runners-up 1965, 1970, 1973.

Football League Cup: Winners 1968; Runners-up 1996.

European Competitions: *European Cup:* 1969–70, 1974–75 (runners-up). *Champions League:* 1992–93, 2000–01 (semi-finalists). *European Cup-Winners' Cup:* 1972–73 (runners-up). *European Fairs Cup:* 1965–66, 1966–67 (runners-up), 1967–68 (winners), 1968–69, 1970–71 (winners). *UEFA Cup:* 1971–72, 1973–74, 1979–80, 1995–96, 1998–99, 1999–2000 (semi-finalists), 2001–02, 2002–03.

SKY SPORTS FACT FILE

The first Leeds United player to score as many as four goals in an FA Cup tie was Allan Clarke in a 6–0 fourth round win at Sutton United on 24 January 1970. He was in his first season at Elland Road. Peter Lorimer added the other two Leeds goals.

MANAGERS

Dick Ray 1919–20
Arthur Fairclough 1920–27
Dick Ray 1927–35
Bill Hampson 1935–47
Willis Edwards 1947–48
Major Frank Buckley 1948–53
Raich Carter 1953–58
Bill Lambton 1958–59
Jack Taylor 1959–61
Don Revie OBE 1961–74
Brian Clough 1974
Jimmy Armfield 1974–78
Jock Stein CBE 1978
Jimmy Adamson 1978–80
Allan Clarke 1980–82
Eddie Gray MBE 1982–85
Billy Bremner 1985–88
Howard Wilkinson 1988–96
George Graham 1996–98
David O'Leary 1998–2002
Terry Venables 2002–03
Peter Reid 2003
Eddie Gray *(Caretaker)* 2003–04
Kevin Blackwell 2004–06
Dennis Wise November 2006–

Record League Victory: 8–0 v Leicester C, Division 1, 7 April 1934 – Moore; George Milburn, Jack Milburn; Edwards, Hart, Copping; Mahon (2), Firth (2), Duggan (2), Furness (2), Cochrane.

Record Cup Victory: 10–0 v Lyn (Oslo), European Cup 1st rd 1st leg, 17 September 1969 – Sprake; Reaney, Cooper, Bremner (2), Charlton, Hunter, Madeley, Clarke (2), Jones (3), Giles (2) (Bates), O'Grady (1).

Record Defeat: 1–8 v Stoke C, Division 1, 27 August 1934.

Most League Points (2 for a win): 67, Division 1, 1968–69.

Most League Points (3 for a win): 85, Division 2, 1989–90.

Most League Goals: 98, Division 2, 1927–28.

Highest League Scorer in Season: John Charles, 42, Division 2, 1953–54.

Most League Goals in Total Aggregate: Peter Lorimer, 168, 1965–79 and 1983–86.

Most League Goals in One Match: 5, Gordon Hodgson v Leicester C, Division 1, 1 October 1938.

Most Capped Player: Lucas Radebe, 58 (70), South Africa.

Most League Appearances: Jack Charlton, 629, 1953–73.

Youngest League Player: Peter Lorimer, 15 years 289 days v Southampton, 29 September 1962.

Record Transfer Fee Received: £29,250,000 from Manchester U for Rio Ferdinand, July 2002 (see Manchester United page 255).

Record Transfer Fee Paid: £18,000,000 to West Ham United for Rio Ferdinand, November 2000.

Football League Record: 1920 Elected to Division 2; 1924–27 Division 1; 1927–28 Division 2; 1928–31 Division 1; 1931–32 Division 2; 1932–47 Division 1; 1947–56 Division 2; 1956–60 Division 1; 1960–64 Division 2; 1964–82 Division 1; 1982–90 Division 2; 1990–92 Division 1; 1992–2004 FA Premier League; 2004–07 FL C; 2007– FL 1.

LATEST SEQUENCES

Longest Sequence of League Wins: 9, 26.9.1931 – 21.11.1931.

Longest Sequence of League Defeats: 6, 28.12.2003 – 7.2.2004.

Longest Sequence of League Draws: 5, 19.4.1997 – 9.8.1997.

Longest Sequence of Unbeaten League Matches: 34, 26.10.1968 – 26.8.1969.

Longest Sequence Without a League Win: 17, 1.2.1947 – 26.5.1947.

Successive Scoring Runs: 30 from 27.8.1927.

Successive Non-scoring Runs: 6 from 30.1.1982.

TEN YEAR LEAGUE RECORD

		P	W	D	L	F	A	Pts	Pos
1997-98	PR Lge	38	17	8	13	57	46	59	5
1998-99	PR Lge	38	18	13	7	62	34	67	4
1999-2000	PR Lge	38	21	6	11	58	43	69	3
2000-01	PR Lge	38	20	8	10	64	43	68	4
2001-02	PR Lge	38	18	12	8	53	37	66	5
2002-03	PR Lge	38	14	5	19	58	57	47	15
2003-04	PR Lge	38	8	9	21	40	79	33	19
2004-05	FL C	46	14	18	14	49	52	60	14
2005-06	FL C	46	21	15	10	57	38	78	5
2006-07	FL C	46	13	7	26	46	72	36*	24

**10 pts deducted for entering administration.*

DID YOU KNOW ?

Two crucial FA Cup goals were lashed in for Leeds United by Percy Whipp. Both were in replays. On 17 January 1923 against Portsmouth he put Leeds on the way to a 3–1 win. The next season on 6 February he scored the only goal of a West Ham United tie.

LEEDS UNITED 2006–07 LEAGUE RECORD

Match No.	Date	Venue	Opponents	Result		H/T Score	Lg. Pos.	Goalscorers	Attendance
1	Aug 5	H	Norwich C	W	1-0	1-0	—	Healy (pen) [41]	22,417
2	8	A	QPR	D	2-2	0-0	—	Lewis [65], Horsfield [82]	13,996
3	13	A	Crystal Palace	L	0-1	0-0	13		17,218
4	19	H	Cardiff C	L	0-1	0-0	18		18,246
5	27	A	Sheffield W	W	1-0	0-0	11	Healy (pen) [70]	23,792
6	Sept 10	H	Wolverhampton W	L	0-1	0-0	16		16,268
7	13	H	Sunderland	L	0-3	0-2	—		23,037
8	16	A	Coventry C	L	0-1	0-1	23		22,146
9	23	H	Birmingham C	W	3-2	2-1	18	Healy 2 (1 pen) [6, 15 (p)], Tebily (og) [85]	18,898
10	30	A	WBA	L	2-4	0-1	20	Horsfield [82], Stone [88]	21,435
11	Oct 14	H	Stoke C	L	0-4	0-1	22		18,173
12	17	H	Leicester C	L	1-2	0-1	—	Butler [87]	16,477
13	21	A	Luton T	L	1-5	1-1	23	Foxe [17]	10,260
14	28	H	Southend U	W	2-0	1-0	21	Moore [40], Blake [88]	19,528
15	31	A	Preston NE	L	1-4	0-2	—	Healy [80]	16,168
16	Nov 4	A	Barnsley	L	2-3	2-1	23	Derry [44], Blake [45]	16,943
17	11	H	Colchester U	W	3-0	1-0	22	Blake 2 (1 pen) [36, 53 (p)], Cresswell [48]	17,678
18	18	H	Southampton	L	0-3	0-1	22		19,647
19	25	A	Plymouth Arg	W	2-1	1-1	21	Blake [3], Lewis [61]	17,088
20	28	A	Burnley	L	1-2	0-0	—	Healy [87]	15,061
21	Dec 2	H	Barnsley	D	2-2	2-2	22	Kandol [8], Ehiogu [45]	21,378
22	9	H	Derby Co	L	0-1	0-1	22		20,087
23	16	A	Ipswich T	L	0-1	0-1	23		23,661
24	23	H	Hull C	D	0-0	0-0	23		22,578
25	26	A	Sunderland	L	0-2	0-0	23		40,116
26	30	A	Stoke C	L	1-3	1-1	23	Moore [41]	18,128
27	Jan 1	H	Coventry C	W	2-1	1-1	23	Healy [15], Douglas [53]	18,158
28	20	H	WBA	L	2-3	1-3	23	Flo [3], Thompson [66]	20,019
29	30	A	Hull C	W	2-1	1-1	—	Heath [21], Thompson [50]	24,311
30	Feb 3	A	Norwich C	L	1-2	1-0	24	Howson [20]	25,018
31	10	H	Crystal Palace	W	2-1	1-0	24	Heath [27], Blake [72]	19,228
32	17	A	Cardiff C	L	0-1	0-1	24		16,544
33	20	H	QPR	D	0-0	0-0	—		29,593
34	24	A	Wolverhampton W	L	0-1	0-0	24		24,314
35	27	A	Birmingham C	L	0-1	0-1	—		18,363
36	Mar 3	H	Sheffield W	L	2-3	0-2	24	Bullen (og) [88], Cresswell [89]	25,297
37	10	H	Luton T	W	1-0	0-0	24	Cresswell [50]	27,138
38	13	A	Leicester C	D	1-1	1-1	—	Blake [45]	25,165
39	17	A	Southend U	D	1-1	0-1	24	Healy [88]	11,274
40	30	H	Preston NE	W	2-1	0-1	—	Blake [51], Healy [90]	18,433
41	Apr 7	H	Plymouth Arg	W	2-1	1-1	21	Healy [45], Michalik [87]	30,034
42	9	A	Colchester U	L	1-2	0-0	22	Lewis [53]	5916
43	14	H	Burnley	W	1-0	1-0	22	Heath [21]	23,528
44	21	A	Southampton	L	0-1	0-0	22		29,012
45	28	H	Ipswich T	D	1-1	1-0	22	Cresswell [12]	31,269
46	May 6	A	Derby Co	L	0-2	0-1	24		31,183

Final League Position: 24

GOALSCORERS

League (46): Healy 10 (3 pens), Blake 8 (1 pen), Cresswell 4, Heath 3, Lewis 3, Horsfield 2, Moore 2, Thompson 2, Butler 1, Derry 1, Douglas 1, Ehiogu 1, Flo 1, Foxe 1, Howson 1, Kandol 1, Michalik 1, Stone 1, own goals 2.
Carling Cup (5): Moore 3, Bakke 1, Blake 1.
FA Cup (1): own goal 1.

Warner T 13	Kelly G 16	Crainey S 18 + 1 / Kishishev R 10	Derry S 23	Butler P 16 / Michalik L 7	Kilgallon M 18 + 1	Stone S 5 + 5 / Gray M 6	Bakke E 2 + 1	Horsfield G 11 + 3	Healy D 31 + 10	Lewis E 40 + 1	Moore I 14 + 19	Westlake I 19 + 8	Carole S 7 + 10	Sullivan N 7 / Bayly R 1	Richardson F 19 + 3	Blake R 27 + 9	Beckford J 1 + 4	Foxe H 12 + 6	Douglas J 34 + 1	Nicholls K 12 + 1	Gregan S 1	Wright A 1 / Elliott T — + 3	Cresswell R 18 + 4	Johnson A 4 + 1 / Delph F — + 1	Stack G 12	Einarsson G — + 3	Heath M 26	Kandol T 11 + 7	Ehiogu U 6	Howson J 6 + 3	Rui Marques M 14 + 3	Elliott R 5 + 2	Armando Sa M 6 + 5	Thompson A 9 + 2	Flo T 1	Ankergren C 14	Johnson J 3 + 2	Match No.
1	2	3^{1}	4	5	6	7	8^{2}	9	10^{3}	11	12	13	14																									1
1	2	3	4	5	6	7	8^{1}	9^{3}	10^{2}	11	14	12	13																									2
1	2	3	4	5	6	7^{2}		9▪	10^{1}	11^{3}	12	8	13		14																							3
1	2	3	4	5	6	7^{1}	12		10	11^{2}		8	13			9^{3}	14																					4
1	2	3	4	5	6				10	11	9	8	7^{1}					12																				5
1	2	3		5	6	12			10	11^{1}	9^{2}	8	7				13		4																			6
1	2	3		5	6	7^{1}		9	10^{2}	11^{3}		8	12			13			4	14																		7
1	2	3		5	6	12		9	10			8^{2}	7^{1}			13			14	11	4^{3}																	8
1	2	3	4^{1}	5	6	12		9^{2}	10	11^{3}	13	14							7	8																		9
1	2^{2}	3	4	5	6	13		9	10	11^{3}	14	12							7	8^{1}																		10
	2		4	5	6	12		9^{3}	10^{2}	11		8^{1}		1		13			7			3	14															11
	2	3	4	5	6▪				10^{3}		11	12		1		13		14	7				9^{2}	8^{1}														12
	2	3	4	5					12	13	14	8^{2}		1		10^{1}		6	7				9^{3}	11														13
	2		4	5	6				10^{2}	3	11^{3}	12			14	13			7				9	8^{1}	1													14
	2		4	5	6			12	10	3	7^{1}	8				13							9	11^{2}	1													15
	2		4	5	6			9^{2}	10	3		8^{1}				11			7^{3}				12	13	1	14												16
		2	8		6			10^{2}		3^{1}	13	12				11	14	4	7				9^{3}		1		5											17
		3	4		6			9^{1}	10	11^{2}	12					8	13	2	7						1		5											18
		3	4		6					11	9^{1}	8	12			10^{2}		2	7						1		5	13										19
		3	4					12	13	11^{2}	9^{1}	8				10^{3}		2▪	7						1		5	14	6									20
		3	4^{3}						12	11	9^{2}	8	13		14	10^{1}			2						1		5	7	6									21
		3	4						10^{1}	11^{2}	12		13			8		2	7						1		5	9	6									22
			4^{3}					12	13	11^{1}	9^{2}	3	14		2			6	7	8▪					1		5	10										23
1			4						12	11		3			2	9^{1}			7								5	10	6	8								24
1			8^{2}		12				13	11	14	3			2		10	4	7								5	9^{3}	6^{1}									25
1			4						10	11	9	3^{1}			2				7								5	12	6	8								26
									10	11	9^{2}	12		1	2^{1}	8^{3}		5	7	4								13		14	6	3						27
									10	11	12			1		7^{1}		5		4						13		14			6	3^{3}	2	8^{2}	9			28
		12							10^{2}	11^{1}				1	3	13			7							14	5	9		4	6		2^{3}	8				29
											12			1	2	10			7	4^{2}		13					5	9^{1}		8	6		3	11				30
										3^{3}	9	8			2	11^{2}		13	7	4			12				5	10^{1}			6		14			1		31
									12	3	9	8^{3}				11^{1}		13	7	4			14				5	10			6^{2}		2			1		32
									10	3						8^{2}		12	7	4			9				5			14	6		2^{1}	11^{3}		1	13	33
									10	3	12		11^{1}		2	8^{2}			7	4		13	9				5				6					1		34
									10^{2}	3	12				2	11^{3}			7	4			9		1		5			8^{1}	6		14				13	35
		11^{2}							10	3	8		13		2	12			7				9		1		5			4^{1}	6							36
		11		6					12	3	13		4^{3}		2	8^{2}			7				9				5						14			1	10^{1}	37
		11		6					12		14		4^{2}		2	8			7				9				5						3	13^{3}		1	10^{1}	38
		4		6					12	11^{2}	13				2	8^{1}			7				9				5	10				3				1		39
		4		6		3			10^{1}	11					2	8^{2}			7				9				5				13	12				1		40
		4		6		3^{2}			10	11	12				2^{3}	8^{1}			7				9				5				13			14		1		41
		4		6		3			10^{1}	11						12			7								5	9			2			8		1		42
		4		6		3			10^{2}	11					2	7^{1}							9				5				12		13	8		1		43
		4							10^{2}	11^{3}					2	7^{1}		12					9				5	14			6	3	13	8▪		1		44
		4				3^{2}			10	11^{3}	12				2	7^{1}		5					9					13			6	14		8		1		45
													7^{1}	4▪		10^{2}		5^{3}				1	9	13						12	2	6		8		1	11	46

FA Cup

Third Round	WBA	(a)	1-3

Carling Cup

First Round	Chester C	(h)	1-0
Second Round	Barnet	(h)	3-1
Third Round	Southend U	(h)	1-3

LEICESTER CITY — FL Championship

FOUNDATION

In 1884 a number of young footballers who were mostly old boys of Wyggeston School, held a meeting at a house on the Roman Fosse Way and formed Leicester Fosse FC. They collected 9d (less than 4p) towards the cost of a ball, plus the same amount for membership. Their first professional, Harry Webb from Stafford Rangers, was signed in 1888 for 2s 6d (12p) per week, plus travelling expenses.

The Walkers Stadium, Filbert Way, Leicester LE2 7FL.

Telephone: 0870 040 6000.

Fax: (0116) 291 1254.

Ticket Office: 0870 499 1884.

Website: www.lcfc.co.uk

Ground Capacity: 32,500.

Record Attendance: 47,298 v Tottenham H, FA Cup 5th rd, 18 February 1928.

Pitch Measurements: 110yd × 74yd.

Chairman: Milan Mandaric.

Chief Executive: Tim Davies.

Secretary: Andrew Neville.

Manager: Martin Allen.

Assistant Manager: Mike Stowell.

Physio: David Rennie.

Colours: Blue shirts, blue shorts, blue stockings.

Change Colours: White shirts, light blue and black diagonal stripe, black shorts, black stockings.

Year Formed: 1884.

Turned Professional: 1888.

Ltd Co: 1897.

Previous Name: 1884, Leicester Fosse; 1919, Leicester City.

Club Nickname: 'Foxes'.

Grounds: 1884, Victoria Park; 1887, Belgrave Road; 1888, Victoria Park; 1891, Filbert Street; 2002, Walkers Stadium.

First Football League Game: 1 September 1894, Division 2, v Grimsby T (a) L 3–4 – Thraves; Smith, Bailey; Seymour, Brown, Henrys; Hill, Hughes, McArthur (1), Skea (2), Priestman.

Record League Victory: 10–0 v Portsmouth, Division 1, 20 October 1928 – McLaren; Black, Brown; Findlay, Carr, Watson; Adcock, Hine (3), Chandler (6), Lochhead, Barry (1).

Record Cup Victory: 8–1 v Coventry C (a), League Cup 5th rd, 1 December 1964 – Banks; Sjoberg, Norman (2); Roberts, King, McDerment; Hodgson (2), Cross, Goodfellow, Gibson (1), Stringfellow (2), (1 og).

HONOURS

Football League: Division 1 – Runners-up 1928–29; Promoted from Division 1 1993–94 (play-offs) and 1995–96 (play-offs); Division 2 – Champions 1924–25, 1936–37, 1953–54, 1956–57, 1970–71, 1979–80; Runners-up 1907–08.

FA Cup: Runners-up 1949, 1961, 1963, 1969.

Football League Cup: Winners 1964, 1997, 2000; Runners-up 1965, 1999.

European Competitions: *European Cup-Winners' Cup:* 1961–62. *UEFA Cup:* 1997–98, 2000–01.

SKY SPORTS FACT FILE

As Leicester Fosse the club achieved a remarkable 13–0 FA Cup qualifying round victory over Notts Olympic on 13 October 1894. Three players had hat-tricks: David Skea, "Tout" Miller and Willie McArthur (both four goals). Johnny Hill scored twice.

Record Defeat: 0–12 (as Leicester Fosse) v Nottingham F, Division 1, 21 April 1909.

Most League Points (2 for a win): 61, Division 2, 1956–57.

Most League Points (3 for a win): 92, Division 1, 2002–03.

Most League Goals: 109, Division 2, 1956–57.

Highest League Scorer in Season: Arthur Rowley, 44, Division 2, 1956–57.

Most League Goals in Total Aggregate: Arthur Chandler, 259, 1923–35.

Most League Goals in One Match: 6, John Duncan v Port Vale, Division 2, 25 December 1924; 6, Arthur Chandler v Portsmouth, Division 1, 20 October 1928.

Most Capped Player: John O'Neill, 39, Northern Ireland.

Most League Appearances: Adam Black, 528, 1920–35.

Youngest League Player: Dave Buchanan, 16 years 192 days v Oldham Ath, 1 January 1979.

Record Transfer Fee Received: £11,750,000 from Liverpool for Emile Heskey, February 2000.

Record Transfer Fee Paid: £5,000,000 to Wolverhampton W for Ade Akinbiyi, July 2000.

Football League Record: 1894 Elected to Division 2; 1908–09 Division 1; 1909–25 Division 2; 1925–35 Division 1; 1935–37 Division 2; 1937–39 Division 1; 1946–54 Division 2; 1954–55 Division 1; 1955–57 Division 2; 1957–69 Division 1; 1969–71 Division 2; 1971–78 Division 1; 1978–80 Division 2; 1980–81 Division 1; 1981–83 Division 2; 1983–87 Division 1; 1987–92 Division 2; 1992–94 Division 1; 1994–95 FA Premier League; 1995–96 Division 1; 1996–2002 FA Premier League; 2002–03 Division 1; 2003–04 FA Premier League; 2004– FL C.

MANAGERS

Frank Gardner 1884–92
Ernest Marson 1892–94
J. Lee 1894–95
Henry Jackson 1895–97
William Clark 1897–98
George Johnson 1898–1912
Jack Bartlett 1912–14
Louis Ford 1914–15
Harry Linney 1915–19
Peter Hodge 1919–26
Willie Orr 1926–32
Peter Hodge 1932–34
Arthur Lochhead 1934–36
Frank Womack 1936–39
Tom Bromilow 1939–45
Tom Mather 1945–46
John Duncan 1946–49
Norman Bullock 1949–55
David Halliday 1955–58
Matt Gillies 1958–68
Frank O'Farrell 1968–71
Jimmy Bloomfield 1971–77
Frank McLintock 1977–78
Jock Wallace 1978–82
Gordon Milne 1982–86
Bryan Hamilton 1986–87
David Pleat 1987–91
Gordon Lee 1991
Brian Little 1991–94
Mark McGhee 1994–95
Martin O'Neill 1995–2000
Peter Taylor 2000–01
Dave Bassett 2001–02
Micky Adams 2002–04
Craig Levein 2004–06
Robert Kelly 2006–07
Martin Allen May 2007–

LATEST SEQUENCES

Longest Sequence of League Wins: 7, 28.2.1993 – 27.3.1993.

Longest Sequence of League Defeats: 8, 17.3.2001 – 28.4.2001.

Longest Sequence of League Draws: 6, 21.8.1976 – 18.9.1976.

Longest Sequence of Unbeaten League Matches: 19, 6.2.1971 – 18.8.1971.

Longest Sequence Without a League Win: 18, 12.4.1975 – 1.11.1975.

Successive Scoring Runs: 31 from 12.11.1932.

Successive Non-scoring Runs: 7 from 21.11.1987.

TEN YEAR LEAGUE RECORD

		P	*W*	*D*	*L*	*F*	*A*	*Pts*	*Pos*
1997-98	PR Lge	38	13	14	11	51	41	53	10
1998-99	PR Lge	38	12	13	13	40	46	49	10
1999-2000	PR Lge	38	16	7	15	55	55	55	8
2000-01	PR Lge	38	14	6	18	39	51	48	13
2001-02	PR Lge	38	5	13	20	30	64	28	20
2002-03	Div 1	46	26	14	6	73	40	92	2
2003-04	PR Lge	38	6	15	17	48	65	33	18
2004-05	FL C	46	12	21	13	49	46	57	15
2005-06	FL C	46	13	15	18	51	59	54	16
2006-07	FL C	46	13	14	19	49	64	53	19

DID YOU KNOW ?

While Peter Shilton who conceded only 379 goals in 339 games for Leicester City ranks the best goalkeeper on average goals (1.12 per match), George Hebden (1921–25) with 118 in 104 matches and Kasey Keller (1996–99) on 143 in 125, come close runners-up.

LEICESTER CITY 2006–07 LEAGUE RECORD

Match No.	*Date*	*Venue*	*Opponents*	*Result*		*H/T Score*	*Lg. Pos.*	*Goalscorers*	*Atten-dance*
1	Aug 5	A	Luton T	L	0-2	0-1	—		8131
2	8	H	Burnley	L	0-1	0-1	—		19,035
3	12	H	Ipswich T	W	3-1	1-0	17	Kisnorbo [8], Hughes [50], Hume [90]	18,820
4	18	A	Coventry C	D	0-0	0-0	—		20,261
5	26	H	Southend U	W	1-0	1-0	12	Kisnorbo [40]	19,427
6	Sept 9	A	WBA	L	0-2	0-0	18		19,322
7	12	H	Hull C	L	0-1	0-0	—		18,677
8	16	A	Sunderland	D	1-1	0-0	20	Fryatt [48]	35,104
9	23	H	Colchester U	D	0-0	0-0	—		22,449
10	30	A	Birmingham C	D	1-1	0-0	19	Hammond [86]	18,002
11	Oct 14	H	Southampton	W	3-2	1-1	16	Hume 2 [35, 62], Stearman [65]	21,347
12	17	A	Leeds U	W	2-1	1-0	—	Tiatto [29], Hume [81]	16,477
13	21	H	Crystal Palace	D	1-1	1-1	16	Hume (pen) [37]	28,762
14	28	A	QPR	D	1-1	1-0	16	Kisnorbo [7]	12,430
15	31	H	Stoke C	W	2-1	1-1	—	Hume [45], Hughes [64]	21,107
16	Nov 4	A	Sheffield W	L	1-2	0-1	15	Fryatt [72]	22,451
17	11	H	Plymouth Arg	D	2-2	1-1	14	Hume [29], Porter [75]	21,703
18	18	H	Preston NE	L	0-1	0-1	18		22,721
19	25	A	Derby Co	L	0-1	0-0	18		28,315
20	28	A	Norwich C	L	1-3	1-1	—	McCarthy [23]	23,896
21	Dec 2	H	Sheffield W	L	1-4	0-1	20	Hughes [57]	22,693
22	9	A	Wolverhampton W	W	2-1	1-0	18	Hammond [38], Porter [90]	18,600
23	16	H	Barnsley	W	2-0	1-0	17	Hammond [45], Porter [52]	30,457
24	23	H	Cardiff C	D	0-0	0-0	18		22,274
25	26	A	Hull C	W	2-1	0-1	16	Kisnorbo [55], Williams [68]	18,523
26	30	A	Southampton	L	0-2	0-1	17		24,447
27	Jan 1	H	Sunderland	L	0-2	0-0	18		21,975
28	13	A	Colchester U	D	1-1	1-0	18	Hume [19]	5915
29	27	A	Cardiff C	L	2-3	0-1	—	Kisnorbo [71], Hammond [89]	12,057
30	Feb 3	H	Luton T	D	1-1	1-1	18	Yeates [6]	20,410
31	10	A	Ipswich T	W	2-0	1-0	17	McAuley 2 [28, 56]	21,221
32	17	H	Coventry C	W	3-0	3-0	14	Horsfield 2 [11, 26], Johnson [18]	25,816
33	20	A	Burnley	W	1-0	0-0	—	McGreal (og) [67]	10,274
34	24	H	WBA	D	1-1	1-1	13	McAuley [35]	25,581
35	Mar 3	A	Southend U	D	2-2	1-0	14	Hume 2 [9, 81]	10,528
36	10	A	Crystal Palace	L	0-2	0-1	16		16,969
37	13	H	Leeds U	D	1-1	1-1	—	Hume [45]	25,165
38	17	H	QPR	L	1-3	0-0	17	Hume (pen) [90]	24,558
39	31	A	Stoke C	L	2-4	1-2	17	Kenton [16], Hammond [58]	13,303
40	Apr 6	H	Derby Co	D	1-1	0-1	—	Fryatt [68]	24,704
41	9	A	Plymouth Arg	L	0-3	0-1	19		10,900
42	14	H	Norwich C	L	1-2	1-0	19	Kenton [1]	21,483
43	17	H	Birmingham C	L	1-2	0-2	—	Newton [82]	24,290
44	21	A	Preston NE	W	1-0	0-0	19	Johansson [90]	14,725
45	28	A	Barnsley	W	1-0	0-0	17	Austin (og) [49]	20,012
46	May 6	H	Wolverhampton W	L	1-4	1-2	19	Hume [3]	30,282

Final League Position: 19

GOALSCORERS

League (49): Hume 13 (2 pens), Hammond 5, Kisnorbo 5, Fryatt 3, Hughes 3, McAuley 3, Porter 3, Horsfield 2, Kenton 2, Johansson 1, Johnson 1, McCarthy 1, Newton 1, Stearman 1, Tiatto 1, Williams 1, Yeates 1, own goals 2.
Carling Cup (7): Stearman 2, Hammond 1, Hume 1 (pen), Kisnorbo 1, McCarthy 1, O'Grady 1.
FA Cup (5): Cadamarteri 1, Fryatt 1, Kisnorbo 1, McAuley 1, Wesolowski 1.

Henderson P 28	Maybury A 25 + 2	Johansson N 36	Kenton D 20 + 3	McCarthy P 20 + 2	Johnson A 21 + 1	Stearman R 23 + 12	Williams G 12 + 2	Hume I 39 + 6	Fryatt M 21 + 11	Tiatto D 24 + 1	O'Grady C 6 + 4	Hammond E 17 + 14	Hughes S 34 + 7	Low J 12 + 4	Kisnorbo P 40	Porter L 26 + 8	Wesolowski J 11 + 8	Logan C 18	McAuley G 27 + 3	Sylla M 3 + 3	Welsh A 4 + 3	Cadamarteri D — + 9	Yeates M 5 + 4	Horsfield G 9 + 4	Glombard L — + 1	Jarrett J 13	Newton S 9	Mattock J 3 + 1	*Match No.*
1	2^{1}	3	4	5	6	7	8	9^{2}	10	11^{3}	12	13	14																1
1	2^{3}		4	5	6	7	8^{1}	9	10	11^{2}		13	12	14	3														2
1		5	2	6	4			12	10	11^{2}		9^{1}	8	7	3	13^{3}	14												3
1		5	2^{1}	6	4	12		13	10			9^{2}	8	7	3	11^{3}	14												4
1		6	2	5	8	12		13	10^{2}	11^{3}	9		4	7^{1}	3	14													5
1		6	2	5	4	12		13	10^{2}		9		8	7^{1}	3	11^{3}	14												6
1		6	2^{1}	5	4	12		9	10		13		8	7^{2}	3	11													7
1		6	2	5	4				10		9		8		3	11	7												8
		3	2^{1}	5	8	12		13	10		9^{2}		4^{3}	14		11	7	1	6										9
		3	2	5	6^{1}		12	9		11^{3}	10^{2}	13	8	7		14		1	4										10
		3	2^{1}	5	6	12	8	9		11	14	10^{3}	13	7^{2}				1	4										11
	12	6				2	8^{3}	9		11^{2}		10	4	7^{1}	3			1	5	13	14								12
		6				2		9		11		10	4	7^{1}	3			1	5	12	8								13
	12	6	4	14		2		9	13	11		10^{3}			3		7^{1}	1	5■		8^{2}								14
		3	4	5	6	2		9	12	11		10^{1}	8					1		7									15
		3	4	5	6^{2}	7		9	12	11^{3}		10^{1}	8					1	2	14	13								16
	2	6		5		7		9	10				4		3	12		1		11	8^{1}								17
	2	6				7^{3}		9	10^{1}	11		12	4	13	3	14		1	5	8^{2}									18
	2^{2}	6		5		7		9	10^{1}	11		12	4		3	14		1	13		8^{3}								19
	2			5^{3}		7^{2}		9^{1}	12	11	13	10	4	8	3	6		1	14										20
	2			5■		7	12	9	13	11^{1}		10^{2}	4	8^{3}	3	6		1	14										21
1	2					7	8	9		11^{1}		10	4	13	3	6	12^{2}		5										22
1		6				2	8	9^{1}	12	11^{2}		10	7		3	4	13		5										23
1	2	6					8	9	12	11^{3}		10^{1}		7^{2}	3	4	14		5		13								24
1	2^{1}	4				12	8	9^{2}	13	11^{3}		10	7		3	6	14		5										25
1	2	6^{1}		14		12	8	9^{3}	13	11^{2}		10	7		3	4			5										26
1			4	5		2	8	12	10		9^{1}		7		3	6	11^{2}					13							27
1	2			5			8	9	10^{1}	11			7		3	6			4			12							28
1	2			5	13		8	9	10^{1}			12	4		3	11^{3}	7^{2}		6			14							29
1	2	6			8	12		9				13	4^{1}		3	11			5				7^{2}	10					30
1	2	6	12		8			9^{2}				13			3	7			5				11^{3}	10^{1}	14	4			31
1	2	6			8	12		9^{3}				13			3	11			5			14	7^{1}	10^{2}		4			32
1	2	6			8	12		9^{2}				13	14		3	11^{1}			5				7^{3}	10		4			33
1	2	6			8			9					7^{1}		3	11			5				12	10		4			34
1	2				6	7		9^{2}				12	8		3	11^{3}			5			13	14	10^{1}		4			35
1		6^{1}	12		7^{3}	2		9				13	8		3	11			5				14	10^{2}		4			36
1	2	6						9				12	8		3	11			5					10^{1}		4	7		37
1	2	6	5					9		12		13	8^{1}		3		14						11	10^{2}		4^{3}	7		38
1	2^{1}		5		8^{2}	6		9	12	11^{3}		10	13		3	14										4	7		39
1	2		5			7		9	12	11		10^{1}	8^{2}		3	6							13			4			40
1	2	6	5					9	10				12		3	11^{2}	8							13		4	7^{1}		41
		6	2^{1}			12		9	10^{2}						3	11	8	1	5^{3}					13		4	7	14	42
	5^{2}	6				2		9	10^{3}				12		3		8	1				14		13		4^{1}	7	11	43
		6				2		9	10^{2}				4		3		8	1	5^{1}			13		12			7	11	44
		6				2		9	10^{1}				4		3		8	1	5			12					7	11	45
		6	12			2^{1}		9	10^{3}	11^{2}			4		3■	13	8	1	5			14					7		46

FA Cup

Third Round	Fulham	(h)	2-2
		(a)	3-4

Carling Cup

First Round	Macclesfield T	(h)	2-0
Second Round	Hereford U	(a)	3-1
Third Round	Aston Villa	(h)	2-3

LEYTON ORIENT — FL Championship 1

FOUNDATION

There is some doubt about the foundation of Leyton Orient, and, indeed, some confusion with clubs like Leyton and Clapton over their early history. As regards the foundation, the most favoured version is that Leyton Orient was formed originally by members of Homerton Theological College who established Glyn Cricket Club in 1881 and then carried on through the following winter playing football. Eventually many employees of the Orient Shipping Line became involved and so the name Orient was chosen in 1888.

Matchroom Stadium, Brisbane Road, Leyton, London E10 5NF.

Telephone: 0871 310 1881.

Fax: 0871 310 1882.

Ticket Office: 0871 310 1883.

Website: www.leytonorient.com

Email: info@leytonorient.net

Ground Capacity: 7,872 (rising to approx 9,000 by 2007).

Record Attendance: 34,345 v West Ham U, FA Cup 4th rd, 25 January 1964.

Pitch Measurements: 110yd × 80yd.

Chairman: Barry Hearn.

Vice-chairman: Nick Levene.

Chief Executive: Matthew Porter.

Secretary: Lindsey Martin.

Manager: Martin Ling.

Assistant Manager: Dean Smith.

Physio: Lewis Manning.

Colours: Red and white. ***Change Colours:*** Blue and white.

Year Formed: 1881. ***Turned Professional:*** 1903.

Ltd Co.: 1906.

Previous Names: 1881, Glyn Cricket and Football Club; 1886, Eagle Football Club; 1888, Orient Football Club; 1898, Clapton Orient; 1946, Leyton Orient; 1966, Orient; 1987, Leyton Orient.

Club Nickname: 'The O's'.

Grounds: 1884, Glyn Road; 1896, Whittles Athletic Ground; 1900, Millfields Road; 1930, Lea Bridge Road; 1937, Brisbane Road.

First Football League Game: 2 September 1905, Division 2, v Leicester Fosse (a) L 1–2 – Butler; Holmes, Codling; Lamberton, Boden, Boyle; Kingaby (1), Wootten, Leigh, Evenson, Bourne.

Record League Victory: 8–0 v Crystal Palace, Division 3 (S), 12 November 1955 – Welton; Lee, Earl; Blizzard, Aldous, McKnight; White (1), Facey (3), Burgess (2), Heckman, Hartburn (2). 8–0 v Rochdale, Division 4, 20 October 1987 – Wells; Howard, Dickenson (1), Smalley (1), Day, Hull, Hales (2), Castle (Sussex), Shinners (2), Godfrey (Harvey), Comfort (2). 8–0 v Colchester U,

HONOURS

Football League: Division 1 best season: 22nd, 1962–63; Division 2 – Runners-up 1961–62; Division 3 – Champions 1969–70; Division 3 (S) – Champions 1955–56; Runners-up 1954–55; Promoted from Division 4 1988–89 (play-offs); Promoted from FL 2 (3rd) 2005–06.

FA Cup: Semi-final 1978.

Football League Cup: best season: 5th rd, 1963.

SKY SPORTS FACT FILE

After six reserve games as an amateur centre-forward Dennis Pacey turned professional with Leyton Orient. A week later he made his debut in an FA Cup second round replay against Gorleston on 3 December 1951 at Highbury scoring a hat-trick in a 5–4 victory.

Division 4, 15 October 1988 – Wells; Howard, Dickenson, Hales (1p), Day (1), Sitton (1), Baker (1), Ward, Hull (3), Juryeff, Comfort (1). 8–0 v Doncaster R, Division 3, 28 December 1997 – Hyde; Channing, Naylor, Smith (1p), Hicks, Clark, Ling, Joseph R, Griffiths (3) (Harris), Richards (2) (Baker (1)), Inglethorpe (1) (Simpson).

Record Cup Victory: 9–2 v Chester, League Cup 3rd rd, 15 October 1962 – Robertson; Charlton, Taylor; Gibbs, Bishop, Lea; Deeley (1), Waites (3), Dunmore (2), Graham (3), Wedge.

Record Defeat: 0–8 v Aston Villa, FA Cup 4th rd, 30 January 1929.

Most League Points (2 for a win): 66, Division 3 (S), 1955–56.

Most League Points (3 for a win): 81, FL 2, 2005–06.

Most League Goals: 106, Division 3 (S), 1955–56.

Highest League Scorer in Season: Tom Johnston, 35, Division 2, 1957–58.

Most League Goals in Total Aggregate: Tom Johnston, 121, 1956–58, 1959–61.

Most League Goals in One Match: 4, Wally Leigh v Bradford C, Division 2, 13 April 1906; 4, Albert Pape v Oldham Ath, Division 2, 1 September 1924; 4, Peter Kitchen v Millwall, Division 3, 21 April 1984.

Most Capped Players: Tunji Banjo, 7 (7), Nigeria; John Chiedozie, 7 (9), Nigeria; Tony Grealish, 7 (45), Eire.

Most League Appearances: Peter Allen, 432, 1965–78.

Youngest League Player: Paul Went, 15 years 327 days v Preston NE, 4 September 1965.

Record Transfer Fee Received: £1,000,000 from Fulham for Gabriel Zakuani, July 2006.

Record Transfer Fee Paid: £175,000 to Wigan Ath for Paul Beesley, October 1989.

Football League Record: 1905 Elected to Division 2; 1929–56 Division 3 (S); 1956–62 Division 2; 1962–63 Division 1; 1963–66 Division 2; 1966–70 Division 3; 1970–82 Division 2; 1982–85 Division 3; 1985–89 Division 4; 1989–92 Division 3; 1992–95 Division 2; 1995–2004 Division 3; 2004–06 FL 2; 2006– FL 1.

MANAGERS

Sam Omerod 1905–06
Ike Ivenson 1906
Billy Holmes 1907–22
Peter Proudfoot 1922–29
Arthur Grimsdell 1929–30
Peter Proudfoot 1930–31
Jimmy Seed 1931–33
David Pratt 1933–34
Peter Proudfoot 1935–39
Tom Halsey 1939
Bill Wright 1939–45
Willie Hall 1945
Bill Wright 1945–46
Charlie Hewitt 1946–48
Neil McBain 1948–49
Alec Stock 1949–59
Les Gore 1959–61
Johnny Carey 1961–63
Benny Fenton 1963–64
Dave Sexton 1965
Dick Graham 1966–68
Jimmy Bloomfield 1968–71
George Petchey 1971–77
Jimmy Bloomfield 1977–81
Paul Went 1981
Ken Knighton 1981
Frank Clark 1982–91 *(Managing Director)*
Peter Eustace 1991–94
Chris Turner/John Sitton 1994–95
Pat Holland 1995–96
Tommy Taylor 1996–2001
Paul Brush 2001–03
Martin Ling January 2004–

LATEST SEQUENCES

Longest Sequence of League Wins: 10, 21.1.1956 – 30.3.1956.

Longest Sequence of League Defeats: 9, 1.4.1995 – 6.5.1995.

Longest Sequence of League Draws: 6, 30.11.1974 – 28.12.1974.

Longest Sequence of Unbeaten League Matches: 13, 30.10.1954 – 19.2.1955.

Longest Sequence Without a League Win: 23, 6.10.1962 – 13.4.1963.

Successive Scoring Runs: 24 from 3.5.2003.

Successive Non-scoring Runs: 8 from 19.11.1994.

TEN YEAR LEAGUE RECORD

		P	W	D	L	F	A	Pts	Pos
1997-98	Div 3	46	19	12	15	62	47	66	11
1998-99	Div 3	46	19	15	12	68	59	72	6
1999-2000	Div 3	46	13	13	20	47	52	52	19
2000-01	Div 3	46	20	15	11	59	51	75	5
2001-02	Div 3	46	13	13	20	55	71	52	18
2002-03	Div 3	46	14	11	21	51	61	53	18
2003-04	Div 3	46	13	14	19	48	65	53	19
2004-05	FL 2	46	16	15	15	65	67	63	11
2005-06	FL 2	46	22	15	9	67	51	81	3
2006-07	FL 1	46	12	15	19	61	77	51	20

DID YOU KNOW ?

On 26 September 2006 Leyton Orient full-back Matt Lockwood rescued a point after Gillingham had taken a 3–0 lead at Brisbane Road in 57 minutes. His first came in 77 minutes from the penalty spot, the second after 85 and the equaliser on 88 minutes.

LEYTON ORIENT 2006–07 LEAGUE RECORD

Match No.	Date		Venue	Opponents	Result		H/T Score	Lg. Pos.	Goalscorers	Attendance
1	Aug	5	A	Port Vale	L	0-3	0-1	—		5631
2		8	H	Millwall	W	2-0	1-0	—	Steele [45], Alexander [78]	6142
3		12	H	Bournemouth	W	3-2	1-0	9	Alexander [28], Steele 2 [67, 90]	4474
4		19	A	Carlisle U	L	1-3	0-1	11	Steele [68]	7160
5		26	H	Swansea C	L	0-1	0-0	13		4162
6	Sept	2	A	Tranmere R	L	0-3	0-2	19		6446
7		9	H	Brentford	D	1-1	1-0	20	Simpson [15]	5420
8		12	A	Bristol C	L	1-2	0-2	—	Lockwood (pen) [66]	9726
9		16	A	Brighton & HA	L	1-4	0-3	22	Lockwood (pen) [83]	6003
10		23	H	Rotherham U	L	2-3	1-2	22	Chambers [20], Miller [68]	4063
11		26	H	Gillingham	D	3-3	0-2	—	Lockwood 3 (1 pen) [77 (p), 85, 88]	4648
12		30	A	Blackpool	L	0-3	0-1	23		5298
13	Oct	7	H	Chesterfield	D	0-0	0-0	23		4309
14		14	A	Oldham Ath	D	3-3	1-0	24	Ibehre [9], Alexander 2 [59, 86]	5014
15		21	H	Cheltenham T	W	2-0	1-0	24	Alexander [6], Lockwood (pen) [66]	4500
16		28	A	Scunthorpe U	L	1-3	1-2	24	Easton [10]	4795
17	Nov	4	A	Doncaster R	D	0-0	0-0	24		5447
18		18	H	Yeovil T	D	0-0	0-0	23		4842
19	Dec	5	H	Bradford C	L	1-2	1-2	—	Thelwell [29]	3529
20		9	H	Huddersfield T	W	1-0	1-0	22	Alexander [28]	4300
21		16	A	Nottingham F	W	3-1	2-0	21	Guttridge [25], Chambers [45], Corden [69]	23,109
22		19	A	Northampton T	W	1-0	0-0	—	Connor [79]	4728
23		23	H	Crewe Alex	D	1-1	0-1	18	Lockwood (pen) [47]	4371
24		26	A	Gillingham	L	1-2	1-0	19	Walker [35]	8216
25		30	A	Rotherham U	D	2-2	1-0	19	Chambers [15], Alexander [52]	4715
26	Jan	1	H	Bristol C	D	1-1	0-0	20	Lockwood (pen) [62]	4814
27		13	A	Brentford	D	2-2	1-0	20	Ibehre [26], Connor [84]	6765
28		20	H	Blackpool	L	0-1	0-0	20		5217
29		27	A	Crewe Alex	W	4-0	1-0	20	Chambers [45], Corden [51], Ibehre [67], Tudor [83]	5280
30	Feb	3	H	Port Vale	W	2-1	0-1	20	Lockwood [68], Ibehre [86]	4295
31		10	A	Bournemouth	L	0-5	0-2	21		5985
32		13	H	Brighton & HA	L	1-4	0-1	—	Demetriou [87]	4670
33		17	H	Carlisle U	D	1-1	0-1	21	Lockwood [47]	4449
34		20	A	Millwall	W	5-2	3-0	—	Alexander [5], Jarvis 3 [7, 12, 76], Walker [90]	10,356
35		24	H	Tranmere R	W	3-1	3-1	18	Miller [18], Jarvis 2 [29, 39]	4832
36	Mar	3	A	Swansea C	D	0-0	0-0	18		12,901
37		10	A	Chesterfield	W	1-0	0-0	18	Tudor [53]	3665
38		17	H	Oldham Ath	D	2-2	1-0	17	Alexander [13], Hooper [70]	5443
39		24	H	Scunthorpe U	D	2-2	1-0	17	Corden [41], Hooper [87]	5869
40		31	A	Cheltenham T	L	1-2	0-1	19	Alexander [63]	4300
41	Apr	7	H	Northampton T	L	0-2	0-2	19		5459
42		9	A	Yeovil T	L	1-2	1-0	19	Jarvis [31]	5206
43		14	H	Doncaster R	D	1-1	1-0	20	Alexander [36]	4697
44		21	A	Bradford C	W	2-0	0-0	18	Alexander [62], Tann [65]	10,665
45		28	H	Nottingham F	L	1-3	1-2	20	Lockwood [9]	7206
46	May	5	A	Huddersfield T	L	1-3	0-3	20	Demetriou [59]	10,842

Final League Position: 20

GOALSCORERS

League (61): Alexander 12, Lockwood 11 (6 pens), Jarvis 6, Chambers 4, Ibehre 4, Steele 4, Corden 3, Connor 2, Demetriou 2, Hooper 2, Miller 2, Tudor 2, Walker 2, Easton 1, Guttridge 1, Simpson 1, Tann 1, Thelwell 1.
Carling Cup (0).
FA Cup (4): Corden 2, Miller 1, Walker 1.
J Paint Trophy (1): Duncan 1.

Garner G 43	Tann A 13 + 8	Lockwood M 41	Easton C 29 + 1	Partridge D 1	Mackie J 33 + 2	Tudor S 28 + 5	Simpson M 15	Alexander G 42 + 2	Steele L 9 + 2	Corden W 36 + 6	McMahon D 3 + 5	Ibehre J 12 + 18	Keith J 8 + 3	Fortune C 9	Barnard D 9 + 10	Connor P 5 + 13	Miller J 28 + 3	Saah B 30 + 2	Morris G 3	Chambers A 36 + 2	Till P 4	Thelwell A 20 + 2	Demetriou J 2 + 13	Guttridge L 15 + 2	Walker J 9 + 5	Duncan D — + 3	Mulryne P 1 + 1	Jarvis R 14	Hooper G 2 + 2	Palmer A 6	Echanomi E — + 3	Shields S — + 1	Page J — + 1	*Match No.*
1	2	3	4	5	6	7	8^{1}	9^{2}	10	11^{3}	12	13	14																					1
1	2	3	4		6	7	8	9	10^{1}			12	11	5																				2
1	2^{1}	3	4		6	7	8	9^{3}	10	13			11^{2}	5	12	14																		3
1	2^{3}	3	4		6	7	8	9^{2}	10	12		13	11^{1}	5	14																			4
1		3	4			7^{3}	8^{1}	9	10			12	11^{2}	5	14	13	$2^{■}$	6																5
	2	3				7^{1}	8	9	10		13		11	5^{3}	4^{2}	12		6	1	14														6
1	5	3					8	9		7		12	11^{2}		13	10^{1}	2	6		4														7
1	2	3			6^{3}	12	8	9		7^{1}		13	11			10^{2}	5	14		4														8
	2	3			$6^{■}$			9^{1}	10^{2}	7^{3}	13	12	11	5	8		14		1	4														9
1		3					8	9^{2}	12	11	7	13		5^{3}	14	10^{1}	2	6		4														10
1		3			5		8	9	10^{2}	12	7	13				11^{1}	2	6		4														11
1	$2^{■}$	3			5^{3}		8	9^{2}	12	11^{1}	7	10	14			13		6		4														12
1		3			6		8	12	10^{1}	11^{2}	13	9		5			2			4	7													13
1		3	12		6		8	9		7^{1}		10		5			2			4	11													14
1		3	4		5	12	8	9		11		10^{2}				13				2	7^{1}	6												15
1		3	4		5^{3}		8	9		11^{2}	12	10				13	14			2	7^{1}	6												16
1		3			5	7		9		11		10^{1}			8	12	2			6		4												17
1		3	4		5	7		9		11		10^{1}			2^{2}	12				6		8	13											18
1		3	4		5^{2}	7^{1}		9		11		12				10^{3}		13		2		6		8	14									19
1		3	4					9		11		12					2	5		7		6		8	10^{1}									20
1		3	4		5	12		9		11^{1}					13		2	6		7				8^{2}	10									21
1		3	4		6	12		9		11^{1}						13	2	5		7				8	10^{2}									22
1		3	4		6	12^{2}		9		11					13	14	2^{1}	5		7				8	10^{3}									23
1		3			6			9^{3}		11^{2}		12			4	13	2	5		7			14	$8^{■}$	10^{1}									24
1		3	4		6			9		11^{1}			12		8^{2}		2	5		7			13		10									25
1		3	4		6			9^{1}		11^{3}		13				12	2	5		7				8	10^{2}	14								26
1		3	4			7^{3}				11^{2}		9			13	12	2	5		8		6	14		10^{1}									27
1		3	4			7		9		11		10^{1}					2	5		8		6			12									28
1	12	3	4			7		9		11		10					2	5		8^{1}		6												29
1		3	4^{2}		12	7		9^{3}		11		10					2^{1}	5		8		6		13	14									30
1		3			12	7		9		11		10^{3}					2^{1}	5		4		6	13	8^{2}	14									31
1		3			5	7		9^{1}		11^{3}					12			2		8		4	13		10	14	6^{2}							32
1	12	3	4		5^{2}	7		9		11^{3}					13		2			8		6^{1}	14					10						33
1	12	3	4		6	7^{1}		9		13					11^{2}		2	5		8					14			10^{3}						34
1		3	4		6	7^{1}		9		11^{2}							2	5		8			12				13	10						35
1	12	3	4		6	7^{3}		9		11^{1}		13					2	5		$8^{■}$				14				10^{2}						36
1	12	3	4		6	7		9		11^{1}							2	5					13	8				10^{2}						37
1	12	3^{1}	4		6	7^{3}		$9^{■}$		11^{2}							2	5				13	8					10	14					38
1	12		4		$6^{■}$	7^{2}				11^{1}							2	5				13	14	8				10	9^{3}	3				39
1	2		4			7		12		11^{2}		13						5		14		6		8^{3}				10	9^{1}	3				40
1			4			7^{2}		9		11^{3}		12					2	5		8		6	13			14		10		3^{1}				41
1	2		4^{3}		11	7		9		12		13						5		8		6	14					10^{2}		3^{1}				42
1	12				6^{2}	7		9		11^{1}								5		4		2	13	8				10^{3}		3	14			43
1	2	3^{1}			5	7		9				13			6		12			11		4		8				10^{2}						44
1	2	3^{3}			5	7^{1}		9		12					4					6		11		8				10^{2}	13		14			45
		3						9		11								5	1	4		2	7	8				10^{1}		6^{2}	12	13^{3}	14	46

FA Cup

First Round	Notts Co	(h)	2-1
Second Round	Torquay U	(a)	1-1
		(h)	1-2

Carling Cup

First Round	WBA	(h)	0-3

J Paint Trophy

Second Round	Bristol C	(h)	1-3

LINCOLN CITY FL Championship 2

FOUNDATION

The original Lincoln Football Club was established in the early 1860's and was one of the first provisional clubs to affiliate to the Football Association. In their early years, they regularly played matches against the famous Sheffield Club and later became known as Lincoln Lindum. The present organisation was formed at a public meeting held in the Monson Arms Hotel in June 1884 and won the Lincolnshire Cup in only their third season. They were founder members of the Midland League in 1889 and that competition's first champions.

Sincil Bank Stadium, Sincil Bank, Lincoln LN5 8LD.

Telephone: 0870 899 2005.

Fax: (01522) 880 020.

Ticket Office: 0870 899 1976.

Website: www.redimps.com

Email: lcfc@redimps.com

Ground Capacity: 10,055.

Record Attendance: 23,196 v Derby Co, League Cup 4th rd, 15 November 1967.

Pitch Measurements: 100m × 65m.

Chairman: Steff Wright.

Vice-chairman: David Beck.

Chief Executive: Dave Roberts.

Secretary (football): Fran Martin.

Head Coach: John Schofield.

Director of Football: John Deehan.

Physio: Michael Wait.

Colours: Red and white.

Change Colours: White.

Year Formed: 1884.

Turned Professional: 1892.

Ltd Co.: 1895.

Club Nickname: 'The Red Imps'.

Grounds: 1883, John O'Gaunt's; 1894, Sincil Bank.

First Football League Game: 3 September 1892, Division 2, v Sheffield U (a) L 2–4 – W. Gresham; Coulton, Neill; Shaw, Mettam, Moore; Smallman, Irving (1), Cameron (1), Kelly, J. Gresham.

Record League Victory: 11–1 v Crewe Alex, Division 3 (N), 29 September 1951 – Jones; Green (1p), Varney; Wright, Emery, Grummett (1); Troops (1), Garvey, Graver (6), Whittle (1), Johnson (1).

Record Cup Victory: 8–1 v Bromley, FA Cup 2nd rd, 10 December 1938 – McPhail; Hartshorne, Corbett; Bean, Leach, Whyte (1); Hancock, Wilson (1), Ponting (3), Deacon (1), Clare (2).

HONOURS

Football League: Division 2 best season: 5th, 1901–02; Promotion from Division 3, 1997–98; Division 3 (N) – Champions 1931–32, 1947–48, 1951–52; Runners-up 1927–28, 1930–31, 1936–37; Division 4 – Champions 1975–76; Runners-up 1980–81.

FA Cup: best season: 1st rd of Second Series (5th rd equivalent), 1887, 2nd rd (5th rd equivalent), 1890, 1902.

Football League Cup: best season: 4th rd, 1968.

GM Vauxhall Conference: Champions 1987–88.

SKY SPORTS FACT FILE

Four goals including two penalties in a 34 minute spell by Jamie Forrester helped Lincoln City to a 4–2 win at Mansfield Town on 26 August 2006. The first such Imps League foursome came from Frank Smallman on 11 February 1893 in a 5–1 win v Burton Swifts.

Record Defeat: 3–11 v Manchester C, Division 2, 23 March 1895.

Most League Points (2 for a win): 74, Division 4, 1975–76.

Most League Points (3 for a win): 77, Division 3, 1981–82.

Most League Goals: 121, Division 3 (N), 1951–52.

Highest League Scorer in Season: Allan Hall, 41, Division 3 (N), 1931–32.

Most League Goals in Total Aggregate: Andy Graver, 143, 1950–55 and 1958–61.

Most League Goals in One Match: 6, Frank Keetley v Halifax T, Division 3N, 16 January 1932; 6, Andy Graver v Crewe Alex, Division 3N, 29 September 1951.

Most Capped Player: Gareth McAuley, 5, Northern Ireland.

Most League Appearances: Grant Brown, 407, 1989–2002.

Youngest League Player: Shane Nicholson, 16 years 172 days v Burnley, 22 November 1986.

Record Transfer Fee Received: £750,000 from Liverpool for Jack Hobbs, August 2005.

Record Transfer Fee Paid: £75,000 to Carlisle U for Dean Walling, September 1997 and £75,000 to Bury for Tony Battersby, August 1998.

Football League Record: 1892 Founder member of Division 2. Remained in Division 2 until 1920 when they failed re-election but also missed seasons 1908–09 and 1911–12 when not re-elected. 1921–32 Division 3 (N); 1932–34 Division 2; 1934–48 Division 3 (N); 1948–49 Division 2; 1949–52 Division 3 (N); 1952–61 Division 2; 1961–62 Division 3; 1962–76 Division 4; 1976–79 Division 3; 1979–81 Division 4; 1981–86 Division 3; 1986–87 Division 4; 1987–88 GM Vauxhall Conference; 1988–92 Division 4; 1992–98 Division 3; 1998–99 Division 2; 1999–2004 Division 3; 2004– FL 2.

MANAGERS

David Calderhead 1900–07
John Henry Strawson 1907–14
(had been Secretary)
George Fraser 1919–21
David Calderhead Jnr. 1921–24
Horace Henshall 1924–27
Harry Parkes 1927–36
Joe McClelland 1936–46
Bill Anderson 1946–65
(General Manager to 1966)
Roy Chapman 1965–66
Ron Gray 1966–70
Bert Loxley 1970–71
David Herd 1971–72
Graham Taylor 1972–77
George Kerr 1977–78
Willie Bell 1977–78
Colin Murphy 1978–85
John Pickering 1985
George Kerr 1985–87
Peter Daniel 1987
Colin Murphy 1987–90
Allan Clarke 1990
Steve Thompson 1990–93
Keith Alexander 1993–94
Sam Ellis 1994–95
Steve Wicks *(Head Coach)* 1995
John Beck 1995–98
Shane Westley 1998
John Reames 1998–99
Phil Stant 2000–01
Alan Buckley 2001–02
Keith Alexander 2002–06
John Schofield June 2006–

LATEST SEQUENCES

Longest Sequence of League Wins: 10, 1.9.1930 – 18.10.1930.

Longest Sequence of League Defeats: 12, 21.9.1896 – 9.1.1897.

Longest Sequence of League Draws: 5, 21.2.1981 – 7.3.1981.

Longest Sequence of Unbeaten League Matches: 18, 11.3.1980 – 13.9.1980.

Longest Sequence Without a League Win: 19, 22.8.1978 – 23.12.1978.

Successive Scoring Runs: 37 from 1.3.1930.

Successive Non-scoring Runs: 5 from 15.11.1913.

TEN YEAR LEAGUE RECORD

		P	*W*	*D*	*L*	*F*	*A*	*Pts*	*Pos*
1997-98	Div 3	46	20	15	11	60	51	72	3
1998-99	Div 2	46	13	7	26	42	74	46	23
1999-2000	Div 3	46	15	14	17	67	69	59	15
2000-01	Div 3	46	12	15	19	58	66	51	18
2001-02	Div 3	46	10	16	20	44	62	46	22
2002-03	Div 3	46	18	16	12	46	37	70	6
2003-04	Div 3	46	19	17	10	68	47	74	7
2004-05	FL 2	46	20	12	14	64	47	72	6
2005-06	FL 2	46	15	21	10	65	53	66	7
2006-07	FL 2	46	21	11	14	70	59	74	5

DID YOU KNOW?

On Good Friday 1939 goalkeeper James Connor was pressed into service at the last minute against Oldham Athletic for his debut as first choice Dan McPhail was ill and Jack Thacker missed his train connection. He kept a clean sheet as Lincoln City won 1–0.

LINCOLN CITY 2006–07 LEAGUE RECORD

Match No.	Date	Venue	Opponents	Result	H/T Score	Lg. Pos.	Goalscorers	Attendance
1	Aug 5	H	Notts Co	D 1-1	1-0	—	Moses [10]	6046
2	8	A	Hereford U	W 2-1	2-0	—	Stallard 2 [11, 29]	4405
3	12	A	Torquay U	W 2-1	0-0	4	Morgan [89], Gritton [90]	3192
4	19	H	Walsall	D 2-2	2-0	7	Kerr [12], Frecklington [22]	4565
5	26	A	Mansfield T	W 4-2	3-0	5	Forrester 4 (2 pens) [15 (p), 23, 29, 49 (p)]	4596
6	Sept 1	H	Accrington S	W 3-1	2-0	—	Gritton [6], Stallard 2 [40, 69]	4999
7	9	A	Shrewsbury T	W 1-0	1-0	2	Frecklington [29]	4083
8	12	H	Macclesfield T	W 2-1	2-1	—	Kerr [14], Beevers [41]	4184
9	16	H	Milton Keynes D	L 2-3	1-2	4	Frecklington [45], Beevers [59]	5310
10	23	A	Wycombe W	W 3-1	1-1	2	Frecklington [45], Stallard 2 [64, 73]	5247
11	27	A	Boston U	L 0-1	0-0	—		4327
12	30	H	Bury	L 0-2	0-1	4		4748
13	Oct 6	H	Hartlepool U	W 2-0	1-0	—	Forrester [39], Hughes [60]	5332
14	14	A	Barnet	W 5-0	3-0	2	Forrester 3 (2 pens) [26, 33 (p), 53 (p)], Beevers [38], Mettam [90]	2409
15	21	H	Rochdale	W 7-1	3-1	2	Forrester 3 [11, 44, 49], Stallard 2 [16, 65], Hughes 2 [56, 77]	5194
16	28	A	Swindon T	W 1-0	0-0	1	Forrester [63]	7685
17	Nov 4	A	Stockport Co	L 0-2	0-0	2		5497
18	18	H	Darlington	L 1-3	0-1	2	Mayo [82]	5292
19	25	A	Wrexham	L 1-2	0-2	3	Stallard [64]	3619
20	Dec 5	H	Bristol R	W 1-0	1-0	—	Forrester (pen) [45]	3913
21	9	A	Chester C	L 1-4	0-1	4	Brown [64]	2142
22	16	H	Grimsby T	W 2-0	1-0	4	Forrester [44], Frecklington [73]	5919
23	23	A	Peterborough U	W 2-1	1-1	3	Amoo 2 [22, 72]	8405
24	26	H	Boston U	W 2-1	1-1	3	Stallard [16], Hughes [60]	6820
25	30	H	Wycombe W	W 1-0	0-0	3	Hughes [72]	5465
26	Jan 1	A	Macclesfield T	L 1-2	1-1	3	Hughes [15]	2869
27	8	A	Milton Keynes D	D 2-2	0-1	—	Forrester (pen) [51], Weir-Daley [84]	7140
28	13	H	Shrewsbury T	D 1-1	1-0	3	Frecklington [17]	4811
29	20	A	Bury	D 2-2	1-1	4	Forrester [37], Frecklington [76]	2476
30	27	H	Peterborough U	W 1-0	0-0	3	Stallard [71]	6606
31	Feb 3	A	Notts Co	L 1-3	0-2	5	Weir-Daley [89]	7019
32	10	H	Torquay U	W 1-0	1-0	4	Stallard [25]	4881
33	16	A	Walsall	W 2-1	2-1	—	Weir-Daley 2 [15, 42]	4885
34	20	H	Hereford U	L 1-4	0-2	—	Weir-Daley [56]	4695
35	24	A	Accrington S	D 2-2	1-1	4	Beevers [15], Kerr [56]	1930
36	Mar 3	H	Mansfield T	L 1-2	0-1	5	Forrester [74]	5316
37	9	A	Hartlepool U	D 1-1	1-0	—	Green [7]	6903
38	17	H	Barnet	W 1-0	0-0	4	Frecklington [51]	4339
39	25	H	Swindon T	L 2-3	1-2	5	Stallard 2 [13, 77]	5741
40	31	A	Rochdale	L 0-2	0-0	5		2911
41	Apr 7	H	Stockport Co	D 0-0	0-0	5		5320
42	9	A	Darlington	D 1-1	0-1	5	Beevers [77]	3878
43	14	H	Wrexham	L 0-3	0-2	5		4279
44	21	A	Bristol R	D 0-0	0-0	5		6828
45	28	A	Grimsby T	D 0-0	0-0	5		6137
46	May 5	H	Chester C	W 2-0	0-0	5	Stallard [64], Forrester (pen) [90]	5267

Final League Position: 5

GOALSCORERS

League (70): Forrester 18 (7 pens), Stallard 15, Frecklington 8, Hughes 6, Beevers 5, Weir-Daley 5, Kerr 3, Amoo 2, Gritton 2, Brown 1, Green 1, Mayo 1, Mettam 1, Morgan 1, Moses 1.
Carling Cup (3): Beevers 1, Frecklington 1, Stallard 1.
FA Cup (1): Frecklington 1.
J Paint Trophy (0).
Play-Offs (4): Hughes 3, Stallard 1.

Marriott A 46	Beevers L 42 + 2	Hughes J 37 + 4	Moses A 26 + 6	Morgan P 27 + 6	Kerr S 44	Frecklington L 38 + 4	Bacon D 1	Stallard M 41	Forrester J 39 + 2	Amoo R 35 + 8	Cryan C — + 4	Semple R — + 4	Mayo P 28 + 6	Gritton M 5 + 12	Ryan O — + 7	Eaden N 32 + 1	Brown N 26 + 2	Mettam L 1 + 3	Nicholson S 7 + 1	Birley M 3 + 1	Weir-Daley S 4 + 7	Green P 11 + 5	N'Guessan D 4 + 5	Warlow O — + 5	Mendes J 4 + 5	Holmes P 5	*Match No.*
1	2	3	4	5	6^{1}	7	8^{2}	9	10^{3}	11	12	13	14														1
1	2	11	4	5	6	7		9	10	8^{1}	12		3														2
1	2^{2}	11^{1}	4	5	6	7		9	10	8		12	3	13													3
1	2	11^{2}	4	5	6^{1}	7		9	10^{3}	8	12	13	3	14													4
1	2	11	4	5	6	7		9^{1}	10^{2}	8			3	12	13												5
1	2		4	5	6	7		9^{1}	10				3	8	12	11											6
1	2	11	4	5	6	7		9	10^{2}	12			3		13	8^{1}											7
1	2^{1}	11	4	5	6	7		9	10^{2}	12	13		3			8											8
1	2^{2}	11	4^{1}	5	6	7		9^{3}	10	12			3	14	13	8											9
1	2	11	4	5	6	7		9^{2}	10	12			3	13		8^{1}											10
1	2^{2}	11^{3}	4	5	6	7		9	10	12			3	13	14	8^{1}											11
1	2	11	4	5	6^{2}	7		9	10	12			3	13		8^{1}											12
1	5	11	4		6	7		9	10	8			3			2											13
1	5	11	4^{2}		6	7^{3}		9^{1}	10	8			3	12		2	13	14									14
1	5	11			6	7^{1}		9	10^{2}	8			3	12		2	4	13									15
1	2	11	4		6	7		9	10	8			3				5										16
1	2^{1}	11	4	12	6	7		9	10	8			3				5										17
1	2		4	5		7		9	10	8		12	3				6	11^{1}									18
1	2		4^{3}	12		7^{1}		9	10	8			3	13		5	14		11^{2}	6							19
1	4		12		6	7		9^{2}	10	8^{1}			14	13		2	5		3	11^{3}							20
1	4		12	13	6^{2}	7		9		8			14	10		2	5		3^{3}	11^{1}							21
1	11	13	12	5	6^{3}	7			10	8				9		2	4^{1}		3^{2}	14							22
1	2	12	13	5	6^{2}			9	10	11				8^{1}		7	4		3								23
1	2	12	14	5	6	13		9	10^{3}	11				8^{2}		7	4		3^{1}								24
1	3	11^{1}		5	6	7		9	10	8						2	4		12								25
1	2	11	4	5	6			9^{1}	10	8				12			7		3^{2}		13						26
1	2	11	12	5■	6^{1}	7		9	10^{2}	8			3				4				13						27
1	2	11	4		6	7		9	10^{1}	8			3				5				12						28
1	2	11	4^{1}	12	6	7			10	8			3				5				9						29
1	2	11	4^{1}	12	6^{2}	7		9	10^{3}	8			3				5					13	14				30
1	2	11	4		6	7^{1}		9^{2}	10■	8			3^{3}			12	5				13		14				31
1	3	11		5	6	7		9		8^{1}						2	4				10^{2}	12	13^{3}	14			32
1	3	11		5	6^{1}	7		9		8						2	4				10^{2}	12		13			33
1		11		5	6	7		9		8^{1}			3^{2}			2	4	12■			10^{3}	14		13			34
1	3	11^{1}		5	6	7		9	10	8^{2}						2	4				12	13					35
1	5■	3	4		6	7^{3}			10	11					12	2					13	8^{1}	9^{2}	14			36
1		11	4		6	7^{1}			10^{2}	8			12			2	5					3	9	13			37
1	12	11^{1}	4		6	7^{2}				8			13			2	5				14	3	9^{3}		10		38
1	12	13		5^{1}	6	7		9	14	8^{2}						2	4					3			10^{3}	11	39
1	5	11^{3}			6	12		9	10	8^{1}						2	4					3	13		14	7^{2}	40
1	5	11			6	7^{2}		9	10^{3}	12			13			2	4■					3			14	8^{1}	41
1	5	11			6			9	12	8			4			2						3	10^{1}		13	7^{2}	42
1	5^{1}	11		12	6			9	10^{3}	8			4			2						3	13		14	7^{2}	43
1	8	11		5	6	12		9	10				4			2						3			7^{1}		44
1	7	11		5	6	12		9	10^{2}				4		13	2						3			8^{1}		45
1	8	11		5	6	7^{1}		9	10	12						2	4					3^{2}			13		46

FA Cup
First Round — Port Vale — (a) 1-2

Carling Cup
First Round — Scunthorpe U — (a) 3-4

J Paint Trophy
First Round — Grimsby T — (h) 0-0

Play-Offs
Semi-Final — Bristol R — (a) 1-2
(h) 3-5

LIVERPOOL

FA Premiership

FOUNDATION

But for a dispute between Everton FC and their landlord at Anfield in 1892, there may never have been a Liverpool club. This dispute persuaded the majority of Evertonians to quit Anfield for Goodison Park, leaving the landlord, Mr John Houlding, to form a new club. He originally tried to retain the name 'Everton' but when this failed, he founded Liverpool Association FC on 15 March 1892.

Anfield, Anfield Road, Liverpool L4 0TH.

Telephone: (0151) 263 2361.

Fax: (0151) 260 8813.

Ticket Office: 0870 220 2345.

Website: www.liverpoolfc.tv

Email: customercontact@liverpoolfc.tv

Ground Capacity: 45,362.

Record Attendance: 61,905 v Wolverhampton W, FA Cup 4th rd, 2 February 1952.

Pitch Measurements: 101m × 68m.

Chairmen: George Gillett, Tom Hicks.

Chief Executive: Rick Parry BSC, FCA.

Secretary: William Bryce Morrison.

Manager: Rafael Benitez.

Assistant Manager: Pako Ayestaran.

Physio: Robert Price.

Colours: Red shirts, red shorts, red stockings.

Change Colours: White shirts, black shorts, white stockings.

Year Formed: 1892.

Turned Professional: 1892.

Ltd Co.: 1892.

Club Nicknames: 'Reds' or 'Pool'.

Ground: 1892, Anfield.

First Football League Game: 2 September 1893, Division 2, v Middlesbrough Ironopolis (a) W 2–0 – McOwen; Hannah, McLean; Henderson, McQue (1), McBride; Gordon, McVean (1), M. McQueen, Stott, H. McQueen.

HONOURS

Football League: Division 1 – Champions 1900–01, 1905–06, 1921–22, 1922–23, 1946–47, 1963–64, 1965–66, 1972–73, 1975–76, 1976–77, 1978–79, 1979–80, 1981–82, 1982–83, 1983–84, 1985–86, 1987–88, 1989–90 (Liverpool have a record number of 18 League Championship wins); Runners-up 1898–99, 1909–10, 1968–69, 1973–74, 1974–75, 1977–78, 1984–85, 1986–87, 1988–89, 1990–91, 2001–02; Division 2 – Champions 1893–94, 1895–96, 1904–05, 1961–62.

FA Cup: Winners 1965, 1974, 1986, 1989, 1992, 2001, 2006; Runners-up 1914, 1950, 1971, 1977, 1988, 1996.

Football League Cup: Winners 1981, 1982, 1983, 1984, 1995, 2001, 2003; Runners-up 1978, 1987, 2005.

League Super Cup: Winners 1986.

European Competitions: *European Cup:* 1964–65, 1966–67, 1973–74, 1976–77 (winners), 1977–78 (winners), 1978–79, 1979–80, 1980–81 (winners), 1981–82, 1982–83, 1983–84 (winners), 1984–85 (runners-up). *Champions League:* 2001–02, 2002–03, 2004–05 (winners), 2005–06, 2006–07 (runners-up). *European Cup-Winners' Cup:* 1965–66 (runners-up), 1971–72, 1974–75, 1992–93, 1996–97 (s-f.). *European Fairs Cup:* 1967–68, 1968–69, 1969–70, 1970–71. *UEFA Cup:* 1972–73 (winners), 1975–76 (winners), 1991–92, 1995–96, 1997–98, 1998–99, 2000–01 (winners), 2002–03, 2003–04. *Super Cup:* 1977 (winners), 1978, 1984, 2001 (winners), 2005 (winners). *World Club Championship:* 1981 (runners-up), 1984 (runners-up). *FIFA Club World Championship:* 2005 (runners-up).

SKY SPORTS FACT FILE

On 20 September 2006 Xabi Alonso scored for Liverpool against Newcastle United from a 65 yard shot. It was his first goal for the club since scoring again from his own half of the field against Luton Town on 6 January in the FA Cup third round.

Record League Victory: 10–1 v Rotherham T, Division 2, 18 February 1896 – Storer; Goldie, Wilkie; McCartney, McQue, Holmes; McVean (3), Ross (2), Allan (4), Becton (1), Bradshaw.

Record Cup Victory: 11–0 v Stromsgodset Drammen, ECWC 1st rd 1st leg, 17 September 1974 – Clemence; Smith (1), Lindsay (1p), Thompson (2), Cormack (1), Hughes (1), Boersma (2), Hall, Heighway (1), Kennedy (1), Callaghan (1).

Record Defeat: 1–9 v Birmingham C, Division 2, 11 December 1954.

Most League Points (2 for a win): 68, Division 1, 1978–79.

Most League Points (3 for a win): 90, Division 1, 1987–88.

Most League Goals: 106, Division 2, 1895–96.

Highest League Scorer in Season: Roger Hunt, 41, Division 2, 1961–62.

Most League Goals in Total Aggregate: Roger Hunt, 245, 1959–69.

Most League Goals in One Match: 5, Andy McGuigan v Stoke C, Division 1, 4 January 1902; 5, John Evans v Bristol R, Division 2, 15 September 1954; 5, Ian Rush v Luton T, Division 1, 29 October 1983.

Most Capped Player: Ian Rush, 67 (73), Wales.

Most League Appearances: Ian Callaghan, 640, 1960–78.

Youngest League Player: Max Thompson, 17 years 128 days v Tottenham H, 8 May 1974.

Record Transfer Fee Received: £12,500,000 from Leeds U for Robbie Fowler, November 2001.

Record Transfer Fee Paid: £14,000,000 (reported figure) to Auxerre for Djibril Cisse, July 2004.

Football League Record: 1893 Elected to Division 2; 1894–95 Division 1; 1895–96 Division 2; 1896–1904 Division 1; 1904–05 Division 2; 1905–54 Division 1; 1954–62 Division 2; 1962–92 Division 1; 1992– FA Premier League.

MANAGERS

W. E. Barclay 1892–96
Tom Watson 1896–1915
David Ashworth 1920–23
Matt McQueen 1923–28
George Patterson 1928–36
(continued as Secretary)
George Kay 1936–51
Don Welsh 1951–56
Phil Taylor 1956–59
Bill Shankly 1959–74
Bob Paisley 1974–83
Joe Fagan 1983–85
Kenny Dalglish 1985–91
Graeme Souness 1991–94
Roy Evans 1994–98
(then Joint Manager)
Gerard Houllier 1998–2004
Rafael Benitez June 2004–

LATEST SEQUENCES

Longest Sequence of League Wins: 12, 21.4.1990 – 6.10.1990.

Longest Sequence of League Defeats: 9, 29.4.1899 – 14.10.1899.

Longest Sequence of League Draws: 6, 19.2.1975 – 19.3.1975.

Longest Sequence of Unbeaten League Matches: 31, 4.5.1987 – 16.3.1988.

Longest Sequence Without a League Win: 14, 12.12.1953 – 20.3.1954.

Successive Scoring Runs: 29 from 27.4.1957.

Successive Non-scoring Runs: 5 from 22.12.1906.

TEN YEAR LEAGUE RECORD

		P	W	D	L	F	A	Pts	Pos
1997-98	PR Lge	38	18	11	9	68	42	65	3
1998-99	PR Lge	38	15	9	14	68	49	54	7
1999-2000	PR Lge	38	19	10	9	51	30	67	4
2000-01	PR Lge	38	20	9	9	71	39	69	3
2001-02	PR Lge	38	24	8	6	67	30	80	2
2002-03	PR Lge	38	18	10	10	61	41	64	5
2003-04	PR Lge	38	16	12	10	55	37	60	4
2004-05	PR Lge	38	17	7	14	52	41	58	5
2005-06	PR Lge	38	25	7	6	57	25	82	3
2006-07	PR Lge	38	20	8	10	57	27	68	3

DID YOU KNOW?

What a talisman for England was Liverpool midfield player Steven Gerrard in his first 21 full international matches from 31 May 2000 to 11 October 2003! He was never on the losing side once and in the matches he missed the country lost eight times.

LIVERPOOL 2006–07 LEAGUE RECORD

Match No.	Date	Venue	Opponents	Result		H/T Score	Lg. Pos.	Goalscorers	Attendance
1	Aug 19	A	Sheffield U	D	1-1	0-0	—	Fowler (pen) [70]	31,726
2	26	H	West Ham U	W	2-1	2-1	7	Agger [42], Crouch [45]	43,965
3	Sept 9	A	Everton	L	0-3	0-2	9		40,004
4	17	A	Chelsea	L	0-1	0-1	15		41,882
5	20	H	Newcastle U	W	2-0	1-0	—	Kuyt [29], Alonso [79]	43,754
6	23	H	Tottenham H	W	3-0	0-0	6	Gonzalez [63], Kuyt [73], Riise [89]	44,330
7	30	A	Bolton W	L	0-2	0-1	10		25,061
8	Oct 14	H	Blackburn R	D	1-1	0-1	10	Bellamy [64]	44,206
9	22	A	Manchester U	L	0-2	0-1	11		75,828
10	28	H	Aston Villa	W	3-1	3-0	8	Kuyt [31], Crouch [38], Luis Garcia [44]	44,117
11	Nov 4	H	Reading	W	2-0	1-0	8	Kuyt 2 [14, 73]	43,741
12	12	A	Arsenal	L	0-3	0-1	9		60,110
13	18	A	Middlesbrough	D	0-0	0-0	10		31,424
14	25	H	Manchester C	W	1-0	0-0	9	Gerrard [67]	44,081
15	29	H	Portsmouth	D	0-0	0-0	—		42,467
16	Dec 2	A	Wigan Ath	W	4-0	4-0	5	Bellamy 2 [9, 26], Kuyt [40], McCulloch (og) [45]	22,089
17	9	H	Fulham	W	4-0	0-0	4	Gerrard [54], Carragher [61], Luis Garcia [66], Gonzalez [90]	43,189
18	16	A	Charlton Ath	W	3-0	1-0	3	Alonso (pen) [3], Bellamy [82], Gerrard [88]	27,111
19	23	H	Watford	W	2-0	0-0	3	Bellamy [47], Alonso [88]	42,807
20	26	A	Blackburn R	L	0-1	0-0	6		29,342
21	30	A	Tottenham H	W	1-0	1-0	4	Luis Garcia [45]	36,170
22	Jan 1	H	Bolton W	W	3-0	0-0	3	Crouch [61], Gerrard [63], Kuyt [83]	41,370
23	13	A	Watford	W	3-0	2-0	3	Bellamy [34], Crouch 2 [40, 48]	19,746
24	20	H.	Chelsea	W	2-0	2-0	3	Kuyt [4], Pennant [18]	44,245
25	30	A	West Ham U	W	2-1	0-0	—	Kuyt [46], Crouch [53]	34,966
26	Feb 3	H	Everton	D	0-0	0-0	3		44,234
27	10	A	Newcastle U	L	1-2	1-1	3	Bellamy [6]	52,305
28	24	H	Sheffield U	W	4-0	2-0	3	Fowler 2 (2 pens) [20, 25], Hyypia [70], Gerrard [73]	44,198
29	Mar 3	H	Manchester U	L	0-1	0-0	3		44,403
30	18	A	Aston Villa	D	0-0	0-0	4		42,551
31	31	H	Arsenal	W	4-1	2-0	3	Crouch 3 [4, 35, 81], Agger [60]	43,958
32	Apr 7	A	Reading	W	2-1	1-0	3	Arbeloa [15], Kuyt [86]	24,121
33	14	A	Manchester C	D	0-0	0-0	3		45,883
34	18	H	Middlesbrough	W	2-0	0-0	—	Gerrard 2 (1 pen) [58, 65 (p)]	41,458
35	21	H	Wigan Ath	W	2-0	1-0	3	Kuyt 2 [30, 68]	44,033
36	28	A	Portsmouth	L	1-2	0-2	3	Hyypia [59]	20,201
37	May 5	A	Fulham	L	0-1	0-0	3		24,554
38	13	H	Charlton Ath	D	2-2	0-1	3	Alonso [62], Kewell (pen) [90]	43,134

Final League Position: 3

GOALSCORERS

League (57): Kuyt 12, Crouch 9, Bellamy 7, Gerrard 7 (1 pen), Alonso 4 (1 pen), Fowler 3 (3 pens), Luis Garcia 3, Agger 2, Gonzalez 2, Hyypia 2, Arbeloa 1, Carragher 1, Kewell 1 (pen), Pennant 1, Riise 1, own goal 1.
Carling Cup (8): Fowler 2, Agger 1, Crouch 1, Gerrard 1, Hyypia 1, Paletta 1, Riise 1.
FA Cup (1): Kuyt 1.
Champions League (22): Crouch 7, Gerrard 3, Luis Garcia 3, Bellamy 2, Fowler 2, Riise 2, Agger 1, Gonzalez 1, Kuyt 1.
Community Shield (2): Crouch 1, Riise 1.

Reina J 35	Kromkamp J 1	Riise J 29 + 4	Sissoko M 15 + 1	Carragher J 34 + 1	Hyypia S 23	Gerrard S 35 + 1	Zenden B 9 + 7	Fowler R 6 + 10	Bellamy C 23 + 4	Fabio Aurelio 10 + 7	Gonzalez J 14 + 11	Agger D 23 + 4	Pennant J 20 + 14	Finnan S 32 + 1	Alonso X 29 + 3	Crouch P 19 + 13	Kuyt D 27 + 7	Luis Garcia 11 + 6	Warnock S 1	Guthrie D — + 3	El Zhar N — + 3	Paletta G 2 + 1	Arbeloa A 8 + 1	Dudek J 2	Mascherano J 7	Insua E 2	Kewell H — + 2	Padelli D 1	*Match No.*
1	2	3^{1}	4	5^{2}	6	7	8	9^{3}	10	11	12	13	14																1
1					6	8	12		10	3	13	5	7^{1}	2	4	9^{3}	14	11^{2}											2
1		12	8^{2}	5	6	7		10^{1}		3			13	2	4	9^{3}	14	11											3
1			8^{2}	5		11	13		10^{1}	14		6	7	2	4	12	9		3^{3}										4
1			8	5		11^{2}			9	3	13	6		2	4	12	10^{1}	7											5
1		3	8	12	6	7			9^{3}	13	11^{2}	5		2	4^{1}		10	14											6
1		3	8^{1}	5	6	11	12		9				7^{3}	2	4	13	10^{2}	14											7
1		11		5	6	8			10	3			7^{1}	2	4	9		12											8
1		3	8	5	6	7					11^{1}		12	2	4^{2}	13	10	9											9
1		3	8	5	6	7^{2}	12	13					14	2	4	9^{3}	10	11^{1}											10
1		3	12	5	6	11	8^{3}	13			14		7	2	4	9^{1}	10^{2}												11
1		3		5	6^{3}	7	8		12		11^{2}	14	13	2	4	9^{1}	10												12
1		3		5		8	12		9		11^{1}	6	7	2	4	13	10^{2}												13
1		11		5	6	4	8	12	13			3	14	2		9^{1}	10^{2}	7^{3}											14
1		3		5	6	8		12				4	7^{2}	2		9^{1}	10	11^{3}		13	14								15
1		3		5	6^{3}	8^{2}			9			4	12	2	7		10	11^{1}		13		14							16
1		3		5		8		12	9^{2}		14	6	7	2	4	13	10^{3}	11^{1}											17
1		3		5	6	8			9	12	11^{3}		7^{2}	2	4	13	10^{1}	14											18
1		3		5		8			9^{1}	13	14	6	7^{3}	2	4	12	10^{2}	11											19
1		3		5	6	7			10^{3}	12	11^{1}	4		2	8	9^{2}	13	14											20
1		3		5		8			9^{2}	11^{1}	12	6	13	2	4	14	10^{3}	7											21
1		3		5	6	8^{1}		13		12	11^{3}		7	2	4	9	10^{2}	14											22
1		12		5	6	7		13	8^{2}	11		3	14	2	4	9^{3}	10^{1}												23
1		3		5		8			12	11	13	6	7	2	4	9^{1}	10^{2}												24
1		11		5	6	8		12	7^{3}		14	3	13	2	4	9^{2}	10^{1}												25
1		3		5		8		12	11^{1}			6	7	2	4	9	10												26
1		3	4	5		8	11^{2}		9			6	7^{3}	2^{1}		12	10			13			14						27
		3		5^{2}	6	8^{3}		10			11	13	7	2	14	9^{1}	12							1	4				28
1		3	8^{3}	5		7			9^{1}	13	11^{2}	6	12	2	4	14	10												29
1		11	8^{3}	5		7^{1}		12	9^{2}	3		6	13	2	14		10								4				30
1		12		5		10^{3}	13			3	11^{2}	6	7		4	9	14						2		8^{1}				31
1		12	8	5	6	7			10^{2}		11^{1}		14	2		9^{3}	13						3		4				32
1		11^{2}		5		9	12				13	6	7^{3}	2	8	14	10						3		4^{1}				33
1		3	8^{2}	5		10^{1}	11				12	6	7			9	13						2		4				34
1		3		5^{3}	6	12	8^{1}		13		11	14	7		4	9^{2}	10						2						35
			7^{2}		6		8	9	10		11^{1}		12		4						13	5	2	1		3			36
1			8		6			9	10		11^{3}		7^{2}	12	4						13	5	2			3^{1}	14		37
		11		5		7	8^{3}	9^{2}				6		2	12	13	10						3^{1}		4		14	1	38

FA Cup

Third Round	Arsenal	(h)	1-3

Carling Cup

Third Round	Reading	(h)	4-3
Fourth Round	Birmingham C	(a)	1-0
Quarter-Final	Arsenal	(h)	3-6

Community Shield

(at Millennium Stadium)	Chelsea		2-1

Champions League

Third Qualifying Round	Maccabi Haifa	(h)	2-1
		(a)	1-1
Group C	PSV Eindhoven	(a)	0-0
	Galatasaray	(h)	3-2
	Bordeaux	(a)	1-0
		(h)	3-0
	PSV Eindhoven	(h)	2-0
	Galatasaray	(a)	2-3
Knock-Out Round	Barcelona	(a)	2-1
		(h)	0-1
Quarter-Final	PSV Eindhoven	(a)	3-0
		(h)	1-0
Semi-Final	Chelsea	(a)	0-1
		(h)	1-0
Final *(in Athens)*	AC Milan		1-2

LUTON TOWN FL Championship 1

FOUNDATION

Formed by an amalgamation of two leading local clubs, Wanderers and Excelsior a works team, at a meeting in Luton Town Hall in April 1885. The Wanderers had three months earlier changed their name to Luton Town Wanderers and did not take too kindly to the formation of another Town club but were talked around at this meeting. Wanderers had already appeared in the FA Cup and the new club entered in its inaugural season.

Kenilworth Stadium, 1 Maple Road, Luton, Beds LU4 8AW.

Telephone: (01582) 411 622.

Fax: (01582) 405 070.

Ticket Office: 0870 017 0656.

Website: www.lutontown.co.uk

Email: clubsec@lutontown.co.uk

Ground Capacity: 10,260.

Record Attendance: 30,069 v Blackpool, FA Cup 6th rd replay, 4 March 1959.

Pitch Measurements: 110yd × 72yd.

Chairman: David Pinkney.

Chief Executive: John Mitchell.

Secretary: Cherry Newbery.

Manager: Kevin Blackwell.

Assistant Manager: Sam Ellis.

Physio: Jon Bowden Bsc MCSP.

Colours: White shirts, black shorts, white stockings.

Change Colours: Orange shirts, white shorts, orange stockings.

Year Formed: 1885.

Turned Professional: 1890.

Ltd Co.: 1897.

Club Nickname: 'The Hatters'.

Grounds: 1885, Excelsior, Dallow Lane; 1897, Dunstable Road; 1905, Kenilworth Road.

First Football League Game: 4 September 1897, Division 2, v Leicester Fosse (a) D 1–1 – Williams; McCartney, McEwen; Davies, Stewart, Docherty; Gallacher, Coupar, Birch, McInnes, Ekins (1).

Record League Victory: 12–0 v Bristol R, Division 3 (S), 13 April 1936 – Dolman; Mackey, Smith; Finlayson, Nelson, Godfrey; Rich, Martin (1), Payne (10), Roberts (1), Stephenson.

Record Cup Victory: 9–0 v Clapton, FA Cup 1st rd (replay after abandoned game), 30 November 1927 – Abbott; Kingham, Graham; Black, Rennie, Fraser; Pointon, Yardley (4), Reid (2), Woods (1), Dennis (2).

HONOURS

Football League: Championship 1 – Winners 2004–05; Division 1 best season: 7th, 1986–87; Division 2 – Champions 1981–82; Runners-up 1954–55, 1973–74; Division 3 – Runners-up 1969–70, 2001–02; Division 4 – Champions 1967–68; Division 3 (S) – Champions 1936–37; Runners-up 1935–36.

FA Cup: Runners-up 1959.

Football League Cup: Winners 1988; Runners-up 1989.

Simod Cup: Runners-up 1988.

SKY SPORTS FACT FILE

Luton Town can claim the unusual distinction of winning two FA Cup ties at Highbury. On 4 December 1930 they beat Clapton Orient – whose ground was out of commission – 4–2 while on 18 February 1952 they beat Brentford 3–2 in a fourth round second replay.

Record Defeat: 0–9 v Small Heath, Division 2, 12 November 1898.

Most League Points (2 for a win): 66, Division 4, 1967–68.

Most League Points (3 for a win): 98, Championship 1 2004–05.

Most League Goals: 103, Division 3 (S), 1936–37.

Highest League Scorer in Season: Joe Payne, 55, Division 3 (S), 1936–37.

Most League Goals in Total Aggregate: Gordon Turner, 243, 1949–64.

Most League Goals in One Match: 10, Joe Payne v Bristol R, Division 3S, 13 April 1936.

Most Capped Player: Mal Donaghy, 58 (91), Northern Ireland.

Most League Appearances: Bob Morton, 495, 1948–64.

Youngest League Player: Mike O'Hara, 16 years 32 days v Stoke C, 1 October 1960.

Record Transfer Fee Received: £3,000,000 from WBA for Curtis Davies, August 2005.

Record Transfer Fee Paid: £850,000 to Odense for Lars Elstrup, August 1989.

Football League Record: 1897 Elected to Division 2; 1900 Failed re-election; 1920 Division 3; 1921–37 Division 3 (S); 1937–55 Division 2; 1955–60 Division 1; 1960–63 Division 2; 1963–65 Division 3; 1965–68 Division 4; 1968–70 Division 3; 1970–74 Division 2; 1974–75 Division 1; 1975–82 Division 2; 1982–96 Division 1; 1996–2001 Division 2; 2001–02 Division 3; 2002–04 Division 2; 2004–05 FL 1; 2005–07 FL C; 2007– FL 1.

MANAGERS

Charlie Green 1901–28
(Secretary-Manager)
George Thomson 1925
John McCartney 1927–29
George Kay 1929–31
Harold Wightman 1931–35
Ted Liddell 1936–38
Neil McBain 1938–39
George Martin 1939–47
Dally Duncan 1947–58
Syd Owen 1959–60
Sam Bartram 1960–62
Bill Harvey 1962–64
George Martin 1965–66
Allan Brown 1966–68
Alec Stock 1968–72
Harry Haslam 1972–78
David Pleat 1978–86
John Moore 1986–87
Ray Harford 1987–89
Jim Ryan 1990–91
David Pleat 1991–95
Terry Westley 1995
Lennie Lawrence 1995–2000
Ricky Hill 2000
Lil Fuccillo 2000
Joe Kinnear 2001–03
Mike Newell 2003–07
Kevin Blackwell March 2007–

LATEST SEQUENCES

Longest Sequence of League Wins: 12, 19.2.2002 – 6.4.2002.

Longest Sequence of League Defeats: 8, 11.11.1899 – 6.1.1900.

Longest Sequence of League Draws: 5, 28.8.1971 – 18.9.1971.

Longest Sequence of Unbeaten League Matches: 19, 8.4.1969 – 7.10.1969.

Longest Sequence Without a League Win: 16, 9.9.1964 – 6.11.1964.

Successive Scoring Runs: 25 from 24.10.1931.

Successive Non-scoring Runs: 5 from 10.4.1973.

TEN YEAR LEAGUE RECORD

		P	W	D	L	F	A	Pts	Pos
1996-97	Div 2	46	21	15	10	71	45	78	3
1997-98	Div 2	46	14	15	17	60	64	57	17
1998-99	Div 2	46	16	10	20	51	60	58	12
1999-2000	Div 2	46	17	10	19	61	65	61	13
2000-01	Div 2	46	9	13	24	52	80	40	22
2001-02	Div 3	46	30	7	9	96	48	97	2
2002-03	Div 2	46	17	14	15	67	62	65	9
2003-04	Div 2	46	17	15	14	69	66	66	10
2004-05	FL 1	46	29	11	6	87	48	98	1
2005-06	FL C	46	17	10	19	66	67	61	10
2006-07	FL C	46	10	10	26	53	81	40	23

DID YOU KNOW?

In 1939 William Redfern was the only Welshman on the professional staff at Luton Town. He was also the sole player who had been recruited from a club in Northern Ireland, Newry Town. Late into English football this inside-forward later went to Derby County.

LUTON TOWN 2006–07 LEAGUE RECORD

Match No.	Date	Venue	Opponents	Result	H/T Score	Lg. Pos.	Goalscorers	Attendance
1	Aug 5	H	Leicester C	W 2-0	1-0	—	Barnett [8], Edwards [79]	8131
2	8	A	Sheffield W	W 1-0	1-0	—	Emanuel [45]	22,613
3	12	A	Norwich C	L 2-3	1-0	6	Vine [15], Morgan [52]	23,863
4	19	H	Stoke C	D 2-2	0-1	5	Barnett [54], Langley (pen) [60]	7727
5	26	A	Wolverhampton W	L 0-1	0-0	10		19,378
6	Sept 9	H	Crystal Palace	W 2-1	1-0	7	Edwards [2], Vine [61]	9187
7	12	H	Colchester U	D 1-1	1-1	—	Parkin [32]	7609
8	16	A	Cardiff C	L 1-4	1-2	12	Vine [45]	14,108
9	23	H	WBA	D 2-2	2-1	12	Vine 2 [27, 36]	9332
10	30	A	Barnsley	W 2-1	0-0	11	Edwards [47], Brkovic [90]	10,175
11	Oct 14	H	Birmingham C	W 3-2	2-1	8	Vine 2 (1 pen) [28 (p), 29], Bell [81]	9275
12	17	A	Hull C	D 0-0	0-0	—		14,895
13	21	H	Leeds U	W 5-1	1-1	5	Edwards 2 [12, 90], Vine [55], Bell [56], Heikkinen [73]	10,260
14	29	A	Ipswich T	L 0-5	0-1	9		20,975
15	31	H	Burnley	L 0-2	0-2	—		7664
16	Nov 4	A	Preston NE	L 0-3	0-0	12		13,094
17	11	H	QPR	L 2-3	2-1	16	Boyd [44], Brkovic [45]	9007
18	18	H	Derby Co	L 0-2	0-0	19		9708
19	25	A	Southampton	L 1-2	0-2	20	Perrett [67]	20,482
20	28	A	Plymouth Arg	L 0-1	0-0	—		9965
21	Dec 2	H	Preston NE	W 2-0	2-0	18	Vine [2], Edwards [19]	7665
22	9	A	Sunderland	L 1-2	1-1	19	Morgan [5]	30,445
23	15	H	Southend U	D 0-0	0-0	—		7468
24	23	H	Coventry C	W 3-1	1-0	19	Brkovic [45], Vine [66], Morgan [68]	8299
25	26	A	Colchester U	L 1-4	0-2	19	Vine (pen) [85]	5427
26	29	A	Birmingham C	D 2-2	1-1	—	Vine [44], Feeney [77]	24,642
27	Jan 1	H	Cardiff C	D 0-0	0-0	19		8004
28	12	A	WBA	L 2-3	0-1	—	Keane [60], Feeney [70]	19,927
29	20	H	Barnsley	L 0-2	0-1	20		7441
30	30	A	Coventry C	L 0-1	0-0	—		18,781
31	Feb 3	A	Leicester C	D 1-1	1-1	20	Morgan [33]	20,410
32	17	A	Stoke C	D 0-0	0-0	19		12,375
33	20	H	Sheffield W	W 3-2	1-1	—	Runstrom [35], Spurr (og) [54], Talbot [63]	8011
34	24	A	Crystal Palace	L 1-2	0-1	19	Hudson (og) [55]	16,177
35	27	H	Norwich C	L 2-3	1-1	—	Runstrom [11], Talbot [48]	8868
36	Mar 3	H	Wolverhampton W	L 2-3	2-1	20	Emanuel [22], Barnett [45]	10,002
37	10	A	Leeds U	L 0-1	0-0	22		27,138
38	13	H	Hull C	L 1-2	0-1	—	Talbot [70]	7777
39	17	H	Ipswich T	L 0-2	0-1	23		8880
40	31	A	Burnley	D 0-0	0-0	24		11,088
41	Apr 7	H	Southampton	L 0-2	0-2	24		9171
42	9	A	QPR	L 2-3	1-1	24	Coyne [45], Bell (pen) [51]	14,360
43	14	H	Plymouth Arg	L 1-2	0-2	24	O'Leary [51]	7601
44	20	A	Derby Co	L 0-1	0-1	—		28,499
45	28	A	Southend U	W 3-1	2-0	24	Andrew [20], Spring [39], Idrizaj [87]	10,276
46	May 6	H	Sunderland	L 0-5	0-2	23		10,260

Final League Position: 23

GOALSCORERS

League (53): Vine 12 (2 pens), Edwards 6, Morgan 4, Barnett 3, Bell 3 (1 pen), Brkovic 3, Talbot 3, Emanuel 2, Feeney 2, Runstrom 2, Andrew 1, Boyd 1, Coyne 1, Heikkinen 1, Idrizaj 1, Keane 1, Langley 1 (pen), O'Leary 1, Parkin 1, Perrett 1, Spring 1, own goals 2.
Carling Cup (4): Boyd 1, Feeney 1, Morgan 1, Vine 1.
FA Cup (3): Feeney 1, Vine 1, own goal 1.

Beresford M 26	Foley K 38 + 1	Davis S 20 + 4	Robinson S 37 + 1	Barnett L 39	Heikkinen M 37	Edwards C 26	Langley R 18 + 11	Vine R 26	Feeney W 15 + 14	Emanuel L 39 + 1	Morgan D 21 + 15	Boyd A 5 + 14	Coyne C 11 + 7	Holmes P 3 + 2	Parkin S 7 + 1	Brkovic A 14 + 6	O'Leary S 5 + 2	Bell D 28 + 6	Keane K 17 + 2	Perrett R 8 + 2	Brill D 9 + 2	Kiely D 11	Spring M 14	Talbot D 13 + 2	Runstrom B 7 + 1	Carlisle C 4 + 1	Idrizaj B 3 + 4	Andrew C 5 + 2	*Match No.*
1	2	3^{1}	4	5	6	7	8	9^{2}	10	11	12	13																	1
1	2	3^{2}	4	5	6	7	8	9^{1}	10	11		12	13																2
1	2	3	4	5	6^{1}	7^{2}	8	9	10	11^{3}	13	14	12																3
1	2	3		5		7	8	9	10^{1}	11	12		6	4															4
1	2	3	4	5	6	7	8	9	10^{2}	11^{1}	12				13														5
1	2	3	4	5	6	7	8	9^{1}	12	11					10														6
1	2	3	4	5	6	7	8	9		11					10														7
1	2	3^{2}	4	5	6	7	8	9		11▮	12		13		10^{1}														8
1	2		4	5	6	7	8^{2}	9	12	3	11				10^{1}	13													9
1	2	12	4	5	6	7	8^{2}	9		3	11^{1}				10	13													10
1	2	3	4	5	6	7		9^{1}	12	11^{2}	13				10		8^{3}	14											11
1	2	3		5	6		8	9			11				10		4	7											12
1	2	3	4^{2}	5	6	7		9	10^{1}		11^{3}	12					13	8	14										13
1	2		4	5		7		9	10^{2}	3^{1}	11^{3}	13				12		8	6	14									14
1			4	5	6	7	8	9	10^{1}		3^{2}	12		2		11		13											15
1▮	2		4	5	6	7	8^{2}	9			11^{6}	10^{1}		3		12		13			15								16
	2		4^{2}	5	6	7		9^{1}	12	3	13	10				11		8			1								17
1	2		4^{3}	5	6	7		9^{1}	12	11	13	10				8^{2}		14		3									18
	2^{2}		8	5	6	7			10	3	12	9^{1}				11		13		4		1							19
	2^{2}		4	5	6	7		9	10^{1}	11	12					8		13		3		1							20
	2		4	5	6	7		9^{2}	12	3	11^{1}	13				8		10				1							21
	2		4	5	6	7		9^{1}	12	3	11^{2}	13				10		8				1							22
	2		4	5	6	7		9^{2}	12	11	3^{1}		13			10		8				1							23
	2		4^{3}	5	6	7	12	9	13	3	11^{2}		14			10^{1}		8				1							24
	2	12		5	6	7^{2}		9	13	3^{1}	11		4			10		8				1							25
	2	12		5	6^{2}	7	8	9	10	3^{1}	11		4	13								1							26
		3	12	5		2	8^{1}	9^{2}	10		11	13		14		7^{3}		4▮		6		1							27
		3	4				12		10	11^{1}	9	13	6			7^{2}		8	2	5		1							28
		3^{1}	4	5^{2}			8		10^{3}	11	9	14	6			12		7	2	13		1							29
	2	3	4							11^{1}	9	12						7	6	5	1		8	10					30
1	2	3	4				12			11^{2}	13	14						7^{1}	6	5			8	10^{3}	9				31
1	2	3▮	4		6		12			13	11	9^{2}						7^{1}	14	5^{3}			8		10				32
1	2		4		6		12			3	11^{1}	13						7	5				8	9^{2}	10				33
1	2		4	5			7▮			3	12							11	6				8	9^{1}	10				34
1	2		4	5	6				12	3								11	7				8	9	10^{1}				35
1	2		4	5	6				12	3								11	7				8^{2}	9^{1}	10	13			36
1		3	4	5	6				9^{1}	11	12							7	2					13	10^{2}	8			37
1^{6}	2	3		5	6		8^{1}		12	11^{2}	13							7	4		15			9		10			38
1	2^{3}		4	5	6				12	3^{2}			13					7	8					9	14	11	10^{1}		39
	12	3^{1}	4	2^{2}	6						10^{3}		13					11	7		1		8	9		5		14	40
	2^{2}		4		6		12			3	10^{3}		5			11			7		1		8	9^{1}			14	13	41
			4		6		13			3	12^{2}		5			7^{1}		11	2		1		8	9^{3}			14	10	42
	2		4	5			12			3^{1}			6				13	11	7		1		8^{2}	9^{3}			14	10	43
	2			5	6		12			3			4				7^{1}	11			1		8	9^{2}			13	10	44
	2	12		5	6		13			3^{1}			4^{2}				7	11			1		8	14			9	10^{3}	45
				5	6		12			3			4			13	7^{1}	11^{2}	2		1		8				9	10	46

FA Cup

Third Round	QPR	(a)	2-2
		(h)	1-0
Fourth Round	Blackburn R	(h)	0-4

Carling Cup

First Round	Bristol R	(a)	1-1
Second Round	Brentford	(a)	3-0
Third Round	Everton	(a)	0-4

MACCLESFIELD TOWN FL Championship 2

FOUNDATION

From the mid-19th Century until 1874, Macclesfield Town FC played under rugby rules. In 1891 they moved to the Moss Rose and finished champions of the Manchester & District League in 1906 and 1908. By 1911, they had carried off the Cheshire Senior Cup five times. Macclesfield were founder members of the Cheshire County League in 1919.

Moss Rose Ground, London Road, Macclesfield, Cheshire SK11 0DQ.

Telephone: (01625) 264 686.

Fax: (01625) 264 692.

Ticket Office: (01625) 264 686.

Website: www.mtfc.co.uk

Email: admin@mtfc.co.uk

Ground Capacity: 6,141.

Record Attendance: 9,008 v Winsford U, Cheshire Senior Cup 2nd rd, 4 February 1948.

Pitch Measurements: 110yds × 72yds.

Chairman: Rob Bickerton.

Chief Executive: Patrick Nelson.

Secretary: Dianne Hehir.

Manager: Ian Brightwell.

Assistant Manager: Asa Hartford.

Physio: Paul Lake.

Colours: Blue shirts, white shorts and blue stockings.

Change Colours: All black.

Year formed: 1874.

Club Nickname: 'The Silkmen'.

Grounds: 1874, Rostron Field; 1891, Moss Rose.

First Football League Game: 9 August 1997, Division 3, v Torquay U (h) W 2–1 – Price; Tinson, Rose, Payne (Edey), Howarth, Sodje (1), Askey, Wood, Landon (1) (Power), Mason, Sorvel.

HONOURS

Football League: Division 3 – Runners-up 1997–98.

FA Cup: best season: 3rd rd, 1968, 1988, 2002, 2003, 2004, 2007.

Football League Cup: never past 2nd rd.

Vauxhall Conference: Champions 1994–95, 1996–97.

FA Trophy: Winners 1969–70, 1995–96; Runners-up 1988–89.

Bob Lord Trophy: Winners 1993–94; Runners-up 1995–96, 1996–97.

Vauxhall Conference Championship Shield: Winners 1996, 1997, 1998.

Northern Premier League: Winners 1968–69, 1969–70, 1986–87; Runners-up 1984–85.

Northern Premier League Challenge Cup: Winners 1986–87; Runners-up 1969–70, 1970–71, 1982–83.

Northern Premier League Presidents Cup: Winners 1986–87; Runners-up 1984–85.

Cheshire Senior Cup: Winners 20 times; Runners-up 11.

SKY SPORTS FACT FILE

In three successive FA Cup ties in 1967–68, Macclesfield Town scored twice in each one through Fred Taberner and builder's labourer Brian Fidler. It began with a 2–1 replay win over Stockport County, the first over Football League opposition.

Record League Victory: 6–0 v Stockport Co, FL 1, 26 December 2005 – Fettis; Harsley, Sandwith, Morley, Swailes (Teague), Navarro, Whitaker (Miles (1)), Bullock (1), Parkin (2), Wijnhard (2) (Townson), McIntyre.

Record Win: 15–0 v Chester St Marys, Cheshire Senior Cup, 2nd rd, 16 February 1886.

Record Defeat: 1–13 v Tranmere R reserves, 3 May 1929.

Most League Points (3 for a win): 82, Division 3, 1997–98.

Most League Goals: 66, Division 3, 1999–2000.

Highest League Scorer in Season: Jon Parkin, 22, League 2, 2004–05.

Most League Goals in Total Aggregate: Matt Tipton, 45, 2002–05; 2006–07.

Most Capped Player: George Abbey, 10, Nigeria.

Most League Appearances: Darren Tinson, 263, 1997–2003.

Youngest League Player: Peter Griffiths, 18 years 44 days v Reading, 26 September 1998.

Record Transfer Fee Received: £300,000 from Stockport Co for Rickie Lambert, April 2002.

Record Transfer Fee Paid: £40,000 to Bury for Danny Swailes, January 2005.

Football League Record: 1997 Promoted to Division 3; 1998–99 Division 2; 1999–2004 Division 3; 2004– FL 2.

MANAGERS

Since 1967
Keith Goalen 1967–68
Frank Beaumont 1968–72
Billy Haydock 1972–74
Eddie Brown 1974
John Collins 1974
Willie Stevenson 1974
John Collins 1975–76
Tony Coleman 1976
John Barnes 1976
Brian Taylor 1976
Dave Connor 1976–78
Derek Partridge 1978
Phil Staley 1978–80
Jimmy Williams 1980–81
Brian Booth 1981–85
Neil Griffiths 1985–86
Roy Campbell 1986
Peter Wragg 1986–93
Sammy McIlroy 1993–2000
Peter Davenport 2000
Gil Prescott 2001
David Moss 2001–03
John Askey 2003–04
Brian Horton 2004–06
Paul Ince 2006–07
Ian Brightwell June 2007–

LATEST SEQUENCES

Longest Sequence of League Wins: 6, 25.1.2005 – 26.2.2005.

Longest Sequence of League Defeats: 6, 26.12.1998 –6.2.1999.

Longest Sequence of League Draws: 4, 26.11.2005 – 17.12.2005.

Longest Sequence of Unbeaten League Matches: 8, 16.10.1999 – 27.11.1999.

Longest Sequence Without a League Win: 19, 5.8.2006 – 25.11.2006.

Successive Scoring Runs: 14 from 11.10.2003.

Successive Non-scoring Runs: 5 from 18.12.1998.

TEN YEAR LEAGUE RECORD

		P	W	D	L	F	A	Pts	Pos
1997-98	Div 3	46	23	13	10	63	44	82	2
1998-99	Div 2	46	11	10	25	43	63	43	24
1999-2000	Div 3	46	18	11	17	66	61	65	13
2000-01	Div 3	46	14	14	18	51	62	56	14
2001-02	Div 3	46	15	13	18	41	52	58	13
2002-03	Div 3	46	14	12	20	57	63	54	16
2003-04	Div 3	46	13	13	20	54	69	52	20
2004-05	FL 2	46	22	9	15	60	49	75	5
2005-06	FL 2	46	12	18	16	60	71	54	17
2006-07	FL 2	46	12	12	22	55	77	48	22

DID YOU KNOW ?

Player-manager Paul Ince made a cameo appearance in what was probably his last Football League game when he came on for Macclesfield Town in the 85th minute against Notts County on 5 May 2007, with escape from relegation already completed.

MACCLESFIELD TOWN 2006–07 LEAGUE RECORD

Match No.	Date	Venue	Opponents	Result		H/T Score	Lg. Pos.	Goalscorers	Attendance
1	Aug 5	A	Darlington	L	0-4	0-3	—		4095
2	8	H	Hartlepool U	D	0-0	0-0	—		1843
3	12	H	Milton Keynes D	L	1-2	0-1	21	McIntyre (pen) 58	1711
4	19	A	Peterborough U	L	1-3	0-0	22	Swailes 90	4136
5	26	H	Wycombe W	L	0-2	0-2	24		1574
6	Sept 1	A	Grimsby T	D	1-1	0-1	—	Teague 49	3638
7	9	H	Barnet	L	2-3	0-0	24	McNeil 52, Tipton 67	1770
8	12	A	Lincoln C	L	1-2	1-2	—	Scott 45	4184
9	16	A	Walsall	L	0-2	0-1	24		4657
10	23	H	Torquay U	D	3-3	1-1	24	Morley 43, Bullock 48, Swailes 90	1836
11	26	H	Chester C	D	1-1	1-0	—	Bullock 10	2022
12	30	A	Hereford U	L	0-1	0-0	24		2705
13	Oct 6	A	Shrewsbury T	L	1-2	0-1	—	Weir-Daley 56	4816
14	14	H	Bury	L	2-3	1-1	24	Scott 28, Weir-Daley 77	2512
15	21	A	Bristol R	D	0-0	0-0	24		5130
16	28	H	Mansfield T	L	2-3	0-0	24	Heath 49, Morley 81	2599
17	Nov 4	A	Wrexham	D	0-0	0-0	24		3568
18	18	H	Boston U	L	2-3	1-3	24	Heath (pen) 17, Regan 90	1895
19	25	A	Stockport Co	D	1-1	1-0	24	McIntyre (pen) 42	6575
20	Dec 5	H	Rochdale	W	1-0	0-0	—	McNeil 52	1472
21	9	A	Notts Co	W	2-1	2-0	24	Heath 25, McIntyre (pen) 33	4036
22	16	H	Accrington S	D	3-3	0-1	24	Tolley 48, Bullock 73, Murphy 89	2242
23	23	H	Swindon T	W	2-1	1-0	24	Murphy 27, Swailes 52	2377
24	26	A	Chester C	W	3-0	1-0	23	Tipton 10, McIntyre 70, Murphy 78	3365
25	30	A	Torquay U	W	1-0	0-0	23	Morley 90	2169
26	Jan 1	H	Lincoln C	W	2-1	1-1	23	McIntyre 2 (2 pens) 6, 65	2869
27	13	A	Barnet	L	0-1	0-1	23		2018
28	20	H	Hereford U	W	3-0	1-0	20	McIntyre (pen) 17, Murphy 2 61, 83	2494
29	27	A	Swindon T	L	0-2	0-1	22		6062
30	30	H	Walsall	L	0-2	0-1	—		2006
31	Feb 3	H	Darlington	D	1-1	0-1	22	Navarro 86	2173
32	17	H	Peterborough U	W	2-1	1-0	21	Bullock 45, Navarro 53	2274
33	20	A	Hartlepool U	L	2-3	0-1	—	Hadfield 65, Regan 70	5242
34	24	H	Grimsby T	W	2-1	2-0	20	McIntyre (pen) 5, Heath 20	2598
35	Mar 3	A	Wycombe W	L	0-3	0-1	20		5450
36	10	H	Shrewsbury T	D	2-2	1-0	20	Tipton 2 29, 52	2928
37	13	A	Milton Keynes D	L	0-3	0-2	—		5681
38	17	A	Bury	D	1-1	0-0	21	McIntyre (pen) 90	2561
39	23	A	Mansfield T	W	2-1	0-0	—	Miles 54, McNeil 66	2414
40	Apr 7	H	Wrexham	W	2-0	1-0	21	McNeil 34, Murphy 62	14,142
41	9	A	Boston U	L	1-4	0-2	21	Holgate 77	1816
42	14	H	Stockport Co	W	2-0	1-0	20	Murphy 19, Miles 69	4451
43	21	A	Rochdale	L	0-5	0-3	21		2989
44	24	H	Bristol R	L	0-1	0-0	—		1940
45	28	A	Accrington S	L	2-3	2-2	22	Miles 30, McNeil 36	3012
46	May 5	H	Notts Co	D	1-1	1-1	22	Miles 6	4114

Final League Position: 22

GOALSCORERS

League (55): McIntyre 9 (8 pens), Murphy 7, McNeil 5, Bullock 4, Heath 4 (1 pen), Miles 4, Tipton 4, Morley 3, Swailes 3, Navarro 2, Regan 2, Scott 2, Weir-Daley 2, Hadfield 1, Holgate 1, Teague 1, Tolley 1.
Carling Cup (0).
FA Cup (4): Murphy 2, McIntyre 1 (pen), McNulty 1.
J Paint Trophy (0).

Lee T 34	Regan C 36 + 2	McNulty J 15	Morley D 35	Swailes D 38	Navarro A 28 + 4	Bullock M 38 + 5	Miles J 23 + 7	McNeil M 29 + 6	Robinson M 5	McIntyre K 43 + 1	Heath C 16 + 9	Hadfield J 30 + 7	Tolley J 22 + 1	Brain J 9	Teague A 10 + 3	Brightwell I 4	Tipton M 15 + 17	Scott R 22 + 4	Weir-Daley S 5 + 2	Murphy J 25 + 4	Wiles S 2 + 5	Begovic A 2 + 1	Jennings J 5 + 4	Reid I 2 + 6	Rouse D 1	Murray A 8 + 3	D'Laryea N 1	Doyle R — + 2	Holgate A 2 + 4	Benjamin R — + 3	Rankin I 1 + 3	Blackman N — + 1	Ince P — + 1	*Match No.*
1	2	3	4	5	6^{1}	7	8^{2}	9	10	11	12	13																						1
1	2	3	4	5	6^{1}	7		9	10	11	12	8																						2
1	2	3	4	5		7		9	10^{1}	11	12	8	6																					3
	2	3		5	12			9	10	11■	8	7	6^{1}	1	4																			4
	12	3		5	13	7	14	9	10^{3}		11^{1}	8	4^{2}	1	6	2																		5
	2	3		5	6	7		9			10^{1}		11	1	8	4	12																	6
	2	3		5	6^{1}	7		9		12			11	1	4^{2}		10	8	13															7
1		3^{3}	4^{1}	5		13		12		11		14	8		6	7^{2}	9	2	10															8
1			4	5		12		9		3		7^{1}	8		2		11	6	10															9
1			4	5		7	10^{1}			11	12	8	6		3		9	2																10
1			4	5		7	8			11	12	10	6		2		9	3^{1}																11
1	2	3^{2}	4	5	6	10^{1}	12			11	13				7		9	8																12
1		3	4	5	6	7■	12			11			8				9^{1}	2	10															13
1		3	4	5	6		7^{2}	9^{1}		11	12	13	8					2	10															14
	3		4	5■	6	7		12		11		8		1			9^{1}	2	10															15
	2		4		6	7				11	10^{2}	8		1	12	3^{1}	9^{3}	5	13	14														16
	2	3	4	5^{1}	8	7		13		11	10^{2}			1	12		9^{3}	6		14														17
	12	3		5	6^{1}	13		9		11	10	8	7^{2}	1	14			2^{3}			4													18
	2	3		5	6	10		9		11		8		1^{6}	4^{1}			12		13	7^{2}	15												19
	2			5	6■	7		10		3	12	8	11					4^{2}		9^{1}		1	13											20
	2			5		7		6		11	10^{1}	8	4				12			9		1	3											21
1	2			5		7	12	10^{2}		3	11^{1}	8	4				13			9			6											22
1			4	5		7		10		3	6^{1}	8	11				12			9				2										23
1	2		4	5	6	7^{3}	8^{2}	12		3		13	11■				10^{1}			9				14										24
1	2		4	5	6	7^{1}	12	10		3	11^{2}	8								9				13										25
1	2		4	5	6	7^{1}		10		3		8	12				9^{2}			13				11										26
	2		4			7	12			3	11^{3}	13	6				10^{1}			9			5	14	1	8^{2}								27
1	2		4	5	12	13	8^{3}	10		3	11^{2}		6^{1}				14			9						7								28
1	2		4		6	7	10^{2}			3			8^{1}				12			9				13		11	5							29
1	2		4^{1}	5	6	7	8^{2}	10		3		14					13	12		9						11^{3}								30
1	2			5	6	7^{3}	8	10^{2}		3	14	12					13	4		9						11^{1}								31
1	2		4	5	6	7	11^{3}			3	10^{2}	8^{1}								9			14	13		12								32
1	2		4	5	6	7^{2}	10			3	11^{1}	8					12			9				13										33
1	2		4	5	6	7	10^{2}			3	11^{1}	8					12			9								13						34
1	2		4	5	6^{2}	7	10^{1}			3	11^{3}	8■					12			9						13		14						35
1	2		4	5	6	7	8^{2}	12		3			11^{3}				10^{1}			9	14		13											36
1	2		4	5		7	12	13		11		8					10^{2}	3^{3}		9	14		6^{1}											37
1	2		4	5	6^{3}	7^{1}	11^{2}	10		3		8						12		9	13								14					38
1	2			5			11^{1}	10		3		8						4		9	12		6^{3}			7^{2}			13	14				39
1	2		4			7^{2}	6	10^{3}		3		8^{1}						5		9						11			12	13	14			40
1	2		4			7^{2}	6	10^{1}		3		8					12	5		9			14			11^{3}			13					41
1	2		4			7^{2}	6	10		3		8					12	5		9^{1}	13					14			11^{3}					42
1	2		4		12	7^{3}	11	10^{2}		3		8					13	5		9									6^{1}		14			43
1	2^{2}		4		6	7^{3}	11	10		3		8					12	5		9^{1}										14	13			44
1		3^{2}	4	5	6^{3}	12	7	10		11		8					13	2													9^{1}	14		45
1	2		4	5	6^{3}	7^{1}	11	10		3			8				12	13		9^{2}													14	46

FA Cup

First Round	Walsall	(h)	0-0
		(a)	1-0
Second Round	Hartlepool U	(h)	2-1
Third Round	Chelsea	(a)	1-6

Carling Cup

First Round	Leicester C	(a)	0-2

J Paint Trophy

First Round	Stockport Co	(h)	0-1

MANCHESTER CITY FA Premiership

FOUNDATION

Manchester City was formed as a Limited Company in 1894 after their predecessors Ardwick had been forced into bankruptcy. However, many historians like to trace the club's lineage as far back as 1880 when St Mark's Church, West Gorton added a football section to their cricket club. They amalgamated with Gorton Athletic in 1884 as Gorton FC. Because of a change of ground they became Ardwick in 1887.

The City of Manchester Stadium, SportCity, Manchester M11 3FF.

Telephone: 0870 062 1894.

Fax: (0161) 438 7999.

Ticket Office: 0870 062 1894.

Club Museum and Ground Tours: 0870 062 1894.

Website: www.mcfc.co.uk

Email: mcfc@mcfc.co.uk

Ground Capacity: 47,715.

Record Attendance: (at Maine Road) 85,569 v Stoke C, FA Cup 6th rd, 3 March 1934 (British record for any game outside London or Glasgow). 47,304 v Chelsea FA Premier League, 28 February 2004 (at City of Manchester Stadium).

Pitch Measurements: 105m × 68m.

Chairman: John Wardle.

Deputy chairman: Bryan Bodek.

Chief Executive: Alistair Mackintosh.

Secretary: J. B. Halford.

Manager: Sven-Göran Eriksson.

Assistant Manager: Hans Backe.

Physio: Ally Beattie.

Colours: Sky blue shirts, white shorts, sky blue stockings.

Change Colours: Purple shirts, purple shorts, purple stockings.

Year Formed: 1887 as Ardwick FC; 1894 as Manchester City.

Turned Professional: 1887 as Ardwick FC.

Ltd Co.: 1894.

Previous Names: 1887, Ardwick FC (formed through the amalgamation of West Gorton and Gorton Athletic, the latter having been formed in 1880); 1894, Manchester City.

Club Nicknames: 'Blues' or 'The Citizens'.

Grounds: 1880, Clowes Street; 1881, Kirkmanshulme Cricket Ground; 1882, Queens Road; 1884, Pink Bank Lane; 1887, Hyde Road (1894–1923 as City); 1923, Maine Road; 2003, City of Manchester Stadium.

First Football League Game: 3 September 1892, Division 2, v Bootle (h) W 7–0 – Douglas; McVickers, Robson; Middleton, Russell, Hopkins; Davies (3), Morris (2), Angus (1), Weir (1), Milarvie.

Record League Victory: 10–1 v Huddersfield T, Division 2, 7 November 1987 – Nixon; Gidman, Hinchcliffe, Clements, Lake, Redmond, White (3), Stewart (3), Adcock (3), McNab (1), Simpson.

HONOURS

Football League: Division 1 – Champions 1936–37, 1967–68, 2001–02; Runners-up 1903–04, 1920–21, 1976–77, 1999–2000; Division 2 – Champions 1898–99, 1902–03, 1909–10, 1927–28, 1946–47, 1965–66; Runners-up 1895–96, 1950–51, 1987–88; Promoted from Division 2 (play-offs) 1998–99.

FA Cup: Winners 1904, 1934, 1956, 1969; Runners-up 1926, 1933, 1955, 1981.

Football League Cup: Winners 1970, 1976; Runners-up 1974.

European Competitions: *European Cup:* 1968–69. *European Cup-Winners' Cup:* 1969–70 (winners), 1970–71. *UEFA Cup:* 1972–73, 1976–77, 1977–78, 1978–79, 2003–04.

SKY SPORTS FACT FILE

Manchester City inside-forward Bobby Marshall achieved the feat in a friendly in Paris against Red Star Olympic on 7 May 1932 of evading five opponents in a memorable run before beating the French international goalkeeper Andre Tassin.

Record Cup Victory: 10–1 v Swindon T, FA Cup 4th rd, 29 January 1930 – Barber; Felton, McCloy; Barrass, Cowan, Heinemann; Toseland, Marshall (5), Tait (3), Johnson (1), Brook (1).

Record Defeat: 1–9 v Everton, Division 1, 3 September 1906.

Most League Points (2 for a win): 62, Division 2, 1946–47.

Most League Points (3 for a win): 99, Division 1, 2001–02.

Most League Goals: 108, Division 2, 1926–27, 108, Division 1, 2001–02.

Highest League Scorer in Season: Tommy Johnson, 38, Division 1, 1928–29.

Most League Goals in Total Aggregate: Tommy Johnson, 158, 1919–30.

Most League Goals in One Match: 5, Fred Williams v Darwen, Division 2, 18 February 1899; 5, Tom Browell v Burnley, Division 2, 24 October 1925; 5, Tom Johnson v Everton, Division 1, 15 September 1928; 5, George Smith v Newport Co, Division 2, 14 June 1947.

Most Capped Player: Colin Bell, 48, England.

Most League Appearances: Alan Oakes, 565, 1959–76.

Youngest League Player: Glyn Pardoe, 15 years 314 days v Birmingham C, 11 April 1962.

Record Transfer Fee Received: £21,000,000 from Chelsea for Shaun Wright-Phillips, July 2005.

Record Transfer Fee Paid: £10,000,000 to Paris St Germain for Nicolas Anelka, June 2002.

Football League Record: 1892 Ardwick elected founder member of Division 2; 1894 Newly-formed Manchester C elected to Division 2; Division 1 1899–1902, 1903–09, 1910–26, 1928–38, 1947–50, 1951–63, 1966–83, 1985–87, 1989–92; Division 2 1902–03, 1909–10, 1926–28, 1938–47, 1950–51, 1963–66, 1983–85, 1987–89; 1992–96 FA Premier League; 1996–98 Division 1; 1998–99 Division 2; 1999–2000 Division 1; 2000–01 FA Premier League; 2001–02 Division 1; 2002– FA Premier League.

MANAGERS

Joshua Parlby 1893–95
(Secretary-Manager)
Sam Omerod 1895–1902
Tom Maley 1902–06
Harry Newbould 1906–12
Ernest Magnall 1912–24
David Ashworth 1924–25
Peter Hodge 1926–32
Wilf Wild 1932–46
(continued as Secretary to 1950)
Sam Cowan 1946–47
John 'Jock' Thomson 1947–50
Leslie McDowall 1950–63
George Poyser 1963–65
Joe Mercer 1965–71
(continued as General Manager to 1972)
Malcolm Allison 1972–73
Johnny Hart 1973
Ron Saunders 1973–74
Tony Book 1974–79
Malcolm Allison 1979–80
John Bond 1980–83
John Benson 1983
Billy McNeill 1983–86
Jimmy Frizzell 1986–87
(continued as General Manager)
Mel Machin 1987–89
Howard Kendall 1990
Peter Reid 1990–93
Brian Horton 1993–95
Alan Ball 1995–96
Steve Coppell 1996
Frank Clark 1996–98
Joe Royle 1998–2001
Kevin Keegan 2001–05
Stuart Pearce 2005–07
Sven-Göran Eriksson July 2007–

LATEST SEQUENCES

Longest Sequence of League Wins: 9, 8.4.1912 – 28.9.1912.

Longest Sequence of League Defeats: 8, 23.8.1995 – 14.10.1995.

Longest Sequence of League Draws: 6, 5.4.1913 – 6.9.1913.

Longest Sequence of Unbeaten League Matches: 22, 16.11.1946 – 19.4.1947.

Longest Sequence Without a League Win: 17, 26.12.1979 – 7.4.1980.

Successive Scoring Runs: 44 from 3.10.1936.

Successive Non-scoring Runs: 6 from 30.1.1971.

TEN YEAR LEAGUE RECORD

		P	*W*	*D*	*L*	*F*	*A*	*Pts*	*Pos*
1997-98	Div 1	46	12	12	22	56	57	48	22
1998-99	Div 2	46	22	16	8	69	33	82	3
1999-2000	Div 1	46	26	11	9	78	40	89	2
2000-01	PR Lge	38	8	10	20	41	65	34	18
2001-02	Div 1	46	31	6	9	108	52	99	1
2002-03	PR Lge	38	15	6	17	47	54	51	9
2003-04	PR Lge	38	9	14	15	55	54	41	16
2004-05	PR Lge	38	13	13	12	47	39	52	8
2005-06	PR Lge	38	13	4	21	43	48	43	15
2006-07	PR Lge	38	11	9	18	29	44	42	14

DID YOU KNOW ?

In the first nine seasons after the end of the Second World War and starting in 1945–46, Manchester City made a profit each time, the highest figure being £21,382 in 1948–49. The total for this period just fell short of £100,000, a healthy figure at the time.

MANCHESTER CITY 2006–07 LEAGUE RECORD

Match No.	Date	Venue	Opponents	Result		H/T Score	Lg. Pos.	Goalscorers	Attendance
1	Aug 20	A	Chelsea	L	0-3	0-2	—		41,953
2	23	H	Portsmouth	D	0-0	0-0	—		37,214
3	26	H	Arsenal	W	1-0	1-0	9	Barton (pen) [41]	40,699
4	Sept 11	A	Reading	L	0-1	0-1	—		24,092
5	17	A	Blackburn R	L	2-4	2-2	17	Barton [39], Ooijer (og) [45]	18,403
6	23	H	West Ham U	W	2-0	0-0	13	Samaras 2 [50, 63]	41,073
7	30	A	Everton	D	1-1	0-1	11	Richards [90]	38,250
8	Oct 14	H	Sheffield U	D	0-0	0-0	11		42,192
9	21	A	Wigan Ath	L	0-4	0-2	14		16,235
10	30	H	Middlesbrough	W	1-0	1-0	—	Dunne [23]	36,720
11	Nov 4	A	Charlton Ath	L	0-1	0-1	14		26,011
12	11	H	Newcastle U	D	0-0	0-0	14		40,571
13	18	H	Fulham	W	3-1	3-0	12	Corradi 2 [12, 32], Barton [45]	35,776
14	25	A	Liverpool	L	0-1	0-0	14		44,081
15	29	A	Aston Villa	W	3-1	2-0	—	Vassell [18], Barton [32], Distin [75]	30,124
16	Dec 4	H	Watford	D	0-0	0-0	—		35,915
17	9	A	Manchester U	L	1-3	0-2	12	Trabelsi [72]	75,858
18	17	H	Tottenham H	L	1-2	0-2	13	Barton [64]	39,825
19	23	H	Bolton W	L	0-2	0-2	15		40,157
20	26	A	Sheffield U	W	1-0	0-0	13	Ireland [78]	32,591
21	30	A	West Ham U	W	1-0	0-0	10	Beasley [83]	34,574
22	Jan 1	H	Everton	W	2-1	0-0	10	Samaras 2 (1 pen) [50, 72 (p)]	39,836
23	13	A	Bolton W	D	0-0	0-0	10		22,334
24	20	H	Blackburn R	L	0-3	0-1	13		36,590
25	Feb 3	H	Reading	L	0-2	0-0	15		38,676
26	10	A	Portsmouth	L	1-2	0-1	16	Corradi [62]	19,344
27	Mar 3	H	Wigan Ath	L	0-1	0-1	17		39,923
28	14	H	Chelsea	L	0-1	0-1	—		39,429
29	17	A	Middlesbrough	W	2-0	0-0	15	Distin [61], Mpenza [74]	26,427
30	31	A	Newcastle U	W	1-0	0-0	13	Mpenza [80]	52,004
31	Apr 6	H	Charlton Ath	D	0-0	0-0	—		41,424
32	9	A	Fulham	W	3-1	2-0	12	Barton [21], Beasley [36], Vassell [59]	22,435
33	14	H	Liverpool	D	0-0	0-0	12		45,883
34	17	A	Arsenal	L	1-3	1-1	—	Beasley [41]	59,913
35	21	A	Watford	D	1-1	0-0	13	Vassell [53]	18,537
36	28	H	Aston Villa	L	0-2	0-1	13		40,799
37	May 5	H	Manchester U	L	0-1	0-1	14		47,244
38	13	A	Tottenham H	L	1-2	1-2	14	Mpenza [40]	35,426

Final League Position: 14

GOALSCORERS

League (29): Barton 6 (1 pen), Samaras 4 (1 pen), Beasley 3, Corradi 3, Mpenza 3, Vassell 3, Distin 2, Dunne 1, Ireland 1, Richards 1, Trabelsi 1, own goal 1.
Carling Cup (1): Samaras 1.
FA Cup (9): Ireland 2, Vassell 2, Ball 1, Barton 1, Beasley 1, Samaras 1 (pen), own goal 1.

Weaver N 25	Richards M 28	Thatcher B 11	Dunne R 38	Distin S 37	Barton J 33	Sinclair T 14 + 4	Dabo O 10 + 3	Samaras G 16 + 20	Corradi B 19 + 6	Reyna C 12 + 3	Vassell D 28 + 4	Dickov P 9 + 7	Ireland S 14 + 10	Jordan S 12 + 1	Miller I 3 + 13	Mills D — + 1	Trabelsi H 16 + 4	Beasley D 11 + 7	Hamann D 12 + 4	Hart J 1	Mills M 1	Johnson M 10	Onuoha N 15 + 3	Isaksson A 12 + 2	Sturridge D — + 2	Jihai S 10 + 3	Ball M 12	Mpenza E 9 + 1	*Match No.*
1	2	3	4	5	6	7	8[1]	9[2]	10■	11[3]	12	13	14																1
1	2	3	4	5	6	7		9[2]		8[1]	11	10	12		13														2
1	2		4	5	6	7	8	12	10[2]		11[3]	9[1]		3	13	14													3
1	2[3]		4	5	6	7	8■	12	10	11[2]		9[1]		3	13		14												4
1	2		4	5	6	11		12	10			9[1]	13	3			7[3]	14	8[2]										5
1	2		4	5	6	7		9[3]	10[2]	12		13	14	3	11[1]				8										6
1	2		4	5	6	7		9	12	13			11[1]	3	10[3]			14	8[2]										7
	2		4	5	6	11		9	10[2]	12		13		3[3]	14		7		8[1]	1									8
1	5		4		6	7		9	10		12	13		3					8[2]		2[1]	11							9
1	2	3	4	5	6	11		9	12	8[3]	13	10[1]					14	7[2]											10
1	2	3	4	5	6	11		9[3]	12	8	13	10[1]					14	7[2]											11
1	2	3	4	5	6	11		12	13	8[2]	10	9[1]					7												12
1	2	3	4	5	6			9[1]	10	8	11	12					7[2]						13						13
1	11	3	4	5	6			12	10	8	9		13				7[2]						2[1]						14
1	2[3]	3	4	5	6			9[2]	10	8	11	12					7[1]		13				14						15
1	2	3	4	5	6			9[2]	10	8[1]	11				13		7		12										16
1[6]	2[2]	3	4	5	6			9	10■	8[1]	11		12				7	13						15					17
1	2[2]		4	5	6		12	9[3]		8[1]	11	10	13	3			7						14						18
1		3[1]	4	5	6■		12	13			9	10[2]	8		11		7						2						19
1	2		4	5	6		8	12	10[1]		9[3]		11	13	14		7						3[2]						20
1	6		4	5			8	12	10[1]		9[2]		11[3]	3	13		7	14					2						21
1	3		4	5			8	12	10[1]		9			11	13		7[2]	6					2						22
1	3		4	5	6	7	8	12	10[1]		9[2]		11		13								2						23
1	2		4	5		7[3]	8	12	10[1]		9		11	6	13		3[2]	14											24
1[6]	2		4	5	6		8[1]	9[2]			10		11				3	7	12					15	13				25
	2		4	5	6		8	12	10		9[3]		7[2]		14			13						1		3[1]	11		26
1	2		4	5	6			9[3]	10				11				7[2]	8							12	13	3[1]	14	27
	2		4	5	6		12	13			10[2]		7		14				8[1]					1		3[3]	11	9	28
	2[1]		4	5	6			12			10[2]							13	8			7		1		3	11	9	29
			4	5	6			12			10						13		8[1]			7	2[2]	1		11	3	9	30
			4	5	6	12		13			10[2]		7[1]									8	2	1		11	3	9	31
			4	5	6	12		13			10[2]							8[1]				7	2	1		11	3	9	32
			4	5	6				12		10[1]		13					8				7	2	1		11	3	9[2]	33
			4	5[2]	6			12	13		9[3]		14					10	8			7	2	1		11[1]	3		34
			4	5	6			14			10		12		13[3]			9[2]	8			7	2	1		11[1]	3		35
			4	5	6	13		9			11		7						8[2]				2[1]	1		12	3	10	36
			4	5		12					10	13	11[2]					7[1]	8[3]			6	2	1		14	3	9	37
			4	5[2]				12			10		7	3				8[1]	13			6	2	1		11		9	38

FA Cup

Third Round	Sheffield W	(a)	1-1
		(h)	2-1
Fourth Round	Southampton	(h)	3-1
Fifth Round	Preston NE	(a)	3-1
Sixth Round	Blackburn R	(a)	0-2

Carling Cup

Second Round	Chesterfield	(a)	1-2

MANCHESTER UNITED FA Premiership

FOUNDATION

Manchester United was formed as comparatively recently as 1902 after their predecessors, Newton Heath, went bankrupt. However, it is usual to give the date of the club's foundation as 1878 when the dining room committee of the carriage and waggon works of the Lancashire and Yorkshire Railway Company formed Newton Heath L and YR Cricket and Football Club. They won the Manchester Cup in 1886 and as Newton Heath FC were admitted to the Second Division in 1892.

Old Trafford, Sir Matt Busby Way, Manchester M16 0RA.

Telephone: (0161) 868 8000.

Fax: (0161) 868 8804.

Ticket Office: 0870 442 1968.

Website: www.manutd.com

Email: enquiries@manutd.co.uk

Ground Capacity: 76,212.

Record Attendance: 76,962 Wolverhampton W v Grimsby T, FA Cup semi-final, 25 March 1939.
Club Record Attendance: 76,098 v Blackburn R, FA Premier League, 31 March 2007.

Pitch Measurements: 105m × 68m.

Chief Executive: David Gill.

Secretary: Ken Ramsden.

Manager: Sir Alex Ferguson CBE.

Assistant Manager: Carlos Queiroz.

Physio: Robert Swire.

Colours: Red shirts, white shorts, black stockings.

Change Colours: All black.

Year Formed: 1878 as Newton Heath LYR; 1902, Manchester United.

Turned Professional: 1885. ***Ltd Co.:*** 1907.

Previous Name: 1880, Newton Heath; 1902, Manchester United.

Club Nickname: 'Red Devils'.

Grounds: 1880, North Road, Monsall Road; 1893, Bank Street; 1910, Old Trafford (played at Maine Road 1941–49).

First Football League Game: 3 September 1892, Division 1, v Blackburn R (a) L 3–4 – Warner; Clements, Brown; Perrins, Stewart, Erentz; Farman (1), Coupar (1), Donaldson (1), Carson, Mathieson.

HONOURS

FA Premier League – Champions 1992–93, 1993–94, 1995–96, 1996–97, 1998–99, 1999–2000, 2000–01, 2002–03, 2006–07; Runners-up 1994–95, 1997–98, 2005–06.

Football League: Division 1 – Champions 1907–08, 1910–11, 1951–52, 1955–56, 1956–57, 1964–65, 1966–67; Runners-up 1946–47, 1947–48, 1948–49, 1950–51, 1958–59, 1963–64, 1967–68, 1979–80, 1987–88, 1991–92. Division 2 – Champions 1935–36, 1974–75; Runners-up 1896–97, 1905–06, 1924–25, 1937–38.

FA Cup: Winners 1909, 1948, 1963, 1977, 1983, 1985, 1990, 1994, 1996, 1999, 2004; Runners-up 1957, 1958, 1976, 1979, 1995, 2005, 2007.

Football League Cup: Winners 1992, 2006; Runners-up 1983, 1991, 1994, 2003.

European Competitions: *European Cup:* 1956–57 (s-f), 1957–58 (s-f), 1965–66 (s-f), 1967–68 (winners), 1968–69 (s-f). *Champions League:* 1993–94, 1994–95, 1996–97 (s-f), 1997–98, 1998–99 (winners), 1999–2000, 2000–01, 2001–02 (s-f), 2002–03, 2003–04, 2004–05, 2005–06, 2006–07 (s-f). *European Cup-Winners' Cup:* 1963–64, 1977–78, 1983–84, 1990–91 (winners). 1991–92. *Inter Cities Fairs Cup:* 1964–65. *UEFA Cup:* 1976–77, 1980–81, 1982–83, 1984–85, 1992–93, 1995–96. *Super Cup:* 1991 (winners), 1999 (runners-up). *Inter-Continental Cup:* 1999 (winners), 1968 (runners-up).

SKY SPORTS FACT FILE

On 6 December 1902 Manchester United met Burnley at Turf Moor. Mitchell and Kenyon filmed the match for showing at a local institute. But United won 2–0 and the evening's screening was cancelled, the footage not being rediscovered until 100 years later.

Record League Victory (as Newton Heath): 10–1 v Wolverhampton W, Division 1, 15 October 1892 – Warner; Mitchell, Clements; Perrins, Stewart (3), Erentz; Farman (1), Hood (1), Donaldson (3), Carson (1), Hendry (1).

Record League Victory (as Manchester U): 9–0 v Ipswich T, FA Premier League, 4 March 1995 – Schmeichel; Keane (1) (Sharpe), Irwin, Bruce (Butt), Kanchelskis, Pallister, Cole (5), Ince (1), McClair, Hughes (2), Giggs.

Record Cup Victory: 10–0 v RSC Anderlecht, European Cup prel. rd 2nd leg, 26 September 1956 – Wood; Foulkes, Byrne; Colman, Jones, Edwards; Berry (1), Whelan (2), Taylor (3), Viollet (4), Pegg.

Record Defeat: 0–7 v Blackburn R, Division 1, 10 April 1926. 0–7 v Aston Villa, Division 1, 27 December 1930. 0–7 v Wolverhampton W, Division 2, 26 December 1931.

Most League Points (2 for a win): 64, Division 1, 1956–57.

Most League Points (3 for a win): 92, FA Premier League, 1993–94.

Most League Goals: 103, Division 1, 1956–57 and 1958–59.

Highest League Scorer in Season: Dennis Viollet, 32, 1959–60.

Most League Goals in Total Aggregate: Bobby Charlton, 199, 1956–73.

Most Capped Player: Bobby Charlton, 106, England.

Most League Appearances: Bobby Charlton, 606, 1956–73.

Youngest League Player: Jeff Whitefoot, 16 years 105 days v Portsmouth, 15 April 1950.

Record Transfer Fee Received: £25,000,000 from Real Madrid for David Beckham, July 2003.

Record Transfer Fee Paid: £30,000,000 to Leeds U for Rio Ferdinand, July 2002 (see also Leeds United page 217).

Football League Record: 1892 Newton Heath elected to Division 1; 1894–1906 Division 2; 1906–22 Division 1; 1922–25 Division 2; 1925–31 Division 1; 1931–36 Division 2; 1936–37 Division 1; 1937–38 Division 2; 1938–74 Division 1; 1974–75 Division 2; 1975–92 Division 1; 1992– FA Premier League.

MANAGERS

J. Ernest Mangnall 1903–12
John Bentley 1912–14
John Robson 1914–21
(Secretary-Manager from 1916)
John Chapman 1921–26
Clarence Hilditch 1926–27
Herbert Bamlett 1927–31
Walter Crickmer 1931–32
Scott Duncan 1932–37
Walter Crickmer 1937–45
(Secretary-Manager)
Matt Busby 1945–69
(continued as General Manager then Director)
Wilf McGuinness 1969–70
Sir Matt Busby 1970–71
Frank O'Farrell 1971–72
Tommy Docherty 1972–77
Dave Sexton 1977–81
Ron Atkinson 1981–86
Sir Alex Ferguson November 1986–

LATEST SEQUENCES

Longest Sequence of League Wins: 14, 15.10.1904 – 3.1.1905.

Longest Sequence of League Defeats: 14, 26.4.1930 – 25.10.1930.

Longest Sequence of League Draws: 6, 30.10.1988 – 27.11.1988.

Longest Sequence of Unbeaten League Matches: 29, 26.12.1998 – 25.9.1999.

Longest Sequence Without a League Win: 16, 19.4.1930 – 25.10.1930.

Successive Scoring Runs: 27 from 11.10.1958.

Successive Non-scoring Runs: 5 from 22.2.1902.

TEN YEAR LEAGUE RECORD

		P	W	D	L	F	A	Pts	Pos
1997-98	PR Lge	38	23	8	7	73	26	77	2
1998-99	PR Lge	38	22	13	3	80	37	79	1
1999-2000	PR Lge	38	28	7	3	97	45	91	1
2000-01	PR Lge	38	24	8	6	79	31	80	1
2001-02	PR Lge	38	24	5	9	87	45	77	3
2002-03	PR Lge	38	25	8	5	74	34	83	1
2003-04	PR Lge	38	23	6	9	64	35	75	3
2004-05	PR Lge	38	22	11	5	58	26	77	3
2005-06	PR Lge	38	25	8	5	72	34	83	2
2006-07	PR Lge	38	28	5	5	83	27	89	1

DID YOU KNOW ?

On 21 October 2006 Paul Scholes made his 500th appearance for Manchester United, the ninth United player to reach this milestone, and celebrated by scoring against Liverpool in 2–0 win.

MANCHESTER UNITED 2006–07 LEAGUE RECORD

Match No.	*Date*	*Venue*	*Opponents*	*Result*		*H/T Score*	*Lg. Pos.*	*Goalscorers*	*Attendance*
1	Aug 20	H	Fulham	W	5-1	4-1	—	Saha [7], Pearce (og) [15], Rooney 2 [16, 64], Ronaldo [19]	75,115
2	23	A	Charlton Ath	W	3-0	0-0	—	Fletcher [49], Saha [80], Solskjaer [90]	25,422
3	26	A	Watford	W	2-1	1-1	1	Silvestre [12], Giggs [52]	19,453
4	Sept 9	H	Tottenham H	W	1-0	1-0	1	Giggs [9]	75,453
5	17	H	Arsenal	L	0-1	0-0	2		75,595
6	23	A	Reading	D	1-1	0-0	3	Ronaldo [73]	24,098
7	Oct 1	H	Newcastle U	W	2-0	1-0	1	Solskjaer 2 [41, 49]	75,664
8	14	A	Wigan Ath	W	3-1	0-1	1	Vidic [62], Saha [66], Solskjaer [90]	20,631
9	22	H	Liverpool	W	2-0	1-0	1	Scholes [39], Ferdinand [66]	75,828
10	28	A	Bolton W	W	4-0	2-0	1	Rooney 3 [10, 16, 89], Ronaldo [82]	27,229
11	Nov 4	H	Portsmouth	W	3-0	2-0	1	Saha (pen) [3], Ronaldo [10], Vidic [66]	76,004
12	11	A	Blackburn R	W	1-0	0-0	1	Saha [64]	26,162
13	18	A	Sheffield U	W	2-1	1-1	1	Rooney 2 [30, 75]	32,584
14	26	H	Chelsea	D	1-1	1-0	1	Saha [29]	75,948
15	29	H	Everton	W	3-0	1-0	—	Ronaldo [39], Evra [63], O'Shea [89]	75,723
16	Dec 2	A	Middlesbrough	W	2-1	1-0	1	Saha (pen) [19], Fletcher [68]	31,238
17	9	H	Manchester C	W	3-1	2-0	1	Rooney [6], Saha [45], Ronaldo [84]	75,858
18	17	A	West Ham U	L	0-1	0-0	1		34,966
19	23	A	Aston Villa	W	3-0	0-0	1	Ronaldo 2 [58, 85], Scholes [64]	42,551
20	26	H	Wigan Ath	W	3-1	0-0	1	Ronaldo 2 [47, 51], Solskjaer [59]	76,018
21	30	H	Reading	W	3-2	1-1	1	Solskjaer [33], Ronaldo 2 [59, 77]	75,910
22	Jan 1	A	Newcastle U	D	2-2	1-1	1	Scholes 2 [40, 46]	52,302
23	13	H	Aston Villa	W	3-1	3-0	1	Park [11], Carrick [13], Ronaldo [35]	76,073
24	21	A	Arsenal	L	1-2	0-0	1	Rooney [53]	60,128
25	31	H	Watford	W	4-0	1-0	—	Ronaldo (pen) [20], Doyley (og) [61], Larsson [70], Rooney [71]	76,032
26	Feb 4	A	Tottenham H	W	4-0	1-0	1	Ronaldo (pen) [45], Vidic [48], Scholes [54], Giggs [77]	36,146
27	10	H	Charlton Ath	W	2-0	1-0	1	Park [24], Fletcher [82]	75,883
28	24	A	Fulham	W	2-1	1-1	1	Giggs [29], Ronaldo [88]	24,459
29	Mar 3	A	Liverpool	W	1-0	0-0	1	O'Shea [90]	44,403
30	17	H	Bolton W	W	4-1	3-0	1	Park 2 [14, 25], Rooney 2 [17, 74]	76,058
31	31	H	Blackburn R	W	4-1	0-1	1	Scholes [61], Carrick [73], Park [83], Solskjaer [90]	76,098
32	Apr 7	A	Portsmouth	L	1-2	0-1	1	O'Shea [90]	20,223
33	17	H	Sheffield U	W	2-0	1-0	—	Carrick [4], Rooney [50]	75,540
34	21	H	Middlesbrough	D	1-1	1-1	1	Richardson [3]	75,967
35	28	A	Everton	W	4-2	0-1	1	O'Shea [61], Neville (og) [68], Rooney [79], Eagles [90]	39,682
36	May 5	A	Manchester C	W	1-0	1-0	1	Ronaldo (pen) [34]	47,244
37	9	A	Chelsea	D	0-0	0-0	—		41,794
38	13	H	West Ham U	L	0-1	0-1	1		75,927

Final League Position: 1

GOALSCORERS

League (83): Ronaldo 17 (3 pens), Rooney 14, Saha 8 (2 pens), Solskjaer 7, Scholes 6, Park 5, Giggs 4, O'Shea 4, Carrick 3, Fletcher 3, Vidic 3, Eagles 1, Evra 1, Ferdinand 1, Larsson 1, Richardson 1, Silvestre 1, own goals 3.
Carling Cup (2): Lee 1, Solskjaer 1.
FA Cup (15): Rooney 5, Ronaldo 3 (2 pens), Solskjaer 2, Carrick 1, Heinze 1, Larsson 1, Richardson 1, Saha 1.
Champions League (23): Rooney 4, Saha 4 (1 pen), Ronaldo 3, Carrick 2, Giggs 2, Evra 1, Larsson 1, O'Shea 1, Richardson 1, Scholes 1, Smith 1, Solskjaer 1, Vidic 1.

Van der Sar E 32	Neville G 24	Evra P 22 + 2	O'Shea J 16 + 16	Ferdinand R 33	Brown W 17 + 5	Ronaldo C 31 + 3	Scholes P 29 + 1	Saha L 18 + 6	Rooney W 33 + 2	Giggs R 25 + 5	Silvestre M 6 + 8	Solskjaer O 9 + 10	Park J 8 + 6	Carrick M 29 + 4	Richardson K 8 + 7	Fletcher D 16 + 8	Kuszczak T 6	Heinze G 17 + 5	Vidic N 25	Larsson H 5 + 2	Smith A 6 + 3	Eagles C 1 + 1	Lee K 1	Dong Fangshou 1	*Match No.*
1	2^1	3	4	5	6	7	8	9^2	10	11^3	12	13	14												1
1		3	4	5	2	10		9		11^1	6	12	8^2	13		7									2
1			3	5	2	7		9		11	6	10^1	12	4^2	13	8									3
1	2	3	4	5	6	7^1		9		11	12		13	8^3	10^2	14									4
	2	12	4	5	6	11	8^2	9	10^3		3^1	14		13		7	1								5
1	2		12	5		9	8	13	10			14		4	11^2	7^3		3^1	6						6
1	2	12		5		11	8		10			9		4		7		3^1	6						7
1		3	4	5	2^1		11	9	10	12		7		8					6						8
1	2^1	3^2	12	5	13		8	9	10	11				4		7			6						9
1	2	3^3	12	5		7	8	9^1	10	11^2				4		13		14	6						10
1	2	3	12	5		7^3	8	9	10^1	11	13			4^2		14			6						11
1	2^1	3^2	12	5		7^3	8	9	10	11	13			4		14			6						12
1	2	3^1		5		7	8	9	10	11				4				12	6						13
1	2		12	5		7^2	8	9^1	10	11				4		13		3	6						14
1	2	3	4	5	12	11^2			10		6			8^1	9	7		13							15
1	2		12	5	13	7^2	8	9	10	11						4^1		3	6						16
1	2		12	5		7	8	9^1	10	11				4				3	6						17
1	2		12	5		7	8	9	10	11^2		13	14	4^1				3^3	6						18
1	2	3	12	5		7	8^3	9	13	11^1	14		10^2			4			6						19
1		3^3	4		2	12	8^2		10		5	9	11		13	7^1		14	6						20
1			4	5	2	7^3			10^2	12	6	9	11^1	8	13	14		3							21
1	2	3		5		7	8	9^1	10	11			12	13		4^2			6						22
1	2	3	12	5		7	8	13	10			14	11^2	4^1					6	9^3					23
1	2	3		5		7^2	8	12	10	11				4				13	6	9^1					24
	2		4	5	12	7			10		13	9^3		8^1	11		1	3	6^2	14					25
1	2	3	12	5		7^3	8	13	10^2	11^1			14	4					6	9					26
	2	3		5			8	9^1	10	11^2			4		12	7	1		6	13					27
1		3^3	12	5	2	7	8	13	10	11	14			4^2					6^1	9					28
1	2	3^3	12	5		7	8■	13	10^1	11	14			4					6	9^2					29
	2^1		4	5	12	7^3			10	9^2			11	8	13		1	3	6		14				30
1			12	5	2	7^2	8		10	9^3		13	11	4				3	6^1		14				31
1			2	5	4	9	8		10	12		13		6^3	11^1	7^2		3			14				32
		3^1			5	7	8		10	11^2		13		4	12	6	1	2			9				33
1			2	5^2	6	7	8		10	12		14		4	11^1	13		3			9^3				34
1		3^2	2		6	12	8		10	11		7^3		4	13			5			9^1	14			35
1			12	5	2	7	8		10^1	11				4		13		3	6		9^2				36
			4		5				12			9		13	11	8	1	3^2			6	7	2	10^1	37
1		3^3	2		6	12	13		10	14		7		4^2	11	8		5			9^1				38

FA Cup

Third Round	Aston Villa	(h)	2-1
Fourth Round	Portsmouth	(h)	2-1
Fifth Round	Reading	(h)	1-1
		(a)	3-2
Sixth Round	Middlesbrough	(a)	2-2
		(h)	1-0
Semi-Final *(at Villa Park)*	Watford		4-1
Final *(at Wembley)*	Chelsea		0-1

Carling Cup

Third Round	Crewe Alex	(a)	2-1
Fourth Round	Southend U	(a)	0-1

Champions League

Group F	Celtic	(h)	3-2
	Benfica	(a)	1-0
	FC Copenhagen	(h)	3-0
		(a)	0-1
	Celtic	(a)	0-1
	Benfica	(h)	3-1
Knock-Out Round	Lille	(a)	1-0
		(h)	1-0
Quarter-Final	Roma	(a)	1-2
		(h)	7-1
Semi-Final	AC Milan	(h)	3-2
		(a)	0-3

MANSFIELD TOWN — FL Championship 2

FOUNDATION

The club was formed as Mansfield Wesleyans in 1897, and changed their name to Mansfield Wesley in 1906 and Mansfield Town in 1910. This was after the Mansfield Wesleyan Chapel trustees had requested that the club change its name as 'it has no longer had any connection with either the chapel or school'. The new club participated in the Notts and Derby District League, but in the following season 1911–12 joined the Central Alliance.

Field Mill Ground, Quarry Lane, Mansfield, Notts NG18 5DA.

Telephone: 0870 756 3160.

Fax: (01623) 482 495.

Ticket Office: 0870 756 3160.

Website: www.mansfieldtown.net

Email: mtfc@stags.plus.com

Ground Capacity: 10,000.

Record Attendance: 24,467 v Nottingham F, FA Cup 3rd rd, 10 January 1953.

Pitch Measurements: 114yd × 70yd.

Chairman: James Derry.

Chief Executive: Keith Haslam.

Secretary: Sharon Roberts.

Manager: Billy Dearden.

Assistant Manager: Paul Holland.

Physio: Paul Madin IIST, SPORTS THERAPY DIP.

Colours: Amber and royal blue.

Change Colours: Sky blue and navy and white.

Year Formed: 1897.

Turned Professional: 1906.

Ltd Co.: 1922.

Previous Name: 1897, Mansfield Wesleyans; 1906, Mansfield Wesley; 1910, Mansfield Town.

Grounds: 1897–99, Westfield Lane; 1899–1901, Ratcliffe Gate; 1901–12, Newgate Lane; 1912–16, Ratcliffe Gate; 1916, Field Mill.

Club Nickname: 'The Stags'.

First Football League Game: 29 August 1931, Division 3 (S), v Swindon T (h) W 3–2 – Wilson; Clifford, England; Wake, Davis, Blackburn; Gilhespy, Readman (1), Johnson, Broom (2), Baxter.

Record League Victory: 9–2 v Rotherham U, Division 3 (N), 27 December 1932 – Wilson; Anthony, England; Davies, S. Robinson, Slack; Prior, Broom, Readman (3), Hoyland (3), Bowater (3).

HONOURS

Football League: Division 2 best season: 21st, 1977–78; Division 3 – Champions 1976–77; Promoted to Division 2 (3rd) 2001–02; Division 4 – Champions 1974–75; Division 3 (N) – Runners-up 1950–51.

FA Cup: best season: 6th rd, 1969.

Football League Cup: best season: 5th rd, 1976.

Freight Rover Trophy: Winners 1987.

SKY SPORTS FACT FILE

Jack Hughes, an outstanding goalkeeper with Mansfield Town from 1937, had been capped at Welsh amateur and full level but had suffered a fractured spine with Blackburn Rovers. Forced to retire full-time he was able to continue in non-league football.

Record Cup Victory: 8–0 v Scarborough (a), FA Cup 1st rd, 22 November 1952 – Bramley; Chessell, Bradley; Field, Plummer, Lewis; Scott, Fox (3), Marron (2), Sid Watson (1), Adam (2).

Record Defeat: 1–8 v Walsall, Division 3 (N), 19 January 1933.

Most League Points (2 for a win): 68, Division 4, 1974–75.

Most League Points (3 for a win): 81, Division 4, 1985–86.

Most League Goals: 108, Division 4, 1962–63.

Highest League Scorer in Season: Ted Harston, 55, Division 3 (N), 1936–37.

Most League Goals in Total Aggregate: Harry Johnson, 104, 1931–36.

Most League Goals in One Match: 7, Ted Harston v Hartlepools U, Division 3N, 23 January 1937.

Most Capped Player: John McClelland, 6 (53), Northern Ireland.

Most League Appearances: Rod Arnold, 440, 1970–83.

Youngest League Player: Cyril Poole, 15 years 351 days v New Brighton, 27 February 1937.

Record Transfer Fee Received: £655,000 from Tottenham H for Colin Calderwood, July 1993.

Record Transfer Fee Paid: £150,000 to Carlisle U for Lee Peacock, October 1997; £150,000 to Wolverhampton W for Colin Larkin, July 2002.

Football League Record: 1931 Elected to Division 3 (S); 1932–37 Division 3 (N); 1937–47 Division 3 (S); 1947–58 Division 3 (N); 1958–60 Division 3; 1960–63 Division 4; 1963–72 Division 3; 1972–75 Division 4; 1975–77 Division 3; 1977–78 Division 2; 1978–80 Division 3; 1980–86 Division 4; 1986–91 Division 3; 1991–92 Division 4; 1992–93 Division 2; 1993–2002 Division 3; 2002–03 Division 2; 2003–04 Division 3; 2004– FL 2.

MANAGERS

John Baynes 1922–25
Ted Davison 1926–28
Jack Hickling 1928–33
Henry Martin 1933–35
Charlie Bell 1935
Harold Wightman 1936
Harold Parkes 1936–38
Jack Poole 1938–44
Lloyd Barke 1944–45
Roy Goodall 1945–49
Freddie Steele 1949–51
George Jobey 1952–53
Stan Mercer 1953–55
Charlie Mitten 1956–58
Sam Weaver 1958–60
Raich Carter 1960–63
Tommy Cummings 1963–67
Tommy Eggleston 1967–70
Jock Basford 1970–71
Danny Williams 1971–74
Dave Smith 1974–76
Peter Morris 1976–78
Billy Bingham 1978–79
Mick Jones 1979–81
Stuart Boam 1981–83
Ian Greaves 1983–89
George Foster 1989–93
Andy King 1993–96
Steve Parkin 1996–99
Billy Dearden 1999–2002
Stuart Watkiss 2002
Keith Curle 2002–05
Carlton Palmer 2005
Peter Shirtliff 2005–06
Billy Dearden December 2006–

LATEST SEQUENCES

Longest Sequence of League Wins: 7, 13.9.1991 – 26.10.1991.

Longest Sequence of League Defeats: 7, 18.1.1947 – 15.3.1947.

Longest Sequence of League Draws: 5, 18.10.1986 – 22.11.1986.

Longest Sequence of Unbeaten League Matches: 20, 14.2.1976 – 21.8.1976.

Longest Sequence Without a League Win: 14, 25.3.2000 – 2.9.2000.

Successive Scoring Runs: 27 from 1.10.1962.

Successive Non-scoring Runs: 8 from 25.3.2000.

TEN YEAR LEAGUE RECORD

		P	*W*	*D*	*L*	*F*	*A*	*Pts*	*Pos*
1997-98	Div 3	46	16	17	13	64	55	65	12
1998-99	Div 3	46	19	10	17	60	58	67	8
1999-2000	Div 3	46	16	8	22	50	65	56	17
2000-01	Div 3	46	15	13	18	64	72	68	13
2001-02	Div 3	46	24	7	15	72	60	79	3
2002-03	Div 2	46	12	8	26	66	97	44	23
2003-04	Div 3	46	22	9	15	76	62	75	5
2004-05	FL 2	46	15	15	16	56	56	60	13
2005-06	FL 2	46	13	15	18	59	66	54	16
2006-07	FL 2	46	14	12	20	58	63	54	17

DID YOU KNOW ?

Mansfield Town owed their election to the Third Division in 1931 by deciding to abandon the attempt to join the Northern Section in favour of the Southern. After six unsuccessful tries they were elected only to be switched north after just one season!

MANSFIELD TOWN 2006–07 LEAGUE RECORD

Match No.	Date	Venue	Opponents	Result		H/T Score	Lg. Pos.	Goalscorers	Attendance
1	Aug 5	A	Shrewsbury T	D	2-2	2-2	—	Hamshaw [17], Brown [43]	5066
2	8	H	Milton Keynes D	W	2-1	2-1	—	Barker [29], Boulding M [37]	4033
3	12	H	Stockport Co	D	1-1	0-1	11	Hamshaw [84]	3856
4	18	A	Grimsby T	D	1-1	0-0	—	Hamshaw [51]	4604
5	26	H	Lincoln C	L	2-4	0-3	14	Reet [66], Barker (pen) [90]	4596
6	Sept 1	A	Wycombe W	L	0-1	0-0	—		4754
7	9	H	Hereford U	W	4-1	2-0	12	Mkandawire (og) [20], Barker 2 (1 pen) [38, 72 (p)], Reet [49]	3242
8	12	A	Hartlepool U	L	0-2	0-0	—		3899
9	16	A	Torquay U	L	0-1	0-1	16		2660
10	23	H	Accrington S	D	2-2	0-1	19	Hamshaw [58], Boulding M [81]	3088
11	26	H	Darlington	W	1-0	0-0	—	Reet [59]	2794
12	30	A	Walsall	L	0-4	0-0	17		5420
13	Oct 7	H	Notts Co	D	2-2	2-0	19	Reet 2 [10, 19]	6182
14	14	A	Boston U	D	1-1	0-1	17	Barker (pen) [71]	2314
15	21	H	Wrexham	W	3-0	2-0	15	Barker 2 [21, 36], Reet [69]	2971
16	28	A	Macclesfield T	W	3-2	0-0	11	Coke [65], Barker 2 (1 pen) [83, 90 (p)]	2599
17	Nov 4	A	Bristol R	L	0-1	0-0	14		5044
18	18	H	Peterborough U	L	0-2	0-1	16		3550
19	25	A	Rochdale	L	0-2	0-2	17		2378
20	Dec 5	H	Swindon T	W	2-0	2-0	—	Barker [3], Brown [38]	2274
21	9	H	Bury	L	0-2	0-1	17		2197
22	16	A	Barnet	L	1-2	0-1	18	Barker [84]	1790
23	26	A	Darlington	W	2-0	1-0	19	Barker [5], Arnold [62]	3808
24	Jan 1	H	Hartlepool U	L	0-1	0-0	20		3531
25	13	A	Hereford U	W	3-1	1-0	17	Conlon [10], Boulding M [79], Gritton [90]	3048
26	16	A	Accrington S	L	2-3	2-1	—	Conlon [32], Dawson [43]	1234
27	20	H	Walsall	W	2-1	1-1	17	Conlon [14], Gritton [57]	3737
28	27	A	Chester C	D	1-1	1-0	17	Buxton [32]	2129
29	30	H	Torquay U	W	5-0	2-0	—	Boulding M [14], Gritton 3 (1 pen) [39, 59, 77 (p)], John-Baptiste [64]	2573
30	Feb 3	H	Shrewsbury T	D	1-1	0-1	16	Brown [60]	3250
31	10	A	Stockport Co	L	0-1	0-1	16		5656
32	17	H	Grimsby T	L	1-2	1-1	16	Boulding M [30]	4033
33	20	A	Milton Keynes D	D	1-1	0-0	—	Arnold [90]	5070
34	24	H	Wycombe W	W	3-2	2-2	15	Mullins [21], Gritton [36], D'Laryea [87]	2711
35	Mar 3	A	Lincoln C	W	2-1	1-0	14	Conlon (pen) [15], Arnold [51]	5316
36	6	H	Chester C	W	2-1	1-1	—	Brown [27], John-Baptiste [82]	2366
37	10	A	Notts Co	D	0-0	0-0	11		10,034
38	17	H	Boston U	L	1-2	1-2	12	Conlon [30]	2790
39	23	H	Macclesfield T	L	1-2	0-0	—	Mullins [68]	2414
40	31	A	Wrexham	D	0-0	0-0	14		7752
41	Apr 7	H	Bristol R	L	0-1	0-1	18		2392
42	9	A	Peterborough U	L	0-2	0-0	18		4276
43	14	H	Rochdale	L	1-2	1-1	18	Hjelde [45]	2023
44	21	A	Swindon T	L	0-2	0-2	18		10,472
45	28	H	Barnet	W	2-1	1-0	17	Conlon [45], Brown [66]	2446
46	May 5	A	Bury	D	1-1	1-0	17	John-Baptiste [25]	3532

Final League Position: 17

GOALSCORERS

League (58): Barker 12 (4 pens), Conlon 6 (1 pen), Gritton 6 (1 pen), Reet 6, Boulding M 5, Brown 5, Hamshaw 4, Arnold 3, John-Baptiste 3, Mullins 2, Buxton 1, Coke 1, D'Laryea 1, Dawson 1, Hjelde 1, own goal 1.
Carling Cup (3): Barker 1, Boulding M 1, Reet 1.
FA Cup (2): Barker 2 (2 pens).
J Paint Trophy (3): Beardsley 2, own goal 1.

Muggleton C 16	Mullins J 39 + 4	Jelleyman G 39 + 1	Coke G 15 + 6	Hjelde J 25 + 3	John-Baptiste A 46	Hamshaw M 38 + 2	D'Laryea J 37	Barker R 24	Brown S 30 + 4	Boulding M 25 + 14	Dawson S 32 + 2	Birchall A 1 + 4	Lloyd C 6 + 13	Buxton J 27 + 3	Beardsley C 3 + 7	Reet D 8 + 13	White J 30	Sheehan A 9 + 1	Arnold N 6 + 16	Charlton A 3 + 1	Conlon B 16 + 1	Gritton M 14 + 5	Boulding R — + 9	Hodge B 9	Sleath D 3 + 4	Kitchen A 4	Wood C 1	McGhee J — + 2	Trimmer L — + 1	*Match No.*
1	2	3	4¹	5	6	7	8	9	10²	11	12	13																		1
1	2	3		5	6	7	8	9	10	11¹	4²	12	13																	2
1	2	3		5²	6	7	8	9	10³	11¹	4	12		13	14															3
1	2	3			6	7	8	9	10²	11¹	4	12		5		13														4
1	2	3			6	7¹	8²	9	10	11	4		13	5		12														5
1	2	3			6	7	8	9	10	11¹	4²		13	5		12														6
	2¹		12		6	7	8	9²	10³	11	4			5	13	14	1	3												7
	2		12		6	7	8	9²		11³	4¹	10		5	13	14	1	3												8
	2	12	4²		6	7	8	9		11¹	13			5	14	10³	1	3												9
	2²	3	4¹		6	7	8	9		12	11			5	10³	14	1	13												10
	12	3	13	4	6	7³	8	9			11²		14	5		10	1	2¹												11
		3	10	4	6	7	8	9					11¹	5		12	1	2²	13											12
		3	12	4	6	7■	8	9			11			5		10	1	2¹												13
1	2	3	12	4	6		8	9			11			5²		10		7¹	13											14
1	2	3	12	5	6	7³	8	9			4¹				13	10²		11	14											15
1	2	11¹	4	5	6	7	8	9		12					13	10²		3												16
1	2	3	4³	5	6	7²	8	9		12	11		14	13		10¹														17
1	2	3	4	5	6	7²	8	9	13	12					10³	14				11¹										18
1	2	3	4²	5	6	7³	8	9	12	11			14	13		10¹														19
1	12	3	4	5	6	7¹	8²	9	10	11³			13	2					14											20
1	12	3	4¹	5	6	7	8³	9	10²	11			14	2		13														21
	2	3	4²	5	6	7	8	9	11				13		10¹	12	1													22
	2	3	4¹		6	7³	8	9	10	11²			12	5	13		1		14											23
	2	3	4		6	7	8	9	10	11¹				5			1		12											24
	2	3	4²		6	7	8			12	11		13	5			1				10¹	9								25
	2	3¹	4²	12	6	7	8		13	14	11			5			1				10	9³								26
	2³	3		12	6¹	7²	8		4	13	11		14	5			1				10	9								27
		3		5	6	7	8		4¹	12	11		13	2			1				10■	9²								28
	12	3		5	6¹	7	8		4²	10	11			2			1		13			9³	14							29
	2	3		5¹	6	7	8		4	10	11						1					9	12							30
	2	3			6	7	8¹		4²	10	11			5			1		12			9	13							31
	2	3			6	7	8		12	11¹	4			5		13	1				10	9²								32
	2	3			6		8		7	11¹	4			5			1		12		10	9²	13							33
	2	3			6		8		11		4			5		12	1		13		10²	9¹		7						34
	2¹	3		12	6	13	8		9	14	11			5			1		7²		10³			4						35
	2	3		5	6	12	8		9	13	11						1		7¹		10³	14		4²						36
	2	3			6	7	8³		10¹	12	11²			5		14	1		13			9		4						37
	2	3³			6	7			8¹	12	11			5			1		13		10	9²		4	14					38
	2	3		5³	6	7			9	12	11						1		8¹		10	13	14		4²					39
	2	3		5²	6	7			10	11¹	8³						1		12	13		9		4	14					40
	2	3			6	7			10¹	12							1		11	5	13	9³	14	4	8²					41
	2	3			6	7			9¹	11			8²				1		12	5³	10	13	14	4						42
1	2			5	6	7¹				9	11²		8³						12		10	13	14	4		3				43
	2			5	6				8	9²			11				1		12		10³		13		7	3	4¹	14		44
	2			5	6				8	9	7		11²				1		4¹		10	12			13	3				45
1	2			5	6				8²	9	11¹		7						4		10³				12	3		13	14	46

FA Cup

First Round	Accrington S	(h)	1-0
Second Round	Doncaster R	(h)	1-1
		(a)	0-2

Carling Cup

First Round	Huddersfield T	(a)	2-0
Second Round	Portsmouth	(h)	1-2

J Paint Trophy

Second Round	Grimsby T	(h)	3-0
Quarter-Final	Darlington	(a)	0-1

MIDDLESBROUGH

FA Premiership

FOUNDATION

A previous belief that Middlesbrough Football Club was founded at a tripe supper at the Corporation Hotel has proved to be erroneous. In fact, members of Middlesbrough Cricket Club were responsible for forming it at a meeting in the gymnasium of the Albert Park Hotel in 1875.

Riverside Stadium, Middlesbrough TS3 6RS.

Telephone: 0844 499 6789.

Fax: (01642) 757 690.

Ticket Office: 0844 499 1234.

Website: www.mfc.co.uk

Email: enquiries@mfc.co.uk

Ground Capacity: 35,041.

Record Attendance: Ayresome Park: 53,536 v Newcastle U, Division 1, 27 December 1949. Riverside Stadium: 34,814 v Newcastle U, FA Premier League, 5 March 2003.

Pitch Measurements: 105m × 68m.

Chairman: Steve Gibson.

Chief Executive: Keith Lamb.

Secretary: Karen Nelson.

Manager: Gareth Southgate.

Assistant Manager: Malcolm Crosby.

Physios: Grant Downie, Chris Moseley

Colours: Red shirts with white trim, red shorts, red stockings.

Change Colours: White shirts with gold trim, gold shorts, gold stockings.

Year Formed: 1876; re-formed 1986.

Turned Professional: 1889; became amateur 1892, and professional again, 1899.

Ltd Co: 1892.

Club Nickname: 'Boro'.

Grounds: 1877, Old Archery Ground, Albert Park; 1879, Breckon Hill; 1882, Linthorpe Road Ground; 1903, Ayresome Park; 1995, Riverside Stadium.

First Football League Game: 2 September 1899, Division 2, v Lincoln C (a) L 0–3 – Smith; Shaw, Ramsey; Allport, McNally, McCracken; Wanless, Longstaffe, Gettins, Page, Pugh.

Record League Victory: 9–0 v Brighton & HA, Division 2, 23 August 1958 – Taylor; Bilcliff, Robinson; Harris (2p), Phillips, Walley; Day, McLean, Clough (5), Peacock (2), Holliday.

Record Cup Victory: 7–0 v Hereford U, Coca-Cola Cup 2nd rd, 1st leg, 18 September 1996 – Miller; Fleming (1), Branco (1), Whyte, Vickers, Whelan, Emerson (1), Mustoe, Stamp, Juninho, Ravanelli (4).

HONOURS

Football League: Division 1 – Champions 1994–95; Runners-up 1997–98; Division 2 – Champions 1926–27, 1928–29, 1973–74; Runners-up 1901–02, 1991–92; Division 3 – Runners-up 1966–67, 1986–87.

FA Cup: Runners-up 1997.

Football League Cup: Winners 2004; Runners-up 1997, 1998.

Amateur Cup: Winners 1895, 1898.

Anglo-Scottish Cup: Winners 1976.

Zenith Data Systems Cup: Runners-up 1990.

European Competitions: *UEFA Cup:* 2004–05, 2005–06 (runners-up).

SKY SPORTS FACT FILE

On 23 March 1974 Middlesbrough beat Oxford United 1–0 at Ayresome Park to clinch promotion to the First Division. It was the quickest elevation in Football League history as they still had five matches to play. Their winning margin was 15 points.

Record Defeat: 0–9 v Blackburn R, Division 2, 6 November 1954.

Most League Points (2 for a win): 65, Division 2, 1973–74.

Most League Points (3 for a win): 94, Division 3, 1986–87.

Most League Goals: 122, Division 2, 1926–27.

Highest League Scorer in Season: George Camsell, 59, Division 2, 1926–27 (Second Division record).

Most League Goals in Total Aggregate: George Camsell, 325, 1925–39.

Most League Goals in One Match: 5, John Wilkie v Gainsborough T, Division 2, 2 March 1901; 5, Andy Wilson v Nottingham F, Division 1, 6 October 1923; 5, George Camsell v Manchester C, Division 2, 25 December 1926; 5, George Camsell v Aston Villa, Division 1, 9 September 1935; 5, Brian Clough v Brighton & HA, Division 2, 22 August 1958.

Most Capped Player: Wilf Mannion, 26, England.

Most League Appearances: Tim Williamson, 563, 1902–23.

Youngest League Player: Stephen Bell, 16 years 323 days v Southampton, 30 January 1982; Sam Lawrie, 16 years 323 days v Arsenal, 3 November 1951.

Record Transfer Fee Received: £12,000,000 from Atletico Madrid for Juninho, July 1997.

Record Transfer Fee Paid: £8,150,000 to Empoli for Massimo Maccarone, August 2002.

Football League Record: 1899 Elected to Division 2; 1902–24 Division 1; 1924–27 Division 2; 1927–28 Division 1; 1928–29 Division 2; 1929–54 Division 1; 1954–66 Division 2; 1966–67 Division 3; 1967–74 Division 2; 1974–82 Division 1; 1982–86 Division 2; 1986–87 Division 3; 1987–88 Division 2; 1988–89 Division 1; 1989–92 Division 2; 1992–93 FA Premier League; 1993–95 Division 1; 1995–97 FA Premier League; 1997–98 Division 1; 1998– FA Premier League.

MANAGERS

John Robson 1899–1905
Alex Mackie 1905–06
Andy Aitken 1906–09
J. Gunter 1908–10
(Secretary-Manager)
Andy Walker 1910–11
Tom McIntosh 1911–19
Jimmy Howie 1920–23
Herbert Bamlett 1923–26
Peter McWilliam 1927–34
Wilf Gillow 1934–44
David Jack 1944–52
Walter Rowley 1952–54
Bob Dennison 1954–63
Raich Carter 1963–66
Stan Anderson 1966–73
Jack Charlton 1973–77
John Neal 1977–81
Bobby Murdoch 1981–82
Malcolm Allison 1982–84
Willie Maddren 1984–86
Bruce Rioch 1986–90
Colin Todd 1990–91
Lennie Lawrence 1991–94
Bryan Robson 1994–2001
Steve McClaren 2001–06
Gareth Southgate June 2006–

LATEST SEQUENCES

Longest Sequence of League Wins: 9, 16.2.1974 – 6.4.1974.

Longest Sequence of League Defeats: 8, 26.12.1995 – 17.2.1996.

Longest Sequence of League Draws: 8, 3.4.1971 – 1.5.1971.

Longest Sequence of Unbeaten League Matches: 24, 8.9.1973 – 19.1.1974.

Longest Sequence Without a League Win: 19, 3.10.1981 – 6.3.1982.

Successive Scoring Runs: 26 from 21.9.1946.

Successive Non-scoring Runs: 4 from 24.11.1923.

TEN YEAR LEAGUE RECORD

		P	W	D	L	F	A	Pts	Pos
1997-98	Div 1	46	27	10	9	77	41	91	2
1998-99	PR Lge	38	12	15	11	48	54	51	9
1999-2000	PR Lge	38	14	10	14	46	52	52	12
2000-01	PR Lge	38	9	15	14	44	44	42	14
2001-02	PR Lge	38	12	9	17	35	47	45	12
2002-03	PR Lge	38	13	10	15	48	44	49	11
2003-04	PR Lge	38	13	9	16	44	52	48	11
2004-05	PR Lge	38	14	13	11	53	46	55	7
2005-06	PR Lge	38	12	9	17	48	58	45	14
2006-07	PR Lge	38	12	10	16	44	49	46	12

DID YOU KNOW ?

Middlesbrough managed to avoid being drawn against non-league opposition in the FA Cup from 1915 until January 1974 when they were drawn away against Grantham Town, then of the Southern League in a first round tie. No banana skin – Boro won 2–0.

MIDDLESBROUGH 2006–07 LEAGUE RECORD

Match No.	Date	Venue	Opponents	Result		H/T Score	Lg. Pos.	Goalscorers	Attendance
1	Aug 19	A	Reading	L	2-3	2-2	—	Downing [11], Yakubu [21]	23,855
2	23	H	Chelsea	W	2-1	0-1	—	Pogatetz [80], Viduka [90]	29,198
3	28	H	Portsmouth	L	0-4	0-1	—		24,834
4	Sept 9	A	Arsenal	D	1-1	1-0	11	Morrison [22]	60,007
5	16	A	Bolton W	D	0-0	0-0	13		21,164
6	23	H	Blackburn R	L	0-1	0-1	16		24,959
7	30	A	Sheffield U	L	1-2	0-1	17	Yakubu [49]	27,483
8	Oct 14	H	Everton	W	2-1	1-0	13	Yakubu (pen) [27], Viduka [71]	27,156
9	22	H	Newcastle U	W	1-0	0-0	12	Yakubu [85]	30,060
10	30	A	Manchester C	L	0-1	0-1	—		36,720
11	Nov 4	A	Watford	L	0-2	0-1	16		18,951
12	11	H	West Ham U	W	1-0	0-0	13	Maccarone [74]	25,898
13	18	H	Liverpool	D	0-0	0-0	14		31,424
14	25	A	Aston Villa	D	1-1	1-1	13	Christie [43]	33,162
15	Dec 2	H	Manchester U	L	1-2	0-1	15	Morrison [66]	31,238
16	5	A	Tottenham H	L	1-2	0-0	—	Huth [80]	34,154
17	9	H	Wigan Ath	D	1-1	0-1	15	Yakubu [67]	23,638
18	18	A	Fulham	L	1-2	0-2	—	Viduka [74]	17,000
19	23	H	Charlton Ath	W	2-0	1-0	14	Yakubu [29], Arca [52]	32,013
20	26	A	Everton	D	0-0	0-0	16		38,126
21	30	A	Blackburn R	L	1-2	0-1	17	Yakubu (pen) [61]	22,653
22	Jan 1	H	Sheffield U	W	3-1	1-1	15	Viduka [36], Yakubu 2 (1 pen) [69, 76 (p)]	27,963
23	13	A	Charlton Ath	W	3-1	1-1	14	Cattermole [45], Arca [63], Yakubu [68]	26,384
24	20	H	Bolton W	W	5-1	4-1	11	Speed (og) [6], Xavier [10], Viduka 2 [23, 84], Downing [43]	24,614
25	30	A	Portsmouth	D	0-0	0-0	—		19,820
26	Feb 3	H	Arsenal	D	1-1	0-0	12	Yakubu (pen) [63]	31,122
27	10	A	Chelsea	L	0-3	0-1	12		41,699
28	24	H	Reading	W	2-1	1-0	12	Viduka [7], Yakubu [69]	26,412
29	Mar 3	A	Newcastle U	D	0-0	0-0	12		52,303
30	17	H	Manchester C	L	0-2	0-0	12		26,427
31	31	A	West Ham U	L	0-2	0-2	12		34,977
32	Apr 7	H	Watford	W	4-1	2-1	12	Viduka 2 [5, 75], Boateng [27], Rochemback [79]	25,534
33	14	H	Aston Villa	L	1-3	1-1	14	Rochemback [13]	26,959
34	18	A	Liverpool	L	0-2	0-0	—		41,458
35	21	A	Manchester U	D	1-1	1-1	14	Viduka [45]	75,967
36	28	H	Tottenham H	L	2-3	0-1	14	Viduka [66], Pogatetz [89]	27,861
37	May 5	A	Wigan Ath	W	1-0	1-0	12	Viduka [29]	21,204
38	13	H	Fulham	W	3-1	2-1	12	Viduka 2 [34, 47], Wheater [45]	29,556

Final League Position: 12

GOALSCORERS

League (44): Viduka 14, Yakubu 12 (4 pens), Arca 2, Downing 2, Morrison 2, Pogatetz 2, Rochemback 2, Boateng 1, Cattermole 1, Christie 1, Huth 1, Maccarone 1, Wheater 1, Xavier 1, own goal 1.
Carling Cup (0).
FA Cup (14): Viduka 5, Yakubu 4 (2 pens), Arca 1, Boateng 1, Cattermole 1, Christie 1, Hines 1.

Schwarzer M 36	Parnaby S 9 + 9	Arca J 18 + 3	Riggott C 5 + 1	Pogatetz E 35	Boateng G 35	Morrison J 15 + 13	Rochemback F 17 + 3	Yakubu A 36 + 1	Viduka M 22 + 7	Downing S 34	Davies A 21 + 2	Johnson A 3 + 9	Mendieta G 4 + 3	Cattermole L 22 + 9	Taylor A 34	Christie M 4 + 9	Woodgate J 30	Euell J 9 + 8	Huth R 8 + 4	Maccarone M 1 + 6	Bates M — + 1	Graham D — + 1	Xavier A 14	Wheater D 1 + 1	Jones B 2	Lee D 3 + 6	Match No.
1	2	3¹	4	5	6	7²	8³	9	10	11	12	13	14														1
1	2		4	5	6		8	9	12	11	7²		10¹	13	3												2
1	2		4	5	6	12	13	9	10³	11			7²	8¹	3	14											3
1	12			5	6■	7¹	10	9²	13	11³	2			14	3		4	8									4
1	12			5		7¹	11	9			2	10²	13	6	3		4	8									5
1	7			5		11¹	8	9	12		2³	14	10²	13	3		4	6									6
1				5		7¹	8	9	10	11	2		12	6	3		4										7
1	12	13		5	6			9	10	11²	2			7¹	3			8	4								8
1				5	6		12	9	10¹	11	2			7	3²		4	8³	13	14							9
1	2³			3	6	12	10²	9		11				8¹			4	7	5	13	14						10
1		3¹		2	6	12		9		11	7			13			4	8²	5	10³		14					11
1				5	6	7	10¹	9		11²	2			8	3		4		13	12							12
1		11		5	6¹	7²	10	9			2³			12	3		4	8	14	13							13
1		11		2	6	7¹		9						12	8	10²	4		5	13			3				14
1	12			2	6	13		9		11				8	7	10³	4²		5	14			3¹				15
1		12		3	6■	13		9	14	11				8³	7¹	10²	4		5				2				16
1	12	3		5¹	6	7		9	10	11					8		4						2				17
1	2³	3¹	4		6	7²		9	10	11	5	13		12	8									14			18
1	12	7		5	6	8¹		9	10²	11	2				3	13	4										19
1	12	7		5	6			9	13	11	2		10²	8¹	3		4										20
1				5	6³	7¹		9	10	11	2²	12		8	3	13	4	14									21
1	12	7²		5	6	13		9	10	11				8	3		4¹						2				22
1		7		5	6¹	12		9³	10²	11				8	3	14	4	13					2				23
1		7		5	6	12		9³	10	11²				8¹	3	14	4	13					2				24
		10		5	6	7¹		9²		11				8	3	12	4	13					2		1		25
		7		5	6	12		9	10²	11				8¹	3	13	4						2		1		26
1		7³		5	6	8²	14	9	10¹	11	2				3	12		13					4				27
1		7		5	6	12		9²	10	11	2			8¹	3		4									13	28
1	2	7²		5	6	12		9³	10	11				8¹	3		4	13								14	29
1	2			5²	6	14		9	12	11	13			8	3			7¹					4			10³	30
1	7³			5²	6		8¹	9	10	11		14			3		4	12	13				2				31
1	12		4		6		8	9²	10³	11		7			3¹	13			5				2			14	32
1			12		6³		8	9		11		7²		13	3	10	4		5¹				2			14	33
1				5	6	7¹	10	9	12	11	2	13		8²	3		4										34
1				5	6		7	9¹	10	11	2			8	3		4									12	35
1		12		5	6		7	9³	10	11	2¹	13		8²	3		4									14	36
1		7		5	6²		8		10¹	11	2	14		13	3		4	12								9³	37
1		7		3	6²	13	8	12	10³	11	2	14					4							5		9¹	38

FA Cup

Third Round	Hull C	(a)	1-1
		(h)	4-3
Fourth Round	Bristol C	(a)	2-2
		(h)	2-2
Fifth Round	WBA	(h)	2-2
		(a)	1-1
Sixth Round	Manchester U	(h)	2-2
		(a)	0-1

Carling Cup

Second Round	Notts Co	(h)	0-1

MILLWALL FL Championship 1

FOUNDATION

Formed in 1885 as Millwall Rovers by employees of Morton & Co, a jam and marmalade factory in West Ferry Road. The founders were predominantly Scotsmen. Their first headquarters was The Islanders pub in Tooke Street, Millwall. Their first trophy was the East End Cup in 1887.

The Den, Zampa Road, London SE16 3LN.

Telephone: (020) 7232 1222.

Fax: (020) 7231 3663.

Ticket Office: (020) 7231 9999.

Website: www.millwallfc.co.uk

Email: questions@millwallplc.com

Ground Capacity: 20,146.

Record Attendance: 20,093 v Arsenal, FA Cup 3rd rd, 10 January 1994.

Pitch Measurements: 105m × 68m.

Chairman: Stewart Till.

Executive Vice-chairman: Heather Rabbatts.

Chief Executive: Andy Ambler.

Secretary: Yvonne Haines.

Manager: Willie Donachie.

Assistant Manager: Pat Holland.

Physio: Terry Standring.

Colours: Blue shirts, white shorts, blue stockings.

Change Colours: All white.

HONOURS

Football League: Division 1 best season: 3rd, 1993–94; Division 2 – Champions 1987–88, 2000–01; Division 3 (S) – Champions 1927–28, 1937–38; Runners-up 1952–53; Division 3 – Runners–up 1965–66, 1984–85; Division 4 – Champions 1961–62; Runners-up 1964–65.

FA Cup: Runners-up 2004; Semi-final 1900, 1903, 1937 (first Division 3 side to reach semi-final).

Football League Cup: best season: 5th rd, 1974, 1977, 1995.

Football League Trophy: Winners 1983.

Auto Windscreens Shield: Runners-up 1999.

European Competitions: *UEFA Cup:* 2004–05.

Year Formed: 1885. ***Turned Professional:*** 1893. ***Ltd Co.:*** 1894.

Previous Names: 1885, Millwall Rovers; 1889, Millwall Athletic; 1899, Millwall; 1985, Millwall Football & Athletic Company.

Club Nickname: 'The Lions'.

Grounds: 1885, Glengall Road, Millwall; 1886, Back of 'Lord Nelson'; 1890, East Ferry Road; 1901, North Greenwich; 1910, The Den, Cold Blow Lane; 1993, The Den, Bermondsey.

First Football League Game: 28 August 1920, Division 3, v Bristol R (h) W 2–0 – Lansdale; Fort, Hodge; Voisey (1), Riddell, McAlpine; Waterall, Travers, Broad (1), Sutherland, Dempsey.

Record League Victory: 9–1 v Torquay U, Division 3 (S), 29 August 1927 – Lansdale, Tilling, Hill, Amos, Bryant (3), Graham, Chance, Hawkins (3), Landells (1), Phillips (2), Black. 9–1 v Coventry C, Division 3 (S), 19 November 1927 – Lansdale, Fort, Hill, Amos, Collins (1), Graham, Chance, Landells (4), Cock (2), Phillips (2), Black.

Record Cup Victory: 7–0 v Gateshead, FA Cup 2nd rd, 12 December 1936 – Yuill; Ted Smith, Inns; Brolly, Hancock, Forsyth; Thomas (1), Mangnall (1), Ken Burditt (2), McCartney (2), Thorogood (1).

SKY SPORTS FACT FILE

From 27 February to 10 April 1926 Millwall kept 11 consecutive clean sheets in Division Three (South), winning nine of the games. They conceded only 39 goals in 42 League matches and overall kept the opposition out 18 times. They finished third.

Record Defeat: 1–9 v Aston Villa, FA Cup 4th rd, 28 January 1946.

Most League Points (2 for a win): 65, Division 3 (S), 1927–28 and Division 3, 1965–66.

Most League Points (3 for a win): 93, Division 2, 2000–01.

Most League Goals: 127, Division 3 (S), 1927–28.

Highest League Scorer in Season: Richard Parker, 37, Division 3 (S), 1926–27.

Most League Goals in Total Aggregate: Neil Harris, 98, 1995–2004; 2006–07.

Most League Goals in One Match: 5, Richard Parker v Norwich C, Division 3S, 28 August 1926.

Most Capped Player: Eamonn Dunphy, 22 (23), Republic of Ireland.

Most League Appearances: Barry Kitchener, 523, 1967–82.

Youngest League Player: Moses Ashikodi, 15 years 240 days v Brighton & HA, 22 February 2003.

Record Transfer Fee Received: £2,300,000 from Liverpool for Mark Kennedy, March 1995.

Record Transfer Fee Paid: £800,000 to Derby Co for Paul Goddard, December 1989.

Football League Record: 1920 Original Members of Division 3; 1921 Division 3 (S); 1928–34 Division 2; 1934–38 Division 3 (S); 1938–48 Division 2; 1948–58 Division 3 (S); 1958–62 Division 4; 1962–64 Division 3; 1964–65 Division 4; 1965–66 Division 3; 1966–75 Division 2; 1975–76 Division 3; 1976–79 Division 2; 1979–85 Division 3; 1985–88 Division 2; 1988–90 Division 1; 1990–92 Division 2; 1992–96 Division 1; 1996–2001 Division 2; 2001–04 Division 1; 2004–06 FL C; 2006– FL 1.

LATEST SEQUENCES

Longest Sequence of League Wins: 10, 10.3.1928 – 25.4.1928.

Longest Sequence of League Defeats: 11, 10.4.1929 – 16.9.1929.

Longest Sequence of League Draws: 5, 22.12.1973 – 12.1.1974.

Longest Sequence of Unbeaten League Matches: 19, 22.8.1959 – 31.10.1959.

Longest Sequence Without a League Win: 20, 26.12.1989 – 5.5.1990.

Successive Scoring Runs: 22 from 8.12.1923.

Successive Non-scoring Runs: 6 from 20.12.1947.

MANAGERS

F. B. Kidd 1894–99
(Hon. Treasurer/Manager)
E. R. Stopher 1899–1900
(Hon. Treasurer/Manager)
George Saunders 1900–11
(Hon. Treasurer/Manager)
Herbert Lipsham 1911–19
Robert Hunter 1919–33
Bill McCracken 1933–36
Charlie Hewitt 1936–40
Bill Voisey 1940–44
Jack Cock 1944–48
Charlie Hewitt 1948–56
Ron Gray 1956–57
Jimmy Seed 1958–59
Reg Smith 1959–61
Ron Gray 1961–63
Billy Gray 1963–66
Benny Fenton 1966–74
Gordon Jago 1974–77
George Petchey 1978–80
Peter Anderson 1980–82
George Graham 1982–86
John Docherty 1986–90
Bob Pearson 1990
Bruce Rioch 1990–92
Mick McCarthy 1992–96
Jimmy Nicholl 1996–97
John Docherty 1997
Billy Bonds 1997–98
Keith Stevens May 1998–2000
(then Joint Manager)
(*plus* Alan McLeary 1999–2000)
Mark McGhee 2000–03
Dennis Wise 2003–05
Steve Claridge 2005
Colin Lee 2005–06
Nigel Spackman 2006
Willie Donachie November 2006–

TEN YEAR LEAGUE RECORD

		P	*W*	*D*	*L*	*F*	*A*	*Pts*	*Pos*
1997-98	Div 2	46	14	13	19	43	54	55	18
1998-99	Div 2	46	17	11	18	52	59	62	10
1999-2000	Div 2	46	23	13	10	76	50	82	5
2000-01	Div 2	46	28	9	9	89	38	93	1
2001-02	Div 1	46	22	11	13	69	48	77	4
2002-03	Div 1	46	19	9	18	59	69	66	9
2003-04	Div 1	46	18	15	13	55	48	69	10
2004-05	FL C	46	18	12	16	51	45	66	10
2005-06	FL C	46	8	17	21	35	61	40	23
2006-07	FL 1	46	19	9	18	59	62	66	10

DID YOU KNOW ?

Former Stockport County winger Johnny Johnson had his career seriously threatened by kidney problems in 1948, but he made a splendid recovery and went on to complete more than 300 League appearances in two spells with the Lions.

MILLWALL 2006–07 LEAGUE RECORD

Match No.	Date	Venue	Opponents	Result	H/T Score	Lg. Pos.	Goalscorers	Attendance
1	Aug 5	H	Yeovil T	D 1-1	0-1	—	Byfield [82]	10,012
2	8	A	Leyton Orient	L 0-2	0-1	—		6142
3	12	A	Chesterfield	L 1-5	0-3	22	Braniff [72]	4136
4	19	H	Oldham Ath	W 1-0	0-0	17	Hubertz [79]	7455
5	26	A	Cheltenham T	L 2-3	2-1	21	McInnes [24], Williams [45]	4386
6	Sept 2	H	Blackpool	D 0-0	0-0	21		7692
7	9	H	Brighton & HA	L 0-1	0-0	23		9372
8	12	A	Gillingham	L 1-2	0-1	—	Hubertz [88]	7934
9	16	A	Crewe Alex	L 0-1	0-0	23		4875
10	23	H	Northampton T	L 0-1	0-1	23		7432
11	26	H	Brentford	D 1-1	1-1	—	Dunne [26]	7618
12	30	A	Rotherham U	W 3-2	1-2	22	Haynes 2 (1 pen) [45 (p), 86], Dunne [90]	4977
13	Oct 7	A	Carlisle U	W 2-1	2-1	22	Dunne [27], Hubertz [39]	8413
14	14	H	Bournemouth	W 1-0	1-0	21	Hackett [45]	9838
15	22	A	Swansea C	L 0-2	0-1	21		13,975
16	28	H	Port Vale	D 1-1	1-0	22	Zebroski [20]	10,189
17	Nov 3	A	Tranmere R	L 1-3	1-2	—	Hackett [41]	7114
18	18	H	Doncaster R	D 2-2	1-1	20	Byfield [40], Hackett [59]	8670
19	25	A	Nottingham F	L 1-3	1-0	22	May [4]	19,410
20	Dec 5	H	Huddersfield T	D 0-0	0-0	—		6251
21	9	H	Bradford C	W 2-0	2-0	20	Morais [6], Byfield (pen) [33]	7588
22	16	A	Bristol C	L 0-1	0-1	23		12,067
23	22	H	Scunthorpe U	L 0-1	0-0	—		7192
24	26	A	Brentford	W 4-1	1-0	20	Hubertz 2 [1, 57], Robinson [62], Byfield (pen) [83]	6925
25	Jan 1	H	Gillingham	W 4-1	1-1	19	Zebroski [38], Byfield 3 (1 pen) [50 (p), 79, 85]	10,055
26	13	A	Brighton & HA	W 1-0	1-0	19	Byfield [22]	6226
27	20	H	Rotherham U	W 4-0	3-0	18	Harris [16], Zebroski [26], Byfield 2 [39, 90]	9534
28	23	A	Northampton T	L 0-3	0-0	—		5834
29	27	A	Scunthorpe U	L 0-3	0-0	19		5001
30	Feb 3	A	Yeovil T	W 1-0	1-0	17	May [12]	5810
31	10	H	Chesterfield	W 2-1	1-0	14	Byfield [10], Hubertz [85]	9711
32	17	A	Oldham Ath	W 2-1	0-0	12	Williams [61], Byfield (pen) [82]	6181
33	20	H	Leyton Orient	L 2-5	0-3	—	Alexander (og) [66], Hubertz [69]	10,356
34	24	A	Blackpool	W 1-0	1-0	14	Brammer [29]	6547
35	Mar 3	H	Cheltenham T	W 2-0	2-0	12	Byfield [33], Brighton [42]	10,261
36	10	H	Carlisle U	W 2-0	0-0	11	Harris 2 [52, 82]	10,415
37	13	H	Crewe Alex	D 2-2	1-1	—	Byfield [44], Hubertz [90]	8867
38	17	A	Bournemouth	L 0-1	0-1	11		7194
39	24	A	Port Vale	L 0-2	0-1	13		3973
40	31	H	Swansea C	W 2-0	1-0	11	Robinson [31], Harris (pen) [70]	9248
41	Apr 7	H	Nottingham F	W 1-0	0-0	11	Harris [53]	12,035
42	9	A	Doncaster R	W 2-1	1-1	10	Williams [38], Hubertz [83]	7870
43	14	H	Tranmere R	D 2-2	0-1	10	Dunne 2 [49, 67]	10,036
44	21	A	Huddersfield T	L 2-4	1-1	11	Byfield [9], Dunne [90]	9406
45	28	H	Bristol C	W 1-0	0-0	9	Robinson [78]	12,547
46	May 5	A	Bradford C	D 2-2	0-1	10	Byfield [46], Craig [71]	7134

Final League Position: 10

GOALSCORERS

League (59): Byfield 16 (4 pens), Hubertz 9, Dunne 6, Harris 5 (1 pen), Hackett 3, Robinson 3, Williams 3, Zebroski 3, Haynes 2 (1 pen), May 2, Brammer 1, Braniff 1, Brighton 1, Craig 1, McInnes 1, Morais 1, own goal 1.
Carling Cup (2): Braniff 1, Hubertz 1.
FA Cup (3): Dunne 1, May 1, own goal 1.
J Paint Trophy (3): Hackett 1, May 1, Robinson 1.

Pidgeley L 42	Ross M 14 + 1	Craig T 30	Elliott M 40 + 2	Shaw R 41	Whitbread Z 13 + 1	Williams M 19 + 10	McInnes D 7 + 6	Brighton T 13 + 3	Byfield D 28 + 3	Morais F 8 + 4	Ardley N 15 + 5	Hackett C 21 + 12	Hubertz P 14 + 20	Phillips M 8 + 4	Braniff K 5 + 2	Robinson P 37 + 1	Day C 4 + 1	Senda D 34 + 2	Dunne A 29 + 3	Trotter L 1 + 1	Fuseini A 5 + 2	Zebroski C 10 + 15	Bakayogo Z 3 + 2	Grant G 1 + 3	Haynes D 5	Mawene S 4	May B 7 + 6	Lee C 4 + 1	Harris N 21	Morris J 1 + 3	Brammer D 17	Smith R 5 + 1	Match No.
1	2	3^1	4^2	5	6	7	8	9	10	11^3	12	13	14																				1
1	2	3■	4	5	6	8^2	11^1	9	10^3	13	7	12	14																				2
1		3^2	4	5	6^3	10	8	9		11		7^1	12	2	13	14																	3
1	2		4	3	6	10	8	9		12	11^1		13		7^2	5																	4
1■	2		4	3	6	10^1	8			11^6	13	7^2	12		9	5	15																5
			4^2	3	6	10	8			11^1	7^3		12		9	5	1	2	13	14													6
			4	3	6	10	8		12	11	7^1		13		9^2	5	1	2															7
	12		4	3	6^1	13			10				14			5	1	2	7		8	9^3	11^2										8
	2		4^2	3	6	11							9		12	5	1		7		8	10^1	13										9
1	2		4	3	6^3								12		9^1	5		14	7		8	10	11^2	13									10
1	2	3	4	6		11^3	12						9			5			7		8^1	13		14	10^2								11
1	2^1	3	4	6		11^2	12					14	9			5			7		8^3	13			10								12
1	6	3	4	5			13					8	9^3	12				2^1	7			14			10	11^2							13
1	5	3	4	6			12					11^1	9^3	13				2^2	7			14			10	8							14
1	5	3^1	4	6			13					7	9	12				2^3		11		14			10	8^2							15
1	2^3	3	4	5		11^2	12		13			7	9	6				14				10				8^1							16
1			4	6	12	11^2				13		7	9^3			5		2				10	3^1	8			14						17
1			4		3	12			10			11	13			5		2	7			9^1					8^2	6					18
1			4		3				10			11	12	6		5^1		2	7				13				9	8^2					19
1	3			6					10	12		11		13		5		2	7			8^1					9	4^2					20
1			4	6	3				10	8^1		11				5		2	7			12					9						21
1			4						10	8^1		11	13	3		5		2	7			12		14			9^2	6^3					22
1			4	6					10	8^2	7^1	11	9			5		2	3		12	13											23
1			4^3	6		12			10		7^2	11	9			5		2	3		13	8^1						14					24
1	3		4	6		8			10		7	11^1	9^2			5			2			12					13						25
1		3	4	6					10^2		7	11^1				5		2	8			12					13		9				26
1		3		6		11^1		12	10		7^3					5		2	4			8^2					13		9	14			27
1		3	4^3	6		11^2		12	10							5		2	7■			8^1					13		9	14			28
1		3	4	6		12		11^1			7					5		2				13					10		9	8^2			29
1		3	4					12	10		7			6		5		2				13					11^2		9^1		8		30
1		3	4			11^1		7	10^3			12	13	6		5		2											9^2	14	8		31
1		3	4	5		12		11^1	10			13	14	6				2	7^2										9^3		8		32
1		3^3	4	5		7		11^1	10			12	13	6				2				14							9^2		8		33
1		3	4	6		12		11^2	10^1		7					5		2				13							9		8		34
1		3	4	6				11^3	10		7^1	13				5		2	12			14							9		8^2		35
1		3	4	6				11	10		7^2	12				5		2	13										9		8^1		36
1		3	4	6				11^1	10			12	13			5		2^2	7										9		8		37
1		3	4	6				11^1	10			7	12			5			2										9		8		38
1		3	4^3	6					10		7^2	12	13			5		2^1	11										9		8	14	39
1		3	12	6					10^3		13	7^1	14			5		2	4^2										9		8	11	40
1		3	4^1	6		13					12		10			5		2	7										9		8	11^2	41
1		3		6		11					12	7^1	10			5		2	4										9		8		42
1		3		6		7^1			12			13	10			5		2	4										9		8	11^2	43
1		3	12	6		13			10			7^1				5		2^2	4										9		8	11	44
1		3	4^3	6		12			10^1			13	14			5		2	7										9		8	11^2	45
1		3	4	6		12			10^1			11^2				5		2	7								13		9		8		46

FA Cup

First Round	Havant & W	(a)	2-1
Second Round	Bradford C	(a)	0-0
		(h)	1-0
Third Round	Stoke C	(a)	0-2

Carling Cup

First Round	Gillingham	(h)	2-1
Second Round	Southampton	(h)	0-4

J Paint Trophy

Second Round	Bournemouth	(h)	2-0
Quarter-Final	Brighton & HA	(h)	1-1

MILTON KEYNES DONS FL Championship 2

FOUNDATION

Old boys from Central School formed this club as Wimbledon Old Centrals in 1889. Their earliest successes were in the Clapham League before switching to the Southern Suburban League in 1902.

Stadium:mk, Way West, Milton Keynes MK1 1ST.

Telephone: (01908) 607 090.

Fax: (01908) 209 449.

Ticket Office: (01908) 609 000.

Website: www.mkdons.com

Email: info@mkdons.com

Ground Capacity: 22,000 (rising to 31,000).

Record Attendance: 30,115 v Manchester U, FA Premier League, 9 May 1993 (at Selhurst Park).

Pitch Measurements: 105m × 68m.

Chairman: Pete Winkelman.

Directors: Berni Winkelman, Sue Dawson, John Cove, Mark Edwards, Mark Turner.

Head of Football Operations: Kirstine Nicholson.

Manager: Paul Ince.

Assistant Manager: Ray Mathias.

Fitness Coach: Duncan Russell.

Colours: White shirts, white shorts, white stockings.

Change Colours: Red shirts, black shorts, black stockings.

Year Formed: 1889.

Turned Professional: 1964.

Ltd Co.: 1964.

Previous Names: 1899–1905, Wimbledon Old Centrals; 1905–2004, Wimbledon.

Grounds: 1899, Plough Lane; 1991, Selhurst Park; 2003, The National Hockey Stadium; 2007, Stadium:mk.

Club Nicknames: 'The Dons', 'The Crazy Gang'.

First Football League Game: 20 August 1977, Division 4, v Halifax T (h) D 3–3 – Guy; Bryant (1), Galvin, Donaldson, Aitken, Davies, Galliers, Smith, Connell (1), Holmes, Leslie (1).

HONOURS

FA Premier League: best season: 6th, 1993–94.

Football League: Division 3 – Runners-up 1983–84; Division 4 – Champions 1982–83.

FA Cup: Winners 1988.

Football League Cup: Semi-final 1996–97, 1998–99.

League Group Cup: Runners-up 1982.

Amateur Cup: Winners 1963; Runners-up 1935, 1947.

European Competitions: *Intertoto Cup:* 1995.

SKY SPORTS FACT FILE

On 26 September 2006 Milton Keynes Dons were trailing 2–0 at half-time to Torquay United. Within five minutes Izale McLeod had reduced the arrears from the penalty spot, levelled it on 59 minutes before Aaron Wilbraham headed the 84th minute equaliser.

MANAGERS

Les Henley 1955–71
Mike Everitt 1971–73
Dick Graham 1973–74
Allen Batsford 1974–78
Dario Gradi 1978–81
Dave Bassett 1981–87
Bobby Gould 1987–90
Ray Harford 1990–91
Peter Withe 1991
Joe Kinnear 1992–99
Egil Olsen 1999–2000
Terry Burton 2000–02
Stuart Murdock 2002–04
Danny Wilson 2004–06
Martin Allen 2006–07
Paul Ince June 2007–

Record League Victory: 6–0 v Newport Co, Division 3, 3 September 1983 – Beasant; Peters, Winterburn, Galliers, Morris, Hatter, Evans (2), Ketteridge (1), Cork (3 incl. 1p), Downes, Hodges (Driver).

Record Cup Victory: 7–2 v Windsor & Eton, FA Cup 1st rd, 22 November 1980 – Beasant; Jones, Armstrong, Galliers, Mick Smith (2), Cunningham (1), Ketteridge, Hodges, Leslie, Cork (1), Hubbick (3).

Record Defeat: 0–8 v Everton, League Cup 2nd rd, 29 August 1978.

Most League Points (2 for a win): 61, Division 4, 1978–79.

Most League Points (3 for a win): 98, Division 4, 1982–83.

Most League Goals: 97, Division 3, 1983–84.

Highest League Scorer in Season: Alan Cork, 29, 1983–84.

Most League Goals in Total Aggregate: Alan Cork, 145, 1977–92.

Most League Goals in One Match: 4, Alan Cork v Torquay U, Division 4, 28 February 1979.

Most Capped Player: Kenny Cunningham, 40 (72), Republic of Ireland.

Most League Appearances: Alan Cork, 430, 1977–92.

Youngest League Player: Kevin Gage, 17 years 15 days v Bury, 2 May 1981.

Record Transfer Fee Received: £7,000,000 from Newcastle U for Carl Cort, July 2000.

Record Transfer Fee Paid: £7,500,000 to West Ham U for John Hartson, January 1999.

Football League Record: 1977 Elected to Division 4; 1979–80 Division 3; 1980–81 Division 4; 1981–82 Division 3; 1982–83 Division 4; 1983–84 Division 3; 1984–86 Division 2; 1986–92 Division 1; 1992–2000 FA Premier League; 2000–04 Division 1; 2004–06 FL 1; 2006– FL 2.

LATEST SEQUENCES

Longest Sequence of League Wins: 7, 4.9.1996 – 19.10.1996.

Longest Sequence of League Defeats: 14, 19.3.2000 – 28.8.2000.

Longest Sequence of League Draws: 4, 24.4.2001 – 6.5.2001.

Longest Sequence of Unbeaten League Matches: 22, 15.1.1983 – 14.5.1983.

Longest Sequence Without a League Win: 14, 19.3.2000 – 28.8.2000.

Successive Scoring Runs: 23 from 18.2.1984.

Successive Non-scoring Runs: 5 from 13.4.1995.

TEN YEAR LEAGUE RECORD

		P	W	D	L	F	A	Pts	Pos
1997-98	PR Lge	38	10	14	14	34	46	44	15
1998-99	PR Lge	38	10	12	16	40	63	42	16
1999-2000	PR Lge	38	7	12	19	46	74	33	18
2000-01	Div 1	46	17	18	11	71	50	69	8
2001-02	Div 1	46	18	13	15	63	57	67	9
2002-03	Div 1	46	18	11	17	76	73	65	10
2003-04	Div 1	46	8	5	33	41	89	29	24
2004-05	FL 1	46	12	15	19	54	68	51	20
2005-06	FL 1	46	12	14	20	45	66	50	22
2006-07	FL 2	46	25	9	12	76	58	84	4

DID YOU KNOW ?

In 1974–75 Wimbledon had two players named Smith with the same initial G. Moreover both were defenders and had connections with Brentford. Gary Smith came on loan at first before being signed, while Graham was actually in his second spell at Plough Lane.

MILTON KEYNES DONS 2006–07 LEAGUE RECORD

Match No.	Date	Venue	Opponents	Result	H/T Score	Lg. Pos.	Goalscorers	Attendance
1	Aug 5	H	Bury	W 2-1	0-0	—	McLeod 2 (1 pen) [59 (p), 83]	5329
2	8	A	Mansfield T	L 1-2	1-2	—	Wilbraham [10]	4033
3	12	A	Macclesfield T	W 2-1	1-0	8	Platt [35], Swailes (og) [80]	1711
4	19	H	Bristol R	W 2-0	1-0	4	Dyer [30], Platt [64]	5125
5	26	A	Boston U	W 1-0	0-0	3	Platt [50]	2032
6	Sept 2	H	Notts Co	W 3-2	1-0	2	Dyer 2 [45, 53], Taylor [73]	6323
7	9	H	Hartlepool U	D 0-0	0-0	4		5630
8	12	A	Swindon T	L 1-2	1-1	—	McGovern [17]	8304
9	16	A	Lincoln C	W 3-2	2-1	5	McLeod (pen) [5], Wilbraham [26], Platt [54]	5310
10	23	H	Chester C	L 1-2	1-0	5	Platt [35]	5476
11	26	H	Torquay U	W 3-2	0-2	—	McLeod 2 (1 pen) [50 (p), 59], Wilbraham [84]	5378
12	30	A	Barnet	D 3-3	1-1	5	O'Hanlon [43], Chorley (pen) [69], Dyer [90]	2819
13	Oct 6	H	Peterborough U	L 0-2	0-0	—		6647
14	14	A	Wrexham	W 2-1	0-1	5	McLeod [46], O'Hanlon [77]	3828
15	21	H	Hereford U	L 1-3	0-2	6	McLeod [59]	5609
16	28	A	Walsall	D 0-0	0-0	6		6275
17	Nov 4	A	Grimsby T	W 3-1	0-0	5	McLeod [53], Wilbraham 2 [60, 79]	3268
18	18	H	Shrewsbury T	W 2-0	1-0	5	Edds [28], Platt [58]	5830
19	25	A	Darlington	L 0-1	0-1	6		4017
20	Dec 5	H	Stockport Co	W 2-0	0-0	—	McLeod 2 [61, 75]	4564
21	9	A	Accrington S	W 4-3	1-2	3	McLeod [16], Wilbraham 2 [54, 58], O'Hanlon [81]	1384
22	16	H	Wycombe W	W 3-1	2-1	3	Andrews [17], McLeod 2 (1 pen) [25 (p), 87]	5977
23	23	H	Rochdale	W 2-1	0-0	2	McLeod [80], Stanton (og) [88]	5459
24	26	A	Torquay U	W 2-0	2-0	2	Platt [27], McLeod (pen) [39]	2715
25	30	A	Chester C	W 3-0	0-0	2	Platt [60], McLeod [65], McGovern [76]	2271
26	Jan 1	H	Swindon T	L 0-1	0-1	2		6797
27	8	H	Lincoln C	D 2-2	1-0	—	McLeod [6], Edds [90]	7140
28	13	A	Hartlepool U	L 0-1	0-0	4		4851
29	20	H	Barnet	W 3-1	1-1	3	Platt 3 [12, 67, 72]	6447
30	27	A	Rochdale	L 0-5	0-3	5		2493
31	Feb 3	A	Bury	W 2-0	1-0	4	Knight [32], Andrews [50]	2325
32	17	A	Bristol R	D 1-1	0-0	5	McGovern [55]	5489
33	20	H	Mansfield T	D 1-1	0-0	—	Taylor [50]	5070
34	24	A	Notts Co	D 2-2	2-1	5	Dyer [26], Lewington [32]	4031
35	Mar 3	H	Boston U	W 3-2	1-2	3	Platt 2 [3, 84], McLeod [75]	6605
36	10	A	Peterborough U	L 0-4	0-2	5		5880
37	13	H	Macclesfield T	W 3-0	2-0	—	McLeod [2], Platt [45], Lee (og) [79]	5681
38	17	H	Wrexham	W 2-1	1-1	3	Andrews (pen) [38], Platt [85]	5712
39	25	H	Walsall	D 1-1	0-0	3	McLeod [52]	8044
40	31	A	Hereford U	D 0-0	0-0	4		2715
41	Apr 7	H	Grimsby T	L 1-2	0-1	4	Andrews [71]	6101
42	9	A	Shrewsbury T	L 1-2	1-0	4	Platt [9]	5238
43	14	H	Darlington	W 1-0	0-0	4	Platt [57]	5730
44	21	A	Stockport Co	W 2-1	1-0	4	Platt [24], Andrews [55]	5681
45	28	A	Wycombe W	W 2-0	0-0	4	Smith G [88], McLeod [90]	7150
46	May 5	H	Accrington S	W 3-1	0-1	4	Andrews (pen) [55], O'Hanlon [69], Stirling [83]	8102

Final League Position: 4

GOALSCORERS

League (76): McLeod 21 (5 pens), Platt 18, Wilbraham 7, Andrews 6 (2 pens), Dyer 5, O'Hanlon 4, McGovern 3, Edds 2, Taylor 2, Chorley 1 (pen), Knight 1, Lewington 1, Smith G 1, Stirling 1, own goals 3.
Carling Cup (3): Wilbraham 2, McLeod 1.
FA Cup (2): McLeod 2 (1 pen).
J Paint Trophy (1): Page 1.
Play-Offs (1): Andrews 1.

Baines A 19	Smith J 16 + 1	Lewington D 45	Diallo D 40	Morgan C 3	Mitchell P 13 + 7	McGovern J 40 + 4	Smith G 9 + 14	Platt C 37 + 5	McLeod I 33 + 1	Dyer L 39 + 2	Crooks L 3 + 9	Wilbraham A 31 + 1	Bankole A 5 + 1	Edds G 26 + 9	Taylor S 6 + 22	Chorley B 12 + 1	O'Hanlon S 33 + 3	Hastings J — + 7	Andrews K 34	Rizzo N — + 3	Tillen J — + 1	Harper L 22	Page S — + 1	Butler P 17	Stirling J 5 + 11	Hayes J — + 11	Knight L 7 + 9	Baldock S — + 1	Blizzard D 8	Jarrett A 2 + 3	Watts A 1 + 1	Match No.
1■	2^1	3	4	5	6^G	7	8^2	9	10	11	12	13	15																			1
		3	4	5^1	6^3	7	14	9	10	11^2	2	8	1	12	13																	2
1		3	4			7	6	9	10	11^1	2	8			12	5																3
1		3	4			7^1	6	9	10^3	11	2	8^2			12	5	13	14														4
1		3	4	5		7	12	9	10■	11^1		8				2	6															5
1		3	4			7	8	9		11		10^3		12	14	6^1	5	13	2^2													6
1		3	4^3		12	7		9		11		10		2	8^2	6		13	5^1	14												7
1		3	4		6^1	7		9^3		11	12	10^2		2	14	5		13	8													8
1		3	4		6^3	7		12	10■		13	9^1		2^2	14	5	11		8													9
1	2	3	4^1		6^2			9		11				7^3	10	5	8	12		14	13											10
1	2	3			6	7		9	10^2	11^1	12	8			13	5	4															11
1	12	3	4		6^2	7		9	10^3	11		8		13	14	5	2^1															12
1	2	3^1	4		6	7		9	10	11		8			12	5																13
1	2	3	4		6	7		9	12	11^2		8			10^1	13	5															14
1	2^3	3	4		6^1	7		12	10	11	13	9^2			14	5			8													15
	2	3	4			7^3		9	10^2	14	12	8^1		11	13		5		6			1										16
	2	3	4		12	6			10^2	11^3		9		7^1	13		5		8			1	14									17
	2	3	4		12	7		9	10^3	11^2	13			8^1	14		5		6			1										18
	2^1	3	4			7		9	10^2	11	12			8^3	13			14	6			1		5								19
		3	4		12	7		13	10^1	11^3		9^2		2			5		8	14		1		6								20
		3^1	4^3			7		13	10	11	12	9		2^2	14		5		8			1		6								21
		3	4		12	7	14	9^2	10^1	11		8		2	13^3				6			1		5								22
		3^2			12	7^1	13	9^3	10	11		8		2	14		5		4			1		6								23
		3	2			7	12	9^2	10^3	11^1		8		13	14		5		4			1		6								24
		3	2			7	12	9	10^3	11^2		8^1		13	14		5		4			1		6								25
		3	2^1			7	13	9^2	10	11		8		12	14		5		4^3			1		6								26
		3	4		6^2	7^3	12	13	10	11^1		9		2			5		8			1			14							27
		3	4^3			12	13	9^1	10■	11^2		8		2			5		7			1		6	14							28
		3				7^1	13	9		11		8		12	10^2		5^3		4			1		6	2	14						29
		3^1				7	13	9		11		8		12	10^2		5^3		4			1		6	2		14					30
1	2	3	4			7		9		12				11^2			13		8					6	5		10^1					31
1	2	3	5		12	7^2						10		11	14		13		8					6	4^1		9^3					32
1		3	2		4	7	11^2							12	10		5		8^1					6	13		9^3	14				33
1	2	3			4^1	7	12	9	10^2	11		8			13		5							6								34
1	2^2	3^3				7^1	12	9	10	11		8					5		4					6	13		14					35
	2^1		3^3			7^2		9	10	11		8					5		4			1		6	12	14	13					36
		3	6			7		9	10^2	11^3		8^1		2			5		4			1			12	14	13					37
		3^2	6			7^3	8	9	10	11				2^1			5		4			1			12	14	13					38
		3	6			7		9	10^1	11^2				2			5		4			1			14	13^3	12		8			39
	2^1	3	6			11		9	10^2					7^3			5		4			1			12	14	13		8			40
		3	6			7^1		9	10	11^3				2			5		4			1			12		13		8^2	14		41
		3^3	6			12	7	9						2^1			5	13	4^2			1			11■	14	10		8			42
		3	6			7	4	9		11^2			1	2			5^3									12	10^1		8	13	14	43
		3	6			12	7^1	9		11^3			1	2					4							13	10^2		8	14	5	44
		3	6				12	9	10	11^2			1	2			5		4							14	13		8^1	7^3		45
		3	6			12			10	11			1	2			5		4						13	14	9^1		8^3	7^2		46

FA Cup

First Round	Farsley C	(a)	0-0
		(h)	2-0
Second Round	Blackpool	(h)	0-2

Play-Offs

Semi-Final	Shrewsbury T	(a)	0-0
		(h)	1-2

Carling Cup

First Round	Colchester U	(h)	1-0
Second Round	Barnsley	(a)	2-1
Third Round	Tottenham H	(h)	0-5

J Paint Trophy

Second Round	Brighton & HA	(a)	1-4

MORECAMBE — FL Championship 2

FOUNDATION

Several attempts to start a senior football club in a rugby stronghold finally succeeded on 7 May 1920 at the West View Hotel, Morecambe and a team competed in the Lancs Combination for 1920–21. The club shared with a local cricket club at Woodhill Lane for the first season and a crowd of 3000 watched the first game. Moved to Roseberry Park whose name was changed to Christie Park after J.B. Christie who as President had purchased the ground.

Christie Park, Morecambe LA4 5TJ.

Telephone: (01524) 411797.

Fax: (01524) 832 230.

Website: www.morecambefc.com

Email: office@morecambefc.com

Ground Capacity: 6,030.

Record Attendance: 9,383 v Weymouth, FA Cup 3rd rd, 6 January 1962.

Chairman: Peter McGuigan.

Vice-chairman: Graham Hodgson.

Chief Executive: Rod Taylor.

Secretary: Neil Marsdin.

Manager: Sammy McIlroy.

Assistant Manager: Mark Lillis.

Physio: David Edge.

Colours: Red shirts, white shorts, white stockings.

Change Colours: All blue.

HONOURS

Conference: Promoted to Football League (play-offs) 2006–07. Semi-finalists – 2002–03, 2005–06.

Northern Premier League: Runners-up – 1994–95.

Presidents Cup: Winners – 1991–92.

FA Trophy: Winners 1973–74.

Lancs Senior Cup: Winners 1967–68.

Lancs Combination: Champions – 1924–25, 1961–62, 1962–63, 1967–68. Runners-up – 1925–26.

Lancs Combination Cup: Winners – 1926–27, 1945–46, 1964–65, 1966–67, 1967–68. Runners-up – 1923–24, 1924–25, 1962–63.

Lancs Junior Cup: Winners – 1927, 1928, 1962, 1963, 1969, 1986, 1987, 1994, 1996, 1999, 2004.

SKY SPORTS FACT FILE

The first time Morecambe won the Lancs Senior Cup was in 1967–68 when they beat Burnley in the final 2–1. The opposition fielded its first team including four full internationals. It was the first occasion a non-league team had won the competition.

Year Formed: 1920.

Club Nickname: The Shrimps.

Grounds: 1920 Woodhill Lane; 1921 Christie Park.

Record League Victory: 16-0 v Rossendale U, Lancashire Combination, September 1967.

Most League Points (3 for a win): 78, Conference, 2002–03.

Most League Goals: 86, Conference 2002–03.

Highest League Scorer in Season: Justin Jackson 29, 1999–2000.

Most League Goals in Total Aggregate: 100, John Norman, 1994–99; 2000–02.

Most League Goals in One Match: 8, Jim Ashworth v Gt Harwood T, 1946–47; 8, Arnold Timmons v Rossendale, 1967–68.

Most League Appearances: 299, Dave McKearney, 1995–2004.

Record Transfer Fee Received: £175,000 from Rushden & D for Justin Jackson, June 2000.

Record Transfer Fee Paid: £25,000 to Northwich Vic for Steve Walton, July 2000.

Football League Record: 2006–07 Promoted from Conference; 2007– FL2.

MANAGERS

Jimmy Milne 1947–48
Albert Dainty 1955–56
Ken Horton 1956–61
Joe Dunn 1961–64
Geoff Twentyman 1964–65
Ken Waterhouse 1965–69
Ronnie Clayton 1969–70
Gerry Irving/Ronnie Mitchell 1970
Ken Waterhouse 1970–72
Dave Roberts 1972–75
Alan Spavin 1975–76
Johnny Johnson 1976–77
Tommy Ferber 1977–78
Mick Hogarth 1978–79
Don Curbage 1979–81
Jim Thompson 1981
Les Rigby 1981–84
Sean Gallagher 1984–85
Joe Wojciechowicz 1985–88
Eric Whalley 1988
Billy Wright 1988–89
Lawrie Milligan 1989
Bryan Griffiths 1989–93
Leighton James 1994
Jim Harvey 1994–2006
Sammy McIlroy May 2006–

LATEST SEQUENCES

Longest Sequence of League Wins: 5, 20.8.98 – 27.9.98

Longest Sequence of League Defeats: 5, 25.3.2001 – 16.4.2001.

TEN YEAR LEAGUE RECORD

		P	W	D	L	F	A	Pts	Pos
1997–98	Conf	42	21	10	11	71	64	73	5
1998–99	Conf	42	15	8	19	60	76	53	14
1999–00	Conf	42	18	16	8	70	48	70	3
2000–01	Conf	42	11	12	19	64	66	45	19
2001–02	Conf	42	17	11	14	63	67	62	6
2002–03	Conf	42	23	9	10	86	42	78	2
2003–04	Conf	42	20	7	15	66	66	67	7
2004–05	Conf	42	19	14	9	69	50	71	7
2005–06	Conf	42	22	8	12	68	41	74	5
2006–07	Conf	46	23	12	11	64	46	81	3

DID YOU KNOW?

In 1961–62 Morecambe registered their first victory over a Football League club in the FA Cup. On 25 November in a second round tie and led by player-manager Joe Dunn, they beat Chester 2–1 at Sealand Road with a goal from Gordon Howarth.

NEWCASTLE UNITED FA Premiership

FOUNDATION

It stemmed from a newly formed club called Stanley in 1881. In October 1882 they changed their name to Newcastle East End to avoid confusion with two other local clubs, Stanley Nops and Stanley Albion. Shortly afterwards another club Rosewood merged with them. Newcastle West End had been formed in August 1882 and they played on a pitch which was part of the Town Moor. Moved to Brandling Park 1885 and St James' Park 1886 (home of Newcastle Rangers). West End went out of existence after a bad run and the remaining committee men invited East End to move to St James' Park. They accepted and, at a meeting in Bath Lane Hall in 1892, changed their name to Newcastle United.

St James' Park, Newcastle-upon-Tyne NE1 4ST.
Telephone: (0191) 201 8400.
Fax: (0191) 201 8600.
Ticket Office: (0191) 261 1571.
Website: www.nufc.co.uk
Email: admin@nufc.co.uk
Ground Capacity: 52,387.
Record Attendance: 68,386 v Chelsea, Division 1, 3 September 1930.
Pitch Measurements: 105m × 68m.
Chairman: Freddy Shepherd.
Vice-chairman: Chris Mort.
Chief Operating Officer: Russell Cushing.
Manager: Sam Allardyce.
First Team Coaches: Steve Round, Nigel Pearson.
Physio: Derek Wright.
Colours: Black and white striped shirts, black shorts, black stockings.
Change Colours: Blue and black shirts, blue and black shorts, blue and black stockings.
Year Formed: 1881.
Turned Professional: 1889.
Ltd Co.: 1890.
Previous Names: 1881, Stanley; 1882, Newcastle East End; 1892, Newcastle United.
Club Nickname: 'The Magpies'.
Grounds: 1881, South Byker; 1886, Chillingham Road, Heaton; 1892, St James' Park.
First Football League Game: 2 September 1893, Division 2, v Royal Arsenal (a) D 2–2 – Ramsay; Jeffery, Miller; Crielly, Graham, McKane; Bowman, Crate (1), Thompson, Sorley (1), Wallace. Graham and not Crate scored according to some reports.

HONOURS

FA Premier League: Runners-up 1995–96, 1996–97; *Football League:* Division 1 – Champions 1904–05, 1906–07, 1908–09, 1926–27, 1992–93; Division 2 – Champions 1964–65; Runners-up 1897–98, 1947–48.

FA Cup: Winners 1910, 1924, 1932, 1951, 1952, 1955; Runners-up 1905, 1906, 1908, 1911, 1974, 1998, 1999.

Football League Cup: Runners-up 1976.

Texaco Cup: Winners 1974, 1975.

European Competitions: *Champions League:* 1997–98, 2002–03, 2003–04. *European Fairs Cup:* 1968–69 (winners), 1969–70, 1970–71. *UEFA Cup:* 1977–78, 1994–95, 1996–97, 1999–2000, 2003–04 (semi-final), 2004–05, 2006–07. *European Cup Winners' Cup:* 1998–99. *Anglo-Italian Cup:* Winners 1972–73. *Intertoto Cup:* 2001 (runners-up), 2005, 2006 (winners).

SKY SPORTS FACT FILE

Monte Wilkinson scored 100 goals for Esh Winning Juniors in one season. At Newcastle United he understudied Hughie Gallacher but once scored a hat-trick against Aston Villa on 10 March 1928 in a pulsating 7–5 win! Later he deputised for Dixie Dean at Everton!

Record League Victory: 13–0 v Newport Co, Division 2, 5 October 1946 – Garbutt; Cowell, Graham; Harvey, Brennan, Wright; Milburn (2), Bentley (1), Wayman (4), Shackleton (6), Pearson.

Record Cup Victory: 9–0 v Southport (at Hillsborough), FA Cup 4th rd, 1 February 1932 – McInroy; Nelson, Fairhurst; McKenzie, Davidson, Weaver (1); Boyd (1), Jimmy Richardson (3), Cape (2), McMenemy (1), Lang (1).

Record Defeat: 0–9 v Burton Wanderers, Division 2, 15 April 1895.

Most League Points (2 for a win): 57, Division 2, 1964–65.

Most League Points (3 for a win): 96, Division 1, 1992–93.

Most League Goals: 98, Division 1, 1951–52.

Highest League Scorer in Season: Hughie Gallacher, 36, Division 1, 1926–27.

Most League Goals in Total Aggregate: Jackie Milburn, 177, 1946–57.

Most League Goals in One Match: 6, Len Shackleton v Newport Co, Division 2, 5 October 1946.

Most Capped Player: Shay Given, 71 (80), Republic of Ireland.

Most League Appearances: Jim Lawrence, 432, 1904–22.

Youngest League Player: Steve Watson, 16 years 223 days v Wolverhampton W, 10 November 1990.

Record Transfer Fee Received: £13,650,000 from Real Madrid for Jonathan Woodgate, August 2004.

Record Transfer Fee Paid: £16,000,000 to Real Madrid for Michael Owen, September 2005.

Football League Record: 1893 Elected to Division 2; 1898–1934 Division 1; 1934–48 Division 2; 1948–61 Division 1; 1961–65 Division 2; 1965–78 Division 1; 1978–84 Division 2; 1984–89 Division 1; 1989–92 Division 2; 1992–93 Division 1; 1993– FA Premier League.

MANAGERS

Frank Watt 1895–32
(Secretary-Manager)
Andy Cunningham 1930–35
Tom Mather 1935–39
Stan Seymour 1939–47
(Hon. Manager)
George Martin 1947–50
Stan Seymour 1950–54
(Hon. Manager)
Duggie Livingstone 1954–56
Stan Seymour 1956–58
(Hon. Manager)
Charlie Mitten 1958–61
Norman Smith 1961–62
Joe Harvey 1962–75
Gordon Lee 1975–77
Richard Dinnis 1977
Bill McGarry 1977–80
Arthur Cox 1980–84
Jack Charlton 1984
Willie McFaul 1985–88
Jim Smith 1988–91
Ossie Ardiles 1991–92
Kevin Keegan 1992–97
Kenny Dalglish 1997–98
Ruud Gullit 1998–99
Sir Bobby Robson 1999–2004
Graeme Souness 2004–06
Glenn Roeder 2006–07
Sam Allardyce May 2007–

LATEST SEQUENCES

Longest Sequence of League Wins: 13, 25.4.1992 – 18.10.1992.

Longest Sequence of League Defeats: 10, 23.8.1977 – 15.10.1977.

Longest Sequence of League Draws: 4, 20.1.1990 – 24.2.1990.

Longest Sequence of Unbeaten League Matches: 14, 22.4.1950 – 30.9.1950.

Longest Sequence Without a League Win: 21, 14.1.1978 – 23.8.1978.

Successive Scoring Runs: 25 from 15.4.1939.

Successive Non-scoring Runs: 6 from 31.12.1938.

TEN YEAR LEAGUE RECORD

		P	W	D	L	F	A	Pts	Pos
1997-98	PR Lge	38	11	11	16	35	44	44	13
1998-99	PR Lge	38	11	13	14	48	54	46	13
1999-2000	PR Lge	38	14	10	14	63	54	52	11
2000-01	PR Lge	38	14	9	15	44	50	51	11
2001-02	PR Lge	38	21	8	9	74	52	71	4
2002-03	PR Lge	38	21	6	11	63	48	69	3
2003-04	PR Lge	38	13	17	8	52	40	56	5
2004-05	PR Lge	38	10	14	14	47	57	44	14
2005-06	PR Lge	38	17	7	14	47	42	58	7
2006-07	PR Lge	38	11	10	17	38	47	43	13

DID YOU KNOW ?

On 2 November 2006 Newcastle United gave debuts to 18 year old Dutchman Tim Krul their fourth-choice goalkeeper and later Andy Carroll as substitute, the youngest United player in Europe at 17 years 267 days in the 1–0 UEFA Cup win against Palermo.

NEWCASTLE UNITED 2006–07 LEAGUE RECORD

Match No.	Date	Venue	Opponents	Result		H/T Score	Lg. Pos.	Goalscorers	Attendance
1	Aug 19	H	Wigan Ath	W	2-1	1-0	—	Parker 38, Ameobi 64	51,569
2	27	A	Aston Villa	L	0-2	0-2	14		35,141
3	Sept 9	H	Fulham	L	1-2	0-0	14	Parker 54	50,365
4	17	A	West Ham U	W	2-0	0-0	9	Duff 50, Martins 75	34,938
5	20	A	Liverpool	L	0-2	0-1	—		43,754
6	24	H	Everton	D	1-1	1-1	12	Ameobi 14	50,107
7	Oct 1	A	Manchester U	L	0-2	0-1	13		75,664
8	15	H	Bolton W	L	1-2	1-0	15	Ameobi (pen) 19	48,145
9	22	A	Middlesbrough	L	0-1	0-0	16		30,060
10	28	H	Charlton Ath	D	0-0	0-0	17		48,642
11	Nov 4	H	Sheffield U	L	0-1	0-0	19		50,188
12	11	A	Manchester C	D	0-0	0-0	18		40,571
13	18	A	Arsenal	D	1-1	1-0	17	Dyer 30	60,058
14	26	H	Portsmouth	W	1-0	0-0	17	Sibierski 69	48,743
15	Dec 6	H	Reading	W	3-2	1-2	—	Sibierski 23, Martins (pen) 57, Emre 84	48,182
16	9	A	Blackburn R	W	3-1	2-0	14	Martins 2 31, 90, Taylor 35	19,225
17	13	A	Chelsea	L	0-1	0-0	—		41,945
18	16	H	Watford	W	2-1	0-0	12	Martins 2 49, 85	49,231
19	23	H	Tottenham H	W	3-1	3-1	11	Dyer 3, Martins 7, Parker 34	52,079
20	26	A	Bolton W	L	1-2	1-1	11	Dyer 8	26,437
21	30	A	Everton	L	0-3	0-1	13		38,682
22	Jan 1	H	Manchester U	D	2-2	1-1	13	Milner 33, Edgar 74	52,302
23	14	A	Tottenham H	W	3-2	1-1	11	Huntington 16, Martins 72, Butt 73	35,942
24	20	H	West Ham U	D	2-2	1-2	12	Milner 45, Solano (pen) 53	52,095
25	31	H	Aston Villa	W	3-1	2-1	—	Milner 5, Dyer 7, Sibierski 90	49,201
26	Feb 3	A	Fulham	L	1-2	0-0	10	Martins 90	24,340
27	10	H	Liverpool	W	2-1	1-1	9	Martins 26, Solano (pen) 70	52,305
28	25	A	Wigan Ath	L	0-1	0-1	11		21,179
29	Mar 3	H	Middlesbrough	D	0-0	0-0	11		52,303
30	18	A	Charlton Ath	L	0-2	0-0	11		27,028
31	31	H	Manchester C	L	0-1	0-0	11		52,004
32	Apr 7	A	Sheffield U	W	2-1	1-0	10	Martins 17, Taylor 80	32,572
33	9	H	Arsenal	D	0-0	0-0	10		52,293
34	14	A	Portsmouth	L	1-2	0-1	11	Emre (pen) 69	20,165
35	22	H	Chelsea	D	0-0	0-0	12		52,056
36	30	A	Reading	L	0-1	0-0	—		24,109
37	May 5	H	Blackburn R	L	0-2	0-1	13		51,226
38	13	A	Watford	D	1-1	1-0	13	Dyer 29	19,830

Final League Position: 13

GOALSCORERS

League (38): Martins 11 (1 pen), Dyer 5, Ameobi 3 (1 pen), Milner 3, Parker 3, Sibierski 3, Emre 2 (1 pen), Solano 2 (2 pens), Taylor 2, Butt 1, Duff 1, Edgar 1, Huntington 1.
Carling Cup (5): Solano 2, Parker 1, Rossi 1, Sibierski 1.
FA Cup (3): Dyer 1, Milner 1, Taylor 1.
Intertoto (4): Ameobi 2, Emre 1, Luque 1.
UEFA Cup (16): Martins 6 (1 pen), Sibierski 4, Bramble 1, Dyer 1, Luque 1, Taylor 1, own goals 2.

Given S 22	Carr S 23	Babayaro C 12	Parker S 28 + 1	Moore C 17	Bramble T 17	Solano N 25 + 3	Butt N 27 + 4	Ameobi F 9 + 3	Emre B 21 + 3	Duff D 20 + 2	Taylor S 26 + 1	N'Zogbia C 10 + 12	Luque A — + 7	Martins O 32 + 1	Milner J 31 + 4	Ramage P 20 + 1	Rossi G 3 + 8	Harper S 15 + 3	Sibierski A 14 + 12	Pattison M 2 + 5	Dyer K 20 + 2	Huntington P 10 + 1	Srnicek P 1 + 1	Edgar D 2 + 1	O'Brien A 1 + 1	Onyewu O 7 + 4	Carroll A — + 4	Owen M 3	*Match No.*
1	2	3	4	5^{1}	6	7	8^{2}	9^{3}	10	11	12	13	14																1
1	2	3^{3}	4	5	6	7^{1}	13		8^{2}	11		12	14	9	10														2
1	2		4^{1}	5	6		12	9	8	7		11		10^{2}		3	13												3
1^{G}	2	3	4	5			12	9^{2}	8^{1}	11				10	7	6		15	13										4
	2	3	4	5				9^{3}	8	11		12		10^{2}	7^{1}	6	13	1	14										5
	2		4	5	6■			9^{2}	8			11		10^{1}	7	3	12	1	13										6
	2		4	5			8^{2}	9	10^{3}	11	3	12		13	7^{1}	6		1		14									7
	2		4	5	6	7^{1}		9	8^{2}	11		12		10		3	13	1											8
	2		4	5			8	12		11	6	13		10	7^{2}	3		1	9^{1}										9
	2	3	4	5	6	7^{1}	8			10		11			12		9	1											10
	2	3	4	5	6	12	8^{2}		13	10		11^{1}	14		7^{3}		9	1											11
	2^{1}		4	5		12		9^{3}	8	11^{2}	6	13			7	3		1	10		14								12
1			4	5^{3}	6	7^{1}	8			11^{2}	2	13		9	12	3			14		10								13
1			4^{1}		6	2	12		8		5	11^{2}	13	9	7^{3}	3			14		10								14
1		3				2	4		8		5	11		9^{1}	7	6	12		10										15
1		3				2^{1}	4		8^{2}		5	11		9	7	6	12		10^{3}	13		14							16
1		3					4				5	11^{2}	12	9	7	6	8		10^{1}	13		2							17
1		3	12				4^{1}		8^{2}	13	5			9	7	6			10		11	2							18
1^{G}			4			2	8		10^{2}		5			9	7	6	12		13		11^{1}	3	15						19
			4				8		12		5			9	7^{2}	6	13		10		11^{1}	3	1	2					20
1			4			2	8		10		5			9	7	6^{1}			12	13	11^{2}	3							21
1			4			2			8^{1}		5			9	7				10	12	11	6		3					22
1						2	4				5			9	7	6			10	8	11	3							23
1^{G}	3		4			2	8							9	7	6^{1}		15			10	5		12	11				24
	2		4		6		8^{1}			11	5			9	7			1	12		10	3							25
	2		4		6	12	8			11^{2}	3			9	7			1	13		10^{1}					5			26
		3	4		6	7^{1}	8			12	2			9	11			1	13		10^{2}					5			27
1			4		6	7^{1}	8			11^{2}	2	13		9	12				10			3^{3}				5	14		28
1			4		6	2	8				3	11		9	7^{1}				12		10					5			29
1			4	5		2			8	3		12		9	7				10		11^{1}					6			30
1	2	3	4	5^{3}		7^{1}	8			11	6			9	12				13		10^{2}					14			31
1	3		4^{1}	5		2^{3}	8		12	11	6			9	7				10^{2}		13					14			32
1^{G}	3					2	4		8^{2}	11	6	12	13	9	7			15			10^{1}					5			33
	3			5^{3}		2	4		8	10^{1}	6	11^{2}	12	9	7			1								14	13		34
	3				5	2	4		8		6			9	7			1	10^{1}		11						12		35
	3				5	2		12	4^{2}		6	13		9	7			1	8^{1}		11							10	36
	3		4		6^{2}	2	8	12						9	7	13		1			11^{1}					5		10	37
1	3					2^{3}	4	9^{2}			6				7	5				8	11				12	14	13	10^{1}	38

FA Cup

Third Round	Birmingham C	(a)	2-2
		(h)	1-5

Carling Cup

Third Round	Portsmouth	(h)	3-0
Fourth Round	Watford	(a)	2-2
Quarter-Final	Chelsea	(h)	0-1

Intertoto Cup

Third Round	Lillestrom	(h)	1-1
		(a)	3-0

UEFA Cup

Second Qualifying Round	Ventspils	(a)	1-0
		(h)	0-0
First Round	Levadia	(a)	1-0
		(h)	2-1
Group H	Fenerbahce	(h)	1-0
	Palermo	(a)	1-0
	Celta Vigo	(h)	2-1
	Eintracht Frankfurt	(a)	0-0
Third Round	Waregem	(a)	3-1
		(h)	1-0
Fourth Round	AZ	(h)	4-2
		(a)	0-2

NORTHAMPTON TOWN FL Championship 1

FOUNDATION

Formed in 1897 by school teachers connected with the Northampton and District Elementary Schools' Association, they survived a financial crisis at the end of their first year when they were £675 in the red and became members of the Midland League – a fast move indeed for a new club. They achieved Southern League membership in 1901.

Sixfields Stadium, Upton Way, Northampton NN5 5QA.

Telephone: 0870 822 1997.

Fax: (01604) 751 613.

Ticket Office: 0870 822 1966.

Website: www.ntfc.co.uk

Email: secretary@ntfc.co.uk

Ground Capacity: 7,653.

Record Attendance: (at County Ground): 24,523 v Fulham, Division 1, 23 April 1966; (at Sixfields Stadium): 7,557 v Manchester C, Division 2, 26 September 1998.

Pitch Measurements: 116yd × 72yd.

Chairman: David Cardoza.

Secretary: Norman Howells.

Manager: Stuart Gray.

Director of Football: Ian Sampson.

Physio: Denis Casey.

Colours: Claret shirts, white shorts, claret stockings.

Change Colours: Indigo shirts, indigo shorts, indigo stockings.

Year Formed: 1897.

Turned Professional: 1901.

Ltd Co.: 1901.

Grounds: 1897, County Ground; 1994, Sixfields Stadium.

Club Nickname: 'The Cobblers'.

First Football League Game: 28 August 1920, Division 3, v Grimsby T (a) L 0–2 – Thorpe; Sproston, Hewison; Jobey, Tomkins, Pease; Whitworth, Lockett, Thomas, Freeman, MacKechnie.

Record League Victory: 10–0 v Walsall, Division 3 (S), 5 November 1927 – Hammond; Watson, Jeffs; Allen, Brett, Odell; Daley, Smith (3), Loasby (3), Hoten (1), Wells (3).

Record Cup Victory: 10–0 v Sutton T, FA Cup prel rd, 7 December 1907 – Cooch; Drennan, Lloyd Davies, Tirrell (1), McCartney, Hickleton, Badenock (3), Platt (3), Lowe (1), Chapman (2), McDiarmid.

HONOURS

Football League: Division 1 best season: 21st, 1965–66; Division 2 – Runners-up 1964–65; Division 3 – Champions 1962–63; Promoted from Division 3 1996–97 (play-offs); Division 3 (S) – Runners-up 1927–28, 1949–50; Division 4 – Champions 1986–87; Runners-up 1975–76; FL 2 – Runners-up 2005–06.

FA Cup: best season: 5th rd, 1934, 1950, 1970.

Football League Cup: best season: 5th rd, 1965, 1967.

SKY SPORTS FACT FILE

Albert Dawes who had scored a hat-trick for Northampton Town in an FA Cup tie against Metropolitan Police on 28 November 1931, hit five in the same round a year later v Lloyds, Sittingbourne.

Record Defeat: 0–11 v Southampton, Southern League, 28 December 1901.

Most League Points (2 for a win): 68, Division 4, 1975–76.

Most League Points (3 for a win): 99, Division 4, 1986–87.

Most League Goals: 109, Division 3, 1962–63 and Division 3 (S), 1952–53.

Highest League Scorer in Season: Cliff Holton, 36, Division 3, 1961–62.

Most League Goals in Total Aggregate: Jack English, 135, 1947–60.

Most League Goals in One Match: 5, Ralph Hoten v Crystal Palace, Division 3S, 27 October 1928.

Most Capped Player: Edwin Lloyd Davies, 12 (16), Wales.

Most League Appearances: Tommy Fowler, 521, 1946–61.

Youngest League Player: Adrian Mann, 16 years 297 days v Bury, 5 May 1984.

Record Transfer Fee Received: £265,000 from Watford for Richard Hill, July 1987.

Record Transfer Fee Paid: £165,000 to Oldham Ath for Josh Low, July 2003.

Football League Record: 1920 Original Member of Division 3; 1921 Division 3 (S); 1958–61 Division 4; 1961–63 Division 3; 1963–65 Division 2; 1965–66 Division 1; 1966–67 Division 2; 1967–69 Division 3; 1969–76 Division 4; 1976–77 Division 3; 1977–87 Division 4; 1987–90 Division 3; 1990–92 Division 4; 1992–97 Division 3; 1997–99 Division 2; 1999–2000 Division 3; 2000–03 Division 2; 2003–04 Division 3; 2004–06 FL 2; 2006– FL 1.

LATEST SEQUENCES

Longest Sequence of League Wins: 8, 27.8.1960 – 19.9.1960.

Longest Sequence of League Defeats: 8, 26.10.1935 – 21.12.1935.

Longest Sequence of League Draws: 6, 18.9.1983 – 15.10.1983.

Longest Sequence of Unbeaten League Matches: 21, 27.9.1986 – 6.2.1987.

Longest Sequence Without a League Win: 18, 26.3.1969 – 20.9.1969.

Successive Scoring Runs: 27 from 23.8.1986.

Successive Non-scoring Runs: 7 from 7.4.1939.

MANAGERS

Arthur Jones 1897–1907
(Secretary-Manager)
Herbert Chapman 1907–12
Walter Bull 1912–13
Fred Lessons 1913–19
Bob Hewison 1920–25
Jack Tresadern 1925–30
Jack English 1931–35
Syd Puddefoot 1935–37
Warney Cresswell 1937–39
Tom Smith 1939–49
Bob Dennison 1949–54
Dave Smith 1954–59
David Bowen 1959–67
Tony Marchi 1967–68
Ron Flowers 1968–69
Dave Bowen 1969–72
(continued as General Manager and Secretary to 1985 when joined the board)
Billy Baxter 1972–73
Bill Dodgin Jnr 1973–76
Pat Crerand 1976–77
Bill Dodgin Jnr 1977
John Petts 1977–78
Mike Keen 1978–79
Clive Walker 1979–80
Bill Dodgin Jnr 1980–82
Clive Walker 1982–84
Tony Barton 1984–85
Graham Carr 1985–90
Theo Foley 1990–92
Phil Chard 1992–93
John Barnwell 1993–95
Ian Atkins 1995–99
Kevin Wilson 1999–2001
Kevan Broadhurst 2001–03
Terry Fenwick 2003
Martin Wilkinson 2003
Colin Calderwood 2003–06
John Gorman 2006
Stuart Gray January 2007–

TEN YEAR LEAGUE RECORD

		P	W	D	L	F	A	Pts	Pos
1997-98	Div 2	46	18	17	11	52	37	71	4
1998-99	Div 2	46	10	18	18	43	57	48	22
1999-2000	Div 3	46	25	7	14	63	45	82	3
2000-01	Div 2	46	15	12	19	46	59	57	18
2001-02	Div 2	46	14	7	25	54	79	49	20
2002-03	Div 2	46	10	9	27	40	79	39	24
2003-04	Div 3	46	22	9	15	58	51	75	6
2004-05	FL 2	46	20	12	14	62	51	72	7
2005-06	FL 2	46	22	17	7	63	37	83	2
2006-07	FL 1	46	15	14	17	48	51	59	14

DID YOU KNOW ?

Maurice Edelston, the former England amateur international inside-forward, made a ten-second, first touch scoring debut for Northampton Town against Exeter City on 4 September 1952 following his transfer from Reading. They went on to win 3–1.

NORTHAMPTON TOWN 2006–07 LEAGUE RECORD

Match No.	Date	Venue	Opponents	Result		H/T Score	Lg. Pos.	Goalscorers	Attendance
1	Aug 5	A	Crewe Alex	D	2-2	2-2	—	McGleish [12], Kirk [42]	5553
2	8	H	Brentford	L	0-1	0-0	—		5707
3	12	H	Nottingham F	L	0-1	0-0	20		7172
4	19	A	Gillingham	W	1-0	1-0	15	Kirk [23]	5654
5	29	H	Bristol C	L	1-3	1-1	—	Kirk [18]	4919
6	Sept 1	A	Rotherham U	W	2-1	0-1	—	McGleish 2 [74, 82]	4971
7	9	A	Carlisle U	D	1-1	0-0	17	McGleish [47]	7602
8	12	H	Yeovil T	D	1-1	1-0	—	Crowe [32]	4853
9	16	H	Tranmere R	L	1-3	0-2	20	McGleish [74]	5334
10	23	A	Millwall	W	1-0	1-0	18	Cole [42]	7432
11	26	A	Cheltenham T	W	2-0	0-0	—	Kirk [67], McGleish (pen) [83]	3224
12	30	H	Port Vale	L	0-2	0-2	16		5316
13	Oct 6	A	Bournemouth	D	0-0	0-0	—		5746
14	13	H	Bradford C	D	0-0	0-0	—		5625
15	21	A	Brighton & HA	D	1-1	0-1	16	Quinn [84]	5862
16	28	H	Swansea C	W	1-0	0-0	13	Chambers [55]	5444
17	Nov 4	H	Blackpool	D	1-1	0-1	16	Jess [62]	5762
18	18	A	Scunthorpe U	L	0-1	0-0	17		4758
19	Dec 6	A	Chesterfield	D	0-0	0-0	—		3341
20	9	H	Doncaster R	L	0-2	0-0	18		5131
21	16	A	Huddersfield T	D	1-1	1-0	18	Burnell [19]	8723
22	19	H	Leyton Orient	L	0-1	0-0	—		4728
23	23	A	Oldham Ath	L	0-3	0-2	19		10,207
24	26	H	Cheltenham T	W	2-0	1-0	18	McGleish 2 (1 pen) [45, 74 (p)]	5239
25	Jan 1	A	Yeovil T	D	0-0	0-0	18		5361
26	6	A	Tranmere R	D	1-1	1-0	18	McGleish [11]	6089
27	13	H	Carlisle U	W	3-2	1-0	17	Kirk [45], McGleish 2 [47, 71]	5549
28	23	H	Millwall	W	3-0	0-0	—	McGleish [46], Holt [71], Brad Johnson [90]	5834
29	28	H	Oldham Ath	L	2-3	1-2	16	Kirk [24], Robertson [88]	5662
30	Feb 3	H	Crewe Alex	L	1-2	0-1	19	Brad Johnson [55]	5262
31	6	A	Port Vale	L	0-1	0-0	—		3353
32	10	A	Nottingham F	L	0-1	0-0	19		24,567
33	16	H	Gillingham	D	1-1	0-0	—	Robertson [86]	5618
34	19	A	Brentford	W	1-0	1-0	—	Crowe [31]	5164
35	24	H	Rotherham U	W	3-0	3-0	16	Deuchar [15], Hughes [21], Taylor [45]	4564
36	Mar 3	A	Bristol C	L	0-1	0-1	17		11,965
37	10	H	Bournemouth	W	3-1	1-0	17	Robertson [17], Deuchar [77], Kirk [85]	5921
38	17	A	Bradford C	W	2-1	0-0	15	Brad Johnson [64], Deuchar [87]	8190
39	24	A	Swansea C	L	1-2	1-1	16	Brad Johnson [6]	11,071
40	31	H	Brighton & HA	L	0-2	0-0	18		6613
41	Apr 7	A	Leyton Orient	W	2-0	2-0	16	Cox [12], Palmer (og) [40]	5459
42	9	H	Scunthorpe U	W	2-1	1-0	13	Pearce [16], Brad Johnson [90]	6361
43	14	A	Blackpool	L	1-4	1-0	15	Cox [42]	7334
44	21	H	Chesterfield	W	1-0	0-0	15	Cox [78]	5730
45	27	H	Huddersfield T	D	1-1	0-0	—	Holt [63]	5842
46	May 5	A	Doncaster R	D	2-2	1-1	14	Crowe [45], Hughes [64]	7534

Final League Position: 14

GOALSCORERS

League (48): McGleish 12 (2 pens), Kirk 7, Brad Johnson 5, Cox 3, Crowe 3, Deuchar 3, Robertson 3, Holt 2, Hughes 2, Burnell 1, Chambers 1, Cole 1, Jess 1, Pearce 1, Quinn 1, Taylor 1, own goal 1.
Carling Cup (2): Kirk 1, Watt 1.
FA Cup (3): Burnell 1, McGleish 1, own goal 1.
J Paint Trophy (0).

Harper L 4	Crowe J 43	Holt A 33 + 2	Chambers L 29	Doig C 39	Taylor I 26 + 7	Bojic P 19 + 7	Burnell J 24	McGleish S 24 + 1	Kirk A 29 + 15	Aiston S 14 + 7	Johnson Brad 21 + 6	Quinn J 5 + 13	Bunn M 42	Jess E 22 + 4	Dyche S 20 + 1	Gilligan R 14 + 10	Watt J 2 + 8	Hunt D 20 + 9	Johnson Brett 2 + 2	Cole M 6 + 2	Wright N 2 + 2	Laird M 2 + 4	Robertson J 9 + 8	Hughes M 17	Deuchar K 14 + 3	Pearce A 15	Cox S 6 + 2	May D 2 + 1	Dolman L 1	Match No.
1	2	3	4	5	6^1	7	8	9	10^2	11	12	13																		1
1	2	3	4	5	6^2	7^1	8	9	10	11	12	13																		2
	2	3	4	5	6^2	7^1	8^3	9▮	10	11	13	12	1	14																3
	2	3	4	5^2	7	12	8		10	11^1	13	9^3	1		6	14														4
	2	3	4^1	5	7^2	13	8		10	11		9^3	1	12	6	14														5
	3		4	5	12	2^1	8	9	10	11^2			1	7	6		13													6
	2		4	5	7	12	8	9	10^2	11^3		13	1		6	14	3^1													7
	2		4	5	7	3	8^3	9	10^1			12	1		6	13	11^2	14												8
	2		4	5	7^2	3^1		9	10			13	1	8	6^3			12	14	11										9
	2		4	5^1	7	3^3		9	10			14	1	8	6		13	12		11^2										10
	2		4	5	7	3		9	10				1	11^1	6			8		12										11
	2		4^3	5	7	12		9	10			14	1	8^1	6		13	3		11^2										12
1	3		4	5	6	2		9	10		12			7				8		11^1										13
1	2^2	12	4	5	6	3		9	10					8		13		7		11^1										14
	2	12	4	5		3	8^3	9	10			14	1	7			13	6^2		11^1										15
	3		4	5	6	2	8^2	9	12			10^1	1	11			13	7												16
	3		4	5	6^2	2	8	9	12			10^1	1	11			13	7^3		14										17
	2	3^2	4	5	7		8	9	10^3			13	1	11^1	6		14	12												18
	2	3	4	5		7^3	8^1	9	10^2			14	1	12		13		6			11									19
	2	3	4	5	12	7^1	8	9	10				1	11		13					6^2									20
	2	3	4		12	7	8^1	9	13				1	11^3	5	10^2		6			14									21
		3	4	5		2^2	8	9	12		13		1	11	6	10^1		7^3			14									22
	2	3	4		12	5^3	8	13	10^2		7		1	11^1		9	14	6												23
	2	3	4	5	7		8	9^1	12	13			1	11	6	10^2														24
	2	3	4	5	6	7	8^1		10			13	1	11^3		9^2		12	14											25
	2	3	4	5	8	12		9^2	10^1		7		1	11	6	13														26
	2	3	4			12	8^1	9	10		7		1	11	6				5											27
	2	3	4	5			8^3	9^1	10	12	7	13	1	11^2	6			14												28
	2	3	4	5			8		10	12	7	9^3	1	11^1	6^2							13	14							29
	2	3		5^1			8		10		7		1	11^2	6							13	12	4	9					30
	2	3			6^2		8^1		10	12	7		1		4			13				11^3	14	5	9					31
	3	2			6				10^1	11	7		1	12		13						8^2		5	9	4				32
	2	3		5					10^1	11	7		1					8					12	6	9	4				33
	2	3		5	12				13	11^1	7		1					8^3				14	10^2	6	9	4				34
	2	3		5	7^2				12	11^1	8		1									13	10	6	9	4				35
	2	3		5	8^2				12	11	7		1					13					10^1	6	9	4				36
	2	3		5	8				12	11^2	7		1			13							10^1	6	9	4				37
	2	3		5	12				13		7		1			11		8					10^2	6	9^1	4				38
	2^3	3		5					12	13	7		1			11		8^2					10^1	6	9	4	14			39
	2	3^1		5	8^2				12	13	7		1			11							10^3	6	9	4	14			40
	2	3		5					10^2		7		1			11		8					12	6	13	4	9^1			41
	2	3		5^1							7▮		1		12	11		8					13	6	9	4	10^2			42
	2					12			13	11^1			1		5	7		8	3^3				14	6	9	4	10^2			43
		3^1		5	12				13		7		1			11		8					14	6	9^2	4	10	2^3		44
		3		5	8^2					12	7		1			11		13					9^3	6	14	4	10^1	2		45
	2	3							12		7		1			11		8					9^1	6	13	4^2	10	14	5^3	46

FA Cup

First Round	Grimsby T	(h)	0-0
		(a)	2-0
Second Round	Barnet	(a)	1-4

Carling Cup

First Round	QPR	(a)	2-3

J Paint Trophy

First Round	Brentford	(h)	0-0

NORWICH CITY FL Championship

FOUNDATION

Formed in 1902, largely through the initiative of two local schoolmasters who called a meeting at the Criterion Cafe, they were shocked by an FA Commission which in 1904 declared the club professional and ejected them from the FA Amateur Cup. However, this only served to strengthen their determination. New officials were appointed and a professional club established at a meeting in the Agricultural Hall in March 1905.

Carrow Road, Norwich NR1 1JE.

Telephone: (01603) 760 760.

Fax: (01603) 613 886.

Ticket Office: 0870 444 1902.

Website: www.canaries.co.uk

Email: reception@ncfc-canaries.co.uk

Ground Capacity: 26,034.

Record Attendance: 43,984 v Leicester C, FA Cup 6th rd, 30 March 1963.

Pitch Measurements: 105m × 67m.

Chairman: Roger Munby.

Chief Executive: Neil Doncaster.

Secretary: Kevan Platt.

Manager: Peter Grant.

Assistant Manager: Jim Duffy.

Physio: Neil Reynolds MCSP, SRP.

Colours: Yellow shirts, green shorts, yellow stockings.

Change Colours: Red shirts, red shorts, red and white stockings. ***Alternative Change Colours:*** White shirts, white shorts, white stockings.

Year Formed: 1902.

Turned Professional: 1905.

Ltd Co.: 1905.

Club Nickname: 'The Canaries'.

Grounds: 1902, Newmarket Road; 1908, The Nest, Rosary Road; 1935, Carrow Road.

First Football League Game: 28 August 1920, Division 3, v Plymouth Arg (a) D 1–1 – Skermer; Gray, Gadsden; Wilkinson, Addy, Martin; Laxton, Kidger, Parker, Whitham (1), Dobson.

Record League Victory: 10–2 v Coventry C, Division 3 (S), 15 March 1930 – Jarvie; Hannah, Graham; Brown, O'Brien, Lochhead (1); Porter (1), Anderson, Hunt (5), Scott (2), Slicer (1).

HONOURS

FA Premier League: best season: 3rd 1992–93.

Football League: Division 1 – Champions 2003–04; Division 2 – Champions 1971–72, 1985–86; Division 3 (S) – Champions 1933–34; Division 3 – Runners-up 1959–60.

FA Cup: Semi-finals 1959, 1989, 1992.

Football League Cup: Winners 1962, 1985; Runners-up 1973, 1975.

European Competitions: *UEFA Cup:* 1993–94.

SKY SPORTS FACT FILE

Percy Varco scored in four FA Cup ties for Norwich City in the late 1920s, but unusually in a sequence of 3, 2, 4 and one in a prolific spree of ten goals. Later found the target in four successive ties while with Exeter City!

Record Cup Victory: 8–0 v Sutton U, FA Cup 4th rd, 28 January 1989 – Gunn; Culverhouse, Bowen, Butterworth, Linighan, Townsend (Crook), Gordon, Fleck (3), Allen (4), Phelan, Putney (1).

Record Defeat: 2–10 v Swindon T, Southern League, 5 September 1908.

Most League Points (2 for a win): 64, Division 3 (S), 1950–51.

Most League Points (3 for a win): 94, Division 1, 2003–04.

Most League Goals: 99, Division 3 (S), 1952–53.

Highest League Scorer in Season: Ralph Hunt, 31, Division 3 (S), 1955–56.

Most League Goals in Total Aggregate: Johnny Gavin, 122, 1945–54, 1955–58.

Most League Goals in One Match: 5, Tommy Hunt v Coventry C, Division 3S, 15 March 1930; 5, Roy Hollis v Walsall, Division 3S, 29 December 1951.

Most Capped Player: Mark Bowen, 35 (41), Wales.

Most League Appearances: Ron Ashman, 592, 1947–64.

Youngest League Player: Ryan Jarvis, 16 years 282 days v Walsall, 19 April 2003.

Record Transfer Fee Received: £7,250,000 from West Ham U for Dean Ashton, January 2006.

Record Transfer Fee Paid: £3,400,000 to Crewe Alex for Dean Ashton, January 2005.

Football League Record: 1920 Original Member of Division 3; 1921 Division 3 (S): 1934–39 Division 2; 1946–58 Division 3 (S); 1958–60 Division 3; 1960–72 Division 2; 1972–74 Division 1; 1974–75 Division 2; 1975–81 Division 1; 1981–82 Division 2; 1982–85 Division 1; 1985–86 Division 2; 1986–92 Division 1; 1992–95 FA Premier League; 1995–2004 Division 1; 2004–05 FA Premier League; 2005– FL C.

MANAGERS

John Bowman 1905–07
James McEwen 1907–08
Arthur Turner 1909–10
Bert Stansfield 1910–15
Major Frank Buckley 1919–20
Charles O'Hagan 1920–21
Albert Gosnell 1921–26
Bert Stansfield 1926
Cecil Potter 1926–29
James Kerr 1929–33
Tom Parker 1933–37
Bob Young 1937–39
Jimmy Jewell 1939
Bob Young 1939–45
Cyril Spiers 1946–47
Duggie Lochhead 1947–50
Norman Low 1950–55
Tom Parker 1955–57
Archie Macaulay 1957–61
Willie Reid 1961–62
George Swindin 1962
Ron Ashman 1962–66
Lol Morgan 1966–69
Ron Saunders 1969–73
John Bond 1973–80
Ken Brown 1980–87
Dave Stringer 1987–92
Mike Walker 1992–94
John Deehan 1994–95
Martin O'Neill 1995
Gary Megson 1995–96
Mike Walker 1996–98
Bruce Rioch 1998–2000
Bryan Hamilton 2000
Nigel Worthington 2001–06
Peter Grant October 2006–

LATEST SEQUENCES

Longest Sequence of League Wins: 10, 23.11.1985 – 25.1.1986.

Longest Sequence of League Defeats: 7, 1.4.1995 – 6.5.1995.

Longest Sequence of League Draws: 7, 15.1.1994 – 26.2.1994.

Longest Sequence of Unbeaten League Matches: 20, 31.8.1950 – 30.12.1950.

Longest Sequence Without a League Win: 25, 22.9.1956 – 23.2.1957.

Successive Scoring Runs: 25 from 31.8.1963.

Successive Non-scoring Runs: 5 from 21.2.1925.

TEN YEAR LEAGUE RECORD

		P	W	D	L	F	A	Pts	Pos
1997-98	Div 1	46	14	13	19	52	69	55	15
1998-99	Div 1	46	15	17	14	62	61	62	9
1999-2000	Div 1	46	14	15	17	45	50	57	12
2000-01	Div 1	46	14	12	20	46	58	54	15
2001-02	Div 1	46	22	9	15	60	51	75	6
2002-03	Div 1	46	19	12	15	60	49	69	8
2003-04	Div 1	46	28	10	8	79	39	94	1
2004-05	PR Lge	38	7	12	19	42	77	33	19
2005-06	FL C	46	18	8	20	56	65	62	9
2006-07	FL C	46	16	9	21	56	71	57	16

DID YOU KNOW ?

On 10 January 1959 Norwich City entertained Manchester United in a third round FA Cup tie at Carrow Road. The post-Munich Busby Babes were well beaten 3–0 with Terry Bly scoring twice and Errol Crossan sandwiching his effort between the pair of them.

NORWICH CITY 2006–07 LEAGUE RECORD

Match No.	*Date*	*Venue*	*Opponents*	*Result*		*H/T Score*	*Lg. Pos.*	*Goalscorers*	*Attendance*
1	Aug 5	A	Leeds U	L	0-1	0-1	—		22,417
2	8	H	Preston NE	W	2-0	0-0	—	St Ledger-Hall (og) [56], Earnshaw [82]	24,676
3	12	H	Luton T	W	3-2	0-1	7	Huckerby [57], Croft [67], Earnshaw [71]	23,863
4	19	A	Derby Co	D	0-0	0-0	6		22,196
5	26	H	Barnsley	W	5-1	2-1	2	Earnshaw 2 (1 pen) [13 (p), 69], Robinson [27], Croft [57], Huckerby [64]	24,876
6	Sept 9	A	Coventry C	L	0-3	0-1	5		20,006
7	12	A	Southend U	D	3-3	2-1	—	Earnshaw 2 [36, 39], Etuhu [47]	11,072
8	16	H	Crystal Palace	L	0-1	0-0	10		24,618
9	23	A	Plymouth Arg	L	1-3	0-1	14	Earnshaw [90]	11,813
10	Oct 1	H	Burnley	L	1-4	0-2	17	Earnshaw [82]	24,717
11	14	A	QPR	D	3-3	1-2	19	Huckerby [4], Dublin [72], Earnshaw (pen) [84]	14,793
12	17	A	Birmingham C	W	1-0	0-0	—	Shackell [66]	20,537
13	21	H	Cardiff C	W	1-0	1-0	11	Etuhu [7]	25,014
14	28	A	Stoke C	L	0-5	0-2	18		13,444
15	31	H	Colchester U	D	1-1	0-0	—	Etuhu [72]	25,065
16	Nov 4	H	Sunderland	W	1-0	0-0	13	Earnshaw [51]	24,652
17	11	A	WBA	W	1-0	0-0	9	Earnshaw [57]	18,718
18	19	A	Ipswich T	L	1-3	1-1	12	Chadwick [26]	27,276
19	25	H	Hull C	D	1-1	0-0	13	Earnshaw [72]	24,129
20	28	H	Leicester C	W	3-1	1-1	—	Robinson [45], Earnshaw [59], McAuley (og) [90]	23,896
21	Dec 2	A	Sunderland	L	0-1	0-0	15		27,934
22	9	H	Sheffield W	L	1-2	0-0	15	Dublin [85]	24,816
23	16	A	Southampton	L	1-2	1-1	16	Earnshaw [21]	25,919
24	23	A	Wolverhampton W	D	2-2	1-1	15	Earnshaw 2 [10, 77]	22,910
25	26	H	Southend U	D	0-0	0-0	17		25,433
26	30	H	QPR	W	1-0	0-0	15	Dublin [69]	25,113
27	Jan 1	A	Crystal Palace	L	1-3	1-3	17	Earnshaw (pen) [45]	16,765
28	13	H	Plymouth Arg	L	1-3	1-0	17	Safri [45]	23,513
29	30	H	Wolverhampton W	L	0-1	0-0	—		23,311
30	Feb 3	H	Leeds U	W	2-1	0-1	16	Dublin [59], Huckerby [78]	25,018
31	20	A	Preston NE	L	1-2	0-2	—	Shackell [62]	11,601
32	24	H	Coventry C	D	1-1	0-1	18	Martin [81]	24,220
33	27	A	Luton T	W	3-2	1-1	—	Martin [26], Shackell [73], Lappin [90]	8868
34	Mar 3	A	Barnsley	W	3-1	3-1	16	Huckerby [7], Croft [26], Martin [41]	11,010
35	6	H	Derby Co	L	1-2	0-0	—	Martin [52]	23,462
36	10	A	Cardiff C	L	0-1	0-1	17		13,276
37	13	H	Birmingham C	W	1-0	0-0	—	Huckerby [47]	23,504
38	17	H	Stoke C	W	1-0	1-0	15	Huckerby [31]	24,293
39	31	A	Colchester U	L	0-3	0-0	16		5851
40	Apr 6	A	Hull C	W	2-1	1-0	—	Huckerby [39], Etuhu [55]	19,053
41	9	H	WBA	L	1-2	0-0	16	Etuhu [58]	25,422
42	14	A	Leicester C	W	2-1	0-1	15	Earnshaw (pen) [74], McAuley (og) [78]	21,483
43	17	A	Burnley	L	0-3	0-1	—		9681
44	22	H	Ipswich T	D	1-1	1-0	15	Etuhu [5]	25,476
45	28	H	Southampton	L	0-1	0-1	16		25,437
46	May 6	A	Sheffield W	L	2-3	0-2	16	Earnshaw [56], Dublin [75]	28,287

Final League Position: 16

GOALSCORERS

League (56): Earnshaw 19 (4 pens), Huckerby 8, Etuhu 6, Dublin 5, Martin 4, Croft 3, Shackell 3, Robinson 2, Chadwick 1, Lappin 1, Safri 1, own goals 3.
Carling Cup (6): Ryan Jarvis 2, Etuhu 1, Fleming 1, McKenzie 1, Thorne 1.
FA Cup (8): Huckerby 5, Dublin 2, Martin 1.

Gallacher P 26 + 1	Colin J 30 + 3	Drury A 39	Shackell J 42 + 1	Doherty G 34	Safri Y 30 + 5	Croft L 33 + 3	Robinson C 26 + 1	Huckerby D 40	Earnshaw R 28 + 2	Etuhu D 42 + 1	Thorne P 4 + 11	McKenzie L — + 4	McVeigh P 6 + 15	Fleming C 4 + 6	Henderson I — + 2	Hughes A 28 + 8	Jarvis Ryan 1 + 4	Boyle P 3	Dublin D 22 + 11	Ashdown J 2	Eagle R 3 + 7	Chadwick L 1 + 3	Camp L 3	Brown C 3 + 1	Marshall D 2	Martin C 13 + 5	Lappin S 14	Fotheringham M 9 + 5	Warner T 13	Renton K 1 + 2	Spillane M 4 + 1	Smart B — + 1	*Match No.*
1	2^{1}	3	4	5	6	7^{2}	8^{3}	9	10	11	12	13	14																				1
1	2^{3}	3	4	5	6	7^{1}	8	9	10^{2}	11		13	12	14																			2
1	2^{3}	3	4	5	6	7^{1}	8	9	10^{2}	11		13	12	14																			3
1	2	3	4	5	6	7^{1}	8	9	10	11			12																				4
1	2	3	4^{3}	5	6	7^{2}	8^{1}	9	10	11		12	13	14																			5
1	2	3	4	5	6	7	8	9^{1}	10	11^{2}			12		13																		6
1	2	3	4	5	6	7^{1}			10	11			9^{2}		12	8	13																7
1	2		4	5	6	7^{1}	8^{2}		10	11	13		9^{3}			12	14	3															8
1	2			5	6^{3}	7^{2}	8		10	11	12		9	4			13	3^{1}	14														9
1	2		12	5▮	6	7^{2}	8	11	10		14			4		13		3^{1}	9^{3}														10
1	2	3	4		12	7^{2}	8^{3}	9	10	11			13	5		6^{1}			14														11
1	2	3^{1}	4	5	6	7^{2}	8	9	10	11			13	12																			12
	2	3	4	5	6^{2}	7	8	9^{1}	10	11			12▮						13	1													13
15	2	3	4	5		7	8^{G}			11	12			6^{1}		10^{2}			9	1▮	13												14
1	2	3	4	5^{2}	6^{1}		8	9	10	11				13		12			14		7^{3}												15
1	2^{2}	3	4		6		8	9	10	11			7^{1}			12			5		13												16
1	2	3	4		6		8	9	10^{2}	11	13		12			7^{1}			5														17
1	2	3	4	5			8	9	10	11						6^{1}			12		13	7^{2}											18
1	2	3	4				6	9	10	11	12		7^{2}			13			5		8^{1}												19
	2	3^{1}	4		12		8	9^{3}	10	11	7^{2}					6	13		5		14		1										20
	2	3	4		6^{1}		8^{2}	9	10	11	12					7			5		13		1										21
	2	3	4				6	9		11	10		12			8	7^{1}		5				1										22
1	2^{1}	3		4		12	8	9^{2}	10	11	7			13		6			5														23
1	12	3	4	5	13	7^{1}	8	9	10^{2}	11	14					6			2^{3}														24
1	2		4	5	12	7	8^{1}	9	10	11						3			6														25
1	2	3	4	5	6^{1}	7^{2}		9	10	11			12			13			8														26
1	2	3	4	5	6^{2}	12	8^{3}	9	10	11	13					7^{1}			14														27
1	2^{1}	3	4	5	6	7	12	9		11			10^{2}						8					13									28
	2	3	4^{1}	5	6	7	8	9		11	10					12^{2}									1	13							29
	2^{1}			5	6	7^{2}		9		11			13			12			4					10^{3}	1	14	3	8					30
1		3	4	2		7					12^{2}		13			6			5^{1}					10		9	11	8					31
1		3	4	5	12	13		9		11			14			2^{1}								10^{2}		8	7	6^{3}					32
1		3	4	5	6	2		9		11^{1}						7										10	8	12					33
	12	3	4	5	6	2^{1}		9		13						7										10	8	11^{2}	1				34
			4	5	6	7		9		11^{1}						2			12							10	3	8	1				35
		3	4	5	6	7^{1}		9		11						2			12							10	8		1				36
		3	4	5	6	7^{2}		9^{3}		11						2			12			13				10^{1}	8	14	1				37
		3^{3}	4	5	6	7^{2}		9		11						2			12			13				10^{1}	8	14	1				38
			4	5	6	7^{1}		9								2			8			12				10	3	11	1				39
		3	4	5	6	7^{2}		9^{1}		11						8			10							12	2	13	1				40
		3	4	5	6^{3}	7^{2}		9		11						2			13		12					10^{1}	8	14	1				41
	2	3^{2}	4			7^{3}		9	12	11						6			5		13					10			1	14	8^{1}		42
		3	4			7			12	11						2			5^{2}		8^{1}					10			1	9	6	13	43
	12	3	4			7^{1}		9	10	11						2			5							13		8	1		6^{2}		44
		3	4					7	9	11						2			5							10^{2}	6^{1}	8	1	12	13		45
		3^{1}	4					9	10	11						2			5							12	6	8	1		7		46

FA Cup

Third Round	Tamworth	(a)	4-1
Fourth Round	Blackpool	(a)	1-1
		(h)	3-2
Fifth Round	Chelsea	(a)	0-4

Carling Cup

First Round	Torquay U	(a)	2-0
Second Round	Rotherham U	(a)	4-2
Third Round	Port Vale	(a)	0-0

NOTTINGHAM FOREST FL Championship 1

FOUNDATION

One of the oldest football clubs in the world, Nottingham Forest was formed at a meeting in the Clinton Arms in 1865. Known originally as the Forest Football Club, the game which first drew the founders together was 'shinney', a form of hockey. When they determined to change to football in 1865, one of their first moves was to buy a set of red caps to wear on the field.

The City Ground, Nottingham NG2 5FJ.

Telephone: (0115) 982 4444.

Fax: (0115) 982 4455.

Ticket Office: 0871 226 1980.

Website: www.nottinghamforest.co.uk

Email: info@nottinghamforest.co.uk

Ground Capacity: 30,602.

Record Attendance: 49,946 v Manchester U, Division 1, 28 October 1967.

Pitch Measurements: 112yd × 74yd.

Chairman: Nigel Doughty.

Chief Executive: Mark Arthur.

Football Administrator: Jane Carnelly.

Manager: Colin Calderwood.

First Team Coaches: David Kerslake, Ian MacParland.

Physios: Gary Fleming, Steve Devine.

Colours: Red shirts, white shorts, red stockings.

Change Colours: White shirts, red shorts, white stockings.

Year Formed: 1865.

Turned Professional: 1889.

Ltd Co.: 1982.

Club Nickname: 'Reds'.

Grounds: 1865, Forest Racecourse; 1879, The Meadows; 1880, Trent Bridge Cricket Ground; 1882, Parkside, Lenton; 1885, Gregory, Lenton; 1890, Town Ground; 1898, City Ground.

First Football League Game: 3 September 1892, Division 1, v Everton (a) D 2–2 – Brown; Earp, Scott; Hamilton, A. Smith, McCracken; McCallum, W. Smith, Higgins (2), Pike, McInnes.

Record League Victory: 12–0 v Leicester Fosse, Division 1, 12 April 1909 – Iremonger; Dudley, Maltby; Hughes (1), Needham, Armstrong; Hooper (3), Marrison, West (3), Morris (2), Spouncer (3 incl. 1p).

Record Cup Victory: 14–0 v Clapton (away), FA Cup 1st rd, 17 January 1891 – Brown; Earp, Scott; A. Smith, Russell, Jeacock; McCallum (2), 'Tich' Smith (1), Higgins (5), Lindley (4), Shaw (2).

Record Defeat: 1–9 v Blackburn R, Division 2, 10 April 1937.

HONOURS

Football League: Division 1 – Champions 1977–78, 1997–98; Runners-up 1966–67, 1978–79; Division 2 – Champions 1906–07, 1921–22; Runners-up 1956–57; Division 3 (S) – Champions 1950–51.

FA Cup: Winners 1898, 1959; Runners-up 1991.

Football League Cup: Winners 1978, 1979, 1989, 1990; Runners-up 1980, 1992.

Anglo-Scottish Cup: Winners 1977;

Simod Cup: Winners 1989.

Zenith Data Systems Cup: Winners: 1992.

European Competitions: *European Cup:* 1978–79 (winners), 1979–80 (winners), 1980–81. *European Fairs Cup:* 1961–62, 1967–68. *UEFA Cup:* 1983–84, 1984–85, 1995–96. *Super Cup:* 1979–80 (winners), 1980–81 (runners-up). *World Club Championship:* 1980.

SKY SPORTS FACT FILE

Ex-miner Tommy Graham had an unsuccessful Newcastle United trial and was then injured in one at Nottingham Forest. Out for seven months and injured in his next, the club persevered and he made over 400 appearances at centre-half to 1944 and won England caps.

Most League Points (2 for a win): 70, Division 3 (S), 1950–51.

Most League Points (3 for a win): 94, Division 1, 1997–98.

Most League Goals: 110, Division 3 (S), 1950–51.

Highest League Scorer in Season: Wally Ardron, 36, Division 3 (S), 1950–51.

Most League Goals in Total Aggregate: Grenville Morris, 199, 1898–1913.

Most League Goals in One Match: 4, Enoch West v Sunderland, Division 1, 9 November 1907; 4, Tommy Gibson v Burnley, Division 2, 25 January 1913; 4, Tom Peacock v Port Vale, Division 2, 23 December 1933; 4, Tom Peacock v Barnsley, Division 2, 9 November 1935; 4, Tom Peacock v Port Vale, Division 2, 23 November 1935; 4, Tom Peacock v Doncaster R, Division 2, 26 December 1935; 4, Tommy Capel v Gillingham, Division 3S, 18 November 1950; 4, Wally Ardron v Hull C, Division 2, 26 December 1952; 4, Tommy Wilson v Barnsley, Division 2, 9 February 1957; 4, Peter Withe v Ipswich T, Division 1, 4 October 1977.

Most Capped Player: Stuart Pearce, 76 (78), England.

Most League Appearances: Bob McKinlay, 614, 1951–70.

Youngest League Player: Craig Westcarr, 16 years 257 days v Burnley, 13 October 2001.

Record Transfer Fee Received: £8,500,000 from Liverpool for Stan Collymore, June 1995.

Record Transfer Fee Paid: £3,500,000 to Celtic for Pierre van Hooijdonk, March 1997.

Football League Record: 1892 Elected to Division 1; 1906–07 Division 2; 1907–11 Division 1; 1911–22 Division 2; 1922–25 Division 1; 1925–49 Division 2; 1949–51 Division 3 (S); 1951–57 Division 2; 1957–72 Division 1; 1972–77 Division 2; 1977–92 Division 1; 1992–93 FA Premier League; 1993–94 Division 1; 1994–97 FA Premier League; 1997–98 Division 1; 1998–99 FA Premier League; 1999–2004 Division 1; 2004–05 FL C; 2005– FL 1.

MANAGERS

Harry Radford 1889–97
(Secretary-Manager)
Harry Haslam 1897–1909
(Secretary-Manager)
Fred Earp 1909–12
Bob Masters 1912–25
John Baynes 1925–29
Stan Hardy 1930–31
Noel Watson 1931–36
Harold Wightman 1936–39
Billy Walker 1939–60
Andy Beattie 1960–63
Johnny Carey 1963–68
Matt Gillies 1969–72
Dave Mackay 1972
Allan Brown 1973–75
Brian Clough 1975–93
Frank Clark 1993–96
Stuart Pearce 1996–97
Dave Bassett 1997–98 *(previously General Manager from February)*
Ron Atkinson 1998–99
David Platt 1999–2001
Paul Hart 2001–04
Joe Kinnear 2004
Gary Megson 2005
Colin Calderwood May 2006–

LATEST SEQUENCES

Longest Sequence of League Wins: 7, 9.5.1979 – 1.9.1979.

Longest Sequence of League Defeats: 14, 21.3.1913 – 27.9.1913.

Longest Sequence of League Draws: 7, 29.4.1978 – 2.9.1978.

Longest Sequence of Unbeaten League Matches: 42, 26.11.1977 – 25.11.1978.

Longest Sequence Without a League Win: 19, 8.9.1998 – 16.1.1999.

Successive Scoring Runs: 22 from 28.3.1931.

Successive Non-scoring Runs: 7 from 13.12.2003.

TEN YEAR LEAGUE RECORD

		P	W	D	L	F	A	Pts	Pos
1997-98	Div 1	46	28	10	8	82	42	94	1
1998-99	PR Lge	38	7	9	22	35	69	30	20
1999-2000	Div 1	46	14	14	18	53	55	56	14
2000-01	Div 1	46	20	8	18	55	53	68	11
2001-02	Div 1	46	12	18	16	50	51	54	16
2002-03	Div 1	46	20	14	12	82	50	74	6
2003-04	Div 1	46	15	15	16	61	58	60	14
2004-05	FL C	46	9	17	20	42	66	44	23
2005-06	FL 1	46	19	12	15	67	52	69	7
2006-07	FL 1	46	23	13	10	65	41	82	4

DID YOU KNOW ?

Nottingham Forest were the champion pre-war escape artists. In 1937–38 they had avoided relegation on goal average of .00208 from Barnsley and in 1938–39 achieved a similar success in the Second Division at the expense of Norwich City by .0481!

NOTTINGHAM FOREST 2006–07 LEAGUE RECORD

Match No.	Date	Venue	Opponents	Result	H/T Score	Lg. Pos.	Goalscorers	Attendance
1	Aug 5	H	Bradford C	W 1-0	1-0	—	Bennett [10]	19,665
2	8	A	Blackpool	W 2-0	1-0	—	Lester [45], Grant Holt [73]	7635
3	12	A	Northampton T	W 1-0	0-0	2	Doig (og) [46]	7172
4	19	H	Brighton & HA	W 2-1	0-1	2	Grant Holt 2 (1 pen) [63 (p), 78]	18,586
5	26	A	Huddersfield T	D 1-1	1-0	1	Grant Holt [34]	11,720
6	Sept 2	H	Chesterfield	W 4-0	2-0	1	Lester [35], Harris [45], Grant Holt (pen) [49], Southall [69]	19,480
7	9	A	Yeovil T	W 1-0	0-0	1	Grant Holt [88]	6925
8	12	H	Oldham Ath	L 0-2	0-2	—		17,446
9	16	H	Carlisle U	D 0-0	0-0	1		19,535
10	23	A	Tranmere R	D 0-0	0-0	1		11,444
11	26	A	Port Vale	D 1-1	1-1	—	Breckin [33]	7388
12	30	H	Swansea C	W 3-1	0-1	1	Perch [54], Commons [56], Agogo [67]	19,034
13	Oct 7	H	Scunthorpe U	L 0-4	0-2	1		22,640
14	14	A	Gillingham	W 1-0	0-0	1	Southall [57]	7800
15	21	H	Bristol C	W 1-0	1-0	1	Southall [9]	23,456
16	28	A	Cheltenham T	W 2-0	2-0	1	Southall 2 [32, 36]	6554
17	Nov 4	H	Brentford	W 2-0	2-0	1	Commons 2 [10, 37]	18,003
18	18	A	Rotherham U	D 1-1	0-0	1	Tyson [88]	7809
19	25	H	Millwall	W 3-1	0-1	1	Agogo [65], Perch [67], Breckin [82]	19,410
20	Dec 5	A	Bournemouth	L 0-2	0-0	—		7067
21	9	A	Crewe Alex	W 4-1	4-1	1	Grant Holt [31], Tyson 3 [37, 43, 45]	7253
22	16	H	Leyton Orient	L 1-3	0-2	1	Breckin [58]	23,109
23	23	A	Doncaster R	L 0-1	0-0	1		8923
24	26	H	Port Vale	W 3-0	1-0	1	Tyson [13], Grant Holt 2 [65, 90]	22,999
25	30	H	Tranmere R	D 1-1	0-0	2	Perch [72]	19,729
26	Jan 1	A	Oldham Ath	L 0-5	0-3	3		9768
27	13	H	Yeovil T	W 1-0	0-0	1	Grant Holt [48]	17,885
28	20	A	Swansea C	D 0-0	0-0	3		16,849
29	31	A	Carlisle U	L 0-1	0-1	—		9022
30	Feb 3	A	Bradford C	D 2-2	2-1	3	Tyson [10], Lester [18]	10,160
31	10	H	Northampton T	W 1-0	0-0	3	Bennett [65]	24,567
32	17	A	Brighton & HA	L 1-2	0-0	4	Lester [55]	7749
33	20	H	Blackpool	D 1-1	1-0	—	Agogo [16]	16,849
34	24	A	Chesterfield	W 2-1	0-0	3	Agogo 2 (1 pen) [56, 62 (p)]	6641
35	Mar 3	H	Huddersfield T	W 5-1	4-0	2	Agogo 2 [6, 60], McGugan [17], Grant Holt [19], Perch [33]	19,070
36	6	H	Doncaster R	L 0-1	0-1	—		16,785
37	10	A	Scunthorpe U	D 1-1	1-0	4	Commons [18]	8906
38	17	H	Gillingham	W 1-0	0-0	3	McGugan [85]	17,950
39	24	H	Cheltenham T	W 3-0	1-0	3	Gary Holt [33], Perch [57], Tyson (pen) [90]	22,640
40	31	A	Bristol C	D 1-1	1-1	3	Grant Holt [5]	19,249
41	Apr 7	A	Millwall	L 0-1	0-0	3		12,035
42	9	H	Rotherham U	D 1-1	1-1	3	Grant Holt (pen) [21]	27,875
43	14	A	Brentford	W 4-2	0-1	3	Prutton [52], Commons 2 [68, 90], Grant Holt (pen) [74]	6637
44	21	H	Bournemouth	W 3-0	1-0	3	Commons 2 [23, 54], Prutton [66]	19,898
45	28	A	Leyton Orient	W 3-1	2-1	3	Lester 2 [18, 58], Commons [29]	7206
46	May 5	H	Crewe Alex	D 0-0	0-0	4		27,472

Final League Position: 4

GOALSCORERS

League (65): Grant Holt 14 (4 pens), Commons 9, Agogo 7 (1 pen), Tyson 7 (1 pen), Lester 6, Perch 5, Southall 5, Breckin 3, Bennett 2, McGugan 2, Prutton 2, Harris 1, Gary Holt 1, own goal 1.
Carling Cup (0).
FA Cup (10): Agogo 3 (1 pen), Commons 3, Tyson 2, Grant Holt 1, Southall 1.
J Paint Trophy (6): Grant Holt 3, Lester 1, Morgan 1, Southall 1.
Play-Offs (4): Commons 1 (pen), Dobie 1, Grant Holt 1, Perch 1 (pen).

Smith P 45	Holt Gary 30 + 9	Bennett J 24 + 6	Cullip D 19 + 1	Breckin I 46	Morgan W 31 + 7	Southall N 26 + 1	Clingan S 25 + 3	Lester J 24 + 11	Tyson N 12 + 12	Perch J 43 + 3	Curtis J 38 + 3	Harris N 11 + 8	Holt Grant 34 + 11	Thompson J 6 + 8	Weir-Daley S — + 1	Agogo J 20 + 9	Dobie S 2 + 17	Commons K 28 + 4	Hughes R — + 2	Pedersen R 1	McGugan L 11 + 2	Prutton D 11 + 1	Chambers L 10 + 4	Wright A 9	Moloney B — + 1	Henry J — + 1	Bastians F — + 2	Match No.
1	2	3	4^{1}	5	6	7	8	9^{2}	10^{3}	11	12	13	14															1
1	2	3^{1}	4	5	6	7	8	9^{3}		11		13	10^{2}	12	14													2
1		3^{1}	4	5	6	7	8	9^{2}		11	12	13	10	2														3
1	2	3	4	5	6^{1}	7	8	9^{2}		11^{3}	12	13	10	14														4
1	2	3	4	5	12	7^{1}	8^{2}	9^{3}		11	6	13	10	14														5
1	2	3	4	5	12	7		9^{3}		11	6^{1}	8^{2}	10	13		14												6
1	2	3	4^{1}	5	12	7	13	9^{3}		11	6^{2}	8	10			14												7
1	2^{1}	3		5	6	7	4	9^{2}		11		8^{3}	10	12		13	14											8
1	2^{2}	3		5	6	7	4	12		11		8^{1}	10^{3}	13		9	14											9
1	2	3		5	6	7^{3}	8	12		11	4	10^{2}	13			9^{1}		14										10
1	2	3		5	6	12	8	13		7^{1}	4	14	10^{2}			9^{3}		11										11
1	2	12		5	6	7	4	13		8	3		10^{2}			9^{3}		11^{1}	14									12
1	2	3		5	6	7		9		8	4	12	10^{1}					11										13
1	2	3	12	5	6	7	13			8	4	10^{3}	14			9^{1}		11^{2}										14
1		12	4	5	6	7	8			3	2	9^{3}	13	14		10^{2}		11^{1}										15
1		12	4	5	6	7	8	13		3	2	10^{1}	14			9^{3}		11^{2}										16
1			4	5	6	7	8	12	13	3	2	10^{3}	14			9^{2}		11^{1}										17
1			4	5	6	7	8^{2}		12	3	2	10^{1}	13			9		11										18
1	12		4^{2}	5	6	7	8		13	3	2	10^{3}	14			9		11^{1}										19
	2^{2}		4	5	6	7	12		9^{3}	8^{1}	3	14	10				13	11		1								20
1	2		4	5	6	7^{1}	8		9^{2}	12	3		10^{3}	14			13	11										21
1	2		4	5	6	7	8		9^{3}	12	3^{2}		10^{1}			13	14	11										22
1	2^{1}		4	5		7	8^{3}		9	12	3		10^{2}	6		13	14	11										23
1	12		4	5		7	8	14	9^{2}	6	3		13	2		10^{1}		11^{3}										24
1	12		4	5		7	8^{1}		9^{3}	6	3		10	2		13	14	11^{2}										25
1	2^{1}		4■	5	12	7	8■	13	14	11	3		10	6^{2}		9^{3}												26
1	2	3		5	6			12	10^{2}	11	4		8	7^{3}		9^{1}	13				14							27
1	2	3		5	6	7		12	10	11	4		8^{2}			9^{1}	13											28
1		3		5	6		8	9^{2}	13	11	2		10			12	4^{1}				7							29
1	12	3		5	6		4^{1}	9	10^{2}	11	2		8^{3}				13					7	14					30
1	2	3		5	6			9^{3}	12	11	4		8^{2}			13	10^{1}	14				7						31
1	2^{3}	3		5	6			9	10■	11	4^{2}		8^{1}			12	13	14				7						32
1	2	3		5	6			9^{2}		11	4		8^{1}			10	12	13				7						33
1	12	3		5	6		4^{3}	9		8	2					10^{2}	13	11^{1}				7	14					34
1	2	3		5	6		7^{2}			8^{3}	4^{1}		10			9		11	14		13		12					35
1	2	3		5^{3}	6				12	8	4		10^{1}			9	13	11			7^{2}		14					36
1	2	3		5	6			10^{2}	12	8			13			9^{1}		11			7		4					37
1	2			5				9^{1}	12	8	6		13			10^{2}		11^{3}			7		4	3	14			38
1	2			5				9	12	8	6		10^{1}				13	11^{3}			7^{2}		4	3		14		39
1	2			5	12			9^{3}	13	8	6^{1}		10					11			7^{2}	14	4	3				40
1	2	13		5	6			9^{1}	12	8			10					11				7	4	3^{2}				41
1		12		5	13			14	9^{3}	8	2		10					11			4^{2}	7	6	3^{1}				42
1	12	14		5	13^{3}			9		8	2		10					11			4^{1}	7	6	3^{2}				43
1	12			5				9		8	2		10^{1}					11			4^{2}	7	6	3			13	44
1	12			5				9		8	2		10^{2}				13	11			4^{1}	7	6	3				45
1	12			5				9		8^{3}	2		10^{2}				13	11			4^{1}	7	6	3			14	46

FA Cup

First Round	Yeading	(h)	5-0
Second Round	Salisbury C	(a)	1-1
		(h)	2-0
Third Round	Charlton Ath	(h)	2-0
Fourth Round	Chelsea	(a)	0-3

Carling Cup

First Round	Accrington S	(a)	0-1

J Paint Trophy

First Round	Gillingham	(a)	2-1
Second Round	Brentford	(h)	2-1
Quarter-Final	Bristol C	(h)	2-2

Play-Offs

Semi-Final	Yeovil T	(a)	2-0
		(h)	2-5

NOTTS COUNTY FL Championship 2

FOUNDATION

According to the official history of Notts County 'the true date of Notts' foundation has to be the meeting at the George Hotel on 7 December 1864'. However, there is documented evidence of continuous play from 1862, when club members played organised matches amongst themselves in The Park in Nottingham.

Meadow Lane Stadium, Meadow Lane, Nottingham NG2 3HJ.

Telephone: (0115) 952 9000.

Fax: (0115) 955 3994.

Ticket Office: (0115) 955 7204 (weekdays), (0115) 955 7210 (match days).

Website: www.nottscountyfc.co.uk

Email: info@nottscountyfc.co.uk

Ground Capacity: 20,300.

Record Attendance: 47,310 v York C, FA Cup 6th rd, 12 March 1955.

Pitch Measurements: 113yd × 72yd.

Chairman: Jeffrey P. Moore.

Vice-chairman: Michael Hammond.

Chief Executive: Geoffrey R. Davey.

Secretary: Tony Cuthbert.

Manager: Steve Thompson.

Assistant Manager: John Gannon.

Physio: John Haselden.

HONOURS

Football League: Division 1 best season: 3rd, 1890–91, 1900–01; Division 2 – Champions 1896–97, 1913–14, 1922–23; Runners-up 1894–95, 1980–81; Promoted from Division 2 1990–91 (play-offs); Division 3 (S) – Champions 1930–31, 1949–50; Runners-up 1936–37; Division 3 – Champions 1997–98; Runners-up 1972–73; Promoted from Division 3 1989–90 (play-offs); Division 4 – Champions 1970–71; Runners-up 1959–60.

FA Cup: Winners 1894; Runners-up 1891.

Football League Cup: best season: 5th rd, 1964, 1973, 1976.

Anglo-Italian Cup: Winners 1995; Runners-up 1994.

Colours: Black and white striped shirts, black shorts, black stockings.

Change Colours: Royal blue and yellow shirts, blue shorts with yellow trim, blue stockings.

Year Formed: 1862* (*see Foundation*). ***Turned Professional:*** 1885. ***Ltd Co.:*** 1890.

Club Nickname: 'Magpies'.

Grounds: 1862, The Park; 1864, The Meadows; 1877, Beeston Cricket Ground; 1880, Castle Ground; 1883, Trent Bridge; 1910, Meadow Lane.

First Football League Game: 15 September 1888, Football League, v Everton (a) L 1–2 – Holland; Guttridge, McLean; Brown, Warburton, Shelton; Hodder, Harker, Jardine, Moore (1), Wardle.

Record League Victory: 11–1 v Newport Co, Division 3 (S), 15 January 1949 – Smith; Southwell, Purvis; Gannon, Baxter, Adamson; Houghton (1), Sewell (4), Lawton (4), Pimbley, Johnston (2).

Record Cup Victory: 15–0 v Rotherham T (at Trent Bridge), FA Cup 1st rd, 24 October 1885 – Sherwin; Snook, H. T. Moore; Dobson (1), Emmett (1), Chapman; Gunn (1), Albert Moore (2), Jackson (3), Daft (2), Cursham (4), (1 og).

SKY SPORTS FACT FILE

On 27 December 1920 Notts County had their then record attendance of 30,578 against Sheffield Wednesday with receipts of £2103. Their share of the 1894 FA Cup final gate of 32,000 when they defeated Bolton Wanderers 4–1 had been just over £199!

Record Defeat: 1–9 v Blackburn R, Division 1, 16 November 1889. 1–9 v Aston Villa, Division 1, 29 September 1888. 1–9 v Portsmouth, Division 2, 9 April 1927.

Most League Points (2 for a win): 69, Division 4, 1970–71.

Most League Points (3 for a win): 99, Division 3, 1997–98.

Most League Goals: 107, Division 4, 1959–60.

Highest League Scorer in Season: Tom Keetley, 39, Division 3 (S), 1930–31.

Most League Goals in Total Aggregate: Les Bradd, 125, 1967–78.

Most League Goals in One Match: 5, Robert Jardine v Burnley, Division 1, 27 October 1888; 5, Daniel Bruce v Port Vale, Division 2, 26 February 1895; 5, Bertie Mills v Barnsley, Division 2, 19 November 1927.

Most Capped Player: Kevin Wilson, 15 (42), Northern Ireland.

Most League Appearances: Albert Iremonger, 564, 1904–26.

Youngest League Player: Tony Bircumshaw, 16 years 54 days v Brentford, 3 April 1961.

Record Transfer Fee Received: £2,500,000 from Derby Co for Craig Short, September 1992.

Record Transfer Fee Paid: £685,000 to Sheffield U for Tony Agana, November 1991.

Football League Record: 1888 Founder Member of the Football League; 1893–97 Division 2; 1897–1913 Division 1; 1913–14 Division 2; 1914–20 Division 1; 1920–23 Division 2; 1923–26 Division 1; 1926–30 Division 2; 1930–31 Division 3 (S); 1931–35 Division 2; 1935–50 Division 3 (S); 1950–58 Division 2; 1958–59 Division 3; 1959–60 Division 4; 1960–64 Division 3; 1964–71 Division 4; 1971–73 Division 3; 1973–81 Division 2; 1981–84 Division 1; 1984–85 Division 2; 1985–90 Division 3; 1990–91 Division 2; 1991–95 Division 1; 1995–97 Division 2; 1997–98 Division 3; 1998–2004 Division 2; 2004– FL 2.

LATEST SEQUENCES

Longest Sequence of League Wins: 10, 3.12.1997 – 31.1.1998.

Longest Sequence of League Defeats: 7, 3.9.1983 – 16.10.1983.

Longest Sequence of League Draws: 5, 2.12.1978 – 26.12.1978.

Longest Sequence of Unbeaten League Matches: 19, 26.4.1930 – 6.12.1930.

Longest Sequence Without a League Win: 20, 3.12.1996 – 31.3.1997.

Successive Scoring Runs: 35 from 26.4.1930.

Successive Non-scoring Runs: 5 from 30.11.1912.

MANAGERS

Albert Fisher 1913–27
Horace Henshall 1927–34
Charlie Jones 1934
David Pratt 1935
Percy Smith 1935–36
Jimmy McMullan 1936–37
Harry Parkes 1938–39
Tony Towers 1939–42
Frank Womack 1942–43
Major Frank Buckley 1944–46
Arthur Stollery 1946–49
Eric Houghton 1949–53
George Poyser 1953–57
Tommy Lawton 1957–58
Frank Hill 1958–61
Tim Coleman 1961–63
Eddie Lowe 1963–65
Tim Coleman 1965–66
Jack Burkitt 1966–67
Andy Beattie *(General Manager)* 1967
Billy Gray 1967–68
Jack Wheeler (*Caretaker Manager*) 1968–69
Jimmy Sirrel 1969–75
Ron Fenton 1975–77
Jimmy Sirrel 1978–82 *(continued as General Manager to 1984)*
Howard Wilkinson 1982–83
Larry Lloyd 1983–84
Richie Barker 1984–85
Jimmy Sirrel 1985–87
John Barnwell 1987–88
Neil Warnock 1989–93
Mick Walker 1993–94
Russell Slade 1994–95
Howard Kendall 1995
Colin Murphy 1995 *(continued as General Manager to 1996)*
Steve Thompson 1996
Sam Allardyce 1997–99
Gary Brazil 1999–2000
Jocky Scott 2000–01
Gary Brazil 2001
Billy Dearden 2002–04
Gary Mills 2004
Ian Richardson 2004–05
Gudjon Thordarson 2005–06
Steve Thompson June 2006–

TEN YEAR LEAGUE RECORD

		P	W	D	L	F	A	Pts	Pos
1997-98	Div 3	46	29	12	5	82	43	99	1
1998-99	Div 2	46	14	12	20	52	61	54	16
1999-2000	Div 2	46	18	11	17	61	55	65	8
2000-01	Div 2	46	19	12	15	62	66	69	8
2001-02	Div 2	46	13	11	22	59	71	50	19
2002-03	Div 2	46	13	16	17	62	70	55	15
2003-04	Div 2	46	10	12	24	50	78	42	23
2004-05	FL 2	46	13	13	20	46	62	52	19
2005-06	FL 2	46	12	16	18	48	63	52	21
2006-07	FL 2	46	16	14	16	55	53	62	13

DID YOU KNOW ?

Centre-half George Walker had won four full Scottish caps and played twice for the Scottish League with St Mirren when Notts County paid £3000 for him in June 1933. He later completed a century of League appearances with Crystal Palace and Watford.

NOTTS COUNTY 2006–07 LEAGUE RECORD

Match No.	Date	Venue	Opponents	Result		H/T Score	Lg. Pos.	Goalscorers	Attendance
1	Aug 5	A	Lincoln C	D	1-1	0-1	—	Hughes (og) [55]	6046
2	8	H	Shrewsbury T	D	1-1	0-0	—	Edwards [53]	4386
3	12	H	Wycombe W	W	1-0	1-0	13	Mendes [17]	4053
4	19	A	Rochdale	W	1-0	0-0	8	White [51]	2321
5	26	H	Peterborough U	D	0-0	0-0	9		6353
6	Sept 2	A	Milton Keynes D	L	2-3	0-1	10	Lee [77], Martin [83]	6323
7	9	H	Accrington S	W	3-2	3-0	7	Edwards [11], Martin 2 [29, 36]	4677
8	12	A	Chester C	D	0-0	0-0	—		1818
9	16	A	Barnet	W	3-2	2-2	6	White [32], Parkinson [37], Lee [55]	2317
10	23	H	Swindon T	D	1-1	0-0	6	White [67]	6079
11	26	H	Stockport Co	W	1-0	1-0	—	Mendes [40]	4021
12	30	A	Torquay U	W	1-0	0-0	6	Dudfield [90]	2815
13	Oct 7	A	Mansfield T	D	2-2	0-2	5	Edwards [71], Dudfield [86]	6182
14	14	H	Bristol R	L	1-2	0-0	6	Mendes [66]	5797
15	21	A	Grimsby T	W	2-0	0-0	5	Mendes [60], Lee [83]	4029
16	28	H	Bury	L	0-1	0-1	5		4770
17	Nov 4	A	Boston U	D	3-3	1-1	6	Lee 2 [28, 48], White [47]	2539
18	18	H	Wrexham	W	2-1	1-0	6	Parkinson [37], Lee [60]	4416
19	25	A	Walsall	L	1-2	0-2	7	Ross [72]	5402
20	Dec 5	H	Hartlepool U	L	0-1	0-1	—		3546
21	9	H	Macclesfield T	L	1-2	0-2	8	Martin [90]	4036
22	16	A	Darlington	W	1-0	0-0	8	White [84]	3253
23	22	H	Hereford U	L	0-1	0-0	—		4106
24	26	A	Stockport Co	L	0-2	0-0	8		5823
25	30	A	Swindon T	D	1-1	1-0	10	Dudfield [35]	6805
26	Jan 1	H	Chester C	L	1-2	1-1	12	Lee [45]	4019
27	13	A	Accrington S	W	2-1	2-1	9	Dudfield [9], Lee [20]	1702
28	20	H	Torquay U	W	5-2	3-2	8	Mendes [23], Smith [39], Parkinson [40], Lee 2 [83, 90]	4311
29	27	A	Hereford U	L	2-3	1-2	8	Lee 2 [7, 64]	3280
30	30	H	Barnet	D	1-1	1-0	—	Dudfield (pen) [17]	3010
31	Feb 3	H	Lincoln C	W	3-1	2-0	8	Smith [2], Lee [45], Dudfield [61]	7019
32	10	A	Wycombe W	D	0-0	0-0	8		4836
33	17	H	Rochdale	L	1-2	0-0	8	Lee [53]	4493
34	20	A	Shrewsbury T	L	0-2	0-2	—		3369
35	24	H	Milton Keynes D	D	2-2	1-2	11	Smith (pen) [40], Hunt [90]	4031
36	Mar 3	A	Peterborough U	L	0-2	0-0	13		5014
37	10	H	Mansfield T	D	0-0	0-0	13		10,034
38	17	A	Bristol R	L	0-2	0-0	15		4642
39	24	A	Bury	W	1-0	1-0	12	N'Toya [40]	2310
40	31	H	Grimsby T	W	2-0	0-0	12	Newey (og) [52], Smith [86]	4724
41	Apr 7	H	Boston U	W	2-0	1-0	11	Lee [11], Somner [70]	4170
42	9	A	Wrexham	W	1-0	0-0	10	Spender (og) [88]	4557
43	14	H	Walsall	L	1-2	1-1	11	Dudfield [41]	7080
44	20	A	Hartlepool U	D	1-1	1-1	—	Parkinson [45]	6174
45	28	H	Darlington	L	0-1	0-0	13		5264
46	May 5	A	Macclesfield T	D	1-1	1-1	13	Parkinson [38]	4114

Final League Position: 13

GOALSCORERS

League (55): Lee 15, Dudfield 7 (1 pen), Mendes 5, Parkinson 5, White 5, Martin 4, Smith 4 (1 pen), Edwards 3, Hunt 1, N'Toya 1, Ross 1, Somner 1, own goals 3.
Carling Cup (5): Dudfield 1, Edwards 1, Lee 1, Martin 1, N'Toya 1.
FA Cup (1): Dudfield 1.
J Paint Trophy (0).

Pilkington K 39	Pipe D 39	McCann A 43	Edwards M 44 + 1	White A 32 + 3	Ross I 26 + 10	Silk G 24 + 6	Sommer M 35 + 3	Lee J 37 + 1	Dudfield L 29 + 12	Parkinson A 40 + 5	Curtis T — + 2	N'Toya T 4 + 17	Mendes J 22 + 15	Sheridan J — + 3	Gleeson D 16 + 1	Martin D 12 + 17	Hunt S 24 + 8	Needham L — + 1	McMahon L 3 + 4	Smith J 25 + 2	Deeney S 7	Walker J 2 + 6	Weston M 1 + 3	Byron M 2 + 1	*Match No.*
1	2	3	4	5	6^{1}	7	8	9^{2}	10^{3}	11	12	13	14												1
1	2	3	4	5	6^{1}	7	8		10^{3}	11^{2}	12	14	9	13											2
1	7	3	4	5	12		8		10^{3}	11^{2}		14	9		2	6^{1}	13								3
1	7	3	4	5	6^{2}		8	9		11^{3}		12	10^{1}		2	13	14								4
1	7^{1}	3	4	5			8	9		11		12	10		2	6									5
1	2^{1}	3	4	5■	12		8■	9	13	11^{3}			10^{2}		6	7	14								6
1	7	3	4		6^{1}	12		9		11^{3}		13	10^{2}		2	5	8	14							7
1	7	3	4	5	12		8	9^{1}	10^{2}	11			13		2	6									8
1	7	3	4	5	12		8^{1}	9	10^{2}	11			13		2	6^{3}	14								9
1	7^{3}	3	4	5	12		8	9^{2}	13	11		14	10		2	6^{1}									10
1	7	3	4	5	6^{2}		8	9^{1}	12	11		14	10^{3}		2		13								11
1	7	3	4	5	12		8	9^{2}	13	11^{1}		14	10^{3}		2		6								12
1	7	3	4	5	6	2^{2}	8^{3}		10	11		12	9^{1}			13	14								13
1	7	3	4	5	6^{3}			9	12	11		10^{2}	13		2^{1}	14	8								14
1	7	3	4	5	6		8	9^{1}	12	11^{2}			10		2^{3}	13	14								15
1	7	3	4^{1}	5	6		8^{2}	9				14	10	13^{3}	2	11	12								16
1		3	4	5	6^{1}	2	8	9	13	11^{2}			10			12	7								17
1	7	3	4	5	6^{2}		8	9	12	11			10^{1}		2^{3}				14	13					18
1	7	3	4	5	6	2^{3}		9	12	11			10^{1}		14				13	8^{2}					19
1	7	3	4	5	6		8^{3}	9^{1}	12	11			13		2^{2}				10	14					20
	7^{1}	3	4	5	6^{2}	2		9	12	11			14			13			10^{3}	8	1				21
		3	4	5	6^{3}	2	8		9^{1}	11		13	10^{2}			12			14	7	1				22
	7	3	4	5	6	2^{1}			9	13		14	10^{3}			12			11^{2}	8	1				23
1	7	3	4	5		2^{2}	8	9	12	11^{1}			10			13				6					24
1	2	3	12	5	6		8	9	10^{2}	11^{3}			13			14	7			4^{1}					25
1	2	3		5	6^{1}	12	8^{2}	9	10^{3}	11			14			13	4			7					26
1	2■		4	5	14	12	8	9	10	11^{2}			13^{3}			3^{1}	6			7					27
1			4	5		2	8	9	10	12			11^{1}			6	3^{2}		13	7					28
1			4	5		3	8	9	10	11			12	13	2^{2}	6^{1}				7					29
1		3	4			2	8	9	10	11			12			6^{1}	5			7					30
1	7^{1}	3	4	12		2	8	9^{2}	10	11			13				5			6					31
1	7^{1}	3	4	13		2	8^{2}	9	10	11			12				5			6					32
1	7	3	4	12		2	8^{1}	9	10	11^{2}			13			14	5^{3}			6					33
1		3	4^{1}	5	6	2	12	9	10	11^{2}			13				7			8					34
	2^{1}	3	4	5	6	12		9		11^{2}		13	10				8			7	1				35
	7	3	4			2^{1}	8		10	11^{2}		13	9			12	5			6	1				36
	2	3	4	5	6^{1}	12			10	11		13	9^{2}				8			7	1				37
	7^{2}	3	4	5	12	2			10	11^{1}		9					6			8	1	13			38
1	2	3	4		6^{2}	7	8	9	10	12		11^{1}				13	5								39
1	2	3	4		6	12	8^{1}	9	10^{3}	13		11^{2}					5			7		14			40
1	2	3	4		6^{1}	7	12	9	10^{2}	11							5			8^{3}		13	14		41
1		3	4		6^{1}	2	8	12	10^{2}	11^{3}		13					5			7		9	14		42
1	2	3	4		12	7^{1}	8^{3}	9	10	13							5			6		11^{2}	14		43
1	2	3	4		6^{3}		8	9	10^{2}	11						12	5■					13	7^{1}	14	44
1	2	3	4		12	7^{2}	8^{1}	9	10^{3}	11						13				6		14		5	45
1	2	3	4			7^{2}	12	9	10^{3}	11						13	5			8		14		6^{1}	46

FA Cup
First Round — Leyton Orient — (a) — 1-2

Carling Cup
First Round — Crystal Palace — (a) — 2-1
Second Round — Middlesbrough — (a) — 1-0
Third Round — Southampton — (h) — 2-0
Fourth Round — Wycombe W — (h) — 0-1

J Paint Trophy
First Round — Barnet — (h) — 0-1

OLDHAM ATHLETIC FL Championship 1

FOUNDATION

It was in 1895 that John Garland, the landlord of the Featherstall and Junction Hotel, decided to form a football club. As Pine Villa they played in the Oldham Junior League. In 1899 the local professional club, Oldham County, went out of existence and one of the liquidators persuaded Pine Villa to take over their ground at Sheepfoot Lane and change their name to Oldham Athletic.

Boundary Park, Furtherwood Road, Oldham OL1 2PA.

Telephone: 0871 226 2235.

Fax: 0871 226 1715.

Ticket Office: 0871 226 2235.

Website: www.oldhamathletic.co.uk

Email: enquiries@oldhamathletic.co.uk

Ground Capacity: 13,595.

Record Attendance: 46,471 v Sheffield W, FA Cup 4th rd, 25 January 1930.

Pitch Measurements: 110yd × 72yd.

Chairman: Simon Blitz.

Vice-chairman: Simon Corney.

Chief Executive/Secretary: Alan Hardy.

Manager: John Sheridan.

Assistant Manager: Tommy Wright.

Physio: Lee Nobes.

Colours: Royal blue shirts with white piping, blue shorts, white stockings.

Change Colours: Tangerine shirts with blue piping, blue shorts, tangerine stockings.

Year Formed: 1895.

Turned Professional: 1899.

Ltd Co.: 1906.

Previous Name: 1895, Pine Villa; 1899, Oldham Athletic.

Club Nickname: 'The Latics'.

Grounds: 1895, Sheepfoot Lane; 1900, Hudson Field; 1906, Sheepfoot Lane; 1907, Boundary Park.

First Football League Game: 9 September 1907, Division 2, v Stoke (a) W 3–1 – Hewitson; Hodson, Hamilton; Fay, Walders, Wilson; Ward, W. Dodds (1), Newton (1), Hancock, Swarbrick (1).

Record League Victory: 11–0 v Southport, Division 4, 26 December 1962 – Bollands; Branagan, Marshall; McCall, Williams, Scott; Ledger (1), Johnstone, Lister (6), Colquhoun (1), Whitaker (3).

HONOURS

Football League: Division 1 – Runners-up 1914–15; Division 2 – Champions 1990–91; Runners-up 1909–10; Division 3 (N) – Champions 1952–53; Division 3 – Champions 1973–74; Division 4 – Runners-up 1962–63.

FA Cup: Semi-final 1913, 1990, 1994.

Football League Cup: Runners-up 1990.

SKY SPORTS FACT FILE

Billy Johnston, a versatile midfield player either in attack or defence, had had two previous spells with Manchester United before joining Oldham Athletic in 1932. A Scottish schoolboy cap his extensive League career finished there after over 250 matches.

Record Cup Victory: 10–1 v Lytham, FA Cup 1st rd, 28 November 1925 – Gray; Wynne, Grundy; Adlam, Heaton, Naylor (1), Douglas, Pynegar (2), Ormston (2), Barnes (3), Watson (2).

Record Defeat: 4–13 v Tranmere R, Division 3 (N), 26 December 1935.

Most League Points (2 for a win): 62, Division 3, 1973–74.

Most League Points (3 for a win): 88, Division 2, 1990–91.

Most League Goals: 95, Division 4, 1962–63.

Highest League Scorer in Season: Tom Davis, 33, Division 3 (N), 1936–37.

Most League Goals in Total Aggregate: Roger Palmer, 141, 1980–94.

Most League Goals in One Match: 7, Eric Gemmell v Chester, Division 3N, 19 January 1952.

Most Capped Player: Gunnar Halle, 24 (64), Norway.

Most League Appearances: Ian Wood, 525, 1966–80.

Youngest League Player: Wayne Harrison, 15 years 11 months v Notts Co, 27 October 1984.

Record Transfer Fee Received: £1,700,000 from Aston Villa for Earl Barrett, February 1992.

Record Transfer Fee Paid: £750,000 to Aston Villa for Ian Olney, June 1992.

Football League Record: 1907 Elected to Division 2; 1910–23 Division 1; 1923–35 Division 2; 1935–53 Division 3 (N); 1953–54 Division 2; 1954–58 Division 3 (N); 1958–63 Division 4; 1963–69 Division 3; 1969–71 Division 4; 1971–74 Division 3; 1974–91 Division 2; 1991–92 Division 1; 1992–94 FA Premier League; 1994–97 Division 1; 1997–2004 Division 2; 2004– FL 1.

MANAGERS

David Ashworth 1906–14
Herbert Bamlett 1914–21
Charlie Roberts 1921–22
David Ashworth 1923–24
Bob Mellor 1924–27
Andy Wilson 1927–32
Jimmy McMullan 1933–34
Bob Mellor 1934–45
(continued as Secretary to 1953)
Frank Womack 1945–47
Billy Wootton 1947–50
George Hardwick 1950–56
Ted Goodier 1956–58
Norman Dodgin 1958–60
Jack Rowley 1960–63
Les McDowall 1963–65
Gordon Hurst 1965–66
Jimmy McIlroy 1966–68
Jack Rowley 1968–69
Jimmy Frizzell 1970–82
Joe Royle 1982–94
Graeme Sharp 1994–97
Neil Warnock 1997–98
Andy Ritchie 1998–2001
Mick Wadsworth 2001–02
Iain Dowie 2002–03
Brian Talbot 2004–05
Ronnie Moore 2005–06
John Sheridan June 2006–

LATEST SEQUENCES

Longest Sequence of League Wins: 10, 12.1.1974 – 12.3.1974.

Longest Sequence of League Defeats: 8, 15.12.1934 – 2.2.1935.

Longest Sequence of League Draws: 5, 26.12.1982 – 15.1.1983.

Longest Sequence of Unbeaten League Matches: 20, 1.5.1990 – 10.11.1990.

Longest Sequence Without a League Win: 17, 4.9.1920 – 18.12.1920.

Successive Scoring Runs: 25 from 15.1.1927.

Successive Non-scoring Runs: 6 from 4.2.1922.

TEN YEAR LEAGUE RECORD

		P	*W*	*D*	*L*	*F*	*A*	*Pts*	*Pos*
1997-98	Div 2	46	15	16	15	62	54	61	13
1998-99	Div 2	46	14	9	23	48	66	51	20
1999-2000	Div 2	46	16	12	18	50	55	60	14
2000-01	Div 2	46	15	13	18	53	65	58	15
2001-02	Div 2	46	18	16	12	77	65	70	9
2002-03	Div 2	46	22	16	8	68	38	82	5
2003-04	Div 2	46	12	21	13	66	60	57	15
2004-05	FL 1	46	14	10	22	60	73	52	19
2005-06	FL 1	46	18	11	17	58	60	65	10
2006-07	FL 1	46	21	12	13	69	47	75	6

DID YOU KNOW?

Twelve years as a professional centre-forward with Huddersfield Town, Lewis Brook joined Oldham Athletic in March 1948 and subsequently filled every position on the field except goalkeeper in making over 200 League and Cup appearances for the Latics.

OLDHAM ATHLETIC 2006–07 LEAGUE RECORD

Match No.	Date	Venue	Opponents	Result		H/T Score	Lg. Pos.	Goalscorers	Attendance
1	Aug 5	A	Tranmere R	L	0-1	0-1	—		8586
2	8	H	Port Vale	L	0-1	0-0	—		4975
3	12	H	Swansea C	W	1-0	0-0	15	Molango [67]	4708
4	19	A	Millwall	L	0-1	0-0	19		7455
5	27	H	Carlisle U	D	0-0	0-0	19		6080
6	Sept 2	A	Bournemouth	L	2-3	0-2	22	Liddell 2 (1 pen) [47 (p), 79]	4838
7	9	H	Scunthorpe U	W	1-0	1-0	18	McDonald [34]	4812
8	12	A	Nottingham F	W	2-0	2-0	—	Porter 2 [29, 45]	17,446
9	16	A	Blackpool	D	2-2	0-1	16	Wellens [63], Porter [72]	6794
10	23	H	Gillingham	W	4-1	2-0	8	Haining [4], Porter 2 [24, 90], Charlton [46]	4652
11	26	H	Rotherham U	W	2-1	0-0	—	Stam [51], Warne [76]	4880
12	30	A	Bristol C	D	0-0	0-0	9		11,656
13	Oct 6	A	Doncaster R	D	1-1	1-1	—	Porter [45]	6241
14	14	H	Leyton Orient	D	3-3	0-1	9	Porter 2 [78, 82], Liddell (pen) [90]	5014
15	21	A	Yeovil T	L	0-1	0-1	11		5471
16	28	H	Brentford	W	3-0	1-0	7	Warne [15], McDonald [47], Wellens [90]	4708
17	Nov 4	A	Cheltenham T	W	2-1	2-0	7	Warne [23], McDonald [41]	4054
18	18	H	Bradford C	W	2-0	0-0	7	Porter 2 [79, 82]	6001
19	25	A	Huddersfield T	W	3-0	1-0	5	McDonald [16], Porter [59], Warne [67]	13,280
20	Dec 5	H	Crewe Alex	W	1-0	1-0	—	Porter [45]	4798
21	9	A	Chesterfield	L	1-2	1-2	5	Eardley [45]	4059
22	16	H	Brighton & HA	D	1-1	1-0	4	Warne [18]	9321
23	23	H	Northampton T	W	3-0	2-0	4	McDonald [22], Porter [37], Liddell [61]	10,207
24	26	A	Rotherham U	W	3-2	2-0	3	Porter 2 [29, 67], Haining [42]	6512
25	30	A	Gillingham	W	3-0	2-0	3	Porter [26], Liddell (pen) [36], Eardley [54]	6790
26	Jan 1	H	Nottingham F	W	5-0	3-0	2	Warne [30], Porter [39], Liddell 2 (2 pens) [43, 68], Rocastle [90]	9768
27	13	A	Scunthorpe U	D	1-1	0-0	3	McDonald [90]	7685
28	20	H	Bristol C	L	0-3	0-2	4		6924
29	28	A	Northampton T	W	3-2	2-1	2	Wellens [2], Warne [44], Porter [58]	5662
30	Feb 3	H	Tranmere R	W	1-0	0-0	1	Hall [90]	6944
31	10	A	Swansea C	W	1-0	1-0	1	Warne [32]	9880
32	17	H	Millwall	L	1-2	0-0	2	Warne [55]	6181
33	20	A	Port Vale	L	0-3	0-1	—		4061
34	24	H	Bournemouth	L	1-2	1-2	5	Liddell (pen) [45]	5429
35	27	H	Blackpool	L	0-1	0-0	—		6956
36	Mar 3	A	Carlisle U	D	1-1	1-0	5	Taylor [13]	7951
37	11	H	Doncaster R	W	4-0	1-0	5	Clarke [8], Rocastle [74], Taylor 2 [76, 90]	6619
38	17	A	Leyton Orient	D	2-2	0-1	5	Taylor [73], Liddell (pen) [81]	5443
39	25	A	Brentford	D	2-2	0-0	5	Clarke 2 (1 pen) [86, 90 (p)]	4720
40	31	H	Yeovil T	W	1-0	1-0	4	McDonald [37]	6035
41	Apr 7	H	Huddersfield T	D	1-1	1-0	4	Porter [23]	7096
42	9	A	Bradford C	D	1-1	0-0	6	Glombard [87]	9940
43	14	H	Cheltenham T	L	0-2	0-2	6		5426
44	21	A	Crewe Alex	L	1-2	0-1	6	Wellens [85]	6304
45	28	A	Brighton & HA	W	2-1	2-0	6	Porter [18], Liddell [40]	7588
46	May 5	H	Chesterfield	W	1-0	0-0	6	Porter [58]	8148

Final League Position: 6

GOALSCORERS

League (69): Porter 21, Liddell 10 (7 pens), Warne 9, McDonald 7, Taylor 4, Wellens 4, Clarke 3 (1 pen), Eardley 2, Haining 2, Rocastle 2, Charlton 1, Glombard 1, Hall 1, Molango 1, Stam 1.
Carling Cup (1): Rocastle 1.
FA Cup (8): Hall 3, Warne 2, Gregan 1, Porter 1, Trotman 1.
J Paint Trophy (0).
Play-Offs (2): Liddell 1 (pen), Wolfenden 1.

Pogliacomi L 40	Wellens R 42	Edwards P 10 + 16	Eardley I 36	Swailes C 4	Haining W 44	Wood N 3 + 2	McDonald G 39 + 4	Liddell A 44 + 2	Molango M 3 + 2	Rocastle C 17 + 18	Warne P 42 + 4	Hall C 2 + 17	Taylor C 40 + 4	Howarth C 2 + 1	Stam S 19 + 3	Charlton S 34	Tierney M 1 + 4	Grabban L 1 + 8	Knight D 2	Smith T — + 1	Porter C 34 + 1	Lomax K 3 + 6	Wolfenden M — + 6	Cywka T — + 4	Trotman N — + 1	Gregan S 27	Pearson M — + 1	Blayney A 2 + 1	Turner B 1	Smalley D — + 2	Clarke L 5	Aljofree H 5	Giombard L 3 + 5	Roque M 1 + 3	Match No.
1	2	3	4■	5	6	7	8	9^{1}	10^{2}	11^{3}	12	13	14■																						1
1^{G}	2	3		5	6	7^{1}	8	9	10^{2}	11	12	13		15	4																				2
	2	3		5	6		8	9	12		11	10^{1}	13	1	4	7^{2}																			3
	7	3		5^{1}	6	12	8	9	10^{3}		11		2^{2}	1	4		13	14																	4
	2	3^{1}	4		6		8	9	13		11^{G}		12		5	7		10^{2}	1■	15															5
	2	3			6^{2}	7^{1}	8	9		13	12		11^{3}		5	4		14	1		10														6
1	2	3	4^{1}		6		8	11		12	10^{2}				5	7		13			9														7
1	2	3^{2}	4		6		8^{1}	11		12	10^{3}		13		5	7		14			9														8
1	2		4^{1}		6	13	8	9		12	10^{3}		3^{2}		5	7		14			11														9
1	2		4		6		8	9		12	10^{2}		3		5	7^{1}		13			11														10
1	2		4		6		8	11		7	10^{1}		3		5			12			9														11
1	2		4		6		8	11			10^{1}		3		5	7		12			9														12
1	2		4		6		8	11		12	10^{2}	13	3^{1}		5	7					9														13
1	2		4		6		8	11		7^{1}	10^{2}	13	3		5		12				9														14
1	2				6		8^{2}	11		4^{1}	10^{3}	12	3		5	7					9	13	14												15
1	2				6		8	11		4^{3}	10	12	3^{2}		5	7	13				9^{1}	14													16
1	2				6		8	11			10^{1}	12	3		5^{2}	7					9	4^{3}		14	13										17
1	2				6		8^{2}	11			10^{1}	12	7				3				9	4		13		5									18
1	2^{3}		4		6		8^{1}	11		12	10		3^{2}			7	13				9			14		5									19
1	2^{1}		4		6		8	11		12	10^{2}		3			7					9		13			5									20
1	2	12	4^{3}		6		8	11^{1}			10	13	3			7					9^{2}		14			5									21
1		12	4		6		8^{2}	11^{3}		7^{1}	10	9	3			2							14	13		5									22
1	2	12	4^{1}				8	11^{2}		13	10^{3}		3		6	7					9		14			5									23
1	2	12	4		6		8^{2}	11		13	10		3^{1}			7					9					5									24
1	2	12	4		6		8	11			10^{2}	13	3^{1}		14	7					9^{3}					5									25
1	2	12	4		6		8	11		13	10		3		14	7^{1}					9^{2}					5^{3}									26
1	2	12	4^{3}		6		8	11		13	10^{2}	14	3^{1}			7					9					5									27
1	2	12	4		6^{2}		8^{1}	11^{3}			10	14	3		13	7					9					5									28
1	2	12	4		6			11		8	10^{2}	13	3^{1}			7					9					5									29
1	2■		4		6		12	11		8^{1}	10^{2}	13	3			7^{3}					9	14				5									30
1			4		6		8	11		7	10^{1}	12	3			2					9					5									31
1		2^{2}	4		6^{3}		8	11^{1}		7	10	12	3		5						9	13					14								32
1■		12	4		6		8	11^{2}		7^{3}	10	13	3		5^{1}	2					9	14													33
	2	12					8^{2}	11		13	10		3^{1}			7^{3}					9	4				5		1	6■	14					34
1	2	12	4		6		8^{1}	11^{3}		13	10		3			7^{2}					9					5				14					35
1	2		4		6		12	11		8^{1}	10		3			7										5					9				36
1	2^{1}		4		6		12	11		8	10		3			7										5					9				37
1	2	12	4		6			11		8	10		3			7^{1}										5					9				38
1	2		4		6		12	11^{2}		8^{1}	10		3													5					9	7	13		39
1	2		4		6		8^{3}	11^{2}			10		3								12					5^{1}					9	7	13	14	40
1	2		4		6		8^{3}	11		12	10		3^{2}								9^{1}					5						7	13	14	41
1	2		4		6		8^{2}	11^{1}		13	12		3								9^{3}					5						7	10	14	42
1^{G}	2	12	4		6		8	13			10		3								9^{2}					5		15				7^{1}	11		43
	2	3			6^{3}			12		8^{1}	10		11			7						14	13			5		1					9^{2}	4	44
1	2	12	4^{2}		6		8	11		13	10		3^{1}			7					9^{3}					5							14		45
1	2	12	4		6		8^{1}	11		13	10		3^{2}			7					9^{3}					5							14		46

FA Cup

First Round	Kettering T	(a)	4-3
Second Round	King's Lynn	(a)	2-0
Third Round	Wolverhampton W	(a)	2-2
		(h)	0-2

Carling Cup

First Round	Rotherham U	(a)	1-3

J Paint Trophy

Second Round	Chesterfield	(h)	0-1

Play-Offs

Semi-Final	Blackpool	(h)	1-2
		(a)	1-3

PETERBOROUGH UNITED FL Championship 2

FOUNDATION

The old Peterborough & Fletton club, founded in 1923, was suspended by the FA during season 1932–33 and disbanded. Local enthusiasts determined to carry on and in 1934 a new professional club, Peterborough United, was formed and entered the Midland League the following year. Peterborough's first success came in 1939–40, but from 1955–56 to 1959–60 they won five successive titles. During the 1958–59 season they were undefeated in the Midland League. They reached the third round of the FA Cup, won the Northamptonshire Senior Cup, the Maunsell Cup and were runners-up in the East Anglian Cup.

London Road Stadium, Peterborough PE2 8AL.

Telephone: (01733) 563 947.

Fax: (01733) 344 140.

Ticket Office: (01733) 865 674.

Website: www.theposh.com

Email: info@theposh.com

Ground Capacity: 15,460.

Record Attendance: 30,096 v Swansea T, FA Cup 5th rd, 20 February 1965.

Pitch Measurements: 112yd × 71yd.

Chairman: Darragh MacAnthony.

Executive Director: Bob Symns.

Secretary: Mary Faxon.

Manager: Darren Ferguson.

Assistant Manager: Kevin Russell.

Physio: Keith Oakes.

Colours: Blue shirts, blue shorts, blue stockings.

Change Colours: Black shirts, black shorts, black stockings.

Year Formed: 1934.

Turned Professional: 1934.

Ltd Co.: 1934.

Club Nickname: 'The Posh'.

Ground: 1934, London Road Stadium.

First Football League Game: 20 August 1960, Division 4, v Wrexham (h) W 3–0 – Walls; Stafford, Walker; Rayner, Rigby, Norris; Hails, Emery (1), Bly (1), Smith, McNamee (1).

Record League Victory: 9–1 v Barnet (a) Division 3, 5 September 1998 – Griemink; Hooper (1), Drury (Farell), Gill, Bodley, Edwards, Davies, Payne, Grazioli (5), Quinn (2) (Rowe), Houghton (Etherington) (1).

HONOURS

Football League: Division 1 best season: 10th, 1992–93; Division 2 1991–92 (play-offs). Promoted from Division 3 1999–2000 (play-offs); Division 4 – Champions 1960–61, 1973–74.

FA Cup: best season: 6th rd, 1965.

Football League Cup: Semi-final 1966.

SKY SPORTS FACT FILE

Denis Emery achieved the remarkable feat of scoring in seven successive FA Cup ties over two seasons from 1955–56. In fact he missed finding the target in only one game in which Peterborough United scored in a run of 13 until 1959–60 producing 17 goals.

Record Cup Victory: 7–0 v Harlow T, FA Cup 1st rd, 16 November 1991 – Barber; Luke, Johnson, Halsall (1), Robinson D, Welsh, Sterling (1) (Butterworth), Cooper G (2 incl. 1p), Riley (1) (Culpin (1)), Charlery (1), Kimble.

Record Defeat: 1–8 v Northampton T, FA Cup 2nd rd (2nd replay), 18 December 1946.

Most League Points (2 for a win): 66, Division 4, 1960–61.

Most League Points (3 for a win): 82, Division 4, 1981–82.

Most League Goals: 134, Division 4, 1960–61.

Highest League Scorer in Season: Terry Bly, 52, Division 4, 1960–61.

Most League Goals in Total Aggregate: Jim Hall, 122, 1967–75.

Most League Goals in One Match: 5, Guiliano Grazioli v Barnet, Division 3, 5 September 1998.

Most Capped Player: James Quinn, 9 (50), Northern Ireland.

Most League Appearances: Tommy Robson, 482, 1968–81.

Youngest League Player: Matthew Etherington, 15 years 262 days v Brentford, 3 May 1997.

Record Transfer Fee Received: £700,000 from Tottenham H for Simon Davies, December 1999.

Record Transfer Fee Paid: £350,000 to Walsall for Martyn O'Connor, July 1996.

Football League Record: 1960 Elected to Division 4; 1961–68 Division 3, when they were demoted for financial irregularities; 1968–74 Division 4; 1974–79 Division 3; 1979–91 Division 4; 1991–92 Division 3; 1992–94 Division 1; 1994–97 Division 2; 1997–2000 Division 3; 2000–04 Division 2; 2004–05 FL 1; 2005– FL 2.

MANAGERS

Jock Porter 1934–36
Fred Taylor 1936–37
Vic Poulter 1937–38
Sam Madden 1938–48
Jack Blood 1948–50
Bob Gurney 1950–52
Jack Fairbrother 1952–54
George Swindin 1954–58
Jimmy Hagan 1958–62
Jack Fairbrother 1962–64
Gordon Clark 1964–67
Norman Rigby 1967–69
Jim Iley 1969–72
Noel Cantwell 1972–77
John Barnwell 1977–78
Billy Hails 1978–79
Peter Morris 1979–82
Martin Wilkinson 1982–83
John Wile 1983–86
Noel Cantwell 1986–88 *(continued as General Manager)*
Mick Jones 1988–89
Mark Lawrenson 1989–90
Chris Turner 1991–92
Lil Fuccillo 1992–93
John Still 1994–95
Mick Halsall 1995–96
Barry Fry 1996–2005
Mark Wright 2005–06
Keith Alexander 2006–07
Darren Ferguson January 2007–

LATEST SEQUENCES

Longest Sequence of League Wins: 9, 1.2.1992 – 14.3.1992.

Longest Sequence of League Defeats: 6, 16.12.2006 – 21.1.2007.

Longest Sequence of League Draws: 8, 18.12.1971 – 12.2.1972.

Longest Sequence of Unbeaten League Matches: 17, 17.12.1960 – 8.4.1961.

Longest Sequence Without a League Win: 17, 23.9.1978 – 30.12.1978.

Successive Scoring Runs: 33 from 20.9.1960.

Successive Non-scoring Runs: 6 from 13.8.2002.

TEN YEAR LEAGUE RECORD

		P	W	D	L	F	A	Pts	Pos
1997-98	Div 3	46	18	13	15	63	51	67	10
1998-99	Div 3	46	18	12	16	72	56	66	9
1999-2000	Div 3	46	22	12	12	63	54	78	5
2000-01	Div 2	46	15	14	17	61	66	59	12
2001-02	Div 2	46	15	10	21	64	59	55	17
2002-03	Div 2	46	14	16	16	51	54	58	11
2003-04	Div 2	46	12	16	18	58	58	52	18
2004-05	FL 1	46	9	12	25	49	73	39	23
2005-06	FL 2	46	17	11	18	57	49	62	9
2006-07	FL 2	46	18	11	17	70	61	65	10

DID YOU KNOW ?

En route to play for Peterborough United against Torquay United in a first round FA Cup tie on 22 November 1952, Paddy Sloan's car broke down. He finished the journey in the first available vehicle – a hearse! He 'lived' to score first in a 2–1 win.

PETERBOROUGH UNITED 2006–07 LEAGUE RECORD

Match No.	Date	Venue	Opponents	Result	H/T Score	Lg. Pos.	Goalscorers	Attendance
1	Aug 5	H	Bristol R	W 4-1	3-0	—	Day [10], Butcher [32], Yeo [35], Opara [77]	4890
2	9	A	Boston U	W 1-0	0-0	—	Yeo [86]	3528
3	12	A	Wrexham	D 0-0	0-0	3		4706
4	19	H	Macclesfield T	W 3-1	0-0	2	Benjamin 2 [46, 48], Teague (og) [62]	4136
5	26	A	Notts Co	D 0-0	0-0	4		6353
6	Sept 3	H	Bury	L 0-1	0-0	6		5561
7	9	H	Darlington	L 1-3	0-3	9	Crow [81]	3848
8	12	A	Walsall	L 0-5	0-3	—		4070
9	16	A	Swindon T	W 1-0	1-0	10	Benjamin [45]	7329
10	23	H	Hartlepool U	L 3-5	0-3	11	Butcher [59], Gain [61], Holden [70]	3916
11	26	H	Barnet	D 1-1	1-0	—	Gain [35]	3193
12	30	A	Stockport Co	W 1-0	0-0	8	Benjamin [46]	4775
13	Oct 6	A	Milton Keynes D	W 2-0	0-0	—	Arber [70], Richards [80]	6647
14	14	H	Shrewsbury T	W 2-1	1-0	7	Benjamin [42], Crow [64]	4171
15	21	A	Wycombe W	L 0-2	0-0	7		4924
16	28	H	Grimsby T	D 2-2	0-0	7	Futcher [61], Benjamin [79]	4203
17	Nov 4	H	Accrington S	W 4-2	0-1	7	Benjamin (pen) [57], Crow 2 [58, 88], McLean [60]	3990
18	18	A	Mansfield T	W 2-0	1-0	7	McLean [39], Crow [67]	3550
19	25	H	Torquay U	W 5-2	3-1	5	Huke [12], Thorpe (og) [26], Futcher [36], McLean [59], Butcher [60]	4452
20	Dec 5	A	Hereford U	D 0-0	0-0	—		2309
21	9	A	Rochdale	W 1-0	0-0	6	McLean [73]	1982
22	16	H	Chester C	L 0-2	0-2	6		4491
23	23	H	Lincoln C	L 1-2	1-1	7	Gain [42]	8405
24	26	A	Barnet	L 0-1	0-1	7		2958
25	30	A	Hartlepool U	L 0-1	0-0	7		4854
26	Jan 1	H	Walsall	L 0-2	0-2	7		4405
27	13	A	Darlington	L 1-3	1-1	10	Smith [23]	2321
28	20	H	Stockport Co	L 0-3	0-2	10		4330
29	27	A	Lincoln C	L 0-1	0-0	13		6606
30	30	H	Swindon T	D 1-1	0-0	—	Gain [71]	3516
31	Feb 3	A	Bristol R	L 2-3	0-1	14	Crow [65], McLean [74]	5700
32	10	H	Wrexham	W 3-0	1-0	11	McLean [23], Boyd [53], Evans (og) [82]	3839
33	17	A	Macclesfield T	L 1-2	0-1	13	McLean [50]	2274
34	20	H	Boston U	D 1-1	0-0	—	Boyd [75]	4882
35	24	A	Bury	W 3-0	0-0	12	Mackail-Smith [53], Futcher [57], Strachan [64]	2085
36	Mar 3	H	Notts Co	W 2-0	0-0	9	Boyd [51], Morgan [55]	5014
37	10	H	Milton Keynes D	W 4-0	2-0	9	Gain [25], Strachan [39], Mackail-Smith [79], Butcher [85]	5880
38	16	A	Shrewsbury T	L 1-2	1-0	—	Gain [22]	4027
39	24	A	Grimsby T	W 2-0	0-0	10	Boyd [46], White [73]	5164
40	31	H	Wycombe W	D 3-3	1-2	10	Mackail-Smith 2 [8, 75], Newton [59]	6062
41	Apr 7	A	Accrington S	L 2-3	1-2	13	Mackail-Smith [43], Low [54]	1808
42	9	H	Mansfield T	W 2-0	0-0	11	Mackail-Smith [87], White [89]	4276
43	14	A	Torquay U	D 1-1	0-1	10	Mackail-Smith (pen) [71]	2106
44	21	H	Hereford U	W 3-0	2-0	8	Mackail-Smith [1], White [13], Strachan [50]	3759
45	28	A	Chester C	D 1-1	0-1	11	Artell (og) [71]	1905
46	May 5	H	Rochdale	D 3-3	2-1	10	Boyd 2 [22, 26], Blanchett [54]	6011

Final League Position: 10

GOALSCORERS

League (70): Mackail-Smith 8 (1 pen), Benjamin 7 (1 pen), McLean 7, Boyd 6, Crow 6, Gain 6, Butcher 4, Futcher 3, Strachan 3, White 3, Yeo 2, Arber 1, Blanchett 1, Day 1, Holden 1, Huke 1, Low 1, Morgan 1, Newton 1, Opara 1, Richards 1, Smith 1, own goals 4.
Carling Cup (3): Branston 2, Benjamin 1 (pen).
FA Cup (7): Crow 3, McLean 3, Butcher 1.
J Paint Trophy (1): Crow 1.

Tyler M 41	Newton A 43	Day J 17 + 7	Arber M 31 + 3	Branston G 23 + 1	Plummer C 7	Holden D 20 + 1	Opara L 6 + 5	Crow D 22 + 13	Yeo S 8 + 5	Butcher R 35 + 8	Stirling J 14 + 8	Benjamin T 15 + 12	Richards J 4 + 9	Huke S 9 + 9	Carden P 1 + 1	Gain P 26 + 8	Ghaichem J 1 + 1	Turner B 7 + 1	Davis L 7	Futcher B 22 + 3	McLean A 16	Smith A 5 + 4	Morgan C 22 + 1	Rachubka P 4	Strachan G 13 + 3	Low J 17 + 2	Hyde M 18	Boyd G 19 + 1	Blackett S 12 + 1	Mackail-Smith C 13 + 2	White A 7	Blanchett D — + 3	Jalal S 1	*Match No.*
1	2	3^1	4	5	6	7	8^2	9	10^3	11	12	13	14																					1
1	2	3^1	4	5	6	7	8■	9^2	10^3	11	12	14	13																					2
1	2	3^1	4	5	6	7		9^2	10	11	12	8	13																					3
1	2	3	4	5^1	6	7			10	11^2		8	9^3	12	13	14																		4
1	2	3^2	4	5	6	7	12		10^1	11	13	8	9^3	14																				5
1	2		4	5	6	7	8^1	12	10^3	11	3	9^2	13			14																		6
1	2		4	5	6^2	7	8	9		11	3	12	10^1			13																		7
1	2	3^3	4	5■		7	8^1	12		10	13	9			6■	11^2	14																	8
1	2	12	4			7				8	5	10	9^2	13		11		6	3^1															9
1	2	12	4			7		9		8	5^1	10				11		6	3															10
1	2	3	12	5		7^2		9		8		10	13			11		6	4^1															11
1	2	3	12	5				9^3		8	4	10^1	13	14		11		6	7^2															12
1	2	3^1	12	5				9^3		8	4	10	13	14		11		6	7^2															13
1	2		4	5		12		9		8	6	10^2	13			11^1		7	3															14
1	2		4^1	5			12	9		7	6	10^2	14			11		8	3^3	13														15
1	2	3	4^1	5		7	12	9		8		10		13		11^2				6														16
1		3^3	4	5		7	12	13		11	14	10		8			2^2			6	9^1													17
1	2		4	5		7	12	9^1		8	3	13		11^3		14				6	10^2													18
1	2	12	4^3	5		7		9		11	3	13		8^1						6	10^2	14												19
1	2		4	5		7		9		8	3	12		11^2		13				6	10^1													20
1			4			7		9		11	3^1	8^3		2		12		13		6	10^2	14	5											21
1	2		4			7	8^1	9	13	10	3^2	12		11^3						6		14	5											22
	2^3	12	4	5^2		7			9	8		13		14		11					10	3^1	6	1										23
	2^1		4	5		7		9	12	8^3	3^2	13				11					10	14	6	1										24
	2		4^2	5				9	8	7	12	13		11^1						6	10		3	1										25
	2		4^2					9	12	8	14	13		11^3						6	10	3	5	1	7^1									26
1	2		4	5^1						11^3		13				14				12	10	3^2	6			7	8	9						27
1	2		4					9	12	13						11^1				6	10	5				7^2	8	3						28
1	2			5^2					12	7				13		11^1				6	10		4		14	3	8^3	9						29
1	2		4					12		7						11				6	10		5			3	8	9^1						30
1	2		4					12		7						11^2				6^3	10		5		13	3	8	9^1	14					31
1	2	3	4					12		11										13	10^1		5			7	8	9^3	6^2	14				32
1	2	3^2	4					12		11^1											10		5		13	7	8	9^3	6	14				33
1	2	3^1	4					9								12							5		11^2	7	8	13	6	10				34
1	2							12								11				6			5		7	3	8	9	4	10^1				35
1	2							12		13						11				4			5		3^2	7	8	9	6	10^1				36
1	2^1	12								13				14		11				4			5		3^2	7	8	9^3	6■	10				37
1	2		4					12								11				6			5		3^1	7	8	9		10				38
1		3								12				4		11				6					2^1	7	8	9		10	5			39
1	2							12		7						11				6			4			3	8	9		10^1	5			40
1	2^1	12						13		14						11				6			5		3^3	7	8	9^2	4	10				41
1	2	12						13		8^2						11				6					3	7^1		9^3	4	10	5	14		42
1	2	3						9		12						11				6^2			13		7^1			8	4	10	5			43
1	2	3^2								12						11							6		7	13	8^1	9	4	10	5			44
1	2									12						11							6		3^1	7	8	9	4	10	5^2	13		45
	2^1			13						7^3												3	6^2		11	12	8	9	4	10	5	14	1	46

FA Cup

First Round	Rotherham U	(h)	3-0
Second Round	Tranmere R	(a)	2-1
Third Round	Plymouth Arg	(h)	1-1
		(a)	1-2

Carling Cup

First Round	Ipswich T	(h)	2-2
Second Round	Everton	(h)	1-2

J Paint Trophy

Second Round	Swansea C	(h)	1-0
Quarter-Final	Bristol R	(a)	0-1

PLYMOUTH ARGYLE FL Championship

FOUNDATION

The club was formed in September 1886 as the Argyle Football Club by former public and private school pupils who wanted to continue playing the game. The meeting was held in a room above the Borough Arms (a Coffee House), Bedford Street, Plymouth. It was common then to choose a local street/terrace as a club name and Argyle or Argyll was a fashionable name throughout the land due to Queen Victoria's great interest in Scotland.

Home Park, Plymouth, Devon PL2 3DQ.

Telephone: (01752) 562 561.

Fax: (01752) 606 167.

Ticket Office: 0845 338 7232.

Website: www.pafc.co.uk

Email: argyle@pafc.co.uk

Ground Capacity: 21,118.

Record Attendance: 43,596 v Aston Villa, Division 2, 10 October 1936.

Pitch Measurements: 112yd × 73yd.

Chairman: Paul Stapleton.

Vice-chairman: Robert Dennerly.

Chief Executive: Michael Dunford.

Secretary: Mrs Carole Rowntree.

Manager: Ian Holloway.

Assistant Manager: Tim Breacker.

Physio: Paul Maxwell.

Colours: Green shirts, white shorts, green stockings.

Change Colours: Yellow shirts, green shorts, yellow stockings.

Year Formed: 1886.

Turned Professional: 1903.

Ltd Co.: 1903.

Previous Name: 1886, Argyle Athletic Club; 1903, Plymouth Argyle.

Club Nickname: 'The Pilgrims'.

Ground: 1886, Home Park.

First Football League Game: 28 August 1920, Division 3, v Norwich C (h) D 1–1 – Craig; Russell, Atterbury; Logan, Dickinson, Forbes; Kirkpatrick, Jack, Bowler, Heeps (1), Dixon.

Record League Victory: 8–1 v Millwall, Division 2, 16 January 1932 – Harper; Roberts, Titmuss; Mackay, Pullan, Reed; Grozier, Bowden (2), Vidler (3), Leslie (1), Black (1), (1 og). 8–1 v Hartlepool U (a), Division 2, 7 May 1994 – Nicholls; Patterson (Naylor), Hill, Burrows, Comyn, McCall (1), Barlow, Castle (1), Landon (3), Marshall (1), Dalton (2).

HONOURS

Football League: Division 2 – Champions 2003–04; Division 3 (S) – Champions 1929–30, 1951–52; Runners-up 1921–22, 1922–23, 1923–24, 1924–25, 1925–26, 1926–27 (record of six consecutive years); Division 3 – Champions 1958–59, 2001–02; Runners-up 1974–75, 1985–86, Promoted 1995–96 (play-offs).

FA Cup: Semi-final 1984.

Football League Cup: Semi-final 1965, 1974.

SKY SPORTS FACT FILE

The first professional player engaged by Plymouth Argyle in 1903 was Bob Jack, a Scot and one-time Bolton Wanderers winger who later became Argyle manager. His two Bolton born sons David and Rollo made their debuts for Plymouth and later moved to Bolton.

Record Cup Victory: 6–0 v Corby T, FA Cup 3rd rd, 22 January 1966 – Leiper; Book, Baird; Williams, Nelson, Newman; Jones (1), Jackson (1), Bickle (3), Piper (1), Jennings.

Record Defeat: 0–9 v Stoke C, Division 2, 17 December 1960.

Most League Points (2 for a win): 68, Division 3 (S), 1929–30.

Most League Points (3 for a win): 102, Division 3, 2001–02.

Most League Goals: 107, Division 3 (S), 1925–26 and 1951–52.

Highest League Scorer in Season: Jack Cock, 32, Division 3 (S), 1926–27.

Most League Goals in Total Aggregate: Sammy Black, 180, 1924–38.

Most League Goals in One Match: 5, Wilf Carter v Charlton Ath, Division 2, 27 December 1960.

Most Capped Player: Moses Russell, 20 (23), Wales.

Most League Appearances: Kevin Hodges, 530, 1978–92.

Youngest League Player: Lee Phillips, 16 years 43 days v Gillingham, 29 October 1996.

Record Transfer Fee Received: £750,000 from Southampton for Michael Evans, March 1997.

Record Transfer Fee Paid: £400,000 to Debrecen for Peter Halmosi, May 2007.

Football League Record: 1920 Original Member of Division 3; 1921–30 Division 3 (S); 1930–50 Division 2; 1950–52 Division 3 (S); 1952–56 Division 2; 1956–58 Division 3 (S); 1958–59 Division 3; 1959–68 Division 2; 1968–75 Division 3; 1975–77 Division 2; 1977–86 Division 3; 1986–95 Division 2; 1995–96 Division 3; 1996–98 Division 2; 1998–2002 Division 3; 2002–04 Division 2; 2004– FL C.

MANAGERS

Frank Brettell 1903–05
Bob Jack 1905–06
Bill Fullerton 1906–07
Bob Jack 1910–38
Jack Tresadern 1938–47
Jimmy Rae 1948–55
Jack Rowley 1955–60
Neil Dougall 1961
Ellis Stuttard 1961–63
Andy Beattie 1963–64
Malcolm Allison 1964–65
Derek Ufton 1965–68
Billy Bingham 1968–70
Ellis Stuttard 1970–72
Tony Waiters 1972–77
Mike Kelly 1977–78
Malcolm Allison 1978–79
Bobby Saxton 1979–81
Bobby Moncur 1981–83
Johnny Hore 1983–84
Dave Smith 1984–88
Ken Brown 1988–90
David Kemp 1990–92
Peter Shilton 1992–95
Steve McCall 1995
Neil Warnock 1995–97
Mick Jones 1997–98
Kevin Hodges 1998–2000
Paul Sturrock 2000–04
Bobby Williamson 2004–05
Tony Pulis 2005–06
Ian Holloway June 2006–

LATEST SEQUENCES

Longest Sequence of League Wins: 9, 8.3.1986 – 12.4.1986.

Longest Sequence of League Defeats: 9, 12.10.1963 – 7.12.1963.

Longest Sequence of League Draws: 5, 26.2.2000 – 14.3.2000.

Longest Sequence of Unbeaten League Matches: 22, 20.4.1929 – 21.12.1929.

Longest Sequence Without a League Win: 13, 27.4.1963 – 2.10.1963.

Successive Scoring Runs: 39 from 15.4.1939.

Successive Non-scoring Runs: 5 from 20.9.1947.

TEN YEAR LEAGUE RECORD

		P	W	D	L	F	A	Pts	Pos
1997-98	Div 2	46	12	13	21	55	70	49	22
1998-99	Div 3	46	17	10	19	58	54	61	13
1999-2000	Div 3	46	16	18	12	55	51	66	12
2000-01	Div 3	46	15	13	18	54	61	58	12
2001-02	Div 3	46	31	9	6	71	28	102	1
2002-03	Div 2	46	17	14	15	63	52	65	8
2003-04	Div 2	46	26	12	8	85	41	90	1
2004-05	FL C	46	14	11	21	52	64	53	17
2005-06	FL C	46	13	17	16	39	46	56	14
2006-07	FL C	46	17	16	13	63	62	67	11

DID YOU KNOW ?

Goalkeeper George Stanbury who was first choice for Plymouth Argyle in the 1927–28 season had been an amateur with Exeter City at only 15 years of age. He also had the unusual distinction of representing English Railways against France, Belgium and Wales.

PLYMOUTH ARGYLE 2006–07 LEAGUE RECORD

Match No.	Date	Venue	Opponents	Result		H/T Score	Lg. Pos.	Goalscorers	Attendance
1	Aug 5	H	Wolverhampton W	D	1-1	1-0	—	Hayles [35]	15,964
2	8	A	Colchester U	W	1-0	1-0	—	Summerfield [30]	4627
3	12	A	Sunderland	W	3-2	2-1	3	Norris [8], Hayles [39], Chadwick [82]	24,377
4	19	H	Sheffield W	L	1-2	1-0	9	Wotton (pen) [43]	14,507
5	26	A	Stoke C	D	1-1	0-1	8	Hayles [78]	11,626
6	Sept 9	H	QPR	D	1-1	1-1	9	Ebanks-Blake [31]	12,138
7	12	H	Cardiff C	D	3-3	0-2	—	McNaughton (og) [69], Hayles [74], Purse (og) [88]	11,655
8	16	A	Southampton	L	0-1	0-0	15		22,514
9	23	H	Norwich C	W	3-1	1-0	9	Doherty (og) [14], Seip [47], Norris [74]	11,813
10	30	A	Coventry C	W	1-0	0-0	8	Samba [82]	19,545
11	Oct 15	H	Derby Co	W	3-1	1-1	5	Wotton 2 (2 pens) [45, 63], Seip [79]	13,622
12	17	A	Barnsley	D	2-2	2-1	—	Ebanks-Blake [29], Hayles [34]	9479
13	21	H	Burnley	D	0-0	0-0	7		12,817
14	28	A	Crystal Palace	W	1-0	1-0	5	Chadwick [39]	17,084
15	31	H	Ipswich T	D	1-1	1-1	—	Wotton [22]	12,210
16	Nov 4	H	Birmingham C	L	0-1	0-0	7		17,008
17	11	A	Leicester C	D	2-2	1-1	7	Nalis [31], Hayles [90]	21,703
18	18	A	Southend U	D	1-1	1-0	9	Djordjic [5]	9469
19	25	H	Leeds U	L	1-2	1-1	12	Djordjic [40]	17,088
20	28	H	Luton T	W	1-0	0-0	—	Djordjic [61]	9965
21	Dec 2	A	Birmingham C	L	0-3	0-3	11		22,592
22	9	H	Hull C	W	1-0	0-0	10	Ebanks-Blake [71]	12,101
23	16	A	Preston NE	L	0-3	0-2	12		13,171
24	23	H	WBA	D	2-2	2-2	12	Hayles [23], Nalis [40]	15,172
25	26	A	Cardiff C	D	2-2	1-0	13	Norris 2 [34, 59]	17,299
26	30	A	Derby Co	L	0-1	0-0	13		25,775
27	Jan 1	H	Southampton	D	1-1	0-1	13	Hayles [66]	15,377
28	13	A	Norwich C	W	3-1	0-1	12	Hayles [59], Buzsaky 2 [63, 75]	23,513
29	22	H	Coventry C	W	3-2	2-1	—	Gallen [18], Buzsaky [32], Hayles [48]	9841
30	31	A	WBA	L	1-2	0-1	—	Fallon [70]	19,894
31	Feb 3	A	Wolverhampton W	D	2-2	2-1	11	Sinclair [27], Timar [36]	19,082
32	10	H	Sunderland	L	0-2	0-0	11		15,247
33	20	H	Colchester U	W	3-0	1-0	—	Norris [12], Ebanks-Blake (pen) [59], Gosling [67]	12,895
34	24	A	QPR	D	1-1	1-0	12	Nalis [32]	13,757
35	Mar 3	H	Stoke C	D	1-1	1-0	12	Ebanks-Blake (pen) [40]	12,539
36	6	A	Sheffield W	D	1-1	0-1	—	Gosling [56]	19,449
37	14	H	Barnsley	L	2-4	2-2	—	Nalis [15], Ebanks-Blake [41]	10,265
38	17	H	Crystal Palace	W	1-0	0-0	13	Sinclair [48]	11,239
39	31	A	Ipswich T	L	0-3	0-2	13		21,078
40	Apr 3	A	Burnley	L	0-4	0-3	—		9793
41	7	A	Leeds U	L	1-2	1-1	15	Halmosi [36]	30,034
42	9	H	Leicester C	W	3-0	1-0	13	Halmosi [15], Ebanks-Blake [46], Hayles [62]	10,900
43	14	A	Luton T	W	2-1	2-0	13	Norris [4], Halmosi [40]	7601
44	21	H	Southend U	W	2-1	1-1	12	Ebanks-Blake [6], Hayles [90]	11,097
45	28	H	Preston NE	W	2-0	0-0	12	Ebanks-Blake (pen) [77], Hayles [85]	13,813
46	May 6	A	Hull C	W	2-1	1-0	11	Halmosi [45], Ebanks-Blake [59]	20,661

Final League Position: 11

GOALSCORERS

League (63): Hayles 13, Ebanks-Blake 10 (3 pens), Norris 6, Halmosi 4, Nalis 4, Wotton 4 (3 pens), Buzsaky 3, Djordjic 3, Chadwick 2, Gosling 2, Seip 2, Sinclair 2, Fallon 1, Gallen 1, Samba 1, Summerfield 1, Timar 1, own goals 3.
Carling Cup (0).
FA Cup (7): Aljofree 2 (2 pens), Sinclair 2, Gallen 1 (pen), Hayles 1, Norris 1.

McCormick L 40	Hodges L 11 + 4	Connolly P 38	Wotton P 21 + 1	Doumbe S 29	Aljofree H 22 + 3	Norris D 41	Nalis L 39 + 3	Chadwick N 9 + 7	Hayles B 37 + 2	Capaldi T 30 + 1	Djordjic B 8 + 9	Ebanks-Blake S 30 + 11	Summerfield L 11 + 12	Sawyer G 19 + 3	Buzsaky A 27 + 9	Reid R 1 + 5	Barness A 1	Seip M 36 + 1	Samba C 1 + 12	Gosling D 8 + 4	Larrieu R 6	Dickson R — + 2	Gallen K 6 + 7	Halmosi P 14 + 2	Fallon R 5 + 10	Sinclair S 8 + 7	Timar K 8 + 1	Match No.
1	2	3	4	5	6	7	8^{1}	9^{2}	10	11	12	13																1
1	2	3	4	5	6	7		9^{1}	10	11^{2}	13	12	8^{3}	14														2
1	2	3	4	5	6	7		12	10	11		9^{1}	8^{2}		13													3
1	2	3	4	5	6	7		9^{2}	10	11^{3}	12	13	8^{1}		14													4
1	2	3	4	5	6	7	8	9^{1}	10	11^{2}		12				13												5
1	2	3	4	5	6	7	8	12	10			9^{2}			11^{1}	13												6
1	2		4^{1}	5	6	7	12	13	10	11		9^{2}	8		14		3^{3}											7
1	2^{1}		12	5	3^{3}	7	8	13	10	11		9	4		6^{2}			14										8
1		2	4	5		7	8	12	10^{1}	3		9^{2}		14	11^{3}	13		6										9
1		2	4	5	12	7	8	9^{2}		3			13		11^{1}	10^{3}		6	14									10
1		2	4	5▪	12^{2}	7	8		10	3		9^{1}	13		11^{3}			6	14									11
1		2	4		5	7	8^{2}		10	11	12	9^{3}	13		6^{1}			3	14									12
1		2	4		5	7	8		10	3		9^{1}			11			6	12									13
1		2	4	5		7	8	10^{1}		3		9^{3}	12	13	11^{2}			6	14									14
1		2	4	5		7	8	10^{1}	12	3		9^{2}			11			6	13									15
1		2	4		5	7	8^{1}	9^{3}	10	3	13	14	12		11^{2}			6										16
1		2	4		5	7	8	9^{1}	10	3	12	13			11^{2}			6										17
1		2	4		5	7	8^{3}	12	10	3	11^{2}	9^{1}	14		13			6										18
1		2	4		5	7	8^{2}	12	10	3^{3}	11^{1}	9	13		14			6										19
1	3	2^{1}	4			7	13		10	12	9^{2}	14	8	5	11^{3}			6										20
1			4	5	12	7	13		10	3	9^{1}		8	2^{2}	11^{3}			6	14									21
1			4^{3}	5			8		10	3	11^{1}	9^{2}	7	2	12			6	13	14								22
1				5	2	7	8		10	3		9	11	6^{1}	12			4^{2}	13									23
				5	6	7	8		10	3	11^{1}	9			4			2	12		1							24
		2^{1}		5	6	7	8		10	3		9			11			4	12		1							25
		2^{1}		5	3	7	8		10	11		9^{2}	12		4^{3}			6	13		1	14						26
				5^{1}		7	8		10▪	11			12	3	4^{3}	13		6	9^{2}	2	1	14						27
1	12				3	7	8		10^{3}				13	5	4	14		6		2^{1}			9	11^{2}				28
1		2			5	7	8		10^{2}			12		3	4^{1}			6					9	11^{3}	13	14		29
1		2			5	7	8		10^{1}	3		12			4			6					9^{2}	11^{3}	13	14		30
1		2					8		10^{1}			12	7	3	13			6		4			14		9^{3}	11^{2}	5	31
1		2		5		7	8			3		9^{2}	12		4^{1}								13	11^{3}	10	14	6	32
1		2				7	8					9^{2}	12	3				6		4^{3}			10^{1}	14	13	11	5	33
1	12	2				7	8▪					9^{1}		3				6		4^{2}				13	10	11	5	34
1	4	2										9^{1}	8^{2}	3				6		13			10	11	12	7	5	35
1	12	2		5	6	7	8^{1}			3	9^{2}									4				11	10	13		36
1		2				7	8		12	3^{2}	13	9^{1}						6					10^{3}	4	14	11	5	37
1	12	2		5		7	8		10			9^{2}		3				6		4^{1}					13	11		38
1		2		5▪			8		10		12	9^{2}		3	4^{3}			6					14	7	13	11^{1}		39
1	4^{2}	2					8		10	3	12	14			13			6		7^{1}					9^{3}	11	5	40
1		2				7	8		10		11^{2}	9^{1}		3				6						4	12	13	5	41
1		2		5		7	8		10^{1}			9^{2}		3	4^{3}			6		12				11	13	14		42
1		2		5		7	8		10^{1}			9^{2}		3	4			6					12	11		13		43
1		2		5		7	8		10			9^{2}		3	4^{1}			6		12			13	11^{3}			14	44
		2		5		7	8		10			9		3	4^{1}			6			1		12	11				45
		2		5		7	8		10^{2}			9		3	4			6			1		12	11^{1}	13			46

FA Cup

Third Round	Peterborough U	(a)	1-1
		(h)	2-1
Fourth Round	Barnet	(a)	2-0
Fifth Round	Derby Co	(h)	2-0
Sixth Round	Watford	(h)	0-1

Carling Cup

First Round	Walsall	(h)	0-1

PORTSMOUTH FA Premiership

FOUNDATION

At a meeting held in his High Street, Portsmouth offices in 1898, solicitor Alderman J. E. Pink and five other business and professional men agreed to buy some ground close to Goldsmith Avenue for £4,950 which they developed into Fratton Park in record breaking time. A team of professionals was signed up by manager Frank Brettell and entry to the Southern League obtained for the new club's September 1899 kick-off.

Fratton Park, Frogmore Road, Portsmouth, Hampshire PO4 8RA.

Telephone: (02392) 731 204.

Fax: (02392) 734 129.

Ticket Office: 0871 230 1898.

Website: www.pompeyfc.co.uk

Email: info@pompeyfc.co.uk

Ground Capacity: 20,328.

Record Attendance: 51,385 v Derby Co, FA Cup 6th rd, 26 February 1949.

Pitch Measurements: 100m × 65m.

Owner: Alexander Gaydamak.

Chief Executive: Peter Storrie.

Secretary: Paul Weld.

Manager: Harry Redknapp.

Assistant Manager: Tony Adams.

Physio: Gary Sadler.

Colours: Blue shirts, white shorts, red stockings.

Change Colours: White with blue trim.

Year Formed: 1898.

Turned Professional: 1898.

Ltd Co.: 1898.

Club Nickname: 'Pompey'.

Ground: 1898, Fratton Park.

First Football League Game: 28 August 1920, Division 3, v Swansea T (h) W 3–0 – Robson; Probert, Potts; Abbott, Harwood, Turner; Thompson, Stringfellow (1), Reid (1), James (1), Beedie.

Record League Victory: 9–1 v Notts Co, Division 2, 9 April 1927 – McPhail; Clifford, Ted Smith; Reg Davies (1), Foxall, Moffat; Forward (1), Mackie (2), Haines (3), Watson, Cook (2).

Record Cup Victory: 7–0 v Stockport Co, FA Cup 3rd rd, 8 January 1949 – Butler; Rookes, Ferrier; Scoular, Flewin, Dickinson; Harris (3), Barlow, Clarke (2), Phillips (2), Froggatt.

HONOURS

Football League: Division 1 – Champions 1948–49, 1949–50, 2002–03; Division 2 – Runners-up 1926–27, 1986–87; Division 3 (S) – Champions 1923–24; Division 3 – Champions 1961–62, 1982–83.

FA Cup: Winners 1939; Runners-up 1929, 1934.

Football League Cup: best season: 5th rd, 1961, 1986.

SKY SPORTS FACT FILE

On 22 April 2007 Portsmouth goalkeeper David James recorded his 142nd Premier League clean sheet in the goalless draw with Aston Villa. He thus overtook the record held by David Seaman of Arsenal. The Pompey last line added another on 13 May, against the Gunners!

Record Defeat: 0–10 v Leicester C, Division 1, 20 October 1928.

Most League Points (2 for a win): 65, Division 3, 1961–62.

Most League Points (3 for a win): 98, Division 1, 2002–03.

Most League Goals: 97, Division 1, 2002–03.

Highest League Scorer in Season: Guy Whittingham, 42, Division 1, 1992–93.

Most League Goals in Total Aggregate: Peter Harris, 194, 1946–60.

Most League Goals in One Match: 5, Alf Strange v Gillingham, Division 3, 27 January 1923; 5, Peter Harris v Aston Villa, Division 1, 3 September 1958.

Most Capped Player: Jimmy Dickinson, 48, England.

Most League Appearances: Jimmy Dickinson, 764, 1946–65.

Youngest League Player: Clive Green, 16 years 259 days v Wrexham, 21 August 1976.

Record Transfer Fee Received: £7,500,000 from Middlesbrough for Ayegbeni Yakubu, July 2005.

Record Transfer Fee Paid: £7,000,000 to Udinese for Sulley Muntari, July 2007.

Football League Record: 1920 Original Member of Division 3; 1921 Division 3 (S); 1924–27 Division 2; 1927–59 Division 1; 1959–61 Division 2; 1961–62 Division 3; 1962–76 Division 2; 1976–78 Division 3; 1978–80 Division 4; 1980–83 Division 3; 1983–87 Division 2; 1987–88 Division 1; 1988–92 Division 2; 1992–2003 Division 1; 2003– FA Premier League.

MANAGERS

Frank Brettell 1898–1901
Bob Blyth 1901–04
Richard Bonney 1905–08
Bob Brown 1911–20
John McCartney 1920–27
Jack Tinn 1927–47
Bob Jackson 1947–52
Eddie Lever 1952–58
Freddie Cox 1958–61
George Smith 1961–70
Ron Tindall 1970–73
(General Manager to 1974)
John Mortimore 1973–74
Ian St John 1974–77
Jimmy Dickinson 1977–79
Frank Burrows 1979–82
Bobby Campbell 1982–84
Alan Ball 1984–89
John Gregory 1989–90
Frank Burrows 1990–91
Jim Smith 1991–95
Terry Fenwick 1995–98
Alan Ball 1998–99
Tony Pulis 2000
Steve Claridge 2000–01
Graham Rix 2001–02
Harry Redknapp 2002–04
Velimir Zajec 2004–05
Alain Perrin 2005
Harry Redknapp December 2005–

LATEST SEQUENCES

Longest Sequence of League Wins: 7, 17.8.2002 – 17.9.2002.

Longest Sequence of League Defeats: 9, 21.10.1975 – 6.12.1975.

Longest Sequence of League Draws: 5, 16.12.2000 – 13.1.2001.

Longest Sequence of Unbeaten League Matches: 15, 18.4.1924 – 18.10.1924.

Longest Sequence Without a League Win: 25, 29.11.1958 – 22.8.1959.

Successive Scoring Runs: 23 from 30.8.1930.

Successive Non-scoring Runs: 6 from 14.1.1939.

TEN YEAR LEAGUE RECORD

		P	W	D	L	F	A	Pts	Pos
1997-98	Div 1	46	13	10	23	51	63	49	20
1998-99	Div 1	46	11	14	21	57	73	47	19
1999-2000	Div 1	46	13	12	21	55	66	51	18
2000-01	Div 1	46	10	19	17	47	59	49	20
2001-02	Div 1	46	13	14	19	60	72	53	17
2002-03	Div 1	46	29	11	6	97	45	98	1
2003-04	PR Lge	38	12	9	17	47	54	45	13
2004-05	PR Lge	38	10	9	19	43	59	39	16
2005-06	PR Lge	38	10	8	20	37	62	38	17
2006-07	PR Lge	38	14	12	12	45	42	54	9

DID YOU KNOW ?

Former Aston Villa and Queens Park Rangers centre-forward Frank Bedingfield scored 55 goals for Portsmouth in two seasons from 1900–01 but collapsed after a cup-tie against Reading in 1902. He was sent to South Africa to recuperate but died two years later.

PORTSMOUTH 2006–07 LEAGUE RECORD

Match No.	Date	Venue	Opponents	Result	H/T Score	Lg. Pos.	Goalscorers	Attendance
1	Aug 19	H	Blackburn R	W 3-0	1-0	—	Todorov [26], Kanu 2 [62, 84]	19,523
2	23	A	Manchester C	D 0-0	0-0	—		37,214
3	28	A	Middlesbrough	W 4-0	1-0	—	Kanu 2 [7, 57], Mwaruwari [50], Todorov [90]	24,834
4	Sept 9	H	Wigan Ath	W 1-0	0-0	2	Mwaruwari [49]	19,508
5	16	A	Charlton Ath	W 1-0	0-0	1	Lua-Lua [74]	26,130
6	25	H	Bolton W	L 0-1	0-1	—		19,105
7	Oct 1	A	Tottenham H	L 1-2	1-2	4	Kanu [40]	36,063
8	14	H	West Ham U	W 2-0	1-0	4	Kanu [24], Cole [82]	20,142
9	21	A	Chelsea	L 1-2	0-0	5	Mwaruwari [69]	41,838
10	28	H	Reading	W 3-1	1-0	4	Gunnarsson (og) [10], Kanu [52], Pedro Mendes [66]	20,146
11	Nov 4	A	Manchester U	L 0-3	0-2	4		76,004
12	11	H	Fulham	D 1-1	0-0	6	Cole [74]	19,563
13	18	H	Watford	W 2-1	1-1	3	Kanu [44], Lua-Lua (pen) [89]	19,738
14	26	A	Newcastle U	L 0-1	0-0	4		48,743
15	29	A	Liverpool	D 0-0	0-0	—		42,467
16	Dec 2	H	Aston Villa	D 2-2	0-1	4	Taylor 2 (1 pen) [52, 80 (p)]	20,042
17	9	H	Everton	W 2-0	2-0	3	Taylor [14], Kanu [26]	19,528
18	16	A	Arsenal	D 2-2	1-0	6	Pamarot [45], Taylor [47]	60,037
19	23	H	Sheffield U	W 3-1	0-1	6	Kozluk (og) [48], Campbell [54], Pamarot [68]	20,164
20	26	A	West Ham U	W 2-1	2-0	5	Primus 2 [16, 38]	34,913
21	30	A	Bolton W	L 2-3	1-2	6	Taylor [2], Cole [89]	22,447
22	Jan 1	H	Tottenham H	D 1-1	1-0	6	Mwaruwari [29]	20,194
23	13	A	Sheffield U	D 1-1	0-1	6	O'Neil [81]	30,269
24	20	H	Charlton Ath	L 0-1	0-0	6		19,567
25	30	H	Middlesbrough	D 0-0	0-0	—		19,820
26	Feb 3	A	Wigan Ath	L 0-1	0-0	7		15,093
27	10	H	Manchester C	W 2-1	1-0	7	Pedro Mendes [5], Kanu [81]	19,344
28	25	A	Blackburn R	L 0-3	0-2	8		17,434
29	Mar 3	H	Chelsea	L 0-2	0-1	9		20,219
30	17	A	Reading	D 0-0	0-0	9		24,087
31	31	A	Fulham	D 1-1	1-0	9	Kranjcar [4]	22,806
32	Apr 7	H	Manchester U	W 2-1	1-0	8	Taylor [30], Ferdinand (og) [89]	20,223
33	9	A	Watford	L 2-4	1-2	8	Taylor [16], Mvuemba [81]	18,119
34	14	H	Newcastle U	W 2-1	1-0	7	Mwaruwari [7], Taylor [59]	20,165
35	22	A	Aston Villa	D 0-0	0-0	8		31,745
36	28	H	Liverpool	W 2-1	2-0	7	Mwaruwari [27], Kranjcar [32]	20,201
37	May 5	A	Everton	L 0-3	0-0	8		39,619
38	13	H	Arsenal	D 0-0	0-0	9		20,188

Final League Position: 9

GOALSCORERS

League (45): Kanu 10, Taylor 8 (1 pen), Mwaruwari 6, Cole 3, Kranjcar 2, Lua-Lua 2 (1 pen), Pamarot 2, Pedro Mendes 2, Primus 2, Todorov 2, Campbell 1, Mvuemba 1, O'Neil 1, own goals 3.
Carling Cup (2): Fernandes 1, Taylor 1.
FA Cup (3): Kanu 2, Cole 1.

James D 38	Johnson G 25 + 1	Stefanovic D 20	Davis S 29 + 2	Primus L 36	Campbell S 32	O'Neil G 35	Pedro Mendes 25 + 1	Mwaruwari B 25 + 6	Todorov S 1 + 3	Taylor M 30 + 5	Thompson D 5 + 7	Kanu N 32 + 4	Hughes R 11 + 7	Pamarot N 21 + 2	Koroman O — + 1	Lua-Lua L 8 + 14	Fernandes M 7 + 3	Cole A 5 + 13	Kranjcar N 11 + 13	O'Brien A 1 + 2	Douala R 1 + 6	Traore D 10	Lauren E 9 + 1	Mvuemba A 1 + 6	Match No.
1	2	3	4	5	6	7	8	9^1	10^2	11	12	13													1
1	2	3	4	5	6	7	8^2	9^1	12	11		10	13												2
1		3	4	5	6	7		9	12	11^2	8^3	10^1	13	2	14										3
1	2	3^2	4	5	6	7	8^1	9		11	12	10^3		13		14									4
1	2	3	4	5	6	7^1	8	9^2		11	12	10				13									5
1	2	3	4	5	6	7	8^1	9^3		11^2	12	10				13	14								6
1	2	3^1	4^2	5	6	7	8	13		12		10^3				9		14	11						7
1	2	3		5	6	7	8	9^2		11		10^1				12	4	13							8
1			12	5	6	7	8^2	9		3	13	10^1		2			4^3	14	11						9
1	2	3	4	5^2	6	7	8	9^1		11		10^3		13		12		14							10
1		6	4			7	8	9^1		3			13	2		12	11^3	14	10^2	5					11
1		3	4	5	6	7^2	8	12		11^3	13	10^1		2		9		14							12
1		3	4	5	6		8				7^1	10		2		9		12	11						13
1		3^1	4	5	6	11	8^2	9^3		12	7	10		2					13		14				14
1				5	6	4	8^2	9^1		3	7	12	11	2			13		10^3	14					15
1	2			5	6	7	8■	12		11		10^2	13	3		9^1	4								16
1	2		4^1	5	6	7		9^3		11		10^2	12	3			8		13		14				17
1	2		4	5	6	7	8			11	9^2	10^1	12	3					13						18
1	2		4	5	6	7^3	8^1	9		11		10^2		3			12	13	14						19
1	2		4	5	6	7	8			11		10^1		3			9	12							20
1	2		4	5^3	6	7^2		12		11	13			3^1			8	9	10	14					21
1	2		4	5	6	7^1	8	9		11		10		3^2				12	13						22
1	2		4^1	5^3	6	7	8	12		11		10^2	13					9	14			3			23
1	2		4^2	5	6		8	12		11		10^1						9			13	3	7		24
1	2			5	6	4	8	9^1		11		10^2				12		13			14	3^3	7		25
1	2			5	6		8	9		12		10^3	4	3^1		13		14			11		7^2		26
1	2		4		6	7	8^3			11		12		5		10		9^1	13			3^2	14		27
1	2		4^1	5	6	7	8^3			11		12		3^2		10		9	13					14	28
1			4	5	6	7				11		10	8	2		9^1		12	13			3^2			29
1	2	3		5	6	7		9		12		10	8						11^1					4	30
1		3	4	5	6	7		9^3	12	13		10^1	8						11^2				2	14	31
1		6	4	5		7		9^1		11		10^2	8			12			13			3	2		32
1		6	4^3	5		7				11		10	8	2		9^2			12		13	3^1		14	33
1		3	4	5	6	7		9^1		11		10^2	8			12			13				2		34
1	12	3		5	6	7		9^3		11		10^2	4			13			8^1				2	14	35
1	2	6	12	5		7		9^1		11^3		10^2	4			13			14			3	8		36
1	2		4	5		7		9				10^2		6		12			11^1		13	3	8^3	14	37
1	2		4^1	5		7^3	12	9^2				10	8	6		13			11			3		14	38

FA Cup

Third Round	Wigan Ath	(h)	2-1
Fourth Round	Manchester U	(a)	1-2

Carling Cup

Second Round	Mansfield T	(a)	2-1
Third Round	Newcastle U	(a)	0-3

PORT VALE — FL Championship 1

FOUNDATION

Formed in 1876 as Port Vale, adopting the prefix 'Burslem' in 1884 upon moving to that part of the city. It was dropped in 1909.

Vale Park, Hamil Road, Burslem, Stoke-on-Trent ST6 1AW.

Telephone: (01782) 655 800.

Fax: (01782) 834 981.

Ticket Office: (01782) 655 832.

Website: www.port-vale.co.uk

Email: enquiries@port-vale.co.uk

Ground Capacity: 18,982.

Record Attendance: 49,768 v Aston Villa, FA Cup 5th rd, 20 February 1960.

Pitch Measurements: 114yd × 75yd.

Chairman/Chief Executive: William A. Bratt.

Vice-chairmen: David Smith, Peter L. Jackson.

Secretary: Bill Lodey.

Manager: Martin Foyle.

Assistant Manager: Dean Glover.

Physio: John Bowers.

Colours: White shirts with black and gold trim, black shorts with white and gold trim, white stockings with black and gold trim.

Change Colours: Sky blue shirts with navy blue trim, navy blue shorts with sky blue trim, sky blue stockings with navy blue trim.

Year Formed: 1876.

Turned Professional: 1885.

Ltd Co.: 1911.

Previous Names: 1876, Port Vale; 1884, Burslem Port Vale; 1909, Port Vale.

Club Nickname: 'Valiants'.

Grounds: 1876, Limekin Lane, Longport; 1881, Westport; 1884, Moorland Road, Burslem; 1886, Athletic Ground, Cobridge; 1913, Recreation Ground, Hanley; 1950, Vale Park.

First Football League Game: 3 September 1892, Division 2, v Small Heath (a) L 1–5 – Frail; Clutton, Elson; Farrington, McCrindle, Delves; Walker, Scarratt, Bliss (1), Jones. (Only 10 men).

Record League Victory: 9–1 v Chesterfield, Division 2, 24 September 1932 – Leckie; Shenton, Poyser; Sherlock, Round, Jones; McGrath, Mills, Littlewood (6), Kirkham (2), Morton (1).

Record Cup Victory: 7–1 v Irthlingborough, FA Cup 1st rd, 12 January 1907 – Matthews; Dunn, Hamilton; Eardley, Baddeley, Holyhead; Carter, Dodds (2), Beats, Mountford (2), Coxon (3).

HONOURS

Football League: Division 2 – Runners-up 1993–94; Division 3 (N) – Champions 1929–30, 1953–54; Runners-up 1952–53; Division 4 – Champions 1958–59; Promoted 1969–70 (4th).

FA Cup: Semi-final 1954, when in Division 3.

Football League Cup: best season: 4th rd 2007.

Autoglass Trophy: Winners 1993.

Anglo-Italian Cup: Runners-up 1996.

LDV Vans Trophy: Winners 2001.

SKY SPORTS FACT FILE

In 1923–24 Port Vale used the services of former England internationals Arthur Bridgett (41) and Tom Holford (45)! Bridgett, in non-league football since released by Sunderland in 1911, actually scored seven goals in his 14 Vale League games.

Record Defeat: 0–10 v Sheffield U, Division 2, 10 December 1892. 0–10 v Notts Co, Division 2, 26 February 1895.

Most League Points (2 for a win): 69, Division 3 (N), 1953–54.

Most League Points (3 for a win): 89, Division 2, 1992–93.

Most League Goals: 110, Division 4, 1958–59.

Highest League Scorer in Season: Wilf Kirkham 38, Division 2, 1926–27.

Most League Goals in Total Aggregate: Wilf Kirkham, 154, 1923–29, 1931–33.

Most League Goals in One Match: 6, Stewart Littlewood v Chesterfield, Division 2, 24 September 1922.

Most Capped Player: Chris Birchall, 22 (26), Trinidad & Tobago.

Most League Appearances: Roy Sproson, 761, 1950–72.

Youngest League Player: Malcolm McKenzie, 15 years 347 days v Newport Co, 12 April 1966.

Record Transfer Fee Received: £2,000,000 from Wimbledon for Gareth Ainsworth, October 1998.

Record Transfer Fee Paid: £500,000 to York C for Jon McCarthy, August 1995 and £500,000 to Lincoln C for Gareth Ainsworth, September 1997.

Football League Record: 1892 Original Member of Division 2. Failed re-election in 1896; Re-elected 1898; Resigned 1907; Returned in Oct, 1919, when they took over the fixtures of Leeds City; 1929–30 Division 3 (N); 1930–36 Division 2; 1936–38 Division 3 (N); 1938–52 Division 3 (S); 1952–54 Division 3 (N); 1954–57 Division 2; 1957–58 Division 3 (S); 1958–59 Division 4; 1959–65 Division 3; 1965–70 Division 4; 1970–78 Division 3; 1978–83 Division 4; 1983–84 Division 3; 1984–86 Division 4; 1986–89 Division 3; 1989–94 Division 2; 1994–2000 Division 1; 2000–04 Division 2; 2004– FL 1.

MANAGERS

Sam Gleaves 1896–1905
(Secretary-Manager)
Tom Clare 1905–11
A. S. Walker 1911–12
H. Myatt 1912–14
Tom Holford 1919–24
(continued as Trainer)
Joe Schofield 1924–30
Tom Morgan 1930–32
Tom Holford 1932–35
Warney Cresswell 1936–37
Tom Morgan 1937–38
Billy Frith 1945–46
Gordon Hodgson 1946–51
Ivor Powell 1951
Freddie Steele 1951–57
Norman Low 1957–62
Freddie Steele 1962–65
Jackie Mudie 1965–67
Sir Stanley Matthews
(General Manager) 1965–68
Gordon Lee 1968–74
Roy Sproson 1974–77
Colin Harper 1977
Bobby Smith 1977–78
Dennis Butler 1978–79
Alan Bloor 1979
John McGrath 1980–83
John Rudge 1984–99
Brian Horton 1999–2004
Martin Foyle February 2004–

LATEST SEQUENCES

Longest Sequence of League Wins: 8, 8.4.1893 – 30.9.1893.

Longest Sequence of League Defeats: 9, 9.3.1957 – 20.4.1957.

Longest Sequence of League Draws: 6, 26.4.1981 – 12.9.1981.

Longest Sequence of Unbeaten League Matches: 19, 5.5.1969 – 8.11.1969.

Longest Sequence Without a League Win: 17, 7.12.1991 – 21.3.1992.

Successive Scoring Runs: 22 from 12.9.1992.

Successive Non-scoring Runs: 4 from 10.2.1896.

TEN YEAR LEAGUE RECORD

		P	W	D	L	F	A	Pts	Pos
1997-98	Div 1	46	13	10	23	56	66	49	19
1998-99	Div 1	46	13	8	25	45	75	47	21
1999-2000	Div 1	46	7	15	24	48	69	36	23
2000-01	Div 2	46	16	14	16	55	49	62	11
2001-02	Div 2	46	16	10	20	51	62	58	14
2002-03	Div 2	46	14	11	21	54	70	53	17
2003-04	Div 2	46	21	10	15	73	63	73	7
2004-05	FL 1	46	17	5	24	49	59	56	18
2005-06	FL 1	46	16	12	18	49	54	60	13
2006-07	FL 1	46	18	6	22	64	65	60	12

DID YOU KNOW ?

In 1953–54 Port Vale had the unusually high goal average of 3.525 in winning the Division Three (North) championship. They scored 74 goals, conceded only 21, kept 30 clean sheets and finished eleven points ahead of the runners-up.

PORT VALE 2006–07 LEAGUE RECORD

Match No.	Date	Venue	Opponents	Result	H/T Score	Lg. Pos.	Goalscorers	Attendance
1	Aug 5	H	Leyton Orient	W 3-0	1-0	—	Constantine 2 [43, 72], Sodje [78]	5631
2	8	A	Oldham Ath	W 1-0	0-0	—	Sodje [66]	4975
3	12	A	Cheltenham T	W 1-0	0-0	1	Constantine [55]	4309
4	19	H	Chesterfield	W 3-2	1-1	1	Constantine 2 [44, 87], Pilkington [77]	5622
5	26	A	Yeovil T	L 0-1	0-1	2		4827
6	Sept 3	H	Doncaster R	L 1-2	1-0	3	Whitaker [43]	4862
7	9	H	Blackpool	W 2-1	1-0	3	Constantine [45], Sodje [68]	5171
8	12	A	Scunthorpe U	L 0-3	0-2	—		3473
9	16	A	Bradford C	L 0-2	0-0	4		7829
10	23	H	Bristol C	L 0-2	0-1	7		5295
11	26	H	Nottingham F	D 1-1	1-1	—	Husbands [1]	7388
12	30	A	Northampton T	W 2-0	2-0	8	Pilkington [12], Moore [32]	5316
13	Oct 8	H	Rotherham U	L 1-3	0-0	10	Constantine (pen) [74]	4810
14	13	A	Tranmere R	W 2-1	2-0	—	Smith J [31], Constantine [45]	7866
15	21	H	Huddersfield T	L 1-2	1-0	10	Constantine [33]	5225
16	28	A	Millwall	D 1-1	0-1	10	Sodje [72]	10,189
17	Nov 4	A	Crewe Alex	L 1-2	1-1	13	Abbey [36]	7632
18	18	H	Swansea C	L 0-2	0-0	14		4615
19	25	A	Carlisle U	L 2-3	2-0	17	Harsley [26], Smith J [40]	7543
20	Dec 5	H	Gillingham	W 2-0	1-0	—	Whitaker [8], Constantine [75]	3077
21	9	A	Bournemouth	W 4-0	2-0	12	Constantine 2 [3, 68], Pilkington [13], Sodje [80]	4538
22	16	H	Brentford	W 1-0	0-0	9	Pilkington [87]	4166
23	23	H	Brighton & HA	W 2-1	2-0	9	Constantine 2 (1 pen) [13, 23 (p)]	4349
24	26	A	Nottingham F	L 0-3	0-1	10		22,999
25	30	A	Bristol C	L 1-2	0-0	11	Smith J [68]	12,776
26	Jan 1	H	Scunthorpe U	D 0-0	0-0	11		4869
27	6	H	Bradford C	L 0-1	0-0	11		4146
28	13	A	Blackpool	L 1-2	0-0	11	Sodje (pen) [90]	6661
29	27	A	Brighton & HA	D 0-0	0-0	13		5177
30	Feb 3	A	Leyton Orient	L 1-2	1-0	15	Gardner [12]	4295
31	6	H	Northampton T	W 1-0	0-0	—	Whitaker [47]	3353
32	17	A	Chesterfield	L 0-3	0-1	16		3752
33	20	H	Oldham Ath	W 3-0	1-0	—	Whitaker [18], Pilkington [49], Constantine (pen) [79]	4061
34	24	A	Doncaster R	L 0-1	0-0	15		7848
35	Mar 3	H	Yeovil T	W 4-2	2-2	13	Constantine 2 [15, 80], Whitaker [17], Rose (og) [49]	4202
36	6	H	Cheltenham T	D 1-1	1-0	—	Kamara [41]	3340
37	10	A	Rotherham U	W 5-1	4-0	12	Sodje 4 [11, 25, 29, 78], Pilkington [44]	3854
38	17	H	Tranmere R	L 2-3	1-2	12	Sonner [36], Constantine [73]	4809
39	24	H	Millwall	W 2-0	1-0	11	Whitaker [11], Sodje [53]	3973
40	31	A	Huddersfield T	D 2-2	1-1	12	Sodje 2 [35, 68]	10,313
41	Apr 7	H	Carlisle U	L 0-2	0-1	12		4882
42	9	A	Swansea C	L 0-3	0-2	14		12,465
43	14	H	Crewe Alex	W 3-0	1-0	12	Hulbert [36], Constantine [59], Rodgers [63]	5740
44	21	A	Gillingham	L 2-3	0-1	14	Whitaker [78], Constantine (pen) [90]	5928
45	28	A	Brentford	L 3-4	0-2	15	Rodgers [55], Constantine 2 [59, 83]	5125
46	May 5	H	Bournemouth	W 2-1	0-0	12	Sodje [51], Rodgers [57]	5080

Final League Position: 12

GOALSCORERS

League (64): Constantine 22 (4 pens), Sodje 14 (1 pen), Whitaker 7, Pilkington 6, Rodgers 3, Smith J 3, Abbey 1, Gardner 1, Harsley 1, Hulbert 1, Husbands 1, Kamara 1, Moore 1, Sonner 1, own goal 1.
Carling Cup (6): Constantine 2, Smith J 1, Sodje 1, Walker 1, Whitaker 1.
FA Cup (2): Sodje 1, Whitaker 1.
J Paint Trophy (2): Constantine 2.

Goodlad M 25	Abbey G 18 + 6	McGregor M 26 + 6	Sonner D 33	Pilkington G 46	Miles C 23 + 6	Cardle J 1 + 6	Hulbert R 16 + 4	Sodje A 38 + 5	Constantine L 41 + 1	Whitaker D 44 + 1	Walker R 12 + 4	Smith J 24 + 3	Harsley P 29 + 3	Husbands M 3 + 20	Walsh M 16 + 2	Talbot J 18 + 4	Moore S 8 + 4	Humphreys R 5 + 2	Lowndes N 1 + 11	Gardner R 12 + 4	Fortune C 11 + 2	Anyon J 21 + 1	Smith C — + 1	Kamara M 14 + 4	Rodgers L 6 + 2	Weston R 15	Match No.
1	2^{1}	3	4	5	6	7^{2}	8^{3}	9	10	11	12	13	14														1
1	2	3	4	5	6^{1}			9	10	7	12	11	8														2
1	2	3	4	5	6			9^{1}	10	7		11	8	12													3
1	2	3	4	5	6^{2}			9^{1}	10	7		11	8	12	13												4
1	2	3	4	5	6^{3}	12		9	10	7		11^{2}	8^{1}	13		14											5
1		2	4	5	3			9^{2}	10	7	12	11	8		6^{1}		13										6
1	2	3	4	5	6			9^{2}	10	7		11^{1}	12	13			8^{3}	14									7
1	2	3	4^{1}	5	6^{2}			9	10	7		13	12	14			8^{3}	11									8
1	2	3		5	6■			9^{1}	10	7^{2}		12	8	14		13	4^{3}	11									9
1		3	4^{3}	5				9^{2}	10	7	6	11	8^{1}	12		2	13	14									10
1		3	4	5					10	7	6		8^{1}	9■		2		11	12								11
1	12	3		5	13			9^{1}	10^{2}	7	6	8				2	4^{3}	11	14								12
1		3	4	5		13			12	7	6	8				2^{1}	10^{2}	11	9								13
1		2	4	5	3^{2}			12	10	7	6	11	8			13	9^{1}										14
1	12	3^{1}	4^{3}	5		13		9	10	7	6	11^{2}	8	14		2											15
1	2		4	5	14	12		9	10	7	6	11^{1}	8^{2}	13^{3}		3											16
1	2		4	5	3			9	10	7	6	11^{1}	8	12													17
1	2		4	5	3^{1}	13		9	10	7	6	11	8			12^{2}											18
1	2			5	3			9	10	7	6	11	8				12			4^{1}							19
1	2		4	5	3				10	7		11	8				12			9^{1}	6						20
1	2		4	5	3			12	10	7		11	8				9^{1}				6						21
1	2		4	5	3			12	10	7		11		13			9^{1}			8^{2}	6						22
1	2		4	5	3			9^{1}	10	7^{2}		11	8	12						13	6						23
1	7	2	4	5	3^{1}			9	10			11	8	12							6						24
1^{6}	2	12^{2}		5	3^{1}		10	9		7	13	11	8							4	6	15					25
				5			12	9		7^{1}	6	11	8	10^{2}	2	4^{3}			13	3		1	14				26
	12			5			14	9		7	6^{1}	11	8	10	2	3			13^{3}	4^{2}		1					27
				5			10^{1}	9		7		11	8	12	2	3				4	6	1					28
	12	2	4	5				13	10	14			8^{2}		6	3				11^{3}		1		7	9^{1}		29
	12	2	4	5			13	14	10^{1}	7					6	3■				11		1		8^{2}	9^{3}		30
		2	4	5	3^{2}		13	9^{1}	10	7				12	6					11		1		8			31
	12		4	5		13		9	10	7				14	6^{1}					8^{2}	2	1		11^{3}		3	32
			4	5			8^{1}	9^{2}	10	7				13	6	3			12	14		1		11^{3}		2	33
		12	4	5			8	9^{2}	10	7				13	6^{1}	3				11^{3}		1		14		2	34
		6	4	5	12		8	9^{3}	10	7				13		3			14			1		11^{2}		2^{1}	35
		6	4	5			8	9	10	7				12		3						1		11^{1}		2	36
		6	4^{1}	5	12		8	9	10	7						3			13			1		11^{2}		2	37
		6^{1}	4	5			8	9	10	7						3			12			1		11		2	38
		6	4	5	12		8	9	10	7						3■						1		11^{1}		2	39
		6	4	5	3		8	9	10	7					12					13		1		11^{2}		2^{1}	40
		12		5	3^{2}		8	9	10	7			4^{3}		6^{1}				13			1		11	14	2	41
		12		5	3^{2}		4	9	10	7			8		6^{1}						13	1		11^{3}	14	2	42
		12		5			4^{3}	9	10	7			8		3				14		6^{1}	1		13	11^{2}	2	43
		12		5			4	9^{2}	10	7			8		6						3^{1}	1		13	11	2	44
				5				9	10	7			8		6				12	13	3	1		4^{1}	11	2^{2}	45
		3		5	12		4	9^{2}	10	7			8		6^{3}						14	1		13	11	2^{1}	46

FA Cup

First Round	Lincoln C	(h)	2-1
Second Round	Hereford U	(a)	0-4

J Paint Trophy

Second Round	Scunthorpe U	(a)	0-0
Quarter-Final	Crewe Alex	(h)	2-3

Carling Cup

First Round	Preston NE	(h)	2-1
Second Round	QPR	(h)	3-2
Third Round	Norwich C	(h)	0-0
Fourth Round	Tottenham H	(a)	1-3

PRESTON NORTH END FL Championship

FOUNDATION

North End Cricket and Rugby Club which was formed in 1863, indulged in most sports before taking up soccer in about 1879. In 1881 they decided to stick to football to the exclusion of other sports and even a 16–0 drubbing by Blackburn Rovers in an invitation game at Deepdale, a few weeks after taking this decision, did not deter them for they immediately became affiliated to the Lancashire FA.

Deepdale Stadium, Sir Tom Finney Way, Deepdale, Preston PR1 6RU.

Telephone: 0870 442 1964.

Fax: (01772) 693 366.

Ticket Office: 0870 442 1966.

Website: www.pne.com

Email: enquiries@pne.com

Ground Capacity: 19,466.

Record Attendance: 42,684 v Arsenal, Division 1, 23 April 1938.

Pitch Measurements: 110yd × 70yd.

Chairman: Derek Shaw.

Vice-chairman: David Taylor.

Secretary: Janet Parr.

Manager: Paul Simpson.

First Team Coach: Rob Kelly.

Physio: Steve Kemp.

Colours: White shirts, navy blue shorts, white stockings.

Change Colours: All red.

Year Formed: 1881.

Turned Professional: 1885. ***Ltd Co.:*** 1893.

Club Nicknames: 'The Lilywhites' or 'North End'.

Ground: 1881, Deepdale.

First Football League Game: 8 September 1888, Football League, v Burnley (h) W 5–2 – Trainer; Howarth, Holmes; Robertson, W. Graham, J. Graham; Gordon (1), Ross (2), Goodall, Dewhurst (2), Drummond.

Record League Victory: 10–0 v Stoke, Division 1, 14 September 1889 – Trainer; Howarth, Holmes; Kelso, Russell (1), Graham; Gordon, Jimmy Ross (2), Nick Ross (3), Thomson (2), Drummond (2).

Record Cup Victory: 26–0 v Hyde, FA Cup 1st rd, 15 October 1887 – Addision; Howarth, Nick Ross; Russell (1), Thomson (5), Graham (1); Gordon (5), Jimmy Ross (8), John Goodall (1), Dewhurst (3), Drummond (2).

Record Defeat: 0–7 v Blackpool, Division 1, 1 May 1948.

Most League Points (2 for a win): 61, Division 3, 1970–71.

Most League Points (3 for a win): 95, Division 2, 1999–2000.

HONOURS

Football League: Division 1 – Champions 1888–89 (first champions) 1889–90; Runners-up 1890–91, 1891–92, 1892–93, 1905–06, 1952–53, 1957–58; Division 2 – Champions 1903–04, 1912–13, 1950–51, 1999–2000; Runners-up 1914–15, 1933–34; Division 3 – Champions 1970–71, 1995–96; Division 4 – Runners-up 1986–87.

FA Cup: Winners 1889, 1938; Runners-up 1888, 1922, 1937, 1954, 1964.

Football League Cup: best season: 4th rd, 2003.

Double Performed: 1888–89.

Football League Cup: best season: 4th rd, 1963, 1966, 1972, 1981.

SKY SPORTS FACT FILE

Legendary inside-left Alex James' arrival at Preston North End coincided with their first season in the Second Division. Such were the changes rung at the club that he was one of 17 to make their debuts in 1925–26, finishing as top scorer with 14 goals.

Most League Goals: 100, Division 2, 1927–28 and Division 1, 1957–58.

Highest League Scorer in Season: Ted Harper, 37, Division 2, 1932–33.

Most League Goals in Total Aggregate: Tom Finney, 187, 1946–60.

Most League Goals in One Match: 4, Jimmy Ross v Stoke, Division 1, 6 October 1888; 4, Nick Ross v Derby Co, Division 1, 11 January 1890; 4, George Drummond v Notts Co, Division 1, 12 December 1891; 4, Frank Becton v Notts Co, Division 1, 31 March 1893; 4, George Harrison v Grimsby T, Division 2, 3 November 1928; 4, Alex Reid v Port Vale, Division 2, 23 February 1929; 4, James McClelland v Reading, Division 2, 6 September 1930; 4, Dick Rowley v Notts Co, Division 2, 16 April 1932; 4, Ted Harper v Burnley, Division 2, 29 August 1932; 4, Ted Harper v Lincoln C, Division 2, 11 March 1933; 4, Charlie Wayman v QPR, Division 2, 25 December 1950; 4, Alex Bruce v Colchester U, Division 3, 28 February 1978.

Most Capped Player: Tom Finney, 76, England.

Most League Appearances: Alan Kelly, 447, 1961–75.

Youngest League Player: Steve Doyle, 16 years 166 days v Tranmere R, 15 November 1974.

Record Transfer Fee Received: £5,000,000 from Manchester C for Jon Macken, February 2002.

Record Transfer Fee Paid: £1,500,000 to Manchester U for David Healy, December 2000.

Football League Record: 1888 Founder Member of League; 1901–04 Division 2; 1904–12 Division 1; 1912–13 Division 2; 1913–14 Division 1; 1914–15 Division 2; 1919–25 Division 1; 1925–34 Division 2; 1934–49 Division 1; 1949–51 Division 2; 1951–61 Division 1; 1961–70 Division 2; 1970–71 Division 3; 1971–74 Division 2; 1974–78 Division 3; 1978–81 Division 2; 1981–85 Division 3; 1985–87 Division 4; 1987–92 Division 3; 1992–93 Division 2; 1993–96 Division 3; 1996–2000 Division 2; 2000–04 Division 1; 2004– FL C.

MANAGERS

Charlie Parker 1906–15
Vincent Hayes 1919–23
Jim Lawrence 1923–25
Frank Richards 1925–27
Alex Gibson 1927–31
Lincoln Hayes 1931–32
Run by committee 1932–36
Tommy Muirhead 1936–37
Run by committee 1937–49
Will Scott 1949–53
Scot Symon 1953–54
Frank Hill 1954–56
Cliff Britton 1956–61
Jimmy Milne 1961–68
Bobby Seith 1968–70
Alan Ball Sr 1970–73
Bobby Charlton 1973–75
Harry Catterick 1975–77
Nobby Stiles 1977–81
Tommy Docherty 1981
Gordon Lee 1981–83
Alan Kelly 1983–85
Tommy Booth 1985–86
Brian Kidd 1986
John McGrath 1986–90
Les Chapman 1990–92
Sam Allardyce 1992 (*Caretaker*)
John Beck 1992–94
Gary Peters 1994–98
David Moyes 1998–2002
Kelham O'Hanlon 2002 (*Caretaker*)
Craig Brown 2002–04
Billy Davies 2004–06
Paul Simpson June 2006–

LATEST SEQUENCES

Longest Sequence of League Wins: 14, 25.12.1950 – 27.3.1951.

Longest Sequence of League Defeats: 8, 22.9.1984 – 27.10.1984.

Longest Sequence of League Draws: 6, 24.2.1979 – 20.3.1979.

Longest Sequence of Unbeaten League Matches: 23, 8.9.1888 – 14.9.1889.

Longest Sequence Without a League Win: 15, 14.4.1923 – 20.10.1923.

Successive Scoring Runs: 30 from 15.11.1952.

Successive Non-scoring Runs: 6 from 8.4.1897.

TEN YEAR LEAGUE RECORD

		P	*W*	*D*	*L*	*F*	*A*	*Pts*	*Pos*
1997-98	Div 2	46	15	14	17	56	56	59	15
1998-99	Div 2	46	22	13	11	78	50	79	5
1999-2000	Div 2	46	28	11	7	74	37	95	1
2000-01	Div 1	46	23	9	14	64	52	78	4
2001-02	Div 1	46	20	12	14	71	59	72	8
2002-03	Div 1	46	16	13	17	68	70	61	12
2003-04	Div 1	46	15	14	17	69	71	59	15
2004-05	FL C	46	21	12	13	67	58	75	5
2005-06	FL C	46	20	20	6	59	30	80	4
2006-07	FL C	46	22	8	16	64	53	74	7

DID YOU KNOW?

On 22 September 1956 Portsmouth scored from the penalty spot after only 35 seconds against Preston North End at Fratton Park and were 2–0 ahead by the third minute. Preston staged a recovery and had equalised at 2–2 at the end of the game.

PRESTON NORTH END 2006–07 LEAGUE RECORD

Match No.	Date	Venue	Opponents	Result	H/T Score	Lg. Pos.	Goalscorers	Attendance
1	Aug 5	H	Sheffield W	D 0-0	0-0	—		15,650
2	8	A	Norwich C	L 0-2	0-0	—		24,676
3	11	A	Wolverhampton W	W 3-1	1-1	—	Nugent 2 [23, 65], Whaley [90]	17,410
4	19	H	QPR	D 1-1	0-1	15	McKenna [86]	11,879
5	26	A	Southampton	D 1-1	0-1	16	Whaley [50]	20,712
6	Sept 9	H	Cardiff C	W 2-1	0-0	10	Agyemang [48], Pugh [65]	12,435
7	12	H	WBA	W 1-0	0-0	—	Agyemang [78]	12,119
8	16	A	Derby Co	D 1-1	1-1	5	Pugh [45]	22,220
9	22	H	Barnsley	W 1-0	1-0	—	Agyemang [30]	11,728
10	30	A	Stoke C	D 1-1	0-1	4	Agyemang [63]	14,342
11	Oct 14	H	Sunderland	W 4-1	3-0	3	Dichio [18], Alexander (pen) [31], Whitehead (og) [35], Whaley [55]	19,603
12	17	A	Ipswich T	W 3-2	0-2	—	Nugent [53], Chilvers [56], Whaley [65]	19,337
13	21	H	Hull C	W 2-1	2-0	2	Dichio 2 [1, 37]	13,728
14	27	A	Burnley	L 2-3	0-1	—	Whaley [77], Ormerod [80]	14,871
15	31	H	Leeds U	W 4-1	2-0	—	Dichio [19], Pugh [22], Nugent [47], Neal [84]	16,168
16	Nov 4	H	Luton T	W 3-0	0-0	2	Alexander (pen) [52], Agyemang [60], Ormerod [87]	13,094
17	11	A	Southend U	D 0-0	0-0	2		9263
18	18	A	Leicester C	W 1-0	1-0	2	Agyemang [15]	22,721
19	25	H	Crystal Palace	D 0-0	0-0	2		14,202
20	28	H	Coventry C	D 1-1	1-0	—	Nugent [35]	13,104
21	Dec 2	A	Luton T	L 0-2	0-2	2		7665
22	9	A	Birmingham C	L 1-3	1-2	4	Ormerod [45]	23,159
23	16	H	Plymouth Arg	W 3-0	2-0	3	Pugh [12], Ormerod [41], Alexander (pen) [56]	13,171
24	23	H	Colchester U	W 1-0	1-0	2	Nugent [33]	14,225
25	26	A	WBA	L 2-4	1-2	2	Alexander (pen) [35], Nugent [67]	22,905
26	30	A	Sunderland	W 1-0	1-0	2	Nugent [36]	30,460
27	Jan 1	H	Derby Co	L 1-2	0-0	3	Nugent [79]	19,204
28	13	A	Barnsley	W 1-0	0-0	3	Chilvers [55]	10,810
29	20	H	Stoke C	W 3-2	0-2	3	McKenna [65], Nugent [74], Wilson [89]	15,151
30	30	A	Colchester U	L 0-1	0-0	—		5085
31	Feb 3	A	Sheffield W	W 3-1	2-1	2	Ormerod [6], Nugent 2 [45, 55]	22,441
32	10	H	Wolverhampton W	L 0-1	0-1	4		15,748
33	20	H	Norwich C	W 2-1	2-0	—	Pergl [28], Dichio [43]	11,601
34	23	A	Cardiff C	L 1-4	0-1	—	Alexander (pen) [53]	12,889
35	Mar 5	H	Southampton	W 3-1	1-0	—	Mellor [45], Nugent [75], Baird (og) [81]	13,060
36	10	A	Hull C	L 0-2	0-1	7		17,118
37	13	H	Ipswich T	W 1-0	1-0	—	Ricketts [6]	13,100
38	17	H	Burnley	W 2-0	1-0	4	Nugent [33], Agyemang [75]	17,666
39	30	A	Leeds U	L 1-2	1-0	—	Ormerod [5]	18,433
40	Apr 3	A	QPR	L 0-1	0-0	—		11,910
41	7	A	Crystal Palace	L 0-3	0-2	4		15,985
42	9	H	Southend U	L 2-3	0-1	6	St Ledger-Hall [51], Alexander (pen) [79]	13,684
43	14	A	Coventry C	W 4-0	2-0	4	Sedgwick [8], Nugent [17], Ormerod 2 [49, 56]	21,117
44	21	H	Leicester C	L 0-1	0-0	4		14,725
45	28	A	Plymouth Arg	L 0-2	0-0	8		13,813
46	May 6	H	Birmingham C	W 1-0	0-0	7	Whaley [85]	16,837

Final League Position: 7

GOALSCORERS

League (64): Nugent 15, Ormerod 8, Agyemang 7, Alexander 6 (6 pens), Whaley 6, Dichio 5, Pugh 4, Chilvers 2, McKenna 2, Mellor 1, Neal 1, Pergl 1, Ricketts 1, Sedgwick 1, St Ledger-Hall 1, Wilson 1, own goals 2.
Carling Cup (1): Whaley 1.
FA Cup (4): Nugent 2, Ormerod 1, Wilson 1.

Nash C 29	Alexander G 42	Hill M 37 + 1	Jarrett J 4 + 1	St Ledger-Hall S 40 + 1	Chilvers L 45	Whaley S 31 + 9	McKenna P 32 + 1	Dichio D 16 + 14	Nugent D 43 + 1	Pugh D 45	Wilson K 13 + 8	Stock B 1 + 1	Agyemang P 10 + 21	Sedgwick C 41 + 2	Neal L 3 + 21	McCormack A — + 3	Anyinsah J — + 3	Ormerod B 16 + 13	Davidson C 12 + 3	Miller T 4 + 3	Ricketts M 7 + 7	Lonergan A 13	Mellor N 2 + 3	Soley S 6	Pergl P 6	Songo'o F 4 + 2	Nowland A — + 1	Henderson W 4	Match No.
1	2	3¹	4²	5	6	7	8	9³	10	11	12	13	14																1
1	2■	3	4	5	6	7	8		10	11¹		9²	12	13															2
1		3	4	5	6	7	8	9²	10¹	11	2		12	13															3
1		2²	4	5	6	9	8		10	11	3³		12	7¹	13	14													4
1	2			5	6	4	8	9¹	10²	11	3		12	7	13														5
1	2	12	13	5	6	4²	8	9³	10■	11	3¹		14	7															6
1	2	3		5	6	4	8	9		11			10¹	7			12												7
1	2	3		5	6	4²	8	9¹	12	11			10	7			13												8
1	2	3		5	6	4²	8	12	10	11³			9¹	7	13	14													9
1	2	3¹		5	6	4²	8	12	10	11			9³	7	13	14													10
1	2	3		5	6	4¹	8	9	10²	11³				7	12			13	14										11
1	2	3		5	6	4	8	9²	10³	11				7¹	12			13	14										12
1	2	3		5	6	4¹	8	9	10²	11				7	12			13											13
1	2	3		5	6	4	8	9²		11¹			10³	7	14			13	12										14
1	2	3		5	6	4	8	9	10¹	11²				7	13			12											15
1	2	3		5³	6	4	8		10¹	11	14		9²	7	12			13											16
1	2	3		5	6	4³	8	9¹	10²	11			12	7	14			13											17
1	2	3		5	6	4³	8	12	10¹	11			9²	7	14			13											18
1	2	3³		5	6	4¹	8	12	10	11			9²	7	14			13											19
1	2			5³	6	4	8	12	10	3	14		9¹	7	13					11²									20
1	2			5	6	4²	8	12	10	3			9¹	7	13			14		11³									21
1	2	3		5	6	4	8	12	10¹	11				7				9											22
1	2	3²		5	6	4	8	12	10	11				7³	13			9¹		14									23
1	2	3		5	6	4¹	8	9³	10²	11	13			7	12					14									24
1	2	3		5	6	4³	8¹	9■	10	11²	12			7				13		14									25
1	2	3		5	6				10¹	8				7	12		13	9²	11	4									26
1	2	3		5	6	12	13		10	8				7¹	14			9	11²	4³									27
1	2	3			6	12	8	13	10¹		5			7	4			9³	11²		14								28
1	2	3			6	12	8		10	11	5			7¹	4			9²			13								29
	2	3²			6	12	8		10	11	5			7	4¹			13			9	1							30
	2	3			6	12	8		10	4	5			7				9			11¹	1							31
	2	3			6	12	8		10	4²	5■			7				9¹			11	1	13						32
		3		12	6	4	8	9²	10³	11	2		13									1	14	5¹	7				33
	2	3		5	6	4	8	9¹	10²	11			12									1	13		7				34
	2			5	6			12	10¹	4	13		14	7					3		11²	1	9³		8				35
	2			5	6				10¹	4			12	7					3		11	1	9		8²	13			36
	2	3		5	6			12	10	4			13	7²				14	11		9¹	1				8³			37
	2	3		5	6			12	10	4			13	7³				9¹	11			1				8²	14		38
				5	6				10	11	2		12	7				9	3¹		13	1			4	8²			39
	2	3³		5	6	4¹		12	10	11	14		13	7							9	1				8²			40
	2			5	6	4³			10²	11	3		12	7				9¹			13	1		8		14			41
	2			5		4²		12	10	11	3		13	7³	14			9¹				1		6	8				42
	2	3		5	6³	12			10²	4	14		13	7				9	11					8¹				1	43
	2	3¹		5	6	12			10	4			13	7²				9³	11		14			8				1	44
	2	3		5	6	12			10³	4			13	7¹				9²	11		14			8				1	45
	2	3		5	6	4			10³	8			12	7²	13			9¹	11		14							1	46

FA Cup

Third Round	Sunderland	(h)	1-0
Fourth Round	Crystal Palace	(a)	2-0
Fifth Round	Manchester C	(h)	1-3

Carling Cup

First Round	Port Vale	(a)	1-2

QUEENS PARK RANGERS FL Championship

FOUNDATION

There is an element of doubt about the date of the foundation of this club, but it is believed that in either 1885 or 1886 it was formed through the amalgamation of Christchurch Rangers and St Jude's Institute FC. The leading light was George Wodehouse, whose family maintained a connection with the club until comparatively recent times. Most of the players came from the Queen's Park district so this name was adopted after a year as St Jude's Institute.

Loftus Road Stadium, South Africa Road, Shepherds Bush, London W12 7PA.

Telephone: (020) 8740 2602. (020) 8740 2541 (press office).

Fax: (020) 740 2525.

Ticket Office: 0870 112 1967.

Website: www.qpr.co.uk

Email: iant@qpr.co.uk (press office).

Ground Capacity: 18,420.

Record Attendance: 35,353 v Leeds U, Division 1, 27 April 1974.

Pitch Measurements: 110yd × 73yd.

Chairman: Gianni Paladini.

QPR Holdings Ltd Chairman: Antonio Caliendo.

Secretary: Mrs Sheila Marson.

Manager: John Gregory.

Assistant Manager: Mick Harford.

Physio: Paul Hunter.

Colours: Blue and white hooped shirts.

Change Colours: Red and black hooped shirts.

Year Formed: 1885* (*see Foundation*).

Turned Professional: 1898. ***Ltd Co.:*** 1899.

Previous Names: 1885, St Jude's; 1887, Queens Park Rangers. ***Club Nicknames:*** 'Rangers' or 'Rs'.

Grounds: 1885* (*see Foundation*), Welford's Fields; 1888–99; London Scottish Ground, Brondesbury, Home Farm, Kensal Rise Green, Gun Club Wormwood Scrubs, Kilburn Cricket Ground; 1899, Kensal Rise Athletic Ground; 1901, Latimer Road, Notting Hill; 1904, Agricultural Society, Park Royal; 1907, Park Royal Ground; 1917, Loftus Road; 1931, White City; 1933, Loftus Road; 1962, White City; 1963, Loftus Road.

First Football League Game: 28 August 1920, Division 3, v Watford (h) L 1–2 – Price; Blackman, Wingrove; McGovern, Grant, O'Brien; Faulkner, Birch (1), Smith, Gregory, Middlemiss.

Record League Victory: 9–2 v Tranmere R, Division 3, 3 December 1960 – Drinkwater; Woods, Ingham; Keen, Rutter, Angell; Lazarus (2), Bedford (2), Evans (2), Andrews (1), Clark (2).

Record Cup Victory: 8–1 v Bristol R (away), FA Cup 1st rd, 27 November 1937 – Gilfillan; Smith, Jefferson; Lowe, James, March; Cape, Mallett, Cheetham (3), Fitzgerald (3) Bott (2). 8–1 v Crewe Alex, Milk Cup 1st rd, 3 October 1983 – Hucker; Neill, Dawes, Waddock (1), McDonald (1), Fenwick, Micklewhite (1), Stewart (1), Allen (1), Stainrod (3), Gregory.

HONOURS

Football League: Division 1 – Runners-up 1975–76; Division 2 – Champions 1982–83; Runners-up 1967–68, 1972–73, 2003–04; Division 3 (S) – Champions 1947–48; Runners-up 1946–47; Division 3 – Champions 1966–67.

FA Cup: Runners-up 1982.

Football League Cup: Winners 1967; Runners-up 1986. (In 1966–67 won Division 3 and Football League Cup).

European Competitions: *UEFA Cup:* 1976–77, 1984–85.

SKY SPORTS FACT FILE

Jack Crawford had established himself as a winger with Hull City and Chelsea prior to joining Queens Park Rangers in May 1934, picking up an England cap at Stamford Bridge, too. A former Scottish AAA sprint champion he later became the QPR coach.

Record Defeat: 1–8 v Mansfield T, Division 3, 15 March 1965. 1–8 v Manchester U, Division 1, 19 March 1969.

Most League Points (2 for a win): 67, Division 3, 1966–67.

Most League Points (3 for a win): 85, Division 2, 1982–83.

Most League Goals: 111, Division 3, 1961–62.

Highest League Scorer in Season: George Goddard, 37, Division 3 (S), 1929–30.

Most League Goals in Total Aggregate: George Goddard, 172, 1926–34.

Most League Goals in One Match: 4, George Goddard v Merthyr T, Division 3S, 9 March 1929; 4, George Goddard v Swindon T, Division 3S, 12 April 1930; 4, George Goddard v Exeter C, Division 3S, 20 December 1930; 4, George Goddard v Watford, Division 3S, 19 September 1931; 4, Tom Cheetham v Aldershot, Division 3S, 14 September 1935; 4, Tom Cheetham v Aldershot, Division 3S, 12 November 1938.

Most Capped Player: Alan McDonald, 52, Northern Ireland.

Most League Appearances: Tony Ingham, 519, 1950–63.

Youngest League Player: Frank Sibley, 16 years 97 days v Bristol C, 10 March 1964.

Record Transfer Fee Received: £6,000,000 from Newcastle U for Les Ferdinand, June 1995.

Record Transfer Fee Paid: £2,350,000 to Stoke C for Mike Sheron, July 1997.

Football League Record: 1920 Original Members of Division 3; 1921–48 Division 3 (S); 1948–52 Division 2; 1952–58 Division 3 (S); 1958–67 Division 3; 1967–68 Division 2; 1968–69 Division 1; 1969–73 Division 2; 1973–79 Division 1; 1979–83 Division 2; 1983–92 Division 1; 1992–96 FA Premier League; 1996–2001 Division 1; 2001–04 Division 2; 2004– FL C.

LATEST SEQUENCES

Longest Sequence of League Wins: 8, 7.11.1931 – 28.12.1931.

Longest Sequence of League Defeats: 9, 25.2.1969 – 5.4.1969.

Longest Sequence of League Draws: 6, 29.1.2000 – 5.3.2000.

Longest Sequence of Unbeaten League Matches: 20, 11.3.1972 – 23.9.1972.

Longest Sequence Without a League Win: 20, 7.12.1968 – 7.4.1969.

Successive Scoring Runs: 33 from 9.12.1961.

Successive Non-scoring Runs: 6 from 18.3.1939.

MANAGERS

James Cowan 1906–13
Jimmy Howie 1913–20
Ted Liddell 1920–24
Will Wood 1924–25
(had been Secretary since 1903)
Bob Hewison 1925–30
John Bowman 1930–31
Archie Mitchell 1931–33
Mick O'Brien 1933–35
Billy Birrell 1935–39
Ted Vizard 1939–44
Dave Mangnall 1944–52
Jack Taylor 1952–59
Alec Stock 1959–65
(General Manager to 1968)
Bill Dodgin Jnr 1968
Tommy Docherty 1968
Les Allen 1968–71
Gordon Jago 1971–74
Dave Sexton 1974–77
Frank Sibley 1977–78
Steve Burtenshaw 1978–79
Tommy Docherty 1979–80
Terry Venables 1980–84
Gordon Jago 1984
Alan Mullery 1984
Frank Sibley 1984–85
Jim Smith 1985–88
Trevor Francis 1988–90
Don Howe 1990–91
Gerry Francis 1991–94
Ray Wilkins 1994–96
Stewart Houston 1996–97
Ray Harford 1997–98
Gerry Francis 1998–2001
Ian Holloway 2001–06
Gary Waddock 2006
John Gregory September 2006–

TEN YEAR LEAGUE RECORD

		P	W	D	L	F	A	Pts	Pos
1997-98	Div 1	46	10	19	17	51	63	49	21
1998-99	Div 1	46	12	11	23	52	61	47	20
1999-2000	Div 1	46	16	18	12	62	53	66	10
2000-01	Div 1	46	7	19	20	45	75	40	23
2001-02	Div 2	46	19	14	13	60	49	71	8
2002-03	Div 2	46	24	11	11	69	45	83	4
2003-04	Div 2	46	22	17	7	80	45	83	2
2004-05	FL C	46	17	11	18	54	58	62	11
2005-06	FL C	46	12	14	20	50	65	50	21
2006-07	FL C	46	14	11	21	54	68	53	18

DID YOU KNOW ?

In 1920–21, the Third Division's inaugural season, Queens Park Rangers finished a creditable third and owed much to the goalscoring trio of Jack Smith (18 goals), Jimmy Birch and Jack Gregory (both 15) from a total of 61 League goals.

QUEENS PARK RANGERS 2006–07 LEAGUE RECORD

Match No.	*Date*	*Venue*	*Opponents*	*Result*		*H/T Score*	*Lg. Pos.*	*Goalscorers*	*Attendance*
1	Aug 5	A	Burnley	L	0-2	0-0	—		12,190
2	8	H	Leeds U	D	2-2	0-0	—	Rowlands (pen) [81], Baidoo [90]	13,996
3	12	H	Southend U	W	2-0	2-0	12	Rowlands [31], Ward [41]	12,368
4	19	A	Preston NE	D	1-1	1-0	14	Ainsworth [5]	11,879
5	25	H	Ipswich T	L	1-3	0-0	—	Gallen [58]	10,918
6	Sept 9	A	Plymouth Arg	D	1-1	1-1	22	Blackstock [17]	12,138
7	12	H	Birmingham C	L	0-2	0-1	—		10,936
8	16	A	Colchester U	L	1-2	0-2	24	Brown (og) [76]	5246
9	23	H	Hull C	W	2-0	0-0	19	Jones R [60], Blackstock [80]	11,381
10	30	A	Southampton	W	2-1	2-1	16	Blackstock [34], Jones R [40]	25,185
11	Oct 14	H	Norwich C	D	3-3	2-1	15	Smith [24], Rowlands 2 [45, 90]	14,793
12	17	H	Derby Co	L	1-2	1-2	—	Smith [7]	10,882
13	21	A	Sheffield W	L	2-3	0-2	19	Blackstock 2 [50, 54]	23,813
14	28	H	Leicester C	D	1-1	0-1	19	Rowlands (pen) [68]	12,430
15	31	A	WBA	D	3-3	1-2	—	Stewart [45], Gallen [48], Nygaard [83]	17,417
16	Nov 4	H	Crystal Palace	W	4-2	1-2	19	Smith 2 [34, 69], Lomas [59], Gallen (pen) [66]	13,989
17	11	A	Luton T	W	3-2	1-2	18	Smith [33], Heikkinen (og) [51], Blackstock [54]	9007
18	17	A	Cardiff C	W	1-0	0-0	—	Jones R [88]	13,250
19	25	H	Coventry C	L	0-1	0-0	15		12,840
20	28	H	Sunderland	L	1-2	0-2	—	Jones R [73]	13,108
21	Dec 2	A	Crystal Palace	L	0-3	0-2	19		17,017
22	9	A	Stoke C	L	0-1	0-1	20		16,487
23	16	H	Wolverhampton W	L	0-1	0-0	20		12,323
24	23	H	Barnsley	W	1-0	1-0	20	Rowlands [15]	11,307
25	26	A	Birmingham C	L	1-2	1-1	—	Cook [31]	29,431
26	30	A	Norwich C	L	0-1	0-0	20		25,113
27	Jan 1	H	Colchester U	W	1-0	1-0	20	Jones R [36]	11,319
28	13	A	Hull C	L	1-2	1-0	20	Blackstock [45]	19,791
29	20	H	Southampton	L	0-2	0-0	21		14,686
30	30	A	Barnsley	L	0-2	0-1	—		9890
31	Feb 3	H	Burnley	W	3-1	1-1	19	Cook [13], Blackstock [55], Lomas [72]	10,811
32	9	A	Southend U	L	0-5	0-1	—		10,217
33	20	A	Leeds U	D	0-0	0-0	—		29,593
34	24	H	Plymouth Arg	D	1-1	0-1	21	Cook [59]	13,757
35	Mar 3	A	Ipswich T	L	1-2	0-1	22	Furlong [71]	21,412
36	10	H	Sheffield W	D	1-1	0-0	21	Rowlands (pen) [72]	15,188
37	13	A	Derby Co	D	1-1	1-0	—	Rowlands [14]	27,567
38	17	A	Leicester C	W	3-1	0-0	21	Idiakez [47], Nygaard 2 (1 pen) [51 (p), 68]	24,558
39	31	H	WBA	L	1-2	0-0	21	Blackstock [63]	14,784
40	Apr 3	H	Preston NE	W	1-0	0-0	—	Blackstock [51]	11,910
41	7	A	Coventry C	W	1-0	0-0	19	Smith [53]	22,850
42	9	H	Luton T	W	3-2	1-1	18	Blackstock 2 (1 pen) [41, 81 (p)], Furlong [90]	14,360
43	14	A	Sunderland	L	1-2	1-1	18	Rowlands (pen) [23]	39,206
44	21	H	Cardiff C	W	1-0	1-0	18	Blackstock [23]	12,710
45	28	A	Wolverhampton W	L	0-2	0-0	19		24,931
46	May 6	H	Stoke C	D	1-1	1-0	18	Rowlands [6]	16,741

Final League Position: 18

GOALSCORERS

League (54): Blackstock 13 (1 pen), Rowlands 10 (4 pens), Smith 6, Jones R 5, Cook 3, Gallen 3 (1 pen), Nygaard 3 (1 pen), Furlong 2, Lomas 2, Ainsworth 1, Baidoo 1, Idiakez 1, Stewart 1, Ward 1, own goals 2.
Carling Cup (5): Cook 1, Gallen 1, Jones R 1, Nygaard 1, Stewart 1.
FA Cup (2): Baidoo 1, Blackstock 1.

Jones P 12	Bignot M 32 + 1	Milanese M 14	Lomas S 26 + 8	Rose M 10 + 1	Stewart D 45	Ainsworth G 18 + 4	Rowlands M 27 + 2	Ward N 11 + 8	Czerkas A 2 + 1	Cook L 37	Jones R 17 + 14	Donnelly S — + 3	Bircham M 12 + 5	Baidoo S 2 + 7	Rehman Z 23 + 2	Blackstock D 37 + 2	Gallen K 9 + 9	Oliseh E 2	Nygaard M 17 + 6	Cole J 3	Kanyuka P 7 + 4	Bailey S 7 + 3	Smith J 22 + 7	Mancienne M 26 + 2	Royce S 20	Furlong P 9 + 13	Timoska S 11 + 3	Bolder A 16	Cullip D 13	Camp L 11	Idiakez I 4 + 1	Ricketts R — + 2	Moore S 3	Shimmin D 1	*Match No.*
1	2	3	4^1	5	6	7	8^2	9	10^3	11	12	13	14																						1
1	2^3	3	4	5	6	7	8^1	9	10^2	11	13		12	14																					2
1		3	12	5	6	7	2^1	9		11	10^2				4	8	13																		3
1		3	12	5	6	7^2	2^1	9		11	10^3			13	4	8	14																		4
1		3^2	4^1	2	6			9		11	10		12	13	5	8	7																		5
1		3	13	2	6			9		11	12		4^2		5	8^1	14	7	10^3																6
1		3		2	6			9		11	12		4	13	5^2	8^1		7	10																7
		3		2	6			9	12	11	8^1	13	4	7^2	5				10	1															8
1	2		12	3^3	6		7	13		11	9		8^2		5	10					14	4^1													9
1	2		12	3^2	6		7			11	9		8^1		5	10					13	4^3	14												10
1	2		4^1	12	6		7			11	9^2		8		5	10	13						3												11
1	2		4^1		6		7			11	9^2	12	8		5	10	13						3												12
1	2^2		4		6		7^1	12		11	9		8^3		5	10	13						3	14											13
	2		4		6	12	7^1			11					5	10	13		9^2		3^3		8	14	1										14
	2		4		6	7				11					5	10^1	9		12				8	3	1										15
	2		4		6	7		12		11					5	10	9^2		13				8^1	3	1										16
	2				6	7		13		11					5	10^1	12^2		9			4	8	3	1										17
	2				6	7^1		12		11	13				5	10^2			9			4	8	3	1										18
	2				6		12	7		11	13				5	10^2	14		9^3			4^1	8	3	1										19
	2				6		4	7		11^1	12				5	10^2	9						8	3	1	13									20
	2				6		4	12			11				5	10^2	7		9^1				8	3	1	13									21
	2	3			6		11^1	12						13		10^3	7		9^2			4	8	5	1	14									22
	2	3					7				9		4^1		5	10	11						8	6	1	12									23
	2	3^2	4		6		7			11	9^3		12		13	10							8^1	5	1	14									24
	2	3^1			6		12			11	13		7^3		5	10^2						14	8	4	1	9									25
	2	3	4		6		8^1	12		11	10					13	7^2							5	1	9									26
	2		4		3			8^1		11	9^2			12		10	7				6			5	1	13									27
	2^3		4		6					11■	9		7^1	12		10^2					3		8	5	1	13	14								28
			4		3						9^1		7^2	11	6	10			12			13	8	5	1		2								29
			4^1		3	12				11	13				6^3	10			14				8	5	1	9^2	2	7							30
			4		3	7	8			11						10								5	1		2	9	6						31
			4		3	7	8			11	12				13	10								5	1		2^2	9	6^1						32
			4		6	7	8			11						10								2			3	9	5	1					33
			4		6	7	8^1			11						10								2		12	3	9	5	1					34
			4^2		6	7^1	8			11	9												13	2		12	3	10	5	1					35
	2				6	12	3			11						10^2			13					4		9		7	5	1	8^1				36
	3		4^3		6	12	7^1			11	13								10				14	2	1	9^2			5		8				37
	3		12		6	7^3				11	13								10				14	2		9^2		4	5	1	8^1				38
	3		12		6	7^3				11						13			10^2					2		9		4	5	1	8^1	14			39
	3		4		6	7				11^1						10			9		14		13	2^3				8	5	1		12^2			40
	12		13		6	7										10			14		2		8			9^3	3^1	4^2	5	1			11		41
	3		4		6	7^2										10			9^1		2^3		13			12	14	8	5	1			11		42
	2		4^2		6		7									10					14		8			12	3	9	5^3	1	13		11^1		43
	2		4		6		8^2			11						10^1			9		5		13			12	3	7		1					44
	2	3	4		6		7				12								10	1	5^3	13	8			9^1	14	11^2							45
	2				6		7				12		13			10^3			9^1	1		4	8			14	3■	11^2						5	46

FA Cup				**Carling Cup**			
Third Round	Luton T	(h)	2-2	First Round	Northampton T	(h)	3-2
		(a)	0-1	Second Round	Port Vale	(a)	2-3

READING — FA Premiership

FOUNDATION

Reading was formed as far back as 1871 at a public meeting held at the Bridge Street Rooms. They first entered the FA Cup as early as 1877 when they amalgamated with the Reading Hornets. The club was further strengthened in 1889 when Earley FC joined them. They were the first winners of the Berks and Bucks Cup in 1878–79.

Madejski Stadium, Junction 11, M4, Reading, Berkshire RG2 0FL.

Telephone: (0118) 968 1100.

Fax: (0118) 968 1101.

Ticket Office: 0870 999 1871.

Website: www.readingfc.co.uk

Email: comments@readingfc.co.uk

Ground Capacity: 24,225.

Record Attendance: Madejski Stadium: 24,122 v Aston Villa, Premiershp, 10 February 2007. Elm Park: 33,042 v Brentford, FA Cup 5th rd, 19 February 1927.

Pitch Measurements: 111yd × 74yd.

Chairman: John Madejski OBE, DL.

Chief Executive: Nigel Howe.

Secretary: Sue Hewett.

Manager: Steve Coppell.

Assistant Manager: Kevin Dillon, Wally Downes.

Physio: Jon Fearn MMACP, MCSP.

Colours: Blue and white hooped shirts, blue shorts, blue stockings.

Change Colours: Black and silver hooped shirts, black shorts, black stockings.

Year Formed: 1871.

Turned Professional: 1895.

Ltd Co.: 1895.

Club Nickname: 'The Royals'.

Grounds: 1871, Reading Recreation; Reading Cricket Ground; 1882, Coley Park; 1889, Caversham Cricket Ground; 1896, Elm Park; 1998, Madejski Stadium.

First Football League Game: 28 August 1920, Division 3, v Newport Co (a) W 1–0 – Crawford; Smith, Horler; Christie, Mavin, Getgood; Spence, Weston, Yarnell, Bailey (1), Andrews.

Record League Victory: 10–2 v Crystal Palace, Division 3 (S), 4 September 1946 – Groves; Glidden, Gulliver; McKenna, Ratcliffe, Young; Chitty, Maurice Edelston (3), McPhee (4), Barney (1), Deverell (2).

HONOURS

FA Premier League: Best season – 8th 2006–07.
Football League: FL C – Champions 2005–06; Division 1 – Runners-up 1994–95; Division 2 – Champions 1993–94; Runners-up 2001–02; Division 3 – Champions 1985–86; Division 3 (S) – Champions 1925–26; Runners-up 1931–32, 1934–35, 1948–49, 1951–52; Division 4 – Champions 1978–79.

FA Cup: Semi-final 1927.

Football League Cup: best season: 5th rd, 1996.

Simod Cup: Winners 1988.

SKY SPORTS FACT FILE

Reading won the Third Division (South) Cup in 1937–38 6–2 on aggregate. After beating Bournemouth, Bristol Rovers and Watford they met Bristol City in the two-legged final held over until the following season. Tony McPhee scored four in the 6–1 home win.

Record Cup Victory: 6–0 v Leyton, FA Cup 2nd rd, 12 December 1925 – Duckworth; Eggo, McConnell; Wilson, Messer, Evans; Smith (2), Braithwaite (1), Davey (1), Tinsley, Robson (2).

Record Defeat: 0–18 v Preston NE, FA Cup 1st rd, 1893–94.

Most League Points (2 for a win): 65, Division 4, 1978–79.

Most League Points (3 for a win): 106, Championship, 2005–06.

Most League Goals: 112, Division 3 (S), 1951–52.

Highest League Scorer in Season: Ronnie Blackman, 39, Division 3 (S), 1951–52.

Most League Goals in Total Aggregate: Ronnie Blackman, 158, 1947–54.

Most League Goals in One Match: 6, Arthur Bacon v Stoke C, Division 2, 3 April 1931.

Most Capped Player: Jimmy Quinn, 17 (46), Northern Ireland.

Most League Appearances: Martin Hicks, 500, 1978–91.

Youngest League Player: Peter Castle, 16 years 49 days v Watford, 30 April 2003.

Record Transfer Fee Received: £2,500,000 (rising to £3,000,000 based on appearances) from Sunderland for Greg Halford, June 2007.

Record Transfer Fee Paid: Undisclosed to Colchester U for Greg Halford, January 2007.

Football League Record: 1920 Original Member of Division 3; 1921–26 Division 3 (S); 1926–31 Division 2; 1931–58 Division 3 (S); 1958–71 Division 3; 1971–76 Division 4; 1976–77 Division 3; 1977–79 Division 4; 1979–83 Division 3; 1983–84 Division 4; 1984–86 Division 3; 1986–88 Division 2; 1988–92 Division 3; 1992–94 Division 2; 1994–98 Division 1; 1998–2002 Division 2; 2002–04 Division 1; 2004–06 FL C; 2006– FA Premier League.

MANAGERS

Thomas Sefton 1897–1901
(Secretary-Manager)
James Sharp 1901–02
Harry Matthews 1902–20
Harry Marshall 1920–22
Arthur Chadwick 1923–25
H. S. Bray 1925–26
(Secretary only since 1922 and 1926–35)
Andrew Wylie 1926–31
Joe Smith 1931–35
Billy Butler 1935–39
John Cochrane 1939
Joe Edelston 1939–47
Ted Drake 1947–52
Jack Smith 1952–55
Harry Johnston 1955–63
Roy Bentley 1963–69
Jack Mansell 1969–71
Charlie Hurley 1972–77
Maurice Evans 1977–84
Ian Branfoot 1984–89
Ian Porterfield 1989–91
Mark McGhee 1991–94
Jimmy Quinn/Mick Gooding 1994–97
Terry Bullivant 1997–98
Tommy Burns 1998–99
Alan Pardew 1999–2003
Steve Coppell October 2003–

LATEST SEQUENCES

Longest Sequence of League Wins: 13, 17.8.1985 – 19.10.1985.

Longest Sequence of League Defeats: 7, 10.4.1998 – 15.8.1998.

Longest Sequence of League Draws: 6, 23.3.2002 – 20.4.2002.

Longest Sequence of Unbeaten League Matches: 33, 9.8.2005 – 14.2.2006.

Longest Sequence Without a League Win: 14, 30.4.1927 – 29.10.1927.

Successive Scoring Runs: 32 from 1.10.1932.

Successive Non-scoring Runs: 6 from 13.4.1925.

TEN YEAR LEAGUE RECORD

		P	*W*	*D*	*L*	*F*	*A*	*Pts*	*Pos*
1997-98	Div 1	46	11	9	26	39	78	42	24
1998-99	Div 2	46	16	13	17	54	63	61	11
1999-2000	Div 2	46	16	14	16	57	63	62	10
2000-01	Div 2	46	25	11	10	86	52	86	3
2001-02	Div 2	46	23	15	8	70	43	84	2
2002-03	Div 1	46	25	4	17	61	46	79	4
2003-04	Div 1	46	20	10	16	55	57	70	9
2004-05	FL C	46	19	13	14	51	44	70	7
2005-06	FL C	46	31	13	2	99	32	106	1
2006-07	PR Lge	38	16	7	15	52	47	55	8

DID YOU KNOW ?

In a highly successful first season in the Premier League, Reading showed their resolve in the opening game against Middlesbrough. Trailing 2–0, they levelled with two goals in as many minutes before the break before Leroy Lita hit a 55th minute winner.

READING 2006–07 LEAGUE RECORD

Match No.	Date	Venue	Opponents	Result		H/T Score	Lg. Pos.	Goalscorers	Attendance
1	Aug 19	H	Middlesbrough	W	3-2	2-2	—	Kitson [43], Sidwell [44], Lita [55]	23,855
2	23	A	Aston Villa	L	1-2	1-1	—	Doyle [4]	37,329
3	26	A	Wigan Ath	L	0-1	0-1	13		14,636
4	Sept 11	H	Manchester C	W	1-0	1-0	—	Ingimarsson [23]	24,092
5	16	A	Sheffield U	W	2-1	2-0	6	Doyle [1], Seol [25]	25,011
6	23	H	Manchester U	D	1-1	0-0	7	Doyle (pen) [48]	24,098
7	Oct 1	A	West Ham U	W	1-0	1-0	7	Seol [2]	34,872
8	14	H	Chelsea	L	0-1	0-1	8		24,025
9	22	H	Arsenal	L	0-4	0-2	9		24,004
10	28	A	Portsmouth	L	1-3	0-1	10	Doyle [84]	20,146
11	Nov 4	A	Liverpool	L	0-2	0-1	12		43,741
12	12	H	Tottenham H	W	3-1	2-1	11	Shorey [38], Sidwell [45], Doyle [79]	24,110
13	18	H	Charlton Ath	W	2-0	1-0	8	Seol [18], Doyle [72]	24,093
14	25	A	Fulham	W	1-0	1-0	7	Doyle (pen) [17]	22,673
15	Dec 2	H	Bolton W	W	1-0	1-0	6	Doyle [33]	23,556
16	6	A	Newcastle U	L	2-3	2-1	—	Harper 2 [37, 42]	48,182
17	9	A	Watford	D	0-0	0-0	7		19,223
18	16	H	Blackburn R	L	1-2	1-0	8	Harper [41]	23,074
19	23	H	Everton	L	0-2	0-1	9		24,053
20	26	A	Chelsea	D	2-2	0-1	9	Lita [67], Essien (og) [85]	41,885
21	30	A	Manchester U	L	2-3	1-1	9	Sonko [38], Lita [90]	75,910
22	Jan 1	H	West Ham U	W	6-0	4-0	9	Gunnarsson [12], Hunt [15], Ferdinand (og) [30], Doyle 2 [36, 78], Lita [53]	24,073
23	14	A	Everton	D	1-1	1-0	9	Lescott (og) [28]	34,722
24	20	H	Sheffield U	W	3-1	1-0	8	Long [44], De la Cruz [50], Hunt [70]	23,956
25	30	H	Wigan Ath	W	3-2	1-1	—	Ingimarsson [31], Long [51], Lita [88]	21,954
26	Feb 3	A	Manchester C	W	2-0	0-0	6	Lita 2 [79, 89]	38,676
27	10	H	Aston Villa	W	2-0	1-0	6	Sidwell 2 [16, 90]	24,122
28	24	A	Middlesbrough	L	1-2	0-1	6	Oster [87]	26,412
29	Mar 3	A	Arsenal	L	1-2	0-0	7	Fabregas (og) [87]	60,132
30	17	H	Portsmouth	D	0-0	0-0	8		24,087
31	Apr 1	A	Tottenham H	L	0-1	0-1	8		36,067
32	7	H	Liverpool	L	1-2	0-1	9	Gunnarsson [47]	24,121
33	9	A	Charlton Ath	D	0-0	0-0	9		26,271
34	14	H	Fulham	W	1-0	1-0	9	Hunt [15]	24,082
35	21	A	Bolton W	W	3-1	0-0	7	Doyle 2 (1 pen) [84 (p), 89], Hunt [90]	23,533
36	30	H	Newcastle U	W	1-0	0-0	—	Kitson [51]	24,109
37	May 5	H	Watford	L	0-2	0-0	7		23,294
38	13	A	Blackburn R	D	3-3	1-1	8	Seol [36], Doyle [58], Gunnarsson [77]	22,671

Final League Position: 8

GOALSCORERS

League (52): Doyle 13 (3 pens), Lita 7, Hunt 4, Seol 4, Sidwell 4, Gunnarsson 3, Harper 3, Ingimarsson 2, Kitson 2, Long 2, De la Cruz 1, Oster 1, Shorey 1, Sonko 1, own goals 4.
Carling Cup (6): Lita 3, Bikey 1, Long 1, Mate 1.
FA Cup (9): Lita 4, Kitson 2, Gunnarsson 1, Long 1, Sodje 1.

Hahnemann M 38	Murty G 23	Shorey N 37	Ingimarsson I 38	Sonko I 23	Harper J 36 + 2	Seol K 22 + 5	Sidwell S 35	Kitson D 9 + 4	Doyle K 28 + 4	Convey B 8 + 1	Gunnarsson B 10 + 13	Lita L 22 + 11	Hunt S 28 + 7	Sodje S 2 + 1	Long S 9 + 12	Oster J 6 + 19	Little G 18 + 6	Bikey A 7 + 8	De la Cruz U 9	Duberry M 8	Halford G 2 + 1	Federici A — + 2	Match No.
1	2	3	4	5	6	7^1	8	9^2	10	11^3	12	13	14										1
1	2	3	4	5■	6	7	8		10^3	11^1	13	9^2	12		14								2
1	2	3	4		6^2	7^1	8		10	11^3		9	12	5	13	14							3
1	2	3	4	5	6	7^1	8		10	11	12	9^2			13								4
1	2	3	4	5	6	7^1	8		10	11^2	12	9^3	13				14						5
1	2^3	3	4	5	6	7^2	8		10	11	12	9^1	13					14					6
1		3	4	5	6	7^1	8		10	11^2	13	9^3	12		14				2				7
1	2^3	3	4	5	6	7^2	8		10			9^1	11		12		13	14■					8
1		3	4	5	6	7^2	8		10		12		11		9^3	13	14		2^1				9
1		3	4	5	6	7^2	8		10	11^1	2	12			9^3	13	14						10
1		3	4	5	6^2	12	8		10		7^1		11	2^3		13	9	14					11
1	2	3	4	5	6	7^1	8		10		13	12	9^3			14	11^2						12
1	2	3	4	5	6	11^3	8		10^1		13	12	9			14	7^2						13
1	2	3	4	5	6	11^1	8^2		10		13	12	9			14	7^3						14
1	2	3	4	5	6	11^2	8		10		12	13	9			7^1							15
1	2^3	3	4	5	6	11	8		10^1			12	9^2			7	13	14					16
1		3	4	5	6		8		10			9^2	11		13	7^1	12	2					17
1	2	3	4	5	6	11^1	8		10			12	9^3		14	13	7^2						18
1	2	3	4	5	6	11^1	8		10^3			12	9^2		14	13	7						19
1	2	3	4	5	6		8		10		11	9					7						20
1	2^3	3	4	5	6	12	8		10^2		11	9	13	14■			7^1						21
1		3	4	5^3	6^1	12	8		10		2	9	11			13	7^2	14					22
1		3	4	5	6		8		10^1			9	11		12		7		2				23
1	2		4	5^3	6	12	8			13		9	11^2		10^1		7	14	3				24
1	2	3	4		6		8	12				9	11		10^1		7	5					25
1	2	3	4		6		8	12				9	11		10^1	13	7^2	5					26
1	2	3	4		6		8	12				9	11		10^1	13	7^2	5					27
1	2	3	4		6		8	12				9	11^2		10^1	13	7			5			28
1	2	3	4		6^2		8	10	12		13	9	11^3			14	7^1	5					29
1	2	3	4		6		8	10	12			9^1	11^3			13	7^2			5	14		30
1^G		3	4		6		8	10	12			9	11^1			13	7^2			5	2	15	31
1		3	4		6		8	9	10		2	12	11			7^1		13		5^2			32
1		3	4		6	7	8					9	11		10			5	2				33
1		3	4		6	7^1		9^2	10		8		11		13	12		5	2				34
1		3	4		12	13	8	9^3	10		6		11		14	7^2			2^1	5			35
1		3	4		12	7		9^2	10		6^1		8		13	11^3		14	2	5			36
1		3	4		6^2	7	8	10^1	12		13	9	11^3			14				5	2		37
1^6		3	4		6	7			10		8	12	11^2		9^1	13			2	5		15	38

FA Cup

Third Round	Burnley	(h)	3-2
Fourth Round	Birmingham C	(a)	3-2
Fifth Round	Manchester U	(a)	1-1
		(h)	2-3

Carling Cup

Second Round	Darlington	(h)	3-3
Third Round	Liverpool	(a)	3-4

ROCHDALE FL Championship 2

FOUNDATION

Considering the love of rugby in their area, it is not surprising that Rochdale had difficulty in establishing an Association Football club. The earlier Rochdale Town club formed in 1900 went out of existence in 1907 when the present club was immediately established and joined the Manchester League, before graduating to the Lancashire Combination in 1908.

Spotland Stadium, Sandy Lane, Rochdale OL11 5DS.

Telephone: (0870) 822 1907.

Fax: (01706) 648 466.

Ticket Office: (0870) 822 1907.

Website: www.rochdaleafc.co.uk

Email: office@rochdaleafc.co.uk

Ground Capacity: 10,208.

Record Attendance: 24,231 v Notts Co, FA Cup 2nd rd, 10 December 1949.

Pitch Measurements: 114yd × 76yd.

Chairman: Chris Dunphy.

Chief Executive/Secretary: Colin Garlick.

Manager: Keith Hill.

Assistant Manager: David Flitcroft.

Physio: Andy Thorpe.

Colours: Black and white striped shirts, white shorts, black stockings.

Change Colours: Yellow shirts, black shorts, black stockings.

Year Formed: 1907.

Turned Professional: 1907.

Ltd Co.: 1910.

Club Nickname: 'The Dale'.

Ground: 1907, St Clements Playing Fields (original name Spotland).

First Football League Game: 27 August 1921, Division 3 (N), v Accrington Stanley (h) W 6–3 – Crabtree; Nuttall, Sheehan; Hill, Farrer, Yarwood; Hoad, Sandiford, Dennison (2), Owens (3), Carney (1).

Record League Victory: 8–1 v Chesterfield, Division 3 (N), 18 December 1926 – Hill; Brown, Ward; Hillhouse, Parkes, Braidwood; Hughes, Bertram, Whitehurst (5), Schofield (2), Martin (1).

Record Cup Victory: 8–2 v Crook T, FA Cup 1st rd, 26 November 1927 – Moody; Hopkins, Ward; Braidwood, Parkes, Barker; Tompkinson, Clennell (3) Whitehurst (4), Hall, Martin (1).

HONOURS

Football League: Division 3 best season: 9th, 1969–70; Division 3 (N) – Runners-up 1923–24, 1926–27.

FA Cup: best season: 5th rd, 1990, 2003.

Football League Cup: Runners-up 1962 (record for 4th Division club).

SKY SPORTS FACT FILE

On 29 August 1931 for the opening game of the season Rochdale attracted a crowd of 6974 for the visit of Accrington Stanley. The attendance was almost twice the size of Manchester United's initial home game v Southampton four days later at Old Trafford – 3507!

Record Defeat: 1–9 v Tranmere R, Division 3 (N), 25 December 1931.

Most League Points (2 for a win): 62, Division 3 (N), 1923–24.

Most League Points (3 for a win): 78, Division 3, 2001–02.

Most League Goals: 105, Division 3 (N), 1926–27.

Highest League Scorer in Season: Albert Whitehurst, 44, Division 3 (N), 1926–27.

Most League Goals in Total Aggregate: Reg Jenkins, 119, 1964–73.

Most League Goals in One Match: 6, Tommy Tippett v Hartlepools U, Division 3N, 21 April 1930.

Most Capped Player: Leo Bertos, 6 (7), New Zealand.

Most League Appearances: Graham Smith, 317, 1966–74.

Youngest League Player: Zac Hughes, 16 years 105 days v Exeter C, 19 September 1987.

Record Transfer Fee Received: £400,000 from West Ham U for Stephen Bywater, August 1998.

Record Transfer Fee Paid: £150,000 to Stoke C for Paul Connor, March 2001.

Football League Record: 1921 Elected to Division 3 (N); 1958–59 Division 3; 1959–69 Division 4; 1969–74 Division 3; 1974–92 Division 4; 1992–2004 Division 3; 2004– FL 2.

MANAGERS

Billy Bradshaw 1920
Run by committee 1920–22
Tom Wilson 1922–23
Jack Peart 1923–30
Will Cameron 1930–31
Herbert Hopkinson 1932–34
Billy Smith 1934–35
Ernest Nixon 1935–37
Sam Jennings 1937–38
Ted Goodier 1938–52
Jack Warner 1952–53
Harry Catterick 1953–58
Jack Marshall 1958–60
Tony Collins 1960–68
Bob Stokoe 1967–68
Len Richley 1968–70
Dick Conner 1970–73
Walter Joyce 1973–76
Brian Green 1976–77
Mike Ferguson 1977–78
Doug Collins 1979
Bob Stokoe 1979–80
Peter Madden 1980–83
Jimmy Greenhoff 1983–84
Vic Halom 1984–86
Eddie Gray 1986–88
Danny Bergara 1988–89
Terry Dolan 1989–91
Dave Sutton 1991–94
Mick Docherty 1995–96
Graham Barrow 1996–99
Steve Parkin 1999–2001
John Hollins 2001–02
Paul Simpson 2002–03
Alan Buckley 2003–04
Steve Parkin 2004–06
Keith Hill January 2007–

LATEST SEQUENCES

Longest Sequence of League Wins: 8, 29.9.1969 – 3.11.1969.

Longest Sequence of League Defeats: 17, 14.11.1931 – 12.3.1932.

Longest Sequence of League Draws: 6, 17.8.1968 – 14.9.1968.

Longest Sequence of Unbeaten League Matches: 20, 15.9.1923 – 19.1.1924.

Longest Sequence Without a League Win: 28, 14.11.1931 – 29.8.1932.

Successive Scoring Runs: 29 from 8.1.1927.

Successive Non-scoring Runs: 9 from 14.3.1980.

TEN YEAR LEAGUE RECORD

		P	*W*	*D*	*L*	*F*	*A*	*Pts*	*Pos*
1997-98	Div 3	46	17	7	22	56	55	58	18
1998-99	Div 3	46	13	15	18	42	55	54	19
1999-2000	Div 3	46	18	14	14	57	54	68	10
2000-01	Div 3	46	18	17	11	59	48	71	8
2001-02	Div 3	46	21	15	10	65	52	78	5
2002-03	Div 3	46	12	16	18	63	70	52	19
2003-04	Div 3	46	12	14	20	49	58	50	21
2004-05	FL 2	46	16	18	12	54	48	66	9
2005-06	FL 2	46	14	14	18	66	69	56	14
2006-07	FL 2	46	18	12	16	70	50	66	9

DID YOU KNOW ?

On 24 March 2007, Rochdale won 7–2 at Stockport County, three weeks after their opponents had established a Football League record of nine consecutive wins without conceding a single goal. Rochdale also hit three 5s and three 4s during the campaign.

ROCHDALE 2006–07 LEAGUE RECORD

Match No.	Date	Venue	Opponents	Result		H/T Score	Lg. Pos.	Goalscorers	Attendance
1	Aug 5	H	Walsall	L	0-1	0-0	—		3218
2	8	A	Torquay U	L	0-1	0-0	—		3039
3	12	A	Swindon T	L	0-1	0-1	23		6771
4	19	H	Notts Co	L	0-1	0-0	23		2321
5	26	A	Accrington S	D	1-1	1-0	23	Dagnall [20]	3045
6	Sept 2	H	Hereford U	D	1-1	0-0	23	Jones (pen) [90]	2146
7	9	A	Bristol R	D	0-0	0-0	23		4689
8	12	H	Grimsby T	W	1-0	0-0	—	Sako [57]	1997
9	16	H	Wycombe W	L	0-2	0-1	22		2313
10	23	A	Boston U	W	3-0	2-0	20	Dagnall 2 [7, 33], Doolan [90]	1709
11	27	A	Wrexham	W	2-1	0-1	—	Dagnall 2 [48, 77]	3577
12	30	H	Shrewsbury T	D	1-1	1-0	16	Sharp [7]	2942
13	Oct 6	A	Darlington	W	5-0	4-0	—	Sako 2 [7, 35], Goodall [20], Dagnall [45], Moyo-Modise [82]	3752
14	14	H	Chester C	D	0-0	0-0	12		3149
15	21	A	Lincoln C	L	1-7	1-3	18	Goodall [23]	5194
16	28	H	Stockport Co	L	1-3	0-2	20	Jones (pen) [53]	3709
17	Nov 4	H	Bury	L	1-3	1-2	21	Dagnall [11]	4499
18	18	A	Barnet	L	2-3	1-1	21	Clarke [22], Murray [59]	1972
19	25	H	Mansfield T	W	2-0	2-0	20	Dagnall [24], Doolan [41]	2378
20	Dec 5	A	Macclesfield T	L	0-1	0-0	—		1472
21	9	H	Peterborough U	L	0-1	0-0	21		1982
22	15	A	Hartlepool U	L	0-1	0-1	—		3659
23	23	A	Milton Keynes D	L	1-2	0-0	22	Harper (og) [58]	5459
24	26	H	Wrexham	D	2-2	0-0	22	Murray [63], Doolan [78]	2837
25	30	H	Boston U	W	4-0	1-0	20	Jones [41], Dagnall [62], Mocquet [65], Murray [70]	2159
26	Jan 1	A	Grimsby T	W	4-0	2-0	19	Ramsden 2 [13, 72], Murray [45], Rundle [66]	4302
27	6	A	Wycombe W	D	1-1	0-0	19	Etuhu [80]	4067
28	13	H	Bristol R	L	0-1	0-0	20		2547
29	27	H	Milton Keynes D	W	5-0	3-0	18	Le Fondre 2 [5, 62], Ramsden [10], Prendergast [16], Etuhu [84]	2493
30	Feb 3	A	Walsall	D	1-1	1-0	18	Ince (og) [5]	5046
31	17	A	Notts Co	W	2-1	0-0	19	Murray [80], Muirhead [83]	4493
32	20	H	Torquay U	W	2-0	1-0	—	Murray [19], Le Fondre (pen) [90]	2456
33	24	A	Hereford U	D	0-0	0-0	18		3090
34	Mar 3	H	Accrington S	W	4-2	3-0	17	Rundle [14], Murray 2 [25, 32], Le Fondre (pen) [82]	3433
35	10	H	Darlington	D	0-0	0-0	18		3256
36	16	A	Chester C	W	1-0	1-0	—	Dodds [5]	2197
37	24	A	Stockport Co	W	7-2	4-2	15	Murray 2 [4, 53], Goodall [11], Rundle (pen) [15], Muirhead 2 [17, 46], Dagnall [89]	6679
38	27	A	Shrewsbury T	L	0-3	0-0	—		4363
39	31	H	Lincoln C	W	2-0	0-0	13	Dagnall [89], Rundle [90]	2911
40	Apr 3	H	Swindon T	D	0-0	0-0	—		2544
41	7	A	Bury	W	1-0	0-0	12	Murray [74]	5075
42	9	H	Barnet	L	0-2	0-2	13		2525
43	14	A	Mansfield T	W	2-1	1-1	12	Murray [9], Dodds [90]	2023
44	21	H	Macclesfield T	W	5-0	3-0	10	Dagnall 3 [20, 41, 45], Murray 2 [47, 59]	2989
45	28	H	Hartlepool U	W	2-0	1-0	9	Murray [2], Dagnall (pen) [76]	5846
46	May 5	A	Peterborough U	D	3-3	1-2	9	Murray [11], Dagnall 2 [63, 69]	6011

Final League Position: 9

GOALSCORERS

League (70): Dagnall 17 (1 pen), Murray 16, Le Fondre 4 (2 pens), Rundle 4 (1 pen), Doolan 3, Goodall 3, Jones 3 (2 pens), Muirhead 3, Ramsden 3, Sako 3, Dodds 2, Etuhu 2, Clarke 1, Mocquet 1, Moyo-Modise 1, Prendergast 1, Sharp 1, own goals 2.
Carling Cup (2): Doolan 1, Rundle 1.
FA Cup (1): Doolan 1.
J Paint Trophy (2): Barker 1, Dagnall 1.

Gilks M 46	Ramsden S 32 + 2	Goodall A 46	Doolan J 40	Stanton N 35	Boardman J 3 + 1	Clarke D 5 + 7	Cooksey E 10 + 9	Lambert R 3	Christie I 4 + 1	Rundle A 20 + 9	Brown G 14 + 7	Dagnall C 32 + 5	Moyo-Modise C 1 + 18	Crooks L 26 + 5	Thompson J 5 + 8	Jackson M 8 + 4	Jones G 26 + 1	Sharp J 12	Barker K 11 + 1	Sako M 14 + 3	Murray G 29 + 2	McArdle R 25	Mocquet W 6 + 1	Warburton C 4	Etuhu C 3 + 1	Perkins D 14 + 4	Reid R — + 2	Le Fondre A 7	Prendergast R 4 + 1	Muirhead B 12	Dodds L 6 + 6	Turnbull S 2 + 2	Reet D — + 6	Poole G 1 + 5	Bates T — + 2	*Match No.*
1	2	3	4	5	6	7^{1}	8	9	10^{2}	11^{3}	12	13	14																						1
1	2	3	4	5		7^{1}	8	9^{2}	10	13	12	11		6																					2
1	2	3	4^{3}	5	6	12	8^{2}		10	11^{1}	13	9		7	14																				3
1	2	3	4	5		12	8		10^{2}	11^{1}	7	9^{3}	13	6	14																				4
1	2	3	4	5		7^{1}	11	9^{2}	12			10	13	8		6																			5
1	2	3	4^{2}	5			11					10^{1}	12	7			13	6	9	8															6
1	2^{1}	3	4	5^{2}			12					10	14	8		13	7	6	9	11^{3}															7
1		3	4	5			12					10^{1}	13	7		2	8	6	9^{2}	11															8
1		3	4	5			12					10^{2}	13	7^{1}		2	8	6	9	11															9
1	12	3	4	5			13					10^{2}	14	8		2^{1}	7	6	9^{3}	11															10
1		3	4^{1}	5			12				2	10	13	7			8	6	9^{2}	11															11
1		3	4	5^{1}	12		13				2	10^{3}	14	7			8	6	9	11^{2}															12
1		3	4	5		12	13				2	10^{1}	14	7^{2}			8	6	9	11^{3}															13
1	2	3		5		12	8					10	13	4			7	6	9^{2}	11^{1}															14
1	2	3	4	5		12						10^{2}	13	7			8	6^{1}	14	11^{3}	9														15
1	12	3	4	5		13						10^{3}	14	7^{2}		2	8	6^{1}		11	9														16
1		3			6■	7^{1}	11			12	2	10	13			5	4		9^{2}	14	8^{3}														17
1		3		5		7^{2}	13			12	4	10				2	8	6		11	9^{1}														18
1		3	4	5		12	11				2	10					8			13	9^{2}	6	7^{1}												19
1		3	4	5			8				2	10	12				7			11^{2}	13	6	9^{1}												20
1		3	4	5						12	2	10					8			13	9^{2}	6	7	11^{1}											21
1	2	3	4	5								10	12				7		9^{2}	11^{1}	13	6		8											22
1	2	3	4	5									12		10		8				9	6	7^{1}	11											23
1	2	3	4	5								10	11^{2}		12		8				9	6	13	7^{1}											24
1	2	3	4^{2}	5						11^{1}	12	10		13	14		8				9	6	7^{3}												25
1	2	3	4	5^{2}						11^{3}	12	10		13	14		8				9	6	7^{1}												26
1	2	3	4							11^{2}	7^{3}	10		5^{1}	13	12	8				9	6			14										27
1	2	3	4^{2}	5			12			11^{1}		10		13	14		7				9	6			8^{3}										28
1	2^{3}	3	4	5						12							8				9^{2}	6			7	14	13	10	11^{1}						29
1	2	3	4	5						12							8				9	6			7^{1}	13	14	10^{3}	11^{2}						30
1	2^{2}	3	4	5						12							8				9	6				13		10	11^{1}	7					31
1		3	4	5						12	2						8^{2}				9	6				13		10	11^{1}	7					32
1		3	4^{1}	5						11	2			12							9	6				8		10^{2}		7	13				33
1	2	3	4							11^{1}				5							9^{2}	6				8		10	12	7	13				34
1	2	3	4							11				5^{1}		12					9					8		10		7^{2}	13	6			35
1	2	5	4							11				12	13						9	6				8				7	10^{2}	3^{1}			36
1	2	3	4	5						11		12		6^{2}							9^{1}					8				7	10^{3}	13	14		37
1	2	3	4	5						11^{3}		12		6^{2}							9					8				7	10^{1}	13	14		38
1	2	3	4	5						11		12									9^{1}	6				8				7	10^{2}		13		39
1	2	3		5						11		9		4								6				8				7^{2}	10^{1}		12	13		40
1	2	3	4							11		10^{3}		5^{1}		12					9	6				8				7^{2}			13	14		41
1	2	3	4							11^{3}		12				5					9	6				8				7^{2}	10^{1}		13	14		42
1	2	3								12	4	10^{2}		5	7^{1}						9	6				8^{3}					13			11	14	43
1	2	3	4							11^{3}	12	10^{2}		5	7^{1}						9	6				8					13			14		44
1	2	3	4■							11	12	10^{1}		5	7						9	6				8										45
1	2	3								11^{3}	4	10		5^{2}	7^{1}						9	6				8					12			14	13	46

FA Cup
First Round — Hartlepool U — (h) 1-1; (a) 0-0

J Paint Trophy
First Round — Wrexham — (a) 1-1
Second Round — Crewe Alex — (h) 1-1

Carling Cup
First Round — Doncaster R — (a) 2-3

ROTHERHAM UNITED FL Championship 2

FOUNDATION

Rotherham were formed in 1870 before becoming Town in the late 1880s. Thornhill United were founded in 1877 and changed their name to Rotherham County in 1905. The Town amalgamated with Rotherham County to form Rotherham United in 1925.

Millmoor Ground, Rotherham S60 1HR.
Telephone: (01709) 512 434.
Fax: (01709) 512 762.
Ticket Office: 0870 443 1884.
Website: www.themillers.co.uk
Email: office@rotherhamunited.net
Ground Capacity: 8,287.
Record Attendance: 25,170 v Sheffield U, Division 2, 13 December 1952.
Pitch Measurements. 108yd × 72yd.
Chairman: Denis Coleman.
Chief Operating Officer/Secretary: Paul Douglas.
Manager: Mark Robins.
Assistant Manager: John Breckin.
Physio: Denis Circuit.
Colours: Red shirts with white band on sleeves and white sides, white shorts, red stockings.
Change Colours: White shirts, black shorts.
Year Formed: 1870.
Turned Professional: 1905.
Ltd Co.: 1920.
Club Nickname: 'The Merry Millers'.
Previous Names: 1877, Thornhill United; 1905, Rotherham County; 1925, amalgamated with Rotherham Town under Rotherham United.
Grounds: 1870, Red House Ground; 1907, Millmoor.
First Football League Game: 2 September 1893, Division 2, Rotherham T v Lincoln C (a) D 1–1 – McKay; Thickett, Watson; Barr, Brown, Broadhead; Longden, Cutts, Leatherbarrow, McCormick, Pickering, (1 og). 30 August 1919, Division 2, Rotherham Co v Nottingham F (h) W 2–0 – Branston; Alton, Baines; Bailey, Coe, Stanton; Lee (1), Cawley (1), Glennon, Lees, Lamb.
Record League Victory: 8–0 v Oldham Ath, Division 3 (N), 26 May 1947 – Warnes; Selkirk, Ibbotson; Edwards, Horace Williams, Danny Williams; Wilson (2), Shaw (1), Ardron (3), Guest (1), Hainsworth (1).
Record Cup Victory: 6–0 v Spennymoor U, FA Cup 2nd rd, 17 December 1977 – McAlister; Forrest, Breckin, Womble, Stancliffe, Green, Finney, Phillips (3), Gwyther (2) (Smith), Goodfellow, Crawford (1). 6–0 v Wolverhampton W, FA Cup 1st rd, 16 November 1985 – O'Hanlon; Forrest, Dungworth, Gooding (1), Smith (1), Pickering, Birch (2), Emerson, Tynan (1), Simmons (1), Pugh. 6–0 v Kings Lynn, FA Cup 2nd rd, 6 December 1997 – Mimms; Clark, Hurst (Goodwin), Garner (1) (Hudson) (1), Warner (Bass), Richardson (1), Berry (1), Thompson, Druce (1), Glover (1), Roscoe.
Record Defeat: 1–11 v Bradford C, Division 3 (N), 25 August 1928.

HONOURS

Football League: Division 2 – runners-up 2000–01; Division 3 – Champions 1980–81; Runners-up 1999–2000; Division 3 (N) – Champions 1950–51; Runners-up 1946–47, 1947–48, 1948–49; Division 4 – Champions 1988–89; Runners-up 1991–92.

FA Cup: best season: 5th rd, 1953, 1968.

Football League Cup: Runners-up 1961.

Auto Windscreens Shield: Winners 1996.

SKY SPORTS FACT FILE

After teenage disappointment at Sheffield Wednesday, full-back Steve Forde made rapid progress with Rotherham United from 1932, even returning on a two-months loan to Wednesday! Transferred to West Ham United in 1937 his career continued there until 1951.

Most League Points (2 for a win): 71, Division 3 (N), 1950–51.

Most League Points (3 for a win): 91, Division 2, 2000–01.

Most League Goals: 114, Division 3 (N), 1946–47.

Highest League Scorer in Season: Wally Ardron, 38, Division 3 (N), 1946–47.

Most League Goals in Total Aggregate: Gladstone Guest, 130, 1946–56.

Most League Goals in One Match: 4, Roland Bastow v York C, Division 3N, 9 November 1935; 4, Roland Bastow v Rochdale, Division 3N, 7 March 1936; 4, Wally Ardron v Crewe Alex, Division 3N, 5 October 1946; 4, Wally Ardron v Carlisle U, Division 3N, 13 September 1947; 4, Wally Ardron v Hartlepools U, Division 3N, 13 October 1948; 4, Ian Wilson v Liverpool, Division 2, 2 May 1955; 4, Carl Gilbert v Swansea C, Division 3, 28 September 1971; 4, Carl Airey v Chester, Division 3, 31 August 1987; 4, Shaun Goater v Hartlepool U, Division 3, 9 April 1994; 4, Lee Glover v Hull C, Division 3, 28 December 1997; 4, Darren Byfield v Millwall, Division 1, 10 August 2002.

Most Capped Player: Shaun Goater 14 (19), Bermuda.

Most League Appearances: Danny Williams, 459, 1946–62.

Youngest League Player: Kevin Eley, 16 years 72 days v Scunthorpe U, 15 May 1984.

Record Transfer Fee Received: £900,000 from Cardiff C for Alan Lee, August 2003.

Record Transfer Fee Paid: £150,000 to Millwall for Tony Towner, August 1980; £150,000 to Port Vale for Lee Glover, August 1996; £150,000 to Burnley for Alan Lee, September 2000; £150,000 to Reading for Martin Butler, September 2003.

MANAGERS

Billy Heald 1925–29 *(Secretary only for long spell)*
Stanley Davies 1929–30
Billy Heald 1930–33
Reg Freeman 1934–52
Andy Smailes 1952–58
Tom Johnston 1958–62
Danny Williams 1962–65
Jack Mansell 1965–67
Tommy Docherty 1967–68
Jimmy McAnearney 1968–73
Jimmy McGuigan 1973–79
Ian Porterfield 1979–81
Emlyn Hughes 1981–83
George Kerr 1983–85
Norman Hunter 1985–87
Dave Cusack 1987–88
Billy McEwan 1988–91
Phil Henson 1991–94
Archie Gemmill/John McGovern 1994–96
Danny Bergara 1996–97
Ronnie Moore 1997–2005
Mick Harford 2005
Alan Knill 2005–07
Mark Robins April 2007–

Football League Record: 1893 Rotherham Town elected to Division 2; 1896 Failed re-election; 1919 Rotherham County elected to Division 2; 1923–51 Division 3 (N); 1951–68 Division 2; 1968–73 Division 3; 1973–75 Division 4; 1975–81 Division 3; 1981–83 Division 2; 1983–88 Division 3; 1988–89 Division 4; 1989–91 Division 3; 1991–92 Division 4; 1992–97 Division 2; 1997–2000 Division 3; 2000–01 Division 2; 2001–04 Division 1; 2004–05 FL C; 2005–07 FL 1; 2007– FL 2.

LATEST SEQUENCES

Longest Sequence of League Wins: 9, 2.2.1982 – 6.3.1982.

Longest Sequence of League Defeats: 8, 7.4.1956 – 18.8.1956.

Longest Sequence of League Draws: 6, 13.10.1969 – 22.11.1969.

Longest Sequence of Unbeaten League Matches: 18, 13.10.1969 – 7.2.1970.

Longest Sequence Without a League Win: 21, 9.5.2004 – 20.11.2004.

Successive Scoring Runs: 30 from 3.4.1954.

Successive Non-scoring Runs: 6 from 21.8.2004.

TEN YEAR LEAGUE RECORD

		P	*W*	*D*	*L*	*F*	*A*	*Pts*	*Pos*
1997-98	Div 3	46	16	19	11	67	61	67	9
1998-99	Div 3	46	20	13	13	79	61	73	5
1999-2000	Div 3	46	24	12	10	72	36	84	2
2000-01	Div 2	46	27	10	9	79	55	91	2
2001-02	Div 1	46	10	19	17	52	66	49	21
2002-03	Div 1	46	15	14	17	62	62	59	15
2003-04	Div 1	46	13	15	18	53	61	54	17
2004-05	FL C	46	5	14	27	35	69	29	24
2005-06	FL 1	46	12	16	18	52	62	52	20
2006-07	FL 1	46	13	9	24	58	75	38	23

DID YOU KNOW ?

From 1945–46, Jack Shaw scored 17 FA Cup goals for Rotherham United. His outstanding performance during this period was on 25 November 1950 when he collected five in a 7–2 win against Darlington. He subsequently moved to neighbours Sheffield Wednesday.

ROTHERHAM UNITED 2006–07 LEAGUE RECORD

Match No.	Date	Venue	Opponents	Result	H/T Score	Lg. Pos.	Goalscorers	Attendance
1	Aug 5	H	Brighton & HA	L 0-1	0-1	—		4998
2	8	A	Huddersfield T	L 0-3	0-2	—		10,161
3	12	A	Blackpool	W 1-0	0-0	24	Hoskins [78]	5677
4	19	H	Scunthorpe U	W 2-1	2-1	24	Bopp [7], Mills [45]	4708
5	26	A	Bradford C	D 1-1	1-0	24	Hoskins [32]	8669
6	Sept 1	H	Northampton T	L 1-2	1-0	—	Hibbert [7]	4971
7	9	A	Chesterfield	L 1-2	1-2	24	Hoskins [11]	4803
8	12	H	Tranmere R	W 2-1	2-1	—	Williamson [18], Hoskins [38]	3732
9	16	H	Doncaster R	D 0-0	0-0	24		6348
10	23	A	Leyton Orient	W 3-2	2-1	24	Sharps [20], Hoskins [45], Wiseman [82]	4063
11	26	A	Oldham Ath	L 1-2	0-0	—	Hoskins [68]	4880
12	30	H	Millwall	L 2-3	2-1	24	Hoskins [30], Sharps [40]	4977
13	Oct 8	A	Port Vale	W 3-1	0-0	24	Cochrane [47], Hibbert [53], Hoskins [85]	4810
14	14	H	Brentford	W 2-0	0-0	23	Williamson 2 (1 pen) [49, 61 (p)]	4722
15	21	A	Bournemouth	W 3-1	3-1	23	Bopp [18], Hoskins [33], Williamson [36]	5544
16	28	H	Crewe Alex	W 5-1	3-1	20	Bopp [32], Partridge 2 [41, 74], Williamson (pen) [45], Hoskins [65]	5407
17	Nov 4	A	Carlisle U	D 1-1	1-0	19	Facey [21]	7247
18	18	H	Nottingham F	D 1-1	0-0	19	Hoskins [59]	7809
19	25	A	Gillingham	L 0-1	0-1	19		5103
20	Dec 2	H	Yeovil T	W 3-2	3-2	—	Facey [11], Skiverton (og) [13], Hoskins (pen) [45]	4823
21	9	H	Bristol C	D 1-1	0-0	19	Facey [53]	4862
22	16	A	Cheltenham T	L 0-2	0-0	19		3525
23	23	A	Swansea C	D 1-1	0-0	20	Bopp [56]	12,327
24	26	H	Oldham Ath	L 2-3	0-2	21	Bopp [54], Hoskins (pen) [81]	6512
25	30	H	Leyton Orient	D 2-2	0-1	20	Hoskins 2 [69, 81]	4715
26	Jan 1	A	Tranmere R	L 1-2	0-2	22	Facey [82]	6675
27	13	H	Chesterfield	L 0-1	0-1	22		5188
28	20	A	Millwall	L 0-4	0-3	23		9534
29	27	A	Doncaster R	L 2-3	1-1	23	Partridge [10], Woods [71]	12,126
30	Feb 3	A	Brighton & HA	D 0-0	0-0	24		5444
31	17	A	Scunthorpe U	L 0-1	0-1	24		5978
32	20	H	Huddersfield T	L 2-3	1-1	—	O'Grady (pen) [31], Facey [71]	4448
33	24	A	Northampton T	L 0-3	0-3	24		4564
34	27	H	Swansea C	L 1-2	0-1	—	Woods [90]	3697
35	Mar 3	H	Bradford C	W 4-1	1-0	24	Facey 2 [4, 72], Woods 2 [66, 88]	4568
36	10	H	Port Vale	L 1-5	0-4	24	Facey [67]	3854
37	17	A	Brentford	W 1-0	1-0	24	Facey [13]	4937
38	24	A	Crewe Alex	L 0-1	0-1	24		5675
39	27	H	Blackpool	W 1-0	0-0	—	O'Grady [60]	4025
40	31	H	Bournemouth	L 0-2	0-2	23		3657
41	Apr 7	H	Gillingham	W 3-2	1-2	23	Facey [7], O'Grady [75], Newsham [86]	3223
42	9	A	Nottingham F	D 1-1	1-1	23	O'Grady [10]	27,875
43	14	H	Carlisle U	L 0-1	0-0	23		4428
44	21	A	Yeovil T	L 0-1	0-1	23		5878
45	28	H	Cheltenham T	L 2-4	2-1	23	Newsham [14], Henderson [22]	3876
46	May 5	A	Bristol C	L 1-3	0-2	23	Newsham [58]	19,517

Final League Position: 23

GOALSCORERS

League (58): Hoskins 15 (2 pens), Facey 10, Bopp 5, Williamson 5 (2 pens), O'Grady 4 (1 pen), Woods 4, Newsham 3, Partridge 3, Hibbert 2, Sharps 2, Cochrane 1, Henderson 1, Mills 1, Wiseman 1, own goal 1.
Carling Cup (5): Hoskins 1, Keane 1, Partridge 1, Sharps 1, Williamson 1 (pen).
FA Cup (0).
J Paint Trophy (1): Facey 1.

Cutler N 41	Worrell D 38 + 3	Hurst P 11 + 1	Partridge R 30 + 3	Sharps I 38	Mills P 27 + 4	Keane M 16 + 6	Bopp E 24 + 5	Facey D 37 + 3	Hibbert D 12 + 9	Williamson L 17 + 2	Wiseman S 9 + 9	Woods M 31 + 5	Taylor R 1 + 9	Hoskins W 22 + 2	Robertson G 16 + 2	Cochrane J 29 + 2	Murdock C 4	Newsham M 3 + 13	Brogan S 19 + 4	King L 4 + 2	Diagouraga T 4 + 3	Henderson I 18	O'Grady C 11 + 2	Fleming C 17	Montgomery G 5 + 1	Streete T 4	Duncum S — + 2	Yates J 2 + 1	Jarvis R 10	Wilson C 5 + 1	Kerr N 1 + 2	Match No.
1	2	3	4	5	6	7^1	8^2	9	10^3	11	12	13	14																			1
1	2	3	4	5	6	7	8	9^2	10	11^1		12		13																		2
1	2		4^1	5	6	7	8	9	10^2	11	12			13	3																	3
1	2		4^2	5	6	7	8	9	12	11	13			10^1	3																	4
1	2	12		5^3	6	7	8^1	9^2	13	4	11	14		10■	3																	5
1	2		4		6	7^1	8	9	10	11	5	12			3																	6
1	2		4	5	6		8	9^1	12	11		7^2		10	3	13																7
1	2		4^1	5	6		8		9	11	12			10	3	7																8
1	2		4^1	5	6	12	8		9^2	11			13	10	3	7																9
1	2			5	6	7	12		9^2	11	14	4^3	13	10^1	3	8																10
1	2		12	5	6	7	13		9^3	11		4^1	14	10	3	8^2																11
1			12	5	6	7	13			11	2	4^2	9	10	3	8^1																12
1	12		4^2	5	6	7	13		9^3	11	2		14	10	3^1	8																13
1	2	3	4	5	6	7^1		13	9^2	11		12	14	10^3		8																14
1	2	3	4^1		6	7	8	9		11	12		13	10^2			5															15
1	2	3	4		6	7	8■	9^1	12	11			13	10^2			5															16
1	2	3	4^1		6	7		9	12	11	13			10^2		8	5															17
1	2	3	4^1	5	6		8	9	12			11		10		7																18
1	2	3^2	4^1	5	6		8	9	12			11		10	13	7^3		14														19
1	2		4^1	5	6		8	9			12	11		10	3	7																20
1	2		4	5	6		8	9				11		10	3	7																21
1	2		4^1	5			8	9	12		13	11		10	3	7^3	6^2	14														22
1	2		4^1	5			8	9			6	11		10	3	7			12													23
1	2		4^1	5			8	9	12		6	11		10	3^2	7^3		13	14													24
1	2		4^1		6^2			9	8	12	5	11		10		7			3	13												25
1	2		4	5				9	8^1	12	6	11		10		7			3													26
1	2		4^2	5	6		8^1	9				11			12			13	3		7	10										27
1	2		4^1	5			8	9^2			6	11				7■			3		12	10	13									28
1	2		4^1	5	6		8	9				11						12	3		7		10									29
1	2			5			8	9				11				7			3			4	10	6								30
1^6	2^1		4	5			8	12				11				7			3			9	10	6	15							31
	2^1		4	5			8	12				11				7			3			9■	10	6	1							32
1			4^1	5	12		13^3	9				11				7^2		14	3		8		10	6		2						33
	12	3	4	5				9^2				7							11		8	10	13	6	1	2^1						34
	12	3	4^2		6			9				7				8		13	11^3		14	10		5	1	2^1						35
		3			6			9				7				8^2		4^1	11	12		10		5	1	2	13					36
1	2			5	13	12^2		9				7						14	11^1	3		10		6				4^3	8			37
1	2			5				9										12	11^3	4	14	10^1		6			13	7^2	8	3		38
1	2			5	13	12		9				7								4		10^2	8	6					11^1	3		39
1	2			5				9^1				7						12	13	4^2		10	8	6					11	3		40
1	2			5		4^2		9				11				12		14	13			10^1	8	6					7	3^3		41
1	2			5^1	12	13		9				7				4^2			3			10	8	6					11			42
1	2				5	12		9				7				4^2		13	3			10^1	8	6					11			43
1	2^3		12	5		7^1		9								4		13	3			10	8^2	6					11		14	44
				5		12		9				7				4^1		8	3			10		6	1				11	13	2^2	45
1				5				9				7	12			4		8^1	3			10^3		6^2				14	11	2	13	46

FA Cup
First Round Peterborough U (a) 0-3

Carling Cup
First Round Oldham Ath (h) 3-1
Second Round Norwich C (h) 2-4

J Paint Trophy
First Round Hartlepool U (a) 1-3

SCUNTHORPE UNITED FL Championship

FOUNDATION

The year of foundation for Scunthorpe United has often been quoted as 1910, but the club can trace its history back to 1899 when Brumby Hall FC, who played on the Old Showground, consolidated their position by amalgamating with some other clubs and changing their name to Scunthorpe United. The year 1910 was when that club amalgamated with North Lindsey United as Scunthorpe and Lindsey United. The link is Mr W. T. Lockwood whose chairmanship covers both years.

Glanford Park, Doncaster Road, Scunthorpe DN15 8TD.

Telephone: (0871) 2211 899.

Fax: (01724) 857 986.

Ticket Office: (0871) 2211 899.

Website: www.scunthorpe-united.co.uk

Email: admin@scunthorpe-united.co.uk

Ground Capacity: 9,182.

Record Attendance: Old Showground: 23,935 v Portsmouth, FA Cup 4th rd, 30 January 1954. Glanford Park: 8,906 v Nottingham F, FL 1, 10 March 2007.

Pitch Measurements: 110yd × 71yd.

Chairman: John Steven Wharton.

Vice-chairman: Rex Garton.

General Manager: Jamie Hammond.

Manager: Nigel Adkins.

Assistant Managers: Ian Baraclough, Andy Crosby.

Physio: Alex Dalton.

Colours: Claret and blue.

Change Colours: White shirts, navy shorts, white and navy stockings.

Year Formed: 1899.

Turned Professional: 1912.

Ltd Co.: 1912.

Club Nickname: 'The Iron'.

Previous Names: Amalgamated first with Brumby Hall then North Lindsey United to become Scunthorpe & Lindsey United, 1910; dropped '& Lindsey' in 1958.

Grounds: 1899, Old Showground; 1988, Glanford Park.

First Football League Game: 19 August 1950, Division 3 (N), v Shrewsbury T (h) D 0–0 – Thompson; Barker, Brownsword; Allen, Taylor, McCormick; Mosby, Payne, Gorin, Rees, Boyes.

HONOURS

Football League: FL 1 – Champions 2006–07; FL 2 – Runners-up 2004–05; Division 3 (N) – Champions 1957–58. Promoted from Division 3 1998–99 (play-offs).

FA Cup: best season: 5th rd, 1958, 1970.

Football League Cup: never past 3rd rd.

SKY SPORTS FACT FILE

Harry Johnson, who had scored 15 goals in six FA Cup ties for Scunthorpe United in 1938–39, figured among the scorers again when the competition resumed in 1945–46. During his service there he became the first United player to achieve 100 goals.

Record League Victory: 8–1 v Luton T, Division 3, 24 April 1965 – Sidebottom; Horstead, Hemstead; Smith, Neale, Lindsey; Bramley (1), Scott, Thomas (5), Mahy (1), Wilson (1). 8–1 v Torquay U (a), Division 3, 28 October 1995 – Samways; Housham, Wilson, Ford (1), Knill (1), Hope (Nicholson), Thornber, Bullimore (Walsh), McFarlane (4) (Young), Eyre (2), Paterson.

Record Cup Victory: 9–0 v Boston U, FA Cup 1st rd, 21 November 1953 – Malan; Hubbard, Brownsword; Sharpe, White, Bushby; Mosby (1), Haigh (3), Whitfield (2), Gregory (1), Mervyn Jones (2).

Record Defeat: 0–8 v Carlisle U, Division 3 (N), 25 December 1952.

Most League Points (2 for a win): 66, Division 3 (N), 1956–57, 1957–58.

Most League Points (3 for a win): 91, FL 1, 2006–07.

Most League Goals: 88, Division 3 (N), 1957–58.

Highest League Scorer in Season: Barrie Thomas, 31, Division 2, 1961–62.

Most League Goals in Total Aggregate: Steve Cammack, 110, 1979–81, 1981–86.

Most League Goals in One Match: 5, Barrie Thomas v Luton T, Division 3, 24 April 1965.

Most Capped Player: Dave Mulligan 1(12), New Zealand.

Most League Appearances: Jack Brownsword, 595, 1950–65.

Youngest League Player: Mike Farrell, 16 years 240 days v Workington, 8 November 1975.

Record Transfer Fee Received: £350,000 from Aston Villa for Neil Cox, February 1991.

Record Transfer Fee Paid: £175,000 to Bristol C for Steve Torpey, February 2000.

Football League Record: 1950 Elected to Division 3 (N); 1958–64 Division 2; 1964–68 Division 3; 1968–72 Division 4; 1972–73 Division 3; 1973–83 Division 4; 1983–84 Division 3; 1984–92 Division 4; 1992–99 Division 3; 1999–2000 Division 2; 2000–04 Division 3; 2004–05 FL 2; 2005–07 FL 1; 2007– FL C.

MANAGERS

Harry Allcock 1915–53
(Secretary-Manager)
Tom Crilly 1936–37
Bernard Harper 1946–48
Leslie Jones 1950–51
Bill Corkhill 1952–56
Ron Suart 1956–58
Tony McShane 1959
Bill Lambton 1959
Frank Soo 1959–60
Dick Duckworth 1960–64
Fred Goodwin 1964–66
Ron Ashman 1967–73
Ron Bradley 1973–74
Dick Rooks 1974–76
Ron Ashman 1976–81
John Duncan 1981–83
Allan Clarke 1983–84
Frank Barlow 1984–87
Mick Buxton 1987–91
Bill Green 1991–93
Richard Money 1993–94
David Moore 1994–96
Mick Buxton 1996–97
Brian Laws 1997–2004; 2004–2006
Nigel Adkins December 2006–

LATEST SEQUENCES

Longest Sequence of League Wins: 7, 27.1.2007 – 3.3.2007.

Longest Sequence of League Defeats: 8, 29.11.1997 – 20.1.1998.

Longest Sequence of League Draws: 6, 2.1.1984 – 25.2.1984.

Longest Sequence of Unbeaten League Matches: 19, 22.12.2006 – 6.4.2007.

Longest Sequence Without a League Win: 14, 22.3.1975 – 6.9.1975.

Successive Scoring Runs: 23 from 18.8.1951.

Successive Non-scoring Runs: 7 from 19.4.1975.

TEN YEAR LEAGUE RECORD

		P	*W*	*D*	*L*	*F*	*A*	*Pts*	*Pos*
1997-98	Div 3	46	19	12	15	56	52	69	8
1998-99	Div 3	46	22	8	16	69	58	74	4
1999-2000	Div 2	46	9	12	25	40	74	39	23
2000-01	Div 3	46	18	11	17	62	52	65	10
2001-02	Div 3	46	19	14	13	74	56	71	8
2002-03	Div 3	46	19	15	12	68	49	72	5
2003-04	Div 3	46	11	16	19	69	72	49	22
2004-05	FL 2	46	22	14	10	69	42	80	2
2005-06	FL 1	46	15	15	16	68	73	60	12
2006-07	FL 1	46	26	13	7	73	35	91	1

DID YOU KNOW ?

The attraction of promotion-seeking rivals Nottingham Forest produced a crowd of 8906 for Scunthorpe United, a record for the Glanford Park enclosure on 10 March 2007. Their highest average attendance had been 12,377 at the Old Show Ground during 1958–59.

SCUNTHORPE UNITED 2006–07 LEAGUE RECORD

Match No.	Date	Venue	Opponents	Result		H/T Score	Lg. Pos.	Goalscorers	Attendance
1	Aug 5	A	Bristol C	L	0-1	0-0	—		13,268
2	8	H	Swansea C	D	2-2	0-1	—	Crosby (pen) [49], Sharp [67]	4187
3	12	H	Crewe Alex	D	2-2	1-1	17	Sharp [39], Crosby (pen) [66]	4329
4	19	A	Rotherham U	L	1-2	1-2	22	Sharp [6]	4708
5	26	H	Brentford	D	1-1	0-1	22	Mousinho (og) [69]	3942
6	Sept 1	A	Gillingham	W	2-0	2-0	—	Hinds [40], Sparrow [45]	5749
7	9	A	Oldham Ath	L	0-1	0-1	21		4812
8	12	H	Port Vale	W	3-0	2-0	—	Sharp 2 [10, 45], Morris [65]	3473
9	16	H	Cheltenham T	W	1-0	0-0	14	Keogh [90]	4288
10	23	A	Bournemouth	D	1-1	1-1	15	MacKenzie [19]	5256
11	27	A	Chesterfield	W	1-0	1-0	—	Sharp [13]	4849
12	30	H	Doncaster R	W	2-0	0-0	7	Sharp [54], Keogh [68]	6441
13	Oct 7	A	Nottingham F	W	4-0	2-0	3	Taylor [28], Keogh [36], Morris [66], Sharp [90]	22,640
14	14	H	Brighton & HA	L	1-2	1-1	4	Sharp [43]	5607
15	21	A	Bradford C	W	1-0	0-0	4	Sharp [79]	8723
16	28	H	Leyton Orient	W	3-1	2-1	3	Sharp 2 [6, 57], Sparrow [38]	4795
17	Nov 4	A	Huddersfield T	D	1-1	0-0	3	Sparrow [55]	10,456
18	18	H	Northampton T	W	1-0	0-0	2	Crosby (pen) [86]	4758
19	25	A	Yeovil T	W	2-0	1-0	2	Sharp 2 [7, 62]	5921
20	Dec 5	H	Tranmere R	D	1-1	1-0	—	Keogh [42]	4572
21	9	A	Carlisle U	W	2-0	0-0	2	Sharp [52], Keogh [90]	6954
22	15	H	Blackpool	L	1-3	0-1	—	Baraclough [90]	4527
23	22	A	Millwall	W	1-0	0-0	—	Torpey [74]	7192
24	26	H	Chesterfield	W	1-0	0-0	2	Sharp [49]	6123
25	30	H	Bournemouth	W	3-2	3-0	1	Crosby [8], Keogh [29], Sharp [44]	4794
26	Jan 1	A	Port Vale	D	0-0	0-0	1		4869
27	13	H	Oldham Ath	D	1-1	0-0	2	Gregan (og) [54]	7685
28	16	A	Cheltenham T	D	1-1	0-1	—	Sharp [79]	3036
29	20	A	Doncaster R	D	2-2	2-0	1	Keogh [15], Talbot [23]	12,414
30	27	H	Millwall	W	3-0	0-0	1	Goodwin [50], Crosby (pen) [53], Beckford [79]	5001
31	Feb 5	H	Bristol C	W	1-0	1-0	—	Sharp [41]	5108
32	17	H	Rotherham U	W	1-0	1-0	1	Beckford [17]	5978
33	20	A	Swansea C	W	2-0	1-0	—	Sharp [3], Beckford [71]	10,746
34	24	H	Gillingham	W	3-1	1-0	1	Hinds [24], Mulligan [65], Morris [90]	5312
35	27	A	Crewe Alex	W	3-1	2-1	—	Sharp 2 [29, 62], Beckford [40]	4842
36	Mar 3	A	Brentford	W	2-0	1-0	1	Beckford [40], Taylor [89]	5645
37	10	H	Nottingham F	D	1-1	0-1	1	Sharp [46]	8906
38	17	A	Brighton & HA	D	1-1	0-0	1	Beckford [64]	6276
39	24	A	Leyton Orient	D	2-2	0-1	1	MacKenzie [51], Sharp [90]	5869
40	31	H	Bradford C	W	2-0	0-0	1	Sharp [56], Beckford [76]	6437
41	Apr 6	H	Yeovil T	W	1-0	1-0	—	Jones (og) [39]	7883
42	9	A	Northampton T	L	1-2	0-1	1	Sharp [57]	6361
43	14	H	Huddersfield T	W	2-0	0-0	1	Sharp 2 (1 pen) [68, 84 (p)]	7518
44	21	A	Tranmere R	W	2-0	0-0	1	Butler [55], Sharp [70]	6721
45	28	A	Blackpool	L	1-3	1-2	1	Sharp [41]	9482
46	May 5	H	Carlisle U	W	3-0	1-0	1	Taylor [41], Sparrow [47], Beckford [64]	8720

Final League Position: 1

GOALSCORERS

League (73): Sharp 30 (1 pen), Beckford 8, Keogh 7, Crosby 5 (4 pens), Sparrow 4, Morris 3, Taylor 3, Hinds 2, MacKenzie 2, Baraclough 1, Butler 1, Goodwin 1, Mulligan 1, Talbot 1, Torpey 1, own goals 3.
Carling Cup (5): Baraclough 1, Mulligan 1, Paul 1, Sharp 1, Torpey 1.
FA Cup (2): Baraclough 1, Sharp 1.
J Paint Trophy (2): Foy 1, Goodwin 1 (pen).

Murphy J 45	Hinds R 37 + 7	Ridley L 15 + 3	Crosby A 36 + 3	Foster S 44	Baraclough I 25 + 8	Mulligan D 20 + 4	Goodwin J 25 + 6	Keogh A 25 + 3	Sharp B 45	Sparrow M 27 + 2	MacKenzie N 10 + 14	Torpey S 5 + 9	Taylor C 42 + 3	Ferretti A — + 4	Byrne C 18 + 6	Williams M 32 + 3	Foy R 1 + 4	Morris I 18 + 10	McBreen D 1 + 6	Lillis J 1	Talbot D 2 + 1	Butler A 4 + 7	Beckford J 17 + 1	Hurst K 11 + 2	Match No.
1	2	3	4	5	6¹	7²	8³	9	10	11	12	13■	14												1
1	8	3	4	5	6¹	2		9	10	11			7	12											2
1	8	3	4	5	6	2		9	10	11¹			7	12											3
1	8	3	4	5	6³	2		9²	10	11	12		7¹	13	14										4
1	6²		4¹	5	12	7		9	10	11			13	14	2	3	8³								5
1	4			5	6	2			10	11		12	7			3		8	9¹						6
1	4			5	6	2		9¹	10	11		12	7²			3		8	13						7
1	4		12	5¹	6	2		13	10	11		9³	7			3		8²	14						8
1	4		12	5¹	6	2		13	10	11		9²	7			3		8							9
1	6		4	5	12			9	10	11¹	8		7		2	3									10
1	2		4¹	5	6²			9³	10	11	13		7		12	3		8	14						11
1	4		12	5	6	2¹		9	10	11			7			3		8²	13						12
1	2		4	5	6¹			9	10	11	12		7			3²		8	13						13
1	2		4	5■	6²	12		9	10	11	13	14	7			3¹		8³							14
1	5		4		6	2		12	10²	11		9	7			3		8¹	13						15
1	5		4		6	2¹	13	9	10	11²		14	7		12	3		8³							16
1	2		4	5	6			9	10	11			7			3		8							17
1	2¹		4	5	6		13	9	10	11			7²		12	3	14	8³							18
1	2		4	5	6	12	8¹	9	10²	11		13	7		3										19
1	2		4	5	6²		13	9	10	11			7		12	3		8¹							20
1	6		4	5	12		8	9	10²	11³		13	7¹		2	3		14							21
1	6		4	5³	12		8	9	10			13	7		2	3¹	14	11²							22
	4	12		5	6³		8	9	10¹		14	13	7		2	3		11²		1					23
1	6		4	5	12		8³	9	10		13	11¹	7²		2	3		14							24
1	12	13	4	5	6		8	9	10				7		2	3²		11¹							25
1	2		4	5	6¹		12	9	10		8²		7³		3	11	14	13							26
1	2¹		4	5	6		8	9	10³				7■		12■	3		11²			14	13			27
1	2	12	4	5	6²		8	9	10		7					3¹	13				11				28
1	6¹	3	4	5		12	8	9			13		7			2					11³	14	10²		29
1		3	4	5		2	8		10		6		7			11							9		30
1	6	3	4	5			8		10¹				7		2			13				12	9	11²	31
1	6	3	4	5		12	8		10		13		7³		2¹			14					9	11²	32
1	6	3	4	5³		2	8		10		12		7²					13				14	9	11¹	33
1	6	3	4	5		2	8²		10	12	13		7¹					14					9	11³	34
1	6	3	4	5		2	8		10	11¹	12		7			13							9²		35
1	4	3²		5		2	8		10		12		7			13						6	9	11¹	36
1	6	3	4	5		2	8		10	11			7										9		37
1	6	3	4	5		2¹	8		10	11■	13		7²					12				14	9³		38
1	12	3²	4	5		2	8¹		10		11		7³			13		6					9	14	39
1	12		4	5²	14		8		10		6		7¹		2	3						13	9	11³	40
1	12		4	5	13		8		10		6		7¹		2	3							9	11²	41
1	6		4	5			8		10		7¹		12		2	3						13	9	11²	42
1	12			5	13		8²		10	14	4¹		7³		2	3						6	9	11	43
1	12			5			13		10¹	4	8²		7		2	3		14				6	9	11³	44
1				5	6		12		10	8			7¹		2	3		13				4	9	11²	45
1	12		4	5	6		8		10²	11		9³	7		2	3¹							14	13	46

FA Cup

First Round	Cheltenham T	(a)	0-0
		(h)	2-0
Second Round	Wrexham	(h)	0-2

Carling Cup

First Round	Lincoln C	(h)	4-3
Second Round	Aston Villa	(h)	1-2

J Paint Trophy

First Round	Bradford C	(a)	2-1
Second Round	Port Vale	(h)	0-0

SHEFFIELD UNITED FL Championship

FOUNDATION

In March 1889, Yorkshire County Cricket Club formed Sheffield United six days after an FA Cup semi-final between Preston North End and West Bromwich Albion had finally convinced Charles Stokes, a member of the cricket club, that the formation of a professional football club would prove successful at Bramall Lane. The United's first secretary, Mr J. B. Wostinholm was also secretary of the cricket club.

Bramall Lane Ground, Cherry Street, Bramall Lane, Sheffield S2 4SU.

Telephone: 0870 787 1960.

Fax: 0870 787 3345.

Ticket Office: 0870 787 1799.

Website: www.sufc.co.uk

Email: info@sufc.co.uk

Ground Capacity: 32,609.

Record Attendance: 68,287 v Leeds U, FA Cup 5th rd, 15 February 1936.

Pitch Measurements: 110yd × 74yd.

Chairman (Plc): Kevin McCabe.

Chairman (Football): Terry Robinson.

Vice-chairman (Plc): Mick Dudley.

Vice-chairman (Football): Chris Steer.

Chief Executive: Jason Rocket.

Secretary: Donna Fletcher.

Manager: Bryan Robson.

Assistant Manager: Brian Kidd.

Physio: Dennis Pettitt.

Colours: Red and white stripes.

Change Colours: Lime.

Year Formed: 1889. ***Turned Professional:*** 1889. ***Ltd Co.:*** 1899.

Club Nickname: 'The Blades'.

Ground: 1889, Bramall Lane.

First Football League Game: 3 September 1892, Division 2, v Lincoln C (h) W 4–2 – Lilley; Witham, Cain; Howell, Hendry, Needham (1); Wallace, Dobson, Hammond (3), Davies, Drummond.

Record League Victory: 10–0 v Burslem Port Vale (a), Division 2, 10 December 1892 – Howlett; Witham, Lilley; Howell, Hendry, Needham; Drummond (1), Wallace (1), Hammond (4), Davies (2), Watson (2).

Record Cup Victory: 6–1 v Lincoln C, League Cup, 22 August 2000 – Tracey; Uhlenbeek, Weber, Woodhouse (Ford), Murphy, Sandford, Devlin (pen), Ribeiro (Santos), Bent (3), Kelly (1) (Thompson), Jagielka, og (1). 6–1 v Loughborough, FA Cup 4th qualifying rd, 6 December 1890; 6–1 v Scarborough (a), FA Cup 1st qualifying rd, 5 October 1889.

HONOURS

Football League: FL C – Runners-up 2005–06; Division 1 – Champions 1897–98; Runners-up 1896–97, 1899–1900; Division 2 – Champions 1952–53; Runners-up 1892–93, 1938–39, 1960–61, 1970–71, 1989–90; Division 4 – Champions 1981–82.

FA Cup: Winners 1899, 1902, 1915, 1925; Runners-up 1901, 1936.

Football League Cup: semi-final 2003.

SKY SPORTS FACT FILE

Sheffield United were declared Champions of Great Britain in 1898 when in challenge matches against the Scottish champions Celtic they won 1–0 at Bramall Lane with a Ralph Gaudie goal and drew 1–1 at Parkhead when Jack Almond equalised.

Record Defeat: 0–13 v Bolton W, FA Cup 2nd rd, 1 February 1890.

Most League Points (2 for a win): 60, Division 2, 1952–53.

Most League Points (3 for a win): 96, Division 4, 1981–82.

Most League Goals: 102, Division 1, 1925–26.

Highest League Scorer in Season: Jimmy Dunne, 41, Division 1, 1930–31.

Most League Goals in Total Aggregate: Harry Johnson, 205, 1919–30.

Most League Goals in One Match: 5, Harry Hammond v Bootle, Division 2, 26 November 1892; 5, Harry Johnson v West Ham U, Division 1, 26 December 1927.

Most Capped Player: Billy Gillespie, 25, Northern Ireland.

Most League Appearances: Joe Shaw, 629, 1948–66.

Youngest League Player: Steve Hawes, 17 years 47 days v WBA, 2 September 1995.

Record Transfer Fee Received: £3,000,000 (dependant on appearances) from Derby Co for Lee Morris, October 1999.

Record Transfer Fee Paid: £3,000,000 to Preston NE for Claude Davis, July 2006.

Football League Record: 1892 Elected to Division 2; 1893–1934 Division 1; 1934–39 Division 2; 1946–49 Division 1; 1949–53 Division 2; 1953–56 Division 1; 1956–61 Division 2; 1961–68 Division 1; 1968–71 Division 2; 1971–76 Division 1; 1976–79 Division 2; 1979–81 Division 3; 1981–82 Division 4; 1982–84 Division 3; 1984–88 Division 2; 1988–89 Division 3; 1989–90 Division 2; 1990–92 Division 1; 1992–94 FA Premier League; 1994–2004 Division 1; 2004–06 FL C; 2006–07 FA Premier League; 2007– FL C.

MANAGERS

J. B. Wostinholm 1889–99
(Secretary-Manager)
John Nicholson 1899–1932
Ted Davison 1932–52
Reg Freeman 1952–55
Joe Mercer 1955–58
Johnny Harris 1959–68
(continued as General Manager to 1970)
Arthur Rowley 1968–69
Johnny Harris *(General Manager resumed Team Manager duties)* 1969–73
Ken Furphy 1973–75
Jimmy Sirrel 1975–77
Harry Haslam 1978–81
Martin Peters 1981
Ian Porterfield 1981–86
Billy McEwan 1986–88
Dave Bassett 1988–95
Howard Kendall 1995–97
Nigel Spackman 1997–98
Steve Bruce 1998–99
Adrian Heath 1999
Neil Warnock 1999–2007
Bryan Robson May 2007–

LATEST SEQUENCES

Longest Sequence of League Wins: 8, 14.9.1960 – 22.10.1960.

Longest Sequence of League Defeats: 7, 19.8.1975 – 20.9.1975.

Longest Sequence of League Draws: 6, 6.5.2001 – 8.9.2001.

Longest Sequence of Unbeaten League Matches: 22, 2.9.1899 – 13.1.1900.

Longest Sequence Without a League Win: 19, 27.9.1975 – 7.2.1976.

Successive Scoring Runs: 34 from 30.3.1956.

Successive Non-scoring Runs: 6 from 4.12.1993.

TEN YEAR LEAGUE RECORD

		P	W	D	L	F	A	Pts	Pos
1997-98	Div 1	46	19	17	10	69	54	74	6
1998-99	Div 1	46	18	13	15	71	66	67	8
1999-2000	Div 1	46	13	15	18	59	71	54	16
2000-01	Div 1	46	19	11	16	52	49	68	10
2001-02	Div 1	46	15	15	16	53	54	60	13
2002-03	Div 1	46	23	11	12	72	52	80	3
2003-04	Div 1	46	20	11	15	65	56	71	8
2004-05	FL C	46	18	13	15	57	56	67	8
2005-06	FL C	46	26	12	8	76	46	90	2
2006-07	PR Lge	38	10	8	20	32	55	38	18

DID YOU KNOW?

Wartime regional football robbed Dennis Thompson of the official tag as the youngest player to turn out for Sheffield United. The right winger was 16 years 103 days when he made his debut against Mansfield Town on 13 September 1941.

SHEFFIELD UNITED 2006–07 LEAGUE RECORD

Match No.	Date	Venue	Opponents	Result	H/T Score	Lg. Pos.	Goalscorers	Attendance
1	Aug 19	H	Liverpool	D 1-1	0-0	—	Hulse [46]	31,726
2	22	A	Tottenham H	L 0-2	0-2	—		35,287
3	26	A	Fulham	L 0-1	0-1	19		18,362
4	Sept 9	H	Blackburn R	D 0-0	0-0	18		29,876
5	16	H	Reading	L 1-2	0-2	20	Hulse [61]	25,011
6	23	A	Arsenal	L 0-3	0-0	20		59,912
7	30	H	Middlesbrough	W 2-1	1-0	18	Hulse [35], Jagielka [90]	27,483
8	Oct 14	A	Manchester C	D 0-0	0-0	16		42,192
9	21	A	Everton	L 0-2	0-2	17		37,900
10	28	H	Chelsea	L 0-2	0-1	19		32,321
11	Nov 4	A	Newcastle U	W 1-0	0-0	18	Webber [68]	50,188
12	11	H	Bolton W	D 2-2	0-1	17	Hulse [70], Kazim-Richards [73]	28,294
13	18	H	Manchester U	L 1-2	1-1	18	Gillespie [13]	32,584
14	25	A	West Ham U	L 0-1	0-1	18		34,454
15	28	A	Watford	W 1-0	0-0	—	Webber [88]	18,887
16	Dec 2	H	Charlton Ath	W 2-1	0-1	16	Morgan [64], Gillespie [88]	27,368
17	11	H	Aston Villa	D 2-2	0-1	—	Quinn S [50], Webber [64]	30,957
18	16	A	Wigan Ath	W 1-0	1-0	14	Hulse [45]	16,322
19	23	A	Portsmouth	L 1-3	1-0	16	Hulse [4]	20,164
20	26	H	Manchester C	L 0-1	0-0	17		32,591
21	30	H	Arsenal	W 1-0	1-0	15	Nade [41]	32,086
22	Jan 1	A	Middlesbrough	L 1-3	1-1	16	Jagielka (pen) [45]	27,963
23	13	H	Portsmouth	D 1-1	1-0	16	Quinn S [22]	30,269
24	20	A	Reading	L 1-3	0-1	16	Nade [77]	23,956
25	30	H	Fulham	W 2-0	2-0	—	Stead [23], Tonge [28]	27,540
26	Feb 3	A	Blackburn R	L 1-2	1-1	16	Stead [25]	20,917
27	10	H	Tottenham H	W 2-1	1-1	15	Hulse [27], Jagielka (pen) [62]	32,144
28	24	A	Liverpool	L 0-4	0-2	16		44,198
29	Mar 3	H	Everton	D 1-1	0-0	16	Hulse [52]	32,019
30	17	A	Chelsea	L 0-3	0-2	17		41,897
31	31	A	Bolton W	L 0-1	0-0	17		24,312
32	Apr 7	H	Newcastle U	L 1-2	0-1	18	Nade [74]	32,572
33	14	H	West Ham U	W 3-0	1-0	17	Tonge [39], Jagielka [68], Stead [78]	31,593
34	17	A	Manchester U	L 0-2	0-1	—		75,540
35	21	A	Charlton Ath	D 1-1	0-0	17	Stead [69]	27,111
36	28	H	Watford	W 1-0	1-0	15	Powell (og) [44]	30,690
37	May 5	A	Aston Villa	L 0-3	0-2	16		42,551
38	13	H	Wigan Ath	L 1-2	1-2	18	Stead [38]	32,604

Final League Position: 18

GOALSCORERS

League (32): Hulse 8, Stead 5, Jagielka 4 (2 pens), Nade 3, Webber 3, Gillespie 2, Quinn S 2, Tonge 2, Kazim-Richards 1, Morgan 1, own goal 1.
Carling Cup (3): Akinbiyi 1, Montgomery 1, Nade 1.
FA Cup (0).

Kenny P 34	Geary D 26	Unsworth D 5	Jagielka P 38	Bromby L 12 + 5	Morgan C 21 + 3	Ifill P 3	Tonge M 23 + 4	Hulse R 28 + 1	Webber D 13 + 9	Armstrong C 24 + 3	Leigertwood M 16 + 3	Gillespie K 27 + 4	Akinbiyi A 2 + 1	Sommeil D 4 + 1	Montgomery N 22 + 4	Nade C 7 + 18	Quinn A 11 + 8	Kazim-Richards C 15 + 12	Bennett I 2	Kozluk R 17 + 2	Davis C 18 + 3	Kabba S — + 7	Wright A 1	Law N 2 + 2	Quinn S 15	Gerrard P 2	Luccketti C 8	Stead J 12 + 2	Fathi A 2 + 1	Kilgallon M 6	Shelton L 2 + 2	*Match No.*
1	2	3	4	5^1	6	7^2	8	9^3	10	11	12	13	14																			1
1		3^2	4	5	6		8		10	11		7^3	9	2^1	12	13	14															2
1		3	4	2^3	6		8^2	9	10	11	5			14	7^1	12	13															3
1		3	4		6	7^3	8^1	9	10^2	11	5			2		13	12	14														4
		3^1	8	5^2	6	7^3		9		11	4	12	10	2		13	14		1													5
	3^2		4					9		8	5	7		2^1			12	10^3	1	13	6	14	11									6
1			4	2			8	9	12	3	5	7^2				13	11^3	10^1			6	14										7
1			4	2			8	9	12	3	5	7					11	10^1			6											8
1			4	2	12		8	9	13	3	5	7^3					11^1	10^2			6■	14										9
1			4	2^3			8^2	9	10	3	5	7^1			13		11			14	6	12										10
1	3		4					9	10^1		5	7			8		11^3	13		2	6	12^2		14								11
1	3		4		6			9	10		5	7^2			8^3	12	11^1	13		2				14								12
1	3		4					9			5	7				12	11^2	10^1		2	6	13		8								13
1	3		4					9			5	7^3			10^2	12	11^1	14		2	6	13		8								14
1	3		4	12	6			9	13		8	7				10^2	11^3	14		2	5^1											15
1	3		4	5	6			9	12			7			8	10^1		13		2					11^2							16
1	3		4	5	6			9	10^1			7			8	12				2					11							17
1	3		4	12	6		8^2	9	10^1	14		7			13					2	5				11^3							18
1	3		4		6		8^2	9^1	10^3			7			13	12		14		2	5				11							19
1	3^2		4	12	6		8	9	10^3	13		7				14				2	5^1				11							20
1^1			4		6		12	13		3	5^3	7			8	9^2	11	10		2	14											21
			4		6		8	9	10^1	3		7^3				12	13	14		2	5				11^2	1						22
	3		4				12	9				7			8	13				2	5				11^1	1	6	10^2				23
1	3^3		4	12				9		7		14■			8	13				2	5^1				11		6	10^2				24
1	2		4				8	9		3					6			7							11		5	10				25
1	2		4				8	9		7					6					3					11		5	10				26
1	2		4	12			8	9^1		3					6			7^2							11		5	10	13			27
1	2		4		12		8	9		3					6			13		7^2					11^3		5^1	14	10			28
1	2		4		6^1			9		3						13	12	7			5				11			10^2	8			29
1	2		4		6		12	9^2		3		7			8	13	11^1	10			5											30
1			4	3			11				5	7^2			8	9^1		10									6	12		2	13	31
1			4	2			12		13	3	5^1	7			8	14		10							11^3		6	9^2				32
1	2		4		12		11		13	3		7			6	10^3	14	8^2			5^1							9				33
1	2		4		6		11		9	12		13			7	14		10^2		3^1										5	8^3	34
1	2^1		4		6		11			3	12	7			8			13										9		5	10^2	35
1	2		4		6		11			3		7^2			8	10^1		12			13							9		5		36
1	2		4		6		11		12	3^3	13	7			8^2			10										9^1		5	14	37
1	2		4		5		8		12			7			6^3	10^1		13			14				11^2			9		3		38

FA Cup
Third Round Swansea C (h) 0-3

Carling Cup
Second Round Bury (h) 1-0
Third Round Birmingham C (h) 2-4

SHEFFIELD WEDNESDAY FL Championship

FOUNDATION

Sheffield being one of the principal centres of early Association Football, this club was formed as long ago as 1867 by the Sheffield Wednesday Cricket Club (formed 1825) and their colours from the start were blue and white. The inaugural meeting was held at the Adelphi Hotel and the original committee included Charles Stokes who was subsequently a founder member of Sheffield United.

Hillsborough, Sheffield S6 1SW.

Telephone: 0870 999 1867.

Fax: (0114) 221 2122.

Ticket Office: 0870 230 1867.

Website: www.swfc.co.uk

Email: enquiries@swfc.co.uk

Ground Capacity: 39,812.

Record Attendance: 72,841 v Manchester C, FA Cup 5th rd, 17 February 1934.

Pitch Measurements: 116yd × 71yd.

Chairman: Dave E. D. Allen.

Chief Executive: Kaven B. Walker

Company Secretary: Paul D. Johnson.

Manager: Brian Laws.

Assistant Manager: Russ Wilcox.

Physio: M. Palmer.

Colours: Blue and white stripes.

Change Colours: Orange.

Year Formed: 1867 (fifth oldest League club).

Turned Professional: 1887.

Ltd Co.: 1899.

Former Names: The Wednesday until 1929.

Club Nickname: 'The Owls'.

Grounds: 1867, Highfield; 1869, Myrtle Road; 1877, Sheaf House; 1887, Olive Grove; 1899, Owlerton (since 1912 known as Hillsborough). Some games were played at Endcliffe in the 1880s. Until 1895 Bramall Lane was used for some games.

First Football League Game: 3 September 1892, Division 1, v Notts Co (a) W 1–0 – Allan; Tom Brandon (1), Mumford; Hall, Betts, Harry Brandon; Spiksley, Brady, Davis, R. N. Brown, Dunlop.

Record League Victory: 9–1 v Birmingham, Division 1, 13 December 1930 – Brown; Walker, Blenkinsop; Strange, Leach, Wilson; Hooper (3), Seed (2), Ball (2), Burgess (1), Rimmer (1).

HONOURS

Football League: Division 1 – Champions 1902–03, 1903–04, 1928–29, 1929–30; Runners-up 1960–61; Promotion from Championship 1 2004–05 (play-offs); Division 2 – Champions 1899–1900, 1925–26, 1951–52, 1955–56, 1958–59; Runners-up 1949–50, 1983–84.

FA Cup: Winners 1896, 1907, 1935; Runners-up 1890, 1966, 1993.

Football League Cup: Winners 1991; Runners-up 1993.

European Competitions: *European Fairs Cup:* 1961–62, 1963–64. *UEFA Cup:* 1992–93. *Intertoto Cup:* 1995.

SKY SPORTS FACT FILE

In nine successive seasons from 1887–88 to 1895–96 inclusive Sheffield Wednesday reached the last eight of the FA Cup each time. In 1889–90 they became the first non-league club to reach the final as they were still members of the Football Alliance.

Record Cup Victory: 12–0 v Halliwell, FA Cup 1st rd, 17 January 1891 – Smith; Thompson, Brayshaw; Harry Brandon (1), Betts, Cawley (2); Winterbottom, Mumford (2), Bob Brandon (1), Woolhouse (5), Ingram (1).

Record Defeat: 0–10 v Aston Villa, Division 1, 5 October 1912.

Most League Points (2 for a win): 62, Division 2, 1958–59.

Most League Points (3 for a win): 88, Division 2, 1983–84.

Most League Goals: 106, Division 2, 1958–59.

Highest League Scorer in Season: Derek Dooley, 46, Division 2, 1951–52.

Most League Goals in Total Aggregate: Andrew Wilson, 199, 1900–20.

Most League Goals in One Match: 6, Doug Hunt v Norwich C, Division 2, 19 November 1938.

Most Capped Player: Nigel Worthington, 50 (66), Northern Ireland.

Most League Appearances: Andrew Wilson, 501, 1900–20.

Youngest League Player: Peter Fox, 15 years 269 days v Orient, 31 March 1973.

Record Transfer Fee Received: £2,750,000 from Blackburn R for Paul Warhurst, September 1993.

Record Transfer Fee Paid: £4,500,000 to Celtic for Paolo Di Canio, August 1997.

Football League Record: 1892 Elected to Division 1; 1899–1900 Division 2; 1900–20 Division 1; 1920–26 Division 2; 1926–37 Division 1; 1937–50 Division 2; 1950–51 Division 1; 1951–52 Division 2; 1952–55 Division 1; 1955–56 Division 2; 1956–58 Division 1; 1958–59 Division 2; 1959–70 Division 1; 1970–75 Division 2; 1975–80 Division 3; 1980–84 Division 2; 1984–90 Division 1; 1990–91 Division 2; 1991–92 Division 1; 1992–2000 FA Premier League; 2000–03 Division 1; 2003–04 Division 2; 2004–05 FL 1; 2005– FL C.

MANAGERS

Arthur Dickinson 1891–1920 *(Secretary-Manager)*
Robert Brown 1920–33
Billy Walker 1933–37
Jimmy McMullan 1937–42
Eric Taylor 1942–58 *(continued as General Manager to 1974)*
Harry Catterick 1958–61
Vic Buckingham 1961–64
Alan Brown 1964–68
Jack Marshall 1968–69
Danny Williams 1969–71
Derek Dooley 1971–73
Steve Burtenshaw 1974–75
Len Ashurst 1975–77
Jackie Charlton 1977–83
Howard Wilkinson 1983–88
Peter Eustace 1988–89
Ron Atkinson 1989–91
Trevor Francis 1991–95
David Pleat 1995–97
Ron Atkinson 1997–98
Danny Wilson 1998–2000
Peter Shreeves (Acting) 2000
Paul Jewell 2000–01
Peter Shreeves 2001
Terry Yorath 2001–02
Chris Turner 2002–04
Paul Sturrock 2004–06
Brian Laws November 2006–

LATEST SEQUENCES

Longest Sequence of League Wins: 9, 23.4.1904 – 15.10.1904.

Longest Sequence of League Defeats: 8, 9.9.2000 – 17.10.2000.

Longest Sequence of League Draws: 5, 24.10.1992 – 28.11.1992.

Longest Sequence of Unbeaten League Matches: 19, 10.12.1960 – 8.4.1961.

Longest Sequence Without a League Win: 20, 11.1.1975 – 30.8.1975.

Successive Scoring Runs: 40 from 14.11.1959.

Successive Non-scoring Runs: 8 from 8.3.1975.

TEN YEAR LEAGUE RECORD

		P	*W*	*D*	*L*	*F*	*A*	*Pts*	*Pos*
1997-98	PR Lge	38	12	8	18	52	67	44	16
1998-99	PR Lge	38	13	7	18	41	42	46	12
1999-2000	PR Lge	38	8	7	23	38	70	31	19
2000-01	Div 1	46	15	8	23	52	71	53	17
2001-02	Div 1	46	12	14	20	49	71	50	20
2002-03	Div 1	46	10	16	20	56	73	46	22
2003-04	Div 2	46	13	14	19	48	64	53	16
2004-05	FL 1	46	19	15	12	77	59	72	5
2005-06	FL C	46	13	13	20	39	52	52	19
2006-07	FL C	46	20	11	15	70	66	71	9

DID YOU KNOW ?

Versatile Harry Brandon was signed prior to his debut in the first Sheffield Wednesday v Sheffield United match on 15 December 1890. He played for the Football Alliance v Football League and his cousins, the brothers Tom, Jim and Bob were also Owls.

SHEFFIELD WEDNESDAY 2006–07 LEAGUE RECORD

Match No.	*Date*	*Venue*	*Opponents*	*Result*		*H/T Score*	*Lg. Pos.*	*Goalscorers*	*Attendance*
1	Aug 5	A	Preston NE	D	0-0	0-0	—		15,650
2	8	H	Luton T	L	0-1	0-1	—		22,613
3	12	H	Burnley	D	1-1	0-0	20	MacLean (pen) [67]	22,425
4	19	A	Plymouth Arg	W	2-1	0-1	16	McAllister [52], O'Brien [83]	14,507
5	27	H	Leeds U	L	0-1	0-0	18		23,792
6	Sept 9	A	Southend U	D	0-0	0-0	19		9639
7	12	H	Stoke C	D	1-1	1-1	—	Brunt (pen) [40]	19,966
8	15	A	Hull C	L	1-2	1-2	—	Burton (pen) [4]	17,685
9	23	H	Derby Co	L	1-2	0-0	23	Brunt [62]	23,659
10	30	A	Sunderland	L	0-1	0-0	24		36,764
11	Oct 14	H	Barnsley	W	2-1	1-0	21	Whelan [4], Brunt [90]	28,687
12	18	A	Colchester U	L	0-4	0-1	—		5097
13	21	H	QPR	W	3-2	2-0	20	Tudgay 2 [13, 45], MacLean (pen) [70]	23,813
14	28	A	Wolverhampton W	D	2-2	1-1	20	Small [36], Brunt [53]	20,637
15	31	H	Crystal Palace	W	3-2	1-1	—	Tudgay [45], Coughlan [73], MacLean [90]	19,034
16	Nov 4	H	Leicester C	W	2-1	1-0	16	Tudgay 2 [34, 55]	22,451
17	11	A	Ipswich T	W	2-0	1-0	13	Tudgay [11], Bougherra [82]	21,830
18	18	A	Coventry C	L	1-3	1-1	17	Brunt [22]	19,489
19	25	H	Cardiff C	D	0-0	0-0	17		23,935
20	28	H	WBA	W	3-1	2-0	—	Whelan [11], Bougherra [15], MacLean (pen) [90]	21,695
21	Dec 2	A	Leicester C	W	4-1	1-0	13	Brunt 2 (1 pen) [43 (p), 53], Whelan [70], Tudgay [72]	22,693
22	9	A	Norwich C	W	2-1	0-0	12	Camp (og) [80], Burton [83]	24,816
23	16	H	Birmingham C	L	0-3	0-1	13		26,083
24	23	H	Southampton	D	3-3	1-2	13	Whelan 2 [28, 69], Crossley [90]	23,739
25	26	A	Stoke C	W	2-1	1-0	12	MacLean [35], Burton [79]	23,003
26	30	A	Barnsley	W	3-0	1-0	9	Andrews [11], Brunt [60], MacLean [68]	21,253
27	Jan 1	H	Hull C	L	1-2	0-1	11	Burton [53]	28,600
28	13	A	Derby Co	L	0-1	0-0	11		28,936
29	20	H	Sunderland	L	2-4	0-2	11	Brunt [82], Small [87]	29,103
30	31	A	Southampton	L	1-2	0-1	—	MacLean [52]	20,230
31	Feb 3	H	Preston NE	L	1-3	1-2	13	Burton [4]	22,441
32	10	A	Burnley	D	1-1	0-0	13	Burton [58]	12,745
33	20	A	Luton T	L	2-3	1-1	—	Burton [25], Whelan [60]	8011
34	24	H	Southend U	W	3-2	2-1	14	Tudgay [16], Prior (og) [29], MacLean (pen) [90]	24,116
35	Mar 3	A	Leeds U	W	3-2	2-0	13	Tudgay [7], Brunt [37], Johnson [54]	25,297
36	6	H	Plymouth Arg	D	1-1	1-0	—	MacLean [21]	19,449
37	10	A	QPR	D	1-1	0-0	13	Brunt [56]	15,188
38	13	H	Colchester U	W	2-0	2-0	—	Simek [27], Mills (og) [35]	18,752
39	17	H	Wolverhampton W	D	2-2	1-1	12	Burton [22], MacLean [47]	24,181
40	31	A	Crystal Palace	W	2-1	0-0	11	Burton [57], Tudgay [85]	21,523
41	Apr 7	A	Cardiff C	W	2-1	1-1	11	Clarke [39], Burton [67]	13,621
42	9	H	Ipswich T	W	2-0	0-0	11	Whelan [47], MacLean [59]	23,232
43	13	A	WBA	W	1-0	0-0	—	Burton [59]	20,415
44	21	H	Coventry C	W	2-1	1-1	10	Tudgay [17], MacLean [70]	23,632
45	28	A	Birmingham C	L	0-2	0-0	10		29,317
46	May 6	H	Norwich C	W	3-2	2-0	9	Johnson [26], Burton [45], Etuhu (og) [50]	28,287

Final League Position: 9

GOALSCORERS

League (70): Burton 12 (1 pen), MacLean 12 (4 pens), Brunt 11 (2 pens), Tudgay 11, Whelan 7, Bougherra 2, Johnson 2, Small 2, Andrews 1, Clarke 1, Coughlan 1, Crossley 1, McAllister 1, O'Brien 1, Simek 1, own goals 4.
Carling Cup (1): Whelan 1.
FA Cup (2): Bullen 1, MacLean 1.

Jones B 15	Simek F 41	Hills J 15 + 1	Whelan G 35 + 3	Coughlan G 14 + 4	Bougherra M 28	Folly Y 20 + 9	O'Brien B 13 + 9	MacLean S 20 + 21	Brunt C 42 + 2	Bullen L 33 + 5	Small W 13 + 7	McAllister S — + 6	Spurr T 31 + 5	Lunt K 30 + 7	McArdle R — + 1	Boden L — + 1	Adamson C 3 + 1	Burton D 35 + 7	Sam L 4	Adams S 2 + 1	Tudgay M 37 + 3	Talbot D 2 + 6	Corr B — + 1	Crossley M 17	Andrews W 7 + 2	Graham D — + 4	Clarke L 3 + 7	Beevers M 2	Watson S 11	Johnson J 5 + 2	Turner I 11	Wood R 12	Gilbert P 5 + 1	Lekaj R — + 2	Match No.
1	2	3	4	5	6	7	8	9^{1}	10^{2}	11■	12	13																								1
1	2	3	4	5	6	7^{2}	8^{1}	9	10		14	13	12	11^{3}																						2
1	2	3	4	5	6		8	9^{1}	10		13	12	7	11^{2}																						3
1	2	3	4	5^{2}	6		8		10		9^{1}	12	11	7^{3}	13	14																				4
1■	2	3^{6}	4	5	6		8		11^{1}	13			7	12			15	10	9^{2}																5
1	2		4	5	6		8		12	13			11	14				10	7^{1}	3^{2}	9^{3}														6
1	2		4^{1}	5	6		8		11	13		14	3	12				10	7^{3}		9^{2}														7
1	2		4	5	6		8		12	13			3^{1}	14				10	7^{2}	11^{3}	9														8
	2		4	5	6		8	12	11				3	7^{2}			1	10^{1}			9^{3}	13	14												9
1	2			5	6	7^{2}	4	12	11		14		3					10^{3}		13	9	8^{1}													10
1	2	3	4^{1}		6	7	12	9^{2}	11		8		5					13			14	10^{3}													11
1	2	3		5	6	7	11	9^{2}		4^{1}	8			12				13			10^{3}	14													12
1	2	3			6	7		12	11		8		5	4				10^{1}			9^{2}	13													13
1	2	3	12		6	7		13	11		8^{1}		5	4				10^{2}			9^{3}	14													14
1	2	3		5^{2}	6	7		12	11	13	8			4				10^{1}			9														15
1	2	3			6	7		12	11	5	8^{2}			4				10			9^{1}	13													16
	2	3	12		6	7	13	14	11^{2}	5	8^{1}			4				10^{3}			9			1											17
	2^{1}	3		12	6	7	13	14	11■	5	8■			4				10^{2}			9^{3}			1											18
	2	3	12	13	6^{2}	7	8	14		5				4				10^{3}			9			1	11^{1}										19
	2	3^{3}	4		6		12	13	11	5			14	7				10^{2}			9			1	8^{1}										20
	2		4	12	6^{1}	7	13	14	11	5			3^{2}					10^{3}			9			1	8										21
	2^{1}		4	12	6	13		14	11	5			3	7^{2}				10			9			1	8^{3}										22
	2				6	7^{1}	12	13	11	5			3	4				10^{3}			9	14		1	8^{2}										23
	2		4		6	7^{2}		12	11	5			3	8				10^{1}			9			1	13										24
	2		4		6		12	9	11^{1}	5			3	8				13			10			1	7^{2}										25
	2		4		6	12	13	9^{1}	11^{2}	5			3	8				14			10			1	7^{3}										26
	2		4		6	7	12	13	11	5			3^{1}	8^{3}				10			9^{2}			1	14										27
	2		4		6			9^{2}	11^{1}	5	12		3	7				10			8			1		13									28
			4	5^{2}		7	8^{3}	9^{1}	11	2	3	13		6				12			10			1			14								29
	2		4			7		9^{1}	11	5	8^{2}		3					12			10			1			13	6							30
	2		4			12		13	11	5	8^{2}		3	7^{1}				10			9^{3}			1			14	6							31
	6					7		9^{1}	11	5	8^{2}		3	4				10			12			1			13		2						32
	2		4			12		9^{2}	11	5			3	7^{1}				10			13			1		14			6	8^{3}					33
	2		4	6				12	11^{2}	5			3					10^{1}			9						13		7	8	1				34
	2		4					12	11	5	13		3					10^{1}			9■								7	8^{2}	1	6			35
	2		4					9	11	5	12		3					10^{2}								13			7	8^{1}	1	6			36
	2		4					9^{2}	11	5			3	12				10			8					13			7^{1}		1	6			37
	2		4^{1}			12		9^{3}	11	5			13	7				10			8										1	6	3^{2}	14	38
	2■		4					9^{1}	11	5			13	12				10			8								7		1	6	3^{2}		39
			4			12		9	11^{2}	5			13	7				10^{1}			8								2		1	6	3		40
			4			12		13	11	5				7^{1}				10^{2}			8						9^{3}		2		1	6	3	14	41
			4			12		9	11	5			3	7^{1}				13			8						10^{2}		2		1	6			42
	2^{1}	12	4^{2}			13		9^{3}	11	5			3	7				10			8						14				1	6			43
	2		4					12	11	5			3					10^{3}			8^{2}						9^{1}		7	13	1	6	14		44
	2^{1}		4					9	11	5			3	7^{2}			1	10			8						12			13		6			45
			4			2		12	11	5				7			1	10			9									8^{1}		6	3		46

FA Cup
Third Round Manchester C (h) 1-1
(a) 1-2

Carling Cup
First Round Wrexham (h) 1-4

SHREWSBURY TOWN FL Championship 2

FOUNDATION

Shrewsbury School having provided a number of the early England and Wales international players it is not surprising that there was a Town club as early as 1876 which won the Birmingham Senior Cup in 1879. However, the present Shrewsbury Town club was formed in 1886 and won the Welsh FA Cup as early as 1891.

New Meadow Stadium, Oteley Road, Shrewsbury, Shropshire SY2 6ST.

Telephone: (01743) 360 111.

Fax: (01743) 236 384.

Ticket Office: (01743) 360 111.

Website: www.shrewsburytown.com

Email: info@shrewsburytown.co.uk

Ground Capacity: 10,000.

Record Attendance: 18,917 v Walsall, Division 3, 26 April 1961.

Pitch Measurements: 114yd × 73yd.

Chairman: Roland Wycherley.

Vice-chairman: Keith Sayfritz.

Chief Executive: Steve Wellbeloved.

Secretary: John Howarth.

Manager: Gary Peters.

First Team Coach: John McMahon.

Physio: Joe Hinnigan MCSP.

Colours: Blue and amber.

Change Colours: Red and blue.

Year Formed: 1886.

Turned Professional: 1896.

Ltd Co.: 1936.

Club Nickname: 'Town', 'Blues' or 'Salop'. The name 'Salop' is a colloquialism for the county of Shropshire. Since Shrewsbury is the only club in Shropshire, cries of 'Come on Salop' are frequently used!

Grounds: 1886, Old Shrewsbury Racecourse; 1910, Gay Meadow; 2007, New Meadow Stadium.

First Football League Game: 19 August 1950, Division 3 (N), v Scunthorpe U (a) D 0–0 – Egglestone; Fisher, Lewis; Wheatley, Depear, Robinson; Griffin, Hope, Jackson, Brown, Barker.

Record League Victory: 7–0 v Swindon T, Division 3 (S), 6 May 1955 – McBride; Bannister, Skeech; Wallace, Maloney, Candlin; Price, O'Donnell (1), Weigh (4), Russell, McCue (2).

HONOURS

Football League: Division 2 best season: 8th, 1983–84, 1984–85; Division 3 – Champions 1978–79, 1993–94; Division 4 – Runners-up 1974–75.

Conference: Promotion 2003–04 (play-offs)

FA Cup: best season: 6th rd, 1979, 1982.

Football League Cup: Semi-final 1961.

Welsh Cup: Winners 1891, 1938, 1977, 1979, 1984, 1985; Runners-up 1931, 1948, 1980.

Auto Windscreens Shield: Runners-up 1996.

SKY SPORTS FACT FILE

Gay Meadow was something of an FA Cup fortress for Shrewsbury Town from 1955–56 to 1968–69 inclusive. During this period they had 21 home ties, winning 12 of them and drawing the other nine. Even Arsenal needed a Highbury replay before progressing.

Record Cup Victory: 11–2 v Marine, FA Cup 1st rd, 11 November 1995 – Edwards, Seabury (Dempsey (1)), Withe (1), Evans (1), Whiston (2), Scott (1), Woods, Stevens (1), Spink (3) (Anthrobus), Walton, Berkley, (1 og).

Record Defeat: 1–8 v Norwich C, Division 3 (S), 13 September 1952. 1–8 v Coventry C, Division 3, 22 October 1963.

Most League Points (2 for a win): 62, Division 4, 1974–75.

Most League Points (3 for a win): 79, Division 3, 1993–94.

Most League Goals: 101, Division 4, 1958–59.

Highest League Scorer in Season: Arthur Rowley, 38, Division 4, 1958–59.

Most League Goals in Total Aggregate: Arthur Rowley, 152, 1958–65 (thus completing his League record of 434 goals).

Most League Goals in One Match: 5, Alf Wood v Blackburn R, Division 3, 2 October 1971.

Most Capped Player: Jimmy McLaughlin, 5 (12), Northern Ireland; Bernard McNally, 5, Northern Ireland.

Most League Appearances: Mickey Brown, 418, 1986–91; 1992–94; 1996–2001.

Youngest League Player: Graham French, 16 years 177 days v Reading, 30 September 1961.

Record Transfer Fee Received: £600,000 from Manchester C for Joe Hart, May 2006.

Record Transfer Fee Paid: £100,000 to Aldershot for John Dungworth, November 1979 and £100,000 to Southampton for Mark Blake, August 1990.

Football League Record: 1950 Elected to Division 3 (N); 1951–58 Division 3 (S); 1958–59 Division 4; 1959–74 Division 3; 1974–75 Division 4; 1975–79 Division 3; 1979–89 Division 2; 1989–94 Division 3; 1994–97 Division 2; 1997–2003 Division 3; 2003–04 Conference; 2004– FL 2.

MANAGERS

W. Adams 1905–12
(Secretary-Manager)
A. Weston 1912–34
(Secretary-Manager)
Jack Roscamp 1934–35
Sam Ramsey 1935–36
Ted Bousted 1936–40
Leslie Knighton 1945–49
Harry Chapman 1949–50
Sammy Crooks 1950–54
Walter Rowley 1955–57
Harry Potts 1957–58
Johnny Spuhler 1958
Arthur Rowley 1958–68
Harry Gregg 1968–72
Maurice Evans 1972–73
Alan Durban 1974–78
Richie Barker 1978
Graham Turner 1978–84
Chic Bates 1984–87
Ian McNeill 1987–90
Asa Hartford 1990–91
John Bond 1991–93
Fred Davies 1994–97
(previously Caretaker-Manager 1993–94)
Jake King 1997–99
Kevin Ratcliffe 1999–2003
Jimmy Quinn 2003–04
Gary Peters November 2004–

LATEST SEQUENCES

Longest Sequence of League Wins: 7, 28.10.1995 – 16.12.1995.

Longest Sequence of League Defeats: 11, 9.4.2003 – 14.8.2004.

Longest Sequence of League Draws: 6, 30.10.1963 – 14.12.1963.

Longest Sequence of Unbeaten League Matches: 16, 30.10.1993 – 26.2.1994.

Longest Sequence Without a League Win: 18, 8.3.2003 – 14.8.2004.

Successive Scoring Runs: 28 from 7.9.1960.

Successive Non-scoring Runs: 6 from 1.1.1991.

TEN YEAR LEAGUE RECORD

		P	*W*	*D*	*L*	*F*	*A*	*Pts*	*Pos*
1997-98	Div 3	46	16	13	17	61	62	61	13
1998-99	Div 3	46	14	14	18	52	63	56	15
1999-2000	Div 3	46	9	13	24	40	67	40	22
2000-01	Div 3	46	15	10	21	49	65	55	15
2001-02	Div 3	46	20	10	16	64	53	70	9
2002-03	Div 3	46	9	14	23	62	92	41	24
2003-04	Conf.	42	20	14	8	67	42	74	3
2004-05	FL 2	46	11	16	19	48	53	49	21
2005-06	FL 2	46	16	13	17	55	55	61	10
2006-07	FL 2	46	18	17	11	68	46	71	7

DID YOU KNOW ?

In 1933–34 Joe Taylor scored 68 goals in all first team competitions for Shrewsbury Town. His haul included two double hat-tricks, a four and three trebles. It launched him onto a Football League career with four different clubs.

SHREWSBURY TOWN 2006–07 LEAGUE RECORD

Match No.	*Date*	*Venue*	*Opponents*	*Result*	*H/T Score*	*Lg. Pos.*	*Goalscorers*	*Attendance*
1	Aug 5	H	Mansfield T	D 2-2	2-2	—	Drummond [22], Edwards [31]	5066
2	8	A	Notts Co	D 1-1	0-0	—	Davies [46]	4386
3	12	A	Bury	W 2-1	0-1	12	Langmead [67], Davies (pen) [78]	2329
4	19	H	Boston U	W 5-0	2-0	5	Davies (pen) [27], Asamoah 2 [42, 67], Symes [83], Edwards [90]	3502
5	26	A	Bristol R	L 0-1	0-1	10		4774
6	Sept 9	H	Lincoln C	L 0-1	0-1	13		4083
7	12	A	Stockport Co	W 3-0	1-0	—	Cooke 3 [44, 57, 78]	4089
8	16	A	Hartlepool U	W 3-0	1-0	8	Daly (og) [11], Drummond [77], Symes [81]	4291
9	23	H	Darlington	D 2-2	0-1	8	Symes [64], Davies (pen) [85]	3931
10	26	H	Walsall	D 1-1	1-1	—	Sorvel [28]	6593
11	30	A	Rochdale	D 1-1	0-1	9	Cooke [62]	2942
12	Oct 6	H	Macclesfield T	W 2-1	1-0	—	Herd [1], Langmead [90]	4816
13	14	A	Peterborough U	L 1-2	0-1	8	Davies (pen) [83]	4171
14	21	H	Swindon T	L 1-2	0-1	8	Davies [68]	5218
15	28	A	Torquay U	D 0-0	0-0	9		2262
16	Nov 4	H	Wycombe W	D 0-0	0-0	12		4116
17	18	A	Milton Keynes D	L 0-2	0-1	14		5830
18	25	H	Chester C	W 2-1	0-1	14	Davies [50], Symes (pen) [90]	4464
19	Dec 2	A	Accrington S	D 3-3	2-1	—	Asamoah (pen) [4], Fortune-West [40], Symes [84]	1602
20	9	A	Grimsby T	L 1-2	0-1	15	Symes [53]	4076
21	16	H	Hereford U	W 3-0	1-0	12	Cooke 2 [35, 66], Edwards [78]	4177
22	22	H	Barnet	L 0-1	0-0	—		3620
23	26	A	Walsall	L 0-1	0-0	16		8345
24	30	A	Darlington	W 2-1	1-0	14	Symes [45], Edwards [87]	2825
25	Jan 1	H	Stockport Co	W 4-2	2-0	10	Davies [4], Cooke 3 [21, 48, 90]	4569
26	6	H	Hartlepool U	D 1-1	0-1	9	Symes [78]	4334
27	13	A	Lincoln C	D 1-1	0-1	11	Jones M [63]	4811
28	Feb 3	A	Mansfield T	D 1-1	1-0	15	Asamoah [13]	3250
29	17	A	Boston U	W 3-0	2-0	14	Burton [5], Cooke [45], Davies [66]	1571
30	20	H	Notts Co	W 2-0	2-0	—	Asamoah [32], Fortune-West [45]	3369
31	25	A	Wrexham	W 3-1	2-0	10	Fortune-West 2 [8, 51], Asamoah [38]	5605
32	Mar 2	H	Bristol R	D 0-0	0-0	—		4227
33	10	A	Macclesfield T	D 2-2	0-1	10	Swailes (og) [63], Fortune-West [73]	2928
34	16	H	Peterborough U	W 2-1	0-1	—	Davies [61], Asamoah [81]	4027
35	20	A	Barnet	D 0-0	0-0	—		1672
36	24	H	Torquay U	W 1-0	0-0	9	Asamoah [77]	4678
37	27	H	Rochdale	W 3-0	0-0	—	Fortune-West [48], Edwards [65], Drummond [78]	4363
38	31	A	Swindon T	L 1-2	1-0	8	Fortune-West [40]	7335
39	Apr 3	H	Bury	L 1-3	1-1	—	Asamoah [45]	4419
40	7	A	Wycombe W	D 1-1	1-1	8	Symes [37]	5299
41	9	H	Milton Keynes D	W 2-1	0-1	7	Asamoah [53], Ashton [75]	5238
42	15	A	Chester C	D 0-0	0-0	7		3266
43	21	H	Accrington S	W 2-1	1-1	6	Ashton [33], Davies [62]	5438
44	24	H	Wrexham	L 0-1	0-0	—		6749
45	28	A	Hereford U	W 1-0	1-0	6	Drummond [45]	4359
46	May 5	H	Grimsby T	D 2-2	0-1	7	Davies (pen) [63], Langmead [74]	7782

Final League Position: 7

GOALSCORERS

League (68): Davies 12 (5 pens), Asamoah 10 (1 pen), Cooke 10, Symes 9 (1 pen), Fortune-West 7, Edwards 5, Drummond 4, Langmead 3, Ashton 2, Burton 1, Herd 1, Jones M 1, Sorvel 1, own goals 2.
Carling Cup (0).
FA Cup (0).
J Paint Trophy (7): Symes 4, Asamoah 1, Edwards 1, own goal 1.
Play-Offs (3): Cooke 2, Drummond 1.

Esson R 6	Hall D 21 + 6	Ashton N 42 + 1	Drummond S 43 + 1	Hope R 33	Burton S 26 + 2	Davies B 43	Edwards D 39 + 6	Langmead K 45	Herd B 29 + 2	Sorvel N 15 + 3	Williams D — + 2	Symes M 20 + 13	Asamoah D 34 + 5	Leslie S 1 + 4	Cooke A 21 + 13	Humphrey C — + 12	MacKenzie C 20	Hogg S — + 1	Cowan G 3 + 1	Shearer S 20	Keith J 1	Fortune-West L 10 + 9	Jones L 4 + 3	Thomas D 3 + 3	Canoville L 6 + 1	Jones M 3 + 10	Tierney M 18	*Match No.*
1	2	3	4	5	6	7	8^1	9^2	10^3	11	12	13	14															1
1	12	3	4^1	5	6	7	8	9	2	11			10															2
1	2^1	3		5	6	7	8	9	4	11	12		10															3
1	4^2	3		5	6	7	8	9	2	11		12	10^1	13														4
1	4	3^2	12	5	6^1	7	8	9^3	2	11			10	13	14													5
1	5	3	4		6^1	7	12	9	2^2	11			10		8	13												6
	2	3	4	5		7	12	9	6	11			10		8^1		1											7
	6	3	4	5		7	12	9	2	11		13	10^1		8^2		1											8
	2^1	3	4	5		7	12	6	8	11^2		9	10			13	1											9
		3	4	5	2	7	8	6		11		9^1	10		12		1											10
		3	4	5	2	7	8^2	6		11		9^1	10		12	13	1											11
		3	4	5	2		8	6	7^2	11		12		10^1	9	13	1											12
		3	4	5	2	11	12	6	7^1	8^2		13	10	14	9^3		1											13
	2		4	5^1	3	7	8	6		11^3		10	13		9^2		1	14	12									14
	2	3^1	4		5	7	8	9	12			10^2	13		11				6	1								15
		3	4^1			7	8	5	2	12		9	10		13				6	1	11^2							16
		3	4		5	7	8	9^1	2	11			12		10^2				6	1		13						17
	5^1	3	4		6	7	8	11	2			9	10			12				1								18
	7	3	4	5			8	6	2			12	10			13				1		9^1	11^2					19
	11	3	4	5		7	8	6	2^1			9	10		12					1								20
		3	4	5		7	8	6	2			9	10^2		11^1					1			12	13				21
		3	4	5		7	8	6	2			9			10	12				1				11^1				22
		3	4	5^1	6	7	8	9	2^3	12		11			10^2					1		13		14				23
	11	3	4		5	7	8	6	2			9			10^1					1				12				24
	3		4	5	6	7	8		2	12		9			10^2	13				1				11^1				25
		3	4	5	6^1	7	8	11	2			9			10^2	13				1		12						26
	12	11	4	5	6^1	7	8	3	2			9			10^2					1						13		27
		3^2	4		5	7	8	6	12			9	10^3		13		1							11	2^1	14		28
		3	4		5	7	8	6	2				10^2		9^1		1					12				13	11	29
			4	5	6	7	8	11	2				10^2			12	1					9^1				13	3	30
	12	13	4	5^3	6	7	8	2	3				10^1				1					9				14	11^2	31
		6	4		2	7	8	11	5			12	10				1					9^1					3	32
	12	11	4		5^1	7	8^3	6				9	10^2				1					13			2	14	3	33
	5	11	4			7	12	6	2				10^2		14	13	1					9^3				8^1	3	34
	5	11	4		12	7		6	2^1				10		14	13	1					9^3				8^2	3	35
	2	11	4	5		7	8	6					12		10^1		1					9^2				13	3	36
	2	11	4^2	5		7	8	6				12	10^1		14		1					9^3				13	3	37
	2	11	4	5		7	8^3	6				12	10^1		13		1					9^2				14	3	38
	2^3	11^2	4		5	7	8	6				12	10		13		1					9^1			14		3	39
		11	4	5		7	8	6				9^1	10		12					1					2		3	40
		11	4	5		7^3	8	6				9^1	10							1		12	13		2^2	14	3	41
	12	11	4	5			8^1	6				9^3	10		13					1		14			2	7^2	3	42
	12	11	4	5^3		7	8	6				13	10		9^2					1			14		2^1		3	43
		11	4	5^2		7	8	6				12	10		9^1					1		13	2				3	44
		11	4	5		7	8^2	6				12	10^1	13	9					1			2				3	45
		11	4	5^2	12	7	8	6					10^1		9					1		13	2				3	46

FA Cup

First Round	Hereford U	(h)	0-0
		(a)	0-2

Play-Offs

Semi-Final	Milton Keynes D	(h)	0-0
		(a)	2-1
Final *(at Wembley)*	Bristol R		1-3

Carling Cup

First Round	Birmingham C	(a)	0-1

J Paint Trophy

First Round	Hereford U	(a)	2-1
Second Round	Yeovil T	(h)	2-1
Quarter-Final	Cheltenham T	(a)	3-2
Semi-Final	Bristol R	(h)	0-1

SOUTHAMPTON FL Championship

FOUNDATION

The club was formed by members of the St Mary's Church of England Young Men's Association at a meeting of the Y.M.A. in November 1885 and it was named as such. For the sake of brevity this was usually shortened to St Mary's Y.M.A. The rector Canon Albert Basil Orme Wilberforce was elected president. The name was changed to plain St Mary's during 1887–88 and did not become Southampton St Mary's until 1894, the inaugural season in the Southern League

St Mary's Stadium, Britannia Road, Southampton SO14 5FP.

Telephone: 0845 688 9448.

Fax: 0845 688 9445.

Ticket Office: 0800 2800 050 (sales), 0845 688 9288 (info).

Website: www.saintsfc.co.uk

Email: sfc@saintsfc.co.uk

Ground Capacity: 32,689.

Record Attendance: 32,104 v Liverpool, FA Premier League, 18 January 2003.

Pitch Measurements: 112yd × 72yd.

Chairman (PLC Board): Ken Dulieu.

Acting Chairman (Football Board): Leon Crouch.

Chief Executive: Jim Hone.

Secretary: Liz Coley.

Manager: George Burley.

Assistant Manager: Malcolm Webster.

Physio: Andy Barr.

Colours: Red and white striped shirts, black shorts, white with red stockings.

Change Colours: Yellow shirts, yellow shorts, yellow stockings.

Year Formed: 1885.

Turned Professional: 1894.

Ltd Co.: 1897.

Previous Name: 1885, St Mary's Young Men's Association; 1887–88, St Mary's; 1894–95 Southampton St Mary's; 1897, Southampton.

Club Nickname: 'The Saints'.

Grounds: 1885, 'The Common' (from 1887 also used the County Cricket Ground and Antelope Cricket Ground); 1889, Antelope Cricket Ground; 1896 The County Cricket Ground; 1898, The Dell; 2001, St Mary's.

First Football League Game: 28 August 1920, Division 3, v Gillingham (a) D 1–1 – Allen; Parker, Titmuss; Shelley, Campbell, Turner; Barratt, Dominy (1), Rawlings, Moore, Foxall.

HONOURS

Football League: Division 1 – Runners-up 1983–84; Division 2 – Runners-up 1965–66, 1977–78; Division 3 (S) – Champions 1921–22; Division 3 – Champions 1959–60: Runners-up 1920–21.

FA Cup: Winners 1976; Runners-up 1900, 1902, 2003.

Football League Cup: Runners-up 1979.

Zenith Data Systems Cup: Runners-up 1992.

European Competitions: *European Fairs Cup:* 1969–70. *UEFA Cup:* 1971–72, 1981–82, 1982–83, 1984–85, 2003–04. *European Cup-Winners' Cup:* 1976–77.

SKY SPORTS FACT FILE

Art Dominy, like many of his generation, lost crucial playing years in the First World War. Leading scorer for Southampton in 1914–15 with 30 Southern League goals, he resumed his career with them in League football and later variously scouted, became part-time team manager and leading figure in the Saints Supporters Club.

Record League Victory: 9–3 v Wolverhampton W, Division 2, 18 September 1965 – Godfrey; Jones, Williams; Walker, Knapp, Huxford; Paine (2), O'Brien (1), Melia, Chivers (4), Sydenham (2).

Record Cup Victory: 7–1 v Ipswich T, FA Cup 3rd rd, 7 January 1961 – Reynolds; Davies, Traynor; Conner, Page, Huxford; Paine (1), O'Brien (3 incl. 1p), Reeves, Mulgrew (2), Penk (1).

Record Defeat: 0–8 v Tottenham H, Division 2, 28 March 1936. 0–8 v Everton, Division 1, 20 November 1971.

Most League Points (2 for a win): 61, Division 3 (S), 1921–22 and Division 3, 1959–60.

Most League Points (3 for a win): 77, Division 1, 1983–84.

Most League Goals: 112, Division 3 (S), 1957–58.

Highest League Scorer in Season: Derek Reeves, 39, Division 3, 1959–60.

Most League Goals in Total Aggregate: Mike Channon, 185, 1966–77, 1979–82.

Most League Goals in One Match: 5, Charlie Wayman v Leicester C, Division 2, 23 October 1948.

Most Capped Player: Peter Shilton, 49 (125), England.

Most League Appearances: Terry Paine, 713, 1956–74.

Youngest League Player: Theo Walcott, 16 years 143 days v Wolverhampton W, 6 August 2005.

Record Transfer Fee Received: £8,000,000 from Tottenham H for Dean Richards, October 2001.

Record Transfer Fee Paid: £4,000,000 to Derby Co for Rory Delap, July 2001.

Football League Record: 1920 Original Member of Division 3; 1921–22 Division 3 (S); 1922–53 Division 2; 1953–58 Division 3 (S); 1958–60 Division 3; 1960–66 Division 2; 1966–74 Division 1; 1974–78 Division 2; 1978–92 Division 1; 1992–2005 FA Premier League; 2005– FL C.

MANAGERS

Cecil Knight 1894–95
(Secretary-Manager)
Charles Robson 1895–97
Er Arnfield 1897–1911
(Secretary-Manager)
(continued as Secretary)
George Swift 1911–12
Er Arnfield 1912–19
Jimmy McIntyre 1919–24
Arthur Chadwick 1925–31
George Kay 1931–36
George Gross 1936–37
Tom Parker 1937–43
J. R. Sarjantson stepped down from the board to act as Secretary-Manager 1943–47 with the next two listed being team Managers during this period
Arthur Dominy 1943–46
Bill Dodgin Snr 1946–49
Sid Cann 1949–51
George Roughton 1952–55
Ted Bates 1955–73
Lawrie McMenemy 1973–85
Chris Nicholl 1985–91
Ian Branfoot 1991–94
Alan Ball 1994–95
Dave Merrington 1995–96
Graeme Souness 1996–97
Dave Jones 1997–2000
Glenn Hoddle 2000–01
Stuart Gray 2001
Gordon Strachan 2001–04
Paul Sturrock 2004
Steve Wigley 2004
Harry Redknapp 2004–05
George Burley December 2005–

LATEST SEQUENCES

Longest Sequence of League Wins: 6, 3.3.1992 – 4.4.1992.

Longest Sequence of League Defeats: 5, 16.8.1998 – 12.9.1998.

Longest Sequence of League Draws: 8, 29.8.2005 – 15.10.2005.

Longest Sequence of Unbeaten League Matches: 19, 5.9.1921 – 31.12.1921.

Longest Sequence Without a League Win: 20, 30.8.1969 – 27.12.1969.

Successive Scoring Runs: 24 from 5.9.1966.

Successive Non-scoring Runs: 5 from 1.9.1937.

TEN YEAR LEAGUE RECORD

		P	W	D	L	F	A	Pts	Pos
1997-98	PR Lge	38	14	6	18	50	55	48	12
1998-99	PR Lge	38	11	8	19	37	64	41	17
1999-2000	PR Lge	38	12	8	18	45	62	44	15
2000-01	PR Lge	38	14	10	14	40	48	52	10
2001-02	PR Lge	38	12	9	17	46	54	45	11
2002-03	PR Lge	38	13	13	12	43	46	52	8
2003-04	PR Lge	38	12	11	15	44	45	47	12
2004-05	PR Lge	38	6	14	18	45	66	32	20
2005-06	FL C	46	13	19	14	49	50	58	12
2006-07	FL C	46	21	12	13	77	53	75	6

DID YOU KNOW ?

Versatile Charlie Sillett who joined Southampton in the 1930s had a background of Army service and non-league football. He had been middleweight boxing champion of the King's Royal Rifle Corps for three years but was killed on active service in 1945.

SOUTHAMPTON 2006–07 LEAGUE RECORD

Match No.	Date	Venue	Opponents	Result	H/T Score	Lg. Pos.	Goalscorers	Atten-dance
1	Aug 6	A	Derby Co	D 2-2	0-1	—	Bale [62], Wright-Phillips [68]	21,939
2	9	H	Coventry C	W 2-0	0-0	—	Bale [61], Rasiak (pen) [86]	21,088
3	12	H	WBA	D 0-0	0-0	9		24,233
4	19	A	Barnsley	D 2-2	0-1	11	Rasiak 2 (1 pen) [47, 74 (p)]	11,306
5	26	H	Preston NE	D 1-1	1-0	9	Rasiak [43]	20,712
6	Sept 9	A	Ipswich T	L 1-2	1-0	13	Jones [3]	21,422
7	12	A	Crystal Palace	W 2-0	1-0	—	Jones [2], Rasiak [48]	17,084
8	16	H	Plymouth Arg	W 1-0	0-0	4	Rasiak [52]	22,514
9	23	A	Burnley	W 3-2	1-2	3	Rasiak 2 [18, 73], Skacel [54]	13,051
10	30	H	QPR	L 1-2	1-2	6	Wright [3]	25,185
11	Oct 14	A	Leicester C	L 2-3	1-1	10	Viafara [45], Idiakez [64]	21,347
12	17	A	Cardiff C	L 0-1	0-0	—		19,345
13	21	H	Stoke C	W 1-0	0-0	9	Licka [54]	20,531
14	28	A	Colchester U	L 0-2	0-1	12		5893
15	Nov 1	H	Wolverhampton W	W 2-0	1-0	—	Wright-Phillips [39], Jones [70]	18,979
16	4	H	Hull C	D 0-0	0-0	10		20,560
17	11	A	Sunderland	D 1-1	0-0	12	Bale [90]	25,667
18	18	A	Leeds U	W 3-0	1-0	8	Rasiak 2 [29, 75], Skacel [69]	19,647
19	25	H	Luton T	W 2-1	2-0	7	Baird [15], Rasiak (pen) [38]	20,482
20	29	H	Birmingham C	W 4-3	3-0	—	Jones 2 [14, 17], Skacel [19], Wright-Phillips [78]	21,889
21	Dec 2	A	Hull C	W 4-2	2-2	5	Rasiak 2 [19, 75], Bale [25], Wright-Phillips [82]	15,697
22	9	A	Southend U	L 1-2	0-1	6	Rasiak [87]	10,867
23	16	H	Norwich C	W 2-1	1-1	4	Bale [41], Jones [65]	25,919
24	23	A	Sheffield W	D 3-3	2-1	5	Rasiak [14], Jones [26], Wright-Phillips [50]	23,739
25	26	H	Crystal Palace	D 1-1	0-0	4	Baird [47]	30,548
26	30	H	Leicester C	W 2-0	1-0	4	Pele [9], Prutton [53]	24,447
27	Jan 1	A	Plymouth Arg	D 1-1	1-0	4	Rasiak [5]	15,377
28	13	H	Burnley	D 0-0	0-0	5		20,486
29	20	A	QPR	W 2-0	0-0	5	Rasiak [81], Wright-Phillips [90]	14,686
30	31	H	Sheffield W	W 2-1	1-0	—	Jones 2 [7, 58]	20,230
31	Feb 3	H	Derby Co	L 0-1	0-0	5		27,656
32	10	A	WBA	D 1-1	1-1	5	Jones [18]	21,138
33	17	H	Barnsley	W 5-2	1-1	4	Surman 3 (1 pen) [11, 80, 90 (p)], Jones 2 (1 pen) [48, 73 (p)]	22,460
34	20	A	Coventry C	L 1-2	1-2	—	Saganowski [14]	17,194
35	24	H	Ipswich T	W 1-0	1-0	5	Saganowski [1]	27,974
36	Mar 5	A	Preston NE	L 1-3	0-1	—	Rasiak [57]	13,060
37	10	A	Stoke C	L 1-2	1-1	8	Saganowski [17]	13,404
38	13	H	Cardiff C	D 2-2	2-0	—	Baird [30], Wright-Phillips [44]	20,383
39	16	H	Colchester U	L 1-2	1-2	—	Saganowski [26]	18,736
40	31	A	Wolverhampton W	W 6-0	3-0	7	Saganowski 3 [24, 36, 83], Breen (og) [27], Best [55], Surman [79]	24,804
41	Apr 7	A	Luton T	W 2-0	2-0	6	Viafara [44], Saganowski [45]	9171
42	9	H	Sunderland	L 1-2	0-0	8	Saganowski [67]	25,766
43	14	A	Birmingham C	L 1-2	0-1	8	Saganowski [85]	19,754
44	21	H	Leeds U	W 1-0	0-0	7	Wright-Phillips [84]	29,012
45	28	A	Norwich C	W 1-0	1-0	6	Best [30]	25,437
46	May 6	H	Southend U	W 4-1	1-1	6	Jones 2 [29, 81], Best 2 [48, 80]	32,008

Final League Position: 6

GOALSCORERS

League (77): Rasiak 18 (3 pens), Jones 14 (1 pen), Saganowski 10, Wright-Phillips 8, Bale 5, Best 4, Surman 4 (1 pen), Baird 3, Skacel 3, Viafara 2, Idiakez 1, Licka 1, Pele 1, Prutton 1, Wright 1, own goal 1.
Carling Cup (9): Wright-Phillips 3, Belmadi 1, Dyer 1, Jones 1, McGoldrick 1, Skacel 1, own goal 1.
FA Cup (3): Rasiak 2, Jones 1.
Play-Offs (4): Viafara 2, Rasiak 1, Surman 1.

Davis K 38	Baird C 44	Bale G 38	Viafara J 29 + 7	Lundekvam C 33	Pele 34 + 3	Belmadi D 9 + 5	Wright J 41 + 1	Rasiak G 32 + 7	Fuller R 1	Skacel R 32 + 5	Ostlund A 17 + 3	Wright-Phillips B 15 + 24	Surman A 26 + 11	Cranie M — + 1	Jones K 25 + 9	Dyer N 10 + 8	Makin C 19 + 3	Lallana A 1	Idiakez I 12 + 2	Licka M 7 + 8	McGoldrick D 1 + 8	Prutton D 1 + 2	Powell D 8	Saganowski M 11 + 2	Guthrie D 8 + 2	Best L 6 + 3	Bialkowski B 8	Match No.
1	2	3	4	5¹	6	7	8	9	10²	11³	12	13	14															1
1	5	3¹	4		6	7	8	9		11²	2	10³	13	12	14													2
1	5	3	4		6	7	8	9²		11¹	2	10	12		13													3
1	5	3³	4		6		8	9		12	2	10²	11		13	7¹	14											4
1	5	3	4		6		12	9²		11		10	7³		13	14	2	8¹										5
1	5		4		6		8	9		11		12	13		10¹	2²	3		7									6
1	5		4		2		8	9²		11	12	14	13		10	7³	3		6¹									7
1	5		4		6	12	2	9		11		13			10²	7¹	3		8									8
1	5		4		6	7³	2	9		11²		10¹	13		12	14	3		8									9
1	5	3	4		6¹		8³	9		11		10²	13		12	14	2			7								10
1	5		4	6			7²	9		11¹	2	10³	12				3		8	13	14							11
1	5	3	4	6			2	9		12			11¹		10				8	7								12
1	5	3		6			2	9		11¹			4		10	12			8	7								13
1	5	3	4³	6			2	9¹		13		12	11²		10	7			8	14								14
1	5	3		6			4			11¹		9	12		10	7²	2		8	13								15
1	5	3		6			4			11		9			10	12	2		8¹	7								16
1	5	3		6	4		8	12		11³		13	14		10¹	9	2			7²								17
1	5	3	12	6	4		8	9²		7		10¹	11				2				13							18
1	5	3	4¹	6	10		8	9		11²			7		12		2			13								19
1	5	3	12	6	4		8	9		11³	2	13	7¹		10²					14								20
1	5	3		6	4		8	9		11	2	12	7²		10¹							13						21
1	5	3		6	4		8	9		11		10³	7¹		12		2²		13	14								22
1	5	3	12	6	4		8	9²		11¹	2	13	7		10													23
1	5	3	12	6¹	4		8	9		11	2	13	7		10²													24
1	5	3		6	4		8	9		11	2	12	7¹		10													25
1	5	3	12	6	4		8	9²		11¹	2	10				7³					13	14						26
1	5	3		6	4		8	9		11³	2	10²					12			14	13	7¹						27
1	2	3		6	4		8	9				12			10¹					7	11		5					28
1	2	3	8	6	4		11	9				12			10¹					7²	13		5					29
1	2	3	8	6	4		7	9		11²		12			10¹				14		13		5³					30
1	2	3	8	5	4		7	9²		11³		12				13			6		14			10¹				31
1	5	3	4	6			8	9¹		11			7		10		2							12				32
1	5	3	4	6		13	8	12		11²	2	14	7		10¹									9³				33
1	5	3	4	6	2²	12	8	14		11¹	13		7		10³									9				34
1	5	3	4	6	12	7¹	8					13	11		10		2							9²				35
1	5	3	4	6		7	8	9				12	11²		10¹		2³							13	14			36
1	2	3	4	6	12		8¹	9²		14		13	11										5	10	7³			37
1	2	3	4	6	8					11¹		9	7			12	13						5²	10³		14		38
	2¹	3	12	5	4		8	13				9	11			7³								10²	6	14	1	39
					6		8			11¹	2	13	7			12²	3			14			5	9	4	10³	1	40
		3	4		6	12	8	13				14	7¹				2						5	9³	11	10²	1	41
	5	3	4		6	11	8	12			2	13				7³								9¹	14	10²	1	42
	5		4		12	11²	8¹				2		13		14		3						6	9	7	10³	1	43
	2		4²	6	5	12		9³		11		13	3		10				8¹						7	14	1	44
	5	3	8	6	4						2	12	11		9¹						13				7	10²	1	45
	5	3	12	6¹	4	7³		13		14	2		11		9²										8	10	1	46

FA Cup
Third Round — Torquay U — (a) 2-0
Fourth Round — Manchester C — (a) 1-3

Carling Cup
First Round — Yeovil T — (h) 5-2
Second Round — Millwall — (a) 4-0
Third Round — Notts Co — (a) 0-2

Play-Offs
Semi-Final — Derby Co — (h) 1-2
(a) 3-2

SOUTHEND UNITED FL Championship 1

FOUNDATION

The leading club in Southend around the turn of the century was Southend Athletic, but they were an amateur concern. Southend United was a more ambitious professional club when they were founded in 1906, employing Bob Jack as secretary-manager and immediately joining the Second Division of the Southern League.

Roots Hall, Victoria Avenue, Southend-on-Sea, Essex SS2 6NQ.

Telephone: (01702) 304 050.

Fax: (01702) 304 124.

Ticket Office: (08444) 770 077.

Website: www.southendunited.co.uk

Email: info@southend-united.co.uk

Ground Capacity: 12,260.

Record Attendance: 31,090 v Liverpool, FA Cup 3rd rd, 10 January 1979.

Pitch Measurements: 110yd × 74yd.

Chairman: Ron Martin.

Chief Executive: Geoffrey King.

Secretary: Mrs Helen Norbury.

Manager: Steve Tilson.

Assistant Manager: Paul Brush.

Physio: John Stannard.

Club Nickname: 'The Blues' or 'The Shrimpers'.

Colours: Navy blue shirts with white piping, navy blue shorts.

Change Colours: White shirts with blue piping, white shorts.

Year Formed: 1906.

Turned Professional: 1906. ***Ltd Co.:*** 1919.

Grounds: 1906, Roots Hall, Prittlewell; 1920, Kursaal; 1934, Southend Stadium; 1955, Roots Hall Football Ground.

First Football League Game: 28 August 1920, Division 3, v Brighton & HA (a) W 2–0 – Capper; Reid, Newton; Wileman, Henderson, Martin; Nicholls, Nuttall, Fairclough (2), Myers, Dorsett.

Record League Victory: 9–2 v Newport Co, Division 3 (S), 5 September 1936 – McKenzie; Nelson, Everest (1); Deacon, Turner, Carr; Bolan, Lane (1), Goddard (4), Dickinson (2), Oswald (1).

Record Cup Victory: 10–1 v Golders Green, FA Cup 1st rd, 24 November 1934 – Moore; Morfitt, Kelly; Mackay, Joe Wilson, Carr (1); Lane (1), Johnson (5), Cheesmuir (2), Deacon (1), Oswald. 10–1 v Brentwood, FA Cup 2nd rd, 7 December 1968 – Roberts; Bentley, Birks; McMillan (1) Beesley, Kurila; Clayton, Chisnall, Moore (4), Best (5), Hamilton. 10–1 v Aldershot, Leyland Daf Cup Prel rd, 6 November 1990 – Sansome; Austin, Powell, Cornwell, Prior (1), Tilson (3), Cawley, Butler, Ansah (1), Benjamin (1), Angell (4).

HONOURS

Football League: FL 1 – Champions 2005–06; Division 1 best season: 13th, 1994–95; Promoted from FL 2 2004–05 (play-offs); Division 3 – Runners-up 1990–91; Division 4 – Champions 1980–81; Runners-up 1971–72, 1977–78.

FA Cup: best season: old 3rd rd, 1921; 5th rd, 1926, 1952, 1976, 1993.

Football League Cup: Quarter final 2007.

LDV Vans Trophy: Runners-up 2004, 2005.

SKY SPORTS FACT FILE

Southern League Second Division champions 1906–07 and 1907–08, Southend United unearthed centre-forward Harold Halse from Wanstead. In the first season he scored 91 goals in all competitions, joined Manchester United and played for England.

Record Defeat: 1–9 v Brighton & HA, Division 3, 27 November 1965.

Most League Points (2 for a win): 67, Division 4, 1980–81.

Most League Points (3 for a win): 85, Division 3, 1990–91.

Most League Goals: 92, Division 3 (S), 1950–51.

Highest League Scorer in Season: Jim Shankly, 31, 1928–29; Sammy McCrory, 1957–58, both in Division 3 (S).

Most League Goals in Total Aggregate: Roy Hollis, 122, 1953–60.

Most League Goals in One Match: 5, Jim Shankly v Merthyr T, Division 3S, 1 March 1930.

Most Capped Player: George Mackenzie, 9, Eire.

Most League Appearances: Sandy Anderson, 452, 1950–63.

Youngest League Player: Phil O'Connor, 16 years 76 days v Lincoln C, 26 December 1969.

Record Transfer Fee Received: £3,570,000 from Nottingham F for Stan Collymore, June 1993.

Record Transfer Fee Paid: £750,000 to Crystal Palace for Stan Collymore, November 1992.

Football League Record: 1920 Original Member of Division 3; 1921–58 Division 3 (S); 1958–66 Division 3; 1966–72 Division 4; 1972–76 Division 3; 1976–78 Division 4; 1978–80 Division 3; 1980–81 Division 4; 1981–84 Division 3; 1984–87 Division 4; 1987–89 Division 3; 1989–90 Division 4; 1990–91 Division 3; 1991–92 Division 2; 1992–97 Division 1; 1997–98 Division 2; 1998–2004 Division 3; 2004–05 FL 2; 2005–06 FL 1; 2006–07 FL C; 2007– FL 1.

MANAGERS

Bob Jack 1906–10
George Molyneux 1910–11
O. M. Howard 1911–12
Joe Bradshaw 1912–19
Ned Liddell 1919–20
Tom Mather 1920–21
Ted Birnie 1921–34
David Jack 1934–40
Harry Warren 1946–56
Eddie Perry 1956–60
Frank Broome 1960
Ted Fenton 1961–65
Alvan Williams 1965–67
Ernie Shepherd 1967–69
Geoff Hudson 1969–70
Arthur Rowley 1970–76
Dave Smith 1976–83
Peter Morris 1983–84
Bobby Moore 1984–86
Dave Webb 1986–87
Dick Bate 1987
Paul Clark 1987–88
Dave Webb *(General Manager)* 1988–92
Colin Murphy 1992–93
Barry Fry 1993
Peter Taylor 1993–95
Steve Thompson 1995
Ronnie Whelan 1995–97
Alvin Martin 1997–99
Alan Little 1999–2000
David Webb 2000–01
Rob Newman 2001–03
Steve Wignall 2003–04
Steve Tilson May 2004–

LATEST SEQUENCES

Longest Sequence of League Wins: 8, 29.8.2005 – 9.10.2005.

Longest Sequence of League Defeats: 6, 29.8.1987 – 19.9.1987.

Longest Sequence of League Draws: 6, 30.1.1982 – 19.2.1982.

Longest Sequence of Unbeaten League Matches: 16, 20.2.1932 – 29.8.1932.

Longest Sequence Without a League Win: 17, 31.12.1983 – 14.4.1984.

Successive Scoring Runs: 24 from 23.3.1929.

Successive Non-scoring Runs: 6 from 28.10.1933.

TEN YEAR LEAGUE RECORD

		P	W	D	L	F	A	Pts	Pos
1997-98	Div 2	46	11	10	25	47	79	43	24
1998-99	Div 3	46	14	12	20	52	58	54	18
1999-2000	Div 3	46	15	11	20	53	61	56	16
2000-01	Div 3	46	15	18	13	55	53	63	11
2001-02	Div 3	46	15	13	18	51	54	58	12
2002-03	Div 3	46	17	3	26	47	59	54	17
2003-04	Div 3	46	14	12	20	51	63	54	17
2004-05	FL 2	46	22	12	12	65	46	78	4
2005-06	FL 1	46	23	13	10	72	43	82	1
2006-07	FL C	46	10	12	24	47	80	42	22

DID YOU KNOW ?

Southend United defeated Manchester United 1–0 in the Carling Cup fourth round on 7 November 2006 at Roots Hall with a 27th minute goal from Freddy Eastwood, the day after Sir Alex Ferguson celebrated his 20th year at Old Trafford.

SOUTHEND UNITED 2006–07 LEAGUE RECORD

Match No.	Date	Venue	Opponents	Result	H/T Score	Lg. Pos.	Goalscorers	Attendance
1	Aug 5	H	Stoke C	W 1-0	1-0	—	Eastwood (pen) [14]	8971
2	8	A	Crystal Palace	L 1-3	1-0	—	Eastwood [42]	18,072
3	12	A	QPR	L 0-2	0-2	19		12,368
4	19	H	Sunderland	W 3-1	1-0	12	Barrett 2 [46, 68], Bradbury [89]	9848
5	26	A	Leicester C	L 0-1	0-1	17		19,427
6	Sept 9	H	Sheffield W	D 0-0	0-0	17		9639
7	12	H	Norwich C	D 3-3	1-2	—	Eastwood [9], Hammell [68], Gower [90]	11,072
8	16	A	WBA	D 1-1	0-0	18	Harrold [82]	19,576
9	24	H	Cardiff C	L 0-3	0-2	21		7901
10	30	A	Derby Co	L 0-3	0-1	22		22,395
11	Oct 13	H	Coventry C	L 2-3	1-1	—	Eastwood 2 (1 pen) [30 (p), 73]	9821
12	17	A	Burnley	D 0-0	0-0	—		10,461
13	21	H	Ipswich T	L 1-3	0-1	22	Francis [65]	11,415
14	28	A	Leeds U	L 0-2	0-1	23		19,528
15	31	H	Hull C	L 2-3	1-1	—	Harrold [28], Eastwood [51]	10,234
16	Nov 4	A	Wolverhampton W	L 1-3	0-3	24	Harrold [57]	17,904
17	11	H	Preston NE	D 0-0	0-0	24		9263
18	18	H	Plymouth Arg	D 1-1	0-1	24	Gower [59]	9469
19	25	A	Colchester U	L 0-3	0-0	24		5954
20	28	A	Barnsley	L 0-2	0-1	—		9588
21	Dec 2	H	Wolverhampton W	L 0-1	0-0	24		9411
22	9	H	Southampton	W 2-1	1-0	24	Eastwood [22], McCormack [64]	10,867
23	15	A	Luton T	D 0-0	0-0	—		7468
24	23	H	Birmingham C	L 0-4	0-2	24		9781
25	26	A	Norwich C	D 0-0	0-0	24		25,433
26	30	A	Coventry C	D 1-1	0-1	24	Gower [54]	16,623
27	Jan 1	H	WBA	W 3-1	3-0	24	Campbell-Ryce 2 [11, 28], Hunt [42]	9907
28	13	A	Cardiff C	W 1-0	1-0	24	Bradbury [23]	13,822
29	20	H	Derby Co	L 0-1	0-1	24		10,745
30	30	A	Birmingham C	W 3-1	1-1	—	Maher [22], Eastwood [48], Gower [84]	19,177
31	Feb 3	A	Stoke C	D 1-1	0-1	23	Eastwood [86]	23,017
32	9	H	QPR	W 5-0	1-0	—	Bradbury [9], Gower [70], Sodje [79], Maher 2 [89, 90]	10,217
33	17	A	Sunderland	L 0-4	0-2	23		33,576
34	20	H	Crystal Palace	L 0-1	0-0	—		10,419
35	24	A	Sheffield W	L 2-3	1-2	23	Hunt [15], Eastwood [61]	24,116
36	Mar 3	H	Leicester C	D 2-2	0-1	23	Eastwood [53], McCormack [90]	10,528
37	10	A	Ipswich T	W 2-0	2-0	23	Gower [35], Clarke [42]	24,051
38	13	H	Burnley	W 1-0	0-0	—	Foran [90]	8855
39	17	H	Leeds U	D 1-1	1-0	22	Gower [24]	11,274
40	31	A	Hull C	L 0-4	0-1	22		19,629
41	Apr 6	H	Colchester U	L 0-3	0-1	—		10,552
42	9	A	Preston NE	W 3-2	1-0	23	Maher 2 [41, 90], McCormack [88]	13,684
43	14	H	Barnsley	L 1-3	0-2	23	Gower [69]	10,089
44	21	A	Plymouth Arg	L 1-2	1-1	23	Clarke [25]	11,097
45	28	H	Luton T	L 1-3	0-2	23	Bradbury [66]	10,276
46	May 6	A	Southampton	L 1-4	1-1	22	Barrett [13]	32,008

Final League Position: 22

GOALSCORERS

League (47): Eastwood 11 (2 pens), Gower 8, Maher 5, Bradbury 4, Barrett 3, Harrold 3, McCormack 3, Campbell-Ryce 2, Clarke 2, Hunt 2, Foran 1, Francis 1, Hammell 1, Sodje 1.
Carling Cup (10): Eastwood 4 (1 pen), Hooper 2, Gower 1, Hammell 1 (pen), Hunt 1, Paynter 1.
FA Cup (4): Bradbury 1, Eastwood 1 (pen), Gower 1, Maher 1.

Flahavan D 46	Francis S 32 + 8	Hammell S 38 + 1	Maher K 41	Prior S 15 + 2	Barrett A 26 + 2	Campbell-Ryce J 38 + 5	Guttridge L 15 + 2	Bradbury L 28 + 3	Eastwood F 41 + 1	Gower M 43	Paynter B 5 + 4	Clarke P 34 + 4	Hunt L 30 + 5	Collis S — + 1	Lawson J — + 2	Cole M 1 + 3	Harrold M 13 + 23	Hooper G 3 + 16	Ricketts M — + 2	Sodje E 23 + 1	McCormack A 20 + 2	Arnau C 1 + 1	Foran R 9 + 6	Moussa F 2 + 2	Wilson C 2	Sam L — + 2	Ademeno C — + 1	Match No.
1	2	3	4	5	6	7^1	8^2	9	10	11^3	12	13	14															1
1	2	3	4	5	6	7	8	9	10	11^1	12																	2
1^G	2	3	4	5	6	7	8	9^1	10	11	12			15														3
1	2	3	4	5^1	6	7^3	8	9	10^2	11		12	13		14													4
1	2	3	4	12	6	7^2	8		10	11^3	9^1	5			13	14												5
1	2	3	4		6	7	8		10^1	11	9^2	5					13	12										6
1	2	3	4		6	7^2	8^1		10	11	9^3	5	12				14	13										7
1	2	3	4		6	7^3	8^1		10	11	9^2	5	12				14	13										8
1	2	3	4		6	7^2	12		10	11^3	9^1	5	8					13	14									9
1	2^1	3	4		6	12	8		10	11		5	7					9^2	13									10
1	2	3	4	5	6	12	8		10	11			7^1				9^2	13										11
1	2	3	4	5^1	6		8		10	11		12	7				9											12
1	7	3	4		6		8		10^1	11	12	5	2				9^2			13								13
1		3	4		6	12	8^1		10	11		7	2				13	9^2		5								14
1	8^2	3	4		6		12		10	11		7^1	2				9	13		5								15
1	8^1	3	4	6		12			10	11		7	2				9			5								16
1	2	3		5		7^1	8		10	11		4				12	9			6								17
1	2	3	4	5^1	12	7^3			10	11		8^2					9	13		6	14							18
1	2	3	4■	5		7		12	10^2	11■							9^1	13		6	8^3	14						19
1	2	3		5		7^2		12	10				4			11^1	9	13		6	8							20
1	2	3		5		7		9^1	10^2	11^3			4			14	12	13		6	8							21
1	2	3		5		7^1		9	10	11		12	4							6	8							22
1		3	4	5		7^1		9^2	10	11			2				13	12		6	8							23
1	12	3	4			7^3		9	10^2	11		5	2				14	13		6	8^1							24
1		3	4		12	7		9		11		5	2				10^2	13		6■		8^1						25
1	12	3	4		6	7		9	13	11		5	2				10^2				8^1							26
1	12	3	4		6	7		9^2	10^3	11^1		5	2				13	14			8							27
1	12	3	4		6	7^3	8	9^2	10^1	11		5	2				13	14										28
1		3	4		6	7		9^1	10	11^2		5	2				12	13			8							29
1	12	3	4		6	7		9^2	10	11		5	2				13				8^1							30
1	2	3^2	4			7		9^1	10	11		5	8				12			6			13					31
1	12		4		3	7		9	10^2	11^3		5	2				13			6^1	8		14					32
1		3	4			7		9^1	10	11^2		5	2				12			6	8^3		13	14				33
1	12		4			7^1		9	10	11		5	2				13			6			8		3^2			34
1	12		4	5		7		9	10	11			2							6			8		3^1			35
1	2		4			7		9^2	10	11		5	3				12			6^1	13		8■					36
1	3	12	4			7		9^2	10^3	11^1		5	2				13			6	8			14				37
1	2		4			7^3		9^2	10	11^1		5	3				12			6	8		13			14		38
1	2		4			7^1		9	10^2	11		5	3				12			6			8			13		39
1	2		4			7^1		9	10	11		5	3				12			6			8					40
1		3^2	4			12		9	10	11		5	2				13			6	7		8^1					41
1	2	3	4		6	7			10^1	11		5					9				8		12					42
1	2	3	4		6	7		12		11		5					9				8		10^1					43
1	2	3	4		6	7		9	10^1	11^2		5					12				8		13					44
1	2	3	4^2	12	6	11		9				5^1	13								8		10^3	7			14	45
1	2	3			6	11		9				5					12	7^1			8		10	4				46

FA Cup

Third Round	Barnsley	(h)	1-1
		(a)	2-0
Fourth Round	Tottenham H	(a)	1-3

Carling Cup

First Round	Bournemouth	(a)	3-1
Second Round	Brighton & HA	(h)	3-2
Third Round	Leeds U	(a)	3-1
Fourth Round	Manchester U	(h)	1-0
Quarter-Final	Tottenham H	(a)	0-1

STOCKPORT COUNTY FL Championship 2

FOUNDATION

Formed at a meeting held at Wellington Road South by members of Wycliffe Congregational Chapel in 1883, they called themselves Heaton Norris Rovers until changing to Stockport County in 1890, a year before joining the Football Combination.

Edgeley Park, Hardcastle Road, Edgeley, Stockport, Cheshire SK3 9DD.

Telephone: (0161) 286 8888.

Fax: (0161) 286 8900.

Ticket Office: 08712 220 120.

Website: www.stockportcounty.com

Email: stockport.county@btinternet.com

Ground Capacity: 10,651.

Record Attendance: 27,833 v Liverpool, FA Cup 5th rd, 11 February 1950.

Pitch Measurements: 111yd × 71yd.

Chairman: Norman Beverley.

Vice-chairman: Grahame White.

Chief Executive: Mark Maguire.

Secretary: David James.

Manager: Jim Gannon.

Assistant Manager: Peter Ward.

Physio: Rodger Wylde.

Colours: Blue shirts, blue shorts, white stockings.

Change Colours: White shirts, blue shorts, white stockings.

Year Formed: 1883.

Turned Professional: 1891.

Ltd Co.: 1908.

Previous Names: 1883, Heaton Norris Rovers; 1888, Heaton Norris; 1890, Stockport County.

Club Nicknames: 'County' or 'Hatters'.

Grounds: 1883 Heaton Norris Recreation Ground; 1884 Heaton Norris Wanderers Cricket Ground; 1885 Chorlton's Farm, Chorlton's Lane; 1886 Heaton Norris Cricket Ground; 1887 Wilkes' Field, Belmont Street; 1889 Nursery Inn, Green Lane; 1902 Edgeley Park.

First Football League Game: 1 September 1900, Division 2, v Leicester Fosse (a) D 2–2 – Moores; Earp, Wainwright; Pickford, Limond, Harvey; Stansfield, Smith (1), Patterson, Foster, Betteley (1).

Record League Victory: 13–0 v Halifax T, Division 3 (N), 6 January 1934 – McGann; Vincent (1p), Jenkinson; Robinson, Stevens, Len Jones; Foulkes (1), Hill (3), Lythgoe (2), Stevenson (2), Downes (4).

Record Cup Victory: 5–0 v Lincoln C, FA Cup 1st rd, 11 November 1995 – Edwards; Connelly, Todd, Bennett, Flynn, Gannon (Dinning), Beaumont, Oliver, Ware, Eckhardt (3), Armstrong (1) (Mike), Chalk, (1 og).

HONOURS

Football League: Division 1 best season: 8th, 1997–98; Division 2 – Runners-up 1996–97; Division 3 (N) – Champions 1921–22, 1936–37; Runners-up 1928–29, 1929-30, 1996–97; Division 4 – Champions 1966–67; Runners-up 1990–91.

FA Cup: best season: 5th rd, 1935, 1950, 2001.

Football League Cup: Semi-final 1997.

Autoglass Trophy: Runners-up 1992, 1993.

SKY SPORTS FACT FILE

When Adam Le Fondre scored four of the Stockport County goals in their 5–2 win over Wrexham on 16 September 2006 it was his first hat-trick in the League. Their first foursome had been credited to Joe Foster in the 4–1 win over Walsall on 22 September 1900.

Record Defeat: 1–8 v Chesterfield, Division 2, 19 April 1902.

Most League Points (2 for a win): 64, Division 4, 1966–67.

Most League Points (3 for a win): 85, Division 2, 1993–94.

Most League Goals: 115, Division 3 (N), 1933–34.

Highest League Scorer in Season: Alf Lythgoe, 46, Division 3 (N), 1933–34.

Most League Goals in Total Aggregate: Jack Connor, 132, 1951–56.

Most League Goals in One Match: 5, Joe Smith v Southport, Division 3N, 7 January 1928; 5, Joe Smith v Lincoln C, Division 3N, 15 September 1928; 5, Frank Newton v Nelson, Division 3N, 21 September 1929; 5, Alf Lythgoe v Southport, Division 3N, 25 August 1934; 5, Billy McNaughton v Mansfield T, Division 3N, 14 December 1935; 5, Jack Connor v Workington, Division 3N, 8 November 1952; 5, Jack Connor v Carlisle U, Division 3N, 7 April 1956.

Most Capped Player: Jarkko Wiss, 9 (43), Finland.

Most League Appearances: Andy Thorpe, 489, 1978–86, 1988–92.

Youngest League Player: Paul Turnbull, 16 years 97 days v Wrexham, 30 April 2005.

Record Transfer Fee Received: £1,600,000 from Middlesbrough for Alun Armstrong, February 1998.

Record Transfer Fee Paid: £800,000 to Nottingham F for Ian Moore, July 1998.

Football League Record: 1900 Elected to Division 2; 1904 Failed re-election; 1905–21 Division 2; 1921–22 Division 3 (N); 1922–26 Division 2; 1926–37 Division 3 (N); 1937–38 Division 2; 1938–58 Division 3 (N); 1958–59 Division 3; 1959–67 Division 4; 1967–70 Division 3; 1970–91 Division 4; 1991–92 Division 3; 1992–97 Division 2; 1997–2002 Division 1; 2002–04 Division 2; 2004–05 FL 1; 2005– FL 2.

MANAGERS

Fred Stewart 1894–1911
Harry Lewis 1911–14
David Ashworth 1914–19
Albert Williams 1919–24
Fred Scotchbrook 1924–26
Lincoln Hyde 1926–31
Andrew Wilson 1932–33
Fred Westgarth 1934–36
Bob Kelly 1936–38
George Hunt 1938–39
Bob Marshall 1939–49
Andy Beattie 1949–52
Dick Duckworth 1952–56
Billy Moir 1956–60
Reg Flewin 1960–63
Trevor Porteous 1963–65
Bert Trautmann *(General Manager)* 1965–66
Eddie Quigley *(Team Manager)* 1965–66
Jimmy Meadows 1966–69
Wally Galbraith 1969–70
Matt Woods 1970–71
Brian Doyle 1972–74
Jimmy Meadows 1974–75
Roy Chapman 1975–76
Eddie Quigley 1976–77
Alan Thompson 1977–78
Mike Summerbee 1978–79
Jimmy McGuigan 1979–82
Eric Webster 1982–85
Colin Murphy 1985
Les Chapman 1985–86
Jimmy Melia 1986
Colin Murphy 1986–87
Asa Hartford 1987–89
Danny Bergara 1989–95
Dave Jones 1995–97
Gary Megson 1997–99
Andy Kilner 1999–2001
Carlton Palmer 2001–03
Sammy McIlroy 2003–04
Chris Turner 2004–05
Jim Gannon January 2006–

LATEST SEQUENCES

Longest Sequence of League Wins: 9, 13.1.2007 – 3.3.2007.

Longest Sequence of League Defeats: 10, 24.11.2001 – 13.01.2002.

Longest Sequence of League Draws: 7, 17.3.1989 – 14.4.1989.

Longest Sequence of Unbeaten League Matches: 18, 28.1.1933 – 28.8.1933.

Longest Sequence Without a League Win: 19, 28.12.1999 – 22.4.2000.

Successive Scoring Runs: 24 from 8.9.1928.

Successive Non-scoring Runs: 7 from 10.3.1923.

TEN YEAR LEAGUE RECORD

		P	W	D	L	F	A	Pts	Pos
1997-98	Div 1	46	19	8	19	71	69	65	8
1998-99	Div 1	46	12	17	17	49	60	53	16
1999-2000	Div 1	46	13	15	18	55	67	54	17
2000-01	Div 1	46	11	18	17	58	65	51	19
2001-02	Div 1	46	6	8	32	42	102	26	24
2002-03	Div 2	46	15	10	21	65	70	55	14
2003-04	Div 2	46	11	19	16	62	70	52	19
2004-05	FL 1	46	6	8	32	49	98	26	24
2005-06	FL 2	46	11	19	16	57	78	52	22
2006-07	FL 2	46	21	8	17	65	54	71	8

DID YOU KNOW ?

Colin Gleave, a Stockport County defender who was signed in February 1938 an played in early years of wartime regional football, was later captured in Italy but escaped to Switzerlan where for a time he playe League football before repatriation!

STOCKPORT COUNTY 2006–07 LEAGUE RECORD

Match No.	Date	Venue	Opponents	Result	H/T Score	Lg. Pos.	Goalscorers	Attendance
1	Aug 5	H	Hereford U	L 0-2	0-1	—		5297
2	8	A	Walsall	L 0-2	0-1	—		4877
3	12	A	Mansfield T	D 1-1	1-0	20	Briggs [24]	3856
4	18	H	Accrington S	D 1-1	1-0	—	Murray [12]	5291
5	26	A	Swindon T	L 0-2	0-1	22		6868
6	Sept 3	H	Bristol R	W 2-1	1-0	20	Murray 2 [39, 53]	4846
7	9	A	Boston U	L 1-2	1-2	22	Taylor [28]	1796
8	12	H	Shrewsbury T	L 0-3	0-1	—		4089
9	16	H	Wrexham	W 5-2	2-1	20	Robinson (pen) [23], Le Fondre 4 [24, 54, 85, 87]	4884
10	23	A	Grimsby T	W 1-0	1-0	16	Briggs [37]	4708
11	26	A	Notts Co	L 0-1	0-1	—		4021
12	30	H	Peterborough U	L 0-1	0-0	22		4775
13	Oct 7	H	Barnet	W 2-0	1-0	20	Poole [31], Le Fondre [51]	4133
14	14	A	Hartlepool U	D 1-1	1-1	18	Griffin [30]	4372
15	21	H	Torquay U	W 1-0	1-0	16	Le Fondre [38]	4663
16	28	A	Rochdale	W 3-1	2-0	12	Williams [19], Robinson (pen) [45], Bramble [80]	3709
17	Nov 4	H	Lincoln C	W 2-0	0-0	10	Rose [56], Malcolm [90]	5497
18	17	A	Chester C	D 1-1	1-0	—	Poole [27]	3624
19	25	H	Macclesfield T	D 1-1	0-1	12	Proudlock [75]	6575
20	Dec 5	A	Milton Keynes D	L 0-2	0-0	—		4564
21	9	H	Darlington	W 5-2	4-2	10	Bramble 2 [18, 36], Proudlock [24], Dinning [32], Gleeson [62]	4564
22	16	A	Bury	L 0-2	0-1	13		4466
23	23	A	Wycombe W	L 0-2	0-1	15		4559
24	26	H	Notts Co	W 2-0	0-0	11	Pilkinton [47], Dickinson [90]	5823
25	30	H	Grimsby T	W 3-0	2-0	9	Barnes (og) [8], Dickinson [29], Malcolm [78]	5032
26	Jan 1	A	Shrewsbury T	L 2-4	0-2	11	Pilkinton 2 [49, 69]	4569
27	13	H	Boston U	W 2-0	1-0	8	Proudlock [25], Bramble [79]	4568
28	20	A	Peterborough U	W 3-0	2-0	7	Elding [20], Rose [31], Griffin [90]	4330
29	27	H	Wycombe W	W 2-0	1-0	7	Elding [21], Gleeson [47]	5353
30	30	A	Wrexham	W 1-0	0-0	—	Dickinson [90]	4060
31	Feb 3	A	Hereford U	W 2-0	2-0	6	Bramble [33], Elding [38]	3310
32	10	H	Mansfield T	W 1-0	1-0	6	Elding [17]	5656
33	17	A	Accrington S	W 1-0	1-0	6	Griffin [45]	3004
34	20	H	Walsall	W 1-0	0-0	—	Elding [52]	6005
35	Mar 3	H	Swindon T	W 3-0	1-0	6	Elding 2 [16, 50], Dickinson [84]	6594
36	10	A	Barnet	L 1-3	1-1	6	Bramble [33]	2647
37	17	H	Hartlepool U	D 3-3	3-1	6	Le Fondre (pen) [24], Elding [28], Dickinson [36]	7860
38	20	A	Bristol R	L 1-2	0-1	—	Rose [68]	4725
39	24	H	Rochdale	L 2-7	2-4	6	Elding [32], Dickinson [35]	6679
40	31	A	Torquay U	L 0-1	0-0	6		3005
41	Apr 7	A	Lincoln C	D 0-0	0-0	6		5320
42	9	H	Chester C	W 2-0	1-0	6	Pilkinton [22], Dinning [47]	5719
43	14	A	Macclesfield T	L 0-2	0-1	6		4451
44	21	H	Milton Keynes D	L 1-2	0-1	7	Pilkinton [80]	5681
45	28	H	Bury	D 0-0	0-0	8		7246
46	May 5	A	Darlington	W 5-0	1-0	8	Elding 2 (1 pen) [35 (p), 80], Poole 2 [49, 68], Dickinson [61]	5184

Final League Position: 8

GOALSCORERS

League (65): Elding 11 (1 pen), Dickinson 7, Le Fondre 7 (1 pen), Bramble 6, Pilkinton 5, Poole 4, Griffin 3, Murray 3, Proudlock 3, Rose 3, Briggs 2, Dinning 2, Gleeson 2, Malcolm 2, Robinson 2 (2 pens), Taylor 1, Williams 1, own goal 1.
Carling Cup (0).
FA Cup (5): Proudlock 3 (1 pen), Bramble 1, Poole 1.
Paint Trophy (1): Malcolm 1.

Spencer J 15	Williams A 46	Rose M 22 + 3	Dinning T 27 + 5	Raynes M 7 + 2	Owen G 39	Briggs K 16 + 4	Taylor J 44 + 1	Murray G 11	Le Fondre A 14 + 7	Malcolm M 10 + 8	Dickinson L 11 + 22	Allen D 1 + 6	Robinson M 11 + 2	Griffin A 29 + 13	Bramble T 19 + 12	Clare R 29 + 1	Proudlock A 14 + 9	Bowler M 5 + 3	Crowther R 1	Ruddy J 11	Poole D 30 + 1	Ellis D — + 2	Kane T 4	Gleeson S 14	Tunnicliffe J 4 + 1	Treacy K 2 + 2	Pilkinton A 18 + 6	Hennessey W 15	Elding A 20	Blizzard D 7	Nolan E 2 + 2	Rowe T 1 + 3	Lewis J 5	Tansey G 2 + 1	*Match No.*
1	2	3	4	5^{1}	6	7	8^{2}	9	10	11	12	13																							1
1	5	2^{2}	4		6	7	8	9	12	11	10	13	3^{1}																						2
1	5	2	4	12	6	7^{1}	8	9^{2}			13		3	11	10^{3}	14																			3
1	5		4		6	7^{1}	8	9	10^{2}	12			3	11		2	13																		4
1	5	12	4		6	7	8	9^{2}		11^{3}	13		3	10^{1}	14			2																	5
1	5	3	4	8	6	7	12	9^{2}			14		13	11	10^{3}			2^{1}																	6
1	5	12	4^{2}	7	6	2	8	9^{3}	10		14		3	11^{1}	13																				7
1	5		4	6		12	8	9	10	11^{2}			3	14	13			2^{1}	7^{3}																8
	5			4	6	2	8	9^{2}	10	11^{1}			3	14	13		12			1	7^{3}														9
	5				6	7	8	9	10^{1}	11^{2}	12		3	13		2	14			1	4^{3}														10
	5				6	4	8		10	11^{1}	9^{2}		3	12		2	13			1	7														11
	5				6	4	8	9^{1}		11	12		3^{3}	14	13	2	10^{2}			1	7														12
	5		4		6	12	8		10		13		14	3	9^{2}	2	11^{3}			1	7^{1}														13
	5		4		6	7^{2}	8		10		12	13		3	9^{1}	2				1	11														14
	5		4		6	7	8		10	11^{2}	12			3	9^{1}	2				1		13													15
	5	12	4		6^{3}		8		10^{2}	13	14	11^{1}	3		9	2				1	7														16
	5	3	12			6^{1}	8		13	11	10^{2}				9	4				1	7		2												17
	5		4			12	8		10^{2}					3	9	6^{1}	13			1	7		2	11											18
	5						8		12	13				3	9		10			1	7^{2}		2	4	6^{1}	11									19
1	5■	3^{2}	4			7^{3}	8			12				13	9^{1}	2■	10				11			6		14									20
1	5		4				8^{1}							3	9		10	12			7		2	11	6										21
1	5		4				8				12			3	9	6	10^{2}	2^{1}			7			11^{3}	13	14									22
1	2		4^{3}		6	12	8			13	14			3	9^{2}									11	5	10	7^{1}								23
1	2	3	4		6	8^{1}					10			12	9									11	5		7								24
1	2	3	4^{2}		6		8			12	10^{1}	13		11		5						14		9			7^{3}								25
1	2■	3^{1}	4		6		8			12	10			11		5								9			7								26
	5	3			6		8					12		13	14	2	10^{3}				4^{1}			11			7^{2}	1	9						27
	5	3			6		8					12		13	14	2	10^{3}				4^{1}			11			7^{2}	1	9						28
	5	3			6		8				12			13	14	2	10^{1}				4			11			7^{2}	1	9^{3}						29
	5	3^{3}			6		8				12			11	13	2	10^{2}				4			7			14	1	9^{1}						30
	5	3			6		8				12			11	10^{2}	2	13				4^{3}			7			14	1	9^{1}						31
	5	3			6		8				12			13		2	10^{2}				7						11	1	9^{1}	4					32
	5	3			6		8				12			11	13	2					7^{2}						10	1	9^{1}	4					33
	5	3	12		6		8				13			11	10^{2}	2											7	1	9^{1}	4					34
	5	3	12		6		8				13			11		2	10^{2}				14						7^{3}	1	9^{1}	4					35
	5	3	12		6		8				13			11^{3}	10^{2}	2					7^{1}						14	1	9	4					36
	5	3			6		8		10^{1}		11^{2}			12	13	2					7^{3}						14	1	9	4					37
	5	3			6		8		10^{2}		13			11	12						7^{3}						14	1	9^{1}	4	2				38
	5	3^{2}	4^{1}	14	6		8		12		10^{3}			13													7	1	9		2	11			39
	5		12	4^{1}	6		8							3	10	2^{3}	13				7^{2}						11	1	9		14				40
	5		4		6		8			12	10■			3		2	13				7^{2}						11^{1}	1	9						41
	5		4		6		8				10^{2}			3		2	12				7^{1}						11		9		13		1		42
	5		4	10^{2}	6		8		12					3		2^{1}		13			7						11		9				1		43
	5		4		6		8		12					3			10^{2}				7^{1}						11		9			13	1	2	44
	5		4		6		8		12					3			10^{1}	13			7^{3}						11		9			14	1	2^{2}	45
	5		4		6		8				11			3	10^{1}			2^{3}			7^{2}						12		9			13	1	14	46

FA Cup

First Round	Exeter C	(a)	2-1
Second Round	Wycombe W	(h)	2-1
Third Round	Watford	(a)	1-4

Carling Cup

First Round	Derby Co	(h)	0-1

J Paint Trophy

First Round	Macclesfield T	(a)	1-0
Second Round	Chester C	(a)	0-3

STOKE CITY — FL Championship

FOUNDATION

The date of the formation of this club has long been in doubt. The year 1863 was claimed, but more recent research by Wade Martin has uncovered nothing earlier than 1868, when a couple of Old Carthusians, who were apprentices at the local works of the old North Staffordshire Railway Company, met with some others from that works, to form Stoke Ramblers. It should also be noted that the old Stoke club went bankrupt in 1908 when a new club was formed.

Britannia Stadium, Stanley Matthews Way, Stoke-on-Trent, Staffs ST4 4EG.

Telephone: (01782) 592 222.

Fax: (01782) 592 221.

Ticket Office: (01782) 592 204.

Website: www.stokecityfc.com

Email: info@stokecityfc.com

Ground Capacity: 28,218.

Record Attendance: 51,380 v Arsenal, Division 1, 29 March 1937 (at Victoria Ground).

Pitch Measurements: 115yd × 72yd.

Chairman: Peter Coates.

Chief Executive: Tony Scholes.

Football Administrator: Eddie Harrison.

Manager: Tony Pulis.

Assistant Manager: Dave Kemp.

Physio: Dave Watson.

Colours: Red and white striped shirts, white shorts, white stockings.

Change Colours: White shirts with black and blue trim, black shorts, black stockings.

Year Formed: 1863* (*see Foundation*).

Turned Professional: 1885. ***Ltd Co.:*** 1908.

Previous Names: 1868, Stoke Ramblers; 1870, Stoke; 1925, Stoke City.

Club Nickname: 'The Potters'.

Grounds: 1875, Sweeting's Field; 1878, Victoria Ground (previously known as the Athletic Club Ground); 1997, Britannia Stadium.

First Football League Game: 8 September 1888, Football League, v WBA (h) L 0–2 – Rowley; Clare, Underwood; Ramsey, Shutt, Smith; Sayer, McSkimming, Staton, Edge, Tunnicliffe.

Record League Victory: 10–3 v WBA, Division 1, 4 February 1937 – Doug Westland; Brigham, Harbot; Tutin, Turner (1p), Kirton; Matthews, Antonio (2), Freddie Steele (5), Jimmy Westland, Johnson (2).

HONOURS

Football League: Division 1 best season: 4th, 1935–36, 1946–47; Division 2 – Champions 1932–33, 1962–63, 1992–93; Runners-up 1921–22; Promoted 1978–79 (3rd), Promoted from Division 2 (play-offs) 2001–02; Division 3 (N) – Champions 1926–27.

FA Cup: Semi-finals 1899, 1971, 1972.

Football League Cup: Winners 1972.

Autoglass Trophy: Winners: 1992.

Auto Windscreens Shield: Winners: 2000.

European Competitions: *UEFA Cup:* 1972–73, 1974–75.

SKY SPORTS FACT FILE

Goalkeeper Norman Wilkinson's career at Stoke City spanned the Second World War. He was a miner and centre-half with West Stanley before an emergency switch of positions. Played over 200 peacetime League and Cup games after three years at Huddersfield Town.

Record Cup Victory: 7–1 v Burnley, FA Cup 2nd rd (replay), 20 February 1896 – Clawley; Clare, Eccles; Turner, Grewe, Robertson; Willie Maxwell, Dickson, A. Maxwell (3), Hyslop (4), Schofield.

Record Defeat: 0–10 v Preston NE, Division 1, 14 September 1889.

Most League Points (2 for a win): 63, Division 3 (N), 1926–27.

Most League Points (3 for a win): 93, Division 2, 1992–93.

Most League Goals: 92, Division 3 (N), 1926–27.

Highest League Scorer in Season: Freddie Steele, 33, Division 1, 1936–37.

Most League Goals in Total Aggregate: Freddie Steele, 142, 1934–49.

Most League Goals in One Match: 7, Neville Coleman v Lincoln C, Division 2, 23 February 1957.

Most Capped Player: Gordon Banks, 36 (73), England.

Most League Appearances: Eric Skeels, 506, 1958–76.

Youngest League Player: Peter Bullock, 16 years 163 days v Swansea C, 19 April 1958.

Record Transfer Fee Received: £2,750,000 from QPR for Mike Sheron, July 1997.

Record Transfer Fee Paid: Undisclosed to Standard Liege for Sambegou Bangoura, August 2005.

Football League Record: 1888 Founder Member of Football League; 1890 Not re-elected; 1891 Re-elected; relegated in 1907, and after one year in Division 2, resigned for financial reasons; 1919 re-elected to Division 2; 1922–23 Division 1; 1923–26 Division 2; 1926–27 Division 3 (N); 1927–33 Division 2; 1933–53 Division 1; 1953–63 Division 2; 1963–77 Division 1; 1977–79 Division 2; 1979–85 Division 1; 1985–90 Division 2; 1990–92 Division 3; 1992–93 Division 2; 1993–98 Division 1; 1998–2002 Division 2; 2002–04 Division 1; 2004– FL C.

MANAGERS

Tom Slaney 1874–83
(Secretary-Manager)
Walter Cox 1883–84
(Secretary-Manager)
Harry Lockett 1884–90
Joseph Bradshaw 1890–92
Arthur Reeves 1892–95
William Rowley 1895–97
H. D. Austerberry 1897–1908
A. J. Barker 1908–14
Peter Hodge 1914–15
Joe Schofield 1915–19
Arthur Shallcross 1919–23
John 'Jock' Rutherford 1923
Tom Mather 1923–35
Bob McGrory 1935–52
Frank Taylor 1952–60
Tony Waddington 1960–77
George Eastham 1977–78
Alan A'Court 1978
Alan Durban 1978–81
Richie Barker 1981–83
Bill Asprey 1984–85
Mick Mills 1985–89
Alan Ball 1989–91
Lou Macari 1991–93
Joe Jordan 1993–94
Lou Macari 1994–97
Chic Bates 1997–98
Chris Kamara 1998
Brian Little 1998–99
Gary Megson 1999
Gudjon Thordarson 1999–2002
Steve Cotterill 2002
Tony Pulis 2002–05
Johan Boskamp 2005–06
Tony Pulis June 2006–

LATEST SEQUENCES

Longest Sequence of League Wins: 8, 30.3.1895 – 21.9.1895.

Longest Sequence of League Defeats: 11, 6.4.1985 – 17.8.1985.

Longest Sequence of League Draws: 5, 21.3.1987 – 11.4.1987.

Longest Sequence of Unbeaten League Matches: 25, 5.9.1992 – 20.2.1993.

Longest Sequence Without a League Win: 17, 22.4.1989 – 14.10.1989.

Successive Scoring Runs: 21 from 24.12.1921.

Successive Non-scoring Runs: 8 from 29.12.1984.

TEN YEAR LEAGUE RECORD

		P	*W*	*D*	*L*	*F*	*A*	*Pts*	*Pos*
1997-98	Div 1	46	11	13	22	44	74	46	23
1998-99	Div 2	46	21	6	19	59	63	69	8
1999-2000	Div 2	46	23	13	10	68	42	82	6
2000-01	Div 2	46	21	14	11	74	49	77	5
2001-02	Div 2	46	23	11	12	67	40	80	5
2002-03	Div 1	46	12	14	20	45	69	50	21
2003-04	Div 1	46	18	12	16	58	55	66	11
2004-05	FL C	46	17	10	19	36	38	61	12
2005-06	FL C	46	17	7	22	54	63	58	13
2006-07	FL C	46	19	16	11	62	41	73	8

DID YOU KNOW ?

The first Stoke City player to score as many as four goals in a League match was Jimmy Broad on 3 December 1921 in a 5–1 victory over Crystal Palace. He finished the season with 25 from a total of 62 in three seasons there in a career of many other clubs.

STOKE CITY 2006–07 LEAGUE RECORD

Match No.	Date	Venue	Opponents	Result	H/T Score	Lg. Pos.	Goalscorers	Attendance
1	Aug 5	A	Southend U	L 0-1	0-1	—		8971
2	8	H	Derby Co	W 2-0	1-0	—	Pericard [18], Russell [58]	20,013
3	12	H	Birmingham C	D 0-0	0-0	11		12,347
4	19	A	Luton T	D 2-2	1-0	13	Sweeney [10], Chadwick [70]	7727
5	26	H	Plymouth Arg	D 1-1	1-0	15	Sidibe [39]	11,626
6	Sept 9	A	Barnsley	D 2-2	2-0	14	Hill [3], Chadwick [23]	10,464
7	12	A	Sheffield W	D 1-1	1-1	—	Paterson [34]	19,966
8	16	H	Burnley	L 0-1	0-1	19		12,247
9	23	A	Wolverhampton W	L 0-2	0-1	22		19,489
10	30	H	Preston NE	D 1-1	1-0	21	Fuller [41]	14,342
11	Oct 14	A	Leeds U	W 4-0	1-0	18	Hendrie [7], Griffin [58], Higginbotham [62], Fuller [88]	18,173
12	17	H	Sunderland	W 2-1	0-1	—	Hendrie [50], Pericard [54]	14,482
13	21	A	Southampton	L 0-1	0-0	18		20,531
14	28	H	Norwich C	W 5-0	2-0	15	Hendrie [22], Fuller [38], Higginbotham (pen) [74], Chadwick [79], Russell [90]	13,444
15	31	A	Leicester C	L 1-2	1-1	—	Fuller [42]	21,107
16	Nov 6	H	Coventry C	W 1-0	0-0	—	Griffin [60]	19,055
17	11	A	Crystal Palace	W 1-0	1-0	10	Russell [38]	18,868
18	18	A	Hull C	W 2-0	1-0	7	Higginbotham [2], Russell [80]	16,940
19	25	H	WBA	W 1-0	1-0	6	Higginbotham (pen) [40]	18,282
20	28	H	Cardiff C	W 3-0	0-0	—	Fuller [60], Lawrence [63], Sidibe [65]	15,039
21	Dec 2	A	Coventry C	D 0-0	0-0	7		19,073
22	9	H	QPR	W 1-0	1-0	5	Higginbotham (pen) [17]	16,487
23	16	A	Colchester U	L 0-3	0-2	7		5345
24	23	A	Ipswich T	W 1-0	0-0	4	Lawrence [71]	20,369
25	26	H	Sheffield W	L 1-2	0-1	8	Sidibe [60]	23,003
26	30	H	Leeds U	W 3-1	1-1	7	Sidibe [12], Ehiogu (og) [54], Fuller [77]	18,128
27	Jan 13	H	Wolverhampton W	D 1-1	0-0	7	Hill [85]	15,882
28	20	A	Preston NE	L 2-3	2-0	9	Lawrence [2], Sidibe [7]	15,151
29	23	A	Burnley	W 1-0	1-0	—	Sidibe [24]	12,109
30	30	H	Ipswich T	D 0-0	0-0	—		11,812
31	Feb 3	H	Southend U	D 1-1	1-0	8	Fuller [31]	23,017
32	11	A	Birmingham C	L 0-1	0-0	10		15,854
33	17	H	Luton T	D 0-0	0-0	10		12,375
34	21	A	Derby Co	W 2-0	2-0	—	Higginbotham (pen) [15], Matteo [26]	24,897
35	26	H	Barnsley	L 0-1	0-1	—		13,114
36	Mar 3	A	Plymouth Arg	D 1-1	0-1	9	Russell [55]	12,539
37	10	H	Southampton	W 2-1	1-1	9	Fortune [34], Martin [72]	13,404
38	13	A	Sunderland	D 2-2	2-1	—	Russell [22], Hoefkens [45]	31,358
39	17	A	Norwich C	L 0-1	0-1	9		24,293
40	31	H	Leicester C	W 4-2	2-1	9	Parkin [18], Fuller (pen) [29], Sidibe [79], Lawrence [90]	13,303
41	Apr 7	A	WBA	W 3-1	3-0	8	Fuller [14], Greening (og) [21], Parkin [22]	20,386
42	9	H	Crystal Palace	W 2-1	2-1	7	Parkin [20], Fuller [27]	13,616
43	14	A	Cardiff C	D 1-1	1-0	7	Hoefkens [30]	11,664
44	21	H	Hull C	D 1-1	1-0	8	Lawrence [45]	17,109
45	28	H	Colchester U	W 3-1	0-1	7	Russell [53], Sidibe [57], Higginbotham [62]	20,108
46	May 6	A	QPR	D 1-1	0-1	8	Sidibe [84]	16,741

Final League Position: 8

GOALSCORERS

League (62): Fuller 10 (1 pen), Sidibe 9, Higginbotham 7 (4 pens), Russell 7, Lawrence 5, Chadwick 3, Hendrie 3, Parkin 3, Griffin 2, Hill 2, Hoefkens 2, Pericard 2, Fortune 1, Martin 1, Matteo 1, Paterson 1, Sweeney 1, own goals 2.
Carling Cup (1): Pericard 1.
FA Cup (2): Fuller 1, own goal 1.

Simonsen S 46	Hoefkens C 42 + 3	Higginbotham D 44	Russell D 40 + 3	Duberry M 29	Hill C 15 + 3	Chadwick L 13 + 2	Brammer D 11 + 11	Sidibe M 42 + 1	Pericard V 17 + 12	Sweeney P 10 + 3	Sigurdsson H — + 2	Eustace J 7 + 8	Dickinson C 5 + 8	Paterson M — + 9	Whitley J — + 3	Harper K — + 3	Griffin A 32 + 1	Pulis A — + 1	Rooney A — + 10	Bangoura S 1 + 3	Fuller R 25 + 5	Hendrie L 26 + 2	Delap R 2	Diao S 27	Lawrence L 27	Berger P 1 + 6	Buxton L 1	Wilkinson A 2 + 2	Matteo D 9	Martin L 4 + 9	Fortune J 14	Zakuani G 9	Parkin J 5 + 1	*Match No.*
1	2	3	4	5	6	7^1	8	9	10	11^2	12	13																						1
1	2	3^2	4	5	6^1	7^3	8	9	10	11	12		13	14																				2
1	2		4	5	6	7^1	8	9	10	11			3	12																				3
1	2		4	5	6	7^1	8	9	10	11			3		12																			4
1	2	3	4	5	6	7^2	8	9	10	11^1					13	12																		5
1		3	4	5	6	7^2	8	9	10	11^1					13	12	2																	6
1	12	3	4	5	6	7^1	8	9	10^2	11^3				13			2	14																7
1	12	3	4	5	6	7^3	8	9		11^1				13			2		14	10^2														8
1	12	3	4	5	6■	7^1	8	9		11^2				13			2		14		10^3													9
1	6	3	4	5			8	9		11^2				13			2			12	10^1	7												10
1	2	6	4	5		12	13	9	10^3								3				14	7^1	8	11^2										11
1	2	6	4	5		12	13	9^3	10								3				14	11^2	7^1	8										12
1	2	4	7	5	6^1				10^2	12							3			13	9	11		8										13
1	2	6	4	5		7	14	9	12	13							3				10^1	11^2		8^3										14
1	2	6^2	4	5	13	7^1		9	12								3				10	11		8										15
1	2	6	4	5		7^1	12	9^2	13								3				10■	11		8										16
1	2	6	4	5		7^1	12	9	10								3					11		8										17
1	2	6	4	5	12		13	9	10^2								3^1			14		11		8	7^3									18
1	2	6	4	5	12			9	10^2								3					11^1		8	7	13								19
1	2	6	4	5			12	9	10^2								3				13	11^1		8	7^3	14								20
1	2	6	4	5			12	9	13								3				10^2	7		8		11^1								21
1	2	6	4	5			12	9	13								3				10^2	11^3		8^1	7	14								22
1	2	6	4^1	5	3		8^3	9^2	13			12									10	11			7	14								23
1	2	6	4		5		12	9					13								10	11^1		8	7		3^2							24
1	2	3	4	5	6^2			9^1	12				13								10	11^3		8	7	14								25
1	2	6	4	5	3			9	12												10^1	11^2		8	7	13								26
1	2^3	6	4	5	3			9	10^1	12^2									13		11			8	7			14						27
1	7	6	4	5			12	9	10^2								3		13						11			2^1	8					28
1	7	6	4	5				9									3				10				11			2	8					29
1	2	6	4	5				9									3		12		10			8	7					11^1				30
1	2	6	4					9									3^1				10	11		8	7			12			5			31
1	2	6						9^2				4				13	3		12		10				7				8	11^1	5			32
1	2	6	4^3					9^2					12				3^1		13		10■	11		8	7					14	5			33
1	2	6	4					9^2				12	14				3		13			10^3		8	7				11^1			5		34
1	2	6	4^2					9				12					3		13			10		8	7^3				11^1	14	5			35
1	2^1	6	4					9				11	12	13			3					10^3		8	7^2					14		5		36
1	2	6	4					9				12		13			3		14					8	7^3					11^1	5		10^2	37
1	2	6	4					9^1				12	13				3				14			8	7						11	5^2	10^3	38
1	2	6	4					9				12					3■				13			8^1	7					14	11	5^3	10^2	39
1	2	3	4^2					12				8	13								10	14			7					11^3	6	5	9^1	40
1	2	3						9^1				4	11								10^3	13			7				8	14	6	5	12^2	41
1	2	3							12			4	8								10^1	11^2			7					13	6	5	9	42
1	2	3	12						10^3			4	11	14			13				9				7				8^1		6^2	5		43
1	2	6	12					9^2	13			4^1					3				10	11^3			7				8	14	5			44
1	2	6	4					9	12			13					3				10^1	11		8^3	7^2					14	5			45
1	2	6	12					9	13								3				10	11^3		8^1					7	14	4	5^2		46

FA Cup
Third Round Millwall (h) 2-0
Fourth Round Fulham (a) 0-3

Carling Cup
First Round Darlington (h) 1-2

SUNDERLAND — FA Premiership

FOUNDATION

A Scottish schoolmaster named James Allan, working at Hendon Board School, took the initiative in the foundation of Sunderland in 1879 when they were formed as The Sunderland and District Teachers' Association FC at a meeting in the Adults School, Norfolk Street. Due to financial difficulties, they quickly allowed members from outside the teaching profession and so became Sunderland AFC in October 1880.

Stadium of Light, Sunderland, Tyne and Wear SR5 1SU.

Telephone: (0191) 551 5000.

Fax: (0191) 551 5123.

Ticket Office: 0845 671 1973.

Website: www.safc.com

Ground Capacity: 49,000.

Record Attendance: Stadium of Light: 48,353 v Liverpool, FA Premier League, 13 April 2002. FA Premier League figure (46,062). Roker Park: 75,118 v Derby Co, FA Cup 6th rd replay, 8 March 1933.

Pitch Measurements: 105m × 68m.

Chairman: Niall Quinn.

Vice-chairman: John Hays.

Chief Executive: Peter Walker.

Club Secretary: Margaret Byrne.

Manager: Roy Keane.

Head Coach: Tony Loughlin.

First Team Coach: Neil Bailey.

Head of Sports Therapy: Pete Friar.

Colours: Red and white striped shirts, black shorts, black and red stockings.

Change Colours: All white with red and black trim.

Year Formed: 1879.

Turned Professional: 1886.

Ltd Co.: 1906.

Club Nickname: Black Cats.

Previous Name: 1879, Sunderland and District Teacher's AFC; 1880, Sunderland.

Grounds: 1879, Blue House Field, Hendon; 1882, Groves Field, Ashbrooke; 1883, Horatio Street; 1884, Abbs Field, Fulwell; 1886, Newcastle Road; 1898, Roker Park; 1997, Stadium of Light.

First Football League Game: 13 September 1890, Football League, v Burnley (h) L 2–3 – Kirtley; Porteous, Oliver; Wilson, Auld, Gibson; Spence (1), Miller, Campbell (1), Scott, D. Hannah.

Record League Victory: 9–1 v Newcastle U (a), Division 1, 5 December 1908 – Roose; Forster, Melton; Daykin, Thomson, Low; Mordue (1), Hogg (3), Brown, Holley (3), Bridgett (2).

HONOURS

Football League: FL C – Champions 2004–05, 2006–07; Division 1 – Champions 1891–92, 1892–93, 1894–95, 1901–02, 1912–13, 1935–36, 1995–96, 1998–99; Runners-up 1893–94, 1897–98, 1900–01, 1922–23, 1934–35; Division 2 – Champions 1975–76; Runners-up 1963–64, 1979–80; 1989–90 (play-offs). Division 3 – Champions 1987–88.

FA Cup: Winners 1937, 1973; Runners-up 1913, 1992.

Football League Cup: Runners-up 1985.

European Competitions: *European Cup-Winners' Cup:* 1973–74.

SKY SPORTS FACT FILE

Like many others of the era, Jack Poole's Football League career was delayed by the First World War. A left-half he was stationed at Roker with the Sherwood Foresters and was spotted by manager Bob Kyle playing on the beach. He had five successful seasons.

Record Cup Victory: 11–1 v Fairfield, FA Cup 1st rd, 2 February 1895 – Doig; McNeill, Johnston; Dunlop, McCreadie (1), Wilson; Gillespie (1), Millar (5), Campbell, Hannah (3), Scott (1).

Record Defeat: 0–8 v Sheff Wed, Division 1, 26 December 1911. 0–8 v West Ham U, Division 1, 19 October 1968. 0–8 v Watford, Division 1, 25 September 1982.

Most League Points (2 for a win): 61, Division 2, 1963–64.

Most League Points (3 for a win): 105, Division 1, 1998–99 (Football League Record).

Most League Goals: 109, Division 1, 1935–36.

Highest League Scorer in Season: Dave Halliday, 43, Division 1, 1928–29.

Most League Goals in Total Aggregate: Charlie Buchan, 209, 1911–25.

Most League Goals in One Match: 5, Charlie Buchan v Liverpool, Division 1, 7 December 1919; 5, Bobby Gurney v Bolton W, Division 1, 7 December 1935; 5, Dominic Sharkey v Norwich C, Division 2, 20 February 1962.

Most Capped Player: Charlie Hurley, 38 (40), Republic of Ireland.

Most League Appearances: Jim Montgomery, 537, 1962–77.

Youngest League Player: Derek Forster, 15 years 184 days v Leicester C, 22 August 1964.

Record Transfer Fee Received: £5,500,000 from Leeds U for Michael Bridges, July 1999.

Record Transfer Fee Paid: £8,000,000 to Rangers for Tore Andre Flo, August 2002.

Football League Record: 1890 Elected to Division 1; 1958–64 Division 2; 1964–70 Division 1; 1970–76 Division 2; 1976–77 Division 1; 1977–80 Division 2; 1980–85 Division 1; 1985–87 Division 2; 1987–88 Division 3; 1988–90 Division 2; 1990–91 Division 1; 1991–92 Division 2; 1992–96 Division 1; 1996–97 FA Premier League; 1997–99 Division 1; 1999–2003 FA Premier League; 2003–04 Division 1; 2004–05 FL C; 2005–06 FA Premier League; 2006–07 FL C; 2007– FA Premier League.

MANAGERS

Tom Watson 1888–96
Bob Campbell 1896–99
Alex Mackie 1899–1905
Bob Kyle 1905–28
Johnny Cochrane 1928–39
Bill Murray 1939–57
Alan Brown 1957–64
George Hardwick 1964–65
Ian McColl 1965–68
Alan Brown 1968–72
Bob Stokoe 1972–76
Jimmy Adamson 1976–78
Ken Knighton 1979–81
Alan Durban 1981–84
Len Ashurst 1984–85
Lawrie McMenemy 1985–87
Denis Smith 1987–91
Malcolm Crosby 1992–93
Terry Butcher 1993
Mick Buxton 1993–95
Peter Reid 1995–2002
Howard Wilkinson 2002–03
Mick McCarthy 2003–06
Niall Quinn 2006
Roy Keane August 2006–

LATEST SEQUENCES

Longest Sequence of League Wins: 13, 14.11.1891 – 2.4.1892.

Longest Sequence of League Defeats: 17, 18.1.2003 – 16.8.2003.

Longest Sequence of League Draws: 6, 26.3.1949 – 19.4.1949.

Longest Sequence of Unbeaten League Matches: 19, 3.5.1998 – 14.11.1998.

Longest Sequence Without a League Win: 22, 21.12.2002 – 16.8.2003.

Successive Scoring Runs: 29 from 8.11.1997.

Successive Non-scoring Runs: 10 from 27.11.1976.

TEN YEAR LEAGUE RECORD

		P	W	D	L	F	A	Pts	Pos
1997-98	Div 1	46	26	12	8	86	50	90	3
1998-99	Div 1	46	31	12	3	91	28	105	1
1999-2000	PR Lge	38	16	10	12	57	56	58	7
2000-01	PR Lge	38	15	12	11	46	41	57	7
2001-02	PR Lge	38	10	10	18	29	51	40	17
2002-03	PR Lge	38	4	7	27	21	65	19	20
2003-04	Div 1	46	22	13	11	62	45	79	3
2004-05	FL C	46	29	7	10	76	41	94	1
2005-06	PR Lge	38	3	6	29	26	69	15	20
2006-07	FL C	46	27	7	12	76	47	88	1

DID YOU KNOW ?

Left-winger Albert McInroy turned goalkeeper at school. A packer at Preston Co-op, he played two North End reserve games in two years, then turned professional with Leyland Motors 1922. In May 1923 he went to Sunderland, won an England cap and never looked back.

SUNDERLAND 2006–07 LEAGUE RECORD

Match No.	Date	Venue	Opponents	Result		H/T Score	Lg. Pos.	Goalscorers	Attendance
1	Aug 6	A	Coventry C	L	1-2	0-0	—	Murphy [52]	22,366
2	9	H	Birmingham C	L	0-1	0-1	—		26,668
3	12	H	Plymouth Arg	L	2-3	1-2	21	Murphy [1], Elliott S [67]	24,377
4	19	A	Southend U	L	1-3	0-1	24	Stead [90]	9848
5	28	H	WBA	W	2-0	1-0	—	Whitehead [33], Collins N [47]	24,242
6	Sept 9	A	Derby Co	W	2-1	0-1	21	Brown [62], Wallace [64]	26,502
7	13	A	Leeds U	W	3-0	2-0	—	Miller L [28], Kavanagh [45], Elliott S [48]	23,037
8	16	H	Leicester C	D	1-1	0-0	14	Hysen [66]	35,104
9	23	A	Ipswich T	L	1-3	1-1	17	De Vos (og) [29]	23,311
10	30	H	Sheffield W	W	1-0	0-0	14	Leadbitter [58]	36,764
11	Oct 14	A	Preston NE	L	1-4	0-3	17	Varga [56]	19,603
12	17	A	Stoke C	L	1-2	1-0	—	Yorke [28]	14,482
13	21	H	Barnsley	W	2-0	0-0	17	Whitehead [82], Brown [88]	27,918
14	28	A	Hull C	W	1-0	0-0	14	Wallace [90]	25,512
15	31	H	Cardiff C	L	1-2	1-2	—	Brown [10]	26,528
16	Nov 4	A	Norwich C	L	0-1	0-0	17		24,652
17	11	H	Southampton	D	1-1	0-0	19	Wallace [62]	25,667
18	18	H	Colchester U	W	3-1	1-0	16	Elliott S 2 [45, 53], Connolly [90]	25,197
19	24	A	Wolverhampton W	D	1-1	0-1	—	Elliott S [80]	27,203
20	28	A	QPR	W	2-1	2-0	—	Murphy [17], Leadbitter [45]	13,108
21	Dec 2	H	Norwich C	W	1-0	0-0	14	Murphy [76]	27,934
22	9	H	Luton T	W	2-1	1-1	13	Murphy [9], Connolly [53]	30,445
23	16	A	Burnley	D	2-2	0-1	11	Leadbitter [80], Connolly [90]	14,798
24	22	A	Crystal Palace	L	0-1	0-1	—		17,439
25	26	H	Leeds U	W	2-0	0-0	11	Connolly [65], Leadbitter [81]	40,116
26	30	H	Preston NE	L	0-1	0-1	12		30,460
27	Jan 1	A	Leicester C	W	2-0	0-0	10	Hysen [79], Connolly [83]	21,975
28	13	H	Ipswich T	W	1-0	1-0	9	Connolly [13]	27,604
29	20	A	Sheffield W	W	4-2	2-0	7	Yorke [21], Hysen [45], Connolly [58], Edwards [89]	29,103
30	30	H	Crystal Palace	D	0-0	0-0	—		26,958
31	Feb 3	H	Coventry C	W	2-0	1-0	7	Yorke [19], Edwards [84]	33,591
32	10	A	Plymouth Arg	W	2-0	0-0	7	Stokes [69], Connolly [71]	15,247
33	17	H	Southend U	W	4-0	2-0	5	Connolly [4], Hysen [13], John 2 [77, 78]	33,576
34	20	A	Birmingham C	D	1-1	1-0	—	Edwards [27]	20,941
35	24	H	Derby Co	W	2-1	1-0	4	Connolly (pen) [27], Miller L [90]	36,049
36	Mar 3	A	WBA	W	2-1	1-0	4	Yorke [23], John [49]	23,252
37	10	A	Barnsley	W	2-0	0-0	3	Leadbitter [66], Connolly [90]	18,207
38	13	H	Stoke C	D	2-2	1-2	—	Whitehead [24], Murphy [90]	31,358
39	17	H	Hull C	W	2-0	1-0	3	Evans [3], John [90]	38,448
40	31	A	Cardiff C	W	1-0	0-0	3	Wallace [72]	19,353
41	Apr 7	H	Wolverhampton W	W	2-1	1-0	2	Murphy [15], Wallace [63]	40,748
42	9	A	Southampton	W	2-1	0-0	1	Edwards [77], Leadbitter [87]	25,766
43	14	H	QPR	W	2-1	1-1	1	Whitehead [7], Leadbitter [76]	39,206
44	21	A	Colchester U	L	1-3	0-1	2	Yorke [55]	6042
45	27	H	Burnley	W	3-2	1-1	—	Murphy [14], Connolly (pen) [54], Edwards [80]	44,448
46	May 6	A	Luton T	W	5-0	2-0	1	Stokes [4], Murphy 2 [6, 46], Wallace [77], Connolly [86]	10,260

Final League Position: 1

GOALSCORERS

League (76): Connolly 13 (2 pens), Murphy 10, Leadbitter 7, Wallace 6, Edwards 5, Elliott S 5, Yorke 5, Hysen 4, John 4, Whitehead 4, Brown 3, Miller L 2, Stokes 2, Collins N 1, Evans 1, Kavanagh 1, Stead 1, Varga 1, own goal 1.
Carling Cup (0).
FA Cup (0).

Alnwick B 11	Delap R 6	Collins D 36 + 2	Miller L 24 + 6	Cunningham K 11	Caldwell S 11	Leadbitter G 24 + 20	Whitehead D 43 + 2	Murphy D 27 + 11	Elliott S 15 + 9	Lawrence L 10 + 2	Kyle K — + 2	Stead J 1 + 4	Clarke C 2 + 2	Brown C 10 + 6	Wright S 2 + 1	Elliott R 7	Collins N 6 + 1	Arnau C — + 1	Nosworthy N 27 + 2	Hysen T 15 + 11	Kavanagh G 10 + 4	Varga S 20	Connolly D 30 + 6	Wallace R 20 + 12	Yorke D 28 + 4	Ward D 30	Nyatanga L 9 + 2	Fulop M 5	Hartley P — + 1	Miller T 3 + 1	Evans J 18	Edwards C 15	Stokes A 7 + 7	Simpson D 13 + 1	John S 10 + 5	Match No.
1	2	3		5	6	7^1	8	9^2	10	11	12	13																		4						1
1	2	3		5	6^1	7	8	9	10	11^2		13	12																	4						2
1	2	3		5		7	8	9	10	11^1		12	6^3	13	14															4^2						3
1	4^1			5		7^2	8	9	10		12	11			2	3	6	13																		4
1	2			5		7^3	8	12	10	4		13		9^2		3	6		14	11^1																5
1	2		4	5			8		12					9		3					7	6	10^1	11												6
1			4	5		13	8^3	9	12^2	14						3	2				7	6	10^1	11												7
1			4^2	5		12	8	9^3						10		3	2^1			13	7	6		11	14											8
1			4	5		12	8^1			13				9^3		3	2^2			14	7	6		11■	10											9
1		3	12	5		7	8	9^2		4				13					2	11^1		6	14		10^3											10
1		5				7	8	9^2		4			3						2	11^1		6	10	12	13											11
		5	4			7	8^3	12					13	14		3^2			2			6	10	11^1	9	1										12
		3		5^3		12	8	9^2		4				11					2			6	10^1	13	7	1	14									13
		5				7	8	9		2^2				10^1			12					6	13	11■	4	1	3									14
		5				12	8	9	13	7^1				10^2			2^3			11	14	6			4	1	3									15
		5			6	12	2	13	14	7				9						11^2	4^1		10^3		8	1	3									16
		5			6	12	8	9^2	14					13					2		4^3		10^1	11	7	1	3									17
		5	4			7^1	2		10					9^3						13	12	6	14	11^2	8	1	3									18
		5	4^1			7	2		9										13	14	12	6	10	11^2	8^3	1	3									19
		3	4^2		5	7^1	12	9	10										2		8	6	13	11		1										20
		6	4		5	7^2	2	9	10											12	8			11^1	13	1	3									21
		3	4		5	12	2	9	7												8	6	10^1	11				1								22
		3	12		5	4	2	9^2	7											13	14	6	10	11^3	8^1	1										23
		3	4^3		5	7^2	8	9^1						12					2		11	6	10	13	14	1										24
		12	4		5	11	2	9^2	7^3											13		6	10	14	8	1	3^1									25
			4		5^3	7	2	9	12					13					3			6	10	11^2	8^1	1	14									26
			4			12	2	13	7					9^2						11^3		6	10	3	8^1	1	5		14							27
		12				4	2	13	14										6	11^2			10	3^1	8	1					5	7	9^3			28
		3	4^1			12	5	13	10										6	11^3			9^2	14	8	1					2	7				29
		3	4^2			12	2	13											5	11^3			10	14	8	1					6	7^1	9			30
		3				4^3	2	9^2											5	12		6		11^1	8	1						7	13	14	10	31
		3	12			13	4												5	11^3			10		8			1			6	7	14	2^1	9^2	32
		3	4			12	8^1												5	11^3			10^2	13				1			6	7	14	2	9	33
		3	12			13	4												5	14			10		8			1			6	7	11^2	2^1	9^3	34
		3	4			12		13											5	11^1			10		8	1					6	7		2	9^2	35
		3	13				4	12											5	14			10		8^2	1					6	7^3	11	2	9^1	36
		3	4^2			7	8	12											5				10	11		1				13	6			2	9^1	37
		3	12			4	7	13											5	11			10	14	8^1	1					6^3			2	9^2	38
		3	4^2			12	7	9											5				10^3	13	8	1					6		11^1	2	14	39
		3	4			7^3	8	9^2											5	11^1			10	12		1					6		14	2	13	40
		3	4			12	8	9	13										5				14	11^3		1					6	7		2^1	10^2	41
		3	4^1			13	12		9^3										5	11			10		8^2	1					6	7	14	2		42
		3				12	4	9^3											5				10	11^2	8^1	1					6	7	14	2	13	43
		3				4^1	2	9^3	12										5				10	13	8	1					6	7	14		11^2	44
		3	4^1			12	8	9											5	13			10^3			1					6	7	11^2	2	14	45
		3				4	11^1	9^3							2				5				12	13	8			1			6	7^2	10		14	46

FA Cup
Third Round — Preston NE — (a) — 0-1

Carling Cup
First Round — Bury — (a) — 0-2

SWANSEA CITY FL Championship 1

FOUNDATION

The earliest Association Football in Wales was played in the Northern part of the country and no international took place in the South until 1894, when a local paper still thought it necessary to publish an outline of the rules and an illustration of the pitch markings. There had been an earlier Swansea club, but this has no connection with Swansea Town (now City) formed at a public meeting in June 1912.

Liberty Stadium, Landore, Swansea SA1 2FA.

Telephone: (01792) 616 600.

Fax: (01792) 616 606.

Ticket Office: (0870) 040 0004.

Website: www.swanseacity.net

Email: jackie@swanseacity

Ground Capacity: 20,520.

Record Attendance: 32,796 v Arsenal, FA Cup 4th rd, 17 February 1968 (at Vetch Field).

Pitch Measurements: 115yd × 74yd.

Chairman: Huw Jenkins.

Vice-chairman: Leigh Dineen.

General Manager: Alun Cowie.

Secretary: Jackie Rockey.

Manager: Roberto Martinez.

Assistant Manager: Graeme Jones.

Physio: Richard Evans.

Colours: All white.

Change Colours: Sky and navy blue.

Year Formed: 1912. ***Turned Professional:*** 1912.

Ltd Co.: 1912.

Previous Name: 1912, Swansea Town; 1970, Swansea City.

Club Nicknames: 'The Swans', 'The Jacks'.

Grounds: 1912, Vetch Field; 2005, Liberty Stadium.

First Football League Game: 28 August 1920, Division 3, v Portsmouth (a) L 0–3 – Crumley; Robson, Evans; Smith, Holdsworth, Williams; Hole, I. Jones, Edmundson, Rigsby, Spottiswood.

Record League Victory: 8–0 v Hartlepool U, Division 4, 1 April 1978 – Barber; Evans, Bartley, Lally (1) (Morris), May, Bruton, Kevin Moore, Robbie James (3 incl. 1p), Curtis (3), Toshack (1), Chappell.

Record Cup Victory: 12–0 v Sliema W (Malta), ECWC 1st rd 1st leg, 15 September 1982 – Davies; Marustik, Hadziabdic (1), Irwin (1), Kennedy, Rajkovic (1), Loveridge (2) (Leighton James), Robbie James, Charles (2), Stevenson (1), Latchford (1) (Walsh (3)).

HONOURS

Football League: Championship 2 – promoted 2004–05 (3rd); Division 1 best season: 6th, 1981–82; Division 2 – Promoted 1980–81 (3rd); Division 3 (S) – Champions 1924–25, 1948–49; Division 3 – Champions 1999–2000; Promoted 1978–79 (3rd); Division 4 – Promoted 1969–70 (3rd), 1977–78 (3rd), 1987–88 (play-offs).

FA Cup: Semi-finals 1926, 1964.

Football League Cup: best season: 4th rd, 1965, 1977.

Welsh Cup: Winners 11 times; Runners-up 8 times.

Autoglass Trophy: Winners 1994, 2006.

Football League Trophy: Winners 2006.

European Competitions: *European Cup-Winners' Cup:* 1961–62, 1966–67, 1981–82, 1982–83, 1983–84, 1989–90, 1991–92.

SKY SPORTS FACT FILE

On 8 January 1915 Southern League Swansea Town met First Division champions Blackburn Rovers in the FA Cup. A home crowd of 16,000 saw Benny Benyon the only amateur on the pitch score the lone goal after 20 minutes. The Swans survived a late missed penalty.

Record Defeat: 0–8 v Liverpool, FA Cup 3rd rd, 9 January 1990. 0–8 v Monaco, ECWC, 1st rd 2nd leg, 1 October 1991.

Most League Points (2 for a win): 62, Division 3 (S), 1948–49.

Most League Points (3 for a win): 85, Division 3, 1999–2000.

Most League Goals: 90, Division 2, 1956–57.

Highest League Scorer in Season: Cyril Pearce, 35, Division 2, 1931–32.

Most League Goals in Total Aggregate: Ivor Allchurch, 166, 1949–58, 1965–68.

Most League Goals in One Match: 5, Jack Fowler v Charlton Ath, Division 3S, 27 December 1924.

Most Capped Player: Ivor Allchurch, 42 (68), Wales.

Most League Appearances: Wilfred Milne, 585, 1919–37.

Youngest League Player: Nigel Dalling, 15 years 289 days v Southport, 6 December 1974.

Record Transfer Fee Received: £400,000 from Bristol C for Steve Torpey, August 1997.

Record Transfer Fee Paid: £340,000 to Liverpool for Colin Irwin, August 1981.

Football League Record: 1920 Original Member of Division 3; 1921–25 Division 3 (S); 1925–47 Division 2; 1947–49 Division 3 (S); 1949–65 Division 2; 1965–67 Division 3; 1967–70 Division 4; 1970–73 Division 3; 1973–78 Division 4; 1978–79 Division 3; 1979–81 Division 2; 1981–83 Division 1; 1983–84 Division 2; 1984–86 Division 3; 1986–88 Division 4; 1988–92 Division 3; 1992–96 Division 2; 1996–2000 Division 3; 2000–01 Division 2; 2001–04 Division 3; 2004–05 FL 2; 2005– FL 1.

MANAGERS

Walter Whittaker 1912–14
William Bartlett 1914–15
Joe Bradshaw 1919–26
Jimmy Thomson 1927–31
Neil Harris 1934–39
Haydn Green 1939–47
Bill McCandless 1947–55
Ron Burgess 1955–58
Trevor Morris 1958–65
Glyn Davies 1965–66
Billy Lucas 1967–69
Roy Bentley 1969–72
Harry Gregg 1972–75
Harry Griffiths 1975–77
John Toshack 1978–83
(resigned October re-appointed in December) 1983–84
Colin Appleton 1984
John Bond 1984–85
Tommy Hutchison 1985–86
Terry Yorath 1986–89
Ian Evans 1989–90
Terry Yorath 1990–91
Frank Burrows 1991–95
Bobby Smith 1995
Kevin Cullis 1996
Jan Molby 1996–97
Micky Adams 1997
Alan Cork 1997–98
John Hollins 1998–2001
Colin Addison 2001–02
Nick Cusack 2002
Brian Flynn 2002–04
Kenny Jackett 2004–07
Roberto Martinez February 2007–

LATEST SEQUENCES

Longest Sequence of League Wins: 9, 27.11.1999 – 22.01.2000.

Longest Sequence of League Defeats: 9, 26.1.1991 – 19.3.1991.

Longest Sequence of League Draws: 5, 5.1.1993 – 5.2.1993.

Longest Sequence of Unbeaten League Matches: 19, 19.10.1970 – 9.3.1971.

Longest Sequence Without a League Win: 15, 25.3.1989 – 2.9.1989.

Successive Scoring Runs: 27 from 28.8.1947.

Successive Non-scoring Runs: 6 from 6.2.1996.

TEN YEAR LEAGUE RECORD

		P	W	D	L	F	A	Pts	Pos
1997-98	Div 3	46	13	11	22	49	62	50	20
1998-99	Div 3	46	19	14	13	56	48	71	7
1999-2000	Div 3	46	24	13	9	51	30	85	1
2000-01	Div 2	46	8	13	25	47	73	37	23
2001-02	Div 3	46	13	12	21	53	77	51	20
2002-03	Div 3	46	12	13	21	48	65	49	21
2003-04	Div 3	46	15	14	17	58	61	59	10
2004-05	FL 2	46	24	8	14	62	43	80	3
2005-06	FL 1	46	18	17	11	78	55	71	6
2006-07	FL 1	46	20	12	14	69	53	72	7

DID YOU KNOW ?

Few players can claim to have played their last official first class match when captaining his country. Goalkeeper and one-time defender Roy John led Wales against England on 11 November 1939 in a wartime match. Later made guest appearances for various clubs.

SWANSEA CITY 2006–07 LEAGUE RECORD

Match No.	Date	Venue	Opponents	Result		H/T Score	Lg. Pos.	Goalscorers	Attendance
1	Aug 5	H	Cheltenham T	L	1-2	0-0	—	Knight [77]	15,199
2	8	A	Scunthorpe U	D	2-2	1-0	—	Robinson [45], Fallon [78]	4187
3	12	A	Oldham Ath	L	0-1	0-0	19		4708
4	19	H	Doncaster R	W	2-0	0-0	13	Trundle 2 [83, 90]	12,218
5	26	A	Leyton Orient	W	1-0	0-0	11	Knight [54]	4162
6	Sept 1	H	Yeovil T	D	1-1	0-0	—	Trundle (pen) [64]	14,513
7	9	H	Bradford C	W	1-0	0-0	7	Robinson [73]	11,481
8	12	A	Brentford	W	2-0	1-0	—	Knight 2 [37, 55]	5392
9	16	A	Gillingham	L	1-3	0-2	8	Knight [85]	5500
10	23	H	Huddersfield T	L	1-2	0-0	10	Knight [81]	12,202
11	26	H	Crewe Alex	W	2-1	1-1	—	Fallon [24], Knight [53]	10,031
12	30	A	Nottingham F	L	1-3	1-0	12	Fallon [42]	19,034
13	Oct 6	H	Tranmere R	D	0-0	0-0	—		12,347
14	14	A	Chesterfield	W	3-2	2-0	8	Britton [4], Trundle 2 (1 pen) [35, 67 (p)]	3915
15	22	H	Millwall	W	2-0	1-0	5	Lawrence [17], Britton [51]	13,975
16	28	A	Northampton T	L	0-1	0-0	6		5444
17	Nov 3	H	Bournemouth	W	4-2	1-0	—	Iriekpen [4], Fallon 2 [58, 60], Trundle [90]	11,795
18	18	A	Port Vale	W	2-0	0-0	6	Trundle [89], Butler [90]	4615
19	26	H	Bristol C	D	0-0	0-0	6		15,531
20	Dec 5	A	Brighton & HA	L	2-3	0-1	—	Lawrence [59], Fallon [90]	5209
21	9	A	Blackpool	D	1-1	1-0	7	Dickinson (og) [21]	6216
22	16	H	Carlisle U	W	5-0	3-0	6	Lawrence [8], Fallon 2 [15, 62], Robinson [27], Pratley [59]	12,550
23	23	H	Rotherham U	D	1-1	0-0	5	Akinfenwa [90]	12,327
24	26	A	Crewe Alex	W	3-1	2-0	5	Trundle 2 [3, 23], Lawrence [47]	6083
25	30	A	Huddersfield T	L	2-3	2-0	7	Trundle 2 (1 pen) [9 (p), 43]	9399
26	Jan 1	H	Brentford	W	2-0	2-0	5	Akinfenwa [29], Osborne (og) [41]	12,554
27	13	A	Bradford C	D	2-2	1-1	7	O'Leary [33], Akinfenwa [52]	7347
28	20	H	Nottingham F	D	0-0	0-0	8		16,849
29	23	H	Gillingham	W	2-0	1-0	—	Akinfenwa [6], Robinson [72]	9675
30	Feb 3	A	Cheltenham T	L	1-2	1-1	6	Trundle [17]	5221
31	10	H	Oldham Ath	L	0-1	0-1	7		9880
32	17	A	Doncaster R	D	2-2	2-1	7	Akinfenwa [20], Trundle (pen) [45]	7900
33	20	H	Scunthorpe U	L	0-2	0-1	—		10,746
34	24	A	Yeovil T	L	0-1	0-0	9		5984
35	27	A	Rotherham U	W	2-1	1-0	—	Abbott [20], Trundle [61]	3697
36	Mar 3	H	Leyton Orient	D	0-0	0-0	7		12,901
37	10	A	Tranmere R	W	2-0	1-0	8	Robinson [6], Trundle [52]	7467
38	16	H	Chesterfield	W	2-0	0-0	—	Robinson (pen) [76], Iriekpen [78]	11,384
39	24	H	Northampton T	W	2-1	1-1	7	Lawrence [45], Robinson [46]	11,071
40	31	A	Millwall	L	0-2	0-1	7		9248
41	Apr 7	A	Bristol C	D	0-0	0-0	7		14,025
42	9	H	Port Vale	W	3-0	2-0	7	Trundle [19], Duffy D 2 [26, 59]	12,465
43	14	A	Bournemouth	D	2-2	0-1	8	Tate [83], Trundle [88]	6786
44	21	H	Brighton & HA	W	2-1	2-1	7	Duffy D 2 [21, 41]	11,972
45	28	A	Carlisle U	W	2-1	1-0	7	Trundle [1], Duffy D [90]	10,578
46	May 5	H	Blackpool	L	3-6	1-2	7	Iriekpen 2 [14, 55], Trundle [47]	18,903

Final League Position: 7

GOALSCORERS

League (69): Trundle 19 (4 pens), Fallon 8, Knight 7, Robinson 7 (1 pen), Akinfenwa 5, Duffy D 5, Lawrence 5, Iriekpen 4, Britton 2, Abbott 1, Butler 1, O'Leary 1, Pratley 1, Tate 1, own goals 2.
Carling Cup (2): Pratley 1, own goal 1.
FA Cup (9): Britton 3 (1 pen), Butler 2, Akinfenwa 1, Iriekpen 1, Robinson 1, Trundle 1.
J Paint Trophy (1): Tudur-Jones 1.

Gueret W 42	Amankwaah K 23 + 6	Williams T 17 + 12	O'Leary K 19 + 4	Monk G 2	Iriekpen E 31 + 1	Pratley D 25 + 3	Robinson A 33 + 6	Knight L 10 + 1	Fallon R 22 + 2	Butler T 17 + 13	Britton L 39 + 2	Akinfenwa A 12 + 13	McLeod K 2 + 2	Tate A 36 + 2	Austin K 26 + 4	Trundle L 31 + 3	Lawrence D 37 + 2	Macdonald S 3 + 5	Way D 4 + 5	Oakes A 4	Tudur Jones O 3 + 1	Jones C — + 7	Painter M 22 + 1	Craney I 24 + 3	Watt S — + 1	Meslien S — + 1	Duffy R 8 + 3	Abbott P 9 + 9	Duffy D 5 + 3	Allen J — + 1	*Match No.*
1	2	3	4[1]	5	6	7	8	9	10[2]	11[3]	12	13	14																		1
1	2	3		5[1]	6	7	8	9[3]	10	13			11[2]	4■	12	14															2
1	2	3[1]	4		6	7		9[2]	10	13	8		12		5	11															3
1	2	12	13		6	7			10[3]	11[2]	4	14	8[1]		5	9	3														4
1	2	3[1]	4		6	7		9■	10[2]	13		12		5	11			8[3]	14												5
1	2	11[3]			6	7	8		10[2]	12	4[1]	13		5	3	9			14												6
1	2				6	7	12	13		11[3]	8[1]	10		4	5	9[2]	3		14												7
1	2				6	7	12	9	13	11[1]	8	10[2]		4	5		3														8
1	2	12			6	7[3]	11	9		13	8[2]	10		4	5[1]		3		14												9
1	2[3]	12			6	7	8	9		11[2]	13	10		4	5[1]		3		14												10
		3			6	7	8	9	10		4			2			5		11	1											11
	12	3			6	7	8	9[2]	10		4[1]	13		2			5[3]	14	11	1											12
1	2	3			6	7	8	9[1]	10		4[2]			5		12		13	11												13
1		3[1]			6	7	8[2]		10	12	4			2	5	9	13		11[3]		14										14
1		3			6	7	11[1]		10[2]	12	4	13		2		9[3]	5				8	14									15
1		3			6		11		10[1]		4■	12		2		9	5	8[2]			7	13									16
1	12	3			6	7[1]	11[2]		10		4			2	13	9	5	14			8[3]										17
	2		8[1]				11[2]		10	13	7			4	5	9	6	12		1			3								18
1	2[3]				12	7	11		10[2]		8	13		4	5	9	6[1]						3	14							19
1	2					7■	11		12		4	9[2]		5	3		6	10[1]				13		8							20
1	2				6[3]		11		10[1]		7[2]	12		4	3	9	5	13						8	14						21
1						7	11		10		4			5	2	9	6						3[1]	8		12					22
1		12				7			10	11[1]	4	13		5	3	9	6						2[2]	8							23
1			14			7	11		10[2]	12	4	13		2	5	9[1]	6						3	8[3]							24
1	2[1]		12			7	13		10[3]	11[2]		14		4	5	9■	6						3	8							25
1	12					7[2]	11[1]		10	13	4	9		2	5		6						3	8							26
1		8	4■						10	11	7	9			5		6						3				2				27
1		3					12			11[1]	7	10		4	5	9	6							8			2				28
1		3				12	13			11	7[1]	10[3]		4	5	9[2]	6							8			2	14			29
1			4[1]			7	11				8	10[2]		2	5	9	6						3	12				13			30
1					6	7	11				4[1]	13		3[3]	12	9	5						14	8			2	10[2]			31
1	12		4		6	13	7[2]			11		10[3]				9	5						3	8			2[1]	14			32
1			4		6[2]	12	7			11		10[3]		13		9	5						3	8[1]			2	14			33
	2		4				11				7			8	5[1]	9	6			1		13	3	12				10[2]			34
1	2	12	4				11[2]			13	7			5		9[1]	6						3	8				10			35
1		2[1]	4		6		11			12	7			5		9						13	3	8				10[2]			36
1	2	12	4[2]		6		11[1]				7			5		9■	13					14	3	8				10[3]			37
1	2[3]	12			6		8			11[1]	7			4			5					13	3	10			14	9[2]			38
1	2[1]	13	12		6		10[3]			11[2]	7			4			5						3	8				9	14		39
1			4		6		8			11	7[3]			2■		12	5						3	10[2]			13	9[1]	14		40
1	2[2]		4		6		12			11[1]	7					9	5						3	8			13	10[3]	14		41
1	12	11	4							13	7[2]				5[1]	9[3]	6						3	8			2	14	10		42
1		12	4[2]		6					11[1]	7			13		9	5						3	8			2[3]	14	10		43
1		12	4		6		11[2]				7			2	13	9	5						3[1]	8				14	10[3]		44
1	12	13	4		6		11[3]				7			3[1]	2[2]	9	5							8				14	10		45
1	2[2]	12	4[1]		6		11[3]				7				3	9	5							8				13	10	14	46

FA Cup

First Round	Newport Co	(a)	3-1
Second Round	Darlington	(a)	3-1
Third Round	Sheffield U	(a)	3-0
Fourth Round	Ipswich T	(a)	0-1

Carling Cup

First Round	Wycombe W	(h)	2-3

J Paint Trophy

First Round	Walsall	(a)	1-1
Second Round	Peterborough U	(a)	0-1

SWINDON TOWN FL Championship 1

FOUNDATION

It is generally accepted that Swindon Town came into being in 1881, although there is no firm evidence that the club's founder, Rev. William Pitt, captain of the Spartans (an offshoot of a cricket club) changed his club's name to Swindon Town before 1883, when the Spartans amalgamated with St Mark's Young Men's Friendly Society.

County Ground, County Road, Swindon, Wiltshire SN1 2ED.

Telephone: 0870 443 1969.

Fax: (01793) 333 703.

Ticket Office: 0870 443 1894.

Website: www.swindontownfc.co.uk

Email: enquiries@swindontownfc.co.uk

Ground Capacity: 14,800 (approx).

Record Attendance: 32,000 v Arsenal, FA Cup 3rd rd, 15 January 1972.

Pitch Measurements: 110yd × 75yd.

Chairman: Willie Carson.

Acting Chief Executive: Martyn Starnes.

Secretary: Louise Fletcher.

Manager: Paul Sturrock.

Assistant Manager: Kevin Summerfield.

Physio: Dick Mackey.

Colours: Red shirts, red shorts, red stockings.

Change Colours: White shirts with red flash, white shorts, white socks.

Year Formed: 1881* (*see Foundation*).

Turned Professional: 1894.

Ltd Co.: 1894.

Club Nickname: 'Robins'.

Grounds: 1881, The Croft; 1896, County Ground.

First Football League Game: 28 August 1920, Division 3, v Luton T (h) W 9–1 – Nash; Kay, Macconachie; Langford, Hawley, Wareing; Jefferson (1), Fleming (4), Rogers, Batty (2), Davies (1), (1 og).

Record League Victory: 9–1 v Luton T, Division 3 (S), 28 August 1920 – Nash; Kay, Macconachie; Langford, Hawley, Wareing; Jefferson (1), Fleming (4), Rogers, Batty (2), Davies (1), (1 og).

HONOURS

Football League: Promoted to FA Premier League from Division 1 – 1992–93 (play-offs); Promoted from FL 2 (3rd) 2006–07.

Division 2 – Champions 1995–96; Division 3 – Runners-up 1962–63, 1968–69; Division 4 – Champions 1985–86 (with record 102 points).

FA Cup: Semi-finals 1910, 1912.

Football League Cup: Winners 1969.

Anglo-Italian Cup: Winners 1970.

SKY SPORTS FACT FILE

Peter Brezovan, loan goalkeeper signing from FC Brno, made an outstanding debut for Swindon Town against Hartlepool United on 5 August 2006. He saved one penalty diving to his right and the point-blank rebound, a second to his left in the 2–1 victory.

Record Cup Victory: 10–1 v Farnham U Breweries (away), FA Cup 1st rd (replay), 28 November 1925 – Nash; Dickenson, Weston, Archer, Bew, Adey; Denyer (2), Wall (1), Richardson (4), Johnson (3), Davies.

Record Defeat: 1–10 v Manchester C, FA Cup 4th rd (replay), 25 January 1930.

Most League Points (2 for a win): 64, Division 3, 1968–69.

Most League Points (3 for a win): 102, Division 4, 1985–86.

Most League Goals: 100, Division 3 (S), 1926–27.

Highest League Scorer in Season: Harry Morris, 47, Division 3 (S), 1926–27.

Most League Goals in Total Aggregate: Harry Morris, 216, 1926–33.

Most League Goals in One Match: 5, Harry Morris v QPR, Division 3S, 18 December 1926; 5, Harry Morris v Norwich C, Division 3S, 26 April 1930; 5, Keith East v Mansfield T, Division 3, 20 November 1965.

Most Capped Player: Rod Thomas, 30 (50), Wales.

Most League Appearances: John Trollope, 770, 1960–80.

Youngest League Player: Paul Rideout, 16 years 107 days v Hull C, 29 November 1980.

Record Transfer Fee Received: £1,500,000 from Manchester C for Kevin Horlock, January 1997.

Record Transfer Fee Paid: £800,000 to West Ham U for Joey Beauchamp, August 1994.

Football League Record: 1920 Original Member of Division 3; 1921–58 Division 3 (S); 1958–63 Division 3; 1963–65 Division 2; 1965–69 Division 3; 1969–74 Division 2; 1974–82 Division 3; 1982–86 Division 4; 1986–87 Division 3; 1987–92 Division 2; 1992–93 Division 1; 1993–94 FA Premier League; 1994–95 Division 1; 1995–96 Division 2; 1996–2000 Division 1; 2000–04 Division 2; 2004–06 FL 1; 2006–07 FL 2; 2007– FL 1.

MANAGERS

Sam Allen 1902–33
Ted Vizard 1933–39
Neil Harris 1939–41
Louis Page 1945–53
Maurice Lindley 1953–55
Bert Head 1956–65
Danny Williams 1965–69
Fred Ford 1969–71
Dave Mackay 1971–72
Les Allen 1972–74
Danny Williams 1974–78
Bobby Smith 1978–80
John Trollope 1980–83
Ken Beamish 1983–84
Lou Macari 1984–89
Ossie Ardiles 1989–91
Glenn Hoddle 1991–93
John Gorman 1993–94
Steve McMahon 1994–99
Jimmy Quinn 1999–2000
Colin Todd 2000
Andy King 2000–01
Roy Evans 2001
Andy King 2002–06
Iffy Onuora 2006
Dennis Wise 2006
Paul Sturrock November 2006–

LATEST SEQUENCES

Longest Sequence of League Wins: 8, 12.1.1986 – 15.3.1986.

Longest Sequence of League Defeats: 8, 29.8.2005 – 8.10.2005.

Longest Sequence of League Draws: 6, 22.11.1991 – 28.12.1991.

Longest Sequence of Unbeaten League Matches: 22, 12.1.1986 – 23.8.86.

Longest Sequence Without a League Win: 19, 30.10.1999 – 4.3.2000.

Successive Scoring Runs: 31 from 17.4.1926.

Successive Non-scoring Runs: 5 from 16.11.1963.

TEN YEAR LEAGUE RECORD

		P	*W*	*D*	*L*	*F*	*A*	*Pts*	*Pos*
1997-98	Div 1	46	14	10	22	42	73	52	18
1998-99	Div 1	46	13	11	22	59	81	50	17
1999-2000	Div 1	46	8	12	26	38	77	36	24
2000-01	Div 2	46	13	13	20	47	65	52	20
2001-02	Div 2	46	15	14	17	46	56	59	13
2002-03	Div 2	46	16	12	18	59	63	60	10
2003-04	Div 2	46	20	13	13	76	58	73	5
2004-05	FL 1	46	17	12	17	66	68	63	12
2005-06	FL 1	46	11	15	20	46	65	48	23
2006-07	FL 2	46	25	10	11	58	38	85	3

DID YOU KNOW ?

Swindon Town enjoyed a successful tour of South America in 1912 remaining unbeaten in eight games, two of which were drawn. Of the 21 goals registered, Archie Bown scored 11. The Argentina League were held 2–2, and the Uruguayan League beaten 3–0.

SWINDON TOWN 2006–07 LEAGUE RECORD

Match No.	Date	Venue	Opponents	Result	H/T Score	Lg. Pos.	Goalscorers	Attendance
1	Aug 5	A	Hartlepool U	W 1-0	1-0	—	Peacock [11]	4690
2	8	H	Barnet	W 2-1	0-1	—	Shakes [54], Brownlie [90]	7475
3	12	H	Rochdale	W 1-0	1-0	2	Goodall (og) [44]	6771
4	19	A	Darlington	W 2-1	2-1	1	Evans [6], Roberts [21]	4571
5	26	H	Stockport Co	W 2-0	1-0	1	Brown [34], Roberts [63]	6868
6	Sept 1	A	Chester C	W 2-0	0-0	—	Peacock 2 [48, 74]	3382
7	9	A	Wrexham	L 1-2	1-0	1	Evans [28]	5257
8	12	H	Milton Keynes D	W 2-1	1-1	—	Smith J (pen) [45], Evans (pen) [56]	8304
9	16	H	Peterborough U	L 0-1	0-1	2		7329
10	23	A	Notts Co	D 1-1	0-0	4	Onibuje [47]	6079
11	26	A	Wycombe W	D 1-1	0-0	—	Brownlie [51]	6090
12	30	H	Boston U	D 1-1	1-0	2	Monkhouse [25]	6074
13	Oct 7	A	Accrington S	D 1-1	0-1	4	Peacock [67]	3083
14	14	H	Grimsby T	W 3-0	2-0	3	Pook [33], Monkhouse [44], Peacock [88]	5719
15	21	A	Shrewsbury T	W 2-1	1-0	3	Onibuje [12], Brown [81]	5218
16	28	H	Lincoln C	L 0-1	0-0	4		7685
17	Nov 4	H	Hereford U	L 1-2	1-1	4	Roberts [32]	6910
18	18	A	Torquay U	W 1-0	0-0	3	Roberts (pen) [62]	4029
19	25	H	Bury	W 2-1	1-1	2	Roberts [34], Fitzgerald (og) [90]	5628
20	Dec 5	A	Mansfield T	L 0-2	0-2	—		2274
21	9	A	Walsall	W 2-0	1-0	2	Jutkiewicz [23], Roberts (pen) [69]	6812
22	16	H	Bristol R	W 2-1	2-1	2	Jutkiewicz [15], Weston [17]	10,010
23	23	A	Macclesfield T	L 1-2	0-1	4	Peacock [64]	2377
24	26	H	Wycombe W	W 2-1	1-0	4	Jutkiewicz [45], Peacock [53]	8878
25	30	H	Notts Co	D 1-1	0-1	4	Timlin [77]	6805
26	Jan 1	A	Milton Keynes D	W 1-0	1-0	4	Peacock [31]	6797
27	13	H	Wrexham	W 2-1	1-1	2	Zaaboub [9], Roberts (pen) [71]	6130
28	20	A	Boston U	W 3-1	1-1	2	Roberts [10], Pook [59], Sturrock [88]	2101
29	27	H	Macclesfield T	W 2-0	1-0	2	Shakes [45], Peacock [52]	6062
30	30	A	Peterborough U	D 1-1	0-0	—	Sturrock [88]	3516
31	Feb 3	H	Hartlepool U	L 0-1	0-0	2		6841
32	17	H	Darlington	D 1-1	1-0	4	Nicholas [9]	5570
33	20	A	Barnet	L 0-1	0-1	—		2639
34	24	H	Chester C	W 1-0	1-0	3	Smith J (pen) [9]	5462
35	Mar 3	A	Stockport Co	L 0-3	0-1	4		6594
36	10	H	Accrington S	W 2-0	1-0	3	Smith J (pen) [45], Nicholas [48]	6197
37	17	A	Grimsby T	L 0-1	0-0	5		4595
38	25	A	Lincoln C	W 3-2	2-1	4	Roberts [17], Corr [34], Peacock [49]	5741
39	31	H	Shrewsbury T	W 2-1	0-1	3	Corr [67], Roberts [73]	7335
40	Apr 3	A	Rochdale	D 0-0	0-0	—		2544
41	7	A	Hereford U	D 0-0	0-0	3		4740
42	9	H	Torquay U	W 2-1	1-0	3	Sturrock [2], Jutkiewicz [83]	7389
43	14	A	Bury	W 1-0	0-0	3	Jutkiewicz [85]	2401
44	21	H	Mansfield T	W 2-0	2-0	3	Corr [4], Hjelde (og) [38]	10,472
45	28	A	Bristol R	L 0-1	0-1	3		9902
46	May 5	H	Walsall	D 1-1	0-0	3	Ifil [52]	14,731

Final League Position: 3

GOALSCORERS

League (58): Peacock 10, Roberts 10 (3 pens), Jutkiewicz 5, Corr 3, Evans 3 (1 pen), Smith J 3 (3 pens), Sturrock 3, Brown 2, Brownlie 2, Monkhouse 2, Nicholas 2, Onibuje 2, Pook 2, Shakes 2, Ifil 1, Timlin 1, Weston 1, Zaaboub 1, own goals 3.
Carling Cup (2): Evans 1, Nicholas 1.
FA Cup (5): Roberts 3 (1 pen), Ifil 1, own goal 1.
J Paint Trophy (0).

Brezovan P 14	Smith J 41	Vincent J 34	Weston C 21 + 6	Ifil J 40	Nicholas A 30 + 5	Shakes R 26 + 6	Pook M 32 + 6	Roberts C 39 + 3	Peacock L 40 + 2	Monkhouse A 9 + 1	Evans P 11 + 4	Onibuje F 6 + 8	Jutkiewicz L 13 + 20	Brownlie R 6 + 8	Williams A 27	Holgate A — + 1	Caton A 3 + 2	Brown A 13 + 17	Comyn-Platt C 2	Ince P 2 + 1	Rhodes A — + 4	Smith P 31	Lonergan A 1	Zaaboub S 23 + 4	Timlin M 18 + 6	Wells B — + 1	Sturrock B 7 + 12	Noubissie P 1 + 2	Westwood A 8 + 1	James K — + 2	Corr B 8	Grimes A — + 4	*Match No.*
1	2	3	4^{1}	5	6	7	8	9^{2}	10^{3}	11	12	13	14																				1
1	2	3	4	5	6	7^{1}	8^{2}	9	10^{3}	11	13	14		12																			2
1	2	3	12	5		7^{1}	8	9^{3}	10^{2}	11	4		13	14	6																		3
1	2	3	4	5	12	7		9^{3}	10^{2}	11^{1}	8			13	6	14																	4
1	2		4	5	3	7	12	9	10^{2}		8^{1}	13			6		11^{3}	14															5
1	2		4^{3}	5■	3	7	12	9^{1}	10^{2}		8	13					14	11	6														6
1	2		4^{3}		6	7^{1}		9	10		8			12	3		13	11^{2}	5	14													7
1	2^{1}		7	5	6	12		9^{2}	10^{3}		8	13		14	3		11			4													8
1			7^{3}	5	6	2		9	10		8	12		14	3		11^{1}	13		4^{2}													9
1	2	3		5			7	12	10	13	8	9^{2}	14	4^{3}	6			11^{1}															10
1	2	3	12	5			8	13	10^{2}	11	4^{1}	9^{3}	14	7	6																		11
1	2	3	4^{3}	5			8	9^{1}	10	11^{2}		12	14	7	6			13															12
1	2	3	4	5			8^{2}	12	10	11	13	9		7^{1}	6																		13
1^{6}	2	3	4	5	15	12	8		10	11		9^{2}		7^{1}	6						13												14
	2	3	4	5		7	8		10^{2}	11^{1}		9			6			12			13	1											15
	2	3	4		6	7^{1}	8		10			9		12	5			11^{2}			13	1											16
	2	3		5	6	4^{2}	7	9^{1}	10		8	12						11			13		1										17
	2		4	5	3	7	12	9^{3}	13		8^{1}		14	11^{2}	6							1		10									18
	2		4	5	6	7		9	10^{1}				12		3			11^{2}				1		13	8								19
	2		4	5	3	7^{1}		9^{2}					10	13^{3}	6			12				1		11	8	14							20
	2	3	4	5	12	13	14	9^{2}					10		6			7^{3}				1		11^{1}	8								21
	2	3	4^{1}	5	13	12		9^{2}	14				10		6			7^{3}				1		11	8								22
		3	4	5	12	2			9		13^{3}		10		6			7^{1}				1		11^{2}	8		14						23
	2	3		5		12	7	9^{2}	4				10^{1}		6							1		11	8		13						24
	2	3^{2}		5		12	7	9	4^{3}				10^{1}		6			13				1		11	8		14						25
	2	3		5		4^{1}	7	9^{2}	10				13		6			12				1		11	8								26
	2	3	4^{3}	5		8	7	9^{2}	10				13		6			12				1		11^{1}			14						27
	2		12	5	3	4	7^{1}	9^{2}	10				13		6							1		11^{3}	8		14						28
	2			5	3	4	7	9	10						6							1		11	8								29
	2			5	3^{2}	4^{1}	7	9	10				12		6			13				1		11^{3}	8		14						30
	2		12	5	3^{1}	4^{3}	7^{2}	9	10				13		6							1		11	8		14						31
	2	3		5	6	4	7^{2}	9^{1}	10				12					11^{3}				1		14	8		13						32
	2	3	4^{1}	5	6^{2}	7^{3}	12	9					10					11				1		13	8		14						33
	2	3	12	5	6		7^{3}	9^{2}					10					13				1		11^{1}	8		4	14					34
	2^{2}	3		5■		6^{3}	12	9	10				13					14				1			8		11^{1}	7	4				35
	2	3			4	6^{1}	7	9^{3}	10				12					11^{2}				1		13	8		14		5				36
	2	3^{3}			6	4^{1}	7	9	10				12					11^{2}				1			8■		13	14	5				37
	2	3	12	5	6		7	9^{2}	10				8^{3}									1		11						13	4^{1}	14	38
	2	3		5	6		7	9^{1}	10				8^{3}					12				1		11^{2}	13		14				4		39
	2	3		5	6		7	9	10				8^{2}					12				1		11^{1}	13						4		40
	2	3			6		7	9	10^{1}				8^{3}					12				1		11^{2}	13				5		4	14	41
	2	3			6		7	9^{1}	10				13					12				1		11^{3}	14		8^{2}		5		4		42
		3		5	6		7	9^{2}	10				12					13				1		11			8^{3}		2		4^{1}	14	43
		3		5	6		7	9^{2}	10				12					13				1		11^{3}	14		8^{1}		2		4		44
		3		5	6		7	9	10				8^{2}									1		11^{3}	12		4^{1}		2	14		13	45
	2^{2}	3		5	6		7	9	10				12									1		11			8		13		4^{1}		46

FA Cup

First Round	Carlisle U	(h)	3-1
Second Round	Morecambe	(h)	1-0
Third Round	Crystal Palace	(a)	1-2

Carling Cup

First Round	Brentford	(h)	2-2

J Paint Trophy

First Round	Wycombe W	(a)	0-1

TORQUAY UNITED Blue Square Premier

FOUNDATION

The idea of establishing a Torquay club was agreed by old boys of Torquay College and Torbay College, while sitting in Princess Gardens listening to the band. A proper meeting was subsequently held at Tor Abbey Hotel at which officers were elected. This was on 1 May 1899 and the club's first competition was the Eastern League (later known as the East Devon League). As an amateur club it played at Teignmouth Road, Torquay Recreation Ground and Cricket Field Road before settling down for four years at Torquay Cricket Ground where the rugby club now plays. They became Torquay United in 1921 after merging with Babbacombe FC.

Plainmoor Ground, Torquay, Devon TQ1 3PS.

Telephone: (01803) 328 666.

Fax: (01803) 323 976.

Ticket Office: (01803) 328 666.

Website: www.torquayunited.com

Email: gullsfc@aol.com

Ground Capacity: 6,117.

Record Attendance: 21,908 v Huddersfield T, FA Cup 4th rd, 29 January 1955.

Pitch Measurements: 110yd × 74yd.

Chairman: Michael Bateson.

Vice-chairman: Mervyn Benney.

Chief Executive: Colin Lee.

Secretary: Deborah Hancox.

Manager: Paul Buckle.

Physio: Darren James.

Colours: Yellow shirts, yellow shorts, yellow stockings.

Change Colours: Blue shirts, blue shorts, blue stockings.

Year Formed: 1899.

Turned Professional: 1921.

Ltd Co.: 1921.

Previous Name: 1910, Torquay Town; 1921, Torquay United.

Club Nickname: 'The Gulls'.

Grounds: 1899, Teignmouth Road; 1900, Torquay Recreation Ground; 1904, Cricket Field Road; 1906, Torquay Cricket Ground; 1910, Plainmoor Ground.

First Football League Game: 27 August 1927, Division 3 (S), v Exeter C (h) D 1–1 – Millsom; Cook, Smith; Wellock, Wragg, Connor, Mackey, Turner (1), Jones, McGovern, Thomson.

HONOURS

Football League: Division 3 – Promoted 2003–04 (3rd); Division 3 (S) – Runners-up 1956–57; Division 4 – Promoted 1959–60 (3rd), 1965–66 (3rd), 1990–91 (play-offs).

FA Cup: best season: 4th rd, 1949, 1955, 1971, 1983, 1990.

Football League Cup: never past 3rd rd.

Sherpa Van Trophy: Runners-up 1989.

SKY SPORTS FACT FILE

Winger Ralph Birkett was snapped up by Torquay United from Dartmouth in 1929, transferred to Arsenal in April 1933 and later played for Middlesbrough and Newcastle United. A pre-war England cap, he had wartime and Football League honours, too.

Record League Victory: 9–0 v Swindon T, Division 3 (S), 8 March 1952 – George Webber; Topping, Ralph Calland; Brown, Eric Webber, Towers; Shaw (1), Marchant (1), Northcott (2), Collins (3), Edds (2).

Record Cup Victory: 7–1 v Northampton T, FA Cup 1st rd, 14 November 1959 – Gill; Penford, Downs; Bettany, George Northcott, Rawson; Baxter, Cox, Tommy Northcott (1), Bond (3), Pym (3).

Record Defeat: 2–10 v Fulham, Division 3 (S), 7 September 1931. 2–10 v Luton T, Division 3 (S), 2 September 1933.

Most League Points (2 for a win): 60, Division 4, 1959–60.

Most League Points (3 for a win): 81, Division 3, 2003–04.

Most League Goals: 89, Division 3 (S), 1956–57.

Highest League Scorer in Season: Sammy Collins, 40, Division 3 (S), 1955–56.

Most League Goals in Total Aggregate: Sammy Collins, 204, 1948–58.

Most League Goals in One Match: 5, Robin Stubbs v Newport Co, Division 4, 19 October 1963.

Most Capped Player: Rodney Jack, (71), St Vincent.

Most League Appearances: Dennis Lewis, 443, 1947–59.

Youngest League Player: David Byng, 16 years 36 days v Walsall, 14 August 1993.

Record Transfer Fee Received: £400,000 from Crystal Palace for Matthew Greg, October 1998.

Record Transfer Fee Paid: £500,000 to Crewe Alex for Rodney Jack, August 1998.

Football League Record: 1927 Elected to Division 3 (S); 1958–60 Division 4; 1960–62 Division 3; 1962–66 Division 4; 1966–72 Division 3; 1972–91 Division 4; 1991–2004 Division 3; 2004–05 FL 1; 2005–07 FL 2; 2007– Blue Square Pr.

LATEST SEQUENCES

Longest Sequence of League Wins: 8, 24.1.1998 – 3.3.1998.

Longest Sequence of League Defeats: 8, 30.9.1995 – 18.11.1995.

Longest Sequence of League Draws: 8, 25.10.1969 – 13.12.1969.

Longest Sequence of Unbeaten League Matches: 15, 5.5.1990 – 3.11.1990.

Longest Sequence Without a League Win: 19, 23.9.2006 – 20.1.2007.

Successive Scoring Runs: 19 from 3.10.1953.

Successive Non-scoring Runs: 7 from 8.1.1972.

MANAGERS

Percy Mackrill 1927–29
A. H. Hoskins 1929
(Secretary-Manager)
Frank Womack 1929–32
Frank Brown 1932–38
Alf Steward 1938–40
Billy Butler 1945–46
Jack Butler 1946–47
John McNeil 1947–50
Bob John 1950
Alex Massie 1950–51
Eric Webber 1951–65
Frank O'Farrell 1965–68
Alan Brown 1969–71
Jack Edwards 1971–73
Malcolm Musgrove 1973–76
Mike Green 1977–81
Frank O'Farrell 1981–82
(continued as General Manager to 1983)
Bruce Rioch 1982–84
Dave Webb 1984–85
John Sims 1985
Stuart Morgan 1985–87
Cyril Knowles 1987–89
Dave Smith 1989–91
John Impey 1991–92
Ivan Golac 1992
Paul Compton 1992–93
Don O'Riordan 1993–95
Eddie May 1995–96
Kevin Hodges *(Head Coach)* 1996–98
Wes Saunders 1998–2001
Roy McFarland 2001–02
Leroy Rosenior 2002–06
Ian Atkins 2006
Lubos Kubik 2006–07
Keith Curle 2007
Leroy Rosenior 2007
Paul Buckle June 2007–

TEN YEAR LEAGUE RECORD

		P	W	D	L	F	A	Pts	Pos
1997-98	Div 3	46	21	11	14	68	59	74	5
1998-99	Div 3	46	12	17	17	47	58	53	20
1999-2000	Div 3	46	19	12	15	62	52	69	9
2000-01	Div 3	46	12	13	21	52	77	49	21
2001-02	Div 3	46	12	15	19	46	63	51	19
2002-03	Div 3	46	16	18	12	71	71	66	9
2003-04	Div 3	46	23	12	11	68	44	81	3
2004-05	FL 1	46	12	15	19	55	79	51	21
2005-06	FL 2	46	13	13	20	53	66	52	20
2006-07	FL 2	46	7	14	25	36	63	35	24

DID YOU KNOW ?

One-time England schoolboy cap centre-forward Tommy Tait, signed from Reading in 1939, played in the three abortive pre-war matches and the two FA Cup ties in 1945–46 as his only first class appearances for the club outside of wartime regional games.

TORQUAY UNITED 2006–07 LEAGUE RECORD

Match No.	*Date*	*Venue*	*Opponents*	*Result*		*H/T Score*	*Lg. Pos.*	*Goalscorers*	*Atten- dance*
1	Aug 5	A	Barnet	W	1-0	0-0	—	Thorpe [90]	2827
2	8	H	Rochdale	W	1-0	0-0	—	Mansell [87]	3039
3	12	H	Lincoln C	L	1-2	0-0	9	Garner [52]	3192
4	19	A	Hartlepool U	D	1-1	1-0	10	Phillips [5]	3688
5	26	H	Chester C	D	2-2	1-0	11	Ward 2 [43, 74]	2541
6	Sept 1	A	Darlington	D	1-1	1-1	—	Thorpe (pen) [33]	4007
7	9	A	Bury	W	1-0	1-0	8	Evans [33]	2317
8	13	H	Bristol R	D	0-0	0-0	—		3145
9	16	H	Mansfield T	W	1-0	1-0	7	Ward [37]	2660
10	23	A	Macclesfield T	D	3-3	1-1	7	Mansell [33], Thorpe [67], Ward [85]	1836
11	26	A	Milton Keynes D	L	2-3	2-0	—	Ward 2 [8, 45]	5378
12	30	H	Notts Co	L	0-1	0-0	10		2815
13	Oct 6	A	Wycombe W	L	0-2	0-1	—		4769
14	14	H	Accrington S	L	0-2	0-0	16		2743
15	21	A	Stockport Co	L	0-1	0-1	19		4663
16	28	H	Shrewsbury T	D	0-0	0-0	18		2262
17	Nov 4	A	Walsall	L	0-1	0-0	19		5806
18	18	H	Swindon T	L	0-1	0-0	20		4029
19	25	A	Peterborough U	L	2-5	1-3	22	Mansell [7], Robertson J [90]	4452
20	Dec 5	H	Wrexham	D	1-1	0-1	—	Robertson J [51]	1588
21	9	A	Hereford U	D	1-1	1-1	23	Angus [2]	3078
22	16	H	Boston U	L	0-1	0-1	23		2107
23	22	A	Grimsby T	L	0-2	0-1	—		4666
24	26	H	Milton Keynes D	L	0-2	0-2	24		2715
25	30	H	Macclesfield T	L	0-1	0-0	24		2169
26	Jan 1	A	Bristol R	L	0-1	0-0	24		6475
27	13	H	Bury	D	2-2	1-0	24	Ward 2 (2 pens) [32, 49]	2063
28	20	A	Notts Co	L	2-5	2-3	24	Cooke [25], Dickson [35]	4311
29	26	H	Grimsby T	W	4-1	2-0	—	Ward [3], Thorpe 3 (1 pen) [44, 59, 83 (p)]	2095
30	30	A	Mansfield T	L	0-5	0-2	—		2573
31	Feb 3	H	Barnet	D	1-1	1-0	24	Taylor [45]	1942
32	10	A	Lincoln C	L	0-1	0-1	24		4881
33	17	H	Hartlepool U	L	0-1	0-1	24		2194
34	20	A	Rochdale	L	0-2	0-1	—		2456
35	24	H	Darlington	L	0-1	0-0	24		2109
36	Mar 2	A	Chester C	D	1-1	0-0	—	Thorpe (pen) [90]	1996
37	10	H	Wycombe W	W	3-0	2-0	24	Kerry [20], Williams [40], Robertson C [76]	3060
38	17	A	Accrington S	L	0-1	0-0	24		4004
39	24	A	Shrewsbury T	L	0-1	0-0	24		4678
40	31	H	Stockport Co	W	1-0	0-0	24	Reid [90]	3005
41	Apr 7	H	Walsall	L	1-2	0-2	24	Reid [58]	4047
42	9	A	Swindon T	L	1-2	0-1	24	Thorpe (pen) [82]	7389
43	14	H	Peterborough U	D	1-1	1-0	24	Hill [45]	2106
44	21	A	Wrexham	L	0-1	0-0	24		6057
45	28	A	Boston U	D	1-1	0-0	24	Mansell [49]	2664
46	May 5	H	Hereford U	D	0-0	0-0	24		2942

Final League Position: 24

GOALSCORERS

League (36): Ward 9 (2 pens), Thorpe 8 (4 pens), Mansell 4, Reid 2, Robertson J 2, Angus 1, Cooke 1, Dickson 1, Evans 1, Garner 1, Hill 1, Kerry 1, Phillips 1, Robertson C 1, Taylor 1, Williams 1.
Carling Cup (0).
FA Cup (5): Robertson J 2, Ward 2 (1 pen), McPhee 1.
J Paint Trophy (0).

Abbey N 24	Andrews L 46	Reed S 10+5 / Williams M 2	Garner D 8	Taylor C 11+2 / Robertson C 9	Angus S 33+3	Phillips M 10+4	Mansell L 43+2	Thorpe L 39+2	Evans M 14	Hill K 24+12	Hockley M 25+12	Ward J 21+4	Villis M 3+3	McPhee C 11+26	Woods S 32	Murray A 21 / Oliver D — +1	Fortune-West L 2+3	Critchell K 6+1 / Graham D 7	Leary M — +2	Motteram C 1+6	Robertson J 5+4	Horsell M 5+1 / Reid R 4+3	Easter J 8+2	McKoy N 1+3	Dickson R 7+2	Hapgood L — +1	Cooke S 9+4	Miller K 7	Robinson M 18	Jarvis R 2+2	Smith P 5+3	Baxter D — +1	Halliday M 3	Kerry L 6+1	Gordon D 8	John A 6+1	Rayner S 10	Match No.
1	2	3	4^1	5	6	7^2	8	9	10^3	11	12	13	14																									1
1	2	3	4^2	5	6	7^1	8	9	10^3	11	13	12		14																								2
1	2		4	5	6^2	7^1	8	9	10	11		12	13		3																							3
1	2		4		6	7^1	8	9	10	3	12	11^2		13	5																							4
1	2		4^1		6	7^2	8	9	10	3	12	11		13	5																							5
1	2	12	4		6	7	8^2	9	10	3^1	13				5	11																						6
1	2		4^1		6		8	9	10	3	12	11^2		13	5	7																						7
1	2				6	12	8	9	10	3	4^1	11			5	7																						8
1	2	3		13			8	9	10	11	4	6^1		12	5	7^2																						9
1	2	12		5	6	7^3	8	9	10		13	11		14	3^1	4^2																						10
1	2			13	6	12	8	9■	10^2	3^1	4^3	11		14	5	7																						11
1	2			5	6	12	8			3		11		10^1	4	7	9																					12
1	2	12		5	6^1		8	9^3		11	4^2	10		13	3	7	14																					13
1	2			5	6	7^2	12	9	10^3		4	11		13	3	8^1	14																					14
1	2		4^2		6	12	8	9	10^3	3^1		11		13	5	7	14																					15
1	2				6	7^1	8	9				3		12	5	11	10	4																				16
1	2^2				3	11^3	8	5				10	12	9	6	7^1		4	13	14																		17
1	2	12			3^1		8	6	10^3	11		9		13	5	7^2		4			14																	18
1	2	3					8	6		11	12	10		9^2	5	7^1		4^3	14		13																	19
1	2	3					8	9^1		11^3	4^2		6	12	5	7		13		14	10																	20
1	2	3			8^2		13			11	12		6	9	5	7		4^1		14	10^3																	21
1	2	3^2			4		8	10				11	6^1	12	5	7				13	9																	22
1	2	3			6		8	12		11^2	4^3	13		9	5	7				14	10^1																	23
1^6	2	3^1			6		8			12	4	10		9	5	7				11^2	13	15																24
	2	12			6		8			3	4	10^2		13	5	7		11^1			9	1																25
	2	3^1			6		8	9			4^2	10		11	5	7				13	12	1																26
	2				6		8	9		3	4	10^1		12	5							1	7^2	13	11													27
	2^2			5	6		8	9		11^1				12	4							1	10		3	13	7											28
	2			5	12		8^1	9			4	10^2			6								13		11^3		7	1	3	14								29
	2			5	6		8	10			4^2			9^3									7				11^1	1	3	12	13	14						30
	2			5	6		8	10		12				13									9^2				11^1	1	3	7	4							31
	2				6■		8	9^3		12	13				5								10				14	1	3	11^2	7^1		4					32
	2						8	9		11	4^3			12									10^2				13	1	5		14		7^1	3	6			33
	2				6		8	9		12	13			14									10					1	11		7^1		3^2	4^3	5			34
	2				6^3		8	9		12	4^1												13	14				1	3		11			10	5	7^2		35
	2				6		8	9		12	13												10^3				14		11		7			4^2	5	3^1	1	36
	2	10^1		6			8	9^3			4			12		14											7^2		3		13			11	5		1	37
	2	10		6			8■	9		12	4			13													11^3		3^2					7^1	5	14	1	38
	2			6				9		12	4			13				10						11	8^1				3						5	7^2	1	39
	2			5	6		8	9		12	4							10				13			11^2				3							7^1	1	40
	2			5	6^1		8	9		12	4^2			13				10				7							3					14		11^3	1	41
	2				12		8	9		13	4			14				7				10			11^2				6^1						5	3^3	1	42
	2^1			6	12		8	13		11	4			7	5			9^3				10^2					14		3								1	43
	2			6			8	9			4			7^2	5			11^1				13			12		10		3								1	44
	2			6			8	9■		12	4			13	5			10^1				14			7^3		11^2		3								1	45
	2			6			8			11	4			9^2	5							10		12	13		7^1		3									46

FA Cup

First Round	Leatherhead	(h)	2-1
Second Round	Leyton Orient	(h)	1-1
		(a)	2-1
Third Round	Southampton	(h)	0-2

Carling Cup

First Round	Norwich C	(h)	0-2

J Paint Trophy

First Round	Bristol R	(a)	0-1

TOTTENHAM HOTSPUR FA Premiership

FOUNDATION

The Hotspur Football Club was formed from an older cricket club in 1882. Most of the founders were old boys of St John's Presbyterian School and Tottenham Grammar School. The Casey brothers were well to the fore as the family provided the club's first goalposts (painted blue and white) and their first ball. They soon adopted the local YMCA as their meeting place, but after a couple of moves settled at the Red House, which is still their headquarters, although now known simply as 748 High Road.

White Hart Lane, Bill Nicholson Way, 748 High Road, Tottenham, London N17 0AP.

Telephone: 0870 420 5000.

Fax: (020) 8365 5175.

Ticket Office: 0870 420 5000.

Website: www.tottenhamhotspur.co.uk

Email: email@tottenhamhotspur.co.uk

Ground Capacity: 36,310.

Record Attendance: 75,038 v Sunderland, FA Cup 6th rd. 5 March 1938.

Pitch Measurements: 100m × 67m.

Chairman: Daniel Levy.

Vice-chairman: Paul Kemsley.

Secretary: John Alexander.

Manager: Martin Jol.

First Team Coach: Chris Hughton.

Head of Medical Services: Dr Kalpesh Parmar.

Colours: White shirts, white shorts, white stockings.

Change Colours: Insignia blue shirts, insignia blue shorts, insignia blue stockings. ***Alternative Change Colours:*** Yellow shirts, yellow shorts, yellow stockings.

Year Formed: 1882.

Turned Professional: 1895.

Ltd Co.: 1898.

Previous Name: 1882, Hotspur Football Club; 1884, Tottenham Hotspur.

Club Nickname: 'Spurs'.

Grounds: 1882, Tottenham Marshes; 1888, Northumberland Park; 1899, White Hart Lane.

First Football League Game: 1 September 1908, Division 2, v Wolverhampton W (h) W 3–0 – Hewitson; Coquet, Burton; Morris (1), D. Steel, Darnell; Walton, Woodward (2), Macfarlane, R. Steel, Middlemiss.

HONOURS

Football League: Division 1 – Champions 1950–51, 1960–61; Runners-up 1921–22, 1951–52, 1956–57, 1962–63; Division 2 – Champions 1919–20, 1949–50; Runners-up 1908–09, 1932–33; Promoted 1977–78 (3rd).

FA Cup: Winners 1901 (as non-League club), 1921, 1961, 1962, 1967, 1981, 1982, 1991; Runners-up 1987.

Football League Cup: Winners 1971, 1973, 1999; Runners-up 1982, 2002.

European Competitions: *European Cup:* 1961–62. *European Cup-Winners' Cup:* 1962–63 (winners), 1963–64, 1967–68, 1981–82, 1982–83, 1991–92. *UEFA Cup:* 1971–72 (winners), 1972–73, 1973–74 (runners-up), 1983–84 (winners), 1984–85, 1999–2000, 2006–07. *Intertoto Cup:* 1995.

SKY SPORTS FACT FILE

On 14 September 2006 the 38th minute goal by Jermaine Jenas for Tottenham Hotspur away to Slavia Prague in the UEFA Cup, was the first away in Europe since Gordon Durie in the Cup-Winners' Cup against Stockerau (Austria) in Vienna 21 August 1991.

Record League Victory: 9–0 v Bristol R, Division 2, 22 October 1977 – Daines; Naylor, Holmes, Hoddle (1), McAllister, Perryman, Pratt, McNab, Moores (3), Lee (4), Taylor (1).

Record Cup Victory: 13–2 v Crewe Alex, FA Cup 4th rd (replay), 3 February 1960 – Brown; Hills, Henry; Blanchflower, Norman, Mackay; White, Harmer (1), Smith (4), Allen (5), Jones (3 incl. 1p).

Record Defeat: 0–8 v Cologne, UEFA Intertoto Cup, 22 July 1995.

Most League Points (2 for a win): 70, Division 2, 1919–20.

Most League Points (3 for a win): 77, Division 1, 1984–85.

Most League Goals: 115, Division 1, 1960–61.

Highest League Scorer in Season: Jimmy Greaves, 37, Division 1, 1962–63.

Most League Goals in Total Aggregate: Jimmy Greaves, 220, 1961–70.

Most League Goals in One Match: 5, Ted Harper v Reading, Division 2, 30 August 1930; 5, Alf Stokes v Birmingham C, Division 1, 18 September 1957; 5, Bobby Smith v Aston Villa, Division 1, 29 March 1958.

Most Capped Player: Pat Jennings, 74 (119), Northern Ireland.

Most League Appearances: Steve Perryman, 655, 1969–86.

Youngest League Player: Ally Dick, 16 years 301 days v Manchester C, 20 February 1982.

Record Transfer Fee Received: £18,600,000 from Manchester U for Michael Carrick, July 2006.

Record Transfer Fee Paid: £16,500,000 to Charlton Ath for Darren Bent, May 2007.

Football League Record: 1908 Elected to Division 2; 1909–15 Division 1; 1919–20 Division 2; 1920–28 Division 1; 1928–33 Division 2; 1933–35 Division 1; 1935–50 Division 2; 1950–77 Division 1; 1977–78 Division 2; 1978–92 Division 1; 1992– FA Premier League.

MANAGERS

Frank Brettell 1898–99
John Cameron 1899–1906
Fred Kirkham 1907–08
Peter McWilliam 1912–27
Billy Minter 1927–29
Percy Smith 1930–35
Jack Tresadern 1935–38
Peter McWilliam 1938–42
Arthur Turner 1942–46
Joe Hulme 1946–49
Arthur Rowe 1949–55
Jimmy Anderson 1955–58
Bill Nicholson 1958–74
Terry Neill 1974–76
Keith Burkinshaw 1976–84
Peter Shreeves 1984–86
David Pleat 1986–87
Terry Venables 1987–91
Peter Shreeves 1991–92
Doug Livermore 1992–93
Ossie Ardiles 1993–94
Gerry Francis 1994–97
Christian Gross *(Head Coach)* 1997–98
George Graham 1998–2001
Glenn Hoddle 2001–03
David Pleat (*Caretaker*) 2003–04
Jacques Santini 2004
Martin Jol November 2004–

LATEST SEQUENCES

Longest Sequence of League Wins: 13, 23.4.1960 – 1.10.1960.

Longest Sequence of League Defeats: 7, 1.1.1994 – 27.2.1994.

Longest Sequence of League Draws: 6, 9.1.1999 – 27.2.1999.

Longest Sequence of Unbeaten League Matches: 22, 31.8.1949 – 31.12.1949.

Longest Sequence Without a League Win: 16, 29.12.1934 – 13.4.1935.

Successive Scoring Runs: 32 from 24.2.1962.

Successive Non-scoring Runs: 6 from 28.12.1985.

TEN YEAR LEAGUE RECORD

		P	*W*	*D*	*L*	*F*	*A*	*Pts*	*Pos*
1997-98	PR Lge	38	11	11	16	44	56	44	14
1998-99	PR Lge	38	11	14	13	47	50	47	11
1999-2000	PR Lge	38	15	8	15	57	49	53	10
2000-01	PR Lge	38	13	10	15	47	54	49	12
2001-02	PR Lge	38	14	8	16	49	53	50	9
2002-03	PR Lge	38	14	8	16	51	62	50	10
2003-04	PR Lge	38	13	6	19	47	57	45	14
2004-05	PR Lge	38	14	10	14	47	41	52	9
2005-06	PR Lge	38	18	11	9	53	38	65	5
2006-07	PR Lge	38	17	9	12	57	54	60	5

DID YOU KNOW?

On 5 November 2006 Tottenham Hotspur beat Chelsea 2–1 at White Hart Lane to record their first win over their London rivals in 33 attempts. On 10 February 1990 Spurs had won 2–1 at Stamford Bridge with goals from David Howells and Gary Lineker.

TOTTENHAM HOTSPUR 2006–07 LEAGUE RECORD

Match No.	Date	Venue	Opponents	Result		H/T Score	Lg. Pos.	Goalscorers	Attendance
1	Aug 19	A	Bolton W	L	0-2	0-2	—		22,899
2	22	H	Sheffield U	W	2-0	2-0	—	Berbatov [7], Jenas [17]	35,287
3	26	H	Everton	L	0-2	0-0	15		35,540
4	Sept 9	A	Manchester U	L	0-1	0-1	15		75,453
5	17	H	Fulham	D	0-0	0-0	16		36,131
6	23	A	Liverpool	L	0-3	0-0	17		44,330
7	Oct 1	H	Portsmouth	W	2-1	2-1	14	Murphy [2], Defoe (pen) [35]	36,063
8	14	A	Aston Villa	D	1-1	0-0	14	Angel (og) [76]	42,551
9	22	H	West Ham U	W	1-0	1-0	13	Mido [45]	36,162
10	28	A	Watford	D	0-0	0-0	12		19,660
11	Nov 5	H	Chelsea	W	2-1	1-1	10	Dawson [25], Lennon [52]	36,070
12	12	A	Reading	L	1-3	1-2	12	Keane (pen) [24]	24,110
13	19	A	Blackburn R	D	1-1	0-1	13	Defoe (pen) [62]	18,083
14	26	H	Wigan Ath	W	3-1	2-1	10	Defoe [43], Berbatov [44], Lennon [90]	35,205
15	Dec 2	A	Arsenal	L	0-3	0-2	12		60,115
16	5	H	Middlesbrough	W	2-1	0-0	—	Berbatov [48], Keane [84]	34,154
17	9	H	Charlton Ath	W	5-1	2-1	8	Berbatov 2 [31, 66], Tainio [33], Malbranque [55], Defoe [63]	35,565
18	17	A	Manchester C	W	2-1	2-0	7	Davenport [16], Huddlestone [24]	39,825
19	23	A	Newcastle U	L	1-3	1-3	7	Taylor (og) [15]	52,079
20	26	H	Aston Villa	W	2-1	0-0	7	Defoe 2 [58, 77]	35,293
21	30	H	Liverpool	L	0-1	0-1	8		36,170
22	Jan 1	A	Portsmouth	D	1-1	0-1	7	Malbranque [50]	20,194
23	14	H	Newcastle U	L	2-3	1-1	8	Defoe [14], Berbatov [54]	35,942
24	20	A	Fulham	D	1-1	0-0	9	Chimbonda [88]	23,580
25	Feb 4	H	Manchester U	L	0-4	0-1	11		36,146
26	10	A	Sheffield U	L	1-2	1-1	11	Jenas [2]	32,144
27	21	A	Everton	W	2-1	1-1	—	Berbatov [35], Jenas [89]	34,121
28	25	H	Bolton W	W	4-1	3-1	9	Keane 2 [11, 22], Jenas [19], Lennon [90]	35,747
29	Mar 4	A	West Ham U	W	4-3	0-2	8	Defoe (pen) [51], Tainio [63], Berbatov [89], Stalteri [90]	34,966
30	17	H	Watford	W	3-1	1-0	7	Jenas [41], Robinson [63], Ghaly [85]	36,051
31	Apr 1	H	Reading	W	1-0	1-0	6	Keane (pen) [41]	36,067
32	7	A	Chelsea	L	0-1	0-0	7		41,864
33	15	A	Wigan Ath	D	3-3	2-2	8	Berbatov [4], Keane 2 (1 pen) [35 (p), 68]	16,506
34	21	H	Arsenal	D	2-2	1-0	9	Keane [30], Jenas [90]	36,050
35	28	A	Middlesbrough	W	3-2	1-0	8	Keane 2 [12, 83], Berbatov [47]	27,861
36	May 7	A	Charlton Ath	W	2-0	1-0	—	Berbatov [7], Defoe [90]	26,339
37	10	H	Blackburn R	D	1-1	0-1	—	Defoe [67]	35,974
38	13	H	Manchester C	W	2-1	2-1	5	Keane [10], Berbatov [32]	35,426

Final League Position: 5

GOALSCORERS

League (57): Berbatov 12, Keane 11 (3 pens), Defoe 10 (3 pens), Jenas 6, Lennon 3, Malbranque 2, Tainio 2, Chimbonda 1, Davenport 1, Dawson 1, Ghaly 1, Huddlestone 1, Mido 1, Murphy 1, Robinson 1, Stalteri 1, own goal 2.
Carling Cup (12): Defoe 4, Mido 3, Huddlestone 2, Berbatov 1, Keane 1, own goals 2.
FA Cup (15): Keane 5 (1 pen), Berbatov 3, Defoe 1, Ghaly 1, Jenas 1, Lennon 1, Malbranque 1, Mido 1, own goal 1.
UEFA Cup (20): Berbatov 7, Keane 5, Defoe 3, Malbranque 2, Ghaly 1, Jenas 1, Lennon 1.

Robinson P 38	Lee Y 20 + 1	Assou-Ekotto B 16	Zokora D 26 + 5	Dawson M 37	Davenport C 8 + 2	Lennon A 22 + 4	Jenas J 24 + 1	Berbatov D 30 + 3	Defoe J 20 + 14	Davids E 6 + 3	Huddlestone T 15 + 6	Keane R 18 + 9	Tainio T 20 + 1	Chimbonda P 33	Murphy D 5 + 7	Ziegler R — + 1	Ghaly H 17 + 4	Mido7 + 5	King L 21	Stalteri P 1 + 5	Malbranque S 18 + 7	Gardner A 6 + 2	Ricardo Rocha 9	Taarabt A — + 2	Ifil P 1	Match No.
1	2^{1}	3	4^{2}	5	6	7	8	9	10	11	12	13														1
1	2	3	12	5	6	7	8	9	13	11		10^{2}	4^{1}													2
1	2^{2}	3	12	5	6	7	8	9	13	11		10	4^{1}													3
1		3	4	5			8		12	11^{3}		10^{1}		2	13	14	7	9	6^{2}							4
1		3	4	5			8		12	13		10	11^{1}	2	7^{2}			9	6							5
1		3	4	5			8		10	12		9	11^{1}	2	7^{2}			13	6							6
1		3	4	5^{2}	13		8	9^{1}	10		14	12		2^{3}	7		11		6							7
1		3	4	5^{3}	6■	12	8	9^{2}	10	13				2	7		11^{1}			14						8
1		3		5		7^{2}	8		10^{1}	11	4	12		2			13	9	6							9
1		3		5		7	8	9	12		4	10^{1}		2	13		11^{2}		6							10
1		3	4	5		7	8	9	12			10^{1}		2			11		6							11
1	2^{1}	3	4^{2}	5		7	8	9	12		13	10					11		6							12
1	2	3	4	5				12	10^{1}	11^{2}	8						7■	9	6		13					13
1		3	4	5		7		9	10^{1}		8	12		2					6		11					14
1	12	3^{1}	4	5		7	13	9	14			10	11^{3}	2					6		8^{2}					15
1	3		4■	5		7		9	10^{1}		8	13^{3}	12	2	14				6		11^{2}					16
1	3			5		7		9^{1}	10		4		11	2^{3}	13			12	6	14	8^{2}					17
1	3				5			9	10^{1}		4		11	2			7	12	6		8					18
1	3		4^{1}	5				9			8			2	7		11	12	6		10					19
1	3		4	5	12			9	10^{1}		8			2	13		11^{2}		6		7					20
1	3		4^{2}	5	6			12	10		8			2	13		11	9^{1}			7					21
1	3			5	6			9	10		4		11	2	12		7^{1}				8^{2}	13				22
1	3		12	5	6^{2}	7		9	10		4	14	11^{1}	2			13				8^{3}					23
1	3		12	5		13		9	10^{3}		4	14	11^{1}	2			7^{2}				8	6				24
1	3		4^{2}	5		7		9	10^{1}		8	12		2			13				11	6				25
1		3	4	5			8	9	12			10	11^{1}	2				13			7^{2}		6			26
1	3		4	5		7^{1}	8	9				10	11	2							12	6				27
1	3		4^{2}	5		7	8	9				10■	11^{1}	2						13	12		6			28
1	3			5		7	8^{2}	9	10		12		4	2^{3}			11^{1}			13		6		14		29
1	3^{2}			5		12	8		10		4			2			7	9		13	11^{1}		6			30
1	3		4	5		7	8	9	12		13	10^{1}		2							11^{2}		6			31
1			12	5			8^{1}	13	10				11^{3}	3			7	9^{2}		2	4		6	14		32
1			4	5		7^{1}	8	9	12			10	11^{2}	2							13		6		3	33
1			4^{1}	5		7^{2}	8	9	12		13	10	11^{3}	2					6		14		3			34
1			4	5		12	8	9				10		2			7^{1}		6		11		3			35
1			4	5		7^{2}	8	9	12			10^{1}	11	2					6		13	14	3^{3}			36
1			4	5		7		9	10			13	11	2			12^{2}		6		8^{1}	3				37
1			4	5		7^{2}	8	9	12			10^{1}	11	2					6		13	3				38

FA Cup

Third Round	Cardiff C	(a)	0-0
		(h)	4-0
Fourth Round	Southend U	(h)	3-1
Fifth Round	Fulham	(a)	4-0
Sixth Round	Chelsea	(a)	3-3
		(h)	1-2

Carling Cup

Third Round	Milton Keynes D	(a)	5-0
Fourth Round	Port Vale	(h)	3-1
Quarter-Final	Southend U	(h)	1-0
Semi-Final	Arsenal	(h)	2-2
		(a)	1-3

UEFA Cup

First Round	Slavia Prague	(a)	1-0
		(h)	1-0
Group B	Besiktas	(a)	2-0
	FC Brugge	(h)	3-1
	Leverkusen	(a)	1-0
	Dinamo Bucharest	(h)	3-1
Third Round Bye	(Feyenoord removed)		
Fourth Round	Braga	(a)	3-2
		(h)	3-2
Quarter-Final	Sevilla	(a)	1-2
		(h)	2-1

TRANMERE ROVERS FL Championship 1

FOUNDATION

Formed in 1884 as Belmont they adopted their present title the following year and eventually joined their first league, the West Lancashire League in 1889–90, the same year as their first success in the Wirral Challenge Cup. The club almost folded in 1899–1900 when all the players left en bloc to join a rival club, but they survived the crisis and went from strength to strength winning the 'Combination' title in 1907–08 and the Lancashire Combination in 1913–14. They joined the Football League in 1921 from the Central League.

Prenton Park, Prenton Road West, Birkenhead, Merseyside CH42 9PY.

Telephone: 0870 460 3333.

Fax: (0151) 608 6144.

Ticket Office: 0870 460 3332.

Website: www.tranmererovers.co.uk

Email: info@tranmererovers.co.uk

Ground Capacity: 16,567.

Record Attendance: 24,424 v Stoke C, FA Cup 4th rd, 5 February 1972.

Pitch Measurements: 110yd × 70yd.

Chairperson: Lorraine Rogers.

Chief Executive/Secretary: Mick Horton.

Manager: Ronnie Moore.

Assistant Manager: Peter Shirtliff.

Physio: Les Parry.

Colours: White.

Change Colours: Black.

Year Formed: 1884.

Turned Professional: 1912.

Ltd Co.: 1920.

Previous Name: 1884, Belmont AFC; 1885, Tranmere Rovers.

Club Nickname: 'The Rovers'.

Grounds: 1884, Steeles Field; 1887, Ravenshaws Field/Old Prenton Park; 1912, Prenton Park.

First Football League Game: 27 August 1921, Division 3 (N), v Crewe Alex (h) W 4–1 – Bradshaw; Grainger, Stuart (1); Campbell, Milnes (1), Heslop; Moreton, Groves (1), Hyam, Ford (1), Hughes.

Record League Victory: 13–4 v Oldham Ath, Division 3 (N), 26 December 1935 – Gray; Platt, Fairhurst; McLaren, Newton, Spencer; Eden, MacDonald (1), Bell (9), Woodward (2), Urmson (1).

HONOURS

Football League Division 1 best season: 4th, 1992–93; Promoted from Division 3 1990–91 (play-offs); Division 3 (N) – Champions 1937–38; Promotion to 3rd Division: 1966–67, 1975–76; Division 4 – Runners-up 1988–89.

FA Cup: best season: 6th rd, 2000, 2001, 2004.

Football League Cup: Runners-up, 2000.

Welsh Cup: Winners 1935; Runners-up 1934.

Leyland Daf Cup: Winners 1990; Runners-up 1991.

SKY SPORTS FACT FILE

On 2 September 2006 Tranmere Rovers took the lead against Leyton Orient with a wind-assisted effort from goalkeeper Gavin Ward. Just outside his own penalty area, his free-kick bounced high over his opposite number into the net. They went on to win 3–0.

Record Cup Victory: 13–0 v Oswestry U, FA Cup 2nd prel rd, 10 October 1914 – Ashcroft; Stevenson, Bullough, Hancock, Taylor, Holden (1), Moreton (1), Cunningham (2), Smith (5), Leck (3), Gould (1).

Record Defeat: 1–9 v Tottenham H, FA Cup 3rd rd (replay), 14 January 1953.

Most League Points (2 for a win): 60, Division 4, 1964–65.

Most League Points (3 for a win): 80, Division 4, 1988–89; Division 3, 1989–90; Division 2, 2002–03.

Most League Goals: 111, Division 3 (N), 1930–31.

Highest League Scorer in Season: Bunny Bell, 35, Division 3 (N), 1933–34.

Most League Goals in Total Aggregate: Ian Muir, 142, 1985–95.

Most League Goals in One Match: 9, Bunny Bell v Oldham Ath, Division 3N, 26 December 1935.

Most Capped Player: John Aldridge, 30 (69), Republic of Ireland.

Most League Appearances: Harold Bell, 595, 1946–64 (incl. League record 401 consecutive appearances).

Youngest League Player: Iain Hume, 16 years 167 days v Swindon T, 15 April 2000.

Record Transfer Fee Received: £2,500,000 from WBA for Jason Koumas, August 2002.

Record Transfer Fee Paid: £450,000 to Aston Villa for Shaun Teale, August 1995.

Football League Record: 1921 Original Member of Division 3 (N): 1938–39 Division 2; 1946–58 Division 3 (N); 1958–61 Division 3; 1961–67 Division 4; 1967–75 Division 3; 1975–76 Division 4; 1976–79 Division 3; 1979–89 Division 4; 1989–91 Division 3; 1991–92 Division 2; 1992–2001 Division 1; 2001–04 Division 2; 2004– FL 1.

MANAGERS

Bert Cooke 1912–35
Jackie Carr 1935–36
Jim Knowles 1936–39
Bill Ridding 1939–45
Ernie Blackburn 1946–55
Noel Kelly 1955–57
Peter Farrell 1957–60
Walter Galbraith 1961
Dave Russell 1961–69
Jackie Wright 1969–72
Ron Yeats 1972–75
John King 1975–80
Bryan Hamilton 1980–85
Frank Worthington 1985–87
Ronnie Moore 1987
John King 1987–96
John Aldridge 1996–2001
Dave Watson 2001–02
Ray Mathias 2002–03
Brian Little 2003–06
Ronnie Moore June 2006–

LATEST SEQUENCES

Longest Sequence of League Wins: 9, 9.2.1990 – 19.3.1990.

Longest Sequence of League Defeats: 8, 29.10.1938 – 17.12.1938.

Longest Sequence of League Draws: 5, 26.12.1997 – 31.1.1998.

Longest Sequence of Unbeaten League Matches: 18, 16.3.1970 – 4.9.1970.

Longest Sequence Without a League Win: 16, 8.11.1969 – 14.3.1970.

Successive Scoring Runs: 32 from 24.2.1934.

Successive Non-scoring Runs: 7 from 20.12.1997.

TEN YEAR LEAGUE RECORD

		P	W	D	L	F	A	Pts	Pos
1997-98	Div 1	46	14	14	18	54	57	56	14
1998-99	Div 1	46	12	20	14	63	61	56	15
1999-2000	Div 1	46	15	12	19	57	68	57	13
2000-01	Div 1	46	9	11	26	46	77	38	24
2001-02	Div 2	46	16	15	15	63	60	63	12
2002-03	Div 2	46	23	11	12	66	57	80	7
2003-04	Div 2	46	17	16	13	59	56	67	8
2004-05	FL 1	46	22	13	11	73	55	79	3
2005-06	FL 1	46	13	15	18	50	52	54	18
2006-07	FL 1	46	18	13	15	58	53	67	9

DID YOU KNOW ?

Centre-forward Stan Rowlands was capped for Wales against England on 15 March 1914 before Tranmere Rovers were in the Football League. He spent most of his lengthy career in the north-west and made 17 different moves, several times returning to former clubs.

TRANMERE ROVERS 2006–07 LEAGUE RECORD

Match No.	*Date*	*Venue*	*Opponents*	*Result*		*H/T Score*	*Lg. Pos.*	*Goalscorers*	*Attendance*
1	Aug 5	H	Oldham Ath	W	1-0	1-0	—	Greenacre [24]	8586
2	8	A	Cheltenham T	L	0-1	0-1	—		3875
3	12	A	Doncaster R	D	0-0	0-0	13		6014
4	19	H	Yeovil T	W	2-1	1-1	9	Ellison [35], Mullin [54]	6023
5	26	A	Chesterfield	W	2-0	1-0	4	Downes (og) [45], Taylor [68]	4163
6	Sept 2	H	Leyton Orient	W	3-0	2-0	2	Ward [9], Greenacre 2 [12, 80]	6446
7	8	H	Bristol C	W	1-0	0-0	—	Mullin [85]	8111
8	12	A	Rotherham U	L	1-2	1-2	—	Ellison [28]	3732
9	16	A	Northampton T	W	3-1	2-0	2	Zola [14], Taylor [35], Mullin (pen) [58]	5334
10	23	H	Nottingham F	D	0-0	0-0	2		11,444
11	26	H	Huddersfield T	D	2-2	2-0	—	Zola [11], Greenacre [37]	6702
12	30	A	Bradford C	L	0-2	0-0	5		8877
13	Oct 6	A	Swansea C	D	0-0	0-0	—		12,347
14	13	H	Port Vale	L	1-2	0-2	—	Greenacre [57]	7866
15	21	A	Carlisle U	L	0-1	0-1	9		7328
16	28	H	Bournemouth	W	1-0	1-0	5	Ellison [41]	6076
17	Nov 3	H	Millwall	W	3-1	2-1	—	Taylor [19], McCready [22], Shuker [89]	7114
18	18	A	Brighton & HA	W	1-0	1-0	4	Greenacre [20]	6069
19	24	H	Blackpool	W	2-0	1-0	3	Greenacre [2], Davies [67]	8247
20	Dec 5	A	Scunthorpe U	D	1-1	0-1	—	Cansdell-Sheriff [53]	4572
21	9	A	Brentford	D	1-1	1-1	4	Shuker [45]	4878
22	23	H	Gillingham	L	2-3	2-3	6	Greenacre [2], Shuker [5]	6407
23	26	A	Huddersfield T	D	2-2	1-1	8	Greenacre 2 [39, 51]	10,228
24	30	A	Nottingham F	D	1-1	0-0	8	Taylor [49]	19,729
25	Jan 1	H	Rotherham U	W	2-1	2-0	8	Cansdell-Sheriff [28], Taylor [43]	6675
26	6	H	Northampton T	D	1-1	0-1	7	Mullin [87]	6089
27	13	A	Bristol C	L	2-3	2-0	9	McCombe (og) [25], McLaren [44]	10,822
28	16	H	Crewe Alex	W	1-0	1-0	—	Taylor [19]	5708
29	19	H	Bradford C	D	1-1	1-1	—	Taylor [9]	6567
30	26	A	Gillingham	L	0-2	0-2	—		5378
31	Feb 3	A	Oldham Ath	L	0-1	0-0	9		6944
32	10	H	Doncaster R	W	1-0	1-0	6	Greenacre [6]	5965
33	17	A	Yeovil T	W	2-0	0-0	6	Shuker 2 [53, 83]	5168
34	20	H	Cheltenham T	D	2-2	0-2	—	Shuker [49], Greenacre [90]	5576
35	24	A	Leyton Orient	L	1-3	1-3	6	Greenacre [34]	4832
36	Mar 2	H	Chesterfield	W	2-0	1-0	—	Mullin [21], Greenacre [73]	6254
37	10	H	Swansea C	L	0-2	0-1	7		7467
38	17	A	Port Vale	W	3-2	2-1	7	Greenacre 2 (1 pen) [3, 35 (p)], Ellison [83]	4809
39	24	A	Bournemouth	L	0-2	0-1	8		5640
40	30	H	Carlisle U	L	0-2	0-1	—		7289
41	Apr 7	A	Blackpool	L	2-3	1-2	9	Zola 2 [29, 46]	8091
42	9	H	Brighton & HA	W	2-1	0-1	9	Curran [76], Greenacre (pen) [90]	5528
43	14	A	Millwall	D	2-2	1-0	9	Cansdell-Sheriff [9], Zola [69]	10,036
44	21	H	Scunthorpe U	L	0-2	0-0	9		6721
45	28	A	Crewe Alex	D	1-1	0-0	10	Harrison [49]	5777
46	May 5	H	Brentford	W	3-1	3-1	9	Curran 3 [5, 7, 36]	6529

Final League Position: 9

GOALSCORERS

League (58): Greenacre 17 (2 pens), Taylor 7, Shuker 6, Mullin 5 (1 pen), Zola 5, Curran 4, Ellison 4, Cansdell-Sheriff 3, Davies 1, Harrison 1, McCready 1, McLaren 1, Ward 1, own goals 2.
Carling Cup (1): Cansdell-Sheriff 1.
FA Cup (5): Greenacre 2, Taylor 2, Cansdell-Sheriff 1.
J Paint Trophy (2): Jennings 1, Shuker 1.

Ward G 36 + 2	Stockdale R 35 + 1	Cansdell-Sheriff S 40 + 3	McLaren P 42	McCready C 42	Goodison I 40	Mullin J 39 + 1	Shuker C 45 + 1	Taylor G 36 + 1	Greenacre C 39 + 5	Ellison K 26 + 8	Zola C 15 + 14	Tremarco C 14 + 9	McAteer J 10 + 8	Jennings S — + 2	Davies S 16 + 12	Harrison D 7 + 5	Thompson J 12	Achterberg J 3 + 1	Hart J 6	Curran C 2 + 2	Hinchliffe B 1 + 1	Match No.
1	2	3	4	5	6	7	8	9^{1}	10	11^{2}	12	13										1
1	2^{1}	3	4	5	6	7^{2}	8	9	10		12	11	13									2
1	2	3	4	5	6	7	8	9	10^{1}	11^{2}	12	13										3
1	2	3	4^{1}	5	6	7	8	9	10	11			12									4
1	2	3	4	5	6	7	8^{1}	9	10	11^{2}		13	12									5
1	2	3	4^{1}	5	6	7	8	9	10	11			12									6
1	2	3	4	5	6	7	8	9	10	11												7
1	2	3	4	5	6	7	8	9	10	11												8
1	2		4^{2}	5	6	7	8	9		11^{1}	10	3		13	12							9
1	2		4	5	6	7	8	9	12	11	10^{1}	3										10
1	2	12	4	5^{1}	6	7^{2}	8		10	11	9	3		13								11
1	2	5			6	7	8		10	11^{1}	9	3	4		12							12
1	2	6	4	5		7	8		10	11		3			9							13
1	2	3	4	5	6	7	8		10	11					9							14
1	2	3	4	5	6	7^{3}	8	12	10	11^{2}			9^{1}		13	14						15
1		3	4	5	6	7	8	9	10^{2}	11^{1}			12		13		2					16
1		3	4	5	6	7	8	9	10			12			11^{1}		2					17
1		3	4	5	6	7	8	9	10				12		11^{1}		2					18
1		3	4	5	6	7	8	9	10		12				11^{1}		2					19
1	12	3	4	5	6	7	8^{1}		10	11	9						2					20
1	2^{2}	3	4	5	6	7	8	9	10^{1}	11	12	13										21
1	2^{1}	3	4	5	6	7	8	9	10	11^{2}	12				13							22
1^{G}	2	3^{2}	4	5	6	7	8	9	10		12	13			11^{1}			15				23
15	2	3	4	5^{1}	6	7	8	9	10	12		13			11^{2}			1^{G}				24
	2	3	4	5	6	7	8	9	10			12			11^{1}				1			25
	2	3	4	5	6	7	8	9	10^{2}	12	13				11^{1}				1			26
		3	4	5	6		8^{1}	9		12	10	2			11^{2}	7			1	13		27
	2	3	4	5	6	7	8	9	12		10^{1}				11				1			28
	2	3	4	5	6^{3}	7	8	9	12	13	10^{1}	14			11^{2}				1			29
	2	3	4	5		7	8	9	10		12	6			11^{1}				1			30
1	2		4	5		7	8^{1}	9	10	11		3			12		6					31
	2	12	4	5			8	9	10	11^{2}		3	6			13	7^{1}	1				32
15	2^{1}	3	4	5	6	7	8	9	10^{2}	13			11			12		1^{G}				33
1		3	4	5	6	7	8	9	10		12	2^{1}	11^{2}		13							34
1		3	4			7	8	9	10	12	11	5	6^{1}			2						35
1	2	3	4	5	6	7^{2}	8	9^{1}	10	11^{3}	12		13		14							36
1	2	3^{1}	4	5	6	7	8	9	10	11^{2}	12				13							37
1	2	3	4	5	6	7	8	9	10	11												38
1	2	3		5	6■	7^{1}	8^{2}	9	10	11	12		4			13						39
1	2	3		5		7^{1}	8	9	10	11^{2}	12	6	4		13							40
1	2	12		5	6	7■	8^{3}	9^{2}	10	13	11	3^{1}	4■			14						41
1	2	3	4		6		8^{2}		10	11^{1}	9				12	7	5			13		42
1	2	3	4		6		8	9^{1}	10		11				12	7	5					43
1		3	4	5^{1}	6		12		10		9				11	7	2			8		44
1■		3	4^{1}	2	6	12	8^{G}		13		10^{2}		7		9	11	5				15	45
		3	4	2	6		8^{2}		12	14	10^{1}		13		11	7	5			9^{3}	1	46

FA Cup

First Round	Woking	(h)	4-2
Second Round	Peterborough U	(h)	1-2

Carling Cup

First Round	Hull C	(a)	1-2

J Paint Trophy

First Round	Bury	(a)	2-0
Second Round	Darlington	(h)	0-1

WALSALL — FL Championship 1

FOUNDATION

Two of the leading clubs around Walsall in the 1880s were Walsall Swifts (formed 1877) and Walsall Town (formed 1879). The Swifts were winners of the Birmingham Senior Cup in 1881, while the Town reached the 4th round (5th round modern equivalent) of the FA Cup in 1883. These clubs amalgamated as Walsall Town Swifts in 1888, becoming simply Walsall in 1895.

Banks's Stadium, Bescot Crescent, Walsall WS1 4SA.

Telephone: 0870 221 0442.

Fax: (01922) 613 202.

Ticket Office: 0870 663 0111 or 0871 663 0222.

Website: www.saddlers.co.uk

Email: info@walsallfc.co.uk

Ground Capacity: 11,300.

Record Attendance: 11,037 v Wolverhampton W, Division 1, 11 January 2003.

Pitch Measurements: 110yd × 73yd.

Chairman: Jeff W. Bonser.

Chief Executive/Secretary: Roy Whalley.

Manager: Richard Money.

Assistant Manager: Eric McManus.

Physio: John Whitney.

Colours: White shirts with red band, red shorts, red stockings.

Change Colours: Blue shirts with yellow trim, yellow shorts, blue stockings.

Year Formed: 1888.

Turned Professional: 1888.

Ltd Co.: 1921.

Previous Names: Walsall Swifts (founded 1877) and Walsall Town (founded 1879) amalgamated in 1888 and were known as Walsall Town Swifts until 1895.

Club Nickname: 'The Saddlers'.

Grounds: 1888, Fellows Park; 1990, Bescot Stadium.

First Football League Game: 3 September 1892, Division 2, v Darwen (h) L 1–2 – Hawkins; Withington, Pinches; Robinson, Whitrick, Forsyth; Marshall, Holmes, Turner, Gray (1), Pangbourn.

Record League Victory: 10–0 v Darwen, Division 2, 4 March 1899 – Tennent; E. Peers (1), Davies; Hickinbotham, Jenkyns, Taggart; Dean (3), Vail (2), Aston (4), Martin, Griffin.

Record Cup Victory: 7–0 v Macclesfield T (a), FA Cup 2nd rd, 6 December 1997 – Walker; Evans, Marsh, Viveash (1), Ryder, Peron, Boli (2 incl. 1p) (Ricketts), Porter (2), Keates, Watson (Platt), Hodge (2 incl. 1p).

Record Defeat: 0–12 v Small Heath, 17 December 1892. 0–12 v Darwen, 26 December 1896, both Division 2.

HONOURS

Football League: Division 2: Runners-up, 1998–99, Promoted to Division 1 – 2000–01 (play-offs); FL 2 – Champions 2006–07; Division 3 – Runners-up 1960–61, 1994–95; Division 4 – Champions 1959–60; Runners-up 1979–80.

FA Cup: best season: 5th rd, 1939, 1975, 1978, 1987, 2002, 2003 and last 16 1889.

Football League Cup: Semi-final 1984.

SKY SPORTS FACT FILE

Record scoring Walsall legend Colin Taylor was a Stourbridge player when one evening while he was buying gramophone discs in a shop he was approached by Walsall officials who persuaded him to sign for the Fellows Park club in February 1958.

Most League Points (2 for a win): 65, Division 4, 1959–60.

Most League Points (3 for a win): 89, FL 2, 2006–07.

Most League Goals: 102, Division 4, 1959–60.

Highest League Scorer in Season: Gilbert Alsop, 40, Division 3 (N), 1933–34 and 1934–35.

Most League Goals in Total Aggregate: Tony Richards, 184, 1954–63; Colin Taylor, 184, 1958–63, 1964–68, 1969–73.

Most League Goals in One Match: 5, Gilbert Alsop v Carlisle U, Division 3N, 2 February 1935; 5, Bill Evans v Mansfield T, Division 3N, 5 October 1935; 5, Johnny Devlin v Torquay U, Division 3S, 1 September 1949.

Most Capped Player: Mick Kearns, 15 (18), Republic of Ireland.

Most League Appearances: Colin Harrison, 467, 1964–82.

Youngest League Player: Geoff Morris, 16 years 218 days v Scunthorpe U, 14 September 1965.

Record Transfer Fee Received: £600,000 from West Ham U for David Kelly, July 1988.

Record Transfer Fee Paid: £175,000 to Birmingham C for Alan Buckley, June 1979.

Football League Record: 1892 Elected to Division 2; 1895 Failed re-election; 1896–1901 Division 2; 1901 Failed re-election; 1921 Original Member of Division 3 (N); 1927–31 Division 3 (S); 1931–36 Division 3 (N); 1936–58 Division 3 (S); 1958–60 Division 4; 1960–61 Division 3; 1961–63 Division 2; 1963–79 Division 3; 1979–80 Division 4; 1980–88 Division 3; 1988–89 Division 2; 1989–90 Division 3; 1990–92 Division 4; 1992–95 Division 3; 1995–99 Division 2; 1999–2000 Division 1; 2000–01 Division 2; 2001–04 Division 1; 2004–06 FL 1; 2006–07 FL 2; 2007– FL 1.

LATEST SEQUENCES

Longest Sequence of League Wins: 7, 10.10.1959 – 21.11.1959.

Longest Sequence of League Defeats: 15, 29.10.1988 – 4.2.1989.

Longest Sequence of League Draws: 5, 7.5.1988 – 17.9.1988.

Longest Sequence of Unbeaten League Matches: 21, 6.11.1979 – 22.3.1980.

Longest Sequence Without a League Win: 18, 15.10.1988 – 4.2.1989.

Successive Scoring Runs: 27 from 9.2.1928.

Successive Non-scoring Runs: 5 from 8.10.1927.

MANAGERS

H. Smallwood 1888–91 *(Secretary-Manager)*
A. G. Burton 1891–93
J. H. Robinson 1893–95
C. H. Ailso 1895–96 *(Secretary-Manager)*
A. E. Parsloe 1896–97 *(Secretary-Manager)*
L. Ford 1897–98 *(Secretary-Manager)*
G. Hughes 1898–99 *(Secretary-Manager)*
L. Ford 1899–1901 *(Secretary-Manager)*
J. E. Shutt 1908–13 *(Secretary-Manager)*
Haydn Price 1914–20
Joe Burchell 1920–26
David Ashworth 1926–27
Jack Torrance 1927–28
James Kerr 1928–29
Sid Scholey 1929–30
Peter O'Rourke 1930–32
Bill Slade 1932–34
Andy Wilson 1934–37
Tommy Lowes 1937–44
Harry Hibbs 1944–51
Tony McPhee 1951
Brough Fletcher 1952–53
Major Frank Buckley 1953–55
John Love 1955–57
Billy Moore 1957–64
Alf Wood 1964
Reg Shaw 1964–68
Dick Graham 1968
Ron Lewin 1968–69
Billy Moore 1969–72
John Smith 1972–73
Doug Fraser 1973–77
Dave Mackay 1977–78
Alan Ashman 1978
Frank Sibley 1979
Alan Buckley 1979–86
Neil Martin *(Joint Manager with Buckley)* 1981–82
Tommy Coakley 1986–88
John Barnwell 1989–90
Kenny Hibbitt 1990–94
Chris Nicholl 1994–97
Jan Sorensen 1997–98
Ray Graydon 1998–2002
Colin Lee 2002–04
Paul Merson 2004–06
Richard Money May 2006–

TEN YEAR LEAGUE RECORD

		P	W	D	L	F	A	Pts	Pos
1997-98	Div 2	46	14	12	20	43	52	54	19
1998-99	Div 2	46	26	9	11	63	47	87	2
1999-2000	Div 1	46	11	13	22	52	77	46	22
2000-01	Div 2	46	23	12	11	79	50	81	4
2001-02	Div 1	46	13	12	21	51	71	51	18
2002-03	Div 1	46	15	9	22	57	69	54	17
2003-04	Div 1	46	13	12	21	45	65	51	22
2004-05	FL 1	46	16	12	18	65	69	60	14
2005-06	FL 1	46	11	14	21	47	70	47	24
2006-07	FL 2	46	25	14	7	66	34	89	1

DID YOU KNOW ?

George 'Paddy' Reid was the first Walsall player to score a goal in Division Three (North) and finished as leading marksman in 1921–22 with 24 League and Cup goals. His tally included hat-tricks in the last two games. Later capped for Northern Ireland.

WALSALL 2006–07 LEAGUE RECORD

Match No.	*Date*	*Venue*	*Opponents*	*Result*		*H/T Score*	*Lg. Pos.*	*Goalscorers*	*Attendance*
1	Aug 5	A	Rochdale	W	1-0	0-0	—	Butler [48]	3218
2	8	H	Stockport Co	W	2-0	1-0	—	Butler [16], Roper [48]	4877
3	12	H	Hartlepool U	W	2-0	2-0	1	Keates 2 [18, 29]	5637
4	19	A	Lincoln C	D	2-2	0-2	3	Taylor [79], Fangueiro [90]	4565
5	26	H	Darlington	W	1-0	1-0	2	Butler [45]	4651
6	Sept 2	A	Barnet	D	1-1	0-1	4	Keates [58]	2356
7	9	A	Grimsby T	L	1-2	1-1	5	Butler [9]	3669
8	12	H	Peterborough U	W	5-0	3-0	—	Fox [7], Dobson 2 [17, 27], Butler 2 [75, 79]	4070
9	16	H	Macclesfield T	W	2-0	1-0	3	Sam [38], Dann [89]	4657
10	23	A	Bristol R	W	2-1	2-0	1	Dann [8], Fox [28]	5260
11	26	A	Shrewsbury T	D	1-1	1-1	—	Bedeau [5]	6593
12	30	H	Mansfield T	W	4-0	0-0	1	Wright M [51], Keates 2 [62, 76], Gerrard [90]	5420
13	Oct 6	A	Chester C	D	0-0	0-0	—		3241
14	14	H	Wycombe W	W	2-0	1-0	1	Sam [34], Kinsella [59]	6745
15	21	A	Accrington S	W	2-1	1-0	1	Sam [40], Wright M [85]	3142
16	28	H	Milton Keynes D	D	0-0	0-0	2		6275
17	Nov 4	H	Torquay U	W	1-0	0-0	1	Roper [53]	5806
18	18	A	Hereford U	W	1-0	0-0	1	Westwood [63]	4462
19	25	H	Notts Co	W	2-1	2-0	1	Wright T [27], Keates [45]	5402
20	Dec 5	A	Bury	W	2-1	0-0	—	Roper [75], Sam [85]	2148
21	9	H	Swindon T	L	0-2	0-1	1		6812
22	16	A	Wrexham	D	1-1	1-0	1	Sam [27]	4270
23	23	A	Boston U	D	1-1	0-0	1	Wright T [72]	2083
24	26	H	Shrewsbury T	W	1-0	0-0	1	Wright M [50]	8345
25	30	H	Bristol R	D	2-2	0-0	1	Sam [45], Dann [88]	5941
26	Jan 1	A	Peterborough U	W	2-0	2-0	1	Fox [14], Westwood [23]	4405
27	15	H	Grimsby T	W	2-0	1-0	—	Butler 2 [28, 79]	4889
28	20	A	Mansfield T	L	1-2	1-1	1	Roper [9]	3737
29	27	H	Boston U	D	1-1	1-1	1	Butler [19]	5058
30	30	A	Macclesfield T	W	2-0	1-0	—	Keates 2 (1 pen) [2 (p), 90]	2006
31	Feb 3	H	Rochdale	D	1-1	0-1	1	Dann [90]	5046
32	10	A	Hartlepool U	L	1-3	1-0	1	Butler [3]	5847
33	16	H	Lincoln C	L	1-2	1-2	—	Sam [16]	4885
34	20	A	Stockport Co	L	0-1	0-0	—		6005
35	24	H	Barnet	W	4-1	1-1	2	Hendon (og) [33], Dobson [54], Harper 2 [65, 77]	4635
36	Mar 3	A	Darlington	D	0-0	0-0	2		3745
37	10	H	Chester C	W	1-0	0-0	2	Keates (pen) [67]	5282
38	17	A	Wycombe W	D	0-0	0-0	2		5625
39	25	A	Milton Keynes D	D	1-1	0-0	2	Wrack [77]	8044
40	31	H	Accrington S	W	3-2	1-1	2	Harper [21], Keates (pen) [75], Butler [85]	6062
41	Apr 7	A	Torquay U	W	2-1	2-0	2	Benjamin [10], Keates (pen) [16]	4047
42	9	H	Hereford U	W	1-0	0-0	2	Keates [83]	5658
43	14	A	Notts Co	W	2-1	1-1	2	Harper [17], Benjamin [84]	7080
44	21	H	Bury	L	0-1	0-1	2		6568
45	28	H	Wrexham	W	1-0	0-0	1	Demontagnac [61]	7057
46	May 5	A	Swindon T	D	1-1	0-0	1	Keates [90]	14,731

Final League Position: 1

GOALSCORERS

League (66): Keates 13 (4 pens), Butler 11, Sam 7, Dann 4, Harper 4, Roper 4, Dobson 3, Fox 3, Wright M 3, Benjamin 2, Westwood 2, Wright T 2, Bedeau 1, Demontagnac 1, Fangueiro 1, Gerrard 1, Kinsella 1, Taylor 1, Wrack 1, own goal 1.
Carling Cup (2): Butler 1, Dann 1.
FA Cup (0).
J Paint Trophy (1): Wrack 1.

Ince C 45	Pead C 26 + 15	Fox D 44	Gerrard A 31 + 4	Picken A 1 + 1	Dobson M 39	Wright M 31 + 6	Kinsella M 8 + 3	Butler M 44	Sam H 28 + 14	Taylor K 27 + 8	Keates D 36 + 3	Constable J 2 + 4	Westwood C 38 + 2	Roper I 27	Demontagnac I 2 + 17	Fangueiro C 2 + 3	Dann S 24 + 6	Bedeau A 8 + 10	Bossu B 1	Wrack D 7 + 11	Wright T 5 + 1	Bradley M — + 1	Cederqvist P 3 + 8	Harper K 10	Cooper K 8	Benjamin T 8	Smith E 1 + 2	Deeney T — + 1	*Match No.*
1	2	3	4	5	6	7	8^{1}	9	10^{2}	11	12	13																	1
1	2^{1}	3	4		6	7	8^{2}	9	10^{3}	11	13	14	12	5															2
1	12	3	4			7	8^{1}	9^{3}	10^{2}	11	6	13	2	5	14														3
1	12	3^{2}	4			7^{3}	8^{1}	9	10	11	6		2	5	13	14													4
1	7^{3}	3	4			11		9	12	13	8	10^{2}	2	5		6^{1}	14												5
1	2	3	4		7	12		9	10^{1}	11^{3}	8		5	6^{2}	14	13													6
1	2^{2}	3^{3}	4		6	7		9	10	12	8		13	5	14	11^{1}													7
1		3	4■		6	7	12	9^{3}	10^{1}	11	8^{2}		2	5	13			14											8
1	2^{1}	3		12	6	7^{2}		9	10^{3}	11	8		4	5			13	14											9
1	12	3			6	7^{2}		9	10^{3}	11	8		4	5^{1}		14	2	13											10
1	12	3	4		6	7^{2}		9	13	11	8^{1}		2				5	10											11
1	12	3^{2}	4		6	7^{3}		9	10^{1}	11	8		2	5	13			14											12
	12	3	4		6	7^{1}		9		11^{2}	8		2	5	13		14	10^{3}	1										13
1	2	3	4		6	7^{3}	12	9	10^{2}	11^{1}	8	13					5	14											14
1	2	3	4			7	12		10^{3}	11^{1}	8	9^{2}		5	13		6			14									15
1	2	3	4		6	7^{3}		9	10^{1}	11	8^{2}			5	13		12	14											16
1	2	3			6	7^{3}		9^{1}	10	12	8		4^{2}	5			13	14		11									17
1		3			6	12	8	9	10^{2}		7		2	5	13		4			11^{1}									18
1					6	7^{2}	8	9	12	3	11		2	5			4	13			10^{1}								19
1	12	3	13			7^{2}	6	9	14	11			2	5			4	8^{1}			10^{3}								20
1	12	3	13		6	7^{3}	8^{1}	9	14	11			2^{2}	5			4				10								21
1	6^{1}	3	4			7		9	10^{2}	11			2	5	12			8^{3}			13	14							22
1	12	3	4^{1}		6	7			10^{2}	11			2		13		5	8			9								23
1	12	3			6	7		9		11			2	5			4	8^{1}			10■								24
1	8	3			6	7		9	10	11			2	5			4												25
1	2	3			6	7		9	10^{1}	11			4	5			8	12											26
1	11		12		6	7		9	10^{3}	3	8^{2}		2	5^{1}	13		4						14						27
1	2	3^{2}			6	7^{3}		9	12	11	14		4	5			8	13					10^{1}						28
1	8	3	12		6	7		9	10^{3}		11^{2}		2	5^{1}	13		4						14						29
1	2	3	8		6	12		9^{2}	10^{1}		11		5				4			7			13						30
1	11	3	4^{2}		6	12		9	10^{3}		8		2		13		5			7^{1}			14						31
1	2	3			6	7		9	12	13	11^{3}		5		14		4	8^{2}					10^{1}						32
1	2	3			6^{2}	7		9	10^{3}	11^{1}	8		4	5			13			12			14						33
1	12	3	7		6			9	10^{2}		8		2	5^{1}			4			13			11						34
1	12	3	4		6	13		9	10^{2}		8		2^{1}				5						14	7^{3}	11				35
1	2	3	5					9	10^{2}	12	8						4			11			13	7	6^{1}				36
1	2	3	5		6			9	12	13	8						4			7^{1}				10^{2}	11				37
1	12	3	5		6			9	10^{1}		8		2				4			13			14	7^{2}	11^{3}				38
1	12	3	5		6			9	13		8		2				4^{1}			14				7	11^{3}	10^{2}			39
1	2	3	4		6			9	12		8		5							13				7	11^{2}	10^{1}			40
1	2^{2}	3	4		6	12		9^{3}		11	8		5							7^{1}						10	13	14	41
1		3	4		6	7^{3}		9	12	13	8		2							14				11^{2}		10^{1}	5		42
1	2^{3}	3	4^{1}		6			9		12	8		5							13				7	11^{2}	10	14		43
1		5	4		6^{1}			9	12	3	8		2		13					14				7	11^{2}	10^{3}			44
1	12	3	4		6	7		9	13		8		5		11^{3}			2^{1}		14						10^{2}			45
1	2	3	4		6			9	12		8		5		11^{1}					13				7		10^{2}			46

FA Cup

First Round	Macclesfield T	(a)	0-0
		(h)	0-1

Carling Cup

First Round	Plymouth Arg	(a)	1-0
Second Round	Bolton W	(h)	1-3

J Paint Trophy

First Round	Swansea C	(h)	1-1

WATFORD FL Championship

FOUNDATION

The club was formed as Watford Rovers in 1881. The name was changed to West Herts in 1893 and then the name Watford was adopted after rival club Watford St Mary's was absorbed in 1898.

Vicarage Road Stadium, Vicarage Road, Watford, Herts WD18 0ER.

Telephone: 0870 111 1881.

Fax: (01923) 496 001.

Ticket Office: 0870 111 1881.

Website: www.watfordfc.com

Email: yourvoice@watfordfc.com

Ground Capacity: 19,920.

Record Attendance: 34,099 v Manchester U, FA Cup 4th rd (replay), 3 February 1969.

Pitch Measurements: 115yd × 75yd.

Chairman: Graham Simpson.

Chief Executive: Mark Ashton.

Secretary: Michelle Ives.

Manager: Adrian Boothroyd.

Assistant Manager: Keith Burkinshaw.

Physio: Andy Rolls.

Colours: Yellow shirts, red shorts, red stockings.

Change Colours: Blue shirts, blue shorts, blue stockings.

Year Formed: 1881.

Turned Professional: 1897.

Ltd Co.: 1909.

Club Nickname: 'The Hornets'.

Previous Names: 1881, Watford Rovers; 1893, West Herts; 1898, Watford.

Grounds: 1883, Vicarage Meadow, Rose and Crown Meadow; 1889, Colney Butts; 1890, Cassio Road; 1922, Vicarage Road.

First Football League Game: 28 August 1920, Division 3, v QPR (a) W 2–1 – Williams; Horseman, F. Gregory; Bacon, Toone, Wilkinson; Bassett, Ronald (1), Hoddinott, White (1), Waterall.

Record League Victory: 8–0 v Sunderland, Division 1, 25 September 1982 – Sherwood; Rice, Rostron, Taylor, Terry, Bolton, Callaghan (2), Blissett (4), Jenkins (2), Jackett, Barnes.

Record Cup Victory: 10–1 v Lowestoft T, FA Cup 1st rd, 27 November 1926 – Yates; Prior, Fletcher (1); F. Smith, 'Bert' Smith, Strain; Stephenson, Warner (3), Edmonds (3), Swan (1), Daniels (1), (1 og).

Record Defeat: 0–10 v Wolverhampton W, FA Cup 1st rd (replay), 24 January 1912.

HONOURS

Football League: Division 1 – Runners-up 1982–83, promoted from Division 1 1998–99 (play-offs); promoted from FL C (play-offs) 2005–06; Division 2 – Champions 1997–98; Runners-up 1981–82; Division 3 – Champions 1968–69; Runners-up 1978–79; Division 4 – Champions 1977–78; Promoted 1959–60 (4th).

FA Cup: Runners-up 1984, semi-finals 1970, 1984, 1987, 2003, 2007.

Football League Cup: Semi-final 1979.

European Competitions: *UEFA Cup:* 1983–84.

SKY SPORTS FACT FILE

Right-winger Billy Chapman was Murton born, started with the local Democrat Club, was with Sheffield Wednesday and Manchester United, joined Watford in 1928 making over 200 League appearances and then returned to his home town to play for Murton Colliery.

Most League Points (2 for a win): 71, Division 4, 1977–78.

Most League Points (3 for a win): 88, Division 2, 1997–98.

Most League Goals: 92, Division 4, 1959–60.

Highest League Scorer in Season: Cliff Holton, 42, Division 4, 1959–60.

Most League Goals in Total Aggregate: Luther Blissett, 148, 1976–83, 1984–88, 1991–92.

Most League Goals in One Match: 5, Eddie Mummery v Newport Co, Division 3S, 5 January 1924.

Most Capped Player: John Barnes, 31 (79), England and Kenny Jackett, 31, Wales.

Most League Appearances: Luther Blissett, 415, 1976–83, 1984–88, 1991–92.

Youngest League Player: Keith Mercer, 16 years 125 days v Tranmere R, 16 February 1973.

Record Transfer Fee Received: £9,600,000 from Aston V for Ashley Young, January 2007.

Record Transfer Fee Paid: £2,250,000 to Tottenham H for Allan Nielsen, August 2000.

Football League Record: 1920 Original Member of Division 3; 1921–58 Division 3 (S); 1958–60 Division 4; 1960–69 Division 3; 1969–72 Division 2; 1972–75 Division 3; 1975–78 Division 4; 1978–79 Division 3; 1979–82 Division 2; 1982–88 Division 1; 1988–92 Division 2; 1992–96 Division 1; 1996–98 Division 2; 1998–99 Division 1; 1999–2000 FA Premier League; 2000–04 Division 1; 2004–06 FL C; 2006–07 FA Premier League; 2007– FL C.

MANAGERS

John Goodall 1903–10
Harry Kent 1910–26
Fred Pagnam 1926–29
Neil McBain 1929–37
Bill Findlay 1938–47
Jack Bray 1947–48
Eddie Hapgood 1948–50
Ron Gray 1950–51
Haydn Green 1951–52
Len Goulden 1952–55
(General Manager to 1956)
Johnny Paton 1955–56
Neil McBain 1956–59
Ron Burgess 1959–63
Bill McGarry 1963–64
Ken Furphy 1964–71
George Kirby 1971–73
Mike Keen 1973–77
Graham Taylor 1977–87
Dave Bassett 1987–88
Steve Harrison 1988–90
Colin Lee 1990
Steve Perryman 1990–93
Glenn Roeder 1993–96
Kenny Jackett 1996–97
Graham Taylor 1997–2001
Gianluca Vialli 2001–02
Ray Lewington 2002–05
Adrian Boothroyd March 2005–

LATEST SEQUENCES

Longest Sequence of League Wins: 7, 28.8.2000 – 14.10.2000.

Longest Sequence of League Defeats: 9, 26.12.1972 – 27.2.1973.

Longest Sequence of League Draws: 7, 30.11.1996 – 27.1.1997.

Longest Sequence of Unbeaten League Matches: 22, 1.10.1996 – 1.3.1997.

Longest Sequence Without a League Win: 19, 27.11.1971 – 8.4.1972.

Successive Scoring Runs: 22 from 20.8.1985.

Successive Non-scoring Runs: 7 from 18.12.1971.

TEN YEAR LEAGUE RECORD

		P	W	D	L	F	A	Pts	Pos
1997-98	Div 2	46	24	16	6	67	41	88	1
1998-99	Div 1	46	21	14	11	65	56	77	5
1999-2000	PR Lge	38	6	6	26	35	77	24	20
2000-01	Div 1	46	20	9	17	76	67	69	9
2001-02	Div 1	46	16	11	19	62	56	59	14
2002-03	Div 1	46	17	9	20	54	70	60	13
2003-04	Div 1	46	15	12	19	54	68	57	16
2004-05	FL C	46	12	16	18	52	59	52	18
2005-06	FL C	46	22	15	9	77	53	81	3
2006-07	PR Lge	38	5	13	20	29	59	28	20

DID YOU KNOW ?

The first time the nickname of The Hornets was used by Watford coincided with their promotion in 1959–60. They were formerly known as The Brewers through the generosity of the Benskins whose parting financial gesture was typical of the previous relationship.

WATFORD 2006–07 LEAGUE RECORD

Match No.	Date	Venue	Opponents	Result	H/T Score	Lg. Pos.	Goalscorers	Attendance
1	Aug 19	A	Everton	L 1-2	0-1	—	Stubbs (og) [90]	39,691
2	22	H	West Ham U	D 1-1	0-0	—	King [63]	18,344
3	26	H	Manchester U	L 1-2	1-1	18	Francis [34]	19,453
4	Sept 9	A	Bolton W	L 0-1	0-0	20		21,140
5	16	H	Aston Villa	D 0-0	0-0	19		18,620
6	23	A	Wigan Ath	D 1-1	0-1	18	Bouazza [63]	16,359
7	Oct 2	H	Fulham	D 3-3	1-0	—	King [23], Young 2 [46, 89]	17,982
8	14	A	Arsenal	L 0-3	0-2	19		60,018
9	21	A	Charlton Ath	D 0-0	0-0	18		27,011
10	28	H	Tottenham H	D 0-0	0-0	18		19,660
11	Nov 4	H	Middlesbrough	W 2-0	1-0	17	Bouazza [6], Young [60]	18,951
12	11	A	Chelsea	L 0-4	0-2	19		41,936
13	18	A	Portsmouth	L 1-2	1-1	19	DeMerit [32]	19,738
14	28	H	Sheffield U	L 0-1	0-0	—		18,887
15	Dec 4	A	Manchester C	D 0-0	0-0	—		35,915
16	9	H	Reading	D 0-0	0-0	20		19,223
17	16	A	Newcastle U	L 1-2	0-0	20	Bouazza [57]	49,231
18	23	A	Liverpool	L 0-2	0-0	20		42,807
19	26	H	Arsenal	L 1-2	1-1	20	Smith [23]	19,750
20	Jan 1	A	Fulham	D 0-0	0-0	20		19,698
21	13	H	Liverpool	L 0-3	0-2	20		19,746
22	20	A	Aston Villa	L 0-2	0-0	20		35,892
23	23	H	Blackburn R	W 2-1	1-1	—	Emerton (og) [12], DeMerit [70]	13,760
24	31	A	Manchester U	L 0-4	0-1	—		76,032
25	Feb 3	H	Bolton W	L 0-1	0-0	20		18,722
26	10	A	West Ham U	W 1-0	1-0	20	Henderson (pen) [12]	34,625
27	21	H	Wigan Ath	D 1-1	1-1	—	Henderson [24]	18,338
28	24	H	Everton	L 0-3	0-2	20		18,761
29	Mar 3	H	Charlton Ath	D 2-2	2-0	19	Bouazza [15], Francis [21]	19,782
30	17	A	Tottenham H	L 1-3	0-1	20	Henderson [89]	36,051
31	31	H	Chelsea	L 0-1	0-0	20		19,793
32	Apr 7	A	Middlesbrough	L 1-4	1-2	20	Francis [23]	25,534
33	9	H	Portsmouth	W 4-2	2-1	20	Bouazza 2 (1 pen) [28 (p), 73], Mahon [45], Priskin [51]	18,119
34	18	A	Blackburn R	L 1-3	1-3	—	Rinaldi [21]	16,035
35	21	H	Manchester C	D 1-1	0-0	20	Priskin [75]	18,537
36	28	A	Sheffield U	L 0-1	0-1	20		30,690
37	May 5	A	Reading	W 2-0	0-0	20	Shittu [60], King [85]	23,294
38	13	H	Newcastle U	D 1-1	0-1	20	King (pen) [52]	19,830

Final League Position: 20

GOALSCORERS

League (29): Bouazza 6 (1 pen), Francis 3, King 4 (1 pen), Henderson 3 (1 pen), Young 3, DeMerit 2, Priskin 2, Mahon 1, Rinaldi 1, Shittu 1, Smith 1, own goals 2.
Carling Cup (4): Francis 1, Priskin 1, Shittu 1, Young 1.
FA Cup (8): Bouazza 2, Mackay 2, Ashikodi 1, Francis 1, McNamee 1, Smith 1.

Foster B 29	Doyley L 17 + 4	Powell C 9 + 6	Francis D 28 + 4	Shittu D 27 + 3	Mariappa A 17 + 2	Chambers J 8 + 4	Mahon G 33 + 1	Henderson D 24 + 11	King M 12 + 1	Young A 20	DeMerit J 29 + 3	Bouazza H 27 + 5	Priskin T 7 + 9	Lee R 9 + 1	Bangura A 12 + 4	Stewart J 30 + 1	Spring M 2 + 4	MacKay M 13 + 1	Smith T 32	Jarrett A — + 1	McNamee A 4 + 3	Hoskins W 4 + 5	Ashikodi M — + 2	Williamson L 4 + 1	Kabba S 6 + 5	Williams G 2 + 1	Cavalli J 2 + 1	Rinaldi D 6 + 1	Carlisle C 4	Avinel C 1	Chamberlain A — + 1	Robinson T — + 1	*Match No.*
1	2	3	4	5	6^{1}	7^{2}	8	9^{3}	10	11	12	13	14																				1
1	2	3	4	5			8^{2}	9	10	11	6	7^{1}	12				13																2
	2	3	4	5			8^{2}	9^{1}	10	7	6	11^{3}		1	13	12	14																3
1	2		4	5			8	9	10	11						3		6	7^{1}	12													4
1	2^{1}		4	5			8	9^{2}	10	11	12	13	14			3		6	7^{3}														5
1			4	5			8	12	10	11	2	9^{2}				3	13	6	7^{1}														6
1			4^{1}	5			8	12	10	7	2	9				3	13	6	11^{2}														7
1	2	12	4	5			8	13	10	9	6	11^{1}				3			7^{2}														8
1	2	12	4	5			8	9		10	6	11^{1}				3			7														9
1	2		4	5			8	9		10	6	11				3			7														10
	2		4	5			8	9		10	6	11		1		3			7														11
1	2	12	4	5			8	9		10	6	11^{1}			13	3			7^{2}														12
1^{G}	2					12	8	9^{1}		10	6	11^{2}	13	15		3	4	5	7														13
	12	3■	7	13		2	8	9			6			1			4^{1}	5	10		11^{2}												14
			4	5		2	8	9		10	6	11		1		3			7														15
		12	4	5		2		9		10	6	11		1	8	3			7^{1}														16
			12	5	13	2^{2}	8	9		10	6	11		1	4	3			7^{1}														17
1			12	5	2		8	9^{2}		10	6	11			4^{1}	3			7		13												18
1			12	5^{3}	2		8	13		10	6	9^{1}	14		4	3			7		11^{2}												19
1			12	5^{3}	2		8	13		10	6		9■		4	3		14	7^{2}		11^{1}												20
1					2		8	12		10	6	9			4^{1}	3		5	7		11^{2}	13											21
1		12	4	5	2		8	13				11^{1}	9^{2}			3		6	7			10^{3}	14										22
1		12	4	5^{2}	2			9			13	11			8	3		6	7			10^{1}											23
	5	11^{1}	4		2			9^{3}			6	10		1	8	3			7^{2}			12		13	14								24
1			4^{3}		2		8	9			6	11^{1}				3		5			12	10		7^{2}	14	13							25
1			4	12	2		8	9^{1}			6				13	3		5	7				14		10^{3}		11^{2}						26
1			4		2		8	9			6	12				3		5	7			13			10^{2}		11^{1}						27
	12		4		2		8	9^{3}			6	11^{2}	14	1		3		5^{1}	7		13				10								28
	12		4^{2}	5	2		8	14			6	11	9^{3}	1		3^{1}			7							10	13						29
1	4	3		5	2	6^{2}	8	12				10	9^{1}						7						13	11^{3}		14					30
1			4	5		2	8	9^{2}			6	12	13			3			7						10^{1}			11					31
1			4	5		2	8^{1}	9^{2}			6	13	12			3			7						10			11					32
1	12		4		2	13	8^{3}				6	11^{2}	9		14	3			7						10				5^{1}				33
1			4		2	12^{2}	8		13		6	10	9			3			7^{1}						14			11^{3}	5				34
1	2	3	4^{2}	12			8		9		6	10	14		7										13^{3}			11^{1}	5				35
1	2	3^{2}		6		13	8	12	10			11	9^{1}		4							14		7^{3}					5				36
1	2	3		5	12		13	9^{3}	10						4				7			14		8				11^{2}		6^{1}			37
1^{G}	6			5	2			12	9						4	3			7^{2}			10^{1}		8				11			15	13	38

FA Cup

Third Round	Stockport Co	(h)	4-1
Fourth Round	West Ham U	(a)	1-0
Fifth Round	Ipswich T	(h)	1-0
Sixth Round	Plymouth Arg	(a)	1-0
Semi-Final	Manchester U		1-4
(at Villa Park)			

Carling Cup

Second Round	Accrington S	(h)	0-0
Third Round	Hull C	(h)	2-1
Fourth Round	Newcastle U	(h)	2-2

WEST BROMWICH ALBION FL Championship

FOUNDATION

There is a well known story that when employees of Salter's Spring Works in West Bromwich decided to form a football club, they had to send someone to the nearby Association Football stronghold of Wednesbury to purchase a football. A weekly subscription of 2d (less than 1p) was imposed and the name of the new club was West Bromwich Strollers.

The Hawthorns, West Bromwich, West Midlands B71 4LF.

Telephone: 0871 271 1100.

Fax: 0871 271 9861.

Ticket Office: 0871 271 9780.

Website: www.wbafc.co.uk

Email: enquiries@wbafc.co.uk

Ground Capacity: 27,877.

Record Attendance: 64,815 v Arsenal, FA Cup 6th rd, 6 March 1937.

Pitch Measurements: 115yd × 74yd.

Chairman: Jeremy Peace.

Club Secretary: Darren Eales.

Manager: Tony Mowbray.

Assistant Manager: Mark Venus.

Physio: Nick Worth.

Colours: Navy blue and white striped shirts, white shorts, navy blue stockings.

Change Colours: Yellow and green striped shirts, green shorts yellow stockings. ***Alternative Change Colours:*** Black shirts, black shorts, black stockings.

Year Formed: 1878.

Turned Professional: 1885.

Ltd Co.: 1892.

Plc: 1996.

Previous Name: 1878, West Bromwich Strollers; 1881, West Bromwich Albion.

Club Nicknames: 'Throstles', 'Baggies', 'Albion'.

Grounds: 1878, Coopers Hill; 1879, Dartmouth Park; 1881, Bunns Field, Walsall Street; 1882, Four Acres (Dartmouth Cricket Club); 1885, Stoney Lane; 1900, The Hawthorns.

First Football League Game: 8 September 1888, Football League, v Stoke (a) W 2–0 – Roberts; J. Horton, Green; E. Horton, Perry, Bayliss; Bassett, Woodhall (1), Hendry, Pearson, Wilson (1).

Record League Victory: 12–0 v Darwen, Division 1, 4 April 1892 – Reader; J. Horton, McCulloch; Reynolds (2), Perry, Groves; Bassett (3), McLeod, Nicholls (1), Pearson (4), Geddes (1), (1 og).

HONOURS

Football League: Division 1 – Champions 1919–20; Runners-up 1924–25, 1953–54, 2001–02, 2003–04; Division 2 – Champions 1901–02, 1910–11; Runners-up 1930–31, 1948–49; Promoted to Division 1 1975–76 (3rd); 1992–93 (play-offs); Promoted to FA Premier League 2001–02.

FA Cup: Winners 1888, 1892, 1931, 1954, 1968; Runners-up 1886, 1887, 1895, 1912, 1935.

Football League Cup: Winners 1966; Runners-up 1967, 1970.

European Competitions: *European Cup-Winners' Cup:* 1968–69. *European Fairs Cup:* 1966–67. *UEFA Cup:* 1978–79, 1979–80, 1981–82.

SKY SPORTS FACT FILE

Midway through the 1948–49 season West Bromwich Albion goalkeeper Jim Sanders had the excellent record of saving no fewer than 15 of the 19 penalty kicks he had faced in the four seasons he had been with the club.

Record Cup Victory: 10–1 v Chatham (away), FA Cup 3rd rd, 2 March 1889 – Roberts; J. Horton, Green; Timmins (1), Charles Perry, E. Horton; Bassett (2), Perry (1), Bayliss (2), Pearson, Wilson (3), (1 og).

Record Defeat: 3–10 v Stoke C, Division 1, 4 February 1937.

Most League Points (2 for a win): 60, Division 1, 1919–20.

Most League Points (3 for a win): 89, Division 1, 2001–02.

Most League Goals: 105, Division 2, 1929–30.

Highest League Scorer in Season: William 'Ginger' Richardson, 39, Division 1, 1935–36.

Most League Goals in Total Aggregate: Tony Brown, 218, 1963–79.

Most League Goals in One Match: 6, Jimmy Cookson v Blackpool, Division 2, 17 September 1927.

Most Capped Player: Stuart Williams, 33 (43), Wales.

Most League Appearances: Tony Brown, 574, 1963–80.

Youngest League Player: Charlie Wilson, 16 years 73 days v Oldham Ath, 1 October 1921.

Record Transfer Fee Received: £6,000,000 from Fulham for Diomansy Kamara, July 2007.

Record Transfer Fee Paid: £3,500,000 to Cardiff C for Robert Earnshaw, August 2004.

Football League Record: 1888 Founder Member of Football League; 1901–02 Division 2; 1902–04 Division 1; 1904–11 Division 2; 1911–27 Division 1; 1927–31 Division 2; 1931–38 Division 1; 1938–49 Division 2; 1949–73 Division 1; 1973–76 Division 2; 1976–86 Division 1; 1986–91 Division 2; 1991–92 Division 3; 1992–93 Division 2; 1993–2002 Division 1; 2002–03 FA Premier League; 2003–04 Division 1; 2004–06 FA Premier League; 2006– FL C.

MANAGERS

Louis Ford 1890–92
(Secretary-Manager)
Henry Jackson 1892–94
(Secretary-Manager)
Edward Stephenson 1894–95
(Secretary-Manager)
Clement Keys 1895–96
(Secretary-Manager)
Frank Heaven 1896–1902
(Secretary-Manager)
Fred Everiss 1902–48
Jack Smith 1948–52
Jesse Carver 1952
Vic Buckingham 1953–59
Gordon Clark 1959–61
Archie Macaulay 1961–63
Jimmy Hagan 1963–67
Alan Ashman 1967–71
Don Howe 1971–75
Johnny Giles 1975–77
Ronnie Allen 1977
Ron Atkinson 1978–81
Ronnie Allen 1981–82
Ron Wylie 1982–84
Johnny Giles 1984–85
Ron Saunders 1986–87
Ron Atkinson 1987–88
Brian Talbot 1988–91
Bobby Gould 1991–92
Ossie Ardiles 1992–93
Keith Burkinshaw 1993–94
Alan Buckley 1994–97
Ray Harford 1997
Denis Smith 1997–2000
Brian Little 2000
Gary Megson 2000–04
Bryan Robson 2004–06
Tony Mowbray October 2006–

LATEST SEQUENCES

Longest Sequence of League Wins: 11, 5.4.1930 – 8.9.1930.

Longest Sequence of League Defeats: 11, 28.10.1995 – 26.12.1995.

Longest Sequence of League Draws: 5, 30.8.1999 – 3.10.1999.

Longest Sequence of Unbeaten League Matches: 17, 7.9.1957 – 7.12.1957.

Longest Sequence Without a League Win: 15, 16.10.2004 – 25.9.2004.

Successive Scoring Runs: 36 from 26.4.1958.

Successive Non-scoring Runs: 4 from 15.2.1913.

TEN YEAR LEAGUE RECORD

		P	W	D	L	F	A	Pts	Pos
1997-98	Div 1	46	16	13	17	50	56	61	10
1998-99	Div 1	46	16	11	19	69	76	59	12
1999-2000	Div 1	46	10	19	17	43	60	49	21
2000-01	Div 1	46	21	11	14	60	52	74	6
2001-02	Div 1	46	27	8	11	61	29	89	2
2002-03	PR Lge	38	6	8	24	29	65	26	19
2003-04	Div 1	46	25	11	10	64	42	86	2
2004-05	PR Lge	38	6	16	16	36	61	34	17
2005-06	PR Lge	38	7	9	22	31	58	30	19
2006-07	FL C	46	22	10	14	81	55	76	4

DID YOU KNOW ?

Harold Pearson, son of Hubert another West Bromwich Albion goalkeeper, succeeded cousin Harry Hibbs at Tamworth Castle and turned professional in 1927. Another cousin Horace was Coventry City custodian and Harold deputised for Hibbs for England.

WEST BROMWICH ALBION 2006–07 LEAGUE RECORD

Match No.	*Date*	*Venue*	*Opponents*	*Result*		*H/T Score*	*Lg. Pos.*	*Goalscorers*	*Attendance*
1	Aug 5	H	Hull C	W	2-0	0-0	—	Hartson 2 [57, 90]	20,682
2	8	A	Cardiff C	D	1-1	1-1	—	Gera [4]	18,506
3	12	A	Southampton	D	0-0	0-0	10		24,233
4	19	H	Colchester U	W	2-1	2-0	4	Ellington (pen) [11], Wallwork [41]	17,509
5	28	A	Sunderland	L	0-2	0-1	—		24,242
6	Sept 9	H	Leicester C	W	2-0	0-0	4	Kenton (og) [83], Phillips (pen) [86]	19,322
7	12	A	Preston NE	L	0-1	0-0	—		12,119
8	16	H	Southend U	D	1-1	0-0	9	Ellington [61]	19,576
9	23	A	Luton T	D	2-2	1-2	10	Carter [34], Gera [61]	9332
10	30	H	Leeds U	W	4-2	1-0	7	Albrechtsen [40], Kamara 2 [65, 90], Phillips [79]	21,435
11	Oct 14	A	Ipswich T	W	5-1	2-1	4	Kamara 2 [29, 56], Phillips 3 [40, 54, 90]	22,581
12	17	A	Crystal Palace	W	2-0	1-0	—	Gera [45], Kamara [48]	16,105
13	22	H	Wolverhampton W	W	3-0	2-0	3	Greening [11], Kamara [27], Hartson (pen) [85]	26,606
14	28	A	Birmingham C	L	0-2	0-1	3		21,009
15	31	H	QPR	D	3-3	2-1	—	Ellington [8], Kamara 2 [40, 54]	17,417
16	Nov 4	A	Derby Co	L	1-2	1-0	5	Chaplow [26]	25,342
17	11	H	Norwich C	L	0-1	0-0	6		18,718
18	18	H	Burnley	W	3-0	3-0	6	Koumas [5], Ellington [7], Carter [45]	18,707
19	25	A	Stoke C	L	0-1	0-1	8		18,282
20	28	A	Sheffield W	L	1-3	0-2	—	Koumas [89]	21,695
21	Dec 2	H	Derby Co	W	1-0	0-0	8	Hartson [89]	20,494
22	10	A	Barnsley	D	1-1	1-1	9	Koumas [30]	9512
23	16	H	Coventry C	W	5-0	3-0	8	Kamara 2 (1 pen) [1, 33 (p)], Koumas [39], Phillips [57], Robinson [83]	20,370
24	23	A	Plymouth Arg	D	2-2	2-2	7	Phillips 2 [44, 45]	15,172
25	26	H	Preston NE	W	4-2	2-1	6	Koumas [6], Kamara [25], Ellington 2 [75, 87]	22,905
26	30	H	Ipswich T	W	2-0	0-0	5	Kamara [53], Koumas [67]	20,328
27	Jan 1	A	Southend U	L	1-3	0-3	5	Hartson [63]	9907
28	12	H	Luton T	W	3-2	1-0	—	Koumas [45], Phillips 2 [88, 90]	19,927
29	20	A	Leeds U	W	3-2	3-1	4	Greening [7], Kamara 2 [19, 45]	20,019
30	31	H	Plymouth Arg	W	2-1	1-0	—	Kamara 2 (1 pen) [41 (p), 50]	19,894
31	Feb 3	A	Hull C	W	1-0	0-0	3	Kamara [59]	18,005
32	10	H	Southampton	D	1-1	1-1	3	Phillips [45]	21,138
33	13	A	Colchester U	W	2-1	0-0	—	McShane [51], Kamara [52]	5611
34	20	H	Cardiff C	W	1-0	0-0	—	Ellington [66]	18,802
35	24	A	Leicester C	D	1-1	1-1	1	Kamara (pen) [27]	25,581
36	Mar 3	H	Sunderland	L	1-2	0-1	3	Carter [72]	23,252
37	11	A	Wolverhampton W	L	0-1	0-0	5		28,016
38	14	H	Crystal Palace	L	2-3	1-2	—	Clement [26], Phillips [76]	17,960
39	18	H	Birmingham C	D	1-1	0-0	6	McShane [64]	21,434
40	31	A	QPR	W	2-1	0-0	5	Phillips [48], Gera [84]	14,784
41	Apr 7	H	Stoke C	L	1-3	0-3	5	Koumas [74]	20,386
42	9	A	Norwich C	W	2-1	0-0	4	Sodje [73], Kamara [90]	25,422
43	13	H	Sheffield W	L	0-1	0-0	—		20,415
44	23	A	Burnley	L	2-3	2-1	—	Koumas [6], Thomas (og) [8]	12,500
45	28	A	Coventry C	W	1-0	1-0	4	Robinson [37]	26,343
46	May 6	H	Barnsley	W	7-0	4-0	4	Phillips 3 [21, 53, 71], Ellington 2 (1 pen) [25 (p), 36], Koren [40], Gera [75]	23,568

Final League Position: 4

GOALSCORERS

League (81): Kamara 20 (3 pens), Phillips 16 (1 pen), Ellington 9 (2 pens), Koumas 9, Gera 5, Hartson 5 (1 pen), Carter 3, Greening 2, McShane 2, Robinson 2, Albrechtsen 1, Chaplow 1, Clement 1, Koren 1, Sodje 1, Wallwork 1, own goals 2.
Carling Cup (6): Nicholson 2 (1 pen), Carter 1, Ellington 1 (pen), Greening 1, Wallwork 1.
FA Cup (9): Phillips 3, Kamara 2, Carter 1, Gera 1, Hartson 1, McShane 1.
Play-Offs (4): Phillips 3, Kamara 1.

Zuberbuhler P 15	Watson S 10 + 2	Robinson P 42	Wallwork R 9 + 1	Davies C 32	Perry C 23	Gera Z 28 + 12	Quashie N 17 + 3	Ellington N 19 + 15	Hartson J 14 + 7	Greening J 40 + 2	Inamoto J — + 3	Carter D 19 + 14	Albrechtsen M 26 + 5	Chaplow R 16 + 12	Phillips K 31 + 5	McShane P 31 + 1	Koumas J 34 + 5	Nicholson S — + 2	Kamara D 33 + 1	Hoult R 14	Hodgkiss J — + 5	Clement N 14 + 6	Koren R 15 + 3	Kiely D 17	MacDonald S — + 9	Sodje S 7	*Match No.*
1	2	3	4^1	5	6	7^2	8	9	10	11^3	12	13	14														1
1	2	3	4^1	5	6	7	8	9^2	10	11^3	12	13		14													2
1	2	3	4^3	5	6	7	8	9^2	10	11^1	12	13		14													3
1	2	3	4^2	5	6	7^1	8	9^3	10	11		12	13	14													4
1	2	3	12	5	6	7	8	9^3	10	11^2		13		4^1	14												5
1		3	4		6		8^2	12	10^1	11^3		7	2	13	9	5	14										6
1		3	4		6	7	8	12	10^1			11^2	2		9	5	13										7
1		3	4		6	7	8	9		12		11^2	2^1		10	5	13										8
1	2^1	3	4		6	12	8^2	9^3		13		11			10	5	7	14									9
1		3			6	7^1			10^2	11		4	2	12	9	5■	8		13								10
1		3		5	6	7^2	12	13		11		8	2		9		4^1		10								11
1		3		5	6	7	12	9^1		11		8	2				4		10								12
1	12	3		5	6	7^1	8	9^2	13	11			2	14			4^3		10								13
1		3■		5	6	7	8^1	9	12	11			2				4		10								14
1	2		4^1	5	6	7		9^2	12	11			3		13		8		10								15
	2			5	6	7^1		9^2	12	11			3	4	13		8		10	1							16
	7^1			5	6			12		11		8	3		9	2^2	4		10	1	13						17
		3		5	6		8	9^1				4	2	12	10		11		7	1							18
		3		5	6	12	8	13		11		4	2^1		10		7		9^2	1							19
		3		5	6^2	12	8			11		4^1	2		10	13	9		7	1							20
		3		5		7	8		12	11			2		10	6	4^2		9^1	1		13					21
		3		5		7^1	8	12	10^2	11		13	2		9	6^3	4			1		14					22
		3		5		12	8	13	10^2	11			2		9	6	4^3		7^1	1		14					23
		3		5		12		13	10^2	11		4	2^3		9	6	7^1		8	1		14■					24
		3		5			12	13	10^1	11		4^2	2	14	9^3	6	8		7	1							25
	12			5		7^2				11		4	2	13	9	6	8		10^1	1		3					26
		3		5		7^2		13	12	11		4	2^3		9^1	6	8		10	1		14					27
	2	3		5^2		12			10^1	11				4	9		8		7^3	1	13	6	14				28
		3		5		7				11				4	9	2		12	10^1	1		6	8				29
		3		5		12				11		13		4	9^2	2	7^1		10^3			6	8	1	14		30
		3		5		12		13		11		14		4	9^2	2	7^1		10^3			6	8	1			31
		3		5		7^2		12				13		4	9^1	2	11		10^3			6	8	1	14		32
		3		5		7			10^1			11		4		2			9			6	8	1	12		33
		3						12	13	11		14	2	4^2	9^1	5	7^3		10			6	8	1			34
		3		5		12		13		11				4	9^2	2	7^1		10			6	8	1			35
		3■		5		12				11^2		13		4	9^3	2	7		10			6	8^1	1	14		36
		3		5		7				11		12	13	4^1	9^3	2^2	8		10			6		1	14		37
		3		5^1		7				11			12■	4^2	9	2	8		10			6	13	1			38
		3				7^2		9		11		12				2	4^1		10			6	8	1	13	5	39
		3				12		13		11		4^2		14	9^1	2	7		10^3			6	8	1		5	40
		3						10		11^1		12	2	4	9^2	5	7				14		8	1	13	6^3	41
		3				7^3		9^1		11		4^2	2	12		5	13		10		14		8	1		6	42
		3				7^1		9		11^2		4■	2		12	5	13		10			14■	8	1		6^3	43
		3			6	7		9^2		11			2	13	12	5■	4		10^1				8	1			44
		3			6	7				11			12	4^2	9^3	2	8		10■				13	1	14	5^1	45
		3			6	12		10^2		11				4	9	2^3	7^1				14		8	1	13	5	46

FA Cup

Third Round	Leeds U	(h)	3-1
Fourth Round	Wolverhampton W	(a)	3-0
Fifth Round	Middlesbrough	(a)	2-2
		(h)	1-1

Carling Cup

First Round	Leyton Orient	(a)	3-0
Second Round	Cheltenham T	(h)	3-1
Third Round	Arsenal	(h)	0-2

Play-Offs

Semi-Final	Wolverhampton W	(a)	3-2
		(h)	1-0
Final *(at Wembley)*	Derby Co		0-1

WEST HAM UNITED FA Premiership

FOUNDATION

Thames Iron Works FC was formed by employees of this famous shipbuilding company in 1895 and entered the FA Cup in their initial season at Chatham and the London League in their second. The committee wanted to introduce professional players, so Thames Iron Works was wound up in June 1900 and relaunched a month later as West Ham United.

The Boleyn Ground, Upton Park, Green Street, London E13 9AZ.

Telephone: (020) 8548 2748.

Fax: (020) 8548 2758.

Ticket Office: 0870 112 2700.

Website: www.whufc.co.uk

Email: yourcomments@westhamunited.co.uk

Ground Capacity: 35,300.

Record Attendance: 42,322 v Tottenham H, Division 1, 17 October 1970.

Pitch Measurements: 100.58m × 66.75m.

Chairman/CEO: Eggert Magnusson.

Deputy Chief Executive: Scott Duxbury.

Secretary: Peter Barnes.

Manager: Alan Curbishley.

Assistant Managers: Mervyn Day, Keith Peacock.

Physio: Steve Allen.

Colours: Claret and blue shirts, white shorts, white stockings.

Change Colours: White shirts, claret shorts, claret stockings.

Year Formed: 1895.

Turned Professional: 1900.

Ltd Co.: 1900.

Previous Name: 1895, Thames Iron Works FC; 1900, West Ham United.

Club Nicknames: 'The Hammers', 'The Irons'.

Grounds: 1895, Memorial Recreation Ground, Canning Town; 1904, Boleyn Ground.

First Football League Game: 30 August 1919, Division 2, v Lincoln C (h) D 1–1 – Hufton; Cope, Lee; Lane, Fenwick, McCrae; D. Smith, Moyes (1), Puddefoot, Morris, Bradshaw.

HONOURS

Football League: Promotion from Championship 2004–05 (play-offs); Division 2 – Champions 1957–58, 1980–81; Runners-up 1922–23, 1990–91.

FA Cup: Winners 1964, 1975, 1980; Runners-up 1923, 2006.

Football League Cup: Runners-up 1966, 1981.

European Competitions: *European Cup-Winners' Cup:* 1964–65 (winners), 1965–66, 1975–76 (runners-up), 1980–81. *UEFA Cup:* 1999–2000; 2006–07. *Intertoto Cup:* 1999 (winners).

SKY SPORTS FACT FILE

Thanks for research by John Northcutt, Billy Williams was the youngest League debutant and goalscorer for West Ham United at 16 years 221 days on 6 May 1922 against Blackpool. Chris Cohen on 13 December 2003 had been 16 years 283 days on his debut.

Record League Victory: 8–0 v Rotherham U, Division 2, 8 March 1958 – Gregory; Bond, Wright; Malcolm, Brown, Lansdowne; Grice, Smith (2), Keeble (2), Dick (4), Musgrove. 8–0 v Sunderland, Division 1, 19 October 1968 – Ferguson; Bonds, Charles; Peters, Stephenson, Moore (1); Redknapp, Boyce, Brooking (1), Hurst (6), Sissons.

Record Cup Victory: 10–0 v Bury, League Cup 2nd rd (2nd leg), 25 October 1983 – Parkes; Stewart (1), Walford, Bonds (Orr), Martin (1), Devonshire (2), Allen, Cottee (4), Swindlehurst, Brooking (2), Pike.

Record Defeat: 2–8 v Blackburn R, Division 1, 26 December 1963.

Most League Points (2 for a win): 66, Division 2, 1980–81.

Most League Points (3 for a win): 88, Division 1, 1992–93.

Most League Goals: 101, Division 2, 1957–58.

Highest League Scorer in Season: Vic Watson, 42, Division 1, 1929–30.

Most League Goals in Total Aggregate: Vic Watson, 298, 1920–35.

Most League Goals in One Match: 6, Vic Watson v Leeds U, Division 1, 9 February 1929; 6, Geoff Hurst v Sunderland, Division 1, 19 October 1968.

Most Capped Player: Bobby Moore, 108, England.

Most League Appearances: Billy Bonds, 663, 1967–88.

Youngest League Player: Billy Williams, 16 years 221 days v Blackpool, 6 May 1922.

Record Transfer Fee Received: £18,000,000 from Leeds U for Rio Ferdinand, November 2000.

Record Transfer Fee Paid: £7,500,000 to Liverpool for Craig Bellamy, July 2007.

Football League Record: 1919 Elected to Division 2; 1923–32 Division 1; 1932–58 Division 2; 1958–78 Division 1; 1978–81 Division 2; 1981–89 Division 1; 1989–91 Division 2; 1991–93 Division 1; 1993–2003 FA Premier League; 2003–04 Division 1; 2004–05 FL C; 2005– FA Premier League.

MANAGERS

Syd King 1902–32
Charlie Paynter 1932–50
Ted Fenton 1950–61
Ron Greenwood 1961–74
(continued as General Manager to 1977)
John Lyall 1974–89
Lou Macari 1989–90
Billy Bonds 1990–94
Harry Redknapp 1994–2001
Glenn Roeder 2001–03
Alan Pardew 2003–06
Alan Curbishley December 2006–

LATEST SEQUENCES

Longest Sequence of League Wins: 9, 19.10.1985 – 14.12.1985.

Longest Sequence of League Defeats: 9, 28.3.1932 – 29.8.1932.

Longest Sequence of League Draws: 5, 15.10.2003 – 1.11.2003.

Longest Sequence of Unbeaten League Matches: 27, 27.12.80 – 10.10.81.

Longest Sequence Without a League Win: 17, 31.1.1976 – 21.8.1976.

Successive Scoring Runs: 27 from 5.10.1957.

Successive Non-scoring Runs: 5 from 1.5.1971.

TEN YEAR LEAGUE RECORD

		P	W	D	L	F	A	Pts	Pos
1997-98	PR Lge	38	16	8	14	56	57	56	8
1998-99	PR Lge	38	16	9	13	46	53	57	5
1999-2000	PR Lge	38	15	10	13	52	53	55	9
2000-01	PR Lge	38	10	12	16	45	50	42	15
2001-02	PR Lge	38	15	8	15	48	57	53	7
2002-03	PR Lge	38	10	12	16	42	59	42	18
2003-04	Div 1	46	19	17	10	67	45	74	4
2004-05	FL C	46	21	10	15	66	56	73	6
2005-06	PR Lge	38	16	7	15	52	55	55	9
2006-07	PR Lge	38	12	5	21	35	59	41	15

DID YOU KNOW ?

On 26 December 2006 Teddy Sheringham became the oldest goalscorer in Premier League history when he scored against Portsmouth aged 40 years 268 days, thus breaking his own landmark first recorded on 13 August 2005 and broken earlier on 29 October 2006 versus Blackburn.

WEST HAM UNITED 2006–07 LEAGUE RECORD

Match No.	Date	Venue	Opponents	Result		H/T Score	Lg. Pos.	Goalscorers	Attendance
1	Aug 19	H	Charlton Ath	W	3-1	0-1	—	Zamora 2 [52, 66], Cole [90]	34,937
2	22	A	Watford	D	1-1	0-0	—	Zamora [65]	18,344
3	26	A	Liverpool	L	1-2	1-2	6	Zamora [12]	43,965
4	Sept 10	H	Aston Villa	D	1-1	0-1	8	Zamora [52]	34,576
5	17	H	Newcastle U	L	0-2	0-0	11		34,938
6	23	A	Manchester C	L	0-2	0-0	15		41,073
7	Oct 1	H	Reading	L	0-1	0-1	16		34,872
8	14	A	Portsmouth	L	0-2	0-1	18		20,142
9	22	A	Tottenham H	L	0-1	0-1	19		36,162
10	29	H	Blackburn R	W	2-1	1-0	16	Sheringham [21], Mullins [80]	33,833
11	Nov 5	H	Arsenal	W	1-0	0-0	15	Harewood [89]	34,969
12	11	A	Middlesbrough	L	0-1	0-0	16		25,898
13	18	A	Chelsea	L	0-1	0-1	16		41,916
14	25	H	Sheffield U	W	1-0	1-0	15	Mullins [36]	34,454
15	Dec 3	A	Everton	L	0-2	0-0	17		32,968
16	6	H	Wigan Ath	L	0-2	0-0	—		33,805
17	9	A	Bolton W	L	0-4	0-1	18		22,283
18	17	H	Manchester U	W	1-0	0-0	18	Reo-Coker [75]	34,966
19	23	A	Fulham	D	0-0	0-0	18		22,452
20	26	H	Portsmouth	L	1-2	0-2	18	Sheringham [81]	34,913
21	30	H	Manchester C	L	0-1	0-0	18		34,574
22	Jan 1	A	Reading	L	0-6	0-4	18		24,073
23	13	H	Fulham	D	3-3	1-1	18	Zamora [28], Benayoun 2 [46, 64]	34,977
24	20	A	Newcastle U	D	2-2	2-1	18	Cole [18], Harewood [22]	52,095
25	30	H	Liverpool	L	1-2	0-0	—	Kepa [77]	34,966
26	Feb 3	A	Aston Villa	L	0-1	0-1	18		41,202
27	10	H	Watford	L	0-1	0-1	18		34,625
28	24	A	Charlton Ath	L	0-4	0-3	19		27,111
29	Mar 4	H	Tottenham H	L	3-4	2-0	20	Noble [16], Tevez [41], Zamora [85]	34,966
30	17	A	Blackburn R	W	2-1	0-0	19	Tevez (pen) [71], Zamora [75]	18,591
31	31	H	Middlesbrough	W	2-0	2-0	19	Zamora [2], Tevez [45]	34,977
32	Apr 7	A	Arsenal	W	1-0	1-0	19	Zamora [45]	60,098
33	14	A	Sheffield U	L	0-3	0-1	19		31,593
34	18	H	Chelsea	L	1-4	1-2	—	Tevez [35]	34,966
35	21	H	Everton	W	1-0	1-0	19	Zamora [13]	34,945
36	28	A	Wigan Ath	W	3-0	1-0	18	Boa Morte [30], Benayoun [57], Harewood [82]	24,726
37	May 5	H	Bolton W	W	3-1	3-0	17	Tevez 2 [10, 21], Noble [29]	34,404
38	13	A	Manchester U	W	1-0	1-0	15	Tevez [45]	75,927

Final League Position: 15

GOALSCORERS

League (35): Zamora 11, Tevez 7 (1 pen), Benayoun 3, Harewood 3, Cole 2, Mullins 2, Noble 2, Sheringham 2, Boa Morte 1, Kepa 1, Reo-Coker 1.
Carling Cup (1): Harewood 1.
FA Cup (3): Cole 1, Mullins 1, Noble 1.
UEFA Cup (0).

Carroll R 12	Mears T 3 + 2	Konchesky P 22	Gabbidon D 18	Ferdinand A 31	Mullins H 21 + 9	Bowyer L 18 + 2	Reo-Coker N 35	Harewood M 19 + 13	Zamora B 27 + 5	Benayoun Y 25 + 4	Pantsil J 3 + 2	Cole C 5 + 12	Sheringham T 4 + 13	Collins J 16	Etherington M 24 + 3	Tevez C 19 + 7	Mascherano J 3 + 2	Dailly C 10 + 4	Spector J 17 + 8	Green R 26	McCartney G 16 + 6	Newton S — + 3	Boa Morte L 8 + 6	Quashie N 7	Davenport C 5 + 1	Kepa 1 + 7	Upson M 2	Neill L 11	Noble M 10	*Match No.*
1	2^{1}	3	4	5	6	7	8	9^{2}	10^{3}	11	12	13	14																	1
1		3	4^{2}	5	6	7	8	9^{1}	10^{3}	13	2	14	12	11																2
1	12	3^{1}	4	5	6	7	8^{2}	9^{3}	10	11	2	14	13																	3
1	2	3	4	5	6	7^{2}	8	9^{3}	10^{1}	11		12			13	14														4
1	2^{1}	3	4	5	12	7	8	13	9	14					11	10^{2}	6^{3}													5
1		3	4	5^{1}	12		8	9^{3}	10^{2}	7		13			11	14	6	2												6
1		3	4		6		8^{1}	12	13	7		9^{2}	14		11	10^{3}		5	2											7
1		3	4	5	6		8	12	9^{1}	7^{3}		13	10^{2}		11		14		2											8
		3	4	5	6		8	9^{3}	10	7^{1}	2	12				13	11^{2}	14		1										9
			4	5	6	12	8	13	9	7^{1}			10^{2}		11			14	2	1	3^{3}									10
		3	4	5^{3}	6	10^{2}	8	12	9^{1}	7			13		11				2	1	14									11
		3	4		6		8	9^{2}		7^{1}		12	10	5	11	13			2	1										12
		3	4	5	6	7^{2}	8	12	9^{1}				13		11^{3}	10			2	1	14									13
		3	4^{3}	5	6	7	8	12	9^{1}				13		11	10^{2}			2	1	14									14
		3		5	6	7^{2}	8	12	9^{1}				13	4	11	10	14		2^{3}	1										15
		3		5^{3}	6	12	8	9		7^{2}			13	4	11^{1}	10			2	1	14									16
		3			6		8	9			12		13	5	11	10^{2}		7	2^{1}	1	4									17
		3		5	6^{1}	7	8	9	10^{2}	12			13	4	11^{3}				2	1	14									18
		3■		5	6	7^{1}	8	9^{3}	10^{2}	12			13		11			4	2	1	14									19
		3	4	5	6		8	9^{1}	10	7			12		11^{2}	13		14	2^{3}	1										20
	12		4^{1}	5	6	8		9		7		13	10^{2}		11^{3}	14		2	3	1										21
		3	4	5	6	7^{3}	8	9^{2}	10	11^{1}		12						2	13	1		14								22
1			4^{3}				8■		12■	7		9		5^{2}		10^{1}		2	13		3	14	11	6						23
1				5^{2}			8	9		7		10^{1}			12			2	13		3		11	4	6					24
1							8	9^{2}	12	7		10^{1}						5	2		3		11	4	6	13				25
1							8	12	10	7					13			14	2		3		11^{2}	4	6	9^{1}	5^{3}			26
				5			8	9	10^{2}	7					11	13			12	1	3		14	4^{3}	6			2^{1}		27
		3		5	6^{2}			12		7		9^{3}			11^{1}	10		2		1		13		8	4	14				28
		3		5		7		9	12						11^{1}	10				1				4^{3}	13	14	6^{2}	2	8	29
				5	12	7	8	9^{2}	13					4	11	10^{3}				1	3		14					2	6^{1}	30
				5	12	7	8^{1}		9^{3}					6	11	10^{2}				1	3		13			14		2	4	31
				5		7	8		9^{1}					6	11	10^{3}			13	1	3^{2}		12			14		2	4	32
				5	12	7^{1}	8		9					6	11^{2}	10				1	3		13			14		2	4^{3}	33
					12		8^{1}		9^{2}	7		13		4		10^{3}			2	1	3		11			14		5	6	34
				5			8		9^{1}	7		12		4	11^{2}	10				1	3		13					2	6	35
				5	12		8^{1}	13	9^{2}	7				4		10^{3}			14	1	3		11					2	6	36
				5	12		8^{1}	13	9^{2}	7				4		10			14	1	3		11^{3}					2	6	37
				5	12		8	13	9^{2}	7				4		10^{1}			14	1	3^{3}		11					2	6	38

FA Cup

Third Round	Brighton & HA	(h)	3-0
Fourth Round	Watford	(h)	0-1

UEFA Cup

First Round	Palermo	(h)	0-1
		(a)	0-3

Carling Cup

Third Round	Chesterfield	(a)	1-2

WIGAN ATHLETIC FA Premiership

FOUNDATION

Following the demise of Wigan Borough and their resignation from the Football League in 1931, a public meeting was called in Wigan at the Queen's Hall in May 1932 at which a new club, Wigan Athletic, was founded in the hope of carrying on in the Football League. With this in mind, they bought Springfield Park for £2,250, but failed to gain admission to the Football League until 46 years later.

JJB Stadium, Robin Park, Newtown, Wigan WN5 0UZ.

Telephone: (01942) 774 000.

Fax: (01942) 770 477.

Ticket Office: 0871 6633 252.

Website: www.wiganathletic.tv

Email: feedback@jjbstadium.co.uk

Ground Capacity: 25,138.

Record Attendance: 27,526 v Hereford U, 12 December 1953 (at Springfield Park).

Pitch Measurements: 105m × 68m.

Chairman: David Whelan.

Vice-chairman: Phillip Williams.

Chief Executive: Brenda Spencer.

Secretary: Stuart Hayton.

Manager: Chris Hutchings.

Assistant Manager: Frank Barlow.

Physio: Alan Tomlinson.

Colours: Blue and white striped shirts, blue shorts, white stockings.

Change Colours: White shirts, flint shorts, flint stockings.

Year Formed: 1932.

Grounds: 1932, Springfield Park; 1999, JJB Stadium.

Club Nickname: 'The Latics'.

First Football League Game: 19 August 1978, Division 4, v Hereford U (a) D 0–0 – Brown; Hinnigan, Gore, Gillibrand, Ward, Davids, Corrigan, Purdie, Houghton, Wilkie, Wright.

Record League Victory: 7–1 v Scarborough, Division 3, 11 March 1997 – Butler L, Butler J, Sharp (Morgan), Greenall, McGibbon (Biggins (1)), Martinez (1), Diaz (2), Jones (Lancashire (1)), Lowe (2), Rogers, Kilford.

Record Cup Victory: 6–0 v Carlisle U (away), FA Cup 1st rd, 24 November 1934 – Caunce; Robinson, Talbot; Paterson, Watson, Tufnell; Armes (2), Robson (1), Roberts (2), Felton, Scott (1).

HONOURS

Football League: Championship – Runners-up 2004–05; Division 2 Champions, 2002–03; Division 3 Champions, 1996–97; Division 4 – Promoted (3rd) 1981–82.

FA Cup: best season: 6th rd, 1987.

Football League Cup: Runners up: 2006.

Freight Rover Trophy: Winners 1985.

Auto Windscreens Shield: Winners 1999.

SKY SPORTS FACT FILE

Jack "Nipper" Roberts had had League experience with Southport and Liverpool when he joined Wigan Athletic and held the club's scoring record for 30 years with 66 League and Cup goals in 1934–35. Later at Port Vale he had a leg amputated after injury.

Record Defeat: 1–6 v Bristol R, Division 3, 3 March 1990.

Most League Points (2 for a win): 55, Division 4, 1978–79 and 1979–80.

Most League Points (3 for a win): 100, Division 2, 2002–03.

Most League Goals: 84, Division 3, 1996–97.

Highest League Scorer in Season: Graeme Jones, 31, Division 3, 1996–97.

Most League Goals in Total Aggregate: Andy Liddell, 70, 1998–2004.

Most League Goals in One Match: Not more than three goals by one player.

Most Capped Player: Lee McCulloch, 11, Scotland.

Most League Appearances: Kevin Langley, 317, 1981–86, 1990–94.

Youngest League Player: Steve Nugent, 16 years 132 days v Leyton Orient, 16 September 1989.

Record Transfer Fee Received: £4,500,000 from Tottenham H for Pascal Chimbonda, August 2006.

Record Transfer Fee Paid: £5,500,000 to Birmingham C for Emile Heskey, July 2006.

Football League Record: 1978 Elected to Division 4; 1982–92 Division 3; 1992–93 Division 2; 1993–97 Division 3; 1997–2003 Division 2; 2003–04 Division 1; 2004–05 FL C; 2005– FA Premier League.

MANAGERS

Charlie Spencer 1932–37
Jimmy Milne 1946–47
Bob Pryde 1949–52
Ted Goodier 1952–54
Walter Crook 1954–55
Ron Suart 1955–56
Billy Cooke 1956
Sam Barkas 1957
Trevor Hitchen 1957–58
Malcolm Barrass 1958–59
Jimmy Shirley 1959
Pat Murphy 1959–60
Allenby Chilton 1960
Johnny Ball 1961–63
Allan Brown 1963–66
Alf Craig 1966–67
Harry Leyland 1967–68
Alan Saunders 1968
Ian McNeill 1968–70
Gordon Milne 1970–72
Les Rigby 1972–74
Brian Tiler 1974–76
Ian McNeill 1976–81
Larry Lloyd 1981–83
Harry McNally 1983–85
Bryan Hamilton 1985–86
Ray Mathias 1986–89
Bryan Hamilton 1989–93
Dave Philpotts 1993
Kenny Swain 1993–94
Graham Barrow 1994–95
John Deehan 1995–98
Ray Mathias 1998–99
John Benson 1999–2000
Bruce Rioch 2000–01
Steve Bruce 2001
Paul Jewell 2001–07
Chris Hutchings May 2007

LATEST SEQUENCES

Longest Sequence of League Wins: 11, 2.11.2002 – 18.1.2003.

Longest Sequence of League Defeats: 8, 13.12.2006 – 30.1.2007.

Longest Sequence of League Draws: 6, 11.12.2001 – 5.1.2002.

Longest Sequence of Unbeaten League Matches: 25, 8.5.1999 – 3.1.2000.

Longest Sequence Without a League Win: 14, 9.5.1989 – 17.10.1989.

Successive Scoring Runs: 24 from 27.4.1996.

Successive Non-scoring Runs: 4 from 15.4.1995.

TEN YEAR LEAGUE RECORD

		P	*W*	*D*	*L*	*F*	*A*	*Pts*	*Pos*
1997-98	Div 2	46	17	11	18	64	66	62	11
1998-99	Div 2	46	22	10	14	75	48	76	6
1999-2000	Div 2	46	22	17	7	72	38	83	4
2000-01	Div 2	46	19	18	9	53	42	75	6
2001-02	Div 2	46	16	16	14	66	51	64	10
2002-03	Div 2	46	29	13	4	68	25	100	1
2003-04	Div 1	46	18	17	11	60	45	71	7
2004-05	FL C	46	25	12	9	79	35	87	2
2005-06	PR Lge	38	15	6	17	45	52	51	10
2006-07	PR Lge	38	10	8	20	37	59	38	17

DID YOU KNOW ?

Scottish international defender Andy Webster created history by cancelling his contract with Hearts in the third year of a four-year deal thanks to EU law. His move on 4 September 2006 to Wigan Athletic was another unprecedented one past the transfer window.

WIGAN ATHLETIC 2006–07 LEAGUE RECORD

Match No.	Date	Venue	Opponents	Result		H/T Score	Lg. Pos.	Goalscorers	Attendance
1	Aug 19	A	Newcastle U	L	1-2	0-1	—	McCulloch [59]	51,569
2	26	H	Reading	W	1-0	1-0	12	Heskey [38]	14,636
3	Sept 9	A	Portsmouth	L	0-1	0-0	13		19,508
4	16	A	Everton	D	2-2	0-0	14	Scharner 2 [62, 68]	37,117
5	23	H	Watford	D	1-1	1-0	14	Camara [29]	16,359
6	Oct 1	A	Blackburn R	L	1-2	1-1	15	Heskey [2]	17,859
7	14	H	Manchester U	L	1-3	1-0	17	Baines [5]	20,631
8	21	H	Manchester C	W	4-0	2-0	15	Heskey [2], Dunne (og) [4], Camara [65], Valencia [67]	16,235
9	28	A	Fulham	W	1-0	0-0	13	Camara [83]	22,882
10	Nov 4	A	Bolton W	W	1-0	0-0	11	McCulloch [79]	21,255
11	11	H	Charlton Ath	W	3-2	2-0	8	McCulloch [13], Camara [41], Jackson [78]	16,572
12	19	H	Aston Villa	D	0-0	0-0	9		18,455
13	26	A	Tottenham H	L	1-3	1-2	11	Camara [25]	35,205
14	Dec 2	H	Liverpool	L	0-4	0-4	13		22,089
15	6	A	West Ham U	W	2-0	0-0	—	Cotterill [51], Spector (og) [58]	33,805
16	9	A	Middlesbrough	D	1-1	1-0	11	Camara (pen) [24]	23,638
17	13	H	Arsenal	L	0-1	0-0	—		15,311
18	16	H	Sheffield U	L	0-1	0-1	11		16,322
19	23	H	Chelsea	L	2-3	1-2	13	Heskey 2 [45, 75]	22,077
20	26	A	Manchester U	L	1-3	0-0	14	Baines (pen) [90]	76,018
21	Jan 1	H	Blackburn R	L	0-3	0-1	17		14,864
22	13	A	Chelsea	L	0-4	0-1	17		40,846
23	21	H	Everton	L	0-2	0-0	17		18,149
24	30	A	Reading	L	2-3	1-1	—	Heskey [3], Landzaat [90]	21,954
25	Feb 3	H	Portsmouth	W	1-0	0-0	17	McCulloch [68]	15,093
26	11	A	Arsenal	L	1-2	1-0	17	Landzaat [35]	60,049
27	21	A	Watford	D	1-1	1-1	—	Folan [40]	18,338
28	25	H	Newcastle U	W	1-0	1-0	17	Taylor [40]	21,179
29	Mar 3	A	Manchester C	W	1-0	1-0	15	Folan [18]	39,923
30	17	H	Fulham	D	0-0	0-0	16		16,001
31	31	A	Charlton Ath	L	0-1	0-0	16		26,500
32	Apr 7	H	Bolton W	L	1-3	1-1	16	Hunt (og) [32]	18,610
33	9	A	Aston Villa	D	1-1	1-0	16	Heskey [21]	31,920
34	15	H	Tottenham H	D	3-3	2-2	15	Heskey [2], Baines [30], Kilbane [60]	16,506
35	21	A	Liverpool	L	0-2	0-1	16		44,033
36	28	H	West Ham U	L	0-3	0-1	17		24,726
37	May 5	H	Middlesbrough	L	0-1	0-1	18		21,204
38	13	A	Sheffield U	W	2-1	2-1	17	Scharner [14], Unsworth (pen) [45]	32,604

Final League Position: 17

GOALSCORERS

League (37): Heskey 8, Camara 6 (1 pen), McCulloch 4, Baines 3 (1 pen), Scharner 3, Folan 2, Landzaat 2, Cotterill 1, Jackson 1, Kilbane 1, Taylor 1, Unsworth 1 (pen), Valencia 1, own goals 3.
Carling Cup (0).
FA Cup (1): McCulloch 1.

Kirkland C 26	Boyce E 34	Baines L 35	Landzaat D 29 + 4	Hall F 22 + 2	De Zeeuw A 21	Valencia L 17 + 5	Scharner P 22 + 3	Camara H 18 + 5	Heskey E 33 + 1	McCulloch L 25 + 4	Kavanagh G — + 2	Connolly D — + 2	Chimbonda P — + 1	Teale G 7 + 5	Cotterill D 5 + 11	Johansson A 4 + 8	Wright D 6 + 6	Kilbane K 26 + 5	Jackson M 17 + 3	Todorov S 2 + 3	Skoko J 24 + 4	Webster A 3 + 1	Pollitt M 2 + 1	Unsworth D 6 + 4	Taylor R 12 + 4	Haestad K 1 + 1	Folan C 8 + 5	Aghahowa J 3 + 3	Filan J 10	*Match No.*
1	2	3	4^{1}	5	6	7^{2}	8	9	10	11	12	13																		1
1	2	3	4^{2}	5	6	7	8	9^{1}	10^{3}	11	13	12	14																	2
1	2	3	4	5	6	7	8	9^{1}	10					11^{2}	13	12														3
1	2	3	4^{2}	5	6	7^{1}	8		10					12		9	13	11												4
1	2	3	4	5	6	7^{1}	8	9	10					12				11												5
1	2	3	4		6	7^{2}	8	9^{3}	10	12				13				11^{1}	5	14										6
1	2	3	4	5	6	12	8	9^{2}	10	13				7^{1}				11^{3}		14										7
1	2	3	12	5^{3}	6	7^{2}	8	9	10					13				11			4^{1}	14								8
1	2	3	4^{2}		6		8	9	10^{1}	12				7		13		11	14			5^{3}								9
1	2	3	4		6		8	9^{2}	10^{1}	12				7^{3}	14	13		11				5								10
1	2	3	4^{3}		6	12	8	9		10					7^{1}		14	11	13			5^{2}								11
1	2		12		6		8	9		10				7^{2}	13		3	11	5		4^{1}									12
1	6	3		12			8	9	13	10				7^{2}	14		2^{1}	11^{3}	5		4									13
1	2	3		6			8	9	10	7					12		13	11^{1}	5^{2}		4									14
1	6	3	12	5			8	13	9	10					7^{2}		2	11			4^{1}									15
1^{6}	6	3		5		12^{2}	8	9		10					7^{1}	13	2	11			4		15							16
1	6	3	4	5				9	10^{1}	8						12	2	11			7									17
1	2^{1}	3	4	5	6			9^{2}	10	8					13		12	11^{3}		14	7									18
1	2	3	4^{2}	5	6				10					12	14	8^{3}	13	11		9^{1}	7									19
1	2	3		5^{2}					10					7^{1}	12	8	4	11	6	9	13									20
1	2	3	4	5	6				10						7	9	12	11			8^{1}									21
1	2	3	12	5					9^{2}	10					7^{3}	13		11			8			6	14	4^{1}				22
1	2	3	4	5^{2}		7^{1}			9	10					12			11			8			6	13					23
1	5	3	4			7			9^{3}	10^{1}						12		14	13		8			6^{2}	2		11			24
1	6		4	12		7^{1}				11						13			5		8			3	2		9	10^{2}		25
1	2	3	4	5^{3}		12			9	11								13	6		8				7^{1}	14		10^{2}		26
	6	3	4	2■					10	11								12	5		8				7		9^{1}		1	27
	6	3	4			7^{2}		13	10^{1}	11								12	5		8				2		9		1	28
	6^{2}	3	4			7^{3}			10^{1}	11								12	5		8			13	2		9	14	1	29
			4^{1}		6	7	12	13	10									11	5		8			3	2		9^{2}		1	30
		3	4	2	6	12	13		10	11									5		8^{2}				7^{1}		9		1	31
		3		6		7	8	12	10	11					13				5		4^{2}				2		9^{1}		1	32
		3	4	5^{1}		7■	8		9^{3}	10								11	6		12			2^{2}	13		14		1	33
	2	3	4		6		8	9	10^{3}	7^{2}								11	5^{1}		12				13		14		1	34
	2	3	4^{3}		6		10	12	9^{2}									11	5		8				7^{1}		13	14	1	35
	2	3	4^{1}		6^{2}		12	9	10	7								11^{3}	5		8			13				14	1	36
	5	3^{2}	4^{1}			7	6		10	11					12						8		1	13	2		14	9^{3}		37
	5	3	4^{3}		6^{1}	7	8		9	10■								11			12		1	13	2^{2}		14			38

FA Cup
Third Round Portsmouth (a) 1-2

Carling Cup
Second Round Crewe Alex (a) 0-2

WOLVERHAMPTON WANDERERS FL Championship

FOUNDATION

Enthusiasts of the game at St Luke's School, Blakenhall formed a club in 1877. In the same neighbourhood a cricket club called Blakenhall Wanderers had a football section. Several St Luke's footballers played cricket for them and shortly before the start of the 1879–80 season the two amalgamated and Wolverhampton Wanderers FC was brought into being.

Molineux, Waterloo Road, Wolverhampton WV1 4QR.

Telephone: 0871 880 8442.

Fax: (01902) 687 006.

Ticket Office: 0871 880 8433

Website: wolves.co.uk

Email: info@wolves.co.uk

Ground Capacity: 28,576.

Record Attendance: 61,315 v Liverpool, FA Cup 5th rd, 11 February 1939.

Pitch Measurements: 110yd × 75yd.

Chief Executive: Jez Moxey.

Secretary: Richard Skirrow.

Manager: Mick McCarthy.

Assistant Manager: Ian Evans.

Physio: Barry Holmes.

Colours: Gold and black.

Change Colours: Navy blue with gold trim.

Year Formed: 1877* (*see Foundation*).

Turned Professional: 1888.

Ltd Co.: 1923 (but current club is WWFC (1986) Ltd).

Previous Names: 1879, St Luke's combined with Wanderers Cricket Club to become Wolverhampton Wanderers (1923) Ltd. New limited companies followed in 1982 and 1986 (current).

Club Nickname: 'Wolves'.

Grounds: 1877, Windmill Field; 1879, John Harper's Field; 1881, Dudley Road; 1889, Molineux.

First Football League Game: 8 September 1888, Football League, v Aston Villa (h) D 1–1 – Baynton; Baugh, Mason; Fletcher, Allen, Lowder; Hunter, Cooper, Anderson, White, Cannon, (1 og).

Record League Victory: 10–1 v Leicester C, Division 1, 15 April 1938 – Sidlow; Morris, Dowen; Galley, Cullis, Gardiner; Maguire (1), Horace Wright, Westcott (4), Jones (1), Dorsett (4).

HONOURS

Football League: Division 1 – Champions 1953–54, 1957–58, 1958–59; Runners-up 1937–38, 1938–39, 1949–50, 1954–55, 1959–60; 2002–03 (play-offs). Division 2 – Champions 1931–32, 1976–77; Runners-up 1966–67, 1982–83; Division 3 (N) – Champions 1923–24; Division 3 – Champions 1988–89; Division 4 – Champions 1987–88.

FA Cup: Winners 1893, 1908, 1949, 1960; Runners-up 1889, 1896, 1921, 1939.

Football League Cup: Winners 1974, 1980.

Texaco Cup: Winners 1971.

Sherpa Van Trophy: Winners 1988.

European Competitions: *European Cup:* 1958–59, 1959–60. *European Cup-Winners' Cup:* 1960–61. *UEFA Cup:* 1971–72 (runners-up), 1973–74, 1974–75, 1980–81.

SKY SPORTS FACT FILE

Dennis Willshaw who had been recalled from loan to Walsall by Wolverhampton Wanderers scored a 20 minute second half hat-trick on his League debut for them on 12 March 1949 against Newcastle United standing in for injured Jimmy Mullen at outside-left.

Record Cup Victory: 14–0 v Crosswell's Brewery, FA Cup 2nd rd, 13 November 1886 – I. Griffiths; Baugh, Mason; Pearson, Allen (1), Lowder; Hunter (4), Knight (2), Brodie (4), B. Griffiths (2), Wood. Plus one goal 'scrambled through'.

Record Defeat: 1–10 v Newton Heath, Division 1, 15 October 1892.

Most League Points (2 for a win): 64, Division 1, 1957–58.

Most League Points (3 for a win): 92, Division 3, 1988–89.

Most League Goals: 115, Division 2, 1931–32.

Highest League Scorer in Season: Dennis Westcott, 38, Division 1, 1946–47.

Most League Goals in Total Aggregate: Steve Bull, 250, 1986–99.

Most League Goals in One Match: 5, Joe Butcher v Accrington, Division 1, 19 November 1892; 5, Tom Phillipson v Barnsley, Division 2, 26 April 1926; 5, Tom Phillipson v Bradford C, Division 2, 25 December 1926; 5, Billy Hartill v Notts Co, Division 2, 12 October 1929; 5, Billy Hartill v Aston Villa, Division 1, 3 September 1934.

Most Capped Player: Billy Wright, 105, England (70 consecutive).

Most League Appearances: Derek Parkin, 501, 1967–82.

Youngest League Player: Jimmy Mullen, 16 years 43 days v Leeds U, 18 February 1939.

Record Transfer Fee Received: £6,000,000 from Coventry C for Robbie Keane, August 1999.

Record Transfer Fee Paid: £3,500,000 to Bristol C for Ade Akinbiyi, September 1999.

Football League Record: 1888 Founder Member of Football League: 1906–23 Division 2; 1923–24 Division 3 (N); 1924–32 Division 2; 1932–65 Division 1; 1965–67 Division 2; 1967–76 Division 1; 1976–77 Division 2; 1977–82 Division 1; 1982–83 Division 2; 1983–84 Division 1; 1984–85 Division 2; 1985–86 Division 3; 1986–88 Division 4; 1988–89 Division 3; 1989–92 Division 2; 1992–2003 Division 1; 2003–04 FA Premier League; 2004– FL C.

MANAGERS

George Worrall 1877–85
(Secretary-Manager)
John Addenbrooke 1885–1922
George Jobey 1922–24
Albert Hoskins 1924–26
(had been Secretary since 1922)
Fred Scotchbrook 1926–27
Major Frank Buckley 1927–44
Ted Vizard 1944–48
Stan Cullis 1948–64
Andy Beattie 1964–65
Ronnie Allen 1966–68
Bill McGarry 1968–76
Sammy Chung 1976–78
John Barnwell 1978–81
Ian Greaves 1982
Graham Hawkins 1982–84
Tommy Docherty 1984–85
Bill McGarry 1985
Sammy Chapman 1985–86
Brian Little 1986
Graham Turner 1986–94
Graham Taylor 1994–95
Mark McGhee 1995–98
Colin Lee 1998–2000
Dave Jones 2001–04
Glenn Hoddle 2004–2006
Mick McCarthy July 2006–

LATEST SEQUENCES

Longest Sequence of League Wins: 8, 15.10.1988 – 26.11.1988.

Longest Sequence of League Defeats: 8, 5.12.1981 – 13.2.1982.

Longest Sequence of League Draws: 6, 22.4.1995 – 20.8.1995.

Longest Sequence of Unbeaten League Matches: 21, 15.1.2005 – 13.8.2005.

Longest Sequence Without a League Win: 19, 1.12.1984 – 6.4.1985.

Successive Scoring Runs: 41 from 20.12.1958.

Successive Non-scoring Runs: 7 from 2.2.1985.

TEN YEAR LEAGUE RECORD

		P	W	D	L	F	A	Pts	Pos
1997-98	Div 1	46	18	11	17	57	53	65	9
1998-99	Div 1	46	19	16	11	64	43	73	7
1999-2000	Div 1	46	21	11	14	64	48	74	7
2000-01	Div 1	46	14	13	19	45	48	55	12
2001-02	Div 1	46	25	11	10	76	43	86	3
2002-03	Div 1	46	20	16	10	81	44	76	5
2003-04	PR Lge	38	7	12	19	38	77	33	20
2004-05	FL C	46	15	21	10	72	59	66	9
2005-06	FL C	46	16	19	11	50	42	67	7
2006-07	FL C	46	22	10	14	59	56	76	5

DID YOU KNOW ?

Bob Hatton was probably destined to become a prolific goalscorer when he scored 30 seconds into his debut for Wolverhampton Wanderers against Portsmouth on 8 October 1966. Nine clubs in total, 18 League seasons and over 200 League goals followed.

WOLVERHAMPTON WANDERERS 2006–07 LEAGUE RECORD

Match No.	*Date*	*Venue*	*Opponents*	*Result*	*H/T Score*	*Lg. Pos.*	*Goalscorers*	*Attendance*
1	Aug 5	A	Plymouth Arg	D 1-1	0-1	—	Doumbe (og) [47]	15,964
2	8	H	Ipswich T	W 1-0	1-0	—	Bothroyd [27]	19,199
3	11	H	Preston NE	L 1-3	1-1	—	Bothroyd [14]	17,410
4	19	A	Burnley	W 1-0	1-0	10	Johnson [19]	12,245
5	26	H	Luton T	W 1-0	0-0	5	Johnson [47]	19,378
6	Sept 10	A	Leeds U	W 1-0	0-0	3	Bothroyd [90]	16,268
7	12	H	Derby Co	L 0-1	0-1	—		21,546
8	16	A	Barnsley	L 0-1	0-1	8		11,350
9	23	H	Stoke C	W 2-0	1-0	6	Clarke [21], Olofinjana [68]	19,489
10	30	A	Cardiff C	L 0-4	0-1	9		19,915
11	Oct 14	H	Colchester U	W 1-0	0-0	6	Bothroyd [51]	19,318
12	17	H	Coventry C	W 1-0	1-0	—	Ward (og) [20]	19,823
13	22	A	WBA	L 0-3	0-2	6		26,606
14	28	H	Sheffield W	D 2-2	1-1	7	Clarke 2 [30, 73]	20,637
15	Nov 1	A	Southampton	L 0-2	0-1	—		18,979
16	4	H	Southend U	W 3-1	3-0	6	Clarke 2 [10, 22], Craddock [12]	17,904
17	11	A	Hull C	L 0-2	0-1	8		16,962
18	18	A	Birmingham C	D 1-1	0-1	10	Craddock [89]	22,256
19	24	H	Sunderland	D 1-1	1-0	—	Johnson [43]	27,203
20	28	H	Crystal Palace	D 1-1	0-0	—	Gobern [63]	17,806
21	Dec 2	A	Southend U	W 1-0	0-0	9	Craddock [61]	9411
22	9	H	Leicester C	L 1-2	0-1	14	Gobern [81]	18,600
23	16	A	QPR	W 1-0	0-0	10	Kightly [49]	12,323
24	23	H	Norwich C	D 2-2	1-1	10	Henry [36], Craddock [90]	22,910
25	26	A	Derby Co	W 2-0	0-0	9	Olofinjana [66], Kightly [90]	31,920
26	30	A	Colchester U	L 1-2	0-2	10	Collins [90]	5893
27	Jan 1	H	Barnsley	W 2-0	0-0	9	Henry [52], Olofinjana [78]	20,064
28	13	A	Stoke C	D 1-1	0-0	10	Collins [63]	15,882
29	20	H	Cardiff C	L 1-2	0-1	10	Olofinjana [58]	16,772
30	30	A	Norwich C	W 1-0	0-0	—	Kightly [53]	23,311
31	Feb 3	H	Plymouth Arg	D 2-2	1-2	10	Ward [33], Olofinjana [69]	19,082
32	10	A	Preston NE	W 1-0	1-0	9	Olofinjana [8]	15,748
33	17	H	Burnley	W 2-1	2-0	8	Kightly [5], Ward [40]	19,521
34	20	A	Ipswich T	W 1-0	1-0	—	Ward [33]	20,602
35	24	H	Leeds U	W 1-0	0-0	8	Kightly [76]	24,314
36	Mar 3	A	Luton T	W 3-2	1-2	5	Breen [10], Keogh [53], Henry [66]	10,002
37	11	H	WBA	W 1-0	0-0	4	Bothroyd [83]	28,016
38	13	A	Coventry C	L 1-2	1-1	—	Kightly [45]	22,099
39	17	A	Sheffield W	D 2-2	1-1	5	McIndoe [35], Keogh [90]	24,181
40	31	H	Southampton	L 0-6	0-3	6		24,804
41	Apr 7	A	Sunderland	L 1-2	0-1	7	Keogh [65]	40,748
42	9	H	Hull C	W 3-1	2-0	5	Bothroyd 2 [18, 47], Olofinjana [39]	20,772
43	14	A	Crystal Palace	D 2-2	2-2	6	Bothroyd 2 [13, 22]	17,981
44	22	H	Birmingham C	L 2-3	0-0	6	McIndoe 2 [67, 71]	22,754
45	28	H	QPR	W 2-0	0-0	5	Keogh [57], Kightly [64]	24,931
46	May 6	A	Leicester C	W 4-1	2-1	5	Olofinjana [25], Kightly [33], McAuley (og) [53], Keogh (pen) [86]	30,282

Final League Position: 5

GOALSCORERS

League (59): Bothroyd 9, Kightly 8, Olofinjana 8, Clarke 5, Keogh 5 (1 pen), Craddock 4, Henry 3, Johnson 3, McIndoe 3, Ward 3, Collins 2, Gobern 2, Breen 1, own goals 3.
Carling Cup (0).
FA Cup (4): Davies C 2, Olofinjana 1, Potter 1.
Play-Offs (2): Craddock 1, Olofinjana 1.

Murray M 44	Clyde M 3	Naylor L 3	Clapham J 21 + 5	Breen G 40	Craddock J 28 + 6	O'Connor K 3	Henry K 34	Cort C 7 + 3	Bothroyd J 19 + 14	Ricketts R 15 + 4	Edwards R 24 + 9	Davies C 6 + 17	Gobern L 6 + 6	Olofinjana S 41 + 3	Clarke L 11 + 11	Jones D 8	Johnson J 14 + 6	Potter D 35 + 3	Ikeme C — + 1	Mulgrew C 5 + 1	Little M 19 + 7	Wheater D 1	McIndoe M 25 + 2	Kightly M 24	McNamara J 19	Collins N 20 + 2	Davies M — + 7	Fleming C 1	Ward S 11 + 7	Keogh A 17	Budtz J 2 + 2	Gleeson S — + 3	*Match No.*
1	2	3	4	5^{1}	6	7	8	9	10^{2}	11^{3}	12	13	14																				1
1	2^{1}	3^{2}	4	5	6	7	8	9■	10^{3}	11	12	14		13																			2
1	2^{1}	3	4	5	6	7	8		10	11^{2}	12	9^{3}		13	14																		3
1			3	5	6		8			7^{2}	2	12		4	9	11	10^{1}	13															4
1^{G}			3	5	6		8	9		12	2			4	13	11	10^{2}	7^{1}	15														5
1				5	6		8	9^{2}	13		2			4	12	11	10^{1}	7		3^{3}	14												6
1				5	6		8^{3}	12	10^{1}	13	2			4	14	11^{2}	9	7			3												7
1				5	6			12	10^{2}	11	3^{3}		8^{1}	4	13		9	7		14	2												8
1				5	6		8			11	2	12	13	4	10^{1}		9^{2}	7		3													9
1			12	5■	6		8		13	11^{3}	2	14		4	9^{1}		10^{2}	7		3													10
1			3	5	6		8		10^{1}	11^{2}	2	12	14	4	13		9^{3}	7															11
1			3	5	6		8		10^{2}	11	2	12		4	13		9^{1}	7															12
1			3	5	6		8		10	11	2^{3}	12		4	13		9^{2}	7^{1}			14												13
1			3	5	6^{3}		8	12	10^{1}	11	2		13	4	9			7^{2}			14												14
1			3	5			8	9		11	2^{3}		12	4	10^{2}		13	7^{1}			14	6											15
1			3	5	6		8	9	12	11^{3}	2		7^{2}	4	10^{1}			13			14												16
1			4	5	6		8	9		11^{2}	2	13	12		10^{3}		14	7		3^{1}													17
1				5	6		8		10	12	13		11	4		9^{1}	14	7^{3}		3^{2}	2												18
1			3	5	6		8		10^{2}			12	7	4	13	11	9^{1}				2												19
1			3	5	6		8					12	7	4	10	11^{2}	9^{1}				2		13										20
1			3	5	6^{3}		8		10^{1}		14	13		4	12		9^{2}				2		11	7									21
1			3	5	6		8		10			12	7	4			9^{1}				2		11										22
1				5	6				10			9^{1}		4	12			8			2		11	7	3								23
1				5	6		8			12		9^{2}		4^{3}	10		13	14			2		11	7	3^{1}								24
1				5			8					12		4	9^{1}			10			2		11	7	3	6							25
1			12	5			8			7^{2}	13	14		4^{3}	9			10			2		11		3^{1}	6							26
1				5			8				12	9^{2}		4			13	7			2		11	10^{3}	3^{1}	6	14						27
1			12	5			8				13	9		4				7			2		11^{2}	10	3^{1}	6							28
1			3				8					9^{2}		4			12	7			2		11^{1}	10		6		5	13				29
1				5■			8		12		13			4				7^{3}			2		11^{2}	10	3■	6			14	9^{1}			30
1			3				4		12		5			13		11^{3}		7			2^{2}		14	8		6			10^{1}	9			31
1							2				5			4				8					11^{1}	7	3	6	12		10	9			32
1					12		2		13		5			4				8					11^{2}	7^{1}	3	6	14		10	9^{3}			33
1					13		2		12		5			4				8					11	7^{1}	3	6	14		10^{3}	9^{2}			34
1					12		2		13		5			4				8					11^{1}	7^{2}	3	6			10	9			35
1				5			8		12		2			4									11	7	3	6			10^{1}	9			36
1				5^{1}	12				13		2			4				8					11^{2}	7^{3}	3	6	14		10	9			37
1			12	5					13		2			4				8					11^{3}	7^{1}	3■	6	14		10^{2}	9			38
1^{G}			3	5	12				13		2^{1}			4				8					11	7		6			10^{2}	9	15		39
1			3^{1}	5	12				13		2^{2}	14		4				8					11	7		6			10^{3}	9			40
1^{G}			3	5					12			13		4				8			2		11	7^{1}		6			10^{2}	9	15		41
				5	6				10^{2}					4				8			2		11^{3}	7	3^{1}	12			13	9	1	14	42
				5	6				10^{3}					4				8			2■		11^{2}	7^{1}	3	13	12		14	9	1		43
1			12	5^{1}	6				10^{2}					4				8					11	7	3	2			13	9			44
1				5	6				10^{2}					4				8			12		11	7^{3}	2	3			13	9^{1}		14	45
1				5	6				10^{3}					4				8^{2}			12		11	7	2^{1}	3			14	9		13	46

FA Cup

Third Round	Oldham Ath	(h)	2-2
		(a)	2-0
Fourth Round	WBA	(h)	0-3

Carling Cup

First Round	Chesterfield	(a)	0-0

Play-Offs

Semi-Final	WBA	(h)	2-3
		(a)	0-1

WREXHAM FL Championship 2

FOUNDATION

The club was formed on 28 September 1872 by members of Wrexham Cricket Club, so they could continue playing a sport during the winter months. This meeting was held at the Turf Hotel, which although rebuilt since, still stands at one corner of the present ground. Their first game was a few weeks later and matches often included 17 players on either side! By 1875 team formations were reduced to 11 men and a year later the club was among the founder members of the Cambrian Football Association, which quickly changed its title to the Football Association of Wales.

Racecourse Ground, Mold Road, Wrexham LL11 2AH.

Telephone: (01978) 262 129.

Fax: (01978) 357 821.

Ticket Office: (01978) 262 129.

Website: www.wrexhamafc.co.uk

Email: info@wrexhamafc.co.uk

Ground Capacity: 15,500.

Record Attendance: 34,445 v Manchester U, FA Cup 4th rd, 26 January 1957.

Pitch Measurements: 111yd × 75yd.

Chairman: Neville Dickens.

Vice-chairman: Geoff Moss.

Chief Executive: Anthony Fairclough.

Secretary: Geraint Parry.

Manager: Brian Carey.

First Team Coach: Steve Weaver.

Physio: Mel Pejic BSc (Hons).

Colours: Red shirts, white shorts, white stockings.

Change Colours: Blue shirts, blue shorts, blue stockings.

Year Formed: 1872 (oldest club in Wales).

Turned Professional: 1912.

Ltd Co.: 1912.

Club Nickname: 'Red Dragons'.

Grounds: 1872, Racecourse Ground; 1883, Rhosddu Recreation Ground; 1887, Racecourse Ground.

First Football League Game: 27 August 1921, Division 3 (N), v Hartlepools U (h) L 0–2 – Godding; Ellis, Simpson; Matthias, Foster, Griffiths; Burton, Goode, Cotton, Edwards, Lloyd.

Record League Victory: 10–1 v Hartlepool U, Division 4, 3 March 1962 – Keelan; Peter Jones, McGavan; Tecwyn Jones, Fox, Ken Barnes; Ron Barnes (3), Bennion (1), Davies (3), Ambler (3), Ron Roberts.

HONOURS

Football League: Division 3 – Champions 1977–78; Runners-up 1992–93; Promoted (3rd) 2002–03; Division 3 (N) – Runners-up 1932–33; Division 4 – Runners-up 1969–70.

FA Cup: best season: 6th rd, 1974, 1978, 1997.

Football League Cup: best season: 5th rd, 1961, 1978.

Welsh Cup: Winners 22 times (joint record); Runners-up 22 times (record).

FAW Premier Cup: Winners 1998, 2000, 2001, 2003.

LDV Vans Trophy: Winners 2005

European Competition: *European Cup-Winners' Cup:* 1972–73, 1975–76, 1978–79, 1979–80, 1984–85, 1986–87, 1990–91, 1995–96.

SKY SPORTS FACT FILE

On 25 October 1972 in a European Cup-Winners' Cup second round first leg tie against Hajduk Split, Wrexham accomplished the feat of winning 3–1 with goals from Brian Tinnion, David Smallman and an opponent before a crowd of 19,013.

Record Cup Victory: 11–1 v New Brighton, Football League Northern Section Cup 1st rd, 3 January 1934 – Foster; Alfred Jones, Hamilton, Bulling, McMahon, Lawrence, Bryant (3), Findlay (1), Bamford (5), Snow, Waller (1), (o.g. 1).

Record Defeat: 0–9 v Brentford, Division 3, 15 October 1963.

Most League Points (2 for a win): 61, Division 4, 1969–70 and Division 3, 1977–78.

Most League Points (3 for a win): 84, Division 3, 2002–03.

Most League Goals: 106, Division 3 (N), 1932–33.

Highest League Scorer in Season: Tom Bamford, 44, Division 3 (N), 1933–34.

Most League Goals in Total Aggregate: Tom Bamford, 175, 1928–34.

Most League Goals in One Match: 5, Tom Bamford v Carlisle U, Division 3N, 17 March 1934; 5, Lee Jones v Cambridge U, Division 2, 6 April 2002; 5 Juan Ugarte v Hartlepool U, League Championship 1, 5 March 2005.

Most Capped Player: Joey Jones, 29 (72), Wales.

Most League Appearances: Arfon Griffiths, 592, 1959–61, 1962–79.

Youngest League Player: Ken Roberts, 15 years 158 days v Bradford PA, 1 September 1951.

Record Transfer Fee Received: £800,000 from Birmingham C for Bryan Hughes, March 1997.

Record Transfer Fee Paid: £210,000 to Liverpool for Joey Jones, October 1978.

Football League Record: 1921 Original Member of Division 3 (N); 1958–60 Division 3; 1960–62 Division 4; 1962–64 Division 3; 1964–70 Division 4; 1970–78 Division 3; 1978–82 Division 2; 1982–83 Division 3; 1983–92 Division 4; 1992–93 Division 3; 1993–2002 Division 2; 2002–03 Division 3; 2003–04 Division 2; 2004–05 FL 1; 2005– FL 2.

MANAGERS

Selection Committee 1872–1924
Charlie Hewitt 1924–25
Selection Committee 1925–29
Jack Baynes 1929–31
Ernest Blackburn 1932–37
James Logan 1937–38
Arthur Cowell 1938
Tom Morgan 1938–42
Tom Williams 1942–49
Les McDowell 1949–50
Peter Jackson 1950–55
Cliff Lloyd 1955–57
John Love 1957–59
Cliff Lloyd 1959–60
Billy Morris 1960–61
Ken Barnes 1961–65
Billy Morris 1965
Jack Rowley 1966–67
Alvan Williams 1967–68
John Neal 1968–77
Arfon Griffiths 1977–81
Mel Sutton 1981–82
Bobby Roberts 1982–85
Dixie McNeil 1985–89
Brian Flynn 1989–2001
Denis Smith 2001–07
Brian Carey January 2007–

LATEST SEQUENCES

Longest Sequence of League Wins: 8, 5.4.2003 – 3.5.2003.

Longest Sequence of League Defeats: 9, 2.10.1963 – 30.10.1963.

Longest Sequence of League Draws: 6, 12.11.1999 – 26.12.1999.

Longest Sequence of Unbeaten League Matches: 18, 8.3.2003 – 25.8.2003.

Longest Sequence Without a League Win: 16, 25.9.1999 – 3.1.2000.

Successive Scoring Runs: 25 from 5.5.1928.

Successive Non-scoring Runs: 6 from 12.9.1973.

TEN YEAR LEAGUE RECORD

		P	*W*	*D*	*L*	*F*	*A*	*Pts*	*Pos*
1997-98	Div 2	46	18	16	12	55	51	70	7
1998-99	Div 2	46	13	14	19	43	62	53	17
1999-2000	Div 2	46	17	11	18	52	61	62	11
2000-01	Div 2	46	17	12	17	65	71	63	10
2001-02	Div 2	46	11	10	25	56	89	43	23
2002-03	Div 3	46	23	15	8	84	50	84	3
2003-04	Div 2	46	17	9	20	50	60	60	13
2004-05	FL 1	46	13	14	19	62	80	43*	22
2005-06	FL 2	46	15	14	17	61	54	59	13
2006-07	FL 2	46	13	12	21	43	65	51	19

**10 points deducted for entering administration.*

DID YOU KNOW ?

Left-winger Gordon Gunson joined Wrexham from Nelson in 1926. Two years later he received a letter from the Welsh FA informing him that he had been selected to play for the national team. However, he had been born in Chester and had to decline the honour.

WREXHAM 2006–07 LEAGUE RECORD

Match No.	Date	Venue	Opponents	Result		H/T Score	Lg. Pos.	Goalscorers	Attendance
1	Aug 5	A	Wycombe W	D	1-1	1-1	—	Mark Jones [32]	4763
2	8	H	Grimsby T	W	3-0	2-0	—	Evans S [16], Llewellyn [34], Done [68]	5180
3	12	H	Peterborough U	D	0-0	0-0	10		4706
4	20	A	Chester C	W	2-1	1-0	6	Roberts (pen) [42], Mark Jones [52]	4206
5	26	H	Barnet	D	1-1	1-0	7	Mark Jones [15]	4304
6	Sept 9	H	Swindon T	W	2-1	0-1	6	Valentine (pen) [68], Mark Jones [69]	5257
7	13	A	Accrington S	L	0-5	0-1	—		2689
8	16	A	Stockport Co	L	2-5	1-2	12	Williams D 2 [43, 61]	4884
9	24	H	Hereford U	W	1-0	1-0	10	Evans S [28]	4705
10	27	H	Rochdale	L	1-2	1-0	—	Llewellyn [12]	3577
11	30	A	Hartlepool U	L	0-3	0-2	15		4452
12	Oct 14	H	Milton Keynes D	L	1-2	1-0	19	Roberts [20]	3828
13	21	A	Mansfield T	L	0-3	0-2	20		2971
14	28	H	Bristol R	W	2-0	1-0	19	Llewellyn [22], Craddock [90]	3803
15	Nov 4	H	Macclesfield T	D	0-0	0-0	18		3568
16	7	A	Bury	L	0-1	0-1	—		2506
17	18	A	Notts Co	L	1-2	0-1	19	Llewellyn [65]	4416
18	25	H	Lincoln C	W	2-1	2-0	15	Mark Jones [24], Llewellyn [44]	3619
19	Dec 5	A	Torquay U	D	1-1	1-0	—	Smith [7]	1588
20	9	A	Boston U	L	0-4	0-1	18		1706
21	16	H	Walsall	D	1-1	0-1	19	Llewellyn [68]	4270
22	23	H	Darlington	W	1-0	1-0	18	Holloway (og) [19]	3401
23	26	A	Rochdale	D	2-2	0-0	18	McEvilly [48], Llewellyn [55]	2837
24	30	A	Hereford U	L	0-2	0-1	18		3444
25	Jan 1	H	Accrington S	L	1-3	1-1	18	Johnson [45]	3805
26	13	A	Swindon T	L	1-2	1-1	21	Marc Williams [8]	6130
27	20	H	Hartlepool U	D	1-1	0-1	21	Llewellyn [64]	3828
28	27	A	Darlington	D	1-1	1-1	21	Spender [31]	3301
29	30	H	Stockport Co	L	0-1	0-0	—		4060
30	Feb 3	H	Wycombe W	L	0-2	0-1	23		3607
31	10	A	Peterborough U	L	0-3	0-1	23		3839
32	18	H	Chester C	D	0-0	0-0	22		6801
33	20	A	Grimsby T	L	1-2	1-1	—	McEvilly [28]	5850
34	25	H	Shrewsbury T	L	1-3	0-2	19	Williams D [55]	5605
35	Mar 3	A	Barnet	W	2-1	0-1	22	McEvilly 2 [57, 60]	2180
36	9	H	Bury	D	1-1	1-0	—	McEvilly [33]	7030
37	17	A	Milton Keynes D	L	1-2	1-1	23	McEvilly [12]	5712
38	24	A	Bristol R	W	1-0	0-0	23	Jeff Whitley [87]	5209
39	31	H	Mansfield T	D	0-0	0-0	22		7752
40	Apr 7	A	Macclesfield T	L	0-2	0-1	22		14,142
41	9	H	Notts Co	L	0-1	0-0	23		4557
42	14	A	Lincoln C	W	3-0	2-0	22	Spender [18], Kerr (og) [29], McEvilly [52]	4279
43	21	H	Torquay U	W	1-0	0-0	22	Roberts [79]	6057
44	24	A	Shrewsbury T	W	1-0	0-0	—	Proctor [79]	6749
45	28	A	Walsall	L	0-1	0-0	21		7057
46	May 5	H	Boston U	W	3-1	0-1	19	Valentine (pen) [56], Llewellyn [87], Proctor [90]	12,374

Final League Position: 19

GOALSCORERS

League (43): Llewellyn 9, McEvilly 7, Mark Jones 5, Roberts 3 (1 pen), Williams D 3, Evans S 2, Proctor 2, Spender 2, Valentine 2 (2 pens), Craddock 1, Done 1, Johnson 1, Smith 1, Jeff Whitley 1, Marc Williams 1, own goals 2.
Carling Cup (5): Llewellyn 2, Done 1, Mark Jones 1, Roberts 1.
FA Cup (4): Mark Jones 1, McEvilly 1, Smith 1, Williams D 1.
J Paint Trophy (1): Crowell 1.

Ingham M 31	Spender S 23 + 2	Valentine R 32 + 2	Williams D 40	Evans S 34 + 1	Lawrence D 3	Jones Mark 29 + 1	Ferguson D 19 + 1	Roberts N 17 + 2	Llewellyn C 39	Done M 27 + 7	Johnson J 10 + 12	Crowell M 10 + 5	Williams Mike 20 + 11	Mackin L 1 + 7	Pejic S 33	Newby J 2 + 9	Roche L 26 + 2	Williams Marc 11 + 5	Evans G 9 + 3	Jones Michael 1	Reed J — + 4	McAliskey J 3 / Walker R 3	Morgan C 1	Craddock T 1 / Proctor M 9	Smith K 5 + 3	Molango M 3	McEvilly L 18 + 10	Ugarte J — + 2	Mitchell P 5	Fleming A 1 + 1	Garret R 10	Samba C 1 + 2	Ruddy J 5	Barron S 3	Carvill M 1 + 5	Whitley Jeff 11	Williams T 9	*Match No.*
1	2	3	4	5	6	7	8	9	10	11																												1
1	2	3	4	5	6	7^{1}	8^{2}	9	10	11	12	13																										2
1	2^{2}	3	4^{3}	5	6	7		9	10	11^{1}	12	8	13	14																								3
1	2^{1}	3	4	5■		7		9	10	11^{2}		8	12		6	13																						4
1	2^{1}	3	4^{3}	5		7		9	10	11^{2}		8	12	14	6	13																						5
1		3	4	5		7	8^{1}	9^{2}	10	11		12			6	13	2																					6
1	2^{1}	3	4	5		7	8		10	11^{2}	13		12		6	9^{3}		14																				7
	12	2^{1}	4	5		7	8		10			13	3			9^{3}		11^{2}	6	1	14																	8
1		3	4	5		7^{1}	8		10	11	12	6					2					9																9
1		3	4	5		7	8		10	11^{1}	12	6^{2}	13			14	2					9^{3}																10
1	2^{1}	3	4	5		7			10	11^{2}		6	12			13	8					9																11
1	12			5^{3}		7	8	9^{2}	10	11		4	3	14		13	2^{1}		6																			12
1		3	4	5		7	8		10	11^{3}	9^{1}	12	13			14	2^{2}						6															13
1		2	4	5		7	8		10■	11			3		6									9														14
1		2	4	5		7	8			11			3		6	12									9^{1}	10												15
1		2^{1}	4	5		7				11	13	8^{2}	3		6	14	12								9^{3}	10												16
1			4	5		7	8		11		9		3		6		2								12	10^{1}												17
1			4	5		7	8		10		11		3		6		2								9^{1}		12											18
1		12	4	5		7^{2}	8		10		9^{1}		3		6		2								11^{3}		13	14										19
1		12	4	5■			8	13	10		9^{3}		3	7^{1}	6		2								11^{2}			14										20
1		3	4				8		10	11	7^{1}		5		6		2	9									12											21
1		3	4				8		10	11	7^{1}		6				2	9	5								12											22
1		3	4				8		10	11	7^{1}	12	5		6		2	9^{2}									13											23
1	2						12		10	11	7^{2}	8^{1}	4		6		3	9^{3}	5						13		14											24
1		3		5			8^{1}		10	11^{2}	7	4	12		6		2	9^{3}							13		14											25
1	7	3	4	5					10		12				6		2	11^{2}	13								9^{1}		8									26
1	7^{1}	3	4						11	12					6		2	9	5								10		8									27
1	7^{1}	3	4	5^{3}					11	12					6		2	9^{2}			13						10		8	14								28
1		3	4						7	11					6		2	9^{2}			12						10^{1}		8		5	13						29
1		3	4	5					10	12					6		2	9^{3}			13						14		8^{2}		11	7^{1}						30
	2		4	5		7^{3}		9^{1}		13	12		3		6^{2}			14									10				11		1	8				31
	2		4	5					10	12			3					13	6								9^{2}			7^{3}	11		1	8^{1}	14			32
		3	4	5		7			10								2		6								9^{1}				11	12	1		8			33
			2	5■		7		9^{2}	10				12				3		6								13				11^{3}		1	8^{1}	14	4		34
1			5^{1}			7		9	11				3		6		2		12								10				8					4		35
		3■				7^{1}		9	11■				12		6		2		5								10				8		1			4		36
1	8		3^{2}			7^{1}		9			12		5	14	6		2■		13								10				11^{3}					4		37
	2		4			7^{1}		9		12			3		6							5		11^{2}			10								13	8	1	38
	2^{1}		4			13		9^{3}		11			3		6		12					5		7^{2}			10				8				14		1	39
	2^{3}			12		7				11	13		5		6		3	14				4^{1}		9^{2}			10									8	1	40
	2	3		5		7^{3}			9^{2}	11	12			14	6			13						4^{1}			10									8	1	41
	2	3	4^{3}	5					9	11^{2}	12		13	14	6									7^{1}			10									8	1	42
	2	3	4^{2}	5				12	9	11				13	6									7^{1}			10									8	1	43
	2	3	4	5				9	11						6									7			10									8	1	44
	2	3	4	5				9^{2}	11	12					6									7			10^{1}								13	8	1	45
	2	3	4	5		7		9^{1}	10	11					6									8			12										1	46

FA Cup

First Round	Stevenage B	(h)	1-0
Second Round	Scunthorpe U	(a)	2-0
Third Round	Derby Co	(a)	1-3

Carling Cup

First Round	Sheffield W	(a)	4-1
Second Round	Birmingham C	(a)	1-4

J Paint Trophy

First Round	Rochdale	(h)	1-1

WYCOMBE WANDERERS FL Championship 2

FOUNDATION

In 1887 a group of young furniture trade workers called a meeting at the Steam Engine public house with the aim of forming a football club and entering junior football. It is thought that they were named after the famous FA Cup winners, The Wanderers who had visited the town in 1877 for a tie with the original High Wycombe club. It is also possible that they played informally before their formation, although there is no proof of this.

Adams Park, Hillbottom Road, Sands, High Wycombe HP12 4HJ.

Telephone: (01494) 472 100.

Fax: (01494) 527 633.

Ticket Office: (01494) 441 118.

Website: www.wwfc.com

Email: wwfc@wwfc.com

Ground Capacity: 10,000.

Record Attendance: 9,921 v Fulham, FA Cup 3rd rd, 9 January 2002.

Pitch Measurements: 115yd × 75yd.

Chairman: Ivor L. Beeks.

Vice-chairman: Brian Kane.

Managing Director: Steve Hayes.

Secretary: Keith J. Allen.

Manager: Paul Lambert.

Assistant Manager: Steve Brown.

Physio: Shay Connolly.

Colours: Light blue and dark blue quarters.

Change Colours: Red and white quarters.

Year Formed: 1887.

Turned Professional: 1974.

Club Nicknames: 'Chairboys' (after High Wycombe's tradition of furniture making), 'The Blues'.

Grounds: 1887, The Rye; 1893, Spring Meadow; 1895, Loakes Park; 1899, Daws Hill Park; 1901, Loakes Park; 1990, Adams Park.

First Football League Game: 14 August 1993, Division 3 v Carlisle U (a) D 2–2: Hyde; Cousins, Horton (Langford), Kerr, Crossley, Ryan, Carroll, Stapleton, Thompson, Scott, Guppy (1) (Hutchinson), (1 og).

Record League Victory: 5–0 v Burnley, Division 2, 15 April 1997 – Parkin; Cousins, Bell, Kavanagh, McCarthy, Forsyth, Carroll (2p) (Simpson), Scott (Farrell), Stallard (1), McGavin (1) (Read (1)), Brown.

HONOURS

Football League: Division 2 best season: 6th, 1994–95. Division 3 1993–94 (play-offs).

FA Amateur Cup: Winners 1931.

FA Trophy: Winners 1991, 1993.

GM Vauxhall Conference: Winners 1992–93.

FA Cup: semi-final 2001.

Football League Cup: semi-final 2007.

SKY SPORTS FACT FILE

In the early 1900s right-back Alf Gilson, who had played for a variety of clubs including Aston Villa and Bristol City, took up residence locally and played for Wycombe Wanderers as a reinstated amateur.

Record Cup Victory: 5–0 v Hitchin T (a), FA Cup 2nd rd, 3 December 1994 – Hyde; Cousins, Brown, Crossley, Evans, Ryan (1), Carroll, Bell (1), Thompson, Garner (3) (Hemmings), Stapleton (Langford).

Record Defeat: 0–5 v Walsall, Auto Windscreens Shield 1st rd, 7 November 1995.

Most League Points (3 for a win): 78, Division 2, 1994–95.

Most League Goals: 72, FL 2, 2005–06.

Highest League Goalscorer in Season: Sean Devine, 23, 1999–2000.

Most League Goals in Total Aggregate: Nathan Tyson, 42, 2004–06.

Most League Goals in One Match: 3, Miquel Desouza v Bradford C, Division 2, 2 September 1995; 3, John Williams v Stockport Co, Division 2, 24 February 1996; 3, Mark Stallard v Walsall, Division 2, 21 October 1997; 3, Sean Devine v Reading, Division 2, 2 October 1999; 3, Sean Divine v Bury, Division 2, 26 February 2000; 3, Nathan Tyson v Lincoln C, FL 2, 5 March 2005; 3 Nathan Tyson v Kidderminster H, FL 2, 2 April 2005; 3 Nathan Tyson v Stockport Co, FL 2, 10 September 2005; 3 Kevin Betsy v Mansfield T 24 September 2005.

Most Capped Player: Mark Rogers, 7, Canada.

Most League Appearances: Steve Brown, 371, 1994–2004.

Youngest League Player: Ikechi Anya, 16 years 279 days v Scunthorpe U, 8 October 2004.

Record Transfer Fee Received: £600,000 from Nottingham F for Nathan Tyson, January 2006.

Record Transfer Fee Paid: £200,000 to Barnet for Sean Devine, 15 April 1999.

Football League Record: Promoted to Division 3 from GM Vauxhall Conference in 1993; 1993–94 Division 3; 1994–2004 Division 2; 2004– FL 2.

MANAGERS

First coach appointed 1951.
Prior to Brian Lee's appointment in 1969 the team was selected by a Match Committee which met every Monday evening.

James McCormack 1951–52
Sid Cann 1952–61
Graham Adams 1961–62
Don Welsh 1962–64
Barry Darvill 1964–68
Brian Lee 1969–76
Ted Powell 1976–77
John Reardon 1977–78
Andy Williams 1978–80
Mike Keen 1980–84
Paul Bence 1984–86
Alan Gane 1986–87
Peter Suddaby 1987–88
Jim Kelman 1988–90
Martin O'Neill 1990–95
Alan Smith 1995–96
John Gregory 1996–98
Neil Smillie 1998–99
Lawrie Sanchez 1999–2003
Tony Adams 2003–04
John Gorman 2004–06
Paul Lambert June 2006–

LATEST SEQUENCES

Longest Sequence of League Wins: 6, 19.8.2006 – 16.9.2006.

Longest Sequence of League Defeats: 6, 18.3.2006 – 17.4.2006.

Longest Sequence of League Draws: 5, 24.1.2004 – 21.2.2004.

Longest Sequence of Unbeaten League Matches: 21, 6.8.2005 – 10.12.2005.

Longest Sequence Without a League Win: 13, 16.8.2003 – 18.10.2003 and 10.1.2004 – 20.3.2004.

Successive Scoring Runs: 15 from 28.12.2004.

Successive Non-scoring Runs: 5 from 15.10.1996.

TEN YEAR LEAGUE RECORD

		P	*W*	*D*	*L*	*F*	*A*	*Pts*	*Pos*
1997-98	Div 2	46	14	18	14	51	53	60	14
1998-99	Div 2	46	13	12	21	52	58	51	19
1999-2000	Div 2	46	16	13	17	56	53	61	12
2000-01	Div 2	46	15	14	17	46	53	59	13
2001-02	Div 2	46	17	13	16	58	64	64	11
2002-03	Div 2	46	13	13	20	59	66	52	18
2003-04	Div 2	46	6	19	21	50	75	37	24
2004-05	FL 2	46	17	14	15	58	52	65	10
2005-06	FL 2	46	18	17	11	72	56	71	6
2006-07	FL 2	46	16	14	16	52	47	62	12

DID YOU KNOW ?

Centre-forward Paul Bates signed for Wycombe Wanderers in 1953–54 scoring 45 goals for the reserves. He made his first team debut in the Amateur Cup v Leytonstone and by his 416th and last match on 21 October 1967 the England Amateur cap had scored 309 goals.

WYCOMBE WANDERERS 2006–07 LEAGUE RECORD

Match No.	Date	Venue	Opponents	Result		H/T Score	Lg. Pos.	Goalscorers	Attendance
1	Aug 5	H	Wrexham	D	1-1	1-1	—	Mooney [6]	4763
2	8	A	Bristol R	W	2-1	0-0	—	Betsy [50], Mooney [59]	5349
3	12	A	Notts Co	L	0-1	0-1	14		4053
4	19	H	Bury	W	3-0	0-0	9	Easter 3 [60, 72, 85]	4184
5	26	A	Macclesfield T	W	2-0	2-0	6	Easter [16], Mooney [36]	1574
6	Sept 1	H	Mansfield T	W	1-0	0-0	—	Easter [59]	4754
7	9	H	Chester C	W	1-0	1-0	3	Betsy [28]	4277
8	12	A	Hereford U	W	2-1	1-0	—	Easter 2 [33, 74]	2585
9	16	A	Rochdale	W	2-0	1-0	1	Mooney [16], Dixon [90]	2313
10	23	H	Lincoln C	L	1-3	1-1	3	Mooney [9]	5247
11	26	H	Swindon T	D	1-1	0-0	—	Mooney [90]	6090
12	30	A	Accrington S	L	1-2	0-1	3	Antwi [55]	2243
13	Oct 6	H	Torquay U	W	2-0	1-0	—	Mooney [5], Martin [80]	4769
14	14	A	Walsall	L	0-2	0-1	4		6745
15	21	H	Peterborough U	W	2-0	0-0	4	Betsy [64], Easter [84]	4924
16	28	A	Boston U	W	1-0	0-0	3	Bloomfield [90]	1762
17	Nov 4	A	Shrewsbury T	D	0-0	0-0	3		4116
18	18	H	Grimsby T	D	1-1	0-0	4	Golbourne [77]	5037
19	25	A	Hartlepool U	L	0-2	0-1	4		3711
20	Dec 5	H	Darlington	W	1-0	1-0	—	Easter [3]	3885
21	9	H	Barnet	D	1-1	0-0	5	Mooney [80]	4711
22	16	A	Milton Keynes D	L	1-3	1-2	5	Mooney [31]	5977
23	23	H	Stockport Co	W	2-0	1-0	5	Betsy [2], Easter [63]	4559
24	26	A	Swindon T	L	1-2	0-1	6	Easter [81]	8878
25	30	A	Lincoln C	L	0-1	0-0	6		5465
26	Jan 1	H	Hereford U	D	0-0	0-0	6		4851
27	6	H	Rochdale	D	1-1	0-0	6	Easter [51]	4067
28	13	A	Chester C	W	1-0	0-0	6	Easter [88]	2336
29	20	H	Accrington S	D	1-1	0-0	6	Betsy [59]	5884
30	27	A	Stockport Co	L	0-2	0-1	6		5353
31	Feb 3	A	Wrexham	W	2-0	1-0	7	Williamson [23], Easter [52]	3607
32	10	H	Notts Co	D	0-0	0-0	7		4836
33	17	A	Bury	W	4-0	2-0	7	Doherty [38], McGleish [43], Mooney [65], Easter [90]	1988
34	24	A	Mansfield T	L	2-3	2-2	7	McGleish 2 [27, 37]	2711
35	Mar 3	H	Macclesfield T	W	3-0	1-0	7	Doherty [40], Martin [54], Bloomfield [65]	5450
36	10	A	Torquay U	L	0-3	0-2	7		3060
37	17	H	Walsall	D	0-0	0-0	7		5625
38	23	H	Boston U	D	0-0	0-0	—		4417
39	27	H	Bristol R	L	0-1	0-1	—		4299
40	31	A	Peterborough U	D	3-3	2-1	7	Bloomfield [23], Stockley [28], Mooney (pen) [86]	6062
41	Apr 7	H	Shrewsbury T	D	1-1	1-1	7	Mooney [32]	5299
42	9	A	Grimsby T	D	2-2	2-0	8	McGleish [22], Easter [25]	4271
43	14	H	Hartlepool U	L	0-1	0-0	8		5540
44	21	A	Darlington	L	2-3	1-1	11	Bloomfield [11], Easter [50]	2727
45	28	H	Milton Keynes D	L	0-2	0-0	12		7150
46	May 5	A	Barnet	L	1-2	1-0	12	McGleish [32]	2707

Final League Position: 12

GOALSCORERS

League (52): Easter 17, Mooney 12 (1 pen), Betsy 5, McGleish 5, Bloomfield 4, Doherty 2, Martin 2, Antwi 1, Dixon 1, Golbourne 1, Stockley 1, Williamson 1.
Carling Cup (10): Easter 6, Oakes 2, Mooney 1 (pen), Williamson 1.
FA Cup (3): Antwi 1, Easter 1, Oakes 1.
J Paint Trophy (1): Stonebridge 1.

Batista R 29	Stockley S 33 + 1	Martin R 32 + 10	Palmer C 22 + 10	Antwi W 25	Williamson M 33	Grant A 39 + 1	Bloomfield M 39 + 2	Mooney T 41 + 1	Easter J 30 + 8	Betsy K 29	Oakes S 29 + 6	Dixon J 1 + 9	Torres S 8 + 12	Golbourne S 31 + 3	Young J 17 + 2	Gregory S — + 3	Anya I 1 + 12	Doherty T 23 + 3	Fernandez V 1	Stonebridge I 1 + 8	O'Halloran S 9 + 2	McParland A 1 + 3	Onibuje F 1 + 4	Crooks L 11	McGleish S 11 + 3	Christon L 5 + 1	Ainsworth L 3 + 4	Barnes-Homer M — + 1	Pettigrew A 1	Match No.
1	2	3	4	5	6	7^{1}	8	9	10^{2}	11	12	13																		1
1	2	3	4^{1}	5	6	7	8	9^{2}	13	11	10		12																	2
1	2	3^{1}	4^{2}	5	6	7■	8	9	12	11	10^{3}	13	14																	3
1	2	12	4	5	6		8^{2}	9^{3}	13	11	10	14	7^{1}	3																4
1	2	12	4	5	6	7		9^{2}	10	11^{3}	3	13	8^{1}	14																5
	2		4^{2}	5	6	3		9^{1}	10	11	8	12	7	13	1															6
1	2			5	6	7■	12	9^{1}	10^{2}	11	4	13	8	3																7
1	2	3		5	6		8		10	11	4^{1}	9^{2}		7		12	13													8
1	2	3		5	6		8^{3}	9^{1}	10	11		12		4		13	14	7^{2}												9
1		12	4^{2}	5	6	7	8	9	10	11				3				13	2^{1}											10
1		3	4	5	6	7^{2}	8	9	10^{1}	11		12		2				13												11
1		3	4	5	6	7^{1}	8	9		11				2		12	13	10^{2}												12
	2	12	4^{2}	5	6	7^{1}	8	9		11	10^{3}			3	1		14	13												13
	2	12	4^{3}	5	6^{1}	7	8	9		10	11^{2}			3	1		13			14										14
1	2	12		5	6	7^{2}	8	9^{3}	14	10	4^{1}			3				11		13										15
1	2	12		5	6	7^{1}	8	9	10^{2}	11				3				4■		13										16
1	2	3	12	5■	6	7	8	9^{1}	10^{2}	11				4						13										17
1	2		12	5	6		8	9	10	11	4^{1}			3				7												18
1	2		12	5	6	7	8	9	10^{3}	11	13							4^{2}		14	3^{1}									19
	2	12		5	6	7^{3}	8	9	10^{2}	11	4^{1}				1			3		13	14									20
	2	12		5	6	7^{1}	8	9		11	4				1		13	3^{2}		10^{3}	14									21
	2^{2}	13		5	6	7^{3}	8^{1}	9	10	11	12				1		14	4■			3									22
		2		5	6	7^{3}	8	9^{1}	10^{2}	11	4	12			1		14			13	3									23
		2		5	6	7^{1}	8	9	10	11	4				1		12				3									24
		2	5		6	7^{1}	8	9	10^{2}	11	4				1		12			13	3									25
1		2	12	5^{1}	6	13	8	14	10^{3}	11	4										3	7^{2}	9							26
1		2	4			7	8	9^{2}	10	11			12					6^{1}			3	13		5						27
1		2	4^{3}		6	7			10	11	8^{1}		12	3			13	9^{2}			5		14							28
1		2	4^{1}		6	7			10	11	12		13	3			9^{2}	8^{3}			5		14							29
1	2	5	12		6	7	13	9	10^{2}		14		4^{3}	3				11^{1}							8					30
1■	2	5			6	7^{1}	8	9^{2}	10^{G}		4		12	3	15			11							13					31
		2	7		6		8^{1}	9	10		4			3	1			11				12		5						32
	12	2	4		6		8	9^{2}	13		7^{3}			3	1			11^{1}				14		5	10					33
		2	4		6^{3}	7^{2}	8	9	12				13	3	1									5	10^{1}	14	11			34
1^{G}	2	6	12			7	8	9^{2}	13					3	15			4						5	10		11^{1}			35
1	2	6	12			7^{1}	8	9	13					3				4						5	10		11^{2}			36
1	2	6				7		9	10		4			3				8						5	11^{1}		12			37
	2	6	12			7^{2}	8	9			4^{1}			3	1			11						5	10		13			38
	2	6	12			7^{2}	8	9					13	3	1			11						5	10^{3}			14	4^{1}	39
	2	6	4			7^{1}	8	9			10^{2}		12	3	1			11								5	13			40
1	2	6	4			7	8	9^{2}	10		11^{1}		12	3											13	5				41
1	2	6	4^{1}			7^{2}	8		10^{3}		11		12	3									14	5	9		13			42
1	2	6				7	8	9	10		12		13	3				4^{1}					14		11^{2}	5^{3}				43
1	2	3	4^{1}			7	8	9	10^{2}		6		11^{3}	12			14							5	13					44
	2	6				7	8	9	10■		4		11	3	1											5				45
	2	6	12			7	8^{1}	9			4		11	3	1										10	5				46

FA Cup

First Round	Oxford U	(h)	2-1
Second Round	Stockport Co	(a)	1-2

J Paint Trophy

First Round	Swindon T	(h)	1-0
Second Round	Bristol R	(h)	0-2

Carling Cup

First Round	Swansea C	(a)	3-2
Second Round	Fulham	(a)	2-1
Third Round	Doncaster R	(h)	2-2
Fourth Round	Notts Co	(a)	1-0
Quarter-Final	Charlton Ath	(a)	1-0
Semi-Final	Chelsea	(h)	1-1
		(a)	0-4

YEOVIL TOWN FL Championship 1

FOUNDATION

One of the prime movers of Yeovil football was Ernest J. Sercombe. His association with the club began in 1895 as a playing member of Yeovil Casuals, of which team he became vice-captain and in his last season 1899–1900, he was chosen to play for Somerset against Devon. Upon the reorganisation of the club, he became secretary of the old Yeovil Town FC and with the amalgamation with Petters United in 1914, he continued to serve until his resignation in 1930.

Huish Park, Lufton Way, Yeovil, Somerset BA22 8YF.

Telephone: (01935) 423 662.

Fax: (01935) 473 956.

Ticket Office: (01935) 847 888.

Website: www.ytfc.net

Email: jcotton@ytfc.co.uk

Ground Capacity: 9,665.

Record Attendance: 9,348 v Liverpool, FA Cup 3rd rd, 4 January 2004 (16,318 v Sunderland at Huish).

Pitch Measurements: 110m × 69m.

Chairman/Chief Executive: John R. Fry.

Secretary: Jean Cotton.

Manager: Russell Slade.

First Team Coach: Steve Thompson.

Physio: Jim Joyce.

Colours: Green and white hooped shirts, white shorts, white stockings.

Change Colours: Black shirts, amber shorts, black stockings with amber trim.

Year Formed: 1895.

Turned Professional: 1921.

Ltd Co.: 1923.

Club Nickname: 'Glovers'.

Previous Names: 1895, Yeovil Casuals; 1907, Yeovil Town; 1915, Yeovil & Petters United; 1946, Yeovil Town.

Grounds: 1895, Pen Mill Ground; 1921, Huish; 1990, Huish Park.

HONOURS

FL Championship 2 winners 2004–05.

Conference: Champions 2002–03.

FA Cup: 5th rd 1949.

League Cup: 2nd rd 2006.

Southern League: Champions 1954–55, 1963–64, 1970–71; Runners-up: 1923–24, 1931–32, 1934–35, 1969–70, 1972–73.

Southern League Cup: Winners 1948–49, 1954–55, 1960–61, 1965–66; Runners-up: 1946–47, 1955–56.

Isthmian League: Winners 1987–88; Runners-up: 1985–86, 1986–87, 1996–97.

AC Delco Cup: Winners 1987–88.

Bob Lord Trophy: Winners 1989–90.

FA Trophy: Winners 2002.

London Combination: Runners-up 1930–31, 1932–33.

SKY SPORTS FACT FILE

Scottish born half-back David Pratt was appointed player-manager of Yeovil & Petters United in July 1929 after service with Celtic, Bradford City, Liverpool and Bury. He transformed the club's fortunes in four successful seasons.

First Football League Game: 9 August 2003, Division 3 v Rochdale (a) W 3-1: Weale; Williams (Lindegaard), Crittenden, Lockwood, O'Brien, Pluck (Rodrigues), Gosling (El Kholti), Way, Jackson, Gall (2), Johnson (1).

Record League Victory: 10–0 v Kidderminster H, Southern League, 27 December 1955. 10–0 v Bedford T, Southern League, 4 March 1961.

Record Cup Victory: 12–1 v Westbury United, FA Cup 1st qual rd, 1923–24.

Record Defeat: 0–8 v Manchester United, FA Cup 5th rd, 12 February 1949.

Most League Points (3 for a win): – 83, FL 2, 2004–05.

Most League Goals: 90, FL 2, 2004–05.

Highest League Goalscorer in Season: Phil Jevons, 27, 2004–05

Most League Goals in Total Aggregate: Phil Jevons, 42, 2004–06

Most Capped Player: Andrejs Stolcers, 1 (81) Latvia and Arron Davies, 1, Wales.

Most League Appearances: Terry Skiverton, 139, 2003–.

Record Transfer Fee Received: Undisclosed from West Ham U for Gavin Williams, December 2004.

Record Transfer Fee Paid: Undisclosed to Atletico Penarol de Rafaela (Argentina) for Pablo Bastianini, August 2005.

Football League Record: 2003 Promoted to Division 3 from Conference; 2003–04 Division 3; 2004–05 FL 2; 2005– FL 1.

LATEST SEQUENCES

Longest Sequence of League Wins: 7, 7.12.2004 – 15.1.2005.

Longest Sequence of League Defeats: 5, 29.10.05 – 6.12.05.

Longest Sequence of Unbeaten League Matches: 7, 7.12.2004 – 15.1.2005.

Longest Sequence Without a League Win: 6, 6.8.05 – 29.8.05.

Successive Scoring Runs: 22 from 30.10.2004.

Successive Non-scoring Runs: 3 from 21.1.2006.

MANAGERS

Jack Gregory 1922–28
Tommy Lawes 1928–29
Dave Pratt 1929–33
Louis Page 1933–35
Dave Halliday 1935–38
Billy Kingdon 1938–46
Alec Stock 1946–49
George Patterson 1949–51
Harry Lowe 1951–53
Ike Clarke 1953–57
Norman Dodgin 1957
Jimmy Baldwin 1957–60
Basil Hayward 1960–64
Glyn Davies 1964–65
Joe McDonald 1965–67
Ron Saunders 1967–69
Mike Hughes 1969–72
Cecil Irwin 1972–75
Stan Harland 1975–81
Barry Lloyd 1978–81
Malcolm Allison 1981
Jimmy Giles 1981–83
Trevor Finnigan/Mike Hughes 1983
Steve Coles 1983–84
Ian McFarlane 1984
Gerry Gow 1984–87
Brian Hall 1987–90
Clive Whitehead 1990–91
Steve Rutter 1991–93
Brian Hall 1994–95
Graham Roberts 1995–98
Colin Lippiatt 1998–99
Steve Thompson 1999–2000
Dave Webb 2000
Gary Johnson 2001–05
Steve Thompson 2005–06
Russell Slade June 2006–

TEN YEAR LEAGUE RECORD

		P	W	D	L	F	A	Pts	Pos
1997–98	Conf.	42	17	8	17	73	63	59	11
1998–99	Conf.	42	20	11	11	68	54	71	5
1999–2000	Conf.	42	18	10	14	60	63	64	7
2000–01	Conf.	42	24	8	10	73	50	80	2
2001–02	Conf.	42	19	13	10	66	53	70	3
2002–03	Conf.	42	28	11	3	100	37	95	1
2003–04	Div 3	46	23	5	18	70	57	74	8
2004–05	FL 2	46	25	8	13	90	65	83	1
2005–06	FL 1	46	15	11	20	54	62	56	15
2006–07	FL 1	46	23	10	13	55	39	79	5

DID YOU KNOW ?

During the period overlapping the 1920s and 1930s an outstanding display by Welsh international Wilf Lewis, in which he scored an FA Cup hat-trick against Dartford on 1 December 1932, helped relaunch his Football League career with Cardiff City.

YEOVIL TOWN 2006–07 LEAGUE RECORD

Match No.	*Date*	*Venue*	*Opponents*	*Result*	*H/T Score*	*Lg. Pos.*	*Goalscorers*	*Attendance*
1	Aug 5	A	Millwall	D 1-1	1-0	—	Gray ^{35}	10,012
2	8	H	Bournemouth	D 0-0	0-0	—		6451
3	12	H	Carlisle U	W 2-1	2-1	10	Cohen ^{16}, Welsh ^{42}	4709
4	19	A	Tranmere R	L 1-2	1-1	12	Cohen ^{44}	6023
5	26	H	Port Vale	W 1-0	1-0	9	Terry ^{5}	4827
6	Sept 1	A	Swansea C	D 1-1	0-0	—	Stewart ^{53}	14,513
7	9	H	Nottingham F	L 0-1	0-0	12		6925
8	12	A	Northampton T	D 1-1	0-1	—	Stewart ^{68}	4853
9	16	A	Huddersfield T	W 3-2	1-1	11	Morris ^{14}, Davies ^{51}, Cohen ^{77}	9573
10	23	H	Crewe Alex	W 2-0	1-0	6	Williams (og) ^{45}, Terry ^{71}	5333
11	26	H	Brighton & HA	W 2-0	1-0	—	Stewart ^{6}, Gray ^{82}	5243
12	30	A	Brentford	W 2-1	0-0	2	Skiverton ^{57}, Cohen ^{88}	5770
13	Oct 6	H	Cheltenham T	L 0-1	0-0	—		6220
14	14	A	Blackpool	D 1-1	0-0	3	Stewart ^{86}	6812
15	21	H	Oldham Ath	W 1-0	1-0	2	Skiverton ^{45}	5471
16	28	A	Chesterfield	D 1-1	0-0	4	Stewart ^{89}	5413
17	Nov 4	H	Bristol C	W 2-1	0-0	2	Davies ^{78}, Gray ^{89}	9009
18	18	A	Leyton Orient	D 0-0	0-0	5		4842
19	25	H	Scunthorpe U	L 0-2	0-1	7		5921
20	Dec 2	A	Rotherham U	L 2-3	2-3	—	Best ^{25}, Morris ^{31}	4823
21	9	H	Gillingham	W 2-0	1-0	6	Best ^{17}, Cohen ^{59}	4933
22	23	H	Bradford C	D 0-0	0-0	8		6208
23	26	A	Brighton & HA	W 3-1	1-0	7	Best ^{38}, Morris ^{47}, Davies ^{59}	6554
24	30	A	Crewe Alex	W 3-2	2-0	6	Best 2 $^{5, 8}$, Morris ^{70}	5450
25	Jan 1	H	Northampton T	D 0-0	0-0	6		5361
26	5	H	Huddersfield T	W 3-1	3-0	—	Morris ^{4}, Best ^{23}, Hardy (og) ^{36}	5554
27	13	A	Nottingham F	L 0-1	0-0	5		17,885
28	20	H	Brentford	W 1-0	0-0	5	Best ^{56}	5373
29	27	A	Bradford C	W 2-0	1-0	5	Davies 2 $^{5, 67}$	7474
30	Feb 3	H	Millwall	L 0-1	0-1	5		5810
31	10	A	Carlisle U	W 4-1	0-1	4	Gray ^{49}, Best 2 $^{72, 89}$, Cohen ^{90}	7112
32	17	H	Tranmere R	L 0-2	0-0	5		5168
33	20	A	Bournemouth	W 2-0	1-0	—	Gray ^{30}, Best ^{77}	7285
34	24	H	Swansea C	W 1-0	0-0	2	Stewart ^{56}	5984
35	27	A	Doncaster R	D 0-0	0-0	—		8046
36	Mar 3	A	Port Vale	L 2-4	2-2	4	Gray ^{37}, Stewart ^{38}	4202
37	10	A	Cheltenham T	W 2-1	1-0	3	Gray 2 $^{20, 63}$	5314
38	17	H	Blackpool	L 0-1	0-0	4		6012
39	24	H	Chesterfield	W 1-0	0-0	4	Jones ^{89}	4735
40	31	A	Oldham Ath	L 0-1	0-1	5		6035
41	Apr 6	A	Scunthorpe U	L 0-1	0-1	—		7883
42	9	H	Leyton Orient	W 2-1	0-1	5	Gray (pen) ^{77}, Davies ^{83}	5206
43	14	A	Bristol C	L 0-2	0-1	5		19,002
44	21	H	Rotherham U	W 1-0	1-0	5	Stewart ^{45}	5878
45	28	H	Doncaster R	W 1-0	0-0	5	Gray ^{72}	6253
46	May 5	A	Gillingham	W 2-0	0-0	5	Kamudimba Kalala ^{63}, Gray ^{68}	7484

Final League Position: 5

GOALSCORERS

League (55): Gray 11 (1 pen), Best 10, Stewart 8, Cohen 6, Davies 6, Morris 5, Skiverton 2, Terry 2, Jones 1, Kamudimba Kalala 1, Welsh 1, own goals 2.
Carling Cup (2): Gray 1, Harrold 1.
FA Cup (1): Cohen 1.
J Paint Trophy (1): Barry 1.
Play-Offs (5): Davies 2, Morris 1, Stewart 1, own goal 1.

Match No.	Mildenhall S 46	Lindegaard A 12+2	Jones N 42	Terry P 20	Skiverton T 39	Forbes T 46	Barry A 13+11	Davies A 34+5	Gray W 24+22	Harrold M 2+3	Cohen C 44	James K 2+4	Poole D 1+3	Morris L 23+10	Kamudimba Kalala J 35+3	Welsh I 4+14	Lynch M 17
1	1	2	3	4	5	6	7^{1}	8	9^{2}	10	11	12	13				
2	1	2	3	4	5	6	7^{1}	8^{2}	9	10^{3}	11	14	12	13			
3	1	2	3	4^{3}	5	6		12	9	13	11	10^{2}	8^{1}		14	7	
4	1	2	3	4	5	6		12	9^{2}	13	11	10^{1}	14		8	7^{3}	
5	1		3	4	5	6	12		9^{2}	13	11	14		10^{3}	8	7^{1}	2
6	1		3	4	5	6	12		9^{3}		11	14		7^{2}	8^{1}	13	2
7	1		3	4	5	6		13	9^{1}		11			7^{3}	8	14	2
8	1		3	4	5	6			9^{2}		11			7^{1}	8	13	2
9	1		3	4^{2}	5	6	13	7	12		11			9^{1}	8		2
10	1		3	4	5	6		7	12		11			9^{1}	8	13	2
11	1		3	4	5	6	12	9^{3}	13		11			7^{2}	8^{1}	14	2
12	1		3	4	5	6		9^{1}	12		11				8	13	2
13	1		3	4	5	6	12		9		11				8^{1}	13	2
14	1		3	4^{1}	5	6	13	9	12		7			14	8^{2}		2
15	1		3	4	5^{2}	6		9	12		11			7^{1}	8		2
16	1		3	4^{1}	5	6	13	9^{2}	12		11				8	14	2
17	1		3^{1}	4	5^{3}	6	7	12	9		11			8^{2}			2
18	1		3	4^{1}		6	7^{2}	8^{3}	12		11			14	13		5
19	1		3^{1}	4		6	7^{3}	8^{2}	12		11			13			2
20	1		3	4^{2}	5	6	14		12		11			8^{1}		13	2
21	1		3		5	6		9	12		11			4^{1}	8	13	
22	1		3		5	6		9^{2}	12		11			4^{1}	8	13	
23	1		3		5	6		9	12		11			4^{1}	8		
24	1		3		5^{3}	6		9	12		11			4^{1}	8		
25	1		3			6	8	9	12		11			4^{1}		13	
26	1	2	3			6	12	7	13		11			4	8		
27	1	2			5	6	7^{3}	11	12					4^{2}	8	13	
28	1	2	3		5	6		7	11^{1}		4				8	12	
29	1	2	3		5	6	7^{1}	11	12		4				8		
30	1	2^{1}	3			6		7^{3}	12		4			13	8		
31	1	2^{3}	3		5	6^{2}		11	12		4				8		
32	1		3^{2}		5	6		7	9^{1}		11						
33	1		3		5	7		11^{1}	9		4				8		
34	1		3		5	6		12	9		2			13	8		
35	1		3		5	6		11^{2}	9		4			12	8		
36	1		3^{2}		5	6			9		4			12	8		
37	1				5	2		11	9		4				8		
38	1				5	2		11	9^{1}		4			12	8		
39	1		3		5	6		7	9^{2}		4			11	8		
40	1		3		5	6	7^{2}	9	12		4			11	8		
41	1		3		5	6	12	7^{1}	9^{2}		4			11	8		
42	1		3		5	6	12	7^{2}	9		4			11^{1}	8		
43	1	12	3		5^{3}	6	11	7	9^{2}		4			13	8^{1}		
44	1	12	3			6	7	8	13		4			11^{3}			
45	1	2	3		5^{2}	6	7	8	9		4			11^{1}	12		
46	1	3				6	4		10^{2}						8	11^{3}	2

Match No.	Stewart M 31	Webb D —+4	Cooper K 4	Tonkin A 1+4	Guyett S 10+6	Brittain M 12+3	Cranie M 11+1	Best L 14+1	Maher S —+1	Sweeney P 5+3	Law N 5+1	Rose M 7+2	Rooney A 1+2	Knights D —+4	Clarke T 1	McCallum G —+1	Alcock C —+1
1																	
2																	
3																	
4																	
5																	
6	10																
7	10	12^{2}															
8	10	12															
9	10																
10	10^{2}																
11	10																
12	10		7^{2}														
13	10		7^{2}														
14	10		11^{3}														
15	10			13													
16	10		7^{3}														
17				13	14■	10											
18	10					9	2										
19	10					9	5	14									
20						9	7^{3}	10									
21						7^{2}	2	10									
22						7	2	10									
23						7	2	10									
24				13	14	7^{2}	2	10									
25					5	7^{2}	2	10									
26	9^{1}				5			10^{2}									
27	9^{1}			3				10	14								
28	9							10									
29	9							10									
30	9^{2}				5	14		10		11							
31	9^{1}			14	13			10		7							
32		13			4	12		10		8	2						
33					6			10		12	2						
34	10				4^{3}	7^{1}				11^{2}		14					
35	10^{1}									13	7	2					
36	10					7^{1}	13			11^{3}	14	2					
37	10				6^{1}		3				7	12					
38	10				6^{3}	13	3				7^{2}		14				
39	10^{1}						2			12			13				
40	10^{1}											2		13			
41	10											2		13			
42	10^{3}				13							2		14			
43	10				14■							2					
44	10				5							2^{1}	9^{2}	14			
45	10				13												
46		12			5	7									9^{1}	13	14

FA Cup
First Round Rushden & D (a) 1-3

Carling Cup
First Round Southampton (a) 2-5

J Paint Trophy
Second Round Shrewsbury T (a) 1-2

Play-Offs
Semi-Final Nottingham F (h) 0-2
(a) 5-2
Final Blackpool 0-2
(at Wembley)

ENGLISH LEAGUE PLAYERS DIRECTORY

Players listed represent those with their clubs during the 2006–07 season.

Players are listed alphabetically on pages 563–569.
The number alongside each player corresponds to the team number heading. (Abbey, George 63 = team 63 (Port Vale))

ACCRINGTON S (1)

ALMEIDA, Mauro (D) 5 0
H: 6 0 W: 11 05 b.Viseu 29-1-82

2006–07	Accrington S	5	0	**5**	**0**

BAINS, Rikki (D) 3 0
H: 6 1 W: 13 00 b.Coventry 3-2-88
Source: Scholar.

2006–07	Coventry C	0	0		
2006–07	Accrington S	3	0	**3**	**0**

BOCO, Romuald (F) 32 3
H: 5 10 W: 10 12 b.Bernay 8-7-85
Source: Niort. *Honours:* Benin 17 full caps.

2006–07	Accrington S	32	3	**32**	**3**

BROWN, David (F) 150 28
H: 5 10 W: 11 02 b.Bolton 2-10-78
Source: Trainee.

1995–96	Manchester U	0	0		
1996–97	Manchester U	0	0		
1997–98	Manchester U	0	0		
1997–98	*Hull C*	7	2		
1998–99	Hull C	42	11		
1999–2000	Hull C	45	6		
2000–01	Hull C	37	4	**131**	**23**
2001–02	Torquay U	2	0	**2**	**0**
From Chester C, Telford U, Hereford U.					
2006–07	Accrington S	17	5	**17**	**5**

BYROM, Joel (M) 1 0
H: 6 0 W: 12 04 b.Oswaldtwistle 14-9-86
Source: Scholar.

2004–05	Blackburn R	0	0		
2005–06	Blackburn R	0	0		
2006–07	Accrington S	1	0	**1**	**0**

CAVANAGH, Paul (D) 26 4
H: 5 11 W: 11 09 b.Liverpool 14-10-81
Source: Liverpool Scholar.

2006–07	Accrington S	26	4	**26**	**4**

DOHERTY, Sean (M) 27 1
H: 5 8 W: 10 08 b.Basingstoke 10-5-85
Source: Scholar. *Honours:* England Youth, Under-20.

2001–02	Fulham	0	0		
2002–03	Fulham	0	0		
2003–04	Fulham	0	0		
2003–04	*Blackpool*	1	0	**1**	**0**
2004–05	Fulham	0	0		
2005–06	Den Haag	0	0		
2005–06	Port Vale	6	0	**6**	**0**
2006–07	Accrington S	20	1	**20**	**1**

DUNBAVIN, Ian (G) 119 0
H: 6 1 W: 12 10 b.Knowsley 27-5-80
Source: Trainee.

1998–99	Liverpool	0	0		
1999–2000	Liverpool	0	0		
1999–2000	Shrewsbury T	7	0		
2000–01	Shrewsbury T	22	0		
2001–02	Shrewsbury T	34	0		
2002–03	Shrewsbury T	33	0		
2003–04	Shrewsbury T	0	0	**96**	**0**
From Halifax T.					
2006–07	Accrington S	23	0	**23**	**0**

EDWARDS, Phil (D) 33 1
H: 5 8 W: 11 03 b.Bootle 8-11-85
Source: Scholar.

2005–06	Wigan Ath	0	0		
2006–07	Accrington S	33	1	**33**	**1**

GRANT, Robert (M) 1 0
H: 5 11 W: 12 00 b.Blackpool 27-3-87
Source: Scholar.

2006–07	Accrington S	1	0	**1**	**0**

GRANT, Tony (M) 260 6
H: 5 9 W: 11 00 b.Liverpool 14-11-74
Source: From Trainee. *Honours:* England Under-21.

1993–94	Everton	0	0		
1994–95	Everton	5	0		
1995–96	Everton	13	1		
1995–96	*Swindon T*	3	1	**3**	**1**
1996–97	Everton	18	0		
1997–98	Everton	7	1		
1998–99	Everton	16	0		
1999–2000	Everton	2	0	**61**	**2**
1999–2000	*Tranmere R*	9	0	**9**	**0**
1999–2000	Manchester C	8	0		
2000–01	Manchester C	10	0		
2000–01	*WBA*	5	0	**5**	**0**
2001–02	Manchester C	3	0	**21**	**0**
2001–02	Burnley	28	0		
2002–03	Burnley	34	1		
2003–04	Burnley	37	0		
2004–05	Burnley	42	2	**141**	**3**
2005–06	Bristol C	0	0		
2005–06	Crewe Alex	10	0		
2006–07	Crewe Alex	4	0	**14**	**0**
2006–07	Accrington S	6	0	**6**	**0**

HARRIS, James (M) 32 2
H: 5 7 W: 11 06 b.Liverpool 15-4-87

2005–06	Everton	0	0		
2005–06	Everton	0	0		
2006–07	Accrington S	32	2	**32**	**2**

MANGAN, Andrew (M) 36 4
H: 5 9 W: 10 03 b.Liverpool 30-8-86
Source: Scholar.

2003–04	Blackpool	2	0		
2004–05	Blackpool	0	0	**2**	**0**
2006–07	Accrington S	34	4	**34**	**4**

McGIVERN, Leighton (M) 32 2
H: 5 8 W: 11 01 b.Liverpool 2-6-84
Source: From Vauxhall Motors.

2004–05	Rochdale	25	1		
2005–06	Rochdale	0	0	**25**	**1**
2006–07	Accrington S	7	1	**7**	**1**

MULLIN, Paul (F) 46 14
H: 6 0 W: 12 01 b.Bury 16-3-74
Source: Clitheroe, Darwen, Radcliffe Borough.

2006–07	Accrington S	46	14	**46**	**14**

N'DA, Julien (M) 3 0
H: 5 10 W: 11 05 b.Niort 15-8-85
Source: Rouen.

2006–07	Accrington S	3	0	**3**	**0**

PROCTOR, Andy (M) 43 3
H: 6 0 W: 12 04 b.Blackburn 13-3-83
Source: Great Harwood T.

2006–07	Accrington S	43	3	**43**	**3**

RICHARDSON, Leam (D) 143 0
H: 5 7 W: 11 04 b.Leeds 19-11-79
Source: Trainee.

1997–98	Blackburn R	0	0		
1998–99	Blackburn R	0	0		
1999–2000	Blackburn R	0	0		
2000–01	Bolton W	12	0		
2001–02	Bolton W	1	0		
2001–02	*Notts Co*	21	0	**21**	**0**
2002–03	Bolton W	0	0	**13**	**0**
2002–03	*Blackpool*	20	0		
2003–04	Blackpool	28	0		
2004–05	Blackpool	23	0	**71**	**0**
2006–07	Accrington S	38	0	**38**	**0**

ROGERS, Alan (D) 329 18
H: 5 9 W: 12 10 b.Liverpool 3-1-77
Source: Trainee. *Honours:* England Under-21.

1995–96	Tranmere R	26	2		
1996–97	Tranmere R	31	0	**57**	**2**
1997–98	Nottingham F	46	1		
1998–99	Nottingham F	34	3		
1999–2000	Nottingham F	37	9		
2000–01	Nottingham F	17	3		
2001–02	Nottingham F	3	0		
2001–02	Leicester C	13	0		
2002–03	Leicester C	41	0		
2003–04	Leicester C	8	0	**62**	**0**
2003–04	*Wigan Ath*	5	0	**5**	**0**
2003–04	*Nottingham F*	12	0		
2004–05	Nottingham F	33	0		
2005–06	Nottingham F	0	0	**182**	**16**
2005–06	*Hull C*	9	0	**9**	**0**
2006–07	Bradford C	8	0	**8**	**0**
2006–07	Accrington S	6	0	**6**	**0**

TODD, Andrew (M) 47 10
H: 6 0 W: 11 03 b.Nottingham 22-2-79
Source: Eastwood T.

1995–96	Nottingham F	0	0		
1996–97	Nottingham F	0	0		
1997–98	Nottingham F	0	0		
1998–99	Nottingham F	0	0		
1998–99	Scarborough	1	0	**1**	**0**
From Etwd T, Wksop, Hucknall, Burton Alb					
2006–07	Accrington S	46	10	**46**	**10**

TRETTON, Andy (D) 111 6
H: 6 0 W: 12 08 b.Derby 9-10-76
Source: Trainee.

1993–94	Derby Co	0	0		
1994–95	Derby Co	0	0		
1995–96	Derby Co	0	0		
1996–97	Derby Co	0	0		
1997–98	Chesterfield	0	0		
1997–98	Shrewsbury T	14	1		
1998–99	Shrewsbury T	23	0		
1999–2000	Shrewsbury T	33	3		
2000–01	Shrewsbury T	22	2		
2001–02	Shrewsbury T	19	0		
2002–03	Shrewsbury T	0	0		
2003–04	Shrewsbury T	0	0		
2004–05	Shrewsbury T	0	0		
2005–06	Shrewsbury T	0	0	**111**	**6**
2006–07	Accrington S	0	0		

VENTRE, Danny (D) 6 0
b.Chester 23-1-86
Source: Chester C.

2006–07	Accrington S	6	0	**6**	**0**

WELCH, Michael (D) 145 8
H: 6 3 W: 11 12 b.Winsford 11-1-82
Source: Barnsley Scholar.

2001–02	Macclesfield T	6	0		
2002–03	Macclesfield T	39	3		
2003–04	Macclesfield T	38	0		
2004–05	Macclesfield T	31	2	**114**	**5**
2006–07	Accrington S	31	3	**31**	**3**

WHALLEY, Shaun (F) 23 2
H: 5 9 W: 10 07 b.Prescot 7-8-87

2004–05	Chester C	3	0	**3**	**0**
From Witton Alb.					
2006–07	Accrington S	20	2	**20**	**2**

WILLIAMS, Robbie (D) 43 3
H: 5 10 W: 12 00 b.Liverpool 12-4-79
Source: St Dominics.

2006–07	Accrington S	43	3	**43**	**3**

ARSENAL (2)

ADEBAYOR, Emmanuel (F) **164 45**
H: 6 4 W: 11 08 b.Lome 26-2-84
Source: Lome. *Honours:* Togo 37 full caps, 16 goals.

2001–02	Metz	10	2		
2002–03	Metz	34	13	**44**	**15**
2003–04	Monaco	31	8		
2004–05	Monaco	34	9		
2005–06	Monaco	13	1	**78**	**18**
2005–06	Arsenal	13	4		
2006–07	Arsenal	29	8	**42**	**12**

ALIADIERE, Jeremie (F) **50 3**
H: 6 0 W: 11 00 b.Rambouillet 30-3-83
Source: Scholarship. *Honours:* France Under-21.

1999–2000	Arsenal	0	0		
2000–01	Arsenal	0	0		
2001–02	Arsenal	1	0		
2002–03	Arsenal	3	1		
2003–04	Arsenal	10	0		
2004–05	Arsenal	4	0		
2005–06	Arsenal	0	0		
2005–06	*West Ham U*	7	0	**7**	**0**
2005–06	*Wolverhampton W*	14	2	**14**	**2**
2006–07	Arsenal	11	0	**29**	**1**

ALMUNIA, Manuel (G) **144 0**
H: 6 3 W: 13 00 b.Pamplona 19-5-77

1997–98	Osasuna B	31	0		
1998–99	Osasuna B	13	0	**44**	**0**
1999–2000	Cartagonova	3	0	**3**	**0**
2000–01	Sabadell	25	0	**25**	**0**
2001–02	Celta Vigo	0	0		
2001–02	*Eibar*	35	0	**35**	**0**
2002–03	*Recreativo*	2	0	**2**	**0**
2003–04	Albacete	24	0	**24**	**0**
2004–05	Arsenal	10	0		
2005–06	Arsenal	0	0		
2006–07	Arsenal	1	0	**11**	**0**

BAPTISTA, Julio (M) **194 58**
H: 6 0 W: 11 05 b.Sao Paulo 1-10-81
Honours: Brazil 22 full caps, 3 goals.

2000	Sao Paulo	14	0		
2001	Sao Paulo	25	4		
2002	Sao Paulo	21	3		
2003	Sao Paulo	15	2	**75**	**9**
2003–04	Sevilla	30	20		
2004–05	Sevilla	33	18	**63**	**38**
2005–06	Real Madrid	32	8	**32**	**8**
2006–07	Arsenal	24	3	**24**	**3**

BENDTNER, Nicklas (F) **42 11**
H: 6 2 W: 13 00 b.Copenhagen 16-1-88
Source: Scholar. *Honours:* Denmark Youth, Under-21, 6 full caps, 3 goals.

2005–06	Arsenal	0	0		
2006–07	Arsenal	0	0		
2006–07	*Birmingham C*	42	11	**42**	**11**

CLICHY, Gael (D) **61 0**
H: 5 9 W: 10 04 b.Toulouse 26-7-85
Source: Cannes. *Honours:* France Under-21.

2003–04	Arsenal	12	0		
2004–05	Arsenal	15	0		
2005–06	Arsenal	7	0		
2006–07	Arsenal	27	0	**61**	**0**

CONNOLLY, Matthew (D) **5 1**
H: 6 1 W: 11 03 b.Barnet 24-9-87
Source: Scholar. *Honours:* England Youth.

2005–06	Arsenal	0	0		
2006–07	Arsenal	0	0		
2006–07	*Bournemouth*	5	1	**5**	**1**

DENILSON (M) **22 0**
H: 5 10 W: 10 10 b.Sao Paulo 16-2-88
Honours: Brazil Youth, Under-20.

2005	Sao Paulo	10	0		
2006	Sao Paulo	2	0	**12**	**0**
2006–07	Arsenal	10	0	**10**	**0**

DIABY, Vassiriki (M) **34 3**
H: 6 2 W: 12 04 b.Paris 11-5-86
Honours: France Youth, Under-21, 2 full caps.

2004–05	Auxerre	5	0		
2005–06	Auxerre	5	1	**10**	**1**
2005–06	Arsenal	12	1		
2006–07	Arsenal	12	1	**24**	**2**

DJOUROU, Johan (D) **28 0**
H: 6 2 W: 12 05 b.Ivory Coast 18-1-87
Source: Scholar. *Honours:* Switzerland Youth, Under-20, Under-21, 8 full caps.

2004–05	Arsenal	0	0		
2005–06	Arsenal	7	0		
2006–07	Arsenal	21	0	**28**	**0**

EBOUE, Emmanuel (D) **113 4**
H: 5 10 W: 11 08 b.Abidjan 4-6-83
Honours: Ivory Coast 14 full caps.

2002–03	Beveren	23	0		
2003–04	Beveren	30	2		
2004–05	Beveren	17	2	**70**	**4**
2004–05	Arsenal	1	0		
2005–06	Arsenal	18	0		
2006–07	Arsenal	24	0	**43**	**0**

FABREGAS, Francesc (M) **106 7**
H: 5 11 W: 11 01 b.Vilessoc de Mar 4-5-87
Source: Barcelona. *Honours:* Spain Youth, Under-21, 16 full caps.

2003–04	Arsenal	0	0		
2004–05	Arsenal	33	2		
2005–06	Arsenal	35	3		
2006–07	Arsenal	38	2	**106**	**7**

FLAMINI, Mathieu (M) **86 4**
H: 5 11 W: 11 10 b.Marseille 7-3-84
Source: Marseille. *Honours:* France Under-21.

2003–04	Marseille	14	0	**14**	**0**
2004–05	Arsenal	21	1		
2005–06	Arsenal	31	0		
2006–07	Arsenal	20	3	**72**	**4**

GALLAS, William (D) **283 17**
H: 6 0 W: 12 12 b.Asnieres 17-8-77
Honours: France Under-21, 54 full caps, 2 goals.

1996–97	Caen	18	0	**18**	**0**
1997–98	Marseille	3	0		
1998–99	Marseille	30	0		
1999–2000	Marseille	22	0		
2000–01	Marseille	30	2	**85**	**2**
2001–02	Chelsea	30	1		
2002–03	Chelsea	38	4		
2003–04	Chelsea	29	0		
2004–05	Chelsea	28	2		
2005–06	Chelsea	34	5		
2006–07	Chelsea	0	0	**159**	**12**
2006–07	Arsenal	21	3	**21**	**3**

GARRY, Ryan (D) **1 0**
H: 6 0 W: 11 05 b.Hornchurch 29-9-83
Source: Scholar. *Honours:* England Youth, Under-20.

2001–02	Arsenal	0	0		
2002–03	Arsenal	1	0		
2003–04	Arsenal	0	0		
2004–05	Arsenal	0	0		
2005–06	Arsenal	0	0		
2006–07	Arsenal	0	0	**1**	**0**

GILBERT, Kerrea (D) **26 0**
H: 5 6 W: 11 03 b.Hammersmith 28-2-87
Source: Scholar. *Honours:* England Youth.

2005–06	Arsenal	2	0		
2006–07	Arsenal	0	0	**2**	**0**
2006–07	*Cardiff C*	24	0	**24**	**0**

HENRY, Thierry (F) **375 197**
H: 6 2 W: 13 05 b.Paris 17-8-77
Honours: France 92 full caps, 39 goals.

1994–95	Monaco	8	3		
1995–96	Monaco	18	3		
1996–97	Monaco	36	9		
1997–98	Monaco	30	4		
1998–99	Monaco	13	1	**105**	**20**
1998–99	Juventus	16	3	**16**	**3**
1999–2000	Arsenal	31	17		
2000–01	Arsenal	35	17		
2001–02	Arsenal	33	24		
2002–03	Arsenal	37	24		
2003–04	Arsenal	37	30		
2004–05	Arsenal	32	25		
2005–06	Arsenal	32	27		
2006–07	Arsenal	17	10	**254**	**174**

HLEB, Aleksandr (M) **237 26**
H: 5 10 W: 11 07 b.Minsk 1-5-81
Honours: Belarus 27 full caps, 4 goals.

1999	BATE	13	1		
2000	BATE	12	3	**25**	**4**
2000–01	Stuttgart B	17	4	**17**	**4**
2000–01	Stuttgart	6	0		
2001–02	Stuttgart	32	2		
2002–03	Stuttgart	34	4		
2003–04	Stuttgart	31	5		
2004–05	Stuttgart	34	2	**137**	**13**
2005–06	Arsenal	25	3		
2006–07	Arsenal	33	2	**58**	**5**

HOYTE, Justin (D) **56 2**
H: 5 11 W: 11 00 b.Waltham Forest 20-11-84
Source: Scholar. *Honours:* England Youth, Under-20, Under-21.

2002–03	Arsenal	1	0		
2003–04	Arsenal	1	0		
2004–05	Arsenal	5	0		
2005–06	Arsenal	0	0		
2005–06	*Sunderland*	27	1	**27**	**1**
2006–07	Arsenal	22	1	**29**	**1**

LEHMANN, Jens (G) **474 2**
H: 6 4 W: 13 05 b.Essen 10-11-69
Honours: Germany Youth, Under-21, 44 full caps.

1991–92	Schalke	37	0		
1992–93	Schalke	8	0		
1993–94	Schalke	21	0		
1994–95	Schalke	34	1		
1995–96	Schalke	32	0		
1996–97	Schalke	34	0		
1997–98	Schalke	34	1	**200**	**2**
1998–99	AC Milan	5	0	**5**	**0**
1998–99	Borussia Dortmd	13	0		
1999–2000	Borussia Dortmd	31	0		
2000–01	Borussia Dortmd	31	0		
2001–02	Borussia Dortmd	30	0		
2002–03	Borussia Dortmd	24	0	**129**	**0**
2003–04	Arsenal	38	0		
2004–05	Arsenal	28	0		
2005–06	Arsenal	38	0		
2006–07	Arsenal	36	0	**140**	**0**

LJUNGBERG, Frederik (M) **295 56**
H: 5 9 W: 11 00 b.Vittsjo 16-4-77
Honours: Sweden Under-21, 67 full caps, 13 goals.

1994	Halmstad	1	0		
1995	Halmstad	16	1		
1996	Halmstad	20	2		
1997	Halmstad	24	5		
1998	Halmstad	18	2	**79**	**10**
1998–99	Arsenal	16	1		
1999–2000	Arsenal	26	6		
2000–01	Arsenal	30	6		
2001–02	Arsenal	25	12		
2002–03	Arsenal	20	6		
2003–04	Arsenal	30	4		
2004–05	Arsenal	26	10		
2005–06	Arsenal	25	1		
2006–07	Arsenal	18	0	**216**	**46**

LUPOLI, Arturo (F) **36 7**
H: 5 7 W: 11 04 b.Brescia 24-6-87
Source: Parma. *Honours:* Italy Youth, Under-21.

2004–05	Arsenal	0	0		
2005–06	Arsenal	1	0		
2006–07	Arsenal	0	0	**1**	**0**
2006–07	*Derby Co*	35	7	**35**	**7**

MANNONE, Vito (G) **2 0**
H: 6 0 W: 11 08 b.Desio 2-3-88
Source: Atalanta.

2005–06	Arsenal	0	0		
2006–07	Arsenal	0	0		
2006–07	*Barnsley*	2	0	**2**	**0**

MERIDA PEREZ, Fran (M) **0 0**
H: 5 11 W: 13 00 b.Barcelona 4-3-90
Source: Scholar.

2006–07	Arsenal	0	0		

O'CEARUILL, Joe (D) 8 0
H: 5 11 W: 12 11 b.Edmonton 9-2-87
Source: From Watford Youth. *Honours:* Eire B, Under-21, 2 full caps.

2006–07	Arsenal	0	0		
2006–07	*Brighton & HA*	8	0	**8**	**0**

PARISIO, Carl (D) 0 0
b.Cannes 7-8-89
Source: Scholar.

2006–07	Arsenal	0	0

POOM, Mart (G) 250 1
H: 6 4 W: 14 02 b.Tallinn 3-2-72
Honours: Estonia 104 full caps.

1992–93	Flora Tallinn	11	0		
1993–94	Flora Tallinn	11	0		
1994–95	Portsmouth	0	0		
1995–96	Portsmouth	4	0		
1995–96	Flora Tallinn	7	0		
1996–97	Portsmouth	0	0	**4**	**0**
1996–97	Flora Tallinn	12	0	**41**	**0**
1996–97	Derby Co	4	0		
1997–98	Derby Co	36	0		
1998–99	Derby Co	17	0		
1999–2000	Derby Co	28	0		
2000–01	Derby Co	33	0		
2001–02	Derby Co	15	0		
2002–03	Derby Co	13	0	**146**	**0**
2002–03	Sunderland	4	0		
2003–04	Sunderland	43	1		
2004–05	Sunderland	11	0		
2005–06	Sunderland	0	0	**58**	**1**
2005–06	Arsenal	0	0		
2006–07	Arsenal	1	0	**1**	**0**

RANDALL, Mark (M) 0 0
b.Milton Keynes 28-9-89
Source: Scholar.

2006–07	Arsenal	0	0

REYES, Jose Antonio (F) 216 45
H: 5 9 W: 12 01 b.Utrera 1-9-83
Honours: Spain 21 full caps, 4 goals.

1999–2000	Sevilla B	32	1		
1999–2000	Sevilla	1	0		
2000–01	Sevilla B	0	0	**32**	**1**
2000–01	Sevilla	1	0		
2001–02	Sevilla	29	8		
2002–03	Sevilla	34	9		
2003–04	Sevilla	20	5	**85**	**22**
2003–04	Arsenal	13	2		
2004–05	Arsenal	30	9		
2005–06	Arsenal	26	5		
2006–07	Arsenal	0	0	**69**	**16**
2006–07	*Real Madrid*	30	6	**30**	**6**

ROSICKY, Tomas (M) 216 30
H: 5 10 W: 10 10 b.Prague 4-10-80
Honours: Czech Republic 62 full caps, 17 goals.

1998–99	Sparta Prague	3	0		
1999–2000	Sparta Prague	24	5		
2000–01	Sparta Prague	14	3	**41**	**8**
2000–01	Borussia Dortmund	15	0		
2001–02	Borussia Dortmund	30	5		
2002–03	Borussia Dortmund	30	3		
2003–04	Borussia Dortmund	19	2		
2004–05	Borussia Dortmund	27	4		
2005–06	Borussia Dortmund	28	5	**149**	**19**
2006–07	Arsenal	26	3	**26**	**3**

SENDEROS, Philippe (D) 73 5
H: 6 1 W: 13 10 b.Geneva 14-2-85
Honours: Switzerland Youth, Under-20, Under-21, 16 full caps, 3 goals.

2001–02	Servette	3	0		
2002–03	Servette	23	3	**26**	**3**
2003–04	Arsenal	0	0		
2004–05	Arsenal	13	0		
2005–06	Arsenal	20	2		
2006–07	Arsenal	14	0	**47**	**2**

SILVA, Gilberto (M) 174 19
H: 6 3 W: 12 04 b.Lagoa da Prata 7-10-76
Honours: Brazil 54 full caps, 3 goals.

2000	Atletico Mineiro	1	0		
2001	Atletico Mineiro	26	3	**27**	**3**
2002–03	Arsenal	35	0		
2003–04	Arsenal	32	4		
2004–05	Arsenal	13	0		
2005–06	Arsenal	33	2		
2006–07	Arsenal	34	10	**147**	**16**

SONG BILLONG, Alexandre (M) 19 0
H: 5 11 W: 12 04 b.Douala 9-9-87
Source: Bastia. *Honours:* France Youth, Cameroon Youth..

2005–06	Arsenal	5	0		
2006–07	Arsenal	2	0	**7**	**0**
2006–07	*Charlton Ath*	12	0	**12**	**0**

TOURE, Kolo (D) 166 6
H: 5 10 W: 13 08 b.Sokuora Bouake 19-3-81
Source: ASEC Mimosas. *Honours:* Ivory Coast 45 full caps, 2 goals.

2001–02	Arsenal	0	0		
2002–03	Arsenal	26	2		
2003–04	Arsenal	37	1		
2004–05	Arsenal	35	0		
2005–06	Arsenal	33	0		
2006–07	Arsenal	35	3	**166**	**6**

TRAORE, Armand (D) 0 0
H: 6 1 W: 12 12 b.Paris 8-10-89
Source: Monaco.

2006–07	Arsenal	0	0

VAN DEN BERG, Vincent (M) 0 0
b.Holland 19-1-89
Source: Heerenveen.

2006–07	Arsenal	0	0

VAN PERSIE, Robin (F) 133 35
H: 6 0 W: 11 00 b.Rotterdam 6-8-83
Honours: Holland Under-21, 19 full caps, 7 goals.

2001–02	Feyenoord	10	0		
2002–03	Feyenoord	23	8		
2003–04	Feyenoord	28	6	**61**	**14**
2004–05	Arsenal	26	5		
2005–06	Arsenal	24	5		
2006–07	Arsenal	22	11	**72**	**21**

WALCOTT, Theo (F) 37 4
H: 5 9 W: 11 01 b.Compton 16-3-89
Source: Scholar. *Honours:* England Youth, B, 1 full cap.

2005–06	Southampton	21	4	**21**	**4**
2005–06	Arsenal	0	0		
2006–07	Arsenal	16	0	**16**	**0**

Scholars
Barazite, Nacer; Dunne, James William; Fonte, Rui Pedro Da Rocha; Gibbs, Kieran James Ricardo; Hoyte, Gavin Andrew; Ogogo, Abu; Rodgers, Paul; Simpson, Jay-Alistaire Frederick; Steer, Rene; Szczesny, Wojciech Tomasz.

ASTON VILLA (3)

AGATHE, Didier (M) 193 24
H: 5 11 W: 12 00 b.Saint Pierre 16-8-75

1995–96	Montpellier	0	0		
1996–97	Ales	29	4	**29**	**4**
1997–98	Montpellier	0	0		
1998–99	Montpellier	2	0	**2**	**0**
1999–2000	Raith R	30	7	**30**	**7**
1999–2000	Hibernian	0	0		
2000–01	Hibernian	5	4	**5**	**4**
2000–01	Celtic	27	3		
2001–02	Celtic	21	1		
2002–03	Celtic	27	0		
2003–04	Celtic	27	5		
2004–05	Celtic	16	0		
2005–06	Celtic	4	0	**122**	**9**
2006–07	Aston Villa	5	0	**5**	**0**

AGBONLAHOR, Gabriel (F) 57 10
H: 5 11 W: 12 05 b.Birmingham 13-10-86
Source: Scholar. *Honours:* England Under-20, Under-21.

2005–06	Aston Villa	9	1		
2005–06	*Watford*	2	0	**2**	**0**
2005–06	*Sheffield W*	8	0	**8**	**0**
2006–07	Aston Villa	38	9	**47**	**10**

ANGEL, Juan Pablo (F) 266 89
H: 6 0 W: 12 10 b.Medellin 24-10-75
Source: Nacional. *Honours:* Colombia 33 full caps, 9 goals.

1997–98	River Plate	12	2		
1998–99	River Plate	27	11		
1999–2000	River Plate	34	19		
2000–01	River Plate	18	13	**91**	**45**
2000–01	Aston Villa	9	1		
2001–02	Aston Villa	29	12		
2002–03	Aston Villa	15	1		
2003–04	Aston Villa	33	16		
2004–05	Aston Villa	35	7		
2005–06	Aston Villa	31	3		
2006–07	Aston Villa	23	4	**175**	**44**

To New York Red Bull April 2007

BAROS, Milan (F) 171 39
H: 6 0 W: 12 00 b.Valasske Mezirici 28-10-81
Honours: Czech Republic Youth, Under-21, 57 full caps, 31 goals.

1998–99	Banik Ostrava	6	0		
1999–2000	Banik Ostrava	29	6		
2000–01	Banik Ostrava	26	5	**61**	**11**
2001–02	Liverpool	0	0		
2002–03	Liverpool	27	9		
2003–04	Liverpool	13	1		
2004–05	Liverpool	26	9		
2005–06	Liverpool	2	0	**68**	**19**
2005–06	Aston Villa	25	8		
2006–07	Aston Villa	17	1	**42**	**9**

To Lyon January 2007

BARRY, Gareth (D) 290 27
H: 5 11 W: 12 06 b.Hastings 23-2-81
Source: Trainee. *Honours:* England Youth, B, Under-21, 9 full caps.

1997–98	Aston Villa	2	0		
1998–99	Aston Villa	32	2		
1999–2000	Aston Villa	30	1		
2000–01	Aston Villa	30	0		
2001–02	Aston Villa	20	0		
2002–03	Aston Villa	35	3		
2003–04	Aston Villa	36	3		
2004–05	Aston Villa	34	7		
2005–06	Aston Villa	36	3		
2006–07	Aston Villa	35	8	**290**	**27**

BELLON, Damien (M) 0 0
H: 5 8 W: 11 05 b.St Gallen 28-8-89
Source: Scholar.

2006–07	Aston Villa	0	0

BELLON, Yago (M) 0 0
H: 5 8 W: 10 11 b.St Gallen 28-8-89
Source: Scholar.

2006–07	Aston Villa	0	0

BERGER, Patrik (M) 342 66
H: 6 1 W: 12 06 b.Prague 10-11-73
Honours: Czechoslovakia 2 full caps.Czech Republic Under-21, 44 full caps, 18 goals.

1991–92	Slavia Prague	20	3		
1992–93	Slavia Prague	29	10		
1993–94	Slavia Prague	12	4		
1994–95	Slavia Prague	28	7	**89**	**24**
1995–96	Borussia Dortmund	25	4	**25**	**4**
1996–97	Liverpool	23	6		
1997–98	Liverpool	22	3		
1998–99	Liverpool	32	7		
1999–2000	Liverpool	34	9		
2000–01	Liverpool	14	2		
2001–02	Liverpool	21	1		
2002–03	Liverpool	2	0	**148**	**28**
2003–04	Portsmouth	20	5		
2004–05	Portsmouth	32	3	**52**	**8**
2005–06	Aston Villa	8	0		
2006–07	Aston Villa	13	2	**21**	**2**
2006–07	*Stoke C*	7	0	**7**	**0**

BOUMA, Wilfred (D) 296 37
H: 5 10 W: 13 01 b.Helmond 15-6-78
Honours: Holland 24 full caps, 2 goals.

1994–95	PSV Eindhoven	1	0		
1995–96	PSV Eindhoven	4	0		
1996–97	PSV Eindhoven	1	0		
1996–97	MVV	18	7		
1997–98	MVV	33	6	**51**	**13**
1998–99	Fortuna Sittard	33	5	**33**	**5**

1999–2000	PSV Eindhoven	27	9		
2000–01	PSV Eindhoven	20	0		
2001–02	PSV Eindhoven	27	3		
2002–03	PSV Eindhoven	27	1		
2003–04	PSV Eindhoven	32	5		
2004–05	PSV Eindhoven	28	1	**167**	**19**
2005–06	Aston Villa	20	0		
2006–07	Aston Villa	25	0	**45**	**0**

BOYLE, Lee (G) 0 0
H: 5 11 W: 10 08 b.Donegal 22-1-88
Source: Scholar.

2005–06	Aston Villa	0	0		
2006–07	Aston Villa	0	0		

BRIDGES, Scott (D) 0 0
H: 5 7 W: 13 08 b.Oxford 3-5-88
Source: Scholar.

2005–06	Aston Villa	0	0		
2006–07	Aston Villa	0	0		

CAHILL, Gary (D) 54 2
H: 6 2 W: 12 06 b.Dronfield 19-12-85
Source: Trainee. *Honours:* England Youth, Under-20, Under-21.

2003–04	Aston Villa	0	0		
2004–05	Aston Villa	0	0		
2004–05	*Burnley*	27	1	**27**	**1**
2005–06	Aston Villa	7	1		
2006–07	Aston Villa	20	0	**27**	**1**

CAREW, John (F) 225 86
H: 6 5 W: 14 11 b.Lorenskog 5-9-79
Source: Lorenskog. *Honours:* Norway Youth, Under-21, 63 full caps, 17 goals.

1998	Valerenga	18	7		
1999	Valerenga	15	7	**33**	**14**
1999	Rosenborg	8	10		
2000	Rosenborg	10	8	**18**	**18**
2000–01	Valencia	37	11		
2001–02	Valencia	15	1		
2002–03	Valencia	32	8	**84**	**20**
2003–04	Roma	20	8	**20**	**8**
2004–05	Besiktas	24	13	**24**	**13**
2005–06	Lyon	26	9		
2006–07	Lyon	9	1	**35**	**10**
2006–07	Aston Villa	11	3	**11**	**3**

DAVIS, Steve (M) 91 5
H: 5 7 W: 9 07 b.Ballymena 1-1-85
Source: Scholar. *Honours:* Northern Ireland Schools, Youth, Under-21, Under-23, 20 full caps, 1 goal.

2001–02	Aston Villa	0	0		
2002–03	Aston Villa	0	0		
2003–04	Aston Villa	0	0		
2004–05	Aston Villa	28	1		
2005–06	Aston Villa	35	4		
2006–07	Aston Villa	28	0	**91**	**5**

DELANEY, Mark (D) 186 2
H: 6 1 W: 11 07 b.Haverfordwest 13-5-76
Source: Carmarthen T. *Honours:* Wales 36 full caps.

1998–99	Cardiff C	28	0	**28**	**0**
1998–99	Aston Villa	2	0		
1999–2000	Aston Villa	28	1		
2000–01	Aston Villa	19	0		
2001–02	Aston Villa	30	0		
2002–03	Aston Villa	12	0		
2003–04	Aston Villa	25	0		
2004–05	Aston Villa	30	0		
2005–06	Aston Villa	12	1		
2006–07	Aston Villa	0	0	**158**	**2**

DJEMBA-DJEMBA, Eric (M) 88 1
H: 5 8 W: 12 07 b.Douala 4-5-81
Source: Kadji Sport, UCB Douala. *Honours:* Cameroon 26 full caps, 2 goals.

2001–02	Nantes	14	0		
2002–03	Nantes	28	1	**42**	**1**
2003–04	Manchester U	15	0		
2004–05	Manchester U	5	0	**20**	**0**
2004–05	Aston Villa	6	0		
2005–06	Aston Villa	4	0		
2006–07	Aston Villa	1	0	**11**	**0**
2006–07	*Burnley*	15	0	**15**	**0**

GARDNER, Craig (M) 21 2
H: 5 10 W: 11 13 b.Solihull 25-11-86
Source: Scholar.

2004–05	Aston Villa	0	0		
2005–06	Aston Villa	8	0		
2006–07	Aston Villa	13	2	**21**	**2**

GREEN, Philip (D) 0 0
H: 5 11 W: 10 13 b.Redditch 10-3-88
Source: Scholar.

2006–07	Aston Villa	0	0		

HENDERSON, Stephen (G) 0 0
H: 6 3 W: 11 00 b.Dublin 2-5-88
Source: Scholar.

2005–06	Aston Villa	0	0		
2006–07	Aston Villa	0	0		

HENDRIE, Lee (M) 279 30
H: 5 10 W: 11 00 b.Birmingham 18-5-77
Source: Trainee. *Honours:* England Youth, Under-21, B, 1 full cap.

1993–94	Aston Villa	0	0		
1994–95	Aston Villa	0	0		
1995–96	Aston Villa	3	0		
1996–97	Aston Villa	4	0		
1997–98	Aston Villa	17	3		
1998–99	Aston Villa	32	3		
1999–2000	Aston Villa	29	1		
2000–01	Aston Villa	32	6		
2001–02	Aston Villa	29	2		
2002–03	Aston Villa	27	4		
2003–04	Aston Villa	32	2		
2004–05	Aston Villa	29	5		
2005–06	Aston Villa	16	1		
2006–07	Aston Villa	1	0	**251**	**27**
2006–07	*Stoke C*	28	3	**28**	**3**

HUGHES, Aaron (D) 259 4
H: 6 0 W: 11 02 b.Cookstown 8-11-79
Source: Trainee. *Honours:* Northern Ireland Youth, B, 54 full caps.

1996–97	Newcastle U	0	0		
1997–98	Newcastle U	4	0		
1998–99	Newcastle U	14	0		
1999–2000	Newcastle U	27	2		
2000–01	Newcastle U	35	0		
2001–02	Newcastle U	34	0		
2002–03	Newcastle U	35	1		
2003–04	Newcastle U	34	0		
2004–05	Newcastle U	22	1	**205**	**4**
2005–06	Aston Villa	35	0		
2006–07	Aston Villa	19	0	**54**	**0**

LAURSEN, Martin (D) 160 6
H: 6 2 W: 12 05 b.Farvoug 26-7-77
Honours: Denmark Youth, Under-21, 41 full caps, 1 goal.

1995–96	Silkeborg	1	0		
1996–97	Silkeborg	12	0		
1997–98	Silkeborg	22	1	**35**	**1**
1998–99	Verona	6	0		
1999–2000	Verona	19	2		
2000–01	Verona	31	0	**56**	**2**
2001–02	AC Milan	22	2		
2002–03	AC Milan	10	0		
2003–04	AC Milan	10	0	**42**	**2**
2004–05	Aston Villa	12	1		
2005–06	Aston Villa	1	0		
2006–07	Aston Villa	14	0	**27**	**1**

LUND, Eric (D) 0 0
H: 6 1 W: 12 00 b.Gothenburg 6-11-88
Source: Scholar.

2006–07	Aston Villa	0	0		

MALONEY, Shaun (M) 112 27
H: 5 7 W: 10 01 b.Miri 24-1-83
Honours: Scotland Under-20, Under-21, 6 full caps, 1 goal.

1999–2000	Celtic	0	0		
2000–01	Celtic	4	0		
2001–02	Celtic	16	5		
2002–03	Celtic	20	3		
2003–04	Celtic	17	5		
2004–05	Celtic	2	0		
2005–06	Celtic	36	13		
2006–07	Celtic	9	0	**104**	**26**
2006–07	Aston Villa	8	1	**8**	**1**

McCANN, Gavin (M) 237 11
H: 5 11 W: 11 00 b.Blackpool 10-1-78
Source: Trainee. *Honours:* England 1 full cap.

1995–96	Everton	0	0		
1996–97	Everton	0	0		
1997–98	Everton	11	0		
1998–99	Everton	0	0	**11**	**0**
1998–99	Sunderland	11	0		
1999–2000	Sunderland	24	4		
2000–01	Sunderland	22	3		
2001–02	Sunderland	29	0		
2002–03	Sunderland	30	1	**116**	**8**
2003–04	Aston Villa	28	0		
2004–05	Aston Villa	20	1		
2005–06	Aston Villa	32	1		
2006–07	Aston Villa	30	1	**110**	**3**

McGURK, Adam (F) 0 0
H: 5 9 W: 12 13 b.St Helier 24-1-89
Source: Scholar.

2005–06	Aston Villa	0	0		
2006–07	Aston Villa	0	0		

MELLBERG, Olof (D) 360 6
H: 6 1 W: 12 10 b.Amncharad 3-9-77
Honours: Sweden Under-21, 74 full caps, 3 goals.

1996	Degerfors	22	0		
1997	Degerfors	25	0	**47**	**0**
1998	AIK Stockholm	17	0	**17**	**0**
1998–99	Santander	25	0		
1999–2000	Santander	37	0		
2000–01	Santander	36	0	**98**	**0**
2001–02	Aston Villa	32	0		
2002–03	Aston Villa	38	1		
2003–04	Aston Villa	33	1		
2004–05	Aston Villa	30	3		
2005–06	Aston Villa	27	0		
2006–07	Aston Villa	38	1	**198**	**6**

MIKAELSSON, Tobias (F) 0 0
H: 6 3 W: 11 04 b.Jorlanda 17-11-88
Source: Scholar.

2005–06	Aston Villa	0	0		
2006–07	Aston Villa	0	0		

MOORE, Luke (F) 78 17
H: 5 11 W: 11 13 b.Birmingham 13-2-86
Source: Trainee. *Honours:* FA Schools, England Youth, Under-21.

2002–03	Aston Villa	0	0		
2003–04	Aston Villa	7	0		
2003–04	*Wycombe W*	6	4	**6**	**4**
2004–05	Aston Villa	25	1		
2005–06	Aston Villa	27	8		
2006–07	Aston Villa	13	4	**72**	**13**

O'HALLORAN, Stephen (D) 11 0
H: 6 0 W: 11 07 b.Cork 29-11-87
Source: Scholar. *Honours:* Eire Under-21, 2 full caps.

2005–06	Aston Villa	0	0		
2006–07	Aston Villa	0	0		
2006–07	*Wycombe W*	11	0	**11**	**0**

OLEJNIK, Robert (G) 0 0
H: 6 0 W: 15 06 b.Vienna 26-11-86
Source: Scholar.

2004–05	Aston Villa	0	0		
2005–06	Aston Villa	0	0		
2006–07	Aston Villa	0	0		

OSBOURNE, Isaiah (M) 11 0
H: 6 2 W: 12 07 b.Birmingham 5-11-87
Source: Scholar.

2005–06	Aston Villa	0	0		
2006–07	Aston Villa	11	0	**11**	**0**

PETROV, Stilian (M) 296 58
H: 5 11 W: 11 09 b.Sofia 5-7-79
Source: FC Montana. *Honours:* Bulgaria 71 full caps, 7 goals.

1997–98	CSKA Sofia	10	0		
1998–99	CSKA Sofia	29	3	**39**	**3**
1999–2000	Celtic	29	1		
2000–01	Celtic	28	7		
2001–02	Celtic	27	6		
2002–03	Celtic	34	12		
2003–04	Celtic	35	6		
2004–05	Celtic	37	11		

2005–06 Celtic 37 10 **227 53**
2006–07 Aston Villa 30 2 **30 2**

RIDGEWELL, Liam (D) 84 6
H: 5 10 W: 10 03 b.Bexley 21-7-84
Source: Scholar. *Honours:* England Youth, Under-20, Under-21.
2001–02 Aston Villa 0 0
2002–03 Aston Villa 0 0
2002–03 *Bournemouth* 5 0 **5 0**
2003–04 Aston Villa 11 0
2004–05 Aston Villa 15 0
2005–06 Aston Villa 32 5
2006–07 Aston Villa 21 1 **79 6**

SAMUEL, J Lloyd (D) 177 2
H: 5 11 W: 11 04 b.Trinidad 29-3-81
Source: Charlton Ath Trainee. *Honours:* England Youth, Under-20, Under-21.
1998–99 Aston Villa 0 0
1999–2000 Aston Villa 9 0
2000–01 Aston Villa 3 0
2001–02 *Gillingham* 8 0 **8 0**
2001–02 Aston Villa 23 0
2002–03 Aston Villa 38 0
2003–04 Aston Villa 38 2
2004–05 Aston Villa 35 0
2005–06 Aston Villa 19 0
2006–07 Aston Villa 4 0 **169 2**

SORENSEN, Thomas (G) 310 0
H: 6 4 W: 13 10 b.Fredericia 12-6-76
Source: Odense. *Honours:* Denmark Youth, Under-21, B, 64 full caps.
1998–99 Sunderland 45 0
1999–2000 Sunderland 37 0
2000–01 Sunderland 34 0
2001–02 Sunderland 34 0
2002–03 Sunderland 21 0 **171 0**
2003–04 Aston Villa 38 0
2004–05 Aston Villa 36 0
2005–06 Aston Villa 36 0
2006–07 Aston Villa 29 0 **139 0**

STIEBER, Zoltan (M) 0 0
H: 5 8 W: 9 10 b.Savar 16-10-88
Source: Scholar.
2006–07 Aston Villa 0 0

SUTTON, Chris (F) 408 148
H: 6 3 W: 13 08 b.Nottingham 10-3-73
Source: From Trainee. *Honours:* England Under-21, B, 1 full cap.
1990–91 Norwich C 2 0
1991–92 Norwich C 21 2
1992–93 Norwich C 38 8
1993–94 Norwich C 41 25 **102 35**
1994–95 Blackburn R 40 15
1995–96 Blackburn R 13 0
1996–97 Blackburn R 25 11
1997–98 Blackburn R 35 18
1998–99 Blackburn R 17 3 **130 47**
1999–2000 Chelsea 28 1 **28 1**
2000–01 Celtic 24 11
2001–02 Celtic 18 4
2002–03 Celtic 28 15
2003–04 Celtic 25 19
2004–05 Celtic 27 12
2005–06 Celtic 8 2 **130 63**
2005–06 Birmingham C 10 1
2006–07 Birmingham C 0 0 **10 1**
2006–07 Aston Villa 8 1 **8 1**

TAYLOR, Stuart (G) 56 0
H: 6 5 W: 13 07 b.Romford 28-11-80
Source: Trainee. *Honours:* FA Schools, England Youth, Under-21.
1998–99 Arsenal 0 0
1999–2000 Arsenal 0 0
1999–2000 *Bristol R* 4 0 **4 0**
2000–01 Arsenal 0 0
2000–01 *Crystal Palace* 10 0 **10 0**
2000–01 *Peterborough U* 6 0 **6 0**
2001–02 Arsenal 10 0
2002–03 Arsenal 8 0
2003–04 Arsenal 0 0
2004–05 Arsenal 0 0 **18 0**
2004–05 *Leicester C* 10 0 **10 0**
2005–06 Aston Villa 2 0
2006–07 Aston Villa 6 0 **8 0**

WILLIAMS, Sam (M) 18 3
H: 5 11 W: 10 08 b.London 9-6-87
Source: Scholar.
2004–05 Aston Villa 0 0
2005–06 Aston Villa 0 0
2005–06 *Wrexham* 15 2 **15 2**
2006–07 Aston Villa 0 0
2006–07 *Brighton & HA* 3 1 **3 1**

YOUNG, Ashley (M) 111 21
H: 5 10 W: 10 03 b.Stevenage 9-7-85
Source: Juniors. *Honours:* England Under-21.
2002–03 Watford 0 0
2003–04 Watford 5 3
2004–05 Watford 34 0
2005–06 Watford 39 13
2006–07 Watford 20 3 **98 19**
2006–07 Aston Villa 13 2 **13 2**

Scholars
Albrighton, Marc Kevin; Bannan, Barry; Bevan, David; Clancy, Steven; Clark, Ciaran; Collins, Jordan; Earls, Daniel; Griffiths, Aaron; Herd, Christopher; Hogg, Jonathan; Lowry, Shane Thomas; Parish, Elliott Charles; Ricketts, William Jonathan; Roome, Matthew John; Simmonds, Sam.

BARNET (4)

ALLEN, Oliver (F) 14 4
H: 5 9 W: 10 05 b.Essex 7-9-86
Source: Scholar.
2005–06 Birmingham C 0 0
2006–07 Birmingham C 0 0
2006–07 Barnet 14 4 **14 4**

BAILEY, Nicky (M) 89 12
H: 5 10 W: 12 06 b.Hammersmith 10-6-84
Source: Sutton U.
2005–06 Barnet 45 7
2006–07 Barnet 44 5 **89 12**

BIRCHALL, Adam (F) 71 12
H: 5 7 W: 10 09 b.Maidstone 2-12-84
Source: Trainee. *Honours:* Wales Under-21.
2002–03 Arsenal 0 0
2003–04 Arsenal 0 0
2004–05 Arsenal 0 0
2004–05 *Wycombe W* 12 4 **12 4**
2005–06 Mansfield T 31 2
2006–07 Mansfield T 5 0 **36 2**
2006–07 Barnet 23 6 **23 6**

CAREW, Ashley (M) 0 0
b.Lambeth 17-12-85
2006–07 Barnet 0 0

CHARLES, Anthony (D) 57 0
H: 6 1 W: 12 07 b.Isleworth 11-3-81
Source: Brook House.
1999–2000 Crewe Alex 0 0
2000–01 Crewe Alex 0 0
From Farnborough T
2005–06 Barnet 40 0
2006–07 Barnet 17 0 **57 0**

COGAN, Barry (F) 63 3
H: 5 9 W: 9 0 b.Sligo 4-11-84
Source: Scholar. *Honours:* Eire Under-21.
2001–02 Millwall 0 0
2002–03 Millwall 0 0
2003–04 Millwall 3 0
2004–05 Millwall 7 0
2005–06 Millwall 14 0 **24 0**
2006–07 Barnet 39 3 **39 3**

DEVERA, Joe (D) 26 0
H: 6 2 W: 12 00 b.Southgate 6-2-87
2005–06 Barnet 0 0
2006–07 Barnet 26 0 **26 0**

FLITNEY, Ross (G) 53 0
H: 6 3 W: 12 07 b.Hitchin 1-6-84
Source: Scholar.
2003–04 Fulham 0 0
2003–04 *Brighton & HA* 3 0 **3 0**
2004–05 Fulham 0 0
2004–05 *Doncaster R* 0 0
2005–06 Barnet 35 0
2006–07 Barnet 15 0 **50 0**

GRAHAM, Richard (M) 51 3
H: 5 10 W: 11 10 b.Newry 5-8-79
Source: Trainee. *Honours:* Northern Ireland Youth, Under-21.
1996–97 QPR 0 0
1997–98 QPR 0 0
1998–99 QPR 2 0
1999–2000 QPR 0 0
2000–01 QPR 0 0 **2 0**
From Chesham, Billericay, Kettering
2004–05 Barnet 0 0
2005–06 Barnet 15 1
2006–07 Barnet 34 2 **49 3**

GRAZIOLI, Giuliano (F) 199 54
H: 5 10 W: 12 00 b.Marylebone 23-3-75
Source: Wembley.
1995–96 Peterborough U 3 1
1996–97 Peterborough U 4 0
1997–98 Peterborough U 0 0
1998–99 Peterborough U 34 15 **41 16**
1999–2000 Swindon T 19 8
2000–01 Swindon T 28 2
2001–02 Swindon T 31 8 **78 18**
2002–03 Bristol R 34 11 **34 11**
2003–04 Barnet 0 0
2004–05 Barnet 0 0
2005–06 Barnet 29 7
2006–07 Barnet 17 2 **46 9**

GROSS, Adam (D) 47 1
H: 5 10 W: 10 09 b.Greenwich 16-2-86
Source: Charlton Ath Scholar.
2005–06 Barnet 20 0
2006–07 Barnet 27 1 **47 1**

HARRISON, Lee (G) 303 0
H: 6 2 W: 11 13 b.Billericay 12-9-71
Source: Trainee.
1990–91 Charlton Ath 0 0
1991–92 Charlton Ath 0 0
1991–92 *Fulham* 0 0
1991–92 *Gillingham* 2 0 **2 0**
1992–93 Charlton Ath 0 0
1992–93 *Fulham* 0 0
1993–94 Fulham 0 0
1994–95 Fulham 7 0
1995–96 Fulham 5 0 **12 0**
1996–97 Barnet 21 0
1997–98 Barnet 46 0
1998–99 Barnet 43 0
1999–2000 Barnet 43 0
2000–01 Barnet 30 0
2001–02 Barnet 0 0
2002–03 Peterborough U 12 0
2002–03 Leyton Orient 6 0
2003–04 Leyton Orient 20 0
2004–05 Leyton Orient 34 0 **60 0**
2005–06 Peterborough U 6 0 **18 0**
2006–07 Barnet 28 0 **211 0**

HATCH, Liam (F) 66 5
H: 6 4 W: 13 09 b.Hitchin 3-4-84
Source: Herne Bay, Gravesend & N.
2005–06 Barnet 35 2
2006–07 Barnet 31 3 **66 5**

HENDON, Ian (D) 414 25
H: 6 1 W: 13 02 b.Ilford 5-12-71
Source: Trainee. *Honours:* England Youth, Under-21.
1989–90 Tottenham H 0 0
1990–91 Tottenham H 2 0
1991–92 Tottenham H 2 0
1991–92 *Portsmouth* 4 0 **4 0**
1991–92 *Leyton Orient* 6 0
1992–93 Tottenham H 0 0 **4 0**
1992–93 *Barnsley* 6 0 **6 0**
1993–94 Leyton Orient 36 2
1994–95 Leyton Orient 29 0
1994–95 *Birmingham C* 4 0 **4 0**
1995–96 Leyton Orient 38 2
1996–97 Leyton Orient 28 1 **137 5**
1996–97 Notts Co 12 0
1997–98 Notts Co 38 0
1998–99 Notts Co 32 6 **82 6**
1998–99 Northampton T 7 0
1999–2000 Northampton T 44 2
2000–01 Northampton T 9 1 **60 3**

2000–01	Sheffield W	31	2		
2001–02	Sheffield W	9	0		
2002–03	Sheffield W	9	0	**49**	**2**
2002–03	Peterborough U	7	1	**7**	**1**
2004–05	Barnet	0	0		
2005–06	Barnet	35	4		
2006–07	Barnet	26	4	**61**	**8**

HESSENTHALER, Andy (M) 548 33
H: 5 7 W: 11 10 b.Gravesend 17-8-65
Source: Dartford, Redbridge Forest.

1991–92	Watford	35	1		
1992–93	Watford	45	3		
1993–94	Watford	42	5		
1994–95	Watford	43	2		
1995–96	Watford	30	0	**195**	**11**
1996–97	Gillingham	38	2		
1997–98	Gillingham	42	0		
1998–99	Gillingham	39	7		
1999–2000	Gillingham	42	5		
2000–01	Gillingham	23	2		
2001–02	Gillingham	17	0		
2002–03	Gillingham	33	1		
2003–04	Gillingham	36	2		
2004–05	Gillingham	17	0		
2004–05	*Hull C*	10	0	**10**	**0**
2005–06	Gillingham	16	1	**303**	**20**
2005–06	Barnet	16	1		
2006–07	Barnet	24	1	**40**	**2**

IOANNOU, Nicky (D) 2 0
H: 5 11 W: 11 00 b.Camden 3-7-87
Source: Scholar.

2005–06	Rushden & D	0	0		
2006–07	Barnet	2	0	**2**	**0**

JAIME RUIZ, Mikhael (G) 0 0
H: 6 1 W: 12 02 b.Merida 12-7-84
Source: Northwood.

2006–07	Barnet	0	0		

KING, Simon (D) 79 2
H: 6 0 W: 13 00 b.Oxford 11-4-83
Source: Scholar.

2000–01	Oxford U	2	0		
2001–02	Oxford U	2	0		
2002–03	Oxford U	0	0		
2003–04	Oxford U	0	0		
2004–05	Oxford U	0	0	**4**	**0**
2005–06	Barnet	32	0		
2006–07	Barnet	43	2	**75**	**2**

LEWIS, Stuart (M) 4 0
H: 5 10 W: 11 06 b.Welwyn 15-10-87
Source: Scholar.

2005–06	Tottenham H	0	0		
2006–07	Tottenham H	0	0		
2006–07	Barnet	4	0	**4**	**0**

NICOLAU, Nicky (D) 58 2
H: 5 8 W: 10 03 b.Camden 12-10-83
Source: Trainee.

2002–03	Arsenal	0	0		
2003–04	Arsenal	0	0		
2003–04	*Southend U*	9	0		
2004–05	Southend U	22	1	**31**	**1**
2005–06	Swindon T	5	0	**5**	**0**
2006–07	Barnet	22	1	**22**	**1**

NORVILLE, Jason (F) 39 3
H: 6 0 W: 11 03 b.Trinidad 9-9-83
Source: Scholar.

2001–02	Watford	2	0		
2002–03	Watford	12	1		
2003–04	Watford	0	0		
2004–05	Watford	0	0	**14**	**1**
2005–06	Barnet	22	2		
2006–07	Barnet	3	0	**25**	**2**

PUNCHEON, Jason (M) 71 6
H: 5 9 W: 12 05 b.Croydon 26-6-86
Source: Scholar.

2003–04	Wimbledon	8	0	**8**	**0**
2004–05	Milton Keynes D	25	1		
2005–06	Milton Keynes D	1	0	**26**	**1**
2006–07	Barnet	37	5	**37**	**5**

SINCLAIR, Dean (M) 88 8
H: 5 10 W: 11 03 b.St Albans 17-12-84
Source: Scholar.

2002–03	Norwich C	2	0		
2003–04	Norwich C	0	0	**2**	**0**
2004–05	Barnet	0	0		
2005–06	Barnet	44	2		
2006–07	Barnet	42	6	**86**	**8**

VIEIRA, Magno (F) 31 5
H: 5 9 W: 11 00 b.Bahia 13-2-85
Source: Juniors.

2003–04	Wigan Ath	0	0		
2003–04	*Northampton T*	10	2	**10**	**2**
2004–05	Wigan Ath	0	0		

From Carlisle U (loan).

2006–07	Barnet	21	3	**21**	**3**

WARHURST, Paul (D) 372 18
H: 6 1 W: 13 00 b.Stockport 26-9-69
Source: Trainee. *Honours:* England Under-21.

1987–88	Manchester C	0	0		
1988–89	Oldham Ath	4	0		
1989–90	Oldham Ath	30	1		
1990–91	Oldham Ath	33	1	**67**	**2**
1991–92	Sheffield W	33	0		
1992–93	Sheffield W	29	6		
1993–94	Sheffield W	4	0	**66**	**6**
1993–94	Blackburn R	9	0		
1994–95	Blackburn R	27	2		
1995–96	Blackburn R	10	0		
1996–97	Blackburn R	11	2	**57**	**4**
1997–98	Crystal Palace	22	3		
1998–99	Crystal Palace	5	1	**27**	**4**
1998–99	Bolton W	20	0		
1999–2000	Bolton W	19	0		
2000–01	Bolton W	20	0		
2001–02	Bolton W	25	0		
2002–03	Bolton W	7	0	**91**	**0**
2002–03	*Stoke C*	5	1	**5**	**1**
2003–04	Chesterfield	4	0	**4**	**0**
2003–04	Barnsley	4	0	**4**	**0**
2003–04	Carlisle U	1	0	**1**	**0**
2003–04	Grimsby T	7	0		
2004–05	Grimsby T	0	0	**7**	**0**
2004–05	Blackpool	4	0	**4**	**0**

From Forest Green R.

2005–06	Wrexham	11	1	**11**	**1**
2005–06	Barnet	9	0		
2006–07	Barnet	19	0	**28**	**0**

YAKUBU, Ismail (D) 55 2
H: 6 1 W: 13 09 b.Kano 8-4-85
Source: Trainee.

2005–06	Barnet	26	1		
2006–07	Barnet	29	1	**55**	**2**

BARNSLEY (5)

ATKINSON, Rob (D) 8 0
H: 6 1 W: 12 00 b.Beverley 29-4-87
Source: Scholar.

2003–04	Barnsley	1	0		
2004–05	Barnsley	1	0		
2005–06	Barnsley	0	0		
2006–07	Barnsley	6	0	**8**	**0**

AUSTIN, Neil (D) 148 0
H: 5 10 W: 11 09 b.Barnsley 26-4-83
Source: Trainee. *Honours:* England Youth, Under-20.

1999–2000	Barnsley	0	0		
2000–01	Barnsley	0	0		
2001–02	Barnsley	0	0		
2002–03	Barnsley	34	0		
2003–04	Barnsley	37	0		
2004–05	Barnsley	15	0		
2005–06	Barnsley	38	0		
2006–07	Barnsley	24	0	**148**	**0**

COLGAN, Nick (G) 247 0
H: 6 1 W: 12 00 b.Drogheda 19-9-73
Source: Drogheda. *Honours:* Eire Under-21, 9 full caps.

1992–93	Chelsea	0	0		
1993–94	Chelsea	0	0		
1993–94	*Crewe Alex*	0	0		
1994–95	Chelsea	0	0		
1994–95	*Grimsby T*	0	0		
1995–96	Chelsea	0	0		
1995–96	*Millwall*	0	0		
1996–97	Chelsea	1	0		
1997–98	Chelsea	0	0	**1**	**0**
1997–98	*Brentford*	5	0	**5**	**0**
1997–98	*Reading*	5	0	**5**	**0**
1998–99	Bournemouth	0	0		
1999–2000	Hibernian	24	0		
2000–01	Hibernian	37	0		
2001–02	Hibernian	30	0		
2002–03	Hibernian	30	0		
2003–04	Hibernian	0	0	**121**	**0**
2003–04	*Stockport Co*	15	0	**15**	**0**
2004–05	Barnsley	13	0		
2005–06	Barnsley	43	0		
2006–07	Barnsley	44	0	**100**	**0**

COULSON, Michael (F) 2 0
H: 5 10 W: 10 00 b.Scarborough 4-4-88
Source: Scarborough.

2006–07	Barnsley	2	0	**2**	**0**

DEVANEY, Martin (M) 282 49
H: 5 11 W: 12 00 b.Cheltenham 1-6-80
Source: Trainee.

1997–98	Coventry C	0	0		
1998–99	Coventry C	0	0		
1999–2000	Cheltenham T	26	6		
2000–01	Cheltenham T	34	10		
2001–02	Cheltenham T	25	1		
2002–03	Cheltenham T	40	6		
2003–04	Cheltenham T	40	5		
2004–05	Cheltenham T	38	10	**203**	**38**
2005–06	Watford	0	0		
2005–06	Barnsley	38	6		
2006–07	Barnsley	41	5	**79**	**11**

FERENCZI, Istvan (F) 224 84
H: 6 3 W: 13 10 b.Gyor 14-9-77
Honours: Hungary 8 full caps, 2 goals.

1995–96	Gyor	8	0		
1996–97	Gyor	8	0		
1997–98	Gyor	18	5		
1998–99	Zalaegerszeg	24	8		
1999–2000	Zalaegerszeg	12	7	**36**	**15**
1999–2000	Gyor	14	3	**48**	**8**
2000–01	MTK	31	14		
2001–02	MTK	28	14		
2001–02	Levski	4	3	**4**	**3**
2002–03	MTK	19	7	**78**	**35**
2003–04	Osnabruck	0	0		
2004–05	Vasas	15	8	**15**	**8**
2005–06	Debrecen	11	5	**11**	**5**
2006–07	Zalaergerszeg	16	5	**16**	**5**
2006–07	Barnsley	16	5	**16**	**5**

HARBAN, Thomas (D) 0 0
H: 6 0 W: 11 09 b.Barnsley 12-11-85
Source: Scholar.

2005–06	Barnsley	0	0		
2006–07	Barnsley	0	0		

HASSELL, Bobby (D) 266 7
H: 5 10 W: 12 00 b.Derby 4-6-80
Source: Trainee.

1997–98	Mansfield T	9	0		
1998–99	Mansfield T	3	0		
1999–2000	Mansfield T	11	1		
2000–01	Mansfield T	40	1		
2001–02	Mansfield T	43	1		
2002–03	Mansfield T	20	0		
2003–04	Mansfield T	34	0	**160**	**3**
2004–05	Barnsley	39	0		
2005–06	Barnsley	28	2		
2006–07	Barnsley	39	2	**106**	**4**

HAYES, Paul (F) 178 40
H: 6 0 W: 12 12 b.Dagenham 20-9-83
Source: Norwich C Scholar.

2002–03	Scunthorpe U	18	8		
2003–04	Scunthorpe U	35	2		
2004–05	Scunthorpe U	46	18	**99**	**28**
2005–06	Barnsley	45	6		
2006–07	Barnsley	30	5	**75**	**11**
2006–07	*Huddersfield T*	4	1	**4**	**1**

HEALY, Colin (M) 85 5
H: 6 1 W: 12 13 b.Cork 14-3-80
Source: Wilton U. *Honours:* Eire Youth, Under-21, 13 full caps, 1 goal.

1998–99	Celtic	3	0		
1999–2000	Celtic	10	1		
2000–01	Celtic	11	0		
2001–02	Celtic	4	0		

2001–02	*Coventry C*	17	2	**17**	**2**
2002–03	Celtic	0	0	**28**	**1**
2003–04	Sunderland	20	0		
2004–05	Sunderland	0	0	**20**	**0**
2005–06	Livingston	10	2	**10**	**2**
2006–07	Barnsley	8	0	**8**	**0**
2006–07	*Bradford C*	2	0	**2**	**0**

HECKINGBOTTOM, Paul (D) **298 11**
H: 6 0 W: 13 01 b.Barnsley 17-7-77
Source: Manchester U Trainee.

1995–96	Sunderland	0	0		
1996–97	Sunderland	0	0		
1997–98	Sunderland	0	0		
1997–98	*Scarborough*	29	0	**29**	**0**
1998–99	Sunderland	0	0		
1998–99	*Hartlepool U*	5	1	**5**	**1**
1998–99	*Darlington*	10	0		
1999–2000	Darlington	45	1		
2000–01	Darlington	18	1		
2001–02	Darlington	42	3	**115**	**5**
2002–03	Norwich C	15	0	**15**	**0**
2003–04	Bradford C	43	0	**43**	**0**
2004–05	Sheffield W	38	4		
2005–06	Sheffield W	4	0	**42**	**4**
2005–06	Barnsley	18	1		
2006–07	Barnsley	31	0	**49**	**1**

HESLOP, Simon (M) **1 0**
H: 5 11 W: 11 00 b.York 1-5-87
Source: Scholar.

2005–06	Barnsley	0	0		
2006–07	Barnsley	1	0	**1**	**0**

HOLT, Stefan (M) **0 0**
Source: Scholar.

2006–07	Barnsley	0	0		

HOWARD, Brian (M) **143 22**
H: 5 8 W: 11 00 b.Winchester 23-1-83
Source: From Trainee. *Honours:* England Schools, Youth, Under-20.

1999–2000	Southampton	0	0		
2000–01	Southampton	0	0		
2001–02	Southampton	0	0		
2002–03	Southampton	0	0		
2003–04	Swindon T	35	4		
2004–05	Swindon T	35	5	**70**	**9**
2005–06	Barnsley	31	5		
2006–07	Barnsley	42	8	**73**	**13**

JARMAN, Nathan (F) **17 0**
H: 5 11 W: 11 03 b.Scunthorpe 19-9-86
Source: Scholar.

2004–05	Barnsley	6	0		
2005–06	Barnsley	9	0		
2005–06	*Bury*	2	0	**2**	**0**
2006–07	Barnsley	0	0	**15**	**0**

JOYNES, Nathan (F) **11 1**
H: 6 1 W: 12 02 b.Hoyland 7-8-85
Source: Scholar.

2004–05	Barnsley	1	0		
2005–06	Barnsley	0	0		
2006–07	Barnsley	0	0	**1**	**0**
2006–07	*Boston U*	10	1	**10**	**1**

KAY, Antony (D) **174 11**
H: 5 11 W: 11 08 b.Barnsley 21-10-82
Source: Trainee. *Honours:* England Youth.

1999–2000	Barnsley	0	0		
2000–01	Barnsley	7	0		
2001–02	Barnsley	1	0		
2002–03	Barnsley	16	0		
2003–04	Barnsley	43	3		
2004–05	Barnsley	39	6		
2005–06	Barnsley	36	1		
2006–07	Barnsley	32	1	**174**	**11**

LAIGHT, Ryan (D) **1 0**
H: 6 2 W: 11 09 b.Barnsley 16-11-85
Source: Scholar.

2002–03	Barnsley	0	0		
2003–04	Barnsley	0	0		
2004–05	Barnsley	0	0		
2005–06	Barnsley	1	0		
2006–07	Barnsley	0	0	**1**	**0**

LETHEREN, Kyle (G) **0 0**
H: 6 2 W: 12 02 b.Swansea 26-12-87
Source: Swansea C Scholar. *Honours:* Wales Under-21.

2006–07	Barnsley	0	0		

LUCAS, David (G) **212 0**
H: 6 1 W: 13 07 b.Preston 23-11-77
Source: Trainee. *Honours:* England Youth.

1995–96	Preston NE	1	0		
1995–96	*Darlington*	6	0		
1996–97	Preston NE	2	0		
1996–97	*Darlington*	7	0	**13**	**0**
1996–97	*Scunthorpe U*	6	0	**6**	**0**
1997–98	Preston NE	6	0		
1998–99	Preston NE	30	0		
1999–2000	Preston NE	6	0		
2000–01	Preston NE	29	0		
2001–02	Preston NE	24	0		
2002–03	Preston NE	21	0		
2003–04	Preston NE	2	0	**121**	**0**
2003–04	*Sheffield W*	17	0		
2004–05	Sheffield W	34	0		
2005–06	Sheffield W	18	0		
2006–07	Sheffield W	0	0	**69**	**0**
2006–07	Barnsley	3	0	**3**	**0**

MATTIS, Dwayne (M) **169 13**
H: 6 1 W: 11 12 b.Huddersfield 31-7-81
Source: Trainee. *Honours:* Eire Under-21.

1998–99	Huddersfield T	2	0		
1999–2000	Huddersfield T	0	0		
2000–01	Huddersfield T	0	0		
2001–02	Huddersfield T	29	1		
2002–03	Huddersfield T	33	1		
2003–04	Huddersfield T	5	0	**69**	**2**
2004–05	Bury	39	5		
2005–06	Bury	36	5		
2006–07	Bury	22	1	**97**	**11**
2006–07	Barnsley	3	0	**3**	**0**

McCANN, Grant (M) **221 35**
H: 5 10 W: 11 00 b.Belfast 14-4-80
Source: Trainee. *Honours:* Northern Ireland Youth, Under-21, 15 full caps, 1 goal.

1998–99	West Ham U	0	0		
1999–2000	West Ham U	0	0		
2000–01	West Ham U	1	0		
2000–01	*Notts Co*	2	0	**2**	**0**
2000–01	*Cheltenham T*	30	3		
2001–02	West Ham U	3	0		
2002–03	West Ham U	0	0	**4**	**0**
2002–03	Cheltenham T	27	6		
2003–04	Cheltenham T	43	8		
2004–05	Cheltenham T	39	4		
2005–06	Cheltenham T	39	8		
2006–07	Cheltenham T	15	5	**193**	**34**
2006–07	Barnsley	22	1	**22**	**1**

McGRORY, Scott (F) **0 0**
H: 5 11 W: 10 11 b.Aberdeen 5-4-87
Source: Scholar.

2006–07	Barnsley	0	0		

MEYNELL, Rhys (D) **0 0**
H: 5 11 W: 12 03 b.Barnsley 17-8-88
Source: Scholar.

2006–07	Barnsley	0	0		

NARDIELLO, Daniel (F) **112 28**
H: 5 11 W: 11 04 b.Coventry 22-10-82
Source: From Trainee. *Honours:* Wales 1 full cap.

1999–2000	Manchester U	0	0		
2000–01	Manchester U	0	0		
2001–02	Manchester U	0	0		
2002–03	Manchester U	0	0		
2003–04	Manchester U	0	0		
2003–04	*Swansea C*	4	0	**4**	**0**
2003–04	*Barnsley*	16	7		
2004–05	Manchester U	0	0		
2004–05	*Barnsley*	28	7		
2005–06	Barnsley	34	5		
2006–07	Barnsley	30	9	**108**	**28**

POTTER, Luke (D) **1 0**
H: 6 2 W: 12 07 b.Barnsley 13-7-89
Source: Scholar.

2006–07	Barnsley	1	0	**1**	**0**

RAJCZI, Peter (F) **102 48**
H: 6 0 W: 12 07 b.LLenyeakoti 3-4-81
Honours: Hungary 9 full caps, 3 goals.

2003–04	Ujpest	22	6		
2004–05	Ujpest	28	13		
2005–06	Ujpest	24	23		
2006–07	Ujpest	13	4	**87**	**46**
2006–07	Barnsley	15	2	**15**	**2**

REID, Paul (D) **183 6**
H: 6 2 W: 11 08 b.Carlisle 18-2-82
Source: Trainee. *Honours:* England Youth, Under-20.

1998–99	Carlisle U	0	0		
1999–2000	Carlisle U	19	0	**19**	**0**
2000–01	Rangers	0	0		
2001–02	Rangers	0	0		
2001–02	*Preston NE*	1	1	**1**	**1**
2002–03	Rangers	0	0		
2002–03	*Northampton T*	19	0		
2003–04	Northampton T	33	2	**52**	**2**
2004–05	Barnsley	41	3		
2005–06	Barnsley	33	0		
2006–07	Barnsley	37	0	**111**	**3**

RICHARDS, Marc (F) **158 37**
H: 6 2 W: 12 06 b.Wolverhampton 8-7-82
Source: Trainee. *Honours:* England Youth, Under-20.

1999–2000	Blackburn R	0	0		
2000–01	Blackburn R	0	0		
2001–02	Blackburn R	0	0		
2001–02	*Crewe Alex*	4	0	**4**	**0**
2001–02	*Oldham Ath*	5	0	**5**	**0**
2001–02	*Halifax T*	5	0	**5**	**0**
2002–03	Blackburn R	0	0		
2002–03	*Swansea C*	17	7	**17**	**7**
2003–04	Northampton T	41	8		
2004–05	Northampton T	12	2		
2004–05	*Rochdale*	5	2	**5**	**2**
2005–06	Northampton T	0	0	**53**	**10**
2005–06	Barnsley	38	12		
2006–07	Barnsley	31	6	**69**	**18**

TOGWELL, Sam (D) **84 3**
H: 5 11 W: 12 04 b.Beaconsfield 14-10-84
Source: Scholar.

2002–03	Crystal Palace	1	0		
2003–04	Crystal Palace	0	0		
2004–05	Crystal Palace	0	0		
2004–05	*Oxford U*	4	0	**4**	**0**
2004–05	*Northampton T*	8	0	**8**	**0**
2005–06	Crystal Palace	0	0	**1**	**0**
2005–06	*Port Vale*	27	2	**27**	**2**
2006–07	Barnsley	44	1	**44**	**1**

TONGE, Dale (D) **48 0**
H: 5 10 W: 10 06 b.Doncaster 7-5-85
Source: Scholar.

2003–04	Barnsley	1	0		
2004–05	Barnsley	14	0		
2005–06	Barnsley	24	0		
2006–07	Barnsley	6	0	**45**	**0**
2006–07	*Gillingham*	3	0	**3**	**0**

WILLIAMS, Robbie (D) **75 8**
H: 5 10 W: 11 13 b.Pontefract 2-10-84
Source: Scholar.

2002–03	Barnsley	8	0		
2003–04	Barnsley	4	1		
2004–05	Barnsley	17	1		
2005–06	Barnsley	22	2		
2006–07	Barnsley	15	0	**66**	**4**
2006–07	*Blackpool*	9	4	**9**	**4**

WROE, Nicky (M) **54 1**
H: 5 11 W: 10 02 b.Sheffield 28-9-85
Source: Scholar.

2002–03	Barnsley	1	0		
2003–04	Barnsley	2	1		
2004–05	Barnsley	31	0		
2005–06	Barnsley	12	0		
2006–07	Barnsley	3	0	**49**	**1**
2006–07	*Bury*	5	0	**5**	**0**

BIRMINGHAM C (6)

ALUKO, Sone (F) 0 0
H: 5 8 W: 9 11 b.Birmingham 19-2-89
Source: Scholar. *Honours:* England Schools, Youth.

2005–06	Birmingham C	0	0		
2006–07	Birmingham C	0	0		

BIRLEY, Matt (M) 5 0
H: 5 8 W: 11 01 b.Bromsgrove 26-7-86
Source: Scholar.

2005–06	Birmingham C	1	0		
2006–07	Birmingham C	0	0	**1**	**0**
2006–07	*Lincoln C*	4	0	**4**	**0**

BLAKE, James (D) 0 0
H: 5 11 W: 12 00 b.Redditch 20-10-86
Source: Scholar.

2006–07	Birmingham C	0	0		

BURGE, Ryan (M) 0 0
H: 5 10 W: 10 03 b.Cheltenham 12-10-88
Source: Scholar.

2005–06	Birmingham C	0	0		
2006–07	Birmingham C	0	0		

CAMPBELL, Dudley (F) 66 18
H: 5 10 W: 11 00 b.London 12-11-81
Source: Aston Villa Trainee, QPR, Chesham U, Stevenage B, Yeading.

2005–06	Brentford	23	9	**23**	**9**
2005–06	Birmingham C	11	0		
2006–07	Birmingham C	32	9	**43**	**9**

CLEMENCE, Stephen (M) 211 10
H: 6 0 W: 12 09 b.Liverpool 31-3-78
Source: Trainee. *Honours:* England Schools, Youth, Under-21.

1994–95	Tottenham H	0	0		
1995–96	Tottenham H	0	0		
1996–97	Tottenham H	0	0		
1997–98	Tottenham H	17	0		
1998–99	Tottenham H	18	0		
1999–2000	Tottenham H	20	1		
2000–01	Tottenham H	29	1		
2001–02	Tottenham H	6	0		
2002–03	Tottenham H	0	0	**90**	**2**
2002–03	Birmingham C	15	2		
2003–04	Birmingham C	35	2		
2004–05	Birmingham C	22	0		
2005–06	Birmingham C	15	0		
2006–07	Birmingham C	34	4	**121**	**8**

DANNS, Neil (M) 126 25
H: 5 10 W: 10 12 b.Liverpool 23-11-82
Source: Scholar.

2000–01	Blackburn R	0	0		
2001–02	Blackburn R	0	0		
2002–03	Blackburn R	2	0		
2003–04	Blackpool	12	2	**12**	**2**
2003–04	Blackburn R	1	0		
2003–04	*Hartlepool U*	9	1	**9**	**1**
2004–05	Blackburn R	0	0	**3**	**0**
2004–05	Colchester U	32	11		
2005–06	Colchester U	41	8	**73**	**19**
2006–07	Birmingham C	29	3	**29**	**3**

DICKER, Gary (M) 68 5
H: 6 0 W: 12 00 b.Dublin 31-7-86
Honours: Eire Under-21.

2004	UCD	9	1		
2005	UCD	31	2		
2006	UCD	28	2	**68**	**5**
2006–07	Birmingham C	0	0		

DOYLE, Colin (G) 36 0
H: 6 5 W: 14 05 b.Cork 12-8-85
Honours: Eire Youth, Under-21, 1 full cap.

2004–05	Birmingham C	0	0		
2004–05	*Chester C*	0	0		
2004–05	*Nottingham F*	3	0	**3**	**0**
2005–06	Birmingham C	0	0		
2005–06	*Millwall*	14	0	**14**	**0**
2006–07	Birmingham C	19	0	**19**	**0**

FORSSELL, Mikael (F) 189 50
H: 5 10 W: 10 10 b.Steinfurt 15-3-81
Honours: Finland Youth, Under-20, Under-21, 47 full caps, 16 goals.

1997	HJK Helsinki	1	0		
1998	HJK Helsinki	16	1	**17**	**1**
1998–99	Chelsea	10	1		
1999–2000	Chelsea	0	0		
1999–2000	*Crystal Palace*	13	3		
2000–01	Chelsea	0	0		
2000–01	*Crystal Palace*	39	13	**52**	**16**
2001–02	Chelsea	22	4		
2002–03	*M'gladbach*	16	7	**16**	**7**
2002–03	Chelsea	0	0		
2003–04	Chelsea	0	0		
2003–04	*Birmingham C*	32	17		
2004–05	Chelsea	1	0	**33**	**5**
2004–05	*Birmingham C*	4	0		
2005–06	Birmingham C	27	3		
2006–07	Birmingham C	8	1	**71**	**21**

GRAY, Julian (M) 195 13
H: 6 1 W: 11 00 b.Lewisham 21-9-79
Source: Trainee.

1998–99	Arsenal	0	0		
1999–2000	Arsenal	1	0	**1**	**0**
2000–01	Crystal Palace	23	1		
2001–02	Crystal Palace	43	2		
2002–03	Crystal Palace	35	5		
2003–04	Crystal Palace	24	2	**125**	**10**
2003–04	*Cardiff C*	9	0	**9**	**0**
2004–05	Birmingham C	32	2		
2005–06	Birmingham C	21	1		
2006–07	Birmingham C	7	0	**60**	**3**

HALL, Asa (M) 12 0
H: 6 2 W: 11 09 b.Sandwell 29-11-86
Source: Scholar. *Honours:* England Youth, Under-20.

2004–05	Birmingham C	0	0		
2005–06	Birmingham C	0	0		
2005–06	*Boston U*	12	0	**12**	**0**
2006–07	Birmingham C	0	0		

HARTHILL, Oliver (M) 0 0
H: 5 11 W: 11 05 b.Birmingham 7-9-88
Source: Scholar.

2005–06	Birmingham C	0	0		
2006–07	Birmingham C	0	0		

HOWLAND, David (M) 0 0
H: 5 11 W: 10 08 b.Ballynahinch 17-9-86
Source: Scholar. *Honours:* Northern Ireland Under-21.

2004–05	Birmingham C	0	0		
2005–06	Birmingham C	0	0		
2006–07	Birmingham C	0	0		

JAIDI, Radhi (D) 81 14
H: 6 2 W: 14 00 b.Tunis 30-8-75
Source: Esperance. *Honours:* Tunisia 92 full caps, 6 goals.

2004–05	Bolton W	27	5		
2005–06	Bolton W	16	3	**43**	**8**
2006–07	Birmingham C	38	6	**38**	**6**

JEROME, Cameron (F) 111 31
H: 6 1 W: 13 06 b.Huddersfield 14-8-86
Honours: England Under-21.

2004–05	Cardiff C	29	6		
2005–06	Cardiff C	44	18	**73**	**24**
2005–06	Birmingham C	0	0		
2006–07	Birmingham C	38	7	**38**	**7**

JOHNSON, Damien (M) 232 7
H: 5 9 W: 11 09 b.Lisburn 18-11-78
Source: Trainee. *Honours:* Northern Ireland Youth, Under-21, 46 full caps.

1995–96	Blackburn R	0	0		
1996–97	Blackburn R	0	0		
1997–98	Blackburn R	0	0		
1997–98	*Nottingham F*	6	0	**6**	**0**
1998–99	Blackburn R	21	1		
1999–2000	Blackburn R	16	1		
2000–01	Blackburn R	16	0		
2001–02	Blackburn R	7	1	**60**	**3**
2001–02	Birmingham C	8	1		
2002–03	Birmingham C	30	1		
2003–04	Birmingham C	35	1		
2004–05	Birmingham C	36	0		
2005–06	Birmingham C	31	0		
2006–07	Birmingham C	26	1	**166**	**4**

KELLY, Stephen (D) 103 2
H: 6 0 W: 12 04 b.Dublin 6-9-83
Source: Juniors. *Honours:* Eire Youth, Under-21, 5 full caps.

2000–01	Tottenham H	0	0		
2001–02	Tottenham H	0	0		
2002–03	Tottenham H	0	0		
2002–03	*Southend U*	10	0	**10**	**0**
2002–03	*QPR*	7	0	**7**	**0**
2003–04	Tottenham H	11	0		
2003–04	*Watford*	13	0	**13**	**0**
2004–05	Tottenham H	17	2		
2005–06	Tottenham H	9	0	**37**	**2**
2006–07	Birmingham C	36	0	**36**	**0**

KILKENNY, Neil (M) 53 4
H: 5 8 W: 10 08 b.Enfield 19-12-85
Source: Arsenal Trainee. *Honours:* England Youth, Under-20, Australia Under-23, 1 full cap.

2003–04	Birmingham C	0	0		
2004–05	Birmingham C	0	0		
2004–05	*Oldham Ath*	27	4	**27**	**4**
2005–06	Birmingham C	18	0		
2006–07	Birmingham C	8	0	**26**	**0**

KRYSIAK, Artur (G) 0 0
H: 6 1 W: 12 08 b.Lodz 11-8-89
Source: LKS Lodz.

2006–07	Birmingham C	0	0		

LARSSON, Sebastian (M) 46 4
H: 5 11 W: 11 02 b.Eskilstuna 6-6-85
Source: From Trainee. *Honours:* Sweden Under-21.

2002–03	Arsenal	0	0		
2003–04	Arsenal	0	0		
2004–05	Arsenal	0	0		
2005–06	Arsenal	3	0		
2006–07	Arsenal	0	0	**3**	**0**
2006–07	Birmingham C	43	4	**43**	**4**

LEGZDINS, Adam (G) 0 0
H: 6 1 W: 14 02 b.Stafford 28-11-86
Source: Scholar.

2006–07	Birmingham C	0	0		

McPIKE, James (F) 0 0
H: 5 10 W: 11 02 b.Birmingham 4-10-88
Source: Scholar.

2005–06	Birmingham C	0	0		
2006–07	Birmingham C	0	0		

McSHEFFREY, Gary (F) 211 68
H: 5 8 W: 10 06 b.Coventry 13-8-82
Source: Trainee. *Honours:* England Youth, Under-20.

1998–99	Coventry C	1	0		
1999–2000	Coventry C	3	0		
2000–01	Coventry C	0	0		
2001–02	*Stockport Co*	5	1	**5**	**1**
2001–02	Coventry C	8	1		
2002–03	Coventry C	29	4		
2003–04	Coventry C	19	11		
2003–04	*Luton T*	18	9		
2004–05	Coventry C	37	12		
2004–05	*Luton T*	5	1	**23**	**10**
2005–06	Coventry C	43	15		
2006–07	Coventry C	3	1	**143**	**44**
2006–07	Birmingham C	40	13	**40**	**13**

MUAMBA, Fabrice (M) 34 0
H: 6 1 W: 11 10 b.DR Congo 6-4-88
Source: Scholar. *Honours:* England Youth.

2005–06	Arsenal	0	0		
2006–07	Arsenal	0	0		
2006–07	Birmingham C	34	0	**34**	**0**

N'GOTTY, Bruno (D) 540 25
H: 6 1 W: 13 07 b.Lyon 10-6-71
Honours: France Youth, Under-21, Under-23, B, 6 full caps.

1989–90	Lyon	27	0		
1990–91	Lyon	37	2		
1991–92	Lyon	36	1		
1992–93	Lyon	36	3		
1993–94	Lyon	36	3		
1994–95	Lyon	35	3	**207**	**12**
1995–96	Paris St Germain	24	1		
1996–97	Paris St Germain	30	4		
1997–98	Paris St Germain	26	2	**80**	**7**

1998–99	AC Milan	25	1		
1999–2000	AC Milan	9	0	**34**	**1**
1999–2000	Venezia	16	0	**16**	**0**
2000–01	Marseille	30	0	**30**	**0**
2001–02	Bolton W	26	1		
2002–03	Bolton W	23	1		
2003–04	Bolton W	33	2		
2004–05	Bolton W	37	0		
2005–06	Bolton W	29	0	**148**	**4**
2006–07	Birmingham C	25	1	**25**	**1**

NAFTI, Mehdi (M) **199** **4**
H: 5 10 W: 12 02 b.Toulouse 28-11-78
Honours: Tunisia 32 full caps, 1 goal.

1998–99	Toulouse	11	0		
1999–2000	Toulouse	13	1	**24**	**1**
2000–01	Santander B	21	0	**21**	**0**
2000–01	Santander	3	0		
2001–02	Santander	30	0		
2002–03	Santander	31	2		
2003–04	Santander	31	1		
2004–05	Santander	16	0	**111**	**3**
2004–05	Birmingham C	10	0		
2005–06	Birmingham C	1	0		
2006–07	Birmingham C	32	0	**43**	**0**

OJI, Sam (D) **9** **0**
H: 6 0 W: 14 05 b.Westminster 9-10-85

2003–04	Birmingham C	0	0		
2004–05	Birmingham C	0	0		
2005–06	Birmingham C	0	0		
2005–06	*Doncaster R*	4	0	**4**	**0**
2006–07	Birmingham C	0	0		
2006–07	*Bristol R*	5	0	**5**	**0**

PEARCE, Kaystian (D) **0** **0**
H: 6 1 W: 13 05 b.Birmingham 5-1-90
Source: Scholar.

2006–07	Birmingham C	0	0

PRICE, Jamie (M) **0** **0**
H: 5 7 W: 11 00 b.Hereford 22-7-88
Source: Scholar.

2006–07	Birmingham C	0	0

SADLER, Matthew (D) **53** **0**
H: 5 11 W: 11 08 b.Birmingham 26-2-85
Source: From Scholar. *Honours:* England Youth.

2001–02	Birmingham C	0	0		
2002–03	Birmingham C	2	0		
2003–04	Birmingham C	0	0		
2003–04	*Northampton T*	7	0	**7**	**0**
2004–05	Birmingham C	0	0		
2005–06	Birmingham C	8	0		
2006–07	Birmingham C	36	0	**46**	**0**

TAYLOR, Maik (G) **405** **0**
H: 6 4 W: 14 02 b.Hildeshein 4-9-71
Source: Farnborough T. *Honours:* Northern Ireland Under-21, B, 60 full caps.

1995–96	Barnet	45	0		
1996–97	Barnet	25	0	**70**	**0**
1996–97	Southampton	18	0		
1997–98	Southampton	0	0	**18**	**0**
1997–98	Fulham	28	0		
1998–99	Fulham	46	0		
1999–2000	Fulham	46	0		
2000–01	Fulham	44	0		
2001–02	Fulham	1	0		
2002–03	Fulham	19	0		
2003–04	Fulham	0	0	**184**	**0**
2003–04	Birmingham C	34	0		
2004–05	Birmingham C	38	0		
2005–06	Birmingham C	34	0		
2006–07	Birmingham C	27	0	**133**	**0**

TAYLOR, Martin (D) **170** **6**
H: 6 4 W: 15 00 b.Ashington 9-11-79
Source: Trainee. *Honours:* England Youth, Under-21.

1997–98	Blackburn R	0	0		
1998–99	Blackburn R	3	0		
1999–2000	Blackburn R	6	0		
1999–2000	*Darlington*	4	0	**4**	**0**
1999–2000	*Stockport Co*	7	0	**7**	**0**
2000–01	Blackburn R	16	3		
2001–02	Blackburn R	19	0		
2002–03	Blackburn R	33	2		
2003–04	Blackburn R	11	0	**88**	**5**
2003–04	Birmingham C	12	1		
2004–05	Birmingham C	7	0		
2005–06	Birmingham C	21	0		
2006–07	Birmingham C	31	0	**71**	**1**

TEBILY, Oliver (D) **140** **1**
H: 6 0 W: 13 05 b.Abidjan 19-12-75
Source: Chateauroux. *Honours:* France Under-21. Ivory Coast 18 full caps.

1997–98	Chateauroux	11	1	**11**	**1**
1998–99	Sheffield U	8	0	**8**	**0**
1999–2000	Celtic	23	0		
2000–01	Celtic	4	0		
2001–02	Celtic	11	0	**38**	**0**
2001–02	Birmingham C	7	0		
2002–03	Birmingham C	12	0		
2003–04	Birmingham C	27	0		
2004–05	Birmingham C	15	0		
2005–06	Birmingham C	16	0		
2006–07	Birmingham C	6	0	**83**	**0**

VINE, Rowan (F) **209** **48**
H: 5 11 W: 12 10 b.Basingstoke 21-9-82
Source: Scholar.

2000–01	Portsmouth	2	0		
2001–02	Portsmouth	11	0		
2002–03	Portsmouth	0	0		
2002–03	*Brentford*	42	10	**42**	**10**
2003–04	Portsmouth	0	0		
2003–04	*Colchester U*	35	6	**35**	**6**
2004–05	Portsmouth	0	0	**13**	**0**
2004–05	*Luton T*	45	9		
2005–06	Luton T	31	10		
2006–07	Luton T	26	12	**102**	**31**
2006–07	Birmingham C	17	1	**17**	**1**

WRIGHT, Nick (M) **8** **0**
H: 6 2 W: 12 00 b.Birmingham 25-11-87
Source: Scholar.

2006–07	Birmingham C	0	0		
2006–07	*Bristol C*	4	0	**4**	**0**
2006–07	*Northampton T*	4	0	**4**	**0**

BLACKBURN R (7)

BARKER, Keith (F) **12** **0**
H: 6 2 W: 12 12 b.Accrington 21-10-86
Source: Scholar. *Honours:* England Youth, Under-20.

2004–05	Blackburn R	0	0		
2005–06	Blackburn R	0	0		
2006–07	Blackburn R	0	0		
2006–07	*Rochdale*	12	0	**12**	**0**

To CS Brugge (loan) January 2006

BENTLEY, David (F) **92** **9**
H: 5 10 W: 11 03 b.Peterborough 27-8-84
Source: Scholar. *Honours:* England Youth, Under-20, Under-21, B.

2001–02	Arsenal	0	0		
2002–03	Arsenal	0	0		
2003–04	Arsenal	1	0		
2004–05	Arsenal	0	0		
2004–05	*Norwich C*	26	2	**26**	**2**
2005–06	Arsenal	0	0	**1**	**0**
2005–06	Blackburn R	29	3		
2006–07	Blackburn R	36	4	**65**	**7**

BERNER, Bruno (M) **182** **6**
H: 6 1 W: 12 13 b.Zurich 21-11-77
Honours: Switzerland Youth, Under-20, Under-21, 16 full caps.

1997–98	Grasshoppers	2	0		
1998–99	Grasshoppers	21	0		
1999–2000	Grasshoppers	6	1		
1999–2000	*Oviedo*	1	1	**1**	**1**
2000–01	Grasshoppers	27	1		
2001–02	Grasshoppers	16	0	**72**	**2**
2002–03	Freiburg	31	2		
2003–04	Freiburg	33	1		
2004–05	Freiburg	12	0	**76**	**3**
2005–06	Basle	17	0		
2006–07	Basle	15	0	**32**	**0**
2006–07	Blackburn R	1	0	**1**	**0**

BROWN, Jason (G) **127** **0**
H: 6 0 W: 15 07 b.Southwark 18-5-82
Source: Charlton Ath Scholar. *Honours:* Wales Youth, Under-21, 2 full caps.

2000–01	Gillingham	0	0		
2001–02	Gillingham	10	0		
2002–03	Gillingham	39	0		
2003–04	Gillingham	22	0		
2004–05	Gillingham	16	0		
2005–06	Gillingham	39	0	**126**	**0**
2006–07	Blackburn R	1	0	**1**	**0**

DE VITA, Raffaele (F) **0** **0**
H: 6 0 W: 11 09 b.Rome 23-9-87
Source: Scholar.

2005–06	Blackburn R	0	0
2006–07	Blackburn R	0	0

DERBYSHIRE, Matt (F) **51** **15**
H: 5 10 W: 11 01 b.Gt Harwood 14-4-86
Source: Gt Harwood T. *Honours:* England Under-21.

2003–04	Blackburn R	0	0		
2004–05	Blackburn R	1	0		
2005–06	Blackburn R	0	0		
2005–06	*Plymouth Arg*	12	0	**12**	**0**
2005–06	*Wrexham*	16	10	**16**	**10**
2006–07	Blackburn R	22	5	**23**	**5**

DUNN, David (M) **205** **37**
H: 5 9 W: 12 03 b.Gt Harwood 27-12-79
Source: Trainee. *Honours:* England Youth, Under-21, 1 full cap.

1997–98	Blackburn R	0	0		
1998–99	Blackburn R	15	1		
1999–2000	Blackburn R	22	2		
2000–01	Blackburn R	42	12		
2001–02	Blackburn R	29	7		
2002–03	Blackburn R	28	8		
2003–04	Birmingham C	21	2		
2004–05	Birmingham C	11	2		
2005–06	Birmingham C	15	2		
2006–07	Birmingham C	11	1	**58**	**7**
2006–07	Blackburn R	11	0	**147**	**30**

EMERTON, Brett (M) **324** **34**
H: 6 1 W: 13 05 b.Bankstown 22-2-79
Honours: Australia Youth, Under-20, Under-23, 57 full caps, 12 goals.

1996–97	Sydney Olympic	18	2		
1997–98	Sydney Olympic	24	3		
1998–99	Sydney Olympic	21	2		
1999–2000	Sydney Olympic	31	9	**94**	**16**
2000–01	Feyenoord	28	2		
2001–02	Feyenoord	31	6		
2002–03	Feyenoord	33	3	**92**	**11**
2003–04	Blackburn R	37	2		
2004–05	Blackburn R	37	4		
2005–06	Blackburn R	30	1		
2006–07	Blackburn R	34	0	**138**	**7**

ENCKELMAN, Peter (G) **133** **0**
H: 6 2 W: 12 05 b.Turku 10-3-77
Source: TPS Turku. *Honours:* Finland Under-21, 7 full caps.

1995	TPS Turku	6	0		
1996	TPS Turku	24	0		
1997	TPS Turku	25	0		
1998	TPS Turku	24	0	**79**	**0**
1998–99	Aston Villa	0	0		
1999–2000	Aston Villa	10	0		
2000–01	Aston Villa	0	0		
2001–02	Aston Villa	9	0		
2002–03	Aston Villa	33	0		
2003–04	Aston Villa	0	0	**52**	**0**
2003–04	Blackburn R	2	0		
2004–05	Blackburn R	0	0		
2005–06	Blackburn R	0	0		
2006–07	Blackburn R	0	0	**2**	**0**

FIELDING, Frank (G) **0** **0**
b.Blackburn 4-4-88
Source: Scholar. *Honours:* England Youth.

2006–07	Blackburn R	0	0

FRIEDEL, Brad (G) **313** **1**
H: 6 3 W: 14 00 b.Lakewood 18-5-71
Honours: USA 82 full caps.

1996	Columbus Crew	9	0		
1997	Columbus Crew	29	0	**38**	**0**
1997–98	Liverpool	11	0		
1998–99	Liverpool	12	0		
1999–2000	Liverpool	2	0		
2000–01	Liverpool	0	0	**25**	**0**
2000–01	Blackburn R	27	0		
2001–02	Blackburn R	36	0		

2002–03	Blackburn R	37	0		
2003–04	Blackburn R	36	1		
2004–05	Blackburn R	38	0		
2005–06	Blackburn R	38	0		
2006–07	Blackburn R	38	0	**250**	**1**

GALLAGHER, Paul (F) 97 17
H: 6 1 W: 11 00 b.Glasgow 9-8-84
Source: Trainee. *Honours:* Scotland Under-21, B, 1 full cap.

2002–03	Blackburn R	1	0		
2003–04	Blackburn R	26	3		
2004–05	Blackburn R	16	2		
2005–06	Blackburn R	1	0		
2005–06	*Stoke C*	37	11	**37**	**11**
2006–07	Blackburn R	16	1	**60**	**6**

GARNER, Joe (F) 18 5
H: 5 10 W: 11 02 b.Blackburn 12-4-88
Source: Scholar. *Honours:* England Schools, Youth.

2004–05	Blackburn R	0	0		
2005–06	Blackburn R	0	0		
2006–07	Blackburn R	0	0		
2006–07	*Carlisle U*	18	5	**18**	**5**

GRAY, Michael (D) 443 16
H: 5 8 W: 10 07 b.Sunderland 3-8-74
Source: Trainee. *Honours:* England 3 full caps.

1992–93	Sunderland	27	2		
1993–94	Sunderland	22	1		
1994–95	Sunderland	16	0		
1995–96	Sunderland	46	4		
1996–97	Sunderland	34	3		
1997–98	Sunderland	44	2		
1998–99	Sunderland	37	2		
1999–2000	Sunderland	33	0		
2000–01	Sunderland	36	1		
2001–02	Sunderland	35	0		
2002–03	Sunderland	32	1		
2003–04	Sunderland	1	0	**363**	**16**
2003–04	Blackburn R	14	0		
2004–05	Blackburn R	9	0		
2004–05	*Leeds U*	10	0		
2005–06	Blackburn R	30	0		
2006–07	Blackburn R	11	0	**64**	**0**
2006–07	*Leeds U*	6	0	**16**	**0**

GRIFFITHS, Rostyn (M) 0 0
H: 6 2 W: 12 08 b.Stoke 10-3-88
Source: Scholar.

2005–06	Blackburn R	0	0		
2006–07	Blackburn R	0	0		

HENCHOZ, Stephane (D) 389 3
H: 6 1 W: 12 08 b.Billens 7-9-74
Source: Bulle. *Honours:* Switzerland 72 full caps.

1992–93	Neuchatel Xamax	35	0		
1993–94	Neuchatel Xamax	21	1		
1994–95	Neuchatel Xamax	35	0	**91**	**1**
1995–96	Hamburg	31	2		
1996–97	Hamburg	18	0	**49**	**2**
1997–98	Blackburn R	36	0		
1998–99	Blackburn R	34	0		
1999–2000	Liverpool	29	0		
2000–01	Liverpool	32	0		
2001–02	Liverpool	37	0		
2002–03	Liverpool	19	0		
2003–04	Liverpool	18	0	**135**	**0**
2004–05	*Celtic*	6	0	**6**	**0**
2005–06	Wigan Ath	26	0		
2006–07	Wigan Ath	0	0	**26**	**0**
2006–07	Blackburn R	12	0	**82**	**0**

HODGE, Bryan (M) 9 0
H: 5 11 W: 11 07 b.Hamilton 23-9-87
Source: Scholar.

2004–05	Blackburn R	0	0		
2005–06	Blackburn R	0	0		
2006–07	Blackburn R	0	0		
2006–07	*Mansfield T*	9	0	**9**	**0**

JEFFERS, Francis (F) 136 29
H: 5 10 W: 11 02 b.Liverpool 25-1-81
Source: Trainee. *Honours:* England Schools, Youth, Under-21, 1 full cap, 1 goal.

1997–98	Everton	1	0		
1998–99	Everton	15	6		
1999–2000	Everton	21	6		
2000–01	Everton	12	6		
2001–02	Arsenal	6	2		
2002–03	Arsenal	16	2		
2003–04	Arsenal	0	0	**22**	**4**
2003–04	*Everton*	18	0	**67**	**18**
2004–05	Charlton Ath	20	3		
2005–06	Charlton Ath	0	0	**20**	**3**
2005–06	*Rangers*	8	0	**8**	**0**
2006–07	Blackburn R	10	0	**10**	**0**
2006–07	*Ipswich T*	9	4	**9**	**4**

JONES, Zak (G) 0 0
H: 5 11 W: 12 08 b.Darwen 24-11-88
Source: Scholar. *Honours:* England Youth.

2005–06	Blackburn R	0	0		
2006–07	Blackburn R	0	0		

JUDGE, Alan (F) 0 0
b.Dublin 11-11-88

2006–07	Blackburn R	0	0		

KANE, Tony (D) 4 0
H: 5 11 W: 11 00 b.Belfast 29-8-87
Source: Scholar. *Honours:* Eire Under-21.

2004–05	Blackburn R	0	0		
2005–06	Blackburn R	0	0		
2006–07	Blackburn R	0	0		
2006–07	*Stockport Co*	4	0	**4**	**0**

KEITA, Mamadi (M) 0 0
b. 14-11-89

2006–07	Blackburn R	0	0		

KHIZANISHVILI, Zurab (D) 173 6
H: 6 1 W: 12 08 b.Tbilisi 6-10-81
Honours: Georgia 44 full caps.

1998–99	Dynamo Tbilisi B	17	3	**17**	**3**
1998–99	Dynamo Tbilisi	2	1	**2**	**1**
1999–2000	Tbilisi	9	0	**9**	**0**
1999–2000	Lokomotivi	5	1		
2000–01	Lokomotivi	11	0	**16**	**1**
2000–01	Dundee	6	0		
2001–02	Dundee	18	0		
2002–03	Dundee	19	0	**43**	**0**
2003–04	Rangers	26	0		
2004–05	Rangers	16	0		
2005–06	Rangers	0	0	**42**	**0**
2005–06	*Blackburn R*	26	1		
2006–07	Blackburn R	18	0	**44**	**1**

McCARTHY, Benni (F) 280 137
H: 6 0 W: 12 08 b.Ciudad de Cabo 11-12-77
Honours: South Africa 65 caps, 28 goals.

1995–96	Seven Stars	29	27		
1996–97	Seven Stars	20	12	**49**	**39**
1997–98	Cape Town Spurs	7	4	**7**	**4**
1997–98	Ajax	17	9		
1998–99	Ajax	19	11	**36**	**20**
1999–2000	Celta Vigo	31	8		
2000–01	Celta Vigo	19	0		
2001–02	Celta Vigo	2	0		
2001–02	Porto	11	12		
2002–03	Celta Vigo	14	2	**66**	**10**
2003–04	Porto	29	20		
2004–05	Porto	23	11		
2005–06	Porto	23	3	**86**	**46**
2006–07	Blackburn R	36	18	**36**	**18**

MOKOENA, Aaron (D) 131 2
H: 6 2 W: 14 00 b.Johannesburg 25-11-80
Honours: South Africa 57 full caps, 1 goal.

2000–01	Ajax	0	0		
2000–01	Antwerp	6	0		
2001–02	Antwerp	13	1		
2002–03	Antwerp	29	1	**48**	**2**
2003–04	Genk	18	0	**18**	**0**
2004–05	Blackburn R	16	0		
2005–06	Blackburn R	22	0		
2006–07	Blackburn R	27	0	**65**	**0**

NELSEN, Ryan (D) 139 7
H: 5 11 W: 14 02 b.Christchurch, NZ 18-10-77
Honours: New Zealand Under-23, 28 full caps, 6 goals.

2001	DC United	19	0		
2002	DC United	20	4		
2003	DC United	25	1		
2004	DC United	17	2	**81**	**7**
2004–05	Blackburn R	15	0		
2005–06	Blackburn R	31	0		
2006–07	Blackburn R	12	0	**58**	**0**

NOLAN, Eddie (D) 4 0
H: 6 0 W: 13 05 b.Waterford 5-8-88
Source: Scholar.

2005–06	Blackburn R	0	0		
2006–07	Blackburn R	0	0		
2006–07	*Stockport Co*	4	0	**4**	**0**

NONDA, Shabani (F) 294 135
H: 6 0 W: 12 02 b.Bujumbura 6-3-77
Source: Esperance, Young Africans, Vaal Professionals. *Honours:* DR Congo 5 full caps, 1 goal.

1995–96	Zurich	10	4		
1996–97	Zurich	31	8		
1997–98	Zurich	34	24	**75**	**36**
1998–99	Rennes	32	15		
1999–2000	Rennes	30	16	**62**	**31**
2000–01	Monaco	29	12		
2001–02	Monaco	30	14		
2002–03	Monaco	35	26		
2003–04	Monaco	11	5		
2004–05	Monaco	10	0	**115**	**57**
2005–06	Roma	16	4	**16**	**4**
2006–07	Blackburn R	26	7	**26**	**7**

O'KEEFE, Josh (M) 0 0
H: 6 1 W: 11 05 b.Whalley 22-12-88
Source: Scholar.

2005–06	Blackburn R	0	0		
2006–07	Blackburn R	0	0		

OLSSON, Martin (D) 0 0
b.Sweden 17-5-88
Source: Hogaborg.

2005–06	Blackburn R	0	0		
2006–07	Blackburn R	0	0		

OOIJER, Andre (D) 319 32
H: 6 0 W: 11 13 b.Amsterdam 11-7-74
Source: SDW, SDZ, Ajax.Holland 29 full caps, 2 goals.

1994–95	Volendam	32	4	**32**	**4**
1995–96	Roda JC	23	1		
1996–97	Roda JC	33	2		
1997–98	Roda JC	19	6	**75**	**9**
1997–98	PSV Eindhoven	12	2		
1998–99	PSV Eindhoven	21	2		
1999–2000	PSV Eindhoven	18	1		
2000–01	PSV Eindhoven	20	2		
2001–02	PSV Eindhoven	26	5		
2002–03	PSV Eindhoven	32	3		
2003–04	PSV Eindhoven	15	2		
2004–05	PSV Eindhoven	24	2		
2005–06	PSV Eindhoven	24	0	**192**	**19**
2006–07	Blackburn R	20	0	**20**	**0**

PEDERSEN, Morten (F) 252 64
H: 5 11 W: 11 00 b.Vadso 8-9-81
Honours: Norway Youth, Under-21, 31 full caps, 7 goals.

2004	Tromso	18	7		
1997	Norlid	21	0		
1998	Pola	20	4	**20**	**4**
1999	Norlid	19	0	**40**	**0**
2000	Tromso	10	3		
2001	Tromso	26	5		
2002	Tromso	23	18		
2003	Tromso	26	8	**103**	**41**
2004–05	Blackburn R	19	4		
2005–06	Blackburn R	34	9		
2006–07	Blackburn R	36	6	**89**	**19**

PETER, Sergio (M) 17 0
H: 5 8 W: 11 00 b.Ludwigshafen 12-10-86
Source: Scholar. *Honours:* Germany Youth, Under-21.

2004–05	Blackburn R	0	0		
2005–06	Blackburn R	8	0		
2006–07	Blackburn R	9	0	**17**	**0**

PEZZONI, Kevin (D) 0 0
b. 22-3-89

2006–07	Blackburn R	0	0		

REID, Steven (M) 220 24
H: 6 0 W: 12 07 b.Kingston 10-3-81
Source: Trainee. *Honours:* England Youth. Eire 22 full caps, 2 goals.

1997–98	Millwall	1	0		

1998–99	Millwall	25	0		
1999–2000	Millwall	21	0		
2000–01	Millwall	37	7		
2001–02	Millwall	35	5		
2002–03	Millwall	20	6	**139**	**18**
2003–04	Blackburn R	16	0		
2004–05	Blackburn R	28	2		
2005–06	Blackburn R	34	4		
2006–07	Blackburn R	3	0	**81**	**6**

ROBERTS, Jason (F) 305 111
H: 6 0 W: 14 01 b.Park Royal 25-1-78
Source: Hayes. *Honours:* Grenada 6 full caps.

1997–98	Wolverhampton W	0	0		
1997–98	*Torquay U*	14	6	**14**	**6**
1997–98	*Bristol C*	3	1	**3**	**1**
1998–99	Bristol R	37	16		
1999–2000	Bristol R	41	22	**78**	**38**
2000–01	WBA	43	14		
2001–02	WBA	14	7		
2002–03	WBA	32	3		
2003–04	WBA	0	0	**89**	**24**
2003–04	*Portsmouth*	10	1	**10**	**1**
2003–04	Wigan Ath	14	8		
2004–05	Wigan Ath	45	21		
2005–06	Wigan Ath	34	8	**93**	**37**
2006–07	Blackburn R	18	4	**18**	**4**

SAMBA, Christopher (D) 38 2
H: 6 5 W: 13 03 b.Creteil 28-3-84
Source: Issy-les-Moulineaux, Rouen.DR Congo 20 full caps.

2001–02	Sedan	1	0		
2002–03	Sedan	0	0		
2003–04	Sedan	3	0	**4**	**0**
2004–05	Hertha Berlin	0	0		
2005–06	Hertha Berlin	12	0		
2006–07	Hertha Berlin	8	0	**20**	**0**
2006–07	Blackburn R	14	2	**14**	**2**

SAVAGE, Robbie (M) 395 30
H: 5 11 W: 11 00 b.Wrexham 18-10-74
Source: Trainee. *Honours:* Wales Schools, Youth, Under-21, 39 full caps, 2 goals.

1993–94	Manchester U	0	0		
1994–95	Crewe Alex	6	2		
1995–96	Crewe Alex	30	7		
1996–97	Crewe Alex	41	1	**77**	**10**
1997–98	Leicester C	35	2		
1998–99	Leicester C	34	1		
1999–2000	Leicester C	35	1		
2000–01	Leicester C	33	4		
2001–02	Leicester C	35	0	**172**	**8**
2002–03	Birmingham C	33	4		
2003–04	Birmingham C	31	3		
2004–05	Birmingham C	18	4	**82**	**11**
2004–05	Blackburn R	9	0		
2005–06	Blackburn R	34	1		
2006–07	Blackburn R	21	0	**64**	**1**

TAYLOR, Andy (D) 18 0
H: 5 11 W: 11 07 b.Blackburn 14-3-86
Source: Scholar. *Honours:* England Youth, Under-20.

2004–05	Blackburn R	0	0		
2005–06	Blackburn R	0	0		
2005–06	*QPR*	3	0	**3**	**0**
2005–06	*Blackpool*	3	0	**3**	**0**
2006–07	Blackburn R	0	0		
2006–07	*Crewe Alex*	4	0	**4**	**0**
2006–07	*Huddersfield T*	8	0	**8**	**0**

THOMSON, Stephen (D) 0 0
b.Edinburgh 7-3-88
Source: Scholar.

2005–06	Blackburn R	0	0		
2006–07	Blackburn R	0	0		

TODD, Andy (D) 252 10
H: 5 11 W: 13 04 b.Derby 21-9-74
Source: Trainee.

1991–92	Middlesbrough	0	0		
1992–93	Middlesbrough	0	0		
1993–94	Middlesbrough	3	0		
1994–95	Middlesbrough	5	0	**8**	**0**
1994–95	*Swindon T*	13	0	**13**	**0**
1995–96	Bolton W	12	2		
1996–97	Bolton W	15	0		
1997–98	Bolton W	25	0		
1998–99	Bolton W	20	0		
1999–2000	Bolton W	12	0	**84**	**2**
1999–2000	Charlton Ath	12	0		
2000–01	Charlton Ath	23	1		
2001–02	Charlton Ath	5	0	**40**	**1**
2001–02	*Grimsby T*	12	3	**12**	**3**
2002–03	Blackburn R	12	1		
2003–04	Blackburn R	19	0		
2003–04	*Burnley*	7	0	**7**	**0**
2004–05	Blackburn R	26	1		
2005–06	Blackburn R	22	2		
2006–07	Blackburn R	9	0	**88**	**4**

TREACY, Keith (M) 4 0
H: 6 0 W: 13 02 b.Dublin 13-9-88
Source: Scholar.

2005–06	Blackburn R	0	0		
2006–07	Blackburn R	0	0		
2006–07	*Stockport Co*	4	0	**4**	**0**

TUGAY, Kerimoglu (M) 501 45
H: 5 9 W: 11 07 b.Istanbul 24-8-70
Honours: Turkey Youth, Under-21, Under-23, 93 full caps, 2 goals.

1988–89	Galatasaray	16	0		
1989–90	Galatasaray	23	0		
1990–91	Galatasaray	12	0		
1991–92	Galatasaray	26	3		
1992–93	Galatasaray	25	6		
1993–94	Galatasaray	25	12		
1994–95	Galatasaray	23	1		
1995–96	Galatasaray	30	3		
1996–97	Galatasaray	33	4		
1997–98	Galatasaray	30	2		
1998–99	Galatasaray	22	2		
1999–2000	Galatasaray	10	1	**275**	**34**
1999–2000	Rangers	16	1		
2000–01	Rangers	26	3	**42**	**4**
2001–02	Blackburn R	33	3		
2002–03	Blackburn R	37	1		
2003–04	Blackburn R	36	1		
2004–05	Blackburn R	21	0		
2005–06	Blackburn R	27	1		
2006–07	Blackburn R	30	1	**184**	**7**

WARNOCK, Stephen (D) 109 6
H: 5 7 W: 11 09 b.Ormskirk 12-12-81
Source: Trainee. *Honours:* England Schools, Youth.

1998–99	Liverpool	0	0		
1999–2000	Liverpool	0	0		
2000–01	Liverpool	0	0		
2001–02	Liverpool	0	0		
2002–03	Liverpool	0	0		
2002–03	*Bradford C*	12	1	**12**	**1**
2003–04	Liverpool	0	0		
2003–04	*Coventry C*	44	3	**44**	**3**
2004–05	Liverpool	19	0		
2005–06	Liverpool	20	1		
2006–07	Liverpool	1	0	**40**	**1**
2006–07	Blackburn R	13	1	**13**	**1**

WINNARD, Dean (D) 0 0
b.Wigan 20-8-89

2006–07	Blackburn R	0	0		

WOODS, Ryan (M) 0 0
b.Preston 16-5-88
Source: Scholar. *Honours:* England Youth.

2005–06	Blackburn R	0	0		
2006–07	Blackburn R	0	0		

Scholars
Arestidou, Andreas; Bateson, Jonathan; Clarke, Jamie Andre; Griffiths, Brent Reece; Haworth, Andrew Alan David; Kavanagh, Conor Myles; King, Mark; McCubbin, Martin Kenneth; O'Connor, Michael Anthony; Paterson, Kris Andrew; Roberts, Joe Alexander; Skidmore, Alex William; Tuffy, Darragh Patrick.

BLACKPOOL (8)

BARKER, Shaun (D) 168 10
H: 6 2 W: 12 08 b.Nottingham 19-9-82
Source: Scholar.

2002–03	Rotherham U	11	0		
2003–04	Rotherham U	36	2		
2004–05	Rotherham U	33	2		
2005–06	Rotherham U	43	3	**123**	**7**
2006–07	Blackpool	45	3	**45**	**3**

BEAN, Marcus (M) 107 4
H: 5 11 W: 11 06 b.Hammersmith 2-11-84
Source: Scholar.

2002–03	QPR	7	0		
2003–04	QPR	31	1		
2004–05	QPR	20	1		
2004–05	*Swansea C*	8	0		
2005–06	QPR	9	0	**67**	**2**
2005–06	*Swansea C*	9	1	**17**	**1**
2005–06	Blackpool	17	1		
2006–07	Blackpool	6	0	**23**	**1**

BLINKHORN, Matthew (F) 56 5
H: 5 11 W: 10 10 b.Blackpool 2-3-85
Source: Scholar.

2001–02	Blackpool	3	0		
2002–03	Blackpool	7	2		
2003–04	Blackpool	12	1		
2004–05	Blackpool	4	0		
2004–05	*Luton T*	2	0	**2**	**0**
2005–06	Blackpool	16	2		
2006–07	Blackpool	2	0	**44**	**5**
2006–07	*Bury*	10	0	**10**	**0**

BURGESS, Ben (F) 195 63
H: 6 3 W: 14 04 b.Buxton 9-11-81
Source: Trainee. *Honours:* Eire Under-21.

1998–99	Blackburn R	0	0		
1999–2000	Blackburn R	2	0		
2000–01	Blackburn R	0	0		
2000–01	Northern Spirit	27	16	**27**	**16**
2001–02	Blackburn R	0	0	**2**	**0**
2001–02	*Brentford*	43	17	**43**	**17**
2002–03	Stockport Co	19	4	**19**	**4**
2002–03	*Oldham Ath*	7	0	**7**	**0**
2002–03	Hull C	7	4		
2003–04	Hull C	44	18		
2004–05	Hull C	2	0		
2005–06	Hull C	14	2		
2006–07	Hull C	3	0	**70**	**24**
2006–07	Blackpool	27	2	**27**	**2**

BURNS, Jamie (F) 48 1
H: 5 9 W: 10 11 b.Blackpool 6-3-84
Source: Scholar.

2002–03	Blackpool	7	0		
2003–04	Blackpool	11	0		
2004–05	Blackpool	23	0		
2005–06	Blackpool	6	1		
2005–06	*Bury*	1	0	**1**	**0**
2006–07	Blackpool	0	0	**47**	**1**

COID, Danny (D) 232 9
H: 5 11 W: 11 07 b.Liverpool 3-10-81
Source: Trainee.

1998–99	Blackpool	1	0		
1999–2000	Blackpool	21	1		
2000–01	Blackpool	46	1		
2001–02	Blackpool	27	3		
2002–03	Blackpool	36	1		
2003–04	Blackpool	35	3		
2004–05	Blackpool	35	0		
2005–06	Blackpool	13	0		
2006–07	Blackpool	18	0	**232**	**9**

DONNELLY, Ciaran (M) 41 2
H: 5 10 W: 11 08 b.Blackpool 2-4-84
Source: Scholar. *Honours:* England Youth.

2001–02	Blackburn R	0	0		
2002–03	Blackburn R	0	0		
2003–04	*Blackpool*	9	0		
2004–05	Blackburn R	0	0		
2004–05	Blackpool	8	0		
2005–06	Blackpool	24	2		
2006–07	Blackpool	0	0	**41**	**2**

DOUGHTY, Phil (D) 0 0
H: 6 2 W: 13 02 b.Kirkham 6-9-86
Source: Scholar.

2003–04	Blackpool	0	0		
2004–05	Blackpool	0	0		
2005–06	Blackpool	0	0		
2006–07	Blackpool	0	0		

EDGE, Lewis (G) 4 0
H: 6 1 W: 12 10 b.Lancaster 12-1-87
Source: Scholar.

2003–04	Blackpool	1	0		

2004–05	Blackpool	0	0		
2005–06	Blackpool	1	0		
2006–07	Blackpool	1	0	**3**	**0**
2006–07	*Bury*	1	0	**1**	**0**

EVANS, Rhys (G) **172** **0**
H: 6 1 W: 13 12 b.Swindon 27-1-82
Source: Trainee. *Honours:* England Schools, Youth, Under-20, Under-21.

1998–99	Chelsea	0	0		
1999–2000	Chelsea	0	0		
1999–2000	*Bristol R*	4	0	**4**	**0**
2000–01	Chelsea	0	0		
2001–02	Chelsea	0	0		
2001–02	*QPR*	11	0	**11**	**0**
2002–03	Chelsea	0	0		
2002–03	*Leyton Orient*	7	0	**7**	**0**
2003–04	Swindon T	41	0		
2004–05	Swindon T	45	0		
2005–06	Swindon T	32	0	**118**	**0**
2006–07	Blackpool	32	0	**32**	**0**

EVATT, Ian (D) **200** **9**
H: 6 3 W: 13 12 b.Coventry 19-11-81
Source: Trainee.

1998–99	Derby Co	0	0		
1999–2000	Derby Co	0	0		
2000–01	Derby Co	1	0		
2001–02	*Northampton T*	11	0	**11**	**0**
2001–02	Derby Co	3	0		
2002–03	Derby Co	30	0	**34**	**0**
2003–04	Chesterfield	43	5		
2004–05	Chesterfield	41	4	**84**	**9**
2005–06	QPR	27	0		
2006–07	QPR	0	0	**27**	**0**
2006–07	Blackpool	44	0	**44**	**0**

FARRELLY, Gareth (M) **188** **11**
H: 6 0 W: 12 07 b.Dublin 28-8-75
Source: Home Farm. *Honours:* Eire Under-21, 6 full caps.

1992–93	Aston Villa	0	0		
1993–94	Aston Villa	0	0		
1994–95	Aston Villa	0	0		
1994–95	*Rotherham U*	10	2		
1995–96	Aston Villa	5	0		
1996–97	Aston Villa	3	0	**8**	**0**
1997–98	Everton	26	1		
1998–99	Everton	1	0		
1999–2000	Everton	0	0	**27**	**1**
1999–2000	Bolton W	11	1		
2000–01	Bolton W	41	3		
2001–02	Bolton W	18	0		
2002–03	Bolton W	8	1		
2002–03	*Rotherham U*	6	0	**16**	**2**
2003–04	Bolton W	0	0	**78**	**5**
2003–04	*Burnley*	12	0	**12**	**0**
2003–04	*Bradford C*	14	0	**14**	**0**
2003–04	Wigan Ath	7	0	**7**	**0**
2004	Bohemians	4	0		
2005	Bohemians	21	3		
2006	Bohemians	0	0	**25**	**3**
2006–07	Blackpool	1	0	**1**	**0**

FORBES, Adrian (F) **287** **34**
H: 5 8 W: 11 10 b.Greenford 23-1-79
Source: Trainee. *Honours:* England Youth.

1996–97	Norwich C	10	0		
1997–98	Norwich C	33	4		
1998–99	Norwich C	15	0		
1999–2000	Norwich C	25	1		
2000–01	Norwich C	29	3	**112**	**8**
2001–02	Luton T	40	4		
2002–03	Luton T	5	1		
2003–04	Luton T	27	9	**72**	**14**
2004–05	Swansea C	40	7		
2005–06	Swansea C	29	4	**69**	**11**
2006–07	Blackpool	34	1	**34**	**1**

FOX, David (M) **48** **6**
H: 5 9 W: 11 08 b.Leek 13-12-83
Source: Scholar. *Honours:* England Youth, Under-20.

2000–01	Manchester U	0	0		
2001–02	Manchester U	0	0		
2002–03	Manchester U	0	0		
2003–04	Manchester U	0	0		
2004–05	Manchester U	0	0		
2004–05	*Shrewsbury T*	4	1	**4**	**1**
2005–06	Manchester U	0	0		
2005–06	Blackpool	7	1		
2006–07	Blackpool	37	4	**44**	**5**

GORKSS, Kaspars (D) **121** **6**
H: 6 3 W: 13 05 b.Riga 6-11-81
Honours: Latvia 6 full caps.

2002	Auda Riga	28	0	**28**	**0**
2003	Oster	8	0		
2004	Oster	24	1	**32**	**1**
2005	Assyriska	23	0	**23**	**0**
2006	Ventspils	28	5	**28**	**5**
2006–07	Blackpool	10	0	**10**	**0**

HOOLAHAN, Wes (M) **161** **17**
H: 5 6 W: 10 03 b.Dublin 10-8-83
Honours: Eire Under-21.

2001–02	Shelbourne	20	3		
2002–03	Shelbourne	23	0		
2004	Shelbourne	31	2		
2005	Shelbourne	29	4	**103**	**9**
2005–06	Livingston	16	0	**16**	**0**
2006–07	Blackpool	42	8	**42**	**8**

JACKSON, Mike (D) **508** **35**
H: 6 0 W: 13 08 b.Runcorn 4-12-73
Source: Trainee.

1991–92	Crewe Alex	1	0		
1992–93	Crewe Alex	4	0	**5**	**0**
1993–94	Bury	39	0		
1994–95	Bury	24	2		
1995–96	Bury	31	4		
1996–97	Bury	31	3	**125**	**9**
1996–97	Preston NE	7	0		
1997–98	Preston NE	40	2		
1998–99	Preston NE	44	8		
1999–2000	Preston NE	46	5		
2000–01	Preston NE	30	1		
2001–02	Preston NE	13	0		
2002–03	Preston NE	22	1		
2002–03	*Tranmere R*	6	0		
2003–04	Preston NE	43	0	**245**	**17**
2004–05	Tranmere R	43	5		
2005–06	Tranmere R	41	3	**90**	**8**
2006–07	Blackpool	43	1	**43**	**1**

JORGENSEN, Claus (M) **237** **34**
H: 5 10 W: 10 06 b.Holstebro 27-4-76
Source: Resen-Humlum, Struer BK, Holstebro, Aarhus, AC Horsens. *Honours:* Faroe Islands 9 full caps, 1 goal.

1999–2000	Bournemouth	44	6		
2000–01	Bournemouth	43	8		
2001–02	Bradford C	18	1		
2002–03	Bradford C	32	11	**50**	**12**
2003–04	Coventry C	8	0		
2003–04	*Bournemouth*	17	0	**104**	**14**
2004–05	Coventry C	17	3		
2005–06	Coventry C	27	3	**52**	**6**
2006–07	Blackpool	31	2	**31**	**2**

JOSEPH, Marc (D) **330** **3**
H: 6 0 W: 12 05 b.Leicester 10-11-76
Source: Trainee.

1995–96	Cambridge U	12	0		
1996–97	Cambridge U	8	0		
1997–98	Cambridge U	41	0		
1998–99	Cambridge U	29	0		
1999–2000	Cambridge U	33	0		
2000–01	Cambridge U	30	0	**153**	**0**
2001–02	Peterborough U	44	2		
2002–03	Peterborough U	17	0	**61**	**2**
2002–03	Hull C	23	0		
2003–04	Hull C	32	1		
2004–05	Hull C	29	0		
2005–06	Hull C	5	0	**89**	**1**
2005–06	*Bristol C*	3	0	**3**	**0**
2005–06	Blackpool	16	0		
2006–07	Blackpool	8	0	**24**	**0**

KAY, Matty (M) **1** **0**
H: 5 9 W: 11 00 b.Blackpool 12-10-89

2005–06	Blackpool	1	0		
2006–07	Blackpool	0	0	**1**	**0**

LAWLOR, Matthew (M) **0** **0**
b.Kirkham 20-8-88

2006–07	Blackpool	0	0		

MORRELL, Andy (F) **248** **73**
H: 5 11 W: 12 00 b.Doncaster 28-9-74
Source: Newcastle Blue Star.

1998–99	Wrexham	7	0		
1999–2000	Wrexham	13	1		
2000–01	Wrexham	20	3		
2001–02	Wrexham	25	2		
2002–03	Wrexham	45	34	**110**	**40**
2003–04	Coventry C	30	9		
2004–05	Coventry C	34	6		
2005–06	Coventry C	34	2		
2006–07	Coventry C	0	0	**98**	**17**
2006–07	Blackpool	40	16	**40**	**16**

PARKER, Keigan (F) **252** **55**
H: 5 7 W: 10 05 b.Livingston 8-6-82
Source: St Johnstone BC. *Honours:* Scotland Youth, Under-21.

1998–99	St Johnstone	2	0		
1999–2000	St Johnstone	10	2		
2000–01	St Johnstone	37	9		
2001–02	St Johnstone	21	1		
2002–03	St Johnstone	31	1		
2003–04	St Johnstone	31	8	**132**	**21**
2004–05	Blackpool	35	9		
2005–06	Blackpool	40	12		
2006–07	Blackpool	45	13	**120**	**34**

PATERSON, Sean (M) **2** **0**
H: 5 11 W: 11 05 b.Greenock 26-3-87
Source: Scholar.

2004–05	Blackpool	2	0		
2005–06	Blackpool	0	0		
2006–07	Blackpool	0	0	**2**	**0**

SOUTHERN, Keith (M) **174** **16**
H: 5 10 W: 12 06 b.Gateshead 24-4-81
Source: Trainee.

1998–99	Everton	0	0		
1999–2000	Everton	0	0		
2000–01	Everton	0	0		
2001–02	Everton	0	0		
2002–03	Everton	0	0		
2002–03	Blackpool	38	1		
2003–04	Blackpool	28	2		
2004–05	Blackpool	27	6		
2005–06	Blackpool	42	2		
2006–07	Blackpool	39	5	**174**	**16**

TIERNEY, Paul (D) **76** **1**
H: 5 10 W: 12 05 b.Salford 15-9-82
Source: Scholar. *Honours:* Eire Under-21.

2000–01	Manchester U	0	0		
2000–01	Manchester U	0	0		
2001–02	Manchester U	0	0		
2002–03	Manchester U	0	0		
2002–03	*Crewe Alex*	17	1	**17**	**1**
2003–04	Manchester U	0	0		
2003–04	*Colchester U*	2	0	**2**	**0**
2004–05	Manchester U	0	0		
2004–05	*Bradford C*	16	0	**16**	**0**
2005–06	Livingston	31	0	**31**	**0**
2006–07	Blackpool	10	0	**10**	**0**

VERNON, Scott (F) **141** **36**
H: 6 1 W: 11 06 b.Manchester 13-12-83
Source: Scholar.

2002–03	Oldham Ath	8	1		
2003–04	Oldham Ath	45	12		
2004–05	Oldham Ath	22	7	**75**	**20**
2004–05	*Blackpool*	4	3		
2005–06	Blackpool	17	1		
2005–06	*Colchester U*	7	1	**7**	**1**
2006–07	Blackpool	38	11	**59**	**15**

WILES, Simon (F) **38** **3**
H: 5 11 W: 11 04 b.Preston 22-4-85
Source: Scholar.

2003–04	Blackpool	4	0		
2004–05	Blackpool	0	0		
2005–06	Blackpool	27	3		
2006–07	Blackpool	0	0	**31**	**3**
2006–07	*Macclesfield T*	7	0	**7**	**0**

BOLTON W (9)

AL-HABSI, Ali (G) 62 0
H: 6 4 W: 12 06 b.Oman 30-12-81
Source: Al-Nasser, Al-Mudhaibi. *Honours:* Oman full caps.

2003	Lyn	13	0		
2004	Lyn	24	0		
2005	Lyn	25	0	62	0
2005–06	Bolton W	0	0		
2006–07	Bolton W	0	0		

ANELKA, Nicolas (F) 316 102
H: 6 1 W: 13 03 b.Versailles 14-3-79
Honours: France Youth, Under-21, 38 full caps, 10 goals.

1995–96	Paris St Germain	2	0		
1996–97	Paris St Germain	8	1		
1996–97	Arsenal	4	0		
1997–98	Arsenal	26	6		
1998–99	Arsenal	35	17	65	23
1999–2000	Real Madrid	19	2	19	2
2000–01	Paris St Germain	27	8		
2001–02	Paris St Germain	12	2	49	11
2001–02	Liverpool	20	4	20	4
2002–03	Manchester C	38	14		
2003–04	Manchester C	32	16		
2004–05	Manchester C	19	7	89	37
2004–05	Fenerbahce	14	4		
2005–06	Fenerbahce	25	10	39	14
2006–07	Bolton W	35	11	35	11

AUGUSTYN, Blazej (M) 0 0
H: 6 3 W: 13 00 b.Strzelin 26-1-88
Source: Scholar. *Honours:* Poland Youth.

2006–07	Bolton W	0	0

BEN HAIM, Tal (D) 174 3
H: 5 11 W: 11 09 b.Rishon Le Zion 31-3-82
Source: Maccabi Tel Aviv. *Honours:* Israel Under-21, 33 full caps.

2000–01	Maccabi Tel Aviv	1	0		
2001–02	Maccabi Tel Aviv	29	1		
2002–03	Maccabi Tel Aviv	30	0		
2003–04	Maccabi Tel Aviv	26	1	86	2
2004–05	Bolton W	21	1		
2005–06	Bolton W	35	0		
2006–07	Bolton W	32	0	88	1

CAMPO, Ivan (M) 314 19
H: 6 1 W: 12 10 b.San Sebastian 21-2-74
Honours: Spain 4 full caps.

1993–94	Alaves	11	1		
1994–95	Alaves	23	1		
1995–96	Alaves	11	0	45	2
1995–96	Valladolid	24	2	24	2
1996–97	Valencia	7	1	7	1
1997–98	Mallorca	33	1	33	1
1998–99	Real Madrid	27	1		
1999–2000	Real Madrid	20	0		
2000–01	Real Madrid	10	0		
2001–02	Real Madrid	3	0	60	1
2002–03	Bolton W	31	2		
2003–04	Bolton W	38	4		
2004–05	Bolton W	27	0		
2005–06	Bolton W	15	2		
2006–07	Bolton W	34	4	145	12

DAVIES, Kevin (F) 408 77
H: 6 0 W: 12 10 b.Sheffield 26-3-77
Source: Trainee. *Honours:* England Youth, Under-21.

1993–94	Chesterfield	24	4		
1994–95	Chesterfield	41	11		
1995–96	Chesterfield	30	4		
1996–97	Chesterfield	34	3	129	22
1996–97	Southampton	0	0		
1997–98	Southampton	25	9		
1998–99	Blackburn R	21	1		
1999–2000	Blackburn R	2	0	23	1
1999–2000	Southampton	23	6		
2000–01	Southampton	27	1		
2001–02	Southampton	23	2		
2002–03	Southampton	9	1	107	19
2002–03	*Millwall*	9	3	9	3
2003–04	Bolton W	38	9		
2004–05	Bolton W	35	8		
2005–06	Bolton W	37	7		
2006–07	Bolton W	30	8	140	32

DIAGNE-FAYE, Aboulaye (M) 153 7
H: 6 2 W: 13 10 b.Dakar 26-2-78
Source: Ndiambour Louga. *Honours:* Senegal 9 full caps, 1 goal.

2001–02	Jeanne D'Arc	32	4	32	4
2002–03	Lens	15	0		
2003–04	Lens	19	0	34	0
2004–05	Istres	28	0	28	0
2005–06	Bolton W	27	1		
2006–07	Bolton W	32	2	59	3

DIOUF, El Hadji (F) 232 39
H: 5 11 W: 11 11 b.Dakar 15-1-81
Honours: Senegal 41 full caps, 16 goals.

1998–99	Sochaux	15	0	15	0
1999–2000	Rennes	28	1	28	1
2000–01	Lens	28	8		
2001–02	Lens	26	10	54	18
2002–03	Liverpool	29	3		
2003–04	Liverpool	26	0		
2004–05	Liverpool	0	0	55	3
2004–05	*Bolton W*	27	9		
2005–06	Bolton W	20	3		
2006–07	Bolton W	33	5	80	17

FOJUT, Jaroslaw (D) 1 0
H: 6 2 W: 13 00 b.Legionowo 17-10-87
Source: Scholar. *Honours:* Poland Youth.

2005–06	Bolton W	1	0		
2006–07	Bolton W	0	0	1	0

FORTUNE, Quinton (F) 178 13
H: 5 10 W: 12 09 b.Cape Town 21-5-77
Source: Kaizer Chiefs, Tottenham H schoolboy. *Honours:* South Africa Under-23, 53 full caps, 2 goals.

1995–96	Mallorca	8	1	8	1
1995–96	Atletico Madrid	3	0		
1996–97	Atletico Madrid B	30	2		
1996–97	Atletico Madrid	2	0		
1997–98	Atletico Madrid B	31	1		
1997–98	Atletico Madrid	0	0		
1998–99	Atletico Madrid	2	0		
1998–99	Atletico Madrid B	20	4	7	0
1999–2000	Manchester U	6	2		
2000–01	Manchester U	7	2		
2001–02	Manchester U	14	1		
2002–03	Manchester U	9	0		
2003–04	Manchester U	23	0		
2004–05	Manchester U	17	0		
2005–06	Manchester U	0	0	76	5
2006–07	Bolton W	6	0	6	0

GARDNER, Ricardo (D) 257 15
H: 5 9 W: 11 00 b.St Andrews 25-9-78
Source: Harbour View. *Honours:* Jamaica 58 full caps, 4 goals.

1998–99	Bolton W	30	2		
1999–2000	Bolton W	29	5		
2000–01	Bolton W	32	3		
2001–02	Bolton W	31	3		
2002–03	Bolton W	32	2		
2003–04	Bolton W	22	0		
2004–05	Bolton W	33	0		
2005–06	Bolton W	30	0		
2006–07	Bolton W	18	0	257	15

GIANNAKOPOULOS, Stelios (M) 428 114
H: 5 8 W: 11 00 b.Athens 12-7-74
Honours: Greece 68 full caps, 12 goals.

1992–93	Ethnikos	32	6	32	6
1993–94	Paniliakos	26	9		
1994–95	Paniliakos	31	10		
1995–96	Paniliakos	27	7	84	26
1996–97	Olympiakos	31	7		
1997–98	Olympiakos	31	3		
1998–99	Olympiakos	23	7		
1999–2000	Olympiakos	29	10		
2000–01	Olympiakos	26	11		
2001–02	Olympiakos	21	11		
2002–03	Olympiakos	29	15	190	64
2003–04	Bolton W	31	2		
2004–05	Bolton W	34	7		
2005–06	Bolton W	34	9		
2006–07	Bolton W	23	0	122	18

HARSANYI, Zoltan (D) 11 1
H: 6 1 W: 12 00 b.Bratislava 1-6-87
Honours: Slovakia Youth, Under-20.

2006–07	Senec	11	1	11	1
2006–07	Bolton W	0	0		

HOWARTH, Chris (G) 3 0
H: 6 2 W: 12 10 b.Bolton 23-5-86
Source: Scholar. *Honours:* England Youth.

2005–06	Bolton W	0	0		
2005–06	*Stockport Co*	0	0		
2006–07	Bolton W	0	0		
2006–07	*Oldham Ath*	3	0	3	0

HUNT, Nicky (D) 114 1
H: 6 1 W: 13 07 b.Westhoughton 3-9-83
Source: Scholar. *Honours:* England Under-21.

2000–01	Bolton W	1	0		
2001–02	Bolton W	0	0		
2002–03	Bolton W	0	0		
2003–04	Bolton W	31	1		
2004–05	Bolton W	29	0		
2005–06	Bolton W	20	0		
2006–07	Bolton W	33	0	114	1

JAASKELAINEN, Jussi (G) 435 0
H: 6 3 W: 12 10 b.Vaasa 19-4-75
Honours: Finland Youth, Under-21, 34 full caps.

1992	MP	6	0		
1993	MP	6	0		
1994	MP	26	0		
1995	MP	26	0	64	0
1996	VPS	27	0		
1997	VPS	27	0	54	0
1997–98	Bolton W	0	0		
1998–99	Bolton W	34	0		
1999–2000	Bolton W	34	0		
2000–01	Bolton W	27	0		
2001–02	Bolton W	34	0		
2002–03	Bolton W	38	0		
2003–04	Bolton W	38	0		
2004–05	Bolton W	36	0		
2005–06	Bolton W	38	0		
2006–07	Bolton W	38	0	317	0

KAZIMIERCZAK, Prezemek (G) 8 0
H: 6 0 W: 12 02 b.Lodz 22-2-88
Source: Scholar.

2006–07	Bolton W	0	0		
2006–07	*Accrington S*	8	0	8	0

MARTIN, Cesar (D) 227 10
H: 6 1 W: 12 11 b.Oviedo 2-4-77
Honours: Spain Under-21, 12 full caps, 2 goals.

1994–95	Oviedo	2	0		
1994–95	Oviedo B	29	3		
1995–96	Oviedo	20	1		
1996–97	Oviedo	19	0		
1997–98	Oviedo	29	1		
1998–99	Oviedo	31	4	101	6
1999–2000	La Coruna	11	1		
2000–01	La Coruna	8	0		
2001–02	La Coruna	17	0		
2002–03	La Coruna	20	0		
2003–04	La Coruna	16	0		
2004–05	La Coruna	14	0		
2005–06	La Coruna	7	0	93	1
2006–07	Levante	3	0	3	0
2006–07	Bolton W	1	0	1	0

MEITE, Abdoulaye (D) 155 2
H: 6 1 W: 12 13 b.Paris 6-10-80
Honours: Ivory Coast 20 full caps.

1998–99	Red Star 93	4	1		
1999–2000	Red Star 93	0	0	4	1
2000–01	Marseille	1	0		
2001–02	Marseille	10	0		
2002–03	Marseille	28	0		
2003–04	Marseille	30	0		
2004–05	Marseille	34	1		
2005–06	Marseille	13	0	116	1
2006–07	Bolton W	35	0	35	0

MICHALIK, Lubomir (D) 31 4
H: 6 4 W: 13 00 b.Cadca 13-8-83
Source: Cadca, Martin. *Honours:* Slovakia 2 full caps, 1 goal.

2005–06	Senec	8	1		
2006–07	Senec	12	1	20	2
2006–07	*Leeds U*	7	1	7	1
2006–07	Bolton W	4	1	4	1

NOLAN, Kevin (M) 243 35
H: 6 0 W: 14 00 b.Liverpool 24-6-82
Source: Scholar. *Honours:* England Youth, Under-20, Under-21.

1999–2000	Bolton W	4	0		
2000–01	Bolton W	31	1		
2001–02	Bolton W	35	8		
2002–03	Bolton W	33	1		
2003–04	Bolton W	37	9		
2004–05	Bolton W	36	4		
2005–06	Bolton W	36	9		
2006–07	Bolton W	31	3	**243**	**35**

O'BRIEN, Joey (M) 39 2
H: 5 11 W: 10 13 b.Dublin 17-2-86
Source: Scholar. *Honours:* Eire Youth, Under-21, 1 full cap.

2004–05	Bolton W	1	0		
2004–05	*Sheffield W*	15	2	**15**	**2**
2005–06	Bolton W	23	0		
2006–07	Bolton W	0	0	**24**	**0**

OBADEYI, Temitope (M) 0 0
b.Birmingham
Source: Coventry C.

2006–07	Bolton W	0	0		

PEDERSEN, Henrik (F) 265 84
H: 6 1 W: 13 03 b.Copenhagen 10-6-75
Honours: Denmark 3 full caps.

1995–96	Silkeborg	12	4		
1996–97	Silkeborg	2	0		
1997–98	Silkeborg	15	9		
1998–99	Silkeborg	33	16		
1999–2000	Silkeborg	28	13		
2000–01	Silkeborg	32	20	**122**	**62**
2001–02	Bolton W	11	0		
2002–03	Bolton W	33	7		
2003–04	Bolton W	33	7		
2004–05	Bolton W	27	6		
2005–06	Bolton W	21	1		
2006–07	Bolton W	18	1	**143**	**22**

SINCLAIR, James (F) 2 0
H: 5 6 W: 10 05 b.Newcastle 22-10-87
Source: Scholar.

2005–06	Bolton W	0	0		
2006–07	Bolton W	2	0	**2**	**0**

SISSONS, Robert (M) 0 0
H: 5 8 W: 11 02 b.Stockport 29-9-88
Source: Scholar. *Honours:* England Youth.

2005–06	Bolton W	0	0		
2006–07	Bolton W	0	0		

SMITH, Johann (M) 15 1
H: 5 11 W: 12 06 b.Hartford 25-4-87
Source: Scholar. *Honours:* USA Youth.

2005–06	Bolton W	0	0		
2006–07	Bolton W	1	0	**1**	**0**
2006–07	*Carlisle U*	14	1	**14**	**1**

SPEED, Gary (M) 626 97
H: 5 10 W: 12 10 b.Deeside 8-9-69
Source: Trainee. *Honours:* Wales Youth, Under-21, 85 full caps, 7 goals.

1988–89	Leeds U	1	0		
1989–90	Leeds U	25	3		
1990–91	Leeds U	38	7		
1991–92	Leeds U	41	7		
1992–93	Leeds U	39	7		
1993–94	Leeds U	36	10		
1994–95	Leeds U	39	3		
1995–96	Leeds U	29	2	**248**	**39**
1996–97	Everton	37	9		
1997–98	Everton	21	7	**58**	**16**
1997–98	Newcastle U	13	1		
1998–99	Newcastle U	38	4		
1999–2000	Newcastle U	36	9		
2000–01	Newcastle U	35	5		
2001–02	Newcastle U	29	5		
2002–03	Newcastle U	24	2		
2003–04	Newcastle U	38	3	**213**	**29**
2004–05	Bolton W	38	1		
2005–06	Bolton W	31	4		
2006–07	Bolton W	38	8	**107**	**13**

TAL, Idan (M) 221 39
H: 5 10 W: 10 13 b.Petah Tikva 13-9-75
Source: Hapoel Jerusalem. *Honours:* Israel Under-21, 64 full caps, 5 goals.

1996–97	Maccabi Petah T	27	1		
1997–98	Maccabi Petah T	29	6		
1998–99	Maccabi Petah T	15	3		
1998–99	Hapoel Tel Aviv	14	2	**14**	**2**
1999–2000	Merida	36	5	**36**	**5**
2000–01	Maccabi Petah T	7	1	**78**	**11**
2000–01	Everton	22	2		
2001–02	Everton	7	0	**29**	**2**
2002–03	Maccabi Haifa	16	6		
2003–04	Maccabi Haifa	0	0		
2004–05	Maccabi Haifa	32	13		
2005–06	Maccabi Haifa	0	0	**48**	**19**
2006–07	Bolton W	16	0	**16**	**0**

TEIMOURIAN, Andranik (M) 17 2
H: 5 11 W: 11 07 b.Tehran 6-3-83
Source: Ararat, Keshavirz, Esteghal, Oghab, ABV Moslem. *Honours:* Iran 19 full caps, 1 goal.

2006–07	Bolton W	17	2	**17**	**2**

THOMPSON, David (M) 218 27
H: 5 7 W: 10 00 b.Birkenhead 12-9-77
Source: Trainee. *Honours:* England Youth, Under-21.

1994–95	Liverpool	0	0		
1995–96	Liverpool	0	0		
1996–97	Liverpool	2	0		
1997–98	Liverpool	5	1		
1997–98	*Swindon T*	10	0	**10**	**0**
1998–99	Liverpool	14	1		
1999–2000	Liverpool	27	3	**48**	**5**
2000–01	Coventry C	25	3		
2001–02	Coventry C	37	12		
2002–03	Coventry C	4	0	**66**	**15**
2002–03	Blackburn R	23	4		
2003–04	Blackburn R	11	1		
2004–05	Blackburn R	24	0		
2005–06	Blackburn R	6	0	**64**	**5**
2005–06	Wigan Ath	10	2	**10**	**2**
2006–07	Portsmouth	12	0	**12**	**0**
2006–07	Bolton W	8	0	**8**	**0**

VAZ TE, Ricardo (F) 61 3
H: 6 2 W: 12 07 b.Lisbon 1-10-86
Source: Trainee. *Honours:* Portugal Youth, Under-20, Under-21.

2003–04	Bolton W	1	0		
2004–05	Bolton W	7	0		
2005–06	Bolton W	22	3		
2006–07	Bolton W	25	0	**55**	**3**
2006–07	*Hull C*	6	0	**6**	**0**

WALKER, Ian (G) 401 0
H: 6 2 W: 13 01 b.Watford 31-10-71
Source: Trainee. *Honours:* England Youth, Under-21, B, 4 full caps.

1989–90	Tottenham H	0	0		
1990–91	Tottenham H	1	0		
1990–91	*Oxford U*	2	0	**2**	**0**
1990–91	*Ipswich T*	0	0		
1991–92	Tottenham H	18	0		
1992–93	Tottenham H	17	0		
1993–94	Tottenham H	11	0		
1994–95	Tottenham H	41	0		
1995–96	Tottenham H	38	0		
1996–97	Tottenham H	37	0		
1997–98	Tottenham H	29	0		
1998–99	Tottenham H	25	0		
1999–2000	Tottenham H	38	0		
2000–01	Tottenham H	4	0	**259**	**0**
2001–02	Leicester C	35	0		
2002–03	Leicester C	46	0		
2003–04	Leicester C	37	0		
2004–05	Leicester C	22	0	**140**	**0**
2005–06	Bolton W	0	0		
2006–07	Bolton W	0	0		

Scholars
Basham, Christopher Paul; Brooks, Tom Michael; Cassidy, Matthew Stephen; Charlesworth, Mark; Ellis, Mark Ian; Gbemie, David; Jamieson, Scott; Lainton, Robert; Sheridan, Samuel; Sinclair, James Alexander; Thompson, Leslie; Wolze, Kevin; Woolfe, Nathan Bret.

BOSTON U (10)

ALBRIGHTON, Mark (D) 85 4
H: 6 1 W: 12 07 b.Nuneaton 6-3-76
Source: Atherstone U, Nuneaton B, Telford U.

2003–04	Doncaster R	28	3		
2004–05	Doncaster R	17	1		
2005–06	Doncaster R	16	0	**61**	**4**
2005–06	*Chester C*	9	0	**9**	**0**
2006–07	Boston U	12	0	**12**	**0**
2006–07	*Darlington*	3	0	**3**	**0**

CANOVILLE, Lee (D) 180 3
H: 6 1 W: 12 00 b.Ealing 14-3-81
Source: Trainee. *Honours:* FA Schools, England Youth.

1998–99	Arsenal	0	0		
1999–2000	Arsenal	0	0		
2000–01	Arsenal	0	0		
2000–01	*Northampton T*	2	0	**2**	**0**
2001–02	Torquay U	12	1		
2002–03	Torquay U	36	0		
2003–04	Torquay U	33	1		
2004–05	Torquay U	31	0	**112**	**2**
2005–06	Boston U	43	1		
2006–07	Boston U	16	0	**59**	**1**
2006–07	*Shrewsbury T*	7	0	**7**	**0**

CLARKE, Jamie (D) 149 5
H: 6 2 W: 12 03 b.Sunderland 18-9-82
Source: Scholar.

2001–02	Mansfield T	1	0		
2002–03	Mansfield T	21	1		
2003–04	Mansfield T	12	0	**34**	**1**
2004–05	Rochdale	41	1		
2005–06	Rochdale	22	0	**63**	**1**
2005–06	Boston U	15	1		
2006–07	Boston U	37	2	**52**	**3**

COOKSEY, Ernie (M) 140 12
H: 5 6 W: 12 04 b.Bishop's Stortford 11-6-80
Source: Crawley T.

2003–04	Oldham Ath	36	4		
2004–05	Oldham Ath	1	0	**37**	**4**
2004–05	Rochdale	34	5		
2005–06	Rochdale	34	3		
2006–07	Rochdale	19	0	**87**	**8**
2006–07	Boston U	16	0	**16**	**0**

COTTON, Daniel (M) 2 0
H: 5 7 W: 10 12 b.Stamford 8-4-88
Source: Blackstones.

2006–07	Boston U	2	0	**2**	**0**

CRYAN, Colin (D) 61 0
H: 5 9 W: 11 08 b.Dublin 23-3-81
Source: From Scholar. *Honours:* Eire Under-21.

1999–2000	Sheffield U	0	0		
2000–01	Sheffield U	1	0		
2001–02	Sheffield U	1	0		
2002–03	Sheffield U	2	0		
2003–04	Sheffield U	1	0		
2004–05	Sheffield U	0	0	**5**	**0**
2005–06	Lincoln C	37	0		
2006–07	Lincoln C	4	0	**41**	**0**
2006–07	Boston U	15	0	**15**	**0**

DAVIDSON, Robert (F) 11 0
H: 5 8 W: 11 09 b.Rutherglen 25-3-86
Source: Rangers.

2003–04	Rangers	1	0		
2004–05	Rangers	1	0		
2005–06	Rangers	0	0	**2**	**0**
2006–07	Boston U	9	0	**9**	**0**

ELLENDER, Paul (D) 179 8
H: 6 1 W: 12 07 b.Scunthorpe 21-10-74
Source: Trainee.

1992–93	Scunthorpe U	0	0		
1993–94	Scunthorpe U	0	0		
From Altrincham, Scarborough					
2002–03	Boston U	26	0		
2003–04	Boston U	42	4		
2004–05	Boston U	39	2		
2005–06	Boston U	25	1		
2005–06	*Chester C*	5	0	**5**	**0**
2006–07	Boston U	42	1	**174**	**8**

FARRELL, Dave (M) **447** **52**
H: 5 11 W: 11 08 b.Birmingham 11-11-71
Source: Redditch U.

1992–93	Aston Villa	2	0		
1992–93	*Scunthorpe U*	5	1	**5**	**1**
1993–94	Aston Villa	4	0		
1994–95	Aston Villa	0	0		
1995–96	Aston Villa	0	0	**6**	**0**
1995–96	Wycombe W	33	7		
1996–97	Wycombe W	27	1	**60**	**8**
1997–98	Peterborough U	42	6		
1998–99	Peterborough U	37	4		
1999–2000	Peterborough U	35	3		
2000–01	Peterborough U	44	7		
2001–02	Peterborough U	38	6		
2002–03	Peterborough U	37	3		
2003–04	Peterborough U	44	5		
2004–05	Peterborough U	31	2		
2005–06	Peterborough U	29	6	**337**	**42**
2006–07	Boston U	39	1	**39**	**1**

FORBES, Nathan (M) **1** **0**
H: 5 5 W: 10 00 b.Sheffield 29-12-89
Source: Scholar.

2006–07	Boston U	1	0	**1**	**0**

GALBRAITH, David (M) **71** **3**
H: 5 8 W: 11 03 b.Luton 20-12-83
Source: Trainee.

2003–04	Tottenham H	0	0		
2003–04	Northampton T	0	0		
2004–05	Northampton T	25	1		
2005–06	Northampton T	4	0	**29**	**1**
2005–06	Boston U	12	0		
2006–07	Boston U	30	2	**42**	**2**

GREAVES, Mark (D) **335** **15**
H: 6 1 W: 13 00 b.Hull 22-1-75
Source: Brigg Town.

1996–97	Hull C	30	2		
1997–98	Hull C	25	2		
1998–99	Hull C	25	0		
1999–2000	Hull C	38	3		
2000–01	Hull C	30	2		
2001–02	Hull C	26	1		
2002–03	Hull C	3	0	**177**	**10**
2002–03	Boston U	26	1		
2003–04	Boston U	37	0		
2004–05	Boston U	22	0		
2005–06	Boston U	34	1		
2006–07	Boston U	39	3	**158**	**5**

GREEN, Francis (F) **253** **37**
H: 5 9 W: 11 04 b.Nottingham 25-4-80
Source: Ilkeston T.

1997–98	Peterborough U	4	1		
1998–99	Peterborough U	7	1		
1999–2000	Peterborough U	20	1		
2000–01	Peterborough U	32	6		
2001–02	Peterborough U	23	3		
2002–03	Peterborough U	19	2		
2003–04	Peterborough U	3	0	**108**	**14**
2003–04	Lincoln C	35	7		
2004–05	Lincoln C	37	8		
2005–06	Lincoln C	28	3	**100**	**18**
2005–06	*Boston U*	6	1		
2006–07	Boston U	39	4	**45**	**5**

HOLLAND, Chris (M) **279** **2**
H: 5 9 W: 11 05 b.Clitheroe 11-9-75
Source: Trainee. *Honours:* England Youth, Under-21.

1993–94	Preston NE	1	0	**1**	**0**
1993–94	Newcastle U	3	0		
1994–95	Newcastle U	0	0		
1995–96	Newcastle U	0	0		
1996–97	Newcastle U	0	0	**3**	**0**
1996–97	Birmingham C	32	0		
1997–98	Birmingham C	10	0		
1998–99	Birmingham C	14	0		
1999–2000	Birmingham C	14	0	**70**	**0**
1999–2000	Huddersfield T	17	1		
2000–01	Huddersfield T	29	0		
2001–02	Huddersfield T	37	1		
2002–03	Huddersfield T	34	0		
2003–04	Huddersfield T	3	0	**120**	**2**
2003–04	Boston U	5	0		
2004–05	Boston U	32	0		
2005–06	Boston U	34	0		
2006–07	Boston U	14	0	**85**	**0**

MARRIOTT, Andy (G) **457** **0**
H: 6 2 W: 13 07 b.Sutton-in-Ashfield 11-10-70
Source: Trainee. *Honours:* England Schools, FA Schools, Youth, Under-21, Wales 5 full caps.

1988–89	Arsenal	0	0		
1989–90	Nottingham F	0	0		
1989–90	WBA	3	0	**3**	**0**
1989–90	*Blackburn R*	2	0	**2**	**0**
1989–90	*Colchester U*	10	0	**10**	**0**
1990–91	Nottingham F	0	0		
1991–92	Nottingham F	6	0		
1991–92	*Burnley*	15	0	**15**	**0**
1992–93	Nottingham F	5	0		
1993–94	Nottingham F	0	0	**11**	**0**
1993–94	Wrexham	36	0		
1994–95	Wrexham	46	0		
1995–96	Wrexham	46	0		
1996–97	Wrexham	43	0		
1997–98	Wrexham	42	0		
1998–99	Wrexham	0	0	**213**	**0**
1998–99	Sunderland	1	0		
1999–2000	Sunderland	1	0		
2000–01	Sunderland	0	0	**2**	**0**
2000–01	*Wigan Ath*	0	0		
2000–01	Barnsley	0	0		
2001–02	Barnsley	18	0		
2002–03	Barnsley	36	0	**54**	**0**
2002–03	Birmingham C	1	0	**1**	**0**
2003–04	Beira Mar	24	0	**24**	**0**
2004–05	Bury	19	0	**19**	**0**
2004–05	Torquay U	11	0		
2005–06	Torquay U	46	0	**57**	**0**
2006–07	Boston U	46	0	**46**	**0**

MAYLETT, Brad (M) **173** **10**
H: 5 8 W: 10 04 b.Manchester 24-12-80
Source: Trainee.

1998–99	Burnley	17	0		
1999–2000	Burnley	0	0		
2000–01	Burnley	12	0		
2001–02	Burnley	10	0		
2002–03	Burnley	6	0	**45**	**0**
2002–03	*Swansea C*	6	0		
2003–04	Swansea C	33	5		
2004–05	Swansea C	16	0	**55**	**5**
2004–05	*Boston U*	9	3		
2005–06	Boston U	38	1		
2006–07	Boston U	21	0	**68**	**4**
2006–07	*Chester C*	5	1	**5**	**1**

NUNN, Ben (D) **1** **0**
H: 5 8 W: 10 00 b.Cambridge 25-10-89
Source: Scholar.

2006–07	Boston U	1	0	**1**	**0**

ROWNTREE, Adam (F) **3** **0**
H: 5 7 W: 11 02 b.Lincoln 23-11-88
Source: Scholar.

2006–07	Boston U	3	0	**3**	**0**

RUSK, Simon (M) **105** **8**
H: 5 11 W: 12 08 b.Peterborough 17-12-81
Source: Peterborough U.

2002–03	Boston U	18	2		
2003–04	Boston U	19	0		
2004–05	Boston U	31	3		
2005–06	Boston U	34	3		
2006–07	Boston U	3	0	**105**	**8**

RYAN, Richie (M) **28** **0**
H: 5 10 W: 10 07 b.Kilkenny 6-1-85
Source: Scholar.

2001–02	Sunderland	0	0		
2002–03	Sunderland	2	0		
2003–04	Sunderland	0	0		
2004–05	Sunderland	0	0	**2**	**0**
2004–05	*Scunthorpe U*	0	0		
2005–06	Scunthorpe U	13	0	**13**	**0**
2006–07	Boston U	13	0	**13**	**0**

STEVENS, Jamie (D) **12** **2**
H: 5 11 W: 11 05 b.Holbeach 25-2-89
Source: Scholar.

2006–07	Boston U	12	2	**12**	**2**

TAIT, Paul (F) **214** **30**
H: 6 2 W: 12 05 b.Newcastle 24-10-74
Source: Trainee.

1993–94	Everton	0	0		
1994–95	Wigan Ath	5	0		
1995–96	Wigan Ath	0	0	**5**	**0**
From Northwich Vic.					
1999–2000	Crewe Alex	33	6		
2000–01	Crewe Alex	18	0		
2001–02	*Hull C*	2	0	**2**	**0**
2001–02	Crewe Alex	12	0	**63**	**6**
2002–03	Bristol R	41	7		
2003–04	Bristol R	33	12	**74**	**19**
2004–05	Rochdale	36	2		
2005–06	Rochdale	11	1	**47**	**3**
2005–06	Chester C	9	0	**9**	**0**
2006–07	Boston U	14	2	**14**	**2**

TALBOT, Stewart (M) **356** **24**
H: 6 0 W: 13 07 b.Birmingham 14-6-73
Source: Doncaster R, Moor Green.

1994–95	Port Vale	2	0		
1995–96	Port Vale	20	0		
1996–97	Port Vale	34	4		
1997–98	Port Vale	42	6		
1998–99	Port Vale	33	0		
1999–2000	Port Vale	6	0	**137**	**10**
2000–01	Rotherham U	38	5		
2001–02	Rotherham U	38	1		
2002–03	Rotherham U	15	1		
2002–03	*Shrewsbury T*	5	0	**5**	**0**
2003–04	Rotherham U	23	1	**114**	**8**
2003–04	Brentford	15	2		
2004–05	Brentford	37	1	**52**	**3**
2005–06	Boston U	30	2		
2006–07	Boston U	18	1	**48**	**3**

VAUGHAN, Stephen (D) **65** **0**
H: 5 6 W: 11 11 b.Liverpool 22-1-85
Source: Scholar.

2001–02	Liverpool	0	0		
2002–03	Liverpool	0	0		
2003–04	Liverpool	0	0		
2004–05	Chester C	21	0		
2005–06	Chester C	17	0		
2006–07	Chester C	20	0	**58**	**0**
2006–07	Boston U	7	0	**7**	**0**

BOURNEMOUTH (11)

ALLEN, Curtis (F) **0** **0**
H: 5 9 W: 10 03 b.Belfast 22-2-88
Source: Scholar.

2006–07	Bournemouth	0	0		

ANDERTON, Darren (M) **433** **51**
H: 6 1 W: 12 05 b.Southampton 3-3-72
Source: From Trainee. *Honours:* England Youth, Under-21, B, 30 full caps, 7 goals.

1989–90	Portsmouth	0	0		
1990–91	Portsmouth	20	0		
1991–92	Portsmouth	42	7	**62**	**7**
1992–93	Tottenham H	34	6		
1993–94	Tottenham H	37	6		
1994–95	Tottenham H	37	5		
1995–96	Tottenham H	8	2		
1996–97	Tottenham H	16	3		
1997–98	Tottenham H	15	0		
1998–99	Tottenham H	32	3		
1999–2000	Tottenham H	22	3		
2000–01	Tottenham H	23	2		
2001–02	Tottenham H	35	3		
2002–03	Tottenham H	20	0		
2003–04	Tottenham H	20	1	**299**	**34**
2004–05	Birmingham C	20	3		
2005–06	Birmingham C	0	0	**20**	**3**
2005–06	Wolverhampton W	24	1	**24**	**1**
2006–07	Bournemouth	28	6	**28**	**6**

BROADHURST, Karl (D) **192** **3**
H: 6 1 W: 11 07 b.Portsmouth 18-3-80
Source: Trainee.

1998–99	Bournemouth	0	0		
1999–2000	Bournemouth	16	0		
2000–01	Bournemouth	30	0		
2001–02	Bournemouth	23	0		
2002–03	Bournemouth	21	1		
2003–04	Bournemouth	39	1		

2004–05	Bournemouth	29	1		
2005–06	Bournemouth	7	0		
2006–07	Bournemouth	27	0	**192**	**3**

BROWNING, Marcus (M) **480 24**
H: 6 0 W: 12 10 b.Bristol 22-4-71
Source: Trainee. *Honours:* Wales 5 full caps.

1989–90	Bristol R	1	0		
1990–91	Bristol R	0	0		
1991–92	Bristol R	11	0		
1992–93	Bristol R	19	1		
1992–93	*Hereford U*	7	5	**7**	**5**
1993–94	Bristol R	31	4		
1994–95	Bristol R	41	2		
1995–96	Bristol R	45	4		
1996–97	Bristol R	26	2	**174**	**13**
1996–97	Huddersfield T	13	0		
1997–98	Huddersfield T	14	0		
1998–99	Huddersfield T	6	0	**33**	**0**
1998–99	Gillingham	4	0		
1999–2000	Gillingham	1	0		
2000–01	Gillingham	31	0		
2001–02	Gillingham	42	3	**78**	**3**
2002–03	Bournemouth	43	1		
2003–04	Bournemouth	42	0		
2004–05	Bournemouth	40	0		
2005–06	Bournemouth	42	0		
2006–07	Bournemouth	21	2	**188**	**3**

CLARIDGE, Steve (F) **641 194**
H: 6 0 W: 12 10 b.Portsmouth 10-4-66
Source: Portsmouth, Fareham T.

1984–85	Bournemouth	6	1		
1985–86	Bournemouth	1	0		
From Weymouth, Basingstoke T					
1988–89	Crystal Palace	0	0		
1988–89	Aldershot	37	9		
1989–90	Aldershot	25	10	**62**	**19**
1989–90	Cambridge U	20	4		
1990–91	Cambridge U	30	12		
1991–92	Cambridge U	29	12		
1992–93	Luton T	16	2	**16**	**2**
1992–93	Cambridge U	29	7		
1993–94	Cambridge U	24	11	**132**	**46**
1993–94	Birmingham C	18	7		
1994–95	Birmingham C	42	20		
1995–96	Birmingham C	28	8	**88**	**35**
1995–96	Leicester C	14	5		
1996–97	Leicester C	32	11		
1997–98	Leicester C	17	0	**63**	**16**
1997–98	*Portsmouth*	10	2		
1997–98	Wolverhampton W	5	0	**5**	**0**
1998–99	Portsmouth	39	9		
1999–2000	Portsmouth	34	14		
2000–01	Portsmouth	31	11	**114**	**36**
2000–01	*Millwall*	6	3		
2001–02	Millwall	41	17		
2002–03	Millwall	44	9	**91**	**29**
From Weymouth					
2004–05	Brighton & HA	5	0	**5**	**0**
2004–05	Brentford	4	0	**4**	**0**
2004–05	*Wycombe W*	19	4	**19**	**4**
2005–06	Gillingham	1	0	**1**	**0**
2005–06	Bradford C	26	5	**26**	**5**
2005–06	*Walsall*	7	1	**7**	**1**
2006–07	Bournemouth	1	0	**8**	**1**

COOKE, Stephen (M) **73 4**
H: 5 8 W: 9 02 b.Walsall 15-2-83
Source: Scholar. *Honours:* England Youth, Under-20.

1999–2000	Aston Villa	0	0		
2000–01	Aston Villa	0	0		
2001–02	Aston Villa	0	0		
2001–02	*Bournemouth*	7	0		
2002–03	Aston Villa	3	0		
2003–04	Aston Villa	0	0		
2003–04	*Bournemouth*	3	0		
2004–05	Aston Villa	0	0	**3**	**0**
2004–05	*Wycombe W*	6	0	**6**	**0**
2005–06	Bournemouth	31	2		
2006–07	Bournemouth	10	1	**51**	**3**
2006–07	*Torquay U*	13	1	**13**	**1**

COOPER, Shaun (D) **94 0**
H: 5 10 W: 10 05 b.Newport (IW) 5-10-83
Source: School.

2000–01	Portsmouth	0	0		
2001–02	Portsmouth	7	0		
2002–03	Portsmouth	0	0		
2003–04	Portsmouth	0	0		
2003–04	*Leyton Orient*	9	0	**9**	**0**
2004–05	Portsmouth	0	0		
2004–05	*Kidderminster H*	10	0	**10**	**0**
2005–06	Portsmouth	0	0	**7**	**0**
2005–06	Bournemouth	35	0		
2006–07	Bournemouth	33	0	**68**	**0**

COUTTS, James (M) **12 0**
H: 5 6 W: 9 01 b.Weymouth 15-4-87
Source: Southampton Juniors.

2004–05	Bournemouth	1	0		
2005–06	Bournemouth	11	0		
2006–07	Bournemouth	0	0	**12**	**0**

CUMMINGS, Warren (D) **150 5**
H: 5 9 W: 11 05 b.Aberdeen 15-10-80
Source: Trainee. *Honours:* Scotland Under-21, 1 full cap.

1999–2000	Chelsea	0	0		
2000–01	Chelsea	0	0		
2000–01	*Bournemouth*	10	1		
2000–01	*WBA*	3	0		
2001–02	Chelsea	0	0		
2001–02	*WBA*	14	0	**17**	**0**
2002–03	Chelsea	0	0		
2002–03	Bournemouth	20	0		
2003–04	Bournemouth	42	2		
2004–05	Bournemouth	30	2		
2005–06	Bournemouth	0	0		
2006–07	Bournemouth	31	0	**133**	**5**

FLETCHER, Steve (F) **525 92**
H: 6 2 W: 14 09 b.Hartlepool 26-7-72
Source: Trainee.

1990–91	Hartlepool U	14	2		
1991–92	Hartlepool U	18	2	**32**	**4**
1992–93	Bournemouth	31	4		
1993–94	Bournemouth	36	6		
1994–95	Bournemouth	40	6		
1995–96	Bournemouth	7	1		
1996–97	Bournemouth	35	7		
1997–98	Bournemouth	42	12		
1998–99	Bournemouth	39	8		
1999–2000	Bournemouth	36	7		
2000–01	Bournemouth	45	9		
2001–02	Bournemouth	2	0		
2002–03	Bournemouth	35	5		
2003–04	Bournemouth	41	9		
2004–05	Bournemouth	36	9		
2005–06	Bournemouth	27	4		
2006–07	Bournemouth	41	1	**493**	**88**

FOLEY-SHERIDAN, Steven (M) **53 6**
H: 5 4 W: 9 00 b.Dublin 10-2-86
Source: Trainee. *Honours:* Eire Youth.

2002–03	Aston Villa	0	0		
2003–04	Aston Villa	0	0		
2004–05	Aston Villa	0	0		
2005–06	Aston Villa	0	0		
2005–06	Bournemouth	35	5		
2006–07	Bournemouth	18	1	**53**	**6**

GOWLING, Josh (D) **59 1**
H: 6 3 W: 12 08 b.Coventry 29-11-83
Source: WBA Scholar.

2004–05	Herfolge	13	0	**13**	**0**
2005–06	Bournemouth	13	0		
2006–07	Bournemouth	33	1	**46**	**1**

HART, Callum (D) **47 0**
H: 6 0 W: 11 00 b.Cardiff 21-12-85
Source: Bristol C Scholar.

2005–06	Bournemouth	39	0		
2006–07	Bournemouth	8	0	**47**	**0**

HAYTER, James (F) **358 94**
H: 5 9 W: 10 13 b.Newport (IW) 9-4-79
Source: Trainee.

1996–97	Bournemouth	2	0		
1997–98	Bournemouth	5	0		
1998–99	Bournemouth	20	2		
1999–2000	Bournemouth	31	2		
2000–01	Bournemouth	40	11		
2001–02	Bournemouth	44	7		
2002–03	Bournemouth	45	9		
2003–04	Bournemouth	44	14		
2004–05	Bournemouth	39	19		
2005–06	Bournemouth	46	20		
2006–07	Bournemouth	42	10	**358**	**94**

HOLLANDS, Danny (M) **43 2**
H: 6 0 W: 11 11 b.Ashford 6-11-85
Source: Trainee.

2003–04	Chelsea	0	0		
2004–05	Chelsea	0	0		
2005–06	Chelsea	0	0		
2005–06	*Torquay U*	10	1	**10**	**1**
2006–07	Bournemouth	33	1	**33**	**1**

HOWE, Eddie (D) **272 12**
H: 5 11 W: 11 10 b.Amersham 29-11-77
Source: Trainee. *Honours:* England Under-21.

1995–96	Bournemouth	5	0		
1996–97	Bournemouth	13	0		
1997–98	Bournemouth	40	1		
1998–99	Bournemouth	45	2		
1999–2000	Bournemouth	28	1		
2000–01	Bournemouth	31	2		
2001–02	Bournemouth	38	4		
2001–02	Portsmouth	1	0		
2002–03	Portsmouth	1	0		
2003–04	Portsmouth	0	0		
2003–04	*Swindon T*	0	0		
2004–05	Portsmouth	0	0	**2**	**0**
2004–05	Bournemouth	35	1		
2005–06	Bournemouth	20	0		
2006–07	Bournemouth	15	1	**270**	**12**

MAHER, Shaun (D) **183 7**
H: 6 2 W: 13 06 b.Dublin 20-6-78
Source: Bohemians.

1996–97	Bohemians	2	0		
1997–98	Fulham	0	0		
1997–98	Bohemians	11	0		
1998–99	Bohemians	25	1		
1999–2000	Bohemians	28	1		
2000–01	Bohemians	0	0	**66**	**2**
2001–02	Bournemouth	31	0		
2002–03	Bournemouth	8	2		
2003–04	Bournemouth	29	1		
2004–05	Bournemouth	36	2		
2005–06	Bournemouth	6	0		
2006–07	Bournemouth	7	0	**117**	**5**

McQUOID, Josh (M) **2 0**
H: 5 9 W: 10 10 b.Southampton 15-12-89
Source: Scholar.

2006–07	Bournemouth	2	0	**2**	**0**

MOSS, Neil (G) **211 0**
H: 6 0 W: 13 10 b.New Milton 10-5-75
Source: Trainee.

1992–93	Bournemouth	1	0		
1993–94	Bournemouth	6	0		
1994–95	Bournemouth	8	0		
1995–96	Bournemouth	7	0		
1995–96	Southampton	0	0		
1996–97	Southampton	3	0		
1997–98	Southampton	0	0		
1997–98	*Gillingham*	10	0	**10**	**0**
1998–99	Southampton	7	0		
1999–2000	Southampton	9	0		
2000–01	Southampton	3	0		
2001–02	Southampton	2	0		
2002–03	Southampton	0	0	**24**	**0**
2002–03	Bournemouth	33	0		
2003–04	Bournemouth	46	0		
2004–05	Bournemouth	46	0		
2005–06	Bournemouth	4	0		
2006–07	Bournemouth	26	0	**177**	**0**

PITMAN, Brett (M) **48 6**
H: 6 0 W: 11 00 b.Jersey 31-1-88

2005–06	Bournemouth	19	1		
2006–07	Bournemouth	29	5	**48**	**6**

PLATT, Conal (F) **0 0**
H: 5 10 W: 11 07 b.Preston 14-10-86
Source: Liverpool.

2006–07	Bournemouth	0	0		

PURCHES, Stephen (D) **244 10**
H: 5 11 W: 11 13 b.Ilford 14-1-80

1998–99	West Ham U	0	0		
1999–2000	West Ham U	0	0		
2000–01	Bournemouth	34	0		
2001–02	Bournemouth	41	2		
2002–03	Bournemouth	44	3		
2003–04	Bournemouth	42	3		

2004–05	Bournemouth	14	1		
2005–06	Bournemouth	26	0		
2006–07	Bournemouth	43	1	**244**	**10**

STANDING, Michael (M) **83 6**
H: 5 10 W: 10 07 b.Shoreham 20-3-81
Source: Trainee. *Honours:* England Schools.

1997–98	Aston Villa	0	0		
1998–99	Aston Villa	0	0		
1999–2000	Aston Villa	0	0		
2000–01	Aston Villa	0	0		
2001–02	Aston Villa	0	0		
2001–02	Bradford C	0	0		
2002–03	Bradford C	24	2		
2003–04	Bradford C	6	0	**30**	**2**
2004–05	Walsall	32	4		
2005–06	Walsall	20	0	**52**	**4**
2006–07	Bournemouth	1	0	**1**	**0**

STEWART, Gareth (G) **146 0**
H: 6 0 W: 12 08 b.Preston 3-2-80
Source: Trainee. *Honours:* England Schools, Youth.

1996–97	Blackburn R	0	0		
1997–98	Blackburn R	0	0		
1998–99	Blackburn R	0	0		
1999–2000	Bournemouth	3	0		
2000–01	Bournemouth	35	0		
2001–02	Bournemouth	45	0		
2002–03	Bournemouth	1	0		
2003–04	Bournemouth	0	0		
2004–05	Bournemouth	0	0		
2005–06	Bournemouth	42	0		
2006–07	Bournemouth	20	0	**146**	**0**

VOKES, Sam (F) **13 4**
H: 6 1 W: 13 10 b.Southampton 21-10-89
Source: Scholar. *Honours:* Wales Under-21.

2006–07	Bournemouth	13	4	**13**	**4**

YOUNG, Neil (D) **408 4**
H: 5 9 W: 12 04 b.Harlow 31-8-73
Source: Trainee.

1991–92	Tottenham H	0	0		
1992–93	Tottenham H	0	0		
1993–94	Tottenham H	0	0		
1994–95	Bournemouth	32	0		
1995–96	Bournemouth	41	0		
1996–97	Bournemouth	44	0		
1997–98	Bournemouth	44	2		
1998–99	Bournemouth	44	1		
1999–2000	Bournemouth	37	0		
2000–01	Bournemouth	7	0		
2001–02	Bournemouth	11	0		
2002–03	Bournemouth	32	1		
2003–04	Bournemouth	10	0		
2004–05	Bournemouth	30	0		
2005–06	Bournemouth	42	0		
2006–07	Bournemouth	34	0	**408**	**4**

BRADFORD C (12)

AINGE, Simon (D) **9 0**
H: 6 1 W: 12 02 b.Shipley 18-2-88
Source: Scholar.

2005–06	Bradford C	0	0		
2006–07	Bradford C	9	0	**9**	**0**

BARRAU, Xavi (M) **16 4**
H: 5 10 W: 11 00 b.Lyon 26-8-82
Source: Lyon.

2006–07	Airdrie U	13	2	**13**	**2**
2006–07	Bradford C	3	2	**3**	**2**

BENTHAM, Craig (D) **27 0**
H: 5 9 W: 11 06 b.Bingley 7-3-85
Source: Scholar.

2004–05	Bradford C	2	0		
2005–06	Bradford C	7	0		
2006–07	Bradford C	18	0	**27**	**0**

BOWER, Mark (D) **237 11**
H: 5 10 W: 11 00 b.Bradford 23-1-80
Source: Trainee.

1997–98	Bradford C	3	0		
1998–99	Bradford C	0	0		
1999–2000	Bradford C	0	0		
1999–2000	*York C*	15	1		
2000–01	Bradford C	0	0		
2000–01	*York C*	21	1	**36**	**2**
2001–02	Bradford C	10	2		
2002–03	Bradford C	37	0		
2003–04	Bradford C	14	0		
2004–05	Bradford C	46	2		
2005–06	Bradford C	45	2		
2006–07	Bradford C	46	3	**201**	**9**

BRIDGE-WILKINSON, Marc (M) **241 45**
H: 5 6 W: 11 00 b.Coventry 16-3-79
Source: Trainee.

1996–97	Derby Co	0	0		
1997–98	Derby Co	0	0		
1998–99	Derby Co	1	0		
1998–99	*Carlisle U*	7	0	**7**	**0**
1999–2000	Derby Co	0	0	**1**	**0**
2000–01	Port Vale	42	9		
2001–02	Port Vale	19	6		
2002–03	Port Vale	31	9		
2003–04	Port Vale	32	7	**124**	**31**
2004–05	Stockport Co	22	2	**22**	**2**
2004–05	*Bradford C*	12	3		
2005–06	Bradford C	36	5		
2006–07	Bradford C	39	4	**87**	**12**

BROWN, Joe (M) **19 1**
H: 5 10 W: 11 04 b.Bradford 3-4-88
Source: Scholar.

2005–06	Bradford C	13	1		
2006–07	Bradford C	6	0	**19**	**1**

CLARKE, Matthew (D) **248 15**
H: 6 3 W: 13 00 b.Leeds 18-12-80
Source: Wolverhampton W Trainee.

1999–2000	Halifax T	19	0		
2000–01	Halifax T	19	1		
2001–02	Halifax T	31	1	**69**	**2**
2002–03	Darlington	38	3		
2003–04	Darlington	45	4		
2004–05	Darlington	43	3		
2005–06	Darlington	43	3		
2006–07	Bradford C	8	0	**8**	**0**
2006–07	*Darlington*	2	0	**171**	**13**

COLBECK, Joe (M) **43 0**
H: 5 10 W: 10 12 b.Bradford 29-11-86
Source: Scholar.

2004–05	Bradford C	0	0		
2005–06	Bradford C	11	0		
2006–07	Bradford C	32	0	**43**	**0**

DALEY, Omar (M) **34 2**
H: 5 10 W: 11 03 b.Kingston, Jamaica 25-4-81
Source: Portmore U. *Honours:* Jamaica Under-20, 52 full caps, 4 goals.

2003–04	Reading	6	0	**6**	**0**
2004–05	Preston NE	14	0	**14**	**0**

From Charleston B, Portmore U.

2006–07	Bradford C	14	2	**14**	**2**

EDGHILL, Richard (D) **268 2**
H: 5 9 W: 12 01 b.Oldham 23-9-74
Source: Trainee. *Honours:* England Under-21, B.

1992–93	Manchester C	0	0		
1993–94	Manchester C	22	0		
1994–95	Manchester C	14	0		
1995–96	Manchester C	13	0		
1996–97	Manchester C	0	0		
1997–98	Manchester C	36	0		
1998–99	Manchester C	38	0		
1999–2000	Manchester C	41	1		
2000–01	Manchester C	6	0		
2000–01	*Birmingham C*	3	0	**3**	**0**
2001–02	Manchester C	11	0	**181**	**1**
2002–03	Wigan Ath	0	0		
2002–03	Sheffield U	1	0	**1**	**0**
2003–04	QPR	20	0		
2004–05	QPR	20	0	**40**	**0**
2005–06	Bradford C	19	1		
2006–07	Bradford C	24	0	**43**	**1**

HOWARTH, Russell (G) **31 0**
H: 6 2 W: 14 05 b.York 27-3-82
Source: Scholar. *Honours:* England Youth, Under-20.

1999–2000	York C	6	0		
2000–01	York C	0	0		
2001–02	York C	2	0		
2002–03	York C	0	0	**8**	**0**
2002–03	Tranmere R	3	0		
2003–04	Tranmere R	1	0		
2004–05	Tranmere R	8	0	**12**	**0**
2005–06	Bradford C	11	0		
2006–07	Bradford C	0	0	**11**	**0**

JOHNSON, Eddie (F) **80 13**
H: 5 10 W: 13 05 b.Chester 20-9-84
Source: Scholar. *Honours:* England Youth, Under-20.

2001–02	Manchester U	0	0		
2002–03	Manchester U	0	0		
2003–04	Manchester U	0	0		
2004–05	Manchester U	0	0		
2004–05	*Coventry C*	26	5	**26**	**5**
2005–06	Manchester U	0	0		
2005–06	*Crewe Alex*	22	5	**22**	**5**
2006–07	Bradford C	32	3	**32**	**3**

McGUIRE, Patrick (M) **0 0**
H: 5 10 W: 10 07 b.Baildon 29-7-87
Source: Scholar.

2005–06	Bradford C	0	0		
2006–07	Bradford C	0	0		

MUIRHEAD, Ben (M) **124 7**
H: 5 9 W: 11 02 b.Doncaster 5-1-83
Source: Trainee. *Honours:* England Youth.

1999–2000	Manchester U	0	0		
2000–01	Manchester U	0	0		
2001–02	Manchester U	0	0		
2002–03	Manchester U	0	0		
2002–03	Bradford C	8	0		
2003–04	Bradford C	28	2		
2004–05	Bradford C	40	1		
2005–06	Bradford C	32	1		
2006–07	Bradford C	4	0	**112**	**4**
2006–07	*Rochdale*	12	3	**12**	**3**

OSBORNE, Leon (F) **1 0**
H: 5 10 W: 10 10 b.Doncaster 28-10-89
Source: Scholar.

2006–07	Bradford C	1	0	**1**	**0**

PENFORD, Tom (M) **23 0**
H: 5 10 W: 11 03 b.Leeds 5-1-85
Source: Scholar.

2002–03	Bradford C	3	0		
2003–04	Bradford C	4	0		
2004–05	Bradford C	3	0		
2005–06	Bradford C	10	0		
2006–07	Bradford C	3	0	**23**	**0**

RICKETTS, Donovan (G) **86 0**
H: 6 1 W: 11 05 b.Kingston 7-6-77
Source: Village U. *Honours:* Jamaica Under-23, 46 full caps.

2003–04	Bolton W	0	0		
2004–05	Bolton W	0	0		
2004–05	Bradford C	4	0		
2005–06	Bradford C	36	0		
2006–07	Bradford C	46	0	**86**	**0**

SCHUMACHER, Steven (M) **121 13**
H: 5 10 W: 11 00 b.Liverpool 30-4-84
Source: Scholar. *Honours:* England Youth.

2000–01	Everton	0	0		
2001–02	Everton	0	0		
2002–03	Everton	0	0		
2003–04	Everton	0	0		
2003–04	*Carlisle U*	4	0	**4**	**0**
2004–05	Bradford C	43	6		
2005–06	Bradford C	30	1		
2006–07	Bradford C	44	6	**117**	**13**

SMITH, Nick (F) **0 0**
H: 5 8 W: 10 00 b.Leeds 25-3-88
Source: Farsley C.

2006–07	Bradford C	0	0		

SWIFT, John (D) **12 0**
H: 5 7 W: 10 06 b.Leeds 20-9-84
Source: Scholar.

2004–05	Bradford C	5	0		
2005–06	Bradford C	5	0		
2006–07	Bradford C	2	0	**12**	**0**

WETHERALL, David (D) **460 28**
H: 6 3 W: 13 12 b.Sheffield 14-3-71
Source: School. *Honours:* England Schools.

1989–90	Sheffield W	0	0		
1990–91	Sheffield W	0	0		

1991–92	Leeds U	1	0		
1992–93	Leeds U	13	1		
1993–94	Leeds U	32	1		
1994–95	Leeds U	38	3		
1995–96	Leeds U	34	4		
1996–97	Leeds U	29	0		
1997–98	Leeds U	34	3		
1998–99	Leeds U	21	0	**202**	**12**
1999–2000	Bradford C	38	2		
2000–01	Bradford C	18	1		
2001–02	Bradford C	19	2		
2002–03	Bradford C	17	0		
2003–04	Bradford C	34	1		
2004–05	Bradford C	45	4		
2005–06	Bradford C	46	5		
2006–07	Bradford C	41	1	**258**	**16**

WINDASS, Dean (F) 575 186
H: 5 10 W: 12 03 b.North Ferriby 1-4-69
Source: N Ferriby U.

1991–92	Hull C	32	6		
1992–93	Hull C	41	7		
1993–94	Hull C	43	23		
1994–95	Hull C	44	17		
1995–96	Hull C	16	4		
1995–96	Aberdeen	20	6		
1996–97	Aberdeen	29	10		
1997–98	Aberdeen	24	5	**73**	**21**
1998–99	Oxford U	33	15	**33**	**15**
1998–99	Bradford C	12	3		
1999–2000	Bradford C	38	10		
2000–01	Bradford C	24	3		
2000–01	Middlesbrough	8	2		
2001–02	Middlesbrough	27	1		
2001–02	*Sheffield W*	2	0	**2**	**0**
2002–03	Middlesbrough	2	0	**37**	**3**
2002–03	Sheffield U	20	6	**20**	**6**
2003–04	Bradford C	36	6		
2004–05	Bradford C	41	27		
2005–06	Bradford C	40	16		
2006–07	Bradford C	25	11	**216**	**76**
2006–07	*Hull C*	18	8	**194**	**65**

BRENTFORD (13)

ABBEY, Nathan (G) 208 0
H: 6 1 W: 11 13 b.Islington 11-7-78
Source: Trainee.

1995–96	Luton T	0	0		
1996–97	Luton T	0	0		
1997–98	Luton T	0	0		
1998–99	Luton T	2	0		
1999–2000	Luton T	33	0		
2000–01	Luton T	20	0		
2001–02	Chesterfield	46	0	**46**	**0**
2002–03	Northampton T	5	0	**5**	**0**
2003–04	Luton T	0	0	**55**	**0**
2003–04	Macclesfield T	0	0		
2003–04	Ipswich T	0	0		
2003–04	Burnley	0	0		
2004–05	Boston U	44	0		
2005–06	Boston U	17	0	**61**	**0**
2005–06	*Leyton Orient*	0	0		
2005–06	Bristol C	1	0	**1**	**0**
2006–07	Torquay U	24	0	**24**	**0**
2006–07	Brentford	16	0	**16**	**0**

BROOKER, Paul (M) 305 23
H: 5 8 W: 10 00 b.Hammersmith 25-11-76
Source: Trainee.

1995–96	Fulham	20	2		
1996–97	Fulham	26	2		
1997–98	Fulham	9	0		
1998–99	Fulham	1	0		
1999–2000	Fulham	0	0	**56**	**4**
1999–2000	*Brighton & HA*	15	2		
2000–01	Brighton & HA	41	3		
2001–02	Brighton & HA	41	4		
2002–03	Brighton & HA	37	6	**134**	**15**
2003–04	Leicester C	3	0	**3**	**0**
2003–04	*Reading*	11	0		
2004–05	Reading	31	0	**42**	**0**
2005–06	Brentford	36	4		
2006–07	Brentford	34	0	**70**	**4**

CARDER-ANDREWS, Karle (M) 5 0
H: 5 11 W: 10 08 b.Feltham 13-3-89
Source: Scholar.

2006–07	Brentford	5	0	**5**	**0**

CHARLES, Darius (M) 20 1
H: 6 1 W: 13 05 b.Ealing 10-12-87
Source: Scholar.

2004–05	Brentford	1	0		
2005–06	Brentford	2	0		
2006–07	Brentford	17	1	**20**	**1**

DARK, Lewis (M) 3 0
H: 5 8 W: 11 06 b.Harlow 10-4-89
Source: Scholar.

2006–07	Brentford	3	0	**3**	**0**

ENGLAND, Jamie (M) 0 0
H: 5 11 W: 11 12 b.Epsom 27-5-88
Source: Milton Keynes D Scholar.

2006–07	Brentford	0	0		

FRAMPTON, Andrew (D) 162 4
H: 5 11 W: 10 10 b.Wimbledon 3-9-79
Source: Trainee.

1998–99	Crystal Palace	6	0		
1999–2000	Crystal Palace	9	0		
2000–01	Crystal Palace	10	0		
2001–02	Crystal Palace	2	0		
2002–03	Crystal Palace	1	0	**28**	**0**
2002–03	Brentford	15	0		
2003–04	Brentford	16	0		
2004–05	Brentford	35	0		
2005–06	Brentford	36	3		
2006–07	Brentford	32	1	**134**	**4**

GRIFFITHS, Adam (D) 71 2
H: 6 2 W: 12 13 b.Sydney 21-8-79

2004–05	Ostend	27	0	**27**	**0**
2005–06	Watford	0	0		
2005–06	Bournemouth	7	1	**7**	**1**
2006–07	Brentford	37	1	**37**	**1**

HEYWOOD, Matthew (D) 248 11
H: 6 3 W: 14 00 b.Chatham 26-8-79
Source: Trainee.

1998–99	Burnley	13	0		
1999–2000	Burnley	0	0		
2000–01	Burnley	0	0	**13**	**0**
2000–01	Swindon T	21	2		
2001–02	Swindon T	44	3		
2002–03	Swindon T	46	1		
2003–04	Swindon T	40	1		
2004–05	Swindon T	32	1	**183**	**8**
2005–06	Bristol C	24	2	**24**	**2**
2006–07	Brentford	28	1	**28**	**1**

IDE, Charlie (M) 27 7
H: 5 9 W: 11 00 b.Sunbury 10-5-88

2004–05	Brentford	1	0		
2005–06	Brentford	0	0		
2006–07	Brentford	26	7	**27**	**7**

KEITH, Joe (M) 283 27
H: 5 7 W: 11 02 b.Plaistow 1-10-78
Source: Trainee.

1997–98	West Ham U	0	0		
1998–99	West Ham U	0	0		
1999–2000	Colchester U	45	1		
2000–01	Colchester U	27	3		
2001–02	Colchester U	41	4		
2002–03	Colchester U	36	9		
2003–04	Colchester U	28	2		
2004–05	Colchester U	31	4	**208**	**23**
2004–05	*Bristol C*	3	0	**3**	**0**
2005–06	Leyton Orient	42	2		
2006–07	Leyton Orient	11	0	**53**	**2**
2006–07	*Shrewsbury T*	1	0	**1**	**0**
2006–07	Brentford	18	2	**18**	**2**

MASTERS, Clark (G) 11 0
H: 6 3 W: 13 12 b.Hastings 31-5-87
Source: Scholar.

2005–06	Brentford	0	0		
2006–07	Brentford	11	0	**11**	**0**

MONTAGUE, Ross (F) 4 0
H: 6 0 W: 12 11 b.Twickenham 1-11-88

2006–07	Brentford	4	0	**4**	**0**

MOORE, Chris (F) 16 2
H: 5 9 W: 11 05 b.Middlesex 13-1-80
Source: Northwood, Dagenham & R.

2006–07	Brentford	16	2	**16**	**2**

MOUSINHO, John (D) 41 0
H: 6 1 W: 12 07 b.Buckingham 30-4-86
Source: Univ of Notre Dame.

2005–06	Brentford	7	0		
2006–07	Brentford	34	0	**41**	**0**

NELSON, Stuart (G) 116 0
H: 6 1 W: 12 12 b.Stroud 17-9-81
Source: Doncaster R, Hucknall T.

2003–04	Brentford	9	0		
2004–05	Brentford	43	0		
2005–06	Brentford	45	0		
2006–07	Brentford	19	0	**116**	**0**

O'CONNOR, Kevin (F) 236 22
H: 5 11 W: 12 00 b.Blackburn 24-2-82
Source: Trainee. *Honours:* Eire Under-21.

1999–2000	Brentford	6	0		
2000–01	Brentford	11	1		
2001–02	Brentford	25	0		
2002–03	Brentford	45	5		
2003–04	Brentford	43	1		
2004–05	Brentford	37	2		
2005–06	Brentford	30	7		
2006–07	Brentford	39	6	**236**	**22**

OSBORNE, Karleigh (D) 23 0
H: 6 2 W: 12 04 b.Southall 19-3-88
Source: Scholar.

2004–05	Brentford	1	0		
2005–06	Brentford	1	0		
2006–07	Brentford	21	0	**23**	**0**

OSEI-KUFFOUR, Jo (F) 198 43
H: 5 8 W: 11 11 b.Edmonton 17-11-81
Source: Scholar.

2000–01	Arsenal	0	0		
2001–02	Arsenal	0	0		
2001–02	*Swindon T*	11	2	**11**	**2**
2002–03	Torquay U	30	5		
2003–04	Torquay U	41	10		
2004–05	Torquay U	34	6		
2005–06	Torquay U	43	8	**148**	**29**
2006–07	Brentford	39	12	**39**	**12**

OWUSU, Lloyd (F) 306 95
H: 6 2 W: 14 00 b.Slough 12-12-76
Source: Slough T.

1998–99	Brentford	46	22		
1999–2000	Brentford	41	12		
2000–01	Brentford	33	10		
2001–02	Brentford	44	20		
2002–03	Sheffield W	32	4		
2003–04	Sheffield W	20	5	**52**	**9**
2003–04	Reading	16	4		
2004–05	Reading	25	6	**41**	**10**
2005–06	Brentford	42	12		
2006–07	Brentford	7	0	**213**	**76**

PETERS, Ryan (F) 43 2
H: 5 8 W: 10 05 b.Wandsworth 21-8-87
Source: Scholar.

2000–01	Southampton	0	0		
2001–02	Southampton	0	0		
2001–02	Brentford	0	0		
2002–03	Brentford	11	1		
2003–04	Brentford	9	0		
2004–05	Brentford	0	0		
2005–06	Brentford	10	1		
2006–07	Brentford	13	0	**43**	**2**

PINAULT, Thomas (M) 203 13
H: 5 10 W: 12 00 b.Grasse 4-12-81
Source: Cannes.

1999–2000	Colchester U	4	0		
2000–01	Colchester U	5	1		
2001–02	Colchester U	42	0		
2002–03	Colchester U	42	4		
2003–04	Colchester U	40	0	**133**	**5**
2004–05	Grimsby T	43	7		
2005–06	Grimsby T	0	0	**43**	**7**
2006–07	Brentford	27	1	**27**	**1**

RHODES, Alex (F) 61 5
H: 5 9 W: 10 04 b.Cambridge 23-1-82
Source: Newmarket T.

2003–04	Brentford	3	1		
2004–05	Brentford	22	3		
2005–06	Brentford	17	1		
2006–07	Brentford	15	0	**57**	**5**
2006–07	*Swindon T*	4	0	**4**	**0**

SHIPPERLEY, Neil (F) 446 120
H: 6 1 W: 13 12 b.Chatham 30-10-74
Source: Trainee. *Honours:* England Under-21.

1992–93	Chelsea	3	1		
1993–94	Chelsea	24	4		
1994–95	Chelsea	10	2	**37**	**7**
1994–95	*Watford*	6	1	**6**	**1**
1994–95	Southampton	19	4		
1995–96	Southampton	37	7		
1996–97	Southampton	10	1	**66**	**12**
1996–97	Crystal Palace	32	12		
1997–98	Crystal Palace	26	7		
1998–99	Crystal Palace	3	1		
1998–99	Nottingham F	20	1	**20**	**1**
1999–2000	Barnsley	39	13		
2000–01	Barnsley	39	14	**78**	**27**
2001–02	Wimbledon	41	12		
2002–03	Wimbledon	46	20	**87**	**32**
2003–04	Crystal Palace	40	9		
2004–05	Crystal Palace	1	0	**102**	**29**
2005–06	Sheffield U	39	11		
2006–07	Sheffield U	0	0	**39**	**11**
2006–07	Brentford	11	0	**11**	**0**

SKULASON, Olafur-Ingi (M) 12 1
H: 6 0 W: 11 10 b.Reykjavik 1-4-83
Source: Fylkir. *Honours:* Iceland Youth, Under-21, 2 full caps.

2001–02	Arsenal	0	0		
2002–03	Arsenal	0	0		
2003–04	Arsenal	0	0		
2004–05	Arsenal	0	0		
2005–06	Brentford	2	0		
2006–07	Brentford	10	1	**12**	**1**

To Helsingborg February 2007

TILLEN, Sam (D) 67 1
H: 5 10 W: 11 09 b.Reading 16-4-85
Source: Trainee. *Honours:* England Youth.

2002–03	Chelsea	0	0		
2003–04	Chelsea	0	0		
2004–05	Chelsea	0	0		
2005–06	Brentford	33	0		
2006–07	Brentford	34	1	**67**	**1**

TOMLIN, Gavin (F) 12 0
H: 6 0 W: 12 02 b.Kent 21-8-83
Source: Staines T, Yeading.

2006–07	Brentford	12	0	**12**	**0**

WIJNHARD, Clyde (F) 314 101
H: 5 11 W: 11 11 b.Paramaribo 1-11-73

1992–93	Ajax	4	2		
1993–94	Groningen	23	3	**23**	**3**
1994–95	Ajax	0	0	**4**	**2**
1995–96	RKC	33	8		
1996–97	RKC	17	10	**50**	**18**
1997–98	Willem II	29	14	**29**	**14**
1998–99	Leeds U	18	3	**18**	**3**
1999–2000	Huddersfield T	45	15		
2000–01	Huddersfield T	4	0		
2001–02	Huddersfield T	13	1	**62**	**16**
2001–02	Preston NE	6	3	**6**	**3**
2002–03	Oldham Ath	25	10	**25**	**10**
2003–04	Beira Mar	29	9	**29**	**9**
2004–05	Darlington	31	14		
2005–06	Darlington	8	1	**39**	**15**
2005–06	Macclesfield T	20	8		
2006–07	Macclesfield T	0	0	**20**	**8**
2006–07	Brentford	9	0	**9**	**0**

WILLOCK, Calum (F) 133 27
H: 6 1 W: 12 08 b.Lambeth 29-10-81
Source: Scholar. *Honours:* England Schools. St Kitts & Nevis 2 full caps, 2 goals.

2000–01	Fulham	1	0		
2001–02	Fulham	2	0		
2002–03	Fulham	2	0		
2002–03	*QPR*	3	0	**3**	**0**
2003–04	Fulham	0	0	**5**	**0**
2003–04	*Bristol R*	5	0	**5**	**0**
2003–04	Peterborough U	29	8		
2004–05	Peterborough U	35	12		
2005–06	Peterborough U	15	3	**79**	**23**
2005–06	Brentford	13	1		
2006–07	Brentford	28	3	**41**	**4**

BRIGHTON & HA (14)

BERTIN, Alexis (M) 132 2
H: 5 8 W: 11 04 b.Le Havre 13-5-80

2000–01	Le Havre	4	0		
2001–02	Le Havre	16	1		
2002–03	Le Havre	10	0		
2003–04	Le Havre	35	1		
2004–05	Le Havre	27	0		
2005–06	Le Havre	24	0	**116**	**2**
2006–07	Brighton & HA	16	0	**16**	**0**

BREACH, Chris (D) 0 0
H: 5 10 W: 12 04 b.Brighton 19-4-86
Source: Scholar.

2005–06	Brighton & HA	0	0		
2006–07	Brighton & HA	0	0		

BUTTERS, Guy (D) 533 34
H: 6 3 W: 13 00 b.Hillingdon 30-10-69
Source: Trainee. *Honours:* England Under-21.

1988–89	Tottenham H	28	1		
1989–90	Tottenham H	7	0	**35**	**1**
1989–90	*Southend U*	16	3	**16**	**3**
1990–91	Portsmouth	23	0		
1991–92	Portsmouth	33	2		
1992–93	Portsmouth	15	1		
1993–94	Portsmouth	15	1		
1994–95	Portsmouth	24	0		
1994–95	*Oxford U*	3	1	**3**	**1**
1995–96	Portsmouth	37	2		
1996–97	Portsmouth	7	0	**154**	**6**
1996–97	Gillingham	30	0		
1997–98	Gillingham	31	7		
1998–99	Gillingham	23	3		
1999–2000	Gillingham	40	2		
2000–01	Gillingham	12	3		
2001–02	Gillingham	23	1	**159**	**16**
2002–03	Brighton & HA	6	0		
2003–04	Brighton & HA	43	3		
2004–05	Brighton & HA	41	2		
2005–06	Brighton & HA	45	2		
2006–07	Brighton & HA	31	0	**166**	**7**

CARPENTER, Richard (M) 507 32
H: 6 0 W: 13 00 b.Sheerness 30-9-72
Source: Trainee.

1990–91	Gillingham	9	1		
1991–92	Gillingham	3	0		
1992–93	Gillingham	28	0		
1993–94	Gillingham	40	3		
1994–95	Gillingham	29	0		
1995–96	Gillingham	12	0		
1996–97	Gillingham	1	0	**122**	**4**
1996–97	Fulham	34	5		
1997–98	Fulham	24	2	**58**	**7**
1998–99	Cardiff C	42	1		
1999–2000	Cardiff C	33	1	**75**	**2**
2000–01	Brighton & HA	42	6		
2001–02	Brighton & HA	45	3		
2002–03	Brighton & HA	44	2		
2003–04	Brighton & HA	42	4		
2004–05	Brighton & HA	32	3		
2005–06	Brighton & HA	32	1		
2006–07	Brighton & HA	15	0	**252**	**19**

CHAMBERLAIN, Scott (M) 0 0
H: 5 9 W: 10 08 b.Eastbourne 15-1-88
Source: Scholar.

2006–07	Brighton & HA	0	0		

COX, Dean (M) 43 6
H: 5 4 W: 9 08 b.Cuckfield 12-8-87
Source: Scholar.

2005–06	Brighton & HA	1	0		
2006–07	Brighton & HA	42	6	**43**	**6**

EL-ABD, Adam (D) 98 1
H: 5 10 W: 13 05 b.Brighton 11-9-84
Source: Scholar.

2003–04	Brighton & HA	11	0		
2004–05	Brighton & HA	16	0		
2005–06	Brighton & HA	29	0		
2006–07	Brighton & HA	42	1	**98**	**1**

ELDER, Nathan (F) 13 1
H: 6 1 W: 13 12 b.Hornchurch 5-4-85
Source: Billericay T.

2006–07	Brighton & HA	13	1	**13**	**1**

ELPHICK, Tommy (M) 4 0
H: 5 11 W: 11 07 b.Brighton 7-9-87
Source: Scholar.

2005–06	Brighton & HA	1	0		
2006–07	Brighton & HA	3	0	**4**	**0**

FOGDEN, Wes (F) 0 0
H: 5 8 W: 10 04 b.Brighton 12-4-88
Source: Scholar.

2006–07	Brighton & HA	0	0		

FRASER, Tom (M) 28 1
H: 5 10 W: 11 00 b.Brighton 5-12-87
Source: Bognor Regis T.

2006–07	Brighton & HA	28	1	**28**	**1**

FRUTOS, Alexandre (M) 46 3
H: 5 9 W: 10 03 b.Vitry-le-Francois 23-4-82
Source: Chateauroux, Metz. *Honours:* France Youth.

2005–06	Brighton & HA	36	3		
2006–07	Brighton & HA	10	0	**46**	**3**

GATTING, Joe (D) 35 4
H: 5 11 W: 12 04 b.Brighton 25-11-87
Source: Scholar.

2005–06	Brighton & HA	12	0		
2006–07	Brighton & HA	23	4	**35**	**4**

HAMMOND, Dean (M) 120 16
H: 6 0 W: 11 09 b.Hastings 7-3-83
Source: Scholar.

2002–03	Brighton & HA	4	0		
2003–04	Brighton & HA	0	0		
2003–04	*Leyton Orient*	8	0	**8**	**0**
2004–05	Brighton & HA	30	4		
2005–06	Brighton & HA	41	4		
2006–07	Brighton & HA	37	8	**112**	**16**

HART, Gary (F) 335 44
H: 5 9 W: 12 03 b.Harlow 21-9-76
Source: Stansted.

1998–99	Brighton & HA	44	12		
1999–2000	Brighton & HA	43	9		
2000–01	Brighton & HA	45	7		
2001–02	Brighton & HA	39	4		
2002–03	Brighton & HA	36	4		
2003–04	Brighton & HA	42	3		
2004–05	Brighton & HA	26	2		
2005–06	Brighton & HA	35	1		
2006–07	Brighton & HA	25	2	**335**	**44**

HINSHELWOOD, Adam (D) 84 1
H: 5 10 W: 12 10 b.Oxford 8-1-84
Source: Scholar.

2002–03	Brighton & HA	7	0		
2003–04	Brighton & HA	17	0		
2004–05	Brighton & HA	38	1		
2005–06	Brighton & HA	11	0		
2006–07	Brighton & HA	11	0	**84**	**1**

HINSHELWOOD, Paul (D) 0 0
H: 5 8 W: 11 00 b.Chatham 11-10-87
Source: Scholar.

2006–07	Brighton & HA	0	0		

KUIPERS, Michels (G) 172 0
H: 6 2 W: 14 03 b.Amsterdam 26-6-74
Source: SDW Amsterdam.

1998–99	Bristol R	1	0		
1999–2000	Bristol R	0	0	**1**	**0**
2000–01	Brighton & HA	34	0		
2001–02	Brighton & HA	39	0		
2002–03	Brighton & HA	21	0		
2003–04	Brighton & HA	10	0		
2003–04	*Hull C*	3	0	**3**	**0**
2004–05	Brighton & HA	30	0		
2005–06	Brighton & HA	5	0		
2005–06	*Boston U*	15	0	**15**	**0**
2006–07	Brighton & HA	14	0	**153**	**0**

LOFT, Doug (M) 14 2
H: 6 0 W: 12 01 b.Maidstone 25-12-86
Source: Hastings U.

2005–06	Brighton & HA	3	1		
2006–07	Brighton & HA	11	1	**14**	**2**

LYNCH, Joel (G) 55 1
H: 6 1 W: 12 10 b.Eastbourne 3-10-87
Source: Scholar. *Honours:* England Youth.

2005–06	Brighton & HA	16	1		
2006–07	Brighton & HA	39	0	**55**	**1**

MARTIN, Richard (G) 0 0
H: 6 2 W: 12 13 b.Chelmsford 1-9-87
Source: Scholar.

2005–06	Brighton & HA	0	0		
2006–07	Brighton & HA	0	0		

MAYO, Kerry (D) 351 12
H: 5 10 W: 12 08 b.Haywards Heath 21-9-77
Source: Trainee.

1996–97	Brighton & HA	24	0		
1997–98	Brighton & HA	44	6		
1998–99	Brighton & HA	25	1		
1999–2000	Brighton & HA	31	1		
2000–01	Brighton & HA	45	1		
2001–02	Brighton & HA	33	0		
2002–03	Brighton & HA	41	1		
2003–04	Brighton & HA	33	0		
2004–05	Brighton & HA	27	1		
2005–06	Brighton & HA	18	1		
2006–07	Brighton & HA	30	0	**351**	**12**

MOLANGO, Maheta (F) 24 2
H: 6 1 W: 12 06 b.St Imier 24-7-82
Source: SV Burghausen.

2004–05	Brighton & HA	5	1		
2005–06	Brighton & HA	0	0		
2005–06	*Lincoln C*	10	0	**10**	**0**
2006–07	Brighton & HA	1	0	**6**	**1**
2006–07	*Oldham Ath*	5	1	**5**	**1**
2006–07	*Wrexham*	3	0	**3**	**0**

To UB Conquense (loan) January 2006

OATWAY, Charlie (M) 383 10
H: 5 7 W: 10 10 b.Hammersmith 28-11-73
Source: Yeading.

1994–95	Cardiff C	30	0		
1995–96	Cardiff C	2	0	**32**	**0**
1995–96	Torquay U	24	0		
1996–97	Torquay U	41	1		
1997–98	Torquay U	2	0	**67**	**1**
1997–98	Brentford	33	0		
1998–99	Brentford	24	0	**57**	**0**
1998–99	*Lincoln C*	3	0	**3**	**0**
1999–2000	Brighton & HA	42	4		
2000–01	Brighton & HA	38	0		
2001–02	Brighton & HA	32	1		
2002–03	Brighton & HA	29	1		
2003–04	Brighton & HA	31	1		
2004–05	Brighton & HA	34	1		
2005–06	Brighton & HA	18	1		
2006–07	Brighton & HA	0	0	**224**	**9**

REID, Paul (M) 193 22
H: 5 10 W: 10 10 b.Sydney 6-7-79
Honours: Australia Under-20.

1998–99	Wollongong Wolves	22	2		
1999–2000	Wollongong Wolves	31	3		
2000–01	Wollongong Wolves	30	7		
2001–02	Wollongong Wolves	15	3	**98**	**15**
2002–03	Bradford C	8	2		
2003–04	Bradford C	0	0	**8**	**2**
2003–04	Brighton & HA	5	0		
2004–05	Brighton & HA	34	2		
2005–06	Brighton & HA	38	2		
2006–07	Brighton & HA	10	1	**87**	**5**

RENTS, Sam (D) 25 0
H: 5 9 W: 11 03 b.Brighton 22-6-87
Source: Scholar.

2006–07	Brighton & HA	25	0	**25**	**0**

REVELL, Alex (F) 95 12
H: 6 3 W: 13 00 b.Cambridge 7-7-83
Source: Scholar.

2000–01	Cambridge U	4	0		
2001–02	Cambridge U	24	2		
2002–03	Cambridge U	9	0		
2003–04	Cambridge U	20	3	**57**	**5**

From Braintree T.

2006–07	Brighton & HA	38	7	**38**	**7**

ROBINSON, Jake (F) 84 8
H: 5 7 W: 10 10 b.Brighton 23-10-86
Source: Scholar.

2003–04	Brighton & HA	9	0		
2004–05	Brighton & HA	10	1		
2005–06	Brighton & HA	27	1		
2006–07	Brighton & HA	38	6	**84**	**8**

SANTOS, Georges (M) 261 16
H: 6 3 W: 14 00 b.Marseille 15-8-70
Source: Toulon.

1998–99	Tranmere R	37	1		
1999–2000	Tranmere R	10	1	**47**	**2**
1999–2000	WBA	8	0	**8**	**0**
2000–01	Sheffield U	31	4		
2001–02	Sheffield U	30	2	**61**	**6**
2002–03	Grimsby T	26	1	**26**	**1**
2003–04	Ipswich T	34	1	**34**	**1**
2004–05	QPR	43	5		
2005–06	QPR	31	1	**74**	**6**
2006–07	Brighton & HA	11	0	**11**	**0**

SAVAGE, Bas (F) 77 8
H: 6 3 W: 13 08 b.London 7-1-82
Source: Walton & Hersham.

2001–02	Reading	1	0		
2002–03	Reading	0	0		
2003–04	Reading	15	0		
2004–05	Reading	0	0	**16**	**0**
2004–05	*Wycombe W*	4	0	**4**	**0**
2004–05	*Bury*	5	0	**5**	**0**
2005–06	Bristol C	23	1		
2006–07	Bristol C	0	0	**23**	**1**
2006–07	Gillingham	14	1	**14**	**1**
2006–07	Brighton & HA	15	6	**15**	**6**

SULLIVAN, John (M) 0 0
H: 5 10 W: 11 04 b.Brighton 8-3-88
Source: Scholar. *Honours:* England Youth.

2005–06	Brighton & HA	0	0		
2006–07	Brighton & HA	0	0		

BRISTOL C (15)

ARTUS, Frankie (M) 0 0
H: 6 0 W: 11 02 b.Bristol 27-9-88
Source: Scholar.

2005–06	Bristol C	0	0		
2006–07	Bristol C	0	0		

BASSO, Adriano (G) 74 0
H: 6 1 W: 11 07 b.Jundiai 18-4-75
Source: Woking.

2005–06	Bristol C	29	0		
2006–07	Bristol C	45	0	**74**	**0**

BENYON, Elliot (M) 0 0
b.Wycombe 29-8-87
Source: Scholar.

2005–06	Bristol C	0	0		
2006–07	Bristol C	0	0		

BETSY, Kevin (M) 246 36
H: 6 1 W: 12 00 b.Seychelles 20-3-78
Source: Woking.

1998–99	Fulham	7	1		
1999–2000	Fulham	2	0		
1999–2000	*Bournemouth*	5	0	**5**	**0**
1999–2000	*Hull C*	2	0	**2**	**0**
2000–01	Fulham	5	0		
2001–02	Fulham	1	0	**15**	**1**
2001–02	Barnsley	10	0		
2002–03	Barnsley	39	5		
2003–04	Barnsley	45	10		
2004–05	Barnsley	0	0	**94**	**15**
2004–05	*Hartlepool U*	6	1	**6**	**1**
2004–05	Oldham Ath	36	5	**36**	**5**
2005–06	Wycombe W	42	8		
2006–07	Wycombe W	29	5	**71**	**13**
2006–07	Bristol C	17	1	**17**	**1**

BROOKER, Stephen (F) 225 69
H: 6 0 W: 14 00 b.Newport Pagnell 21-5-81
Source: Trainee.

1999–2000	Watford	1	0		
2000–01	Watford	0	0	**1**	**0**
2000–01	Port Vale	23	8		
2001–02	Port Vale	41	9		
2002–03	Port Vale	26	5		
2003–04	Port Vale	32	8		
2004–05	Port Vale	9	5	**131**	**35**
2004–05	Bristol C	33	16		
2005–06	Bristol C	37	16		
2006–07	Bristol C	23	2	**93**	**34**

CAREY, Louis (D) 425 10
H: 5 10 W: 11 00 b.Bristol 20-1-77
Source: Trainee. *Honours:* Scotland Under-21.

1995–96	Bristol C	23	0		
1996–97	Bristol C	42	0		
1997–98	Bristol C	38	0		
1998–99	Bristol C	41	0		
1999–2000	Bristol C	22	0		
2000–01	Bristol C	46	3		
2001–02	Bristol C	35	0		
2002–03	Bristol C	24	1		
2003–04	Bristol C	41	1		
2004–05	Coventry C	23	0	**23**	**0**
2004–05	Bristol C	14	0		
2005–06	Bristol C	38	3		
2006–07	Bristol C	38	2	**402**	**10**

FONTAINE, Liam (D) 71 0
H: 5 11 W: 11 09 b.Beckenham 7-1-86
Source: Trainee. *Honours:* England Youth, Under-20.

2003–04	Fulham	0	0		
2004–05	Fulham	1	0		
2004–05	*Yeovil T*	15	0		
2005–06	Fulham	0	0	**1**	**0**
2005–06	*Yeovil T*	10	0	**25**	**0**
2005–06	*Bristol C*	15	0		
2006–07	Bristol C	30	0	**45**	**0**

GRUBB, Dean (M) 0 0
H: 5 9 W: 11 11 b.Weston-Super-Mare 4-10-87
Honours: Wales Under-21.

2006–07	Bristol C	0	0		

JEVONS, Phil (F) 220 74
H: 5 11 W: 12 00 b.Liverpool 1-8-79
Source: Trainee.

1996–97	Everton	0	0		
1997–98	Everton	0	0		
1998–99	Everton	1	0		
1999–2000	Everton	3	0		
2000–01	Everton	4	0	**8**	**0**
2001–02	Grimsby T	31	6		
2002–03	Grimsby T	3	0		
2002–03	*Hull C*	24	3	**24**	**3**
2003–04	Grimsby T	29	12	**63**	**18**
2004–05	Yeovil T	46	27		
2005–06	Yeovil T	38	15	**84**	**42**
2006–07	Bristol C	41	11	**41**	**11**

JOHNSON, Lee (M) 161 19
H: 5 6 W: 10 07 b.Newmarket 7-6-81
Source: Trainee.

1998–99	Watford	0	0		
1999–2000	Watford	0	0		
2000–01	Brighton & HA	0	0		
2000–01	Brentford	0	0		
2001–02	Brentford	0	0		
2003–04	Yeovil T	45	5		
2004–05	Yeovil T	44	7		
2005–06	Yeovil T	26	2	**115**	**14**
2005–06	Hearts	4	0	**4**	**0**
2006–07	Bristol C	42	5	**42**	**5**

KEOGH, Richard (M) 43 3
H: 6 0 W: 11 02 b.Harlow 11-8-86
Source: Scholar. *Honours:* Eire Under-21.

2004–05	Stoke C	0	0		
2005–06	Bristol C	9	1		
2005–06	*Wycombe W*	3	0	**3**	**0**
2006–07	Bristol C	31	2	**40**	**3**

LAMB, Shaun (D) 0 0
b.Bristol 17-11-86
Source: Scholar.

2005–06	Bristol C	0	0		
2006–07	Bristol C	0	0		

McALLISTER, Jamie (D) **279** **2**
H: 5 10 W: 11 00 b.Glasgow 26-4-78
Honours: Scotland1 full cap.

1995–96	Q of S	2	0		
1996–97	Q of S	6	0		
1997–98	Q of S	15	0		
1998–99	Q of S	27	0	**50**	**0**
1999–2000	Aberdeen	34	0		
2000–01	Aberdeen	25	0		
2001–02	Aberdeen	29	0		
2002–03	Aberdeen	29	0	**117**	**0**
2003–04	Livingston	34	1	**34**	**1**
2004–05	Hearts	30	0		
2005–06	Hearts	17	0	**47**	**0**
2006–07	Bristol C	31	1	**31**	**1**

McCOMBE, Jamie (D) **191** **12**
H: 6 5 W: 12 05 b.Scunthorpe 1-1-83
Source: Scholar.

2001–02	Scunthorpe U	17	0		
2002–03	Scunthorpe U	31	1		
2003–04	Scunthorpe U	15	0	**63**	**1**
2003–04	Lincoln C	8	0		
2004–05	Lincoln C	41	3		
2005–06	Lincoln C	38	4	**87**	**7**
2006–07	Bristol C	41	4	**41**	**4**

MURRAY, Scott (M) **375** **76**
H: 5 9 W: 11 00 b.Aberdeen 26-5-74
Source: Fraserburgh. *Honours:* Scotland B.

1993–94	Aston Villa	0	0		
1994–95	Aston Villa	0	0		
1995–96	Aston Villa	3	0		
1996–97	Aston Villa	1	0		
1997–98	Aston Villa	0	0	**4**	**0**
1997–98	Bristol C	23	0		
1998–99	Bristol C	32	3		
1999–2000	Bristol C	41	6		
2000–01	Bristol C	46	10		
2001–02	Bristol C	37	8		
2002–03	Bristol C	45	19		
2003–04	Reading	34	5	**34**	**5**
2003–04	Bristol C	6	0		
2004–05	Bristol C	42	8		
2005–06	Bristol C	37	10		
2006–07	Bristol C	28	7	**337**	**71**

MYRIE-WILLIAMS, Jennison (F) **26** **2**
H: 5 11 W: 12 08 b.London 17-5-88
Source: Scholar.

2005–06	Bristol C	1	0		
2006–07	Bristol C	25	2	**26**	**2**

NOBLE, David (M) **125** **10**
H: 6 0 W: 12 04 b.Hitchin 2-2-82
Source: Scholar. *Honours:* England Youth, Under-20. Scotland Under-21, B.

2000–01	Arsenal	0	0		
2001–02	Arsenal	0	0		
2001–02	*Watford*	15	1	**15**	**1**
2002–03	Arsenal	0	0		
2002–03	West Ham U	0	0		
2003–04	West Ham U	3	0	**3**	**0**
2003–04	Boston U	14	2		
2004–05	Boston U	32	3		
2005–06	Boston U	11	0	**57**	**5**
2005–06	Bristol C	24	1		
2006–07	Bristol C	26	3	**50**	**4**

ORR, Bradley (M) **114** **5**
H: 6 0 W: 11 11 b.Liverpool 1-11-82
Source: Scholar.

2001–02	Newcastle U	0	0		
2002–03	Newcastle U	0	0		
2003–04	Newcastle U	0	0		
2003–04	*Burnley*	4	0	**4**	**0**
2004–05	Bristol C	37	0		
2005–06	Bristol C	38	1		
2006–07	Bristol C	35	4	**110**	**5**

PARTRIDGE, David (D) **178** **2**
H: 6 1 W: 13 06 b.Westminster 26-11-78
Source: Trainee. *Honours:* Wales Under-21, 7 full caps.

1997–98	West Ham U	0	0		
1998–99	Dundee U	1	0		
1999–2000	Dundee U	29	0		
2000–01	Dundee U	19	0		
2001–02	Dundee U	13	0	**62**	**0**
2001–02	*Leyton Orient*	7	0		
2002–03	Motherwell	32	1		
2003–04	Motherwell	15	0		
2004–05	Motherwell	29	1	**76**	**2**
2005–06	Bristol C	11	0	**11**	**0**
2005–06	*Milton Keynes D*	18	0	**18**	**0**
2006–07	*Leyton Orient*	1	0	**8**	**0**
2006–07	*Brentford*	3	0	**3**	**0**
2006–07	*Swindon T*	0	0		

RIBEIRO, Christian (D) **0** **0**
H: 5 11 W: 12 02 b.Neath 14-12-89
Source: Scholar.

2006–07	Bristol C	0	0		

RUSSELL, Alex (M) **391** **49**
H: 5 10 W: 11 07 b.Crosby 17-3-73
Source: Burscough.

1994–95	Rochdale	7	1		
1995–96	Rochdale	25	0		
1996–97	Rochdale	39	9		
1997–98	Rochdale	31	4	**102**	**14**
1998–99	Cambridge U	37	6		
1999–2000	Cambridge U	15	0		
2000–01	Cambridge U	29	2	**81**	**8**
2001–02	Torquay U	33	7		
2002–03	Torquay U	39	9		
2003–04	Torquay U	43	2		
2004–05	Torquay U	38	3	**153**	**21**
2005–06	Bristol C	27	4		
2006–07	Bristol C	28	2	**55**	**6**

SHOWUNMI, Enoch (F) **135** **24**
H: 6 3 W: 14 11 b.Kilburn 21-4-82
Source: Willesden Constantine. *Honours:* Nigeria 2 full caps.

2003–04	Luton T	26	7		
2004–05	Luton T	35	6		
2005–06	Luton T	41	1	**102**	**14**
2006–07	Bristol C	33	10	**33**	**10**

SKUSE, Cole (M) **87** **2**
H: 6 1 W: 11 05 b.Bristol 29-3-86
Source: Scholar.

2004–05	Bristol C	7	0		
2005–06	Bristol C	38	2		
2006–07	Bristol C	42	0	**87**	**2**

SLOCOMBE, Martin (M) **0** **0**
b.Weston-Super-Mare

2006–07	Bristol C	0	0		

SMITH, Andy (F) **34** **0**
H: 5 11 W: 12 02 b.Lisburn 25-9-80
Honours: Northern Ireland B, 18 full caps.

2004–05	Preston NE	14	0		
2004–05	*Stockport Co*	1	0	**1**	**0**
2005–06	*Motherwell*	7	0	**7**	**0**
2005–06	Preston NE	0	0		
2006–07	Preston NE	0	0	**14**	**0**
2006–07	*Cheltenham T*	2	0	**2**	**0**
2006–07	Bristol C	10	0	**10**	**0**

WALKER, Jordan (M) **0** **0**
b.Bristol

2006–07	Bristol C	0	0		

WEALE, Chris (G) **99** **0**
H: 6 2 W: 13 03 b.Yeovil 9-2-82
Source: Juniors.

2003–04	Yeovil T	35	0		
2004–05	Yeovil T	38	0		
2005–06	Yeovil T	25	0	**98**	**0**
2006–07	Bristol C	1	0	**1**	**0**

WILSON, Brian (D) **150** **14**
H: 5 10 W: 11 00 b.Manchester 9-5-83
Source: Scholar.

2001–02	Stoke C	1	0		
2002–03	Stoke C	3	0		
2003–04	Stoke C	2	0	**6**	**0**
2003–04	Cheltenham T	14	0		
2004–05	Cheltenham T	43	3		
2005–06	Cheltenham T	43	9		
2006–07	Cheltenham T	25	2	**125**	**14**
2006–07	Bristol C	19	0	**19**	**0**

WILSON, James (D) **0** **0**
H: 6 2 W: 11 05 b.Chepstow 26-2-89
Source: Scholar.

2005–06	Bristol C	0	0		
2006–07	Bristol C	0	0		

WOODMAN, Craig (D) **122** **3**
H: 5 9 W: 10 11 b.Tiverton 22-12-82
Source: Trainee.

1999–2000	Bristol C	0	0		
2000–01	Bristol C	2	0		
2001–02	Bristol C	6	0		
2002–03	Bristol C	10	0		
2003–04	Bristol C	21	0		
2004–05	Bristol C	3	0		
2004–05	*Mansfield T*	8	1	**8**	**1**
2004–05	*Torquay U*	22	1		
2005–06	Bristol C	37	1		
2005–06	*Torquay U*	2	0	**24**	**1**
2006–07	Bristol C	11	0	**90**	**1**

WRING, Danny (M) **1** **0**
H: 5 10 W: 10 03 b.Portishead 26-10-86
Source: Scholar.

2004–05	Bristol C	1	0		
2005–06	Bristol C	0	0		
2006–07	Bristol C	0	0	**1**	**0**

BRISTOL R (16)

ANTHONY, Byron (D) **23** **0**
H: 6 1 W: 11 02 b.Newport 20-9-84
Source: Scholar. *Honours:* Wales Youth, Under-21.

2003–04	Cardiff C	0	0		
2004–05	Cardiff C	0	0		
2005–06	Cardiff C	0	0		
2006–07	Bristol R	23	0	**23**	**0**

CAMPBELL, Stuart (M) **298** **14**
H: 5 10 W: 10 08 b.Corby 9-12-77
Source: Trainee. *Honours:* Scotland Under-21.

1996–97	Leicester C	10	0		
1997–98	Leicester C	11	0		
1998–99	Leicester C	12	0		
1999–2000	Leicester C	4	0		
1999–2000	*Birmingham C*	2	0	**2**	**0**
2000–01	Leicester C	0	0	**37**	**0**
2000–01	*Grimsby T*	38	2		
2001–02	Grimsby T	33	3		
2002–03	Grimsby T	45	6		
2003–04	Grimsby T	39	1	**155**	**12**
2004–05	Bristol R	25	0		
2005–06	Bristol R	38	1		
2006–07	Bristol R	41	1	**104**	**2**

CARRUTHERS, Chris (M) **157** **2**
H: 5 10 W: 12 00 b.Kettering 19-8-83
Source: Scholar. *Honours:* England Under-20.

2000–01	Northampton T	3	0		
2001–02	Northampton T	13	1		
2002–03	Northampton T	33	0		
2003–04	Northampton T	24	0		
2004–05	Northampton T	1	0	**74**	**1**
2004–05	*Bristol R*	5	0		
2005–06	Bristol R	40	1		
2006–07	Bristol R	38	0	**83**	**1**

DISLEY, Craig (M) **256** **32**
H: 5 10 W: 10 13 b.Worksop 24-8-81
Source: Trainee.

1999–2000	Mansfield T	5	0		
2000–01	Mansfield T	24	0		
2001–02	Mansfield T	36	7		
2002–03	Mansfield T	42	4		
2003–04	Mansfield T	34	5	**141**	**16**
2004–05	Bristol R	28	4		
2005–06	Bristol R	42	8		
2006–07	Bristol R	45	4	**115**	**16**

ELLIOTT, Steve (D) **226** **10**
H: 6 1 W: 14 00 b.Derby 29-10-78
Source: Trainee. *Honours:* England Under-21.

1996–97	Derby Co	0	0		
1997–98	Derby Co	3	0		
1998–99	Derby Co	11	0		
1999–2000	Derby Co	20	0		
2000–01	Derby Co	6	0		
2001–02	Derby Co	6	0		
2002–03	Derby Co	23	1		
2003–04	Derby Co	4	0	**73**	**1**
2003–04	Blackpool	28	0	**28**	**0**

2004–05	Bristol R	41	2		
2005–06	Bristol R	45	2		
2006–07	Bristol R	39	5	**125**	**9**

GREEN, Mike (G) 0 0
H: 6 1 W: 13 01 b.Bristol 23-7-89
Source: Scholar.

2006–07	Bristol R	0	0		

GREEN, Ryan (M) 68 0
H: 5 7 W: 10 10 b.Cardiff 20-10-80
Source: From Danes Court. *Honours:* Wales Youth, Under-21, 2 full caps.

1997–98	Wolverhampton W	0	0		
1998–99	Wolverhampton W	1	0		
1999–2000	Wolverhampton W	0	0		
2000–01	Wolverhampton W	7	0		
2000–01	*Torquay U*	10	0	**10**	**0**
2001–02	Wolverhampton W	0	0	**8**	**0**
2001–02	Millwall	13	0	**13**	**0**
2002–03	Cardiff C	0	0		
2002–03	Sheffield W	4	0	**4**	**0**
From Hereford U.					
2006–07	Bristol R	33	0	**33**	**0**

HALDANE, Lewis (F) 115 14
H: 6 0 W: 11 03 b.Trowbridge 13-3-85
Source: Scholar. *Honours:* Wales Under-21.

2003–04	Bristol R	27	5		
2004–05	Bristol R	13	0		
2005–06	Bristol R	30	3		
2006–07	Bristol R	45	6	**115**	**14**

HINTON, Craig (D) 277 3
H: 6 0 W: 12 00 b.Wolverhampton 26-11-77
Source: Trainee.

1996–97	Birmingham C	0	0		
1997–98	Birmingham C	0	0		
2000–01	Kidderminster H	46	2		
2001–02	Kidderminster H	41	0		
2002–03	Kidderminster H	44	0		
2003–04	Kidderminster H	42	1	**173**	**3**
2004–05	Bristol R	38	0		
2005–06	Bristol R	36	0		
2006–07	Bristol R	30	0	**104**	**0**

HUNT, James (M) 381 20
H: 5 8 W: 10 03 b.Derby 17-12-76
Source: Trainee.

1994–95	Notts Co	0	0		
1995–96	Notts Co	10	1		
1996–97	Notts Co	9	0	**19**	**1**
1997–98	Northampton T	21	0		
1998–99	Northampton T	35	2		
1999–2000	Northampton T	37	1		
2000–01	Northampton T	41	1		
2001–02	Northampton T	38	4	**172**	**8**
2002–03	Oxford U	39	1		
2003–04	Oxford U	41	2	**80**	**3**
2004–05	Bristol R	41	4		
2005–06	Bristol R	40	1		
2006–07	Bristol R	14	1	**95**	**6**
2006–07	*Grimsby T*	15	2	**15**	**2**

IGOE, Sammy (M) 384 29
H: 5 6 W: 10 00 b.Staines 30-9-75
Source: Trainee.

1993–94	Portsmouth	0	0		
1994–95	Portsmouth	1	0		
1995–96	Portsmouth	22	0		
1996–97	Portsmouth	40	2		
1997–98	Portsmouth	31	3		
1998–99	Portsmouth	40	5		
1999–2000	Portsmouth	26	1	**160**	**11**
1999–2000	Reading	6	0		
2000–01	Reading	31	6		
2001–02	Reading	35	1		
2002–03	Reading	15	0	**87**	**7**
2002–03	*Luton T*	2	0	**2**	**0**
2003–04	Swindon T	36	5		
2004–05	Swindon T	43	4	**79**	**9**
2005–06	Millwall	5	0	**5**	**0**
2005–06	*Bristol R*	11	1		
2006–07	Bristol R	40	1	**51**	**2**

LAMBERT, Ricky (F) 245 62
H: 6 2 W: 14 08 b.Liverpool 16-2-82
Source: Trainee.

1999–2000	Blackpool	3	0		
2000–01	Blackpool	0	0	**3**	**0**
2000–01	Macclesfield T	9	0		
2001–02	Macclesfield T	35	8	**44**	**8**
2001–02	Stockport Co	0	0		
2002–03	Stockport Co	29	2		
2003–04	Stockport Co	40	12		
2004–05	Stockport Co	29	4	**98**	**18**
2004–05	Rochdale	15	6		
2005–06	Rochdale	46	22		
2006–07	Rochdale	3	0	**64**	**28**
2006–07	Bristol R	36	8	**36**	**8**

LESCOTT, Aaron (M) 219 1
H: 5 8 W: 10 09 b.Birmingham 2-12-78
Source: Trainee. *Honours:* England Schools.

1996–97	Aston Villa	0	0		
1997–98	Aston Villa	0	0		
1998–99	Aston Villa	0	0		
1999–2000	Aston Villa	0	0		
1999–2000	*Lincoln C*	5	0	**5**	**0**
2000–01	Aston Villa	0	0		
2000–01	Sheffield W	30	0		
2001–02	Sheffield W	7	0	**37**	**0**
2001–02	Stockport Co	17	0		
2002–03	Stockport Co	41	1		
2003–04	Stockport Co	14	0	**72**	**1**
2003–04	*Bristol R*	8	0		
2004–05	Bristol R	26	0		
2005–06	Bristol R	37	0		
2006–07	Bristol R	34	0	**105**	**0**

LINES, Chris (M) 11 0
H: 6 2 W: 12 00 b.Bristol 30-11-85

2005–06	Bristol R	4	0		
2006–07	Bristol R	7	0	**11**	**0**

MULLINGS, Darren (M) 4 0
H: 6 1 W: 12 00 b.Bristol 3-3-87

2005–06	Bristol R	4	0		
2006–07	Bristol R	0	0	**4**	**0**

PALMER, James (M) 0 0
H: 5 7 W: 11 04 b.Bristol 30-3-88
Source: Scholar.

2006–07	Bristol R	0	0		

PARRINELLO, Tom (D) 0 0
H: 5 6 W: 10 07 b.Parkway 11-11-89
Source: Scholar.

2006–07	Bristol R	0	0		

PHILLIPS, Steve (G) 301 0
H: 6 1 W: 11 10 b.Bath 6-5-78
Source: Paulton R.

1996–97	Bristol C	0	0		
1997–98	Bristol C	0	0		
1998–99	Bristol C	15	0		
1999–2000	Bristol C	21	0		
2000–01	Bristol C	42	0		
2001–02	Bristol C	22	0		
2002–03	Bristol C	46	0		
2003–04	Bristol C	46	0		
2004–05	Bristol C	46	0		
2005–06	Bristol C	19	0	**257**	**0**
2006–07	Bristol R	44	0	**44**	**0**

RIGG, Sean (F) 18 1
H: 5 9 W: 12 01 b.Bristol 1-10-88
Source: Forest Green R.

2006–07	Bristol R	18	1	**18**	**1**

SANDELL, Andy (M) 36 3
H: 5 11 W: 11 09 b.Calne 8-9-83
Source: Bath C.

2005–06	Bristol R	0	0		
2006–07	Bristol R	36	3	**36**	**3**

SHEARER, Scott (G) 167 0
H: 6 3 W: 12 00 b.Glasgow 15-2-81
Source: Tower Hearts. *Honours:* Scotland Under-21, B.

2000–01	Albion R	3	0		
2001–02	Albion R	10	0		
2002–03	Albion R	36	0	**49**	**0**
2003–04	Coventry C	30	0		
2004–05	Coventry C	8	0	**38**	**0**
2004–05	*Rushden & D*	13	0	**13**	**0**
2005–06	Bristol R	45	0		
2006–07	Bristol R	2	0	**47**	**0**
2006–07	*Shrewsbury T*	20	0	**20**	**0**

WALKER, Richard (F) 254 69
H: 6 0 W: 12 04 b.Sutton Coldfield 8-11-77
Source: Trainee.

1995–96	Aston Villa	0	0		
1996–97	Aston Villa	0	0		
1997–98	Aston Villa	1	0		
1998–99	Aston Villa	0	0		
1998–99	*Cambridge U*	21	3	**21**	**3**
1999–2000	Aston Villa	5	2		
2000–01	Aston Villa	0	0		
2000–01	*Blackpool*	18	3		
2001–02	Aston Villa	0	0	**6**	**2**
2001–02	*Wycombe W*	12	3	**12**	**3**
2001–02	Blackpool	21	8		
2002–03	Blackpool	32	4		
2003–04	Blackpool	9	0	**80**	**15**
2003–04	*Northampton T*	12	4	**12**	**4**
2003–04	Oxford U	4	0	**4**	**0**
2004–05	Bristol R	27	10		
2005–06	Bristol R	46	20		
2006–07	Bristol R	46	12	**119**	**42**

BURNLEY (17)

AKINBIYI, Ade (F) 429 128
H: 6 1 W: 13 08 b.Hackney 10-10-74
Source: Trainee. *Honours:* Nigeria 1 full cap.

1992–93	Norwich C	0	0		
1993–94	Norwich C	2	0		
1993–94	*Hereford U*	4	2	**4**	**2**
1994–95	Norwich C	13	0		
1994–95	*Brighton & HA*	7	4	**7**	**4**
1995–96	Norwich C	22	3		
1996–97	Norwich C	12	0	**49**	**3**
1996–97	Gillingham	19	7		
1997–98	Gillingham	44	21	**63**	**28**
1998–99	Bristol C	44	19		
1999–2000	Bristol C	3	2	**47**	**21**
1999–2000	Wolverhampton W	37	16	**37**	**16**
2000–01	Leicester C	37	9		
2001–02	Leicester C	21	2	**58**	**11**
2001–02	Crystal Palace	14	2		
2002–03	Crystal Palace	10	1		
2002–03	*Stoke C*	4	2		
2003–04	Crystal Palace	0	0	**24**	**3**
2003–04	Stoke C	30	10		
2004–05	Stoke C	29	7	**63**	**19**
2004–05	Burnley	10	4		
2005–06	Burnley	29	12		
2005–06	Sheffield U	15	3		
2006–07	Sheffield U	3	0	**18**	**3**
2006–07	Burnley	20	2	**59**	**18**

BRANCH, Graham (F) 387 31
H: 6 2 W: 12 02 b.Liverpool 12-2-72
Source: Heswall.

1991–92	Tranmere R	4	0		
1992–93	Tranmere R	3	0		
1992–93	*Bury*	4	1	**4**	**1**
1993–94	Tranmere R	13	0		
1994–95	Tranmere R	1	0		
1995–96	Tranmere R	21	2		
1996–97	Tranmere R	35	5		
1997–98	Tranmere R	25	3	**102**	**10**
1997–98	*Wigan Ath*	3	0	**3**	**0**
1998–99	Stockport Co	14	3	**14**	**3**
1998–99	Burnley	20	1		
1999–2000	Burnley	44	3		
2000–01	Burnley	35	5		
2001–02	Burnley	10	0		
2002–03	Burnley	32	0		
2003–04	Burnley	38	3		
2004–05	Burnley	43	3		
2005–06	Burnley	37	2		
2006–07	Burnley	5	0	**264**	**17**

CALDWELL, Steven (D) 149 6
H: 6 2 W: 13 12 b.Stirling 12-9-80
Source: Trainee. *Honours:* Scotland Youth, Under-21, B, 9 full caps.

1997–98	Newcastle U	0	0		
1998–99	Newcastle U	0	0		
1999–2000	Newcastle U	0	0		
2000–01	Newcastle U	9	0		
2001–02	Newcastle U	0	0		
2001–02	*Blackpool*	6	0	**6**	**0**
2001–02	*Bradford C*	9	0	**9**	**0**

2002–03	Newcastle U	14	1		
2003–04	Newcastle U	5	0	**28**	**1**
2003–04	*Leeds U*	13	1	**13**	**1**
2004–05	Sunderland	41	4		
2005–06	Sunderland	24	0		
2006–07	Sunderland	11	0	**76**	**4**
2006–07	Burnley	17	0	**17**	**0**

COYNE, Danny (G) **336 0**
H: 6 0 W: 13 00 b.Prestatyn 27-8-73
Source: Trainee. *Honours:* Wales Schools, Youth, Under-21, B, 15 full caps.

1991–92	Tranmere R	0	0		
1992–93	Tranmere R	1	0		
1993–94	Tranmere R	5	0		
1994–95	Tranmere R	5	0		
1995–96	Tranmere R	46	0		
1996–97	Tranmere R	21	0		
1997–98	Tranmere R	16	0		
1998–99	Tranmere R	17	0	**111**	**0**
1999–2000	Grimsby T	44	0		
2000–01	Grimsby T	46	0		
2001–02	Grimsby T	45	0		
2002–03	Grimsby T	46	0	**181**	**0**
2003–04	Leicester C	4	0	**4**	**0**
2004–05	Burnley	20	0		
2005–06	Burnley	8	0		
2006–07	Burnley	12	0	**40**	**0**

DUFF, Michael (D) **328 14**
H: 6 1 W: 11 08 b.Belfast 11-1-78
Source: Trainee. *Honours:* Northern Ireland 17 full caps.

1999–2000	Cheltenham T	31	2		
2000–01	Cheltenham T	39	5		
2001–02	Cheltenham T	45	3		
2002–03	Cheltenham T	44	2		
2003–04	Cheltenham T	42	0	**201**	**12**
2004–05	Burnley	42	0		
2005–06	Burnley	41	0		
2006–07	Burnley	44	2	**127**	**2**

ELLIOTT, Wade (M) **298 38**
H: 5 10 W: 10 03 b.Southampton 14-12-78

1999–2000	Bournemouth	12	3		
2000–01	Bournemouth	36	9		
2001–02	Bournemouth	46	8		
2002–03	Bournemouth	44	4		
2003–04	Bournemouth	39	3		
2004–05	Bournemouth	43	4	**220**	**31**
2005–06	Burnley	36	3		
2006–07	Burnley	42	4	**78**	**7**

FOSTER, Stephen (D) **235 15**
H: 6 0 W: 11 05 b.Warrington 10-9-80
Source: Trainee. *Honours:* England Schools.

1998–99	Crewe Alex	1	0		
1999–2000	Crewe Alex	0	0		
2000–01	Crewe Alex	30	0		
2001–02	Crewe Alex	34	5		
2002–03	Crewe Alex	35	4		
2003–04	Crewe Alex	45	2		
2004–05	Crewe Alex	34	1		
2005–06	Crewe Alex	39	3	**218**	**15**
2006–07	Burnley	17	0	**17**	**0**

GRAY, Andy (F) **301 65**
H: 6 1 W: 13 00 b.Harrogate 15-11-77
Source: Trainee. *Honours:* Scotland Youth, B, 2 full caps.

1995–96	Leeds U	15	0		
1996–97	Leeds U	7	0		
1997–98	Leeds U	0	0		
1997–98	*Bury*	6	1	**6**	**1**
1998–99	Leeds U	0	0	**22**	**0**
1998–99	Nottingham F	8	0		
1998–99	*Preston NE*	5	0	**5**	**0**
1998–99	*Oldham Ath*	4	0	**4**	**0**
1999–2000	Nottingham F	22	0		
2000–01	Nottingham F	18	0		
2001–02	Nottingham F	16	1	**64**	**1**
2002–03	Bradford C	44	15		
2003–04	Bradford C	33	5	**77**	**20**
2003–04	Sheffield U	14	9		
2004–05	Sheffield U	43	15		
2005–06	Sheffield U	1	1	**58**	**25**
2005–06	Sunderland	21	1	**21**	**1**
2005–06	Burnley	9	3		
2006–07	Burnley	35	14	**44**	**17**

GUDJONSSON, Joey (M) **181 21**
H: 5 9 W: 12 04 b.Akranes 25-5-80
Honours: Iceland Youth, Under-21, 30 full caps, 1 goal.

1998–99	Genk	5	0	**5**	**0**
1999–2000	MVV	19	5	**19**	**5**
2000–01	RKC	31	4	**31**	**4**
2001–02	Betis	11	0	**11**	**0**
2002–03	Aston Villa	11	2	**11**	**2**
2003–04	Wolverhampton W	11	0	**11**	**0**
2004–05	Leicester C	35	2		
2005–06	Leicester C	42	8	**77**	**10**
2006–07	AZ	5	0	**5**	**0**
2006–07	Burnley	11	0	**11**	**0**

HARLEY, Jon (D) **224 12**
H: 5 8 W: 10 03 b.Maidstone 26-9-79
Source: Trainee. *Honours:* England Under-21.

1996–97	Chelsea	0	0		
1997–98	Chelsea	3	0		
1998–99	Chelsea	0	0		
1999–2000	Chelsea	17	2		
2000–01	Chelsea	10	0	**30**	**2**
2000–01	*Wimbledon*	6	2	**6**	**2**
2001–02	Fulham	10	0		
2002–03	Fulham	11	1		
2002–03	*Sheffield U*	9	1		
2003–04	Fulham	4	0	**25**	**1**
2003–04	*Sheffield U*	5	0		
2003–04	*West Ham U*	15	1	**15**	**1**
2004–05	Sheffield U	44	2		
2005–06	Sheffield U	4	0	**62**	**3**
2005–06	Burnley	41	2		
2006–07	Burnley	45	1	**86**	**3**

JENSEN, Brian (G) **190 0**
H: 6 1 W: 12 04 b.Copenhagen 8-6-75
Source: Hvidovre, B93.

1997–98	AZ	0	0		
1998–99	AZ	1	0	**1**	**0**
1999–2000	WBA	12	0		
2000–01	WBA	33	0		
2001–02	WBA	1	0		
2002–03	WBA	0	0	**46**	**0**
2003–04	Burnley	46	0		
2004–05	Burnley	27	0		
2005–06	Burnley	39	0		
2006–07	Burnley	31	0	**143**	**0**

JONES, Steve (F) **209 45**
H: 5 10 W: 10 05 b.Derry 25-10-76
Source: Leigh RMI. *Honours:* Northern Ireland B, 27 full caps, 1 goal.

2001–02	*Rochdale*	9	1	**9**	**1**
2001–02	Crewe Alex	6	0		
2002–03	Crewe Alex	31	9		
2003–04	Crewe Alex	45	15		
2004–05	Crewe Alex	36	10		
2005–06	Crewe Alex	41	5	**159**	**39**
2006–07	Burnley	41	5	**41**	**5**

LAFFERTY, Kyle (F) **55 8**
H: 6 4 W: 11 02 b.Belfast 21-7-87
Source: Scholar. *Honours:* Northern Ireland Youth, Under-21, 10 full caps, 1 goal.

2005–06	Burnley	11	1		
2005–06	*Darlington*	9	3	**9**	**3**
2006–07	Burnley	35	4	**46**	**5**

MAHON, Alan (M) **263 28**
H: 5 8 W: 12 03 b.Dublin 4-4-78
Source: Crumplin U. *Honours:* Eire Under-21, 2 full caps.

1994–95	Tranmere R	0	0		
1995–96	Tranmere R	2	0		
1996–97	Tranmere R	25	2		
1997–98	Tranmere R	18	1		
1998–99	Tranmere R	39	6		
1999–2000	Tranmere R	36	4	**120**	**13**
2000–01	Sporting Lisbon	1	0	**1**	**0**
2000–01	Blackburn R	18	0		
2001–02	Blackburn R	13	1		
2002–03	Blackburn R	2	0		
2002–03	*Cardiff C*	15	2	**15**	**2**
2003–04	Blackburn R	3	0	**36**	**1**
2003–04	*Ipswich T*	11	1	**11**	**1**
2003–04	Wigan Ath	14	1		
2004–05	Wigan Ath	27	7		
2005–06	Wigan Ath	6	1	**47**	**9**

2005–06	Burnley	8	0		
2006–07	Burnley	25	2	**33**	**2**

McCANN, Chris (M) **61 7**
H: 6 1 W: 11 11 b.Dublin 21-7-87
Source: Scholar. *Honours:* Eire Youth.

2005–06	Burnley	23	2		
2006–07	Burnley	38	5	**61**	**7**

McGREAL, John (D) **414 6**
H: 5 11 W: 12 08 b.Birkenhead 2-6-72
Source: Trainee.

1990–91	Tranmere R	3	0		
1991–92	Tranmere R	0	0		
1992–93	Tranmere R	0	0		
1993–94	Tranmere R	15	1		
1994–95	Tranmere R	43	0		
1995–96	Tranmere R	32	0		
1996–97	Tranmere R	24	0		
1997–98	Tranmere R	42	0		
1998–99	Tranmere R	36	0	**195**	**1**
1999–2000	Ipswich T	34	0		
2000–01	Ipswich T	28	1		
2001–02	Ipswich T	27	1		
2002–03	Ipswich T	16	1		
2003–04	Ipswich T	18	1	**123**	**4**
2004–05	Burnley	39	1		
2005–06	Burnley	35	0		
2006–07	Burnley	22	0	**96**	**1**

NOEL-WILLIAMS, Gifton (F) **316 65**
H: 6 3 W: 13 06 b.Islington 21-1-80
Source: Trainee. *Honours:* England Youth.

1996–97	Watford	25	2		
1997–98	Watford	38	7		
1998–99	Watford	26	10		
1999–2000	Watford	3	0		
2000–01	Watford	32	8		
2001–02	Watford	29	6		
2002–03	Watford	16	0	**169**	**33**
2003–04	Stoke C	42	10		
2004–05	Stoke C	46	13	**88**	**23**
2005–06	Burnley	29	2		
2005–06	*Brighton & HA*	7	2	**7**	**2**
2006–07	Burnley	23	5	**52**	**7**

To Real Murcia January 2007

O'CONNOR, Gareth (M) **235 35**
H: 5 10 W: 11 00 b.Dublin 10-11-78
Source: Bohemians.

1998–99	Shamrock R	8	0	**8**	**0**
1999–2000	Bohemians	22	4	**22**	**4**
2000–01	Bournemouth	22	1		
2001–02	Bournemouth	28	0		
2002–03	Bournemouth	41	8		
2003–04	Bournemouth	37	2		
2004–05	Bournemouth	40	13	**168**	**24**
2005–06	Burnley	29	7		
2006–07	Burnley	8	0	**37**	**7**

O'CONNOR, James (M) **316 24**
H: 5 8 W: 11 00 b.Dublin 1-9-79
Source: Trainee. *Honours:* Eire Under-21.

1996–97	Stoke C	0	0		
1997–98	Stoke C	0	0		
1998–99	Stoke C	4	0		
1999–2000	Stoke C	42	6		
2000–01	Stoke C	44	8		
2001–02	Stoke C	43	2		
2002–03	Stoke C	43	0	**176**	**16**
2003–04	WBA	30	0		
2004–05	WBA	0	0	**30**	**0**
2004–05	Burnley	21	2		
2005–06	Burnley	46	3		
2006–07	Burnley	43	3	**110**	**8**

SINCLAIR, Frank (D) **444 12**
H: 5 8 W: 12 09 b.Lambeth 3-12-71
Source: Trainee. *Honours:* Jamaica 28 full caps, 1 goal.

1989–90	Chelsea	0	0		
1990–91	Chelsea	4	0		
1991–92	Chelsea	8	1		
1991–92	*WBA*	6	1	**6**	**1**
1992–93	Chelsea	32	0		
1993–94	Chelsea	35	0		
1994–95	Chelsea	35	3		
1995–96	Chelsea	13	1		
1996–97	Chelsea	20	1		
1997–98	Chelsea	22	1	**169**	**7**

1998–99 Leicester C 31 1
1999–2000 Leicester C 34 0
2000–01 Leicester C 17 0
2001–02 Leicester C 35 0
2002–03 Leicester C 33 1
2003–04 Leicester C 14 1 **164 3**
2004–05 Burnley 36 1
2005–06 Burnley 37 0
2006–07 Burnley 19 0 **92 1**
2006–07 *Huddersfield T* 13 0 **13 0**

SPICER, John (M) 88 10
H: 5 11 W: 11 07 b.Romford 13-9-83
Source: Scholar. *Honours:* England Schools, Youth, Under-20.
2001–02 Arsenal 0 0
2002–03 Arsenal 0 0
2003–04 Arsenal 0 0
2004–05 Arsenal 0 0
2004–05 Bournemouth 39 6
2005–06 Bournemouth 4 0 **43 6**
2005–06 Burnley 34 3
2006–07 Burnley 11 1 **45 4**

THOMAS, Mitchell (D) 619 15
H: 6 2 W: 14 00 b.Luton 2-10-64
Source: Apprentice. *Honours:* England Youth, Under-21, B.
1982–83 Luton T 4 0
1983–84 Luton T 26 0
1984–85 Luton T 36 0
1985–86 Luton T 41 1
1986–87 Tottenham H 39 4
1987–88 Tottenham H 36 0
1988–89 Tottenham H 25 1
1989–90 Tottenham H 26 1
1990–91 Tottenham H 31 0 **157 6**
1991–92 West Ham U 35 3
1992–93 West Ham U 3 0
1993–94 West Ham U 0 0 **38 3**
1993–94 Luton T 20 1
1994–95 Luton T 36 0
1995–96 Luton T 27 0
1996–97 Luton T 42 3
1997–98 Luton T 28 1
1998–99 Luton T 32 0 **292 6**
1999–2000 Burnley 44 0
2000–01 Burnley 43 0
2001–02 Burnley 12 0
2002–03 Burnley 0 0
2003–04 Burnley 0 0
2004–05 Burnley 0 0
2005–06 Burnley 0 0
2006–07 Burnley 33 0 **132 0**

THOMAS, Wayne (D) 328 13
H: 6 2 W: 14 12 b.Gloucester 17-5-79
Source: Trainee.
1995–96 Torquay U 6 0
1996–97 Torquay U 12 0
1997–98 Torquay U 21 1
1998–99 Torquay U 44 1
1999–2000 Torquay U 40 3 **123 5**
2000–01 Stoke C 34 0
2001–02 Stoke C 40 2
2002–03 Stoke C 41 0
2003–04 Stoke C 39 3
2004–05 Stoke C 35 2 **189 7**
2005–06 Burnley 16 1
2006–07 Burnley 0 0 **16 1**

BURY (18)

ADAMS, Nicky (F) 34 2
H: 5 10 W: 11 00 b.Bolton 16-10-86
Source: Scholar.
2005–06 Bury 15 1
2006–07 Bury 19 1 **34 2**

BAKER, Richie (M) 39 5
H: 5 10 W: 11 05 b.Burnley 29-12-87
Source: Preston NE Scholar.
2006–07 Bury 39 5 **39 5**

BARRY-MURPHY, Brian (M) 273 12
H: 5 10 W: 13 01 b.Cork 27-7-78
Honours: Eire Under-21.
1995–96 Cork City 13 0
1996–97 Cork City 25 0
1997–98 Cork City 15 1
1998–99 Cork City 27 1 **80 2**
1999–2000 Preston NE 1 0
2000–01 Preston NE 14 0
2001–02 Preston NE 4 0
2001–02 *Southend U* 8 1 **8 1**
2002–03 Preston NE 2 0 **21 0**
2002–03 *Hartlepool U* 7 0 **7 0**
2002–03 Sheffield W 17 0
2003–04 Sheffield W 41 0 **58 0**
2004–05 Bury 45 6
2005–06 Bury 40 3
2006–07 Bury 14 0 **99 9**

BISHOP, Andy (F) 98 25
H: 6 0 W: 10 10 b.Stone 19-10-82
Source: Scholar.
2002–03 Walsall 0 0
2002–03 *Kidderminster H* 29 5
2003–04 *Kidderminster H* 11 2 **40 7**
2003–04 *Rochdale* 10 1 **10 1**
2003–04 *Yeovil T* 5 2 **5 2**
From York C.
2006–07 Bury 43 15 **43 15**

BRASS, Chris (M) 306 6
H: 5 10 W: 11 13 b.Easington 24-7-75
Source: Trainee.
1993–94 Burnley 0 0
1994–95 Burnley 5 0
1994–95 *Torquay U* 7 0 **7 0**
1995–96 Burnley 9 0
1996–97 Burnley 39 0
1997–98 Burnley 40 1
1998–99 Burnley 34 0
1999–2000 Burnley 7 0
2000–01 Burnley 0 0 **134 1**
2000–01 *Halifax T* 6 0 **6 0**
2000–01 York C 10 1
2001–02 York C 41 2
2002–03 York C 40 1
2003–04 York C 39 1
2004–05 York C 0 0 **130 5**
2005–06 Bury 7 0
2006–07 Bury 22 0 **29 0**

BUCHANAN, David (M) 67 0
H: 5 7 W: 11 03 b.Rochdale 6-5-86
Source: Scholar. *Honours:* Northern Ireland Youth, Under-21.
2004–05 Bury 3 0
2005–06 Bury 23 0
2006–07 Bury 41 0 **67 0**

CHALLINOR, Dave (D) 368 9
H: 6 1 W: 12 06 b.Chester 2-10-75
Source: Brombrough Pool. *Honours:* England Schools, Youth.
1994–95 Tranmere R 0 0
1995–96 Tranmere R 0 0
1996–97 Tranmere R 5 0
1997–98 Tranmere R 32 1
1998–99 Tranmere R 34 2
1999–2000 Tranmere R 41 3
2000–01 Tranmere R 22 0
2001–02 Tranmere R 6 0 **140 6**
2001–02 Stockport Co 18 0
2002–03 Stockport Co 46 1
2003–04 Stockport Co 17 0 **81 1**
2003–04 *Bury* 15 0
2004–05 Bury 43 1
2005–06 Bury 46 1
2006–07 Bury 43 0 **147 2**

FETTIS, Alan (G) 382 2
H: 6 1 W: 13 09 b.Belfast 1-2-71
Source: Ards. *Honours:* Northern Ireland Schools, Youth, B, 25 full caps.
1991–92 Hull C 43 0
1992–93 Hull C 20 0
1993–94 Hull C 37 0
1994–95 Hull C 28 2
1995–96 Hull C 7 0
1995–96 *WBA* 3 0 **3 0**
1996–97 Nottingham F 4 0
1997–98 Nottingham F 0 0 **4 0**
1997–98 Blackburn R 8 0
1998–99 Blackburn R 2 0
1999–2000 Blackburn R 1 0 **11 0**
1999–2000 *Leicester C* 0 0
1999–2000 York C 13 0
2000–01 York C 46 0
2001–02 York C 45 0
2002–03 York C 21 0 **125 0**
2002–03 Hull C 17 0
2003–04 Hull C 3 0 **155 2**
2003–04 *Sheffield U* 3 0 **3 0**
2003–04 *Grimsby T* 11 0 **11 0**
2004–05 Macclesfield T 28 0
2005–06 Macclesfield T 33 0 **61 0**
2006–07 Bury 9 0 **9 0**

FITZGERALD, John (D) 64 3
H: 6 2 W: 12 13 b.Dublin 10-2-84
Source: Scholar. *Honours:* Eire Youth, Under-21.
2000–01 Blackburn R 0 0
2001–02 Blackburn R 0 0
2002–03 Blackburn R 0 0
2003–04 Blackburn R 0 0
2004–05 Blackburn R 0 0
2004–05 *Bury* 14 0
2005–06 Bury 27 0
2006–07 Bury 23 3 **64 3**

FLITCROFT, David (M) 452 28
H: 5 11 W: 14 05 b.Bolton 14-1-74
Source: Trainee.
1991–92 Preston NE 0 0
1992–93 Preston NE 8 2
1993–94 Preston NE 0 0 **8 2**
1993–94 *Lincoln C* 2 0 **2 0**
1993–94 Chester C 8 1
1994–95 Chester C 32 0
1995–96 Chester C 9 1
1996–97 Chester C 32 6
1997–98 Chester C 44 4
1998–99 Chester C 42 6 **167 18**
1999–2000 Rochdale 43 2
2000–01 Rochdale 41 0
2001–02 Rochdale 35 0
2002–03 Rochdale 41 2 **160 4**
2003–04 Macclesfield T 15 0 **15 0**
2003–04 Bury 17 0
2004–05 Bury 36 3
2005–06 Bury 43 1
2006–07 Bury 4 0 **100 4**

GOODFELLOW, Marc (M) 115 15
H: 5 10 W: 11 00 b.Swadlincote 20-9-81
1998–99 Stoke C 0 0
1999–2000 Stoke C 0 0
2000–01 Stoke C 7 0
2001–02 Stoke C 23 5
2002–03 Stoke C 20 1
2003–04 Stoke C 4 0 **54 6**
2003–04 Bristol C 15 4
2004–05 Bristol C 5 0 **20 4**
2004–05 *Port Vale* 5 0 **5 0**
2004–05 *Swansea C* 6 3
2004–05 *Colchester U* 5 1 **5 1**
2005–06 Swansea C 11 0 **17 3**
2005–06 Grimsby T 10 1 **10 1**
2006–07 Bury 4 0 **4 0**

GRUNDY, Aaron (G) 2 0
H: 6 1 W: 12 07 b.Bolton 21-1-88
Source: Scholar.
2005–06 Bury 1 0
2006–07 Bury 1 0 **2 0**

HURST, Glynn (F) 295 103
H: 5 10 W: 11 06 b.Barnsley 17-1-76
Source: Tottenham H Trainee.
1994–95 Barnsley 2 0
1995–96 Barnsley 5 0
1995–96 *Swansea C* 2 1 **2 1**
1996–97 Barnsley 1 0 **8 0**
1996–97 *Mansfield T* 6 0 **6 0**
1998–99 Ayr U 34 18
1999–2000 Ayr U 25 14 **59 32**
2000–01 Stockport Co 11 0
2001–02 Stockport Co 15 4 **26 4**
2001–02 Chesterfield 23 9
2002–03 Chesterfield 32 7
2003–04 Chesterfield 29 13 **84 29**
2004–05 Notts Co 41 14
2005–06 Notts Co 18 9 **59 23**
2005–06 Shrewsbury T 16 3

2006–07 Shrewsbury T 0 0 **16 3**
2006–07 Bury 35 11 **35 11**

KENNEDY, Tom (D) 143 5
H: 5 10 W: 11 01 b.Bury 24-6-85
Source: Scholar.
2002–03 Bury 0 0
2003–04 Bury 27 0
2004–05 Bury 46 1
2005–06 Bury 33 4
2006–07 Bury 37 0 **143 5**

PARRISH, Andy (D) 17 0
H: 6 0 W: 11 00 b.Bolton 22-6-88
Source: Scholar.
2005–06 Bury 8 0
2006–07 Bury 9 0 **17 0**

PUGH, Marc (M) 41 4
H: 5 11 W: 11 04 b.Burnley 2-4-87
Source: Scholar.
2005–06 Burnley 0 0
2005–06 Bury 6 1
2006–07 Bury 35 3 **41 4**

QUIGLEY, Damien (M) 1 0
H: 5 8 W: 11 06 b.Rochdale 20-9-87
Source: Scholar.
2005–06 Bury 1 0
2006–07 Bury 0 0 **1 0**

ROUSE, Domaine (F) 2 0
H: 5 6 W: 10 10 b.Stretford 4-7-89
Source: Scholar.
2006–07 Bury 2 0 **2 0**

SCOTT, Paul (D) 142 6
H: 5 11 W: 12 00 b.Wakefield 5-11-79
Source: Trainee.
1998–99 Huddersfield T 0 0
1999–2000 Huddersfield T 0 0
2000–01 Huddersfield T 0 0
2001–02 Huddersfield T 0 0
2002–03 Huddersfield T 13 0
2003–04 Huddersfield T 19 2
2004–05 Huddersfield T 0 0 **32 2**
2004–05 Bury 23 0
2005–06 Bury 41 2
2006–07 Bury 46 2 **110 4**

SPEIGHT, Jake (F) 30 2
H: 5 7 W: 11 02 b.Sheffield 28-9-85
Source: Sheffield W Scholar.
From Scarborough.
2005–06 Bury 17 2
2006–07 Bury 13 0 **30 2**

STEPHENS, Dale (M) 3 0
H: 5 7 W: 11 04 b.Bolton 12-12-87
Source: Scholar.
2006–07 Bury 3 0 **3 0**

TAYLOR, Daryl (F) 34 3
H: 5 10 W: 11 03 b.Birmingham 14-11-84
Source: Scholar.
2004–05 Walsall 19 3
2005–06 Walsall 11 0 **30 3**
2006–07 Bury 4 0 **4 0**

TIPTON, Matt (F) 303 63
H: 5 10 W: 11 02 b.Bangor 29-6-80
Source: Trainee. *Honours:* Wales Youth, Under-21.
1997–98 Oldham Ath 3 0
1998–99 Oldham Ath 28 2
1999–2000 Oldham Ath 29 3
2000–01 Oldham Ath 30 5
2001–02 Oldham Ath 22 5 **112 15**
2001–02 Macclesfield T 13 3
2002–03 Macclesfield T 36 10
2003–04 Macclesfield T 38 16
2004–05 Macclesfield T 44 12
2005–06 Mansfield T 4 0 **4 0**
2005–06 Bury 24 3
2006–07 Bury 0 0 **24 3**
2006–07 *Macclesfield T* 32 4 **163 45**

WARRINGTON, Andy (G) 170 0
H: 6 3 W: 12 13 b.Sheffield 10-6-76
Source: Trainee.
1994–95 York C 0 0
1995–96 York C 6 0
1996–97 York C 27 0
1997–98 York C 17 0
1998–99 York C 11 0 **61 0**
2003–04 Doncaster R 46 0
2004–05 Doncaster R 34 0
2005–06 Doncaster R 9 0
2006–07 Doncaster R 0 0 **89 0**
2006–07 Bury 20 0 **20 0**

WOODTHORPE, Colin (D) 549 12
H: 6 0 W: 11 08 b.Ellesmere Pt 13-1-69
Source: Apprentice.
1986–87 Chester C 30 2
1987–88 Chester C 35 0
1988–89 Chester C 44 3
1989–90 Chester C 46 1 **155 6**
1990–91 Norwich C 1 0
1991–92 Norwich C 15 1
1992–93 Norwich C 7 0
1993–94 Norwich C 20 0 **43 1**
1994–95 Aberdeen 14 0
1995–96 Aberdeen 15 1
1996–97 Aberdeen 19 0 **48 1**
1997–98 Stockport Co 32 1
1998–99 Stockport Co 37 2
1999–2000 Stockport Co 26 0
2000–01 Stockport Co 24 1
2001–02 Stockport Co 34 0
2002–03 Stockport Co 0 0 **153 4**
2002–03 Bury 32 0
2003–04 Bury 39 0
2004–05 Bury 30 0
2005–06 Bury 33 0
2006–07 Bury 16 0 **150 0**

WORRALL, David (M) 1 0
H: 6 0 W: 11 03 b.Manchester 12-6-90
Source: Scholar.
2006–07 Bury 1 0 **1 0**

YOUNGS, Tom (F) 235 51
H: 5 9 W: 11 13 b.Bury St Edmunds 31-8-79
Source: Trainee.
1997–98 Cambridge U 4 0
1998–99 Cambridge U 10 0
1999–2000 Cambridge U 21 8
2000–01 Cambridge U 38 14
2001–02 Cambridge U 42 11
2002–03 Cambridge U 35 10 **150 43**
2002–03 Northampton T 5 0
2003–04 Northampton T 12 0
2004–05 Northampton T 9 0 **26 0**
2004–05 Leyton Orient 10 1 **10 1**
2005–06 Bury 30 3
2006–07 Bury 19 4 **49 7**

CARDIFF C (19)

ALEXANDER, Neil (G) 321 0
H: 6 1 W: 12 08 b.Edinburgh 10-3-78
Source: Edina Hibs. *Honours:* Scotland Under-21, B, 3 full caps.
1996–97 Stenhousemuir 12 0
1997–98 Stenhousemuir 36 0 **48 0**
1998–99 Livingston 21 0
1999–2000 Livingston 13 0
2000–01 Livingston 26 0 **60 0**
2001–02 Cardiff C 46 0
2002–03 Cardiff C 40 0
2003–04 Cardiff C 25 0
2004–05 Cardiff C 17 0
2005–06 Cardiff C 46 0
2006–07 Cardiff C 39 0 **213 0**

BARKER, Chris (D) 314 3
H: 6 2 W: 13 08 b.Sheffield 2-3-80
Source: Alfreton.
1998–99 Barnsley 0 0
1999–2000 Barnsley 29 0
2000–01 Barnsley 40 0
2001–02 Barnsley 44 3 **113 3**
2002–03 Cardiff C 40 0
2003–04 Cardiff C 39 0
2004–05 *Stoke C* 4 0 **4 0**
2004–05 Cardiff C 39 0
2005–06 Cardiff C 41 0
2006–07 Cardiff C 0 0 **159 0**
2006–07 *Colchester U* 38 0 **38 0**

BLAKE, Darcy (M) 11 0
H: 5 10 W: 12 05 b.Caerphilly 13-12-88
Source: Scholar. *Honours:* Wales Youth, Under-21.
2005–06 Cardiff C 1 0
2006–07 Cardiff C 10 0 **11 0**

BYRNE, Jason (F) 260 133
H: 5 11 W: 11 11 b.Dublin 23-2-78
Honours: Eire 2 full caps.
1998–99 Bray W 17 5
1999–2000 Bray W 31 7
2000–01 Bray W 30 11
2001–02 Bray W 30 14
2002–03 Bray W 20 12 **128 49**
2003 Shelbourne 32 21
2004 Shelbourne 33 25
2005 Shelbourne 31 22
2006 Shelbourne 26 15 **122 83**
2006–07 Cardiff C 10 1 **10 1**

CAMPBELL, Kevin (F) 499 148
H: 6 0 W: 13 08 b.Lambeth 4-2-70
Source: Trainee. *Honours:* England Youth, Under-21, B.
1987–88 Arsenal 1 0
1988–89 Arsenal 0 0
1988–89 *Leyton Orient* 16 9 **16 9**
1989–90 Arsenal 15 2
1989–90 *Leicester C* 11 5 **11 5**
1990–91 Arsenal 22 9
1991–92 Arsenal 31 13
1992–93 Arsenal 37 4
1993–94 Arsenal 37 14
1994–95 Arsenal 23 4 **166 46**
1995–96 Nottingham F 21 3
1996–97 Nottingham F 17 6
1997–98 Nottingham F 42 23 **80 32**
1998–99 Trabzonspor 17 5 **17 5**
1998–99 Everton 8 9
1999–2000 Everton 26 12
2000–01 Everton 29 9
2001–02 Everton 23 4
2002–03 Everton 36 10
2003–04 Everton 17 1
2004–05 Everton 6 0 **145 45**
2004–05 WBA 16 3
2005–06 WBA 29 3 **45 6**
2006–07 Cardiff C 19 0 **19 0**

CHOPRA, Michael (F) 112 45
H: 5 9 W: 10 10 b.Newcastle 23-12-83
Source: Scholar. *Honours:* England Youth, Under-20, Under-21.
2000–01 Newcastle U 0 0
2001–02 Newcastle U 0 0
2002–03 Newcastle U 1 0
2002–03 *Watford* 5 5 **5 5**
2003–04 Newcastle U 6 0
2003–04 *Nottingham F* 5 0 **5 0**
2004–05 Newcastle U 1 0
2004–05 *Barnsley* 39 17 **39 17**
2005–06 Newcastle U 13 1 **21 1**
2006–07 Cardiff C 42 22 **42 22**

COOMBES, Gregg (M) 0 0
H: 6 0 W: 12 02 b.Porth 1-3-88
Source: Scholar.
2005–06 Cardiff C 0 0
2006–07 Cardiff C 0 0

COOPER, Kevin (M) 346 45
H: 5 8 W: 10 04 b.Derby 8-2-75
Source: Trainee.
1993–94 Derby Co 0 0
1994–95 Derby Co 1 0
1995–96 Derby Co 1 0
1996–97 Derby Co 0 0 **2 0**
1996–97 *Stockport Co* 12 3
1997–98 Stockport Co 38 8
1998–99 Stockport Co 38 1
1999–2000 Stockport Co 46 4
2000–01 Stockport Co 34 5 **168 21**
2000–01 Wimbledon 11 3
2001–02 Wimbledon 40 10 **51 13**
2001–02 Wolverhampton W 5 0
2002–03 Wolverhampton W 26 3
2003–04 Wolverhampton W 1 0
2003–04 *Sunderland* 1 0 **1 0**

2003–04 *Norwich C* 10 0 **10 0**
2004–05 Wolverhampton W 30 6 **62 9**
2005–06 Cardiff C 36 2
2006–07 Cardiff C 4 0 **40 2**
2006–07 *Yeovil T* 4 0 **4 0**
2006–07 *Walsall* 8 0 **8 0**

EASTER, Jamal (F) 13 0
H: 5 8 W: 11 00 b.Cardiff 15-11-87
Source: Scholar.
2006–07 Cardiff C 0 0
2006–07 *Bristol R* 3 0 **3 0**
2006–07 *Torquay U* 10 0 **10 0**

FERRETTI, Andrea (F) 9 0
H: 5 10 W: 11 10 b.Parma 18-9-86
Source: Parma.
2005–06 Cardiff C 4 0
2006–07 Cardiff C 1 0 **5 0**
2006–07 *Scunthorpe U* 4 0 **4 0**

FLOOD, Willo (M) 53 3
H: 5 7 W: 10 05 b.Dublin 10-4-85
Source: Trainee. *Honours:* Eire Youth, Under-21.
2001–02 Manchester C 0 0
2002–03 Manchester C 0 0
2003–04 Manchester C 0 0
2003–04 *Rochdale* 6 0 **6 0**
2004–05 Manchester C 9 1
2005–06 Manchester C 5 0 **14 1**
2005–06 *Coventry C* 8 1 **8 1**
2006–07 Cardiff C 25 1 **25 1**

FORDE, David (G) 7 0
H: 6 3 W: 13 06 b.Galway 20-12-79
Source: Barry T.
2001–02 West Ham U 0 0
2002–03 West Ham U 0 0
2003–04 West Ham U 0 0
2004–05 West Ham U 0 0
2005–06 West Ham U 0 0
2006–07 Cardiff C 7 0 **7 0**

GLOMBARD, Luigi (F) 44 3
H: 5 10 W: 11 11 b.Montreuil-sous-Bois 21-8-84
Honours: France Youth.
2002–03 Nantes 4 0
2003–04 Nantes 7 1
2004–05 Nantes 2 0
2005–06 Nantes 16 1 **29 2**
2006–07 Cardiff C 6 0 **6 0**
2006–07 *Leicester C* 1 0 **1 0**
2006–07 *Oldham Ath* 8 1 **8 1**

GREEN, Matt (F) 6 0
H: 5 5 W: 10 06 b.Bath 2-1-87
Source: Newport Co.
2006–07 Cardiff C 6 0 **6 0**

GUNTER, Chris (D) 15 0
H: 5 11 W: 11 02 b.Newport 21-7-89
Source: From Scholar. *Honours:* Wales Under-21, 1 full cap.
2006–07 Cardiff C 15 0 **15 0**

HOWARD, Mark (G) 8 0
H: 6 2 W: 12 00 b.Southwark 21-9-86
Source: Scholar. *Honours:* England Under-20.
2004–05 Arsenal 0 0
2005–06 Falkirk 8 0 **8 0**
2006–07 Cardiff C 0 0
2006–07 *Swansea C* 0 0

JACOBSON, Joe (D) 18 1
H: 5 11 W: 12 06 b.Cardiff 17-11-86
Source: Scholar. *Honours:* Wales Under-21.
2005–06 Cardiff C 1 0
2006–07 Cardiff C 0 0 **1 0**
2006–07 *Accrington S* 6 1 **6 1**
2006–07 *Bristol R* 11 0 **11 0**

JOHNSON, Roger (D) 189 21
H: 6 3 W: 11 00 b.Ashford 28-4-83
Source: Trainee.
1999–2000 Wycombe W 1 0
2000–01 Wycombe W 1 0
2001–02 Wycombe W 7 1
2002–03 Wycombe W 33 3
2003–04 Wycombe W 28 2
2004–05 Wycombe W 42 6
2005–06 Wycombe W 45 7 **157 19**
2006–07 Cardiff C 32 2 **32 2**

LEDLEY, Joe (M) 116 8
H: 6 0 W: 11 07 b.Cardiff 23-1-87
Source: Scholar. *Honours:* Wales Youth, Under-21, 12 full caps.
2004–05 Cardiff C 28 3
2005–06 Cardiff C 42 3
2006–07 Cardiff C 46 2 **116 8**

LOOVENS, Glenn (D) 125 5
H: 6 1 W: 12 11 b.Doetinchem 22-9-83
Honours: Holland Youth, Under-21.
2001–02 Feyenoord 8 0
2002–03 Feyenoord 12 0
2003–04 Feyenoord 1 0
2003–04 Excelsior 24 2 **24 2**
2004–05 Feyenoord 6 0 **27 0**
2004–05 De Graafschap 11 0 **11 0**
2005–06 Cardiff C 33 2
2006–07 Cardiff C 30 1 **63 3**

MARGETSON, Martyn (G) 166 0
H: 6 0 W: 14 00 b.West Neath 8-9-71
Source: Trainee. *Honours:* Wales Schools, Youth, Under-21, B, 1 full cap.
1990–91 Manchester C 2 0
1991–92 Manchester C 3 0
1992–93 Manchester C 1 0
1993–94 Manchester C 0 0
1993–94 *Bristol R* 3 0 **3 0**
1993–94 *Bolton W* 0 0
1994–95 Manchester C 0 0
1994–95 *Luton T* 0 0
1995–96 Manchester C 0 0
1996–97 Manchester C 17 0
1997–98 Manchester C 28 0 **51 0**
1998–99 Southend U 32 0 **32 0**
1999–2000 Huddersfield T 0 0
2000–01 Huddersfield T 2 0
2001–02 Huddersfield T 46 0 **48 0**
2002–03 Cardiff C 6 0
2003–04 Cardiff C 22 0
2004–05 Cardiff C 4 0
2005–06 Cardiff C 0 0
2006–07 Cardiff C 0 0 **32 0**

McDONALD, Curtis (M) 1 0
H: 5 10 W: 10 08 b.Cardiff 24-3-88
Source: Scholar. *Honours:* Wales Youth, Under-21.
2005–06 Cardiff C 1 0
2006–07 Cardiff C 0 0 **1 0**

McKOY, Nick (M) 23 0
H: 6 0 W: 12 06 b.Newham 3-9-86
Source: Scholar.
2003–04 Wimbledon 3 0 **3 0**
2004–05 Milton Keynes D 0 0
2005–06 Milton Keynes D 16 0 **16 0**
2006–07 Cardiff C 0 0
2006–07 *Torquay U* 4 0 **4 0**

McNAUGHTON, Kevin (D) 217 3
H: 5 10 W: 10 06 b.Dundee 28-8-82
Honours: Scotland Under-21, 3 full caps.
1999–2000 Aberdeen 0 0
2000–01 Aberdeen 33 0
2001–02 Aberdeen 34 0
2002–03 Aberdeen 22 1
2003–04 Aberdeen 17 0
2004–05 Aberdeen 35 2
2005–06 Aberdeen 34 0 **175 3**
2006–07 Cardiff C 42 0 **42 0**

McPHAIL, Stephen (M) 208 7
H: 5 8 W: 11 04 b.Westminster 9-12-79
Source: Trainee. *Honours:* Eire B, Under-21, 10 full caps, 1 goal.
1996–97 Leeds U 0 0
1997–98 Leeds U 4 0
1998–99 Leeds U 17 0
1999–2000 Leeds U 24 2
2000–01 Leeds U 7 0
2001–02 Leeds U 1 0
2001–02 *Millwall* 3 0 **3 0**
2002–03 Leeds U 13 0
2003–04 Leeds U 12 1 **78 3**
2003–04 *Nottingham F* 14 0 **14 0**
2004–05 Barnsley 36 2
2005–06 Barnsley 34 2 **70 4**
2006–07 Cardiff C 43 0 **43 0**

PARRY, Paul (M) 110 12
H: 5 11 W: 12 12 b.Chepstow 19-8-80
Source: Hereford U. *Honours:* Wales 11 full caps, 1 goal.
2003–04 Cardiff C 17 1
2004–05 Cardiff C 24 4
2005–06 Cardiff C 27 1
2006–07 Cardiff C 42 6 **110 12**

PURSE, Darren (D) 374 26
H: 6 2 W: 12 08 b.Stepney 14-2-77
Source: Trainee. *Honours:* England Under-21.
1993–94 Leyton Orient 5 0
1994–95 Leyton Orient 38 3
1995–96 Leyton Orient 12 0 **55 3**
1996–97 Oxford U 31 1
1997–98 Oxford U 28 4 **59 5**
1997–98 Birmingham C 8 0
1998–99 Birmingham C 20 0
1999–2000 Birmingham C 38 2
2000–01 Birmingham C 37 3
2001–02 Birmingham C 36 3
2002–03 Birmingham C 20 1
2003–04 Birmingham C 9 0 **168 9**
2004–05 WBA 22 0 **22 0**
2005–06 Cardiff C 39 5
2006–07 Cardiff C 31 4 **70 9**

RAMSEY, Aaron (M) 1 0
H: 5 9 W: 10 07 b.Caerphilly 26-12-90
2006–07 Cardiff C 1 0 **1 0**

REDAN, Iwan (F) 122 36
H: 5 11 W: 12 04 b.Rotterdam 21-8-80
Source: Germinal, Neptunus, Sparta Rotterdam.
1999–2000 Vitesse 0 0
1999–2000 RBC 9 2 **9 2**
2000–01 RKC Waalwijk 24 5
2001–02 RKC Waalwijk 0 0
2002–03 RKC Waalwijk 5 0
2003–04 RKC Waalwijk 18 8
2003–04 Roda JC 11 5 **11 5**
2004–05 RKC Waalwijk 0 0 **47 13**
2004–05 Willem II 26 6
2005–06 Willem II 11 8
2006–07 Willem II 16 2 **53 16**
2006–07 Cardiff C 2 0 **2 0**

SCIMECA, Riccardo (D) 341 16
H: 6 1 W: 12 09 b.Leamington Spa 13-6-75
Source: Trainee. *Honours:* England Under-21, B.
1993–94 Aston Villa 0 0
1994–95 Aston Villa 0 0
1995–96 Aston Villa 17 0
1996–97 Aston Villa 17 0
1997–98 Aston Villa 21 0
1998–99 Aston Villa 18 2 **73 2**
1999–2000 Nottingham F 38 0
2000–01 Nottingham F 36 4
2001–02 Nottingham F 37 0
2002–03 Nottingham F 40 3 **151 7**
2003–04 Leicester C 29 1 **29 1**
2004–05 WBA 33 0
2005–06 WBA 2 0 **35 0**
2005–06 Cardiff C 18 1
2006–07 Cardiff C 35 5 **53 6**

THOMPSON, Steven (F) 248 45
H: 6 2 W: 12 05 b.Paisley 14-10-78
Source: Dundee U BC. *Honours:* Scotland Under-21, 16 full caps, 3 goals.
1996–97 Dundee U 1 0
1997–98 Dundee U 8 0
1998–99 Dundee U 15 1
1999–2000 Dundee U 27 1
2000–01 Dundee U 31 4
2001–02 Dundee U 32 6
2002–03 Dundee U 20 6 **134 18**
2002–03 Rangers 8 2
2003–04 Rangers 16 8
2004–05 Rangers 19 5
2005–06 Rangers 14 2 **57 17**
2005–06 Cardiff C 14 4
2006–07 Cardiff C 43 6 **57 10**

WHITLEY, Jeff (M) **266 14**
H: 5 8 W: 11 06 b.Zambia 28-1-79
Source: Trainee. *Honours:* England Youth, Northern Ireland Under-21, B, 20 full caps, 2 goals.

1995–96	Manchester C	0	0		
1996–97	Manchester C	23	1		
1997–98	Manchester C	17	1		
1998–99	Manchester C	8	1		
1998–99	*Wrexham*	9	2		
1999–2000	Manchester C	42	4		
2000–01	Manchester C	31	1		
2001–02	Manchester C	2	0		
2001–02	*Notts Co*	6	0		
2002–03	Manchester C	0	0	**123**	**8**
2002–03	*Notts Co*	12	0	**18**	**0**
2003–04	Sunderland	33	2		
2004–05	Sunderland	35	0	**68**	**2**
2005–06	Cardiff C	34	1		
2006–07	Cardiff C	0	0	**34**	**1**
2006–07	*Stoke C*	3	0	**3**	**0**
2006–07	*Wrexham*	11	1	**20**	**3**

WHITTINGHAM, Peter (D) **93 5**
H: 5 10 W: 9 13 b.Nuneaton 8-9-84
Source: Trainee. *Honours:* England Youth, Under-20, Under-21.

2002–03	Aston Villa	4	0		
2003–04	Aston Villa	32	0		
2004–05	Aston Villa	13	1		
2004–05	*Burnley*	7	0	**7**	**0**
2005–06	Aston Villa	4	0		
2005–06	*Derby Co*	11	0	**11**	**0**
2006–07	Aston Villa	3	0	**56**	**1**
2006–07	Cardiff C	19	4	**19**	**4**

CARLISLE U (20)

ARANALDE, Zigor (D) **279 11**
H: 6 1 W: 13 03 b.Ibarra 28-2-73
Source: Logrones.

2000–01	Walsall	45	0		
2001–02	Walsall	45	2		
2002–03	Walsall	39	3		
2003–04	Walsall	36	0		
2004–05	Walsall	30	0	**195**	**5**
2004–05	Sheffield W	2	0	**2**	**0**
2005–06	Carlisle U	39	5		
2006–07	Carlisle U	43	1	**82**	**6**

ARNISON, Paul (D) **155 4**
H: 5 10 W: 10 12 b.Hartlepool 18-9-77
Source: Trainee.

1995–96	Newcastle U	0	0		
1996–97	Newcastle U	0	0		
1997–98	Newcastle U	0	0		
1998–99	Newcastle U	0	0		
1999–2000	Newcastle U	0	0		
1999–2000	Hartlepool U	8	1		
2000–01	Hartlepool U	27	1		
2001–02	Hartlepool U	19	0		
2002–03	Hartlepool U	19	1		
2003–04	Hartlepool U	4	0	**77**	**3**
2003–04	Carlisle U	26	1		
2004–05	Carlisle U	0	0		
2005–06	Carlisle U	41	0		
2006–07	Carlisle U	11	0	**78**	**1**

ATKIN, Liam (D) **0 0**
H: 6 1 W: 12 00 b.Ashington 12-12-86
Source: Newcastle U.

2006–07	Carlisle U	0	0		

BILLY, Chris (M) **500 25**
H: 5 11 W: 11 08 b.Huddersfield 2-1-73
Source: Trainee.

1991–92	Huddersfield T	10	2		
1992–93	Huddersfield T	13	0		
1993–94	Huddersfield T	34	0		
1994–95	Huddersfield T	37	2	**94**	**4**
1995–96	Plymouth Arg	32	4		
1996–97	Plymouth Arg	45	3		
1997–98	Plymouth Arg	41	2	**118**	**9**
1998–99	Notts Co	6	0	**6**	**0**
1998–99	Bury	37	0		
1999–2000	Bury	36	4		
2000–01	Bury	46	0		
2001–02	Bury	21	3		
2002–03	Bury	38	4	**178**	**11**
2003–04	Carlisle U	39	1		
2004–05	Carlisle U	0	0		
2005–06	Carlisle U	45	0		
2006–07	Carlisle U	20	0	**104**	**1**

BRADLEY, Adam (G) **0 0**
H: 6 0 W: 12 06 b.Carlisle 25-8-88

2005–06	Carlisle U	0	0		
2006–07	Carlisle U	0	0		

EARL, James (M) **0 0**
H: 5 11 W: 11 08 b.Carlisle 29-11-87
Source: Scholar.

2006–07	Carlisle U	0	0		

GALL, Kevin (F) **218 26**
H: 5 9 W: 10 08 b.Merthyr 4-2-82
Source: From Trainee. *Honours:* Wales Schools, Youth, Under-21.

1998–99	Newcastle U	0	0		
1999–2000	Newcastle U	0	0		
2000–01	Newcastle U	0	0		
2000–01	Bristol R	10	2		
2001–02	Bristol R	31	3		
2002–03	Bristol R	9	0	**50**	**5**
2003–04	Yeovil T	43	8		
2004–05	Yeovil T	43	3		
2005–06	Yeovil T	37	2	**123**	**13**
2006–07	Carlisle U	45	8	**45**	**8**

GRAY, Kevin (D) **484 19**
H: 6 0 W: 14 00 b.Sheffield 7-1-72
Source: Trainee.

1988–89	Mansfield T	1	0		
1989–90	Mansfield T	16	0		
1990–91	Mansfield T	31	1		
1991–92	Mansfield T	18	0		
1992–93	Mansfield T	33	0		
1993–94	Mansfield T	42	2	**141**	**3**
1994–95	Huddersfield T	5	0		
1995–96	Huddersfield T	38	0		
1996–97	Huddersfield T	39	1		
1997–98	Huddersfield T	35	1		
1998–99	Huddersfield T	34	1		
1999–2000	Huddersfield T	18	2		
2000–01	*Stockport Co*	1	0	**1**	**0**
2000–01	Huddersfield T	17	0		
2001–02	Huddersfield T	44	1	**230**	**6**
2002–03	Tranmere R	10	1		
2003–04	Tranmere R	2	0	**12**	**1**
2003–04	Carlisle U	25	3		
2004–05	Carlisle U	0	0		
2005–06	Carlisle U	44	3		
2006–07	Carlisle U	31	3	**100**	**9**

HACKNEY, Simon (M) **48 8**
H: 5 8 W: 9 13 b.Manchester 5-2-84
Source: Woodley Sports.

2005–06	Carlisle U	30	6		
2006–07	Carlisle U	18	2	**48**	**8**

HAWLEY, Karl (F) **107 43**
H: 5 8 W: 12 02 b.Walsall 6-12-81
Source: Scholar.

2000–01	Walsall	0	0		
2001–02	Walsall	1	0		
2002–03	Walsall	0	0		
2002–03	*Raith R*	17	7		
2003–04	Walsall	0	0	**1**	**0**
2003–04	*Raith R*	11	2	**28**	**9**
2004–05	Carlisle U	0	0		
2005–06	Carlisle U	46	22		
2006–07	Carlisle U	32	12	**78**	**34**

HINDMARCH, Stephen (F) **7 0**
H: 5 10 W: 11 11 b.Keswick 16-11-89

2006–07	Carlisle U	7	0	**7**	**0**

HOLMES, Derek (F) **237 40**
H: 6 2 W: 13 00 b.Lanark 18-10-78
Source: Royal Albert.

1995–96	Hearts	0	0		
1996–97	Hearts	1	0		
1997–98	Hearts	1	1		
1997–98	Cowdenbeath	13	5	**13**	**5**
1998–99	Hearts	6	0	**8**	**1**
1999–2000	Ross Co	25	8		
2000–01	Ross Co	0	0	**25**	**8**
2001–02	Bournemouth	37	9		
2002–03	Bournemouth	29	3		
2003–04	Bournemouth	26	2		
2004–05	Bournemouth	23	2	**115**	**16**
2004–05	Carlisle U	0	0		
2005–06	Carlisle U	40	7		
2006–07	Carlisle U	36	3	**76**	**10**

JOYCE, Luke (M) **16 1**
H: 5 11 W: 12 03 b.Bolton 9-7-87
Source: Scholar.

2005–06	Wigan Ath	0	0		
2005–06	Carlisle U	0	0		
2006–07	Carlisle U	16	1	**16**	**1**

KIRKUP, Dan (D) **0 0**
H: 6 3 W: 12 07 b.Hexham 19-5-88
Source: Scholar.

2006–07	Carlisle U	0	0		

LIVESEY, Danny (D) **94 5**
H: 6 3 W: 13 01 b.Salford 31-12-84
Source: Trainee.

2002–03	Bolton W	2	0		
2003–04	Bolton W	0	0		
2003–04	*Notts Co*	11	0	**11**	**0**
2003–04	*Rochdale*	13	0	**13**	**0**
2004–05	Bolton W	0	0	**2**	**0**
2004–05	*Blackpool*	1	0	**1**	**0**
2005–06	Carlisle U	36	4		
2006–07	Carlisle U	31	1	**67**	**5**

LUMSDON, Chris (M) **186 23**
H: 5 11 W: 10 06 b.Newcastle 15-12-79
Source: Trainee.

1997–98	Sunderland	1	0		
1998–99	Sunderland	0	0		
1999–2000	Sunderland	1	0		
1999–2000	*Blackpool*	6	1	**6**	**1**
2000–01	Sunderland	0	0		
2000–01	*Crewe Alex*	16	0	**16**	**0**
2001–02	Sunderland	0	0	**2**	**0**
2001–02	Barnsley	32	7		
2002–03	Barnsley	25	3		
2003–04	Barnsley	28	3		
2004–05	Barnsley	0	0	**85**	**13**
2005–06	Carlisle U	38	7		
2006–07	Carlisle U	39	2	**77**	**9**

McDERMOTT, Neale (M) **31 5**
H: 5 9 W: 10 11 b.Newcastle 8-3-85
Source: Scholar. *Honours:* England Youth.

2001–02	Newcastle U	0	0		
2002–03	Newcastle U	0	0		
2002–03	Fulham	0	0		
2003–04	Fulham	0	0		
2004–05	Fulham	0	0		
2005–06	Fulham	0	0		
2005–06	*Swindon T*	13	2	**13**	**2**
2005–06	*Darlington*	3	0	**3**	**0**
2006–07	Carlisle U	15	3	**15**	**3**

MURPHY, Peter (M) **220 8**
H: 5 10 W: 12 10 b.Dublin 27-10-80
Source: Trainee. *Honours:* Eire Under-21, 1 full cap.

1998–99	Blackburn R	0	0		
1999–2000	Blackburn R	0	0		
2000–01	Blackburn R	0	0		
2000–01	*Halifax T*	21	1	**21**	**1**
2001–02	Blackburn R	0	0		
2001–02	Carlisle U	40	0		
2002–03	Carlisle U	40	2		
2003–04	Carlisle U	35	1		
2004–05	Carlisle U	0	0		
2005–06	Carlisle U	44	2		
2006–07	Carlisle U	40	2	**199**	**7**

MURRAY, Paul (M) **308 26**
H: 5 9 W: 10 08 b.Carlisle 31-8-76
Source: Trainee. *Honours:* England Youth, Under-21, B.

1993–94	Carlisle U	8	0		
1994–95	Carlisle U	5	0		
1995–96	Carlisle U	28	1		
1995–96	QPR	1	0		
1996–97	QPR	32	5		
1997–98	QPR	32	1		
1997–98	QPR	0	0		
1998–99	QPR	39	1		
1999–2000	QPR	30	0		
2000–01	QPR	6	0	**140**	**7**
2001–02	Southampton	1	0	**1**	**0**

2001–02	Oldham Ath	24	5		
2002–03	Oldham Ath	30	1		
2003–04	Oldham Ath	41	9	**95**	**15**
2004–05	Beira Mar	17	2	**17**	**2**
2005–06	Carlisle U	0	0		
2006–07	Carlisle U	14	1	**55**	**2**

RAVEN, David (D) 48 0
H: 6 0 W: 11 04 b.Birkenhead 10-3-85
Source: Scholar. *Honours:* England Youth, Under-20.

2001–02	Liverpool	0	0		
2002–03	Liverpool	0	0		
2003–04	Liverpool	0	0		
2004–05	Liverpool	1	0		
2005–06	Liverpool	0	0	**1**	**0**
2005–06	*Tranmere R*	11	0	**11**	**0**
2006–07	Carlisle U	36	0	**36**	**0**

SMITH, Jeff (M) 125 8
H: 5 11 W: 11 10 b.Middlesbrough 28-6-80
Source: Trainee.

1998–99	Hartlepool U	3	0		
1999–2000	Hartlepool U	0	0	**3**	**0**
From Bishop Auckland					
2000–01	Bolton W	1	0		
2001–02	*Macclesfield T*	8	2	**8**	**2**
2001–02	Bolton W	1	0		
2002–03	Bolton W	0	0		
2003–04	Bolton W	0	0	**2**	**0**
2003–04	*Scunthorpe U*	1	0	**1**	**0**
2003–04	*Rochdale*	1	0	**1**	**0**
2003–04	Preston NE	5	0	**5**	**0**
2004–05	Port Vale	34	1		
2005–06	Port Vale	27	1		
2006–07	Port Vale	27	3	**88**	**5**
2006–07	Carlisle U	17	1	**17**	**1**

THIRLWELL, Paul (M) 170 1
H: 5 11 W: 12 08 b.Springwell 13-2-79
Source: Trainee. *Honours:* England Under-21.

1996–97	Sunderland	0	0		
1997–98	Sunderland	0	0		
1998–99	Sunderland	2	0		
1999–2000	Sunderland	8	0		
1999–2000	*Swindon T*	12	0	**12**	**0**
2000–01	Sunderland	5	0		
2001–02	Sunderland	14	0		
2002–03	Sunderland	19	0		
2003–04	Sunderland	29	0	**77**	**0**
2004–05	Sheffield U	30	1	**30**	**1**
2005–06	Derby Co	21	0		
2006–07	Derby Co	0	0	**21**	**0**
2006–07	Carlisle U	30	0	**30**	**0**

VIPOND, Shaun (M) 4 0
H: 5 11 W: 11 04 b.Hexham 25-12-88
Source: Scholar.

2006–07	Carlisle U	4	0	**4**	**0**

WESTWOOD, Keiren (G) 81 0
H: 6 1 W: 13 10 b.Manchester 23-10-84

2001–02	Manchester C	0	0		
2002–03	Manchester C	0	0		
2003–04	Manchester C	0	0		
2003–04	*Oldham Ath*	0	0		
2004–05	Manchester C	0	0		
2005–06	Manchester C	0	0		
2005–06	Carlisle U	35	0		
2006–07	Carlisle U	46	0	**81**	**0**

WILLIAMS, Tony (G) 241 0
H: 6 2 W: 13 09 b.Maesteg 20-9-77
Source: Trainee. *Honours:* Wales Youth, Under-21.

1996–97	Blackburn R	0	0		
1997–98	Blackburn R	0	0		
1997–98	*QPR*	0	0		
1998–99	Blackburn R	0	0		
1998–99	*Macclesfield T*	4	0		
1998–99	*Huddersfield T*	0	0		
1998–99	*Bristol R*	9	0	**9**	**0**
1999–2000	Blackburn R	0	0		
1999–2000	*Gillingham*	2	0	**2**	**0**
1999–2000	*Macclesfield T*	11	0	**15**	**0**
2000–01	Hartlepool U	41	0		
2001–02	Hartlepool U	43	0		
2002–03	Hartlepool U	46	0		
2003–04	Hartlepool U	1	0	**131**	**0**
2003–04	*Swansea C*	0	0		
2003–04	*Stockport Co*	15	0	**15**	**0**
2004–05	Grimsby T	46	0	**46**	**0**
2005–06	Carlisle U	11	0		
2005–06	*Bury*	3	0	**3**	**0**
2006–07	Carlisle U	0	0	**11**	**0**
2006–07	*Wrexham*	9	0	**9**	**0**

CHARLTON ATH (21)

AMBROSE, Darren (M) 121 19
H: 6 0 W: 11 00 b.Harlow 29-2-84
Source: Scholar. *Honours:* England Youth, Under-20, Under-21.

2001–02	Ipswich T	1	0		
2002–03	Ipswich T	29	8	**30**	**8**
2002–03	Newcastle U	1	0		
2003–04	Newcastle U	24	2		
2004–05	Newcastle U	12	3	**37**	**5**
2005–06	Charlton Ath	28	3		
2006–07	Charlton Ath	26	3	**54**	**6**

ANDERSEN, Stephan (G) 17 0
H: 6 2 W: 13 07 b.Copenhagen 26-11-81
Source: AB Copenhagen. *Honours:* Denmark Youth, Under-20, Under-21, 1 full cap.

2004–05	Charlton Ath	2	0		
2005–06	Charlton Ath	15	0		
2006–07	Charlton Ath	0	0	**17**	**0**

To Brondby January 2007

ASHTON, Nathan (D) 0 0
H: 5 8 W: 9 07 b.Plaistow 30-1-87
Source: Scholar. *Honours:* England Youth, Under-20.

2004–05	Charlton Ath	0	0		
2005–06	Charlton Ath	0	0		
2006–07	Charlton Ath	0	0		
2006–07	*Millwall*	0	0		

BENT, Darren (F) 190 80
H: 5 11 W: 12 07 b.Wandsworth 6-2-84
Source: Scholar. *Honours:* England Youth, Under-21, 2 full caps.

2001–02	Ipswich T	5	1		
2002–03	Ipswich T	35	12		
2003–04	Ipswich T	37	16		
2004–05	Ipswich T	45	20	**122**	**49**
2005–06	Charlton Ath	36	18		
2006–07	Charlton Ath	32	13	**68**	**31**

BENT, Marcus (F) 398 82
H: 6 2 W: 13 03 b.Hammersmith 19-5-78
Source: Trainee. *Honours:* England Under-21.

1995–96	Brentford	12	1		
1996–97	Brentford	34	3		
1997–98	Brentford	24	4	**70**	**8**
1997–98	Crystal Palace	16	5		
1998–99	Crystal Palace	12	0	**28**	**5**
1998–99	Port Vale	15	0		
1999–2000	Port Vale	8	1	**23**	**1**
1999–2000	Sheffield U	32	15		
2000–01	Sheffield U	16	5	**48**	**20**
2000–01	Blackburn R	28	8		
2001–02	Blackburn R	9	0	**37**	**8**
2001–02	Ipswich T	25	9		
2002–03	Ipswich T	32	11		
2003–04	Ipswich T	4	1	**61**	**21**
2003–04	*Leicester C*	33	9	**33**	**9**
2004–05	Everton	37	6		
2005–06	Everton	18	1	**55**	**7**
2005–06	Charlton Ath	13	2		
2006–07	Charlton Ath	30	1	**43**	**3**

BOUGHERRA, Madjid (D) 93 4
H: 6 2 W: 14 00 b.Dijon 7-10-82
Source: Longvic. *Honours:* Algeria 13 full caps.

2002–03	Gueugnon	1	0		
2003–04	Gueugnon	8	1		
2004–05	Gueugnon	30	0		
2005–06	Gueugnon	10	0	**49**	**1**
2005–06	Crewe Alex	11	1	**11**	**1**
2006–07	Sheffield W	28	2	**28**	**2**
2006–07	Charlton Ath	5	0	**5**	**0**

DIAWARA, Souleymane (D) 218 6
H: 6 1 W: 12 08 b.Gabou 24-12-78
Source: Frileuse. *Honours:* Senegal 12 full caps.

1997–98	Le Havre	6	0		
1998–99	Le Havre	4	0		
1999–2000	Le Havre	25	0		
2000–01	Le Havre	14	0		
2001–02	Le Havre	30	1		
2002–03	Le Havre	32	1	**111**	**2**
2003–04	Sochaux	29	2		
2004–05	Sochaux	29	1		
2005–06	Sochaux	23	1		
2006–07	Sochaux	3	0	**84**	**4**
2006–07	Charlton Ath	23	0	**23**	**0**

DICKSON, Christopher (F) 0 0
b.East Dulwich 28-12-84
Source: Dulwich H.

2006–07	Charlton Ath	0	0		

EL KARKOURI, Talal (D) 161 8
H: 6 1 W: 12 03 b.Casablanca 8-7-76
Source: Casablanca School of Sportsmen. *Honours:* Morocco 31 full caps, 1 goal.

1999–2000	Paris St Germain	10	0		
2000–01	Paris St Germain	11	0		
2000–01	Aris Salonika	11	0	**11**	**0**
2001–02	Paris St Germain	16	0		
2002–03	Sunderland	8	0	**8**	**0**
2003–04	Paris St Germain	27	0	**64**	**0**
2004–05	Charlton Ath	32	5		
2005–06	Charlton Ath	10	0		
2006–07	Charlton Ath	36	3	**78**	**8**

ELLIOT, Rob (G) 11 0
H: 6 3 W: 14 10 b.Greenwich 30-4-86
Source: Scholar.

2004–05	Charlton Ath	0	0		
2004–05	*Notts Co*	4	0	**4**	**0**
2005–06	Charlton Ath	0	0		
2006–07	Charlton Ath	0	0		
2006–07	*Accrington S*	7	0	**7**	**0**

FAYE, Amdy (M) 186 3
H: 6 1 W: 12 06 b.Dakar 12-3-77
Source: Frejus. *Honours:* Senegal 18 full caps.

1998–99	Auxerre	0	0		
1999–2000	Auxerre	3	0		
2000–01	Auxerre	23	0		
2001–02	Auxerre	20	0		
2002–03	Auxerre	34	2	**80**	**2**
2003–04	Portsmouth	27	0		
2004–05	Portsmouth	20	0	**47**	**0**
2004–05	Newcastle U	9	0		
2005–06	Newcastle U	22	0	**31**	**0**
2006–07	Charlton Ath	28	1	**28**	**1**

FORTUNE, Jon (D) 155 6
H: 6 2 W: 12 12 b.Islington 23-8-80
Source: Trainee.

1998–99	Charlton Ath	0	0		
1999–2000	Charlton Ath	0	0		
1999–2000	*Mansfield T*	4	0		
2000–01	Charlton Ath	0	0		
2000–01	*Mansfield T*	14	0	**18**	**0**
2001–02	Charlton Ath	19	0		
2002–03	Charlton Ath	26	1		
2003–04	Charlton Ath	28	2		
2004–05	Charlton Ath	31	2		
2005–06	Charlton Ath	11	0		
2006–07	Charlton Ath	8	0	**123**	**5**
2006–07	*Stoke C*	14	1	**14**	**1**

GIBBS, Cory (D) 106 6
H: 6 3 W: 12 12 b.Fort Lauderdale 14-1-80
Source: Brown Univ. *Honours:* USA Under-21, Under-23, 19 full caps.

2001–02	St Pauli II	5	1	**5**	**1**
2001–02	St Pauli	25	1		
2002–03	St Pauli	21	0		
2003–04	St Pauli	14	3	**60**	**4**
2004	Dallas Burn	21	0	**21**	**0**
2004–05	Feyenoord	15	1	**15**	**1**
2005–06	*Den Haag*	5	0	**5**	**0**
2006–07	Charlton Ath	0	0		

GISLASON, Rurik (M) **0 0**

H: 6 0 W: 11 04 b.Reykjavik 25-2-88

Source: Kopavogur, Anderlecht. *Honours:* Iceland 1 full cap.

2005–06	Charlton Ath	0	0		
2006–07	Charlton Ath	0	0		

HASSELBAINK, Jimmy Floyd (F) **382 183**

H: 5 10 W: 13 10 b.Paramaribo 27-3-72

Honours: Holland 23 full caps, 9 goals.

1995–96	Campomairorense	31	12	**31**	**12**
1996–97	Boavista	29	20	**29**	**20**
1997–98	Leeds U	33	16		
1998–99	Leeds U	36	18	**69**	**34**
1999–2000	Atletico Madrid	34	24	**34**	**24**
2000–01	Chelsea	35	23		
2001–02	Chelsea	35	23		
2002–03	Chelsea	36	11		
2003–04	Chelsea	30	12	**136**	**69**
2004–05	Middlesbrough	36	13		
2005–06	Middlesbrough	22	9	**58**	**22**
2006–07	Charlton Ath	25	2	**25**	**2**

HOLLAND, Matt (M) **489 67**

H: 5 10 W: 12 03 b.Bury 11-4-74

Source: Trainee. *Honours:* Eire B, 49 full caps, 5 goals.

1992–93	West Ham U	0	0		
1993–94	West Ham U	0	0		
1994–95	West Ham U	0	0		
1994–95	Bournemouth	16	1		
1995–96	Bournemouth	43	10		
1996–97	Bournemouth	45	7	**104**	**18**
1997–98	Ipswich T	46	10		
1998–99	Ipswich T	46	5		
1999–2000	Ipswich T	46	10		
2000–01	Ipswich T	38	3		
2001–02	Ipswich T	38	3		
2002–03	Ipswich T	45	7	**259**	**38**
2003–04	Charlton Ath	38	6		
2004–05	Charlton Ath	32	3		
2005–06	Charlton Ath	23	1		
2006–07	Charlton Ath	33	1	**126**	**11**

HREIDARSSON, Hermann (D) **402 19**

H: 6 3 W: 12 12 b.Reykjavik 11-7-74

Honours: Iceland Under-21, 65 full caps, 4 goals.

1993	IBV	2	0		
1994	IBV	18	2		
1995	IBV	18	1		
1996	IBV	17	2		
1997	IBV	11	0	**66**	**5**
1997–98	Crystal Palace	30	2		
1998–99	Crystal Palace	7	0	**37**	**2**
1998–99	Brentford	33	4		
1999–2000	Brentford	8	2	**41**	**6**
1999–2000	Wimbledon	24	1	**24**	**1**
2000–01	Ipswich T	36	1		
2001–02	Ipswich T	38	1		
2002–03	Ipswich T	28	0	**102**	**2**
2002–03	Charlton Ath	0	0		
2003–04	Charlton Ath	33	2		
2004–05	Charlton Ath	34	1		
2005–06	Charlton Ath	34	0		
2006–07	Charlton Ath	31	0	**132**	**3**

HUGHES, Bryan (M) **416 51**

H: 5 10 W: 11 08 b.Liverpool 19-6-76

Source: Trainee.

1993–94	Wrexham	11	0		
1994–95	Wrexham	38	9		
1995–96	Wrexham	22	0		
1996–97	Wrexham	23	3	**94**	**12**
1996–97	Birmingham C	11	0		
1997–98	Birmingham C	40	5		
1998–99	Birmingham C	28	3		
1999–2000	Birmingham C	45	10		
2000–01	Birmingham C	45	4		
2001–02	Birmingham C	31	7		
2002–03	Birmingham C	22	2		
2003–04	Birmingham C	26	3	**248**	**34**
2004–05	Charlton Ath	17	1		
2005–06	Charlton Ath	33	3		
2006–07	Charlton Ath	24	1	**74**	**5**

JOHN, Alistair (M) **11 0**

H: 6 0 W: 14 00 b.London 28-11-87

Source: Scholar.

2005–06	Charlton Ath	0	0		
2006–07	Charlton Ath	0	0		
2006–07	*Brighton & HA*	4	0	**4**	**0**
2006–07	*Torquay U*	7	0	**7**	**0**

KEMENES, Szabolcs (G) **0 0**

H: 6 2 W: 12 12 b.Budapest 18-5-86

Source: ferencvaros.

2004–05	Charlton Ath	0	0		
2005–06	Charlton Ath	0	0		
2006–07	Charlton Ath	0	0		

KISHISHEV, Radostin (D) **382 19**

H: 5 11 W: 12 03 b.Bourgas 30-7-74

Honours: Bulgaria 74 full caps.

1991–92	Chernomorets	6	1		
1992–93	Chernomorets	23	2		
1993–94	Chernomorets	23	1	**52**	**4**
1994–95	Neftochimik	14	0		
1995–96	Neftochimik	30	0		
1996–97	Neftochimik	30	6		
1997–98	Neftochimik	1	0	**75**	**6**
1997–98	Bursaspor	20	3	**20**	**3**
1997–98	Litets Lovech	5	0		
1998–99	Litets Lovech	26	2		
1999–2000	Litets Lovech	15	2	**46**	**4**
2000–01	Charlton Ath	27	0		
2001–02	Charlton Ath	3	0		
2002–03	Charlton Ath	34	2		
2003–04	Charlton Ath	33	0		
2004–05	Charlton Ath	31	0		
2005–06	Charlton Ath	37	0		
2006–07	Charlton Ath	14	0	**179**	**2**
2006–07	*Leeds U*	10	0	**10**	**0**

LISBIE, Kevin (F) **179 22**

H: 5 10 W: 11 06 b.Hackney 17-10-78

Source: Trainee. *Honours:* England Youth. Jamaica 10 full caps, 2 goals.

1996–97	Charlton Ath	25	1		
1997–98	Charlton Ath	17	1		
1998–99	Charlton Ath	1	0		
1998–99	*Gillingham*	7	4	**7**	**4**
1999–2000	Charlton Ath	0	0		
1999–2000	*Reading*	2	0	**2**	**0**
2000–01	Charlton Ath	18	0		
2000–01	*QPR*	2	0	**2**	**0**
2001–02	Charlton Ath	22	5		
2002–03	Charlton Ath	32	4		
2003–04	Charlton Ath	9	4		
2004–05	Charlton Ath	17	1		
2005–06	Charlton Ath	6	0		
2005–06	*Norwich C*	6	1	**6**	**1**
2005–06	*Derby Co*	7	1	**7**	**1**
2006–07	Charlton Ath	8	0	**155**	**16**

MYHRE, Thomas (G) **277 0**

H: 6 4 W: 14 02 b.Sarpsborg 16-10-73

Source: Norway Youth, Under-21, 56 full caps.

1993	Viking	22	0		
1994	Viking	22	0		
1995	Viking	24	0		
1996	Viking	0	0		
1997	Viking	26	0	**94**	**0**
1997–98	Everton	22	0		
1998–99	Everton	38	0		
1999–2000	Everton	4	0		
1999–2000	*Rangers*	3	0	**3**	**0**
1999–2000	*Birmingham C*	7	0	**7**	**0**
2000–01	Everton	6	0		
2000–01	*Tranmere R*	3	0	**3**	**0**
2000–01	FC Copenhagen	14	0	**14**	**0**
2001–02	Everton	0	0	**70**	**0**
2001–02	Besiktas	13	0	**13**	**0**
2002–03	Sunderland	2	0		
2003–04	Sunderland	4	0		
2003–04	*Crystal Palace*	15	0	**15**	**0**
2004–05	Sunderland	31	0	**37**	**0**
2005–06	Charlton Ath	20	0		
2006–07	Charlton Ath	1	0	**21**	**0**

POUSO, Omar (M) **169 19**

H: 6 0 W: 11 11 b.Montevideo 28-2-80

Honours: Uruguay 8 full caps, 1 goal.

1998	Danubio	3	0		
1999	Danubio	9	0		
2000	Danubio	32	9		
2001	Danubio	21	1		
2002	Danubio	29	4		
2003	Danubio	39	3		
2004	Danubio	15	2		
2005	Danubio	12	0	**160**	**19**
2006	Penarol	8	0	**8**	**0**
2006–07	Charlton Ath	1	0	**1**	**0**

To Penarol February 2007

RANDOLPH, Darren (G) **4 0**

H: 6 2 W: 14 00 b.Dublin 12-5-87

Source: Ardmore R Scholar, Eire B, Under-21.

2004–05	Charlton Ath	0	0		
2005–06	Charlton Ath	0	0		
2006–07	Charlton Ath	1	0	**1**	**0**
2006–07	*Gillingham*	3	0	**3**	**0**

REID, Andy (M) **186 24**

H: 5 9 W: 12 08 b.Dublin 29-7-82

Source: Trainee. *Honours:* Eire Youth, Under-21, 22 full caps, 4 goals.

1999–2000	Nottingham F	0	0		
2000–01	Nottingham F	14	2		
2001–02	Nottingham F	29	0		
2002–03	Nottingham F	30	1		
2003–04	Nottingham F	46	13		
2004–05	Nottingham F	25	5	**144**	**21**
2004–05	Tottenham H	13	1		
2005–06	Tottenham H	13	0	**26**	**1**
2006–07	Charlton Ath	16	2	**16**	**2**

RICKETTS, Mark (D) **5 0**

H: 6 0 W: 11 02 b.Sidcup 7-10-84

Source: Scholar.

2005–06	Charlton Ath	0	0		
2005–06	*Milton Keynes D*	5	0	**5**	**0**
2006–07	Charlton Ath	0	0		

ROMMEDAHL, Dennis (F) **279 38**

H: 5 9 W: 11 08 b.Copenhagen 22-7-78

Honours: Denmark Youth, Under-21, 67 full caps, 15 goals.

1995–96	Lyngby	9	0	**9**	**0**
1996–97	PSV Eindhoven	2	0		
1997–98	RKC	34	5	**34**	**5**
1998–99	PSV Eindhoven	19	2		
1999–2000	PSV Eindhoven	23	0		
2000–01	PSV Eindhoven	31	5		
2001–02	PSV Eindhoven	34	12		
2002–03	PSV Eindhoven	33	6		
2003–04	PSV Eindhoven	19	4	**161**	**29**
2004–05	Charlton Ath	26	2		
2005–06	Charlton Ath	21	2		
2006–07	Charlton Ath	28	0	**75**	**4**

SAM, Lloyd (F) **26 0**

H: 5 10 W: 11 00 b.Leeds 27-9-84

Honours: England Youth, Under-20.

2002–03	Charlton Ath	0	0		
2003–04	Charlton Ath	0	0		
2003–04	*Leyton Orient*	10	0	**10**	**0**
2004–05	Charlton Ath	1	0		
2005–06	Charlton Ath	2	0		
2006–07	Charlton Ath	7	0	**10**	**0**
2006–07	*Sheffield W*	4	0	**4**	**0**
2006–07	*Southend U*	2	0	**2**	**0**

SANKOFA, Osei (D) **22 0**

H: 6 0 W: 12 04 b.London 19-3-85

Source: Scholar. *Honours:* England Youth, Under-20.

2002–03	Charlton Ath	1	0		
2003–04	Charlton Ath	0	0		
2004–05	Charlton Ath	0	0		
2005–06	Charlton Ath	4	0		
2005–06	*Bristol C*	8	0	**8**	**0**
2006–07	Charlton Ath	9	0	**14**	**0**

SORONDO, Gonzalo (D) **122 6**

H: 5 11 W: 12 08 b.Montevideo 9-10-79

Honours: Uruguay 27 full caps, 1 goal.

1998	Defensor	4	0		
1999	Defensor	12	0		
2000	Defensor	27	4		
2001	Defensor	17	0	**60**	**4**
2001–02	Internazionale	11	0		
2002–03	Internazionale	0	0		
2003–04	Internazionale	0	0	**11**	**0**

2003–04	Standard Liege	23	2	**23**	**2**
2004–05	Crystal Palace	20	0	**20**	**0**
2005–06	Charlton Ath	7	0		
2006–07	Charlton Ath	1	0	**8**	**0**

STAUNTON, Mark (D) **0 0**
H: 5 11 W: 12 00 b.Glasgow 30-1-89
Source: Celtic.

2006–07	Charlton Ath	0	0		

TANSKA, Jani (D) **0 0**
H: 6 4 W: 12 12 b.Anjalankoski 29-7-88
Source: Scholar.

2005–06	Charlton Ath	0	0		
2006–07	Charlton Ath	0	0		

THATCHER, Ben (D) **299 2**
H: 5 10 W: 12 07 b.Swindon 30-11-75
Source: Trainee. *Honours:* England Youth, Under-21, Wales 7 full caps.

1992–93	Millwall	0	0		
1993–94	Millwall	8	0		
1994–95	Millwall	40	1		
1995–96	Millwall	42	0	**90**	**1**
1996–97	Wimbledon	9	0		
1997–98	Wimbledon	26	0		
1998–99	Wimbledon	31	0		
1999–2000	Wimbledon	20	0	**86**	**0**
2000–01	Tottenham H	12	0		
2001–02	Tottenham H	12	0		
2002–03	Tottenham H	12	0	**36**	**0**
2003–04	Leicester C	29	1	**29**	**1**
2004–05	Manchester C	18	0		
2005–06	Manchester C	18	0		
2006–07	Manchester C	11	0	**47**	**0**
2006–07	Charlton Ath	11	0	**11**	**0**

THOMAS, Jerome (M) **80 10**
H: 5 9 W: 11 09 b.Wembley 23-3-83
Source: Scholar. *Honours:* England Youth, Under-20, Under-21.

2001–02	Arsenal	0	0		
2001–02	*QPR*	4	1		
2002–03	Arsenal	0	0		
2002–03	*QPR*	6	2	**10**	**3**
2003–04	Arsenal	0	0		
2003–04	Charlton Ath	1	0		
2004–05	Charlton Ath	24	3		
2005–06	Charlton Ath	25	1		
2006–07	Charlton Ath	20	3	**70**	**7**

VARNEY, Alex (F) **1 0**
H: 5 11 W: 11 13 b.Bromley 27-12-84
Source: Trainee.

2003–04	Charlton Ath	0	0		
2004–05	Charlton Ath	0	0		
2005–06	Charlton Ath	0	0		
2005–06	*Barnet*	1	0	**1**	**0**
2006–07	Charlton Ath	0	0		

WALKER, James (F) **30 3**
H: 5 10 W: 11 10 b.Hackney 25-11-87
Source: Scholar. *Honours:* England Youth.

2004–05	Charlton Ath	0	0		
2005–06	Charlton Ath	0	0		
2005–06	*Hartlepool U*	4	0	**4**	**0**
2006–07	Charlton Ath	0	0		
2006–07	*Bristol R*	4	1	**4**	**1**
2006–07	*Leyton Orient*	14	2	**14**	**2**
2006–07	*Notts Co*	8	0	**8**	**0**

WALTON, Simon (D) **59 6**
H: 6 1 W: 13 05 b.Sherburn-in-Elmet 13-9-87
Source: Scholar. *Honours:* England Youth.

2004–05	Leeds U	30	3		
2005–06	Leeds U	4	0	**34**	**3**
2006–07	Charlton Ath	0	0		
2006–07	*Ipswich T*	19	3	**19**	**3**
2006–07	*Cardiff C*	6	0	**6**	**0**

WESTON, Myles (F) **4 0**
H: 5 11 W: 12 05 b.Lewisham 12-3-88
Source: Scholar.

2006–07	Charlton Ath	0	0		
2006–07	*Notts Co*	4	0	**4**	**0**

YOUGA, Kelly (D) **15 0**
H: 6 1 W: 12 00 b.Bangui 22-9-85
Source: Lyon.

2005–06	Charlton Ath	0	0		
2005–06	*Bristol C*	4	0	**4**	**0**
2006–07	Charlton Ath	0	0		
2006–07	*Bradford C*	11	0	**11**	**0**

YOUNG, Luke (D) **245 4**
H: 6 0 W: 12 04 b.Harlow 19-7-79
Source: Trainee. *Honours:* England Youth, Under-21, 7 full caps.

1997–98	Tottenham H	0	0		
1998–99	Tottenham H	15	0		
1999–2000	Tottenham H	20	0		
2000–01	Tottenham H	23	0	**58**	**0**
2001–02	Charlton Ath	34	0		
2002–03	Charlton Ath	32	0		
2003–04	Charlton Ath	24	0		
2004–05	Charlton Ath	36	2		
2005–06	Charlton Ath	32	1		
2006–07	Charlton Ath	29	1	**187**	**4**

ZHENG-ZHI (M) **132 44**
H: 5 11 W: 11 11 b.Shenyang 20-8-80
Honours: China 37 full caps, 11 goals.

2001	Shenzhen	23	3		
2002	Shenzhen	22	6		
2003	Shenzhen	16	3		
2004	Shenzhen	16	2	**77**	**14**
2005	Shandong Luneng	17	8		
2006	Shandong Luneng	26	21	**43**	**29**
2006–07	Charlton Ath	12	1	**12**	**1**

Scholars
Arter, Harry Nicolas; Basey, Grant William; Coleman, Rhys Deor; Harkin, Ruairi; Saunders, Christopher Michael; Thomas, Aswad; Wagstaff, Scott Andrew; Woolley, Joe; Wright, Josh; Yussuff, Rashid Toks.

CHELSEA (22)

BALLACK, Michael (M) **324 97**
H: 6 2 W: 12 08 b.Gorlitz 26-9-76
Source: Motor Karl-Marx-Stadt.Germany Under-21, 77 full caps, 35 goals.

1995–96	Chemnitzer	15	0		
1996–97	Chemnitzer	34	10	**49**	**10**
1997–98	Kaiserslautern A	17	8	**17**	**8**
1997–98	Kaiserslautern	16	0		
1998–99	Kaiserslautern	30	4	**46**	**4**
1999–2000	Leverkusen	23	3		
2000–01	Leverkusen	27	7		
2001–02	Leverkusen	29	17	**79**	**27**
2002–03	Bayern Munich	26	10		
2003–04	Bayern Munich	28	7		
2004–05	Bayern Munich	27	13		
2005–06	Bayern Munich	26	13	**107**	**43**
2006–07	Chelsea	26	5	**26**	**5**

BERTRAND, Ryan (D) **5 0**
H: 5 10 W: 11 00 b.Southwark 5-8-89
Source: Scholar.

2006–07	Chelsea	0	0		
2006–07	*Bournemouth*	5	0	**5**	**0**

BOULAHROUZ, Khalid (D) **129 5**
H: 6 0 W: 12 10 b.Maassluis 28-12-81
Source: Excelsior Maassluis, Ajax, Haarlem. *Honours:* Holland 19 full caps.

2001–02	RKC Waalwijk	1	0		
2002–03	RKC Waalwijk	31	0		
2003–04	RKC Waalwijk	29	4		
2004–05	RKC Waalwijk	3	0	**64**	**4**
2004–05	Hamburg	24	1		
2005–06	Hamburg	28	0	**52**	**1**
2006–07	Chelsea	13	0	**13**	**0**

BRIDGE, Wayne (D) **234 3**
H: 5 10 W: 12 13 b.Southampton 5-8-80
Source: Trainee. *Honours:* England Youth, Under-21, 25 full caps, 1 goal.

1997–98	Southampton	0	0		
1998–99	Southampton	23	0		
1999–2000	Southampton	19	1		
2000–01	Southampton	38	0		
2001–02	Southampton	38	0		
2002–03	Southampton	34	1	**152**	**2**
2003–04	Chelsea	33	1		
2004–05	Chelsea	15	0		
2005–06	Chelsea	0	0		
2005–06	*Fulham*	12	0	**12**	**0**
2006–07	Chelsea	22	0	**70**	**1**

CECH, Petr (G) **217 0**
H: 6 5 W: 14 07 b.Plzen 20-5-82
Honours: Czech Republic Youth, Under-20, Under-21, 52 full caps.

1998–99	Viktoria Plzen	0	0		
1999–2000	Chmel	1	0		
2000–01	Chmel	26	0	**27**	**0**
2001–02	Sparta Prague	26	0	**26**	**0**
2002–03	Rennes	37	0		
2003–04	Rennes	38	0	**75**	**0**
2004–05	Chelsea	35	0		
2005–06	Chelsea	34	0		
2006–07	Chelsea	20	0	**89**	**0**

COLE, Ashley (D) **193 9**
H: 5 8 W: 10 05 b.Stepney 20-12-80
Source: Trainee. *Honours:* England Youth, Under-21, B, 58 full caps.

1998–99	Arsenal	0	0		
1999–2000	Arsenal	1	0		
1999–2000	*Crystal Palace*	14	1	**14**	**1**
2000–01	Arsenal	17	3		
2001–02	Arsenal	29	2		
2002–03	Arsenal	31	1		
2003–04	Arsenal	32	0		
2004–05	Arsenal	35	2		
2005–06	Arsenal	11	0		
2006–07	Arsenal	0	0	**156**	**8**
2006–07	Chelsea	23	0	**23**	**0**

COLE, Joe (M) **236 26**
H: 5 9 W: 11 09 b.Islington 8-11-81
Source: Trainee. *Honours:* England Schools, Youth, Under-21, B, 40 full caps, 7 goals.

1998–99	West Ham U	8	0		
1999–2000	West Ham U	22	1		
2000–01	West Ham U	30	5		
2001–02	West Ham U	30	0		
2002–03	West Ham U	36	4	**126**	**10**
2003–04	Chelsea	35	1		
2004–05	Chelsea	28	8		
2005–06	Chelsea	34	7		
2006–07	Chelsea	13	0	**110**	**16**

CORK, Jack (D) **7 0**
H: 6 0 W: 10 12 b.Carshalton 25-6-89
Source: Scholar.

2006–07	Chelsea	0	0		
2006–07	*Bournemouth*	7	0	**7**	**0**

CRESPO, Hernan (F) **358 174**
H: 6 0 W: 12 11 b.Florida, Arg 5-7-75
Honours: Argentina 59 full caps, 32 goals.

1993–94	River Plate	25	13		
1994–95	River Plate	18	5		
1995–96	River Plate	21	5	**64**	**23**
1996–97	Parma	27	12		
1997–98	Parma	25	12		
1998–99	Parma	30	16		
1999–2000	Parma	34	22	**116**	**62**
2000–01	Lazio	32	26		
2001–02	Lazio	22	13	**54**	**39**
2002–03	Internazionale	18	7		
2003–04	Chelsea	19	10		
2004–05	*AC Milan*	28	10	**28**	**10**
2005–06	Chelsea	30	10		
2006–07	Internazionale	29	13	**47**	**20**
2006–07	Chelsea	0	0	**49**	**20**

CUDICINI, Carlo (G) **213 0**
H: 6 1 W: 12 08 b.Milan 6-9-73
Honours: Italy Under-21.

1991–92	AC Milan	0	0		
1992–93	AC Milan	0	0		
1993–94	Como	6	0	**6**	**0**
1994–95	AC Milan	0	0		
1995–96	AC Milan	0	0		
1995–96	Prato	30	0	**30**	**0**
1996–97	Lazio	1	0	**1**	**0**
1997–98	Castel di Sangro	14	0		
1998–99	Castel di Sangro	32	0	**46**	**0**
1999–2000	Chelsea	1	0		
2000–01	Chelsea	24	0		
2001–02	Chelsea	28	0		
2002–03	Chelsea	36	0		
2003–04	Chelsea	26	0		
2004–05	Chelsea	3	0		
2005–06	Chelsea	4	0		
2006–07	Chelsea	8	0	**130**	**0**

DIARRA, Lassana (M) **13 0**
H: 5 8 W: 11 02 b.Paris 10-3-85
Source: Le Havre. *Honours:* France Youth, Under-21, Under-23, 3 full caps.

2005–06	Chelsea	3	0		
2006–07	Chelsea	10	0	**13**	**0**

DROGBA, Didier (F) **235 91**
H: 6 2 W: 14 05 b.Abidjan 11-3-78
Honours: Ivory Coast 40 full caps, 28 goals.

1998–99	Le Mans	2	0		
1999–2000	Le Mans	30	6		
2000–01	Le Mans	11	0		
2001–02	Le Mans	21	5	**64**	**11**
2001–02	Guingamp	11	3		
2002–03	Guingamp	34	17	**45**	**20**
2003–04	Marseille	35	18	**35**	**18**
2004–05	Chelsea	26	10		
2005–06	Chelsea	29	12		
2006–07	Chelsea	36	20	**91**	**42**

ELMER, Jonas (D) **0 0**
b.Zurich 28-2-88
Source: Grasshoppers, Chelsea Scholar.

2005–06	Chelsea	0	0		
2006–07	Chelsea	0	0		

ESSIEN, Michael (M) **201 22**
H: 5 10 W: 13 06 b.Accra 3-12-82
Honours: Ghana 25 full caps, 5 goals.

2000–01	Bastia	13	1		
2001–02	Bastia	24	4		
2002–03	Bastia	29	6	**66**	**11**
2003–04	Lyon	34	3		
2004–05	Lyon	37	4	**71**	**7**
2005–06	Chelsea	31	2		
2006–07	Chelsea	33	2	**64**	**4**

FERNANDES, Ricardo (M) **0 0**
b.Leiria 20-4-78
Source: Scholar.

2006–07	Chelsea	0	0		

FERREIRA, Fabio (M) **0 0**
b.Barreiro 3-5-89
Source: Scholar.

2006–07	Chelsea	0	0		

GEREMI (M) **213 20**
H: 5 9 W: 13 01 b.Bafoussam 20-12-78
Source: From Racing Bafousam. *Honours:* Cameroon 66 full caps, 2 goals.

1997	Cerro Porteno	6	0	**6**	**0**
1997–98	Genclerbirligi	28	4		
1998–99	Genclerbirligi	29	5	**57**	**9**
1999–2000	Real Madrid	20	0		
2000–01	Real Madrid	16	0		
2001–02	Real Madrid	9	0	**45**	**0**
2002–03	Middlesbrough	33	7	**33**	**7**
2003–04	Chelsea	25	1		
2004–05	Chelsea	13	0		
2005–06	Chelsea	15	2		
2006–07	Chelsea	19	1	**72**	**4**

GRANT, Anthony (M) **43 0**
H: 5 10 W: 11 01 b.Lambeth 4-6-87
Source: Scholar. *Honours:* England Youth.

2004–05	Chelsea	1	0		
2005–06	Chelsea	0	0		
2005–06	*Oldham Ath*	2	0	**2**	**0**
2006–07	Chelsea	0	0	**1**	**0**
2006–07	*Wycombe W*	40	0	**40**	**0**

HAMANN, Nick (G) **0 0**
H: 6 2 W: 12 00 b.Dresden 5-9-87
Source: Scholar. *Honours:* Germany Youth.

2006–07	Chelsea	0	0		

HEDMAN, Magnus (G) **261 0**
H: 6 3 W: 14 00 b.Stockholm 19-3-73
Honours: Sweden 56 full caps.

1990	AIK Stockholm	2	0		
1991	AIK Stockholm	2	0		
1992	AIK Stockholm	7	0		
1993	AIK Stockholm	26	0		
1994	AIK Stockholm	26	0		
1995	AIK Stockholm	25	0		
1996	AIK Stockholm	26	0		
1997	AIK Stockholm	13	0	**127**	**0**
1997–98	Coventry C	14	0		
1998–99	Coventry C	36	0		
1999–2000	Coventry C	35	0		
2000–01	Coventry C	15	0		
2001–02	Coventry C	34	0		
2002–03	Coventry C	0	0		
2003–04	Coventry C	0	0		
2004–05	Coventry C	0	0		
2005–06	Coventry C	0	0	**134**	**0**
2006–07	Chelsea	0	0		

HILARIO (G) **166 0**
H: 6 2 W: 13 05 b.San Pedro da Cova 21-10-75
Honours: Portugal Under-21, B.

1997–98	Porto	3	0		
1998–99	Amadora	27	0	**27**	**0**
1999–2000	Porto	19	0		
2000–01	Porto	0	0		
2001–02	Varzim	24	0	**24**	**0**
2002–03	Porto	0	0	**22**	**0**
2002–03	Academica	10	0	**10**	**0**
2003–04	Nacional	29	0		
2004–05	Nacional	32	0		
2005–06	Nacional	11	0	**72**	**0**
2006–07	Chelsea	11	0	**11**	**0**

HURRELL, Sam (D) **0 0**
b.Hillingdon 13-7-88

2005–06	Chelsea	0	0		
2006–07	Chelsea	0	0		

HUTCHINSON, Sam (M) **1 0**
H: 6 0 W: 11 07 b.Windsor 3-8-89
Source: Scholar.

2006–07	Chelsea	1	0	**1**	**0**

JOHNSON, Glen (D) **89 3**
H: 6 0 W: 13 04 b.Greenwich 23-8-84
Source: From Scholar. *Honours:* England Youth, Under-20, Under-21, 5 full caps.

2001–02	West Ham U	0	0		
2002–03	West Ham U	15	0	**15**	**0**
2002–03	*Millwall*	8	0	**8**	**0**
2003–04	Chelsea	19	3		
2004–05	Chelsea	17	0		
2005–06	Chelsea	4	0		
2006–07	Chelsea	0	0	**40**	**3**
2006–07	*Portsmouth*	26	0	**26**	**0**

KALOU, Salomon (F) **111 46**
H: 6 0 W: 12 02 b.Oume 5-8-85
Source: Oume, ASEC Abidjan. *Honours:* Ivory Coast 2 full caps, 1 goal.

2003–04	Excelsior	11	4	**11**	**4**
2003–04	Feyenoord	2	0		
2004–05	Feyenoord	31	20		
2005–06	Feyenoord	34	15	**67**	**35**
2006–07	Chelsea	33	7	**33**	**7**

LAMPARD, Frank (M) **380 85**
H: 6 0 W: 14 02 b.Romford 20-6-78
Source: Trainee. *Honours:* England Youth, Under-21, B, 55 full caps, 12 goals.

1994–95	West Ham U	0	0		
1995–96	West Ham U	2	0		
1995–96	*Swansea C*	9	1	**9**	**1**
1996–97	West Ham U	13	0		
1997–98	West Ham U	31	4		
1998–99	West Ham U	38	5		
1999–2000	West Ham U	34	7		
2000–01	West Ham U	30	7	**148**	**23**
2001–02	Chelsea	37	5		
2002–03	Chelsea	38	6		
2003–04	Chelsea	38	10		
2004–05	Chelsea	38	13		
2005–06	Chelsea	35	16		
2006–07	Chelsea	37	11	**223**	**61**

MA KALAMBAY, Yves (G) **0 0**
H: 6 5 W: 14 10 b.Brussels 31-1-86
Source: PSV Eindhoven. *Honours:* Belgium Youth, Under-21.

2003–04	Chelsea	0	0		
2004–05	Chelsea	0	0		
2005–06	Chelsea	0	0		
2005–06	*Watford*	0	0		
2006–07	Chelsea	0	0		

MAGNAY, Carl (D) **0 0**
b.Durham 27-1-89

2006–07	Chelsea	0	0		

MAKELELE, Claude (M) **492 18**
H: 5 7 W: 10 05 b.Kinshasa 18-2-73
Source: Brest. *Honours:* France Under-20, Under-21, Under-23, B, 58 full caps.

1992–93	Nantes	34	1		
1993–94	Nantes	30	0		
1994–95	Nantes	36	3		
1995–96	Nantes	33	0		
1996–97	Nantes	36	5	**169**	**9**
1997–98	Marseille	33	4	**33**	**4**
1998–99	Celta Vigo	36	2		
1999–2000	Celta Vigo	34	1	**70**	**3**
2000–01	Real Madrid	33	0		
2001–02	Real Madrid	32	0		
2002–03	Real Madrid	29	0	**94**	**0**
2003–04	Chelsea	30	0		
2004–05	Chelsea	36	1		
2005–06	Chelsea	31	0		
2006–07	Chelsea	29	1	**126**	**2**

MANCIENNE, Michael (D) **28 0**
H: 6 0 W: 11 09 b.Isleworth 8-1-88
Source: Scholar. *Honours:* England Youth.

2005–06	Chelsea	0	0		
2006–07	Chelsea	0	0		
2006–07	*QPR*	28	0	**28**	**0**

MIKEL, John Obi (M) **28 1**
H: 6 0 W: 13 05 b.Plateau State 22-4-87
Source: Plateau U. *Honours:* Nigeria Youth, 6 full caps, 1 goal.

2005	Lyn	6	1	**6**	**1**
2006–07	Chelsea	22	0	**22**	**0**

NUNO MORAIS (D) **53 3**
H: 6 0 W: 12 04 b.Penafiel 29-1-84
Honours: Portugal Youth, Under-21.

2003–04	Penafiel	32	3	**32**	**3**
2004–05	Chelsea	2	0		
2005–06	Chelsea	0	0		
2005–06	Maritimo	17	0	**17**	**0**
2006–07	Chelsea	2	0	**4**	**0**

PAULO FERREIRA (D) **239 4**
H: 6 0 W: 11 13 b.Cascais 18-1-79
Honours: Portugal Under-21, 40 full caps.

1997–98	Estoril	1	0		
1998–99	Estoril	16	0		
1999–2000	Estoril	18	2	**35**	**2**
2000–01	Vitoria Setubal	34	2		
2001–02	Vitoria Setubal	34	0	**68**	**2**
2002–03	Porto	30	0		
2003–04	Porto	32	0	**62**	**0**
2004–05	Chelsea	29	0		
2005–06	Chelsea	21	0		
2006–07	Chelsea	24	0	**74**	**0**

PETTIGREW, Adrian (D) **1 0**
H: 6 0 W: 13 01 b.Hackney 12-11-86
Source: Scholar.

2004–05	Chelsea	0	0		
2005–06	Chelsea	0	0		
2006–07	Chelsea	0	0		
2006–07	*Wycombe W*	1	0	**1**	**0**

RICARDO CARVALHO (D) **228 12**
H: 6 0 W: 12 04 b.Amarante 18-5-78
Honours: Portugal Under-21, 38 full caps, 4 goals.

1996–97	Leca	0	0		
1997–98	Leca	22	1	**22**	**1**
1998–99	Porto	1	0		
1999–2000	Vitoria Setubal	25	2	**25**	**2**
2000–01	Alverca	29	1	**29**	**1**
2001–02	Porto	25	0		
2002–03	Porto	17	1		
2003–04	Porto	29	2	**72**	**3**
2004–05	Chelsea	25	1		
2005–06	Chelsea	24	1		
2006–07	Chelsea	31	3	**80**	**5**

ROBBEN, Arjen (F) **174 40**
H: 5 11 W: 12 08 b.Bedum 23-1-84
Honours: Holland 29 full caps, 8 goals.

2000–01	Groningen	18	2		
2001–02	Groningen	28	6	**46**	**8**
2002–03	PSV Eindhoven	33	12		
2003–04	PSV Eindhoven	28	5	**61**	**17**
2004–05	Chelsea	18	7		

2005–06	Chelsea	28	6		
2006–07	Chelsea	21	2	**67**	**15**

RUSSELL, James (G) **0 0**
b.Welwyn 19-9-87
Source: Scholar. *Honours:* Eire Under-21.

2006–07	Chelsea	0	0		

SAHAR, Ben (F) **3 0**
H: 5 10 W: 12 05 b.Holon 10-8-89
Honours: Israel Under-21, 3 full caps, 2 goals.

2006–07	Chelsea	3	0	**3**	**0**

SARKI, Emmanuel (M) **7 0**
b.Nigeria 26-12-87

2005–06	Chelsea	0	0		
2005–06	*Westerlo*	7	0	**7**	**0**
2006–07	Chelsea	0	0		

SHEVCHENKO, Andriy (F) **356 191**
H: 6 0 W: 11 05 b.Dvirkivshchyna 29-9-76
Honours: Ukraine Under-21, 73 full caps, 33 goals.

1994–95	Dynamo Kiev	16	1		
1995–96	Dynamo Kiev	31	16		
1996–97	Dynamo Kiev	20	6		
1997–98	Dynamo Kiev	23	19		
1998–99	Dynamo Kiev	28	18	**118**	**60**
1999–2000	AC Milan	32	24		
2000–01	AC Milan	34	24		
2001–02	AC Milan	29	14		
2002–03	AC Milan	24	5		
2003–04	AC Milan	32	24		
2004–05	AC Milan	29	17		
2005–06	AC Milan	28	19	**208**	**127**
2006–07	Chelsea	30	4	**30**	**4**

SIMMONDS, James (M) **0 0**
b.Hammersmith 3-12-87
Source: Scholar. *Honours:* Eire Under-21.

2005–06	Chelsea	0	0		
2006–07	Chelsea	0	0		

SINCLAIR, Scott (F) **19 2**
H: 5 10 W: 10 00 b.Bath 26-3-89
Source: Bristol R Schoolboy, England Youth.

2004–05	Bristol R	2	0	**2**	**0**
2005–06	Chelsea	0	0		
2006–07	Chelsea	2	0	**2**	**0**
2006–07	*Plymouth Arg*	15	2	**15**	**2**

SMITH, Jimmy (M) **30 6**
H: 6 0 W: 10 03 b.Newham 7-1-87
Source: Scholar. *Honours:* England Youth.

2004–05	Chelsea	0	0		
2005–06	Chelsea	1	0		
2006–07	Chelsea	0	0	**1**	**0**
2006–07	*QPR*	29	6	**29**	**6**

TERRY, John (D) **220 15**
H: 6 1 W: 14 02 b.Barking 7-12-80
Source: Trainee. *Honours:* England Under-21, 39 full caps, 3 goals.

1997–98	Chelsea	0	0		
1998–99	Chelsea	2	0		
1999–2000	Chelsea	4	0		
1999–2000	*Nottingham F*	6	0	**6**	**0**
2000–01	Chelsea	22	1		
2001–02	Chelsea	33	1		
2002–03	Chelsea	20	3		
2003–04	Chelsea	33	2		
2004–05	Chelsea	36	3		
2005–06	Chelsea	36	4		
2006–07	Chelsea	28	1	**214**	**15**

VERON, Juan Sebastian (M) **354 43**
H: 5 11 W: 12 04 b.La Plata 9-3-75
Honours: Argentina 58 full caps, 9 goals.

1993–94	Estudiantes	7	0		
1994–95	Estudiantes	38	5		
1995–96	Estudiantes	15	2		
1995–96	Boca Juniors	17	4	**17**	**4**
1996–97	Sampdoria	32	5		
1997–98	Sampdoria	29	2	**61**	**7**
1998–99	Parma	26	1	**26**	**1**
1999–2000	Lazio	31	8		
2000–01	Lazio	22	3	**53**	**11**
2001–02	Manchester U	26	5		
2002–03	Manchester U	25	2	**51**	**7**
2003–04	Chelsea	7	1		
2004–05	*Internazionale*	24	3		
2005–06	*Internazionale*	25	0	**49**	**3**
2006–07	*Estudiantes*	30	2	**90**	**9**
2006–07	Chelsea	0	0	**7**	**1**

WEIHRAUCH, Per (F) **0 0**
b.Copenhagen 3-7-88
Source: Ajax.

2006–07	Chelsea	0	0		

WOODS, Michael (M) **0 0**
H: 6 0 W: 12 07 b.York 6-4-90
Source: From Scholar. *Honours:* England Youth. Scotland B.

2006–07	Chelsea	0	0		

WORLEY, Harry (D) **10 0**
H: 6 3 W: 13 00 b.Warrington 25-11-88
Source: Scholar.

2005–06	Chelsea	0	0		
2006–07	Chelsea	0	0		
2006–07	*Doncaster R*	10	0	**10**	**0**

WRIGHT-PHILLIPS, Shaun (F) **207 28**
H: 5 5 W: 10 01 b.Lewisham 25-10-81
Source: Scholar. *Honours:* England Under-21, 12 full caps, 1 goal.

1998–99	Manchester C	0	0		
1999–2000	Manchester C	4	0		
2000–01	Manchester C	15	0		
2001–02	Manchester C	35	8		
2002–03	Manchester C	31	1		
2003–04	Manchester C	34	7		
2004–05	Manchester C	34	10	**153**	**26**
2005–06	Chelsea	27	0		
2006–07	Chelsea	27	2	**54**	**2**

YOUNGHUSBAND, Phil (F) **0 0**
H: 5 10 W: 10 08 b.Ashford 4-8-87
Source: Scholar.

2004–05	Chelsea	0	0		
2005–06	Chelsea	0	0		
2006–07	Chelsea	0	0		

Scholars
Bridcutt, Liam Robert; Cummings, Shaun; Nelson, Morten; Ofori-Twumasi, Seth Nana; Rodriquez, Sergio Tejera; Sahar, Ben; Sawyer, Lee Thomas; Stoch, Miroslav; Taiwo, Thomas James William; Taylor, Rhys Francis; Woods, Michael.

CHELTENHAM T (23)

ARMSTRONG, Craig (M) **317 9**
H: 5 11 W: 12 09 b.South Shields 23-5-75
Source: Trainee.

1992–93	Nottingham F	0	0		
1993–94	Nottingham F	0	0		
1994–95	Nottingham F	0	0		
1994–95	*Burnley*	4	0	**4**	**0**
1995–96	Nottingham F	0	0		
1995–96	*Bristol R*	14	0	**14**	**0**
1996–97	Nottingham F	0	0		
1996–97	*Gillingham*	10	0	**10**	**0**
1996–97	*Watford*	15	0	**15**	**0**
1997–98	Nottingham F	18	0		
1998–99	Nottingham F	22	0	**40**	**0**
1998–99	Huddersfield T	13	1		
1999–2000	Huddersfield T	39	0		
2000–01	Huddersfield T	44	3		
2001–02	Huddersfield T	11	1	**107**	**5**
2001–02	Sheffield W	8	0		
2002–03	Sheffield W	17	1		
2003–04	Sheffield W	10	0		
2003–04	*Grimsby T*	9	1	**9**	**1**
2004–05	Sheffield W	0	0	**35**	**1**
2004–05	Bradford C	7	0	**7**	**0**
2005–06	Cheltenham T	34	2		
2006–07	Cheltenham T	42	0	**76**	**2**

BELL, Mickey (D) **594 52**
H: 5 9 W: 12 02 b.Newcastle 15-11-71
Source: Trainee.

1989–90	Northampton T	6	0		
1990–91	Northampton T	28	0		
1991–92	Northampton T	30	4		
1992–93	Northampton T	39	5		
1993–94	Northampton T	38	0		
1994–95	Northampton T	12	1	**153**	**10**
1994–95	Wycombe W	31	3		
1995–96	Wycombe W	41	1		
1996–97	Wycombe W	46	2	**118**	**6**
1997–98	Bristol C	44	10		
1998–99	Bristol C	33	5		
1999–2000	Bristol C	36	5		
2000–01	Bristol C	41	4		
2001–02	Bristol C	42	7		
2002–03	Bristol C	38	2		
2003–04	Bristol C	27	0		
2004–05	Bristol C	31	1	**292**	**34**
2005–06	Port Vale	15	2	**15**	**2**
2005–06	Cheltenham T	9	0		
2006–07	Cheltenham T	7	0	**16**	**0**

BIRD, David (M) **139 3**
H: 5 9 W: 12 00 b.Gloucester 26-12-84
Source: Cinderford T.

2001–02	Cheltenham T	0	0		
2002–03	Cheltenham T	14	0		
2003–04	Cheltenham T	24	0		
2004–05	Cheltenham T	34	0		
2005–06	Cheltenham T	36	1		
2006–07	Cheltenham T	31	2	**139**	**3**

BROWN, Scott (M) **67 5**
H: 5 9 W: 10 03 b.Runcorn 8-5-85
Source: Scholar. *Honours:* England Youth.

2001–02	Everton	0	0		
2002–03	Everton	0	0		
2003–04	Everton	0	0		
2004–05	Bristol C	19	0		
2005–06	Bristol C	29	1		
2006–07	Bristol C	15	4	**63**	**5**
2006–07	Cheltenham T	4	0	**4**	**0**

BROWN, Scott P (G) **12 0**
H: 6 2 W: 13 01 b.Wolverhampton 26-4-85
Source: Wolverhampton W Trainee. From Welshpool T

2003–04	Bristol C	0	0		
2004–05	Cheltenham T	0	0		
2005–06	Cheltenham T	1	0		
2006–07	Cheltenham T	11	0	**12**	**0**

CAINES, Gavin (D) **107 4**
H: 6 1 W: 12 00 b.Birmingham 20-9-83
Source: Scholar.

2003–04	Walsall	0	0		
2004–05	Cheltenham T	29	2		
2005–06	Cheltenham T	39	2		
2006–07	Cheltenham T	39	0	**107**	**4**

CONNOLLY, Adam (M) **17 1**
H: 5 9 W: 12 04 b.Manchester 10-4-86
Source: Scholar.

2004–05	Cheltenham T	4	0		
2005–06	Cheltenham T	5	1		
2006–07	Cheltenham T	8	0	**17**	**1**

CONNOR, Paul (F) **262 64**
H: 6 2 W: 11 08 b.Bishop Auckland 12-1-79
Source: Trainee.

1996–97	Middlesbrough	0	0		
1997–98	Middlesbrough	0	0		
1997–98	*Hartlepool U*	5	0	**5**	**0**
1998–99	Middlesbrough	0	0		
1998–99	*Stoke C*	3	2		
1999–2000	Stoke C	26	5		
2000–01	Stoke C	7	0	**36**	**7**
2000–01	*Cambridge U*	13	5	**13**	**5**
2000–01	Rochdale	14	10		
2001–02	Rochdale	17	1		
2002–03	Rochdale	39	12		
2003–04	Rochdale	24	5	**94**	**28**
2003–04	Swansea C	12	5		
2004–05	Swansea C	40	10		
2005–06	Swansea C	13	1	**65**	**16**
2005–06	Leyton Orient	16	5		
2006–07	Leyton Orient	18	2	**34**	**7**
2006–07	Cheltenham T	15	1	**15**	**1**

DUFF, Shane (D) **132 2**
H: 6 1 W: 12 10 b.Wroughton 2-4-82
Source: Juniors. *Honours:* Northern Ireland Under-21.

2000–01	Cheltenham T	0	0		
2001–02	Cheltenham T	0	0		
2002–03	Cheltenham T	18	0		
2003–04	Cheltenham T	15	1		
2004–05	Cheltenham T	45	1		

2005–06 Cheltenham T 20 0
2006–07 Cheltenham T 34 0 **132 2**

FINNIGAN, John (M) 336 21
H: 5 8 W: 10 09 b.Wakefield 29-3-76
Source: Trainee.
1992–93 Nottingham F 0 0
1993–94 Nottingham F 0 0
1994–95 Nottingham F 0 0
1995–96 Nottingham F 0 0
1996–97 Nottingham F 0 0
1997–98 Nottingham F 0 0
1997–98 *Lincoln C* 6 0
1998–99 Lincoln C 37 1
1999–2000 Lincoln C 37 2
2000–01 Lincoln C 40 0
2001–02 Lincoln C 23 0 **143 3**
2001–02 Cheltenham T 12 2
2002–03 Cheltenham T 37 1
2003–04 Cheltenham T 33 1
2004–05 Cheltenham T 32 3
2005–06 Cheltenham T 39 4
2006–07 Cheltenham T 40 7 **193 18**

FOLEY, Sam (M) 0 0
H: 6 0 W: 10 08 b.Upton-on-Severn 17-10-86
Source: Scholar.
2005–06 Cheltenham T 0 0
2006–07 Cheltenham T 0 0

GALLINAGH, Andy (D) 2 0
H: 5 8 W: 11 08 b.Sutton Coldfield 16-3-85
Source: Stratford T.
2004–05 Cheltenham T 0 0
2005–06 Cheltenham T 1 0
2006–07 Cheltenham T 1 0 **2 0**

GILL, Jeremy (D) 233 0
H: 5 11 W: 12 00 b.Clevedon 8-9-70
Source: Yeovil T.
1997–98 Birmingham C 3 0
1998–99 Birmingham C 3 0
1999–2000 Birmingham C 11 0
2000–01 Birmingham C 29 0
2001–02 Birmingham C 14 0
2002–03 Birmingham C 0 0 **60 0**
2002–03 Northampton T 41 0
2003–04 Northampton T 0 0 **41 0**
2003–04 Cheltenham T 7 0
2004–05 Cheltenham T 44 0
2005–06 Cheltenham T 42 0
2006–07 Cheltenham T 39 0 **132 0**

GILLESPIE, Steven (F) 61 16
H: 5 9 W: 11 02 b.Liverpool 4-6-84
Source: Liverpool Scholar.
2004–05 Bristol C 8 0
2004–05 *Cheltenham T* 12 5
2005–06 Bristol C 4 1 **12 1**
2005–06 Cheltenham T 14 5
2006–07 Cheltenham T 23 5 **49 15**

GUINAN, Stephen (F) 194 34
H: 6 1 W: 13 02 b.Birmingham 24-12-75
Source: Trainee.
1992–93 Nottingham F 0 0
1993–94 Nottingham F 0 0
1994–95 Nottingham F 0 0
1995–96 Nottingham F 2 0
1995–96 *Darlington* 3 1 **3 1**
1996–97 Nottingham F 2 0
1996–97 *Burnley* 6 0 **6 0**
1997–98 Nottingham F 2 0
1997–98 *Crewe Alex* 3 0 **3 0**
1998–99 Nottingham F 0 0
1998–99 *Halifax T* 12 2 **12 2**
1998–99 *Plymouth Arg* 11 7
1999–2000 Nottingham F 1 0 **7 0**
1999–2000 *Scunthorpe U* 3 1 **3 1**
1999–2000 Cambridge U 6 0 **6 0**
1999–2000 Plymouth Arg 8 2
2000–01 Plymouth Arg 22 1
2001–02 Plymouth Arg 0 0 **41 10**
2001–02 Shrewsbury T 5 0
2002–03 Shrewsbury T 0 0
2003–04 Shrewsbury T 0 0 **5 0**
2004–05 Cheltenham T 43 6
2005–06 Cheltenham T 30 7
2006–07 Cheltenham T 19 0 **92 13**

2006–07 *Hereford U* 16 7 **16 7**

HIGGS, Shane (G) 191 0
H: 6 3 W: 14 06 b.Oxford 13-5-77
Source: Trainee.
1994–95 Bristol R 0 0
1995–96 Bristol R 0 0
1996–97 Bristol R 2 0
1997–98 Bristol R 8 0 **10 0**
From Worcester C.
1999–2000 Cheltenham T 0 0
2000–01 Cheltenham T 1 0
2001–02 Cheltenham T 1 0
2002–03 Cheltenham T 10 0
2003–04 Cheltenham T 42 0
2004–05 Cheltenham T 46 0
2005–06 Cheltenham T 45 0
2006–07 Cheltenham T 36 0 **181 0**

MELLIGAN, John (M) 179 28
H: 5 9 W: 11 02 b.Dublin 11-2-82
Source: Trainee. *Honours:* Eire Under-21.
2000–01 Wolverhampton W 0 0
2001–02 Wolverhampton W 0 0
2001–02 *Bournemouth* 8 0 **8 0**
2002–03 Wolverhampton W 2 0
2002–03 *Kidderminster H* 29 10
2003–04 Wolverhampton W 0 0 **2 0**
2003–04 *Kidderminster H* 5 1 **34 11**
2003–04 *Doncaster R* 21 2 **21 2**
2004–05 Cheltenham T 29 2
2005–06 Cheltenham T 42 6
2006–07 Cheltenham T 43 7 **114 15**

ODEJAYI, Kayode (F) 154 30
H: 6 2 W: 12 02 b.Ibadon 21-2-82
Source: Scholarship.
1999–2000 Bristol C 3 0
2000–01 Bristol C 3 0
2001–02 Bristol C 0 0
2002–03 Bristol C 0 0 **6 0**
2003–04 Cheltenham T 30 5
2004–05 Cheltenham T 32 1
2005–06 Cheltenham T 41 11
2006–07 Cheltenham T 45 13 **148 30**

PAUL, Shane (F) 0 0
H: 5 6 W: 10 07 b.Walsall 25-1-87
Source: Scholar. *Honours:* England Youth.
2004–05 Aston Villa 0 0
2005–06 Aston Villa 0 0
2006–07 Cheltenham T 0 0

PUDDY, Will (G) 0 0
H: 5 10 W: 11 07 b.Salisbury 4-10-87
Source: Scholar.
2005–06 Cheltenham T 0 0
2006–07 Cheltenham T 0 0

REID, Craig (F) 6 0
H: 5 10 W: 11 10 b.Coventry 17-12-85
Honours: Ipswich T Scholar.
2004–05 Coventry C 0 0
2005–06 Coventry C 0 0
2006–07 Coventry C 0 0
2006–07 Cheltenham T 6 0 **6 0**

SPENCER, Damien (F) 199 30
H: 6 1 W: 14 00 b.Ascot 19-9-81
Source: Scholarship.
1999–2000 Bristol C 9 1
2000–01 Bristol C 4 0
2000–01 *Exeter C* 6 0 **6 0**
2001–02 Bristol C 0 0 **13 1**
2002–03 Cheltenham T 30 6
2003–04 Cheltenham T 36 9
2004–05 Cheltenham T 41 8
2005–06 Cheltenham T 46 3
2006–07 Cheltenham T 27 3 **180 29**

TOWNSEND, Michael (D) 61 1
H: 6 1 W: 13 12 b.Walsall 17-5-86
Source: Wolverhampton W scholar.
2004–05 Cheltenham T 0 0
2005–06 Cheltenham T 31 0
2006–07 Cheltenham T 30 1 **61 1**

VICTORY, Jamie (D) 274 23
H: 5 10 W: 12 13 b.Hackney 14-11-75
Source: Trainee.
1994–95 West Ham U 0 0
1995–96 Bournemouth 16 1
1996–97 Bournemouth 0 0 **16 1**
1999–2000 Cheltenham T 46 4
2000–01 Cheltenham T 3 1
2001–02 Cheltenham T 46 7
2002–03 Cheltenham T 45 2
2003–04 Cheltenham T 44 2
2004–05 Cheltenham T 42 3
2005–06 Cheltenham T 22 2
2006–07 Cheltenham T 10 1 **258 22**

VINCENT, Ashley (F) 44 3
H: 5 10 W: 11 08 b.Oldbury 26-5-85
Source: Wolverhampton W Scholar.
2004–05 Cheltenham T 26 1
2005–06 Cheltenham T 13 2
2006–07 Cheltenham T 5 0 **44 3**

WHITTINGTON, Michael (F) 0 0
H: 5 8 W: 11 00 b.Bristol 16-12-86
Source: Scholar.
2005–06 Cheltenham T 0 0
2006–07 Cheltenham T 0 0

WYLDE, Michael (M) 8 0
H: 6 2 W: 13 02 b.Birmingham 6-1-87
Source: Scholar.
2005–06 Cheltenham T 1 0
2006–07 Cheltenham T 7 0 **8 0**

YAO, Sosthene (M) 18 0
H: 5 4 W: 11 09 b.Ivory Coast 7-8-87
Source: West Ham U Scholar.
2005–06 Cheltenham T 3 0
2006–07 Cheltenham T 15 0 **18 0**

CHESTER C (24)

ALLEN, Graham (D) 240 12
H: 6 1 W: 12 00 b.Bolton 8-4-77
Source: Trainee. *Honours:* England Youth.
1994–95 Everton 0 0
1995–96 Everton 0 0
1996–97 Everton 1 0
1997–98 Everton 5 0
1998–99 Everton 0 0 **6 0**
1998–99 Tranmere R 41 5
1999–2000 Tranmere R 24 0
2000–01 Tranmere R 22 0
2001–02 Tranmere R 31 1
2002–03 Tranmere R 41 3
2003–04 Tranmere R 41 1 **200 10**
2004–05 Rushden & D 26 1
2005–06 Rushden & D 5 1 **31 2**
2006–07 Chester C 3 0 **3 0**

ARTELL, Dave (D) 190 13
H: 6 3 W: 14 01 b.Rotherham 22-11-80
Source: Trainee.
1999–2000 Rotherham U 1 0
2000–01 Rotherham U 36 4
2001–02 Rotherham U 0 0
2002–03 Rotherham U 0 0 **37 4**
2002–03 *Shrewsbury T* 28 1 **28 1**
2003–04 Mansfield T 26 3
2004–05 Mansfield T 19 2 **45 5**
2005–06 Chester C 37 2
2006–07 Chester C 43 1 **80 3**

BENNETT, Dean (M) 252 19
H: 5 11 W: 11 00 b.Wolverhampton 13-12-77
Source: Aston Villa Juniors.
1996–97 WBA 1 0
1997–98 WBA 0 0 **1 0**
2000–01 Kidderminster H 42 4
2001–02 Kidderminster H 42 8
2002–03 Kidderminster H 32 1
2003–04 Kidderminster H 38 3 **154 16**
2002–03 Wrexham 18 0
2003–04 Wrexham 0 0
2004–05 Wrexham 14 0
2005–06 Wrexham 33 2 **65 2**
2006–07 Chester C 32 1 **32 1**

BOLLAND, Phil (D) 121 4
H: 6 4 W: 13 03 b.Liverpool 26-8-76
Source: Altrincham, Knowsley U, Trafford, Salford C, Altrincham, Southport.
2001–02 Oxford U 20 1 **20 1**

2001–02	Chester C	0	0		
2002–03	Chester C	0	0		
2003–04	Chester C	0	0		
2004–05	Chester C	42	1		
2005–06	Chester C	16	1		
2005–06	Peterborough U	17	0	**17**	**0**
2006–07	Chester C	26	1	**84**	**3**

BRANCH, Michael (F) 219 38
H: 5 9 W: 12 08 b.Liverpool 18-10-78
Source: Trainee. *Honours:* England Schools, Youth, Under-21.

1995–96	Everton	3	0		
1996–97	Everton	25	3		
1997–98	Everton	6	0		
1998–99	Everton	7	0		
1998–99	*Manchester C*	4	0	**4**	**0**
1999–2000	Everton	0	0	**41**	**3**
2000–01	Wolverhampton W	38	4		
1999–2000	Wolverhampton W	27	6		
2001–02	Wolverhampton W	7	0		
2001–02	*Reading*	2	0	**2**	**0**
2002–03	Wolverhampton W	0	0	**72**	**10**
2002–03	*Hull C*	7	3	**7**	**3**
2003–04	Bradford C	33	6	**33**	**6**
2004–05	Chester C	33	11		
2005–06	Chester C	27	5		
2006–07	Chester C	0	0	**60**	**16**

BROUGHTON, Drewe (F) 287 56
H: 6 3 W: 12 01 b.Hitchin 25-10-78
Source: Trainee.

1996–97	Norwich C	8	1		
1997–98	Norwich C	1	0		
1997–98	*Wigan Ath*	4	0	**4**	**0**
1998–99	Norwich C	0	0	**9**	**1**
1998–99	Brentford	1	0	**1**	**0**
1998–99	Peterborough U	25	7		
1999–2000	Peterborough U	10	1		
2000–01	Peterborough U	0	0	**35**	**8**
2000–01	Kidderminster H	19	7		
2001–02	Kidderminster H	38	8		
2002–03	Kidderminster H	37	4	**94**	**19**
2003–04	Southend U	35	2		
2004–05	Southend U	9	0	**44**	**2**
2004–05	Rushden & D	21	6		
2004–05	*Wycombe W*	3	0	**3**	**0**
2005–06	Rushden & D	37	10	**58**	**16**
2006–07	Chester C	14	2	**14**	**2**
2006–07	*Boston U*	25	8	**25**	**8**

CARROLL, Neil (M) 0 0
b.Cheltenham 21-9-88

2006–07	Chester C	0	0

CRONIN, Glenn (M) 73 0
H: 5 8 W: 10 08 b.Dublin 14-9-81
Source: Trainee.

2000–01	Exeter C	0	0		
2001–02	Exeter C	30	0		
2002–03	Exeter C	39	0		
2003–04	Exeter C	0	0		
2004–05	Exeter C	0	0		
2005–06	Exeter C	0	0	**69**	**0**
2006–07	Chester C	4	0	**4**	**0**

DANBY, John (G) 94 0
H: 6 2 W: 14 06 b.Stoke 20-9-83
Source: Juniors.

2001–02	Kidderminster H	2	0		
2002–03	Kidderminster H	0	0		
2003–04	Kidderminster H	9	0		
2004–05	Kidderminster H	37	0		
2005–06	Kidderminster H	0	0	**48**	**0**
2006–07	Chester C	46	0	**46**	**0**

HAND, Jamie (M) 129 2
H: 6 0 W: 11 08 b.Uxbridge 7-2-84
Source: Scholar. *Honours:* England Youth.

2001–02	Watford	10	0		
2002–03	Watford	23	0		
2003–04	Watford	22	0		
2004–05	Watford	0	0		
2004–05	*Oxford U*	11	0	**11**	**0**
2005–06	Watford	0	0	**55**	**0**
2005–06	*Peterborough U*	9	0	**9**	**0**
From Fisher Ath.					
2005–06	*Northampton T*	11	0	**11**	**0**
2006–07	Chester C	43	2	**43**	**2**

HESSEY, Sean (D) 140 2
H: 5 11 W: 12 08 b.Whiston 19-9-78
Source: Liverpool Trainee.

1997–98	Wigan Ath	0	0		
1997–98	Leeds U	0	0		
1997–98	Huddersfield T	1	0		
1998–99	Huddersfield T	10	0	**11**	**0**
1999–2000	Kilmarnock	11	0		
2000–01	Kilmarnock	6	0		
2001–02	Kilmarnock	15	0		
2002–03	Kilmarnock	5	0		
2003–04	Kilmarnock	7	1	**44**	**1**
2003–04	Blackpool	6	0	**6**	**0**
2004–05	Chester C	34	1		
2005–06	Chester C	19	0		
2006–07	Chester C	26	0	**79**	**1**

HOLROYD, Chris (M) 22 0
H: 5 11 W: 12 03 b.Macclesfield 24-10-86

2005–06	Chester C	0	0		
2006–07	Chester C	22	0	**22**	**0**

KELLY, Shaun (D) 2 0
H: 6 1 W: 11 04 b.Southampton 4-7-86
Source: Scholar.

2006–07	Chester C	2	0	**2**	**0**

LINWOOD, Paul (D) 90 1
H: 6 2 W: 13 03 b.Birkenhead 24-10-83
Source: Scholar.

2001–02	Tranmere R	0	0		
2002–03	Tranmere R	0	0		
2003–04	Tranmere R	20	0		
2004–05	Tranmere R	10	0		
2005–06	Tranmere R	14	0	**44**	**0**
2005–06	*Wrexham*	9	0	**9**	**0**
2006–07	Chester C	37	1	**37**	**1**

MARPLES, Simon (D) 73 0
H: 5 10 W: 11 00 b.Sheffield 30-7-75
Source: Stocksbridge Park Steels.

2003–04	Doncaster R	16	0		
2004–05	Doncaster R	12	0		
2005–06	Doncaster R	15	0	**43**	**0**
2006–07	Chester C	30	0	**30**	**0**

MARSH-EVANS, Robert (D) 0 0
H: 6 3 W: 12 08 b.Abergele 13-10-86
Source: Ruthin T.

2006–07	Chester C	0	0

MARTINEZ, Roberto (M) 363 24
H: 5 9 W: 12 02 b.Balaguer 13-7-73
Source: Balaguer.

1995–96	Wigan Ath	42	9		
1996–97	Wigan Ath	43	4		
1997–98	Wigan Ath	33	1		
1998–99	Wigan Ath	10	0		
1999–2000	Wigan Ath	25	3		
2000–01	Wigan Ath	34	0	**187**	**17**
2001–02	Motherwell	17	0	**17**	**0**
2002–03	Walsall	6	0	**6**	**0**
2002–03	Swansea C	19	2		
2003–04	Swansea C	27	0		
2004–05	Swansea C	37	0		
2005–06	Swansea C	39	2	**122**	**4**
2006–07	Chester C	31	3	**31**	**3**

McSPORRAN, Jermaine (M) 195 31
H: 5 10 W: 10 12 b.Manchester 1-1-77
Source: Oxford C.

1998–99	Wycombe W	26	4		
1999–2000	Wycombe W	38	9		
2000–01	Wycombe W	20	2		
2001–02	Wycombe W	32	7		
2002–03	Wycombe W	9	1		
2003–04	Wycombe W	33	7	**158**	**30**
2003–04	Walsall	6	0	**6**	**0**
2004–05	Doncaster R	26	1		
2005–06	Doncaster R	2	0	**28**	**1**
2005–06	*Boston U*	2	0	**2**	**0**
2006–07	Chester C	1	0	**1**	**0**

MEECHAN, Alex (F) 22 4
H: 5 8 W: 10 06 b.Plymouth 29-1-80
Source: Trainee.

1997–98	Swindon T	1	0	**1**	**0**
1998–99	Bristol C	1	0		
1999–2000	Bristol C	12	4	**13**	**4**
From Dagenham, Leigh, Halifax, For Green					
2006–07	Chester C	8	0	**8**	**0**

NEWTON, Sean (M) 0 0
b.Liverpool 23-9-88

2006–07	Chester C	0	0

ROBERTS, Kevin (D) 0 0
H: 6 2 W: 14 00 b.Chester 10-3-87

2006–07	Chester C	0	0

RUTHERFORD, Paul (M) 15 0
H: 5 9 W: 11 07 b.Moreton 10-7-87
Source: Greenleas.

2005–06	Chester C	6	0		
2006–07	Chester C	9	0	**15**	**0**

SANDWITH, Kevin (D) 110 7
H: 5 11 W: 12 05 b.Workington 30-4-78
Source: Trainee.

1996–97	Carlisle U	0	0		
1997–98	Carlisle U	3	0		
1998–99	Carlisle U	0	0	**3**	**0**
From Halifax T					
2003–04	Lincoln C	3	0		
2004–05	Lincoln C	37	2	**40**	**2**
2005–06	Macclesfield T	35	3	**35**	**3**
2006–07	Chester C	32	2	**32**	**2**

STEELE, Lee (F) 296 77
H: 5 8 W: 12 05 b.Liverpool 2-12-73
Source: Bootle, Northwich V.

1997–98	Shrewsbury T	38	13		
1998–99	Shrewsbury T	38	13		
1999–2000	Shrewsbury T	37	11	**113**	**37**
2000–01	Brighton & HA	23	2		
2001–02	Brighton & HA	37	9	**60**	**11**
2002–03	Oxford U	10	3		
2003–04	Oxford U	16	1	**26**	**4**
2004–05	Leyton Orient	39	16		
2005–06	Leyton Orient	27	4		
2006–07	Leyton Orient	11	4	**77**	**24**
2006–07	Chester C	20	1	**20**	**1**

VAUGHAN, James (D) 6 0
H: 5 10 W: 12 09 b.Liverpool 6-12-86

2005–06	Chester C	0	0		
2006–07	Chester C	6	0	**6**	**0**

WESTWOOD, Ashley (D) 265 21
H: 6 0 W: 12 09 b.Bridgnorth 31-8-76
Source: Trainee. *Honours:* England Youth.

1994–95	Manchester U	0	0		
1995–96	Crewe Alex	33	4		
1996–97	Crewe Alex	44	2		
1997–98	Crewe Alex	21	3	**98**	**9**
1998–99	Bradford C	19	2		
1999–2000	Bradford C	5	0		
2000–01	Bradford C	0	0	**24**	**2**
2000–01	Sheffield W	33	2		
2001–02	Sheffield W	26	1		
2002–03	Sheffield W	23	2	**82**	**5**
2003–04	Northampton T	9	0		
2004–05	Northampton T	19	2		
2005–06	Northampton T	3	0	**31**	**2**
2006–07	Chester C	21	3	**21**	**3**
2006–07	*Swindon T*	9	0	**9**	**0**

WILSON, Laurence (M) 56 2
H: 5 10 W: 10 09 b.Huyton 10-10-86
Source: Scholar. *Honours:* England Youth.

2004–05	Everton	0	0		
2005–06	Everton	0	0		
2005–06	*Mansfield T*	15	1	**15**	**1**
2006–07	Chester C	41	1	**41**	**1**

YEO, Simon (F) 162 48
H: 5 10 W: 11 08 b.Stockport 20-10-73
Source: Hyde U.

2002–03	Lincoln C	37	5		
2003–04	Lincoln C	41	11		
2004–05	Lincoln C	44	21		
From New Zealand Knights					
2005–06	Lincoln C	12	5	**134**	**42**
2006–07	Peterborough U	13	2	**13**	**2**
2006–07	Chester C	15	4	**15**	**4**

CHESTERFIELD (25)

ALLISON, Wayne (F) 743 171
H: 6 0 W: 14 13 b.Huddersfield 16-10-68
Source: Trainee.

1986–87	Halifax T	8	4

1987–88	Halifax T	35	4		
1988–89	Halifax T	41	15	**84**	**23**
1989–90	Watford	7	0	**7**	**0**
1990–91	Bristol C	37	6		
1991–92	Bristol C	43	10		
1992–93	Bristol C	39	4		
1993–94	Bristol C	39	15		
1994–95	Bristol C	37	13	**195**	**48**
1995–96	Swindon T	44	17		
1996–97	Swindon T	41	11		
1997–98	Swindon T	16	3	**101**	**31**
1997–98	Huddersfield T	27	6		
1998–99	Huddersfield T	44	9		
1999–2000	Huddersfield T	3	0	**74**	**15**
1999–2000	Tranmere R	40	16		
2000–01	Tranmere R	36	6		
2001–02	Tranmere R	27	4	**103**	**26**
2002–03	Sheffield U	34	6		
2003–04	Sheffield U	39	1	**73**	**7**
2004–05	Chesterfield	38	6		
2005–06	Chesterfield	32	11		
2006–07	Chesterfield	36	4	**106**	**21**

ALLOTT, Mark (M) **375 42**

H: 5 11 W: 11 07 b.Manchester 3-10-77

Source: Trainee.

1995–96	Oldham Ath	0	0		
1996–97	Oldham Ath	5	1		
1997–98	Oldham Ath	22	2		
1998–99	Oldham Ath	41	7		
1999–2000	Oldham Ath	32	10		
2000–01	Oldham Ath	39	7		
2001–02	Oldham Ath	15	4	**154**	**31**
2001–02	Chesterfield	21	4		
2002–03	Chesterfield	33	0		
2003–04	Chesterfield	40	2		
2004–05	Chesterfield	45	2		
2005–06	Chesterfield	43	3		
2006–07	Chesterfield	39	0	**221**	**11**

BAILEY, Alex (D) **93 1**

H: 5 9 W: 11 08 b.Newham 21-9-83

Source: Scholar. *Honours:* England Youth.

2001–02	Arsenal	0	0		
2002–03	Arsenal	0	0		
2003–04	Arsenal	0	0		
2004–05	Chesterfield	45	1		
2005–06	Chesterfield	18	0		
2006–07	Chesterfield	30	0	**93**	**1**

CRITCHELL, Kyle (D) **17 0**

H: 6 0 W: 12 02 b.Dorchester 18-1-87

Source: Scholar. *Honours:* Wales Under-21.

2005–06	Southampton	0	0		
2006–07	Southampton	0	0		
2006–07	*Torquay U*	7	0	**7**	**0**
2006–07	Chesterfield	10	0	**10**	**0**

DAVIES, Gareth (M) **115 2**

H: 6 1 W: 12 10 b.Chesterfield 4-2-83

Source: Trainee.

2001–02	Chesterfield	0	0		
2002–03	Chesterfield	34	1		
2003–04	Chesterfield	28	0		
2004–05	Chesterfield	19	1		
2005–06	Chesterfield	20	0		
2006–07	Chesterfield	14	0	**115**	**2**

DOWNES, Aaron (D) **76 5**

H: 6 2 W: 13 02 b.Mudgee 15-5-85

Honours: Australia Youth, Under-21.

2004–05	Chesterfield	9	2		
2005–06	Chesterfield	22	0		
2006–07	Chesterfield	45	3	**76**	**5**

GRIMALDI, Sebastien (D) **159 9**

H: 6 1 W: 12 01 b.Gisors 10-9-79

Source: Saint-Romain Engier, Oulins.

1999–2000	Lyon	0	0		
2000–01	Cannes	31	2		
2001–02	Cannes	28	1	**59**	**3**
2002–03	Angers	22	1		
2003–04	Angers	33	3		
2004–05	Angers	28	1	**83**	**5**
2005–06	Mouscron	9	1	**9**	**1**
2006–07	Chesterfield	8	0	**8**	**0**

HALL, Paul (M) **616 108**

H: 5 8 W: 12 00 b.Manchester 3-7-72

Source: Trainee. *Honours:* Jamaica 41 full caps, 9 goals.

1989–90	Torquay U	10	0		
1990–91	Torquay U	17	0		
1991–92	Torquay U	38	1		
1992–93	Torquay U	28	0	**93**	**1**
1992–93	Portsmouth	0	0		
1993–94	Portsmouth	28	4		
1994–95	Portsmouth	43	5		
1995–96	Portsmouth	46	10		
1996–97	Portsmouth	42	13		
1997–98	Portsmouth	29	5	**188**	**37**
1998–99	Coventry C	9	0		
1998–99	*Bury*	7	0	**7**	**0**
1999–2000	Coventry C	1	0	**10**	**0**
1999–2000	*Sheffield U*	4	1	**4**	**1**
1999–2000	*WBA*	4	0	**4**	**0**
1999–2000	Walsall	10	4		
2000–01	Walsall	42	6		
2001–02	Walsall	0	0	**52**	**10**
2001–02	Rushden & D	34	8		
2002–03	Rushden & D	45	16		
2003–04	Rushden & D	33	2	**112**	**26**
2003–04	Tranmere R	9	2		
2004–05	Tranmere R	46	11	**55**	**13**
2005–06	Chesterfield	45	15		
2006–07	Chesterfield	46	5	**91**	**20**

HAZELL, Reuben (D) **198 5**

H: 5 11 W: 12 05 b.Birmingham 24-4-79

Source: Trainee.

1996–97	Aston Villa	0	0		
1997–98	Aston Villa	0	0		
1998–99	Aston Villa	0	0		
1999–2000	Tranmere R	23	1		
2000–01	Tranmere R	13	0		
2001–02	Tranmere R	6	0	**42**	**1**
2001–02	Torquay U	19	0		
2002–03	Torquay U	46	1		
2003–04	Torquay U	19	1		
2004–05	Torquay U	0	0	**84**	**2**
2005–06	Chesterfield	33	0		
2006–07	Chesterfield	39	2	**72**	**2**

HUGHES, Mark (M) **65 2**

H: 5 10 W: 12 05 b.Dungannon 16-9-83

Source: Scholar. *Honours:* Northern Ireland Schools, Youth, Under-21, Under-23, 2 full caps.

2001–02	Tottenham H	0	0		
2002–03	Tottenham H	0	0		
2003–04	Tottenham H	0	0		
2004–05	Tottenham H	0	0		
2004–05	*Northampton T*	3	0	**3**	**0**
2004–05	*Oldham Ath*	27	0		
2005–06	Oldham Ath	33	1		
2006–07	Oldham Ath	0	0	**60**	**1**

From Thurrock.

2006–07	Chesterfield	2	1	**2**	**1**

To Stevenage B January 2007

JACKSON, Jamie (F) **16 0**

H: 5 6 W: 10 04 b.Sheffield 1-11-86

Source: Scholar.

2005–06	Chesterfield	2	0		
2006–07	Chesterfield	14	0	**16**	**0**

JORDAN, Michael (G) **6 0**

H: 6 2 W: 13 02 b.Cheshunt 7-4-86

Source: Scholar.

2003–04	Arsenal	0	0		
2004–05	Arsenal	0	0		
2005–06	Arsenal	0	0		
2005–06	*Yeovil T*	0	0		
2006–07	Chesterfield	6	0	**6**	**0**

KOVACS, Janos (D) **16 0**

H: 6 4 W: 14 10 b.Budapest 11-9-85

Source: MTK.

2005–06	Chesterfield	9	0		
2006–07	Chesterfield	7	0	**16**	**0**

LARKIN, Colin (F) **208 42**

H: 5 9 W: 11 07 b.Dundalk 27-4-82

Source: Trainee.

1998–99	Wolverhampton W	0	0		
1999–2000	Wolverhampton W	1	0		
2000–01	Wolverhampton W	2	0		
2001–02	Wolverhampton W	0	0	**3**	**0**
2001–02	*Kidderminster H*	33	6	**33**	**6**
2002–03	Mansfield T	22	7		
2003–04	Mansfield T	37	7		
2004–05	Mansfield T	33	11	**92**	**25**
2005–06	Chesterfield	41	7		
2006–07	Chesterfield	39	4	**80**	**11**

LOWRY, Jamie (D) **8 0**

H: 6 0 W: 12 00 b.Newquay 18-3-87

Source: Scholar.

2006–07	Chesterfield	8	0	**8**	**0**

NICHOLSON, Shane (D) **523 31**

H: 5 11 W: 12 06 b.Newark 3-6-70

Source: Trainee.

1986–87	Lincoln C	7	0		
1987–88	Lincoln C	0	0		
1988–89	Lincoln C	34	1		
1989–90	Lincoln C	23	0		
1990–91	Lincoln C	40	4		
1991–92	Lincoln C	29	1		
1991–92	Derby Co	0	0		
1992–93	Derby Co	17	0		
1993–94	Derby Co	22	1		
1994–95	Derby Co	15	0		
1995–96	Derby Co	20	0	**74**	**1**
1995–96	WBA	18	0		
1996–97	WBA	18	0		
1997–98	WBA	16	0	**52**	**0**
1998–99	Chesterfield	24	0		
1999–2000	Stockport Co	42	1		
2000–01	Stockport Co	35	2	**77**	**3**
2001–02	Sheffield U	25	3	**25**	**3**
2002–03	Tranmere R	38	4		
2003–04	Tranmere R	16	2	**54**	**6**
2004–05	Chesterfield	43	7		
2005–06	Chesterfield	25	5		
2006–07	Chesterfield	2	0	**94**	**12**
2006–07	*Lincoln C*	8	0	**141**	**6**
2006–07	*Boston U*	6	0	**6**	**0**

NIVEN, Derek (M) **148 10**

H: 5 11 W: 12 05 b.Falkirk 12-12-83

Source: Stenhousemuir.

2000–01	Raith R	1	0	**1**	**0**
2001–02	Bolton W	0	0		
2002–03	Bolton W	0	0		
2003–04	Bolton W	0	0		
2003–04	Chesterfield	22	1		
2004–05	Chesterfield	38	1		
2005–06	Chesterfield	42	5		
2006–07	Chesterfield	45	3	**147**	**10**

O'HARE, Alan (D) **141 3**

H: 6 1 W: 12 09 b.Drogheda 31-7-82

Source: Scholar. *Honours:* Eire Youth.

2001–02	Bolton W	0	0		
2001–02	*Chesterfield*	19	0		
2002–03	Bolton W	0	0		
2002–03	Chesterfield	22	0		
2003–04	Chesterfield	40	1		
2004–05	Chesterfield	21	0		
2005–06	Chesterfield	22	0		
2006–07	Chesterfield	17	2	**141**	**3**

PICKEN, Phil (D) **71 2**

H: 5 9 W: 10 07 b.Droylsden 12-11-85

Source: Scholar.

2004–05	Manchester U	0	0		
2005–06	Manchester U	0	0		
2005–06	*Chesterfield*	32	1		
2006–07	Chesterfield	39	1	**71**	**2**

ROCHE, Barry (G) **94 0**

H: 6 5 W: 14 08 b.Dublin 6-4-82

Source: Trainee.

1999–2000	Nottingham F	0	0		
2000–01	Nottingham F	2	0		
2001–02	Nottingham F	0	0		
2002–03	Nottingham F	1	0		
2003–04	Nottingham F	8	0		
2004–05	Nottingham F	2	0	**13**	**0**
2005–06	Chesterfield	41	0		
2006–07	Chesterfield	40	0	**81**	**0**

SHAW, Paul (F) **374 81**

H: 5 11 W: 12 04 b.Burnham 4-9-73

Source: Trainee.

1991–92	Arsenal	0	0		
1992–93	Arsenal	0	0		

1993–94	Arsenal	0	0		
1994–95	Arsenal	1	0		
1994–95	*Burnley*	9	4	**9**	**4**
1995–96	Arsenal	3	0		
1995–96	*Cardiff C*	6	0	**6**	**0**
1995–96	*Peterborough U*	12	5	**12**	**5**
1996–97	Arsenal	8	2		
1997–98	Arsenal	0	0	**12**	**2**
1997–98	Millwall	40	11		
1998–99	Millwall	34	10		
1999–2000	Millwall	35	5	**109**	**26**
2000–01	Gillingham	33	1		
2001–02	Gillingham	37	7		
2002–03	Gillingham	44	12		
2003–04	Gillingham	21	6	**135**	**26**
2003–04	Sheffield U	13	1		
2004–05	Sheffield U	21	7		
2004–05	*Rotherham U*	9	2		
2005–06	Sheffield U	1	0	**35**	**8**
2005–06	Rotherham U	17	4	**26**	**6**
2006–07	Chesterfield	30	4	**30**	**4**

SMITH, Adam (M) **58 3**
H: 5 11 W: 12 00 b.Huddersfield 20-2-85
Source: Scholar.

2003–04	Chesterfield	3	0		
2004–05	Chesterfield	16	0		
2005–06	Chesterfield	26	3		
2006–07	Chesterfield	13	0	**58**	**3**

WARD, Jamie (M) **43 13**
H: 5 5 W: 9 04 b.Birmingham 12-5-86
Source: Scholar. *Honours:* Northern Ireland Youth, Under-21.

2003–04	Aston Villa	0	0		
2004–05	Aston Villa	0	0		
2005–06	Aston Villa	0	0		
2005–06	*Stockport Co*	9	1	**9**	**1**
2006–07	Torquay U	25	9	**25**	**9**
2006–07	Chesterfield	9	3	**9**	**3**

WIGGINS-THOMAS, Ruben (M) **0 0**
H: 5 11 W: 10 03 b.Nottingham 7-4-88
Source: Scholar.

2006–07	Chesterfield	0	0		

COLCHESTER U (26)

BALDWIN, Pat (D) **124 1**
H: 6 3 W: 12 07 b.City of London 12-11-82
Source: Chelsea Academy.

2002–03	Colchester U	19	0		
2003–04	Colchester U	4	0		
2004–05	Colchester U	38	0		
2005–06	Colchester U	25	0		
2006–07	Colchester U	38	1	**124**	**1**

BROWN, Wayne (D) **241 10**
H: 6 0 W: 12 06 b.Barking 20-8-77
Source: Trainee.

1995–96	Ipswich T	0	0		
1996–97	Ipswich T	0	0		
1997–98	Ipswich T	1	0		
1997–98	*Colchester U*	2	0		
1998–99	Ipswich T	1	0		
1999–2000	Ipswich T	25	0		
2000–01	Ipswich T	4	0		
2000–01	*QPR*	2	0	**2**	**0**
2001–02	Ipswich T	0	0		
2001–02	*Wimbledon*	17	1	**17**	**1**
2001–02	*Watford*	11	3		
2002–03	Ipswich T	9	0	**40**	**0**
2002–03	Watford	13	1		
2003–04	Watford	12	0	**36**	**4**
2003–04	*Gillingham*	4	1	**4**	**1**
2003–04	*Colchester U*	16	0		
2004–05	Colchester U	40	1		
2005–06	Colchester U	38	2		
2006–07	Colchester U	46	1	**142**	**4**

COUSINS, Mark (G) **0 0**
H: 6 2 W: 12 02 b.Chelmsford 9-1-87
Source: Scholar.

2005–06	Colchester U	0	0		
2006–07	Colchester U	0	0		

CURETON, Jamie (F) **441 168**
H: 5 8 W: 10 07 b.Bristol 28-8-75
Source: Trainee. *Honours:* England Youth.

1992–93	Norwich C	0	0		
1993–94	Norwich C	0	0		
1994–95	Norwich C	17	4		
1995–96	Norwich C	12	2		
1995–96	*Bournemouth*	5	0	**5**	**0**
1996–97	Norwich C	0	0	**29**	**6**
1996–97	Bristol R	38	11		
1997–98	Bristol R	43	13		
1998–99	Bristol R	46	25		
1999–2000	Bristol R	46	22		
2000–01	Bristol R	1	1	**174**	**72**
2000–01	Reading	43	26		
2001–02	Reading	38	15		
2002–03	Reading	27	9	**108**	**50**
From Busan Icons.					
2003–04	QPR	13	2		
2004–05	QPR	30	4	**43**	**6**
2005–06	Swindon T	30	7	**30**	**7**
2005–06	*Colchester U*	8	4		
2006–07	Colchester U	44	23	**52**	**27**

DAVISON, Aidan (G) **346 0**
H: 6 2 W: 13 12 b.Sedgefield 11-5-68
Source: Billingham Synthonia. *Honours:* Northern Ireland B, 3 full caps.

1987–88	Notts Co	0	0		
1988–89	Notts Co	1	0		
1989–90	Notts Co	0	0	**1**	**0**
1989–90	*Leyton Orient*	0	0		
1989–90	Bury	0	0		
1989–90	*Chester C*	0	0		
1990–91	Bury	0	0		
1990–91	*Blackpool*	0	0		
1991–92	Millwall	33	0		
1992–93	Millwall	1	0	**34**	**0**
1993–94	Bolton W	31	0		
1994–95	Bolton W	4	0		
1995–96	Bolton W	2	0		
1996–97	Bolton W	0	0	**37**	**0**
1996–97	*Ipswich T*	0	0		
1996–97	*Hull C*	9	0	**9**	**0**
1996–97	Bradford C	10	0		
1997–98	Grimsby T	42	0		
1998–99	Grimsby T	35	0		
1999–2000	Grimsby T	0	0		
1999–2000	Sheffield U	2	0	**2**	**0**
1999–2000	Bradford C	6	0		
2000–01	Bradford C	2	0		
2001–02	Bradford C	9	0		
2002–03	Bradford C	34	0	**61**	**0**
2003–04	Grimsby T	32	0	**109**	**0**
2004–05	Colchester U	33	0		
2005–06	Colchester U	41	0		
2006–07	Colchester U	19	0	**93**	**0**

DUGUID, Karl (M) **348 42**
H: 5 11 W: 11 06 b.Hitchin 21-3-78
Source: Trainee.

1995–96	Colchester U	16	1		
1996–97	Colchester U	20	3		
1997–98	Colchester U	21	3		
1998–99	Colchester U	33	4		
1999–2000	Colchester U	41	12		
2000–01	Colchester U	41	5		
2001–02	Colchester U	41	4		
2002–03	Colchester U	27	3		
2003–04	Colchester U	30	2		
2004–05	Colchester U	0	0		
2005–06	Colchester U	35	0		
2006–07	Colchester U	43	5	**348**	**42**

ELOKOBI, George (D) **27 1**
H: 5 10 W: 13 02 b.Cameroon 31-1-86
Source: Dulwich Hamlet.

2004–05	Colchester U	0	0		
2004–05	*Chester C*	5	0	**5**	**0**
2005–06	Colchester U	12	1		
2006–07	Colchester U	10	0	**22**	**1**

GARCIA, Richard (F) **116 20**
H: 5 11 W: 12 01 b.Perth 4-9-81
Source: Trainee. *Honours:* Australia Under-23.

1998–99	West Ham U	0	0		
1999–2000	West Ham U	0	0		
2000–01	West Ham U	0	0		
2000–01	*Leyton Orient*	18	4	**18**	**4**
2001–02	West Ham U	8	0		
2002–03	West Ham U	0	0		
2003–04	West Ham U	7	0		
2004–05	West Ham U	1	0	**16**	**0**
2004–05	Colchester U	24	4		
2005–06	Colchester U	22	5		
2006–07	Colchester U	36	7	**82**	**16**

GERKEN, Dean (G) **48 0**
H: 6 3 W: 12 08 b.Rochford 22-5-85
Source: Scholar.

2003–04	Colchester U	1	0		
2004–05	Colchester U	13	0		
2005–06	Colchester U	7	0		
2006–07	Colchester U	27	0	**48**	**0**

GUY, Jamie (M) **36 3**
H: 6 1 W: 13 00 b.Barking 1-8-87
Source: Scholar.

2004–05	Colchester U	2	0		
2005–06	Colchester U	2	0		
2006–07	Colchester U	32	3	**36**	**3**

HUGHES, Craig (F) **0 0**
H: 6 0 W: 12 06 b.Canterbury 26-11-87
Source: Scholar.

2005–06	Colchester U	0	0		
2006–07	Colchester U	0	0		

IWELUMO, Chris (F) **264 62**
H: 6 3 W: 15 03 b.Coatbridge 1-8-78

1996–97	St Mirren	14	0		
1997–98	St Mirren	12	0	**26**	**0**
1998–99	Aarhus Fremad	27	4	**27**	**4**
1999–2000	Stoke C	3	0		
2000–01	Stoke C	2	1		
2000–01	*York C*	12	2	**12**	**2**
2000–01	*Cheltenham T*	4	1	**4**	**1**
2001–02	Stoke C	38	10		
2002–03	Stoke C	32	5		
2003–04	Stoke C	9	0	**84**	**16**
2003–04	Brighton & HA	10	4	**10**	**4**
2004–05	Aachen	9	0	**9**	**0**
2005–06	Colchester U	46	17		
2006–07	Colchester U	46	18	**92**	**35**

IZZET, Kem (M) **217 16**
H: 5 7 W: 10 05 b.Mile End 29-9-80
Source: Trainee.

1998–99	Charlton Ath	0	0		
1999–2000	Charlton Ath	0	0		
2000–01	Charlton Ath	0	0		
2000–01	Colchester U	6	1		
2001–02	Colchester U	40	3		
2002–03	Colchester U	45	8		
2003–04	Colchester U	44	3		
2004–05	Colchester U	4	0		
2005–06	Colchester U	33	0		
2006–07	Colchester U	45	1	**217**	**16**

JACKSON, Johnnie (M) **99 6**
H: 6 1 W: 12 00 b.Camden 15-8-82
Source: Trainee. *Honours:* England Youth, Under-20.

1999–2000	Tottenham H	0	0		
2000–01	Tottenham H	0	0		
2001–02	Tottenham H	0	0		
2002–03	Tottenham H	0	0		
2002–03	*Swindon T*	13	1	**13**	**1**
2002–03	*Colchester U*	8	0		
2003–04	Tottenham H	11	1		
2003–04	*Coventry C*	5	2	**5**	**2**
2004–05	Tottenham H	8	0		
2004–05	*Watford*	15	0	**15**	**0**
2005–06	Tottenham H	1	0	**20**	**1**
2005–06	*Derby Co*	6	0	**6**	**0**
2006–07	Colchester U	32	2	**40**	**2**

KING, Robbie (M) **3 0**
H: 5 11 W: 12 05 b.Chelmsford 1-10-86
Source: Scholar.

2005–06	Colchester U	3	0		
2006–07	Colchester U	0	0	**3**	**0**

McLEOD, Kevin (M) **140 16**
H: 5 11 W: 11 00 b.Liverpool 12-9-80
Source: Trainee.

1998–99	Everton	0	0		
1999–2000	Everton	0	0		
2000–01	Everton	5	0		

2001–02 Everton 0 0
2002–03 Everton 0 0
2002–03 *QPR* 8 2
2003–04 Everton 0 0 **5 0**
2003–04 QPR 35 3
2004–05 QPR 24 1 **67 6**
2004–05 Swansea C 11 0
2005–06 Swansea C 29 7
2006–07 Swansea C 4 0 **44 7**
2006–07 Colchester U 24 3 **24 3**

PAINE, Matt (D) **0 0**
H: 6 1 W: 12 12 b.Bexley 22-12-87
Source: Scholar.
2005–06 Colchester U 0 0
2006–07 Colchester U 0 0

RICHARDS, Garry (D) **30 2**
H: 6 3 W: 13 00 b.Romford 11-6-86
Source: Scholar.
2005–06 Colchester U 15 0
2006–07 Colchester U 5 1 **20 1**
2006–07 *Brentford* 10 1 **10 1**

WATSON, Kevin (M) **389 13**
H: 6 0 W: 12 06 b.Hackney 3-1-74
Source: Trainee.
1991–92 Tottenham H 0 0
1992–93 Tottenham H 5 0
1993–94 Tottenham H 0 0
1993–94 *Brentford* 3 0 **3 0**
1994–95 Tottenham H 0 0
1994–95 *Bristol C* 2 0 **2 0**
1994–95 *Barnet* 13 0 **13 0**
1995–96 Tottenham H 0 0 **5 0**
1996–97 Swindon T 27 1
1997–98 Swindon T 18 0
1998–99 Swindon T 18 0 **63 1**
1999–2000 Rotherham U 44 1
2000–01 Rotherham U 46 5
2001–02 Rotherham U 19 1 **109 7**
2001–02 Reading 12 1
2002–03 Reading 32 1
2003–04 Reading 22 0 **66 2**
2004–05 Colchester U 44 2
2005–06 Colchester U 44 0
2006–07 Colchester U 40 1 **128 3**

WHITE, John (D) **71 0**
H: 6 0 W: 12 01 b.Maldon 26-7-86
Source: Scholar.
2004–05 Colchester U 20 0
2005–06 Colchester U 35 0
2006–07 Colchester U 16 0 **71 0**

WILSON, Lawrie (D) **0 0**
H: 5 11 W: 11 06 b.London 11-9-87
Source: Charlton Ath.
2006–07 Colchester U 0 0

COVENTRY C (27)

ADEBOLA, Dele (F) **452 106**
H: 6 3 W: 12 08 b.Lagos 23-6-75
Source: Trainee.
1992–93 Crewe Alex 6 0
1993–94 Crewe Alex 0 0
1994–95 Crewe Alex 30 8
1995–96 Crewe Alex 29 8
1996–97 Crewe Alex 32 16
1997–98 Crewe Alex 27 7 **124 39**
1997–98 Birmingham C 17 7
1998–99 Birmingham C 39 13
1999–2000 Birmingham C 42 5
2000–01 Birmingham C 31 6
2001–02 Birmingham C 0 0 **129 31**
2001–02 *Oldham Ath* 5 0 **5 0**
2002–03 Crystal Palace 39 5 **39 5**
2003–04 Coventry C 28 2
2003–04 *Burnley* 3 1 **3 1**
2004–05 Coventry C 25 5
2004–05 *Bradford C* 15 3 **15 3**
2005–06 Coventry C 44 12
2006–07 Coventry C 40 8 **137 27**

ANDREWS, Wayne (F) **175 39**
H: 5 10 W: 11 06 b.Paddington 25-11-77
Source: Trainee.
1995–96 Watford 1 0
1996–97 Watford 25 4
1997–98 Watford 2 0
1998–99 Watford 0 0 **28 4**
1998–99 *Cambridge U* 2 0 **2 0**
1998–99 *Peterborough U* 10 5 **10 5**
From Aldershot T, Chesham U
2001–02 Oldham Ath 0 0
2002–03 Oldham Ath 37 11 **37 11**
2003–04 Colchester U 41 12
2004–05 Colchester U 5 2 **46 14**
2004–05 Crystal Palace 9 0
2005–06 Crystal Palace 24 1 **33 1**
2006–07 Coventry C 3 1 **3 1**
2006–07 *Sheffield W* 9 1 **9 1**
2006–07 *Bristol C* 7 2 **7 2**

BIRCHALL, Chris (M) **106 9**
H: 5 7 W: 13 05 b.Stafford 5-5-84
Source: Scholar. *Honours:* Trinidad & Tobago 26 full caps, 4 goals.
2001–02 Port Vale 1 0
2002–03 Port Vale 2 0
2003–04 Port Vale 10 0
2004–05 Port Vale 34 6
2005–06 Port Vale 31 1 **78 7**
2006–07 Coventry C 28 2 **28 2**

BISCHOFF, Mikkel (D) **29 1**
H: 6 3 W: 13 11 b.Copenhagen 3-2-82
Honours: Denmark Under-21.
2001–02 AB Copenhagen 10 0 **10 0**
2002–03 Manchester C 1 0
2003–04 Manchester C 0 0
2004–05 Manchester C 0 0
2004–05 *Wolverhampton W* 11 1 **11 1**
2005–06 Manchester C 0 0 **1 0**
2005–06 *Sheffield W* 4 0 **4 0**
2006–07 Coventry C 3 0 **3 0**
To Brondby January 2007

BUNCE, Che (D) **0 0**
H: 6 4 W: 14 00 b. 28-9-75
Source: New Zealand K.
2006–07 Coventry C 0 0

CAMERON, Colin (M) **474 93**
H: 5 8 W: 11 00 b.Kirkcaldy 23-10-72
Source: From Lochore Welfare. *Honours:* Scotland B, 28 full caps, 2 goals.
1990–91 Raith R 0 0
1991–92 *Sligo R* 0 0
1992–93 Raith R 16 1
1993–94 Raith R 41 6
1994–95 Raith R 35 7
1995–96 Raith R 30 9 **122 23**
1995–96 Hearts 4 2
1996–97 Hearts 36 7
1997–98 Hearts 31 8
1998–99 Hearts 11 6
1999–2000 Hearts 32 8
2000–01 Hearts 37 12
2001–02 Hearts 4 3 **155 46**
2001–02 Wolverhampton W 41 4
2002–03 Wolverhampton W 33 7
2003–04 Wolverhampton W 30 4
2004–05 Wolverhampton W 37 3
2005–06 Wolverhampton W 27 4 **168 22**
2005–06 *Millwall* 5 0 **5 0**
2006–07 Coventry C 24 2 **24 2**

DAVIS, Liam (M) **12 0**
H: 5 9 W: 11 07 b.Wandsworth 23-11-86
Source: Scholar.
2005–06 Coventry C 2 0
2006–07 Coventry C 3 0 **5 0**
2006–07 *Peterborough U* 7 0 **7 0**

DOYLE, Micky (M) **168 10**
H: 5 10 W: 11 00 b.Dublin 8-7-81
Source: Celtic. *Honours:* Eire Under-21, 1 full cap.
2003–04 Coventry C 40 5
2004–05 Coventry C 44 2
2005–06 Coventry C 44 0
2006–07 Coventry C 40 3 **168 10**

EL IDRISSI, Faysal (M) **136 19**
H: 5 8 W: 10 03 b.Lille 16-11-77
Honours: Morocco Youth, Under-21, Under-23, full caps.
1996–97 Lille 0 0
1997–98 Mouscron 20 5
1998–99 Mouscron 23 3 **43 8**
1999–2000 Santa Clara 18 3 **18 3**
2000–01 Groningen 13 0
2001–02 Groningen 0 0 **13 0**
From Ronse
2003–04 Saarbrucken 31 8
2004–05 Saarbrucken 30 0
2005–06 Saarbrucken 0 0 **61 8**
2006–07 Coventry C 1 0 **1 0**

FADIGA, Khalilou (M) **225 26**
H: 6 0 W: 12 02 b.Dakar 30-12-74
Honours: Senegal 30 full caps, 3 goals.
1995–96 Lommel 20 0
1996–97 Lommel 28 2 **48 2**
1997–98 FC Brugge 31 3
1998–99 FC Brugge 21 4
1999–2000 FC Brugge 17 2
2000–01 FC Brugge 3 4 **72 13**
2000–01 Auxerre 21 1
2001–02 Auxerre 27 8
2002–03 Auxerre 34 1 **82 10**
2003–04 Internazionale 0 0
2004–05 Bolton W 5 0
2005–06 Bolton W 8 1 **13 1**
2005–06 *Derby Co* 4 0 **4 0**
2006–07 Coventry C 6 0 **6 0**

GIDDINGS, Stuart (M) **16 0**
H: 6 0 W: 11 08 b.Coventry 27-3-86
Source: Scholar. *Honours:* England Youth.
2003–04 Coventry C 1 0
2004–05 Coventry C 12 0
2005–06 Coventry C 2 0
2006–07 Coventry C 1 0 **16 0**

GOODING, Andy (M) **0 0**
H: 5 7 W: 10 05 b.Coventry 30-4-88
Source: Scholar.
2006–07 Coventry C 0 0

HALL, Marcus (D) **301 3**
H: 6 1 W: 12 02 b.Coventry 24-3-76
Source: From Trainee. *Honours:* England Under-21, B.
1994–95 Coventry C 5 0
1995–96 Coventry C 25 0
1996–97 Coventry C 13 0
1997–98 Coventry C 25 1
1998–99 Coventry C 5 0
1999–2000 Coventry C 9 0
2000–01 Coventry C 21 0
2001–02 Coventry C 29 1
2002–03 Nottingham F 1 0 **1 0**
2002–03 Stoke C 24 0
2003–04 Stoke C 35 0
2004–05 Stoke C 20 1 **79 1**
2004–05 Coventry C 10 0
2005–06 Coventry C 39 0
2006–07 Coventry C 40 0 **221 2**

HAWKINS, Colin (D) **238 20**
H: 6 1 W: 12 06 b.Galway 17-8-77
Honours: Eire Youth, Under-20.
1995–96 Coventry C 0 0
1996–97 Coventry C 0 0
1997–98 St Patrick's Ath 32 4
1998–99 St Patrick's Ath 26 7
1999–2000 St Patrick's Ath 27 2 **85 13**
From Doncaster R
2001–02 Bohemians 9 1
2002–03 Bohemians 21 2
2003 Bohemians 30 1
2004 Bohemians 29 1 **89 5**
2005 Shelbourne 26 0
2006 Shelbourne 25 2 **51 2**
2006–07 Coventry C 13 0 **13 0**

HILDRETH, Lee (M) **1 0**
H: 6 0 W: 11 02 b.Nuneaton 22-11-88
Source: Scholar.
2006–07 Coventry C 1 0 **1 0**

HUGHES, Stephen (M) **192 10**
H: 6 0 W: 12 12 b.Wokingham 18-9-76
Source: From Trainee. *Honours:* England Schools, Youth, Under-21.
1994–95 Arsenal 1 0
1995–96 Arsenal 1 0
1996–97 Arsenal 14 1

1997–98	Arsenal	17	2		
1998–99	Arsenal	14	1		
1999–2000	Fulham	3	0	**3**	**0**
1999–2000	Arsenal	2	0	**49**	**4**
1999–2000	Everton	11	1		
2000–01	Everton	18	0	**29**	**1**
2001–02	Watford	15	0		
2002–03	Watford	0	0	**15**	**0**
2003–04	Charlton Ath	0	0		
2004–05	Coventry C	40	4		
2005–06	Coventry C	19	0		
2006–07	Coventry C	37	1	**96**	**5**

HUTCHISON, Don (M) **403** **54**
H: 6 1 W: 11 08 b.Gateshead 9-5-71
Source: Trainee. *Honours:* Scotland B, 26 full caps, 6 goals.

1989–90	Hartlepool U	13	2		
1990–91	Hartlepool U	11	0	**24**	**2**
1990–91	Liverpool	0	0		
1991–92	Liverpool	3	0		
1992–93	Liverpool	31	7		
1993–94	Liverpool	11	0	**45**	**7**
1994–95	West Ham U	23	9		
1995–96	West Ham U	12	2		
1995–96	Sheffield U	19	2		
1996–97	Sheffield U	41	3		
1997–98	Sheffield U	18	0	**78**	**5**
1997–98	Everton	11	1		
1998–99	Everton	33	3		
1999–2000	Everton	31	6	**75**	**10**
2000–01	Sunderland	32	8		
2001–02	Sunderland	2	0	**34**	**8**
2001–02	West Ham U	24	1		
2002–03	West Ham U	10	0		
2003–04	West Ham U	24	4		
2004–05	West Ham U	5	0	**98**	**16**
2005–06	Millwall	11	2	**11**	**2**
2005–06	Coventry C	24	4		
2006–07	Coventry C	14	0	**38**	**4**

KYLE, Kevin (F) **137** **15**
H: 6 4 W: 14 07 b.Stranraer 7-6-81
Source: Ayr Boswell. *Honours:* Scotland Under-21, B, 9 full caps, 1 goal.

1998–99	Sunderland	0	0		
1999–2000	Sunderland	0	0		
2000–01	Sunderland	3	0		
2000–01	*Huddersfield T*	4	0	**4**	**0**
2000–01	*Darlington*	5	1	**5**	**1**
2000–01	*Rochdale*	6	0	**6**	**0**
2001–02	Sunderland	6	0		
2002–03	Sunderland	17	0		
2003–04	Sunderland	44	10		
2004–05	Sunderland	6	0		
2005–06	Sunderland	13	1		
2006–07	Sunderland	2	0	**91**	**11**
2006–07	Coventry C	31	3	**31**	**3**

LEE-BARRETT, Arran (G) **0** **0**
H: 6 2 W: 14 01 b.Ipswich 28-2-84
Source: Norwich C Scholar.

2002–03	Cardiff C	0	0		
2003–04	Cardiff C	0	0		
2004–05	Cardiff C	0	0		
2005–06	Cardiff C	0	0		
From Weymouth					
2006–07	Coventry C	0	0		

LYNCH, Ryan (M) **0** **0**
H: 5 11 W: 11 09 b.Solihull 13-3-87
Source: Scholar.

2005–06	Coventry C	0	0		
2006–07	Coventry C	0	0		

MARSHALL, Andy (G) **372** **0**
H: 6 3 W: 14 08 b.Bury St Edmunds 14-4-75
Source: Trainee. *Honours:* England Under-21.

1993–94	Norwich C	0	0		
1994–95	Norwich C	21	0		
1995–96	Norwich C	3	0		
1996–97	Norwich C	7	0		
1996–97	*Bournemouth*	11	0	**11**	**0**
1996–97	*Gillingham*	5	0	**5**	**0**
1997–98	Norwich C	42	0		
1998–99	Norwich C	37	0		
1999–2000	Norwich C	44	0		
2000–01	Norwich C	41	0	**195**	**0**

2001–02	Ipswich T	13	0		
2002–03	Ipswich T	40	0		
2003–04	Ipswich T	0	0	**53**	**0**
2003–04	Millwall	16	0		
2004–05	Millwall	22	0		
2005–06	Millwall	29	0	**67**	**0**
2006–07	Coventry C	41	0	**41**	**0**

McKENZIE, Leon (F) **302** **87**
H: 5 11 W: 12 11 b.Croydon 17-5-78
Source: Trainee.

1995–96	Crystal Palace	12	0		
1996–97	Crystal Palace	21	2		
1997–98	Crystal Palace	3	0		
1997–98	*Fulham*	3	0	**3**	**0**
1998–99	Crystal Palace	16	1		
1998–99	*Peterborough U*	14	8		
1999–2000	Crystal Palace	25	4		
2000–01	Crystal Palace	8	0	**85**	**7**
2000–01	Peterborough U	30	13		
2001–02	Peterborough U	30	18		
2002–03	Peterborough U	11	5		
2003–04	Peterborough U	19	9	**104**	**53**
2003–04	Norwich C	18	9		
2004–05	Norwich C	37	7		
2005–06	Norwich C	20	4		
2006–07	Norwich C	4	0	**79**	**20**
2006–07	Coventry C	31	7	**31**	**7**

McNAMEE, David (D) **133** **4**
H: 5 11 W: 11 02 b.Glasgow 10-10-80
Source: St Mirren BC. *Honours:* Scotland B, 4 full caps.

1997–98	St Mirren	1	0		
1998–99	St Mirren	31	0	**32**	**0**
1998–99	Blackburn R	0	0		
1999–2000	Blackburn R	0	0		
2000–01	Blackburn R	0	0		
2001–02	Blackburn R	0	0		
2002–03	Livingston	12	0		
2003–04	Livingston	30	3		
2004–05	Livingston	29	1		
2005–06	Livingston	14	0	**85**	**4**
2006–07	Coventry C	16	0	**16**	**0**

MIFSUD, Michael (F) **150** **77**
H: 5 6 W: 10 00 b.Pieta 17-4-81
Honours: Malta 46 full caps, 12 goals.

1997–98	Sliema Wanderers	7	1		
1998–99	Sliema Wanderers	22	8		
1999–2000	Sliema Wanderers	26	21		
2000–01	Sliema Wanderers	25	30	**80**	**60**
2001–02	Kaiserslautern	5	0		
2002–03	Kaiserslautern	16	2		
2003–04	Kaiserslautern	0	0	**21**	**2**
2004	Lillestrom	9	0		
2005	Lillestrom	2	0		
2006	Lillestrom	19	11	**30**	**11**
2006–07	Coventry C	19	4	**19**	**4**

OSBOURNE, Isaac (M) **42** **0**
H: 5 10 W: 11 11 b.Birmingham 22-6-86
Source: Scholar.

2002–03	Coventry C	2	0		
2003–04	Coventry C	0	0		
2004–05	Coventry C	9	0		
2005–06	Coventry C	10	0		
2006–07	Coventry C	19	0	**40**	**0**
2006–07	*Crewe Alex*	2	0	**2**	**0**

PAGE, Robert (D) **402** **4**
H: 6 0 W: 12 05 b.Llwynpia 3-9-74
Source: Trainee. *Honours:* Wales Schools, Youth, Under-21, B, 41 full caps.

1992–93	Watford	0	0		
1993–94	Watford	4	0		
1994–95	Watford	5	0		
1995–96	Watford	19	0		
1996–97	Watford	36	0		
1997–98	Watford	41	0		
1998–99	Watford	39	0		
1999–2000	Watford	36	1		
2000–01	Watford	36	1		
2001–02	Watford	0	0	**216**	**2**
2001–02	Sheffield U	43	0		
2002–03	Sheffield U	34	0		
2003–04	Sheffield U	30	1	**107**	**1**
2004–05	Cardiff C	9	0	**9**	**0**
2004–05	Coventry C	9	0		

2005–06	Coventry C	32	1		
2006–07	Coventry C	29	0	**70**	**1**

RAFA (G) **81** **0**
H: 6 4 W: 13 12 b.Aviles 25-10-70

1993–94	Oviedo	3	0		
1994–95	Oviedo	1	0		
1995–96	Oviedo	1	0		
1996–97	Oviedo	1	0	**6**	**0**
1997–98	Malaga	37	0		
1998–99	Malaga	31	0		
1999–2000	Malaga	1	0		
2000–01	Malaga	3	0		
2001–02	Malaga	2	0		
2002–03	Malaga	1	0	**75**	**0**
From Oviedo					
2006–07	Coventry C	0	0		

TABB, Jay (M) **159** **23**
H: 5 7 W: 10 00 b.Tooting 21-2-84
Source: Trainee. *Honours:* Eire Under-21.

2000–01	Brentford	2	0		
2001–02	Brentford	3	0		
2002–03	Brentford	5	0		
2003–04	Brentford	36	9		
2004–05	Brentford	40	5		
2005–06	Brentford	42	6	**128**	**20**
2006–07	Coventry C	31	3	**31**	**3**

THORNTON, Kevin (M) **27** **1**
H: 5 7 W: 11 00 b.Drogheda 9-7-86
Source: Scholar. *Honours:* Eire Youth.

2003–04	Coventry C	0	0		
2004–05	Coventry C	0	0		
2005–06	Coventry C	16	0		
2006–07	Coventry C	11	1	**27**	**1**

TURNER, Ben (D) **11** **0**
H: 6 4 W: 14 04 b.Birmingham 21-1-88
Source: Scholar.

2005–06	Coventry C	1	0		
2006–07	Coventry C	1	0	**2**	**0**
2006–07	*Peterborough U*	8	0	**8**	**0**
2006–07	*Oldham Ath*	1	0	**1**	**0**

VIRGO, Adam (D) **107** **10**
H: 6 2 W: 13 12 b.Brighton 25-1-83
Source: Juniors. *Honours:* Scotland B.

2000–01	Brighton & HA	6	0		
2001–02	Brighton & HA	6	0		
2002–03	Brighton & HA	3	0		
2002–03	*Exeter C*	9	0	**9**	**0**
2003–04	Brighton & HA	22	1		
2004–05	Brighton & HA	36	8	**73**	**9**
2005–06	Celtic	10	0		
2006–07	Celtic	0	0	**10**	**0**
2006–07	Coventry C	15	1	**15**	**1**

WARD, Elliot (D) **73** **4**
H: 6 2 W: 13 00 b.Harrow 19-1-85
Source: Scholar.

2001–02	West Ham U	0	0		
2002–03	West Ham U	0	0		
2003–04	West Ham U	0	0		
2004–05	West Ham U	11	0		
2004–05	*Bristol R*	3	0	**3**	**0**
2005–06	West Ham U	4	0	**15**	**0**
2005–06	*Plymouth Arg*	16	1	**16**	**1**
2006–07	Coventry C	39	3	**39**	**3**

WHING, Andrew (D) **118** **2**
H: 6 0 W: 12 00 b.Birmingham 20-9-84
Source: Scholar.

2002–03	Coventry C	14	0		
2003–04	Coventry C	28	1		
2004–05	Coventry C	16	1		
2005–06	Coventry C	32	0		
2006–07	Coventry C	16	0	**106**	**2**
2006–07	*Brighton & HA*	12	0	**12**	**0**

CREWE ALEX (28)

BAILEY, James (M) **0** **0**
b.Bollington 18-9-88

2006–07	Crewe Alex	0	0		

BAILEY, Matt (F) **5** **0**
H: 6 4 W: 11 06 b.Crewe 12-3-86
Source: Nantwich T.

2003–04	Stockport Co	0	0		

2004–05 Stockport Co 1 0 **1 0**
2004–05 *Scunthorpe U* 4 0 **4 0**
From Northwich Vic.
2005–06 Crewe Alex 0 0
2006–07 Crewe Alex 0 0

BAUDET, Julien (D) 178 15
H: 6 2 W: 13 07 b.Grenoble 13-1-79
Source: Toulouse.
2001–02 Oldham Ath 20 1
2002–03 Oldham Ath 24 2 **44 3**
2003–04 Rotherham U 11 0 **11 0**
2004–05 Notts Co 39 5
2005–06 Notts Co 42 6 **81 11**
2006–07 Crewe Alex 42 1 **42 1**

BELL, Lee (M) 54 3
H: 5 11 W: 12 04 b.Crewe 26-1-83
Source: Scholar.
2000–01 Crewe Alex 0 0
2001–02 Crewe Alex 0 0
2002–03 Crewe Alex 17 1
2003–04 Crewe Alex 3 0
2004–05 Crewe Alex 17 0
2005–06 Crewe Alex 17 2
2006–07 Crewe Alex 0 0 **54 3**

BIGNOT, Paul (D) 21 0
H: 6 1 W: 12 03 b.Birmingham 14-2-86
Source: Scholar.
2004–05 Crewe Alex 5 0
2005–06 Crewe Alex 5 0
2006–07 Crewe Alex 11 0 **21 0**

BROWN, Junior (M) 0 0
b.Crewe 7-5-89
2006–07 Crewe Alex 0 0

CARRINGTON, Mark (M) 3 0
H: 6 0 W: 11 00 b.Warrington 4-5-87
Source: Scholar.
2006–07 Crewe Alex 3 0 **3 0**

COO, Cavell (D) 1 0
H: 5 9 W: 11 03 b.Manchester 7-8-87
Source: Scholar.
2006–07 Crewe Alex 1 0 **1 0**

COX, Neil (D) 522 37
H: 5 11 W: 13 08 b.Scunthorpe 8-10-71
Source: From Trainee. *Honours:* England Under-21.
1989–90 Scunthorpe U 0 0
1990–91 Scunthorpe U 17 1 **17 1**
1990–91 Aston Villa 0 0
1991–92 Aston Villa 7 0
1992–93 Aston Villa 15 1
1993–94 Aston Villa 20 2 **42 3**
1994–95 Middlesbrough 40 1
1995–96 Middlesbrough 35 2
1996–97 Middlesbrough 31 0 **106 3**
1997–98 Bolton W 21 1
1998–99 Bolton W 44 4
1999–2000 Bolton W 15 2 **80 7**
1999–2000 Watford 21 0
2000–01 Watford 44 5
2001–02 Watford 40 2
2002–03 Watford 40 9
2003–04 Watford 35 4
2004–05 Watford 39 0 **219 20**
2005–06 Cardiff C 27 2 **27 2**
2006–07 Crewe Alex 31 1 **31 1**

DANIEL, Colin (M) 0 0
b.Nottingham
2006–07 Crewe Alex 0 0

DUGDALE, Adam (D) 2 0
H: 6 3 W: 12 07 b.Liverpool 12-9-87
Source: Scholar.
2006–07 Crewe Alex 0 0
2006–07 *Accrington S* 2 0 **2 0**

FARQUHARSON, Nick (M) 0 0
b.Coventry 7-9-88
2006–07 Crewe Alex 0 0

FLYNN, Christopher (M) 1 0
H: 5 11 W: 12 04 b.Bolton 5-11-87
Source: Scholar. *Honours:* Wales Under-21.
2006–07 Crewe Alex 1 0 **1 0**

HIGDON, Michael (F) 81 10
H: 6 2 W: 11 05 b.Liverpool 2-9-83
Source: School.
2000–01 Crewe Alex 0 0
2001–02 Crewe Alex 0 0
2002–03 Crewe Alex 0 0
2003–04 Crewe Alex 10 1
2004–05 Crewe Alex 20 3
2005–06 Crewe Alex 26 3
2006–07 Crewe Alex 25 3 **81 10**

JACK, Rodney (F) 335 72
H: 5 7 W: 10 05 b.Kingston, Jamaica 28-9-72
Source: Lambada. *Honours:* St Vincent 71 full caps.
1995–96 Torquay U 14 2
1996–97 Torquay U 33 10
1997–98 Torquay U 40 12 **87 24**
1998–99 Crewe Alex 39 9
1999–2000 Crewe Alex 23 4
2000–01 Crewe Alex 30 4
2001–02 Crewe Alex 33 7
2002–03 Crewe Alex 38 9
2003–04 Rushden & D 45 12 **45 12**
2004–05 Oldham Ath 10 2
2005–06 Oldham Ath 0 0 **10 2**
2006–07 Crewe Alex 30 1 **193 34**

JONES, Billy (M) 132 8
H: 5 11 W: 13 00 b.Shrewsbury 24-3-87
Source: Scholar. *Honours:* England Youth, Under-20.
2003–04 Crewe Alex 27 1
2004–05 Crewe Alex 20 0
2005–06 Crewe Alex 44 6
2006–07 Crewe Alex 41 1 **132 8**

KEMPSON, Darran (D) 19 0
H: 6 2 W: 13 00 b.Blackpool 6-12-84
Source: Scholar.
2004–05 Preston NE 0 0
From Morecambe.
2006–07 Crewe Alex 7 0 **7 0**
2006–07 *Bury* 12 0 **12 0**

LLOYD, Rob (D) 0 0
H: 6 0 W: 11 10 b.Chester 13-8-86
Source: Scholar.
2005–06 Crewe Alex 0 0
2006–07 Crewe Alex 0 0

LOWE, Ryan (F) 214 45
H: 5 10 W: 12 08 b.Liverpool 18-9-78
Source: Burscough.
2000–01 Shrewsbury T 30 4
2001–02 Shrewsbury T 38 7
2002–03 Shrewsbury T 39 9
2003–04 Shrewsbury T 0 0
2004–05 Shrewsbury T 30 3 **137 23**
2004–05 Chester C 8 4
2005–06 Chester C 32 10 **40 14**
2005–06 Crewe Alex 0 0
2006–07 Crewe Alex 37 8 **37 8**

MATTHEWS, Lee (F) 119 20
H: 6 2 W: 14 02 b.Middlesbrough 16-1-79
Source: Trainee. *Honours:* England Youth.
1995–96 Leeds U 0 0
1996–97 Leeds U 0 0
1997–98 Leeds U 3 0
1998–99 Leeds U 0 0
1998–99 *Notts Co* 5 0 **5 0**
1999–2000 Leeds U 0 0
1999–2000 *Gillingham* 5 0 **5 0**
2000–01 Leeds U 0 0 **3 0**
2000–01 Bristol C 6 3
2001–02 Bristol C 22 3
2002–03 Bristol C 7 1
2003–04 Bristol C 8 2 **43 9**
2003–04 *Darlington* 6 1 **6 1**
2003–04 *Bristol R* 9 0 **9 0**
2003–04 *Yeovil T* 4 0 **4 0**
2004–05 Port Vale 31 10
2005–06 Port Vale 3 0
2006–07 Port Vale 0 0 **34 10**
2006–07 Crewe Alex 10 0 **10 0**

MAYNARD, Nicky (F) 32 17
H: 5 11 W: 11 00 b.Winsford 11-12-86
Source: Scholar.
2005–06 Crewe Alex 1 1
2006–07 Crewe Alex 31 16 **32 17**

MILLER, Shaun (F) 7 3
H: 5 10 W: 11 08 b.Alsager 25-9-87
Source: Scholar.
2006–07 Crewe Alex 7 3 **7 3**

MOORE, Byron (M) 0 0
b.Stoke 24-8-88
2006–07 Crewe Alex 0 0

MOSS, Darren (D) 198 12
H: 5 10 W: 11 00 b.Wrexham 24-5-81
Source: Trainee. *Honours:* Wales Under-21.
1998–99 Chester C 7 0
1999–2000 Chester C 35 0
2000–01 Chester C 0 0 **42 0**
2001–02 Shrewsbury T 31 2
2002–03 Shrewsbury T 40 2
2003–04 Shrewsbury T 0 0
2004–05 Shrewsbury T 26 6 **97 10**
2004–05 Crewe Alex 6 0
2005–06 Crewe Alex 31 0
2006–07 Crewe Alex 22 2 **59 2**

O'CONNOR, Michael (M) 31 0
H: 6 1 W: 11 08 b.Belfast 6-10-87
Source: Scholar. *Honours:* Northern Ireland Youth.
2005–06 Crewe Alex 2 0
2006–07 Crewe Alex 29 0 **31 0**

OTSEMOBOR, John (D) 81 4
H: 5 10 W: 12 07 b.Liverpool 23-3-83
Source: Trainee. *Honours:* England Youth, Under-20.
1999–2000 Liverpool 0 0
2000–01 Liverpool 0 0
2001–02 Liverpool 0 0
2002–03 Liverpool 0 0
2002–03 *Hull C* 9 3 **9 3**
2003–04 Liverpool 4 0
2003–04 *Bolton W* 1 0 **1 0**
2004–05 Liverpool 0 0 **4 0**
2004–05 *Crewe Alex* 14 1
2005–06 Rotherham U 10 0 **10 0**
2005–06 Crewe Alex 16 0
2006–07 Crewe Alex 27 0 **57 1**

POPE, Tom (M) 4 0
H: 6 3 W: 11 03 b.Stoke 27-8-85
Source: Lancaster C.
2005–06 Crewe Alex 0 0
2006–07 Crewe Alex 4 0 **4 0**

RIX, Ben (M) 114 4
H: 5 9 W: 11 13 b.Wolverhampton 11-12-82
Source: Scholar.
2000–01 Crewe Alex 0 0
2001–02 Crewe Alex 21 0
2002–03 Crewe Alex 23 0
2003–04 Crewe Alex 26 2
2004–05 Crewe Alex 0 0
2005–06 Crewe Alex 2 0
2005–06 *Bournemouth* 11 0 **11 0**
2006–07 Crewe Alex 31 2 **103 4**

ROBERTS, Gary (M) 80 5
H: 5 8 W: 10 05 b.Chester 4-2-87
Source: Scholar. *Honours:* England Youth.
2003–04 Crewe Alex 2 0
2004–05 Crewe Alex 2 0
2005–06 Crewe Alex 33 2
2006–07 Crewe Alex 43 3 **80 5**

ROBERTS, Mark (D) 7 0
H: 6 1 W: 12 00 b.Northwich 16-10-83
Source: Scholar.
2002–03 Crewe Alex 0 0
2003–04 Crewe Alex 0 0
2004–05 Crewe Alex 6 0
2005–06 Crewe Alex 0 0
2005–06 *Chester C* 1 0 **1 0**
2006–07 Crewe Alex 0 0 **6 0**

SUHAJ, Pavol (F) **51 5**
H: 6 3 W: 12 00 b.Lipany 16-4-81
Source: Patraikos.

2003–04	Trencin	16	2		
2004–05	Trencin	27	3	**43**	**5**
2005–06	Crewe Alex	6	0		
2006–07	Crewe Alex	2	0	**8**	**0**

SUTTON, Ritchie (D) **0 0**
H: 6 0 W: 11 05 b.Stoke 29-4-86
Source: Scholar.

2005–06	Crewe Alex	0	0		
2006–07	Crewe Alex	0	0		

TOMLINSON, Stuart (G) **11 0**
H: 6 1 W: 11 02 b.Chester 10-5-85
Source: Scholar.

2002–03	Crewe Alex	1	0		
2003–04	Crewe Alex	1	0		
2004–05	Crewe Alex	0	0		
2005–06	Crewe Alex	2	0		
2006–07	Crewe Alex	7	0	**11**	**0**

VARNEY, Luke (F) **95 27**
H: 5 11 W: 11 00 b.Leicester 28-9-82
Source: Quorn.

2002–03	Crewe Alex	0	0		
2003–04	Crewe Alex	8	1		
2004–05	Crewe Alex	26	4		
2005–06	Crewe Alex	27	5		
2006–07	Crewe Alex	34	17	**95**	**27**

VAUGHAN, David (M) **184 18**
H: 5 7 W: 11 00 b.Rhuddlan 18-2-83
Source: Scholar. *Honours:* Wales Youth, Under-21, 10 full caps.

2000–01	Crewe Alex	1	0		
2001–02	Crewe Alex	13	0		
2002–03	Crewe Alex	32	3		
2003–04	Crewe Alex	31	0		
2004–05	Crewe Alex	44	6		
2005–06	Crewe Alex	34	5		
2006–07	Crewe Alex	29	4	**184**	**18**

WARLOW, Adam (M) **0 0**
b.Southport 3-2-87

2006–07	Crewe Alex	0	0		

WILLIAMS, Ben (G) **103 0**
H: 6 0 W: 13 01 b.Manchester 27-8-82
Source: Scholar. *Honours:* England Schools.

2001–02	Manchester U	0	0		
2002–03	Manchester U	0	0		
2002–03	*Coventry C*	0	0		
2002–03	*Chesterfield*	14	0	**14**	**0**
2003–04	Manchester U	0	0		
2003–04	*Crewe Alex*	10	0		
2004–05	Crewe Alex	23	0		
2005–06	Crewe Alex	17	0		
2006–07	Crewe Alex	39	0	**89**	**0**

WILLIAMS, Owain Fon (G) **0 0**
H: 6 1 W: 12 09 b.Gwynedd 17-3-87
Source: Scholar. *Honours:* Wales Under-21.

2005–06	Crewe Alex	0	0		
2006–07	Crewe Alex	0	0		

WOODARDS, Danny (M) **11 0**
H: 5 11 W: 11 01 b.Forest Gate 7-10-83
Source: Trainee.

2003–04	Chelsea	0	0		
2004–05	Chelsea	0	0		
2005–06	Chelsea	0	0		
From Exeter C.					
2006–07	Crewe Alex	11	0	**11**	**0**

CRYSTAL PALACE (29)

BLACK, Tommy (M) **162 17**
H: 5 7 W: 11 10 b.Chigwell 26-11-79
Source: Trainee.

1998–99	Arsenal	0	0		
1999–2000	Arsenal	1	0	**1**	**0**
1999–2000	*Carlisle U*	5	1	**5**	**1**
1999–2000	*Bristol C*	4	0	**4**	**0**
2000–01	Crystal Palace	40	4		
2001–02	Crystal Palace	25	0		
2002–03	Crystal Palace	36	6		
2003–04	Crystal Palace	25	0		
2004–05	Crystal Palace	0	0		
2004–05	*Sheffield U*	4	1	**4**	**1**
2005–06	Crystal Palace	1	0		
2005–06	*Gillingham*	17	5	**17**	**5**
2006–07	Crystal Palace	0	0	**127**	**10**
2006–07	*Bradford C*	4	0	**4**	**0**

BORROWDALE, Gary (D) **98 0**
H: 6 0 W: 12 01 b.Sutton 16-7-85
Source: Scholar. *Honours:* England Youth, Under-20.

2002–03	Crystal Palace	13	0		
2003–04	Crystal Palace	23	0		
2004–05	Crystal Palace	7	0		
2005–06	Crystal Palace	30	0		
2006–07	Crystal Palace	25	0	**98**	**0**

BUTTERFIELD, Danny (D) **263 8**
H: 5 10 W: 11 06 b.Boston 21-11-79
Source: Trainee. *Honours:* England Youth.

1997–98	Grimsby T	7	0		
1998–99	Grimsby T	12	0		
1999–2000	Grimsby T	29	0		
2000–01	Grimsby T	30	1		
2001–02	Grimsby T	46	2	**124**	**3**
2002–03	Crystal Palace	46	1		
2003–04	Crystal Palace	45	4		
2004–05	Crystal Palace	7	0		
2005–06	Crystal Palace	13	0		
2006–07	Crystal Palace	28	0	**139**	**5**

CORT, Leon (D) **260 28**
H: 6 3 W: 13 01 b.Bermondsey 11-9-79
Source: Dulwich H.

1997–98	Millwall	0	0		
1998–99	Millwall	0	0		
1999–2000	Millwall	0	0		
2000–01	Millwall	0	0		
2001–02	Southend U	45	4		
2002–03	Southend U	46	6		
2003–04	Southend U	46	1	**137**	**11**
2004–05	Hull C	44	6		
2005–06	Hull C	42	4	**86**	**10**
2006–07	Crystal Palace	37	7	**37**	**7**

FLETCHER, Carl (M) **277 25**
H: 5 10 W: 11 07 b.Camberley 7-4-80
Source: Trainee. *Honours:* Wales 22 full caps.

1997–98	Bournemouth	1	0		
1998–99	Bournemouth	1	0		
1999–2000	Bournemouth	25	3		
2000–01	Bournemouth	43	6		
2001–02	Bournemouth	35	5		
2002–03	Bournemouth	42	1		
2003–04	Bournemouth	40	2		
2004–05	Bournemouth	6	2	**193**	**19**
2004–05	West Ham U	32	2		
2005–06	West Ham U	12	1	**44**	**3**
2005–06	*Watford*	3	0	**3**	**0**
2006–07	Crystal Palace	37	3	**37**	**3**

FLINDERS, Scott (G) **43 0**
H: 6 4 W: 13 00 b.Rotherham 12-6-86
Source: Scholar. *Honours:* England Youth, Under-20.

2004–05	Barnsley	11	0		
2005–06	Barnsley	3	0	**14**	**0**
2006–07	Crystal Palace	8	0	**8**	**0**
2006–07	*Gillingham*	9	0	**9**	**0**
2006–07	*Brighton & HA*	12	0	**12**	**0**

FRAY, Arron (D) **0 0**
H: 5 11 W: 11 02 b.Bromley 1-5-87
Source: Scholar.

2005–06	Crystal Palace	0	0		
2006–07	Crystal Palace	0	0		

FREEDMAN, Dougie (F) **454 148**
H: 5 9 W: 12 05 b.Glasgow 21-1-74
Source: Trainee. *Honours:* Scotland Schools, Under-21, B, 2 full caps, 1 goal.

1991–92	QPR	0	0		
1992–93	QPR	0	0		
1993–94	QPR	0	0		
1994–95	Barnet	42	24		
1995–96	Barnet	5	3	**47**	**27**
1995–96	Crystal Palace	39	20		
1996–97	Crystal Palace	44	11		
1997–98	Crystal Palace	7	0		
1997–98	Wolverhampton W	29	10	**29**	**10**
1998–99	Nottingham F	31	9		
1999–2000	Nottingham F	34	9		
2000–01	Nottingham F	5	0	**70**	**18**
2000–01	Crystal Palace	26	11		
2001–02	Crystal Palace	40	20		
2002–03	Crystal Palace	29	9		
2003–04	Crystal Palace	35	13		
2004–05	Crystal Palace	20	1		
2005–06	Crystal Palace	34	5		
2006–07	Crystal Palace	34	3	**308**	**93**

GRABBAN, Lewis (F) **17 1**
H: 6 0 W: 11 03 b.Croydon 12-1-88
Source: Scholar.

2005–06	Crystal Palace	0	0		
2006–07	Crystal Palace	8	1	**8**	**1**
2006–07	*Oldham Ath*	9	0	**9**	**0**

GRANVILLE, Danny (D) **324 19**
H: 6 0 W: 12 00 b.Islington 19-1-75
Source: Trainee. *Honours:* England Under-21.

1993–94	Cambridge U	11	5		
1994–95	Cambridge U	16	2		
1995–96	Cambridge U	35	0		
1996–97	Cambridge U	37	0	**99**	**7**
1996–97	Chelsea	5	0		
1997–98	Chelsea	13	0	**18**	**0**
1998–99	Leeds U	9	0		
1999–2000	Leeds U	0	0	**9**	**0**
1999–2000	Manchester C	35	2		
2000–01	Manchester C	19	0		
2000–01	*Norwich C*	6	0	**6**	**0**
2001–02	Manchester C	16	1	**70**	**3**
2001–02	Crystal Palace	16	0		
2002–03	Crystal Palace	35	3		
2003–04	Crystal Palace	21	3		
2004–05	Crystal Palace	35	3		
2005–06	Crystal Palace	0	0		
2006–07	Crystal Palace	15	0	**122**	**9**

GREEN, Stuart (M) **177 31**
H: 5 10 W: 11 01 b.Whitehaven 15-6-81
Source: Trainee.

1999–2000	Newcastle U	0	0		
2000–01	Newcastle U	0	0		
2001–02	Newcastle U	0	0		
2001–02	*Carlisle U*	16	3		
2002–03	Newcastle U	0	0		
2002–03	Hull C	28	6		
2002–03	*Carlisle U*	10	2	**26**	**5**
2003–04	Hull C	42	6		
2004–05	Hull C	29	8		
2005–06	Hull C	38	4		
2006–07	Hull C	0	0	**137**	**24**
2006–07	Crystal Palace	14	2	**14**	**2**

HALL, Ryan (M) **0 0**
H: 5 10 W: 10 04 b.Dulwich 4-1-88
Source: Scholar.

2005–06	Crystal Palace	0	0		
2006–07	Crystal Palace	0	0		

HUDSON, Mark (D) **90 5**
H: 6 1 W: 12 01 b.Guildford 30-3-82
Source: Trainee.

1998–99	Fulham	0	0		
1999–2000	Fulham	0	0		
2000–01	Fulham	0	0		
2001–02	Fulham	0	0		
2002–03	Fulham	0	0		
2003–04	Fulham	0	0		
2003–04	*Oldham Ath*	15	0	**15**	**0**
2003–04	*Crystal Palace*	14	0		
2004–05	Crystal Palace	7	1		
2005–06	Crystal Palace	15	0		
2006–07	Crystal Palace	39	4	**75**	**5**

HUGHES, Michael (M) **436 35**
H: 5 6 W: 10 08 b.Larne 2-8-71
Source: Carrick R. *Honours:* Northern Ireland Schools, Youth, Under-21, Under-23, 71 full caps, 5 goals.

1988–89	Manchester C	1	0		
1989–90	Manchester C	0	0		
1990–91	Manchester C	1	0		
1991–92	Manchester C	24	1	**26**	**1**
1992–93	Strasbourg	36	2		
1993–94	Strasbourg	34	7		
1994–95	Strasbourg	13	0	**83**	**9**
1994–95	*West Ham U*	17	2		
1995–96	*West Ham U*	28	0		

1996–97	West Ham U	33	3		
1997–98	West Ham U	5	0	**83**	**5**
1997–98	Wimbledon	29	4		
1998–99	Wimbledon	30	2		
1999–2000	Wimbledon	20	2		
2000–01	Wimbledon	10	1		
2001–02	Wimbledon	26	4		
2001–02	*Birmingham C*	3	0	**3**	**0**
2002–03	Wimbledon	0	0	**115**	**13**
2003–04	Crystal Palace	34	3		
2004–05	Crystal Palace	36	2		
2005–06	Crystal Palace	40	2		
2006–07	Crystal Palace	16	0	**126**	**7**

IFILL, Paul (M) **285 51**
H: 6 0 W: 12 09 b.Brighton 20-10-79
Source: Trainee. *Honours:* England Youth, Barbados 8 full caps, 6 goals.

1998–99	Millwall	15	1		
1999–2000	Millwall	44	11		
2000–01	Millwall	35	6		
2001–02	Millwall	40	4		
2002–03	Millwall	45	6		
2003–04	Millwall	33	8		
2004–05	Millwall	18	4	**230**	**40**
2005–06	Sheffield U	39	9		
2006–07	Sheffield U	3	0	**42**	**9**
2006–07	Crystal Palace	13	2	**13**	**2**

KENNEDY, Mark (M) **359 32**
H: 5 11 W: 11 09 b.Dublin 15-5-76
Source: Belvedere, Trainee. *Honours:* Eire Under-21, 34 full caps, 3 goals.

1992–93	Millwall	1	0		
1993–94	Millwall	12	4		
1994–95	Millwall	30	5	**43**	**9**
1994–95	Liverpool	6	0		
1995–96	Liverpool	4	0		
1996–97	Liverpool	5	0		
1997–98	Liverpool	1	0	**16**	**0**
1997–98	*QPR*	8	2	**8**	**2**
1997–98	Wimbledon	4	0		
1998–99	Wimbledon	17	0	**21**	**0**
1999–2000	Manchester C	41	8		
2000–01	Manchester C	25	0	**66**	**8**
2001–02	Wolverhampton W	35	5		
2002–03	Wolverhampton W	31	3		
2003–04	Wolverhampton W	31	2		
2004–05	Wolverhampton W	30	0		
2005–06	Wolverhampton W	40	2	**167**	**12**
2006–07	Crystal Palace	38	1	**38**	**1**

KIRALY, Gabor (G) **374 0**
H: 6 3 W: 13 06 b.Szombathely 1-4-76
Honours: Hungary Youth, Under-21, 70 full caps.

1993–94	Haladas	15	0		
1994–95	Haladas	0	0		
1995–96	Haladas	19	0		
1996–97	Haladas	33	0	**67**	**0**
1997–98	Hertha Berlin	27	0		
1998–99	Hertha Berlin	34	0		
1999–2000	Hertha Berlin	27	0		
2000–01	Hertha Berlin	34	0		
2001–02	Hertha Berlin	25	0		
2002–03	Hertha Berlin	33	0		
2003–04	Hertha Berlin	18	0	**198**	**0**
2004–05	Crystal Palace	32	0		
2005–06	Crystal Palace	43	0		
2006–07	Crystal Palace	29	0	**104**	**0**
2006–07	*Aston Villa*	5	0	**5**	**0**

KUQI, Shefki (F) **369 102**
H: 6 2 W: 13 13 b.Albania 10-11-76
Source: Trepka, Miki. *Honours:* Albania 8 full caps, 1 goal, Finland 48 full caps, 5 goals.

1995	MP	24	3		
1996	MP	26	7	**50**	**10**
1997	HJK Helsinki	25	6		
1998	HJK Helsinki	22	1		
1999	HJK Helsinki	25	11	**72**	**18**
From Jokerit					
2000–01	Stockport Co	17	6		
2001–02	Stockport Co	18	5	**35**	**11**
2001–02	Sheffield W	17	6		
2002–03	Sheffield W	40	8		
2003–04	Sheffield W	7	5	**64**	**19**
2003–04	Ipswich T	36	11		
2004–05	Ipswich T	43	19	**79**	**30**
2005–06	Blackburn R	33	7		
2006–07	Blackburn R	1	0	**34**	**7**
2006–07	Crystal Palace	35	7	**35**	**7**

LAWRENCE, Matt (D) **396 5**
H: 6 1 W: 12 12 b.Northampton 19-6-74
Source: Grays Ath. *Honours:* England Schools.

1995–96	Wycombe W	3	0		
1996–97	Wycombe W	13	1		
1996–97	Fulham	15	0		
1997–98	Fulham	43	0		
1998–99	Fulham	1	0	**59**	**0**
1998–99	Wycombe W	34	2		
1999–2000	Wycombe W	29	2	**79**	**5**
1999–2000	Millwall	9	0		
2000–01	Millwall	45	0		
2001–02	Millwall	26	0		
2002–03	Millwall	33	0		
2003–04	Millwall	36	0		
2004–05	Millwall	44	0		
2005–06	Millwall	31	0	**224**	**0**
2006–07	Crystal Palace	34	0	**34**	**0**

MARTIN, David (M) **5 0**
H: 5 9 W: 10 10 b.Erith 3-6-85
Source: Dartford.

2006–07	Crystal Palace	5	0	**5**	**0**

McANUFF, Jobi (M) **227 29**
H: 5 11 W: 11 05 b.Edmonton 9-11-81
Source: From Scholar. *Honours:* Jamaica 1 full cap.

2000–01	Wimbledon	0	0		
2001–02	Wimbledon	38	4		
2002–03	Wimbledon	31	4		
2003–04	Wimbledon	27	5	**96**	**13**
2003–04	West Ham U	12	1		
2004–05	West Ham U	1	0	**13**	**1**
2004–05	Cardiff C	43	2	**43**	**2**
2005–06	Crystal Palace	41	8		
2006–07	Crystal Palace	34	5	**75**	**13**

MORRISON, Clinton (F) **325 101**
H: 6 0 W: 12 00 b.Tooting 14-5-79
Source: Trainee. *Honours:* Eire Under-21, 36 full caps, 9 goals.

1996–97	Crystal Palace	0	0		
1997–98	Crystal Palace	1	1		
1998–99	Crystal Palace	37	12		
1999–2000	Crystal Palace	29	13		
2000–01	Crystal Palace	45	14		
2001–02	Crystal Palace	45	22		
2002–03	Birmingham C	28	6		
2003–04	Birmingham C	32	4		
2004–05	Birmingham C	26	4		
2005–06	Birmingham C	1	0	**87**	**14**
2005–06	Crystal Palace	40	13		
2006–07	Crystal Palace	41	12	**238**	**87**

REICH, Marco (M) **220 17**
H: 6 0 W: 12 00 b.Meisenheim 30-12-77
Honours: Germany Under-21, 1 full cap.

1996–97	Kaiserslautern	0	0		
1997–98	Kaiserslautern	31	1		
1998–99	Kaiserslautern	27	3		
1999–2000	Kaiserslautern	28	2		
2000–01	Kaiserslautern	18	2	**104**	**8**
2001–02	Cologne	24	0	**24**	**0**
2002–03	Werder Bremen	15	0	**15**	**0**
2003–04	Derby Co	13	1		
2004–05	Derby Co	37	6	**50**	**7**
2005–06	Crystal Palace	21	2		
2006–07	Crystal Palace	6	0	**27**	**2**

To Kickers Offenbach January 2007

SCOWCROFT, James (F) **420 79**
H: 6 1 W: 14 07 b.Bury St Edmunds 15-11-75
Source: Trainee. *Honours:* England Under-21.

1994–95	Ipswich T	0	0		
1995–96	Ipswich T	23	2		
1996–97	Ipswich T	41	9		
1997–98	Ipswich T	31	6		
1998–99	Ipswich T	32	13		
1999–2000	Ipswich T	41	13		
2000–01	Ipswich T	34	4		
2001–02	Leicester C	24	5		
2002–03	Leicester C	43	10		
2003–04	Leicester C	35	5		
2004–05	Leicester C	31	4	**133**	**24**
2004–05	*Ipswich T*	9	0	**211**	**47**
2005–06	Coventry C	41	3	**41**	**3**
2006–07	Crystal Palace	35	5	**35**	**5**

SHERINGHAM, Charlie (F) **0 0**
H: 6 1 W: 11 06 b.London 17-4-88

2006–07	Crystal Palace	0	0		

SOARES, Tom (M) **106 4**
H: 6 0 W: 11 04 b.Reading 10-7-86
Source: Scholar. *Honours:* England Youth, Under-20, Under-21.

2003–04	Crystal Palace	3	0		
2004–05	Crystal Palace	22	0		
2005–06	Crystal Palace	44	1		
2006–07	Crystal Palace	37	3	**106**	**4**

SPENCE, Lewis (M) **2 0**
H: 5 9 W: 11 02 b.Lambeth 29-10-87
Source: Scholar.

2006–07	Crystal Palace	2	0	**2**	**0**

SPERONI, Julian (G) **109 0**
H: 6 0 W: 11 00 b.Buenos Aires 18-5-79

1999–2000	Platense	2	0		
2000–01	Platense	0	0	**2**	**0**
2001–02	Dundee	17	0		
2002–03	Dundee	38	0		
2003–04	Dundee	37	0	**92**	**0**
2004–05	Crystal Palace	6	0		
2005–06	Crystal Palace	4	0		
2006–07	Crystal Palace	5	0	**15**	**0**

STARKEY, Phil (D) **0 0**
H: 6 2 W: 12 02 b.Gravesend 10-9-87
Source: Scholar.

2006–07	Crystal Palace	0	0		

WARD, Darren (D) **278 11**
H: 6 3 W: 11 04 b.Kenton 13-9-78
Source: Trainee.

1995–96	Watford	1	0		
1996–97	Watford	7	0		
1997–98	Watford	0	0		
1998–99	Watford	1	0		
1999–2000	Watford	9	1		
1999–2000	*QPR*	14	0	**14**	**0**
2000–01	Watford	40	1		
2001–02	Watford	1	0	**59**	**2**
2001–02	Millwall	14	0		
2002–03	Millwall	39	1		
2003–04	Millwall	46	3		
2004–05	Millwall	43	0	**142**	**4**
2005–06	Crystal Palace	43	5		
2006–07	Crystal Palace	20	0	**63**	**5**

WATSON, Ben (M) **109 8**
H: 5 10 W: 10 11 b.Camberwell 9-7-85
Source: Scholar. *Honours:* England Under-21.

2002–03	Crystal Palace	5	0		
2003–04	Crystal Palace	16	1		
2004–05	Crystal Palace	21	0		
2005–06	Crystal Palace	42	4		
2006–07	Crystal Palace	25	3	**109**	**8**

WIGGINS, Rhoys (D) **0 0**
H: 5 8 W: 11 05 b.Hillingdon 4-11-87
Source: Scholar. *Honours:* Wales Under-21.

2006–07	Crystal Palace	0	0		

WILKINSON, David (G) **0 0**
H: 5 11 W: 12 00 b.Croydon 17-4-88
Source: Scholar.

2006–07	Crystal Palace	0	0		

DARLINGTON (30)

ARMSTRONG, Alun (F) **355 83**
H: 6 0 W: 12 00 b.Gateshead 22-2-75
Source: School.

1993–94	Newcastle U	0	0		
1994–95	Stockport Co	45	14		
1995–96	Stockport Co	46	13		
1996–97	Stockport Co	39	9		
1997–98	Stockport Co	29	12	**159**	**48**
1997–98	Middlesbrough	11	7		
1998–99	Middlesbrough	6	1		
1999–2000	Middlesbrough	12	1		

1999–2000	*Huddersfield T*	6	0	**6**	**0**
2000–01	Middlesbrough	0	0	**29**	**9**
2000–01	Ipswich T	21	7		
2001–02	Ipswich T	32	4		
2002–03	Ipswich T	19	1		
2003–04	Ipswich T	7	2		
2003–04	*Bradford C*	6	1	**6**	**1**
2004–05	Ipswich T	0	0	**79**	**14**
2004–05	Darlington	32	9		
2005–06	Darlington	0	0		
2005–06	Rushden & D	9	0	**9**	**0**
2005–06	Doncaster R	6	0	**6**	**0**
2006–07	Darlington	29	2	**61**	**11**

BLUNDELL, Greg (F) **157 43**
H: 5 10 W: 11 06 b.Liverpool 3-10-77
Source: Tranmere R Trainee, Vauxhall M, Northwich Vic.

2003–04	Doncaster R	44	18		
2004–05	Doncaster R	41	9	**85**	**27**
2005–06	Chester C	30	7		
2006–07	Chester C	27	6	**57**	**13**
2006–07	Darlington	15	3	**15**	**3**

BURGESS, Kevin (D) **1 0**
H: 6 0 W: 12 00 b.Eston 8-1-88
Source: Scholar.

2006–07	Middlesbrough	0	0		
2006–07	Darlington	1	0	**1**	**0**

CLARKE, Wayne (M) **0 0**
b.Crook 30-9-88

2006–07	Darlington	0	0		

CLOSE, Brian (M) **91 1**
H: 5 10 W: 12 03 b.Belfast 27-1-82
Honours: Northern Ireland Under-21.

1999–2000	Middlesbrough	0	0		
2000–01	Middlesbrough	0	0		
2001–02	Middlesbrough	0	0		
2002–03	Middlesbrough	0	0		
2002–03	*Chesterfield*	8	1	**8**	**1**
2003–04	Middlesbrough	0	0		
2003–04	Darlington	12	0		
2004–05	Darlington	38	0		
2005–06	Darlington	6	0		
2006–07	Darlington	27	0	**83**	**0**

COLLINS, Patrick (D) **75 1**
H: 6 2 W: 12 08 b.Oman 4-2-85
Source: Scholar. *Honours:* England Youth, Under-20.

2001–02	Sunderland	0	0		
2002–03	Sunderland	0	0		
2003–04	Sunderland	0	0		
2004–05	Sheffield W	28	1		
2005–06	Sheffield W	3	0	**31**	**1**
2005–06	*Swindon T*	13	0	**13**	**0**
2006–07	Darlington	31	0	**31**	**0**

CUMMINS, Michael (M) **294 35**
H: 6 0 W: 13 06 b.Dublin 1-6-78
Source: Trainee. *Honours:* Eire Youth, Under-21.

1995–96	Middlesbrough	0	0		
1996–97	Middlesbrough	0	0		
1997–98	Middlesbrough	0	0		
1998–99	Middlesbrough	1	0		
1999–2000	Middlesbrough	1	0	**2**	**0**
1999–2000	Port Vale	12	1		
2000–01	Port Vale	45	2		
2001–02	Port Vale	46	8		
2002–03	Port Vale	30	4		
2003–04	Port Vale	42	4		
2004–05	Port Vale	39	2		
2005–06	Port Vale	39	10	**253**	**31**
2006–07	Darlington	39	4	**39**	**4**

DUKE, David (D) **237 8**
H: 5 10 W: 11 00 b.Inverness 7-11-78
Source: Redby CA.

1997–98	Sunderland	0	0		
1998–99	Sunderland	0	0		
1999–2000	Sunderland	0	0		
2000–01	Swindon T	32	1		
2001–02	Swindon T	42	2		
2002–03	Swindon T	44	2		
2003–04	Swindon T	42	1		
2004–05	Swindon T	44	1	**204**	**7**
2005–06	Darlington	20	1		
2006–07	Darlington	13	0	**33**	**1**

GIALLANZA, Gaetano (F) **265 85**
H: 5 11 W: 11 05 b.Basle 6-6-74

1991–92	Old Boys Basle	7	3	**7**	**3**
1992–93	Basle	1	0		
1993–94	Servette	10	1	**10**	**1**
1994–95	Young Boys	33	16		
1995–96	Sion	23	3	**23**	**3**
1996–97	Basle	32	19		
1997–98	Basle	11	4	**44**	**23**
1997–98	Nantes	12	2	**12**	**2**
1997–98	Bolton W	3	0	**3**	**0**
1998–99	Lugano	29	8	**29**	**8**
1999–2000	Norwich C	3	0		
2000–01	Norwich C	11	2		
2001–02	Norwich C	0	0		
2002–03	Norwich C	0	0	**14**	**2**
2003–04	Young Boys	19	5	**52**	**21**
2004–05	Aarau	27	9		
2005–06	Aarau	30	10	**57**	**19**
2006–07	Darlington	14	3	**14**	**3**

HARDMAN, Lewis (D) **1 0**
H: 5 10 W: 11 00 b.Sunderland 12-4-85
Source: Scholar.

2006–07	Darlington	1	0	**1**	**0**

HOLLOWAY, Darren (D) **242 3**
H: 6 0 W: 12 05 b.Crook 3-10-77
Source: From Trainee. *Honours:* England Under-21.

1995–96	Sunderland	0	0		
1996–97	Sunderland	0	0		
1997–98	Sunderland	32	0		
1997–98	*Carlisle U*	5	0	**5**	**0**
1998–99	Sunderland	6	0		
1999–2000	Sunderland	15	0		
1999–2000	*Bolton W*	4	0	**4**	**0**
2000–01	Sunderland	5	0	**58**	**0**
2000–01	Wimbledon	31	0		
2001–02	Wimbledon	32	0		
2002–03	Wimbledon	16	0		
2003–04	Wimbledon	13	0	**92**	**0**
2003–04	*Scunthorpe U*	5	1	**5**	**1**
2004–05	Bradford C	33	1		
2005–06	Bradford C	24	0	**57**	**1**
2006–07	Darlington	21	1	**21**	**1**

HUTCHINSON, Joey (D) **83 0**
H: 5 11 W: 11 11 b.Middlesbrough 2-4-82
Source: Scholar.

2000–01	Birmingham C	0	0		
2001–02	Birmingham C	3	0		
2002–03	Birmingham C	1	0	**4**	**0**
2003–04	Darlington	39	0		
2004–05	Darlington	8	0		
2005–06	Darlington	19	0		
2006–07	Darlington	13	0	**79**	**0**

JAMES, Craig (D) **107 2**
H: 6 0 W: 13 00 b.Middlesbrough 15-11-82
Source: Scholar.

2000–01	Sunderland	0	0		
2001–02	Sunderland	0	0		
2002–03	Sunderland	0	0		
2003–04	Sunderland	1	0	**1**	**0**
2003–04	*Darlington*	10	1		
2003–04	Port Vale	8	0		
2004–05	Port Vale	30	1		
2005–06	Port Vale	35	0	**73**	**1**
2006–07	Darlington	23	0	**33**	**1**

JOACHIM, Julian (F) **413 107**
H: 5 6 W: 12 02 b.Boston 20-9-74
Source: Trainee. *Honours:* England Youth, Under-21.

1992–93	Leicester C	26	10		
1993–94	Leicester C	36	11		
1994–95	Leicester C	15	3		
1995–96	Leicester C	22	1	**99**	**25**
1995–96	Aston Villa	11	1		
1996–97	Aston Villa	15	3		
1997–98	Aston Villa	26	8		
1998–99	Aston Villa	36	14		
1999–2000	Aston Villa	33	6		
2000–01	Aston Villa	20	7	**141**	**39**
2001–02	Coventry C	16	1		
2002–03	Coventry C	11	2		
2003–04	Coventry C	29	8	**56**	**11**
2004–05	Leeds U	27	2	**27**	**2**
2004–05	*Walsall*	8	6	**8**	**6**
2005–06	Boston U	43	14		
2006–07	Boston U	3	3	**46**	**17**
2006–07	Darlington	36	7	**36**	**7**

JOHNSON, Simon (F) **120 17**
H: 5 9 W: 11 09 b.West Bromwich 9-3-83
Source: Scholar. *Honours:* England Youth, Under-20.

2000–01	Leeds U	0	0		
2001–02	Leeds U	0	0		
2002–03	Leeds U	4	0		
2002–03	*Hull C*	12	2	**12**	**2**
2003–04	Leeds U	5	0		
2003–04	*Blackpool*	4	1	**4**	**1**
2004–05	Leeds U	2	0	**11**	**0**
2004–05	*Sunderland*	5	0	**5**	**0**
2004–05	*Doncaster R*	11	3	**11**	**3**
2004–05	*Barnsley*	11	2	**11**	**2**
2005–06	Darlington	42	7		
2006–07	Darlington	24	2	**66**	**9**

JONES, Lee (G) **249 0**
H: 6 3 W: 14 04 b.Pontypridd 9-8-70
Source: Porth.

1993–94	Swansea C	0	0		
1994–95	Swansea C	2	0		
1995–96	Swansea C	1	0		
1995–96	*Crewe Alex*	0	0		
1996–97	Swansea C	1	0		
1997–98	Swansea C	2	0	**6**	**0**
1997–98	Bristol R	8	0		
1998–99	Bristol R	32	0		
1999–2000	Bristol R	36	0	**76**	**0**
2000–01	Stockport Co	27	0		
2001–02	Stockport Co	24	0		
2002–03	Stockport Co	24	0		
2003–04	Stockport Co	0	0	**75**	**0**
2003–04	Blackpool	21	0		
2004–05	Blackpool	29	0		
2005–06	Blackpool	31	0		
2006–07	Blackpool	0	0	**81**	**0**
2006–07	*Bury*	2	0	**2**	**0**
2006–07	Darlington	9	0	**9**	**0**

KELTIE, Clark (M) **134 5**
H: 5 11 W: 11 08 b.Newcastle 31-8-83
Source: Shildon.

2001–02	Darlington	1	0		
2002–03	Darlington	30	3		
2003–04	Darlington	31	1		
2004–05	Darlington	21	0		
2005–06	Darlington	24	0		
2006–07	Darlington	27	1	**134**	**5**

LOGAN, Carlos (M) **55 5**
H: 5 10 W: 12 06 b.Wythenshawe 7-11-85
Source: Scholar.

2004–05	Manchester C	0	0		
2004–05	*Chesterfield*	9	1	**9**	**1**
2005–06	Darlington	33	4		
2006–07	Darlington	9	0	**42**	**4**
2006–07	*Bradford C*	4	0	**4**	**0**

MARTIS, Shelton (D) **64 2**
H: 6 0 W: 11 11 b.Willemstad 29-11-82

2002–03	Excelsior	12	0		
2003–04	Excelsior	10	0	**22**	**0**
2005–06	Darlington	40	2		
2006–07	Darlington	2	0	**42**	**2**

McLEOD, Mark (M) **6 0**
H: 6 0 W: 12 00 b.Sunderland 15-12-86
Source: Scholar.

2005–06	Darlington	4	0		
2006–07	Darlington	2	0	**6**	**0**

NGOMA, Kalusivikako (M) **18 1**
H: 6 4 W: 13 05 b.Kinshasa 3-8-77
Source: Viry-Chatillon, Red Star 93, Aurillac, Libourne/Saint-Seurin.

2006–07	Darlington	18	1	**18**	**1**

RAVENHILL, Ricky (M) **133 12**
H: 5 10 W: 11 02 b.Doncaster 16-1-81
Source: Barnsley Trainee.

2003–04	Doncaster R	36	3		
2004–05	Doncaster R	35	3		
2005–06	Doncaster R	27	3	**98**	**9**
2006–07	Chester C	3	0	**3**	**0**

2006–07	Grimsby T	17	2	**17**	**2**
2006–07	Darlington	15	1	**15**	**1**

REAY, Sean (F) **3** **0**
H: 6 1 W: 12 00 b.Jarrow 20-5-89
Source: Scholar.

2005–06	Darlington	0	0		
2006–07	Darlington	3	0	**3**	**0**

ROWSON, David (M) **239** **13**
H: 5 10 W: 11 10 b.Aberdeen 14-9-76
Source: FC Stoneywood. *Honours:* Scotland Under-21.

1994–95	Aberdeen	0	0		
1995–96	Aberdeen	9	0		
1996–97	Aberdeen	34	2		
1997–98	Aberdeen	30	5		
1998–99	Aberdeen	22	0		
1999–2000	Aberdeen	0	0		
2000–01	Aberdeen	0	0	**95**	**7**
2001–02	Stoke C	13	0		
2002–03	Stoke C	0	0	**13**	**0**
2003–04	Partick T	35	2	**35**	**2**
2004–05	Northampton T	37	2		
2005–06	Northampton T	29	0	**66**	**2**
2006–07	Darlington	24	2	**24**	**2**
2006–07	*Boston U*	6	0	**6**	**0**

RUSSELL, Sam (G) **118** **0**
H: 6 0 W: 10 13 b.Middlesbrough 4-10-82
Source: Scholar.

2000–01	Middlesbrough	0	0		
2001–02	Middlesbrough	0	0		
2002–03	Middlesbrough	0	0		
2002–03	*Darlington*	1	0		
2003–04	Middlesbrough	0	0		
2003–04	*Scunthorpe U*	10	0	**10**	**0**
2004–05	Darlington	46	0		
2005–06	Darlington	30	0		
2006–07	Darlington	31	0	**108**	**0**

RYAN, Tim (D) **153** **11**
H: 5 10 W: 11 00 b.Stockport 10-12-74
Source: Trainee.

1992–93	Scunthorpe U	1	0		
1993–94	Scunthorpe U	1	0		
1994–95	Scunthorpe U	0	0	**2**	**0**
From Buxton.					
1996–97	Doncaster R	28	0		
From Southport					
2003–04	Doncaster R	42	2		
2004–05	Doncaster R	39	4		
2005–06	Doncaster R	7	0	**116**	**6**
2005–06	Peterborough U	7	0	**7**	**0**
2006–07	Boston U	23	4	**23**	**4**
2006–07	Darlington	5	1	**5**	**1**

SMITH, Martin (F) **363** **93**
H: 5 11 W: 12 07 b.Sunderland 13-11-74
Source: Trainee. *Honours:* England Schools, Under-21.

1992–93	Sunderland	0	0		
1993–94	Sunderland	29	8		
1994–95	Sunderland	35	10		
1995–96	Sunderland	20	2		
1996–97	Sunderland	11	0		
1997–98	Sunderland	16	2		
1998–99	Sunderland	8	3	**119**	**25**
1999–2000	Sheffield U	26	10	**26**	**10**
1999–2000	Huddersfield T	12	4		
2000–01	Huddersfield T	30	8		
2001–02	Huddersfield T	0	0		
2002–03	Huddersfield T	38	17	**80**	**29**
2003–04	Northampton T	44	11		
2004–05	Northampton T	34	10		
2005–06	Northampton T	26	3	**104**	**24**
2006–07	Darlington	34	5	**34**	**5**

STAMP, Phil (M) **125** **7**
H: 5 11 W: 13 05 b.Middlesbrough 12-12-75
Source: Trainee. *Honours:* England Youth.

1992–93	Middlesbrough	0	0		
1993–94	Middlesbrough	10	0		
1994–95	Middlesbrough	3	0		
1995–96	Middlesbrough	12	2		
1996–97	Middlesbrough	24	1		
1997–98	Middlesbrough	10	0		
1998–99	Middlesbrough	16	2		
1999–2000	Middlesbrough	16	0		
2000–01	Middlesbrough	19	1		
2001–02	Middlesbrough	6	0		
2001–02	*Millwall*	1	0	**1**	**0**
2002–03	Middlesbrough	0	0		
2003–04	Middlesbrough	0	0		
2004–05	Middlesbrough	0	0	**116**	**6**
2005–06	Darlington	8	1		
2006–07	Darlington	0	0	**8**	**1**

STOCKDALE, David (G) **7** **0**
H: 6 3 W: 13 04 b.Leeds 20-9-85
Source: Scholar.

2002–03	York C	1	0		
2003–04	York C	0	0		
2004–05	York C	0	0		
2005–06	York C	0	0	**1**	**0**
2006–07	Darlington	6	0	**6**	**0**

VAISANEN, Ville (D) **138** **15**
H: 6 3 W: 13 10 b.Finland 19-4-77
Honours: Finland Under-21, 5 full caps, 1 goal.

1997	Jazz	10	2	**10**	**2**
1997–98	De Graafschap	10	0		
1998–99	De Graafschap	4	1		
1999	Tampere	10	1	**10**	**1**
1999	Lahti	1	0	**1**	**0**
1999–2000	De Graafschap	16	1	**30**	**2**
2000–01	Ethnikos	2	0	**2**	**0**
2001	Haka	25	4		
2002	Haka	20	4	**45**	**8**
2005	Jaro	21	0		
2006	Jaro	14	2	**35**	**2**
2006–07	Darlington	5	0	**5**	**0**

WAINWRIGHT, Neil (M) **264** **31**
H: 6 0 W: 12 00 b.Warrington 4-11-77
Source: Trainee.

1996–97	Wrexham	0	0		
1997–98	Wrexham	11	3	**11**	**3**
1998–99	Sunderland	2	0		
1999–2000	Sunderland	0	0		
1999–2000	*Darlington*	17	4		
2000–01	Sunderland	0	0		
2000–01	*Halifax T*	13	0	**13**	**0**
2001–02	Sunderland	0	0	**2**	**0**
2001–02	Darlington	35	4		
2002–03	Darlington	33	1		
2003–04	Darlington	35	7		
2004–05	Darlington	38	4		
2005–06	Darlington	39	3		
2006–07	Darlington	41	5	**238**	**28**

WRIGHT, Josh (F) **1** **0**
H: 5 6 W: 11 02 b.Hartlepool 18-9-88
Source: Scholar.

2006–07	Darlington	1	0	**1**	**0**

WRIGHT, Tommy (F) **112** **19**
H: 6 0 W: 12 02 b.Leicester 28-9-84
Source: From Scholar. *Honours:* England Youth, Under-20.

2001–02	Leicester C	1	0		
2002–03	Leicester C	13	2		
2003–04	Leicester C	0	0		
2003–04	*Brentford*	25	3	**25**	**3**
2004–05	Leicester C	7	0		
2005–06	Leicester C	0	0	**21**	**2**
2005–06	*Blackpool*	13	6	**13**	**6**
2005–06	Barnsley	17	1		
2006–07	Barnsley	17	1	**34**	**2**
2006–07	*Walsall*	6	2	**6**	**2**
2006–07	Darlington	13	4	**13**	**4**

DERBY CO (31)

ADDISON, Miles (D) **2** **0**
H: 6 2 W: 13 03 b.London 7-1-89
Source: Scholar.

2005–06	Derby Co	2	0		
2006–07	Derby Co	0	0	**2**	**0**

AINSWORTH, Lionel (F) **16** **0**
H: 5 9 W: 9 10 b.Nottingham 1-10-87
Source: Scholar. *Honours:* England Youth.

2005–06	Derby Co	2	0		
2006–07	Derby Co	0	0	**2**	**0**
2006–07	*Bournemouth*	7	0	**7**	**0**
2006–07	*Wycombe W*	7	0	**7**	**0**

BARNES, Giles (M) **58** **9**
H: 6 0 W: 12 10 b.Barking 5-8-88
Source: Scholar. *Honours:* England Youth.

2005–06	Derby Co	19	1		
2006–07	Derby Co	39	8	**58**	**9**

BISGAARD, Morten (M) **332** **56**
H: 6 1 W: 12 04 b.Randers 25-6-74
Honours: Denmark Youth, Under-21, 8 full caps, 1 goal.

1993–94	Odense	7	1		
1994–95	Odense	27	4		
1995–96	Odense	25	6		
1996–97	Odense	33	16		
1997–98	Odense	29	8	**121**	**35**
1998–99	Udinese	3	0		
1999–2000	Udinese	20	1		
2000–01	Udinese	13	0	**36**	**1**
2001–02	FC Copenhagen	27	6		
2002–03	FC Copenhagen	27	1		
2003–04	FC Copenhagen	20	3	**74**	**10**
2004–05	Derby Co	36	4		
2005–06	Derby Co	33	4		
2006–07	Derby Co	32	2	**101**	**10**

BOERTIEN, Paul (D) **142** **3**
H: 5 10 W: 11 02 b.Haltwhistle 21-1-79
Source: Trainee.

1996–97	Carlisle U	0	0		
1997–98	Carlisle U	9	0		
1998–99	Carlisle U	8	1	**17**	**1**
1998–99	Derby Co	1	0		
1999–2000	Derby Co	2	0		
1999–2000	*Crewe Alex*	2	0	**2**	**0**
2000–01	Derby Co	8	1		
2001–02	Derby Co	32	0		
2002–03	Derby Co	42	1		
2003–04	Derby Co	18	0		
2003–04	*Notts Co*	5	0	**5**	**0**
2004–05	Derby Co	0	0		
2005–06	Derby Co	0	0		
2006–07	Derby Co	11	0	**114**	**2**
2006–07	*Chesterfield*	4	0	**4**	**0**

BOSSEKOTA, Jeremy (M) **0** **0**
b.Amiens 28-2-88
Source: Amiens.

2006–07	Derby Co	0	0		

BYWATER, Steve (G) **116** **0**
H: 6 2 W: 12 10 b.Manchester 7-6-81
Source: From Trainee. *Honours:* England Youth, Under-20, Under-21.

1997–98	Rochdale	0	0		
1998–99	West Ham U	0	0		
1999–2000	West Ham U	4	0		
1999–2000	*Wycombe W*	2	0	**2**	**0**
1999–2000	*Hull C*	4	0	**4**	**0**
2000–01	West Ham U	1	0		
2001–02	West Ham U	0	0		
2001–02	*Wolverhampton W*	0	0		
2001–02	*Cardiff C*	0	0		
2002–03	West Ham U	0	0		
2003–04	West Ham U	17	0		
2004–05	West Ham U	36	0		
2005–06	West Ham U	1	0		
2005–06	*Coventry C*	14	0	**14**	**0**
2006–07	West Ham U	0	0	**59**	**0**
2006–07	Derby Co	37	0	**37**	**0**

CAMARA, Mo (D) **290** **2**
H: 5 11 W: 11 03 b.Conakry 25-6-75
Honours: Guinea full caps.

1993–94	Beauvais	19	0		
1994–95	Beauvais	0	0		
1995–96	Troyes	13	0	**13**	**0**
1996–97	Beauvais	35	0	**54**	**0**
1997–98	Le Havre	14	0		
1998–99	Lille	34	2	**34**	**2**
1999–2000	Le Havre	2	0	**16**	**0**
2000–01	Wolverhampton W	18	0		
2001–02	Wolverhampton W	27	0		
2002–03	Wolverhampton W	0	0	**45**	**0**
2003–04	Burnley	45	0		
2004–05	Burnley	45	0	**90**	**0**
2005–06	Celtic	18	0		
2006–07	Celtic	1	0	**19**	**0**
2006–07	Derby Co	19	0	**19**	**0**

CAMP, Lee (G) **115 0**
H: 5 11 W: 11 11 b.Derby 22-8-84
Source: Scholar. *Honours:* England Youth, Under-20, Under-21.

2002–03	Derby Co	1	0		
2003–04	Derby Co	0	0		
2003–04	*QPR*	12	0		
2004–05	Derby Co	45	0		
2005–06	Derby Co	40	0		
2006–07	Derby Co	3	0	**89**	**0**
2006–07	*Norwich C*	3	0	**3**	**0**
2006–07	*QPR*	11	0	**23**	**0**

CANN, Steven (G) **0 0**
H: 6 3 W: 13 01 b.South Africa 20-1-88
Source: Scholar. *Honours:* Wales Youth.

2006–07	Derby Co	0	0

CUMBERWORTH, Tom (M) **0 0**
H: 5 8 W: 12 02 b.Dagenham 12-1-88
Source: Scholar.

2006–07	Derby Co	0	0

EDWORTHY, Marc (D) **432 2**
H: 5 10 W: 11 11 b.Barnstaple 24-12-72
Source: Trainee.

1990–91	Plymouth Arg	0	0		
1991–92	Plymouth Arg	15	0		
1992–93	Plymouth Arg	15	0		
1993–94	Plymouth Arg	12	0		
1994–95	Plymouth Arg	27	1	**69**	**1**
1995–96	Crystal Palace	44	0		
1996–97	Crystal Palace	45	0		
1997–98	Crystal Palace	34	0		
1998–99	Crystal Palace	3	0	**126**	**0**
1998–99	Coventry C	22	0		
1999–2000	Coventry C	10	0		
2000–01	Coventry C	24	1		
2001–02	Coventry C	20	0	**76**	**1**
2002–03	Wolverhampton W	22	0	**22**	**0**
2003–04	Norwich C	43	0		
2004–05	Norwich C	28	0	**71**	**0**
2005–06	Derby Co	30	0		
2006–07	Derby Co	38	0	**68**	**0**

FAGAN, Craig (F) **167 34**
H: 5 11 W: 11 11 b.Birmingham 11-12-82
Source: Scholar.

2001–02	Birmingham C	0	0		
2002–03	Birmingham C	1	0		
2002–03	*Bristol C*	6	1	**6**	**1**
2003–04	Birmingham C	0	0	**1**	**0**
2003–04	Colchester U	37	9		
2004–05	Colchester U	26	8	**63**	**17**
2004–05	Hull C	12	4		
2005–06	Hull C	41	5		
2006–07	Hull C	27	6	**80**	**15**
2006–07	Derby Co	17	1	**17**	**1**

GRANT, Lee (G) **91 0**
H: 6 3 W: 13 01 b.Hemel Hempstead 27-1-83
Source: Scholar. *Honours:* England Youth, Under-21.

2000–01	Derby Co	0	0		
2001–02	Derby Co	0	0		
2002–03	Derby Co	29	0		
2003–04	Derby Co	36	0		
2004–05	Derby Co	2	0		
2005–06	Derby Co	0	0		
2005–06	*Burnley*	1	0	**1**	**0**
2005–06	*Oldham Ath*	16	0	**16**	**0**
2006–07	Derby Co	7	0	**74**	**0**

HOLMES, Lee (M) **77 3**
H: 5 8 W: 10 06 b.Mansfield 2-4-87
Source: Scholar. *Honours:* FA Schools, England Youth.

2002–03	Derby Co	2	0		
2003–04	Derby Co	23	2		
2004–05	Derby Co	3	0		
2004–05	*Swindon T*	15	1	**15**	**1**
2005–06	Derby Co	18	0		
2006–07	Derby Co	0	0	**46**	**2**
2006–07	*Bradford C*	16	0	**16**	**0**

HOWARD, Steve (F) **483 156**
H: 6 3 W: 15 00 b.Durham 10-5-76
Source: Tow Law T.

1995–96	Hartlepool U	39	7		
1996–97	Hartlepool U	32	8		
1997–98	Hartlepool U	43	7		
1998–99	Hartlepool U	28	5	**142**	**27**
1998–99	Northampton T	12	0		
1999–2000	Northampton T	41	10		
2000–01	Northampton T	33	8	**86**	**18**
2000–01	Luton T	12	3		
2001–02	Luton T	42	24		
2002–03	Luton T	41	22		
2003–04	Luton T	34	14		
2004–05	Luton T	40	18		
2005–06	Luton T	43	14	**212**	**95**
2006–07	Derby Co	43	16	**43**	**16**

JACKSON, Richard (D) **140 0**
H: 5 8 W: 12 10 b.Whitby 18-4-80
Source: Trainee.

1997–98	Scarborough	2	0		
1998–99	Scarborough	20	0	**22**	**0**
1998–99	Derby Co	0	0		
1999–2000	Derby Co	2	0		
2000–01	Derby Co	2	0		
2001–02	Derby Co	7	0		
2002–03	Derby Co	21	0		
2003–04	Derby Co	36	0		
2004–05	Derby Co	19	0		
2005–06	Derby Co	26	0		
2006–07	Derby Co	5	0	**118**	**0**

JOHNSON, Michael (D) **504 17**
H: 5 11 W: 11 12 b.Nottingham 4-7-73
Source: Trainee. *Honours:* Jamaica 12 full caps.

1991–92	Notts Co	5	0		
1992–93	Notts Co	37	0		
1993–94	Notts Co	34	0		
1994–95	Notts Co	31	0		
1995–96	Notts Co	0	0	**107**	**0**
1995–96	Birmingham C	33	0		
1996–97	Birmingham C	35	0		
1997–98	Birmingham C	38	3		
1998–99	Birmingham C	45	5		
1999–2000	Birmingham C	34	2		
2000–01	Birmingham C	39	2		
2001–02	Birmingham C	32	1		
2002–03	Birmingham C	6	0		
2003–04	Birmingham C	0	0	**262**	**13**
2003–04	Derby Co	39	1		
2004–05	Derby Co	36	1		
2005–06	Derby Co	31	1		
2006–07	Derby Co	29	1	**135**	**4**

JOHNSON, Seth (M) **277 16**
H: 5 10 W: 12 13 b.Birmingham 12-3-79
Source: Trainee. *Honours:* England, Youth, Under-21, 1 full cap.

1996–97	Crewe Alex	11	1		
1997–98	Crewe Alex	40	1		
1998–99	Crewe Alex	42	4	**93**	**6**
1999–2000	Derby Co	36	1		
2000–01	Derby Co	30	1		
2001–02	Derby Co	7	0		
2001–02	Leeds U	14	0		
2002–03	Leeds U	9	1		
2003–04	Leeds U	25	2		
2004–05	Leeds U	6	1	**54**	**4**
2005–06	Derby Co	30	3		
2006–07	Derby Co	27	1	**130**	**6**

JONES, David (M) **69 15**
H: 5 11 W: 10 10 b.Southport 4-11-84
Source: Trainee. *Honours:* England Youth, Under-21.

2003–04	Manchester U	0	0		
2004–05	Manchester U	0	0		
2005–06	Manchester U	0	0		
2005–06	*Preston NE*	24	3	**24**	**3**
2005–06	NEC Nijmegen	17	6	**17**	**6**
2006–07	Manchester U	0	0		
2006–07	Derby Co	28	6	**28**	**6**

LEACOCK, Dean (D) **60 0**
H: 6 2 W: 12 04 b.Croydon 10-6-84
Source: Trainee. *Honours:* England Youth, Under-20.

2002–03	Fulham	0	0		
2003–04	Fulham	4	0		
2004–05	Fulham	0	0		
2004–05	*Coventry C*	13	0	**13**	**0**
2005–06	Fulham	5	0		
2006–07	Fulham	0	0	**9**	**0**
2006–07	Derby Co	38	0	**38**	**0**

MACKEN, Jon (F) **282 76**
H: 5 11 W: 12 04 b.Manchester 7-9-77
Source: Trainee. *Honours:* England Youth. Eire 1 full cap.

1996–97	Manchester U	0	0		
1997–98	Preston NE	29	6		
1998–99	Preston NE	42	8		
1999–2000	Preston NE	44	22		
2000–01	Preston NE	38	19		
2001–02	Preston NE	31	8	**184**	**63**
2001–02	Manchester C	8	5		
2002–03	Manchester C	5	0		
2003–04	Manchester C	15	1		
2004–05	Manchester C	23	1	**51**	**7**
2005–06	Crystal Palace	24	2		
2006–07	Crystal Palace	1	0	**25**	**2**
2006–07	*Ipswich T*	14	4	**14**	**4**
2006–07	Derby Co	8	0	**8**	**0**

MALCOLM, Bob (D) **99 3**
H: 5 11 W: 11 02 b.Glasgow 12-11-80
Honours: Scotland Under-21, B.

1997–98	Rangers	0	0		
1998–99	Rangers	0	0		
1999–2000	Rangers	3	0		
2000–01	Rangers	6	1		
2001–02	Rangers	7	0		
2002–03	Rangers	24	1		
2003–04	Rangers	14	0		
2004–05	Rangers	22	1		
2005–06	Rangers	14	0	**90**	**3**
2006–07	Derby Co	9	0	**9**	**0**

McEVELEY, James (D) **66 2**
H: 6 1 W: 13 03 b.Liverpool 11-2-85
Source: Trainee. *Honours:* England Under-20, Under-21.

2002–03	Blackburn R	9	0		
2003–04	Blackburn R	0	0		
2003–04	*Burnley*	4	0	**4**	**0**
2004–05	Blackburn R	5	0		
2004–05	*Gillingham*	10	1	**10**	**1**
2005–06	Blackburn R	0	0		
2005–06	*Ipswich T*	19	1	**19**	**1**
2006–07	Blackburn R	4	0	**18**	**0**
2006–07	Derby Co	15	0	**15**	**0**

MEREDITH, James (D) **1 0**
H: 6 0 W: 11 09 b.Albury 4-4-88
Source: Scholar.

2006–07	Derby Co	0	0		
2006–07	*Chesterfield*	1	0	**1**	**0**

MOORE, Darren (D) **453 29**
H: 6 2 W: 15 07 b.Birmingham 22-4-74
Source: Trainee. *Honours:* Jamaica 3 full caps.

1991–92	Torquay U	5	1		
1992–93	Torquay U	31	2		
1993–94	Torquay U	37	2		
1994–95	Torquay U	30	3	**103**	**8**
1995–96	Doncaster R	35	2		
1996–97	Doncaster R	41	5	**76**	**7**
1997–98	Bradford C	18	0		
1998–99	Bradford C	44	3		
1999–2000	Bradford C	0	0	**62**	**3**
1999–2000	Portsmouth	25	1		
2000–01	Portsmouth	32	1		
2001–02	Portsmouth	2	0	**59**	**2**
2001–02	WBA	32	2		
2002–03	WBA	29	2		
2003–04	WBA	22	2		
2004–05	WBA	16	0		
2005–06	WBA	5	0	**104**	**6**
2005–06	Derby Co	14	1		
2006–07	Derby Co	35	2	**49**	**3**

NYATANGA, Lewin (D) **52 3**
H: 6 2 W: 12 08 b.Burton 18-8-88
Source: Scholar. *Honours:* Wales Under-21, 12 full caps.

2005–06	Derby Co	24	1		
2006–07	Derby Co	7	1	**31**	**2**
2006–07	*Sunderland*	11	0	**11**	**0**
2006–07	*Barnsley*	10	1	**10**	**1**

OAKLEY, Matthew (M) **298 20**
H: 5 10 W: 12 06 b.Peterborough 17-8-77
Source: Trainee. *Honours:* England Under-21.

1994–95	Southampton	1	0		
1995–96	Southampton	10	0		
1996–97	Southampton	28	3		
1997–98	Southampton	33	1		
1998–99	Southampton	22	2		
1999–2000	Southampton	31	3		
2000–01	Southampton	35	1		
2001–02	Southampton	27	1		
2002–03	Southampton	31	0		
2003–04	Southampton	7	0		
2004–05	Southampton	7	1		
2005–06	Southampton	29	2	**261**	**14**
2006–07	Derby Co	37	6	**37**	**6**

PEARSON, Stephen (M) **145 18**
H: 6 0 W: 11 01 b.Lanark 2-10-82
Honours: Scotland Under-21, B, 6 full caps.

2000–01	Motherwell	6	0		
2001–02	Motherwell	27	2		
2002–03	Motherwell	29	6		
2003–04	Motherwell	18	4	**80**	**12**
2003–04	Celtic	17	3		
2004–05	Celtic	8	0		
2005–06	Celtic	18	2		
2006–07	Celtic	13	1	**56**	**6**
2006–07	Derby Co	9	0	**9**	**0**

PESCHISOLIDO, Paul (F) **443 118**
H: 5 7 W: 10 12 b.Scarborough, Can 25-5-71
Source: Toronto Blizzard. *Honours:* Canada Youth, Under-21, 52 full caps, 10 goals.

1992–93	Birmingham C	19	7		
1993–94	Birmingham C	24	9		
1994–95	Stoke C	40	13		
1995–96	Stoke C	26	6	**66**	**19**
1995–96	Birmingham C	9	1	**52**	**17**
1996–97	WBA	37	15		
1997–98	WBA	8	3	**45**	**18**
1997–98	Fulham	32	13		
1998–99	Fulham	33	7		
1999–2000	Fulham	30	4		
2000–01	Fulham	0	0	**95**	**24**
2000–01	*QPR*	5	1	**5**	**1**
2000–01	*Sheffield U*	5	2		
2000–01	*Norwich C*	5	0	**5**	**0**
2001–02	Sheffield U	29	6		
2002–03	Sheffield U	23	3		
2003–04	Sheffield U	27	8	**84**	**19**
2003–04	Derby Co	11	4		
2004–05	Derby Co	32	8		
2005–06	Derby Co	34	5		
2006–07	Derby Co	14	3	**91**	**20**

RICHARDS, Matthew (M) **0 0**
H: 5 9 W: 11 07 b.Derby 1-12-89
Source: Scholar.

2006–07	Derby Co	0	0		

SMITH, Ryan (M) **38 1**
H: 5 10 W: 11 00 b.Islington 10-11-86
Source: From Scholar. *Honours:* England Youth, Under-20.

2004–05	Arsenal	0	0		
2005–06	Arsenal	0	0		
2005–06	*Leicester C*	17	1	**17**	**1**
2006–07	Derby Co	15	0	**15**	**0**
2006–07	*Millwall*	6	0	**6**	**0**

TEALE, Gary (F) **348 36**
H: 5 11 W: 12 02 b.Glasgow 21-7-78
Honours: Scotland Under-21, B, 8 full caps.

1996–97	Clydebank	33	6		
1997–98	Clydebank	27	6		
1998–99	Clydebank	8	2	**68**	**14**
1998–99	Ayr U	23	4		
1999–2000	Ayr U	32	0		
2000–01	Ayr U	29	5		
2001–02	Ayr U	18	4	**102**	**13**
2001–02	Wigan Ath	23	1		
2002–03	Wigan Ath	38	2		
2003–04	Wigan Ath	28	2		
2004–05	Wigan Ath	37	3		
2005–06	Wigan Ath	24	0		
2006–07	Wigan Ath	12	0	**162**	**8**
2006–07	Derby Co	16	1	**16**	**1**

DONCASTER R (32)

BROWN, Adam (M) **3 1**
H: 5 10 W: 10 07 b.Sunderland 17-12-87
Source: Scholar.

2004–05	Doncaster R	3	1		
2005–06	Doncaster R	0	0		
2006–07	Doncaster R	0	0	**3**	**1**

BUDTZ, Jan (G) **31 0**
H: 6 0 W: 13 05 b.Denmark 20-4-79
Source: B1909 Odense.

2004–05	Nordsjaelland	0	0		
2005–06	Doncaster R	20	0		
2006–07	Doncaster R	7	0	**27**	**0**
2006–07	*Wolverhampton W*	4	0	**4**	**0**

COPPINGER, James (F) **174 19**
H: 5 7 W: 10 03 b.Middlesbrough 10-1-81
Source: Darlington Trainee. *Honours:* England Youth.

1997–98	Newcastle U	0	0		
1998–99	Newcastle U	0	0		
1999–2000	Newcastle U	0	0		
1999–2000	*Hartlepool U*	10	3		
2000–01	Newcastle U	1	0		
2001–02	Newcastle U	0	0	**1**	**0**
2001–02	*Hartlepool U*	14	2	**24**	**5**
2002–03	Exeter C	43	5		
2003–04	Exeter C	0	0	**43**	**5**
2004–05	Doncaster R	31	0		
2005–06	Doncaster R	36	5		
2006–07	Doncaster R	39	4	**106**	**9**

DI PIEDI, Michaelli (F) **47 5**
H: 6 0 W: 13 00 b.Palermo 4-12-80

2000–01	Sheffield W	25	4		
2001–02	Sheffield W	12	1		
2002–03	Sheffield W	2	0	**39**	**5**
2002–03	*Bristol R*	5	0	**5**	**0**
From Apoel, Gela.					
2006–07	Doncaster R	3	0	**3**	**0**

DYER, Bruce (F) **462 119**
H: 6 0 W: 11 03 b.Ilford 13-4-75
Source: Trainee. *Honours:* England Under-21.

1992–93	Watford	2	0		
1993–94	Watford	29	6		
1993–94	Crystal Palace	11	0		
1994–95	Crystal Palace	16	1		
1995–96	Crystal Palace	35	13		
1996–97	Crystal Palace	43	17		
1997–98	Crystal Palace	24	4		
1998–99	Crystal Palace	6	2	**135**	**37**
1998–99	Barnsley	28	7		
1999–2000	Barnsley	32	6		
2000–01	Barnsley	38	15		
2001–02	Barnsley	44	14		
2002–03	Barnsley	40	17	**182**	**59**
2003–04	Watford	32	3		
2004–05	Watford	36	9	**99**	**18**
2005–06	Stoke C	11	0	**11**	**0**
2005–06	*Millwall*	10	2	**10**	**2**
2005–06	Sheffield U	5	1	**5**	**1**
2006–07	Doncaster R	15	1	**15**	**1**
2006–07	*Bradford C*	5	1	**5**	**1**

GREEN, Liam (M) **2 0**
H: 5 9 W: 10 00 b.Grimsby 17-3-88
Source: Scholar.

2006–07	Doncaster R	2	0	**2**	**0**

GREEN, Paul (M) **160 20**
H: 5 9 W: 12 02 b.Pontefract 10-4-83
Source: Trainee.

2003–04	Doncaster R	43	8		
2004–05	Doncaster R	42	7		
2005–06	Doncaster R	34	3		
2006–07	Doncaster R	41	2	**160**	**20**

GRIFFITH, Anthony (M) **10 0**
H: 6 0 W: 12 00 b.Huddersfield 28-10-86

2005–06	Doncaster R	4	0		
2005–06	*Oxford U*	0	0		
2006–07	Doncaster R	2	0	**6**	**0**
2006–07	*Darlington*	4	0	**4**	**0**

GUY, Lewis (F) **76 10**
H: 5 10 W: 10 07 b.Penrith 27-8-85
Source: Trainee. *Honours:* England Youth, Under-20.

2002–03	Newcastle U	0	0		
2003–04	Newcastle U	0	0		
2004–05	Newcastle U	0	0		
2004–05	Doncaster R	9	3		
2005–06	Doncaster R	31	3		
2006–07	Doncaster R	36	4	**76**	**10**

HEFFERNAN, Paul (F) **182 60**
H: 5 10 W: 11 00 b.Dublin 29-12-81
Source: Newton.

1999–2000	Notts Co	2	0		
2000–01	Notts Co	1	0		
2001–02	Notts Co	23	6		
2002–03	Notts Co	36	10		
2003–04	Notts Co	38	20	**100**	**36**
2004–05	Bristol C	27	5	**27**	**5**
2005–06	Doncaster R	26	8		
2006–07	Doncaster R	29	11	**55**	**19**

HORLOCK, Kevin (M) **467 61**
H: 6 0 W: 12 00 b.Erith 1-11-72
Source: Trainee. *Honours:* Northern Ireland B, 32 full caps.

1991–92	West Ham U	0	0		
1992–93	West Ham U	0	0		
1992–93	Swindon T	14	1		
1993–94	Swindon T	38	0		
1994–95	Swindon T	38	1		
1995–96	Swindon T	45	12		
1996–97	Swindon T	28	8	**163**	**22**
1996–97	Manchester C	18	4		
1997–98	Manchester C	25	5		
1998–99	Manchester C	37	9		
1999–2000	Manchester C	38	10		
2000–01	Manchester C	14	2		
2001–02	Manchester C	42	7		
2002–03	Manchester C	30	0	**204**	**37**
2003–04	West Ham U	27	1	**27**	**1**
2004–05	Ipswich T	41	0		
2005–06	Ipswich T	17	0	**58**	**0**
2005–06	*Doncaster R*	13	0		
2006–07	Doncaster R	2	1	**15**	**1**

LEE, Graeme (D) **345 29**
H: 6 2 W: 13 07 b.Middlesbrough 31-5-78
Source: Trainee.

1995–96	Hartlepool U	6	0		
1996–97	Hartlepool U	24	0		
1997–98	Hartlepool U	37	3		
1998–99	Hartlepool U	24	3		
1999–2000	Hartlepool U	38	7		
2000–01	Hartlepool U	6	0		
2001–02	Hartlepool U	39	4		
2002–03	Hartlepool U	45	2	**219**	**19**
2003–04	Sheffield W	30	3		
2004–05	Sheffield W	22	1		
2005–06	Sheffield W	15	1	**67**	**5**
2005–06	Doncaster R	20	1		
2006–07	Doncaster R	39	4	**59**	**5**

LOCKWOOD, Adam (D) **126 9**
H: 6 0 W: 12 07 b.Wakefield 26-10-81
Source: Reading Trainee.

2003–04	Yeovil T	43	4		
2004–05	Yeovil T	10	0		
2005–06	Yeovil T	20	0	**73**	**4**
2005–06	*Torquay U*	9	3	**9**	**3**
2006–07	Doncaster R	44	2	**44**	**2**

McCAMMON, Mark (F) **167 21**
H: 6 2 W: 14 05 b.Barnet 7-8-78
Source: Cambridge C.

1997–98	Cambridge U	2	0		
1998–99	Cambridge U	2	0	**4**	**0**
1998–99	Charlton Ath	0	0		
1999–2000	Charlton Ath	4	0	**4**	**0**
1999–2000	*Swindon T*	4	0	**4**	**0**
2000–01	Brentford	24	3		
2001–02	Brentford	14	0		
2002–03	Brentford	37	7	**75**	**10**
2002–03	Millwall	7	2		
2003–04	Millwall	7	0		
2004–05	Millwall	8	0	**22**	**2**
2004–05	Brighton & HA	18	3		
2005–06	Brighton & HA	7	0	**25**	**3**

2005–06 *Bristol C* 11 4 **11 4**
2006–07 Doncaster R 22 2 **22 2**

McDAID, Sean (D) 55 0
H: 5 6 W: 9 08 b.Harrogate 6-3-86
Source: Trainee.
2002–03 Leeds U 0 0
2003–04 Leeds U 0 0
2004–05 Leeds U 0 0
2005–06 Doncaster R 35 0
2006–07 Doncaster R 20 0 **55 0**

NELTHORPE, Craig (M) 8 1
H: 5 10 W: 11 00 b.Doncaster 10-6-87
Source: Scholar.
2004–05 Doncaster R 1 0
2005–06 Doncaster R 1 0
2006–07 Doncaster R 6 1 **8 1**

O'CONNOR, James (D) 98 2
H: 5 10 W: 12 05 b.Birmingham 20-11-84
Source: Scholar.
2003–04 Aston Villa 0 0
2004–05 Aston Villa 0 0
2004–05 *Port Vale* 13 0 **13 0**
2004–05 Bournemouth 6 0
2005–06 Bournemouth 39 1 **45 1**
2006–07 Doncaster R 40 1 **40 1**

PACEY, Rob (D) 0 0
H: 6 4 W: 12 07 b.Leeds 18-6-87
Source: Scholar.
2005–06 Doncaster R 0 0
2006–07 Doncaster R 0 0

PITTMAN, Jon-Paul (F) 12 1
H: 5 9 W: 11 00 b.Oklahoma City 24-10-86
Source: Scholar.
2005–06 Nottingham F 0 0
2005–06 *Hartlepool U* 3 0 **3 0**
2006–07 Bury 9 1 **9 1**
2006–07 Doncaster R 0 0

PRICE, Jamie (D) 25 0
H: 5 10 W: 11 00 b.Normanton 27-10-81
Source: Trainee.
2003–04 Doncaster R 19 0
2004–05 Doncaster R 6 0
2005–06 Doncaster R 0 0
2006–07 Doncaster R 0 0 **25 0**

PRICE, Jason (M) 325 52
H: 6 2 W: 11 05 b.Pontypridd 12-4-77
Source: Aberaman Ath. *Honours:* Wales Under-21.
1995–96 Swansea C 0 0
1996–97 Swansea C 2 0
1997–98 Swansea C 34 3
1998–99 Swansea C 28 4
1999–2000 Swansea C 39 6
2000–01 Swansea C 41 4 **144 17**
2001–02 Brentford 15 1 **15 1**
2001–02 Tranmere R 24 7
2002–03 Tranmere R 25 4 **49 11**
2003–04 Hull C 33 9
2004–05 Hull C 27 2
2005–06 Hull C 15 2 **75 13**
2005–06 Doncaster R 11 4
2006–07 Doncaster R 31 6 **42 10**

ROBERTS, Gareth (D) 311 14
H: 5 8 W: 11 12 b.Wrexham 6-2-78
Source: Trainee. *Honours:* Wales Under-21, B, 9 full caps.
1995–96 Liverpool 0 0
1996–97 Liverpool 0 0
1997–98 Liverpool 0 0
1998–99 Liverpool 0 0
1999–2000 Tranmere R 37 1
2000–01 Tranmere R 34 0
2001–02 Tranmere R 45 2
2002–03 Tranmere R 37 4
2003–04 Tranmere R 44 1
2004–05 Tranmere R 40 3
2005–06 Tranmere R 44 2 **281 13**
2006–07 Doncaster R 30 1 **30 1**

ROBERTS, Steve (D) 198 7
H: 6 1 W: 11 02 b.Wrexham 24-2-80
Source: Trainee. *Honours:* Wales Youth, Under-21, 1 full cap.
1997–98 Wrexham 0 0
1998–99 Wrexham 0 0
1999–2000 Wrexham 19 0
2000–01 Wrexham 7 0
2001–02 Wrexham 24 1
2002–03 Wrexham 39 2
2003–04 Wrexham 27 0
2004–05 Wrexham 34 3 **150 6**
2005–06 Doncaster R 27 1
2006–07 Doncaster R 21 0 **48 1**

SMITH, Benjamin (G) 13 0
H: 6 1 W: 12 11 b.Newcastle 5-9-86
2006–07 Stockport Co 0 0
2006–07 Doncaster R 13 0 **13 0**

STOCK, Brian (M) 189 20
H: 5 11 W: 11 02 b.Winchester 24-12-81
Source: Trainee. *Honours:* Wales Under-21.
1999–2000 Bournemouth 5 0
2000–01 Bournemouth 1 0
2001–02 Bournemouth 26 2
2002–03 Bournemouth 27 2
2003–04 Bournemouth 19 3
2004–05 Bournemouth 41 6
2005–06 Bournemouth 26 3 **145 16**
2005–06 Preston NE 6 1
2006–07 Preston NE 2 0 **8 1**
2006–07 Doncaster R 36 3 **36 3**

THORNTON, Barry (F) 0 0
H: 6 1 W: 13 00 b.Dublin 21-1-85
Source: Scholar.
2001–02 Coventry C 0 0
2002–03 Coventry C 0 0
2003–04 Coventry C 0 0
2004–05 Coventry C 0 0
2005–06 Doncaster R 0 0
2006–07 Doncaster R 0 0

THORNTON, Sean (M) 122 12
H: 5 10 W: 11 00 b.Drogheda 18-5-83
Source: Scholar. *Honours:* Eire Under-21.
2001–02 Tranmere R 11 1 **11 1**
2002–03 Sunderland 11 1
2002–03 *Blackpool* 3 0 **3 0**
2003–04 Sunderland 22 4
2004–05 Sunderland 16 4 **49 9**
2005–06 Doncaster R 29 2
2006–07 Doncaster R 30 0 **59 2**

WILSON, Mark (M) 93 8
H: 5 10 W: 12 07 b.Scunthorpe 9-2-79
Source: Trainee. *Honours:* England Schools, Under-21.
1995–96 Manchester U 0 0
1996–97 Manchester U 0 0
1997–98 Manchester U 0 0
1997–98 *Wrexham* 13 4 **13 4**
1998–99 Manchester U 0 0
1999–2000 Manchester U 3 0
2000–01 Manchester U 0 0 **3 0**
2001–02 Middlesbrough 10 0
2002–03 Middlesbrough 6 0
2002–03 *Stoke C* 4 0 **4 0**
2003–04 Middlesbrough 0 0
2003–04 *Swansea C* 12 2 **12 2**
2003–04 *Sheffield W* 3 0 **3 0**
2004–05 Middlesbrough 0 0 **16 0**
2004–05 *Doncaster R* 3 0
2004–05 *Livingston* 5 0 **5 0**
2006 Dallas 12 1 **12 1**
2006–07 Doncaster R 22 1 **25 1**

EVERTON (33)

AGARD, Kieran (F) 0 0
b.Newham 10-10-89
Source: Scholar.
2006–07 Everton 0 0

ANDERSON (M) 72 4
H: 6 2 W: 12 11 b.Sao Paulo 29-8-82
2003 Santiago Wanderers18 2 **18 2**
2003–04 Santander 8 0
2004–05 Santander 30 2 **38 2**
2005–06 Malaga 15 0 **15 0**
2006–07 Everton 1 0 **1 0**

ANICHEBE, Victor (F) 21 4
H: 6 1 W: 13 00 b.Nigeria 23-4-88
Source: Scholar.
2005–06 Everton 2 1
2006–07 Everton 19 3 **21 4**

ARTETA, Mikel (M) 171 26
H: 5 9 W: 10 08 b.San Sebastian 26-3-82
Honours: Spain Youth, Under-21.
2000–01 Barcelona B 0 0
2000–01 Paris St Germain 6 1
2001–02 Paris St Germain 25 1 **31 2**
2002–03 Rangers 27 4
2003–04 Rangers 23 8 **50 12**
2004–05 Real Sociedad 14 1 **14 1**
2004–05 Everton 12 1
2005–06 Everton 29 1
2006–07 Everton 35 9 **76 11**

BEATTIE, James (F) 284 81
H: 6 1 W: 13 06 b.Lancaster 27-2-78
Source: Trainee. *Honours:* England Under-21, 5 full caps.
1994–95 Blackburn R 0 0
1995–96 Blackburn R 0 0
1996–97 Blackburn R 1 0
1997–98 Blackburn R 3 0 **4 0**
1998–99 Southampton 35 5
1999–2000 Southampton 18 0
2000–01 Southampton 37 11
2001–02 Southampton 28 12
2002–03 Southampton 38 23
2003–04 Southampton 37 14
2004–05 Southampton 11 3 **204 68**
2004–05 Everton 11 1
2005–06 Everton 32 10
2006–07 Everton 33 2 **76 13**

BOYLE, Patrick (D) 3 0
H: 6 0 W: 12 09 b.Glasgow 20-3-87
Source: Scholar.
2005–06 Everton 0 0
2006–07 Everton 0 0
2006–07 *Norwich C* 3 0 **3 0**

CAHILL, Tim (M) 300 74
H: 5 10 W: 10 12 b.Sydney 6-12-79
Source: Sydney U. *Honours:* Western Samoa Youth, Australia Under-23, 24 full caps, 12 goals.
1997–98 Millwall 1 0
1998–99 Millwall 36 6
1999–2000 Millwall 45 12
2000–01 Millwall 41 9
2001–02 Millwall 43 13
2002–03 Millwall 11 3
2003–04 Millwall 40 9 **217 52**
2004–05 Everton 33 11
2005–06 Everton 32 6
2006–07 Everton 18 5 **83 22**

CARSLEY, Lee (M) 363 30
H: 5 10 W: 12 04 b.Birmingham 28-2-74
Source: Trainee. *Honours:* Eire 34 full caps.
1992–93 Derby Co 0 0
1993–94 Derby Co 0 0
1994–95 Derby Co 23 2
1995–96 Derby Co 35 1
1996–97 Derby Co 24 0
1997–98 Derby Co 34 1
1998–99 Derby Co 22 1 **138 5**
1998–99 Blackburn R 8 0
1999–2000 Blackburn R 30 10
2000–01 Blackburn R 8 0 **46 10**
2000–01 Coventry C 21 2
2001–02 Coventry C 26 2 **47 4**
2001–02 Everton 8 1
2002–03 Everton 24 3
2003–04 Everton 21 2
2004–05 Everton 36 4
2005–06 Everton 5 0
2006–07 Everton 38 1 **132 11**

DENNEHY, Darren (D) 0 0
H: 6 3 W: 11 11 b.Republic of Ireland 21-9-88
Source: Scholar.
2005–06 Everton 0 0
2006–07 Everton 0 0

DOWNES, Aiden (F) 0 0
H: 5 8 W: 11 07 b.Republic of Ireland 24-7-88
Source: Scholar.

2005–06	Everton	0	0		
2006–07	Everton	0	0		

HARPUR, Ryan (M) 0 0
H: 5 9 W: 11 11 b.Craigavon 1-12-88
Source: Scholar.

2005–06	Everton	0	0		
2006–07	Everton	0	0		

HIBBERT, Tony (D) 140 0
H: 5 9 W: 11 05 b.Liverpool 20-2-81
Source: Trainee.

1998–99	Everton	0	0		
1999–2000	Everton	0	0		
2000–01	Everton	3	0		
2001–02	Everton	10	0		
2002–03	Everton	24	0		
2003–04	Everton	25	0		
2004–05	Everton	36	0		
2005–06	Everton	29	0		
2006–07	Everton	13	0	**140**	**0**

HOWARD, Tim (G) 166 0
H: 6 3 W: 14 12 b.North Brunswick 6-3-79
Source: USA Under-21, Under-23, 23 full caps.

1998	NY/NJ MetrStars	1	0		
1999	NY/NJ MetrStars	9	0		
2000	NY/NJ MetrStars	9	0		
2001	NY/NJ MetrStars	26	0		
2002	NY/NJ MetrStars	27	0		
2003	NY/NJ MetrStars	13	0	**85**	**0**
2003–04	Manchester U	32	0		
2004–05	Manchester U	12	0		
2005–06	Manchester U	1	0		
2006–07	Manchester U	0	0	**45**	**0**
2006–07	Everton	36	0	**36**	**0**

INGASON, Thordur (G) 0 0
b.Iceland
Source: Fjolnir.

2005–06	Everton	0	0		
2006–07	Everton	0	0		

IRVING, John (M) 0 0
H: 5 10 W: 11 00 b.Liverpool 17-9-88
Source: Scholar.

2005–06	Everton	0	0		
2006–07	Everton	0	0		

JOHNSON, Andy (F) 255 93
H: 5 7 W: 10 09 b.Bedford 10-2-81
Source: From Trainee. *Honours:* England Youth, Under-20, 7 full caps.

1997–98	Birmingham C	0	0		
1998–99	Birmingham C	4	0		
1999–2000	Birmingham C	22	1		
2000–01	Birmingham C	34	4		
2001–02	Birmingham C	23	3	**83**	**8**
2002–03	Crystal Palace	28	11		
2003–04	Crystal Palace	42	27		
2004–05	Crystal Palace	37	21		
2005–06	Crystal Palace	33	15	**140**	**74**
2006–07	Everton	32	11	**32**	**11**

JUTKIEWICZ, Lucas (F) 38 5
H: 6 1 W: 12 11 b.Southampton 20-3-89
Source: Scholar.

2005–06	Swindon T	5	0		
2006–07	Swindon T	33	5	**38**	**5**
2006–07	Everton	0	0		

KEARNEY, Alan (M) 6 0
H: 6 1 W: 12 06 b.Cork 22-9-87
Source: Scholar.

2005–06	Everton	0	0		
2006–07	Everton	0	0		
2006–07	*Chester C*	6	0	**6**	**0**

KISSOCK, John (M) 0 0
b.Fazackerley 1-12-89
Source: Scholar.

2006–07	Everton	0	0		

LESCOTT, Jolean (D) 250 15
H: 6 2 W: 13 00 b.Birmingham 16-8-82
Source: From Trainee. *Honours:* England Youth, Under-20, Under-21, B.

1999–2000	Wolverhampton W	0	0		
2000–01	Wolverhampton W	37	2		
2001–02	Wolverhampton W	44	5		
2002–03	Wolverhampton W	44	1		
2003–04	Wolverhampton W	0	0		
2004–05	Wolverhampton W	41	4		
2005–06	Wolverhampton W	46	1	**212**	**13**
2006–07	Everton	38	2	**38**	**2**

McFADDEN, James (M) 160 35
H: 6 0 W: 12 11 b.Glasgow 14-4-83
Honours: Scotland Under-21, B, 31 full caps, 10 goals.

2000–01	Motherwell	6	0		
2001–02	Motherwell	24	10		
2002–03	Motherwell	30	13		
2003–04	Motherwell	3	3	**63**	**26**
2003–04	Everton	23	0		
2004–05	Everton	23	1		
2005–06	Everton	32	6		
2006–07	Everton	19	2	**97**	**9**

MOLYNEUX, Lee (D) 0 0
H: 5 10 W: 11 07 b.Liverpool 24-2-89
Source: Scholar. *Honours:* England Schools, Youth.

2005–06	Everton	0	0		
2006–07	Everton	0	0		

MORRISON, Steven (M) 0 0
H: 6 0 W: 10 13 b.Southport 10-9-88
Source: Scholar.

2005–06	Everton	0	0		
2006–07	Everton	0	0		

NAYSMITH, Gary (D) 231 9
H: 5 9 W: 12 01 b.Edinburgh 16-11-78
Source: Whitehill Welfare Colts. *Honours:* Scotland Schools, Under-21, B, 36 full caps, 1 goal.

1995–96	Hearts	1	0		
1996–97	Hearts	10	0		
1997–98	Hearts	16	2		
1998–99	Hearts	26	0		
1999–2000	Hearts	35	1		
2000–01	Hearts	9	0	**97**	**3**
2000–01	Everton	20	2		
2001–02	Everton	24	0		
2002–03	Everton	28	1		
2003–04	Everton	29	2		
2004–05	Everton	11	0		
2005–06	Everton	7	0		
2006–07	Everton	15	1	**134**	**6**

NEVILLE, Phil (M) 332 6
H: 5 11 W: 12 00 b.Bury 21-1-77
Source: Trainee. *Honours:* England Schools, Youth, B, Under-21, 56 full caps.

1994–95	Manchester U	2	0		
1995–96	Manchester U	24	0		
1996–97	Manchester U	18	0		
1997–98	Manchester U	30	1		
1998–99	Manchester U	28	0		
1999–2000	Manchester U	29	0		
2000–01	Manchester U	29	1		
2001–02	Manchester U	28	2		
2002–03	Manchester U	25	1		
2003–04	Manchester U	31	0		
2004–05	Manchester U	19	0	**263**	**5**
2005–06	Everton	34	0		
2006–07	Everton	35	1	**69**	**1**

NUNO VALENTE (D) 269 4
H: 6 0 W: 12 03 b.Lisbon 12-9-74
Honours: Portugal Under-21, 33 full caps, 1 goal.

1993–94	Portimonense	26	1	**26**	**1**
1994–95	Sporting Lisbon	9	0		
1995–96	Sporting Lisbon	9	0		
1996–97	Maritimo	30	0	**30**	**0**
1997–98	Sporting Lisbon	6	0		
1998–99	Sporting Lisbon	12	1	**36**	**1**
1999–2000	Uniao Leiria	28	0		
2000–01	Uniao Leiria	31	2		
2001–02	Uniao Leiria	28	0	**87**	**2**
2002–03	Porto	21	0		
2003–04	Porto	27	0		
2004–05	Porto	8	0	**56**	**0**
2005–06	Everton	20	0		
2006–07	Everton	14	0	**34**	**0**

OSMAN, Leon (F) 133 17
H: 5 8 W: 10 09 b.Billinge 17-5-81
Source: Trainee. *Honours:* England Schools, Youth.

1998–99	Everton	0	0		
1999–2000	Everton	0	0		
2000–01	Everton	0	0		
2001–02	Everton	0	0		
2002–03	Everton	2	0		
2002–03	*Carlisle U*	12	1	**12**	**1**
2003–04	Everton	4	1		
2003–04	*Derby Co*	17	3	**17**	**3**
2004–05	Everton	29	6		
2005–06	Everton	35	3		
2006–07	Everton	34	3	**104**	**13**

PHELAN, Scott (M) 0 0
H: 5 7 W: 10 07 b.Liverpool 13-3-88
Source: Scholar. *Honours:* England Youth.

2005–06	Everton	0	0		
2006–07	Everton	0	0		

PISTONE, Alessandro (D) 249 8
H: 5 11 W: 11 08 b.Milan 27-7-75
Honours: Italy Under-21.

1992–93	Vicenza	0	0		
1993–94	Solbiatese	20	1	**20**	**1**
1994–95	Crevalcore	29	4	**29**	**4**
1995–96	Vicenza	6	0	**6**	**0**
1995–96	Internazionale	19	1		
1996–97	Internazionale	26	0	**45**	**1**
1997–98	Newcastle U	28	0		
1998–99	Newcastle U	3	0		
1999–2000	Newcastle U	15	1	**46**	**1**
2000–01	Everton	7	0		
2001–02	Everton	25	1		
2002–03	Everton	15	0		
2003–04	Everton	21	0		
2004–05	Everton	33	0		
2005–06	Everton	2	0		
2006–07	Everton	0	0	**103**	**1**

RUDDY, John (G) 69 0
H: 6 3 W: 12 07 b.St Ives 24-10-86
Source: Scholar. *Honours:* England Youth.

2003–04	Cambridge U	1	0		
2004–05	Cambridge U	38	0	**39**	**0**
2005–06	Everton	1	0		
2005–06	*Walsall*	5	0	**5**	**0**
2005–06	*Rushden & D*	3	0	**3**	**0**
2005–06	*Chester C*	4	0	**4**	**0**
2006–07	Everton	0	0	**1**	**0**
2006–07	*Stockport Co*	11	0	**11**	**0**
2006–07	*Wrexham*	5	0	**5**	**0**
2006–07	*Bristol C*	1	0	**1**	**0**

SPENCER, Scott (F) 0 0
b.Oldham 1-1-89
Source: Oldham Ath Scholar.

2006–07	Everton	0	0		

STUBBS, Alan (D) 479 18
H: 6 2 W: 14 02 b.Kirkby 6-10-71
Source: From Trainee. *Honours:* England B.

1990–91	Bolton W	23	0		
1991–92	Bolton W	32	1		
1992–93	Bolton W	42	2		
1993–94	Bolton W	41	1		
1994–95	Bolton W	39	1		
1995–96	Bolton W	25	4	**202**	**9**
1996–97	Celtic	20	0		
1997–98	Celtic	29	1		
1998–99	Celtic	23	1		
1999–2000	Celtic	23	0		
2000–01	Celtic	11	1	**106**	**3**
2001–02	Everton	31	2		
2002–03	Everton	35	0		
2003–04	Everton	27	0		
2004–05	Everton	31	1		
2005–06	Sunderland	10	1	**10**	**1**
2005–06	Everton	14	0		
2006–07	Everton	23	2	**161**	**5**

STUBHAUG, Lars (G) **0 0**
b.Haugesund 18-4-90
Source: Vard-Haugesund.

2006–07	Everton	0	0		

TURNER, Iain (G) **45 0**
H: 6 3 W: 12 10 b.Stirling 26-1-84
Source: From Riverside BC. *Honours:* Scotland Youth, Under-21, B.

2002–03	Stirling A	14	0	**14**	**0**
2002–03	Everton	0	0		
2003–04	Everton	0	0		
2004–05	Everton	0	0		
2004–05	*Doncaster R*	8	0	**8**	**0**
2005–06	Everton	3	0		
2005–06	*Wycombe W*	3	0	**3**	**0**
2006–07	Everton	1	0	**4**	**0**
2006–07	*Crystal Palace*	5	0	**5**	**0**
2006–07	*Sheffield W*	11	0	**11**	**0**

VAN DER MEYDE, Andy (M) **173 22**
H: 5 10 W: 12 04 b.Arnhem 30-9-79
Honours: Holland 18 full caps, 1 goal.

1997–98	Ajax	4	0		
1998–99	Ajax	1	0		
1999–2000	Twente	32	2	**32**	**2**
2000–01	Ajax	27	3		
2001–02	Ajax	30	5		
2002–03	Ajax	29	11	**91**	**19**
2003–04	Internazionale	14	1		
2004–05	Internazionale	18	0	**32**	**1**
2005–06	Everton	10	0		
2006–07	Everton	8	0	**18**	**0**

VAUGHAN, James (F) **17 5**
H: 5 11 W: 13 00 b.Birmingham 14-7-88
Source: Scholar. *Honours:* England Youth, Under-21.

2004–05	Everton	2	1		
2005–06	Everton	1	0		
2006–07	Everton	14	4	**17**	**5**

VIDARSSON, Bjarni (M) **6 1**
H: 6 1 W: 11 08 b.Iceland 5-3-88
Source: Scholar. *Honours:* Iceland Youth, Under-21.

2005–06	Everton	0	0		
2006–07	Everton	0	0		
2006–07	*Bournemouth*	6	1	**6**	**1**

WEIR, David (D) **460 25**
H: 6 5 W: 14 03 b.Falkirk 10-5-70
Source: Celtic BC. *Honours:* Scotland 56 full caps, 1 goal.

1992–93	Falkirk	30	1		
1993–94	Falkirk	37	3		
1994–95	Falkirk	32	1		
1995–96	Falkirk	34	3	**133**	**8**
1996–97	Hearts	34	6		
1997–98	Hearts	35	1		
1998–99	Hearts	23	1	**92**	**8**
1998–99	Everton	14	0		
1999–2000	Everton	35	2		
2000–01	Everton	37	1		
2001–02	Everton	36	4		
2002–03	Everton	31	0		
2003–04	Everton	10	0		
2004–05	Everton	34	1		
2005–06	Everton	33	1		
2006–07	Everton	5	0	**235**	**9**

To Rangers January 2007

WRIGHT, Richard (G) **312 0**
H: 6 2 W: 14 04 b.Ipswich 5-11-77
Source: Trainee. *Honours:* England Schools, Youth, Under-21, 2 full caps.

1994–95	Ipswich T	3	0		
1995–96	Ipswich T	23	0		
1996–97	Ipswich T	40	0		
1997–98	Ipswich T	46	0		
1998–99	Ipswich T	46	0		
1999–2000	Ipswich T	46	0		
2000–01	Ipswich T	36	0	**240**	**0**
2001–02	Arsenal	12	0	**12**	**0**
2002–03	Everton	33	0		
2003–04	Everton	4	0		
2004–05	Everton	7	0		
2005–06	Everton	15	0		
2006–07	Everton	1	0	**60**	**0**

YOBO, Joseph (D) **217 7**
H: 6 1 W: 13 00 b.Kano 6-9-80
Source: Mechelen. *Honours:* Nigeria B, 47 full caps, 2 goals.

1998–99	Standard Liege	0	0		
1999–2000	Standard Liege	18	0		
2000–01	Standard Liege	30	2	**48**	**2**
2001–02	Marseille	23	0	**23**	**0**
2002–03	Everton	24	0		
2003–04	Everton	28	2		
2004–05	Everton	27	0		
2005–06	Everton	29	1		
2006–07	Everton	38	2	**146**	**5**

Scholars
Connor, Stephen Jeffrey; Densmore, Shaun Peter; Hall, Walter Alonte James; Imudia, Jeffrey; Jensen, Michael; Jones, Jamie; McEntegart, Michael; Sinnott, Cory.

FULHAM (34)

BATISTA, Ricardo (G) **38 0**
H: 6 2 W: 12 06 b.Portugal 19-11-86
Source: Vitoria Setubal. *Honours:* Portugal Youth, Under-21.

2004–05	Fulham	0	0		
2005–06	Fulham	0	0		
2005–06	*Milton Keynes D*	9	0	**9**	**0**
2006–07	Fulham	0	0		
2006–07	*Wycombe W*	29	0	**29**	**0**

BOCANEGRA, Carlos (D) **181 12**
H: 5 11 W: 12 07 b.Alta Loma 25-5-79
Honours: USA Under-21, Under-23, 49 full caps, 7 goals.

2000	Chicago Fire	27	1		
2001	Chicago Fire	15	1		
2002	Chicago Fire	26	2		
2003	Chicago Fire	19	1	**87**	**5**
2003–04	Fulham	15	0		
2004–05	Fulham	28	1		
2005–06	Fulham	21	1		
2006–07	Fulham	30	5	**94**	**7**

BRIGGS, Matthew (D) **1 0**
H: 6 1 W: 11 12 b.Wandsworth 6-3-91

2006–07	Fulham	1	0	**1**	**0**

BROOKS-MEADE, Corrin (G) **0 0**
b.London 19-3-88
Source: Scholar.

2006–07	Fulham	0	0		

BROWN, Michael (M) **341 32**
H: 5 9 W: 12 04 b.Hartlepool 25-1-77
Source: From Trainee. *Honours:* England Under-21.

1994–95	Manchester C	0	0		
1995–96	Manchester C	21	0		
1996–97	Manchester C	11	0		
1996–97	*Hartlepool U*	6	1	**6**	**1**
1997–98	Manchester C	26	0		
1998–99	Manchester C	31	2		
1999–2000	Manchester C	0	0	**89**	**2**
1999–2000	*Portsmouth*	4	0	**4**	**0**
1999–2000	Sheffield U	24	3		
2000–01	Sheffield U	36	1		
2001–02	Sheffield U	36	5		
2002–03	Sheffield U	40	16		
2003–04	Sheffield U	15	2	**151**	**27**
2003–04	Tottenham H	17	1		
2004–05	Tottenham H	24	1		
2005–06	Tottenham H	9	0	**50**	**2**
2005–06	Fulham	7	0		
2006–07	Fulham	34	0	**41**	**0**

BROWN, Wayne (M) **0 0**
b.Surrey 6-8-88
Source: Scholar.

2006–07	Fulham	0	0		

BULLARD, Jimmy (M) **215 23**
H: 5 10 W: 11 05 b.Newham 23-10-78
Source: Corinthian, Dartford, Gravesend & N.

1998–99	West Ham U	0	0		
1999–2000	West Ham U	0	0		
2000–01	West Ham U	0	0		
2001–02	Peterborough U	40	8		
2002–03	Peterborough U	26	3	**66**	**11**
2002–03	Wigan Ath	17	1		
2003–04	Wigan Ath	46	2		
2004–05	Wigan Ath	46	3		
2005–06	Wigan Ath	36	4	**145**	**10**
2005–06	Fulham	0	0		
2006–07	Fulham	4	2	**4**	**2**

CHRISTANVAL, Philippe (D) **160 2**
H: 6 2 W: 12 10 b.Paris 31-8-78
Honours: France Under-21, 6 full caps.

1997–98	Monaco	10	0		
1998–99	Monaco	23	1		
1999–2000	Monaco	25	0		
2000–01	Monaco	23	0	**81**	**1**
2001–02	Barcelona	26	0		
2002–03	Barcelona	5	0	**31**	**0**
2003–04	Marseille	13	0		
2004–05	Marseille	0	0	**13**	**0**
2005–06	Fulham	15	0		
2006–07	Fulham	20	1	**35**	**1**

COLLINS, Matty (M) **0 0**
H: 5 8 W: 10 10 b.Merthyr 31-3-86
Source: Trainee. *Honours:* Wales Youth, Under-21.

2002–03	Fulham	0	0		
2003–04	Fulham	0	0		
2004–05	Fulham	0	0		
2005–06	Fulham	0	0		
2006–07	Fulham	0	0		

CROSSLEY, Mark (G) **388 1**
H: 6 3 W: 15 09 b.Barnsley 16-6-69
Source: Trainee. *Honours:* England Under-21, B, Wales B, 8 full caps.

1987–88	Nottingham F	0	0		
1988–89	Nottingham F	2	0		
1989–90	Nottingham F	8	0		
1989–90	*Manchester U*	0	0		
1990–91	Nottingham F	38	0		
1991–92	Nottingham F	36	0		
1992–93	Nottingham F	37	0		
1993–94	Nottingham F	37	0		
1994–95	Nottingham F	42	0		
1995–96	Nottingham F	38	0		
1996–97	Nottingham F	33	0		
1997–98	Nottingham F	0	0		
1997–98	*Millwall*	13	0	**13**	**0**
1998–99	Nottingham F	12	0		
1999–2000	Nottingham F	20	0	**303**	**0**
2000–01	Middlesbrough	5	0		
2001–02	Middlesbrough	18	0		
2002–03	Middlesbrough	0	0	**23**	**0**
2002–03	*Stoke C*	12	0	**12**	**0**
2003–04	Fulham	1	0		
2004–05	Fulham	6	0		
2005–06	Fulham	13	0		
2006–07	Fulham	0	0	**20**	**0**
2006–07	*Sheffield W*	17	1	**17**	**1**

DAVIES, Simon (M) **245 22**
H: 5 10 W: 11 07 b.Haverfordwest 23-10-79
Source: Trainee. *Honours:* Wales Youth, Under-21, B, 41 full caps, 5 goals.

1997–98	Peterborough U	6	0		
1998–99	Peterborough U	43	4		
1999–2000	Peterborough U	16	2	**65**	**6**
1999–2000	Tottenham H	3	0		
2000–01	Tottenham H	13	2		
2001–02	Tottenham H	31	4		
2002–03	Tottenham H	36	5		
2003–04	Tottenham H	17	2		
2004–05	Tottenham H	21	0	**121**	**13**
2005–06	Everton	30	1		
2006–07	Everton	15	0	**45**	**1**
2006–07	Fulham	14	2	**14**	**2**

DEMPSEY, Clint (M) **87 27**
H: 6 1 W: 12 02 b.Nacogdoches 9-3-83
Source: Furman Univ. *Honours:* USA Under-21, 32 full caps, 8 goals.

2004	New England Rev	24	7		
2005	New England Rev	30	11		
2006	New England Rev	23	8	**77**	**26**
2006–07	Fulham	10	1	**10**	**1**

DIOP, Papa Bouba (M) 168 23
H: 6 4 W: 14 12 b.Dakar 28-1-78
Source: Espoir, Jaraaf, Vevey Sports.
Honours: Senegal 29 full caps, 9 goals.

1999–2000	Neuchatel Xamax	0	0		
2000–01	Neuchatel Xamax	18	4	**18**	**4**
2000–01	Grasshoppers	11	1		
2001–02	Grasshoppers	18	4	**29**	**5**
2001–02	Lens	5	0		
2002–03	Lens	16	3		
2003–04	Lens	26	3	**47**	**6**
2004–05	Fulham	29	6		
2005–06	Fulham	22	2		
2006–07	Fulham	23	0	**74**	**8**

EHUI, Ismael (F) 3 0
H: 5 5 W: 10 02 b.Lille 10-12-86
Source: Scholar.

2004–05	Fulham	0	0		
2005–06	Fulham	0	0		
2005–06	*Scunthorpe U*	3	0	**3**	**0**
2006–07	Fulham	0	0		

ELLIOTT, Simon (M) 193 11
H: 6 0 W: 13 02 b.Wellington 10-6-74
Source: Waterside Karori, Wellington Coll, Wellington U, Wellington Olympic AFC, Miramar R, Western Suburbs, Stanford Univ, Boston Bulldogs. *Honours:* New Zealand Under-20, Under-23, 48 full caps, 6 goals.

1999	Los Angeles G	23	2		
2000	Los Angeles G	27	5		
2001	Los Angeles G	23	1		
2002	Los Angeles G	25	1		
2003	Los Angeles G	24	1	**122**	**10**
2004	Columbus Crew	27	0		
2005	Columbus Crew	32	1	**59**	**1**
2005–06	Fulham	12	0		
2006–07	Fulham	0	0	**12**	**0**

ELRICH, Ahmed (M) 136 20
H: 5 11 W: 12 00 b.Sydney 30-5-81
Honours: Australia Under-20, Under-23, 17 full caps, 5 goals.

1999–2000	Parramatta Power	21	1		
2000–01	Parramatta Power	24	2		
2001–02	Parramatta Power	22	2		
2002–03	Parramatta Power	32	10		
2003–04	Parramatta Power	21	4	**120**	**19**
2003–04	Busan Icons	10	1		
2004–05	Busan Icons	0	0	**10**	**1**
2005–06	Fulham	6	0		
2006–07	Fulham	0	0	**6**	**0**

HELGUSON, Heidar (F) 275 85
H: 5 10 W: 12 09 b.Akureyri 22-8-77
Source: Throttur. *Honours:* Iceland Youth, Under-21, 39 full caps, 6 goals.

1998	Lillestrom	19	2		
1999	Lillestrom	25	16	**44**	**18**
1999–2000	Watford	16	6		
2000–01	Watford	33	8		
2001–02	Watford	34	6		
2002–03	Watford	30	11		
2003–04	Watford	22	8		
2004–05	Watford	39	16	**174**	**55**
2005–06	Fulham	27	8		
2006–07	Fulham	30	4	**57**	**12**

JAMES, Chris (M) 0 0
H: 5 8 W: 10 12 b.New Zealand 4-7-87
Source: Scholar. *Honours:* England Youth.

2005–06	Fulham	0	0		
2006–07	Fulham	0	0		

JENSEN, Claus (M) 309 42
H: 6 0 W: 13 01 b.Nykobing 29-4-77
Source: Stubbekobing, Nykobing. *Honours:* Denmark Youth, Under-21, 47 full caps, 8 goals.

1995–96	Naestved	4	0	**4**	**0**
1996–97	Lyngby	31	3		
1997–98	Lyngby	31	11	**62**	**14**
1998–99	Bolton W	44	2		
1999–2000	Bolton W	42	6	**86**	**8**
2000–01	Charlton Ath	38	5		
2001–02	Charlton Ath	18	1		
2002–03	Charlton Ath	35	6		
2003–04	Charlton Ath	31	4	**122**	**16**
2004–05	Fulham	12	0		
2005–06	Fulham	11	2		
2006–07	Fulham	12	2	**35**	**4**

JENSEN, Niclas (D) 328 18
H: 5 9 W: 13 00 b.Copenhagen 17-8-74
Honours: Denmark Youth, Under-21, 56 full caps.

1992–93	Lyngby	12	2		
1993–94	Lyngby	21	0		
1994–95	Lyngby	20	1		
1995–96	Lyngby	32	3		
1996–97	Lyngby	7	1	**92**	**7**
1996–97	PSV Eindhoven	2	0		
1997–98	PSV Eindhoven	2	0	**4**	**0**
1997–98	FC Copenhagen	10	0		
1998–99	FC Copenhagen	33	4		
1999–2000	FC Copenhagen	29	1		
2000–01	FC Copenhagen	32	1		
2001–02	FC Copenhagen	18	1	**122**	**7**
2001–02	Manchester C	18	1		
2002–03	Manchester C	33	1	**51**	**2**
2003–04	Bor Dortmund	27	1		
2004–05	Bor Dortmund	16	1	**43**	**2**
2005–06	Fulham	16	0		
2006–07	Fulham	0	0	**16**	**0**

To FC Copenhagen January 2007

JOHN, Collins (F) 128 31
H: 5 11 W: 12 13 b.Zwandru 17-10-85
Source: Holland Youth, Under-21, 2 full caps.

2002–03	Twente	17	2		
2003–04	Twente	18	9	**35**	**11**
2003–04	Fulham	8	4		
2004–05	Fulham	27	4		
2005–06	Fulham	35	11		
2006–07	Fulham	23	1	**93**	**20**

KNIGHT, Zat (D) 154 3
H: 6 6 W: 15 02 b.Solihull 2-5-80
Source: Rushall Olympic. *Honours:* England Under-21, 2 full caps.

1998–99	Fulham	0	0		
1999–2000	Fulham	0	0		
1999–2000	*Peterborough U*	8	0	**8**	**0**
2000–01	Fulham	0	0		
2001–02	Fulham	10	0		
2002–03	Fulham	17	0		
2003–04	Fulham	31	0		
2004–05	Fulham	35	1		
2005–06	Fulham	30	0		
2006–07	Fulham	23	2	**146**	**3**

LASTUVKA, Jan (G) 120 0
H: 6 3 W: 13 10 b.Havirov 7-7-82
Source: Karvina. *Honours:* Czech Republic Youth.

2001–02	Banik Ostrava	24	0		
2002–03	Banik Ostrava	25	0		
2003–04	Banik Ostrava	30	0	**79**	**0**
2004–05	Shakhtjar Donetsk	20	0		
2005–06	Shakhtjar Donetsk	13	0	**33**	**0**
2006–07	Fulham	8	0	**8**	**0**

McBRIDE, Brian (F) 313 96
H: 6 0 W: 12 08 b.Chicago 19-6-72
Source: St Louis Univ. *Honours:* USA 95 full caps, 30 goals.

1994–95	Wolfsburg	12	1	**12**	**1**
1996	Columbus Crew	28	17		
1997	Columbus Crew	13	6		
1998	Columbus Crew	24	10		
1999	Columbus Crew	25	5		
2000	Columbus Crew	18	6		
2000–01	Preston NE	9	1	**9**	**1**
2001	Columbus Crew	15	1		
2002	Columbus Crew	14	5		
2002–03	Everton	8	4	**8**	**4**
2003	Columbus Crew	24	12	**161**	**62**
2003–04	Fulham	16	4		
2004–05	Fulham	31	6		
2005–06	Fulham	38	9		
2006–07	Fulham	38	9	**123**	**28**

MILSOM, Robert (D) 0 0
b.Redhill 2-1-87
Source: Scholar.

2005–06	Fulham	0	0		
2006–07	Fulham	0	0		

MONCUR, Tom (D) 0 0
b.Hackney 23-9-87
Source: Scholar.

2005–06	Fulham	0	0		
2006–07	Fulham	0	0		

MONTELLA, Vincenzo (F) 358 186
H: 5 8 W: 10 12 b.Pomigliano d'Arco 18-6-74
Honours: Italy 20 full caps, 3 goals.

1990–91	Empoli	1	0		
1991–92	Empoli	7	4		
1992–93	Empoli	13	5		
1993–94	Empoli	0	0		
1994–95	Empoli	30	17	**51**	**26**
1995–96	Genoa	34	21	**34**	**21**
1996–97	Sampdoria	28	22		
1997–98	Sampdoria	33	20		
1998–99	Sampdoria	22	12	**83**	**54**
1999–2000	Roma	31	18		
2000–01	Roma	28	13		
2001–02	Roma	19	13		
2002–03	Roma	29	9		
2003–04	Roma	11	5		
2004–05	Roma	37	21		
2005–06	Roma	13	1		
2006–07	Roma	12	3	**180**	**83**
2006–07	Fulham	10	2	**10**	**2**

NIEMI, Antti (G) 397 0
H: 6 1 W: 12 04 b.Oulu 31-5-72
Honours: Finland Youth, Under-21, 66 full caps.

1991	HJK Helsinki	2	0		
1992	HJK Helsinki	28	0		
1993	HJK Helsinki	24	0		
1994	HJK Helsinki	24	0		
1995	HJK Helsinki	24	0	**102**	**0**
1995–96	FC Copenhagen	17	0		
1996–97	FC Copenhagen	30	0	**47**	**0**
1997–98	Rangers	5	0		
1998–99	Rangers	7	0		
1999–2000	Rangers	1	0	**13**	**0**
1999–2000	Hearts	17	0		
2000–01	Hearts	37	0		
2001–02	Hearts	32	0		
2002–03	Hearts	3	0	**89**	**0**
2002–03	Southampton	25	0		
2003–04	Southampton	28	0		
2004–05	Southampton	28	0		
2005–06	Southampton	25	0	**106**	**0**
2005–06	Fulham	9	0		
2006–07	Fulham	31	0	**40**	**0**

OMOZUSI, Elliot (D) 0 0
b.Hackney 15-12-88
Source: Scholar. *Honours:* England Youth.

2005–06	Fulham	0	0		
2006–07	Fulham	0	0		

ORELAJA, Kazeem (M) 0 0
b.Nigeria 21-5-88
Source: Scholar.

2006–07	Fulham	0	0		

OSEI-GYAN, King (M) 0 0
b.Ghana 22-12-88

2006–07	Fulham	0	0		

PEARCE, Ian (D) 264 12
H: 6 3 W: 15 06 b.Bury St Edmunds 7-5-74
Source: School. *Honours:* England Youth, Under-21.

1990–91	Chelsea	1	0		
1991–92	Chelsea	2	0		
1992–93	Chelsea	1	0		
1993–94	Chelsea	0	0	**4**	**0**
1993–94	Blackburn R	5	1		
1994–95	Blackburn R	28	0		
1995–96	Blackburn R	12	1		
1996–97	Blackburn R	12	0		
1997–98	Blackburn R	5	0	**62**	**2**
1997–98	West Ham U	30	1		
1998–99	West Ham U	33	2		
1999–2000	West Ham U	1	0		
2000–01	West Ham U	15	1		
2001–02	West Ham U	9	2		
2002–03	West Ham U	30	2		
2003–04	West Ham U	24	1	**142**	**9**

2003–04	Fulham	13	0		
2004–05	Fulham	11	0		
2005–06	Fulham	10	0		
2006–07	Fulham	22	1	**56**	**1**

PEMBRIDGE, Mark (M) 418 51
H: 5 7 W: 11 13 b.Merthyr 29-11-70
Source: Trainee. *Honours:* Wales Schools, Under-21, B, 54 full caps, 6 goals.

1989–90	Luton T	0	0		
1990–91	Luton T	18	1		
1991–92	Luton T	42	5	**60**	**6**
1992–93	Derby Co	42	8		
1993–94	Derby Co	41	11		
1994–95	Derby Co	27	9	**110**	**28**
1995–96	Sheffield W	25	1		
1996–97	Sheffield W	34	6		
1997–98	Sheffield W	34	4	**93**	**11**
1998–99	Benfica	19	1	**19**	**1**
1999–2000	Everton	31	2		
2000–01	Everton	21	0		
2001–02	Everton	14	1		
2002–03	Everton	21	1		
2003–04	Everton	4	0	**91**	**4**
2003–04	Fulham	12	1		
2004–05	Fulham	28	0		
2005–06	Fulham	5	0		
2006–07	Fulham	0	0	**45**	**1**

QUEUDRUE, Franck (D) 221 14
H: 6 1 W: 12 01 b.Paris 27-8-78
Source: Meaux.

1999–2000	Lens	16	1		
2000–01	Lens	24	1		
2001–02	Lens	2	0	**42**	**2**
2001–02	Middlesbrough	28	2		
2002–03	Middlesbrough	31	1		
2003–04	Middlesbrough	31	0		
2004–05	Middlesbrough	31	5		
2005–06	Middlesbrough	29	3	**150**	**11**
2006–07	Fulham	29	1	**29**	**1**

RADZINSKI, Tomasz (F) 376 129
H: 5 8 W: 11 11 b.Poznan 14-12-73
Source: Toronto Rockets, St Catherines Roma. *Honours:* Canada Under-23, 33 full caps, 9 goals.

1994–95	Ekeren	28	6		
1995–96	Ekeren	22	9		
1996–97	Ekeren	23	8		
1997–98	Ekeren	31	19	**104**	**42**
1998–99	Anderlecht	22	15		
1999–2000	Anderlecht	25	14		
2000–01	Anderlecht	31	23	**78**	**52**
2001–02	Everton	27	6		
2002–03	Everton	30	11		
2003–04	Everton	34	8	**91**	**25**
2004–05	Fulham	35	6		
2005–06	Fulham	33	2		
2006–07	Fulham	35	2	**103**	**10**

ROSENIOR, Liam (D) 111 2
H: 5 10 W: 11 05 b.Wandsworth 9-7-84
Source: Scholar. *Honours:* England Youth, Under-20, Under-21.

2001–02	Bristol C	1	0		
2002–03	Bristol C	21	2		
2003–04	Bristol C	0	0	**22**	**2**
2003–04	Fulham	0	0		
2003–04	*Torquay U*	10	0	**10**	**0**
2004–05	Fulham	17	0		
2005–06	Fulham	24	0		
2006–07	Fulham	38	0	**79**	**0**

RUNSTROM, Bjorn (F) 66 20
H: 6 1 W: 12 08 b.Stockholm 1-3-84
Source: Bologna, Chievo, Fiorentina. *Honours:* Sweden Youth, Under-21.

2004	Hammarby	25	5		
2005	Hammarby	23	9		
2006	Hammarby	9	4	**57**	**18**
2006–07	Fulham	1	0	**1**	**0**
2006–07	*Luton T*	8	2	**8**	**2**

SMERTIN, Alexei (M) 436 27
H: 5 9 W: 10 10 b.Barnaul 1-5-75
Honours: Russia 55 full caps.

1992	Dynamo Barnaul	18	2		
1993	Dynamo Barnaul	24	0	**42**	**2**
1994	Zarya	49	2		
1995	Zarya	37	7		
1996	Zarya	34	4		
1997	Zarya	13	0	**133**	**13**
1997	Uralan	23	0		
1998	Uralan	26	3	**49**	**3**
1999	Loko Moscow	29	6		
2000	Loko Moscow	10	1	**39**	**7**
2000–01	Bordeaux	23	0		
2001–02	Bordeaux	28	0		
2002–03	Bordeaux	33	2	**84**	**2**
2003–04	Chelsea	0	0		
2003–04	*Portsmouth*	26	0	**26**	**0**
2004–05	Chelsea	16	0		
2005–06	Chelsea	0	0	**16**	**0**
2005–06	*Charlton Ath*	18	0	**18**	**0**
2006	Dynamo Moscow	22	0	**22**	**0**
2006–07	Fulham	7	0	**7**	**0**

TIMLIN, Michael (M) 28 1
H: 5 8 W: 11 08 b.Lambeth 19-3-85
Source: Trainee. *Honours:* Eire Youth, Under-21.

2002–03	Fulham	0	0		
2003–04	Fulham	0	0		
2004–05	Fulham	0	0		
2005–06	Fulham	0	0		
2005–06	*Scunthorpe U*	1	0	**1**	**0**
2005–06	*Doncaster R*	3	0	**3**	**0**
2006–07	Fulham	0	0		
2006–07	*Swindon T*	24	1	**24**	**1**

VOLZ, Moritz (D) 126 3
H: 5 10 W: 11 07 b.Siegen 21-1-83
Source: Schalke. *Honours:* Germany Youth, Under-21.

1999–2000	Arsenal	0	0		
2000–01	Arsenal	0	0		
2001–02	Arsenal	0	0		
2002–03	Arsenal	0	0		
2002–03	*Wimbledon*	10	1	**10**	**1**
2003–04	Arsenal	0	0		
2003–04	Fulham	33	0		
2004–05	Fulham	31	0		
2005–06	Fulham	23	0		
2006–07	Fulham	29	2	**116**	**2**

WARNER, Tony (G) 281 0
H: 6 4 W: 15 06 b.Liverpool 11-5-74
Source: School. *Honours:* Trinidad & Tobago 1 full cap.

1993–94	Liverpool	0	0		
1994–95	Liverpool	0	0		
1995–96	Liverpool	0	0		
1996–97	Liverpool	0	0		
1997–98	Liverpool	0	0		
1997–98	*Swindon T*	2	0	**2**	**0**
1998–99	Liverpool	0	0		
1998–99	*Celtic*	3	0	**3**	**0**
1998–99	*Aberdeen*	6	0	**6**	**0**
1999–2000	Millwall	45	0		
2000–01	Millwall	35	0		
2001–02	Millwall	46	0		
2002–03	Millwall	46	0		
2003–04	Millwall	28	0	**200**	**0**
2004–05	Cardiff C	26	0		
2005–06	Cardiff C	0	0	**26**	**0**
2005–06	Fulham	18	0		
2006–07	Fulham	0	0	**18**	**0**
2006–07	*Leeds U*	13	0	**13**	**0**
2006–07	*Norwich C*	13	0	**13**	**0**

WATTS, Adam (D) 2 0
H: 6 1 W: 11 09 b.London 4-3-88
Source: Scholar.

2006–07	Fulham	0	0		
2006–07	*Milton Keynes D*	2	0	**2**	**0**

ZAKUANI, Gaby (D) 96 3
H: 6 1 W: 12 13 b.DR Congo 31-5-86
Source: Scholar. *Honours:* DR Congo full caps.

2002–03	Leyton Orient	1	0		
2003–04	Leyton Orient	10	2		
2004–05	Leyton Orient	33	0		
2005–06	Leyton Orient	43	1	**87**	**3**
2006–07	Fulham	0	0		
2006–07	*Stoke C*	9	0	**9**	**0**

Scholars
Anderson, Joe; Cameron, Tyrone; Cumber, Lewis Perry; Etheridge, Neil; Goncalves, Lino; Hawthorne, Callum; Hudson-Odoi, Bradley; Noble, Max Emanuel; Saunders, Matthew; Smith, Lewis George; Thompson, Ashley; Wilson, Jordan Garfield.

GILLINGHAM (35)

BENTLEY, Mark (M) 134 16
H: 6 2 W: 13 04 b.Hertford 7-1-78
Source: Enfield, Aldershot T, Gravesend & N, Dagenham & R.

2003–04	Southend U	21	2		
2004–05	Southend U	39	5		
2005–06	Southend U	33	5	**93**	**12**
2006–07	Gillingham	41	4	**41**	**4**

CLOHESSY, Sean (D) 26 1
H: 5 11 W: 12 07 b.Croydon 12-12-86
Source: Arsenal Scholar.

2005–06	Gillingham	20	1		
2006–07	Gillingham	6	0	**26**	**1**

COLLIN, Frannie (F) 9 1
H: 5 10 W: 11 07 b.Chatham 20-4-87

2005–06	Gillingham	6	1		
2006–07	Gillingham	3	0	**9**	**1**

COX, Ian (D) 435 26
H: 6 1 W: 12 08 b.Croydon 25-3-71
Source: Carshalton Ath. *Honours:* Trinidad & Tobago 16 full caps.

1993–94	Crystal Palace	0	0		
1994–95	Crystal Palace	11	0		
1995–96	Crystal Palace	4	0	**15**	**0**
1995–96	Bournemouth	8	0		
1996–97	Bournemouth	44	8		
1997–98	Bournemouth	46	3		
1998–99	Bournemouth	46	5		
1999–2000	Bournemouth	28	0	**172**	**16**
1999–2000	Burnley	17	1		
2000–01	Burnley	38	1		
2001–02	Burnley	34	2		
2002–03	Burnley	26	1	**115**	**5**
2003–04	Gillingham	33	0		
2004–05	Gillingham	31	2		
2005–06	Gillingham	36	0		
2006–07	Gillingham	33	3	**133**	**5**

CROFTS, Andrew (D) 124 12
H: 5 10 W: 12 09 b.Chatham 29-5-84
Source: Trainee. *Honours:* Wales Youth, Under-21, 6 full caps.

2000–01	Gillingham	1	0		
2001–02	Gillingham	0	0		
2002–03	Gillingham	0	0		
2003–04	Gillingham	8	0		
2004–05	Gillingham	27	2		
2005–06	Gillingham	45	2		
2006–07	Gillingham	43	8	**124**	**12**

CUMBERS, Luis (M) 1 0
H: 6 0 W: 11 10 b.Chelmsford 6-9-88
Source: Scholar.

2006–07	Gillingham	1	0	**1**	**0**

EASTON, Clint (M) 223 9
H: 5 11 W: 11 00 b.Barking 1-10-77
Source: From Trainee. *Honours:* England Youth.

1996–97	Watford	17	1		
1997–98	Watford	12	0		
1998–99	Watford	7	0		
1999–2000	Watford	17	0		
2000–01	Watford	11	0	**64**	**1**
2001–02	Norwich C	14	1		
2002–03	Norwich C	26	2		
2003–04	Norwich C	10	2	**50**	**5**
2004–05	Wycombe W	33	1		
2005–06	Wycombe W	44	1	**77**	**2**
2006–07	Gillingham	32	1	**32**	**1**

FLYNN, Michael (M) 141 21
H: 5 10 W: 13 04 b.Newport 17-10-80
Source: Barry T.

2002–03	Wigan Ath	17	1		
2003–04	Wigan Ath	8	0		

2004–05	Wigan Ath	13	1	**38**	**2**
2004–05	*Blackpool*	6	0	**6**	**0**
2004–05	Gillingham	16	3		
2005–06	Gillingham	36	6		
2006–07	Gillingham	45	10	**97**	**19**

HOWELL, Luke (D) **1 0**
H: 5 10 W: 10 05 b.Cuckfield 5-1-87
Source: Scholar.

2006–07	Gillingham	1	0	**1**	**0**

JACK, Kelvin (G) **25 0**
H: 6 3 W: 16 00 b.Trinidad 29-4-76
Honours: Holy Cross Coll, Yavapai Coll, Doc's Khelwalaas, W Connection. From San Juan. Trinidad & Tobago Under-23, 33 full caps.

2003–04	Reading	0	0		
2004–05	Dundee	2	0		
2005–06	Dundee	14	0	**16**	**0**
2006–07	Gillingham	9	0	**9**	**0**

JACKMAN, Danny (D) **140 6**
H: 5 4 W: 10 00 b.Worcester 3-1-83
Source: Scholar.

2000–01	Aston Villa	0	0		
2001–02	Aston Villa	0	0		
2001–02	*Cambridge U*	7	1	**7**	**1**
2002–03	Aston Villa	0	0		
2003–04	Aston Villa	0	0		
2003–04	Stockport Co	27	2		
2004–05	Stockport Co	33	2	**60**	**4**
2005–06	Gillingham	42	0		
2006–07	Gillingham	31	1	**73**	**1**

JARVIS, Matthew (M) **110 12**
H: 5 8 W: 11 10 b.Middlesbrough 22-5-86
Source: Scholar.

2003–04	Gillingham	10	0		
2004–05	Gillingham	30	3		
2005–06	Gillingham	35	3		
2006–07	Gillingham	35	6	**110**	**12**

JOHNSON, Leon (M) **146 5**
H: 6 1 W: 13 05 b.Shoreditch 10-5-81
Source: Scholarship.

1999–2000	Southend U	0	0		
2000–01	Southend U	20	1		
2001–02	Southend U	28	2	**48**	**3**
2002–03	Gillingham	18	0		
2003–04	Gillingham	20	0		
2004–05	Gillingham	8	0		
2005–06	Gillingham	28	1		
2006–07	Gillingham	24	1	**98**	**2**

JUPP, Duncan (D) **275 2**
H: 6 0 W: 12 12 b.Guildford 25-1-75
Source: Trainee. *Honours:* Scotland Under-21.

1992–93	Fulham	3	0		
1993–94	Fulham	30	0		
1994–95	Fulham	36	2		
1995–96	Fulham	36	0	**105**	**2**
1996–97	Wimbledon	6	0		
1997–98	Wimbledon	3	0		
1998–99	Wimbledon	6	0		
1999–2000	Wimbledon	9	0		
2000–01	Wimbledon	4	0		
2001–02	Wimbledon	2	0		
2002–03	Wimbledon	0	0	**30**	**0**
2002–03	*Notts Co*	8	0	**8**	**0**
2002–03	Luton T	5	0	**5**	**0**
2003–04	Southend U	40	0		
2004–05	Southend U	31	0		
2005–06	Southend U	29	0	**100**	**0**
2006–07	Gillingham	27	0	**27**	**0**

McDONALD, Dean (F) **45 8**
H: 5 7 W: 11 00 b.Lambeth 19-2-86

2004–05	Ipswich T	0	0		
2005–06	Ipswich T	14	1	**14**	**1**
2005–06	*Hartlepool U*	5	1	**5**	**1**
2006–07	Gillingham	26	6	**26**	**6**

MULLIGAN, Gary (M) **75 12**
H: 6 1 W: 12 03 b.Dublin 23-4-85
Source: Scholar.

2002–03	Wolverhampton W	0	0		
2003–04	Wolverhampton W	0	0		
2004–05	Wolverhampton W	1	0	**1**	**0**
2004–05	*Rushden & D*	13	3	**13**	**3**
2005–06	Sheffield U	0	0		
2005–06	*Port Vale*	10	1	**10**	**1**
2005–06	*Gillingham*	13	1		
2006–07	Gillingham	38	7	**51**	**8**

N'DUMBU NSUNGU, Guylain (F) **113 24**
H: 6 1 W: 12 08 b.Kinshasa 26-12-82
Source: Amiens. *Honours:* DR Congo Under-21, full caps.

2003–04	Sheffield W	24	9		
2004–05	Sheffield W	11	1	**35**	**10**
2004–05	*Preston NE*	6	0	**6**	**0**
2004–05	Colchester U	8	1	**8**	**1**
2005–06	Darlington	21	10	**21**	**10**
2005–06	Cardiff C	11	0	**11**	**0**
2006–07	Gillingham	32	3	**32**	**3**

POUTON, Alan (M) **278 22**
H: 6 2 W: 13 09 b.Newcastle 1-2-77
Source: Newcastle U Trainee.

1995–96	Oxford U	0	0		
1995–96	York C	0	0		
1996–97	York C	22	1		
1997–98	York C	41	5		
1998–99	York C	27	1		
1999–2000	York C	0	0	**90**	**7**
1999–2000	Grimsby T	35	1		
2000–01	Grimsby T	21	1		
2001–02	Grimsby T	35	5		
2002–03	Grimsby T	25	5		
2003–04	Grimsby T	5	0	**121**	**12**
2003–04	Gillingham	19	0		
2004–05	Gillingham	12	0		
2004–05	*Hartlepool U*	5	0	**5**	**0**
2005–06	Gillingham	23	2		
2006–07	Gillingham	8	1	**62**	**3**

PUGH, Andy (F) **3 0**
H: 5 9 W: 12 05 b.Gravesend 28-1-89
Source: Scholar.

2006–07	Gillingham	3	0	**3**	**0**

SANCHO, Brent (D) **93 4**
H: 6 1 W: 14 01 b.Belmont 13-3-77
Source: From Portland T. *Honours:* Trinidad & Tobago 43 full caps.

2003–04	Dundee	21	0		
2004–05	Dundee	27	2	**48**	**2**
2005–06	Gillingham	19	2		
2006–07	Gillingham	26	0	**45**	**2**

SOUTHALL, Nicky (M) **565 62**
H: 5 11 W: 12 04 b.Stockton 28-1-72
Source: Trainee.

1990–91	Hartlepool U	0	0		
1991–92	Hartlepool U	22	3		
1992–93	Hartlepool U	39	6		
1993–94	Hartlepool U	40	9		
1994–95	Hartlepool U	37	6	**138**	**24**
1995–96	Grimsby T	33	2		
1996–97	Grimsby T	34	3		
1997–98	Grimsby T	5	0	**72**	**5**
1997–98	Gillingham	23	2		
1998–99	Gillingham	42	4		
1999–2000	Gillingham	45	9		
2000–01	Gillingham	44	2		
2001–02	Bolton W	18	1		
2002–03	Bolton W	0	0	**18**	**1**
2002–03	*Norwich C*	9	0	**9**	**0**
2002–03	Gillingham	24	1		
2003–04	Gillingham	35	0		
2004–05	Gillingham	33	1		
2005–06	Nottingham F	40	8		
2006–07	Nottingham F	27	5	**67**	**13**
2006–07	Gillingham	15	0	**261**	**19**

SPILLER, Danny (M) **129 6**
H: 5 8 W: 11 00 b.Maidstone 10-10-81
Source: Trainee.

2000–01	Gillingham	0	0		
2001–02	Gillingham	1	0		
2002–03	Gillingham	10	0		
2003–04	Gillingham	39	6		
2004–05	Gillingham	22	0		
2005–06	Gillingham	32	0		
2006–07	Gillingham	25	0	**129**	**6**

STONE, Craig (M) **6 0**
H: 6 0 W: 10 05 b.Rochester 29-12-88
Source: Scholar.

2005–06	Gillingham	3	0		
2006–07	Gillingham	3	0	**6**	**0**

GRIMSBY T (36)

BARNES, Phil (G) **196 0**
H: 6 1 W: 11 01 b.Sheffield 2-3-79
Source: Trainee.

1996–97	Rotherham U	2	0	**2**	**0**
1997–98	Blackpool	1	0		
1998–99	Blackpool	1	0		
1999–2000	Blackpool	12	0		
2000–01	Blackpool	34	0		
2001–02	Blackpool	30	0		
2002–03	Blackpool	44	0		
2003–04	Blackpool	19	0	**141**	**0**
2004–05	Sheffield U	1	0		
2004–05	*Torquay U*	5	0	**5**	**0**
2005–06	Sheffield U	0	0	**1**	**0**
2005–06	*QPR*	1	0	**1**	**0**
2006–07	Grimsby T	46	0	**46**	**0**

BEAGRIE, Peter (M) **670 90**
H: 5 8 W: 12 04 b.Middlesbrough 28-11-65
Source: Local. *Honours:* England Under-21, B.

1983–84	Middlesbrough	0	0		
1984–85	Middlesbrough	7	1		
1985–86	Middlesbrough	26	1	**33**	**2**
1986–87	Sheffield U	41	9		
1987–88	Sheffield U	43	2	**84**	**11**
1988–89	Stoke C	41	7		
1989–90	Stoke C	13	0	**54**	**7**
1989–90	Everton	19	0		
1990–91	Everton	17	2		
1991–92	Everton	27	3		
1991–92	*Sunderland*	5	1	**5**	**1**
1992–93	Everton	22	3		
1993–94	Everton	29	3		
1993–94	Manchester C	9	1		
1994–95	Manchester C	37	2		
1995–96	Manchester C	5	0		
1996–97	Manchester C	1	0	**52**	**3**
1997–98	Bradford C	34	0		
1997–98	*Everton*	6	0	**120**	**11**
1998–99	Bradford C	43	12		
1999–2000	Bradford C	35	7		
2000–01	Bradford C	19	1	**131**	**20**
2000–01	Wigan Ath	10	1	**10**	**1**
2001–02	Scunthorpe U	40	11		
2002–03	Scunthorpe U	34	5		
2003–04	Scunthorpe U	32	11		
2004–05	Scunthorpe U	36	2		
2005–06	Scunthorpe U	30	5	**172**	**34**
2006–07	Grimsby T	9	0	**9**	**0**

BENNETT, Ryan (M) **5 0**
H: 6 2 W: 11 00 b.Orsett 6-3-90
Source: Scholar.

2006–07	Grimsby T	5	0	**5**	**0**

BLOOMER, Matt (D) **121 3**
H: 6 1 W: 13 00 b.Cleethorpes 3-11-78
Source: Trainee.

1997–98	Grimsby T	0	0		
1998–99	Grimsby T	4	0		
1999–2000	Grimsby T	2	0		
2000–01	Grimsby T	6	0		
2001–02	Grimsby T	0	0		
2001–02	Hull C	3	0		
2001–02	*Lincoln C*	5	0		
2002–03	Hull C	0	0	**3**	**0**
2002–03	Lincoln C	13	1		
2003–04	Lincoln C	27	0		
2004–05	Lincoln C	37	2		
2005–06	Lincoln C	12	0		
2005–06	*Grimsby T*	3	0		
2006–07	Lincoln C	0	0	**94**	**3**
2006–07	Grimsby T	9	0	**24**	**0**

BOLLAND, Paul (M) **267 15**
H: 5 10 W: 10 12 b.Bradford 23-12-79
Source: Trainee.

1997–98	Bradford C	10	0		
1998–99	Bradford C	2	0	**12**	**0**

1998–99 Notts Co 13 0
1999–2000 Notts Co 25 1
2000–01 Notts Co 7 0
2001–02 Notts Co 19 0
2002–03 Notts Co 29 3
2003–04 Notts Co 39 1
2004–05 Notts Co 40 1 **172 6**
2005–06 Grimsby T 44 4
2006–07 Grimsby T 39 5 **83 9**

BORE, Peter (M) 32 8
H: 5 11 W: 11 04 b.Grimsby 4-11-87
2006–07 Grimsby T 32 8 **32 8**

BOSHELL, Danny (M) 138 5
H: 5 11 W: 11 09 b.Bradford 30-5-81
Source: Trainee.
1998–99 Oldham Ath 0 0
1999–2000 Oldham Ath 8 0
2000–01 Oldham Ath 18 1
2001–02 Oldham Ath 4 0
2002–03 Oldham Ath 2 0
2003–04 Oldham Ath 22 0
2004–05 Oldham Ath 16 1 **70 2**
2004–05 *Bury* 6 0 **6 0**
2005–06 Stockport Co 33 1 **33 1**
2006–07 Grimsby T 29 2 **29 2**

COHEN, Gary (F) 66 6
H: 5 11 W: 11 02 b.Leyton 20-1-84
Source: Academy.
2002–03 Watford 0 0
From Scarborough
2003–04 Gretna 26 0
2004–05 Gretna 0 0 **26 0**
2005–06 Grimsby T 40 6
2006–07 Grimsby T 0 0 **40 6**

CROFT, Gary (D) 363 8
H: 5 9 W: 11 08 b.Burton-on-Trent 17-2-74
Source: Trainee. *Honours:* England Under-21.
1990–91 Grimsby T 1 0
1991–92 Grimsby T 0 0
1992–93 Grimsby T 32 0
1993–94 Grimsby T 36 1
1994–95 Grimsby T 44 1
1995–96 Grimsby T 36 1
1995–96 Blackburn R 0 0
1996–97 Blackburn R 5 0
1997–98 Blackburn R 23 1
1998–99 Blackburn R 12 0
1999–2000 Blackburn R 0 0 **40 1**
1999–2000 Ipswich T 21 1
2000–01 Ipswich T 8 0
2001–02 Ipswich T 0 0 **29 1**
2001–02 *Wigan Ath* 7 0 **7 0**
2001–02 *Cardiff C* 6 1
2002–03 Cardiff C 43 1
2003–04 Cardiff C 27 1
2004–05 Cardiff C 1 0 **77 3**
2005–06 Grimsby T 33 0
2006–07 Grimsby T 28 0 **210 3**

FENTON, Nick (D) 297 17
H: 6 0 W: 10 02 b.Preston 23-11-79
Source: Trainee. *Honours:* England Youth.
1996–97 Manchester C 0 0
1997–98 Manchester C 0 0
1998–99 Manchester C 15 0
1999–2000 Manchester C 0 0
1999–2000 *Notts Co* 13 1
1999–2000 *Bournemouth* 8 0
2000–01 Manchester C 0 0 **15 0**
2000–01 *Bournemouth* 5 0 **13 0**
2000–01 Notts Co 30 2
2001–02 Notts Co 42 3
2002–03 Notts Co 40 3
2003–04 Notts Co 43 1 **168 10**
2004–05 Doncaster R 38 1
2005–06 Doncaster R 25 2
2006–07 Doncaster R 0 0 **63 3**
2006–07 Grimsby T 38 4 **38 4**

GRAND, Simon (D) 59 4
H: 6 0 W: 10 03 b.Chorley 23-2-84
Source: Scholar.
2002–03 Rochdale 23 2
2003–04 Rochdale 17 0 **40 2**
2004–05 Carlisle U 0 0
2005–06 Carlisle U 8 2
2006–07 Carlisle U 4 0 **12 2**
2006–07 Grimsby T 7 0 **7 0**

HARKINS, Gary (M) 29 1
H: 6 2 W: 12 10 b.Greenock 2-1-85
Source: Trainee.
2003–04 Blackburn R 0 0
2003–04 *Huddersfield T* 3 0 **3 0**
2004–05 Blackburn R 0 0
2004–05 *Bury* 5 0 **5 0**
2005–06 Blackburn R 0 0
2005–06 *Blackpool* 4 1 **4 1**
2006–07 Grimsby T 17 0 **17 0**

HEGARTY, Nick (M) 18 0
H: 5 10 W: 11 00 b.Hemsworth 25-6-86
Source: Scholar.
2004–05 Grimsby T 1 0
2005–06 Grimsby T 2 0
2006–07 Grimsby T 15 0 **18 0**

JONES, Gary (M) 385 67
H: 6 3 W: 15 02 b.Chester 10-5-75
Source: Trainee.
1993–94 Tranmere R 6 2
1994–95 Tranmere R 19 3
1995–96 Tranmere R 23 1
1996–97 Tranmere R 30 6
1997–98 Tranmere R 43 8
1998–99 Tranmere R 26 5
1999–2000 Tranmere R 31 3
2000–01 Nottingham F 31 1
2001–02 Nottingham F 5 1
2002–03 Nottingham F 0 0 **36 2**
2002–03 Tranmere R 40 6
2003–04 Tranmere R 42 9
2004–05 Tranmere R 10 1 **270 44**
2005–06 Grimsby T 40 13
2006–07 Grimsby T 39 8 **79 21**

McDERMOTT, John (D) 647 11
H: 5 7 W: 10 00 b.Middlesbrough 3-2-69
Source: Trainee.
1986–87 Grimsby T 13 0
1987–88 Grimsby T 28 1
1988–89 Grimsby T 38 1
1989–90 Grimsby T 39 0
1990–91 Grimsby T 43 0
1991–92 Grimsby T 39 1
1992–93 Grimsby T 38 2
1993–94 Grimsby T 26 0
1994–95 Grimsby T 12 0
1995–96 Grimsby T 28 1
1996–97 Grimsby T 29 1
1997–98 Grimsby T 41 1
1998–99 Grimsby T 37 0
1999–2000 Grimsby T 26 0
2000–01 Grimsby T 36 0
2001–02 Grimsby T 24 0
2002–03 Grimsby T 35 0
2003–04 Grimsby T 21 0
2004–05 Grimsby T 39 2
2005–06 Grimsby T 32 1
2006–07 Grimsby T 23 0 **647 11**

MURRAY, Robert (M) 0 0
H: 5 8 W: 9 00 b.Leamington Spa 11-7-88
Source: Scholar.
2004–05 Grimsby T 0 0
2005–06 Grimsby T 0 0
2006–07 Grimsby T 0 0

NEWEY, Tom (D) 164 6
H: 5 10 W: 10 02 b.Sheffield 31-10-82
Source: Scholar.
2000–01 Leeds U 0 0
2001–02 Leeds U 0 0
2002–03 Leeds U 0 0
2002–03 *Cambridge U* 6 0
2002–03 *Darlington* 7 1 **7 1**
2003–04 Leyton Orient 34 2
2004–05 Leyton Orient 20 1 **54 3**
2004–05 *Cambridge U* 16 0 **22 0**
2005–06 Grimsby T 38 1
2006–07 Grimsby T 43 1 **81 2**

NORTH, Danny (F) 22 6
H: 5 9 W: 12 08 b.Grimsby 7-9-87
Source: Scholar.
2004–05 Grimsby T 1 0
2005–06 Grimsby T 1 0
2006–07 Grimsby T 20 6 **22 6**

RANKIN, Isiah (F) 239 44
H: 5 10 W: 11 00 b.London 22-5-78
Source: Trainee.
1995–96 Arsenal 0 0
1996–97 Arsenal 0 0
1997–98 Arsenal 1 0 **1 0**
1997–98 *Colchester U* 11 5 **11 5**
1998–99 Bradford C 27 4
1999–2000 Bradford C 9 0
1999–2000 *Birmingham C* 13 4 **13 4**
2000–01 Bradford C 1 0 **37 4**
2000–01 *Bolton W* 16 2 **16 2**
2000–01 Barnsley 9 1
2001–02 Barnsley 9 1
2002–03 Barnsley 9 1
2003–04 Barnsley 20 5 **47 8**
2003–04 Grimsby T 12 4
2004–05 Brentford 41 8
2005–06 Brentford 37 7 **78 15**
2006–07 Grimsby T 20 2 **32 6**
2006–07 *Macclesfield T* 4 0 **4 0**

REDDY, Michael (F) 165 37
H: 6 1 W: 11 07 b.Kilkenny City 24-3-80
Source: Kilkenny C. *Honours:* Eire Under-21.
1999–2000 Sunderland 8 1
2000–01 Sunderland 2 0
2000–01 *Swindon T* 18 4 **18 4**
2001–02 Sunderland 0 0
2001–02 *Hull C* 5 4 **5 4**
2001–02 *Barnsley* 0 0
2002–03 Sunderland 0 0
2002–03 *York C* 11 2 **11 2**
2002–03 *Sheffield W* 15 3
2003–04 Sunderland 0 0 **10 1**
2003–04 *Sheffield W* 12 1 **27 4**
2004–05 Grimsby T 40 9
2005–06 Grimsby T 44 13
2006–07 Grimsby T 10 0 **94 22**

TAYLOR, Andy (F) 11 2
H: 6 2 W: 13 00 b.Caistor 30-10-88
Source: Scholar.
2005–06 Grimsby T 0 0
2006–07 Grimsby T 11 2 **11 2**

THORPE, Tony (F) 384 136
H: 5 9 W: 12 06 b.Leicester 10-4-74
Source: Leicester C.
1992–93 Luton T 0 0
1993–94 Luton T 14 1
1994–95 Luton T 4 0
1995–96 Luton T 33 7
1996–97 Luton T 41 28
1997–98 Luton T 28 14
1997–98 Fulham 13 3 **13 3**
1998–99 Bristol C 16 2
1998–99 *Reading* 6 1 **6 1**
1998–99 *Luton T* 8 4
1999–2000 Bristol C 31 13
1999–2000 *Luton T* 4 1
2000–01 Bristol C 39 19
2001–02 Bristol C 42 16 **128 50**
2002–03 Luton T 30 13
2003–04 Luton T 2 2 **164 70**
2003–04 QPR 31 10
2004–05 QPR 10 0 **41 10**
2004–05 *Rotherham U* 5 1 **5 1**
2005–06 Swindon T 7 1 **7 1**
2005–06 Colchester U 14 0 **14 0**
From Stevenage B.
2006–07 Grimsby T 6 0 **6 0**

TILL, Peter (M) 50 1
H: 5 11 W: 11 04 b.Walsall 7-9-85
Source: Scholar.
2005–06 Birmingham C 0 0
2005–06 *Scunthorpe U* 8 0 **8 0**
2005–06 *Boston U* 16 1 **16 1**
2006–07 Birmingham C 0 0
2006–07 *Leyton Orient* 4 0 **4 0**
2006–07 Grimsby T 22 0 **22 0**

TONER, Ciaran (M) 151 15
H: 6 1 W: 12 02 b.Craigavon 30-6-81
Source: Trainee. *Honours:* Northern Ireland Under-21, 2 full caps.

1999–2000	Tottenham H	0	0		
2000–01	Tottenham H	0	0		
2001–02	Tottenham H	0	0		
2001–02	*Peterborough U*	6	0	**6**	**0**
2001–02	Bristol R	6	0	**6**	**0**
2001–02	Leyton Orient	0	0		
2002–03	Leyton Orient	25	1		
2003–04	Leyton Orient	27	1	**52**	**2**
2004–05	Lincoln C	15	2	**15**	**2**
2004–05	*Cambridge U*	8	0	**8**	**0**
2005–06	Grimsby T	31	3		
2006–07	Grimsby T	33	8	**64**	**11**

WHITTLE, Justin (D) 381 5
H: 6 1 W: 12 12 b.Derby 18-3-71
Source: Celtic.

1994–95	Stoke C	0	0		
1995–96	Stoke C	8	0		
1996–97	Stoke C	37	0		
1997–98	Stoke C	20	0		
1998–99	Stoke C	14	1	**79**	**1**
1998–99	Hull C	24	1		
1999–2000	Hull C	38	0		
2000–01	Hull C	38	0		
2001–02	Hull C	36	0		
2002–03	Hull C	39	1		
2003–04	Hull C	18	0	**193**	**2**
2004–05	Grimsby T	40	1		
2005–06	Grimsby T	32	0		
2006–07	Grimsby T	37	1	**109**	**2**

WOODHOUSE, Curtis (M) 258 20
H: 5 8 W: 11 00 b.Driffield 17-4-80
Source: Trainee. *Honours:* England Youth, Under-21.

1997–98	Sheffield U	9	0		
1998–99	Sheffield U	33	3		
1999–2000	Sheffield U	37	3		
2000–01	Sheffield U	25	0	**104**	**6**
2000–01	Birmingham C	17	2		
2001–02	Birmingham C	28	0		
2002–03	Birmingham C	3	0		
2002–03	*Rotherham U*	11	0	**11**	**0**
2003–04	Birmingham C	0	0	**48**	**2**
2003–04	Peterborough U	27	7		
2004–05	Peterborough U	34	4	**61**	**11**
2005–06	Hull C	18	0	**18**	**0**
2005–06	Grimsby T	16	1		
2006–07	Grimsby T	0	0	**16**	**1**

HARTLEPOOL U (37)

BARKER, Richard (F) 377 96
H: 6 0 W: 14 03 b.Sheffield 30-5-75
Source: Trainee. *Honours:* England Schools.

1993–94	Sheffield W	0	0		
1994–95	Sheffield W	0	0		
1995–96	Sheffield W	0	0		
1995–96	*Doncaster R*	6	0	**6**	**0**
1996–97	Sheffield W	0	0		
From Linfield					
1997–98	Brighton & HA	17	2		
1998–99	Brighton & HA	43	10	**60**	**12**
1999–2000	Macclesfield T	35	16		
2000–01	Macclesfield T	23	7	**58**	**23**
2000–01	Rotherham U	19	1		
2001–02	Rotherham U	35	3		
2002–03	Rotherham U	37	7		
2003–04	Rotherham U	32	1		
2004–05	Rotherham U	17	0	**140**	**12**
2004–05	Mansfield T	28	10		
2005–06	Mansfield T	43	18		
2006–07	Mansfield T	24	12	**95**	**40**
2006–07	Hartlepool U	18	9	**18**	**9**

BARRON, Micky (D) 328 3
H: 5 11 W: 11 10 b.Chester-le-Street 22-12-74
Source: Trainee.

1992–93	Middlesbrough	0	0		
1993–94	Middlesbrough	2	0		
1994–95	Middlesbrough	0	0		
1995–96	Middlesbrough	1	0		
1996–97	Middlesbrough	0	0	**3**	**0**
1996–97	*Hartlepool U*	16	0		
1997–98	Hartlepool U	33	0		
1998–99	Hartlepool U	38	1		
1999–2000	Hartlepool U	40	0		
2000–01	Hartlepool U	28	0		
2001–02	Hartlepool U	39	1		
2002–03	Hartlepool U	42	0		
2003–04	Hartlepool U	32	1		
2004–05	Hartlepool U	13	0		
2005–06	Hartlepool U	15	0		
2006–07	Hartlepool U	29	0	**325**	**3**

BOLAND, Willie (M) 299 3
H: 5 9 W: 12 04 b.Ennis 6-8-75
Source: Trainee. *Honours:* Eire Youth, B, Under-21.

1992–93	Coventry C	1	0		
1993–94	Coventry C	27	0		
1994–95	Coventry C	12	0		
1995–96	Coventry C	3	0		
1996–97	Coventry C	1	0		
1997–98	Coventry C	19	0		
1998–99	Coventry C	0	0	**63**	**0**
1999–2000	Cardiff C	28	1		
2000–01	Cardiff C	25	1		
2001–02	Cardiff C	42	1		
2002–03	Cardiff C	41	0		
2003–04	Cardiff C	37	0		
2004–05	Cardiff C	21	0		
2005–06	Cardiff C	15	0	**209**	**3**
2006–07	Hartlepool U	27	0	**27**	**0**

BRACKSTONE, John (D) 25 0
H: 6 0 W: 11 06 b.Hartlepool 9-2-85
Source: Scholar.

2003–04	Hartlepool U	6	0		
2004–05	Hartlepool U	9	0		
2005–06	Hartlepool U	2	0		
2006–07	Hartlepool U	8	0	**25**	**0**

BROWN, James (F) 40 7
H: 5 11 W: 11 00 b.Newcastle 3-1-87
Source: Cramlington Jun.

2004–05	Hartlepool U	0	0		
2005–06	Hartlepool U	4	1		
2006–07	Hartlepool U	36	6	**40**	**7**

BULLOCK, Lee (M) 259 35
H: 6 0 W: 11 04 b.Stockton 22-5-81
Source: Trainee.

1999–2000	York C	24	0		
2000–01	York C	33	3		
2001–02	York C	40	8		
2002–03	York C	39	6		
2003–04	York C	35	7	**171**	**24**
2003–04	*Cardiff C*	11	3		
2004–05	Cardiff C	21	3	**32**	**6**
2005–06	Hartlepool U	31	4		
2006–07	Hartlepool U	25	1	**56**	**5**

CLARK, Ben (D) 105 3
H: 6 1 W: 13 11 b.Shotley Bridge 24-1-83
Source: Manchester U Trainee. *Honours:* England Youth, Under-20.

2000–01	Sunderland	0	0		
2001–02	Sunderland	0	0		
2002–03	Sunderland	1	0		
2003–04	Sunderland	5	0		
2004–05	Sunderland	2	0	**8**	**0**
2004–05	Hartlepool U	25	0		
2005–06	Hartlepool U	32	0		
2006–07	Hartlepool U	40	3	**97**	**3**

CLARKE, Darrell (M) 298 44
H: 5 10 W: 11 05 b.Mansfield 16-12-77
Source: Trainee.

1995–96	Mansfield T	3	0		
1996–97	Mansfield T	19	2		
1997–98	Mansfield T	35	4		
1998–99	Mansfield T	33	5		
1999–2000	Mansfield T	39	7		
2000–01	Mansfield T	32	6	**161**	**24**
2001–02	Hartlepool U	33	7		
2002–03	Hartlepool U	45	7		
2003–04	Hartlepool U	33	5		
2004–05	Hartlepool U	0	0		
2004–05	*Stockport Co*	1	0	**1**	**0**
2005–06	Hartlepool U	12	0		
2005–06	*Port Vale*	1	0	**1**	**0**
2006–07	Hartlepool U	0	0	**123**	**19**
2006–07	*Rochdale*	12	1	**12**	**1**

DALY, Jon (F) 173 30
H: 6 3 W: 12 00 b.Dublin 8-1-83
Source: Trainee. *Honours:* Eire Under-21.

1999–2000	Stockport Co	4	0		
2000–01	Stockport Co	0	0		
2001–02	Stockport Co	13	1		
2002–03	Stockport Co	35	7		
2003–04	Stockport Co	25	3		
2003–04	*Bury*	7	1		
2004–05	Stockport Co	14	3	**91**	**14**
2004–05	*Grimsby T*	3	1	**3**	**1**
2004–05	Hartlepool U	12	1		
2005–06	Hartlepool U	30	2		
2005–06	*Bury*	11	2	**18**	**3**
2006–07	Hartlepool U	19	9	**61**	**12**

To Dundee U January 2007

DAVISON, Tony (G) 0 0
H: 6 0 W: 12 07 b.Gateshead 1-12-87
Source: Scholar.

2006–07	Hartlepool U	0	0		

FOLEY, David (F) 39 0
H: 5 4 W: 8 09 b.South Shields 12-5-87
Source: Scholar.

2003–04	Hartlepool U	1	0		
2004–05	Hartlepool U	2	0		
2005–06	Hartlepool U	11	0		
2006–07	Hartlepool U	25	0	**39**	**0**

GIBB, Ali (M) 385 6
H: 5 9 W: 11 07 b.Salisbury 17-2-76
Source: Trainee.

1994–95	Norwich C	0	0		
1995–96	Norwich C	0	0		
1995–96	Northampton T	23	2		
1996–97	Northampton T	18	1		
1997–98	Northampton T	35	1		
1998–99	Northampton T	41	0		
1999–2000	Northampton T	14	0	**131**	**4**
1999–2000	Stockport Co	14	0		
2000–01	Stockport Co	39	0		
2001–02	Stockport Co	41	0		
2002–03	Stockport Co	45	1		
2003–04	Stockport Co	26	0	**165**	**1**
2003–04	Bristol R	8	1		
2004–05	Bristol R	23	0		
2005–06	Bristol R	33	0	**64**	**1**
2006–07	Hartlepool U	25	0	**25**	**0**

HIGNETT, Craig (M) 478 125
H: 5 9 W: 12 06 b.Whiston 12-1-70
Source: Liverpool Trainee.

1987–88	Crewe Alex	0	0		
1988–89	Crewe Alex	1	0		
1989–90	Crewe Alex	35	8		
1990–91	Crewe Alex	38	13		
1991–92	Crewe Alex	33	13		
1992–93	Crewe Alex	14	8		
1992–93	Middlesbrough	21	4		
1993–94	Middlesbrough	29	5		
1994–95	Middlesbrough	26	8		
1995–96	Middlesbrough	22	5		
1996–97	Middlesbrough	22	4		
1997–98	Middlesbrough	36	7	**156**	**33**
1998–99	Aberdeen	13	2	**13**	**2**
1998–99	Barnsley	24	9		
1999–2000	Barnsley	42	19	**66**	**28**
2000–01	Blackburn R	30	3		
2001–02	Blackburn R	20	4		
2002–03	Blackburn R	3	1	**53**	**8**
2002–03	*Coventry C*	8	2	**8**	**2**
2003–04	Leicester C	13	1	**13**	**1**
2003–04	*Crewe Alex*	15	0	**136**	**42**
2004–05	Leeds U	0	0		
2004–05	Darlington	19	9	**19**	**9**
2005–06	Apollon	12	0	**12**	**0**
2006–07	Hartlepool U	2	0	**2**	**0**

HUMPHREYS, Richie (M) 364 38
H: 5 11 W: 12 07 b.Sheffield 30-11-77
Source: Trainee. *Honours:* England Youth, Under-21.

1995–96	Sheffield W	5	0		
1996–97	Sheffield W	29	3		
1997–98	Sheffield W	7	0		

1998–99	Sheffield W	19	1		
1999–2000	Sheffield W	0	0		
1999–2000	*Scunthorpe U*	6	2	**6**	**2**
1999–2000	*Cardiff C*	9	2	**9**	**2**
2000–01	Sheffield W	7	0	**67**	**4**
2000–01	Cambridge U	7	3	**7**	**3**
2001–02	Hartlepool U	46	5		
2002–03	Hartlepool U	46	11		
2003–04	Hartlepool U	46	3		
2004–05	Hartlepool U	46	3		
2005–06	Hartlepool U	46	2		
2006–07	Hartlepool U	38	3	**268**	**27**
2006–07	*Port Vale*	7	0	**7**	**0**

JONES, Carl (D) 1 0
H: 6 1 W: 12 02 b.Sunderland 3-9-86
Source: Chester-Le-Street.

2005–06	Hartlepool U	1	0		
2006–07	Hartlepool U	0	0	**1**	**0**

KONSTANTOPOULOS, Dimitrios (G) 117 0
H: 6 4 W: 14 02 b.Kalamata 29-11-78
Source: Farense. *Honours:* Greece Under-21.

2003–04	Hartlepool U	0	0		
2004–05	Hartlepool U	25	0		
2005–06	Hartlepool U	46	0		
2006–07	Hartlepool U	46	0	**117**	**0**

LIDDLE, Gary (D) 42 3
H: 6 1 W: 12 06 b.Middlesbrough 15-6-86
Source: Trainee. *Honours:* England Youth.

2003–04	Middlesbrough	0	0		
2004–05	Middlesbrough	0	0		
2005–06	Middlesbrough	0	0		
2006–07	Hartlepool U	42	3	**42**	**3**

MACKAY, Michael (F) 1 0
H: 6 0 W: 11 06 b.Durham 11-10-82
Source: Consett.

2006–07	Hartlepool U	1	0	**1**	**0**

MAIDENS, Michael (M) 25 1
H: 5 11 W: 11 04 b.Middlesbrough 7-5-87
Source: Scholar.

2004–05	Hartlepool U	1	0		
2005–06	Hartlepool U	20	1		
2006–07	Hartlepool U	4	0	**25**	**1**

MONKHOUSE, Andy (M) 164 18
H: 6 1 W: 11 06 b.Leeds 23-10-80
Source: Trainee.

1998–99	Rotherham U	5	1		
1999–2000	Rotherham U	0	0		
2000–01	Rotherham U	12	0		
2001–02	Rotherham U	38	2		
2002–03	Rotherham U	20	0		
2003–04	Rotherham U	27	3		
2004–05	Rotherham U	14	2		
2005–06	Rotherham U	12	1	**128**	**9**
2006–07	Swindon T	10	2	**10**	**2**
2006–07	Hartlepool U	26	7	**26**	**7**

NELSON, Michael (D) 240 15
H: 6 2 W: 13 03 b.Gateshead 15-3-82

2000–01	Bury	2	1		
2001–02	Bury	31	2		
2002–03	Bury	39	5	**72**	**8**
2003–04	Hartlepool U	40	3		
2004–05	Hartlepool U	43	1		
2005–06	Hartlepool U	43	2		
2006–07	Hartlepool U	42	1	**168**	**7**

PORTER, Joel (F) 204 60
H: 5 9 W: 11 13 b.Adelaide 25-12-78
Honours: Australia 4 full caps, 5 goals.

1998–99	West Adelaide	20	3	**20**	**3**
2000–01	Melbrne Knights	30	12		
2001–02	Melbrne Knights	26	12	**56**	**24**
2002–03	Sydney Olympic	32	8	**32**	**8**
2003–04	Hartlepool U	27	3		
2004–05	Hartlepool U	39	14		
2005–06	Hartlepool U	8	3		
2006–07	Hartlepool U	22	5	**96**	**25**

PROCTOR, Michael (F) 189 41
H: 5 11 W: 11 11 b.Sunderland 3-10-80
Source: Trainee.

1997–98	Sunderland	0	0		
1998–99	Sunderland	0	0		
1999–2000	Sunderland	0	0		
2000–01	Sunderland	0	0		
2000–01	*Halifax T*	12	4	**12**	**4**
2001–02	Sunderland	0	0		
2001–02	*York C*	41	14	**41**	**14**
2002–03	Sunderland	21	2		
2002–03	*Bradford C*	12	4	**12**	**4**
2003–04	Sunderland	17	1	**38**	**3**
2003–04	Rotherham U	17	6		
2004–05	Rotherham U	28	1	**45**	**7**
2004–05	*Swindon T*	4	2	**4**	**2**
2005–06	Hartlepool U	26	5		
2006–07	Hartlepool U	2	0	**28**	**5**
2006–07	*Wrexham*	9	2	**9**	**2**

PROVETT, Jim (G) 66 0
H: 6 0 W: 13 04 b.Stockton 22-12-82
Source: Trainee.

1999–2000	Hartlepool U	0	0		
2000–01	Hartlepool U	0	0		
2001–02	Hartlepool U	0	0		
2002–03	Hartlepool U	0	0		
2003–04	Hartlepool U	45	0		
2004–05	Hartlepool U	21	0		
2005–06	Hartlepool U	0	0		
2006–07	Hartlepool U	0	0	**66**	**0**

RAE, Michael (F) 0 0
H: 5 10 W: 12 04 b.North Cleveland 23-10-87
Source: Scholar.

2006–07	Hartlepool U	0	0		

ROBSON, Matty (D) 89 6
H: 5 10 W: 11 02 b.Durham 23-1-85
Source: Scholar.

2002–03	Hartlepool U	0	0		
2003–04	Hartlepool U	23	1		
2004–05	Hartlepool U	27	2		
2005–06	Hartlepool U	19	1		
2006–07	Hartlepool U	20	2	**89**	**6**

SWEENEY, Anthony (M) 131 23
H: 6 0 W: 11 07 b.Stockton 5-9-83
Source: Scholar.

2001–02	Hartlepool U	2	0		
2002–03	Hartlepool U	4	0		
2003–04	Hartlepool U	11	1		
2004–05	Hartlepool U	44	13		
2005–06	Hartlepool U	35	5		
2006–07	Hartlepool U	35	4	**131**	**23**

TINKLER, Mark (M) 382 43
H: 6 2 W: 12 00 b.Bishop Auckland 24-10-74
Source: Trainee. *Honours:* England Schools, Youth.

1991–92	Leeds U	0	0		
1992–93	Leeds U	7	0		
1993–94	Leeds U	3	0		
1994–95	Leeds U	3	0		
1995–96	Leeds U	9	0		
1996–97	Leeds U	3	0	**25**	**0**
1996–97	York C	9	1		
1997–98	York C	44	5		
1998–99	York C	37	2		
1999–2000	York C	0	0	**90**	**8**
1999–2000	Southend U	41	0		
2000–01	Southend U	15	1	**56**	**1**
2000–01	Hartlepool U	28	3		
2001–02	Hartlepool U	40	9		
2002–03	Hartlepool U	45	13		
2003–04	Hartlepool U	44	6		
2004–05	Hartlepool U	33	2		
2005–06	Hartlepool U	15	1		
2006–07	Hartlepool U	6	0	**211**	**34**

TURNBULL, Philip (M) 0 0
H: 5 11 W: 11 08 b.South Shields 7-1-87
Source: Scholar.

2006–07	Hartlepool U	0	0		

TURNBULL, Stephen (M) 32 0
H: 5 10 W: 11 00 b.South Shields 7-1-87
Source: Scholar.

2004–05	Hartlepool U	2	0		
2005–06	Hartlepool U	21	0		
2006–07	Hartlepool U	0	0	**23**	**0**
2006–07	*Bury*	5	0	**5**	**0**
2006–07	*Rochdale*	4	0	**4**	**0**

WILLIAMS, Darren (D) 304 4
H: 5 11 W: 11 00 b.Middlesbrough 28-4-77
Source: Trainee. *Honours:* England Under-21, B.

1994–95	York C	1	0		
1995–96	York C	18	0		
1996–97	York C	1	0	**20**	**0**
1996–97	Sunderland	11	2		
1997–98	Sunderland	36	2		
1998–99	Sunderland	25	0		
1999–2000	Sunderland	25	0		
2000–01	Sunderland	28	0		
2001–02	Sunderland	28	0		
2002–03	Sunderland	16	0		
2003–04	Sunderland	29	0		
2004–05	Sunderland	1	0	**199**	**4**
2004–05	Cardiff C	20	0	**20**	**0**
2005–06	Hartlepool U	39	0		
2006–07	Hartlepool U	26	0	**65**	**0**

WILLIAMS, Eifion (F) 319 74
H: 5 11 W: 11 02 b.Bangor 15-11-75
Source: Wolverhampton W trainee, Caernarfon T, Barry T. *Honours:* Wales Under-21, B.

1998–99	Torquay U	7	5		
1999–2000	Torquay U	42	9		
2000–01	Torquay U	37	9		
2001–02	Torquay U	25	1	**111**	**24**
2001–02	Hartlepool U	8	4		
2002–03	Hartlepool U	45	15		
2003–04	Hartlepool U	41	13		
2004–05	Hartlepool U	38	5		
2005–06	Hartlepool U	36	7		
2006–07	Hartlepool U	40	6	**208**	**50**

HEREFORD U (38)

BECKWITH, Dean (D) 33 0
H: 6 3 W: 13 04 b.Southwark 18-9-83
Source: Scholar.

2003–04	Gillingham	0	0		
2004–05	Gillingham	1	0	**1**	**0**
2006–07	Hereford U	32	0	**32**	**0**

BROWN, Wayne (G) 147 0
H: 6 0 W: 13 11 b.Southampton 14-1-77
Source: Trainee.

1993–94	Bristol C	1	0		
1994–95	Bristol C	0	0		
1995–96	Bristol C	0	0	**1**	**0**
From Weston-S-Mare					
1996–97	Chester C	2	0		
1997–98	Chester C	13	0		
1998–99	Chester C	23	0		
1999–2000	Chester C	46	0		
2000–01	Chester C	0	0		
2001–02	Chester C	0	0		
2004–05	Chester C	23	0		
2005–06	Chester C	0	0	**107**	**0**
2006–07	Hereford U	39	0	**39**	**0**

CONNELL, Alan (F) 120 24
H: 6 0 W: 12 00 b.Enfield 5-2-83
Source: Ipswich T Trainee.

2002–03	Bournemouth	13	6		
2003–04	Bournemouth	7	0		
2004–05	Bournemouth	34	2	**54**	**8**
2005–06	Torquay U	22	7	**22**	**7**
2006–07	Hereford U	44	9	**44**	**9**

FERRELL, Andrew (M) 21 0
H: 5 9 W: 11 13 b.Newcastle 9-1-84
Source: Trainee.

2002–03	Newcastle U	0	0		
2003–04	Newcastle U	0	0		
2004–05	Watford	0	0		
2006–07	Hereford U	21	0	**21**	**0**

FITZPATRICK, Jordan (M) 1 0
H: 6 0 W: 12 00 b.Stourbridge 15-6-88
Source: Wolverhampton W Scholar.

2006–07	Hereford U	1	0	**1**	**0**

FLEETWOOD, Stuart (F) 38 3
H: 5 10 W: 12 07 b.Gloucester 23-4-86
Source: Scholar. *Honours:* Wales Youth, Under-21.

2003–04	Cardiff C	2	0		

2004–05	Cardiff C	6	0		
2005–06	Cardiff C	0	0	**8**	**0**
2006–07	Hereford U	27	3	**27**	**3**
2006–07	*Accrington S*	3	0	**3**	**0**

GILES, Martyn (D) 18 0
H: 6 0 W: 12 00 b.Cardiff 10-4-83
Source: Scholar. *Honours:* Wales Youth.

2000–01	Cardiff C	5	0		
2001–02	Cardiff C	0	0		
2002–03	Cardiff C	0	0		
2003–04	Cardiff C	0	0	**5**	**0**
From Morecambe.					
2006–07	Hereford U	13	0	**13**	**0**

GULLIVER, Phil (D) 120 4
H: 6 2 W: 13 05 b.Bishop Auckland 12-9-82
Source: Scholar.

2000–01	Middlesbrough	0	0		
2001–02	Middlesbrough	0	0		
2002–03	Middlesbrough	0	0		
2002–03	*Blackpool*	3	0	**3**	**0**
2002–03	*Carlisle U*	1	0	**1**	**0**
2002–03	*Bournemouth*	6	0	**6**	**0**
2003–04	Middlesbrough	0	0		
2003–04	*Bury*	10	0	**10**	**0**
2003–04	*Scunthorpe U*	2	0	**2**	**0**
2004–05	Rushden & D	32	0		
2005–06	Rushden & D	40	4	**72**	**4**
2006–07	Hereford U	26	0	**26**	**0**

GWYNNE, Sam (M) 0 0
b.Hereford 17-12-87
Source: Scholar.

2006–07	Hereford U	0	0		

HARRISON, Paul (G) 5 0
H: 5 9 W: 13 04 b.Liverpool 18-12-84
Source: Scholar.

2003–04	Liverpool	0	0		
2004–05	Liverpool	0	0		
2004–05	*Leeds U*	0	0		
2005–06	Liverpool	0	0		
2005–06	Wolverhampton W	0	0		
2005–06	Chester C	4	0	**4**	**0**
2006–07	Hereford U	1	0	**1**	**0**

JEANNIN, Alex (D) 35 1
H: 6 0 W: 11 06 b.Troyes 30-12-77
Source: Troyes.

2000–01	Darlington	11	0		
2001–02	Darlington	11	0	**22**	**0**
From Exeter C.					
2004–05	Bristol R	1	0	**1**	**0**
2005–06	Hereford U	0	0		
2006–07	Hereford U	12	1	**12**	**1**

McCLENAHAN, Trent (D) 65 1
H: 5 11 W: 12 00 b.Sydney 4-2-85
Source: Scholar. *Honours:* Australia Under-20, Under-23.

2004–05	West Ham U	2	0		
2004–05	*Milton Keynes D*	8	0		
2005–06	West Ham U	0	0	**2**	**0**
2005–06	*Milton Keynes D*	29	0	**37**	**0**
2006–07	Hereford U	26	1	**26**	**1**

MKANDAWIRE, Tamika (D) 39 2
H: 6 1 W: 12 03 b.Malawi 28-5-83
Source: Scholar.

2002–03	WBA	0	0		
2003–04	WBA	0	0		
2006–07	Hereford U	39	2	**39**	**2**

OSBORN, Simon (M) 434 33
H: 5 9 W: 11 04 b.Croydon 19-1-72
Source: Apprentice.

1989–90	Crystal Palace	0	0		
1990–91	Crystal Palace	4	0		
1991–92	Crystal Palace	14	2		
1992–93	Crystal Palace	31	2		
1993–94	Crystal Palace	6	1	**55**	**5**
1994–95	Reading	32	5	**32**	**5**
1995–96	QPR	9	1	**9**	**1**
1995–96	Wolverhampton W	21	2		
1996–97	Wolverhampton W	35	5		
1997–98	Wolverhampton W	24	2		
1998–99	Wolverhampton W	37	2		
1999–2000	Wolverhampton W	25	0		
2000–01	Wolverhampton W	20	0	**162**	**11**
2000–01	Tranmere R	9	1	**9**	**1**
2001–02	Port Vale	7	0	**7**	**0**
2001–02	Gillingham	28	4		
2002–03	Gillingham	18	1	**46**	**5**
2003–04	Walsall	43	3		
2004–05	Walsall	38	0		
2005–06	Walsall	32	2	**113**	**5**
2006–07	Hereford U	1	0	**1**	**0**

PALMER, Marcus (F) 3 0
H: 6 0 W: 11 07 b.Gloucester 22-12-88
Source: Cheltenham T Scholar.

2006–07	Hereford U	3	0	**3**	**0**

PURDIE, Rob (M) 44 6
H: 5 9 W: 11 06 b.Leicester 28-9-82
Source: Leicester C.

2006–07	Hereford U	44	6	**44**	**6**

ROSE, Richard (D) 100 1
H: 6 0 W: 12 04 b.Pembury 8-9-82
Source: Trainee.

2000–01	Gillingham	4	0		
2001–02	Gillingham	3	0		
2002–03	Gillingham	2	0		
2002–03	*Bristol R*	9	0	**9**	**0**
2003–04	Gillingham	17	0		
2004–05	Gillingham	18	0		
2005–06	Gillingham	14	0	**58**	**0**
2006–07	Hereford U	33	1	**33**	**1**

SHELDON, Gareth (F) 114 8
H: 5 10 W: 12 08 b.Birmingham 31-1-80
Source: Trainee.

1997–98	Scunthorpe U	1	0		
1998–99	Scunthorpe U	11	1		
1999–2000	Scunthorpe U	22	2		
2000–01	Scunthorpe U	39	1		
2001–02	Scunthorpe U	14	2	**87**	**6**
2002–03	Exeter C	19	1		
2003–04	Exeter C	0	0		
2004–05	Exeter C	0	0	**19**	**1**
2005–06	Kidderminster H	0	0		
2006–07	Hereford U	8	1	**8**	**1**

SILLS, Tim (F) 49 3
H: 6 1 W: 14 00 b.Romsey 10-9-79
Source: Camberley T, Basingstoke T, Kingstonian, Aldershot T.

2005–06	Oxford U	13	1	**13**	**1**
2006–07	Hereford U	36	2	**36**	**2**

SMITH, Ben (M) 43 5
H: 5 9 W: 11 09 b.Chelmsford 23-11-78
Source: Yeovil T.

2001–02	Southend U	1	0	**1**	**0**
From Hereford U					
2004–05	Shrewsbury T	12	3		
2005–06	Shrewsbury T	12	1	**24**	**4**
From Weymouth.					
2006–07	Hereford U	18	1	**18**	**1**

THOMAS, Danny (M) 165 12
H: 5 7 W: 10 10 b.Leamington Spa 1-5-81
Source: Trainee.

1997–98	Nottingham F	0	0		
1997–98	Leicester C	0	0		
1998–99	Leicester C	0	0		
1999–2000	Leicester C	3	0		
2000–01	Leicester C	0	0		
2001–02	Leicester C	0	0	**3**	**0**
2001–02	Bournemouth	12	0		
2002–03	Bournemouth	37	2		
2003–04	Bournemouth	10	0	**59**	**2**
2003–04	Boston U	8	3		
2004–05	Boston U	39	3		
2005–06	Boston U	35	2		
2006–07	Boston U	0	0	**82**	**8**
2006–07	Shrewsbury T	6	0	**6**	**0**
2006–07	Hereford U	15	2	**15**	**2**

TRAVIS, Simon (D) 66 2
H: 5 7 W: 10 00 b.Preston 22-3-77
Source: Trainee.

1995–96	Torquay U	8	0		
1996–97	Torquay U	0	0	**8**	**0**
From Holywell T.					
1997–98	Stockport Co	13	2		
1998–99	Stockport Co	9	0	**22**	**2**
From Telford U, Forest GR, Stevenage B.					
2006–07	Hereford U	36	0	**36**	**0**

WALLIS, John (M) 19 0
H: 5 7 W: 11 04 b.Gravesend 4-4-86
Source: Scholar.

2005–06	Gillingham	17	0	**17**	**0**
2006–07	Hereford U	2	0	**2**	**0**

WEBB, Luke (M) 21 0
H: 6 0 W: 12 01 b.Nottingham 12-9-86

2005–06	Coventry C	0	0		
2006–07	Hereford U	21	0	**21**	**0**

WILLIAMS, Andy (F) 41 8
H: 5 11 W: 11 09 b.Hereford 14-8-86

2006–07	Hereford U	41	8	**41**	**8**

HUDDERSFIELD T (39)

ADAMS, Danny (D) 255 2
H: 5 8 W: 13 08 b.Manchester 3-1-76
Source: Altrincham.

2000–01	Macclesfield T	37	0		
2001–02	Macclesfield T	39	0		
2002–03	Macclesfield T	45	1		
2003–04	Macclesfield T	27	0	**148**	**1**
2003–04	Stockport Co	12	0		
2004–05	Stockport Co	27	1	**39**	**1**
2004–05	Huddersfield T	5	0		
2005–06	Huddersfield T	40	0		
2006–07	Huddersfield T	23	0	**68**	**0**

AHMED, Adnan (M) 41 1
H: 5 10 W: 11 02 b.Burnley 7-6-84
Source: Scholar.

2003–04	Huddersfield T	1	0		
2004–05	Huddersfield T	18	1		
2005–06	Huddersfield T	13	0		
2006–07	Huddersfield T	9	0	**41**	**1**

AKINS, Lucas (F) 2 0
H: 5 10 W: 11 07 b.Huddersfield 25-2-89
Source: Scholar.

2006–07	Huddersfield T	2	0	**2**	**0**

BECKETT, Luke (F) 316 137
H: 5 11 W: 11 02 b.Sheffield 25-11-76
Source: Trainee.

1995–96	Barnsley	0	0		
1996–97	Barnsley	0	0		
1997–98	Barnsley	0	0		
1998–99	Chester C	28	11		
1999–2000	Chester C	46	14	**74**	**25**
2000–01	Chesterfield	41	16		
2001–02	Chesterfield	21	6	**62**	**22**
2001–02	Stockport Co	19	7		
2002–03	Stockport Co	42	27		
2003–04	Stockport Co	8	4		
2004–05	Stockport Co	15	7	**84**	**45**
2004–05	Sheffield U	5	0		
2004–05	*Huddersfield T*	7	6		
2004–05	*Oldham Ath*	9	6		
2005–06	Sheffield U	0	0	**5**	**0**
2005–06	*Oldham Ath*	34	18	**43**	**24**
2006–07	Huddersfield T	41	15	**48**	**21**

BERRETT, James (M) 2 0
H: 5 10 W: 10 13 b.Halifax 13-1-89
Source: Scholar. *Honours:* Eire Youth.

2006–07	Huddersfield T	2	0	**2**	**0**

BOOTH, Andy (F) 473 145
H: 6 0 W: 12 06 b.Huddersfield 6-12-73
Source: Trainee. *Honours:* England Under-21.

1991–92	Huddersfield T	3	0		
1992–93	Huddersfield T	5	2		
1993–94	Huddersfield T	26	10		
1994–95	Huddersfield T	46	26		
1995–96	Huddersfield T	43	16		
1996–97	Sheffield W	35	10		
1997–98	Sheffield W	23	7		
1998–99	Sheffield W	34	6		
1999–2000	Sheffield W	23	2		
2000–01	Sheffield W	18	3	**133**	**28**
2000–01	*Tottenham H*	4	0	**4**	**0**
2000–01	Huddersfield T	8	3		
2001–02	Huddersfield T	36	11		
2002–03	Huddersfield T	33	6		
2003–04	Huddersfield T	37	13		
2004–05	Huddersfield T	29	10		

2005–06 Huddersfield T 36 13
2006–07 Huddersfield T 34 7 **336 117**

BRANDON, Chris (M) 262 31
H: 5 8 W: 10 00 b.Bradford 7-4-76
Source: Bradford PA.
1999–2000 Torquay U 42 5
2000–01 Torquay U 2 0
2001–02 Torquay U 27 3 **71 8**
2002–03 Chesterfield 36 7
2003–04 Chesterfield 43 4 **79 11**
2004–05 Huddersfield T 44 6
2005–06 Huddersfield T 40 3
2006–07 Huddersfield T 23 1 **107 10**
2006–07 *Blackpool* 5 2 **5 2**

BROADBENT, Daniel (M) 0 0
b.Leeds
2006–07 Huddersfield T 0 0

CLARKE, Nathan (D) 164 2
H: 6 2 W: 12 00 b.Halifax 30-11-83
Source: Scholar.
2001–02 Huddersfield T 36 1
2002–03 Huddersfield T 3 0
2003–04 Huddersfield T 26 1
2004–05 Huddersfield T 37 0
2005–06 Huddersfield T 46 0
2006–07 Huddersfield T 16 0 **164 2**

CLARKE, Tom (D) 38 1
H: 6 0 W: 11 02 b.Halifax 21-12-87
Source: Scholar. *Honours:* England Youth.
2004–05 Huddersfield T 12 0
2005–06 Huddersfield T 17 1
2006–07 Huddersfield T 9 0 **38 1**

COLLINS, Michael (M) 68 5
H: 6 0 W: 11 00 b.Halifax 30-4-86
Source: Scholar. *Honours:* Eire Youth.
2004–05 Huddersfield T 8 0
2005–06 Huddersfield T 17 1
2006–07 Huddersfield T 43 4 **68 5**

EASTWOOD, Simon (G) 0 0
H: 6 2 W: 13 00 b.Luton 26-6-89
Source: Scholar. *Honours:* England Youth.
2005–06 Huddersfield T 0 0
2006–07 Huddersfield T 0 0

GLENNON, Matty (G) 199 0
H: 6 2 W: 14 08 b.Stockport 8-10-78
Source: Trainee.
1997–98 Bolton W 0 0
1998–99 Bolton W 0 0
1999–2000 Bolton W 0 0
1999–2000 *Port Vale* 0 0
1999–2000 *Stockport Co* 0 0
2000–01 Bolton W 0 0
2000–01 *Bristol R* 1 0 **1 0**
2000–01 *Carlisle U* 29 0
2001–02 Hull C 26 0
2002–03 Hull C 9 0 **35 0**
2002–03 Carlisle U 32 0
2003–04 Carlisle U 44 0
2004–05 Carlisle U 0 0 **105 0**
2005–06 St Johnstone 12 0 **12 0**
2006–07 Huddersfield T 46 0 **46 0**

HAND, James (M) 1 0
H: 5 9 W: 11 00 b.Drogheda 22-10-86
b.Halifax 22.11.1988
Source: Scholar. *Honours:* Eire Youth, Under-21.
2005–06 Huddersfield T 0 0
2006–07 Huddersfield T 1 0 **1 0**

HARDY, Aaron (M) 9 0
H: 5 8 W: 11 04 b.Pontefract 26-5-86
Source: Scholar.
2005–06 Huddersfield T 0 0
2006–07 Huddersfield T 9 0 **9 0**

HOLDSWORTH, Andy (D) 153 3
H: 5 9 W: 11 02 b.Pontefract 29-1-84
Source: Scholar.
2003–04 Huddersfield T 36 0
2004–05 Huddersfield T 40 0
2005–06 Huddersfield T 42 1
2006–07 Huddersfield T 35 2 **153 3**

HUDSON, Mark (M) 174 16
H: 5 10 W: 11 03 b.Bishop Auckland 24-10-80
Source: Trainee.
1999–2000 Middlesbrough 0 0
2000–01 Middlesbrough 3 0
2001–02 Middlesbrough 2 0
2002–03 Middlesbrough 0 0 **5 0**
2002–03 *Carlisle U* 15 1 **15 1**
2002–03 Chesterfield 24 3
2003–04 Chesterfield 35 2
2004–05 Chesterfield 34 4 **93 9**
2005–06 Huddersfield T 29 3
2006–07 Huddersfield T 32 3 **61 6**

McALISKEY, John (F) 49 7
H: 6 4 W: 12 01 b.Huddersfield 2-9-84
Source: Scholar. *Honours:* Eire Under-21.
2003–04 Huddersfield T 8 4
2004–05 Huddersfield T 18 2
2005–06 Huddersfield T 9 0
2005–06 *Torquay U* 3 0 **3 0**
2006–07 Huddersfield T 8 1 **43 7**
2006–07 *Wrexham* 3 0 **3 0**

McCOMBE, John (D) 14 0
H: 6 2 W: 13 00 b.Pontefract 7-5-85
Source: Scholar.
2002–03 Huddersfield T 1 0
2003–04 Huddersfield T 0 0
2004–05 Huddersfield T 5 0
2005–06 Huddersfield T 1 0
2005–06 *Torquay U* 0 0
2006–07 Huddersfield T 7 0 **14 0**

McINTOSH, Martin (D) 450 47
H: 6 3 W: 13 07 b.East Kilbride 19-3-71
Honours: Scotland B.
1988–89 St Mirren 2 0
1989–90 St Mirren 2 0
1990–91 St Mirren 0 0 **4 0**
1991–92 Clydebank 28 5
1992–93 Clydebank 33 4
1993–94 Clydebank 4 1 **65 10**
1993–94 Hamilton A 13 2
1994–95 Hamilton A 30 2
1995–96 Hamilton A 23 1
1996–97 Hamilton A 33 7 **99 12**
1997–98 Stockport Co 38 2
1998–99 Stockport Co 41 3
1999–2000 Stockport Co 20 0 **99 5**
1999–2000 Hibernian 9 0
2000–01 Hibernian 0 0
2001–02 Hibernian 0 0 **9 0**
2001–02 Rotherham U 39 4
2002–03 Rotherham U 42 5
2003–04 Rotherham U 18 2
2004–05 Rotherham U 23 5 **122 16**
2005–06 Huddersfield T 22 4
2006–07 Huddersfield T 26 0 **48 4**
2006–07 *Grimsby T* 4 0 **4 0**

MIRFIN, David (M) 132 8
H: 6 3 W: 13 00 b.Sheffield 18-4-85
Source: Scholar.
2002–03 Huddersfield T 1 0
2003–04 Huddersfield T 21 2
2004–05 Huddersfield T 41 4
2005–06 Huddersfield T 31 1
2006–07 Huddersfield T 38 1 **132 8**

RACCHI, Danny (D) 3 0
H: 5 8 W: 10 04
Source: Scholar.
2006–07 Huddersfield T 3 0 **3 0**

RACHUBKA, Paul (G) 119 0
H: 6 1 W: 13 05 b.San Luis Opispo 21-5-81
Source: Trainee. *Honours:* England Youth.
1999–2000 Manchester U 0 0
2000–01 Manchester U 1 0
2001–02 Manchester U 0 0 **1 0**
2001–02 *Oldham Ath* 16 0 **16 0**
2001–02 Charlton Ath 0 0
2002–03 Charlton Ath 0 0
2003–04 Charlton Ath 0 0
2003–04 *Huddersfield T* 13 0
2004–05 Charlton Ath 0 0
2004–05 *Milton Keynes D* 4 0 **4 0**
2004–05 *Northampton T* 10 0 **10 0**
2004–05 Huddersfield T 29 0
2005–06 Huddersfield T 34 0
2006–07 Huddersfield T 0 0 **76 0**
2006–07 *Peterborough U* 4 0 **4 0**
2006–07 *Blackpool* 8 0 **8 0**

SCHOFIELD, Danny (F) 223 37
H: 5 10 W: 11 02 b.Doncaster 10-4-80
Source: Brodsworth.
1998–99 Huddersfield T 1 0
1999–2000 Huddersfield T 2 0
2000–01 Huddersfield T 1 0
2001–02 Huddersfield T 40 8
2002–03 Huddersfield T 30 2
2003–04 Huddersfield T 40 8
2004–05 Huddersfield T 33 5
2005–06 Huddersfield T 41 9
2006–07 Huddersfield T 35 5 **223 37**

SKARZ, Joe (D) 17 0
H: 5 10 W: 11 04 b.Huddersfield 13-7-89
Source: Scholar.
2006–07 Huddersfield T 17 0 **17 0**

SMITHIES, Alex (G) 0 0
H: 6 1 W: 10 01 b.Huddersfield 25-3-90
Source: From Scholar. *Honours:* England Youth.
2006–07 Huddersfield T 0 0

TAYLOR-FLETCHER, Gary (F) 188 49
H: 6 0 W: 11 00 b.Liverpool 4-6-81
Source: Northwich Vic. *Honours:* England Schools.
2000–01 Hull C 5 0 **5 0**
2001–02 Leyton Orient 9 0
2002–03 Leyton Orient 12 1 **21 1**
2003–04 Lincoln C 42 16
2004–05 Lincoln C 38 11 **80 27**
2005–06 Huddersfield T 43 10
2006–07 Huddersfield T 39 11 **82 21**

WILSON, Adam (D) 0 0
H: 6 0 W: 12 01 b.Reading 13-7-88
Source: Scholar.
2006–07 Huddersfield T 0 0

WORTHINGTON, Jon (M) 169 12
H: 5 9 W: 11 05 b.Dewsbury 16-4-83
Source: Scholar.
2001–02 Huddersfield T 0 0
2002–03 Huddersfield T 22 0
2003–04 Huddersfield T 39 3
2004–05 Huddersfield T 39 3
2005–06 Huddersfield T 41 4
2006–07 Huddersfield T 28 2 **169 12**

YOUNG, Matthew (M) 31 2
H: 5 8 W: 11 03 b.Woodlesford 25-10-85
Source: Scholar.
2005–06 Huddersfield T 2 0
2006–07 Huddersfield T 29 2 **31 2**

HULL C (40)

ASHBEE, Ian (M) 355 16
H: 6 1 W: 13 07 b.Birmingham 6-9-76
Source: Trainee. *Honours:* England Youth.
1994–95 Derby Co 1 0
1995–96 Derby Co 0 0
1996–97 Derby Co 0 0 **1 0**
1996–97 Cambridge U 18 0
1997–98 Cambridge U 27 1
1998–99 Cambridge U 31 4
1999–2000 Cambridge U 45 1
2000–01 Cambridge U 44 3
2001–02 Cambridge U 38 2 **203 11**
2002–03 Hull C 31 1
2003–04 Hull C 39 2
2004–05 Hull C 40 1
2005–06 Hull C 6 0
2006–07 Hull C 35 1 **151 5**

ASPDEN, Curtis (G) 0 0
H: 6 1 W: 11 12 b.Darwen 16-11-87
Source: Scholar.
2005–06 Hull C 0 0
2006–07 Hull C 0 0

ATKINSON, William (M) **0 0**
H: 5 10 W: 10 07 b.Beverley 14-10-88
Source: Scholar.

2006–07	Hull C	0	0		

BARMBY, Nick (F) **393 71**
H: 5 7 W: 11 03 b.Hull 11-2-74
Source: From Trainee. *Honours:* England Schools, Youth, Under-21, B, 23 full caps, 4 goals.

1991–92	Tottenham H	0	0		
1992–93	Tottenham H	22	6		
1993–94	Tottenham H	27	5		
1994–95	Tottenham H	38	9	**87**	**20**
1995–96	Middlesbrough	32	7		
1996–97	Middlesbrough	10	1	**42**	**8**
1996–97	Everton	25	4		
1997–98	Everton	30	2		
1998–99	Everton	24	3		
1999–2000	Everton	37	9	**116**	**18**
2000–01	Liverpool	26	2		
2001–02	Liverpool	6	0	**32**	**2**
2002–03	Leeds U	19	4		
2003–04	*Nottingham F*	6	1	**6**	**1**
2003–04	Leeds U	6	0	**25**	**4**
2004–05	Hull C	39	9		
2005–06	Hull C	26	5		
2006–07	Hull C	20	4	**85**	**18**

BENNETT, James (M) **0 0**
H: 5 10 W: 12 03 b.Beverley 4-9-88
Source: Scholar.

2006–07	Hull C	0	0		

BRIDGES, Michael (F) **216 53**
H: 6 1 W: 10 11 b.North Shields 5-8-78
Source: From Trainee. *Honours:* England Schools, Youth, Under-21.

1995–96	Sunderland	15	4		
1996–97	Sunderland	25	3		
1997–98	Sunderland	9	1		
1998–99	Sunderland	30	8		
1999–2000	Leeds U	34	19		
2000–01	Leeds U	7	0		
2001–02	Leeds U	0	0		
2002–03	Leeds U	5	0		
2003–04	Leeds U	10	0	**56**	**19**
2003–04	*Newcastle U*	6	0	**6**	**0**
2004–05	Bolton W	0	0		
2004–05	Sunderland	19	1	**98**	**17**
2005–06	Bristol C	11	0	**11**	**0**
2005–06	Carlisle U	25	15		
2006–07	Carlisle U	5	0	**30**	**15**
2006–07	Hull C	15	2	**15**	**2**

BYRON, Michael (D) **3 0**
H: 6 1 W: 11 03 b.Liverpool 16-8-87
Source: Scholar.

2006–07	Hull C	0	0		
2006–07	*Notts Co*	3	0	**3**	**0**

COLES, Danny (D) **178 5**
H: 6 1 W: 11 05 b.Bristol 31-10-81
Source: Scholarship.

1999–2000	Bristol C	1	0		
2000–01	Bristol C	2	0		
2001–02	Bristol C	23	0		
2002–03	Bristol C	39	2		
2003–04	Bristol C	45	2		
2004–05	Bristol C	38	1	**148**	**5**
2005–06	Hull C	9	0		
2006–07	Hull C	21	0	**30**	**0**

COLLINS, Sam (D) **277 13**
H: 6 2 W: 14 03 b.Pontefract 5-6-77
Source: Trainee.

1994–95	Huddersfield T	0	0		
1995–96	Huddersfield T	0	0		
1996–97	Huddersfield T	4	0		
1997–98	Huddersfield T	10	0		
1998–99	Huddersfield T	23	0	**37**	**0**
1999–2000	Bury	19	0		
2000–01	Bury	34	2		
2001–02	Bury	29	0	**82**	**2**
2002–03	Port Vale	44	5		
2003–04	Port Vale	43	4		
2004–05	Port Vale	33	2		
2005–06	Port Vale	15	0	**135**	**11**
2005–06	Hull C	17	0		
2006–07	Hull C	6	0	**23**	**0**

DAWSON, Andy (D) **318 13**
H: 5 9 W: 11 02 b.Northallerton 20-10-78
Source: Trainee.

1995–96	Nottingham F	0	0		
1996–97	Nottingham F	0	0		
1997–98	Nottingham F	0	0		
1998–99	Nottingham F	0	0		
1998–99	Scunthorpe U	24	0		
1999–2000	Scunthorpe U	43	2		
2000–01	Scunthorpe U	41	4		
2001–02	Scunthorpe U	44	0		
2002–03	Scunthorpe U	43	2	**195**	**8**
2003–04	Hull C	33	3		
2004–05	Hull C	34	0		
2005–06	Hull C	18	0		
2006–07	Hull C	38	2	**123**	**5**

DELANEY, Damien (D) **231 6**
H: 6 3 W: 14 00 b.Cork 20-7-81
Source: Cork C.

2000–01	Leicester C	5	0		
2001–02	Leicester C	3	0		
2001–02	*Stockport Co*	12	1	**12**	**1**
2001–02	*Huddersfield T*	2	0	**2**	**0**
2002–03	Leicester C	0	0	**8**	**0**
2002–03	*Mansfield T*	7	0	**7**	**0**
2002–03	Hull C	30	1		
2003–04	Hull C	46	2		
2004–05	Hull C	43	1		
2005–06	Hull C	46	0		
2006–07	Hull C	37	1	**202**	**5**

DOYLE, Nathan (M) **50 0**
H: 5 11 W: 12 06 b.Derby 12-1-87
Source: Scholar. *Honours:* England Youth, Under-20.

2003–04	Derby Co	2	0		
2004–05	Derby Co	3	0		
2005–06	Derby Co	4	0		
2005–06	*Notts Co*	12	0	**12**	**0**
2006–07	Derby Co	0	0	**9**	**0**
2006–07	*Bradford C*	28	0	**28**	**0**
2006–07	Hull C	1	0	**1**	**0**

DUFFY, Darryl (F) **99 39**
H: 5 11 W: 12 01 b.Glasgow 16-4-84
Honours: Scotland Under-21, B.

2003–04	Rangers	1	0	**1**	**0**
2004–05	Falkirk	35	17		
2005–06	Falkirk	21	9	**56**	**26**
2005–06	Hull C	15	3		
2006–07	Hull C	9	0	**24**	**3**
2006–07	*Hartlepool U*	10	5	**10**	**5**
2006–07	*Swansea C*	8	5	**8**	**5**

DUKE, Matt (G) **13 0**
H: 6 5 W: 13 04 b.Sheffield 16-7-77
Source: Alfreton T.

1999–2000	Sheffield U	0	0		
2000–01	Sheffield U	0	0		
2001–02	Sheffield U	0	0		
2004–05	Hull C	2	0		
2005–06	Hull C	2	0		
2005–06	*Stockport Co*	3	0	**3**	**0**
2005–06	*Wycombe W*	5	0	**5**	**0**
2006–07	Hull C	1	0	**5**	**0**

EDGE, Roland (D) **124 1**
H: 5 9 W: 11 07 b.Gillingham 25-11-78
Source: Trainee.

1997–98	Gillingham	0	0		
1998–99	Gillingham	8	0		
1999–2000	Gillingham	26	1		
2000–01	Gillingham	20	0		
2001–02	Gillingham	14	0		
2002–03	Gillingham	34	0		
2003–04	Gillingham	0	0	**102**	**1**
2004–05	Hull C	14	0		
2005–06	Hull C	8	0		
2006–07	Hull C	0	0	**22**	**0**

ELLIOTT, Stuart (M) **352 114**
H: 5 10 W: 11 09 b.Belfast 23-7-78
Honours: Northern Ireland Under-21, 36 full caps, 4 goals.

1994–95	Glentoran	0	0		
1995–96	Glentoran	1	0		
1996–97	Glentoran	8	1		
1997–98	Glentoran	22	5		
1998–99	Glentoran	31	7		
1999–2000	Glentoran	34	16	**96**	**29**
2000–01	Motherwell	33	10		
2001–02	Motherwell	37	10	**70**	**20**
2002–03	Hull C	36	12		
2003–04	Hull C	42	14		
2004–05	Hull C	36	27		
2005–06	Hull C	40	7		
2006–07	Hull C	32	5	**186**	**65**

FEATHERSTONE, Nicky (F) **2 0**
H: 5 6 W: 11 02 b.North Ferriby 22-9-88
Source: Scholar.

2006–07	Hull C	2	0	**2**	**0**

FORSTER, Nicky (F) **490 147**
H: 5 9 W: 11 05 b.Caterham 8-9-73
Source: From Horley T. *Honours:* England Under-21.

1992–93	Gillingham	26	6		
1993–94	Gillingham	41	18	**67**	**24**
1994–95	Brentford	46	24		
1995–96	Brentford	38	5		
1996–97	Brentford	25	10	**109**	**39**
1996–97	Birmingham C	7	3		
1997–98	Birmingham C	28	3		
1998–99	Birmingham C	33	5	**68**	**11**
1999–2000	Reading	36	10		
2000–01	Reading	9	1		
2001–02	Reading	42	19		
2002–03	Reading	40	16		
2003–04	Reading	30	7		
2004–05	Reading	30	7	**187**	**60**
2005–06	Ipswich T	20	7		
2006–07	Ipswich T	4	1	**24**	**8**
2006–07	Hull C	35	5	**35**	**5**

FRANCE, Ryan (M) **118 6**
H: 5 11 W: 11 11 b.Sheffield 13-12-80
Source: Alfreton T.

2003–04	Hull C	28	2		
2004–05	Hull C	31	2		
2005–06	Hull C	35	2		
2006–07	Hull C	24	0	**118**	**6**

FRY, Russell (M) **2 0**
H: 6 0 W: 12 01 b.Hull 4-12-85
Source: Scholar. *Honours:* England Under-20.

2002–03	Hull C	0	0		
2003–04	Hull C	0	0		
2004–05	Hull C	1	0		
2005–06	Hull C	1	0		
2006–07	Hull C	0	0	**2**	**0**

LIVERMORE, David (M) **298 16**
H: 5 11 W: 12 02 b.Edmonton 20-5-80
Source: Trainee.

1998–99	Arsenal	0	0		
1999–2000	Millwall	32	2		
2000–01	Millwall	39	3		
2001–02	Millwall	43	0		
2002–03	Millwall	41	2		
2003–04	Millwall	36	1		
2004–05	Millwall	41	2		
2005–06	Millwall	41	2	**273**	**12**
2006–07	Hull C	25	4	**25**	**4**

MARNEY, Dean (M) **72 4**
H: 5 10 W: 11 09 b.Barking 31-1-84
Source: Scholar. *Honours:* England Under-21.

2002–03	Tottenham H	0	0		
2002–03	*Swindon T*	9	0	**9**	**0**
2003–04	Tottenham H	3	0		
2003–04	*QPR*	2	0	**2**	**0**
2004–05	Tottenham H	5	2		
2004–05	*Gillingham*	3	0	**3**	**0**
2005–06	Tottenham H	0	0	**8**	**2**
2005–06	*Norwich C*	13	0	**13**	**0**
2006–07	Hull C	37	2	**37**	**2**

McPHEE, Stephen (F) **177 44**
H: 5 7 W: 10 08 b.Glasgow 5-6-81
Honours: Scotland Under-21.

1998–99	Coventry C	0	0		
1999–2000	Coventry C	0	0		
2000–01	Coventry C	0	0		
2001–02	Port Vale	44	11		
2002–03	Port Vale	40	3		
2003–04	Port Vale	46	25	**130**	**39**
2004–05	Beira Mar	31	5	**31**	**5**
2005–06	Hull C	4	0		
2006–07	Hull C	12	0	**16**	**0**

MYHILL, Boaz (G) 178 0

H: 6 3 W: 14 06 b.Modesto 9-11-82

Source: Scholar. *Honours:* England Youth, Under-20.

2000–01	Aston Villa	0	0		
2001–02	Aston Villa	0	0		
2001–02	*Stoke C*	0	0		
2002–03	Aston Villa	0	0		
2002–03	*Bristol C*	0	0		
2002–03	*Bradford C*	2	0	**2**	**0**
2003–04	Aston Villa	0	0		
2003–04	*Macclesfield T*	15	0	**15**	**0**
2003–04	*Stockport Co*	2	0	**2**	**0**
2003–04	Hull C	23	0		
2004–05	Hull C	45	0		
2005–06	Hull C	45	0		
2006–07	Hull C	46	0	**159**	**0**

PARKIN, Jon (F) 203 58

H: 6 4 W: 13 07 b.Barnsley 30-12-81

Source: Scholarship.

1998–99	Barnsley	2	0		
1999–2000	Barnsley	0	0		
2000–01	Barnsley	4	0		
2001–02	Barnsley	4	0	**10**	**0**
2001–02	*Hartlepool U*	1	0	**1**	**0**
2001–02	York C	18	2		
2002–03	York C	41	10		
2003–04	York C	15	2	**74**	**14**
2003–04	Macclesfield T	12	1		
2004–05	Macclesfield T	42	22		
2005–06	Macclesfield T	11	7	**65**	**30**
2005–06	Hull C	18	5		
2006–07	Hull C	29	6	**47**	**11**
2006–07	*Stoke C*	6	3	**6**	**3**

PARLOUR, Ray (M) 400 22

H: 5 10 W: 11 12 b.Romford 7-3-73

Source: Trainee. *Honours:* England Under-21, B, 10 full caps.

1990–91	Arsenal	0	0		
1991–92	Arsenal	6	1		
1992–93	Arsenal	21	1		
1993–94	Arsenal	27	2		
1994–95	Arsenal	30	0		
1995–96	Arsenal	22	0		
1996–97	Arsenal	30	2		
1997–98	Arsenal	34	5		
1998–99	Arsenal	35	6		
1999–2000	Arsenal	30	1		
2000–01	Arsenal	33	4		
2001–02	Arsenal	27	0		
2002–03	Arsenal	19	0		
2003–04	Arsenal	25	0	**339**	**22**
2004–05	Middlesbrough	33	0		
2005–06	Middlesbrough	13	0		
2006–07	Middlesbrough	0	0	**46**	**0**
2006–07	Hull C	15	0	**15**	**0**

PLUMMER, Matthew (D) 0 0

H: 6 1 W: 12 01 b.Hull 18-1-89

Source: Scholar.

2006–07	Hull C	0	0		

RICKETTS, Sam (D) 171 3

H: 6 1 W: 12 01 b.Aylesbury 11-10-81

Source: From Trainee. *Honours:* Wales 19 full caps.

1999–2000	Oxford U	0	0		
2000–01	Oxford U	14	0		
2001–02	Oxford U	29	1		
2002–03	Oxford U	2	0	**45**	**1**
From Telford U					
2004–05	Swansea C	42	0		
2005–06	Swansea C	44	1	**86**	**1**
2006–07	Hull C	40	1	**40**	**1**

TURNER, Michael (D) 141 7

H: 6 4 W: 13 05 b.Lewisham 9-11-83

Source: Scholar.

2001–02	Charlton Ath	0	0		
2002–03	Charlton Ath	0	0		
2002–03	*Leyton Orient*	7	1	**7**	**1**
2003–04	Charlton Ath	0	0		
2004–05	Charlton Ath	0	0		
2004–05	Brentford	45	1		
2005–06	Brentford	46	2	**91**	**3**
2006–07	Hull C	43	3	**43**	**3**

WELSH, John (M) 54 3

H: 5 7 W: 12 02 b.Liverpool 10-1-84

Source: Scholar. *Honours:* England Youth, Under-20, Under-21.

2000–01	Liverpool	0	0		
2001–02	Liverpool	0	0		
2002–03	Liverpool	0	0		
2003–04	Liverpool	1	0		
2004–05	Liverpool	3	0		
2005–06	Liverpool	0	0	**4**	**0**
2005–06	Hull C	32	2		
2006–07	Hull C	18	1	**50**	**3**

WILKINSON, Ben (M) 0 0

H: 5 11 W: 12 01 b.Sheffield 25-4-87

Source: Derby Co Scholar.

2005–06	Hull C	0	0		
2006–07	Hull C	0	0		

WISEMAN, Scott (D) 46 1

H: 6 0 W: 11 06 b.Hull 9-10-85

Source: From Scholar. *Honours:* England Youth, Under-20.

2003–04	Hull C	2	0		
2004–05	Hull C	3	0		
2004–05	*Boston U*	2	0	**2**	**0**
2005–06	Hull C	11	0		
2006–07	Hull C	0	0	**16**	**0**
2006–07	*Rotherham U*	18	1	**18**	**1**
2006–07	*Darlington*	10	0	**10**	**0**

IPSWICH T (41)

BARRON, Scott (D) 18 0

H: 5 9 W: 9 08 b.Preston 2-9-85

Source: Scholar.

2003–04	Ipswich T	0	0		
2004–05	Ipswich T	0	0		
2005–06	Ipswich T	15	0		
2006–07	Ipswich T	0	0	**15**	**0**
2006–07	*Wrexham*	3	0	**3**	**0**

BOWDITCH, Dean (F) 96 11

H: 5 11 W: 11 05 b.Bishops Stortford 15-6-86

Source: Trainee. *Honours:* FA Schools, England Youth.

2002–03	Ipswich T	5	0		
2003–04	Ipswich T	16	4		
2004–05	Ipswich T	21	3		
2004–05	*Burnley*	10	1	**10**	**1**
2005–06	Ipswich T	21	0		
2005–06	*Wycombe W*	11	1	**11**	**1**
2006–07	Ipswich T	9	1	**72**	**8**
2006–07	*Brighton & HA*	3	1	**3**	**1**

BREKKE-SKARD, Vemund (M) 3 0

H: 5 8 W: 13 03 b.Norway 11-9-81

Source: Brumunddal.

2005–06	Ipswich T	3	0		
2006–07	Ipswich T	0	0	**3**	**0**

BRITTAIN, Martin (M) 16 0

H: 5 8 W: 10 07 b.Newcastle 29-12-84

Source: Trainee.

2003–04	Newcastle U	1	0		
2004–05	Newcastle U	0	0		
2005–06	Newcastle U	0	0	**1**	**0**
2006–07	Ipswich T	0	0		
2006–07	*Yeovil T*	15	0	**15**	**0**

BRUCE, Alex (D) 76 0

H: 6 0 W: 11 06 b.Norwich 28-9-84

Source: Trainee. *Honours:* Eire B, Under-21, 1 full cap.

2002–03	Blackburn R	0	0		
2003–04	Blackburn R	0	0		
2004–05	Blackburn R	0	0		
2004–05	*Oldham Ath*	12	0	**12**	**0**
2004–05	Birmingham C	0	0		
2004–05	*Sheffield W*	6	0	**6**	**0**
2005–06	Birmingham C	6	0	**6**	**0**
2005–06	*Tranmere R*	11	0	**11**	**0**
2006–07	Ipswich T	41	0	**41**	**0**

CASEMENT, Chris (M) 5 0

H: 6 0 W: 12 02 b.Belfast 12-1-88

Source: Scholar. *Honours:* Northern Ireland Youth, Under-21.

2005–06	Ipswich T	5	0		
2006–07	Ipswich T	0	0	**5**	**0**

CLARKE, Billy (F) 35 3

H: 5 7 W: 10 01 b.Cork 13-12-87

Source: Scholar. *Honours:* Republic of Ireland Youth, Under-21.

2004–05	Ipswich T	0	0		
2005–06	Ipswich T	2	0		
2005–06	*Colchester U*	6	0	**6**	**0**
2006–07	Ipswich T	27	3	**29**	**3**

CURRIE, Darren (M) 473 55

H: 5 11 W: 12 07 b.Hampstead 29-11-74

Source: Trainee.

1993–94	West Ham U	0	0		
1994–95	West Ham U	0	0		
1994–95	*Shrewsbury T*	17	2		
1995–96	West Ham U	0	0		
1995–96	*Leyton Orient*	10	0	**10**	**0**
1995–96	Shrewsbury T	13	2		
1996–97	Shrewsbury T	37	2		
1997–98	Shrewsbury T	16	4	**83**	**10**
1997–98	Plymouth Arg	7	0	**7**	**0**
1998–99	Barnet	38	4		
1999–2000	Barnet	44	5		
2000–01	Barnet	45	10	**127**	**19**
2001–02	Wycombe W	46	3		
2002–03	Wycombe W	38	4		
2003–04	Wycombe W	42	7	**126**	**14**
2004–05	Brighton & HA	22	2	**22**	**2**
2004–05	Ipswich T	24	3		
2005–06	Ipswich T	46	5		
2006–07	Ipswich T	13	1	**83**	**9**
2006–07	*Coventry C*	8	0	**8**	**0**
2006–07	*Derby Co*	7	1	**7**	**1**

DE VOS, Jason (D) 352 30

H: 6 4 W: 13 07 b.London, Can 2-1-74

Source: Montreal Impact. *Honours:* Canada Youth, Under-23, 49 full caps, 4 goals.

1996–97	Darlington	8	0		
1997–98	Darlington	24	3		
1998–99	Darlington	12	2	**44**	**5**
1998–99	Dundee U	25	0		
1999–2000	Dundee U	35	2		
2000–01	Dundee U	33	0	**93**	**2**
2001–02	Wigan Ath	20	5		
2002–03	Wigan Ath	43	8		
2003–04	Wigan Ath	27	2	**90**	**15**
2004–05	Ipswich T	45	3		
2005–06	Ipswich T	41	3		
2006–07	Ipswich T	39	2	**125**	**8**

DROBNY, Jaroslav (G) 0 0

H: 6 4 W: 14 00 b.Pocatky 19-10-79

Source: Panionios. *Honours:* Czech Republic Youth, Under-20, Under-21.

2005–06	Fulham	0	0		
2006–07	Fulham	0	0		
2006–07	Ipswich T	0	0		

To Bochum January 2007

GARVAN, Owen (M) 59 4

H: 6 0 W: 10 07 b.Dublin 29-1-88

Source: Scholar. *Honours:* Eire Youth.

2005–06	Ipswich T	32	3		
2006–07	Ipswich T	27	1	**59**	**4**

HARDING, Dan (D) 129 1

H: 6 0 W: 11 11 b.Gloucester 23-12-83

Source: Scholar. *Honours:* England Under-21.

2002–03	Brighton & HA	1	0		
2003–04	Brighton & HA	23	0		
2004–05	Brighton & HA	43	1	**67**	**1**
2005–06	Leeds U	20	0	**20**	**0**
2006–07	Ipswich T	42	0	**42**	**0**

HAYNES, Danny (F) 55 12

H: 5 11 W: 12 04 b.London 19-1-88

Source: Scholar. *Honours:* England Youth.

2005–06	Ipswich T	19	3		
2006–07	Ipswich T	31	7	**50**	**10**
2006–07	*Millwall*	5	2	**5**	**2**

KNIGHTS, Darryl (F) **5 0**
H: 5 7 W: 10 01 b.Ipswich 1-5-88
Source: Scholar. *Honours:* England Youth.

2004–05	Ipswich T	1	0		
2005–06	Ipswich T	0	0		
2006–07	Ipswich T	0	0	**1**	**0**
2006–07	*Yeovil T*	4	0	**4**	**0**

KRAUSE, James (D) **3 0**
H: 5 11 W: 10 03 b.Bury St Edmunds 9-1-87
Source: Scholar.

2005–06	Ipswich T	0	0		
2006–07	Ipswich T	0	0		
2006–07	*Carlisle U*	3	0	**3**	**0**

LEE, Alan (F) **285 71**
H: 6 2 W: 13 09 b.Galway 21-8-78
Source: Trainee. *Honours:* Eire Under-21, 10 full caps.

1995–96	Aston Villa	0	0		
1996–97	Aston Villa	0	0		
1997–98	Aston Villa	0	0		
1998–99	Aston Villa	0	0		
1998–99	*Torquay U*	7	2	**7**	**2**
1998–99	*Port Vale*	11	2	**11**	**2**
1999–2000	Burnley	15	0		
2000–01	Burnley	0	0	**15**	**0**
2000–01	Rotherham U	31	13		
2001–02	Rotherham U	38	9		
2002–03	Rotherham U	41	15		
2003–04	Rotherham U	1	0	**111**	**37**
2003–04	Cardiff C	23	3		
2004–05	Cardiff C	38	5		
2005–06	Cardiff C	25	2	**86**	**10**
2005–06	Ipswich T	14	4		
2006–07	Ipswich T	41	16	**55**	**20**

LEGWINSKI, Sylvain (M) **334 28**
H: 6 1 W: 11 07 b.Clermont-Ferrand 6-10-73
Honours: France Under-21.

1992–93	Monaco	2	0		
1993–94	Monaco	0	0		
1994–95	Monaco	21	1		
1995–96	Monaco	29	2		
1996–97	Monaco	37	9		
1997–98	Monaco	22	0		
1998–99	Monaco	14	1	**125**	**13**
1999–2000	Bordeaux	13	1		
2000–01	Bordeaux	32	1		
2001–02	Bordeaux	4	0	**49**	**2**
2001–02	Fulham	33	3		
2002–03	Fulham	35	4		
2003–04	Fulham	32	0		
2004–05	Fulham	15	1		
2005–06	Fulham	13	0		
2006–07	Fulham	0	0	**128**	**8**
2006–07	Ipswich T	32	5	**32**	**5**

MILLER, Ian (M) **20 1**
H: 6 2 W: 12 02 b.Colchester 23-11-83

2006–07	Ipswich T	1	0	**1**	**0**
2006–07	*Boston U*	12	0	**12**	**0**
2006–07	*Darlington*	7	1	**7**	**1**

MOORE, Sammy (M) **1 0**
H: 5 8 W: 9 00 b.Dover 7-9-87
Source: Scholar.

2006–07	Ipswich T	1	0	**1**	**0**

NAYLOR, Richard (D) **305 37**
H: 6 1 W: 13 07 b.Leeds 28-2-77
Source: Trainee.

1995–96	Ipswich T	0	0		
1996–97	Ipswich T	27	4		
1997–98	Ipswich T	5	2		
1998–99	Ipswich T	30	5		
1999–2000	Ipswich T	36	8		
2000–01	Ipswich T	13	1		
2001–02	Ipswich T	14	1		
2001–02	*Millwall*	3	0	**3**	**0**
2001–02	*Barnsley*	8	0	**8**	**0**
2002–03	Ipswich T	17	2		
2003–04	Ipswich T	39	5		
2004–05	Ipswich T	46	6		
2005–06	Ipswich T	42	3		
2006–07	Ipswich T	25	0	**294**	**37**

O'CALLAGHAN, George (M) **138 20**
H: 6 1 W: 10 11 b.Cork 5-9-79
Source: Trainee. *Honours:* Eire Youth.

1998–99	Port Vale	4	0		
1999–2000	Port Vale	11	0		
2000–01	Port Vale	8	1		
2001–02	Port Vale	11	3	**34**	**4**
2002–03	Cork C	26	6		
2003–04	Cork C	0	0		
2004–05	Cork C	35	3		
2005–06	Cork C	32	6	**93**	**15**
2006–07	Ipswich T	11	1	**11**	**1**

PETERS, Jaime (M) **36 2**
H: 5 7 W: 10 12 b.Pickering 4-5-87
Source: Moor Green. *Honours:* Canada Youth, Under-20, Under-23, 14 full caps.

2005–06	Ipswich T	13	0		
2006–07	Ipswich T	23	2	**36**	**2**

PLUMMER, Andrew (G) **0 0**
H: 6 0 W: 12 13 b.Ipswich 3-10-89
Source: Scholar.

2006–07	Ipswich T	0	0		

PRICE, Lewis (G) **74 0**
H: 6 3 W: 13 05 b.Bournemouth 19-7-84
Source: From Southampton Academy. *Honours:* Wales Youth, Under-21, 3 full caps.

2002–03	Ipswich T	0	0		
2003–04	Ipswich T	1	0		
2004–05	Ipswich T	8	0		
2004–05	*Cambridge U*	6	0	**6**	**0**
2005–06	Ipswich T	25	0		
2006–07	Ipswich T	34	0	**68**	**0**

RICHARDS, Matt (D) **147 8**
H: 5 8 W: 11 00 b.Harlow 26-12-84
Source: Scholar. *Honours:* England Under-21.

2001–02	Ipswich T	0	0		
2002–03	Ipswich T	13	0		
2003–04	Ipswich T	44	1		
2004–05	Ipswich T	24	1		
2005–06	Ipswich T	38	4		
2006–07	Ipswich T	28	2	**147**	**8**

ROBERTS, Gary (F) **47 10**
H: 5 10 W: 11 09 b.Wales 18-3-84
Source: Denbigh T, Bangor C.

2006–07	Accrington S	14	8	**14**	**8**
2006–07	Ipswich T	33	2	**33**	**2**

SITO (D) **107 0**
H: 5 8 W: 11 07 b.Coruna 21-5-80

2001–02	Lugo	10	0	**10**	**0**
2001–02	Calahorra	18	0	**18**	**0**
2002–03	Racing Ferrol	12	0		
2003–04	Racing Ferrol	21	0		
2004–05	Racing Ferrol	0	0	**33**	**0**
2005–06	Ipswich T	38	0		
2006–07	Ipswich T	8	0	**46**	**0**

SUPPLE, Shane (G) **34 0**
H: 6 0 W: 11 13 b.Dublin 4-5-87
Source: Scholar. *Honours:* Eire Youth.

2004–05	Ipswich T	0	0		
2005–06	Ipswich T	22	0		
2006–07	Ipswich T	12	0	**34**	**0**

SYNNOTT, Michael (D) **0 0**
H: 5 7 W: 12 03 b.Dublin 20-1-87
Source: Scholar.

2006–07	Ipswich T	0	0		

TROTTER, Liam (M) **3 0**
H: 6 2 W: 12 02 b.Ipswich 24-8-88
Source: Scholar.

2005–06	Ipswich T	1	0		
2006–07	Ipswich T	0	0	**1**	**0**
2006–07	*Millwall*	2	0	**2**	**0**

UPSON, Edward (M) **0 0**
H: 5 10 W: 11 07 b.Bury St Edmunds 21-11-89
Source: Scholar.

2006–07	Ipswich T	0	0		

WALTERS, Jon (F) **143 25**
H: 6 0 W: 12 06 b.Birkenhead 20-9-83
Source: From Blackburn R Scholar. *Honours:* Eire Under-21.

2001–02	Bolton W	0	0		
2002–03	Bolton W	4	0		
2002–03	*Hull C*	11	5		
2003–04	Bolton W	0	0	**4**	**0**
2003–04	Crewe Alex	0	0		
2003–04	*Barnsley*	8	0	**8**	**0**
2003–04	Hull C	16	1		
2004–05	Hull C	21	1	**48**	**7**
2004–05	*Scunthorpe U*	3	0	**3**	**0**
2005–06	Wrexham	38	5	**38**	**5**
2006–07	Chester C	26	9	**26**	**9**
2006–07	Ipswich T	16	4	**16**	**4**

WILLIAMS, Gavin (M) **106 15**
H: 5 10 W: 11 05 b.Pontypridd 20-6-80
Source: Hereford U. *Honours:* Wales 2 full caps.

2003–04	Yeovil T	42	9		
2004–05	Yeovil T	13	2	**55**	**11**
2004–05	West Ham U	10	1		
2005–06	West Ham U	0	0	**10**	**1**
2005–06	Ipswich T	12	1		
2006–07	Ipswich T	29	2	**41**	**3**

WILNIS, Fabian (D) **510 10**
H: 5 8 W: 12 06 b.Paramaribo 23-8-70
Source: Het Noorden, NOC, De Zwervers, Sparta.

1990–91	NAC	7	3		
1991–92	NAC	30	0		
1992–93	NAC	32	0		
1993–94	NAC	34	0		
1994–95	NAC	31	0	**134**	**3**
1995–96	De Graafschap	32	0		
1996–97	De Graafschap	23	0		
1997–98	De Graafschap	33	1		
1998–99	De Graafschap	19	0	**107**	**1**
1998–99	Ipswich T	18	1		
1999–2000	Ipswich T	35	0		
2000–01	Ipswich T	29	2		
2001–02	Ipswich T	14	0		
2002–03	Ipswich T	35	2		
2003–04	Ipswich T	41	0		
2004–05	Ipswich T	41	0		
2005–06	Ipswich T	35	1		
2006–07	Ipswich T	21	0	**269**	**6**

WRIGHT, David (D) **280 4**
H: 5 11 W: 11 01 b.Warrington 1-5-80
Source: Trainee. *Honours:* England Youth.

1997–98	Crewe Alex	3	0		
1998–99	Crewe Alex	20	1		
1999–2000	Crewe Alex	45	0		
2000–01	Crewe Alex	42	0		
2001–02	Crewe Alex	30	0		
2002–03	Crewe Alex	31	1		
2003–04	Crewe Alex	40	1	**211**	**3**
2004–05	Wigan Ath	31	0		
2005–06	Wigan Ath	2	0		
2005–06	*Norwich C*	5	0	**5**	**0**
2006–07	Wigan Ath	12	0	**45**	**0**
2006–07	Ipswich T	19	1	**19**	**1**

LEEDS U (42)

ANKERGREN, Casper (G) **100 0**
H: 6 3 W: 14 07 b.Koge 9-11-79
Source: Koge. *Honours:* Denmark Youth, Under-21.

2001–02	Brondby	1	0		
2002–03	Brondby	16	0		
2003–04	Brondby	1	0		
2004–05	Brondby	32	0		
2005–06	Brondby	18	0		
2006–07	Brondby	18	0	**86**	**0**
2006–07	Leeds U	14	0	**14**	**0**

ARMANDO SA, Miguel (D) **181 4**
H: 5 9 W: 11 02 b.Maputo 16-9-75
Honours: Mozambique 21 full caps.

1995–96	Villafranquense	29	1	**29**	**1**
From Braganca, Vila Real.					
1998–99	Rio Ave	19	0		
1999–2000	Rio Ave	29	1	**48**	**1**
2000–01	Braga	16	0	**16**	**0**
2001–02	Benfica	14	0		
2002–03	Benfica	9	1		
2003–04	Benfica	14	0	**37**	**1**
2004–05	Villarreal	20	0	**20**	**0**

2005–06	Espanyol	20	1		
2006–07	Espanyol	0	0	**20**	**1**
2006–07	Leeds U	11	0	**11**	**0**

BAKKE, Eirik (M) 233 25
H: 6 1 W: 12 08 b.Sogndal 13-9-77
Honours: Norway Youth, Under-20, Under-21, 26 full caps.

1994	Sogndal	5	0		
1995	Sogndal	0	0		
1996	Sogndal	19	8		
1997	Sogndal	25	4		
1998	Sogndal	19	2		
1999	Sogndal	8	3	**76**	**17**
1999–2000	Leeds U	29	2		
2000–01	Leeds U	29	2		
2001–02	Leeds U	27	2		
2002–03	Leeds U	34	1		
2003–04	Leeds U	10	1		
2004–05	Leeds U	1	0		
2005–06	Leeds U	10	0		
2005–06	*Aston Villa*	14	0	**14**	**0**
2006–07	Leeds U	3	0	**143**	**8**

To Brann January 2007

BAYLY, Robert (M) 1 0
H: 5 9 W: 11 09 b.Dublin 22-2-88
Source: Scholar.

2005–06	Leeds U	0	0		
2006–07	Leeds U	1	0	**1**	**0**

BECKFORD, Jermaine (F) 32 9
H: 6 2 W: 13 02 b.London 9-12-83
Source: Wealdstone.

2005–06	Leeds U	5	0		
2006–07	Leeds U	5	0	**10**	**0**
2006–07	*Carlisle U*	4	1	**4**	**1**
2006–07	*Scunthorpe U*	18	8	**18**	**8**

BLAKE, Robbie (F) 440 125
H: 5 9 W: 12 00 b.Middlesbrough 4-3-76
Source: Trainee.

1994–95	Darlington	9	0		
1995–96	Darlington	29	11		
1996–97	Darlington	30	10	**68**	**21**
1996–97	Bradford C	5	0		
1997–98	Bradford C	34	8		
1998–99	Bradford C	39	16		
1999–2000	Bradford C	28	2		
2000–01	Bradford C	21	4		
2000–01	*Nottingham F*	11	1	**11**	**1**
2001–02	Bradford C	26	10	**153**	**40**
2001–02	Burnley	10	0		
2002–03	Burnley	41	13		
2003–04	Burnley	45	19		
2004–05	Burnley	24	10	**120**	**42**
2004–05	Birmingham C	11	2	**11**	**2**
2005–06	Leeds U	41	11		
2006–07	Leeds U	36	8	**77**	**19**

BUTLER, Paul (D) 561 24
H: 6 2 W: 13 00 b.Manchester 2-11-72
Source: Trainee. *Honours:* Eire 1 full cap.

1990–91	Rochdale	2	0		
1991–92	Rochdale	25	0		
1992–93	Rochdale	16	2		
1993–94	Rochdale	38	2		
1994–95	Rochdale	39	3		
1995–96	Rochdale	38	3	**158**	**10**
1996–97	Bury	41	2		
1997–98	Bury	43	2	**84**	**4**
1998–99	Sunderland	44	2		
1999–2000	Sunderland	32	1		
2000–01	Sunderland	3	0	**79**	**3**
2000–01	Wolverhampton W	12	0		
2001–02	Wolverhampton W	43	1		
2002–03	Wolverhampton W	32	1		
2003–04	Wolverhampton W	37	1	**124**	**3**
2004–05	Leeds U	39	0		
2005–06	Leeds U	44	3		
2006–07	Leeds U	16	1	**99**	**4**
2006–07	*Milton Keynes D*	17	0	**17**	**0**

CAMFIELD, Bailey (D) 0 0
b.Wakefield 22-1-88
Source: Scholar.

2005–06	Leeds U	0	0		
2006–07	Leeds U	0	0		

CAROLE, Sebastien (M) 69 3
H: 5 7 W: 11 05 b.Pontoise 8-9-82
Source: Monaco.

2003–04	West Ham U	1	0	**1**	**0**
2004–05	Chateauroux	11	1	**11**	**1**
2005–06	Brighton & HA	40	2	**40**	**2**
2006–07	Leeds U	17	0	**17**	**0**

CRAINEY, Stephen (D) 98 0
H: 5 9 W: 9 11 b.Glasgow 22-6-81
Honours: Scotland B, Under-21, 6 full caps.

1999–2000	Celtic	9	0		
2000–01	Celtic	2	0		
2001–02	Celtic	15	0		
2002–03	Celtic	13	0		
2003–04	Celtic	2	0	**41**	**0**
2003–04	Southampton	5	0	**5**	**0**
2004–05	Leeds U	9	0		
2005–06	Leeds U	24	0		
2006–07	Leeds U	19	0	**52**	**0**

CRESSWELL, Richard (F) 364 82
H: 6 0 W: 11 08 b.Bridlington 20-9-77
Source: Trainee. *Honours:* England Under-21.

1995–96	York C	16	1		
1996–97	York C	17	0		
1996–97	*Mansfield T*	5	1	**5**	**1**
1997–98	York C	26	4		
1998–99	York C	36	16	**95**	**21**
1998–99	Sheffield W	7	1		
1999–2000	Sheffield W	20	1		
2000–01	Sheffield W	4	0	**31**	**2**
2000–01	Leicester C	8	0	**8**	**0**
2000–01	*Preston NE*	11	2		
2001–02	Preston NE	40	13		
2002–03	Preston NE	42	16		
2003–04	Preston NE	45	2		
2004–05	Preston NE	46	16		
2005–06	Preston NE	3	0	**187**	**49**
2005–06	Leeds U	16	5		
2006–07	Leeds U	22	4	**38**	**9**

DELPH, Fabian (D) 1 0
H: 5 8 W: 11 00 b.Bradford 5-5-91

2006–07	Leeds U	1	0	**1**	**0**

DERRY, Shaun (M) 361 11
H: 5 10 W: 10 13 b.Nottingham 6-12-77
Source: Trainee.

1995–96	Notts Co	12	0		
1996–97	Notts Co	39	2		
1997–98	Notts Co	28	2	**79**	**4**
1997–98	Sheffield U	12	0		
1998–99	Sheffield U	26	0		
1999–2000	Sheffield U	34	0	**72**	**0**
1999–2000	Portsmouth	9	1		
2000–01	Portsmouth	28	0		
2001–02	Portsmouth	12	0	**49**	**1**
2002–03	Crystal Palace	39	1		
2003–04	Crystal Palace	37	2		
2004–05	Crystal Palace	7	0	**83**	**3**
2004–05	*Nottingham F*	7	0	**7**	**0**
2004–05	Leeds U	7	2		
2005–06	Leeds U	41	0		
2006–07	Leeds U	23	1	**71**	**3**

DOUGLAS, Jonathan (M) 124 11
H: 5 11 W: 11 11 b.Monaghan 22-11-81
Source: Trainee. *Honours:* Eire Under-21, 7 full caps.

1999–2000	Blackburn R	0	0		
2000–01	Blackburn R	0	0		
2001–02	Blackburn R	0	0		
2002–03	Blackburn R	1	0		
2002–03	*Chesterfield*	7	1	**7**	**1**
2003–04	Blackpool	16	3	**16**	**3**
2003–04	Blackburn R	14	1		
2004–05	Blackburn R	1	0		
2004–05	*Gillingham*	10	0	**10**	**0**
2005–06	Blackburn R	0	0		
2005–06	*Leeds U*	40	5		
2006–07	Blackburn R	0	0	**16**	**1**
2006–07	Leeds U	35	1	**75**	**6**

EINARSSON, Gylfi (M) 124 27
H: 6 1 W: 11 11 b.Iceland 27-10-78
Honours: Iceland Youth, 24 full caps, 1 goal.

1996	Fylkir	2	0		
1997	Fylkir	0	0		
1998	Fylkir	0	0		
1999	Fylkir	0	0		
2000	Fylkir	18	10	**20**	**10**
2000–01	Lille	18	1		
2001–02	Lille	22	1		
2002–03	Lille	17	2		
2003–04	Lille	26	12	**83**	**16**
2004–05	Leeds U	8	1		
2005–06	Leeds U	10	0		
2006–07	Leeds U	3	0	**21**	**1**

ELLIOTT, Robbie (D) 242 16
H: 5 10 W: 10 12 b.Gosforth 25-12-73
Source: Trainee. *Honours:* England Youth, Under-21.

1990–91	Newcastle U	6	0		
1991–92	Newcastle U	9	0		
1992–93	Newcastle U	0	0		
1993–94	Newcastle U	15	0		
1994–95	Newcastle U	14	2		
1995–96	Newcastle U	6	0		
1996–97	Newcastle U	29	7		
1997–98	Bolton W	4	0		
1998–99	Bolton W	22	0		
1999–2000	Bolton W	27	3		
2000–01	Bolton W	33	2	**86**	**5**
2001–02	Newcastle U	27	1		
2002–03	Newcastle U	2	0		
2003–04	Newcastle U	0	0		
2004–05	Newcastle U	17	1		
2005–06	Newcastle U	17	0	**142**	**11**
2006–07	Sunderland	7	0	**7**	**0**
2006–07	Leeds U	7	0	**7**	**0**

ELLIOTT, Tom (F) 3 0
H: 5 10 W: 11 02 b.Leeds 9-9-89

2006–07	Leeds U	3	0	**3**	**0**

FLO, Tore Andre (F) 372 137
H: 6 4 W: 13 08 b.Strin 15-6-73
Honours: Norway Under-21, 76 full caps, 23 goals.

1994	Sogndal	22	5	**22**	**5**
1995	Tromso	26	18	**26**	**18**
1996	Brann	24	19		
1997	Brann	16	9	**40**	**28**
1997–98	Chelsea	34	11		
1998–99	Chelsea	30	10		
1999–2000	Chelsea	34	10		
2000–01	Chelsea	14	3	**112**	**34**
2000–01	Rangers	19	11		
2001–02	Rangers	30	17		
2002–03	Rangers	4	0	**53**	**28**
2002–03	Sunderland	29	4	**29**	**4**
2003–04	Siena	33	8		
2004–05	Siena	32	7	**65**	**15**
2005	Valerenga	8	0		
2006	Valerenga	16	4	**24**	**4**
2006–07	Leeds U	1	1	**1**	**1**

FOXE, Hayden (D) 113 8
H: 6 3 W: 13 05 b.Sydney 23-6-77
Honours: Australia Youth, Under-20, Under-23, 10 full caps, 2 goals.

1997–98	Arminia Bielefeld	1	0	**1**	**0**
1998	Sanfrecce	15	3		
1999	Sanfrecce	22	2	**37**	**5**
2000–01	Mechelen	4	0	**4**	**0**
2000–01	West Ham U	5	0		
2001–02	West Ham U	6	0	**11**	**0**
2002–03	Portsmouth	32	1		
2003–04	Portsmouth	10	1		
2004–05	Portsmouth	0	0		
2005–06	Portsmouth	0	0	**42**	**2**
2006–07	Leeds U	18	1	**18**	**1**

GARDNER, Scott (M) 0 0
b.Luxembourg 1-4-88
Source: Scholar. *Honours:* England Youth.

2005–06	Leeds U	0	0		
2006–07	Leeds U	0	0		

HEALY, David (F) 280 78
H: 5 8 W: 10 09 b.Downpatrick 5-8-79
Source: Trainee. *Honours:* Northern Ireland Schools, Youth, Under-21, B, 56 full caps, 29 goals.

1997–98	Manchester U	0	0		
1998–99	Manchester U	0	0		
1999–2000	Manchester U	0	0		

1999–2000	*Port Vale*	16	3	**16**	**3**
2000–01	Manchester U	1	0	**1**	**0**
2000–01	Preston NE	22	9		
2001–02	Preston NE	44	10		
2002–03	Preston NE	24	5		
2002–03	*Norwich C*	13	2	**13**	**2**
2003–04	Preston NE	38	15		
2004–05	Preston NE	11	5	**139**	**44**
2004–05	Leeds U	28	7		
2005–06	Leeds U	42	12		
2006–07	Leeds U	41	10	**111**	**29**

HEATH, Matt (D) **117** **10**

H: 6 4 W: 13 13 b.Leicester 1-11-81

Source: Scholar.

2000–01	Leicester C	0	0		
2001–02	Leicester C	5	0		
2002–03	Leicester C	11	3		
2003–04	Leicester C	13	0		
2003–04	*Stockport Co*	8	0	**8**	**0**
2004–05	Leicester C	22	3	**51**	**6**
2005–06	Coventry C	25	1		
2006–07	Coventry C	7	0	**32**	**1**
2006–07	Leeds U	26	3	**26**	**3**

HIRD, Samuel (D) **5** **0**

H: 5 7 W: 10 12 b.Askern 7-9-87

Source: Scholar.

2005–06	Leeds U	0	0		
2006–07	Leeds U	0	0		
2006–07	*Doncaster R*	5	0	**5**	**0**

HOWSON, Jonathan (M) **9** **1**

H: 5 11 W: 12 01 b.Morley 21-5-88

Source: Scholar.

2006–07	Leeds U	9	1	**9**	**1**

KANDOL, Tresor (F) **87** **16**

H: 6 0 W: 13 07 b.Banga 30-8-81

Source: Trainee.

1998–99	Luton T	4	0		
1999–2000	Luton T	4	0		
2000–01	Luton T	13	3	**21**	**3**
2001–02	Bournemouth	12	0	**12**	**0**
From Thurrock, Dagenham					
2005–06	*Darlington*	7	2	**7**	**2**
From Dagenham & R.					
2005–06	Barnet	13	4		
2006–07	Barnet	16	6	**29**	**10**
2006–07	Leeds U	18	1	**18**	**1**

KELLY, Gary (D) **430** **2**

H: 5 8 W: 13 03 b.Drogheda 9-7-74

Source: Home Farm. *Honours:* Eire Youth, Under-21, 52 full caps, 2 goals.

1991–92	Leeds U	2	0		
1992–93	Leeds U	0	0		
1993–94	Leeds U	42	0		
1994–95	Leeds U	42	0		
1995–96	Leeds U	34	0		
1996–97	Leeds U	36	2		
1997–98	Leeds U	34	0		
1998–99	Leeds U	0	0		
1999–2000	Leeds U	31	0		
2000–01	Leeds U	24	0		
2001–02	Leeds U	20	0		
2002–03	Leeds U	25	0		
2003–04	Leeds U	37	0		
2004–05	Leeds U	43	0		
2005–06	Leeds U	44	0		
2006–07	Leeds U	16	0	**430**	**2**

LEWIS, Eddie (M) **326** **32**

H: 5 10 W: 11 02 b.Cerritos 17-5-74

Honours: USA 72 full caps, 8 goals.

1996	San Jose Clash	25	0		
1997	San Jose Clash	29	2		
1998	San Jose Clash	32	3		
1999	San Jose Clash	29	4	**115**	**9**
1999–2000	Fulham	8	0		
2000–01	Fulham	7	0		
2001–02	Fulham	1	0	**16**	**0**
2002–03	Preston NE	38	5		
2003–04	Preston NE	33	6		
2004–05	Preston NE	40	4	**111**	**15**
2005–06	Leeds U	43	5		
2006–07	Leeds U	41	3	**84**	**8**

LUND, Jonny (G) **0** **0**

H: 5 10 W: 11 10 b.Leeds 1-11-88

Source: Scholar.

2006–07	Leeds U	0	0		

MADDEN, Simon (D) **0** **0**

b.Dublin 1-5-88

Source: Shelbourne.

2005–06	Leeds U	0	0		
2006–07	Leeds U	0	0		

MOORE, Ian (F) **424** **72**

H: 5 11 W: 12 00 b.Birkenhead 26-8-76

Source: Trainee. *Honours:* England Youth, Under-21.

1994–95	Tranmere R	1	0		
1995–96	Tranmere R	36	9		
1996–97	Tranmere R	21	3	**58**	**12**
1996–97	*Bradford C*	6	0	**6**	**0**
1996–97	Nottingham F	5	0		
1997–98	Nottingham F	10	1	**15**	**1**
1997–98	*West Ham U*	1	0	**1**	**0**
1998–99	Stockport Co	38	3		
1999–2000	Stockport Co	38	10		
2000–01	Stockport Co	17	7	**93**	**20**
2000–01	Burnley	27	5		
2001–02	Burnley	46	11		
2002–03	Burnley	44	8		
2003–04	Burnley	40	9		
2004–05	Burnley	35	4	**192**	**37**
2004–05	Leeds U	6	0		
2005–06	Leeds U	20	0		
2006–07	Leeds U	33	2	**59**	**2**

NICHOLLS, Kevin (M) **232** **33**

H: 5 10 W: 11 13 b.Newham 2-1-79

Source: Trainee. *Honours:* England Youth.

1995–96	Charlton Ath	0	0		
1996–97	Charlton Ath	6	1		
1997–98	Charlton Ath	6	0		
1998–99	Charlton Ath	0	0	**12**	**1**
1998–99	*Brighton & HA*	4	1	**4**	**1**
1999–2000	Wigan Ath	8	0		
2000–01	Wigan Ath	20	0	**28**	**0**
2001–02	Luton T	42	7		
2002–03	Luton T	36	5		
2003–04	Luton T	21	2		
2004–05	Luton T	44	12		
2005–06	Luton T	32	5	**175**	**31**
2006–07	Leeds U	13	0	**13**	**0**

PARKER, Ben (D) **39** **0**

H: 5 11 W: 11 06 b.Pontefract 8-11-87

Source: Scholar. *Honours:* England Youth.

2004–05	Leeds U	0	0		
2005–06	Leeds U	0	0		
2006–07	Leeds U	0	0		
2006–07	*Bradford C*	39	0	**39**	**0**

RICHARDSON, Frazer (D) **100** **3**

H: 5 11 W: 11 12 b.Rotherham 29-10-82

Source: Trainee. *Honours:* England Youth, Under-20.

1999–2000	Leeds U	0	0		
2000–01	Leeds U	0	0		
2001–02	Leeds U	0	0		
2002–03	Leeds U	0	0		
2002–03	*Stoke C*	7	0		
2003–04	Leeds U	4	0		
2003–04	*Stoke C*	6	1	**13**	**1**
2004–05	Leeds U	38	1		
2005–06	Leeds U	23	1		
2006–07	Leeds U	22	0	**87**	**2**

ROTHERY, Gavin (F) **0** **0**

b.Morley 22-9-87

Source: Scholar. *Honours:* England Youth.

2005–06	Leeds U	0	0		
2006–07	Leeds U	0	0		

RUI MARQUES, Manuel (D) **133** **0**

H: 5 11 W: 11 13 b.Luanda 3-9-77

Source: Benfica. *Honours:* Angola 3 full caps.

1998–99	Baden	27	0	**27**	**0**
1999–2000	SSV Ulm	32	0	**32**	**0**
2000–01	Hertha	1	0	**1**	**0**
2000–01	Stuttgart	12	0		
2001–02	Stuttgart	23	0		
2002–03	Stuttgart	12	0		
2003–04	Stuttgart	0	0	**47**	**0**
2004–05	Maritimo	8	0	**8**	**0**
2005–06	Leeds U	0	0		
2005–06	*Hull C*	1	0	**1**	**0**
2006–07	Leeds U	17	0	**17**	**0**

STONE, Steve (F) **368** **37**

H: 5 9 W: 12 07 b.Gateshead 20-8-71

Source: Trainee. *Honours:* England 9 full caps, 2 goals.

1989–90	Nottingham F	0	0		
1990–91	Nottingham F	0	0		
1991–92	Nottingham F	1	0		
1992–93	Nottingham F	12	1		
1993–94	Nottingham F	45	5		
1994–95	Nottingham F	41	5		
1995–96	Nottingham F	34	7		
1996–97	Nottingham F	5	0		
1997–98	Nottingham F	29	2		
1998–99	Nottingham F	26	3	**193**	**23**
1998–99	Aston Villa	10	0		
1999–2000	Aston Villa	24	1		
2000–01	Aston Villa	34	2		
2001–02	Aston Villa	22	1		
2002–03	Aston Villa	0	0	**90**	**4**
2002–03	Portsmouth	18	4		
2003–04	Portsmouth	32	2		
2004–05	Portsmouth	23	3	**73**	**9**
2005–06	Leeds U	2	0		
2006–07	Leeds U	10	1	**12**	**1**

SULLIVAN, Neil (G) **361** **0**

H: 6 2 W: 12 00 b.Sutton 24-2-70

Source: Trainee. *Honours:* Scotland 28 full caps.

1988–89	Wimbledon	0	0		
1989–90	Wimbledon	0	0		
1990–91	Wimbledon	1	0		
1991–92	Wimbledon	1	0		
1991–92	*Crystal Palace*	1	0	**1**	**0**
1992–93	Wimbledon	1	0		
1993–94	Wimbledon	2	0		
1994–95	Wimbledon	11	0		
1995–96	Wimbledon	16	0		
1996–97	Wimbledon	36	0		
1997–98	Wimbledon	38	0		
1998–99	Wimbledon	38	0		
1999–2000	Wimbledon	37	0	**181**	**0**
2000–01	Tottenham H	35	0		
2001–02	Tottenham H	29	0		
2002–03	Tottenham H	0	0	**64**	**0**
2003–04	Chelsea	4	0	**4**	**0**
2004–05	Leeds U	46	0		
2005–06	Leeds U	42	0		
2006–07	Leeds U	7	0	**95**	**0**
2006–07	*Doncaster R*	16	0	**16**	**0**

THOMPSON, Alan (M) **389** **77**

H: 6 0 W: 12 08 b.Newcastle 22-12-73

Source: Trainee. *Honours:* England Youth, Under-21, B, 1 full cap.

1990–91	Newcastle U	0	0		
1991–92	Newcastle U	14	0		
1992–93	Newcastle U	2	0	**16**	**0**
1993–94	Bolton W	27	6		
1994–95	Bolton W	37	7		
1995–96	Bolton W	26	1		
1996–97	Bolton W	34	10		
1997–98	Bolton W	33	9	**157**	**33**
1998–99	Aston Villa	25	2		
1999–2000	Aston Villa	21	2		
2000–01	Aston Villa	30	4	**76**	**8**
2001–02	Celtic	25	6		
2002–03	Celtic	29	8		
2003–04	Celtic	26	11		
2004–05	Celtic	32	7		
2005–06	Celtic	17	2		
2006–07	Celtic	0	0	**129**	**34**
2006–07	Leeds U	11	2	**11**	**2**

WESTLAKE, Ian (M) **141** **15**

H: 5 10 W: 11 06 b.Clacton 10-7-83

Source: Scholar.

2002–03	Ipswich T	4	0		
2003–04	Ipswich T	39	6		
2004–05	Ipswich T	45	7		
2005–06	Ipswich T	26	2	**114**	**15**
2006–07	Leeds U	27	0	**27**	**0**

LEICESTER C (43)

CADAMARTERI, Danny (F) 225 23
H: 5 7 W: 13 05 b.Bradford 12-10-79
Source: Trainee. *Honours:* England Youth, Under-21.

1996–97	Everton	1	0		
1997–98	Everton	26	4		
1998–99	Everton	30	4		
1999–2000	Everton	17	1		
1999–2000	*Fulham*	5	1	**5**	**1**
2000–01	Everton	16	4		
2001–02	Everton	3	0	**93**	**13**
2001–02	Bradford C	14	2		
2002–03	Bradford C	20	0		
2003–04	Bradford C	18	3		
2004–05	Leeds U	0	0		
2004–05	Sheffield U	21	1	**21**	**1**
2005–06	Bradford C	39	2		
2006–07	Bradford C	0	0	**91**	**7**
2006–07	*Doncaster R*	6	1	**6**	**1**
2006–07	Leicester C	9	0	**9**	**0**

CHAMBERS, Ashley (F) 0 0
H: 5 10 W: 11 06 b.Leicester 1-3-90
Honours: England Schools, Youth.

2005–06	Leicester C	0	0
2006–07	Leicester C	0	0

CISAK, Aleksander (G) 0 0
H: 6 3 W: 14 11 b.Krakow 19-5-89
Source: Scholar.

2006–07	Leicester C	0	0

DE VRIES, Mark (F) 183 47
H: 6 3 W: 13 05 b.Surinam 24-8-75

1995–96	Volendam	4	0		
1996–97	Volendam	10	0		
1997–98	Volendam	14	1	**28**	**1**
1998–99	Niort	0	0		
1999–2000	Dordrecht	8	0		
2000–01	Dordrecht	30	11		
2001–02	Dordrecht	0	0	**38**	**11**
2002–03	Hearts	32	15		
2003–04	Hearts	31	12		
2004–05	Hearts	9	1	**72**	**28**
2004–05	Leicester C	16	1		
2005–06	Leicester C	29	6		
2006–07	Leicester C	0	0	**45**	**7**

To Den Haag (loan) January 2007

DODDS, Louis (F) 12 2
H: 5 10 W: 12 04 b.Leicester 8-10-86
Source: Scholar.

2005–06	Leicester C	0	0		
2006–07	Leicester C	0	0		
2006–07	*Rochdale*	12	2	**12**	**2**

DOUGLAS, Rab (G) 329 0
H: 6 3 W: 14 12 b.Lanark 24-4-72
Source: Forth Wanderers. *Honours:* Scotland B, 19 full caps.

1992–93	Meadowbank T	0	0		
1993–94	Meadowbank T	4	0		
1994–95	Meadowbank T	8	0	**12**	**0**
1995–96	Livingston	24	0		
1996–97	Livingston	36	0	**60**	**0**
1997–98	Dundee	36	0		
1998–99	Dundee	35	0		
1999–2000	Dundee	35	0		
2000–01	Dundee	11	0	**117**	**0**
2000–01	Celtic	22	0		
2001–02	Celtic	35	0		
2002–03	Celtic	21	0		
2003–04	Celtic	16	0		
2004–05	Celtic	14	0	**108**	**0**
2005–06	Leicester C	32	0		
2006–07	Leicester C	0	0	**32**	**0**

FRYATT, Matty (F) 131 37
H: 5 10 W: 11 00 b.Nuneaton 5-3-86
Source: Scholar. *Honours:* England Youth.

2002–03	Walsall	0	0		
2003–04	Walsall	11	1		
2003–04	*Carlisle U*	10	1	**10**	**1**
2004–05	Walsall	36	15		
2005–06	Walsall	23	11	**70**	**27**
2005–06	Leicester C	19	6		
2006–07	Leicester C	32	3	**51**	**9**

GERRBRAND, Patrik (D) 82 2
H: 6 2 W: 12 06 b.Stockholm 27-4-81
Source: Alvsjo. *Honours:* Sweden Under-21.

2000	Hammarby	6	0		
2001	Hammarby	5	0		
2002	Hammarby	0	0		
2003	Hammarby	16	1		
2004	Hammarby	25	1		
2005	Hammarby	13	0	**65**	**2**
2005–06	Leicester C	17	0		
2006–07	Leicester C	0	0	**17**	**0**

GRADEL, Max (M) 0 0
H: 5 8 W: 12 03 b.Ivory Coast 30-9-87

2005–06	Leicester C	0	0
2006–07	Leicester C	0	0

HAMMOND, Elvis (F) 100 10
H: 5 10 W: 11 02 b.Accra 6-10-80
Source: Trainee. *Honours:* Ghana 1 full cap.

1999–2000	Fulham	0	0		
2000–01	Fulham	0	0		
2001–02	Fulham	0	0		
2001–02	*Bristol R*	7	0	**7**	**0**
2002–03	Fulham	10	0		
2003–04	Fulham	0	0		
2003–04	*Norwich C*	4	0	**4**	**0**
2004–05	Fulham	1	0		
2004–05	RBC Roosendaal	14	2	**14**	**2**
2005–06	Fulham	0	0	**11**	**0**
2005–06	Leicester C	33	3		
2006–07	Leicester C	31	5	**64**	**8**

HENDERSON, Paul (G) 217 0
H: 6 1 W: 12 06 b.Sydney 22-4-76

1998–99	Northern Spirit	30	0		
1999–2000	Northern Spirit	14	0		
2000–01	Northern Spirit	21	0		
2001–02	Northern Spirit	13	0		
2002–03	Northern Spirit	33	0		
2003–04	Northern Spirit	23	0	**134**	**0**
2004–05	Bradford C	40	0	**40**	**0**
2005–06	Leicester C	15	0		
2006–07	Leicester C	28	0	**43**	**0**

HUGHES, Stephen (M) 154 14
H: 5 11 W: 9 06 b.Motherwell 14-11-82
Honours: Scotland Youth, Under-21.

2000–01	Rangers	1	0		
2001–02	Rangers	17	1		
2002–03	Rangers	12	1		
2003–04	Rangers	22	3		
2004–05	Rangers	11	2	**63**	**7**
2004–05	Leicester C	16	1		
2005–06	Leicester C	34	3		
2006–07	Leicester C	41	3	**91**	**7**

HUME, Iain (F) 232 54
H: 5 7 W: 11 02 b.Brampton 31-10-83
Source: Juniors. *Honours:* Canada Youth, Under-20, 18 full caps, 1 goal.

1999–2000	Tranmere R	3	0		
2000–01	Tranmere R	10	0		
2001–02	Tranmere R	14	0		
2002–03	Tranmere R	35	6		
2003–04	Tranmere R	40	10		
2004–05	Tranmere R	42	15		
2005–06	Tranmere R	6	1	**150**	**32**
2005–06	Leicester C	37	9		
2006–07	Leicester C	45	13	**82**	**22**

JOHANSSON, Nils-Eric (D) 171 1
H: 6 1 W: 12 10 b.Stockholm 13-1-80
Source: Viksjo, Brommapojkana. *Honours:* Sweden 4 full caps.

1998	AIK Stockholm	0	0		
1998–99	Bayern Munich	2	0		
1999–2000	Bayern Munich	0	0		
2000–01	Bayern Munich	0	0	**2**	**0**
2001–02	Nuremberg	8	0	**8**	**0**
2001–02	Blackburn R	20	0		
2002–03	Blackburn R	30	0		
2003–04	Blackburn R	14	0		
2004–05	Blackburn R	22	0	**86**	**0**
2005–06	Leicester C	39	0		
2006–07	Leicester C	36	1	**75**	**1**

JOHNSON, Andy (M) 339 30
H: 6 0 W: 13 00 b.Bristol 2-5-74
Source: Trainee. *Honours:* England Youth, Wales 15 full caps.

1991–92	Norwich C	2	0		
1992–93	Norwich C	2	1		
1993–94	Norwich C	2	0		
1994–95	Norwich C	7	0		
1995–96	Norwich C	26	7		
1996–97	Norwich C	27	5	**66**	**13**
1997–98	Nottingham F	34	4		
1998–99	Nottingham F	28	0		
1999–2000	Nottingham F	25	2		
2000–01	Nottingham F	31	3		
2001–02	Nottingham F	1	0	**119**	**9**
2001–02	WBA	32	4		
2002–03	WBA	32	1		
2003–04	WBA	38	2		
2004–05	WBA	22	0		
2005–06	WBA	8	0	**132**	**7**
2006–07	Leicester C	22	1	**22**	**1**

KENTON, Darren (D) 220 11
H: 5 10 W: 12 06 b.Wandsworth 13-9-78
Source: Trainee.

1997–98	Norwich C	11	0		
1998–99	Norwich C	22	1		
1999–2000	Norwich C	26	1		
2000–01	Norwich C	29	2		
2001–02	Norwich C	33	4		
2002–03	Norwich C	37	1	**158**	**9**
2002–03	Southampton	0	0		
2003–04	Southampton	7	0		
2004–05	Southampton	9	0		
2004–05	*Leicester C*	10	0		
2005–06	Southampton	13	0	**29**	**0**
2006–07	Leicester C	23	2	**33**	**2**

KISNORBO, Patrick (D) 192 10
H: 6 1 W: 11 11 b.Melbourne 24-3-81
Honours: Australia Schools, Under-20, Under-23, 12 full caps.

2000–01	South Melbourne	25	0		
2001–02	South Melbourne	23	2		
2002–03	South Melbourne	19	1	**67**	**3**
2003–04	Hearts	31	0		
2004–05	Hearts	17	1	**48**	**1**
2005–06	Leicester C	37	1		
2006–07	Leicester C	40	5	**77**	**6**

LOGAN, Conrad (G) 31 0
H: 6 2 W: 14 00 b.Letterkenny 18-4-86
Source: Scholar. *Honours:* Eire Youth.

2003–04	Leicester C	0	0		
2004–05	Leicester C	0	0		
2005–06	Leicester C	0	0		
2005–06	*Boston U*	13	0	**13**	**0**
2006–07	Leicester C	18	0	**18**	**0**

LYCETT, Scott (D) 0 0
H: 6 0 W: 11 11 b.Stoke 5-9-87
Source: Scholar.

2006–07	Leicester C	0	0

MATTOCK, Joe (D) 4 0
H: 5 11 W: 12 05 b.Leicester 15-5-90
Source: Scholar.

2006–07	Leicester C	4	0	**4**	**0**

MAYBURY, Alan (D) 222 7
H: 5 8 W: 11 08 b.Dublin 8-8-78
Source: From Trainee. *Honours:* Eire Youth, Under-21, B, 10 full caps.

1995–96	Leeds U	1	0		
1996–97	Leeds U	0	0		
1997–98	Leeds U	12	0		
1998–99	Leeds U	0	0		
1998–99	*Reading*	8	0	**8**	**0**
1999–2000	Leeds U	0	0		
2000–01	Leeds U	0	0		
2000–01	*Crewe Alex*	6	0	**6**	**0**
2001–02	Leeds U	1	0	**14**	**0**
2001–02	Hearts	27	0		
2002–03	Hearts	35	2		
2003–04	Hearts	33	2		
2004–05	Hearts	15	0	**110**	**4**
2004–05	Leicester C	17	2		
2005–06	Leicester C	40	1		
2006–07	Leicester C	27	0	**84**	**3**

McAULEY, Gareth (D) **102** **11**
H: 6 3 W: 13 00 b.Larne 5-12-79
Source: Coleraine. *Honours:* Northern Ireland B, 5 full caps.

2004–05	Lincoln C	37	3		
2005–06	Lincoln C	35	5	**72**	**8**
2006–07	Leicester C	30	3	**30**	**3**

McCARTHY, Patrick (D) **90** **3**
H: 6 2 W: 13 07 b.Dublin 31-5-83
Source: Scholar. *Honours:* Eire Youth, B, Under-21.

2000–01	Manchester C	0	0		
2001–02	Manchester C	0	0		
2002–03	Manchester C	0	0		
2002–03	*Boston U*	12	0	**12**	**0**
2002–03	*Notts Co*	6	0	**6**	**0**
2003–04	Manchester C	0	0		
2004–05	Manchester C	0	0		
2004–05	Leicester C	12	0		
2005–06	Leicester C	38	2		
2006–07	Leicester C	22	1	**72**	**3**

ODHIAMBO, Eric (F) **0** **0**
H: 5 9 W: 11 02 b.Oxford 12-5-89
Source: Scholar.

2006–07	Leicester C	0	0		

PORTER, Levi (F) **34** **3**
H: 5 4 W: 10 05 b.Leicester 6-4-87
Source: From Scholar. *Honours:* England Youth.

2005–06	Leicester C	0	0		
2006–07	Leicester C	34	3	**34**	**3**

SHEEHAN, Alan (D) **13** **0**
H: 5 11 W: 11 02 b.Athlone 14-9-86
Source: Scholar. *Honours:* Eire Youth, Under-21.

2004–05	Leicester C	1	0		
2005–06	Leicester C	2	0		
2006–07	Leicester C	0	0	**3**	**0**
2006–07	*Mansfield T*	10	0	**10**	**0**

STEARMAN, Richard (D) **77** **5**
H: 6 2 W: 10 08 b.Wolverhampton 19-8-87
Source: Scholar. *Honours:* England Youth.

2004–05	Leicester C	8	1		
2005–06	Leicester C	34	3		
2006–07	Leicester C	35	1	**77**	**5**

SYLLA, Momo (M) **155** **10**
H: 6 0 W: 11 09 b.Conakry 13-3-77
Honours: Guinea 2 full caps.

1997–98	Ayr U	3	0	**3**	**0**
1998–99	Le Havre	10	0	**10**	**0**
1999–2000	Le Mans	27	1	**27**	**1**
2000–01	St Johnstone	34	6		
2001–02	St Johnstone	1	0	**35**	**6**
2001–02	Celtic	8	1		
2002–03	Celtic	18	2		
2003–04	Celtic	14	0		
2004–05	Celtic	6	0	**46**	**3**
2005–06	Leicester C	28	0		
2006–07	Leicester C	6	0	**34**	**0**

To Kilmarnock January 2007

TIATTO, Danny (D) **282** **11**
H: 5 8 W: 11 08 b.Melbourne 22-5-73
Honours: Australia Under-23, 23 full caps, 1 goal.

1994–95	Melbourne Knights	25	3		
1995–96	Melbourne Knights	18	0	**43**	**3**
1996–97	Salernitana	11	1	**11**	**1**
1997–98	Stoke C	15	1	**15**	**1**
From Baden					
1998–99	Manchester C	17	0		
1999–2000	Manchester C	35	0		
2000–01	Manchester C	33	2		
2001–02	Manchester C	37	1		
2002–03	Manchester C	13	0		
2003–04	Manchester C	5	0	**140**	**3**
2004–05	Leicester C	30	1		
2005–06	Leicester C	18	1		
2006–07	Leicester C	25	1	**73**	**3**

WESOLOWSKI, James (D) **24** **0**
H: 5 8 W: 11 11 b.Sydney 25-8-87
Source: Scholar. *Honours:* Australia Youth, Under-20.

2004–05	Leicester C	0	0		
2005–06	Leicester C	5	0		
2006–07	Leicester C	19	0	**24**	**0**

LEYTON ORIENT (44)

ALEXANDER, Gary (F) **321** **98**
H: 6 0 W: 13 04 b.Lambeth 15-8-79
Source: Trainee.

1998–99	West Ham U	0	0		
1999–2000	West Ham U	0	0		
1999–2000	*Exeter C*	37	16	**37**	**16**
2000–01	Swindon T	37	7	**37**	**7**
2001–02	Hull C	43	17		
2002–03	Hull C	25	6	**68**	**23**
2002–03	Leyton Orient	17	2		
2003–04	Leyton Orient	44	15		
2004–05	Leyton Orient	28	9		
2005–06	Leyton Orient	46	14		
2006–07	Leyton Orient	44	12	**179**	**52**

BARNARD, Donny (D) **140** **1**
H: 5 10 W: 12 01 b.Forest Gate 1-7-84
Source: Trainee.

2001–02	Leyton Orient	10	0		
2002–03	Leyton Orient	29	0		
2003–04	Leyton Orient	23	0		
2004–05	Leyton Orient	33	1		
2005–06	Leyton Orient	26	0		
2006–07	Leyton Orient	19	0	**140**	**1**

CHAMBERS, Adam (D) **107** **5**
H: 5 10 W: 11 12 b.Sandwell 20-11-80
Source: Trainee. *Honours:* England Youth.

1998–99	WBA	0	0		
1999–2000	WBA	0	0		
2000–01	WBA	11	1		
2001–02	WBA	32	0		
2002–03	WBA	13	0		
2003–04	WBA	0	0		
2003–04	*Sheffield W*	11	0	**11**	**0**
2004–05	WBA	0	0	**56**	**1**
2004–05	Kidderminster H	2	0	**2**	**0**
2006–07	Leyton Orient	38	4	**38**	**4**

CORDEN, Wayne (M) **327** **41**
H: 5 10 W: 11 05 b.Leek 1-11-75
Source: Trainee.

1994–95	Port Vale	1	0		
1995–96	Port Vale	2	0		
1996–97	Port Vale	12	0		
1997–98	Port Vale	33	1		
1998–99	Port Vale	16	0		
1999–2000	Port Vale	2	0	**66**	**1**
2000–01	Mansfield T	34	3		
2001–02	Mansfield T	46	8		
2002–03	Mansfield T	44	13		
2003–04	Mansfield T	44	8		
2004–05	Mansfield T	24	3	**192**	**35**
2004–05	Scunthorpe U	8	0		
2005–06	Scunthorpe U	9	0	**17**	**0**
2005–06	*Chester C*	2	0	**2**	**0**
2005–06	*Leyton Orient*	8	2		
2006–07	Leyton Orient	42	3	**50**	**5**

DEMETRIOU, Jason (M) **18** **2**
H: 5 11 W: 10 08 b.Newham 18-11-87
Source: Scholar.

2005–06	Leyton Orient	3	0		
2006–07	Leyton Orient	15	2	**18**	**2**

DUNCAN, Derek (M) **20** **0**
H: 5 10 W: 10 11 b.Newham 23-4-87
Source: Scholar.

2003–04	Leyton Orient	1	0		
2004–05	Leyton Orient	15	0		
2005–06	Leyton Orient	1	0		
2006–07	Leyton Orient	3	0	**20**	**0**

EASTON, Craig (M) **132** **7**
H: 5 11 W: 11 03 b.Bellshill 26-2-79
Source: Dundee U BC. *Honours:* Scotland Youth, Under-21.

1995–96	Dundee U	0	0		
1996–97	Dundee U	2	0		
1997–98	Dundee U	29	1		
1998–99	Dundee U	30	1		
1999–2000	Dundee U	0	0		
2000–01	Dundee U	0	0		
2001–02	Dundee U	0	0	**61**	**2**
2005–06	Leyton Orient	41	4		
2006–07	Leyton Orient	30	1	**71**	**5**

ECHANOMI, Efe (F) **37** **8**
H: 5 7 W: 11 13 b.Nigeria 27-9-86

2004–05	Leyton Orient	18	5		
2005–06	Leyton Orient	16	3		
2006–07	Leyton Orient	3	0	**37**	**8**

FORTUNE, Clayton (D) **100** **2**
H: 6 3 W: 13 10 b.Forest Gate 10-11-82
Source: Tottenham H Scholar.

2000–01	Bristol C	0	0		
2001–02	Bristol C	1	0		
2002–03	Bristol C	10	0		
2003–04	Bristol C	6	0		
2004–05	Bristol C	30	0		
2005–06	Bristol C	6	0	**53**	**0**
2005–06	*Port Vale*	25	2		
2006–07	Leyton Orient	9	0	**9**	**0**
2006–07	*Port Vale*	13	0	**38**	**2**

GARNER, Glyn (G) **212** **0**
H: 6 2 W: 13 11 b.Pontypool 9-12-76
Source: Llanelli. *Honours:* Wales 1 full cap.

2000–01	Bury	0	0		
2001–02	Bury	7	0		
2002–03	Bury	46	0		
2003–04	Bury	46	0		
2004–05	Bury	27	0	**126**	**0**
2005–06	Leyton Orient	43	0		
2006–07	Leyton Orient	43	0	**86**	**0**

GUTTRIDGE, Luke (M) **217** **23**
H: 5 6 W: 8 07 b.Barnstaple 27-3-82
Source: Trainee.

1999–2000	Torquay U	1	0		
2000–01	Torquay U	0	0	**1**	**0**
2000–01	Cambridge U	1	1		
2001–02	Cambridge U	29	2		
2002–03	Cambridge U	43	3		
2003–04	Cambridge U	46	11		
2004–05	Cambridge U	17	0	**136**	**17**
2004–05	Southend U	5	0		
2005–06	Southend U	41	5		
2006–07	Southend U	17	0	**63**	**5**
2006–07	Leyton Orient	17	1	**17**	**1**

IBEHRE, Jabo (F) **178** **29**
H: 6 2 W: 13 13 b.Islington 28-1-83
Source: Trainee.

1999–2000	Leyton Orient	3	0		
2000–01	Leyton Orient	5	2		
2001–02	Leyton Orient	28	4		
2002–03	Leyton Orient	25	5		
2003–04	Leyton Orient	35	4		
2004–05	Leyton Orient	19	2		
2005–06	Leyton Orient	33	8		
2006–07	Leyton Orient	30	4	**178**	**29**

LOCKWOOD, Matt (D) **391** **51**
H: 5 11 W: 11 10 b.Southend 17-10-76
Source: Trainee.

1994–95	QPR	0	0		
1995–96	QPR	0	0		
1996–97	Bristol R	39	1		
1997–98	Bristol R	24	0	**63**	**1**
1998–99	Leyton Orient	37	3		
1999–2000	Leyton Orient	41	6		
2000–01	Leyton Orient	32	7		
2001–02	Leyton Orient	24	2		
2002–03	Leyton Orient	43	5		
2003–04	Leyton Orient	25	2		
2004–05	Leyton Orient	43	6		
2005–06	Leyton Orient	42	8		
2006–07	Leyton Orient	41	11	**328**	**50**

MACKIE, John (D) **193** **14**
H: 6 1 W: 12 08 b.Enfield 5-7-76
Source: Sutton U.

1999–2000	Reading	0	0		
2000–01	Reading	10	0		
2001–02	Reading	27	2		
2002–03	Reading	25	0		
2003–04	Reading	9	1	**71**	**3**
2003–04	Leyton Orient	20	1		
2004–05	Leyton Orient	27	4		
2005–06	Leyton Orient	40	6		
2006–07	Leyton Orient	35	0	**122**	**11**

McMAHON, Daryl (M) 71 5
H: 6 0 W: 12 07 b.Dublin 10-10-83
Honours: Eire Youth.
2000–01 West Ham U 0 0
2001–02 West Ham U 0 0
2002–03 West Ham U 0 0
2003–04 West Ham U 0 0
2003–04 *Torquay U* 1 0 **1 0**
2004–05 Port Vale 5 0 **5 0**
2004–05 Leyton Orient 24 3
2005–06 Leyton Orient 33 2
2006–07 Leyton Orient 8 0 **65 5**

MILLER, Justin (D) 163 5
H: 6 1 W: 12 12 b.Johannesburg 16-12-80
Source: Academy.
1999–2000 Ipswich T 0 0
2000–01 Ipswich T 0 0
2001–02 Ipswich T 0 0
2002–03 Ipswich T 0 0
2002–03 Leyton Orient 19 0
2003–04 Leyton Orient 34 2
2004–05 Leyton Orient 43 0
2005–06 Leyton Orient 36 1
2006–07 Leyton Orient 31 2 **163 5**

MORRIS, Glenn (G) 71 0
H: 6 0 W: 12 03 b.Woolwich 20-12-83
Source: Scholar.
2001–02 Leyton Orient 2 0
2002–03 Leyton Orient 23 0
2003–04 Leyton Orient 27 0
2004–05 Leyton Orient 12 0
2005–06 Leyton Orient 4 0
2006–07 Leyton Orient 3 0 **71 0**

MULRYNE, Phil (M) 168 18
H: 5 9 W: 11 03 b.Belfast 1-1-78
Source: Trainee. *Honours:* Northern Ireland Youth, Under-21, B, 27 full caps, 3 goals.
1994–95 Manchester U 0 0
1995–96 Manchester U 0 0
1996–97 Manchester U 0 0
1997–98 Manchester U 1 0
1998–99 Manchester U 0 0 **1 0**
1998–99 Norwich C 7 2
1999–2000 Norwich C 9 0
2000–01 Norwich C 28 1
2001–02 Norwich C 40 6
2002–03 Norwich C 33 6
2003–04 Norwich C 34 3
2004–05 Norwich C 10 0 **161 18**
2005–06 Cardiff C 4 0
2006–07 Cardiff C 0 0 **4 0**
2006–07 Leyton Orient 2 0 **2 0**

PAGE, Jack (M) 1 0
H: 6 0 W: 11 07 b.Purley 16-12-89
Source: Scholar.
2006–07 Leyton Orient 1 0 **1 0**

PALMER, Aiden (D) 14 0
H: 5 8 W: 10 10 b.Enfield 2-1-87
Source: Scholar.
2004–05 Leyton Orient 5 0
2005–06 Leyton Orient 3 0
2006–07 Leyton Orient 6 0 **14 0**

SAAH, Brian (M) 53 0
H: 6 3 W: 12 03 b.Rush Green 16-12-86
Source: Scholar.
2003–04 Leyton Orient 6 0
2004–05 Leyton Orient 12 0
2005–06 Leyton Orient 3 0
2006–07 Leyton Orient 32 0 **53 0**

SHIELDS, Solomon (M) 1 0
H: 5 10 W: 12 00 b.Leyton 14-10-89
Source: Scholar.
2006–07 Leyton Orient 1 0 **1 0**

SIMPSON, Michael (M) 451 23
H: 5 8 W: 10 12 b.Nottingham 28-2-74
Source: Trainee.
1992–93 Notts Co 0 0
1993–94 Notts Co 6 1
1994–95 Notts Co 19 2
1995–96 Notts Co 23 0
1996–97 Notts Co 1 0 **49 3**
1996–97 *Plymouth Arg* 12 0 **12 0**
1996–97 Wycombe W 20 1
1997–98 Wycombe W 21 0
1998–99 Wycombe W 33 4
1999–2000 Wycombe W 43 0
2000–01 Wycombe W 45 3
2001–02 Wycombe W 43 1
2002–03 Wycombe W 42 5
2003–04 Wycombe W 38 2 **285 16**
2004–05 Leyton Orient 45 2
2005–06 Leyton Orient 45 1
2006–07 Leyton Orient 15 1 **105 4**

SMITH, Dean (D) 566 54
H: 6 1 W: 13 10 b.West Bromwich 19-3-71
Source: Trainee.
1988–89 Walsall 15 0
1989–90 Walsall 7 0
1990–91 Walsall 33 0
1991–92 Walsall 9 0
1992–93 Walsall 42 1
1993–94 Walsall 36 1 **142 2**
1994–95 Hereford U 35 3
1995–96 Hereford U 40 8
1996–97 Hereford U 42 8 **117 19**
1997–98 Leyton Orient 43 9
1998–99 Leyton Orient 37 9
1999–2000 Leyton Orient 44 4
2000–01 Leyton Orient 43 5
2001–02 Leyton Orient 45 2
2002–03 Leyton Orient 27 3
2002–03 Sheffield W 14 0
2003–04 Sheffield W 41 1 **55 1**
2004–05 Port Vale 13 0 **13 0**
2004–05 Leyton Orient 0 0
2005–06 Leyton Orient 0 0
2006–07 Leyton Orient 0 0 **239 32**

TANN, Adam (D) 157 6
H: 6 0 W: 11 05 b.Fakenham 12-5-82
Source: Scholar. *Honours:* England Youth.
1999–2000 Cambridge U 0 0
2000–01 Cambridge U 1 0
2001–02 Cambridge U 25 0
2002–03 Cambridge U 25 1
2003–04 Cambridge U 34 2
2004–05 Cambridge U 36 1 **121 4**
From Gravesend & N.
2005–06 Notts Co 5 0 **5 0**
2005–06 Leyton Orient 10 1
2006–07 Leyton Orient 21 1 **31 2**

THELWELL, Alton (D) 80 2
H: 6 0 W: 12 05 b.Islington 5-9-80
Source: Trainee. *Honours:* England Under-21.
1998–99 Tottenham H 0 0
1999–2000 Tottenham H 0 0
2000–01 Tottenham H 16 0
2001–02 Tottenham H 2 0
2002–03 Tottenham H 0 0 **18 0**
2003–04 Hull C 26 1
2004–05 Hull C 3 0
2005–06 Hull C 9 0
2006–07 Hull C 2 0 **40 1**
2006–07 Leyton Orient 22 1 **22 1**

TUDOR, Shane (M) 188 27
H: 5 7 W: 11 12 b.Wolverhampton 10-2-82
Source: Trainee.
1999–2000 Wolverhampton W 0 0
2000–01 Wolverhampton W 1 0
2001–02 Wolverhampton W 0 0 **1 0**
2001–02 Cambridge U 32 3
2002–03 Cambridge U 27 9
2003–04 Cambridge U 36 3
2004–05 Cambridge U 26 6 **121 21**
2005–06 Leyton Orient 33 4
2006–07 Leyton Orient 33 2 **66 6**

LINCOLN C (45)

AMOO, Ryan (M) 49 2
H: 5 10 W: 9 12 b.Leicester 11-10-83
Source: Scholar.
2001–02 Aston Villa 0 0
2002–03 Aston Villa 0 0
2003–04 Aston Villa 0 0
2003–04 Northampton T 1 0
2004–05 Northampton T 5 0
2005–06 Northampton T 0 0 **6 0**
2006–07 Lincoln C 43 2 **43 2**

BACON, Danny (F) 46 4
H: 5 10 W: 10 12 b.Mansfield 20-9-80
Source: Trainee.
1999–2000 Mansfield T 8 2
2000–01 Mansfield T 22 1
2001–02 Mansfield T 8 1
2002–03 Mansfield T 6 0 **44 4**
From Hucknall T
2005–06 Lincoln C 1 0
2006–07 Lincoln C 1 0 **2 0**

BEEVERS, Lee (D) 157 9
H: 6 2 W: 11 07 b.Doncaster 4-12-83
Source: Scholar. *Honours:* Wales Youth, Under-21.
2000–01 Ipswich T 0 0
2001–02 Ipswich T 0 0
2002–03 Ipswich T 0 0
2002–03 *Boston U* 1 0
2003–04 Boston U 40 2
2004–05 Boston U 31 1 **72 3**
2004–05 Lincoln C 8 0
2005–06 Lincoln C 33 1
2006–07 Lincoln C 44 5 **85 6**

BIRCH, Gary (F) 151 23
H: 6 0 W: 12 03 b.Birmingham 8-10-81
Source: Trainee.
1998–99 Walsall 0 0
1999–2000 Walsall 0 0
2000–01 Walsall 0 0
2000–01 *Exeter C* 9 2
2001–02 *Exeter C* 15 0 **24 2**
2001–02 Walsall 1 0
2002–03 Walsall 19 1
2003–04 Walsall 35 4
2003–04 *Barnsley* 8 2 **8 2**
2004–05 Walsall 13 2 **68 7**
2004–05 Kidderminster H 14 4 **14 4**
2005–06 Lincoln C 37 8
2006–07 Lincoln C 0 0 **37 8**

BROWN, Nat (F) 143 8
H: 6 2 W: 12 05 b.Sheffield 15-6-81
Source: Trainee.
1999–2000 Huddersfield T 0 0
2000–01 Huddersfield T 0 0
2001–02 Huddersfield T 0 0
2002–03 Huddersfield T 38 0
2003–04 Huddersfield T 21 0
2004–05 Huddersfield T 17 0 **76 0**
2005–06 Lincoln C 39 7
2006–07 Lincoln C 28 1 **67 8**

CLARKE, Shane (D) 0 0
H: 6 1 W: 13 03 b.Lincoln 7-11-87
Source: Scholar.
2006–07 Lincoln C 0 0

DUFFY, Ayden (M) 0 0
H: 5 8 W: 10 12 b.Kettering 16-11-86
Source: Scholar.
2006–07 Lincoln C 0 0

FORRESTER, Jamie (F) 426 128
H: 5 7 W: 11 00 b.Bradford 1-11-74
Source: From Auxerre. *Honours:* England Schools, Youth.
1992–93 Leeds U 6 0
1993–94 Leeds U 3 0
1994–95 Leeds U 0 0
1994–95 *Southend U* 5 0 **5 0**
1994–95 *Grimsby T* 9 1
1995–96 Leeds U 0 0 **9 0**
1995–96 Grimsby T 28 5
1996–97 Grimsby T 13 1 **50 7**
1996–97 Scunthorpe U 10 6
1997–98 Scunthorpe U 45 11
1998–99 Scunthorpe U 46 20 **101 37**
1999–2000 Utrecht 1 0 **1 0**
1999–2000 Walsall 5 0 **5 0**
1999–2000 *Northampton T* 10 6
2000–01 Northampton T 43 17
2001–02 Northampton T 43 17
2002–03 Northampton T 25 5 **121 45**
2002–03 Hull C 11 3
2003–04 Hull C 21 4 **32 7**
2004–05 Bristol R 35 7

2005–06	Bristol R	17	2	**52**	**9**
2005–06	*Lincoln C*	9	5		
2006–07	Lincoln C	41	18	**50**	**23**

FOSTER, Luke (D) 16 1
H: 6 2 W: 12 08 b.Mexborough 8-9-85
Source: Scholar.

2004–05	Sheffield W	0	0		
2005–06	Lincoln C	16	1		
2006–07	Lincoln C	0	0	**16**	**1**

FRECKLINGTON, Lee (M) 63 10
H: 5 8 W: 11 00 b.Lincoln 8-9-85
Source: Scholar. *Honours:* Eire B.

2003–04	Lincoln C	0	0		
2004–05	Lincoln C	3	0		
2005–06	Lincoln C	18	2		
2006–07	Lincoln C	42	8	**63**	**10**

GREEN, Paul (D) 16 1
H: 5 8 W: 10 04 b.Birmingham 15-4-87
Source: Scholar.

2005–06	Aston Villa	0	0		
2006–07	Aston Villa	0	0		
2006–07	Lincoln C	16	1	**16**	**1**

GRITTON, Martin (F) 232 45
H: 6 1 W: 12 02 b.Glasgow 1-6-78
Source: Porthleven.

1998–99	Plymouth Arg	2	0		
1999–2000	Plymouth Arg	30	6		
2000–01	Plymouth Arg	10	1		
2001–02	Plymouth Arg	2	0		
2002–03	Plymouth Arg	0	0	**44**	**7**
2002–03	Torquay U	43	13		
2003–04	Torquay U	31	4		
2004–05	Torquay U	19	6	**93**	**23**
2004–05	Grimsby T	23	4		
2005–06	Grimsby T	26	2	**49**	**6**
2005–06	Lincoln C	10	1		
2006–07	Lincoln C	17	2	**27**	**3**
2006–07	*Mansfield T*	19	6	**19**	**6**

HUGHES, Jeff (D) 113 9
H: 6 1 W: 11 00 b.Larne 29-5-85
Source: Larne Tech Old Boys. *Honours:* Northern Ireland Under-21, 2 full caps.

2003–04	Larne	21	1		
2004–05	Larne	29	0	**50**	**1**
2005–06	Lincoln C	22	2		
2006–07	Lincoln C	41	6	**63**	**8**

JOHN-LEWIS, Leneli (M) 0 0
H: 5 10 W: 11 10 b.Hammersmith 17-5-89
Source: Scholar.

2006–07	Lincoln C	0	0		

KELL, Richard (M) 100 11
H: 6 1 W: 10 13 b.Bishop Auckland 15-9-79
Source: Trainee.

1998–99	Middlesbrough	0	0		
1999–2000	Middlesbrough	0	0		
2000–01	Middlesbrough	0	0		
2000–01	Torquay U	15	3		
2001–02	Torquay U	0	0	**15**	**3**
2001–02	Scunthorpe U	16	1		
2002–03	Scunthorpe U	0	0		
2003–04	Scunthorpe U	24	2		
2004–05	Scunthorpe U	43	5	**83**	**8**
2005–06	Barnsley	2	0	**2**	**0**
2006–07	Lincoln C	0	0		

KERR, Scott (M) 86 5
H: 5 9 W: 10 07 b.Leeds 11-12-81
Source: Scholar.

2000–01	Bradford C	1	0	**1**	**0**
2001–02	Hull C	0	0		
2002–03	Hull C	0	0		
2003–04	Hull C	0	0		
2004–05	Hull C	0	0		
From Scarborough.					
2005–06	Lincoln C	41	2		
2006–07	Lincoln C	44	3	**85**	**5**

MARRIOTT, Alan (G) 317 0
H: 5 11 W: 12 05 b.Bedford 3-9-78
Source: Trainee.

1997–98	Tottenham H	0	0		
1998–99	Tottenham H	0	0		
1999–2000	Lincoln C	18	0		
2000–01	Lincoln C	30	0		
2001–02	Lincoln C	43	0		
2002–03	Lincoln C	46	0		
2003–04	Lincoln C	46	0		
2004–05	Lincoln C	45	0		
2005–06	Lincoln C	43	0		
2006–07	Lincoln C	46	0	**317**	**0**

MAYO, Paul (D) 193 10
H: 5 11 W: 11 09 b.Lincoln 13-10-81
Source: Scholarship.

1999–2000	Lincoln C	19	0		
2000–01	Lincoln C	27	0		
2001–02	Lincoln C	14	0		
2002–03	Lincoln C	15	0		
2003–04	Lincoln C	31	6		
2003–04	Watford	12	0		
2004–05	Watford	13	0	**25**	**0**
2005–06	Lincoln C	28	3		
2006–07	Lincoln C	34	1	**168**	**10**

METTAM, Leon (F) 5 1
H: 5 9 W: 11 01 b.Lincoln 9-12-86
Source: Scholar.

2005–06	Lincoln C	1	0		
2006–07	Lincoln C	4	1	**5**	**1**

MORGAN, Paul (D) 212 2
H: 6 0 W: 11 05 b.Belfast 23-10-78
Source: Trainee. *Honours:* Northern Ireland Under-21.

1997–98	Preston NE	0	0		
1998–99	Preston NE	0	0		
1999–2000	Preston NE	0	0		
2000–01	Preston NE	0	0		
2001–02	Lincoln C	34	1		
2002–03	Lincoln C	45	0		
2003–04	Lincoln C	41	0		
2004–05	Lincoln C	39	0		
2005–06	Lincoln C	20	0		
2006–07	Lincoln C	33	1	**212**	**2**

MOSES, Adi (D) 309 5
H: 5 11 W: 13 01 b.Doncaster 4-5-75
Source: School. *Honours:* England Under-21.

1993–94	Barnsley	0	0		
1994–95	Barnsley	4	0		
1995–96	Barnsley	24	1		
1996–97	Barnsley	28	2		
1997–98	Barnsley	35	0		
1998–99	Barnsley	34	0		
1999–2000	Barnsley	12	0		
2000–01	Barnsley	14	0	**151**	**3**
2000–01	Huddersfield T	12	0		
2001–02	Huddersfield T	17	0		
2002–03	Huddersfield T	40	1	**69**	**1**
2003–04	Crewe Alex	21	0		
2004–05	Crewe Alex	21	0		
2005–06	Crewe Alex	15	0	**57**	**0**
2006–07	Lincoln C	32	1	**32**	**1**

N'GUESSAN, Dany (M) 32 5
H: 6 0 W: 12 13 b.Ivry-sur-Seine 11-8-87
Source: Auxerre, Rangers.

2006–07	Boston U	23	5	**23**	**5**
2006–07	Lincoln C	9	0	**9**	**0**

RAYNER, Simon (G) 14 0
H: 6 4 W: 15 00 b.Vancouver 8-7-83
Source: Bournemouth, Barry T, Port Talbot.
Honours: Canada Under-23.

2004–05	Lincoln C	1	0		
2005–06	Lincoln C	3	0		
2006–07	Lincoln C	0	0	**4**	**0**
2006–07	*Torquay U*	10	0	**10**	**0**

RYAN, Oliver (M) 23 0
H: 5 9 W: 11 00 b.Boston 26-9-85
Source: Scholar.

2004–05	Lincoln C	6	0		
2005–06	Lincoln C	10	0		
2006–07	Lincoln C	7	0	**23**	**0**

SEMPLE, Ryan (M) 48 3
H: 5 11 W: 10 11 b.Belfast 4-7-85
Source: Scholar.

2002–03	Peterborough U	3	0		
2003–04	Peterborough U	2	0		
2004–05	Peterborough U	8	0		
2005–06	Peterborough U	28	3	**41**	**3**
2006–07	Lincoln C	4	0	**4**	**0**
2006–07	*Chester C*	3	0	**3**	**0**

SHERLOCK, Jamie (D) 0 0
H: 6 1 W: 13 00 b.Hull 25-4-83
Source: N.Ferriby U, Brigg T, Scarborough, Gainsborough T.

2005–06	Lincoln C	0	0		
2006–07	Lincoln C	0	0		

STALLARD, Mark (F) 451 133
H: 6 0 W: 13 09 b.Derby 24-10-74
Source: Trainee.

1991–92	Derby Co	3	0		
1992–93	Derby Co	5	0		
1993–94	Derby Co	0	0		
1994–95	Derby Co	16	2		
1994–95	*Fulham*	4	3	**4**	**3**
1995–96	Derby Co	3	0	**27**	**2**
1995–96	Bradford C	21	9		
1996–97	Bradford C	22	1	**43**	**10**
1996–97	*Preston NE*	4	1	**4**	**1**
1996–97	Wycombe W	12	4		
1997–98	Wycombe W	43	17		
1998–99	Wycombe W	15	2	**70**	**23**
1998–99	Notts Co	14	4		
1999–2000	Notts Co	36	14		
2000–01	Notts Co	42	17		
2001–02	Notts Co	26	4		
2002–03	Notts Co	45	24		
2003–04	Notts Co	22	4		
2003–04	Barnsley	10	1		
2004–05	Barnsley	5	0	**15**	**1**
2004–05	*Chesterfield*	9	2	**9**	**2**
2004–05	*Notts Co*	16	3	**201**	**70**
2005–06	Shrewsbury T	37	6	**37**	**6**
2006–07	Lincoln C	41	15	**41**	**15**

WARLOW, Owain (M) 5 0
H: 6 0 W: 12 00 b.Treforest 3-7-88
Source: Scholar. *Honours:* Wales Under-21.

2006–07	Lincoln C	5	0	**5**	**0**

WATT, Phil (F) 0 0
H: 5 11 W: 11 04 b.Rotherham 10-1-88
Source: Scholar.

2006–07	Lincoln C	0	0		

WILKINSON, Tom (D) 1 0
H: 5 7 W: 11 03 b.Lincoln 26-9-85
Source: Scholar.

2005–06	Lincoln C	1	0		
2006–07	Lincoln C	0	0	**1**	**0**

LIVERPOOL (46)

AGGER, Daniel (D) 65 7
H: 6 2 W: 12 06 b.Hvidovre 12-12-84
Honours: Denmark Youth, Under-20, Under-21, 15 full caps, 2 goals.

2004–05	Brondby	26	5		
2005–06	Brondby	8	0	**34**	**5**
2005–06	Liverpool	4	0		
2006–07	Liverpool	27	2	**31**	**2**

AJDAREVIC, Astrit (M) 0 0
b.Kosovo 20-9-90
Source: Falkenberg.

2006–07	Liverpool	0	0		

ALONSO, Xabi (M) 220 18
H: 6 0 W: 12 02 b.Tolosa 25-11-81
Source: Spain Under-21, 37 full caps, 1 goal.
Honours:

1999–2000	Real Sociedad	0	0		
2000–01	Eibar	14	0	**14**	**0**
2000–01	Real Sociedad	18	0		
2001–02	Real Sociedad	29	3		
2002–03	Real Sociedad	33	3		
2003–04	Real Sociedad	35	3	**115**	**9**
2004–05	Liverpool	24	2		
2005–06	Liverpool	35	3		
2006–07	Liverpool	32	4	**91**	**9**

ANDERSON, Paul (M) 0 0
H: 5 9 W: 10 04 b.Leicester 23-7-88
Source: Scholar. *Honours:* England Youth.

2005–06	Hull C	0	0		
2005–06	Liverpool	0	0		
2006–07	Liverpool	0	0		

ANTWI-BIRAGO, Godwin (D) **9 0**
H: 6 1 W: 13 09 b.Tafu 7-6-88
Source: San Gregorio.

2005–06	Liverpool	0	0		
2006–07	Liverpool	0	0		
2006–07	*Accrington S*	9	0	**9**	**0**

ARBELOA, Alvaro (D) **116 2**
H: 6 0 W: 12 06 b.Salamanca 17-1-83
Honours: Spain Under-21.

2003–04	Real Madrid B	22	0		
2004–05	Real Madrid B	28	1	**50**	**1**
2004–05	Real Madrid	2	0		
2005–06	Real Castilla	34	0	**2**	**0**
2006–07	La Coruna	21	0	**21**	**0**
2006–07	Liverpool	9	1	**9**	**1**

BARNETT, Charlie (M) **0 0**
b.Liverpool 19-9-88
Source: Scholar.

2006–07	Liverpool	0	0		

BELLAMY, Craig (F) **277 92**
H: 5 9 W: 10 12 b.Cardiff 13-7-79
Source: From Trainee. *Honours:* Wales Schools, Youth, Under-21, 46 full caps, 13 goals.

1996–97	Norwich C	3	0		
1997–98	Norwich C	36	13		
1998–99	Norwich C	40	17		
1999–2000	Norwich C	4	2		
2000–01	Norwich C	1	0	**84**	**32**
2000–01	Coventry C	34	6	**34**	**6**
2001–02	Newcastle U	27	9		
2002–03	Newcastle U	29	7		
2003–04	Newcastle U	16	4		
2004–05	Newcastle U	21	7	**93**	**27**
2004–05	*Celtic*	12	7	**12**	**7**
2005–06	Blackburn R	27	13	**27**	**13**
2006–07	Liverpool	27	7	**27**	**7**

BROUWER, Jordy (F) **0 0**
b.Den Haag 26-2-88
Source: Ajax.

2006–07	Liverpool	0	0		

CALLISTE, Ramon (F) **0 0**
H: 5 10 W: 11 06 b.Cardiff 16-12-85
Source: From Trainee. *Honours:* Wales Youth, Under-21.

2003–04	Manchester U	0	0		
2004–05	Manchester U	0	0		
2005–06	Liverpool	0	0		
2006–07	Liverpool	0	0		

CARRAGHER, Jamie (D) **325 3**
H: 5 9 W: 12 01 b.Liverpool 28-1-78
Source: Trainee. *Honours:* England Youth, Under-21, B, 34 full caps.

1995–96	Liverpool	0	0		
1996–97	Liverpool	2	1		
1997–98	Liverpool	20	0		
1998–99	Liverpool	34	1		
1999–2000	Liverpool	36	0		
2000–01	Liverpool	34	0		
2001–02	Liverpool	33	0		
2002–03	Liverpool	35	0		
2003–04	Liverpool	22	0		
2004–05	Liverpool	38	0		
2005–06	Liverpool	36	0		
2006–07	Liverpool	35	1	**325**	**3**

CARSON, Scott (G) **52 0**
H: 6 3 W: 14 00 b.Whitehaven 3-9-85
Source: Scholar. *Honours:* England Youth, Under-21, B.

2002–03	Leeds U	0	0		
2003–04	Leeds U	3	0		
2004–05	Leeds U	0	0	**3**	**0**
2004–05	Liverpool	4	0		
2005–06	Liverpool	0	0		
2005–06	*Sheffield W*	9	0	**9**	**0**
2006–07	Liverpool	0	0	**4**	**0**
2006–07	*Charlton Ath*	36	0	**36**	**0**

CISSE, Djibril (F) **177 83**
H: 6 0 W: 13 00 b.Arles 12-8-81
Honours: France 30 full caps, 9 goals.

1998–99	Auxerre	1	0		
1999–2000	Auxerre	2	0		
2000–01	Auxerre	25	8		
2001–02	Auxerre	29	22		
2002–03	Auxerre	33	14		
2003–04	Auxerre	38	26	**128**	**70**
2004–05	Liverpool	16	4		
2005–06	Liverpool	33	9		
2006–07	Liverpool	0	0	**49**	**13**

CROUCH, Peter (F) **222 67**
H: 6 7 W: 13 03 b.Macclesfield 30-1-81
Source: Trainee. *Honours:* England Youth, Under-20, Under-21, B, 19 full caps, 12 goals.

1998–99	Tottenham H	0	0		
1999–2000	Tottenham H	0	0		
2000–01	QPR	42	10	**42**	**10**
2001–02	Portsmouth	37	18	**37**	**18**
2001–02	Aston Villa	7	2		
2002–03	Aston Villa	14	0		
2003–04	Aston Villa	16	4	**37**	**6**
2003–04	*Norwich C*	15	4	**15**	**4**
2004–05	Southampton	27	12	**27**	**12**
2005–06	Liverpool	32	8		
2006–07	Liverpool	32	9	**64**	**17**

DARBY, Stephen (D) **0 0**
H: 5 9 W: 10 00 b.Liverpool 6-10-88
Source: Scholar. *Honours:* England Youth.

2006–07	Liverpool	0	0		

DUDEK, Jerzy (G) **278 0**
H: 6 2 W: 12 08 b.Ribnek 23-3-73
Source: GKS Tychy. *Honours:* Poland 56 full caps.

1995–96	Sokol Tychy	15	0	**15**	**0**
1996–97	Feyenoord	0	0		
1997–98	Feyenoord	34	0		
1998–99	Feyenoord	34	0		
1999–2000	Feyenoord	34	0		
2000–01	Feyenoord	34	0	**136**	**0**
2001–02	Liverpool	35	0		
2002–03	Liverpool	30	0		
2003–04	Liverpool	30	0		
2004–05	Liverpool	24	0		
2005–06	Liverpool	6	0		
2006–07	Liverpool	2	0	**127**	**0**

DURAN VAZQUEZ, Francisco (M) **0 0**
b.Malaga 28-4-88
Source: Malaga.

2006–07	Liverpool	0	0		

EL ZHAR, Nabil (F) **3 0**
H: 5 9 W: 11 05 b.Ales 27-8-86
Source: From St Etienne. *Honours:* France Youth, Morocco Under-20.

2006–07	Liverpool	3	0	**3**	**0**

FABIO AURELIO (M) **165 14**
H: 5 10 W: 11 11 b.Sao Carlos 24-9-79
Honours: Brazil Youth, Under-20, Under-21.

1997	Sao Paulo	15	1		
1998	Sao Paulo	11	1		
1998	Santos	0	0		
1999	Sao Paulo	23	1		
2000	Sao Paulo	4	0	**53**	**3**
2000–01	Valencia	7	0		
2001–02	Valencia	15	1		
2002–03	Valencia	26	8		
2003–04	Valencia	2	0		
2004–05	Valencia	21	0		
2005–06	Valencia	24	2	**95**	**11**
2006–07	Liverpool	17	0	**17**	**0**

FINNAN, Steve (D) **405 15**
H: 6 0 W: 12 03 b.Limerick 24-4-76
Source: Welling U. *Honours:* Eire Under-21, B, 46 full caps, 1 goal.

1995–96	Birmingham C	12	1		
1995–96	*Notts Co*	17	2		
1996–97	Birmingham C	3	0	**15**	**1**
1996–97	Notts Co	23	0		
1997–98	Notts Co	44	5		
1998–99	Notts Co	13	0	**97**	**7**
1998–99	Fulham	22	2		
1999–2000	Fulham	35	2		
2000–01	Fulham	45	2		
2001–02	Fulham	38	0		
2002–03	Fulham	32	0	**172**	**6**
2003–04	Liverpool	22	0		
2004–05	Liverpool	33	1		
2005–06	Liverpool	33	0		
2006–07	Liverpool	33	0	**121**	**1**

FLYNN, Ryan (M) **0 0**
H: 5 8 W: 10 00 b.Scotland 4-9-88
Source: Scholar.

2006–07	Liverpool	0	0		

FOWLER, Robbie (F) **376 163**
H: 5 10 W: 12 05 b.Liverpool 9-4-75
Source: From Trainee. *Honours:* England Youth, B, Under-21, 26 full caps, 7 goals.

1991–92	Liverpool	0	0		
1992–93	Liverpool	0	0		
1993–94	Liverpool	28	12		
1994–95	Liverpool	42	25		
1995–96	Liverpool	38	28		
1996–97	Liverpool	32	18		
1997–98	Liverpool	20	9		
1998–99	Liverpool	25	14		
1999–2000	Liverpool	14	3		
2000–01	Liverpool	27	8		
2001–02	Liverpool	10	3		
2001–02	Leeds U	22	12		
2002–03	Leeds U	8	2	**30**	**14**
2002–03	Manchester C	13	2		
2003–04	Manchester C	31	7		
2004–05	Manchester C	32	11		
2005–06	Manchester C	4	1	**80**	**21**
2005–06	Liverpool	14	5		
2006–07	Liverpool	16	3	**266**	**128**

GERRARD, Steven (M) **268 44**
H: 6 0 W: 12 05 b.Whiston 30-5-80
Source: Trainee. *Honours:* England Youth, Under-21, 57 full caps, 12 goals.

1997–98	Liverpool	0	0		
1998–99	Liverpool	12	0		
1999–2000	Liverpool	29	1		
2000–01	Liverpool	33	7		
2001–02	Liverpool	28	3		
2002–03	Liverpool	34	5		
2003–04	Liverpool	34	4		
2004–05	Liverpool	30	7		
2005–06	Liverpool	32	10		
2006–07	Liverpool	36	7	**268**	**44**

GONZALEZ, Jose Miguel (M) **105 22**
H: 5 9 W: 12 08 b.Malaga 15-11-79
Honours: Chile 16 caps, 3 goals.

2002	Univ Catolica	6	0		
2003	Univ Catolica	28	9		
2004	Univ Catolica	8	1	**42**	**10**
2004–05	Albacete	26	5	**26**	**5**
2005–06	Real Sociedad	12	5	**12**	**5**
2005–06	Liverpool	0	0		
2006–07	Liverpool	25	2	**25**	**2**

GUTHRIE, Danny (M) **13 0**
H: 5 9 W: 11 06 b.Shrewsbury 18-4-87
Source: Scholar. *Honours:* England Schools, Youth.

2004–05	Liverpool	0	0		
2005–06	Liverpool	0	0		
2006–07	Liverpool	3	0	**3**	**0**
2006–07	*Southampton*	10	0	**10**	**0**

HAMMILL, Adam (M) **0 0**
b.Liverpool 25-1-88
Source: Scholar. *Honours:* England Youth.

2005–06	Liverpool	0	0		
2006–07	Liverpool	0	0		

To Dunfermline Ath (loan) January 2007

HOBBS, Jack (D) **1 0**
H: 6 3 W: 13 05 b.Portsmouth 18-8-88
Source: Scholar.

2004–05	Lincoln C	1	0	**1**	**0**
2005–06	Liverpool	0	0		
2006–07	Liverpool	0	0		

HUTH, Ronald (D) **0 0**
b.Asuncion 30-10-89
Source: Tacuary.

2006–07	Liverpool	0	0		

HYYPIA, Sami (D) **438 26**
H: 6 3 W: 13 09 b.Porvoo 7-10-73
Source: From KuMu. *Honours:* Finland Youth, Under-21, 83 full caps, 5 goals.

1993	MyPa 47	12	0		
1994	MyPa 47	25	0		

1995	MyPa 47	26	3	**63**	**3**
1995–96	Willem II	14	0		
1996–97	Willem II	30	1		
1997–98	Willem II	30	0		
1998–99	Willem II	26	2	**100**	**3**
1999–2000	Liverpool	38	2		
2000–01	Liverpool	35	3		
2001–02	Liverpool	37	3		
2002–03	Liverpool	36	3		
2003–04	Liverpool	38	4		
2004–05	Liverpool	32	2		
2005–06	Liverpool	36	1		
2006–07	Liverpool	23	2	**275**	**20**

IDRIZAJ, Bezian (F) **7** **1**

H: 6 2 W: 12 02 b.Austria 12-10-87

Source: LASK Linz.

2005–06	Liverpool	0	0		
2006–07	Liverpool	0	0		
2006–07	*Luton T*	7	1	**7**	**1**

INSUA, Emiliano (D) **2** **0**

H: 5 10 W: 12 08 b.Buenos Aires 7-1-89

Source: Boca Juniors. *Honours:* Argentina Youth.

2006–07	Liverpool	2	0	**2**	**0**

KEWELL, Harry (M) **264** **57**

H: 5 9 W: 12 06 b.Sydney 22-9-78

Source: NSW Soccer Academy. *Honours:* Australia Youth, Under-20, 24 full caps, 8 goals.

1995–96	Leeds U	2	0		
1996–97	Leeds U	1	0		
1997–98	Leeds U	29	5		
1998–99	Leeds U	38	6		
1999–2000	Leeds U	36	10		
2000–01	Leeds U	17	2		
2001–02	Leeds U	27	8		
2002–03	Leeds U	31	14	**181**	**45**
2003–04	Liverpool	36	7		
2004–05	Liverpool	18	1		
2005–06	Liverpool	27	3		
2006–07	Liverpool	2	1	**83**	**12**

KROMKAMP, Jan (D) **214** **11**

H: 6 3 W: 13 06 b.Makkinga 17-8-80

Honours: Holland 11 full caps.

1998–99	Go Ahead	28	1		
1999–2000	Go Ahead	33	4	**61**	**5**
2000–01	AZ	25	2		
2001–02	AZ	22	1		
2002–03	AZ	25	2		
2003–04	AZ	34	0		
2004–05	AZ	27	1	**133**	**6**
2005–06	Villarreal	6	0	**6**	**0**
2005–06	Liverpool	13	0		
2006–07	Liverpool	1	0	**14**	**0**

To PSV Eindhoven August 2006

KUYT, Dirk (F) **295** **134**

H: 6 0 W: 12 02 b.Katwijk 22-7-80

Source: Quick Boys.Holland 29 full caps, 5 goals.

1998–99	Utrecht	28	5		
1999–2000	Utrecht	32	6		
2000–01	Utrecht	32	13		
2001–02	Utrecht	34	7		
2002–03	Utrecht	34	20	**160**	**51**
2003–04	Feyenoord	34	20		
2004–05	Feyenoord	34	29		
2005–06	Feyenoord	33	22	**101**	**71**
2006–07	Liverpool	34	12	**34**	**12**

LE TALLEC, Anthony (M) **105** **11**

H: 6 0 W: 12 00 b.Hennebont 3-10-84

Honours: France Under-21.

2001–02	Le Havre	24	5		
2002–03	Le Havre	30	2	**54**	**7**
2003–04	Liverpool	13	0		
2004–05	Liverpool	4	0		
2004–05	*St Etienne*	7	1	**7**	**1**
2005–06	Liverpool	0	0		
2005–06	*Sunderland*	27	3	**27**	**3**
2006–07	Liverpool	0	0	**17**	**0**

LINDFIELD, Craig (F) **0** **0**

H: 6 0 W: 10 05 b.Wirral 7-9-88

Source: Scholar. *Honours:* England Youth.

2006–07	Liverpool	0	0		

LUIS GARCIA (M) **292** **82**

H: 5 6 W: 10 05 b.Badalona 24-6-78

Honours: Spain 18 full caps, 4 goals.

1997–98	Barcelona B	36	15		
1998–99	Barcelona B	36	10	**72**	**25**
1999–2000	Valladolid	6	0		
1999–2000	Toledo	17	4	**17**	**4**
2000–01	Tenerife	40	16	**40**	**16**
2001–02	Valladolid	25	6	**31**	**6**
2002–03	Atletico Madrid	30	9	**30**	**9**
2003–04	Barcelona	25	4	**25**	**4**
2004–05	Liverpool	29	8		
2005–06	Liverpool	31	7		
2006–07	Liverpool	17	3	**77**	**18**

MANNIX, David (M) **1** **0**

H: 5 8 W: 11 06 b.Winsford 24-9-85

Source: Trainee. *Honours:* England Under-20.

2003–04	Liverpool	0	0		
2004–05	Liverpool	0	0		
2005–06	Liverpool	0	0		
2006–07	Liverpool	0	0		
2006–07	*Accrington S*	1	0	**1**	**0**

To Hamkam January 2007

MARTIN, David (G) **27** **0**

H: 6 1 W: 13 04 b.Romford 22-1-86

Source: Scholar. *Honours:* England Youth, Under-20.

2003–04	Wimbledon	2	0	**2**	**0**
2004–05	Milton Keynes D	15	0		
2005–06	Milton Keynes D	0	0	**15**	**0**
2005–06	Liverpool	0	0		
2006–07	Liverpool	0	0		
2006–07	*Accrington S*	10	0	**10**	**0**

MASCHERANO, Javier (M) **65** **0**

H: 5 7 W: 10 05 b.San Lorenzo 8-6-84

Honours: Argentina Youth, Under-20, Under-23, 24 full caps.

2003–04	River Plate	21	0		
2004–05	River Plate	25	0	**46**	**0**
2005	Corinthians	7	0	**7**	**0**
2006–07	West Ham U	5	0	**5**	**0**
2006–07	Liverpool	7	0	**7**	**0**

O'DONNELL, Daniel (D) **25** **1**

H: 6 2 W: 11 11 b.Livepool 10-3-86

Source: Scholar.

2004–05	Liverpool	0	0		
2005–06	Liverpool	0	0		
2006–07	Liverpool	0	0		
2006–07	*Crewe Alex*	25	1	**25**	**1**

PADELLI, Daniele (G) **35** **0**

H: 6 4 W: 12 13 b.Lecco 25-10-85

Honours: Italy Youth, Under-21.

2004–05	Sampdoria	0	0		
2005–06	Sampdoria	0	0		
2005–06	*Pizzighettone*	33	0	**33**	**0**
2006–07	*Crotone*	1	0	**1**	**0**
2006–07	Liverpool	1	0	**1**	**0**

PALETTA, Gabriel (D) **45** **5**

H: 6 3 W: 12 08 b.Longchamps 15-2-86

Honours: Argentina Under-20.

2004–05	Banfield	9	2		
2005–06	Banfield	33	3	**42**	**5**
2006–07	Liverpool	3	0	**3**	**0**

PELTIER, Lee (F) **7** **0**

H: 5 10 W: 12 00 b.Liverpool 11-12-86

Source: Scholar.

2004–05	Liverpool	0	0		
2005–06	Liverpool	0	0		
2006–07	Liverpool	0	0		
2006–07	*Hull C*	7	0	**7**	**0**

PENNANT, Jermaine (M) **153** **10**

H: 5 9 W: 10 06 b.Nottingham 15-1-83

Honours: England Schools, Youth, Under-21.

1998–99	Notts Co	0	0		
1998–99	Arsenal	0	0		
1999–2000	Arsenal	0	0		
2000–01	Arsenal	0	0		
2001–02	Arsenal	0	0		
2001–02	*Watford*	9	2		
2002–03	Arsenal	5	3		
2002–03	*Watford*	12	0	**21**	**2**
2003–04	Arsenal	0	0		
2003–04	*Leeds U*	36	2	**36**	**2**
2004–05	Arsenal	7	0	**12**	**3**
2004–05	Birmingham C	12	0		
2005–06	Birmingham C	38	2	**50**	**2**
2006–07	Liverpool	34	1	**34**	**1**

REINA, Jose (G) **199** **0**

H: 6 2 W: 14 06 b.Madrid 31-8-82

Honours: Spain Youth, Under-21, 6 full caps.

1999–2000	Barcelona B	30	0	**30**	**0**
2000–01	Barcelona	19	0		
2001–02	Barcelona	11	0	**30**	**0**
2002–03	Villarreal	33	0		
2003–04	Villarreal	38	0		
2004–05	Villarreal	0	0	**71**	**0**
2005–06	Liverpool	33	0		
2006–07	Liverpool	35	0	**68**	**0**

RIISE, John Arne (M) **249** **25**

H: 6 1 W: 14 00 b.Molde 24-9-80

Honours: Norway Youth, Under-21, 62 full caps, 6 goals.

1998–99	Monaco	7	0		
1999–2000	Monaco	21	1		
2000–01	Monaco	16	3	**44**	**4**
2001–02	Liverpool	38	7		
2002–03	Liverpool	37	6		
2003–04	Liverpool	28	0		
2004–05	Liverpool	37	6		
2005–06	Liverpool	32	1		
2006–07	Liverpool	33	1	**205**	**21**

ROQUE, Miguel (D) **4** **0**

H: 6 2 W: 12 03 b.Lleida 8-7-88

Source: EU Lleida.

2005–06	Liverpool	0	0		
2006–07	Liverpool	0	0		
2006–07	*Oldham Ath*	4	0	**4**	**0**

RYAN, James (M) **0** **0**

b.Maghull 6-9-88

Source: Scholar.

2006–07	Liverpool	0	0		

SINAMA-PONGOLLE, Florent (F) **59** **7**

H: 5 7 W: 11 05 b.Saint-Pierre 20-10-84

Honours: France Under-21, Under-23.

2001–02	Le Havre	11	2		
2002–03	Le Havre	0	0	**11**	**2**
2003–04	Liverpool	15	2		
2004–05	Liverpool	16	2		
2005–06	Liverpool	7	0		
2005–06	*Blackburn R*	10	1	**10**	**1**
2006–07	Liverpool	0	0	**38**	**4**

To Huelva (loan) August 2006

SISSOKO, Mohamed (M) **87** **0**

H: 6 2 W: 12 08 b.Mont Saint Aigan 22-1-85

Source: Auxerre. *Honours:* Mali 11 full caps, 2 goals.

2003–04	Valencia	21	0		
2004–05	Valencia	24	0	**45**	**0**
2005–06	Liverpool	26	0		
2006–07	Liverpool	16	0	**42**	**0**

SMITH, James (D) **0** **0**

H: 5 10 W: 11 08 b.Liverpool 17-10-85

2004–05	Liverpool	0	0		
2005–06	Liverpool	0	0		
2006–07	Liverpool	0	0		

To Ross Co January 2007

SPEARING, Jay (D) **0** **0**

b.Wirral 25-11-88

Source: Scholar.

2006–07	Liverpool	0	0		

THRELFALL, Robert (D) **0** **0**

H: 5 11 W: 11 00 b.Liverpool 25-11-88

Source: Scholar.

2006–07	Liverpool	0	0		

ZENDEN, Boudewijn (M) **308** **41**

H: 5 8 W: 11 01 b.Maastricht 15-8-76

Honours: Holland 54 full caps, 7 goals.

1994–95	PSV Eindhoven	27	5		
1995–96	PSV Eindhoven	25	7		
1996–97	PSV Eindhoven	34	8		
1997–98	PSV Eindhoven	25	3	**111**	**23**
1998–99	Barcelona	25	0		
1999–2000	Barcelona	29	2		

2000–01	Barcelona	10	1	**64**	**3**
2001–02	Chelsea	22	3		
2002–03	Chelsea	21	1		
2003–04	Chelsea	0	0	**43**	**4**
2003–04	*Middlesbrough*	31	4		
2004–05	Middlesbrough	36	5	**67**	**9**
2005–06	Liverpool	7	2		
2006–07	Liverpool	16	0	**23**	**2**

Scholars

Awang, Mattone; Burns, Michael; Collins, Michael; Gaughan, Laurence; Hansen, Martin; Kelly, Martin Ronald; Mimms, Josh; O'Connor, Shane; Parsonage, Ben; Putterill, Raymond; Scott, Michael David.

LUTON T (47)

ANDREW, Calvin (F) **27** **3**

H: 6 0 W: 12 11 b.Luton 19-12-86

Source: Scholar.

2004–05	Luton T	8	0		
2005–06	Luton T	1	1		
2005–06	*Grimsby T*	8	1	**8**	**1**
2005–06	*Bristol C*	3	0	**3**	**0**
2006–07	Luton T	7	1	**16**	**2**

BARNETT, Leon (D) **59** **3**

H: 6 0 W: 12 04 b.Stevenage 30-11-85

Source: Scholar.

2003–04	Luton T	0	0		
2004–05	Luton T	0	0		
2005–06	Luton T	20	0		
2006–07	Luton T	39	3	**59**	**3**

BARRETT, Zach (G) **0** **0**

H: 6 2 W: 11 07 b.Stevenage 26-5-88

Source: Scholar.

2006–07	Luton T	0	0

BELL, David (M) **164** **13**

H: 5 10 W: 11 05 b.Kettering 21-1-84

Source: From Trainee. *Honours:* Eire Under-21.

2001–02	Rushden & D	0	0		
2002–03	Rushden & D	30	3		
2003–04	Rushden & D	37	1		
2004–05	Rushden & D	40	3		
2005–06	Rushden & D	14	3	**121**	**10**
2005–06	Luton T	9	0		
2006–07	Luton T	34	3	**43**	**3**

BERESFORD, Marlon (G) **474** **0**

H: 6 1 W: 13 10 b.Lincoln 2-9-69

Source: Trainee.

1987–88	Sheffield W	0	0		
1988–89	Sheffield W	0	0		
1989–90	Sheffield W	0	0		
1989–90	*Bury*	1	0	**1**	**0**
1989–90	*Ipswich T*	0	0		
1990–91	Sheffield W	0	0		
1990–91	*Northampton T*	13	0		
1990–91	*Crewe Alex*	3	0	**3**	**0**
1991–92	Sheffield W	0	0		
1991–92	*Northampton T*	15	0	**28**	**0**
1992–93	Burnley	44	0		
1993–94	Burnley	46	0		
1994–95	Burnley	40	0		
1995–96	Burnley	36	0		
1996–97	Burnley	40	0		
1997–98	Burnley	34	0		
1997–98	Middlesbrough	3	0		
1998–99	Middlesbrough	4	0		
1999–2000	Middlesbrough	1	0		
2000–01	Middlesbrough	1	0		
2000–01	*Sheffield W*	4	0	**4**	**0**
2001–02	Middlesbrough	1	0	**10**	**0**
2001–02	*Wolverhampton W*	0	0		
2001–02	*Burnley*	13	0		
2002–03	York C	6	0	**6**	**0**
2002–03	Burnley	34	0		
2003–04	Burnley	0	0	**287**	**0**
2003–04	Bradford C	5	0	**5**	**0**
2003–04	Luton T	11	0		
2003–04	Barnsley	14	0	**14**	**0**
2004–05	Luton T	38	0		
2005–06	Luton T	41	0		
2006–07	Luton T	26	0	**116**	**0**

BOYD, Adam (F) **177** **58**

H: 5 9 W: 10 12 b.Hartlepool 25-5-82

Source: Scholarship.

1999–2000	Hartlepool U	4	1		
2000–01	Hartlepool U	5	0		
2001–02	Hartlepool U	29	9		
2002–03	Hartlepool U	22	5		
2003–04	Hartlepool U	18	12		
2003–04	*Boston U*	14	4	**14**	**4**
2004–05	Hartlepool U	45	22		
2005–06	Hartlepool U	21	4	**144**	**53**
2006–07	Luton T	19	1	**19**	**1**

BRILL, Dean (G) **29** **0**

H: 6 2 W: 14 05 b.Luton 2-12-85

Source: Scholar.

2003–04	Luton T	5	0		
2004–05	Luton T	0	0		
2005–06	Luton T	5	0		
2006–07	Luton T	11	0	**21**	**0**
2006–07	*Gillingham*	8	0	**8**	**0**

BRKOVIC, Ahmet (M) **262** **39**

H: 5 8 W: 11 11 b.Dubrovnik 23-9-74

Source: Dubrovnik.

1999–2000	Leyton Orient	29	5		
2000–01	Leyton Orient	40	3		
2001–02	Leyton Orient	0	0	**69**	**8**
2001–02	Luton T	21	1		
2002–03	Luton T	36	3		
2003–04	Luton T	32	1		
2004–05	Luton T	42	15		
2005–06	Luton T	42	8		
2006–07	Luton T	20	3	**193**	**31**

COYNE, Chris (D) **232** **14**

H: 6 2 W: 13 10 b.Brisbane 20-12-78

Source: Perth SC. *Honours:* Australia Youth, Under-23.

1995–96	West Ham U	0	0		
1996–97	West Ham U	0	0		
1997–98	West Ham U	0	0		
1998–99	West Ham U	1	0	**1**	**0**
1998–99	*Brentford*	7	0	**7**	**0**
1998–99	*Southend U*	1	0	**1**	**0**
1999–2000	Dundee	2	0		
2000–01	Dundee	18	0	**20**	**0**
2001–02	Luton T	31	3		
2002–03	Luton T	40	1		
2003–04	Luton T	44	2		
2004–05	Luton T	40	5		
2005–06	Luton T	30	2		
2006–07	Luton T	18	1	**203**	**14**

DAVIS, Sol (D) **277** **2**

H: 5 7 W: 12 04 b.Cheltenham 4-9-79

Source: Trainee.

1997–98	Swindon T	6	0		
1998–99	Swindon T	25	0		
1999–2000	Swindon T	29	0		
2000–01	Swindon T	36	0		
2001–02	Swindon T	21	0		
2002–03	Swindon T	0	0	**117**	**0**
2002–03	Luton T	34	0		
2003–04	Luton T	36	0		
2004–05	Luton T	45	2		
2005–06	Luton T	21	0		
2006–07	Luton T	24	0	**160**	**2**

EMANUEL, Lewis (D) **179** **6**

H: 5 8 W: 12 01 b.Bradford 14-10-83

Source: Scholar. *Honours:* England Schools, Youth. Eire B.

2001–02	Bradford C	9	0		
2002–03	Bradford C	29	0		
2003–04	Bradford C	28	2		
2004–05	Bradford C	36	0		
2005–06	Bradford C	37	2	**139**	**4**
2006–07	Luton T	40	2	**40**	**2**

FEENEY, Warren (F) **222** **59**

H: 5 8 W: 12 04 b.Belfast 17-1-81

Source: Trainee. *Honours:* Northern Ireland Schools, Youth, Under-21, 18 full caps, 2 goals.

1997–98	Leeds U	0	0		
1998–99	Leeds U	0	0		
1999–2000	Leeds U	0	0		
2000–01	Leeds U	0	0		
2000–01	*Bournemouth*	10	4		
2001–02	Bournemouth	37	13		
2002–03	Bournemouth	21	7		
2003–04	Bournemouth	40	12	**108**	**36**
2004–05	Stockport Co	31	15	**31**	**15**
2004–05	Luton T	6	0		
2005–06	Luton T	42	6		
2006–07	Luton T	29	2	**77**	**8**
2006–07	*Cardiff C*	6	0	**6**	**0**

FOLEY, Kevin (D) **151** **3**

H: 5 9 W: 11 11 b.Luton 1-11-84

Source: Scholar. *Honours:* Eire B, Under-21.

2002–03	Luton T	2	0		
2003–04	Luton T	33	1		
2004–05	Luton T	39	2		
2005–06	Luton T	38	0		
2006–07	Luton T	39	0	**151**	**3**

HEIKKINEN, Markus (D) **296** **7**

H: 6 1 W: 12 13 b.Katrineholm 13-10-78

Honours: Finland Youth, Under-21, 27 full caps.

1996	TPS Turku	0	0		
1997	TPS Turku	22	0	**22**	**0**
1998	MyPa	14	0		
1999	MyPa	29	1	**43**	**1**
2000	HJK Helsinki	32	0		
2001	HJK Helsinki	33	1		
2002	HJK Helsinki	20	0	**85**	**1**
2002–03	Portsmouth	2	0	**2**	**0**
2003–04	Aberdeen	38	0		
2004–05	Aberdeen	30	2	**68**	**2**
2005–06	Luton T	39	2		
2006–07	Luton T	37	1	**76**	**3**

HOLMES, Peter (M) **120** **12**

H: 5 11 W: 11 13 b.Bishop Auckland 18-11-80

Source: Trainee. *Honours:* England Schools.

1997–98	Sheffield W	0	0		
1998–99	Sheffield W	0	0		
1999–2000	Sheffield W	0	0		
2000–01	Luton T	18	1		
2001–02	Luton T	7	1		
2002–03	Luton T	17	1		
2003–04	Luton T	16	3		
2004–05	Luton T	19	3		
2005–06	Luton T	23	2		
2006–07	Luton T	5	0	**105**	**11**
2006–07	*Chesterfield*	10	1	**10**	**1**
2006–07	*Lincoln C*	5	0	**5**	**0**

KEANE, Keith (M) **61** **3**

H: 5 9 W: 12 02 b.Luton 20-11-86

Source: Scholar. *Honours:* Eire Youth, Under-21.

2003–04	Luton T	15	1		
2004–05	Luton T	17	0		
2005–06	Luton T	10	1		
2006–07	Luton T	19	1	**61**	**3**

LANGLEY, Richard (M) **264** **30**

H: 6 0 W: 11 04 b.Harlesden 27-12-79

Source: Trainee. *Honours:* England Youth, Jamaica 12 full caps, 2 goals.

1996–97	QPR	0	0		
1997–98	QPR	0	0		
1998–99	QPR	8	1		
1999–2000	QPR	41	3		
2000–01	QPR	26	1		
2001–02	QPR	18	3		
2002–03	QPR	39	9		
2003–04	QPR	1	1		
2003–04	Cardiff C	44	6		
2004–05	Cardiff C	25	2		
2005–06	Cardiff C	0	0	**69**	**8**
2005–06	QPR	33	3	**166**	**21**
2006–07	Luton T	29	1	**29**	**1**

LEARY, Michael (M) **69** **3**

H: 6 0 W: 11 11 b.Ealing 17-4-83

Source: Scholar.

2001–02	Luton T	0	0		
2002–03	Luton T	0	0		
2003–04	Luton T	14	2		
2004–05	Luton T	8	0		
2005–06	Luton T	0	0		
2005–06	*Bristol R*	13	0	**13**	**0**
2005–06	*Walsall*	15	1	**15**	**1**
2006–07	Luton T	0	0	**22**	**2**

2006–07	*Torquay U*	2	0	**2**	**0**
2006–07	*Brentford*	17	0	**17**	**0**

MORGAN, Dean (M) **174 19**
H: 5 11 W: 13 00 b.Enfield 3-10-83
Source: Scholar.

2000–01	Colchester U	4	0		
2001–02	Colchester U	30	0		
2002–03	Colchester U	37	6		
2003–04	Colchester U	0	0	**71**	**6**
2003–04	Reading	13	1		
2004–05	Reading	18	2	**31**	**3**
2005–06	Luton T	36	6		
2006–07	Luton T	36	4	**72**	**10**

O'LEARY, Stephen (M) **50 6**
H: 6 0 W: 11 09 b.Barnet 12-2-85
Source: Scholar. *Honours:* Eire Youth.

2003–04	Luton T	5	1		
2004–05	Luton T	17	1		
2005–06	Luton T	0	0		
2005–06	*Tranmere R*	21	3	**21**	**3**
2006–07	Luton T	7	1	**29**	**3**

PARKIN, Sam (F) **216 85**
H: 6 2 W: 13 00 b.Roehampton 14-3-81
Honours: England Schools. Scotland B.

1998–99	Chelsea	0	0		
1999–2000	Chelsea	0	0		
2000–01	Chelsea	0	0		
2000–01	*Millwall*	7	4	**7**	**4**
2000–01	*Wycombe W*	8	1	**8**	**1**
2000–01	*Oldham Ath*	7	3	**7**	**3**
2001–02	Chelsea	0	0		
2001–02	*Northampton T*	40	4	**40**	**4**
2002–03	Swindon T	43	25		
2003–04	Swindon T	40	19		
2004–05	Swindon T	41	23	**124**	**67**
2005–06	Ipswich T	20	5		
2006–07	Ipswich T	2	0	**22**	**5**
2006–07	Luton T	8	1	**8**	**1**

PERRETT, Russell (D) **200 12**
H: 6 1 W: 12 08 b.Barton-on-Sea 18-6-73
Source: AFC Lymington.

1995–96	Portsmouth	9	0		
1996–97	Portsmouth	32	1		
1997–98	Portsmouth	16	1		
1998–99	Portsmouth	15	0	**72**	**2**
1999–2000	Cardiff C	27	1		
2000–01	Cardiff C	2	0	**29**	**1**
2001–02	Luton T	40	3		
2002–03	Luton T	20	2		
2003–04	Luton T	6	2		
2004–05	Luton T	12	1		
2005–06	Luton T	11	0		
2006–07	Luton T	10	1	**99**	**9**

ROBINSON, Steve (M) **430 62**
H: 5 7 W: 11 09 b.Lisburn 10-12-74
Source: Trainee. *Honours:* Northern Ireland Schools, Youth, Under-21, B, 6 full caps.

1992–93	Tottenham H	0	0		
1993–94	Tottenham H	2	0		
1994–95	Tottenham H	0	0	**2**	**0**
1994–95	*Leyton Orient*	0	0		
1994–95	Bournemouth	32	5		
1995–96	Bournemouth	41	7		
1996–97	Bournemouth	40	7		
1997–98	Bournemouth	45	10		
1998–99	Bournemouth	42	13		
1999–2000	Bournemouth	40	9	**240**	**51**
2000–01	Preston NE	22	1		
2001–02	Preston NE	2	0	**24**	**1**
2001–02	*Bristol C*	6	1	**6**	**1**
2002–03	Luton T	29	1		
2003–04	Luton T	34	2		
2004–05	Luton T	31	4		
2005–06	Luton T	26	2		
2006–07	Luton T	38	0	**158**	**9**

ROSS, Shaun (D) **0 0**
H: 5 7 W: 10 07 b. 9-5-87
Source: Horden CW.

2006–07	Luton T	0	0		

SPRING, Matthew (M) **322 35**
H: 5 11 W: 12 05 b.Harlow 17-11-79
Source: Trainee.

1997–98	Luton T	12	0		
1998–99	Luton T	45	3		
1999–2000	Luton T	45	6		
2000–01	Luton T	41	4		
2001–02	Luton T	42	6		
2002–03	Luton T	41	5		
2003–04	Luton T	24	1		
2004–05	Leeds U	13	1		
2005–06	Leeds U	0	0	**13**	**1**
2005–06	Watford	39	8		
2006–07	Watford	6	0	**45**	**8**
2006–07	Luton T	14	1	**264**	**26**

STEVENS, Danny (F) **1 0**
H: 5 5 W: 9 09 b.Enfield 26-11-86
Source: Tottenham H Scholar.

2004–05	Luton T	0	0		
2005–06	Luton T	1	0		
2006–07	Luton T	0	0	**1**	**0**

TALBOT, Drew (F) **47 8**
H: 5 10 W: 11 00 b.Barnsley 19-7-86
Source: Trainee.

2003–04	Sheffield W	0	0		
2004–05	Sheffield W	21	4		
2005–06	Sheffield W	0	0		
2006–07	Sheffield W	8	0	**29**	**4**
2006–07	*Scunthorpe U*	3	1	**3**	**1**
2006–07	Luton T	15	3	**15**	**3**

UNDERWOOD, Paul (M) **177 6**
H: 5 9 W: 12 13 b.Wimbledon 16-8-73
Source: Enfield.

2001–02	Rushden & D	40	0		
2002–03	Rushden & D	40	1		
2003–04	Rushden & D	30	0	**110**	**1**
2003–04	Luton T	1	0		
2004–05	Luton T	37	5		
2005–06	Luton T	29	0		
2006–07	Luton T	0	0	**67**	**5**

MACCLESFIELD T (48)

BENJAMIN, Ronayne (M) **3 0**
H: 5 10 W: 12 00 b.Chiswick 12-5-85
Source: Crawley T.

2006–07	Macclesfield T	3	0	**3**	**0**

BLACKMAN, Nick (F) **1 0**
H: 6 2 W: 11 08 b.Whitefield 11-11-89
Source: Scholar.

2006–07	Macclesfield T	1	0	**1**	**0**

BRAIN, Jonny (G) **68 0**
H: 6 3 W: 13 05 b.Carlisle 11-2-83
Source: Newcastle U Trainee.

2003–04	Port Vale	32	0		
2004–05	Port Vale	27	0		
2005–06	Port Vale	0	0	**59**	**0**
2006–07	Macclesfield T	9	0	**9**	**0**

BRIGHTWELL, Ian (D) **464 18**
H: 5 10 W: 12 07 b.Lutterworth 9-4-68
Source: Congleton T. *Honours:* England Schools, Youth, Under-21.

1986–87	Manchester C	16	1		
1987–88	Manchester C	33	5		
1988–89	Manchester C	26	6		
1989–90	Manchester C	28	2		
1990–91	Manchester C	33	0		
1991–92	Manchester C	40	1		
1992–93	Manchester C	21	1		
1993–94	Manchester C	7	0		
1994–95	Manchester C	30	0		
1995–96	Manchester C	29	0		
1996–97	Manchester C	37	2		
1997–98	Manchester C	21	0	**321**	**18**
1998–99	Coventry C	0	0		
1999–2000	Coventry C	0	0		
1999–2000	Walsall	10	0		
2000–01	Walsall	44	0		
2001–02	Walsall	27	0	**81**	**0**
2001–02	Stoke C	4	0	**4**	**0**
2002–03	Port Vale	35	0		
2003–04	Port Vale	2	0	**37**	**0**
2004–05	Macclesfield T	6	0		
2005–06	Macclesfield T	11	0		
2006–07	Macclesfield T	4	0	**21**	**0**

BULLOCK, Martin (M) **427 20**
H: 5 5 W: 10 07 b.Derby 5-3-75
Source: Eastwood T. *Honours:* England Under-21.

1993–94	Barnsley	0	0		
1994–95	Barnsley	29	0		
1995–96	Barnsley	41	1		
1996–97	Barnsley	28	0		
1997–98	Barnsley	33	0		
1998–99	Barnsley	32	2		
1999–2000	Barnsley	4	0		
1999–2000	*Port Vale*	6	1	**6**	**1**
2000–01	Barnsley	18	1		
2001–02	Barnsley	0	0	**185**	**4**
2001–02	Blackpool	43	2		
2002–03	Blackpool	38	1		
2003–04	Blackpool	44	1		
2004–05	Blackpool	28	0	**153**	**4**
2005–06	Macclesfield T	40	7		
2006–07	Macclesfield T	43	4	**83**	**11**

DOYLE, Robert (F) **117 29**
H: 5 9 W: 12 00 b.Bray 15-4-82
Source: Trainee.

1998–99	Blackburn R	0	0		
1999–2000	Blackburn R	0	0		
2000–01	Blackburn R	0	0		
2001–02	Blackburn R	0	0		
2002–03	UCD	21	7	**21**	**7**
2003	Bohemians	21	8		
2004	Bohemians	11	1	**32**	**9**
2004	St Patrick's Ath	12	5		
2005	St Patrick's Ath	30	7	**42**	**12**
2006	Bray Wanderers	20	1	**20**	**1**
2006–07	Macclesfield T	2	0	**2**	**0**

HADFIELD, Jordan (M) **38 1**
H: 5 10 W: 11 04 b.Swinton 12-8-87
Source: Trainee.

2004–05	Stockport Co	1	0		
2005–06	Stockport Co	0	0	**1**	**0**
2006–07	Macclesfield T	37	1	**37**	**1**

HEATH, Colin (F) **46 5**
H: 6 0 W: 11 13 b.Matlock 31-12-83
Source: Scholar.

2000–01	Manchester U	0	0		
2001–02	Manchester U	0	0		
2002–03	Manchester U	0	0		
2003–04	Manchester U	0	0		
2004–05	Manchester U	0	0		
2004–05	*Cambridge U*	6	0	**6**	**0**
2005–06	Manchester U	0	0		
2005–06	*Swindon T*	11	1	**11**	**1**
2005–06	Chesterfield	4	0	**4**	**0**
2006–07	Macclesfield T	25	4	**25**	**4**

INCE, Paul (M) **609 71**
H: 5 10 W: 12 02 b.Ilford 21-10-67
Source: Trainee. *Honours:* England Youth, Under-21, B, 53 full caps, 2 goals.

1985–86	West Ham U	0	0		
1986–87	West Ham U	10	1		
1987–88	West Ham U	28	3		
1988–89	West Ham U	33	3		
1989–90	West Ham U	1	0	**72**	**7**
1989–90	Manchester U	26	0		
1990–91	Manchester U	31	3		
1991–92	Manchester U	33	3		
1992–93	Manchester U	41	5		
1993–94	Manchester U	39	8		
1994–95	Manchester U	36	5	**206**	**24**
1995–96	Internazionale	30	3		
1996–97	Internazionale	24	6	**54**	**9**
1997–98	Liverpool	31	8		
1998–99	Liverpool	34	6	**65**	**14**
1999–2000	Middlesbrough	32	3		
2000–01	Middlesbrough	30	2		
2001–02	Middlesbrough	31	2	**93**	**7**
2002–03	Wolverhampton W	37	2		
2003–04	Wolverhampton W	32	2		
2004–05	Wolverhampton W	28	3		
2005–06	Wolverhampton W	18	3		
2006–07	Wolverhampton W	0	0	**115**	**10**
2006–07	Swindon T	3	0	**3**	**0**
2006–07	Macclesfield T	1	0	**1**	**0**

JENNINGS, James (D) **9** **0**
H: 5 10 W: 11 02 b.Manchester 2-9-87
Source: Scholar.

2006–07	Macclesfield T	9	0	**9**	**0**

LEE, Tommy (G) **45** **0**
H: 6 2 W: 12 00 b.Keighley 3-1-86
Source: Scholar.

2005–06	Manchester U	0	0		
2005–06	*Macclesfield T*	11	0		
2006–07	Macclesfield T	34	0	**45**	**0**

McDONALD, Marvin (F) **0** **0**
H: 5 7 W: 10 00 b.Wythenshawe 24-8-86
Source: Scholar.

2005–06	Macclesfield T	0	0		
2006–07	Macclesfield T	0	0		

McINTYRE, Kevin (M) **123** **14**
H: 6 0 W: 11 10 b.Liverpool 23-12-77
Source: Trainee.

1996–97	Tranmere R	0	0		
1997–98	Tranmere R	2	0		
1998–99	Tranmere R	0	0		
1999–2000	Tranmere R	0	0		
2000–01	Tranmere R	0	0		
2001–02	Tranmere R	0	0	**2**	**0**
2004–05	Chester C	10	0	**10**	**0**
2004–05	Macclesfield T	23	0		
2005–06	Macclesfield T	44	5		
2006–07	Macclesfield T	44	9	**111**	**14**

McNEIL, Matthew (F) **47** **6**
H: 6 5 W: 14 03 b.Macclesfield 14-7-76
Source: Burnley, Curzon Ashton, Altrincham, Woodley Sp, Stalybridge C, Woking, Runcorn, Hyde U.

2005–06	Macclesfield T	12	1		
2006–07	Macclesfield T	35	5	**47**	**6**

McNULTY, Jim (D) **15** **0**
H: 6 1 W: 12 00 b.Liverpool 13-2-85
Source: Scholar.

2003–04	Wrexham	0	0		
2004–05	Wrexham	0	0		
2005–06	Wrexham	0	0		
2006–07	Macclesfield T	15	0	**15**	**0**

MILES, John (F) **128** **22**
H: 5 10 W: 10 08 b.Fazackerley 28-9-81
Source: Trainee.

1998–99	Liverpool	0	0		
1999–2000	Liverpool	0	0		
2000–01	Liverpool	0	0		
2001–02	Liverpool	0	0		
2001–02	Stoke C	1	0	**1**	**0**
2002–03	Crewe Alex	5	1	**5**	**1**
2002–03	Macclesfield T	8	4		
2003–04	Macclesfield T	29	6		
2004–05	Macclesfield T	30	3		
2005–06	Macclesfield T	25	4		
2006–07	Macclesfield T	30	4	**122**	**21**

MORLEY, Dave (D) **271** **12**
H: 6 1 W: 13 02 b.St Helens 25-9-77
Source: Trainee.

1995–96	Manchester C	0	0		
1996–97	Manchester C	0	0		
1997–98	Manchester C	3	1		
1997–98	*Ayr U*	4	0	**4**	**0**
1998–99	Manchester C	0	0	**3**	**1**
1998–99	Southend U	27	0		
1999–2000	Southend U	32	0		
2000–01	Southend U	17	0	**76**	**0**
2000–01	Carlisle U	23	1		
2001–02	Carlisle U	18	0	**41**	**1**
2001–02	Oxford U	18	3	**18**	**3**
2003–04	Doncaster R	21	1		
2004–05	Doncaster R	9	0	**30**	**1**
2004–05	Macclesfield T	19	2		
2005–06	Macclesfield T	45	1		
2006–07	Macclesfield T	35	3	**99**	**6**

MURPHY, John (F) **384** **110**
H: 6 2 W: 14 00 b.Whiston 18-10-76
Source: Trainee.

1994–95	Chester C	5	0		
1995–96	Chester C	18	3		
1996–97	Chester C	11	1		
1997–98	Chester C	27	4		
1998–99	Chester C	42	12	**103**	**20**
1999–2000	Blackpool	39	10		
2000–01	Blackpool	46	18		
2001–02	Blackpool	37	13		
2002–03	Blackpool	35	16		
2003–04	Blackpool	30	9		
2004–05	Blackpool	31	9		
2005–06	Blackpool	34	8		
2006–07	Blackpool	0	0	**252**	**83**
2006–07	Macclesfield T	29	7	**29**	**7**

MURRAY, Adam (M) **195** **16**
H: 5 8 W: 10 12 b.Birmingham 30-9-81
Source: Trainee. *Honours:* England Youth, Under-20.

1998–99	Derby Co	4	0		
1999–2000	Derby Co	8	0		
2000–01	Derby Co	14	0		
2001–02	Derby Co	6	0		
2001–02	*Mansfield T*	13	7		
2002–03	Derby Co	24	0		
2003–04	Derby Co	0	0	**56**	**0**
2003–04	Kidderminster H	22	3	**22**	**3**
From Burton Alb.					
2003–04	Notts Co	3	0	**3**	**0**
2004–05	Mansfield T	32	5	**45**	**12**
2004–05	Carlisle U	0	0		
2005–06	Carlisle U	37	1		
2006–07	Carlisle U	0	0	**37**	**1**
2006–07	Torquay U	21	0	**21**	**0**
2006–07	Macclesfield T	11	0	**11**	**0**

NAVARRO, Alan (M) **133** **5**
H: 5 10 W: 11 07 b.Liverpool 31-5-81
Source: Trainee.

1998–99	Liverpool	0	0		
1999–2000	Liverpool	0	0		
2000–01	Liverpool	0	0		
2000–01	*Crewe Alex*	8	1		
2001–02	Liverpool	0	0		
2001–02	*Crewe Alex*	7	0	**15**	**1**
2001–02	Tranmere R	21	1		
2002–03	Tranmere R	5	0		
2003–04	Tranmere R	19	0		
2004–05	Tranmere R	0	0		
2004–05	*Chester C*	3	0	**3**	**0**
2004–05	*Macclesfield T*	11	1		
2005–06	Tranmere R	0	0	**45**	**1**
From Accrington S.					
2005–06	Macclesfield T	27	0		
2006–07	Macclesfield T	32	2	**70**	**3**

REGAN, Carl (D) **160** **2**
H: 5 11 W: 11 12 b.Liverpool 14-1-80
Source: Trainee. *Honours:* England Youth.

1997–98	Everton	0	0		
1998–99	Everton	0	0		
1999–2000	Everton	0	0		
2000–01	Barnsley	27	0		
2001–02	Barnsley	10	0		
2002–03	Barnsley	0	0	**37**	**0**
2002–03	Hull C	38	0		
2003–04	Hull C	0	0		
2004–05	Hull C	0	0	**38**	**0**
2004–05	Chester C	6	0		
2005–06	Chester C	41	0	**47**	**0**
2006–07	Macclesfield T	38	2	**38**	**2**

REID, Izak (M) **8** **0**
H: 5 5 W: 10 05 b.Sheffield 8-7-87
Source: Scholar.

2006–07	Macclesfield T	8	0	**8**	**0**

ROBINSON, Marvin (F) **107** **20**
H: 5 11 W: 12 13 b.Crewe 11-4-80
Source: Trainee.

1998–99	Derby Co	1	0		
1999–2000	Derby Co	8	0		
2000–01	Derby Co	0	0		
2000–01	*Stoke C*	3	1	**3**	**1**
2001–02	Derby Co	2	1		
2002–03	Derby Co	1	0	**12**	**1**
2002–03	*Tranmere R*	6	1	**6**	**1**
2003–04	Chesterfield	32	6		
2004–05	Chesterfield	0	0	**32**	**6**
2004–05	Notts Co	2	0	**2**	**0**
2004–05	Rushden & D	2	0	**2**	**0**
2004–05	Walsall	10	4	**10**	**4**
2004–05	Stockport Co	3	0	**3**	**0**
2005–06	Lincoln C	32	7	**32**	**7**
2006–07	Macclesfield T	5	0	**5**	**0**

ROUSE, David (G) **1** **0**
H: 6 0 W: 13 07 b.Stretford 6-3-76

2006–07	Macclesfield T	1	0	**1**	**0**

SCOTT, Rob (D) **331** **36**
H: 6 0 W: 12 09 b.Epsom 15-8-73
Source: Sutton U.

1993–94	Sheffield U	0	0		
1994–95	Sheffield U	1	0		
1994–95	*Scarborough*	8	3	**8**	**3**
1995–96	Sheffield U	5	1	**6**	**1**
1995–96	*Northampton T*	5	0	**5**	**0**
1995–96	Fulham	21	5		
1996–97	Fulham	43	9		
1997–98	Fulham	17	3		
1998–99	Fulham	3	0	**84**	**17**
1998–99	*Carlisle U*	7	3	**7**	**3**
1998–99	Rotherham U	6	1		
1999–2000	Rotherham U	34	1		
2000–01	Rotherham U	39	2		
2001–02	Rotherham U	38	3		
2002–03	Rotherham U	23	0		
2003–04	Rotherham U	10	0		
2004–05	Rotherham U	24	2	**174**	**9**
2005–06	Oldham Ath	21	1		
2006–07	Oldham Ath	0	0	**21**	**1**
2006–07	Macclesfield T	26	2	**26**	**2**

SMART, Andrew (D) **9** **0**
H: 6 1 W: 14 00 b.Altrincham 17-3-86
Source: Scholar.

2004–05	Macclesfield T	0	0		
2005–06	Macclesfield T	9	0		
2006–07	Macclesfield T	0	0	**9**	**0**

SWAILES, Danny (D) **258** **18**
H: 6 3 W: 12 06 b.Bolton 1-4-79
Source: Trainee.

1997–98	Bury	0	0		
1998–99	Bury	0	0		
1999–2000	Bury	24	3		
2000–01	Bury	11	0		
2001–02	Bury	28	1		
2002–03	Bury	39	3		
2003–04	Bury	42	5		
2004–05	Bury	20	1	**164**	**13**
2004–05	Macclesfield T	17	0		
2005–06	Macclesfield T	39	2		
2006–07	Macclesfield T	38	3	**94**	**5**

TEAGUE, Andrew (D) **43** **2**
H: 6 2 W: 12 00 b.Preston 5-2-86
Source: Scholar.

2004–05	Macclesfield T	5	0		
2005–06	Macclesfield T	25	1		
2006–07	Macclesfield T	13	1	**43**	**2**

TOLLEY, Jamie (M) **183** **15**
H: 6 1 W: 11 03 b.Ludlow 12-5-83
Source: Scholarship. *Honours:* Wales Under-21.

1999–2000	Shrewsbury T	2	0		
2000–01	Shrewsbury T	24	2		
2001–02	Shrewsbury T	23	1		
2002–03	Shrewsbury T	39	3		
2003–04	Shrewsbury T	0	0		
2004–05	Shrewsbury T	36	4		
2005–06	Shrewsbury T	36	4	**160**	**14**
2006–07	Macclesfield T	23	1	**23**	**1**

MANCHESTER C (49)

ABDOUN, Djamel (M) **12** **2**
H: 5 9 W: 10 03 b.Montreuil-sous-Bois 14-2-86

2003–04	Ajaccio	1	0		
2004–05	Ajaccio	2	0		
2005–06	Ajaccio	7	2		
2006–07	Ajaccio	2	0	**12**	**2**
2006–07	Manchester C	0	0		

BALL, Michael (D) **202** **9**
H: 5 11 W: 11 12 b.Liverpool 2-10-79
Source: Trainee. *Honours:* England Schools, Youth, Under-21, 1 full cap.

1996–97	Everton	5	0		
1997–98	Everton	25	1		
1998–99	Everton	37	3		
1999–2000	Everton	25	1		

2000–01	Everton	29	3	**121**	**8**
2001–02	Rangers	8	0		
2002–03	Rangers	0	0		
2003–04	Rangers	32	1		
2004–05	Rangers	15	0		
2005–06	Rangers	2	0	**57**	**1**
2005–06	PSV Eindhoven	12	0		
2006–07	PSV Eindhoven	0	0	**12**	**0**
2006–07	Manchester C	12	0	**12**	**0**

BARTON, Joey (M) **130** **15**
H: 5 11 W: 12 05 b.Huyton 2-9-82
Source: Scholar. *Honours:* England Under-21, 1 full cap.

2001–02	Manchester C	0	0		
2002–03	Manchester C	7	1		
2003–04	Manchester C	28	1		
2004–05	Manchester C	31	1		
2005–06	Manchester C	31	6		
2006–07	Manchester C	33	6	**130**	**15**

BEASLEY, DaMarcus (M) **172** **28**
H: 5 7 W: 9 00 b.Fort Wayne 24-5-82
Source: Los Angeles G. *Honours:* USA Youth, Under-23, 68 full caps, 15 goals.

2000	Chicago Fire	18	2		
2001	Chicago Fire	24	3		
2002	Chicago Fire	19	3		
2003	Chicago Fire	22	7		
2004	Chicago Fire	15	0	**98**	**15**
2004–05	PSV Eindhoven	29	6		
2005–06	PSV Eindhoven	27	4	**56**	**10**
2006–07	Manchester C	18	3	**18**	**3**

BREEN, Garry (D) **0** **0**
b.Kilkenny
Source: Scholar.

2006–07	Manchester C	0	0		

CORRADI, Bernardo (F) **371** **85**
H: 6 2 W: 13 08 b.Siena 30-3-76
Source: From Siena. *Honours:* Italy 13 full caps, 2 goals.

1994–95	Poggibonsi	16	1		
1995–96	Poggibonsi	31	8	**47**	**9**
1996–97	Mobilieri	31	6	**31**	**6**
1997–98	Cagliari	2	0		
1997–98	*Montevarchi*	26	5	**26**	**5**
1998–99	Fidelis Andria	31	7	**31**	**7**
1999–2000	Cagliari	20	0	**22**	**0**
2000–01	Chievo	36	12		
2001–02	Chievo	32	10	**68**	**22**
2002–03	Internazionale	0	0		
2002–03	*Lazio*	32	10		
2003–04	Lazio	32	10	**64**	**20**
2004–05	Valencia	21	3		
2005–06	Valencia	0	0	**21**	**3**
2005–06	*Parma*	36	10	**36**	**10**
2006–07	Manchester C	25	3	**25**	**3**

D'LARYEA, Nathan (D) **1** **0**
H: 5 10 W: 12 02 b.Manchester 3-9-85
Source: Trainee.

2003–04	Manchester C	0	0		
2004–05	Manchester C	0	0		
2005–06	Manchester C	0	0		
2006–07	Manchester C	0	0		
2006–07	*Macclesfield T*	1	0	**1**	**0**

DABO, Ousmane (M) **260** **11**
H: 6 1 W: 13 04 b.Laval 8-2-77
Honours: France Under-21, 3 full caps.

1995–96	Rennes	5	1		
1996–97	Rennes	24	1		
1997–98	Rennes	12	1	**41**	**3**
1998–99	Internazionale	5	0		
1998–99	*Vicenza*	13	0		
1999–2000	Internazionale	8	0	**13**	**0**
1999–2000	Parma	16	0	**16**	**0**
2000–01	Monaco	16	0	**16**	**0**
2000–01	Vicenza	17	1	**30**	**1**
2001–02	Atalanta	21	0		
2002–03	Atalanta	31	4	**52**	**4**
2003–04	Lazio	19	0		
2004–05	Lazio	29	1		
2005–06	Lazio	31	2	**79**	**3**
2006–07	Manchester C	13	0	**13**	**0**

DALY, Michael (M) **0** **0**

2006–07	Manchester C	0	0		

DICKOV, Paul (F) **355** **88**
H: 5 6 W: 10 06 b.Livingston 1-11-72
Source: Trainee. *Honours:* Scotland Schools, Youth, Under-21, 10 full caps, 1 goal.

1992–93	Arsenal	3	2		
1993–94	Arsenal	1	0		
1993–94	*Luton T*	15	1	**15**	**1**
1993–94	*Brighton & HA*	8	5	**8**	**5**
1994–95	Arsenal	9	0		
1995–96	Arsenal	7	1		
1996–97	Arsenal	1	0	**21**	**3**
1996–97	Manchester C	29	5		
1997–98	Manchester C	30	9		
1998–99	Manchester C	35	10		
1999–2000	Manchester C	34	5		
2000–01	Manchester C	21	4		
2001–02	Manchester C	7	0		
2001–02	Leicester C	12	4		
2002–03	Leicester C	42	17		
2003–04	Leicester C	35	11	**89**	**32**
2004–05	Blackburn R	29	9		
2005–06	Blackburn R	21	5	**50**	**14**
2006–07	Manchester C	16	0	**172**	**33**

DISTIN, Sylvain (D) **293** **9**
H: 6 3 W: 14 06 b.Bagnolet 16-12-77

1998–99	Tours	26	3	**26**	**3**
1999–2000	Gueugnon	33	1	**33**	**1**
2000–01	Paris St Germain	28	0	**28**	**0**
2001–02	Newcastle U	28	0	**28**	**0**
2002–03	Manchester C	34	0		
2003–04	Manchester C	38	2		
2004–05	Manchester C	38	1		
2005–06	Manchester C	31	0		
2006–07	Manchester C	37	2	**178**	**5**

DUNNE, Richard (D) **287** **7**
H: 6 2 W: 15 10 b.Dublin 21-9-79
Source: Trainee. *Honours:* Eire Schools, Youth, Under-21, B, 35 full caps, 5 goals.

1996–97	Everton	7	0		
1997–98	Everton	3	0		
1998–99	Everton	16	0		
1999–2000	Everton	31	0		
2000–01	Everton	3	0	**60**	**0**
2000–01	Manchester C	25	0		
2001–02	Manchester C	43	1		
2002–03	Manchester C	25	0		
2003–04	Manchester C	29	0		
2004–05	Manchester C	35	2		
2005–06	Manchester C	32	3		
2006–07	Manchester C	38	1	**227**	**7**

ETUHU, Kelvin (F) **4** **2**
H: 5 11 W: 11 02 b.Kano 30-5-88
Source: Scholar.

2005–06	Manchester C	0	0		
2006–07	Manchester C	0	0		
2006–07	*Rochdale*	4	2	**4**	**2**

EVANS, Ched (F) **0** **0**
b. 28-12-88
Honours: Wales Under-21.

2006–07	Manchester C	0	0		

GRIMES, Ashley (M) **4** **0**
H: 6 0 W: 11 02 b.Swinton 9-12-86
Source: Scholar.

2006–07	Manchester C	0	0		
2006–07	*Swindon T*	4	0	**4**	**0**

HAMANN, Dietmar (M) **335** **18**
H: 6 2 W: 13 00 b.Waldasson 27-8-73
Source: Wacker Munich. *Honours:* Germany Youth, Under-21, 59 full caps, 5 goals.

1993–94	Bayern Munich	5	1		
1994–95	Bayern Munich	30	0		
1995–96	Bayern Munich	20	2		
1996–97	Bayern Munich	22	1		
1997–98	Bayern Munich	28	2	**105**	**6**
1998–99	Newcastle U	23	4	**23**	**4**
1999–2000	Liverpool	28	1		
2000–01	Liverpool	30	2		
2001–02	Liverpool	31	1		
2002–03	Liverpool	30	2		
2003–04	Liverpool	25	2		
2004–05	Liverpool	30	0		
2005–06	Liverpool	17	0	**191**	**8**
2006–07	Manchester C	16	0	**16**	**0**

HART, Joe (G) **64** **0**
H: 6 3 W: 13 03 b.Shrewsbury 19-4-87
Source: Scholar, England Youth, Under-21.

2004–05	Shrewsbury T	6	0		
2005–06	Shrewsbury T	46	0	**52**	**0**
2006–07	Manchester C	1	0	**1**	**0**
2006–07	*Tranmere R*	6	0	**6**	**0**
2006–07	*Blackpool*	5	0	**5**	**0**

IRELAND, Stephen (F) **48** **1**
H: 5 8 W: 10 07 b.Cork 22-8-86
Source: Scholar. *Honours:* Eire Youth, Under-21, 5 full caps, 3 goals.

2005–06	Manchester C	24	0		
2006–07	Manchester C	24	1	**48**	**1**

ISAKSSON, Andreas (G) **155** **0**
H: 6 6 W: 13 12 b.Trelleborg 3-10-81
Honours: Sweden Under-21, 46 full caps.

1999	Trelleborg	11	0	**11**	**0**
1999–2000	Juventus	0	0		
2000–01	Juventus	0	0		
2001	Djurgaarden	22	0		
2002	Djurgaarden	20	0		
2003	Djurgaarden	26	0	**68**	**0**
2004–05	Rennes	38	0		
2005–06	Rennes	24	0	**62**	**0**
2006–07	Manchester C	14	0	**14**	**0**

JIHAI, Sun (D) **139** **3**
H: 5 9 W: 12 02 b.Dalian 30-9-77
Source: Dalian Wanda. *Honours:* China 66 full caps, 8 goals.

1998–99	Crystal Palace	23	0	**23**	**0**
From Dalian Wanda.					
2001–02	Manchester C	7	0		
2002–03	Manchester C	28	2		
2003–04	Manchester C	33	1		
2004–05	Manchester C	6	0		
2005–06	Manchester C	29	0		
2006–07	Manchester C	13	0	**116**	**3**

JOHNSON, Michael (M) **10** **0**
H: 6 1 W: 12 07 b.Urmston 3-3-88
Source: Scholar. *Honours:* England Youth.

2005–06	Manchester C	0	0		
2006–07	Manchester C	10	0	**10**	**0**

JORDAN, Stephen (D) **64** **0**
H: 6 1 W: 13 00 b.Warrington 6-3-82
Source: Scholarship.

1998–99	Manchester C	0	0		
1999–2000	Manchester C	0	0		
2000–01	Manchester C	0	0		
2001–02	Manchester C	0	0		
2002–03	Manchester C	1	0		
2002–03	*Cambridge U*	11	0	**11**	**0**
2003–04	Manchester C	2	0		
2004–05	Manchester C	19	0		
2005–06	Manchester C	18	0		
2006–07	Manchester C	13	0	**53**	**0**

LAIRD, Marc (M) **6** **0**
H: 6 1 W: 10 07 b.Edinburgh 23-1-86
Source: Trainee.

2003–04	Manchester C	0	0		
2004–05	Manchester C	0	0		
2005–06	Manchester C	0	0		
2006–07	Manchester C	0	0		
2006–07	*Northampton T*	6	0	**6**	**0**

LOGAN, Shaleum (M) **0** **0**
Source: Scholar.

2006–07	Manchester C	0	0		

MILLER, Ishmael (F) **17** **0**
H: 6 3 W: 14 00 b.Manchester 5-3-87
Source: Scholar.

2005–06	Manchester C	1	0		
2006–07	Manchester C	16	0	**17**	**0**

MILLS, Danny (D) **300** **7**
H: 5 11 W: 12 13 b.Norwich 18-5-77
Source: Trainee. *Honours:* England Youth, Under-21, 19 full caps.

1994–95	Norwich C	0	0		
1995–96	Norwich C	14	0		
1996–97	Norwich C	32	0		
1997–98	Norwich C	20	0	**66**	**0**
1997–98	Charlton Ath	9	1		

1998–99	Charlton Ath	36	2	**45**	**3**
1999–2000	Leeds U	17	1		
2000–01	Leeds U	23	0		
2001–02	Leeds U	28	1		
2002–03	Leeds U	33	1		
2003–04	Leeds U	0	0	**101**	**3**
2003–04	*Middlesbrough*	28	0	**28**	**0**
2004–05	Manchester C	32	0		
2005–06	Manchester C	18	1		
2006–07	Manchester C	1	0	**51**	**1**
2006–07	*Hull C*	9	0	**9**	**0**

MILLS, Matthew (D) **31** **3**

H: 6 3 W: 12 12 b.Swindon 14-7-86

Source: Scholar. *Honours:* England Youth.

2004–05	Southampton	0	0		
2004–05	*Coventry C*	4	0	**4**	**0**
2004–05	*Bournemouth*	12	3	**12**	**3**
2005–06	Southampton	4	0	**4**	**0**
2005–06	Manchester C	1	0		
2006–07	Manchester C	1	0	**2**	**0**
2006–07	*Colchester U*	9	0	**9**	**0**

MOORE, Karl (M) **0** **0**

b.Dublin 9-11-88

Source: Scholar.

2006–07	Manchester C	0	0

MOURITSEN, Christian (M) **0** **0**

b.Faroe Islands

Source: Scholar.

2006–07	Manchester C	0	0

MPENZA, Emile (F) **232** **90**

H: 5 9 W: 10 12 b.Zellik 4-7-78

Honours: Belgium 52 full caps, 17 goals.

1995–96	Kortrijk	0	0		
1996–97	Mouscron	31	12	**31**	**12**
1997–98	Standard Liege	20	6		
1998–99	Standard Liege	17	10		
1999–2000	Standard Liege	11	4		
1999–2000	Schalke	15	6		
2000–01	Schalke	27	13		
2001–02	Schalke	16	4		
2002–03	Schalke	21	5	**79**	**28**
2003–04	Standard Liege	28	21		
2003–04	Standard Liege	0	0	**76**	**41**
2004–05	Hamburg	26	5		
2005–06	Hamburg	10	1	**36**	**6**
From Al Rayyan.					
2006–07	Manchester C	10	3	**10**	**3**

ONUOHA, Nedum (D) **45** **0**

H: 6 2 W: 12 04 b.Warri 12-11-86

Source: Scholar. *Honours:* England Youth, Under-20, Under-21.

2004–05	Manchester C	17	0		
2005–06	Manchester C	10	0		
2006–07	Manchester C	18	0	**45**	**0**

REYNA, Claudio (M) **221** **21**

H: 5 9 W: 11 08 b.New Jersey 20-7-73

Source: Union County SC, Univ Virginia. *Honours:* USA 112 full caps, 8 goals.

1996–97	Leverkusen	5	0	**5**	**0**
1997–98	Wolfsburg	28	4		
1998–99	Wolfsburg	20	2	**48**	**6**
1998–99	Rangers	6	0		
1999–2000	Rangers	29	5		
2000–01	Rangers	18	2		
2001–02	Rangers	10	1	**63**	**8**
2001–02	Sunderland	17	3		
2002–03	Sunderland	11	0		
2003–04	Sunderland	0	0	**28**	**3**
2003–04	Manchester C	23	1		
2004–05	Manchester C	17	2		
2005–06	Manchester C	22	1		
2006–07	Manchester C	15	0	**77**	**4**

To New York Red Bull January 2007

RICHARDS, Micah (D) **41** **1**

H: 5 11 W: 13 00 b.Birmingham 24-6-88

Source: Scholar. *Honours:* England Youth, Under-21, 4 full caps.

2005–06	Manchester C	13	0		
2006–07	Manchester C	28	1	**41**	**1**

SAMARAS, Georgios (F) **136** **33**

H: 6 3 W: 13 07 b.Heraklion 21-2-85

Source: OFI Crete. *Honours:* Greece Under-21, 11 full caps, 3 goals.

2002–03	Heerenveen	15	4		
2003–04	Heerenveen	27	4		
2004–05	Heerenveen	31	11		
2005–06	Heerenveen	13	6	**86**	**25**
2005–06	Manchester C	14	4		
2006–07	Manchester C	36	4	**50**	**8**

SCHMEICHEL, Kasper (G) **48** **0**

H: 6 1 W: 13 00 b.Denmark 5-11-86

Source: Scholar. *Honours:* Denmark Youth, Under-20, Under-21.

2003–04	Manchester C	0	0		
2004–05	Manchester C	0	0		
2005–06	Manchester C	0	0		
2005–06	*Darlington*	4	0	**4**	**0**
2005–06	*Bury*	15	0		
2006–07	Manchester C	0	0		
2006–07	*Falkirk*	15	0	**15**	**0**
2006–07	*Bury*	14	0	**29**	**0**

SINCLAIR, Trevor (M) **538** **73**

H: 5 9 W: 13 05 b.Dulwich 2-3-73

Source: Trainee. *Honours:* England Youth, Under-21, B, 12 full caps.

1989–90	Blackpool	9	0		
1990–91	Blackpool	31	1		
1991–92	Blackpool	27	3		
1992–93	Blackpool	45	11	**112**	**15**
1993–94	QPR	32	4		
1994–95	QPR	33	4		
1995–96	QPR	37	2		
1996–97	QPR	39	3		
1997–98	QPR	26	3	**167**	**16**
1997–98	West Ham U	14	7		
1998–99	West Ham U	36	7		
1999–2000	West Ham U	36	7		
2000–01	West Ham U	19	3		
2001–02	West Ham U	34	5		
2002–03	West Ham U	38	8	**177**	**37**
2003–04	Manchester C	29	1		
2004–05	Manchester C	4	1		
2005–06	Manchester C	31	3		
2006–07	Manchester C	18	0	**82**	**5**

STURRIDGE, Daniel (F) **2** **0**

H: 6 2 W: 12 00 b.Manchester 1-9-89

Source: Scholar. *Honours:* England Youth.

2006–07	Manchester C	2	0	**2**	**0**

TRABELSI, Hatem (D) **119** **3**

H: 5 10 W: 11 02 b.Ariana 25-1-77

Source: Sfaxien. *Honours:* Tunisia 61 full caps, 1 goal.

2001–02	Ajax	21	0		
2002–03	Ajax	26	1		
2003–04	Ajax	8	1		
2004–05	Ajax	24	0		
2005–06	Ajax	20	0	**99**	**2**
2006–07	Manchester C	20	1	**20**	**1**

VASSELL, Darius (F) **230** **46**

H: 5 9 W: 13 00 b.Birmingham 13-6-80

Source: Trainee. *Honours:* England Youth, Under-21, 22 full caps, 6 goals.

1998–99	Aston Villa	6	0		
1999–2000	Aston Villa	11	0		
2000–01	Aston Villa	23	4		
2001–02	Aston Villa	36	12		
2002–03	Aston Villa	33	8		
2003–04	Aston Villa	32	9		
2004–05	Aston Villa	21	2	**162**	**35**
2005–06	Manchester C	36	8		
2006–07	Manchester C	32	3	**68**	**11**

WEAVER, Nick (G) **187** **0**

H: 6 4 W: 14 07 b.Sheffield 2-3-79

Source: Trainee. *Honours:* England Under-21.

1995–96	Mansfield T	1	0		
1996–97	Mansfield T	0	0	**1**	**0**
1996–97	Manchester C	0	0		
1997–98	Manchester C	0	0		
1998–99	Manchester C	45	0		
1999–2000	Manchester C	45	0		
2000–01	Manchester C	31	0		
2001–02	Manchester C	25	0		
2002–03	Manchester C	0	0		
2003–04	Manchester C	0	0		
2004–05	Manchester C	1	0		
2005–06	Manchester C	0	0		
2005–06	*Sheffield W*	14	0	**14**	**0**
2006–07	Manchester C	25	0	**172**	**0**

WILLIAMSON, Samuel (D) **0** **0**

H: 5 8 W: 11 09 b.Macclesfield 15-10-87

Source: Scholar.

2006–07	Manchester C	0	0

Scholars

Ball, David Michael; Brown, Matthew Anthony; Campbell, John Terrance; Clayton, Adam Stephen; Connor, Michael; Daly, Ian; Evans, Chedwyn Michael; Hartley, Gregory; Kay, Scott John David; Marshall, Paul Anthony; McDermott, Donal; McDonald, Clayton; McGivern, Ryan; Mee, Benjamin; Mentel, Filip; Morris, Benjamin Thomas; Obeng, Curtis; Poole, James Alexander; Ramsey, Christopher; Tsiaklis, Angelos; Vidal, Javan; Weiss, Vladimir.

MANCHESTER U (50)

BARDSLEY, Phillip (D) **32** **1**

H: 5 11 W: 11 13 b.Salford 28-6-85

Source: Trainee.

2003–04	Manchester U	0	0		
2004–05	Manchester U	0	0		
2005–06	Manchester U	8	0		
2005–06	*Burnley*	6	0	**6**	**0**
2006–07	Manchester U	0	0	**8**	**0**
2006–07	*Rangers*	5	1	**5**	**1**
2006–07	*Aston Villa*	13	0	**13**	**0**

BARNES, Michael (M) **0** **0**

H: 5 10 W: 11 05 b.Chorley 24-6-88

Source: Lancaster C.

2006–07	Manchester U	0	0

BRANDY, Febian (F) **0** **0**

H: 5 5 W: 10 00 b.Manchester 4-2-89

Source: Scholar.

2006–07	Manchester U	0	0

BROWN, Wes (D) **162** **1**

H: 6 1 W: 13 08 b.Manchester 13-10-79

Source: From Trainee. *Honours:* England Schools, Youth, Under-21, 12 full caps.

1996–97	Manchester U	0	0		
1997–98	Manchester U	2	0		
1998–99	Manchester U	14	0		
1999–2000	Manchester U	0	0		
2000–01	Manchester U	28	0		
2001–02	Manchester U	17	0		
2002–03	Manchester U	22	0		
2003–04	Manchester U	17	0		
2004–05	Manchester U	21	1		
2005–06	Manchester U	19	0		
2006–07	Manchester U	22	0	**162**	**1**

CAMPBELL, Frazier (F) **0** **0**

H: 5 11 W: 12 04 b.Huddersfield 13-9-87

Source: Scholar. *Honours:* England Youth.

2005–06	Manchester U	0	0
2006–07	Manchester U	0	0

CARRICK, Michael (M) **241** **13**

H: 6 1 W: 11 10 b.Wallsend 28-7-81

Source: Trainee. *Honours:* England Youth, Under-21, B, 13 full caps.

1998–99	West Ham U	0	0		
1999–2000	West Ham U	8	1		
1999–2000	*Swindon T*	6	2	**6**	**2**
1999–2000	*Birmingham C*	2	0	**2**	**0**
2000–01	West Ham U	33	1		
2001–02	West Ham U	30	2		
2002–03	West Ham U	30	1		
2003–04	West Ham U	35	1		
2004–05	West Ham U	0	0	**136**	**6**
2004–05	Tottenham H	29	0		
2005–06	Tottenham H	35	2	**64**	**2**
2006–07	Manchester U	33	3	**33**	**3**

CATHCART, Craig (D) **0 0**
H: 6 2 W: 11 06 b.Belfast 6-2-89
Source: Scholar. *Honours:* Northern Ireland Under-21.

2005–06	Manchester U	0	0		
2006–07	Manchester U	0	0		

DONG FANGZHOU (M) **93 54**
H: 6 1 W: 11 09 b.Liaoning 23-1-85
Source: China Under-23, 10 full caps, 1 goal.

2002	Dalian Saidelong	14	20	**14**	**20**
2003	Dalian Shide	8	0	**8**	**0**
2003–04	Manchester U	0	0		
2003–04	*Antwerp*	9	1		
2004–05	*Antwerp*	19	6		
2005–06	*Antwerp*	28	18		
2006–07	*Antwerp*	14	9	**70**	**34**
2006–07	Manchester U	1	0	**1**	**0**

EAGLES, Chris (M) **57 8**
H: 5 10 W: 11 07 b.Hemel Hempstead 19-11-85
Source: Trainee. *Honours:* England Youth.

2003–04	Manchester U	0	0		
2004–05	Manchester U	0	0		
2004–05	*Watford*	13	1		
2005–06	Manchester U	0	0		
2005–06	*Sheffield W*	25	3	**25**	**3**
2005–06	*Watford*	17	3	**30**	**4**
2006–07	Manchester U	2	1	**2**	**1**

ECKERSLEY, Adam (D) **6 0**
H: 5 9 W: 11 13 b.Manchester 7-9-85
Source: Scholar. *Honours:* England Youth.

2004–05	Manchester U	0	0		
2005–06	Manchester U	0	0		
2006–07	Manchester U	0	0		
2006–07	*Barnsley*	6	0	**6**	**0**

EVANS, Jonny (D) **18 1**
H: 6 2 W: 12 02 b.Belfast 3-1-88
Source: Scholar. *Honours:* Northern Ireland Schools, Youth, Under-21, 5 full caps.

2004–05	Manchester U	0	0		
2005–06	Manchester U	0	0		
2006–07	Manchester U	0	0		
2006–07	*Sunderland*	18	1	**18**	**1**

EVANS, Sean (F) **0 0**
H: 5 9 W: 11 00 b.Ludlow 25-9-87
Source: Scholar.

2006–07	Manchester U	0	0		

EVRA, Patrice (D) **221 6**
H: 5 8 W: 11 10 b.Dakar 15-5-81
Honours: France 6 full caps.

1998–99	Marsala	24	3	**24**	**3**
1999–2000	Monza	3	0	**3**	**0**
2000–01	Nice	5	0		
2001–02	Nice	34	1	**39**	**1**
2002–03	Monaco	36	1		
2003–04	Monaco	33	0		
2004–05	Monaco	36	0		
2005–06	Monaco	15	0	**120**	**1**
2005–06	Manchester U	11	0		
2006–07	Manchester U	24	1	**35**	**1**

FAGAN, Chris (F) **0 0**
H: 5 8 W: 10 05 b.Dublin 11-5-89
Source: Scholar.

2006–07	Manchester U	0	0		

FERDINAND, Rio (D) **340 8**
H: 6 2 W: 13 12 b.Peckham 7-11-78
Source: From Trainee. *Honours:* England Youth, Under-21, B, 59 full caps, 1 goal.

1995–96	West Ham U	1	0		
1996–97	West Ham U	15	2		
1996–97	*Bournemouth*	10	0	**10**	**0**
1997–98	West Ham U	35	0		
1998–99	West Ham U	31	0		
1999–2000	West Ham U	33	0		
2000–01	West Ham U	12	0	**127**	**2**
2000–01	Leeds U	23	2		
2001–02	Leeds U	31	0	**54**	**2**
2002–03	Manchester U	28	0		
2003–04	Manchester U	20	0		
2004–05	Manchester U	31	0		
2005–06	Manchester U	37	3		
2006–07	Manchester U	33	1	**149**	**4**

FLETCHER, Darren (M) **91 7**
H: 6 0 W: 11 09 b.Edinburgh 1-2-84
Source: Scholar. *Honours:* Scotland Under-21, B, 29 full caps, 4 goals.

2000–01	Manchester U	0	0		
2001–02	Manchester U	0	0		
2002–03	Manchester U	0	0		
2003–04	Manchester U	22	0		
2004–05	Manchester U	18	3		
2005–06	Manchester U	27	1		
2006–07	Manchester U	24	3	**91**	**7**

FOSTER, Ben (G) **92 0**
H: 6 2 W: 12 08 b.Leamington Spa 3-4-83
Source: Racing Club Warwick. *Honours:* England 1 full cap.

2000–01	Stoke C	0	0		
2001–02	Stoke C	0	0		
2002–03	Stoke C	0	0		
2003–04	Stoke C	0	0		
2004–05	Stoke C	0	0		
2004–05	*Kidderminster H*	2	0	**2**	**0**
2004–05	*Wrexham*	17	0	**17**	**0**
2005–06	Manchester U	0	0		
2005–06	*Watford*	44	0		
2006–07	Manchester U	0	0		
2006–07	*Watford*	29	0	**73**	**0**

GIBSON, Darron (M) **0 0**
H: 6 0 W: 12 04 b.Londonderry 25-10-87
Source: Scholar. *Honours:* Eire Youth, Under-21.

2005–06	Manchester U	0	0		
2006–07	Manchester U	0	0		

GIGGS, Ryan (F) **504 98**
H: 5 11 W: 11 02 b.Cardiff 29-11-73
Source: School. *Honours:* England Schools, Wales Youth, Under-21, 64 full caps, 12 goals.

1990–91	Manchester U	2	1		
1991–92	Manchester U	38	4		
1992–93	Manchester U	41	9		
1993–94	Manchester U	38	13		
1994–95	Manchester U	29	1		
1995–96	Manchester U	33	11		
1996–97	Manchester U	26	3		
1997–98	Manchester U	29	8		
1998–99	Manchester U	24	3		
1999–2000	Manchester U	30	6		
2000–01	Manchester U	31	5		
2001–02	Manchester U	25	7		
2002–03	Manchester U	36	8		
2003–04	Manchester U	33	7		
2004–05	Manchester U	32	5		
2005–06	Manchester U	27	3		
2006–07	Manchester U	30	4	**504**	**98**

GRAY, David (F) **0 0**
H: 5 11 W: 11 02 b.Edinburgh 4-5-88
Source: Scholar.

2005–06	Manchester U	0	0		
2006–07	Manchester U	0	0		

HEATON, Tom (G) **14 0**
H: 6 1 W: 13 12 b.Chester 15-4-86
Source: Trainee. *Honours:* England Youth.

2003–04	Manchester U	0	0		
2004–05	Manchester U	0	0		
2005–06	Manchester U	0	0		
2005–06	*Swindon T*	14	0	**14**	**0**
2006–07	Manchester U	0	0		

HEINZE, Gabriel (D) **218 7**
H: 5 10 W: 12 08 b.Crespo 19-4-78
Source: Union de Crespo. *Honours:* Argentina 35 full caps, 1 goal.

1997–98	Newell's Old Boys	8	0	**8**	**0**
1997–98	Valladolid	0	0		
1998–99	Sporting Lisbon	5	1	**5**	**1**
1999–2000	Valladolid	18	0		
2000–01	Valladolid	36	1	**54**	**1**
2001–02	Paris St Germain	31	0		
2002–03	Paris St Germain	35	2		
2003–04	Paris St Germain	33	2	**99**	**4**
2004–05	Manchester U	26	1		
2005–06	Manchester U	4	0		
2006–07	Manchester U	22	0	**52**	**1**

JONES, Richie (M) **10 0**
H: 6 0 W: 11 00 b.Manchester 26-9-86
Source: Scholar. *Honours:* England Youth.

2004–05	Manchester U	0	0		
2005–06	Manchester U	0	0		
2006–07	Manchester U	0	0		
2006–07	*Colchester U*	6	0	**6**	**0**
2006–07	*Barnsley*	4	0	**4**	**0**

To Antwerp (loan) January 2006

LARSSON, Henrik (F) **503 295**
H: 5 10 W: 11 11 b.Sweden 20-9-71
Honours: Sweden Under-21, B, 93 full caps, 36 goals.

1989	Hogaborg	21	1		
1990	Hogaborg	21	7		
1991	Hogaborg	22	15	**64**	**23**
1992	Helsingborg	31	34		
1993	Helsingborg	25	16		
1993–94	Feyenoord	15	1		
1994–95	Feyenoord	23	8		
1995–96	Feyenoord	32	10		
1996–97	Feyenoord	31	7	**101**	**26**
1997–98	Celtic	35	16		
1998–99	Celtic	35	29		
1999–2000	Celtic	9	7		
2000–01	Celtic	37	35		
2001–02	Celtic	33	29		
2002–03	Celtic	35	28		
2003–04	Celtic	37	30	**221**	**174**
2004–05	Barcelona	11	3		
2005–06	Barcelona	28	10	**39**	**13**
2006	Helsingborg	15	8	**71**	**58**
2006–07	Manchester U	7	1	**7**	**1**

To Helsingborg March 2007

LEE, Kieran (D) **1 0**
H: 6 1 W: 12 00 b.Tameside 22-6-88
Source: Scholar.

2006–07	Manchester U	1	0	**1**	**0**

MARSH, Phil (F) **0 0**
H: 5 10 W: 11 13 b.St Helens 15-11-86
Source: Scholar.

2006–07	Manchester U	0	0		

MARTIN, Lee (M) **20 1**
H: 5 10 W: 10 03 b.Taunton 9-2-87
Source: From Scholar. *Honours:* England Youth.

2004–05	Manchester U	0	0		
2005–06	Manchester U	0	0		
2006–07	Manchester U	0	0		
2006–07	*Rangers*	7	0	**7**	**0**
2006–07	*Stoke C*	13	1	**13**	**1**

NEVILLE, Gary (D) **364 5**
H: 5 11 W: 12 10 b.Bury 18-2-75
Source: Trainee. *Honours:* England Youth, 85 full caps.

1992–93	Manchester U	0	0		
1993–94	Manchester U	1	0		
1994–95	Manchester U	18	0		
1995–96	Manchester U	31	0		
1996–97	Manchester U	31	1		
1997–98	Manchester U	34	0		
1998–99	Manchester U	34	1		
1999–2000	Manchester U	22	0		
2000–01	Manchester U	32	1		
2001–02	Manchester U	34	0		
2002–03	Manchester U	26	0		
2003–04	Manchester U	30	2		
2004–05	Manchester U	22	0		
2005–06	Manchester U	25	0		
2006–07	Manchester U	24	0	**364**	**5**

O'SHEA, John (D) **173 10**
H: 6 3 W: 13 07 b.Waterford 30-4-81
Source: Waterford. *Honours:* Eire Youth, Under-21, 38 full caps, 1 goal.

1998–99	Manchester U	0	0		
1999–2000	Manchester U	0	0		
1999–2000	*Bournemouth*	10	1	**10**	**1**
2000–01	Manchester U	0	0		
2001–02	Manchester U	9	0		
2002–03	Manchester U	32	0		
2003–04	Manchester U	33	2		
2004–05	Manchester U	23	2		
2005–06	Manchester U	34	1		
2006–07	Manchester U	32	4	**163**	**9**

PARK, Ji-Sung (M) **187 30**
H: 5 9 W: 11 06 b.Seoul 25-2-81
Honours: South Korea 67 full caps, 6 goals.

2000	Kyoto Purple S	13	1		
2001	Kyoto Purple S	38	3		
2002	Kyoto Purple S	25	7	**76**	**11**
2002–03	PSV Eindhoven	8	0		
2003–04	PSV Eindhoven	28	6		
2004–05	PSV Eindhoven	28	7	**64**	**13**
2005–06	Manchester U	33	1		
2006–07	Manchester U	14	5	**47**	**6**

PIQUE, Gerard (D) **3 0**
H: 6 3 W: 13 03 b.Barcelona 2-2-87
Source: Scholar. *Honours:* Spain Youth.

2004–05	Manchester U	0	0		
2005–06	Manchester U	3	0		
2006–07	Manchester U	0	0	**3**	**0**

RICHARDSON, Kieran (M) **53 5**
H: 5 9 W: 11 13 b.Greenwich 21-10-84
Source: Scholar. *Honours:* England Under-21, 8 full caps, 2 goals.

2002–03	Manchester U	2	0		
2003–04	Manchester U	0	0		
2004–05	Manchester U	2	0		
2004–05	*WBA*	12	3	**12**	**3**
2005–06	Manchester U	22	1		
2006–07	Manchester U	15	1	**41**	**2**

RONALDO, Cristiano (M) **154 38**
H: 6 1 W: 13 02 b.Funchal 5-2-85
Honours: Portugal Youth, Under-21, 46 full caps, 17 goals.

2002–03	Sporting Lisbon	25	3	**25**	**3**
2003–04	Manchester U	29	4		
2004–05	Manchester U	33	5		
2005–06	Manchester U	33	9		
2006–07	Manchester U	34	17	**129**	**35**

ROONEY, Wayne (F) **167 56**
H: 5 10 W: 12 13 b.Liverpool 24-10-85
Source: Scholar. *Honours:* FA Schools, England Youth, 38 full caps, 12 goals.

2002–03	Everton	33	6		
2003–04	Everton	34	9	**67**	**15**
2004–05	Manchester U	29	11		
2005–06	Manchester U	36	16		
2006–07	Manchester U	35	14	**100**	**41**

ROSE, Danny (M) **0 0**
H: 5 7 W: 10 01 b.Bristol 21-2-88
Source: Scholar. *Honours:* England Youth.

2006–07	Manchester U	0	0		

ROSSI, Giuseppe (F) **16 1**
H: 5 9 W: 11 06 b.New Jersey 1-2-87
Honours: Italy Youth, Under-21.

2004–05	Manchester U	0	0		
2005–06	Manchester U	5	1		
2006–07	Manchester U	0	0	**5**	**1**
2006–07	*Newcastle U*	11	0	**11**	**0**

To Parma (loan) January 2007

SAHA, Louis (F) **244 82**
H: 6 1 W: 12 08 b.Paris 8-8-78
Honours: France Youth, Under-21, 18 full caps, 4 goals.

1997–98	Metz	21	1		
1998–99	Metz	3	0		
1998–99	Newcastle U	11	1	**11**	**1**
1999–2000	Metz	23	4	**47**	**5**
2000–01	Fulham	43	27		
2001–02	Fulham	36	8		
2002–03	Fulham	17	5		
2003–04	Fulham	21	13	**117**	**53**
2003–04	Manchester U	12	7		
2004–05	Manchester U	14	1		
2005–06	Manchester U	19	7		
2006–07	Manchester U	24	8	**69**	**23**

SCHOLES, Paul (M) **371 95**
H: 5 7 W: 11 00 b.Salford 16-11-74
Source: Trainee. *Honours:* England Youth, 66 full caps, 14 goals.

1992–93	Manchester U	0	0		
1993–94	Manchester U	0	0		
1994–95	Manchester U	17	5		
1995–96	Manchester U	26	10		
1996–97	Manchester U	24	3		
1997–98	Manchester U	31	8		
1998–99	Manchester U	31	6		
1999–2000	Manchester U	31	9		
2000–01	Manchester U	32	6		
2001–02	Manchester U	35	8		
2002–03	Manchester U	33	14		
2003–04	Manchester U	28	9		
2004–05	Manchester U	33	9		
2005–06	Manchester U	20	2		
2006–07	Manchester U	30	6	**371**	**95**

SHAWCROSS, Ryan (D) **0 0**
H: 6 3 W: 13 13 b.Chester 4-10-87
Source: Scholar.

2006–07	Manchester U	0	0		

SILVESTRE, Mikael (D) **313 7**
H: 6 0 W: 13 12 b.Chambray les Tours 9-8-77
Honours: France Youth, Under-21, 44 full caps, 3 goals.

1995–96	Rennes	1	0		
1996–97	Rennes	16	0		
1997–98	Rennes	32	0	**49**	**0**
1998–99	Internazionale	18	1	**18**	**1**
1999–2000	Manchester U	31	0		
2000–01	Manchester U	30	1		
2001–02	Manchester U	35	0		
2002–03	Manchester U	34	1		
2003–04	Manchester U	34	0		
2004–05	Manchester U	35	2		
2005–06	Manchester U	33	1		
2006–07	Manchester U	14	1	**246**	**6**

SIMPSON, Danny (D) **14 0**
H: 5 9 W: 11 05 b.Eccles 4-1-87
Source: Scholar.

2005–06	Manchester U	0	0		
2006–07	Manchester U	0	0		
2006–07	*Sunderland*	14	0	**14**	**0**

SMITH, Alan (F) **233 45**
H: 5 10 W: 12 04 b.Rothwell 28-10-80
Source: Trainee. *Honours:* England Youth, Under-21, 17 full caps, 1 goal.

1997–98	Leeds U	0	0		
1998–99	Leeds U	22	7		
1999–2000	Leeds U	26	4		
2000–01	Leeds U	33	11		
2001–02	Leeds U	23	4		
2002–03	Leeds U	33	3		
2003–04	Leeds U	35	9	**172**	**38**
2004–05	Manchester U	31	6		
2005–06	Manchester U	21	1		
2006–07	Manchester U	9	0	**61**	**7**

SOLSKJAER, Ole Gunnar (F) **277 122**
H: 5 10 W: 11 07 b.Kristiansund 26-2-73
Honours: Norway Under-21, 67 full caps, 23 goals.

1995	Molde	26	20		
1996	Molde	16	11	**42**	**31**
1996–97	Manchester U	33	18		
1997–98	Manchester U	22	6		
1998–99	Manchester U	19	12		
1999–2000	Manchester U	28	12		
2000–01	Manchester U	31	10		
2001–02	Manchester U	30	17		
2002–03	Manchester U	37	9		
2003–04	Manchester U	13	0		
2004–05	Manchester U	0	0		
2005–06	Manchester U	3	0		
2006–07	Manchester U	19	7	**235**	**91**

VAN DER SAR, Edwin (G) **489 1**
H: 6 5 W: 14 11 b.Voorhout 29-10-70
Honours: Holland 119 full caps.

1990–91	Ajax	9	0		
1991–92	Ajax	0	0		
1992–93	Ajax	19	0		
1993–94	Ajax	32	0		
1994–95	Ajax	33	0		
1995–96	Ajax	33	0		
1996–97	Ajax	33	0		
1997–98	Ajax	33	1	**192**	**1**
1998–99	Juventus	34	0		
1999–2000	Juventus	32	0		
2000–01	Juventus	34	0	**100**	**0**
2001–02	Fulham	37	0		
2002–03	Fulham	19	0		
2003–04	Fulham	37	0		
2004–05	Fulham	34	0	**127**	**0**
2005–06	Manchester U	38	0		
2006–07	Manchester U	32	0	**70**	**0**

VIDIC, Nemanja (D) **170 25**
H: 6 1 W: 13 02 b.Uzice 21-10-81
Honours: Serbia & Montenegro 25 full caps, 2 goals.

2000–01	Subotica	27	6	**27**	**6**
2001–02	Red Star Belgrade	22	2		
2002–03	Red Star Belgrade	26	5		
2003–04	Red Star Belgrade	20	5	**68**	**12**
2004	Spartak Moscow	12	2		
2005	Spartak Moscow	27	2	**39**	**4**
2005–06	Manchester U	11	0		
2006–07	Manchester U	25	3	**36**	**3**

ZIELER, Ron-Robert (G) **0 0**
H: 6 1 W: 11 07 b.Cologne 12-2-89
Source: Scholar.

2006–07	Manchester U	0	0		

Scholars
Amos, Benjamin Paul; Bryan, Antonio Stefan; Chester, James Grant; Derbyshire, James Jeffrey; Drinkwater, Daniel Noel; Eckersley, Richard John; Eikrem, Magnus Wolff; Evans, Corry John; Galbraith, Daniel; Hewson, Sam; Lea, Michael Robert; McCormack, Conor James.

MANSFIELD T (51)

ARNOLD, Nathan (F) **30 4**
H: 5 8 W: 10 07 b.Mansfield 26-7-87

2005–06	Mansfield T	8	1		
2006–07	Mansfield T	22	3	**30**	**4**

BEARDSLEY, Chris (F) **62 6**
H: 6 0 W: 12 12 b.Derby 28-2-84
Source: Scholar.

2002–03	Mansfield T	5	0		
2003–04	Mansfield T	15	1		
2004–05	Doncaster R	4	0	**4**	**0**
2004–05	Kidderminster H	25	5	**25**	**5**
2005–06	Mansfield T	3	0		
2006–07	Mansfield T	10	0	**33**	**1**

BOULDING, Mick (F) **224 54**
H: 5 10 W: 11 05 b.Sheffield 8-2-76
Source: Hallam.

1999–2000	Mansfield T	33	6		
2000–01	Mansfield T	33	6		
2001–02	Mansfield T	0	0		
2001–02	Grimsby T	35	11		
2002–03	Aston Villa	0	0		
2002–03	*Sheffield U*	6	0	**6**	**0**
2002–03	Grimsby T	12	4		
2003–04	Grimsby T	27	12	**74**	**27**
2003–04	Barnsley	6	0		
2004–05	Barnsley	29	10	**35**	**10**
2004–05	*Cardiff C*	4	0	**4**	**0**
2005–06	Rotherham U	0	0		
2006–07	Mansfield T	39	5	**105**	**17**

BOULDING, Rory (F) **9 0**
H: 6 0 W: 12 02 b.Sheffield 21-7-88
Source: Ilkeston T.

2006–07	Mansfield T	9	0	**9**	**0**

BROWN, Simon (F) **105 19**
H: 5 10 W: 11 00 b.West Bromwich 18-9-83
Source: Scholar.

2003–04	WBA	0	0		
2003–04	*Kidderminster H*	8	2		
2004–05	WBA	0	0		
2004–05	*Kidderminster H*	13	0	**21**	**2**
2004–05	Mansfield T	21	2		
2005–06	Mansfield T	29	10		
2006–07	Mansfield T	34	5	**84**	**17**

BUXTON, Jake (D) **111 3**
H: 6 1 W: 13 05 b.Sutton-in-Ashfield 4-3-85
Source: Scholar.

2002–03	Mansfield T	3	0		
2003–04	Mansfield T	9	1		
2004–05	Mansfield T	30	1		

2005–06	Mansfield T	39	0		
2006–07	Mansfield T	30	1	**111**	**3**

CHARLTON, Asa (D) **4** **0**
H: 5 11 W: 12 00 b.Bridgnorth 1-7-87
Source: Stourport S, Redditch U.

2006–07	Mansfield T	4	0	**4**	**0**

COKE, Gilles (M) **70** **5**
H: 6 0 W: 11 11 b.London 3-6-86
Source: Kingstonian.

2004–05	Mansfield T	9	0		
2005–06	Mansfield T	40	4		
2006–07	Mansfield T	21	1	**70**	**5**

CONLON, Barry (M) **317** **87**
H: 6 3 W: 14 00 b.Drogheda 1-10-78
Source: QPR Trainee. *Honours:* Eire Under-21.

1997–98	Manchester C	7	0		
1997–98	*Plymouth Arg*	13	2	**13**	**2**
1998–99	Manchester C	0	0	**7**	**0**
1998–99	Southend U	34	7	**34**	**7**
1999–2000	York C	40	11		
2000–01	York C	8	0	**48**	**11**
2000–01	*Colchester U*	26	8	**26**	**8**
2001–02	Darlington	35	10		
2002–03	Darlington	41	15		
2003–04	Darlington	39	14		
2004–05	Barnsley	24	6		
2005–06	Barnsley	11	1	**35**	**7**
2005–06	*Rotherham U*	3	1	**3**	**1**
2006–07	Darlington	19	6	**134**	**45**
2006–07	Mansfield T	17	6	**17**	**6**

D'LARYEA, Jonathan (M) **66** **1**
H: 5 10 W: 12 02 b.Manchester 3-9-85
Source: Trainee.

2003–04	Manchester C	0	0		
2004–05	Manchester C	0	0		
2005–06	Manchester C	0	0		
2005–06	Mansfield T	29	0		
2006–07	Mansfield T	37	1	**66**	**1**

DAWSON, Stephen (M) **74** **2**
H: 5 9 W: 11 09 b.Dublin 4-12-85
Source: Scholar. *Honours:* Eire Under-21.

2003–04	Leicester C	0	0		
2004–05	Leicester C	0	0		
2005–06	Mansfield T	40	1		
2006–07	Mansfield T	34	1	**74**	**2**

HAMSHAW, Matt (M) **153** **11**
H: 5 10 W: 11 08 b.Rotherham 1-1-82
Source: Trainee. *Honours:* England Youth, Under-20.

1998–99	Sheffield W	0	0		
1999–2000	Sheffield W	0	0		
2000–01	Sheffield W	18	0		
2001–02	Sheffield W	21	0		
2002–03	Sheffield W	15	1		
2003–04	Sheffield W	0	0		
2004–05	Sheffield W	20	1	**74**	**2**
2005–06	Stockport Co	39	5	**39**	**5**
2006–07	Mansfield T	40	4	**40**	**4**

HJELDE, Jon Olav (D) **257** **7**
H: 6 2 W: 13 07 b.Levanger 30-7-72

1994	Rosenborg	1	0		
1995	Rosenborg	7	0		
1996	Rosenborg	16	1		
1997	Rosenborg	3	0	**27**	**1**
1997–98	Nottingham F	28	1		
1998–99	Nottingham F	17	1		
1999–2000	Nottingham F	33	0		
2000–01	Nottingham F	11	2		
2001–02	Nottingham F	42	0		
2002–03	Nottingham F	26	0		
2003–04	Nottingham F	0	0		
2004–05	Nottingham F	14	0	**171**	**4**
2005–06	Mansfield T	31	1		
2006–07	Mansfield T	28	1	**59**	**2**

JELLEYMAN, Gareth (D) **192** **1**
H: 5 10 W: 10 02 b.Holywell 14-11-80
Source: Trainee. *Honours:* Wales Youth, Under-21.

1998–99	Peterborough U	0	0		
1999–2000	Peterborough U	20	0		
2000–01	Peterborough U	8	0		
2001–02	Peterborough U	10	0		
2002–03	Peterborough U	32	0		
2003–04	Peterborough U	17	0		
2004–05	Peterborough U	14	0	**101**	**0**
2004–05	*Boston U*	3	0	**3**	**0**
2004–05	Mansfield T	14	0		
2005–06	Mansfield T	34	1		
2006–07	Mansfield T	40	0	**88**	**1**

JOHN-BAPTISTE, Alex (D) **149** **5**
H: 6 0 W: 11 11 b.Sutton-in-Ashfield 31-1-86
Source: Scholar.

2002–03	Mansfield T	4	0		
2003–04	Mansfield T	17	0		
2004–05	Mansfield T	41	1		
2005–06	Mansfield T	41	1		
2006–07	Mansfield T	46	3	**149**	**5**

KITCHEN, Ashley (M) **4** **0**
H: 5 11 W: 11 06 b.Edwinstowe 10-10-88
Source: Scholar.

2006–07	Mansfield T	4	0	**4**	**0**

LLOYD, Callum (M) **41** **4**
H: 5 9 W: 11 07 b.Nottingham 1-1-86
Source: Scholar.

2004–05	Mansfield T	10	4		
2005–06	Mansfield T	12	0		
2006–07	Mansfield T	19	0	**41**	**4**

McGHEE, Jamie (M) **2** **0**
H: 5 8 W: 10 07 b.Grantham 28-9-89
Source: Scholar.

2006–07	Mansfield T	2	0	**2**	**0**

McINTOSH, Austin (M) **1** **0**
H: 5 11 W: 10 09 b.Newham 5-11-87
Source: Scholar.

2004–05	Mansfield T	1	0		
2005–06	Mansfield T	0	0		
2006–07	Mansfield T	0	0	**1**	**0**

MUGGLETON, Carl (G) **410** **0**
H: 6 2 W: 14 12 b.Leicester 13-9-68
Source: Apprentice. *Honours:* England Under-21.

1986–87	Leicester C	0	0		
1987–88	Leicester C	0	0		
1987–88	*Chesterfield*	17	0		
1987–88	*Blackpool*	2	0	**2**	**0**
1988–89	Leicester C	3	0		
1988–89	*Hartlepool U*	8	0	**8**	**0**
1989–90	Leicester C	0	0		
1989–90	*Stockport Co*	4	0	**4**	**0**
1990–91	Leicester C	22	0		
1990–91	*Liverpool*	0	0		
1991–92	Leicester C	4	0		
1992–93	Leicester C	17	0		
1993–94	Leicester C	0	0	**46**	**0**
1993–94	*Stoke C*	6	0		
1993–94	*Sheffield U*	0	0		
1993–94	Celtic	12	0	**12**	**0**
1994–95	Stoke C	24	0		
1995–96	Stoke C	6	0		
1995–96	*Rotherham U*	6	0	**6**	**0**
1995–96	*Sheffield U*	1	0	**1**	**0**
1996–97	Stoke C	33	0		
1997–98	Stoke C	34	0		
1998–99	Stoke C	40	0		
1999–2000	Stoke C	0	0		
1999–2000	*Mansfield T*	9	0		
1999–2000	*Chesterfield*	5	0		
2000–01	Stoke C	12	0	**155**	**0**
2000–01	*Cardiff C*	6	0	**6**	**0**
2001–02	Cheltenham T	7	0	**7**	**0**
2001–02	*Bradford C*	4	0	**4**	**0**
2002–03	Chesterfield	26	0		
2003–04	Chesterfield	46	0		
2004–05	Chesterfield	37	0		
2005–06	Chesterfield	3	0	**134**	**0**
2006–07	Mansfield T	16	0	**25**	**0**

MULLINS, John (D) **64** **4**
H: 5 11 W: 12 07 b.Hampstead 6-11-85
Source: Scholar.

2004–05	Reading	0	0		
2004–05	*Kidderminster H*	21	2	**21**	**2**
2005–06	Reading	0	0		
2006–07	Mansfield T	43	2	**43**	**2**

REET, Danny (F) **51** **15**
H: 6 1 W: 14 02 b.Sheffield 31-1-87

2005–06	Sheffield W	0	0		
2005–06	*Bury*	6	4	**6**	**4**
2005–06	Mansfield T	18	5		
2006–07	Mansfield T	21	6	**39**	**11**
2006–07	*Rochdale*	6	0	**6**	**0**

SLEATH, Danny (M) **7** **0**
H: 5 8 W: 9 07 b.Matlock 14-12-86

2005–06	Mansfield T	0	0		
2006–07	Mansfield T	7	0	**7**	**0**

TRIMMER, Lewis (M) **1** **0**
H: 5 7 W: 10 00 b.Norwich 30-10-89

2006–07	Mansfield T	1	0	**1**	**0**

WHITE, Jason (G) **40** **0**
H: 6 2 W: 12 01 b.Sutton-in-Ashfield 28-1-84
Source: Trainee.

2002–03	Mansfield T	1	0		
2003–04	Mansfield T	0	0		
2004–05	Mansfield T	4	0		
2005–06	Mansfield T	5	0		
2006–07	Mansfield T	30	0	**40**	**0**

WOOD, Chris (M) **2** **0**
H: 6 0 W: 10 11 b.Worksop 24-1-87

2004–05	Mansfield T	1	0		
2005–06	Mansfield T	0	0		
2006–07	Mansfield T	1	0	**2**	**0**

MIDDLESBROUGH (52)

ARCA, Julio (M) **214** **20**
H: 5 9 W: 11 13 b.Quilmes 31-1-81
Honours: Argentina Under-21.

1999–2000	Argentinos Jun	19	0		
2000–01	Argentinos Jun	17	1	**36**	**1**
2000–01	Sunderland	27	2		
2001–02	Sunderland	22	1		
2002–03	Sunderland	13	0		
2003–04	Sunderland	31	4		
2004–05	Sunderland	40	9		
2005–06	Sunderland	24	1	**157**	**17**
2006–07	Middlesbrough	21	2	**21**	**2**

BATES, Matthew (D) **25** **0**
H: 5 10 W: 12 03 b.Stockton 10-12-86
Source: Scholar. *Honours:* England Youth, Under-20.

2003–04	Middlesbrough	0	0		
2004–05	Middlesbrough	2	0		
2004–05	*Darlington*	4	0	**4**	**0**
2005–06	Middlesbrough	16	0		
2006–07	Middlesbrough	1	0	**19**	**0**
2006–07	*Ipswich T*	2	0	**2**	**0**

BOATENG, George (M) **376** **16**
H: 5 9 W: 12 06 b.Nkawkaw 5-9-75
Honours: Holland 4 full caps.

1994–95	Excelsior	9	0	**9**	**0**
1995–96	Feyenoord	24	1		
1996–97	Feyenoord	26	0		
1997–98	Feyenoord	18	0	**68**	**1**
1997–98	Coventry C	14	1		
1998–99	Coventry C	33	4	**47**	**5**
1999–2000	Aston Villa	33	2		
2000–01	Aston Villa	33	1		
2001–02	Aston Villa	37	1	**103**	**4**
2002–03	Middlesbrough	28	0		
2003–04	Middlesbrough	35	0		
2004–05	Middlesbrough	25	3		
2005–06	Middlesbrough	26	2		
2006–07	Middlesbrough	35	1	**149**	**6**

CATTERMOLE, Lee (M) **45** **2**
H: 5 10 W: 11 13 b.Stockton 21-3-88
Source: Scholar. *Honours:* England Youth.

2005–06	Middlesbrough	14	1		
2006–07	Middlesbrough	31	1	**45**	**2**

CHRISTIE, Malcolm (F) **159** **37**
H: 6 0 W: 12 06 b.Peterborough 11-4-79
Source: Nuneaton B. *Honours:* England Under-21.

1998–99	Derby Co	2	0		
1999–2000	Derby Co	21	5		
2000–01	Derby Co	34	8		

2001–02	Derby Co	35	9		
2002–03	Derby Co	24	8	**116**	**30**
2002–03	Middlesbrough	12	4		
2003–04	Middlesbrough	10	1		
2004–05	Middlesbrough	2	1		
2005–06	Middlesbrough	6	0		
2006–07	Middlesbrough	13	1	**43**	**7**

CRADDOCK, Tom (F) 2 1
H: 5 11 W: 11 10 b.Durham 14-10-86
Source: Scholar.

2005–06	Middlesbrough	1	0		
2006–07	Middlesbrough	0	0	**1**	**0**
2006–07	*Wrexham*	1	1	**1**	**1**

DAVIES, Andrew (D) 81 3
H: 6 3 W: 14 08 b.Stockton 17-12-84
Source: Scholar. *Honours:* England Youth, Under-20, Under-21.

2002–03	Middlesbrough	1	0		
2003–04	Middlesbrough	10	0		
2004–05	Middlesbrough	3	0		
2004–05	*QPR*	9	0	**9**	**0**
2005–06	Middlesbrough	12	0		
2005–06	*Derby Co*	23	3	**23**	**3**
2006–07	Middlesbrough	23	0	**49**	**0**

DOWNING, Stewart (M) 113 11
H: 5 11 W: 10 04 b.Middlesbrough 22-7-84
Source: Scholar. *Honours:* England Youth, Under-21, B, 14 full caps.

2001–02	Middlesbrough	3	0		
2002–03	Middlesbrough	2	0		
2003–04	Middlesbrough	20	0		
2003–04	*Sunderland*	7	3	**7**	**3**
2004–05	Middlesbrough	35	5		
2005–06	Middlesbrough	12	1		
2006–07	Middlesbrough	34	2	**106**	**8**

EHIOGU, Ugo (D) 371 20
H: 6 2 W: 14 10 b.Hackney 3-11-72
Source: Trainee. *Honours:* England Under-21, B, 4 full caps, 1 goal.

1990–91	WBA	2	0	**2**	**0**
1991–92	Aston Villa	8	0		
1992–93	Aston Villa	4	0		
1993–94	Aston Villa	17	0		
1994–95	Aston Villa	39	3		
1995–96	Aston Villa	36	1		
1996–97	Aston Villa	38	3		
1997–98	Aston Villa	37	2		
1998–99	Aston Villa	25	2		
1999–2000	Aston Villa	31	1		
2000–01	Aston Villa	2	0	**237**	**12**
2000–01	Middlesbrough	21	3		
2001–02	Middlesbrough	29	1		
2002–03	Middlesbrough	32	3		
2003–04	Middlesbrough	16	0		
2004–05	Middlesbrough	10	0		
2005–06	Middlesbrough	18	0		
2006–07	Middlesbrough	0	0	**126**	**7**
2006–07	*Leeds U*	6	1	**6**	**1**

To Rangers January 2007

EUELL, Jason (F) 297 75
H: 5 11 W: 11 13 b.Lambeth 6-2-77
Source: Trainee. *Honours:* England Youth, Under-21, Jamaica 3 full caps, 1 goal.

1995–96	Wimbledon	9	2		
1996–97	Wimbledon	7	2		
1997–98	Wimbledon	19	4		
1998–99	Wimbledon	33	10		
1999–2000	Wimbledon	37	4		
2000–01	Wimbledon	36	19	**141**	**41**
2001–02	Charlton Ath	36	11		
2002–03	Charlton Ath	36	10		
2003–04	Charlton Ath	31	10		
2004–05	Charlton Ath	26	2		
2005–06	Charlton Ath	10	1		
2006–07	Charlton Ath	0	0	**139**	**34**
2006–07	Middlesbrough	17	0	**17**	**0**

GOULON, Herold (M) 0 0
H: 6 4 W: 14 07 b.Paris 12-6-88

2005–06	Lyon	0	0		
2006–07	Middlesbrough	0	0		

GRAHAM, Danny (F) 56 11
H: 5 11 W: 12 05 b.Gateshead 12-8-85
Source: Trainee. *Honours:* England Youth, Under-20.

2003–04	Middlesbrough	0	0		
2003–04	*Darlington*	9	2	**9**	**2**
2004–05	Middlesbrough	11	1		
2005–06	Middlesbrough	3	0		
2005–06	*Derby Co*	14	0	**14**	**0**
2005–06	*Leeds U*	3	0	**3**	**0**
2006–07	Middlesbrough	1	0	**15**	**1**
2006–07	*Blackpool*	4	1	**4**	**1**
2006–07	*Carlisle U*	11	7	**11**	**7**

HINES, Seb (D) 0 0
H: 6 1 W: 12 02 b.Wetherby 29-5-88
Source: Scholar. *Honours:* England Youth.

2005–06	Middlesbrough	0	0		
2006–07	Middlesbrough	0	0		

HUTCHINSON, Ben (F) 0 0
H: 5 11 W: 12 07 b.Nottingham 27-11-87
Source: Arnold T.

2005–06	Middlesbrough	0	0		
2006–07	Middlesbrough	0	0		

HUTH, Robert (D) 54 1
H: 6 3 W: 14 07 b.Berlin 18-8-84
Source: Scholar. *Honours:* Germany Youth, Under-21, 17 full caps, 2 goals.

2001–02	Chelsea	1	0		
2002–03	Chelsea	2	0		
2003–04	Chelsea	16	0		
2004–05	Chelsea	10	0		
2005–06	Chelsea	13	0	**42**	**0**
2006–07	Middlesbrough	12	1	**12**	**1**

JOHNSON, Adam (M) 30 1
H: 5 8 W: 10 00 b.Sunderland 14-7-87
Source: Scholar. *Honours:* England Youth.

2004–05	Middlesbrough	0	0		
2005–06	Middlesbrough	13	1		
2006–07	Middlesbrough	12	0	**25**	**1**
2006–07	*Leeds U*	5	0	**5**	**0**

JONES, Brad (G) 52 0
H: 6 3 W: 12 01 b.Armadale 19-3-82
Source: Trainee. *Honours:* Australia Under-20, Under-23, 1 full cap.

1998–99	Middlesbrough	0	0		
1999–2000	Middlesbrough	0	0		
2000–01	Middlesbrough	0	0		
2001–02	Middlesbrough	0	0		
2002	Shelbourne	2	0	**2**	**0**
2002–03	Middlesbrough	0	0		
2002–03	*Stockport Co*	1	0	**1**	**0**
2003–04	Middlesbrough	1	0		
2003–04	*Blackpool*	5	0		
2003–04	*Rotherham U*	0	0		
2004–05	Middlesbrough	5	0		
2004–05	*Blackpool*	12	0	**17**	**0**
2005–06	Middlesbrough	9	0		
2006–07	Middlesbrough	2	0	**17**	**0**
2006–07	*Sheffield W*	15	0	**15**	**0**

KENNEDY, Jason (M) 29 1
H: 6 1 W: 13 02 b.Stockton 11-9-86
Source: Scholar.

2004–05	Middlesbrough	1	0		
2005–06	Middlesbrough	3	0		
2006–07	Middlesbrough	0	0	**4**	**0**
2006–07	*Boston U*	13	1	**13**	**1**
2006–07	*Bury*	12	0	**12**	**0**

KNIGHT, David (G) 5 0
H: 6 0 W: 11 07 b.Sunderland 15-1-87
Source: Scholar. *Honours:* England Youth.

2004–05	Middlesbrough	0	0		
2005–06	Middlesbrough	0	0		
2005–06	*Darlington*	3	0	**3**	**0**
2006–07	Middlesbrough	0	0		
2006–07	*Oldham Ath*	2	0	**2**	**0**

LEE, Dong-Gook (F) 102 22
H: 6 2 W: 12 13 b.Pohang 29-4-79
Source: Pohang Steelers. *Honours:* South Korea 64 caps, 22 goals.

2000–01	Werder Bremen	7	0	**7**	**0**
From Pohang					
2003	Gwangiu	41	11		
2004	Gwangiu	19	1	**60**	**12**
2005	Pohang	17	3		
2006	Pohang	9	7	**26**	**10**
2006–07	Middlesbrough	9	0	**9**	**0**

MACCARONE, Massimo (F) 133 40
H: 5 10 W: 12 05 b.Galliate 6-9-79
Honours: Italy 2 full caps.

2000–01	Empoli	35	16		
2001–02	Empoli	0	0	**35**	**16**
2002–03	Middlesbrough	34	9		
2003–04	Middlesbrough	23	6		
2004–05	Middlesbrough	0	0		
2004–05	*Siena*	17	6	**17**	**6**
2005–06	Middlesbrough	17	2		
2006–07	Middlesbrough	7	1	**81**	**18**

To Siena January 2007

McMAHON, Tony (D) 16 0
H: 5 10 W: 11 04 b.Bishop Auckland 24-3-86
Source: Scholar. *Honours:* England Youth.

2003–04	Middlesbrough	0	0		
2004–05	Middlesbrough	13	0		
2005–06	Middlesbrough	3	0		
2006–07	Middlesbrough	0	0	**16**	**0**

MENDIETA, Gaizka (M) 409 52
H: 5 9 W: 11 02 b.Bilbao 27-3-74
Honours: Spain 40 full caps, 8 goals.

1991–92	Castellon	16	0	**16**	**0**
1992–93	Valencia B	31	2		
1992–93	Valencia	2	0		
1993–94	Valencia B	17	0	**48**	**2**
1993–94	Valencia	20	0		
1994–95	Valencia	13	1		
1995–96	Valencia	34	0		
1996–97	Valencia	29	1		
1997–98	Valencia	30	10		
1998–99	Valencia	38	7		
1999–2000	Valencia	33	13		
2000–01	Valencia	31	10	**230**	**42**
2001–02	Lazio	20	0	**20**	**0**
2002–03	Barcelona	33	4	**33**	**4**
2003–04	Middlesbrough	31	2		
2004–05	Middlesbrough	7	0		
2005–06	Middlesbrough	17	2		
2006–07	Middlesbrough	7	0	**62**	**4**

MORRISON, James (M) 67 3
H: 5 10 W: 10 06 b.Darlington 25-5-86
Source: Trainee. *Honours:* England Youth, Under-20.

2003–04	Middlesbrough	1	0		
2004–05	Middlesbrough	14	0		
2005–06	Middlesbrough	24	1		
2006–07	Middlesbrough	28	2	**67**	**3**

PARNABY, Stuart (M) 97 2
H: 5 11 W: 11 00 b.Durham 19-7-82
Source: Trainee. *Honours:* England Youth, Under-20, Under-21.

1999–2000	Middlesbrough	0	0		
2000–01	Middlesbrough	0	0		
2000–01	*Halifax T*	6	0	**6**	**0**
2001–02	Middlesbrough	0	0		
2002–03	Middlesbrough	21	0		
2003–04	Middlesbrough	13	0		
2004–05	Middlesbrough	19	0		
2005–06	Middlesbrough	20	2		
2006–07	Middlesbrough	18	0	**91**	**2**

POGATETZ, Emanuel (D) 182 5
H: 6 2 W: 13 05 b.Steinbock 16-1-83
Honours: Austria 20 full caps, 1 goal.

1999–2000	Sturm Graz	0	0		
2000–01	Karntern	33	0	**33**	**0**
2001–02	Leverkusen B	23	0		
2001–02	Leverkusen	0	0		
2002–03	Leverkusen B	3	0	**26**	**0**
2002–03	Leverkusen	0	0		
2002–03	Aarau	11	0	**11**	**0**
2003–04	Graz	31	1		
2004–05	Graz	22	1	**53**	**2**
2005–06	Middlesbrough	24	1		
2006–07	Middlesbrough	35	2	**59**	**3**

RIGGOTT, Chris (D) 162 9
H: 6 2 W: 13 09 b.Derby 1-9-80
Source: Trainee. *Honours:* England Youth, Under-21.

1998–99	Derby Co	0	0		

1999–2000	Derby Co	1	0		
2000–01	Derby Co	31	3		
2001–02	Derby Co	37	0		
2002–03	Derby Co	22	2	**91**	**5**
2002–03	Middlesbrough	5	2		
2003–04	Middlesbrough	17	0		
2004–05	Middlesbrough	21	2		
2005–06	Middlesbrough	22	0		
2006–07	Middlesbrough	6	0	**71**	**4**

ROCHEMBACK, Fabio (M) **153 19**
H: 6 0 W: 13 01 b.Soledade 10-12-81
Honours: Brazil 7 full caps.

2000	Internacional	20	4		
2001	Internacional	0	0	**20**	**4**
2001–02	Barcelona	24	1		
2002–03	Barcelona	21	1	**45**	**2**
2003–04	Sporting Lisbon	21	8		
2004–05	Sporting Lisbon	23	1		
2005–06	Sporting Lisbon	2	0	**46**	**9**
2005–06	Middlesbrough	22	2		
2006–07	Middlesbrough	20	2	**42**	**4**

SCHWARZER, Mark (G) **410 0**
H: 6 4 W: 14 07 b.Sydney 6-10-72
Honours: Australia Youth, Under-20, Under-23, 45 full caps.

1990–91	Marconi Stallions	1	0		
1991–92	Marconi Stallions	9	0		
1992–93	Marconi Stallions	23	0		
1993–94	Marconi Stallions	25	0	**58**	**0**
1994–95	Dynamo Dresden	2	0	**2**	**0**
1995–96	Kaiserslautern	4	0		
1996–97	Kaiserslautern	0	0	**4**	**0**
1996–97	Bradford C	13	0	**13**	**0**
1996–97	Middlesbrough	7	0		
1997–98	Middlesbrough	35	0		
1998–99	Middlesbrough	34	0		
1999–2000	Middlesbrough	37	0		
2000–01	Middlesbrough	31	0		
2001–02	Middlesbrough	21	0		
2002–03	Middlesbrough	38	0		
2003–04	Middlesbrough	36	0		
2004–05	Middlesbrough	31	0		
2005–06	Middlesbrough	27	0		
2006–07	Middlesbrough	36	0	**333**	**0**

SOUTHGATE, Gareth (D) **503 26**
H: 6 0 W: 12 03 b.Watford 3-9-70
Source: Trainee. *Honours:* England 57 full caps, 2 goals.

1988–89	Crystal Palace	0	0		
1989–90	Crystal Palace	0	0		
1990–91	Crystal Palace	1	0		
1991–92	Crystal Palace	30	0		
1992–93	Crystal Palace	33	3		
1993–94	Crystal Palace	46	9		
1994–95	Crystal Palace	42	3	**152**	**15**
1995–96	Aston Villa	31	1		
1996–97	Aston Villa	28	1		
1997–98	Aston Villa	32	0		
1998–99	Aston Villa	38	1		
1999–2000	Aston Villa	31	2		
2000–01	Aston Villa	31	2	**191**	**7**
2001–02	Middlesbrough	37	1		
2002–03	Middlesbrough	36	2		
2003–04	Middlesbrough	27	1		
2004–05	Middlesbrough	36	0		
2005–06	Middlesbrough	24	0		
2006–07	Middlesbrough	0	0	**160**	**4**

TAYLOR, Andrew (D) **71 0**
H: 5 10 W: 11 04 b.Hartlepool 1-8-86
Source: Trainee. *Honours:* England Youth, Under-20, Under-21.

2003–04	Middlesbrough	0	0		
2004–05	Middlesbrough	0	0		
2005–06	Middlesbrough	13	0		
2005–06	*Bradford C*	24	0	**24**	**0**
2006–07	Middlesbrough	34	0	**47**	**0**

TURNBULL, Ross (G) **60 0**
H: 6 4 W: 15 00 b.Bishop Auckland 4-1-85
Source: Trainee. *Honours:* England Youth, Under-20.

2002–03	Middlesbrough	0	0		
2003–04	Middlesbrough	0	0		
2003–04	*Darlington*	1	0	**1**	**0**
2003–04	*Barnsley*	3	0		
2004–05	Middlesbrough	0	0		
2004–05	*Bradford C*	2	0	**2**	**0**
2004–05	*Barnsley*	23	0	**26**	**0**
2005–06	Middlesbrough	2	0		
2005–06	*Crewe Alex*	29	0	**29**	**0**
2006–07	Middlesbrough	0	0	**2**	**0**

VIDUKA, Mark (F) **371 195**
H: 6 2 W: 15 01 b.Melbourne 9-10-75
Honours: Australia Youth, Under-20, Under-23, 39 full caps, 8 goals.

1992–93	Melbourne Knights	4	2		
1993–94	Melbourne Knights	20	17		
1994–95	Melbourne Knights	24	21	**48**	**40**
1995–96	Croatia Zagreb	27	12		
1996–97	Croatia Zagreb	25	18		
1997–98	Croatia Zagreb	25	8		
1998–99	Croatia Zagreb	7	2	**84**	**40**
1998–99	Celtic	9	5		
1999–2000	Celtic	28	25	**37**	**30**
2000–01	Leeds U	34	17		
2001–02	Leeds U	33	11		
2002–03	Leeds U	33	20		
2003–04	Leeds U	30	11	**130**	**59**
2004–05	Middlesbrough	16	5		
2005–06	Middlesbrough	27	7		
2006–07	Middlesbrough	29	14	**72**	**26**

WALKER, Josh (M) **7 0**
H: 5 11 W: 11 13 b.Newcastle 21-2-89
Source: Scholar. *Honours:* England Schools, Youth.

2005–06	Middlesbrough	1	0		
2006–07	Middlesbrough	0	0	**1**	**0**
2006–07	*Bournemouth*	6	0	**6**	**0**

WHEATER, David (D) **31 4**
H: 6 5 W: 12 12 b.Redcar 14-2-87
Source: Scholar. *Honours:* England Youth.

2004–05	Middlesbrough	0	0		
2005–06	Middlesbrough	6	0		
2005–06	*Doncaster R*	7	1	**7**	**1**
2006–07	Middlesbrough	2	1	**8**	**1**
2006–07	*Wolverhampton W*	1	0	**1**	**0**
2006–07	*Darlington*	15	2	**15**	**2**

WILLIAMS, Rhys (D) **0 0**
b.Perth 14-7-88
Source: Scholar. *Honours:* Wales Under-21.

2006–07	Middlesbrough	0	0

WOODGATE, Jonathan (D) **171 4**
H: 6 2 W: 12 06 b.Middlesbrough 22-1-80
Source: Trainee. *Honours:* England Youth, Under-21, 6 full caps.

1996–97	Leeds U	0	0		
1997–98	Leeds U	0	0		
1998–99	Leeds U	25	2		
1999–2000	Leeds U	34	1		
2000–01	Leeds U	14	1		
2001–02	Leeds U	13	0		
2002–03	Leeds U	18	0	**104**	**4**
2002–03	Newcastle U	10	0		
2003–04	Newcastle U	18	0	**28**	**0**
2004–05	Real Madrid	0	0		
2005–06	Real Madrid	9	0	**9**	**0**
2006–07	Middlesbrough	30	0	**30**	**0**

XAVIER, Abel (D) **260 8**
H: 6 3 W: 12 07 b.Mozambique 30-11-72
Honours: Portugal 20 full caps, 2 goals.

1990–91	Amadora	22	0		
1991–92	Amadora	21	0		
1992–93	Amadora	0	0	**43**	**0**
1993–94	Benfica	24	1		
1994–95	Benfica	22	3	**46**	**4**
1995–96	Bari	8	0	**8**	**0**
1996–97	Oviedo	27	0		
1997–98	Oviedo	31	0	**58**	**0**
1998–99	PSV Eindhoven	19	2	**19**	**2**
1999–2000	Everton	20	0		
2000–01	Everton	11	0		
2001–02	Everton	12	0	**43**	**0**
2001–02	Liverpool	10	1		
2002–03	Liverpool	4	0		
2002–03	Galatasaray	11	0	**11**	**0**
2003–04	Liverpool	0	0		
2004–05	Liverpool	0	0	**14**	**1**
2005–06	Middlesbrough	4	0		
2006–07	Middlesbrough	14	1	**18**	**1**

YAKUBU, Ayegbeni (F) **211 82**
H: 6 0 W: 14 07 b.Benin City 22-11-82
Source: Julius Berger. *Honours:* Nigeria Under-21, Under-23, 19 full caps, 5 goals.

1999–2000	Gil Vicente	0	0		
1999–2000	Hapoel Kfar-Sava	23	6	**23**	**6**
2000–01	Maccabi Haifa	14	3		
2001–02	Maccabi Haifa	22	13	**36**	**16**
2002–03	Portsmouth	14	7		
2003–04	Portsmouth	37	16		
2004–05	Portsmouth	30	12	**81**	**35**
2005–06	Middlesbrough	34	13		
2006–07	Middlesbrough	37	12	**71**	**25**

Scholars
Atkinson, Matthew; Bennett, Joseph; Franks, Jonathan Ian; Grounds, Jonathan Martin; Hillerby, David James; Johnson, John James; McArdle, Lewis Andrew; Owens, Graeme Adams; Porritt, Nathan John; Saiko, Shaun; Smith, Lewis James; Steele, Jason; Thompson, Stephen.

MILLWALL (53)

ARDLEY, Neal (M) **414 26**
H: 5 10 W: 12 12 b.Epsom 1-9-72
Source: Trainee. *Honours:* England Under-21.

1990–91	Wimbledon	1	0		
1991–92	Wimbledon	8	0		
1992–93	Wimbledon	26	4		
1993–94	Wimbledon	16	1		
1994–95	Wimbledon	14	1		
1995–96	Wimbledon	6	0		
1996–97	Wimbledon	34	2		
1997–98	Wimbledon	34	2		
1998–99	Wimbledon	23	0		
1999–2000	Wimbledon	17	2		
2000–01	Wimbledon	37	3		
2001–02	Wimbledon	29	3	**245**	**18**
2002–03	Watford	43	2		
2003–04	Watford	38	1		
2004–05	Watford	30	4	**111**	**7**
2004–05	Cardiff C	8	1		
2005–06	Cardiff C	30	0	**38**	**1**
2006–07	Millwall	20	0	**20**	**0**

BAKAYOGO, Zaoumana (D) **5 0**
H: 5 9 W: 10 08 b.Paris 11-8-86
Source: Paris St Germain. *Honours:* Ivory Coast Under-23.

2006–07	Millwall	5	0	**5**	**0**

BRAMMER, Dave (M) **419 22**
H: 5 8 W: 12 00 b.Bromborough 28-2-75
Source: Trainee.

1992–93	Wrexham	2	0		
1993–94	Wrexham	22	2		
1994–95	Wrexham	14	1		
1995–96	Wrexham	11	2		
1996–97	Wrexham	21	1		
1997–98	Wrexham	33	4		
1998–99	Wrexham	34	2	**137**	**12**
1998–99	Port Vale	9	0		
1999–2000	Port Vale	29	0		
2000–01	Port Vale	35	3	**73**	**3**
2001–02	Crewe Alex	30	2		
2002–03	Crewe Alex	41	1		
2003–04	Crewe Alex	16	1	**87**	**4**
2004–05	Stoke C	43	1		
2005–06	Stoke C	40	1		
2006–07	Stoke C	22	0	**105**	**2**
2006–07	Millwall	17	1	**17**	**1**

BRANIFF, Kevin (F) **67 5**
H: 5 11 W: 10 03 b.Belfast 4-3-83
Source: Scholarship. *Honours:* Northern Ireland Schools, Youth, Under-21, Under-23.

1999–2000	Millwall	0	0		
2000–01	Millwall	5	0		
2001–02	Millwall	1	0		
2002–03	Millwall	10	0		
2003–04	Millwall	16	1		
2004–05	Millwall	1	0		
2004–05	*Rushden & D*	12	3	**12**	**3**
2005–06	Millwall	15	0		

2006–07	Millwall	7	1	**55**	**2**

To Portadown January 2007

BRIGHTON, Tom (M) **58** **9**
H: 5 10 W: 11 11 b.Irvine 28-3-84
Honours: Scotland Youth, Under-21.

2001–02	Rangers	1	0		
2002–03	Rangers	0	0		
2003–04	Rangers	0	0	**1**	**0**
2004–05	Scunthorpe U	5	0	**5**	**0**
2005–06	Clyde	36	8	**36**	**8**
2006–07	Millwall	16	1	**16**	**1**

BYFIELD, Darren (F) **285** **77**
H: 5 11 W: 12 07 b.Sutton Coldfield 29-9-76
Source: Trainee. *Honours:* Jamaica 7 full caps.

1993–94	Aston Villa	0	0		
1994–95	Aston Villa	0	0		
1995–96	Aston Villa	0	0		
1996–97	Aston Villa	0	0		
1997–98	Aston Villa	7	0		
1998–99	Aston Villa	0	0		
1998–99	*Preston NE*	5	1	**5**	**1**
1999–2000	Aston Villa	0	0	**7**	**0**
1999–2000	*Northampton T*	6	1	**6**	**1**
1999–2000	*Cambridge U*	4	0	**4**	**0**
1999–2000	*Blackpool*	3	0	**3**	**0**
2000–01	Walsall	40	9		
2001–02	Walsall	37	4	**77**	**13**
2001–02	Rotherham U	3	2		
2002–03	Rotherham U	37	13		
2003–04	Rotherham U	28	7	**68**	**22**
2003–04	Sunderland	17	5	**17**	**5**
2004–05	Gillingham	38	6		
2005–06	Gillingham	29	13	**67**	**19**
2006–07	Millwall	31	16	**31**	**16**

COTTRELL, Adam (D) **0** **0**
H: 5 9 W: 11 05 b.London 15-11-86
Source: Charlton Ath Scholar.

2006–07	Millwall	0	0		

CRAIG, Tony (D) **93** **2**
H: 6 0 W: 10 03 b.Greenwich 20-4-85
Source: Scholar.

2002–03	Millwall	2	1		
2003–04	Millwall	9	0		
2004–05	Millwall	10	0		
2004–05	*Wycombe W*	14	0	**14**	**0**
2005–06	Millwall	28	0		
2006–07	Millwall	30	1	**79**	**2**

DAY, Chris (G) **177** **0**
H: 6 2 W: 13 07 b.Whipps Cross 28-7-75
Source: Trainee. *Honours:* England Under-21.

1992–93	Tottenham H	0	0		
1993–94	Tottenham H	0	0		
1994–95	Tottenham H	0	0		
1995–96	Tottenham H	0	0		
1996–97	Crystal Palace	24	0	**24**	**0**
1997–98	Watford	0	0		
1998–99	Watford	0	0		
1999–2000	Watford	11	0		
2000–01	Watford	0	0	**11**	**0**
2000–01	*Lincoln C*	14	0	**14**	**0**
2001–02	QPR	16	0		
2002–03	QPR	12	0		
2003–04	QPR	29	0		
2004–05	QPR	30	0	**87**	**0**
2004–05	*Preston NE*	6	0	**6**	**0**
2005–06	Oldham Ath	30	0	**30**	**0**
2006–07	Millwall	5	0	**5**	**0**

DUNNE, Alan (D) **104** **9**
H: 5 10 W: 10 13 b.Dublin 23-8-82
Source: Trainee.

1999–2000	Millwall	0	0		
2000–01	Millwall	0	0		
2001–02	Millwall	1	0		
2002–03	Millwall	4	0		
2003–04	Millwall	8	0		
2004–05	Millwall	19	3		
2005–06	Millwall	40	0		
2006–07	Millwall	32	6	**104**	**9**

EDWARDS, Preston (G) **0** **0**
H: 6 0 W: 12 07 b.Edmonton 5-9-89
Source: Scholar.

2006–07	Millwall	0	0		

ELLIOTT, Marvin (M) **144** **3**
H: 6 0 W: 12 02 b.Wandsworth 15-9-84
Source: Scholar.

2001–02	Millwall	0	0		
2002–03	Millwall	1	0		
2003–04	Millwall	21	0		
2004–05	Millwall	41	1		
2005–06	Millwall	39	2		
2006–07	Millwall	42	0	**144**	**3**

FUSEINI, Ali (M) **7** **0**
H: 5 6 W: 9 10 b.Ghana 7-12-88
Source: Scholar.

2006–07	Millwall	7	0	**7**	**0**

GAYNOR, Ross (F) **0** **0**
H: 5 10 W: 11 12 b.Drogheda 9-9-87
Source: From Scholar. *Honours:* Eire Youth, Under-21.

2005–06	Millwall	0	0		
2006–07	Millwall	0	0		

GRANT, Gavin (F) **14** **1**
H: 5 11 W: 11 00 b.Middlesex 27-3-84
Source: Tooting & Mitcham U.

2005–06	Gillingham	10	1	**10**	**1**
2005–06	Millwall	0	0		
2006–07	Millwall	4	0	**4**	**0**

HACKETT, Chris (M) **160** **12**
H: 6 0 W: 12 08 b.Oxford 1-3-83
Source: Scholarship.

1999–2000	Oxford U	2	0		
2000–01	Oxford U	16	2		
2001–02	Oxford U	15	0		
2002–03	Oxford U	12	0		
2003–04	Oxford U	22	1		
2004–05	Oxford U	37	4		
2005–06	Oxford U	21	2	**125**	**9**
2005–06	Hearts	2	0	**2**	**0**
2006–07	Millwall	33	3	**33**	**3**

HARRIS, Neil (F) **326** **106**
H: 5 10 W: 12 08 b.Orsett 12-7-77
Source: Cambridge C.

1997–98	Millwall	3	0		
1998–99	Millwall	39	15		
1999–2000	Millwall	38	25		
2000–01	Millwall	42	27		
2001–02	Millwall	21	4		
2002–03	Millwall	40	12		
2003–04	Millwall	38	9		
2004–05	Millwall	12	1		
2004–05	*Cardiff C*	3	1	**3**	**1**
2004–05	Nottingham F	13	0		
2005–06	Nottingham F	1	0		
2005–06	*Gillingham*	36	6	**36**	**6**
2006–07	Nottingham F	19	1	**33**	**1**
2006–07	Millwall	21	5	**254**	**98**

HUBERTZ, Poul (F) **158** **45**
H: 6 5 W: 14 09 b.Viborg 21-9-76

2000	Frem	25	7		
From Farum					
2003	*Frem*	15	8	**40**	**15**
2003–04	Herfolge	30	7		
2004–05	Herfolge	28	11	**58**	**18**
2005–06	Aalborg	26	3	**26**	**3**
2006–07	Millwall	34	9	**34**	**9**

MAWENE, Samy-Oyame (M) **6** **0**
H: 6 0 W: 12 04 b.Caen 12-11-84

2004–05	Caen	1	0		
2005–06	Caen	1	0	**2**	**0**
2006–07	Millwall	4	0	**4**	**0**

MAY, Ben (F) **141** **23**
H: 6 3 W: 12 12 b.Gravesend 10-3-84
Source: Juniors.

2000–01	Millwall	0	0		
2001–02	Millwall	0	0		
2002–03	Millwall	10	1		
2002–03	*Colchester U*	6	0		
2003–04	Millwall	0	0		
2003–04	*Brentford*	41	7		
2004–05	Millwall	8	1		
2004–05	*Colchester U*	14	1	**20**	**1**
2004–05	Brentford	10	1	**51**	**8**
2005–06	Millwall	39	10		
2006–07	Millwall	13	2	**70**	**14**

McINNES, Derek (M) **447** **30**
H: 5 8 W: 11 05 b.Paisley 5-7-71
Source: Gleniffer Th. *Honours:* Scotland 2 full caps.

1987–88	Greenock Morton	2	0		
1988–89	Greenock Morton	29	1		
1989–90	Greenock Morton	23	1		
1990–91	Greenock Morton	31	3		
1991–92	Greenock Morton	42	7		
1992–93	Greenock Morton	40	2		
1993–94	Greenock Morton	16	1		
1994–95	Greenock Morton	26	3		
1995–96	Greenock Morton	12	1	**221**	**19**
1995–96	Rangers	6	0		
1996–97	Rangers	21	1		
1997–98	Rangers	0	0		
1998–99	Rangers	7	0		
1998–99	*Stockport Co*	13	0	**13**	**0**
1999–2000	Toulouse	3	0	**3**	**0**
1999–2000	Rangers	1	0	**35**	**1**
2000–01	WBA	14	1		
2001–02	WBA	45	3		
2002–03	WBA	29	2	**88**	**6**
2003–04	Dundee U	35	1		
2004–05	Dundee U	27	0		
2005–06	Dundee U	12	2	**74**	**3**
2006–07	Millwall	13	1	**13**	**1**

To St Johnstone January 2007

MORAIS, Filipe (M) **25** **1**
H: 5 9 W: 11 10 b.Lisbon 21-11-85
Source: Trainee. *Honours:* Portugal Youth.

2003–04	Chelsea	0	0		
2004–05	Chelsea	0	0		
2005–06	Chelsea	0	0		
2005–06	*Milton Keynes D*	13	0	**13**	**0**
2006–07	Millwall	12	1	**12**	**1**

MORRIS, Jody (F) **211** **11**
H: 5 5 W: 10 03 b.Hammersmith 22-12-78
Source: Trainee. *Honours:* England Schools, Youth, Under-21.

1995–96	Chelsea	1	0		
1996–97	Chelsea	12	0		
1997–98	Chelsea	12	1		
1998–99	Chelsea	18	1		
1999–2000	Chelsea	30	3		
2000–01	Chelsea	21	0		
2001–02	Chelsea	5	0		
2002–03	Chelsea	25	0	**124**	**5**
2003–04	Leeds U	12	0	**12**	**0**
2003–04	Rotherham U	10	1	**10**	**1**
2004–05	Millwall	37	5		
2005–06	Millwall	24	0		
2006–07	Millwall	4	0	**65**	**5**

PHILLIPS, Mark (D) **75** **1**
H: 6 2 W: 11 00 b.Lambeth 27-1-82
Source: Scholarship.

1999–2000	Millwall	0	0		
2000–01	Millwall	0	0		
2001–02	Millwall	1	0		
2002–03	Millwall	7	0		
2003–04	Millwall	0	0		
2004–05	Millwall	25	1		
2005–06	Millwall	22	0		
2006–07	Millwall	12	0	**67**	**1**
2006–07	*Darlington*	8	0	**8**	**0**

PIDGELEY, Lenny (G) **71** **0**
H: 6 4 W: 14 09 b.Isleworth 7-2-84
Source: Scholar. *Honours:* England Under-20.

2003–04	Chelsea	0	0		
2003–04	*Watford*	27	0	**27**	**0**
2004–05	Chelsea	1	0		
2005–06	Chelsea	1	0	**2**	**0**
2005–06	*Millwall*	0	0		
2006–07	Millwall	42	0	**42**	**0**

ROBINSON, Paul (D) **105** **3**
H: 6 1 W: 11 09 b.Barnet 7-1-82
Source: Scholar.

2000–01	Millwall	0	0		
2001–02	Millwall	0	0		
2002–03	Millwall	14	0		
2003–04	Millwall	9	0		
2004–05	Millwall	0	0		
2004–05	*Torquay U*	12	0	**12**	**0**

2005–06	Millwall	32	0		
2006–07	Millwall	38	3	**93**	**3**

ROSS, Maurice (D) **111** **2**
H: 5 11 W: 11 01 b.Dundee 3-2-81
Honours: Scotland 13 full caps.

1999–2000	Rangers	1	0		
2000–01	Rangers	1	0		
2001–02	Rangers	21	0		
2002–03	Rangers	20	1		
2003–04	Rangers	20	1		
2004–05	Rangers	13	0		
2005–06	Rangers	1	0	**77**	**2**
2005–06	Sheffield W	1	0	**1**	**0**
2005–06	Wolverhampton W	18	0	**18**	**0**
2006–07	Millwall	15	0	**15**	**0**

To Viking January 2007

SENDA, Danny (M) **312** **9**
H: 5 10 W: 10 02 b.Harrow 17-4-81
Source: Southampton Trainee. *Honours:* England Youth.

1998–99	Wycombe W	6	0		
1999–2000	Wycombe W	27	1		
2000–01	Wycombe W	31	2		
2001–02	Wycombe W	43	0		
2002–03	Wycombe W	41	2		
2003–04	Wycombe W	40	0		
2004–05	Wycombe W	44	4		
2005–06	Wycombe W	44	0	**276**	**9**
2006–07	Millwall	36	0	**36**	**0**

SHAW, Richard (D) **569** **4**
H: 5 9 W: 12 08 b.Brentford 11-9-68
Source: Apprentice.

1986–87	Crystal Palace	0	0		
1987–88	Crystal Palace	3	0		
1988–89	Crystal Palace	14	0		
1989–90	Crystal Palace	21	0		
1989–90	*Hull C*	4	0	**4**	**0**
1990–91	Crystal Palace	36	1		
1991–92	Crystal Palace	10	0		
1992–93	Crystal Palace	33	0		
1993–94	Crystal Palace	34	2		
1994–95	Crystal Palace	41	0		
1995–96	Crystal Palace	15	0	**207**	**3**
1995–96	Coventry C	21	0		
1996–97	Coventry C	35	0		
1997–98	Coventry C	33	0		
1998–99	Coventry C	37	0		
1999–2000	Coventry C	29	0		
2000–01	Coventry C	24	0		
2001–02	Coventry C	32	0		
2002–03	Coventry C	29	0		
2003–04	Coventry C	19	1		
2004–05	Coventry C	33	0		
2005–06	Coventry C	25	0	**317**	**1**
2006–07	Millwall	41	0	**41**	**0**

WHITBREAD, Zak (D) **39** **0**
H: 6 2 W: 12 07 b.Houston 4-3-84
Honours: USA Under-23.

2002–03	Liverpool	0	0		
2003–04	Liverpool	0	0		
2004–05	Liverpool	0	0		
2005–06	Liverpool	0	0		
2005–06	*Millwall*	25	0		
2006–07	Millwall	14	0	**39**	**0**

WILLIAMS, Marvin (M) **53** **8**
H: 5 11 W: 11 06 b.London 12-8-87
Source: Scholar.

2005–06	Millwall	22	4		
2006–07	Millwall	29	3	**51**	**7**
2006–07	*Torquay U*	2	1	**2**	**1**

ZEBROSKI, Chris (F) **29** **3**
H: 6 1 W: 11 08 b.Swindon 29-10-86
Source: Cirencester T, Scholar.

2005–06	Plymouth Arg	4	0		
2006–07	Plymouth Arg	0	0	**4**	**0**
2006–07	Millwall	25	3	**25**	**3**

MILTON KEYNES D (54)

ANDREWS, Keith (M) **158** **9**
H: 6 0 W: 12 04 b.Dublin 13-9-80
Source: Trainee. *Honours:* Eire Youth.

1997–98	Wolverhampton W	0	0		
1998–99	Wolverhampton W	0	0		
1999–2000	Wolverhampton W	2	0		
2000–01	Wolverhampton W	22	0		
2000–01	*Oxford U*	4	1	**4**	**1**
2001–02	Wolverhampton W	11	0		
2002–03	Wolverhampton W	9	0		
2003–04	Wolverhampton W	1	0		
2003–04	*Stoke C*	16	0	**16**	**0**
2003–04	*Walsall*	10	2	**10**	**2**
2004–05	Wolverhampton W	20	0	**65**	**0**
2005–06	Hull C	26	0		
2006–07	Hull C	3	0	**29**	**0**
2006–07	Milton Keynes D	34	6	**34**	**6**

BAINES, Adolfo (G) **175** **0**
H: 6 2 W: 14 02 b.Isaba 12-2-72

1998–99	Gimnastic	22	0		
1999–2000	Gimnastic	32	0	**54**	**0**
2000–01	Badajoz	38	0		
2001–02	Badajoz	29	0		
2002–03	Badajoz	31	0	**98**	**0**
2003–04	Tenerife	3	0		
2004–05	Tenerife	1	0		
2005–06	Tenerife	0	0	**4**	**0**
2006–07	Milton Keynes D	19	0	**19**	**0**

BALDOCK, Sam (F) **1** **0**
H: 5 7 W: 10 07 b.Bedford 15-3-89
Source: Scholar.

2005–06	Milton Keynes D	0	0		
2006–07	Milton Keynes D	1	0	**1**	**0**

BANKOLE, Ademola (G) **70** **0**
H: 6 3 W: 13 00 b.Lagos 9-9-69
Source: Leyton Orient.

1996–97	Crewe Alex	3	0		
1997–98	Crewe Alex	3	0		
1998–99	QPR	0	0		
1998–99	*Grimsby T*	0	0		
1999–2000	QPR	1	0	**1**	**0**
1999–2000	*Bradford C*	0	0		
2000–01	Crewe Alex	21	0		
2001–02	Crewe Alex	28	0		
2002–03	Crewe Alex	3	0		
2003–04	Crewe Alex	0	0	**58**	**0**
2004–05	Brentford	3	0		
2005–06	Brentford	2	0	**5**	**0**
2006–07	Milton Keynes D	6	0	**6**	**0**

CHORLEY, Ben (M) **154** **6**
H: 6 3 W: 13 02 b.Sidcup 30-9-82
Source: Scholar.

2001–02	Arsenal	0	0		
2002–03	Arsenal	0	0		
2002–03	*Brentford*	2	0	**2**	**0**
2002–03	Wimbledon	10	0		
2003–04	Wimbledon	35	2	**45**	**2**
2004–05	Milton Keynes D	41	2		
2005–06	Milton Keynes D	26	0		
2006–07	Milton Keynes D	13	1	**80**	**3**
2006–07	*Gillingham*	27	1	**27**	**1**

COLLINS, Sam (M) **0** **0**
H: 6 0 W: 12 06 b.London 25-6-89
Source: Scholar.

2006–07	Milton Keynes D	0	0		

DIALLO, Drissa (D) **110** **1**
H: 6 1 W: 11 13 b.Nouadhibou 4-1-73
Honours: Guinea full caps.

2002–03	Burnley	14	1	**14**	**1**
2003–04	Ipswich T	19	0		
2004–05	Ipswich T	26	0	**45**	**0**
2005–06	Sheffield W	11	0	**11**	**0**
2006–07	Milton Keynes D	40	0	**40**	**0**

DYER, Lloyd (M) **96** **8**
H: 5 8 W: 10 03 b.Birmingham 13-9-82
Source: Aston Villa Juniors.

2001–02	WBA	0	0		
2002–03	WBA	0	0		
2003–04	WBA	17	2		
2003–04	*Kidderminster H*	7	1	**7**	**1**
2004–05	WBA	4	0		
2004–05	*Coventry C*	6	0	**6**	**0**
2005–06	WBA	0	0	**21**	**2**
2005–06	*QPR*	15	0	**15**	**0**
2005–06	Millwall	6	0	**6**	**0**
2006–07	Milton Keynes D	41	5	**41**	**5**

EDDS, Gareth (D) **168** **11**
H: 5 11 W: 11 01 b.Sydney 3-2-81
Source: Trainee. *Honours:* Australia Under-20, Under-23.

1997–98	Nottingham F	0	0		
1998–99	Nottingham F	0	0		
1999–2000	Nottingham F	2	0		
2000–01	Nottingham F	13	1		
2001–02	Nottingham F	1	0	**16**	**1**
2002–03	Swindon T	14	0	**14**	**0**
2003–04	Bradford C	23	0	**23**	**0**
2004–05	Milton Keynes D	39	5		
2005–06	Milton Keynes D	41	3		
2006–07	Milton Keynes D	35	2	**115**	**10**

HARDING, Ben (M) **51** **6**
H: 5 10 W: 11 02 b.Carshalton 6-9-84
Source: Scholar.

2001–02	Wimbledon	0	0		
2002–03	Wimbledon	0	0		
2003–04	Wimbledon	15	0	**15**	**0**
2004–05	Milton Keynes D	26	4		
2005–06	Milton Keynes D	10	2		
2006–07	Milton Keynes D	0	0	**36**	**6**

HARPER, Lee (G) **300** **0**
H: 6 1 W: 15 06 b.Chelsea 30-10-71
Source: Sittingbourne.

1994–95	Arsenal	0	0		
1995–96	Arsenal	0	0		
1996–97	Arsenal	1	0	**1**	**0**
1997–98	QPR	36	0		
1998–99	QPR	15	0		
1999–2000	QPR	38	0		
2000–01	QPR	29	0	**118**	**0**
2001–02	Walsall	3	0	**3**	**0**
2002–03	Northampton T	31	0		
2003–04	Northampton T	39	0		
2004–05	Northampton T	36	0		
2005–06	Northampton T	46	0		
2006–07	Northampton T	4	0	**156**	**0**
2006–07	Milton Keynes D	22	0	**22**	**0**

HASTINGS, John (F) **7** **0**
H: 6 1 W: 11 11 b.London 9-5-98
Source: Hayes, Tooting & Mitcham U.

2006–07	Milton Keynes D	7	0	**7**	**0**

HOWE, Joe (M) **0** **0**
H: 5 10 W: 11 10 b.Sidcup 21-1-88
Source: Scholar.

2006–07	Milton Keynes D	0	0		

KNIGHT, Leon (F) **227** **69**
H: 5 5 W: 9 06 b.Hackney 16-9-82
Source: From Trainee. *Honours:* England Youth, Under-20.

1999–2000	Chelsea	0	0		
2000–01	Chelsea	0	0		
2000–01	*QPR*	11	0	**11**	**0**
2001–02	Chelsea	0	0		
2001–02	*Huddersfield T*	31	16	**31**	**16**
2002–03	Chelsea	0	0		
2002–03	*Sheffield W*	24	3	**24**	**3**
2003–04	Chelsea	0	0		
2003–04	Brighton & HA	44	25		
2004–05	Brighton & HA	39	4		
2005–06	Brighton & HA	25	5	**108**	**34**
2005–06	Swansea C	17	8		
2006–07	Swansea C	11	7	**28**	**15**
2006–07	*Barnsley*	9	0	**9**	**0**
2006–07	Milton Keynes D	16	1	**16**	**1**

LEWINGTON, Dean (D) **161** **5**
H: 5 11 W: 11 07 b.Kingston 18-5-84
Source: Scholar.

2002–03	Wimbledon	1	0		
2003–04	Wimbledon	28	1	**29**	**1**
2004–05	Milton Keynes D	43	2		
2005–06	Milton Keynes D	44	1		
2006–07	Milton Keynes D	45	1	**132**	**4**

LEWIS, Junior (M) **189** **15**
H: 6 2 W: 13 00 b.Wembley 9-10-73
Source: Trainee.

1992–93	Fulham	6	0	**6**	**0**
From Dover, Hendon					
1999–2000	Gillingham	42	6		
2000–01	Gillingham	17	2	**59**	**8**
2000–01	Leicester C	15	0		

2001–02	Leicester C	6	0		
2001–02	*Brighton & HA*	15	3	**15**	**3**
2002–03	Leicester C	9	1		
2002–03	*Swindon T*	9	0		
2003–04	Leicester C	0	0	**30**	**1**
2003–04	*Swindon T*	4	0	**13**	**0**
2003–04	*Hull C*	13	1		
2004–05	Hull C	39	2		
2005–06	Hull C	0	0	**52**	**3**
2005–06	Brentford	14	0	**14**	**0**
2006–07	Milton Keynes D	0	0		

McGOVERN, John-Paul (M) **112 10**
H: 5 10 W: 12 02 b.Glasgow 3-10-80
Source: Celtic BC.

2001–02	Celtic	0	0		
2002–03	Celtic	0	0		
2002–03	*Sheffield U*	15	1	**15**	**1**
2003–04	Celtic	0	0		
2004–05	Sheffield W	46	6		
2005–06	Sheffield W	7	0	**53**	**6**
2006–07	Milton Keynes D	44	3	**44**	**3**

McLEOD, Izale (F) **162 58**
H: 6 1 W: 11 02 b.Birmingham 15-10-84
Source: Scholar. *Honours:* England Under-21.

2002–03	Derby Co	29	3		
2003–04	Derby Co	10	1	**39**	**4**
2003–04	*Sheffield U*	7	0	**7**	**0**
2004–05	Milton Keynes D	43	16		
2005–06	Milton Keynes D	39	17		
2006–07	Milton Keynes D	34	21	**116**	**54**

MITCHELL, Paul (M) **159 0**
H: 5 9 W: 12 01 b.Manchester 26-8-81
Source: Trainee.

2000–01	Wigan Ath	1	0		
2000–01	*Halifax T*	11	0	**11**	**0**
2001–02	Wigan Ath	23	0		
2002–03	Wigan Ath	27	0		
2003–04	Wigan Ath	12	0		
2004–05	Wigan Ath	1	0	**64**	**0**
2004–05	*Swindon T*	7	0	**7**	**0**
2004–05	*Milton Keynes D*	13	0		
2005–06	Milton Keynes D	39	0		
2006–07	Milton Keynes D	20	0	**72**	**0**
2006–07	*Wrexham*	5	0	**5**	**0**

MURPHY, Kieron (D) **0 0**
H: 5 11 W: 10 12 b.Kingston 21-12-87
Honours: Eire Under-21.

2006–07	Milton Keynes D	0	0		

O'HANLON, Sean (D) **135 13**
H: 6 1 W: 12 05 b.Southport 2-1-83
Honours: England Schools, Youth, Under-20.

1999–2000	Everton	0	0		
2000–01	Everton	0	0		
2001–02	Everton	0	0		
2002–03	Everton	0	0		
2003–04	Everton	0	0		
2003–04	Swindon T	19	2		
2004–05	Swindon T	40	3		
2005–06	Swindon T	40	4	**99**	**9**
2006–07	Milton Keynes D	36	4	**36**	**4**

PAGE, Sam (D) **1 0**
H: 6 4 W: 13 02 b.Croydon 30-10-87
Source: Scholar.

2006–07	Milton Keynes D	1	0	**1**	**0**

PLATT, Clive (F) **359 70**
H: 6 4 W: 12 07 b.Wolverhampton 27-10-77
Source: Trainee.

1995–96	Walsall	4	2		
1996–97	Walsall	1	0		
1997–98	Walsall	20	1		
1998–99	Walsall	7	1		
1999–2000	Walsall	0	0	**32**	**4**
1999–2000	Rochdale	41	9		
2000–01	Rochdale	43	8		
2001–02	Rochdale	43	7		
2002–03	Rochdale	42	6	**169**	**30**
2003–04	Notts Co	19	3	**19**	**3**
2003–04	Peterborough U	18	2		
2004–05	Peterborough U	19	4	**37**	**6**
2004–05	Milton Keynes D	20	3		
2005–06	Milton Keynes D	40	6		
2006–07	Milton Keynes D	42	18	**102**	**27**

RIZZO, Nicky (M) **112 7**
H: 5 10 W: 12 00 b.Sydney 9-6-79
Source: Sydney Olympic. *Honours:* Australia Youth, Under-20, Under-23, 1 full cap.

1996–97	Liverpool	0	0		
1997–98	Liverpool	0	0		
1998–99	Crystal Palace	19	1		
1999–2000	Crystal Palace	17	0	**36**	**1**
2000–01	Ternana	0	0		
2001–02	Ternana	1	0		
2002–03	Ternana	0	0	**1**	**0**
2003–04	Prato	20	2	**20**	**2**
2004–05	Milton Keynes D	18	2		
2005–06	Milton Keynes D	29	2		
2006–07	Milton Keynes D	3	0	**50**	**4**
2006–07	*Grimsby T*	1	0	**1**	**0**
2006–07	*Chesterfield*	4	0	**4**	**0**

SMITH, Gary (M) **82 8**
H: 5 8 W: 10 09 b.Middlesbrough 30-1-84
Source: Trainee.

2002–03	Middlesbrough	0	0		
2003–04	Middlesbrough	0	0		
2003–04	*Wimbledon*	11	3	**11**	**3**
2004–05	Milton Keynes D	23	1		
2005–06	Milton Keynes D	25	3		
2006–07	Milton Keynes D	23	1	**71**	**5**

SMITH, Jamie (M) **314 7**
H: 5 6 W: 10 08 b.Birmingham 17-9-74
Source: Trainee.

1993–94	Wolverhampton W	0	0		
1994–95	Wolverhampton W	25	0		
1995–96	Wolverhampton W	13	0		
1996–97	Wolverhampton W	38	0		
1997–98	Wolverhampton W	11	0	**87**	**0**
1997–98	Crystal Palace	18	0		
1998–99	Crystal Palace	26	0		
1998–99	*Fulham*	9	1	**9**	**1**
1999–2000	Crystal Palace	27	0		
2000–01	Crystal Palace	29	0		
2001–02	Crystal Palace	32	4		
2002–03	Crystal Palace	2	0		
2003–04	Crystal Palace	15	0	**149**	**4**
2004–05	Bristol C	39	2		
2005–06	Bristol C	6	0	**45**	**2**
2005–06	*Brentford*	7	0	**7**	**0**
2006–07	Milton Keynes D	17	0	**17**	**0**

STIRLING, Jude (D) **64 1**
H: 6 2 W: 11 12 b.Enfield 29-6-82
Source: Trainee.

1999–2000	Luton T	0	0		
2000–01	Luton T	9	0		
2001–02	Luton T	1	0	**10**	**0**

From Tamworth.

2005–06	Oxford U	10	0	**10**	**0**

From Stevenage B, Hornchurch, Tamworth

2005–06	Lincoln C	6	0	**6**	**0**
2006–07	Peterborough U	22	0	**22**	**0**
2006–07	Milton Keynes D	16	1	**16**	**1**

TAYLOR, Scott (F) **392 78**
H: 5 10 W: 11 04 b.Chertsey 5-5-76
Source: Staines T.

1994–95	Millwall	6	0		
1995–96	Millwall	22	0	**28**	**0**
1995–96	Bolton W	1	0		
1996–97	Bolton W	11	1		
1997–98	Bolton W	0	0		
1997–98	*Rotherham U*	10	3	**10**	**3**
1997–98	*Blackpool*	5	1		
1998–99	Bolton W	0	0	**12**	**1**
1998–99	Tranmere R	36	9		
1999–2000	Tranmere R	35	3		
2000–01	Tranmere R	37	5	**108**	**17**
2001–02	Stockport Co	28	4	**28**	**4**
2001–02	Blackpool	17	2		
2002–03	Blackpool	44	13		
2003–04	Blackpool	31	16		
2004–05	Blackpool	24	12	**121**	**44**
2004–05	Plymouth Arg	16	3		
2005–06	Plymouth Arg	18	1	**34**	**4**
2005–06	Milton Keynes D	17	3		
2006–07	Milton Keynes D	28	2	**45**	**5**
2006–07	*Brentford*	6	0	**6**	**0**

TILLEN, Joe (M) **1 0**
H: 5 10 W: 11 07 b.Reading 15-12-86
Source: Scholar. *Honours:* England Youth.

2004–05	Chelsea	0	0		
2005–06	Chelsea	0	0		
2006–07	Milton Keynes D	1	0	**1**	**0**

WILBRAHAM, Aaron (F) **263 51**
H: 6 3 W: 12 04 b.Knutsford 21-10-79
Source: Trainee.

1997–98	Stockport Co	7	1		
1998–99	Stockport Co	26	0		
1999–2000	Stockport Co	26	4		
2000–01	Stockport Co	36	12		
2001–02	Stockport Co	21	3		
2002–03	Stockport Co	15	7		
2003–04	Stockport Co	41	8	**172**	**35**
2004–05	Hull C	19	2	**19**	**2**
2004–05	*Oldham Ath*	4	2	**4**	**2**
2005–06	Milton Keynes D	31	4		
2005–06	*Bradford C*	5	1	**5**	**1**
2006–07	Milton Keynes D	32	7	**63**	**11**

NEWCASTLE U (55)

AMEOBI, Shola (F) **162 28**
H: 6 3 W: 11 13 b.Zaria 12-10-81
Source: Trainee. *Honours:* England Under-21.

1998–99	Newcastle U	0	0		
1999–2000	Newcastle U	0	0		
2000–01	Newcastle U	20	2		
2001–02	Newcastle U	15	0		
2002–03	Newcastle U	28	5		
2003–04	Newcastle U	26	7		
2004–05	Newcastle U	31	2		
2005–06	Newcastle U	30	9		
2006–07	Newcastle U	12	3	**162**	**28**

BABAYARO, Celestine (D) **254 13**
H: 5 10 W: 11 11 b.Kaduna 29-8-78
Source: Plateau U. *Honours:* Nigeria 26 full caps.

1994–95	Anderlecht	22	0		
1995–96	Anderlecht	28	5		
1996–97	Anderlecht	25	3	**75**	**8**
1997–98	Chelsea	8	0		
1998–99	Chelsea	28	3		
1999–2000	Chelsea	25	0		
2000–01	Chelsea	24	0		
2001–02	Chelsea	18	0		
2002–03	Chelsea	19	1		
2003–04	Chelsea	6	1		
2004–05	Chelsea	4	0	**132**	**5**
2004–05	Newcastle U	7	0		
2005–06	Newcastle U	28	0		
2006–07	Newcastle U	12	0	**47**	**0**

BOUMSONG, Jean-Alain (D) **238 6**
H: 6 3 W: 13 03 b.Douala 14-12-79
Source: US Palaiseau. *Honours:* France 21 full caps, 1 goal.

1997–98	Le Havre	1	0		
1998–99	Le Havre	18	1		
1999–2000	Le Havre	23	0	**42**	**1**
2000–01	Auxerre	32	0		
2001–02	Auxerre	34	1		
2002–03	Auxerre	33	1		
2003–04	Auxerre	32	1	**131**	**3**
2004–05	Rangers	18	2	**18**	**2**
2004–05	Newcastle U	14	0		
2005–06	Newcastle U	33	0		
2006–07	Newcastle U	0	0	**47**	**0**

To Juventus August 2006

BRAMBLE, Titus (D) **155 4**
H: 6 2 W: 13 10 b.Ipswich 31-7-81
Source: Trainee. *Honours:* England Under-21.

1998–99	Ipswich T	4	0		
1999–2000	Ipswich T	0	0		
1999–2000	*Colchester U*	2	0	**2**	**0**
2000–01	Ipswich T	26	1		
2001–02	Ipswich T	18	0	**48**	**1**
2002–03	Newcastle U	16	0		
2003–04	Newcastle U	29	0		
2004–05	Newcastle U	19	1		

2005–06	Newcastle U	24	2		
2006–07	Newcastle U	17	0	**105**	**3**

BUTT, Nicky (M) 343 26
H: 5 10 W: 11 05 b.Manchester 21-1-75
Source: Trainee. *Honours:* England Schools, Youth, Under-21, 39 full caps.

1992–93	Manchester U	1	0		
1993–94	Manchester U	1	0		
1994–95	Manchester U	22	1		
1995–96	Manchester U	32	2		
1996–97	Manchester U	26	5		
1997–98	Manchester U	33	3		
1998–99	Manchester U	31	2		
1999–2000	Manchester U	32	3		
2000–01	Manchester U	28	3		
2001–02	Manchester U	25	1		
2002–03	Manchester U	18	0		
2003–04	Manchester U	21	1	**270**	**21**
2004–05	Newcastle U	18	1		
2005–06	*Birmingham C*	24	3	**24**	**3**
2006–07	Newcastle U	31	1	**49**	**2**

CARR, Stephen (D) 294 8
H: 5 9 W: 11 13 b.Dublin 29-8-76
Source: Trainee. *Honours:* Eire Schools, Youth, Under-21, 43 full caps.

1993–94	Tottenham H	1	0		
1994–95	Tottenham H	0	0		
1995–96	Tottenham H	0	0		
1996–97	Tottenham H	26	0		
1997–98	Tottenham H	38	0		
1998–99	Tottenham H	37	0		
1999–2000	Tottenham H	34	3		
2000–01	Tottenham H	28	3		
2001–02	Tottenham H	0	0		
2002–03	Tottenham H	30	0		
2003–04	Tottenham H	32	1	**226**	**7**
2004–05	Newcastle U	26	1		
2005–06	Newcastle U	19	0		
2006–07	Newcastle U	23	0	**68**	**1**

CARROLL, Andy (F) 4 0
H: 6 4 W: 11 00 b.Gateshead 6-1-89
Source: Scholar.

2006–07	Newcastle U	4	0	**4**	**0**

DUFF, Damien (F) 287 42
H: 5 9 W: 12 06 b.Ballyboden 2-3-79
Source: From Lourdes Celtic. *Honours:* Eire Schools, Youth, Under-20, B, 66 full caps, 7 goals.

1995–96	Blackburn R	0	0		
1996–97	Blackburn R	1	0		
1997–98	Blackburn R	26	4		
1998–99	Blackburn R	28	1		
1999–2000	Blackburn R	39	5		
2000–01	Blackburn R	32	1		
2001–02	Blackburn R	32	7		
2002–03	Blackburn R	26	9	**184**	**27**
2003–04	Chelsea	23	5		
2004–05	Chelsea	30	6		
2005–06	Chelsea	28	3	**81**	**14**
2006–07	Newcastle U	22	1	**22**	**1**

DYER, Kieron (M) 281 32
H: 5 8 W: 10 01 b.Ipswich 29-12-78
Source: Trainee. *Honours:* England Youth, Under-21, B, 32 full caps.

1996–97	Ipswich T	13	0		
1997–98	Ipswich T	41	4		
1998–99	Ipswich T	37	5	**91**	**9**
1999–2000	Newcastle U	30	3		
2000–01	Newcastle U	26	5		
2001–02	Newcastle U	18	3		
2002–03	Newcastle U	35	2		
2003–04	Newcastle U	25	1		
2004–05	Newcastle U	23	4		
2005–06	Newcastle U	11	0		
2006–07	Newcastle U	22	5	**190**	**23**

EDGAR, David (D) 3 1
H: 6 2 W: 12 13 b.Ontario 19-5-87
Source: Scholar. *Honours:* Canada Youth, Under-20.

2005–06	Newcastle U	0	0		
2006–07	Newcastle U	3	1	**3**	**1**

EMRE, Belezoglu (M) 205 20
H: 5 8 W: 10 10 b.Istanbul 7-9-80
Honours: Turkey Youth, Under-21, 44 full caps, 3 goals.

1997–98	Galatasaray	24	2		
1998–99	Galatasaray	27	2		
1999–2000	Galatasaray	24	5		
2000–01	Galatasaray	26	4	**101**	**13**
2001–02	Internazionale	14	0		
2002–03	Internazionale	25	3		
2003–04	Internazionale	21	0		
2004–05	Internazionale	0	0	**60**	**3**
2005–06	Newcastle U	20	2		
2006–07	Newcastle U	24	2	**44**	**4**

GATE, Kris (D) 0 0
H: 5 7 W: 10 03 b.Newcastle 1-1-85
Source: Trainee.

2003–04	Newcastle U	0	0		
2004–05	Newcastle U	0	0		
2005–06	Newcastle U	0	0		
2006–07	Newcastle U	0	0		

GIVEN, Shay (G) 337 0
H: 6 0 W: 13 03 b.Lifford 20-4-76
Source: Celtic. *Honours:* Eire Youth, Under-21, 80 full caps.

1994–95	Blackburn R	0	0		
1994–95	*Swindon T*	0	0		
1995–96	Blackburn R	0	0		
1995–96	*Swindon T*	5	0	**5**	**0**
1995–96	*Sunderland*	17	0	**17**	**0**
1996–97	Blackburn R	2	0	**2**	**0**
1997–98	Newcastle U	24	0		
1998–99	Newcastle U	31	0		
1999–2000	Newcastle U	14	0		
2000–01	Newcastle U	34	0		
2001–02	Newcastle U	38	0		
2002–03	Newcastle U	38	0		
2003–04	Newcastle U	38	0		
2004–05	Newcastle U	36	0		
2005–06	Newcastle U	38	0		
2006–07	Newcastle U	22	0	**313**	**0**

HARPER, Steve (G) 91 0
H: 6 2 W: 13 10 b.Easington 14-3-75
Source: Seaham Red Star.

1993–94	Newcastle U	0	0		
1994–95	Newcastle U	0	0		
1995–96	Newcastle U	0	0		
1995–96	*Bradford C*	1	0	**1**	**0**
1996–97	Newcastle U	0	0		
1996–97	*Stockport Co*	0	0		
1997–98	Newcastle U	0	0		
1997–98	*Hartlepool U*	15	0	**15**	**0**
1997–98	*Huddersfield T*	24	0	**24**	**0**
1998–99	Newcastle U	8	0		
1999–2000	Newcastle U	18	0		
2000–01	Newcastle U	5	0		
2001–02	Newcastle U	0	0		
2002–03	Newcastle U	0	0		
2003–04	Newcastle U	0	0		
2004–05	Newcastle U	2	0		
2005–06	Newcastle U	0	0		
2006–07	Newcastle U	18	0	**51**	**0**

HUNTINGTON, Paul (D) 11 1
H: 6 3 W: 12 08 b.Carlisle 17-9-87
Source: Scholar. *Honours:* England Youth.

2005–06	Newcastle U	0	0		
2006–07	Newcastle U	11	1	**11**	**1**

KRUL, Tim (G) 0 0
H: 6 2 W: 11 08 b.Den Haag 3-4-88
Source: Academy. *Honours:* Holland Youth.

2005–06	Newcastle U	0	0		
2006–07	Newcastle U	0	0		

LUQUE, Alberto (F) 282 78
H: 6 0 W: 11 11 b.Barcelona 11-3-78
Honours: Spain Under-21, 18 full caps, 2 goals.

1997–98	Mallorca B	31	10		
1998–99	Mallorca B	31	15	**62**	**25**
1998–99	Mallorca	5	0		
1999–2000	Malaga	23	3	**23**	**3**
2000–01	Mallorca	32	9		
2001–02	Mallorca	36	14	**73**	**23**
2002–03	La Coruna	32	7		
2003–04	La Coruna	34	8		
2004–05	La Coruna	37	11	**103**	**26**
2005–06	Newcastle U	14	1		
2006–07	Newcastle U	7	0	**21**	**1**

MARTINS, Obafemi (F) 123 38
H: 5 9 W: 10 07 b.Lagos 28-10-84
Honours: Nigeria 17 full caps, 11 goals.

2000–01	Reggiana	2	0	**2**	**0**
2001–02	Internazionale	0	0		
2002–03	Internazionale	4	1		
2003–04	Internazionale	25	7		
2004–05	Internazionale	31	11		
2005–06	Internazionale	28	8	**88**	**27**
2006–07	Newcastle U	33	11	**33**	**11**

MILNER, James (M) 144 12
H: 5 9 W: 11 00 b.Leeds 4-1-86
Source: Trainee. *Honours:* FA Schools, Youth, England Under-20, Under-21.

2002–03	Leeds U	18	2		
2003–04	Leeds U	30	3	**48**	**5**
2003–04	*Swindon T*	6	2	**6**	**2**
2004–05	Newcastle U	25	1		
2005–06	Newcastle U	3	0		
2005–06	*Aston Villa*	27	1	**27**	**1**
2006–07	Newcastle U	35	3	**63**	**4**

MOORE, Craig (D) 237 18
H: 6 1 W: 12 00 b.Canterbury, Australia 12-12-75
Source: Australian Institute of Sport. *Honours:* Australia Schools, Youth, Under-20, Under-23, 38 full caps, 2 goals.

1993–94	Rangers	1	0		
1994–95	Rangers	21	2		
1995–96	Rangers	11	1		
1996–97	Rangers	23	1		
1997–98	Rangers	10	0		
1998–99	Rangers	8	1		
1998–99	Crystal Palace	23	3	**23**	**3**
1999–2000	Rangers	22	1		
2000–01	Rangers	5	0		
2001–02	Rangers	18	3		
2002–03	Rangers	35	3		
2003–04	Rangers	19	2		
2004–05	Rangers	3	0	**176**	**14**
2004–05	M'gladbach	13	1	**13**	**1**
2005–06	Newcastle U	8	0		
2006–07	Newcastle U	17	0	**25**	**0**

N'ZOGBIA, Charles (M) 68 5
H: 5 9 W: 11 00 b.Le Havre 28-5-86
Honours: France Youth.

2004–05	Newcastle U	14	0		
2005–06	Newcastle U	32	5		
2006–07	Newcastle U	22	0	**68**	**5**

O'BRIEN, Alan (M) 10 1
H: 5 10 W: 10 10 b.Dublin 20-2-85
Source: Scholar. *Honours:* Eire Youth, B, Under-21, 5 full caps.

2001–02	Newcastle U	0	0		
2002–03	Newcastle U	0	0		
2003–04	Newcastle U	0	0		
2004–05	Newcastle U	0	0		
2005–06	Newcastle U	3	0		
2005–06	*Carlisle U*	5	1	**5**	**1**
2006–07	Newcastle U	2	0	**5**	**0**

ONYEWU, Oguchi (D) 112 7
H: 6 3 W: 15 06 b.Washington DC 13-5-82
Source: Clemson Univ. *Honours:* USA 17 full caps, 1 goal.

2002–03	Metz	3	0	**3**	**0**
2003–04	La Louviere	24	1	**24**	**1**
2004–05	Standard	30	3		
2005–06	Standard	29	2		
2006–07	Standard	15	1	**74**	**6**
2006–07	Newcastle U	11	0	**11**	**0**

OWEN, Michael (F) 266 138
H: 5 8 W: 10 12 b.Chester 14-12-79
Source: Trainee. *Honours:* England Schools, Youth, Under-21, B, 82 full caps, 37 goals.

1996–97	Liverpool	2	1		
1997–98	Liverpool	36	18		
1998–99	Liverpool	30	18		
1999–2000	Liverpool	27	11		
2000–01	Liverpool	28	16		
2001–02	Liverpool	29	19		
2002–03	Liverpool	35	19		

2003–04	Liverpool	29	16	**216**	**118**
2004–05	Real Madrid	36	13	**36**	**13**
2005–06	Newcastle U	11	7		
2006–07	Newcastle U	3	0	**14**	**7**

PARKER, Scott (M) 204 15
H: 5 9 W: 11 10 b.Lambeth 13-10-80
Source: Trainee. *Honours:* England Schools, Youth, Under-21, 3 full caps.

1997–98	Charlton Ath	3	0		
1998–99	Charlton Ath	4	0		
1999–2000	Charlton Ath	15	1		
2000–01	Charlton Ath	20	1		
2000–01	*Norwich C*	6	1	**6**	**1**
2001–02	Charlton Ath	38	1		
2002–03	Charlton Ath	28	4		
2003–04	Charlton Ath	20	2	**128**	**9**
2003–04	Chelsea	11	1		
2004–05	Chelsea	4	0	**15**	**1**
2005–06	Newcastle U	26	1		
2006–07	Newcastle U	29	3	**55**	**4**

PATTISON, Matt (M) 10 0
H: 5 9 W: 11 00 b.Johannesburg 27-10-86
Source: Scholar.

2005–06	Newcastle U	3	0		
2006–07	Newcastle U	7	0	**10**	**0**

RAMAGE, Peter (D) 48 0
H: 6 3 W: 11 02 b.Whitley Bay 22-11-83
Source: Trainee.

2003–04	Newcastle U	0	0		
2004–05	Newcastle U	4	0		
2005–06	Newcastle U	23	0		
2006–07	Newcastle U	21	0	**48**	**0**

SHANKS, Chris (D) 0 0
H: 6 0 W: 11 00 b.Ashington 16-10-86
Source: Scholar.

2004–05	Newcastle U	0	0		
2005–06	Newcastle U	0	0		
2006–07	Newcastle U	0	0		

SIBIERSKI, Antoine (M) 378 75
H: 6 2 W: 12 04 b.Lille 5-8-74
Honours: France Youth, Under-21, Under-23, B.

1992–93	Lille	6	0		
1993–94	Lille	22	1		
1994–95	Lille	36	7		
1995–96	Lille	33	9	**97**	**17**
1996–97	Auxerre	30	7		
1997–98	Auxerre	12	1	**42**	**8**
1998–99	Nantes	4	0		
1999–2000	Nantes	28	13	**32**	**13**
2000–01	Lens	27	5		
2001–02	Lens	25	6		
2002–03	Lens	37	12	**89**	**23**
2003–04	Manchester C	33	5		
2004–05	Manchester C	35	4		
2005–06	Manchester C	24	2		
2006–07	Manchester C	0	0	**92**	**11**
2006–07	Newcastle U	26	3	**26**	**3**

SOLANO, Nolberto (M) 385 82
H: 5 8 W: 10 07 b.Callao 12-12-74
Honours: Peru 77 full caps, 20 goals.

1994–95	Sporting Cristal	38	12		
1995–96	Sporting Cristal	26	13		
1996–97	Sporting Cristal	11	7	**75**	**32**
1997–98	Boca Juniors	32	5	**32**	**5**
1998–99	Newcastle U	29	6		
1999–2000	Newcastle U	30	3		
2000–01	Newcastle U	33	6		
2001–02	Newcastle U	37	7		
2002–03	Newcastle U	31	7		
2003–04	Newcastle U	12	0		
2003–04	Aston Villa	10	0		
2004–05	Aston Villa	36	8		
2005–06	Aston Villa	3	0	**49**	**8**
2005–06	Newcastle U	29	6		
2006–07	Newcastle U	28	2	**229**	**37**

SRNICEK, Pavel (G) 300 0
H: 6 2 W: 14 09 b.Bohumin 10-3-68
Source: Banik Ostrava. *Honours:* Czech Republic 49 full caps.

1990–91	Newcastle U	7	0		
1991–92	Newcastle U	13	0		
1992–93	Newcastle U	32	0		
1993–94	Newcastle U	21	0		
1994–95	Newcastle U	38	0		
1995–96	Newcastle U	15	0		
1996–97	Newcastle U	22	0		
1997–98	Newcastle U	1	0		
1998–99	Banik Ostrava	6	0	**6**	**0**
1998–99	Sheffield W	24	0		
1999–2000	Sheffield W	20	0	**44**	**0**
2000–01	Brescia	26	0		
2001–02	Brescia	1	0		
2002–03	Brescia	5	0	**32**	**0**
2003–04	Portsmouth	3	0	**3**	**0**
2003–04	West Ham U	3	0	**3**	**0**
2004–05	Beira Mar	29	0		
2005–06	Beira Mar	32	0	**61**	**0**
2006–07	Newcastle U	2	0	**151**	**0**

TAYLOR, Steven (D) 59 2
H: 6 2 W: 13 01 b.Greenwich 23-1-86
Source: Trainee. *Honours:* FA Schools, Youth, England Under-20, Under-21, B.

2002–03	Newcastle U	0	0		
2003–04	Newcastle U	1	0		
2003–04	*Wycombe W*	6	0	**6**	**0**
2004–05	Newcastle U	13	0		
2005–06	Newcastle U	12	0		
2006–07	Newcastle U	27	2	**53**	**2**

TROISI, James (F) 0 0
H: 5 10 W: 11 03 b.Adelaide 3-7-88
Source: Scholar. *Honours:* Australia Under-23.

2006–07	Newcastle U	0	0		

Scholars
Bertram, Mark Joseph; Cook, Mark Daniel; Danquah, Frank Wiafe; Doninger, Mark; Forster, Fraser Gerard; Francis, Alex James; Godsmark, Jonathan; Lough, Darren; Marwood, James William; Morris, Callum Edward; Patterson, Alex.

NORTHAMPTON T (56)

AISTON, Sam (M) 251 10
H: 6 1 W: 14 00 b.Newcastle 21-11-76
Source: Newcastle U Trainee. *Honours:* England Schools.

1995–96	Sunderland	14	0		
1996–97	Sunderland	2	0		
1996–97	*Chester C*	14	0		
1997–98	Sunderland	3	0		
1998–99	Sunderland	1	0		
1998–99	*Chester C*	11	0	**25**	**0**
1999–2000	Sunderland	0	0	**20**	**0**
1999–2000	*Stoke C*	6	0	**6**	**0**
1999–2000	*Shrewsbury T*	10	0		
2000–01	Shrewsbury T	42	2		
2001–02	Shrewsbury T	35	2		
2002–03	Shrewsbury T	21	2		
2003–04	Shrewsbury T	0	0		
2004–05	Shrewsbury T	35	1	**143**	**7**
2005–06	Tranmere R	36	3	**36**	**3**
2006–07	Northampton T	21	0	**21**	**0**

BOJIC, Pedj (D) 114 5
H: 5 11 W: 11 12 b.Sydney 9-4-84
Honours: Australia Youth.

2001–02	Parramatta Power	3	0		
2002–03	Parramatta Power	0	0	**3**	**0**
2003–04	Sydney Olympic	13	1	**13**	**1**
2004–05	Northampton T	36	0		
2005–06	Northampton T	36	4		
2006–07	Northampton T	26	0	**98**	**4**

BUNN, Mark (G) 42 0
H: 6 0 W: 12 02 b.Camden 16-11-84
Source: Scholar.

2004–05	Northampton T	0	0		
2005–06	Northampton T	0	0		
2006–07	Northampton T	42	0	**42**	**0**

BURNELL, Joe (M) 212 2
H: 5 8 W: 12 00 b.Bristol 10-10-80
Source: Trainee.

1999–2000	Bristol C	17	0		
2000–01	Bristol C	23	0		
2001–02	Bristol C	30	0		
2002–03	Bristol C	44	0		
2003–04	Bristol C	17	1	**131**	**1**
2004–05	Wycombe W	24	0		
2005–06	Wycombe W	33	0	**57**	**0**
2006–07	Northampton T	24	1	**24**	**1**

CROWE, Jason (D) 256 14
H: 5 9 W: 10 09 b.Sidcup 30-9-78
Source: Trainee. *Honours:* England Schools, Youth.

1995–96	Arsenal	0	0		
1996–97	Arsenal	0	0		
1997–98	Arsenal	0	0		
1998–99	Arsenal	0	0		
1998–99	*Crystal Palace*	8	0	**8**	**0**
1999–2000	Portsmouth	25	0		
2000–01	Portsmouth	23	0		
2000–01	*Brentford*	9	0	**9**	**0**
2001–02	Portsmouth	22	1		
2002–03	Portsmouth	16	4	**86**	**5**
2003–04	Grimsby T	32	0		
2004–05	Grimsby T	37	4	**69**	**4**
2005–06	Northampton T	41	2		
2006–07	Northampton T	43	3	**84**	**5**

DEUCHAR, Kenny (F) 188 93
H: 6 3 W: 13 00 b.Stirling 8-6-80
Source: Camelon J.

1998–99	Falkirk	0	0		
1999–2000	Falkirk	0	0		
2000–01	Falkirk	12	0		
2001–02	Falkirk	13	1	**25**	**1**
2002–03	East Fife	32	20		
2003–04	East Fife	36	11	**68**	**31**
2004–05	Gretna	36	38		
2005–06	Gretna	34	18		
2006–07	Gretna	8	2	**78**	**58**
2006–07	Northampton T	17	3	**17**	**3**

DOIG, Chris (D) 163 3
H: 6 2 W: 12 06 b.Dumfries 13-2-81
Source: Trainee. *Honours:* Scotland Schools, Youth, Under-21.

1997–98	Nottingham F	0	0		
1998–99	Nottingham F	2	0		
1999–2000	Nottingham F	11	0		
2000–01	Nottingham F	15	0		
2001–02	Nottingham F	8	1		
2002–03	Nottingham F	10	0		
2003–04	Nottingham F	10	0		
2003–04	*Northampton T*	9	0		
2004–05	Nottingham F	21	0	**77**	**1**
2005–06	Northampton T	38	2		
2006–07	Northampton T	39	0	**86**	**2**

DOLMAN, Liam (D) 1 0
H: 6 0 W: 14 05 b.Brixworth 26-9-87
Source: Scholar.

2005–06	Northampton T	0	0		
2006–07	Northampton T	1	0	**1**	**0**

DUNN, Chris (G) 0 0
H: 6 5 W: 13 11 b.Essex 23-10-87
Source: Scholar.

2006–07	Northampton T	0	0		

DYCHE, Sean (D) 459 12
H: 6 0 W: 13 10 b.Kettering 28-6-71
Source: Trainee.

1988–89	Nottingham F	0	0		
1989–90	Nottingham F	0	0		
1989–90	Chesterfield	22	2		
1990–91	Chesterfield	28	2		
1991–92	Chesterfield	42	3		
1992–93	Chesterfield	20	1		
1993–94	Chesterfield	20	0		
1994–95	Chesterfield	22	0		
1995–96	Chesterfield	41	0		
1996–97	Chesterfield	36	0	**231**	**8**
1997–98	Bristol C	11	0		
1998–99	Bristol C	6	0	**17**	**0**
1998–99	*Luton T*	14	1	**14**	**1**
1999–2000	Millwall	1	0		
2000–01	Millwall	33	0		
2001–02	Millwall	35	3	**69**	**3**
2002–03	Watford	24	0		
2003–04	Watford	25	0		
2004–05	Watford	23	0	**72**	**0**
2005–06	Northampton T	35	0		
2006–07	Northampton T	21	0	**56**	**0**

GILLIGAN, Ryan (M) 47 4
H: 5 10 W: 11 07 b.Swindon 18-1-87
Source: Watford Scholar.

2005–06	Northampton T	23	4		
2006–07	Northampton T	24	0	**47**	**4**

HOLT, Andy (M) 327 24
H: 6 1 W: 12 07 b.Stockport 21-5-78
Source: Trainee.

1996–97	Oldham Ath	1	0		
1997–98	Oldham Ath	14	1		
1998–99	Oldham Ath	43	5		
1999–2000	Oldham Ath	46	3		
2000–01	Oldham Ath	20	1	**124**	**10**
2000–01	*Hull C*	10	2		
2001–02	Hull C	30	0		
2002–03	Hull C	6	0		
2002–03	*Barnsley*	7	0	**7**	**0**
2002–03	*Shrewsbury T*	9	0	**9**	**0**
2003–04	Hull C	25	1	**71**	**3**
2004–05	Wrexham	45	6		
2005–06	Wrexham	36	3	**81**	**9**
2006–07	Northampton T	35	2	**35**	**2**

HUGHES, Mark (D) 21 3
H: 6 1 W: 13 03 b.Liverpool 9-12-86
Source: Scholar.

2004–05	Everton	0	0		
2005–06	Everton	0	0		
2005–06	*Stockport Co*	3	1	**3**	**1**
2006–07	Everton	1	0	**1**	**0**
2006–07	Northampton T	17	2	**17**	**2**

HUNT, David (M) 140 4
H: 5 11 W: 11 09 b.Dulwich 10-9-82
Source: Scholar.

2002–03	Crystal Palace	2	0	**2**	**0**
2003–04	Leyton Orient	38	1		
2004–05	Leyton Orient	27	0	**65**	**1**
2004–05	Northampton T	4	0		
2005–06	Northampton T	40	3		
2006–07	Northampton T	29	0	**73**	**3**

JESS, Eoin (M) 548 105
H: 5 10 W: 11 06 b.Aberdeen 13-12-70
Source: Rangers 'S' Form. *Honours:* Scotland Under-21, B, 18 full caps, 2 goals.

1987–88	Aberdeen	0	0		
1988–89	Aberdeen	2	0		
1989–90	Aberdeen	11	3		
1990–91	Aberdeen	27	13		
1991–92	Aberdeen	39	12		
1992–93	Aberdeen	31	12		
1993–94	Aberdeen	41	6		
1994–95	Aberdeen	25	1		
1995–96	Aberdeen	25	3		
1995–96	Coventry C	12	1		
1996–97	Coventry C	27	0	**39**	**1**
1997–98	Aberdeen	34	9		
1998–99	Aberdeen	36	14		
1999–2000	Aberdeen	26	5		
2000–01	Aberdeen	0	0	**297**	**78**
2000–01	Bradford C	17	3		
2001–02	Bradford C	45	14	**62**	**17**
2002–03	Nottingham F	32	3		
2003–04	Nottingham F	34	2		
2004–05	Nottingham F	20	2	**86**	**7**
2005–06	Northampton T	38	1		
2006–07	Northampton T	26	1	**64**	**2**

JOHNSON, Brad (M) 31 5
H: 6 0 W: 12 10 b.Hackney 28-4-87
Source: Cambridge U Juniors.

2004–05	Cambridge U	1	0	**1**	**0**
2005–06	Northampton T	3	0		
2006–07	Northampton T	27	5	**30**	**5**

JOHNSON, Brett (D) 10 0
H: 6 1 W: 13 00 b.Hammersmith 15-8-85
Source: Ashford T, Aldershot T.

2005–06	Northampton T	6	0		
2006–07	Northampton T	4	0	**10**	**0**

KIRK, Andy (F) 270 91
H: 5 11 W: 11 01 b.Belfast 29-5-79
Honours: Northern Ireland Under-21, 8 full caps.

1995–96	Glentoran	1	1		
1996–97	Glentoran	25	8		
1997–98	Glentoran	25	9	**51**	**18**
1998–99	Hearts	5	0		
1999–2000	Hearts	4	0		
2000–01	Hearts	31	13		
2001–02	Hearts	20	1		
2002–03	Hearts	29	10		
2003–04	Hearts	24	8	**113**	**32**
2004–05	Boston U	25	19	**25**	**19**
2004–05	Northampton T	8	7		
2005–06	Northampton T	29	8		
2006–07	Northampton T	44	7	**81**	**22**

MAY, Danny (D) 3 0
H: 5 8 W: 10 09 b.Northampton 19-11-88
Source: Scholar.

2006–07	Northampton T	3	0	**3**	**0**

QUINN, James (M) 342 61
H: 6 1 W: 12 10 b.Coventry 15-12-74
Source: From Trainee. *Honours:* Northern Ireland Youth, Under-21, B, 50 full caps, 4 goals.

1992–93	Birmingham C	4	0	**4**	**0**
1993–94	Blackpool	14	2		
1993–94	*Stockport Co*	1	0	**1**	**0**
1994–95	Blackpool	41	9		
1995–96	Blackpool	44	9		
1996–97	Blackpool	38	13		
1997–98	Blackpool	14	4	**151**	**37**
1997–98	WBA	13	2		
1998–99	WBA	43	6		
1999–2000	WBA	37	0		
2000–01	WBA	14	1		
2001–02	WBA	7	0		
2001–02	*Notts Co*	6	3	**6**	**3**
2001–02	*Bristol R*	6	1	**6**	**1**
2002–03	WBA	0	0		
2003–04	WBA	0	0	**114**	**9**
2004–05	Sheffield W	15	2	**15**	**2**
2005–06	Peterborough U	24	7	**24**	**7**
2005–06	*Bristol C*	3	1	**3**	**1**
2006–07	Northampton T	18	1	**18**	**1**

TAYLOR, Ian (M) 477 79
H: 6 2 W: 11 06 b.Birmingham 4-6-68
Source: Moor Green.

1992–93	Port Vale	41	15		
1993–94	Port Vale	42	13	**83**	**28**
1994–95	Sheffield W	14	1	**14**	**1**
1994–95	Aston Villa	22	1		
1995–96	Aston Villa	25	3		
1996–97	Aston Villa	34	2		
1997–98	Aston Villa	32	6		
1998–99	Aston Villa	33	4		
1999–2000	Aston Villa	29	5		
2000–01	Aston Villa	29	4		
2001–02	Aston Villa	16	3		
2002–03	Aston Villa	13	0	**233**	**28**
2003–04	Derby Co	42	11		
2004–05	Derby Co	39	3	**81**	**14**
2005–06	Northampton T	33	7		
2006–07	Northampton T	33	1	**66**	**8**

WATT, Jerome (M) 10 0
b.Preston 20-10-84
Source: Scholar. *Honours:* England Youth.

2001–02	Blackburn R	0	0		
2002–03	Blackburn R	0	0		
2003–04	Blackburn R	0	0		
2004–05	Blackburn R	0	0		
2005–06	Blackburn R	0	0		
2006–07	Northampton T	10	0	**10**	**0**

NORWICH C (57)

BROWN, Chris (F) 105 20
H: 6 3 W: 13 01 b.Doncaster 11-12-84
Source: Trainee. *Honours:* England Youth.

2002–03	Sunderland	0	0		
2003–04	Sunderland	0	0		
2003–04	*Doncaster R*	22	10	**22**	**10**
2004–05	Sunderland	37	5		
2005–06	Sunderland	13	1		
2005–06	*Hull C*	13	1	**13**	**1**
2006–07	Sunderland	16	3	**66**	**9**
2006–07	Norwich C	4	0	**4**	**0**

CAVE-BROWN, Andrew (D) 0 0
H: 5 10 W: 12 02 b.Gravesend 5-8-88
Source: Scholar. *Honours:* Scotland Youth.

2005–06	Norwich C	0	0		
2006–07	Norwich C	0	0		

CHADWICK, Luke (M) 163 15
H: 5 11 W: 11 08 b.Cambridge 18-11-80
Source: Trainee. *Honours:* England Youth, Under-21.

1998–99	Manchester U	0	0		
1999–2000	Manchester U	0	0		
2000–01	Manchester U	16	2		
2001–02	Manchester U	8	0		
2002–03	Manchester U	1	0		
2002–03	*Reading*	15	1	**15**	**1**
2003–04	Manchester U	0	0	**25**	**2**
2003–04	*Burnley*	36	5	**36**	**5**
2004–05	West Ham U	32	1		
2005–06	West Ham U	0	0	**32**	**1**
2005–06	Stoke C	36	2		
2006–07	Stoke C	15	3	**51**	**5**
2006–07	Norwich C	4	1	**4**	**1**

COLIN, Jurgen (D) 123 1
H: 5 10 W: 11 10 b.Utrecht 20-1-81
Honours: Holland Youth.

2001–02	PSV Eindhoven	4	0		
2001–02	Genk	7	0	**7**	**0**
2002–03	NAC Breda	34	0	**34**	**0**
2003–04	PSV Eindhoven	20	1		
2004–05	PSV Eindhoven	0	0	**24**	**1**
2005–06	Norwich C	25	0		
2006–07	Norwich C	33	0	**58**	**0**

CROFT, Lee (F) 76 4
H: 5 11 W: 13 00 b.Wigan 21-6-85
Source: Scholar. *Honours:* England Youth, Under-20.

2002–03	Manchester C	0	0		
2003–04	Manchester C	0	0		
2004–05	Manchester C	7	0		
2004–05	*Oldham Ath*	12	0	**12**	**0**
2005–06	Manchester C	21	1	**28**	**1**
2006–07	Norwich C	36	3	**36**	**3**

DOHERTY, Gary (D) 230 19
H: 6 3 W: 13 13 b.Carndonagh 31-1-80
Source: Trainee. *Honours:* Eire Youth, Under-20, Under-21, 33 full caps, 4 goals.

1997–98	Luton T	10	0		
1998–99	Luton T	20	6		
1999–2000	Luton T	40	6	**70**	**12**
1999–2000	Tottenham H	2	0		
2000–01	Tottenham H	22	3		
2001–02	Tottenham H	7	0		
2002–03	Tottenham H	15	1		
2003–04	Tottenham H	17	0		
2004–05	Tottenham H	1	0	**64**	**4**
2004–05	Norwich C	20	2		
2005–06	Norwich C	42	1		
2006–07	Norwich C	34	0	**96**	**3**

DRURY, Adam (D) 387 5
H: 5 10 W: 11 09 b.Cambridge 29-8-78
Source: Trainee.

1995–96	Peterborough U	1	0		
1996–97	Peterborough U	5	1		
1997–98	Peterborough U	31	0		
1998–99	Peterborough U	40	0		
1999–2000	Peterborough U	42	1		
2000–01	Peterborough U	29	0	**148**	**2**
2000–01	Norwich C	6	0		
2001–02	Norwich C	35	0		
2002–03	Norwich C	45	2		
2003–04	Norwich C	42	0		
2004–05	Norwich C	33	1		
2005–06	Norwich C	39	0		
2006–07	Norwich C	39	0	**239**	**3**

DUBLIN, Dion (F) 575 176
H: 6 2 W: 15 00 b.Leicester 22-4-69
Source: Oakham U. *Honours:* England 4 full caps.

1987–88	Norwich C	0	0		
1988–89	Cambridge U	21	6		
1989–90	Cambridge U	46	15		
1990–91	Cambridge U	46	16		
1991–92	Cambridge U	43	15	**156**	**52**
1992–93	Manchester U	7	1		

1993–94	Manchester U	5	1	12	2
1994–95	Coventry C	31	13		
1995–96	Coventry C	34	14		
1996–97	Coventry C	34	13		
1997–98	Coventry C	36	18		
1998–99	Coventry C	10	3	145	61
1998–99	Aston Villa	24	11		
1999–2000	Aston Villa	26	12		
2000–01	Aston Villa	33	8		
2001–02	Aston Villa	21	4		
2001–02	*Millwall*	5	2	5	2
2002–03	Aston Villa	28	10		
2003–04	Aston Villa	23	3	155	48
2004–05	Leicester C	37	5		
2005–06	Leicester C	21	0	58	5
2005–06	Celtic	11	1		
2006–07	Celtic	0	0	11	1
2006–07	Norwich C	33	5	33	5

EAGLE, Robert (M) **10 0**

H: 5 7 W: 10 08 b.Leiston 23-2-87

Source: Scholar.

2006–07	Norwich C	10	0	10	0

EARNSHAW, Robert (F) **269 126**

H: 5 6 W: 9 09 b.Mulfulira 6-4-81

Source: From Trainee. *Honours:* Wales Youth, Under-21, 34 full caps, 12 goals.

1997–98	Cardiff C	5	0		
1998–99	Cardiff C	5	1		
1998–99	*Middlesbrough*	0	0		
1999–2000	Cardiff C	6	1		
1999–2000	*Morton*	3	2	3	2
2000–01	Cardiff C	36	19		
2001–02	Cardiff C	30	11		
2002–03	Cardiff C	46	31		
2003–04	Cardiff C	46	21		
2004–05	Cardiff C	4	1	178	85
2004–05	WBA	31	11		
2005–06	WBA	12	1	43	12
2005–06	Norwich C	15	8		
2006–07	Norwich C	30	19	45	27

ETUHU, Dickson (M) **208 23**

H: 6 2 W: 13 04 b.Kano 8-6-82

Source: Scholarship.

1999–2000	Manchester C	0	0		
2000–01	Manchester C	0	0		
2001–02	Manchester C	12	0	12	0
2001–02	Preston NE	16	3		
2002–03	Preston NE	39	6		
2003–04	Preston NE	31	3		
2004–05	Preston NE	35	3		
2005–06	Preston NE	13	2	134	17
2005–06	Norwich C	19	0		
2006–07	Norwich C	43	6	62	6

FISK, Andrew (M) **0 0**

H: 5 7 W: 10 05 b.Diss 22-10-87

Source: Scholar.

2006–07	Norwich C	0	0		

FOTHERINGHAM, Mark (M) **90 4**

H: 5 7 W: 12 00 b.Dundee 22-10-83

Honours: Scotland Youth, Under-20, Under-21, B.

1999–2000	Celtic	2	0		
2000–01	Celtic	1	0		
2001–02	Celtic	0	0		
2002–03	Celtic	0	0	3	0
2003–04	Dundee	24	4		
2004–05	Dundee	27	0	51	4
2005–06	Freiburg	9	0	9	0
2006–07	Aarau	13	0	13	0
2006–07	Norwich C	14	0	14	0

GALLACHER, Paul (G) **153 0**

H: 6 1 W: 12 04 b.Glasgow 16-8-79

Honours: Scotland Under-21, B, 8 full caps.

1999–2000	Dundee U	1	0		
2000–01	Dundee U	15	0		
2001–02	Dundee U	38	0		
2002–03	Dundee U	34	0		
2003–04	Dundee U	23	0	111	0
2004–05	Norwich C	0	0		
2004–05	*Gillingham*	3	0	3	0
2004–05	*Sheffield W*	8	0	8	0
2005–06	Norwich C	4	0		
2006–07	Norwich C	27	0	31	0

HALLIDAY, Matthew (D) **3 0**

H: 6 2 W: 12 05 b.Norwich 21-1-87

Source: Scholar.

2006–07	Norwich C	0	0		
2006–07	*Torquay U*	3	0	3	0

HENDERSON, Ian (F) **86 7**

H: 5 10 W: 11 06 b.Thetford 24-1-85

Source: Scholar. *Honours:* England Youth, Under-20.

2002–03	Norwich C	20	1		
2003–04	Norwich C	19	4		
2004–05	Norwich C	3	0		
2005–06	Norwich C	24	1		
2006–07	Norwich C	2	0	68	6
2006–07	*Rotherham U*	18	1	18	1

HUCKERBY, Darren (F) **403 101**

H: 5 10 W: 12 09 b.Nottingham 23-4-76

Source: Trainee. *Honours:* England Under-21, B.

1993–94	Lincoln C	6	1		
1994–95	Lincoln C	6	2		
1995–96	Lincoln C	16	2	28	5
1995–96	Newcastle U	1	0		
1996–97	Newcastle U	0	0	1	0
1996–97	*Millwall*	6	3	6	3
1996–97	Coventry C	25	5		
1997–98	Coventry C	34	14		
1998–99	Coventry C	34	9		
1999–2000	Coventry C	1	0	94	28
1999–2000	Leeds U	33	2		
2000–01	Leeds U	7	0	40	2
2000–01	Manchester C	13	1		
2001–02	Manchester C	40	20		
2002–03	Manchester C	16	1		
2002–03	*Nottingham F*	9	5	9	5
2003–04	Manchester C	0	0	69	22
2003–04	Norwich C	36	14		
2004–05	Norwich C	37	6		
2005–06	Norwich C	43	8		
2006–07	Norwich C	40	8	156	36

HUGHES, Andy (M) **381 38**

H: 5 11 W: 12 01 b.Stockport 2-1-78

Source: Trainee.

1995–96	Oldham Ath	15	1		
1996–97	Oldham Ath	8	0		
1997–98	Oldham Ath	10	0	33	1
1997–98	Notts Co	15	2		
1998–99	Notts Co	30	3		
1999–2000	Notts Co	35	7		
2000–01	Notts Co	30	5	110	17
2001–02	Reading	39	6		
2002–03	Reading	43	9		
2003–04	Reading	43	3		
2004–05	Reading	41	0	166	18
2005–06	Norwich C	36	2		
2006–07	Norwich C	36	0	72	2

JARVIS, Rossi (D) **17 0**

H: 5 11 W: 11 12 b.Fakenham 11-3-88

Source: Scholar. *Honours:* England Youth.

2005–06	Norwich C	3	0		
2006–07	Norwich C	0	0	3	0
2006–07	*Torquay U*	4	0	4	0
2006–07	*Rotherham U*	10	0	10	0

JARVIS, Ryan (F) **48 9**

H: 6 1 W: 11 11 b.Fakenham 11-7-86

Source: Scholar. *Honours:* FA Schools, England Youth.

2002–03	Norwich C	3	0		
2003–04	Norwich C	12	1		
2004–05	Norwich C	4	1		
2004–05	*Colchester U*	6	0	6	0
2005–06	Norwich C	4	1		
2006–07	Norwich C	5	0	28	3
2006–07	*Leyton Orient*	14	6	14	6

LAPPIN, Simon (M) **14 1**

H: 5 11 W: 9 06 b.Glasgow 25-1-83

Honours: Scotland Under-21.

2006–07	Norwich C	14	1	14	1

LEWIS, Joe (G) **5 0**

H: 6 5 W: 12 10 b.Bury St Edmunds 6-10-87

Source: Scholar. *Honours:* England Youth.

2004–05	Norwich C	0	0		
2005–06	Norwich C	0	0		
2006–07	Norwich C	0	0		
2006–07	*Stockport Co*	5	0	5	0

MARSHALL, David (G) **37 0**

H: 6 3 W: 13 04 b.Glasgow 5-3-85

Source: Celtic Youth. *Honours:* Scotland Youth, Under-21, B, 2 full caps.

2003–04	Celtic	11	0		
2004–05	Celtic	18	0		
2005–06	Celtic	4	0		
2006–07	Celtic	2	0	35	0

Was on loan from Celtic

2006–07	Norwich C	2	0	2	0

MARTIN, Chris (F) **18 4**

H: 6 2 W: 12 06 b.Beccles 4-11-88

Source: Scholar. *Honours:* England Youth.

2006–07	Norwich C	18	4	18	4

McVEIGH, Paul (F) **227 40**

H: 5 7 W: 11 00 b.Belfast 6-12-77

Source: Trainee. *Honours:* Northern Ireland Schools, Youth, Under-21, 20 full caps.

1995–96	Tottenham H	0	0		
1996–97	Tottenham H	3	1		
1997–98	Tottenham H	0	0		
1998–99	Tottenham H	0	0		
1999–2000	Tottenham H	0	0	3	1
1999–2000	Norwich C	1	0		
2000–01	Norwich C	11	1		
2001–02	Norwich C	42	8		
2002–03	Norwich C	44	14		
2003–04	Norwich C	44	5		
2004–05	Norwich C	17	1		
2005–06	Norwich C	36	7		
2006–07	Norwich C	21	0	216	36
2006–07	*Burnley*	8	3	8	3

RENTON, Kris (F) **3 0**

H: 6 3 W: 12 06 b.Musselburgh 12-7-90

Source: Scholar.

2006–07	Norwich C	3	0	3	0

ROBINSON, Carl (M) **319 28**

H: 5 11 W: 12 08 b.Llandrindod Wells 13-10-76

Source: Trainee. *Honours:* Wales Youth, Under-21, B, 39 full caps, 1 goal.

1995–96	Wolverhampton W	0	0		
1995–96	*Shrewsbury T*	4	0	4	0
1996–97	Wolverhampton W	2	0		
1997–98	Wolverhampton W	32	3		
1998–99	Wolverhampton W	34	8		
1999–2000	Wolverhampton W	33	3		
2000–01	Wolverhampton W	40	3		
2001–02	Wolverhampton W	23	2	164	19
2002–03	Portsmouth	15	0		
2002–03	*Sheffield W*	4	1	4	1
2002–03	*Walsall*	11	1	11	1
2003–04	Portsmouth	1	0	16	0
2003–04	*Rotherham U*	14	0	14	0
2003–04	*Sheffield U*	5	0	5	0
2003–04	*Sunderland*	7	1		
2004–05	Sunderland	40	4		
2005–06	Sunderland	5	0	52	5
2005–06	Norwich C	22	0		
2006–07	Norwich C	27	2	49	2

To Toronto Lynx January 2007

SAFRI, Youseff (M) **174 4**

H: 5 9 W: 12 09 b.Casablanca 1-3-77

Source: Raja. *Honours:* Morocco 10 full caps.

2001–02	Coventry C	33	1		
2002–03	Coventry C	27	0		
2003–04	Coventry C	31	0	91	1
2004–05	Norwich C	18	1		
2005–06	Norwich C	30	1		
2006–07	Norwich C	35	1	83	3

SHACKELL, Jason (D) **79 3**

H: 6 4 W: 13 06 b.Stevenage 27-9-83

Source: Scholar.

2002–03	Norwich C	2	0		
2003–04	Norwich C	6	0		
2004–05	Norwich C	11	0		
2005–06	Norwich C	17	0		
2006–07	Norwich C	43	3	79	3

SMART, Bally (M) **1 0**
H: 5 10 W: 10 00 b.Polokwane 27-4-89
Source: Scholar.

2006–07	Norwich C	1	0	**1**	**0**

SPILLANE, Michael (M) **7 0**
H: 5 9 W: 11 10 b.Cambridge 23-3-89
Source: From Scholar. *Honours:* Eire Youth.

2005–06	Norwich C	2	0		
2006–07	Norwich C	5	0	**7**	**0**

THORNE, Peter (F) **408 139**
H: 6 1 W: 13 13 b.Manchester 21-6-73
Source: Trainee.

1991–92	Blackburn R	0	0		
1992–93	Blackburn R	0	0		
1993–94	Blackburn R	0	0		
1993–94	*Wigan Ath*	11	0	**11**	**0**
1994–95	Blackburn R	0	0		
1994–95	Swindon T	20	9		
1995–96	Swindon T	26	10		
1996–97	Swindon T	31	8	**77**	**27**
1997–98	Stoke C	36	12		
1998–99	Stoke C	34	9		
1999–2000	Stoke C	45	24		
2000–01	Stoke C	38	16		
2001–02	Stoke C	5	4	**158**	**65**
2001–02	Cardiff C	26	8		
2002–03	Cardiff C	46	13		
2003–04	Cardiff C	23	13		
2004–05	Cardiff C	31	12	**126**	**46**
2005–06	Norwich C	21	1		
2006–07	Norwich C	15	0	**36**	**1**

NOTTINGHAM F (58)

AGOGO, Junior (F) **178 55**
H: 5 10 W: 11 07 b.Accra 1-8-79
Source: Willesden. *Honours:* Ghana 5 full caps, 2 goals.

1996–97	Sheffield W	0	0		
1997–98	Sheffield W	1	0		
1998–99	Sheffield W	1	0		
1999–2000	Sheffield W	0	0	**2**	**0**
1999–2000	*Oldham Ath*	2	0	**2**	**0**
1999–2000	*Chester C*	10	6	**10**	**6**
1999–2000	*Chesterfield*	4	0	**4**	**0**
1999–2000	*Lincoln C*	3	1	**3**	**1**
From Colorado R, San Jose E.					
2001–02	QPR	2	0	**2**	**0**
2002–03	Barnet	0	0		
2003–04	Bristol R	38	6		
2004–05	Bristol R	43	19		
2005–06	Bristol R	42	16		
2006–07	Bristol R	3	0	**126**	**41**
2006–07	Nottingham F	29	7	**29**	**7**

BASTIANS, Felix (M) **18 1**
H: 6 2 W: 12 00 b.Bochum 9-5-88
Source: Scholar. *Honours:* Germany Youth.

2005–06	Nottingham F	11	0		
2006–07	Nottingham F	2	0	**13**	**0**
2006–07	*Gillingham*	5	1	**5**	**1**

BENCHERIF, Hamza (D) **0 0**
b.France 9-2-88
Source: Scholar.

2006–07	Nottingham F	0	0		

BENNETT, Julian (D) **99 7**
H: 6 1 W: 13 00 b.Nottingham 17-12-84
Source: Scholar.

2003–04	Walsall	1	0		
2004–05	Walsall	31	2		
2005–06	Walsall	19	1	**51**	**3**
2005–06	Nottingham F	18	2		
2006–07	Nottingham F	30	2	**48**	**4**

BRECKIN, Ian (D) **532 25**
H: 6 2 W: 13 05 b.Rotherham 24-2-75
Source: Trainee.

1993–94	Rotherham U	10	0		
1994–95	Rotherham U	41	2		
1995–96	Rotherham U	39	1		
1996–97	Rotherham U	42	3	**132**	**6**
1997–98	Chesterfield	43	1		
1998–99	Chesterfield	44	2		
1999–2000	Chesterfield	38	1		
2000–01	Chesterfield	45	3		
2001–02	Chesterfield	42	1	**212**	**8**
2002–03	Wigan Ath	9	0		
2003–04	Wigan Ath	45	0		
2004–05	Wigan Ath	42	0	**96**	**0**
2005–06	Nottingham F	46	8		
2006–07	Nottingham F	46	3	**92**	**11**

CHAMBERS, Luke (D) **138 1**
H: 6 1 W: 11 13 b.Kettering 29-8-85
Source: Scholar.

2002–03	Northampton T	1	0		
2003–04	Northampton T	24	0		
2004–05	Northampton T	27	0		
2005–06	Northampton T	43	0		
2006–07	Northampton T	29	1	**124**	**1**
2006–07	Nottingham F	14	0	**14**	**0**

CLINGAN, Sammy (M) **79 3**
H: 5 11 W: 11 06 b.Belfast 13-1-84
Source: Scholar. *Honours:* Northern Ireland Schools, Youth, Under-21, Under-23, 8 full caps.

2001–02	Wolverhampton W	0	0		
2002–03	Wolverhampton W	0	0		
2003–04	Wolverhampton W	0	0		
2004–05	Wolverhampton W	0	0		
2004–05	*Chesterfield*	15	2		
2005–06	Wolverhampton W	0	0		
2005–06	*Chesterfield*	21	1	**36**	**3**
2005–06	Nottingham F	15	0		
2006–07	Nottingham F	28	0	**43**	**0**

COMMONS, Kris (M) **140 28**
H: 5 6 W: 9 08 b.Mansfield 30-8-83
Source: Scholar.

2000–01	Stoke C	0	0		
2001–02	Stoke C	0	0		
2002–03	Stoke C	8	1		
2003–04	Stoke C	33	4	**41**	**5**
2004–05	Nottingham F	30	6		
2005–06	Nottingham F	37	8		
2006–07	Nottingham F	32	9	**99**	**23**

CURTIS, John (D) **227 2**
H: 5 10 W: 11 07 b.Nuneaton 3-9-78
Source: Trainee. *Honours:* England Schools, Youth, Under-21, B.

1995–96	Manchester U	0	0		
1996–97	Manchester U	0	0		
1997–98	Manchester U	8	0		
1998–99	Manchester U	4	0		
1999–2000	Manchester U	1	0	**13**	**0**
1999–2000	*Barnsley*	28	2	**28**	**2**
2000–01	Blackburn R	46	0		
2001–02	Blackburn R	10	0		
2002–03	Blackburn R	5	0	**61**	**0**
2002–03	*Sheffield U*	12	0	**12**	**0**
2003–04	Leicester C	15	0	**15**	**0**
2003–04	Portsmouth	6	0		
2004–05	Portsmouth	1	0	**7**	**0**
2004–05	*Preston NE*	12	0	**12**	**0**
2004–05	Nottingham F	11	0		
2005–06	Nottingham F	27	0		
2006–07	Nottingham F	41	0	**79**	**0**

DOBIE, Scott (F) **307 51**
H: 6 1 W: 12 05 b.Workington 10-10-78
Source: Trainee. *Honours:* Scotland 6 full caps, 1 goal.

1996–97	Carlisle U	2	1		
1997–98	Carlisle U	23	0		
1998–99	Carlisle U	33	6		
1998–99	*Clydebank*	6	0	**6**	**0**
1999–2000	Carlisle U	34	7		
2000–01	Carlisle U	44	10	**136**	**24**
2001–02	WBA	43	10		
2002–03	WBA	31	5		
2003–04	WBA	31	5		
2004–05	WBA	5	1	**110**	**21**
2004–05	Millwall	16	3	**16**	**3**
2004–05	Nottingham F	12	1		
2005–06	Nottingham F	8	2		
2006–07	Nottingham F	19	0	**39**	**3**

EADEN, Nicky (D) **550 13**
H: 5 9 W: 12 02 b.Sheffield 12-12-72
Source: Trainee.

1991–92	Barnsley	0	0		
1992–93	Barnsley	2	0		
1993–94	Barnsley	37	2		
1994–95	Barnsley	45	1		
1995–96	Barnsley	46	2		
1996–97	Barnsley	46	3		
1997–98	Barnsley	35	0		
1998–99	Barnsley	40	1		
1999–2000	Barnsley	42	1	**293**	**10**
2000–01	Birmingham C	45	2		
2001–02	Birmingham C	29	1		
2002–03	Birmingham C	0	0	**74**	**3**
2002–03	Wigan Ath	37	0		
2003–04	Wigan Ath	46	0		
2004–05	Wigan Ath	39	0	**122**	**0**
2005–06	Nottingham F	28	0		
2006–07	Nottingham F	0	0	**28**	**0**
2006–07	*Lincoln C*	33	0	**33**	**0**

FERNANDEZ, Vincent (D) **3 0**
H: 6 3 W: 10 11 b.Marseille 19-9-86
Source: Scholar.

2004–05	Nottingham F	0	0		
2005–06	Nottingham F	1	0		
2006–07	Nottingham F	0	0	**1**	**0**
2006–07	*Wycombe W*	1	0	**1**	**0**
2006–07	*Blackpool*	1	0	**1**	**0**

FRIIO, David (M) **189 40**
H: 6 0 W: 11 05 b.Thionville 17-2-73
Source: Epinal, Nimes, ASOA Valence.

2000–01	Plymouth Arg	26	5		
2001–02	Plymouth Arg	41	8		
2002–03	Plymouth Arg	36	6		
2003–04	Plymouth Arg	36	14		
2004–05	Plymouth Arg	28	6	**167**	**39**
2004–05	Nottingham F	5	0		
2005–06	Nottingham F	17	1		
2006–07	Nottingham F	0	0	**22**	**1**

GAMBLE, Paddy (G) **0 0**
b.Nottingham 1-9-88
Source: Scholar. *Honours:* England Youth.

2005–06	Nottingham F	0	0		
2006–07	Nottingham F	0	0		

HEATH, Joe (D) **0 0**
b.Birkenhead 4-10-88

2005–06	Nottingham F	0	0		
2006–07	Nottingham F	0	0		

HOLT, Gary (M) **385 13**
H: 6 0 W: 12 00 b.Irvine 9-3-73
Source: Celtic. *Honours:* Scotland 10 full caps, 1 goal.

1994–95	Stoke C	0	0		
1995–96	Kilmarnock	26	0		
1996–97	Kilmarnock	12	1		
1997–98	Kilmarnock	27	2		
1998–99	Kilmarnock	33	3		
1999–2000	Kilmarnock	35	0		
2000–01	Kilmarnock	19	3	**152**	**9**
2000–01	Norwich C	4	0		
2001–02	Norwich C	46	2		
2002–03	Norwich C	45	0		
2003–04	Norwich C	46	1		
2004–05	Norwich C	27	0	**168**	**3**
2005–06	Nottingham F	26	0		
2006–07	Nottingham F	39	1	**65**	**1**

HOLT, Grant (F) **169 56**
H: 6 1 W: 14 02 b.Carlisle 12-4-81
Source: Workington.

1999–2000	Halifax T	4	0		
2000–01	Halifax T	2	0	**6**	**0**
From Sengkang, Barrow					
2002–03	Sheffield W	7	1		
2003–04	Sheffield W	17	2	**24**	**3**
2003–04	Rochdale	14	4		
2004–05	Rochdale	40	17		
2005–06	Rochdale	21	14	**75**	**35**
2005–06	Nottingham F	19	4		
2006–07	Nottingham F	45	14	**64**	**18**

HUGHES, Robert (M) **2 0**
H: 5 11 W: 11 04 b.Peterborough 1-10-86
Source: Scholar.

2006–07	Nottingham F	2	0	**2**	**0**

JAMES, Kevin (M) **87 5**
H: 5 7 W: 11 12 b.Southwark 3-1-80
Source: Trainee.

1998–99	Charlton Ath	0	0		
1999–2000	Charlton Ath	0	0		

2000–01	Gillingham	7	0		
2001–02	Gillingham	10	0		
2002–03	Gillingham	15	3		
2003–04	Gillingham	17	1	**49**	**4**
2004–05	Nottingham F	7	0		
2004–05	*Boston U*	6	0	**6**	**0**
2005–06	Nottingham F	0	0	**7**	**0**
2005–06	*Walsall*	15	1	**15**	**1**
2006–07	*Yeovil T*	6	0	**6**	**0**
2006–07	*Grimsby T*	2	0	**2**	**0**
2006–07	*Swindon T*	2	0	**2**	**0**

LESTER, Jack (F) **363 63**
H: 5 9 W: 12 08 b.Sheffield 8-10-75
Source: Trainee. *Honours:* England Schools.

1994–95	Grimsby T	7	0		
1995–96	Grimsby T	5	0		
1996–97	Grimsby T	22	5		
1996–97	*Doncaster R*	11	1	**11**	**1**
1997–98	Grimsby T	40	4		
1998–99	Grimsby T	33	4		
1999–2000	Grimsby T	26	4	**133**	**17**
1999–2000	Nottingham F	15	2		
2000–01	Nottingham F	19	7		
2001–02	Nottingham F	32	5		
2002–03	Nottingham F	33	7		
2003–04	Sheffield U	32	12		
2004–05	Sheffield U	12	0	**44**	**12**
2004–05	Nottingham F	3	1		
2005–06	Nottingham F	38	5		
2006–07	Nottingham F	35	6	**175**	**33**

McGUGAN, Lewis (M) **13 2**
H: 5 9 W: 11 06 b.Long Eaton 25-10-88
Source: Scholar.

2006–07	Nottingham F	13	2	**13**	**2**

MOLONEY, Brendan (M) **1 0**
H: 6 1 W: 11 12 b.Killarney 18-1-89
Source: Scholar.

2005–06	Nottingham F	0	0		
2006–07	Nottingham F	1	0	**1**	**0**

MORGAN, Wes (D) **161 6**
H: 6 2 W: 14 00 b.Nottingham 21-1-84
Source: Scholar.

2002–03	Nottingham F	0	0		
2002–03	*Kidderminster H*	5	1	**5**	**1**
2003–04	Nottingham F	32	2		
2004–05	Nottingham F	43	1		
2005–06	Nottingham F	43	2		
2006–07	Nottingham F	38	0	**156**	**5**

NEWBOLD, Adam (F) **0 0**
b.Nottingham 16-11-89
Source: Scholar.

2006–07	Nottingham F	0	0		

PADULA, Gino (D) **122 4**
H: 5 9 W: 12 11 b.Buenos Aires 11-7-76
Source: Xerex.

1999–2000	Bristol R	0	0		
1999–2000	Walsall	25	0	**25**	**0**
2000–01	Wigan Ath	4	0		
2001–02	Wigan Ath	0	0	**4**	**0**
2002–03	QPR	21	1		
2003–04	QPR	36	3		
2004–05	QPR	33	0	**90**	**4**
2005–06	Nottingham F	3	0		
2006–07	Nottingham F	0	0	**3**	**0**

To Montpellier January 2007

PEDERSEN, Rune (G) **58 0**
H: 6 3 W: 13 08 b.Rigshospitalet 9-10-79
Source: Hvidovre. *Honours:* Denmark Youth, Under-21.

1999–2000	FC Copenhagen	0	0		
2000–01	FC Copenhagen	16	0		
2001–02	FC Copenhagen	2	0		
2002–03	FC Copenhagen	14	0	**32**	**0**
2003–04	Aarhus	7	0	**7**	**0**
2005–06	Nottingham F	18	0		
2006–07	Nottingham F	1	0	**19**	**0**

PERCH, James (D) **106 8**
H: 5 11 W: 11 05 b.Mansfield 29-9-85
Source: Scholar.

2002–03	Nottingham F	0	0		
2003–04	Nottingham F	0	0		
2004–05	Nottingham F	22	0		
2005–06	Nottingham F	38	3		
2006–07	Nottingham F	46	5	**106**	**8**

POWER, Alan (M) **0 0**
H: 5 7 W: 11 06 b.Dublin 23-1-88
Source: Scholar.

2005–06	Nottingham F	0	0		
2006–07	Nottingham F	0	0		

REDMOND, Shane (G) **0 0**
b.Dublin 23-3-89
Source: Scholar.

2006–07	Nottingham F	0	0		

ROBERTS, Dale (M) **0 0**
H: 6 3 W: 11 06 b.Horden 22-10-86
Source: Scholar.

2005–06	Nottingham F	0	0		
2006–07	Nottingham F	0	0		

SMITH, Paul (G) **147 0**
H: 6 3 W: 14 00 b.Epsom 17-12-79

1998–99	Charlton Ath	0	0		
1998–99	*Brentford*	0	0		
1999–2000	Charlton Ath	0	0		

From Carshalton Ath.

2000–01	Brentford	2	0		
2001–02	Brentford	18	0		
2002–03	Brentford	43	0		
2003–04	Brentford	24	0	**87**	**0**
2003–04	Southampton	0	0		
2004–05	Southampton	6	0		
2005–06	Southampton	9	0	**15**	**0**
2006–07	Nottingham F	45	0	**45**	**0**

STAPLES, Reece (M) **0 0**
b.Nottingham 10-9-89
Source: Scholar.

2006–07	Nottingham F	0	0		

THOMPSON, John (D) **141 7**
H: 6 0 W: 12 01 b.Dublin 12-10-81
Source: From Home Farm. *Honours:* Eire Youth, Under-21, 1 full cap.

1999–2000	Nottingham F	0	0		
2000–01	Nottingham F	0	0		
2001–02	Nottingham F	8	0		
2002–03	Nottingham F	20	3		
2003–04	Nottingham F	32	1		
2004–05	Nottingham F	20	0		
2005–06	Nottingham F	35	3		
2006–07	Nottingham F	14	0	**129**	**7**
2006–07	*Tranmere R*	12	0	**12**	**0**

TYSON, Nathan (F) **182 62**
H: 5 10 W: 10 02 b.Reading 4-5-82
Source: Trainee. *Honours:* England Under-20.

1999–2000	Reading	1	0		
2000–01	Reading	0	0		
2001–02	Reading	1	0		
2001–02	*Swansea C*	11	1	**11**	**1**
2001–02	*Cheltenham T*	8	1	**8**	**1**
2002–03	Reading	23	1		
2003–04	Reading	8	0	**33**	**1**
2003–04	Wycombe W	21	9		
2004–05	Wycombe W	42	22		
2005–06	Wycombe W	15	11	**78**	**42**
2005–06	Nottingham F	28	10		
2006–07	Nottingham F	24	7	**52**	**17**

WEIR-DALEY, Spencer (F) **30 9**
H: 5 9 W: 10 11 b.Leicester 5-9-85
Source: Scholar.

2003–04	Nottingham F	0	0		
2004–05	Nottingham F	0	0		
2005–06	Nottingham F	6	1		
2006–07	Nottingham F	1	0	**7**	**1**
2006–07	*Macclesfield T*	7	2	**7**	**2**
2006–07	*Lincoln C*	11	5	**11**	**5**
2006–07	*Bradford C*	5	1	**5**	**1**

NOTTS CO (59)

AKERS, Steven (M) **0 0**
H: 5 7 W: 10 07 b.Worksop 26-9-89
Source: Scholar.

2006–07	Notts Co	0	0		

CURTIS, Tom (M) **400 13**
H: 5 8 W: 11 12 b.Exeter 1-3-73
Source: School.

1991–92	Derby Co	0	0		
1992–93	Derby Co	0	0		
1993–94	Chesterfield	36	3		
1994–95	Chesterfield	40	2		
1995–96	Chesterfield	46	0		
1996–97	Chesterfield	40	3		
1997–98	Chesterfield	36	1		
1998–99	Chesterfield	24	3		
1999–2000	Chesterfield	18	0	**240**	**12**
2000–01	Portsmouth	4	0		
2001–02	Portsmouth	9	0		
2001–02	*Walsall*	4	0	**4**	**0**
2002–03	Portsmouth	0	0	**13**	**0**
2002–03	*Tranmere R*	8	0	**8**	**0**
2002–03	Mansfield T	23	0		
2003–04	Mansfield T	38	0		
2004–05	Mansfield T	32	0	**93**	**0**
2005–06	Chester C	40	1	**40**	**1**
2006–07	Notts Co	2	0	**2**	**0**

DEENEY, Saul (G) **49 0**
H: 6 0 W: 12 13 b.Londonderry 12-3-83
Source: Scholar. *Honours:* Eire Youth, Under-21.

2000–01	Notts Co	0	0		
2001–02	Notts Co	0	0		
2002–03	Notts Co	7	0		
2003–04	Notts Co	3	0		
2004–05	Notts Co	32	0		
2005–06	Notts Co	0	0		
2006–07	Notts Co	7	0	**49**	**0**

DUDFIELD, Lawrie (F) **239 42**
H: 6 1 W: 13 05 b.Southwark 7-5-80
Source: Kettering T.

1997–98	Leicester C	0	0		
1998–99	Leicester C	0	0		
1999–2000	Leicester C	2	0		
2000–01	Leicester C	0	0	**2**	**0**
2000–01	*Lincoln C*	3	0	**3**	**0**
2000–01	*Chesterfield*	14	3	**14**	**3**
2001–02	Hull C	38	12		
2002–03	Hull C	21	1	**59**	**13**
2002–03	Northampton T	10	1		
2003–04	Northampton T	19	3		
2003–04	Southend U	13	5		
2004–05	Southend U	36	4	**49**	**9**
2005–06	Northampton T	6	1	**35**	**5**
2005–06	Boston U	36	5	**36**	**5**
2006–07	Notts Co	41	7	**41**	**7**

EDWARDS, Mike (D) **316 17**
H: 6 0 W: 12 10 b.Hessle 25-4-80
Source: Trainee.

1997–98	Hull C	21	0		
1998–99	Hull C	30	0		
1999–2000	Hull C	40	1		
2000–01	Hull C	42	4		
2001–02	Hull C	39	1		
2002–03	Hull C	6	0	**178**	**6**
2002–03	Colchester U	5	0	**5**	**0**
2003–04	Grimsby T	33	1	**33**	**1**
2004–05	Notts Co	9	0		
2005–06	Notts Co	46	7		
2006–07	Notts Co	45	3	**100**	**10**

FROST, Stef (M) **4 0**
H: 6 2 W: 11 05 b.Nottingham 3-7-89
Source: Scholar.

2005–06	Notts Co	4	0		
2006–07	Notts Co	0	0	**4**	**0**

GLEESON, Dan (M) **54 0**
H: 6 3 W: 13 02 b.Cambridge 17-2-85
Source: Scholar.

2003–04	Cambridge U	7	0		
2004–05	Cambridge U	30	0		
2005–06	Cambridge U	0	0	**37**	**0**
2006–07	Notts Co	17	0	**17**	**0**

HUNT, Stephen (D) **54 2**
H: 6 2 W: 13 00 b.Southampton 11-11-84
Source: Southampton Scholar.

2004–05	Colchester U	20	1		
2005–06	Colchester U	2	0	**22**	**1**
2006–07	Notts Co	32	1	**32**	**1**

LEE, Jason (F) **488 106**
H: 6 3 W: 13 08 b.Forest Gate 9-5-71
Source: Trainee.

1989–90	Charlton Ath	1	0		
1990–91	Charlton Ath	0	0		
1990–91	*Stockport Co*	2	0	**2**	**0**
1990–91	Lincoln C	17	3		
1991–92	Lincoln C	35	6		
1992–93	Lincoln C	41	12	**93**	**21**
1993–94	Southend U	24	3	**24**	**3**
1993–94	Nottingham F	13	2		
1994–95	Nottingham F	22	3		
1995–96	Nottingham F	28	8		
1996–97	Nottingham F	13	1	**76**	**14**
1996–97	*Charlton Ath*	8	3	**9**	**3**
1996–97	*Grimsby T*	7	1	**7**	**1**
1997–98	Watford	36	10		
1998–99	Watford	1	1	**37**	**11**
1998–99	Chesterfield	22	1		
1999–2000	Chesterfield	6	0	**28**	**1**
1999–2000	Peterborough U	23	6		
2000–01	Peterborough U	30	8		
2001–02	Peterborough U	0	0		
2002–03	Peterborough U	25	3	**78**	**17**
2003–04	Falkirk	29	8	**29**	**8**
2004–05	Boston U	39	9		
2005–06	Boston U	17	2	**56**	**11**
2005–06	Northampton T	11	1	**11**	**1**
2006–07	Notts Co	38	15	**38**	**15**

MARTIN, Dan (D) **51 8**
H: 6 1 W: 12 13 b.Derby 27-9-86
Source: Scholar. *Honours:* Wales Under-21.

2004–05	Derby Co	0	0		
2005–06	Notts Co	22	4		
2006–07	Notts Co	29	4	**51**	**8**

McCANN, Austin (D) **262 9**
H: 5 9 W: 11 13 b.Alexandria 21-1-80
Source: Wolverhampton W Trainee.

1997–98	Airdrieonians	14	0		
1998–99	Airdrieonians	31	4		
1999–2000	Airdrieonians	29	2		
2000–01	Airdrieonians	20	1	**94**	**7**
2000–01	Hearts	10	0		
2001–02	Hearts	6	0		
2002–03	Hearts	17	1		
2003–04	Hearts	6	0	**39**	**1**
2003–04	Clyde	6	0	**6**	**0**
2004–05	Boston U	45	1		
2005–06	Boston U	35	0	**80**	**1**
2006–07	Notts Co	43	0	**43**	**0**

McMAHON, Lewis (M) **61 2**
H: 5 9 W: 10 10 b.Doncaster 2-5-85
Source: Scholar.

2003–04	Sheffield W	10	0		
2004–05	Sheffield W	15	2	**25**	**2**
2005–06	Notts Co	29	0		
2006–07	Notts Co	7	0	**36**	**0**

MENDES, Junior (F) **316 52**
H: 5 10 W: 11 00 b.Balham 15-9-76
Source: Trainee. *Honours:* Montserrat full caps.

1995–96	Chelsea	0	0		
1995–96	St Mirren	0	0		
1996–97	St Mirren	36	3		
1997–98	St Mirren	29	9		
1998–99	St Mirren	22	4		
1998–99	*Carlisle U*	6	1	**6**	**1**
1999–2000	St Mirren	33	5		
2000–01	Dunfermline Ath	13	0	**13**	**0**
2001–02	Rushden & D	0	0		
2002–03	St Mirren	17	6	**137**	**27**
2002–03	Mansfield T	18	1		
2003–04	Mansfield T	39	11	**57**	**12**
2004–05	Huddersfield T	25	5		
2005–06	Huddersfield T	5	0	**30**	**5**
2005–06	*Northampton T*	12	2	**12**	**2**
2005–06	*Grimsby T*	15	0	**15**	**0**
2006–07	Notts Co	37	5	**37**	**5**
2006–07	*Lincoln C*	9	0	**9**	**0**

N'TOYA, Tcham (F) **77 13**
H: 5 11 W: 12 11 b.Kinshasa 3-11-83
Source: Troyes.

2003–04	Chesterfield	6	0		
2004–05	Chesterfield	38	8		
2005–06	Chesterfield	4	0	**48**	**8**
2005–06	*Oxford U*	8	4	**8**	**4**
2006–07	Notts Co	21	1	**21**	**1**

NEEDHAM, Liam (M) **23 0**
H: 6 1 W: 12 02 b.Sheffield 19-10-85
Source: Scholar.

2004–05	Sheffield W	0	0		
From Gainsborough T.					
2005–06	Notts Co	22	0		
2006–07	Notts Co	1	0	**23**	**0**

PARKINSON, Andy (F) **315 38**
H: 5 8 W: 10 12 b.Liverpool 27-5-79
Source: Liverpool Trainee.

1996–97	Tranmere R	0	0		
1997–98	Tranmere R	18	1		
1998–99	Tranmere R	29	2		
1999–2000	Tranmere R	37	7		
2000–01	Tranmere R	39	6		
2001–02	Tranmere R	31	2		
2002–03	Tranmere R	10	0	**164**	**18**
2003–04	Sheffield U	7	0	**7**	**0**
2003–04	*Notts Co*	14	3		
2004–05	Grimsby T	45	8		
2005–06	Grimsby T	40	4	**85**	**12**
2006–07	Notts Co	45	5	**59**	**8**

PILKINGTON, Kevin (G) **303 0**
H: 6 1 W: 13 00 b.Hitchin 8-3-74
Source: Trainee. *Honours:* England Schools.

1992–93	Manchester U	0	0		
1993–94	Manchester U	0	0		
1994–95	Manchester U	1	0		
1995–96	Manchester U	3	0		
1995–96	*Rochdale*	6	0	**6**	**0**
1996–97	Manchester U	0	0		
1996–97	*Rotherham U*	17	0	**17**	**0**
1997–98	Manchester U	2	0		
1998–99	Manchester U	0	0	**6**	**0**
1998–99	Port Vale	8	0		
1999–2000	Port Vale	15	0	**23**	**0**
2000–01	Macclesfield T	0	0		
2000–01	Wigan Ath	0	0		
2000–01	Mansfield T	2	0		
2001–02	Mansfield T	45	0		
2002–03	Mansfield T	32	0		
2003–04	Mansfield T	46	0		
2004–05	Mansfield T	42	0	**167**	**0**
2005–06	Notts Co	45	0		
2006–07	Notts Co	39	0	**84**	**0**

PIPE, David (M) **162 5**
H: 5 9 W: 12 01 b.Caerphilly 5-11-83
Source: Scholar. *Honours:* Wales Under-21, 1 full cap.

2000–01	Coventry C	0	0		
2001–02	Coventry C	0	0		
2002–03	Coventry C	21	1		
2003–04	Coventry C	0	0	**21**	**1**
2003–04	Notts Co	18	0		
2004–05	Notts Co	41	2		
2005–06	Notts Co	43	2		
2006–07	Notts Co	39	0	**141**	**4**

SHERIDAN, Jake (M) **30 1**
H: 5 9 W: 11 06 b.Nottingham 8-7-86
Source: Dunkirk.

2005–06	Notts Co	27	1		
2006–07	Notts Co	3	0	**30**	**1**

SILK, Gary (M) **66 0**
H: 5 9 W: 13 07 b.Newport (IW) 13-9-84
Source: Scholar.

2003–04	Portsmouth	0	0		
2004–05	Portsmouth	0	0		
2004–05	*Wycombe W*	22	0	**22**	**0**
2005–06	Portsmouth	0	0		
2005–06	*Boston U*	14	0	**14**	**0**
2006–07	Notts Co	30	0	**30**	**0**

SMITH, Jay (M) **95 11**
H: 5 7 W: 12 00 b.Lambeth 24-9-81
Source: Scholar.

2000–01	Aston Villa	0	0		
2001–02	Aston Villa	0	0		
2002–03	Aston Villa	0	0		
2002–03	Southend U	31	5		
2003–04	Southend U	18	1		
2004–05	Southend U	0	0		
2005–06	Southend U	13	1		
2005–06	*Oxford U*	6	0	**6**	**0**
2006–07	Southend U	0	0	**62**	**7**
2006–07	Notts Co	27	4	**27**	**4**

SOMNER, Matt (D) **147 2**
H: 6 0 W: 13 00 b.Isleworth 8-12-82
Source: Trainee. *Honours:* Wales Under-21.

2000–01	Brentford	3	0		
2001–02	Brentford	0	0		
2002–03	Brentford	40	1		
2003–04	Brentford	39	0		
2004–05	Brentford	2	0	**84**	**1**
2004–05	Cambridge U	24	0	**24**	**0**
2005–06	Bristol R	1	0	**1**	**0**
From Aldershot T.					
2006–07	Notts Co	38	1	**38**	**1**

WHITE, Alan (D) **339 19**
H: 6 0 W: 13 04 b.Darlington 22-3-76
Source: Derby Co Schoolboy.

1994–95	Middlesbrough	0	0		
1995–96	Middlesbrough	0	0		
1996–97	Middlesbrough	0	0		
1997–98	Middlesbrough	0	0		
1997–98	Luton T	28	1		
1998–99	Luton T	33	1		
1999–2000	Luton T	19	1	**80**	**3**
1999–2000	*Colchester U*	4	0		
2000–01	Colchester U	32	0		
2001–02	Colchester U	33	3		
2002–03	Colchester U	41	0		
2003–04	Colchester U	33	1	**143**	**4**
2004–05	Leyton Orient	26	0	**26**	**0**
2004–05	Boston U	11	0		
2005–06	Boston U	37	4	**48**	**4**
2006–07	Notts Co	35	5	**35**	**5**
2006–07	*Peterborough U*	7	3	**7**	**3**

WHITLOW, Mike (D) **397 15**
H: 6 0 W: 12 13 b.Northwich 13-1-68
Source: Witton Alb.

1988–89	Leeds U	20	1		
1989–90	Leeds U	29	1		
1990–91	Leeds U	18	1		
1991–92	Leeds U	10	1	**77**	**4**
1991–92	Leicester C	5	0		
1992–93	Leicester C	24	1		
1993–94	Leicester C	31	2		
1994–95	Leicester C	28	2		
1995–96	Leicester C	42	3		
1996–97	Leicester C	17	0		
1997–98	Leicester C	0	0	**147**	**8**
1997–98	Bolton W	13	0		
1998–99	Bolton W	28	0		
1999–2000	Bolton W	37	1		
2000–01	Bolton W	8	1		
2001–02	Bolton W	29	0		
2002–03	Bolton W	17	0	**132**	**2**
2003–04	Sheffield U	17	1	**17**	**1**
2004–05	Notts Co	24	0		
2005–06	Notts Co	0	0		
2006–07	Notts Co	0	0	**24**	**0**

OLDHAM ATH (60)

BAGULEY, Chris (M) **0 0**
H: 5 10 W: 10 09 b.Salford 1-9-87
Source: Trainee.

2006–07	Oldham Ath	0	0		

BARLOW, Matty (F) **10 0**
H: 5 11 W: 10 04 b.Oldham 25-6-87
Source: Scholar.

2003–04	Oldham Ath	1	0		
2004–05	Oldham Ath	9	0		
2005–06	Oldham Ath	0	0		
2006–07	Oldham Ath	0	0	**10**	**0**

BLAYNEY, Alan (G) **53 0**
H: 6 2 W: 13 12 b.Belfast 9-10-81
Source: Scholar. *Honours:* Northern Ireland Under-21, Under-23, 1 full cap.

2001–02	Southampton	0	0		
2002–03	Southampton	0	0		
2002–03	*Stockport Co*	2	0	**2**	**0**
2002–03	*Bournemouth*	2	0	**2**	**0**
2003–04	Southampton	2	0		
2004–05	Southampton	1	0		
2004–05	*Rushden & D*	4	0	**4**	**0**
2004–05	*Brighton & HA*	7	0		
2005–06	Southampton	0	0	**3**	**0**
2005–06	*Brighton & HA*	8	0	**15**	**0**
2005–06	Doncaster R	16	0		

2006–07	Doncaster R	8	0	**24**	**0**
2006–07	Oldham Ath	3	0	**3**	**0**

CHARLTON, Simon (D) 509 6
H: 5 9 W: 12 01 b.Huddersfield 25-10-71
Source: Trainee. *Honours:* FA Schools.

1989–90	Huddersfield T	3	0		
1990–91	Huddersfield T	30	0		
1991–92	Huddersfield T	45	0		
1992–93	Huddersfield T	46	1	**124**	**1**
1993–94	Southampton	33	1		
1994–95	Southampton	25	1		
1995–96	Southampton	26	0		
1996–97	Southampton	27	0		
1997–98	Southampton	3	0	**114**	**2**
1998–99	Birmingham C	28	0		
1997–98	Birmingham C	24	0		
1999–2000	Birmingham C	20	0	**72**	**0**
2000–01	Bolton W	22	0		
2001–02	Bolton W	36	0		
2002–03	Bolton W	31	0		
2003–04	Bolton W	31	0	**120**	**0**
2004–05	Norwich C	24	1		
2005–06	Norwich C	21	1	**45**	**2**
2006–07	Oldham Ath	34	1	**34**	**1**

EARDLEY, Neal (M) 37 2
H: 5 11 W: 11 10 b.Llandudno 6-11-88
Source: Scholar. *Honours:* Wales Under-21.

2005–06	Oldham Ath	1	0		
2006–07	Oldham Ath	36	2	**37**	**2**

EDWARDS, Paul (M) 187 7
H: 5 11 W: 10 12 b.Manchester 1-1-80
Source: Altrincham.

2001–02	Swindon T	20	0	**20**	**0**
2002–03	Wrexham	38	4		
2003–04	Wrexham	41	0	**79**	**4**
2004–05	Blackpool	28	3	**28**	**3**
2005–06	Oldham Ath	34	0		
2006–07	Oldham Ath	26	0	**60**	**0**

GREGAN, Sean (M) 518 18
H: 6 2 W: 14 00 b.Guisborough 29-3-74
Source: Trainee.

1991–92	Darlington	17	0		
1992–93	Darlington	17	1		
1993–94	Darlington	23	1		
1994–95	Darlington	25	2		
1995–96	Darlington	38	0		
1996–97	Darlington	16	0	**136**	**4**
1996–97	Preston NE	21	1		
1997–98	Preston NE	35	2		
1998–99	Preston NE	41	3		
1999–2000	Preston NE	33	3		
2000–01	Preston NE	41	2		
2001–02	Preston NE	41	1	**212**	**12**
2002–03	WBA	36	1		
2003–04	WBA	43	1		
2004–05	WBA	0	0	**79**	**2**
2004–05	Leeds U	35	0		
2005–06	Leeds U	28	0		
2006–07	Leeds U	1	0	**64**	**0**
2006–07	Oldham Ath	27	0	**27**	**0**

HAINING, Will (D) 155 11
H: 6 0 W: 11 02 b.Glasgow 2-10-82
Source: Scholar.

2001–02	Oldham Ath	4	0		
2002–03	Oldham Ath	26	2		
2003–04	Oldham Ath	31	2		
2004–05	Oldham Ath	35	5		
2005–06	Oldham Ath	15	0		
2006–07	Oldham Ath	44	2	**155**	**11**

HALL, Chris (F) 43 1
H: 6 2 W: 11 07 b.Manchester 27-11-86
Source: Scholar.

2003–04	Oldham Ath	1	0		
2004–05	Oldham Ath	6	0		
2005–06	Oldham Ath	17	0		
2006–07	Oldham Ath	19	1	**43**	**1**

LEVER, Chris (D) 0 0
H: 5 11 W: 11 02 b.Oldham 13-2-87
Source: Scholar.

2006–07	Oldham Ath	0	0		

LIDDELL, Andy (F) 523 126
H: 5 7 W: 11 11 b.Leeds 28-6-73
Source: From Trainee. *Honours:* Scotland Under-21.

1990–91	Barnsley	0	0		
1991–92	Barnsley	1	0		
1992–93	Barnsley	21	2		
1993–94	Barnsley	22	1		
1994–95	Barnsley	39	13		
1995–96	Barnsley	43	9		
1996–97	Barnsley	38	8		
1997–98	Barnsley	26	1		
1998–99	Barnsley	8	0	**198**	**34**
1998–99	Wigan Ath	28	10		
1999–2000	Wigan Ath	41	8		
2000–01	Wigan Ath	37	9		
2001–02	Wigan Ath	34	18		
2002–03	Wigan Ath	37	16		
2003–04	Wigan Ath	40	9	**217**	**70**
2004–05	Sheffield U	33	3	**33**	**3**
2005–06	Oldham Ath	29	9		
2006–07	Oldham Ath	46	10	**75**	**19**

LOMAX, Kelvin (D) 19 0
H: 5 11 W: 12 03 b.Bury 12-11-86
Source: Scholar.

2003–04	Oldham Ath	1	0		
2004–05	Oldham Ath	9	0		
2005–06	Oldham Ath	0	0		
2006–07	Oldham Ath	9	0	**19**	**0**

McDONALD, Gary (F) 149 18
H: 6 0 W: 11 06 b.Irvine 10-4-82
Honours: Scotland B.

1999–2000	Kilmarnock	0	0		
2000–01	Kilmarnock	0	0		
2001–02	Kilmarnock	6	0		
2002–03	Kilmarnock	12	2		
2003–04	Kilmarnock	23	3		
2004–05	Kilmarnock	38	3		
2005–06	Kilmarnock	27	3	**106**	**11**
2006–07	Oldham Ath	43	7	**43**	**7**

OWEN, Gareth (D) 90 1
H: 6 1 W: 11 07 b.Stoke 21-9-82
Source: Scholar. *Honours:* Wales Youth.

2001–02	Stoke C	0	0		
2002–03	Stoke C	0	0		
2003–04	Stoke C	3	0		
2003–04	*Oldham Ath*	15	1		
2004–05	Stoke C	2	0	**5**	**0**
2004–05	*Torquay U*	5	0	**5**	**0**
2004–05	*Oldham Ath*	9	0		
2005–06	Oldham Ath	17	0		
2006–07	Oldham Ath	0	0	**41**	**1**
2006–07	*Stockport Co*	39	0	**39**	**0**

PEARSON, Michael (M) 1 0
H: 5 11 W: 11 01 b.Bangor 19-1-88
Source: Scholar.

2006–07	Oldham Ath	1	0	**1**	**0**

POGLIACOMI, Les (G) 280 0
H: 6 4 W: 13 02 b.Sydney 3-5-76
Honours: Australia Schools, Under-20.

1994–95	Marconi Stallions	11	0		
1995–96	Marconi Stallions	1	0		
1996–97	Marconi Stallions	10	0	**22**	**0**
1997–98	Adelaide City	0	0		
1998–99	Wollongong W	22	0		
1999–2000	Wollongong W	34	0	**56**	**0**
2000–01	Parramatta Power	8	0		
2001–02	Parramatta Power	19	0	**27**	**0**
2002–03	Oldham Ath	37	0		
2003–04	Oldham Ath	46	0		
2004–05	Oldham Ath	37	0		
2005–06	Oldham Ath	0	0		
2005–06	Blackpool	15	0	**15**	**0**
2006–07	Oldham Ath	40	0	**160**	**0**

PORTER, Chris (F) 137 46
H: 6 1 W: 12 09 b.Wigan 12-12-83
Source: School.

2002–03	Bury	2	0		
2003–04	Bury	37	9		
2004–05	Bury	32	9	**71**	**18**
2005–06	Oldham Ath	31	7		
2006–07	Oldham Ath	35	21	**66**	**28**

ROCASTLE, Craig (M) 78 3
H: 6 1 W: 13 09 b.Lewisham 17-8-81
Source: Kingstonian.

2003–04	Chelsea	0	0		
2003–04	*Barnsley*	5	0	**5**	**0**
2003–04	*Lincoln C*	2	0	**2**	**0**
2004–05	Chelsea	0	0		
2004–05	Sheffield W	11	1		
2005–06	Sheffield W	17	0	**28**	**1**
2005–06	*Yeovil T*	8	0	**8**	**0**
2006–07	Oldham Ath	35	2	**35**	**2**

SMALLEY, Deane (M) 2 0
H: 6 0 W: 11 10 b.Chadderton 5-9-88
Source: Scholar.

2006–07	Oldham Ath	2	0	**2**	**0**

SMITH, Terry (G) 1 0
H: 6 0 W: 11 00 b.Runcorn 16-9-87
Source: Scholar.

2005–06	Oldham Ath	0	0		
2006–07	Oldham Ath	1	0	**1**	**0**

STAM, Stefan (D) 48 1
H: 6 2 W: 13 02 b.Amersfoort 14-9-79
Honours: Holland Under-21.

2004–05	Oldham Ath	13	0		
2005–06	Oldham Ath	13	0		
2006–07	Oldham Ath	22	1	**48**	**1**

SWAILES, Chris (D) 394 25
H: 6 2 W: 13 09 b.Gateshead 19-10-70
Source: Ipswich T Trainee, Peterborough U, Boston U, Birmingham C, Bridlington T.

1993–94	Doncaster R	17	0		
1994–95	Doncaster R	32	0	**49**	**0**
1995–96	Ipswich T	5	0		
1996–97	Ipswich T	23	1		
1997–98	Ipswich T	5	0	**33**	**1**
1997–98	Bury	13	1		
1998–99	Bury	43	3		
1999–2000	Bury	27	2		
2000–01	Bury	43	4	**126**	**10**
2001–02	Rotherham U	44	6		
2002–03	Rotherham U	43	3		
2003–04	Rotherham U	43	3		
2004–05	Rotherham U	37	2	**167**	**14**
2005–06	Oldham Ath	15	0		
2006–07	Oldham Ath	4	0	**19**	**0**

TAYLOR, Chris (M) 58 4
H: 5 11 W: 11 00 b.Oldham 20-12-86
Source: Scholar.

2005–06	Oldham Ath	14	0		
2006–07	Oldham Ath	44	4	**58**	**4**

TROTMAN, Neal (D) 1 0
H: 6 3 W: 13 08 b.Levenshulme 11-3-87
Source: Burnley Scholar.

2006–07	Oldham Ath	1	0	**1**	**0**

WARNE, Paul (M) 359 50
H: 5 10 W: 11 07 b.Norwich 8-5-73
Source: Wroxham.

1997–98	Wigan Ath	25	2		
1998–99	Wigan Ath	11	1	**36**	**3**
1998–99	Rotherham U	19	8		
1999–2000	Rotherham U	43	10		
2000–01	Rotherham U	44	7		
2001–02	Rotherham U	25	0		
2002–03	Rotherham U	40	1		
2003–04	Rotherham U	35	1		
2004–05	Rotherham U	24	1	**230**	**28**
2004–05	*Mansfield T*	7	1	**7**	**1**
2005–06	Oldham Ath	40	9		
2006–07	Oldham Ath	46	9	**86**	**18**

WELLENS, Richard (M) 275 24
H: 5 9 W: 11 06 b.Manchester 26-3-80
Source: Trainee. *Honours:* England Youth.

1996–97	Manchester U	0	0		
1997–98	Manchester U	0	0		
1998–99	Manchester U	0	0		
1999–2000	Manchester U	0	0		
1999–2000	Blackpool	8	0		
2000–01	Blackpool	36	8		
2001–02	Blackpool	36	1		
2002–03	Blackpool	39	1		
2003–04	Blackpool	41	3		
2004–05	Blackpool	28	3	**188**	**16**

2005–06	Oldham Ath	45	4		
2006–07	Oldham Ath	42	4	**87**	**8**

WOLFENDEN, Matthew (F) **9 0**
H: 5 9 W: 11 02 b.Oldham 23-7-87
Source: Scholar.

2003–04	Oldham Ath	1	0		
2004–05	Oldham Ath	1	0		
2005–06	Oldham Ath	1	0		
2006–07	Oldham Ath	6	0	**9**	**0**

WOOD, Neil (M) **42 2**
H: 5 10 W: 13 02 b.Manchester 4-1-83
Source: Trainee. *Honours:* England Youth.

1999–2000	Manchester U	0	0		
2000–01	Manchester U	0	0		
2001–02	Manchester U	0	0		
2002–03	Manchester U	0	0		
2003–04	Manchester U	0	0		
2003–04	*Peterborough U*	3	1	**3**	**1**
2003–04	*Burnley*	10	1	**10**	**1**
2004–05	Coventry C	13	0		
2005–06	Coventry C	4	0	**17**	**0**
2005–06	Blackpool	7	0	**7**	**0**
2006–07	Oldham Ath	5	0	**5**	**0**

PETERBOROUGH U (61)

ARBER, Mark (D) **309 24**
H: 6 1 W: 11 09 b.Johannesburg 9-10-77
Source: Trainee.

1995–96	Tottenham H	0	0		
1996–97	Tottenham H	0	0		
1997–98	Tottenham H	0	0		
1998–99	Tottenham H	0	0		
1998–99	Barnet	35	2		
1999–2000	Barnet	45	6		
2000–01	Barnet	45	7		
2001–02	Barnet	0	0	**125**	**15**
2002–03	Peterborough U	25	2		
2003–04	Peterborough U	44	3		
2004–05	Oldham Ath	14	1	**14**	**1**
2004–05	Peterborough U	21	0		
2005–06	Peterborough U	46	2		
2006–07	Peterborough U	34	1	**170**	**8**

BENJAMIN, Trevor (F) **324 70**
H: 6 2 W: 13 07 b.Kettering 8-2-79
Source: Trainee. *Honours:* England Under-21, Jamaica 2 full caps.

1995–96	Cambridge U	5	0		
1996–97	Cambridge U	7	1		
1997–98	Cambridge U	25	4		
1998–99	Cambridge U	42	10		
1999–2000	Cambridge U	44	20	**123**	**35**
2000–01	Leicester C	21	1		
2001–02	Leicester C	11	0		
2001–02	*Crystal Palace*	6	1	**6**	**1**
2001–02	*Norwich C*	6	0	**6**	**0**
2001–02	*WBA*	3	1	**3**	**1**
2002–03	Leicester C	35	8		
2003–04	Leicester C	4	0		
2003–04	*Gillingham*	4	1	**4**	**1**
2003–04	*Rushden & D*	6	1	**6**	**1**
2003–04	*Brighton & HA*	10	5	**10**	**5**
2004–05	Leicester C	10	2	**81**	**11**
2004–05	*Northampton T*	5	2	**5**	**2**
2004–05	Coventry C	12	1	**12**	**1**
2005–06	Peterborough U	20	1		
2005–06	*Watford*	2	0	**2**	**0**
2005–06	*Swindon T*	8	2	**8**	**2**
2006–07	Peterborough U	27	7	**47**	**8**
2006–07	*Boston U*	3	0	**3**	**0**
2006–07	*Walsall*	8	2	**8**	**2**

BLACKETT, Shane (D) **13 0**
H: 6 0 W: 12 11 b.Luton 26-6-81
Source: Arlesey, Dagenham & R.

2006–07	Peterborough U	13	0	**13**	**0**

BLANCHETT, Danny (D) **3 1**
H: 5 11 W: 11 12 b.Wembley 12-3-88
Source: Northwood, Hendon, Harrow Borough, Cambridge C.

2006–07	Peterborough U	3	1	**3**	**1**

BOYD, George (M) **20 6**
H: 5 10 W: 11 07 b.Chatham 2-10-85
Source: Stevenage B.

2006–07	Peterborough U	20	6	**20**	**6**

BRANSTON, Guy (D) **235 18**
H: 6 1 W: 15 01 b.Leicester 9-1-79
Source: Trainee.

1997–98	Leicester C	0	0		
1997–98	*Colchester U*	12	1		
1998–99	Leicester C	0	0		
1998–99	*Colchester U*	1	0	**13**	**1**
1998–99	*Plymouth Arg*	7	1	**7**	**1**
1999–2000	Leicester C	0	0		
1999–2000	*Lincoln C*	4	0	**4**	**0**
1999–2000	Rotherham U	30	4		
2000–01	Rotherham U	41	6		
2001–02	Rotherham U	10	1		
2002–03	Rotherham U	15	2		
2003–04	Rotherham U	8	0	**104**	**13**
2003–04	*Wycombe W*	9	0	**9**	**0**
2003–04	*Peterborough U*	14	0		
2004–05	Sheffield W	11	0	**11**	**0**
2004–05	*Peterborough U*	4	1		
2004–05	Oldham Ath	7	1		
2005–06	Oldham Ath	38	1	**45**	**2**
2006–07	Peterborough U	24	0	**42**	**1**

BUTCHER, Richard (M) **187 20**
H: 6 0 W: 13 01 b.Peterborough 22-1-81
Source: Kettering T.

2002–03	Lincoln C	26	3		
2003–04	Lincoln C	32	6		
2004–05	Lincoln C	46	2		
2005–06	Oldham Ath	36	4	**36**	**4**
2005–06	*Lincoln C*	4	1	**108**	**12**
2006–07	Peterborough U	43	4	**43**	**4**

CARDEN, Paul (M) **141 0**
H: 5 9 W: 11 10 b.Liverpool 29-3-79
Source: Trainee.

1996–97	Blackpool	1	0		
1997–98	Blackpool	0	0	**1**	**0**
1997–98	Rochdale	7	0		
1998–99	Rochdale	25	0		
1999–2000	Rochdale	13	0	**45**	**0**
1999–2000	Chester C	11	0		

From Doncaster R.

2004–05	Chester C	40	0	**51**	**0**
2005–06	Peterborough U	42	0		
2006–07	Peterborough U	2	0	**44**	**0**

CROW, Danny (F) **86 23**
H: 5 10 W: 11 00 b.Great Yarmouth 26-1-86
Source: Scholar.

2004–05	Norwich C	3	0	**3**	**0**
2004–05	*Northampton T*	10	2	**10**	**2**
2005–06	Peterborough U	38	15		
2006–07	Peterborough U	35	6	**73**	**21**

DAY, Jamie (M) **50 2**
H: 5 9 W: 10 07 b.Wycombe 7-5-86
Source: Scholar.

2003–04	Peterborough U	0	0		
2004–05	Peterborough U	1	0		
2005–06	Peterborough U	25	1		
2006–07	Peterborough U	24	1	**50**	**2**

FERGUSON, Darren (M) **441 28**
H: 6 0 W: 11 10 b.Glasgow 9-2-72
Source: Trainee. *Honours:* Scotland Youth, Under-21.

1990–91	Manchester U	5	0		
1991–92	Manchester U	4	0		
1992–93	Manchester U	15	0		
1993–94	Manchester U	3	0	**27**	**0**
1993–94	Wolverhampton W	14	0		
1994–95	Wolverhampton W	24	0		
1995–96	Wolverhampton W	33	1		
1996–97	Wolverhampton W	16	3		
1997–98	Wolverhampton W	26	0		
1998–99	Wolverhampton W	4	0		
1999–2000	Wolverhampton W	0	0	**117**	**4**
1999–2000	Wrexham	37	4		
2000–01	Wrexham	43	9		
2001–02	Wrexham	38	3		
2002–03	Wrexham	41	2		
2003–04	Wrexham	39	1		
2004–05	Wrexham	40	3		
2005–06	Wrexham	39	2		
2006–07	Wrexham	20	0	**297**	**24**
2006–07	Peterborough U	0	0		

FUTCHER, Ben (D) **189 18**
H: 6 7 W: 12 05 b.Manchester 20-2-81
Source: Trainee.

1999–2000	Oldham Ath	5	0		
2000–01	Oldham Ath	5	0		
2001–02	Oldham Ath	0	0	**10**	**0**

From Stalybridge C, Doncaster R

2002–03	Lincoln C	43	8		
2003–04	Lincoln C	43	2		
2004–05	Lincoln C	35	3	**121**	**13**
2005–06	Boston U	14	0	**14**	**0**
2005–06	Grimsby T	15	2		
2006–07	Grimsby T	4	0	**19**	**2**
2006–07	Peterborough U	25	3	**25**	**3**

GAIN, Peter (M) **298 30**
H: 5 9 W: 11 07 b.Hammersmith 11-11-76
Source: Trainee.

1995–96	Tottenham H	0	0		
1996–97	Tottenham H	0	0		
1997–98	Tottenham H	0	0		
1998–99	Tottenham H	0	0		
1998–99	Lincoln C	4	0		
1999–2000	Lincoln C	32	2		
2000–01	Lincoln C	24	5		
2001–02	Lincoln C	42	2		
2002–03	Lincoln C	43	5		
2003–04	Lincoln C	42	7		
2004–05	Lincoln C	40	0	**227**	**21**
2005–06	Peterborough U	37	3		
2006–07	Peterborough U	34	6	**71**	**9**

GHAICHEM, Jimmy (M) **2 0**
H: 5 8 W: 12 00 b.Sheffield 11-4-84

2006–07	Peterborough U	2	0	**2**	**0**

HOLDEN, Dean (D) **177 15**
H: 6 1 W: 12 04 b.Salford 15-9-79
Source: Trainee. *Honours:* England Youth.

1997–98	Bolton W	0	0		
1998–99	Bolton W	0	0		
1999–2000	Bolton W	12	0		
2000–01	Bolton W	1	1		
2001–02	Bolton W	0	0	**13**	**1**
2001–02	*Oldham Ath*	23	2		
2002–03	Oldham Ath	6	2		
2003–04	Oldham Ath	39	4		
2004–05	Oldham Ath	40	2	**108**	**10**
2005–06	Peterborough U	35	3		
2006–07	Peterborough U	21	1	**56**	**4**

To Falkirk January 2007

HUKE, Shane (M) **29 1**
H: 5 11 W: 12 07 b.Reading 2-10-85
Source: Scholar.

2003–04	Peterborough U	0	0		
2004–05	Peterborough U	8	0		
2005–06	Peterborough U	3	0		
2006–07	Peterborough U	18	1	**29**	**1**

HYDE, Micah (M) **480 38**
H: 5 10 W: 11 02 b.Newham 10-11-74
Source: Trainee. *Honours:* Jamaica 12 full caps, 1 goal.

1993–94	Cambridge U	18	2		
1994–95	Cambridge U	27	0		
1995–96	Cambridge U	24	4		
1996–97	Cambridge U	38	7	**107**	**13**
1997–98	Watford	40	4		
1998–99	Watford	44	2		
1999–2000	Watford	34	3		
2000–01	Watford	26	6		
2001–02	Watford	39	4		
2002–03	Watford	37	4		
2003–04	Watford	33	1	**253**	**24**
2004–05	Burnley	38	1		
2005–06	Burnley	41	0		
2006–07	Burnley	23	0	**102**	**1**
2006–07	Peterborough U	18	0	**18**	**0**

JALAL, Shwan (G) **1 0**
H: 6 2 W: 14 02 b.Baghdad 14-8-83
Source: Hastings T.

2001–02	Tottenham H	0	0		
2002–03	Tottenham H	0	0		
2003–04	Tottenham H	0	0		

From Woking.

2006–07	*Sheffield W*	0	0		
2006–07	Peterborough U	1	0	**1**	**0**

LOW, Josh (M) 260 26
H: 6 2 W: 14 03 b.Bristol 15-2-79
Source: Trainee. *Honours:* Wales Youth, Under-21.

1995–96	Bristol R	1	0		
1996–97	Bristol R	3	0		
1997–98	Bristol R	10	0		
1998–99	Bristol R	8	0	**22**	**0**
1999–2000	Leyton Orient	5	1	**5**	**1**
1999–2000	Cardiff C	17	2		
2000–01	Cardiff C	36	4		
2001–02	Cardiff C	22	0		
2002–03	Cardiff C	0	0	**75**	**6**
2002–03	Oldham Ath	21	3	**21**	**3**
2003–04	Northampton T	33	3		
2004–05	Northampton T	34	7		
2005–06	Northampton T	35	5	**102**	**15**
2006–07	Leicester C	16	0	**16**	**0**
2006–07	Peterborough U	19	1	**19**	**1**

MACKAIL-SMITH, Craig (F) 15 8
H: 6 3 W: 12 04 b.Hertford 25-2-84
Source: Dagenham & R.

2006–07	Peterborough U	15	8	**15**	**8**

McLEAN, Aaron (F) 56 9
H: 5 9 W: 10 10 b.Hammersmith 25-5-83
Source: Trainee.

1999–2000	Leyton Orient	3	0		
2000–01	Leyton Orient	2	1		
2001–02	Leyton Orient	27	1		
2002–03	Leyton Orient	8	0	**40**	**2**

From Aldershot T, Grays Ath.

2006–07	Peterborough U	16	7	**16**	**7**

MORGAN, Craig (D) 119 2
H: 6 0 W: 11 04 b.St Asaph 18-6-85
Source: Scholar. *Honours:* Wales Youth, Under-21, 1 full cap.

2001–02	Wrexham	2	0		
2002–03	Wrexham	6	1		
2003–04	Wrexham	18	0		
2004–05	Wrexham	26	0		
2005–06	Milton Keynes D	40	0		
2006–07	Milton Keynes D	3	0	**43**	**0**
2006–07	*Wrexham*	1	0	**53**	**1**
2006–07	Peterborough U	23	1	**23**	**1**

NEWTON, Adam (M) 221 10
H: 5 10 W: 11 00 b.Ascot 4-12-80
Source: West Ham U Trainee. *Honours:* England Under-21. St Kitts & Nevis 2 full caps, 1 goal.

1999–2000	West Ham U	2	0		
1999–2000	*Portsmouth*	3	0	**3**	**0**
2000–01	West Ham U	0	0		
2000–01	*Notts Co*	20	1	**20**	**1**
2001–02	West Ham U	0	0	**2**	**0**
2001–02	*Leyton Orient*	10	1	**10**	**1**
2002–03	Peterborough U	36	2		
2003–04	Peterborough U	37	2		
2004–05	Peterborough U	30	0		
2005–06	Peterborough U	40	3		
2006–07	Peterborough U	43	1	**186**	**8**

OPARA, Lloyd (F) 35 3
H: 6 1 W: 12 08 b.Enfield 6-1-84
Source: Scholar.

2001–02	Colchester U	1	0		
2002–03	Colchester U	5	0	**6**	**0**
2002–03	Cambridge U	2	0		
2003–04	Cambridge U	8	1	**10**	**1**

From Grays Ath.

2004–05	Swindon T	0	0		

From Cheshunt.

2005–06	Peterborough U	8	1		
2006–07	Peterborough U	11	1	**19**	**2**

PLUMMER, Chris (D) 114 3
H: 6 2 W: 13 08 b.Isleworth 12-10-76
Source: Trainee. *Honours:* England Youth, Under-21.

1994–95	QPR	0	0		
1995–96	QPR	1	0		
1996–97	QPR	5	0		
1997–98	QPR	0	0		
1998–99	QPR	10	0		
1999–2000	QPR	18	0		
2000–01	QPR	25	2		
2001–02	QPR	1	0		
2002–03	QPR	2	0		
2002–03	*Bristol R*	2	0	**2**	**0**
2003–04	QPR	0	0		
2004–05	QPR	0	0	**62**	**2**
2004–05	Peterborough U	21	0		
2005–06	Peterborough U	22	1		
2006–07	Peterborough U	7	0	**50**	**1**

RICHARDS, Justin (F) 35 1
H: 5 11 W: 11 00 b.Sandwell 16-10-80
Source: Trainee.

1998–99	WBA	1	0		
1999–2000	WBA	0	0		
2000–01	WBA	0	0	**1**	**0**
2000–01	Bristol R	7	0		
2001–02	Bristol R	1	0		
2002–03	Bristol R	8	0	**16**	**0**
2002–03	*Colchester U*	2	0	**2**	**0**

From Stevenage B, Woking.

2006–07	Peterborough U	13	1	**13**	**1**
2006–07	*Boston U*	3	0	**3**	**0**

SMITH, Adam (D) 9 1
H: 5 7 W: 10 05 b.Lingwood 11-9-85
From Kings Lynn.

2006–07	Peterborough U	9	1	**9**	**1**

STRACHAN, Gavin (M) 129 10
H: 5 10 W: 11 07 b.Aberdeen 23-12-78
Source: Trainee. *Honours:* Scotland Youth, Under-21.

1996–97	Coventry C	0	0		
1997–98	Coventry C	9	0		
1998–99	Coventry C	0	0		
1998–99	*Dundee*	6	0	**6**	**0**
1999–2000	Coventry C	3	0		
2000–01	Coventry C	2	0		
2001–02	Coventry C	1	0		
2002–03	Coventry C	1	0	**16**	**0**
2002–03	*Peterborough U*	2	0		
2002–03	Southend U	7	0	**7**	**0**
2003–04	Hartlepool U	36	5		
2004–05	Hartlepool U	29	1		
2005–06	Hartlepool U	9	1		
2005–06	*Stockport Co*	4	0	**4**	**0**
2006–07	Hartlepool U	4	0	**78**	**7**
2006–07	Peterborough U	16	3	**18**	**3**

TYLER, Mark (G) 396 0
H: 6 0 W: 12 09 b.Norwich 2-4-77
Source: Trainee. *Honours:* England Youth, Under-20.

1994–95	Peterborough U	5	0		
1995–96	Peterborough U	0	0		
1996–97	Peterborough U	3	0		
1997–98	Peterborough U	46	0		
1998–99	Peterborough U	27	0		
1999–2000	Peterborough U	32	0		
2000–01	Peterborough U	40	0		
2001–02	Peterborough U	44	0		
2002–03	Peterborough U	29	0		
2003–04	Peterborough U	43	0		
2004–05	Peterborough U	46	0		
2005–06	Peterborough U	40	0		
2006–07	Peterborough U	41	0	**396**	**0**

WHELPDALE, Chris (M) 0 0
b.Harold Wood 27-1-87
Source: Billericay T.

2006–07	Peterborough U	0	0		

WHELPDALE, Chris (M) 0 0
Source: Billericay T.

2006–07	Peterborough U	0	0		

PLYMOUTH ARG (62)

ALJOFREE, Hasney (D) 191 7
H: 6 0 W: 12 00 b.Manchester 11-7-78
Source: Trainee.

1996–97	Bolton W	0	0		
1997–98	Bolton W	2	0		
1998–98	Bolton W	4	0		
1999–2000	Bolton W	8	0	**14**	**0**
2000–01	Dundee U	26	2		
2001–02	Dundee U	27	2	**53**	**4**
2002–03	Plymouth Arg	19	1		
2003–04	Plymouth Arg	24	0		
2004–05	Plymouth Arg	12	1		
2004–05	*Sheffield W*	2	0	**2**	**0**
2005–06	Plymouth Arg	37	1		
2006–07	Plymouth Arg	25	0	**117**	**3**
2006–07	*Oldham Ath*	5	0	**5**	**0**

BARNES, Ashley (F) 0 0
H: 6 0 W: 12 00 b.Bath 30-10-89
Source: Paulton R.

2006–07	Plymouth Arg	0	0		

BARNESS, Anthony (D) 272 4
H: 5 10 W: 13 01 b.Lewisham 25-3-73
Source: Trainee.

1990–91	Charlton Ath	0	0		
1991–92	Charlton Ath	22	1		
1992–93	Charlton Ath	5	0		
1992–93	Chelsea	2	0		
1993–94	Chelsea	0	0		
1993–94	*Middlesbrough*	0	0		
1994–95	Chelsea	12	0		
1995–96	Chelsea	0	0	**14**	**0**
1995–96	*Southend U*	5	0	**5**	**0**
1996–97	Charlton Ath	45	2		
1997–98	Charlton Ath	29	1		
1998–99	Charlton Ath	3	0		
1999–2000	Charlton Ath	19	0	**123**	**4**
2000–01	Bolton W	20	0		
2001–02	Bolton W	25	0		
2002–03	Bolton W	25	0		
2003–04	Bolton W	15	0		
2004–05	Bolton W	8	0	**93**	**0**
2005–06	Plymouth Arg	36	0		
2006–07	Plymouth Arg	1	0	**37**	**0**

BUZSAKY, Akos (M) 85 8
H: 5 11 W: 11 09 b.Hungary 7-5-82
Source: MTK, Porto. *Honours:* Hungary Under-21, 3 full caps.

2004–05	Plymouth Arg	15	1		
2005–06	Plymouth Arg	34	4		
2006–07	Plymouth Arg	36	3	**85**	**8**

CAPALDI, Tony (M) 141 12
H: 6 0 W: 11 08 b.Porsgrunn 12-8-81
Source: Trainee. *Honours:* Northern Ireland Youth, Under-21, 21 full caps.

1999–2000	Birmingham C	0	0		
2000–01	Birmingham C	0	0		
2001–02	Birmingham C	0	0		
2002–03	Birmingham C	0	0		
2002–03	Plymouth Arg	1	0		
2003–04	Plymouth Arg	33	7		
2004–05	Plymouth Arg	35	2		
2005–06	Plymouth Arg	41	3		
2006–07	Plymouth Arg	31	0	**141**	**12**

CHADWICK, Nick (F) 103 15
H: 6 0 W: 12 08 b.Market Drayton 26-10-82
Source: Scholar.

1999–2000	Everton	0	0		
2000–01	Everton	0	0		
2001–02	Everton	9	3		
2002–03	Everton	1	0		
2002–03	*Derby Co*	6	0	**6**	**0**
2003–04	Everton	3	0		
2003–04	*Millwall*	15	4	**15**	**4**
2004–05	Everton	1	0	**14**	**3**
2004–05	Plymouth Arg	15	1		
2005–06	Plymouth Arg	37	5		
2006–07	Plymouth Arg	16	2	**68**	**8**

CLAPHAM, Josh (G) 0 0
H: 6 5 W: 13 00 b.Bristol 6-8-84
Source: Plymouth Univ.

2006–07	Plymouth Arg	0	0		

CONNOLLY, Paul (D) 120 0
H: 6 0 W: 11 09 b.Liverpool 29-9-83
Source: Scholar.

2000–01	Plymouth Arg	1	0		
2001–02	Plymouth Arg	0	0		
2002–03	Plymouth Arg	2	0		
2003–04	Plymouth Arg	29	0		
2004–05	Plymouth Arg	19	0		
2005–06	Plymouth Arg	31	0		
2006–07	Plymouth Arg	38	0	**120**	**0**

DICKSON, Ryan (M) 14 1
H: 5 10 W: 11 05 b.Saltash 14-12-86
Source: Scholar.

2004–05	Plymouth Arg	3	0		
2005–06	Plymouth Arg	0	0		
2006–07	Plymouth Arg	2	0	**5**	**0**
2006–07	*Torquay U*	9	1	**9**	**1**

DJORDJIC, Bojan (M) 68 4
H: 5 10 W: 11 01 b.Belgrade 6-2-82
Honours: Sweden Under-21.

1998–99	Manchester U	0	0		
1999–2000	Manchester U	0	0		
2000–01	Manchester U	1	0		
2001–02	Manchester U	0	0		
2001–02	*Sheffield W*	5	0	**5**	**0**
2002–03	Manchester U	0	0		
2003–04	*Red St Belgrade*	19	0	**19**	**0**
2004–05	Manchester U	0	0	**1**	**0**
2004–05	Rangers	4	0	**4**	**0**
2005–06	Plymouth Arg	22	1		
2006–07	Plymouth Arg	17	3	**39**	**4**

DOUMBE, Stephen (D) 143 5
H: 6 1 W: 12 05 b.Paris 28-10-79
Source: Paris St Germain. *Honours:* France Youth.

2001–02	Hibernian	0	0		
2002–03	Hibernian	12	0		
2003–04	Hibernian	33	2	**45**	**2**
2004–05	Plymouth Arg	26	2		
2005–06	Plymouth Arg	43	1		
2006–07	Plymouth Arg	29	0	**98**	**3**

EBANKS-BLAKE, Sylvan (F) 41 10
H: 5 10 W: 13 04 b.Cambridge 29-3-86
Source: Scholar.

2004–05	Manchester U	0	0		
2005–06	Manchester U	0	0		
2006–07	Plymouth Arg	41	10	**41**	**10**

FALLON, Rory (F) 200 46
H: 6 2 W: 11 09 b.Gisbourne 20-3-82
Source: North Shore U. *Honours:* England Youth.

1998–99	Barnsley	0	0		
1999–2000	Barnsley	0	0		
2000–01	Barnsley	1	0		
2001–02	Barnsley	9	0		
2001–02	*Shrewsbury T*	11	0	**11**	**0**
2002–03	Barnsley	26	7		
2003–04	Barnsley	16	4	**52**	**11**
2003–04	Swindon T	19	6		
2004–05	Swindon T	31	3		
2004–05	*Yeovil T*	6	1	**6**	**1**
2005–06	Swindon T	25	12	**75**	**21**
2005–06	Swansea C	17	4		
2006–07	Swansea C	24	8	**41**	**12**
2006–07	Plymouth Arg	15	1	**15**	**1**

GOSLING, Dan (M) 12 2
H: 6 0 W: 11 00 b.Brixham 2-2-90
Source: Scholar. *Honours:* England Youth.

2006–07	Plymouth Arg	12	2	**12**	**2**

HALMOSI, Peter (M) 210 31
H: 5 10 W: 10 12 b.Szombathely 25-9-79
Honours: Hungary 11 full caps.

1998–99	Haladas	2	0		
1999–2000	Haladas	26	2		
2000–01	Haladas	14	2		
2001–02	Haladas	38	2	**80**	**6**
2002–03	Graz	17	3	**17**	**3**
2003–04	Debrecen	29	5		
2004–05	Debrecen	28	5		
2005–06	Debrecen	26	7		
2006–07	Debrecen	14	1	**97**	**18**
2006–07	Plymouth Arg	16	4	**16**	**4**

HAYLES, Barry (F) 335 105
H: 5 10 W: 12 11 b.Lambeth 17-5-72
Source: Stevenage Bor. *Honours:* Jamaica 10 full caps.

1997–98	Bristol R	45	23		
1998–99	Bristol R	17	9	**62**	**32**
1998–99	Fulham	30	8		
1999–2000	Fulham	35	5		
2000–01	Fulham	35	18		
2001–02	Fulham	35	8		
2002–03	Fulham	14	1		
2003–04	Fulham	26	4	**175**	**44**
2004–05	Sheffield U	4	0	**4**	**0**
2004–05	Millwall	32	12		
2005–06	Millwall	23	4	**55**	**16**
2006–07	Plymouth Arg	39	13	**39**	**13**

HODGES, Lee (M) 367 49
H: 6 0 W: 12 01 b.Epping 4-9-73
Source: Trainee.

1991–92	Tottenham H	0	0		
1992–93	Tottenham H	4	0		
1992–93	*Plymouth Arg*	7	2		
1993–94	Tottenham H	0	0	**4**	**0**
1993–94	*Wycombe W*	4	0	**4**	**0**
1994–95	Barnet	34	4		
1995–96	Barnet	40	17		
1996–97	Barnet	31	5	**105**	**26**
1997–98	Reading	24	6		
1998–99	Reading	1	0		
1999–2000	Reading	25	2		
2000–01	Reading	29	2		
2001–02	Reading	0	0	**79**	**10**
2001–02	Plymouth Arg	45	6		
2002–03	Plymouth Arg	39	2		
2003–04	Plymouth Arg	37	3		
2004–05	Plymouth Arg	19	0		
2005–06	Plymouth Arg	13	0		
2006–07	Plymouth Arg	15	0	**175**	**13**

LAIRD, Scott (D) 0 0
H: 5 11 W: 11 05 b.Taunton 15-5-88
Source: Scholar.

2006–07	Plymouth Arg	0	0		

LARRIEU, Romain (G) 197 0
H: 6 4 W: 13 01 b.Mont-de-Marsan 31-8-76
Source: Montpellier, ASOA Valence.
Honours: France Youth.

2000–01	Plymouth Arg	15	0		
2001–02	Plymouth Arg	45	0		
2002–03	Plymouth Arg	43	0		
2003–04	Plymouth Arg	6	0		
2004–05	Plymouth Arg	23	0		
2005–06	Plymouth Arg	45	0		
2006–07	Plymouth Arg	6	0	**183**	**0**
2006–07	*Gillingham*	14	0	**14**	**0**

McCORMICK, Luke (G) 110 0
H: 6 0 W: 13 12 b.Coventry 15-8-83
Source: Scholar.

2000–01	Plymouth Arg	1	0		
2001–02	Plymouth Arg	0	0		
2002–03	Plymouth Arg	3	0		
2003–04	Plymouth Arg	40	0		
2004–05	Plymouth Arg	23	0		
2004–05	*Boston U*	2	0	**2**	**0**
2005–06	Plymouth Arg	1	0		
2006–07	Plymouth Arg	40	0	**108**	**0**

NALIS, Lilian (M) 379 32
H: 6 1 W: 11 00 b.Nogent sur Marne 29-9-71

1992–93	Auxerre	0	0		
1993–94	Caen	16	0		
1994–95	Caen	4	0	**20**	**0**
1995–96	Laval	42	4		
1996–97	Laval	39	8	**81**	**12**
1997–98	Guingamp	30	0	**30**	**0**
1998–99	Le Havre	27	3	**27**	**3**
1999–2000	Bastia	28	1		
2000–01	Bastia	28	1		
2001–02	Bastia	26	2	**82**	**4**
2002–03	Chievo	8	0	**8**	**0**
2003–04	Leicester C	20	1		
2004–05	Leicester C	39	5	**59**	**6**
2005–06	Sheffield U	4	0	**4**	**0**
2005–06	*Coventry C*	6	2	**6**	**2**
2005–06	Plymouth Arg	20	1		
2006–07	Plymouth Arg	42	4	**62**	**5**

NORRIS, David (M) 205 23
H: 5 7 W: 11 06 b.Stamford 22-2-81
Source: Boston U.

1999–2000	Bolton W	0	0		
2000–01	Bolton W	0	0		
2001–02	Bolton W	0	0		
2001–02	*Hull C*	6	1	**6**	**1**
2002–03	Bolton W	0	0		
2002–03	Plymouth Arg	33	6		
2003–04	Plymouth Arg	45	5		
2004–05	Plymouth Arg	35	3		
2005–06	Plymouth Arg	45	2		
2006–07	Plymouth Arg	41	6	**199**	**22**

REID, Reuben (F) 16 2
H: 6 0 W: 12 02 b.Bristol 26-7-88

2005–06	Plymouth Arg	1	0		
2006–07	Plymouth Arg	6	0	**7**	**0**
2006–07	*Rochdale*	2	0	**2**	**0**
2006–07	*Torquay U*	7	2	**7**	**2**

SAMBA, Cherno (M) 21 1
H: 5 10 W: 10 01 b.Gambia 10-1-85
Source: Scholar. *Honours:* England Youth, Under-20.

2001–02	Millwall	0	0		
2002–03	Millwall	0	0		
2003–04	Millwall	0	0		
2004–05	Cadiz	1	0	**1**	**0**
2005–06	Malaga B	4	0	**4**	**0**
2006–07	Plymouth Arg	13	1	**13**	**1**
2006–07	*Wrexham*	3	0	**3**	**0**

SAWYER, Gary (D) 22 0
H: 6 0 W: 11 08 b.Bideford 5-7-85
Source: Scholar.

2004–05	Plymouth Arg	0	0		
2005–06	Plymouth Arg	0	0		
2006–07	Plymouth Arg	22	0	**22**	**0**

SEIP, Marcel (D) 159 4
H: 6 0 W: 11 03 b.Winschoten 5-4-82

1999–2000	Veendam	9	0		
2000–01	Veendam	18	0	**27**	**0**
2001–02	Heerenveen	0	0		
2002–03	Heerenveen	6	0		
2003–04	Heerenveen	31	1		
2004–05	Heerenveen	30	1		
2005–06	Heerenveen	28	0	**95**	**2**
2006–07	Plymouth Arg	37	2	**37**	**2**

SUMMERFIELD, Luke (M) 32 2
H: 6 0 W: 11 00 b.Ivybridge 6-12-87
Source: Scholar.

2004–05	Plymouth Arg	1	0		
2005–06	Plymouth Arg	0	0		
2006–07	Plymouth Arg	23	1	**24**	**1**
2006–07	*Bournemouth*	8	1	**8**	**1**

TIMAR, Krisztian (D) 90 8
H: 6 3 W: 13 08 b.Budapest 4-10-79
Source: Ferencvaros, MTK, Elore. *Honours:* Hungary Youth, Under-21, Under-23.

2001–02	Videoton	31	4		
2002–03	Videoton	15	0	**46**	**4**
2003	Jokerit	0	0		
2003–04	Tatabanya	0	0		
2004–05	Nyiregyhaza	12	0	**12**	**0**
2005–06	Ferencvaros	23	3	**23**	**3**
2006–07	Plymouth Arg	9	1	**9**	**1**

WOTTON, Paul (D) 386 53
H: 5 11 W: 12 00 b.Plymouth 17-8-77
Source: Trainee.

1994–95	Plymouth Arg	7	0		
1995–96	Plymouth Arg	1	0		
1996–97	Plymouth Arg	9	1		
1997–98	Plymouth Arg	34	1		
1998–99	Plymouth Arg	36	1		
1999–2000	Plymouth Arg	23	0		
2000–01	Plymouth Arg	42	4		
2001–02	Plymouth Arg	46	5		
2002–03	Plymouth Arg	43	8		
2003–04	Plymouth Arg	38	9		
2004–05	Plymouth Arg	40	12		
2005–06	Plymouth Arg	45	8		
2006–07	Plymouth Arg	22	4	**386**	**53**

PORT VALE (63)

ABBEY, George (D) 162 2
H: 5 10 W: 12 04 b.Port Harcourt 20-10-78
Source: Sharks. *Honours:* Nigeria 16 full caps.

1999–2000	Macclesfield T	18	0		
2000–01	Macclesfield T	18	0		
2001–02	Macclesfield T	17	0		
2002–03	Macclesfield T	22	1		
2003–04	Macclesfield T	25	0		
2004–05	Macclesfield T	0	0	**100**	**1**
2004–05	Port Vale	18	0		
2005–06	Port Vale	20	0		
2006–07	Port Vale	24	1	**62**	**1**

ANYON, Joe (G) **22 0**
H: 6 1 W: 12 11 b.Poulton-le-Fylde 29-12-86
Source: Scholar.

2005–06	Port Vale	0	0		
2006–07	Port Vale	22	0	**22**	**0**

BRISCOE, Louie (F) **0 0**
H: 6 0 W: 13 07 b.Burton-on-Trent 2-4-88
Source: Scholar.

2006–07	Port Vale	0	0		

CARDLE, Joe (M) **13 0**
H: 5 8 W: 9 05 b.Blackpool 27-2-87
Source: Scholar.

2005–06	Port Vale	6	0		
2006–07	Port Vale	7	0	**13**	**0**

CONSTANTINE, Leon (F) **198 67**
H: 6 2 W: 12 00 b.Hackney 24-2-78
Source: Edgware T.

2000–01	Millwall	1	0		
2001–02	Millwall	0	0	**1**	**0**
2001–02	*Leyton Orient*	10	3	**10**	**3**
2001–02	*Partick T*	2	0	**2**	**0**
2002–03	Brentford	17	0	**17**	**0**
2003–04	Southend U	43	21	**43**	**21**
2004–05	Peterborough U	11	1	**11**	**1**
2004–05	Torquay U	27	9		
2005–06	Torquay U	15	1	**42**	**10**
2005–06	Port Vale	30	10		
2006–07	Port Vale	42	22	**72**	**32**

GARDNER, Ross (M) **44 1**
H: 5 8 W: 10 06 b.South Shields 15-12-85
Source: Scholar. *Honours:* England Youth, Under-20.

2001–02	Newcastle U	0	0		
2002–03	Newcastle U	0	0		
2003–04	Nottingham F	2	0		
2004–05	Nottingham F	14	0		
2005–06	Nottingham F	12	0		
2006–07	Nottingham F	0	0	**28**	**0**
2006–07	Port Vale	16	1	**16**	**1**

GOODLAD, Mark (G) **215 0**
H: 6 1 W: 14 05 b.Barnsley 9-9-79
Source: Trainee.

1996–97	Nottingham F	0	0		
1997–98	Nottingham F	0	0		
1998–99	Nottingham F	0	0		
1998–99	*Scarborough*	3	0	**3**	**0**
1999–2000	Nottingham F	0	0		
1999–2000	Port Vale	1	0		
2000–01	Port Vale	40	0		
2001–02	Port Vale	43	0		
2002–03	Port Vale	37	0		
2003–04	Port Vale	0	0		
2004–05	Port Vale	20	0		
2005–06	Port Vale	46	0		
2006–07	Port Vale	25	0	**212**	**0**

HARSLEY, Paul (M) **371 30**
H: 5 8 W: 11 05 b.Scunthorpe 29-5-78
Source: Trainee.

1996–97	Grimsby T	0	0		
1997–98	Scunthorpe U	15	1		
1998–99	Scunthorpe U	34	0		
1999–2000	Scunthorpe U	46	3		
2000–01	Scunthorpe U	33	1	**128**	**5**
2001–02	Halifax T	45	11	**45**	**11**
2002–03	Northampton T	45	2		
2003–04	Northampton T	14	0	**59**	**2**
2003–04	Macclesfield T	16	2		
2004–05	Macclesfield T	46	3		
2005–06	Macclesfield T	45	6	**107**	**11**
2006–07	Port Vale	32	1	**32**	**1**

HULBERT, Robin (M) **120 1**
H: 5 9 W: 12 02 b.Plymouth 14-3-80
Source: Trainee. *Honours:* England Youth.

1997–98	Swindon T	1	0		
1997–98	*Newcastle U*	0	0		
1998–99	Swindon T	16	0		
1999–2000	Swindon T	12	0	**29**	**0**
1999–2000	Bristol C	2	0		
2000–01	Bristol C	19	0		
2001–02	Bristol C	11	0		
2002–03	Bristol C	7	0		
2002–03	*Shrewsbury T*	7	0	**7**	**0**
2003–04	Bristol C	0	0	**39**	**0**
2004–05	Port Vale	24	0		
2005–06	Port Vale	1	0		
2006–07	Port Vale	20	1	**45**	**1**

HUSBANDS, Michael (F) **62 5**
H: 5 8 W: 10 10 b.Birmingham 13-11-83
Source: Scholar.

2001–02	Aston Villa	0	0		
2002–03	Aston Villa	0	0		
2003–04	Southend U	9	0		
2004–05	Southend U	2	0	**11**	**0**
2005–06	Bristol R	0	0		
2005–06	Walsall	4	0	**4**	**0**
From Rushall Olympic.					
2005–06	Port Vale	24	4		
2006–07	Port Vale	23	1	**47**	**5**

KAMARA, Malvin (M) **110 7**
H: 5 11 W: 13 00 b.Southwark 17-11-83
Source: Scholar.

2002–03	Wimbledon	2	0		
2003–04	Wimbledon	27	2	**29**	**2**
2004–05	Milton Keynes D	25	1		
2005–06	Milton Keynes D	23	2	**48**	**3**
2006–07	Cardiff C	15	1	**15**	**1**
2006–07	Port Vale	18	1	**18**	**1**

LOWNDES, Nathan (F) **206 33**
H: 6 0 W: 11 10 b.Salford 2-6-77
Source: Trainee.

1994–95	Leeds U	0	0		
1995–96	Leeds U	0	0		
1995–96	Watford	0	0		
1996–97	Watford	3	0		
1997–98	Watford	4	0	**7**	**0**
1998–99	St Johnstone	29	2		
1999–2000	St Johnstone	25	10		
2000–01	St Johnstone	10	2	**64**	**14**
2001–02	Livingston	21	3	**21**	**3**
2001–02	*Rotherham U*	2	0	**2**	**0**
2002–03	Plymouth Arg	16	2		
2003–04	Plymouth Arg	33	8		
2004–05	Plymouth Arg	4	0	**53**	**10**
2004–05	Port Vale	12	1		
2005–06	Port Vale	35	5		
2006–07	Port Vale	12	0	**59**	**6**

McGREGOR, Mark (D) **403 13**
H: 5 11 W: 11 05 b.Chester 16-2-77
Source: Trainee.

1994–95	Wrexham	1	0		
1995–96	Wrexham	32	1		
1996–97	Wrexham	38	1		
1997–98	Wrexham	42	2		
1998–99	Wrexham	43	1		
1999–2000	Wrexham	45	1		
2000–01	Wrexham	43	5		
2001–02	Wrexham	0	0	**244**	**11**
2001–02	Burnley	1	0		
2002–03	Burnley	30	1		
2003–04	Burnley	23	1	**54**	**2**
2004–05	Blackpool	38	0		
2005–06	Blackpool	21	0	**59**	**0**
2005–06	Port Vale	14	0		
2006–07	Port Vale	32	0	**46**	**0**

MILES, Colin (D) **121 4**
H: 6 0 W: 13 10 b.Edmonton 6-9-78
Source: Trainee.

1996–97	Watford	0	0		
1997–98	Watford	1	0		
1998–99	Watford	0	0	**1**	**0**
1999–2000	Morton	4	0	**4**	**0**
From Dover Ath					
2003–04	Yeovil T	36	4		
2004–05	Yeovil T	21	0		
2005–06	Yeovil T	30	0	**87**	**4**
2006–07	Port Vale	29	0	**29**	**0**

PILKINGTON, George (D) **186 9**
H: 5 11 W: 12 05 b.Rugeley 7-11-81
Source: Trainee. *Honours:* England Youth.

1998–99	Everton	0	0		
1999–2000	Everton	0	0		
2000–01	Everton	0	0		
2001–02	Everton	0	0		
2002–03	Everton	0	0		
2002–03	*Exeter C*	7	0	**7**	**0**
2003–04	Port Vale	44	1		
2004–05	Port Vale	43	0		
2005–06	Port Vale	46	2		
2006–07	Port Vale	46	6	**179**	**9**

PROSSER, Luke (M) **0 0**
H: 6 2 W: 12 04 b.Enfield 28-5-88
Source: Scholar.

2006–07	Port Vale	0	0		

RODGERS, Luke (F) **188 64**
H: 5 8 W: 11 00 b.Birmingham 1-1-82
Source: Trainee.

1999–2000	Shrewsbury T	6	1		
2000–01	Shrewsbury T	26	7		
2001–02	Shrewsbury T	38	22		
2002–03	Shrewsbury T	36	16		
2003–04	Shrewsbury T	0	0		
2004–05	Shrewsbury T	36	6	**142**	**52**
2005–06	Crewe Alex	26	6		
2006–07	Crewe Alex	12	3	**38**	**9**
2006–07	Port Vale	8	3	**8**	**3**

SMITH, Christian (M) **1 0**
H: 6 2 W: 13 02 b.Crewe 10-12-87
Source: Scholar.

2006–07	Port Vale	1	0	**1**	**0**

SOBOLJEW, Mark (M) **0 0**
H: 6 0 W: 11 12 b.Stoke 24-9-87
Source: Scholar.

2006–07	Port Vale	0	0		

SODJE, Akpo (F) **93 23**
H: 6 2 W: 12 08 b.Greenwich 31-1-81
Source: QPR, Stevenage B, Margate, Gravesend & N, Erith & Belvedere.

2004–05	Huddersfield T	7	0	**7**	**0**
2004–05	*Darlington*	7	1		
2005–06	Darlington	36	8	**43**	**9**
2006–07	Port Vale	43	14	**43**	**14**

SONNER, Danny (M) **303 17**
H: 6 0 W: 12 03 b.Wigan 9-1-72
Source: Wigan Ath. *Honours:* Northern Ireland B, 13 full caps.

1990–91	Burnley	2	0		
1991–92	Burnley	3	0		
1992–93	Burnley	1	0	**6**	**0**
1992–93	*Bury*	5	3	**5**	**3**
From Erzgebirge Aue					
1996–97	Ipswich T	29	2		
1997–98	Ipswich T	23	1		
1998–99	Ipswich T	4	0	**56**	**3**
1998–99	Sheffield W	26	3		
1999–2000	Sheffield W	27	0	**53**	**3**
2000–01	Birmingham C	26	1		
2001–02	Birmingham C	15	1	**41**	**2**
2002–03	Walsall	24	4	**24**	**4**
2003–04	Nottingham F	28	0		
2004–05	Nottingham F	0	0	**28**	**0**
2004–05	Peterborough U	15	0	**15**	**0**
2004–05	*Port Vale*	13	0		
2005–06	Port Vale	29	1		
2006–07	Port Vale	33	1	**75**	**2**

TALBOT, Jason (D) **37 0**
H: 5 8 W: 10 01 b.Irlam 30-9-85
Source: Scholar.

2004–05	Bolton W	0	0		
2004–05	*Derby Co*	2	0	**2**	**0**
2004–05	*Mansfield T*	2	0		
2005–06	Mansfield T	6	0	**8**	**0**
2005–06	*Port Vale*	5	0		
2006–07	Port Vale	22	0	**27**	**0**

WALKER, Richard (D) **119 6**
H: 6 2 W: 12 08 b.Stafford 17-9-80
Source: Brook House.

1999–2000	Crewe Alex	0	0		
2000–01	Crewe Alex	3	0		
2001–02	Crewe Alex	1	0		
2002–03	Crewe Alex	35	2		
2003–04	Crewe Alex	20	1		
2004–05	Crewe Alex	23	2		
2005–06	Crewe Alex	18	1	**100**	**6**
2006–07	Port Vale	16	0	**16**	**0**
2006–07	*Wrexham*	3	0	**3**	**0**

WALSH, Michael (D) **276 5**
H: 5 11 W: 13 11 b.Rotherham 5-8-77
Source: Trainee.

1994–95	Scunthorpe U	3	0		
1995–96	Scunthorpe U	25	0		
1996–97	Scunthorpe U	36	0		
1997–98	Scunthorpe U	39	1	**103**	**1**
1998–99	Port Vale	19	1		

1999–2000	Port Vale	12	1		
2000–01	Port Vale	39	1		
2001–02	Port Vale	28	0		
2002–03	Port Vale	17	1		
2003–04	Port Vale	13	0		
2004–05	Port Vale	23	0		
2005–06	Port Vale	4	0		
2006–07	Port Vale	18	0	**173**	**4**

WESTON, Rhys (D) **198 2**
H: 6 1 W: 12 12 b.Kingston 27-10-80
Source: Trainee. *Honours:* England Schools, Youth, Wales Under-21, 7 full caps.

1999–2000	Arsenal	1	0		
2000–01	Arsenal	0	0	**1**	**0**
2000–01	Cardiff C	28	0		
2001–02	Cardiff C	37	0		
2002–03	Cardiff C	38	2		
2003–04	Cardiff C	24	0		
2004–05	Cardiff C	25	0		
2005–06	Cardiff C	30	0	**182**	**2**
2006–07	Port Vale	15	0	**15**	**0**

WHITAKER, Danny (M) **216 30**
H: 5 10 W: 11 00 b.Manchester 14-11-80
Source: Wilmslow Sports.

2000–01	Macclesfield T	0	0		
2001–02	Macclesfield T	16	2		
2002–03	Macclesfield T	41	10		
2003–04	Macclesfield T	36	5		
2004–05	Macclesfield T	36	2		
2005–06	Macclesfield T	42	4	**171**	**23**
2006–07	Port Vale	45	7	**45**	**7**

PORTSMOUTH (64)

ASHDOWN, Jamie (G) **69 0**
H: 6 1 W: 13 05 b.Reading 30-11-80
Source: Scholar.

1999–2000	Reading	0	0		
2000–01	Reading	1	0		
2001–02	Reading	1	0		
2001–02	*Arsenal*	0	0		
2002–03	Reading	1	0		
2002–03	*Bournemouth*	2	0	**2**	**0**
2003–04	Reading	10	0	**13**	**0**
2003–04	*Rushden & D*	19	0	**19**	**0**
2004–05	Portsmouth	16	0		
2005–06	Portsmouth	17	0		
2006–07	Portsmouth	0	0	**33**	**0**
2006–07	*Norwich C*	2	0	**2**	**0**

BEGOVIC, Asmir (G) **3 0**
H: 6 5 W: 13 01 b.Trebinje 20-6-87
Source: La Louviere. *Honours:* Canada Under-20.

2006–07	Portsmouth	0	0		
2006–07	*Macclesfield T*	3	0	**3**	**0**

CAMPBELL, Sol (D) **422 19**
H: 6 2 W: 15 07 b.Newham 18-9-74
Source: Trainee. *Honours:* England Youth, Under-21, B, 69 full caps, 1 goal.

1992–93	Tottenham H	1	1		
1993–94	Tottenham H	34	0		
1994–95	Tottenham H	30	0		
1995–96	Tottenham H	31	1		
1996–97	Tottenham H	38	0		
1997–98	Tottenham H	34	0		
1998–99	Tottenham H	37	6		
1999–2000	Tottenham H	29	0		
2000–01	Tottenham H	21	2	**255**	**10**
2001–02	Arsenal	31	2		
2002–03	Arsenal	33	2		
2003–04	Arsenal	35	1		
2004–05	Arsenal	16	1		
2005–06	Arsenal	20	2	**135**	**8**
2006–07	Portsmouth	32	1	**32**	**1**

COLE, Andy (F) **479 223**
H: 5 11 W: 12 11 b.Nottingham 15-10-71
Source: Trainee. *Honours:* England Schools, Youth, Under-21, B, 15 full caps, 1 goal. Football League.

1989–90	Arsenal	0	0		
1990–91	Arsenal	1	0		
1991–92	Arsenal	0	0	**1**	**0**
1991–92	*Fulham*	13	3		
1991–92	*Bristol C*	12	8		
1992–93	Bristol C	29	12	**41**	**20**
1992–93	Newcastle U	12	12		
1993–94	Newcastle U	40	34		
1994–95	Newcastle U	18	9	**70**	**55**
1994–95	Manchester U	18	12		
1995–96	Manchester U	34	11		
1996–97	Manchester U	20	6		
1997–98	Manchester U	33	15		
1998–99	Manchester U	32	17		
1999–2000	Manchester U	28	19		
2000–01	Manchester U	19	9		
2001–02	Manchester U	11	4	**195**	**93**
2001–02	Blackburn R	15	9		
2002–03	Blackburn R	34	7		
2003–04	Blackburn R	34	11	**83**	**27**
2004–05	Fulham	31	12	**44**	**15**
2005–06	Manchester C	22	9	**22**	**9**
2006–07	Portsmouth	18	3	**18**	**3**
2006–07	*Birmingham C*	5	1	**5**	**1**

DAVIS, Sean (M) **218 15**
H: 5 10 W: 12 00 b.Clapham 20-9-79
Source: Trainee. *Honours:* England Under-21.

1996–97	Fulham	1	0		
1997–98	Fulham	0	0		
1998–99	Fulham	6	0		
1999–2000	Fulham	26	0		
2000–01	Fulham	40	6		
2001–02	Fulham	30	0		
2002–03	Fulham	28	3		
2003–04	Fulham	24	5	**155**	**14**
2004–05	Tottenham H	15	0		
2005–06	Tottenham H	0	0	**15**	**0**
2005–06	Portsmouth	17	1		
2006–07	Portsmouth	31	0	**48**	**1**

DOUALA, Rudolphe (F) **220 34**
H: 5 9 W: 11 11 b.Douala 25-9-78
Honours: Cameroon 11 full caps, 1 goal.

1998–99	Boavista	26	5		
1999–2000	Boavista	14	1	**40**	**6**
2000–01	Desportes Aves	28	4	**28**	**4**
2001–02	Gil Vicente	32	4	**32**	**4**
2002–03	Uniao Leiria	33	5		
2003–04	Uniao Leiria	33	10	**66**	**15**
2004–05	Sporting Lisbon	22	4		
2005–06	Sporting Lisbon	25	1	**47**	**5**
2006–07	Portsmouth	7	0	**7**	**0**

DUFFY, Richard (D) **96 2**
H: 5 9 W: 10 03 b.Swansea 30-8-85
Source: Scholar. *Honours:* Wales Youth, Under-21, 12 full caps.

2002–03	Swansea C	0	0		
2003–04	Swansea C	18	1		
2003–04	Portsmouth	1	0		
2004–05	Portsmouth	0	0		
2004–05	*Burnley*	7	1	**7**	**1**
2004–05	*Coventry C*	14	0		
2005–06	Portsmouth	0	0		
2005–06	*Coventry C*	32	0		
2006–07	Portsmouth	0	0	**1**	**0**
2006–07	*Coventry C*	13	0	**59**	**0**
2006–07	*Swansea C*	11	0	**29**	**1**

FERNANDES, Manuel (M) **86 5**
H: 5 9 W: 10 12 b.Lisbon 5-2-86
Honours: Portugal Youth, Under-20, 2 full caps, 1 goal.

2003–04	Benfica	10	1		
2004–05	Benfica	29	1		
2005–06	Benfica	28	1	**67**	**3**
2006–07	Portsmouth	10	0	**10**	**0**
2006–07	*Everton*	9	2	**9**	**2**

To Benfica January 2007

FORDYCE, Daryl (M) **3 0**
H: 6 0 W: 11 08 b.Belfast 2-1-87
Source: Scholar. *Honours:* Northern Ireland Youth, Under-21.

2005–06	Portsmouth	0	0		
2005–06	*Bournemouth*	3	0	**3**	**0**
2006–07	Portsmouth	0	0		

GRIFFIN, Andy (D) **210 6**
H: 5 9 W: 10 10 b.Billinge 7-3-79
Source: Trainee. *Honours:* England Youth, Under-21.

1996–97	Stoke C	34	1		
1997–98	Stoke C	23	1		
1997–98	Newcastle U	4	0		
1998–99	Newcastle U	14	0		
1999–2000	Newcastle U	3	1		
2000–01	Newcastle U	19	0		
2001–02	Newcastle U	4	0		
2002–03	Newcastle U	27	1		
2003–04	Newcastle U	5	0	**76**	**2**
2004–05	Portsmouth	22	0		
2005–06	Portsmouth	22	0		
2006–07	Portsmouth	0	0	**44**	**0**
2006–07	*Stoke C*	33	2	**90**	**4**

HARRIS, Scott (M) **0 0**
b.Worthing 24-7-85
Source: Scholar.

2004–05	Portsmouth	0	0
2005–06	Portsmouth	0	0
2006–07	Portsmouth	0	0

HUGHES, Richard (M) **220 15**
H: 6 0 W: 13 03 b.Glasgow 25-6-79
Source: Atalanta. *Honours:* Scotland Youth, Under-21, 5 full caps.

1997–98	Arsenal	0	0		
1998–99	Bournemouth	44	2		
1999–2000	Bournemouth	21	2		
2000–01	Bournemouth	44	8		
2001–02	Bournemouth	22	2	**131**	**14**
2002–03	Portsmouth	6	0		
2002–03	*Grimsby T*	12	1	**12**	**1**
2003–04	Portsmouth	11	0		
2004–05	Portsmouth	16	0		
2005–06	Portsmouth	26	0		
2006–07	Portsmouth	18	0	**77**	**0**

JAMES, David (G) **592 0**
H: 6 5 W: 15 07 b.Welwyn 1-8-70
Source: Trainee. *Honours:* England Youth, Under-21, B, 34 full caps.

1988–89	Watford	0	0		
1989–90	Watford	0	0		
1990–91	Watford	46	0		
1991–92	Watford	43	0	**89**	**0**
1992–93	Liverpool	29	0		
1993–94	Liverpool	14	0		
1994–95	Liverpool	42	0		
1995–96	Liverpool	38	0		
1996–97	Liverpool	38	0		
1997–98	Liverpool	27	0		
1998–99	Liverpool	26	0	**214**	**0**
1999–2000	Aston Villa	29	0		
2000–01	Aston Villa	38	0	**67**	**0**
2001–02	West Ham U	26	0		
2002–03	West Ham U	38	0		
2003–04	West Ham U	27	0	**91**	**0**
2003–04	Manchester C	17	0		
2004–05	Manchester C	38	0		
2005–06	Manchester C	38	0	**93**	**0**
2006–07	Portsmouth	38	0	**38**	**0**

KANU, Nwankwo (F) **334 88**
H: 6 5 W: 12 08 b.Owerri 1-8-76
Honours: Nigeria 62 full caps, 11 goals.

1991–92	Federation Works	30	9	**30**	**9**
1992–93	Iwanyanwu	30	6	**30**	**6**
1993–94	Ajax	6	2		
1994–95	Ajax	18	10		
1995–96	Ajax	30	13	**54**	**25**
1996–97	Internazionale	0	0		
1997–98	Internazionale	11	1		
1998–99	Internazionale	1	0	**12**	**1**
1998–99	Arsenal	12	6		
1999–2000	Arsenal	31	12		
2000–01	Arsenal	27	3		
2001–02	Arsenal	23	3		
2002–03	Arsenal	16	5		
2003–04	Arsenal	10	1	**119**	**30**
2004–05	WBA	28	2		
2005–06	WBA	25	5	**53**	**7**
2006–07	Portsmouth	36	10	**36**	**10**

KEENE, James (F) **24** **3**
H: 5 11 W: 11 08 b.Wells 26-12-85
Source: Portsmouth Scholar.

2004–05	*Kidderminster H*	5	0	**5**	**0**
2004–05	Portsmouth	2	0		
2005–06	Portsmouth	0	0		
2005–06	*Bournemouth*	11	2	**11**	**2**
2005–06	*Boston U*	6	1	**6**	**1**
2006–07	Portsmouth	0	0	**2**	**0**

To Elfsborg January 2007

KOROMAN, Ognjen (D) **90** **12**
H: 5 9 W: 11 00 b.Sarajevo 19-9-78
Honours: Serbia & Montenegro 26 full caps, 1 goal.

2002	Dynamo Moscow	24	6	**24**	**6**
2003	Kryliya	6	1		
2004	Kryliya	24	2		
2005	Kryliya	26	1	**56**	**4**
2005	Terek Grozny	6	1	**6**	**1**
2005–06	Portsmouth	3	1		
2006–07	Portsmouth	1	0	**4**	**1**

To Terek Grozny February 2007

KRANJCAR, Niko (M) **159** **35**
H: 6 1 W: 12 13 b.Zagreb 13-8-84
Honours: Croatia Youth, Under-21, 35 full caps, 3 goals.

2001–02	Dynamo Zagreb	24	3		
2002–03	Dynamo Zagreb	21	4		
2003–04	Dynamo Zagreb	24	10		
2004–05	Dynamo Zagreb	16	2	**85**	**19**
2004–05	Hajduk Split	13	1		
2005–06	Hajduk Split	32	10		
2006–07	Hajduk Split	5	3	**50**	**14**
2006–07	Portsmouth	24	2	**24**	**2**

LAUREN, Etame-Mayer (D) **312** **24**
H: 5 11 W: 11 07 b.Londi Kribi 19-1-77
Honours: Cameroon 25 full caps, 1 goal.

1995–96	Utrera	30	5	**30**	**5**
1996–97	Sevilla B	17	3	**17**	**3**
1997–98	Levante	34	6	**34**	**6**
1998–99	Mallorca	32	1		
1999–2000	Mallorca	30	3	**62**	**4**
2000–01	Arsenal	18	2		
2001–02	Arsenal	27	2		
2002–03	Arsenal	27	1		
2003–04	Arsenal	32	0		
2004–05	Arsenal	33	1		
2005–06	Arsenal	22	0		
2006–07	Arsenal	0	0	**159**	**6**
2006–07	Portsmouth	10	0	**10**	**0**

LUA-LUA, Lomano (F) **207** **39**
H: 5 8 W: 12 02 b.Kinshasa 28-12-80
Honours: DR Congo 6 full caps, 1 goal.

1998–99	Colchester U	13	1		
1999–2000	Colchester U	41	12		
2000–01	Colchester U	7	2	**61**	**15**
2000–01	Newcastle U	21	0		
2001–02	Newcastle U	20	3		
2002–03	Newcastle U	11	2		
2003–04	Newcastle U	7	0	**59**	**5**
2003–04	*Portsmouth*	15	4		
2004–05	Portsmouth	25	6		
2005–06	Portsmouth	25	7		
2006–07	Portsmouth	22	2	**87**	**19**

MBESUMA, Collins (F) **4** **0**
H: 6 0 W: 12 04 b.Luanshya 3-2-84
Source: Kaizer Chiefs. *Honours:* Zambia full caps.

2005–06	Portsmouth	4	0		
2006–07	Portsmouth	0	0	**4**	**0**

MORNAR, Ivica (F) **253** **67**
H: 6 0 W: 12 04 b.Split 12-1-74
Honours: Croatia 22 full caps, 1 goal.

1992–93	Hajduk Split	21	7		
1993–94	Hajduk Split	27	8		
1994–95	Hajduk Split	9	3		
1995–96	Hajduk Split	1	0	**58**	**18**
1995–96	Eintracht Frankfurt	19	1	**19**	**1**
1996–97	Sevilla	11	2	**11**	**2**
1997–98	Ourense	28	8	**28**	**8**
1998–99	Standard Liege	15	3		
1999–2000	Standard Liege	24	8		
2000–01	Standard Liege	30	12	**69**	**23**
2001–02	Anderlecht	23	8		
2002–03	Anderlecht	20	6	**43**	**14**
2003–04	Portsmouth	8	1		

2004–05	*Rennes*	15	0	**15**	**0**
2005–06	Portsmouth	2	0		
2006–07	Portsmouth	0	0	**10**	**1**

MVUEMBA, Arnold (M) **40** **2**
H: 5 8 W: 10 07 b.Alencon 28-1-85
Honours: France Under-21.

2003–04	Rennes	8	0		
2004–05	Rennes	8	0		
2005–06	Rennes	16	1		
2006–07	Rennes	1	0	**33**	**1**
2006–07	Portsmouth	7	1	**7**	**1**

MWARUWARI, Benjamin (F) **189** **47**
H: 6 2 W: 12 03 b.Harare 13-8-78
Honours: Zimbabwe 33 full caps, 9 goals.

1999–2000	Jomo Cosmos	15	7		
2000–01	Jomo Cosmos	30	13	**45**	**20**
2001–02	Grasshoppers	25	1	**25**	**1**
2002–03	Auxerre	27	7		
2003–04	Auxerre	3	0		
2004–05	Auxerre	31	11		
2005–06	Auxerre	11	1	**72**	**19**
2005–06	Portsmouth	16	1		
2006–07	Portsmouth	31	6	**47**	**7**

O'BRIEN, Andy (D) **285** **9**
H: 6 2 W: 11 13 b.Harrogate 29-6-79
Source: Trainee. *Honours:* England Youth, Under-21, Eire Under-21, 26 full caps, 1 goal.

1996–97	Bradford C	22	2		
1997–98	Bradford C	26	0		
1998–99	Bradford C	31	0		
1999–2000	Bradford C	36	1		
2000–01	Bradford C	18	0	**133**	**3**
2000–01	Newcastle U	9	1		
2001–02	Newcastle U	34	2		
2002–03	Newcastle U	26	0		
2003–04	Newcastle U	28	1		
2004–05	Newcastle U	23	2	**120**	**6**
2005–06	Portsmouth	29	0		
2006–07	Portsmouth	3	0	**32**	**0**

O'NEIL, Gary (M) **189** **17**
H: 5 10 W: 11 00 b.Bromley 18-5-83
Source: Scholar. *Honours:* England Youth, Under-20, Under-21.

1999–2000	Portsmouth	1	0		
2000–01	Portsmouth	10	1		
2001–02	Portsmouth	33	1		
2002–03	Portsmouth	31	3		
2003–04	Portsmouth	3	2		
2003–04	*Walsall*	7	0	**7**	**0**
2004–05	Portsmouth	24	2		
2004–05	*Cardiff C*	9	1	**9**	**1**
2005–06	Portsmouth	36	6		
2006–07	Portsmouth	35	1	**173**	**16**

PAMAROT, Noe (D) **205** **11**
H: 5 11 W: 13 07 b.Fontenay-sous-Bois 14-4-79
Source: Martigues, Nice.

1997–98	Martigues	25	2		
1998–99	Martigues	0	0	**25**	**2**
1999–2000	Nice	0	0		
1999–2000	Portsmouth	2	0		
2000–01	Nice	23	0		
2001–02	Nice	33	3		
2002–03	Nice	33	1		
2003–04	Nice	33	2	**122**	**6**
2004–05	Tottenham H	23	1		
2005–06	Tottenham H	2	0	**25**	**1**
2005–06	Portsmouth	8	0		
2006–07	Portsmouth	23	2	**33**	**2**

PEARCE, Jason (D) **0** **0**
H: 5 11 W: 12 00 b.Hampshire 6-12-87
Source: Scholar.

2006–07	Portsmouth	0	0		

PEDRO MENDES (M) **210** **15**
H: 5 9 W: 12 04 b.Guimaraes 26-2-79
Honours: Portugal Under-21, 2 full caps.

1998–99	Felgueiras	31	2	**31**	**2**
1999–2000	Guimaraes	13	1		
2000–01	Guimaraes	12	0		
2001–02	Guimaraes	26	0		
2002–03	Guimaraes	32	6	**83**	**7**
2003–04	Porto	26	0	**26**	**0**
2004–05	Tottenham H	24	1		
2005–06	Tottenham H	6	0	**30**	**1**
2005–06	Portsmouth	14	3		
2006–07	Portsmouth	26	2	**40**	**5**

PRIMUS, Linvoy (D) **423** **13**
H: 5 10 W: 12 04 b.Forest Gate 14-9-73
Source: Trainee.

1992–93	Charlton Ath	4	0		
1993–94	Charlton Ath	0	0	**4**	**0**
1994–95	Barnet	39	0		
1995–96	Barnet	42	4		
1996–97	Barnet	46	3	**127**	**7**
1997–98	Reading	36	1		
1998–99	Reading	31	0		
1999–2000	Reading	28	0	**95**	**1**
2000–01	Portsmouth	23	0		
2001–02	Portsmouth	22	2		
2002–03	Portsmouth	40	0		
2003–04	Portsmouth	21	0		
2004–05	Portsmouth	35	1		
2005–06	Portsmouth	20	0		
2006–07	Portsmouth	36	2	**197**	**5**

SONGO'O, Frank (M) **12** **0**
H: 6 2 W: 12 06 b.Yaounde 14-5-87
Source: Barcelona. *Honours:* France Youth.

2005–06	Portsmouth	2	0		
2006–07	Portsmouth	0	0	**2**	**0**
2006–07	*Bournemouth*	4	0	**4**	**0**
2006–07	*Preston NE*	6	0	**6**	**0**

STEFANOVIC, Dejan (D) **318** **20**
H: 6 2 W: 13 01 b.Belgrade 28-10-74
Honours: Serbia-Montenegro 23 full caps.

1992–93	Red Star Belgrade	14	0		
1993–94	Red Star Belgrade	2	0		
1994–95	Red Star Belgrade	30	9	**46**	**9**
1995–96	Sheffield W	6	0		
1996–97	Sheffield W	29	2		
1997–98	Sheffield W	20	2		
1998–99	Sheffield W	11	0	**66**	**4**
1999–2000	Perugia	0	0		
1999–2000	OFK Belgrade	0	0		
1999–2000	Vitesse	14	0		
2000–01	Vitesse	27	1		
2001–02	Vitesse	25	3		
2002–03	Vitesse	28	0	**94**	**4**
2003–04	Portsmouth	32	3		
2004–05	Portsmouth	32	0		
2005–06	Portsmouth	28	0		
2006–07	Portsmouth	20	0	**112**	**3**

TAYLOR, Matthew (D) **295** **38**
H: 5 11 W: 12 03 b.Oxford 27-11-81
Source: Trainee. *Honours:* England Youth, Under-21.

1998–99	Luton T	0	0		
1999–2000	Luton T	41	4		
2000–01	Luton T	45	1		
2001–02	Luton T	43	11	**129**	**16**
2002–03	Portsmouth	35	7		
2003–04	Portsmouth	30	0		
2004–05	Portsmouth	32	1		
2005–06	Portsmouth	34	6		
2006–07	Portsmouth	35	8	**166**	**22**

TODOROV, Svetoslav (F) **179** **73**
H: 5 8 W: 11 11 b.Dobrich 30-8-78
Honours: Bulgaria Youth, 42 full caps, 6 goals.

1996–97	Dobrudzha	12	2	**12**	**2**
1997–98	Litets Lovech	19	9		
1998–99	Litets Lovech	11	2		
1999–2000	Litets Lovech	26	19		
2000–01	Litets Lovech	15	7	**71**	**37**
2000–01	West Ham U	8	1		
2001–02	West Ham U	6	0	**14**	**1**
2001–02	Portsmouth	3	1		
2002–03	Portsmouth	45	26		
2003–04	Portsmouth	1	0		
2004–05	Portsmouth	0	0		
2005–06	Portsmouth	24	4		
2006–07	Portsmouth	4	2	**77**	**33**
2006–07	*Wigan Ath*	5	0	**5**	**0**

TRAORE, Djimi (D) **128** **0**
H: 6 2 W: 12 07 b.Saint-Ouen 1-3-80
Source: Laval. *Honours:* France Youth, Under-21, Mali 5 full caps, 1 goal.

1998–99	Liverpool	0	0		
1999–2000	Liverpool	0	0		
2000–01	Liverpool	8	0		
2001–02	Liverpool	0	0		

2001–02	Lens	19	0	**19**	**0**
2002–03	Liverpool	32	0		
2003–04	Liverpool	7	0		
2004–05	Liverpool	26	0		
2005–06	Liverpool	15	0	**88**	**0**
2006–07	Charlton Ath	11	0	**11**	**0**
2006–07	Portsmouth	10	0	**10**	**0**

WILSON, Marc (M) 21 3
H: 6 2 W: 12 07 b.Belfast 17-8-87
Source: Scholar. *Honours:* Eire Under-21.

2005–06	Portsmouth	0	0		
2005–06	*Yeovil T*	2	0	**2**	**0**
2006–07	Portsmouth	0	0		
2006–07	*Bournemouth*	19	3	**19**	**3**

Scholars
Harris, Richard Leslie; Jordan, Nicholas; Oastler, Joseph; Page, Jonathan Edward; Ritchie, Matthew Thomas; Walker, Stephen Lee; Ward, Joel.

PRESTON NE (65)

AGYEMANG, Patrick (F) 266 45
H: 6 1 W: 12 00 b.Walthamstow 29-9-80
Source: Trainee. *Honours:* Ghana 3 full caps, 1 goal.

1998–99	Wimbledon	0	0		
1999–2000	Wimbledon	0	0		
1999–2000	*Brentford*	12	0	**12**	**0**
2000–01	Wimbledon	29	4		
2001–02	Wimbledon	33	4		
2002–03	Wimbledon	33	5		
2003–04	Wimbledon	26	7	**121**	**20**
2003–04	Gillingham	20	6		
2004–05	Gillingham	13	2	**33**	**8**
2004–05	Preston NE	27	4		
2005–06	Preston NE	42	6		
2006–07	Preston NE	31	7	**100**	**17**

ALEXANDER, Graham (D) 658 85
H: 5 10 W: 12 07 b.Coventry 10-10-71
Source: Trainee. *Honours:* Scotland B, 30 full caps.

1989–90	Scunthorpe U	0	0		
1990–91	Scunthorpe U	1	0		
1991–92	Scunthorpe U	36	5		
1992–93	Scunthorpe U	41	5		
1993–94	Scunthorpe U	41	4		
1994–95	Scunthorpe U	40	4	**159**	**18**
1995–96	Luton T	37	1		
1996–97	Luton T	45	2		
1997–98	Luton T	39	8		
1998–99	Luton T	29	4	**150**	**15**
1998–99	Preston NE	10	0		
1999–2000	Preston NE	46	6		
2000–01	Preston NE	34	5		
2001–02	Preston NE	45	6		
2002–03	Preston NE	45	10		
2003–04	Preston NE	45	9		
2004–05	Preston NE	42	7		
2005–06	Preston NE	40	3		
2006–07	Preston NE	42	6	**349**	**52**

ANYINSAH, Joe (M) 16 0
H: 5 8 W: 11 00 b.Bristol 8-10-84
Source: Scholar.

2001–02	Bristol C	0	0		
2002–03	Bristol C	0	0		
2003–04	Bristol C	0	0		
2004–05	Bristol C	7	0	**7**	**0**
2005–06	Preston NE	3	0		
2005–06	*Bury*	3	0	**3**	**0**
2006–07	Preston NE	3	0	**6**	**0**

CHILVERS, Liam (D) 174 6
H: 6 2 W: 12 03 b.Chelmsford 6-11-81
Source: Scholar.

2000–01	Arsenal	0	0		
2000–01	*Northampton T*	7	0	**7**	**0**
2001–02	Arsenal	0	0		
2001–02	*Notts Co*	9	1	**9**	**1**
2002–03	Arsenal	0	0		
2002–03	*Colchester U*	6	0		
2003–04	Arsenal	0	0		
2003–04	*Colchester U*	32	0		
2004–05	Colchester U	41	1		
2005–06	Colchester U	34	2	**113**	**3**
2006–07	Preston NE	45	2	**45**	**2**

DAVIDSON, Callum (D) 271 12
H: 5 10 W: 11 08 b.Stirling 25-6-76
Source: 'S' Form. *Honours:* Scotland Under-21, 17 full caps.

1994–95	St Johnstone	7	1		
1995–96	St Johnstone	2	0		
1996–97	St Johnstone	20	2		
1997–98	St Johnstone	15	1	**44**	**4**
1997–98	Blackburn R	1	0		
1998–99	Blackburn R	34	1		
1999–2000	Blackburn R	30	0	**65**	**1**
2000–01	Leicester C	28	1		
2001–02	Leicester C	30	0		
2002–03	Leicester C	30	1		
2003–04	Leicester C	13	0	**101**	**2**
2004–05	Preston NE	19	1		
2005–06	Preston NE	27	4		
2006–07	Preston NE	15	0	**61**	**5**

DICHIO, Danny (F) 345 71
H: 6 3 W: 12 03 b.Hammersmith 19-10-74
Source: Trainee. *Honours:* England Schools, Under-21.

1993–94	QPR	0	0		
1993–94	*Barnet*	9	2	**9**	**2**
1994–95	QPR	9	3		
1995–96	QPR	29	10		
1996–97	QPR	37	7	**75**	**20**
1997–98	Sampdoria	0	0		
1997–98	Lecce	4	1	**4**	**1**
1997–98	Sunderland	13	0		
1998–99	Sunderland	36	10		
1999–2000	Sunderland	12	0		
2000–01	Sunderland	15	1		
2001–02	Sunderland	0	0	**76**	**11**
2001–02	WBA	27	9		
2002–03	WBA	28	5		
2003–04	WBA	11	0	**66**	**14**
2003–04	*Derby Co*	6	1	**6**	**1**
2003–04	Millwall	15	7		
2004–05	Millwall	31	10	**46**	**17**
2005–06	Preston NE	33	0		
2006–07	Preston NE	30	5	**63**	**5**

To Toronto Lynx April 2007

HENDERSON, Wayne (G) 70 0
H: 5 11 W: 12 02 b.Dublin 16-9-83
Source: Scholar. *Honours:* Eire Youth, Under-21, 5 full caps.

2000–01	Aston Villa	0	0		
2001–02	Aston Villa	0	0		
2002–03	Aston Villa	0	0		
2003–04	Aston Villa	0	0		
2003–04	*Wycombe W*	3	0	**3**	**0**
2004–05	Aston Villa	0	0		
2004–05	*Notts Co*	11	0	**11**	**0**
2005–06	Aston Villa	0	0		
2005–06	Brighton & HA	32	0		
2006–07	Brighton & HA	20	0	**52**	**0**
2006–07	Preston NE	4	0	**4**	**0**

HIBBERT, Dave (F) 48 4
H: 6 2 W: 12 00 b.Eccleshall 28-1-86
Source: Scholar.

2004–05	Port Vale	9	2	**9**	**2**
2005–06	Preston NE	10	0		
2006–07	Preston NE	0	0	**10**	**0**
2006–07	*Rotherham U*	21	2	**21**	**2**
2006–07	*Bradford C*	8	0	**8**	**0**

HILL, Matt (D) 276 6
H: 5 7 W: 12 06 b.Bristol 26-3-81
Source: Trainee.

1998–99	Bristol C	3	0		
1999–2000	Bristol C	14	0		
2000–01	Bristol C	34	0		
2001–02	Bristol C	40	1		
2002–03	Bristol C	42	3		
2003–04	Bristol C	42	2		
2004–05	Bristol C	23	0	**198**	**6**
2004–05	Preston NE	14	0		
2005–06	Preston NE	26	0		
2006–07	Preston NE	38	0	**78**	**0**

HINCHLIFFE, Ben (G) 2 0
H: 5 10 W: 11 07 b.Preston 9-10-88
Source: Scholar.

2006–07	Preston NE	0	0		
2006–07	*Tranmere R*	2	0	**2**	**0**

JARRETT, Jason (M) 211 6
H: 6 1 W: 13 10 b.Bury 14-9-79
Source: Trainee.

1998–99	Blackpool	2	0		
1999–2000	Blackpool	0	0	**2**	**0**
1999–2000	Wrexham	1	0	**1**	**0**
2000–01	Bury	25	2		
2001–02	Bury	37	2	**62**	**4**
2001–02	Wigan Ath	5	0		
2002–03	Wigan Ath	35	0		
2003–04	Wigan Ath	41	1		
2004–05	Wigan Ath	14	0	**95**	**1**
2004–05	*Stoke C*	2	0	**2**	**0**
2005–06	Norwich C	11	0	**11**	**0**
2005–06	*Plymouth Arg*	7	0	**7**	**0**
2005–06	*Preston NE*	10	1		
2006–07	Preston NE	5	0	**15**	**1**
2006–07	*Hull C*	3	0	**3**	**0**
2006–07	*Leicester C*	13	0	**13**	**0**

LONERGAN, Andrew (G) 50 1
H: 6 4 W: 13 02 b.Preston 19-10-83
Source: Scholar. *Honours:* Eire Youth, England Youth, Under-20.

2000–01	Preston NE	1	0		
2001–02	Preston NE	0	0		
2002–03	Preston NE	0	0		
2002–03	*Darlington*	2	0	**2**	**0**
2003–04	Preston NE	8	0		
2004–05	Preston NE	23	1		
2005–06	Preston NE	0	0		
2005–06	*Wycombe W*	2	0	**2**	**0**
2006–07	Preston NE	13	0	**45**	**1**
2006–07	*Swindon T*	1	0	**1**	**0**

MAWENE, Youl (D) 137 4
H: 6 2 W: 12 06 b.Caen 16-7-79

1999–2000	Lens	6	0	**6**	**0**
2000–01	Derby Co	8	0		
2001–02	Derby Co	17	1		
2002–03	Derby Co	0	0		
2003–04	Derby Co	30	0	**55**	**1**
2004–05	Preston NE	46	2		
2005–06	Preston NE	30	1		
2006–07	Preston NE	0	0	**76**	**3**

McGRAIL, Chris (F) 2 0
H: 6 0 W: 13 05 b.Preston 25-2-88
Source: Scholar.

2006–07	Preston NE	0	0		
2006–07	*Accrington S*	2	0	**2**	**0**

McKENNA, Paul (M) 345 28
H: 5 7 W: 11 12 b.Eccleston 20-10-77
Source: Trainee.

1995–96	Preston NE	0	0		
1996–97	Preston NE	5	1		
1997–98	Preston NE	5	0		
1998–99	Preston NE	36	0		
1999–2000	Preston NE	24	2		
2000–01	Preston NE	44	5		
2001–02	Preston NE	38	4		
2002–03	Preston NE	41	3		
2003–04	Preston NE	39	6		
2004–05	Preston NE	39	3		
2005–06	Preston NE	41	2		
2006–07	Preston NE	33	2	**345**	**28**

MELLOR, Neil (F) 36 6
H: 6 0 W: 13 05 b.Sheffield 4-11-82
Source: Scholar.

2001–02	Liverpool	0	0		
2002–03	Liverpool	3	0		
2003–04	Liverpool	0	0		
2003–04	*West Ham U*	16	2	**16**	**2**
2004–05	Liverpool	9	2		
2005–06	Liverpool	0	0		
2005–06	*Wigan Ath*	3	1	**3**	**1**
2006–07	Liverpool	0	0	**12**	**2**
2006–07	Preston NE	5	1	**5**	**1**

NASH, Carlo (G) 233 0
H: 6 5 W: 14 01 b.Bolton 13-9-73
Source: Clitheroe.

1996–97	Crystal Palace	21	0		
1997–98	Crystal Palace	0	0	**21**	**0**
1998–99	Stockport Co	43	0		
1999–2000	Stockport Co	38	0		
2000–01	Stockport Co	8	0	**89**	**0**
2000–01	Manchester C	6	0		
2001–02	Manchester C	23	0		
2002–03	Manchester C	9	0	**38**	**0**
2003–04	Middlesbrough	1	0		
2004–05	Middlesbrough	2	0	**3**	**0**
2004–05	Preston NE	7	0		
2005–06	Preston NE	46	0		
2006–07	Preston NE	29	0	**82**	**0**

NEAL, Chris (G) 1 0
H: 6 2 W: 12 04 b.St Albans 23-10-85
Source: Scholar.

2004–05	Preston NE	1	0		
2005–06	Preston NE	0	0		
2006–07	Preston NE	0	0	**1**	**0**

NEAL, Lewis (M) 118 5
H: 5 10 W: 11 02 b.Leicester 14-7-81
Source: Juniors.

1998–99	Stoke C	0	0		
1999–2000	Stoke C	0	0		
2000–01	Stoke C	1	0		
2001–02	Stoke C	11	0		
2002–03	Stoke C	16	0		
2003–04	Stoke C	19	1		
2004–05	Stoke C	23	1	**70**	**2**
2005–06	Preston NE	24	2		
2006–07	Preston NE	24	1	**48**	**3**

NOWLAND, Adam (M) 162 15
H: 5 11 W: 11 06 b.Preston 6-7-81
Source: Trainee.

1997–98	Blackpool	1	0		
1998–99	Blackpool	37	2		
1999–2000	Blackpool	21	3		
2000–01	Blackpool	10	0	**69**	**5**
2001–02	Wimbledon	7	0		
2002–03	Wimbledon	24	2		
2003–04	Wimbledon	25	3	**56**	**5**
2003–04	West Ham U	11	0		
2004–05	West Ham U	4	1	**15**	**1**
2004–05	*Gillingham*	3	1	**3**	**1**
2004–05	Nottingham F	5	0		
2005–06	Nottingham F	0	0	**5**	**0**
2005–06	Preston NE	13	3		
2006–07	Preston NE	1	0	**14**	**3**

NUGENT, Dave (F) 182 51
H: 5 11 W: 12 13 b.Liverpool 2-5-85
Source: Scholar. *Honours:* England Youth, Under-20, Under-21, 1 full cap, 1 goal.

2001–02	Bury	5	0		
2002–03	Bury	31	4		
2003–04	Bury	26	3		
2004–05	Bury	26	11	**88**	**18**
2004–05	Preston NE	18	8		
2005–06	Preston NE	32	10		
2006–07	Preston NE	44	15	**94**	**33**

ORMEROD, Brett (F) 283 71
H: 5 11 W: 11 12 b.Blackburn 18-10-76
Source: Blackburn R Trainee, Accrington S.

1996–97	Blackpool	4	0		
1997–98	Blackpool	9	2		
1998–99	Blackpool	40	8		
1999–2000	Blackpool	13	5		
2000–01	Blackpool	41	17		
2001–02	Blackpool	21	13	**128**	**45**
2001–02	Southampton	18	1		
2002–03	Southampton	31	5		
2003–04	Southampton	22	5		
2004–05	Southampton	9	0		
2004–05	*Leeds U*	6	0	**6**	**0**
2004–05	*Wigan Ath*	6	2	**6**	**2**
2005–06	Southampton	19	1	**99**	**12**
2005–06	Preston NE	15	4		
2006–07	Preston NE	29	8	**44**	**12**

PERGL, Pavel (D) 157 12
H: 5 11 W: 12 04 b.Prague 14-11-77
Source: Sparta, Pelikan.

1998–99	Chmel	21	1		
1999–2000	Chmel	6	0	**27**	**1**
1999–2000	Petra	9	1	**9**	**1**
2000–01	Drnovice	13	0		
2001–02	Drnovice	14	2	**27**	**2**
2001–02	Marila	6	1		
2002–03	Marila	14	2	**20**	**3**
2002–03	Sparta	7	1		
2003–04	Sparta	23	1		
2004–05	Sparta	12	1		
2005–06	Sparta	9	0	**51**	**3**
2005–06	Dynamo Dresden	17	1	**17**	**1**
2006–07	Preston NE	6	1	**6**	**1**

PUGH, Danny (M) 96 9
H: 6 0 W: 12 10 b.Manchester 19-10-82
Source: Scholar.

2000–01	Manchester U	0	0		
2001–02	Manchester U	0	0		
2002–03	Manchester U	1	0		
2003–04	Manchester U	0	0	**1**	**0**
2004–05	Leeds U	38	5		
2005–06	Leeds U	12	0	**50**	**5**
2006–07	Preston NE	45	4	**45**	**4**

RICKETTS, Michael (F) 288 62
H: 6 2 W: 11 12 b.Birmingham 4-12-78
Source: Trainee. *Honours:* England 1 full cap.

1995–96	Walsall	1	1		
1996–97	Walsall	11	1		
1997–98	Walsall	24	1		
1998–99	Walsall	8	0		
1999–2000	Walsall	32	11	**76**	**14**
2000–01	Bolton W	39	19		
2001–02	Bolton W	37	12		
2002–03	Bolton W	22	6	**98**	**37**
2002–03	Middlesbrough	9	1		
2003–04	Middlesbrough	23	2	**32**	**3**
2004–05	Leeds U	21	0		
2004–05	*Stoke C*	11	0	**11**	**0**
2005–06	Leeds U	4	0	**25**	**0**
2005–06	*Cardiff C*	17	5	**17**	**5**
2005–06	*Burnley*	13	2	**13**	**2**
2006–07	Southend U	2	0	**2**	**0**
2006–07	Preston NE	14	1	**14**	**1**

SEDGWICK, Chris (M) 356 25
H: 5 11 W: 11 10 b.Sheffield 28-4-80
Source: Trainee.

1997–98	Rotherham U	4	0		
1998–99	Rotherham U	33	4		
1999–2000	Rotherham U	38	5		
2000–01	Rotherham U	21	2		
2001–02	Rotherham U	44	1		
2002–03	Rotherham U	43	1		
2003–04	Rotherham U	40	2		
2004–05	Rotherham U	20	2	**243**	**17**
2004–05	Preston NE	24	3		
2005–06	Preston NE	46	4		
2006–07	Preston NE	43	1	**113**	**8**

SOLEY, Seyfo (D) 136 3
H: 6 3 W: 13 12 b.Lamin 16-2-80
Source: Banjul Hawks, Sint Niklaas. *Honours:* Gambia 37 full caps.

2000–01	Lokeren	25	0		
2001–02	Lokeren	23	0	**48**	**0**
2002–03	Genk	28	0		
From Al Hilali					
2003–04	Genk	11	1		
2004–05	Genk	19	0		
2005–06	Genk	24	2	**82**	**3**
2006–07	Preston NE	6	0	**6**	**0**

ST LEDGER-HALL, Sean (D) 120 2
H: 6 0 W: 11 09 b.Solihull 28-12-84
Source: Scholar.

2002–03	Peterborough U	1	0		
2003–04	Peterborough U	2	0		
2004–05	Peterborough U	33	0		
2005–06	Peterborough U	43	1	**79**	**1**
2006–07	Preston NE	41	1	**41**	**1**

WHALEY, Simon (M) 129 20
H: 5 10 W: 11 11 b.Bolton 7-6-85
Source: Scholar.

2002–03	Bury	2	0		
2003–04	Bury	10	1		
2004–05	Bury	38	3		
2005–06	Bury	23	7	**73**	**11**
2005–06	Preston NE	16	3		
2006–07	Preston NE	40	6	**56**	**9**

WILSON, Kelvin (D) 105 4
H: 6 2 W: 12 12 b.Nottingham 3-9-85
Source: Scholar.

2003–04	Notts Co	3	0		
2004–05	Notts Co	41	2		
2005–06	Notts Co	34	1	**78**	**3**
2005–06	*Preston NE*	6	0		
2006–07	Preston NE	21	1	**27**	**1**

QPR (66)

AINSWORTH, Gareth (M) 400 86
H: 5 10 W: 12 05 b.Blackburn 10-5-73
Source: Blackburn R Trainee.

1991–92	Preston NE	5	0		
1992–93	Cambridge U	4	1	**4**	**1**
1992–93	Preston NE	26	0		
1993–94	Preston NE	38	11		
1994–95	Preston NE	16	1		
1995–96	Preston NE	2	0		
1995–96	Lincoln C	31	12		
1996–97	Lincoln C	46	22		
1997–98	Lincoln C	6	3	**83**	**37**
1997–98	Port Vale	40	5		
1998–99	Port Vale	15	5	**55**	**10**
1998–99	Wimbledon	8	0		
1999–2000	Wimbledon	2	2		
2000–01	Wimbledon	12	2		
2001–02	Wimbledon	2	0		
2001–02	*Preston NE*	5	1	**92**	**13**
2002–03	Wimbledon	12	2	**36**	**6**
2002–03	*Walsall*	5	1	**5**	**1**
2002–03	Cardiff C	9	0	**9**	**0**
2003–04	QPR	29	6		
2004–05	QPR	22	2		
2005–06	QPR	43	9		
2006–07	QPR	22	1	**116**	**18**

BAIDOO, Shabazz (M) 28 3
H: 5 8 W: 10 07 b.Hackney 13-4-88
Source: Scholar.

2004–05	QPR	4	0		
2005–06	QPR	15	2		
2006–07	QPR	9	1	**28**	**3**

BAILEY, Stefan (M) 17 0
H: 5 11 W: 12 08 b.Brent 10-11-87
Source: Scholar.

2004–05	QPR	2	0		
2005–06	QPR	5	0		
2006–07	QPR	10	0	**17**	**0**

BIGNOT, Marcus (D) 369 4
H: 5 7 W: 11 04 b.Birmingham 22-8-74
Source: Kidderminster H.

1997–98	Crewe Alex	42	0		
1998–99	Crewe Alex	26	0		
1999–2000	Crewe Alex	27	0	**95**	**0**
2000–01	Bristol R	26	1	**26**	**1**
2000–01	QPR	9	1		
2001–02	QPR	45	0		
2002–03	Rushden & D	33	0		
2003–04	Rushden & D	35	2	**68**	**2**
2003–04	QPR	6	0		
2004–05	QPR	43	0		
2005–06	QPR	44	0		
2006–07	QPR	33	0	**180**	**1**

BIRCHAM, Marc (M) 256 10
H: 5 11 W: 11 06 b.Wembley 11-5-78
Source: Trainee. *Honours:* Canada 17 full caps, 1 goal.

1996–97	Millwall	6	0		
1997–98	Millwall	4	0		
1998–99	Millwall	28	0		
1999–2000	Millwall	22	1		
2000–01	Millwall	20	2		
2001–02	Millwall	24	0	**104**	**3**
2002–03	QPR	36	2		
2003–04	QPR	38	2		
2004–05	QPR	35	1		
2005–06	QPR	26	2		
2006–07	QPR	17	0	**152**	**7**

BLACKSTOCK, Dexter (F) **90 24**
H: 6 2 W: 13 00 b.Oxford 20-5-86
Source: Scholar. *Honours:* England Youth, Under-20.

2004–05	Southampton	9	1		
2004–05	*Plymouth Arg*	14	4	**14**	**4**
2005–06	Southampton	19	3	**28**	**4**
2005–06	*Derby Co*	9	3	**9**	**3**
2006–07	QPR	39	13	**39**	**13**

BOLDER, Adam (M) **202 11**
H: 5 9 W: 10 08 b.Hull 25-10-80
Source: Trainee.

1998–99	Hull C	1	0		
1999–2000	Hull C	19	0	**20**	**0**
1999–2000	Derby Co	0	0		
2000–01	Derby Co	2	0		
2001–02	Derby Co	11	0		
2002–03	Derby Co	45	6		
2003–04	Derby Co	24	1		
2004–05	Derby Co	36	2		
2005–06	Derby Co	35	2		
2006–07	Derby Co	13	0	**166**	**11**
2006–07	QPR	16	0	**16**	**0**

COLE, Jake (G) **6 0**
H: 6 2 W: 13 00 b.Hammersmith 11-9-85
Source: Scholar.

2005–06	QPR	3	0		
2006–07	QPR	3	0	**6**	**0**

COOK, Lee (M) **198 18**
H: 5 8 W: 11 10 b.Hammersmith 3-8-82
Source: Aylesbury U.

1999–2000	Watford	0	0		
2000–01	Watford	4	0		
2001–02	Watford	10	0		
2002–03	Watford	4	0		
2002–03	*York C*	7	1	**7**	**1**
2002–03	*QPR*	13	1		
2003–04	Watford	41	7	**59**	**7**
2004–05	QPR	42	2		
2005–06	QPR	40	4		
2006–07	QPR	37	3	**132**	**10**

CULLIP, Danny (D) **341 9**
H: 6 0 W: 12 12 b.Bracknell 17-9-76
Source: Trainee.

1995–96	Oxford U	0	0		
1996–97	Fulham	29	1		
1997–98	Fulham	21	1	**50**	**2**
1997–98	Brentford	13	0		
1998–99	Brentford	2	0		
1999–2000	Brentford	0	0	**15**	**0**
1999–2000	Brighton & HA	33	2		
2000–01	Brighton & HA	38	2		
2001–02	Brighton & HA	44	0		
2002–03	Brighton & HA	44	2		
2003–04	Brighton & HA	40	1		
2004–05	Brighton & HA	18	0	**217**	**7**
2004–05	Sheffield U	11	0	**11**	**0**
2004–05	*Watford*	4	0	**4**	**0**
2005–06	Nottingham F	11	0		
2006–07	Nottingham F	20	0	**31**	**0**
2006–07	QPR	13	0	**13**	**0**

CZERKAS, Adam (F) **29 3**
H: 6 1 W: 12 00 b.Sokolow Podlask 13-7-84
Source: Korona Kielce.

2005–06	Odra	26	3	**26**	**3**
2006–07	QPR	3	0	**3**	**0**

To Korona Kielce January 2007

DOHERTY, Tom (M) **230 9**
H: 5 8 W: 10 06 b.Bristol 17-3-79
Source: Trainee. *Honours:* Northern Ireland 9 full caps.

1997–98	Bristol C	30	2		
1998–99	Bristol C	23	1		
1999–2000	Bristol C	1	0		
2000–01	Bristol C	0	0		
2001–02	Bristol C	34	1		
2002–03	Bristol C	38	0		
2003–04	Bristol C	33	2		
2004–05	Bristol C	29	1	**188**	**7**
2005–06	QPR	15	0		
2005–06	*Yeovil T*	1	0	**1**	**0**
2006–07	QPR	0	0	**15**	**0**
2006–07	*Wycombe W*	26	2	**26**	**2**

DONNELLY, Scott (M) **13 0**
H: 5 8 W: 11 10 b.Hammersmith 25-12-87
Source: Scholar.

2004–05	QPR	2	0		
2005–06	QPR	8	0		
2006–07	QPR	3	0	**13**	**0**

FURLONG, Paul (F) **486 163**
H: 6 0 W: 13 11 b.Wood Green 1-10-68
Source: Enfield.

1991–92	Coventry C	37	4	**37**	**4**
1992–93	Watford	41	19		
1993–94	Watford	38	18	**79**	**37**
1994–95	Chelsea	36	10		
1995–96	Chelsea	28	3	**64**	**13**
1996–97	Birmingham C	43	10		
1997–98	Birmingham C	25	15		
1998–99	Birmingham C	29	13		
1999–2000	Birmingham C	19	11		
2000–01	Birmingham C	4	0		
2000–01	*QPR*	3	1		
2001–02	Birmingham C	11	1		
2001–02	*Sheffield U*	4	2	**4**	**2**
2002–03	Birmingham C	0	0	**131**	**50**
2002–03	QPR	33	13		
2003–04	QPR	36	16		
2004–05	QPR	40	18		
2005–06	QPR	37	7		
2006–07	QPR	22	2	**171**	**57**

GALLEN, Kevin (F) **425 103**
H: 5 11 W: 13 05 b.Hammersmith 21-9-75
Source: Trainee. *Honours:* England Schools, Youth, Under-21.

1992–93	QPR	0	0		
1993–94	QPR	0	0		
1994–95	QPR	37	10		
1995–96	QPR	30	8		
1996–97	QPR	2	3		
1997–98	QPR	27	3		
1998–99	QPR	44	8		
1999–2000	QPR	31	4		
2000–01	Huddersfield T	38	10	**38**	**10**
2001–02	Barnsley	9	2	**9**	**2**
2001–02	QPR	25	7		
2002–03	QPR	42	13		
2003–04	QPR	45	17		
2004–05	QPR	46	10		
2005–06	QPR	18	4		
2006–07	QPR	18	3	**365**	**90**
2006–07	*Plymouth Arg*	13	1	**13**	**1**

HOWELL, Andrew (D) **0 0**
H: 5 11 W: 12 01 b.Gt Yarmouth 18-3-89
Source: Scholar.

2005–06	QPR	0	0		
2006–07	QPR	0	0		

JONES, Paul (G) **338 0**
H: 6 3 W: 15 02 b.Chirk 18-4-67
Source: Bridgnorth, Kidderminster H. *Honours:* Wales 50 full caps.

1991–92	Wolverhampton W	0	0		
1992–93	Wolverhampton W	16	0		
1993–94	Wolverhampton W	0	0		
1994–95	Wolverhampton W	9	0		
1995–96	Wolverhampton W	8	0		
1996–97	Stockport Co	46	0	**46**	**0**
1997–98	Southampton	38	0		
1998–99	Southampton	31	0		
1999–2000	Southampton	31	0		
2000–01	Southampton	35	0		
2001–02	Southampton	36	0		
2002–03	Southampton	14	0		
2003–04	Southampton	8	0	**193**	**0**
2003–04	*Liverpool*	2	0	**2**	**0**
2003–04	Wolverhampton W	16	0		
2004–05	Wolverhampton W	10	0		
2004–05	*Watford*	9	0	**9**	**0**
2005–06	Wolverhampton W	0	0	**59**	**0**
2005–06	*Millwall*	3	0	**3**	**0**
2005–06	QPR	14	0		
2006–07	QPR	12	0	**26**	**0**

JONES, Ray (F) **33 5**
H: 6 4 W: 14 05 b.Newham 28-8-88
Source: Scholar.

2005–06	QPR	2	0		
2006–07	QPR	31	5	**33**	**5**

KANYUKA, Patrick (D) **12 0**
H: 6 0 W: 12 06 b.Kinshasa 19-7-87
Source: QPR Juniors.

2004–05	QPR	1	0		
2005–06	QPR	0	0		
2006–07	QPR	11	0	**12**	**0**

LOMAS, Steve (M) **353 20**
H: 6 0 W: 12 08 b.Hanover 18-1-74
Source: Trainee. *Honours:* Northern Ireland Schools, Youth, B, 45 full caps, 3 goals.

1991–92	Manchester C	0	0		
1992–93	Manchester C	0	0		
1993–94	Manchester C	23	0		
1994–95	Manchester C	20	2		
1995–96	Manchester C	33	3		
1996–97	Manchester C	35	3	**111**	**8**
1996–97	West Ham U	7	0		
1997–98	West Ham U	33	2		
1998–99	West Ham U	30	1		
1999–2000	West Ham U	25	1		
2000–01	West Ham U	20	1		
2001–02	West Ham U	15	4		
2002–03	West Ham U	29	0		
2003–04	West Ham U	5	0		
2004–05	West Ham U	23	1		
2005–06	West Ham U	0	0	**187**	**10**
2005–06	QPR	21	0		
2006–07	QPR	34	2	**55**	**2**

MILANESE, Mauro (D) **410 22**
H: 6 1 W: 13 01 b.Trieste 17-9-71

1989–90	Triestina	0	0		
1990–91	Monfalcone	33	5	**33**	**5**
1991–92	Massese	22	2	**22**	**2**
1992–93	Triestina	25	2		
1993–94	Triestina	25	1	**50**	**3**
1994–95	Cremonese	27	3	**27**	**3**
1995–96	Torino	31	0	**31**	**0**
1996–97	Napoli	29	1	**29**	**1**
1997–98	Parma	6	0	**6**	**0**
1997–98	Internazionale	9	1		
1998–99	Internazionale	7	0	**16**	**1**
1999–2000	Perugia	25	0		
2000–01	Perugia	4	0		
2001–02	Perugia	30	1		
2002–03	Perugia	31	1		
2003–04	Ancona	27	1	**27**	**1**
2004–05	Perugia	39	4	**129**	**6**
2005–06	QPR	26	0		
2006–07	QPR	14	0	**40**	**0**

MINTO-ST AIMIE, Kieron (M) **0 0**
b.Wembley

2006–07	QPR	0	0		

MOORE, Stefan (F) **77 5**
H: 5 10 W: 10 12 b.Birmingham 28-9-83
Source: Scholar. *Honours:* England Youth.

2000–01	Aston Villa	0	0		
2001–02	Aston Villa	0	0		
2001–02	*Chesterfield*	2	0	**2**	**0**
2002–03	Aston Villa	13	1		
2003–04	Aston Villa	8	1		
2004–05	Aston Villa	1	0	**22**	**2**
2004–05	*Millwall*	6	0	**6**	**0**
2004–05	*Leicester C*	7	0	**7**	**0**
2005–06	QPR	25	2		
2006–07	QPR	3	0	**28**	**2**
2006–07	*Port Vale*	12	1	**12**	**1**

NYGAARD, Marc (F) **225 38**
H: 6 5 W: 14 05 b.Copenhagen 1-9-76
Source: FC Copenhagen. *Honours:* Denmark Youth, Under-21, 6 full caps.

1995–96	Heerenveen	6	1		
1996–97	Heerenveen	20	5	**26**	**6**
1997–98	MVV	34	3	**34**	**3**
1998–99	Roda JC	30	10		
1999–2000	Roda JC	2	0		
2000–01	Roda JC	24	1		
2001–02	Roda JC	21	1	**77**	**12**
2002–03	Lommel	4	1	**4**	**1**
2002–03	Excelsior	8	1	**8**	**1**
2003–04	Catania	12	3	**12**	**3**
2003–04	Vicenza	4	0	**4**	**0**
2004–05	Brescia	10	0	**10**	**0**
2005–06	QPR	27	9		
2006–07	QPR	23	3	**50**	**12**

OLISEH, Egutu (M) **172 3**
H: 6 0 W: 11 09 b.Lagos 18-11-80

1998–99	Nancy	4	0		
1999–2000	Nancy	8	0		
1999–2000	Louhans-Cuiseaux	8	0	**8**	**0**
2000–01	Nancy	4	0		
2001–02	Beauvais	34	0	**34**	**0**
2002–03	Nancy	30	0	**46**	**0**
2003–04	Grenoble	18	0		
2004–05	Grenoble	33	2	**51**	**2**
2005–06	La Louviere	31	1	**31**	**1**
2006–07	QPR	2	0	**2**	**0**

To Montpellier January 2007

REHMAN, Zesh (D) **70 2**
H: 6 2 W: 12 08 b.Birmingham 14-10-83
Source: Scholar. *Honours:* England Youth, Pakistan full caps.

2001–02	Fulham	0	0		
2002–03	Fulham	0	0		
2003–04	Fulham	1	0		
2003–04	*Brighton & HA*	11	2		
2004–05	Fulham	17	0		
2005–06	Fulham	3	0	**21**	**0**
2005–06	*Norwich C*	5	0	**5**	**0**
2006–07	QPR	25	0	**25**	**0**
2006–07	*Brighton & HA*	8	0	**19**	**2**

ROWLANDS, Martin (M) **269 45**
H: 5 9 W: 10 10 b.Hammersmith 8-2-79
Source: Farnborough T. *Honours:* Eire Under-21, 3 full caps.

1998–99	Brentford	36	4		
1999–2000	Brentford	40	6		
2000–01	Brentford	32	2		
2001–02	Brentford	23	7		
2002–03	Brentford	18	1	**149**	**20**
2003–04	QPR	42	10		
2004–05	QPR	35	3		
2005–06	QPR	14	2		
2006–07	QPR	29	10	**120**	**25**

ROYCE, Simon (G) **267 0**
H: 6 2 W: 12 10 b.Forest Gate 9-9-71
Source: Heybridge Swifts.

1991–92	Southend U	1	0		
1992–93	Southend U	3	0		
1993–94	Southend U	6	0		
1994–95	Southend U	13	0		
1995–96	Southend U	46	0		
1996–97	Southend U	43	0		
1997–98	Southend U	37	0	**149**	**0**
1998–99	Charlton Ath	8	0		
1999–2000	Charlton Ath	0	0		
2000–01	Leicester C	19	0		
2001–02	Leicester C	0	0		
2001–02	*Brighton & HA*	6	0	**6**	**0**
2001–02	*Manchester C*	0	0		
2002–03	Leicester C	0	0	**19**	**0**
2002–03	*QPR*	16	0		
2003–04	Charlton Ath	1	0		
2004–05	Charlton Ath	0	0	**9**	**0**
2004–05	*Luton T*	2	0	**2**	**0**
2004–05	*QPR*	13	0		
2005–06	QPR	30	0		
2006–07	QPR	20	0	**79**	**0**
2006–07	*Gillingham*	3	0	**3**	**0**

SHIMMIN, Dominic (D) **3 0**
H: 6 0 W: 12 06 b.Bermondsey 13-10-87
Source: Arsenal Scholar.

2004–05	QPR	0	0		
2005–06	QPR	2	0		
2006–07	QPR	1	0	**3**	**0**

STEWART, Damion (D) **68 2**
H: 6 3 W: 13 10 b.Jamaica 18-8-80
Source: Harbour View. *Honours:* Jamaica 35 full caps, 2 goals.

2005–06	Bradford C	23	1	**23**	**1**
2006–07	QPR	45	1	**45**	**1**

TCHAKOUNTE, Armel (M) **0 0**
H: 6 3 W: 13 08 b.Cameroon 22-12-78
Source: Carshalton Ath.

2006–07	QPR	0	0

THOMAS, Sean (G) **0 0**
H: 6 1 W: 12 03 b.Edgware 5-9-87
Source: Scholar.

2005–06	QPR	0	0
2006–07	QPR	0	0

TIMOSKA, Sampsa (D) **148 8**
H: 6 1 W: 11 11 b.Kokemaki 12-2-79
Honours: Finland Under-21, 2 full caps.

1998	MyPa	1	0		
1999	MyPa	14	0		
2000	MyPa	16	0		
2001	MyPa	19	1		
2002	MyPa	26	1		
2003	MyPa	18	1		
2004	MyPa	23	3		
2005	MyPa	17	2	**134**	**8**
2006–07	QPR	14	0	**14**	**0**

WARD, Nick (M) **27 2**
H: 6 0 W: 12 06 b.Perth 24-3-85
Honours: Australia Under-21.

2006–07	QPR	19	1	**19**	**1**
2006–07	*Brighton & HA*	8	1	**8**	**1**

READING (67)

ANDERSEN, Mikkel (G) **0 0**
H: 6 5 W: 12 08 b.Herlev 17-12-88
Source: AB Copenhagen. *Honours:* Denmark Youth.

2006–07	Reading	0	0

BENNETT, Alan (D) **0 0**
H: 6 2 W: 12 08 b.Kilkenny 4-10-81
Honours: Eire Under-21, 2 full caps.

2006–07	Reading	0	0

BIKEY, Andre (M) **42 1**
H: 6 0 W: 12 08 b.Douala 8-1-85
Source: Espanyol, Marco. *Honours:* Cameroon 4 caps.

2003–04	Pacos de Ferreira	2	0	**2**	**0**
2004–05	Dep Aves	0	0		
2005	Shinnik	11	1	**11**	**1**
2005	Loko Moscow	9	0		
2006	Loko Moscow	5	0	**14**	**0**
2006–07	Reading	15	0	**15**	**0**

BOZANIC, Oliver (M) **0 0**
H: 6 0 W: 12 00 b.Melbourne 8-1-89
Source: Central Coast M.

2006–07	Reading	0	0

BROWN, Aaron (D) **4 0**
H: 6 4 W: 14 07 b.Birmingham 23-6-83
Source: Tamworth.

2005–06	Reading	0	0		
2005–06	*Bournemouth*	4	0	**4**	**0**
2006–07	Reading	0	0		

CONVEY, Bobby (M) **72 7**
H: 5 8 W: 10 12 b.Philadelphia 27-5-83
Source: DC United. *Honours:* USA Youth, Under-21, 43 full caps, 1 goal.

2004–05	Reading	18	0		
2005–06	Reading	45	7		
2006–07	Reading	9	0	**72**	**7**

COX, Simon (M) **23 3**
H: 5 10 W: 10 12 b.Reading 28-4-87
Source: Scholar.

2005–06	Reading	2	0		
2006–07	Reading	0	0	**2**	**0**
2006–07	*Brentford*	13	0	**13**	**0**
2006–07	*Northampton T*	8	3	**8**	**3**

DAVIES, Scott (M) **0 0**
H: 5 11 W: 12 00 b.Dublin 10-3-88
Source: Scholar.

2006–07	Reading	0	0

DE LA CRUZ, Ulises (D) **298 27**
H: 5 8 W: 12 10 b.Piqulucho 8-2-74
Source: From Cruzeiro. *Honours:* Ecuador Youth, Under-23, 94 full caps, 5 goals.

1996	Aucas	32	3	**32**	**3**
1997	LDU Quito	38	4		
1998	LDU Quito	42	7		
1999	LDU Quito	22	4		
1999	Cruzeiro	4	0	**4**	**0**
2000	LDU Quito	30	5	**132**	**20**
2001–02	Hibernian	32	2	**32**	**2**
2002–03	Aston Villa	20	1		
2003–04	Aston Villa	28	0		
2004–05	Aston Villa	34	0		
2005–06	Aston Villa	7	0	**89**	**1**
2006–07	Reading	9	1	**9**	**1**

DOYLE, Kevin (F) **120 51**
H: 5 11 W: 12 06 b.Adamstown 18-9-83
Source: Adamstown, Wexford, St Patrick's Ath. *Honours:* Eire Under-21, 9 full caps, 3 goals.

2004	Cork C	32	13		
2005	Cork C	11	7	**43**	**20**
2005–06	Reading	45	18		
2006–07	Reading	32	13	**77**	**31**

DUBERRY, Michael (D) **254 6**
H: 6 1 W: 13 10 b.Enfield 14-10-75
Source: Trainee. *Honours:* England Under-21.

1993–94	Chelsea	1	0		
1994–95	Chelsea	0	0		
1995–96	Chelsea	22	0		
1995–96	*Bournemouth*	7	0	**7**	**0**
1996–97	Chelsea	15	1		
1997–98	Chelsea	23	0		
1998–99	Chelsea	25	0	**86**	**1**
1999–2000	Leeds U	13	1		
2000–01	Leeds U	5	0		
2001–02	Leeds U	3	0		
2002–03	Leeds U	14	0		
2003–04	Leeds U	19	3		
2004–05	Leeds U	4	0	**58**	**4**
2004–05	Stoke C	25	0		
2005–06	Stoke C	41	1		
2006–07	Stoke C	29	0	**95**	**1**
2006–07	Reading	8	0	**8**	**0**

FEDERICI, Adam (G) **2 0**
H: 6 2 W: 14 02 b.Nowra 31-1-85
Honours: Australia Youth, Under-21.

2005–06	Reading	0	0		
2006–07	Reading	2	0	**2**	**0**

GOLBOURNE, Scott (M) **49 1**
H: 5 8 W: 11 08 b.Bristol 29-2-88
Source: Scholar. *Honours:* England Youth.

2004–05	Bristol C	9	0		
2005–06	Bristol C	5	0	**14**	**0**
2005–06	Reading	1	0		
2006–07	Reading	0	0	**1**	**0**
2006–07	*Wycombe W*	34	1	**34**	**1**

GUNNARSSON, Brynjar (M) **290 29**
H: 6 1 W: 12 01 b.Reykjavik 16-10-75
Honours: Iceland Youth, Under-21, 55 full caps, 3 goals.

1995	KR	16	1		
1996	KR	18	0		
1997	KR	16	0	**50**	**1**
1998	Moss	5	2	**5**	**2**
1999–2000	Stoke C	22	1		
2000–01	Stoke C	46	5		
2001–02	Stoke C	23	5		
2002–03	Stoke C	40	5		
2003–04	Nottingham F	13	0	**13**	**0**
2003–04	*Stoke C*	3	0	**134**	**16**
2004–05	Watford	36	3	**36**	**3**
2005–06	Reading	29	4		
2006–07	Reading	23	3	**52**	**7**

HAHNEMANN, Marcus (G) **285 0**
H: 6 3 W: 13 03 b.Seattle 15-6-72
Honours: USA 6 full caps.

1997	Colorado Rapids	25	0		
1998	Colorado Rapids	28	0		
1999	Colorado Rapids	13	0	**66**	**0**
1999–2000	Fulham	0	0		
2000–01	Fulham	2	0		
2001–02	Fulham	0	0	**2**	**0**
2001–02	*Rochdale*	5	0	**5**	**0**
2001–02	*Reading*	6	0		
2002–03	Reading	41	0		
2003–04	Reading	36	0		
2004–05	Reading	46	0		
2005–06	Reading	45	0		
2006–07	Reading	38	0	**212**	**0**

HALFORD, Greg (D) **139 18**
H: 6 4 W: 12 10 b.Chelmsford 8-12-84
Source: Scholar. *Honours:* England Youth, Under-20.

2002–03	Colchester U	1	0		
2003–04	Colchester U	18	4		
2004–05	Colchester U	44	4		
2005–06	Colchester U	45	7		
2006–07	Colchester U	28	3	**136**	**18**
2006–07	Reading	3	0	**3**	**0**

HALLS, John (M) **76 3**
H: 6 0 W: 11 11 b.Islington 14-2-82
Source: Scholar. *Honours:* England Youth, Under-20.

2000–01	Arsenal	0	0		
2001–02	Arsenal	0	0		
2001–02	*Colchester U*	6	0	**6**	**0**
2002–03	Arsenal	0	0		
2003–04	Arsenal	0	0		
2003–04	Stoke C	34	0		
2004–05	Stoke C	22	0		
2005–06	Stoke C	13	2	**69**	**2**
2005–06	Reading	1	1		
2006–07	Reading	0	0	**1**	**1**

HAMER, Ben (G) **0 0**
H: 5 11 W: 12 04 b.Reading 20-11-87
Source: Crawley T.

2006–07	Reading	0	0		

HARPER, James (M) **240 18**
H: 5 10 W: 11 02 b.Chelmsford 9-11-80
Source: Trainee.

1999–2000	Arsenal	0	0		
2000–01	Arsenal	0	0		
2000–01	*Cardiff C*	3	0	**3**	**0**
2000–01	Reading	12	1		
2001–02	Reading	26	1		
2002–03	Reading	36	2		
2003–04	Reading	39	1		
2004–05	Reading	41	3		
2005–06	Reading	45	7		
2006–07	Reading	38	3	**237**	**18**

HAYES, Jonathan (M) **11 0**
H: 5 7 W: 11 00 b.Dublin 9-7-87
Source: Scholar. *Honours:* Eire Under-21.

2004–05	Reading	0	0		
2005–06	Reading	0	0		
2006–07	Reading	0	0		
2006–07	*Milton Keynes D*	11	0	**11**	**0**

HENRY, James (M) **1 0**
H: 6 1 W: 11 11 b.Reading 10-6-89
Source: Scholar. *Honours:* England Youth.

2006–07	Reading	0	0		
2006–07	*Nottingham F*	1	0	**1**	**0**

HUNT, Steve (M) **212 31**
H: 5 9 W: 10 10 b.Port Laoise 1-8-80
Source: Trainee. *Honours:* Eire Under-21, B, 5 full caps.

1999–2000	Crystal Palace	3	0		
2000–01	Crystal Palace	0	0	**3**	**0**
2001–02	Brentford	35	4		
2002–03	Brentford	42	7		
2003–04	Brentford	40	11		
2004–05	Brentford	19	3	**136**	**25**
2005–06	Reading	38	2		
2006–07	Reading	35	4	**73**	**6**

INGIMARSSON, Ivar (D) **379 31**
H: 6 0 W: 12 07 b.Reykjavik 20-8-77
Honours: Iceland Youth, Under-21, 18 full caps.

1995	Valur	12	0		
1996	Valur	17	2		
1997	Valur	16	3	**45**	**5**
1998	IBV	18	1		
1999	IBV	18	4	**36**	**5**
1999–2000	Torquay U	4	1	**4**	**1**
1999–2000	Brentford	25	1		
2000–01	Brentford	42	3		
2001–02	Brentford	46	6	**113**	**10**
2002–03	Wolverhampton W	13	2		
2002–03	*Brighton & HA*	15	0	**15**	**0**
2003–04	Wolverhampton W	0	0	**13**	**2**
2003–04	Reading	25	1		
2004–05	Reading	44	3		
2005–06	Reading	46	2		
2006–07	Reading	38	2	**153**	**8**

KITSON, Dave (F) **203 84**
H: 6 3 W: 12 07 b.Hitchin 21-1-80
Source: Arlesey.

2000–01	Cambridge U	8	1		
2001–02	Cambridge U	33	9		
2002–03	Cambridge U	44	20		
2003–04	Cambridge U	17	10	**102**	**40**
2003–04	Reading	17	5		
2004–05	Reading	37	19		
2005–06	Reading	34	18		
2006–07	Reading	13	2	**101**	**44**

LITA, Leroy (F) **144 49**
H: 5 7 W: 11 12 b.DR Congo 28-12-84
Source: Scholar. *Honours:* England Under-21.

2002–03	Bristol C	15	2		
2003–04	Bristol C	26	5		
2004–05	Bristol C	44	24	**85**	**31**
2005–06	Reading	26	11		
2006–07	Reading	33	7	**59**	**18**

LITTLE, Glen (M) **356 40**
H: 6 3 W: 13 00 b.Wimbledon 15-10-75
Source: Trainee.

1994–95	Crystal Palace	0	0		
1995–96	Crystal Palace	0	0		
1996–97	Glentoran	6	2	**6**	**2**
1996–97	Burnley	9	0		
1997–98	Burnley	24	4		
1998–99	Burnley	34	5		
1999–2000	Burnley	41	3		
2000–01	Burnley	34	3		
2001–02	Burnley	37	9		
2002–03	Burnley	33	5		
2002–03	*Reading*	6	1		
2003–04	Burnley	34	3	**246**	**32**
2003–04	*Bolton W*	4	0	**4**	**0**
2004–05	Reading	35	0		
2005–06	Reading	35	5		
2006–07	Reading	24	0	**100**	**6**

LONG, Shane (F) **33 5**
H: 5 10 W: 11 02 b.Gortnahoe 22-1-87
Honours: Eire Youth, B, Under-21, 4 full caps, 1 goal.

2005	Cork C	1	0	**1**	**0**
2005–06	Reading	11	3		
2006–07	Reading	21	2	**32**	**5**

MATE, Peter (D) **79 10**
H: 6 4 W: 14 13 b.Debrecen 2-12-84
Source: Tunet, Olasz. *Honours:* Hungary Under-21, 3 full caps.

2000–01	Debrecen	2	0		
2001–02	Debrecen	1	0		
2002–03	Debrecen	11	1		
2003–04	Diosgyor	14	1		
2004–05	Diosgyor	26	3	**40**	**4**
2005–06	Debrecen	25	5	**39**	**6**
2006–07	Reading	0	0		

MURTY, Graeme (D) **395 9**
H: 5 10 W: 11 10 b.Saltburn 13-11-74
Source: Trainee. *Honours:* Scotland B, 3 full caps.

1992–93	York C	0	0		
1993–94	York C	1	0		
1994–95	York C	20	2		
1995–96	York C	35	2		
1996–97	York C	27	2		
1997–98	York C	34	1	**117**	**7**
1998–99	Reading	9	0		
1999–2000	Reading	17	0		
2000–01	Reading	23	1		
2001–02	Reading	43	0		
2002–03	Reading	44	0		
2003–04	Reading	38	0		
2004–05	Reading	41	0		
2005–06	Reading	40	1		
2006–07	Reading	23	0	**278**	**2**

OSANO, Curtis (M) **0 0**
H: 5 11 W: 11 04 b.Nakuru 8-3-87
Source: Scholar.

2005–06	Reading	0	0		
2006–07	Reading	0	0		

OSTER, John (M) **232 19**
H: 5 9 W: 10 08 b.Boston 8-12-78
Source: From Trainee. *Honours:* Wales Youth, Under-21, B, 13 full caps.

1996–97	Grimsby T	24	3		
1997–98	Everton	31	1		
1998–99	Everton	9	0	**40**	**1**
1999–2000	Sunderland	10	0		
2000–01	Sunderland	8	0		
2001–02	Sunderland	0	0		
2001–02	*Barnsley*	2	0	**2**	**0**
2002–03	Sunderland	3	0		
2002–03	*Grimsby T*	17	6	**41**	**9**
2003–04	Sunderland	38	5		
2004–05	Sunderland	9	0	**68**	**5**
2004–05	*Leeds U*	8	1	**8**	**1**
2004–05	Burnley	15	1	**15**	**1**
2005–06	Reading	33	1		
2006–07	Reading	25	1	**58**	**2**

PEARCE, Alex (D) **15 1**
H: 6 0 W: 11 10 b.Wallingford 9-11-88
Source: Scholar. *Honours:* Scotland Youth.

2006–07	Reading	0	0		
2006–07	*Northampton T*	15	1	**15**	**1**

SEOL, Ki-Hyun (F) **192 40**
H: 6 0 W: 11 07 b.South Korea 8-1-79
Honours: South Korea 75 full caps, 16 goals.

2000–01	Antwerp	25	10	**25**	**10**
2001–02	Anderlecht	20	3		
2002–03	Anderlecht	32	12		
2003–04	Anderlecht	19	3	**71**	**18**
2004–05	Wolverhampton W	37	4		
2005–06	Wolverhampton W	32	4	**69**	**8**
2006–07	Reading	27	4	**27**	**4**

SHOREY, Nicky (D) **246 10**
H: 5 9 W: 10 08 b.Romford 19-2-81
Source: Trainee. *Honours:* England B, 1 full cap.

1999–2000	Leyton Orient	7	0		
2000–01	Leyton Orient	8	0	**15**	**0**
2000–01	Reading	0	0		
2001–02	Reading	32	0		
2002–03	Reading	43	2		
2003–04	Reading	35	2		
2004–05	Reading	44	3		
2005–06	Reading	40	2		
2006–07	Reading	37	1	**231**	**10**

SIDWELL, Steve (M) **210 38**
H: 5 10 W: 11 00 b.Wandsworth 14-12-82
Source: Scholar. *Honours:* England Under-20, Under-21.

2001–02	Arsenal	0	0		
2001–02	*Brentford*	30	4	**30**	**4**
2002–03	Arsenal	0	0		
2002–03	*Brighton & HA*	12	5	**12**	**5**
2002–03	Reading	13	2		
2003–04	Reading	43	8		
2004–05	Reading	44	5		
2005–06	Reading	33	10		
2006–07	Reading	35	4	**168**	**29**

SODJE, Sam (D) **93 13**
H: 6 0 W: 12 00 b.Greenwich 29-5-79
Source: Stevenage B, Margate. *Honours:* Nigeria full caps.

2004–05	Brentford	40	7		
2005–06	Brentford	43	5	**83**	**12**
2006–07	Reading	3	0	**3**	**0**
2006–07	*WBA*	7	1	**7**	**1**

SONKO, Ibrahima (D) **188 13**
H: 6 3 W: 13 07 b.Bignola 22-1-81
Source: St Etienne, Grenoble. *Honours:* Senegal Under-21.

2002–03	Brentford	37	5		
2003–04	Brentford	43	3	**80**	**8**
2004–05	Reading	39	1		
2005–06	Reading	46	3		
2006–07	Reading	23	1	**108**	**5**

STACK, Graham (G) **39 0**
H: 6 2 W: 12 07 b.Hampstead 26-9-81
Honours: Eire Under-21.

2000–01	Arsenal	0	0		
2001–02	Arsenal	0	0		
2002–03	Arsenal	0	0		

2003–04	Arsenal	0	0		
2004–05	Arsenal	0	0		
2004–05	*Millwall*	26	0	**26**	**0**
2005–06	Arsenal	0	0		
2005–06	Reading	1	0		
2006–07	Reading	0	0	**1**	**0**
2006–07	*Leeds U*	12	0	**12**	**0**

Scholars
Bayley, Harrison; Bignall, Nicholas; Bygrave, Adam Michael; Church, Simon Richard; Cox, Patrick; Hateley, Tom; Illugason, Viktor; Karacan, Jem Paul; Kelly, Julian James; Kitteridge, Ross Harrison; McCarthy, Alex; Osano, Curtis; Piotrowski, Thomas Richard; Robson-Kanu, Hal; Sigurdsson, Gylfi; Small, Jamal Forde; Spence, Daniel; Webb, Josh; Williams, Luke.

ROCHDALE (68)

BATES, Tom (M) 3 0
H: 5 10 W: 12 00 b.Coventry 31-10-85

2002–03	Coventry C	1	0		
2003–04	Coventry C	0	0		
2004–05	Coventry C	0	0	**1**	**0**
From Leamington.					
2006–07	Rochdale	2	0	**2**	**0**

BOARDMAN, Jon (D) 25 1
H: 6 2 W: 12 09 b.Reading 27-1-81
Source: Trainee.

1999–2000	Crystal Palace	0	0		
2000–01	Crystal Palace	0	0		
2001–02	Crystal Palace	0	0		
From Woking.					
2005–06	Rochdale	21	1		
2006–07	Rochdale	4	0	**25**	**1**

BROWN, Gary (D) 38 0
H: 5 6 W: 10 00 b.Darwen 29-10-85
Source: Scholar.

2004–05	Rochdale	1	0		
2005–06	Rochdale	16	0		
2006–07	Rochdale	21	0	**38**	**0**

CHRISTIE, Iyseden (F) 243 58
H: 5 10 W: 12 02 b.Coventry 14-11-76
Source: Trainee.

1994–95	Coventry C	0	0		
1995–96	Coventry C	1	0		
1996–97	Coventry C	0	0	**1**	**0**
1996–97	*Bournemouth*	4	0	**4**	**0**
1996–97	*Mansfield T*	8	0		
1997–98	Mansfield T	39	10		
1998–99	Mansfield T	42	8		
1999–2000	Leyton Orient	36	7		
2000–01	Leyton Orient	7	2		
2001–02	Leyton Orient	15	3	**58**	**12**
2002–03	Mansfield T	37	18		
2003–04	Mansfield T	27	8	**153**	**44**
2004–05	Kidderminster H	8	0		
2005–06	Kidderminster H	0	0	**8**	**0**
2005–06	Rochdale	14	2		
2006–07	Rochdale	5	0	**19**	**2**

COLEMAN, Theo (M) 1 0
H: 5 11 W: 10 07 b.Manchester 5-5-89

2005–06	Rochdale	1	0		
2006–07	Rochdale	0	0	**1**	**0**

COMYN-PLATT, Charlie (D) 28 1
H: 6 2 W: 12 00 b.Salford 2-10-85
Source: Scholar.

2003–04	Bolton W	0	0		
2004–05	Bolton W	0	0		
2004–05	*Wycombe W*	4	0	**4**	**0**
2005–06	Swindon T	22	1		
2006–07	Swindon T	2	0	**24**	**1**
2006–07	Rochdale	0	0		

CROOKS, Lee (M) 242 4
H: 6 2 W: 12 01 b.Wakefield 14-1-78
Source: Trainee. *Honours:* England Youth.

1994–95	Manchester C	0	0		
1995–96	Manchester C	0	0		
1996–97	Manchester C	15	0		
1997–98	Manchester C	5	0		
1998–99	Manchester C	34	1		
1999–2000	Manchester C	20	1		
2000–01	Manchester C	2	0	**76**	**2**
2000–01	*Northampton T*	3	0	**3**	**0**
2000–01	Barnsley	0	0		
2001–02	Barnsley	26	0		
2002–03	Barnsley	18	0		
2003–04	Barnsley	23	0	**67**	**0**
2004–05	Bradford C	32	1		
2005–06	Bradford C	15	0	**47**	**1**
2005–06	*Notts Co*	18	1	**18**	**1**
2006–07	Rochdale	31	0	**31**	**0**

DAGNALL, Chris (F) 97 27
H: 5 8 W: 12 03 b.Liverpool 15-4-86
Source: Scholar.

2003–04	Tranmere R	10	1		
2004–05	Tranmere R	23	6		
2005–06	Tranmere R	6	0	**39**	**7**
2005–06	Rochdale	21	3		
2006–07	Rochdale	37	17	**58**	**20**

DOOLAN, John (M) 419 22
H: 6 1 W: 13 00 b.Liverpool 7-5-74
Source: Trainee.

1992–93	Everton	0	0		
1993–94	Everton	0	0		
1994–95	Mansfield T	24	1		
1995–96	Mansfield T	42	2		
1996–97	Mansfield T	41	6		
1997–98	Mansfield T	24	1	**131**	**10**
1997–98	Barnet	17	0		
1998–99	Barnet	42	2		
1999–2000	Barnet	44	2		
2000–01	Barnet	31	3		
2001–02	Barnet	0	0		
2002–03	Barnet	0	0	**134**	**7**
2003–04	Doncaster R	39	0		
2004–05	Doncaster R	38	2	**77**	**2**
2005–06	Blackpool	19	0	**19**	**0**
2005–06	Rochdale	18	0		
2006–07	Rochdale	40	3	**58**	**3**

GILKS, Matthew (G) 176 0
H: 6 3 W: 13 12 b.Rochdale 4-6-82
Source: Scholar.

2000–01	Rochdale	3	0		
2001–02	Rochdale	19	0		
2002–03	Rochdale	20	0		
2003–04	Rochdale	12	0		
2004–05	Rochdale	30	0		
2005–06	Rochdale	46	0		
2006–07	Rochdale	46	0	**176**	**0**

GOODALL, Alan (D) 120 8
H: 5 7 W: 11 08 b.Birkenhead 2-12-81
Source: Bangor C.

2004–05	Rochdale	34	2		
2005–06	Rochdale	40	3		
2006–07	Rochdale	46	3	**120**	**8**

JACKSON, Mark (D) 198 4
H: 5 11 W: 12 00 b.Barnsley 30-9-77
Source: Trainee. *Honours:* England Youth.

1995–96	Leeds U	1	0		
1996–97	Leeds U	17	0		
1997–98	Leeds U	1	0		
1998–99	Leeds U	0	0		
1998–99	*Huddersfield T*	5	0	**5**	**0**
1999–2000	Leeds U	0	0	**19**	**0**
1999–2000	*Barnsley*	1	0	**1**	**0**
1999–2000	Scunthorpe U	6	0		
2000–01	Scunthorpe U	32	1		
2001–02	Scunthorpe U	45	3		
2002–03	Scunthorpe U	33	0		
2003–04	Scunthorpe U	17	0		
2004–05	Scunthorpe U	3	0	**136**	**4**
2004–05	Kidderminster H	13	0		
2005–06	Kidderminster H	0	0	**13**	**0**
2005–06	Rochdale	12	0		
2006–07	Rochdale	12	0	**24**	**0**

JONES, Gary (M) 338 43
H: 5 11 W: 12 05 b.Birkenhead 3-6-77
Source: Caernarfon T.

1997–98	Swansea C	8	0	**8**	**0**
1997–98	Rochdale	17	2		
1998–99	Rochdale	20	0		
1999–2000	Rochdale	39	7		
2000–01	Rochdale	44	8		
2001–02	Rochdale	20	5		
2001–02	Barnsley	25	1		
2002–03	Barnsley	31	1		
2003–04	Barnsley	0	0	**56**	**2**
2003–04	Rochdale	26	4		
2004–05	Rochdale	39	8		
2005–06	Rochdale	42	4		
2006–07	Rochdale	27	3	**274**	**41**

McARDLE, Rory (D) 45 1
H: 6 1 W: 11 11 b.Doncaster 1-5-87
Source: Scholar. *Honours:* Northern Ireland Youth, Under-21.

2004–05	Sheffield W	0	0		
2005–06	Sheffield W	0	0		
2005–06	*Rochdale*	19	1		
2006–07	Sheffield W	1	0	**1**	**0**
2006–07	Rochdale	25	0	**44**	**1**

MOYO-MODISE, Clive (F) 28 1
H: 5 10 W: 11 00 b.London 20-9-87

2005–06	Rochdale	9	0		
2006–07	Rochdale	19	1	**28**	**1**

MURRAY, Glenn (F) 69 22
H: 6 1 W: 12 12 b.Maryport 25-9-83
Source: Wilmington Hammerheads, Workington.

2005–06	Carlisle U	26	3		
2006–07	Carlisle U	1	0	**27**	**3**
2006–07	*Stockport Co*	11	3	**11**	**3**
2006–07	Rochdale	31	16	**31**	**16**

PERKINS, David (D) 18 0
H: 5 6 W: 11 06 b.St Asaph 21-6-82

2006–07	Rochdale	18	0	**18**	**0**

POOLE, Glenn (M) 6 0
H: 5 7 W: 11 04 b.Essex 3-2-81
Source: Thurrock, Grays Ath.

2006–07	Rochdale	6	0	**6**	**0**

PRENDERGAST, Rory (F) 45 1
H: 5 8 W: 12 00 b.Pontefract 6-4-78
Source: Rochdale.

1995–96	Barnsley	0	0		
1996–97	Barnsley	0	0		
1997–98	Barnsley	0	0		
1998–99	York C	3	0	**3**	**0**
1998–99	Oldham Ath	0	0		
From Accrington S					
2005–06	Blackpool	24	0		
2006–07	Blackpool	5	0	**29**	**0**
2006–07	Rochdale	5	1	**5**	**1**
2006–07	*Darlington*	8	0	**8**	**0**

RAMSDEN, Simon (D) 118 4
H: 6 0 W: 12 06 b.Bishop Auckland 17-12-81
Source: Scholar.

2000–01	Sunderland	0	0		
2001–02	Sunderland	0	0		
2002–03	Sunderland	0	0		
2002–03	*Notts Co*	32	0	**32**	**0**
2003–04	Sunderland	0	0		
2004–05	Grimsby T	25	0		
2005–06	Grimsby T	12	0	**37**	**0**
2005–06	Rochdale	15	1		
2006–07	Rochdale	34	3	**49**	**4**

RUNDLE, Adam (F) 143 14
H: 5 8 W: 11 02 b.Durham 8-7-84
Source: Scholar.

2001–02	Darlington	12	0		
2002–03	Darlington	5	0	**17**	**0**
2002–03	Carlisle U	21	1		
2003–04	Carlisle U	23	0		
2004–05	Carlisle U	0	0	**44**	**1**
2004–05	Mansfield T	18	4		
2005–06	Mansfield T	35	5	**53**	**9**
2006–07	Rochdale	29	4	**29**	**4**

SAKO, Morike (M) 42 6
H: 6 7 W: 12 00 b.Paris 17-11-81
Source: Delemont.

2005–06	Torquay U	25	3	**25**	**3**
2006–07	Rochdale	17	3	**17**	**3**

To St Pauli January 2007

SHARP, James (D) 127 4
H: 6 1 W: 13 00 b.Reading 2-1-76
Source: Reading, Florida Tech, Aldershot T, Wokingham, Andover T.

2000–01	Hartlepool U	34	2		

2001–02 Hartlepool U 15 0
2002–03 Hartlepool U 0 0 **49 2**
2003–04 Falkirk 30 1
2004–05 Falkirk 4 0 **34 1**
2005–06 Torquay U 32 0 **32 0**
2006–07 Shrewsbury T 0 0
2006–07 Rochdale 12 1 **12 1**

STANTON, Nathan (D) 272 0
H: 5 9 W: 12 06 b.Nottingham 6-5-81
Source: Trainee. *Honours:* England Youth.
1997–98 Scunthorpe U 1 0
1998–99 Scunthorpe U 4 0
1999–2000 Scunthorpe U 34 0
2000–01 Scunthorpe U 38 0
2001–02 Scunthorpe U 42 0
2002–03 Scunthorpe U 42 0
2003–04 Scunthorpe U 33 0
2004–05 Scunthorpe U 21 0
2005–06 Scunthorpe U 22 0 **237 0**
2006–07 Rochdale 35 0 **35 0**

THOMPSON, Joe (M) 14 0
H: 6 0 W: 9 07 b.Rochdale 5-3-89
Source: Scholar.
2005–06 Rochdale 1 0
2006–07 Rochdale 13 0 **14 0**

WARBURTON, Callum (M) 4 0
H: 5 9 W: 11 00 b.Stockport 25-2-89
Source: Scholar.
2006–07 Rochdale 4 0 **4 0**

ROTHERHAM U (69)

BOPP, Eugene (M) 106 13
H: 5 11 W: 12 03 b.Kiev 5-9-83
Source: Bayern Munich.
2000–01 Nottingham F 0 0
2001–02 Nottingham F 19 1
2002–03 Nottingham F 13 2
2003–04 Nottingham F 15 1
2004–05 Nottingham F 18 3
2005–06 Nottingham F 12 1 **77 8**
2006–07 Rotherham U 29 5 **29 5**

BROGAN, Stephen (D) 26 0
H: 5 7 W: 10 04 b.Rotherham 12-4-88
Source: Scholar.
2005–06 Rotherham U 3 0
2006–07 Rotherham U 23 0 **26 0**

COCHRANE, Justin (M) 109 2
H: 5 11 W: 11 07 b.Hackney 26-1-82
Source: Scholarship.
1999–2000 QPR 0 0
2000–01 QPR 1 0
2001–02 QPR 0 0
2002–03 QPR 0 0 **1 0**
From Hayes.
2003–04 Crewe Alex 39 0
2004–05 Crewe Alex 29 0
2005–06 Crewe Alex 4 0 **72 0**
2005–06 *Gillingham* 5 1 **5 1**
2006–07 Rotherham U 31 1 **31 1**

CUTLER, Neil (G) 208 0
H: 6 1 W: 12 00 b.Cannock 3-9-76
Source: Trainee. *Honours:* England Schools, Youth.
1993–94 WBA 0 0
1994–95 WBA 0 0
1995–96 WBA 0 0
1995–96 *Coventry C* 0 0
1995–96 *Chester C* 1 0
1996–97 Crewe Alex 0 0
1996–97 *Chester C* 5 0
1997–98 Crewe Alex 0 0
1998–99 Chester C 23 0
1999–2000 Chester C 0 0 **29 0**
1999–2000 Aston Villa 1 0
2000–01 Aston Villa 0 0
2000–01 *Oxford U* 11 0 **11 0**
2001–02 Aston Villa 0 0 **1 0**
2001–02 Stoke C 36 0
2002–03 Stoke C 20 0
2002–03 *Swansea C* 13 0 **13 0**
2003–04 Stoke C 13 0 **69 0**
2004–05 Stockport Co 22 0 **22 0**

2005–06 Rotherham U 22 0
2006–07 Rotherham U 41 0 **63 0**

DUNCUM, Sam (M) 5 0
H: 5 9 W: 11 02 b.Sheffield 18-2-87
Source: Scholar.
2004–05 Rotherham U 2 0
2005–06 Rotherham U 1 0
2006–07 Rotherham U 2 0 **5 0**

FACEY, Delroy (F) 225 44
H: 6 0 W: 15 02 b.Huddersfield 22-4-80
Source: Trainee.
1996–97 Huddersfield T 3 0
1997–98 Huddersfield T 3 0
1998–99 Huddersfield T 20 3
1999–2000 Huddersfield T 2 0
2000–01 Huddersfield T 34 10
2001–02 Huddersfield T 13 2
2002–03 Huddersfield T 0 0
2002–03 *Bradford C* 6 1 **6 1**
2002–03 Bolton W 9 1
2003–04 Bolton W 1 0 **10 1**
2003–04 *Burnley* 14 5 **14 5**
2003–04 WBA 9 0 **9 0**
2004–05 Hull C 21 4 **21 4**
2004–05 *Huddersfield T* 4 0 **79 15**
2004–05 Oldham Ath 6 0
2005–06 Oldham Ath 3 0 **9 0**
2005–06 Tranmere R 37 8 **37 8**
2006–07 Rotherham U 40 10 **40 10**

FLEMING, Craig (D) 582 13
H: 6 0 W: 12 11 b.Halifax 6-10-71
Source: Trainee.
1988–89 Halifax T 1 0
1989–90 Halifax T 10 0
1990–91 Halifax T 46 0 **57 0**
1991–92 Oldham Ath 32 1
1992–93 Oldham Ath 24 0
1993–94 Oldham Ath 37 0
1994–95 Oldham Ath 5 0
1995–96 Oldham Ath 22 0
1996–97 Oldham Ath 44 0 **164 1**
1997–98 Norwich C 22 1
1998–99 Norwich C 37 3
1999–2000 Norwich C 39 3
2000–01 Norwich C 39 0
2001–02 Norwich C 46 0
2002–03 Norwich C 30 0
2003–04 Norwich C 46 3
2004–05 Norwich C 38 1
2005–06 Norwich C 36 1
2006–07 Norwich C 10 0 **343 12**
2006–07 *Wolverhampton W* 1 0 **1 0**
2006–07 Rotherham U 17 0 **17 0**

HURST, Paul (D) 422 13
H: 5 4 W: 9 04 b.Sheffield 25-9-74
Source: Trainee.
1993–94 Rotherham U 4 0
1994–95 Rotherham U 13 0
1995–96 Rotherham U 40 1
1996–97 Rotherham U 30 3
1997–98 Rotherham U 30 0
1998–99 Rotherham U 32 2
1999–2000 Rotherham U 30 2
2000–01 Rotherham U 44 3
2001–02 Rotherham U 45 0
2002–03 Rotherham U 44 1
2003–04 Rotherham U 28 1
2004–05 Rotherham U 39 0
2005–06 Rotherham U 31 0
2006–07 Rotherham U 12 0 **422 13**

KEANE, Michael (M) 144 8
H: 5 7 W: 10 10 b.Dublin 29-12-82
Source: Scholar. *Honours:* Eire Under-21.
2000–01 Preston NE 2 0
2001–02 Preston NE 20 2
2002–03 Preston NE 5 0
2002–03 *Grimsby T* 7 2 **7 2**
2003–04 Preston NE 30 1 **57 3**
2004–05 Hull C 20 3 **20 3**
2004–05 Rotherham U 10 0
2005–06 Rotherham U 28 0
2006–07 Rotherham U 22 0 **60 0**

KERR, Natt (D) 3 0
H: 6 0 W: 10 10 b.Manchester 31-10-87
Source: Crewe Alex Scholar.
2006–07 Rotherham U 3 0 **3 0**

KING, Liam (D) 6 0
H: 5 9 W: 10 02 b.Rainworth 3-12-87
Source: Scholar.
2005–06 Rotherham U 0 0
2006–07 Rotherham U 6 0 **6 0**

MILLS, Pablo (D) 119 2
H: 5 9 W: 11 04 b.Birmingham 27-5-84
Source: Trainee. *Honours:* England Youth.
2002–03 Derby Co 16 0
2003–04 Derby Co 19 0
2004–05 Derby Co 22 0
2005–06 Derby Co 1 0 **58 0**
2005–06 *Milton Keynes D* 16 1 **16 1**
2005–06 *Walsall* 14 0 **14 0**
2006–07 Rotherham U 31 1 **31 1**

MONTGOMERY, Gary (G) 45 0
H: 5 11 W: 13 08 b.Leamington Spa 8-10-82
Source: Scholar.
2000–01 Coventry C 0 0
2001–02 Coventry C 0 0
2001–02 *Crewe Alex* 0 0
2001–02 *Kidderminster H* 2 0 **2 0**
2002–03 Coventry C 8 0 **8 0**
2003–04 Rotherham U 4 0
2004–05 Rotherham U 1 0
2005–06 Rotherham U 24 0
2006–07 Rotherham U 6 0 **35 0**

MURDOCK, Colin (D) 273 11
H: 6 2 W: 13 00 b.Ballymena 2-7-75
Source: Trainee. *Honours:* Northern Ireland Schools, Youth, B, 34 full caps, 1 goal.
1992–93 Manchester U 0 0
1993–94 Manchester U 0 0
1994–95 Manchester U 0 0
1995–96 Manchester U 0 0
1996–97 Manchester U 0 0
1997–98 Preston NE 27 1
1998–99 Preston NE 33 1
1999–2000 Preston NE 33 2
2000–01 Preston NE 37 0
2001–02 Preston NE 23 2
2002–03 Preston NE 24 0 **177 6**
2003–04 Hibernian 32 3
2004–05 Hibernian 5 0 **37 3**
2004–05 Crewe Alex 16 0 **16 0**
2005–06 Rotherham U 39 2
2006–07 Rotherham U 4 0 **43 2**

NEWSHAM, Mark (F) 23 3
H: 5 10 W: 9 11 b.Hatfield 24-3-87
Source: Scholar.
2004–05 Rotherham U 4 0
2005–06 Rotherham U 3 0
2006–07 Rotherham U 16 3 **23 3**

O'GRADY, Chris (F) 68 9
H: 6 3 W: 12 04 b.Nottingham 25-1-86
Source: Trainee. *Honours:* England Youth.
2002–03 Leicester C 1 0
2003–04 Leicester C 0 0
2004–05 Leicester C 0 0
2004–05 *Notts Co* 9 0 **9 0**
2005–06 Leicester C 13 1
2005–06 *Rushden & D* 22 4 **22 4**
2006–07 Leicester C 10 0 **24 1**
2006–07 Rotherham U 13 4 **13 4**

PARTRIDGE, Richie (M) 84 8
H: 5 8 W: 11 00 b.Dublin 12-9-80
Source: Trainee. *Honours:* Eire Under-21.
1998–99 Liverpool 0 0
1999–2000 Liverpool 0 0
2000–01 Liverpool 0 0
2000–01 *Bristol R* 6 1 **6 1**
2001–02 Liverpool 0 0
2002–03 Liverpool 0 0
2002–03 *Coventry C* 27 4 **27 4**
2003–04 Liverpool 0 0
2004–05 Liverpool 0 0
2005–06 Sheffield W 18 0 **18 0**
2006–07 Rotherham U 33 3 **33 3**

ROBERTSON, Gregor (D) **89** **1**
H: 6 0 W: 12 04 b.Edinburgh 19-1-84
Honours: Scotland Under-21.

2000–01	Nottingham F	0	0		
2001–02	Nottingham F	0	0		
2002–03	Nottingham F	0	0		
2003–04	Nottingham F	16	0		
2004–05	Nottingham F	20	0	**36**	**0**
2005–06	Rotherham U	35	1		
2006–07	Rotherham U	18	0	**53**	**1**

SHARPS, Ian (D) **208** **8**
H: 6 3 W: 14 07 b.Warrington 23-10-80
Source: Trainee.

1998–99	Tranmere R	1	0		
1999–2000	Tranmere R	0	0		
2000–01	Tranmere R	0	0		
2001–02	Tranmere R	29	0		
2002–03	Tranmere R	30	3		
2003–04	Tranmere R	27	1		
2004–05	Tranmere R	44	1		
2005–06	Tranmere R	39	1	**170**	**6**
2006–07	Rotherham U	38	2	**38**	**2**

STREETE, Theo (D) **10** **1**
H: 6 2 W: 13 05 b.Birmingham 23-11-87
Source: Scholar.

2006–07	Derby Co	0	0		
2006–07	*Doncaster R*	6	1	**6**	**1**
2006–07	Rotherham U	4	0	**4**	**0**

TAYLOR, Ryan (F) **11** **0**
H: 6 2 W: 10 10 b.Rotherham 4-5-88
Source: Scholar.

2005–06	Rotherham U	1	0		
2006–07	Rotherham U	10	0	**11**	**0**

WOODS, Martin (M) **50** **4**
H: 5 11 W: 11 13 b.Airdrie 1-1-86
Source: Trainee. *Honours:* Scotland Youth, Under-21.

2002–03	Leeds U	0	0		
2003–04	Leeds U	0	0		
2004–05	Leeds U	1	0	**1**	**0**
2004–05	*Hartlepool U*	6	0	**6**	**0**
2005–06	Sunderland	7	0	**7**	**0**
2006–07	Rotherham U	36	4	**36**	**4**

WORRELL, David (D) **246** **0**
H: 5 11 W: 12 04 b.Dublin 12-1-78
Source: Trainee. *Honours:* Eire Youth, Under-21.

1994–95	Blackburn R	0	0		
1995–96	Blackburn R	0	0		
1996–97	Blackburn R	0	0		
1997–98	Blackburn R	0	0		
1998–99	Blackburn R	0	0		
1998–99	Dundee U	4	0		
1999–2000	Dundee U	13	0	**17**	**0**
2000–01	Plymouth Arg	14	0		
2001–02	Plymouth Arg	42	0		
2002–03	Plymouth Arg	43	0		
2003–04	Plymouth Arg	18	0		
2004–05	Plymouth Arg	30	0	**147**	**0**
2005–06	Rotherham U	41	0		
2006–07	Rotherham U	41	0	**82**	**0**

YATES, Jamie (F) **3** **0**
H: 5 7 W: 10 11 b.Sheffield 24-12-88
Source: Scholar.

2006–07	Rotherham U	3	0	**3**	**0**

SCUNTHORPE U (70)

ALLANSON, Ashley (M) **1** **0**
H: 5 11 W: 12 00 b.Hull 13-11-86
Source: Hull C Scholar.

2005–06	Scunthorpe U	1	0		
2006–07	Scunthorpe U	0	0	**1**	**0**

BARACLOUGH, Ian (M) **587** **40**
H: 6 1 W: 12 09 b.Leicester 4-12-70
Source: Trainee.

1988–89	Leicester C	0	0		
1989–90	Leicester C	0	0		
1989–90	*Wigan Ath*	9	2	**9**	**2**
1990–91	Leicester C	0	0		
1990–91	*Grimsby T*	4	0		
1991–92	Grimsby T	0	0		
1992–93	Grimsby T	1	0	**5**	**0**
1992–93	Lincoln C	36	5		
1993–94	Lincoln C	37	5	**73**	**10**
1994–95	Mansfield T	36	3		
1995–96	Mansfield T	11	2	**47**	**5**
1995–96	Notts Co	35	2		
1996–97	Notts Co	38	2		
1997–98	Notts Co	38	6		
1997–98	QPR	8	0		
1998–99	QPR	43	1		
1999–2000	QPR	45	0		
2000–01	QPR	29	0	**125**	**1**
2001–02	Notts Co	33	3		
2002–03	Notts Co	34	2		
2003–04	Notts Co	34	0	**212**	**15**
2004–05	Scunthorpe U	45	3		
2005–06	Scunthorpe U	38	3		
2006–07	Scunthorpe U	33	1	**116**	**7**

BUTLER, Andy (D) **103** **14**
H: 6 0 W: 13 00 b.Doncaster 4-11-83
Source: Scholar.

2003–04	Scunthorpe U	35	2		
2004–05	Scunthorpe U	37	10		
2005–06	Scunthorpe U	16	1		
2006–07	Scunthorpe U	11	1	**99**	**14**
2006–07	*Grimsby T*	4	0	**4**	**0**

BYRNE, Cliff (D) **137** **3**
H: 6 0 W: 12 11 b.Dublin 27-4-82
Honours: Eire Under-21.

1999–2000	Sunderland	0	0		
2000–01	Sunderland	0	0		
2001–02	Sunderland	0	0		
2002–03	Sunderland	0	0		
2002–03	*Scunthorpe U*	13	0		
2003–04	Scunthorpe U	39	1		
2004–05	Scunthorpe U	29	1		
2005–06	Scunthorpe U	32	1		
2006–07	Scunthorpe U	24	0	**137**	**3**

CROSBY, Andy (D) **581** **35**
H: 6 2 W: 13 13 b.Rotherham 3-3-73
Source: Leeds U Trainee.

1991–92	Doncaster R	22	0		
1992–93	Doncaster R	29	0		
1993–94	Doncaster R	0	0	**51**	**0**
1993–94	Darlington	25	0		
1994–95	Darlington	35	0		
1995–96	Darlington	45	1		
1996–97	Darlington	42	1		
1997–98	Darlington	34	1	**181**	**3**
1998–99	Chester C	41	4	**41**	**4**
1999–2000	Brighton & HA	36	3		
2000–01	Brighton & HA	34	2		
2001–02	Brighton & HA	2	0	**72**	**5**
2001–02	Oxford U	23	1		
2002–03	Oxford U	46	6		
2003–04	Oxford U	42	5	**111**	**12**
2004–05	Scunthorpe U	44	3		
2005–06	Scunthorpe U	42	3		
2006–07	Scunthorpe U	39	5	**125**	**11**

FOSTER, Steve (D) **359** **9**
H: 6 1 W: 13 00 b.Mansfield 3-12-74
Source: Trainee.

1993–94	Mansfield T	5	0	**5**	**0**
From Telford U, Woking					
1997–98	Bristol R	34	0		
1998–99	Bristol R	43	1		
1999–2000	Bristol R	43	1		
2000–01	Bristol R	44	4		
2001–02	Bristol R	33	1	**197**	**7**
2002–03	Doncaster R	0	0		
2003–04	Doncaster R	44	1		
2004–05	Doncaster R	34	1		
2005–06	Doncaster R	17	0	**95**	**2**
2005–06	Scunthorpe U	18	0		
2006–07	Scunthorpe U	44	0	**62**	**0**

FOY, Robbie (F) **35** **3**
H: 5 9 W: 10 07 b.Edinburgh 29-10-85
Source: Trainee. *Honours:* Scotland Under-21.

2002–03	Liverpool	0	0		
2003–04	Liverpool	0	0		
2004–05	Liverpool	0	0		
2004–05	*Chester C*	13	0	**13**	**0**
2005–06	Liverpool	0	0		
2005–06	*Wrexham*	17	3	**17**	**3**
2006–07	Scunthorpe U	5	0	**5**	**0**

GOODWIN, Jim (M) **147** **10**
H: 5 9 W: 12 01 b.Waterford 20-11-81
Source: Tramore. *Honours:* Eire Under-21, 1 full cap.

2001–02	Celtic	0	0		
2002–03	Stockport Co	33	3		
2003–04	Stockport Co	34	4		
2004–05	Stockport Co	36	0	**103**	**7**
2005–06	Scunthorpe U	13	2		
2006–07	Scunthorpe U	31	1	**44**	**3**

HINDS, Richard (D) **193** **9**
H: 6 2 W: 12 02 b.Sheffield 22-8-80
Source: Schoolboy.

1998–99	Tranmere R	2	0		
1999–2000	Tranmere R	6	0		
2000–01	Tranmere R	29	0		
2001–02	Tranmere R	10	0		
2002–03	Tranmere R	8	0	**55**	**0**
2003–04	Hull C	39	1		
2004–05	Hull C	6	0	**45**	**1**
2004–05	*Scunthorpe U*	7	0		
2005–06	Scunthorpe U	42	6		
2006–07	Scunthorpe U	44	2	**93**	**8**

LILLIS, Josh (G) **1** **0**
H: 6 0 W: 12 08 b.Derby 24-6-87
Source: Scholar.

2006–07	Scunthorpe U	1	0	**1**	**0**

MACKENZIE, Neil (M) **251** **15**
H: 6 2 W: 12 05 b.Birmingham 15-4-76
Source: WBA schoolboy.

1996–97	Stoke C	22	1		
1997–98	Stoke C	12	0		
1998–99	Stoke C	6	0		
1998–99	*Cambridge U*	4	1		
1999–2000	Stoke C	2	0	**42**	**1**
1999–2000	Cambridge U	22	0		
2000–01	Cambridge U	6	0	**32**	**1**
2000–01	Kidderminster H	23	3	**23**	**3**
2001–02	Blackpool	14	1	**14**	**1**
2002–03	Mansfield T	24	1		
2003–04	Mansfield T	32	2		
2004–05	Mansfield T	15	1	**71**	**4**
2004–05	Macclesfield T	18	0		
2005–06	Macclesfield T	6	1	**24**	**1**
2005–06	Scunthorpe U	14	2		
2006–07	Scunthorpe U	24	2	**38**	**4**
2006–07	*Hereford U*	7	0	**7**	**0**

McBREEN, Daniel (F) **132** **31**
H: 6 1 W: 13 01 b.Newcastle, Aus 23-4-77
Source: Toronto-Awaba, Edgeworth.

2000–01	Newcastle U (Aus)	23	6		
2001–02	Newcastle U (Aus)	13	3	**36**	**9**
2002–03	Uni Craiova	13	1		
2003–04	Uni Craiova	20	2	**33**	**3**
2004–05	Falkirk	23	13		
2005–06	Falkirk	33	6	**56**	**19**
2006–07	Scunthorpe U	7	0	**7**	**0**

MORRIS, Ian (D) **58** **6**
H: 6 0 W: 11 05 b.Dublin 27-2-87
Source: Scholar. *Honours:* Eire Under-21.

2003–04	Leeds U	0	0		
2004–05	Leeds U	0	0		
2005–06	Leeds U	0	0		
2005–06	*Blackpool*	30	3	**30**	**3**
2006–07	Leeds U	0	0		
2006–07	Scunthorpe U	28	3	**28**	**3**

MULLIGAN, Dave (D) **166** **6**
H: 5 8 W: 9 13 b.Bootle 24-3-82
Source: Scholar. *Honours:* New Zealand Youth, Under-20, Under-23, 12 full caps.

2000–01	Barnsley	0	0		
2001–02	Barnsley	28	0		
2002–03	Barnsley	33	1		
2003–04	Barnsley	4	0	**65**	**1**
2003–04	Doncaster R	14	1		
2004–05	Doncaster R	31	1		
2005–06	Doncaster R	32	2	**77**	**4**
2006–07	Scunthorpe U	24	1	**24**	**1**

MURPHY, Joe (G) **152 0**
H: 6 2 W: 13 06 b.Dublin 21-8-81
Source: Trainee. *Honours:* Eire Under-21, 1 full cap.

1999–2000	Tranmere R	21	0		
2000–01	Tranmere R	20	0		
2001–02	Tranmere R	22	0	**63**	**0**
2002–03	WBA	2	0		
2003–04	WBA	3	0		
2004–05	WBA	0	0	**5**	**0**
2004–05	*Walsall*	25	0		
2005–06	Sunderland	0	0		
2005–06	*Walsall*	14	0	**39**	**0**
2006–07	Scunthorpe U	45	0	**45**	**0**

RIDLEY, Lee (D) **100 2**
H: 5 9 W: 11 11 b.Scunthorpe 5-12-81
Source: Scholar.

2000–01	Scunthorpe U	2	0		
2001–02	Scunthorpe U	4	0		
2002–03	Scunthorpe U	11	0		
2003–04	Scunthorpe U	18	1		
2004–05	Scunthorpe U	44	0		
2005–06	Scunthorpe U	3	1		
2006–07	Scunthorpe U	18	0	**100**	**2**

SHARP, Billy (F) **100 62**
H: 5 9 W: 11 00 b.Sheffield 5-2-86
Source: Scholar.

2004–05	Sheffield U	2	0		
2004–05	*Rushden & D*	16	9	**16**	**9**
2005–06	Sheffield U	0	0	**2**	**0**
2005–06	Scunthorpe U	37	23		
2006–07	Scunthorpe U	45	30	**82**	**53**

SPARROW, Matt (M) **238 31**
H: 5 11 W: 10 06 b.Wembley 3-10-81
Source: Scholarship.

1999–2000	Scunthorpe U	11	0		
2000–01	Scunthorpe U	11	4		
2001–02	Scunthorpe U	24	1		
2002–03	Scunthorpe U	42	9		
2003–04	Scunthorpe U	38	3		
2004–05	Scunthorpe U	44	5		
2005–06	Scunthorpe U	39	5		
2006–07	Scunthorpe U	29	4	**238**	**31**

TAYLOR, Cleveland (M) **157 15**
H: 5 8 W: 10 07 b.Leicester 9-9-83
Source: Scholar.

2001–02	Bolton W	0	0		
2002–03	Bolton W	0	0		
2002–03	*Exeter C*	3	0	**3**	**0**
2003–04	Bolton W	0	0		
2003–04	Scunthorpe U	20	3		
2004–05	Scunthorpe U	44	6		
2005–06	Scunthorpe U	45	3		
2006–07	Scunthorpe U	45	3	**154**	**15**

TORPEY, Steve (F) **580 139**
H: 6 3 W: 13 06 b.Islington 8-12-70
Source: Trainee.

1988–89	Millwall	0	0		
1989–90	Millwall	7	0		
1990–91	Millwall	0	0	**7**	**0**
1990–91	Bradford C	29	7		
1991–92	Bradford C	43	10		
1992–93	Bradford C	24	5	**96**	**22**
1993–94	Swansea C	40	9		
1994–95	Swansea C	41	11		
1995–96	Swansea C	42	15		
1996–97	Swansea C	39	9	**162**	**44**
1997–98	Bristol C	29	8		
1998–99	Bristol C	21	4		
1998–99	*Notts Co*	6	1	**6**	**1**
1999–2000	Bristol C	20	1	**70**	**13**
1999–2000	Scunthorpe U	15	1		
2000–01	Scunthorpe U	40	10		
2001–02	Scunthorpe U	39	13		
2002–03	Scunthorpe U	28	10		
2003–04	Scunthorpe U	33	11		
2004–05	Scunthorpe U	34	12		
2005–06	Scunthorpe U	26	1		
2006–07	Scunthorpe U	14	1	**239**	**59**

WILLIAMS, Marcus (D) **69 0**
H: 5 8 W: 10 07 b.Doncaster 8-4-86
Source: Scholar.

2003–04	Scunthorpe U	1	0		
2004–05	Scunthorpe U	4	0		
2005–06	Scunthorpe U	29	0		
2006–07	Scunthorpe U	35	0	**69**	**0**

WINN, Peter (M) **0 0**
H: 6 0 W: 11 09 b.Cleethorpes 19-12-88
Source: Scholar.

2006–07	Scunthorpe U	0	0		

SHEFFIELD U (71)

ABDI, Liban (M) **0 0**
b.Somalia

2006–07	Sheffield U	0	0		

ANNERSON, Jamie (G) **0 0**
H: 6 2 W: 13 02 b.Sheffield 21-6-88
Source: Scholar. *Honours:* England Youth.

2005–06	Sheffield U	0	0		
2006–07	Sheffield U	0	0		

ARMSTRONG, Chris (D) **166 5**
H: 5 9 W: 11 00 b.Newcastle 5-8-82
Source: Scholar. *Honours:* England Under-20.

2000–01	Bury	22	1		
2001–02	Bury	11	0	**33**	**1**
2001–02	Oldham Ath	32	0		
2002–03	Oldham Ath	33	1	**65**	**1**
2003–04	Sheffield U	12	1		
2004–05	Sheffield U	0	0		
2005–06	Sheffield U	24	2		
2005–06	*Blackpool*	5	0	**5**	**0**
2006–07	Sheffield U	27	0	**63**	**3**

ASHMORE, James (M) **0 0**
H: 5 8 W: 11 00 b.Sheffield 2-3-86
Source: Scholar.

2004–05	Sheffield U	0	0		
2005–06	Sheffield U	0	0		
2006–07	Sheffield U	0	0		

BENNETT, Ian (G) **376 0**
H: 6 0 W: 12 10 b.Worksop 10-10-71
Source: Newcastle U Trainee.

1991–92	Peterborough U	7	0		
1992–93	Peterborough U	46	0		
1993–94	Peterborough U	19	0	**72**	**0**
1993–94	Birmingham C	22	0		
1994–95	Birmingham C	46	0		
1995–96	Birmingham C	24	0		
1996–97	Birmingham C	40	0		
1997–98	Birmingham C	45	0		
1998–99	Birmingham C	10	0		
1999–2000	Birmingham C	21	0		
2000–01	Birmingham C	45	0		
2001–02	Birmingham C	18	0		
2002–03	Birmingham C	10	0		
2003–04	Birmingham C	6	0		
2004–05	Birmingham C	0	0	**287**	**0**
2004–05	*Sheffield U*	5	0		
2004–05	*Coventry C*	6	0	**6**	**0**
2005–06	Leeds U	4	0		
2006–07	Leeds U	0	0	**4**	**0**
2006–07	Sheffield U	2	0	**7**	**0**

BINNION, Travis (M) **0 0**
H: 5 10 W: 11 02 b.Derby 10-11-86
Source: Scholar.

2005–06	Sheffield U	0	0		
2006–07	Sheffield U	0	0		

BROMBY, Leigh (D) **213 9**
H: 5 11 W: 11 06 b.Dewsbury 2-6-80
Honours: England Schools.

1998–99	Sheffield W	0	0		
1999–2000	Sheffield W	0	0		
1999–2000	*Mansfield T*	10	1	**10**	**1**
2000–01	Sheffield W	18	0		
2001–02	Sheffield W	26	1		
2002–03	Sheffield W	27	0		
2002–03	*Norwich C*	5	0	**5**	**0**
2003–04	Sheffield W	29	1	**100**	**2**
2004–05	Sheffield U	46	5		
2005–06	Sheffield U	35	1		
2006–07	Sheffield U	17	0	**98**	**6**

CRESSWELL, Ryan (D) **0 0**
b.Rotherham 22-12-87
Source: Scholar.

2006–07	Sheffield U	0	0		

DAVIS, Claude (D) **115 4**
H: 6 3 W: 14 04 b.Kingston, Jam 6-3-79
Source: From Portmore U. *Honours:* Jamaica 47 full caps, 2 goals.

2003–04	Preston NE	22	1		
2004–05	Preston NE	32	0		
2005–06	Preston NE	40	3	**94**	**4**
2006–07	Sheffield U	21	0	**21**	**0**

DONNELLY, Martin (M) **0 0**
b.Belfast 28-8-88
Source: Scholar. *Honours:* Northern Ireland Youth, Under-21.

2006–07	Sheffield U	0	0		

FATHI, Ahmed (M) **3 0**
H: 5 9 W: 11 05 b.Egypt 11-10-84
Source: Ismaily SC. *Honours:* Egypt Youth, 11 full caps, 1 goal.

2006–07	Sheffield U	3	0	**3**	**0**

FORTE, Jonathan (M) **95 14**
H: 6 0 W: 12 02 b.Sheffield 25-7-86
Source: Scholar. *Honours:* England Youth.

2003–04	Sheffield U	7	0		
2004–05	Sheffield U	22	1		
2005–06	Sheffield U	1	0		
2005–06	*Doncaster R*	13	4		
2005–06	*Rotherham U*	11	4	**11**	**4**
2006–07	Sheffield U	0	0	**30**	**1**
2006–07	*Doncaster R*	41	5	**54**	**9**

GEARY, Derek (D) **182 1**
H: 5 6 W: 10 00 b.Dublin 19-6-80

1997–98	Sheffield W	0	0		
1998–99	Sheffield W	0	0		
1999–2000	Sheffield W	0	0		
2000–01	Sheffield W	5	0		
2001–02	Sheffield W	32	0		
2002–03	Sheffield W	26	0		
2003–04	Sheffield W	41	0	**104**	**0**
2004–05	Stockport Co	13	0	**13**	**0**
2004–05	Sheffield U	19	1		
2005–06	Sheffield U	20	0		
2006–07	Sheffield U	26	0	**65**	**1**

GERRARD, Paul (G) **320 1**
H: 6 2 W: 13 11 b.Heywood 22-1-73
Source: Trainee. *Honours:* England Under-21.

1991–92	Oldham Ath	0	0		
1992–93	Oldham Ath	25	0		
1993–94	Oldham Ath	16	0		
1994–95	Oldham Ath	42	0		
1995–96	Oldham Ath	36	1	**119**	**1**
1996–97	Everton	5	0		
1997–98	Everton	4	0		
1998–99	Everton	0	0		
1998–99	*Oxford U*	16	0	**16**	**0**
1999–2000	Everton	34	0		
2000–01	Everton	32	0		
2001–02	Everton	13	0		
2002–03	Everton	2	0		
2002–03	*Ipswich T*	5	0	**5**	**0**
2003–04	Everton	0	0	**90**	**0**
2003–04	*Sheffield U*	16	0		
2003–04	*Nottingham F*	8	0		
2004–05	Nottingham F	42	0		
2005–06	Nottingham F	22	0		
2006–07	Nottingham F	0	0	**72**	**0**
2006–07	Sheffield U	2	0	**18**	**0**

GILLESPIE, Keith (M) **351 25**
H: 5 10 W: 11 03 b.Larne 18-2-75
Source: Trainee. *Honours:* Northern Ireland Schools, Youth, Under-21, 75 full caps, 2 goals.

1992–93	Manchester U	0	0		
1993–94	Manchester U	0	0		
1993–94	*Wigan Ath*	8	4		
1994–95	Manchester U	9	1	**9**	**1**
1994–95	Newcastle U	17	2		
1995–96	Newcastle U	28	4		
1996–97	Newcastle U	32	1		
1997–98	Newcastle U	29	4		
1998–99	Newcastle U	7	0	**113**	**11**
1998–99	Blackburn R	16	1		
1999–2000	Blackburn R	22	2		
2000–01	Blackburn R	18	0		
2000–01	*Wigan Ath*	5	0	**13**	**4**

2001–02 Blackburn R 32 2
2002–03 Blackburn R 25 0 **113 5**
2003–04 Leicester C 12 0
2004–05 Leicester C 30 2 **42 2**
2005–06 Sheffield U 30 0
2006–07 Sheffield U 31 2 **61 2**

GYAKI, Ryan (G) 0 0
H: 5 10 W: 11 02 b.Toronto 6-12-85
Source: Scholar. *Honours:* Canada Under-20.
2005–06 Sheffield U 0 0
2006–07 Sheffield U 0 0

HAIDONG, Hao (F) 0 0
H: 5 11 W: 11 00 b.Qingdao 9-5-70
Source: Dalian Shide. *Honours:* China 115 full caps, 41 goals.
2004–05 Sheffield U 0 0
2005–06 Sheffield U 0 0
2006–07 Sheffield U 0 0

HORSFIELD, Geoff (F) 302 78
H: 6 0 W: 11 07 b.Barnsley 1-11-73
1992–93 Scarborough 6 1
1993–94 Scarborough 6 0 **12 1**
From Witton Alb
1998–99 Halifax T 10 7 **10 7**
1998–99 Fulham 28 15
1999–2000 Fulham 31 7 **59 22**
2000–01 Birmingham C 34 7
2001–02 Birmingham C 40 11
2002–03 Birmingham C 31 5
2003–04 Birmingham C 3 0 **108 23**
2003–04 Wigan Ath 16 7 **16 7**
2003–04 WBA 20 7
2004–05 WBA 29 3
2005–06 WBA 18 4
2005–06 *Sheffield U* 3 0
2006–07 WBA 0 0 **67 14**
2006–07 Sheffield U 0 0 **3 0**
2006–07 *Leeds U* 14 2 **14 2**
2006–07 *Leicester C* 13 2 **13 2**

HORWOOD, Evan (D) 31 0
H: 6 0 W: 10 06 b.Billingham 10-3-86
Source: Scholar.
2004–05 Sheffield U 0 0
2004–05 *Stockport Co* 10 0 **10 0**
2005–06 Sheffield U 0 0
2005–06 *Scunthorpe U* 0 0
2005–06 *Chester C* 1 0 **1 0**
2006–07 Sheffield U 0 0
2006–07 *Darlington* 20 0 **20 0**

HULSE, Rob (F) 235 82
H: 6 1 W: 12 04 b.Crewe 25-10-79
Source: Trainee.
1998–99 Crewe Alex 0 0
1999–2000 Crewe Alex 4 1
2000–01 Crewe Alex 33 11
2001–02 Crewe Alex 41 12
2002–03 Crewe Alex 38 22 **116 46**
2003–04 WBA 33 10
2004–05 WBA 5 0 **38 10**
2004–05 *Leeds U* 13 6
2005–06 Leeds U 39 12 **52 18**
2006–07 Sheffield U 29 8 **29 8**

HURST, Kevan (M) 97 9
H: 5 10 W: 11 07 b.Chesterfield 27-8-85
Source: Sheffield U Scholar.
2003–04 *Boston U* 7 1 **7 1**
2004–05 Sheffield U 1 0
2004–05 *Stockport Co* 14 1 **14 1**
2005–06 Sheffield U 0 0
2005–06 *Chesterfield* 37 4
2006–07 Sheffield U 0 0 **1 0**
2006–07 *Chesterfield* 25 3 **62 7**
2006–07 *Scunthorpe U* 13 0 **13 0**

JAGIELKA, Phil (D) 254 18
H: 6 0 W: 13 01 b.Manchester 17-8-82
Source: Scholar. *Honours:* England Youth, Under-20, Under-21, B.
1999–2000 Sheffield U 1 0
2000–01 Sheffield U 15 0
2001–02 Sheffield U 23 3
2002–03 Sheffield U 42 0
2003–04 Sheffield U 43 3
2004–05 Sheffield U 46 0
2005–06 Sheffield U 46 8
2006–07 Sheffield U 38 4 **254 18**

KAZIM-RICHARDS, Colin (F) 100 10
H: 6 1 W: 10 10 b.Leyton 26-8-86
Source: Scholar. *Honours:* Turkey Under-21.
2004–05 Bury 30 3 **30 3**
2005–06 Brighton & HA 42 6
2006–07 Brighton & HA 1 0 **43 6**
2006–07 Sheffield U 27 1 **27 1**

KENNY, Paddy (G) 325 0
H: 6 1 W: 14 01 b.Halifax 17-5-78
Source: Bradford PA. *Honours:* Eire 7 full caps.
1998–99 Bury 0 0
1999–2000 Bury 46 0
2000–01 Bury 46 0
2001–02 Bury 41 0
2002–03 Bury 0 0 **133 0**
2002–03 Sheffield U 45 0
2003–04 Sheffield U 27 0
2004–05 Sheffield U 40 0
2005–06 Sheffield U 46 0
2006–07 Sheffield U 34 0 **192 0**

KERRY, Lloyd (M) 7 1
H: 6 2 W: 12 04 b.Chesterfield 22-1-88
Source: Scholar.
2006–07 Sheffield U 0 0
2006–07 *Torquay U* 7 1 **7 1**

KILGALLON, Matthew (D) 89 3
H: 6 1 W: 12 10 b.York 8-1-84
Source: Scholar. *Honours:* England Youth, Under-20, Under-21.
2000–01 Leeds U 0 0
2001–02 Leeds U 0 0
2002–03 Leeds U 2 0
2003–04 Leeds U 8 2
2003–04 *West Ham U* 3 0 **3 0**
2004–05 Leeds U 26 0
2005–06 Leeds U 25 1
2006–07 Leeds U 19 0 **80 3**
2006–07 Sheffield U 6 0 **6 0**

KOZLUK, Rob (D) 244 2
H: 5 8 W: 10 02 b.Mansfield 5-8-77
Source: Trainee. *Honours:* England Under-21.
1995–96 Derby Co 0 0
1996–97 Derby Co 0 0
1997–98 Derby Co 9 0
1998–99 Derby Co 7 0 **16 0**
1998–99 Sheffield U 10 0
1999–2000 Sheffield U 39 0
2000–01 Sheffield U 27 0
2000–01 *Huddersfield T* 14 0 **14 0**
2001–02 Sheffield U 8 0
2002–03 Sheffield U 32 1
2003–04 Sheffield U 42 1
2004–05 Sheffield U 9 0
2004–05 *Preston NE* 1 0 **1 0**
2005–06 Sheffield U 27 0
2006–07 Sheffield U 19 0 **213 2**

LAW, Nicky (M) 10 0
H: 5 10 W: 11 06 b.Nottingham 29-3-88
Source: Scholar. *Honours:* England Youth.
2005–06 Sheffield U 0 0
2006–07 Sheffield U 4 0 **4 0**
2006–07 *Yeovil T* 6 0 **6 0**

LEIGERTWOOD, Mikele (D) 142 3
H: 6 1 W: 11 04 b.Enfield 12-11-82
Source: Scholar.
2001–02 Wimbledon 1 0
2001–02 *Leyton Orient* 8 0 **8 0**
2002–03 Wimbledon 28 0
2003–04 Wimbledon 27 2 **56 2**
2003–04 Crystal Palace 12 0
2004–05 Crystal Palace 20 1
2005–06 Crystal Palace 27 0 **59 1**
2006–07 Sheffield U 19 0 **19 0**

LI TIE (M) 34 0
H: 6 0 W: 11 10 b.Liaoning 18-9-77
Source: Liaoning Bodao. *Honours:* China 87 full caps, 5 goals.
2002–03 Everton 29 0
2003–04 Everton 5 0
2004–05 Everton 0 0
2005–06 Everton 0 0 **34 0**
2006–07 Sheffield U 0 0

LUCKETTI, Chris (D) 582 21
H: 6 1 W: 13 06 b.Rochdale 28-9-71
Source: Trainee.
1988–89 Rochdale 1 0
1989–90 Rochdale 0 0 **1 0**
1990–91 Stockport Co 0 0
1991–92 Halifax T 36 0
1992–93 Halifax T 42 2 **78 2**
1993–94 Bury 27 1
1994–95 Bury 39 3
1995–96 Bury 42 1
1996–97 Bury 38 0
1997–98 Bury 46 2
1998–99 Bury 43 1 **235 8**
1999–2000 Huddersfield T 26 0
2000–01 Huddersfield T 40 1
2001–02 Huddersfield T 2 0 **68 1**
2001–02 Preston NE 40 2
2002–03 Preston NE 43 2
2003–04 Preston NE 37 1
2004–05 Preston NE 41 4
2005–06 Preston NE 28 1 **189 10**
2005–06 *Sheffield U* 3 0
2006–07 Sheffield U 8 0 **11 0**

MARRISON, Colin (F) 16 0
H: 6 1 W: 12 05 b.Sheffield 23-9-85
Source: Scholar.
2005–06 Sheffield U 0 0
2005–06 *Bury* 16 0 **16 0**
2006–07 Sheffield U 0 0

MONTGOMERY, Nick (M) 207 7
H: 5 9 W: 11 08 b.Leeds 28-10-81
Source: Scholar. *Honours:* Scotland Under-21, B.
2000–01 Sheffield U 27 0
2001–02 Sheffield U 31 2
2002–03 Sheffield U 23 0
2003–04 Sheffield U 36 3
2004–05 Sheffield U 25 1
2005–06 Sheffield U 39 1
2006–07 Sheffield U 26 0 **207 7**

MORGAN, Chris (D) 321 14
H: 6 1 W: 12 03 b.Barnsley 9-11-77
Source: Trainee.
1996–97 Barnsley 0 0
1997–98 Barnsley 11 0
1998–99 Barnsley 19 0
1999–2000 Barnsley 37 0
2000–01 Barnsley 40 1
2001–02 Barnsley 42 4
2002–03 Barnsley 36 2 **185 7**
2003–04 Sheffield U 32 1
2004–05 Sheffield U 41 2
2005–06 Sheffield U 39 3
2006–07 Sheffield U 24 1 **136 7**

NADE, Christian (F) 93 11
H: 6 0 W: 12 08 b.Montmorency 18-9-84
Honours: France Under-21.
1999–2000 Troyes 3 0
2000–01 Troyes 0 0
2001–02 Troyes 0 0
2002–03 Troyes 5 1
2003–04 Troyes 25 6
2004–05 Troyes 1 0
2004–05 *Le Havre* 17 1 **17 1**
2005–06 Troyes 17 0 **51 7**
2006–07 Sheffield U 25 3 **25 3**

NAUGHTON, Kyle (M) 0 0
b.Sheffield 11-11-88
2006–07 Sheffield U 0 0

OLIVER, Dean (F) 1 0
H: 6 0 W: 12 05 b.Derby 4-12-87
Source: Scholar.
2006–07 Sheffield U 0 0
2006–07 *Torquay U* 1 0 **1 0**

QUINN, Alan (M) 252 27
H: 5 9 W: 10 06 b.Dublin 13-6-79
Source: Cherry Orchard. *Honours:* Eire Youth, Under-21, 8 full caps.
1997–98 Sheffield W 1 0

1998–99 Sheffield W 1 0
1999–2000 Sheffield W 19 3
2000–01 Sheffield W 37 2
2001–02 Sheffield W 38 2
2002–03 Sheffield W 37 5
2003–04 Sheffield W 24 4 **157 16**
2003–04 *Sunderland* 6 0 **6 0**
2004–05 Sheffield U 43 7
2005–06 Sheffield U 27 4
2006–07 Sheffield U 19 0 **89 11**

QUINN, Keith (M) 0 0
b.Dublin 22-9-88
Source: Scholar. *Honours:* Eire Under-21.
2006–07 Sheffield U 0 0

QUINN, Stephen (M) 46 2
H: 5 6 W: 9 08 b.Dublin 4-4-86
Source: Trainee.
2005–06 Sheffield U 0 0
2005–06 *Milton Keynes D* 15 0 **15 0**
2005–06 *Rotherham U* 16 0 **16 0**
2006–07 Sheffield U 15 2 **15 2**

ROBERTSON, Jordan (F) 26 5
H: 6 0 W: 12 06 b.Sheffield 12-2-88
Source: Scholar.
2006–07 Sheffield U 0 0
2006–07 *Torquay U* 9 2 **9 2**
2006–07 *Northampton T* 17 3 **17 3**

ROSS, Ian (M) 57 5
H: 5 10 W: 11 00 b.Sheffield 23-1-86
Source: Scholar. *Honours:* England Under-20.
2004–05 Sheffield U 0 0
2005–06 Sheffield U 0 0
2005–06 *Boston U* 14 4 **14 4**
2005–06 *Bury* 7 0 **7 0**
2006–07 Sheffield U 0 0
2006–07 *Notts Co* 36 1 **36 1**

SECK, Mamadou (M) 0 0
H: 6 4 W: 12 13 b.Rufisgue 23-8-79
Honours: Senegal 6 full caps.
2006–07 Sheffield U 0 0

SHELTON, Luton (F) 23 9
H: 5 11 W: 11 11 b.Jamaica 11-11-85
Source: Harbour View, Jamaica Youth, Under-20, Under-23, 11 full caps, 2 goals.
2006 Helsingborg 19 9 **19 9**
2006–07 Sheffield U 4 0 **4 0**

SHORT, Craig (D) 565 31
H: 6 1 W: 13 08 b.Bridlington 25-6-68
Source: Pickering T.
1987–88 Scarborough 21 2
1988–89 Scarborough 42 5 **63 7**
1989–90 Notts Co 44 2
1990–91 Notts Co 0 0
1990–91 Notts Co 43 0
1991–92 Notts Co 38 3
1992–93 Notts Co 3 1 **128 6**
1992–93 Derby Co 38 3
1993–94 Derby Co 43 3
1994–95 Derby Co 37 3 **118 9**
1995–96 Everton 23 2
1996–97 Everton 23 2
1997–98 Everton 31 0
1998–99 Everton 22 0 **99 4**
1999–2000 Blackburn R 17 0
2000–01 Blackburn R 35 1
2001–02 Blackburn R 22 0
2002–03 Blackburn R 27 1
2003–04 Blackburn R 19 1
2004–05 Blackburn R 14 1 **134 4**
2005–06 Sheffield U 23 1
2006–07 Sheffield U 0 0 **23 1**

SOMMEIL, David (D) 332 7
H: 5 10 W: 12 12 b.Ponte-a-Pitre 10-8-74
Honours: France B.
1993–94 Caen 1 0
1994–95 Caen 25 0
1995–96 Caen 30 0
1996–97 Caen 25 0
1997–98 Caen 38 1 **119 1**
1998–99 Rennes 33 0
1999–2000 Rennes 30 1 **63 1**
2000–01 Bordeaux 29 0
2001–02 Bordeaux 31 0
2002–03 Bordeaux 17 1 **77 1**
2002–03 Manchester C 14 1
2003–04 Manchester C 18 1
2003–04 *Marseille* 19 0 **19 0**
2004–05 Manchester C 1 0
2005–06 Manchester C 16 2 **49 4**
2006–07 Sheffield U 5 0 **5 0**

STAROSTA, Ben (D) 0 0
b.Sheffield 7-1-87
Source: Scholar.
2006–07 Sheffield U 0 0

STEAD, Jon (F) 176 40
H: 6 3 W: 13 03 b.Huddersfield 7-4-83
Source: From Scholar. *Honours:* England Under-21.
2001–02 Huddersfield T 0 0
2002–03 Huddersfield T 42 6
2003–04 Huddersfield T 26 16 **68 22**
2003–04 Blackburn R 13 6
2004–05 Blackburn R 29 2 **42 8**
2005–06 Sunderland 30 1
2006–07 Sunderland 5 1 **35 2**
2006–07 *Derby Co* 17 3 **17 3**
2006–07 Sheffield U 14 5 **14 5**

TONGE, Michael (M) 213 20
H: 6 0 W: 11 10 b.Manchester 7-4-83
Source: Scholar. *Honours:* England Under-20, Under-21.
2000–01 Sheffield U 2 0
2001–02 Sheffield U 30 3
2002–03 Sheffield U 44 6
2003–04 Sheffield U 46 4
2004–05 Sheffield U 34 2
2005–06 Sheffield U 30 3
2006–07 Sheffield U 27 2 **213 20**

TRAVIS, Nicky (M) 0 0
H: 6 0 W: 12 01 b.Sheffield 12-3-87
Source: Scholar.
2004–05 Sheffield U 0 0
2005–06 Sheffield U 0 0
2006–07 Sheffield U 0 0

WEBBER, Danny (F) 140 37
H: 5 10 W: 11 04 b.Manchester 28-12-81
Source: Trainee. *Honours:* England Youth, Under-20.
1998–99 Manchester U 0 0
1999–2000 Manchester U 0 0
2000–01 Manchester U 0 0
2001–02 Manchester U 0 0
2001–02 *Port Vale* 4 0 **4 0**
2001–02 *Watford* 5 2
2002–03 Manchester U 0 0
2002–03 *Watford* 12 2
2003–04 Watford 27 5
2004–05 Watford 28 12 **72 21**
2004–05 *Sheffield U* 7 3
2005–06 Sheffield U 35 10
2006–07 Sheffield U 22 3 **64 16**

WEDGBURY, Samuel (M) 0 0
b.Oldbury 26-2-89
2006–07 Sheffield U 0 0

WRIGHT, Alan (D) 503 7
H: 5 4 W: 9 09 b.Ashton-under-Lyme 28-9-71
Source: Trainee. *Honours:* England Schools, Youth, Under-21.
1987–88 Blackpool 1 0
1988–89 Blackpool 16 0
1989–90 Blackpool 24 0
1990–91 Blackpool 45 0
1991–92 Blackpool 12 0 **98 0**
1991–92 Blackburn R 33 1
1992–93 Blackburn R 24 0
1993–94 Blackburn R 12 0
1994–95 Blackburn R 5 0 **74 1**
1994–95 Aston Villa 8 0
1995–96 Aston Villa 38 2
1996–97 Aston Villa 38 1
1997–98 Aston Villa 37 0
1998–99 Aston Villa 38 0
1999–2000 Aston Villa 32 1
2000–01 Aston Villa 36 1
2001–02 Aston Villa 23 0
2002–03 Aston Villa 10 0 **260 5**
2003–04 Middlesbrough 2 0 **2 0**
2003–04 Sheffield U 21 1
2004–05 Sheffield U 14 0
2005–06 Sheffield U 6 0
2005–06 *Derby Co* 7 0 **7 0**
2006–07 Sheffield U 1 0 **42 1**
2006–07 *Leeds U* 1 0 **1 0**
2006–07 *Cardiff C* 7 0 **7 0**
2006–07 *Doncaster R* 3 0 **3 0**
2006–07 *Nottingham F* 9 0 **9 0**

Scholars
Askham, Lee Raymond; Boden, Scott David; Booker, Ryan; Chapman, Adam; Eagers, Jordan William; Furniss, Marc; Gordon, Sean; Hancock, Steven; Hernandez, Stephen James; Hilton, Antony; Lowton, Matthew John; Okoko, Mark; Reid, Elijah; Tahar, Aymer; Walker, Kyle Andrew; Yates, Adam Philip.

SHEFFIELD W (72)

ADAMS, Steve (M) 177 7
H: 6 0 W: 12 03 b.Plymouth 25-9-80
Source: Trainee.
1999–2000 Plymouth Arg 1 0
2000–01 Plymouth Arg 17 0
2001–02 Plymouth Arg 46 2
2002–03 Plymouth Arg 37 2
2003–04 Plymouth Arg 36 2
2004–05 Plymouth Arg 20 1 **157 7**
2004–05 Sheffield W 9 0
2005–06 Sheffield W 8 0
2006–07 Sheffield W 3 0 **20 0**

ADAMSON, Chris (G) 33 0
H: 6 2 W: 13 07 b.Ashington 4-11-78
Source: Trainee.
1997–98 WBA 3 0
1998–99 WBA 0 0
1998–99 *Mansfield T* 2 0 **2 0**
1999–2000 WBA 9 0
1999–2000 *Halifax T* 7 0 **7 0**
2000–01 WBA 0 0
2001–02 WBA 0 0 **12 0**
2001–02 *Plymouth Arg* 1 0 **1 0**
From St Patrick's At
2004–05 Sheffield W 2 0
2005–06 Sheffield W 5 0
2006–07 Sheffield W 4 0 **11 0**

BEEVERS, Mark (D) 2 0
H: 6 4 W: 13 00 b.Barnsley 21-11-89
Source: Scholar.
2006–07 Sheffield W 2 0 **2 0**

BODEN, Luke (F) 1 0
H: 6 1 W: 12 00 b.Sheffield 26-11-88
Source: Scholar.
2006–07 Sheffield W 1 0 **1 0**

BOWMAN, Matthew (F) 0 0
H: 5 8 W: 11 11 b.Barnsley 31-1-90
Source: Scholar.
2006–07 Sheffield W 0 0

BROADBENT, Andrew (M) 0 0
H: 5 8 W: 11 00 b.Nuneaton 2-1-88
Source: Scholar.
2006–07 Sheffield W 0 0

BRUNT, Chris (M) 139 24
H: 6 1 W: 13 04 b.Belfast 14-12-84
Source: From Trainee. *Honours:* Northern Ireland Under-21, Under-23, 10 full caps.
2002–03 Middlesbrough 0 0
2003–04 Middlesbrough 0 0
2003–04 Sheffield W 9 2
2004–05 Sheffield W 42 4
2005–06 Sheffield W 44 7
2006–07 Sheffield W 44 11 **139 24**

BULLEN, Lee (D) 365 86
H: 6 1 W: 12 07 b.Edinburgh 29-3-71
1990–91 Meadowbank T 3 0 **3 0**
1991–92 Stenhousemuir 35 22
1992–93 Stenhousemuir 35 24 **70 46**
From Stanmore, Golden, South China.
1997–98 Kalamata 18 4
1998–99 Kalamata 27 7

1999–2000	Kalamata	5	0	**50**	**11**
1999–2000	Dunfermline Ath	13	7		
2000–01	Dunfermline Ath	24	4		
2001–02	Dunfermline Ath	31	4		
2002–03	Dunfermline Ath	35	5		
2003–04	Dunfermline Ath	27	2	**130**	**22**
2004–05	Sheffield W	46	7		
2005–06	Sheffield W	28	0		
2006–07	Sheffield W	38	0	**112**	**7**

BURTON, Deon (F) 353 81
H: 5 9 W: 11 09 b.Ashford 25-10-76
Source: Trainee. *Honours:* Jamaica 49 full caps, 8 goals.

1993–94	Portsmouth	2	0		
1994–95	Portsmouth	7	2		
1995–96	Portsmouth	32	7		
1996–97	Portsmouth	21	1		
1996–97	*Cardiff C*	5	2	**5**	**2**
1997–98	Derby Co	29	3		
1998–99	Derby Co	21	9		
1998–99	*Barnsley*	3	0	**3**	**0**
1999–2000	Derby Co	19	4		
2000–01	Derby Co	32	5		
2001–02	Derby Co	17	1		
2001–02	*Stoke C*	12	2	**12**	**2**
2002–03	Derby Co	7	3	**125**	**25**
2002–03	Portsmouth	15	4		
2003–04	Portsmouth	1	0	**78**	**14**
2003–04	*Walsall*	3	0	**3**	**0**
2003–04	*Swindon T*	4	1	**4**	**1**
2004–05	Brentford	40	10	**40**	**10**
2005–06	Rotherham U	24	12	**24**	**12**
2005–06	Sheffield W	17	3		
2006–07	Sheffield W	42	12	**59**	**15**

CLARKE, Leon (F) 99 17
H: 6 2 W: 14 02 b.Birmingham 10-2-85
Source: Scholar.

2003–04	Wolverhampton W	0	0		
2003–04	*Kidderminster H*	4	0	**4**	**0**
2004–05	Wolverhampton W	28	7		
2005–06	Wolverhampton W	24	1		
2005–06	*QPR*	1	0	**1**	**0**
2005–06	*Plymouth Arg*	5	0	**5**	**0**
2006–07	Wolverhampton W	22	5	**74**	**13**
2006–07	Sheffield W	10	1	**10**	**1**
2006–07	*Oldham Ath*	5	3	**5**	**3**

CORR, Barry (F) 28 3
H: 6 3 W: 12 07 b.Co. Wicklow 2-4-85
Honours: Eire Youth.

2001–02	Leeds U	0	0		
2002–03	Leeds U	0	0		
2003–04	Leeds U	0	0		
2004–05	Leeds U	0	0		
2005–06	Sheffield W	16	0		
2006–07	Sheffield W	1	0	**17**	**0**
2006–07	*Bristol C*	3	0	**3**	**0**
2006–07	*Swindon T*	8	3	**8**	**3**

COUGHLAN, Graham (D) 289 32
H: 6 2 W: 13 07 b.Dublin 18-11-74
Source: Bray Wanderers.

1995–96	Blackburn R	0	0		
1996–97	Blackburn R	0	0		
1996–97	*Swindon T*	3	0	**3**	**0**
1997–98	Blackburn R	0	0		
1998–99	Livingston	6	0		
1999–2000	Livingston	29	0		
2000–01	Livingston	21	2	**56**	**2**
2001–02	Plymouth Arg	46	11		
2002–03	Plymouth Arg	42	5		
2003–04	Plymouth Arg	46	7		
2004–05	Plymouth Arg	43	2	**177**	**25**
2005–06	Sheffield W	33	4		
2006–07	Sheffield W	18	1	**51**	**5**
2006–07	*Burnley*	2	0	**2**	**0**

FOLLY, Yoann (M) 60 0
H: 5 9 W: 11 04 b.Togo 6-6-85
Source: St Etienne. *Honours:* France Youth, Under-21.

2003–04	Southampton	9	0		
2004–05	Southampton	3	0		
2004–05	*Nottingham F*	1	0	**1**	**0**
2004–05	*Preston NE*	2	0	**2**	**0**
2005–06	Southampton	2	0	**14**	**0**
2005–06	*Sheffield W*	14	0		
2006–07	Sheffield W	29	0	**43**	**0**

GILBERT, Peter (D) 110 1
H: 5 11 W: 12 00 b.Newcastle 31-7-83
Source: Scholar. *Honours:* Wales Under-21.

2001–02	Birmingham C	0	0		
2002–03	Birmingham C	0	0		
2003–04	Birmingham C	0	0		
2003–04	Plymouth Arg	40	1		
2004–05	Plymouth Arg	38	0	**78**	**1**
2005–06	Leicester C	5	0	**5**	**0**
2005–06	Sheffield W	17	0		
2006–07	Sheffield W	6	0	**23**	**0**
2006–07	*Doncaster R*	4	0	**4**	**0**

GRAHAM, David (F) 266 66
H: 5 10 W: 11 02 b.Edinburgh 6-10-78
Source: Rangers SABC. *Honours:* Scotland Under-21.

1995–96	Rangers	0	0		
1996–97	Rangers	0	0		
1997–98	Rangers	0	0		
1998–99	Rangers	3	0	**3**	**0**
1998–99	Dunfermline Ath	21	2		
1999–2000	Dunfermline Ath	15	2		
2000–01	Dunfermline Ath	4	0	**40**	**4**
2000–01	Torquay U	5	2		
2001–02	Torquay U	36	8		
2002–03	Torquay U	34	15		
2003–04	Torquay U	45	22		
2004–05	Wigan Ath	30	1		
2005–06	Wigan Ath	0	0	**30**	**1**
2005–06	Sheffield W	24	2		
2005–06	*Huddersfield T*	16	9	**16**	**9**
2006–07	Sheffield W	4	0	**28**	**2**
2006–07	*Bradford C*	22	3	**22**	**3**
2006–07	*Torquay U*	7	0	**127**	**47**

HILLS, John (D) 278 19
H: 5 9 W: 12 08 b.St Annes-on-Sea 21-4-78
Source: Trainee.

1995–96	Blackpool	0	0		
1995–96	Everton	0	0		
1996–97	Everton	3	0		
1996–97	*Swansea C*	11	0		
1997–98	Everton	0	0	**3**	**0**
1997–98	*Swansea C*	7	1	**18**	**1**
1997–98	Blackpool	19	1		
1998–99	Blackpool	28	1		
1999–2000	Blackpool	33	2		
2000–01	Blackpool	18	2		
2001–02	Blackpool	37	5		
2002–03	Blackpool	27	5	**162**	**16**
2003–04	Gillingham	29	2		
2004–05	Gillingham	23	0	**52**	**2**
2005–06	Sheffield W	27	0		
2006–07	Sheffield W	16	0	**43**	**0**

JOHNSON, Jermaine (M) 85 15
H: 5 11 W: 11 05 b.Kingston, Jamaica 25-6-80
Source: Tivoli Gardens. *Honours:* Jamaica 40 full caps, 5 goals.

2001–02	Bolton W	10	0		
2002–03	Bolton W	2	0		
2003–04	Bolton W	0	0	**12**	**0**
2003–04	Oldham Ath	20	5		
2004–05	Oldham Ath	19	4		
2005–06	Oldham Ath	0	0	**39**	**9**
2006–07	Bradford C	27	4	**27**	**4**
2006–07	Sheffield W	7	2	**7**	**2**

LEKAJ, Rocky (M) 2 0
H: 5 10 W: 10 05 b.Kosovo 12-10-89
Source: Scholar.

2006–07	Sheffield W	2	0	**2**	**0**

LUNT, Kenny (M) 410 35
H: 5 10 W: 10 05 b.Runcorn 20-11-79
Source: From Trainee. *Honours:* England Schools, Youth.

1997–98	Crewe Alex	41	2		
1998–99	Crewe Alex	18	1		
1999–2000	Crewe Alex	43	3		
2000–01	Crewe Alex	46	1		
2001–02	Crewe Alex	45	5		
2002–03	Crewe Alex	46	7		
2003–04	Crewe Alex	45	7		
2004–05	Crewe Alex	46	5		
2005–06	Crewe Alex	43	4	**373**	**35**
2006–07	Sheffield W	37	0	**37**	**0**

MACLEAN, Steve (F) 128 55
H: 5 11 W: 12 06 b.Edinburgh 23-8-82
Honours: Scotland Under-21.

2002–03	Rangers	3	0	**3**	**0**
2003–04	Scunthorpe U	42	23	**42**	**23**
2004–05	Sheffield W	36	18		
2005–06	Sheffield W	6	2		
2006–07	Sheffield W	41	12	**83**	**32**

McALLISTER, Sean (M) 8 1
H: 5 8 W: 10 07 b.Bolton 15-8-87
Source: Scholar.

2005–06	Sheffield W	2	0		
2006–07	Sheffield W	6	1	**8**	**1**

McCLEMENTS, David (M) 0 0
H: 5 7 W: 10 01 b.Ballymoney 14-1-89
Source: Scholar. *Honours:* Northern Ireland Youth.

2006–07	Sheffield W	0	0		

O'BRIEN, Burton (M) 187 19
H: 5 10 W: 11 09 b.South Africa 10-6-81
Source: S Form. *Honours:* Scotland Youth, Under-21.

1998–99	St Mirren	22	1	**22**	**1**
1998–99	Blackburn R	0	0		
1999–2000	Blackburn R	0	0		
2000–01	Blackburn R	0	0		
2001–02	Blackburn R	0	0		
2002–03	Livingston	28	1		
2003–04	Livingston	33	6		
2004–05	Livingston	38	8	**99**	**15**
2005–06	Sheffield W	44	2		
2006–07	Sheffield W	22	1	**66**	**3**

SIMEK, Frankie (D) 97 2
H: 6 0 W: 11 06 b.St Louis 13-10-84
Source: Trainee. *Honours:* USA 5 full caps.

2002–03	Arsenal	0	0		
2003–04	Arsenal	0	0		
2004–05	Arsenal	0	0		
2004–05	*QPR*	5	0	**5**	**0**
2004–05	*Bournemouth*	8	0	**8**	**0**
2005–06	Sheffield W	43	1		
2006–07	Sheffield W	41	1	**84**	**2**

SMALL, Wade (M) 119 14
H: 5 8 W: 11 05 b.Croydon 23-2-84
Source: Scholar.

2003–04	Wimbledon	27	1	**27**	**1**
2004–05	Milton Keynes D	44	10		
2005–06	Milton Keynes D	28	1	**72**	**11**
2006–07	Sheffield W	20	2	**20**	**2**

SPURR, Tommy (D) 38 0
H: 6 1 W: 11 05 b.Leeds 13-9-87
Source: Scholar.

2005–06	Sheffield W	2	0		
2006–07	Sheffield W	36	0	**38**	**0**

TUDGAY, Marcus (F) 150 33
H: 5 10 W: 12 04 b.Worthing 3-2-83
Source: Trainee.

2002–03	Derby Co	8	0		
2003–04	Derby Co	29	6		
2004–05	Derby Co	34	9		
2005–06	Derby Co	21	2	**92**	**17**
2005–06	Sheffield W	18	5		
2006–07	Sheffield W	40	11	**58**	**16**

WHELAN, Glenn (M) 130 10
H: 5 11 W: 12 07 b.Dublin 13-1-84
Source: Scholar. *Honours:* Eire Youth, Under-21.

2000–01	Manchester C	0	0		
2001–02	Manchester C	0	0		
2002–03	Manchester C	0	0		
2003–04	Manchester C	0	0		
2003–04	*Bury*	13	0	**13**	**0**
2004–05	Sheffield W	36	2		
2005–06	Sheffield W	43	1		
2006–07	Sheffield W	38	7	**117**	**10**

WOOD, Richard (D) 91 3
H: 6 3 W: 12 13 b.Wakefield 5-7-85
Source: Scholar.

2002–03	Sheffield W	3	1		
2003–04	Sheffield W	12	0		
2004–05	Sheffield W	34	1		
2005–06	Sheffield W	30	1		
2006–07	Sheffield W	12	0	**91**	**3**

SHREWSBURY T (73)

ASAMOAH, Derek (F) **234 35**
H: 5 6 W: 10 04 b.Ghana 1-5-81
Source: Slough T. *Honours:* Ghana 2 full caps.

2001–02	Northampton T	40	3		
2002–03	Northampton T	42	4		
2003–04	Northampton T	31	3	**113**	**10**
2004–05	Mansfield T	30	5	**30**	**5**
2004–05	Lincoln C	10	0		
2005–06	Lincoln C	25	2	**35**	**2**
2005–06	*Chester C*	17	8	**17**	**8**
2006–07	Shrewsbury T	39	10	**39**	**10**

ASHTON, Neil (M) **112 3**
H: 5 8 W: 12 04 b.Liverpool 15-1-85
Source: Scholar.

2002–03	Tranmere R	0	0		
2003–04	Tranmere R	1	0		
2004–05	Tranmere R	0	0	**1**	**0**
2004–05	*Shrewsbury T*	24	0		
2005–06	Shrewsbury T	44	1		
2006–07	Shrewsbury T	43	2	**111**	**3**

BURTON, Sagi (D) **261 12**
H: 6 2 W: 14 02 b.Birmingham 25-11-77
Source: Trainee. *Honours:* St Kitts & Nevis 3 full caps.

1995–96	Crystal Palace	0	0		
1996–97	Crystal Palace	0	0		
1997–98	Crystal Palace	2	0		
1998–99	Crystal Palace	23	1	**25**	**1**
1999–2000	Colchester U	9	0	**9**	**0**
1999–2000	Sheffield U	0	0		
1999–2000	Port Vale	20	2		
2000–01	Port Vale	29	0		
2001–02	Port Vale	37	0	**86**	**2**
2002–03	Crewe Alex	1	0	**1**	**0**
2002–03	Peterborough U	31	0		
2003–04	Peterborough U	30	1		
2004–05	Peterborough U	16	1		
2005–06	Peterborough U	19	2	**96**	**4**
2005–06	Shrewsbury T	16	4		
2006–07	Shrewsbury T	28	1	**44**	**5**

COOKE, Andy (F) **344 91**
H: 6 0 W: 12 07 b.Shrewsbury 20-1-74
Source: Newtown.

1994–95	Burnley	0	0		
1995–96	Burnley	23	5		
1996–97	Burnley	31	13		
1997–98	Burnley	34	16		
1998–99	Burnley	36	9		
1999–2000	Burnley	36	7		
2000–01	Burnley	11	2	**171**	**52**
2000–01	Stoke C	22	6		
2001–02	Stoke C	35	9		
2002–03	Stoke C	31	6		
2003–04	Stoke C	0	0	**88**	**21**
From Pusan Icons.					
2004–05	Bradford C	20	4		
2005–06	Bradford C	17	1	**37**	**5**
2005–06	*Darlington*	14	3	**14**	**3**
2006–07	Shrewsbury T	34	10	**34**	**10**

COWAN, Gavin (D) **24 1**
H: 6 4 W: 14 04 b.Hanover 24-5-81
Source: Braintree T, Canvey Island.

2004–05	Shrewsbury T	5	0		
2005–06	Shrewsbury T	15	1		
2006–07	Shrewsbury T	4	0	**24**	**1**

DAVIES, Ben (M) **144 21**
H: 5 7 W: 12 03 b.Birmingham 27-5-81
Source: Walsall trainee.

2000–01	Kidderminster H	3	0		
2001–02	Kidderminster H	9	0	**12**	**0**
2004–05	Chester C	44	2		
2005–06	Chester C	45	7	**89**	**9**
2006–07	Shrewsbury T	43	12	**43**	**12**

DRUMMOND, Stuart (M) **131 16**
H: 6 2 W: 13 08 b.Preston 11-12-75
Source: Morecambe.

2004–05	Chester C	45	6		
2005–06	Chester C	42	6	**87**	**12**
2006–07	Shrewsbury T	44	4	**44**	**4**

EDWARDS, Dave (M) **103 12**
H: 5 11 W: 11 04 b.Shrewsbury 3-2-86
Source: Scholar. *Honours:* Wales Youth, Under-21.

2002–03	Shrewsbury T	1	0		
2003–04	Shrewsbury T	0	0		
2004–05	Shrewsbury T	27	5		
2005–06	Shrewsbury T	30	2		
2006–07	Shrewsbury T	45	5	**103**	**12**

ESSON, Ryan (G) **104 0**
H: 6 1 W: 12 06 b.Aberdeen 19-3-80
Honours: Scotland Youth, Under-21.

1999–2000	Aberdeen	1	0		
2000–01	Aberdeen	36	0		
2001–02	Aberdeen	9	0		
2001–02	Aberdeen	9	0		
2001–02	*Rotherham U*	0	0		
2002–03	Aberdeen	0	0		
2003–04	Aberdeen	2	0		
2004–05	Aberdeen	23	0		
2005–06	Aberdeen	18	0	**98**	**0**
2006–07	Shrewsbury T	6	0	**6**	**0**

FORTUNE-WEST, Leo (F) **362 98**
H: 6 4 W: 13 10 b.Stratford 9-4-71
Source: Tiptree, Dagenham, Dartford, Bishops Stortford, Stevenage Bor.

1995–96	Gillingham	40	12		
1996–97	Gillingham	7	2		
1996–97	*Leyton Orient*	5	0	**5**	**0**
1997–98	Gillingham	20	4	**67**	**18**
1998–99	Lincoln C	9	1	**9**	**1**
1998–99	Brentford	11	0	**11**	**0**
1998–99	Rotherham U	20	12		
1999–2000	Rotherham U	39	17		
2000–01	Rotherham U	5	1	**64**	**30**
2000–01	Cardiff C	37	12		
2001–02	Cardiff C	36	9		
2002–03	Cardiff C	19	2	**92**	**23**
2003–04	Doncaster R	39	11		
2004–05	Doncaster R	24	6		
2005–06	Doncaster R	27	2	**90**	**19**
From Rushden & D.					
2006–07	*Torquay U*	5	0	**5**	**0**
2006–07	Shrewsbury T	19	7	**19**	**7**

On loan to Shrewsbury T.

HALL, Danny (D) **91 1**
H: 6 0 W: 12 02 b.Ashton-under-Lyne 14-11-83
Source: Scholar.

2002–03	Oldham Ath	2	0		
2003–04	Oldham Ath	31	1		
2004–05	Oldham Ath	21	0		
2005–06	Oldham Ath	10	0	**64**	**1**
2006–07	Shrewsbury T	27	0	**27**	**0**

HERD, Ben (D) **77 3**
H: 5 9 W: 10 12 b.Welwyn 21-6-85
Source: Scholar.

2002–03	Watford	0	0		
2003–04	Watford	0	0		
2004–05	Watford	0	0		
2005–06	Shrewsbury T	46	2		
2006–07	Shrewsbury T	31	1	**77**	**3**

HOGG, Steven (M) **13 0**
H: 6 3 W: 11 11 b.Bury 1-10-85
Source: Manchester U Scholar.

2005–06	Shrewsbury T	12	0		
2006–07	Shrewsbury T	1	0	**13**	**0**

HOPE, Richard (D) **337 12**
H: 6 2 W: 12 06 b.Stockton 22-6-78
Source: Trainee.

1995–96	Blackburn R	0	0		
1996–97	Blackburn R	0	0		
1996–97	Darlington	20	0		
1997–98	Darlington	35	1		
1998–99	Darlington	8	0	**63**	**1**
1998–99	Northampton T	19	0		
1999–2000	Northampton T	17	0		
2000–01	Northampton T	33	0		
2001–02	Northampton T	43	6		
2002–03	Northampton T	23	1	**135**	**7**
2003–04	York C	36	2	**36**	**2**
2004–05	Chester C	28	0	**28**	**0**
2005–06	Shrewsbury T	42	2		
2006–07	Shrewsbury T	33	0	**75**	**2**

HUMPHREY, Chris (M) **12 0**
H: 5 10 W: 10 08 b.Walsall 19-9-87
Source: WBA Scholar.

2006–07	Shrewsbury T	12	0	**12**	**0**

JONES, Luke (D) **7 0**
H: 5 9 W: 11 09 b.Darwen 10-4-87
Source: Scholar.

2005–06	Blackburn R	0	0		
2006–07	Shrewsbury T	7	0	**7**	**0**

LANGMEAD, Kelvin (F) **137 17**
H: 6 1 W: 12 00 b.Coventry 23-3-85
Source: Scholar.

2003–04	Preston NE	0	0		
2003–04	*Carlisle U*	11	1	**11**	**1**
2004–05	Preston NE	1	0	**1**	**0**
2004–05	*Kidderminster H*	10	1	**10**	**1**
2004–05	Shrewsbury T	28	3		
2005–06	Shrewsbury T	42	9		
2006–07	Shrewsbury T	45	3	**115**	**15**

LESLIE, Steven (M) **6 0**
H: 5 10 W: 11 02 b.Shrewsbury 5-11-87

2005–06	Shrewsbury T	1	0		
2006–07	Shrewsbury T	5	0	**6**	**0**

MACKENZIE, Chris (G) **164 1**
H: 5 11 W: 14 02 b.Northampton 14-5-72
Source: Corby T.

1994–95	Hereford U	22	0		
1995–96	Hereford U	38	1		
1996–97	Hereford U	0	0	**60**	**1**
1997–98	Leyton Orient	4	0		
1998–99	Leyton Orient	26	0	**30**	**0**
From Telford U					
2004–05	Chester C	24	0		
2005–06	Chester C	30	0	**54**	**0**
2006–07	Shrewsbury T	20	0	**20**	**0**

SORVEL, Neil (M) **408 25**
H: 5 10 W: 11 04 b.Whiston 2-3-73
Source: Trainee.

1991–92	Crewe Alex	9	0		
1992–93	Crewe Alex	0	0		
1997–98	Macclesfield T	45	3		
1998–99	Macclesfield T	41	4	**86**	**7**
1999–2000	Crewe Alex	46	6		
2000–01	Crewe Alex	46	1		
2001–02	Crewe Alex	38	0		
2002–03	Crewe Alex	43	3		
2003–04	Crewe Alex	31	0		
2004–05	Crewe Alex	46	3	**259**	**13**
2005–06	Shrewsbury T	45	4		
2006–07	Shrewsbury T	18	1	**63**	**5**

SYMES, Michael (F) **53 13**
H: 6 3 W: 12 04 b.Gt Yarmouth 31-10-83
Source: Scholar.

2001–02	Everton	0	0		
2002–03	Everton	0	0		
2003–04	Everton	0	0		
2003–04	*Crewe Alex*	4	1	**4**	**1**
2004–05	Bradford C	12	2		
2004–05	*Darlington*	0	0		
2005–06	Bradford C	3	1		
2005–06	*Stockport Co*	1	0	**1**	**0**
2006–07	Bradford C	0	0	**15**	**3**
2006–07	Shrewsbury T	33	9	**33**	**9**

TIERNEY, Marc (D) **55 0**
H: 5 11 W: 11 04 b.Manchester 7-9-86
Source: Trainee.

2003–04	Oldham Ath	2	0		
2004–05	Oldham Ath	11	0		
2005–06	Oldham Ath	19	0		
2006–07	Oldham Ath	5	0	**37**	**0**
2006–07	Shrewsbury T	18	0	**18**	**0**

WHITEHEAD, Stuart (D) **238 2**
H: 6 0 W: 12 04 b.Bromsgrove 17-7-76
Source: Bromsgrove R.

1995–96	Bolton W	0	0		
1996–97	Bolton W	0	0		
1997–98	Bolton W	0	0		
1998–99	Carlisle U	37	0		
1999–2000	Carlisle U	29	0		
2000–01	Carlisle U	45	1		
2001–02	Carlisle U	32	1		
2002–03	Carlisle U	9	0	**152**	**2**
2002–03	Darlington	23	0	**23**	**0**

From Telford U

2004–05	Shrewsbury T	40	0		
2005–06	Shrewsbury T	23	0		
2006–07	Shrewsbury T	0	0	**63**	**0**

WILLIAMS, Dale (F) **3** **0**
H: 6 0 W: 11 04 b.Neath 26-3-87
Source: Scholar. *Honours:* Wales Youth, Under-21.

2004–05	Yeovil T	0	0		
2005–06	Yeovil T	1	0	**1**	**0**
2006–07	Shrewsbury T	2	0	**2**	**0**

SOUTHAMPTON (74)

BAIRD, Chris (D) **86** **3**
H: 5 10 W: 11 11 b.Ballymoney 25-2-82
Source: Scholar. *Honours:* Northern Ireland Youth, Under-21, 25 full caps.

2000–01	Southampton	0	0		
2001–02	Southampton	0	0		
2002–03	Southampton	3	0		
2003–04	Southampton	4	0		
2003–04	*Walsall*	10	0	**10**	**0**
2003–04	*Watford*	8	0	**8**	**0**
2004–05	Southampton	0	0		
2005–06	Southampton	17	0		
2006–07	Southampton	44	3	**68**	**3**

BALE, Gareth (D) **40** **5**
H: 6 0 W: 11 10 b.Cardiff 16-7-89
Source: Scholar. *Honours:* Wales Youth, Under-21, 6 full caps, 2 goals.

2005–06	Southampton	2	0		
2006–07	Southampton	38	5	**40**	**5**

BASEYA, Cedric (M) **0** **0**
b.Bretigny 19-12-87

2006–07	Southampton	0	0		

BELMADI, Djamel (M) **175** **26**
H: 5 7 W: 11 00 b.Champigny-sur-Marne 27-3-76
Honours: Algeria 21 full caps, 5 goals.

1995–96	Paris St Germain	1	0	**1**	**0**
1996–97	Martigues	31	8	**31**	**8**
1997–98	Marseille	0	0		
1998–99	Cannes	26	6	**26**	**6**
1999–2000	Marseille	9	1		
1999–2000	Celta Vigo	10	0	**10**	**0**
2000–01	Marseille	29	8		
2001–02	Marseille	10	0		
2002–03	Marseille	15	0	**63**	**9**
2002–03	Manchester C	8	0		
2003–04	Manchester C	0	0		
2004–05	Manchester C	0	0	**8**	**0**
2005–06	Southampton	22	3		
2006–07	Southampton	14	0	**36**	**3**

BEST, Leon (F) **63** **19**
H: 6 1 W: 13 03 b.Nottingham 19-9-86
Source: Scholar. *Honours:* Eire Youth.

2004–05	Southampton	3	0		
2004–05	*QPR*	5	0	**5**	**0**
2005–06	Southampton	3	0		
2005–06	*Sheffield W*	13	2	**13**	**2**
2006–07	Southampton	9	4	**15**	**4**
2006–07	*Bournemouth*	15	3	**15**	**3**
2006–07	*Yeovil T*	15	10	**15**	**10**

BIALKOWSKI, Bartosz (G) **20** **0**
H: 6 3 W: 12 10 b.Braniewo 6-7-87
Honours: Poland Under-21.

2004–05	Gornik Zabrze	7	0	**7**	**0**
2005–06	Southampton	5	0		
2006–07	Southampton	8	0	**13**	**0**

CONDESSO, Feliciano (M) **0** **0**
H: 6 0 W: 11 13 b.Congo 6-4-87

2005–06	Southampton	0	0		
2006–07	Southampton	0	0		

CRANIE, Martin (D) **31** **0**
H: 6 1 W: 12 09 b.Yeovil 23-9-86
Source: Scholar. *Honours:* England Youth, Under-20.

2003–04	Southampton	1	0		
2004–05	Southampton	3	0		
2004–05	*Bournemouth*	3	0	**3**	**0**
2005–06	Southampton	11	0		
2006–07	Southampton	1	0	**16**	**0**
2006–07	*Yeovil T*	12	0	**12**	**0**

DAVIES, Kyle (M) **0** **0**
b.Oakland

2006–07	Southampton	0	0		

DAVIS, Kelvin (G) **382** **0**
H: 6 1 W: 11 05 b.Bedford 29-9-76
Source: Trainee. *Honours:* England Youth, Under-21.

1993–94	Luton T	1	0		
1994–95	Luton T	9	0		
1994–95	*Torquay U*	2	0	**2**	**0**
1995–96	Luton T	6	0		
1996–97	Luton T	0	0		
1997–98	Luton T	32	0		
1997–98	*Hartlepool U*	2	0	**2**	**0**
1998–99	Luton T	44	0	**92**	**0**
1999–2000	Wimbledon	0	0		
2000–01	Wimbledon	45	0		
2001–02	Wimbledon	40	0		
2002–03	Wimbledon	46	0	**131**	**0**
2003–04	Ipswich T	45	0		
2004–05	Ipswich T	39	0	**84**	**0**
2005–06	Sunderland	33	0	**33**	**0**
2006–07	Southampton	38	0	**38**	**0**

DUTTON-BLACK, Josh (M) **0** **0**
b.Oxford 29-12-87
Source: Oxford U, Southampton Scholar.

2005–06	Southampton	0	0		
2006–07	Southampton	0	0		

DYER, Nathan (M) **40** **2**
H: 5 5 W: 9 00 b.Trowbridge 29-11-87
Source: Scholar. *Honours:* England Youth.

2005–06	Southampton	17	0		
2005–06	*Burnley*	5	2	**5**	**2**
2006–07	Southampton	18	0	**35**	**0**

GIALLOMBARDO, Andrew (M) **0** **0**
H: 5 9 W: 12 02 b.New York 15-3-89
Source: Scholar.

2006–07	Southampton	0	0		

GILLETT, Simon (M) **40** **2**
H: 5 6 W: 11 07 b.London 6-11-85
Source: From Trainee. *Honours:* Luxembourg full caps.

2003–04	Southampton	0	0		
2004–05	Southampton	0	0		
2005–06	Southampton	0	0		
2005–06	*Walsall*	2	0	**2**	**0**
2006–07	Southampton	0	0		
2006–07	*Blackpool*	31	1	**31**	**1**
2006–07	*Bournemouth*	7	1	**7**	**1**

HATCH, Jamie (M) **0** **0**
b.Hampshire 21-9-89
Source: Scholar.

2006–07	Southampton	0	0		

IDIAKEZ, Inigo (M) **426** **77**
H: 6 0 W: 12 02 b.San Sebastian 8-11-73

1992–93	Real Sociedad	1	0		
1993–94	Real Sociedad B	25	13		
1993–94	Real Sociedad	2	0		
1994–95	Real Sociedad	26	4		
1995–96	Real Sociedad	33	4		
1996–97	Real Sociedad	31	4		
1997–98	Real Sociedad	16	1		
1998–99	Real Sociedad	29	7		
1999–2000	Real Sociedad	27	4		
2000–01	Real Sociedad	33	7		
2001–02	Real Sociedad	34	2	**232**	**33**
2002–03	Oviedo	33	4	**33**	**4**
2003–04	Rayo Vallecano	29	5	**29**	**5**
2004–05	Derby Co	41	9		
2005–06	Derby Co	42	11		
2006–07	Derby Co	5	0	**88**	**20**
2006–07	Southampton	14	1	**14**	**1**
2006–07	*QPR*	5	1	**5**	**1**

JAMES, Lloyd (M) **0** **0**
H: 5 11 W: 11 01 b.Bristol 16-2-88
Source: Scholar. *Honours:* Wales Under-21.

2005–06	Southampton	0	0		
2006–07	Southampton	0	0		

JONES, Kenwyne (F) **90** **28**
H: 6 2 W: 13 06 b.Trinidad & Tobago 5-10-84
Source: W Connection. *Honours:* Trindad & Tobago Youth, Under-23, 33 full caps, 3 goals.

2004–05	Southampton	2	0		
2004–05	*Sheffield W*	7	7	**7**	**7**
2004–05	*Stoke C*	13	3	**13**	**3**
2005–06	Southampton	34	4		
2006–07	Southampton	34	14	**70**	**18**

LALLANA, Adam (M) **1** **0**
b.St Albans 10-5-88
Source: Scholar. *Honours:* England Youth.

2005–06	Southampton	0	0		
2006–07	Southampton	1	0	**1**	**0**

LANCASHIRE, Oliver (D) **0** **0**
H: 6 1 W: 11 10 b.Basingstoke 13-12-88
Source: Scholar.

2006–07	Southampton	0	0		

LICKA, Mario (M) **108** **14**
H: 5 10 W: 11 11 b.Ostrava 30-4-82

2002–03	Banik Ostrava	25	7		
2003–04	Banik Ostrava	29	4		
2004–05	Banik Ostrava	11	1	**65**	**12**
2005–06	Slovacko	28	1	**28**	**1**
2006–07	Southampton	15	1	**15**	**1**

LUNDEKVAM, Claus (D) **410** **3**
H: 6 3 W: 13 05 b.Austevoll 22-2-73
Honours: Norway Youth, Under-21, 40 full caps, 2 goals.

1993	Brann	3	0		
1994	Brann	20	0		
1995	Brann	14	0		
1996	Brann	16	1	**53**	**1**
1996–97	Southampton	29	0		
1997–98	Southampton	31	0		
1998–99	Southampton	33	0		
1999–2000	Southampton	27	0		
2000–01	Southampton	38	0		
2001–02	Southampton	34	0		
2002–03	Southampton	33	0		
2003–04	Southampton	31	1		
2004–05	Southampton	34	0		
2005–06	Southampton	34	1		
2006–07	Southampton	33	0	**357**	**2**

MAKIN, Chris (D) **404** **7**
H: 5 11 W: 11 02 b.Manchester 8-5-73
Source: Trainee. *Honours:* England Schools, Youth, Under-21.

1991–92	Oldham Ath	0	0		
1992–93	Oldham Ath	0	0		
1992–93	*Wigan Ath*	15	2	**15**	**2**
1993–94	Oldham Ath	27	1		
1994–95	Oldham Ath	28	1		
1995–96	Oldham Ath	39	2	**94**	**4**
1996–97	Marseille	29	0	**29**	**0**
1997–98	Sunderland	25	0		
1998–99	Sunderland	38	0		
1999–2000	Sunderland	34	1		
2000–01	Sunderland	23	0	**120**	**1**
2000–01	Ipswich T	10	0		
2001–02	Ipswich T	30	0		
2002–03	Ipswich T	33	0		
2003–04	Ipswich T	5	0	**78**	**0**
2004–05	Leicester C	21	0	**21**	**0**
2004–05	*Derby Co*	13	0	**13**	**0**
2005–06	Reading	12	0	**12**	**0**
2006–07	Southampton	22	0	**22**	**0**

McGOLDRICK, David (F) **32** **6**
H: 6 1 W: 11 10 b.Nottingham 29-11-87
Source: Schoolboy.

2003–04	Notts Co	4	0		
2004–05	Notts Co	0	0		
2005–06	Southampton	1	0		
2005–06	*Notts Co*	6	0	**10**	**0**
2006–07	Southampton	9	0	**10**	**0**
2006–07	*Bournemouth*	12	6	**12**	**6**

MILLER, Kevin (G) **628** **0**
H: 6 1 W: 13 00 b.Falmouth 15-3-69
Source: Newquay.

1988–89	Exeter C	3	0		
1989–90	Exeter C	28	0		

1990–91	Exeter C	46	0		
1991–92	Exeter C	42	0		
1992–93	Exeter C	44	0		
1993–94	Birmingham C	24	0	**24**	**0**
1994–95	Watford	44	0		
1995–96	Watford	42	0		
1996–97	Watford	42	0	**128**	**0**
1997–98	Crystal Palace	38	0		
1998–99	Crystal Palace	28	0		
1999–2000	Crystal Palace	0	0	**66**	**0**
1999–2000	Barnsley	41	0		
2000–01	Barnsley	46	0		
2001–02	Barnsley	28	0	**115**	**0**
2002–03	Exeter C	46	0	**209**	**0**
2003–04	Bristol R	44	0		
2004–05	*Derby Co*	0	0		
2004–05	Bristol R	28	0	**72**	**0**
2005–06	Southampton	7	0		
2006–07	Southampton	0	0	**7**	**0**
2006–07	*Torquay U*	7	0	**7**	**0**

MILLS, Joseph (F) **0 0**
H: 5 9 W: 11 00 b.Swindon 30-10-89
Source: Scholar.

2006–07	Southampton	0	0		

OSTLUND, Alexander (D) **245 9**
H: 5 11 W: 11 13 b.Akersborg 2-11-78
Honours: Sweden Under-21, 22 full caps.

1994	AIK Stockholm	3	1		
1995	AIK Stockholm	17	1		
1996	AIK Stockholm	2	0		
1997	Brommapojkarna	13	2	**13**	**2**
1998	AIK Stockholm	24	1	**46**	**3**
1998–99	Guimaraes	0	0		
1999	Norrkoping	11	1		
2000	Norrkoping	22	1		
2001	Norrkoping	21	1		
2002	Norrkoping	23	0	**77**	**3**
2003	Hammarby	20	0		
2004	Hammarby	25	0	**45**	**0**
2004–05	Feyenoord	16	0		
2005–06	Feyenoord	16	1	**32**	**1**
2005–06	Southampton	12	0		
2006–07	Southampton	20	0	**32**	**0**

PELE (D) **282 12**
H: 6 1 W: 13 08 b.Albufeira 2-5-78

1997–98	Imortal	15	0		
1998–99	Imortal	20	0		
1999–2000	Imortal	29	2		
2000–01	Imortal	25	3		
2001–02	Imortal	38	2	**127**	**7**
2002–03	Farense	28	2	**28**	**2**
2003–04	Belenenses	25	1		
2004–05	Belenenses	33	1		
2005–06	Belenenses	32	0	**90**	**2**
2006–07	Southampton	37	1	**37**	**1**

POKE, Michael (G) **0 0**
H: 6 1 W: 13 12 b.Spelthorne 21-11-85
Source: Trainee.

2003–04	Southampton	0	0		
2004–05	Southampton	0	0		
2005–06	Southampton	0	0		
2005–06	*Oldham Ath*	0	0		
2005–06	*Northampton T*	0	0		
2006–07	Southampton	0	0		

POWELL, Darren (D) **221 10**
H: 6 2 W: 13 07 b.Hammersmith 10-3-76
Source: Hampton.

1998–99	Brentford	33	2		
1999–2000	Brentford	36	2		
2000–01	Brentford	18	1		
2001–02	Brentford	41	1	**128**	**6**
2002–03	Crystal Palace	39	1		
2003–04	Crystal Palace	10	0		
2004–05	Crystal Palace	6	1	**55**	**2**
2004–05	*West Ham U*	5	1	**5**	**1**
2005–06	Southampton	25	1		
2006–07	Southampton	8	0	**33**	**1**

PRUTTON, David (M) **237 12**
H: 5 10 W: 13 00 b.Hull 12-9-81
Source: Trainee. *Honours:* England Youth, Under-21.

1998–99	Nottingham F	0	0		
1999–2000	Nottingham F	34	2		
2000–01	Nottingham F	42	1		
2001–02	Nottingham F	43	3		
2002–03	Nottingham F	24	1		
2002–03	Southampton	12	0		
2003–04	Southampton	27	1		
2004–05	Southampton	23	1		
2005–06	Southampton	17	0		
2006–07	Southampton	3	1	**82**	**3**
2006–07	*Nottingham F*	12	2	**155**	**9**

RASIAK, Grzegorz (F) **195 83**
H: 6 3 W: 13 03 b.Szczecin 12-1-79
Source: Warta, GKS. *Honours:* Poland 35 full caps, 8 goals.

2000–01	Odra	28	9	**28**	**9**
2001–02	Groclin	26	14		
2002–03	Groclin	22	10		
2003–04	Groclin	18	10	**66**	**34**
2003–04	Siena	0	0		
2004–05	Derby Co	35	16		
2005–06	Derby Co	6	2	**41**	**18**
2005–06	Tottenham H	8	0	**8**	**0**
2005–06	Southampton	13	4		
2006–07	Southampton	39	18	**52**	**22**

RUDD, Sean (D) **0 0**
H: 6 2 W: 11 03 b.Oxford 23-10-87
Source: Scholar. *Honours:* England Youth.

2005–06	Southampton	0	0		
2006–07	Southampton	0	0		

SAGANOWSKI, Marek (F) **276 99**
H: 5 10 W: 12 04 b.Lodz 31-10-78
Honours: Poland 16 full caps, 3 goals.

1994–95	Lodz	3	0		
1995–96	Lodz	29	11		
1996–97	Lodz	2	1		
1996–97	Hamburg	3	0	**3**	**0**
1996–97	Feyenoord	7	0	**7**	**0**
1997–98	Lodz	22	11		
1998–99	Lodz	15	1		
1999–2000	Lodz	24	6	**95**	**30**
2000–01	Plock	23	4	**23**	**4**
2001–02	Odra	27	2		
2002–03	Odra	3	0	**30**	**2**
2002–03	Legia	17	10		
2003–04	Legia	24	17		
2004–05	Legia	26	14	**67**	**41**
2005–06	Guimaraes	32	12	**32**	**12**
2006–07	Troyes	6	0	**6**	**0**
2006–07	Southampton	13	10	**13**	**10**

SARMIENTO, Marcelo (M) **0 0**
H: 6 0 W: 12 00 b.Cordoba 24-8-79
Source: Instituto, Las Flores, Talleres, Litets, Olimpo Bahia, Argentinos Juniors.

2006–07	Southampton	0	0		

To Racing Cordoba January 2007

SKACEL, Rudi (M) **169 38**
H: 5 10 W: 12 01 b.Trutnov 17-7-79
Honours: Czech Republic Under-21, 3 full caps, 1 goal.

1998–99	Hradec Kralove	0	0		
1999–2000	Hradec Kralove	3	0		
2000–01	Hradec Kralove	0	0		
2001–02	Hradec Kralove	18	6	**21**	**6**
2001–02	Slavia Prague	12	3		
2002–03	Slavia Prague	28	8	**40**	**11**
2003–04	Marseille	20	1	**20**	**1**
2004–05	Panathinaikos	16	1	**16**	**1**
2005–06	Hearts	35	16	**35**	**16**
2006–07	Southampton	37	3	**37**	**3**

SPARV, Tim (M) **0 0**
H: 6 4 W: 12 05 b.Vasa 20-2-87
Source: Scholar.

2004–05	Southampton	0	0		
2005–06	Southampton	0	0		
2006–07	Southampton	0	0		

To Halmstad December 2006

SURMAN, Andrew (M) **87 14**
H: 5 10 W: 11 06 b.Johannesburg 20-8-86
Source: Trainee.

2003–04	Southampton	0	0		
2004–05	Southampton	0	0		
2004–05	*Walsall*	14	2	**14**	**2**
2005–06	Southampton	12	2		
2005–06	*Bournemouth*	24	6	**24**	**6**
2006–07	Southampton	37	4	**49**	**6**

SVENSSON, Michael (D) **245 11**
H: 6 2 W: 12 02 b.Varnamo 25-11-75
Honours: Sweden 25 full caps.

1992	Skillingaryds	21	0	**21**	**0**
1993	Varnamo	20	0		
1994	Varnamo	20	0		
1995	Varnamo	17	1		
1996	Varnamo	0	0	**57**	**1**
1997	Halmstad	0	0		
1998	Halmstad	14	2		
1999	Halmstad	20	0		
2000	Halmstad	25	2		
2001	Halmstad	18	1	**77**	**5**
2001–02	Troyes	23	1	**23**	**1**
2002–03	Southampton	34	2		
2003–04	Southampton	26	2		
2004–05	Southampton	0	0		
2005–06	Southampton	7	0		
2006–07	Southampton	0	0	**67**	**4**

THOMSON, Jake (M) **0 0**
H: 5 11 W: 11 05 b.Southsea 12-5-89
Source: Scholar.

2006–07	Southampton	0	0		

VIAFARA, John (M) **246 14**
H: 6 0 W: 13 01 b.Robles 27-10-78
Honours: Colombia full caps.

1999	Pasto	44	2		
2000	America	27	0		
2001	America	10	0	**37**	**0**
2001	Pasto	18	0	**62**	**2**
2002	Once Caldas	37	2		
2003	Once Caldas	32	4		
2004	Once Caldas	17	3	**86**	**9**
2005–06	Portsmouth	14	1	**14**	**1**
2005–06	Real Sociedad	11	0	**11**	**0**
2006–07	Southampton	36	2	**36**	**2**

WHITE, Jamie (F) **0 0**
H: 5 8 W: 10 07 b.Southampton 21-9-89
Source: Scholar.

2006–07	Southampton	0	0		

WRIGHT-PHILLIPS, Bradley (M) **71 10**
H: 5 10 W: 10 07 b.Lewisham 12-3-85
Source: From Scholar. *Honours:* England Youth, Under-20.

2002–03	Manchester C	0	0		
2003–04	Manchester C	0	0		
2004–05	Manchester C	14	1		
2005–06	Manchester C	18	1	**32**	**2**
2006–07	Southampton	39	8	**39**	**8**

WRIGHT, Jermaine (M) **374 21**
H: 5 9 W: 11 09 b.Greenwich 21-10-75
Source: Trainee. *Honours:* England Youth.

1992–93	Millwall	0	0		
1993–94	Millwall	0	0		
1994–95	Millwall	0	0		
1994–95	Wolverhampton W	6	0		
1995–96	Wolverhampton W	7	0		
1995–96	*Doncaster R*	13	0	**13**	**0**
1996–97	Wolverhampton W	3	0		
1997–98	Wolverhampton W	4	0	**20**	**0**
1997–98	Crewe Alex	5	0		
1998–99	Crewe Alex	44	5	**49**	**5**
1999–2000	Ipswich T	34	1		
2000–01	Ipswich T	37	2		
2001–02	Ipswich T	29	1		
2002–03	Ipswich T	39	1		
2003–04	Ipswich T	45	5	**184**	**10**
2004–05	Leeds U	35	3		
2005–06	Leeds U	3	0	**38**	**3**
2005–06	*Millwall*	15	2	**15**	**2**
2005–06	*Southampton*	13	0		
2006–07	Southampton	42	1	**55**	**1**

SOUTHEND U (75)

ADEMENO, Charles (F) **2 0**
H: 5 10 W: 11 13 b.Milton Keynes 12-12-88
Source: Scholar.

2005–06	Southend U	1	0		
2006–07	Southend U	1	0	**2**	**0**

BARRETT, Adam (D) 295 26
H: 5 10 W: 12 00 b.Dagenham 29-11-79
Source: Leyton Orient Trainee.

1998–99	Plymouth Arg	1	0		
1999–2000	Plymouth Arg	42	3		
2000–01	Plymouth Arg	9	0	**52**	**3**
2000–01	Mansfield T	8	1		
2001–02	Mansfield T	29	0	**37**	**1**
2002–03	Bristol R	45	1		
2003–04	Bristol R	45	4	**90**	**5**
2004–05	Southend U	43	11		
2005–06	Southend U	45	3		
2006–07	Southend U	28	3	**116**	**17**

BRADBURY, Lee (F) 381 82
H: 6 0 W: 12 07 b.Isle of Wight 3-7-75
Source: Cowes. *Honours:* England Under-21.

1995–96	Portsmouth	12	0		
1995–96	*Exeter C*	14	5	**14**	**5**
1996–97	Portsmouth	42	15		
1997–98	Manchester C	27	7		
1998–99	Manchester C	13	3	**40**	**10**
1998–99	Crystal Palace	22	4		
1998–99	*Birmingham C*	7	0	**7**	**0**
1999–2000	Crystal Palace	10	2	**32**	**6**
1999–2000	Portsmouth	35	10		
2000–01	Portsmouth	39	10		
2001–02	Portsmouth	22	7		
2002–03	Portsmouth	3	1		
2002–03	*Sheffield W*	11	3	**11**	**3**
2003–04	Portsmouth	0	0	**153**	**43**
2003–04	*Derby Co*	7	0	**7**	**0**
2003–04	Walsall	8	1	**8**	**1**
2004–05	Oxford U	41	4		
2005–06	Oxford U	22	5	**63**	**9**
2005–06	Southend U	15	1		
2006–07	Southend U	31	4	**46**	**5**

BYRNE, Paul (M) 125 11
H: 5 11 W: 13 00 b.Dublin 30-6-72
Source: Trainee. *Honours:* Eire Youth.

1989–90	Oxford U	3	0		
1990–91	Oxford U	2	0		
1991–92	Oxford U	1	0	**6**	**0**
From Bangor					
1993–94	Celtic	22	2		
1994–95	Celtic	6	2	**28**	**4**
1994–95	*Brighton & HA*	8	1	**8**	**1**
1995–96	Southend U	41	5		
1996–97	Southend U	32	1		
1997–98	Southend U	10	0		
1998–99	Southend U	0	0		
1999–2000	Southend U	0	0		
2000–01	Southend U	0	0		
2001–02	Southend U	0	0		
2002–03	Southend U	0	0		
2003–04	Southend U	0	0		
2004–05	Southend U	0	0		
2005–06	Southend U	0	0		
2006–07	Southend U	0	0	**83**	**6**

CAMPBELL-RYCE, Jamal (M) 129 4
H: 5 7 W: 12 03 b.Lambeth 6-4-83
Source: Scholar. *Honours:* Jamaica 6 full caps.

2002–03	Charlton Ath	1	0		
2002–03	*Leyton Orient*	17	2	**17**	**2**
2003–04	Charlton Ath	2	0		
2003–04	*Wimbledon*	4	0	**4**	**0**
2004–05	Charlton Ath	0	0	**3**	**0**
2004–05	*Chesterfield*	14	0	**14**	**0**
2004–05	Rotherham U	24	0		
2005–06	Rotherham U	7	0	**31**	**0**
2005–06	*Southend U*	13	0		
2005–06	*Colchester U*	4	0	**4**	**0**
2006–07	Southend U	43	2	**56**	**2**

CLARKE, Peter (D) 165 17
H: 6 0 W: 12 00 b.Southport 3-1-82
Source: Trainee. *Honours:* England Schools, Youth, Under-20, Under-21.

1998–99	Everton	0	0		
1999–2000	Everton	0	0		
2000–01	Everton	1	0		
2001–02	Everton	7	0		
2002–03	Everton	0	0		
2002–03	*Blackpool*	16	3		
2002–03	*Port Vale*	13	1	**13**	**1**
2003–04	Everton	1	0		
2003–04	*Coventry C*	5	0	**5**	**0**
2004–05	Everton	0	0	**9**	**0**
2004–05	Blackpool	38	5		
2005–06	Blackpool	46	6	**100**	**14**
2006–07	Southend U	38	2	**38**	**2**

COLE, Mitchell (M) 41 2
H: 5 11 W: 11 05 b.London 6-10-85
Source: Trainee. *Honours:* England Youth.

2002–03	West Ham U	0	0		
2003–04	West Ham U	0	0		
2004–05	West Ham U	0	0		
From Grays Ath.					
2005–06	Southend U	29	1		
2006–07	Southend U	4	0	**33**	**1**
2006–07	*Northampton T*	8	1	**8**	**1**

COLLIS, Steve (G) 44 0
H: 6 3 W: 12 05 b.Harrow 18-3-81
Source: Barnet Juniors.

1999–2000	Barnet	0	0		
2000–01	Nottingham F	0	0		
2001–02	Nottingham F	0	0		
2003–04	Yeovil T	11	0		
2004–05	Yeovil T	9	0		
2005–06	Yeovil T	23	0	**43**	**0**
2006–07	Southend U	1	0	**1**	**0**

EASTWOOD, Freddy (F) 115 53
H: 5 11 W: 12 04 b.Epsom 29-10-83
Source: West Ham U Trainee, Grays Ath.

2004–05	Southend U	33	19		
2005–06	Southend U	40	23		
2006–07	Southend U	42	11	**115**	**53**

FLAHAVAN, Darryl (G) 265 0
H: 5 11 W: 12 05 b.Southampton 28-11-78
Source: Trainee.
From Woking.

2000–01	Southend U	29	0		
2001–02	Southend U	41	0		
2002–03	Southend U	41	0		
2003–04	Southend U	37	0		
2004–05	Southend U	28	0		
2005–06	Southend U	43	0		
2006–07	Southend U	46	0	**265**	**0**

FORAN, Richie (F) 228 60
H: 6 1 W: 13 00 b.Dublin 16-6-80
Honours: Eire Under-21.

2000–01	Shelbourne	28	11	**28**	**11**
2001–02	Carlisle U	37	14		
2002–03	Carlisle U	31	7		
2003–04	Carlisle U	23	4	**91**	**25**
2003–04	*Oxford U*	4	0	**4**	**0**
2004–05	Motherwell	35	5		
2005–06	Motherwell	32	11		
2006–07	Motherwell	23	7	**90**	**23**
2006–07	Southend U	15	1	**15**	**1**

FRANCIS, Simon (D) 129 3
H: 6 0 W: 12 06 b.Nottingham 16-2-85
Source: Scholar. *Honours:* England Youth, Under-20.

2002–03	Bradford C	25	1		
2003–04	Bradford C	30	0	**55**	**1**
2003–04	Sheffield U	5	0		
2004–05	Sheffield U	6	0		
2005–06	Sheffield U	1	0	**12**	**0**
2005–06	*Grimsby T*	5	0	**5**	**0**
2005–06	*Tranmere R*	17	1	**17**	**1**
2006–07	Southend U	40	1	**40**	**1**

GOWER, Mark (M) 184 28
H: 5 11 W: 11 12 b.Edmonton 5-10-78
Source: Trainee. *Honours:* England Schools, Youth.

1996–97	Tottenham H	0	0		
1997–98	Tottenham H	0	0		
1998–99	Tottenham H	0	0		
1998–99	*Motherwell*	9	1	**9**	**1**
1999–2000	Tottenham H	0	0		
2000–01	Tottenham H	0	0		
2000–01	Barnet	14	1		
2001–02	Barnet	0	0		
2002–03	Barnet	0	0	**14**	**1**
2003–04	Southend U	40	6		
2004–05	Southend U	38	6		
2005–06	Southend U	40	6		
2006–07	Southend U	43	8	**161**	**26**

HAMMELL, Steven (D) 254 3
H: 5 9 W: 11 11 b.Rutherglen 18-2-82
Honours: Scotland Under-21, 1 full cap.

1999–2000	Motherwell	4	0		
2000–01	Motherwell	34	0		
2001–02	Motherwell	38	1		
2002–03	Motherwell	37	0		
2003–04	Motherwell	37	1		
2004–05	Motherwell	32	0		
2005–06	Motherwell	33	0	**215**	**2**
2006–07	Southend U	39	1	**39**	**1**

HARROLD, Matt (F) 121 16
H: 6 1 W: 11 10 b.Leyton 25-7-84
Source: Harlow T.

2003–04	Brentford	13	2		
2004–05	Brentford	19	0	**32**	**2**
2004–05	*Grimsby T*	6	2	**6**	**2**
2005–06	Yeovil T	42	9		
2006–07	Yeovil T	5	0	**47**	**9**
2006–07	Southend U	36	3	**36**	**3**

HOOPER, Gary (M) 23 2
H: 5 10 W: 12 07 b.Loughton 26-1-88
Source: Grays Ath.

2006–07	Southend U	19	0	**19**	**0**
2006–07	*Leyton Orient*	4	2	**4**	**2**

HUNT, Lewis (D) 133 2
H: 5 11 W: 12 09 b.Birmingham 25-8-82
Source: Scholar.

2000–01	Derby Co	0	0		
2001–02	Derby Co	0	0		
2002–03	Derby Co	10	0		
2003–04	Derby Co	1	0	**11**	**0**
2003–04	*Southend U*	26	0		
2004–05	Southend U	31	0		
2005–06	Southend U	30	0		
2006–07	Southend U	35	2	**122**	**2**

LAWSON, James (M) 31 2
H: 6 0 W: 11 07 b.Basildon 21-1-87
Source: Scholar.

2004–05	Southend U	1	0		
2005–06	Southend U	23	2		
2006–07	Southend U	2	0	**26**	**2**
2006–07	*Grimsby T*	1	0	**1**	**0**
2006–07	*Bournemouth*	4	0	**4**	**0**

MAHER, Kevin (M) 364 22
H: 6 0 W: 12 13 b.Ilford 17-10-76
Source: Trainee. *Honours:* Eire Under-21.

1995–96	Tottenham H	0	0		
1996–97	Tottenham H	0	0		
1997–98	Tottenham H	0	0		
1997–98	Southend U	18	1		
1998–99	Southend U	34	4		
1999–2000	Southend U	24	0		
2000–01	Southend U	41	2		
2001–02	Southend U	36	5		
2002–03	Southend U	42	2		
2003–04	Southend U	42	1		
2004–05	Southend U	42	1		
2005–06	Southend U	44	1		
2006–07	Southend U	41	5	**364**	**22**

McCORMACK, Alan (M) 74 7
H: 5 8 W: 11 00 b.Dublin 10-1-84

2002–03	Preston NE	0	0		
2003–04	Preston NE	5	0		
2003–04	*Leyton Orient*	10	0	**10**	**0**
2004–05	Preston NE	3	0		
2004–05	*Southend U*	7	2		
2005–06	Preston NE	0	0		
2005–06	*Motherwell*	24	2	**24**	**2**
2006–07	Preston NE	3	0	**11**	**0**
2006–07	Southend U	22	3	**29**	**5**

MOUSSA, Franck (M) 5 0
H: 5 8 W: 10 08 b.Brussels 24-9-87
Source: Scholar.

2005–06	Southend U	1	0		
2006–07	Southend U	4	0	**5**	**0**

PAYNTER, Billy (F) 190 37
H: 6 1 W: 14 01 b.Liverpool 13-7-84
Source: Schoolboy.

2000–01	Port Vale	1	0		
2001–02	Port Vale	7	0		
2002–03	Port Vale	31	5		
2003–04	Port Vale	44	13		

2004–05	Port Vale	45	10		
2005–06	Port Vale	16	2	**144**	**30**
2005–06	Hull C	22	3	**22**	**3**
2006–07	Southend U	9	0	**9**	**0**
2006–07	*Bradford C*	15	4	**15**	**4**

PRIOR, Spencer (D) **513** **13**
H: 6 3 W: 13 04 b.Rochford 22-4-71
Source: Trainee.

1988–89	Southend U	14	1		
1989–90	Southend U	15	1		
1990–91	Southend U	19	0		
1991–92	Southend U	42	1		
1992–93	Southend U	45	0		
1993–94	Norwich C	13	0		
1994–95	Norwich C	17	0		
1995–96	Norwich C	44	1	**74**	**1**
1996–97	Leicester C	34	0		
1997–98	Leicester C	30	0	**64**	**0**
1998–99	Derby Co	34	1		
1999–2000	Derby Co	20	0	**54**	**1**
1999–2000	Manchester C	9	3		
2000–01	Manchester C	21	1	**30**	**4**
2001–02	Cardiff C	37	2		
2002–03	Cardiff C	37	0		
2003–04	Cardiff C	7	0	**81**	**2**
2004–05	Southend U	41	2		
2005–06	Southend U	17	0		
2006–07	Southend U	17	0	**210**	**5**

SODJE, Efe (D) **322** **19**
H: 6 1 W: 12 00 b.Greenwich 5-10-72
Source: Delta Steel Pioneer, Stevenage Bor. *Honours:* Nigeria 9 full caps, 1 goal.

1997–98	Macclesfield T	41	3		
1998–99	Macclesfield T	42	3	**83**	**6**
1999–2000	Luton T	9	0	**9**	**0**
1999–2000	Colchester U	3	0	**3**	**0**
2000–01	Crewe Alex	32	0		
2001–02	Crewe Alex	36	2		
2002–03	Crewe Alex	30	1	**98**	**3**
2003–04	Huddersfield T	39	4		
2004–05	Huddersfield T	28	1	**67**	**5**
2004–05	Yeovil T	6	2		
2005–06	Yeovil T	19	1	**25**	**3**
2005–06	Southend U	13	1		
2006–07	Southend U	24	1	**37**	**2**

WILSON, Che (D) **206** **2**
H: 5 9 W: 11 04 b.Ely 17-1-79
Source: Trainee.

1997–98	Norwich C	0	0		
1998–99	Norwich C	17	0		
1999–2000	Norwich C	5	0	**22**	**0**
2000–01	Bristol R	37	0		
2001–02	Bristol R	38	0		
2002–03	Bristol R	0	0	**75**	**0**
From Cambridge C.					
2003–04	Southend U	14	0		
2004–05	Southend U	40	0		
2005–06	Southend U	44	2		
2006–07	Southend U	2	0	**100**	**2**
2006–07	*Brentford*	3	0	**3**	**0**
2006–07	*Rotherham U*	6	0	**6**	**0**

STOCKPORT CO (76)

ALLEN, Damien (M) **50** **1**
H: 5 11 W: 11 04 b.Cheadle 1-8-86
Source: Trainee.

2004–05	Stockport Co	21	1		
2005–06	Stockport Co	22	0		
2006–07	Stockport Co	7	0	**50**	**1**

BOWLER, Michael (M) **8** **0**
H: 5 11 W: 12 00 b.Glossop 8-9-87

2006–07	Stockport Co	8	0	**8**	**0**

BRAMBLE, Tes (F) **216** **43**
H: 6 2 W: 13 05 b.Ipswich 20-7-80
Source: Cambridge C. *Honours:* Monserrat 1 full cap, 1 goal.

2000–01	Southend U	16	6		
2001–02	Southend U	35	9		
2002–03	Southend U	34	9		
2003–04	Southend U	34	4		
2004–05	Southend U	20	1	**139**	**29**
2004–05	*Cambridge U*	9	3	**9**	**3**
2005–06	Stockport Co	37	5		
2006–07	Stockport Co	31	6	**68**	**11**

BRIGGS, Keith (D) **143** **10**
H: 6 0 W: 11 00 b.Glossop 11-12-81
Source: Trainee.

1999–2000	Stockport Co	7	1		
2000–01	Stockport Co	0	0		
2001–02	Stockport Co	32	0		
2002–03	Stockport Co	19	1		
2002–03	Norwich C	2	0		
2003–04	Norwich C	3	0		
2004–05	Norwich C	0	0	**5**	**0**
2004–05	*Crewe Alex*	3	0	**3**	**0**
2004–05	Stockport Co	16	2		
2005–06	Stockport Co	41	4		
2006–07	Stockport Co	20	2	**135**	**10**

CLARE, Rob (D) **204** **5**
H: 6 2 W: 13 00 b.Belper 28-2-83
Source: Trainee. *Honours:* England Under-20.

1999–2000	Stockport Co	0	0		
2000–01	Stockport Co	22	0		
2001–02	Stockport Co	23	0		
2002–03	Stockport Co	36	0		
2003–04	Stockport Co	36	3		
2004–05	Blackpool	23	0	**23**	**0**
2005–06	Stockport Co	34	2		
2006–07	Stockport Co	30	0	**181**	**5**

COWARD, Chris (F) **0** **0**
H: 6 1 W: 11 07 b.Manchester 23-7-89
Source: Scholar.

2005–06	Stockport Co	0	0		
2006–07	Stockport Co	0	0		

CROWTHER, Ryan (M) **2** **0**
H: 5 11 W: 11 00 b.Stockport 17-9-88
Source: Scholar.

2005–06	Stockport Co	1	0		
2006–07	Stockport Co	1	0	**2**	**0**

DICKINSON, Liam (F) **54** **14**
H: 6 4 W: 11 07 b.Salford 4-10-85
Source: Woodley Sports.

2005–06	Stockport Co	21	7		
2006–07	Stockport Co	33	7	**54**	**14**

DINNING, Tony (M) **430** **53**
H: 6 0 W: 13 05 b.Wallsend 12-4-75
Source: Trainee.

1993–94	Newcastle U	0	0		
1994–95	Stockport Co	40	1		
1995–96	Stockport Co	10	1		
1996–97	Stockport Co	20	2		
1997–98	Stockport Co	30	4		
1998–99	Stockport Co	41	5		
1999–2000	Stockport Co	44	12		
2000–01	Stockport Co	6	0		
2000–01	Wolverhampton W	31	6		
2001–02	Wolverhampton W	4	0	**35**	**6**
2001–02	Wigan Ath	33	5		
2001–02	*Stoke C*	5	0	**5**	**0**
2002–03	Wigan Ath	38	7		
2003–04	Wigan Ath	13	0		
2003–04	*Walsall*	5	0	**5**	**0**
2003–04	*Blackpool*	10	3	**10**	**3**
2004–05	Wigan Ath	0	0	**84**	**12**
2004–05	*Ipswich T*	7	0	**7**	**0**
2004–05	*Bristol C*	19	0	**19**	**0**
2004–05	*Port Vale*	7	3		
2005–06	Port Vale	35	2	**42**	**5**
2006–07	Stockport Co	32	2	**223**	**27**

ELDING, Anthony (F) **47** **16**
H: 6 1 W: 12 02 b.Boston 16-4-82
Source: Trainee.

2002–03	Boston U	8	0		
From Stevenage B, Kettering T.					
2006–07	Boston U	19	5	**27**	**5**
2006–07	Stockport Co	20	11	**20**	**11**

ELLIS, Dan (M) **5** **0**
H: 5 10 W: 12 07 b.Stockport 18-11-88
Source: Scholar.

2005–06	Stockport Co	3	0		
2006–07	Stockport Co	2	0	**5**	**0**

GRIFFIN, Adam (D) **134** **8**
H: 5 7 W: 10 04 b.Salford 26-8-84
Source: Scholar.

2001–02	Oldham Ath	1	0		
2002–03	Oldham Ath	0	0		
2003–04	Oldham Ath	26	1		
2004–05	Oldham Ath	35	2		
2005–06	Oldham Ath	0	0	**62**	**3**
2005–06	*Oxford U*	9	0	**9**	**0**
2005–06	*Stockport Co*	21	2		
2006–07	Stockport Co	42	3	**63**	**5**

HAVERN, Gianluca (F) **0** **0**
H: 6 1 W: 13 00 b.Manchester 24-9-88
Source: Scholar.

2006–07	Stockport Co	0	0		

LE FONDRE, Adam (F) **70** **21**
H: 5 9 W: 11 04 b.Stockport 2-12-86
Source: Trainee.

2004–05	Stockport Co	20	4		
2005–06	Stockport Co	22	6		
2006–07	Stockport Co	21	7	**63**	**17**
2006–07	*Rochdale*	7	4	**7**	**4**

MALCOLM, Michael (F) **41** **5**
H: 5 10 W: 11 07 b.Harrow 13-10-85
Source: Trainee. *Honours:* England Youth.

2002–03	Tottenham H	0	0		
2003–04	Tottenham H	0	0		
2004–05	Tottenham H	0	0		
2005–06	Stockport Co	23	3		
2006–07	Stockport Co	18	2	**41**	**5**

PILKINGTON, Anthony (M) **24** **5**
H: 5 11 W: 12 00 b.Manchester 3-11-87
Source: Atherton CW.

2006–07	Stockport Co	24	5	**24**	**5**

POOLE, David (M) **60** **6**
H: 5 8 W: 12 00 b.Manchester 25-11-84
Source: Trainee.

2002–03	Manchester U	0	0		
2003–04	Manchester U	0	0		
2004–05	Manchester U	0	0		
2005–06	Yeovil T	25	2		
2006–07	Yeovil T	4	0	**29**	**2**
2006–07	Stockport Co	31	4	**31**	**4**

PROUDLOCK, Adam (F) **170** **31**
H: 6 0 W: 13 07 b.Wellington 9-5-81
Source: Trainee.

1999–2000	Wolverhampton W	0	0		
2000–01	*Clyde*	4	4	**4**	**4**
2000–01	Wolverhampton W	35	8		
2001–02	Wolverhampton W	19	3		
2001–02	*Nottingham F*	3	0	**3**	**0**
2002–03	Wolverhampton W	17	2		
2002–03	*Tranmere R*	5	0	**5**	**0**
2002–03	*Sheffield W*	5	2		
2003–04	Wolverhampton W	0	0	**71**	**13**
2003–04	Sheffield W	30	3		
2004–05	Sheffield W	14	6		
2005–06	Sheffield W	6	0	**55**	**11**
2005–06	Ipswich T	9	0		
2006–07	Ipswich T	0	0	**9**	**0**
2006–07	Stockport Co	23	3	**23**	**3**

RAYNES, Michael (D) **53** **1**
H: 6 4 W: 12 00 b.Wythenshawe 15-10-87
Source: Scholar.

2004–05	Stockport Co	19	0		
2005–06	Stockport Co	25	1		
2006–07	Stockport Co	9	0	**53**	**1**

ROSE, Michael (D) **84** **4**
H: 5 11 W: 12 04 b.Salford 28-7-82
Source: Trainee.

1999–2000	Manchester U	0	0		
2000–01	Manchester U	0	0		
2001–02	Manchester U	0	0		
From Hereford U					
2004–05	Yeovil T	40	1		
2005–06	Yeovil T	1	0	**41**	**1**
2005–06	*Cheltenham T*	3	0	**3**	**0**
2005–06	*Scunthorpe U*	15	0	**15**	**0**
2006–07	Stockport Co	25	3	**25**	**3**

ROWE, Tommy (M) **4 0**
H: 5 11 W: 12 11 b.Manchester 1-5-89
Source: Scholar.

2006–07	Stockport Co	4	0	**4**	**0**

SPENCER, James (G) **91 0**
H: 6 3 W: 15 04 b.Stockport 11-4-85
Source: Trainee.

2001–02	Stockport Co	2	0		
2002–03	Stockport Co	1	0		
2003–04	Stockport Co	15	0		
2004–05	Stockport Co	24	0		
2005–06	Stockport Co	34	0		
2006–07	Stockport Co	15	0	**91**	**0**

TANSEY, Greg (M) **3 0**
H: 6 1 W: 12 03 b.Huyton 21-11-88
Source: Scholar.

2006–07	Stockport Co	3	0	**3**	**0**

TAYLOR, Jason (M) **54 1**
H: 6 1 W: 11 03 b.Ashton-under-Lyne 28-1-87
Source: Scholar.

2005–06	Oldham Ath	0	0		
2005–06	*Stockport Co*	9	0		
2006–07	Stockport Co	45	1	**54**	**1**

TUNNICLIFFE, James (D) **6 0**
H: 6 4 W: 12 03 b.Denton 17-1-89
Source: Scholar.

2005–06	Stockport Co	1	0		
2006–07	Stockport Co	5	0	**6**	**0**

TURNBULL, Paul (F) **1 0**
H: 6 0 W: 12 07 b.Handforth 23-1-89
Source: Scholar.

2004–05	Stockport Co	1	0		
2005–06	Stockport Co	0	0		
2006–07	Stockport Co	0	0	**1**	**0**

WILLIAMS, Ashley (D) **136 3**
H: 6 0 W: 11 02 b.Wolverhampton 23-8-84
Source: Hednesford T.

2003–04	Stockport Co	10	0		
2004–05	Stockport Co	44	1		
2005–06	Stockport Co	36	1		
2006–07	Stockport Co	46	1	**136**	**3**

STOKE C (77)

BANGOURA, Sammy (F) **162 70**
H: 6 0 W: 12 02 b.Guinea 3-4-82
Source: Kindia, AS Kaloum. *Honours:* Guinea 11 full caps, 3 goals.

2000–01	Lokeren	30	13		
2001–02	Lokeren	25	12		
2002–03	Lokeren	29	16	**84**	**41**
2003–04	Standard Liege	20	5		
2004–05	Standard Liege	30	15	**50**	**20**
2005–06	Stoke C	24	9		
2006–07	Stoke C	4	0	**28**	**9**

To Standard Liege (loan) January 2007

BROOMES, Marlon (D) **188 4**
H: 6 0 W: 12 12 b.Birmingham 28-11-77
Source: Trainee. *Honours:* England Schools, Youth, Under-21.

1994–95	Blackburn R	0	0		
1995–96	Blackburn R	0	0		
1996–97	Blackburn R	0	0		
1996–97	*Swindon T*	12	1	**12**	**1**
1997–98	Blackburn R	4	0		
1998–99	Blackburn R	13	0		
1999–2000	Blackburn R	13	1		
2000–01	Blackburn R	1	0		
2000–01	*QPR*	5	0	**5**	**0**
2001–02	Blackburn R	0	0	**31**	**1**
2001–02	*Grimsby T*	15	0	**15**	**0**
2001–02	Sheffield W	19	0	**19**	**0**
2002–03	Preston NE	28	0		
2003–04	Preston NE	30	0		
2004–05	Preston NE	11	0	**69**	**0**
2005–06	Stoke C	37	2		
2006–07	Stoke C	0	0	**37**	**2**

BUXTON, Lewis (D) **126 1**
H: 6 1 W: 13 11 b.Newport (IW) 10-12-83
Source: School.

2000–01	Portsmouth	0	0		
2001–02	Portsmouth	29	0		
2002–03	Portsmouth	1	0		
2002–03	*Exeter C*	4	0	**4**	**0**
2002–03	*Bournemouth*	17	0		
2003–04	Portsmouth	0	0		
2003–04	*Bournemouth*	26	0	**43**	**0**
2004–05	Portsmouth	0	0	**30**	**0**
2004–05	Stoke C	16	0		
2005–06	Stoke C	32	1		
2006–07	Stoke C	1	0	**49**	**1**

DELAP, Rory (M) **314 24**
H: 6 3 W: 13 00 b.Sutton Coldfield 6-7-76
Source: Trainee. *Honours:* Eire Under-21, B, 11 full caps.

1992–93	Carlisle U	1	0		
1993–94	Carlisle U	1	0		
1994–95	Carlisle U	3	0		
1995–96	Carlisle U	19	3		
1996–97	Carlisle U	32	4		
1997–98	Carlisle U	9	0	**65**	**7**
1997–98	Derby Co	13	0		
1998–99	Derby Co	23	0		
1999–2000	Derby Co	34	8		
2000–01	Derby Co	33	3	**103**	**11**
2001–02	Southampton	28	2		
2002–03	Southampton	24	0		
2003–04	Southampton	27	1		
2004–05	Southampton	37	2		
2005–06	Southampton	16	0	**132**	**5**
2005–06	Sunderland	6	1		
2006–07	Sunderland	6	0	**12**	**1**
2006–07	Stoke C	2	0	**2**	**0**

DIAO, Salif (M) **154 1**
H: 6 1 W: 12 08 b.Kedougou 10-2-77
Honours: Senegal 39 full caps, 4 goals.

1996–97	Epinal	2	0	**2**	**0**
1996–97	Monaco	0	0		
1997–98	Monaco	12	0		
1998–99	Monaco	14	0		
1999–2000	Monaco	1	0	**27**	**0**
2000–01	Sedan	26	0		
2001–02	Sedan	22	0	**48**	**0**
2002–03	Liverpool	26	1		
2003–04	Liverpool	3	0		
2004–05	Liverpool	8	0		
2004–05	*Birmingham C*	2	0	**2**	**0**
2005–06	Liverpool	0	0		
2005–06	*Portsmouth*	11	0	**11**	**0**
2006–07	Liverpool	0	0	**37**	**1**
2006–07	Stoke C	27	0	**27**	**0**

DICKINSON, Carl (D) **26 0**
H: 6 1 W: 12 04 b.Swadlincote 31-3-87
Source: Scholar.

2004–05	Stoke C	1	0		
2005–06	Stoke C	5	0		
2006–07	Stoke C	13	0	**19**	**0**
2006–07	*Blackpool*	7	0	**7**	**0**

DUGGAN, Robert (G) **0 0**
H: 6 1 W: 12 07 b.Dublin 1-4-87
Source: Scholar. *Honours:* Eire Youth.

2005–06	Stoke C	0	0		
2006–07	Stoke C	0	0		

EUSTACE, John (M) **154 13**
H: 5 11 W: 11 12 b.Solihull 3-11-79
Source: Trainee.

1996–97	Coventry C	0	0		
1997–98	Coventry C	0	0		
1998–99	Coventry C	0	0		
1998–99	Dundee U	11	1	**11**	**1**
1999–2000	Coventry C	16	1		
2000–01	Coventry C	32	2		
2001–02	Coventry C	6	0		
2002–03	Coventry C	32	4	**86**	**7**
2002–03	*Middlesbrough*	1	0	**1**	**0**
2003–04	Stoke C	26	5		
2004–05	Stoke C	7	0		
2005–06	Stoke C	0	0		
2006–07	Stoke C	15	0	**48**	**5**
2006–07	*Hereford U*	8	0	**8**	**0**

FULLER, Ricardo (F) **188 57**
H: 6 3 W: 12 10 b.Kingston, Jamaica 31-10-79
Source: Tivoli Gardens. *Honours:* Jamaica 32 full caps, 4 goals.

2000–01	Crystal Palace	8	0	**8**	**0**
2001–02	Hearts	27	8	**27**	**8**
From Tivoli Gardens.					
2002–03	Preston NE	18	9		
2003–04	Preston NE	38	17		
2004–05	Preston NE	2	1	**58**	**27**
2004–05	Portsmouth	31	1	**31**	**1**
2005–06	Southampton	30	9		
2005–06	*Ipswich T*	3	2	**3**	**2**
2006–07	Southampton	1	0	**31**	**9**
2006–07	Stoke C	30	10	**30**	**10**

GARRETT, Robert (M) **12 0**
H: 5 7 W: 11 05 b.Belfast 5-5-88
Source: Scholar. *Honours:* Northern Ireland Youth, Under-21.

2005–06	Stoke C	2	0		
2006–07	Stoke C	0	0	**2**	**0**
2006–07	*Wrexham*	10	0	**10**	**0**

HARPER, Kevin (M) **310 31**
H: 5 6 W: 10 09 b.Oldham 15-1-76
Source: Hutcheson Vale BC. *Honours:* Scotland Schools, Under-21, B.

1993–94	Hibernian	2	0		
1994–95	Hibernian	23	5		
1995–96	Hibernian	16	3		
1996–97	Hibernian	26	5		
1997–98	Hibernian	27	1		
1998–99	Hibernian	2	1	**96**	**15**
1998–99	Derby Co	27	1		
1999–2000	Derby Co	5	0	**32**	**1**
1999–2000	*Walsall*	9	1		
1999–2000	Portsmouth	12	2		
2000–01	Portsmouth	24	2		
2001–02	Portsmouth	39	1		
2002–03	Portsmouth	37	4		
2003–04	Portsmouth	7	0		
2003–04	*Norwich C*	9	0	**9**	**0**
2004–05	Portsmouth	0	0	**119**	**9**
2004–05	*Leicester C*	2	0	**2**	**0**
2004–05	Stoke C	9	0		
2005–06	Stoke C	14	1		
2006–07	Stoke C	3	0	**26**	**1**
2006–07	*Carlisle U*	7	0	**7**	**0**
2006–07	*Walsall*	10	4	**19**	**5**

HAZLEY, Matthew (M) **1 0**
H: 5 10 W: 12 03 b.Banbridge 30-12-87
Source: Scholar. *Honours:* Northern Ireland Youth, Under-21.

2005–06	Stoke C	1	0		
2006–07	Stoke C	0	0	**1**	**0**

HIGGINBOTHAM, Danny (D) **228 14**
H: 6 2 W: 13 01 b.Manchester 29-12-78
Source: Trainee.

1997–98	Manchester U	1	0		
1998–99	Manchester U	0	0		
1999–2000	Manchester U	3	0	**4**	**0**
2000–01	Derby Co	26	0		
2001–02	Derby Co	37	1		
2002–03	Derby Co	23	2	**86**	**3**
2002–03	Southampton	9	0		
2003–04	Southampton	27	0		
2004–05	Southampton	21	1		
2005–06	Southampton	37	3	**94**	**4**
2006–07	Stoke C	44	7	**44**	**7**

HILL, Clint (D) **232 20**
H: 6 0 W: 11 06 b.Liverpool 19-10-78
Source: Trainee.

1997–98	Tranmere R	14	0		
1998–99	Tranmere R	33	4		
1999–2000	Tranmere R	29	5		
2000–01	Tranmere R	34	5		
2001–02	Tranmere R	30	2	**140**	**16**
2002–03	Oldham Ath	17	1	**17**	**1**
2003–04	Stoke C	12	0		
2004–05	Stoke C	32	1		
2005–06	Stoke C	13	0		
2006–07	Stoke C	18	2	**75**	**3**

HOEFKENS, Carl (D) **315 13**
H: 6 1 W: 12 13 b.Lier 6-10-78
Honours: Belgium 16 full caps, 1 goal.

1996–97	Lierse	17	0		
1997–98	Lierse	27	1		
1998–99	Lierse	30	0		
1999–2000	Lierse	31	0		
2000–01	Lierse	27	0	**132**	**1**
2001–02	Lommel	33	3		
2002–03	Lommel	22	0	**55**	**3**
2002–03	Westerlo	7	0	**7**	**0**
2003–04	Beerschot	32	4		
2004–05	Beerschot	0	0	**32**	**4**
2005–06	Stoke C	44	3		
2006–07	Stoke C	45	2	**89**	**5**

HOULT, Russell (G) **392 0**
H: 6 3 W: 14 09 b.Ashby 22-11-72
Source: Trainee.

1990–91	Leicester C	0	0		
1991–92	Leicester C	0	0		
1991–92	*Lincoln C*	2	0		
1991–92	*Blackpool*	0	0		
1992–93	Leicester C	10	0		
1993–94	Leicester C	0	0		
1993–94	*Bolton W*	4	0	**4**	**0**
1994–95	Leicester C	0	0	**10**	**0**
1994–95	*Lincoln C*	15	0	**17**	**0**
1994–95	*Derby Co*	15	0		
1995–96	Derby Co	41	0		
1996–97	Derby Co	32	0		
1997–98	Derby Co	2	0		
1998–99	Derby Co	23	0		
1999–2000	Derby Co	10	0	**123**	**0**
1999–2000	Portsmouth	18	0		
2000–01	Portsmouth	22	0	**40**	**0**
2000–01	WBA	13	0		
2001–02	WBA	45	0		
2002–03	WBA	37	0		
2003–04	WBA	44	0		
2004–05	WBA	36	0		
2005–06	WBA	1	0		
2005–06	*Nottingham F*	8	0	**8**	**0**
2006–07	WBA	14	0	**190**	**0**
2006–07	Stoke C	0	0		

LAWRENCE, Liam (M) **236 49**
H: 5 11 W: 12 06 b.Retford 14-12-81
Source: Trainee.

1999–2000	Mansfield T	2	0		
2000–01	Mansfield T	18	4		
2001–02	Mansfield T	32	2		
2002–03	Mansfield T	43	10		
2003–04	Mansfield T	41	18	**136**	**34**
2004–05	Sunderland	32	7		
2005–06	Sunderland	29	3		
2006–07	Sunderland	12	0	**73**	**10**
2006–07	Stoke C	27	5	**27**	**5**

MATTEO, Dominic (D) **286 4**
H: 6 1 W: 13 08 b.Dumfries 28-4-74
Source: Trainee. *Honours:* England Youth, Under-21, B, Scotland 6 full caps.

1992–93	Liverpool	0	0		
1993–94	Liverpool	11	0		
1994–95	Liverpool	7	0		
1994–95	*Sunderland*	1	0	**1**	**0**
1995–96	Liverpool	5	0		
1996–97	Liverpool	26	0		
1997–98	Liverpool	26	0		
1998–99	Liverpool	20	1		
1999–2000	Liverpool	32	0		
2000–01	Liverpool	0	0	**127**	**1**
2000–01	Leeds U	30	0		
2001–02	Leeds U	32	0		
2002–03	Leeds U	20	0		
2003–04	Leeds U	33	2	**115**	**2**
2004–05	Blackburn R	28	0		
2005–06	Blackburn R	6	0		
2006–07	Blackburn R	0	0	**34**	**0**
2006–07	Stoke C	9	1	**9**	**1**

PATERSON, Martin (F) **30 7**
H: 5 9 W: 10 11 b.Tunstall 13-5-87
Source: Scholar. *Honours:* Northern Ireland Youth, Under-21.

2004–05	Stoke C	3	0		
2005–06	Stoke C	3	0		
2006–07	Stoke C	9	1	**15**	**1**
2006–07	*Grimsby T*	15	6	**15**	**6**

PERICARD, Vincent de Paul (F) **99 17**
H: 6 1 W: 13 08 b.Efok 3-10-82
Source: Juventus.

2002–03	Portsmouth	32	9		
2003–04	Portsmouth	6	0		
2004–05	Portsmouth	0	0		
2005–06	Portsmouth	6	0	**44**	**9**
2005–06	*Sheffield U*	11	2	**11**	**2**
2005–06	*Plymouth Arg*	15	4	**15**	**4**
2006–07	Stoke C	29	2	**29**	**2**

PULIS, Anthony (M) **18 0**
H: 5 10 W: 10 10 b.Bristol 21-7-84
Source: Scholar. *Honours:* Wales Under-21.

2002–03	Portsmouth	0	0		
2003–04	Portsmouth	0	0		
2004–05	Portsmouth	0	0		
2004–05	Stoke C	0	0		
2004–05	*Torquay U*	3	0	**3**	**0**
2005–06	Stoke C	0	0		
2005–06	*Plymouth Arg*	5	0	**5**	**0**
2006–07	Stoke C	1	0	**1**	**0**
2006–07	*Grimsby T*	9	0	**9**	**0**

ROONEY, Adam (F) **18 4**
H: 5 10 W: 12 03 b.Dublin 21-4-87
Source: Scholar. *Honours:* Eire Youth, Under-21.

2005–06	Stoke C	5	4		
2006–07	Stoke C	10	0	**15**	**4**
2006–07	*Yeovil T*	3	0	**3**	**0**

RUSSELL, Darel (M) **303 23**
H: 5 10 W: 11 09 b.Mile End 22-10-80
Source: Trainee. *Honours:* England Youth.

1997–98	Norwich C	1	0		
1998–99	Norwich C	13	1		
1999–2000	Norwich C	33	4		
2000–01	Norwich C	41	2		
2001–02	Norwich C	23	0		
2002–03	Norwich C	21	0	**132**	**7**
2003–04	Stoke C	46	4		
2004–05	Stoke C	45	2		
2005–06	Stoke C	37	3		
2006–07	Stoke C	43	7	**171**	**16**

SHOTTON, Ryan (M) **0 0**
b.Stoke 30-9-88

2006–07	Stoke C	0	0		

SIDIBE, Mamady (F) **222 32**
H: 6 4 W: 12 02 b.Bamako 18-12-79
Source: CA Paris. *Honours:* Mali 7 full caps.

2001–02	Swansea C	31	7	**31**	**7**
2002–03	Gillingham	30	3		
2003–04	Gillingham	41	5		
2004–05	Gillingham	35	2	**106**	**10**
2005–06	Stoke C	42	6		
2006–07	Stoke C	43	9	**85**	**15**

SIGURDSSON, Hannes (F) **105 17**
H: 6 2 W: 13 02 b.Reykjavik 10-4-83
Honours: Iceland Youth, Under-21, 5 full caps, 1 goal.

2001	FH	11	1	**11**	**1**
2002	Viking	12	4		
2003	Viking	23	5		
2004	Viking	20	3		
2005	Viking	14	3	**69**	**15**
2005–06	Stoke C	23	1		
2006–07	Stoke C	2	0	**25**	**1**

To Brondby August 2006

SIMONSEN, Steve (G) **187 0**
H: 6 2 W: 12 08 b.South Shields 3-4-79
Source: Trainee. *Honours:* England Youth, Under-21.

1996–97	Tranmere R	0	0		
1997–98	Tranmere R	30	0		
1998–99	Tranmere R	5	0	**35**	**0**
1998–99	Everton	0	0		
1999–2000	Everton	1	0		
2000–01	Everton	1	0		
2001–02	Everton	25	0		
2002–03	Everton	2	0		
2003–04	Everton	1	0	**30**	**0**
2004–05	Stoke C	31	0		
2005–06	Stoke C	45	0		
2006–07	Stoke C	46	0	**122**	**0**

SWEENEY, Peter (M) **97 7**
H: 6 0 W: 12 11 b.Glasgow 25-9-84
Source: Scholar. *Honours:* Scotland Youth, Under-21, B.

2001–02	Millwall	1	0		
2002–03	Millwall	5	1		
2003–04	Millwall	29	2		
2004–05	Millwall	24	2	**59**	**5**
2005–06	Stoke C	17	1		
2006–07	Stoke C	13	1	**30**	**2**
2006–07	*Yeovil T*	8	0	**8**	**0**

VASS, Adam (M) **0 0**
H: 5 11 W: 11 00 b.Hungary 9-9-88
Source: Scholar. *Honours:* Hungary 2 full caps.

2006–07	Stoke C	0	0		

WILKINSON, Andy (D) **30 0**
H: 5 11 W: 11 00 b.Stone 6-8-84
Source: Scholar.

2001–02	Stoke C	0	0		
2002–03	Stoke C	0	0		
2003–04	Stoke C	3	0		
2004–05	Stoke C	1	0		
2004–05	*Shrewsbury T*	9	0	**9**	**0**
2005–06	Stoke C	6	0		
2006–07	Stoke C	4	0	**14**	**0**
2006–07	*Blackpool*	7	0	**7**	**0**

SUNDERLAND (78)

ARNAU, Caldentey (M) **3 0**
H: 5 9 W: 11 07 b.Manacor 1-10-81
Source: Mallorca, Barcelona B.

2006–07	Sunderland	1	0	**1**	**0**
2006–07	*Southend U*	2	0	**2**	**0**

CARSON, Trevor (G) **0 0**
H: 6 0 W: 14 11 b.Downpatrick 5-3-88
Source: Scholar. *Honours:* Northern Ireland Under-21.

2006–07	Sunderland	0	0		

CLARKE, Clive (D) **241 9**
H: 5 11 W: 12 03 b.Dublin 14-1-80
Source: Trainee. *Honours:* Eire Under-21, 2 full caps.

1996–97	Stoke C	0	0		
1997–98	Stoke C	0	0		
1998–99	Stoke C	2	0		
1999–2000	Stoke C	42	1		
2000–01	Stoke C	21	0		
2001–02	Stoke C	43	1		
2002–03	Stoke C	31	3		
2003–04	Stoke C	42	3		
2004–05	Stoke C	42	1	**223**	**9**
2005–06	West Ham U	2	0	**2**	**0**
2006–07	Sunderland	4	0	**4**	**0**
2006–07	*Coventry C*	12	0	**12**	**0**

COLLINS, Danny (D) **87 2**
H: 6 2 W: 11 13 b.Buckley 6-8-80
Source: Buckley T. *Honours:* Wales 6 full caps.

2004–05	Chester C	12	1	**12**	**1**
2004–05	Sunderland	14	0		
2005–06	Sunderland	23	1		
2006–07	Sunderland	38	0	**75**	**1**

CONNOLLY, David (F) **321 135**
H: 5 9 W: 11 00 b.Willesden 6-6-77
Source: Trainee. *Honours:* Eire Under-21, 41 full caps, 9 goals.

1994–95	Watford	2	0		
1995–96	Watford	11	8		
1996–97	Watford	13	2	**26**	**10**
1997–98	Feyenoord	10	2		
1998–99	Wolverhampton W	32	6	**32**	**6**
1999–2000	Excelsior	32	29	**32**	**29**
2000–01	Feyenoord	15	5	**25**	**7**
2001–02	Wimbledon	35	18		
2002–03	Wimbledon	28	24	**63**	**42**
2003–04	West Ham U	39	10	**39**	**10**
2004–05	Leicester C	44	13		
2005–06	Leicester C	5	4	**49**	**17**
2005–06	Wigan Ath	17	1		
2006–07	Wigan Ath	2	0	**19**	**1**
2006–07	Sunderland	36	13	**36**	**13**

CUNNINGHAM, Kenny (D) 531 1
H: 5 11 W: 12 07 b.Dublin 28-6-71
Source: Tolka R. *Honours:* Eire Youth, Under-21, B, 72 full caps.

1989–90	Millwall	5	0		
1990–91	Millwall	23	0		
1991–92	Millwall	17	0		
1992–93	Millwall	37	0		
1993–94	Millwall	39	1		
1994–95	Millwall	15	0	**136**	**1**
1994–95	Wimbledon	28	0		
1995–96	Wimbledon	33	0		
1996–97	Wimbledon	36	0		
1997–98	Wimbledon	32	0		
1998–99	Wimbledon	35	0		
1999–2000	Wimbledon	37	0		
2000–01	Wimbledon	15	0		
2001–02	Wimbledon	34	0	**250**	**0**
2002–03	Birmingham C	31	0		
2003–04	Birmingham C	36	0		
2004–05	Birmingham C	36	0		
2005–06	Birmingham C	31	0	**134**	**0**
2006–07	Sunderland	11	0	**11**	**0**

DENNEHY, Billy (F) 0 0
H: 5 8 W: 11 10 b.Tralee 17-2-87
Honours: Eire Under-21.

2004–05	Sunderland	0	0		
2005–06	Sunderland	0	0		
2006–07	Sunderland	0	0		

EDWARDS, Carlos (M) 249 36
H: 5 8 W: 11 02 b.Port of Spain 24-10-78
Source: Defence Force. *Honours:* Trinidad & Tobago 57 full caps, 1 goal.

2000–01	Wrexham	36	4		
2001–02	Wrexham	26	5		
2002–03	Wrexham	44	8		
2003–04	Wrexham	42	5		
2004–05	Wrexham	18	1	**166**	**23**
2005–06	Luton T	42	2		
2006–07	Luton T	26	6	**68**	**8**
2006–07	Sunderland	15	5	**15**	**5**

ELLIOTT, Stephen (F) 83 22
H: 5 8 W: 11 07 b.Dublin 6-1-84
Source: School. *Honours:* Eire Youth, Under-21, 9 full caps, 1 goal.

2000–01	Manchester C	0	0		
2001–02	Manchester C	0	0		
2002–03	Manchester C	0	0		
2003–04	Manchester C	2	0	**2**	**0**
2004–05	Sunderland	42	15		
2005–06	Sunderland	15	2		
2006–07	Sunderland	24	5	**81**	**22**

FULOP, Marton (G) 43 0
H: 6 6 W: 14 07 b.Budapest 3-5-83
Source: MTK, Elore, Bodajk. *Honours:* Hungary Under-21, 4 full caps.

2004–05	Tottenham H	0	0		
2004–05	*Chesterfield*	7	0	**7**	**0**
2005–06	Tottenham H	0	0		
2005–06	*Coventry C*	31	0	**31**	**0**
2006–07	Tottenham H	0	0		
2006–07	Sunderland	5	0	**5**	**0**

HARTLEY, Peter (D) 1 0
H: 6 0 W: 12 06 b.Hartlepool 3-4-88
Source: Scholar.

2006–07	Sunderland	1	0	**1**	**0**

HYSEN, Tobias (M) 158 34
H: 5 10 W: 11 11 b.Gothenburg 9-3-82
Source: From Lundby. *Honours:* Sweden Under-21, 5 full caps.

1999	Hacken	0	0		
2000	Hacken	1	0		
2001	Hacken	13	1		
2002	Hacken	25	7		
2003	Hacken	28	5	**67**	**13**
2004	Djurgaarden	25	3		
2005	Djurgaarden	25	9		
2006	Djurgaarden	15	5	**65**	**17**
2006–07	Sunderland	26	4	**26**	**4**

JOHN, Stern (F) 304 108
H: 6 1 W: 12 13 b.Tunapuna 30-10-76
Honours: Trinidad & Tobago 100 full caps, 67 goals.

1998	Columbus Crew	27	26		
1999	Columbus Crew	28	18	**55**	**44**
1999–2000	Nottingham F	17	3		
2000–01	Nottingham F	29	2		
2001–02	Nottingham F	26	13	**72**	**18**
2001–02	Birmingham C	15	7		
2002–03	Birmingham C	30	5		
2003–04	Birmingham C	29	4		
2004–05	Birmingham C	3	0	**77**	**16**
2004–05	Coventry C	30	11		
2005–06	Coventry C	25	10		
2005–06	*Derby Co*	7	0	**7**	**0**
2006–07	Coventry C	23	5	**78**	**26**
2006–07	Sunderland	15	4	**15**	**4**

KAVANAGH, Graham (M) 450 67
H: 5 10 W: 13 03 b.Dublin 2-12-73
Source: Home Farm. *Honours:* Eire Schools, Youth, Under-21, B, 16 full caps, 1 goal.

1991–92	Middlesbrough	0	0		
1992–93	Middlesbrough	10	0		
1993–94	Middlesbrough	11	2		
1993–94	*Darlington*	5	0	**5**	**0**
1994–95	Middlesbrough	7	0		
1995–96	Middlesbrough	7	1		
1996–97	Middlesbrough	0	0	**35**	**3**
1996–97	Stoke C	38	4		
1997–98	Stoke C	44	5		
1998–99	Stoke C	36	11		
1999–2000	Stoke C	45	7		
2000–01	Stoke C	43	8	**206**	**35**
2001–02	Cardiff C	43	13		
2002–03	Cardiff C	44	5		
2003–04	Cardiff C	27	7		
2004–05	Cardiff C	28	3	**142**	**28**
2004–05	Wigan Ath	11	0		
2005–06	Wigan Ath	35	0		
2006–07	Wigan Ath	2	0	**48**	**0**
2006–07	Sunderland	14	1	**14**	**1**

LEADBITTER, Grant (M) 61 8
H: 5 9 W: 11 06 b.Sunderland 7-1-86
Source: Trainee. *Honours:* FA Schools, England Youth, Under-20.

2002–03	Sunderland	0	0		
2003–04	Sunderland	0	0		
2004–05	Sunderland	0	0		
2005–06	Sunderland	12	0		
2005–06	*Rotherham U*	5	1	**5**	**1**
2006–07	Sunderland	44	7	**56**	**7**

MILLER, Liam (M) 111 11
H: 5 7 W: 10 05 b.Cork 13-2-81
Honours: Eire Under-21, 13 full caps, 1 goal.

1999–2000	Celtic	1	0		
2000–01	Celtic	0	0		
2001–02	Celtic	0	0		
2001–02	Aarhus	18	6	**18**	**6**
2002–03	Celtic	0	0		
2003–04	Celtic	25	2	**26**	**2**
2004–05	Manchester U	8	0		
2005–06	Manchester U	1	0	**9**	**0**
2005–06	*Leeds U*	28	1	**28**	**1**
2006–07	Sunderland	30	2	**30**	**2**

MILLER, Tommy (M) 294 68
H: 6 0 W: 11 07 b.Easington 8-1-79
Source: Trainee.

1997–98	Hartlepool U	13	1		
1998–99	Hartlepool U	34	4		
1999–2000	Hartlepool U	44	14		
2000–01	Hartlepool U	46	16		
2001–02	Hartlepool U	0	0	**137**	**35**
2001–02	Ipswich T	8	0		
2002–03	Ipswich T	30	6		
2003–04	Ipswich T	34	11		
2004–05	Ipswich T	45	13	**117**	**30**
2005–06	Sunderland	29	3		
2006–07	Sunderland	4	0	**33**	**3**
2006–07	*Preston NE*	7	0	**7**	**0**

MOCQUET, William (M) 101 9
H: 5 10 W: 10 07 b.Valognes 23-1-83
Honours: France Under-21.

2000–01	Le Havre	1	0		
2001–02	Le Havre	6	0		
2002–03	Le Havre	7	0		
2003–04	Le Havre	15	1		
2004–05	Le Havre	29	1	**58**	**2**
2005–06	Louhans-Cuiseaux	27	6	**27**	**6**
2006–07	Sunderland	0	0		
2006–07	*Rochdale*	7	1	**7**	**1**
2006–07	*Bury*	9	0	**9**	**0**

MURPHY, Daryl (F) 60 11
H: 6 2 W: 13 12 b.Waterford 15-3-83
Honours: Eire Youth, Under-21, 2 full caps.

2000–01	Luton T	0	0		
2001–02	Luton T	0	0		
2005–06	Sunderland	18	1		
2005–06	*Sheffield W*	4	0	**4**	**0**
2006–07	Sunderland	38	10	**56**	**11**

NOSWORTHY, Nayron (D) 233 5
H: 6 0 W: 12 08 b.Brixton 11-10-80
Source: Trainee.

1998–99	Gillingham	3	0		
1999–2000	Gillingham	29	1		
2000–01	Gillingham	10	0		
2001–02	Gillingham	29	0		
2002–03	Gillingham	39	2		
2003–04	Gillingham	27	2		
2004–05	Gillingham	37	0	**174**	**5**
2005–06	Sunderland	30	0		
2006–07	Sunderland	29	0	**59**	**0**

RICHARDSON, Jake (M) 0 0
H: 5 8 W: 10 00 b.Watford 22-10-88

2006–07	Sunderland	0	0		

SMITH, Kevin (F) 8 1
H: 5 11 W: 11 09 b.Edinburgh 20-3-87
Source: Scholar.

2003–04	Leeds U	0	0		
2004–05	Leeds U	0	0		
2005–06	Leeds U	0	0		
2005–06	Sunderland	0	0		
2006–07	Sunderland	0	0		
2006–07	*Wrexham*	8	1	**8**	**1**

To Dundee January 2007

STOKES, Anthony (F) 30 16
H: 5 11 W: 11 06 b.Dublin 25-7-88
Source: Scholar. *Honours:* Eire Youth, B, Under-21, 3 full caps.

2005–06	Arsenal	0	0		
2006–07	Arsenal	0	0		
2006–07	*Falkirk*	16	14	**16**	**14**
2006–07	Sunderland	14	2	**14**	**2**

VARGA, Stanislav (D) 287 34
H: 6 5 W: 14 09 b.Lipany 8-10-72
Honours: Slovakia 56 full caps, 1 goal.

1993–94	Tatran Presov	12	2		
1994–95	Tatran Presov	25	2		
1995–96	Tatran Presov	21	2		
1996–97	Tatran Presov	22	3		
1997–98	Tatran Presov	26	1	**106**	**10**
1998–99	Slovan Bratislava	28	3		
1999–2000	Slovan Bratislava	28	9	**56**	**12**
2000–01	Sunderland	12	1		
2001–02	Sunderland	9	0		
2001–02	*WBA*	4	0	**4**	**0**
2002–03	Celtic	1	0		
2003–04	Celtic	35	6		
2004–05	Celtic	34	3		
2005–06	Celtic	10	1	**80**	**10**
2006–07	Sunderland	20	1	**41**	**2**

WALLACE, Ross (M) 69 7
H: 5 6 W: 9 12 b.Dundee 23-5-85
Source: Celtic S Form. *Honours:* Scotland Youth, Under-21.

2001–02	Celtic	0	0		
2002–03	Celtic	0	0		
2003–04	Celtic	8	1		
2004–05	Celtic	16	0		
2005–06	Celtic	11	0		
2006–07	Celtic	2	0	**37**	**1**
2006–07	Sunderland	32	6	**32**	**6**

WARD, Darren (G) 486 0
H: 6 0 W: 13 09 b.Worksop 11-5-74
Source: Trainee. *Honours:* Wales Under-21, B, 5 full caps.

1992–93	Mansfield T	13	0		

1993–94	Mansfield T	33	0		
1994–95	Mansfield T	35	0	**81**	**0**
1995–96	Notts Co	46	0		
1996–97	Notts Co	38	0		
1997–98	Notts Co	44	0		
1998–99	Notts Co	43	0		
1999–2000	Notts Co	45	0		
2000–01	Notts Co	35	0	**251**	**0**
2000–01	Nottingham F	0	0		
2001–02	Nottingham F	46	0		
2002–03	Nottingham F	45	0		
2003–04	Nottingham F	32	0		
2004–05	Nottingham F	0	0	**123**	**0**
2004–05	Norwich C	1	0		
2005–06	Norwich C	0	0	**1**	**0**
2006–07	Sunderland	30	0	**30**	**0**

WELSH, Andy (M) 119 7
H: 5 8 W: 10 03 b.Manchester 24-11-83
Source: Scholar. *Honours:* Scotland Youth.

2001–02	Stockport Co	15	0		
2002–03	Stockport Co	13	2		
2002–03	*Macclesfield T*	6	2	**6**	**2**
2003–04	Stockport Co	34	1		
2004–05	Stockport Co	13	0	**75**	**3**
2004–05	Sunderland	7	1		
2005–06	Sunderland	14	0		
2005–06	*Leicester C*	10	1		
2006–07	Sunderland	0	0	**21**	**1**
2006–07	*Leicester C*	7	0	**17**	**1**

To Toronto Lynx March 2007

WHITEHEAD, Dean (M) 246 21
H: 5 11 W: 12 06 b.Oxford 12-1-82
Source: Trainee.

1999–2000	Oxford U	0	0		
2000–01	Oxford U	20	0		
2001–02	Oxford U	40	1		
2002–03	Oxford U	18	1		
2003–04	Oxford U	44	7	**122**	**9**
2004–05	Sunderland	42	5		
2005–06	Sunderland	37	3		
2006–07	Sunderland	45	4	**124**	**12**

WRIGHT, Stephen (D) 129 2
H: 6 0 W: 12 06 b.Liverpool 8-2-80
Source: Trainee. *Honours:* England Youth, Under-21.

1997–98	Liverpool	0	0		
1998–99	Liverpool	0	0		
1999–2000	Liverpool	0	0		
1999–2000	*Crewe Alex*	23	0	**23**	**0**
2000–01	Liverpool	2	0		
2001–02	Liverpool	12	0	**14**	**0**
2002–03	Sunderland	26	0		
2003–04	Sunderland	22	1		
2004–05	Sunderland	39	1		
2005–06	Sunderland	2	0		
2006–07	Sunderland	3	0	**92**	**2**

YORKE, Dwight (F) 454 147
H: 5 10 W: 12 04 b.Canaan 3-11-71
Source: St Clair's, Tobago. *Honours:* Trinidad & Tobago 58 full caps, 16 goals.

1989–90	Aston Villa	2	0		
1990–91	Aston Villa	18	2		
1991–92	Aston Villa	32	11		
1992–93	Aston Villa	27	6		
1993–94	Aston Villa	12	2		
1994–95	Aston Villa	37	6		
1995–96	Aston Villa	35	17		
1996–97	Aston Villa	37	17		
1997–98	Aston Villa	30	12		
1998–99	Aston Villa	1	0	**231**	**73**
1998–99	Manchester U	32	18		
1999–2000	Manchester U	32	20		
2000–01	Manchester U	22	9		
2001–02	Manchester U	10	1	**96**	**48**
2002–03	Blackburn R	33	8		
2003–04	Blackburn R	23	4		
2004–05	Blackburn R	4	0	**60**	**12**
2004–05	Birmingham C	13	2	**13**	**2**
2005–06	Sydney	22	7	**22**	**7**
2006–07	Sunderland	32	5	**32**	**5**

SWANSEA C (79)

ABBOTT, Pawel (F) 171 61
H: 6 2 W: 13 10 b.York 5-5-82
Source: LKS Lodz. *Honours:* Poland Under-21.

2000–01	Preston NE	0	0		
2001–02	Preston NE	0	0		
2002–03	Preston NE	16	4		
2002–03	*Bury*	17	6	**17**	**6**
2003–04	Preston NE	9	2	**25**	**6**
2003–04	Huddersfield T	13	5		
2004–05	Huddersfield T	44	26		
2005–06	Huddersfield T	36	12		
2006–07	Huddersfield T	18	5	**111**	**48**
2006–07	Swansea C	18	1	**18**	**1**

AKINFENWA, Adebayo (F) 132 37
H: 5 11 W: 13 07 b.Nigeria 10-5-82

2001	Atlantas	19	4		
2002	Atlantas	4	1	**23**	**5**
From Barry T					
2003–04	Boston U	3	0	**3**	**0**
2003–04	Leyton Orient	1	0	**1**	**0**
2003–04	Rushden & D	0	0		
2003–04	Doncaster R	9	4	**9**	**4**
2004–05	Torquay U	37	14	**37**	**14**
2005–06	Swansea C	34	9		
2006–07	Swansea C	25	5	**59**	**14**

ALLEN, Joe (M) 1 0
H: 5 6 W: 9 10 b.Carmarthen 14-3-90

2006–07	Swansea C	1	0	**1**	**0**

AMANKWAAH, Kevin (D) 154 2
H: 6 1 W: 12 12 b.Harrow 19-5-82
Source: Scholar. *Honours:* England Youth.

1999–2000	Bristol C	5	0		
2000–01	Bristol C	14	0		
2001–02	Bristol C	24	1		
2002–03	Bristol C	1	0		
2002–03	*Torquay U*	6	0	**6**	**0**
2003–04	Bristol C	5	0		
2003–04	*Cheltenham T*	12	0	**12**	**0**
2004–05	Bristol C	5	0	**54**	**1**
2004–05	Yeovil T	15	0		
2005–06	Yeovil T	38	1	**53**	**1**
2006–07	Swansea C	29	0	**29**	**0**

AUSTIN, Kevin (D) 404 5
H: 6 1 W: 14 08 b.Hackney 12-2-73
Source: Saffron Walden. *Honours:* Trinidad & Tobago 1 full cap.

1993–94	Leyton Orient	30	0		
1994–95	Leyton Orient	39	2		
1995–96	Leyton Orient	40	1	**109**	**3**
1996–97	Lincoln C	44	1		
1997–98	Lincoln C	46	0		
1998–99	Lincoln C	39	1	**129**	**2**
1999–2000	Barnsley	3	0		
2000–01	Barnsley	0	0	**3**	**0**
2000–01	*Brentford*	3	0	**3**	**0**
2001–02	Cambridge U	6	0	**6**	**0**
2002–03	Bristol R	33	0		
2003–04	Bristol R	23	0	**56**	**0**
2004–05	Swansea C	42	0		
2005–06	Swansea C	26	0		
2006–07	Swansea C	30	0	**98**	**0**

BRITTON, Leon (M) 176 10
H: 5 6 W: 10 00 b.Merton 16-9-82
Source: Trainee. *Honours:* England Youth.

1999–2000	West Ham U	0	0		
2000–01	West Ham U	0	0		
2001–02	West Ham U	0	0		
2002–03	West Ham U	0	0		
2002–03	*Swansea C*	25	0		
2003–04	Swansea C	42	3		
2004–05	Swansea C	30	1		
2005–06	Swansea C	38	4		
2006–07	Swansea C	41	2	**176**	**10**

BUTLER, Thomas (M) 118 3
H: 5 7 W: 12 00 b.Dublin 25-4-81
Source: Trainee. *Honours:* Eire Under-21, 2 full caps.

1998–99	Sunderland	0	0		
1999–2000	Sunderland	1	0		
2000–01	Sunderland	4	0		
2000–01	*Darlington*	8	0	**8**	**0**
2001–02	Sunderland	7	0		
2002–03	Sunderland	7	0		
2003–04	Sunderland	12	0	**31**	**0**
2004–05	Dunfermline Ath	12	0	**12**	**0**
2004–05	Hartlepool U	9	1		
2005–06	Hartlepool U	28	1	**37**	**2**
2006–07	Swansea C	30	1	**30**	**1**

CRANEY, Ian (M) 45 5
H: 5 10 W: 12 00 b.Liverpool 21-7-82
Source: Runcorn, Altrincham.

2006–07	Accrington S	18	5	**18**	**5**
2006–07	Swansea C	27	0	**27**	**0**

EVANS, Scott (M) 0 0
H: 6 0 W: 11 07 b.Swansea 6-1-89
Source: Manchester C Scholar.

2006–07	Swansea C	0	0		

GUERET, Willy (G) 146 0
H: 6 1 W: 13 02 b.Saint Claude 3-8-73
Source: Le Mans.

2000–01	Millwall	11	0		
2001–02	Millwall	1	0		
2002–03	Millwall	0	0		
2003–04	Millwall	2	0	**14**	**0**
2004–05	Swansea C	44	0		
2005–06	Swansea C	46	0		
2006–07	Swansea C	42	0	**132**	**0**

IRIEKPEN, Ezomo (D) 141 9
H: 6 1 W: 12 02 b.East London 14-5-82
Source: Trainee. *Honours:* England Youth.

1998–99	West Ham U	0	0		
1999–2000	West Ham U	0	0		
2000–01	West Ham U	0	0		
2001–02	West Ham U	0	0		
2002–03	West Ham U	0	0		
2002–03	*Leyton Orient*	5	1	**5**	**1**
2002–03	*Cambridge U*	13	1	**13**	**1**
2003–04	Swansea C	34	1		
2004–05	Swansea C	29	2		
2005–06	Swansea C	28	0		
2006–07	Swansea C	32	4	**123**	**7**

JONES, Chris (F) 7 0
H: 5 7 W: 10 00 b.Swansea 12-9-89
Honours: Wales Under-21.

2006–07	Swansea C	7	0	**7**	**0**

LAWRENCE, Dennis (D) 237 19
H: 6 7 W: 11 13 b.Trinidad 1-8-74
Source: Defence Force. *Honours:* Trinidad & Tobago 69 full caps, 4 goals.

2000–01	Wrexham	3	0		
2001–02	Wrexham	32	2		
2002–03	Wrexham	32	1		
2003–04	Wrexham	45	5		
2004–05	Wrexham	44	4		
2005–06	Wrexham	39	2		
2006–07	Wrexham	3	0	**198**	**14**
2006–07	Swansea C	39	5	**39**	**5**

MACDONALD, Shaun (M) 15 0
H: 6 1 W: 11 04 b.Swansea 17-6-88
Source: Scholar. *Honours:* Wales Under-21.

2005–06	Swansea C	7	0		
2006–07	Swansea C	8	0	**15**	**0**

MESLIEN, Sylvain (D) 20 0
H: 5 10 W: 11 05 b.Bondy 7-8-81

2000–01	St Etienne	4	0		
2001–02	St Etienne	2	0		
2002–03	St Etienne	2	0		
2003–04	St Etienne	2	0		
2004–05	Troyes	9	0		
2005–06	Troyes	0	0	**9**	**0**
2006–07	St Etienne	0	0	**10**	**0**
2006–07	Swansea C	1	0	**1**	**0**

MONK, Garry (D) 130 1
H: 6 0 W: 12 10 b.Bedford 6-3-79
Source: Trainee.

1995–96	Torquay U	5	0		
1996–97	Southampton	0	0		
1997–98	Southampton	0	0		
1998–99	Southampton	4	0		
1998–99	*Torquay U*	6	0	**11**	**0**
1999–2000	Southampton	2	0		
1999–2000	*Stockport Co*	2	0	**2**	**0**
2000–01	Southampton	2	0		

2000–01	*Oxford U*	5	0	**5**	**0**
2001–02	Southampton	2	0		
2002–03	Southampton	1	0		
2002–03	*Sheffield W*	15	0	**15**	**0**
2003–04	Southampton	0	0	**11**	**0**
2003–04	Barnsley	17	0	**17**	**0**
2004–05	Swansea C	34	0		
2005–06	Swansea C	33	1		
2006–07	Swansea C	2	0	**69**	**1**

O'LEARY, Kristian (M) 278 11
H: 5 11 W: 12 09 b.Port Talbot 30-8-77
Source: Trainee. *Honours:* Wales Youth.

1995–96	Swansea C	1	0		
1996–97	Swansea C	12	1		
1997–98	Swansea C	29	0		
1998–99	Swansea C	19	2		
1999–2000	Swansea C	20	0		
2000–01	Swansea C	24	2		
2001–02	Swansea C	31	2		
2002–03	Swansea C	33	0		
2003–04	Swansea C	34	0		
2004–05	Swansea C	32	1		
2005–06	Swansea C	15	1		
2006–07	Swansea C	23	1	**273**	**10**
2006–07	*Cheltenham T*	5	1	**5**	**1**

OAKES, Andy (G) 101 0
H: 6 3 W: 12 04 b.Northwich 11-1-77
Source: Burnley Trainee.

1995–96	Bury	0	0		
1996–97	Bury	0	0		
1997–98	Bury	0	0		
From Winsford U.					
1998–99	Hull C	19	0	**19**	**0**
1999–2000	Derby Co	0	0		
1999–2000	*Port Vale*	0	0		
2000–01	Derby Co	6	0		
2001–02	Derby Co	20	0		
2002–03	Derby Co	7	0		
2003–04	Derby Co	10	0		
2004–05	Derby Co	0	0	**43**	**0**
2004–05	*Bolton W*	1	0	**1**	**0**
2004–05	Walsall	9	0		
2005–06	Walsall	25	0	**34**	**0**
2006–07	Swansea C	4	0	**4**	**0**

PAINTER, Marcos (D) 28 0
H: 5 11 W: 12 04 b.Solihull 17-8-86
Source: Scholar. *Honours:* Eire Youth, Under-21.

2005–06	Birmingham C	4	0		
2006–07	Birmingham C	1	0	**5**	**0**
2006–07	Swansea C	23	0	**23**	**0**

PRATLEY, Darren (M) 75 6
H: 6 1 W: 10 12 b.Barking 22-4-85
Source: Scholar.

2001–02	Fulham	0	0		
2002–03	Fulham	0	0		
2003–04	Fulham	1	0		
2004–05	Fulham	0	0		
2004–05	*Brentford*	14	1		
2005–06	Fulham	0	0	**1**	**0**
2005–06	*Brentford*	32	4	**46**	**5**
2006–07	Swansea C	28	1	**28**	**1**

ROBINSON, Andy (M) 152 35
H: 5 8 W: 11 04 b.Birkenhead 3-11-79
Source: Cammell Laird.

2002–03	Tranmere R	0	0		
2003–04	Swansea C	37	8		
2004–05	Swansea C	37	8		
2005–06	Swansea C	39	12		
2006–07	Swansea C	39	7	**152**	**35**

TATE, Alan (D) 157 2
H: 6 1 W: 13 05 b.Easington 2-9-82
Source: Scholar.

2000–01	Manchester U	0	0		
2001–02	Manchester U	0	0		
2002–03	Manchester U	0	0		
2002–03	*Swansea C*	27	0		
2003–04	Manchester U	0	0		
2003–04	Swansea C	26	1		
2004–05	Swansea C	23	0		
2005–06	Swansea C	43	0		
2006–07	Swansea C	38	1	**157**	**2**

TRUNDLE, Lee (F) 237 104
H: 6 0 W: 11 06 b.Liverpool 10-10-76
Source: Rhyl.

2000–01	Wrexham	14	8		
2001–02	Wrexham	36	8		
2002–03	Wrexham	44	11	**94**	**27**
2003–04	Swansea C	31	16		
2004–05	Swansea C	42	22		
2005–06	Swansea C	36	20		
2006–07	Swansea C	34	19	**143**	**77**

TUDUR JONES, Owain (M) 25 3
H: 6 2 W: 12 00 b.Bangor 15-10-84
Source: Bangor C. *Honours:* Wales Under-21.

2005–06	Swansea C	21	3		
2006–07	Swansea C	4	0	**25**	**3**

WATT, Steven (D) 7 1
H: 6 2 W: 12 09 b.Aberdeen 1-5-85
Source: Trainee. *Honours:* Scotland Under-21, B.

2002–03	Chelsea	0	0		
2003–04	Chelsea	0	0		
2004–05	Chelsea	1	0		
2005–06	Chelsea	0	0	**1**	**0**
2005–06	*Barnsley*	3	1	**3**	**1**
2005–06	Swansea C	2	0		
2006–07	Swansea C	1	0	**3**	**0**

WAY, Darren (M) 113 13
H: 5 7 W: 11 00 b.Plymouth 21-11-79
Source: Norwich C Trainee.

2003–04	Yeovil T	39	5		
2004–05	Yeovil T	45	7		
2005–06	Yeovil T	15	1	**99**	**13**
2005–06	Swansea C	5	0		
2006–07	Swansea C	9	0	**14**	**0**

WILLIAMS, Tom (M) 190 4
H: 5 11 W: 12 06 b.Carshalton 8-7-80
Source: Walton & Hersham.

1999–2000	West Ham U	0	0		
2000–01	West Ham U	0	0		
2000–01	*Peterborough U*	2	0		
2001–02	Peterborough U	34	2		
2001–02	Birmingham C	4	0		
2002–03	Birmingham C	0	0		
2002–03	*QPR*	26	1		
2003–04	Birmingham C	0	0	**4**	**0**
2003–04	*QPR*	5	0	**31**	**1**
2003–04	*Peterborough U*	21	1	**57**	**3**
2004–05	Barnsley	39	0	**39**	**0**
2005–06	Gillingham	13	0	**13**	**0**
2005–06	Swansea C	17	0		
2006–07	Swansea C	29	0	**46**	**0**

SWINDON T (80)

BREZOVAN, Peter (G) 41 0
H: 6 6 W: 14 13 b.Bratislava 9-12-79
Source: PS Bratislava, Vinohrady, Devin, Slovan Breclav, Zigma Olomouc. *Honours:* Slovakia Under-21.

2002–03	Brno	10	0		
2003–04	Brno	2	0		
2004–05	Inter Bratislava	8	0	**8**	**0**
2005–06	Brno	7	0	**19**	**0**
2006–07	Swindon T	14	0	**14**	**0**

BROWN, Aaron (M) 233 17
H: 5 10 W: 11 11 b.Bristol 14-3-80
Source: Trainee. *Honours:* England Schools.

1997–98	Bristol C	0	0		
1998–99	Bristol C	14	0		
1999–2000	Bristol C	13	2		
1999–2000	*Exeter C*	5	1	**5**	**1**
2000–01	Bristol C	35	2		
2001–02	Bristol C	36	1		
2002–03	Bristol C	32	2		
2003–04	Bristol C	30	5	**160**	**12**
2004–05	QPR	1	0		
2004–05	*Torquay U*	5	0	**5**	**0**
2005–06	QPR	2	0	**3**	**0**
2005–06	*Cheltenham T*	3	0	**3**	**0**
2005–06	Swindon T	27	2		
2006–07	Swindon T	30	2	**57**	**4**

BROWNLIE, Royce (F) 18 2
H: 6 0 W: 13 12 b.Coffs Harbour 28-1-80

2006–07	Swindon T	14	2	**14**	**2**
2006–07	*Chester C*	4	0	**4**	**0**

CATON, Andy (M) 13 1
H: 6 0 W: 12 03 b.Oxford 3-12-87
Source: Scholar.

2004–05	Swindon T	8	1		
2005–06	Swindon T	0	0		
2006–07	Swindon T	5	0	**13**	**1**

EVANS, Paul (M) 446 70
H: 5 8 W: 12 06 b.Oswestry 1-9-74
Source: Trainee. *Honours:* Wales Youth, Under-21, 2 full caps.

1991–92	Shrewsbury T	2	0		
1992–93	Shrewsbury T	4	0		
1993–94	Shrewsbury T	13	0		
1994–95	Shrewsbury T	32	5		
1995–96	Shrewsbury T	34	3		
1996–97	Shrewsbury T	42	6		
1997–98	Shrewsbury T	39	6		
1998–99	Shrewsbury T	32	6	**198**	**26**
1998–99	Brentford	14	3		
1999–2000	Brentford	33	7		
2000–01	Brentford	43	7		
2001–02	Brentford	40	14	**130**	**31**
2002–03	Bradford C	19	2		
2002–03	*Blackpool*	10	1	**10**	**1**
2003–04	Bradford C	23	3	**42**	**5**
2003–04	Nottingham F	8	0		
2004–05	Nottingham F	39	4		
2005–06	Nottingham F	0	0	**47**	**4**
2005–06	*Rotherham U*	4	0	**4**	**0**
2006–07	Swindon T	15	3	**15**	**3**

GNAPKA, Claude (D) 0 0
H: 6 0 W: 13 05 b.Marseille 9-6-83
Source: Montpellier, Santander, Alaves, Vaduz.

2006–07	Swindon T	0	0		

HOLGATE, Ashan (F) 15 1
H: 6 2 W: 12 00 b.Swindon 9-11-86
Source: Scholar.

2004–05	Swindon T	2	0		
2005–06	Swindon T	6	0		
2006–07	Swindon T	1	0	**9**	**0**
2006–07	*Macclesfield T*	6	1	**6**	**1**

IFIL, Jerel (D) 149 1
H: 6 1 W: 12 10 b.Wembley 27-6-82
Source: Academy.

1999–2000	Watford	0	0		
2000–01	Watford	0	0		
2001–02	Watford	0	0		
2001–02	*Huddersfield T*	2	0	**2**	**0**
2002–03	Watford	1	0		
2002–03	*Swindon T*	9	0		
2003–04	Watford	10	0	**11**	**0**
2003–04	*Swindon T*	16	0		
2004–05	Swindon T	35	0		
2005–06	Swindon T	36	0		
2006–07	Swindon T	40	1	**136**	**1**

NICHOLAS, Andrew (D) 120 3
H: 6 2 W: 12 08 b.Liverpool 10-10-83
Honours: Liverpool Trainee.

2003–04	Swindon T	31	1		
2004–05	Swindon T	16	0		
2004–05	*Chester C*	5	0	**5**	**0**
2005–06	Swindon T	33	0		
2006–07	Swindon T	35	2	**115**	**3**

NOUBISSIE, Patrick (D) 5 0
H: 5 11 W: 11 04 b.Bois-Colombes 25-6-83
Source: Bretigny-sur-Orge, Le Mee-sur-Seine.

2001–02	Sedan	1	0		
2002–03	Sedan	0	0		
2003–04	Sedan	1	0	**2**	**0**
From Roye Foot Picardie.					
2006–07	Crewe Alex	0	0		
2006–07	Swindon T	3	0	**3**	**0**

PEACOCK, Lee (F) 425 112
H: 6 0 W: 12 08 b.Paisley 9-10-76
Source: Trainee. *Honours:* Scotland Youth, Under-21.

1993–94	Carlisle U	1	0		
1994–95	Carlisle U	7	0		

1995–96	Carlisle U	22	2		
1996–97	Carlisle U	44	9		
1997–98	Carlisle U	2	0	**76**	**11**
1997–98	Mansfield T	32	5		
1998–99	Mansfield T	45	17		
1999–2000	Mansfield T	12	7	**89**	**29**
1999–2000	Manchester C	8	0	**8**	**0**
2000–01	Bristol C	35	13		
2001–02	Bristol C	31	15		
2002–03	Bristol C	37	12		
2003–04	Bristol C	41	14	**144**	**54**
2004–05	Sheffield W	29	4		
2005–06	Sheffield W	22	2	**51**	**6**
2005–06	Swindon T	15	2		
2006–07	Swindon T	42	10	**57**	**12**

POOK, Michael (M) **73 2**
H: 5 11 W: 11 10 b.Swindon 22-10-85
Source: Scholar.

2003–04	Swindon T	0	0		
2004–05	Swindon T	5	0		
2005–06	Swindon T	30	0		
2006–07	Swindon T	38	2	**73**	**2**

ROBERTS, Chris (F) **280 58**
H: 5 11 W: 12 08 b.Cardiff 22-10-79
Source: Trainee. *Honours:* Wales Youth, Under-21.

1997–98	Cardiff C	11	3		
1998–99	Cardiff C	4	0		
1999–2000	Cardiff C	8	0	**23**	**3**
2000–01	Exeter C	42	8		
2001–02	Exeter C	37	11	**79**	**19**
2001–02	Bristol C	4	0		
2002–03	Bristol C	44	13		
2003–04	Bristol C	38	6		
2004–05	Bristol C	8	1	**94**	**20**
2004–05	Swindon T	21	3		
2005–06	Swindon T	21	3		
2006–07	Swindon T	42	10	**84**	**16**

SHAKES, Ricky (M) **77 7**
H: 5 10 W: 12 00 b.Brixton 26-1-85
Source: Scholar. *Honours:* Trinidad & Tobago 1 full cap.

2003–04	Bolton W	0	0		
2004–05	Bolton W	0	0		
2004–05	*Bristol R*	1	0	**1**	**0**
2004–05	*Bury*	7	2	**7**	**2**
2005–06	Swindon T	37	3		
2006–07	Swindon T	32	2	**69**	**5**

SMITH, Jack (D) **104 5**
H: 5 11 W: 11 05 b.Hemel Hempstead 14-10-83
Source: Scholar.

2001–02	Watford	0	0		
2002–03	Watford	1	0		
2003–04	Watford	17	2		
2004–05	Watford	7	0	**25**	**2**
2005–06	Swindon T	38	0		
2006–07	Swindon T	41	3	**79**	**3**

SMITH, Phil (G) **36 0**
H: 6 1 W: 13 11 b.Harrow 14-12-79
Source: Trainee.

1997–98	Millwall	0	0		
1998–99	Millwall	5	0	**5**	**0**
From Folkestone, Dover, Margate, Crawley					
2006–07	Swindon T	31	0	**31**	**0**

STURROCK, Blair (F) **162 22**
H: 5 10 W: 12 09 b.Dundee 25-8-81
Source: Dundee U.

2000–01	Brechin C	27	6	**27**	**6**
2001–02	Plymouth Arg	19	1		
2002–03	Plymouth Arg	20	1		
2003–04	Plymouth Arg	24	0		
2004–05	Plymouth Arg	0	0	**63**	**2**
2004–05	Kidderminster H	22	5	**22**	**5**
2005–06	Rochdale	31	6		
2006–07	Rochdale	0	0	**31**	**6**
2006–07	Swindon T	19	3	**19**	**3**

VINCENT, Jamie (D) **332 10**
H: 5 10 W: 11 08 b.Wimbledon 18-6-75
Source: Trainee.

1993–94	Crystal Palace	0	0		
1994–95	Crystal Palace	0	0		
1994–95	*Bournemouth*	8	0		
1995–96	Crystal Palace	25	0		
1996–97	Crystal Palace	0	0	**25**	**0**
1996–97	Bournemouth	29	0		
1997–98	Bournemouth	44	3		
1998–99	Bournemouth	32	2	**113**	**5**
1998–99	Huddersfield T	7	0		
1999–2000	Huddersfield T	36	2		
2000–01	Huddersfield T	16	0	**59**	**2**
2000–01	Portsmouth	14	0		
2001–02	Portsmouth	34	1		
2002–03	Portsmouth	0	0		
2003–04	Portsmouth	0	0	**48**	**1**
2003–04	*Walsall*	12	0	**12**	**0**
2003–04	Derby Co	7	1		
2004–05	Derby Co	15	1	**22**	**2**
2005–06	Millwall	19	0	**19**	**0**
2005–06	Yeovil T	0	0		
2006–07	Swindon T	34	0	**34**	**0**

WELLS, Ben (M) **6 0**
H: 5 9 W: 10 07 b.Basingstoke 26-3-88
Source: Scholar.

2004–05	Swindon T	1	0		
2005–06	Swindon T	4	0		
2006–07	Swindon T	1	0	**6**	**0**

WESTON, Curtis (M) **31 1**
H: 5 11 W: 11 09 b.Greenwich 24-1-87
Source: Scholar.

2003–04	Millwall	1	0		
2004–05	Millwall	3	0		
2005–06	Millwall	0	0	**4**	**0**
2006–07	Swindon T	27	1	**27**	**1**

WHALLEY, Gareth (M) **363 14**
H: 5 10 W: 11 06 b.Manchester 19-12-73
Source: Trainee.

1992–93	Crewe Alex	25	1		
1993–94	Crewe Alex	15	1		
1994–95	Crewe Alex	40	1		
1995–96	Crewe Alex	44	2		
1996–97	Crewe Alex	38	3		
1997–98	Crewe Alex	18	1		
1998–99	Bradford C	45	2		
1999–2000	Bradford C	16	1		
2000–01	Bradford C	19	0		
2001–02	Bradford C	23	0	**103**	**3**
2001–02	*Crewe Alex*	7	0	**187**	**9**
2002–03	Cardiff C	19	0		
2003–04	Cardiff C	22	2		
2004–05	Cardiff C	0	0	**41**	**2**
2004–05	Wigan Ath	8	0	**8**	**0**
2005–06	Swindon T	24	0		
2006–07	Swindon T	0	0	**24**	**0**

WILLIAMS, Ady (D) **434 21**
H: 6 2 W: 13 02 b.Reading 16-8-71
Source: Trainee. *Honours:* Wales 13 full caps, 1 goal.

1988–89	Reading	8	0		
1989–90	Reading	16	2		
1990–91	Reading	7	0		
1991–92	Reading	40	4		
1992–93	Reading	31	4		
1993–94	Reading	41	0		
1994–95	Reading	22	1		
1995–96	Reading	31	3		
1996–97	Wolverhampton W	6	0		
1997–98	Wolverhampton W	20	0		
1998–99	Wolverhampton W	0	0		
1999–2000	Wolverhampton W	1	0	**27**	**0**
1999–2000	*Reading*	15	1		
2000–01	Reading	5	0		
2001–02	Reading	35	1		
2002–03	Reading	38	1		
2003–04	Reading	33	1		
2004–05	Reading	11	0	**333**	**18**
2004–05	Coventry C	21	2		
2005–06	Coventry C	14	0	**35**	**2**
2005–06	*Millwall*	12	1	**12**	**1**
2006–07	Swindon T	27	0	**27**	**0**

ZAABOUB, Sofiane (D) **47 2**
H: 5 11 W: 11 09 b.Melun 23-1-83
Source: Montereau, St Etienne, Modena, Sora, Real Jaen.

2005–06	FC Brussels	20	1	**20**	**1**
2006–07	Swindon T	27	1	**27**	**1**

TORQUAY U (81)

ANDREWS, Lee (D) **153 0**
H: 6 0 W: 10 12 b.Carlisle 23-4-83
Source: Scholar.

2001–02	Carlisle U	39	0		
2002–03	Carlisle U	15	0		
2002–03	*Rochdale*	8	0	**8**	**0**
2003–04	Carlisle U	37	0		
2004–05	Carlisle U	0	0		
2005–06	Carlisle U	1	0	**92**	**0**
2005–06	*Torquay U*	7	0		
2006–07	Torquay U	46	0	**53**	**0**

ANGUS, Stevland (D) **191 2**
H: 6 0 W: 12 00 b.Westminster 16-9-80
Source: Trainee.

1999–2000	West Ham U	0	0		
2000–01	West Ham U	0	0		
2000–01	*Bournemouth*	9	0	**9**	**0**
2001–02	Cambridge U	41	0		
2002–03	Cambridge U	40	0		
2003–04	Cambridge U	40	1		
2004–05	Cambridge U	14	0	**135**	**1**
2004–05	*Hull C*	2	0	**2**	**0**
2004–05	*Scunthorpe U*	9	0	**9**	**0**
From Grays Ath					
2005–06	Barnet	0	0		
2006–07	Torquay U	36	1	**36**	**1**

BAXTER, Darren (M) **1 0**
H: 5 7 W: 12 00 b.Brighton 26-10-81

2006–07	Torquay U	1	0	**1**	**0**

EVANS, Micky (F) **504 87**
H: 6 1 W: 13 04 b.Plymouth 1-1-73
Source: Trainee. *Honours:* Eire 1 full cap.

1990–91	Plymouth Arg	4	0		
1991–92	Plymouth Arg	13	0		
1992–93	Plymouth Arg	23	1		
1992–93	*Blackburn R*	0	0		
1993–94	Plymouth Arg	22	9		
1994–95	Plymouth Arg	23	4		
1995–96	Plymouth Arg	45	12		
1996–97	Plymouth Arg	33	12		
1996–97	Southampton	12	4		
1997–98	Southampton	10	0	**22**	**4**
1997–98	WBA	10	1		
1998–99	WBA	20	2		
1999–2000	WBA	33	3		
2000–01	WBA	0	0	**63**	**6**
2000–01	Bristol R	21	4	**21**	**4**
2000–01	Plymouth Arg	10	4		
2001–02	Plymouth Arg	38	7		
2002–03	Plymouth Arg	42	4		
2003–04	Plymouth Arg	44	11		
2004–05	Plymouth Arg	42	4		
2005–06	Plymouth Arg	45	4	**384**	**72**
2006–07	Torquay U	14	1	**14**	**1**

GARNER, Darren (M) **351 27**
H: 5 10 W: 12 02 b.Plymouth 10-12-71
Source: Trainee.

1988–89	Plymouth Arg	1	0		
1989–90	Plymouth Arg	1	0		
1990–91	Plymouth Arg	5	1		
1991–92	Plymouth Arg	10	0		
1992–93	Plymouth Arg	10	0		
1993–94	Plymouth Arg	0	0	**27**	**1**
From Dorchester T.					
1995–96	Rotherham U	31	1		
1996–97	Rotherham U	30	2		
1997–98	Rotherham U	40	3		
1998–99	Rotherham U	40	4		
1999–2000	Rotherham U	35	9		
2000–01	Rotherham U	31	1		
2001–02	Rotherham U	0	0		
2002–03	Rotherham U	26	3		
2003–04	Rotherham U	13	0		
2004–05	Rotherham U	18	0	**264**	**23**
2004–05	*Torquay U*	9	0		
2005–06	Torquay U	43	2		
2006–07	Torquay U	8	1	**60**	**3**

GORDON, Dean (D) **357 31**
H: 5 11 W: 13 08 b.Croydon 10-2-73
Source: Trainee. *Honours:* England Under-21.

1991–92	Crystal Palace	4	0		
1992–93	Crystal Palace	10	0		
1993–94	Crystal Palace	45	5		

1994–95	Crystal Palace	41	2		
1995–96	Crystal Palace	34	8		
1996–97	Crystal Palace	30	3		
1997–98	Crystal Palace	37	2	**201**	**20**
1998–99	Middlesbrough	38	3		
1999–2000	Middlesbrough	4	0		
2000–01	Middlesbrough	20	1		
2001–02	Middlesbrough	1	0	**63**	**4**
2001–02	*Cardiff C*	7	2	**7**	**2**
2002–03	Coventry C	30	1		
2003–04	Coventry C	5	0	**35**	**1**
2003–04	*Reading*	3	0	**3**	**0**
2004–05	Grimsby T	20	2	**20**	**2**
2004–05	Apoel	8	0	**8**	**0**
From Crook T.					
2005–06	Blackpool	1	0	**1**	**0**
From Lewes, Worksop, Albany U					
2006–07	Auckland C	5	2	**5**	**2**
2006–07	NZ Knights	6	0	**6**	**0**
2006–07	Torquay U	8	0	**8**	**0**

HANCOX, Richard (F) **83** **10**

H: 5 10 W: 12 06 b.Stourbridge 4-10-70

Source: Stourbridge S.

1992–93	Torquay U	7	0		
1993–94	Torquay U	3	0		
1994–95	Torquay U	36	9		
1995–96	Torquay U	25	1		
1996–97	Torquay U	11	0		
1997–98	Torquay U	0	0		
1998–99	Torquay U	0	0		
2005–06	Torquay U	1	0		
2006–07	Torquay U	0	0	**83**	**10**

HAPGOOD, Leon (F) **41** **3**

H: 5 6 W: 10 00 b.Torbay 7-8-79

Source: Trainee.

1999–2000	*Yeovil T*	0	0		
1996–97	Torquay U	1	0		
1997–98	Torquay U	22	3		
1998–99	Torquay U	17	0		
1999–2000	Plymouth Arg	0	0		
1999–2000	*Yeovil T*	0	0		
From Clevedon T.					
2006–07	Torquay U	1	0	**41**	**3**

HILL, Kevin (M) **404** **49**

H: 5 8 W: 10 06 b.Exeter 6-3-76

Source: Torrington.

1997–98	Torquay U	37	7		
1998–99	Torquay U	35	5		
1999–2000	Torquay U	43	2		
2000–01	Torquay U	44	9		
2001–02	Torquay U	44	2		
2002–03	Torquay U	39	4		
2003–04	Torquay U	45	5		
2004–05	Torquay U	39	5		
2005–06	Torquay U	42	9		
2006–07	Torquay U	36	1	**404**	**49**

HOCKLEY, Matthew (D) **210** **9**

H: 5 10 W: 12 04 b.Paignton 5-6-82

Source: Trainee.

2000–01	Torquay U	6	1		
2001–02	Torquay U	12	0		
2002–03	Torquay U	40	2		
2003–04	Torquay U	45	5		
2004–05	Torquay U	34	1		
2005–06	Torquay U	36	0		
2006–07	Torquay U	37	0	**210**	**9**

HORSELL, Martin (G) **6** **0**

H: 6 0 W: 12 00 b.Torquay 10-12-86

Source: Scholar.

2005–06	Bristol R	0	0		
2006–07	Torquay U	6	0	**6**	**0**

MANSELL, Lee (D) **136** **13**

H: 5 10 W: 11 10 b.Gloucester 28-10-82

Source: Scholar.

2000–01	Luton T	18	5		
2001–02	Luton T	11	1		
2002–03	Luton T	1	0		
2003–04	Luton T	16	2		
2004–05	Luton T	1	0	**47**	**8**
2005–06	Oxford U	44	1	**44**	**1**
2006–07	Torquay U	45	4	**45**	**4**

McPHEE, Chris (F) **105** **4**

H: 5 11 W: 11 09 b.Eastbourne 20-3-83

Source: Scholarship.

1999–2000	Brighton & HA	4	0		
2000–01	Brighton & HA	0	0		
2001–02	Brighton & HA	2	0		
2002–03	Brighton & HA	2	0		
2003–04	Brighton & HA	29	4		
2004–05	Brighton & HA	16	0		
2005–06	Brighton & HA	7	0	**60**	**4**
2005–06	*Swindon T*	8	0	**8**	**0**
2006–07	Torquay U	37	0	**37**	**0**

MOTTERAM, Carl (M) **7** **0**

H: 5 8 W: 9 11 b.Birmingham 3-9-84

Source: Scholar.

2004–05	Birmingham C	0	0		
2005–06	Birmingham C	0	0		
2006–07	Torquay U	7	0	**7**	**0**

PHILLIPS, Martin (M) **288** **22**

H: 5 10 W: 11 10 b.Exeter 13-3-76

Source: Trainee.

1992–93	Exeter C	6	0		
1993–94	Exeter C	9	0		
1994–95	Exeter C	24	2		
1995–96	Exeter C	13	3		
1995–96	Manchester C	11	0		
1996–97	Manchester C	4	0		
1997–98	Manchester C	0	0		
1997–98	*Scunthorpe U*	3	0	**3**	**0**
1997–98	*Exeter C*	8	0	**60**	**5**
1998–99	Manchester C	0	0	**15**	**0**
1998–99	Portsmouth	17	1		
1998–99	*Bristol R*	2	0	**2**	**0**
1999–2000	Portsmouth	7	0	**24**	**1**
2000–01	Plymouth Arg	42	1		
2001–02	Plymouth Arg	39	6		
2002–03	Plymouth Arg	24	2		
2003–04	Plymouth Arg	9	1	**114**	**10**
2004–05	Torquay U	30	2		
2005–06	Torquay U	26	3		
2006–07	Torquay U	14	1	**70**	**6**

REED, Steve (D) **34** **0**

H: 5 8 W: 12 02 b.Barnstaple 18-6-85

Source: Juniors.

2003–04	Yeovil T	5	0		
2004–05	Yeovil T	3	0		
2005–06	Yeovil T	0	0	**8**	**0**
2005–06	*Torquay U*	11	0		
2006–07	Torquay U	15	0	**26**	**0**

ROBERTSON, Chris (D) **10** **1**

H: 6 3 W: 11 08 b.Dundee 11-10-85

Source: Scholar.

2005–06	Sheffield U	0	0		
2005–06	*Chester C*	1	0	**1**	**0**
2006–07	Sheffield U	0	0		
2006–07	Torquay U	9	1	**9**	**1**

ROBINSON, Mark (D) **162** **4**

H: 5 9 W: 11 00 b.Guisborough 24-7-81

Source: Trainee.

1999–2000	Hartlepool U	0	0		
2000–01	Hartlepool U	6	0		
2001–02	Hartlepool U	37	0		
2002–03	Hartlepool U	38	0		
2003–04	Hartlepool U	4	0	**85**	**0**
From Hereford U					
2005–06	Stockport Co	46	2		
2006–07	Stockport Co	13	2	**59**	**4**
2006–07	Torquay U	18	0	**18**	**0**

SMITH, Paul (M) **549** **34**

H: 5 11 W: 14 00 b.East Ham 18-9-71

Source: Trainee.

1989–90	Southend U	10	1		
1990–91	Southend U	2	0		
1991–92	Southend U	0	0		
1992–93	Southend U	8	0	**20**	**1**
1993–94	Brentford	32	3		
1994–95	Brentford	35	3		
1995–96	Brentford	46	4		
1996–97	Brentford	46	1	**159**	**11**
1997–98	Gillingham	46	3		
1998–99	Gillingham	45	6		
1999–2000	Gillingham	44	1		
2000–01	Gillingham	42	3		
2001–02	Gillingham	46	2		
2002–03	Gillingham	45	3		
2003–04	Gillingham	33	0		
2004–05	Gillingham	41	3		
2005–06	Walsall	8	1	**8**	**1**
2005–06	*Gillingham*	3	0	**345**	**21**
2005–06	Swindon T	9	0		
2006–07	Swindon T	0	0	**9**	**0**
2006–07	Torquay U	8	0	**8**	**0**

TAYLOR, Craig (D) **271** **14**

H: 6 2 W: 13 00 b.Plymouth 24-1-74

Source: Dorchester T.

1996–97	Swindon T	0	0		
1997–98	Swindon T	32	2		
1998–99	Swindon T	21	0		
1998–99	*Plymouth Arg*	6	1		
1999–2000	Swindon T	2	0	**55**	**2**
1999–2000	Plymouth Arg	41	3		
2000–01	Plymouth Arg	39	3		
2001–02	Plymouth Arg	1	0		
2002–03	Plymouth Arg	1	0	**88**	**7**
2002–03	*Torquay U*	5	0		
2003–04	Torquay U	43	4		
2004–05	Torquay U	36	0		
2005–06	Torquay U	31	0		
2006–07	Torquay U	13	1	**128**	**5**

THORPE, Lee (F) **375** **88**

H: 6 0 W: 11 06 b.Wolverhampton 14-12-75

Source: Trainee.

1993–94	Blackpool	1	0		
1994–95	Blackpool	1	0		
1995–96	Blackpool	1	0		
1996–97	Blackpool	9	0	**12**	**0**
1997–98	Lincoln C	44	14		
1998–99	Lincoln C	38	8		
1999–2000	Lincoln C	42	16		
2000–01	Lincoln C	31	7		
2001–02	Lincoln C	37	13	**192**	**58**
2001–02	Leyton Orient	0	0		
2002–03	Leyton Orient	38	8		
2003–04	Leyton Orient	17	4	**55**	**12**
2003–04	*Grimsby T*	6	0	**6**	**0**
2003–04	Bristol R	10	1		
2004–05	Bristol R	25	3	**35**	**4**
2004–05	Swansea C	15	3		
2005–06	Swansea C	3	0	**18**	**3**
2005–06	*Peterborough U*	6	0	**6**	**0**
2005–06	*Torquay U*	10	3		
2006–07	Torquay U	41	8	**51**	**11**

VILLIS, Matt (D) **40** **0**

H: 6 2 W: 12 00 b.Bridgwater 13-4-84

Source: Bridgwater T.

2002–03	Plymouth Arg	0	0		
2003–04	Plymouth Arg	0	0		
2004–05	Plymouth Arg	0	0		
2004–05	*Torquay U*	22	0		
2005–06	Torquay U	12	0		
2006–07	Torquay U	6	0	**40**	**0**

WOODS, Steve (D) **263** **10**

H: 6 1 W: 13 00 b.Northwich 15-12-76

Source: Trainee.

1995–96	Stoke C	0	0		
1996–97	Stoke C	0	0		
1997–98	Stoke C	1	0		
1997–98	*Plymouth Arg*	5	0	**5**	**0**
1998–99	Stoke C	33	0	**34**	**0**
1999–2000	Chesterfield	25	0		
2000–01	Chesterfield	0	0	**25**	**0**
2001–02	Torquay U	38	2		
2002–03	Torquay U	9	0		
2003–04	Torquay U	46	6		
2004–05	Torquay U	36	2		
2005–06	Torquay U	38	0		
2006–07	Torquay U	32	0	**199**	**10**

TOTTENHAM H (82)

ALNWICK, Ben (G) **19** **0**

H: 6 2 W: 13 12 b.Prudhoe 1-1-87

Source: Scholar. *Honours:* England Youth.

2003–04	Sunderland	0	0		
2004–05	Sunderland	3	0		
2005–06	Sunderland	5	0		
2006–07	Sunderland	11	0	**19**	**0**
2006–07	Tottenham H	0	0		

ASSOU-EKOTTO, Benoit (M) 82 0
H: 5 10 W: 10 12 b.Arras 24-3-84
Honours: Cameroon B, full caps.

2003–04	Lens	3	0		
2004–05	Lens	29	0		
2005–06	Lens	34	0	**66**	**0**
2006–07	Tottenham H	16	0	**16**	**0**

BARCHAM, Andy (F) 0 0
H: 5 8 W: 11 10 b.Basildon 16-12-86
Source: Scholar.

2005–06	Tottenham H	0	0		
2006–07	Tottenham H	0	0		

BARNARD, Lee (F) 19 0
H: 5 10 W: 10 10 b.Romford 18-7-84
Source: Trainee.

2002–03	Tottenham H	0	0		
2002–03	*Exeter C*	3	0	**3**	**0**
2003–04	Tottenham H	0	0		
2004–05	Tottenham H	0	0		
2004–05	*Leyton Orient*	8	0	**8**	**0**
2004–05	*Northampton T*	5	0	**5**	**0**
2005–06	Tottenham H	3	0		
2006–07	Tottenham H	0	0	**3**	**0**

BERBATOV, Dimitar (F) 237 106
H: 6 2 W: 12 06 b.Blagoevgrad 30-1-81
Honours: Bulgaria 58 full caps, 35 goals.

1998–99	CSKA Sofia	11	3		
1999–2000	CSKA Sofia	27	14		
2000–01	CSKA Sofia	12	8	**50**	**25**
2000–01	Leverkusen	6	0		
2001–02	Leverkusen	24	8		
2002–03	Leverkusen	24	4		
2003–04	Leverkusen	33	16		
2004–05	Leverkusen	33	20		
2005–06	Leverkusen	34	21	**154**	**69**
2006–07	Tottenham H	33	12	**33**	**12**

BURCH, Rob (G) 6 0
H: 6 2 W: 12 13 b.Yeovil 8-10-83
Source: Trainee. *Honours:* England Under-20.

2002–03	Tottenham H	0	0		
2003–04	Tottenham H	0	0		
2004–05	Tottenham H	0	0		
2004–05	*West Ham U*	0	0		
2005–06	Tottenham H	0	0		
2005–06	*Bristol C*	0	0		
2006–07	Tottenham H	0	0		
2006–07	*Barnet*	6	0	**6**	**0**

BUTTON, David (G) 0 0
H: 6 3 W: 13 00 b.Stevenage 27-2-89
Source: Scholar. *Honours:* England Youth.

2005–06	Tottenham H	0	0		
2006–07	Tottenham H	0	0		

CERNY, Radek (G) 3 0
H: 6 1 W: 14 02 b.Prague 18-2-74
Source: Slavia Prague. *Honours:* Czech Republic 3 full caps.

2004–05	Tottenham H	3	0		
2005–06	Tottenham H	0	0		
2006–07	Tottenham H	0	0	**3**	**0**

CHIMBONDA, Pascal (D) 223 12
H: 5 10 W: 11 05 b.Les Abymes 21-2-79
Honours: France 1 full cap.

1999–2000	Le Havre	2	0		
2000–01	Le Havre	32	1		
2001–02	Le Havre	27	2		
2002–03	Le Havre	24	2	**85**	**5**
2003–04	Bastia	31	1		
2004–05	Bastia	36	3	**67**	**4**
2005–06	Wigan Ath	37	2		
2006–07	Wigan Ath	1	0	**38**	**2**
2006–07	Tottenham H	33	1	**33**	**1**

DANIELS, Charlie (M) 2 0
H: 6 1 W: 12 12 b.Harlow 7-9-86
Source: Scholar.

2005–06	Tottenham H	0	0		
2006–07	Tottenham H	0	0		
2006–07	*Chesterfield*	2	0	**2**	**0**

DAVIDS, Edgar (M) 355 34
H: 5 7 W: 10 10 b.Paramaribo 13-3-73
Honours: Holland Under-21, 74 full caps, 6 goals.

1991–92	Ajax	13	9		
1992–93	Ajax	28	1		
1993–94	Ajax	15	2		
1994–95	Ajax	22	5		
1995–96	Ajax	28	7	**106**	**24**
1996–97	AC Milan	15	0		
1997–98	AC Milan	3	0	**18**	**0**
1997–98	Juventus	20	1		
1998–99	Juventus	27	2		
1999–2000	Juventus	27	1		
2000–01	Juventus	26	1		
2001–02	Juventus	28	2		
2002–03	Juventus	26	1		
2003–04	Juventus	5	0	**159**	**8**
2003–04	Barcelona	18	1	**18**	**1**
2004–05	Internazionale	14	0	**14**	**0**
2005–06	Tottenham H	31	1		
2006–07	Tottenham H	9	0	**40**	**1**

DAVIS, Jamie (M) 0 0
H: 5 7 W: 10 10 b.Braintree 25-10-88
Source: Scholar. *Honours:* England Youth.

2005–06	Tottenham H	0	0		
2006–07	Tottenham H	0	0		

DAWKINS, Simon (F) 0 0
H: 5 10 W: 11 01 b.Edgware 1-12-87
Source: Scholar.

2005–06	Tottenham H	0	0		
2006–07	Tottenham H	0	0		

DAWSON, Michael (D) 157 8
H: 6 2 W: 12 02 b.Northallerton 18-11-83
Source: School. *Honours:* England Youth, Under-21, B.

2000–01	Nottingham F	0	0		
2001–02	Nottingham F	1	0		
2002–03	Nottingham F	38	5		
2003–04	Nottingham F	30	1		
2004–05	Nottingham F	14	1	**83**	**7**
2004–05	Tottenham H	5	0		
2005–06	Tottenham H	32	0		
2006–07	Tottenham H	37	1	**74**	**1**

DEFENDI, Rodrigo (D) 0 0
H: 6 2 W: 13 01 b.Ribeirao Preto 16-6-86
Source: Cruzeiro.

2004–05	Tottenham H	0	0		
2005–06	Tottenham H	0	0		
2006–07	Tottenham H	0	0		

DEFOE, Jermain (F) 242 86
H: 5 7 W: 10 04 b.Beckton 7-10-82
Source: Charlton Ath. *Honours:* England Youth, Under-21, B, 24full caps, 3 goals.

1999–2000	West Ham U	0	0		
2000–01	West Ham U	1	0		
2000–01	*Bournemouth*	29	18	**29**	**18**
2001–02	West Ham U	35	10		
2002–03	West Ham U	38	8		
2003–04	West Ham U	19	11	**93**	**29**
2003–04	Tottenham H	15	7		
2004–05	Tottenham H	35	13		
2005–06	Tottenham H	36	9		
2006–07	Tottenham H	34	10	**120**	**39**

DERVITE, Dorian (D) 0 0
b.Lille 25-7-88
Honours: France Youth.

2006–07	Tottenham H	0	0		

DIXON, Terry (F) 0 0
b.Holloway 15-1-90
Honours: Eire Youth, Under-21.

2006–07	Tottenham H	0	0		

FORECAST, Tommy (G) 0 0
H: 6 6 W: 11 10 b.Newham 15-10-86
Source: Scholar.

2005–06	Tottenham H	0	0		
2006–07	Tottenham H	0	0		

GARDNER, Anthony (D) 151 5
H: 6 3 W: 14 00 b.Stone 19-9-80
Source: Trainee. *Honours:* England Under-21, 1 full cap.

1998–99	Port Vale	15	1		
1999–2000	Port Vale	26	3	**41**	**4**
1999–2000	Tottenham H	0	0		
2000–01	Tottenham H	8	0		
2001–02	Tottenham H	15	0		
2002–03	Tottenham H	12	1		
2003–04	Tottenham H	33	0		
2004–05	Tottenham H	17	0		
2005–06	Tottenham H	17	0		
2006–07	Tottenham H	8	0	**110**	**1**

GHALY, Hossam (M) 64 4
H: 5 11 W: 12 04 b.Cairo 15-12-81
Honours: Egypt 21 full caps, 5 goals.

2003–04	Feyenoord	13	0		
2004–05	Feyenoord	20	1		
2005–06	Feyenoord	10	2	**43**	**3**
2005–06	Tottenham H	0	0		
2006–07	Tottenham H	21	1	**21**	**1**

HALLFREDSSON, Emil (M) 35 9
H: 6 1 W: 13 01 b.Iceland 29-6-84
Honours: Iceland Under-21.

2004	FH	16	4	**16**	**4**
2004–05	Tottenham H	0	0		
2005–06	Tottenham H	0	0		
2006	Malmo	19	5	**19**	**5**
2006–07	Tottenham H	0	0		

HAMED, Radwan (F) 0 0
b. 19-12-88
Source: Scholar.

2006–07	Tottenham H	0	0		

HUDDLESTONE, Tom (M) 126 2
H: 6 2 W: 11 02 b.Nottingham 28-12-86
Source: From Scholar. *Honours:* England Youth, Under-20, Under-21.

2003–04	Derby Co	43	0		
2004–05	Derby Co	45	0	**88**	**0**
2005–06	Tottenham H	4	0		
2005–06	*Wolverhampton W*	13	1	**13**	**1**
2006–07	Tottenham H	21	1	**25**	**1**

IFIL, Phil (D) 19 0
H: 5 10 W: 12 02 b.Willesden 18-11-86
Honours: England Youth, Under-20.

2004–05	Tottenham H	2	0		
2005–06	Tottenham H	0	0		
2005–06	*Millwall*	16	0	**16**	**0**
2006–07	Tottenham H	1	0	**3**	**0**

JENAS, Jermaine (M) 194 25
H: 5 11 W: 11 00 b.Nottingham 18-2-83
Source: Scholar. *Honours:* England Youth, Under-21, B, 17 full caps.

1999–2000	Nottingham F	0	0		
2000–01	Nottingham F	1	0		
2001–02	Nottingham F	28	4	**29**	**4**
2001–02	Newcastle U	12	0		
2002–03	Newcastle U	32	6		
2003–04	Newcastle U	31	2		
2004–05	Newcastle U	31	1		
2005–06	Newcastle U	4	0	**110**	**9**
2005–06	Tottenham H	30	6		
2006–07	Tottenham H	25	6	**55**	**12**

KEANE, Robbie (F) 317 114
H: 5 9 W: 12 02 b.Dublin 8-7-80
Source: Trainee. *Honours:* Eire Youth, B, 72 full caps, 29 goals.

1997–98	Wolverhampton W	38	11		
1998–99	Wolverhampton W	33	11		
1999–2000	Wolverhampton W	2	2	**73**	**24**
1999–2000	Coventry C	31	12	**31**	**12**
2000–01	Internazionale	6	0	**6**	**0**
2000–01	Leeds U	18	9		
2001–02	Leeds U	25	3		
2002–03	Leeds U	3	1	**46**	**13**
2002–03	Tottenham H	29	13		
2003–04	Tottenham H	34	14		
2004–05	Tottenham H	35	11		
2005–06	Tottenham H	36	16		
2006–07	Tottenham H	27	11	**161**	**65**

KING, Ledley (D) 193 7
H: 6 2 W: 14 05 b.Bow 12-10-80
Source: Trainee. *Honours:* England Youth, B, Under-21, 19 full caps, 1 goal.

1998–99	Tottenham H	1	0		
1999–2000	Tottenham H	3	0		
2000–01	Tottenham H	18	1		

2001–02	Tottenham H	32	0		
2002–03	Tottenham H	25	0		
2003–04	Tottenham H	29	1		
2004–05	Tottenham H	38	2		
2005–06	Tottenham H	26	3		
2006–07	Tottenham H	21	0	**193**	**7**

LEE, Charlie (M) 5 0
H: 5 11 W: 11 07 b.Whitechapel 5-1-87
Source: Scholar.

2005–06	Tottenham H	0	0		
2006–07	Tottenham H	0	0		
2006–07	*Millwall*	5	0	**5**	**0**

LEE, Young-Pyo (D) 130 1
H: 5 8 W: 10 10 b.Hong Chung 23-4-77
Source: Anyang Cheetahs. *Honours:* South Korea 93 full caps, 5 goals.

2002–03	PSV Eindhoven	15	0		
2003–04	PSV Eindhoven	32	0		
2004–05	PSV Eindhoven	31	1	**78**	**1**
2005–06	Tottenham H	31	0		
2006–07	Tottenham H	21	0	**52**	**0**

LENNON, Aaron (M) 91 6
H: 5 6 W: 10 03 b.Leeds 16-4-87
Source: Trainee. *Honours:* England Youth, Under-21, B, 9 full caps.

2003–04	Leeds U	11	0		
2004–05	Leeds U	27	1	**38**	**1**
2005–06	Tottenham H	27	2		
2006–07	Tottenham H	26	3	**53**	**5**

LIVERMORE, Jake (M) 0 0
b.Enfield 14-11-89

2006–07	Tottenham H	0	0		

MAGHOMA, Jacques (M) 0 0
H: 5 9 W: 11 06 b.Lubumbashi 23-10-87
Source: Scholar.

2005–06	Tottenham H	0	0		
2006–07	Tottenham H	0	0		

MALBRANQUE, Steed (M) 274 39
H: 5 7 W: 11 07 b.Mouscron 6-1-80
Honours: France Under-21.

1997–98	Lyon	2	0		
1998–99	Lyon	21	0		
1999–2000	Lyon	28	3		
2000–01	Lyon	26	2	**77**	**5**
2001–02	Fulham	37	8		
2002–03	Fulham	37	6		
2003–04	Fulham	38	6		
2004–05	Fulham	26	6		
2005–06	Fulham	34	6	**172**	**32**
2006–07	Tottenham H	25	2	**25**	**2**

MARTIN, Joe (M) 0 0
H: 6 0 W: 12 13 b.Dagenham 29-11-88
Source: Scholar. *Honours:* England Youth.

2005–06	Tottenham H	0	0		
2006–07	Tottenham H	0	0		

McKENNA, Kieran (M) 0 0
H: 5 10 W: 10 07 b.London 14-5-86
Source: Academy. *Honours:* Northern Ireland Under-21.

2003–04	Tottenham H	0	0		
2004–05	Tottenham H	0	0		
2005–06	Tottenham H	0	0		
2006–07	Tottenham H	0	0		

MIDO (F) 151 60
H: 6 2 W: 14 09 b.Cairo 23-2-83
Honours: Egypt 44 full caps, 18 goals.

1999–2000	Zamalek	4	3	**4**	**3**
2000–01	Gent	21	11	**21**	**11**
2001–02	Ajax	24	12		
2002–03	Ajax	16	9	**40**	**21**
2002–03	Celta Vigo	8	4	**8**	**4**
2003–04	Marseille	22	7	**22**	**7**
2004–05	Roma	8	0	**8**	**0**
2004–05	Tottenham H	9	2		
2005–06	Tottenham H	27	11		
2006–07	Tottenham H	12	1	**48**	**14**

MILLS, Leigh (D) 0 0
H: 6 2 W: 13 00 b.Winchester 8-2-88
Source: Scholar. *Honours:* England Youth.

2005–06	Tottenham H	0	0		
2006–07	Tottenham H	0	0		

MURPHY, Danny (M) 398 61
H: 5 10 W: 11 09 b.Chester 18-3-77
Source: Trainee. *Honours:* England Schools, Youth, Under-21, 9 full caps, 1 goal.

1993–94	Crewe Alex	12	2		
1994–95	Crewe Alex	35	5		
1995–96	Crewe Alex	42	10		
1996–97	Crewe Alex	45	10		
1997–98	Liverpool	16	0		
1998–99	Liverpool	1	0		
1998–99	*Crewe Alex*	16	1	**150**	**28**
1999–2000	Liverpool	23	3		
2000–01	Liverpool	27	4		
2001–02	Liverpool	36	6		
2002–03	Liverpool	36	7		
2003–04	Liverpool	31	5	**170**	**25**
2004–05	Charlton Ath	38	3		
2005–06	Charlton Ath	18	4	**56**	**7**
2005–06	Tottenham H	10	0		
2006–07	Tottenham H	12	1	**22**	**1**

O'HARA, Jamie (M) 19 5
H: 5 11 W: 12 04 b.South London 25-9-86
Source: Scholar. *Honours:* England Youth.

2004–05	Tottenham H	0	0		
2005–06	Tottenham H	0	0		
2005–06	*Chesterfield*	19	5	**19**	**5**
2006–07	Tottenham H	0	0		

OLSEN, Alex (F) 0 0
b.Gjovik 9-9-89
Source: Gjovik.

2006–07	Tottenham H	0	0		

PEKHART, Tomas (F) 0 0
b.Susice 26-5-89
Honours: Czech Republic Youth.

2006–07	Tottenham H	0	0		

RICARDO ROCHA (D) 168 5
H: 6 0 W: 12 08 b.Santo Tirso 3-10-78
Honours: Portugal 6 full caps.

2000–01	Braga	19	0		
2001–02	Braga	25	2	**44**	**2**
2002–03	Benfica	27	0		
2003–04	Benfica	25	0		
2004–05	Benfica	25	0		
2005–06	Benfica	26	0		
2006–07	Benfica	12	3	**115**	**3**
2006–07	Tottenham H	9	0	**9**	**0**

RILEY, Chris (D) 0 0
b.London 2-2-88
Source: Scholar. *Honours:* England Youth.

2006–07	Tottenham H	0	0		

ROBINSON, Paul (G) 207 1
H: 6 1 W: 14 07 b.Beverley 15-10-79
Source: Trainee. *Honours:* England Under-21, 36 full caps.

1996–97	Leeds U	0	0		
1997–98	Leeds U	0	0		
1998–99	Leeds U	5	0		
1999–2000	Leeds U	0	0		
2000–01	Leeds U	16	0		
2001–02	Leeds U	0	0		
2002–03	Leeds U	38	0		
2003–04	Leeds U	36	0	**95**	**0**
2003–04	Tottenham H	0	0		
2004–05	Tottenham H	36	0		
2005–06	Tottenham H	38	0		
2006–07	Tottenham H	38	1	**112**	**1**

ROUTLEDGE, Wayne (M) 150 10
H: 5 6 W: 11 02 b.Sidcup 7-1-85
Source: Scholar. *Honours:* England Youth, Under-20, Under-21.

2001–02	Crystal Palace	2	0		
2002–03	Crystal Palace	26	4		
2003–04	Crystal Palace	44	6		
2004–05	Crystal Palace	38	0	**110**	**10**
2005–06	Tottenham H	3	0		
2005–06	*Portsmouth*	13	0	**13**	**0**
2006–07	Tottenham H	0	0	**3**	**0**
2006–07	*Fulham*	24	0	**24**	**0**

STALTERI, Paul (D) 189 8
H: 5 11 W: 11 13 b.Etobicoke 18-10-77
Source: Malton Bullets, Toronto Lynx. *Honours:* Canada Youth, Under-20, Under-23, 58 full caps, 7 goals.

1999–2000	Werder Bremen	0	0		
2000–01	Werder Bremen	31	1		
2001–02	Werder Bremen	22	3		
2002–03	Werder Bremen	33	0		
2003–04	Werder Bremen	33	2		
2004–05	Werder Bremen	31	0	**150**	**6**
2005–06	Tottenham H	33	1		
2006–07	Tottenham H	6	1	**39**	**2**

TAARABT, Adel (M) 3 0
H: 5 9 W: 10 12 b.Berre-l'Etang 24-5-89
Honours: France Youth.

2006–07	Lens	1	0	**1**	**0**
2006–07	Tottenham H	2	0	**2**	**0**

TAINIO, Teemu (M) 189 19
H: 5 9 W: 11 09 b.Tornio 27-11-79
Honours: Finland Youth, Under-21, 35 full caps, 5 goals.

1996	Haka	20	4	**20**	**4**
1997–98	Auxerre	1	0		
1998–99	Auxerre	13	1		
1999–2000	Auxerre	25	3		
2000–01	Auxerre	10	1		
2001–02	Auxerre	28	3		
2002–03	Auxerre	25	1		
2003–04	Auxerre	22	3		
2004–05	Auxerre	0	0	**124**	**12**
2005–06	Tottenham H	24	1		
2006–07	Tottenham H	21	2	**45**	**3**

YEATES, Mark (F) 74 6
H: 5 8 W: 13 03 b.Dublin 11-1-85
Source: Trainee. *Honours:* Eire Youth, Under-21.

2002–03	Tottenham H	0	0		
2003–04	Tottenham H	1	0		
2003–04	*Brighton & HA*	9	0	**9**	**0**
2004–05	Tottenham H	2	0		
2004–05	*Swindon T*	4	0	**4**	**0**
2005–06	Tottenham H	0	0		
2005–06	*Colchester U*	44	5	**44**	**5**
2006–07	Tottenham H	0	0	**3**	**0**
2006–07	*Hull C*	5	0	**5**	**0**
2006–07	*Leicester C*	9	1	**9**	**1**

ZIEGLER, Reto (M) 80 1
H: 6 0 W: 12 06 b.Nyon 16-1-86
Source: FC Gland, Servette, Terre-Sainte, Lausanne. *Honours:* Switzerland Under-21, 5 full caps.

2002–03	Grasshoppers	10	0		
2003–04	Grasshoppers	28	0	**38**	**0**
2004–05	Tottenham H	23	1		
2005–06	Tottenham H	0	0		
2005–06	*Hamburg*	8	0	**8**	**0**
2005–06	*Wigan Ath*	10	0	**10**	**0**
2006–07	Tottenham H	1	0	**24**	**1**

To Sampdoria (loan) January 2007

ZOKORA, Didier (D) 221 1
H: 5 10 W: 11 00 b.Abidjan 14-12-80
Honours: Ivory Coast 41 full caps.

2000–01	Genk	28	0		
2001–02	Genk	30	0		
2002–03	Genk	33	0		
2003–04	Genk	33	1	**124**	**1**
2004–05	St Etienne	35	0		
2005–06	St Etienne	31	0	**66**	**0**
2006–07	Tottenham H	31	0	**31**	**0**

Scholars
Archibald-Henville, Troy Patrick; Casey, Chris; Fraser-Allen, Kyle; Hughton, Cian James; Hutchins, Daniel Sean; Hutton, David; Medley, Luke Anthony Cleve; Mtandari, Takura Ndinadzo; Wells, Matthew Elliott.

TRANMERE R (83)

ACHTERBERG, John (G) 286 0
H: 6 1 W: 14 03 b.Utrecht 8-7-71
Source: VV RUC, Utrecht.

1993–94	NAC	1	0		

1994–95	NAC	2	0		
1995–96	NAC	6	0	**9**	**0**
1996–97	Eindhoven	32	0	**32**	**0**

From Utrecht.

1998–99	Tranmere R	24	0		
1999–2000	Tranmere R	26	0		
2000–01	Tranmere R	25	0		
2001–02	Tranmere R	25	0		
2002–03	Tranmere R	38	0		
2003–04	Tranmere R	45	0		
2004–05	Tranmere R	39	0		
2005–06	Tranmere R	19	0		
2006–07	Tranmere R	4	0	**245**	**0**

BEAHON, Thomas (M) 0 0

H: 5 8 W: 10 02 b.Wirral 18-9-88

Source: Scholar.

2006–07	Tranmere R	0	0		

CANSDELL-SHERIFF, Shane (D) 128 10

H: 5 11 W: 11 08 b.Sydney 10-11-82

Source: From NSW Academy. *Honours:* Australia Youth, Under-23.

1999–2000	Leeds U	0	0		
2000–01	Leeds U	0	0		
2001–02	Leeds U	0	0		
2002–03	Leeds U	0	0		
2002–03	*Rochdale*	3	0	**3**	**0**
2003–04	Aarhus	29	4		
2004–05	Aarhus	26	2		
2005–06	Aarhus	27	1	**82**	**7**
2006–07	Tranmere R	43	3	**43**	**3**

CURRAN, Craig (F) 4 4

H: 5 9 W: 11 09 b.Liverpool 23-9-89

Source: Scholar.

2006–07	Tranmere R	4	4	**4**	**4**

DAVIES, Steve (F) 50 3

H: 6 0 W: 12 00 b.Liverpool 29-12-87

Source: Scholar.

2005–06	Tranmere R	22	2		
2006–07	Tranmere R	28	1	**50**	**3**

ELLISON, Kevin (M) 157 17

H: 6 0 W: 12 00 b.Liverpool 23-2-79

Source: Altrincham.

2000–01	Leicester C	1	0		
2001–02	Leicester C	0	0	**1**	**0**
2001–02	Stockport Co	11	0		
2002–03	Stockport Co	23	1		
2003–04	Stockport Co	14	1	**48**	**2**
2003–04	*Lincoln C*	11	0	**11**	**0**
2004–05	Chester C	24	9	**24**	**9**
2004–05	Hull C	16	1		
2005–06	Hull C	23	1	**39**	**2**
2006–07	Tranmere R	34	4	**34**	**4**

GOODISON, Ian (D) 204 3

H: 6 1 W: 13 04 b.St James, Jamaica 21-11-72

Source: Olympic Gardens. *Honours:* Jamaica 100 full caps, 9 goals.

1999–2000	Hull C	18	0		
2000–01	Hull C	36	1		
2001–02	Hull C	16	0		
2002–03	Hull C	0	0	**70**	**1**

From Seba U.

2003–04	Tranmere R	12	0		
2004–05	Tranmere R	44	1		
2005–06	Tranmere R	38	1		
2006–07	Tranmere R	40	0	**134**	**2**

GREENACRE, Chris (F) 320 94

H: 5 9 W: 12 09 b.Halifax 23-12-77

Source: Trainee.

1995–96	Manchester C	0	0		
1996–97	Manchester C	4	0		
1997–98	Manchester C	3	1		
1997–98	*Cardiff C*	11	2	**11**	**2**
1997–98	*Blackpool*	4	0	**4**	**0**
1998–99	Manchester C	1	0		
1998–99	*Scarborough*	12	2	**12**	**2**
1999–2000	Manchester C	0	0	**8**	**1**
1999–2000	Mansfield T	31	9		
2000–01	Mansfield T	46	19		
2001–02	Mansfield T	44	21	**121**	**49**
2002–03	Stoke C	30	4		
2003–04	Stoke C	13	2		
2004–05	Stoke C	32	1	**75**	**7**
2005–06	Tranmere R	45	16		
2006–07	Tranmere R	44	17	**89**	**33**

HARRISON, Danny (M) 124 5

H: 5 11 W: 12 04 b.Liverpool 4-11-82

Source: Scholar.

2001–02	Tranmere R	1	0		
2002–03	Tranmere R	12	0		
2003–04	Tranmere R	32	2		
2004–05	Tranmere R	32	0		
2005–06	Tranmere R	35	2		
2006–07	Tranmere R	12	1	**124**	**5**

HENRY, Paul (M) 0 0

H: 5 8 W: 11 06 b.Liverpool 28-1-88

Source: Scholar.

2005–06	Tranmere R	0	0		
2006–07	Tranmere R	0	0		

JAMES, Olly (D) 1 0

H: 6 0 W: 11 10 b.Birkenhead 13-1-87

Source: Scholar.

2004–05	Tranmere R	0	0		
2005–06	Tranmere R	1	0		
2006–07	Tranmere R	0	0	**1**	**0**

JENNINGS, Steven (M) 66 1

H: 5 7 W: 11 11 b.Liverpool 28-10-84

Source: Scholar.

2002–03	Tranmere R	0	0		
2003–04	Tranmere R	4	0		
2004–05	Tranmere R	11	0		
2005–06	Tranmere R	38	1		
2006–07	Tranmere R	2	0	**55**	**1**
2006–07	*Hereford U*	11	0	**11**	**0**

JOHNSTON, Michael (D) 0 0

H: 5 9 W: 12 03 b.Birkenhead 16-12-87

Source: Scholar.

2005–06	Tranmere R	0	0		
2006–07	Tranmere R	0	0		

JONES, Mike (M) 14 1

H: 5 11 W: 12 04 b.Birkenhead 15-8-87

Source: Scholar.

2005–06	Tranmere R	1	0		
2006–07	Tranmere R	0	0	**1**	**0**
2006–07	*Shrewsbury T*	13	1	**13**	**1**

McATEER, Jason (M) 420 24

H: 5 11 W: 13 01 b.Birkenhead 18-6-71

Source: Marine. *Honours:* Eire B, 52 full caps, 3 goals.

1991–92	Bolton W	0	0		
1992–93	Bolton W	21	0		
1993–94	Bolton W	46	3		
1994–95	Bolton W	43	5		
1995–96	Bolton W	4	0	**114**	**8**
1995–96	Liverpool	29	0		
1996–97	Liverpool	37	1		
1997–98	Liverpool	21	2		
1998–99	Liverpool	13	0	**100**	**3**
1998–99	Blackburn R	13	1		
1999–2000	Blackburn R	28	2		
2000–01	Blackburn R	27	1		
2001–02	Blackburn R	4	0	**72**	**4**
2001–02	Sunderland	26	2		
2002–03	Sunderland	9	1		
2003–04	Sunderland	18	2	**53**	**5**
2004–05	Tranmere R	34	4		
2005–06	Tranmere R	29	0		
2006–07	Tranmere R	18	0	**81**	**4**

McCREADY, Chris (D) 118 1

H: 6 1 W: 12 05 b.Ellesmere Port 5-9-81

Source: Scholar.

2000–01	Crewe Alex	0	0		
2001–02	Crewe Alex	1	0		
2002–03	Crewe Alex	8	0		
2003–04	Crewe Alex	22	0		
2004–05	Crewe Alex	20	0		
2005–06	Crewe Alex	25	0	**76**	**0**
2006–07	Tranmere R	42	1	**42**	**1**

McLAREN, Paul (M) 377 17

H: 6 0 W: 13 04 b.High Wycombe 17-11-76

Source: Trainee.

1993–94	Luton T	1	0		
1994–95	Luton T	0	0		
1995–96	Luton T	12	1		
1996–97	Luton T	24	0		
1997–98	Luton T	43	0		
1998–99	Luton T	23	0		
1999–2000	Luton T	29	1		
2000–01	Luton T	35	2	**167**	**4**
2001–02	Sheffield W	35	2		
2002–03	Sheffield W	36	4		
2003–04	Sheffield W	25	2	**96**	**8**
2004–05	Rotherham U	33	1		
2005–06	Rotherham U	39	3	**72**	**4**
2006–07	Tranmere R	42	1	**42**	**1**

MULLIN, John (M) 363 31

H: 6 0 W: 11 10 b.Bury 11-8-75

Source: School.

1992–93	Burnley	0	0		
1993–94	Burnley	6	1		
1994–95	Burnley	12	1		
1995–96	Sunderland	10	1		
1996–97	Sunderland	10	1		
1997–98	Sunderland	6	0		
1997–98	*Preston NE*	7	0	**7**	**0**
1997–98	*Burnley*	6	0		
1998–99	Sunderland	9	2	**35**	**4**
1999–2000	Burnley	37	5		
2000–01	Burnley	36	3		
2001–02	Burnley	4	0	**101**	**10**
2001–02	Rotherham U	34	2		
2002–03	Rotherham U	34	3		
2003–04	Rotherham U	38	4		
2004–05	Rotherham U	31	1		
2005–06	Rotherham U	43	2	**180**	**12**
2006–07	Tranmere R	40	5	**40**	**5**

PALETHORPE, Philip (G) 0 0

H: 6 2 W: 11 08 b.Wallasey 17-9-86

Source: Scholar.

2003–04	Tranmere R	0	0		
2004–05	Tranmere R	0	0		
2005–06	Tranmere R	0	0		
2006–07	Tranmere R	0	0		

SHUKER, Chris (M) 193 26

H: 5 5 W: 9 03 b.Liverpool 9-5-82

Source: Scholarship.

1999–2000	Manchester C	0	0		
2000–01	Manchester C	0	0		
2000–01	*Macclesfield T*	9	1	**9**	**1**
2001–02	Manchester C	2	0		
2002–03	Manchester C	3	0		
2002–03	*Walsall*	5	0	**5**	**0**
2003–04	Manchester C	0	0	**5**	**0**
2003–04	*Rochdale*	14	1	**14**	**1**
2003–04	*Hartlepool U*	14	1	**14**	**1**
2003–04	Barnsley	9	0		
2004–05	Barnsley	45	7		
2005–06	Barnsley	46	10	**100**	**17**
2006–07	Tranmere R	46	6	**46**	**6**

STOCKDALE, Robbie (D) 184 3

H: 6 0 W: 11 03 b.Middlesbrough 30-11-79

Source: Trainee. *Honours:* England Under-21, B, Scotland 5 full caps.

1997–98	Middlesbrough	1	0		
1998–99	Middlesbrough	19	0		
1999–2000	Middlesbrough	11	1		
2000–01	Middlesbrough	0	0		
2000–01	*Sheffield W*	6	0	**6**	**0**
2001–02	Middlesbrough	28	1		
2002–03	Middlesbrough	14	0		
2003–04	Middlesbrough	2	0	**75**	**2**
2003–04	*West Ham U*	7	0	**7**	**0**
2003–04	*Rotherham U*	16	1		
2004–05	Rotherham U	27	0	**43**	**1**
2004–05	Hull C	14	0		
2005–06	Hull C	0	0	**14**	**0**
2005–06	*Darlington*	3	0	**3**	**0**
2006–07	Tranmere R	36	0	**36**	**0**

TAYLOR, Gareth (F) 441 118

H: 6 2 W: 13 07 b.Weston-Super-Mare 25-2-73

Source: Southampton Trainee. *Honours:* Wales Under-21, 15 full caps, 1 goal.

1991–92	Bristol R	1	0		
1992–93	Bristol R	0	0		
1993–94	Bristol R	0	0		
1994–95	Bristol R	39	12		
1995–96	Bristol R	7	4	**47**	**16**
1995–96	Crystal Palace	20	1	**20**	**1**
1995–96	Sheffield U	10	2		
1996–97	Sheffield U	34	12		
1997–98	Sheffield U	28	10		

1998–99	Sheffield U	12	1	**84**	**25**
1998–99	Manchester C	26	4		
1999–2000	Manchester C	17	5		
1999–2000	*Port Vale*	4	0	**4**	**0**
1999–2000	*QPR*	6	1	**6**	**1**
2000–01	Manchester C	0	0	**43**	**9**
2000–01	*Burnley*	15	4		
2001–02	Burnley	40	16		
2002–03	Burnley	40	16		
2003–04	Burnley	0	0	**95**	**36**
2003–04	Nottingham F	34	8		
2004–05	Nottingham F	36	7		
2005–06	Nottingham F	20	4	**90**	**19**
2005–06	*Crewe Alex*	15	4	**15**	**4**
2006–07	Tranmere R	37	7	**37**	**7**

TREMARCO, Carl (D) **44** **1**

H: 5 8 W: 11 11 b.Liverpool 11-10-85

Source: Scholar.

2003–04	Tranmere R	0	0		
2004–05	Tranmere R	3	0		
2005–06	Tranmere R	18	1		
2006–07	Tranmere R	23	0	**44**	**1**

WARD, Gavin (G) **316** **1**

H: 6 3 W: 14 12 b.Sutton Coldfield 30-6-70

Source: Aston Villa Trainee.

1988–89	Shrewsbury T	0	0		
1989–90	WBA	0	0		
1989–90	Cardiff C	2	0		
1990–91	Cardiff C	1	0		
1991–92	Cardiff C	24	0		
1992–93	Cardiff C	32	0	**59**	**0**
1993–94	Leicester C	32	0		
1994–95	Leicester C	6	0	**38**	**0**
1995–96	Bradford C	36	0	**36**	**0**
1995–96	Bolton W	5	0		
1996–97	Bolton W	11	0		
1997–98	Bolton W	6	0		
1998–99	Bolton W	0	0	**22**	**0**
1998–99	*Burnley*	17	0	**17**	**0**
1998–99	Stoke C	6	0		
1999–2000	Stoke C	46	0		
2000–01	Stoke C	17	0		
2001–02	Stoke C	10	0	**79**	**0**
2002–03	Walsall	7	0	**7**	**0**
2003–04	Coventry C	12	0	**12**	**0**
2003–04	*Barnsley*	1	0	**1**	**0**
2004–05	Preston NE	7	0		
2005–06	Preston NE	0	0	**7**	**0**
2006–07	Tranmere R	38	1	**38**	**1**

ZOLA, Calvin (F) **91** **16**

H: 6 3 W: 14 06 b.Kinshasa 31-12-84

Source: Scholar.

2001–02	Newcastle U	0	0		
2002–03	Newcastle U	0	0		
2003–04	Newcastle U	0	0		
2003–04	*Oldham Ath*	25	5	**25**	**5**
2004–05	Tranmere R	15	2		
2005–06	Tranmere R	22	4		
2006–07	Tranmere R	29	5	**66**	**11**

WALSALL (84)

BEDEAU, Anthony (F) **330** **59**

H: 5 10 W: 10 06 b.Hammersmith 24-3-79

Source: Trainee. *Honours:* Grenada full caps.

1995–96	Torquay U	4	0		
1996–97	Torquay U	8	1		
1997–98	Torquay U	34	5		
1998–99	Torquay U	36	9		
1999–2000	Torquay U	38	16		
2000–01	Torquay U	34	5		
2001–02	Torquay U	21	4		
2001–02	*Barnsley*	3	0	**3**	**0**
2002–03	Torquay U	40	6		
2003–04	Torquay U	24	1		
2004–05	Torquay U	35	2		
2005–06	Torquay U	31	9	**305**	**58**
2006–07	Walsall	18	1	**18**	**1**
2006–07	*Bury*	4	0	**4**	**0**

BOSSU, Bertrand (G) **18** **0**

H: 6 7 W: 14 00 b.Calais 14-10-80

1999–2000	Barnet	0	0		
2000–01	Barnet	0	0		
2001–02	Barnet	0	0		
2002–03	Barnet	0	0		

From Hayes.

2003–04	Gillingham	4	0		
2004–05	Gillingham	2	0	**6**	**0**
2004–05	*Torquay U*	2	0	**2**	**0**
2004–05	*Oldham Ath*	0	0		
2005–06	Darlington	9	0	**9**	**0**
2006–07	Walsall	1	0	**1**	**0**

BRADLEY, Mark (D) **5** **0**

H: 6 0 W: 11 05 b.Dudley 14-1-88

Source: Scholar. *Honours:* Wales Youth, Under-21.

2004–05	Walsall	1	0		
2005–06	Walsall	3	0		
2006–07	Walsall	1	0	**5**	**0**

BUTLER, Martin (F) **421** **120**

H: 5 11 W: 11 09 b.Wordsley 15-9-74

Source: Trainee.

1993–94	Walsall	15	3		
1994–95	Walsall	8	0		
1995–96	Walsall	28	4		
1996–97	Walsall	23	1		
1997–98	Cambridge U	31	10		
1998–99	Cambridge U	46	17		
1999–2000	Cambridge U	26	14	**103**	**41**
1999–2000	Reading	17	4		
2000–01	Reading	45	24		
2001–02	Reading	17	2		
2002–03	Reading	21	2		
2003–04	Reading	3	0	**103**	**32**
2003–04	Rotherham U	37	15		
2004–05	Rotherham U	21	6		
2005–06	Rotherham U	39	7	**97**	**28**
2006–07	Walsall	44	11	**118**	**19**

CEDERQVIST, Par (F) **11** **0**

H: 6 2 W: 12 13 b.Sweden 10-3-80

Source: Raufoss.

2006–07	Walsall	11	0	**11**	**0**

CONSTABLE, James (F) **23** **3**

H: 6 2 W: 12 12 b.Malmesbury 4-10-84

Source: Chippenham T.

2005–06	Walsall	17	3		
2006–07	Walsall	6	0	**23**	**3**

DANN, Scott (D) **31** **4**

H: 6 2 W: 12 00 b.Liverpool 14-2-87

Source: Scholar.

2004–05	Walsall	1	0		
2005–06	Walsall	0	0		
2006–07	Walsall	30	4	**31**	**4**

DEENEY, Troy (F) **1** **0**

H: 5 11 W: 12 00 b.Chelmsley 29-6-88

Source: Chelmsley T.

2006–07	Walsall	1	0	**1**	**0**

DEMONTAGNAC, Ishmel (F) **43** **3**

H: 5 10 W: 11 05 b.London 15-6-88

Source: Charlton Ath Scholar. *Honours:* England Youth.

2005–06	Walsall	24	2		
2006–07	Walsall	19	1	**43**	**3**

DOBSON, Michael (D) **217** **6**

H: 6 0 W: 12 04 b.Isleworth 9-4-81

Source: Trainee.

1999–2000	Brentford	0	0		
2000–01	Brentford	26	0		
2001–02	Brentford	39	0		
2002–03	Brentford	46	1		
2003–04	Brentford	42	1		
2004–05	Brentford	18	1		
2005–06	Brentford	6	0	**177**	**3**
2005–06	*Reading*	1	0	**1**	**0**
2006–07	Walsall	39	3	**39**	**3**

FANGUEIRO, Carlos (M) **288** **51**

H: 5 9 W: 11 05 b.Matosinhos 19-12-76

1995–96	Leixoes	29	8		
1996–97	Leixoes	32	7	**61**	**15**
1997–98	Guimaraes	19	1		
1998–99	Maia	30	3	**30**	**3**
1999–2000	Gil Vicente	31	7	**31**	**7**
2000–01	Guimaraes	30	4		
2001–02	Guimaraes	30	10		
2002–03	Guimaraes	27	7		
2003–04	Guimaraes	17	2	**123**	**24**
2004–05	Uniao Leiria	29	1	**29**	**1**
2005–06	Millwall	9	0	**9**	**0**
2006–07	Walsall	5	1	**5**	**1**

To Ionikos January 2007

FOX, Daniel (D) **88** **4**

H: 5 11 W: 12 06 b.Crewe 29-5-86

Source: Scholar.

2004–05	Everton	0	0		
2004–05	*Stranraer*	11	1	**11**	**1**
2005–06	Walsall	33	0		
2006–07	Walsall	44	3	**77**	**3**

GERRARD, Anthony (D) **77** **1**

H: 6 2 W: 13 07 b.Liverpool 6-2-86

Source: Scholar. *Honours:* Eire Youth.

2004–05	Everton	0	0		
2004–05	*Walsall*	8	0		
2005–06	Walsall	34	0		
2006–07	Walsall	35	1	**77**	**1**

GILMARTIN, Rene (G) **2** **0**

H: 6 5 W: 13 06 b.Dublin 31-5-87

Source: St Patrick's BC. *Honours:* Eire Youth, Under-21.

2005–06	Walsall	2	0		
2006–07	Walsall	0	0	**2**	**0**

INCE, Clayton (G) **169** **0**

H: 6 3 W: 13 03 b.Trinidad 13-7-72

Source: Defence Force. *Honours:* Trinidad & Tobago 63 full caps.

1999–2000	Crewe Alex	1	0		
2000–01	Crewe Alex	1	0		
2001–02	Crewe Alex	19	0		
2002–03	Crewe Alex	43	0		
2003–04	Crewe Alex	36	0		
2004–05	Crewe Alex	23	0	**123**	**0**
2005–06	Coventry C	1	0	**1**	**0**
2006–07	Walsall	45	0	**45**	**0**

KEATES, Dean (M) **332** **39**

H: 5 6 W: 10 06 b.Walsall 30-6-78

Source: Trainee.

1996–97	Walsall	2	0		
1997–98	Walsall	33	1		
1998–99	Walsall	43	2		
1999–2000	Walsall	35	1		
2000–01	Walsall	33	4		
2001–02	Walsall	13	1		
2002–03	Hull C	36	4		
2003–04	Hull C	14	0	**50**	**4**
2003–04	Kidderminster H	8	2		
2004–05	Kidderminster H	41	5	**49**	**7**
2005–06	Lincoln C	21	4	**21**	**4**
2005–06	Walsall	14	2		
2006–07	Walsall	39	13	**212**	**24**

KINSELLA, Mark (M) **469** **48**

H: 5 8 W: 11 04 b.Dublin 12-8-72

Source: Home Farm. *Honours:* Eire 48 full caps, 3 goals.

1989–90	Colchester U	6	0		
1990–91	Colchester U	0	0		
1991–92	Colchester U	0	0		
1992–93	Colchester U	38	6		
1993–94	Colchester U	42	8		
1994–95	Colchester U	42	6		
1995–96	Colchester U	45	5		
1996–97	Colchester U	7	2	**180**	**27**
1996–97	Charlton Ath	37	6		
1997–98	Charlton Ath	46	6		
1998–99	Charlton Ath	38	2		
1999–2000	Charlton Ath	38	3		
2000–01	Charlton Ath	32	2		
2001–02	Charlton Ath	17	0		
2002–03	Charlton Ath	0	0	**208**	**19**
2002–03	Aston Villa	19	0		
2003–04	Aston Villa	2	0	**21**	**0**
2003–04	WBA	18	1	**18**	**1**
2004–05	Walsall	22	0		
2005–06	Walsall	9	0		
2006–07	Walsall	11	1	**42**	**1**

McDERMOTT, David (M) **1** **0**

H: 5 5 W: 10 00 b.Stourbridge 6-2-88

Source: Scholar.

2004–05	Walsall	0	0		
2005–06	Walsall	1	0		
2006–07	Walsall	0	0	**1**	**0**

McKEOWN, James (G) **0** **0**

H: 6 1 W: 13 07 b.Birmingham 24-7-89

Source: Scholar.

2005–06	Walsall	0	0		
2006–07	Walsall	0	0		

NICHOLLS, Alex (F) **8 0**
H: 5 10 W: 11 00 b.Stourbridge 9-12-87
Source: Scholar.

2005–06	Walsall	8	0		
2006–07	Walsall	0	0	**8**	**0**

PEAD, Craig (M) **135 3**
H: 5 9 W: 11 06 b.Bromsgrove 15-9-81
Source: Trainee. *Honours:* England Youth, Under-20.

1998–99	Coventry C	0	0		
1999–2000	Coventry C	0	0		
2000–01	Coventry C	0	0		
2001–02	Coventry C	1	0		
2002–03	Coventry C	24	2		
2003–04	Coventry C	17	1		
2004–05	Coventry C	0	0	**42**	**3**
2004–05	*Notts Co*	5	0	**5**	**0**
2004–05	*Walsall*	8	0		
2005–06	Walsall	39	0		
2006–07	Walsall	41	0	**88**	**0**

PICKEN, Allan (D) **2 0**
H: 6 2 W: 13 12 b.Sydney 17-1-81
Source: Newcastle U Jets.

2006–07	Walsall	2	0	**2**	**0**

ROPER, Ian (D) **306 6**
H: 6 3 W: 14 00 b.Nuneaton 20-6-77
Source: Trainee.

1994–95	Walsall	0	0		
1995–96	Walsall	5	0		
1996–97	Walsall	11	0		
1997–98	Walsall	21	0		
1998–99	Walsall	32	1		
1999–2000	Walsall	34	1		
2000–01	Walsall	25	0		
2001–02	Walsall	27	0		
2002–03	Walsall	40	0		
2003–04	Walsall	33	0		
2004–05	Walsall	26	0		
2005–06	Walsall	25	0		
2006–07	Walsall	27	4	**306**	**6**

SAM, Hector (F) **196 42**
H: 5 10 W: 12 07 b.Mount Hope 25-2-78
Source: San Juan Jabloteh. *Honours:* Trinidad & Tobago Under-21, 20 full caps, 2 goals.

2000–01	Wrexham	20	6		
2001–02	Wrexham	29	5		
2002–03	Wrexham	26	5		
2003–04	Wrexham	37	10		
2004–05	Wrexham	38	9	**150**	**35**
2005–06	Port Vale	4	0	**4**	**0**
2006–07	Walsall	42	7	**42**	**7**

SANSARA, Netan (D) **0 0**
H: 6 0 W: 12 00 b.Walsall 3-8-89
Source: Scholar. *Honours:* England Youth.

2006–07	Walsall	0	0

SMITH, Emmanuel (D) **3 0**
H: 6 2 W: 12 03 b.Birmingham 8-11-88
Source: Scholar.

2005–06	Walsall	0	0		
2006–07	Walsall	3	0	**3**	**0**

TAYLOR, Kris (M) **80 6**
H: 5 9 W: 11 05 b.Stafford 12-1-84
Source: Scholar. *Honours:* England Schools, Youth.

2000–01	Manchester U	0	0		
2001–02	Manchester U	0	0		
2002–03	Manchester U	0	0		
2002–03	Walsall	0	0		
2003–04	Walsall	11	1		
2004–05	Walsall	12	2		
2005–06	Walsall	22	2		
2006–07	Walsall	35	1	**80**	**6**

WESTWOOD, Chris (D) **323 13**
H: 5 11 W: 12 10 b.Dudley 13-2-77
Source: Trainee.

1995–96	Wolverhampton W	0	0		
1996–97	Wolverhampton W	0	0		
1997–98	Wolverhampton W	4	1		
1998–99	Wolverhampton W	0	0	**4**	**1**
1998–99	Hartlepool U	4	0		
1999–2000	Hartlepool U	37	0		
2000–01	Hartlepool U	46	1		
2001–02	Hartlepool U	35	1		
2002–03	Hartlepool U	46	1		
2003–04	Hartlepool U	45	0		
2004–05	Hartlepool U	37	4	**250**	**7**
2005–06	Walsall	29	3		
2006–07	Walsall	40	2	**69**	**5**

WRACK, Darren (M) **342 47**
H: 5 9 W: 12 02 b.Cleethorpes 5-5-76
Source: Trainee.

1994–95	Derby Co	16	1		
1995–96	Derby Co	10	0	**26**	**1**
1996–97	Grimsby T	12	1		
1996–97	*Shrewsbury T*	4	0	**4**	**0**
1997–98	Grimsby T	1	0	**13**	**1**
1998–99	Walsall	46	13		
1999–2000	Walsall	44	4		
2000–01	Walsall	28	4		
2001–02	Walsall	43	4		
2002–03	Walsall	43	6		
2003–04	Walsall	27	6		
2004–05	Walsall	43	7		
2005–06	Walsall	7	0		
2006–07	Walsall	18	1	**299**	**45**

WRIGHT, Mark (M) **124 9**
H: 5 11 W: 11 00 b.Wolverhampton 24-2-82
Source: Scholar.

2000–01	Walsall	4	0		
2001–02	Walsall	0	0		
2002–03	Walsall	5	0		
2003–04	Walsall	11	2		
2004–05	Walsall	37	2		
2005–06	Walsall	30	2		
2006–07	Walsall	37	3	**124**	**9**

WATFORD (85)

ASHIKODI, Moses (M) **20 2**
H: 6 0 W: 11 09 b.Lagos 27-6-87
Honours: FA Schools, England Youth.

2002–03	Millwall	5	0		
2003–04	Millwall	0	0	**5**	**0**
2004–05	West Ham U	0	0		
2005–06	West Ham U	0	0		
2005–06	*Gillingham*	4	0	**4**	**0**
2005–06	Rangers	1	0		
2006–07	Rangers	0	0	**1**	**0**
2006–07	Watford	2	0	**2**	**0**
2006–07	*Bradford C*	8	2	**8**	**2**

AVINEL, Cedric (D) **2 0**
H: 6 2 W: 13 03 b.Paris 11-9-86

2006–07	Creteil	1	0	**1**	**0**
2006–07	Watford	1	0	**1**	**0**

BANGURA, Alhassan (M) **53 1**
H: 5 11 W: 10 07 b.Freetown 24-1-88
Source: Scholar.

2004–05	Watford	2	0		
2005–06	Watford	35	1		
2006–07	Watford	16	0	**53**	**1**

BLIZZARD, Dominic (M) **44 2**
H: 6 2 W: 12 04 b.High Wycombe 2-9-83
Source: Scholar.

2001–02	Watford	0	0		
2002–03	Watford	0	0		
2003–04	Watford	2	1		
2004–05	Watford	17	1		
2005–06	Watford	10	0		
2006–07	Watford	0	0	**29**	**2**
2006–07	*Stockport Co*	7	0	**7**	**0**
2006–07	*Milton Keynes D*	8	0	**8**	**0**

BOUAZZA, Hameur (F) **96 11**
H: 5 10 W: 12 01 b.Evry 22-2-85
Source: Scholar. *Honours:* Algeria 1 full cap.

2003–04	Watford	9	1		
2004–05	Watford	28	1		
2005–06	Watford	14	1		
2005–06	*Swindon T*	13	2	**13**	**2**
2006–07	Watford	32	6	**83**	**9**

CAMPANA, Alex (M) **0 0**
H: 5 11 W: 12 01 b.Harrow 11-10-88
Source: Scholar.

2005–06	Watford	0	0
2006–07	Watford	0	0

CARLISLE, Clarke (D) **265 20**
H: 6 2 W: 14 11 b.Preston 14-10-79
Source: Trainee. *Honours:* England Under-21.

1997–98	Blackpool	11	2		
1998–99	Blackpool	39	1		
1999–2000	Blackpool	43	4	**93**	**7**
2000–01	QPR	27	3		
2001–02	QPR	0	0		
2002–03	QPR	36	2		
2003–04	QPR	33	1	**96**	**6**
2004–05	Leeds U	35	4	**35**	**4**
2005–06	Watford	32	3		
2006–07	Watford	4	0	**36**	**3**
2006–07	*Luton T*	5	0	**5**	**0**

CAVALLI, Johann (M) **119 13**
H: 5 6 W: 10 03 b.Ajaccio 12-9-81
Source: Nantes. *Honours:* France Youth.

2001–02	Lorient	3	0		
2002–03	Lorient	17	0		
2003–04	Creteil	30	6		
2003–04	Lorient	1	0	**21**	**0**
2004–05	Mallorca	0	0		
2004–05	Creteil	14	5	**44**	**11**
2005–06	Istres	35	1		
2006–07	Istres	16	1	**51**	**2**
2006–07	Watford	3	0	**3**	**0**

CHAMBERLAIN, Alec (G) **679 0**
H: 6 1 W: 14 01 b.March 20-6-64
Source: Ramsey T.

1981–82	Ipswich T	0	0		
1982–83	Colchester U	4	0		
1983–84	Colchester U	46	0		
1984–85	Colchester U	46	0		
1985–86	Colchester U	46	0		
1986–87	Colchester U	46	0	**188**	**0**
1987–88	Everton	0	0		
1987–88	*Tranmere R*	15	0	**15**	**0**
1988–89	Luton T	6	0		
1989–90	Luton T	38	0		
1990–91	Luton T	38	0		
1991–92	Luton T	24	0		
1992–93	Luton T	32	0	**138**	**0**
1992–93	*Chelsea*	0	0		
1993–94	Sunderland	43	0		
1994–95	Sunderland	18	0		
1994–95	*Liverpool*	0	0		
1995–96	Sunderland	29	0	**90**	**0**
1996–97	Watford	4	0		
1997–98	Watford	46	0		
1998–99	Watford	46	0		
1999–2000	Watford	27	0		
2000–01	Watford	21	0		
2001–02	Watford	32	0		
2002–03	Watford	42	0		
2003–04	Watford	21	0		
2004–05	Watford	5	0		
2005–06	Watford	3	0		
2006–07	Watford	1	0	**248**	**0**

CHAMBERS, James (D) **170 0**
H: 5 10 W: 11 11 b.West Bromwich 20-11-80
Source: Trainee. *Honours:* England Youth.

1998–99	WBA	0	0		
1999–2000	WBA	12	0		
2000–01	WBA	31	0		
2001–02	WBA	5	0		
2002–03	WBA	8	0		
2003–04	WBA	17	0		
2004–05	WBA	0	0	**73**	**0**
2004–05	Watford	40	0		
2005–06	Watford	38	0		
2006–07	Watford	12	0	**90**	**0**
2006–07	*Cardiff C*	7	0	**7**	**0**

DEMERIT, Jay (D) **88 7**
H: 6 2 W: 12 13 b.Green Bay 4-12-79
Source: Chicago Fire, Univ of Illinois, Northwood. *Honours:* USA 3 full caps.

2004–05	Watford	24	3		
2005–06	Watford	32	2		
2006–07	Watford	32	2	**88**	**7**

DIAGOURAGA, Toumani (M) **16 0**
H: 6 2 W: 11 05 b.Corbeil-Essones 10-6-87
Source: Scholar.

2004–05	Watford	0	0		
2005–06	Watford	1	0		
2005–06	*Swindon T*	8	0	**8**	**0**
2006–07	Watford	0	0	**1**	**0**
2006–07	*Rotherham U*	7	0	**7**	**0**

DOYLEY, Lloyd (D) **145 0**
H: 5 10 W: 12 13 b.Whitechapel 1-12-82
Source: Scholar.

2000–01	Watford	0	0		
2001–02	Watford	20	0		
2002–03	Watford	22	0		
2003–04	Watford	9	0		
2004–05	Watford	29	0		
2005–06	Watford	44	0		
2006–07	Watford	21	0	**145**	**0**

FRANCIS, Damien (M) **222 33**
H: 6 0 W: 11 10 b.Wandsworth 27-2-79
Source: Trainee. *Honours:* Jamaica 1 full cap.

1996–97	Wimbledon	0	0		
1997–98	Wimbledon	2	0		
1998–99	Wimbledon	0	0		
1999–2000	Wimbledon	9	0		
2000–01	Wimbledon	29	8		
2001–02	Wimbledon	23	1		
2002–03	Wimbledon	34	6	**97**	**15**
2003–04	Norwich C	41	7		
2004–05	Norwich C	32	7	**73**	**14**
2005–06	Wigan Ath	20	1	**20**	**1**
2006–07	Watford	32	3	**32**	**3**

GILL, Ben (M) **0 0**
H: 5 9 W: 10 11 b.Harrow 9-10-87
Source: Scholar.

2005–06	Watford	0	0		
2006–07	Watford	0	0		

GRANT, Joel (F) **7 0**
H: 6 0 W: 12 01 b.Hammersmith 26-8-87
Source: Scholar.

2005–06	Watford	7	0		
2006–07	Watford	0	0	**7**	**0**

HENDERSON, Darius (F) **188 44**
H: 6 3 W: 14 03 b.Sutton 7-9-81
Source: Trainee.

1999–2000	Reading	6	0		
2000–01	Reading	4	0		
2001–02	Reading	38	7		
2002–03	Reading	22	4		
2003–04	Reading	1	0	**71**	**11**
2003–04	*Brighton & HA*	10	2	**10**	**2**
2003–04	Gillingham	4	0		
2004–05	Gillingham	32	9	**36**	**9**
2004–05	*Swindon T*	6	5	**6**	**5**
2005–06	Watford	30	14		
2006–07	Watford	35	3	**65**	**17**

HOSKINS, Will (F) **82 23**
H: 5 11 W: 11 02 b.Nottingham 6-5-86
Source: Scholar. *Honours:* England Youth, Under-20.

2003–04	Rotherham U	4	2		
2004–05	Rotherham U	22	2		
2005–06	Rotherham U	23	4		
2006–07	Rotherham U	24	15	**73**	**23**
2006–07	Watford	9	0	**9**	**0**

JARRETT, Albert (M) **49 3**
H: 6 1 W: 10 07 b.Sierra Leone 23-10-84
Source: Dulwich Hamlet.

2002–03	Wimbledon	0	0		
2003–04	Wimbledon	9	0	**9**	**0**
2004–05	Brighton & HA	12	1		
2005–06	Brighton & HA	11	0	**23**	**1**
2005–06	*Swindon T*	6	0	**6**	**0**
2006–07	Watford	1	0	**1**	**0**
2006–07	*Boston U*	5	2	**5**	**2**
2006–07	*Milton Keynes D*	5	0	**5**	**0**

KABBA, Steven (F) **115 25**
H: 5 10 W: 11 03 b.Lambeth 7-3-81
Source: Trainee.

1999–2000	Crystal Palace	1	0		
2000–01	Crystal Palace	1	0		
2001–02	Crystal Palace	4	0		
2001–02	*Luton T*	3	0	**3**	**0**
2002–03	Crystal Palace	4	1	**10**	**1**
2002–03	*Grimsby T*	13	6	**13**	**6**
2002–03	Sheffield U	25	7		
2003–04	Sheffield U	1	0		
2004–05	Sheffield U	11	2		
2005–06	Sheffield U	34	9		
2006–07	Sheffield U	7	0	**78**	**18**
2006–07	Watford	11	0	**11**	**0**

KAMARA, Sheku (D) **0 0**
b.Lambeth 15-11-87
Source: Charlton Ath Scholar.

2006–07	Watford	0	0		

KING, Marlon (F) **267 89**
H: 5 10 W: 12 10 b.Dulwich 26-4-80
Source: From Trainee. *Honours:* Jamaica 12 full caps, 4 goals.

1998–99	Barnet	22	6		
1999–2000	Barnet	31	8	**53**	**14**
2000–01	Gillingham	38	15		
2001–02	Gillingham	42	17		
2002–03	Gillingham	10	4		
2003–04	Gillingham	11	4	**101**	**40**
2003–04	Nottingham F	24	5		
2004–05	Nottingham F	26	5		
2004–05	*Leeds U*	9	0	**9**	**0**
2005–06	Nottingham F	0	0	**50**	**10**
2005–06	Watford	41	21		
2006–07	Watford	13	4	**54**	**25**

LEE, Richard (G) **47 0**
H: 6 0 W: 12 06 b.Oxford 5-10-82
Source: Scholar. *Honours:* England Under-20.

2000–01	Watford	0	0		
2001–02	Watford	0	0		
2002–03	Watford	4	0		
2003–04	Watford	0	0		
2004–05	Watford	33	0		
2005–06	Watford	0	0		
2005–06	*Blackburn R*	0	0		
2006–07	Watford	10	0	**47**	**0**

LOACH, Scott (G) **0 0**
H: 6 1 W: 13 01 b.Nottingham 27-5-88
Source: Lincoln C.

2006–07	Watford	0	0		

MACKAY, Malky (D) **389 30**
H: 6 2 W: 14 07 b.Bellshill 19-2-72
Source: From Queen's Park Youth. *Honours:* Scotland 5 full caps.

1990–91	Queen's Park	10	0		
1991–92	Queen's Park	27	3		
1992–93	Queen's Park	33	3	**70**	**6**
1993–94	Celtic	0	0		
1994–95	Celtic	1	0		
1995–96	Celtic	11	1		
1996–97	Celtic	20	1		
1997–98	Celtic	4	1		
1998–99	Celtic	1	1	**37**	**4**
1998–99	Norwich C	27	1		
1999–2000	Norwich C	21	0		
2000–01	Norwich C	38	1		
2001–02	Norwich C	44	3		
2002–03	Norwich C	37	6		
2003–04	Norwich C	45	4		
2004–05	Norwich C	0	0	**212**	**15**
2004–05	West Ham U	18	2		
2005–06	West Ham U	0	0	**18**	**2**
2005–06	Watford	38	3		
2006–07	Watford	14	0	**52**	**3**

MAHON, Gavin (M) **322 15**
H: 5 11 W: 13 07 b.Birmingham 2-1-77
Source: Trainee.

1995–96	Wolverhampton W	0	0		
1996–97	Hereford U	11	1		
1997–98	Hereford U	0	0		
1998–99	Hereford U	0	0	**11**	**1**
1998–99	Brentford	29	4		
1999–2000	Brentford	37	3		
2000–01	Brentford	40	1		
2001–02	Brentford	35	0	**141**	**8**
2001–02	Watford	6	0		
2002–03	Watford	17	0		
2003–04	Watford	32	2		
2004–05	Watford	43	0		
2005–06	Watford	38	3		
2006–07	Watford	34	1	**170**	**6**

MARIAPPA, Adrian (D) **22 0**
H: 5 10 W: 11 12 b.Harrow 3-10-86
Source: Scholar.

2005–06	Watford	3	0		
2006–07	Watford	19	0	**22**	**0**

McNAMEE, Anthony (M) **96 2**
H: 5 6 W: 10 03 b.Kensington 13-7-84
Source: Scholar. *Honours:* England Youth, Under-20.

2001–02	Watford	7	1		
2002–03	Watford	23	0		
2003–04	Watford	2	0		
2004–05	Watford	14	0		
2005–06	Watford	38	1		
2006–07	Watford	7	0	**91**	**2**
2006–07	*Crewe Alex*	5	0	**5**	**0**

OSBORNE, Junior (D) **2 0**
H: 5 11 W: 11 13 b.Watford 12-2-88
Source: Scholar.

2004–05	Watford	1	0		
2005–06	Watford	1	0		
2006–07	Watford	0	0	**2**	**0**

PARKES, Jordan (D) **0 0**
H: 6 0 W: 12 00 b.Hemel Hempstead 26-7-89
Source: Scholar. *Honours:* England Youth.

2006–07	Watford	0	0		

POWELL, Chris (D) **631 5**
H: 5 11 W: 11 12 b.Lambeth 8-9-69
Source: Trainee. *Honours:* England 5 full caps.

1987–88	Crystal Palace	0	0		
1988–89	Crystal Palace	3	0		
1989–90	Crystal Palace	0	0	**3**	**0**
1989–90	*Aldershot*	11	0	**11**	**0**
1990–91	Southend U	45	1		
1991–92	Southend U	44	0		
1992–93	Southend U	42	2		
1993–94	Southend U	46	0		
1994–95	Southend U	44	0		
1995–96	Southend U	27	0	**248**	**3**
1995–96	Derby Co	19	0		
1996–97	Derby Co	35	0		
1997–98	Derby Co	37	1	**91**	**1**
1998–99	Charlton Ath	38	0		
1999–2000	Charlton Ath	40	0		
2000–01	Charlton Ath	33	0		
2001–02	Charlton Ath	36	1		
2002–03	Charlton Ath	37	0		
2003–04	Charlton Ath	16	0		
2004–05	Charlton Ath	0	0		
2004–05	West Ham U	36	0	**36**	**0**
2005–06	Charlton Ath	27	0	**227**	**1**
2006–07	Watford	15	0	**15**	**0**

PRISKIN, Tamas (F) **84 26**
H: 6 2 W: 13 03 b.Komarno 27-9-86
Honours: Hungary Under-21, 8 full caps, 6 goals.

2002–03	Gyor	3	0		
2003–04	Gyor	17	5		
2004–05	Gyor	23	8		
2005–06	Gyor	25	11	**68**	**24**
2006–07	Watford	16	2	**16**	**2**

RINALDI, Douglas (D) **7 1**
H: 6 0 W: 12 03 b.Erval Seco 10-2-84
Source: Veranopolis.

2006–07	Watford	7	1	**7**	**1**

ROBINSON, Theo (M) **2 0**
H: 5 9 W: 10 03 b.Birmingham 22-1-89
Source: Scholar.

2005–06	Watford	1	0		
2006–07	Watford	1	0	**2**	**0**

SEANLA, Claude (F) **0 0**
b.Ivory Coast 2-6-88
Source: Scholar.

2006–07	Watford	0	0		

SHITTU, Dan (D) **216 20**
H: 6 2 W: 16 03 b.Lagos 2-9-80
Honours: Nigeria 3 full caps.

1999–2000	Charlton Ath	0	0		
2000–01	Charlton Ath	0	0		
2000–01	*Blackpool*	17	2	**17**	**2**

2001–02 Charlton Ath 0 0
2001–02 QPR 27 2
2002–03 QPR 43 7
2003–04 QPR 20 0
2004–05 QPR 34 4
2005–06 QPR 45 4 **169 17**
2006–07 Watford 30 1 **30 1**

SMITH, Tommy (F) 306 58
H: 5 8 W: 11 04 b.Hemel Hempstead 22-5-80
Source: Trainee. *Honours:* England Youth, Under-21.
1997–98 Watford 1 0
1998–99 Watford 8 2
1999–2000 Watford 22 2
2000–01 Watford 43 11
2001–02 Watford 40 11
2002–03 Watford 35 7
2003–04 Watford 0 0
2003–04 Sunderland 35 4 **35 4**
2004–05 Derby Co 42 11
2005–06 Derby Co 43 8
2006–07 Derby Co 5 1 **90 20**
2006–07 Watford 32 1 **181 34**

STEWART, Jordan (D) 180 6
H: 6 0 W: 12 09 b.Birmingham 3-3-82
Source: Trainee. *Honours:* England Youth, Under-21.
1999–2000 Leicester C 1 0
1999–2000 *Bristol R* 4 0 **4 0**
2000–01 Leicester C 0 0
2001–02 Leicester C 12 0
2002–03 Leicester C 37 4
2003–04 Leicester C 25 1
2004–05 Leicester C 35 1 **110 6**
2005–06 Watford 35 0
2006–07 Watford 31 0 **66 0**

WILLIAMS, Gareth (M) 223 12
H: 6 1 W: 12 03 b.Glasgow 16-12-81
Source: Trainee. *Honours:* Scotland Youth, B, Under-21, 5 full caps.
1998–99 Nottingham F 0 0
1999–2000 Nottingham F 2 0
2000–01 Nottingham F 17 0
2001–02 Nottingham F 44 0
2002–03 Nottingham F 40 3
2003–04 Nottingham F 39 6 **142 9**
2004–05 Leicester C 33 1
2005–06 Leicester C 31 1
2006–07 Leicester C 14 1 **78 3**
2006–07 Watford 3 0 **3 0**

WILLIAMSON, Lee (M) 242 12
H: 5 10 W: 10 04 b.Derby 7-6-82
Source: Trainee.
1999–2000 Mansfield T 4 0
2000–01 Mansfield T 15 0
2001–02 Mansfield T 46 3
2002–03 Mansfield T 40 0
2003–04 Mansfield T 35 0
2004–05 Mansfield T 4 0 **144 3**
2004–05 Northampton T 37 0 **37 0**
2005–06 Rotherham U 37 4
2006–07 Rotherham U 19 5 **56 9**
2006–07 Watford 5 0 **5 0**

Scholars
Beech, Aaron; Bennett, Dale Owen; Brown, Raphael; Clarke, Ewan; Forbes, Kieron; Henderson, Liam Marc; Maxwell, Loren; Morgan, Aaron; Young, Lewis.

WBA (86)

ALBRECHTSEN, Martin (D) 247 5
H: 6 1 W: 12 13 b.Copenhagen 31-3-80
Source: Denmark Youth, Under-21, 4 full caps.
1998–99 Aalborg 9 1
1999–2000 Aalborg 31 1
2000–01 Aalborg 30 0
2001–02 Aalborg 19 1 **89 3**
2001–02 FC Copenhagen 14 0
2002–03 FC Copenhagen 27 0
2003–04 FC Copenhagen 31 0 **72 0**
2004–05 WBA 24 0
2005–06 WBA 31 1
2006–07 WBA 31 1 **86 2**

CARTER, Darren (M) 108 8
H: 6 2 W: 12 11 b.Solihull 18-12-83
Source: Scholar. *Honours:* England Youth, Under-20.
2001–02 Birmingham C 13 1
2002–03 Birmingham C 12 0
2003–04 Birmingham C 5 0
2004–05 Birmingham C 15 2 **45 3**
2004–05 *Sunderland* 10 1 **10 1**
2005–06 WBA 20 1
2006–07 WBA 33 3 **53 4**

CHAPLOW, Richard (M) 115 9
H: 5 9 W: 9 03 b.Accrington 2-2-85
Source: Scholar. *Honours:* England Youth, Under-20, Under-21.
2002–03 Burnley 5 0
2003–04 Burnley 39 5
2004–05 Burnley 21 2 **65 7**
2004–05 WBA 4 0
2005–06 WBA 7 0
2005–06 *Southampton* 11 1 **11 1**
2006–07 WBA 28 1 **39 1**

CLEMENT, Neil (D) 279 22
H: 6 0 W: 12 03 b.Reading 3-10-78
Source: Trainee. *Honours:* England Schools, Youth.
1995–96 Chelsea 0 0
1996–97 Chelsea 1 0
1997–98 Chelsea 0 0
1998–99 Chelsea 0 0
1998–99 *Reading* 11 1 **11 1**
1998–99 *Preston NE* 4 0 **4 0**
1999–2000 Chelsea 0 0 **1 0**
1999–2000 *Brentford* 8 0 **8 0**
1999–2000 *WBA* 8 0
2000–01 WBA 45 5
2001–02 WBA 45 6
2002–03 WBA 36 3
2003–04 WBA 35 2
2004–05 WBA 35 3
2005–06 WBA 31 1
2006–07 WBA 20 1 **255 21**

DANIELS, Luke (G) 0 0
H: 6 1 W: 12 10 b.Bolton 5-1-88
Source: Manchester U Scholar.
2006–07 WBA 0 0

DAVIES, Curtis (D) 121 4
H: 6 2 W: 11 13 b.Waltham Forest 15-3-85
Source: From Scholar. *Honours:* England Under-21.
2003–04 Luton T 6 0
2004–05 Luton T 44 1
2005–06 Luton T 6 1 **56 2**
2005–06 WBA 33 2
2006–07 WBA 32 0 **65 2**

DAVIES, Rob (M) 0 0
H: 5 9 W: 11 02 b.Tywyn 24-3-87
Source: Scholar. *Honours:* Wales Under-21.
2005–06 WBA 0 0
2006–07 WBA 0 0

ELLINGTON, Nathan (F) 315 108
H: 5 10 W: 13 01 b.Bradford 2-7-81
Source: Walton & Hersham.
1998–99 Bristol R 10 1
1999–2000 Bristol R 37 4
2000–01 Bristol R 42 15
2001–02 Bristol R 27 15 **116 35**
2001–02 Wigan Ath 3 2
2002–03 Wigan Ath 42 15
2003–04 Wigan Ath 44 18
2004–05 Wigan Ath 45 24 **134 59**
2005–06 WBA 31 5
2006–07 WBA 34 9 **65 14**

ELVINS, Rob (F) 5 0
H: 6 2 W: 12 04 b.Alvechurch 17-9-86
Source: Scholar.
2005–06 WBA 0 0
2006–07 WBA 0 0
2006–07 *Cheltenham T* 5 0 **5 0**

FORSYTH, Jeff (D) 0 0
H: 5 10 W: 12 02 b.Hexham 14-10-87
Source: Scholar.
2005–06 WBA 0 0
2006–07 WBA 0 0

GERA, Zoltan (M) 223 49
H: 6 0 W: 11 11 b.Pecs 22-4-79
Source: From Hakarny. *Honours:* Hungary 42 full caps, 13 goals.
1999–2000 Pecsi 15 4 **15 4**
2000–01 Ferencvaros 32 7
2001–02 Ferencvaros 27 8
2002–03 Ferencvaros 26 6
2003–04 Ferencvaros 30 11 **115 32**
2004–05 WBA 38 6
2005–06 WBA 15 2
2006–07 WBA 40 5 **93 13**

GREENING, Jonathan (M) 252 10
H: 5 11 W: 11 00 b.Scarborough 2-1-79
Source: Trainee. *Honours:* England Youth, Under-21.
1996–97 York C 5 0
1997–98 York C 20 2 **25 2**
1997–98 Manchester U 0 0
1998–99 Manchester U 3 0
1999–2000 Manchester U 4 0
2000–01 Manchester U 7 0 **14 0**
2001–02 Middlesbrough 36 1
2002–03 Middlesbrough 38 2
2003–04 Middlesbrough 25 1 **99 4**
2004–05 WBA 34 0
2005–06 WBA 38 2
2006–07 WBA 42 2 **114 4**

HARTSON, John (F) 395 167
H: 6 0 W: 13 07 b.Swansea 5-4-75
Source: Trainee. *Honours:* Wales Under-21, 51 full caps, 14 goals.
1992–93 Luton T 0 0
1993–94 Luton T 34 6
1994–95 Luton T 20 5 **54 11**
1994–95 Arsenal 15 7
1995–96 Arsenal 19 4
1996–97 Arsenal 19 3 **53 14**
1996–97 West Ham U 11 5
1997–98 West Ham U 32 15
1998–99 West Ham U 17 4 **60 24**
1998–99 Wimbledon 14 2
1999–2000 Wimbledon 16 9
2000–01 Wimbledon 19 8 **49 19**
2000–01 Coventry C 12 6 **12 6**
2001–02 Celtic 31 19
2002–03 Celtic 27 18
2003–04 Celtic 15 8
2004–05 Celtic 38 25
2005–06 Celtic 35 18 **146 88**
2006–07 WBA 21 5 **21 5**

HODGKISS, Jared (M) 6 0
H: 5 6 W: 11 02 b.Stafford 15-11-86
Source: Scholar.
2005–06 WBA 1 0
2006–07 WBA 5 0 **6 0**

INAMOTO, Junichi (M) 201 20
H: 6 0 W: 11 11 b.Kagoshima 18-9-79
Honours: Japan 66 full caps, 4 goals.
1997 Gamba Osaka 27 3
1998 Gamba Osaka 28 6
1999 Gamba Osaka 22 1
2000 Gamba Osaka 28 4
2001 Gamba Osaka 13 2 **118 16**
2001–02 Arsenal 0 0
2002–03 Fulham 19 2
2003–04 Fulham 22 2 **41 4**
2004–05 WBA 3 0
2004–05 *Cardiff C* 14 0 **14 0**
2005–06 WBA 22 0
2006–07 WBA 3 0 **28 0**
To Galatasaray August 2006

KAMARA, Diomansy (F) 172 43
H: 6 0 W: 11 05 b.Paris 8-11-80
Honours: Senegal 3 full caps.
1999–2000 Catanzaro 11 4
2000–01 Catanzaro 23 5 **34 9**
2001–02 Chievo 0 0
2001–02 Modena 24 4

2002–03	Modena	29	5	**53**	**9**
2004–05	Portsmouth	25	4	**25**	**4**
2005–06	WBA	26	1		
2006–07	WBA	34	20	**60**	**21**

KIELY, Dean (G) 612 0
H: 6 1 W: 13 10 b.Salford 10-10-70
Source: WBA School. *Honours:* England Schools, FA Schools, Youth, Eire B, 8 full caps.

1987–88	Coventry C	0	0		
1988–89	Coventry C	0	0		
1989–90	Coventry C	0	0		
1989–90	*Ipswich T*	0	0		
1989–90	*York C*	0	0		
1990–91	York C	17	0		
1991–92	York C	21	0		
1992–93	York C	40	0		
1993–94	York C	46	0		
1994–95	York C	46	0		
1995–96	York C	40	0	**210**	**0**
1996–97	Bury	46	0		
1997–98	Bury	46	0		
1998–99	Bury	45	0	**137**	**0**
1999–2000	Charlton Ath	45	0		
2000–01	Charlton Ath	25	0		
2001–02	Charlton Ath	38	0		
2002–03	Charlton Ath	38	0		
2003–04	Charlton Ath	37	0		
2004–05	Charlton Ath	36	0		
2005–06	Charlton Ath	3	0	**222**	**0**
2005–06	Portsmouth	15	0		
2006–07	Portsmouth	0	0	**15**	**0**
2006–07	*Luton T*	11	0	**11**	**0**
2006–07	WBA	17	0	**17**	**0**

KOREN, Robert (M) 233 53
H: 5 10 W: 11 03 b.Ljubljana 20-9-80
Honours: Slovenia Under-21, 21 full caps, 1 goal.

1999–2000	Dravograd	31	2		
2000–01	Dravograd	31	9	**62**	**11**
2001–02	Publikum	31	5		
2002–03	Publikum	32	12		
2003–04	Publikum	15	5	**78**	**22**
2004	Lillestrom	23	1		
2005	Lillestrom	26	8		
2006	Lillestrom	26	10	**75**	**19**
2006–07	WBA	18	1	**18**	**1**

KOUMAS, Jason (M) 294 60
H: 5 10 W: 11 02 b.Wrexham 25-9-79
Source: Trainee. *Honours:* Wales 23 full caps, 5 goals.

1997–98	Tranmere R	0	0		
1998–99	Tranmere R	23	3		
1999–2000	Tranmere R	23	2		
2000–01	Tranmere R	39	10		
2001–02	Tranmere R	38	8		
2002–03	Tranmere R	4	2	**127**	**25**
2002–03	WBA	32	4		
2003–04	WBA	42	10		
2004–05	WBA	10	0		
2005–06	WBA	0	0		
2005–06	*Cardiff C*	44	12	**44**	**12**
2006–07	WBA	39	9	**123**	**23**

KUSZCZAK, Tomasz (G) 37 0
H: 6 3 W: 13 03 b.Krosno Odrzansia 20-3-82
Source: Uerdingen. *Honours:* Poland Youth, Under-21, 4 full caps.

2001–02	Hertha Berlin	0	0		
2002–03	Hertha Berlin	0	0		
2003–04	Hertha Berlin	0	0		
2004–05	WBA	3	0		
2005–06	WBA	28	0		
2006–07	WBA	0	0	**31**	**0**
2006–07	*Manchester U*	6	0	**6**	**0**

MACDONALD, Sherjill (F) 95 20
H: 6 0 W: 12 06 b.Amsterdam 20-11-84
Source: Ajax youth. *Honours:* Holland Youth, Under-21.

2001–02	Anderlecht	11	1		
2002–03	Anderlecht	9	0		
2003–04	Anderlecht	6	0	**26**	**1**
2004–05	Heracles	17	4	**17**	**4**
2005–06	Hamburg II	22	4	**22**	**4**
2006–07	Apeldoorn	21	11	**21**	**11**
2006–07	WBA	9	0	**9**	**0**

McSHANE, Paul (D) 74 6
H: 6 0 W: 11 05 b.Wicklow 6-1-86
Source: Trainee. *Honours:* Eire Youth, Under-21, 5 full caps.

2002–03	Manchester U	0	0		
2003–04	Manchester U	0	0		
2004–05	Manchester U	0	0		
2004–05	*Walsall*	4	1	**4**	**1**
2005–06	Manchester U	0	0		
2005–06	*Brighton & HA*	38	3	**38**	**3**
2006–07	WBA	32	2	**32**	**2**

NARDIELLO, Michael (F) 0 0
H: 5 10 W: 11 09 b.Torquay 9-5-89
Source: Liverpool Scholar.

2006–07	WBA	0	0		

NICHOLSON, Stuart (F) 28 6
H: 5 10 W: 11 09 b.Newcastle 3-2-86
Source: From Scholar. *Honours:* England Youth.

2005–06	WBA	4	0		
2006–07	WBA	2	0	**6**	**0**
2006–07	*Bristol R*	22	6	**22**	**6**

PERRY, Chris (D) 386 8
H: 5 8 W: 11 03 b.Carshalton 26-4-73
Source: Trainee.

1991–92	Wimbledon	0	0		
1992–93	Wimbledon	0	0		
1993–94	Wimbledon	2	0		
1994–95	Wimbledon	22	0		
1995–96	Wimbledon	37	0		
1996–97	Wimbledon	37	1		
1997–98	Wimbledon	35	1		
1998–99	Wimbledon	34	0	**167**	**2**
1999–2000	Tottenham H	37	1		
2000–01	Tottenham H	32	1		
2001–02	Tottenham H	33	0		
2002–03	Tottenham H	18	1		
2003–04	Tottenham H	0	0	**120**	**3**
2003–04	Charlton Ath	29	1		
2004–05	Charlton Ath	19	1		
2005–06	Charlton Ath	28	1	**76**	**3**
2006–07	WBA	23	0	**23**	**0**

PHILLIPS, Kevin (F) 390 179
H: 5 7 W: 11 00 b.Hitchin 25-7-73
Source: Baldock T. *Honours:* England B, 8 full caps.

1994–95	Watford	16	9		
1995–96	Watford	27	11		
1996–97	Watford	16	4	**59**	**24**
1997–98	Sunderland	43	29		
1998–99	Sunderland	26	23		
1999–2000	Sunderland	36	30		
2000–01	Sunderland	34	14		
2001–02	Sunderland	37	11		
2002–03	Sunderland	32	6	**208**	**113**
2003–04	Southampton	34	12		
2004–05	Southampton	30	10	**64**	**22**
2005–06	Aston Villa	23	4		
2006–07	Aston Villa	0	0	**23**	**4**
2006–07	WBA	36	16	**36**	**16**

ROBINSON, Paul (D) 355 11
H: 5 9 W: 11 12 b.Watford 14-12-78
Source: Trainee. *Honours:* England Under-21.

1996–97	Watford	12	0		
1997–98	Watford	22	2		
1998–99	Watford	29	0		
1999–2000	Watford	32	0		
2000–01	Watford	39	0		
2001–02	Watford	38	3		
2002–03	Watford	37	3		
2003–04	Watford	10	0	**219**	**8**
2003–04	WBA	31	0		
2004–05	WBA	30	1		
2005–06	WBA	33	0		
2006–07	WBA	42	2	**136**	**3**

STEELE, Luke (G) 39 0
H: 6 2 W: 12 00 b.Peterborough 24-9-84
Source: Scholar. *Honours:* England Youth, Under-20.

2001–02	Peterborough U	2	0	**2**	**0**
2001–02	Manchester U	0	0		
2002–03	Manchester U	0	0		
2003–04	Manchester U	0	0		
2004–05	Manchester U	0	0		
2004–05	*Coventry C*	32	0		
2005–06	Manchester U	0	0		
2006–07	WBA	0	0		
2006–07	*Coventry C*	5	0	**37**	**0**

WALLWORK, Ronnie (M) 138 7
H: 5 10 W: 12 09 b.Manchester 10-9-77
Source: Trainee. *Honours:* England Youth, Under-20.

1994–95	Manchester U	0	0		
1995–96	Manchester U	0	0		
1996–97	Manchester U	0	0		
1997–98	Manchester U	1	0		
1997–98	*Carlisle U*	10	1	**10**	**1**
1997–98	*Stockport Co*	7	0	**7**	**0**
1998–99	Manchester U	0	0		
1999–2000	Manchester U	5	0		
2000–01	Manchester U	12	0		
2001–02	Manchester U	1	0	**19**	**0**
2002–03	WBA	27	0		
2003–04	WBA	5	0		
2003–04	*Bradford C*	7	4	**7**	**4**
2004–05	WBA	20	1		
2005–06	WBA	31	0		
2006–07	WBA	10	1	**93**	**2**
2006–07	*Barnsley*	2	0	**2**	**0**

WATSON, Steve (D) 428 27
H: 6 0 W: 12 07 b.North Shields 1-4-74
Source: Trainee. *Honours:* England Youth, Under-21, B.

1990–91	Newcastle U	24	0		
1991–92	Newcastle U	28	1		
1992–93	Newcastle U	2	0		
1993–94	Newcastle U	32	2		
1994–95	Newcastle U	27	4		
1995–96	Newcastle U	23	3		
1996–97	Newcastle U	36	1		
1997–98	Newcastle U	29	1		
1998–99	Newcastle U	7	0	**208**	**12**
1998–99	Aston Villa	27	0		
1999–2000	Aston Villa	14	0	**41**	**0**
2000–01	Everton	34	0		
2001–02	Everton	25	4		
2002–03	Everton	18	5		
2003–04	Everton	24	5		
2004–05	Everton	25	0	**126**	**14**
2005–06	WBA	30	1		
2006–07	WBA	12	0	**42**	**1**
2006–07	*Sheffield W*	11	0	**11**	**0**

ZUBERBUHLER, Pascal (G) 431 0
H: 6 5 W: 15 08 b.Frauenfeld 8-1-71
Honours: Switzerland 47 full caps.

1991–92	Grasshoppers	9	0		
1992–93	Grasshoppers	21	0		
1993–94	Grasshoppers	0	0		
1994–95	Grasshoppers	33	0		
1995–96	Grasshoppers	24	0		
1996–97	Grasshoppers	36	0		
1997–98	Grasshoppers	28	0		
1998–99	Grasshoppers	36	0	**187**	**0**
1999–2000	Basle	36	0		
2000–01	Basle	3	0		
2000–01	Leverkusen	13	0	**13**	**0**
2000–01	Aarau	2	0	**2**	**0**
2001–02	Basle	36	0		
2002–03	Basle	35	0		
2003–04	Basle	35	0		
2004–05	Basle	33	0		
2005–06	Basle	36	0	**214**	**0**
2006–07	WBA	15	0	**15**	**0**

To Neuchatel Xamax February 2007

WEST HAM U (87)

ASHTON, Dean (F) 214 80
H: 6 2 W: 14 07 b.Crewe 24-11-83
Source: Schoolboy. *Honours:* England Youth, Under-20, Under-21.

2000–01	Crewe Alex	21	8		
2001–02	Crewe Alex	31	7		
2002–03	Crewe Alex	39	9		
2003–04	Crewe Alex	44	19		
2004–05	Crewe Alex	24	17	**159**	**60**
2004–05	Norwich C	16	7		

2005–06	Norwich C	28	10	44	17
2005–06	West Ham U	11	3		
2006–07	West Ham U	0	0	11	3

BENAYOUN, Yossi (M) 284 89
H: 5 10 W: 11 00 b.Beer Sheva 6-6-80
Honours: Israel 49 full caps, 11 goals.

1997–98	Hapoel Beer Sheva	25	15	25	15
1998–99	Maccabi Haifa	29	16		
1999–2000	Maccabi Haifa	38	19		
2000–01	Maccabi Haifa	37	13		
2001–02	Maccabi Haifa	26	7	130	55
2002–03	Santander	31	4		
2003–04	Santander	35	7		
2004–05	Santander	0	0	66	11
2005–06	West Ham U	34	5		
2006–07	West Ham U	29	3	63	8

BLACKMORE, David (G) 0 0
H: 6 1 W: 13 00 b.Chelmsford 23-3-89
Source: Scholar.

2006–07	West Ham U	0	0		

BOA MORTE, Luis (F) 258 46
H: 5 9 W: 12 06 b.Lisbon 4-8-77
Source: Sporting Lisbon, Lourihanense (loan). *Honours:* Portugal Youth, Under-21, 26 full caps, 1 goal.

1997–98	Arsenal	15	0		
1998–99	Arsenal	8	0		
1999–2000	Arsenal	2	0	25	0
1999–2000	Southampton	14	1		
2000–01	Southampton	0	0	14	1
2000–01	*Fulham*	39	18		
2001–02	Fulham	23	1		
2002–03	Fulham	29	2		
2003–04	Fulham	33	9		
2004–05	Fulham	31	8		
2005–06	Fulham	35	6		
2006–07	Fulham	15	0	205	44
2006–07	West Ham U	14	1	14	1

BOWYER, Lee (M) 358 52
H: 5 9 W: 10 12 b.Canning Town 3-1-77
Source: Trainee. *Honours:* England Youth, Under-21, 1 full cap.

1993–94	Charlton Ath	0	0		
1994–95	Charlton Ath	5	0		
1995–96	Charlton Ath	41	8	46	8
1996–97	Leeds U	32	4		
1997–98	Leeds U	25	3		
1998–99	Leeds U	35	9		
1999–2000	Leeds U	33	5		
2000–01	Leeds U	38	9		
2001–02	Leeds U	25	5		
2002–03	Leeds U	15	3	203	38
2002–03	West Ham U	10	0		
2003–04	Newcastle U	24	2		
2004–05	Newcastle U	27	3		
2005–06	Newcastle U	28	1	79	6
2006–07	West Ham U	20	0	30	0

CARROLL, Roy (G) 261 0
H: 6 2 W: 13 12 b.Enniskillen 30-9-77
Source: Trainee. *Honours:* Northern Ireland Youth, Under-21, 19 full caps.

1995–96	Hull C	23	0		
1996–97	Hull C	23	0	46	0
1996–97	Wigan Ath	0	0		
1997–98	Wigan Ath	29	0		
1998–99	Wigan Ath	43	0		
1999–2000	Wigan Ath	34	0		
2000–01	Wigan Ath	29	0	135	0
2001–02	Manchester U	7	0		
2002–03	Manchester U	10	0		
2003–04	Manchester U	6	0		
2004–05	Manchester U	26	0	49	0
2005–06	West Ham U	19	0		
2006–07	West Ham U	12	0	31	0

COLE, Carlton (F) 97 14
H: 6 3 W: 14 02 b.Croydon 12-11-83
Source: Scholar. *Honours:* England Youth, Under-20, Under-21.

2000–01	Chelsea	0	0		
2001–02	Chelsea	3	1		
2002–03	Chelsea	13	3		
2002–03	*Wolverhampton W*	7	1	7	1
2003–04	Chelsea	0	0		
2003–04	*Charlton Ath*	21	4	21	4
2004–05	Chelsea	0	0		
2004–05	*Aston Villa*	27	3	27	3
2005–06	Chelsea	9	0	25	4
2006–07	West Ham U	17	2	17	2

COLLINS, James (D) 96 5
H: 6 2 W: 14 05 b.Newport 23-8-83
Source: Scholar. *Honours:* Wales Youth, Under-21, 19 full caps.

2000–01	Cardiff C	3	0		
2001–02	Cardiff C	7	1		
2002–03	Cardiff C	2	0		
2003–04	Cardiff C	20	1		
2004–05	Cardiff C	34	1	66	3
2005–06	West Ham U	14	2		
2006–07	West Ham U	16	0	30	2

DAILLY, Christian (D) 436 28
H: 6 1 W: 12 10 b.Dundee 23-10-73
Source: 'S' Form. *Honours:* Scotland Schools, Youth, Under-21, B, 65 full caps, 6 goals.

1990–91	Dundee U	18	5		
1991–92	Dundee U	8	0		
1992–93	Dundee U	14	4		
1993–94	Dundee U	38	4		
1994–95	Dundee U	33	4		
1995–96	Dundee U	30	1	141	18
1996–97	Derby Co	36	3		
1997–98	Derby Co	30	1		
1998–99	Derby Co	1	0	67	4
1998–99	Blackburn R	17	0		
1999–2000	Blackburn R	43	4		
2000–01	Blackburn R	10	0	70	4
2000–01	West Ham U	12	0		
2001–02	West Ham U	38	0		
2002–03	West Ham U	26	0		
2003–04	West Ham U	43	2		
2004–05	West Ham U	3	0		
2005–06	West Ham U	22	0		
2006–07	West Ham U	14	0	158	2

DAVENPORT, Calum (D) 128 5
H: 6 4 W: 14 00 b.Bedford 1-1-83
Source: Trainee. *Honours:* England Youth, Under-20, Under-21.

1999–2000	Coventry C	0	0		
2000–01	Coventry C	1	0		
2001–02	Coventry C	3	0		
2002–03	Coventry C	32	3		
2003–04	Coventry C	33	0		
2004–05	Coventry C	6	0	75	3
2004–05	*Southampton*	7	0	7	0
2004–05	Tottenham H	1	0		
2004–05	*West Ham U*	10	0		
2005–06	Tottenham H	4	0		
2005–06	*Norwich C*	15	1	15	1
2006–07	Tottenham H	10	1	15	1
2006–07	West Ham U	6	0	16	0

EPHRAIM, Hogan (F) 21 1
H: 5 9 W: 10 06 b.Islington 31-3-88
Source: Scholar. *Honours:* England Youth.

2004–05	West Ham U	0	0		
2005–06	West Ham U	0	0		
2006–07	West Ham U	0	0		
2006–07	*Colchester U*	21	1	21	1

ETHERINGTON, Matthew (M) 243 19
H: 5 10 W: 10 12 b.Truro 14-8-81
Source: School. *Honours:* England Youth, Under-21.

1996–97	Peterborough U	1	0		
1997–98	Peterborough U	2	0		
1998–99	Peterborough U	29	3		
1999–2000	Peterborough U	19	3	51	6
1999–2000	Tottenham H	5	0		
2000–01	Tottenham H	6	0		
2001–02	*Bradford C*	13	1	13	1
2001–02	Tottenham H	11	0		
2002–03	Tottenham H	23	1	45	1
2003–04	West Ham U	35	5		
2004–05	West Ham U	39	4		
2005–06	West Ham U	33	2		
2006–07	West Ham U	27	0	134	11

FERDINAND, Anton (D) 113 3
H: 6 2 W: 11 00 b.Peckham 18-2-85
Source: Trainee. *Honours:* England Youth, Under-20, Under-21.

2002–03	West Ham U	0	0		
2003–04	West Ham U	20	0		
2004–05	West Ham U	29	1		
2005–06	West Ham U	33	2		
2006–07	West Ham U	31	0	113	3

FITZGERALD, Lorcan (D) 0 0
H: 5 9 W: 10 09 b.Republic of Ireland 3-1-89
Source: Scholar.

2005–06	West Ham U	0	0		
2006–07	West Ham U	0	0		

GABBIDON, Daniel (D) 267 10
H: 6 0 W: 13 05 b.Cwmbran 8-8-79
Source: Trainee. *Honours:* Wales Youth, Under-21, 33 full caps.

1998–99	WBA	2	0		
1999–2000	WBA	18	0		
2000–01	WBA	0	0	20	0
2000–01	Cardiff C	43	3		
2001–02	Cardiff C	44	3		
2002–03	Cardiff C	24	0		
2003–04	Cardiff C	41	3		
2004–05	Cardiff C	45	1	197	10
2005–06	West Ham U	32	0		
2006–07	West Ham U	18	0	50	0

GREEN, Rob (G) 249 0
H: 6 3 W: 14 09 b.Chertsey 18-1-80
Source: Trainee. *Honours:* England Youth, B, 1 full cap.

1997–98	Norwich C	0	0		
1998–99	Norwich C	2	0		
1999–2000	Norwich C	3	0		
2000–01	Norwich C	5	0		
2001–02	Norwich C	41	0		
2002–03	Norwich C	46	0		
2003–04	Norwich C	46	0		
2004–05	Norwich C	38	0		
2005–06	Norwich C	42	0	223	0
2006–07	West Ham U	26	0	26	0

HALES, Lee (M) 0 0
H: 5 9 W: 11 00 b.Sidcup 15-2-89
Source: Scholar. *Honours:* England Schools, Youth.

2005–06	West Ham U	0	0		
2006–07	West Ham U	0	0		

HAREWOOD, Marlon (F) 330 99
H: 6 1 W: 13 07 b.Hampstead 25-8-79
Source: Trainee.

1996–97	Nottingham F	0	0		
1997–98	Nottingham F	1	0		
1998–99	Nottingham F	23	1		
1998–99	*Ipswich T*	6	1	6	1
1999–2000	Nottingham F	34	4		
2000–01	Nottingham F	33	3		
2001–02	Nottingham F	28	11		
2002–03	Nottingham F	44	20		
2003–04	Nottingham F	19	12	182	51
2003–04	West Ham U	28	13		
2004–05	West Ham U	45	17		
2005–06	West Ham U	37	14		
2006–07	West Ham U	32	3	142	47

KATAN, Yaniv (F) 229 40
H: 6 1 W: 12 13 b.Kiryat Ata 27-1-81
Honours: Israel 24 full caps, 5 goals.

1998–99	Maccabi Haifa	26	1		
1999–2000	Maccabi Haifa	36	3		
2000–01	Maccabi Haifa	35	5		
2001–02	Maccabi Haifa	19	5		
2002–03	Maccabi Haifa	32	6		
2003–04	Maccabi Haifa	28	7		
2004–05	Maccabi Haifa	32	8		
2005–06	Maccabi Haifa	15	5	223	40
2005–06	West Ham U	6	0		
2006–07	West Ham U	0	0	6	0

KEPA (F) 41 10
H: 5 9 W: 12 11 b.Marbella 13-1-84
Honours: Spain Under-21.

2004–05	Sevilla	2	0		
2005–06	Sevilla	23	6		
2006–07	Sevilla	8	3	33	9
2006–07	West Ham U	8	1	8	1

KONCHESKY, Paul (D) **220 6**
H: 5 10 W: 11 07 b.Barking 15-5-81
Source: Trainee. *Honours:* England Youth, Under-20, Under-21, 2 full caps.

1997–98	Charlton Ath	3	0		
1998–99	Charlton Ath	2	0		
1999–2000	Charlton Ath	8	0		
2000–01	Charlton Ath	23	0		
2001–02	Charlton Ath	34	1		
2002–03	Charlton Ath	30	3		
2003–04	Charlton Ath	21	0		
2003–04	*Tottenham H*	12	0	**12**	**0**
2004–05	Charlton Ath	28	1	**149**	**5**
2005–06	West Ham U	37	1		
2006–07	West Ham U	22	0	**59**	**1**

McCARTNEY, George (D) **156 0**
H: 5 11 W: 11 02 b.Belfast 29-4-81
Source: Trainee. *Honours:* Northern Ireland Schools, Youth, Under-21, 20 full caps, 1 goal.

1998–99	Sunderland	0	0		
1999–2000	Sunderland	0	0		
2000–01	Sunderland	2	0		
2001–02	Sunderland	18	0		
2002–03	Sunderland	24	0		
2003–04	Sunderland	41	0		
2004–05	Sunderland	36	0		
2005–06	Sunderland	13	0	**134**	**0**
2006–07	West Ham U	22	0	**22**	**0**

MEARS, Tyrone (D) **89 5**
H: 5 11 W: 11 10 b.Stockport 18-2-83
Source: Manchester C Juniors.

2000–01	Manchester C	0	0		
2001–02	Manchester C	1	0	**1**	**0**
2002–03	Preston NE	22	1		
2003–04	Preston NE	12	1		
2004–05	Preston NE	4	0		
2005–06	Preston NE	32	2	**70**	**4**
2006–07	West Ham U	5	0	**5**	**0**
2006–07	*Derby Co*	13	1	**13**	**1**

MULLINS, Hayden (D) **351 21**
H: 5 11 W: 11 12 b.Reading 27-3-79
Source: Trainee. *Honours:* England Under-21.

1996–97	Crystal Palace	0	0		
1997–98	Crystal Palace	0	0		
1998–99	Crystal Palace	40	5		
1999–2000	Crystal Palace	45	10		
2000–01	Crystal Palace	41	1		
2001–02	Crystal Palace	43	0		
2002–03	Crystal Palace	43	2		
2003–04	Crystal Palace	10	0	**222**	**18**
2003–04	West Ham U	27	0		
2004–05	West Ham U	37	1		
2005–06	West Ham U	35	0		
2006–07	West Ham U	30	2	**129**	**3**

NEILL, Lucas (D) **351 18**
H: 6 0 W: 12 03 b.Sydney 9-3-78
Source: NSW Soccer Academy. *Honours:* Australia Under-20, Under-23, 34 full caps.

1995–96	Millwall	13	0		
1996–97	Millwall	39	3		
1997–98	Millwall	6	0		
1998–99	Millwall	35	6		
1999–2000	Millwall	31	1		
2000–01	Millwall	24	2		
2001–02	Millwall	4	1	**152**	**13**
2001–02	Blackburn R	31	1		
2002–03	Blackburn R	34	0		
2003–04	Blackburn R	32	2		
2004–05	Blackburn R	36	1		
2005–06	Blackburn R	35	1		
2006–07	Blackburn R	20	0	**188**	**5**
2006–07	West Ham U	11	0	**11**	**0**

NEWTON, Shaun (M) **419 34**
H: 5 8 W: 11 00 b.Camberwell 20-8-75
Source: Trainee. *Honours:* England Under-21.

1992–93	Charlton Ath	2	0		
1993–94	Charlton Ath	19	2		
1994–95	Charlton Ath	26	0		
1995–96	Charlton Ath	41	5		
1996–97	Charlton Ath	43	3		
1997–98	Charlton Ath	41	5		
1998–99	Charlton Ath	16	0		
1999–2000	Charlton Ath	42	5		
2000–01	Charlton Ath	10	0	**240**	**20**
2001–02	Wolverhampton W	45	8		
2002–03	Wolverhampton W	33	3		
2003–04	Wolverhampton W	28	0		
2004–05	Wolverhampton W	24	1	**130**	**12**
2004–05	West Ham U	11	0		
2005–06	West Ham U	26	1		
2006–07	West Ham U	3	0	**40**	**1**
2006–07	*Leicester C*	9	1	**9**	**1**

NOBLE, Mark (M) **46 3**
H: 5 11 W: 12 00 b.West Ham 8-5-87
Source: Scholar. *Honours:* England Youth, Under-21.

2004–05	West Ham U	13	0		
2005–06	West Ham U	5	0		
2005–06	*Hull C*	5	0	**5**	**0**
2006–07	West Ham U	10	2	**28**	**2**
2006–07	*Ipswich T*	13	1	**13**	**1**

PANTSIL, John (D) **93 3**
H: 5 10 W: 12 08 b.Berekum 15-6-81
Source: Liberty Professionals, Berkum Arsenals. *Honours:* Ghana Youth, Under-20, 29 full caps.

2002–03	Maccabi Tel Aviv	17	0		
2003–04	Maccabi Tel Aviv	29	0	**46**	**0**
2004–05	Hapoel Tel Aviv	15	1		
2005–06	Hapoel Tel Aviv	27	2	**42**	**3**
2006–07	West Ham U	5	0	**5**	**0**

QUASHIE, Nigel (M) **322 24**
H: 6 0 W: 13 10 b.Peckham 20-7-78
Source: Trainee. *Honours:* England Youth, Under-21, B, Scotland 14 full caps, 1 goal.

1995–96	QPR	11	0		
1996–97	QPR	13	0		
1997–98	QPR	33	3		
1998–99	QPR	0	0	**57**	**3**
1998–99	Nottingham F	16	0		
1999–2000	Nottingham F	28	2	**44**	**2**
2000–01	Portsmouth	31	5		
2001–02	Portsmouth	35	2		
2002–03	Portsmouth	42	5		
2003–04	Portsmouth	21	1		
2004–05	Portsmouth	19	0	**148**	**13**
2004–05	Southampton	13	1		
2005–06	Southampton	24	4	**37**	**5**
2005–06	WBA	9	1		
2006–07	WBA	20	0	**29**	**1**
2006–07	West Ham U	7	0	**7**	**0**

REED, Matthew (G) **4 0**
H: 6 0 W: 11 00 b.Dartford 24-12-86

2005–06	West Ham U	0	0		
2005–06	*Barnet*	4	0	**4**	**0**
2006–07	West Ham U	0	0		

REID, Kyel (M) **28 2**
H: 5 10 W: 12 05 b.South London 26-11-87
Source: Scholar. *Honours:* England Youth.

2004–05	West Ham U	0	0		
2005–06	West Ham U	2	0		
2006–07	West Ham U	0	0	**2**	**0**
2006–07	*Barnsley*	26	2	**26**	**2**

REO-COKER, Nigel (M) **178 17**
H: 5 8 W: 12 03 b.Southwark 14-5-84
Source: Scholar. *Honours:* England Youth, Under-20, Under-21.

2001–02	Wimbledon	1	0		
2002–03	Wimbledon	32	2		
2003–04	Wimbledon	25	4	**58**	**6**
2003–04	West Ham U	15	2		
2004–05	West Ham U	39	3		
2005–06	West Ham U	31	5		
2006–07	West Ham U	35	1	**120**	**11**

SHERINGHAM, Teddy (F) **715 272**
H: 6 0 W: 12 05 b.Highams Park 2-4-66
Source: Apprentice. *Honours:* England Youth, Under-21, 51 full caps, 11 goals.

1983–84	Millwall	7	1		
1984–85	Millwall	0	0		
1984–85	*Aldershot*	5	0	**5**	**0**
1985–86	Millwall	18	4		
1986–87	Millwall	42	13		
1987–88	Millwall	43	22		
1988–89	Millwall	33	11		
1989–90	Millwall	31	9		
1990–91	Millwall	46	33	**220**	**93**
1991–92	Nottingham F	39	13		
1992–93	Nottingham F	3	1	**42**	**14**
1992–93	Tottenham H	38	21		
1993–94	Tottenham H	19	13		
1994–95	Tottenham H	42	18		
1995–96	Tottenham H	38	16		
1996–97	Tottenham H	29	7		
1997–98	Manchester U	31	9		
1998–99	Manchester U	17	2		
1999–2000	Manchester U	27	5		
2000–01	Manchester U	29	15	**104**	**31**
2001–02	Tottenham H	34	10		
2002–03	Tottenham H	36	12	**236**	**97**
2003–04	Portsmouth	32	9	**32**	**9**
2004–05	West Ham U	33	20		
2005–06	West Ham U	26	6		
2006–07	West Ham U	17	2	**76**	**28**

SPECTOR, Jonathan (D) **48 0**
H: 6 0 W: 12 08 b.Arlington Heights 1-3-86
Source: Chicago Sockers, USA Youth, 9 full caps.

2003–04	Manchester U	0	0		
2004–05	Manchester U	3	0		
2005–06	Manchester U	0	0	**3**	**0**
2005–06	*Charlton Ath*	20	0	**20**	**0**
2006–07	West Ham U	25	0	**25**	**0**

STOKES, Tony (M) **25 0**
H: 5 10 W: 11 10 b.East London 7-1-87
Source: Scholar.

2005–06	West Ham U	0	0		
2005–06	*Rushden & D*	19	0	**19**	**0**
2006–07	West Ham U	0	0		
2006–07	*Brighton & HA*	6	0	**6**	**0**

TEVEZ, Carlos (F) **130 53**
H: 5 8 W: 11 11 b.Cuidadela 5-2-84
Source: All Boys. *Honours:* Argentina Youth, Under-20, Under-23, 29 full caps, 6 goals.

2001–02	Boca Juniors	11	1		
2002–03	Boca Juniors	32	11		
2003–04	Boca Juniors	23	12		
2004–05	Boca Juniors	9	2	**75**	**26**
2005	Corinthians	29	20	**29**	**20**
2006–07	West Ham U	26	7	**26**	**7**

TOMKINS, James (D) **0 0**
H: 6 3 W: 11 10 b.Basildon 29-3-89
Source: Scholar. *Honours:* England Schools, Youth.

2005–06	West Ham U	0	0		
2006–07	West Ham U	0	0		

UPSON, Matthew (D) **172 5**
H: 6 1 W: 11 04 b.Stowmarket 18-4-79
Source: Trainee. *Honours:* England Youth, Under-21, 7 full caps.

1995–96	Luton T	0	0		
1996–97	Luton T	1	0	**1**	**0**
1996–97	Arsenal	0	0		
1997–98	Arsenal	5	0		
1998–99	Arsenal	5	0		
1999–2000	Arsenal	8	0		
2000–01	Arsenal	2	0		
2000–01	*Nottingham F*	1	0	**1**	**0**
2000–01	*Crystal Palace*	7	0	**7**	**0**
2001–02	Arsenal	14	0		
2002–03	Arsenal	0	0	**34**	**0**
2002–03	*Reading*	14	0	**14**	**0**
2002–03	Birmingham C	14	0		
2003–04	Birmingham C	30	0		
2004–05	Birmingham C	36	2		
2005–06	Birmingham C	24	1		
2006–07	Birmingham C	9	2	**113**	**5**
2006–07	West Ham U	2	0	**2**	**0**

WALKER, Jim (G) **416 0**
H: 5 11 W: 13 04 b.Sutton-in-Ashfield 9-7-73
Source: Trainee.

1991–92	Notts Co	0	0		
1992–93	Notts Co	0	0		
1993–94	Walsall	31	0		
1994–95	Walsall	4	0		
1995–96	Walsall	26	0		
1996–97	Walsall	36	0		
1997–98	Walsall	46	0		
1998–99	Walsall	46	0		

1999–2000	Walsall	43	0		
2000–01	Walsall	44	0		
2001–02	Walsall	43	0		
2002–03	Walsall	41	0		
2003–04	Walsall	43	0	**403**	**0**
2004–05	West Ham U	10	0		
2005–06	West Ham U	3	0		
2006–07	West Ham U	0	0	**13**	**0**

ZAMORA, Bobby (F) 262 105
H: 6 1 W: 11 11 b.Barking 16-1-81
Source: Trainee. *Honours:* England Under-21.

1999–2000	Bristol R	4	0	**4**	**0**
1999–2000	*Brighton & HA*	6	6		
2000–01	Brighton & HA	43	28		
2001–02	Brighton & HA	41	28		
2002–03	Brighton & HA	35	14	**125**	**76**
2003–04	Tottenham H	16	0	**16**	**0**
2003–04	West Ham U	17	5		
2004–05	West Ham U	34	7		
2005–06	West Ham U	34	6		
2006–07	West Ham U	32	11	**117**	**29**

Scholars
Blackwell, Robbie; Bowes, Gary; Collison, Jack David; Hales, Lee Adam; Harvey, Thomas; Hines, Zavon; Hunt, Ben; Jeffery, Jack; Miller, Ashley Donnelly; Ngala, Bondz; O'neill, Ryan; Sears, Fred; Spence, Jordan; Stanislas, Junior; Stech, Marek; Widdowson, Joseph.

WIGAN ATH (88)

AGHAHOWA, Julius (F) 95 32
H: 5 10 W: 11 07 b.Benin City 12-2-82
Source: Esperance. *Honours:* Nigeria 32 full caps, 14 goals.

2000–01	Shakhtjar Donetsk	8	7		
2001–02	Shakhtjar Donetsk	17	7		
2002–03	Shakhtjar Donetsk	10	1		
2003–04	Shakhtjar Donetsk	17	6		
2004–05	Shakhtjar Donetsk	14	7		
2005–06	Shakhtjar Donetsk	8	0		
2006–07	Shakhtjar Donetsk	15	4	**89**	**32**
2006–07	Wigan Ath	6	0	**6**	**0**

BAINES, Leighton (D) 145 4
H: 5 8 W: 11 00 b.Liverpool 11-12-84
Source: Trainee. *Honours:* England Under-21.

2002–03	Wigan Ath	6	0		
2003–04	Wigan Ath	26	0		
2004–05	Wigan Ath	41	1		
2005–06	Wigan Ath	37	0		
2006–07	Wigan Ath	35	3	**145**	**4**

BOYCE, Emmerson (D) 289 10
H: 6 0 W: 12 03 b.Aylesbury 24-9-79
Source: Trainee.

1997–98	Luton T	0	0		
1998–99	Luton T	1	0		
1999–2000	Luton T	30	1		
2000–01	Luton T	42	3		
2001–02	Luton T	37	0		
2002–03	Luton T	34	0		
2003–04	Luton T	42	4	**186**	**8**
2004–05	Crystal Palace	27	0		
2005–06	Crystal Palace	42	2	**69**	**2**
2006–07	Wigan Ath	34	0	**34**	**0**

CAMARA, Henri (F) 215 79
H: 5 9 W: 10 08 b.Dakar 10-5-77
Honours: Senegal 72 full caps, 21 goals.

1999–2000	Neuchatel Xamax	20	12		
2000–01	Neuchatel Xamax	12	5	**32**	**17**
2000–01	Grasshoppers	11	3	**11**	**3**
2001–02	Sedan	25	8		
2002–03	Sedan	34	14	**59**	**22**
2003–04	Wolverhampton W	30	7		
2004–05	Wolverhampton W	0	0	**30**	**7**
2004–05	*Celtic*	18	8	**18**	**8**
2004–05	*Southampton*	13	4	**13**	**4**
2005–06	Wigan Ath	29	12		
2006–07	Wigan Ath	23	6	**52**	**18**

COTTERILL, David (F) 78 9
H: 5 9 W: 11 02 b.Cardiff 4-12-87
Source: Scholar. *Honours:* Wales Youth, Under-21, 8 full caps.

2004–05	Bristol C	12	0		
2005–06	Bristol C	45	7		
2006–07	Bristol C	5	1	**62**	**8**
2006–07	Wigan Ath	16	1	**16**	**1**

CYWKA, Thomasz (M) 4 0
H: 5 10 W: 11 09 b.Gliwice 27-6-88
Source: Gwarek Zabrze. *Honours:* Poland Youth, Under-21.

2006–07	Wigan Ath	0	0		
2006–07	*Oldham Ath*	4	0	**4**	**0**

DE ZEEUW, Arjan (D) 524 23
H: 6 0 W: 13 06 b.Castricum 16-4-70
Source: Vitesse 22.

1992–93	Telstar	30	1		
1993–94	Telstar	31	2		
1994–95	Telstar	29	1		
1995–96	Telstar	12	1	**102**	**5**
1995–96	Barnsley	31	1		
1996–97	Barnsley	43	2		
1997–98	Barnsley	26	0		
1998–99	Barnsley	38	4	**138**	**7**
1999–2000	Wigan Ath	39	3		
2000–01	Wigan Ath	45	1		
2001–02	Wigan Ath	42	2		
2002–03	Portsmouth	38	1		
2003–04	Portsmouth	36	1		
2004–05	Portsmouth	32	3	**106**	**5**
2005–06	Wigan Ath	31	0		
2006–07	Wigan Ath	21	0	**178**	**6**

FILAN, John (G) 417 0
H: 6 2 W: 14 07 b.Sydney 8-2-70
Honours: Australia Under-20, Under-23, 2 full caps.

1989–90	St George	26	0		
1990–91	St George	26	0	**52**	**0**
1991–92	Wollongong Wolves	23	0		
1992–93	Wollongong Wolves	6	0	**29**	**0**
1992–93	Cambridge U	6	0		
1993–94	Cambridge U	46	0		
1994–95	Cambridge U	16	0	**68**	**0**
1994–95	*Nottingham F*	0	0		
1994–95	Coventry C	2	0		
1995–96	Coventry C	13	0		
1996–97	Coventry C	1	0	**16**	**0**
1997–98	Blackburn R	7	0		
1998–99	Blackburn R	26	0		
1999–2000	Blackburn R	16	0		
2000–01	Blackburn R	13	0		
2001–02	Blackburn R	0	0	**62**	**0**
2001–02	Wigan Ath	25	0		
2002–03	Wigan Ath	46	0		
2003–04	Wigan Ath	45	0		
2004–05	Wigan Ath	46	0		
2005–06	Wigan Ath	15	0		
2006–07	Wigan Ath	10	0	**187**	**0**
2006–07	*Doncaster R*	3	0	**3**	**0**

FOLAN, Caleb (F) 122 17
H: 6 2 W: 14 07 b.Leeds 26-10-82
Source: Trainee.

1999–2000	Leeds U	0	0		
2000–01	Leeds U	0	0		
2001–02	Leeds U	0	0		
2001–02	*Rushden & D*	6	0	**6**	**0**
2001–02	*Hull C*	1	0	**1**	**0**
2002–03	Leeds U	0	0		
2002–03	Chesterfield	13	1		
2003–04	Chesterfield	7	0		
2004–05	Chesterfield	32	6		
2005–06	Chesterfield	27	0		
2006–07	Chesterfield	23	8	**102**	**15**
2006–07	Wigan Ath	13	2	**13**	**2**

GRANQVIST, Andreas (D) 0 0
H: 6 3 W: 13 03 b.Helsingborg 16-4-85
Honours: Sweden Under-21, 1 full cap.

2006–07	Wigan Ath	0	0		

HAESTAD, Kristofer (M) 135 18
H: 5 9 W: 11 10 b.Kristiansand 9-12-83
Honours: Norway Youth, Under-21, 15 full caps, 1 goal.

2001	Start	8	1		
2002	Start	25	2		
2003	Start	25	0		
2004	Start	30	9		
2005	Start	23	3		
2006	Start	22	3	**133**	**18**
2006–07	Wigan Ath	2	0	**2**	**0**

To Start March 2007

HALL, Fitz (D) 154 8
H: 6 3 W: 13 00 b.Leytonstone 20-12-80
Source: Barnet Trainee, Chesham U.

2001–02	Oldham Ath	4	1		
2002–03	Oldham Ath	40	4	**44**	**5**
2003–04	Southampton	11	0	**11**	**0**
2004–05	Crystal Palace	36	2		
2005–06	Crystal Palace	39	1	**75**	**3**
2006–07	Wigan Ath	24	0	**24**	**0**

HESKEY, Emile (F) 406 101
H: 6 2 W: 13 12 b.Leicester 11-1-78
Source: Trainee. *Honours:* England Youth, Under-21, B, 43 full caps, 5 goals.

1994–95	Leicester C	1	0		
1995–96	Leicester C	30	7		
1996–97	Leicester C	35	10		
1997–98	Leicester C	35	10		
1998–99	Leicester C	30	6		
1999–2000	Leicester C	23	7	**154**	**40**
1999–2000	Liverpool	12	3		
2000–01	Liverpool	36	14		
2001–02	Liverpool	35	9		
2002–03	Liverpool	32	6		
2003–04	Liverpool	35	7	**150**	**39**
2004–05	Birmingham C	34	10		
2005–06	Birmingham C	34	4	**68**	**14**
2006–07	Wigan Ath	34	8	**34**	**8**

JACKSON, Matt (D) 504 14
H: 6 1 W: 14 00 b.Leeds 19-10-71
Source: School. *Honours:* England Schools, Under-21.

1990–91	Luton T	0	0		
1990–91	*Preston NE*	4	0	**4**	**0**
1991–92	Luton T	9	0	**9**	**0**
1991–92	Everton	30	1		
1992–93	Everton	27	3		
1993–94	Everton	38	0		
1994–95	Everton	29	0		
1995–96	Everton	14	0		
1995–96	*Charlton Ath*	8	0	**8**	**0**
1996–97	Everton	0	0	**138**	**4**
1996–97	*QPR*	7	0	**7**	**0**
1996–97	*Birmingham C*	10	0	**10**	**0**
1996–97	Norwich C	19	2		
1997–98	Norwich C	41	3		
1998–99	Norwich C	37	1		
1999–2000	Norwich C	38	0		
2000–01	Norwich C	26	0		
2001–02	Norwich C	0	0	**161**	**6**
2001–02	Wigan Ath	26	0		
2002–03	Wigan Ath	45	1		
2003–04	Wigan Ath	24	1		
2004–05	Wigan Ath	36	1		
2005–06	Wigan Ath	16	0		
2006–07	Wigan Ath	20	1	**167**	**4**

JOHANSSON, Andreas (M) 259 71
H: 5 11 W: 12 05 b.Vanersborg 5-7-78
Honours: Sweden Under-21, 13 full caps.

1993	Melleruds	2	0		
1994	Melleruds	15	1		
1995	Melleruds	21	10	**38**	**11**
1996	Degerfors	10	1		
1997	Degerfors	23	4		
1998	Degerfors	23	5	**56**	**10**
1999	AIK	12	1	**12**	**1**
2000	Djurgaarden	24	7		
2001	Djurgaarden	25	5		
2002	Djurgaarden	26	10		
2003	Djurgaarden	26	12		
2004	Djurgaarden	23	11	**124**	**45**
2004–05	Wigan Ath	1	0		
2005–06	Wigan Ath	16	4		
2006–07	Wigan Ath	12	0	**29**	**4**

KILBANE, Kevin (M) 401 31
H: 6 1 W: 13 05 b.Preston 1-2-77
Source: Trainee. *Honours:* Eire Under-21, 80 full caps, 7 goals.

1993–94	Preston NE	0	0		

1994–95	Preston NE	0	0		
1995–96	Preston NE	11	1		
1996–97	Preston NE	36	2	**47**	**3**
1997–98	WBA	43	4		
1998–99	WBA	44	6		
1999–2000	WBA	19	5	**106**	**15**
1999–2000	Sunderland	20	1		
2000–01	Sunderland	30	4		
2001–02	Sunderland	28	2		
2002–03	Sunderland	30	1		
2003–04	Sunderland	5	0	**113**	**8**
2003–04	Everton	30	3		
2004–05	Everton	38	1		
2005–06	Everton	34	0		
2006–07	Everton	2	0	**104**	**4**
2006–07	Wigan Ath	31	1	**31**	**1**

KIRKLAND, Christopher (G) 85 0
H: 6 5 W: 14 08 b.Leicester 2-5-81
Source: Trainee. *Honours:* England Youth, Under-21, 1 full cap.

1997–98	Coventry C	0	0		
1998–99	Coventry C	0	0		
1999–2000	Coventry C	0	0		
2000–01	Coventry C	23	0		
2001–02	Coventry C	1	0	**24**	**0**
2001–02	Liverpool	1	0		
2002–03	Liverpool	8	0		
2003–04	Liverpool	6	0		
2004–05	Liverpool	10	0		
2005–06	Liverpool	0	0		
2005–06	*WBA*	10	0	**10**	**0**
2006–07	Liverpool	0	0	**25**	**0**
2006–07	Wigan Ath	26	0	**26**	**0**

KUPISZ, Tomasz (M) 0 0
b.Radom 2-1-90
Source: Piaseczno.

2006–07	Wigan Ath	0	0

LANDZAAT, Denny (M) 354 72
H: 5 10 W: 11 00 b.Amsterdam 6-5-76
Honours: Holland 36 full caps, 1 goal.

1995–96	Ajax	1	0	**1**	**0**
1996–97	MVV	34	2		
1997–98	MVV	34	4		
1998–99	MVV	34	4	**102**	**10**
1999–2000	Willem II	25	3		
2000–01	Willem II	33	12		
2001–02	Willem II	34	16		
2002–03	Willem II	34	5		
2003–04	Willem II	13	2	**139**	**38**
2003–04	AZ	17	3		
2004–05	AZ	33	10		
2005–06	AZ	29	9	**79**	**22**
2006–07	Wigan Ath	33	2	**33**	**2**

McCULLOCH, Lee (F) 346 66
H: 6 1 W: 13 07 b.Bellshill 14-5-78
Source: Cumbernauld U. *Honours:* Scotland Youth, Under-21, B, 11 full caps.

1995–96	Motherwell	1	0		
1996–97	Motherwell	15	0		
1997–98	Motherwell	25	2		
1998–99	Motherwell	26	3		
1999–2000	Motherwell	29	9		
2000–01	Motherwell	26	8	**122**	**22**
2000–01	Wigan Ath	10	3		
2001–02	Wigan Ath	34	6		
2002–03	Wigan Ath	38	6		
2003–04	Wigan Ath	41	6		
2004–05	Wigan Ath	42	14		
2005–06	Wigan Ath	30	5		
2006–07	Wigan Ath	29	4	**224**	**44**

McMILLAN, Steve (D) 244 6
H: 5 9 W: 12 05 b.Edinburgh 19-1-76
Source: Troon Juniors. *Honours:* Scotland Under-21

1993–94	Motherwell	1	0		
1994–95	Motherwell	3	0		
1995–96	Motherwell	12	0		
1996–97	Motherwell	16	0		
1997–98	Motherwell	34	1		
1998–99	Motherwell	30	2		
1999–2000	Motherwell	31	3		
2000–01	Motherwell	25	0	**152**	**6**
2000–01	Wigan Ath	6	0		
2001–02	Wigan Ath	29	0		
2002–03	Wigan Ath	32	0		
2003–04	Wigan Ath	15	0		
2004–05	Wigan Ath	8	0		
2005–06	Wigan Ath	2	0		
2006–07	Wigan Ath	0	0	**92**	**0**

MONTROSE, Lewis (M) 0 0
H: 6 0 W: 12 00 b.Manchester 17-11-88
Source: Scholar.

2006–07	Wigan Ath	0	0

POLLITT, Mike (G) 494 0
H: 6 4 W: 15 03 b.Farnworth 29-2-72
Source: Trainee.

1990–91	Manchester U	0	0		
1990–91	*Oldham Ath*	0	0		
1991–92	Bury	0	0		
1992–93	Lincoln C	27	0		
1993–94	Lincoln C	30	0	**57**	**0**
1994–95	Darlington	40	0		
1995–96	Darlington	15	0	**55**	**0**
1995–96	Notts Co	0	0		
1996–97	Notts Co	8	0		
1997–98	Notts Co	2	0	**10**	**0**
1997–98	*Oldham Ath*	16	0	**16**	**0**
1997–98	*Gillingham*	6	0	**6**	**0**
1997–98	*Brentford*	5	0	**5**	**0**
1997–98	Sunderland	0	0		
1998–99	Rotherham U	46	0		
1999–2000	Rotherham U	46	0		
2000–01	Chesterfield	46	0	**46**	**0**
2001–02	Rotherham U	46	0		
2002–03	Rotherham U	41	0		
2003–04	Rotherham U	43	0		
2004–05	Rotherham U	45	0	**267**	**0**
2005–06	Wigan Ath	24	0		
2006–07	Wigan Ath	3	0	**27**	**0**
2006–07	*Ipswich T*	1	0	**1**	**0**
2006–07	*Burnley*	4	0	**4**	**0**

SCHARNER, Paul (D) 175 19
H: 6 3 W: 12 09 b.Scheibbs 11-3-80
Source: St Polten. *Honours:* Austria 15 full caps.

1998–99	FK Austria	4	0		
1999–2000	FK Austria	12	0		
2000–01	FK Austria	14	0		
2001–02	FK Austria	16	1		
2002–03	FK Austria	29	1		
2003–04	FK Austria	9	1	**84**	**3**
2003–04	Salzburg	13	2		
2004–05	Salzburg	5	1	**18**	**3**
2004	Brann	7	1		
2005	Brann	25	6	**32**	**7**
2005–06	Wigan Ath	16	3		
2006–07	Wigan Ath	25	3	**41**	**6**

SKOKO, Josip (M) 304 32
H: 5 9 W: 12 02 b.Mount Gambier 10-12-75
Honours: Australia Under-20, Under-23, 50 full caps, 9 goals.

1995–96	Hajduk Split	14	1		
1996–97	Hajduk Split	27	10		
1997–98	Hajduk Split	26	5		
1998–99	Hajduk Split	24	3		
1999–2000	Hajduk Split	15	0	**106**	**19**
1999–2000	Genk	9	1		
2000–01	Genk	28	3		
2001–02	Genk	32	2		
2002–03	Genk	29	1	**98**	**7**
2003–04	Genclerbirligi	28	2		
2004–05	Genclerbirligi	30	2	**58**	**4**
2005–06	Wigan Ath	5	0		
2005–06	*Stoke C*	9	2	**9**	**2**
2006–07	Wigan Ath	28	0	**33**	**0**

TAYLOR, Ryan (M) 125 15
H: 5 8 W: 10 04 b.Liverpool 19-8-84
Source: Scholar. *Honours:* England Youth, Under-21.

2001–02	Tranmere R	0	0		
2002–03	Tranmere R	25	1		
2003–04	Tranmere R	30	5		
2004–05	Tranmere R	43	8	**98**	**14**
2005–06	Wigan Ath	11	0		
2006–07	Wigan Ath	16	1	**27**	**1**

UNSWORTH, Dave (D) 416 44
H: 6 1 W: 13 07 b.Chorley 16-10-73
Source: Trainee. *Honours:* England Youth, Under-21, 1 full cap.

1991–92	Everton	2	1		
1992–93	Everton	3	0		
1993–94	Everton	8	0		
1994–95	Everton	38	3		
1995–96	Everton	31	2		
1996–97	Everton	34	5		
1997–98	West Ham U	32	2	**32**	**2**
1998–99	Aston Villa	0	0		
1998–99	Everton	34	1		
1999–2000	Everton	33	6		
2000–01	Everton	29	5		
2001–02	Everton	33	3		
2002–03	Everton	33	5		
2003–04	Everton	26	3	**304**	**34**
2004–05	Portsmouth	15	2		
2004–05	*Ipswich T*	16	1	**16**	**1**
2005–06	Portsmouth	0	0	**15**	**2**
2005–06	Sheffield U	34	4		
2006–07	Sheffield U	5	0	**39**	**4**
2006–07	Wigan Ath	10	1	**10**	**1**

VALENCIA, Luis (M) 84 10
H: 5 10 W: 12 04 b.Lago Agrio 5-8-85
Honours: Ecuador Under-21, Under-23, 19 full caps, 3 goals.

2003	El Nacional	42	5		
2004	El Nacional	14	4	**56**	**9**
2004–05	Villarreal	0	0		
2005–06	Villarreal	2	0	**2**	**0**
2005–06	*Recreativo*	4	0	**4**	**0**
2006–07	Wigan Ath	22	1	**22**	**1**

WEBSTER, Andy (D) 169 7
H: 6 0 W: 11 13 b.Dundee 23-4-82
Honours: Scotland Under-21, B, 22 full caps, 1 goal.

1999–2000	Arbroath	4	0		
2000–01	Arbroath	13	1	**17**	**1**
2000–01	Hearts	4	0		
2001–02	Hearts	26	1		
2002–03	Hearts	21	1		
2003–04	Hearts	32	2		
2004–05	Hearts	35	1		
2005–06	Hearts	30	1	**148**	**6**
2006–07	Wigan Ath	4	0	**4**	**0**

Scholars
Ashworth, Luke Alexander; Field, Lewis; Hampson, Matthew; Holt, Joseph; Horn, Timothy; King, Kristofer; Mahon, Craig; McArdle, Scott; McCaughtrie, Christopher; Montrose, Lewis Robert Egerton; Moore, Peter Francis; Pearson, Andrew David; Saunders, Russell.

WOLVERHAMPTON W (89)

BAILEY, Matthew (M) 0 0
H: 5 10 W: 9 11 b.Birmingham 24-9-88
Source: Scholar.

2006–07	Wolverhampton W	0	0

BENNETT, Elliott (M) 0 0
H: 5 9 W: 10 11 b.Telford 18-12-88
Source: Scholar.

2006–07	Wolverhampton W	0	0

BOTHROYD, Jay (F) 160 30
H: 6 3 W: 14 13 b.Islington 7-5-82
Source: From Trainee. *Honours:* England Schools, Youth, Under-20, Under-21.

1999–2000	Arsenal	0	0		
2000–01	Coventry C	8	0		
2001–02	Coventry C	31	6		
2002–03	Coventry C	33	8	**72**	**14**
2003–04	*Perugia*	26	4	**26**	**4**
2004–05	Blackburn R	11	1	**11**	**1**
2005–06	Charlton Ath	18	2	**18**	**2**
2006–07	Wolverhampton W	33	9	**33**	**9**

BREEN, Gary (D) 486 13
H: 6 3 W: 13 03 b.Hendon 12-12-73
Source: Charlton Ath. *Honours:* Eire Under-21, 63 full caps, 7 goals.

1991–92	Maidstone U	19	0	**19**	**0**

1992–93	Gillingham	29	0		
1993–94	Gillingham	22	0	**51**	**0**
1994–95	Peterborough U	44	1		
1995–96	Peterborough U	25	0	**69**	**1**
1995–96	Birmingham C	18	1		
1996–97	Birmingham C	22	1	**40**	**2**
1996–97	Coventry C	9	0		
1997–98	Coventry C	30	1		
1998–99	Coventry C	25	0		
1999–2000	Coventry C	21	0		
2000–01	Coventry C	31	1		
2001–02	Coventry C	30	0	**146**	**2**
2002–03	West Ham U	14	0	**14**	**0**
2003–04	Sunderland	32	4		
2004–05	Sunderland	40	2		
2005–06	Sunderland	35	1	**107**	**7**
2006–07	Wolverhampton W	40	1	**40**	**1**

CLAPHAM, Jamie (M) 329 11
H: 5 9 W: 11 09 b.Lincoln 7-12-75
Source: Trainee.

1994–95	Tottenham H	0	0		
1995–96	Tottenham H	0	0		
1996–97	Tottenham H	1	0		
1996–97	*Leyton Orient*	6	0	**6**	**0**
1996–97	*Bristol R*	5	0	**5**	**0**
1997–98	Tottenham H	0	0	**1**	**0**
1997–98	Ipswich T	22	0		
1998–99	Ipswich T	46	3		
1999–2000	Ipswich T	46	2		
2000–01	Ipswich T	35	2		
2001–02	Ipswich T	32	2		
2002–03	Ipswich T	26	1	**207**	**10**
2002–03	Birmingham C	16	0		
2003–04	Birmingham C	25	0		
2004–05	Birmingham C	27	0		
2005–06	Birmingham C	16	1	**84**	**1**
2006–07	Wolverhampton W	26	0	**26**	**0**

CLYDE, Mark (D) 51 0
H: 6 1 W: 13 00 b.Limavady 27-12-82
Source: Scholar. *Honours:* Northern Ireland Under-21, 3 full caps.

2001–02	Wolverhampton W	0	0		
2002–03	Wolverhampton W	17	0		
2002–03	*Kidderminster H*	4	0	**4**	**0**
2003–04	Wolverhampton W	9	0		
2004–05	Wolverhampton W	18	0		
2005–06	Wolverhampton W	0	0		
2006–07	Wolverhampton W	3	0	**47**	**0**

COLLINS, Lee (D) 0 0
H: 6 1 W: 11 10 b.Telford 23-9-83
Source: Scholar.

2006–07	Wolverhampton W	0	0		

COLLINS, Neill (D) 160 7
H: 6 3 W: 12 07 b.Irvine 2-9-83
Honours: Scoland Under-21.

2000–01	Queen's Park	4	0		
2001–02	Queen's Park	28	0	**32**	**0**
2002–03	Dumbarton	33	2		
2003–04	Dumbarton	30	2	**63**	**4**
2004–05	Sunderland	11	0		
2005–06	Sunderland	1	0		
2005–06	*Hartlepool U*	22	0	**22**	**0**
2005–06	*Sheffield U*	2	0	**2**	**0**
2006–07	Sunderland	7	1	**19**	**1**
2006–07	Wolverhampton W	22	2	**22**	**2**

CORNES, Chris (M) 10 3
H: 5 8 W: 14 02 b.Worcester 20-12-86
Source: Scholar.

2004–05	Wolverhampton W	0	0		
2005–06	*Port Vale*	10	3	**10**	**3**
2005–06	Wolverhampton W	0	0		
2006–07	Wolverhampton W	0	0		

CORT, Carl (F) 195 55
H: 6 4 W: 12 04 b.Southwark 1-11-77
Source: Trainee. *Honours:* England Under-21.

1996–97	Wimbledon	1	0		
1996–97	*Lincoln C*	6	1	**6**	**1**
1997–98	Wimbledon	22	4		
1998–99	Wimbledon	16	3		
1999–2000	Wimbledon	34	9	**73**	**16**
2000–01	Newcastle U	13	6		
2001–02	Newcastle U	8	1		
2002–03	Newcastle U	1	0		
2003–04	Newcastle U	0	0	**22**	**7**
2003–04	Wolverhampton W	16	5		
2004–05	Wolverhampton W	37	15		
2005–06	Wolverhampton W	31	11		
2006–07	Wolverhampton W	10	0	**94**	**31**

CRADDOCK, Jody (D) 427 12
H: 6 0 W: 12 04 b.Redditch 25-7-75
Source: Christchurch.

1993–94	Cambridge U	20	0		
1994–95	Cambridge U	38	0		
1995–96	Cambridge U	46	3		
1996–97	Cambridge U	41	1	**145**	**4**
1997–98	Sunderland	32	0		
1998–99	Sunderland	6	0		
1999–2000	Sunderland	19	0		
1999–2000	*Sheffield U*	10	0	**10**	**0**
2000–01	Sunderland	34	0		
2001–02	Sunderland	30	1		
2002–03	Sunderland	25	1	**146**	**2**
2003–04	Wolverhampton W	32	1		
2004–05	Wolverhampton W	42	1		
2005–06	Wolverhampton W	18	0		
2006–07	Wolverhampton W	34	4	**126**	**6**

DAVIES, Craig (F) 71 8
H: 6 2 W: 13 05 b.Burton-on-Trent 9-1-86
Source: Manchester C.Wales Youth, Under-21, 4 full caps.

2004–05	Oxford U	28	6		
2005–06	Oxford U	20	2	**48**	**8**
2005–06	Verona	0	0		
2006–07	Wolverhampton W	23	0	**23**	**0**

DAVIES, Mark (M) 27 1
H: 5 11 W: 11 08 b.Wolverhampton 18-2-88
Source: Scholar. *Honours:* England Youth.

2004–05	Wolverhampton W	0	0		
2005–06	Wolverhampton W	20	1		
2006–07	Wolverhampton W	7	0	**27**	**1**

EDWARDS, Rob (D) 118 2
H: 6 1 W: 11 10 b.Telford 25-12-82
Source: Trainee. *Honours:* Wales Youth, 15 full caps.

1999–2000	Aston Villa	0	0		
2000–01	Aston Villa	0	0		
2001–02	Aston Villa	0	0		
2002–03	Aston Villa	8	0		
2003–04	Aston Villa	0	0	**8**	**0**
2003–04	*Crystal Palace*	7	1	**7**	**1**
2003–04	*Derby Co*	11	1	**11**	**1**
2004–05	Wolverhampton W	17	0		
2005–06	Wolverhampton W	42	0		
2006–07	Wolverhampton W	33	0	**92**	**0**

FRANKOWSKI, Tomasz (F) 199 119
H: 5 8 W: 10 01 b.Poland 16-8-74
Source: Bialystok, Strasbourg, Grampus Eight, Poitiers, Martigues. *Honours:* Poland 20 full caps, 10 goals.

1998–99	Wisla Krakow	29	21		
1999–2000	Wisla Krakow	26	17		
2000–01	Wisla Krakow	28	18		
2001–02	Wisla Krakow	26	9		
2002–03	Wisla Krakow	12	6		
2003–04	Wisla Krakow	22	15		
2004–05	Wisla Krakow	26	25	**169**	**111**
2005–06	Elche	14	8	**14**	**8**
2005–06	Wolverhampton W	16	0		
2006–07	Wolverhampton W	0	0	**16**	**0**

To Tenerife (loan) August 2006

GLEESON, Stephen (M) 17 2
H: 6 2 W: 11 00 b.Dublin 3-8-88
Source: Scholar. *Honours:* Eire 2 full caps.

2006–07	Wolverhampton W	3	0	**3**	**0**
2006–07	*Stockport Co*	14	2	**14**	**2**

GOBERN, Lewis (M) 29 4
H: 5 10 W: 11 07 b.Birmingham 28-1-85
Source: Scholar.

2003–04	Wolverhampton W	0	0		
2004–05	Wolverhampton W	0	0		
2004–05	*Hartlepool U*	1	0	**1**	**0**
2005–06	Wolverhampton W	1	0		
2005–06	*Blackpool*	8	1	**8**	**1**
2005–06	*Bury*	7	1	**7**	**1**
2006–07	Wolverhampton W	12	2	**13**	**2**

GYEPES, Gabor (D) 134 12
H: 6 3 W: 13 01 b.Hungary 26-6-81
Honours: Hungary 22 full caps, 1 goal.

1999–2000	Ferencvaros	2	0		
2000–01	Ferencvaros	29	2		
2001–02	Ferencvaros	33	3		
2002–03	Ferencvaros	17	2		
2003–04	Ferencvaros	7	0		
2004–05	Ferencvaros	26	5	**114**	**12**
2005–06	Wolverhampton W	20	0		
2006–07	Wolverhampton W	0	0	**20**	**0**

HENNESSEY, Wayne (G) 15 0
H: 6 0 W: 11 06 b.Anglesey 24-1-87
Source: Scholar. *Honours:* Wales Schools, Youth, Under-21, 2 full caps.

2004–05	Wolverhampton W	0	0		
2005–06	Wolverhampton W	0	0		
2006–07	Wolverhampton W	0	0		
2006–07	*Bristol C*	0	0		
2006–07	*Stockport Co*	15	0	**15**	**0**

HENRY, Karl (M) 163 5
H: 6 0 W: 12 00 b.Wolverhampton 26-11-82
Source: Trainee. *Honours:* England Youth, Under-20.

1999–2000	Stoke C	0	0		
2000–01	Stoke C	0	0		
2001–02	Stoke C	24	0		
2002–03	Stoke C	18	1		
2003–04	Stoke C	20	0		
2003–04	*Cheltenham T*	9	1	**9**	**1**
2004–05	Stoke C	34	0		
2005–06	Stoke C	24	0	**120**	**1**
2006–07	Wolverhampton W	34	3	**34**	**3**

HUGHES, Liam (F) 0 0
H: 6 2 W: 11 09 b.Gornal 11-9-88
Source: Scholar.

2006–07	Wolverhampton W	0	0		

IKEME, Carl (G) 10 0
H: 6 2 W: 13 09 b.Sutton Coldfield 8-6-86
Source: Scholar.

2005–06	Wolverhampton W	0	0		
2005–06	*Stockport Co*	9	0	**9**	**0**
2006–07	Wolverhampton W	1	0	**1**	**0**

JOHNSON, Jemal (F) 43 7
H: 5 8 W: 11 09 b.New Jersey 3-5-84
Source: Scholar.

2001–02	Blackburn R	0	0		
2002–03	Blackburn R	0	0		
2003–04	Blackburn R	0	0		
2004–05	Blackburn R	3	0		
2005–06	Blackburn R	3	0		
2005–06	*Preston NE*	3	1	**3**	**1**
2005–06	*Darlington*	9	3	**9**	**3**
2006–07	Blackburn R	0	0	**6**	**0**
2006–07	Wolverhampton W	20	3	**20**	**3**
2006–07	*Leeds U*	5	0	**5**	**0**

JONES, Daniel (D) 9 0
H: 6 2 W: 13 00 b.Wordsley 14-7-86
Source: Scholar.

2005–06	Wolverhampton W	1	0		
2006–07	Wolverhampton W	8	0	**9**	**0**

KEOGH, Andy (F) 119 28
H: 6 0 W: 11 00 b.Dublin 16-5-86
Source: Scholar. *Honours:* Eire Youth, B, Under-21, 1 full cap.

2003–04	Leeds U	0	0		
2004–05	Leeds U	0	0		
2004–05	*Bury*	4	2	**4**	**2**
2004–05	Scunthorpe U	25	3		
2005–06	Scunthorpe U	45	11		
2006–07	Scunthorpe U	28	7	**98**	**21**
2006–07	Wolverhampton W	17	5	**17**	**5**

KIGHTLY, Michael (F) 37 8
H: 5 10 W: 10 10 b.Basildon 24-1-86
Source: Scholar.

2002–03	Southend U	1	0		
2003–04	Southend U	11	0		
2004–05	Southend U	1	0	**13**	**0**

From Grays Ath.

2006–07	Wolverhampton W	24	8	**24**	**8**

LITTLE, Mark (D) 26 0
H: 6 1 W: 12 10 b.Worcester 20-8-88
Source: Scholar. *Honours:* England Youth.

2005–06	Wolverhampton W	0	0		
2006–07	Wolverhampton W	26	0	**26**	**0**

LOWE, Keith (D) **51 1**
H: 6 2 W: 13 03 b.Wolverhampton 13-9-85
Source: Scholar.

2004–05	Wolverhampton W	11	0		
2005–06	Wolverhampton W	3	0		
2005–06	*Burnley*	16	0	**16**	**0**
2005–06	*QPR*	1	0	**1**	**0**
2005–06	*Swansea C*	4	0	**4**	**0**
2006–07	Wolverhampton W	0	0	**14**	**0**
2006–07	*Brighton & HA*	0	0		
2006–07	*Cheltenham T*	16	1	**16**	**1**

McINDOE, Michael (M) **214 35**
H: 5 8 W: 11 00 b.Edinburgh 2-12-79
Source: Trainee. *Honours:* Scotland B.

1997–98	Luton T	0	0		
1998–99	Luton T	22	0		
1999–2000	Luton T	17	0	**39**	**0**

Fr Hereford, Yeovil

2003–04	Doncaster R	45	10		
2004–05	Doncaster R	44	10		
2005–06	Doncaster R	33	8	**122**	**28**
2005–06	*Derby Co*	8	0	**8**	**0**
2006–07	Barnsley	18	4	**18**	**4**
2006–07	Wolverhampton W	27	3	**27**	**3**

McNAMARA, Jackie (D) **364 13**
H: 5 9 W: 10 04 b.Glasgow 24-10-73
Source: Gairdoch U. *Honours:* Scotland B, Under-21, 33 full caps.

1991–92	Dunfermline Ath	0	0		
1992–93	Dunfermline Ath	3	0		
1993–94	Dunfermline Ath	39	0		
1994–95	Dunfermline Ath	30	2		
1995–96	Dunfermline Ath	7	1	**79**	**3**
1995–96	Celtic	26	1		
1996–97	Celtic	30	1		
1997–98	Celtic	31	2		
1998–99	Celtic	16	0		
1999–2000	Celtic	23	0		
2000–01	Celtic	30	3		
2001–02	Celtic	20	0		
2002–03	Celtic	19	1		
2003–04	Celtic	27	1		
2004–05	Celtic	34	1	**256**	**10**
2005–06	Wolverhampton W	10	0		
2006–07	Wolverhampton W	19	0	**29**	**0**

MULGREW, Charlie (D) **19 2**
H: 6 2 W: 13 01 b.Glasgow 6-3-86
Honours: Scotland Youth, Under-21.

2002–03	Celtic	0	0		
2003–04	Celtic	0	0		
2004–05	Celtic	0	0		
2005–06	Celtic	0	0		
2005–06	*Dundee U*	13	2	**13**	**2**
2006–07	Wolverhampton W	6	0	**6**	**0**

MURRAY, Matt (G) **89 0**
H: 6 4 W: 13 10 b.Solihull 2-5-81
Source: Trainee. *Honours:* England Youth, Under-21.

1997–98	Wolverhampton W	0	0		
1998–99	Wolverhampton W	0	0		
1999–2000	Wolverhampton W	0	0		
2000–01	Wolverhampton W	0	0		
2001–02	Wolverhampton W	0	0		
2002–03	Wolverhampton W	40	0		
2003–04	Wolverhampton W	1	0		
2004–05	Wolverhampton W	1	0		
2005–06	Wolverhampton W	1	0		
2005–06	*Tranmere R*	2	0	**2**	**0**
2006–07	Wolverhampton W	44	0	**87**	**0**

NAYLOR, Lee (D) **293 7**
H: 5 9 W: 11 03 b.Walsall 19-3-80
Source: Trainee. *Honours:* England Youth, Under-21.

1997–98	Wolverhampton W	16	0		
1998–99	Wolverhampton W	23	1		
1999–2000	Wolverhampton W	30	2		
2000–01	Wolverhampton W	46	1		
2001–02	Wolverhampton W	27	0		
2002–03	Wolverhampton W	32	1		
2003–04	Wolverhampton W	38	0		
2004–05	Wolverhampton W	38	1		
2005–06	Wolverhampton W	40	1		
2006–07	Wolverhampton W	3	0	**293**	**7**

O'CONNOR, Kevin (M) **10 1**
H: 5 11 W: 12 02 b.Dublin 19-10-85
Source: Scholar. *Honours:* Eire Under-21.

2003–04	Wolverhampton W	0	0		
2004–05	Wolverhampton W	0	0		
2005–06	Wolverhampton W	0	0		
2005–06	*Stockport Co*	7	1	**7**	**1**
2006–07	Wolverhampton W	3	0	**3**	**0**

OAKES, Michael (G) **251 0**
H: 6 2 W: 14 06 b.Northwich 30-10-73
Source: Trainee. *Honours:* England Under-21.

1991–92	Aston Villa	0	0		
1992–93	Aston Villa	0	0		
1993–94	Aston Villa	0	0		
1993–94	*Scarborough*	1	0	**1**	**0**
1993–94	*Tranmere R*	0	0		
1994–95	Aston Villa	0	0		
1995–96	Aston Villa	0	0		
1996–97	Aston Villa	20	0		
1997–98	Aston Villa	8	0		
1998–99	Aston Villa	23	0		
1999–2000	Aston Villa	0	0	**51**	**0**
1999–2000	Wolverhampton W	28	0		
2000–01	Wolverhampton W	46	0		
2001–02	Wolverhampton W	46	0		
2002–03	Wolverhampton W	6	0		
2003–04	Wolverhampton W	21	0		
2004–05	Wolverhampton W	35	0		
2005–06	Wolverhampton W	17	0		
2006–07	Wolverhampton W	0	0	**199**	**0**

OLOFINJANA, Seyi (M) **133 24**
H: 6 4 W: 11 10 b.Lagos 30-6-80
Source: Kwara United Ilorin. *Honours:* Nigeria 11 full caps.

2003	Brann	25	9		
2004	Brann	9	2	**34**	**11**
2004–05	Wolverhampton W	42	5		
2005–06	Wolverhampton W	13	0		
2006–07	Wolverhampton W	44	8	**99**	**13**

POTTER, Darren (M) **50 0**
H: 6 0 W: 10 08 b.Liverpool 21-12-84
Source: Scholar. *Honours:* Eire Youth, B, Under-21, 2 full caps.

2001–02	Liverpool	0	0		
2002–03	Liverpool	0	0		
2003–04	Liverpool	0	0		
2004–05	Liverpool	2	0		
2005–06	Liverpool	0	0		
2005–06	*Southampton*	10	0	**10**	**0**
2006–07	Liverpool	0	0	**2**	**0**
2006–07	Wolverhampton W	38	0	**38**	**0**

RICKETTS, Rohan (M) **89 2**
H: 5 10 W: 11 07 b.Clapham 22-12-82
Source: Scholar. *Honours:* England Youth, Under-20.

2001–02	Arsenal	0	0		
2002–03	Tottenham H	0	0		
2003–04	Tottenham H	24	1		
2004–05	Tottenham H	6	0	**30**	**1**
2004–05	*Coventry C*	6	0	**6**	**0**
2004–05	*Wolverhampton W*	7	1		
2005–06	Wolverhampton W	25	0		
2006–07	Wolverhampton W	19	0	**51**	**1**
2006–07	*QPR*	2	0	**2**	**0**

RILEY, Martin (D) **0 0**
H: 6 0 W: 12 01 b.Wolverhampton 5-12-86
Source: Scholar. *Honours:* England Under-20.

2004–05	Wolverhampton W	0	0		
2005–06	Wolverhampton W	0	0		
2006–07	Wolverhampton W	0	0		

ROSA, Denes (M) **198 29**
H: 5 8 W: 10 05 b.Hungary 7-4-77
Honours: Hungary 10 full caps.

1996–97	BVSC	12	0		
1997–98	BVSC	26	5		
1998–99	BVSC	13	4		
1999–2000	BVSC	0	0		
1999–2000	Gyor	8	1		
2000–01	Gyor	25	1		
2001–02	BVSC	0	0	**51**	**9**
2001–02	Gyor	12	1	**45**	**3**
2002–03	Dunaferr	14	0	**14**	**0**
2002–03	Ujpest	9	1	**9**	**1**
2003–04	Ferencvaros	25	2		
2004–05	Ferencvaros	27	8		
2005–06	Ferencvaros	14	4	**66**	**14**
2005–06	Wolverhampton W	9	2		
2006–07	Wolverhampton W	0	0	**9**	**2**
2006–07	*Cheltenham T*	4	0	**4**	**0**

SALMON, Mark (M) **0 0**
H: 5 10 W: 10 07 b.Dublin 31-10-88
Source: Scholar.

2006–07	Wolverhampton W	0	0		

WARD, Stephen (F) **90 14**
H: 5 11 W: 12 02 b.Dublin 20-8-85
Honours: Eire Youth, Under-21.

2003	Bohemians	6	0		
2004	Bohemians	16	2		
2005	Bohemians	29	7		
2006	Bohemians	21	2	**72**	**11**
2006–07	Wolverhampton W	18	3	**18**	**3**

WREXHAM (90)

CARVILL, Michael (F) **6 0**
H: 5 10 W: 10 10 b.Belfast 3-4-88
Source: Scholar. *Honours:* Northern Ireland Youth.

2005–06	Charlton Ath	0	0		
2006–07	Charlton Ath	0	0		
2006–07	Wrexham	6	0	**6**	**0**

CROWELL, Matt (M) **87 4**
H: 5 11 W: 10 10 b.Bridgend 3-7-84
Source: Scholar. *Honours:* Wales Youth, Under-21.

2001–02	Southampton	0	0		
2002–03	Southampton	0	0		
2003–04	Wrexham	15	1		
2004–05	Wrexham	28	0		
2005–06	Wrexham	29	3		
2006–07	Wrexham	15	0	**87**	**4**

DONE, Matt (M) **40 1**
H: 5 10 W: 10 04 b.Oswestry 22-6-88
Source: Scholar.

2005–06	Wrexham	6	0		
2006–07	Wrexham	34	1	**40**	**1**

EVANS, Gareth (D) **12 0**
H: 6 1 W: 12 12 b.Wrexham 10-1-87
Source: Scholar.

2005–06	Wrexham	0	0		
2006–07	Wrexham	12	0	**12**	**0**

EVANS, Steve (D) **186 26**
H: 6 5 W: 13 05 b.Wrexham 26-2-79
Honours: Wales 5 full caps.

1999–2000	TNS	14	4		
2000–01	TNS	8	0		
2001–02	TNS	16	2		
2002–03	TNS	27	7		
2003–04	TNS	20	8		
2004–05	TNS	33	0		
2005–06	TNS	33	3	**151**	**24**
2006–07	Wrexham	35	2	**35**	**2**

FLEMING, Andy (M) **2 0**
H: 6 1 W: 12 00 b.Liverpool 1-4-87
Source: Scholar.

2006–07	Wrexham	2	0	**2**	**0**

INGHAM, Michael (G) **130 0**
H: 6 4 W: 13 10 b.Preston 7-9-80
Source: From Malachians. *Honours:* Northern Ireland Youth, Under-21, 3 full caps.

1998–99	Cliftonville	18	0	**18**	**0**
1999–2000	Sunderland	0	0		
1999–2000	*Carlisle U*	7	0	**7**	**0**
2000–01	Sunderland	0	0		
2001–02	Sunderland	0	0		
2001–02	*Stoke C*	0	0		
2002–03	Sunderland	0	0		
2002–03	*Darlington*	3	0	**3**	**0**
2002–03	*York C*	17	0	**17**	**0**
2003–04	Sunderland	0	0		
2003–04	*Wrexham*	11	0		
2004–05	Sunderland	2	0	**2**	**0**
2004–05	*Doncaster R*	1	0	**1**	**0**
2005–06	Wrexham	40	0		
2006–07	Wrexham	31	0	**82**	**0**

JOHNSON, Josh (M) **22 1**
H: 5 5 W: 10 07 b.Carenage 16-4-81
Source: San Juan Jabloteh. *Honours:* Trinidad & Tobago Under-20, Under-21, full caps.

2006–07	Wrexham	22	1	**22**	**1**

JONES, Mark (M) **112 22**
H: 5 11 W: 10 12 b.Wrexham 15-8-83
Source: Scholar. *Honours:* Wales Under-21, 1 full cap.

2002–03	Wrexham	1	0		
2003–04	Wrexham	13	1		
2004–05	Wrexham	26	3		
2005–06	Wrexham	42	13		
2006–07	Wrexham	30	5	**112**	**22**

JONES, Michael (G) **9 0**
H: 6 4 W: 12 05 b.Liverpool 3-12-87
Source: Scholar.

2004–05	Wrexham	1	0		
2005–06	Wrexham	7	0		
2006–07	Wrexham	1	0	**9**	**0**

LLEWELLYN, Chris (F) **315 44**
H: 5 11 W: 11 06 b.Swansea 29-8-79
Source: Trainee. *Honours:* Wales Youth, Under-21, B, 6 full caps, 1 goal.

1996–97	Norwich C	0	0		
1997–98	Norwich C	15	4		
1998–99	Norwich C	31	2		
1999–2000	Norwich C	36	3		
2000–01	Norwich C	42	8		
2001–02	Norwich C	13	0		
2002–03	Norwich C	5	0	**142**	**17**
2002–03	*Bristol R*	14	3	**14**	**3**
2003–04	Wrexham	46	8		
2004–05	Wrexham	45	7		
2005–06	Hartlepool U	29	0	**29**	**0**
2006–07	Wrexham	39	9	**130**	**24**

MACKIN, Levi (M) **36 0**
H: 6 1 W: 11 04 b.Chester 4-4-86
Source: Scholar. *Honours:* Wales Under-21.

2003–04	Wrexham	1	0		
2004–05	Wrexham	10	0		
2005–06	Wrexham	17	0		
2006–07	Wrexham	8	0	**36**	**0**

McEVILLY, Lee (F) **136 39**
H: 6 0 W: 13 00 b.Liverpool 15-4-82
Source: Burscough. *Honours:* Northern Ireland Under-21, 1 full cap.

2001–02	Rochdale	18	4		
2002–03	Rochdale	37	15		
2003–04	Rochdale	30	6	**85**	**25**
From Accrington S					
2005–06	Wrexham	23	7		
2006–07	Wrexham	28	7	**51**	**14**

NEWBY, Jon (F) **207 26**
H: 5 11 W: 11 00 b.Warrington 28-11-78
Source: Trainee.

1998–99	Liverpool	0	0		
1999–2000	Liverpool	1	0		
1999–2000	*Crewe Alex*	6	0	**6**	**0**
2000–01	Liverpool	0	0	**1**	**0**
2000–01	*Sheffield U*	13	0	**13**	**0**
2000–01	Bury	17	5		
2001–02	Bury	46	6		
2002–03	Bury	46	10		
2003–04	Huddersfield T	14	0	**14**	**0**
2003–04	*York C*	7	0	**7**	**0**
2004–05	Bury	36	4		
2005–06	Bury	10	1	**155**	**26**
2006–07	Wrexham	11	0	**11**	**0**

PEJIC, Shaun (D) **155 0**
H: 6 0 W: 11 07 b.Hereford 16-11-82
Source: Trainee. *Honours:* Wales Youth, Under-21.

2000–01	Wrexham	1	0		
2001–02	Wrexham	12	0		
2002–03	Wrexham	27	0		
2003–04	Wrexham	21	0		
2004–05	Wrexham	35	0		
2005–06	Wrexham	26	0		
2006–07	Wrexham	33	0	**155**	**0**

REED, Jamie (F) **14 0**
H: 5 11 W: 11 07 b.Deeside 13-8-87
Source: Scholar.

2005–06	Wrexham	3	0		
2005–06	*Glentoran*	7	0	**7**	**0**
2006–07	Wrexham	4	0	**7**	**0**

ROBERTS, Neil (F) **289 48**
H: 5 10 W: 11 00 b.Wrexham 7-4-78
Source: Trainee. *Honours:* Wales Youth, Under-21, B, 4 full caps.

1996–97	Wrexham	0	0		
1997–98	Wrexham	34	8		
1998–99	Wrexham	22	3		
1999–2000	Wrexham	19	6		
1999–2000	Wigan Ath	9	1		
2000–01	Wigan Ath	34	6		
2001–02	*Hull C*	6	0	**6**	**0**
2001–02	Wigan Ath	17	4		
2002–03	Wigan Ath	37	6		
2003–04	Wigan Ath	28	2		
2004–05	Wigan Ath	0	0	**125**	**19**
2004–05	*Bradford C*	3	1	**3**	**1**
2004–05	Doncaster R	31	6		
2005–06	Doncaster R	30	2	**61**	**8**
2006–07	Wrexham	19	3	**94**	**20**

ROCHE, Lee (D) **141 3**
H: 5 10 W: 10 11 b.Bolton 28-10-80
Source: Trainee. *Honours:* England Youth, Under-21.

1998–99	Manchester U	0	0		
1999–2000	Manchester U	0	0		
2000–01	Manchester U	0	0		
2000–01	*Wrexham*	41	0		
2001–02	Manchester U	0	0		
2002–03	Manchester U	1	0	**1**	**0**
2003–04	Burnley	25	1		
2004–05	Burnley	29	1	**54**	**2**
2005–06	Wrexham	17	1		
2006–07	Wrexham	28	0	**86**	**1**

SPENDER, Simon (D) **63 4**
H: 5 11 W: 11 00 b.Mold 15-11-85
Source: Scholar. *Honours:* Wales Youth, Under-21.

2003–04	Wrexham	6	0		
2004–05	Wrexham	13	0		
2005–06	Wrexham	19	2		
2006–07	Wrexham	25	2	**63**	**4**

UGARTE, Juan (F) **37 17**
H: 5 10 W: 10 08 b.San Sebastian 7-11-80

2001–02	Real Sociedad	1	0		
2002–03	Real Sociedad	0	0		
2003–04	Real Sociedad	0	0	**1**	**0**
From Dorchester T					
2004–05	Wrexham	30	17		
2005–06	Crewe Alex	2	0	**2**	**0**
2005–06	*Wrexham*	2	0		
2006–07	Wrexham	2	0	**34**	**17**

VALENTINE, Ryan (D) **196 6**
H: 5 10 W: 11 05 b.Wrexham 19-8-82
Source: Trainee. *Honours:* Wales Youth, Under-21.

1999–2000	Everton	0	0		
2000–01	Everton	0	0		
2001–02	Everton	0	0		
2002–03	Darlington	43	1		
2003–04	Darlington	40	2		
2004–05	Darlington	36	1		
2005–06	Darlington	43	0	**162**	**4**
2006–07	Wrexham	34	2	**34**	**2**

WILLIAMS, Danny (M) **262 19**
H: 6 1 W: 13 00 b.Wrexham 12-7-79
Source: Trainee. *Honours:* Wales Under-21.

1996–97	Liverpool	0	0		
1997–98	Liverpool	0	0		
1998–99	Liverpool	0	0		
1998–99	Wrexham	0	0		
1999–2000	Wrexham	24	1		
2000–01	Wrexham	15	2		
2001–02	Kidderminster H	38	1		
2002–03	Kidderminster H	45	2		
2003–04	Kidderminster H	28	5	**111**	**8**
2003–04	Bristol R	6	1	**6**	**1**
2004–05	Wrexham	21	0		
2005–06	Wrexham	45	4		
2006–07	Wrexham	40	3	**145**	**10**

WILLIAMS, Marc (F) **20 1**
H: 5 10 W: 11 12 b.Colwyn Bay 27-7-88
Source: Scholar. *Honours:* Wales Youth, Under-21.

2005–06	Wrexham	4	0		
2006–07	Wrexham	16	1	**20**	**1**

WILLIAMS, Mike (D) **43 0**
H: 5 11 W: 12 00 b.Colwyn Bay 27-10-86
Source: Scholar. *Honours:* Wales Under-21.

2005–06	Wrexham	12	0		
2006–07	Wrexham	31	0	**43**	**0**

WYCOMBE W (91)

ANTWI, Will (D) **34 1**
H: 6 2 W: 12 08 b.Epsom 19-10-82
Source: Scholar. *Honours:* Ghana 1 full cap.

2002–03	Crystal Palace	4	0		
2003–04	Crystal Palace	0	0	**4**	**0**
From Aldershot T					
2005–06	Wycombe W	5	0		
2006–07	Wycombe W	25	1	**30**	**1**

ANYA, Ikechi (M) **18 0**
H: 5 5 W: 11 04 b.Glasgow 3-1-88
Source: Scholar.

2004–05	Wycombe W	3	0		
2005–06	Wycombe W	2	0		
2006–07	Wycombe W	13	0	**18**	**0**

BARNES-HOMER, Matthew (M) **1 0**
H: 5 11 W: 12 05 b.Dudley 25-1-86
From Willenhall T.

2006–07	Wycombe W	1	0	**1**	**0**

BLOOMFIELD, Matt (M) **118 12**
H: 5 9 W: 11 00 b.Ipswich 8-2-84
Source: Scholar. *Honours:* England Youth, Under-20.

2001–02	Ipswich T	0	0		
2002–03	Ipswich T	0	0		
2003–04	Ipswich T	0	0		
2003–04	Wycombe W	12	1		
2004–05	Wycombe W	26	2		
2005–06	Wycombe W	39	5		
2006–07	Wycombe W	41	4	**118**	**12**

CADMORE, Tom (D) **0 0**
b.Rickmansworth 26-1-88
Source: Scholar.

2005–06	Wycombe W	0	0		
2006–07	Wycombe W	0	0		

CHRISTON, Lewis (D) **6 0**
H: 6 0 W: 12 02 b.Milton Keynes 24-1-89
Source: Scholar.

2005–06	Wycombe W	0	0		
2006–07	Wycombe W	6	0	**6**	**0**

CROOKS, Leon (M) **63 0**
H: 6 0 W: 11 12 b.Greenwich 21-11-85
Source: Scholar.

2004–05	Milton Keynes D	17	0		
2005–06	Milton Keynes D	23	0		
2006–07	Milton Keynes D	12	0	**52**	**0**
2006–07	Wycombe W	11	0	**11**	**0**

DIXON, Jonny (F) **73 7**
H: 5 9 W: 11 01 b.Murcia 16-1-84
Source: Scholar.

2002–03	Wycombe W	22	5		
2003–04	Wycombe W	8	0		
2004–05	Wycombe W	16	1		
2005–06	Wycombe W	17	0		
2006–07	Wycombe W	10	1	**73**	**7**

EASTER, Jermaine (F) **147 40**
H: 5 9 W: 12 02 b.Cardiff 15-1-82
Source: Trainee. *Honours:* Wales Youth, 3 full caps.

2000–01	Wolverhampton W	0	0		
2000–01	Hartlepool U	4	0		
2001–02	Hartlepool U	12	2		
2002–03	Hartlepool U	8	0		
2003–04	Hartlepool U	3	0	**27**	**2**
2003–04	*Cambridge U*	15	2		
2004–05	Cambridge U	24	6	**39**	**8**
2004–05	Boston U	9	3	**9**	**3**
2005–06	Stockport Co	19	8	**19**	**8**
2005–06	Wycombe W	15	2		
2006–07	Wycombe W	38	17	**53**	**19**

FAULKNER, James (F) **0 0**
b.Aylesbury 22-11-87
Source: Scholar.
2005–06 Wycombe W 0 0
2006–07 Wycombe W 0 0

GREGORY, Steven (D) **4 0**
H: 6 1 W: 12 04 b.Aylesbury 19-3-87
Source: Scholar.
2005–06 Wycombe W 1 0
2006–07 Wycombe W 3 0 **4 0**

GRIFFIN, Charlie (F) **50 5**
H: 6 0 W: 12 07 b.Bath 25-6-79
Source: Bristol R Schoolboy.
1998–99 Swindon T 5 1
1999–2000 Swindon T 21 1
2000–01 Swindon T 2 0 **28 2**
From Forest Green R.
2005–06 Wycombe W 22 3
2006–07 Wycombe W 0 0 **22 3**

MARTIN, Russell (M) **72 5**
H: 6 0 W: 11 08 b.Brighton 4-1-86
2004–05 Wycombe W 7 0
2005–06 Wycombe W 23 3
2006–07 Wycombe W 42 2 **72 5**

MASSEY, Alan (D) **0 0**
b.High Wycombe 11-1-89
Source: Scholar.
2006–07 Wycombe W 0 0

McGLEISH, Scott (F) **489 142**
H: 5 9 W: 11 09 b.Barnet 10-2-74
Source: Edgware T.
1994–95 Charlton Ath 6 0 **6 0**
1994–95 *Leyton Orient* 6 1
1995–96 Peterborough U 12 0
1995–96 *Colchester U* 15 6
1996–97 Peterborough U 1 0 **13 0**
1996–97 *Cambridge U* 10 7 **10 7**
1996–97 Leyton Orient 28 7
1997–98 Leyton Orient 8 0 **42 8**
1997–98 Barnet 37 13
1998–99 Barnet 36 8
1999–2000 Barnet 42 10
2000–01 Barnet 19 5 **134 36**
2000–01 Colchester U 21 5
2001–02 Colchester U 46 15
2002–03 Colchester U 43 8
2003–04 Colchester U 34 10 **159 44**
2004–05 Northampton T 44 13
2005–06 Northampton T 42 17
2006–07 Northampton T 25 12 **111 42**
2006–07 Wycombe W 14 5 **14 5**

McPARLAND, Anthony (M) **12 0**
H: 5 7 W: 10 07 b.Rutherglen 20-9-82
Source: Celtic. *Honours:* Scotland Under-21.
2005–06 Barnsley 8 0
2006–07 Barnsley 0 0 **8 0**
2006–07 Wycombe W 4 0 **4 0**

MOONEY, Tommy (F) **602 174**
H: 5 10 W: 13 05 b.Billingham 11-8-71
Source: Trainee.
1989–90 Aston Villa 0 0
1990–91 Scarborough 27 13
1991–92 Scarborough 40 8
1992–93 Scarborough 40 9 **107 30**
1993–94 Southend U 14 5 **14 5**
1993–94 *Watford* 10 2
1994–95 Watford 29 3
1995–96 Watford 42 6
1996–97 Watford 37 13
1997–98 Watford 45 6
1998–99 Watford 36 9
1999–2000 Watford 12 2
2000–01 Watford 39 19 **250 60**
2001–02 Birmingham C 33 13
2002–03 Birmingham C 1 0 **34 13**
2002–03 *Stoke C* 12 3 **12 3**
2002–03 *Sheffield U* 3 0 **3 0**
2002–03 *Derby Co* 8 0 **8 0**
2003–04 Swindon T 45 19 **45 19**
2004–05 Oxford U 42 15 **42 15**
2005–06 Wycombe W 45 17
2006–07 Wycombe W 42 12 **87 29**

OAKES, Stefan (M) **193 9**
H: 6 1 W: 13 07 b.Leicester 6-9-78
Source: Trainee.
1997–98 Leicester C 0 0
1998–99 Leicester C 3 0
1999–2000 Leicester C 22 1
2000–01 Leicester C 13 0
2001–02 Leicester C 21 1
2002–03 Leicester C 5 0 **64 2**
2002–03 *Crewe Alex* 7 0 **7 0**
2003–04 Walsall 5 0 **5 0**
2003–04 Notts Co 14 0
2004–05 Notts Co 31 5 **45 5**
2005–06 Wycombe W 37 2
2006–07 Wycombe W 35 0 **72 2**

ONIBUJE, Fola (F) **28 2**
H: 6 7 W: 12 00 b.Lagos 25-9-84
2002–03 Preston NE 0 0
2003–04 Preston NE 0 0
2003–04 *Huddersfield T* 2 0 **2 0**
2004–05 Barnsley 3 0 **3 0**
2004–05 Peterborough U 2 0 **2 0**
From Cambridge U.
2006–07 Swindon T 14 2 **14 2**
2006–07 *Brentford* 2 0 **2 0**
2006–07 Wycombe W 5 0 **5 0**

PALMER, Chris (M) **86 5**
H: 5 7 W: 11 00 b.Derby 16-10-83
Source: Scholar.
2003–04 Derby Co 0 0
2004–05 Notts Co 25 4
2005–06 Notts Co 29 1 **54 5**
2006–07 Wycombe W 32 0 **32 0**

STOCKLEY, Sam (D) **405 6**
H: 6 0 W: 12 08 b.Tiverton 5-9-77
Source: Trainee.
1996–97 Southampton 0 0
1996–97 Barnet 21 0
1997–98 Barnet 41 0
1998–99 Barnet 41 0
1999–2000 Barnet 34 1
2000–01 Barnet 45 1 **182 2**
2001–02 Oxford U 41 0
2002–03 Oxford U 0 0 **41 0**
2002–03 Colchester U 33 1
2003–04 Colchester U 44 0
2004–05 Colchester U 37 1
2005–06 Colchester U 27 1 **141 3**
2005–06 *Blackpool* 7 0 **7 0**
2006–07 Wycombe W 34 1 **34 1**

STONEBRIDGE, Ian (F) **248 44**
H: 6 0 W: 11 04 b.Lewisham 30-8-81
Source: Tottenham H Trainee. *Honours:* England Youth.
1999–2000 Plymouth Arg 31 9
2000–01 Plymouth Arg 31 11
2001–02 Plymouth Arg 42 8
2002–03 Plymouth Arg 37 5
2003–04 Plymouth Arg 30 5 **171 38**
2004–05 Wycombe W 38 4
2005–06 Wycombe W 27 2
2005–06 *Torquay U* 3 0 **3 0**
2006–07 Wycombe W 9 0 **74 6**

TALIA, Frank (G) **273 0**
H: 6 1 W: 13 06 b.Melbourne 20-7-72
Honours: Australia Schools, Under-20.
1990–91 Sunshine 11 0
1991–92 Sunshine 0 0 **11 0**
1992–93 Blackburn R 0 0
1992–93 *Hartlepool U* 14 0 **14 0**
1993–94 Blackburn R 0 0
1994–95 Blackburn R 0 0
1995–96 Blackburn R 0 0
1995–96 Swindon T 16 0
1996–97 Swindon T 15 0
1997–98 Swindon T 2 0
1998–99 Swindon T 43 0
1999–2000 Swindon T 31 0 **107 0**
2000–01 Wolverhampton W 0 0
2000–01 Sheffield U 6 0 **6 0**
2001–02 Antwerp 3 0 **3 0**
2001–02 Reading 0 0
2002–03 Wycombe W 35 0
2003–04 Wycombe W 17 0
2004–05 Wycombe W 45 0
2005–06 Wycombe W 35 0
2006–07 Wycombe W 0 0 **132 0**

THORNTON, Dean (G) **0 0**
b.Hillingdon 17-12-87
Source: Scholar.
2006–07 Wycombe W 0 0

TORRES, Sergio (M) **44 1**
H: 6 2 W: 12 04 b.Mar del Plata 8-11-83
Source: Basingstoke T.
2005–06 Wycombe W 24 1
2006–07 Wycombe W 20 0 **44 1**

WILLIAMS, Steve (G) **21 0**
H: 6 6 W: 13 10 b.Oxford 21-4-83
Source: Scholar.
2001–02 Wycombe W 0 0
2002–03 Wycombe W 0 0
2003–04 Wycombe W 19 0
2004–05 Wycombe W 1 0
2005–06 Wycombe W 1 0
2006–07 Wycombe W 0 0 **21 0**

WILLIAMSON, Mike (D) **123 8**
H: 6 4 W: 13 03 b.Stoke 8-11-83
Source: Trainee.
2001–02 Torquay U 3 0
2001–02 Southampton 0 0
2002–03 Southampton 0 0
2003–04 Southampton 0 0
2003–04 *Torquay U* 11 0 **14 0**
2003–04 *Doncaster R* 0 0
2004–05 Southampton 0 0
2004–05 *Wycombe W* 37 2
2005–06 Wycombe W 39 5
2006–07 Wycombe W 33 1 **109 8**

YOUNG, Jamie (G) **40 0**
H: 5 11 W: 13 00 b.Brisbane 25-8-85
Source: Scholar. *Honours:* England Youth, Under-20.
2003–04 Reading 1 0
2004–05 Reading 0 0
2005–06 Reading 0 0 **1 0**
2005–06 *Rushden & D* 20 0 **20 0**
2006–07 Wycombe W 19 0 **19 0**

YEOVIL T (92)

ALCOCK, Craig (D) **1 0**
H: 5 8 W: 11 00 b.Cornwall 8-12-87
Source: Youth.
2006–07 Yeovil T 1 0 **1 0**

BARKER, Danny (G) **0 0**
H: 6 1 W: 11 05 b.Oxford 30-1-87
2005–06 Yeovil T 0 0
2006–07 Yeovil T 0 0

BARRY, Anthony (M) **28 0**
H: 5 7 W: 10 00 b.Liverpool 29-5-86
Source: Everton.
2004–05 Coventry C 0 0
From Accrington S.
2005–06 Yeovil T 4 0
2006–07 Yeovil T 24 0 **28 0**

BEHCET, Darren (M) **0 0**
H: 6 0 W: 11 07 b.London 18-10-86
Source: Scholar.
2005–06 West Ham U 0 0
2006–07 Yeovil T 0 0

CLARKE, Tom (F) **1 0**
H: 5 8 W: 9 13 b.Worthing 2-1-89
Source: Youth.
2006–07 Yeovil T 1 0 **1 0**

COHEN, Chris (M) **92 7**
H: 5 11 W: 10 11 b.Norwich 5-3-87
Source: From Scholar. *Honours:* England Youth.
2003–04 West Ham U 7 0
2004–05 West Ham U 11 0
2005–06 West Ham U 0 0 **18 0**
2005–06 *Yeovil T* 30 1
2006–07 Yeovil T 44 6 **74 7**

DAVIES, Arron (M) **105 22**
H: 5 9 W: 11 00 b.Cardiff 22-6-84
Source: Trainee. *Honours:* Wales Under-21, 1 full cap.

2002–03	Southampton	0	0		
2003–04	Southampton	0	0		
2003–04	*Barnsley*	4	0	**4**	**0**
2004–05	Southampton	0	0		
2004–05	Yeovil T	23	8		
2005–06	Yeovil T	39	8		
2006–07	Yeovil T	39	6	**101**	**22**

FORBES, Terrell (D) **235 0**
H: 5 11 W: 12 07 b.Southwark 17-8-81
Source: Trainee.

1999–2000	West Ham U	0	0		
1999–2000	*Bournemouth*	3	0	**3**	**0**
2000–01	West Ham U	0	0		
2001–02	QPR	43	0		
2002–03	QPR	38	0		
2003–04	QPR	30	0		
2004–05	QPR	3	0	**114**	**0**
2004–05	Grimsby T	33	0	**33**	**0**
2005–06	Oldham Ath	39	0	**39**	**0**
2006–07	Yeovil T	46	0	**46**	**0**

GRAY, Wayne (F) **238 45**
H: 5 10 W: 11 05 b.Dulwich 7-11-80
Source: Trainee.

1998–99	Wimbledon	0	0		
1999–2000	Wimbledon	1	0		
1999–2000	*Swindon T*	12	2	**12**	**2**
2000–01	Wimbledon	11	0		
2000–01	*Port Vale*	3	0	**3**	**0**
2001–02	Wimbledon	0	0		
2001–02	*Leyton Orient*	15	5	**15**	**5**
2001–02	*Brighton & HA*	4	1	**4**	**1**
2002–03	Wimbledon	30	2		
2003–04	Wimbledon	33	4	**75**	**6**
2004–05	Southend U	44	11		
2005–06	Southend U	39	9	**83**	**20**
2006–07	Yeovil T	46	11	**46**	**11**

GUYETT, Scott (D) **77 2**
H: 6 2 W: 13 06 b.Ascot 20-1-76
Source: Brisbane C, Gresley R, Southport.

2001–02	Oxford U	22	0	**22**	**0**
From Chester C.					
2004–05	Yeovil T	18	2		
2005–06	Yeovil T	21	0		
2006–07	Yeovil T	16	0	**55**	**2**

JONES, Nathan (M) **352 10**
H: 5 6 W: 10 06 b.Rhondda 28-5-73
Source: Cardiff C Trainee, Maesteg Park, Ton Pentre, Merthyr T.

1995–96	Luton T	0	0		
Badajoz, Numaicia					
1997–98	Southend U	39	0		
1998–99	Southend U	17	0		
1998–99	*Scarborough*	9	0	**9**	**0**
1999–2000	Southend U	43	2	**99**	**2**
2000–01	Brighton & HA	40	4		
2001–02	Brighton & HA	36	2		
2002–03	Brighton & HA	28	1		
2003–04	Brighton & HA	36	0		
2004–05	Brighton & HA	19	0	**159**	**7**
2005–06	Yeovil T	43	0		
2006–07	Yeovil T	42	1	**85**	**1**

KAMUD'A KALALA, Jean-Paul (M) **61 6**
H: 5 10 W: 12 02 b.Lubumbashi 16-2-82
Honours: DR Congo 8 full caps.

2003–04	Nice	2	0		
2004–05	Nice	0	0	**2**	**0**
2005–06	Grimsby T	21	5	**21**	**5**
2006–07	Yeovil T	38	1	**38**	**1**

LINDEGAARD, Andy (M) **89 3**
H: 5 8 W: 11 04 b.Taunton 10-9-80
Source: Westland Sp.

2003–04	Yeovil T	23	2		
2004–05	Yeovil T	29	1		
2005–06	Yeovil T	23	0		
2006–07	Yeovil T	14	0	**89**	**3**

LYNCH, Mark (D) **64 0**
H: 5 11 W: 11 03 b.Manchester 2-9-81
Source: Trainee.

1999–2000	Manchester U	0	0		
2000–01	Manchester U	0	0		
2001–02	Manchester U	0	0		
2001–02	*St Johnstone*	20	0	**20**	**0**
2002–03	Manchester U	0	0		
2003–04	Manchester U	0	0		
2004–05	Sunderland	11	0	**11**	**0**
2005–06	Hull C	16	0		
2006–07	Hull C	0	0	**16**	**0**
2006–07	Yeovil T	17	0	**17**	**0**

MAHER, Stephen (M) **1 0**
H: 5 10 W: 11 01 b.Dublin 3-3-88
Source: Shelbourne.

2006–07	Yeovil T	1	0	**1**	**0**

McCALLUM, Gavin (M) **1 0**
H: 5 9 W: 12 00 b.Mississauga 24-8-87
Honours: Canada Under-20.

2005–06	Yeovil T	0	0		
2006–07	Yeovil T	1	0	**1**	**0**

MILDENHALL, Steve (G) **207 1**
H: 6 4 W: 14 01 b.Swindon 13-5-78
Source: Trainee.

1996–97	Swindon T	1	0		
1997–98	Swindon T	4	0		
1998–99	Swindon T	0	0		
1999–2000	Swindon T	5	0		
2000–01	Swindon T	23	0	**33**	**0**
2001–02	Notts Co	26	0		
2002–03	Notts Co	21	0		
2003–04	Notts Co	28	0		
2004–05	Notts Co	1	0	**76**	**0**
2004–05	Oldham Ath	6	0	**6**	**0**
2005–06	Grimsby T	46	1	**46**	**1**
2006–07	Yeovil T	46	0	**46**	**0**

MORRIS, Lee (F) **165 29**
H: 5 10 W: 11 07 b.Blackpool 30-4-80
Source: Trainee. *Honours:* England Youth.

1997–98	Sheffield U	5	0		
1998–99	Sheffield U	20	6		
1999–2000	Sheffield U	1	0	**26**	**6**
1999–2000	Derby Co	3	0		
2000–01	Derby Co	20	0		
2000–01	*Huddersfield T*	5	1	**5**	**1**
2001–02	Derby Co	15	4		
2002–03	Derby Co	30	8		
2003–04	Derby Co	23	5	**91**	**17**
2003–04	Leicester C	0	0		
2004–05	Leicester C	10	0		
2005–06	Leicester C	0	0	**10**	**0**
2006–07	Yeovil T	33	5	**33**	**5**

ROSE, Matthew (D) **256 8**
H: 5 11 W: 12 02 b.Dartford 24-9-75
Source: Trainee. *Honours:* England Under-21.

1994–95	Arsenal	0	0		
1995–96	Arsenal	4	0		
1996–97	Arsenal	1	0	**5**	**0**
1997–98	QPR	16	0		
1998–99	QPR	29	0		
1999–2000	QPR	29	1		
2000–01	QPR	27	0		
2001–02	QPR	39	3		
2002–03	QPR	28	2		
2003–04	QPR	20	0		
2004–05	QPR	28	2		
2005–06	QPR	15	0		
2006–07	QPR	11	0	**242**	**8**
2006–07	Yeovil T	9	0	**9**	**0**

SKIVERTON, Terry (D) **159 15**
H: 6 1 W: 13 06 b.Mile End 26-6-75
Source: Trainee.

1993–94	Chelsea	0	0		
1994–95	Chelsea	0	0		
1994–95	*Wycombe W*	10	0		
1995–96	Chelsea	0	0		
1995–96	Wycombe W	4	1		
1996–97	Wycombe W	6	0	**20**	**1**
From Welling U					
2003–04	Yeovil T	26	2		
2004–05	Yeovil T	38	4		
2005–06	Yeovil T	36	6		
2006–07	Yeovil T	39	2	**139**	**14**

SMEETON, Jake (D) **0 0**
H: 5 7 W: 12 06 b.Yeovil 9-8-88
Source: Youth.

2006–07	Yeovil T	0	0		

STEWART, Marcus (F) **543 186**
H: 5 10 W: 11 00 b.Bristol 7-11-72
Source: From Trainee. *Honours:* England Schools, Football League.

1991–92	Bristol R	33	5		
1992–93	Bristol R	38	11		
1993–94	Bristol R	29	5		
1994–95	Bristol R	27	15		
1995–96	Bristol R	44	21	**171**	**57**
1996–97	Huddersfield T	20	7		
1997–98	Huddersfield T	41	15		
1998–99	Huddersfield T	43	22		
1999–2000	Huddersfield T	29	14	**133**	**58**
1999–2000	Ipswich T	10	2		
2000–01	Ipswich T	34	19		
2001–02	Ipswich T	28	6		
2002–03	Ipswich T	3	0	**75**	**27**
2002–03	Sunderland	19	1		
2003–04	Sunderland	40	14		
2004–05	Sunderland	43	16	**102**	**31**
2005–06	Bristol C	27	5		
2005–06	*Preston NE*	4	0	**4**	**0**
2006–07	Bristol C	0	0	**27**	**5**
2006–07	Yeovil T	31	8	**31**	**8**

TERRY, Paul (M) **135 10**
H: 5 10 W: 12 06 b.Barking 3-4-79
Source: Dagenham & R.

2003–04	Yeovil T	34	1		
2004–05	Yeovil T	39	6		
2005–06	Yeovil T	42	1		
2006–07	Yeovil T	20	2	**135**	**10**

THOMAS, Bradley (D) **11 2**
H: 6 2 W: 13 02 b.Forest Green 29-3-84
Source: Scholar.

2003–04	Peterborough U	0	0		
2004–05	Peterborough U	0	0		
From Eastleigh.					
2005–06	Yeovil T	0	0		
2006–07	Yeovil T	0	0		
2006–07	*Boston U*	11	2	**11**	**2**

TONKIN, Anthony (D) **117 0**
H: 5 11 W: 12 02 b.Newlyn 17-1-80
Source: Yeovil T.

2002–03	Stockport Co	24	0		
2003–04	Stockport Co	0	0	**24**	**0**
2003–04	Crewe Alex	26	0		
2004–05	Crewe Alex	35	0		
2005–06	Crewe Alex	27	0	**88**	**0**
2006–07	Yeovil T	5	0	**5**	**0**

WEBB, Daniel (F) **118 9**
H: 6 1 W: 11 08 b.Poole 2-7-83

2000–01	Southend U	15	1		
2001–02	Southend U	16	2		
2001–02	*Brighton & HA*	12	1		
2002–03	Southend U	0	0	**31**	**3**
2002–03	*Brighton & HA*	3	0	**15**	**1**
2002–03	Hull C	12	0		
2002–03	*Lincoln C*	5	1	**5**	**1**
2003–04	Hull C	4	0	**16**	**0**
2003–04	Cambridge U	21	3		
2004–05	Cambridge U	22	1		
2005–06	Cambridge U	0	0	**43**	**4**
2005–06	Yeovil T	4	0		
2006–07	Yeovil T	4	0	**8**	**0**

WELSH, Ishmael (F) **18 1**
H: 5 7 W: 10 11 b.Leicester 4-9-87
Source: West Ham U Scholar.

2006–07	Yeovil T	18	1	**18**	**1**

ENGLISH LEAGUE PLAYERS – INDEX

Abbey, George 63
Abbey, Nathan 13
Abbott, Pawel 79
Abdi, Liban 71
Abdoun, Djamel 49
Achterberg, John 83
Adams, Danny 39
Adams, Nicky 18
Adams, Steve 72
Adamson, Chris 72
Addison, Miles 31
Adebayor, Emmanuel 2
Adebola, Dele 27
Ademeno, Charles 75
Agard, Kieran 33
Agard, Kieran 33
Agathe, Didier 3
Agbonlahor, Gabriel 3
Agger, Daniel 46
Aghahowa, Julius 88
Agogo, Junior 58
Agyemang, Patrick 65
Ahmed, Adnan 39
Ainge, Simon 12
Ainsworth, Gareth 66
Ainsworth, Lionel 31
Aiston, Sam 56
Ajdarevic, Astrit 46
Akers, Steven 59
Akinbiyi, Ade 17
Akinfenwa, Adebayo 79
Akins, Lucas 39
Al-Habsi, Ali 9
Albrechtsen, Martin 86
Albrighton, Mark 10
Alcock, Craig 92
Alexander, Gary 44
Alexander, Graham 65
Alexander, Neil 19
Aliadiere, Jeremie 2
Aljofree, Hasney 62
Allanson, Ashley 70
Allen, Curtis 11
Allen, Damien 76
Allen, Graham 24
Allen, Joe 79
Allen, Oliver 4
Allison, Wayne 25
Allott, Mark 25
Almeida, Mauro 1
Almunia, Manuel 2
Alnwick, Ben 82
Alonso, Xabi 46
Aluko, Sone 6
Amankwaah, Kevin 79
Ambrose, Darren 21
Ameobi, Shola 55
Amoo, Ryan 45
Andersen, Mikkel 67
Andersen, Stephan 21
Anderson 33
Anderson, Paul 46
Anderton, Darren 11
Andrew, Calvin 47
Andrews, Keith 54
Andrews, Lee 81
Andrews, Wayne 27
Anelka, Nicolas 9
Angel, Juan Pablo 3
Angus, Stevland 81
Anichebe, Victor 33
Ankergren, Casper 42
Annerson, Jamie 71
Anthony, Byron 16
Antwi-Birago, Godwin 46
Antwi, Will 91
Anya, Ikechi 91
Anyinsah, Joe 65
Anyon, Joe 63
Aranalde, Zigor 20
Arbeloa, Alvaro 46
Arber, Mark 61
Arca, Julio 52
Ardley, Neal 53
Armando Sa, Miguel 42
Armstrong, Alun 30
Armstrong, Chris 71
Armstrong, Craig 23
Arnau, Caldentey 78
Arnison, Paul 20
Arnold, Nathan 51
Artell, Dave 24
Arteta, Mikel 33
Artus, Frankie 15
Asamoah, Derek 73
Ashbee, Ian 40
Ashdown, Jamie 64
Ashikodi, Moses 85
Ashmore, James 71
Ashton, Dean 87
Ashton, Nathan 21
Ashton, Neil 73
Aspden, Curtis 40
Assou-Ekotto, Benoit 82
Atkin, Liam 20
Atkinson, Rob 5
Atkinson, William 40
Augustyn, Blazej 9
Austin, Kevin 79
Austin, Neil 5
Avinel, Cedric 85

Babayaro, Celestine 55
Bacon, Danny 45
Baguley, Chris 60
Baidoo, Shabazz 66
Bailey, Alex 25
Bailey, James 28
Bailey, Matt 28
Bailey, Matthew 89
Bailey, Nicky 4
Bailey, Stefan 66
Baines, Adolfo 54
Baines, Leighton 88
Bains, Rikki 1
Baird, Chris 74
Bakayogo, Zaoumana 53
Baker, Richie 18
Bakke, Eirik 42
Baldock, Sam 54
Baldwin, Pat 26
Bale, Gareth 74
Ball, Michael 49
Ballack, Michael 22
Bangoura, Sammy 77
Bangura, Alhassan 85
Bankole, Ademola 54
Baptista, Julio 2
Baraclough, Ian 70
Barcham, Andy 82
Bardsley, Phillip 50
Barker, Chris 19
Barker, Danny 92
Barker, Keith 7
Barker, Richard 37
Barker, Shaun 8
Barlow, Matty 60
Barmby, Nick 40
Barnard, Donny 44
Barnard, Lee 82
Barnes-Homer, Matthew 91
Barnes, Ashley 62
Barnes, Giles 31
Barnes, Michael 50
Barnes, Phil 36
Barness, Anthony 62
Barnett, Charlie 46
Barnett, Leon 47
Baros, Milan 3
Barrau, Xavi 12
Barrett, Adam 75
Barrett, Zach 47
Barron, Micky 37
Barron, Scott 41
Barry-Murphy, Brian 18
Barry, Anthony 92
Barry, Gareth 3
Barton, Joey 49
Baseya, Cedric 74
Basso, Adriano 15
Bastians, Felix 58
Bates, Matthew 52
Bates, Tom 68
Batista, Ricardo 34
Baudet, Julien 28
Baxter, Darren 81
Bayly, Robert 42
Beagrie, Peter 36
Beahon, Thomas 83
Bean, Marcus 8
Beardsley, Chris 51
Beasley, DaMarcus 49
Beattie, James 33
Beckett, Luke 39
Beckford, Jermaine 42
Beckwith, Dean 38
Bedeau, Anthony 84
Beevers, Lee 45
Beevers, Mark 72
Begovic, Asmir 64
Behcet, Darren 92
Bell, David 47
Bell, Lee 28
Bell, Mickey 23
Bellamy, Craig 46
Bellon, Damien 3
Bellon, Yago 3
Belmadi, Djamel 74
Ben Haim, Tal 9
Benayoun, Yossi 87
Bencherif, Hamza 58
Bendtner, Nicklas 2
Benjamin, Ronayne 48
Benjamin, Trevor 61
Bennett, Alan 67
Bennett, Dean 24
Bennett, Elliott 89
Bennett, Ian 71
Bennett, James 40
Bennett, Julian 58
Bennett, Ryan 36
Bent, Darren 21
Bent, Marcus 21
Bentham, Craig 12
Bentley, David 7
Bentley, Mark 35
Benyon, Elliot 15
Berbatov, Dimitar 82
Beresford, Marlon 47
Berger, Patrik 3
Berner, Bruno 7
Berrett, James 39
Bertin, Alexis 14
Bertrand, Ryan 22
Best, Leon 74
Betsy, Kevin 15
Bialkowski, Bartosz 74
Bignot, Marcus 66
Bignot, Paul 28
Bikey, Andre 67
Billy, Chris 20
Binnion, Travis 71
Birch, Gary 45
Birchall, Adam 4
Birchall, Chris 27
Bircham, Marc 66
Bird, David 23
Birley, Matt 6
Bischoff, Mikkel 27
Bisgaard, Morten 31
Bishop, Andy 18
Black, Tommy 29
Blackett, Shane 61
Blackman, Nick 48
Blackmore, David 87
Blackstock, Dexter 66
Blake, Darcy 19
Blake, James 6
Blake, Robbie 42
Blanchett, Danny 61
Blayney, Alan 60
Blinkhorn, Matthew 8
Blizzard, Dominic 85
Bloomer, Matt 36
Bloomfield, Matt 91
Blundell, Greg 30
Boa Morte, Luis 87
Boardman, Jon 68
Boateng, George 52
Bocanegra, Carlos 34
Boco, Romuald 1
Boden, Luke 72
Boertien, Paul 31
Bojic, Pedj 56
Boland, Willie 37
Bolder, Adam 66
Bolland, Paul 36
Bolland, Phil 24
Booth, Andy 39
Bopp, Eugene 69
Bore, Peter 36
Borrowdale, Gary 29
Boshell, Danny 36
Bossekota, Jeremy 31
Bossu, Bertrand 84
Bothroyd, Jay 89
Bouazza, Hameur 85
Bougherra, Madjid 21
Boulahrouz, Khalid 22
Boulding, Mick 51
Boulding, Rory 51
Bouma, Wilfred 3
Boumsong, Jean-Alain 55
Bowditch, Dean 41
Bower, Mark 12
Bowler, Michael 76
Bowman, Matthew 72
Bowyer, Lee 87
Boyce, Emmerson 88
Boyd, Adam 47
Boyd, George 61
Boyle, Lee 3
Boyle, Patrick 33
Bozanic, Oliver 67
Brackstone, John 37
Bradbury, Lee 75
Bradley, Adam 20
Bradley, Mark 84
Brain, Jonny 48
Bramble, Tes 76
Bramble, Titus 55
Brammer, Dave 53
Branch, Graham 17
Branch, Michael 24
Brandon, Chris 39
Brandy, Febian 50
Braniff, Kevin 53
Branston, Guy 61
Brass, Chris 18
Breach, Chris 14
Breckin, Ian 58
Breen, Garry 49
Breen, Gary 89
Brekke-Skard, Vemund 41
Brezovan, Peter 80
Bridge-Wilkinson, Marc 12
Bridge, Wayne 22
Bridges, Michael 40
Bridges, Scott 3
Briggs, Keith 76
Briggs, Matthew 34
Brighton, Tom 53
Brightwell, Ian 48
Brill, Dean 47
Briscoe, Louie 63
Brittain, Martin 41
Britton, Leon 79
Brkovic, Ahmet 47
Broadbent, Andrew 72
Broadbent, Daniel 39
Broadhurst, Karl 11
Brogan, Stephen 69
Bromby, Leigh 71
Brooker, Paul 13
Brooker, Stephen 15
Brooks-Meade, Corrin 34
Broomes, Marlon 77
Broughton, Drewe 24
Brouwer, Jordy 46
Brown, Aaron 67
Brown, Aaron 80
Brown, Adam 32
Brown, Chris 57
Brown, David 1
Brown, Gary 68
Brown, James 37
Brown, Jason 7
Brown, Joe 12
Brown, Junior 28
Brown, Michael 34
Brown, Nat 45
Brown, Scott 23
Brown, Scott P 23
Brown, Simon 51
Brown, Wayne 38
Brown, Wayne 26
Brown, Wayne 34
Brown, Wes 50
Browning, Marcus 11
Brownlie, Royce 80
Bruce, Alex 41
Brunt, Chris 72
Buchanan, David 18
Budtz, Jan 32
Bullard, Jimmy 34
Bullen, Lee 72
Bullock, Lee 37
Bullock, Martin 48
Bunce, Che 27
Bunn, Mark 56
Burch, Rob 82
Burge, Ryan 6
Burgess, Ben 8
Burgess, Kevin 30
Burnell, Joe 56
Burns, Jamie 8
Burton, Deon 72
Burton, Sagi 73
Butcher, Richard 61
Butler, Andy 70
Butler, Martin 84
Butler, Paul 42
Butler, Thomas 79
Butt, Nicky 55
Butterfield, Danny 29
Butters, Guy 14
Button, David 82
Buxton, Jake 51
Buxton, Lewis 77
Buzsaky, Akos 62
Byfield, Darren 53
Byrne, Cliff 70
Byrne, Jason 19
Byrne, Paul 75
Byrom, Joel 1
Byron, Michael 40
Bywater, Steve 31

Cadamarteri, Danny 43
Cadmore, Tom 91
Cahill, Gary 3
Cahill, Tim 33
Caines, Gavin 23
Caldwell, Steven 17
Calliste, Ramon 46
Camara, Henri 88

Camara, Mo 31
Cameron, Colin 27
Camfield, Bailey 42
Camp, Lee 31
Campana, Alex 85
Campbell-Ryce, Jamal 75
Campbell, Dudley 6
Campbell, Frazier 50
Campbell, Kevin 19
Campbell, Sol 64
Campbell, Stuart 16
Campo, Ivan 9
Cann, Steven 31
Canoville, Lee 10
Cansdell-Sheriff, Shane 83
Capaldi, Tony 62
Carden, Paul 61
Carder-Andrews, Karle 13
Cardle, Joe 63
Carew, Ashley 4
Carew, John 3
Carey, Louis 15
Carlisle, Clarke 85
Carole, Sebastien 42
Carpenter, Richard 14
Carr, Stephen 55
Carragher, Jamie 46
Carrick, Michael 50
Carrington, Mark 28
Carroll, Andy 55
Carroll, Neil 24
Carroll, Roy 87
Carruthers, Chris 16
Carsley, Lee 33
Carson, Scott 46
Carson, Trevor 78
Carter, Darren 86
Carvill, Michael 90
Casement, Chris 41
Cathcart, Craig 50
Caton, Andy 80
Cattermole, Lee 52
Cavalli, Johann 85
Cavanagh, Paul 1
Cave-Brown, Andrew 57
Cech, Petr 22
Cederqvist, Par 84
Cerny, Radek 82
Chadwick, Luke 57
Chadwick, Nick 62
Challinor, Dave 18
Chamberlain, Alec 85
Chamberlain, Scott 14
Chambers, Adam 44
Chambers, Ashley 43
Chambers, James 85
Chambers, Luke 58
Chaplow, Richard 86
Charles, Anthony 4
Charles, Darius 13
Charlton, Asa 51
Charlton, Simon 60
Chilvers, Liam 65
Chimbonda, Pascal 82
Chopra, Michael 19
Chorley, Ben 54
Christanval, Philippe 34
Christie, Iyseden 68
Christie, Malcolm 52
Christon, Lewis 91
Cisak, Aleksander 43
Cisse, Djibril 46
Clapham, Jamie 89
Clapham, Josh 62
Clare, Rob 76
Claridge, Steve 11
Clark, Ben 37
Clarke, Billy 41
Clarke, Clive 78
Clarke, Darrell 37
Clarke, Jamie 10
Clarke, Leon 72
Clarke, Matthew 12
Clarke, Nathan 39
Clarke, Peter 75
Clarke, Shane 45
Clarke, Tom 39
Clarke, Tom 92
Clarke, Wayne 30
Clemence, Stephen 6
Clement, Neil 86
Clichy, Gael 2
Clingan, Sammy 58
Clohessy, Sean 35
Close, Brian 30
Clyde, Mark 89
Cochrane, Justin 69
Cogan, Barry 4
Cohen, Chris 92
Cohen, Gary 36
Coid, Danny 8
Coke, Gilles 51
Colbeck, Joe 12
Cole, Andy 64
Cole, Ashley 22
Cole, Carlton 87
Cole, Jake 66
Cole, Joe 22
Cole, Mitchell 75
Coleman, Theo 68
Coles, Danny 40
Colgan, Nick 5
Colin, Jurgen 57
Collin, Frannie 35
Collins, Danny 78
Collins, James 87
Collins, Lee 89
Collins, Matty 34
Collins, Michael 39
Collins, Neill 89
Collins, Patrick 30
Collins, Sam 40
Collins, Sam 54
Collis, Steve 75
Commons, Kris 58
Comyn-Platt, Charlie 68
Condesso, Feliciano 74
Conlon, Barry 51
Connell, Alan 38
Connolly, Adam 23
Connolly, David 78
Connolly, Matthew 2
Connolly, Paul 62
Connor, Paul 23
Constable, James 84
Constantine, Leon 63
Convey, Bobby 67
Coo, Cavell 28
Cook, Lee 66
Cooke, Andy 73
Cooke, Stephen 11
Cooksey, Ernie 10
Coombes, Gregg 19
Cooper, Kevin 19
Cooper, Shaun 11
Coppinger, James 32
Corden, Wayne 44
Cork, Jack 22
Cornes, Chris 89
Corr, Barry 72
Corradi, Bernardo 49
Cort, Carl 89
Cort, Leon 29
Cotterill, David 88
Cotton, Daniel 10
Cottrell, Adam 53
Coughlan, Graham 72
Coulson, Michael 5
Cousins, Mark 26
Coutts, James 11
Cowan, Gavin 73
Coward, Chris 76
Cox, Dean 14
Cox, Ian 35
Cox, Neil 28
Cox, Simon 67
Coyne, Chris 47
Coyne, Danny 17
Craddock, Jody 89
Craddock, Tom 52
Craig, Tony 53
Crainey, Stephen 42
Craney, Ian 79
Cranie, Martin 74
Crespo, Hernan 22
Cresswell, Richard 42
Cresswell, Ryan 71
Critchell, Kyle 25
Croft, Gary 36
Croft, Lee 57
Crofts, Andrew 35
Cronin, Glenn 24
Crooks, Lee 68
Crooks, Leon 91
Crosby, Andy 70
Crossley, Mark 34
Crouch, Peter 46
Crow, Danny 61
Crowe, Jason 56
Crowell, Matt 90
Crowther, Ryan 76
Cryan, Colin 10
Cudicini, Carlo 22
Cullip, Danny 66
Cumbers, Luis 35
Cumberworth, Tom 31
Cummings, Warren 11
Cummins, Michael 30
Cunningham, Kenny 78
Cureton, Jamie 26
Curran, Craig 83
Currie, Darren 41
Curtis, John 58
Curtis, Tom 59
Cutler, Neil 69
Cywka, Thomasz 88
Czerkas, Adam 66

D'Laryea, Jonathan 51
D'Laryea, Nathan 49
Dabo, Ousmane 49
Dagnall, Chris 68
Dailly, Christian 87
Daley, Omar 12
Daly, Jon 37
Daly, Michael 49
Danby, John 24
Daniel, Colin 28
Daniels, Charlie 82
Daniels, Luke 86
Dann, Scott 84
Danns, Neil 6
Darby, Stephen 46
Dark, Lewis 13
Davenport, Calum 87
Davids, Edgar 82
Davidson, Callum 65
Davidson, Robert 10
Davies, Andrew 52
Davies, Arron 92
Davies, Ben 73
Davies, Craig 89
Davies, Curtis 86
Davies, Gareth 25
Davies, Kevin 9
Davies, Kyle 74
Davies, Mark 89
Davies, Rob 86
Davies, Scott 67
Davies, Simon 34
Davies, Steve 83
Davis, Claude 71
Davis, Jamie 82
Davis, Kelvin 74
Davis, Liam 27
Davis, Sean 64
Davis, Sol 47
Davis, Steve 3
Davison, Aidan 26
Davison, Tony 37
Dawkins, Simon 82
Dawson, Andy 40
Dawson, Michael 82
Dawson, Stephen 51
Day, Chris 53
Day, Jamie 61
De Vita, Raffaele 7
De Vos, Jason 41
De Vries, Mark 43
De Zeeuw, Arjan 88
De la Cruz, Ulises 67
DeMerit, Jay 85
Deeney, Saul 59
Deeney, Troy 84
Defendi, Rodrigo 82
Defoe, Jermain 82
Delaney, Damien 40
Delaney, Mark 3
Delap, Rory 77
Delph, Fabian 42
Demetriou, Jason 44
Demontagnac, Ishmel 84
Dempsey, Clint 34
Denilson 2
Dennehy, Billy 78
Dennehy, Darren 33
Derbyshire, Matt 7
Derry, Shaun 42
Dervite, Dorian 82
Deuchar, Kenny 56
Devaney, Martin 5
Devera, Joe 4
Di Piedi, Michaelli 32
Diaby, Vassiriki 2
Diagne-Faye, Aboulaye 9
Diagouraga, Toumani 85
Diallo, Drissa 54
Diao, Salif 77
Diarra, Lassana 22
Diawara, Souleymane 21
Dichio, Danny 65
Dicker, Gary 6
Dickinson, Carl 77
Dickinson, Liam 76
Dickov, Paul 49
Dickson, Christopher 21
Dickson, Ryan 62
Dinning, Tony 76
Diop, Papa Bouba 34
Diouf, El Hadji 9
Disley, Craig 16
Distin, Sylvain 49
Dixon, Jonny 91
Dixon, Terry 82
Djemba-Djemba, Eric 3
Djordjic, Bojan 62
Djourou, Johan 2
Dobie, Scott 58
Dobson, Michael 84
Dodds, Louis 43
Doherty, Gary 57
Doherty, Sean 1
Doherty, Tom 66
Doig, Chris 56
Dolman, Liam 56
Done, Matt 90
Dong Fangzhou 50
Donnelly, Ciaran 8
Donnelly, Martin 71
Donnelly, Scott 66
Doolan, John 68
Douala, Rudolphe 64
Doughty, Phil 8
Douglas, Jonathan 42
Douglas, Rab 43
Doumbe, Stephen 62
Downes, Aaron 25
Downes, Aiden 33
Downing, Stewart 52
Doyle, Colin 6
Doyle, Kevin 67
Doyle, Micky 27
Doyle, Nathan 40
Doyle, Robert 48
Doyley, Lloyd 85
Drobny, Jaroslav 41
Drogba, Didier 22
Drummond, Stuart 73
Drury, Adam 57
Duberry, Michael 67
Dublin, Dion 57
Dudek, Jerzy 46
Dudfield, Lawrie 59
Duff, Damien 55
Duff, Michael 17
Duff, Shane 23
Duffy, Ayden 45
Duffy, Darryl 40
Duffy, Richard 64
Dugdale, Adam 28
Duggan, Robert 77
Duguid, Karl 26
Duke, David 30
Duke, Matt 40
Dunbavin, Ian 1
Duncan, Derek 44
Duncum, Sam 69
Dunn, Chris 56
Dunn, David 7
Dunne, Alan 53
Dunne, Richard 49
Duran Vazquez, Francisco 46
Dutton-Black, Josh 74
Dyche, Sean 56
Dyer, Bruce 32
Dyer, Kieron 55
Dyer, Lloyd 54
Dyer, Nathan 74

Eaden, Nicky 58
Eagle, Robert 57
Eagles, Chris 50
Eardley, Neal 60
Earl, James 20
Earnshaw, Robert 57
Easter, Jamal 19
Easter, Jermaine 91
Easton, Clint 35
Easton, Craig 44
Eastwood, Freddy 75
Eastwood, Simon 39
Ebanks-Blake, Sylvan 62
Eboue, Emmanuel 2
Echanomi, Efe 44
Eckersley, Adam 50
Edds, Gareth 54
Edgar, David 55
Edge, Lewis 8
Edge, Roland 40
Edghill, Richard 12
Edwards, Carlos 78
Edwards, Dave 73
Edwards, Mike 59
Edwards, Paul 60
Edwards, Phil 1
Edwards, Preston 53
Edwards, Rob 89
Edworthy, Marc 31
Ehiogu, Ugo 52
Ehui, Ismael 34
Einarsson, Gylfi 42
El Idrissi, Faysal 27
El Karkouri, Talal 21
El Zhar, Nabil 46
El-Abd, Adam 14
Elder, Nathan 14
Elding, Anthony 76
Ellender, Paul 10
Ellington, Nathan 86
Elliot, Rob 21
Elliott, Marvin 53
Elliott, Robbie 42
Elliott, Simon 34
Elliott, Stephen 78
Elliott, Steve 16
Elliott, Stuart 40
Elliott, Tom 42
Elliott, Wade 17
Ellis, Dan 76
Ellison, Kevin 83
Elmer, Jonas 22
Elokobi, George 26
Elphick, Tommy 14
Elrich, Ahmed 34

Elvins, Rob 86
Emanuel, Lewis 47
Emerton, Brett 7
Emre, Belezoglu 55
Enckelman, Peter 7
England, Jamie 13
Ephraim, Hogan 87
Essien, Michael 22
Esson, Ryan 73
Etherington, Matthew 87
Etuhu, Dickson 57
Etuhu, Kelvin 49
Euell, Jason 52
Eustace, John 77
Evans, Ched 49
Evans, Gareth 90
Evans, Jonny 50
Evans, Micky 81
Evans, Paul 80
Evans, Rhys 8
Evans, Scott 79
Evans, Sean 50
Evans, Steve 90
Evatt, Ian 8
Evra, Patrice 50

Fabio Aurelio 46
Fabregas, Francesc 2
Facey, Delroy 69
Fadiga, Khalilou 27
Fagan, Chris 50
Fagan, Craig 31
Fallon, Rory 62
Fangueiro, Carlos 84
Farquharson, Nick 28
Farrell, Dave 10
Farrelly, Gareth 8
Fathi, Ahmed 71
Faulkner, James 91
Faye, Amdy 21
Featherstone, Nicky 40
Federici, Adam 67
Feeney, Warren 47
Fenton, Nick 36
Ferdinand, Anton 87
Ferdinand, Rio 50
Ferenczi, Istvan 5
Ferguson, Darren 61
Fernandes, Manuel 64
Fernandes, Ricardo 22
Fernandez, Vincent 58
Ferreira, Fabio 22
Ferrell, Andrew 38
Ferretti, Andrea 19
Fettis, Alan 18
Fielding, Frank 7
Filan, John 88
Finnan, Steve 46
Finnigan, John 23
Fisk, Andrew 57
Fitzgerald, John 18
Fitzgerald, Lorcan 87
Fitzpatrick, Jordan 38
Flahavan, Darryl 75
Flamini, Mathieu 2
Fleetwood, Stuart 38
Fleming, Andy 90
Fleming, Craig 69
Fletcher, Carl 29
Fletcher, Darren 50
Fletcher, Steve 11
Flinders, Scott 29
Flitcroft, David 18
Flitney, Ross 4
Flo, Tore Andre 42
Flood, Willo 19
Flynn, Christopher 28
Flynn, Michael 35
Flynn, Ryan 46
Fogden, Wes 14
Fojut, Jaroslaw 9
Folan, Caleb 88
Foley-Sheridan, Steven 11
Foley, David 37
Foley, Kevin 47
Foley, Sam 23
Folly, Yoann 72
Fontaine, Liam 15
Foran, Richie 75
Forbes, Adrian 8
Forbes, Nathan 10
Forbes, Terrell 92
Forde, David 19
Fordyce, Daryl 64
Forecast, Tommy 82
Forrester, Jamie 45
Forssell, Mikael 6
Forster, Nicky 40
Forsyth, Jeff 86
Forte, Jonathan 71
Fortune-West, Leo 73
Fortune, Clayton 44
Fortune, Jon 21
Fortune, Quinton 9
Foster, Ben 50
Foster, Luke 45
Foster, Stephen 17
Foster, Steve 70
Fotheringham, Mark 57
Fowler, Robbie 46
Fox, Daniel 84
Fox, David 8
Foxe, Hayden 42
Foy, Robbie 70
Frampton, Andrew 13
France, Ryan 40
Francis, Damien 85
Francis, Simon 75
Frankowski, Tomasz 89
Fraser, Tom 14
Fray, Arron 29
Frecklington, Lee 45
Freedman, Dougie 29
Friedel, Brad 7
Friio, David 58
Frost, Stef 59
Frutos, Alexandre 14
Fry, Russell 40
Fryatt, Matty 43
Fuller, Ricardo 77
Fulop, Marton 78
Furlong, Paul 66
Fuseini, Ali 53
Futcher, Ben 61

Gabbidon, Daniel 87
Gain, Peter 61
Galbraith, David 10
Gall, Kevin 20
Gallacher, Paul 57
Gallagher, Paul 7
Gallas, William 2
Gallen, Kevin 66
Gallinagh, Andy 23
Gamble, Paddy 58
Garcia, Richard 26
Gardner, Anthony 82
Gardner, Craig 3
Gardner, Ricardo 9
Gardner, Ross 63
Gardner, Scott 42
Garner, Darren 81
Garner, Glyn 44
Garner, Joe 7
Garrett, Robert 77
Garry, Ryan 2
Garvan, Owen 41
Gate, Kris 55
Gatting, Joe 14
Gaynor, Ross 53
Geary, Derek 71
Gera, Zoltan 86
Geremi 22
Gerken, Dean 26
Gerrard, Anthony 84
Gerrard, Paul 71
Gerrard, Steven 46
Gerrbrand, Patrik 43
Ghaichem, Jimmy 61
Ghaly, Hossam 82
Giallanza, Gaetano 30
Giallombardo, Andrew 74
Giannakopoulos, Stelios 9
Gibb, Ali 37
Gibbs, Cory 21
Gibson, Darron 50
Giddings, Stuart 27
Giggs, Ryan 50
Gilbert, Kerrea 2
Gilbert, Peter 72
Giles, Martyn 38
Gilks, Matthew 68
Gill, Ben 85
Gill, Jeremy 23
Gillespie, Keith 71
Gillespie, Steven 23
Gillett, Simon 74
Gilligan, Ryan 56
Gilmartin, Rene 84
Gislason, Rurik 21
Given, Shay 55
Gleeson, Dan 59
Gleeson, Stephen 89
Glennon, Matty 39
Glombard, Luigi 19
Gnapka, Claude 80
Gobern, Lewis 89
Golbourne, Scott 67
Gonzalez, Jose Miguel 46
Goodall, Alan 68
Goodfellow, Marc 18
Gooding, Andy 27
Goodison, Ian 83
Goodlad, Mark 63
Goodwin, Jim 70
Gordon, Dean 81
Gorkss, Kaspars 8
Gosling, Dan 62
Goulon, Herold 52
Gower, Mark 75
Gowling, Josh 11
Grabban, Lewis 29
Gradel, Max 43
Graham, Danny 52
Graham, David 72
Graham, Richard 4
Grand, Simon 36
Granqvist, Andreas 88
Grant, Anthony 22
Grant, Gavin 53
Grant, Joel 85
Grant, Lee 31
Grant, Robert 1
Grant, Tony 1
Granville, Danny 29
Gray, Andy 17
Gray, David 50
Gray, Julian 6
Gray, Kevin 20
Gray, Michael 7
Gray, Wayne 92
Grazioli, Giuliano 4
Greaves, Mark 10
Green, Francis 10
Green, Liam 32
Green, Matt 19
Green, Mike 16
Green, Paul 45
Green, Paul 32
Green, Philip 3
Green, Rob 87
Green, Ryan 16
Green, Stuart 29
Greenacre, Chris 83
Greening, Jonathan 86
Gregan, Sean 60
Gregory, Steven 91
Griffin, Adam 76
Griffin, Andy 64
Griffin, Charlie 91
Griffith, Anthony 32
Griffiths, Adam 13
Griffiths, Rostyn 7
Grimaldi, Sebastien 25
Grimes, Ashley 49
Gritton, Martin 45
Gross, Adam 4
Grubb, Dean 15
Grundy, Aaron 18
Gudjonsson, Joey 17
Gueret, Willy 79
Guinan, Stephen 23
Gulliver, Phil 38
Gunnarsson, Brynjar 67
Gunter, Chris 19
Guthrie, Danny 46
Guttridge, Luke 44
Guy, Jamie 26
Guy, Lewis 32
Guyett, Scott 92
Gwynne, Sam 38
Gyaki, Ryan 71
Gyepes, Gabor 89

Hackett, Chris 53
Hackney, Simon 20
Hadfield, Jordan 48
Haestad, Kristofer 88
Hahnemann, Marcus 67
Haidong, Hao 71
Haining, Will 60
Haldane, Lewis 16
Hales, Lee 87
Halford, Greg 67
Hall, Asa 6
Hall, Chris 60
Hall, Danny 73
Hall, Fitz 88
Hall, Marcus 27
Hall, Paul 25
Hall, Ryan 29
Hallfredsson, Emil 82
Halliday, Matthew 57
Halls, John 67
Halmosi, Peter 62
Hamann, Dietmar 49
Hamann, Nick 22
Hamed, Radwan 82
Hamer, Ben 67
Hammell, Steven 75
Hammill, Adam 46
Hammond, Dean 14
Hammond, Elvis 43
Hamshaw, Matt 51
Hancox, Richard 81
Hand, James 39
Hand, Jamie 24
Hapgood, Leon 81
Harban, Thomas 5
Harding, Ben 54
Harding, Dan 41
Hardman, Lewis 30
Hardy, Aaron 39
Harewood, Marlon 87
Harkins, Gary 36
Harley, Jon 17
Harper, James 67
Harper, Kevin 77
Harper, Lee 54
Harper, Steve 55
Harpur, Ryan 33
Harris, James 1
Harris, Neil 53
Harris, Scott 64
Harrison, Danny 83
Harrison, Lee 4
Harrison, Paul 38
Harrold, Matt 75
Harsanyi, Zoltan 9
Harsley, Paul 63
Hart, Callum 11
Hart, Gary 14
Hart, Joe 49
Harthill, Oliver 6
Hartley, Peter 78
Hartson, John 86
Hasselbaink, Jimmy Floyd 21
Hassell, Bobby 5
Hastings, John 54
Hatch, Jamie 74
Hatch, Liam 4
Havern, Gianluca 76
Hawkins, Colin 27
Hawley, Karl 20
Hayes, Jonathan 67
Hayes, Paul 5
Hayles, Barry 62
Haynes, Danny 41
Hayter, James 11
Hazell, Reuben 25
Hazley, Matthew 77
Healy, Colin 5
Healy, David 42
Heath, Colin 48
Heath, Joe 58
Heath, Matt 42
Heaton, Tom 50
Heckingbottom, Paul 5
Hedman, Magnus 22
Heffernan, Paul 32
Hegarty, Nick 36
Heikkinen, Markus 47
Heinze, Gabriel 50
Helguson, Heidar 34
Henchoz, Stephane 7
Henderson, Darius 85
Henderson, Ian 57
Henderson, Paul 43
Henderson, Stephen 3
Henderson, Wayne 65
Hendon, Ian 4
Hendrie, Lee 3
Hennessey, Wayne 89
Henry, James 67
Henry, Karl 89
Henry, Paul 83
Henry, Thierry 2
Herd, Ben 73
Heskey, Emile 88
Heslop, Simon 5
Hessenthaler, Andy 4
Hessey, Sean 24
Heywood, Matthew 13
Hibbert, Dave 65
Hibbert, Tony 33
Higdon, Michael 28
Higginbotham, Danny 77
Higgs, Shane 23
Hignett, Craig 37
Hilario 22
Hildreth, Lee 27
Hill, Clint 77
Hill, Kevin 81
Hill, Matt 65
Hills, John 72
Hinchliffe, Ben 65
Hindmarch, Stephen 20
Hinds, Richard 70
Hines, Seb 52
Hinshelwood, Adam 14
Hinshelwood, Paul 14
Hinton, Craig 16
Hird, Samuel 42
Hjelde, Jon Olav 51
Hleb, Aleksandr 2
Hobbs, Jack 46
Hockley, Matthew 81
Hodge, Bryan 7
Hodges, Lee 62
Hodgkiss, Jared 86
Hoefkens, Carl 77
Hogg, Steven 73
Holden, Dean 61
Holdsworth, Andy 39
Holgate, Ashan 80
Holland, Chris 10
Holland, Matt 21
Hollands, Danny 11
Holloway, Darren 30
Holmes, Derek 20
Holmes, Lee 31
Holmes, Peter 47
Holroyd, Chris 24
Holt, Andy 56
Holt, Gary 58

Holt, Grant 58
Holt, Stefan 5
Hoolahan, Wes 8
Hooper, Gary 75
Hope, Richard 73
Horlock, Kevin 32
Horsell, Martin 81
Horsfield, Geoff 71
Horwood, Evan 71
Hoskins, Will 85
Hoult, Russell 77
Howard, Brian 5
Howard, Mark 19
Howard, Mark 19
Howard, Steve 31
Howard, Tim 33
Howarth, Chris 9
Howarth, Russell 12
Howe, Eddie 11
Howe, Joe 54
Howell, Andrew 66
Howell, Luke 35
Howland, David 6
Howson, Jonathan 42
Hoyte, Justin 2
Hreidarsson, Hermann 21
Hubertz, Poul 53
Huckerby, Darren 57
Huddlestone, Tom 82
Hudson, Mark 39
Hudson, Mark 29
Hughes, Aaron 3
Hughes, Andy 57
Hughes, Bryan 21
Hughes, Craig 26
Hughes, Jeff 45
Hughes, Liam 89
Hughes, Mark 56
Hughes, Mark 25
Hughes, Michael 29
Hughes, Richard 64
Hughes, Robert 58
Hughes, Stephen 27
Hughes, Stephen 43
Huke, Shane 61
Hulbert, Robin 63
Hulse, Rob 71
Hume, Iain 43
Humphrey, Chris 73
Humphreys, Richie 37
Hunt, David 56
Hunt, James 16
Hunt, Lewis 75
Hunt, Nicky 9
Hunt, Stephen 59
Hunt, Steve 67
Huntington, Paul 55
Hurrell, Sam 22
Hurst, Glynn 18
Hurst, Kevan 71
Hurst, Paul 69
Husbands, Michael 63
Hutchinson, Ben 52
Hutchinson, Joey 30
Hutchinson, Sam 22
Hutchison, Don 27
Huth, Robert 52
Huth, Ronald 46
Hyde, Micah 61
Hysen, Tobias 78
Hyypia, Sami 46

Ibehre, Jabo 44
Ide, Charlie 13
Idiakez, Inigo 74
Idrizaj, Bezian 46
Ifil, Jerel 80
Ifil, Phil 82
Ifill, Paul 29
Igoe, Sammy 16
Ikeme, Carl 89
Inamoto, Junichi 86
Ince, Clayton 84
Ince, Paul 48
Ingason, Thordur 33
Ingham, Michael 90
Ingimarsson, Ivar 67
Insua, Emiliano 46
Ioannou, Nicky 4
Ireland, Stephen 49
Iriekpen, Ezomo 79
Irving, John 33
Isaksson, Andreas 49
Iwelumo, Chris 26
Izzet, Kem 26

Jaaskelainen, Jussi 9
Jack, Kelvin 35
Jack, Rodney 28
Jackman, Danny 35
Jackson, Jamie 25
Jackson, Johnnie 26
Jackson, Mark 68
Jackson, Matt 88
Jackson, Mike 8
Jackson, Richard 31
Jacobson, Joe 19
Jagielka, Phil 71
Jaidi, Radhi 6
Jaime Ruiz, Mikhael 4
Jalal, Shwan 61
James, Chris 34
James, Craig 30
James, David 64
James, Kevin 58
James, Lloyd 74
James, Olly 83
Jarman, Nathan 5
Jarrett, Albert 85
Jarrett, Jason 65
Jarvis, Matthew 35
Jarvis, Rossi 57
Jarvis, Ryan 57
Jeannin, Alex 38
Jeffers, Francis 7
Jelleyman, Gareth 51
Jenas, Jermaine 82
Jennings, James 48
Jennings, Steven 83
Jensen, Brian 17
Jensen, Claus 34
Jensen, Niclas 34
Jerome, Cameron 6
Jess, Eoin 56
Jevons, Phil 15
Jihai, Sun 49
Joachim, Julian 30
Johansson, Andreas 88
Johansson, Nils-Eric 43
John-Baptiste, Alex 51
John-Lewis, Leneli 45
John, Alistair 21
John, Collins 34

John, Stern 78
Johnson, Adam 52
Johnson, Andy 33
Johnson, Andy 43
Johnson, Brad 56
Johnson, Brett 56
Johnson, Damien 6
Johnson, Eddie 12
Johnson, Glen 22
Johnson, Jemal 89
Johnson, Jermaine 72
Johnson, Josh 90
Johnson, Lee 15
Johnson, Leon 35
Johnson, Michael 31
Johnson, Michael 49
Johnson, Roger 19
Johnson, Seth 31
Johnson, Simon 30
Johnston, Michael 83
Jones, Billy 28
Jones, Brad 52
Jones, Carl 37
Jones, Chris 79
Jones, Daniel 89
Jones, David 31
Jones, Gary 68
Jones, Gary 36
Jones, Kenwyne 74
Jones, Lee 30
Jones, Luke 73
Jones, Mark 90
Jones, Michael 90
Jones, Mike 83
Jones, Nathan 92
Jones, Paul 66
Jones, Ray 66
Jones, Richie 50
Jones, Steve 17
Jones, Zak 7
Jordan, Michael 25
Jordan, Stephen 49
Jorgensen, Claus 8
Joseph, Marc 8
Joyce, Luke 20
Joynes, Nathan 5
Judge, Alan 7
Jupp, Duncan 35
Jutkiewicz, Lucas 33

Kabba, Steven 85
Kalou, Salomon 22
Kamara, Diomansy 86
Kamara, Malvin 63
Kamara, Sheku 85
Kamud'a Kalala, Jean-Paul 92
Kandol, Tresor 42
Kane, Tony 7
Kanu, Nwankwo 64
Kanyuka, Patrick 66
Katan, Yaniv 87
Kavanagh, Graham 78
Kay, Antony 5
Kay, Matty 8
Kazim-Richards, Colin 71
Kazimierczak, Prezemek 9
Keane, Keith 47
Keane, Michael 69
Keane, Robbie 82
Kearney, Alan 33

Keates, Dean 84
Keene, James 64
Keita, Mamadi 7
Keith, Joe 13
Kell, Richard 45
Kelly, Gary 42
Kelly, Shaun 24
Kelly, Stephen 6
Keltie, Clark 30
Kemenes, Szabolcs 21
Kempson, Darran 28
Kennedy, Jason 52
Kennedy, Mark 29
Kennedy, Tom 18
Kenny, Paddy 71
Kenton, Darren 43
Keogh, Andy 89
Keogh, Richard 15
Kepa 87
Kerr, Natt 69
Kerr, Scott 45
Kerry, Lloyd 71
Kewell, Harry 46
Khizanishvili, Zurab 7
Kiely, Dean 86
Kightly, Michael 89
Kilbane, Kevin 88
Kilgallon, Matthew 71
Kilkenny, Neil 6
King, Ledley 82
King, Liam 69
King, Marlon 85
King, Robbie 26
King, Simon 4
Kinsella, Mark 84
Kiraly, Gabor 29
Kirk, Andy 56
Kirkland, Christopher 88
Kirkup, Dan 20
Kishishev, Radostin 21
Kisnorbo, Patrick 43
Kissock, John 33
Kissock, John 33
Kitchen, Ashley 51
Kitson, Dave 67
Knight, David 52
Knight, Leon 54
Knight, Zat 34
Knights, Darryl 41
Konchesky, Paul 87
Konstantopoulos, Dimitrios 37
Koren, Robert 86
Koroman, Ognjen 64
Koumas, Jason 86
Kovacs, Janos 25
Kozluk, Rob 71
Kranjcar, Niko 64
Krause, James 41
Kromkamp, Jan 46
Krul, Tim 55
Krysiak, Artur 6
Kuipers, Michels 14
Kupisz, Tomasz 88
Kuqi, Shefki 29
Kuszczak, Tomasz 86
Kuyt, Dirk 46
Kyle, Kevin 27

Lafferty, Kyle 17
Laight, Ryan 5

Laird, Marc 49
Laird, Scott 62
Lallana, Adam 74
Lamb, Shaun 15
Lambert, Ricky 16
Lampard, Frank 22
Lancashire, Oliver 74
Landzaat, Denny 88
Langley, Richard 47
Langmead, Kelvin 73
Lappin, Simon 57
Larkin, Colin 25
Larrieu, Romain 62
Larsson, Henrik 50
Larsson, Sebastian 6
Lastuvka, Jan 34
Lauren, Etame-Mayer 64
Laursen, Martin 3
Law, Nicky 71
Lawlor, Matthew 8
Lawrence, Dennis 79
Lawrence, Liam 77
Lawrence, Matt 29
Lawson, James 75
Le Fondre, Adam 76
Le Tallec, Anthony 46
Leacock, Dean 31
Leadbitter, Grant 78
Leary, Michael 47
Ledley, Joe 19
Lee-Barrett, Arran 27
Lee, Alan 41
Lee, Charlie 82
Lee, Dong-Gook 52
Lee, Graeme 32
Lee, Jason 59
Lee, Kieran 50
Lee, Richard 85
Lee, Tommy 48
Lee, Young-Pyo 82
Legwinski, Sylvain 41
Legzdins, Adam 6
Lehmann, Jens 2
Leigertwood, Mikele 71
Lekaj, Rocky 72
Lennon, Aaron 82
Lescott, Aaron 16
Lescott, Jolean 33
Leslie, Steven 73
Lester, Jack 58
Letheren, Kyle 5
Lever, Chris 60
Lewington, Dean 54
Lewis, Eddie 42
Lewis, Joe 57
Lewis, Junior 54
Lewis, Stuart 4
Li Tie 71
Licka, Mario 74
Liddell, Andy 60
Liddle, Gary 37
Lillis, Josh 70
Lindegaard, Andy 92
Lindfield, Craig 46
Lines, Chris 16
Linwood, Paul 24
Lisbie, Kevin 21
Lita, Leroy 67
Little, Glen 67
Little, Mark 89
Livermore, David 40

Livermore, Jake 82
Livesey, Danny 20
Ljungberg, Frederik 2
Llewellyn, Chris 90
Lloyd, Callum 51
Lloyd, Rob 28
Loach, Scott 85
Lockwood, Adam 32
Lockwood, Matt 44
Loft, Doug 14
Logan, Carlos 30
Logan, Conrad 43
Logan, Shaleum 49
Lomas, Steve 66
Lomax, Kelvin 60
Lonergan, Andrew 65
Long, Shane 67
Loovens, Glenn 19
Low, Josh 61
Lowe, Keith 89
Lowe, Ryan 28
Lowndes, Nathan 63
Lowry, Jamie 25
Lua-Lua, Lomano 64
Lucas, David 5
Lucketti, Chris 71
Luis Garcia 46
Lumsdon, Chris 20
Lund, Eric 3
Lund, Jonny 42
Lundekvam, Claus 74
Lunt, Kenny 72
Lupoli, Arturo 2
Luque, Alberto 55
Lycett, Scott 43
Lynch, Joel 14
Lynch, Mark 92
Lynch, Ryan 27

Ma Kalambay, Yves 22
MacDonald, Sherjill 86
MacKay, Malky 85
MacKay, Michael 37
MacKenzie, Chris 73
MacKenzie, Neil 70
MacLean, Steve 72
Maccarone, Massimo 52
Macdonald, Shaun 79
Mackail-Smith, Craig 61
Macken, Jon 31
Mackie, John 44
Mackin, Levi 90
Madden, Simon 42
Maghoma, Jacques 82
Magnay, Carl 22
Maher, Kevin 75
Maher, Shaun 11
Maher, Stephen 92
Mahon, Alan 17
Mahon, Gavin 85
Maidens, Michael 37
Makelele, Claude 22
Makin, Chris 74
Malbranque, Steed 82
Malcolm, Bob 31
Malcolm, Michael 76
Maloney, Shaun 3
Mancienne, Michael 22
Mangan, Andrew 1
Mannix, David 46
Mannone, Vito 2

Mansell, Lee 81
Margetson, Martyn 19
Mariappa, Adrian 85
Marney, Dean 40
Marples, Simon 24
Marriott, Alan 45
Marriott, Andy 10
Marrison, Colin 71
Marsh-Evans, Robert 24
Marsh, Phil 50
Marshall, Andy 27
Marshall, David 57
Martin, Cesar 9
Martin, Chris 57
Martin, Dan 59
Martin, David 46
Martin, David 29
Martin, Joe 82
Martin, Lee 50
Martin, Richard 14
Martin, Russell 91
Martinez, Roberto 24
Martins, Obafemi 55
Martis, Shelton 30
Mascherano, Javier 46
Massey, Alan 91
Masters, Clark 13
Mate, Peter 67
Matteo, Dominic 77
Matthews, Lee 28
Mattis, Dwayne 5
Mattock, Joe 43
Mawene, Samy-Oyame 53
Mawene, Youl 65
May, Ben 53
May, Danny 56
Maybury, Alan 43
Maylett, Brad 10
Maynard, Nicky 28
Mayo, Kerry 14
Mayo, Paul 45
Mbesuma, Collins 64
McAliskey, John 39
McAllister, Jamie 15
McAllister, Sean 72
McAnuff, Jobi 29
McArdle, Rory 68
McAteer, Jason 83
McAuley, Gareth 43
McBreen, Daniel 70
McBride, Brian 34
McCallum, Gavin 92
McCammon, Mark 32
McCann, Austin 59
McCann, Chris 17
McCann, Gavin 3
McCann, Grant 5
McCarthy, Benni 7
McCarthy, Patrick 43
McCartney, George 87
McClements, David 72
McClenahan, Trent 38
McCombe, Jamie 15
McCombe, John 39
McCormack, Alan 75
McCormick, Luke 62
McCready, Chris 83
McCulloch, Lee 88
McDaid, Sean 32
McDermott, David 84
McDermott, John 36
McDermott, Neale 20
McDonald, Curtis 19
McDonald, Dean 35
McDonald, Gary 60
McDonald, Marvin 48
McEveley, James 31
McEvilly, Lee 90
McFadden, James 33
McGhee, Jamie 51
McGivern, Leighton 1
McGleish, Scott 91
McGoldrick, David 74
McGovern, John-Paul 54
McGrail, Chris 65
McGreal, John 17
McGregor, Mark 63
McGrory, Scott 5
McGugan, Lewis 58
McGuire, Patrick 12
McGurk, Adam 3
McIndoe, Michael 89
McInnes, Derek 53
McIntosh, Austin 51
McIntosh, Martin 39
McIntyre, Kevin 48
McKenna, Kieran 82
McKenna, Paul 65
McKenzie, Leon 27
McKeown, James 84
McKoy, Nick 19
McLaren, Paul 83
McLean, Aaron 61
McLeod, Izale 54
McLeod, Kevin 26
McLeod, Mark 30
McMahon, Daryl 44
McMahon, Lewis 59
McMahon, Tony 52
McMillan, Steve 88
McNamara, Jackie 89
McNamee, Anthony 85
McNamee, David 27
McNaughton, Kevin 19
McNeil, Matthew 48
McNulty, Jim 48
McParland, Anthony 91
McPhail, Stephen 19
McPhee, Chris 81
McPhee, Stephen 40
McPike, James 6
McQuoid, Josh 11
McShane, Paul 86
McSheffrey, Gary 6
McSporran, Jermaine 24
McVeigh, Paul 57
Mears, Tyrone 87
Meechan, Alex 24
Meite, Abdoulaye 9
Mellberg, Olof 3
Melligan, John 23
Mellor, Neil 65
Mendes, Junior 59
Mendieta, Gaizka 52
Meredith, James 31
Merida Perez, Fran 2
Meslien, Sylvain 79
Mettam, Leon 45
Meynell, Rhys 5
Michalik, Lubomir 9
Mido 82
Mifsud, Michael 27
Mikaelsson, Tobias 3
Mikel, John Obi 22
Milanese, Mauro 66
Mildenhall, Steve 92
Miles, Colin 63
Miles, John 48
Miller, Ian 41
Miller, Ishmael 49
Miller, Justin 44
Miller, Kevin 74
Miller, Liam 78
Miller, Shaun 28
Miller, Tommy 78
Mills, Danny 49
Mills, Joseph 74
Mills, Leigh 82
Mills, Matthew 49
Mills, Pablo 69
Milner, James 55
Milsom, Robert 34
Minto-St Aimie, Kieron 66
Mirfin, David 39
Mitchell, Paul 54
Mkandawire, Tamika 38
Mocquet, William 78
Mokoena, Aaron 7
Molango, Maheta 14
Moloney, Brendan 58
Molyneux, Lee 33
Moncur, Tom 34
Monk, Garry 79
Monkhouse, Andy 37
Montague, Ross 13
Montella, Vincenzo 34
Montgomery, Gary 69
Montgomery, Nick 71
Montrose, Lewis 88
Mooney, Tommy 91
Moore, Byron 28
Moore, Chris 13
Moore, Craig 55
Moore, Darren 31
Moore, Ian 42
Moore, Karl 49
Moore, Luke 3
Moore, Sammy 41
Moore, Stefan 66
Morais, Filipe 53
Morgan, Chris 71
Morgan, Craig 61
Morgan, Dean 47
Morgan, Paul 45
Morgan, Wes 58
Morley, Dave 48
Mornar, Ivica 64
Morrell, Andy 8
Morris, Glenn 44
Morris, Ian 70
Morris, Jody 53
Morris, Lee 92
Morrison, Clinton 29
Morrison, James 52
Morrison, Steven 33
Moses, Adi 45
Moss, Darren 28
Moss, Neil 11
Motteram, Carl 81
Mouritsen, Christian 49
Mousinho, John 13
Moussa, Franck 75
Moyo-Modise, Clive 68
Mpenza, Emile 49
Muamba, Fabrice 6
Muggleton, Carl 51
Muirhead, Ben 12
Mulgrew, Charlie 89
Mulligan, Dave 70
Mulligan, Gary 35
Mullin, John 83
Mullin, Paul 1
Mullings, Darren 16
Mullins, Hayden 87
Mullins, John 51
Mulryne, Phil 44
Murdock, Colin 69
Murphy, Danny 82
Murphy, Daryl 78
Murphy, Joe 70
Murphy, John 48
Murphy, Kieron 54
Murphy, Peter 20
Murray, Adam 48
Murray, Glenn 68
Murray, Matt 89
Murray, Paul 20
Murray, Robert 36
Murray, Scott 15
Murty, Graeme 67
Mvuemba, Arnold 64
Mwaruwari, Benjamin 64
Myhill, Boaz 40
Myhre, Thomas 21
Myrie-Williams, Jennison 15

N'Da, Julien 1
N'Dumbu Nsungu, Guylain 35
N'Gotty, Bruno 6
N'Guessan, Dany 45
N'Toya, Tcham 59
N'Zogbia, Charles 55
Nade, Christian 71
Nafti, Mehdi 6
Nalis, Lilian 62
Nardiello, Daniel 5
Nardiello, Michael 86
Nash, Carlo 65
Naughton, Kyle 71
Navarro, Alan 48
Naylor, Lee 89
Naylor, Richard 41
Naysmith, Gary 33
Neal, Chris 65
Neal, Lewis 65
Needham, Liam 59
Neill, Lucas 87
Nelsen, Ryan 7
Nelson, Michael 37
Nelson, Stuart 13
Nelthorpe, Craig 32
Neville, Gary 50
Neville, Phil 33
Newbold, Adam 58
Newby, Jon 90
Newey, Tom 36
Newsham, Mark 69
Newton, Adam 61
Newton, Sean 24
Newton, Shaun 87
Ngoma, Kalusivikako 30
Nicholas, Andrew 80
Nicholls, Alex 84
Nicholls, Kevin 42
Nicholson, Shane 25
Nicholson, Stuart 86
Nicolau, Nicky 4
Niemi, Antti 34
Niven, Derek 25
Noble, David 15
Noble, Mark 87
Noel-Williams, Gifton 17
Nolan, Eddie 7
Nolan, Kevin 9
Nonda, Shabani 7
Norris, David 62
North, Danny 36
Norville, Jason 4
Nosworthy, Nayron 78
Noubissie, Patrick 80
Nowland, Adam 65
Nugent, Dave 65
Nunn, Ben 10
Nuno Morais 22
Nuno Valente 33
Nyatanga, Lewin 31
Nygaard, Marc 66

O'Brien, Alan 55
O'Brien, Andy 64
O'Brien, Burton 72
O'Brien, Joey 9
O'Callaghan, George 41
O'Cearuill, Joe 2
O'Connor, Gareth 17
O'Connor, James 32
O'Connor, James 17
O'Connor, Kevin 13
O'Connor, Kevin 89
O'Connor, Michael 28
O'Donnell, Daniel 46
O'Grady, Chris 69
O'Halloran, Stephen 3
O'Hanlon, Sean 54
O'Hara, Jamie 82
O'Hare, Alan 25
O'Keefe, Josh 7
O'Leary, Kristian 79
O'Leary, Stephen 47
O'Neil, Gary 64
O'Shea, John 50
Oakes, Andy 79
Oakes, Michael 89
Oakes, Stefan 91
Oakley, Matthew 31
Oatway, Charlie 14
Obadeyi, Temitope 9
Odejayi, Kayode 23
Odhiambo, Eric 43
Oji, Sam 6
Olejnik, Robert 3
Oliseh, Egutu 66
Oliver, Dean 71
Olofinjana, Seyi 89
Olsen, Alex 82
Olsson, Martin 7
Omozusi, Elliot 34
Onibuje, Fola 91
Onuoha, Nedum 49
Onyewu, Oguchi 55
Ooijer, Andre 7
Opara, Lloyd 61
Orelaja, Kazeem 34
Ormerod, Brett 65
Orr, Bradley 15
Osano, Curtis 67
Osborn, Simon 38
Osborne, Junior 85
Osborne, Karleigh 13
Osborne, Leon 12
Osbourne, Isaac 27
Osbourne, Isaiah 3
Osei-Gyan, King 34
Osei-Kuffour, Jo 13
Osman, Leon 33
Oster, John 67
Ostlund, Alexander 74
Otsemobor, John 28
Owen, Gareth 60
Owen, Michael 55
Owusu, Lloyd 13

Pacey, Rob 32
Padelli, Daniele 46
Padula, Gino 58
Page, Jack 44
Page, Robert 27
Page, Sam 54
Paine, Matt 26
Painter, Marcos 79
Palethorpe, Philip 83
Paletta, Gabriel 46
Palmer, Aiden 44
Palmer, Chris 91
Palmer, James 16
Palmer, Marcus 38
Pamarot, Noe 64
Pantsil, John 87
Parisio, Carl 2
Park, Ji-Sung 50
Parker, Ben 42
Parker, Keigan 8
Parker, Scott 55
Parkes, Jordan 85
Parkin, Jon 40
Parkin, Sam 47
Parkinson, Andy 59
Parlour, Ray 40
Parnaby, Stuart 52
Parrinello, Tom 16
Parrish, Andy 18
Parry, Paul 19
Partridge, David 15
Partridge, Richie 69
Paterson, Martin 77
Paterson, Sean 8
Pattison, Matt 55
Paul, Shane 23
Paulo Ferreira 22
Paynter, Billy 75
Peacock, Lee 80
Pead, Craig 84
Pearce, Alex 67
Pearce, Ian 34
Pearce, Jason 64
Pearce, Kaystian 6
Pearson, Michael 60
Pearson, Stephen 31
Pedersen, Henrik 9
Pedersen, Morten 7
Pedersen, Rune 58
Pedro Mendes 64
Pejic, Shaun 90
Pekhart, Tomas 82

Pele 74
Peltier, Lee 46
Pembridge, Mark 34
Penford, Tom 12
Pennant, Jermaine 46
Perch, James 58
Pergl, Pavel 65
Pericard, Vincent de Paul 77
Perkins, David 68
Perrett, Russell 47
Perry, Chris 86
Peschisolido, Paul 31
Peter, Sergio 7
Peters, Jaime 41
Peters, Ryan 13
Petrov, Stilian 3
Pettigrew, Adrian 22
Pezzoni, Kevin 7
Phelan, Scott 33
Phillips, Kevin 86
Phillips, Mark 53
Phillips, Martin 81
Phillips, Steve 16
Picken, Allan 84
Picken, Phil 25
Pidgeley, Lenny 53
Pilkington, Anthony 76
Pilkington, George 63
Pilkington, Kevin 59
Pinault, Thomas 13
Pipe, David 59
Pique, Gerard 50
Pistone, Alessandro 33
Pitman, Brett 11
Pittman, Jon-Paul 32
Platt, Clive 54
Platt, Conal 11
Plummer, Andrew 41
Plummer, Chris 61
Plummer, Matthew 40
Pogatetz, Emanuel 52
Pogliacomi, Les 60
Poke, Michael 74
Pollitt, Mike 88
Pook, Michael 80
Poole, David 76
Poole, Glenn 68
Poom, Mart 2
Pope, Tom 28
Porter, Chris 60
Porter, Joel 37
Porter, Levi 43
Potter, Darren 89
Potter, Luke 5
Pouso, Omar 21
Pouton, Alan 35
Powell, Chris 85
Powell, Darren 74
Power, Alan 58
Pratley, Darren 79
Prendergast, Rory 68
Price, Jamie 32
Price, Jamie 6
Price, Jason 32
Price, Lewis 41
Primus, Linvoy 64
Prior, Spencer 75
Priskin, Tamas 85
Proctor, Andy 1
Proctor, Michael 37
Prosser, Luke 63
Prosser, Luke 63
Proudlock, Adam 76
Provett, Jim 37
Prutton, David 74
Puddy, Will 23
Pugh, Andy 35
Pugh, Danny 65
Pugh, Marc 18
Pulis, Anthony 77
Puncheon, Jason 4
Purches, Stephen 11
Purdie, Rob 38
Purse, Darren 19

Quashie, Nigel 87
Queudrue, Franck 34
Quigley, Damien 18
Quinn, Alan 71
Quinn, James 56
Quinn, Keith 71
Quinn, Stephen 71

Racchi, Danny 39
Rachubka, Paul 39
Radzinski, Tomasz 34
Rae, Michael 37
Rafa 27
Rajczi, Peter 5
Ramage, Peter 55
Ramsden, Simon 68
Ramsey, Aaron 19
Randall, Mark 2
Randolph, Darren 21
Rankin, Isiah 36
Rasiak, Grzegorz 74
Raven, David 20
Ravenhill, Ricky 30
Rayner, Simon 45
Raynes, Michael 76
Reay, Sean 30
Redan, Iwan 19
Reddy, Michael 36
Redmond, Shane 58
Reed, Jamie 90
Reed, Matthew 87
Reed, Steve 81
Reet, Danny 51
Regan, Carl 48
Rehman, Zesh 66
Reich, Marco 29
Reid, Andy 21
Reid, Craig 23
Reid, Izak 48
Reid, Kyel 87
Reid, Paul 5
Reid, Paul 14
Reid, Reuben 62
Reid, Steven 7
Reina, Jose 46
Renton, Kris 57
Rents, Sam 14
Reo-Coker, Nigel 87
Revell, Alex 14
Reyes, Jose Antonio 2
Reyna, Claudio 49
Rhodes, Alex 13
Ribeiro, Christian 15
Ricardo Carvalho 22
Ricardo Rocha 82
Richards, Garry 26
Richards, Justin 61
Richards, Marc 5
Richards, Matt 41
Richards, Matthew 31
Richards, Micah 49
Richardson, Frazer 42
Richardson, Jake 78
Richardson, Kieran 50
Richardson, Leam 1
Ricketts, Donovan 12
Ricketts, Mark 21
Ricketts, Michael 65
Ricketts, Rohan 89
Ricketts, Sam 40
Ridgewell, Liam 3
Ridley, Lee 70
Rigg, Sean 16
Riggott, Chris 52
Riise, John Arne 46
Riley, Chris 82
Riley, Martin 89
Rinaldi, Douglas 85
Rix, Ben 28
Rizzo, Nicky 54
Robben, Arjen 22
Roberts, Chris 80
Roberts, Dale 58
Roberts, Gareth 32
Roberts, Gary 28
Roberts, Gary 41
Roberts, Jason 7
Roberts, Kevin 24
Roberts, Mark 28
Roberts, Neil 90
Roberts, Steve 32
Robertson, Chris 81
Robertson, Gregor 69
Robertson, Jordan 71
Robinson, Andy 79
Robinson, Carl 57
Robinson, Jake 14
Robinson, Mark 81
Robinson, Marvin 48
Robinson, Paul 53
Robinson, Paul 82
Robinson, Paul 86
Robinson, Steve 47
Robinson, Theo 85
Robson, Matty 37
Rocastle, Craig 60
Roche, Barry 25
Roche, Lee 90
Rochemback, Fabio 52
Rodgers, Luke 63
Rogers, Alan 1
Rommedahl, Dennis 21
Ronaldo, Cristiano 50
Rooney, Adam 77
Rooney, Wayne 50
Roper, Ian 84
Roque, Miguel 46
Rosa, Denes 89
Rose, Danny 50
Rose, Matthew 92
Rose, Michael 76
Rose, Richard 38
Rosenior, Liam 34
Rosicky, Tomas 2
Ross, Ian 71
Ross, Maurice 53
Ross, Shaun 47
Rossi, Giuseppe 50
Rothery, Gavin 42
Rouse, David 48
Rouse, Domaine 18
Routledge, Wayne 82
Rowe, Tommy 76
Rowlands, Martin 66
Rowntree, Adam 10
Rowson, David 30
Royce, Simon 66
Rudd, Sean 74
Ruddy, John 33
Rui Marques, Manuel 42
Rundle, Adam 68
Runstrom, Bjorn 34
Rusk, Simon 10
Russell, Alex 15
Russell, Darel 77
Russell, James 22
Russell, Sam 30
Rutherford, Paul 24
Ryan, James 46
Ryan, Oliver 45
Ryan, Richie 10
Ryan, Tim 30

Saah, Brian 44
Sadler, Matthew 6
Safri, Youseff 57
Saganowski, Marek 74
Saha, Louis 50
Sahar, Ben 22
Sako, Morike 68
Salmon, Mark 89
Sam, Hector 84
Sam, Lloyd 21
Samaras, Georgios 49
Samba, Cherno 62
Samba, Christopher 7
Samuel, J Lloyd 3
Sancho, Brent 35
Sandell, Andy 16
Sandwith, Kevin 24
Sankofa, Osei 21
Sansara, Netan 84
Santos, Georges 14
Sarki, Emmanuel 22
Sarmiento, Marcelo 74
Savage, Bas 14
Savage, Robbie 7
Sawyer, Gary 62
Scharner, Paul 88
Schmeichel, Kasper 49
Schofield, Danny 39
Scholes, Paul 50
Schumacher, Steven 12
Schwarzer, Mark 52
Scimeca, Riccardo 19
Scott, Paul 18
Scott, Rob 48
Scowcroft, James 29
Seanla, Claude 85
Seck, Mamadou 71
Sedgwick, Chris 65
Seip, Marcel 62
Semple, Ryan 45
Senda, Danny 53
Senderos, Philippe 2
Seol, Ki-Hyun 67
Shackell, Jason 57
Shakes, Ricky 80
Shanks, Chris 55
Sharp, Billy 70
Sharp, James 68
Sharps, Ian 69
Shaw, Paul 25
Shaw, Richard 53
Shawcross, Ryan 50
Shearer, Scott 16
Sheehan, Alan 43
Sheldon, Gareth 38
Shelton, Luton 71
Sheridan, Jake 59
Sheringham, Charlie 29
Sheringham, Teddy 87
Sherlock, Jamie 45
Shevchenko, Andriy 22
Shields, Solomon 44
Shimmin, Dominic 66
Shipperley, Neil 13
Shittu, Dan 85
Shorey, Nicky 67
Short, Craig 71
Shotton, Ryan 77
Showunmi, Enoch 15
Shuker, Chris 83
Sibierski, Antoine 55
Sidibe, Mamady 77
Sidwell, Steve 67
Sigurdsson, Hannes 77
Silk, Gary 59
Sills, Tim 38
Silva, Gilberto 2
Silvestre, Mikael 50
Simek, Frankie 72
Simmonds, James 22
Simonsen, Steve 77
Simpson, Danny 50
Simpson, Michael 44
Sinama-Pongolle, Florent 46
Sinclair, Dean 4
Sinclair, Frank 17
Sinclair, James 9
Sinclair, Scott 22
Sinclair, Trevor 49
Sissoko, Mohamed 46
Sissons, Robert 9
Sito 41
Skacel, Rudi 74
Skarz, Joe 39
Skiverton, Terry 92
Skoko, Josip 88
Skulason, Olafur-Ingi 13
Skuse, Cole 15
Sleath, Danny 51
Slocombe, Martin 15
Small, Wade 72
Smalley, Deane 60
Smart, Andrew 48
Smart, Bally 57
Smeeton, Jake 92
Smertin, Alexei 34
Smith, Adam 25
Smith, Adam 61
Smith, Alan 50
Smith, Andy 15
Smith, Ben 38
Smith, Benjamin 32
Smith, Christian 63
Smith, Dean 44
Smith, Emmanuel 84
Smith, Gary 54
Smith, Jack 80
Smith, James 46
Smith, Jamie 54
Smith, Jay 59
Smith, Jeff 20
Smith, Jimmy 22
Smith, Johann 9
Smith, Kevin 78
Smith, Martin 30
Smith, Nick 12
Smith, Paul 81
Smith, Paul 58
Smith, Phil 80
Smith, Ryan 31
Smith, Terry 60
Smith, Tommy 85
Smithies, Alex 39
Soares, Tom 29
Soboljew, Mark 63
Sodje, Akpo 63
Sodje, Efe 75
Sodje, Sam 67
Solano, Nolberto 55
Soley, Seyfo 65
Solskjaer, Ole Gunnar 50
Sommeil, David 71
Somner, Matt 59
Song Billong, Alexandre 2
Songo'o, Frank 64
Sonko, Ibrahima 67
Sonner, Danny 63
Sorensen, Thomas 3
Sorondo, Gonzalo 21
Sorvel, Neil 73
Southall, Nicky 35
Southern, Keith 8
Southgate, Gareth 52
Sparrow, Matt 70
Sparv, Tim 74
Spearing, Jay 46
Spector, Jonathan 87
Speed, Gary 9
Speight, Jake 18
Spence, Lewis 29
Spencer, Damien 23
Spencer, James 76
Spencer, Scott 33
Spender, Simon 90
Speroni, Julian 29
Spicer, John 17
Spillane, Michael 57
Spiller, Danny 35
Spring, Matthew 47
Spurr, Tommy 72
Srnicek, Pavel 55
St Ledger-Hall, Sean 65
Stack, Graham 67
Stallard, Mark 45
Stalteri, Paul 82
Stam, Stefan 60
Stamp, Phil 30
Standing, Michael 11
Stanton, Nathan 68
Staples, Reece 58
Starkey, Phil 29
Starosta, Ben 71
Staunton, Mark 21
Stead, Jon 71
Stearman, Richard 43
Steele, Lee 24

Steele, Luke 86
Stefanovic, Dejan 64
Stephens, Dale 18
Stevens, Danny 47
Stevens, Jamie 10
Stewart, Damion 66
Stewart, Gareth 11
Stewart, Jordan 85
Stewart, Marcus 92
Stieber, Zoltan 3
Stirling, Jude 54
Stock, Brian 32
Stockdale, David 30
Stockdale, Robbie 83
Stockley, Sam 91
Stokes, Anthony 78
Stokes, Tony 87
Stone, Craig 35
Stone, Steve 42
Stonebridge, Ian 91
Strachan, Gavin 61
Streete, Theo 69
Stubbs, Alan 33
Stubhaug, Lars 33
Sturridge, Daniel 49
Sturrock, Blair 80
Suhaj, Pavol 28
Sullivan, John 14
Sullivan, Neil 42
Summerfield, Luke 62
Supple, Shane 41
Surman, Andrew 74
Sutton, Chris 3
Sutton, Ritchie 28
Svensson, Michael 74
Swailes, Chris 60
Swailes, Danny 48
Sweeney, Anthony 37
Sweeney, Peter 77
Swift, John 12
Sylla, Momo 43
Symes, Michael 73
Synnott, Michael 41

Taarabt, Adel 82
Tabb, Jay 27
Tainio, Teemu 82
Tait, Paul 10
Tal, Idan 9
Talbot, Drew 47
Talbot, Jason 63
Talbot, Stewart 10
Talia, Frank 91
Tann, Adam 44
Tansey, Greg 76
Tanska, Jani 21
Tate, Alan 79
Taylor-Fletcher, Gary 39
Taylor, Andrew 52
Taylor, Andy 7
Taylor, Andy 36
Taylor, Chris 60
Taylor, Cleveland 70
Taylor, Craig 81
Taylor, Daryl 18
Taylor, Gareth 83
Taylor, Ian 56
Taylor, Jason 76
Taylor, Kris 84
Taylor, Maik 6
Taylor, Martin 6
Taylor, Matthew 64
Taylor, Ryan 69
Taylor, Ryan 88
Taylor, Scott 54
Taylor, Steven 55
Taylor, Stuart 3
Tchakounte, Armel 66
Teague, Andrew 48
Teale, Gary 31
Tebily, Oliver 6
Teimourian, Andranik 9
Terry, John 22
Terry, Paul 92
Tevez, Carlos 87
Thatcher, Ben 21
Thelwell, Alton 44
Thirlwell, Paul 20
Thomas, Bradley 92
Thomas, Danny 38
Thomas, Jerome 21
Thomas, Mitchell 17
Thomas, Sean 66
Thomas, Wayne 17
Thompson, Alan 42
Thompson, David 9
Thompson, Joe 68
Thompson, John 58
Thompson, Steven 19
Thomson, Jake 74
Thomson, Stephen 7
Thorne, Peter 57
Thornton, Barry 32
Thornton, Dean 91
Thornton, Kevin 27
Thornton, Sean 32
Thorpe, Lee 81
Thorpe, Tony 36
Threlfall, Robert 46
Tiatto, Danny 43
Tierney, Marc 73
Tierney, Paul 8
Till, Peter 36
Tillen, Joe 54
Tillen, Sam 13
Timar, Krisztian 62
Timlin, Michael 34
Timoska, Sampsa 66
Tinkler, Mark 37
Tipton, Matt 18
Todd, Andrew 1
Todd, Andy 7
Todorov, Svetoslav 64
Togwell, Sam 5
Tolley, Jamie 48
Tomkins, James 87
Tomlin, Gavin 13
Tomlinson, Stuart 28
Toner, Ciaran 36
Tonge, Dale 5
Tonge, Michael 71
Tonkin, Anthony 92
Torpey, Steve 70
Torres, Sergio 91
Toure, Kolo 2
Townsend, Michael 23
Trabelsi, Hatem 49
Traore, Armand 2
Traore, Djimi 64
Travis, Nicky 71
Travis, Simon 38
Treacy, Keith 7
Tremarco, Carl 83
Tretton, Andy 1
Trimmer, Lewis 51
Troisi, James 55
Trotman, Neal 60
Trotter, Liam 41
Trundle, Lee 79
Tudgay, Marcus 72
Tudor, Shane 44
Tudur Jones, Owain 79
Tugay, Kerimoglu 7
Tunnicliffe, James 76
Turnbull, Paul 76
Turnbull, Philip 37
Turnbull, Ross 52
Turnbull, Stephen 37
Turner, Ben 27
Turner, Iain 33
Turner, Michael 40
Tyler, Mark 61
Tyson, Nathan 58

Ugarte, Juan 90
Underwood, Paul 47
Unsworth, Dave 88
Upson, Edward 41
Upson, Matthew 87

Vaisanen, Ville 30
Valencia, Luis 88
Valentine, Ryan 90
Van Den Berg, Vincent 2
Van Persie, Robin 2
Van der Meyde, Andy 33
Van der Sar, Edwin 50
Varga, Stanislav 78
Varney, Alex 21
Varney, Luke 28
Vass, Adam 77
Vassell, Darius 49
Vaughan, David 28
Vaughan, James 24
Vaughan, James 33
Vaughan, Stephen 10
Vaz Te, Ricardo 9
Ventre, Danny 1
Vernon, Scott 8
Veron, Juan Sebastian 22
Viafara, John 74
Victory, Jamie 23
Vidarsson, Bjarni 33
Vidic, Nemanja 50
Viduka, Mark 52
Vieira, Magno 4
Villis, Matt 81
Vincent, Ashley 23
Vincent, Jamie 80
Vine, Rowan 6
Vipond, Shaun 20
Virgo, Adam 27
Vokes, Sam 11
Volz, Moritz 34
Wainwright, Neil 30
Walcott, Theo 2
Walker, Ian 9
Walker, James 21
Walker, Jim 87
Walker, Jordan 15
Walker, Josh 52
Walker, Richard 16
Walker, Richard 63
Wallace, Ross 78
Wallis, John 38
Wallwork, Ronnie 86
Walsh, Michael 63
Walters, Jon 41
Walton, Simon 21
Warburton, Callum 68
Ward, Darren 29
Ward, Darren 78
Ward, Elliot 27
Ward, Gavin 83
Ward, Jamie 25
Ward, Nick 66
Ward, Stephen 89
Warhurst, Paul 4
Warlow, Adam 28
Warlow, Owain 45
Warne, Paul 60
Warner, Tony 34
Warnock, Stephen 7
Warrington, Andy 18
Watson, Ben 29
Watson, Kevin 26
Watson, Steve 72
Watt, Jerome 56
Watt, Phil 45
Watt, Steven 79
Watts, Adam 34
Way, Darren 79
Weale, Chris 15
Weaver, Nick 49
Webb, Daniel 92
Webb, Luke 38
Webber, Danny 71
Webster, Andy 88
Wedgbury, Samuel 71
Weihrauch, Per 22
Weir-Daley, Spencer 58
Weir, David 33
Welch, Michael 1
Wellens, Richard 60
Wells, Ben 80
Welsh, Andy 78
Welsh, Ishmael 92
Welsh, John 40
Wesolowski, James 43
Westlake, Ian 42
Weston, Curtis 80
Weston, Myles 21
Weston, Rhys 63
Westwood, Ashley 24
Westwood, Chris 84
Westwood, Keiren 20
Wetherall, David 12
Whaley, Simon 65
Whalley, Gareth 80
Whalley, Shaun 1
Wheater, David 52
Whelan, Glenn 72
Whelpdale, Chris 61
Whelpdale, Chris 61
Whing, Andrew 27
Whitaker, Danny 63
Whitbread, Zak 53
White, Alan 59
White, Jamie 74
White, Jason 51
White, John 26
Whitehead, Dean 78
Whitehead, Stuart 73
Whitley, Jeff 19
Whitlow, Mike 59
Whittingham, Peter 19
Whittington, Michael 23
Whittle, Justin 36
Wiggins-Thomas, Ruben 25
Wiggins, Rhoys 29
Wijnhard, Clyde 13
Wilbraham, Aaron 54
Wiles, Simon 8
Wilkinson, Andy 77
Wilkinson, Ben 40
Wilkinson, David 29
Wilkinson, Tom 45
Williams, Ady 80
Williams, Andy 38
Williams, Ashley 76
Williams, Ben 28
Williams, Dale 73
Williams, Danny 90
Williams, Darren 37
Williams, Eifion 37
Williams, Gareth 85
Williams, Gavin 41
Williams, Marc 90
Williams, Marcus 70
Williams, Marvin 53
Williams, Mike 90
Williams, Owain Fon 28
Williams, Rhys 52
Williams, Robbie 5
Williams, Robbie 1
Williams, Sam 3
Williams, Steve 91
Williams, Tom 79
Williams, Tony 20
Williamson, Lee 85
Williamson, Mike 91
Williamson, Samuel 49
Willock, Calum 13
Wilnis, Fabian 41
Wilson, Adam 39
Wilson, Brian 15
Wilson, Che 75
Wilson, James 15
Wilson, Kelvin 65
Wilson, Laurence 24
Wilson, Lawrie 26
Wilson, Marc 64
Wilson, Mark 32
Windass, Dean 12
Winn, Peter 70
Winnard, Dean 7
Wiseman, Scott 40
Wolfenden, Matthew 60
Wood, Chris 51
Wood, Neil 60
Wood, Richard 72
Woodards, Danny 28
Woodgate, Jonathan 52
Woodhouse, Curtis 36
Woodman, Craig 15
Woods, Martin 69
Woods, Michael 22
Woods, Ryan 7
Woods, Steve 81
Woodthorpe, Colin 18
Worley, Harry 22
Worrall, David 18
Worrell, David 69
Worthington, Jon 39
Wotton, Paul 62
Wrack, Darren 84
Wright-Phillips, Bradley 74
Wright-Phillips, Shaun 22
Wright, Alan 71
Wright, David 41
Wright, Jermaine 74
Wright, Josh 30
Wright, Mark 84
Wright, Nick 6
Wright, Richard 33
Wright, Stephen 78
Wright, Tommy 30
Wring, Danny 15
Wroe, Nicky 5
Wylde, Michael 23

Xavier, Abel 52

Yakubu, Ayegbeni 52
Yakubu, Ismail 4
Yao, Sosthene 23
Yates, Jamie 69
Yeates, Mark 82
Yeo, Simon 24
Yobo, Joseph 33
Yorke, Dwight 78
Youga, Kelly 21
Young, Ashley 3
Young, Jamie 91
Young, Luke 21
Young, Matthew 39
Young, Neil 11
Younghusband, Phil 22
Youngs, Tom 18

Zaaboub, Sofiane 80
Zakuani, Gaby 34
Zamora, Bobby 87
Zebroski, Chris 53
Zenden, Boudewijn 46
Zheng-Zhi 21
Ziegler, Reto 82
Zieler, Ron-Robert 50
Zokora, Didier 82
Zola, Calvin 83
Zuberbuhler, Pascal 86

TRANSFERS 2006–07

JUNE 2006	From	To	Fee in £
3 Baudet, Julien	Notts County	Crewe Alexandra	undisclosed
12 Bowyer, Lee D.	Newcastle United	West Ham United	250,000
26 Butcher, Richard T.	Oldham Athletic	Peterborough United	undisclosed
30 Cort, Leon	Hull City	Crystal Palace	1,250,000
27 Danns, Neil A.	Colchester United	Birmingham City	500,000
14 Davis, Claude	Preston North End	Sheffield United	2,500,000
13 Francis, Simon C.	Sheffield United	Southend United	undisclosed
2 Gray, Andrew D.	Sunderland	Burnley	750,000
30 Hall, Fitz	Crystal Palace	Wigan Athletic	3,000,000
2 Johnson, Andrew	Crystal Palace	Everton	8,600,000
15 Lescott, Joleon P.	Wolverhampton Wanderers	Everton	5,000,000
1 Lucketti, Christopher J.	Preston North End	Sheffield United	300,000
1 Lunt, Kenny V.	Crewe Alexandra	Sheffield Wednesday	Free
3 McCombe, Jamie	Lincoln City	Bristol City	undisclosed
28 Morais, Filipe A.	Chelsea	Millwall	undisclosed
9 Pidgeley, Leonard J.	Chelsea	Millwall	undisclosed
1 Small, Wade K.	Milton Keynes Dons	Sheffield Wednesday	nominal
16 Spector, Jonathan M.	Manchester United	West Ham United	500,000
19 Ward, Elliot L.	West Ham United	Coventry City	1,000,000
13 Whitbread, Zak B.	Liverpool	Millwall	undisclosed

JULY 2006			
7 Barnes, Philip K.	Sheffield United	Grimsby Town	undisclosed
5 Beckett, Luke J.	Sheffield United	Huddersfield Town	undisclosed
7 Bellamy, Craig D.	Blackburn Rovers	Liverpool	6,000,000
27 Bennett, Ian M.	Leeds United	Sheffield United	100,000
31 Boyd, Adam M.	Hartlepool United	Luton Town	500,000
7 Cohen, Christopher D.	West Ham United	Yeovil Town	undisclosed
6 Cole, Carlton	Chelsea	West Ham United	2,000,000
6 Collins, Patrick	Sheffield Wednesday	Darlington	undisclosed
31 Croft, Lee	Manchester City	Norwich City	700,000
21 Davis, Kelvin G.	Sunderland	Southampton	1,000,000
6 Day, Christopher N.	Oldham Athletic	Millwall	undisclosed
26 Duff, Damien A.	Chelsea	Newcastle United	5,000,000
17 Ebanks-Blake, Sylvan	Manchester United	Plymouth Argyle	200,000
3 Ellison, Kevin	Hull City	Tranmere Rovers	undisclosed
29 Fletcher, Carl N.	West Ham United	Crystal Palace	400,000
13 Flinders, Scott L.	Barnsley	Crystal Palace	500,000
12 Folly, Yoann	Southampton	Sheffield Wednesday	undisclosed
13 Francis, Damien J.	Wigan Athletic	Watford	1,000,000
11 Hamann, Dietmar	Liverpool	Bolton Wanderers	Free
12 Hamann, Dietmar	Bolton Wanderers	Manchester City	400,000
20 Hayles, Barrington	Millwall	Plymouth Argyle	100,000
14 Heskey, Emile I.	Birmingham City	Wigan Athletic	5,500,000
3 Horsfield, Geoffrey M.	West Bromwich Albion	Sheffield United	1,200,000
26 Hulse, Robert W.	Leeds United	Sheffield United	2,200,000
4 Kelly, Stephen M.	Tottenham Hotspur	Birmingham City	750,000
19 Leigertwood, Mikele B.	Crystal Palace	Sheffield United	600,000
21 Livermore, David	Millwall	Leeds United	400,000
18 Mansell, Lee R.S.	Oxford United	Torquay United	undisclosed
14 Marney, Dean E.	Tottenham Hotspur	Hull City	1,000,000
17 McIndoe, Michael	Doncaster Rovers	Barnsley	undisclosed
6 Mears, Tyrone	Preston North End	West Ham United	1,000,000
27 Nicholls, Kevin J.	Luton Town	Leeds United	700,000
4 Opara, Lloyd	Cheshunt	Peterborough United	undisclosed
27 Pennant, Jermaine	Birmingham City	Liverpool	6,700,000
20 Phillips, Steven J.	Bristol City	Bristol Rovers	undisclosed
28 Queudrue, Franck	Middlesbrough	Fulham	2,000,000
13 Raven, David H.	Liverpool	Carlisle United	undisclosed
4 Ricketts, Michael B.	Leeds United	Southend United	undisclosed
3 Roberts, Jason A.D.	Wigan Athletic	Blackburn Rovers	3,000,000
26 Scowcroft, James B.	Coventry City	Crystal Palace	500,000
27 Semple, Ryan D.	Peterborough United	Lincoln City	undisclosed
12 Seol, Ki-Hyeon	Wolverhampton Wanderers	Reading	1,000,000
11 Smith, Paul	Southampton	Nottingham Forest	500,000
14 Sodje, Samuel	Brentford	Reading	350,000
10 St Ledger-Hall, Sean P.	Peterborough United	Preston North End	225,000
19 Togwell, Samuel J.	Crystal Palace	Barnsley	undisclosed
5 Turner, Michael T.	Brentford	Hull City	350,000
10 Walton, Simon W.	Leeds United	Charlton Athletic	500,000
5 Wright-Phillips, Bradley E.	Manchester City	Southampton	1,000,000
12 Zakuani, Gabriel A.	Leyton Orient	Fulham	1,000,000

TEMPORARY TRANSFERS

27 Clarke, Darrell J. – Hartlepool United – Rochdale; 19 Forte, Jonathan – Sheffield United – Doncaster Rovers; 29 Graham, David – Sheffield Wednesday – Bradford City; 26 Grant, Anthony P.S. – Chelsea – Wycombe Wanderers; 14 Griffin, Charles – Wycombe Wanderers – Forest Green Rovers; 27 Heywood, Matthew S. – Bristol City – Brentford; 5 Howard, Timothy M. – Manchester United – Everton; 20 Hurst, Kevan – Sheffield United – Chesterfield; 11 Johnson, Glen M.C. – Chelsea – Portsmouth; 22 Kirkland, Christopher E. – Liverpool – Wigan Athletic; 31 Muamba, Fabrice – Arsenal – Birmingham City; 30 Nade, Raphael – Carlisle United – Weymouth; 3 Owen, Gareth J. – Oldham Athletic – Stockport County; 28 Parker, Ben B.C. – Leeds United – Bradford City; 27 Partridge, David W. – Bristol City – Leyton Orient; 28 Ravenhill, Richard J. – Doncaster Rovers – Chester City; 21 Roberts, Dale – Nottingham Forest – Alfreton Town; 17 Ross, Ian – Sheffield United – Notts County; 10 Wiseman, Scott N.K. – Hull City – Rotherham United

AUGUST 2006

29 Agogo, Manuel	Bristol Rovers	Nottingham Forest	undisclosed
9 Arca, Julio A.	Sunderland	Middlesbrough	1,750,000
2 Barker, Shaun	Rotherham United	Blackpool	undisclosed
7 Birchall, Chris	Port Vale	Coventry City	undisclosed
10 Blackstock, Dexter A.	Southampton	Queens Park Rangers	undisclosed
15 Boyce, Emmerson O.	Crystal Palace	Wigan Athletic	1,000,000
31 Bridges, Michael	Carlisle United	Hull City	350,000
3 Bruce, Alex	Birmingham City	Ipswich Town	Free
31 Burgess, Benjamin K.	Hull City	Blackpool	undisclosed
29 Bywater, Stephen	West Ham United	Derby County	undisclosed
1 Carrick, Michael	Tottenham Hotspur	Manchester United	18,600,000
31 Chimbonda, Pascal	Wigan Athletic	Tottenham Hotspur	undisclosed
8 Clarke, Clive	West Ham United	Sunderland	exch.
2 Clarke, Peter M.	Blackpool	Southend United	undisclosed
11 Cogan, Barry	Millwall	Barnet	undisclosed
3 Cole, Andrew A.	Manchester City	Portsmouth	500,000
31 Connolly, David J.	Wigan Athletic	Sunderland	1,400,000
31 Cotterill, David	Bristol City	Wigan Athletic	2,000,000
31 Douglas, Jonathan	Blackburn Rovers	Leeds United	undisclosed
31 Euell, Jason J.	Charlton Athletic	Middlesbrough	300,000
10 Faye, Amdy M.	Newcastle United	Charlton Athletic	2,000,000
24 Fenton, Nicholas L.	Doncaster Rovers	Grimsby Town	undisclosed
31 Forster, Nicholas	Ipswich Town	Hull City	250,000
31 Fuller, Ricardo	Southampton	Stoke City	undisclosed
24 Futcher, Benjamin P.	Grimsby Town	Peterborough United	undisclosed
18 Green, Robert P.	Norwich City	West Ham United	2,000,000
31 Green, Stuart	Hull City	Crystal Palace	75,000
11 Griffin, Adam	Oldham Athletic	Stockport County	undisclosed
4 Harding, Daniel A.	Leeds United	Ipswich Town	exch.
31 Harrold, Matthew	Yeovil Town	Southend United	undisclosed
18 Heywood, Matthew S.	Bristol City	Brentford	undisclosed
3 Higginbotham, Daniel J.	Southampton	Stoke City	225,000
31 Idiakez-Barkaiztegi, Inigo	Derby County	Southampton	250,000
4 Jaidi, Radhi B.A.	Bolton Wanderers	Birmingham City	500,000
15 James, David B.	Manchester City	Portsmouth	1,200,000
16 Jarrett, Albert O.	Brighton & Hove Albion	Watford	Free
15 Joachim, Julian K.	Boston United	Darlington	undisclosed
17 Johnson, Jemal J.	Blackburn Rovers	Wolverhampton Wanderers	undisclosed
31 Jorgensen, Claus B.	Coventry City	Blackpool	undisclosed
31 Kavanagh, Graham A.	Wigan Athletic	Sunderland	500,000
31 Kazim-Richards, Colin	Brighton & Hove Albion	Sheffield United	undisclosed
31 Kilbane, Kevin	Everton	Wigan Athletic	2,000,000
25 Kyle, Kevin	Sunderland	Coventry City	600,000
31 Lambert, Rickie L.	Rochdale	Bristol Rovers	undisclosed
17 Lawrence, Dennis W.	Wrexham	Swansea City	undisclosed
2 Lawrence, Matthew J.	Millwall	Crystal Palace	undisclosed
11 Leacock, Dean	Fulham	Derby County	375,000
18 Liddle, Gary D.	Middlesbrough	Hartlepool United	undisclosed
4 Llewellyn, Christopher M.	Hartlepool United	Wrexham	undisclosed
31 Lynch, Mark J.	Hull City	Yeovil Town	undisclosed
16 Makin, Christopher	Reading	Southampton	Free
31 Malbranque, Steed	Fulham	Tottenham Hotspur	undisclosed
31 McKenzie, Leon M.	Norwich City	Coventry City	1,000,000
30 McLeod, Kevin A.	Swansea City	Colchester United	Free
10 McShane, Paul D.	Manchester United	West Bromwich Albion	exch.
17 McSheffrey, Gary	Coventry City	Birmingham City	4,000,000
30 Mellor, Neil A.	Liverpool	Preston North End	undisclosed
31 Miller, Liam W.	Manchester United	Sunderland	Free
16 Morrell, Andrew J.	Coventry City	Blackpool	undisclosed
31 Morris, Ian	Leeds United	Scunthorpe United	undisclosed
31 Murray, Adam D.	Carlisle United	Torquay United	undisclosed
25 Parkin, Sam	Ipswich Town	Luton Town	340,000
7 Paynter, William P.	Hull City	Southend United	undisclosed
22 Phillips, Kevin	Aston Villa	West Bromwich Albion	700,000
31 Ravenhill, Richard J.	Doncaster Rovers	Grimsby Town	undisclosed
8 Rehman, Zeshan	Fulham	Queens Park Rangers	500,000

17 Reid, Andrew M.	Tottenham Hotspur	Charlton Athletic	3,000,000
31 Robinson, Marvin L.S.C.	Macclesfield Town	Oxford United	undisclosed
7 Shittu, Daniel O.	Queens Park Rangers	Watford	1,600,000
4 Smith, Ryan C.M.	Arsenal	Derby County	undisclosed
10 Steele, Luke D.	Manchester United	West Bromwich Albion	exch.
31 Symes, Michael	Bradford City	Shrewsbury Town	undisclosed
3 Taylor, Jason J.F.	Oldham Athletic	Stockport County	undisclosed
11 Tolley, Jamie	Shrewsbury Town	Macclesfield Town	undisclosed
10 Traore, Djimi	Liverpool	Charlton Athletic	2,000,000
4 Viafara, John E.	Portsmouth	Southampton	undisclosed
4 Westlake, Ian J.	Ipswich Town	Leeds United	exch.

TEMPORARY TRANSFERS

3 Ainsworth, Lionel – Derby County – AFC Bournemouth; 11 Aspden, Curtis – Hull City – Scarborough; 25 Baldock, Samuel – Milton Keynes Dons – Arlesey Town; 31 Barker, Keith H.D. – Blackburn Rovers – Rochdale; 4 Bendtner, Nicklas – Arsenal – Birmingham City; 2 Best, Leon J. – Southampton – AFC Bournemouth; 10 Birch, Gary S. – Lincoln City – Tamworth; 5 Birchall, Chris – Port Vale – Coventry City; 11 Bonner, Tom E. – Northampton Town – Nuneaton Borough; 11 Bostwick, Michael – Millwall – Crawley Town; 18 Boulding, Rory J. – Mansfield Town – Ilkeston Town; 12 Bywater, Stephen – West Ham United – Derby County; 14 Carson, Scott P. – Liverpool – Charlton Athletic; 4 Batista, Ricardo – Fulham – Wycombe Wanderers; 31 Christie, Iyseden – Rochdale – Kidderminster Harriers; 10 Cowan, Gavin P. – Shrewsbury Town – Kidderminster Harriers; 18 Davison, Tony – Hartlepool United – Newcastle Blue Star; 31 Deakin, Graham – Walsall – Tamworth; 2 Doyle, Nathan – Derby County – Bradford City; 31 Eaden, Nicholas J. – Nottingham Forest – Lincoln City; 1 Edge, Lewis J.S. – Blackpool – Rochdale; 2 Elliot, Robert – Charlton Athletic – Accrington Stanley; 3 Evatt, Ian R. – Queens Park Rangers – Blackpool; 29 Federici, Adam – Reading – Bristol City; 30 Fernandez, Vincent – Nottingham Forest – Wycombe Wanderers; 25 Fitzgerald, Scott – Brentford – AFC Wimbledon; 10 Foster, Benjamin – Manchester United – Watford; 14 Fry, Adam G. – Peterborough United – Kettering Town; 24 Fry, Russell H. – Hull City – Halifax Town; 8 Gillett, Simon J. – Southampton – Blackpool; 18 Golbourne, Scott J. – Reading – Wycombe Wanderers; 17 Grabban, Lewis – Crystal Palace – Oldham Athletic; 1 Graham, Daniel A.W. – Middlesbrough – Blackpool; 31 Grant, Joel V. – Watford – Aldershot Town; 18 Hamer, Ben – Reading – Crawley Town; 31 Harding, Benjamin S. – Milton Keynes Dons – Aldershot Town; 31 Hennessey, Wayne R. – Wolverhampton Wanderers – Bristol City; 10 Henry, Leigh – Swindon Town – Weston-Super-Mare; 1 Hibbert, David J. – Preston North End – Rotherham United; 18 Hinchliffe, Ben – Preston North End – Kendal Town; 19 Hinshelwood, Paul – Brighton & Hove Albion – Burgess Hill Town; 2 Holmes, Lee D. – Derby County – Bradford City; 4 Horsfield, Geoffrey M. – Sheffield United – Leeds United; 4 Howarth, Christopher – Bolton Wanderers – Oldham Athletic; 25 Howe, Joe D.W. – Milton Keynes Dons – Walton & Hersham; 3 James, Kevin E. – Nottingham Forest – Yeovil Town; 4 Jones, Bradley – Middlesbrough – Sheffield Wednesday; 10 Kemp, Thomas J.R. – Lincoln City – Tamworth; 25 Knight, David – Middlesbrough – Oldham Athletic; 10 Kuszczak, Tomasz – West Bromwich Albion – Manchester United; 4 Larsson, Sebastien – Arsenal – Birmingham City; 1 Lowe, Keith S. – Wolverhampton Wanderers – Brighton & Hove Albion; 18 Lupoli, Arturo – Arsenal – Derby County; 22 Lynch, Mark J. – Hull City – Yeovil Town; 31 Macken, Jonathan P. – Crystal Palace – Ipswich Town; 18 Mannone, Vito – Arsenal – Barnsley; 10 Martin, Richard W. – Brighton & Hove Albion – Dorchester Town; 24 Matthews, Thomas M. – Hull City – Halifax Town; 23 McCallum, Gavin K. – Yeovil Town – Tamworth; 8 McCartney, George – Sunderland – West Ham United; 17 McIntosh, Martin W. – Huddersfield Town – Grimsby Town; 25 McShane, Luke – Peterborough United – Kettering Town; 4 Molango, Maheta – Brighton & Hove Albion – Oldham Athletic; 30 Moore, Stefan – Queens Park Rangers – Port Vale; 18 Murphy, Kieran – Milton Keynes Dons – Aylesbury United; 1 Murray, Glenn – Carlisle United – Stockport County; 18 Noble, Mark – West Ham United – Ipswich Town; 8 O'Donnell, Daniel – Liverpool – Crewe Alexandra; 18 Page, Sam T. – Milton Keynes Dons – Aylesbury United; 4 Paynter, William P. – Hull City – Southend United; 18 Pearce, Jason D. – Portsmouth – Bognor Regis Town; 4 Pittman, Jon P. – Nottingham Forest – Bury; 10 Pope, Thomas J. – Crewe Alexandra – Barrow; 15 Potter, Darren M. – Liverpool – Wolverhampton Wanderers; 18 Rae, Michael E. – Hartlepool United – Newcastle Blue Star; 18 Randolph, Darren E. – Charlton Athletic – Gillingham; 4 Roberts, Mark A. – Crewe Alexandra – Halifax Town; 31 Rossi, Giuseppe – Manchester United – Newcastle United; 31 Routledge, Wayne N.A. – Tottenham Hotspur – Fulham; 24 Sam, Lloyd E. – Charlton Athletic – Sheffield Wednesday; 24 Schmeichel, Kasper – Manchester City – Bury; 31 Sibierski, Antoine – Manchester City – Newcastle United; 4 Steele, Luke D. – Manchester United – Coventry City; 30 Stewart, Marcus P. – Bristol City – Yeovil Town; 3 Stokes, Tony – West Ham United – Brighton & Hove Albion; 9 Sutton, Richard A. – Crewe Alexandra – Stafford Rangers; 4 Symes, Michael – Bradford City – Shrewsbury Town; 23 Thomas, Bradley M. – Yeovil Town – Tamworth; 31 Tipton, Matthew – Bury – Macclesfield Town; 31 Todorov, Svetoslav – Portsmouth – Wigan Athletic; 31 Trotter, Liam – Ipswich Town – Millwall; 11 Wall, Stuart J. – Peterborough United – Alfreton Town; 18 Walton, Simon W. – Charlton Athletic – Ipswich Town; 18 Warlow, Adam T. – Crewe Alexandra – Witton Albion; 4 Warner, Anthony R. – Fulham – Leeds United; 18 Webb, Robert D. – Milton Keynes Dons – Thurrock; 31 Weir-Daley, Spencer J.A. – Nottingham Forest – Macclesfield Town; 1 Williams, Steven – Wycombe Wanderers – Forest Green Rovers; 10 Yeates, Mark – Tottenham Hotspur – Hull City

SEPTEMBER 2006

1 Cole, Ashley	Arsenal	Chelsea	undisclosed
1 Gallas, William	Chelsea	Arsenal	undisclosed
1 Huth, Robert	Chelsea	Middlesbrough	6,000,000
21 McCartney, George	Sunderland	West Ham United	undisclosed
23 Miller, Ian	Bury Town	Ipswich Town	undisclosed

TEMPORARY TRANSFERS

21 Bacon, Daniel S. – Lincoln City – Worksop Town; 22 Barker, Daniel G. – Yeovil Town – Clyst Rovers; 14 Boyle, Patrick – Everton – Norwich City; 12 Brooks, Alan – Millwall – Beckenham Town; 8 Camp, Lee M.J. – Derby County – Norwich City; 11 Carrington, Mark R. – Crewe Alexandra – Kidsgrove Athletic; 14 Cole, Mitchell J. – Southend United – Northampton Town; 11 Cox, Simon – Reading – Brentford; 15 Cross, Scott – Northampton Town – Bedford Town; 22 Davies, Scott – Reading – Yeading; 15 Davis, Liam L. – Coventry City – Peterborough United; 14 Doherty, Thomas

– Queens Park Rangers – Wycombe Wanderers; 8 Duffy, Ayden – Lincoln City – Worksop Town; 5 Duncan, Derek – Leyton Orient – Lewes; 8 Elvins, Robert – West Bromwich Albion – Cheltenham Town; 8 Flinders, Scott L. – Crystal Palace – Gillingham; 29 Fortune-West, Leo P.D. – Rushden & Diamonds – Torquay United; 28 Fry, Adam G. – Peterborough United – Kings Lynn; 11 Gaynor, Ross – Millwall – Sutton United; 22 Green, Michael J. – Bristol Rovers – Mangotsfield United; 9 Griffin, Andrew – Portsmouth – Stoke City; 26 Haynes, Danny – Ipswich Town – Millwall; 29 Hendrie, Lee A. – Aston Villa – Stoke City; 11 Higgins, Ben – Grimsby Town – Eastwood Town; 8 Humphreys, Richie J. – Hartlepool United – Port Vale; 22 Hurst, Glynn – Shrewsbury Town – Bury; 11 Ide, Charles – Brentford – Sutton United; 1 Joseph-Dubois, Pierre – Reading – Tooting & Mitcham United; 28 Kirkup, Daniel – Carlisle United – Southport; 8 Laird, Scott – Plymouth Argyle – Tiverton Town; 22 Lawson, James P. – Southend United – Grimsby Town; 26 Ledgister, Joel – Southend United – Lewes; 29 Logan, Richard A. – Darlington – Gateshead; 8 Lowe, Keith S. – Wolverhampton Wanderers – Cheltenham Town; 19 McAliskey, John J. – Huddersfield Town – Wrexham; 1 McDonald, Marvin M. – Macclesfield Town – Mossley; 14 Mills, Daniel J. – Manchester City – Hull City; 22 Muckles, Neil – Hartlepool United – Newcastle Blue Star; 22 Neal, Christopher M. – Preston North End – Shrewsbury Town; 25 Page, Sam T. – Milton Keynes Dons – Hendon; 15 Poole, David A. – Yeovil Town – Stockport County; 12 Pooley, Dean – Millwall – Beckenham Town; 14 Ruddy, John T.G. – Everton – Stockport County; 8 Sheehan, Alan – Leicester City – Mansfield Town; 27 Smith, James D. – Chelsea – Queens Park Rangers; 12 Stock, Brian B. – Preston North End – Doncaster Rovers; 22 Streete, Theo – Derby County – Doncaster Rovers; 29 Stroud, David – Swindon Town – Basingstoke Town; 8 Thirlwell, Paul – Derby County – Carlisle United; 26 Thorpe, Anthony L. – Stevenage Borough – Grimsby Town; 15 Turner, Ben H. – Coventry City – Peterborough United; 15 Ujah, Curtis – Reading – Slough Town; 27 Walker, James L.N. – Charlton Athletic – Bristol Rovers; 1 Watt, Philip A. – Lincoln City – Grantham Town; 29 Wells, Benjamin – Swindon Town – Basingstoke Town; 29 Wheater, David J. – Middlesbrough – Wolverhampton Wanderers; 14 Whittington, Michael J. – Cheltenham Town – Gloucester City; 29 Williams, Sam – Aston Villa – Brighton & Hove Albion

OCTOBER 2006

27 Kirkland, Christopher E.	Liverpool	Wigan Athletic	undisclosed

TEMPORARY TRANSFERS

13 Alcock, Craig – Yeovil Town – Weston-Super-Mare; 20 Ashdown, Jamie – Portsmouth – Norwich City; 17 Beattie, Warren S. – Preston North End – Kendal Town; 5 Beckford, Jermaine P. – Leeds United – Carlisle United; 10 Benyon, Elliot P. – Bristol City – St Albans City; 3 Bignot, Paul J. – Crewe Alexandra – Kidderminster Harriers; 27 Birch, Gary S. – Lincoln City – Hucknall Town; 9 Bowler, Michael – Stockport County – Witton Albion; 31 Brittain, Martin – Ipswich Town – Yeovil Town; 26 Broughton, Drewe O. – Chester City – Boston United; 6 Butler, Andrew P. – Scunthorpe United – Grimsby Town; 17 Byron, Michael J. – Hull City – Hinckley United; 10 Chamberlain, Miles – Grimsby Town – Eastwood Town; 14 Charles, Wesley D.D. – Brentford – Staines Town; 26 Chorley, Benjamin F. – Milton Keynes Dons – Gillingham; 6 Clapham, Joshua T. – Plymouth Argyle – Tiverton Town; 23 Clarke, Clive – Sunderland – Coventry City; 26 Clarke, Matthew P. – Bradford City – Darlington; 26 Corr, Barry – Sheffield Wednesday – Bristol City; 31 Cywka, Tomasz – Wigan Athletic – Oldham Athletic; 12 Delap, Rory J. – Sunderland – Stoke City; 12 Diao, Salif – Liverpool – Stoke City; 20 Dickinson, Carl – Stoke City – Blackpool; 9 Dodds, Louis – Leicester City – Northwich Victoria; 23 Duffy, Richard – Portsmouth – Coventry City; 2 Eaden, Nicholas J. – Nottingham Forest – Lincoln City; 13 Edge, Lewis J.S. – Blackpool – Bury; 13 Eustace, John M. – Stoke City – Hereford United; 5 Federici, Adam – Reading – Bristol City; 20 Ferris, Peter – Carlisle United – Workington; 6 Filan, John R. – Wigan Athletic – Doncaster Rovers; 5 Foster, Luke J. – Lincoln City – York City; 5 Gill, Benjamin D. – Watford – Cambridge United; 13 Gunn, Andrew P. – Oxford United – Didcot Town; 2 Harban, Thomas J. – Barnsley – Tamworth; 20 Harper, Kevin P. – Stoke City – Carlisle United; 27 Harper, Lee C.P. – Northampton Town – Milton Keynes Dons; 12 Horwood, Evan D. – Sheffield United – Darlington; 13 Hutchinson, Ben L.P. – Middlesbrough – Billingham Synthonia; 27 James, Kevin E. – Nottingham Forest – Grimsby Town; 16 Johnson, Adam – Middlesbrough – Leeds United; 27 Jones, Richard G. – Manchester United – Colchester United; 31 Keith, Joseph R. – Leyton Orient – Shrewsbury Town; 2 Laight, Ryan D. – Barnsley – Tamworth; 27 Legzdins, Adam R. – Birmingham City – Oldham Athletic; 12 Lloyd, Robert F. – Crewe Alexandra – Witton Albion; 26 MacKenzie, Neil – Scunthorpe United – Hereford United; 16 Mancienne, Michael I. – Chelsea – Queens Park Rangers; 9 Matthews, Thomas M. – Hull City – Halifax Town; 6 McCallum, Gavin K. – Yeovil Town – Tamworth; 31 McLean, Aaron – Grays Athletic – Peterborough United; 19 Meredith, James G. – Derby County – Cambridge United; 5 Moore, Stefan – Queens Park Rangers – Port Vale; 26 Mullings, Darren – Bristol Rovers – Clevedon Town; 27 Murphy, John J. – Blackpool – Macclesfield Town; 20 Murray, Glenn – Carlisle United – Rochdale; 9 Nelthorpe, Craig R. – Doncaster Rovers – Kidderminster Harriers; 19 Nyatanga, Lewin J. – Derby County – Sunderland; 20 O'Halloran, Stephen – Aston Villa – Wycombe Wanderers; 20 Osbourne, Isaac S. – Coventry City – Crewe Alexandra; 20 Paterson, Sean P. – Blackpool – Southport; 27 Pendleton, Chris – Luton Town – Hitchin Town; 12 Plummer, Christopher S. – Peterborough United – Grays Athletic; 20 Powell, Lewis – Bristol Rovers – Mangotsfield United; 2 Rae, Michael E. – Hartlepool United – Gateshead; 5 Reid, Reuben – Plymouth Argyle – Kidderminster Harriers; 10 Rhodes, Alexander – Brentford – Swindon Town; 17 Roberts, Gary – Accrington Stanley – Ipswich Town; 20 Schmeichel, Kasper – Manchester City – Bury; 25 Shearer, Scott – Bristol Rovers – Shrewsbury Town; 2 Sherlock, James – Lincoln City – Ilkeston Town; 13 Sleath, Danny – Mansfield Town – Gresley Rovers; 20 Songo'o, Franck S. – Portsmouth – AFC Bournemouth; 27 Stack, Graham – Reading – Leeds United; 13 Stead, Jonathan – Sunderland – Derby County; 30 Steele, Lee A.J. – Leyton Orient – Chester City; 27 Tait, Paul – Boston United – Southport; 20 Taylor, Andrew – Blackburn Rovers – Crewe Alexandra; 21 Thelwell, Alton A. – Hull City – Leyton Orient; 6 Thomas, Bradley M. – Yeovil Town – Tamworth; 25 Thompson, John – Nottingham Forest – Tranmere Rovers; 6 Till, Peter – Birmingham City – Leyton Orient; 13 Tillen, Joseph E. – Milton Keynes Dons – Thurrock; 12 Ventre, Daniel – Accrington Stanley – Southport; 16 Welsh, Andrew P.D. – Sunderland – Leicester City; 7 Whing, Andrew J. – Coventry City – Brighton & Hove Albion; 31 Wiles, Simon P. – Blackpool – Macclesfield Town; 12 Wright, Alan – Sheffield United – Leeds United; 12 Wright, Nicholas – Birmingham City – Bristol City

NOVEMBER 2006

9 Sibierski, Antoine	Manchester City	Newcastle United	undisclosed

TEMPORARY TRANSFERS

23 Albrighton, Mark – Boston United – Darlington; 23 Andrews, Wayne M.A. – Coventry City – Sheffield Wednesday; 23 Arnau – Sunderland – Southend United; 14 Atkinson, Robert – Barnsley – Halifax Town; 3 Bacon, Daniel S. – Lincoln City – Worksop Town; 23 Bains, Rikki L. – Accrington Stanley – Leek Town; 23 Barlow, Matthew J. – Oldham Athletic – Stafford Rangers; 6 Barrett, Zach – Luton Town – Kettering Town; 2 Bastians, Felix – Nottingham Forest –

Northwich Victoria; 17 Bates, Matthew D. – Middlesbrough – Ipswich Town; 15 Beechers, Billy J. – Oxford United – Oxford City; 23 Begovic, Asmir – Portsmouth – Macclesfield Town; 23 Berger, Patrik – Aston Villa – Stoke City; 3 Bertrand, Ryan D. – Chelsea – AFC Bournemouth; 23 Best, Leon J. – Southampton – Yeovil Town; 22 Birchall, Adam S. – Mansfield Town – Barnet; 23 Birley, Matthew – Birmingham City – Lincoln City; 16 Black, Thomas R. – Crystal Palace – Bradford City; 22 Blinkhorn, Matthew D. – Blackpool – Bury; 1 Bowditch, Dean – Ipswich Town – Brighton & Hove Albion; 16 Brown, David A. – Accrington Stanley – Burton Albion; 23 Burns, Jamie D. – Blackpool – Morecambe; 21 Butler, Paul J. – Leeds United – Milton Keynes Dons; 14 Chadwick, Luke H. – Stoke City – Norwich City; 2 Collins, Neill – Sunderland – Wolverhampton Wanderers; 23 Comyn-Platt, Charlie – Swindon Town – Grays Athletic; 23 Connolly, Matthew T. – Arsenal – AFC Bournemouth; 23 Constable, James A. – Walsall – Kidderminster Harriers; 3 Cork, Jack F.P. – Chelsea – AFC Bournemouth; 3 Cousins, Mark – Colchester United – Yeading; 17 Coutts, James R. – AFC Bournemouth – Grays Athletic; 22 Cox, Simon – Reading – Brentford; 8 Cranie, Martin J. – Southampton – Yeovil Town; 7 Critchell, Kyle A.R. – Southampton – Torquay United; 8 Crossley, Mark G. – Fulham – Sheffield Wednesday; 23 Currie, Darren – Ipswich Town – Coventry City; 17 Davies, Robert – West Bromwich Albion – Kidderminster Harriers; 23 Dillon, John G. – Crewe Alexandra – Leigh RMI; 22 Doherty, Sean – Accrington Stanley – Southport; 23 Donnelly, Ciaran – Blackpool – Southport; 22 Dubourdeau, Francois – Accrington Stanley – Southport; 3 Duffy, Darryl A. – Hull City – Hartlepool United; 23 Dugdale, Adam – Crewe Alexandra – Accrington Stanley; 23 Ehiogu, Ugochuku – Middlesbrough – Leeds United; 23 Ephraim, Hogan – West Ham United – Colchester United; 23 Fernandez, Vincent – Nottingham Forest – Blackpool; 10 Fitzgerald, Scott – Brentford – AFC Wimbledon; 23 Fortune, Clayton A. – Leyton Orient – Port Vale; 6 Fortune-West, Leo P.D. – Rushden & Diamonds – Shrewsbury Town; 23 Fulop, Marton – Tottenham Hotspur – Sunderland; 8 Gardner, Ross – Nottingham Forest – Port Vale; 22 Gillett, Simon J. – Southampton – AFC Bournemouth; 3 Gleeson, Stephen M. – Wolverhampton Wanderers – Stockport County; 8 Gregan, Sean M. – Leeds United – Oldham Athletic; 23 Griffiths, Anthony J. – Doncaster Rovers – Darlington; 23 Guttridge, Luke – Southend United – Leyton Orient; 3 Hannigan, Thomas J. – Notts County – Alfreton Town; 9 Healy, Colin – Barnsley – Bradford City; 9 Heath, Matthew P. – Coventry City – Leeds United; 16 Heslop, Simon – Barnsley – Tamworth; 23 Hicks, Rodney D. – Peterborough United – Kings Lynn; 23 Hinchliffe, Ben – Preston North End – Kendal Town; 3 Howell, Luke A. – Gillingham – Folkestone Invicta; 3 Hughes, Mark A. – Thurrock – Chesterfield; 23 Jalal, Shwan S. – Woking – Sheffield Wednesday; 10 Janes, Alex – Darlington – Whitby Town; 2 Jarrett, Jason L. – Preston North End – Hull City; 23 John, Alistair A. – Charlton Athletic – Brighton & Hove Albion; 16 Johnson, Bradley – Northampton Town – Stevenage Borough; 17 Jones, David F.L. – Manchester United – Derby County; 14 Joynes, Nathan – Barnsley – Halifax Town; 23 Kamara, Sheku – Watford – Grays Athletic; 23 Kandol, Tresor O. – Barnet – Leeds United; 2 Kane, Anthony M. – Blackburn Rovers – Stockport County; 2 Kennedy, Jason – Middlesbrough – Boston United; 23 Kiely, Dean L. – Portsmouth – Luton Town; 16 Kightly, Michael J. – Grays Athletic – Wolverhampton Wanderers; 17 Kiraly, Gabor F. – Crystal Palace – West Ham United; 22 Kirkup, Daniel – Carlisle United – Southport; 22 Krause, James – Ipswich Town – Carlisle United; 18 Lawrence, Liam – Sunderland – Stoke City; 3 Leary, Michael – Luton Town – Torquay United; 16 Lee, Charlie – Tottenham Hotspur – Millwall; 2 Lonergan, Andrew – Preston North End – Swindon Town; 20 Mancienne, Michael I. – Chelsea – Queens Park Rangers; 23 Mannix, David – Liverpool – Accrington Stanley; 7 McArdle, Rory A. – Sheffield Wednesday – Rochdale; 23 McCallum, Gavin K. – Yeovil Town – Crawley Town; 23 McCann, Grant S. – Cheltenham Town – Barnsley; 17 McCormack, Alan – Preston North End – Southend United; 23 McIndoe, Michael – Barnsley – Wolverhampton Wanderers; 24 McLeod, Mark – Darlington – Workington; 13 McMahon, Daryl – Leyton Orient – Notts County; 3 McShane, Luke – Peterborough United – Worksop Town; 3 Miller, Ian – Ipswich Town – Boston United; 14 Miller, Thomas W. – Sunderland – Preston North End; 23 Mocquet, William – Sunderland – Rochdale; 23 Monkhouse, Andrew W. – Swindon Town – Hartlepool United; 23 Morgan, Craig – Milton Keynes Dons – Peterborough United; 10 Munday, John – Queens Park Rangers – Hendon; 17 Murphy, Kieran – Milton Keynes Dons – Maidenhead United; 16 Needham, Liam P. – Notts County – Gainsborough Trinity; 17 Nelthorpe, Craig R. – Doncaster Rovers – Gateshead; 23 Nicholson, Shane M. – Chesterfield – Lincoln City; 16 Nicholson, Stuart I. – West Bromwich Albion – Bristol Rovers; 10 Onibuje, Fola – Swindon Town – Brentford; 21 Paterson, Sean P. – Blackpool – Southport; 23 Patterson, Martin – Stoke City – Grimsby Town; 8 Pearce, Jason D. – Portsmouth – Bognor Regis Town; 15 Peters, Ryan V. – Brentford – Crawley Town; 3 Platt, Conal J. – AFC Bournemouth – Morecambe; 17 Plummer, Christopher S. – Peterborough United – Rushden & Diamonds; 23 Poke, Michael H. – Southampton – Woking; 15 Pollitt, Michael F. – Wigan Athletic – Ipswich Town; 23 Pulis, Anthony J. – Stoke City – Grimsby Town; 23 Reid, Kyel – West Ham United – Barnsley; 3 Richards, Justin D. – Peterborough United – Grays Athletic; 3 Robertson, Jordan – Sheffield United – Torquay United; 22 Rowson, David – Darlington – Boston United; 23 Semple, Ryan D. – Lincoln City – Chester City; 17 Slabber, Jamie – Grays Athletic – Oxford United; 3 Smith, Andrew W. – Preston North End – Cheltenham Town; 1 Smith, James D. – Chelsea – Queens Park Rangers; 16 Smith, Jay A. – Southend United – Notts County; 28 Sullivan, Neil – Leeds United – Doncaster Rovers; 23 Till, Peter – Birmingham City – Grimsby Town; 23 Timlin, Michael – Fulham – Swindon Town; 23 Treacy, Keith P. – Blackburn Rovers – Stockport County; 22 Turnbull, Stephen – Hartlepool United – Bury; 16 Turner, Iain R. – Everton – Crystal Palace; 23 Walker, James L.N. – Charlton Athletic – Leyton Orient; 3 Wallis, Jonathan – Hereford United – Dover Athletic; 23 Wallwork, Ronald – West Bromwich Albion – Barnsley; 9 Webb, Robert D. – Milton Keynes Dons – Fisher Athletic; 8 Whalley, Shaun – Witton Albion – Accrington Stanley; 3 Whittington, Michael J. – Cheltenham Town – Gloucester City; 23 Wilkinson, Andrew G. – Stoke City – Blackpool; 23 Wright, Nicholas – Birmingham City – Northampton Town; 23 Wright, Thomas – Barnsley – Walsall.

DECEMBER 2006

29 Elder, Nathan	Billericay Town	Brighton & Hove Albion	undisclosed

TEMPORARY TRANSFERS

29 Abbey, Nathanael – Torquay United – Brentford; 8 Allanson, Ashley G. – Scunthorpe United – Farsley Celtic; 8 Barnes, Oliver J.P. – Bristol Rovers – Gloucester City; 1 Beattie, Warren S. – Preston North End – Lancaster City; 1 Breach, Christopher B. – Brighton & Hove Albion – Bognor Regis Town; 8 Brill, Dean M. – Luton Town – Gillingham; 21 Cave-Brown, Andrew – Norwich City – King's Lynn; 30 Cecila Batista, Ricardo J. – Fulham – Wycombe Wanderers; 1 Coo, Cavell S. – Crewe Alexandra – Woodley Sports; 29 Cresswell, Ryan – Sheffield United – Ilkeston Town; 8 Cross, Scott – Northampton Town – Basingstoke Town; 28 Curtis, Thomas D. – Notts County – Nuneaton Borough; 1 Duffy, Ayden – Lincoln City – Worksop Town; 21 Fisk, Andrew – Norwich City – Kings Lynn; 5 Fry, Russell H. – Hull City – Hinckley United; 22 Green, Liam T. – Doncaster Rovers – Guiseley; 29 Hall, Ryan – Crystal Palace – Lewes; 7 Hendrie, Lee A. – Aston Villa – Stoke City; 30 Horwood, Evan D. – Sheffield United – Darlington;

8 Jones, Lee – Blackpool – Bury; 14 Kiraly, Gabor F. – Crystal Palace – Aston Villa; 16 Logan, Richard A. – Darlington – Durham City; 31 McParland, Anthony – Barnsley – Wycombe Wanderers; 15 Miller, Shaun R. – Crewe Alexandra – Witton Albion; 22 Murphy, Kieran – Milton Keynes Dons – Hendon; 20 Peacock, Anthony L. – Darlington – Blyth Spartans; 22 Rachubka, Paul S. – Huddersfield Town – Peterborough United; 29 Serrant, Ryan P. – Leeds United – Guiseley; 8 Smeeton, Jake – Yeovil Town – Chard Town; 1 Smith, Nicholas – Bradford City – Farsley Celtic; 22 Steele, Luke D. – West Bromwich Albion – Coventry City; 20 Thornton, Dean – Wycombe Wanderers – Banbury United; 29 Vaughan, James – Chester City – Droylsden; 7 Wilkinson, Alistair B. – Hull City – Harrogate Town; 8 Wilson, Lawrie – Colchester United – Welling United

JANUARY 2007

22 Abbott, Pawel T.H.	Huddersfield Town	Swansea City	undisclosed
3 Akinbiyi, Adeola P.	Sheffield United	Burnley	750,000
2 Alnwick, Ben	Sunderland	Tottenham Hotspur	1,300,000
5 Barker, Richard I.	Mansfield Town	Hartlepool United	undisclosed
31 Beardsley, Christopher K.	Mansfield Town	Rushden & Diamonds	undisclosed
27 Betsy, Kevin	Wycombe Wanderers	Bristol City	undisclosed
31 Billy, Christopher A.	Carlisle United	Halifax Town	undisclosed
4 Birchall, Adam S.	Mansfield Town	Barnet	undisclosed
18 Bisan-Etame Mayer, Laurean	Arsenal	Portsmouth	undisclosed
29 Blackett, Shane J.	Dagenham & Redbridge	Peterborough United	undisclosed
31 Blundell, Gregg	Chester City	Darlington	undisclosed
5 Boa Morte, Luis	Fulham	West Ham United	undisclosed
29 Bougherra, Madjid	Sheffield Wednesday	Charlton Athletic	2,500,000
8 Boyd, George	Stevenage Borough	Peterborough United	undisclosed
29 Brammer, David	Stoke City	Millwall	undisclosed
11 Brown, Christopher	Sunderland	Norwich City	undisclosed
30 Brown, Scott	Bristol City	Cheltenham Town	undisclosed
30 Burns, Jamie D.	Blackpool	Morecambe	undisclosed
31 Caldwell, Stephen	Sunderland	Burnley	400,000
30 Chambers, Luke	Northampton Town	Nottingham Forest	undisclosed
16 Clarke, Leon M.	Wolverhampton Wanderers	Sheffield Wednesday	undisclosed
26 Cole, Mitchell J.	Southend United	Stevenage Borough	undisclosed
5 Collins, Neill	Sunderland	Wolverhampton Wanderers	150,000
16 Connor, Paul	Leyton Orient	Cheltenham Town	undisclosed
30 Constable, James A.	Walsall	Kidderminster Harriers	undisclosed
9 Craney, Ian T.W.	Accrington Stanley	Swansea City	undisclosed
19 Critchell, Kyle A.R.	Southampton	Chesterfield	Free
5 Crooks, Leon E.G.	Milton Keynes Dons	Wycombe Wanderers	undisclosed
18 Davenport, Calum R.P.	Tottenham Hotspur	West Ham United	undisclosed
24 Davies, Simon	Everton	Fulham	undisclosed
29 Delap, Rory J.	Sunderland	Stoke City	Free
25 Diao, Salif	Liverpool	Stoke City	Free
11 Dixon, Jonathan J.	Wycombe Wanderers	Aldershot Town	6000
31 Doyle, Nathan	Derby County	Hull City	undisclosed
31 Duberry, Michael W.	Stoke City	Reading	undisclosed
17 Dunn, David J.I.	Birmingham City	Blackburn Rovers	undisclosed
2 Edwards, Akhenaton C.	Luton Town	Sunderland	1,400,000
3 Elding, Anthony L.	Boston United	Stockport County	undisclosed
3 Elliott, Robert J.	Sunderland	Leeds United	Free
10 Fagan, Craig	Hull City	Derby County	750,000
19 Fallon, Rory M.	Swansea City	Plymouth Argyle	300,000
22 Ferguson, Darren	Wrexham	Peterborough United	undisclosed
31 Fleming, Craig	Norwich City	Rotherham United	Free
26 Folan, Caleb C.	Chesterfield	Wigan Athletic	undisclosed
2 Fulop, Marton	Tottenham Hotspur	Sunderland	500,000
12 Grand, Simon	Carlisle United	Grimsby Town	undisclosed
31 Guttridge, Luke	Sheffield United	Leyton Orient	undisclosed
30 Halford, Gregory	Colchester United	Reading	2,500,000
9 Harris, Neil	Nottingham Forest	Millwall	undisclosed
31 Henderson, Wayne	Brighton & Hove Albion	Preston North End	200,000
31 Holland, Christopher J.	Boston United	Southport	undisclosed
8 Hoskins, William	Rotherham United	Watford	undisclosed
31 Hoult, Russell	West Bromwich Albion	Stoke City	Free
31 Hughes, Mark A.	Everton	Northampton Town	undisclosed
3 Hurst, Glynn	Shrewsbury Town	Bury	undisclosed
11 Hyde, Micah A.	Burnley	Peterborough United	75,000
8 Ifill, Paul E.	Sheffield United	Crystal Palace	750,000
10 Jalal, Shwan S.	Woking	Peterborough United	undisclosed
29 John, Stern	Coventry City	Sunderland	undisclosed
30 Johnson, Jermaine	Bradford City	Sheffield Wednesday	250,000
3 Jones, David F.L.	Manchester United	Derby County	1,000,000
31 Jones, Lee	Blackpool	Darlington	undisclosed
25 Kabba, Steven	Sheffield United	Watford	undisclosed
4 Kandol, Tresor O.	Barnet	Leeds United	undisclosed
23 Keogh, Andrew D.	Scunthorpe United	Wolverhampton Wanderers	850,000
30 Kiely, Dean L.	Portsmouth	West Bromwich Albion	Free
3 Kightly, Michael J.	Grays Athletic	Wolverhampton Wanderers	nominal
10 Kilgallon, Matthew	Leeds United	Sheffield United	1,750,000

22 Knight, Leon L.	Swansea City	Milton Keynes Dons	undisclosed
31 Larsson, Sebastien	Arsenal	Birmingham City	1,000,000
3 Lawrence, Liam	Sunderland	Stoke City	500,000
31 Lee-Barrett, Arran	Weymouth	Coventry City	Free
5 Low, Joshua D.	Leicester City	Peterborough United	100,000
29 Mackail-Smith, Craig	Dagenham & Redbridge	Peterborough United	undisclosed
22 Martin, David	Dartford	Crystal Palace	25,000
19 Matteo, Dominic	Blackburn Rovers	Stoke City	undisclosed
11 Mattis, Dwayne A.	Bury	Barnsley	50,000
8 McArdle, Rory A.	Sheffield Wednesday	Rochdale	undisclosed
5 McCann, Grant S.	Cheltenham Town	Barnsley	100,000
3 McCormack, Alan	Preston North End	Southend United	undisclosed
29 McEveley, James	Blackburn Rovers	Derby County	800,000
26 McGleish, Scott	Northampton Town	Wycombe Wanderers	undisclosed
4 McIndoe, Michael	Barnsley	Wolverhampton Wanderers	250,000
1 McLean, Aaron	Grays Athletic	Peterborough United	undisclosed
29 McParland, Anthony	Barnsley	Wycombe Wanderers	undisclosed
12 Monkhouse, Andrew W.	Swindon Town	Hartlepool United	undisclosed
10 Murray, Adam D.	Torquay United	Macclesfield Town	undisclosed
4 Murray, Glenn	Carlisle United	Rochdale	undisclosed
23 Neill, Lucas E.	Blackburn Rovers	West Ham United	undisclosed
26 O'Grady, Christopher	Leicester City	Rotherham United	65,000
5 Onibuje, Fola	Swindon Town	Wycombe Wanderers	undisclosed
31 Painter, Marcos	Birmingham City	Swansea City	undisclosed
22 Perkins, David	Morecambe	Rochdale	undisclosed
3 Poole, David A.	Yeovil Town	Stockport County	undisclosed
19 Potter, Darren M.	Liverpool	Wolverhampton Wanderers	200,000
9 Quashie, Nigel F.	West Bromwich Albion	West Ham United	1,500,000
19 Ravenhill, Richard J.	Grimsby Town	Darlington	undisclosed
2 Roberts, Gareth M.	Accrington Stanley	Ipswich Town	undisclosed
17 Rodgers, Luke J.	Crewe Alexandra	Port Vale	undisclosed
9 Ryan, Tim J.	Boston United	Darlington	undisclosed
29 Smith, Jeff	Port Vale	Carlisle United	undisclosed
31 Southall, Leslie N.	Nottingham Forest	Gillingham	undisclosed
18 Spring, Matthew	Watford	Luton Town	200,000
11 Stead, Jonathan	Sunderland	Sheffield United	750,000
5 Steele, Lee A.J.	Leyton Orient	Chester City	undisclosed
9 Stirling, Jude B.	Peterborough United	Milton Keynes Dons	undisclosed
1 Stock, Brian B.	Preston North End	Doncaster Rovers	undisclosed
11 Stokes, Anthony	Arsenal	Sunderland	2,000,000
26 Tait, Paul	Boston United	Southport	undisclosed
26 Talbot, Andrew	Sheffield Wednesday	Luton Town	250,000
11 Teale, Gary	Wigan Athletic	Derby County	600,000
11 Thatcher, Benjamin D.	Manchester City	Charlton Athletic	undisclosed
3 Thelwell, Alton A.	Hull City	Leyton Orient	undisclosed
31 Thompson, David A.	Portsmouth	Bolton Wanderers	undisclosed
15 Tierney, Marc	Oldham Athletic	Shrewsbury Town	undisclosed
5 Till, Peter	Birmingham City	Grimsby Town	Free
11 Traore, Djimi	Charlton Athletic	Portsmouth	undisclosed
5 Unsworth, David G.	Sheffield United	Wigan Athletic	undisclosed
31 Upson, Matthew J.	Birmingham City	West Ham United	7,500,000
19 Vaughan, Stephen J.	Chester City	Boston United	undisclosed
12 Vine, Rowan	Luton Town	Birmingham City	2,500,000
27 Walters, Jonathan R.	Chester City	Ipswich Town	undisclosed
31 Ward, Jamie J.	Torquay United	Chesterfield	undisclosed
23 Warnock, Stephen	Liverpool	Blackburn Rovers	undisclosed
10 Whalley, Shaun	Witton Albion	Accrington Stanley	undisclosed
11 Whittingham, Peter M.	Aston Villa	Cardiff City	undisclosed
31 Williams, Gareth J.G.	Leicester City	Watford	undisclosed
8 Williamson, Lee	Rotherham United	Watford	undisclosed
12 Wilson, Brian	Cheltenham Town	Bristol City	undisclosed
31 Woodards, Daniel M.	Exeter City	Crewe Alexandra	undisclosed
12 Wright, David	Wigan Athletic	Ipswich Town	undisclosed
19 Wright, Thomas	Barnsley	Darlington	undisclosed
31 Yeo, Simon J.	Peterborough United	Chester City	undisclosed
23 Young, Ashley	Watford	Aston Villa	undisclosed

TEMPORARY TRANSFERS

22 Ainsworth, Lionel – Derby County – Halifax Town; 31 Albrighton, Mark – Boston United – Rushden & Diamonds; 31 Andrews, Wayne M.H. – Coventry City – Bristol City; 11 Bailey, Matthew – Crewe Alexandra – Barrow; 25 Bakayoko, Zoumana – Millwall – Brighton & Hove Albion; 8 Bardsley, Phillip A. – Manchester United – Aston Villa; 7 Barnes, Oliver J.P. – Bristol Rovers – Gloucester City; 26 Bastians, Felix – Nottingham Forest – Halifax Town; 19 Beardsley, Christopher K. – Mansfield Town – Rushden & Diamonds; 19 Beckford, Jermaine P. – Leeds United – Scunthorpe United; 3 Bendtner, Niklas – Arsenal – Birmingham City; 25 Benyon, Elliot P. – Bristol City – Crawley Town; 18 Bertrand, Ryan D. – Chelsea – AFC Bournemouth; 2 Best, Leon J. – Southampton – Yeovil Town; 3 Blinkhorn, Matthew D. – Blackpool – Bury; 31 Brittain, Martin – Ipswich Town – Yeovil Town; 4 Broughton, Drewe O. – Chester City – Boston United; 12 Brown, Scott – Bristol City – Cheltenham Town; 26 Budtz, Jan – Doncaster Rovers – Wolverhampton Wanderers; 30 Burch, Robert K. – Tottenham Hotspur – Barnet; 5 Cadmore, Tom – Wycombe

Wanderers – Yeading; 30 Canoville, Lee – Boston United – Shrewsbury Town; 10 Chorley, Benjamin F. – Milton Keynes Dons – Gillingham; 15 Connor, Paul – Leyton Orient – Cheltenham Town; 15 Cooke, Stephen L. – AFC Bournemouth – Torquay United; 29 Cork, Jack F.P. – Chelsea – AFC Bournemouth; 19 Coutts, James R. – AFC Bournemouth – Weymouth; 5 Crossley, Mark G. – Fulham – Sheffield Wednesday; 11 Dawson, Tony – Hartlepool United – Gateshead; 11 Diagouraga, Toumani – Watford – Rotherham United; 12 Dickson, Ryan A. – Plymouth Argyle – Torquay United; 12 Djemba-Djemba, Eric D. – Aston Villa – Burnley; 19 D'Laryea, Nathan A. – Manchester City – Macclesfield Town; 2 Doherty, Thomas – Queens Park Rangers – Wycombe Wanderers; 5 Donnelly, Ciaran – Blackpool – Southport; 5 Doyle, Nathan – Derby County – Bradford City; 19 Dugdale, Adam – Crewe Alexandra – Southport; 31 Dyer, Bruce A. – Doncaster Rovers – Bradford City; 30 Eaden, Nicholas J. – Nottingham Forest – Lincoln City; 8 Eckersley, Adam – Manchester United – Barnsley; 31 Edge, Lewis J.S. – Blackpool – Rochdale; 1 Elliott, Robert J. – Sunderland – Leeds United; 31 Elvins, Robert – West Bromwich Albion – York City; 5 Etuhu, Kelvin – Manchester City – Rochdale; 4 Evans, Jonathan – Manchester United – Sunderland; 2 Fernandez, Vincent – Nottingham Forest – Grays Athletic; 4 Ferris, Peter – Carlisle United – Kendal Town; 31 Fleetwood, Stuart K. – Hereford United – Accrington Stanley; 19 Fleming, Craig – Norwich City – Wolverhampton Wanderers; 20 Forte, Jonathan – Sheffield United – Doncaster Rovers; 12 Fortune, Clayton A. – Leyton Orient – Port Vale; 31 Fortune, Jonathan J. – Charlton Athletic – Stoke City; 1 Fortune-West, Leopold D. – Rushden & Diamonds – Shrewsbury Town; 5 Frost, Stef – Notts County – Gainsborough Trinity; 11 Gallen, Kevin A. – Queens Park Rangers – Plymouth Argyle; 19 Garner, Joseph A. – Blackburn Rovers – Carlisle United; 9 Gilbert, Peter – Sheffield Wednesday – Doncaster Rovers; 31 Gillett, Simon J. – Southampton – Blackpool; 12 Golbourne, Scott J. – Reading – Wycombe Wanderers; 1 Graham, Daniel A.W. – Middlesbrough – Carlisle United; 9 Grand, Simon – Carlisle United – Grimsby Town; 31 Grant, Gavin – Millwall – Grays Athletic; 19 Griffin, Andrew – Portsmouth – Stoke City; 26 Griffiths, Anthony J. – Doncaster Rovers – Stafford Rangers; 12 Gritton, Martin – Lincoln City – Mansfield Town; 25 Guinan, Stephen – Cheltenham Town – Hereford United; 26 Halliday, Matthew R. – Norwich City – Torquay United; 9 Harding, Benjamin S. – Milton Keynes Dons – Grays Athletic; 1 Hart, Charles J.J. – Manchester City – Tranmere Rovers; 10 Hayes, Jonathan – Reading – Milton Keynes Dons; 12 Henderson, Ian – Norwich City – Rotherham United; 12 Hennessey, Wayne R. – Wolverhampton Wanderers – Stockport County; 4 Hibbert, David J. – Preston North End – Bradford City; 31 Holgate, Ashan – Swindon Town – Macclesfield Town; 12 Holmes, Peter J. – Luton Town – Chesterfield; 31 Horsfield, Geoffrey M. – Sheffield United – Leicester City; 5 Hunt, James M. – Bristol Rovers – Grimsby Town; 31 Hurst, Kevan – Sheffield United – Scunthorpe United; 5 Ifill, Paul E. – Sheffield United – Crystal Palace; 26 Jarvis, Rossi – Norwich City – Torquay United; 31 Jennings, Steven J. – Tranmere Rovers – Hereford United; 8 Jones, Lee – Blackpool – Darlington; 8 Jones, Michael D. – Tranmere Rovers – Shrewsbury Town; 31 Joynes, Nathan – Barnsley – Boston United; 31 Kazmierczak, Przemyslaw – Bolton Wanderers – Accrington Stanley; 26 Kearns, Callum S.B. – Southend United – Chelmsford City; 12 King, Robert – Colchester United – Heybridge Swifts; 21 Krause, James – Ipswich Town – Carlisle United; 26 Laird, Marc – Manchester City – Northampton Town; 31 Lamb, Shaun A. – Bristol City – Forest Green Rovers; 22 Larrieu, Romain – Plymouth Argyle – Gillingham; 5 Lawson, James P. – Southend United – AFC Bournemouth; 4 Leary, Michael – Luton Town – Brentford; 19 Ledgister, Joel – Southend United – Gravesend & Northfleet; 12 Lee-Barrett, Aaran – Weymouth – Coventry City; 19 Le Fondre, Adam – Stockport County – Rochdale; 11 Legzdins, Adam R. – Birmingham City – Macclesfield Town; 11 Logan, Carlos S. – Darlington – Bradford City; 5 Lowe, Keith S. – Wolverhampton Wanderers – Cheltenham Town; 19 Maidens, Michael D. – Hartlepool United – York City; 17 Mancienne, Michael I. – Chelsea – Queens Park Rangers; 26 Martin, Lee R. – Manchester United – Stoke City; 4 McDermott, David A. – Walsall – Halesowen Town; 22 McShane, Luke – Peterborough United – Gravesend & Northfleet; 31 Mears, Tyrone – West Ham United – Derby County; 24 Miller, Kevin – Southampton – Torquay United; 26 Mills, Matthew C. – Manchester City – Colchester United; 4 Murphy, John J. – Blackpool – Macclesfield Town; 18 Nicholson, Shane M. – Chesterfield – Boston United; 4 O'Cearuill, Joseph – Arsenal – Brighton & Hove Albion; 1 O'Donnell, Daniel – Liverpool – Crewe Alexandra; 1 O'Halloran, Stephen – Aston Villa – Wycombe Wanderers; 12 Oliver, Dean – Sheffield United – Hednesford Town; 1 Onibuje, Fola – Swindon Town – Wycombe Wanderers; 4 Opara, Lloyd – Peterborough United – Burton Albion; 31 Pacey, Robert – Doncaster Rovers – Gateshead; 26 Paine, Matthew S. – Colchester United – Thurrock; 4 Parker, Ben B.C. – Leeds United – Bradford City; 4 Partridge, David W. – Bristol City – Brentford; 31 Paterson, Sean P. – Blackpool – Southport; 2 Patterson, Martin – Stoke City – Grimsby Town; 31 Paynter, William P. – Southend United – Bradford City; 5 Pearce, Jason D. – Portsmouth – Woking; 11 Pollitt, Michael F. – Wigan Athletic – Burnley; 2 Price, Jamie – Birmingham City – Tamworth; 30 Prutton, David T. – Southampton – Nottingham Forest; 2 Pulis, Anthony J. – Stoke City – Grimsby Town; 26 Quigley, Damien – Bury – Hyde United; 31 Rachubka, Paul S. – Huddersfield Town – Blackpool; 16 Ravenhill, Richard J. – Grimsby Town – Darlington; 26 Reid, Reuben – Plymouth Argyle – Rochdale; 5 Rizzo, Nicholas A. – Milton Keynes Dons – Grimsby Town; 4 Roberts, Mark A. – Crewe Alexandra – Northwich Victoria; 26 Robertson, Jordan – Sheffield United – Northampton Town; 31 Rose, Daniel S. – Manchester United – Hereford United; 4 Rose, Daniel S. – Manchester United – Oxford United; 26 Ross, Ian – Sheffield United – Notts County; 29 Runstrom, Bjorn – Fulham – Luton Town; 5 Santos, George – Brighton & Hove Albion – Oxford United; 29 Shearer, Scott – Bristol Rovers – Shrewsbury Town; 29 Simpson, Daniel P. – Manchester United – Sunderland; 17 Sinclair, Scott A. – Chelsea – Plymouth Argyle; 25 Smart, Andrew J. – Macclesfield Town – Northwich Victoria; 25 Smith, Christian D. – Port Vale – Cambridge United; 4 Smith, Emmanuele – Walsall – Halesowen Town; 1 Smith, James D. – Chelsea – Queens Park Rangers; 26 Smith, Jeff – Port Vale – Carlisle United; 31 Smith, Johann – Bolton Wanderers – Carlisle United; 30 Song Billong, Alexandre D. – Arsenal – Charlton Athletic; 28 Stack, Graham – Reading – Leeds United; 4 Steele, Luke D. – West Bromwich Albion – Coventry City; 8 Stirling, Jude B. – Peterborough United – Milton Keynes Dons; 1 Strachan, Gavin D. – Hartlepool United – Peterborough United; 1 Sutton, Richard A. – Crewe Alexandra – Stafford Rangers; 31 Sweeney, Peter – Stoke City – Yeovil Town; 12 Talbot, Andrew – Sheffield Wednesday – Scunthorpe United; 31 Taylor, Andrew – Blackburn Rovers – Huddersfield Town; 5 Thomas, Bradley M. – Yeovil Town – Boston United; 3 Thomas, Sean I.S. – Queens Park Rangers – Bristol City; 31 Thompson, John – Nottingham Forest – Tranmere Rovers; 24 Thorpe, Anthony L. – Stevenage Borough – Grimsby Town; 3 Timlin, Michael – Fulham – Swindon Town; 1 Tipton, Matthew – Bury – Macclesfield Town; 4 Trotman, Neal – Oldham Athletic – Halifax Town; 2 Vaughan, Stephen J. – Chester City – Rochdale; 5 Walker, James L.N. – Charlton Athletic – Leyton Orient; 31 Ward, Nicholas – Queens Park Rangers – Brighton & Hove Albion; 26 Watt, Jerome – Northampton Town – Morecambe; 4 Webb, Daniel J. – Yeovil Town – Rushden & Diamonds; 1 Weir-Daley, Spencer J.A. – Nottingham Forest – Lincoln City; 1 Wheater, David J. – Middlesbrough – Darlington; 19 Whittington, Michael J. – Cheltenham Town – Weston-Super-Mare; 31 Wiles, Simon P. – Blackpool – Macclesfield Town; 31 Wilkinson, Thomas – Lincoln City – Grays Athletic; 16 Wilson, Che C.A. – Southend United – Brentford; 5 Wilson, Marc D. – Portsmouth – AFC Bournemouth; 18 Windass, Dean – Braford City – Hull City; 17 Wiseman, Scott N.K. – Hull City – Rotherham United; 16 Wright, Thomas – Barnsley – Darlington; 31 Yeates, Mark – Tottenham Hotspur – Leicester City; 31 Youga, Kelly A. – Charlton Athletic – Bradford City; 30 Zakuani, Gabriel A. – Fulham – Stoke City

FEBRUARY 2007

14 Howard, Timothy M.	Manchester United	Everton	undisclosed

TEMPORARY TRANSFERS

22 Ainsworth, Lionel – Derby County – Wycombe Wanderers; 2 Alcock, Craig – Yeovil Town – Taunton Town; 1 Allen, Curtis L. – AFC Bournemouth – Leyton; 2 Barlow, Matthew J. – Oldham Athletic – Stalybridge Celtic; 23 Beattie, Warren S. – Preston North End – Hednesford Town; 23 Bedeau, Anthony C. – Walsall – Bury; 9 Benjamin, Trevor J. – Peterborough United – Boston United; 8 Blizzard, Dominic J. – Watford – Stockport County; 13 Camp, Lee M.J. – Derby County – Queens Park Rangers; 2 Chamberlain, Scott D. – Brighton & Hove Albion – Bognor Regis Town; 20 Charles, Anthony D. – Barnet – Aldershot Town; 9 Charles, Wesley D.D. – Brentford – Crawley Town; 2 Clarke, Tom – Yeovil Town – Taunton Town; 15 Cottrell, Adam – Millwall – Weymouth; 20 Dodds, Louis – Leicester City – Rochdale; 23 Duggan, Robert – Stoke City – Stafford Rangers; 20 Flinders, Scott L. – Crystal Palace – Brighton & Hove Albion; 17 Gilmartin, Rene – Walsall – Worcester City; 23 Harper, Kevin P. – Stoke City – Walsall; 23 Hays, Paul – Barnsley – Huddersfield Town; 23 Hinchliffe, Ben – Preston North End – Tranmere Rovers; 8 Hird, Adrian S. – Leeds United – Doncaster Rovers; 22 Hodge, Bryan – Blackburn Rovers – Mansfield Town; 16 Jarman, Nathan G. – Barnsley – Worksop Town; 16 Jarrett, Albert O. – Watford – Boston United; 8 Jarrett, Jason L. – Preston North End – Leicester City; 15 Jarvis, Ryan – Norwich City – Leyton Orient; 23 John, Alastair A. – Charlton Athletic – Torquay United; 19 Johnson, Jemal J. – Wolverhampton Wanderers – Leeds United; 9 Jones, Richard G. – Manchester United – Barnsley; 13 Kearney, Alan – Everton – Chester City; 23 Kempson, Darren – Crewe Alexandra – Bury; 16 Kerry, Lloyd – Sheffield United – Torquay United; 23 Knights, Darryl – Ipswich Town – Yeovil Town; 16 Law, Nicholas – Sheffield United – Yeovil Town; 16 Lawson, James P. – Southend United – Dagenham & Redbridge; 19 Le Fondre, Adam – Stockport County – Rochdale; 2 Malsom, Sam A. – Plymouth Argyle – Tiverton Town; 23 Martin, David E. – Liverpool – Accrington Stanley; 23 Martin, Richard W. – Brighton & Hove Albion – Folkestone Invicta; 16 McGoldrick, David J. – Southampton – AFC Bournemouth; 19 Meredith, James G. – Derby County – Chesterfield; 9 Miller, Ian – Ipswich Town – Darlington; 9 Moyo-Modise, Clive – Rochdale – Mossley; 8 Muirhead, Ben R. – Bradford City – Rochdale; 19 Nash, Carlo J. – Preston North End – Wigan Athletic; 22 Nicholls, Alex – Walsall – Burton Albion; 13 Nyatanga, Lewin J. – Derby County – Barnsley; 16 Oji, Samuel U.U. – Birmingham City – Bristol Rovers; 9 Page, Sam T. – Milton Keynes Dons – Cambridge United; 9 Pearce, Alex – Reading – Northampton Town; 15 Platt, Conal J. – AFC Bournemouth – Weymouth; 9 Richards, Gary – Colchester United – Brentford; 16 Robinson, Theo – Watford – Wealdstone; 2 Russell, James P. – Chelsea – Walton & Hersham; 1 Serrant, Ryan P. – Leeds United – Guiseley; 8 Sinclair, Frank M. – Burnley – Huddersfield Town; 2 Sleath, Danny – Mansfield Town – Alfreton Town; 25 Smart, Andrew J. – Macclesfield Town – Northwich Victoria; 16 Smith, Nicholas – Bradford City – North Ferriby United; 19 Sullivan, Neil – Leeds United – Doncaster Rovers; 23 Turnbull, Philip – Hartlepool United – Blyth Spartans; 23 Turner, Ben H. – Coventry City – Oldham Athletic; 23 Turner, Iain R. – Everton – Sheffield Wednesday; 8 Vidarsson, Bjarni T. – Everton – AFC Bournemouth; 19 Wallis, Jonathan – Hereford United – Dagenham & Redbridge; 9 Watson, Steven C. – West Bromwich Albion – Sheffield Wednesday; 23 Whittington, Michael J. – Cheltenham Town – Mangotsfield United; 8 Wilkinson, David M. – Crystal Palace – Welling United; 16 Wright, Alan – Sheffield United – Doncaster Rovers; 9 Wroe, Nicholas – Barnsley – Bury

MARCH 2007

22 Barnes, Ashley L.	Paulton Rovers	Plymouth Argyle	undisclosed
12 Dickson, Christopher M.	Dulwich Hamlet	Charlton Athletic	undisclosed

TEMPORARY TRANSFERS

28 Alcock, Craig – Yeovil Town – Tiverton Town; 21 Aljofree, Hasney – Plymouth Arygle – Oldham Athletic; 29 Allanson, Ashley G. – Scunthorpe United – Farsley Celtic; 13 Antwi-Birago, Godwin – Liverpool – Accrington Stanley; 22 Arber, Mark A. – Peterborough United – Dagenham & Redbridge; 6 Ashikodi, Moses – Watford – Bradford City; 15 Ashton, Nathan – Charlton Athletic – Millwall; 22 Baldock, Samuel – Milton Keynes Dons – Walton & Hersham; 22 Bastians, Felix – Nottingham Forest – Gillingham; 22 Benjamin, Trevor J. – Peterborough United – Walsall; 2 Blinkhorn, Matthew D. – Blackpool – Morecambe; 22 Blizzard, Dominic J. – Watford – Milton Keynes Dons; 22 Boertien, Paul – Derby County – Chesterfield; 21 Brandon, Christopher – Huddersfield Town – Blackpool; 2 Brownlie, Royce – Swindon Town – Chester City; 18 Cadamarteri, Daniel L. – Leicester City – Doncaster Rovers; 1 Carlisle, Clarke J. – Watford – Luton Town; 22 Casement, Christopher – Ipswich Town – Millwall; 5 Chamberlain, Scott D. – Brighton & Hove Albion – Bognor Regis Town; 1 Clarke, Leon M. – Sheffield Wednesday – Oldham Athletic; 9 Clarke, Wayne J. – Darlington – Whitby Town; 22 Cole, Andrew A. – Portsmouth – Birmingham City; 19 Corr, Barry – Sheffield Wednesday – Swindon Town; 22 Coughlan, Graham – Sheffield Wednesday – Burnley; 3 Cowley, David K. – Southend United – Heybridge Swifts; 22 Cox, Simon – Reading – Northampton Town; 2 Cranie, Martin J. – Southampton – Yeovil Town; 15 Currie, Darren – Ipswich Town – Derby County; 9 Daniels, Charlie – Tottenham Hotspur – Chesterfield; 22 Dickson, Ryan A. – Plymouth Argyle – Torquay United; 22 Donnelly, Ciaran – Blackpool – Macclesfield Town; 29 Doughty, Philip M. – Blackpool – Barrow; 6 Elvins, Robert – West Bromwich Albion – York City; 9 Faulkner, James – Wycombe Wanderers – Leighton Town; 22 Ferrell, Andrew E. – Hereford United – Kidderminster Harriers; 16 Flynn, Christopher P. – Crewe Alexandra – Cambridge United; 10 Fortune, Jonathan J. – Charlton Athletic – Stoke City; 26 Gamble, Patrick J. – Nottingham Forest – York City; 15 Gleeson, Daniel E. – Notts County – Cambridge United; 21 Graham, David – Sheffield Wednesday – Torquay United; 4 Grant, Gavin – Millwall – Grays Athletic; 22 Gray, Michael – Blackburn Rovers – Leeds United; 22 Grimes, Ashley – Manchester City – Swindon Town; 4 Guinan, Stephen – Cheltenham Town – Hereford United; 3 Guthrie, Danny S. – Liverpool – Southampton; 30 Hall, Asa – Birmingham City – Ashford Town; 1 Hastings, John – Milton Keynes Dons – St Albans City; 22 Henry, James – Reading – Nottingham Forest; 22 Holmes, Peter J. – Luton Town – Lincoln City; 15 Hooper, Gary – Southend United – Leyton Orient; 21 Howarth, Christopher – Bolton Wanderers – Carlisle United; 22 Hughes, Craig – Colchester United – Cambridge United; 16 Hurst, Kevan – Sheffield United – Scunthorpe United; 10 Idiakez, Inigo – Southampton – Queens Park Rangers; 16 Idrizaj, Besian – Liverpool – Luton Town; 22 James, Craig P. – Darlington – York City; 22 James, Kevin E. – Nottingham Forest – Swindon Town; 21 Jarrett, Albert O. – Watford – Milton Keynes Dons; 13 Jarvis, Rossi – Norwich City – Rotherham United; 2 Jeffers, Francis – Blackburn Rovers – Ipswich Town; 6 Joynes, Nathan – Barnsley – Boston United; 1 Kazimierczak, Przemyslaw – Bolton Wanderers – Accrington Stanley; 1 Kennedy, Jason – Middlesbrough – Bury; 2 Kishishev, Radostin – Charlton Athletic – Leeds United; 1 Kovacs, Janos – Chesterfield – York City; 21 Laight, Ryan D. – Barnsley – Alfreton Town; 23 Laird, Scott – Plymouth Argyle –

Tiverton Town; 4 Lamb, Shaun A. – Bristol City – Forest Green Rovers; 6 Larrieu, Romain – Plymouth Argyle – Gillingham; 22 Lever, Christopher D. – Oldham Athletic – Stalybridge Celtic; 22 Lewis, Joseph – Norwich City – Stockport County; 22 Lynch, Ryan P. – Coventry City – Tamworth; 9 Marrison, Colin – Sheffield United – Hinckley United; 27 Massey, Alan – Wycombe Wanderers – Chesham United; 16 Masters, Clark J. – Brentford – AFC Wimbledon; 2 Maylett, Bradley – Boston United – Chester City; 2 McCallum, Gavin K. – Yeovil Town – Dorchester Town; 21 McNamee, Anthony – Watford – Crewe Alexandra; 22 McVeigh, Paul F. – Norwich City – Burnley; 16 Mendes, Albert J.H.A. – Notts County – Lincoln City; 9 Meynell, Rhys – Barnsley – Ossett Albion; 9 Michalik, Lubomir – Bolton Wanderers – Leeds United; 22 Mocquet, William – Sunderland – Bury; 22 Murphy, Kieran – Milton Keynes Dons – Walton & Hersham; 9 Newton, Shaun O. – West Ham United – Leicester City; 16 Nolan, Edward W. – Blackburn Rovers – Stockport County; 8 Olejnik, Robert – Aston Villa – Lincoln City; 1 Oliver, Dean – Sheffield United – Torquay United; 10 Parkin, Jonathan – Hull City – Stoke City; 22 Partridge, David W. – Bristol City – Swindon Town; 6 Paynter, William P. – Southend United – Bradford City; 16 Peltier, Lee A. – Liverpool – Hull City; 22 Peters, Ryan V. – Brentford – AFC Wimbledon; 2 Pettigrew, Adrian R.J. – Chelsea – Wycombe Wanderers; 22 Phillips, Mark I. – Millwall – Darlington; 22 Poole, Glenn S. – Grays Athletic – Rochdale; 22 Prendergast, Rory – Rochdale – Darlington; 22 Quinn, James S. – Northampton Town – Scunthorpe United; 22 Rankin, Isaiah – Grimsby Town – Macclesfield Town; 1 Rayner, Simon – Lincoln City – Torquay United; 22 Reet, Daniel – Mansfield Town – Rochdale; 22 Rehman, Zeshan – Queens Park Rangers – Brighton & Hove Albion; 22 Reid, Reuben – Plymouth Argyle – Torquay United; 9 Rhodes, Alexander – Brentford – Grays Athletic; 22 Ricketts, Rohan A. – Wolverhampton Wanderers – Queens Park Rangers; 22 Rizzo, Nicholas A. – Milton Keynes Dons – Chesterfield; 16 Rooney, Adam – Stoke City – Yeovil Town; 22 Roque, Miguel – Liverpool – Oldham Athletic; 10 Rosa, Denes – Wolverhampton Wanderers – Cheltenham Town; 2 Runstrom, Bjorn – Fulham – Luton Town; 12 Sam, Lloyd E. – Charlton Athletic – Southend United; 8 Serrant, Ryan P. – Leeds United – Farsley Celtic; 29 Sherlock, James – Lincoln City – Hinckley United; 7 Smith, Christian D. – Port Vale – Cambridge United; 21 Smith, Christian D. – Port Vale – Northwich Victoria; 21 Smith, Ryan C.M. – Derby County – Millwall; 12 Smith, Terence – Oldham Athletic – Southport; 16 Sodje, Samuel – Reading – West Bromwich Albion; 8 Songo'o, Franck S. – Portsmouth – Preston North End; 20 Summerfield, Luke – Plymouth Argyle – AFC Bournemouth; 5 Taylor, Andrew – Blackburn Rovers – Huddersfield Town; 8 Taylor, Scott J. – Milton Keynes Dons – Brentford; 20 Tonge, Dale – Barnsley – Gillingham; 2 Tonkin, Anthony – Yeovil Town – Grays Athletic; 1 Turnbull, Stephen – Hartlepool United – Rochdale; 9 Vaz Te, Ricardo J. – Bolton Wanderers – Hull City; 15 Walker, James L.N. – Charlton Athletic – Notts County; 9 Walker, Joshua – Middlesbrough – AFC Bournemouth; 2 Warner, Anthony R. – Fulham – Norwich City; 22 Watt, Jerome – Northampton Town – Salisbury City; 22 Watts, Adam – Fulham – Milton Keynes Dons; 12 Webb, Daniel J. – Yeovil Town – Woking; 22 Weir-Daley, Spencer J.A. – Nottingham Forest – Bradford City; 2 Welsh, Ishmael – Yeovil Town – Weymouth; 15 Weston, Myles – Charlton Athletic – Notts County; 2 Westwood, Ashley M. – Chester City – Swindon Town; 5 Wheater, David J. – Middlesbrough – Darlington; 20 White, Alan – Notts County – Peterborough United; 8 Wiggins-Thomas, Ruben S. – Chesterfield – Bradford Park Avenue; 6 Williams, Marvin T. – Millwall – Torquay United; 21 Williams, Robert I. – Barnsley – Blackpool; 9 Wilson, Bobby – Notts County – Hucknall Town; 22 Wilson, Che C.A. – Southend United – Rotherham United; 8 Wiseman, Scott N.K. – Hull City – Darlington; 26 Wood, Christopher H. – Mansfield Town – Ilkeston Town; 6 Worley, Harry J. – Chelsea – Doncaster Rovers; 16 Wright, Alan – Sheffield United – Nottingham Forest; 30 Wright, Nicholas – Birmingham City – Ashford Town; 8 Youga, Kelly A. – Charlton Athletic – Bradford City; 21 Zebroski, Christopher – Millwall – Oxford United

APRIL 2007

TEMPORARY TRANSFERS

8 Hart, Charles J.J. – Manchester City – Blackpool; 19 Royce, Simon E. – Queens Park Rangers – Gillingham; 21 Ruddy, John T.G. – Everton – Bristol City.

MAY 2007

29 Bale, Gareth	Southampton	Tottenham Hotspur	5,000,000
8 Daniel, Colin	Eastwood Town	Crewe Alexandra	undisclosed
29 Jackson, Matthew A.	Wigan Athletic	Watford	Free
29 Jones, William K.	Exeter City	Crewe Alexandra	undisclosed
18 Jutkiewicz, Lucas I.P.	Swindon Town	Everton	undisclosed
18 Muamba, Fabrice	Arsenal	Birmingham City	4,000,000
30 Poom, Mart	Arsenal	Watford	Free
29 Schumacher, Steven T.	Bradford City	Crewe Alexandra	nominal
21 Varney, Luke I.	Crewe Alexandra	Charlton Athletic	2,000,000

TEMPORARY TRANSFERS

8 Blizzard, Dominic J. – Watford – Milton Keynes Dons; 8 Currie, Darren – Ipswich Town – Derby County; 7 Eaden, Nicholas J. – Nottingham Forest – Lincoln City; 8 Hayes, Jonathan – Reading – Milton Keynes Dons; 9 Jarrett, Albert O. – Watford – Milton Keynes Dons; 14 Neal, Christopher M. – Preston North End – Morecambe; 6 Roque, Miguel – Liverpool – Oldham Athletic; 8 Watts, Adam – Fulham – Milton Keynes Dons; 10 Wright, Alan – Sheffield United – Nottingham Forest

THE NEW FOREIGN LEGION 2006–07

JULY 2006	*From*	*To*	*Fee in £*
14 Assou-Ekotto, Benoit	Lens	Tottenham Hotspur	undisclosed
20 Aurelio, Fabio	Valencia	Liverpool	undisclosed
17 Ballack, Michael	Bayern Munich	Chelsea	Free
12 Berbatov, Dimitar	Leverkusen	Tottenham Hotspur	10,890,000
28 Corradi, Bernardo	Valencia	Manchester City	2,000,000
7 Dabo, Ousmane	Lazio	Manchester City	undisclosed
13 Gonzalez, Mark	Albacete	Liverpool	4,000,000
10 Hilario	Nacional	Chelsea	undisclosed
13 Kalou, Salomon	Feyenoord	Chelsea	3,000,000
21 Landzaat, Denny	AZ	Wigan Athletic	2,500,000
18 Mikel, Jon O.	Manchester United/Lyn	Chelsea	12,000,000
6 Nade, Christopher	Troyes	Sheffield United	undisclosed
14 Paletta, Gabriel A.	Atletico Banfield	Liverpool	2,000,000
4 Shevchenko, Andriy	AC Milan	Chelsea	29,500,000
7 Zokora, Didier A.	St Etienne	Tottenham Hotspur	8,200,000
AUGUST 2006			
31 Beasley, Damarcus	PSV Eindhoven	Manchester City	loan
1 Bikey, Andre	Lokomotiv Moscow	Reading	undisclosed
23 Boulahrouz, Khalid	Hamburg	Chelsea	7,000,000
31 Denilson	Sao Paulo	Arsenal	3,400,000
30 Diawara Souleymane	Souchaux	Charlton Athletic	3,700,000
31 Douala, Rudolphe	Sporting Lisbon	Portsmouth	loan
30 Fernandes, Manuel	Benfica	Portsmouth	loan
17 Isaksson, Andreas	Rennes	Manchester City	2,000,000
31 Julio Baptista	Real Madrid	Arsenal	exch
31 Kranjcar, Niko	Hajduk Split	Portsmouth	3,500,000
18 Kuyt, Dirk	Feyenoord	Liverpool	7,000,000
31 Lastuvka, Jan	Shakhtar Donetsk	Fulham	loan
25 Martins, Obafemi	Internazionale	Newcastle United	10,000,000
31 Mascherano, Javier	Corinthians	West Ham United	undisclosed
2 McCarthy, Benni	Porto	Blackburn Rovers	2,500,000
10 Meite, Abdoulaye	Marseille	Bolton Wanderers	1,000,000
30 Mido	Roma	Tottenham Hotspur	4,500,000
31 Nonda, Shabani	Roma	Blackburn R	loan
25 Ooijer, Andre A.M.	PSV Eindhoven	Blackburn Rovers	undisclosed
7 Pantsil, John	Hapoel Tel Aviv	West Ham United	1,000,000
30 Petrov, Stilian A.	Celtic	Aston Villa	6,500,000
31 Pouso, Omar	Penarol	Charlton Athletic	loan
1 Priskin, Tamas	Gyor	Watford	undisclosed
7 Runstrom, Bjorn	Hammarby	Fulham	700,000
31 Tevez, Carlos	Corinthians	West Ham United	undisclosed
31 Teimourian, Andranik	Abu Moslem	Bolton Wanderers	undisclosed
10 Trabelsi, Hatem	Ajax	Manchester City	Free
10 Valencia, Luis	Villarreal	Wigan Athletic	loan
31 Webster, Andy	Hearts	Wigan Athletic	undisclosed
SEPTEMBER 2006			
12 Agathe, Didier	Celtic	Aston Villa	undisclosed
8 Teimourian, Andranik	Aboo Moslem	Bolton Wanderers	undisclosed
OCTOBER 2006			
1El Zhar, Nabil	St Etienne	Liverpool	undisclosed
JANUARY 2007			
31 Aghahowa, Julius	Shakhtar Donetsk	Wigan Athletic	2,100,000
2 Anderson	Santander	Everton	undisclosed
31 Arbeloa, Alvaro	La Coruna	Liverpool	2,600,000
31 Avinel, Cedric	Creteil	Watford	Free
30 Berner, Bruno	Basle	Blackburn Rovers	loan
22 Carew, John	Lyon	Aston Villa	undisclosed
31 Cavalli, Johann	Istres	Watford	Free
10 Dempsey, Clint	New England Rev	Fulham	1,500,000
12 Dong Fangzhou	Dalian Schide	Manchester United	500,000
31 Dong-Gook Lee	Pohang Steelers	Middlesbrough	Free
31 Fernandes, Manuel	Benfica	Everton	loan
1 Haestad, Kristofer	Start	Wigan Athletic	loan
1 Insua, Emiliano	Boca Juniors	Liverpool	loan
22 Kepa	Sevilla	West Ham United	loan
31 Maloney, Shaun	Celtic	Aston Villa	1,000,000
25 Michalik, Lubomir	Senec	Bolton Wanderers	undisclosed
25 Samba, Christopher	Hertha Berlin	Blackburn Rovers	Free
4 Montella, Vincenzo	Roma	Fulham	loan
11 Mvuemba, Arnold	Rennes	Portsmouth	loan
30 Onyewu, Oguchi	Standard Liege	Newcastle United	loan
1 Padelli, Daniele	Sampdoria	Liverpool	loan
23 Ricardo Rocha	Benfica	Tottenham Hotspur	3,300,000
31 Rinaldi, Douglas	Veranopolis	Watford	loan
25 Shelton, Luton	Helsingborg	Sheffield United	1,850,000
2 Taarabt, Adel	Lens	Tottenham Hotspur	originally loan
1 Zheng-Zhi	Shandong	Charlton Athletic	loan
FEBRUARY 2007			
20 Cesar Martin	Levante	Bolton Wanderers	Free
16 Mpenza, Emile	Hamburg	Manchester City	Free

REFEREEING AND THE LAWS OF THE GAME

For the forthcoming season there are less Law changes and directions than for many years. Indeed almost all there is to consider is tidying up exercises and reminders. Jewellery is the one most highlighted with the taping up of rings being permitted if it renders them entirely safe and only if they cannot be removed. Also as a result of players increasingly becoming injured by opponents' studs and blades referees are now instructed to carry out inspections prior to every match. There is a further reiteration of the intended punishments for the offences of making racist remarks, attempts to indulge in simulation and surrounding of referees to challenge their decisions and reminders that players bleeding from wounds or having blood-stained apparel must leave the field.

As to the Law changes themselves there is almost a distinction without a difference where it is stated that there shall be no advertising on the ground within the Technical Area or one meter from the touchline. Previously it was merely stated that there was to be no advertising in the technical area. One can only assume that this is to deter ingenious advertisers or their agents. There are some references in the equipment section to underwear becoming outerwear since a new practice appears to have occurred of wearing under-shorts as an alternative to thermal ones so these too must be the same main colour as the shorts. Furthermore undershirts are also becoming increasingly popular and these too are brought into the framework since their sleeves must also be the same main colour as the outer jersey or shirt. It would appear that undershirts do seem to be causing FIFA some concern since the aspect of revealing them for one reason or another is to be punished more considerably. Any hint of players revealing any political, religious or personal statements on such undershirts or indeed on any of the basic compulsory players' equipment will be severely sanctioned. Whereas previously the breach by a player was only to be sanctioned by the competition organiser, against him or her now it is the "Team" of the player who will be so sanctioned and in addition FIFA have given themselves the power to get involved.

At senior level where there is likely to be Fourth Official he normally takes the place of an injured colleague. This is changing since if a reserve Assistant Referee is appointed for the game he can only now replace an Assistant Referee who cannot continue or alternatively to replace the Fourth Official as required.

The change most likely to affect players relates to goal celebrations. Certain acts have for some time been cautionable, but a powerful new one has been added which indicates that if a player "covers his head or face with a mask or other similar item to celebrate a goal" he must be cautioned. Without doubt this will lead to both uncertainty and controversy and will almost certainly have to be clarified and altered next year. This is because it has to be unclear whether reference is being made literally to a mask as donned by Fecundo Savva when he scored for Fulham or the covering of the face by a shirt or undershirt. Of 18 definitions of "mark" culled from an internet dictionary only one might apply namely "a protective covering for the face or head".

However the 3 great categories of controversy in the Laws namely Offside; Handball and goal-line technology have not been tackled. On the last named, experiments are taking place in junior competitions, whilst Hawk-Eye the British company behind cricket and tennis technology are expecting to demonstrate their own goal-line technology to FIFA shortly. On offsides the interpretation of the Law still causes immense problems to the media, the public, the participants playing or managing and worse still on many occasions to Assistant Referees. Finally the interpretation of hand-ball is having the same adverse affect. Too many cannot grasp the concept of accidental hand-ball, whilst cunning players are deliberately ensuring the ball strikes their hands or arms and claiming that it is accidental. There must come a time when consideration is given to making all hand-ball an offence to simplify both the Law and its interpretation.

In reference to the Referees themselves, two high profile of their number have retired from the National List. The first one mentioned Dermot Gallagher was the oldest and the second Graham Poll was arguably the most controversial. Certainly Graham Poll's exit fell into that category as he retired a year earlier than was required whilst Dermot Gallagher retired a year after the cut-off point, allowed to remain under the age discrimination laws. Although the mild of temperament Gallagher bowed out without a word except perhaps for a "thank you" the more volatile Poll did not go quietly and fired a broadside at a number of people. He remonstrated saying that referees "were losing the war" against badly behaved Premiership Managers and players and went on to add "My 27th and final season as a referee was not enjoyable." However the Professional Game Match Officials (PGMO) an organisation set up some years ago to manage match officials who officiate at the professional game level did not support Poll's arguments and as can be seen below there are several new members both at Referee and Assistant Referee level who are delighted to be in a position to take the flack. Apart from the two referees mentioned above six more have left the list and eight new ones have been appointed. These consist of Messrs – Atwell, Cook, East, Evans, Haines, Horwood, Lewis (G) and Ward. The Board itself consists of the Chief Executives of the FA, the FA Premier League, and the Football League. Keith Hackett the General Manager heads a list of 2 other Senior Managers, 3 Divisional Managers and a team of 10 coaches. They control what is known as the Select Group of Referees dealing with their fitness, performance, monitoring and improvement and game understanding of on-field management of players. They have fortnightly training sessions and meetings and work with 2 sports scientists as well as a host of medical back-ups. The FA's Head of Senior Referee Development is Neale Barry a former Premier League Referee who is charged principally with recruitment and retention of referees.

Steve Bennett (Kent) refereed the FA Cup Final in 2007 whilst Howard Webb (Yorks) was not only his Fourth Official for that game but also Refereed the 2007 Carling Cup Final.

KEN GOLDMAN

NATIONAL LIST OF REFEREES FOR SEASON 2007–08

Armstrong, P (Paul) – Berkshire
Atkinson, M (Martin) – W. Yorkshire
Attwell, SB (Stuart) – Warwickshire
Bates, A (Tony) – Staffordshire
Beeby, RJ (Richard) – Northamptonshire
Bennett, SG (Steve) – Kent
Booth, RJ (Russell) – Nottinghamshire
Boyeson, C (Carl) – E. Yorkshire
Bratt, SJ (Steve) – West Midlands
Clattenburg, M (Mark) – Tyne & Wear
Cook, SD (Steven) – Surrey
Crossley, PT (Phil) – Kent
Deadman, D (Darren) – Cambridgeshire
Dean, ML (Mike) – Wirral
Dorr, SJ (Steve) – Worcestershire
Dowd, P (Phil) – Staffordshire
Drysdale, D (Darren) – Lincolnshire
D'Urso, AP (Andy) – Essex
East, R (Roger) – Wiltshire
Evans, KG (Karl) – Gtr Manchester
Foster, D (David) – Tyne & Wear
Foy, CJ (Chris) – Merseyside
Friend, KA (Kevin) – Leicestershire
Graham F (Fred) – Essex
Haines, A (Andy) – Tyne & Wear
Hall, AR (Andy) – W. Midlands
Halsey, MR (Mark) – Lancashire
Haywood, M (Mark) – W. Yorkshire
Hegley, GK (Grant) – Hertfordshire
Hill, KD (Keith) – Hertfordshire
Horwood, GD (Graham) – Bedfordshire
Ilderton, EL (Eddie) – Tyne & Wear
Jones, MJ (Michael) – Cheshire
Joslin, PJ (Phil) – Nottinghamshire
Kettle, TM (Trevor) – Rutland
Knight, B (Barry) – Kent
Laws, G (Graham) – Tyne & Wear
Lee, R (Ray) – Essex
Lewis, GJ (Gary) – Cambridgeshire
Lewis, RL (Rob) – Shropshire
McDermid, D (Danny) – London
Marriner, AM (Andre) – W. Midlands
Mason, LS (Lee) – Lancashire
Mathieson, SW (Scott) – Cheshire
Mellin, PW (Paul) – Surrey
Miller, NS (Nigel) – Durham
Miller, P (Pat) – Bedfordshire
Moss, J (Jon) – W. Yorkshire
Oliver, CW (Clive) – Northumberland
Oliver, M (Michael) – Northumberland
Penn, AM (Andy) – W. Midlands
Penton, C (Clive) – Sussex
Pike, MS (Mike) – Cumbria
Probert, LW (Lee) – Wiltshire
Rennie, UD (Uriah) – S. Yorkshire
Riley, MA (Mike) – W. Yorkshire
Russell, MP (Mike) – Hertfordshire
Salisbury, G (Graham) – Lancashire
Shoebridge, RL (Rob) – Derbyshire
Singh, J (Jarnail) – Middlesex
Stroud, KP (Keith) – Hampshire
Styles, R (Rob) – Hampshire
Swarbrick, ND (Neil) – Lancashire
Tanner, SJ (Steve) – Somerset
Taylor, A (Anthony) – Gtr Manchester
Taylor, P (Paul) – Hertfordshire
Thorpe, M (Mike) – Suffolk
Walton, P (Peter) – Northamptonshire
Ward, GL (Gavin) – Surrey
Webb, HM (Howard) – S. Yorkshire
Webster, CH (Colin) – Tyne & Wear
Whitestone, D (Dean) – Northamptonshire
Wiley, AG (Alan) – Staffordshire
Williamson, IG (Iain) – Berkshire
Woolmer, KA (Andy) – Northamptonshire
Wright, KK (Kevin) – Cambridgeshire

ASSISTANT REFEREES

Artis, SG (Stephen) – Norfolk
Astley, MA (Mark) – Gtr Manchester
Atkin, W (Warren) – W. Sussex
Atkins, G (Graeme) – W. Yorkshire
Babski, DS (Dave) – Lincolnshire
Bannister, N (Nigel) – E. Yorkshire
Barnes, PW (Paul) – Cambridgeshire
Barratt, W (Wayne) – Worcestershire
Barrow, SJ (Simon) – Staffordshire
Beale, GA (Guy) – Somerset
Beck, SP (Simon) – Essex
Beevor, R (Richard) – Suffolk
Belbin, D (David) – Middlesex
Bennett, A (Andrew) – Devon
Bentley, IF (Ian) – Kent
Benton, DK (David) – S. Yorkshire
Berry, CJ (Carl) – Surrey
Beswick, G (Gary) – Co. Durham
Birkett, DJ (Dave) – Lincolnshire
Blackledge, M (Mike) – Cambridgeshire
Bond, DS (Darren) – Lancashire
Bramley, P (Philip) – W. Yorkshire
Brittain, GM (Gary) – S. Yorkshire
Brown, M (Mark) – E. Yorkshire
Brumwell, CA (Chris) – Cumbria
Bryan, DS (Dave) – Lincolnshire
Buck, D (David) – Kent
Bull, M (Michael) – Essex
Bull, W (William) – Hampshire
Burt, S (Stuart) – Northamptonshire
Burton, R (Roy) – Staffordshire
Bushell, DD (David) – London
Butler, AN (Andrew) – Lancashire
Cairns, MJ (Mike) – Somerset
Canadine, P (Paul) – S. Yorkshire
Cann, DJ (Darren) – Norfolk
Castle, S (Steve) – W. Midlands
Child, SA (Stephen) – Kent
Collin, J (Jake) – Merseyside
Comley, JG (Justin) – Berkshire
Cook, SJ (Steve) – Derbyshire
Cooke, SG (Stephen) – Nottinghamshire
Cooper, IJ (Ian) – Kent
Coote, DH (David) – Nottinghamshire
Cox, JL (James) – Worcestershire
Creighton, SW (Steve) – Berkshire
Cummins, SP (Steven) – Cheshire
Curry, PE (Paul) – Northumberland
Davies, A (Andy) – Hampshire
Davies, PP (Peter) – Cheshire
Denton, MJ (Michael) – Lancashire
Devine, JP (Jim) – Cleveland
Dexter, MC (Martin) – Leicestershire
Duncan, SAJ (Scott) – Tyne & Wear
Dunn, C (Carl) – Staffordshire
Evans, C (Craig) – Lincolnshire
Evans, IA (Ian) – W. Midlands
Evetts, GS (Gary) – Hertfordshire
Farries, J (John) – Oxfordshire
Fletcher, R (Russell) – Derbyshire
Flynn, J (John) – Wiltshire
Foley, MJ (Matt) – S. Yorkshire
Ford, D (Declan) – Leicestershire
Francis, CJ (Chris) – Cambridgeshire
Ganfield, RS (Ron) – Somerset
Garratt, AM (Andy) – W. Midlands
Gibbs, PN (Phil) – W. Midlands
George, M (Mike) – Norfolk
Gosling, IJ (Ian) – Kent
Graham, P (Paul) – Gtr Manchester
Green, RC (Russell) – Lancashire
Greenwood, AH (Alf) – Yorkshire
Grove, PJ (Peter) – W. Midlands
Grunnill, W (Wayne) – E. Yorkshire

Halliday, A (Andy) – London
Hambling, GS (Glenn) – Norfolk
Hamilton, IJ (Ian) – Gloucestershire
Handley, D (Darren) – Lancashire
Harrington, T (Tony) – Cleveland
Harwood, CN (Colin) – Gtr Manchester
Hay, J (John) – Lancashire
Haycock, KW (Ken) – W. Yorkshire
Hayto, JM (John) – Essex
Hendley, AR (Andy) – W. Midlands
Hewitt, RT (Richard) – N. Yorkshire
Heywood, M (Mark) – Cheshire
Hilton, G (Gary) – Lancashire
Hobbis, N (Nick) – W. Midlands
Holderness, BC (Barry) – Essex
Hooper, SA (Simon) – Wiltshire
Hopkins, JD (John) – Essex
Horton, AJ (Tony) – W. Midlands
Hutchinson, AD (Andrew) – Cheshire
Hutchinson, SM (Mark) – Nottinghamshire
Ihringova, A (Sasa) – Shropshire
Jerden, GJN (Gary) – Essex
Joyce, R (Ross) – Cleveland
Keane, PJ (Patrick) – W. Midlands
Kettlewell, PT (Paul) – Lancashire
Khatib, B (Billy) – Tyne & Wear
Kinseley, N (Nick) – Essex
Kirkup, PJ (Peter) – Northamptonshire
Knapp, SC (Simon) – S. Gloucestershire
Langford, O (Oliver) – W. Midlands
Laver, AA (Andrew) – Hampshire
Law, GC (Geoff) – Leicestershire
Lawson, KD (Keith) – Lincolnshire
Lawson, MR (Mark) – Northumberland
Ledger, S (Scott) – S. Yorkshire
Lennard, HW (Harry) – E. Sussex
Linington, JJ (James) – Isle of Wight
Long, SJ (Simon) – Suffolk
McCallum, DA (Dave) – Tyne & Wear
McCoy, MT (Michael) – Kent
McDonough, M (Mick – Tyne & Wear
McIntosh, WA (Wayne) – Lincolnshire
McLaughlin, M (Mathew) – Bedfordshire
Mackrell, EB (Eric) – Hampshire
Magill, JP (John) – Essex
Malone, B (Brendan) – Wiltshire
Margetts, DS (David) – Essex
Martin, PC (Paul) – Northamptonshire
Martin, RW (Rob) – S. Yorkshire
Mason, T (Tony) – Kent
Massey, T (Trevor) – Cheshire
Matadar, M (Mo) – Lancashire
Matthews, A (Adrian) – Wiltshire
Mattocks, KJ (Kevin) – Lancashire
Mellor, G (Glyn) – Derbyshire
Merchant, R (Rob) – Staffordshire
Metcalfe, RL (Lee) – Lancashire
Mohareb, D (Dean) – Cheshire
Mullarkey, M (Mike) – Devon
Murphy, ME (Michael) – W. Midlands
Murphy, N (Nigel) – Nottinghamshire
Naylor, D (Dave) – Nottinghamshire
Naylor, MA (Michael) – S. Yorkshire
Newbold, AM (Andrew) – Leicestershire
Newell, AC (Andy) – Lancashire
Nolan, I (Ian) – Lancashire
Norman, PV (Paul) – Dorset
Norris, P (Paul) – Cheshire
Pardoe, SA (Steve) – Cheshire
Parker, AR (Alan) – Derbyshire
Parry, B (Brian) – Co. Durham
Pawson, CL (Craig) – S. Yorkshire
Pearce, JE (John) – Norfolk
Phillips, D (David) – Sussex
Philpott, M (Mark) – Cornwall
Phipps, SJ (Stephen) – Oxfordshire
Pike, K (Kevin) – Dorset
Pollock, RM (Bob) – Merseyside
Porter, W (Wayne) – Lincolnshire
Procter-Green, SRM (Shaun) – Lincolnshire
Quinn, P (Peter) – Cleveland
Radford, N (Neil) – Worcestershire
Rayner, AE (Amy) – Leicestershire
Reeves, CL (Christopher) – E. Yorkshire
Richards, DC (Ceri) – Carmarthenshire
Richardson, D (David) – W. Yorkshire
Roberts, B (Bob) – Lancashire
Roberts, DJ (Danny) – Gtr Manchester
Rock, DK (David) – Hertfordshire
Rodda, A (Andrew – Devon
Ross, SJ (Stephen) – Lincolnshire
Rowbury, J (John) – Kent
Rowley, MD (Michael) – Berkshire
Rubery, SP (Steve) – Essex
Rushton, SJ (Steven) Staffordshire
Russell, GR (Geoff) – Northamptonshire
Sainsbury, A (Andrew) – Wiltshire
Saliy, O (Oleksandr) – London
Salt, RA (Richard) – N. Yorkshire
Sarginson, CD (Christopher) – Staffordshire
Scarr, IK (Ian) – W. Midlands
Scholes, MS (Mark) – Buckinghamshire
Scott, GD (Graham) – Oxfordshire
Scregg, AJ (Andrew) – Merseyside
Sharp, PR (Phil) – Hertfordshire
Sheffield, JA (Alan) – W. Midlands
Sheldrake, D (Darren) – Surrey
Siddall, I (Iain) – Lancashire
Simpson, J (Jeremy) – Lancashire
Simpson, P (Paul) – Co. Durham
Slaughter, A (Ashley) – Sussex
Smallwood, W (William) – Cheshire
Smedley, I (Ian) – Derbyshire
Smith, AN (Andrew) – W. Yorkshire
Smith, EI (Eamonn) – Surrey
Smith, N (Nigel) – Derbyshire
Smith, RH (Richard) – W. Midlands
Snartt, SP (Simon) – Gloucestershire
Stewart, M (Matt) – Essex
Stokes, JD (John) – Wirral
Storrie, D (David) – W. Yorkshire
Stott, GT (Gary) – Gtr Manchester
Street, DR (Duncan) – W. Yorkshire
Stretton, GS (Guy) – Leicestershire
Sutton, GJ (Gary) – Lincolnshire
Sutton, MA (Mark) – Derbyshire
Swabey, L (Lee) – Devon
Sygmuta, BC (Barry) – N. Yorkshire
Tattan, BJ (Brian) – Merseyside
Thompson, MF (Marvin) – Middlesex
Thompson, PI (Paul) – Derbyshire
Tierney, P (Paul) – Lancashire
Tincknell, SW (Steve) – Hertfordshire
Tingey, M (Mike) – Buckinghamshire
Tomlinson, SD (Stephen) – Hampshire
Turner, A (Andrew) – Devon
Turner, GB (Glenn) – Derbyshire
Tyas, J (Jason) – W. Yorkshire
Unsworth, D (David) – Gtr Manchester
Varley, PC (Paul) – W. Yorkshire
Vaughan, RG (Roger) – N. Somerset
Wallace, G (Garry) – Tyne & Wear
Waring, J (Jim) – Lancashire
Watts, AS (Adam) – Worcestershire
Waugh, J (Jock) – S. Yorkshire
Weaver, M (Mark) – W. Midlands
Webb, D (David) – Co. Durham
West, MG (Malcolm) – Cornwall
West, RJ (Richard) – E. Yorkshire
Whitton, RP (Rob) – Essex
Wigglesworth, RJ (Richard) – S. Yorkshire
Wilkinson, K (Keith) – Northumberland
Williams, MA (Andy) – Herefordshire
Woodward, IJ (Irvine) – E. Sussex
Yates, NA (Neil) – Lancashire
Yeo, KG (Keith) – Essex
Yerby, MS (Martin) – Kent
Young, GR (Gary) – Bedfordshire

THE THINGS THEY SAID . . .

Sir Alex Ferguson was quietly confident even before the season started:
"I am producing a team that will last years. When you have an old team maybe all the challenges have gone for them. But the youngsters have a hunger to achieve."

Notwithstanding that, the pre-season era had its problems left over from the World Cup with Cristiano Ronaldo and his alleged involvement with the dismissal of Wayne Rooney for England. An Old Trafford spokesman told the *Sunday People*:
"We don't yet know what will happen until Ronaldo actually arrives. The manager is playing things down and insists there won't be a problem either between Wayne or Cristiano or a security issue."

Portsmouth manager Harry Redknapp after Mark Taylor's wonder goal against Everton:
"He's scored from 45 yards . . . Bloody hell, I don't go that far on my holidays!"

Roy Keane on his appointment as manager of Sunderland:
"I haven't helped myself over the years with my image and that was part of the scene I had with Manchester United and Ireland. Maybe I was football mad. Maybe psycho is probably too strong a word, but football means a lot to me. It was like an acting job. I would drive up to Old Trafford for any game and I would turn into this mean machine."

Internacional coach Abel Braga on his motivation skills which enabled the Brazilians to win the World Club Championship in Tokyo beating Barcelona:
"We shut the players in a room for 15 minutes to get their spirits up."

Stuart Pearce on the eve of Manchester City playing and winning at West Ham, who had recently beaten Manchester United there:
"I think (Curbishley) has inherited a squad that, if you take the Bobby Moore era out, is certainly the best there has ever been."

On the 20th anniversary of Sir Alex Ferguson taking over at Old Trafford, Paul Scholes offered his personal opinion:
"Who knows how long he will go on? He is not looking any older and he still enjoys coming out of the training ground every day. He loves it even in the freezing cold."

Sir Alex on the same occasion with his own view of the period:
"I'm proud of what we've achieved here in 20 years. We've also done it the right way, the Manchester United way."

Aston Villa under new manager Martin O'Neill succeeded in remaining unbeaten longer than any other team in the Premiership during 2006–07. His opinion in September went this way;
"I'm disappointed we are not leading the league."

Liverpool manager Rafa Benitez commenting after Everton's goalless draw:
"Our team wanted to win, the other wanted not to lose. they put nine men behind the ball and played narrow and compact. That's what small clubs do when they come to Anfield."

Reading manager Steve Coppell getting his priorities right when picking his best player:
"Ronaldo is probably the player every manager in the league would like."

Portsmouth goalkeeper David James on beating David Seaman's record of 141 clean sheets in the Premier League:
"I'm delighted and feel proud. It was a tough game and to keep a clean sheet at Villa against my old club makes me very happy."

Sir Alex Ferguson on the growing confidence about the resting place of the championship in 2006–07 on the last day of April:
"The fans are starting to smell it and the players taste it."

Following the final score of Bolton Wanderers 1 Reading 3, Steve Coppell revealed his earlier anguish:
"At 1-0 down, I would have ripped someone's arm off for a point."

Adrian Boothroyd, manager of Watford after defeat at Arsenal's new Emirates Stadium headquarters:
"I want to come back here again next year – that's if Arsenal stay up!"

Harry Redknapp the Portsmouth manager with his finger on the statistics pulse as ever:
"Kanu's 47 years old but has six goals in eight games – it takes some doing."

Ashley Cole on the brink of leaving Arsenal for Chelsea:
"People think I am a greedy pig. But I am genuine. It's never been about money. For me it's about respect."

Despite losing the relegation battle against West Ham, Paul Jewell still had expectations for Wigan Athletic:
"It was a poor day at the office but we can still stay up."

West Ham, too, were faced with the daunting prospect of playing their last game away at Old Trafford against the newly crowned Premier League champions. Manager Alan Curbishley said:
"We need a result at United but we've given ourselves a chance."

While Chelsea were fighting for their lives at Arsenal, Sir Alex viewed the affair thus:
"I was twiddling my thumbs. I watched the last 15 minutes at the Emirates and was in agony, my heart was in my mouth. It was a great effort by Chelsea, we've got to give them great credit."

As the likelihood of Chelsea retaining their title appeared to be slipping away, Liverpool manager Rafa Benitez reflected:
"It will be really difficult for Chelsea. Last week they were talking about trophies, trophies, trophies, then one week later it's different. You can't change things by just talking."

Jose Mourinho singing the praises of his central defender Ricardo Carvalho after scoring against Tottenham Hotspur:
"Ricardo has been unbelievable this season. When all the players were out injured, he was there for us. And I could not be happier that he was the one to score today."

On the day West Ham United were knocked out of the FA Cup on their own ground by Watford, manager Alan Curbishley pointed to apparently insoluble problems:
"The problem is if we get in front or fall behind we seem to panic. It's a frustrating time at the moment."

FIFA head honcho Sepp Blatter pouring cold water on Gordon Brown's theory for the World Cup coming back to England in the not-too-distant future:
"I can understand the eagerness of the English FA supported by politicians to stage the finals, but it is not definite, the finals will come to Europe in 2018."

When events were making it harder and harder for Chelsea to be sure of retaining their Premier League title in February, manager Jose Mourinho was still Blue, through and through:
"Walk away? No chance. Zero. I would never do that to Chelsea, to my players to the supporters."

French born Arsene Wenger talking about foreigners in charge of English clubs:
"What was traditionally true in England is that the people who were the owners were the supporters. But that looks to be a period of the past. That was really reassuring for the fans because it looked that the heart of the owner was like their heart. It looks as if that period has gone."

While he was still manager of Bolton Wanderers, Sam Allardyce hit out at the BBC Panorama programme which alleged he was implicated in the "bungs" controversy:
"Those individuals never thought their lies would be exposed in the way that they have been and have apologised to me. As a result of their greed my good name has been tarnished by deceit and innuendo."

Carlos Queiroz, Sir Alex's assistant at Manchester United, extolling the virtures of evergreen Ryan Giggs:
"He is one of the best players I have seen in my life and he is one of the few players who have a right to a place in the history of the game."

Tottenham Hotspur manager Martin Jol on discovering what the ingredients are for a truly successful team:
"All we need to win the title is a couple of Rooneys."

Liverpool's new co-owner Tom Hicks, fresh from the USA:
"To feel the passion of a Premiership game and the noise – I found that very exciting."

Before he decided that his future was no longer in the Emerald Isle in charge of Northern Ireland, Lawrie Sanchez on his first thoughts at Fulham:
"Over the next couple of weeks, Fulham get to test-drive a manager and I get to see if I fancy it."

Arsenal manager Arsene Wenger was involved in more than his share of FA Cup replays during the season:
"I'd be happy to stop replays, but I don't think everybody would be."

Alan Curbishley explaining why he decided it was time to leave Charlton Athletic:
"I thought it had reached the point where even the fans needed a break from me. That's not a healthy situation."

Sir Clive Woodward talking about his contribution to football as a coach:
"I think football has been really good to me and when I look at Southampton now I think they are a far better club than they were when I arrived."

Glenn Roeder as manager of Newcastle United in some of the better days earlier on in the season for the Toon and two goals for Obi Martins against Watford:
"It's pleasing to see him score goals and they were magnificent finishes. It's nice to be proved right."

Before Tottenham Hotspur began their march towards a place in the UEFA Cup for 2007–08, Martin Jol pinpointed their problem:
"We must grow up if we went to do well. We must put this right."

Jose Mourinho the Special One at Chelsea in an interview reported in the *Daily Telegraph*:
"Roman Abramovich respects me and my opinions. I don't care about my image. I don't care about the consequences of what I say or do."

After a 2-0 victory at White Hart Lane against Tottenham Hostpur, Everton manager David Moyes was succinct in his appraisal:
"That was excellent, despite having ten men and having not won here for 21 years."

Swansea City's FA Cup giant-killing act against Premier League Sheffield United yielded this comment from their manager Kenny Jackett:
"Even though we were missing players, I thought we had a chance."

Gianfranco Zola, one of the best foreign ambassadors to play in English football:
"Italian football's best years were when we were allowed three foreigners per team."

Crack agent Pini Zahavi reacted furiously to the bung allegations in which his name was mentioned:
"I did so much for English football and I will not let them destroy my name."

Harry Redknapp on reaching – or maybe passing – the milestone of 1000 matches as a manager:
"They said it was 1000 for me against Sheffield United. Now I hear it's about 1030. When I first took over at Bournemouth all those years ago, I lost my first game 9-0 at Lincoln on a frozen pitch and they soon brought in somebody else."

Source: National Press.

ENGLISH LEAGUE HONOURS 1888 TO 2007

FA PREMIER LEAGUE

MAXIMUM POINTS: ***a*** **126;** ***b*** **114.**

**Won or placed on goal average (ratio), goal difference or most goals scored. ††Not promoted after play-offs.*

	First	*Pts*	*Second*	*Pts*	*Third*	*Pts*
1992–93*a*	Manchester U	84	Aston Villa	74	Norwich C	72
1993–94*a*	Manchester U	92	Blackburn R	84	Newcastle U	77
1994–95*a*	Blackburn R	89	Manchester U	88	Nottingham F	77
1995–96*b*	Manchester U	82	Newcastle U	78	Liverpool	71
1996–97*b*	Manchester U	75	Newcastle U*	68	Arsenal*	68
1997–98*b*	Arsenal	78	Manchester U	77	Liverpool	65
1998–99*b*	Manchester U	79	Arsenal	78	Chelsea	75
1999–2000*b*	Manchester U	91	Arsenal	73	Leeds U	69
2000–01	Manchester U	80	Arsenal	70	Liverpool	69
2001–02	Arsenal	87	Liverpool	80	Manchester U	77
2002–03	Manchester U	83	Arsenal	78	Newcastle U	69
2003–04	Arsenal	90	Chelsea	79	Manchester U	75
2004–05	Chelsea	95	Arsenal	83	Manchester U	77
2005–06	Chelsea	91	Manchester U	83	Liverpool	82
2006–07	Manchester U	89	Chelsea	83	Liverpool*	68

FOOTBALL LEAGUE CHAMPIONSHIP

MAXIMUM POINTS: 138

2004–05	Sunderland	94	Wigan Ath	87	Ipswich T††	85
2005–06	Reading	106	Sheffield U	90	Watford	81
2006–07	Sunderland	88	Birmingham C	86	Derby Co	84

FIRST DIVISION

MAXIMUM POINTS: 138

1992–93	Newcastle U	96	West Ham U*	88	Portsmouth††	88
1993–94	Crystal Palace	90	Nottingham F	83	Millwall††	74
1994–95	Middlesbrough	82	Reading††	79	Bolton W	77
1995–96	Sunderland	83	Derby Co	79	Crystal Palace††	75
1996–97	Bolton W	98	Barnsley	80	Wolverhampton W††	76
1997–98	Nottingham F	94	Middlesbrough	91	Sunderland††	90
1998–99	Sunderland	105	Bradford C	87	Ipswich T††	86
1999–2000	Charlton Ath	91	Manchester C	89	Ipswich T	87
2000–01	Fulham	101	Blackburn R	91	Bolton W	87
2001–02	Manchester C	99	WBA	89	Wolverhampton W††	86
2002–03	Portsmouth	98	Leicester C	92	Sheffield U††	80
2003–04	Norwich C	94	WBA	86	Sunderland††	79

FOOTBALL LEAGUE CHAMPIONSHIP 1

MAXIMUM POINTS: 138

2004–05	Luton T	98	Hull C	86	Tranmere R††	79
2005–06	Southend U	82	Colchester U	79	Brentford††	76
2006–07	Scunthorpe U	91	Bristol C	85	Blackpool	83

SECOND DIVISION

MAXIMUM POINTS: 138

1992–93	Stoke C	93	Bolton W	90	Port Vale††	89
1993–94	Reading	89	Port Vale	88	Plymouth Arg*††	85
1994–95	Birmingham C	89	Brentford††	85	Crewe Alex††	83
1995–96	Swindon T	92	Oxford U	83	Blackpool††	82
1996–97	Bury	84	Stockport Co	82	Luton T††	78
1997–98	Watford	88	Bristol C	85	Grimsby T	72
1998–99	Fulham	101	Walsall	87	Manchester C	82
1999–2000	Preston NE	95	Burnley	88	Gillingham	85
2000–01	Millwall	93	Rotherham U	91	Reading††	86
2001–02	Brighton & HA	90	Reading	84	Brentford*††	83
2002–03	Wigan Ath	100	Crewe Alex	86	Bristol C††	83
2003–04	Plymouth Arg	90	QPR	83	Bristol C††	82

FOOTBALL LEAGUE CHAMPIONSHIP 2

MAXIMUM POINTS: 138

2004–05	Yeovil T	83	Scunthorpe U*	80	Swansea C	80
2005–06	Carlisle U	86	Northampton T	83	Leyton Orient	81
2006–07	Walsall	89	Hartlepool U	88	Swindon T	85

THIRD DIVISION

MAXIMUM POINTS: ***a*** **126;** ***b*** **138.**

1992–93*a*	Cardiff C	83	Wrexham	80	Barnet	79
1993–94*a*	Shrewsbury T	79	Chester C	74	Crewe Alex	73
1994–95*a*	Carlisle U	91	Walsall	83	Chesterfield	81
1995–96*b*	Preston NE	86	Gillingham	83	Bury	79
1996–97*b*	Wigan Ath*	87	Fulham	87	Carlisle U	84
1997–98*b*	Notts Co	99	Macclesfield T	82	Lincoln C	72
1998–99*b*	Brentford	85	Cambridge U	81	Cardiff C	80
1999–2000*b*	Swansea C	85	Rotherham U	84	Northampton T	82
2000–01	Brighton & HA	92	Cardiff C	82	Chesterfield¶	80
2001–02	Plymouth Arg	102	Luton T	97	Mansfield T	79
2002–03	Rushden & D	87	Hartlepool U	85	Wrexham	84
2003–04	Doncaster R	92	Hull C	88	Torquay U*	81

¶9pts deducted for irregularities.

FOOTBALL LEAGUE

MAXIMUM POINTS: *a* 44; *b* 60

	First	Pts	Second	Pts	Third	Pts
1888–89*a*	Preston NE	40	Aston Villa	29	Wolverhampton W	28
1889–90*a*	Preston NE	33	Everton	31	Blackburn R	27
1890–91*a*	Everton	29	Preston NE	27	Notts Co	26
1891–92*b*	Sunderland	42	Preston NE	37	Bolton W	36

FIRST DIVISION to 1991–92

MAXIMUM POINTS: *a* 44; *b* 52; *c* 60; *d* 68; *e* 76; *f* 84; *g* 126; *h* 120; *k* 114.

	First	Pts	Second	Pts	Third	Pts
1892–93*c*	Sunderland	48	Preston NE	37	Everton	36
1893–94*c*	Aston Villa	44	Sunderland	38	Derby Co	36
1894–95*c*	Sunderland	47	Everton	42	Aston Villa	39
1895–96*c*	Aston Villa	45	Derby Co	41	Everton	39
1896–97*c*	Aston Villa	47	Sheffield U*	36	Derby Co	36
1897–98*c*	Sheffield U	42	Sunderland	37	Wolverhampton W*	35
1898–99*d*	Aston Villa	45	Liverpool	43	Burnley	39
1899–1900*d*	Aston Villa	50	Sheffield U	48	Sunderland	41
1900–01*d*	Liverpool	45	Sunderland	43	Notts Co	40
1901–02*d*	Sunderland	44	Everton	41	Newcastle U	37
1902–03*d*	The Wednesday	42	Aston Villa*	41	Sunderland	41
1903–04*d*	The Wednesday	47	Manchester C	44	Everton	43
1904–05*d*	Newcastle U	48	Everton	47	Manchester C	46
1905–06*e*	Liverpool	51	Preston NE	47	The Wednesday	44
1906–07*e*	Newcastle U	51	Bristol C	48	Everton*	45
1907–08*e*	Manchester U	52	Aston Villa*	43	Manchester C	43
1908–09*e*	Newcastle U	53	Everton	46	Sunderland	44
1909–10*e*	Aston Villa	53	Liverpool	48	Blackburn R*	45
1910–11*e*	Manchester U	52	Aston Villa	51	Sunderland*	45
1911–12*e*	Blackburn R	49	Everton	46	Newcastle U	44
1912–13*e*	Sunderland	54	Aston Villa	50	Sheffield W	49
1913–14*e*	Blackburn R	51	Aston Villa	44	Middlesbrough*	43
1914–15*e*	Everton	46	Oldham Ath	45	Blackburn R*	43
1919–20*f*	WBA	60	Burnley	51	Chelsea	49
1920–21*f*	Burnley	59	Manchester C	54	Bolton W	52
1921–22*f*	Liverpool	57	Tottenham H	51	Burnley	49
1922–23*f*	Liverpool	60	Sunderland	54	Huddersfield T	53
1923–24*f*	Huddersfield T*	57	Cardiff C	57	Sunderland	53
1924–25*f*	Huddersfield T	58	WBA	56	Bolton W	55
1925–26*f*	Huddersfield T	57	Arsenal	52	Sunderland	48
1926–27*f*	Newcastle U	56	Huddersfield T	51	Sunderland	49
1927–28*f*	Everton	53	Huddersfield T	51	Leicester C	48
1928–29*f*	Sheffield W	52	Leicester C	51	Aston Villa	50
1929–30*f*	Sheffield W	60	Derby Co	50	Manchester C*	47
1930–31*f*	Arsenal	66	Aston Villa	59	Sheffield W	52
1931–32*f*	Everton	56	Arsenal	54	Sheffield W	50
1932–33*f*	Arsenal	58	Aston Villa	54	Sheffield W	51
1933–34*f*	Arsenal	59	Huddersfield T	56	Tottenham H	49
1934–35*f*	Arsenal	58	Sunderland	54	Sheffield W	49
1935–36*f*	Sunderland	56	Derby Co*	48	Huddersfield T	48
1936–37*f*	Manchester C	57	Charlton Ath	54	Arsenal	52
1937–38*f*	Arsenal	52	Wolverhampton W	51	Preston NE	49
1938–39*f*	Everton	59	Wolverhampton W	55	Charlton Ath	50
1946–47*f*	Liverpool	57	Manchester U*	56	Wolverhampton W	56
1947–48*f*	Arsenal	59	Manchester U*	52	Burnley	52
1948–49*f*	Portsmouth	58	Manchester U*	53	Derby Co	53
1949–50*f*	Portsmouth*	53	Wolverhampton W	53	Sunderland	52
1950–51*f*	Tottenham H	60	Manchester U	56	Blackpool	50
1951–52*f*	Manchester U	57	Tottenham H*	53	Arsenal	53
1952–53*f*	Arsenal*	54	Preston NE	54	Wolverhampton W	51
1953–54*f*	Wolverhampton W	57	WBA	53	Huddersfield T	51
1954–55*f*	Chelsea	52	Wolverhampton W*	48	Portsmouth*	48
1955–56*f*	Manchester U	60	Blackpool*	49	Wolverhampton W	49
1956–57*f*	Manchester U	64	Tottenham H*	56	Preston NE	56
1957–58*f*	Wolverhampton W	64	Preston NE	59	Tottenham H	51
1958–59*f*	Wolverhampton W	61	Manchester U	55	Arsenal*	50
1959–60*f*	Burnley	55	Wolverhampton W	54	Tottenham H	53
1960–61*f*	Tottenham H	66	Sheffield W	58	Wolverhampton W	57
1961–62*f*	Ipswich T	56	Burnley	53	Tottenham H	52
1962–63*f*	Everton	61	Tottenham H	55	Burnley	54
1963–64*f*	Liverpool	57	Manchester U	53	Everton	52
1964–65*f*	Manchester U*	61	Leeds U	61	Chelsea	56
1965–66*f*	Liverpool	61	Leeds U*	55	Burnley	55
1966–67*f*	Manchester U	60	Nottingham F*	56	Tottenham H	56
1967–68*f*	Manchester C	58	Manchester U	56	Liverpool	55
1968–69*f*	Leeds U	67	Liverpool	61	Everton	57
1969–70*f*	Everton	66	Leeds U	57	Chelsea	55
1970–71*f*	Arsenal	65	Leeds U	64	Tottenham H*	52
1971–72*f*	Derby Co	58	Leeds U*	57	Liverpool*	57
1972–73*f*	Liverpool	60	Arsenal	57	Leeds U	53
1973–74*f*	Leeds U	62	Liverpool	57	Derby Co	48
1974–75*f*	Derby Co	53	Liverpool*	51	Ipswich T	51
1975–76*f*	Liverpool	60	QPR	59	Manchester U	56
1976–77*f*	Liverpool	57	Manchester C	56	Ipswich T	52
1977–78*f*	Nottingham F	64	Liverpool	57	Everton	55

	First	Pts	Second	Pts	Third	Pts
1978–79*f*	Liverpool	68	Nottingham F	60	WBA	59
1979–80*f*	Liverpool	60	Manchester U	58	Ipswich T	52
1980–81*f*	Aston Villa	60	Ipswich T	56	Arsenal	53
1981–82*g*	Liverpool	87	Ipswich T	83	Manchester U	78
1982–83*g*	Liverpool	82	Watford	71	Manchester U	70
1983–84*g*	Liverpool	80	Southampton	77	Nottingham F*	74
1984–85*g*	Everton	90	Liverpool*	77	Tottenham H	77
1985–86*g*	Liverpool	88	Everton	86	West Ham U	84
1986–87*g*	Everton	86	Liverpool	77	Tottenham H	71
1987–88*h*	Liverpool	90	Manchester U	81	Nottingham F	73
1988–89*k*	Arsenal*	76	Liverpool	76	Nottingham F	64
1989–90*k*	Liverpool	79	Aston Villa	70	Tottenham H	63
1990–91*k*	Arsenal†	83	Liverpool	76	Crystal Palace	69
1991–92*g*	Leeds U	82	Manchester U	78	Sheffield W	75

No official competition during 1915–19 and 1939–46; Regional Leagues operated. †2 pts deducted.

SECOND DIVISION to 1991–92

MAXIMUM POINTS: ***a*** **44;** ***b*** **56;** ***c*** **60;** ***d*** **68;** ***e*** **76;** ***f*** **84;** ***g*** **126;** ***h*** **132;** ***k*** **138.**

	First	Pts	Second	Pts	Third	Pts
1892–93*a*	Small Heath	36	Sheffield U	35	Darwen	30
1893–94*b*	Liverpool	50	Small Heath	42	Notts Co	39
1894–95*c*	Bury	48	Notts Co	39	Newton Heath*	38
1895–96*c*	Liverpool*	46	Manchester C	46	Grimsby T*	42
1896–97*c*	Notts Co	42	Newton Heath	39	Grimsby T	38
1897–98*c*	Burnley	48	Newcastle U	45	Manchester C	39
1898–99*d*	Manchester C	52	Glossop NE	46	Leicester Fosse	45
1899–1900*d*	The Wednesday	54	Bolton W	52	Small Heath	46
1900–01*d*	Grimsby T	49	Small Heath	48	Burnley	44
1901–02*d*	WBA	55	Middlesbrough	51	Preston NE*	42
1902–03*d*	Manchester C	54	Small Heath	51	Woolwich A	48
1903–04*d*	Preston NE	50	Woolwich A	49	Manchester U	48
1904–05*d*	Liverpool	58	Bolton W	56	Manchester U	53
1905–06*e*	Bristol C	66	Manchester U	62	Chelsea	53
1906–07*e*	Nottingham F	60	Chelsea	57	Leicester Fosse	48
1907–08*e*	Bradford C	54	Leicester Fosse	52	Oldham Ath	50
1908–09*e*	Bolton W	52	Tottenham H*	51	WBA	51
1909–10*e*	Manchester C	54	Oldham Ath*	53	Hull C*	53
1910–11*e*	WBA	53	Bolton W	51	Chelsea	49
1911–12*e*	Derby Co*	54	Chelsea	54	Burnley	52
1912–13*e*	Preston NE	53	Burnley	50	Birmingham	46
1913–14*e*	Notts Co	53	Bradford PA*	49	Woolwich A	49
1914–15*e*	Derby Co	53	Preston NE	50	Barnsley	47
1919–20*f*	Tottenham H	70	Huddersfield T	64	Birmingham	56
1920–21*f*	Birmingham*	58	Cardiff C	58	Bristol C	51
1921–22*f*	Nottingham F	56	Stoke C*	52	Barnsley	52
1922–23*f*	Notts Co	53	West Ham U*	51	Leicester C	51
1923–24*f*	Leeds U	54	Bury*	51	Derby Co	51
1924–25*f*	Leicester C	59	Manchester U	57	Derby Co	55
1925–26*f*	Sheffield W	60	Derby Co	57	Chelsea	52
1926–27*f*	Middlesbrough	62	Portsmouth*	54	Manchester C	54
1927–28*f*	Manchester C	59	Leeds U	57	Chelsea	54
1928–29*f*	Middlesbrough	55	Grimsby T	53	Bradford PA*	48
1929–30*f*	Blackpool	58	Chelsea	55	Oldham Ath	53
1930–31*f*	Everton	61	WBA	54	Tottenham H	51
1931–32*f*	Wolverhampton W	56	Leeds U	54	Stoke C	52
1932–33*f*	Stoke C	56	Tottenham H	55	Fulham	50
1933–34*f*	Grimsby T	59	Preston NE	52	Bolton W*	51
1934–35*f*	Brentford	61	Bolton W*	56	West Ham U	56
1935–36*f*	Manchester U	56	Charlton Ath	55	Sheffield U*	52
1936–37*f*	Leicester C	56	Blackpool	55	Bury	52
1937–38*f*	Aston Villa	57	Manchester U*	53	Sheffield U	53
1938–39*f*	Blackburn R	55	Sheffield U	54	Sheffield W	53
1946–47*f*	Manchester C	62	Burnley	58	Birmingham C	55
1947–48*f*	Birmingham C	59	Newcastle U	56	Southampton	52
1948–49*f*	Fulham	57	WBA	56	Southampton	55
1949–50*f*	Tottenham H	61	Sheffield W*	52	Sheffield U*	52
1950–51*f*	Preston NE	57	Manchester C	52	Cardiff C	50
1951–52*f*	Sheffield W	53	Cardiff C*	51	Birmingham C	51
1952–53*f*	Sheffield U	60	Huddersfield T	58	Luton T	52
1953–54*f*	Leicester C*	56	Everton	56	Blackburn R	55
1954–55*f*	Birmingham C*	54	Luton T*	54	Rotherham U	54
1955–56*f*	Sheffield W	55	Leeds U	52	Liverpool*	48
1956–57*f*	Leicester C	61	Nottingham F	54	Liverpool	53
1957–58*f*	West Ham U	57	Blackburn R	56	Charlton Ath	55
1958–59*f*	Sheffield W	62	Fulham	60	Sheffield U*	53
1959–60*f*	Aston Villa	59	Cardiff C	58	Liverpool*	50
1960–61*f*	Ipswich T	59	Sheffield U	58	Liverpool	52
1961–62*f*	Liverpool	62	Leyton Orient	54	Sunderland	53
1962–63*f*	Stoke C	53	Chelsea*	52	Sunderland	52
1963–64*f*	Leeds U	63	Sunderland	61	Preston NE	56
1964–65*f*	Newcastle U	57	Northampton T	56	Bolton W	50
1965–66*f*	Manchester C	59	Southampton	54	Coventry C	53
1966–67*f*	Coventry C	59	Wolverhampton W	58	Carlisle U	52
1967–68*f*	Ipswich T	59	QPR*	58	Blackpool	58

	First	Pts	Second	Pts	Third	Pts
1968–69*f*	Derby Co	63	Crystal Palace	56	Charlton Ath	50
1969–70*f*	Huddersfield T	60	Blackpool	53	Leicester C	51
1970–71*f*	Leicester C	59	Sheffield U	56	Cardiff C*	53
1971–72*f*	Norwich C	57	Birmingham C	56	Millwall	55
1972–73*f*	Burnley	62	QPR	61	Aston Villa	50
1973–74*f*	Middlesbrough	65	Luton T	50	Carlisle U	49
1974–75*f*	Manchester U	61	Aston Villa	58	Norwich C	53
1975–76*f*	Sunderland	56	Bristol C*	53	WBA	53
1976–77*f*	Wolverhampton W	57	Chelsea	55	Nottingham F	52
1977–78*f*	Bolton W	58	Southampton	57	Tottenham H*	56
1978–79*f*	Crystal Palace	57	Brighton & HA*	56	Stoke C	56
1979–80*f*	Leicester C	55	Sunderland	54	Birmingham C*	53
1980–81*f*	West Ham U	66	Notts Co	53	Swansea C*	50
1981–82*g*	Luton T	88	Watford	80	Norwich C	71
1982–83*g*	QPR	85	Wolverhampton W	75	Leicester C	70
1983–84*g*	Chelsea*	88	Sheffield W	88	Newcastle U	80
1984–85*g*	Oxford U	84	Birmingham C	82	Manchester C	74
1985–86*g*	Norwich C	84	Charlton Ath	77	Wimbledon	76
1986–87*g*	Derby Co	84	Portsmouth	78	Oldham Ath††	75
1987–88*h*	Millwall	82	Aston Villa*	78	Middlesbrough	78
1988–89*k*	Chelsea	99	Manchester C	82	Crystal Palace	81
1989–90*k*	Leeds U*	85	Sheffield U	85	Newcastle U††	80
1990–91*k*	Oldham Ath	88	West Ham U	87	Sheffield W	82
1991–92*k*	Ipswich T	84	Middlesbrough	80	Derby Co	78

No official competition during 1915–19 and 1939–46; Regional Leagues operated.

THIRD DIVISION to 1991–92

MAXIMUM POINTS: 92; 138 FROM 1981–82.

	First	Pts	Second	Pts	Third	Pts
1958–59	Plymouth Arg	62	Hull C	61	Brentford*	57
1959–60	Southampton	61	Norwich C	59	Shrewsbury T*	52
1960–61	Bury	68	Walsall	62	QPR	60
1961–62	Portsmouth	65	Grimsby T	62	Bournemouth*	59
1962–63	Northampton T	62	Swindon T	58	Port Vale	54
1963–64	Coventry C*	60	Crystal Palace	60	Watford	58
1964–65	Carlisle U	60	Bristol C*	59	Mansfield T	59
1965–66	Hull C	69	Millwall	65	QPR	57
1966–67	QPR	67	Middlesbrough	55	Watford	54
1967–68	Oxford U	57	Bury	56	Shrewsbury T	55
1968–69	Watford*	64	Swindon T	64	Luton T	61
1969–70	Orient	62	Luton T	60	Bristol R	56
1970–71	Preston NE	61	Fulham	60	Halifax T	56
1971–72	Aston Villa	70	Brighton & HA	65	Bournemouth*	62
1972–73	Bolton W	61	Notts Co	57	Blackburn R	55
1973–74	Oldham Ath	62	Bristol R*	61	York C	61
1974–75	Blackburn R	60	Plymouth Arg	59	Charlton Ath	55
1975–76	Hereford U	63	Cardiff C	57	Millwall	56
1976–77	Mansfield T	64	Brighton & HA	61	Crystal Palace*	59
1977–78	Wrexham	61	Cambridge U	58	Preston NE*	56
1978–79	Shrewsbury T	61	Watford*	60	Swansea C	60
1979–80	Grimsby T	62	Blackburn R	59	Sheffield W	58
1980–81	Rotherham U	61	Barnsley*	59	Charlton Ath	59
1981–82	Burnley*	80	Carlisle U	80	Fulham	78
1982–83	Portsmouth	91	Cardiff C	86	Huddersfield T	82
1983–84	Oxford U	95	Wimbledon	87	Sheffield U*	83
1984–85	Bradford C	94	Millwall	90	Hull C	87
1985–86	Reading	94	Plymouth Arg	87	Derby Co	84
1986–87	Bournemouth	97	Middlesbrough	94	Swindon T	87
1987–88	Sunderland	93	Brighton & HA	84	Walsall	82
1988–89	Wolverhampton W	92	Sheffield U*	84	Port Vale	84
1989–90	Bristol R	93	Bristol C	91	Notts Co	87
1990–91	Cambridge U	86	Southend U	85	Grimsby T*	83
1991–92	Brentford	82	Birmingham C	81	Huddersfield T	78

FOURTH DIVISION (1958–1992)

MAXIMUM POINTS: 92; 138 FROM 1981–82.

	First	Pts	Second	Pts	Third	Pts	Fourth	Pts
1958–59	Port Vale	64	Coventry C*	60	York C	60	Shrewsbury T	58
1959–60	Walsall	65	Notts Co*	60	Torquay U	60	Watford	57
1960–61	Peterborough U	66	Crystal Palace	64	Northampton T*	60	Bradford PA	60
1961–62†	Millwall	56	Colchester U	55	Wrexham	53	Carlisle U	52
1962–63	Brentford	62	Oldham Ath*	59	Crewe Alex	59	Mansfield T*	57
1963–64	Gillingham*	60	Carlisle U	60	Workington	59	Exeter C	58
1964–65	Brighton & HA	63	Millwall*	62	York C	62	Oxford U	61
1965–66	Doncaster R*	59	Darlington	59	Torquay U	58	Colchester U*	56
1966–67	Stockport Co	64	Southport*	59	Barrow	59	Tranmere R	58
1967–68	Luton T	66	Barnsley	61	Hartlepools U	60	Crewe Alex	58
1968–69	Doncaster R	59	Halifax T	57	Rochdale*	56	Bradford C	56
1969–70	Chesterfield	64	Wrexham	61	Swansea C	60	Port Vale	59
1970–71	Notts Co	69	Bournemouth	60	Oldham Ath	59	York C	56
1971–72	Grimsby T	63	Southend U	60	Brentford	59	Scunthorpe U	57
1972–73	Southport	62	Hereford U	58	Cambridge U	57	Aldershot*	56
1973–74	Peterborough U	65	Gillingham	62	Colchester U	60	Bury	59

	First	*Pts*	*Second*	*Pts*	*Third*	*Pts*	*Fourth*	*Pts*
1974–75	Mansfield T	68	Shrewsbury T	62	Rotherham U	59	Chester*	57
1975–76	Lincoln C	74	Northampton T	68	Reading	60	Tranmere R	58
1976–77	Cambridge U	65	Exeter C	62	Colchester U*	59	Bradford C	59
1977–78	Watford	71	Southend U	60	Swansea C*	56	Brentford	56
1978–79	Reading	65	Grimsby T*	61	Wimbledon*	61	Barnsley	61
1979–80	Huddersfield T	66	Walsall	64	Newport Co	61	Portsmouth*	60
1980–81	Southend U	67	Lincoln C	65	Doncaster R	56	Wimbledon	55
1981–82	Sheffield U	96	Bradford C*	91	Wigan Ath	91	Bournemouth	88
1982–83	Wimbledon	98	Hull C	90	Port Vale	88	Scunthorpe U	83
1983–84	York C	101	Doncaster R	85	Reading*	82	Bristol C	82
1984–85	Chesterfield	91	Blackpool	86	Darlington	85	Bury	84
1985–86	Swindon T	102	Chester C	84	Mansfield T	81	Port Vale	79
1986–87	Northampton T	99	Preston NE	90	Southend U	80	Wolverhampton W††	79
1987–88	Wolverhampton W	90	Cardiff C	85	Bolton W	78	Scunthorpe U††	77
1988–89	Rotherham U	82	Tranmere R	80	Crewe Alex	78	Scunthorpe U††	77
1989–90	Exeter C	89	Grimsby T	79	Southend U	75	Stockport Co††	74
1990–91	Darlington	83	Stockport Co*	82	Hartlepool U	82	Peterborough U	80
1991–92†*	Burnley	83	Rotherham U*	77	Mansfield T	77	Blackpool	76

†*Maximum points:* 88 owing to Accrington Stanley's resignation.
†**Maximum points:* 126 owing to Aldershot being expelled (and only 23 teams started the competition).

THIRD DIVISION—SOUTH (1920–1958)

1920–21 SEASON AS THIRD DIVISION. MAXIMUM POINTS: *a* 84; *b* 92.

	First	*Pts*	*Second*	*Pts*	*Third*	*Pts*
1920–21*a*	Crystal Palace	59	Southampton	54	QPR	53
1921–22*a*	Southampton*	61	Plymouth Arg	61	Portsmouth	53
1922–23*a*	Bristol C	59	Plymouth Arg*	53	Swansea T	53
1923–24*a*	Portsmouth	59	Plymouth Arg	55	Millwall	54
1924–25*a*	Swansea T	57	Plymouth Arg	56	Bristol C	53
1925–26*a*	Reading	57	Plymouth Arg	56	Millwall	53
1926–27*a*	Bristol C	62	Plymouth Arg	60	Millwall	56
1927–28*a*	Millwall	65	Northampton T	55	Plymouth Arg	53
1928–29*a*	Charlton Ath*	54	Crystal Palace	54	Northampton T*	52
1929–30*a*	Plymouth Arg	68	Brentford	61	QPR	51
1930–31*a*	Notts Co	59	Crystal Palace	51	Brentford	50
1931–32*a*	Fulham	57	Reading	55	Southend U	53
1932–33*a*	Brentford	62	Exeter C	58	Norwich C	57
1933–34*a*	Norwich C	61	Coventry C*	54	Reading*	54
1934–35*a*	Charlton Ath	61	Reading	53	Coventry C	51
1935–36*a*	Coventry C	57	Luton T	56	Reading	54
1936–37*a*	Luton T	58	Notts Co	56	Brighton & HA	53
1937–38*a*	Millwall	56	Bristol C	55	QPR*	53
1938–39*a*	Newport Co	55	Crystal Palace	52	Brighton & HA	49
1939–46	Competition cancelled owing to war. Regional Leagues operated.					
1946–47*a*	Cardiff C	66	QPR	57	Bristol C	51
1947–48*a*	QPR	61	Bournemouth	57	Walsall	51
1948–49*a*	Swansea T	62	Reading	55	Bournemouth	52
1949–50*a*	Notts Co	58	Northampton T*	51	Southend U	51
1950–51*b*	Nottingham F	70	Norwich C	64	Reading*	57
1951–52*b*	Plymouth Arg	66	Reading*	61	Norwich C	61
1952–53*b*	Bristol R	64	Millwall*	62	Northampton T	62
1953–54*b*	Ipswich T	64	Brighton & HA	61	Bristol C	56
1954–55*b*	Bristol C	70	Leyton Orient	61	Southampton	59
1955–56*b*	Leyton Orient	66	Brighton & HA	65	Ipswich T	64
1956–57*b*	Ipswich T*	59	Torquay U	59	Colchester U	58
1957–58*b*	Brighton & HA	60	Brentford*	58	Plymouth Arg	58

THIRD DIVISION—NORTH (1921–1958)

MAXIMUM POINTS: *a* 76; *b* 84; *c* 80; *d* 92.

	First	*Pts*	*Second*	*Pts*	*Third*	*Pts*
1921–22*a*	Stockport Co	56	Darlington*	50	Grimsby T	50
1922–23*a*	Nelson	51	Bradford PA	47	Walsall	46
1923–24*b*	Wolverhampton W	63	Rochdale	62	Chesterfield	54
1924–25*b*	Darlington	58	Nelson*	53	New Brighton	53
1925–26*b*	Grimsby T	61	Bradford PA	60	Rochdale	59
1926–27*b*	Stoke C	63	Rochdale	58	Bradford PA	55
1927–28*b*	Bradford PA	63	Lincoln C	55	Stockport Co	54
1928–29*b*	Bradford C	63	Stockport Co	62	Wrexham	52
1929–30*b*	Port Vale	67	Stockport Co	63	Darlington*	50
1930–31*b*	Chesterfield	58	Lincoln C	57	Wrexham*	54
1931–32*c*	Lincoln C*	57	Gateshead	57	Chester	50
1932–33*b*	Hull C	59	Wrexham	57	Stockport Co	54
1933–34*b*	Barnsley	62	Chesterfield	61	Stockport Co	59
1934–35*b*	Doncaster R	57	Halifax T	55	Chester	54
1935–36*b*	Chesterfield	60	Chester*	55	Tranmere R	55
1936–37*b*	Stockport Co	60	Lincoln C	57	Chester	53
1937–38*b*	Tranmere R	56	Doncaster R	54	Hull C	53
1938–39*b*	Barnsley	67	Doncaster R	56	Bradford C	52
1939–46	Competition cancelled owing to war. Regional Leagues operated.					
1946–47*b*	Doncaster R	72	Rotherham U	60	Chester	56
1947–48*b*	Lincoln C	60	Rotherham U	59	Wrexham	50
1948–49*b*	Hull C	65	Rotherham U	62	Doncaster R	50
1949–50*b*	Doncaster R	55	Gateshead	53	Rochdale*	51
1950–51*d*	Rotherham U	71	Mansfield T	64	Carlisle U	62

	First	*Pts*	*Second*	*Pts*	*Third*	*Pts*
1951–52*d*	Lincoln C	69	Grimsby T	66	Stockport Co	59
1952–53*d*	Oldham Ath	59	Port Vale	58	Wrexham	56
1953–54*d*	Port Vale	69	Barnsley	58	Scunthorpe U	57
1954–55*d*	Barnsley	65	Accrington S	61	Scunthorpe U*	58
1955–56*d*	Grimsby T	68	Derby Co	63	Accrington S	59
1956–57*d*	Derby Co	63	Hartlepools U	59	Accrington S*	58
1957–58*d*	Scunthorpe U	66	Accrington S	59	Bradford C	57

PROMOTED AFTER PLAY-OFFS

(NOT ACCOUNTED FOR IN PREVIOUS SECTION)

1986–87 Aldershot to Division 3.
1987–88 Swansea C to Division 3.
1988–89 Leyton Orient to Division 3.
1989–90 Sunderland to Division 1; Notts Co to Division 2; Cambridge U to Division 3.
1990–91 Notts Co to Division 1; Tranmere R to Division 2; Torquay U to Division 3.
1991–92 Blackburn R to Premier League; Peterborough U to Division 1.
1992–93 Swindon T to Premier League; WBA to Division 1; York C to Division 2.
1993–94 Leicester C to Premier League; Burnley to Division 1; Wycombe W to Division 2.
1994–95 Huddersfield T to Division 1.
1995–96 Leicester C to Premier League; Bradford C to Division 1; Plymouth Arg to Division 2.
1996–97 Crystal Palace to Premier League; Crewe Alex to Division 1; Northampton T to Division 2.
1997–98 Charlton Ath to Premier League; Colchester U to Division 2.
1998–99 Watford to Premier League; Scunthorpe U to Division 2.
1999–2000 Peterborough U to Division 2
2000–01 Walsall to Division 1; Blackpool to Division 2
2001–02 Birmingham C to Premier League; Stoke C to Division 1; Cheltenham T to Division 2
2002–03 Wolverhampton W to Premier League; Cardiff C to Division 1; Bournemouth to Division 2
2003–04 Crystal Palace to Premier League; Brighton & HA to Division 1; Huddersfield T to Division 2
2004–05 West Ham U to Premier League; Sheffield W to Championship; Southend U to Championship 1
2005–06 Watford to Premier League; Barnsley to Championship; Cheltenham T to Championship 1
2006–07 Derby Co to Premier League; Blackpool to Championship; Bristol R to Championship 1

LEAGUE TITLE WINS

FA PREMIER LEAGUE – Manchester U 9, Arsenal 3, Chelsea 2, Blackburn R 1.

FOOTBALL LEAGUE CHAMPIONSHIP – Sunderland 2, Reading 1.

LEAGUE DIVISION 1 – Liverpool 18, Arsenal 10, Everton 9, Sunderland 8, Aston Villa 7, Manchester U 7, Newcastle U 5, Sheffield W 4, Huddersfield T 3, Leeds U 3, Manchester C 3, Portsmouth 3, Wolverhampton W 3, Blackburn R 2, Burnley 2, Derby Co 2, Nottingham F 2, Preston NE 2, Tottenham H 2; Bolton W, Charlton Ath, Chelsea, Crystal Palace, Fulham, Ipswich T, Middlesbrough, Norwich C, Sheffield U, WBA 1 each.

FOOTBALL LEAGUE CHAMPIONSHIP 1 – Luton T 1, Scunthorpe U 1, Southend U 1.

LEAGUE DIVISION 2 – Leicester C 6, Manchester C 6, Birmingham C (one as Small Heath) 5, Sheffield W 5, Derby Co 4, Liverpool 4, Preston NE 4, Ipswich T 3, Leeds U 3, Middlesbrough 3, Notts Co 3, Stoke C 3, Aston Villa 2, Bolton W 2, Burnley 2, Bury 2, Chelsea 2, Fulham 2, Grimsby T 2, Manchester U 2, Millwall 2, Norwich C 2, Nottingham F 2, Tottenham H 2, WBA 2, West Ham U 2, Wolverhampton W 2; Blackburn R, Blackpool, Bradford C, Brentford, Brighton & HA, Bristol C, Coventry C, Crystal Palace, Everton, Huddersfield T, Luton T, Newcastle U, QPR, Oldham Ath, Oxford U, Plymouth Arg, Reading, Sheffield U, Sunderland, Swindon T, Watford, Wigan Ath 1 each.

FOOTBALL LEAGUE CHAMPIONSHIP 2 – Carlisle U 1, Walsall 1, Yeovil T 1.

LEAGUE DIVISION 3 – Brentford 2, Carlisle U 2, Oxford U 2, Plymouth Arg 2, Portsmouth 2, Preston NE 2, Shrewsbury T 2; Aston Villa, Blackburn R, Bolton W, Bournemouth, Bradford C, Brighton & HA, Bristol R, Burnley, Bury, Cambridge U, Cardiff C, Coventry C, Doncaster R. Grimsby T, Hereford U, Hull C, Leyton Orient, Mansfield T, Northampton T, Notts Co, Oldham Ath, QPR, Reading, Rotherham U, Rushden & D Southampton, Sunderland, Swansea C, Watford, Wigan Ath, Wolverhampton W, Wrexham 1 each.

LEAGUE DIVISION 4 – Chesterfield 2, Doncaster R 2, Peterborough U 2; Brentford, Brighton & HA, Burnley, Cambridge U, Darlington, Exeter C, Gillingham, Grimsby T, Huddersfield T, Lincoln C, Luton T, Mansfield T, Millwall, Northampton T, Notts Co, Port Vale, Reading, Rotherham U, Sheffield U, Southend U, Southport, Stockport Co, Swindon T, Walsall, Watford, Wimbledon, Wolverhampton W, York C 1 each.

TO 1957–58

DIVISION 3 (South) – Bristol C 3, Charlton Ath 2, Ipswich T 2, Millwall 2, Notts Co 2, Plymouth Arg 2, Swansea T 2; Brentford, Brighton & HA, Bristol R, Cardiff C, Coventry C, Crystal Palace, Fulham, Leyton Orient, Luton T, Newport Co, Norwich C, Nottingham F, Portsmouth, QPR, Reading, Southampton 1 each.

DIVISION 3 (North) – Barnsley 3, Doncaster R 3, Lincoln C 3, Chesterfield 2, Grimsby T 2, Hull C 2, Port Vale 2, Stockport Co 2; Bradford C, Bradford PA, Darlington, Derby Co, Nelson, Oldham Ath, Rotherham U, Scunthorpe U, Stoke C, Tranmere R, Wolverhampton W 1 each.

RELEGATED CLUBS

1891–92 League extended. Newton Heath, Sheffield W and Nottingham F admitted. *Second Division formed* including Darwen.
1892–93 In Test matches, Sheffield U and Darwen won promotion in place of Notts Co and Accrington S.
1893–94 In Tests, Liverpool and Small Heath won promotion. Newton Heath and Darwen relegated.
1894–95 After Tests, Bury promoted, Liverpool relegated.
1895–96 After Tests, Liverpool promoted, Small Heath relegated.
1896–97 After Tests, Notts Co promoted, Burnley relegated.
1897–98 Test system abolished after success of Stoke C and Burnley. League extended. Blackburn R and Newcastle U elected to First Division. *Automatic promotion and relegation introduced.*

FA PREMIER LEAGUE TO DIVISION 1

1992–93 Crystal Palace, Middlesbrough, Nottingham F
1993–94 Sheffield U, Oldham Ath, Swindon T
1994–95 Crystal Palace, Norwich C, Leicester C, Ipswich T
1995–96 Manchester C, QPR, Bolton W
1996–97 Sunderland, Middlesbrough, Nottingham F
1997–98 Bolton W, Barnsley, Crystal Palace
1998–99 Charlton Ath, Blackburn R, Nottingham F
1999–2000 Wimbledon, Sheffield W, Watford
2000–01 Manchester C, Coventry C, Bradford C
2001–02 Ipswich T, Derby Co, Leicester C
2002–03 West Ham U, WBA, Sunderland
2003–04 Leicester C, Leeds U, Wolverhampton W.

FA PREMIER LEAGUE TO CHAMPIONSHIP

2004–05 Crystal Palace, Norwich C, Southampton
2005–06 Birmingham C, WBA, Sunderland
2006–07 Sheffield U, Charlton Ath, Watford

DIVISION 1 TO DIVISION 2

1898–99 Bolton W and Sheffield W
1899–1900 Burnley and Glossop
1900–01 Preston NE and WBA
1901–02 Small Heath and Manchester C
1902–03 Grimsby T and Bolton W
1903–04 Liverpool and WBA
1904–05 League extended. Bury and Notts Co, two bottom clubs in First Division, re-elected.
1905–06 Nottingham F and Wolverhampton W
1906–07 Derby Co and Stoke C
1907–08 Bolton W and Birmingham C
1908–09 Manchester C and Leicester Fosse
1909–10 Bolton W and Chelsea
1910–11 Bristol C and Nottingham F
1911–12 Preston NE and Bury
1912–13 Notts Co and Woolwich Arsenal
1913–14 Preston NE and Derby Co
1914–15 Tottenham H and Chelsea*
1919–20 Notts Co and Sheffield W
1920–21 Derby Co and Bradford PA
1921–22 Bradford C and Manchester U
1922–23 Stoke C and Oldham Ath
1923–24 Chelsea and Middlesbrough
1924–25 Preston NE and Nottingham F
1925–26 Manchester C and Notts Co
1926–27 Leeds U and WBA
1927–28 Tottenham H and Middlesbrough
1928–29 Bury and Cardiff C
1929–30 Burnley and Everton
1930–31 Leeds U and Manchester U
1931–32 Grimsby T and West Ham U
1932–33 Bolton W and Blackpool
1933–34 Newcastle U and Sheffield U
1934–35 Leicester C and Tottenham H
1935–36 Aston Villa and Blackburn R
1936–37 Manchester U and Sheffield W
1937–38 Manchester C and WBA
1938–39 Birmingham C and Leicester C
1946–47 Brentford and Leeds U
1947–48 Blackburn R and Grimsby T
1948–49 Preston NE and Sheffield U
1949–50 Manchester C and Birmingham C
1950–51 Sheffield W and Everton
1951–52 Huddersfield T and Fulham
1952–53 Stoke C and Derby Co
1953–54 Middlesbrough and Liverpool
1954–55 Leicester C and Sheffield W
1955–56 Huddersfield T and Sheffield U
1956–57 Charlton Ath and Cardiff C
1957–58 Sheffield W and Sunderland
1958–59 Portsmouth and Aston Villa
1959–60 Luton T and Leeds U
1960–61 Preston NE and Newcastle U
1961–62 Chelsea and Cardiff C
1962–63 Manchester C and Leyton Orient
1963–64 Bolton W and Ipswich T
1964–65 Wolverhampton W and Birmingham C
1965–66 Northampton T and Blackburn R
1966–67 Aston Villa and Blackpool
1967–68 Fulham and Sheffield U
1968–69 Leicester C and QPR
1969–70 Sunderland and Sheffield W
1970–71 Burnley and Blackpool
1971–72 Huddersfield T and Nottingham F
1972–73 Crystal Palace and WBA
1973–74 Southampton, Manchester U, Norwich C
1974–75 Luton T, Chelsea, Carlisle U
1975–76 Wolverhampton W, Burnley, Sheffield U
1976–77 Sunderland, Stoke C, Tottenham H
1977–78 West Ham U, Newcastle U, Leicester C
1978–79 QPR, Birmingham C, Chelsea
1979–80 Bristol C, Derby Co, Bolton W
1980–81 Norwich C, Leicester C, Crystal Palace
1981–82 Leeds U, Wolverhampton W, Middlesbrough
1982–83 Manchester C, Swansea C, Brighton & HA
1983–84 Birmingham C, Notts Co, Wolverhampton W
1984–85 Norwich C, Sunderland, Stoke C
1985–86 Ipswich T, Birmingham C, WBA
1986–87 Leicester C, Manchester C, Aston Villa
1987–88 Chelsea**, Portsmouth, Watford, Oxford U
1988–89 Middlesbrough, West Ham U, Newcastle U
1989–90 Sheffield W, Charlton Ath, Millwall
1990–91 Sunderland and Derby Co
1991–92 Luton T, Notts Co, West Ham U
1992–93 Brentford, Cambridge U, Bristol R
1993–94 Birmingham C, Oxford U, Peterborough U
1994–95 Swindon T, Burnley, Bristol C, Notts Co
1995–96 Millwall, Watford, Luton T
1996–97 Grimsby T, Oldham Ath, Southend U
1997–98 Manchester C, Stoke C, Reading
1998–99 Bury, Oxford U, Bristol C
1999–2000 Walsall, Port Vale, Swindon T
2000–01 Huddersfield T, QPR, Tranmere R
2001–02 Crewe Alex, Barnsley, Stockport Co
2002–03 Sheffield W, Brighton & HA, Grimsby T
2003–04 Walsall, Bradford C, Wimbledon

***Relegated after play-offs.*
**Subsequently re-elected to Division 1 when League was extended after the War.*

FOOTBALL LEAGUE CHAMPIONSHIP TO FOOTBALL LEAGUE CHAMPIONSHIP 1

2004–05 Gillingham, Nottingham F, Rotherham U
2005–06 Crewe Alex, Millwall, Brighton & HA
2006–07 Southend U, Luton T, Leeds U

DIVISION 2 TO DIVISION 3

1920–21 Stockport Co
1921–22 Bradford PA and Bristol C
1922–23 Rotherham Co and Wolverhampton W
1923–24 Nelson and Bristol C
1924–25 Crystal Palace and Coventry C
1925–26 Stoke C and Stockport Co
1926–27 Darlington and Bradford C
1927–28 Fulham and South Shields
1928–29 Port Vale and Clapton Orient
1929–30 Hull C and Notts Co
1930–31 Reading and Cardiff C
1931–32 Barnsley and Bristol C
1932–33 Chesterfield and Charlton Ath
1933–34 Millwall and Lincoln C
1934–35 Oldham Ath and Notts Co
1935–36 Port Vale and Hull C
1936–37 Doncaster R and Bradford C
1937–38 Barnsley and Stockport Co
1938–39 Norwich C and Tranmere R
1946–47 Swansea T and Newport Co
1947–48 Doncaster R and Millwall
1948–49 Nottingham F and Lincoln C
1949–50 Plymouth Arg and Bradford PA
1950–51 Grimsby T and Chesterfield
1951–52 Coventry C and QPR
1952–53 Southampton and Barnsley
1953–54 Brentford and Oldham Ath
1954–55 Ipswich T and Derby Co

1955–56 Plymouth Arg and Hull C
1956–57 Port Vale and Bury
1957–58 Doncaster R and Notts Co
1958–59 Barnsley and Grimsby T
1959–60 Bristol C and Hull C
1960–61 Lincoln C and Portsmouth
1961–62 Brighton & HA and Bristol R
1962–63 Walsall and Luton T
1963–64 Grimsby T and Scunthorpe U
1964–65 Swindon T and Swansea T
1965–66 Middlesbrough and Leyton Orient
1966–67 Northampton T and Bury
1967–68 Plymouth Arg and Rotherham U
1968–69 Fulham and Bury
1969–70 Preston NE and Aston Villa
1970–71 Blackburn R and Bolton W
1971–72 Charlton Ath and Watford
1972–73 Huddersfield T and Brighton & HA
1973–74 Crystal Palace, Preston NE, Swindon T
1974–75 Millwall, Cardiff C, Sheffield W
1975–76 Oxford U, York C, Portsmouth
1976–77 Carlisle U, Plymouth Arg, Hereford U
1977–78 Blackpool, Mansfield T, Hull C
1978–79 Sheffield U, Millwall, Blackburn R
1979–80 Fulham, Burnley, Charlton Ath
1980–81 Preston NE, Bristol C, Bristol R
1981–82 Cardiff C, Wrexham, Orient
1982–83 Rotherham U, Burnley, Bolton W
1983–84 Derby Co, Swansea C, Cambridge U
1984–85 Notts Co, Cardiff C, Wolverhampton W
1985–86 Carlisle U, Middlesbrough, Fulham
1986–87 Sunderland**, Grimsby T, Brighton & HA
1987–88 Huddersfield T, Reading, Sheffield U**
1988–89 Shrewsbury T, Birmingham C, Walsall
1989–90 Bournemouth, Bradford C, Stoke C
1990–91 WBA and Hull C
1991–92 Plymouth Arg, Brighton & HA, Port Vale
1992–93 Preston NE, Mansfield T, Wigan Ath, Chester C
1993–94 Fulham, Exeter C, Hartlepool U, Barnet
1994–95 Cambridge U, Plymouth Arg, Cardiff C, Chester C, Leyton Orient
1995–96 Carlisle U, Swansea C, Brighton & HA, Hull C
1996–97 Peterborough U, Shrewsbury T, Rotherham U, Notts Co
1997–98 Brentford, Plymouth Arg, Carlisle U, Southend U
1998–99 York C, Northampton T, Lincoln C, Macclesfield T
1999–2000 Cardiff C, Blackpool, Scunthorpe U, Chesterfield
2000–01 Bristol R, Luton T, Swansea C, Oxford U
2001–02 Bournemouth, Bury, Wrexham, Cambridge U
2002–03 Cheltenham T, Huddersfield T, Mansfield T Northampton T
2003–04 Grimsby T, Rushden & D, Notts Co, Wycombe W

FOOTBALL LEAGUE CHAMPIONSHIP 1 TO FOOTBALL LEAGUE CHAMPIONSHIP 2

2004–05 Torquay U, Wrexham, Peterborough U, Stockport Co
2005–06 Hartlepool U, Milton Keynes D, Swindon T, Walsall
2006–07 Chesterfield, Bradford C, Rotherham U, Brentford

DIVISION 3 TO DIVISION 4

1958–59 Stockport Co, Doncaster R, Notts Co, Rochdale
1959–60 York C, Mansfield T, Wrexham, Accrington S
1960–61 Tranmere R, Bradford C, Colchester U, Chesterfield
1961–62 Torquay U, Lincoln C, Brentford, Newport Co
1962–63 Bradford PA, Brighton & HA, Carlisle U, Halifax T
1963–64 Millwall, Crewe Alex, Wrexham, Notts Co
1964–65 Luton T, Port Vale, Colchester U, Barnsley
1965–66 Southend U, Exeter C, Brentford, York C
1966–67 Swansea T, Darlington, Doncaster R, Workington
1967–68 Grimsby T, Colchester U, Scunthorpe U, Peterborough U (demoted)
1968–69 Northampton T, Hartlepool, Crewe Alex, Oldham Ath
1969–70 Bournemouth, Southport, Barrow, Stockport Co
1970–71 Reading, Bury, Doncaster R, Gillingham
1971–72 Mansfield T, Barnsley, Torquay U, Bradford C
1972–73 Rotherham U, Brentford, Swansea C, Scunthorpe U
1973–74 Cambridge U, Shrewsbury T, Southport, Rochdale
1974–75 Bournemouth, Tranmere R, Watford, Huddersfield T
1975–76 Aldershot, Colchester U, Southend U, Halifax T
1976–77 Reading, Northampton T, Grimsby T, York C
1977–78 Port Vale, Bradford C, Hereford U, Portsmouth
1978–79 Peterborough U, Walsall, Tranmere R, Lincoln C
1979–80 Bury, Southend U, Mansfield T, Wimbledon
1980–81 Sheffield U, Colchester U, Blackpool, Hull C
1981–82 Wimbledon, Swindon T, Bristol C, Chester
1982–83 Reading, Wrexham, Doncaster R, Chesterfield
1983–84 Scunthorpe U, Southend U, Port Vale, Exeter C
1984–85 Burnley, Orient, Preston NE, Cambridge U
1985–86 Lincoln C, Cardiff C, Wolverhampton W, Swansea C
1986–87 Bolton W**, Carlisle U, Darlington, Newport Co
1987–88 Rotherham U**, Grimsby T, York C, Doncaster R
1988–89 Southend U, Chesterfield, Gillingham, Aldershot
1989–90 Cardiff C, Northampton T, Blackpool, Walsall
1990–91 Crewe Alex, Rotherham U, Mansfield T
1991–92 Bury, Shrewsbury T, Torquay U, Darlington

** *Relegated after play-offs.*

APPLICATIONS FOR RE-ELECTION

FOURTH DIVISION

Eleven: Hartlepool U.
Seven: Crewe Alex.
Six: Barrow (lost League place to Hereford U 1972), Halifax T, Rochdale, Southport (lost League place to Wigan Ath 1978), York C.
Five: Chester C, Darlington, Lincoln C, Stockport Co, Workington (lost League place to Wimbledon 1977).
Four: Bradford PA (lost League place to Cambridge U 1970), Newport Co, Northampton T.
Three: Doncaster R, Hereford U.
Two: Bradford C, Exeter C, Oldham Ath, Scunthorpe U, Torquay U.
One: Aldershot, Colchester U, Gateshead (lost League place to Peterborough U 1960), Grimsby T, Swansea C, Tranmere R, Wrexham, Blackpool, Cambridge U, Preston NE.
Accrington S resigned and Oxford U were elected 1962.
Port Vale were forced to re-apply following expulsion in 1968.
Aldershot expelled March 1992. Maidstone U resigned August 1992.

THIRD DIVISIONS NORTH & SOUTH

Seven: Walsall.
Six: Exeter C, Halifax T, Newport Co.
Five: Accrington S, Barrow, Gillingham, New Brighton, Southport.
Four: Rochdale, Norwich C.
Three: Crystal Palace, Crewe Alex, Darlington, Hartlepool U, Merthyr T, Swindon T.
Two: Aberdare Ath, Aldershot, Ashington, Bournemouth, Brentford, Chester, Colchester U, Durham C, Millwall, Nelson, QPR, Rotherham U, Southend U, Tranmere R, Watford, Workington.
One: Bradford C, Bradford PA, Brighton & HA, Bristol R, Cardiff C, Carlisle U, Charlton Ath, Gateshead, Grimsby T, Mansfield T, Shrewsbury T, Torquay U, York C.

LEAGUE STATUS FROM 1986–87

RELEGATED FROM LEAGUE
1986–87 Lincoln C 1987–88 Newport Co;
1988–89 Darlington 1989–90 Colchester U
1990–91 — 1991–92 —
1992–93 Halifax T 1993–94 —
1994–95 — 1995–96 —
1996–97 Hereford U 1997–98 Doncaster R
1998–99 Scarborough 1999–2000 Chester C
2000–01 Barnet 2001–02 Halifax T
2002–03 Shrewsbury T, Exeter C
2003–04 Carlisle U, York C
2004–05 Kidderminster H, Cambridge U
2005–06 Oxford U, Rushden & D
2006–07 Boston U, Torquay U

PROMOTED TO LEAGUE
1986–87 Scarborough 1987–88 Lincoln C
1988–89 Maidstone U 1989–90 Darlington
1990–91 Barnet 1991–92 Colchester U
1992–93 Wycombe W 1993–94 —
1994–95 — 1995–96 —
1996–97 Macclesfield T 1997–98 Halifax T
1998–99 Cheltenham T 1999–2000 Kidderminster H
2000–01 Rushden & D 2001–02 Boston U
2002–03 Yeovil T, Doncaster R
2003–04 Chester C, Shrewsbury T
2004–05 Barnet, Carlisle U
2005–06 Accrington S, Hereford U
2006–07 Dagenham & R, Morecambe

FOOTBALL LEAGUE COMPETITION ATTENDANCES

LEAGUE CUP ATTENDANCES

Season	*Attendances*	*Games*	*Average*
1960–61	1,204,580	112	10,755
1961–62	1,030,534	104	9,909
1962–63	1,029,893	102	10,097
1963–64	945,265	104	9,089
1964–65	962,802	98	9,825
1965–66	1,205,876	106	11,376
1966–67	1,394,553	118	11,818
1967–68	1,671,326	110	15,194
1968–69	2,064,647	118	17,497
1969–70	2,299,819	122	18,851
1970–71	2,035,315	116	17,546
1971–72	2,397,154	123	19,489
1972–73	1,935,474	120	16,129
1973–74	1,722,629	132	13,050
1974–75	1,901,094	127	14,969
1975–76	1,841,735	140	13,155
1976–77	2,236,636	147	15,215
1977–78	2,038,295	148	13,772
1978–79	1,825,643	139	13,134
1979–80	2,322,866	169	13,745
1980–81	2,051,576	161	12,743
1981–82	1,880,682	161	11,681
1982–83	1,679,756	160	10,498
1983–84	1,900,491	168	11,312
1984–85	1,876,429	167	11,236
1985–86	1,579,916	163	9,693
1986–87	1,531,498	157	9,755
1987–88	1,539,253	158	9,742
1988–89	1,552,780	162	9,585
1989–90	1,836,916	168	10,934
1990–91	1,675,496	159	10,538
1991–92	1,622,337	164	9,892
1992–93	1,558,031	161	9,677
1993–94	1,744,120	163	10,700
1994–95	1,530,478	157	9,748
1995–96	1,776,060	162	10,963
1996–97	1,529,321	163	9,382
1997–98	1,484,297	153	9,701
1998–99	1,555,856	153	10,169
1999–2000	1,354,233	153	8,851
2000–01	1,501,304	154	9,749
2001–02	1,076,390	93	11,574
2002–03	1,242,478	92	13,505
2003–04	1,267,729	93	13,631
2004–05	1,313,693	93	14,216
2005–06	1,072,362	93	11,531

CARLING CUP 2006–07

Round	*Aggregate*	*Games*	*Average*
One	177,988	36	4,944
Two	162,949	24	6,790
Three	238,999	16	14,937
Four	172,900	8	21,613
Quarter-finals	132,771	4	33,193
Semi-finals	142,723	4	35,681
Final	70,073	1	70,073
Total	1,098,403	93	11,811

JOHNSTONE'S PAINT TROPHY 2006–07

Round	*Aggregate*	*Games*	*Average*
One	30,115	16	1,882
Two	28,207	16	1,763
Area Quarter-finals	25,142	8	3,143
Area Semi-finals	21,107	4	5,277
Area finals	47,452	4	11,863
Final	59,024	1	59,024
Total	211,047	49	4,307

LEAGUE ATTENDANCES SINCE 1946–47

Season	*Matches*	*Total*	*Div. 1*	*Div. 2*	*Div. 3 (S)*	*Div. 3 (N)*
1946–47	1848	35,604,606	15,005,316	11,071,572	5,664,004	3,863,714
1947–48	1848	40,259,130	16,732,341	12,286,350	6,653,610	4,586,829
1948–49	1848	41,271,414	17,914,667	11,353,237	6,998,429	5,005,081
1949–50	1848	40,517,865	17,278,625	11,694,158	7,104,155	4,440,927
1950–51	2028	39,584,967	16,679,454	10,780,580	7,367,884	4,757,109
1951–52	2028	39,015,866	16,110,322	11,066,189	6,958,927	4,880,428
1952–53	2028	37,149,966	16,050,278	9,686,654	6,704,299	4,708,735
1953–54	2028	36,174,590	16,154,915	9,510,053	6,311,508	4,198,114
1954–55	2028	34,133,103	15,087,221	8,988,794	5,996,017	4,051,071
1955–56	2028	33,150,809	14,108,961	9,080,002	5,692,479	4,269,367
1956–57	2028	32,744,405	13,803,037	8,718,162	5,622,189	4,601,017
1957–58	2028	33,562,208	14,468,652	8,663,712	6,097,183	4,332,661

		Total	*Div. 1*	*Div. 2*	*Div. 3*	*Div. 4*
1958–59	2028	33,610,985	14,727,691	8,641,997	5,946,600	4,276,697
1959–60	2028	32,538,611	14,391,227	8,399,627	5,739,707	4,008,050
1960–61	2028	28,619,754	12,926,948	7,033,936	4,784,256	3,874,614
1961–62	2015	27,979,902	12,061,194	7,453,089	5,199,106	3,266,513
1962–63	2028	28,885,852	12,490,239	7,792,770	5,341,362	3,261,481
1963–64	2028	28,535,022	12,486,626	7,594,158	5,419,157	3,035,081
1964–65	2028	27,641,168	12,708,752	6,984,104	4,436,245	3,512,067
1965–66	2028	27,206,980	12,480,644	6,914,757	4,779,150	3,032,429
1966–67	2028	28,902,596	14,242,957	7,253,819	4,421,172	2,984,648
1967–68	2028	30,107,298	15,289,410	7,450,410	4,013,087	3,354,391
1968–69	2028	29,382,172	14,584,851	7,382,390	4,339,656	3,075,275
1969–70	2028	29,600,972	14,868,754	7,581,728	4,223,761	2,926,729
1970–71	2028	28,194,146	13,954,337	7,098,265	4,377,213	2,764,331
1971–72	2028	28,700,729	14,484,603	6,769,308	4,697,392	2,749,426
1972–73	2028	25,448,642	13,998,154	5,631,730	3,737,252	2,081,506
1973–74	2027	24,982,203	13,070,991	6,326,108	3,421,624	2,163,480
1974–75	2028	25,577,977	12,613,178	6,955,970	4,086,145	1,992,684
1975–76	2028	24,896,053	13,089,861	5,798,405	3,948,449	2,059,338
1976–77	2028	26,182,800	13,647,585	6,250,597	4,152,218	2,132,400
1977–78	2028	25,392,872	13,255,677	6,474,763	3,332,042	2,330,390
1978–79	2028	24,540,627	12,704,549	6,153,223	3,374,558	2,308,297
1979–80	2028	24,623,975	12,163,002	6,112,025	3,999,328	2,349,620
1980–81	2028	21,907,569	11,392,894	5,175,442	3,637,854	1,701,379
1981–82	2028	20,006,961	10,420,793	4,750,463	2,836,915	1,998,790
1982–83	2028	18,766,158	9,295,613	4,974,937	2,943,568	1,552,040
1983–84	2028	18,358,631	8,711,448	5,359,757	2,729,942	1,557,484
1984–85	2028	17,849,835	9,761,404	4,030,823	2,667,008	1,390,600
1985–86	2028	16,488,577	9,037,854	3,551,968	2,490,481	1,408,274
1986–87	2028	17,379,218	9,144,676	4,168,131	2,350,970	1,715,441
1987–88	2030	17,959,732	8,094,571	5,341,599	2,751,275	1,772,287
1988–89	2036	18,464,192	7,809,993	5,887,805	3,035,327	1,791,067
1989–90	2036	19,445,442	7,883,039	6,867,674	2,803,551	1,891,178
1990–91	2036	19,508,202	8,618,709	6,285,068	2,835,759	1,768,666
1991–92	2064*	20,487,273	9,989,160	5,809,787	2,993,352	1,694,974

		Total	*FA Premier*	*Div. 1*	*Div. 2*	*Div. 3*
1992–93	2028	20,657,327	9,759,809	5,874,017	3,483,073	1,540,428
1993–94	2028	21,683,381	10,644,551	6,487,104	2,972,702	1,579,024
1994–95	2028	21,856,020	11,213,168	6,044,293	3,037,752	1,560,807
1995–96	2036	21,844,416	10,469,107	6,566,349	2,843,652	1,965,308
1996–97	2036	22,783,163	10,804,762	6,931,539	3,195,223	1,851,639
1997–98	2036	24,692,608	11,092,106	8,330,018	3,503,264	1,767,220
1998–99	2036	25,435,542	11,620,326	7,543,369	4,169,697	2,102,150
1999-2000	2036	25,341,090	11,668,497	7,810,208	3,700,433	2,161,952
2000–01	2036	26,030,167	12,472,094	7,909,512	3,488,166	2,160,395
2001–02	2036	27,756,977	13,043,118	8,352,128	3,963,153	2,398,578
2002–03	2036	28,343,386	13,468,965	8,521,017	3,892,469	2,460,935
2003–04	2036	29,197,510	13,303,136	8,772,780	4,146,495	2,975,099

		Total	*FA Premier*	*Championship*	*Championship 1*	*Championship 2*
2004–05	2036	29,245,870	12,878,791	9,612,761	4,270,674	2,483,644
2005–06	2036	29,089,084	12,871,643	9,719,204	4,183,011	2,315,226
2006–07	2036	29,541,949	13,058,115	10,057,813	4,135,599	2,290,422

**Figures include matches played by Aldershot.*
Football League official total for their three divisions in 2001–02 was 14,716,162.
The official Premiership total was 13,094,307 for 2006–07.

ENGLISH LEAGUE ATTENDANCES 2006–07

FA BARCLAYCARD PREMIERSHIP ATTENDANCES

	Average Gate			*Season 2006–07*	
	2005–06	2006–07	+/–%	Highest	Lowest
Arsenal	38,186	60,045	+57.24	60,132	59,912
Aston Villa	34,059	36,214	+6.33	42,551	27,450
Blackburn Rovers	21,015	21,275	+1.24	29,342	16,035
Bolton Wanderers	25,265	23,606	–6.57	27,229	21,140
Charlton Athletic	26,196	26,195	–0.00	27,111	23,423
Chelsea	41,902	41,542	–0.86	41,953	38,000
Everton	36,860	36,739	–0.33	40,004	32,968
Fulham	20,654	22,279	+7.87	24,554	17,000
Liverpool	44,236	43,563	–1.52	44,403	41,370
Manchester City	42,856	39,997	–6.67	47,244	35,776
Manchester United	68,765	75,826	+10.27	76,098	75,115
Middlesbrough	28,463	27,730	–2.58	32,013	23,638
Newcastle United	52,032	50,686	–2.59	52,305	48,145
Portsmouth	19,840	19,862	+0.11	20,223	19,105
Reading	20,207	23,829	+17.92	24,122	21,954
Sheffield United	23,650	30,512	+29.01	32,604	25,011
Tottenham Hotspur	36,074	35,739	–0.93	36,170	34,154
Watford	15,415	18,750	+21.63	19,830	13,760
West Ham United	33,743	34,719	+2.89	34,977	33,805
Wigan Athletic	20,610	18,159	–11.89	24,726	14,636

TOTAL ATTENDANCES:	13,058,115 (380 games) Average 34,363 (+1.45%)
HIGHEST:	76,098 Manchester United v Blackburn Rovers
LOWEST:	13,760 Watford v Blackburn Rovers
HIGHEST AVERAGE:	75,826 Manchester United
LOWEST AVERAGE:	18,159 Wigan Athletic

FOOTBALL LEAGUE: CHAMPIONSHIP ATTENDANCES

	Average Gate			*Season 2006–07*	
	2005–06	2006–07	+/–%	Highest	Lowest
Barnsley	9,054	12,733	+40.6	21,253	9,479
Birmingham City	27,392	22,274	–18.7	29,431	15,854
Burnley	12,462	11,956	–4.1	15,061	9,681
Cardiff City	11,720	15,219	+29.9	20,109	11,549
Colchester United	3,969	5,466	+37.7	6,065	4,249
Coventry City	21,302	20,342	–4.5	27,212	16,178
Crystal Palace	19,457	17,541	–9.8	21,523	15,985
Derby County	24,166	25,945	+7.4	31,920	21,295
Hull City	19,841	18,758	–5.5	25,512	14,895
Ipswich Town	24,253	22,445	–7.5	28,355	19,337
Leeds United	22,355	21,613	–3.3	31,269	16,268
Leicester City	22,234	23,206	+4.4	30,457	18,677
Luton Town	9,139	8,580	–6.1	10,260	7,441
Norwich City	24,952	24,545	–1.6	25,476	23,311
Plymouth Argyle	13,776	13,012	–5.5	17,088	9,841
Preston North End	14,617	14,430	–1.3	19,603	11,601
Queens Park Rangers	13,441	12,936	–3.8	16,741	10,811
Sheffield Wednesday	24,853	23,638	–4.9	29,103	18,752
Southampton	23,614	23,556	–0.2	32,008	18,736
Southend United	8,053	10,024	+24.5	11,415	7,901
Stoke City	14,432	15,749	+9.1	23,017	11,626
Sunderland	33,904	31,887	–5.9	44,448	24,242
West Bromwich Albion	25,404	20,472	–19.4	26,606	17,417
Wolverhampton Wanderers	23,624	20,968	–11.2	28,016	16,772

TOTAL ATTENDANCES:	10,057,813 (552 games) Average 18,221 (+3.5%)
HIGHEST:	44,448 Sunderland v Burnley
LOWEST:	4,249 Colchester United v Barnsley
HIGHEST AVERAGE:	31,887 Sunderland
LOWEST AVERAGE:	5,466 Colchester United

Premiership and Football League attendance averages and highest crowd figures for 2006–07 are unofficial. The official Premiership total was 13,094,307.

FOOTBALL LEAGUE: CHAMPIONSHIP 1 ATTENDANCES

	Average Gate			*Season 2006–07*	
	2005–06	2006–07	+/–%	Highest	Lowest
Blackpool	5,820	6,877	+18.2	9,482	4,600
AFC Bournemouth	6,458	6,028	–6.7	8,001	4,538
Bradford City	8,265	8,694	+5.2	14,925	7,134
Brentford	6,775	5,600	–17.3	7,023	4,296
Brighton & Hove Albion	6,802	6,048	–11.1	7,749	5,146
Bristol City	11,725	12,818	+9.3	19,517	9,726
Carlisle United	7,218	7,907	+9.5	12,031	6,087
Cheltenham Town	3,453	4,359	+26.2	6,554	3,036
Chesterfield	4,772	4,235	–11.3	6,641	3,341
Crewe Alexandra	6,732	5,462	–18.9	7,632	4,062
Doncaster Rovers	6,139	7,746	+26.2	14,470	5,190
Gillingham	6,671	6,282	–5.8	8,216	5,103
Huddersfield Town	13,058	10,573	–19.0	14,772	8,723
Leyton Orient	4,699	4,857	+3.4	7,206	3,529
Millwall	9,529	9,234	–3.1	12,547	6,251
Northampton Town	5,935	5,573	–6.1	7,172	4,564
Nottingham Forest	20,257	20,612	+1.8	27,875	16,785
Oldham Athletic	5,797	6,334	+9.3	10,207	4,652
Port Vale	4,657	4,725	+1.5	7,388	3,077
Rotherham United	5,306	4,763	–10.2	7,809	3,223
Scunthorpe United	5,171	5,669	+9.6	8,906	3,473
Swansea City	14,112	12,720	–9.9	18,903	9,675
Tranmere Rovers	7,211	6,930	–3.9	11,444	5,528
Yeovil Town	6,668	5,765	–13.5	9,009	4,709

TOTAL ATTENDANCES: 4,135,599 (552 games)
Average 7,492 (–1.1%)
HIGHEST: 27,875 Nottingham Forest v Rotherham United
LOWEST: 3,036 Cheltenham Town v Scunthorpe United
HIGHEST AVERAGE: 20,612 Nottingham Forest
LOWEST AVERAGE: 4,235 Chesterfield

FOOTBALL LEAGUE: CHAMPIONSHIP 2 ATTENDANCES

	Average Gate			*Season 2006–07*	
	2005–06	2006–07	+/–%	Highest	Lowest
Accrington Stanley	1,895	2,260	+19.3	4,004	1,234
Barnet	2,578	2,279	–11.6	2,958	1,461
Boston United	2,519	2,152	–14.6	4,327	1,571
Bristol Rovers	5,989	5,480	–8.5	9,902	4,327
Bury	2,594	2,588	–0.2	5,075	1,775
Chester City	2,964	2,473	–16.6	4,206	1,527
Darlington	4,199	3,814	–9.2	9,987	2,321
Grimsby Town	5,151	4,379	–15.0	6,137	3,012
Hartlepool United	4,812	5,096	+5.9	7,629	3,659
Hereford United	2,793	3,328	+19.2	5,201	2,176
Lincoln City	4,739	5,176	+9.2	6,820	3,913
Macclesfield Town	2,275	2,863	+25.8	14,142	1,472
Mansfield Town	3,560	3,176	–10.8	6,182	2,023
Milton Keynes Dons	5,776	6,034	+4.5	8,102	4,564
Notts County	5,467	4,974	–9.0	10,034	3,010
Peterborough United	4,364	4,662	+6.8	8,405	3,193
Rochdale	2,808	2,898	+3.2	5,846	1,982
Shrewsbury Town	3,997	4,730	+18.3	7,782	3,369
Stockport County	4,772	5,514	+15.5	7,860	4,089
Swindon Town	5,951	7,419	+24.7	14,731	5,462
Torquay United	2,851	2,633	–7.6	4,047	1,588
Walsall	5,392	5,643	+4.7	8,345	4,070
Wrexham	4,478	5,030	+12.3	12,374	3,401
Wycombe Wanderers	5,445	4,983	–8.5	7,150	3,885

TOTAL ATTENDANCES: 2,290,422 (552 games)
Average 4,149 (–1.1%)
HIGHEST: 14,731 Swindon Town v Walsall
LOWEST: 1,234 Accrington Stanley v Mansfield Town
HIGHEST AVERAGE: 7,419 Swindon Town
LOWEST AVERAGE: 2,152 Boston United

LEAGUE CUP FINALISTS 1961–2007

Played as a two-leg final until 1966. All subsequent finals at Wembley until 2000, then at Millennium Stadium, Cardiff.

Year	*Winners*	*Runners-up*	*Score*
1961	Aston Villa	Rotherham U	0-2, 3-0 (aet)
1962	Norwich C	Rochdale	3-0, 1-0
1963	Birmingham C	Aston Villa	3-1, 0-0
1964	Leicester C	Stoke C	1-1, 3-2
1965	Chelsea	Leicester C	3-2, 0-0
1966	WBA	West Ham U	1-2, 4-1
1967	QPR	WBA	3-2
1968	Leeds U	Arsenal	1-0
1969	Swindon T	Arsenal	3-1 (aet)
1970	Manchester C	WBA	2-1 (aet)
1971	Tottenham H	Aston Villa	2-0
1972	Stoke C	Chelsea	2-1
1973	Tottenham H	Norwich C	1-0
1974	Wolverhampton W	Manchester C	2-1
1975	Aston Villa	Norwich C	1-0
1976	Manchester C	Newcastle U	2-1
1977	Aston Villa	Everton	0-0, 1-1 (aet), 3-2 (aet)
1978	Nottingham F	Liverpool	0-0 (aet), 1-0
1979	Nottingham F	Southampton	3-2
1980	Wolverhampton W	Nottingham F	1-0
1981	Liverpool	West Ham U	1-1 (aet), 2-1

MILK CUP

1982	Liverpool	Tottenham H	3-1 (aet)
1983	Liverpool	Manchester U	2-1 (aet)
1984	Liverpool	Everton	0-0 (aet), 1-0
1985	Norwich C	Sunderland	1-0
1986	Oxford U	QPR	3-0

LITTLEWOODS CUP

1987	Arsenal	Liverpool	2-1
1988	Luton T	Arsenal	3-2
1989	Nottingham F	Luton T	3-1
1990	Nottingham F	Oldham Ath	1-0

RUMBELOWS LEAGUE CUP

1991	Sheffield W	Manchester U	1-0
1992	Manchester U	Nottingham F	1-0

COCA-COLA CUP

1993	Arsenal	Sheffield W	2-1
1994	Aston Villa	Manchester U	3-1
1995	Liverpool	Bolton W	2-1
1996	Aston Villa	Leeds U	3-0
1997	Leicester C	Middlesbrough	1-1 (aet), 1-0 (aet)
1998	Chelsea	Middlesbrough	2-0 (aet)

WORTHINGTON CUP

1999	Tottenham H	Leicester C	1-0
2000	Leicester C	Tranmere R	2-1
2001	Liverpool	Birmingham C	1-1 (aet)
Liverpool won 5-4 on penalties			
2002	Blackburn R	Tottenham H	2-1
2003	Liverpool	Manchester U	2-0

CARLING CUP

2004	Middlesbrough	Bolton W	2-1
2005	Chelsea	Liverpool	3-2 (aet)
2006	Manchester U	Wigan Ath	4-0
2007	Chelsea	Arsenal	2-1

LEAGUE CUP WINS

Liverpool 7, Aston Villa 5, Chelsea 4, Nottingham F 4, Leicester C 3, Tottenham H 3, Arsenal 2, Manchester C 2, Manchester U 2, Norwich C 2, Wolverhampton W 2, Birmingham C 1, Blackburn R 1, Leeds U 1, Luton T 1, Middlesbrough 1, Oxford U 1, QPR 1, Sheffield W 1, Stoke C 1, Swindon T 1, WBA 1.

APPEARANCES IN FINALS

Liverpool 10, Aston Villa 7, Arsenal 6, Manchester U 6, Nottingham F 6, Chelsea 5, Leicester C 5, Tottenham H 5, Norwich C 4, Manchester C 3, Middlesbrough 3, WBA 3, Birmingham C 2, Bolton W 2, Everton 2, Leeds U 2, Luton T 2, QPR 2, Sheffield W 2, Stoke C 2, West Ham U 2, Wolverhampton W 2, Blackburn R 1, Newcastle U 1, Oldham Ath 1, Oxford U 1, Rochdale 1, Rotherham U 1, Southampton 1, Sunderland 1, Swindon T 1, Tranmere R 1, Wigan Ath 1.

APPEARANCES IN SEMI-FINALS

Liverpool 13, Arsenal 12, Aston Villa 12, Tottenham H 11, Manchester U 10, Chelsea 9, West Ham U 7, Nottingham F 6, Blackburn R 5, Leeds U 5, Leicester C 5, Manchester C 5, Middlesbrough 5, Norwich C 5, Birmingham C 4, Bolton W 4, Sheffield W 4, WBA 4, Burnley 3, Crystal Palace 3, Everton 3, Ipswich T 3, QPR 3, Sunderland 3, Swindon T 3, Wolverhampton W 3, Bristol C 2, Coventry C 2, Luton T 2, Oxford U 2, Plymouth Arg 2, Southampton 2, Stoke C 2, Tranmere R 2, Watford 2, Wimbledon 2, Blackpool 1, Bury 1, Cardiff C 1, Carlisle U 1, Chester C 1, Derby Co 1, Huddersfield T 1, Newcastle U 1, Oldham Ath 1, Peterborough U 1, Rochdale 1, Rotherham U 1, Sheffield U 1, Shrewsbury T 1, Stockport Co 1, Walsall 1, Wigan Ath 1, Wycombe W 1.

CARLING CUP 2006–07

▪ *Denotes player sent off.*

FIRST ROUND

Monday, 21 August 2006

Accrington S (0) 1 *(Mullin 61)*

Nottingham F (0) 0 2146

Accrington S: Dunbavin; Cavanagh, Richardson, Harris (Edwards), Williams, Welch, Todd, Craney, Boco, Mullin, Roberts (N'Da).
Nottingham F: Smith; Gary Holt, Padula, Cullip, Breckin, Morgan (Southall), Curtis, Clingan (Grant Holt), Harris, Weir-Daley (Lester), Thompson.

Tuesday, 22 August 2006

Birmingham C (0) 1 *(Larsson 83)*

Shrewsbury T (0) 0 12,428

Birmingham C: Doyle; Larsson, Gray, Clemence, Martin Taylor, Jaidi, Kilkenny, Muamba (Kelly), Forssell (Campbell), Jerome (Bendtner), Danns.
Shrewsbury T: MacKenzie; Herd, Hogg (Leslie), Hall, Hope, Burton (Sharp), Davies, Edwards, Symes (Langmead), Asamoah, Sorvel.

Blackpool (0) 2 *(Vernon 70, 120)*

Barnsley (0) 2 *(Williams 53 (pen), Devaney 117)* 3938

Blackpool: Evans; Evatt, Tierney, Fox (Bean), Jackson, Barker, Hoolahan (Coid), Southern, Vernon, Morrell, Prendergast (Parker).
Barnsley: Mannone; Tonge, Williams, Reid P, Hassell, Wroe (Hayes), McParland (Devaney), Healy, Jarman, Wright, Coulson (McIndoe).
aet; Barnsley won 4-2 on penalties.

Bournemouth (0) 1 *(Fletcher 47)*

Southend U (1) 3 *(Gower 33, Eastwood 56 (pen), 67)* 3764

Bournemouth: Moss; Purches, Hart (Cummings), Cooper, Broadhurst, Gowling, Cooke (Platt), Fletcher, Hayter, Best, Foley-Sheridan (Hollands).
Southend U: Flahavan; Francis, Hammell, Maher, Clarke, Barrett, Campbell-Ryce, Guttridge (Hunt), Lawson (Hooper), Eastwood, Gower (Cole).

Bristol R (0) 1 *(Walker R 61)*

Luton T (1) 1 *(Boyd 3)* 2882

Bristol R: Phillips; Green, Carruthers (Lescott), Campbell, Anthony, Elliott, Sandell, Disley, Walker R, Haldane (Rigg), Igoe.
Luton T: Beresford; Keane, Davis, O'Leary (Foley), Barnett, Coyne, Bell, Holmes (Edwards), Boyd (Vine), Morgan, Brkovic.
aet; Luton T won 5-3 on penalties.

Burnley (0) 0

Hartlepool U (0) 1 *(Porter 78 (pen))* 3853

Burnley: Jensen; Thomas▪, Harley, McCann (Hyde), Foster (Elliott), Duff, O'Connor J, Mahon (Sinclair), Lafferty, Gray, Jones.
Hartlepool U: Konstantopoulos; Williams D, Brackstone, Liddle, Nelson, Bullock, Williams E (Brown), Sweeney, Porter, Proctor (Foley), Robson.

Bury (0) 2 *(Fitzgerald 82, Bishop 88)*

Sunderland (0) 0 2930

Bury: Fettis; Scott, Brass (Parrish), Fitzgerald▪, Woodthorpe, Adams, Baker, Mattis (Barry-Murphy), Pittman (Youngs), Bishop, Buchanan.
Sunderland: Alnwick; Delap (Collins D), Wright (Lawrence), Collins N, Cunningham, Elliott R (Stead), Whitehead, Leadbitter, Murphy, Elliott S, Arnau▪.

Cardiff C (0) 0

Barnet (1) 2 *(Kandol 32, 54)* 3305

Cardiff C: Howard; Gunter, Jacobson, Cooper (Ledley), Johnson, Weston (Blake), Flood, McKoy, Campbell, Glombard, Kamara (Parry).
Barnet: Flitney; Devera, Gross, Cogan, Warhurst, Charles, Bailey, Sinclair, Vieira (Norville), Kandol (Hatch), Puncheon (Nicolau).

Carlisle U (1) 1 *(Holmes 31)*

Bradford C (0) 1 *(Johnson E 81)* 4757

Carlisle U: Williams; Arnison, Aranalde, Grand, Gray, Livesey, McDermott (Murphy), Hackney (Westwood), Holmes (Bridges), Hawley, Lumsdon.
Bradford C: Ricketts; Doyle, Rogers, Schumacher, Wetherall, Bower, Johnson J, Bridge-Wilkinson, Johnson E, Windass, Holmes.
aet; Carlisle U won 4-3 on penalties.

Cheltenham T (2) 2 *(Guinan 24, Wilson 33)*

Bristol C (1) 1 *(Cotterill 39)* 3713

Cheltenham T: Higgs; Gill, Armstrong, Victory, Caines, McCann, Melligan (Vincent), Finnigan, Guinan (Gillespie), Odejayi, Wilson.
Bristol C: Basso; Keogh (Brown), McAllister, Johnson, Carey, Fontaine, Cotterill, Noble (Skuse), Jevons, Showunmi, Murray (Myrie-Williams).

Crystal Palace (1) 1 *(Hughes 17)*

Notts Co (1) 2 *(Dudfield 23, Martin 84)* 4481

Crystal Palace: Flinders; Lawrence, Borrowdale, Ward, Hudson, Watson, Reich (Spence), Hughes, Morrison, Macken (Black), Freedman.
Notts Co: Deeney; Edwards, Hunt (Gleeson), Ross (Mendes), White, Martin, Silk, Curtis, N'Toya, Dudfield, Sheridan (Needham).

Doncaster R (0) 3 *(McCammon 55, 67, Coppinger 56)*

Rochdale (1) 2 *(Rundle 45, Doolan 79)* 3690

Doncaster R: Blayney; O'Connor, McDaid, Lockwood, Fenton, Green P, Price (Coppinger), Thornton, Guy (Heffernan), McCammon, Forte.
Rochdale: Gilks; Ramsden, Goodall, Doolan, Stanton, Boardman, Crooks, Cooksey, Christie (Moyo-Modise), Dagnall, Rundle (Brown).

Grimsby T (0) 0

Crewe Alex (1) 3 *(Maynard 38, O'Connor 73, Lowe 89 (pen))* 1635

Grimsby T: Barnes; Croft, Newey, Toner, Futcher, Whittle, Bore, Bolland, Rankin, Jones (Reddy), Beagrie.
Crewe Alex: Tomlinson; Otsemobor, Jones, O'Connor, Baudet, O'Donnell (Kempson), Rix, Lowe, Maynard, Varney, Vaughan.

Hereford U (1) 3 *(Fleetwood 1, 57, 64)*

Coventry C (0) 1 *(Adebola 59)* 3404

Hereford U: Tynan; McClenahan, Rose, Purdie, Mkandawire, Beckwith, Travis, Ferrell, Fleetwood (Williams), Sills, Giles.
Coventry C: Marshall; Whing (Thornton), Hall, Hughes, Heath, Ward, Cameron, Birchall, Adebola, John, El Idrissi.

Huddersfield T (0) 0

Mansfield T (1) 2 *(Boulding M 45, Barker 48)* 5111

Huddersfield T: Glennon; Holdsworth, Adams, Hudson, Mirfin, Clarke N, Taylor-Fletcher (Booth), Collins, Abbott, Beckett, Schofield.
Mansfield T: White; Mullins, Jelleyman, Dawson, Buxton, John-Baptiste, Hamshaw, D'Laryea, Barker, Brown (Beardsley), Boulding M.

Hull C (0) 2 *(Burgess 56, Duffy 110)*

Tranmere R (1) 1 *(Cansdell-Sheriff 31)* 6075

Hull C: Myhill; Ricketts, Dawson, Marney (Welsh), Collins, Turner, France, Livermore, Fagan, Elliott (Duffy), Burgess (Parkin).
Tranmere R: Ward; Stockdale, Cansdell-Sheriff, McAteer (Jennings), McCready, Goodison, Shuker (Zola), Mullin, Taylor, Greenacre, Ellison (Davies).
aet.

Leeds U (0) 1 *(Bakke 57)*
Chester C (0) 0 10,013
Leeds U: Sullivan; Richardson, Crainey, Bakke, Foxe (Kilgallon), Gregan, Carole, Westlake, Beckford (Moore), Blake (Healy), Lewis.
Chester C: Danby; Vaughan, Wilson, Linwood, Westwood, Artell, Blundell, Martinez (Rutherford), Broughton (Holroyd), Walters, Hand.

Leicester C (1) 2 *(O'Grady 24, McCarthy 89)*
Macclesfield T (0) 0 6298
Leicester C: Logan; Stearman, Maybury, Wesolowski (Hughes), McCarthy, McAuley, Low, Williams, Hume, O'Grady, Porter.
Macclesfield T: Brain; Regan (Hadfield), McNulty, Brightwell, Swailes, Teague, Heath, Navarro (McDonald), Miles, Robinson, Tolley.

Millwall (1) 2 *(Braniff 39, Hubertz 85)*
Gillingham (0) 1 *(Crofts 81)* 5040
Millwall: Pidgeley; Ross, Bakayogo (Craig), Elliott, Robinson, Whitbread, Hackett, Mawene (Hubertz), Brighton, Braniff, Ardley (Morais).
Gillingham: Randolph; Jupp, Jackman, Flynn, Cox, Sancho, Easton, Bentley (Crofts), Ndumbu-Nsungu, McDonald (Mulligan), Jarvis.

Milton Keynes D (0) 1 *(McLeod 94)*
Colchester U (0) 0 2747
Milton Keynes D: Bankole; Edds, Tillen (McLeod), Morgan, O'Hanlon, Chorley, Mitchell, Howe (Dyer), Taylor, Hastings, Harding (McGovern).
Colchester U: Gerken; Halford, White, Baldwin, Brown, Watson, Izzet, Garcia, Iwelumo, Guy (Cureton), Duguid.
aet.

Peterborough U (1) 2 *(Benjamin 45 (pen), Branston 95)*
Ipswich T (0) 2 *(De Vos 90, Clarke 105)* 4792
Peterborough U: Tyler; Newton, Day (Carden), Arber, Branston, Plummer, Holden, Benjamin, Richards (Stirling), Yeo (Gain), Butcher.
Ipswich T: Price; Wilnis (Casement), Harding, Bruce, De Vos, Naylor, Currie (Clarke), Haynes, Bowditch, Forster (Brittain), Richards.
aet; Peterborough U won 4-2 on penalties.

Plymouth Arg (0) 0
Walsall (0) 1 *(Dann 85)* 6407
Plymouth Arg: McCormick; Connolly, Barness, Wotton, Doumbe, Aljofree, Norris, Nalis, Chadwick (Reid), Ebanks-Blake, Capaldi (Buzsaky).
Walsall: Ince; Pead, Fox, Fangueiro (Dann), Roper, Westwood, Gerrard, Keates, Sam (Wright), Constable (Demontagnac), Taylor.

QPR (1) 3 *(Cook 18, Gallen 50, Jones R 87)*
Northampton T (0) 2 *(Watt 55, Kirk 78)* 4569
QPR: Cole; Bignot, Howell, Bailey, Rehman, Stewart (Kanyuka), Baidoo, Bircham (Jones R), Gallen (Oliseh), Blackstock, Cook.
Northampton T: Bunn; Crowe, Brett Johnson (Bojic), Burnell, Dyche, Chambers, Brad Johnson (Watt), Jess, Quinn (Gilligan), Kirk, Aiston.

Rotherham U (0) 3 *(Sharps 48, Hoskins 54, Partridge 88)*
Oldham Ath (1) 1 *(Rocastle 41)* 3065
Rotherham U: Cutler; Worrell, Robertson, Woods, Sharps, Mills, Partridge, Bopp, Facey, Hoskins (Hibbert), Wiseman (Keane).
Oldham Ath: Howarth (Smith); Wellens, Edwards, Eardley, Stam (Tierney), Haining, Wood, Rocastle, Grabban, Warne (Molango), Liddell.

Scunthorpe U (1) 4 *(Torpey 7, Mulligan 58, Paul 111, Baraclough 112)*
Lincoln C (0) 3 *(Stallard 69, Frecklington 80, Beevers 92)* 3455
Scunthorpe U: Murphy; Byrne, Williams, Crosby, Foster, Hinds, Mulligan (Taylor), Foy (Baraclough), Torpey (Paul), Sharp, Sparrow.
Lincoln C: Rayner; Beevers, Mayo, Moses, Morgan, Kerr, Frecklington, Amoo, Stallard, Forrester, Hughes.
aet.

Stockport Co (0) 0
Derby Co (1) 1 *(Johnson M 44)* 3394
Stockport Co: Spencer; Bowler, Rose, Dinning, Williams, Owen, Allen (Briggs), Taylor, Proudlock (Le Fondre), Dickinson (Raynes), Griffin.
Derby Co: Camp; Edworthy, Camara, Bolder, Johnson M, Nyatanga, Bisgaard (Idiakez), Barnes, Howard, Smith T (Lupoli), Smith R (Peschisolido).

Stoke C (1) 1 *(Pericard 29)*
Darlington (1) 2 *(Logan 45, Joachim 54)* 3573
Stoke C: Simonsen; Russell, Dickinson, Hill, Duberry, Pulis, Harper (Paterson), Whitley (Eustace), Sidibe (Sigurdsson), Pericard, Sweeney.
Darlington: Stockdale; Close, James■, Collins, Holloway, Ngoma, Duke, Johnson (Giallanza), Logan (Rowson), Joachim (Wainwright), Cummins.

Swansea C (0) 2 *(Williamson 72 (og), Pratley 81)*
Wycombe W (0) 3 *(Easter 50, Oakes 64, Williamson 113)* 5892
Swansea C: Gueret; Amankwaah, Lawrence (Williams), Britton, Austin, Iriekpen, Pratley, O'Leary, Trundle, Fallon (Butler), McLeod (Akinfenwa).
Wycombe W: Young; Stockley, Martin (Gregory), Palmer, Antwi, Williamson, Grant, Oakes, Easter (Dixon), Torres (Anya), Betsy.
aet.

Swindon T (1) 2 *(Nicholas 38, Evans 72)*
Brentford (2) 2 *(O'Connor 10, Osei-Kuffour 25)* 5582
Swindon T: Smith P; Smith J, Nicholas, Holgate, Ifil, Vincent (Weston), Shakes, Evans, Onibuje, Brownlie■, Brown (Caton).
Brentford: Nelson; O'Connor (Osborne), Tillen, Pinault, Heywood, Griffiths, Brooker, Mousinho, Moore (Ide), Osei-Kuffour, Rhodes (Charles).
aet; Brentford won 4-3 on penalties.

Wednesday, 23 August 2006

Brighton & HA (0) 1 *(Reid 73)*
Boston U (0) 0 2533
Brighton & HA: Kuipers; Reid, Mayo, Carpenter, Lynch, Santos, Cox, Hammond, Robinson (Gatting), Revell, Stokes (Loft).
Boston U: Marriott; Canoville, Ryan, Talbot (Forbes), Greaves, Ellender (Farrell), N'Guessan, Galbraith (Clarke), Tait, Davidson, Holland.

Chesterfield (0) 0
Wolverhampton W (0) 0 4136
Chesterfield: Roche; Picken, O'Hare, Hazell, Downes, Niven, Hall (Bailey), Allott, Larkin (Allison), Shaw (Folan), Hurst.
Wolverhampton W: Ikeme; Edwards, Little, Olofinjana, Craddock, Clapham, Potter, Rosa (Henry), Davies C (Clarke), Frankowski (Johnson), Ricketts.
aet; Chesterfield won 6-5 on penalties.

Port Vale (0) 2 *(Sodje 52, Constantine 82)*
Preston NE (0) 1 *(Whaley 72)* 3522
Port Vale: Goodlad; Abbey (Talbot), McGregor, Sonner, Pilkington, Walsh (Walker), Whitaker, Harsley, Sodje, Constantine, Smith J.
Preston NE: Nash; Hill, Wilson, Whaley, St Ledger-Hall, Chilvers, Sedgwick, McKenna, Jarrett (Agyemang), Nugent, Pugh.

Sheffield W (0) 1 *(Whelan 79)*
Wrexham (2) 4 *(Roberts 33, Llewellyn 39, Done 63, Mark Jones 84)* 8047
Sheffield W: Adamson; Simek, Hills, Whelan, Bullen, Bougherra, Spurr, McAllister (McClements), Boden (Bowman), Brunt, Lunt.
Wrexham: Ingham; Spender (Evans G), Valentine, Williams D, Mike Williams, Pejic (Roche), Mark Jones, Crowell (Mackin), Roberts, Llewellyn, Done.

Southampton (3) 5 *(Cohen 25 (og), Skacel 32, Wright-Phillips 37, Dyer 69, Jones 78)*

Yeovil T (1) 2 *(Gray 30, Harrold 90)* 20,653

Southampton: Davis; Makin, Bale, Viafara, Baird, Pele, Surman, Lallana (Dyer), Jones, Wright-Phillips (Fuller), Skacel (Sarmiento).
Yeovil T: Mildenhall; Lynch, Jones, Terry (James), Skiverton, Forbes, Davies, Kamudimba Kalala, Gray (Morris), Welsh (Harrold), Cohen.

Torquay U (0) 0

Norwich C (0) 2 *(McKenzie 48, Etuhu 64)* 3100

Torquay U: Abbey; Andrews, Hill, Garner (Hockley), Woods, Angus, McPhee (Motteram), Mansell, Thorpe, Evans, Ward.
Norwich C: Gallacher; Cave-Brown (Spillane), Drury (Halliday), Fleming, Doherty, Hughes, Robinson, Ryan Jarvis, Henderson, McKenzie, Etuhu.

Thursday, 24 August 2006

Leyton Orient (0) 0

WBA (1) 3 *(Nicholson 41, Carter 71, Greening 76)* 3058

Leyton Orient: Garner; Miller (McMahon), Lockwood, Easton, Saah, Fortune, Tudor, Barnard, Connor (Steele), Ibehre (Alexander), Corden.
WBA: Zuberbuhler; Albrechtsen, Robinson, Wallwork, Davies C, McShane, Carter, Chaplow, Phillips (Hartson), Nicholson, Greening.

SECOND ROUND

Tuesday, 19 September 2006

Barnsley (0) 1 *(McIndoe 66)*

Milton Keynes D (1) 2 *(Wilbraham 28, 90)* 4411

Barnsley: Mannone; Tonge, Williams, Wroe, Kay, Austin, McParland (McIndoe), Healy, Wright, Coulson, Jarman.
Milton Keynes D: Baines; Crooks, Lewington, Diallo, Chorley, Mitchell, Edds, McGovern, Platt, Taylor (Hastings), Wilbraham.

Birmingham C (1) 4 *(Jerome 41, McSheffrey 102, 113, Bendtner 117)*

Wrexham (1) 1 *(Llewellyn 29)* 10,491

Birmingham C: Doyle; Kelly, Painter, Muamba (Dunn), Martin Taylor, Tebily, Larsson, Kilkenny, Forssell (Campbell), Jerome (Bendtner), McSheffrey.
Wrexham: Ingham; Roche, Mike Williams, Williams D, Evans S, Crowell, Mark Jones (Mackin), Ferguson, McAliskey (Evans G), Llewellyn, Johnson (Newby).
aet.

Brentford (0) 0

Luton T (1) 3 *(Morgan 10, Feeney 53, Vine 90)* 3005

Brentford: Nelson; Osborne, Charles, Pinault, Heywood, Mousinho (Willock), Brooker, Cox (England), Tomlin (Moore■), Osei-Kuffour, Tillen.
Luton T: Beresford; Brkovic (Foley), Bell, O'Leary, Barnett■, Keane, Edwards, Holmes, Boyd (Vine), Feeney, Morgan (Langley).

Charlton Ath (0) 1 *(Bent D 57)*

Carlisle U (0) 0 8190

Charlton Ath: Myhre; Young, Ashton, Faye, El-Karkouri, Fortune, Kishishev (Sankofa), Ambrose, Bent M (Lisbie), Bent D, Rommedahl.
Carlisle U: Williams; Arnison, Aranalde, Billy, Livesey, Murphy, Hackney, Gall (McDermott), Holmes (Thirlwell), Hawley, Lumsdon (Hindmarch).

Crewe Alex (1) 2 *(Jack 42, Maynard 90)*

Wigan Ath (0) 0 3907

Crewe Alex: Williams; Otsemobor, Jones, Roberts, Baudet, Cox, O'Connor, Jack (Rix), Maynard (O'Donnell), Varney, Vaughan.
Wigan Ath: Pollitt; Wright, Baines, Landzaat, Hall (De Zeeuw), Jackson, Teale, Scharner, Johansson (Heskey), Cywka (Montrose), Kilbane.

Hereford U (0) 1 *(Purdie 56 (pen))*

Leicester C (1) 3 *(Hammond 27, Stearman 66, Hume 76 (pen))* 4073

Hereford U: Brown; Travis, Rose, Purdie, Mkandawire, Beckwith, McClenahan■, Williams, Fleetwood (Connell), Sills, Giles.
Leicester C: Logan; Stearman, Kisnorbo■, Wesolowski (Sylla), Maybury, McAuley, Low, Porter, Hume (Johansson), Hammond, Tiatto.

Hull C (0) 0

Hartlepool U (0) 0 6392

Hull C: Myhill; Dawson, Ricketts, Marney, Collins, Turner, France (Parkin), Welsh, Fagan, Barmby (Duffy), Yeates (Elliott).
Hartlepool U: Konstantopoulos; Williams D, Brackstone, Liddle, Nelson, Clark, Gibb, Sweeney (Bullock), Porter (Foley), Daly, Robson (Brown).
aet; Hull C won 3-2 on penalties.

Leeds U (1) 3 *(Blake 7, Moore 55, 74)*

Barnet (0) 1 *(Vieira 78)* 7220

Leeds U: Sullivan; Kelly, Crainey, Douglas, Foxe, Kilgallon, Stone (Howson), Nicholls (Derry), Horsfield (Moore), Blake, Lewis.
Barnet: Flitney; Devera, Nicolau, Bailey, Warhurst, Yakubu (Hessenthaler), Graham, Sinclair, Grazioli (Kandol), Hatch (Vieira), Puncheon.

Mansfield T (0) 1 *(Reet 81)*

Portsmouth (2) 2 *(Fernandes 5, Taylor 33)* 6646

Mansfield T: White; Mullins, Jelleyman, Coke (Boulding M), Buxton, John-Baptiste, Hamshaw, D'Laryea, Barker, Beardsley (Reet), Dawson (Lloyd).
Portsmouth: Kiely; Duffy, Taylor, Fernandes, Pamarot, O'Brien, Koroman (Douala), Kranjcar (Thompson), Cole, Lua-Lua (Mwaruwari), Hughes.

Millwall (0) 0

Southampton (2) 4 *(Belmadi 20, Wright-Phillips 43, 89, McGoldrick 90)* 5492

Millwall: Day; Ross, Shaw, Elliott, Robinson, Whitbread, Dunne, McInnes, Hubertz, Zebroski (Braniff), Bakayogo (Grant).
Southampton: Davis; Ostlund, Bale, Sarmiento, Baird, Pele, Belmadi (Dyer), Wright (Licka), Jones (McGoldrick), Wright-Phillips, Surman.

Peterborough U (0) 1 *(Benjamin 56)*

Everton (1) 2 *(Stirling 24 (og), Cahill 87)* 10,756

Peterborough U: Tyler; Newton, Davis (Crow), Arber, Stirling, Turner, Holden, Butcher (Huke), Richards, Benjamin, Gain (Branston).
Everton: Wright; Neville, Nuno Valente, Hughes, Lescott, Van der Meyde (Cahill), Davies, Carsley, Beattie, Anichebe, Naysmith (Arteta).

Port Vale (2) 3 *(Smith J 19, Whitaker 28, Walker 61)*

QPR (1) 2 *(Nygaard 9, Stewart 78)* 3550

Port Vale: Goodlad; Talbot, McGregor, Sonner (Husbands), Pilkington, Walker, Whitaker, Harsley, Sodje, Constantine, Smith J.
QPR: Cole; Bignot, Milanese (Rose), Bailey, Kanyuka, Stewart, Bircham, Ward (Baidoo), Nygaard (Jones R), Czerkas, Cook.

Reading (2) 3 *(Lita 31, 35, Mate 86)*

Darlington (2) 3 *(Johnson 19 (pen), Joachim 34, 52)* 10,353

Reading: Stack; Halls (Harper), De La Cruz, Gunnarsson, Bikey, Mate, Little, Hunt, Lita (Doyle), Long, Oster.
Darlington: Stockdale; Duke■, James, Holloway, Hutchinson (Close), Ngoma, Johnson, Rowson, Logan (Wainwright), Joachim, McLeod (Cummins).
aet; Reading won 4-2 on penalties.

Rotherham U (1) 2 *(Keane 24, Williamson 49 (pen))*
Norwich C (1) 4 *(Thorne 6, Ryan Jarvis 53, 90, Fleming 54)* 3958
Rotherham U: Cutler; Worrell (Wiseman), Robertson, Woods, Sharps, Mills, Keane, Cochrane, Taylor, Hoskins, Williamson.
Norwich C: Gallacher; Colin, Rossi Jarvis, Shackell, Fleming, Eagle, Hughes, Robinson (Etuhu), Thorne (McVeigh), Ryan Jarvis, Henderson (Spillane).

Sheffield U (1) 1 *(Nade 16)*
Bury (0) 0 6273
Sheffield U: Bennett; Kozluk, Wright (Quinn S), Li Tie, Short (Lucketti), Davis, Quinn A, Law, Nade, Kazim-Richards, Akinbiyi (Marrison).
Bury: Fettis (Grundy); Scott, Kennedy T, Fitzgerald, Challinor, Adams (Goodfellow), Baker, Mattis, Taylor, Bishop, Buchanan (Pugh).

Southend U (0) 3 *(Paynter 87, Hunt 88, Eastwood 89)*
Brighton & HA (0) 2 *(Cox 71, El-Abd 90)* 4819
Southend U: Flahavan; Francis, Hammell, Maher, Sodje, Barrett, Campbell-Ryce (Hooper), Hunt, Paynter, Eastwood, Gower.
Brighton & HA: Kuipers; Reid (Butters), Mayo, El-Abd, Lynch, Fraser, Cox, Hammond, Hart (Robinson), Revell, Frutos (Loft).

WBA (0) 3 *(Wallwork 48, Ellington 60 (pen), Nicholson 68 (pen))*
Cheltenham T (1) 1 *(Odejayi 45)* 10,974
WBA: Zuberbuhler; Hodgkiss, Robinson, Wallwork (Greening), McShane, Perry, Carter (Gera), Chaplow, Ellington, Nicholson (Kamara), Koumas.
Cheltenham T: Higgs; Gill, Bell (Yao), Lowe, Caines, McCann, Wilson, Finnigan, Guinan (Wylde), Odejayi (Spencer), Armstrong.

Walsall (0) 1 *(Butler 74)*
Bolton W (0) 3 *(Nolan 68, Campo 88, Anelka 90)* 6243
Walsall: Ince; Pead, Fox (Demontagnac), Westwood, Roper, Dobson, Wright, Keates, Butler, Sam, Taylor.
Bolton W: Walker; Hunt, Teimourian (Nolan), Campo, Tal, Meite, Giannakopoulos (Diouf), Speed, Anelka, Vaz Te, Fojut.

Watford (0) 0
Accrington Stanley (0) 0 8368
Watford: Lee; Chambers, Parkes, Spring, Blizzard (Kamara), Mariappa, Jarrett, Bangura (Seanla), Diagouraga, Priskin, McNamee.
Accrington Stanley: Dunbavin (Elliot); Cavanagh, Richardson, Proctor, Williams, Edwards, Todd, Craney, Roberts, Mullin, Doherty (Boco).
aet; Watford 6-5 on penalties.

Wednesday, 20 September 2006
Chesterfield (0) 2 *(Folan 51, Niven 67)*
Manchester C (1) 1 *(Samaras 40)* 7960
Chesterfield: Roche; Picken, Bailey, Hazell, Downes, Niven, Hall, Allott, Shaw (Allison), Folan, Hurst.
Manchester C: Weaver; Richards, Jordan (Dickov), Dunne, Distin, Barton, Reyna (Miller), Hamann (Ireland), Samaras, Corradi, Sinclair.

Doncaster R (2) 3 *(Forte 6, 57, Stock 29)*
Derby Co (0) 3 *(Howard 74, Moore 78, Lupoli 90)* 5598
Doncaster R: Budtz; Lockwood, Roberts G, Roberts S (Griffith), O'Connor, Stock, Forte (Price), Green P, Heffernan (Thornton), Guy, McDaid.
Derby Co: Grant; Jackson, Camara, Barnes (Smith R), Moore, Nyatanga, Bolder, Oakley, Howard, Peschisolido (Lupoli■), Malcolm (Johnson S).
aet; Doncaster R won 8-7 on penalties.

Fulham (0) 1 *(Helguson 47)*
Wycombe W (2) 2 *(Easter 8, Mooney 41 (pen))* 6620
Fulham: Lastuvka; Volz, Jensen N (Rosenior), Jensen C, Zakuani, Bocanegra (Omozusi), Routledge, Radzinski, Helguson, Runstrom (John), Timlin.
Wycombe W: Young; Fernandez (Martin), Golbourne, Palmer (Doherty), Antwii, Williamson, Grant, Bloomfield, Mooney (Dixon), Easter, Betsy.

Middlesbrough (0) 0
Notts Co (1) 1 *(N'Toya 26)* 11,148
Middlesbrough: Turnbull; McMahon (Morrison), Taylor, Cattermole (Euell), Bates, Huth, Parnaby, Mendieta, Maccarone, Viduka, Johnson.
Notts Co: Deeney; Silk, McCann, Ross, Hunt, Edwards, Curtis, Somner, N'Toya (Needham), Dudfield (Gleeson), Sheridan (Mendes).

Scunthorpe U (0) 1 *(Sharp 73)*
Aston Villa (1) 2 *(Angel 42, 64)* 6502
Scunthorpe U: Murphy; Mulligan, Williams, Hinds, Foster, Baraclough, Taylor, Morris, Keogh, Sharp, Sparrow.
Aston Villa: Sorensen; Hughes, Barry, Davis, Mellberg, Ridgewell, Agbonlahor, McCann (Whittingham), Angel, Moore (Baros), Petrov.

THIRD ROUND

Tuesday, 24 October 2006
Chesterfield (0) 2 *(Larkin 54, Folan 87)*
West Ham U (1) 1 *(Harewood 4)* 7787
Chesterfield: Roche; Bailey (Lowry), O'Hare, Hazell, Downes, Niven, Hall, Allott, Folan, Larkin (Allison), Hurst.
West Ham U: Green; Pantsil, McCartney (Konchesky), Gabbidon, Ferdinand, Mullins, Dailly, Reo-Coker, Harewood (Sheringham), Zamora, Reid (Etherington).

Everton (2) 4 *(Cahill 23, Keane 34 (og), McFadden 53, Anichebe 83)*
Luton T (0) 0 27,149
Everton: Turner; Davies (Anichebe), Lescott, Weir (Hughes), Stubbs, Carsley, Osman, Cahill, McFadden, Johnson (Beattie), Arteta.
Luton T: Beresford; Foley, Davis, Robinson, Barnett, Keane, Edwards, Bell, Vine (Boyd), Feeney, Morgan (Brkovic).

Leeds U (1) 1 *(Moore 44)*
Southend U (2) 3 *(Hammell 34 (pen), Hooper 36, 64)* 10,449
Leeds U: Warner; Kelly, Crainey (Cresswell), Westlake, Butler, Kilgallon, Douglas, Richardson, Moore (Blake), Healy, Lewis (Bayly).
Southend U: Flahavan; Hunt, Hammell, Maher, Sodje, Barrett, Francis, Clarke, Paynter (Guttridge), Hooper (Wilson), Gower.

Leicester C (1) 2 *(Stearman 42, Kisnorbo 85)*
Aston Villa (2) 3 *(Angel 5, Barry 45 (pen), Agbonlahor 119)* 27,288
Leicester C: Henderson; Stearman, Kisnorbo, Maybury, McAuley, Johansson, Sylla (Kenton), Wesolowski, Hume, Hammond (Odhiambo), Welsh (Low).
Aston Villa: Taylor; Hughes, Barry, Davis (Agathe), Mellberg, Ridgewell, Agbonlahor, Osbourne (Bouma), Angel, Baros (Sutton), Petrov.
aet.

Notts Co (2) 2 *(Edwards 13, Lee 44)*
Southampton (0) 0 6731
Notts Co: Deeney; Silk (Gleeson), Hunt, Somner, White, Edwards, Pipe, Ross (Martin), Lee, Mendes, Parkinson (N'Toya).
Southampton: Davis; Makin (Wright), Bale, Viafara, Baird, Pele (Dyer), Licka, Sarmiento, Rasiak, Wright-Phillps, Skacel (Surman).

Port Vale (0) 0
Norwich C (0) 0 4518
Port Vale: Goodlad; Abbey, Talbot, Sonner (Husbands) (Moore), Pilkington, Walker, Whitaker, Harsley, Sodje, Constantine, Smith J.
Norwich C: Gallacher; Colin, Drury, Shackell, Doherty, Safri (Eagle), Croft, Ryan Jarvis (Thorne), Earnshaw (Dublin), Robinson, Etuhu.
aet; Port Vale won 3-2 on penalties.

Sheffield U (1) 2 *(Akinbiyi 21, Montgomery 85)*
Birmingham C (1) 4 *(Campbell 41, Bendtner 70, Jerome 79, Larsson 90)* 10,584
Sheffield U: Bennett; Sommeil, Unsworth, Law, Morgan, Short, Ifill, Montgomery, Akinbiyi (Nade), Kabba, Webber (Geary).
Birmingham C: Doyle; Kelly, Sadler, Muamba, Martin Taylor, Jaidi, Larsson, Danns, Jerome (Kilkenny), Campbell (Bendtner), Gray.

WBA (0) 0
Arsenal (1) 2 *(Aliadiere 34 (pen), 49)* 21,566
WBA: Hoult; Watson, Robinson, Chaplow (Gera), Davies C, McShane, Carter (Kamara), Quashie (Albrechtsen), Ellington, Hartson, Greening.
Arsenal: Almunia; Connolly, Clichy, Denilson (Randall), Djourou, Senderos, Song-Billong, Walcott, Adebayor (Traore), Aliadiere, Flamini.

Watford (1) 2 *(Young 2, Priskin 54)*
Hull C (0) 1 *(Barmby 71)* 8274
Watford: Foster; Doyley, Stewart, Francis, Shittu (Mackay), Demerit, Young, Mahon, Henderson, Priskin (Spring), Bouazza.
Hull C: Myhill; Ricketts, Dawson, Ashbee, Turner, Delaney, France (Yeates), Marney (Duffy), Parkin, Elliott (Barmby), Welsh.

Wycombe W (0) 2 *(Oakes 71, Easter 116)*
Doncaster R (0) 2 *(Forte 65, Grant 97 (og))* 3308
Wycombe W: Batista; Stockley, Golbourne, Oakes■, Martin, Williamson, Grant (Stonebridge), Doherty (Palmer), Easter, Bloomfield, Betsy.
Doncaster R: Smith; O'Connor, Lockwood, Roberts S (Streete), Lee, Stock, Forte (Coppinger), Green P, Price (Heffernan), Guy, McDaid.
aet; Wycombe W won 3-2 on penalties.

Wednesday, 25 October 2006

Blackburn R (0) 0
Chelsea (0) 2 *(Cole J 53, Kalou 81)* 14,732
Blackburn R: Friedel; Emerton, Neill, Mokoena, Khizanishvili, Henchoz, Bentley, McEveley, Nonda (Roberts), McCarthy (Jeffers), Pedersen (Peter).
Chelsea: Hilario; Geremi, Cole A, Essien, Terry, Boulahrouz, Cole J (Wright-Phillips), Makelele, Kalou, Ballack (Lampard), Robben (Drogba).

Charlton Ath (1) 1 *(Bent M 17)*
Bolton W (0) 0 10,788
Charlton Ath: Myhre; Young, Hreidarsson, Holland, El-Karkouri (Sankofa), Fortune, Kishishev (Rommedahl), Hughes, Hasselbaink, Bent M, Thomas (Ambrose).
Bolton W: Walker; Hunt, Teimourian (Smith), Tal, Ben-Haim, Meite, Giannakopoulos, Speed (Campo), Davies, Vaz Te, Pedersen (Fojut).

Crewe Alex (0) 1 *(Varney 73)*
Manchester U (1) 2 *(Solskjaer 26, Lee 119)* 10,046
Crewe Alex: Williams; Otsemobor, Taylor (Bell), Osbourne, Baudet (O'Donnell), Cox, Rix, Lowe, Maynard, Varney, Vaughan.
Manchester U: Kuszczak; Gray (Lee), Heinze, Jones D, Brown, Silvestre, Marsh (Barnes) (Shawcross), Jones R, Smith, Solskjaer, Richardson.
aet.

Liverpool (2) 4 *(Fowler 44, Riise 45, Paletta 50, Crouch 77)*
Reading (0) 3 *(Bikey 75, Lita 81, Long 85)* 42,445
Liverpool: Reina; Peltier (Smith), Warnock, Sissoko (Guthrie), Agger, Paletta, Pennant, Zenden, Crouch, Fowler, Riise (Kuyt).
Reading: Stack; De la Cruz, Halls, Ingimarsson, Bikey, Gunnarsson (Sodje), Little, Hunt, Lita, Long, Oster.

Milton Keynes D (0) 0
Tottenham H (2) 5 *(Mido 36, 60, Defoe 44, 51, Keane 90)* 8306
Milton Keynes D: Baines; Smith J, Lewington, Diallo, O'Hanlon, Andrews (Edds), McGovern, Wilbraham, Platt (Taylor), McLeod, Dyer (Crooks).
Tottenham H: Cerny; Stalteri, Ziegler, Huddlestone (Lennon), Gardner, Davenport (Dawson), Murphy, Davids, Mido, Defoe (Keane), Ghaly.

Newcastle U (0) 3 *(Rossi 48, Solano 53, 90)*
Portsmouth (0) 0 25,028
Newcastle U: Harper; Taylor (Ramage), Babayaro, Butt (Dyer), Moore, Bramble, Solano, Milner, Martins (Duff), Rossi, N'Zogbia.
Portsmouth: James; Pamarot, Taylor, Davis (Hughes), Primus, O'Brien, Thompson (Koroman), Fernandes, Cole, Lua Lua, Kranjcar (Douala).

FOURTH ROUND

Tuesday, 7 November 2006

Chesterfield (1) 3 *(Larkin 3, Folan 47, Allison 120)*
Charlton Ath (1) 3 *(Hasselbaink 40, 93, Bent D 73)* 7000
Chesterfield: Roche; Lowry, O'Hare, Hazell, Downes, Niven, Hall (Smith), Allott, Folan (Allison), Larkin (Davies), Hurst.
Charlton Ath: Carson; Young, Hreidarsson, Hughes (Ambrose), Fortune, Diawara, Kishishev (Faye), Bent M (Bent D), Hasselbaink, Thomas, Reid.
aet; Charlton Ath won 4-3 on penalties.

Notts Co (0) 0
Wycombe W (0) 1 *(Easter 49)* 7395
Notts Co: Deeney; Silk, McCann, Edwards, White, Ross, Pipe (N'Toya), Somner (Martin), Lee, Mendes, Parkinson (Dudfield).
Wycombe W: Batista; Stockley, Golbourne, Oakes (Palmer), Martin, Williamson, Grant, Bloomfield, Mooney, Easter, Betsy.

Southend U (1) 1 *(Eastwood 27)*
Manchester U (0) 0 11,532
Southend U: Flahavan; Hunt (Francis), Hammell, Maher, Prior, Sodje, Campbell-Ryce, Clarke, Hooper (Lawson), Eastwood, Gower.
Manchester U: Kuszczak; O'Shea (Lee), Heinze, Jones D (Shawcross), Brown, Silvestre, Ronaldo, Fletcher, Smith (Evra), Rooney, Richardson.

Watford (0) 2 *(Francis 69, Shittu 108)*
Newcastle U (1) 2 *(Sibierski 3, Parker 116)* 16,791
Watford: Lee; Doyley, Stewart, Spring, Shittu, Demerit, Francis, Priskin (Bangura), Henderson, Young, Bouazza.
Newcastle U: Harper; Carr, Babayaro, Parker, Ramage, Taylor, Milner, Emre, Rossi (Solano), Sibierski (N'Zogbia), Duff.
aet; Newcastle U won 5-4 on penalties.

Wednesday, 8 November 2006

Birmingham C (0) 0
Liverpool (1) 1 *(Agger 45)* 23,061
Birmingham C: Maik Taylor; Kelly, Sadler, Nafti (Muamba), Martin Taylor, Jaidi, Larsson, Danns, Jerome (Bendtner), Campbell (McSheffrey), Gray.
Liverpool: Dudek; Peltier, Warnock, Sissoko (Xabi Alonso), Agger, Paletta, Pennant, Zenden, Fowler (Kuyt), Bellamy (Guthrie), Gonzalez.

Chelsea (1) 4 *(Lampard 32, Shevchenko 65, Essien 82, Drogba 84)*
Aston Villa (0) 0 41,516
Chelsea: Cudicini; Geremi, Bridge, Makelele (Diarra), Boulahrouz, Ricardo Carvalho, Essien, Lampard, Drogba, Shevchenko (Kalou), Ballack (Cole J).
Aston Villa: Sorensen; Hughes, Bouma, Davis (Baros), Mellberg, Laursen (Ridgewell), Petrov, McCann, Angel, Agbonlahor, Barry (Berger).

Everton (0) 0
Arsenal (0) 1 *(Adebayor 85)* 31,045
Everton: Howard; Neville, Nuno Valente, Yobo, Lescott, Carsley (Anichebe), Osman, Cahill, Johnson, McFadden■, Arteta.
Arsenal: Almunia (Poom); Eboue, Flamini, Song Billong, Djourou, Senderos, Walcott, Denilson (Randall), Adebayor, Aliadiere, Traore.

Tottenham H (0) 3 *(Huddlestone 80, 99, Defoe 107)*
Port Vale (0) 1 *(Constantine 64)* 34,560
Tottenham H: Cerny; Ifil, Lee, Huddlestone, Dawson, Dervite, Murphy (Ghaly), Malbranque (Lennon), Barcham (Berbatov), Defoe, Davids.
Port Vale: Goodlad; Abbey, Miles, Sonner (Gardner), Pilkington, Walker, Whitaker, Harsley, Sodje (Husbands), Constantine, Smith J (Cardle).
aet.

QUARTER-FINALS

Tuesday, 19 December 2006
Charlton Ath (0) 0
Wycombe W (1) 1 *(Easter 35)* 16,940
Charlton Ath: Carson; Sankofa (Hasselbaink), Traore, Hughes, Fortune, Diawara, Rommedahl, Faye (Holland), Bent M, Bent D, Thomas (Sam).
Wycombe W: Young; Martin, O'Halloran, Oakes, Antwii, Williamson, Grant (Palmer), Bloomfield, Mooney (Stonebridge), Easter, Betsy.

Wednesday, 20 December 2006
Newcastle U (0) 0
Chelsea (0) 1 *(Drogba 79)* 37,406
Newcastle U: Given; Solano, Huntington, Parker, Taylor, Ramage, Milner (Sibierski), Butt, Martins, Emre, Dyer.
Chelsea: Hilario; Paulo Ferreira, Bridge, Makelele (Lampard), Boulahrouz, Ricardo Carvalho, Essien, Kalou, Mikel (Ballack), Shevchenko (Drogba), Robben.

Tottenham H (0) 1 *(Defoe 115)*
Southend U (0) 0 35,811
Tottenham H: Robinson; Stalteri, Assou-Ekotto, Huddlestone, Dawson, Davenport, Murphy (Berbatov), Malbranque, Mido, Defoe, Tainio (Davids).
Southend U: Flahavan; Hunt, Hammell, Maher, Prior (Clarke), Sodje, Campbell-Ryce (Hooper), McCormack (Francis), Bradbury, Eastwood, Gower.
aet.

QUARTER-FINAL

Tuesday, 9 January 2007
Liverpool (1) 3 *(Fowler 33, Gerrard 68, Hyypia 80)*
Arsenal (4) 6 *(Aliadiere 27, Julio Baptista 40, 45, 60, 84, Song Billong 44)* 42,614
Liverpool: Dudek; Peltier, Warnock (Xabi Alonso), Fabio Aurelio, Paletta, Hyypia, Guthrie, Gerrard, Fowler, Bellamy, Gonzalez (Luis Garcia) (Carragher).
Arsenal: Almunia; Hoyte, Traore (Connolly), Song Billong, Toure, Djourou, Walcott (Diaby), Fabregas, Aliadiere, Julio Baptista, Denilson.

SEMI-FINAL FIRST LEG

Wednesday, 10 January 2007
Wycombe W (0) 1 *(Easter 77)*
Chelsea (1) 1 *(Bridge 36)* 9775
Wycombe W: Batista; Martin, O'Halloran, Oakes, Antwii, Williamson, Doherty, Bloomfield (Torres), Mooney (Dixon), Easter, Betsy.
Chelsea: Hilario; Geremi, Cole A, Makelele, Paulo Ferreira, Bridge (Lampard), Essien, Mikel, Kalou (Sinclair), Wright-Phillips (Sahar), Ballack.

SEMI-FINAL SECOND LEG

Tuesday, 23 January 2007
Chelsea (2) 4 *(Shevchenko 22, 43, Lampard 69, 90)*
Wycombe W (0) 0 41,591
Chelsea: Cech; Diarra, Cole A (Morais), Makelele, Essien, Ricardo Carvalho, Mikel, Lampard, Drogba, Shevchenko (Kalou), Ballack (Wright-Phillips).
Wycombe W: Batista; Martin, Golbourne, Oakes (Anya), Antwi (Stockley), Williamson, Doherty, Bloomfield (Torres), Mooney, Easter, Betsy.

SEMI-FINAL FIRST LEG

Wednesday, 24 January 2007
Tottenham H (2) 2 *(Berbatov 12, Julio Baptista 21 (og))*
Arsenal (0) 2 *(Julio Baptista 64, 77)* 35,485
Tottenham H: Robinson; Chimbonda, Assou-Ekotto, Zokora, Dawson, Gardner, Lennon, Huddlestone, Berbatov (Keane), Defoe (Mido), Malbranque.
Arsenal: Almunia; Hoyte, Traore, Diaby (Hleb) (Flamini), Toure, Senderos, Denilson, Fabregas, Aliadiere (Eboue), Walcott, Julio Baptista.

SEMI-FINAL SECOND LEG

Wednesday, 31 January 2007
Arsenal (0) 3 *(Adebayor 77, Aliadiere 105, 113 (og))*
Tottenham H (0) 1 *(Mido 85)* 55,872
Arsenal: Almunia; Hoyte, Traore (Clichy), Silva, Toure, Senderos, Walcott (Rosicky), Denilson, Adebayor, Aliadiere, Diaby (Fabregas).
Tottenham H: Robinson; Chimbonda, Assou-Ekotto, Zokora, Dawson, Gardner (Rocha), Ghaly (Huddlestone), Jenas, Keane, Defoe, Malbranque (Mido).
aet.

CARLING CUP FINAL

Sunday, 25 February 2007
(at Millennium Stadium, Cardiff, attendance 70,073)

Chelsea (1) 2 Arsenal (1) 1

Chelsea: Cech; Diarra, Bridge, Makelele (Robben), Terry (Mikel■), Ricardo Carvalho, Essien, Lampard, Drogba, Shevchenko (Kalou), Ballack.

Scorers: Drogba 20, 84.

Arsenal: Almunia; Hoyte, Traore (Eboue), Denilson, Toure■, Senderos, Walcott, Fabregas, Aliadiere (Adebayor■), Julio Baptista, Diaby (Hleb).

Scorer: Walcott 12.

Referee: H. Webb (South Yorkshire).

JOHNSTONE'S PAINT TROPHY 2006–07

▪ *Denotes player sent off.*

NORTHERN SECTION FIRST ROUND

Tuesday, 17 October 2006

Accrington S (0) 1 *(Lumsdon 53 (og))*
Carlisle U (1) 1 *(Holmes 41)* 850

Accrington S: Elliot; Edwards, Richardson, Doherty, Williams, Welch (N'Da), Todd, Craney, Boco (Brown), Mangan, Byrom (Harris).
Carlisle U: Williams; Arnison, Aranalde, Thirlwell, Grand, Livesey, Murray G (Gall), Holmes, Hackney, Beckford (Hindmarch), Lumsdon.
Accrington S won 3-1 on penalties.

Bradford C (0) 1 *(Brown 88)*
Scunthorpe U (0) 2 *(Foy 48, Goodwin 73 (pen))* 1936

Bradford C: Howarth; Edghill, Parker, Schumacher, Doyle (Ainge), Clarke▪, Colbeck, Holmes, Graham (Brown), Johnson E, Rogers (McGuire).
Scunthorpe U: Murphy; Mulligan (Hinds), Ridley, Goodwin, Byrne, Williams (Crosby), Foy, MacKenzie, McBreen, Torpey, Winn (Allanson).

Bury (0) 0
Tranmere R (1) 2 *(Shuker 22, Jennings 87)* 1093

Bury: Edge; Parrish, Woodthorpe (Kennedy T), Fitzgerald, Challinor, Flitcroft, Barry-Murphy, Pugh (Speight), Youngs, Adams, Buchanan (Goodfellow).
Tranmere R: Achterberg; Stockdale, Cansdell-Sheriff, McAteer, McCready, Goodison, Harrison (Jennings), Shuker, Davies (Mullin), Greenacre, Ellison (Tremarco).

Hartlepool U (2) 3 *(Bullock 12, Foley 43, Humphreys 67)*
Rotherham U (1) 1 *(Facey 28)* 1832

Hartlepool U: Provett; Turnbull P, Brackstone, Strachan, Nelson, Clark, Foley, Bullock, Brown (Maidens), Daly (Porter), Robson (Humphreys).
Rotherham U: Cutler; Worrell, Hurst, Partridge (Brogan), Sharps▪, Mills (Murdock), Wiseman, Woods▪, Facey, Taylor (Newsham), Williamson.

Huddersfield T (0) 1 *(Booth 61)*
Doncaster R (1) 2 *(Price 26, Guy 87)* 3629

Huddersfield T: Glennon (Rachubka); Hardy, Adams, Ahmed (Collins), Clarke N, McCombe, Worthington, Brandon, Booth, Abbott, Schofield.
Doncaster R: Filan; Streete (Green P), McDaid, Roberts S, Lee, Griffith (Roberts G), Lockwood, Thornton, Heffernan, Guy, Price.

Lincoln C (0) 0
Grimsby T (0) 0 2019

Lincoln C: Marriott (Rayner); Cryan, Mayo, Brown, Beevers, Kerr, Frecklington, Amoo, Gritton, Mettam (Forrester), Ryan (Stallard).
Grimsby T: Barnes; McDermott (Croft), Newey, Ravenhill, Fenton, Whittle, Bore (Thorpe), Boshell, Hegarty, Jones, Toner.
Grimsby T won 5-3 on penalties.

Macclesfield T (0) 0
Stockport Co (0) 1 *(Malcolm 65)* 1792

Macclesfield T: Brain; Scott, McNulty (McNeil), Morley, Swailes, Navarro, Hadfield (Regan), Tolley (Teague), Heath, Weir-Daley, McIntyre.
Stockport Co: Spencer; Clare, Tansey, Dinning, Owen, Allen (Rose), Briggs, Taylor (Poole), Robinson, Dickinson, Malcolm (Ellis).

Wrexham (0) 1 *(Crowell 80)*
Rochdale (1) 1 *(Dagnall 40)* 1209

Wrexham: Ingham; Valentine, Mike Williams, Williams D, Evans S, Morgan, Mark Jones, Crowell, Johnson (Newby), Llewellyn, Done.
Rochdale: Gilks; Ramsden, Goodall, Doolan, Sharp, Boardman, Crooks (Cooksey), Jones, Barker, Dagnall, Moyo-Modise (Sako).
Rochdale won 5-3 on penalties.

SOUTHERN SECTION FIRST ROUND

Tuesday, 17 October 2006

Brighton & HA (1) 2 *(Robinson 41, Hammond 65)*
Boston U (0) 0 1740

Brighton & HA: Henderson; Whing, Mayo, Hinshelwood, Butters (Lynch), El-Abd, Cox, Hammond, Williams (Revell), Robinson (Fraser), Gatting.
Boston U: Marriott; Galbraith, Ryan T, Ellender, Greaves, Albrighton (Talbot) (N'Guessan), Cotton, Holland, Davidson (Elding), Farrell, Rusk.

Bristol R (0) 1 *(Anthony 89)*
Torquay U (0) 0 2672

Bristol R: Shearer; Lescott, Carruthers, Campbell, Anthony, Elliott, Sandell (Rigg), Disley, Walker R, Walker J, Haldane.
Torquay U: Abbey; Andrews, Reed, Garner (Hockley), Woods, Thorpe, Murray, Mansell, McPhee (Ward), Evans (Fortune-West), Hill.

Gillingham (0) 1 *(Mulligan 73)*
Nottingham F (1) 2 *(Lester 7, Grant Holt 55)* 1817

Gillingham: Flinders; Howell (Savage), Easton, Flynn, Jupp, Johnson, Crofts (Stone), Bentley, McDonald (Mulligan), Ndumbu-Nsungu, Jarvis.
Nottingham F: Pedersen; Thompson, Bennett (Fernandez), Cullip, Morgan, Clingan, Perch, Hughes (Harris), Lester, Grant Holt, Commons (McGugan).

Hereford U (0) 1 *(Williams 79)*
Shrewsbury T (1) 2 *(Symes 22, 77)* 2007

Hereford U: Thompson; Travis (Purdie), Gulliver, Webb, Mkandawire, Beckwith, McClenahan, Connell, Fleetwood, Sills (Williams), Ferrell (Rose).
Shrewsbury T: Neal; Herd, Hall, Ashton, Langmead, Cowan, Edwards, Hogg, Symes, Asamoah (Humphrey), Leslie (Williams).

Northampton T (0) 0
Brentford (0) 0 2088

Northampton T: Bunn; Crowe (Brett Johnson), Holt, Chambers, Bojic, Hunt (Watt), Jess, Burnell, McGleish, Kirk, Cole (Gilligan).
Brentford: Masters; O'Connor, Frampton, Osborne (Mousinho), Heywood, Carder-Andrews, Peters, Skulason, Moore (Brooker), Osei-Kuffour (Wijnhard), Tomlin.
Brentford won 4-2 on penalties.

Notts Co (0) 0
Barnet (1) 1 *(Kandol 16)* 1291

Notts Co: Deeney; Silk (Gleeson), Needham, Martin, White, Hunt, Mendes (Sheridan), Somner, Dudfield (Akers), N'Toya, Ross.
Barnet: Flitney; Devera, Nicolau, Hessenthaler, Yakubu, Charles, Bailey, Sinclair, Vieira (Hatch), Kandol, Puncheon.

Walsall (0) 1 *(Wrack 90)*
Swansea C (0) 1 *(Tudur-Jones 89)* 2557

Walsall: Ince; Pead, Fox, Gerrard, Roper, Dann, Wright (Wrack), Kinsella (Constable), Bedeau (Demontagnac), Sam, Taylor.
Swansea C: Oakes; Amankwaah (Williams), Austin, Tudur-Jones, Tate, Lawrence, Pratley, MacDonald (Britton), Trundle, Robinson, Butler (Jones).
Swansea C won 4-3 on penalties.

Wycombe W (1) 1 *(Stonebridge 13)*
Swindon T (0) 0 1583
Wycombe W: Batista; Stockley, Golbourne, Palmer, Antwii, Martin, Grant (Bloomfield), Stonebridge, Dixon (Anya), Betsy, Doherty (Oakes).
Swindon T: Smith P; Smith J, Vincent, Whalley (Monkhouse), Ifil, Shakes, Brown, Brownlie (Onibuje), Jutkiewicz, Weston (Pook), Nicholas.

NORTHERN SECTION SECOND ROUND

Monday, 30 October 2006
Scunthorpe U (0) 0
Port Vale (0) 0 3421
Scunthorpe U: Murphy (Lillis); Byrne, Ridley, Crosby, Foster, Hinds, Mulligan, Goodwin, McBreen (Foy), Torpey, Williams (Winn).
Port Vale: Anyon; Abbey, Talbot■, Sonner, Walsh, Walker, Cardle (Smith J), Harsley, Husbands (Sodje), Constantine, Whitaker (Pilkington).
Port Vale won 5-3 on penalties.

Tuesday, 31 October 2006
Accrington S (1) 4 *(Craney 44, Todd 59, Mullin 65, Williams 90)*
Blackpool (1) 4 *(Gillett 31, Barker 54, Burgess 75 (pen), 85)* 1344
Accrington S: Elliot; Cavanagh, Richardson, Proctor, Williams, Welch (Edwards), Todd, Craney, Doherty (Mangan), Mullin (Brown), Harris.
Blackpool: Evans; Joseph, Dickinson, Bean (Donnelly), Evatt, Barker, Forbes (Burgess), Gillett, Blinkhorn, Parker, Jorgensen.
Accrington S won 4-2 on penalties.

Chester C (1) 3 *(Hand 42, Blundell 83, Wilson 85)*
Stockport Co (0) 0 1229
Chester C: Danby; Wilson, Bennett, Bolland, Artell, Hessey, Marples, Sandwith, Blundell, Steele (Walters), Hand.
Stockport Co: Spencer; Williams, Robinson, Dinning, Clare, Tansey, Poole, Allen (Bramble), Dickinson (Ellis), Malcolm (Taylor), Rose.

Hartlepool U (0) 1 *(Liddle 90)*
Doncaster R (0) 3 *(Heffernan 54, 55, Price 86)* 1853
Hartlepool U: Provett; Williams D, Brackstone (Robson), Liddle, Nelson, Clark, Maidens, Bullock, Porter (Williams E), Daly (Brown), Humphreys.
Doncaster R: Smith; Streete (Lee), Roberts G, Roberts S, Lockwood, Thornton, Griffith (Stock), Green P, Heffernan, McCammon, Forte (Price).

Mansfield T (1) 3 *(Butler 37 (og), Beardsley 79, 85)*
Grimsby T (0) 0 1761
Mansfield T: White; Mullins (Wood), Sheehan, Coke, Buxton, John-Baptiste, Hamshaw (Brown), D'Laryea, Boulding M, Beardsley, Lloyd (Boulding R).
Grimsby T: Barnes; McDermott, Croft (Harkins), Ravenhill, Fenton, Butler, James (Hegarty), Boshell, Rankin, Bore (North), Toner.

Rochdale (0) 1 *(Barker 60)*
Crewe Alex (1) 1 *(Varney 39)* 1148
Rochdale: Gilks; Brown, Goodall, Doolan (Jackson), Stanton, Crooks, Jones, Cooksey, Barker, Dagnall, Moyo-Modise.
Crewe Alex: Tomlinson; Dugdale, Flynn, Roberts (Coo), O'Donnell, Kempson, Rix, Lowe, Maynard, Varney, Osbourne.
Crewe Alex won 2-0 on penalties.

Tranmere R (0) 0
Darlington (0) 1 *(Giallanza 67 (pen))* 2036
Tranmere R: Achterberg; Jennings (Goodison), Cansdell-Sheriff, McAteer, McCready, Tremarco, Mullin, Shuker, Taylor, Davies (Harrison), Ellison (Greenacre).
Darlington: Russell; Rowson, Duke, Collins, Holloway, Ngoma, Johnson (McLeod), Keltie (Cummins), Conlon (Wainwright), Giallanza, Logan.

SOUTHERN SECTION SECOND ROUND

Tuesday, 31 October 2006
Cheltenham T (3) 3 *(McCann 17, 28 (pen), Melligan 20)*
Barnet (1) 2 *(Kandol 6, 66)* 964
Cheltenham T: Higgs; Gallinagh, Armstrong, Lowe, Caines, McCann, Melligan (Yao), Bird (Wylde), Odejayi (Guinan), Spencer, Wilson.
Barnet: Flitney; Devera, Nicolau, Cogan, Yakubu, King, Bailey, Sinclair, Vieira (Warhurst), Kandol, Puncheon.

Millwall (1) 2 *(Hackett 20, May 46)*
Bournemouth (0) 0 1905
Millwall: Pidgeley; Senda, Bakayoko, Grant, Craig (Elliott), Shaw (Robinson), Hackett, Mawene, Williams, Zebroski (May), Morais.
Bournemouth: Moss; Purches, Cummings (Songo'o), Hollands, Young, Hart, Ainsworth (Foley-Sheridan), Anderton, Hayter, Best, Gowling.

Nottingham F (0) 2 *(Southall 47, Grant Holt 56)*
Brentford (1) 1 *(Osei-Kuffour 39)* 2031
Nottingham F: Pedersen; Curtis, Bennett, Clingan (McGugan), Fernandez, Morgan, Southall (Hughes), Grant Holt, Agogo (Commons), Lester, Perch.
Brentford: Masters; O'Connor, Frampton, Pinault (Wijnhard), Heywood, Tillen, Brooker (Tomlin), Mousinho, Ide, Osei-Kuffour (Peters), Skulason.

Peterborough U (1) 1 *(Crow 3)*
Swansea C (0) 0 1432
Peterborough U: Tyler; Ghaichem (Richards), Day (Stirling), Arber, Branston, Futcher, Holden, Huke, Crow (Opara), McLean, Butcher.
Swansea C: Gueret; Amankwaah (Trundle), Austin, Tate, Lawrence, Watt, O'Leary (Williams), MacDonald, Akinfenwa, Jones, Butler (Tudur-Jones).

Shrewsbury T (0) 2 *(Edwards 75, Symes 84)*
Yeovil T (0) 1 *(Barry 67)* 1759
Shrewsbury T: MacKenzie; Herd, Ashton, Edwards, Hall, Cowan, Davies, Sorvel, Symes, Asamoah, Keith.
Yeovil T: Mildenhall; Lynch, Tonkin, Terry (Kamudimba Kalala), Forbes, Guyett, Barry, Welsh (Cohen), Webb, Gray (Brittain), Davies.

Wycombe W (0) 0
Bristol R (1) 2 *(Easter 30, Igoe 87)* 1314
Wycombe W: Batista; Stockley, O'Halloran, Palmer (Grant), Antwii, Williamson, Martin, Bloomfield, Stonebridge (Anya), Easter, Betsy.
Bristol R: Phillips; Green, Carruthers, Campbell, Anthony, Hinton, Sandell, Disley, Walker R, Easter (Rigg), Igoe.

NORTHERN SECTION SECOND ROUND

Wednesday, 1 November 2006
Oldham Ath (0) 0
Chesterfield (1) 1 *(Smith 19)* 2118
Oldham Ath: Pogliacomi (Legzdins); Wood (Wellens), Taylor, Lomax, Stam, Haining, Cywka, Tierney, Hall, Warne (Barlow), Liddell.
Chesterfield: Roche; Lowry, O'Hare, Standing (Nicholson), Downes, Kovacs, Wiggins-Thomas, Davies, Larkin, Allison, Smith (Jackson).

SOUTHERN SECTION SECOND ROUND

Wednesday, 1 November 2006
Brighton & HA (2) 4 *(Cox 14, Revell 37, 82, Hammond 87)*
Milton Keynes D (0) 1 *(Page 84)* 2774
Brighton & HA: Henderson; Whing, Mayo (Lynch), Hinshelwood, Butters, El-Abd, Cox, Hammond, Robinson, Revell (Gatting), Fraser (Bowditch).
Milton Keynes D: Baines; Crooks, Page, Mitchell, O'Hanlon (Collins), Murphy, McGovern, Hastings, Taylor, McLeod (Howe) (Baldock), Rizzo.

Leyton Orient (0) 1 *(Duncan 63)*

Bristol C (0) 3 *(Corr 71, Jevons 80, Keogh 90)* 1118

Leyton Orient: Garner; Lockwood, Barnard, Chambers, Mackie, Thelwell, Till (Demetriou), Simpson (Miller), Connor, Ibehre (Alexander), Duncan.
Bristol C: Basso; Keogh, Woodman, Fontaine, McCombe, Russell, Wright (Carey), Noble, Corr (Johnson), Jevons, Myrie-Williams (McAllister).

NORTHERN QUARTER-FINALS

Tuesday, 28 November 2006

Darlington (0) 1 *(Smith 75)*

Mansfield T (0) 0 2059

Darlington: Russell; Duke, James, Close, Collins, Ngoma, Wainwright, Conlon (Armstrong), Logan (Smith), Joachim (Johnson), Cummins.
Mansfield T: Muggleton; Buxton, Charlton, Lloyd (Wood), Hjelde, John-Baptiste, Arnold, D'Laryea, Brown (Boulding R), Beardsley (Reet), Boulding M.

Doncaster R (2) 2 *(Heffernan 13, Thornton 28)*

Accrington S (0) 0 3209

Doncaster R: Smith; Streete, Roberts G, Lockwood (Green P), Lee, Thornton, Coppinger, Forte (Guy), Heffernan, McCammon, McDaid (Wilson).
Accrington S: Elliot; Ventre, Jacobson, Proctor, Edwards, Welch, Todd (McDonald), Williams, Mangan, Mullin (McGivern), Whalley■.

SOUTHERN QUARTER-FINALS

Tuesday, 28 November 2006

Cheltenham T (1) 2 *(Odejayi 6, Finnigan 69)*

Shrewsbury T (1) 3 *(Asamoah 45, Gill 57 (og), Symes 88)* 1379

Cheltenham T: Higgs; Gill, Wilson, Duff, Caines, Bird, Melligan, Finnigan, Odejayi, Spencer, Armstrong.
Shrewsbury T: MacKenzie; Jones L, Ashton (Cowan), Humphrey (Herd), Hope, Langmead (Hogg), Davies, Sorvel, Symes, Asamoah, Thomas.

Millwall (1) 1 *(Robinson 41)*

Brighton & HA (0) 1 *(Robinson 88)* 3659

Millwall: Day; Phillips, Bakayogo (Zebroski), Elliott (Trotter), Robinson, Whitbread, Hackett, Lee, May, Byfield, Grant (Senda).
Brighton & HA: Henderson; Whing, Lynch, Hinshelwood, Butters■, El-Abd (John), Cox, Hammond, Robinson, Revell (Gatting), Fraser (Mayo).
Brighton & HA won 3-2 on penalties.

NORTHERN QUARTER-FINALS

Wednesday, 29 November 2006

Chesterfield (2) 4 *(Shaw 1, Folan 15, Downes 51, 70)*

Chester C (2) 4 *(Linwood 21, Wilson 27, Blundell 48, Bolland 86)* 2414

Chesterfield: Roche; Bailey, O'Hare (Picken), Hazell, Downes, Niven, Hall, Allott, Folan, Shaw, Hurst.
Chester C: Danby; Vaughan S (Vaughan J), Wilson (Rutherford), Linwood, Westwood, Bolland, Hessey, Martinez, Blundell, Bennett, Semple (Holroyd).
Chesterfield won 3-1 on penalties.

Port Vale (0) 2 *(Constantine 78, 88)*

Crewe Alex (1) 3 *(Lowe 38 (pen), Jack 48, Varney 57)* 4694

Port Vale: Goodlad; Abbey, Miles, Sonner, Pilkington■, Fortune, Whitaker, Harsley, Sodje (Moore), Constantine, Gardner.
Crewe Alex: Williams; Otsemobor, Taylor (Baudet), Roberts, O'Donnell, Jones, Rix, Lowe (Maynard), Jack (Bignot), Varney, Vaughan.

SOUTHERN QUARTER-FINALS

Wednesday, 29 November 2006

Bristol R (1) 1 *(Nicholson 29)*

Peterborough U (0) 0 3621

Bristol R: Phillips; Green, Carruthers, Campbell, Anthony, Elliott, Igoe, Disley, Lambert, Nicholson, Haldane (Sandell).
Peterborough U: Tyler; Newton (Stirling), Day (Opara), Arber, Futcher, Turner (Smith), Holden, Butcher, Crow, Benjamin, Gain.

Nottingham F (1) 2 *(Morgan 45, Grant Holt 79)*

Bristol C (0) 2 *(Jevons 58, Showunmi 63)* 4107

Nottingham F: Pedersen; Gary Holt, Bennett (Harris), Clingan, Breckin, Morgan, Southall, Lester (Dobie), Tyson (Commons), Grant Holt, Perch.
Bristol C: Basso; Orr, McAllister, Fontaine, Carey, Skuse (Keogh), Murray, Johnson (Russell), Jevons, Showunmi (Brown), Myrie-Williams.
Bristol C won 4-2 on penalties.

NORTHERN SEMI-FINALS

Tuesday, 9 January 2007

Doncaster R (0) 2 *(Heffernan 54, Price 89)*

Darlington (0) 0 8009

Doncaster R: Smith; Lockwood, Gilbert (Pittman), Thornton, Roberts S, Stock, Dyer (Coppinger), Green P, Heffernan, Guy (Wilson), Price.
Darlington: Jones; Close, Horwood (James), Collins (Holloway), Wheater, Keltie, Rowson, Johnson, Armstrong (Reay), Joachim, Wainwright.

Wednesday, 10 January 2007

Chesterfield (1) 2 *(Niven 31, Hall 84)*

Crewe Alex (1) 4 *(Maynard 20, Varney 54, 89, 90)* 3414

Chesterfield: Roche; Picken, Davies, Hazell, Downes, Niven, Hall, Allott, Folan, Allison (Larkin), Smith (Shaw).
Crewe Alex: Williams; Moss, Bignot, Roberts, Baudet, Jones, Rix, Lowe (Higdon), Maynard, Varney, O'Connor.

SOUTHERN SEMI-FINAL

Tuesday, 23 January 2007

Bristol C (1) 2 *(Showunmi 41, Andrews 68)*

Brighton & HA (0) 0 6485

Bristol C: Basso; Orr, McAllister, McCombe, Carey (Keogh), Skuse, Murray, Johnson (Russell), Andrews, Showunmi (Fontaine), Myrie-Williams.
Brighton & HA: Kuipers; Hart (O'Cearuill), Rents, Lynch, Butters (Frutos), El-Abd, Cox, Hammond, Robinson, Gatting, Fraser (Chamberlain).

NORTHERN FINAL FIRST LEG

Tuesday, 30 January 2007

Crewe Alex (0) 3 *(Moss 51, Lowe 63, Varney 86)*

Doncaster R (2) 3 *(Heffernan 29 (pen), 74, Stock 40)* 4631

Crewe Alex: Williams; Otsemobor, Jones, Roberts, Baudet, Cox, Moss, Lowe, Varney, O'Connor, Vaughan.
Doncaster R: Smith; O'Connor, Roberts G, Roberts S, Lee, Stock, Guy, Wilson, Heffernan, McCammon (Lockwood), Price (Green P).

SOUTHERN SEMI-FINAL

Tuesday, 30 January 2007

Shrewsbury T (0) 0

Bristol R (0) 1 *(Walker R 53)* 3199

Shrewsbury T: MacKenzie; Jones L (Jones M), Burton, Drummond, Hall (Humphrey), Langmead, Davies, Edwards, Symes, Asamoah, Ashton.
Bristol R: Phillips; Green, Carruthers, Campbell, Hinton, Elliott, Sandell, Disley, Walker R, Lambert (Haldane), Igoe.

NORTHERN FINAL SECOND LEG

Monday, 12 February 2007
Doncaster R (0) 3 *(Heffernan 63, 83 (pen), Price 89)*
Crewe Alex (2) 2 *(Varney 32, Lowe 36)* 12,561
Doncaster R: Smith; Lockwood, Roberts G (Green P), Roberts S (Nelthorpe), Lee, Stock (Thornton), Coppinger, Wilson, Heffernan, Price, O'Connor.
Crewe Alex: Williams; Otsemobor, Bignot, Roberts (Higdon), Baudet, Jones, Rix, O'Connor, Lowe (Maynard), Varney, Vaughan.

SOUTHERN FINAL FIRST LEG

Wednesday, 21 February 2007
Bristol C (0) 0
Bristol R (0) 0 18,730
Bristol C: Basso; Orr, Woodman (Myrie-Williams), Keogh, Carey, Fontaine, Noble (Jevons), Johnson, Brooker, Andrews, Murray (Skuse).
Bristol R: Phillips; Lescott, Carruthers, Campbell, Hinton, Elliott, Igoe, Disley, Walker R (Nicholson), Lambert, Haldane (Sandell).

SOUTHERN FINAL SECOND LEG

Tuesday, 27 February 2007
Bristol R (0) 1 *(Lambert 65)*
Bristol C (0) 0 11,530
Bristol R: Phillips; Lescott, Carruthers, Campbell, Hinton, Elliott, Igoe, Disley, Walker R (Nicholson), Lambert (Sandell), Haldane.
Bristol C: Basso; Orr, Keogh (Smith), McCombe, Carey, Fontaine, Noble, Johnson, Brooker, Jevons (Andrews), Showunmi (Skuse).

JOHNSTONE'S PAINT TROPHY FINAL

Sunday, 1 April 2007
(at Millennium Stadium, Cardiff, attendance 59,024)
Bristol R (0) 2 Doncaster R (2) 3

Bristol R: Phillips; Lescott, Carruthers, Campbell, Hinton, Elliott, Igoe (Sandell), Disley, Walker R (Nicholson), Lambert, Haldane (Lines).

Scorers: Walker R 49 (pen), Igoe 62.

Doncaster R: Sullivan; O'Connor, McDaid, Lockwood, Lee, Stock (Wilson), Coppinger, Green P, Heffernan, Price (Thornton), Forte (Guy).
aet.

Scorers: Forte 1, Heffernan 5, Lee 110.

Referee: G. Laws (Tyne & Wear).

FA CUP FINALS 1872–2007

1872 and 1874–92	Kennington Oval	1910	Replay at Everton
1873	Lillie Bridge	1911	Replay at Old Trafford
1886	Replay at Derby (Racecourse Ground)	1912	Replay at Bramall Lane
		1915	Old Trafford, Manchester
1893	Fallowfield, Manchester	1920–22	Stamford Bridge
1894	Everton	1923 to 2000	Wembley
1895–1914	Crystal Palace	1970	Replay at Old Trafford
1901	Replay at Bolton	2001 to date	Millennium Stadium, Cardiff

Year	*Winners*	*Runners-up*	*Score*
1872	Wanderers	Royal Engineers	1-0
1873	Wanderers	Oxford University	2-0
1874	Oxford University	Royal Engineers	2-0
1875	Royal Engineers	Old Etonians	2-0 (after 1-1 draw aet)
1876	Wanderers	Old Etonians	3-0 (after 1-1 draw aet)
1877	Wanderers	Oxford University	2-1 (aet)
1878	Wanderers*	Royal Engineers	3-1
1879	Old Etonians	Clapham R	1-0
1880	Clapham R	Oxford University	1-0
1881	Old Carthusians	Old Etonians	3-0
1882	Old Etonians	Blackburn R	1-0
1883	Blackburn Olympic	Old Etonians	2-1 (aet)
1884	Blackburn R	Queen's Park, Glasgow	2-1
1885	Blackburn R	Queen's Park, Glasgow	2-0
1886	Blackburn R†	WBA	2-0 (after 0-0 draw)
1887	Aston Villa	WBA	2-0
1888	WBA	Preston NE	2-1
1889	Preston NE	Wolverhampton W	3-0
1890	Blackburn R	The Wednesday	6-1
1891	Blackburn R	Notts Co	3-1
1892	WBA	Aston Villa	3-0
1893	Wolverhampton W	Everton	1-0
1894	Notts Co	Bolton W	4-1
1895	Aston Villa	WBA	1-0
1896	The Wednesday	Wolverhampton W	2-1
1897	Aston Villa	Everton	3-2
1898	Nottingham F	Derby Co	3-1
1899	Sheffield U	Derby Co	4-1
1900	Bury	Southampton	4-0
1901	Tottenham H	Sheffield U	3-1 (after 2-2 draw)
1902	Sheffield U	Southampton	2-1 (after 1-1 draw)
1903	Bury	Derby Co	6-0
1904	Manchester C	Bolton W	1-0
1905	Aston Villa	Newcastle U	2-0
1906	Everton	Newcastle U	1-0
1907	The Wednesday	Everton	2-1
1908	Wolverhampton W	Newcastle U	3-1
1909	Manchester U	Bristol C	1-0
1910	Newcastle U	Barnsley	2-0 (after 1-1 draw)
1911	Bradford C	Newcastle U	1-0 (after 0-0 draw)
1912	Barnsley	WBA	1-0 (aet, after 0-0 draw)
1913	Aston Villa	Sunderland	1-0
1914	Burnley	Liverpool	1-0
1915	Sheffield U	Chelsea	3-0
1920	Aston Villa	Huddersfield T	1-0 (aet)
1921	Tottenham H	Wolverhampton W	1-0
1922	Huddersfield T	Preston NE	1-0
1923	Bolton W	West Ham U	2-0
1924	Newcastle U	Aston Villa	2-0
1925	Sheffield U	Cardiff C	1-0
1926	Bolton W	Manchester C	1-0
1927	Cardiff C	Arsenal	1-0
1928	Blackburn R	Huddersfield T	3-1
1929	Bolton W	Portsmouth	2-0
1930	Arsenal	Huddersfield T	2-0
1931	WBA	Birmingham	2-1
1932	Newcastle U	Arsenal	2-1
1933	Everton	Manchester C	3-0
1934	Manchester C	Portsmouth	2-1
1935	Sheffield W	WBA	4-2

Year	*Winners*	*Runners-up*	*Score*
1936	Arsenal	Sheffield U	1-0
1937	Sunderland	Preston NE	3-1
1938	Preston NE	Huddersfield T	1-0 (aet)
1939	Portsmouth	Wolverhampton W	4-1
1946	Derby Co	Charlton Ath	4-1 (aet)
1947	Charlton Ath	Burnley	1-0 (aet)
1948	Manchester U	Blackpool	4-2
1949	Wolverhampton W	Leicester C	3-1
1950	Arsenal	Liverpool	2-0
1951	Newcastle U	Blackpool	2-0
1952	Newcastle U	Arsenal	1-0
1953	Blackpool	Bolton W	4-3
1954	WBA	Preston NE	3-2
1955	Newcastle U	Manchester C	3-1
1956	Manchester C	Birmingham C	3-1
1957	Aston Villa	Manchester U	2-1
1958	Bolton W	Manchester U	2-0
1959	Nottingham F	Luton T	2-1
1960	Wolverhampton W	Blackburn R	3-0
1961	Tottenham H	Leicester C	2-0
1962	Tottenham H	Burnley	3-1
1963	Manchester U	Leicester C	3-1
1964	West Ham U	Preston NE	3-2
1965	Liverpool	Leeds U	2-1 (aet)
1966	Everton	Sheffield W	3-2
1967	Tottenham H	Chelsea	2-1
1968	WBA	Everton	1-0 (aet)
1969	Manchester C	Leicester C	1-0
1970	Chelsea	Leeds U	2-1 (aet)
	(after 2-2 draw, after extra time)		
1971	Arsenal	Liverpool	2-1 (aet)
1972	Leeds U	Arsenal	1-0
1973	Sunderland	Leeds U	1-0
1974	Liverpool	Newcastle U	3-0
1975	West Ham U	Fulham	2-0
1976	Southampton	Manchester U	1-0
1977	Manchester U	Liverpool	2-1
1978	Ipswich T	Arsenal	1-0
1979	Arsenal	Manchester U	3-2
1980	West Ham U	Arsenal	1-0
1981	Tottenham H	Manchester C	3-2
	(after 1-1 draw, after extra time)		
1982	Tottenham H	QPR	1-0
	(after 1-1 draw, after extra time)		
1983	Manchester U	Brighton & HA	4-0
	(after 2-2 draw, after extra time)		
1984	Everton	Watford	2-0
1985	Manchester U	Everton	1-0 (aet)
1986	Liverpool	Everton	3-1
1987	Coventry C	Tottenham H	3-2 (aet)
1988	Wimbledon	Liverpool	1-0
1989	Liverpool	Everton	3-2 (aet)
1990	Manchester U	Crystal Palace	1-0
	(after 3-3 draw, after extra time)		
1991	Tottenham H	Nottingham F	2-1 (aet)
1992	Liverpool	Sunderland	2-0
1993	Arsenal	Sheffield W	2-1 (aet)
	(after 1-1 draw, after extra time)		
1994	Manchester U	Chelsea	4-0
1995	Everton	Manchester U	1-0
1996	Manchester U	Liverpool	1-0
1997	Chelsea	Middlesbrough	2-0
1998	Arsenal	Newcastle U	2-0
1999	Manchester U	Newcastle U	2-0
2000	Chelsea	Aston Villa	1-0
2001	Liverpool	Arsenal	2-1
2002	Arsenal	Chelsea	2-0
2003	Arsenal	Southampton	1-0
2004	Manchester U	Millwall	3-0
2005	Arsenal	Manchester U	0-0 (aet)
	(Arsenal won 5-4 on penalties)		
2006	Liverpool	West Ham U	3-3 (aet)
	(Liverpool won 3-1 on penalties)		
2007	Chelsea	Manchester U	1-0 (aet)

* *Won outright, but restored to the Football Association.* † *A special trophy was awarded for third consecutive win.*

FA CUP WINS

Manchester U 11, Arsenal 10, Tottenham H 8, Aston Villa 7, Liverpool 7, Blackburn R 6, Newcastle U 6, Everton 5, The Wanderers 5, WBA 5, Bolton W 4, Chelsea 4, Manchester C 4, Sheffield U 4, Wolverhampton W 4, Sheffield W 3, West Ham U 3, Bury 2, Nottingham F 2, Old Etonians 2, Preston NE 2, Sunderland 2, Barnsley 1, Blackburn Olympic 1, Blackpool 1, Bradford C 1, Burnley 1, Cardiff C 1, Charlton Ath 1, Clapham R 1, Coventry C 1, Derby Co 1, Huddersfield T 1, Ipswich T 1, Leeds U 1, Notts Co 1, Old Carthusians 1, Oxford University 1, Portsmouth 1, Royal Engineers 1, Southampton 1, Wimbledon 1.

APPEARANCES IN FINALS

Manchester U 18, Arsenal 17, Liverpool 13, Newcastle U 13, Everton 12, Aston Villa 10, WBA 10, Tottenham H 9, Blackburn R 8, Chelsea 8, Manchester C 8, Wolverhampton W 8, Bolton W 7, Preston NE 7, Old Etonians 6, Sheffield U 6, Sheffield W 6, Huddersfield T 5, *The Wanderers 5, West Ham U 5, Derby Co 4, Leeds U 4, Leicester C 4, Oxford University 4, Royal Engineers 4, Southampton 4, Sunderland 4, Blackpool 3, Burnley 3, Nottingham F 3, Portsmouth 3, Barnsley 2, Birmingham C 2, *Bury 2, Cardiff C 2, Charlton Ath 2, Clapham R 2, Notts Co 2, Queen's Park (Glasgow) 2, *Blackburn Olympic 1, *Bradford C 1, Brighton & HA 1, Bristol C 1, *Coventry C 1, Crystal Palace 1, Fulham 1, *Ipswich T 1, Luton T 4, Middlesbrough 1, Millwall 1, *Old Carthusians 1, QPR 1, Watford 1, *Wimbledon 1.
** Denotes undefeated.*

APPEARANCES IN SEMI-FINALS

Arsenal 25, Manchester U 25, Everton 23, Liverpool 22, Aston Villa 19, WBA 19, Blackburn R 18, Chelsea 17, Newcastle U 17, Tottenham H 17, Sheffield W 16, Wolverhampton W 14, Bolton W 13, Derby Co 13, Sheffield U 13, Nottingham F 12, Sunderland 12, Southampton 11, Manchester C 10, Preston NE 10, Birmingham C 9, Burnley 8, Leeds U 8, Leicester C 8, Huddersfield T 7, West Ham U 7, Old Etonians 6, Fulham 6, Oxford University 6, Notts Co 5, Portsmouth 5, The Wanderers 5, Watford 5, Luton T 4, Millwall 4, Queen's Park (Glasgow) 4, Royal Engineers 4, Blackpool 3, Cardiff C 3, Clapham R 3, Crystal Palace (professional club) 3, Ipswich T 3, Middlesbrough 3, Norwich C 3, Old Carthusians 3, Oldham Ath 3, Stoke C 3, The Swifts 3, Barnsley 2, Blackburn Olympic 2, Bristol C 2, Bury 2, Charlton Ath 2, Grimsby T 2, Swansea T 2, Swindon T 2, Wimbledon 2, Bradford C 1, Brighton & HA 1, Cambridge University 1, Chesterfield 1, Coventry C 1, Crewe Alex 1, Crystal Palace (amateur club) 1, Darwen 1, Derby Junction 1, Glasgow R 1, Hull C 1, Marlow 1, Old Harrovians 1, Orient 1, Plymouth Arg 1, Port Vale 1, QPR 1, Reading 1, Shropshire W 1, Wycombe W 1, York C 1.

FA CUP ATTENDANCES 1969–2007

	1st Round	*2nd Round*	*3rd Round*	*4th Round*	*5th Round*	*6th Round*	*Semi-finals & Final*	*Total*	*No. of matches*	*Average per match*
2006–07	168,884	113,924	708,628	478,924	340,612	230,064	177,810	2,218,846	158	14,043
2005–06	188,876	107,456	654,570	388,339	286,225	163,449	177,723	1,966,638	160	12,291
2004–05	161,197	98,702	602,152	477,472	339,082	127,914	193,233	1,999,752	146	13,697
2003–04	162,738	117,967	624,732	347,964	292,521	156,780	167,401	1,870,103	149	12,551
2002–03	189,905	104,103	577,494	404,599	242,483	156,244	175,498	1,850,326	150	12,336
2001–02	198,369	119,781	566,284	330,434	249,190	173,757	171,278	1,809,093	148	12,224
2000–01	171,689	122,061	577,204	398,241	256,899	100,663	177,778	1,804,535	151	11,951
1999–2000	181,485	127,728	514,030	374,795	182,511	105,443	214,921	1,700,913	158	10,765
1998–99	191,954	132,341	609,486	431,613	359,398	181,005	202,150	2,107,947	155	13,599
1997–98	204,803	130,261	629,127	455,557	341,290	192,651	172,007	2,125,696	165	12,883
1996–97	209,521	122,324	651,139	402,293	199,873	67,035	191,813	1,843,998	151	12,211
1995–96	185,538	115,669	748,997	391,218	274,055	174,142	156,500	2,046,199	167	12,252
1994–95	219,511	125,629	640,017	438,596	257,650	159,787	174,059	2,015,249	161	12,517
1993–94	190,683	118,031	691,064	430,234	172,196	134,705	228,233	1,965,146	159	12,359
1992–93	241,968	174,702	612,494	377,211	198,379	149,675	293,241	2,047,670	161	12,718
1991–92	231,940	117,078	586,014	372,576	270,537	155,603	201,592	1,935,340	160	12,095
1990–91	194,195	121,450	594,592	530,279	276,112	124,826	196,434	2,038,518	162	12,583
1989–90	209,542	133,483	683,047	412,483	351,423	123,065	277,420	2,190,463	170	12,885
1988–89	212,775	121,326	690,199	421,255	206,781	176,629	167,353	1,966,318	164	12,173
1987–88	204,411	104,561	720,121	443,133	281,461	119,313	177,585	2,050,585	155	13,229
1986–87	209,290	146,761	593,520	349,342	263,550	119,396	195,533	1,877,400	165	11,378
1985–86	171,142	130,034	486,838	495,526	311,833	184,262	192,316	1,971,951	168	11,738
1984–85	174,604	137,078	616,229	320,772	269,232	148,690	242,754	1,909,359	157	12,162
1983–84	192,276	151,647	625,965	417,298	181,832	185,382	187,000	1,941,400	166	11,695
1982–83	191,312	150,046	670,503	452,688	260,069	193,845	291,162	2,209,625	154	14,348
1981–82	236,220	127,300	513,185	356,987	203,334	124,308	279,621	1,840,955	160	11,506
1980–81	246,824	194,502	832,578	534,402	320,530	288,714	339,250	2,756,800	169	16,312
1979–80	267,121	204,759	804,701	507,725	364,039	157,530	355,541	2,661,416	163	16,328
1978–79	243,773	185,343	880,345	537,748	243,683	263,213	249,897	2,604,002	166	15,687
1977–78	258,248	178,930	881,406	540,164	400,751	137,059	198,020	2,594,578	160	16,216
1976–77	379,230	192,159	942,523	631,265	373,330	205,379	258,216	2,982,102	174	17,139
1975–76	255,533	178,099	867,880	573,843	471,925	206,851	205,810	2,759,941	161	17,142
1974–75	283,956	170,466	914,994	646,434	393,323	268,361	291,369	2,968,903	172	17,261
1973–74	214,236	125,295	840,142	747,909	346,012	233,307	273,051	2,779,952	167	16,646
1972–73	259,432	169,114	938,741	735,825	357,386	241,934	226,543	2,928,975	160	18,306
1971–72	277,726	236,127	986,094	711,399	486,378	230,292	248,546	3,158,562	160	19,741
1970–71	329,687	230,942	956,683	757,852	360,687	304,937	279,644	3,220,432	162	19,879
1969–70	345,229	195,102	925,930	651,374	319,893	198,537	390,700	3,026,765	170	17,805

THE FA CUP 2006–07

PRELIMINARY AND QUALIFYING ROUNDS

EXTRA PRELIMINARY ROUND

New Mills v Atherton Collieries	2-1
Sunderland Nissan v Darlington Railway Athletic	5-0
Glasshoughton Welfare v Bacup Borough	2-0
Hall Road Rangers v Durham City	0-1
Atherton LR v Parkgate	5-1
Congleton Town v Winsford United	1-0
Dunston FB v Holker Old Boys	4-0
Cheadle Town v Crook Town	3-1
Whickham v Marske United	1-2
Jarrow Roofing Boldon CA v Billingham Synthonia	5-2
Whitley Bay v Northallerton Town	2-1
Hebburn Town v Alnwick Town	3-1
Selby Town v Morpeth Town	3-3, 1-3
Salford City v Shildon	0-1
Billingham Town v Borrowash Victoria	5-2
Bishop Auckland v Squires Gate	3-1
Thackley v Ramsbottom United	1-1, 1-0
Prudhoe Town v Consett	0-5
Blackpool Mechanics v Armthorpe Welfare	2-0
Blackpool Mechanics fielded a suspended player; Armthorpe Welfare reinstated.	
Ashington v Thornaby	0-0, 2-3
Daisy Hill v Winterton Rangers	1-1, 0-3
West Allotment Celtic v Norton & Stockton Ancients	1-1, 1-6
Brandon United v Seaham Red Star	3-5
Liversedge v Nelson	2-0
Oldham Town v Trafford	1-3
Pickering Town v Formby	4-0
Chadderton v Rossington Main	2-1
Retford United v Tadcaster Albion	6-0
Garforth Town v Penrith	2-0
Silsden v Hallam	1-1, 2-3
Tow Law Town v St Helens Town	1-1, 1-2
Glossop North End v North Shields	2-0
Norton United v Colne	1-5
Newcastle Blue Star v South Shields	3-1
Teversal v Loughborough Dynamo	0-3
Blackstones v Oadby Town	1-1, 2-3
Quorn v Arnold Town	6-0
Mickleover Sports v Glapwell	1-0
Staveley MW v Boston Town	1-5
Atherstone Town v Carlton Town	3-2
Eccleshall v Pegasus Juniors	1-1, 3-0
Ford Sports Daventry v Racing Club Warwick	2-2, 1-4
Deeping Rangers v Lincoln Moorlands	5-4
Coalville Town v Studley	4-0
St Margaretsbury v Eton Manor	1-1, 1-1
Eton Manor won 4-1 on penalties.	
Dereham Town v Brentwood Town	3-1
Sawbridgeworth Town v St Neots Town	1-2
Haverhill Rovers v Welling Garden City	2-0
Felixstowe & Walton United v Potton United	0-1
Holmer Green v Wootton Blue Cross	1-3
Halstead Town v Harefield United	0-0, 1-3
Broxbourne Borough V&E v Colney Heath	1-0
Fakenham Town v Norwich United	4-0
Stanway Rovers v Leverstock Green	0-1
Wembley v Thame United	3-0
Hertford Town v Stotfold	1-2
Cogenhoe United v Saffron Walden Town	2-2, 2-6
Needham Market v Desborough Town	2-1
Bowers & Pitsea v Haringey Borough	2-0
Ruislip Manor v Aylesbury Vale	3-1
Mildenhall Town v Kirkley	8-2
Lowestoft Town v Stansted	3-1
Barkingside v Clacton Town	2-1
Biggleswade Town v Clapton	4-2
Chalfont St Peter v Hullbridge Sports	0-1
Langford v Ely City	2-4
Gorleston v Tiptree United	0-1
March Town United v St Ives Town	3-3, 1-2
Stowmarket Town v Soham Town Rangers	1-1, 4-1
Walsham Le Willows v Leiston	1-4
Long Melford v Cornard United	1-3
Long Buckby v London APSA	2-1
Tring Athletic v Diss Town	2-1
Royston Town v Harwich & Parkeston	2-2, 1-4
Newport Pagnell Town v Romford	0-1
Oxhey Jets v Concord Rangers	3-0
Ipswich Wanderers v Woodbridge Town	2-2, 3-1
London Colney v Raunds Town	0-1
Newmarket Town v Southend Manor	4-1
Arundel v Dorking	5-0
Farnham Town v Three Bridges	0-1
Moneyfields v Oakwood	2-1
Croydon v Sandhurst Town	1-2
Wick v Westfield	1-1, 0-0
Westfield won 5-3 on penalties.	
East Preston v Milton United	3-1
Ash United v Deal Town	5-0
Chessington & Hook United v Mile Oak	3-1
Saltdean United v Lancing	0-1
North Leigh w.o.v AFC Newbury removed.	
Henley Town removed v Epsom & Ewell w.o.	
Brockenhurst v Hamble ASSC	1-2
Guildford City v Whitstable Town	0-1
Reading Town v Thamesmead Town	3-4
Egham Town v Hungerford Town	2-3
Rye United v Bedfont Green	0-2
Hassocks v Wantage Town	1-0
Frimley Green v VT	1-5
Lymington Town v Sidley United	0-4
Sporting Bengal United v Slade Green	0-2
Selsey v AFC Totton	0-5
Redhill v Cowes Sports	1-2
Eastbourne United v Cobham	0-0, 1-2
Abingdon Town v Camberley Town	3-0
Raynes Park Vale v Shoreham	1-6
Hythe Town v Lordswood	2-2, 6-0
Herne Bay v Erith & Belvedere	1-6
Erith Town v Hailsham Town	0-2
Banstead Athletic v Worthing United	1-2
Carterton v Gosport Borough	1-0
Devizes Town v Calne Town	3-0
Almondsbury Town v Odd Down	0-1
Christchurch v Bitton	3-1
Shortwood United v Backwell United	4-2
Fairford Town v Harrow Hill	2-0
Westbury United v Slimbridge	2-3
Welton Rovers v Wimborne Town	2-0
St Blazey v Bodmin Town	1-0
Corsham Town v Shepton Mallet	4-0
Melksham Town v Torrington	2-1
Bemerton Heath Harlequins v Downton	1-3
Bristol Manor Farm v Barnstaple Town	0-0, 3-5
Liskeard Athletic v Sherborne Town	4-1
Witney United v Highworth Town	2-1
Bournemouth v Minehead	2-0
Wadebridge Town v Elmore	1-1, 2-3
Brislington v Dawlish Town	0-1
Hamworthy United v Hallen	1-2
Penzance v Clevedon United	1-2
Porthleven v Newquay	0-1

PRELIMINARY ROUND

Pontefract Collieries v Woodley Sports	0-3
Spennymoor Town v Bamber Bridge	3-1
Trafford v Brodsworth MW	4-1
Bridlington Town v Bishop Auckland	1-2
Cammell Laird v Morpeth Town	2-0
Norton & Stockton Ancients v Darwen	5-1
Consett v Rossendale United	1-1, 1-2
Eccleshill United v Glasshoughton Welfare	2-1
Garforth Town v Chorley	1-2
Guisborough Town v Hallam	0-3
Goole v Bradford Park Avenue	5-3
Pickering Town v New Mills	0-1
Atherton LR v Clitheroe	0-3
Glossop North End v Seaham Red Star	2-1
Shildon v Harrogate Railway Athletic	0-3
Bedlington Terriers v Curzon Ashton	1-4
St Helens Town v Skelmersdale United	0-3
Alsager Town v Cheadle Town	6-0
Sheffield v Retford United	0-0, 1-1
Sheffield won 3-0 on penalties.	

Liversedge v Newcastle Blue Star	2-2, 2-3
Yorkshire Amateur v Warrington Town	1-5
Abbey Hey v Chadderton	1-2
Thornaby v Chester-Le-Street Town	0-2
Jarrow Roofing Boldon CA v Thackley	5-4
Colwyn Bay v Ossett Albion	1-1, 2-4
Whitley Bay v Stocksbridge Park Steels	1-0
Maine Road v Armthorpe Welfare	1-2
Sunderland Nissan v Horden CW	3-2
Winterton Rangers v West Auckland Town	3-0
Marske United v Brigg Town	3-1
Hebburn Town v Flixton	3-3, 0-3
Padiham v Colne	3-2
Billingham Town v Congleton Town	4-0
Long Eaton United v Washington	1-0
Wakefield v Dunston FB	3-2
Newcastle Benfield (Bay Plastics) v Ryton	3-3, 2-0
Esh Winning v Durham City	3-5
Rocester v Oldbury United	1-0
Eccleshall v Shepshed Dynamo	0-2
Kidsgrove Athletic v Spalding United	2-0
Tipton Town v Rushall Olympic	1-0
Coalville Town v Chasetown	0-0, 1-3
Nantwich Town v Deeping Rangers	1-2
Gresley Rovers v South Normanton Athletic	1-1, 1-1
Gresley Rovers won 5-3 on penalties.	
Stratford Town v Bourne Town	2-2, 3-2
Buxton v Atherstone Town	4-1
Eastwood Town v Bromsgrove Rovers	5-5, 0-2
Gedling Town v Holbeach United	4-0
Newcastle Town v Stourbridge	2-1
Sutton Coldfield Town v Leek CSOB	3-0
Alvechurch v Bedworth United	1-2
Solihull Borough v Sutton Town	6-2
Belper Town v Boston Town	2-2, 2-1
Shirebrook Town v Barwell	3-1
Westfields v Racing Club Warwick	3-0
Quorn v Malvern Town	3-0
Romulus v Stourport Swifts	0-0, 5-0
Oadby Town v Cradley Town	7-0
Biddulph Victoria v Boldmere St Michaels	2-2, 0-7
Loughborough Dynamo v Willenhall Town	1-2
Leamington v Stone Dominoes	6-0
Causeway United v Mickleover Sports	3-2
Great Yarmouth Town v Needham Market	0-2
Tilbury v Romford	0-2
Cornard United v St Ives Town	1-3
Wroxham v Aylesbury United	1-1, 2-1
Arlesey Town v Ilford	2-2, 2-1
Harefield United v Wivenhoe Town	1-4
Broxbourne Borough V&E v Stotfold	1-1, 4-0
Long Buckby v Flackwell Heath	3-2
Harwich & Parkeston v Leiston	0-4
Marlow v Waltham Forest	0-2
Barkingside v Maldon Town	0-2
Haverhill Rovers v Wootton Blue Cross	3-0
Uxbridge v Potton United	0-2
Wisbech Town v Mildenhall Town	4-1
Biggleswade United v AFC Hornchurch	2-4
Raunds Town v Enfield	1-1, 2-1
Bowers & Pitsea v Dunstable Town	0-1
Leverstock Green v Beaconsfield SYCOB	2-3
Stowmarket Town v Dereham Town	0-2
Northampton Spencer v Chesham United	2-3
St Neots Town v Brackley Town	2-2, 0-4
Hadleigh United v Rothwell Town	2-3
Great Wakering Rovers v Newmarket Town	4-1
Hullbridge Sports v Yaxley	0-2
Tiptree United v Ipswich Wanderers	2-1
Lowestoft Town v Witham Town	2-0
Barton Rovers v Barking	0-1
Biggleswade Town v Leighton Town	0-0, 0-2
Potters Bar Town v Waltham Abbey	2-2, 2-1
Ruislip Manor v Enfield Town	2-1
Hanwell Town v Buckingham Town	2-2, 2-3
Ely City v Woodford United	0-3
Bury Town v Brook House	6-1
Berkhamsted Town v AFC Sudbury	2-6
Eton Manor v Wingate & Finchley	0-2
Hillingdon Borough v Tring Athletic	1-2
Burnham Ramblers v Ware	0-0, 2-1
Harlow Town v Saffron Walden Town	0-1
Aveley v Oxhey Jets	0-1
Canvey Island v Fakenham Town	4-1
Wembley v Redbridge	0-3
Hailsham Town v AFC Totton	0-1
Kingstonian v Pagham	3-1
Hungerford Town v Littlehampton Town	1-0
Croydon Athletic v Arundel	4-2
Fareham Town v Carterton	1-2
Cowes Sports v Sandhurst Town	1-0
Dover Athletic v Bracknell Town	3-0
Whyteleafe v Ash United	3-2
Fleet Town v Thatcham Town	1-0
Walton Casuals v Cray Wanderers	2-3
Sevenoaks Town v Moneyfields	1-3
Dulwich Hamlet v Three Bridges	3-0
Colliers Wood United v Chipstead	1-1, 2-1
AFC Wallingford v Burnham	1-0
Peacehaven & Telscombe v Whitehawk	0-1
Ashford Town v Bedfont Green	7-0
Epsom & Ewell v Leatherhead	0-2
Bedfont v Whitstable Town	0-1
Maidstone United v Burgess Hill Town	2-1
Godalming Town v North Greenford United	1-1, 2-4
Slade Green v Cobham	2-2, 0-2
Sittingbourne v Thamesmead Town	3-1
Eastbourne Town v VCD Athletic	2-2, 0-1
Hassocks v Newport (IW)	2-0
Ardley United v Ringmer	3-0
Hythe Town v VT	1-3
Lymington & New Milton v Shoreham	4-2
Cove v Tooting & Mitcham United	0-6
Oxford City v Abingdon United	2-2, 4-3
Hastings United v Merstham	0-0, 4-2
Sidley United v Worthing United	0-1
Winchester City v Chatham Town	4-3
Horsham YMCA v Molesey	1-2
Lancing v North Leigh	3-1
East Preston w.o. v Hawley Town removed.	
Andover v Corinthian Casuals	1-1, 4-3
Windsor & Eton v Bashley	1-2
Metropolitan Police v Chessington & Hook United	7-0
Chertsey Town v Abingdon Town	3-2
Hamble ASSC v East Grinstead Town	1-1, 3-1
Tunbridge Wells v Dartford	0-5
Westfield v Alton Town	2-5
Dicot Town v Erith & Belvedere	2-1
Penryn Athletic v Slimbridge	2-3
Liskeard Athletic v Welton Rovers	1-0
Saltash United v Barnstaple Town	3-3, 1-0
Odd Down v Bridgwater Town	0-1
Downton v Christchurch	2-1
Radstock Town v Elmore	3-1
Melksham Town v Cinderford Town	1-2
Street v Bishop's Cleeve	0-1
Tavistock v Bridport	4-2
Fairford Town v Bournemouth	3-1
Poole Town v Taunton Town	0-1
Evesham United v Clevedon United	6-0
Bideford v Hallen	2-1
Falmouth Town v Bishop Sutton	1-2
Paulton Rovers v Witney United	1-1, 2-1
Devizes Town v Swindon Supermarine	1-1, 0-3
Chard Town v Willand Rovers	0-4
Shortwood United v Truro City	0-5
Corsham Town v Dawlish Town	3-1
Newquay v St Blazey	1-1, 1-3

FIRST QUALIFYING ROUND

Chorley v North Ferriby United	1-3
Durham City v Alsager Town	2-0
Eccleshill United v Flixton	1-2
Witton Albion v Sheffield	3-2
Armthorpe Welfare v Burscough	1-3
Cammell Laird v Newcastle Benfield (Bay Plastics)	0-2
Fleetwood Town v Jarrow Roofing Boldon CA	3-0
Guiseley v Mossley	2-1
Long Eaton United v Warrington Town	1-3
Glossop North End v New Mills	3-1
Chadderton v Trafford	1-1, 1-3
Winterton Rangers v Kendal Town	0-5
Hallam v Sunderland Nissan	2-1
Clitheroe v Marine	0-2
Radcliffe Borough v Skelmersdale United	1-2
Whitby Town v Frickley Athletic	2-4
Harrogate Railway Athletic v Marske United	3-4
Gateshead v Rossendale United	3-1
Whitley Bay v Norton & Stockton Ancients	3-2
Newcastle Blue Star v Prescot Cables	0-4
Chester-Le-Street Town v Wakefield	0-1

Woodley Sports v Bishop Auckland	4-0
Ossett Town v Ossett Albion	1-2
Curzon Ashton v Billingham Town	4-2
Goole v Spennymoor Town	4-1
Ashton United v Padiham	4-2
Sutton Coldfield Town v Newcastle Town	3-0
Oadby Town v Grantham Town	4-2
Bedworth United v Matlock Town	1-3
AFC Telford United v Halesowen Town	2-4
Gresley Rovers v Quorn	0-1
Rugby Town v Deeping Rangers	4-1
Kidsgrove Athletic v Leek Town	0-0, 1-0
Romulus v Shirebrook Town	6-0
Hednesford Town v Gedling Town	1-1, 0-1
Shepshed Dynamo v Chasetown	0-2
Causeway United v Boldmere St Michaels	2-0
Tipton Town v Buxton	1-1, 1-2
Belper Town v Westfields	4-0
Rocester v Leamington	1-0
Ilkeston Town v Bromsgrove Rovers	1-1, 1-0
Corby Town v Solihull Borough	1-3
Lincoln United v Stamford	2-2, 2-1
Willenhall Town v Stratford Town	2-3
Canvey Island v Lowestoft Town	1-3
Boreham Wood v St Ives Town	8-2
Hendon v Arlesey Town	4-0
Potters Bar Town v Wealdstone	2-1
Hitchin Town v Saffron Walden Town	1-1, 1-1
Hitchin Town won 4-1 on penalties.	
Hemel Hempstead Town v Leyton	6-3
AFC Sudbury v Waltham Forest	1-0
Woodford United v Wroxham	3-1
Great Wakering Rovers v Burnham Ramblers	2-1
Redbridge v AFC Hornchurch	1-2
Heybridge Swifts v Potton United	6-1
Buckingham Town v Raunds Town	1-4
Hampton & Richmond Borough v Billericay Town	1-1, 0-0
Billericay Town won 4-1 on penalties.	
Dunstable Town v Leiston	3-2
Haverhill Rovers v Broxbourne Borough V&E	3-1
Banbury United v Beaconsfield SYCOB	5-1
Wingate & Finchley v East Thurrock United	1-2
Tiptree United v Brackley Town	0-4
Maldon Town v Staines Town	2-1
Tring Athletic v King's Lynn	1-5
Wivenhoe Town v Yaxley	1-2
Long Buckby v Rothwell Town	1-2
Bury Town v Wisbech Town	0-2
Oxhey Jets v Ruislip Manor	1-0
Harrow Borough v Northwood	2-0
Romford v Leighton Town	3-0
Chesham United v Cheshunt	2-3
Barking v Chelmsford City	1-4
Needham Market v Dereham Town	3-4
Worthing v Colliers Wood United	3-0
Ashford Town v Tonbridge Angels	1-3
Cobham v Slough Town	1-2
Sittingbourne v Hassocks	3-0
Margate v Fleet Town	0-0, 1-0
Maidenhead United v Carterton	1-1, 3-2
Dover Athletic v Alton Town	6-1
Dartford v Hastings United	0-2
Whyteleafe v Folkestone Invicta	1-2
Ashford Town (Middlesex) v Maidstone United	4-0
Molesey v Leatherhead	1-1, 0-3
Hungerford Town v Ardley United	3-0
Tooting & Mitcham United v Lancing	6-0
Bromley v AFC Totton	4-0
Cowes Sports v Lymington & New Milton	1-2
Oxford City v Chertsey Town	5-0
North Greenford United v VT	0-1
Kingstonian v Ramsgate	1-2
Andover v Carshalton Athletic	0-2
Walton & Hersham v Dulwich Hamlet	3-0
Whitstable Town v Croydon Athletic	1-0
Winchester City v Cray Wanderers	2-2, 2-2
Cray Wanderers won 5-4 on penalties.	
Bashley v VCD Athletic	5-0
AFC Wimbledon v Horsham	1-0
Worthing United v Hamble ASSC	3-2
Didcot Town v Whitehawk	6-1
Moneyfields v AFC Wallingford	3-1
East Preston v Metropolitan Police	1-3
Fairford Town v Cinderford Town	0-3
Downton v Team Bath	0-7
St Blazey v Saltash United	3-1
Cirencester Town v Merthyr Tydfil	2-3
Bishop Sutton v Bishop's Cleeve	0-0, 1-5
Radstock Town v Evesham United	1-6
Mangotsfield United v Paulton Rovers	1-0
Taunton Town v Swindon Supermarine	2-2, 3-2
Bath City v Tiverton Town	0-0, 3-1
Bideford v Bridgwater Town	2-2, 2-0
Willand Rovers v Tavistock	4-0
Clevedon Town v Truro City	1-1, 1-0
Gloucester City v Liskeard Athletic	0-0, 3-0
Yate Town v Slimbridge	1-2
Chippenham Town v Corsham Town	2-0

SECOND QUALIFYING ROUND

Moor Green v Hinckley United	4-2
North Ferriby United v Whitley Bay	0-2
Leigh RMI v Woodley Sports	0-2
Droylsden v Worksop Town	2-0
Burscough v Blyth Spartans	1-2
Trafford v Glossop North End	5-0
Marske United v Skelmersdale United	0-2
Farsley Celtic v Wakefield	3-0
Witton Albion v Vauxhall Motors	3-0
Prescot Cables v Marine	1-2
Hyde United v Newcastle Benfield (Bay Plastics)	0-2
Scarborough v Lancaster City	1-1, 2-1
Ashton United v Gainsborough Trinity	0-2
Durham City v Hallam	5-1
Flixton v Barrow	1-2
Ossett Albion v Workington	2-1
Curzon Ashton v Harrogate Town	0-2
Guiseley v Gateshead	1-0
Fleetwood Town v Goole	4-2
Stalybridge Celtic v Frickley Athletic	1-1, 1-0
Kendal Town v Warrington Town	1-1, 2-3
Raunds Town v Stratford Town	1-2
Halesowen Town v Chasetown	3-1
Sutton Coldfield Town v Cambridge City	0-2
Worcester City v Romulus	2-2, 3-1
Solihull Borough v Alfreton Town	1-1, 3-1
Histon v Matlock Town	0-1
Lincoln United v Hucknall Town	0-2
Redditch United v Wisbech Town	2-3
Oadby Town v Nuneaton Borough	0-6
Kidsgrove Athletic v Rothwell Town	6-0
Gedling Town v Rocester	0-2
Belper Town v Quorn	1-1, 1-3
King's Lynn v Causeway United	3-1
Ilkeston Town v Rugby Town	1-3
Kettering Town v Yaxley	5-1
Buxton v Woodford United	0-1
East Thurrock United v Maidenhead United	1-2
Cray Wanderers v Leatherhead	1-1, 2-4
Ramsgate v Yeading	0-1
Heybridge Swifts v Didcot Town	2-2, 3-1
Braintree Town v Brackley Town	0-2
Hemel Hempstead Town v Harrow Borough	4-2
AFC Wimbledon v Oxhey Jets	3-0
Worthing United v Romford	4-2
Hastings United v Metropolitan Police	1-1, 1-5
Hendon v Lewes	0-2
Fisher Athletic v Sittingbourne	7-1
Maldon Town v Potters Bar Town	0-0, 2-3
Sutton United v Bishop's Stortford	1-3
Haverhill Rovers v Eastbourne Borough	1-0
Farnborough Town v Slough Town	2-0
Worthing v Cheshunt	0-0, 0-1
Great Wakering Rovers v Carshalton Athletic	0-1
Lowestoft Town v Bromley	0-1
Tooting & Mitcham United v AFC Sudbury	2-3
Folkestone Invicta v Welling United	1-1, 1-3
Whitstable Town v Margate	1-2
Walton & Hersham v Ashford Town (Middlesex)	2-2, 1-3
Billericay Town v Hayes	0-0, 1-2
Thurrock v Dover Athletic	0-3
Tonbridge Angels v Banbury United	1-1, 2-1
Bedford Town v Dunstable Town	3-2
Hitchin Town v Bognor Regis Town	0-0, 1-0
Boreham Wood v AFC Hornchurch	0-2
Dereham Town v Chelmsford City	2-2, 0-4
Dorchester Town v Cinderford Town	3-0
Bishop's Cleeve v Oxford City	3-1
Eastleigh v Gloucester City	3-2
Clevedon Town v Willand Rovers	3-1

Slimbridge v Chippenham Town	3-1
Lymington & New Milton v Basingstoke Town	0-0, 0-1
Bideford v Newport County	0-3
Bashley v Taunton Town	3-1
Moneyfields v Evesham United	0-4
Bath City v Merthyr Tydfil	0-0, 2-3
Havant & Waterlooville v Team Bath	3-1
VT v Salisbury City	0-3
Weston-Super-Mare v Hungerford Town	1-2
Mangotsfield United v St Blazey	3-1

THIRD QUALIFYING ROUND

Ossett Albion v Scarborough	1-1, 0-2
Durham City v Barrow	0-1
Woodley Sports v Gainsborough Trinity	0-2
Droylsden v Skelmersdale United	3-2
Whitley Bay v Blyth Spartans	2-2, 2-1
Trafford v Harrogate Town	0-1
Guiseley v Newcastle Benfield (Bay Plastics)	0-1
Marine v Stalybridge Celtic	3-2
Witton Albion v Farsley Celtic	1-1, 0-1
Fleetwood Town v Warrington Town	2-0
Halesowen Town v King's Lynn	1-2
Nuneaton Borough v Hucknall Town	0-1
Bedford Town v Moor Green	0-2
Solihull Borough v Wisbech Town	1-2
Cambridge City v Matlock Town	0-0, 3-2
Woodford United v AFC Sudbury	1-3
Kettering Town v Rocester	2-1
Worcester City v Hemel Hempstead Town	1-1, 2-0
Bishop's Stortford v Stratford Town	2-0
Rugby Town v Chelmsford City	1-3
Haverhill Rovers v Kidsgrove Athletic	2-1
Quorn v Brackley Town	0-0, 1-2
Mangotsfield United v Leatherhead	1-1, 1-4
Bashley v Hungerford Town	1-2
Maidenhead United v Worthing	3-1
Dorchester Town v Lewes	0-4
Heybridge Swifts v Dover Athletic	2-3
Hayes v Bromley	1-3
Margate v Potters Bar Town	1-2
AFC Hornchurch v Welling United	1-1, 1-3
Clevedon Town v Hitchin Town	1-1, 2-2
Clevedon Town won 4-3 on penalties.	

Fisher Athletic v Metropolitan Police	6-1
Cheshunt v Tonbridge Angels	1-2
Eastleigh v Salisbury City	0-1
Newport County v Bishop's Cleeve	4-2
AFC Wimbledon v Evesham United	2-1
Merthyr Tydfil v Slimbridge	2-0
Havant & Waterlooville v Carshalton Athletic	2-0
Farnborough Town v Yeading	1-1, 0-3
Basingstoke Town v Ashford Town (Middlesex)	3-0

FOURTH QUALIFYING ROUND

Newcastle Benfield (Bay Plastics) v York City	0-1
Barrow v Marine	3-2
Stafford Rangers v Scarborough	3-0
Tamworth v Harrogate Town	3-1
Gainsborough Trinity v Whitley Bay	2-0
King's Lynn v Hucknall Town	3-0
Fleetwood Town v Wisbech Town	3-0
Rushden & Diamonds v Altrincham	3-0
Burton Albion v Halifax Town	1-0
Northwich Victoria v Cambridge United	2-0
Farsley Celtic v Cambridge City	2-1
Southport v Kettering Town	0-1
Kidderminster Harriers v Droylsden	5-1
Moor Green v Morecambe	1-2
Worcester City v Basingstoke Town	1-1, 1-1
Basingstoke Town won 7-6 on penalties.	
Crawley Town v Lewes	2-3
Dover Athletic v Bishop's Stortford	0-0, 2-3
Hungerford Town v Weymouth	0-3
Woking v Potters Bar Town	3-2
Maidenhead United v Merthyr Tydfil	1-0
Welling United v Clevedon Town	0-3
Stevenage Borough v Forest Green Rovers	4-1
Tonbridge Angels v Newport County	0-1
Dagenham & Redbridge v Oxford United	0-1
Yeading v St Albans City	2-1
Haverhill Rovers v Aldershot Town	0-4
Exeter City v AFC Wimbledon	2-1
AFC Sudbury v Leatherhead	1-2
Chelmsford City v Gravesend & Northfleet	1-0
Grays Athletic v Bromley	1-2
Fisher Athletic v Salisbury City	0-1
Brackley Town v Havant & Waterlooville	0-2

Didier Drogba scores the winner past Edwin van der Sar in the FA Cup Final victory for Chelsea against Manchester United in the first FA Cup final at the new Wembley. (Phil Cole/Getty Images)

THE E.ON FA CUP 2006–07

COMPETITION PROPER

■ *Denotes player sent off.*

FIRST ROUND

Friday, 10 November 2006

Cheltenham T (0) 0

Scunthorpe U (0) 0 2721

Cheltenham T: Higgs; Gill, Armstrong, McCann, Caines, Duff, Melligan, Bird (Wylde), Spencer, Smith (Odejayi), Wilson.
Scunthorpe U: Murphy; Hinds, Williams, Crosby, Foster, Baraclough, Taylor (Byrne), Morris, Keogh, Sharp (McBreen), Sparrow (Goodwin).

Saturday, 11 November 2006

Barrow (0) 2 *(Pope 69, Rogan 77)*

Bristol R (1) 3 *(Walker R 35, Disley 62, Anthony 67)* 2939

Barrow: Speare; Bond, Cotterill, Ridley, Butler (Eckersley), Howson (Rogan), Brown, Jones, Taylor, Pope, Stringfellow (Flitcroft).
Bristol R: Phillips; Green, Carruthers, Campbell, Anthony, Elliott, Sandell (Haldane), Disley, Walker R, Rigg (Lambert), Igoe (Hinton).

Bishop's Stortford (2) 3 *(Essandoh 36, Morgan 40, Martin 81)*

King's Lynn (2) 5 *(Smith 27, 45, Frew 55, 61, O'Halloran 71)* 1750

Bishop's Stortford: Wright; Collis, Stanbrook (Mason), Howell (Lockett), Gwillim, Porter, Gillman, Morgan, Martin, Midson, Essandoh (Innocent).
King's Lynn: Marshall; West, Cooper, Defty J (Nolan), Smith, Warren, Camm, McMahon, O'Halloran (Defty C), Notman (Norris), Frew.

Bournemouth (2) 4 *(Fletcher 5, 42, Hayter 59, Hollands 90)*

Boston U (0) 0 4263

Bournemouth: Moss; Purches, Bertrand, Hollands, Young, Maher, Cork, Anderton, Hayter, Fletcher, Foley-Sheridan (Hart).
Boston U: Marriott; Clarke, Ryan T, Ellender, Greaves, Albrighton, N'Guessan (Farrell), Holland (Ryan R), Broughton, Green (Elding), Galbraith.

Bradford C (1) 4 *(Bridge-Wilkinson 3, Schumacher 61, Windass 70, Kempson 77 (og))*

Crewe Alex (0) 0 3483

Bradford C: Ricketts; Doyle, Ainge, Schumacher (Bentham), Wetherall, Bower, Johnson J (Muirhead), Bridge-Wilkinson (McGuire), Johnson E, Windass, Healy.
Crewe Alex: Tomlinson; Otsemobor, Bignot, Roberts, O'Donnell, Cox (Kempson), Rix, Grant, Rodgers, Higdon, Jack (Miller).

Brentford (0) 0

Doncaster R (1) 1 *(Guy 32)* 3607

Brentford: Masters; O'Connor, Tillen, Mousinho, Frampton, Griffiths, Brooker, Skulason (Pinault), Osei-Kuffour, Ide (Wijnhard), Onibuje (Moore).
Doncaster R: Smith; O'Connor, Roberts G, Roberts S, Lockwood, Stock, Price, Green P, Guy (Streete), McCammon (Thornton), Forte (Heffernan).

Brighton & HA (2) 8 *(Cox 8, 90, Robinson 18, 55, 78, Revell 64, Gatting 82, Rents 89)*

Northwich Vic (0) 0 4487

Brighton & HA: Kuipers; Lynch, Mayo, Hinshelwood, Butters, El Abd, Cox, Hammond, Robinson (Rents), Revell (Gatting), Fraser (Frutos).
Northwich Vic: Senior; McCarthy (Byrne), Brown, Griffiths, Elliott, Payne, Carr, Bastians, Brayson, Townson (Sale), Mayman.

Burton Alb (0) 1 *(Clare 49)*

Tamworth (0) 2 *(Poole 59 (og), Stevenson 90)* 4150

Burton Alb: Poole; Corbett, Austin (Harrad), Stride, Tinson, Rowett, Carden, Fowler (Shaw), Clare, Ducros, Gilroy.
Tamworth: Da Viega; Laight (Law), Kendrick, Smith, Weaver, Kemp, Taylor (Storer), Stevenson, Williams, Atieno (Burton), McGrath.

Chelmsford C (0) 1 *(Minton 51 (pen))*

Aldershot T (0) 1 *(Chenery 59 (og))* 2838

Chelmsford C: McKinney; Conroy, Duffy, Manuella, Chenery, Ward, Noto, Minton, Ibe (Hallett), Holmes, Knight (Ainsley).
Aldershot T: Bull; Smith, Barnard, Newman (Soares), Day, Edwards (Anderson), Lee, Molesley, John Grant, Gayle, Joel Grant (Williams).

Chesterfield (0) 0

Basingstoke T (1) 1 *(Warner 25)* 3539

Chesterfield: Roche; Lowry, O'Hare, Kovacs, Downes, Niven, Hall (Jackson), Hughes (Davies), Larkin (Folan), Allison, Smith.
Basingstoke T: Searle; Watkins, Bruce, Surey, Wells, Dolan, Hay, Taylor, Stroud, Levis (Roach), Warner.

Clevedon T (0) 1 *(Pitcher 90)*

Chester C (1) 4 *(Wilson 7, Hand 49, Walters 60, Blundell 74)* 2261

Clevedon T: Greaves; Witcombe, Scott, Hapgood, Bater, Jacobs (Rawlins), Clark, Mullings, Haines, Pitcher, Page.
Chester C: Danby; Wilson (Vaughan S), Bennett, Bolland, Artell, Hessey, Sandwith, Martinez, Walters (Blundell), Steele (Holroyd), Hand.

Exeter C (1) 1 *(Phillips 45)*

Stockport Co (1) 2 *(Bramble 21, Proudlock 82)* 4454

Exeter C: Jones P; Woodards, Jones B, Gill, Edwards, Todd, Taylor (Ada), Buckle (Cozic), Stansfield (Mackie), Phillips, Challinor.
Stockport Co: Spencer; Clare, Griffin (Ellis), Dinning, Williams, Rose, Malcolm, Taylor, Bramble (Robinson), Le Fondre (Proudlock), Gleeson.

Gainsborough T (0) 1 *(Ellis 75)*

Barnet (1) 3 *(Sinclair 14, Kandol 78, 90 (pen))* 1914

Gainsborough T: Sollitt; Purkiss, Caudwell, Lancaster (Bird), Ellis■, Pell, Graves (Smith), Anson, Parker, Bett, Wood.
Barnet: Harrison; Devera, Nicolau, Hessenthaler, Yakubu, King, Bailey, Cogan, Warhurst (Kandol), Sinclair, Puncheon.

Gillingham (1) 4 *(Bentley 31, 59, Ndumbu-Nsungu 84, 90)*

Bromley (0) 1 *(McDonnell 70)* 5547

Gillingham: Jack; Jupp, Easton, Flynn, Cox, Johnson (Sancho), Pouton (Crofts), Bentley, Mulligan, McDonald (Ndumbu-Nsungu), Jarvis.
Bromley: Walker; Duku, Adeniyi, Moore (Williams), Henriques, O'Sullivan, Bowry (Greenway), Watts (Osborn), Blackman, McDonnell, Wood.

Huddersfield T (0) 0

Blackpool (0) 1 *(Hoolahan 70 (pen))* 6597

Huddersfield T: Glennon; Holdsworth, Skarz, Hudson, McCombe, Clarke N, Worthington, Collins (Beckett), Booth, Taylor-Fletcher, Schofield (Young).
Blackpool: Evans; Evatt, Dickinson, Fox (Jorgensen), Jackson, Barker, Forbes, Southern, Morrell, Parker (Vernon), Hoolahan.

Kettering T (0) 3 *(McIlwain 52, Abbey 62, Solkhon 84)*
Oldham Ath (1) 4 *(Gregan 43, Warne 56, Trotman 60, Hall 90)* 3481
Kettering T: Musselwhite; Nicoll, McIlwain, Hall, McKie, Graham, Solkhon, Baucaud (Howe), Makofo (Caskey), Westcarr, Abbey.
Oldham Ath: Pogliacomi; Wellens, Taylor, Lomax, Gregan, Haining (Trotman), Charlton (Tierney), McDonald, Porter (Hall), Warne, Liddell.

Lewes (0) 1 *(Farrell 79)*
Darlington (1) 4 *(Smith 38, 90, Collins 62, Ngoma 82)* 1500
Lewes: Crane; Hooper, Hamilton, Holloway, Robinson, Simpemba, Drury, Kennett (Kadi■), Booth, Sigere (Farrell), Wormull (Storey).
Darlington: Russell; Close, James, Collins, Holloway, Keltie, Wainwright (Logan), Conlon (Armstrong), Johnson, Smith, Cummins (Ngoma).

Leyton Orient (1) 2 *(Corden 12, Miller 58)*
Notts Co (0) 1 *(Dudfield 90)* 3011
Leyton Orient: Garner; Miller (Demetriou), Lockwood, Barnard, Mackie, Thelwell, Tudor (Duncan), Easton, Alexander, Ibehre (Connor), Corden.
Notts Co: Pilkington; Silk (Gleeson), McCann, Edwards, White, Ross, Pipe (N'Toya), Somner, Lee (Dudfield), Mendes, Parkinson.

Mansfield T (1) 1 *(Barker 44 (pen))*
Accrington S (0) 0 3909
Mansfield T: Muggleton; Mullins, Jelleyman, Coke, Hjelde, John-Baptiste, Hamshaw (Brown), D'Laryea, Barker, Beardsley (Reet), Boulding M (Dawson).
Accrington S: Dunbavin; Ventre (McGivern), Richardson, Welch, Edwards, Doherty, Craney, Mangan, Todd, Mullin, Harris.

Morecambe (1) 2 *(Curtis 44 (pen), Twiss 73)*
Kidderminster H (0) 1 *(Hurren 89)* 1673
Morecambe: Drench; Yates, Howard, McLachlan, Blackburn, Bentley, Thompson, Curtis, Twiss, Rigoglioso, Perkins.
Kidderminster H: Bevan; Kenna, Blackwood, Hurren, Creighton, Whitehead, Smikle (Reynolds), Penn, White (Taylor B), Christie, Nelthorpe (McGrath).

Newport Co (0) 1 *(Hillier 48)*
Swansea C (3) 3 *(Trundle 7, Iriekpen 31, Britton 45)* 4660
Newport Co: Ovendale; Hillier, Brewer (Evans), Bowen, Cochlin, Brough, Davies, Collier (Garner), Hughes, Alsop, O'Sullivan (Green).
Swansea C: Gueret; Amankwaah, Austin, Tate, Lawrence, Iriekpen, Britton (O'Leary), MacDonald, Trundle (Butler), Fallon (Akinfenwa), Robinson.

Northampton T (0) 0
Grimsby T (0) 0 4092
Northampton T: Bunn; Bojic (Holt), Crowe, Chambers, Doig, Taylor, Watt (Quinn), Hunt (Burnell), McGleish, Kirk, Jess.
Grimsby T: Barnes; Croft (McDermott), Newey, Harkins, Fenton, Whittle, Toner, Bolland, North (Taylor), Boshell, Hegarty.

Nottingham F (3) 5 *(Commons 19, 32, 45, Agogo 54 (pen), 63)*
Yeading (0) 0 7704
Nottingham F: Smith; Gary Holt (Grant Holt), Curtis, Cullip (Lester), Breckin, Morgan, Southall, Clingan, Agogo, Harris (Tyson), Commons.
Yeading: Cousins; Behzadi, Hudell, Brown (Haule), Goddard, Bowden-Haase, Allen-Page (Everitt), Quamina, Morgan, Louis (Goulding), Patterson.

Peterborough U (1) 3 *(Butcher 29, McLean 59, Crow 73)*
Rotherham U (0) 0 4281
Peterborough U: Tyler; Newton, Stirling, Arber, Branston, Futcher, Holden, Butcher, Crow, McLean, Huke (Opara).
Rotherham U: Cutler; Worrell, Hurst (Sharps), Partridge, Murdock, Mills, Keane (Taylor), Bopp, Facey, Hoskins, Williamson (Cochrane).

Port Vale (2) 2 *(Whitaker 29, Sodje 38)*
Lincoln C (0) 1 *(Frecklington 84)* 3884
Port Vale: Goodlad; Abbey (Gardner), Miles, Sonner, Pilkington, Walker, Whitaker, Harsley, Sodje, Constantine, Smith J.
Lincoln C: Marriott; Beevers, Mayo, Moses, Brown, Kerr (Morgan), Frecklington, Amoo, Stallard, Forrester, Cryan (John-Lewis).

Rochdale (0) 1 *(Doolan 62)*
Hartlepool U (1) 1 *(Brown 41)* 2098
Rochdale: Gilks; Brown, Jackson, Doolan, Stanton, Sharp, Jones, Cooksey (Sako), Murray (Barker), Dagnall, Rundle.
Hartlepool U: Konstantopoulos; Williams D, Humphreys, Liddle, Nelson, Clark, Gibb, Boland, Brown (Williams E), Daly, Robson.

Rushden & D (1) 3 *(Hope 28, Rankine 54, 75)*
Yeovil T (0) 1 *(Cohen 82)* 2530
Rushden & D: Tynan; Wilson, Watson, Shaw (Sedgemore), Hope, Hatswell, Savage, Berry, Rankine (Chillingworth), Tomlin (Jackson), Kelly.
Yeovil T: Mildenhall; Lynch, Jones, Terry, Forbes, Tonkin (Thomas), Barry, Morris (Welsh), Davies, Gray (Webb), Cohen.

Salisbury C (1) 3 *(Tubbs 12, Holmes 60, Bartlett 69)*
Fleetwood T (0) 0 2684
Salisbury C: Clarke; Bass, Beswetherick, Holmes (Clay), Cook, Bond, Prince, Turk, Tubbs (McGregor), Sales (Matthews), Bartlett.
Fleetwood T: Hale; Hardiker, Fitzgerald, Pond, Robinson (Reed), Moran, Beech (Haddow), Milligan, Denney, Saunders (Bell), Pryers.

Shrewsbury T (0) 0
Hereford U (0) 0 5574
Shrewsbury T: Shearer; Herd, Ashton, Drummond, Langmead, Cowan, Davies, Sorvel, Symes (Cooke), Asamoah, Edwards.
Hereford U: Brown; Gulliver, Jeannin, Purdie, Mkandawire, Beckwith, Ferrell, Connell, Williams, Sills, Rose.

Stafford R (1) 1 *(Daniel 13)*
Maidenhead U (0) 1 *(Lee 52)* 1526
Stafford R: Alcock; Sutton, Talbott, Murphy (Olaoye), Daniel, McAughtrie, Edwards, Lovatt, Grayson, Madjo, Gibson (Street).
Maidenhead U: Ramos; Nisbet, Parsons, Osman (Johnson), Witt, Sterling■, David Clarke, O'Connor■, Newman (Romeo), Lee, Dwain Clarke (Gorman).

Swindon T (1) 3 *(Lumsdon 9 (og), Roberts 70, 90)*
Carlisle U (1) 1 *(Gray 43)* 4308
Swindon T: Smith P; Smith J, Williams, Weston, Ifil, Nicholas, Shakes, Evans, Roberts, Brownlie (Jutkiewicz), Brown (Zaaboub).
Carlisle U: Westwood; Raven (Livesey), Aranalde, Thirlwell, Gray, Murphy, Harper, Gall, Holmes (Hindmarch), Hawley, Lumsdon.

Torquay U (0) 2 *(Ward 57, McPhee 72)*
Leatherhead (1) 1 *(Hendry 2)* 2218
Torquay U: Abbey; Critchell, Reed, Leary (Andrews), Woods, Thorpe, Murray (McPhee), Mansell, Ward, Evans, Hill.
Leatherhead: Gibson; Beer, Duncan (Thompson), Sargent, Hendry, Doherty, Gray (Carpenter), Holmes, Stevens, Charles-Smith, Bennetts.

Tranmere R (2) 4 *(Taylor 18, 48, Greenacre 37, 83)*
Woking (0) 2 *(Jackson 63, McAllister 69)* 4591
Tranmere R: Ward; Thompson, Cansdell-Sheriff, McAteer, McCready, Goodison, Mullin, McLaren (Jones), Taylor, Greenacre, Davies.
Woking: Jalal; Jackson, El Salahi, Murray, Hutchinson, MacDonald, Ferguson, Berquez, Sole, McAllister, Smith (Evans).

Wrexham (1) 1 *(Williams D 40)*
Stevenage B (0) 0 2863
Wrexham: Ingham; Roche, Mike Williams, Williams D, Evans S, Pejic, Mark Jones, Ferguson (Mackin), Smith (Marc Williams), Molango, Done.
Stevenage B: Julian; Fuller, Nutter, Miller, Gaia, Henry, Beard, Binns (Dobson), Morison, Nurse (Oliver), Boyd.

Wycombe W (0) 2 *(Antwi 58, Oakes 86)*
Oxford U (1) 1 *(Johnson 85)* 6279
Wycombe W: Young; Stockley, Martin, Oakes, Antwi, Williamson, Palmer, Grant (Gregory), Bloomfield, Mooney (Dixon), Betsy.
Oxford U: Turley; Anaclet (Dempster), Brevett (Day), Gilchrist, Willmott, Quinn, Pettefer, Hargreaves, Basham, Odubade, Hutchinson (Johnson).

York C (0) 0
Bristol C (0) 1 *(McCombe 53)* 3525
York C: Evans; Craddock, Lloyd, Bowey, Foster, Goodliffe, Bishop, Panther, Donaldson, Farrell (Stamp), Woolford.
Bristol C: Basso; Keogh, McAllister (Brown), Fontaine, McCombe, Skuse, Russell, Johnson, Jevons (Myrie-Williams), Showunmi, Woodman.

Sunday, 12 November 2006
Farsley C (0) 0
Milton Keynes D (0) 0 2200
Farsley C: Cuss; Stabb, Serrant, Watson (Krief), Pemberton, Crossley, Knowles, Bambrook, Midgley (Reeves), Grant (Thackray), Stamer.
Milton Keynes D: Harper; Smith J (Platt), Lewington, Diallo, O'Hanlon, Andrews, McGovern, Dyer (Taylor), Wilbraham, McLeod (Crooks), Edds.

Weymouth (0) 2 *(Weatherstone 50, Logan 55)*
Bury (1) 2 *(Pugh 26, Bishop 75)* 2503
Weymouth: Lee-Barrett; Downer (Wilkinson), El Kholti, O'Brien, Vickers, Smith, Crittenden (Tully), Weatherstone, Logan, Nade (Purser), Elam.
Bury: Grundy; Scott, Kennedy T, Fitzgerald, Challinor, Pugh, Baker, Mattis, Hurst (Speight), Bishop, Buchanan (Adams).

Monday, 13 November 2006
Havant & Waterlooville (0) 1 *(Baptiste 57)*
Millwall (1) 2 *(May 6, Dunne 71)* 5793
Havant & Waterlooville: Gore; Wanfer, Jordan, Byles, Gregory (Holdsworth), Harkin (Watkins), Collins (Simpson), Taggart, Poate, Pacquette, Baptiste.
Millwall: Pidgeley; Senda (Ross), Whitbread, Elliott, Robinson, Shaw, Dunne, McInnes (Mawene), May (Byfield), Zebroski, Hackett.
at Portsmouth.

Macclesfield T (0) 0
Walsall (0) 0 2018
Macclesfield T: Brain; Scott, Wiles (Tolley), Morley (McNulty), Swailes, Navarro, Bullock, Hadfield, Murphy, Heath (McNeil), McIntyre.
Walsall: Ince; Pead■, Fox, Dann, Roper, Dobson, Wright (Bedeau), Keates, Butler, Sam (Wrack), Taylor.

FIRST ROUND REPLAYS

Monday, 20 November 2006
Hartlepool U (0) 0
Rochdale (0) 0 2788
Hartlepool U: Konstantopoulos; Williams D (Barron), Humphreys, Liddle, Nelson, Clark, Brown (Bullock), Boland, Williams E, Daly, Robson (Gibb).
Rochdale: Gilks; Brown, Goodall, Jones, Stanton, McArdle, Rundle (Warburton), Cooksey, Murray (Barker), Dagnall, Sako (Boardman).
aet; Hartlepool U won 4-2 on penalties.

Tuesday, 21 November 2006
Aldershot T (0) 2 *(Barnard 53 (pen), John Grant 80)*
Chelmsford C (0) 0 2731
Aldershot T: Bull; Smith, Barnard, Newman, Day, Lee, Soares, Molesley, John Grant, Gayle (Joel Grant), Williams (Harding).
Chelmsford C: McKinney; Conroy, Duffy, Ward, Chenery, Manuella (Heeroo), Noto, Minton, Ibe, Holmes, Knight (Hallett).

Bury (2) 4 *(Mattis 10, 67, Bishop 23, 74)*
Weymouth (3) 3 *(Downer 16, Purser 20, Tully 30)* 2231
Bury: Grundy; Scott, Kennedy T (Woodthorpe), Fitzgerald, Challinor, Adams (Buchanan), Pugh, Mattis, Speight, Bishop, Baker.
Weymouth: Lee-Barrett; Tully, El Kholti, Downer (Nade), Vickers, James, Smith, Weatherstone (Tindall), Logan, Purser (Wilkinson), Elam.

Grimsby T (0) 0
Northampton T (1) 2 *(Burnell 45, Whittle 80 (og))* 2657
Grimsby T: Barnes; McDermott, Croft, Harkins (Ravenhill), Fenton, Whittle, Boshell, Bolland, North, Jones (Rankin), Hegarty (Bore).
Northampton T: Bunn; Crowe (Bojic), Holt, Chambers, Doig (Taylor), Dyche, Hunt, Burnell, McGleish, Quinn (Gilligan), Jess.

Hereford U (0) 2 *(Connell 85, Webb 88)*
Shrewsbury T (0) 0 4224
Hereford U: Brown; Gulliver, Jeannin, Purdie, Mkandawire, Beckwith, Webb, Ferrell (Travis), Sheldon (Williams), Sills, Connell.
Shrewsbury T: Shearer; Herd, Ashton, Drummond, Burton (Jones L), Cowan, Hall, Edwards, Symes (Asamoah), Cooke (Fortune-West), Davies.

Maidenhead U (0) 0
Stafford R (1) 2 *(Murray 9, 78)* 1934
Maidenhead U: Ramos; Nisbet (Johnson), Parsons, David Clarke, Lee, Sterling, Osman (Fotheringham), Witt, Newman, O'Connor (Allen), Smith.
Stafford R: Alcock; Sutton, Talbott, Murphy, Daniel, Murray, Street, Lovatt (Oldfield), Grayson (Gibson), Madjo, Edwards.

Milton Keynes D (0) 2 *(McLeod 63, 76 (pen))*
Farsley C (0) 0 2676
Milton Keynes D: Baines; Smith J, Lewington, Diallo, Crooks, Mitchell, McGovern, Andrews (Taylor), Platt (Hastings), McLeod (Rizzo), Edds.
Farsley C: Cuss; Stabb, Pemberton (Nestor), Bambrook■, Crossley, Serrant, Watson (Midgeley), Knowles, Grant, Reeves (Walls), Stamer■.

Scunthorpe U (1) 2 *(Baraclough 26, Sharp 74)*
Cheltenham T (0) 0 3074
Scunthorpe U: Murphy; Hinds, Williams, Crosby (Byrne), Foster, Baraclough (Goodwin), Taylor, Foy (Mulligan), Keogh, Sharp, Sparrow.
Cheltenham T: Higgs; Gill, Armstrong, McCann, Caines, Duff, Melligan (Spencer), Bird, Guinan■, Odejayi, Wilson.

Walsall (0) 0
Macclesfield T (0) 1 *(McNulty 83)* 3114
Walsall: Ince; Wright, Fox, Dann, Roper, Dobson, Bedeau (Constable), Keates, Butler, Sam (Demontagnac), Taylor.
Macclesfield T: Brain; Regan, McNulty, Teague, Swailes, Navarro, Wiles (Jennings), Tolley (Hadfield), Bullock, Heath (McNeil), McIntyre.

SECOND ROUND

Friday, 1 December 2006

Bradford C (0) 0

Millwall (0) 0 4346

Bradford C: Ricketts; Doyle, Ainge, Schumacher, Wetherall, Bower, Johnson J, Bridge-Wilkinson, Johnson E, Holmes, Healy (Black).
Millwall: Pidgeley; Senda, Whitbread, Ross, Robinson, Shaw, Dunne, Zebroski, May, Byfield (Morais), Hackett.

King's Lynn (0) 0

Oldham Ath (1) 2 *(Porter 10, Hall 82)* 5444

King's Lynn: Marshall; West, Cooper, Defty J (Hicks), Defty C, Warren, Camm, McMahon, O'Halloran (Nolan), Notman, Frew.
Oldham Ath: Pogliacomi; Wellens, Taylor, Eardley, Gregan, Haining, Charlton, McDonald, Porter (Rocastle), Warne (Hall), Liddell (Edwards).

Stockport Co (1) 2 *(Proudlock 43 (pen), 75)*

Wycombe W (1) 1 *(Easter 34)* 3821

Stockport Co: Spencer; Briggs, Rose, Dinning, Williams, Clare, Poole (Ellis), Taylor, Proudlock, Bramble (Le Fondre), Gleeson (Malcolm).
Wycombe W: Young; Stockley, Martin, Oakes (Palmer), Antwi, Williamson, Grant, Bloomfield, Mooney, Easter, Betsy.

Saturday, 2 December 2006

Aldershot T (0) 1 *(John Grant 77)*

Basingstoke T (1) 1 *(Bruce 45)* 4525

Aldershot T: Bull; Smith, Barnard, Scott, Day, Newman, Soares, Lee (Hylton), John Grant, Molesley, Williams.
Basingstoke T: Searle; Ray, McKay (Quarm), Howell (Harris), Dolan, Bruce, Watkins, Surey, Roach (Levis), Taylor, Warner.

Barnet (0) 4 *(Birchall 49, Sinclair 53, Hendon 67 (pen), Vieira 87)*

Northampton T (1) 1 *(McGleish 45)* 2786

Barnet: Harrison; Hendon, King, Cogan, Yakubu, Gross (Devera), Bailey, Birchall (Vieira), Hatch, Sinclair, Puncheon.
Northampton T: Bunn; Holt, Chambers, Hunt (Watt), Doig, Dyche, Taylor, Burnell, McGleish, Quinn (Kirk), Jess (Wright).

Brighton & HA (1) 3 *(Hammond 18, Revell 66, Robinson 90)*

Stafford R (0) 0 5741

Brighton & HA: Henderson; Rents, Mayo, Hinshelwood, Lynch, Fraser (Carpenter), Cox, Hammond, Robinson, Revell (Gatting), Frutos (John).
Stafford R: Alcock; Sutton, Talbott, Murphy, Daniel, Murray, Street (Gibson), Lovatt (Basham), Grayson, Madjo (Olaoye), Edwards.

Bristol R (1) 1 *(Walker R 45 (pen))*

Bournemouth (0) 1 *(Hayter 73)* 6252

Bristol R: Phillips; Lescott, Carruthers, Campbell, Anthony, Elliott, Igoe, Disley, Walker R, Lambert, Haldane.
Bournemouth: Moss; Purches, Bertrand (Pitman), Hollands (Foley-Sheridan), Broadhurst, Young,Cork, Cooper (Howe), Hayter, Fletcher, Connolly.

Bury (0) 2 *(Bishop 66, Baker 69)*

Chester C (0) 2 *(Steele 63, 73)* 3428

Bury: Warrington; Scott, Kennedy T, Fitzgerald, Challinor, Pugh, Baker, Mattis, Hurst (Speight), Bishop, Buchanan.
Chester C: Danby; Vaughan S, Wilson, Linwood, Westwood, Artell, Sandwith (Bennett), Martinez, Walters, Semple (Steele■), Hand.

Darlington (1) 1 *(Smith 2)*

Swansea C (1) 3 *(Britton 15, Robinson 52, Akinfenwa 79)* 4183

Darlington: Russell; Duke (Joachim), James, Close, Collins, Keltie, Wainwright, Johnson (Conlon), Armstrong, Smith (Logan), Cummins.
Swansea C: Gueret; Meslien (Amankwaah), Austin, Tate, Lawrence, Britton, Pratley, Robinson, Trundle (Fallon), MacDonald, Butler (Akinfenwa).

Hereford U (1) 4 *(Webb 41, Purdie 49 (pen), 51, Ferrell 83)*

Port Vale (0) 0 4076

Hereford U: Brown; Gulliver, Jeannin, Purdie, Mkandawire, Beckwith, Webb, Ferrell, Williams (Fleetwood), Sills (Rose), Connell (Sheldon).
Port Vale: Goodlad; Abbey, Miles (McGregor), Sonner, Fortune, Gardner, Whitaker, Harsley, Moore (Briscoe), Constantine, Smith J (Cardle).

Macclesfield T (1) 2 *(McIntyre 45 (pen), Murphy 52)*

Hartlepool U (1) 1 *(Regan 8 (og))* 1992

Macclesfield T: Begovic; Regan, McIntyre, Scott, Swailes, Navarro, Bullock, Tolley, Murphy, McNeil (Heath), Hadfield.
Hartlepool U: Konstantopoulos; Barron (Tinkler), Humphreys, Boland (Maidens), Nelson, Clark, Gibb (Robson), Sweeney■, Williams E, Daly, Bullock.

Mansfield T (1) 1 *(Barker 23 (pen))*

Doncaster R (0) 1 *(Stock 90)* 4837

Mansfield T: Muggleton; Buxton, Jelleyman, Coke, Hjelde, John-Baptiste, Hamshaw, D'Laryea, Barker, Brown (Reet), Boulding M.
Doncaster R: Smith; O'Connor, Roberts G, Lockwood, Lee, Stock, Price, Thornton, McCammon (Heffernan), Guy (Coppinger), Forte (Dyer).

Milton Keynes D (0) 0

Blackpool (1) 2 *(Parker 31, Morrell 48)* 3837

Milton Keynes D: Harper; Crooks, Lewington, McGovern, O'Hanlon, Butler, Andrews, Wilbraham, Platt (Edds), Taylor (Hastings), Dyer.
Blackpool: Evans; Evatt, Dickinson, Fox (Bean), Jackson, Barker, Jorgensen, Southern, Morrell (Fernandez), Parker, Forbes.

Rushden & D (0) 1 *(Shaw 85)*

Tamworth (1) 2 *(Burton 42, McGrath 77)* 2815

Rushden & D: Tynan; Wilson (Chillingworth), Watson, Woodhouse, Hope, Hatswell, Savage, Berry, Rankine, Tomlin, Kelly (Shaw).
Tamworth: Da Veiga; Law, Laight, Heslop, Weaver, Smith, Stevenson, Taylor, Burton, Atieno, McGrath (Storer).

Scunthorpe U (0) 0

Wrexham (0) 2 *(Mark Jones 49, Smith 66)* 5054

Scunthorpe U: Murphy; Hinds (Williams), Byrne, Crosby, Foster, Baraclough, Taylor, Morris (Torpey), Keogh, Sharp, Sparrow.
Wrexham: Ingham; Roche, Mike Williams, Williams D, Evans S, Pejic, Mark Jones, Ferguson, Johnson (Ugarte), Smith (McEvilly), Llewellyn.

Swindon T (0) 1 *(Roberts 89 (pen))*

Morecambe (0) 0 5942

Swindon T: Smith P; Smith J, Williams, Nicholas, Ifil, Shakes (Jutkiewicz), Brown (Zaaboub), Weston, Roberts, Peacock, Whalley (Pook).
Morecambe: Drench; Yates, Brannan, McLachlan, Howard (Platt), Bentley, Thompson (Burns), Stanley, Twiss, Rigoglioso, Perkins.

Torquay U (0) 1 *(Ward 60 (pen))*

Leyton Orient (0) 1 *(Corden 76)* 2392

Torquay U: Abbey; Andrews (Critchell), Reed, Hockley, Woods, Villis, McPhee (Robertson J), Mansell, Ward (Motteram), Thorpe, Hill.
Leyton Orient: Garner; Chambers, Lockwood, Easton, Mackie (Saah), Thelwell, Tudor, Demetriou, Alexander (Walker), Ibehre (Connor), Corden.

Tranmere R (1) 1 *(Cansdell-Sheriff 30)*
Peterborough U (1) 2 *(Crow 45, 70)* 6308
Tranmere R: Ward; Thompson, Cansdell-Sheriff, McLaren, McCready, Goodison, Shuker, Ellison (Zola), Taylor, Greenacre, Davies.
Peterborough U: Tyler; Newton, Stirling, Arber, Branston, Futcher, Holden, Huke (Morgan), Crow, McLean (Benjamin), Butcher (Gain).

Sunday, 3 December 2006
Bristol C (3) 4 *(Jevons 21, 44, 45, Showunmi 64)*
Gillingham (0) 3 *(Mulligan 49, Flynn 66, 90 (pen))* 5663
Bristol C: Basso; Keogh, McAllister (Fontaine), McCombe, Carey, Skuse (Murray), Russell, Johnson, Jevons (Brown), Showunmi, Myrie-Williams.
Gillingham: Jack (Spiller); Jupp, Easton, Flynn, Johnson, Sancho, Crofts, Bentley, Mulligan, McDonald (Ndumbu-Nsungu), Jarvis.

Salisbury C (0) 1 *(Tubbs 61)*
Nottingham F (1) 1 *(Tyson 27)* 3100
Salisbury C: Clarke; Bass, Browne (Middleton), Clay, Cook, Bond, Turk, Holmes, Sales (Matthews), Tubbs (McGregor), Prince.
Nottingham F: Pedersen; Gary Holt, Curtis, Cullip, Breckin, Morgan, Southall, Perch, Tyson (Dobie), Grant Holt (Harris), Commons.

SECOND ROUND REPLAYS

Tuesday, 12 December 2006
Basingstoke T (1) 1 *(Roach 4)*
Aldershot T (2) 3 *(Soares 14, 30, Barnard 51)* 3300
Basingstoke T: Searle; Ray, Bruce, Watkins, Dolan, McKay (Townsend), Levis, Surey, Roach, Taylor, Warner.
Aldershot T: Bull; Smith, Barnard, Scott, Day, Anderson, Soares, Molesley, John Grant (Pritchard), Joel Grant, Williams (Harding).

Bournemouth (0) 0
Bristol R (0) 1 *(Walker R 64)* 4153
Bournemouth: Moss; Young, Hart (Vokes), Hollands, Broadhurst, Gowling, Cooper (Ainsworth), Anderton, Hayter, Fletcher (Pitman), Connolly.
Bristol R: Phillips; Lescott, Carruthers, Campbell, Anthony, Elliott, Igoe, Disley, Walker R, Lambert (Sandell), Haldane.

Chester C (1) 1 *(Wilson 3)*
Bury (1) 3 *(Bishop 36, Hurst 48, Mattis 54)* 2810
Chester C: Danby; Vaughan S, Wilson, Marples (Steele), Bolland, Artell, Sandwith (Linwood), Martinez, Walters, Blundell (Semple), Hand.
Bury: Fettis; Scott, Brass, Woodthorpe, Challinor, Pugh, Turnbull (Barry-Murphy), Mattis, Hurst (Speight), Bishop, Buchanan (Kennedy T).
Chester C reinstated; Bury removed for fielding an ineligible player.

Doncaster R (1) 2 *(McCammon 23, Heffernan 50)*
Mansfield T (0) 0 5338
Doncaster R: Smith; Streete, Roberts G, Lockwood, Lee, Stock, Coppinger, Green P, Forte (Guy), McCammon (Thornton), Price (Heffernan).
Mansfield T: Muggleton; Buxton (Mullins), Jelleyman, Coke, Hjelde, John-Baptiste, Hamshaw, D'Laryea, Barker (Beardsley), Brown (Boulding M), Arnold.

Leyton Orient (0) 1 *(Walker 58)*
Torquay U (0) 2 *(Robertson J 52, 81)* 2384
Leyton Orient: Garner; Miller, Lockwood, Easton, Saah, Thelwell (Ibehre), Chambers, Demetriou (Keith), Alexander (Connor), Walker, Corden.
Torquay U: Abbey; Andrews, Reed, Angus (Critchell), Woods, Villis, Murray, Mansell, McPhee, Robertson J, Hill (Motteram) (Thorpe).

Millwall (0) 1 *(Doyle 114 (og))*
Bradford C (0) 0 3220
Millwall: Pidgeley; Senda, Whitbread (Phillips), Elliott, Robinson, Shaw, Dunne, Zebroski (Fuseini), May, Byfield, Morais (Hubertz).
Bradford C: Ricketts; Doyle (Bentham), Parker (Clarke), Schumacher, Wetherall, Bower, Johnson J, Bridge-Wilkinson, Johnson E, Windass, Black (Colbeck).
aet.

Nottingham F (0) 2 *(Tyson 53, Southall 81)*
Salisbury C (0) 0 6177
Nottingham F: Smith; Gary Holt, Bennett, Cullip, Morgan, Clingan, Perch, Grant Holt, Tyson (Lester), Agogo (Southall), Commons (Dobie).
Salisbury C: Clarke; Bass, Browne, Holmes (McGregor), Cook, Bond, Turk, Clay (Bartlett), Sales (Matthews), Tubbs, Prince.

THIRD ROUND

Friday, 5 January 2007
Bristol R (1) 1 *(Walker R 23 (pen))*
Hereford U (0) 0 8978
Bristol R: Phillips; Lescott, Carruthers, Campbell, Hinton, Elliott, Sandell, Disley, Lambert (Haldane), Walker R, Igoe.
Hereford U: Brown; Travis, Rose, Purdie, Mkandawire, Gulliver, McClenahan, Ferrell (Fleetwood), Connell, Sills, Webb (Williams).

Stoke C (0) 2 *(Elliott 82 (og), Fuller 87)*
Millwall (0) 0 8024
Stoke C: Simonsen; Hoefkens, Hill, Russell, Duberry, Higginbotham, Eustace (Brammer), Diao (Fuller), Sidibe, Pericard, Sweeney (Rooney).
Millwall: Pidgeley; Senda, Ross (Bakayogo), Elliott, Robinson, Shaw, Ardley, Williams (Fuseini), May (Hubertz), Byfield, Zebroski.

Saturday, 6 January 2007
Birmingham C (1) 2 *(Campbell 15, Larsson 86)*
Newcastle U (1) 2 *(Taylor 40, Dyer 54)* 16,444
Birmingham C: Maik Taylor; Kelly (Martin Taylor), Sadler, Muamba, Upson, Jaidi■, Johnson, Larsson, Bendtner (Kilkenny), Campbell (Danns), McSheffrey.
Newcastle U: Given; Solano, Edgar, Butt, Taylor, Huntington, Milner, Pattison, Martins, Sibierski (O'Brien), Dyer.

Blackpool (2) 4 *(Vernon 4, Morrell 7, 73, Burgess 80 (pen))*
Aldershot T (1) 2 *(John Grant 27, Pritchard 88)* 6355
Blackpool: Evans; Evatt, Tierney (Gorkss), Fox (Bean), Jackson, Barker, Forbes, Southern, Morrell, Vernon, Farrelly (Burgess).
Aldershot T: Bull; Newman, Barnard, Scott (Smith), Day, Edwards (Lee), Soares, Molesley, John Grant, Gayle, Williams (Pritchard).

Bristol C (3) 3 *(Brooker 14, Showunmi 18, Jevons 21)*
Coventry C (2) 3 *(Cameron 13, McKenzie 33, John 81)* 13,336
Bristol C: Basso; Orr, McAllister, McCombe, Keogh, Russell, Murray, Johnson, Brooker, Jevons (Skuse), Showunmi.
Coventry C: Steele; Whing, Virgo, Doyle, Page, Turner, Osbourne, Cameron, Adebola (John), Kyle (Andrews), McKenzie.

Chelsea (2) 6 *(Lampard 16, 41, 51 (pen), Wright-Phillips 68, Mikel 82, Ricardo Carvalho 86)*
Macclesfield T (1) 1 *(Murphy 40)* 41,434
Chelsea: Hilario; Geremi, Cole A (Woods), Lampard (Morais), Paulo Ferreira, Ricardo Carvalho, Wright-Phillips, Mikel, Kalou (Sahar), Shevchenko, Bridge.
Macclesfield T: Lee■; Regan, McIntyre, Morley, Swailes, Navarro, Bullock, Hadfield (Tolley), Murphy, McNeil (Jennings), Heath (Miles).

Chester C (0) 0
Ipswich T (0) 0 4330
Chester C: Danby; Marples, Wilson, Bolland, Westwood, Artell, Hessey (Bennett), Martinez, Walters, Blundell, Hand.
Ipswich T: Supple; Bruce (Casement), Harding, Garvan, De Vos, Naylor, Roberts, Legwinski, Lee, Clarke (Haynes), Richards (Williams).

Crystal Palace (1) 2 *(Kuqi 8, McAnuff 70)*
Swindon T (0) 1 *(Ifil 85)* 10,238
Crystal Palace: Flinders; Lawrence, Ward, Fletcher (Butterfield), Hudson, Cort, McAnuff, Hughes (Kennedy), Freedman (Morrison), Kuqi, Green.
Swindon T: Smith P; Smith J, Vincent, Williams, Ifil, Shakes, Pook (Sturrock), Timlin, Roberts (Brown), Peacock, Zaaboub (Jutkiewicz).

Derby Co (1) 3 *(Lupoli 32, 56, 85)*
Wrexham (0) 1 *(McEvilly 61)* 15,609
Derby Co: Bywater; Edworthy, Camara, Oakley (Peschisolido), Moore, Johnson M, Bisgaard (Barnes), Malcolm (Smith R), Howard, Lupoli, Jones.
Wrexham: Ingham; Valentine, Mike Williams, Williams D, Evans S, Pejic, Crowell (Johnson), Ferguson, McEvilly, Llewellyn, Done.

Doncaster R (0) 0
Bolton W (3) 4 *(Davies 8, Teymourian 22, 49, Tal 33)* 14,297
Doncaster R: Smith; Lockwood (Roberts S), O'Connor, Green P, Lee, Stock, Coppinger, Wilson, Heffernan, McCammon (Price), Forte (Guy).
Bolton W: Walker; Hunt, Gardner, Diagne-Faye, Meite (Augustyn), Teymourian, Tal, Vaz Te, Davies (Anelka), Fortune (Smith), Giannakopoulos.

Hull C (0) 1 *(Forster 79)*
Middlesbrough (0) 1 *(Viduka 73)* 17,520
Hull C: Myhill; Dawson, Ricketts, Ashbee, Coles, Turner, France (Featherstone), McPhee (Forster), Elliott (Duffy), Parkin, Livermore.
Middlesbrough: Jones; Xavier, Taylor, Riggott, Pogatetz, Boateng, Arca, Cattermole (Morrison), Yakubu, Viduka, Downing.

Leicester C (0) 2 *(Kisnorbo 80, Cadamarteri 90)*
Fulham (0) 2 *(McBride 69, Volz 83)* 15,499
Leicester C: Henderson; Maybury, Kisnorbo, Hughes, McCarthy, McAuley, Williams, Porter, Hume (Cadamarteri), Fryatt, Tiatto (Wesolowski).
Fulham: Lastuvka; Rosenior, Omozusi, Volz, Bocanegra, Pearce (Zakuani), Routledge, Radzinski, McBride, Helguson (Montella), Brown.

Liverpool (0) 1 *(Kuyt 71)*
Arsenal (2) 3 *(Rosicky 37, 45, Henry 84)* 43,619
Liverpool: Dudek; Finnan, Riise (Fabio Aurelio), Xabi Alonso, Carragher, Agger, Pennant, Gerrard, Crouch, Kuyt, Luis Garcia.
Arsenal: Almunia; Eboue (Hoyte), Clichy, Silva, Toure, Senderos, Hleb, Flamini, Van Persie (Julio Bapstista), Henry (Walcott), Rosicky.

Nottingham F (2) 2 *(Agogo 28, Grant Holt 32)*
Charlton Ath (0) 0 19,017
Nottingham F: Smith; Gary Holt, Bennett, Curtis, Breckin, Morgan, Southall, Grant Holt (Lester), Agogo (Dobie), Tyson (McGugan), Perch.
Charlton Ath: Myhre; Kishishev (Sam), Traore, Holland, El Karkouri, Fortune, Rommedahl (Thomas), Faye (Diawara), Bent M, Hasselbaink, Ambrose.

Peterborough U (0) 1 *(McLean 78)*
Plymouth Arg (0) 1 *(Aljofree 74 (pen))* 6255
Peterborough U: Tyler; Newton, Day (Yeo), Arber, Morgan, Futcher (Branston), Low, Butcher, Crow, McLean, Strachan (Benjamin).
Plymouth Arg: McCormick; Connolly■, Aljofree, Buzsaky (Dickson), Sawyer, Seip, Norris, Nalis, Samba (Summerfield), Reid (Hodges), Capaldi.

Portsmouth (0) 2 *(Cole 64, Kanu 90)*
Wigan Ath (0) 1 *(McCulloch 83)* 14,336
Portsmouth: James; Johnson, Taylor, Davis, Primus, Campbell, O'Neil, Pedro Mendes, Mwaruwari (Kanu), Cole, Kranjcar (Thompson).
Wigan Ath: Pollitt; Hall, Baines, Landzaat (Haestad), Boyce, Granqvist (Jackson), Cotterill, Johansson, Heskey, McCulloch, Kilbane (Teale).

Preston NE (1) 1 *(Ormerod 31)*
Sunderland (0) 0 10,318
Preston NE: Nash; Alexander, Hill (Whaley), Pugh, Wilson, Chilvers, Sedgwick (Neal), McKenna, Ormerod (Anyinsah), Nugent, Davidson.
Sunderland: Ward; Whitehead, Wallace, Miller L■, Evans, Varga, Elliott S, Leadbitter (Collins D), Murphy (Edwards), Connolly, Hysen (Yorke).

QPR (1) 2 *(Blackstock 32, Baidoo 76)*
Luton T (1) 2 *(Vine 45, Feeney 46)* 10,064
QPR: Royce; Bignot, Kanyuka, Lomas (Bircham), Mancienne, Stewart, Ward (Baidoo), Smith, Jones R (Furlong), Blackstock, Cook.
Luton T: Beresford; Barnett, Davis, Robinson, Perrett, Coyne, Brkovic, Langley, Vine, Feeney, Morgan.

Sheffield U (0) 0
Swansea C (0) 3 *(Butler 53, 59, Britton 67 (pen))* 15,896
Sheffield U: Gerrard; Geary, Armstrong, Montgomery, Bromby, Sommeil, Kazim-Richards, Hurst (Law), Nade (Quinn S), Webber (Tonge), Quinn A.
Swansea C: Gueret; Amankwaah (Iriekpen), Williams, O'Leary, Austin, Lawrence, Britton, Tate, Akinfenwa, Fallon, Butler.

Southend U (0) 1 *(Gower 58)*
Barnsley (0) 1 *(Coulson 90)* 5485
Southend U: Flahavan; Hunt, Hammell, Maher, Clarke, Barrett, Campbell-Ryce, McCormack (Guttridge), Bradbury, Eastwood, Gower.
Barnsley: Colgan; Hassell, Austin, Reid P, Atkinson, Howard, Hayes (Coulson), Togwell, Richards, Nardiello, Devaney.

Tamworth (0) 1 *(Storer 68)*
Norwich C (2) 4 *(Dublin 40, 62, Huckerby 42, 51)* 3165
Tamworth: Da Veiga; Smith, Heslop (Law), Storer, Weaver, Kemp, Taylor, Laight, Burton (Atieno), Williams (Price), McGrath.
Norwich C: Gallacher; Colin, Drury, Shackell, Doherty, Safri (Hughes), Croft (Robinson), Dublin (Thorne), Huckerby, Earnshaw, Etuhu.

Torquay U (0) 0
Southampton (1) 2 *(Rasiak 43, 72)* 5396
Torquay U: Horsell; Andrews, Hill (Motteram), Hockley (Easter), Woods, Angus, Murray, Mansell, McPhee, Thorpe, McKoy.
Southampton: Davis; Wright, Makin (Cranie), Pele, Baird, Powell, Sarmiento (Licka), Viafara, Rasiak, Wright-Phillips (Prutton), McGoldrick.

WBA (2) 3 *(McShane 6, Hartson 15, Phillips 82)*
Leeds U (0) 1 *(Robinson 90 (og))* 16,957
WBA: Hoult; McShane, Robinson, Chaplow (Carter), Davies C, Clement, Kamara (Koren), Koumas, Phillips, Hartson, Greening.
Leeds U: Sullivan; Rui Marques, Elliott, Nicholls, Foxe, Heath (Armando Sa), Blake, Howson (Derry), Moore (Flo), Healy, Lewis.

Watford (1) 4 *(Mackay 30, 76, Smith 48, Ashikodi 82)*
Stockport Co (1) 1 *(Poole 23)* 11,745
Watford: Foster; Mariappa, Stewart, Bangura, Mackay (Doyley), Demerit, Smith, Francis (Diagouraga), Henderson (Young), Ashikodi, McNamee.
Stockport Co: Spencer; Clare, Tunnicliffe, Dinning (Rowe), Poole (Le Fondre), Owen, Gleeson, Taylor, Malcolm (Bramble), Dickinson, Griffin.

West Ham U (0) 3 *(Noble 49, Cole 58, Mullins 90)*
Brighton & HA (0) 0 32,874

West Ham U: Carroll; Dailly, McCartney, Gabbidon, Ferdinand (Spector), Mullins, Benayoun, Noble, Cole (Zamora), Tevez, Boa Morte (Newton).
Brighton & HA: Henderson; O'Cearuill, Mayo, Lynch, Butters, El Abd, Fraser (Hart), Hammond, Robinson, Revell (Gatting), Frutos (Rents).

Wolverhampton W (2) 2 *(Olofinjana 35, Davies C 42)*
Oldham Ath (1) 2 *(Warne 19, Hall 78)* 14,524

Wolverhampton W: Murray; Little, McNamara, Olofinjana, Breen (Edwards), Collins, Potter, Henry, Davies C, Ricketts (Davies M), McIndoe (Johnson).
Oldham Ath: Pogliacomi; Wellens, Edwards, Eardley, Stam, Haining, Charlton, McDonald (Rocastle), Wolfenden (Hall), Warne, Liddell.

Sunday, 7 January 2007

Cardiff C (0) 0
Tottenham H (0) 0 20,376

Cardiff C: Alexander; Gilbert, McNaughton, Scimeca, Purse, Loovens, Flood, McPhail, Thompson, Chopra, Ledley.
Tottenham H: Robinson; Chimbonda, Lee (Gardner), Huddlestone, Dawson, Davenport, Murphy (Lennon), Malbranque, Berbatov, Defoe (Keane), Tainio.

Everton (0) 1 *(Johnson 69 (pen))*
Blackburn R (3) 4 *(Derbyshire 5, Pedersen 21, Gallagher 38, McCarthy 90)* 24,426

Everton: Howard; Neville, Nuno Valente (Naysmith), Yobo (Vaughan), Lescott, Carsley, Osman, Van der Meyde, Anichebe, Johnson, Arteta.
Blackburn R: Friedel; Ooijer, McEveley, Mokoena, Khizanishvili (Henchoz), Todd, Bentley, Tugay, Gallagher (Emerton), Derbyshire (McCarthy), Pedersen.

Manchester U (0) 2 *(Larsson 55, Solskjaer 90)*
Aston Villa (0) 1 *(Baros 74)* 74,924

Manchester U: Kuszczak; Neville, Evra, Park (Fletcher), Ferdinand, Brown, Ronaldo, Carrick (O'Shea), Larsson (Solskjaer), Rooney, Giggs.
Aston Villa: Kiraly; Hughes, Bouma, Osbourne, Cahill, Ridgewell, Petrov (Samuel), McCann, Angel (Baros), Agbonlahor, Barry.

Sheffield W (0) 1 *(MacLean 78)*
Manchester C (0) 1 *(Samaras 78 (pen))* 28,487

Sheffield W: Crossley; Simek, Spurr, Whelan, Bullen, Coughlan, Lunt, Tudgay (Small), MacLean, Burton, Brunt.
Manchester C: Weaver; Trabelsi (Sinclair), Onuoha, Dunne, Distin, Jordan, Richards, Dabo (Dickov), Samaras, Vassell, Beasley (Miller).

Tuesday, 9 January 2007

Barnet (0) 2 *(Yakubu 62, Puncheon 80)*
Colchester U (1) 1 *(Cureton 35)* 3075

Barnet: Harrison; Hendon, Nicolau, Cogan (Hatch), Yakubu, King, Bailey, Sinclair, Birchall, Graham, Puncheon.
Colchester U: Gerken; Halford, Barker, Baldwin, Brown, Watson, Izzet (Jackson), Garcia, Iwelumo (Guy), Cureton, McLeod (Duguid).

Reading (2) 3 *(Lita 27, Long 37, Sodje 55)*
Burnley (0) 2 *(Akinbiyi 69, O'Connor G 90)* 11,514

Reading: Federici; De la Cruz, Golbourne, Ingimarsson (Pearce), Sodje, Bikey, Seol, Oster, Lita (Kitson), Long, Convey.
Burnley: Jensen; Thomas, Harley, McCann, Foster, McGreal, O'Connor J, Jones (Mahon), Akinbiyi, Noel-Williams (Lafferty), Elliott (O'Connor G).

THIRD ROUND REPLAYS

Tuesday, 16 January 2007

Barnsley (0) 0
Southend U (1) 2 *(Maher 22, Bradbury 58)* 4944

Barnsley: Colgan; Hassell, Heckingbottom, Reid P, Atkinson, Howard, Hayes, Togwell, Coulson, Nardiello (Richards), Devaney.
Southend U: Flahavan; Hunt, Hammell, Maher, Clarke, Barrett, Campbell-Ryce (Guttridge), McCormack, Bradbury (Harrold), Eastwood, Gower.

Coventry C (0) 0
Bristol C (1) 2 *(Murray 39, Showunmi 54)* 13,055

Coventry C: Steele; Whing, Hall, Doyle, Page, Turner, Tabb (Birchall), Osbourne (Thornton), Kyle (Adebola), John, McKenzie.
Bristol C: Basso; Orr, McAllister, McCombe, Carey, Skuse (Russell), Murray, Johnson, Brooker (Keogh), Jevons (Myrie-Williams), Showunmi.

Ipswich T (0) 1 *(Richards 84)*
Chester C (0) 0 11,732

Ipswich T: Price; Wilnis, Harding, Williams, Bruce, Naylor, Peters, Legwinski (Richards), Lee, Haynes (Clarke), Roberts.
Chester C: Danby; Marples, Wilson, Bennett, Bolland, Artell, Hessey, Martinez, Walters, Blundell, Hand.

Manchester C (1) 2 *(Ireland 44, Vassell 56)*
Sheffield W (0) 1 *(Bullen 51)* 25,621

Manchester C: Weaver; Richards, Jordan, Dunne, Distin, Barton, Sinclair, Dabo, Vassell (Beasley), Corradi (Samaras), Ireland.
Sheffield W: Crossley; Simek (Wood), Spurr, Whelan, Coughlan, Bullen, Lunt (Folly), Tudgay, MacLean, Burton (Small), Brunt.

Middlesbrough (1) 4 *(Hines 32, Viduka 49, 64, Yakubu 57 (pen))*
Hull C (0) 3 *(Dawson 59, 69, Parkin 63 (pen))* 16,702

Middlesbrough: Schwarzer; Davies, Arca, Woodgate, Xavier (Ehiogu), Hines, Morrison, Cattermole, Yakubu (Christie), Viduka, Downing.
Hull C: Myhill; Dawson, Ricketts, Marney, Delaney, Turner, McPhee (Elliott), Ashbee, Forster, Parkin, Livermore (France).

Oldham Ath (0) 0
Wolverhampton W (0) 2 *(Potter 56, Davies C 75)* 9628

Oldham Ath: Pogliacomi; Wellens, Taylor, Eardley, Stam (Edwards), Haining, Charlton, McDonald, Porter, Warne (Hall), Liddell.
Wolverhampton W: Murray; Little, Clapham (Edwards), Olofinjana, Breen, Collins, Ricketts, Henry, Davies C (Johnson), Potter, McIndoe (Davies M).

Plymouth Arg (2) 2 *(Hayles 18, Norris 27)*
Peterborough U (1) 1 *(McLean 13)* 9973

Plymouth Arg: McCormick; Connolly, Sawyer, Buzsaky (Summerfield), Aljofree, Seip, Norris, Nalis, Reid (Ebanks-Blake), Hayles, Capaldi.
Peterborough U: Tyler; Newton, Huke (Yeo), Arber, Morgan, Strachan (Gain), Low (Benjamin), Day, Crow, McLean, Butcher.

Wednesday, 17 January 2007

Fulham (1) 4 *(McBride 35, Montella 51, 60, Routledge 90)*
Leicester C (2) 3 *(Fryatt 13, McAuley 45, Wesolowski 47)* 11,222

Fulham: Warner; Rosenior, Queudrue, Volz, Bocanegra, Christanval, Routledge, Radzinski, McBride (Montella), Helguson, Brown.
Leicester C: Henderson; Maybury, Kisnorbo, Williams, McCarthy, McAuley (Stearman), Hughes (Cadamarteri), Porter, Hume, Fryatt, Tiatto (Wesolowski).

Newcastle U (0) 1 *(Milner 56)*

Birmingham C (2) 5 *(McSheffrey 5, Solano 45 (og), N'Gotty 59, Larsson 83, Campbell 89)* 26,099

Newcastle U: Given; Solano, Huntington, Butt, Taylor■, Ramage, Milner, Pattison (O'Brien), Martins, Sibierski (Carroll), Dyer.
Birmingham C: Maik Taylor; N'Gotty, Sadler, Muamba (Nafti), Upson, Martin Taylor, Larsson (Danns), Jerome, Campbell, Johnson, McSheffrey (Kilkenny).

Tottenham H (3) 4 *(Lennon 27, Keane 30, Malbranque 41, Defoe 81)*

Cardiff C (0) 0 27,641

Tottenham H: Robinson; Chimbonda, Assou-Ekotto, Huddlestone, Dawson, Gardner, Zokora (Tainio), Malbranque (Ghali), Berbatov (Defoe), Keane, Lennon.
Cardiff C: Alexander; Gilbert, McNaughton, Scimeca, Purse, Loovens, Flood (Cooper), McPhail, Thompson, Chopra (Ferretti), Ledley.

THIRD ROUND REPLAY

Tuesday, 23 January 2007

Luton T (0) 1 *(Rehman 80 (og))*

QPR (0) 0 7494

Luton T: Brill; Foley, Davis, Robinson, Perrett, Coyne, Bell, Langley, Boyd, Brkovic (Morgan), Emanuel.
QPR: Royce; Rehman, Milanese, Bailey■, Mancienne, Stewart, Lomas, Smith (Ainsworth), Nygaard (Jones R), Blackstock, Cook.

FOURTH ROUND

Saturday, 27 January 2007

Barnet (0) 0

Plymouth Arg (0) 2 *(Aljofree 67 (pen), Sinclair 83)* 5204

Barnet: Flitney; Devera (Allen), Nicolau, Cogan (Hatch), Yakubu, King, Bailey, Hessenthaler, Birchall, Graham, Puncheon.
Plymouth Arg: McCormick; Connolly, Capaldi, Buzsaky (Summerfield), Aljofree, Seip, Norris, Nalis, Gallen, Hayles, Halmosi (Sinclair).

Birmingham C (0) 2 *(Martin Taylor 47, Larsson 90)*

Reading (2) 3 *(Kitson 3, Lita 41, 82)* 20,041

Birmingham C: Maik Taylor; N'Gotty (Danns), Sadler, Muamba (Kilkenny), Upson, Martin Taylor, Larsson, Johnson, Jerome, Campbell (Bendtner), McSheffrey.
Reading: Federici; Murty, De la Cruz, Bikey, Sodje, Harper (Osano), Seol, Oster, Lita, Kitson (Cox), Convey.

Blackpool (0) 1 *(Evatt 52)*

Norwich C (1) 1 *(Huckerby 45)* 9491

Blackpool: Evans; Evatt, Gorkss, Fox (Jorgensen), Jackson, Barker, Forbes (Burgess), Southern, Morrell, Vernon (Parker), Hoolahan.
Norwich C: Marshall; Colin, Drury, Dublin (McVeigh), Doherty, Safri, Croft (Thorne), Robinson, Huckerby, Brown■, Etuhu.

Bristol C (0) 2 *(Keogh 53, Murray 59)*

Middlesbrough (2) 2 *(Yakubu 4, Christie 23)* 19,008

Bristol C: Basso; Orr, Fontaine (Woodman), Keogh, Carey, Skuse (Russell), Murray, Johnson, Showunmi, McAllister, Noble (Myrie-Williams).
Middlesbrough: Schwarzer; Xavier, Taylor, Cattermole, Pogatetz, Woodgate, Arca, Morrison (Johnson), Yakubu, Christie (Euell), Downing.

Crystal Palace (0) 0

Preston NE (0) 2 *(Nugent 46, Wilson 83)* 8422

Crystal Palace: Flinders; Lawrence, Butterfield (Freedman), Fletcher, Hudson, Ward, McAnuff, Green (Ifill), Scowcroft (Kuqi), Morrison, Kennedy.
Preston NE: Lonergan; Alexander, Hill, Neal, Wilson, Chilvers, Sedgwick (Whaley), McKenna, Ricketts (Ormerod), Nugent (Mellor), Pugh.

Derby Co (0) 1 *(Peschisolido 82)*

Bristol R (0) 0 25,033

Derby Co: Bywater; Jackson, Camara, Barnes, Moore, Johnson M, Fagan (Bisgaard), Malcolm (Smith R), Howard, Lupoli (Peschisolido), Johnson S.
Bristol R: Phillips; Lescott■, Carruthers, Campbell, Hinton, Elliott, Sandell (Haldane), Disley, Walker R (Green), Lambert, Igoe (Rigg).

Fulham (2) 3 *(Montella 11, McBride 39, Radzinski 54)*

Stoke C (0) 0 11,059

Fulham: Lastuvka; Rosenior (Davies), Queudrue, Volz, Bocanegra, Christianval, Routledge, Radzinski, McBride (Jensen), Montella (Dempsey), Brown.
Stoke C: Simonsen; Hoefkens, Griffin (Wilkinson), Russell, Duberry, Higginbotham, Lawrence, Matteo (Diao), Sidibe, Fuller (Rooney), Martin.

Ipswich T (0) 1 *(Lee 64 (pen))*

Swansea C (0) 0 16,635

Ipswich T: Price; Sito, Harding, Williams (Haynes), Wilnis, Naylor (Casement), Peters, Legwinski, Lee, Clarke (Garvan), Roberts.
Swansea C: Gueret; Duffy R, Williams (Painter), Tate, Lawrence, Iriekpen, Britton, Pratley (Trundle), Akinfenwa (Abbott), Robinson, Butler.

Luton T (0) 0

Blackburn R (2) 4 *(Derbyshire 10, 56, McCarthy 37, Pedersen 74)* 5887

Luton T: Beresford; Foley, Davis, Robinson, Perrett, Coyne (Keane), Bell (Morgan), Langley, Boyd, Talbot (O'Leary), Emanuel.
Blackburn R: Friedel; Khizanishvili (Gallagher), Warnock, Mokoena, Nelsen (Samba), Henchoz, Emerton, Bentley, Derbyshire, McCarthy (Jeffers), Pedersen.

Manchester U (0) 2 *(Rooney 77, 83)*

Portsmouth (0) 1 *(Kanu 87)* 71,137

Manchester U: Kuszczak; Neville, Evra, Park, Ferdinand, Vidic, Carrick, Scholes, Larsson, Solskjaer (Rooney), Giggs (Fletcher).
Portsmouth: James; Johnson, Hughes (Douala), O'Neil, Primus, Campbell, Lauren, Pedro Mendes, Cole (Kanu), Kranjcar (Mwaruwai), Taylor.

Tottenham H (1) 3 *(Keane 12, Jenas 50, Mido 76)*

Southend U (0) 1 *(Eastwood 69 (pen))* 33,406

Tottenham H: Cerny; Stalteri, Lee, Zokora, Dawson, Rocha, Ghaly (Malbranque), Jenas, Mido (Huddlestone), Keane (Defoe), Lennon.
Southend U: Flahavan; Hunt, Hammell, Maher, Clarke, Barrett, Campbell-Ryce, McCormack (Guttridge), Bradbury (Harrold), Eastwood, Gower (Hooper).

West Ham U (0) 0

Watford (1) 1 *(McNamee 42)* 31,168

West Ham U: Carroll; Neill (Pantsil), McCartney, Quashie, Spector, Dailly, Newton (Sheringham), Reo-Coker, Cole, Zamora, Boa Morte (Etherington).
Watford: Foster; Mariappa, Stewart, Francis, Mackay, Demerit, Smith, Bangura, Henderson, Bouazza, McNamee (Powell).

Sunday, 28 January 2007

Arsenal (0) 1 *(Toure 78)*

Bolton W (0) 1 *(Nolan 50)* 59,778

Arsenal: Almunia; Hoyte (Julio Baptista), Clichy, Flamini, Toure, Senderos, Walcott (Aliadiere), Fabregas, Adebayor, Henry, Rosicky.
Bolton W: Jaaskelainen; Hunt, Gardner (Pedersen), Campo, Diagne-Faye, Meite, Nolan, Speed, Anelka, Davies, Giannakopoulos (Vaz Te).

Chelsea (3) 3 *(Shevchenko 9, Drogba 18, Mikel 45)*
Nottingham F (0) 0 41,516
Chelsea: Cech; Geremi, Bridge, Diarra, Essien, Ricardo Carvalho, Wright-Phillips (Morais), Lampard (Woods), Drogba (Kalou), Shevchenko, Mikel.
Nottingham F: Smith; Gary Holt, Bennett, Curtis, Breckin, Morgan, Southall, Grant Holt (Clingan), Agogo (Lester), Tyson, Perch (Dobie).

Manchester C (2) 3 *(Vassell 26, Barton 45, Beasley 70)*
Southampton (1) 1 *(Jones 23)* 26,496
Manchester C: Weaver; Richards, Beasley, Dunne, Distin, Barton (Hamann), Trabelsi, Dabo, Samaras (Miller), Vassell (Abdoun), Ireland.
Southampton: Davis; Ostlund (Licka), Bale, Pele, Baird, Powell, McGoldrick, Viafara, Rasiak (Wright-Phillips), Jones, Wright.

Wolverhampton W (0) 0
WBA (1) 3 *(Kamara 44, Phillips 49, Gera 78)* 28,107
Wolverhampton W: Murray; Little, McNamara, Olofinjana (Johnson), Breen, Collins, Potter, Henry, Davies C (Davies M), Ricketts (Ward), McIndoe.
WBA: Zuberbuhler; McShane, Robinson, Chaplow, Davies C, Clement, Koumas, Koren (Gera), Phillips, Kamara (Carter), Greening.

FOURTH ROUND REPLAYS

Tuesday, 13 February 2007

Middlesbrough (0) 2 *(Viduka 69, Yakubu 102)*
Bristol C (1) 2 *(Noble 23, McCombe 117)* 26,328
Middlesbrough: Schwarzer; Hines (Davies), Taylor, Xavier, Pogatetz, Boateng, Rochemback, Cattermole (Johnson), Yakubu, Christie (Viduka), Downing.
Bristol C: Weale; Orr, Fontaine (Partridge), McCombe, Keogh, Russell, Murray, Johnson, Jevons, Noble (Myrie-Williams), McAllister (Woodman).
aet; Middlesbrough won 5-4 on penalties.

Norwich C (0) 3 *(Huckerby 78, 95, Martin 112)*
Blackpool (1) 2 *(Jackson 37, Barker 108)* 19,120
Norwich C: Marshall; Colin (Martin), Drury, Shackell, Dublin, Safri (Doherty), Croft, Hughes, Huckerby, Brown, Etuhu.
Blackpool: Evans; Evatt, Tierney (Gorkss), Fox, Jackson, Barker, Forbes (Jorgensen), Southern, Vernon (Burgess), Parker, Hoolahan.
aet.

Wednesday, 14 February 2007

Bolton W (0) 1 *(Meite 90)*
Arsenal (1) 3 *(Adebayor 13, 120, Ljungberg 108)* 21,088
Bolton W: Jaaskelainen; Campo, Gardner (Pedersen), Teymourian (Tal), Ben Haim■, Meite, Giannakopoulos (Vaz Te), Speed, Anelka, Diouf, Nolan.
Arsenal: Almunia; Diaby, Clichy, Silva, Toure, Djourou (Hoyte), Hleb (Ljungberg), Denilson, Adebayor, Julio Baptista, Rosicky (Aliadiere).
aet.

FIFTH ROUND

Saturday, 17 February 2007

Arsenal (0) 0
Blackburn R (0) 0 56,761
Arsenal: Almunia; Hoyte, Gallas (Clichy), Flamini, Toure, Senderos, Walcott (Adebayor), Fabregas, Aliadiere, Henry, Ljungberg (Rosicky).
Blackburn R: Friedel; Emerton, Warnock, Mokoena, Nelsen, Khizanishvili, Bentley, Samba, Nonda (Roberts), Berner (Derbyshire), Dunn (Todd).

Chelsea (1) 4 *(Wright-Phillips 39, Drogba 51, Essien 89, Shevchenko 90)*
Norwich C (0) 0 41,537
Chelsea: Cech; Paulo Ferreira, Diarra, Mikel, Terry, Boulahrouz (Essien), Geremi,Lampard (Shevchenko), Drogba (Kalou), Robben, Wright-Phillips.
Norwich C: Marshall (Gallacher); Hughes, Drury, Shackell, Dublin, Safri, Croft, Lappin (Martin), Huckerby, Brown, Etuhu (Fotheringham).

Manchester U (1) 1 *(Carrick 45)*
Reading (0) 1 *(Gunnarsson 67)* 70,608
Manchester U: Kuszczak; Brown, Heinze (Evra), Carrick, Silvestre, Vidic, Ronaldo, Fletcher, Saha, Solskjaer (Larsson), Park (Scholes).
Reading: Federici; De la Cruz, Shorey, Ingimarsson, Bikey, Gunnarsson, Seol (Little), Sidwell, Kitson, Oster (Sodje), Convey (Hunt).

Middlesbrough (2) 2 *(Arca 29, Yakubu 45 (pen))*
WBA (1) 2 *(Kamara 41, Phillips 58)* 31,491
Middlesbrough: Schwarzer; Xavier, Taylor, Woodgate, Pogatetz, Boateng, Arca, Johnson (Morrison), Yakubu (Christie), Viduka, Downing.
WBA: Kiely; McShane, Robinson, Chaplow, Davies C■, Clement, Koumas (Gera), Koren, Phillips (Ellington), Kamara (Albrechtsen), Greening.

Plymouth Arg (1) 2 *(Gallen 14 (pen), Sinclair 83)*
Derby Co (0) 0 18,026
Plymouth Arg: McCormick; Connolly, Sawyer, Gosling (Halmosi), Timar, Seip, Norris, Nalis, Ebanks-Blake, Gallen, Sinclair.
Derby Co: Bywater; Mears, Camara, Pearson, Moore■, Leacock, Bisgaard, Jones (Barnes), Howard, Johnson S (Johnson M), Smith R (Macken).

Watford (0) 1 *(Francis 88)*
Ipswich T (0) 0 17,016
Watford: Lee; Mariappa, Powell, Francis, Shittu, Demerit, Smith, Mahon, Henderson, Kabba (Priskin), Cavalli (Bouazza).
Ipswich T: Price; Wright, Harding, Bruce, Casement, O'Callaghan■, Roberts, Legwinski, Haynes (Clarke), Peters (Trotter), Richards.

Sunday, 18 February 2007

Fulham (0) 0
Tottenham H (1) 4 *(Keane 6, 68, Berbatov 77, 90)* 18,655
Fulham: Lastuvka; Volz, Queudrue, Diop, Knight, Christianval, Smertin, Radzinski (Dempsey), McBride (John), Helguson (Montella■), Davies.
Tottenham H: Robinson; Chimbonda, Lee, Zokora, Dawson, Gardner, Lennon (Ghaly), Malbranque, Mido (Berbatov), Keane, Tainio.

Preston NE (1) 1 *(Nugent 8)*
Manchester C (1) 3 *(Ball 35, Hill 85 (og), Ireland 90)* 18,890
Preston NE: Lonergan; Alexander, Hill, Soley, Chilvers, Pugh, Sedgwick, McKenna, Ricketts (Agyemang), Nugent, Whaley (Mellor).
Manchester C: Weaver; Richards, Ball, Dunne, Distin, Barton, Trabelsi, Dabo, Samaras, Corradi, Ireland.

FIFTH ROUND REPLAYS

Tuesday, 27 February 2007

Reading (1) 2 *(Kitson 23, Lita 84)*
Manchester U (3) 3 *(Heinze 2, Saha 4, Solskjaer 6)* 23,821
Reading: Federici; De la Cruz, Shorey, Ingimarsson, Bikey, Gunnarsson, Oster, Sidwell, Kitson, Doyle (Lita), Seol (Little).
Manchester U: Van der Sar; Silvestre, Heinze, O'Shea, Ferdinand, Brown, Park, Fletcher, Saha (Rooney), Solskjaer (Ronaldo), Richardson.

WBA (1) 1 *(Carter 26)*
Middlesbrough (0) 1 *(Viduka 63)* 24,925
WBA: Kiely; McShane, Robinson, Chaplow (Koren), Davies C, Clement, Gera (MacDonald), Carter, Ellington■, Koumas (Kamara), Greening.
Middlesbrough: Jones; Davies (Parnaby), Taylor, Woodgate, Pogatetz, Boateng, Arca, Cattermole (Morrison), Yakubu, Viduka (Lee), Downing.
aet; Middlesbrough won 5-4 on penalties.

Wednesday, 28 February 2007
Blackburn R (0) 1 *(McCarthy 87)*
Arsenal (0) 0 18,882

Blackburn R: Friedel; Emerton, Warnock (Khizanishvili), Tugay (Dunn), Nelsen, Samba, Bentley, Mokoena, Nonda (McCarthy), Derbyshire, Pedersen.
Arsenal: Almunia; Eboue (Walcott), Traore (Clichy), Silva, Gallas, Senderos, Hleb, Denilson, Aliadiere, Julio Baptista, Ljungberg.

SIXTH ROUND

Saturday, 10 March 2007
Middlesbrough (1) 2 *(Cattermole 45, Boateng 47)*
Manchester United (1) 2 *(Rooney 23, Ronaldo 68 (pen))* 33,308

Middlesbrough: Schwarzer; Parnaby, Taylor, Woodgate, Pogatetz, Boateng (Euell), Arca, Cattermole (Morrison), Yakubu, Viduka (Lee), Downing.
Manchester United: Kuszczak; Neville, Heinze, O'Shea, Ferdinand, Vidic, Ronaldo, Carrick, Larsson, Rooney, Giggs.

Sunday, 11 March 2007
Blackburn Rovers (1) 2 *(Mokoena 28, Derbyshire 90)*
Manchester City (0) 0 27,743

Blackburn Rovers: Friedel; Emerton, Warnock, Tugay (Peter), Nelsen (Khizanishvili), Samba, Bentley, Mokoena■, Derbyshire, McCarthy (Roberts), Pedersen.
Manchester City: Weaver; Richards, Jihai (Beasley), Dunne, Distin, Barton, Ireland, Hamann (Samaras), Vassell, Corradi (Mpenza), Ball.

Chelsea (1) 3 *(Lampard 22, 71, Kalou 86)*
Tottenham Hotspur (3) 3 *(Berbatov 5, Essien 28 (og), Ghaly 36)* 41,517

Chelsea: Cech; Paulo Ferreira (Wright-Phillips), Cole A (Kalou), Diarra (Boulahrouz), Essien, Ricardo Carvalho, Ballack, Lampard, Drogba, Shevchenko, Robben.
Tottenham Hotspur: Cerny; Stalteri, Lee, Zokora, Dawson, Ricardo Rocha, Lennon (Malbranque), Tainio, Berbatov (Mido), Defoe, Ghaly (Gardner).

Plymouth Arg (0) 0
Watford (1) 1 *(Bouazza 21)* 20,652

Plymouth Arg: McCormick; Connolly, Sawyer (Halmosi), Gosling (Hayles), Timar, Seip, Norris, Nalis, Ebanks-Blake, Gallen, Sinclair (Capaldi).
Watford: Foster; Mariappa, Powell, Francis, Shittu, Demerit, Smith, Mahon, Priskin (Henderson), Kabba (Chambers), Bouazza.

SIXTH ROUND REPLAYS

Monday, 19 March 2007
Manchester U (0) 1 *(Ronaldo 76 (pen))*
Middlesbrough (0) 0 71,325

Manchester U: Kuszczak; Brown, Heinze, Carrick, Ferdinand, Vidic, Ronaldo, Richardson (Park), Smith (O'Shea), Rooney, Giggs.
Middlesbrough: Schwarzer; Xavier, Taylor (Huth), Woodgate, Pogatetz, Boateng, Arca (Rochemback), Cattermole (Morrison■), Yakubu, Viduka, Downing.

Tottenham H (0) 1 *(Keane 79 (pen))*
Chelsea (0) 2 *(Shevchenko 55, Wright-Phillips 61)* 35,519

Tottenham H: Robinson; Chimbonda, Lee, Zokora, Dawson, Ricardo Rocha (Stalteri), Lennon, Jenas, Berbatov, Keane, Malbranque (Defoe).
Chelsea: Cech; Diarra (Paulo Ferreira), Cole A, Mikel, Terry, Ricardo Carvalho, Wright-Phillips (Kalou), Lampard, Drogba, Shevchenko (Robben), Ballack.

SEMI-FINALS

Saturday, 14 April 2007 (at Villa Park)
Watford (1) 1 *(Bouazza 26)*
Manchester U (2) 4 *(Rooney 7, 66, Ronaldo 28, Richardson 82)* 37,425

Watford: Lee; Mariappa (Doyley), Stewart, Chambers (Kabba), Carlisle, DeMerit, Smith, Mahon, Priskin (King), Bouazza, Francis.
Manchester U: Van der Sar; Evra, Heinze, Carrick, Ferdinand (Fletcher), Brown, Ronaldo (Richardson), Scholes, Smith, Rooney, Giggs (Solskjaer).

Sunday, 15 April 2007 (at Old Trafford)
Blackburn R (0) 1 *(Roberts 64)*
Chelsea (1) 2 *(Lampard 16, Ballack 109)* 50,559

Blackburn R: Friedel; Emerton, Warnock, Mokoena, Nelsen, Samba, Bentley (Derbyshire), Dunn (Peter), Roberts, McCarthy, Pedersen.
Chelsea: Cech; Essien, Cole A, Makelele (Mikel), Terry, Ricardo Carvalho, Ballack, Lampard, Drogba, Shevchenko (Kalou), Cole J (Wright-Phillips).
aet.

THE FA CUP FINAL

Saturday, 19 May 2007
(at Wembley Stadium, attendance 89,826)

Chelsea (0) 1 **Manchester U (0) 0**

Chelsea: Cech; Paulo Ferreira, Bridge, Makelele, Terry, Essien, Wright-Phillips (Kalou), Lampard, Drogba, Mikel, Cole J (Robben) (Cole A).

Scorer: Drogba 116.

Manchester U: Van der Sar; Brown, Heinze, Carrick (O'Shea), Ferdinand, Vidic, Ronaldo, Scholes, Rooney, Fletcher (Smith), Giggs (Solskjaer).

aet.

Referee: S. Bennett (Kent).

NATIONWIDE CONFERENCE 2006–07

At last, Dagenham & Redbridge have made it to the Football League following their disappointment five years ago when they lost out on goal difference to Boston United. But had the four points subsequently deducted from Boston at the start of 2002–03 been applied to the Conference, the Essex club could well have made it much earlier. Ironically, of course they now take the place of relegated Boston, demoted to the Northern Section, too.

However, it did not start off too well for the Daggers, especially in only the second game and first at Victoria Road when highly fancied Oxford United arrived and left with the three points.

Results did pick up, but in successive weeks late in October Kidderminster Harriers came to Dagenham and won 3-1, then Oxford repeated their earlier success by the same margin of victory at the same venue in the FA Cup.

Early departure from this competition might have proved a blessing as did losing at Redditch United later on in the Trophy. But when Dagenham transferred Craig Mackail-Smith and Shane Blackett to Peterborough United for a club record transfer fee and lost at home to Rushden & Diamonds, one wondered whether the wheels might come off at Dagenham.

But it was just a blip and they did not lose the next ten including a 2-2 draw at Oxford, who by this time were drawing far too many matches. Then in front of 4,044, their best crowd of the season, on 7 April they won, albeit shakily, 2-1 against Aldershot to clinch automatic promotion and the championship.

In fact, Oxford's first defeat of the season had come in that FA Cup game previously mentioned. But they had completed 17 Conference matches without losing. Then on 18 November they lost 1-0 at Gravesend & Northfleet which precipitated something of a crisis for the club.

A week later they did account for lowly Tamworth, but they failed to win any of the next eleven and not until the return with Gravesend on 17 February did they manage another Conference win.

Oxford eventually finished in second place, but consigned to the play-offs along with Morecambe, York City and Exeter City. So three of the contenders were former Football League clubs.

The odd men out were Morecambe, certainly one of the most consistent of the teams not quite making it in the last half dozen years. This time they were separated from second place by goal difference with York a further point away lying fourth.

However, Morecambe faltered from the start, losing at home to Burton Albion. Of their opening 11 matches, the Shrimps won just three. Naturally results had a healthier glow later on.

York had lost to Morecambe in September, though the result was reversed on New Year's Day. However, from the middle of March a run of four without a win finished any lingering hopes of first place.

Exeter opening their campaign with a goalless draw against York and drew the return 1-1 in March. Always in or around the top five from mid-February, City had shown their usual confidence.

So, to the play-offs and Exeter were shaken when Oxford took a first leg lead from their visit to Devon in front of a crowd of 8,659. At York, Morecambe managed a goalless draw with 6,660 present. In the return games, Oxford seemed well on the way to Wembley when they took the lead again, only for Exeter to force a 2-1 win and then succeed in the penalty shoot-out 4-3. The attendance was 10,691. York, too, thought optimistically, when they led at Morecambe but were also beaten 2-1 with the crowd 5,567.

At Wembley again it was the losing team which led, Lee Phillips scoring. Wayne Curtis then had a penalty kick saved by Paul Jones before Garry Thompson finally levelled the scores after 42 minutes. Danny Carlton clinched it for the Shrimps with a late winner with 40,043 watching.

Of the others, Burton and Gravesend (before becoming Ebbsfleet United), threatened seriously as did Weymouth before their financial crisis. Stevenage Borough and Kidderminster had the Trophy final as a consolation game.

Rushden had been expected to do better, Northwich surprised pleasantly but it was another disappointing season for Aldershot, Woking and particularly Grays Athletic. Cambridge United and Halifax Town made late runs out of trouble, Forest Green Rovers looked in improved shape and Crawley Town made light of a ten point deduction.

Erratic Altrincham were reprieved from the drop again through the Boston affair. Stafford Rangers escaped as well. Tamworth, Southport and St Albans City were not as fortunate.

However, for the 2007–08 season it is all change with the Conference bowing out and Blue Square Premier blowing in. The participating newcomers from the North and South are Droylsden from the Manchester area, joined by Farsley Celtic, with runaway South winners Histon linking up with Salisbury City the runners-up, who also enjoyed a fine FA Cup run.

Scarborough, a Football League club only eight years ago, were one of two clubs with a ten-point deduction. The others Lancaster City finished with just one point. Scarborough were subsequently wound up and re-formed as Scarborough Athletic.

Farnborough Town with financial worries of their own and similarly in administration, made light of their ten-point penalty and finished 11th in the South, to be known as Blue Square South of course.

NATIONWIDE CONFERENCE 2006–07 FINAL LEAGUE TABLE

			Home					*Away*					*Total*						
		P	*W*	*D*	*L*	*F*	*A*	*W*	*D*	*L*	*F*	*A*	*W*	*D*	*L*	*F*	*A*	*GD*	*Pts*
1	Dagenham & R	46	16	4	3	50	20	12	7	4	43	28	28	11	7	93	48	45	95
2	Oxford U	46	11	9	3	33	16	11	6	6	33	17	22	15	9	66	33	33	81
3	Morecambe	46	11	7	5	29	20	12	5	6	35	26	23	12	11	64	46	18	81
4	York C	46	10	6	7	29	22	13	5	5	36	23	23	11	12	65	45	20	80
5	Exeter C	46	14	7	2	39	19	8	5	10	28	29	22	12	12	67	48	19	78
6	Burton Alb	46	13	3	7	28	21	9	6	8	24	26	22	9	15	52	47	5	75
7	Gravesend & N	46	12	6	5	33	25	9	5	9	30	31	21	11	14	63	56	7	74
8	Stevenage B	46	12	4	7	46	30	8	6	9	30	36	20	10	16	76	66	10	70
9	Aldershot T	46	11	7	5	40	31	7	4	12	24	31	18	11	17	64	62	2	65
10	Kidderminster H	46	7	5	11	19	26	10	7	6	24	24	17	12	17	43	50	–7	63
11	Weymouth	46	12	6	5	35	26	6	3	14	21	47	18	9	19	56	73	–17	63
12	Rushden & D	46	10	5	8	34	24	7	6	10	24	30	17	11	18	58	54	4	62
13	Northwich Vic	46	9	2	12	26	33	9	2	12	25	36	18	4	24	51	69	–18	58
14	Forest Green R	46	10	5	8	34	33	3	13	7	25	31	13	18	15	59	64	–5	57
15	Woking	46	8	8	7	34	26	7	4	12	22	35	15	12	19	56	61	–5	57
16	Halifax T	46	12	8	3	40	22	3	2	18	15	40	15	10	21	55	62	–7	55
17	Cambridge U	46	8	4	11	34	33	7	6	10	23	33	15	10	21	57	66	–9	55
18	Crawley T*	46	10	6	7	27	20	7	6	10	25	32	17	12	17	52	52	0	53
19	Grays Ath	46	8	9	6	29	21	5	4	14	27	34	13	13	20	56	55	1	52
20	Stafford R	46	7	4	12	25	33	7	6	10	24	38	14	10	22	49	71	–22	52
21	Altrincham	46	9	4	10	28	32	4	8	11	25	35	13	12	21	53	67	–14	51
22	Tamworth	46	8	6	9	24	27	5	3	15	19	34	13	9	24	43	61	–18	48
23	Southport	46	7	4	12	29	30	4	10	9	28	37	11	14	21	57	67	–10	47
24	St Albans C	46	5	5	13	28	49	5	5	13	29	40	10	10	26	57	89	–32	40

**Deducted 10 points for entering administration.*

NATIONWIDE CONFERENCE LEADING GOALSCORERS 2006–07

	League	*FA Cup*	*Trophy*	*Total*
Paul Benson *(Dagenham & R)*	28	0	2	30
Charlie MacDonald *(Gravesend & N)*	27	0	2	29
Clayton Donaldson *(York C)*	24	1	1	26
Steve Morison *(Stevenage B)*	23	2	8	33
Simeon Jackson *(Rushden & D)*	19	1	0	20
Robert Duffy *(Oxford U)*	18	1	2	21
John Grant *(Aldershot T)*	17	5	1	23
Robbie Simpson *(Cambridge U)*	17	0	0	17
Daryl Clare *(Burton Alb)*	16	2	0	18
Craig McAllister *(Woking)*	15	1	1	17
Craig Mackail-Smith *(Dagenham & R)*	15	0	1	16
Neil Grayson *(Stafford R)*	13	0	0	13
Aaron McLean *(Grays Ath)*	13	0	0	13

ATTENDANCES BY CLUB 2006–07

	Aggregate 2006–07	*Average 2006–07*	*Highest Attendance 2006–07*
Oxford United	145,634	6,332	11,065 v Woking
Exeter City	83,427	3,627	6,670 v Southport
York City	65,764	2,859	5,378 v Oxford United
Cambridge United	64,747	2,815	6,021 v Tamworth
Aldershot Town	54,284	2,360	3,621 v Oxford United
Stevenage Borough	48,898	2,126	3,058 v Exeter City
Rushden & Diamonds	47,028	2,045	3,270 v Oxford United
Weymouth	45,269	1,968	5,244 v Oxford United
Burton Albion	43,045	1,872	2,910 v Rushden & Diamonds
Woking	40,808	1,774	3,725 v Aldershot Town
Dagenham & Redbridge	40,390	1,756	4,044 v Aldershot Town
Halifax Town	38,138	1,658	2,515 v Stevenage Borough
Kidderminster Harriers	37,345	1,624	2,264 v Oxford United
Morecambe	36,763	1,598	2,412 v Halifax Town
Tamworth	29,282	1,273	2,411 v Altrincham
Southport	27,593	1,200	3,206 v York City
Forest Green Rovers	27,258	1,185	3,021 v Oxford United
Stafford Rangers	27,164	1,181	1,795 v Oxford United
Altrincham	26,818	1,166	2,330 v Northwich Victoria
Gravesend & Northfleet	26,804	1,165	2,019 v Oxford United
Crawley Town	26,638	1,158	2,101 v Oxford United
St Albans City	26,300	1,143	2,878 v Stevenage Borough
Grays Athletic	24,772	1,077	1,759 v Oxford United
Northwich Victoria	22,352	972	1,552 v Oxford United

NATIONWIDE CONFERENCE PLAY-OFFS 2006–07

CONFERENCE SEMI-FINAL FIRST LEG

Friday, 4 May 2007

Exeter C (0) 0
Oxford U (1) 1 *(Taylor 40 (og))* 8659

Exeter C: Rice; Tully, Jones B, Gill, Edwards (Richardson), Todd, Carlisle (Challinor), Taylor, Stansfield, Logan, Elam (Mackie).
Oxford U: Turley; Anaclet (Brevett), Gilchrist, Foster M, Day, Quinn, Rose, Hargreaves, Zebroski, Odubade (Duffy), Burgess.

York C (0) 0
Morecambe (0) 0 6660

York C: Evans; Lloyd, James, Bishop, McGurk, Parslow, Woolford, Panther, Donaldson, Farrell (Brodie), Bowey.
Morecambe: Drench; Yates, Adams, Brannan (Hunter), Bentley, Blackburn, Thompson (Lloyd), Sorvel, Twiss, Carlton (Curtis), Stanley.

CONFERENCE SEMI-FINAL SECOND LEG

Monday, 7 May 2007

Morecambe (1) 2 *(Curtis 40, 48)*
York C (1) 1 *(Bowey 20 (pen))* 5567

Morecambe: Drench (Davies); Yates, Adams, Stanley, Bentley, Blackburn, Lloyd (Hunter), Sorvel, Twiss, Carlton, Curtis (McNiven).
York C: Evans; Lloyd, James (Peat), Bishop, McGurk, Parslow, Woolford, Panther, Donaldson (Brodie), Farrell, Bowey (Convery).

Tuesday, 8 May 2007

Oxford U (1) 1 *(Odubade 27)*
Exeter C (1) 2 *(Phillips 39, Stansfield 70)* 10,691

Oxford U: Turley; Anaclet (Duffy), Gilchrist, Foster M (Pettefer), Day, Quinn, Rose (Johnson), Hargreaves, Zebroski, Odubade, Burgess.
Exeter C: Rice; Tully, Jones B, Gill, Edwards, Todd, Carlisle (Stansfield), Taylor, Phillips (Mackie), Challinor, Elam (Logan).
aet; Exeter C won 4-3 on penalties.

CONFERENCE FINAL (AT WEMBLEY)

Sunday, 20 May 2007

Exeter C (1) 1 *(Phillips 8)*
Morecambe (1) 2 *(Thompson 42, Carlton 82)* 40,043

Exeter C: Jones P; Tully, Jones B, Gill■, Edwards, Todd, Carlisle (Logan), Taylor, Phillips (Stansfield), Challinor, Elam (Mackie).
Morecambe: Davies; Yates, Adams, Stanley, Bentley, Blackburn, Thompson (Brannan), Sorvel, Twiss (Hunter), Carlton (McNiven), Curtis.
Referee: M. Oliver (Ashington).

CONFERENCE SECOND DIVISION PLAY-OFFS

NORTH PLAY-OFF SEMI-FINAL FIRST LEG

Hinckley United 0, Workington 0
Farsley Celtic 1 *(Reeves 17)*, Kettering Town 1 *(Solkhon 75)*

SEMI-FINAL SECOND LEG

Kettering Town 0, Farsley Celtic 0
aet; Farsley Celtic won 4-2 on penalties.
Workington 1 *(Hewson 87)*, Hinckley United 2 *(Jackson 43, Marrison 47)*

FINAL

Farsley Celtic 4 *(Grant 15, Reeves 79, 89 (pen), Crossley 87)*, Hinckley United 3 *(Shilton 19, Cartwright 21, 83)*

SOUTH PLAY-OFF SEMI-FINAL FIRST LEG

Havant & Waterlooville 1 *(Louis 88)*, Braintree Town 1 *(Baker 45)*
Bishop's Stortford 1 *(Pearson 54)*, Salisbury City 1 *(Matthews 64)*

SEMI-FINAL SECOND LEG

Braintree Town 1 *(Hawes 75)*, Havant & Waterlooville 1 *(Collins 89 (pen))*
aet; Braintree Town won 4-2 on penalties.
Salisbury City 3 *(Tubbs 18, Matthews 100, Fowler 118)*, Bishop's Stortford 1 *(Porter 34)*

FINAL

Braintree Town 0, Salisbury City 1 *(Tubbs 84)*

NATIONWIDE CONFERENCE SECOND DIVISION 2006–07

NATIONWIDE CONFERENCE NORTH FINAL LEAGUE TABLE

			Home					*Away*					*Total*						
		P	*W*	*D*	*L*	*F*	*A*	*W*	*D*	*L*	*F*	*A*	*W*	*D*	*L*	*F*	*A*	*GD*	*Pts*
1	Droylsden	42	16	4	1	54	25	7	5	9	31	30	23	9	10	85	55	30	78
2	Kettering Town	42	11	6	4	41	27	9	7	5	34	31	20	13	9	75	58	17	73
3	Workington	42	12	5	4	33	17	8	5	8	28	29	20	10	12	61	46	15	70
4	Hinckley United	42	10	8	3	40	24	9	4	8	28	30	19	12	11	68	54	14	69
5	Farsley Celtic	42	10	5	6	27	21	9	6	6	31	30	19	11	12	58	51	7	68
6	Harrogate Town	42	8	8	5	27	18	10	5	6	31	23	18	13	11	58	41	17	67
7	Blyth Spartans	42	10	5	6	30	21	9	4	8	26	29	19	9	14	56	50	6	66
8	Hyde United	42	12	5	4	47	24	6	6	9	32	38	18	11	13	79	62	17	65
9	Worcester City	42	9	8	4	41	28	7	6	8	26	26	16	14	12	67	54	13	62
10	Nuneaton Borough	42	8	9	4	19	13	7	6	8	35	32	15	15	12	54	45	9	60
11	Moor Green	42	8	6	7	30	23	8	5	8	23	28	16	11	15	53	51	2	59
12	Gainsborough Trinity	42	9	5	7	30	26	6	6	9	21	31	15	11	16	51	57	–6	56
13	Hucknall Town	42	8	4	9	40	37	7	5	9	29	32	15	9	18	69	69	0	54
14	Alfreton Town	42	8	6	7	24	21	6	6	9	20	29	14	12	16	44	50	–6	54
15	Vauxhall Motors	42	6	6	9	29	31	6	9	6	33	33	12	15	15	62	64	–2	51
16	Barrow	42	7	6	8	23	23	5	8	8	24	25	12	14	16	47	48	–1	50
17	Leigh RMI	42	9	4	8	31	32	4	6	11	16	29	13	10	19	47	61	–14	49
18	Stalybridge Celtic	42	7	6	8	38	45	6	4	11	26	36	13	10	19	64	81	–17	49
19	Redditch United	42	6	7	8	32	35	5	8	8	30	32	11	15	16	62	67	–5	48
20	Scarborough*	42	6	6	9	21	21	7	10	4	29	24	13	16	13	50	45	5	45
21	Worksop Town	42	6	6	9	24	29	6	3	12	20	33	12	9	21	44	62	–18	45
22	Lancaster City*	42	0	2	19	10	49	2	3	16	17	61	2	5	35	27	110	–83	1

**Deducted 10 points for entering administration.*

NATIONWIDE CONFERENCE SOUTH FINAL LEAGUE TABLE

			Home					*Away*					*Total*						
		P	*W*	*D*	*L*	*F*	*A*	*W*	*D*	*L*	*F*	*A*	*W*	*D*	*L*	*F*	*A*	*GD*	*Pts*
1	Histon	42	18	0	3	47	20	12	4	5	38	24	30	4	8	85	44	41	94
2	Salisbury City	42	10	7	4	26	14	11	5	5	39	23	21	12	9	65	37	28	75
3	Braintree Town	42	9	7	5	27	19	12	4	5	24	19	21	11	10	51	38	13	74
4	Havant & Waterlooville	42	15	4	2	52	20	5	9	7	23	26	20	13	9	75	46	29	73
5	Bishop's Stortford	42	11	7	3	37	26	10	3	8	35	35	21	10	11	72	61	11	73
6	Newport County	42	15	1	5	52	24	6	6	9	31	33	21	7	14	83	57	26	70
7	Eastbourne Borough	42	11	8	2	29	15	7	7	7	29	27	18	15	9	58	42	16	69
8	Welling United	42	11	3	7	37	23	10	3	8	28	28	21	6	15	65	51	14	69
9	Lewes	42	11	7	3	41	25	4	10	7	26	27	15	17	10	67	52	15	62
10	Fisher Athletic	42	11	5	5	49	33	4	6	11	29	47	15	11	16	78	80	–2	56
11	Farnborough Town*	42	14	4	3	36	20	5	4	12	23	32	19	8	15	59	52	7	55
12	Bognor Regis Town	42	6	10	5	29	23	7	3	11	27	39	13	13	16	56	62	–6	52
13	Cambridge City	42	8	4	9	25	21	7	3	11	19	31	15	7	20	44	52	–8	52
14	Sutton United	42	8	8	5	30	26	6	1	14	28	37	14	9	19	58	63	–5	51
15	Eastleigh	42	8	6	7	26	26	3	9	9	22	27	11	15	16	48	53	–5	48
16	Yeading	42	6	9	6	27	28	6	0	15	29	50	12	9	21	56	78	–22	45
17	Dorchester Town	42	6	2	13	26	44	5	10	6	23	33	11	12	19	49	77	–28	45
18	Thurrock	42	6	6	9	34	41	5	5	11	27	39	11	11	20	61	80	–19	44
19	Basingstoke Town	42	4	6	11	18	26	5	10	6	28	32	9	16	17	46	58	–12	43
20	Hayes	42	5	4	12	25	37	6	6	9	22	36	11	10	21	47	73	–26	43
21	Weston-Super-Mare	42	4	4	13	25	45	4	7	10	24	32	8	11	23	49	77	–28	35
22	Bedford Town	42	5	5	11	25	36	3	2	16	18	46	8	7	27	43	82	–39	31

**Deducted 10 points for entering administration.*

NATIONWIDE CONFERENCE SECOND DIVISION NORTH RESULTS 2006–07

	Alfreton Town	Barrow	Blyth Spartans	Droylsden	Farsley Celtic	Gainsborough Trinity	Harrogate Town	Hinckley United	Hucknall Town	Hyde United	Kettering Town	Lancaster City	Leigh RMI	Moor Green	Nuneaton Borough	Redditch United	Scarborough	Stalybridge Celtic	Vauxhall Motors	Worcester City	Workington	Worksop Town
Alfreton Town	—	1-0	0-1	1-3	0-1	3-1	0-0	0-1	2-1	2-2	1-1	2-1	1-0	3-0	0-3	0-0	1-1	1-2	2-0	0-2	1-1	3-0
Barrow	1-1	—	0-2	2-1	2-2	3-0	2-3	1-0	1-0	1-2	0-1	3-0	2-0	1-1	0-1	0-4	1-1	2-1	0-0	0-1	0-0	1-2
Blyth Spartans	3-0	1-0	—	0-3	4-1	2-0	0-0	3-1	2-2	0-0	2-2	3-0	1-0	0-1	1-2	1-2	2-0	1-0	1-2	2-2	0-2	2-0
Droylsden	1-1	2-1	0-0	—	4-1	2-1	2-0	3-1	5-3	4-2	1-1	6-1	2-2	1-0	4-2	2-1	1-3	6-1	1-0	2-1	2-1	3-2
Farsley Celtic	1-1	2-2	3-0	0-3	—	1-0	1-0	0-2	1-0	1-1	2-1	3-1	1-1	0-1	0-1	4-0	0-2	1-1	3-2	1-0	1-2	1-0
Gainsborough Trinity	4-0	1-0	0-2	3-2	0-0	—	1-3	1-0	2-3	2-3	2-3	1-0	0-0	1-0	1-1	2-2	3-1	2-0	1-2	1-3	1-0	1-1
Harrogate Town	0-1	1-1	1-2	1-1	1-0	1-1	—	2-0	1-1	1-2	2-3	3-0	2-1	1-1	1-1	2-2	0-1	0-0	1-0	1-0	4-0	1-0
Hinckley United	2-2	1-1	2-1	2-1	2-1	1-1	0-1	—	1-1	2-0	3-1	5-0	3-1	2-0	2-2	3-1	1-1	2-3	1-1	3-3	2-1	0-1
Hucknall Town	0-2	1-3	1-2	2-2	0-1	3-3	0-3	1-2	—	4-2	1-2	5-0	1-3	3-2	2-1	2-2	0-1	2-1	2-2	4-2	2-1	4-0
Hyde United	2-1	1-1	5-1	2-1	3-4	3-0	4-0	2-0	1-0	—	3-5	5-0	2-0	4-1	3-2	0-2	1-1	3-1	1-1	0-0	1-1	1-2
Kettering Town	0-1	3-2	1-1	1-0	3-2	4-2	3-1	1-2	0-0	1-0	—	3-3	4-0	1-1	3-2	3-1	3-1	2-1	0-1	1-1	2-3	2-2
Lancaster City	0-2	0-2	0-2	1-2	1-2	0-1	0-2	1-4	0-1	2-3	0-1	—	0-0	0-3	0-4	1-2	1-5	0-1	2-2	0-2	1-5	0-3
Leigh RMI	2-0	0-3	3-1	2-2	1-3	2-0	1-3	2-3	4-3	2-0	1-2	0-1	—	2-2	1-0	0-0	1-1	1-3	0-3	2-1	2-0	2-1
Moor Green	2-0	0-0	0-2	5-2	1-1	2-1	0-1	0-1	1-2	1-1	1-2	3-1	0-0	—	1-1	1-1	1-2	2-1	5-2	3-1	1-0	0-1
Nuneaton Borough	1-0	3-0	1-1	1-0	1-1	0-1	0-0	0-1	2-1	0-0	2-1	1-0	0-1	0-1	—	1-0	1-1	3-2	1-1	1-1	0-0	0-0
Redditch United	3-2	1-1	0-2	0-0	1-4	1-1	2-1	1-3	1-2	2-1	4-4	2-2	2-1	0-1	2-0	—	1-1	1-2	3-3	1-2	4-1	0-1
Scarborough	0-1	1-1	0-1	1-0	0-0	0-0	1-1	3-0	1-2	1-2	1-1	1-2	1-1	3-0	1-3	3-2	—	0-1	0-1	1-0	0-1	2-1
Stalybridge Celtic	3-2	0-4	3-2	1-2	0-2	0-2	0-2	2-2	2-2	3-7	0-0	3-1	2-1	2-3	4-3	3-2	2-2	—	3-3	1-1	1-2	3-0
Vauxhall Motors	1-2	0-1	2-0	2-3	1-2	0-1	1-5	2-2	1-2	1-0	1-1	4-1	2-1	1-1	1-3	1-1	1-1	2-2	—	2-0	1-2	2-0
Worcester City	0-0	3-0	3-2	3-1	0-1	1-1	2-3	3-1	2-0	2-2	2-0	4-1	1-2	0-1	3-3	1-1	3-2	1-1	3-3	—	2-2	2-1
Workington	1-1	1-1	3-0	0-0	3-0	1-2	3-2	1-1	1-0	3-1	2-0	1-1	0-1	3-2	2-0	1-0	0-1	2-1	2-0	0-1	—	3-2
Worksop Town	2-0	2-0	1-1	0-2	2-2	1-2	0-0	1-1	1-3	3-1	0-2	3-1	2-0	0-1	0-0	2-3	0-0	2-1	1-4	0-2	1-3	—

NATIONWIDE CONFERENCE SECOND DIVISION SOUTH RESULTS 2006–07

	Basingstoke Town	Bedford Town	Bishop's Stortford	Bognor Regis Town	Braintree Town	Cambridge City	Dorchester Town	Eastbourne Borough	Eastleigh	Farnborough Town	Fisher Athletic	Havant & Waterlooville	Hayes	Histon	Lewes	Newport County	Salisbury City	Sutton United	Thurrock	Welling United	Weston-Super-Mare	Yeading
Basingstoke Town	—	0-1	1-0	4-0	1-2	0-0	2-2	0-1	0-1	0-2	2-1	2-1	1-1	1-2	0-0	0-1	1-1	0-2	1-1	1-3	0-1	1-3
Bedford Town	0-0	—	3-1	2-3	1-2	0-1	1-1	1-1	1-1	0-2	1-4	2-1	1-2	0-2	0-2	0-2	1-2	2-0	3-1	2-2	2-1	2-5
Bishop's Stortford	3-1	2-2	—	0-1	0-2	2-1	4-3	1-0	1-1	2-1	2-2	1-0	3-1	0-0	3-0	2-2	1-1	3-2	2-1	1-3	2-2	2-0
Bognor Regis Town	1-2	1-0	2-4	—	1-2	0-1	3-0	1-1	0-0	1-1	1-1	0-0	5-1	0-0	1-1	1-1	1-1	0-4	3-0	1-1	3-1	3-1
Braintree Town	1-0	2-0	3-1	1-2	—	2-1	3-1	1-1	1-1	2-1	2-2	0-0	0-1	1-1	1-1	2-1	0-0	0-1	0-1	2-1	0-1	3-1
Cambridge City	0-1	0-0	0-1	2-0	1-0	—	0-1	1-0	2-0	1-1	0-0	3-0	2-2	0-1	1-0	2-1	1-3	2-3	2-3	0-1	2-3	3-0
Dorchester Town	1-2	1-3	0-1	0-1	0-0	3-1	—	0-0	1-0	4-1	1-3	1-3	0-2	1-2	1-5	0-4	0-3	5-4	3-1	0-1	1-5	3-2
Eastbourne Borough	1-1	0-3	2-1	2-0	1-2	2-1	1-1	—	0-0	0-0	3-1	1-1	0-0	1-1	2-1	2-1	1-0	2-0	3-1	0-0	3-0	2-0
Eastleigh	3-1	2-0	1-1	0-4	0-3	0-1	1-1	1-1	—	3-1	4-0	0-1	2-1	1-0	0-0	3-1	0-1	1-0	1-1	1-3	1-1	1-4
Farnborough Town	1-1	3-2	3-1	3-1	2-1	2-1	1-1	1-0	1-0	—	2-0	2-1	1-3	2-3	1-1	1-0	0-1	4-0	2-1	2-1	0-0	2-1
Fisher Athletic	3-3	3-0	0-1	3-0	3-0	3-0	1-1	0-3	3-1	3-0	—	3-3	3-0	1-4	5-1	3-3	1-4	2-1	3-5	2-1	1-1	3-1
Havant & Waterlooville	1-0	4-0	5-4	2-2	1-1	2-3	2-0	2-1	1-1	2-0	1-3	—	6-0	2-1	1-1	3-1	3-1	1-0	3-0	4-0	2-1	4-0
Hayes	1-1	3-1	1-2	2-3	2-3	0-1	4-0	1-1	2-1	1-1	4-3	0-1	—	1-3	1-4	0-1	0-4	0-4	1-1	0-1	1-0	0-1
Histon	4-2	1-0	0-2	2-1	2-0	2-1	3-0	1-2	1-0	2-1	2-1	4-0	5-0	—	3-2	1-0	4-2	2-1	3-1	1-0	3-2	1-2
Lewes	2-2	5-1	2-3	1-1	0-1	1-1	2-2	1-1	0-3	1-0	2-0	1-1	2-0	3-1	—	2-0	1-0	3-1	1-1	4-2	4-2	3-2
Newport County	3-0	2-0	4-1	3-1	0-1	1-2	0-1	4-0	3-1	3-4	4-2	1-0	2-0	5-1	1-1	—	4-3	3-1	1-3	3-1	1-0	4-1
Salisbury City	0-0	3-1	3-1	2-1	0-1	2-0	1-1	1-2	1-0	0-1	3-0	1-1	0-0	0-3	1-1	2-1	—	1-0	0-0	1-0	0-0	4-0
Sutton United	3-3	3-1	1-1	3-2	0-0	2-2	0-0	3-1	2-2	1-0	2-2	0-1	1-0	1-0	0-2	1-1	0-1	—	2-1	1-2	3-1	1-3
Thurrock	2-2	2-1	0-3	1-1	0-1	1-0	2-3	2-4	1-1	1-4	5-1	1-1	0-1	0-4	3-2	2-2	1-5	3-0	—	1-2	2-2	1-0
Welling United	0-2	5-0	2-3	3-0	4-1	1-0	1-2	1-0	2-1	1-0	2-0	1-1	1-1	2-4	0-0	2-3	1-2	1-0	1-2	—	1-0	5-1
Weston-Super-Mare	1-3	2-1	1-2	1-3	0-0	0-1	1-2	2-4	3-3	2-1	0-1	1-5	0-5	1-2	1-1	3-4	1-1	0-2	2-1	1-2	—	2-1
Yeading	1-1	2-1	1-1	2-0	0-1	5-0	0-0	2-5	1-4	2-1	1-1	1-1	1-1	1-3	1-0	1-1	1-3	2-2	2-1	0-1	0-0	—

ALDERSHOT TOWN — Blue Square Premier

Ground: Recreation Ground, High Street, Aldershot, Hampshire GU11 1TW. *Tel:* (01252) 320 211.
Year Formed: 1992 (formerly 1926). *Record Gate:* 7,500 (2000 v Brighton & Hove Albion, FA Cup First Round) (in Football League 19,138). *Nickname:* Shots. *Manager:* Gary Waddock. *Secretary:* Graham Hortop.
Colours: Red shirts with blue trim, red shorts, red stockings with blue trim.

ALDERSHOT TOWN 2006–07 LEAGUE RECORD

Match No.	Date	Venue	Opponents	Result		H/T Score	Lg. Pos.	Goalscorers	Attendance
1	Aug 12	H	Gravesend & N	W	3-2	0-1	—	John Grant 2 [53, 63], Scott [90]	2487
2	15	A	Weymouth	L	0-1	0-0	—		3583
3	19	A	St Albans C	W	5-3	1-0	8	Barnard (pen) [45], Williams [58], John Grant 2 [60, 73], Gayle [75]	1373
4	26	H	Dagenham & R	D	1-1	0-0	7	Soares [87]	2657
5	28	A	Stafford R	W	3-0	1-0	6	Gayle [31], John Grant [68], Williams [88]	1720
6	Sept 2	H	Halifax T	W	1-0	0-0	5	Barnard [89]	2330
7	9	A	Exeter C	D	0-0	0-0	4		3933
8	12	H	Stevenage Bor	W	4-0	2-0	—	Joel Grant 2 [44, 80], John Grant [45], Soares [76]	2371
9	16	H	Northwich Vic	L	1-3	0-1	5	Williams [55]	2588
10	19	A	Grays Ath	W	2-1	0-0	—	Winfield [61], Williams [84]	1279
11	22	A	Cambridge U	L	0-2	0-2	—		2535
12	30	H	Altrincham	D	0-0	0-0	4		2433
13	Oct 3	H	Tamworth	D	3-3	1-2	—	Joel Grant [19], Gayle 2 [50, 52]	2084
14	6	A	York C	L	0-1	0-1	—		2679
15	9	A	Woking	L	0-2	0-1	—		3725
16	14	H	Kidderminster H	W	4-2	1-2	7	John Grant [8], Gayle 3 [67, 71, 77]	2182
17	21	H	Morecambe	L	0-1	0-1	10		2394
18	Nov 3	A	Oxford U	L	0-2	0-0	11		8185
19	18	H	Southport	D	2-2	1-0	10	John Grant 2 [6, 90]	2290
20	25	A	Rushden & D	W	1-0	0-0	9	John Grant [88]	2128
21	Dec 9	A	Burton Alb	W	3-1	2-1	9	Day [37], Corbett (og) [41], John Grant [47]	1876
22	26	H	Forest Green R	W	2-1	1-0	8	Soares [45], Barnard [89]	2216
23	Jan 1	A	Stevenage Bor	L	2-3	1-1	—	Beckford [36], Hudson [90]	2683
24	13	H	Crawley T	L	0-2	0-1	—		2349
25	20	A	Northwich Vic	W	3-1	1-0	11	Williams [36], Dixon [53], Molesley [87]	890
26	23	A	Forest Green R	L	0-3	0-0	—		951
27	27	H	Burton Alb	W	3-2	2-2	11	Williams 2 (1 pen) [26 (p), 78], John Grant [37]	1970
28	Feb 6	H	Grays Ath	W	1-0	0-0	—	Dixon [87]	1924
29	10	H	Oxford U	D	1-1	0-1	9	Hudson [85]	3621
30	17	A	Southport	L	0-1	0-1	9		1160
31	24	H	Rushden & D	D	2-2	2-0	9	John Grant [8], Dixon [16]	2189
32	Mar 3	A	Crawley T	W	2-1	0-0	9	Pritchard [47], Dixon [51]	1737
33	6	A	Tamworth	L	0-2	0-1	—		1086
34	10	H	York C	L	0-2	0-1	9		2435
35	13	H	Woking	D	2-2	1-1	—	Hudson [40], John Grant [73]	2739
36	20	A	Morecambe	L	1-2	0-2	—	Hudson [83]	1165
37	23	A	Gravesend & N	D	1-1	1-0	—	John Grant [6]	1103
38	27	H	Weymouth	W	1-0	0-0	—	Day [55]	2224
39	31	H	St Albans C	W	2-0	1-0	10	Barnard (pen) [26], John Grant [72]	1749
40	Apr 3	H	Exeter C	W	3-2	1-1	—	Day [22], Dixon 2 [46, 63]	2250
41	7	A	Dagenham & R	L	1-2	0-1	9	Dixon [66]	4044
42	9	H	Stafford R	W	4-2	2-2	—	Williams 2 [6, 61], John Grant [35], Dixon [70]	1734
43	14	A	Halifax T	L	0-2	0-1	9		1611
44	17	A	Kidderminster H	D	0-0	0-0	—		1215
45	21	H	Cambridge U	L	0-1	0-0	9		3068
46	28	A	Altrincham	D	0-0	0-0	9		2005

Final League Position: 9

GOALSCORERS

League (64): John Grant 17, Williams 9 (1 pen), Dixon 8, Gayle 7, Barnard 4 (2 pens), Hudson 4, Day 3, Joel Grant 3, Soares 3, Beckford 1, Molesley 1, Pritchard 1, Scott 1, Winfield 1, own goal 1.
FA Cup (13): John Grant 5, Barnard 3 (1 pen), Soares 3, Pritchard 1, own goal 1.
Trophy (1): John Grant 1.

Bull 46	Smith 36 + 5	Barnard 40 + 1	Newman 37	Day 36 + 1	Gayle 18 + 6	Soares 32 + 8	Molesley 33	Grant John 39 + 2	Pritchard 2 + 21	Williams 45 + 1	Hudson 9 + 17	Scott 18 + 14	Anderson 6 + 6	Okuonghae 2	Edwards 15 + 2	Winfield 14 + 8	Grant Joel 8 + 6	Harding 8 + 8	Lee 9 + 3	Osano 9 + 1	Hylton — + 1	Beckford 10 + 9	Dixon 21 + 1	Charles 13	Wells — + 1	*Match No.*
1	2	3	4	5	6	7	8^{3}	9	10^{2}	11^{1}	12	13	14													1
1	2	3	4^{1}	5	10^{3}	7	8	9	14	11^{2}	12	13		6												2
1	2	3^{1}	4	5	10^{3}	7	8^{2}	9	14	11		13	12	6												3
1	2	3	4	5	10^{2}	7		9	13	11^{1}	12	8			6											4
1	2^{1}	3	4	5	10	7		9^{2}	13	11		8			6	12										5
1		3	4	5	10^{3}	7		9		11^{2}		13	2^{1}		6	12	14	8								6
1	2		4^{1}	5	10^{2}	7		9		11		8	3		6		13	12								7
1	2	3^{2}		5^{1}	12	7		9^{3}	14	11		8	13			6	10	4								8
1	2^{1}	13			12	7^{2}		9^{3}	14	11		8	3		6	5	10	4								9
1	2		4			7		9		11^{1}		8	3		6	5	10	12								10
1	2		4^{2}		14	7^{1}		9^{3}	13	11		8	3		6	5	10	12								11
1	2	3	4^{1}		10^{3}	7		14		11		12			6	5	9	8^{2}	13							12
1	2	3	4^{1}		10	7		14		11		13			6	5	9^{3}	12	8^{2}							13
1	12	3■			10	13		9		14		8			6	5	11^{3}	4^{2}	7^{1}	2						14
1	2		4		10	7^{1}		9^{3}		11^{2}					6	5	13	12	8	3	14					15
1	14	3	4		13	7^{1}		9		11^{2}					6	5	12	10^{3}	8	2						16
1	13	3			10	12	8^{2}	9		11^{3}					6	5	14	7	4	2^{1}						17
1	2	3		12	10	13	8			11					6	5^{1}	9		4^{2}	7						18
1	6	3	4	5	10	12	8^{1}	9		11^{3}	14							13	7^{2}	2						19
1	2	3^{1}	4	5		7^{2}	8	9		11		14					13	6	10^{3}	12						20
1	12	3	4■	5		7	8	9^{2}		11^{1}	10	6						13		2						21
1		3	4^{1}	5		7	8^{2}	9	14	11	10^{3}	6			12			13		2						22
1	2	3	4	5	12	7	8^{3}	9		11^{2}	13				6^{1}				14			10				23
1			4	5	10		8	9		11	13	6	3		12^{2}					2^{1}		7^{3}	14			24
1		3	2	5	6	7^{1}	8	9	13	11	12	4											10^{2}			25
1	2	3	4	5		7^{1}	8^{2}	9	14	11		6							12			13	10^{3}			26
1	14	3	2	5	6	7^{1}	8	9■		11^{3}		12							4^{2}			13	10			27
1	2	3	4	5		7	8		12	11^{2}	13	6										9^{1}	10			28
1	2	3^{1}	4	5		7	8		14	11^{2}	13	6	12									9^{3}	10			29
1	2	3	4^{1}	5		7	8		14	11	9^{3}	6^{2}				12						13	10			30
1	2	3	4	5			8	9		11	12											7^{1}	10	6		31
1	2	3	4	5^{1}			8		9^{3}	11	14	13				12						7^{2}	10	6		32
1	2	3^{1}	4^{3}	5			8	9	12	11	14	13										7^{2}	10	6		33
1	2	3	4	5			8	9^{2}	13	11	7^{1}											12	10	6		34
1	2	3	4^{1}	5			8	9	13	11	7											12	10^{2}	6		35
1	2	3^{1}		5		13	8	9	14	11^{2}	7					12						4	10^{3}	6		36
1	2	3		5^{1}		13	8	9		11^{3}	7^{2}	14				12						4	10	6		37
1	2	3		5		14	8	9	12	11^{2}	7^{1}	13										4	10^{3}	6		38
1	2	3	4^{1}	5		7^{2}	8	9	14	11		12										13	10^{3}	6		39
1^{6}	2	3	4	5		7^{1}	8	9		11		12■											10	6	15	40
1	2	3	4	5		7^{1}	8^{2}	9		11	12					14						13	10^{3}	6		41
1		3	4	5		2	8	9	12	11	7												10^{1}	6		42
1	2	3	4^{3}	5		7^{2}	8	9		11	13					12						14	10	6^{1}		43
1	2	3^{1}	4	5		7	8^{3}	9	13	11	12^{2}					6						14	10			44
1	2	3^{1}		5	13	7^{2}	8	9		11	14	4	12			6							10^{3}			45
1	2	3	4^{1}	5	10	12	8	9		11^{3}	14	7^{2}	13			6										46

FA Cup

Fourth Qualifying Round			
	Haverhill R	(a)	4-0
First Round	Chelmsford C	(a)	1-1
		(h)	2-0
Second Round	Basingstoke T	(h)	1-1
		(a)	3-1
Third Round	Blackpool	(a)	2-4

Trophy

First Round	AFC Wimbledon	(h)	1-2

ALTRINCHAM

Blue Square Premier

Ground: Moss Lane, Altrincham WA15 8AP. *Tel:* (0161) 928 1045. *Year Formed:* 1903. *Record Gate:* 10,275 (1991 Altrincham Boys v Sunderland Boys, ESFA Shield). *Nickname:* The Robins. *Manager:* Graham Heathcote. *Secretary:* Graham Heathcote. *Colours:* Red and white striped shirts, black shorts, red stockings.

ALTRINCHAM 2006–07 LEAGUE RECORD

Match No.	Date	Venue	Opponents	Result		H/T Score	Lg. Pos.	Goalscorers	Attendance
1	Aug 12	H	Stevenage Bor	W	2-1	2-0	—	Little [14], Aspinall (pen) [40]	1035
2	15	A	Stafford R	L	0-1	0-0	—		1410
3	19	A	Exeter C	L	1-2	1-1	14	Lawton [3]	3345
4	26	H	St Albans C	W	2-0	1-0	10	Peyton [45], Talbot [65]	890
5	28	A	Gravesend & N	L	1-3	0-0	12	Aspinall (pen) [79]	900
6	Sept 3	H	Dagenham & R	L	0-5	0-2	16		951
7	9	A	Rushden & D	L	0-3	0-2	18		1680
8	12	H	Halifax T	W	1-0	1-0	—	Little [7]	1036
9	16	H	Woking	L	2-3	2-1	18	Bushell [5], Lawton [18]	886
10	19	A	Forest Green R	D	2-2	0-2	—	Thornley [52], Lugsden [59]	910
11	23	H	Tamworth	W	2-0	2-0	13	Thornley [5], O'Neill [33]	882
12	30	A	Aldershot T	D	0-0	0-0	14		2433
13	Oct 3	A	Cambridge U	D	2-2	1-1	—	Aspinall (pen) [35], Lawton [65]	2680
14	7	H	Weymouth	D	0-0	0-0	14		1214
15	10	H	Morecambe	L	0-2	0-1	—		1085
16	14	A	Oxford U	D	1-1	0-0	16	Aspinall (pen) [86]	5938
17	21	H	Southport	W	2-1	2-0	14	Jackson (og) [19], Munroe [44]	1336
18	Nov 5	A	York C	L	0-1	0-0	15		2726
19	18	H	Crawley T	D	1-1	0-0	18	Chalmers [50]	1033
20	25	A	Grays Ath	D	1-1	1-0	18	Owen [23]	725
21	Dec 2	H	Burton Alb	L	2-3	1-2	20	Owen [21], Little [90]	1212
22	9	A	Kidderminster H	L	2-3	1-2	21	Little [24], O'Neill [60]	1455
23	26	H	Northwich Vic	W	3-0	1-0	17	Thornley [25], Aspinall (pen) [80], Lawton [81]	2330
24	30	H	Forest Green R	D	2-2	0-0	16	Chalmers [68], Owen [88]	912
25	Jan 1	A	Halifax T	D	1-1	1-1	—	Thompson [10]	1791
26	6	H	Rushden & D	W	2-1	1-0	14	O'Neill 2 [28, 89]	1111
27	20	A	Woking	L	0-2	0-0	17		1612
28	27	H	Kidderminster H	L	0-1	0-1	21		1116
29	Feb 3	A	Southport	L	1-2	0-1	21	Chalmers [86]	1145
30	10	H	York C	L	0-4	0-2	22		1327
31	17	A	Crawley T	D	1-1	1-1	23	Okuonghae (og) [45]	1180
32	20	A	Northwich Vic	D	1-1	0-0	—	Senior [90]	1290
33	Mar 2	A	Burton Alb	L	1-2	0-1	—	Chalmers [64]	1441
34	6	H	Cambridge U	W	5-0	1-0	—	Peyton [22], Chalmers [46], Little [57], O'Neill [68], Senior [77]	891
35	10	A	Weymouth	W	2-1	1-0	19	Little 2 [45, 73]	1503
36	13	A	Morecambe	W	1-0	1-0	—	Little [21]	1403
37	17	H	Oxford U	L	0-3	0-2	18		1497
38	20	H	Grays Ath	W	1-0	1-0	—	O'Neill [29]	829
39	24	A	Stevenage Bor	W	1-0	1-0	13	Senior [24]	1913
40	27	H	Stafford R	L	0-1	0-1	—		1150
41	31	H	Exeter C	L	1-2	1-0	17	Chalmers [19]	1100
42	Apr 7	A	St Albans C	W	5-1	4-1	16	Lawton [3], Little 3 [12, 21, 45], Thornley [90]	680
43	9	H	Gravesend & N	L	0-2	0-1	—		990
44	14	A	Dagenham & R	L	1-4	1-1	17	Little [21]	1473
45	21	A	Tamworth	L	0-1	0-1	19		2411
46	28	H	Aldershot T	D	0-0	0-0	21		2005

Final League Position: 21

GOALSCORERS

League (53): Little 12, Chalmers 6, O'Neill 6, Aspinall 5 (5 pens), Lawton 5, Thornley 4, Owen 3, Senior 3, Peyton 2, Bushell 1, Lugsden 1, Munroe 1, Talbot 1, Thompson 1, own goals 2.
FA Cup (0).
Trophy (1): Little 1.

Coburn 36	Aspinall 29 + 6	Scott G 20 + 6	Band 34 + 3	Talbot 10 + 11	Bushell 34 + 1	Lawton 46	Owen 28 + 1	Little 34	O'Neill 41 + 3	Peyton 45 + 1	Hendley — + 8	Chalmers 40 + 5	Thornley 12 + 20	Bowler — + 7	Munroe 37 + 2	Rose 25 + 3	Potts 8 + 3	Acton 10 + 1	Hussin — + 3	Lugsden 1 + 4	McFadden 1 + 19	Thompson 2 + 6	Senior 8 + 7	Scott A 5 + 1	*Match No.*
1	2	3	4	5	6	7^{1}	8	9	10^{2}	11	12	13													1
1	2	3	4	5	6	7^{1}	8	9	10^{2}	11	13	12													2
1	2	3	4	5^{1}	6	7	8	9^{3}	10^{2}	11		12	13	14											3
1	2	3	4^{1}	5	6	7	8	9	10^{2}	11			13		12										4
1	2	3		5	6	7	8^{2}	9	10	11^{3}		13		14	4^{1}	12									5
1	2^{1}	3	4^{2}	5	6	7	8	9	10^{3}	11	14	13		12											6
1	12	3^{1}		5	6^{2}	7	8■	9	10^{3}	11	13	4	14		2										7
1	2	3			6^{1}	7		9^{2}	10	11	13	4		12	5	8									8
1	2	3^{2}	14		6^{3}	7			10	11	13	4	12		5	8^{1}	9								9
	2					7			10	11	13	4	9^{2}		5	3	6^{1}	1	12	8^{3}	14				10
	2	12				7	8		10	11		4^{2}	9^{3}		5	3	6^{1}	1	13	14					11
	2		12			7	8		10	11		4	9^{2}		5	3	6^{1}	1		13					12
	2		4			7	8		10	11	12^{2}	6		14	5	3^{1}	9^{3}	1		13					13
	2		4			7	8		10^{2}	11		6			5	3	9^{1}	1		13	12				14
	2		4		12	7	8		10^{3}	11		3^{1}		13	5	9	6^{2}	1			14				15
	2	12	4^{1}			7	8		10^{3}	11		3	9^{2}		5	6		1	14		13				16
	2	12	4^{1}			7	8		10^{3}	11		6	9^{2}		5	3	14	1			13				17
1		3			6	7		9^{2}	10	11		4	8^{1}		5	2	12				13				18
1	2				6	7	8	9^{1}	10^{2}	11		4	12		5	3						13			19
1	2	3^{1}			6	7	8	9^{2}	12	11		10			5	4						13			20
1	2^{1}	3^{2}	14		6	7	8	9		11		10^{3}	13		5	4	12								21
1		3	4	12	6	7	8	9	10^{3}	11		5^{2}	13			2^{1}						14			22
1	2	12	4		6	7		9■	10^{2}	11		3	8^{1}		5						13				23
1	2	3^{1}	4		6	7	12		10^{3}	11		8	9^{2}		5						13	14			24
1	2	12	4		6^{1}	7	8		14	11		3		13	5						9^{2}	10^{3}			25
1	2		4			7	8		10	11		3	6^{1}		5	13					12	9^{2}			26
1	2		4			7	8	9^{2}	10	11		3	14		5^{1}	12						13	6^{3}		27
1	2		4			7	8^{2}	9	10^{3}	11		6	13		5							14	12	3^{1}	28
1	2^{1}	12	4			7^{2}		9	10	11		6	14		5						13		8^{3}	3	29
1	2		4		6^{2}	7		9	14	13		8	11^{1}		5						12		10^{3}	3	30
1		3	4	13	6	7	8	9^{2}	10	11		2^{1}			5								12		31
1		2	4	14	6	7^{1}	8	9^{3}	10	11		3^{2}	13		5								12		32
1		3	4		6	7^{1}	8	9^{3}	10	11		2^{2}	13			5					12		14		33
1		3^{1}	4	12	6	7	8	9^{2}	10^{3}	11		5	13			2							14		34
1		3^{1}	4		6	7	8^{2}	9	10	11		5^{3}	14		12	2							13		35
1			4		6	7		9^{2}	10	11		3	13		5	2					12		8^{1}		36
1	2^{1}			12	6	7		9	10	3		4	13		5	8							11^{2}		37
1			4	12	6	7		9^{1}	10	11		3			5	2					13		8^{2}		38
1			4	12	6^{1}	7		9^{2}	10	3		8			5	2					14		11^{3}	13	39
1			4	12	6	7		9	10	3		8			5	2■							11^{1}		40
1	12		4	2^{1}	6^{2}	7		9	10	11		8	14		5								13^{3}	3	41
1	12		4	2	6^{1}	7		9^{2}	10^{3}	11		3	14		5		8				13				42
	13		4	2^{1}	6	7		9	10^{3}	11		8	12		5			1			14			3^{2}	43
	12		4	14	6^{1}	7		9	10	3		2	11^{2}		5^{3}	8		1			13				44
1	13		4	12	6^{2}	7	8	9	10^{3}	11		3	14		5	2^{1}									45
1^{6}	2	3^{1}	4	12	6	7		9		11		8	10^{2}		5			15			13				46

FA Cup
Fourth Qualifying Round
Rushden & D (a) 0-3

Trophy
First Round Tamworth (h) 0-0
(a) 1-2

BURTON ALBION

Blue Square Premier

Ground: Eton Park, Princess Way, Burton-on-Trent DE14 2RU. *Tel:* (01283) 565 938. *Year Formed:* 1950.
Record Gate: 5,806 (1964 v Weymouth, Southern League Cup Final). *Nickname:* Brewers. *Manager:* Nigel Clough.
Secretary: Tony Kirkland. *Colours:* All yellow with black trim.

BURTON ALBION 2006–07 LEAGUE RECORD

Match No.	*Date*	*Venue*	*Opponents*	*Result*		*H/T Score*	*Lg. Pos.*	*Goalscorers*	*Attendance*
1	Aug 12	A	Morecambe	W	1-0	0-0	—	Webster (pen) [77]	1907
2	15	H	Kidderminster H	D	1-1	1-0	—	Clare [45]	1880
3	18	H	Oxford U	L	1-2	1-0	—	Clare [15]	2501
4	25	A	York C	L	2-3	0-1	—	Ducros [50], Rowett [73]	2812
5	28	H	Southport	L	0-1	0-0	17		1831
6	Sept 1	A	Grays Ath	W	1-0	0-0	—	Ducros [70]	1367
7	9	H	Weymouth	D	1-1	1-0	15	Clare [9]	1523
8	12	A	Stafford R	D	1-1	1-0	—	Webster [11]	1554
9	16	A	St Albans C	W	1-0	1-0	13	Scoffham [13]	1111
10	19	H	Cambridge U	W	2-1	1-0	—	Corbett [34], Clare [60]	1612
11	23	H	Northwich Vic	W	2-0	2-0	9	Hall [24], Clare [45]	1817
12	30	A	Rushden & D	W	2-1	2-1	6	Webster [3], Clare [25]	2179
13	Oct 3	H	Crawley T	W	2-1	1-0	—	Webster [39], Stride [81]	1768
14	6	A	Woking	D	0-0	0-0	—		1651
15	10	A	Forest Green R	L	0-1	0-1	—		888
16	14	H	Gravesend & N	L	0-1	0-0	9		1766
17	21	A	Halifax T	W	2-1	1-1	5	Webster [10], Roberts (og) [81]	1844
18	Nov 3	H	Stevenage Bor	W	2-1	0-1	—	Gilroy [55], Carden [89]	1907
19	18	A	Dagenham & R	L	0-3	0-1	7		1581
20	27	H	Exeter C	W	1-0	1-0	—	Corbett [29]	1819
21	Dec 2	A	Altrincham	W	3-2	2-1	3	Clare 2 [17, 50], Fowler [33]	1212
22	9	H	Aldershot T	L	1-3	1-2	5	Fowler [26]	1876
23	26	A	Tamworth	W	1-0	0-0	5	Clare (pen) [77]	2029
24	30	A	Cambridge U	W	2-1	0-0	3	Duncan (og) [81], Clare (pen) [90]	3375
25	Jan 1	H	Stafford R	D	0-0	0-0	—		2570
26	20	H	St Albans C	W	1-0	1-0	5	Webster [45]	1632
27	27	A	Aldershot T	L	2-3	2-2	6	Clare [1], Corbett [14]	1970
28	Feb 3	A	Weymouth	D	1-1	1-0	6	Harrad [38]	1370
29	10	A	Stevenage Bor	L	1-2	0-0	7	Holmes [89]	2154
30	17	H	Dagenham & R	L	0-2	0-1	8		1809
31	20	H	Tamworth	W	1-0	0-0	—	Shaw [72]	1953
32	24	A	Exeter C	L	0-3	0-0	8		3475
33	Mar 2	H	Altrincham	W	2-1	1-0	—	Clare 2 [9, 79]	1441
34	6	A	Crawley T	L	0-1	0-1	—		663
35	10	H	Woking	W	2-1	1-1	6	Stride [40], Brayford [54]	1603
36	12	H	Forest Green R	W	1-0	0-0	—	Holmes [52]	1522
37	17	A	Gravesend & N	D	0-0	0-0	5		1069
38	24	H	Morecambe	W	2-1	2-0	4	Shaw [27], Clare [29]	1732
39	27	A	Kidderminster H	D	0-0	0-0	—		1635
40	31	A	Oxford U	D	0-0	0-0	5		6187
41	Apr 7	H	York C	L	1-2	0-0	6	Corbett [19]	2718
42	9	A	Southport	L	1-3	1-0	—	Ducros [23]	1552
43	14	H	Grays Ath	W	3-0	2-0	6	Webster 2 (1 pen) [22, 90 (p)], Clare [29]	1419
44	17	H	Halifax T	W	1-0	0-0	—	Goodfellow [82]	1436
45	21	A	Northwich Vic	W	3-0	3-0	6	Shaw [5], Ducros [22], Clare [44]	1218
46	28	H	Rushden & D	L	1-2	1-1	6	Shaw [38]	2910

Final League Position: 6

GOALSCORERS

League (52): Clare 16 (2 pens), Webster 8 (2 pens), Corbett 4, Ducros 4, Shaw 4, Fowler 2, Holmes 2, Stride 2, Brayford 1, Carden 1, Gilroy 1, Goodfellow 1, Hall 1, Harrad 1, Rowett 1, Scoffham 1, own goals 2.
FA Cup (2): Clare 2.
Trophy (5): Shaw 2, Ducros 1, Harrad 1, own goal 1.

Poole 46	Rowett 26	Webster 36	Corbett 43 + 2	Tinson 33 + 2	Austin 33 + 4	Holmes 21 + 12	Fowler 20 + 2	Clare 41	Harrad 13 + 28	Ducros 25 + 5	Shaw 23 + 13	Scoffham 4 + 6	Stride 36 + 3	Gilroy 20 + 5	Brayford 21 + 4	Hall 7 + 5	Henshaw 1 + 8	Liversage — + 1	Carden 27 + 1	Brown 4	Opara 1	Goodfellow 2 + 4	Bell 9 + 3	Nicholls 14	*Match No.*
1	2	3	4	5	6	7	8	9^{1}	10^{2}	11	12	13													1
1	2	3	4	5	6	12	8^{2}	9	10^{3}	7	14		13	11^{1}											2
1	2	3	4	5	6		8	9		10^{1}		12	7	11											3
1	2	3	4^{1}	5	6▪	12	8	9	14	11^{2}		10^{3}	7	13											4
1		3			6	7	8^{1}	9	10^{3}		12	14	5	11^{2}	2	4	13								5
1		3	4			7	8	9^{1}	12	11	10		5		2	6									6
1		3	4		6	12		9^{2}	13	8	10^{3}	14	2	11^{1}	5	7									7
1	2	3	4	5	6	7		9		11^{1}	10		8			12									8
1	2	3	4^{1}	5	6	7	12		14		10	9^{3}	8		13	11^{2}									9
1	2	3	4	5	6	7^{1}	8^{2}	9			10		11		13	12									10
1	2	3^{2}	4	5^{1}	6	12	8	9	14			10^{3}	7		13	11									11
1	2	3	4	5	6	13	8	9^{2}	10^{3}	11^{1}		14	7			12									12
1	2	3	4	5	6	12	8^{1}	9	10^{3}	11^{2}		14	7			13									13
1	2	3	4	5	6		8	9	12			10^{1}	7			11									14
1		3	4	5	6	7	8^{1}	9	10		13		2			11^{2}		12							15
1	2	3	4	5	6		8	9	13	11^{1}	10^{2}		7			12									16
1	2	3	4	5	6	13		9^{2}	10^{3}	12	14		7	11^{1}					8						17
1		3▪	4	5	6	13	8	9^{1}	12	10^{2}				11	2				7						18
1	2	3	4	5			8	9	13		12		6^{1}	11					7	10^{2}					19
1	2	3	4	5		12	8	9^{2}	14	11^{1}	13		6						7	10^{3}					20
1	2	3	4	5		12	8^{1}	9	14	11^{2}	13		6						7	10^{3}					21
1	2		4	5^{1}	12	7	8	9	14	11^{2}	13		3						6	10^{3}					22
1	2		4	5^{1}	12	13^{3}	8	9		7^{2}	10		6		3		14		11						23
1	2		4		6		12	9	14	8^{2}	10^{3}		5	13	3		7^{1}		11						24
1	2		4		6		8	9	10		5			11	3				7						25
1	2	3	4	5		7		9	12				6	11					8		10^{1}				26
1		3	4	5^{1}		7		9	10		12		6	11^{2}	2				8			13			27
1	2	3	4	5		7			10				6		11		12		8				9^{1}		28
1	2	3	4	5		7		9^{2}	10^{3}	12	14		6		13				11				8^{1}		29
1	9	3	4	5	12	7^{2}			10	11	13		6^{1}		2		14						8^{3}		30
1	2^{1}		4	5	6			9	12	11	10				3		13		8				7^{2}		31
1			4	5	6			9^{2}	12	11	10				2▪		13		8				7^{1}	3	32
1	2		4	5	6			9^{2}	13	8	10		12	11									7^{1}	3	33
1			4		6			9	14	11	10		5	12	2		13		8^{2}				7^{1}	3^{3}	34
1			4		6	12		9^{3}	14	13	10		5	11^{2}	2				8				7^{1}	3	35
1			4		6	7^{1}		9^{2}		13	10		5	11	2				8				12	3	36
1		3	4		6	7^{2}		9^{3}	12		10		5		2		14		8				13	11^{1}	37
1		3	12	13	6	7		9^{3}	14		10^{2}		5	11	2				8					4^{1}	38
1		3	12		6	7		9^{2}	13		10		5	11^{1}	2				8					4	39
1		3	4		6	7			12		10^{1}		5	11	2				8					9	40
1		3	4	12	6	7^{2}			14		10^{3}		5^{1}	11	2				8				13	9	41
1		3	4	5	6^{1}			9	10	11				12	2				14			13	7^{3}	8^{2}	42
1		3	4	5	6	7		9^{2}	14	10^{3}	13			11					8			12		2^{1}	43
1		3	4	5	6^{1}	7▪		9^{2}	14	13	10^{3}		12	11					8			2			44
1		3	4	5^{1}	12			9	14	11	10^{3}		6	13					8			7^{2}		2	45
1		3	4	5				9	12	7	10		6	11^{2}					8			13		2^{1}	46

FA Cup

Fourth Qualifying Round	Halifax T	(h)	1-0
First Round	Tamworth	(h)	1-2

Trophy

First Round	Gateshead	(a)	4-0
Second Round	Worcester C	(a)	1-2

CAMBRIDGE UNITED — Blue Square Premier

Ground: Abbey Stadium, Newmarket Road, Cambridge CB5 8LN. *Tel:* (01223) 566 500. *Year Formed:* 1912.
Record Gate: 14,000 (1970 v Chelsea, Friendly). *Nickname:* The 'U's'. *Manager:* Jimmy Quinn.
Secretary: Andrew Pincher. *Colours:* Navy and sky blue shirts, sky blue shorts, sky blue stockings.

CAMBRIDGE UNITED 2006–07 LEAGUE RECORD

Match No.	Date	Venue	Opponents	Result		H/T Score	Lg. Pos.	Goalscorers	Attendance
1	Aug 12	H	Northwich Vic	L	0-1	0-0	—		2506
2	15	A	St Albans C	D	0-0	0-0	—		1916
3	19	A	Weymouth	L	1-2	0-1	19	Simpson R [62]	1766
4	26	H	Halifax T	L	1-2	0-1	22	Jaszczun [90]	2056
5	28	A	Dagenham & R	L	0-2	0-0	23		1539
6	Sept 1	H	Exeter C	L	1-3	1-1	—	Peters [20]	2315
7	9	A	Forest Green R	D	1-1	0-1	24	Carey-Bertram [90]	1139
8	12	H	Kidderminster H	D	1-1	0-0	—	Brady [71]	1860
9	16	H	Stevenage Bor	W	1-0	1-0	19	Richardson [32]	2696
10	19	A	Burton Alb	L	1-2	0-1	—	Marum [46]	1612
11	22	H	Aldershot T	W	2-0	2-0	—	Newman (og) [28], Marum [39]	2535
12	30	A	Tamworth	W	1-0	1-0	17	Richardson (pen) [3]	1233
13	Oct 3	H	Altrincham	D	2-2	1-1	—	Marum [13], Richardson [54]	2680
14	7	A	Gravesend & N	L	0-2	0-0	19		1132
15	10	A	York C	W	2-1	0-1	—	Sedgemore [69], Brady [87]	2614
16	14	H	Crawley T	L	1-2	0-0	18	Brady [90]	3445
17	20	H	Oxford U	L	0-3	0-1	—		3932
18	Nov 3	A	Grays Ath	D	1-1	1-1	20	Simpson R [17]	1163
19	11	H	Gravesend & N	W	3-0	1-0	14	Gash [45], Pitt [47], Bridges [73]	1933
20	18	H	Morecambe	L	1-3	0-1	19	Carey-Bertram (pen) [90]	3142
21	25	A	Southport	W	2-1	0-1	15	Bridges [60], Carey-Bertram [64]	1106
22	Dec 2	H	St Albans C	L	0-2	0-1	18		2131
23	9	A	Woking	W	1-0	0-0	16	Smith S [80]	1886
24	26	H	Rushden & D	L	0-1	0-1	16		3000
25	30	H	Burton Alb	L	1-2	0-0	17	Gash [56]	3375
26	Jan 1	A	Kidderminster H	L	0-1	0-0	—		1922
27	13	H	Stafford R	L	0-1	0-1	—		2056
28	20	A	Stevenage Bor	L	1-4	1-0	21	Holdsworth [26]	2759
29	23	A	Rushden & D	L	1-3	0-1	—	Morrison [90]	2239
30	27	H	Woking	W	3-0	2-0	22	Simpson R 2 [15, 35], Brown [74]	2206
31	Feb 3	A	Oxford U	D	1-1	1-0	22	Duncan [32]	5613
32	10	H	Grays Ath	W	2-0	1-0	17	Simpson R 2 (1 pen) [45 (p), 84]	2842
33	17	A	Morecambe	D	2-2	1-0	17	Chillingworth [28], Ademeno [74]	1493
34	24	H	Southport	D	2-2	1-2	19	Simpson R 2 (1 pen) [4 (p), 74]	3444
35	27	H	Forest Green R	D	1-1	0-1	—	Pitt [65]	2127
36	Mar 3	A	Stafford R	W	2-1	1-1	17	Bridges [42], Smith C [88]	1096
37	6	A	Altrincham	L	0-5	0-1	—		891
38	13	H	York C	L	0-5	0-2	—		2428
39	17	A	Crawley T	D	1-1	1-0	20	Simpson R [41]	1177
40	25	A	Northwich Vic	W	4-0	2-0	18	Simpson R 3 [5, 81, 84], Chillingworth [24]	1156
41	31	H	Weymouth	W	7-0	4-0	18	Gleeson [6], Chillingworth 3 [10, 18, 69], Simpson R 2 [38, 64], Smith S [82]	2698
42	Apr 7	A	Halifax T	L	0-1	0-1	20		1942
43	9	H	Dagenham & R	W	4-2	3-2	—	Peters [24], Simpson R [32], Pitt [37], Wolleaston [54]	3319
44	14	A	Exeter C	L	0-2	0-1	19		4364
45	21	A	Aldershot T	W	1-0	0-0	17	Simpson R [78]	3068
46	28	H	Tamworth	W	1-0	0-0	17	Simpson R (pen) [59]	6021

Final League Position: 17

GOALSCORERS

League (57): Simpson R 17 (3 pens), Chillingworth 5, Brady 3, Bridges 3, Carey-Bertram 3 (1 pen), Marum 3, Pitt 3, Richardson 3 (1 pen), Gash 2, Peters 2, Smith S 2, Ademeno 1, Brown 1, Duncan 1, Gleeson 1, Holdsworth 1, Jaszczun 1, Morrison 1, Sedgemore 1, Smith C 1, Wolleaston 1, own goal 1.
FA Cup (0).
Trophy (0).

Crichton 33	Smith S 16 + 7	Jaszczun 10 + 1	Morrison 46	Bloomer 16 + 2	Hanlon 11 + 2	Brady 31 + 4	Wolleaston 34 + 3	Simpson R 28 + 5	Carey-Bertram 8 + 9	Pitt 40 + 3	Simpson J 11 + 8	Gash 7 + 9	Bridges 19 + 12	Lawrence — + 1	Quinton 3 + 4	Richardson 17 + 3 / Collins A 10 + 1	Davies 1	Marum 7 + 9 / Gleeson 8	Gier 15 + 2	Peters 19 + 4	Robinson 7 + 2	Sedgemore 3 + 1 / Flynn 1	Gill 3 + 1	Gordon 1 / Hughes — + 5	Duncan 20	Meredith 1	Brown 24	Herbert 13	Collins J 6 + 1	Purser 5 + 5	Holdsworth 3	Hooper 2 + 1	Hyem — + 1	Smith C 5 + 1	Ademeno 1 + 5	Chillingworth 15 + 1	Page 6 + 2	*Match No.*
1	2^{1}	3	4	5	6	7	8	9	10	11^{2}	12	13																										1
1	2	3	4	5	6^{2}	13	8	9	10■	11	7^{1}		12																									2
1	2^{1}	3	4	5		7	8	9		11	10	13	6^{2}	12																								3
1	2^{1}	3	4	5		7	8^{2}	9		11	13	12			6	10																						4
1	2	3■	4	5		12				13	9	10			6	8	7^{1}	11^{2}																				5
1			4	5^{1}	6■	7	8		10^{3}	11		13				9^{2}		14	2	3	12																	6
1	6^{2}		4			7^{1}	8	9^{3}	14	11		12	13			10			2	5	3																	7
1			4		6	7	8	13	10^{2}	11		12				9^{1}			2	5	3																	8
1			4		6	7^{1}	8	9^{3}		11		13	14			10^{2}		12	2	5	3																	9
1		13	4	12		7	8			11		14	6			9		10^{3}	2	5^{1}	3^{2}																	10
1		3	4	5		7	8			11		12	6			9		10^{1}	2																			11
1	13	3^{1}	4	5		7	8		14	11^{2}			6			9		10^{3}	2		12																	12
1	12		4	5		7	8		13	11^{1}			6			9		10^{2}	2		3																	13
1			4	5	6^{2}	7^{1}	8		14	12			11			9		10^{3}	2		3■	13																14
1			4	5^{1}	6	7	8		13	11			14			9		10^{2}	12			2^{3}	3															15
1			4		12	7	8		13	11^{3}			14			9			2		3	6^{1}	5	10^{2}														16
1			4			7	8		10	11			13			9^{3}		14	12			6^{2}	2		5^{1}	3												17
1		3	4	5	6	7		9^{3}		11		10^{2}	8			13		14	2^{1}				12															18
1		3^{1}	4	2	6		12	9^{3}	13	11		10^{2}	7			14									5		8											19
1		3	4	2	6		12		13	11		10	7^{1}			9^{2}									5		8											20
1			4	2			8		10	11	7		6			9^{1}		12		5							3											21
1■			4	2	13	7^{1}	8	12	10		9		6^{2}			11^{3}		14		5							3											22
	2		4		6	7	8	9	10^{1}	11								12		5							3	1										23
1	12		4			7	8^{1}	9^{3}	13	11	6	10^{2}						14	2						5				3									24
1■			4			7	8^{1}	9		11^{2}	12	10^{3}				14			2	13					5		6		3									25
			4			7	8	9		11		10^{2}						13	2^{1}	12					5		6	1	3									26
	6		4				8	13		11	7^{2}								2	12					5			1	3^{1}	10	9							27
			4			7	8^{1}	13		11	6									5					3			1		10	9^{2}	2	12					28
1	13		4	12		7	8	14		11										5					3				6^{2}	10	9^{3}	2^{1}						29
	13		4			7		9		11	12		8							5					2		6^{2}	1		10^{3}				3^{1}	14			30
			4			7	13	9		11	12		6^{1}			2									5		8	1						3■		10^{2}		31
			4			7	8^{1}	9		11^{2}	6					2											3	1				13			12	10	5	32
	14		4			7		9^{3}		11^{2}	6		8^{1}			2									5		3	1							13	10	12	33
			4			7		9^{3}		11^{2}	8^{1}		6			2									5		3	1		14					13	10	12	34
			2			7		9		11	13		8^{2}			4^{1}									5		6	1						12	10^{3}	14	3	35
	2		4			12		9		11^{1}			8												5		6	1		13				7		10^{2}	3	36
	2^{2}		4			7				12	13		3^{1}							14					5		11	1		9				8		10^{3}	6	37
	2^{2}		4			7^{3}		9			14		12		13										5		8	1	3^{1}					11		10	6	38
1			4			12	8	9					6			13		3		2^{2}					5^{1}		7			14						10^{3}	11	39
1	13		4				8^{1}	9		11			12			5		3		2		7^{2}		14			6									10^{3}		40
1	2		4				8	9^{3}		11^{1}						6		3		5				14			7		12	13						10^{2}		41
1	2^{1}		4				8	9		11			12			6		3		5				13			7									10^{2}		42
1	2^{2}		4				8	9		11			12		13	6		3^{1}		5				14			7									10^{3}		43
1	7^{2}		4				8	9		11			12		13	2^{1}		3		5				14			6									10^{3}		44
1	2^{1}		4				8	9		11					12			3		5					7		6								13	10^{4}		45
1			4				8	9		11			12		7			3		5					6		2^{1}			13						10^{2}		46

FA Cup
Fourth Qualifying Round Northwich Vic (a) 0-2

Trophy
First Round Histon (a) 0-5

CRAWLEY TOWN — Blue Square Premier

Ground: Broadfield Ground, Broadfield Stadium, Brighton Road, West Sussex RH11 9RX. *Tel:* (01293) 410 000.
Year Formed: 1896. *Record Gate:* 4,522 (2004 v Weymouth, Dr Martens League). *Nickname:* The Reds.
Manager: Steve Evans. *Secretary:* Barry Munn. *Colours:* All red.

CRAWLEY TOWN 2006–07 LEAGUE RECORD

Match No.	Date	Venue	Opponents	Result		H/T Score	Lg. Pos.	Goalscorers	Attendance
1	Aug 12	H	Rushden & D	W	1-0	0-0	—	Strevens [62]	1088
2	15	A	Woking	W	2-1	1-1	—	Strevens (pen) [12], Woozley [59]	1750
3	19	A	Stevenage Bor	W	3-2	0-1	24	Bostwick 2 [57, 83], Strevens (pen) [67]	1751
4	26	H	Stafford R	L	1-2	1-1	24	Judge [17]	929
5	28	A	Exeter C	D	1-1	1-0	24	Blackburn [21]	3403
6	Sept 2	H	Northwich Vic	L	0-2	0-0	24		778
7	9	H	York C	W	3-0	1-0	22	Edwards [23], Bulman [59], Blackburn [62]	932
8	12	A	Dagenham & R	L	1-2	0-1	—	Rendell [88]	1138
9	16	A	Southport	L	1-3	0-3	23	Strevens [63]	1025
10	18	H	Oxford U	L	0-1	0-0	—		2101
11	23	H	Grays Ath	L	0-1	0-0	24		974
12	30	A	Kidderminster H	W	1-0	0-0	24	Rendell (pen) [49]	1458
13	Oct 3	A	Burton Alb	L	1-2	0-1	—	Bulman [68]	1768
14	7	H	Morecambe	W	4-0	2-0	23	Rendell 3 (1 pen) [13, 45, 51 (p)], Scully [90]	890
15	10	H	Weymouth	L	0-3	0-0	—		1218
16	14	A	Cambridge U	W	2-1	0-0	23	Rendell 2 [68, 77]	3445
17	21	A	Forest Green R	L	0-1	0-0	23		1128
18	Nov 4	H	St Albans C	W	2-1	0-1	22	Bulman [57], Edwards [85]	840
19	18	A	Altrincham	D	1-1	0-0	23	Peters [49]	1033
20	25	H	Halifax T	W	2-0	1-0	22	Scully [18], Blackburn [55]	1062
21	Dec 9	H	Tamworth	W	1-0	0-0	19	Rendell (pen) [53]	957
22	26	A	Gravesend & N	L	0-1	0-1	21		1062
23	30	A	Oxford U	D	1-1	1-0	19	Scully [45]	6368
24	Jan 1	H	Dagenham & R	D	0-0	0-0	—		1486
25	6	A	York C	L	0-5	0-3	21		2590
26	13	A	Aldershot T	W	2-0	1-0	—	Woozley [37], Bull [70]	2349
27	20	H	Southport	W	2-1	1-0	16	Rendell [12], Bull [90]	1152
28	23	H	Gravesend & N	D	1-1	0-0	—	Woozley [89]	816
29	27	A	Tamworth	W	1-0	0-0	14	Wright [54]	1101
30	Feb 3	H	Forest Green R	W	3-1	0-0	13	Evans [56], Rendell [63], Scully [89]	1076
31	10	A	St Albans C	D	2-2	1-1	12	Okuonghae [12], Benyon [90]	857
32	17	H	Altrincham	D	1-1	1-1	12	Benyon [31]	1180
33	Mar 3	H	Aldershot T	L	1-2	0-0	15	Benyon [59]	1737
34	6	H	Burton Alb	W	1-0	1-0	—	Woozley [2]	663
35	10	A	Morecambe	L	0-1	0-1	14		1374
36	13	A	Weymouth	L	2-3	0-0	—	Rendell [57], Scully [81]	1310
37	17	H	Cambridge U	D	1-1	0-1	14	Richardson [90]	1177
38	23	A	Rushden & D	D	1-1	1-0	—	Blackburn [25]	1974
39	27	H	Woking	D	0-0	0-0	—		1098
40	31	H	Stevenage Bor	W	3-0	1-0	13	Bulman (pen) [11], Scully [53], Richardson [74]	1258
41	Apr 7	A	Stafford R	W	1-0	1-0	13	Evans [8]	967
42	9	H	Exeter C	L	0-3	0-2	—		1562
43	14	A	Northwich Vic	L	1-2	1-1	15	Okuonghae [17]	706
44	21	A	Grays Ath	D	0-0	0-0	16		1131
45	24	A	Halifax T	L	1-2	0-0	—	Scully [90]	1561
46	28	H	Kidderminster H	D	0-0	0-0	18		1664

Final League Position: 18

GOALSCORERS

League (52): Rendell 11 (3 pens), Scully 7, Blackburn 4, Bulman 4 (1 pen), Strevens 4 (2 pens), Woozley 4, Benyon 3, Bostwick 2, Bull 2, Edwards 2, Evans 2, Okuonghae 2, Richardson 2, Judge 1, Peters 1, Wright 1.
FA Cup (2): Bostwick 1, Rendell 1.
Trophy (0).

Hamer 45	Hiley 42 + 2	Brown 13 + 1	Woozley 44 + 1	Judge 29 + 1	Mills 17 + 4	Bostwick 24	Blackburn 39 + 2	Edwards 16 + 5	Strevens 13 + 2	Scully 36 + 4	Sappleton 2 + 7	Rendell 26 + 16	Bulman 36 + 1	Townsend — + 1	Macleod 5 + 6	Lovegrove 4 + 1	Obersteller — + 1	Baker — + 1	Dadson — + 1	Match No.
1	2	3	4	5	6^{1}	7	8	9	10^{2}	11	12	13								1
1	2	3	4	5	6	7	8	9^{1}	10	11		12								2
1	2	3	4	5^{1}	6	7	8	9	10	11	12									3
1	2^{1}	3	4	5^{2}	6	7	8	9	10	11	13	12								4
1	2	3	4	5	6^{1}	7	8	9	10	11	12									5
1	2^{1}	3	4	5	6^{2}	7	8	9^{3}	10	11		14	12	13						6
1	2	3^{1}	4	5	13	7	8^{2}	9	10^{3}	11	12	14	6							7
1	2	3^{1}	4	5	13	7^{2}	8^{3}	9	10	11	12	14	6							8
1	2^{1}	3^{3}	4^{2}	5	14	7	8	9	10	11		12	6		13					9
1	2	3		5		7	8	9^{1}	10	11	6	12	4							10
1	2	3^{1}	14		6	7	8^{2}		13	11	4	9^{3}	10		5	12				11
1	2		4	5	6	7	8					9	11		10	3				12
1	2		4	5	6	7	8^{3}			13		9	11		10^{2}	3^{1}		12	14	13
1	2	12	4	5	6	7^{2}	8	14	10^{3}	13		9	11			3^{1}				14
1	2		4	5^{1}	6^{3}	7	14	9	13	11	12	10	8			3^{2}				15
1	2	3	4	5		7	8	9	10^{2}			11	6^{1}		13					16
1	2	3	4	5	13	7^{1}	8	9	10			11^{2}	6							17
1	2^{1}		4	5	6	7	8	9^{2}		11		10	3		12					18
1	2^{1}		4	5	6	7	8			11		10	3		12					19
1			4	5	6	7	8	12		11			2							20
1	12		4	5	6^{2}	7	8	14		11		10								21
1	2		4	5	6		8	13		11		9								22
1	2		4	5	6	7	8	9^{2}		11		10								23
1	2		4	5		7	8	9		11		13								24
1^{G}	2		4	5		7	8^{1}	13		11		9	6							25
	2		4							11^{2}		9	8		13					26
1	2		4				8					9	7		6					27
1	2^{1}		4				8			13		9	7		6^{2}					28
1	2		4	5^{1}						12		9	7							29
1	2		4				8■			11^{1}		9^{2}	7		12					30
1	2		4							11		9	7							31
1	2		4							11		10^{2}	7							32
1	2^{1}		4							11		13	7							33
1	2		4				8^{1}			11		13	7							34
1	2^{1}		4				8					10	7							35
1	2		4				12			11		9	7							36
1			4				8^{1}			11		9	7^{2}							37
1	2		4				8			11		9^{1}	7							38
1	2		4				8			11		10^{2}	7							39
1	2		4				8			11■		13	7							40
1	2		4				8					13	7							41
1	2^{1}		4	12			8			11		13	7							42
1	2		4	5^{1}			8^{2}			11		12	7							43
1	2		4	5^{1}			8			11		9^{3}	7				12			44
1	2^{2}		4	5^{1}			8			11		12	7							45
1	12		4	5			8			11			7							46

Marshall 3 + 12	Peters 3	Wright 9	Kember 1	Benjamin — + 3	McCallum 2	Rowaye — + 1	Blackman 9 + 7	Tolfrey 1 + 1	Okuonghae 21	Evans 14 + 2	Bull 16 + 1	Nayee — + 2	Richardson 11 + 7	Benyon 12 + 3	England 2 + 1	Charles 5 + 1	Suliaman — + 2	Berry 6 + 2	Match No.
																			1
																			2
																			3
																			4
																			5
																			6
																			7
																			8
																			9
																			10
																			11
																			12
																			13
																			14
																			15
12																			16
12																			17
13																			18
13	9^{2}																		19
13	9^{1}	3	10^{2}																20
	9^{3}	3^{1}		13	2														21
14		3^{1}			7^{2}	12	10^{3}												22
		3^{1}		12			13												23
6		3^{1}		12			10^{2}												24
12		3^{2}					10	15											25
12■		5^{1}					10^{3}	1	6	7	3	14							26
		3^{1}					10		5		11		12						27
11■							10		5		3		12						28
		8					10^{2}		6	11	3			13					29
									5	6	3	13	10^{3}		14				30
							10^{2}		5		3		8	13	6^{1}	12			31
							13		5	6	3		12	9	8^{1}				32
8^{2}							12		5	6			10	9		3			33
12									5	6			10^{2}	9		3			34
							12		5	6	11			9		3			35
									5	8	3		10^{2}			6^{1}	13		36
12									5	2	3		14	10		6^{3}	13		37
									5		3		12	10				6	38
									5	12	3		13	9				6^{1}	39
12									5		3		10^{2}	9				6^{1}	40
12									5	11	3		10^{2}	9				6^{1}	41
									5	14	3^{2}		10	9				6^{3}	42
							14		6	3			10^{3}	9				13	43
							14		6	3			10^{2}	13					44
							14		6	3	13		10					9^{3}	45
							10^{3}		6	2^{2}	3^{1}		14	9				13	46

FA Cup
Fourth Qualifying Round
Lewes (h) 2-3

Trophy
First Round Dagenham & R (a) 0-2

DAGENHAM & REDBRIDGE FL Championship 2

Ground: The London Borough of Barking and Dagenham Stadium, Victoria Road, Dagenham, Essex RM10 7XL. *Tel:* (0208) 592 7194. *Year Formed:* 1992. *Record Gate:* 5,500 (1992 v Leyton Orient, FA Cup, First Round). *Nickname:* Daggers. *Manager:* John Still. *Secretary:* Derek Almond. *Colours:* Red shirts, white shorts, red stockings.

DAGENHAM & REDBRIDGE 2006–07 LEAGUE RECORD

Match No.	Date	Venue	Opponents	Result		H/T Score	Lg. Pos.	Goalscorers	Attendance
1	Aug 12	A	Forest Green R	W	1-0	1-0	—	Uddin [37]	1067
2	15	H	Oxford U	L	0-1	0-0	—		2022
3	19	H	Tamworth	W	4-0	2-0	7	Uddin [4], Sloma [14], Akurang 2 [54, 67]	947
4	26	A	Aldershot T	D	1-1	0-0	6	Benson [85]	2657
5	28	H	Cambridge U	W	2-0	0-0	5	Benson [64], Sloma [68]	1539
6	Sept 3	A	Altrincham	W	5-0	2-0	3	Rainford [11], Southam [12], Saunders [66], Benson [70], Mackail-Smith [73]	951
7	9	A	Woking	D	2-2	1-1	3	Uddin [11], Akurang (pen) [89]	1724
8	12	H	Crawley T	W	2-1	1-0	—	Benson 2 [8, 67]	1138
9	16	H	Morecambe	W	2-1	1-1	2	Rainford 2 [18, 52]	1237
10	19	A	Halifax T	L	1-3	0-2	—	Rainford (pen) [53]	1268
11	23	H	Weymouth	W	4-1	3-1	2	Downer (og) [5], Benson 2 [28, 38], Southam (pen) [76]	1602
12	30	A	Gravesend & N	D	0-0	0-0	2		1524
13	Oct 3	A	Stafford R	W	2-1	1-1	—	Southam (pen) [22], Benson [59]	1143
14	7	H	Northwich Vic	W	5-0	3-0	2	Benson 2 [21, 29], Southam [41], Mackail-Smith [78], Sloma [86]	1235
15	10	H	St Albans C	W	4-2	3-0	—	Benson [8], Mackail-Smith 2 [26, 85], Rainford [45]	1508
16	14	A	Stevenage Bor	W	2-1	1-1	2	Sloma 2 [10, 60]	2362
17	21	H	Kidderminster H	L	1-3	1-0	2	Mackail-Smith [6]	1874
18	Nov 3	A	Rushden & D	W	3-2	3-2	2	Mackail-Smith 2 [6, 45], Benson [10]	2039
19	18	H	Burton Alb	W	3-0	1-0	2	Mackail-Smith [34], Benson [85], Rainford (pen) [90]	1581
20	25	A	York C	W	3-2	1-1	2	Mackail-Smith 2 [31, 77], Southam [64]	3050
21	Dec 2	H	Southport	D	0-0	0-0	2		1285
22	9	A	Exeter C	L	2-3	1-1	2	Benson [4], Rainford [65]	2928
23	26	H	Grays Ath	D	0-0	0-0	2		1855
24	30	H	Halifax T	W	1-0	0-0	1	Mackail-Smith [80]	1261
25	Jan 1	A	Crawley T	D	0-0	0-0	—		1486
26	6	H	Woking	W	3-2	2-2	1	Mackail-Smith 2 [13, 38], Benson [76]	1389
27	20	A	Morecambe	D	1-1	0-1	1	Benson [72]	1711
28	23	A	Grays Ath	W	1-0	1-0	—	Mackail-Smith [11]	1504
29	27	H	Exeter C	W	4-1	0-0	1	Benson 3 [46, 55, 90], Mackail-Smith [69]	1816
30	Feb 10	H	Rushden & D	L	1-2	1-1	1	Benson [33]	1817
31	17	A	Burton Alb	W	2-0	1-0	1	Sloma 2 [18, 86]	1809
32	20	A	Kidderminster H	W	4-1	1-1	—	Benson 2 [10, 62], Kenna (og) [59], Strevens [84]	1383
33	24	H	York C	W	2-1	1-0	1	Boardman 2 [23, 55]	2252
34	Mar 3	A	Southport	W	4-1	2-0	1	Boardman [7], Southam [42], Saunders [66], Moore [87]	1245
35	6	H	Stafford R	D	1-1	0-0	—	Moore [63]	1710
36	13	A	St Albans C	W	2-1	2-1	—	Benson [28], Rainford [38]	1170
37	17	H	Forest Green R	D	1-1	1-0	1	Benson [39]	1800
38	20	H	Stevenage Bor	W	2-0	0-0	—	Strevens [76], Rainford [87]	1984
39	26	A	Oxford U	D	2-2	1-0	—	Benson [17], Sloma [90]	6836
40	31	A	Tamworth	W	2-0	1-0	1	Rainford [45], Strevens [82]	1269
41	Apr 7	H	Aldershot T	W	2-1	1-0	1	Benson [12], Rainford (pen) [60]	4044
42	9	A	Cambridge U	L	2-4	2-3	—	Benson 2 [8, 11]	3319
43	11	A	Northwich Vic	L	0-2	0-0	—		757
44	14	H	Altrincham	W	4-1	1-1	1	Taylor [11], Southam [59], Moore (pen) [82], Saunders [88]	1473
45	21	A	Weymouth	D	1-1	0-1	1	Strevens [89]	1655
46	28	H	Gravesend & N	W	2-1	2-1	1	Strevens 2 [18, 36]	3021

Final League Position: 1

GOALSCORERS

League (93): Benson 28, Mackail-Smith 15, Rainford 11 (3 pens), Sloma 8, Southam 7 (2 pens), Strevens 6, Akurang 3 (1 pen), Boardman 3, Moore 3 (1 pen), Saunders 3, Uddin 3, Taylor 1, own goals 2.
FA Cup (0).
Trophy (4): Benson 2, Mackail-Smith 1, Sloma 1.

Roberts 45	Griffiths 44 + 1	Olayle 2	Rainford 40	Uddin 42 + 1	Leberl 28 + 9	Saunders 37 + 5	Southam 42 + 1	Benson 45 + 1	Akurang 10 + 17	Sloma 40 + 4	Atieno — + 3	Batt — + 4	Foster 45	Mackail-Smith 27 + 1	Lettejallon — + 3	Hogan — + 1	Bruce 1 + 12	Cole 3 + 1	Blackett 17	Strevens 10 + 10	Vernazza 4 + 6	Boardman 9	Moore 6 + 9	Wallis — + 2	Lawson — + 3	Taylor 2 + 2	Arber 6	Eyre 1	Match No.
1	2	3[1]	4	5	6	7	8	9	10	11	12[2]	13																	1
1	2		4	5	6	7	8	9[2]	10	11[1]	12		3	13															2
1	13		4	5	6	7[1]	8	9	10[3]	11	12		2	3[2]	14														3
1	2		4	5	6[1]	7	8	12	10	11		13	3	9[2]															4
1	2		4	5	6	7	8	9		11			3	10															5
1[G]	2		4	5	6	7	8	9[2]	13	11[1]			3	10		15	12												6
1	2		4	5	6	7		9	10	11[1]			3	8			12												7
1	2		4	5	6	7		9	8	11			3	10															8
1	2		4	5	6	7		9	8	11			3	10															9
1	2		4	5	6	7	13	9	8[1]	11[2]		14	3	10[3]			12												10
1	2		4[2]	5	6	7[1]	8	9	12	11[3]			3	10	13		14												11
1	2		4	5		7	8	9	12	11[2]			3	10			13	6[1]											12
1	2		4	5		7	8	9	12	11[1]			3	10[2]			13		6										13
1	2		4	5	12	7	8	9[3]	14	11		13	3[1]	10[2]					6										14
1	2		4	5	12	7[1]	8	9[3]	14	11[2]			3	10			13		6										15
1	2		4	5	12	7[2]	8	9	14	11[1]			3	10[3]			13		6										16
1	2		4	5	12	7[3]	8	9	14	11[2]			3[1]	10			13		6										17
1	2		4	5		7[1]	8	9	12	11			3	10					6										18
1	2		4	5		7[2]	8	9	13	11[1]			3	10			12		6										19
1	2			5	6	7[1]	8	9	12[2]	11[3]			3	10	13		14		4										20
1	2		4	5[1]	12	7	8	9[3]	14	11[2]			3	10			13		6										21
1			4		6	7[1]	8	9	12				2	10			11	3	5										22
1	2		4		6	7	8	9	12	11[1]			3	10					5										23
1	2		4	5			8[1]	9	10	11[2]			3	7					6	12	13								24
1	2		4■	5	12		8[1]	9	10	11[2]			3	7					6		13								25
1	2			5	6		8	9		11			3	10					4	12	7[1]								26
1	2			5	6	7	8	9	12	11[1]			3	10					4										27
1	2		4	5	6	7[2]	8	9[1]	12	13			3	10[3]					11	14									28
1	2		4	5	6	13	8[1]	9	12	11[2]			3	10[3]					7	14									29
1	2		4	5	6	13	8	9		11[1]			7							12		3	10[2]						30
1	2		4	5		7	8	9		11			3							12		6	10[1]						31
1	2		4	5	13	7	8[2]	9		11			3							10[1]		6	12						32
1	2			5	6	7[1]	8	9		11[2]			3							10[3]		4	14	12	13				33
1	2			5	6	7[1]	8	9		11[2]			3							10[3]		4	14	12	13				34
1	2	10[2]	4	5		7	8	9		11[1]			3									6	13			12			35
1	2		4	5	12	7[1]	8	9		11			3							13		6	10[2]						36
1	2		4	5		7	8	9		11[1]			3							10		6			12				37
1	2		4	5	6		8	9					3							10	12	7[1]	11						38
1	2		4[1]	5	6	13	8[2]	9		14			3							10	12		11[3]				7		39
1	2		4	5	6	12	8[1]	9		11			3							10							7		40
1	2		4	5	14	7[1]	8[2]	9		11[3]			3							10	12		13				6		41
	2			5	6	7[1]	8[2]	9		12			3							14	11		10[3]			13	4	1	42
1	2		4	5	6	13	8	9		11[1]			3							10[2]	7		12						43
1	2		4		6	7	8	9[2]		11[1]			3					5		12	13		14			10[3]			44
1	2		4	5		7[1]	8	9		12			3							13	11[2]		14			10[3]	6		45
1	2		4	14	6[1]	7	8	9[3]		11[2]			3					12		10			13				5		46

FA Cup

Fourth Qualifying Round				
	Oxford U	(h)	0-1	

Trophy

First Round	Crawley T	(h)	2-0
Second Round	Redditch U	(a)	2-3

EBBSFLEET UNITED

Blue Square Premier

(Formerly Gravesend and Northfleet)

Ground: Stonebridge Road, Northfleet, Kent DA11 9BA. *Tel:* (01474) 533 796. *Year Formed:* 1946.
Record Gate: 12,036 (1963 v Sunderland, FA Cup Fourth Round). *Nickname:* The Fleet. *Manager:* Liam Daish.
Secretary: Roly Edwards. *Colours:* Red shirts, white shorts, red stockings.

GRAVESEND & NORTHFLEET 2006–07 LEAGUE RECORD

Match No.	Date	Venue	Opponents	Result		H/T Score	Lg. Pos.	Goalscorers	Attendance
1	Aug 12	A	Aldershot T	L	2-3	1-0	—	De Bolla [24], MacDonald (pen) [50]	2487
2	15	H	Tamworth	W	4-1	2-1	—	MacDonald 2 [7, 67], De Bolla 2 [35, 53]	936
3	19	H	York C	L	0-1	0-1	13		1036
4	26	A	Forest Green R	W	1-0	1-0	9	Moore [28]	881
5	28	H	Altrincham	W	3-1	0-0	8	MacDonald 2 [58, 76], Moore [66]	900
6	Sept 2	A	Southport	D	2-2	2-2	9	De Bolla [12], Moore [37]	861
7	9	A	Halifax T	D	1-1	1-1	8	MacDonald [2]	1435
8	12	H	Grays Ath	W	2-0	1-0	—	MacDonald [22], De Bolla [63]	1200
9	16	H	Exeter C	D	2-2	0-2	7	Sodje [56], Smith R [78]	1167
10	19	A	Rushden & D	D	0-0	0-0	—		1879
11	23	A	St Albans C	W	3-2	0-0	7	MacDonald 2 (2 pens) [51, 60], De Bolla [90]	987
12	30	H	Dagenham & R	D	0-0	0-0	9		1524
13	Oct 4	A	Weymouth	L	1-2	1-1	—	MacDonald [17]	2153
14	7	H	Cambridge U	W	2-0	0-0	7	MacDonald (pen) [69], Sodje [82]	1132
15	10	H	Stafford R	L	1-4	0-1	—	MacDonald [64]	857
16	14	A	Burton Alb	W	1-0	0-0	6	Slatter [69]	1766
17	21	H	Woking	W	1-0	0-0	4	MacDonald [75]	1208
18	Nov 3	A	Morecambe	L	0-1	0-1	7		1429
19	11	A	Cambridge U	L	0-3	0-1	7		1933
20	18	H	Oxford U	W	1-0	0-0	5	Sodje [69]	2019
21	25	A	Northwich Vic	W	2-1	2-1	3	Sodje [43], Slatter [45]	813
22	Dec 2	H	Kidderminster H	L	1-3	0-2	6	Hawkins [87]	1160
23	9	A	Stevenage Bor	L	0-3	0-1	7		2014
24	26	H	Crawley T	W	1-0	1-0	7	Moore [41]	1062
25	30	H	Rushden & D	W	1-0	0-0	6	Sodje [83]	1110
26	Jan 4	A	Grays Ath	W	2-0	1-0	—	Coleman [40], MacDonald [90]	1071
27	20	A	Exeter C	W	3-1	3-0	4	MacDonald 2 [18, 41], Moore [29]	3287
28	23	A	Crawley T	D	1-1	0-0	—	MacDonald [66]	816
29	27	H	Stevenage Bor	D	1-1	1-1	4	MacDonald [33]	1409
30	Feb 10	H	Morecambe	W	2-1	1-1	4	MacDonald (pen) [10], Ledgister [56]	1156
31	17	A	Oxford U	L	0-1	0-1	4		5615
32	20	A	Woking	D	2-2	0-1	—	MacDonald [73], Varney [83]	851
33	Mar 3	A	Kidderminster H	W	2-1	1-0	4	Long [13], Sodje [84]	1508
34	6	H	Weymouth	L	1-3	1-0	—	Moore [35]	1098
35	13	A	Stafford R	L	1-3	0-2	—	Varney [69]	524
36	17	H	Burton Alb	D	0-0	0-0	8		1069
37	23	H	Aldershot T	D	1-1	0-1	—	MacDonald [84]	1103
38	27	A	Tamworth	L	1-2	0-1	—	MacDonald [81]	1044
39	31	A	York C	W	2-0	1-0	7	MacDonald [17], Sodje [83]	2709
40	Apr 3	H	Halifax T	W	2-0	1-0	—	Smith R [17], Sodje [80]	946
41	7	H	Forest Green R	D	1-1	1-1	7	Sodje [26]	1063
42	9	A	Altrincham	W	2-0	1-0	—	Ledgister [6], Eribenne [58]	990
43	14	H	Southport	L	0-4	0-2	7		1432
44	19	H	Northwich Vic	W	3-0	2-0	—	MacDonald 2 (1 pen) [43, 45 (p)], Moore [74]	1182
45	21	H	St Albans C	W	3-2	1-0	7	MacDonald 2 (1 pen) [19 (p), 74], McCarthy [50]	1035
46	28	A	Dagenham & R	L	1-2	1-2	7	Smith R [33]	3021

Final League Position: 7

GOALSCORERS

League (63): MacDonald 27 (7 pens), Sodje 9, Moore 7, De Bolla 6, Smith R 3, Ledgister 2, Slatter 2, Varney 2, Coleman 1, Eribenne 1, Hawkins 1, Long 1, McCarthy 1.
FA Cup (0).
Trophy (4): MacDonald 2 (1 pen), De Bolla 1, Long 1.

Cronin 43	Hawkins 29 + 4	Opinel 31 + 1	Smith R 42	Smith J 22 + 2	Quinn 42	Slatter 38 + 3	Ekoku 1 + 5	De Bolla 25 + 6	MacDonald 41	Keeling 26 + 11	Ricketts 26 + 5	Purcell 1 + 9	McCarthy 38	Roberts — + 1	Moore 30 + 8	McKenna — + 1	Coleman 10 + 20	Sodje 14 + 25	Anderson — + 1	Long 27 + 2	McShane 3	Ledgister 6 + 7	Howe — + 1	Varney 2 + 2	Eribenne 9 + 1	*Match No.*
1	2■	3^{1}	4	5	6	7	8	9^{2}	10	11	12	13														1
1			4	5	6	7^{1}		9	10^{2}	11	2	12	3	13	8^{3}	14										2
1			4	5	6	7	12	9	10	11	2^{1}		3		8											3
1			4	5	6	7^{1}	13	9	10	11	2		3		8^{2}		12									4
1	12		4	5	6	7^{1}		9	10	11^{2}	2		3		8^{3}		13	14								5
1			4	5	6	7^{2}		9	10	11	2^{1}		3		8		13	12								6
1	12		4	5	6	7^{2}		9	10	11	2		3^{1}		8^{3}		13	14								7
1	12		4	5	6			9	10	11	2^{1}		3		8^{2}		7	13								8
1	2		4	5	6	12		9	10	11	3				8^{2}		7^{1}	13								9
1	12		4^{2}	5	6	7		9	10	11	2		3^{1}		8		13^{3}	14								10
1	2		4	5	6	7		9	10	11^{2}	3	13^{3}			8^{1}		14	12								11
1		12	4	5	6	7		9	10	11^{1}	2		3		8^{2}			13								12
1		3^{2}	4	5	6	7	12	9^{3}	10		2^{1}	13	11		8			14								13
1	2	3		5	6	7			10		4		11		8^{1}		12	9								14
1	2^{1}	3		5	6	7			10		11^{2}	12	4		8			9	13							15
1	2	3		5	6	7			10		11		4		8^{1}		9	12								16
1		3^{2}	4	5	6	7			10	13	2		11		8^{3}		9^{1}	14		12						17
1	2	3^{1}	4	5	6	7	13		10	12	11^{2}						14	9		8^{3}						18
1	2	3	4		5	7^{1}	14	13	10	11	6	12						9^{3}		8^{2}						19
1	2	3	4			7			10	11	6		8					9		5						20
1	2	3	4		6	7		12	10	11^{1}			5					9		8						21
1	2	3^{3}	5		6^{2}	7		13	10	11^{1}		12	4		14			9		8						22
1	2		5		6^{2}	7		9	10	11			4		13		12	8		3^{1}						23
1	2	3	4		6	7			10	12			5		9^{2}		11^{1}	13		8						24
1	2	3^{2}	4		6	7		12		13^{3}		14	5		10		11^{1}	9		8						25
1	2	3	4	12	6	7		13	10				5^{1}		9^{3}		11^{2}	14		8						26
1	2	3	4		6	7^{1}		9^{2}	10^{3}		12		5		8		13	14		11						27
	2	3■	4		6	7^{1}		9^{2}	10				5		8^{3}		13	14		11	1	12				28
	2		4		6	7		9	10			11^{1}	5		8^{2}			13		3	1	12				29
	2	3	4		6			9^{2}	10		13		5		8^{3}		12	14		11	1	7^{1}				30
1	2■	3	4		5			9^{2}	10	12			6		8^{3}		13	14		7^{1}		11				31
1		11	4	5	6				10	12	8^{2}		2				7	9^{3}				3^{1}	13	14		32
1		3	4		6	7^{1}		9^{2}		11	12		5		8			14		2		13		10^{3}		33
1		3	4		6^{1}	7		9	10	11	2				8^{2}			13		5		12				34
1		3	4	5	6	7				11^{2}	2				10^{3}		13	9		8^{1}		12		14		35
1		3	4	5	6	7^{1}			10	13	2						12	14		8		11^{2}		9^{3}		36
1		3	4		6^{1}	7		13	10	11^{3}			5		12		2			8^{2}		14			9	37
1	2	3	4		6	7^{1}		9^{3}	10	12			5		13		11^{2}			14					8	38
1	2	3	4		6			9^{2}	10	11^{1}			5				13	14		8		12			7^{3}	39
1	2	3	4		6	12		9	10^{2}	11^{1}			5		13			14		8					7^{3}	40
1	2	3	4^{1}		6	13		9^{2}		11			5		14		12	10		8					7^{3}	41
1	2^{1}	3		5	6	7				13	12		4		14			10		8		11^{2}			9^{3}	42
1	2^{1}	3■	4		6^{3}	7			10	13			5		12			9		8		11^{2}			14	43
1	2		4	12		7			10	11^{2}	3^{3}	13	5^{1}		8		14			6					9	44
1	2		4			7			10	11^{1}	3		5		8		12	13		6					9^{2}	45
1	2	3	4			7			10	13	11^{2}		5		8^{3}		12	14		6^{1}					9	46

FA Cup

Fourth Qualifying Round — Chelmsford C (a) 0-1

Trophy

First Round	Havant & W	(a)	2-1
Second Round	AFC Wimbledon	(h)	0-1
AFC Wimbledon removed from the competition.			
Third Round	Rushden & D	(h)	2-1
Fourth Round	Northwich Vic	(a)	0-3

EXETER CITY

Blue Square Premier

Ground: St James Park, Exeter EX4 6PX. *Tel:* (01392) 411 243. *Year Formed:* 1904.
Record Gate: 20,984 (1931 v Sunderland, FA Cup Sixth Round Replay). *Nickname:* The Grecians.
Manager: Paul Tisdale. *Secretary:* Sally Cooke. *Colours:* Red and white shirts, white shorts, white stockings.

EXETER CITY 2006–07 LEAGUE RECORD

Match No.	Date	Venue	Opponents	Result		H/T Score	Lg. Pos.	Goalscorers	Attendance
1	Aug 12	A	York C	D	0-0	0-0	—		2789
2	15	H	Forest Green R	W	1-0	1-0	—	Stansfield [40]	3527
3	19	H	Altrincham	W	2-1	1-1	4	Todd [39], Challinor [86]	3345
4	26	A	Tamworth	L	0-1	0-0	8		1242
5	28	H	Crawley T	D	1-1	0-1	9	Moxey [58]	3403
6	Sept 1	A	Cambridge U	W	3-1	1-1	—	Phillips [40], Challinor [55], Crichton (og) [64]	2315
7	9	H	Aldershot T	D	0-0	0-0	7		3933
8	12	A	Oxford U	L	0-1	0-1	—		6083
9	16	A	Gravesend & N	D	2-2	2-0	10	Edwards [19], Smith J (og) [40]	1167
10	19	H	St Albans C	W	4-2	1-0	—	Cozic [44], Gill [65], Phillips [81], Jones B (pen) [87]	2494
11	23	H	Stevenage Bor	D	1-1	0-0	10	Jones B [87]	3194
12	30	A	Southport	W	1-0	0-0	10	Buckle [60]	1163
13	Oct 3	A	Grays Ath	D	2-2	1-0	—	Challinor [39], Jones B [90]	1157
14	7	H	Halifax T	W	4-1	1-1	6	Challinor 2 [25, 90], Stansfield [75], Mackie [89]	3114
15	10	H	Northwich Vic	D	1-1	0-1	—	Phillips [48]	2928
16	14	A	Morecambe	D	2-2	1-1	5	Mackie [1], Stansfield [57]	1582
17	21	H	Stafford R	L	1-2	0-0	7	Stansfield [55]	3977
18	Nov 3	A	Woking	W	2-0	2-0	6	Buckle [19], Mackie [31]	2590
19	18	H	Kidderminster H	D	1-1	1-1	8	Jones B [28]	3082
20	27	A	Burton Alb	L	0-1	0-1	—		1819
21	Dec 9	H	Dagenham & R	W	3-2	1-1	8	Stansfield [38], Mackie [60], Blackett (og) [90]	2928
22	26	A	Weymouth	L	1-2	0-1	9	Jones B [51]	4294
23	30	A	St Albans C	W	2-1	0-0	8	Carlisle [50], Moxey [88]	1314
24	Jan 1	H	Oxford U	W	2-1	1-0	—	Brevett (og) [14], Mackie [76]	4720
25	20	H	Gravesend & N	L	1-3	0-3	9	Challinor [84]	3287
26	23	H	Weymouth	W	4-0	1-0	—	Elam 3 [45, 60, 74], Challinor [81]	3474
27	27	A	Dagenham & R	L	1-4	0-0	9	Carlisle [61]	1816
28	Feb 3	A	Stafford R	W	1-0	1-0	7	Phillips [29]	970
29	10	H	Woking	W	1-0	0-0	5	Challinor [53]	3363
30	17	A	Kidderminster H	W	2-0	0-0	5	Challinor [54], Elam [88]	2033
31	20	H	Rushden & D	D	0-0	0-0	—		3135
32	24	H	Burton Alb	W	3-0	0-0	3	Jones B (pen) [69], Logan (pen) [76], Stansfield [90]	3475
33	Mar 3	A	Rushden & D	L	0-3	0-2	5		2344
34	6	H	Grays Ath	W	2-1	1-0	—	Buckle [39], Jones B [90]	2894
35	10	A	Halifax T	L	1-2	0-1	5	Jones B [58]	1599
36	17	H	Morecambe	W	1-0	0-0	4	Logan [74]	3530
37	20	A	Northwich Vic	L	0-1	0-0	—		784
38	24	H	York C	D	1-1	1-0	5	Jones B (pen) [25]	4410
39	27	A	Forest Green R	L	1-2	1-1	—	Elam [45]	1691
40	31	A	Altrincham	W	2-1	0-1	6	Logan [50], Jones B (pen) [80]	1100
41	Apr 3	A	Aldershot T	L	2-3	1-1	—	Elam [8], Seaborne [65]	2250
42	7	H	Tamworth	W	1-0	0-0	5	Carlisle [74]	4180
43	9	A	Crawley T	W	3-0	2-0	—	Elam [3], Carlisle 2 [34, 51]	1562
44	14	H	Cambridge U	W	2-0	1-0	4	Logan [32], Stansfield [56]	4364
45	21	A	Stevenage Bor	D	0-0	0-0	5		3058
46	28	H	Southport	W	2-1	0-1	5	Stansfield 2 [68, 71]	6670

Final League Position: 5

GOALSCORERS

League (67): Jones B 10 (4 pens), Challinor 9, Stansfield 9, Elam 7, Carlisle 5, Mackie 5, Logan 4 (1 pen), Phillips 4, Buckle 3, Moxey 2, Cozic 1, Edwards 1, Gill 1, Seaborne 1, Todd 1, own goals 4.
FA Cup (3): Challinor 1, Phillips 1, Taylor 1.
Trophy (3): Cozic 1, Gill 1, Jones B 1.
Play-Offs (3): Phillips 2, Stansfield 1.

Rice 25 + 1	Woodards 21 + 1	Jones B 46	Gill 46	Edwards 43	Todd 35	Taylor 26 + 4	Buckle 26 + 3	Stansfield 26 + 12	Mackie 22 + 18	Challinor 32 + 10	Cozic 15 + 15	Moxey 11 + 12	Phillips 21 + 15	Friend — + 2	Richardson 13 + 6	Clay 2 + 3	Seaborne 3 + 1	Ada 5 + 1	Jones P 21	Carlisle 21 + 3	Tully 17	Elam 19 + 1	Logan 10 + 7	Match No.
1	2	3	4	5	6	7	8	9	10^{1}	11^{2}	12	13												1
1	2	3	4	5	6	7	8^{1}	9	10^{3}	11^{2}	12	13	14											2
1	2^{1}	3	4	5	6	7	8^{2}	9^{3}	10	11	12	13	14											3
1	2	3	4	5	6	7	8	9^{3}	10^{2}	11^{1}	14	12	13											4
1	2^{1}	3	4	5	6	7		9^{3}	14	12	8	11^{2}	10	13										5
1		3	4	5	6	2	14	13	9^{2}	7^{1}	8	11	10^{3}	12										6
1	2	3	4	5^{1}	6	7^{2}		14	10^{3}	13	8	11	9		12									7
1	2	3	4	5	6^{1}	13		9^{3}	14	7	8	11^{2}	10		12									8
1	2	3	4	5	6	7		13	10^{2}	11^{1}	8	12	9											9
1	2	3	4	5		7	12		10		8^{1}	11	9		6									10
1	2	3	4	5		7^{1}	8^{2}	14	10^{3}	12		11	9		6	13								11
1	2	3	4	5		14	12	9^{3}	13	7	8^{1}	11^{2}	10		6									12
1	2	3	4			7	8^{2}	9^{3}	13	11		14	10		6		5^{1}	12						13
1	2	3	4	5		7		9	12	11			10^{1}		6	8								14
1	2	3	4	5		7^{1}		9	13	11		12	10^{2}		6	8								15
1	2	3	4	5		7	8	9^{3}	10^{2}	12		11^{1}	14		6	13								16
1	2	3	4	5		7^{1}	8^{2}	9^{3}	10	11		12	14		6	13								17
		3	4	5	6	7	8	12	9^{1}	11	13		10^{2}					2	1					18
	2	3	4	5	6	7^{1}	8	9^{2}	13	11		12	10						1					19
	2	3	4	5		7^{1}	8	9	14	11^{2}	12	13	10^{3}		6				1					20
	2^{1}	3	4	5		7	8	9	10	11					6				1	12				21
	12	3	4	5		7^{2}	8	9	10	11^{3}	14				6			2^{1}	1	13				22
	2	3	4	5	6		8		10	11^{1}	9^{2}	12			13				1	7				23
	2	3	4	5	6		8		10^{1}	13	9^{2}	11	12						1	7				24
1		3	4	5	6^{1}			12	10^{2}	11	8	13	9							7	2			25
1		3	4	5	6		8	13	14	10^{2}	12		9^{3}							7	2	11^{1}		26
1		3	4	5	6	7^{1}	8^{2}			9	13	11^{3}	10							12	2	14		27
		3	4^{1}	5	6		8			10	12		9						1	7	2	11		28
		3	4	5	6		8		13	10^{1}			9^{2}						1	7	2	11	12	29
		3	4	5	6		8		10	9									1	7	2	11		30
		3	4^{2}	5	6		8	12	10^{3}	9	13								1	7^{1}	2	11	14	31
		3	4	5	6		8^{2}	14	10^{3}	9	13	11							1	7^{1}	2		12	32
		3	4	5	6		8^{1}	9^{2}	13		12		14						1	7	2	11	10^{3}	33
		3	4	5	6		8^{2}	14	10^{3}	9	12								1	7^{1}	2	11	13	34
		3	4	5	6^{1}		8	13	10^{2}	9^{3}					12				1	7	2	11	14	35
		3	4	5	6		8^{1}			10^{2}	12		9		2				1	7		11	13	36
		3	4	5	6	12		13		10^{2}	8^{1}		9^{3}		2				1	7		11	14	37
		3	4	5	6			9^{3}	14	12	8		13					2	1	7^{1}		11^{2}	10	38
		3	4	5	6			9^{2}	14	12	8		13					2	1	7^{1}		11	10^{3}	39
		3	4	5	6	12		9^{2}	14	7	8		13						1		2	11^{1}	10^{3}	40
15		3	4	5^{1}	6			9	13	7	8						12		1■		2	11^{2}	10^{G}	41
1		3	4		6	8		9					12				5			7	2	11	10^{1}	42
1		3	4^{1}		6	8		9^{3}	14	12			13				5			7	2	11	10^{2}	43
1		3	4	5	6	8		9^{3}	14				13		12					7	2^{1}	11	10^{2}	44
1		3	4	5	6	8		9^{2}	13	12			14					2		7		11^{1}	10^{3}	45
1		3	4	5	6^{1}	8		9		12			14		13					7	2	11^{2}	10^{3}	46

FA Cup
Fourth Qualifying Round — AFC Wimbledon (h) 2-1
First Round — Stockport Co (h) 1-2

Trophy
First Round — Heybridge S (h) 3-0
Second Round — Kidderminster H (h) 0-1

Play-Offs
Semi-Final — Oxford U (h) 0-1; (a) 2-1
Final *(at Wembley)* — Morecambe 1-2

FOREST GREEN ROVERS Blue Square Premier

Ground: The Lawn, Nympsfield Road, Forest Green, Nailsworth GL6 0ET. *Tel:* (01453) 834 860.
Year Formed: 1890. *Record Gate:* 3,002 (1999 v St Albans City, FA Umbro Trophy). *Nickname:* Rovers.
Manager: Jim Harvey. *Secretary:* David Honeybill. *Colours:* Black and white striped shirts, black shorts, red stockings.

FOREST GREEN ROVERS 2006–07 LEAGUE RECORD

Match No.	Date	Venue	Opponents	Result		H/T Score	Lg. Pos.	Goalscorers	Attendance
1	Aug 12	H	Dagenham & R	L	0-1	0-1	—		1067
2	15	A	Exeter C	L	0-1	0-1	—		3527
3	19	A	Rushden & D	L	0-2	0-1	22		1693
4	26	H	Gravesend & N	L	0-1	0-1	23		881
5	28	A	Stevenage Bor	D	3-3	2-2	22	Russell [24], Clist [38], Butler [54]	1905
6	Sept 1	H	Woking	L	2-3	1-2	—	Evans (og) [28], Meechan [61]	1228
7	9	H	Cambridge U	D	1-1	1-0	23	Russell [17]	1139
8	12	A	Weymouth	L	0-1	0-0	—		1568
9	16	A	Tamworth	D	1-1	0-1	24	Clist [47]	1215
10	19	H	Altrincham	D	2-2	2-0	—	Rigoglioso [6], Clist [35]	910
11	23	A	Halifax T	D	2-2	1-2	23	Nicholson (pen) [42], Pitman [52]	1561
12	30	H	Stafford R	W	2-1	1-0	23	Russell [17], Rigoglioso [54]	945
13	Oct 3	A	St Albans C	D	0-0	0-0	—		806
14	6	H	Oxford U	L	1-5	1-2	—	Russell [38]	3021
15	10	H	Burton Alb	W	1-0	1-0	—	Rigoglioso [33]	888
16	14	A	Grays Ath	D	1-1	1-1	22	Stuart (og) [40]	910
17	21	H	Crawley T	W	1-0	0-0	20	Griffin [82]	1128
18	Nov 3	A	Kidderminster H	D	2-2	2-1	19	Meechan [15], Clist [45]	1661
19	11	H	St Albans C	D	2-2	1-1	19	Clist [44], Russell [61]	1003
20	18	H	Northwich Vic	W	2-1	1-0	16	Brough [34], Stonehouse [72]	869
21	25	A	Morecambe	D	1-1	1-1	17	Robinson M [28]	1561
22	Dec 2	H	York C	L	0-1	0-1	19		1125
23	9	H	Southport	L	1-2	0-1	20	Nicholson [90]	1090
24	26	A	Aldershot T	L	1-2	0-1	22	Nicholson [69]	2216
25	30	A	Altrincham	D	2-2	0-0	21	Giles [60], Butler [76]	912
26	Jan 1	H	Weymouth	W	3-2	3-0	—	Giles [18], Beesley [32], Afful [35]	1245
27	20	H	Tamworth	W	2-0	0-0	19	Nicholson (pen) [63], Williams D [68]	1049
28	23	H	Aldershot T	W	3-0	0-0	—	Nicholson (pen) [57], Beesley 2 [66, 82]	951
29	27	A	Southport	W	2-1	2-1	13	Clist [6], Beesley [19]	1104
30	Feb 3	A	Crawley T	L	1-3	0-0	14	Rigoglioso [79]	1076
31	10	H	Kidderminster H	W	2-1	0-1	14	Rigoglioso 2 [72, 85]	1211
32	17	A	Northwich Vic	L	0-2	0-0	15		773
33	24	H	Morecambe	L	1-3	1-2	15	Lawless [10]	1292
34	27	A	Cambridge U	D	1-1	1-0	—	Carey-Bertram [16]	2127
35	Mar 3	A	York C	D	0-0	0-0	14		2923
36	10	A	Oxford U	W	2-0	1-0	13	Carey-Bertram 2 [45, 59]	6157
37	12	A	Burton Alb	L	0-1	0-0	—		1522
38	17	A	Dagenham & R	D	1-1	0-1	13	Brough [74]	1800
39	27	H	Exeter C	W	2-1	1-1	—	Hardiker 2 [11, 90]	1691
40	31	H	Rushden & D	L	0-2	0-0	16		1110
41	Apr 3	H	Grays Ath	D	0-0	0-0	—		782
42	7	A	Gravesend & N	D	1-1	1-1	17	Carey-Bertram [34]	1063
43	9	H	Stevenage Bor	D	4-4	3-1	—	Clist [16], Stonehouse [19], Beesley [21], Dodgson [90]	969
44	14	A	Woking	D	3-3	3-0	16	Carey-Bertram 2 [13, 44], Nicholson [45]	1578
45	21	H	Halifax T	W	2-0	1-0	14	Carey-Bertram [21], Afful [77]	1664
46	28	A	Stafford R	W	1-0	0-0	14	Preece [54]	1791

Final League Position: 14

GOALSCORERS

League (59): Carey-Bertram 7, Clist 7, Nicholson 6 (3 pens), Rigoglioso 6, Beesley 5, Russell 5, Afful 2, Brough 2, Butler 2, Giles 2, Hardiker 2, Meechan 2, Stonehouse 2, Dodgson 1, Griffin 1, Lawless 1, Pitman 1, Preece 1, Robinson M 1, Williams D 1, own goals 2.
FA Cup (1): Nicholson 1.
Trophy (0).

Williams S 26	Lawless 33 + 5	Nicholson 44	Clist 44 + 1	Butler 6 + 3	Edwards 9 + 1	Pitman 23 + 9	Meechan 26 + 3	Russell 15 + 5	Griffin 5 + 9	Afful 25 + 16	Preece 19 + 11	Beesley 24 + 7	Zarczynski — + 3	Brough 39 + 1	Stonehouse 8 + 18	Williams D 11 + 7	Jones 40	Ipoua 2 + 5	Rigoglioso 9 + 2	Robinson M 11 + 1	Wanless 3 + 5	Giles 22 + 1	Hardiker 23	Carey-Bertram 14 + 6	Dodgson 4 + 9	Lamb 1 + 4	Harrison 2 + 1	Robinson R 18	*Match No.*
1	2	3	4	5	6^{1}	7	8^{2}	9^{3}	10	11	12	13	14																1
1	2	3	4^{1}	5		7	8	9	12	11^{2}	6			10	13														2
1	2	3	4^{1}	5		7	8	14	10^{3}	12	6	9^{2}	13	11															3
1	2	3	13	5	6	7^{2}	8	9	10^{3}	11^{1}						12	4	14											4
1	2	3	4	5	6	12	8	9		13				7^{1}			11	10^{2}											5
1	2^{1}	3	4^{2}	5	6	12	8	9		14				7		13	11	10^{3}											6
1	2	3	4		6	7	8	9^{3}		11^{1}				13	10^{2}	12	5	14											7
1	2	3	4		6	7	8	9^{3}	12	11^{1}				10^{2}	13		5	14											8
1	2	3	4		6	7	8	9^{3}	14	11^{1}			13	10^{2}	12		5												9
1	2	3	4		6	7	8	9^{2}		14				11^{1}	12		5	13	10^{3}										10
1	2	3	4		6^{1}	7	8	9^{2}		13	12			11			5	14	10^{3}										11
1	2	3	4			7	8^{1}	9^{2}		12	6	13		11			5		10^{3}	14									12
1		3	4			7^{1}	8	9		13	6	10^{3}		2	12^{2}		5			11	14								13
1	2	3	4				8	9		13	6	10^{2}		7^{1}	12		5			11									14
1	2	3	4				8			11^{2}	6	14		7	12	13	5		10^{3}	9^{1}									15
1	2	3	4	13			8	14		11^{1}	6			7^{2}		12	5		10^{3}	9									16
1	2	3^{1}	4				8^{3}		13	11	6			7	12	10^{2}	5			9	14								17
1	2	3	4^{2}		13		8		14	11^{1}	6	12		7		9^{3}	5			10									18
1	2	3^{1}	4				8	14	10^{3}	11	6	13		7			5			9		12^{2}							19
1	2	3^{1}	4				8	14	13	11^{2}		9^{3}		7	12		5			10		6							20
1	2	3	4				12	9^{2}	13	11^{1}	6						5			10		8	7						21
1	12		4				13	9	14	11		10^{3}		6	7^{2}		5			3		8	2^{1}						22
1	2	3					8	13	10^{3}	12				6		14	5			9^{2}	7^{1}	4	11						23
1		3	4	12			8^{3}			11	6^{1}	14		7	13	9					10^{2}	5	2						24
1		3	4	12■			13		14	11^{3}		9^{2}		7		8	5				10^{1}	6	2						25
1		3	4^{1}				8			11^{2}	14	9		7	13^{3}	10	5				12	6	2						26
	13	3	4			12^{2}	8^{3}			11		9		7^{1}		10	5					6	2	14				1	27
	13	3	4			7^{2}	8^{3}			11^{1}		9				10	5					6	2	12	14			1	28
	2^{2}	3^{1}	4			13	8^{3}			11		9				10	5		12			6	7	14				1	29
			4			7				11		9^{2}		6		8			13		12	3■	2	10^{3}	14■	5^{1}		1	30
		3^{1}	4			7				13		9		8		6	5		11				2	10^{2}		12		1	31
	2^{1}	3	4			7^{2}				11	12	9^{3}		8		13	5		10				6	14				1	32
	2^{1}	3	4							11	12	9^{3}		8	13	7^{2}	5		10				6	14				1	33
		3	4			7^{1}				14	13	9		8			5		11^{3}			6^{2}	2	10	12			1	34
		3	4			7				11^{2}	12	9		8	13		5^{1}					6	2	10^{3}	14			1	35
	2	3	4			7				14	12	9^{2}		8	13		5					6	11^{1}	10^{3}				1	36
	2	3	4			7^{2}				12	14	9		8	13		5					11	6^{1}	10^{3}				1	37
	2	3	4			7^{2}				11	6^{1}	14		10	9^{3}		5					8		12	13			1	38
	14	3	4			7^{3}					12	9		11	13		5					6^{1}	2	10	8^{2}			1	39
	2	3	4			7^{1}				12	14			8	13		5					6	11	10^{3}	9^{2}			1	40
	2	3	4			12					7	9^{3}		8^{1}	14		5					6		10	11^{2}	13		1	41
	2^{1}	3	4			7					8				9^{2}		5					6	11	10	12	13	15	1^{6}	42
	14	3	4			13					6	9		7^{1}	8^{3}		5■					11	2	10^{2}	12		1		43
	2	3^{2}	4			14					6	9		7	8							5^{1}	11	10^{3}	12	13	1		44
	2	3	4			12				13	6	9^{1}		7	8^{3}		5						11	10^{2}	14			1	45
	2^{1}	3	4			13				14	6	9		7^{2}	11^{3}		5				12			10	8			1	46

FA Cup
Fourth Qualifying Round — Stevenage B (a) 1-4

Trophy
First Round — Yeading (h) 0-1

GRAYS ATHLETIC

Blue Square Premier

Ground: Recreation Ground, Bridge Road, Grays RM17 6BZ. *Tel:* (01375) 391 649. *Year Formed:* 1890.
Record Gate: 9,500 (1959 v Chelmsford City, FA Cup). *Nickname:* The Blues. *Manager:* Justin Edinburgh.
Secretary: Phil O'Reilly. *Colours:* All sky blue.

GRAYS ATHLETIC 2006–07 LEAGUE RECORD

Match No.	Date	Venue	Opponents	Result		H/T Score	Lg. Pos.	Goalscorers	Attendance
1	Aug 12	H	Stafford R	D	1-1	1-1	—	Kightly [6]	1049
2	15	A	Rushden & D	W	3-1	1-1	—	Poole [30], McLean [61], Kightly [85]	2015
3	19	A	Halifax T	W	2-0	2-0	3	McLean [17], Kightly [42]	1589
4	26	H	Woking	W	3-0	2-0	3	McLean 2 [3, 44], Kightly [51]	1116
5	28	A	Northwich Vic	W	3-0	1-0	1	McLean [35], Stuart [51], Slabber [79]	874
6	Sept 1	H	Burton Alb	L	0-1	0-0	—		1367
7	9	H	Southport	W	4-0	3-0	2	McLean 2 [20, 29], Kightly 2 [42, 87]	1024
8	12	A	Gravesend & N	L	0-2	0-1	—		1200
9	16	A	Oxford U	D	1-1	1-1	4	McLean [38]	6504
10	19	H	Aldershot T	L	1-2	0-0	—	Kightly [71]	1279
11	23	A	Crawley T	W	1-0	0-0	4	McLean [63]	974
12	30	H	Morecambe	L	0-1	0-0	8		1056
13	Oct 3	H	Exeter C	D	2-2	0-1	—	Slabber [52], McLean [79]	1157
14	7	A	Kidderminster H	L	1-2	1-1	10	McLean [27]	1316
15	10	A	Tamworth	L	2-4	0-3	—	McLean [78], Green [87]	907
16	14	H	Forest Green R	D	1-1	1-1	11	Kightly [12]	910
17	21	A	St Albans C	W	6-0	1-0	9	Kightly 2 [41, 90], Green [56], McLean [58], Poole 2 [64, 65]	1045
18	Nov 3	H	Cambridge U	D	1-1	1-1	9	Boylan [45]	1163
19	18	A	Stevenage Bor	L	0-1	0-1	9		2207
20	25	H	Altrincham	D	1-1	0-1	11	Oli [67]	725
21	Dec 2	A	Weymouth	L	2-3	2-2	11	Boylan 2 [16, 38]	1451
22	9	H	York C	D	0-0	0-0	11		1139
23	26	A	Dagenham & R	D	0-0	0-0	12		1855
24	Jan 4	H	Gravesend & N	L	0-2	0-1	—		1071
25	6	A	Southport	L	1-3	0-2	15	Stuart [58]	810
26	20	H	Oxford U	D	2-2	0-1	15	Poole [63], Williamson [81]	1759
27	23	H	Dagenham & R	L	0-1	0-1	—		1504
28	27	A	York C	D	2-2	1-2	17	Poole [15], Harding [77]	2689
29	Feb 6	A	Aldershot T	L	0-1	0-0	—		1924
30	10	A	Cambridge U	L	0-2	0-1	20		2842
31	17	H	Stevenage Bor	L	0-2	0-1	21		1552
32	27	H	St Albans C	W	2-1	1-1	—	Oli [5], Grant [86]	803
33	Mar 3	H	Weymouth	D	2-2	1-0	20	Griffiths [43], Grant [79]	1003
34	6	A	Exeter C	L	1-2	0-1	—	Poole [48]	2894
35	13	H	Tamworth	W	1-0	1-0	—	Grant [42]	779
36	20	A	Altrincham	L	0-1	0-1	—		829
37	24	A	Stafford R	L	2-4	0-3	22	Thurgood (pen) [49], Rhodes [85]	865
38	27	H	Rushden & D	W	3-1	0-0	—	O'Connor 2 [48, 50], Oli [51]	762
39	31	H	Halifax T	W	1-0	0-0	20	O'Connor [66]	801
40	Apr 3	A	Forest Green R	D	0-0	0-0	—		782
41	7	A	Woking	L	0-1	0-1	21		1834
42	9	H	Northwich Vic	W	1-0	1-0	—	O'Connor [45]	776
43	14	A	Burton Alb	L	0-3	0-2	21		1419
44	21	H	Crawley T	D	0-0	0-0	20		1131
45	24	H	Kidderminster H	W	3-0	2-0	—	Thurgood (pen) [7], Downer [43], Griffiths [90]	846
46	28	A	Morecambe	L	0-1	0-1	19		2303

Final League Position: 19

GOALSCORERS

League (56): McLean 13, Kightly 10, Poole 6, O'Connor 4, Boylan 3, Grant 3, Oli 3, Green 2, Griffiths 2, Slabber 2, Stuart 2, Thurgood 2 (2 pens), Downer 1, Harding 1, Rhodes 1, Williamson 1.
FA Cup (1): Boylan 1.
Trophy (13): Martin 5, Turner 2, Boylan 1, Cadamarteri 1, Grant 1, Poole 1, Rhodes 1, Thurgood 1.

Bayes 36	Sambrook 36	Green 17 + 1	Stuart 46	Smith 20 + 2	Nicholls 33 + 2	Kightly 18	Martin 31 + 5	Boylan 16 + 5	McLean 17	Poole 30 + 6	Oli 31 + 5	Slabber 2 + 10	Williamson 11 + 7	Turner 1 + 10	Mawer 8 + 2	Sangere 6 + 2 / Tonkin 11 + 1	Thurgood 20 + 3	Plummer 3 / Barness 3 + 3	Bull 3	Richards 5 / Rhodes 6 + 6	Coutts — + 1	Comyn-Platt 4 / Joseph-Dubois — + 1	Kamara 2 + 2	Cadamarteri 1 / Downer	Bodkin 9 + 3	Cowan 8	Harding 11 + 8	Fernandez 1 + 1	O'Connor 14 + 1	El Kholti 4 + 2	Knowles 10 + 1	Howell 3 + 6	Grant 7	Molango 1 + 1	Eribenne 2 + 2	Griffiths 6 + 7	Kemp 4	Match No.
1	2	3	4	5	6	7	8	9^1	10	11	12																											1
1	2	3	4	5	6	7	8	9^1	10	11	12																											2
1	2	3	4	5	6	7	8	9^2	10^1	11	13	12																										3
1	2	3	4	5	6	7	8		10^2	11^1	9^3	13	12	14																								4
1	2	3	4	5	6	7	8		10^2	11	9^1	12		13																								5
1	2	3	4	5^1	6	7	8^2	12	10	11	9	13																										6
1		3	4	5	6	7	8^1	13	10^3	11	9^2		12	14	2																							7
1	2	3^1	4	5	6	7	8	12	10	11	9																											8
1	2	3	4	5■	6	7		9^3	10^2	11	8^1	13	12			14																						9
1		3^2	4		6	7		9	10	11	8	13	12		2^1	5																						10
1		3	4		6	7		9^2	10	11	8	13	12		2^1	5																						11
1	2	3^1	4		6	7	13	9	10	11^2	8	12				5																						12
1	2		4	5	6	7		13	10	12	8^1	9^2	11			3																						13
1	2		4	5^1	6	7	13	9^2	10	11		8	3			12																						14
1	2	3	4		6	7	8^1		10	11	9					5	12																					15
1	2	3	4		6^2	7^1	8		10	11	9	12					13	5																				16
1	2	3	4		6	7	8^1	14	10^3	11^2	9	13					12	5																				17
1			4	5	12	7^2	8	9		13	11						6	2	3^1	10																		18
1		3^1	4	5			8	9		11	7			13		6	2			10^2	12																	19
1		3	4	5			8^1	9^2		11	7		12	13			2			10		6																20
1	2	13	4	5			12	9^2		11	7^1		8				6			10		3																21
1	2		4	5^1	6		14			11	13^3		3				8			10^2		7	12	9														22
1	2		4		6		8^1	9^2		12			7	13					3			5	11		10													23
1	2		4		6^2			9^3		11			7	12					3				8^1		10	5	13	14										24
1	2		4		12		8			11			7	6^3									13		10^2	5	14	3^1	9									25
1	2		4	5^1	6			9		11			13	14			7^2								12	3	8		10^3									26
1	2		4				12	9		11			6	13											7^1	5	8		10^2	3								27
	2		4	12	6		8			11				13	14										9^3	5^1	7		10^2	3	1							28
1	2		4		6		8			11					7^1											5	3					12	10^2	13	9			29
1	2		4	5	6^2		8			12	14																13			3		11	10	7^1	9^3			30
1	2■		4		6		8			14	10^3				12											5^1			13	3		11	7^2			9		31
1			4	5			8			11^2	10^3		6^1		2		7									3	12			13			9			14		32
1			6	5^1			8			11					3	12	7										4^2						9		13	10	2	33
1			4	12			8			11^2					2	3	6										7					13	9^3		14	10	5^1	34
1	2		4				8^1			13	10^3				5	3	6	12		9							11^2						7			14		35
1	2		4		6					11	10					3				9^2					7^1		8					12				13	5	36
1	2		4								10					3	6			13		14			7^2		8		9^3		12	11					5^1	37
	2		4		6		8^2				11					3	7	12		10^3				5^1			13		9		1					14		38
	2		4		6		8^1				11					3	7			13				5			12		9		1					10^2		39
	2		4								7		11			3	6			13				5			8		9^2		1	12				10^1		40
	2		4								7		11^1				6	3		13				5			8		9		1	12				10^2		41
			4		6		8				10^3					3	7	2		11^1				5			14		9^2		1	12				13		42
	2		4		6		8				10					3■	7			11^1				5	12				9		1							43
	2		4		6		8				10						7	3		11^2				5^1	13				9	12	1							44
	2		4		6		8				10^2					3	7	12		14				5^1	11^3				9		1					13		45
	2		4		6^1		8				10^2					3	7			13				5	11^3		12		9		1					14		46

FA Cup
Fourth Qualifying Round Bromley (h) 1-2

Trophy

First Round	Weymouth	(a)	2-1
Second Round	Weston-Super-Mare	(a)	4-0
Third Round	Yeading	(h)	2-1
Fourth Round	Welling U	(a)	4-1
Semi-Final	Stevenage B	(h)	0-1
		(a)	1-2

HALIFAX TOWN

Blue Square Premier

Ground: The Shay Stadium, Shay Syke, Halifax, West Yorkshire HX1 2YS. *Tel:* (01422) 341 222.
Year Formed: 1911. *Record Gate:* 36,885 (1953 v Tottenham Hotspur, FA Cup Fifth Round).
Nickname: The Shaymen. *Manager:* Chris Wilder *Secretary:* Jenna Helliwell. *Colours:* All blue.

HALIFAX TOWN 2006–07 LEAGUE RECORD

Match No.	Date	Venue	Opponents	Result		H/T Score	Lg. Pos.	Goalscorers	Attendance
1	Aug 12	A	Oxford U	L	0-2	0-1	—		5785
2	15	H	Southport	D	1-1	0-0	—	Smeltz [90]	2002
3	19	H	Grays Ath	L	0-2	0-2	20		1589
4	26	A	Cambridge U	W	2-1	1-0	16	Roberts [14], Quinn [66]	2056
5	28	H	Morecambe	D	1-1	1-0	16	Torpey [45]	1909
6	Sept 2	A	Aldershot T	L	0-1	0-0	19		2330
7	9	H	Gravesend & N	D	1-1	1-1	16	Sugden [45]	1435
8	12	A	Altrincham	L	0-1	0-1	—		1036
9	16	A	Weymouth	L	0-1	0-1	20		1910
10	19	H	Dagenham & R	W	3-1	2-0	—	Wright [42], Sugden [45], Forrest [73]	1268
11	23	H	Forest Green R	D	2-2	2-1	19	Sugden [25], Forrest [34]	1561
12	30	A	Stevenage Bor	L	1-2	1-1	21	Sugden [32]	1904
13	Oct 3	H	Kidderminster H	W	2-0	1-0	—	Campbell [37], Wright [84]	1438
14	7	A	Exeter C	L	1-4	1-1	18	Killeen [17]	3114
15	10	A	Rushden & D	W	1-0	1-0	—	Torpey [2]	1839
16	14	H	Tamworth	W	3-1	2-1	14	Torpey 2 [11, 49], Sugden [34]	1646
17	21	H	Burton Alb	L	1-2	1-1	16	Torpey [30]	1844
18	Nov 3	A	Northwich Vic	L	2-3	2-0	17	Forrest [15], Torpey [27]	1150
19	18	H	Stafford R	W	3-1	1-0	15	Joynes [3], Killeen 2 [53, 68]	1681
20	25	A	Crawley T	L	0-2	0-1	16		1062
21	Dec 2	H	Woking	W	3-0	1-0	14	Uhlenbeek [38], Joynes [75], Forrest [78]	1536
22	9	H	St Albans C	W	4-1	1-1	12	Atkinson 2 [20, 61], Smeltz [79], Senior [89]	1617
23	23	A	York C	L	0-2	0-1	—		3588
24	30	A	Dagenham & R	L	0-1	0-0	14		1261
25	Jan 1	H	Altrincham	D	1-1	1-1	—	Joynes [42]	1791
26	23	H	York C	D	1-1	0-0	—	Ainsworth [69]	2308
27	27	A	St Albans C	L	2-3	1-2	19	Bastians [35], Stamp [90]	1009
28	Feb 17	A	Stafford R	W	3-2	3-1	19	Stamp [25], Bastians [32], Trotman [45]	1062
29	20	H	Weymouth	W	4-1	1-1	—	Bastians [34], Trotman [50], Uhlenbeek 2 [63, 90]	1277
30	27	H	Northwich Vic	L	0-2	0-0	—		1221
31	Mar 3	A	Woking	D	2-2	1-0	18	Bastians [22], Hutchinson (og) [90]	1419
32	6	A	Kidderminster H	L	0-1	0-1	—		1203
33	10	H	Exeter C	W	2-1	1-0	15	Strong [5], Forrest [79]	1599
34	13	H	Rushden & D	D	0-0	0-0	—		1314
35	17	A	Tamworth	L	0-1	0-1	17		1337
36	21	H	Oxford U	D	1-1	0-0	—	Forrest [71]	1473
37	27	A	Southport	D	1-1	0-1	—	Stamp [90]	936
38	31	A	Grays Ath	L	0-1	0-0	22		801
39	Apr 3	A	Gravesend & N	L	0-2	0-1	—		946
40	7	H	Cambridge U	W	1-0	1-0	19	Torpey [33]	1942
41	9	A	Morecambe	L	0-4	0-1	—		2412
42	14	H	Aldershot T	W	2-0	1-0	18	Campbell [45], Forrest [90]	1611
43	17	A	Burton Alb	L	0-1	0-0	—		1436
44	21	A	Forest Green R	L	0-2	0-1	21		1664
45	24	H	Crawley T	W	2-1	0-0	—	Stamp [60], Quinn [72]	1561
46	28	H	Stevenage Bor	W	2-1	1-0	16	Campbell 2 [36, 83]	2515

Final League Position: 16

GOALSCORERS

League (55): Forrest 7, Torpey 7, Sugden 5, Bastians 4, Campbell 4, Stamp 4, Joynes 3, Killeen 3, Uhlenbeek 3, Atkinson 2, Quinn 2, Smeltz 2, Trotman 2, Wright 2, Ainsworth 1, Roberts 1, Senior 1, Strong 1, own goal 1.
FA Cup (0).
Trophy (11): Killeen 2, Smeltz 2, Stamp 2, Atkinson 1, Foster 1 (pen), Joynes 1, Senior 1, Trotman 1.

Mawson 46	Haslam 20	Doughty 29 + 4	Foster 20 + 3	Roberts 12 + 1	Quinn 31 + 1	Smeltz 13 + 18	Forrest 38 + 2	Senior 4 + 14	Sugden 16 + 7	Thompson 33 + 5	Campbell 12 + 10	Torpey 17 + 10	Wright 22 + 5	Uhlenbeek 23 + 7	Killeen 39 + 4	Fry 2 + 2	Young 10 + 1	Kearney 28 + 2	Gray 2 + 5	Toulson 11 + 4	Matthews 3	Atkinson 4	Joynes 5 + 2	Trotman 11	Ainsworth 2	Bastians 8 + 1	Stamp 14 + 4	Cresswell 14 + 1	Billy 10 + 3	Parke — + 3	Strong 7 + 1	*Match No.*
1	2	3	4	5	6	7	8	9^1	10^2	11	12	13																				1
1	2	3	4	5	6	7	8	9^1	10^2	11	13	12																				2
1	2		4	5	6	7^3	8	9^2	14	11^1	13		3	12	10																	3
1			4	5	6	7^3	8^1		13	11	10^2		3	2	9	12	14															4
1		3	4	5	6	12	8		10^3	11^2	14	7^1		2	9	13																5
1		12	4	5	6	14	8^2		10^3		11	13	3^1	2	9	7																6
1		3	4	5	6			14	10	13	11^3	7^1	12	2	9	8^2																7
1		11^1	4	5	6	14		13	10^2	7	9^3	12	3	2	8																	8
1			4	5^1	6	14	8^2	13	10^3	11	12		3	2	9		7															9
1			4		6	12	8	13	10^1	11	9^2		3	2	7		5															10
1		12	4		6	13	8		10^2	11	9		3^1	2	7		5															11
1			4	5			8	12	10		9^2		3	2	11		6	7^1	13													12
1			4		6		8	14	10		9^3	11^2	3	2	13		5	7^1	12													13
1					6	12	8	13	10	11		7^2	3		9		5		4	2^1												14
1		3	4	12	6	7^3	8		14	11		10^2			9		5^1		13		2											15
1		3	4	5	6	14	8^1	12	10^3	11		7^2			9			13			2											16
1		3	4	5	6	13	8	12	10^2	11		7^1			9						2											17
1		3			6	13	8	14	10^3	11		7^1	5		9^2			4	12	2												18
1		3			6	7^2	12	14	13	11				8^1	9			4		2		5	10^3									19
1					6	7^3	12	13	14	11			3	8^1	9			4		2		5	10^2									20
1		3	13		6		8	12	14	11				7^1	9^2			4		2		5	10^3									21
1		3	4		6	13	8	12		11					9			7^1		2		5	10^2									22
1		3	12		6	7^2	10■			11				8^1	9		5	4		2			13									23
1		3	14		6	7			10^1	11^2		13		8	9		5	2	4^3				12									24
1		3	4		6			10^3	14			8	12	7^2	9		5^1	2		13			11									25
1		3	4		6	7	8								9			11^1	12	2				5	10							26
1		3^1	4		6		8^2			12				14	9			11		2				5	10^3	7	13					27
1		3			6^1	14	8			11				2	9			4						5		7^2	10^3	12	13			28
1	2	3					8			11■			14	7	9^3			12						5		10^2		6	4^1	13		29
1	2	12											3	7	9			8						5^1		11	10^2	6	4	13		30
1	2	3				14	8					13	5		9			7		12						11^2	10^3	6^1	4			31
1	2	3				7	8			11		9^2	5	10^1				4		6						13				12		32
1	2					14	8			12			3	13	9			4								11^2	10^3	6	7^1		5	33
1	2					7^3	8			11			3	12	9			4								10^1	13	6			5	34
1	2					12	8			11		13	3		9^1											7^2	10	6	4		5	35
1	2						8			13	14	12	3	7^1	9			4									10^3	6	11^2		5	36
1	2				12		8				14	13	3	7^2	9^3			4									10	6	11		5^1	37
1	2	12					8			11	13	9^3	3		14			4									10	6	7^2		5^1	38
1	2	3				12	8			7	14	13	11^2		9^3												10	6	4		5^1	39
1	2	3			6		8^1			11	13	7^2	12	14	9			4						5			10^3					40
1		3			6		8			14	9^3	10		7^1	12			4		2							13	5	11^2			41
1	2	3				13	8			11	9^3	10^1			12			4						6			7^2	5	14			42
1	2	3				12	8			11	10■				9			4						6			7^1	5				43
1	2	3				7	8			11		10^2	12		9			4						6			13	5^1				44
1	2	3			6		8^1			11		10^2		12	9			4		14				5			7^3				13	45
1	2	3			6					11	8^3	10^1		12	9			4		13				5			7^2		14			46

FA Cup

Fourth Qualifying Round	Burton Alb	(a)	0-1

Trophy

First Round	Hyde U	(h)	3-1
Second Round	Oxford U	(a)	2-2
		(h)	2-1
Third Round	Redditch U	(h)	3-1
Fourth Round	Kidderminster H	(a)	1-3

KIDDERMINSTER HARRIERS Blue Square Premier

Ground: Aggborough Stadium, Hoo Road, Kidderminster DY10 1NB. *Tel:* (01562) 823 951. *Year Formed:* 1886. *Record Gate:* 9,155 (1948 v Hereford U). *Nickname:* Harriers. *Manager:* Mark Yates. *Secretary:* Roger Barlow. *Colours:* Red shirts, white shorts, red stockings.

KIDDERMINSTER HARRIERS 2006–07 LEAGUE RECORD

Match No.	Date	Venue	Opponents	Result	H/T Score	Lg. Pos.	Goalscorers	Attendance
1	Aug 12	H	St Albans C	L 1-3	0-3	—	Kenna [90]	1806
2	15	A	Burton Alb	D 1-1	0-1	—	Penn [57]	1880
3	19	A	Northwich Vic	W 1-0	1-0	12	Reynolds [35]	976
4	26	H	Weymouth	L 0-1	0-1	15		1753
5	28	A	Woking	L 0-3	0-2	18		1544
6	Sept 1	H	Rushden & D	D 0-0	0-0	—		1850
7	9	H	Tamworth	L 0-2	0-0	21		1641
8	12	A	Cambridge U	D 1-1	0-0	—	Russell [89]	1860
9	16	A	York C	L 0-1	0-1	21		2181
10	19	H	Southport	W 2-0	0-0	—	White [49], Hurren [74]	1258
11	23	A	Morecambe	W 1-0	0-0	15	Christie [73]	1496
12	30	H	Crawley T	L 0-1	0-0	18		1458
13	Oct 3	A	Halifax T	L 0-2	0-1	—		1438
14	7	H	Grays Ath	W 2-1	1-1	15	Reid [15], Christie (pen) [63]	1316
15	10	H	Oxford U	D 0-0	0-0	—		2264
16	14	A	Aldershot T	L 2-4	2-1	19	Christie 2 [42, 44]	2182
17	21	A	Dagenham & R	W 3-1	0-1	17	Russell [50], Reid [71], White [89]	1874
18	Nov 3	H	Forest Green R	D 2-2	1-2	14	Christie 2 (1 pen) [23, 90 (p)]	1661
19	18	A	Exeter C	D 1-1	1-1	17	Penn [2]	3082
20	25	H	Stevenage Bor	L 1-2	0-1	19	Christie [47]	1584
21	Dec 2	A	Gravesend & N	W 3-1	2-0	16	Harkness 2 [20, 57], Constable [22]	1160
22	9	H	Altrincham	W 3-2	2-1	14	Constable [29], Christie (pen) [41], Harkness [65]	1455
23	26	A	Stafford R	W 2-1	1-0	11	Constable 2 [42, 57]	1758
24	30	A	Southport	W 1-0	0-0	11	Reynolds [84]	1016
25	Jan 1	H	Cambridge U	W 1-0	0-0	—	Hurren [65]	1922
26	20	H	York C	W 2-1	1-0	10	Constable [14], Blackwood [56]	2073
27	23	H	Stafford R	W 2-0	1-0	—	Russell [9], Penn [53]	1573
28	27	A	Altrincham	W 1-0	1-0	7	Smikle [13]	1116
29	Feb 10	A	Forest Green R	L 1-2	1-0	10	Harkness [23]	1211
30	17	H	Exeter C	L 0-2	0-0	10		2033
31	20	H	Dagenham & R	L 1-4	1-1	—	Blackwood [8]	1383
32	Mar 3	H	Gravesend & N	L 1-2	0-1	11	Reynolds [54]	1508
33	6	H	Halifax T	W 1-0	1-0	—	Toulson (og) [31]	1203
34	13	A	Oxford U	W 1-0	0-0	—	Russell [86]	4542
35	20	A	Tamworth	D 0-0	0-0	—		1115
36	24	A	St Albans C	D 1-1	1-1	10	Constable [34]	821
37	27	H	Burton Alb	D 0-0	0-0	—		1635
38	31	H	Northwich Vic	L 0-1	0-1	11		1621
39	Apr 3	A	Stevenage Bor	W 2-1	2-0	—	Penn [21], Christie (pen) [32]	1753
40	7	A	Weymouth	D 1-1	1-1	11	Hurren [12]	1439
41	9	H	Woking	L 0-1	0-1	—		1479
42	14	A	Rushden & D	W 1-0	1-0	11	Penn [41]	1925
43	17	H	Aldershot T	D 0-0	0-0	—		1215
44	21	H	Morecambe	L 0-1	0-1	11		1654
45	24	A	Grays Ath	L 0-3	0-2	—		846
46	28	A	Crawley T	D 0-0	0-0	10		1664

Final League Position: 10

GOALSCORERS

League (43): Christie 9 (4 pens), Constable 6, Penn 5, Harkness 4, Russell 4, Hurren 3, Reynolds 3, Blackwood 2, Reid 2, White 2, Kenna 1, Smikle 1, own goal 1.
FA Cup (6): White 2, Christie 1, Hurren 1, Nelthorpe 1, Penn 1.
Trophy (21): Constable 9, Christie 2, Hurren 2, Penn 2, Russell 2, Blackwood 1, Creighton 1, Reynolds 1, White 1.

Bevan 40	Kenna 29	Cowan 5	Lee 5	Creighton 46	Whitehead 43	McClen 5	Penn 40 + 1	White 10 + 16	Sturridge 2 + 4	Blackwood 38 + 6	Russell 34 + 8	Smikle 11 + 17	Reynolds 12 + 28	Hurren 34 + 5	Sedgemore 23 + 7	Harkness 29 + 2	Christie 32 + 2	McGrath 7 + 6	Taylor B 4 + 2	Eaton 1 + 1	Bignot 3	Reid 6	Nelthorpe 4	Davies 4	Constable 21 + 2	Craven — + 1	Hay 3 + 7	Ferrell 1	Brady 6 + 3	Wilson 6	Taylor S 2 + 1	*Match No.*
1	2	3	4^{1}	5	6	7^{2}	8	9^{3}	10	11	12	13	14																			1
1	2^{1}	3	4	5	6		8	13		11		10	9^{2}	12	7																	2
1		3	4^{1}	5	6		8	13	12^{2}	11	14	10^{3}	9	2	7																	3
1	2	3	4	5	6		8	14	13	11	12	7^{1}	9^{3}		10^{2}																	4
1		3^{1}	4^{2}	5	6		8	9^{3}	10	11	7	13	14	2		12																5
1	2			5	6	7^{1}	8		13	11		10	12		4	3	9^{2}															6
1	2			5	6		8		13^{3}	11		7	9^{2}	14	4	3^{1}	10	12														7
1	2			5	6	7^{1}	8	14			12		9^{2}	4		3	10^{3}	11	13													8
1	2^{1}			5	6	7^{2}	8			14	13		9	4	12	3	10	11^{3}														9
1				5	6		8	9^{3}		13	7^{1}	12		2	4	3	10	11^{2}		14												10
1				5	6		8	9^{3}		13	7^{1}	12	14	4	2	3	10	11^{2}														11
1				5	6	7^{2}		9^{3}		11	8	13	14	4	2^{1}	3	10		12													12
1				5	6		8	9^{3}		12	11	7^{2}	14	4	2	3^{1}	10	13														13
1				5	6		8	14		11	7	13		4	12		10	3^{2}			2^{1}	9^{3}										14
1				5	6		8			11	7			4	12		10				2■	9	3^{1}									15
1				5	6		8	12		11	7^{1}		13	2	3		10	14				9^{2}	4^{3}									16
1				5	6		8	14		3	7	12	13	4	2		10^{2}					9^{3}	11^{1}									17
1				5	6		8	14		3	7	13	12	4			10				2^{1}	9^{3}	11^{2}									18
1	2			5	6		8			3	7			4			10					9■		11								19
1	2^{1}			5	6^{2}		8	14		3	7	12		4		13	10							11^{3}	9							20
1	2			5			8	12		11	6		13	4		3	10^{1}							7	9^{2}							21
1	2			5			8			11	7		12	4		3	10^{1}							6	9							22
1	2			5	6		8	12		11	7		13	4		3	10^{1}								9^{2}							23
1	2			5	6		8	13		11	7^{1}	12	14	4		3	10^{2}								9^{3}							24
1	2			5	6		8	14		11^{2}	7^{1}	12	10^{3}	4		3		13							9							25
1	2			5	6		8	14		11	7^{1}	12	13	4		3	10^{2}								9^{3}							26
1	2			5	6		8	9^{3}		11	7	12	14	4^{2}	13	3^{1}									10							27
1	2			5	6			9^{3}		11	7	3	14	4^{1}	8			13							10	12^{2}						28
1				5	6		8	9^{1}		11	7	2	12		4	3									10							29
1	2			5	6		8	9^{2}		11	7^{1}	12	14	4		3									10^{3}		13					30
1	2			5	6		8	14		11	7^{1}	12	13	4		3									10^{2}		9^{3}					31
1	2			5			8			11	7		9	4	6	3									10							32
1	2			5	6		8	14		11	7		13	4^{1}	12	3	9^{2}								10^{3}							33
	2			5	6		8			11	7	12	14	4	13	3^{1}	9^{3}		1						10^{2}							34
	2			5	6		8			11	7^{1}	12	13		4	3	9^{2}		1						10^{3}		14					35
				5	6■		8			11^{2}	12		13			3	9		1						10■			7	4^{1}	2		36
	2			5	6		8			11^{1}	7		10^{2}	4		3	9		1								13		12			37
1				5	6		8			14	7		10	4^{2}	13	3	9										12		11^{3}	2^{1}		38
1	2			5	6		8			11	7^{2}		13	12	4	3^{1}	9													10		39
1	2			5	6		8^{2}			11	7		14	4	3		9^{3}								13				12	10^{1}		40
1	2			5	6^{1}		13			11^{3}	14			4	8^{2}		9								10		12		7	3		41
1				5	6		8			12		7	13	4	2	3	9^{2}								10^{3}		14		11^{1}			42
1				5	6						8	7	9^{3}	12	4	3■	14								13		10^{2}		11^{1}	2		43
1■	2			5	6					11	8^{G}	7^{1}	13	4	3		9^{2}	12							10						15	44
	2			5	6					11	7		14		4	3■	9^{3}	8^{1}							10^{2}		12		13		1	45
				5	6		8			11^{1}	13		9	12	4		14	7		3^{2}							10^{3}		2		1	46

FA Cup

Fourth Qualifying Round — Droylsden (h) 5-1

First Round — Morecambe (a) 1-2

Second Round — Exeter C (a) 1-0

Third Round — Braintree T (h) 0-0, (a) 3-1

Fourth Round — Halifax T (h) 3-1

Semi-Final — Northwich Vic (h) 2-0, (a) 2-3

Final *(at Wembley)* — Stevenage B 2-3

Trophy

First Round — Vauxhall M (h) 4-4, (a) 4-0

MORECAMBE

FL Championship 2

Ground: Christie Park, Lancaster Road, Morecambe, Lancashire LA4 5TJ. *Tel:* (01524) 411 797. *Year Formed:* 1920. *Record Gate:* 9,326 (1962 v Weymouth, FA Cup Third Round). *Nickname:* The Shrimps. *Manager:* Sammy McIlroy. *Secretary:* Neil Marsdin. *Colours:* Red shirts, white shorts, black stockings.

MORECAMBE 2006–07 LEAGUE RECORD

Match No.	Date	Venue	Opponents	Result		H/T Score	Lg. Pos.	Goalscorers	Attendance
1	Aug 12	H	Burton Alb	L	0-1	0-0	—		1907
2	15	A	Northwich Vic	W	2-0	1-0	—	Twiss 2 28, 90	1346
3	19	A	Woking	D	1-1	0-0	9	McNiven 90	1222
4	26	H	Stevenage Bor	D	3-3	1-2	12	Twiss 2 24, 48, Carlton 50	1524
5	28	A	Halifax T	D	1-1	0-1	11	Twiss 61	1909
6	Sept 2	H	Weymouth	W	2-0	1-0	10	Meadowcroft 30, Curtis 61	1333
7	9	H	Oxford U	L	0-3	0-2	13		2314
8	12	A	York C	W	3-2	2-0	—	Twiss 2 20, 75, Thompson 40	2233
9	16	A	Dagenham & R	L	1-2	1-1	12	Carlton 43	1237
10	19	H	Tamworth	D	0-0	0-0	—		1248
11	23	H	Kidderminster H	L	0-1	0-0	12		1496
12	30	A	Grays Ath	W	1-0	0-0	11	McNiven 57	1056
13	Oct 3	H	Rushden & D	W	1-0	0-0	—	Carlton 52	1252
14	7	A	Crawley T	L	0-4	0-2	11		890
15	10	A	Altrincham	W	2-0	1-0	—	McLachlan 23, Carlton 81	1085
16	14	H	Exeter C	D	2-2	1-1	10	Carlton 38, Stanley 75	1582
17	21	A	Aldershot T	W	1-0	1-0	8	Osano (og) 45	2394
18	Nov 3	H	Gravesend & N	W	1-0	1-0	8	Smith R (og) 43	1429
19	18	A	Cambridge U	W	3-1	1-0	6	Twiss 2 14, 64, Curtis 59	3142
20	25	H	Forest Green R	D	1-1	1-1	6	Thompson 14	1561
21	Dec 9	H	Stafford R	W	1-0	1-0	6	Thompson 40	1373
22	26	A	Southport	W	2-1	0-1	6	Blackburn 77, Yates 80	1804
23	30	A	Tamworth	W	1-0	0-0	5	Curtis 64	1029
24	Jan 1	H	York C	L	1-3	0-1	—	Blackburn 77	2203
25	6	A	Oxford U	D	0-0	0-0	6		5489
26	20	H	Dagenham & R	D	1-1	1-0	6	Thompson 27	1711
27	23	H	Southport	D	0-0	0-0	—		1484
28	27	A	Stafford R	W	3-1	3-0	5	Twiss 10, Yates 32, Thompson 40	957
29	Feb 10	A	Gravesend & N	L	1-2	1-1	6	Stanley 14	1156
30	17	H	Cambridge U	D	2-2	0-1	6	Bentley 61, Lloyd 82	1493
31	24	A	Forest Green R	W	3-1	2-1	6	Lloyd 23, Carlton 36, Thompson 87	1292
32	Mar 3	H	St Albans C	W	2-0	1-0	6	Blinkhorn 16, Thompson 90	1415
33	6	A	Rushden & D	D	2-2	0-1	—	Hope (og) 74, Curtis 76	1701
34	10	H	Crawley T	W	1-0	1-0	4	Thompson 34	1374
35	13	H	Altrincham	L	0-1	0-1	—		1403
36	17	A	Exeter C	L	0-1	0-0	6		3530
37	20	H	Aldershot T	W	2-1	2-0	—	Blinkhorn 9, Sorvel 19	1165
38	24	A	Burton Alb	L	1-2	0-2	6	Curtis (pen) 81	1732
39	27	H	Northwich Vic	W	2-1	1-0	—	Blinkhorn 20, Blackburn 72	1315
40	31	H	Woking	W	2-0	1-0	3	Blinkhorn 2 15, 48	1466
41	Apr 3	A	St Albans C	W	2-0	1-0	—	McNiven 37, Blinkhorn 81	613
42	7	A	Stevenage Bor	D	3-3	1-1	3	Curtis 45, Fuller (og) 53, Thompson 65	1845
43	9	H	Halifax T	W	4-0	1-0	—	Blinkhorn 2 39, 89, Sorvel 60, Thompson 87	2412
44	14	A	Weymouth	L	1-2	1-1	3	Carlton 42	1206
45	21	A	Kidderminster H	W	1-0	1-0	3	Thompson (pen) 42	1654
46	28	H	Grays Ath	W	1-0	1-0	3	Lloyd 2	2303

Final League Position: 3

GOALSCORERS

League (64): Thompson 11 (1 pen), Twiss 10, Blinkhorn 8, Carlton 7, Curtis 6 (1 pen), Blackburn 3, Lloyd 3, McNiven 3, Sorvel 2, Stanley 2, Yates 2, Bentley 1, McLachlan 1, Meadowcroft 1, own goals 4.
FA Cup (4): Curtis 1 (pen), McNiven 1, Stanley 1, Twiss 1.
Trophy (8): Twiss 3, Curtis 1, Howard 1, Hunter 1, Thompson 1 (pen), Walker 1.
Play-Offs (4): Curtis 2, Carlton 1, Thompson 1.

Drench 41	Brannan 17 + 14	Howard 31 + 1	Stanley 37 + 6	Bentley 31	Blackburn 39 + 1	Thompson 35	Hunter 27 + 7	Twiss 30	Carlton 27 + 5	Perkins 20	Yates 43 + 1	McNiven 13 + 14	Rigoglioso 7 + 3	Meadowcroft 7 + 5	McLachlan 10 + 5	Davies 1 + 2	Robinson 4	Curtis 28 + 2	Shaw — + 4	Lloyd 4 + 4	Platt 1 + 3	Burns 4 + 10	Walmsley — + 1	Walker 1 + 4	Sorvel 19	Watt 1 + 2	Adams 16	Blinkhorn 12	*Match No.*
1	2^{1}	3	4	5	6	7^{2}	8^{3}	9	10	11	12	13	14																1
1	12	3	4		6	7	8	9	10	11^{2}	2			5^{1}	13														2
1^{6}	12	3	4		6	7	8	9	10^{2}	11^{1}	2	13		5		15													3
		3	4		6	7	8	9	10		2			5			1	11											4
	13	3■	4		6	7^{2}	8	9	10		2	12		5			1	11^{1}											5
			4		6	7	8	9	10^{1}	3	2	12		5			1	11											6
			4		6	7^{1}	8	9	10	3	2	12		5			1	11											7
1	2	12	4		6	7	8	9	10^{2}	3	5				13			11^{1}											8
1	2		4		6	7	8	9	10	3	5	12						11^{1}											9
1	2	3^{1}	4		6	7	8^{2}	9	10	11	5				13				12										10
1	2				6^{1}	7^{2}	8	9	10	3	5	11		12	4				13										11
1	2	3	4		6		12	9	10	11	5	8^{1}			7														12
1	2	3	4		6		13	9	10^{1}	11	5	8^{2}			7				12										13
1	2	3	4		6■		12	9	10^{2}	11	5	8^{3}		14	7^{1}				13										14
1	2	3	4	5		7■	12	9	10	11	6				8^{1}														15
1	2^{1}	3	4	5^{2}	6			9	10	11	7	14		13	8^{3}					12									16
1	2	3	4		6			9	10^{2}	11	5	13	8^{1}	12	7														17
1		3	4	5	6	7^{1}		9		11	2		10^{2}		13			8			12								18
1	12	3^{1}	4^{2}	5	6	7		9		11	2		10		13			8^{3}			14								19
1		3	4	5	6	7^{1}		9		11	2		10^{2}					8			13	12							20
1		3	4	5	6	7		9		11	2		10^{1}		8							12							21
1		3	4	5	6			9		11■	2	13	8^{2}					10			7^{1}	12							22
1	12	3	4	5	6		8^{1}	9			2		13		7			10				11^{2}							23
1	13	3	4	5	6		8^{1}	9			2	14	10^{3}		7^{2}			11					12						24
1	2	3	4	5	6		8	9			7	11^{1}	12					10											25
1	2	3	4	5	6	7	8^{1}	9			11							10						12					26
1	2^{1}	3	4	5	6	7	8	9			11	12						10^{2}						13					27
1	12	3	4	5	6	7^{2}	8	9			11													13	2	10^{1}			28
1	2	3	4	5	6^{1}	7	8	9						12						13				10^{3}	11^{2}	14			29
1	2	3	4	5		7	8^{2}		10^{3}		6							9^{1}		12				13	11	14			30
1		3	4			7	13		10^{1}		2			5				9^{2}		11		12			8		6		31
1	13	3	4	5	12	7			10^{3}		2							11^{2}				14			8		6^{1}	9	32
1		3	4	5		7			10		2							11							8		6	9	33
1		3	4	5		7^{1}	12		10^{2}		2							11				13			8		6	9	34
1		3	4	5		7			10^{1}		2							11				12			8		6	9	35
1		3	4	5	6	7	12		13			10										11			8^{1}		2	9^{2}	36
1	13			5	6	7^{2}	8		14		2	10^{3}						12				11			4		3^{1}	9	37
1				5	6	7^{1}	8		12		2	10						13				11^{2}			4		3	9	38
1			13	5	6		8		10^{3}		2	14						11		7^{1}		12			4^{2}		3	9	39
1	13		12	5	6	7	8				2	10^{2}						11							4^{1}		3	9	40
1	12		13	5	6	7	8				2	10^{3}						11^{2}				14			4^{1}		3	9	41
1^{9}			13	5	6	7	8		12		2	10^{1}				15		11							4		3	9^{2}	42
	12		13	5	6	7	8^{2}		14		2	10^{3}				1		11							4^{1}		3	9	43
1	12		13	5	6^{1}	7	8^{2}		9		2	10						11^{3}		14					4		3		44
1	2		4	5	6	7			10^{1}		11	12								9					8		3		45
1	12		4	5^{1}	6			9^{3}	10		2	14						11		7^{2}		13			8		3		46

FA Cup

Fourth Qualifying Round	Moor Green	(a)	2-1
First Round	Kidderminster H	(h)	2-1
Second Round	Swindon T	(a)	0-1
Third Round	Stevenage B	(h)	1-1
		(a)	0-3

Trophy

First Round	York C	(h)	2-1
Second Round	Mangotsfield U	(h)	5-0

Play-Offs

Semi-Final	York C	(a)	0-0
		(h)	2-1
Final *(at Wembley)*	Exeter C		2-1

NORTHWICH VICTORIA Blue Square Premier

Ground: Victoria Stadium, Wincham Avenue, Northwich, Cheshire CW9 6GB. *Tel:* (01606) 815 200
Year Formed: 1874. *Record Gate:* 12,000 (1977 v Watford, FA Cup Fourth Round). *Nickname:* The Vics.
Manager: Neil Redfearn. *Secretary:* Derek Nuttall. *Colours:* Green and white hooped shirts, white shorts, white stockings.

NORTHWICH VICTORIA 2006–07 LEAGUE RECORD

Match No.	Date	Venue	Opponents	Result		H/T Score	Lg. Pos.	Goalscorers	Attendance
1	Aug 12	A	Cambridge U	W	1-0	0-0	—	Townson 48	2506
2	15	H	Morecambe	L	0-2	0-1	—		1346
3	19	H	Kidderminster H	L	0-1	0-1	16		976
4	26	A	Oxford U	L	1-5	0-2	17	Brayson 76	5364
5	28	H	Grays Ath	L	0-3	0-1	20		874
6	Sept 2	A	Crawley T	W	2-0	0-0	17	Mayman 48, Brayson 64	778
7	9	H	St Albans C	L	0-3	0-3	19		717
8	16	A	Aldershot T	W	3-1	1-0	17	Byrne 45, Brayson 49, Allan 53	2588
9	19	H	Stafford R	W	4-0	2-0	—	Byrne 2 1, 64, Brayson 37, Townson 86	971
10	23	A	Burton Alb	L	0-2	0-2	16		1817
11	26	A	Southport	W	2-1	1-0	—	Carr 2 13, 51	1059
12	30	H	Woking	L	0-2	0-1	13		990
13	Oct 3	H	York C	L	1-2	0-1	—	Charnock 52	1021
14	7	A	Dagenham & R	L	0-5	0-3	16		1235
15	10	A	Exeter C	D	1-1	1-0	—	Brayson 42	2928
16	14	H	Rushden & D	W	4-1	3-0	15	Griffiths 19, Brayson 37, Gallimore 38, Dodds 49	853
17	21	A	Stevenage Bor	W	2-0	1-0	13	Elliott (pen) 22, Dodds 70	1773
18	Nov 3	H	Halifax T	W	3-2	0-2	13	Carr 58, Brayson 81, Dodds 90	1150
19	18	A	Forest Green R	L	1-2	0-1	13	Bastians 55	869
20	25	H	Gravesend & N	L	1-2	1-2	14	Roca 11	813
21	Dec 9	H	Weymouth	L	0-1	0-1	17		874
22	26	A	Altrincham	L	0-3	0-1	18		2330
23	Jan 1	H	Southport	W	3-1	0-1	—	Allan 2 57, 90, Brayson 69	1056
24	6	A	St Albans C	W	3-1	2-0	13	Byrne 14, Allan 34, Carr 59	767
25	20	H	Aldershot T	L	1-3	0-1	14	Brayson 90	890
26	27	A	Weymouth	D	1-1	0-0	15	Allan 81	1451
27	Feb 17	H	Forest Green R	W	2-0	0-0	16	Jones (og) 70, Dean 90	773
28	20	H	Altrincham	D	1-1	0-0	—	Dean 67	1290
29	27	A	Halifax T	W	2-0	0-0	—	Shaw 69, Brayson 86	1221
30	Mar 3	H	Tamworth	L	0-1	0-0	16		1070
31	6	A	York C	L	1-2	1-0	—	Smart 40	2132
32	20	H	Exeter C	W	1-0	0-0	—	Carr (pen) 77	784
33	25	H	Cambridge U	L	0-4	0-2	20		1156
34	27	A	Morecambe	L	1-2	0-1	—	Mayman 69	1315
35	31	A	Kidderminster H	W	1-0	1-0	19	Byrne 15	1621
36	Apr 3	A	Tamworth	W	1-0	0-0	—	Byrne 50	1006
37	7	H	Oxford U	W	1-0	1-0	14	Dean 7	1552
38	9	A	Grays Ath	L	0-1	0-1	—		776
39	11	H	Dagenham & R	W	2-0	0-0	—	Dean 63, Brayson 69	757
40	14	H	Crawley T	W	2-1	1-1	12	Roberts 36, Brayson 57	706
41	17	A	Stafford R	L	0-2	0-0	—		1049
42	19	A	Gravesend & N	L	0-3	0-2	—		1182
43	21	H	Burton Alb	L	0-3	0-3	12		1218
44	23	A	Rushden & D	L	0-1	0-0	—		1533
45	25	H	Stevenage Bor	D	0-0	0-0	—		515
46	28	A	Woking	L	2-3	1-1	13	Byrne (pen) 31, Townson 90	1753

Final League Position: 13

GOALSCORERS

League (51): Brayson 12, Byrne 7 (1 pen), Allan 5, Carr 5 (1 pen), Dean 4, Dodds 3, Townson 3, Mayman 2, Bastians 1, Charnock 1, Elliott 1 (pen), Gallimore 1, Griffiths 1, Roberts 1, Roca 1, Shaw 1, Smart 1, own goal 1.
FA Cup (2): Brayson 1, Carr 1.
Trophy (12): Brayson 3, Carr 2 (1 pen), Roca 2, Shaw 2, Allan 1, Battersby 1, Griffiths 1.

Senior 26	Battersby 34 + 5	Gallimore 12 + 1	Griffiths 25 + 3	Elliott 25 + 1	Charnock 42	Byrne 26 + 12	Carr 37 + 1	Allan 21 + 1	Townson 15 + 17	Williams 3 + 3	McCarthy 17 + 11	Roca 15 + 13	Brayson 33 + 7	Sale 2 + 7	Payne 11 + 4	Barwick 14 + 7	Connett 20	Brown 21 + 2	Mayman 24 + 2	Dodds 6	Bastians 3 + 1	Young 3	Roberts 22 + 1	Beaumont 5	Dean 15 + 5	Smart 17 + 1	Shaw 9 + 4	Warburton — + 2	Smith 3	Rutter — + 2	Match No.
1	2	3	4	5	6	7[1]	8	9	10	11	12																				1
1	2	3	4	5[2]	6	7[1]	8	9[3]	10	11	13	12	14																		2
1	2[1]	3	4		6	7	8	9	10	11[3]		14	13	12	5[2]																3
1	2[1]	3	4	5	6	7[2]	8	9	10[3]		12		11		13	14															4
	2[1]		4	5	6	14	8[3]	9				7[2]	10	13	11	12	1	3													5
	2		4	5	6	14	8[3]	9	13		12		10[2]			11	1	3	7[1]												6
	2		4[1]	5	6	13	8[3]	9	14				10		12	11	1	3	7[2]												7
1	12			5	6	7	8[2]	9■	14		3		10[3]		4	13		2	11[1]												8
1	12			5	6	7	8		10		2		9		4			3	11[1]												9
1	13			5	6	7	8	14	10[3]		2[1]		9		4	12		3	11[2]												10
1	2	13	4	5	6	7[2]	8	9	14				10[3]			12		3[1]	11												11
1	2	3	4[1]	5	6	7[2]	8	9	14				10[3]	13	12				11												12
1	2	3		5	6	7[1]		9	13				10[2]	12	4	8			11												13
	2		12	13	6[1]	7[3]		9	14				10	11	3	4[2]	1	5	8												14
1	2	3	6	5				9	12		13		10		7	11[2]		4		8[1]											15
1	2	3	4	5			8[1]	9[2]	13		12		10		7	14		11		6[3]											16
1		3	4	5		13	8	9	12				10[1]		2			6	7	11[2]											17
1		3	4	5		13	8		10[2]				9		6			7[1]	11	2	12										18
1			4	5	6	14	8		10[3]		2[1]	13		12					11[2]	9	7	3									19
1			4[2]	5	6	14	8				2[1]	7[3]	10	12	13					9	11	3									20
1	2			5	6	13	8	9			3[1]	7	10						12		11[2]	4									21
	13	3		5[2]	6	12	8	9			2	11[3]	10	14			1	4[1]	7												22
	4	3		5[1]	6	7	8	9			2	12	13	10[2]		11	1														23
	13			5	6	7[1]	8	9			2	12	10[2]			11	1						4	3							24
					6	7[2]	8	9			2	13	10			11[1]	1	3					5	4	12						25
	2		12	5	6		8	9	13			11[3]	10			7	1						4[1]	3[2]		14					26
	2		4	5	6		8■				12	13	9[3]				1		7				14	11[1]	3	10[2]					27
	2		4	5	6				14		12	13	9[3]			3[1]	1		7				8		10	11[2]					28
			4		6		8				2	12	9				1		7				5		10[1]	3	11				29
	2[1]		4		6		8				12	11	9				1		7				5		13	3	10[2]				30
			4		6		12		10[2]		2	11	13			8	1						5	7[1]	9	3					31
	2		4[1]		6	14	8		13		11	10[2]	9[3]				1		12				5			3	7				32
	2				6	13	8[1]				11	10[3]	9				1	3					5		14		7	12	4[2]		33
	2				6	11	8				3	12	9[2]				1		7				5		13		10		4[1]		34
1	2				6	11	8		14			4[1]	9[2]						7				5		13	3	10[3]	12			35
1	2		4		6	7	8		10[1]				12						11				5		9	3					36
1	2[1]		4		6	7	8		10[3]			12	14						11[2]				5		9	3	13				37
1	2		4■		6	7[2]	8		10		13	14											5		3	9[3]	12		11[1]		38
1	2				6	7	8				11	10[1]	12					3					5		4	9					39
1	2		13		6	7[1]	8		14			11[2]	9					12	4				5		10[3]	3					40
	2		4[1]		6	13	8		10		11						1	12	7				5		9[3]	3[2]	14				41
	2				6	7	8[1]		14		13	12	9				1	4	11[2]				5		10[3]	3					42
1	2				6	7			10[2]			11[1]				12		3					5		9	4	8			13	43
1	2				6	7			10	13		11[2]				8		3					5		9[1]	4	12				44
	2				6	7				12			9			8	1	3					5		10	4	11[1]				45
1	2				6	7[3]			13	12		11[1]	9			8		3					5		10		4[2]			14	46

FA Cup

Fourth Qualifying Round	Cambridge U	(h)	2-0
First Round	Brighton & HA	(a)	0-8

Trophy

First Round	Farsley C	(h)	3-1
Second Round	Eastbourne B	(a)	1-0
Third Round	Histon	(a)	2-1
Fourth Round	Gravesend & N	(h)	3-0
Semi-Final	Kidderminster H	(a)	0-2
		(h)	3-2

OXFORD UNITED

Blue Square Premier

Ground: The Kassam Stadium, Grenoble Road, Oxford OX4 4XP. *Tel:* (01865) 337 500. *Year Formed:* 1893.
Record Gate: 22,730 (1964 v Preston NE, FA Cup Sixth Round). *Nickname:* The U's. *Manager:* Jim Smith.
Secretary: Mick Brown. *Colours:* Yellow with navy trim shirts, navy shorts, navy stockings.

OXFORD UNITED 2006–07 LEAGUE RECORD

Match No.	*Date*	*Venue*	*Opponents*	*Result*		*H/T Score*	*Lg. Pos.*	*Goalscorers*	*Attendance*
1	Aug 12	H	Halifax T	W	2-0	1-0	—	Duffy (pen) [16], Burgess [70]	5785
2	15	A	Dagenham & R	W	1-0	0-0	—	Odubade [57]	2022
3	18	A	Burton Alb	W	2-1	0-1	—	Duffy 2 (1 pen) [75, 86 (p)]	2501
4	26	H	Northwich Vic	W	5-1	2-0	1	Duffy [16], Pettefer [45], Basham [47], Johnson [66], Odubade [82]	5364
5	28	A	Weymouth	D	1-1	0-0	2	Hargreaves [90]	5244
6	Sept 1	H	St Albans C	W	2-1	0-0	—	Odubade [69], Day [84]	6190
7	9	A	Morecambe	W	3-0	2-0	1	Basham [22], Gilchrist [34], Burgess [90]	2314
8	12	H	Exeter C	W	1-0	1-0	—	Basham [7]	6083
9	16	H	Grays Ath	D	1-1	1-1	1	Basham [20]	6504
10	18	A	Crawley T	W	1-0	0-0	—	Day [90]	2101
11	23	A	Stafford R	W	1-0	0-0	1	Duffy [60]	1795
12	30	H	York C	W	2-0	1-0	1	Duffy [14], Burgess [67]	6602
13	Oct 3	H	Southport	D	2-2	0-1	—	Duffy 2 (2 pens) [54, 90]	5844
14	6	A	Forest Green R	W	5-1	2-1	—	Duffy 3 [26, 44, 89], Odubade [83], Hargreaves [90]	3021
15	10	A	Kidderminster H	D	0-0	0-0	—		2264
16	14	H	Altrincham	D	1-1	0-0	1	Day [54]	5938
17	20	A	Cambridge U	W	3-0	1-0	—	Odubade 2 [27, 63], Hargreaves [56]	3932
18	Nov 3	H	Aldershot T	W	2-0	0-0	1	Burgess 2 (1 pen) [74 (p), 84]	8185
19	18	A	Gravesend & N	L	0-1	0-0	1		2019
20	25	H	Tamworth	W	2-1	0-0	1	Day [52], Duffy (pen) [80]	6614
21	Dec 2	A	Stevenage Bor	D	2-2	0-2	1	Duffy [54], Hargreaves [59]	3008
22	9	A	Rushden & D	L	0-1	0-1	1		3270
23	26	H	Woking	D	0-0	0-0	1		11,065
24	30	H	Crawley T	D	1-1	0-1	2	Duffy [79]	6368
25	Jan 1	A	Exeter C	L	1-2	0-1	—	Burgess (pen) [89]	4720
26	6	H	Morecambe	D	0-0	0-0	2		5489
27	20	A	Grays Ath	D	2-2	1-0	2	Duffy 2 (1 pen) [4, 73 (p)]	1759
28	23	A	Woking	L	0-1	0-1	—		2228
29	30	H	Rushden & D	L	0-1	0-0	—		5654
30	Feb 3	H	Cambridge U	D	1-1	0-1	2	Anaclet [57]	5613
31	10	A	Aldershot T	D	1-1	1-0	2	Odubade [40]	3621
32	17	H	Gravesend & N	W	1-0	1-0	2	Duffy [36]	5615
33	24	A	Tamworth	W	3-1	2-0	2	Odubade [11], Duffy (pen) [21], Anaclet [90]	2089
34	Mar 3	H	Stevenage Bor	W	2-0	1-0	2	Day [45], Beard (og) [59]	6410
35	6	A	Southport	W	1-0	0-0	—	Rose [60]	1054
36	10	H	Forest Green R	L	0-2	0-1	2		6157
37	13	H	Kidderminster H	L	0-1	0-0	—		4542
38	17	A	Altrincham	W	3-0	2-0	2	Anaclet [25], Corcoran [39], Robinson [89]	1497
39	21	A	Halifax T	D	1-1	0-0	—	Robinson [49]	1473
40	26	H	Dagenham & R	D	2-2	0-1	—	Odubade 2 [70, 72]	6836
41	31	H	Burton Alb	D	0-0	0-0	2		6187
42	Apr 7	A	Northwich Vic	L	0-1	0-1	2		1552
43	9	H	Weymouth	W	4-1	1-1	—	Zebroski [23], Hargreaves [78], Robinson [81], Quinn [83]	5582
44	14	A	St Albans C	W	2-0	1-0	2	Odubade [26], Foster L [90]	1713
45	21	H	Stafford R	W	2-0	1-0	2	Zebroski [40], Daniel (og) [60]	7007
46	28	A	York C	L	0-1	0-1	2		5378

Final League Position: 2

GOALSCORERS

League (66): Duffy 18 (7 pens), Odubade 11, Burgess 6 (2 pens), Day 5, Hargreaves 5, Basham 4, Anaclet 3, Robinson 3, Zebroski 2, Corcoran 1, Foster L 1, Gilchrist 1, Johnson 1, Pettefer 1, Quinn 1, Rose 1, own goals 2.
FA Cup (2): Duffy 1, Johnson 1.
Trophy (4): Duffy 2 (1 pen), Robinson 1, Rose 1.
Play-Offs (2): Odubade 1, own goal 1.

Turley 42	Anaclet 41 + 3	Johnson 23 + 7	Gilchrist 36	Day 21 + 16	Quinn 40 + 1	Pettefer 34 + 4	Dempster 8 + 9	Duffy 33 + 3	Hutchinson 8 + 10	Burgess 32 + 7	Odubade 19 + 25	Hargreaves 30 + 8	Basham 17 + 3	Willmott 17	Robinson 10 + 11	Brevett 19 + 2	Slabber 2 + 1	Tardif 4 + 1	Kennet — + 1	Santos 3	Rose 19 + 1	Gunn 1 + 2	Grebis 3 + 1	Coombes 1	Corcoran 16	Foster M 13	Foster L 7 + 2	Zebroski 7 + 1	*Match No.*
1	2	3	4	5	6	7	8	9^{1}	10^{2}	11^{3}	13	14	12																1
1	2	3	4	5	6▮	7	8	9	10^{1}	11^{2}	13	12																	2
1	2	3	4	5		7	8^{1}	9	12	11	13	6	10^{2}																3
1	2	3^{1}	4	12	6	7		9^{3}	13	11	14	8^{2}	10	5															4
1	2^{1}	3	4	12	6	7^{2}		9	13	11	14	8	10^{3}	5															5
1	2	3^{1}	4	12	6	7		9^{3}	14	11	13	8▮		5	10^{2}														6
1	2^{1}		4	12	6	7	13		10^{2}	11	14		9^{3}	5	8	3													7
1	2			5	6	7	12		10^{1}	11	13		9^{2}	4	8	3													8
1	2		4		6^{1}	7			10	8	12		9	5	11	3													9
1	2			5	6	7	12	13		11	14	8	9^{2}	4	10^{3}	3^{1}													10
1	2			5	6	7	8^{1}	9^{2}	13		12	11	10	4		3													11
1	2		4	13	6	7	12	9^{3}	10	11^{1}	14		8	5		3^{2}													12
1	2		4^{1}	12	6	7		9	10^{2}	11	14	13	8^{3}	5		3													13
1	2		4	5	6	7	13	9^{2}		11	12	8	10^{1}	3															14
1	2		4	12	6	7		9	14	11^{2}	13	8	10^{3}	5		3^{1}													15
1	2		4	5	6	7	3	9		11	10	8																	16
1	2^{1}		4	13	6	7^{3}	12		14	11	10	8	9	5		3^{2}													17
1	2	12	4		6	7		9^{3}	13	11	10^{2}	8	14	5		3^{1}													18
1	2	13	4	12	6	7				11	14	8	9^{3}	5		3^{1}	10^{2}												19
1	2	3		5	6	12		9	7^{1}	11	13	8		4			10^{2}												20
1^{6}	2	3	4	5	6	7^{2}	13	9		11	12	8		10^{1}				15											21
1	2	3	4	12^{2}	6^{1}	7	5	9		11	14	8^{3}	10				13												22
1	2		4	5	6	7	8^{1}	9	12^{2}	11	14	13	10^{3}			3													23
1	2^{2}	3^{3}	4	5^{1}	6	7	12	9		11	10	8	14			13													24
1	2	14	4^{1}	5	6	7	8			11		10	9^{3}			3^{2}			13			12							25
1	2	3	4^{1}	12	6	7		9		11	10									5	8								26
1	2^{1}		4	12	6	7		9			13	8				3				5	11		10^{2}						27
1		3	4	5^{2}	6	7^{3}	12	9			13	8			14					2^{1}	11		10						28
	2	12	4		6			9		11	14				13	3^{1}		1			8	5	10^{3}	7^{2}					29
	2^{2}	12	4		6			9		14	10	8			13	3^{1}		1			11^{3}				5	7			30
	2^{1}	3	4					9^{3}		13	7	8			11			1			10^{2}	12	14		5	6			31
1	2^{1}	3	4		6	12		9^{3}		13	10	8			14						11^{2}				5	7			32
1	2	3	4	12	6^{1}			9^{3}		13	10	8			14						7^{2}				5	11			33
1	2	3	4	5		12		9^{2}		11	10				13						8				6	7^{1}			34
1	2	3	4^{2}	5^{1}	13			9^{3}		11	10	14			12						7				6	8			35
1	2	3^{1}	4	5				9^{2}		11	10	12			13						7				6	8			36
1	13		4			7		9^{3}		12	10	14			11	3					8^{2}				5	6^{1}	2		37
1	2^{1}	3		12	6	13				14	10^{3}	8			9						11				5	7^{2}	4		38
1	2				6	7						8			9	11					3				5		4	10	39
1	2	3	4		6	7^{2}		12		11	10	14			13						8^{3}						5	9^{1}	40
1	2	13^{3}		14	6^{1}			9		11^{2}	10	8									12				5	4	3	7	41
1	12			2	6	7^{1}		13			10	8			9^{3}	3▮					11^{2}				5	4		14	42
1	2^{1}	3^{2}	4	12	6						10	8			14						7^{3}				5	11	13	9	43
1		3^{1}	4	5	6	7				13	10^{3}	8			14						11^{2}				2		12	9	44
1	12	13		5	6^{1}	7^{2}		9^{3}		11	14	8													2	4	3	10	45
	2^{1}	3^{3}		5	6	7		9	13		12					14		1			8				4		11^{2}	10	46

FA Cup

Fourth Qualifying Round	Dagenham & R	(a)	1-0
First Round	Wycombe W	(a)	1-2

Play-Offs

Semi-Final	Exeter C	(a)	1-0
		(h)	1-2

Trophy

First Round	Lewes	(a)	0-0
		(h)	1-0
Second Round	Halifax T	(h)	2-2
		(a)	1-2

RUSHDEN & DIAMONDS Blue Square Premier

Ground: Nene Park, Irthlingborough, Northants NN9 5QF. *Tel:* (01933) 652 000. *Year Formed:* 1992.
Record Gate: 6,431 (1999 v Leeds U, FA Cup Third Round). *Nickname:* The Diamonds. *Manager:* Garry Hill.
Secretary: Matt Wild. *Colours:* White shirts, white shorts, white stockings.

RUSHDEN & DIAMONDS 2006–07 LEAGUE RECORD

Match No.	Date	Venue	Opponents	Result		H/T Score	Lg. Pos.	Goalscorers	Attendance
1	Aug 12	A	Crawley T	L	0-1	0-0	—		1088
2	15	H	Grays Ath	L	1-3	1-1	—	Rankine [43]	2015
3	19	H	Forest Green R	W	2-0	1-0	15	Chillingworth [20], Jackson [75]	1693
4	26	A	Southport	W	2-1	2-0	11	Chillingworth [29], Watson [35]	1083
5	28	H	York C	L	0-1	0-0	13		2416
6	Sept 1	A	Kidderminster H	D	0-0	0-0	—		1850
7	9	H	Altrincham	W	3-0	2-0	10	Jackson 3 [33, 35, 88]	1680
8	12	A	Tamworth	W	4-1	1-0	—	Jackson 3 [11, 62, 72], Ashton (pen) [67]	1105
9	16	A	Stafford R	D	1-1	1-0	9	Hope [6]	1054
10	19	H	Gravesend & N	D	0-0	0-0	—		1879
11	23	A	Woking	L	0-3	0-3	11		2084
12	30	H	Burton Alb	L	1-2	1-2	12	Kelly [30]	2179
13	Oct 3	A	Morecambe	L	0-1	0-0	—		1252
14	6	H	Stevenage Bor	D	2-2	2-1	—	Hatswell [37], Hope [45]	2309
15	10	H	Halifax T	L	0-1	0-1	—		1839
16	14	A	Northwich Vic	L	1-4	0-3	17	Jackson [49]	853
17	21	A	Weymouth	D	1-1	1-1	18	Tomlin [21]	2148
18	Nov 3	H	Dagenham & R	L	2-3	2-3	18	Kelly [1], Watson (pen) [41]	2039
19	18	A	St Albans C	L	2-3	0-3	22	Tomlin [47], Kelly [62]	1236
20	25	H	Aldershot T	L	0-1	0-0	23		2128
21	Dec 9	H	Oxford U	W	1-0	1-0	22	Woodhouse [7]	3270
22	26	A	Cambridge U	W	1-0	1-0	19	Kelly [44]	3000
23	30	A	Gravesend & N	L	0-1	0-0	20		1110
24	Jan 1	H	Tamworth	D	1-1	1-0	—	Savage [43]	1872
25	6	A	Altrincham	L	1-2	0-1	22	Tomlin [90]	1111
26	20	H	Stafford R	W	2-1	0-0	20	Cook [53], Jackson [54]	1837
27	23	H	Cambridge U	W	3-1	1-0	—	Jackson [7], Beardsley [75], Rankine [80]	2239
28	30	A	Oxford U	W	1-0	0-0	—	Beardsley [54]	5654
29	Feb 10	A	Dagenham & R	W	2-1	1-1	15	Jackson [32], Hope [77]	1817
30	17	H	St Albans C	W	1-0	0-0	13	Maamria [76]	2488
31	20	A	Exeter C	D	0-0	0-0	—		3135
32	24	A	Aldershot T	D	2-2	0-2	12	Jackson [52], Charles (og) [57]	2189
33	Mar 3	H	Exeter C	W	3-0	2-0	12	Jackson [11], Albrighton [19], Woodhouse [52]	2344
34	6	H	Morecambe	D	2-2	1-0	—	Rankine [34], Kelly [66]	1701
35	13	A	Halifax T	D	0-0	0-0	—		1314
36	23	H	Crawley T	D	1-1	0-1	—	Tomlin [78]	1974
37	27	A	Grays Ath	L	1-3	0-0	—	Jackson [90]	762
38	31	A	Forest Green R	W	2-0	0-0	12	Jackson [48], Ashton [85]	1110
39	Apr 3	H	Weymouth	W	4-1	1-0	—	Williams [44], Weatherstone (og) [73], Rankine 2 [85, 90]	1624
40	7	H	Southport	L	2-3	1-2	12	Jackson [8], Rankine [90]	2122
41	10	A	York C	L	1-3	1-1	—	Jackson [3]	2955
42	14	H	Kidderminster H	L	0-1	0-1	14		1925
43	17	A	Stevenage Bor	L	0-1	0-0	—		1715
44	21	H	Woking	W	2-0	1-0	13	Rankine [45], Jackson [64]	1922
45	23	H	Northwich Vic	W	1-0	0-0	—	Woodhouse [62]	1533
46	28	A	Burton Alb	W	2-1	1-1	12	Jackson [45], Woodhouse [58]	2910

Final League Position: 12

GOALSCORERS

League (58): Jackson 19, Rankine 7, Kelly 5, Tomlin 4, Woodhouse 4, Hope 3, Ashton 2 (1 pen), Beardsley 2, Chillingworth 2, Watson 2 (1 pen), Albrighton 1, Cook 1, Hatswell 1, Maamria 1, Savage 1, Williams 1, own goals 2.
FA Cup (7): Rankine 2, Shaw 2, Hope 1, Jackson 1, Tomlin 1.
Trophy (5): Ashton 1, Chillingworth 1, Rankine 1, Tomlin 1, Woodhouse 1.

Eyre 19	Wilson 27 + 4	Watson 37 + 3	Ashton 40	Hope 45	Hatswell 34 + 1	Savage 25 + 10	Rankine 32 + 8	Fortune-West 2 + 4	Chillingworth 12 + 5	Kelly 33 + 1	Tomlin 10 + 15	Berry 14 + 9	Jackson 35 + 10	Shaw 14 + 6	Pearson 3 + 4	Rigby 2	Grainger 2 + 1	Sedgemore 1	Tynan 21	Plummer 2	Woodhouse 15 + 1	Ghaichem — + 1	Cook 7 + 1	Webb 1	Albrighton 16 + 1	Mills 15 + 2	Beardsley 5 + 7	Perpetuini 3 + 2	Bostwick 5 + 3	Goodlife 5 + 2	Maamria 3 + 1	Williams 12	Baker 6	Lambley 1 + 5	Wright 2 + 1	Beecroft — + 1	Match No.
1	2	3	4	5	6	7^{1}	8	9^{2}	10^{3}	11	12	13	14																								1
1	2	3	4	5	6	7	8	9^{2}	10^{1}	11		12	13																								2
1	2	3	4	5	6	7	8		10	11	12		9^{1}																								3
1	2	3^{1}	4	5	6	7	8		10	11			9	12																							4
1	2	3	4	5	6	7	8^{2}	13	12		11^{1}	10	9																								5
1	2	3	4	5	6	12	8		10^{1}	11		14	9^{3}	7^{2}	13																						6
1	2	3	4^{1}	5	6	12	8^{2}	13	10^{3}	11		14	9	7																							7
1	2	3	4^{1}	5	6	12	8			11		10	9	7																							8
1	2	3	4	5	6	12	8^{2}			11^{1}		10	9	7■	13																						9
1	2	3	4	5	6	7	8■	12		11		10	9^{1}																								10
1	2	3	4	5	6	7		12	10^{2}	11		8	9^{1}		13																						11
1	2	3	4	5	6	7	13			11		12	9		10^{2}	8^{1}																					12
1	2	3	4	5	6	7	8			11		13	9^{1}		12	10^{2}																					13
1	12	3	4	5	6				10	11		8	13	7	9^{2}		2^{1}																				14
1	12	3	4	5	6^{2}	13			10	11		8	14	7	9^{3}		2^{1}																				15
1	2	3	4	5^{1}	6	7	13		10^{3}		14	8	9	11^{2}			12																				16
1	2	3	4	5	6	7			13	11^{1}	10^{2}	8	9	12																							17
1	2	3		5	6	7			13	11^{2}	10	8	9	12				4^{1}																			18
		3^{1}		5	6	7	8^{2}		12	11	10	4	13	9					1	2																	19
	2	3		5		7	13			11	10^{2}	8	9	12					1	6	4^{1}																20
1		3	4	5	6	7	9^{2}		13	11		10^{1}	12	8							2																21
	2	3	4	5	6	7	8		10^{2}	11		13	9^{1}						1		12																22
	2	3	4^{1}	5	6	7	8		10^{3}	11	13	14	12^{2}						1		9																23
		3	4	5	6	7	8			11^{1}	9^{2}	10	12	13					1		2																24
	2		4	5	6	7^{2}	8^{3}				13	14	9	3^{1}					1			12	11	10													25
	2	13	4	5	6		12			11^{2}			9^{3}						1				7^{1}		3	8	10	14									26
	2^{1}		4	5	6	12	14			11^{2}			9^{3}						1				7		3	8	10	13									27
	2^{1}	3	4		6	12				13	14		9^{3}						1				7		5	8	10	11^{2}									28
	2			5	6		13						9^{1}						1				7		4	8	10^{2}		3	12	11						29
	2^{1}		4	5	6		14			11^{2}			9						1				7		3	8	10^{3}		12		13						30
			4	5	6		8^{1}						9^{2}						1				13		3	7	12	11	2		10						31
	13		4	5	6		12						9^{3}						1				7^{1}		3	8	14	11^{2}	2■		10						32
		3	4	5			8^{2}			11	12		9^{1}						1		6				2	7	13					10					33
		3	4	5			8			11	12		9						1		6				2	7^{2}			13			10^{1}					34
		3	2	5		12	8^{3}			11	13		9^{2}						1		4^{1}						14		7	6		10					35
		3	4	5			8^{3}			11	12		9						1		6					13	14		10^{2}	2		7^{1}					36
		3	4	5		7^{1}	8			11	9^{3}		12						1		10^{2}				2	14			13	6							37
		3	4	5			8			11	12		9^{1}						1		6				2	10						7					38
		3	4	5		12	8			11	13		9^{2}						1		6				2	7^{1}						10					39
		3^{1}	4	5			8			11	13		9	14					1		6				2	7^{3}				12		10^{2}					40
		13	4^{1}	5		7	8^{3}				14		9	10											2	6				3			1	12	11^{2}		41
		3	4	5	12	13	8						9	10												6^{2}				2^{1}		7	1	14	11^{3}		42
		3	4^{1}	5	6^{2}	7	8				10			11											12	2^{3}	13					9	1	14			43
	2	3		5	6	7	8^{2}				12		9^{3}	11^{1}							4						13					10	1	14			44
	2^{1}	3		5		7^{3}	8				10		13								6				4							9	1	11^{2}	14	12	45
	14	12	4	5	6	7	8				10^{1}		9^{3}								11				2							3^{2}	1	13			46

FA Cup

Fourth Qualifying Round	Altrincham	(h)	3-0
First Round	Yeovil T	(h)	3-1
Second Round	Tamworth	(h)	1-2

Trophy

First Round	Scarborough	(h)	3-2
Second Round	Witton Alb	(a)	1-0
Third Round	Gravesend & N	(a)	1-2

ST ALBANS CITY

Blue Square South

Ground: Clarence Park, St Albans, Herts AL1 4PL. *Tel:* (01727) 864 296. *Year formed:* 1908.
Record gate: 9,757 (1926 v Ferryhill Ath, FA Amateur Cup). *Nickname:* The Saints. *Manager:* Ritchie Hanlon.
Secretary: Steve Eames. *Colours:* Yellow with blue trim.

ST ALBANS CITY 2006–07 LEAGUE RECORD

Match No.	Date	Venue	Opponents	Result		H/T Score	Lg. Pos.	Goalscorers	Attendance
1	Aug 12	A	Kidderminster H	W	3-1	3-0	—	Hakim [9], Theobald [21], Clarke (pen) [43]	1806
2	15	H	Cambridge U	D	0-0	0-0	—		1916
3	19	H	Aldershot T	L	3-5	0-1	10	Marwa [49], Davis (pen) [88], Cracknell [90]	1373
4	26	A	Altrincham	L	0-2	0-1	14		890
5	28	H	Tamworth	W	1-0	1-0	10	Hakim [32]	1184
6	Sept 1	A	Oxford U	L	1-2	0-0	—	Theobald [83]	6190
7	9	A	Northwich Vic	W	3-0	3-0	11	Hakim [9], Flynn [31], Theobald [41]	717
8	12	H	Woking	L	0-1	0-0	—		1018
9	16	H	Burton Alb	L	0-1	0-1	14		1111
10	19	A	Exeter C	L	2-4	0-1	—	Jackman [57], Clarke [90]	2494
11	23	H	Gravesend & N	L	2-3	0-0	18	Davis (pen) [77], Hakim [89]	987
12	30	A	Weymouth	L	1-2	0-0	20	Hakim [59]	1676
13	Oct 3	H	Forest Green R	D	0-0	0-0	—		806
14	7	A	Southport	D	1-1	0-0	21	Batt D [64]	1005
15	10	A	Dagenham & R	L	2-4	0-3	—	Batt D [66], Hakim [80]	1508
16	14	H	York C	W	4-2	1-1	21	Cracknell [32], McBean [49], Hakim [52], Benyon [90]	1237
17	21	H	Grays Ath	L	0-6	0-1	22		1045
18	Nov 4	A	Crawley T	L	1-2	1-0	24	Hakim [27]	840
19	11	A	Forest Green R	D	2-2	1-1	22	Walshe [42], Benyon [68]	1003
20	18	H	Rushden & D	W	3-2	3-0	21	Benyon 2 [1, 12], Clarke [3]	1236
21	25	A	Stafford R	D	2-2	1-0	20	Benyon [24], Clarke [68]	1030
22	Dec 2	A	Cambridge U	W	2-0	1-0	17	Marwa [22], Davis (pen) [56]	2131
23	9	A	Halifax T	L	1-4	1-1	18	Benyon [7]	1617
24	26	H	Stevenage Bor	L	2-3	0-1	20	Clarke [47], Flynn [86]	2878
25	30	H	Exeter C	L	1-2	0-0	22	Hann [60]	1314
26	Jan 1	A	Woking	W	2-1	0-1	—	Marwa [56], Davis [81]	2178
27	6	H	Northwich Vic	L	1-3	0-2	20	Clarke (pen) [63]	767
28	20	A	Burton Alb	L	0-1	0-1	22		1632
29	23	A	Stevenage Bor	W	2-1	0-0	—	Hakim [70], Clarke [73]	2141
30	27	H	Halifax T	W	3-2	2-1	16	Clarke [22], Archer [24], Davis [59]	1009
31	Feb 10	H	Crawley T	D	2-2	1-1	18	Marwa [18], Archer [58]	857
32	17	A	Rushden & D	L	0-1	0-0	20		2488
33	24	H	Stafford R	L	0-3	0-2	20		883
34	27	A	Grays Ath	L	1-2	1-1	—	Archer [10]	803
35	Mar 3	A	Morecambe	L	0-2	0-1	21		1415
36	10	H	Southport	D	2-2	0-1	23	Watters [56], Elphick [83]	948
37	13	H	Dagenham & R	L	1-2	1-2	—	Archer [20]	1170
38	17	A	York C	D	0-0	0-0	23		2927
39	24	H	Kidderminster H	D	1-1	1-1	23	Archer [19]	821
40	31	A	Aldershot T	L	0-2	0-1	24		1749
41	Apr 3	H	Morecambe	L	0-2	0-1	—		613
42	7	H	Altrincham	L	1-5	1-4	24	Archer [10]	680
43	9	A	Tamworth	D	1-1	1-0	—	Clarke [15]	966
44	14	H	Oxford U	L	0-2	0-1	24		1713
45	21	A	Gravesend & N	L	2-3	0-1	24	Sangare [57], Martin B [90]	1035
46	28	H	Weymouth	W	1-0	0-0	24	Sangare [57]	734

Final League Position: 24

GOALSCORERS

League (57): Clarke 9 (2 pens), Hakim 9, Archer 6, Benyon 6, Davis 5 (3 pens), Marwa 4, Theobald 3, Batt D 2, Cracknell 2, Flynn 2, Sangare 2, Elphick 1, Hann 1, Jackman 1, Martin B 1, McBean 1, Walshe 1, Watters 1.
FA Cup (1): Davis 1 (pen).
Trophy (2): Clarke 1, own goal 1.

Bastock 44	Seeby 40 + 3	Flynn 16 + 4	Marwa 23 + 6	Elphick 36 + 1	Theobald 22	Hann 30 + 8	Davis 39 + 1	Clarke 39 + 5	Hakim 21 + 2	Wilde 7 + 3	Norris 2 + 7	Martin S 5 + 9	Martin B 2 + 6	Sozzo 2 + 4	Lewis 1	Cracknell 18 + 11	Batt D 22	Okuonghae 15 + 4	Jackman 3 + 3	Husnu 1 / Cousins 5	Nicolas 6	Simpson 2 + 2	Roddis — + 2	Benyon 10 + 2	McBean 2	Perks 2	Batt S 2	Walshe 6	Sangare 16 + 1	Archer 15 + 2	Watters 7 + 4	Ada 11	Deen 15	Basse — + 3	Buari 9 + 4	Hastings 5 + 1	Lopez 5 + 5	Match No.
1	2	3	4	5■	6	7^1	8	9	10^2	11^3	12	13	14																									1
1	2	3	4	5■	6	7	8	9	10^2	11^1			12	13																								2
1	2	3	4^2		6	7^1	8	9^3	10	11	12			14	5	13																						3
1	2	3	12	5	6	7	8	9^2	10	11^1	13					4																						4
1	2	3		5	6	7	8	9	10	11		12		4^1																								5
1	2	3		5^2	6	7	8	9	10	11		12					4^1	13																				6
1	2	3		5	6	14	8	9	10		12	11^2		13^3			7^1	4																				7
1	2	3		5^1	6	7	8	9	10	12				11^2		13		4																				8
1	2	3			6	7^1	8	9	10	11^2	12			13			5	4																				9
1	2	3			6		8	9	10^2	13	12					7^1	5	4	11																			10
1	2	3		12	6^1		8	9^3	10	13	7						5	4	14	11^2																		11
1	2	3	7^2	5^1	6			9	10		12					13		4	11		8																	12
1	12	3	4^2	5^1	6		8	14	10								11	2	9^3		7	13																13
1	2	3			6		8	9^2	10			11^1				13	5	4			7		12															14
1	2	3^2			6		8	9	10			7^3				12	5	4^1	14		11	13																15
1	2				6		8		10			12				7	5		13		11	3		4^1	9^2													16
1	2		14		6	13	8		10				12			7^2	5				4^3	3^1		11	9													17
	2		4^1		6	7	8	12	10				13				3	5						14		1	9^3	11^2										18
	2			5	6	7	8	9	10								3							12		1	4^1	11										19
1	2	13	4	5	6	7	8^1	9^3								12	3	14						10				11^2										20
1	2	13	4	5	6	7	8	9^2									3	12						10				11^1										21
1	2	13	4^1	5	6	7	8	9									3	12						10				11^2										22
1	2		4	5		7	8	9									3	6						10				11										23
1	2^1	14	12	5		7	8	9	10^3			13				6^2	3	4						11														24
1	2		13	5		7	8	9			6^1	12				11^2	3	4						10														25
1	2		4	5		7	8	9								11	3■	6						10														26
1	2	3^1	4^3	5		7		9				14				11^2		6						10					12	13	8							27
1	2^1		4	5		7		9^2	13			14				6	3												8	10^3	12	11						28
1				5		7	8	9	12							11	3												6	10	4^1	2						29
1	12		13	5		7	8	9	10^2							4■	3^1												6	11		2						30
1	2		4	5		7	8	9																					6	10	11	3						31
1	14		4	5		7^2	8	9				10				12													6		11^3	2	3^1	13				32
1			4^1	5		13	8	9								12													6	10	11^2	2	3		7			33
1	2		12	5		7	8	9				10				6^1														11^2		4	3		13			34
1	2^1		4	5		7		9				12																	6^2		14	11	3	13	10^3	8		35
1				5		7	8	9								4^1													6	13	11^2	2	3			10	12	36
1	2^1			5		13	8	12																					6	9	14	3	11^3		7^2	10	4	37
1	2			5		13	8	12																					6	9^2		3	11		7^1	10	4	38
1	2^1			5		7	8	12								14													6	9	13		3		11^2	10	4^3	39
1	2		3	5		7^1	8^2	9								4													6	10^3			11		12	14	13	40
1	2		4^3	5		13	14	9								12													6	10	11^2		3		7		8^1	41
1	2		4	5		14	8	9								13				11^3										10			3	12	7^1		6^2	42
1	2		4■				8	9					5			6				11										10			3		7^1		12	43
1	2			5		14	8	9					12			4				11^2									6	10^3			3		7^1		13	44
1	2		4	5^1		7		9					12			8				11									6	10^2			3		13			45
1	2		4^3	5		7^1		9					10			8^2				11			14						6				3		12		13	46

FA Cup
Fourth Qualifying Round
Yeading (a) 1-2

Trophy
First Round Bishop's Stortford (a) 2-3

SOUTHPORT

Blue Square North

Ground: Haig Avenue, Southport PR8 6JZ. *Tel:* (01704) 533 422. *Year Formed:* 1881.
Record Gate: 20,010 (1932 v Newcastle U, FA Cup). *Nickname:* Sandgrounders. *Manager:* Peter Davenport.
Secretary: Ken Hilton. *Colours:* Old gold and black.

SOUTHPORT 2006–07 LEAGUE RECORD

Match No.	*Date*	*Venue*	*Opponents*	*Result*		*H/T Score*	*Lg. Pos.*	*Goalscorers*	*Attendance*
1	Aug 12	H	Woking	D	0-0	0-0	—		1305
2	15	A	Halifax T	D	1-1	0-0	—	Blakeman [48]	2002
3	19	A	Stafford R	L	0-1	0-0	18		1081
4	26	H	Rushden & D	L	1-2	0-2	19	Baker (pen) [85]	1083
5	28	A	Burton Alb	W	1-0	0-0	15	Boyd [61]	1831
6	Sept 2	H	Gravesend & N	D	2-2	2-2	15	Boyd [32], Powell [44]	861
7	9	A	Grays Ath	L	0-4	0-3	17		1024
8	16	H	Crawley T	W	3-1	3-0	16	Smith A [4], Maamria 2 (1 pen) [20, 45 (p)]	1025
9	19	A	Kidderminster H	L	0-2	0-0	—		1258
10	23	A	York C	D	2-2	2-1	20	Gray [1], Blakeman [34]	2446
11	26	H	Northwich Vic	L	1-2	0-1	—	Fowler [56]	1059
12	30	H	Exeter C	L	0-1	0-0	22		1163
13	Oct 3	A	Oxford U	D	2-2	1-0	—	Maamria 2 [3, 75]	5844
14	7	H	St Albans C	D	1-1	0-0	22	Gray [71]	1005
15	10	H	Stevenage Bor	L	1-2	1-0	—	Boyd [39]	1010
16	14	A	Weymouth	L	0-2	0-1	24		1865
17	21	A	Altrincham	L	1-2	0-2	24	Paterson [77]	1336
18	Nov 3	H	Tamworth	W	1-0	0-0	23	Blakeman [65]	1014
19	18	A	Aldershot T	D	2-2	0-1	24	Maamria [60], Day (og) [89]	2290
20	25	H	Cambridge U	L	1-2	1-0	24	Gray [30]	1106
21	Dec 2	A	Dagenham & R	D	0-0	0-0	24		1285
22	9	A	Forest Green R	W	2-1	1-0	23	Hoolickin [43], Doherty [59]	1090
23	26	H	Morecambe	L	1-2	1-0	23	Baker [37]	1804
24	30	H	Kidderminster H	L	0-1	0-0	23		1016
25	Jan 1	A	Northwich Vic	L	1-3	1-0	—	Maamria [43]	1056
26	6	H	Grays Ath	W	3-1	2-0	23	Donnelly [2], Gray [18], Baker [47]	810
27	20	A	Crawley T	L	1-2	0-1	23	Gray [46]	1152
28	23	A	Morecambe	D	0-0	0-0	—		1484
29	27	H	Forest Green R	L	1-2	1-2	23	Paterson [20]	1104
30	Feb 3	H	Altrincham	W	2-1	1-0	23	Baker [45], Newby [66]	1145
31	10	A	Tamworth	D	1-1	1-1	23	Baker [23]	1056
32	17	H	Aldershot T	W	1-0	1-0	22	Blakeman [26]	1160
33	24	A	Cambridge U	D	2-2	2-1	21	Blakeman [10], Duffy [44]	3444
34	Mar 3	H	Dagenham & R	L	1-4	0-2	22	Powell [83]	1245
35	6	H	Oxford U	L	0-1	0-0	—		1054
36	10	A	St Albans C	D	2-2	1-0	24	Blakeman [35], Duffy [69]	948
37	13	A	Stevenage Bor	L	1-3	1-0	—	Tait [25]	1653
38	17	H	Weymouth	L	0-1	0-0	24		918
39	24	A	Woking	D	1-1	0-1	24	Gray [63]	1276
40	27	H	Halifax T	D	1-1	1-0	—	Baker [13]	936
41	31	H	Stafford R	W	5-1	3-0	23	Baker 2 [33, 47], Maamria 2 [37, 71], Boyd [41]	1012
42	Apr 7	A	Rushden & D	W	3-2	2-1	23	Birch [4], Baker [28], Gray [74]	2122
43	9	H	Burton Alb	W	3-1	0-1	—	Baker (pen) [50], Duffy [78], Paterson [90]	1552
44	14	A	Gravesend & N	W	4-0	2-0	22	Duffy [9], Gray 2 [17, 85], Baker (pen) [75]	1432
45	21	H	York C	L	0-1	0-0	23		3206
46	28	A	Exeter C	L	1-2	1-0	23	Tait [40]	6670

Final League Position: 23

GOALSCORERS

League (57): Baker 11 (3 pens), Gray 9, Maamria 8 (1 pen), Blakeman 6, Boyd 4, Duffy 4, Paterson 3, Powell 2, Tait 2, Birch 1, Doherty 1, Donnelly 1, Fowler 1, Hoolickin 1, Newby 1, Smith A 1, own goal 1.
FA Cup (0).
Trophy (2): Baker 1, Gray 1.

Robinson 16	Lane 29 + 4	Hoolickin 22 + 3	Rowland 32 + 2	Lee 32	Boyd 35 + 6	Baker 36 + 4	Blakeman 24 + 10	Jackson 7 + 2	Maamria 26 + 1	Smith A 10	Booth 4 + 3	Powell 28 + 10	Fowler 5 + 13	Martin 6 + 1	Clancy 6 + 5	Olsen 12 + 7	Barlow — + 1	Owen — + 1	Barry — + 3	Harrison 17 + 2	Gray 26 + 8	Douglas — + 5	Kirkup 11 + 1	Ventre 3	Paterson 4 + 10	Tait 6 + 9	Donnelly 11	Doherty 6	Dubourdeau 3	Dugdale 7 + 1	Birch 19	Newby 7 + 4	Hocking 14	Holland 17	Duffy 15 + 2	Smith T 10	*Match No.*
1	2	3	4	5	6	7^{1}	8^{2}	9^{3}	10	11	12	13	14																							1
1■	2	3		5	6	7^{1}	8	13	10^{2}	11			12	4	9^{3}	14																				2
	2	3		5	6	7	8	9^{3}			13	11^{1}	12	4■	10^{2}		14			1																3
	2	3^{1}		5	6	7	8^{2}	9^{3}			11	4			12	10		13	14	1																4
	2	3	4	5	6		8				7^{1}	11		9		10			12	1																5
	2	3	4	5	6	13	8				9^{2}	7■		11^{3}	12	10^{1}				1	14															6
	2	3	4	5	6	12	8	14	10^{3}		9^{2}			13		7^{1}				1	11															7
1	2	3	4	5	6	7^{1}	8^{2}		10^{3}	9	12	13			11						14															8
1	2	7^{3}	4	5^{1}	6		8^{2}	9	10	11		12			3						13	14														9
1	12	3	4^{1}		6^{3}		8		10	11		2	7^{2}	5		14					9	13														10
1		3	4		6^{2}	14	8		10	11		2	7^{1}	5		13					9^{3}	12														11
1	2		4		6^{2}	7^{1}	13		10	11		12	8^{3}			3					9	14	5													12
1	2	12	4			7			10	11		8	6			3					9^{1}		5													13
1	2	12	4^{1}		14	7	13		10^{3}	11		6	8^{2}			3					9		5													14
1	2■	3^{2}			6^{1}	7		9^{3}		11		4	14		8	12					10	13	5													15
1		3	12		6	7	8	9^{3}				4	14		10^{1}	11^{2}			13				5	2												16
1	12	3^{2}	4	5^{1}	6		8	9^{3}				7	14			13							11	2	10											17
1	2	3			6	7	8		10^{1}			4	12								9^{2}			5	13	11										18
1	2	3	4		6	7^{2}	8^{1}		10			11	13			5					12					9										19
1	2		4	5	6	12	8^{2}						13								10		3			9	7^{1}	11								20
1	2	13	4	5	12	7^{2}	8^{1}		10^{3}			6				3										14	11	9								21
	2	11		5		7			10			8	12			3				15			6				4	9^{1}	1^{G}							22
	2	3^{3}	4^{1}	5	13	7			10			6^{2}	14								12		8				11	9	1							23
	2	3	4	5		7			10^{2}			8^{1}								15	12		6			13	11	9	1^{G}							24
	2	3^{2}	4	5	12	7			10^{3}			8^{1}								1	14		6			13	11	9								25
	2	3	4^{1}	5	6^{2}	7						8			13	9				1	10^{3}		12		14		11									26
	2	11	4	5	6	7						13				12				1	9				8^{1}		10^{2}			3							27
	2^{1}		4	5	6	7						8	12			13				1	9^{3}				14		10^{2}			3	11						28
	2		4	5	6	7						8^{2}	13							1					12		10^{1}			3	11	9					29
	14		4		6^{2}	7	13					12								1					10					5	2	9	3^{1}	8	11^{3}		30
			4		6	7	12													1	13				9^{2}					3	2	10	5	8	11^{1}		31
	2		4	5	6	7	8^{2}								13					1					12						3	10		11	9^{1}		32
	2■			5	6		8					12								1	9										3	10	4	7	11^{1}		33
			4	5^{1}		7	8					14								1	9					13				12	2	10^{3}	3	6	11^{2}		34
			4^{1}	5	6	7	8													1	9^{2}					12					2	10	3	11	13		35
	2		4^{1}		6	7^{2}	8^{3}		10			12								1	9					14					3		5	11	13		36
	2^{1}		12		14		13		10^{3}			6									9					8				5	3		4	7^{2}	11	1	37
			4			7	8		12												9^{2}				13	10				5	2		3^{1}	6	11	1	38
			4^{1}	5	12	7^{2}			10			6									9										2	13	3	8	11	1	39
			4■	5	6	7	13		10^{3}			12									9^{2}										2	14	3	8	11^{1}	1	40
	12			5^{1}	6^{2}	7	13		10^{3}			3									9					14					2		4	8	11	1	41
				5	6	7^{2}	13		10			3									9					12					2		4	8	11^{1}	1	42
				5	6	7			10^{2}			2									9^{1}				13	12	4				3			8	11	1	43
				5^{1}	6	7	13		10^{3}			8			12						9^{2}				14						2		4	11	3	1	44
				5	6	7	12		10^{3}			2■									9^{2}				14						3	13	4	8	11^{1}	1	45
			4	5^{1}	6	7	8														10				12	9					2	13		3	11^{2}	1	46

FA Cup
Fourth Qualifying Round Kettering T (h) 0-1

Trophy
First Round Droylsden (h) 1-0
Second Round Salisbury C (a) 1-2

STAFFORD RANGERS — Blue Square Premier

Ground: Marston Road, Stafford ST16 3BX. *Tel:* (01785) 602 430. *Year formed:* 1876.
Record gate: 8,536 (1975 v Rotherham U, FA Cup. *Nickname:* The Boro. *Manager:* Phil Robinson.
Secretary: Michael Hughes. *Colours:* Black and white striped shirts, black shorts, black stockings.

STAFFORD RANGERS 2006–07 LEAGUE RECORD

Match No.	Date	Venue	Opponents	Result		H/T Score	Lg. Pos.	Goalscorers	Attendance
1	Aug 12	A	Grays Ath	D	1-1	1-1	—	Grayson (pen) [9]	1049
2	15	H	Altrincham	W	1-0	0-0	—	Madjo [81]	1410
3	19	H	Southport	W	1-0	0-0	5	Grayson [81]	1081
4	26	A	Crawley T	W	2-1	1-1	5	Talbott [16], Street [78]	929
5	28	H	Aldershot T	L	0-3	0-1	7		1720
6	Sept 1	A	York C	D	0-0	0-0	—		2955
7	9	A	Stevenage Bor	L	0-6	0-4	9		1708
8	12	H	Burton Alb	D	1-1	0-1	—	Grayson (pen) [89]	1554
9	16	H	Rushden & D	D	1-1	0-1	11	Olaoye [90]	1054
10	19	A	Northwich Vic	L	0-4	0-2	—		971
11	23	H	Oxford U	L	0-1	0-0	14		1795
12	30	A	Forest Green R	L	1-2	0-1	15	Gibson R [54]	945
13	Oct 3	H	Dagenham & R	L	1-2	1-1	—	Grayson [45]	1143
14	7	A	Tamworth	D	0-0	0-0	17		1249
15	10	A	Gravesend & N	W	4-1	1-0	—	McCarthy (og) [11], Grayson 2 [50, 88], Madjo [70]	857
16	14	H	Woking	W	1-0	1-0	12	Madjo [8]	1033
17	21	A	Exeter C	W	2-1	0-0	12	Grayson 2 [71, 90]	3977
18	Nov 3	H	Weymouth	W	2-0	2-0	10	Gibson R [37], Grayson (pen) [41]	1056
19	18	A	Halifax T	L	1-3	0-1	11	Madjo [80]	1681
20	25	H	St Albans C	D	2-2	0-1	12	Madjo [64], Olaoye [90]	1030
21	Dec 9	A	Morecambe	L	0-1	0-1	15		1373
22	26	H	Kidderminster H	L	1-2	0-1	15	McAughtrie [82]	1758
23	Jan 1	A	Burton Alb	D	0-0	0-0	—		2570
24	13	A	Cambridge U	W	1-0	1-0	—	Olaoye [30]	2056
25	20	A	Rushden & D	L	1-2	0-0	13	Olaoye [90]	1837
26	23	A	Kidderminster H	L	0-2	0-1	—		1573
27	27	H	Morecambe	L	1-3	0-3	18	Madjo [54]	957
28	Feb 3	H	Exeter C	L	0-1	0-1	19		970
29	10	A	Weymouth	W	2-1	2-1	16	Reid [25], McNiven [45]	1371
30	17	H	Halifax T	L	2-3	1-3	18	McNiven 2 [7, 69]	1062
31	20	H	Stevenage Bor	L	1-3	1-2	—	McNiven [15]	653
32	24	A	St Albans C	W	3-0	2-0	16	McAughtrie [15], Grayson 2 [20, 90]	883
33	Mar 3	H	Cambridge U	L	1-2	1-1	19	McNiven [20]	1096
34	6	A	Dagenham & R	D	1-1	0-0	—	McNiven [89]	1710
35	10	H	Tamworth	L	0-4	0-3	20		1303
36	13	H	Gravesend & N	W	3-1	2-0	—	McNiven 3 [21, 37, 57]	524
37	17	A	Woking	D	1-1	0-0	16	Gibson R [51]	1294
38	24	H	Grays Ath	W	4-2	3-0	15	Grayson 2 [20, 45], McAughtrie [44], Madjo [59]	865
39	27	A	Altrincham	W	1-0	1-0	—	Madjo [43]	1150
40	31	A	Southport	L	1-5	0-3	14	Edwards [77]	1012
41	Apr 7	H	Crawley T	L	0-1	0-1	18		967
42	9	A	Aldershot T	L	2-4	2-2	—	Madjo 2 [29, 45]	1734
43	14	H	York C	D	0-0	0-0	20		1293
44	17	H	Northwich Vic	W	2-0	0-0	—	Madjo 2 [73, 87]	1049
45	21	A	Oxford U	L	0-2	0-1	18		7007
46	28	H	Forest Green R	L	0-1	0-0	20		1791

Final League Position: 20

GOALSCORERS

League (49): Grayson 13 (3 pens), Madjo 12, McNiven 9, Olaoye 4, Gibson R 3, McAughtrie 3, Edwards 1, Reid 1, Street 1, Talbott 1, own goal 1.
FA Cup (6): Madjo 2, Murray 2, Daniel 1, McAughtrie 1.
Trophy (0).

Williams 9	Sutton 37	Talbot 43	Murphy 34 + 4	Daniel 46	Murray 18 + 2	Downes 11 + 1	Street 20	Grayson 38 + 6	Madjo 37 + 5	Gibson R 37 + 6	Lovatt 30 + 6	Olaoye 5 + 12	Quailey 4 + 8	McAughtrie 38 + 1	Bailey 2	Dacres 1 + 1	Oldfield 5 + 7	Alcock 23 + 1	Robinson 2	Edwards 5 + 17	Basham 3	Barlow 1 + 1	Griffith 20	McNiven 8 + 1	Ridgeway 1 + 1	Reid 10 + 3	Gibson A 3 + 1	Duggan 14	Lorougnon — + 4	White 1 + 5	Match No.
1	2	3	4^{1}	5	6	7	8	9	10	11	12																				1
1	2	3	4	5	6	7	8	9	10	11^{1}		12																			2
1	2	3	4	5	6	7	8	9	10	11^{1}			12																		3
1	2	3	4	5	6	7	8	9	10^{1}	11		12																			4
1	2	3^{1}	4	5	6	7^{2}	8	9^{3}	10	11		13	14	12																	5
1			4	5	6	7	8	9	10^{2}	11	12		13	3	2^{1}																6
1		3	4■	5	12	7	8	9^{2}	10^{3}	11			14	2	6^{1}	13															7
1		3^{1}		5	6	7^{3}	8	9		11	13	12	10	2		4^{2}	14														8
1^{6}				5	6^{1}	7^{2}	8	9		11	4	12	10	2			13	15	3												9
				5	6	13	8	9^{2}	10^{3}	11	4^{1}	14	7	3			12	1	2												10
		3	4	5		7	8	9	10^{3}	11^{1}	6^{2}	14		2			13	1		12											11
		3	4	5		7^{2}	2	9	10^{3}	11	8^{1}		13	6			12	1		14											12
	2	3	4^{2}	5			8	9	13	11	7	14	12	6^{1}				1		10^{3}											13
	6	3	4	5			8	9	12	11^{2}	7		10^{1}	2				1		13											14
	2	3	4	5			8	9	10	11	7			6				1													15
	2	3	4	5			8	9	10^{2}	11	7^{1}			6			12	1		13											16
	2	3	4^{2}	5			8	9	10	11^{1}	7			6			13	1		12											17
	2	3	4	5^{1}	12		8^{2}	9	10	11	7			6				1		13											18
	2	3	4	5			8^{1}	9^{3}	10	12	7	13	14	6				1		11^{2}											19
	2	3	4	5	6		8		10	12		13	14					1		11^{2}	7^{1}	9^{3}									20
	2	3	4	5	6			9^{1}	10		7	8						1		12	11										21
	2	3	4	5				9	10^{2}	11		12		6				1		8^{1}	7	13									22
	2	3	4	5	6			9	10^{1}	11		12		7			8	1													23
	2	3	4	5	6			9		11		10		7			8	1													24
	2	3	4^{2}	5	6			9	14	11^{1}	12	10		7			8^{3}	1		13											25
	2	3		5	6			13	10	11^{1}	7	9^{2}		4			8	1		12											26
	2	3		5				9	10	12	7	11^{2}		4			8^{1}	1		13			6								27
	2^{1}	3	12	5				9	10		7			4				1		6^{2}			11	13	8^{3}	14					28
		3	4^{1}	5					10	12	2			6				1					11	9		8	7				29
	2	3	4	5	6			13	10	12								1					11^{2}	9		8	7^{1}				30
	2■	3	13	5				9		11^{1}	7^{2}			4				1		12			6	10	14	8^{3}					31
		3	4	5				9	13	11	12			8									6	10^{2}		7^{1}	2	1			32
	2	3	4	5				9^{3}	14	11	13			6						12			8^{1}	10		7^{2}		1			33
	2	3^{2}	4^{1}	5	6			13	10		7			11									8	9		12		1			34
	2	3	4^{3}	5	6^{1}			12	10	13	7			11									8^{2}	9		14		1			35
	2	3	12	5				13	10	11^{1}	7			4									6	9^{2}		8		1			36
	2	3		5				9	10	11	7			4									6			8		1			37
	2	3	12	5				9	10	11	7			4									6			8^{1}		1			38
	2	3	4	5				9	10^{1}	11	7			6									8					1	12		39
	2	3	4	5				9^{2}	10	11^{1}	7			6						12			8					1		13	40
	2	3^{1}		5				9	10	11	7			6						12			4			8^{2}		1		13	41
	2	3		5				13	10	11	7^{1}			4						14			6			8^{2}	12	1		9^{3}	42
	2	3	4	5				9^{1}	10	11	7			6									8					1		12	43
	2	3	4^{1}	5				9	10	11	7			6									8					1	12		44
	2	3	4^{1}	5				9	10	11^{2}	7			6						13			8					1^{6}	12	15	45
	2	3	4	5^{1}				9^{3}	10	11^{2}	7			6				1		12			8						14	13	46

FA Cup

Fourth Qualifying Round	Scarborough	(h)	3-0
First Round	Maidenhead U	(h)	1-1
		(a)	2-0
Second Round	Brighton & HA	(a)	0-3

Trophy

First Round	Kettering T	(a)	0-1

STEVENAGE BOROUGH Blue Square Premier

Ground: Broadhall Way Stadium, Broadhall Way, Stevenage, Hertfordshire SG2 8RH. *Tel:* (01438) 223 223.
Year Formed: 1976. *Record Gate:* 6,489 (1997 v Kidderminster Harriers, Conference). *Nickname:* The Boro.
Manager: Mark Stimson. *Secretary:* Roger Austin. *Colours:* Red and white shirts, black shorts, white stockings.

STEVENAGE BOROUGH 2006–07 LEAGUE RECORD

Match No.	*Date*	*Venue*	*Opponents*	*Result*		*H/T Score*	*Lg. Pos.*	*Goalscorers*	*Attendance*
1	Aug 12	A	Altrincham	L	1-2	0-2	—	Boyd [51]	1035
2	15	H	York C	L	1-2	1-1	—	Miller (pen) [21]	2306
3	19	H	Crawley T	L	2-3	1-0	21	Miller [40], Morison [58]	1751
4	26	A	Morecambe	D	3-3	2-1	21	Morison 3 [1, 26, 60]	1524
5	28	H	Forest Green R	D	3-3	2-2	21	Morison 2 [6, 90], Boyd [12]	1905
6	Sept 2	A	Tamworth	L	1-2	0-1	21	Boyd [57]	1034
7	9	H	Stafford R	W	6-0	4-0	20	Boyd 3 [25, 34, 61], Dobson 2 [43, 63], Morison [45]	1708
8	12	A	Aldershot T	L	0-4	0-2	—		2371
9	16	A	Cambridge U	L	0-1	0-1	22		2696
10	19	H	Weymouth	W	1-0	1-0	—	Beard [44]	1674
11	23	A	Exeter C	D	1-1	0-0	21	Guppy [58]	3194
12	30	H	Halifax T	W	2-1	1-1	16	Morison [19], Boyd [51]	1904
13	Oct 3	H	Woking	W	3-2	1-1	—	Lee [5], Nutter (pen) [84], Dobson [90]	2410
14	6	A	Rushden & D	D	2-2	1-2	—	Hatswell (og) [20], Nurse [49]	2309
15	10	A	Southport	W	2-1	0-1	—	Morison [49], Nurse [54]	1010
16	14	H	Dagenham & R	L	1-2	1-1	13	Morison [45]	2362
17	21	H	Northwich Vic	L	0-2	0-1	15		1773
18	Nov 3	A	Burton Alb	L	1-2	1-0	—	Nurse [16]	1907
19	18	H	Grays Ath	W	1-0	1-0	14	Miller [42]	2207
20	25	A	Kidderminster H	W	2-1	1-0	13	Oliver [8], Boyd [55]	1584
21	Dec 2	H	Oxford U	D	2-2	2-0	13	Morison 2 [16, 31]	3008
22	9	H	Gravesend & N	W	3-0	1-0	10	Nutter (pen) [27], Morison [73], Nurse [78]	2014
23	26	A	St Albans C	W	3-2	1-0	10	Miller [34], Boyd [77], Morison [83]	2878
24	30	A	Weymouth	W	1-0	1-0	10	Nurse [36]	1906
25	Jan 1	H	Aldershot T	W	3-2	1-1	—	Boyd 2 [32, 73], Morison [53]	2683
26	20	H	Cambridge U	W	4-1	0-1	8	Nutter (pen) [57], Beard [72], Binns [75], Morison [88]	2759
27	23	H	St Albans C	L	1-2	0-0	—	Binns [48]	2141
28	27	A	Gravesend & N	D	1-1	1-1	10	Morison [28]	1409
29	Feb 10	H	Burton Alb	W	2-1	0-0	8	Nutter [56], Miller [62]	2154
30	17	A	Grays Ath	W	2-0	1-0	7	Fuller [35], Morison [57]	1552
31	20	A	Stafford R	W	3-1	2-1	—	Morison 2 [17, 66], Hughes [42]	653
32	Mar 3	A	Oxford U	L	0-2	0-1	8		6410
33	6	A	Woking	W	1-0	1-0	—	Hughes [15]	1407
34	13	H	Southport	W	3-1	0-1	—	Nurse [49], Beard [89], Birch (og) [90]	1653
35	20	A	Dagenham & R	L	0-2	0-0	—		1984
36	24	H	Altrincham	L	0-1	0-1	9		1913
37	27	A	York C	W	1-0	0-0	—	Hakim [54]	2969
38	31	A	Crawley T	L	0-3	0-1	8		1258
39	Apr 3	H	Kidderminster H	L	1-2	0-2	—	Henry [46]	1753
40	7	H	Morecambe	D	3-3	1-1	8	Nurse [27], Morison [46], Hakim [52]	1845
41	9	A	Forest Green R	D	4-4	1-3	—	Dobson [33], Cole [59], Nutter (pen) [78], Morison [81]	969
42	14	H	Tamworth	W	3-0	1-0	8	Cole [11], Oliver [56], Morison [80]	2202
43	17	H	Rushden & D	W	1-0	0-0	—	Nutter (pen) [62]	1715
44	21	H	Exeter C	D	0-0	0-0	8		3058
45	25	A	Northwich Vic	D	0-0	0-0	—		515
46	28	A	Halifax T	L	1-2	0-1	8	Nurse [60]	2515

Final League Position: 8

GOALSCORERS

League (76): Morison 23, Boyd 11, Nurse 8, Nutter 6 (5 pens), Miller 5 (1 pen), Dobson 4, Beard 3, Binns 2, Cole 2, Hakim 2, Hughes 2, Oliver 2, Fuller 1, Guppy 1, Henry 1, Lee 1, own goals 2.
FA Cup (4): Morison 2, Boyd 1, Miller 1.
Trophy (23): Morison 8, Boyd 4, Dobson 2, Slabber 2, Cole 1, Gaia 1, Guppy 1, McMahon 1, Miller 1, Nurse 1, Oliver 1.

Potter 4	Henry 37 + 3	Nutter 46	Miller 24 + 5	Gaia 38 + 1	Oliver 19 + 9	Dobson 23 + 15	Fuller 38	Stamp 1 + 3	Thorpe 2 + 2	Boyd 25	Sullivan — + 6	Nurse 23 + 9	Bulman 1	Goodliffe 7 + 1	Hicks 4	Guppy 25 + 2	Julian 42 + 1	Morison 42 + 1	Lee 10 + 2	Beard 37 + 2	Deen 2 + 5	Binns 3 + 6	Johnson 4	Scaley — + 1	Bradshaw — + 1	Hatton — + 1	Hughes 8 + 2	Slabber 2 + 2	Cole 14 + 5	Batt 5 + 3	McMahon 12	Hakim 5 + 7	Lewis 3 + 5	*Match No.*
1	2	3	4	5	6	7	8	9^1	10^2	11	12	13																						1
1	12	3	4	5^1	6	7	2		10^2	11	13	9	8																					2
1■		3	4		6	7^1	2			11	12	13		5	8	10^6	15	9^2																3
	13	3	4		6	7^1	2		12	11				5	8^2	10	1	9																4
		3	4	5		7^1	2	12		11				6	8	10	1	9																5
	13	3	4	5		12	2^1	14		11^3				6	8^2	10	1	9	7															6
		3	4^2	5	6	7	2^1			11^3	14			8		10	1	9	13	12														7
		3	4■	5	6	7^1	8^2			11	14			2		10^3	1	9	13	12														8
		3		5	13	7^3	8		12	11	14			4^2		10	1	9	6	2^1														9
	2	3		5		7	8			11						10	1	9	4	6														10
	2	3		5		7	8	12		11						10	1	9^1	6	4														11
	2	3		5		7	4			11		12				10^1	1	9	6	8^2	13													12
	2	3		5		7	8			11		12				10^1	1	9	6	4														13
	2	3		5		7	8			11		10					1	9	6	4														14
	2	3		5	6^1	12	8			11		10^2					1	9	7	4	13													15
	2	3	13	5		7	8^1			11		10					1	9	4^2	6	12													16
	2	3	12	5		7^2	8			11		10					1	9	6^1	4^3	14	13												17
1	2	3	4	5			8			11		10						9		7		6												18
	2	3	4	5		12	8			11		10^1					1	9		7			6											19
	2	3	4		6	13	8^1			11^2						10	1	9^3		7	12		5	14										20
	2	3	4	12	6■	13				11						10^1	1	9		7^2	5■		8											21
	2	3	4^1	5		7^3				11		14				10^2	1	9		8		12	6		13									22
	2	3	4	5	14	13	8			11^2		7				10^1	1	9^3		6		12												23
	2	3	4	5	13	12	8			11^1		7				10	1	9^2		6														24
	2	3^1	4^2	5	12	14	8			11^3		7				10	1	9		6						13								25
	2	3	4	5	14		8^1					7				11^2	1	9		6		13					12	10^3						26
	2	3	4	5	13		8^1					7					1	9		6		11					12	10^2						27
	2	3	4	5	6^3	14						7		12			1	9		8		11^2					10^1		13					28
	2	3	4	5			8^1					7				13	1	9		10^3									11^2	12	6	14		29
	2	3		5			8					7					1	9		6		13					10^1	12	11^2		4			30
	2	3		5		13	8					11^2				10^1	1	9		7							6		12		4			31
	2	3		5		13	8^1					9					1			6							7^2	14	11	12	4	10^3		32
	2	3		5								10					1	9		7^1		13					4		11^2	6	8	12		33
	2	3		5■	13							7					1	9		8							10		11^1	6	4^2	12		34
	2	3			6	13	8					7^1					1	9		5							10		11		4^2	12		35
	2	3			6	12						14				10^1	1	9		8									11	4	5^2	7^3	13	36
	2	3			6											10	1	9		7									11	5	4	8		37
	2	3	13■		6	14										10^1	1	9^3		7									11	5	4^2	8	12	38
	2	3		5	13	7^2	8					11				10^3	1	9		4							6^1		14				12	39
	2	3^1		5		7^2	8					10					1	9		6									11	12		13	4	40
	2	3	4	5	12	7^2	8					13					1	9		6									11			10^1		41
	2	3	4	5	6	7^1	8									13	1	9^3		10									11^2			14	12	42
	2	3	4	5	6^3	7^1	8					12					1	9		10^2									11			14	13	43
	2	3	4	5	6	12	8										1	9		10^1									11				7	44
	2	3	13	5	6	7^1	8					14				10	1	9^3											12		4^2		11	45
		3	13	5	6^3	7^1	8					9^2				10	1	14		2	11								12		4			46

FA Cup

Fourth Qualifying Round	Forest Green R	(h)	4-1
First Round	Wrexham	(a)	0-1

Trophy

First Round	Merthyr T	(h)	7-0
Second Round	Leigh RMI	(h)	3-1
Third Round	Morecambe	(a)	1-1
		(h)	3-0
Fourth Round	Salisbury C	(h)	3-0
Semi-Final	Grays Ath	(a)	1-0
		(h)	2-1
Final *(at Wembley)*	Kidderminster H		3-2

TAMWORTH

Blue Square North

Ground: The Lamb Ground, Kettlebrook, Tamworth, Staffordshire B77 1AA. *Tel:* (01827) 65798.
Year Formed: 1933. *Record Gate:* 4,920 (1948 v Atherstone Town, Birmingham Combination). *Nickname:* The Lambs. *Manager:* Gary Mills. *Secretary:* Russell Moore. *Colours:* Red shirts, red shorts, white stockings.

TAMWORTH 2006–07 LEAGUE RECORD

Match No.	Date	Venue	Opponents	Result		H/T Score	Lg. Pos.	Goalscorers	Attendance
1	Aug 12	H	Weymouth	L	1-3	0-2	—	Williams [86]	1409
2	15	A	Gravesend & N	L	1-4	1-2	—	Stevenson [15]	936
3	19	A	Dagenham & R	L	0-4	0-2	23		947
4	26	H	Exeter C	W	1-0	0-0	18	Smith [80]	1242
5	28	A	St Albans C	L	0-1	0-1	19		1184
6	Sept 2	H	Stevenage Bor	W	2-1	1-0	18	Nutter (og) [32], Atieno [52]	1034
7	9	A	Kidderminster H	W	2-0	0-0	14	Atieno [53], Thomas [64]	1641
8	12	H	Rushden & D	L	1-4	0-1	—	Williams [50]	1105
9	16	H	Forest Green R	D	1-1	1-0	15	Atieno [12]	1215
10	19	A	Morecambe	D	0-0	0-0	—		1248
11	23	A	Altrincham	L	0-2	0-2	17		882
12	30	H	Cambridge U	L	0-1	0-1	19		1233
13	Oct 3	A	Aldershot T	D	3-3	2-1	—	Burton [43], Weaver [45], Storer [64]	2084
14	7	H	Stafford R	D	0-0	0-0	20		1249
15	10	H	Grays Ath	W	4-2	3-0	—	McGrath [2], Atieno 2 [10, 18], Thomas [50]	907
16	14	A	Halifax T	L	1-3	1-2	20	Burton (pen) [43]	1646
17	21	H	York C	D	2-2	1-2	19	Williams 2 [25, 61]	1311
18	Nov 3	A	Southport	L	0-1	0-0	21		1014
19	18	H	Woking	W	3-1	2-1	20	McGrath [17], Taylor [21], Burton [90]	1039
20	25	A	Oxford U	L	1-2	0-0	21	Atieno [62]	6614
21	Dec 9	A	Crawley T	L	0-1	0-0	24		957
22	26	H	Burton Alb	L	0-1	0-0	24		2029
23	30	H	Morecambe	L	0-1	0-0	24		1029
24	Jan 1	A	Rushden & D	D	1-1	0-1	—	Atieno [73]	1872
25	20	A	Forest Green R	L	0-2	0-0	24		1049
26	27	H	Crawley T	L	0-1	0-0	24		1101
27	Feb 3	A	York C	W	2-0	1-0	24	Edwards [21], Atieno [86]	2477
28	10	H	Southport	D	1-1	1-1	24	McGrath [35]	1056
29	17	A	Woking	W	2-0	0-0	24	Edwards [51], Heslop [82]	1411
30	20	A	Burton Alb	L	0-1	0-0	—		1953
31	24	H	Oxford U	L	1-3	0-2	24	Williams [89]	2089
32	Mar 3	A	Northwich Vic	W	1-0	0-0	24	Taylor [74]	1070
33	6	H	Aldershot T	W	2-0	1-0	—	Taylor [42], Edwards [90]	1086
34	10	A	Stafford R	W	4-0	3-0	21	Atieno 2 [13, 24], Edwards 2 [43, 65]	1303
35	13	A	Grays Ath	L	0-1	0-1	—		779
36	17	H	Halifax T	W	1-0	1-0	19	Taylor [3]	1337
37	20	H	Kidderminster H	D	0-0	0-0	—		1115
38	24	A	Weymouth	L	1-3	1-1	21	Atieno [41]	1369
39	27	H	Gravesend & N	W	2-1	1-0	—	Edwards 2 [45, 61]	1044
40	31	H	Dagenham & R	L	0-2	0-1	21		1269
41	Apr 3	H	Northwich Vic	L	0-1	0-0	—		1006
42	7	A	Exeter C	L	0-1	0-0	22		4180
43	9	H	St Albans C	D	1-1	0-1	—	Law (pen) [78]	966
44	14	A	Stevenage Bor	L	0-3	0-1	23		2202
45	21	H	Altrincham	W	1-0	1-0	22	Atieno [14]	2411
46	28	A	Cambridge U	L	0-1	0-0	22		6021

Final League Position: 22

GOALSCORERS

League (43): Atieno 12, Edwards 7, Williams 5, Taylor 4, Burton 3 (1 pen), McGrath 3, Thomas 2, Heslop 1, Law 1 (pen), Smith 1, Stevenson 1, Storer 1, Weaver 1, own goal 1.
FA Cup (8): McGrath 2, Atieno 1, Burton 1, Stevenson 1, Storer 1, Williams 1, own goal 1.
Trophy (4): Edwards 1, Heslop 1, Stevenson 1, Taylor 1.

Match No.	Bowles 15 + 1	Smith 35 + 1	Bampton 3 + 6	Friars 19 + 2	Redmile 2	Kemp 20 + 1	Ward 5 + 5 / Briscoe 15 + 2	Storer 22 + 8	Moore 3 + 2	Birch 1	McGrath 41 + 1	Law 23 + 5	Stevenson 13 + 14	Williams 18 + 14	Neilson 4 + 3	Dormand 1	Weaver 36 + 2	Thomas 11	McCallum 12 + 1	Atieno 37 + 2
1	1	2	3	4	5	6[1]	7	8[2]	9	10[3]	11	12	13	14						
2	1	2	3[1]		5		7	12	9		11	4	6	10	8					
3	15	2[1]		4		12	7	8	9		11[2]	3	6	10	13	1[G]	5			
4	1	2				6	7				11	12	9[2]	13	8[1]		5	3	4	10
5	1	2				6	7[2]		13		11[1]	4	9[3]	14	12		5	3	8	10
6	1	4				6	14	13	12		11[1]			9[3]	7■		5	2	8	10
7	1	2	12			6		8			11			9[3]			5	3	7[2]	10
8	1	2[1]	14			6		8[2]			3			9			5	4	11	10
9	1					6							12	9[2]	7		5	3	11■	10[3]
10	1	2		12		3		8					9	14			5			7[2]
11	1	2				3		8			12		4[2]	13			5	6	9[3]	7
12	1	2		4[1]		6		8[2]			11	3		9■			5		7	10[3]
13	1			4[1]		6	13[3]	8			11	3[2]			14		5			10
14	1	13				6	14	8[2]			11		9[3]				5	7	3[1]	10
15	1	2				6	13				11		14				5[1]	3	7	10
16	1	2[2]				6	13				11		14	12			5	3	7	10[3]
17		2				6		13			11[2]			7			5	4[1]	14	10
18		2				6		12			11		13	9[2]			5		8[1]	10[3]
19		2						14			11	12	7[2]	13			5			10
20		2						13			11	12	7[2]				5			10
21		2									11	3	9[2]	13			5[1]			10
22		2				6		8					12	9[G]			5			10[2]
23		2				6		13			11		12	14			5			10[3]
24		2				6		4			11		12	10[2]			5			13
25		2				6		8[1]			11■		9				5			13
26				4				8			11[1]	2	9[3]	14			5			10
27		2		4				8				11		7			5			10
28		2		4				8			11[1]	12		7			5			10
29		2		4				8			11			6			5			10[1]
30				4[1]			12	8			11[2]	2	13	7			5			10■
31		2		4			12	8			11		14	7			5			
32		2		4			6				11	7	9[2]				5			
33		2	12	4[1]			8				11	7		10[3]			5			
34		2[3]	12	4			8				11	7					5[1]			10
35							8				11	2					5[1]			10
36		2[1]	12	4			8				11	7								10
37				4			6	8			11	2								10
38				4			7	8[2]			11	2	12							10
39		6	12	4			5	13			11	2								10[2]
40		8		4			5				11	2	13							10[2]
41							5	4[2]			11	2	14	10[3]			13			
42							5	6			11	2		14						10
43		2		4[2]			6				11	7	13				5[1]			10
44		2					6				11	7[1]		13			12			10
45		2					6				11	7		12			5			10
46			4[G]	15			6				11			12			5			10

Match No.	Deakin 5	Burton 12 + 14	Kendrick 9 + 6	Touhy 4 + 5	Devlin 1 + 3 / Quistin — + 9	Bradley 2	Harban 4 / Lynch 3	Laight 12 + 1	Ghent 1 / Ujah 1	Da Viega 28	Taylor 21 + 2	Heslop 24 + 3	Belford D — + 1	Belford C 1	Bains 21	Cooper — + 1	Price 1 + 1	Edwards 20 + 1
1																		
2																		
3																		
4																		
5																		
6	3[2]																	
7	4[1]	14	13															
8	7[3]	13	12															
9	8	14	4	2[1]	13													
10	6	10[3]	4[1]		13	11												
11		14	11[1]		10													
12		13		12	14													
13		9	12				2	7										
14			12				2	4										
15		9[3]	12				8[2]	4										
16		9					8[1]	4										
17		9[3]	3	12				8	1									
18		14	3			7				1	4							
19		9[3]	3					4[1]		1	6	8						
20		9	3[1]					4		1	6	8						
21		7	12					4		1	8	6						
22		13	3					4[1]		1■	7	11	15					
23		9	3[2]					4			7[1]	8		1				
24		9						3		1	7[1]	8						
25										1		7			3	12	4[2]	10
26		13						3		1		7					12	6[2]
27		13						12		1		6			3[1]			9[2]
28		13								1		6			3			9[2]
29		13		12						1		7			3			9[2]
30		9[3]		14						1		6			3			
31		9[2]								1	13	6[1]			3			10[3]
32		12			13					1	8				3			10[1]
33		13								1	6[2]	14			3			9
34					13					1	6[2]	14			3			9
35		13		6	12					1	7	4			3			9[2]
36					13					1	6[2]	5			3			9
37										1	7	9			3			5
38					13					1	5	9			3			6[1]
39										1	7	8[1]			3			9
40					12					1	6	7[1]			3			9
41					12		6			1	7[1]	8			3			9
42					12		4[1]		7[2]	1	13	8			3			9[3]
43					14■					1	8	12			3			9[3]
44				5[2]						1	4	8			3			9
45				13						1	4[1]	8			3			9[2]
46				9[2]			2			1■	7[1]	8			3			13

FA Cup

Round	Opponents	Venue	Result
Fourth Qualifying Round	Harrogate T	(h)	3-1
First Round	Burton Alb	(a)	2-1
Second Round	Rushden & D	(a)	2-1
Third Round	Norwich C	(h)	1-4

Trophy

Round	Opponents	Venue	Result
First Round	Altrincham	(a)	0-0
		(h)	2-1
Second Round	Welling U	(h)	1-1
		(a)	1-2

WEYMOUTH

Blue Square Premier

Ground: Wessex Stadium, Radipole Road, Weymouth, Dorset DT4 9XJ. *Tel:* (01305) 785 558. *Year formed:* 1890.
Record gate: 6,680 (2005 v Nottingham F, FA Cup). *Nickname:* The Terras. *Manager:* Jason Tindall.
Secretary: Pete Saxby. *Colours:* Claret and sky blue.

WEYMOUTH 2006–07 LEAGUE RECORD

Match No.	Date	Venue	Opponents	Result		H/T Score	Lg. Pos.	Goalscorers	Attendance
1	Aug 12	A	Tamworth	W	3-1	2-0	—	Smith [1], Tully [13], Downer [53]	1409
2	15	H	Aldershot T	W	1-0	0-0	—	Downer [83]	3583
3	19	H	Cambridge U	W	2-1	1-0	1	Eribenne [24], Smith [59]	1766
4	26	A	Kidderminster H	W	1-0	1-0	2	Eribenne (pen) [10]	1753
5	28	H	Oxford U	D	1-1	0-0	3	Johnson (og) [85]	5244
6	Sept 2	A	Morecambe	L	0-2	0-1	6		1333
7	9	A	Burton Alb	D	1-1	0-1	5	Nade [90]	1523
8	12	H	Forest Green R	W	1-0	0-0	—	Crittenden [60]	1568
9	16	H	Halifax T	W	1-0	1-0	3	Weatherstone [3]	1910
10	19	A	Stevenage Bor	L	0-1	0-1	—		1674
11	23	A	Dagenham & R	L	1-4	1-3	6	Smith [40]	1602
12	30	H	St Albans C	W	2-1	0-0	3	Purser 2 [80, 85]	1676
13	Oct 4	H	Gravesend & N	W	2-1	1-1	—	Smith [18], Logan [64]	2153
14	7	A	Altrincham	D	0-0	0-0	3		1214
15	10	A	Crawley T	W	3-0	0-0	—	Logan [51], Smith [69], Elam [81]	1218
16	14	H	Southport	W	2-0	1-0	3	Elam [44], Logan (pen) [65]	1865
17	21	H	Rushden & D	D	1-1	1-1	3	Smith [36]	2148
18	Nov 3	A	Stafford R	L	0-2	0-2	3		1056
19	18	H	York C	L	1-2	0-0	3	Purser [71]	1774
20	25	A	Woking	L	0-4	0-2	4		1884
21	Dec 2	H	Grays Ath	W	3-2	2-2	4	Logan [18], Nade [33], Eribenne [77]	1451
22	9	A	Northwich Vic	W	1-0	1-0	3	Smith [17]	874
23	26	H	Exeter C	W	2-1	1-0	3	Logan [14], Smith [82]	4294
24	30	H	Stevenage Bor	L	0-1	0-1	4		1906
25	Jan 1	A	Forest Green R	L	2-3	0-3	—	Smith 2 [50, 83]	1245
26	23	A	Exeter C	L	0-4	0-1	—		3474
27	27	H	Northwich Vic	D	1-1	0-0	8	Beavon [63]	1451
28	Feb 3	H	Burton Alb	D	1-1	0-1	9	Beavon [90]	1370
29	10	H	Stafford R	L	1-2	1-2	11	Tindall (pen) [41]	1371
30	17	A	York C	L	0-1	0-0	11		2769
31	20	A	Halifax T	L	1-4	1-1	—	Beavon [2]	1277
32	Mar 3	A	Grays Ath	D	2-2	0-1	10	Beavon 2 [70, 76]	1003
33	6	A	Gravesend & N	W	3-1	0-1	—	Coutts 2 [52, 63], James (pen) [88]	1098
34	10	H	Altrincham	L	1-2	0-1	10	Nade [90]	1503
35	13	H	Crawley T	W	3-2	0-0	—	Beavon [49], Okuonghae (og) [72], Coutts [90]	1310
36	17	A	Southport	W	1-0	0-0	9	Matthews [89]	918
37	20	H	Woking	L	2-3	2-0	—	Nade [15], Weatherstone [33]	1257
38	24	H	Tamworth	W	3-1	1-1	8	Crittenden [25], James (pen) [53], Bains (og) [68]	1369
39	27	A	Aldershot T	L	0-1	0-0	—		2224
40	31	A	Cambridge U	L	0-7	0-4	9		2698
41	Apr 3	A	Rushden & D	L	1-4	0-1	—	Crittenden [68]	1624
42	7	H	Kidderminster H	D	1-1	1-1	10	Crittenden [21]	1439
43	9	A	Oxford U	L	1-4	1-1	—	Nade [40]	5582
44	14	H	Morecambe	W	2-1	1-1	10	Beavon [38], James (pen) [53]	1206
45	21	H	Dagenham & R	D	1-1	1-0	10	Nade [9]	1655
46	28	A	St Albans C	L	0-1	0-0	11		734

Final League Position: 11

GOALSCORERS

League (56): Smith 10, Beavon 7, Nade 6, Logan 5 (1 pen), Crittenden 4, Coutts 3, Eribenne 3 (1 pen), James 3 (3 pens), Purser 3, Downer 2, Elam 2, Weatherstone 2, Matthews 1, Tindall 1 (pen), Tully 1, own goals 3.
FA Cup (8): Purser 2, Downer 1, Elam 1, Logan 1, O'Brien 1, Tully 1, Weatherstone 1.
Trophy (1): Logan 1 (pen).

Lee-Barrett 19	Tully 23 + 2	El Kholti 23	O'Brien 15 + 4	Downer 15 + 2	Smith 25	Crittenden 30 + 2	Weatherstone 38 + 4	Nade 32 + 5	Eribenne 16 + 8	Elam 23	Purser 7 + 5	Logan 14 + 9	Vickers 26 + 4	Tindall 5 + 13	James 26 + 7	Wilkinson 10 + 5	Howell 11 + 6	Williams — + 2	Challis 17 + 5	Matthews 25	Beavon 18 + 2	Coutts 16 + 5	Dutton 7 + 7	Bernard 9 + 3	Hartman 3 + 1	Dixon 1 + 2	Ross-Jennings — + 1	Cottrell 16 + 1	Platt 6 + 5	Phillips 7 + 4	Welsh 9	Crawley 2 + 3	Rink — + 1	Robinson 10 + 2	Bell — + 3	Jones 2	Ironside — + 1	*Match No.*
1	2	3	4	5	6	7	8	9^{1}	10^{2}	11	12	13																										1
1	2	3		5	6	7	8	9^{2}	10^{3}	11^{1}	13	14	4	12																								2
1	2	3		5	6	7	8	9^{2}	10^{3}	11^{1}	12	14	4		13																							3
1	2	3		5^{1}	6	7	8	9	10^{3}	11^{2}		13	4		12	14																						4
1	2	3		5	6	7	8	9^{1}	10^{2}	11	12	13	4																									5
1	2	3^{1}		5	6	7	8	9	10	11^{3}		12	4^{2}		13		14																					6
1	2	3		5	6	7^{2}	8	14	10^{3}	11		9	4^{1}	13			12																					7
1	2	3		12^{2}	6	7	8	9		11		10^{3}	4^{1}	14	5		13																					8
1	2	3	14	5^{1}	6	7^{2}	8	9	10	11				12	4		13^{3}																					9
1	2	3		12	7		8^{3}	9	10	11				5^{1}	4	14	6^{2}	13																				10
1	2	3	13	5^{1}	6		8	9■	10	11			4^{2}			7^{3}	12	14																				11
1	2	3^{2}	4	5	6		8		10		9^{3}	13			7^{1}	12	11		14																			12
1	12	3	4	5^{1}	6		13		14	11	9^{3}	10			2	8^{2}	7																					13
1	12	3	4	5^{1}	6		13	9^{3}	14	11		10			2	8^{2}	7																					14
1	2	3	4	5	6		13	9^{3}	14	11^{1}		10^{2}				8	7■		12																			15
1	2	3	4		6		8	9^{3}	14	11^{2}		10	5^{1}	12		7			13																			16
1	2	3	4		6		8	14	10^{3}	11	13	9^{2}	5			12	7^{1}																					17
1	2		4		6	7^{3}	8			11	10	9	5^{1}	13	12	14			3^{2}																			18
	2	3	4		6		8			11	10^{3}	9	5^{1}	14	12	7^{2}			13	1																		19
1	2	3^{1}	4	5	6			9	13	11^{2}	10			7		8■			12																			20
	2	3	4		6		8	9	14		11^{2}	10^{3}	5		13		12		7^{1}	1																		21
	2	7^{1}		5	6		8	9^{3}	13	11	10^{2}	14	4		12				3■	1																		22
	2	3^{1}	13		6	12		14	10^{3}	11^{2}		9	5		4	8	7			1																		23
	2	3^{1}			6	14	13	12	10	11		9	5		4	8^{2}	7^{3}			1																		24
	2		4^{1}		6		8	9	13	11^{3}		14	12		5	10^{2}	7		3	1																		25
			4^{1}			7	8	9	10			6	12	14	2		11^{3}		3^{2}	1	13	5																26
						7	8		10^{2}			9	5■	12	6		4			1	13	2^{1}	3	11														27
						7	8							5	6				3	1	9	2	4	11	10													28
			12			7	8						5	10					4^{1}	1	9	6	2	3^{2}	11^{3}	13	14											29
			4			7							5	10					3	1	9	8	13		12			2	11^{1}	6^{2}								30
			4			7^{2}	8						12■	13	5				3	1	10	11	14					2^{1}	9■	6^{3}								31
						7	8	12							5				3	1	9	11^{2}	4^{1}			13		2		6	10							32
						7	8	9^{3}							5				3	1	10	12	13	14		4^{1}		2		6^{2}	11							33
						7	8^{1}	9							5				3	1	10	11^{3}	4^{2}	14				2			6	12	13					34
						7	8	9^{2}							5				3	1	10	4						2	12		11	6^{1}		13				35
						7	8	9							5				3	1	10	4^{1}		13^{3}				2	14		11	6^{2}		12				36
						7	8	9					14		5				3	1	10	13						2^{1}	4^{3}	12	6^{2}			11				37
						7	8	9					6		5					1	10^{3}	13	12					2	4^{1}		11^{2}			3	14			38
						7	8^{3}	9					6^{1}		5					1	10	13	12					2	4^{2}	14	11			3				39
						7	8	9^{3}					6^{1}	13	5					1	10	4^{2}	12					2		14	11			3				40
						7	8	9					6		5					1	10	4^{3}	13	3				2^{1}	14	12				11^{2}				41
						7		9					6		5						10	4		3				2		11				8		1		42
						7	8	9					6^{1}	12	5						10	13		3				2	14	4^{2}				11^{3}		1		43
						7	8	9							5^{1}					1	10^{3}	2	6	3				12	14	4^{2}				11			13	44
						7	8	9^{1}											5	1		4	6■	3				2	10^{2}			13		11	12			45
							8	9^{3}					5	14					6	1	10^{2}	4		3	7^{1}			2				12		11	13			46

FA Cup

Fourth Qualifying Round			
	Hungerford T	(a)	3-0
First Round	Bury	(h)	2-2
		(a)	3-4

Trophy

First Round	Grays Ath	(h)	1-2

WOKING

Blue Square Premier

Ground: Kingfield Sports Ground, Kingfield, Woking, Surrey GU22 9AA. *Tel:* (01483) 772 470. *Year Formed:* 1889.
Record Gate: 6,084 (1997 v Coventry City, FA Cup Third Round). *Nickname:* The Cards. *Manager:* Frank Gray.
Secretary: Phil Ledger. *Colours:* Red and white shirts, black shorts, red stockings.

WOKING 2006–07 LEAGUE RECORD

Match No.	Date	Venue	Opponents	Result		H/T Score	Lg. Pos.	Goalscorers	Attendance
1	Aug 12	A	Southport	D	0-0	0-0	—		1305
2	15	H	Crawley T	L	1-2	1-1	—	McAllister [45]	1750
3	19	H	Morecambe	D	1-1	0-0	17	Sole [89]	1222
4	26	A	Grays Ath	L	0-3	0-2	20		1116
5	28	H	Kidderminster H	W	3-0	2-0	14	McAllister [27], Sole [32], Ferguson [77]	1544
6	Sept 1	A	Forest Green R	W	3-2	2-1	—	Nurse [18], McAllister 2 [27, 83]	1228
7	9	H	Dagenham & R	D	2-2	1-1	12	Sole [33], Hutchinson [90]	1724
8	12	A	St Albans C	W	1-0	0-0	—	Sole [62]	1018
9	16	A	Altrincham	W	3-2	1-2	8	Lambu 2 [31, 57], McAllister [64]	886
10	19	H	York C	L	1-2	0-2	—	Nurse [54]	1907
11	23	H	Rushden & D	W	3-0	3-0	8	McAllister 2 (1 pen) [5, 10 (p)], Sole [27]	2084
12	30	A	Northwich Vic	W	2-0	1-0	5	McAllister (pen) [45], Bunce [84]	990
13	Oct 3	A	Stevenage Bor	L	2-3	1-1	—	Murray [16], Berquez [79]	2410
14	6	H	Burton Alb	D	0-0	0-0	—		1651
15	9	H	Aldershot T	W	2-0	1-0	—	Evans [30], Sole [88]	3725
16	14	A	Stafford R	L	0-1	0-1	8		1033
17	21	A	Gravesend & N	L	0-1	0-0	11		1208
18	Nov 3	H	Exeter C	L	0-2	0-2	12		2590
19	18	A	Tamworth	L	1-3	1-2	12	Ferguson [3]	1039
20	25	H	Weymouth	W	4-0	2-0	10	Sole [11], Hutchinson [39], McAllister [64], Lambu [67]	1884
21	Dec 2	A	Halifax T	L	0-3	0-1	10		1536
22	9	H	Cambridge U	L	0-1	0-0	13		1886
23	26	A	Oxford U	D	0-0	0-0	13		11,065
24	29	A	York C	W	1-0	0-0	—	Taylor [81]	3173
25	Jan 1	H	St Albans C	L	1-2	1-0	—	Sharpling [5]	2178
26	6	A	Dagenham & R	L	2-3	2-2	12	Blackett (og) [5], Pearce [32]	1389
27	20	H	Altrincham	W	2-0	0-0	12	McAllister 2 [64, 76]	1612
28	23	H	Oxford U	W	1-0	1-0	—	Smith [13]	2228
29	27	A	Cambridge U	L	0-3	0-2	12		2206
30	Feb 10	A	Exeter C	L	0-1	0-0	13		3363
31	17	H	Tamworth	L	0-2	0-0	14		1411
32	20	H	Gravesend & N	D	2-2	1-0	—	Sole 2 [38, 90]	851
33	Mar 3	H	Halifax T	D	2-2	0-1	13	Murray [51], Berquez [56]	1419
34	6	H	Stevenage Bor	L	0-1	0-1	—		1407
35	10	A	Burton Alb	L	1-2	1-1	16	McAllister [44]	1603
36	13	A	Aldershot T	D	2-2	1-1	—	Webb [8], McAllister [63]	2739
37	17	H	Stafford R	D	1-1	0-0	15	McAllister [79]	1294
38	20	A	Weymouth	W	3-2	0-2	—	Hutchinson [61], McAllister [76], Sole [79]	1257
39	24	H	Southport	D	1-1	1-0	14	Sole [12]	1276
40	27	A	Crawley T	D	0-0	0-0	—		1098
41	31	A	Morecambe	L	0-2	0-1	15		1466
42	Apr 7	H	Grays Ath	W	1-0	1-0	15	Hutchinson [12]	1834
43	9	A	Kidderminster H	W	1-0	1-0	—	Marum [40]	1479
44	14	H	Forest Green R	D	3-3	0-3	13	Marum [81], Hutchinson [88], Sole [90]	1578
45	21	A	Rushden & D	L	0-2	0-1	15		1922
46	28	H	Northwich Vic	W	3-2	1-1	15	Marum [22], Hutchinson [54], Smith [71]	1753

Final League Position: 15

GOALSCORERS

League (56): McAllister 15 (2 pens), Sole 12, Hutchinson 6, Lambu 3, Marum 3, Berquez 2, Ferguson 2, Murray 2, Nurse 2, Smith 2, Bunce 1, Evans 1, Pearce 1, Sharpling 1, Taylor 1, Webb 1, own goal 1.
FA Cup (5): Smith 2, Jackson 1, McAllister 1, Sole 1.
Trophy (1): McAllister 1.

Jalal 23	Jackson 11 + 5	Bunce 34 + 2	Oyedele 9 + 10	Hutchinson 34	MacDonald 28	Ferguson 7 + 16	Berquez 17 + 11	Cockerill L 2	McAllister 44	Evans 14 + 3	Sole 33 + 9	Smith 40 + 1	El-Salahi 12 + 3	Murray 42 + 1	Lambu 31 + 8	Nurse 8	Sankoh 1 + 15	Ruby 8 + 1	Poke 3	Sharpling 2 + 1	Taylor 9 + 2	Pearce 16 + 3	Marum 6 + 8	Cockerill S 1 + 3	Bittner 12	Barrett 6 + 1	Green 15 + 2	Gier 7	Osano 13 + 1	Selley 3 + 3	Webb 7 + 1	Gindre 8	Match No.
1	2	3	4	5	6	7	8	9[1]	10	11	12																						1
1	2	3	4[3]	5[■]	6	7	8	9[2]	10		14	11[1]	12	13																			2
1	2	3	4		6	9[2]	8		10		12	11[1]	5	7	13																		3
1	2	3	4[1]		6	13	8		10[2]		12		5	7	11	9																	4
1		3		5	6	14	12		10	11[2]	7	2[1]	13	4	8	9[3]																	5
1		3	13	5	6[1]				10	11	7[2]	2	12	4	8	9[3]	14																6
1		3		5	6	12			10	11	7[2]	2		4	8[1]	9	13																7
1	12	3	4	5	6	13			10		11[3]	8[2]		2	7[1]	9	14																8
1	13	3	4	5	6	14			10		11[2]	8		2	7[1]	9[3]	12																9
1	2	3	4[3]		6[1]	12	13		10		14	7[2]	5	11	8	9																	10
1		3		5	6	12			10		11	8	2	4	7[1]	9[2]	13																11
1	12	3		5[1]	6	14	8		10		11[3]	7	2	4	9[2]		13																12
1	2[1]	3	13		6	14	8		10	12	9	7[2]	5	4	11[3]																		13
1		3		5	6[1]		8		10		9	7	2	4	11		12																14
1	12	3	13	5		14	8		10	11[2]	9[3]	6[1]	2	4	7																		15
1	2	3	14	5		13	8		10	11[3]	9	4[2]	6		7[1]		12																16
1		3	12	5		14	8		10	11[1]	9	7	6	2	13[3]		4[2]																17
1	14	3	4[3]	5		12	8[1]		10	11[2]	9	6	2	7			13																18
1	2[2]		13	5		9	8		10	11[3]	12	7	3[1]	4			14	6															19
	2	3	13	5		7			10[3]	12	9	8[2]		4	11[1]		14	6	1														20
	2	3	12	5		8	13		10	11[1]	9[3]	4[2]			7		14	6	1														21
	2	3		5	6	9			10	12		8[1]		4	7				1	11[2]	13												22
1		3		5	6	12			10[1]	11	9	4		2	7						8												23
1		3	12	5					10	11	9	4[1]		2	7			6		13	8[2]												24
1		3	4[1]	5		13				11	9			2	7[2]		14	6		10[3]	8			12									25
1		3				12				11	9			2	7		13	6[1]			8	5	10[2]	4									26
		3			6[1]				10[2]		9	2		4	12						11	5	13	14	1	7[3]	8						27
		3					13		10		9	7[1]		4	11[2]						8[3]	5	14	12	1	6	2						28
		3[1]					13		10[3]		12	7[2]		4	11						14	5	9		1	6	8	2					29
		3[1]					13		10			6		4	7[2]						9		12		1	8	11	2	5				30
							12		10		9	11		4	7						8	5			1	6[1]	3		2				31
							8		10		12	11		4	13			14			9[3]	5			1	7[1]	3[■]	6[2]	2				32
		3		5			8		10		9			4	7[1]			6				11	12		1				2				33
		12		5			8		10		9	11[3]		4	7[2]			6[1]				3	13		1		14		2				34
				5	6		8		10[2]		9	7[1]		4	13							3			1		11		2	12			35
				5	6[■]		13		10[2]		9[1]	7		4	12							3	14		1		8		2		11[3]		36
		12		5					10		9[2]	7		4	13							6[1]			1		3		2	8	11		37
				5	6[1]		12		10		9	7		4								3			1		11		2		8		38
				5	6				10		9	7		4								3					11		2		8	1	39
				5	6				10		9	7		4								3					8		2		11	1	40
		11[3]		5	6		13		10		9[1]	7[2]		4	14							3	12						2		8	1	41
		11[2]		5	6		12		10[3]		13	8		4	7								14				3	2[1]			9	1	42
		11[1]		5	6				10[2]			8		4	7							14	9[3]				3	2		12	13	1	43
				5	6[2]		8[3]		10		9	12		4	7							13	11				3	2[1]		14		1	44
			13		6				10			11		4	7		14					5	9[3]				12	2[1]	3[2]	8		1	45
		3		5[1]	6				10		9	11[3]		4	7[2]							12	8			14			13	2		1	46

FA Cup
Fourth Qualifying Round
Potters Bar T (h) 3-2
First Round Tranmere R (a) 2-4

Trophy
First Round Salisbury C (a) 1-3

YORK CITY

Blue Square Premier

Ground: KitKat Crescent, York YO30 7AQ. *Tel:* (01904) 624 447. *Year Formed:* 1922.
Record Gate: 28,123 (1938 v Huddersfield T, FA Cup Sixth Round). *Nickname:* Minster Men.
Manager: Billy McEwan. *Colours:* Red shirts, navy shorts, navy stockings.

YORK CITY 2006–07 LEAGUE RECORD

Match No.	Date	Venue	Opponents	Result		H/T Score	Lg. Pos.	Goalscorers	Attendance
1	Aug 12	H	Exeter C	D	0-0	0-0	—		2789
2	15	A	Stevenage Bor	W	2-1	1-1	—	Donaldson [6], Bowey [64]	2306
3	19	A	Gravesend & N	W	1-0	1-0	6	Donaldson [33]	1036
4	25	H	Burton Alb	W	3-2	1-0	—	Donaldson [8], Convery [61], Peat [90]	2812
5	28	A	Rushden & D	W	1-0	0-0	4	Donaldson [49]	2416
6	Sept 1	H	Stafford R	D	0-0	0-0	—		2955
7	9	A	Crawley T	L	0-3	0-1	6		932
8	12	H	Morecambe	L	2-3	0-2	—	Woolford [49], Donaldson (pen) [75]	2233
9	16	H	Kidderminster H	W	1-0	1-0	6	Donaldson [43]	2181
10	19	A	Woking	W	2-1	2-0	—	Woolford 2 [28, 41]	1907
11	23	H	Southport	D	2-2	1-2	3	Farrell [21], Hoolickin (og) [77]	2446
12	30	A	Oxford U	L	0-2	0-1	7		6602
13	Oct 3	A	Northwich Vic	W	2-1	1-0	—	Donaldson [31], Peat [90]	1021
14	6	H	Aldershot T	W	1-0	1-0	—	Convery [12]	2679
15	10	H	Cambridge U	L	1-2	1-0	—	Donaldson [22]	2614
16	14	A	St Albans C	L	2-4	1-1	4	Farrell 2 [25, 66]	1237
17	21	A	Tamworth	D	2-2	2-1	6	Donaldson 2 [10, 32]	1311
18	Nov 5	H	Altrincham	W	1-0	0-0	5	Donaldson [47]	2726
19	18	A	Weymouth	W	2-1	0-0	4	Panther [60], Goodliffe [81]	1774
20	25	H	Dagenham & R	L	2-3	1-1	5	Woolford [10], Donaldson [47]	3050
21	Dec 2	A	Forest Green R	W	1-0	1-0	5	Donaldson [9]	1125
22	9	A	Grays Ath	D	0-0	0-0	4		1139
23	23	H	Halifax T	W	2-0	1-0	—	Donaldson 2 (1 pen) [5, 67 (p)]	3588
24	29	H	Woking	L	0-1	0-0	—		3173
25	Jan 1	A	Morecambe	W	3-1	1-0	—	Donaldson [45], Farrell [47], Bowey [61]	2203
26	6	H	Crawley T	W	5-0	3-0	3	Donaldson 2 (1 pen) [20 (p), 53], Bowey [21], Panther [32], Farrell [73]	2590
27	20	A	Kidderminster H	L	1-2	0-1	3	Farrell [83]	2073
28	23	A	Halifax T	D	1-1	0-0	—	Woolford [57]	2308
29	27	H	Grays Ath	D	2-2	2-1	3	Bowey [5], McMahon [13]	2689
30	Feb 3	H	Tamworth	L	0-2	0-1	3		2477
31	10	A	Altrincham	W	4-0	2-0	3	Bishop [1], Bowey [8], Brodie [66], Woolford [90]	1327
32	17	H	Weymouth	W	1-0	0-0	3	Bowey [90]	2769
33	24	A	Dagenham & R	L	1-2	0-1	4	Bishop [62]	2252
34	Mar 3	H	Forest Green R	D	0-0	0-0	3		2923
35	6	H	Northwich Vic	W	2-1	0-1	—	Charnock (og) [55], Woolford [69]	2132
36	10	A	Aldershot T	W	2-0	1-0	3	Farrell [25], Panther [90]	2435
37	13	A	Cambridge U	W	5-0	2-0	—	Farrell [21], Donaldson 3 [33, 63, 72], Kovacs [47]	2428
38	17	H	St Albans C	D	0-0	0-0	3		2927
39	24	A	Exeter C	D	1-1	0-1	3	Farrell [58]	4410
40	27	H	Stevenage Bor	L	0-1	0-0	—		2969
41	31	H	Gravesend & N	L	0-2	0-1	4		2709
42	Apr 7	A	Burton Alb	W	2-1	0-0	4	Woolford [71], Farrell [80]	2718
43	10	H	Rushden & D	W	3-1	1-1	—	Donaldson 2 [41, 50], Bowey [54]	2955
44	14	A	Stafford R	D	0-0	0-0	5		1293
45	21	A	Southport	W	1-0	0-0	4	Donaldson (pen) [56]	3206
46	28	H	Oxford U	W	1-0	1-0	4	Bishop [38]	5378

Final League Position: 4

GOALSCORERS

League (65): Donaldson 24 (4 pens), Farrell 10, Woolford 8, Bowey 7, Bishop 3, Panther 3, Convery 2, Peat 2, Brodie 1, Goodliffe 1, Kovacs 1, McMahon 1, own goals 2.
FA Cup (1): Donaldson 1 (pen).
Trophy (1): Donaldson 1.
Play-Offs (1): Bowey 1 (pen).

Evans 45	Craddock 32 + 3	Peat 22 + 3	Bishop 42 + 3	McGurk 38	Dudgeon 9 + 4	Convery 15 + 9	Panther 42 + 2	Donaldson 43	Farrell 44 + 2	Bowey 42	Lloyd 23 + 7	Greenwood 2 + 10	Webster — + 2	McMahon 8 + 11	Woolford 26 + 14	Reid 1 + 1	Parslow 21 + 3	Foster 4 + 1	Goodliffe 11	Stamp 5 + 5	Maidens 1 + 2	Elvins 4 + 5	Brodie 3 + 9	Kovacs 8	James 8	Purkiss 7 + 1	Bell — + 1	Match No.
1	2	3	4	5	6	7	8	9	10	11																		1
1	2	3[1]	4[2]	5	6	7	8	9	10[3]	11	12	13	14															2
1	2	3[1]	4[2]	5	6	7	8	9[3]	10	11	12	14	13															3
1	2	3	4	5	6	7	8	9	10	11																		4
1	2	3	4	5	6	7	8	9	10[1]	11■		12																5
1	2	3	4[1]	5	6	7	8	9	10			11[2]		12	13													6
1■	2	3	4	5	6[1]	7[2]	8	9	10					13	11[G]	15	12											7
	2	3[2]	4	5	6[1]	7	8[3]	9	10		13			14	11	1	12											8
1	2		4	5		12		9	10[1]	11	3			8	7		6											9
1	2		4	5[1]	12	13		9	10[2]	11	3			8	7		6											10
1	2	3	4[1]			13	12	9	10	11	5			8[2]	7		6											11
1	2		4[1]	5		13	8	9	10	11	3			7[2]	12		6											12
1	2	3	12	5			8	9	10	11				4[1]	7		6											13
1	2	3	13			7	8	9	10[2]	11				12	4[1]		6	5										14
1	2[1]	3				7	8	9	10	11	12				4		6	5										15
1	2■	3	12			13	8[1]	9	10	11	14			4[2]	7[3]		6	5										16
1		3	4				8	9	10	11	2						6	12	5[1]	7								17
1	2		4				12	9	10	11	3				7			5	6	8[1]								18
1	2	3	4	5			8	9[1]	10	11					7				6	12								19
1	2[1]		4[3]	5			8	9	10	11	3[2]	12		13	7				6	14								20
1	2		4[1]	5			8	9	10	11	3			12	7[2]				6	13								21
1		3	4	5			8	9	10	11	2				7[1]				6	12								22
1	13	3	4	5	12		8	9[2]	10	11	2				14				6[1]	7[3]								23
1	12	3[1]	4	5			8	9	10	11[2]	2				7				6	13								24
1	2		4				8	9	10	11[1]	3			12	13		5		6	7[2]								25
1	2		4[1]				8	9	10[3]	11[2]	3	13		12	14		5		6	7								26
1	2[1]		4	5			8	9■	10	11	3	12			14		13		6[2]		7[3]							27
1	2		4	5			8		10	11	3			6	7		9											28
1	2[1]	12	4	5	13		8		10	11	3			7[3]	9		6[2]				14							29
1	12	3[1]	4	5	6		8		10	11	2			13	9[3]						14	7[2]						30
1	2		4	5[1]	12		8	9	10	11[2]	3				13		6					7[3]	14					31
1	2		4	5			8[2]	9	10[1]	11	3			13	12		6					7[3]	14					32
1	2	12	4	5			8	9	10	11[2]	3[1]				14		6					13	7[3]					33
1	2		4[1]	5			8	9	12	11	3				7							10[2]	13	6				34
1	2	12	4	5		7[2]	8	9[3]	10	11	3[1]				13							14		6				35
1	2	3	4	5		7[1]	8	9[2]	10	11					12							13		6				36
1	2[1]	3	4	5		7[2]	8[3]	9	10		12	14			11							13		6				37
1		3	4	5		7[1]	8	9	10	11[3]	2				14							13	12[2]	6				38
1			4	5		12	8	9[3]	10[1]	11		2■			14								7[2]	6	3	13		39
1			4	5		7[1]	8[2]	9	10	11[3]				13	14								12	6	3	2		40
1			4	5			8	9	14	11[2]		12			7								10[3]	6	3	2[1]	13	41
1			4[1]	5			8	9	10	11[2]		12			7		6						13		3	2		42
1			4[1]	5		13	8	9	10[3]	11[2]		12			7		6						14		3	2		43
1			4	5		13	8	9	10	11[1]					7		6						12[2]		3	2		44
1			4	5			8	9	10	11					7		6								3	2		45
1			4	5		13	8	9	10[3]	11	12				7[2]		6						14		3	2[1]		46

FA Cup

Fourth Qualifying Round	Newcastle Benfield	(a)	1-0
First Round	Bristol C	(h)	0-1

Trophy

First Round	Morecambe	(a)	1-2

Play-Offs

Semi-Final	Morecambe	(h)	0-0
		(a)	1-2

REVIEW OF THE SCOTTISH SEASON 2006–07

'Why is it,' said that famous musician, Sir Thomas Beecham, 'that we have so many third-rate foreign conductors with our orchestras when we have so many second-rate ones of our own?'

In the early part of the season there were fun and games in the two cups: Queen's Park took out Aberdeen, Albion Rovers beat Partick Thistle, St Johnstone beat Elgin City 4-0 – which might have been expected, but not after extra time! And so on. The League Challenge Cup was won by Ross County after a struggle in the final with Clyde which ended in a large number of penalties. In the CIS Cup, St Johnstone were prominent, and disposed of Rangers on their way to the semi-finals, whilst Falkirk had the better of a penalty shoot-out against Celtic. Hibs carried all before, and stood no nonsense from last season's giant-killers, Gretna. They won convincingly in the final against a stalwart Kilmarnock.

In Europe we enjoyed the luxury of having two teams left in the competitions in the New Year, Celtic in the Champions League, and Rangers in the UEFA Cup. Both went out in their next games, but only narrowly.

For Rangers, in particular, the European venture was a face-saver. Back at home they were never at ease with their new manager. He is clearly a most competent and successful manager, but he failed to fit in at Ibrox, and a series of draws and defeats meant that Rangers were never in the hunt for the Premier League title, and they departed from the Cups with little ceremony. With the arrival of Walter Smith (together with the enthusiastic Ally McCoist) in the New Year, there was soon a more business-like and cheerful atmosphere. Celtic had rocketed away in the League, and established a vast lead over the other teams. The fight was on for the next three places. Rangers moved comfortably into second place, but the third (and important) place was hotly contested by Aberdeen, who had a good season, and Hearts, who lost some of their better players. Aberdeen won the race.

In the Divisions, play-off matches were interesting. No one doubts the strain that they put on players and managers at the end of a long season, but it certainly does enliven the later stages of the programme with vital games involving most teams as some strive to reach fourth place, or to avoid ninth. The other clubs have few meaningless games – a contrast to the lower half of the Premier League.

At the foot of the First Division, Ross County and Airdrie disputed the bottom place and certain relegation, whilst Queen of the South – who spent much of the season in the depths – found some form and emerged from danger.

The leaders are often decided: in the Second Division this time, Morton, who have fiddled about in the last few years, made no mistake, and they move up a stage – as perhaps they should have done before. At the foot, Forfar lost touch by mid-season. The Third Division found Berwick Rangers comfortably placed at the top. Morton and Berwick were joined in promotion after the play-offs by two worthy teams – Stirling Albion and Queen's Park.

At the top of the First Division were Gretna after a nail-biting last day when St Johnstone almost managed to displace them. Gretna thus complete a remarkable ascent from the depths in quick time. There was the usual talk in the Premier League of blocking Gretna's progress, but it came to nothing.

Down from the top flight go Dunfermline. The Pars had an unfortunate league season, including a run of nine games when they failed to score. A spirited fight in the last months saw them almost achieve safety at the expense of St Mirren, but it was not to be. So different was their progress in the Scottish Cup, where they disposed of Rangers, Hearts, and Hibs on the way to the final against Celtic. St Johnstone reached semi-finals of both the Scottish Cup and the CIS Cup, also with some notable scalps, and mention must be made of Highland League Deveronvale who reached the Fourth Round, and lost there to Partick by a single goal. Celtic won the Cup in the end, but the Pars put up a dogged fight, and it was very late on that they conceded the single goal.

Clubs which have failed to stay in the Premier League are, not unnaturally, unhappy to lose their status. There have been all sorts of plans and discussions to bring further changes in the present leagues set-up. It does seem a pity that what was, only a few years ago, a flourishing situation is now involved in this sort of self-destruction. It was 'All in the best interests of Scottish Football', we were told.

Qualification for the next European Nations Cup looked pretty difficult immediately the draw was made. With Walter Smith at the helm, Scottish teams at last looked to be on the way up, and some fine results put us at the head of the table. When he left for the ailing Ibrox, there were those who were highly critical of his move: they perhaps forgot how much he had done for us. He left behind a promising situation, much better than had at one time looked possible. His successor, Alex McLeish, is totally committed to his team, and for sure he is in no doubt of the immensity of his task. He has made a good start, but there are formidable matches ahead. He and his team deserve our full support; and I hope they will get it.

ALAN ELLIOTT

SCOTTISH LEAGUE TABLES 2006–07

SCOTTISH PREMIER LEAGUE

			Home					Away					Total						
		P	W	D	L	F	A	W	D	L	F	A	W	D	L	F	A	GD	Pts
1	Celtic	38	16	1	2	36	13	10	5	4	29	21	26	6	6	65	34	31	84
2	Rangers	38	11	6	2	35	10	10	3	6	26	22	21	9	8	61	32	29	72
3	Aberdeen	38	11	3	5	33	21	8	5	6	22	17	19	8	11	55	38	17	65
4	Hearts	38	9	4	6	26	19	8	6	5	21	16	17	10	11	47	35	12	61
5	Kilmarnock	38	7	5	6	24	22	9	2	9	23	32	16	7	15	47	54	−7	55
6	Hibernian	38	9	6	4	32	20	4	4	11	24	26	13	10	15	56	46	10	49
7	Falkirk	38	10	2	8	24	19	5	3	10	25	28	15	5	18	49	47	2	50
8	Inverness CT	38	8	6	5	25	20	3	7	9	17	28	11	13	14	42	48	−6	46
9	Dundee U	38	5	8	6	17	24	5	4	10	23	35	10	12	16	40	59	−19	42
10	Motherwell	38	5	3	11	25	34	5	5	9	16	27	10	8	20	41	61	−20	38
11	St Mirren	38	3	6	10	13	23	5	6	8	18	28	8	12	18	31	51	−20	36
12	Dunfermline Ath	38	6	4	9	17	28	2	4	13	9	27	8	8	22	26	55	−29	32

After 33 matches, the first six clubs play once against each other; bottom six likewise. Thus the finishing position of Falkirk moves them from sixth to seventh place.

SCOTTISH FOOTBALL LEAGUE FIRST DIVISION

			Home					Away					Total						
		P	W	D	L	F	A	W	D	L	F	A	W	D	L	F	A	GD	Pts
1	Gretna	36	10	4	4	35	18	9	5	4	35	22	19	9	8	70	40	30	66
2	St Johnstone	36	13	3	2	39	17	6	5	7	26	25	19	8	9	65	42	23	65
3	Dundee	36	11	2	5	27	19	5	3	10	21	23	16	5	15	48	42	6	53
4	Hamilton A	36	9	7	2	30	17	5	4	9	16	30	14	11	11	46	47	−1	53
5	Clyde	36	8	4	6	24	14	3	10	5	22	21	11	14	11	46	35	11	47
6	Livingston	36	3	7	8	20	24	8	5	5	21	22	11	12	13	41	46	−5	45
7	Partick Th	36	6	6	6	25	33	6	3	9	22	30	12	9	15	47	63	−16	45
8	Queen of the S	36	6	6	6	19	24	4	5	9	15	30	10	11	15	34	54	−20	41
9	Airdrie U	36	6	3	9	19	25	5	4	9	20	25	11	7	18	39	50	−11	40
10	Ross Co	36	6	6	6	22	25	3	4	11	18	32	9	10	17	40	57	−17	37

SCOTTISH FOOTBALL LEAGUE SECOND DIVISION

			Home					Away					Total						
		P	W	D	L	F	A	W	D	L	F	A	W	D	L	F	A	GD	Pts
1	Morton	36	13	4	1	41	13	11	1	6	35	19	24	5	7	76	32	44	77
2	Stirling A	36	12	2	4	37	17	9	4	5	30	22	21	6	9	67	39	28	69
3	Raith R	36	7	5	6	22	18	11	3	4	28	15	18	8	10	50	33	17	62
4	Brechin C	36	9	2	7	30	24	9	4	5	31	21	18	6	12	61	45	16	60
5	Ayr U	36	7	3	8	21	23	7	5	6	25	24	14	8	14	46	47	−1	50
6	Cowdenbeath	36	7	4	7	36	35	6	2	10	23	21	13	6	17	59	56	3	45
7	Alloa Ath	36	5	6	7	24	27	6	3	9	23	43	11	9	16	47	70	−23	42
8	Peterhead	36	6	5	7	34	27	5	3	10	26	35	11	8	17	60	62	−2	41
9	Stranraer	36	8	2	8	29	38	2	7	9	16	36	10	9	17	45	74	−29	39
10	Forfar Ath	36	4	3	11	21	31	0	4	14	16	59	4	7	25	37	90	−53	19

SCOTTISH FOOTBALL LEAGUE THIRD DIVISION

			Home					Away					Total						
		P	W	D	L	F	A	W	D	L	F	A	W	D	L	F	A	GD	Pts
1	Berwick R	36	12	3	3	29	14	12	0	6	22	15	24	3	9	51	29	22	75
2	Arbroath	36	9	4	5	27	20	13	0	5	34	13	22	4	10	61	33	28	70
3	Queen's Park	36	12	3	3	33	13	9	2	7	24	15	21	5	10	57	28	29	68
4	East Fife	36	10	4	4	26	15	10	3	5	33	22	20	7	9	59	37	22	67
5	Dumbarton	36	12	2	4	30	15	6	3	9	22	22	18	5	13	52	37	15	59
6	Albion R	36	8	2	8	30	29	6	4	8	26	32	14	6	16	56	61	−5	48
7	Stenhousemuir	36	9	1	8	36	31	4	4	10	17	32	13	5	18	53	63	−10	44
8	Montrose	36	6	2	10	20	27	5	2	11	22	35	11	4	21	42	62	−20	37
9	Elgin C	36	7	0	11	24	30	2	2	14	15	39	9	2	25	39	69	−30	29
10	East Stirling	36	3	1	14	11	37	3	2	13	16	41	6	3	27	27	78	−51	21

ABERDEEN — Premier League

Year Formed: 1903. *Ground & Address:* Pittodrie Stadium, Pittodrie St, Aberdeen AB24 5QH. *Telephone:* 01224 650400. *Fax:* 01224 644173. *E-mail:* davidj@afc.co.uk. *Website:* www.afc.co.uk
Ground Capacity: all seated: 21,421. *Size of Pitch:* 115yd × 72yd.
Chairman: Stewart Milne. *Executive Director:* Duncan Fraser. *Director of Football:* Willie Miller. *Secretary:* David Johnston. *Operations Manager:* John Morgan.
Manager: Jimmy Calderwood. *Assistant Manager:* Jimmy Nichol. *U-19 Manager:* Neil Cooper. *Physios:* David Wylie, John Sharp. *Reserve Team Coach:* Sandy Clark.
Managers since 1975: Ally MacLeod, Billy McNeill, Alex Ferguson, Ian Porterfield, Alex Smith and Jocky Scott, Willie Miller, Roy Aitken, Alex Miller, Paul Hegarty, Ebbe Skovdahl, Steve Paterson. *Club Nicknames(s):* The Dons.
Previous Grounds: None.
Record Attendance: 45,061 v Hearts, Scottish Cup 4th rd, 13 Mar 1954.
Record Transfer Fee received: £1.75 million for Eoin Jess to Coventry City (February 1996).
Record Transfer Fee paid: £1m+ for Paul Bernard from Oldham Athletic (September 1995).
Record Victory: 13-0 v Peterhead, Scottish Cup, 9 Feb 1923.
Record Defeat: 0-8 v Celtic, Division 1, 30 Jan 1965.
Most Capped Player: Alex McLeish, 77 (Scotland).
Most League Appearances: 556: Willie Miller, 1973-90.
Most League Goals in Season (Individual): 38: Benny Yorston, Division I, 1929-30.
Most Goals Overall (Individual): 199: Joe Harper.

ABERDEEN 2006–07 LEAGUE RECORD

Match No.	Date	Venue	Opponents	Result	H/T Score	Lg. Pos.	Goalscorers	Attendance
1	Jul 29	A	Hibernian	D 1-1	1-1	—	Crawford [19]	15,047
2	Aug 5	H	Inverness CT	D 1-1	1-0	7	Crawford [29]	11,955
3	12	A	Motherwell	W 2-0	1-0	5	Mackie 2 [33, 62]	5186
4	19	A	St Mirren	D 1-1	1-0	7	Crawford [33]	5344
5	26	H	Dunfermline Ath	W 1-0	0-0	4	Severin [67]	9889
6	Sept 9	H	Celtic	L 0-1	0-0	5		15,304
7	16	A	Falkirk	W 2-0	0-0	4	Dempsey [51], Daal [82]	5812
8	24	H	Hearts	L 1-3	0-0	4	Daal [80]	11,160
9	Oct 1	A	Rangers	L 0-1	0-0	5		50,488
10	14	A	Kilmarnock	L 0-1	0-0	8		5744
11	21	H	Dundee U	W 3-1	1-0	7	Mackie [38], Nicholson 2 [47, 71]	10,747
12	30	H	Hibernian	W 2-1	0-0	4	Miller [55], Severin [90]	11,179
13	Nov 6	A	Inverness CT	D 1-1	0-0	4	Lovell [89]	5744
14	11	H	Motherwell	W 2-1	0-0	4	Smith J [55], Miller [85]	10,527
15	18	H	St Mirren	W 2-0	0-0	3	Mackie 2 [78, 84]	11,426
16	25	A	Dunfermline Ath	W 3-0	0-0	3	Miller [53], Mackie 2 [83, 85]	6501
17	Dec 2	A	Celtic	L 0-1	0-0	3		58,911
18	9	H	Falkirk	W 2-1	2-0	3	Mackie [17], Clark [43]	10,594
19	16	A	Hearts	W 1-0	0-0	2	Lovell [87]	17,274
20	23	H	Rangers	L 1-2	0-2	3	Lovell [83]	20,045
21	26	H	Kilmarnock	W 3-1	2-0	—	Maguire [5], Nicholson [9], Lovell [86]	11,887
22	30	A	Dundee U	L 1-3	0-0	2	Severin [55]	12,329
23	Jan 2	A	Hibernian	D 0-0	0-0	—		16,278
24	13	H	Inverness CT	D 1-1	0-1	3	Lovell [90]	10,300
25	27	A	St Mirren	W 2-0	2-0	3	Considine 2 [8, 36]	4921
26	Feb 10	H	Dunfermline Ath	W 3-0	1-0	3	Mackie [33], Nicholson (pen) [57], Lovell [83]	9379
27	17	H	Celtic	L 1-2	0-2	3	Mackie [88]	16,711
28	Mar 3	A	Falkirk	W 2-1	1-0	3	Dempsey [15], Foster [64]	5825
29	10	H	Hearts	W 1-0	1-0	3	Lovell [6]	13,964
30	13	A	Motherwell	W 2-0	1-0	—	Fitzpatrick (og) [32], Foster [90]	4530
31	17	A	Rangers	L 0-3	0-3	3		50,354
32	31	A	Kilmarnock	W 2-1	0-0	3	Fowler (og) [58], Anderson [70]	7236
33	Apr 7	H	Dundee U	L 2-4	2-3	3	Lovell [6], Mackie (pen) [8]	12,148
34	21	H	Hibernian	D 2-2	1-2	3	Anderson [25], Foster [80]	9753
35	28	H	Kilmarnock	W 3-0	1-0	3	Nicholson (pen) [6], Miller [48], Mackie [61]	10,046
36	May 6	A	Hearts	D 1-1	0-1	3	Nicholson [89]	17,208
37	12	A	Celtic	L 1-2	1-1	3	Mackie [41]	59,510
38	20	H	Rangers	W 2-0	2-0	3	Severin [21], Lovell [32]	20,010

Final League Position: 3

Honours
League Champions: Division I 1954-55. Premier Division 1979-80, 1983-84, 1984-85; *Runners-up:* Division I 1910-11, 1936-37, 1955-56, 1970-71, 1971-72. Premier Division 1977-78, 1980-81, 1981-82, 1988-89, 1989-90, 1990-91, 1992-93, 1993-94.
Scottish Cup Winners: 1947, 1970, 1982, 1983, 1984, 1986, 1990; *Runners-up:* 1937, 1953, 1954, 1959, 1967, 1978, 1993, 2000.
League Cup Winners: 1955-56, 1976-77, 1985-86, 1989-90, (Coca-Cola cup) 1995-96; *Runners-up:* 1946-47, 1978-79, 1979-80, 1987-88, 1988-89, 1992-93, 1999-2000.
Drybrough Cup Winners: 1971, 1980.

European: *European Cup:* 12 matches (1980-81, 1984-85, 1985-86); *Cup Winners' Cup:* 39 matches (1967-68, 1970-71, 1978-79, 1982-83 winners, 1983-84 semi-finals, 1986-87, 1990-91, 1993-94); *UEFA Cup:* 48 matches (*Fairs Cup:* 1968-69. *UEFA Cup:* 1971-72, 1972-73, 1973-74, 1977-78, 1979-80, 1981-82, 1987-88, 1988-89, 1989-90, 1991-92, 1994-95, 1996-97, 2000-01, 2002-03).

Club colours: Shirt, Shorts, Stockings: Red.

Goalscorers: *League* (55): Mackie 13 (1 pen), Lovell 9, Nicholson 6 (2 pens), Miller 4, Severin 4, Crawford 3, Foster 3, Anderson 2, Considine 2, Daal 2, Dempsey 2, Clark 1, Maguire 1, Smith J 1, own goals 2.
Scottish Cup (3): Nicholson 2, Brewster 1.
CIS Cup (0).

Langfield J 38	Hart M 34	Byrne R 4 + 1	Anderson R 35	Foster R 35 + 2	Touzani K 6 + 5	Nicholson B 31	Clark C 37	Smith J 20 + 2	Lovell S 15 + 12	Crawford S 4	Mackie D 31 + 5	Stewart J 1 + 3	Dempsey G 20 + 6	Severin S 34 + 2	Diamond A 13 + 8	Considine A 23 + 9	Smith D 2 + 3	Maguire C 3 + 16	Daal D 1 + 6	Miller L 25 + 7	Brewster C 6 + 6	*Match No.*
1	2	3	4	5	6	7	8	9	10^{1}	11^{2}	12	13										1
1	2	3	4	5	6	7^{1}	8	9	10^{2}	11^{3}	13		12	14								2
1	2		4	12	3	7	8	9		11^{3}	10^{2}	13	6^{1}	14	5							3
1			4	12		7	6	9		11^{1}	10	13	8		5	2	3^{2}					4
1			4	2	8^{1}	7	9				11	3^{2}	13	6	5	12		14	10^{3}			5
1	3^{3}		4	2		7	9				11		8^{1}	6	5		12	13	14	10^{2}		6
1	3		4	5		7	9				11		8	6		2			12	10^{1}		7
1	3	13	4	5^{2}		7	9				11		8	6		2^{1}			12	10		8
1	3		4^{1}	5		7	9				11^{2}		8	6	12	2			13	10		9
1	3			4		7	9				11		8^{1}	6	5	2^{2}	13	14	12	10^{3}		10
1	3		4	2		7	9	8^{1}			11^{2}		5	6		13		12		10		11
1	3		4	2		7	9				11		8^{2}	6	5^{1}	12		13		10		12
1	3		4	2		7	9^{1}	8	13		11^{3}		5^{2}	6		12		14		10		13
1	3		4	2		7	9	8	11^{1}		12		5^{2}	6				13		10		14
1	3		4	2		7^{3}	9	8	11^{2}		13		5	6		12				10		15
1	3		4	5	12	7	9				11		8^{1}	6		2		13		10^{2}		16
1	3		4	5		7	9	12	13		11		8^{1}	6		2^{2}				10		17
1	3		4	2^{1}	14	7	9	8	13		11		5^{2}	6		12				10^{3}		18
1	3		4	5		7	9	8	12		11			6		2				10^{1}		19
1	3		4	5		7^{3}	9	8^{1}	13		11			6	12	2^{1}		14		10		20
1	3		4^{1}	5		7	9^{3}		13		11		14	6	12	2		8^{2}		10		21
1	3■			5	13		9		12		11		7	6	4	2		8^{1}		10^{2}		22
1			4	3			9		8^{2}		11		7	6	5	2		13		10^{1}	12	23
1	3		4	2		7	9		14		11		13	6		12		5^{2}		10^{3}	8^{1}	24
1	3		4	5	8	7	9		10^{1}		11			6		2				12		25
1	3		4	5		7	9^{3}		10^{2}		11		14	6		2	8^{1}		13	12		26
1	3		4	5		7	9^{1}		10^{2}		11			6		2	13	12		8		27
1	3		4	5		7	9	12	10^{2}		11		8^{1}	6	14	2^{3}					13	28
1	3		4	5		7^{1}	9	8	10^{2}				13	6	12	2				14	11^{3}	29
1	3		4	5	7^{1}		9	8	10^{2}		13			6	12	2				14	11^{3}	30
1	3		4	5			9^{1}	8	10^{2}				7	6	12	2		14		11^{3}	13	31
1		3	4				9	8^{1}	12		11		7	6	5	2				13	10^{2}	32
1	7	3	4^{1}	5			8		9		11			6	13	2^{2}		12		14	10^{3}	33
1	3		4	5		7	9^{3}	8	13		11			6		2^{1}		12		14	10^{2}	34
1	3		4	2^{2}		7	9	8^{1}	12		11			6	5	13		14		10^{3}		35
1	3			5^{3}	12	7■	9	8	14		11			6	4	2^{1}				10^{2}	13	36
1	3		4	2			8	7	9^{2}		11			6	5			13		10^{1}	12	37
1	3^{1}		4	2	12	7		8	9		11			6^{3}	5	14				10^{2}	13	38

AIRDRIE UNITED — Second Division

Year Formed: 2002. *Ground & Address:* Shyberry Excelsior Stadium, Broomfield Park, Craigneuk Avenue, Airdrie ML6 8QZ. *Telephone:* (Stadium) 01236 622000. *Postal Address:* 60 St Enoch Square, Glasgow G1 4AG.
E-mail: enquiries@airdrieunitedfc.com. *Website:* www.airdrieunited.com
Ground Capacity: all seated: 10,000. *Size of Pitch:* 112yd × 76yd.
Chairman: James Ballantyne. *Secretary:* Ann Marie Ballantyne. *Commercial Manager:* Les Jones.
Manager: Kenny Black. *Management team:* Jimmy Boyle, Michael McLaughlin, John Donnelly.
Previous Manager: Sandy Stewart.
Record Attendance: 5704 v Morton, Second Division, 15 May 2004.
Record Victory: 7-0 v Dundee, First Division, 11 March 2006.
Record Defeat: 1-6 v Morton, Second Division, 1 Nov 2003.
Most League Appearances: 101, Mark McGeown, 2002-05.
Most League Goals in Season (Individual): 18, Jerome Vareille, 2002-03.
Most Goals Overall (Individual): 28, Jerome Vareille, 2002-04.

AIRDRIE UNITED 2006–07 LEAGUE RECORD

Match No.	*Date*	*Venue*	*Opponents*	*Result*		*H/T Score*	*Lg. Pos.*	*Goalscorers*	*Attendance*
1	Aug 5	H	Ross Co	L	0-2	0-1	—		1292
2	12	A	Partick Th	L	2-4	0-2	10	McKeown (pen) [57], Taylor [87]	3473
3	19	H	Queen of the S	D	2-2	0-0	10	McPhee [65], Tierney [89]	1298
4	26	H	Hamilton A	L	1-2	0-0	9	Taylor [88]	1416
5	Sept 9	A	Livingston	L	0-3	0-2	10		1754
6	16	A	St Johnstone	L	0-1	0-1	10		2178
7	23	H	Dundee	L	0-1	0-1	9		1249
8	30	A	Gretna	W	2-0	1-0	9	McKenna [41], McPhee [46]	1492
9	Oct 14	H	Clyde	W	2-1	0-0	9	Barrau [51], McDonald [72]	1397
10	21	H	Partick Th	L	1-2	1-1	9	Taylor [37]	2351
11	28	A	Ross Co	L	1-2	0-2	9	Lovering [58]	2010
12	Nov 4	H	Livingston	L	0-1	0-0	10		1455
13	11	A	Hamilton A	L	1-2	1-1	10	Prunty [38]	1724
14	18	H	St Johnstone	W	2-1	1-0	10	Barrau (pen) [39], Smyth [59]	1550
15	25	A	Dundee	L	0-1	0-1	10		3528
16	Dec 2	A	Clyde	D	0-0	0-0	10		1347
17	9	H	Gretna	W	4-2	1-1	9	McDougall [42], Twigg 3 [61, 70, 79]	1169
18	16	A	Queen of the S	D	1-1	0-0	9	Prunty [88]	1577
19	26	H	Ross Co	L	0-1	0-1	—		1301
20	30	A	Livingston	W	3-1	1-1	9	Twigg 2 [12, 80], Holmes [71]	1645
21	Jan 2	H	Hamilton A	W	1-0	1-0	—	Twigg [8]	1414
22	20	A	St Johnstone	L	3-4	0-2	9	Koudou 2 [53, 57], Twigg [75]	2106
23	27	H	Clyde	W	1-0	1-0	9	Twigg [37]	1340
24	Feb 3	H	Dundee	L	0-3	0-1	9		1404
25	10	A	Gretna	D	0-0	0-0	9		1299
26	17	H	Queen of the S	L	0-3	0-2	9		1805
27	Mar 3	A	Hamilton A	L	0-3	0-2	10		1714
28	10	H	Livingston	W	3-1	0-1	9	Holmes [60], Taylor [78], Proctor [88]	1162
29	17	H	St Johnstone	L	1-2	1-1	10	Holmes [36]	1138
30	25	A	Partick Th	W	1-0	1-0	10	Harty [35]	2211
31	Apr 1	A	Dundee	L	1-2	1-1	10	Harty [16]	2837
32	4	H	Gretna	D	0-0	0-0	—		1209
33	7	A	Clyde	W	1-0	1-0	9	McDonald [15]	1306
34	14	A	Ross Co	D	1-1	1-1	9	Twigg [7]	2717
35	21	H	Partick Th	D	1-1	1-1	9	Twigg [7]	2178
36	28	A	Queen of the S	W	3-0	2-0	9	Taylor [10], Harty [20], Lovering [60]	3012

Final League Position: 9

Honours
League Champions: Second Division 2003-04.
Bell's League Challenge Cup runners-up: 2003-04.

Club colours: Shirt: White with red diamond. Shorts: White with two red horizontal stripes. Stockings: White with red hoops.

Goalscorers: *League* (39): Twigg 10, Taylor 5, Harty 3, Holmes 3, Barrau 2 (1 pen), Koudou 2, Lovering 2, McDonald 2, McPhee 2, Prunty 2, McDougall 1, McKenna 1, McKeown 1 (1 pen), Proctor 1, Smyth 1, Tierney 1.
Play-Offs (10): Harty 3 (2 pens), McDonald 2, McKeown 2, Twigg 2, Taylor 1.
Scottish Cup (0).
CIS Cup (2): McLaren 1, Prunty 1.
Challenge Cup (0).

Robertson S 36	McKenna S 26 + 5	Lovering P 29 + 1	Smyth M 29	Christie K 9 + 1	Holmes G 34 + 1	McDougall S 27 + 6	McKeown S 21 + 9	Prunty B 18 + 8	Twigg G 27 + 6	McLaren W 3 + 1	McPhee B 10 + 15	Taylor S 23 + 8	Watson G 3 + 4	McGowan N 23 + 4	Tierney G 6 + 8	Barrau X 14 + 1	McDonald K 23 + 1	Koudou A 3 + 3	Potter C 3 + 2	Proctor D 12	Lukoszewski M 7 + 2	Harty I 7 + 4	McGuire D 3 + 2	*Match No.*
1	2^{2}	3	4	5	6	7	8^{3}	9	10^{1}	11	12	13	14											1
1	2	3	4	5^{2}	6	7	8^{3}	9	10^{1}	11	12	14		13										2
1		3^{3}	2	5	6	7	8^{1}	9		14	10	11	12	4^{2}	13									3
1		3	2	5		12	8	9	14	11	10^{1}	4	7^{3}	13	6^{2}									4
1	2	3	4		10	7^{1}	8	9	12		11	6		13	5^{2}									5
1	13		2	4	8^{2}	7		9^{1}	10			6		3	5	11	12							6
1	14		2	4	8	7	12	13	10^{3}		9^{2}	6		3■	5^{1}	11								7
1	2	3	4		6	7	13	12	10^{1}		9	5				11	8^{2}							8
1	2	3	4		6^{2}	7		12	10^{1}		9	5		13		11	8							9
1	2	3	4		12	7^{2}	8^{1}	9	13		10	5				11	6							10
1	2	3	4		7^{2}	13	8	9^{1}	12		10^{3}	5			14	11■	6							11
1	2		4	14	7	11	8	12	10^{3}		9^{1}	5		3^{2}	13		6							12
1	2		4		10	7	8	9			12	5		3			6	11^{1}						13
1	13	14	2	5	8	7	12	9^{1}			10^{2}	4		3		11^{3}	6							14
1		3	2		5	7	10^{3}	9^{2}	13			4		6^{1}	12	11	8	14						15
1	12	3	2■		8^{3}	7^{1}	10	14	9^{2}		13	5		6		11	4							16
1	2	3		5^{1}	8	7^{2}	10	14	9^{3}		13			6	12	11	4							17
1	2^{3}	3			10	7	8	14	9		13	5		6^{1}	12	11^{2}	4							18
1	2	3		5^{3}	10	7	8		9^{2}		13	4^{1}		6	14	11		12■						19
1	5	3	2		10	7	8		9		12	4		6		11^{1}								20
1	5	3	2		10	7	8^{1}		9^{3}		13	4	12	6		11^{2}		14						21
1	5	3^{2}	2■		10	7	8	14	9^{3}			4^{1}	12		6	13		11						22
1	5	3			10	7	4	8^{2}	9^{3}		13		2	6^{1}	12			11	14					23
1	5	3			10	11^{2}	8	7	9		12		2		6		4^{1}		13					24
1	12	3	5		10	11	8	7^{1}	9					6			4			2				25
1		3^{1}	5		10	11	8	7	9^{3}			14		6			4^{2}			2	12	13		26
1		3^{3}	4^{1}		10	7^{2}	14	9	12			11		6			8			2	5	13		27
1	11	3^{1}	5		10	12		8	9			14		6			4^{3}		7^{2}	2		13		28
1	11	3	5		10	13		8^{3}	9					6^{1}			4		7^{2}	2	12	14		29
1	3		4		10				9			7		6			11			2	5	8		30
1	3		4		10	12	13		9			8		6^{3}			11^{2}			2^{1}	5	7	14	31
1	11	3^{3}	4		10	7^{1}			9		13	14					6			2	5	8^{2}	12	32
1	11	3	4		10		12		9^{2}		14	13					6			2	5	8^{3}	7^{1}	33
1	11	3^{2}	4		10		12		9			13					6			2	5	8	7^{1}	34
1	4	3			10	11^{3}	13		9		14	12		6						2	5^{1}	8	7^{2}	35
1	5^{2}	3			11	12	13		9^{3}		14	8		6			4		7	2		10^{1}		36

ALBION ROVERS — Third Division

Year Formed: 1882. *Ground & Address:* Cliftonhill Stadium, Main St, Coatbridge ML5 3RB. *Telephone/Fax:* 01236 606334.
Ground capacity: 1249 (seated 489). *Size of Pitch:* 110yd × 72yd.
Chairman and Secretary: Frank Meade ACMA. *General Manager:* John Reynolds. *Commercial Manager:* Patrick Rollink.
Manager: John McCormack. *Assistant Manager:* Graham Diamond. *Physio:* Derek Kelly.
Managers since 1975: G. Caldwell, S. Goodwin, H. Hood, J. Baker, D. Whiteford, M. Ferguson, W. Wilson, B. Rooney, A. Ritchie, T. Gemmell, D. Provan, M. Oliver, B. McLaren, T. Gemmell, T Spence, J. Crease, V. Moore, B. McLaren, J. McVeigh, P. Hetherston, K. McAllister, J. Chapman.
Club Nickname(s): The Wee Rovers. *Previous Grounds:* Cowheath Park, Meadow Park, Whifflet.
Record Attendance: 27,381 v Rangers, Scottish Cup 2nd rd, 8 Feb 1936.
Record Transfer Fee received: £40,000 from Motherwell for Bruce Cleland.
Record Transfer Fee paid: £7000 for Gerry McTeague to Stirling Albion, September 1989.
Record Victory: 12-0 v Airdriehill, Scottish Cup, 3 Sept 1887.
Record Defeat: 1-11 v Partick Th, League Cup, 11 Aug 1993.
Most Capped Player: Jock White, 1 (2), Scotland.
Most League Appearances: 399, Murdy Walls, 1921-36.
Most League Goals in Season (Individual): 41: Jim Renwick, Division II, 1932-33.
Most Goals Overall (Individual): 105: Bunty Weir, 1928-31.

ALBION ROVERS 2006–07 LEAGUE RECORD

Match No.	Date	Venue	Opponents	Result		H/T Score	Lg. Pos.	Goalscorers	Attendance
1	Aug 5	A	Berwick R	D	1-1	0-1	—	Chaplain [89]	457
2	12	H	East Fife	L	0-1	0-0	8		334
3	19	A	East Stirling	W	1-0	0-0	5	Chaplain [79]	263
4	26	H	Queen's Park	D	1-1	0-0	7	Savage [89]	501
5	Sept 3	A	Montrose	L	1-2	0-0	8	Sim [83]	245
6	9	A	Arbroath	W	3-2	1-0	6	Donnelly (pen) [40], Doyle [51], Walker [78]	610
7	16	H	Elgin C	W	3-1	2-0	4	Chisholm [10], Savage [15], Chaplain [63]	276
8	23	A	Dumbarton	L	1-3	1-2	7	Chisholm [62]	639
9	30	H	Stenhousemuir	L	2-5	2-2	8	Donnelly [12], Chaplain [24]	383
10	Oct 14	H	Berwick R	L	0-1	0-1	8		437
11	21	A	East Fife	D	2-2	2-1	8	Lennox [7], Creaney [18]	594
12	28	H	Montrose	W	3-1	2-0	8	Lennox [8], Chaplain [41], Creaney [55]	485
13	Nov 4	A	Queen's Park	L	1-2	0-0	8	Chaplain [57]	543
14	11	A	Elgin C	W	3-0	1-0	7	Lennon [45], Donnelly [48], Felvus [80]	440
15	25	H	Arbroath	L	1-3	0-2	7	Creaney [88]	409
16	Dec 2	H	Dumbarton	W	2-1	2-0	7	Watson [2], Chaplain [4]	504
17	16	A	Stenhousemuir	L	2-3	0-3	7	Murie (og) [54], Chaplain (pen) [71]	332
18	23	A	Berwick R	L	0-3	0-2	7		415
19	30	H	East Stirling	W	4-0	3-0	7	McFarlane [1], Walker 2 [5, 44], Felvus [87]	518
20	Jan 2	H	Queen's Park	W	2-1	0-0	—	Walker 2 [50, 82]	409
21	6	A	Stenhousemuir	W	4-0	2-0	6	Chaplain 3 [10, 28, 56], Walker [47]	341
22	13	A	Montrose	W	3-2	1-1	5	Walker 2 [22, 90], Nicoll [53]	249
23	20	H	Elgin C	W	6-2	3-1	3	Chisholm [20], Walker [28], Low (og) [38], Chaplain 2 [48, 89], McFarlane [80]	425
24	27	A	Arbroath	D	0-0	0-0	3		602
25	Feb 3	A	Dumbarton	L	1-3	1-1	6	McFarlane [26]	746
26	17	A	East Stirling	D	0-0	0-0	6		298
27	24	H	East Fife	L	0-3	0-3	6		420
28	Mar 3	A	Queen's Park	L	0-5	0-1	6		654
29	10	H	Montrose	D	2-2	1-1	6	Chaplain 2 (2 pens) [11, 77]	412
30	17	A	Elgin C	L	0-3	0-1	7		339
31	20	H	Stenhousemuir	W	2-1	1-1	—	Felvus [30], Chaplain [66]	319
32	31	H	Arbroath	L	0-3	0-1	6		488
33	Apr 7	H	Dumbarton	L	0-1	0-1	6		619
34	14	H	Berwick R	L	0-1	0-1	6		382
35	21	A	East Fife	W	3-1	3-1	6	Smith [26], Lennon [31], Walker [42]	542
36	28	H	East Stirling	W	2-1	0-1	6	Chaplain 2 [75, 85]	398

Final League Position: 6

Honours
League Champions: Division II 1933-34, Second Division 1988-89; *Runners-up:* Division II 1913-14, 1937-38, 1947-48.
Scottish Cup Runners-up: 1920.

Club colours: Shirt: Primrose yellow. Shorts: Red. Stockings: Red.

Goalscorers: *League* (56): Chaplain 18 (3 pens), Walker 10, Chisholm 3, Creaney 3, Donnelly 3 (1 pen), Felvus 3, McFarlane 3, Lennon 2, Lennox 2, Savage 2, Doyle 1, Nicoll 1, Sim 1, Smith 1, Watson 1, own goals 2.
Scottish Cup (1): Felvus 1.
CIS Cup (1): Chaplain 1.
Challenge Cup (11): Chaplain 4, Savage 2, Chisholm 1, Donnelly 1, Higgins 1, Lennon 1, McBride 1.

Ewings J 23	Nicoll K 25 + 1	Lennox T 25 + 1	Lennon G 33	Watson P 17 + 1	Donnelly C 33	Friel S 9	Chaplain S 35	Felvus B 16 + 11	Bonnar M 5 + 3	Sichi L 3	Chisholm I 14 + 12	Walker P 21 + 10	McBride M 5 + 7	McGhee G 4	Doyle J 15	Clearie A — + 1	Moffat G 20 + 3	Savage J 7 + 1	Creaney P 11 + 15	Sim A 4 + 12	Bollan G 2	Smith B 28 + 3	Donachy S — + 2	McFarlane D 16 + 1	Thomson R 9 + 1	Thompson L 7 + 3	Hadden K — + 1	McGoldrick J — + 4	Scott D 6	McGeogh J 3 + 3	Brown A — + 3	*Match No.*
1	2^{1}	3^{2}	4	5	6	7	8	9	10	11^{3}	12	13	14																			1
1			4	5	6		8		10^{1}	11^{3}	2	9	12	3^{2}	7	13	14															2
1	2		4		5	6^{1}	8	9			13		11	3	7			10^{2}	12													3
1			4		5	6	8	9				14	11^{3}	3^{1}	7^{2}		2	10	13	12												4
1		3^{1}	4		5	6^{3}	8	9			12	13	11		7			10	2^{2}	14												5
1			4		5	6	8				9^{2}	12	11^{1}		7		2	10^{3}		13	3	14										6
1			4		5	6	8^{2}				9	11^{1}	12		7		2	10^{3}	14		3	13										7
1			4		5	6	8			11^{2}	10	13		3^{3}	7		2		14	9^{1}		12										8
1	2	3	4		5	6	8	12	14		9^{1}				7^{2}			10	13			11^{3}										9
1	3		4	2	5	6^{1}	8	12	10^{2}			14						9^{1}	13	7^{3}		11										10
1	3	7^{1}	4	2	5		8	9	13						6^{2}				10	12		11										11
1	3	7	4	2	5		8	9	13			12			6				10^{2}			11^{1}										12
1	3	7^{1}	4	2	5		8	9							6				10^{2}	13		11	12									13
1	3	7	4	2	5		8^{3}	9					13		6		14	12	10^{1}			11^{2}										14
1	3	14	4	2^{2}	5		8	9	10			12			6^{1}				13	7^{3}		11										15
1^{3}	3	7^{2}	4	2	5		8	12	6			10^{1}							14			11	13	9								16
1	3	7	4	2^{3}	5^{1}		8	13				10^{2}			6				14	12		11		9								17
1	3		4	2	5		8	10^{1}			14	12	7^{3}		6^{2}		13					11		9								18
1	6	3	4		5			13			12	10^{3}	14				2			7^{1}		11		9^{2}	8							19
1	6^{3}	3	4		5		8^{1}	14			12	10^{2}	13				2					11		9	7							20
	6	3	4		5		8^{1}	13				10^{2}	14				2			12		11		9^{3}	7	1						21
	6^{2}	3	4		5		8				12	10					2		13			11		9	7^{1}	1						22
		3	4		5		8	13			7	10^{1}					2		12			11		9^{2}	6^{3}	1	14					23
	6^{2}	3	4	5			8	14			7^{1}	10^{3}					2		13	12		11		9		1						24
	6^{1}	3	4		5		8				7^{3}	10^{2}					2		12	14		11		9		1		13				25
	12	3	4		5		8				13	10^{2}					2		6^{1}	15		11		9	7	1^{6}						26
	6	3	4	14	5^{3}		8				7^{1}	10^{2}					2			13		11		9		1		12				27
	4	3^{2}		5			8	9			13	10					2		6^{1}			11			7			12	1			28
	4	3		5^{1}			8	9			7	10							6			11			2				1	12		29
			3	5	4		8	9^{3}			14	12					6		10^{2}			11			2			13	1	7^{1}		30
	6	3		4	5		8	9^{2}			12	10^{3}					2			13		7				14			1	11^{1}		31
	6	3	4		5^{3}		8	9^{2}			14	10^{1}					2					7		13					1	11^{1}	12	32
	6^{3}		4	2	5		8	11^{1}			3^{2}	10							14			7		9		12			1		13	33
1	6^{3}	3	4		5		8	13			7^{2}	10^{1}					2		14			11		9						12		34
1		3	4		5		8	12			7	10^{1}					2		6^{2}			11		9	13							35
1		3^{2}	4		5		8				7	10					2^{1}		6^{3}			11		9		12				13	14	36

ALLOA ATHLETIC Second Division

Year Formed: 1878. *Ground & Address:* Recreation Park, Clackmannan Rd, Alloa FK10 1RY. *Telephone:* 01259 722695. *Fax:* 01259 210886. *E-mail:* fcadmin@alloaathletic.co.uk. *Website:* www.alloaathletic.co.uk
Ground Capacity: total: 3100, seated: 400. *Size of Pitch:* 110yd × 75yd.
Chairman: Ian Henderson. *Secretary:* Ewen G. Cameron.
Manager: Allan Maitland. *Physios:* Vanessa Smith & Stuart Murphy.
Managers since 1975: H. Wilson, A. Totten, W. Garner, J. Thomson, D. Sullivan, G. Abel, B. Little, H. McCann, W. Lamont, P. McAuley, T. Hendrie, T. Christie, T. Hendrie.
Club Nickname(s): The Wasps. *Previous Grounds:* West End Public Park, Gabberston Park, Belleview Park.
Record Attendance: 13,000 v Dunfermline Athletic, Scottish Cup 3rd rd replay, 26 Feb 1939.
Record Transfer Fee received: £100,000 for Martin Cameron to Bristol Rovers.
Record Transfer Fee paid: £26,000 for Ross Hamilton from Stenhousemuir.
Record Victory: 9-0 v Selkirk, Scottish Cup First Round, 28 November 2005.
Record Defeat: 0-10 v Dundee, Division II, 8 Mar 1947 v Third Lanark, League Cup, 8 Aug 1953.
Most Capped Player: Jock Hepburn, 1, Scotland.
Most League Goals in Season (Individual): 49: 'Wee' Willie Crilley, Division II, 1921-22.

ALLOA ATHLETIC 2006–07 LEAGUE RECORD

Match No.	Date	Venue	Opponents	Result		H/T Score	Lg. Pos.	Goalscorers	Attendance
1	Aug 5	A	Cowdenbeath	L	1-6	0-2	—	Hamilton 46	717
2	12	H	Peterhead	D	1-1	1-1	9	Hamilton 36	462
3	19	A	Forfar Ath	W	2-0	1-0	8	Hamilton 36, Grant 80	502
4	26	H	Stirling A	L	1-2	1-1	8	Sloan 2	991
5	Sept 3	A	Morton	L	0-4	0-2	8		2226
6	9	A	Brechin C	L	0-2	0-0	10		451
7	16	H	Ayr U	L	0-1	0-0	10		556
8	23	A	Raith R	D	0-0	0-0	10		1517
9	30	H	Stranraer	D	1-1	0-0	9	Burns (og) 87	479
10	Oct 14	H	Cowdenbeath	W	2-1	2-1	9	Hamilton 4, McClune 44	543
11	21	A	Peterhead	W	2-1	0-0	7	Brown 75, Payo 88	491
12	28	H	Morton	W	3-2	3-1	6	Brown 2 24, 40, Clark 29	1138
13	Nov 4	A	Stirling A	L	0-5	0-4	6		1227
14	11	A	Ayr U	W	1-0	0-0	6	Brown (pen) 65	1097
15	25	H	Brechin C	D	2-2	1-0	5	Brown 20, Sloan 50	415
16	Dec 2	H	Raith R	L	1-2	0-1	6	Brown 51	786
17	16	A	Stranraer	D	2-2	1-2	8	Malcolm 14, Snowdon (og) 60	276
18	23	A	Cowdenbeath	L	2-5	1-2	8	McKeown (pen) 25, Mackie 63	418
19	30	H	Forfar Ath	W	2-0	1-0	7	McAnespie 25, Grant 60	469
20	Jan 2	H	Stirling A	D	1-1	0-0	—	Bolochoweckyj 90	1050
21	13	A	Morton	L	1-2	1-0	7	Mackie 10	2067
22	20	H	Ayr U	D	1-1	0-1	8	McAulay 90	501
23	27	A	Brechin C	W	3-2	2-2	7	Grant 2 23, 32, Stuart Ferguson (og) 64	438
24	Feb 3	A	Raith R	L	0-3	0-1	7		1763
25	10	H	Stranraer	W	1-0	1-0	5	Mackie 37	344
26	17	A	Forfar Ath	W	2-0	1-0	5	McAnespie 14, Mackie 64	413
27	24	H	Peterhead	L	2-4	0-1	5	Forrest 49, McClune 72	440
28	Mar 3	A	Stirling A	L	0-4	0-0	5		969
29	10	H	Morton	L	0-3	0-1	7		983
30	17	A	Ayr U	L	3-4	3-1	7	Bolochoweckyj 14, Forrest 24, McKeown (pen) 43	922
31	31	H	Brechin C	L	2-3	1-3	8	McKeown 2 (2 pens) 7, 89	400
32	Apr 3	A	Stranraer	W	4-3	1-3	—	Mackie 19, Clark 2 46, 67, Townsley 80	279
33	7	H	Raith R	L	2-3	0-3	8	McAnespie 56, Sloan 62	825
34	14	H	Cowdenbeath	D	0-0	0-0	8		536
35	21	A	Peterhead	D	0-0	0-0	8		769
36	28	H	Forfar Ath	W	2-0	0-0	7	Sloan 74, Bolochoweckyj 80	499

Final League Position: 7

Honours
League Champions: Division II 1921-22; Third Division 1997-98. *Runners-up:* Division II 1938-39. Second Division 1976-77, 1981-82, 1984-85, 1988-89, 1999-2000, 2001-02.
Bell's League Challenge Winners: 1999-2000; *Runners-up:* 2001-02.

Club colours: Shirt: Gold with black trim. Shorts: Black with gold stripe. Stockings: Gold with black hoop on top.

Goalscorers: *League* (47): Brown 6 (1 pen), Mackie 5, Grant 4, Hamilton 4, McKeown 4 (4 pens), Sloan 4, Bolochoweckyj 3, Clark 3, McAnespie 3, Forrest 2, McClune 2, McAulay 1, Malcolm 1, Payo 1, Townsley 1, own goals 3.
Scottish Cup (2): McAnespie 2.
CIS Cup (4): Brown 2, Forrest 1, Grant 1.
Challenge Cup (1): Townsley 1.

Creer A 31 + 1	Bolochoweckyj M 19 + 8	Clark R 20 + 2	Townsley C 11 + 1	Malcolm S 23	Grant J 30 + 2	Hamilton R 11 + 9	Sloan R 24 + 9	Brown G 18 + 2	McAnespie K 25 + 1	McCallum N 5 + 3	Thomson P — + 1	Comrie A 4 + 12	Hazeldine M 2 + 4	Forrest F 29	McKeown S 30	Johnston J — + 2	McAulay P 2 + 6	McColligan B 22 + 3	Ovenstone J 20 + 3	McClune D 22	Payo X 5 + 1	Stuart M 3 + 7	Mackie C 14 + 1	Thomson S 14	Coult L 6 + 3	Caine D — + 1	Coleman P 1 + 2	Findlay S 1 + 1	McEwan D 4	Kelly F — + 1	Match No.
1	2	3^{1}	4	5	6	7	8	9^{2}	10	11^{3}	12	13	14																		1
1	2		4	5	8	7^{2}	11	9^{1}		12		10		3	6	13															2
1	2		4	5	8	7^{3}	10	9^{1}	11^{2}			13		3	6	12	14														3
1	2		4	5	8^{1}	7	10	9^{2}		12		14	13	3^{3}	11			6													4
1	2		4	5	12	7^{1}	11^{3}	9^{2}	10	14			13		8			6	3												5
1	2		4^{1}	5	8	12	10	9					11	3	7			6													6
1	2		4	5	8	7	10	9^{2}				11^{1}	12		6			3	13												7
1	12			5	8	7	11	13					10^{2}	4^{1}	2		9	14	3	6^{3}											8
1				2	4	9^{1}	3	7	13			14		5	6		10^{2}	12	11^{3}	8											9
1		12		4	6	7^{1}	11	9^{2}	10					5	2		13		3	8											10
1		13		4	6	7^{1}	11	9^{2}	10^{3}			14		5	2				3	8	12										11
1		7^{2}		4	6	13	12	9^{3}	11			14		5	2				3	8	10^{1}										12
1	12	7		4■	6	14	13	9^{3}	11^{2}					5	2				3	8	10^{1}										13
1		7^{3}			6	13	4	9^{1}	11			14		5	2			12	3	8	10^{2}										14
1		3		4	7	12	11^{2}	9^{1}	8			13			2			6	5		10										15
1	14	3^{1}		4	7	12	11	9						5	2■			6^{2}	8^{3}		10	13									16
1	2^{1}	6		4	8	7	11		10	9^{2}		13		5			12		3												17
1	14	7■		4^{3}	8		11			9^{2}				5	2			6	3	10^{1}		13	12								18
1	3			2	6		12		11^{2}	10^{1}		14		4				8	5	7		13	9^{3}								19
1	2	7		4	12		11^{1}		6	9^{2}				5				8	3	10		13									20
1	3^{1}	7		5	8		12		11					4	2			6^{2}		10		13	9								21
1	13	3		4	7		11		10					5^{2}	2		12	6		8^{1}			9								22
1	12	3			7		13		11^{3}			14		5	2			6		8			9^{2}	4	10^{1}						23
1	12			3	7		11		10					5	2					6		13	9^{2}	4	8^{1}						24
1	3								11					5	2			6		8		7	9	4	10^{1}	12					25
1	3			5	8				11			13			2			6		7^{2}		12	9	4	10^{1}						26
1	3				7		13		11					5	2^{2}			6	12	8			9	4	10^{1}						27
1	3^{1}	7			8■		13		11					5	2			6		10			9^{2}	4	12						28
1^{6}	3	8					12		11					5	2			6	13	10				4	9^{1}		7^{2}	15			29
	9■				7				11					5	2		13	6	3^{3}	10^{2}		8^{1}		4	14		12	1			30
		3			7		10		11					5	2		12	6		8^{1}			9	4					1		31
		10	12		7		13		11					5	2^{1}			6	3	8^{2}			9	4					1		32
		2	5^{2}		8	13	10	12	11									6	3			7^{1}	9	4					1		33
15	12	7	2		8	13	11	10^{1}						5				6	3				9^{2}	4					1^{G}		34
1	4	7	2				11	9				8			6				3				10^{1}	5	12						35
1	10	7^{3}	2^{1}			12	11	9				8^{2}		5	6				3					4			14			13	36

ARBROATH — Third Division

Year Formed: 1878. *Ground & Address:* Gayfield Park, Arbroath DD11 1QB. *Telephone:* 01241 872157. *Fax:* 01241 431125. *E-mail:* AFCwebmaster@arbroathfc.co.uk. *Website:* www.arbroathfc.co.uk
Ground Capacity: 8488. *Size of Pitch:* 115yd × 71yd.
President: John D. Christison. *Secretary:* Dr Gary Callon. *Administrator:* Mike Cargill.
Manager: John McGlashan. *Assistant Manager:* Robbie Raeside. *Physio:* Jim Crosby.
Managers since 1975: A. Henderson, I. J. Stewart, G. Fleming, J. Bone, J. Young, W. Borthwick, M. Lawson, D. McGrain MBE, J. Scott, J. Brogan, T. Campbell, G. Mackie, D. Baikie, J. Brownlie, S. Kirk, H. Cairney.
Club Nickname(s): The Red Lichties. *Previous Grounds:* None.
Record Attendance: 13,510 v Rangers, Scottish Cup 3rd rd, 23 Feb 1952.
Record Transfer Fee received: £120,000 for Paul Tosh to Dundee (Aug 1993).
Record Transfer Fee paid: £20,000 for Douglas Robb from Montrose (1981).
Record Victory: 36-0 v Bon Accord, Scottish Cup 1st rd, 12 Sept 1885.
Record Defeat: 1-9 v Celtic, League Cup 3rd rd, 25 Aug 1993.
Most Capped Player: Ned Doig, 2 (5), Scotland.
Most League Appearances: 445: Tom Cargill, 1966-81.
Most League Goals in Season (Individual): 45: Dave Easson, Division II, 1958-59.
Most Goals Overall (Individual): 120: Jimmy Jack, 1966-71.

ARBROATH 2006–07 LEAGUE RECORD

Match No.	Date	Venue	Opponents	Result	H/T Score	Lg. Pos.	Goalscorers	Attendance
1	Aug 5	A	Queen's Park	W 3-0	1-0	—	Sellars [43], Scott 2 [72, 82]	634
2	12	H	Berwick R	L 0-1	0-0	5		646
3	19	A	East Fife	L 1-2	1-1	8	Martin [32]	670
4	26	H	Montrose	W 3-1	1-1	5	Black [17], Stein [50], Voigt [62]	1010
5	Sept 3	A	Dumbarton	W 2-0	2-0	4	Sellars [23], Brazil [40]	720
6	9	H	Albion R	L 2-3	0-1	5	Raeside [50], Sellars [55]	610
7	16	A	East Stirling	W 2-0	1-0	3	Scott [5], Martin [70]	300
8	23	A	Stenhousemuir	W 2-1	1-0	2	Martin (pen) [32], Sellars [53]	382
9	30	H	Elgin C	W 2-1	1-1	2	Rennie [35], Brazil [60]	610
10	Oct 14	H	Queen's Park	L 1-2	0-2	2	Sellars [70]	627
11	21	A	Berwick R	L 2-3	0-1	5	Martin (pen) [62], Scott [73]	434
12	28	H	Dumbarton	D 0-0	0-0	5		718
13	Nov 4	A	Montrose	W 1-0	1-0	4	Martin [18]	1143
14	11	H	East Stirling	L 1-2	1-0	6	Sellars [31]	560
15	25	A	Albion R	W 3-1	2-0	5	Bishop [11], Stein [19], Raeside [61]	409
16	Dec 2	H	Stenhousemuir	W 2-0	1-0	2	Martin [31], Scott [82]	649
17	16	A	Elgin C	W 4-0	2-0	2	Scott [9], Sellars 2 [24, 82], Martin (pen) [50]	411
18	23	A	Queen's Park	L 0-1	0-1	4		475
19	30	H	East Fife	D 1-1	1-1	4	Watson [26]	950
20	Jan 2	H	Montrose	W 1-0	1-0	—	Reilly [32]	1295
21	27	H	Albion R	D 0-0	0-0	6		602
22	Feb 3	A	Stenhousemuir	W 2-1	0-0	4	Raeside [80], Webster [90]	337
23	17	A	East Fife	W 2-1	2-0	3	Brazil [3], Reilly [44]	654
24	24	H	Berwick R	W 1-0	0-0	3	Reilly [90]	650
25	Mar 3	A	Montrose	W 1-0	1-0	3	Reilly [8]	1256
26	7	H	Elgin C	W 2-1	1-1	—	Black [7], Dobbins [90]	447
27	10	H	Dumbarton	D 2-2	0-2	3	Rennie [56], Stein [66]	810
28	14	A	East Stirling	W 5-1	1-0	—	Rennie [3], Sellars [46], Brazil [47], Smith [53], Bishop [88]	275
29	24	A	Elgin C	W 1-0	0-0	2	Reilly [75]	305
30	27	H	East Stirling	W 3-2	1-0	—	Reilly [31], Bishop [47], Raeside [74]	657
31	31	A	Albion R	W 3-0	1-0	2	McCulloch [25], Scott [78], Webster [81]	488
32	Apr 3	A	Dumbarton	L 0-1	0-0	—		528
33	7	H	Stenhousemuir	W 4-1	0-0	2	Martin [70], Rennie [78], Scott [86], Smith [90]	751
34	14	H	Queen's Park	W 1-0	1-0	2	Reilly [27]	957
35	21	A	Berwick R	L 0-1	0-1	2		2054
36	28	H	East Fife	L 1-3	1-2	2	Martin (pen) [6]	825

Final League Position: 2

Honours
League Runners-up: Division II 1934-35, 1958-59, 1967-68, 1971-72; Second Division 2000-01; Third Division 1997-98.
Scottish Cup: Quarter-finals 1993.

Club colours: Shirt: Maroon with white trim. Shorts: White. Stockings: Maroon.

Goalscorers: *League* (61): Martin 9 (3 pens), Sellars 9, Scott 8, Reilly 7, Brazil 4, Raeside 4, Rennie 4, Bishop 3, Stein 3, Black 2, Smith 2, Webster 2, Dobbins 1, McCulloch 1, Voigt 1, Watson 1.
Play-Offs (1): Tosh 1.
Scottish Cup (2): Martin 2.
CIS Cup (0).
Challenge Cup (2): Cook 1, Rennie 1.

Peat M 35	Rennie S 27 + 3	Black R 17 + 3	Raeside R 30	Bishop J 33	Dobbins I 26 + 1	McMullan K 26 + 4	Smith N 17 + 10	Martin W 27 + 3	Sellars B 22	Stein J 27 + 5	Scott B 10 + 16	Brazil A 27 + 3	Cook S 2 + 5	McCulloch M 28 + 2	Voigt J — + 7	Watson P 11 + 3	Reilly A 15 + 14	McGlashan J 1	Masson T — + 2	Gardiner R 4	Doyle J 2 + 1	Savage J — + 3	Webster K 4 + 8	Tosh P 4 + 1	Morrison S 1	*Match No.*
1	2	3	4	5	6	7^{3}	8^{1}	9^{2}	10	11	12	13	14													1
1	2		4	5	6	7^{1}	8	9^{3}		11	13	10^{2}	12	3	14											2
1	2	11	4		5	14		9	10	13	8^{1}		7^{3}	3	12	6^{2}										3
1	2	7^{3}	4	5	6		14	9^{1}	10	11		8^{2}		3	12		13									4
1	2	7	4	5	6			8^{3}	10	11^{1}		9^{2}		3	13	12	14									5
1	2	7	4	5	6		13	8^{3}	10	11^{2}	12	9^{1}		3	14											6
1	4	7^{1}			5	2		8	10	11^{3}	6	9^{2}	13	3		12	14									7
1	2			5	4	7^{1}	13	8	10	11	9^{3}	12		3		6^{2}	14									8
1	2			5	4	7	12	8	10	11^{3}		9^{2}	14	3^{1}		6	13									9
1	2^{2}			5	4	7	12	8^{3}	10	11		9	13	3		6^{1}	14									10
1	2		4	5	6	7^{2}	12	8	10	11^{1}	13	9		3												11
1	2		4	5	6	7^{2}	11	8		13		9		3				10^{1}	12							12
1	14	3	4	5	6	2	13	8■		11^{2}	12	9^{3}		10			7^{1}									13
1		8	4	5	6^{2}	2	13		10	11	12	9		3			7^{1}									14
1	2		4	5		7	6	8^{2}	10	11	13	9^{1}		3			12									15
1	2		4	5		7	6^{2}	8	10	11	9^{1}			3		13	12									16
1			4	5		2	6	8^{2}	10	11	9^{1}				13	7^{3}	12		14	3						17
1	2		4	5		7	6	8^{2}	10	11^{1}	9				13		12			3						18
1	2		4	5	12	7	6^{1}	8	10	11						9^{2}	13			3						19
1	2		4	5	6	7		8^{1}	10	11^{3}	12	13		14			9^{2}			3						20
1	14		4	5		2	6	8^{1}		11^{3}		10		3			9^{2}				7	12	13			21
1			4	5	6	2		8	10	11^{1}	7^{2}	9		3			13						12			22
1	2		4	5	6	7			10		12	9				3	11^{1}						8			23
1	2	12	4	5	6	7^{3}		13	10			9		14		3^{1}	11						8^{2}			24
1	2	7	4	5	6			8^{2}	10			9		3			11^{1}					13	12			25
1	2	7^{1}	4	5	6			8^{3}		12		9		3		10■	11^{2}				13	14■				26
1	2	7	4	5		6^{1}	13			11	8	9		3							10^{2}		12			27
1	2	13	4	5		12	6	14	10^{2}	11	7^{1}	9		3			8^{3}									28
1		7	4	5	6	2	13	8^{1}			14	9		3		10^{2}	11^{3}						12			29
1		13	4	5	7	2	6			11^{2}	14	9^{3}		3			8^{1}						12	10		30
1	2	7	4		5	12	6			11^{3}	13	9^{1}		3			8						14	10^{2}		31
1		11	4^{2}	5	8	2	6			13	14	9		3			12						7^{1}	10^{3}		32
1	2	7	4	5			6	12		11^{2}	13	9		3			8^{1}							10■		33
1	2	7		5	4	12	6^{1}	10		11	13	9		3			8^{2}									34
1	2	7^{3}	4	5		6^{1}	10	8		14	12	9■		3			11^{2}						13			35
	14			5	4	3	6	8^{2}		11	9^{1}		2^{3}			10	13						7	12	1	36

AYR UNITED — Second Division

Year Formed: 1910. *Ground & Address:* Somerset Park, Tryfield Place, Ayr KA8 9NB. *Telephone:* 01292 263435.
E-mail: info@ayrunitedfc.co.uk. *Website:* ayrunitedfc.co.uk
Ground Capacity: 10,185, seated: 1549. *Size of Pitch:* 110yd × 72yd.
Chairman: Donald Cameron. *Managing Director:* Lachlan Cameron. *Administrator:* Lachlan Cameron.
Manager: Neil Watt. *Assistant Manager:* Stuart Millar. *Physio:* Karen MacLellan.
Managers since 1975: Alex Stuart, Ally MacLeod, Willie McLean, George Caldwell, Ally MacLeod, George Burley, Simon Stainrod, Gordon Dalziel, Mark Shanks, Campbell Money, Robert Connor. *Club Nickname(s):* The Honest Men. *Previous Grounds:* None.
Record Attendance: 25,225 v Rangers, Division I, 13 Sept 1969.
Record Transfer Fee received: £300,000 for Steven Nicol to Liverpool (Oct 1981).
Record Transfer Fee paid: £90,000 for Mark Campbell from Stranraer (March 1999).
Record Victory: 11-1 v Dumbarton, League Cup, 13 Aug 1952.
Record Defeat: 0-9 in Division I v Rangers (1929); v Hearts (1931); B Division v Third Lanark (1954).
Most Capped Player: Jim Nisbet, 3, Scotland.
Most League Appearances: 459, John Murphy, 1963-78.
Most League League and Cup Goals in Season (Individual): 66, Jimmy Smith, 1927-28.
Most League and Cup Goals Overall (Individual): 213, Peter Price, 1955-61.

AYR UNITED 2006–07 LEAGUE RECORD

Match No.	Date	Venue	Opponents	Result	H/T Score	Lg. Pos.	Goalscorers	Attendance
1	Aug 5	A	Stirling A	W 3-1	0-0	—	Vareille 2 [52, 65], Robertson [81]	993
2	12	H	Cowdenbeath	L 0-4	0-1	5		1199
3	19	A	Morton	D 0-0	0-0	7		2681
4	26	H	Stranraer	L 0-2	0-2	9		1265
5	Sept 3	A	Forfar Ath	W 1-0	1-0	6	Miller [38]	449
6	9	H	Peterhead	L 1-2	1-0	7	Wardlaw [26]	1002
7	16	A	Alloa Ath	W 1-0	0-0	5	Weaver [62]	556
8	23	A	Brechin C	W 2-0	1-0	4	Weaver [30], Vareille [60]	509
9	30	H	Raith R	W 1-0	0-0	3	Pettigrew [81]	1281
10	Oct 14	H	Stirling A	D 0-0	0-0	3		1208
11	21	A	Cowdenbeath	D 1-1	0-1	3	Strain [80]	685
12	28	H	Forfar Ath	W 5-0	2-0	3	Stevenson [35], Robertson [38], Vareille [53], Wardlaw [56], Strain [61]	988
13	Nov 4	A	Stranraer	W 3-1	3-0	3	Strain [2], Wardlaw [9], Vareille [20]	940
14	11	H	Alloa Ath	L 0-1	0-0	3		1097
15	25	A	Peterhead	L 1-3	1-2	4	Vareille [45]	628
16	Dec 2	H	Brechin C	L 1-2	0-2	4	Friels [83]	1028
17	16	A	Raith R	L 0-1	0-0	4		1186
18	23	A	Stirling A	L 2-4	0-2	5	Weaver [54], Caddis [88]	952
19	30	H	Morton	L 0-1	0-0	5		1987
20	Jan 2	H	Stranraer	W 1-0	0-0	—	Wardlaw [90]	1105
21	13	A	Forfar Ath	D 1-1	1-0	5	Caddis [26]	370
22	20	A	Alloa Ath	D 1-1	1-0	5	Strain [13]	501
23	27	H	Peterhead	D 0-0	0-0	5		953
24	Feb 3	A	Brechin C	L 0-2	0-0	5		488
25	17	A	Morton	L 2-4	1-1	6	Waddell [29], Wardlaw [83]	2601
26	21	H	Raith R	L 0-2	0-0	—		853
27	24	H	Cowdenbeath	L 0-2	0-1	8		862
28	Mar 3	A	Stranraer	W 3-0	3-0	6	Wardlaw [27], McLaren A [28], Forrest [35]	667
29	10	H	Forfar Ath	W 3-1	1-1	5	Forrest [16], Waddell [79], McLaren A [86]	955
30	17	H	Alloa Ath	W 4-3	1-3	5	Lowing [27], Waddell 2 [64, 74], Forrest [70]	922
31	31	A	Peterhead	D 2-2	1-0	6	Forrest [44], McLaren F [90]	679
32	Apr 3	A	Raith R	W 1-0	0-0	—	Robertson [65]	1546
33	7	H	Brechin C	D 1-1	1-1	5	Shields [44]	1361
34	14	H	Stirling A	W 3-2	1-1	5	Lowing [20], Shields 2 [50, 56]	1007
35	21	A	Cowdenbeath	L 1-3	0-2	5	Wardlaw [64]	344
36	28	H	Morton	W 1-0	0-0	5	Stevenson [87]	1998

Final League Position: 5

Honours
League Champions: Division II 1911-12, 1912-13, 1927-28, 1936-37, 1958-59, 1965-66. Second Division 1987-88, 1996-97;
Runners-up: Division II 1910-11, 1955-56, 1968-69.
Scottish Cup: Semi-finals 2002.
League Cup: Runners-up: 2001-02.
B&Q Cup Runners-up: 1990-91, 1991-92.

Club colours: Shirt: White with black trim. Shorts: Black. Stockings: White with black.

Goalscorers: *League* (46): Wardlaw 7, Vareille 6, Forrest 4, Strain 4, Waddell 4, Robertson 3, Shields 3, Weaver 3, Caddis 2, Lowing 2, McLaren A 2, Stevenson 2, Friels 1, McLaren F 1, Miller 1, Pettigrew 1.
Scottish Cup (3): Dunn 1, Stevenson 1, Vareille 1.
CIS Cup (2): Caddis 1, Casey 1.
Challenge Cup (4): Robertson 1, Strain 1, Vareille 1, Weaver 1.

McGeown M 32	McKinstry J 2	Lowing D 31	Forrest E 36	Robertson C 28+1	Casey M 25+2	Caddis R 14+11	Weaver P 25+4	Vareille J 29+3	Friels G 3+7	Dunn D 29+3	Logan R 2+2	Reid A —+2	Strain C 18+3	Campbell M 13+2	Wardlaw G 14+10	Pettigrew C 9+8	Walker P —+9	Miller G 14+1	Reid B 15	Hyslop P 3+7	Stevenson R 24	Templeton P 1+2	Waddell R 8+2	Harty I 1	Johnston D —+1	Brown A 4	McLaren A 9	Shields P 5	McLaren F 2+3	Match No.
1	2	3^{1}	4	5	6	7^{2}	8	9	10	11^{3}	12	13	14																	1
1	2	3	4	5	6^{1}	7	8	9	10^{2}	11	12	13																		2
1		3	4	5	8	11^{2}	10	9^{1}	13		6		7	2	12															3
1		3	4	5	8	11^{2}	10	9		14	6^{3}		7		12	2^{1}	13													4
1		3	4	5	6	13	8	9	12	11			7^{2}		10^{1}			2												5
1		3■	4	5	6	12	8	9^{3}	14	11^{2}			7^{1}		10		13	2												6
1			4	5	10	11	8	9^{2}		3			7^{3}		13	12		2	6^{1}	14										7
1		3	4	5	6	11	8	9		10			7					2												8
1		3	4	5	6^{1}	11	8	9^{2}		10			7		13	12		2												9
1		3	4	5	6	11^{2}	8^{1}	9		10			7		13		12	2												10
1		3	4	5^{1}	6	11^{2}		9		10			7^{3}	12	13	14		2			8									11
1		3	4	5	12			9		11^{1}			7^{2}	14	10		13	2	6^{3}		8									12
1		3	4	5^{1}	12	13		9		11^{2}			7		10			2	6		8									13
1			4	5				9^{2}		11			7	3	10	12	13	2	6^{1}		8									14
1			4	5		13	6	9		11^{3}			7^{2}	3	10^{1}	14	12	2			8									15
1		3	4	10		13	7	9^{1}	12	11				5^{3}			14	2	6^{2}		8									16
1		3	4	6		2^{1}	10	9		11			7^{2}	5			13	12			8									17
1		3	4	6^{2}		12	10	9	13	11				5				2^{3}	7^{1}	14	8									18
1		3	4	12	6^{3}	7	10	9	11	14			13	5^{1}				2^{2}			8									19
1		3	4	2		12	10	9		6			7	5	11						8^{1}									20
1		3	4		5	13	10		12	11■			7^{3}		9^{1}	6				2^{2}	8■	14								21
1		3	4		5	13	10		12	11■			7^{3}		9^{1}	6				2^{2}	8■	14								22
1		3	4	5	6	7^{2}	10						8		9	2	13			12			11^{1}							23
1		3	4	5	6■	7^{1}	10			8			12		13	2							11^{2}	9						24
1		3	4	5^{1}		13	14	9		6				2^{3}	10	12				7^{2}	8		11							25
1^{6}		3	4			12	7	9		6^{1}				2	10				5		8		11		15					26
		3	4	9			7	12		6				2	10				5^{1}		8		11			1				27
		3	2^{2}		8			7		6				4	9	13			5		10		12			1	11^{1}			28
		3	2		8		13	7		6				4					5	12	10		9^{1}			1	11^{2}			29
		3	2		8		12	7		6						4^{1}			5^{2}	13	10		9			1	11			30
1		3	2	4	8			7^{1}											5	12	6		11^{2}				10	9	13	31
1		3	2	4	8		7	13											5^{1}	12	6						10	9^{2}	11	32
1		3	4	5	8		7	12		14					13	2^{3}					6						10	9^{2}	11^{1}	33
1		3	4	5■	8			7		11						2					6						10	9^{1}	12	34
1			5		8		4^{1}	7		11					13	2			3		6		12				10^{2}	9^{3}	14	35
1			3	4	2	7^{1}	14	9		11					12	13			5		6	8^{2}					10^{3}			36

BERWICK RANGERS Second Division

Year Formed: 1881. *Ground & Address:* Shielfield Park, Tweedmouth, Berwick-upon-Tweed TD15 2EF. *Telephone:* 01289 307424. *Fax:* 01289 309424. *E-mail:* dennismccleary133.fsnet.co.uk. *Website:* berwickrangers.co.uk
Ground Capacity: 4131, seated: 1366. *Size of Pitch:* 110yd × 70yd.
Chairman: Robert L. Wilson. *Vice-chairman:* Moray McLaren. *Company Secretary:* Ross Hood. *Football Secretary:* Dennis McCleary. *Treasurer:* J. N. Simpson.
Manager: John Coughlin. *Coach:* Ian Smith. *Physios:* Ian Smith, Ian Oliver. *Ground/Kit:* Ian Oliver.
Managers since 1975: H. Melrose, G. Haig, W. Galbraith, D. Smith, F. Connor, J. McSherry, E. Tait, J. Thomson, J. Jefferies, R. Callachan, J. Anderson, J. Crease, T. Hendrie, I. Ross, J. Thomson, P. Smith, S. Clark.
Club Nickname(s): The Borderers. *Previous Grounds:* Bull Stob Close, Pier Field, Meadow Field, Union Park, Old Shielfield.
Record Attendance: 13,365 v Rangers, Scottish Cup 1st rd, 28 Jan 1967.
Record Victory: 8-1 v Forfar Ath, Division II, 25 Dec 1965; v Vale of Leithen, Scottish Cup, Dec 1966.
Record Defeat: 1-9 v Hamilton A, First Division, 9 Aug 1980.
Most League Appearances: 435: Eric Tait, 1970-87.
Most League Goals in Season (Individual): 33: Ken Bowron, Division II, 1963-64.
Most Goals Overall (Individual): 115: Eric Tait, 1970-87.

BERWICK RANGERS 2006–07 LEAGUE RECORD

Match No.	Date	Venue	Opponents	Result	H/T Score	Lg. Pos.	Goalscorers	Attendance
1	Aug 5	H	Albion R	D 1-1	1-0	—	Horn [6]	457
2	12	A	Arbroath	W 1-0	0-0	3	Greenhill D [63]	646
3	19	H	Stenhousemuir	L 0-1	0-1	6		522
4	26	H	Dumbarton	W 3-0	1-0	2	Smith [42], Paliczka [48], Fraser [72]	465
5	Sept 3	H	Queen's Park	W 1-0	1-0	2	Thomson [37]	448
6	9	H	East Stirling	D 2-2	1-0	3	Manson 2 [11, 56]	403
7	16	A	East Fife	L 0-2	0-2	5		622
8	23	A	Elgin C	W 2-1	0-1	3	McLaughlin [52], Haynes [58]	359
9	30	H	Montrose	L 1-2	1-0	5	Thomson [35]	386
10	Oct 14	A	Albion R	W 1-0	1-0	3	Fraser [25]	437
11	21	H	Arbroath	W 3-2	1-0	2	McLaughlin (pen) [1], Wood [48], Thomson [59]	434
12	28	A	Queen's Park	L 0-1	0-1	4		564
13	Nov 4	A	Dumbarton	L 0-2	0-1	6		740
14	11	H	East Fife	W 2-1	2-0	5	Wood 2 [18, 27]	485
15	Dec 2	H	Elgin C	W 3-1	3-0	5	Haynes (pen) [26], Wood [36], McNicoll [45]	343
16	16	A	Montrose	W 1-0	1-0	4	Haynes (pen) [41]	451
17	23	H	Albion R	W 3-0	2-0	3	Wood 2 [9, 84], Thomson [37]	415
18	30	A	Stenhousemuir	W 3-2	3-1	2	Fraser [5], Thomson [16], Greenhill G [22]	463
19	Jan 13	A	Queen's Park	W 2-0	2-0	2	Haynes [39], Greenhill D [42]	491
20	20	A	East Fife	W 2-0	0-0	1	Horn [48], Haynes [50]	628
21	27	H	East Stirling	W 2-0	2-0	1	Greenhill D [8], Diack [29]	517
22	Feb 3	A	Elgin C	L 1-2	0-2	1	McNicoll [77]	370
23	10	H	Montrose	W 1-0	1-0	1	Diack [40]	323
24	17	H	Stenhousemuir	W 2-1	1-0	1	Diack [11], Thomson [59]	537
25	24	A	Arbroath	L 0-1	0-0	1		650
26	Mar 3	A	Dumbarton	W 2-1	1-1	1	Manson [20], Diack [49]	866
27	7	H	Dumbarton	W 2-1	1-1	—	Wood [42], Haynes [83]	425
28	10	H	Queen's Park	L 0-2	0-0	1		704
29	17	H	East Fife	W 2-0	1-0	1	Wood [42], Diack [55]	623
30	20	A	East Stirling	W 1-0	0-0	—	Diack [83]	234
31	25	A	Montrose	W 2-1	1-1	1	Wood 2 [38, 49]	441
32	31	A	East Stirling	W 3-0	2-0	1	Haynes [23], Horn [38], Notman [87]	304
33	Apr 7	H	Elgin C	D 0-0	0-0	1		636
34	14	A	Albion R	W 1-0	1-0	1	Fraser [12]	382
35	21	H	Arbroath	W 1-0	1-0	1	Diack [20]	2054
36	28	A	Stenhousemuir	L 0-2	0-1	1		654

Final League Position: 1

Honours
League Champions: Second Division 1978-79. Third Division 2006-07; *Runners-up:* Second Division 1993-94. Third Division 1999-2000.
Scottish Cup: Quarter-finals 1953-54, 1979-80.
League Cup: Semi-finals 1963-64.
Bell's League Challenge: Quarter-finals 2004-05

Club colours: Shirt: Black with broad gold vertical stripes. Shorts: Black with white trim. Stockings: Gold with black and white trim.

Goalscorers: *League* (51): Wood 10, Diack 7, Haynes 7 (2 pens), Thomson 6, Fraser 4, Greenhill D 3, Horn 3, Manson 3, McLaughlin 2 (1 pen), McNicoll 2, Greenhill G 1, Notman 1, Paliczka 1, Smith 1.
Scottish Cup (5): Haynes 2 (1 pen), Wood 2, McLaughlin 1.
CIS Cup (0).
Challenge Cup (1): Horn 1.

O'Connor G 31	Notman S 12 + 5	Campbell N 6 + 6	Wood G 23	Horn R 31	Thomson I 31 + 3	Manson R 32 + 2	Fraser S 29 + 1	McCallum R 6 + 7	Paliczka S 5 + 11	Noble S 24 + 7	Greenhill G 20 + 6	Smith J 22	McNicoll G 22 + 1	Greenhill D 28 + 5	Britton T 7 + 2	Haynes K 17 + 5	Manini S — + 1	Lucas S 2 + 11	Shand C 5 + 3	McLaughlin D 5 + 5	Flockhart C 5	McGroarty C 15 + 2	Diack I 15 + 1	Swanson D 1 + 2	Little I 2 + 2	*Match No.*
1	2	3^1	4	5	6	7	8	9	10	11	12															1
1	2		9	5	8	7	10	13		3		4	6^1	11^2	12											2
1		12			7	2	8	10^3	14	3^2	13	5	6^1	11	4	9▪										3
1		12		5	7^3	2	8	10	11^2	3		6		9^1	4		13	14								4
1		14		5	7	2	8^1	10^3	11	3	12	6		9^2	4	13										5
1				5	7	2	8^3	10^2	11	3	14	6		9	4^1	13			12							6
1		3	9	5	11	7	8^2	14	10^3			4^1	6	13	12				2							7
1		3	10	4^1	8	7	6	14		11			5^2	12		9^3			2	13						8
1		3^1	4	5	7	12	6	14	13	11				8		9^3			2	10^2						9
1			9	5	7	2	6	12	14	3	8^2			10^1	4			13		11^3						10
1			9	5^2	7	2	6^1		14	3	8			11	4			12	13	10^3						11
1			9		8	2	6	11^2	13	3	10		5	12	4^1					7						12
1			9		7^1	2	6			3	8	5	4	10		12				11						13
1			10	4		2	8			3	7	6	5	11		9^1				12						14
			10	4	7	2	12			3	8^1	5	6	11		9^2				13	1					15
	13		10^3	4	7	2	8	14		3		5	6	11^2		9^1				12	1					16
		3^1	10	4	7^3	2	8					5	6	11		9^2		12	14	13	1					17
	8^3			4	7	3	6	13		12	10^1	5	2	11		9^2		14			1					18
1	10^2			5	7	2	4		13	6	8		3^1	11		9						12				19
1	10^1	13		5	7	2			14	3	8^2	4	6	11		9^3						12				20
1				4	7	12			13	11	6	5	2	8^1		9▪						3	10^2			21
1			9	4^2	7	2			14	3^1	12	5	6	11^3								8	10	13		22
1			9	4		2	8^1			11	6	5		7				12				3	10			23
1		13	9	4	7	2	8		14		6^2		5^1	11▪				12				3	10^3			24
1		13	9▪	5	8	7^2	4		12	11								6	2^1			3	10			25
1	6^2			4	12	7	2			11	8^1		5	10				13				3	9			26
1	2		9	4	8	7^1	11^2			12	6		5	13		14						3	10^3			27
1	2		9		8	11	4			12	6^3		5	7^1		13		14				3	10^2			28
1	13		10	4	12	2	8				6		5	7^1		9^2						3	11			29
1	8^1		10	4	7	2				13	6		5			9^2		12				3	11			30
1	13		9	5	7	2				12	8^3	4	6^1	11				14				3	10^2			31
1	13			4	7	2	6			12	8^1	5		11^2		9^3						3	10		14	32
1	2			4	7		6			12	8^1	5		11		9▪						3	10			33
1	2			4	7	8	6^1			11		5		10^2								3	9	13	12	34
1	8^3			4	7	2	6				13	5	14	12		9^1						3	10		11^2	35
	12	3^2	4^1		14					6		5		7		9^3		10	2		1		13	8	11	36

BRECHIN CITY — Second Division

Year Formed: 1906. *Ground & Address:* Glebe Park, Trinity Rd, Brechin, Angus DD9 6BJ. *Telephone:* 01356 622856.
Fax (to Secretary): 01356 625524. *Website:* www.brechincity.com
Ground Capacity: total: 3960, seated: 1519. *Size of Pitch:* 110yd × 67yd.
Chairman: David Birse. *Vice-Chairman:* Hugh Campbell Adamson. *Secretary:* Ken Ferguson.
Manager: Michael O'Neill. *Physio:* Tom Gilmartin.
Managers since 1975: C. Dunn, I. Stewart, D. Houston, I. Fleming, J. Ritchie, I. Redford, J. Young, R. Campbell, I. Campbell.
Club Nickname(s): The City. *Previous Grounds:* Nursery Park.
Record Attendance: 8122 v Aberdeen, Scottish Cup 3rd rd, 3 Feb 1973.
Record Transfer Fee received: £100,000 for Scott Thomson to Aberdeen (1991) and Chris Templeman to Morton (2004).
Record Transfer Fee paid: £16,000 for Sandy Ross from Berwick Rangers (1991).
Record Victory: 12-1 v Thornhill, Scottish Cup 1st rd, 28 Jan 1926.
Record Defeat: 0-10 v Airdrieonians, Albion R and Cowdenbeath, all in Division II, 1937-38.
Most League Appearances: 459: David Watt, 1975-89.
Most League Goals in Season (Individual): 26: W. McIntosh, Division II, 1959-60.
Most Goals Overall (Individual): 131: Ian Campbell.

BRECHIN CITY 2006–07 LEAGUE RECORD

Match No.	Date	Venue	Opponents	Result	H/T Score	Lg. Pos.	Goalscorers	Attendance
1	Aug 5	A	Peterhead	D 1-1	0-0	—	Walker R ^{58}	645
2	12	H	Stirling A	L 0-1	0-1	7		476
3	19	A	Cowdenbeath	W 3-1	0-1	3	Connolly 2 $^{47, 67}$, Johnson ^{52}	707
4	26	H	Forfar Ath	W 4-2	2-1	3	Geddes 2 $^{11, 89}$, Callaghan (pen) ^{36}, Hampshire ^{59}	622
5	Sept 3	A	Stranraer	L 1-3	1-1	4	Callaghan (pen) ^{15}	411
6	9	H	Alloa Ath	W 2-0	0-0	4	Callaghan ^{63}, Walker R ^{89}	451
7	16	A	Raith R	D 1-1	1-0	4	Fairbairn (og) ^{17}	1818
8	23	H	Ayr U	L 0-2	0-1	5		509
9	30	A	Morton	L 0-1	0-1	6		2526
10	Oct 14	H	Peterhead	W 1-0	1-0	5	King ^{42}	483
11	21	A	Stirling A	L 1-2	0-1	5	Smith ^{53}	701
12	28	H	Stranraer	W 3-0	1-0	4	Smith ^{7}, Russell 2 (1 pen) $^{60 (p), 62}$	407
13	Nov 4	A	Forfar Ath	W 2-1	0-0	4	Russell ^{46}, Walker S ^{79}	687
14	11	H	Raith R	W 1-0	1-0	4	King ^{4}	745
15	25	A	Alloa Ath	D 2-2	0-1	3	Connolly ^{60}, Ward ^{77}	415
16	Dec 2	A	Ayr U	W 2-1	2-0	3	Callaghan ^{20}, Russell ^{30}	1028
17	16	H	Morton	L 2-3	1-3	3	Russell 2 $^{23, 76}$	606
18	23	A	Peterhead	W 4-1	3-0	3	Russell 2 $^{5, 77}$, Walker S ^{11}, Smith ^{21}	615
19	30	H	Cowdenbeath	W 4-2	1-1	3	Callaghan ^{4}, Russell ^{55}, Hampshire ^{69}, Byers ^{90}	544
20	Jan 2	H	Forfar Ath	D 2-2	1-1	—	Hampshire ^{6}, Russell ^{57}	804
21	13	A	Stranraer	W 2-0	0-0	3	Hampshire ^{50}, Smith ^{67}	212
22	20	A	Raith R	L 0-1	0-0	3		1445
23	27	H	Alloa Ath	L 2-3	2-2	3	Smith ^{24}, Connolly ^{45}	438
24	Feb 3	H	Ayr U	W 2-0	0-0	3	Russell ^{69}, Connolly ^{83}	488
25	10	A	Morton	W 2-0	0-0	3	Russell 2 $^{50, 85}$	2134
26	17	A	Cowdenbeath	W 3-0	1-0	3	Russell 2 $^{29, 52}$, Hampshire ^{80}	419
27	24	H	Stirling A	L 1-4	0-2	3	Russell ^{61}	588
28	Mar 3	A	Forfar Ath	L 2-3	2-0	3	Russell 2 $^{5, 26}$	583
29	10	H	Stranraer	D 1-1	1-0	3	Russell ^{34}	415
30	17	H	Raith R	L 1-2	0-1	4	Steven Ferguson ^{80}	909
31	31	A	Alloa Ath	W 3-2	3-1	3	King ^{2}, Russell ^{24}, Ward ^{37}	400
32	Apr 3	H	Morton	L 0-1	0-1	—		776
33	7	A	Ayr U	D 1-1	1-1	4	Russell ^{15}	1361
34	14	H	Peterhead	W 3-1	1-1	4	White ^{21}, Byers ^{76}, Hampshire ^{81}	504
35	21	A	Stirling A	W 1-0	0-0	4	Hampshire ^{66}	564
36	28	H	Cowdenbeath	W 1-0	0-0	4	Connolly ^{72}	475

Final League Position: 4

Honours
League Champions: C Division 1953-54. Second Division 1982-83, 1989-90, 2004-05. Third Division 2001-02. *Runners-up:* Second Division 1992-93, 2002-03. Third Division 1995-96. Second Division 2004-05.
Bell's League Challenge: Runners-up 2002-03. Semi-finals 2001-02.

Club colours: Shirt, Shorts, Stockings: Red with white trimmings.

Goalscorers: *League* (61): Russell 21 (1 pen), Hampshire 7, Connolly 6, Callaghan 5 (2 pens), Smith 5, King 3, Byres 2, Geddes 2, Walker R 2, Walker S 2, Ward 2, Steven Ferguson 1, Johnson 1, White 1, own goal 1.
Play-Offs (1): Russell 1.
Scottish Cup (6): Byres 1, Callaghan 1 (pen), Connolly 1, Hampshire 1, Russell 1, own goal 1.
CIS Cup (2): Callaghan 1, Geddes 1.
Challenge Cup (1): Callaghan 1.

Nelson C 36	McEwan C 8 + 2	Ferguson Stuart 8 + 2	Walker S 27 + 2	White D 30 + 1	Ferguson Steven 19 + 2	Johnson G 11 + 1	Callaghan S 34	Geddes C 8 + 8	Connolly P 20 + 12	Smith D 31	Walker R 21 + 7	Russell I 24 + 9	Ward J 22	Byers K 20 + 7	Archibald R 15	Devlin S 3 + 6	Hampshire S 26 + 5	King C 16 + 10	McManus S — + 2	Flynn M 5 + 2	Murie D 12	Hughes C — + 2	Hillcoat J — + 2	*Match No.*
1	2	3	4	5	6^{1}	7	8	9	10	11	12^{2}	13												1
1	2^{1}	3	6	5		7^{2}	8	9	10^{3}	11	13	14	4	12										2
1	2^{2}			5		6	8	9^{1}	10^{3}	11		14	4	7	3	12	13							3
1				5		6	3	10	9^{2}	11^{1}	2	12	4	7		13	8							4
1				5		6	3	10	9^{1}	11	2^{2}	12	4		7		8	13						5
1			5	6			3	10^{1}	9^{3}	11	13	12	4		2	7^{2}	8	14						6
1	2		5	6			3	10^{1}	9	11	12	13	4			7^{3}	8^{2}	14						7
1	2^{2}		3	5		7^{1}	6	10	9^{3}	11	13	14	4			12	8							8
1		3	6^{2}	5			8	13	14	11	2	9^{3}	4			7^{1}	10	12						9
1		3^{1}	12	5^{3}			6	13		11	7	9^{2}	4	14	2		10	8						10
1	12		5	3			6	13	9	11	2^{2}		4	7^{1}			10	8						11
1	2		5	3^{1}	8		6		9	11^{2}		10^{3}	4	7			14	12	13					12
1	2		5	3	8^{1}		6		9^{2}	11		10	4	7		12	13							13
1	2		6	5	8^{2}		3	12				10	4	7		13	9^{1}	11						14
1			5	13	8^{1}		6		10	11	2		4	7	3^{2}		9		12					15
1	13		12	6			3		10	11^{1}	2	8^{2}	4	7			9			5				16
1		13	4	5■			3		12	11	2	10		6			9^{1}	8		7^{2}				17
1		12	5^{3}		13		3		14	11^{1}	2	10		6	4		9	8		7^{2}				18
1		3		5			7		13	11	2	10		6	4		9^{2}	8^{1}		12				19
1		3		5	12		7			11	2	10		6	4		9	8^{1}						20
1				5	7		3	12	13	11		10^{1}	4	6	2		9^{2}	8						21
1		3	4	5	7		6^{1}	12	8	11		10			2^{3}		9^{2}	13		14				22
1		3^{1}	4	5	7		6	12	9	11	2	10^{2}		8				13						23
1			4	5	7		6		9	11^{1}	2	10		8				12			3			24
1			4	5	7		6		9	11	2	10		8^{1}				12			3			25
1			4		7		6	13	9^{1}	11	2^{3}	10^{2}			5	14	12	8			3			26
1			4				6		9	11■	2	10		7^{1}	5		13	8			3^{2}	12		27
1			4	5	7^{3}		6		14		11	10		12^{2}	2^{1}		9	8			3		13	28
1			4	5	7^{3}		6		14		11	10		12^{2}	2^{1}		9	8			3		13	29
1			4	5	6		3		12		2	10		11			9	8		7^{1}				30
1			5		6	12	3		13	11	7^{1}	10	4				9^{2}	8			2			31
1			5		6^{1}	7	3^{3}		13	11	14	10	4	12			9	8^{2}			2			32
1			5	3	6	7^{1}	8		13	11		10	4	12			9^{2}				2			33
1			5	3	6	7^{1}	8			11		10	4	12			9				2			34
1			5	3	6	8			13	11	12		4	7^{1}			10^{2}	9			2			35
1				5		7			10^{3}		8^{2}	13	4	6	3		9	12		11^{1}	2	14		36

CELTIC

Premier League

Year Formed: 1888. *Ground & Address:* Celtic Park, Glasgow G40 3RE. *Telephone:* 0871 226 1888. *Fax:* 0141 551 8106. *E-mail:* customerservices@celticfc.co.uk. *Website:* www.celticfc.net
Ground Capacity: all seated: 60,355. *Size of Pitch:* 105m × 68m.
Chairman: Brian Quinn. *Chief Executive:* Peter Lawwell. *Secretary:* Robert Howat.
Manager: Gordon Strachan. *Assistant Manager:* Garry Pendrey. *Youth Development Manager:* Tommy Burns. *Head Youth Coach:* Willie McStay. *Physio:* Tim Williamson. *Club Doctor:* Derek McCormack. *Kit Manager:* John Clark.
Managers since 1975: Jock Stein, Billy McNeill, David Hay, Billy McNeill, Liam Brady, Lou Macari, Tommy Burns, Wim Jansen, Dr Jozef Venglos, John Barnes, Martin O'Neill. *Club Nickname(s):* The Bhoys. *Previous Grounds:* None.
Record Attendance: 92,000 v Rangers, Division I, 1 Jan 1938.
Record Transfer Fee received: £4,700,000 for Paolo Di Canio to Sheffield W (August 1997).
Record Transfer Fee paid: £6,000,000 for Chris Sutton from Chelsea (July 2000).
Record Victory: 11-0 Dundee, Division I, 26 Oct 1895.
Record Defeat: 0-8 v Motherwell, Division I, 30 Apr 1937.
Most Capped Player: Pat Bonner 80, Republic of Ireland.
Most League Appearances: 486: Billy McNeill, 1957-75.
Most League Goals in Season (Individual): 50: James McGrory, Division I, 1935-36.
Most Goals Overall (Individual): 397: James McGrory, 1922-39.

Honours

League Champions: (41 times) Division I 1892-93, 1893-94, 1895-96, 1897-98, 1904-05, 1905-06, 1906-07, 1907-08, 1908-09, 1909-10, 1913-14, 1914-15, 1915-16, 1916-17, 1918-19, 1921-22, 1925-26, 1935-36, 1937-38, 1953-54, 1965-66, 1966-67, 1967-68, 1968-69, 1969-70, 1970-71, 1971-72, 1972-73, 1973-74. Premier Division 1976-77, 1978-79, 1980-81, 1981-82, 1985-86, 1987-88, 1997-98, 2000-01, 2001-02, 2003-04, 2005-06, 2006-07. *Runners-up:* 27 times.

CELTIC 2006–07 LEAGUE RECORD

Match No.	Date	Venue	Opponents	Result	H/T Score	Lg. Pos.	Goalscorers	Attendance
1	Jul 29	H	Kilmarnock	W 4-1	2-0	—	Zurawski 2 [24, 90], Jarosik [37], Nakamura [76]	54,620
2	Aug 6	A	Hearts	L 1-2	0-0	5	Petrov [65]	16,822
3	12	H	St Mirren	W 2-0	1-0	3	McManus [28], Petrov [68]	56,579
4	20	A	Inverness CT	D 1-1	1-0	2	Pearson [25]	7332
5	26	H	Hibernian	W 2-1	0-1	1	Zurawski [63], Vennegoor [67]	58,078
6	Sept 9	A	Aberdeen	W 1-0	0-0	1	Vennegoor [78]	15,304
7	16	H	Dunfermline Ath	W 1-0	1-0	1	McManus [34]	55,894
8	23	H	Rangers	W 2-0	1-0	1	Gravesen [33], Miller [73]	59,341
9	Oct 1	A	Falkirk	W 1-0	0-0	1	McGeady [84]	7139
10	14	A	Dundee U	W 4-1	1-1	1	Nakamura 3 [43, 48, 57], Vennegoor [52]	10,504
11	21	H	Motherwell	W 2-1	1-0	1	Zurawski 2 [16, 65]	57,742
12	29	A	Kilmarnock	W 2-1	0-0	1	Nakamura [55], Miller [75]	10,083
13	Nov 4	H	Hearts	W 2-1	0-0	1	Jarosik [85], Gordon (og) [90]	58,971
14	12	A	St Mirren	W 3-1	2-0	1	Gravesen 3 [1, 20, 68]	8445
15	18	H	Inverness CT	W 3-0	1-0	1	Dods (og) [42], Vennegoor [71], Jarosik [84]	56,637
16	26	A	Hibernian	D 2-2	0-1	1	Sno [69], McGeady [73]	16,747
17	Dec 2	H	Aberdeen	W 1-0	0-0	1	Zurawski [72]	58,911
18	10	A	Dunfermline Ath	W 2-1	0-0	1	McGeady [49], Zurawski [68]	7080
19	17	A	Rangers	D 1-1	1-0	1	Gravesen [38]	50,418
20	23	H	Falkirk	W 1-0	1-0	1	Gravesen [23]	55,000
21	26	H	Dundee U	D 2-2	0-1	—	O'Dea [78], Nakamura [80]	57,343
22	30	A	Motherwell	D 1-1	1-0	—	Riordan [36]	9769
23	Jan 2	H	Kilmarnock	W 2-0	1-0	—	O'Dea [38], McGeady [89]	57,236
24	14	A	Hearts	W 2-1	0-1	1	Vennegoor [59], Jarosik [81]	17,129
25	20	H	St Mirren	W 5-1	1-0	1	Vennegoor 3 (1 pen) [16, 60 (p), 75], McGeady [70], Miller [82]	58,382
26	28	A	Inverness CT	W 2-1	1-0	1	Riordan [37], Vennegoor [89]	7484
27	Feb 10	H	Hibernian	W 1-0	0-0	1	Beattie [54]	59,659
28	17	A	Aberdeen	W 2-1	2-0	1	Beattie [8], Nakamura [19]	16,711
29	Mar 3	H	Dunfermline Ath	W 2-1	1-0	1	Miller [4], Vennegoor [77]	59,131
30	11	H	Rangers	L 0-1	0-0	1		59,425
31	18	A	Falkirk	L 0-1	0-1	1		6438
32	31	A	Dundee U	D 1-1	0-0	1	Nakamura [47]	11,363
33	Apr 7	H	Motherwell	W 1-0	0-0	1	Riordan [53]	58,654
34	22	A	Kilmarnock	W 2-1	1-0	1	Vennegoor [24], Nakamura [90]	13,673
35	29	H	Hearts	L 1-3	0-0	1	Pressley [63]	59,510
36	May 5	A	Rangers	L 0-2	0-1	1		50,384
37	12	H	Aberdeen	W 2-1	1-1	1	Vennegoor 2 [32, 48]	59,510
38	20	A	Hibernian	L 1-2	0-0	1	Riordan [56]	13,885

Final League Position: 1

Scottish Cup Winners: (34 times) 1892, 1899, 1900, 1904, 1907, 1908, 1911, 1912, 1914, 1923, 1925, 1927, 1931, 1933, 1937, 1951, 1954, 1965, 1967, 1969, 1971, 1972, 1974, 1975, 1977, 1980, 1985, 1988, 1989, 1995, 2001, 2004, 2005, 2007. *Runners-up:* 18 times.
League Cup Winners: (13 times) 1956-57, 1957-58, 1965-66, 1966-67, 1967-68, 1968-69, 1969-70, 1974-75, 1982-83, 1997-98, 1999-2000, 2000-01, 2005-06. *Runners-up:* 13 times.

European: *European Cup:* 112 matches (1966-67 winners, 1967-68, 1968-69, 1969-70 runners-up, 1970-71, 1971-72 semi-finals, 1972-73, 1973-74 semi-finals, 1974-75, 1977-78, 1979-80, 1981-82, 1982-83, 1986-87, 1988-89, 1998-99, 2001-02, 2002-03, 2003-04, 2005-06, 2006-07). *Cup Winners' Cup:* 39 matches (1963-64 semi-finals, 1965-66 semi-finals, 1975-76, 1980-81, 1984-85, 1985-86, 1989-90, 1995-96). *UEFA Cup:* 73 matches (*Fairs Cup:* 1962-63, 1964-65. *UEFA Cup:* 1976-77, 1983-84, 1987-88, 1991-92, 1992-93, 1993-94, 1996-97, 1997-98, 1998-99, 1999-2000, 2000-01, 2001-02, 2002-03 runners-up, 2003-04 quarter-finals).

Club colours: Shirt: Emerald green and white hoops. Shorts: White with emerald trim. Stockings: White.

Goalscorers: *League* (65): Vennegoor of Hesselink 13 (1 pen), Nakamura 9, Zurawski 7, Gravesen 6, McGeady 5, Jarosik 4, Miller 4, Riordan 4, Beattie 2, McManus 2, O'Dea 2, Petrov 2, Pearson 1, Pressley 1, Sno 1, own goals 2.
Scottish Cup (12): Vennegoor of Hesselink 4 (1 pen), Riordan 3, Zurawski 2, Miller 1, O'Dea 1, Pressley 1.
CIS Cup (3): Zurawski 2, Beattie 1.

Boruc A 36	Wilson M 12	Camara M 1	Caldwell G 20 + 1	McManus S 31	Petrov S 3	Jarosik J 18 + 7	McGeady A 22 + 12	Nakamura S 37	Miller K 20 + 11	Zurawski M 19 + 7	Sno E 7 + 11	Riordan D 6 + 11	Telfer P 20 + 1	Lennon N 30 + 1	Pearson S 3 + 9	Wallace R 2	Beattie C 9 + 7	Marshall D 1 + 1	Naylor L 32	Vennegoor J 17 + 4	Gravesen T 18 + 4	Maloney S 7 + 2	O'Dea D 9 + 5	Balde B 6	Pressley S 14	Hartley P 10	Doumbe J 3 + 1	Kennedy J 3	Brown M 1	Bjarnason T 1	Sheridan C — + 1	*Match No.*
1	2	3	4	5	6	7^{1}	8	9	10^{2}	11	12	13																				1
1	2		4	5	6	7	9	8^{2}	11^{1}	10			3	12	13																	2
1	2		4	5	6	7	9	8	11	10^{2}					12	3^{1}	13															3
1^{6}	2		4	5		6^{1}	10	9	11^{2}	12				7	8	3	13	15														4
	2		4	5			9	8^{2}	11^{1}	10	13			7	6			1	3	12												5
1	2		4	5			9	8	12	10^{1}				7	13				3	11^{2}	6											6
1			4	5			12	8	10^{2}	13			2	7					3	11	6	9^{1}										7
1			4	5			9	8^{1}	10^{2}	13	12		2	7	14				3	11	6^{3}											8
1			4	5			9	8^{1}	11^{3}	10	12		2	7			14		3		6^{2}	13										9
1			4	5		6		9	12		8	13	2	7^{3}	14				3	11^{1}		10^{2}										10
1			4	5		13	12	8	11^{2}	10	6^{3}		2	7	14				3			9^{1}										11
1			4	5		6^{1}	12	9^{3}	13	10^{2}	14		2	7	8				3			11										12
1			4	5		13	9^{3}	8	11	10^{1}	6^{2}		2	7					3	12		14										13
1			4	5		14		8	10^{1}	12	13		2	7					3	11^{3}	6	9^{2}										14
1			4^{1}	5		13	14	8		10			2	7					3	11	6^{2}	9^{3}	12									15
1				5		6	13	8	11	10^{1}	12		2	7					3			9^{2}		4								16
1				5		9	10	8	11^{2}	12			2	7	13				3		6^{1}			4								17
1	2					6^{3}	9	8^{1}	11	10^{2}	14	13		7					3		12		5	4								18
1	2			5		8^{1}	11	9^{2}	12	10				7	13				3		6			4								19
1				5		8	11^{3}	9	12	10^{1}	13	14	2	7■					3		6^{2}			4								20
1				5		8^{2}	11^{3}	9	13	10	7	14	2						3		6		12	4^{1}								21
1				5			13	8	11^{2}	10^{1}		9^{3}	2	7	14		12		3		6		4									22
1						6	13	8	14	10^{3}		9^{2}	2	7			11^{1}		3	12			5		4							23
1						6		8		10^{1}	9		2				12		3	11	7		5		4							24
1						6^{1}	11^{2}	8	14		12	13	2				9^{3}		3	10	7		5		4							25
1				5		14		8	13^{3}			11	2	7			9^{2}		3	10■	6		12		4^{1}							26
1	2			5			11	8	10^{1}					7			9		3		12				4	6						27
1	2			5		6	13	8^{3}			12		14	7			11^{2}		3	10^{1}					4	9						28
1				5^{2}			9	8	10^{3}		7	14	2				11^{1}		3	12	6		13		4							29
1	2			5		12	9	8	10^{1}		6^{3}	14		7					3	11			13		4^{2}							30
1	2^{3}			5■		6^{1}	12	8	10^{2}	13				7			11		3		14				4	9						31
1			2				9	8		12				7			10^{1}		3	11			5		4	6						32
1			2				9	8		10^{1}		12		7			13		3	11^{2}			5		4	6						33
1			2			13	12	8				10		7						11	6^{1}		5		4	9^{2}		3				34
1				5		6^{1}	10^{3}	8	12			14		7^{2}					3	11	13				4	9	2					35
1			2^{2}	5			10^{3}	8	12			14		7					3	11	6^{1}				4	9	13					36
1			14	5			12	8	10^{2}			9^{1}		7^{3}			13		3	11						6	2	4				37
			6	5			12					11					10^{2}				7^{1}		3			9	2	4	1	8	13	38

CLYDE

First Division

Year Formed: 1877. *Ground & Address:* Broadwood Stadium, Cumbernauld, G68 9NE. *Telephone:* 01236 451511.
E-mail: info@clydefc.co.uk. *Website:* www.clydefc.co.uk
Ground Capacity: all seated: 8200. *Size of Pitch:* 112yd × 76yd.
Chairman: Len McGuire. *Secretary:* John D. Taylor.
Manager: Colin Hendry. *Physio:* Ian McKinlay.
Managers since 1975: S. Anderson, C. Brown, J. Clark, A. Smith, G. Speirs, A. Maitland, A. Kernaghan, B. Reid, G. Roberts, J. Miller.
Club Nickname(s): The Bully Wee. *Previous Grounds:* Barrowfield Park 1877-97, Shawfield Stadium 1897-1986.
Record Attendance: 52,000 v Rangers, Division I, 21 Nov 1908.
Record Transfer Fee received: £175,000 for Scott Howie to Norwich City (Aug 1993).
Record Transfer Fee paid: £14,000 for Harry Hood from Sunderland (1966).
Record Victory: 11-1 v Cowdenbeath, Division II, 6 Oct 1951.
Record Defeat: 0-11 v Dumbarton, Scottish Cup 4th rd, 22 Nov, 1879; v Rangers, Scottish Cup 4th rd, 13 Nov 1880.
Most Capped Player: Tommy Ring, 12, Scotland.
Most League Appearances: 428: Brian Ahern.
Most League Goals in Season (Individual): 32: Bill Boyd, 1932-33.

CLYDE 2006–07 LEAGUE RECORD

Match No.	Date	Venue	Opponents	Result		H/T Score	Lg. Pos.	Goalscorers	Attendance
1	Aug 5	A	St Johnstone	D	0-0	0-0	—		2572
2	13	H	Gretna	L	1-2	1-1	7	Imrie [25]	1348
3	20	A	Dundee	L	0-3	0-2	9		3417
4	26	H	Partick Th	D	0-0	0-0	8		2956
5	Sept 16	H	Ross Co	W	3-0	0-0	8	McHale (pen) [49], Ferguson [63], Imrie [85]	993
6	23	A	Queen of the S	W	2-0	1-0	7	Imrie 2 [23, 79]	1770
7	30	H	Livingston	D	1-1	0-0	7	Ferguson [47]	1607
8	Oct 14	A	Airdrie U	L	1-2	0-0	7	O'Donnell [54]	1397
9	17	A	Hamilton A	L	1-3	1-3	—	Masterton [33]	1253
10	21	A	Gretna	D	3-3	1-1	7	Higgins [23], O'Donnell [65], Masterton [69]	1124
11	28	H	St Johnstone	W	1-0	0-0	7	Imrie [85]	1427
12	Nov 4	H	Hamilton A	W	2-1	0-0	6	McGregor N [77], Malone [81]	1364
13	18	A	Ross Co	D	1-1	0-1	7	McKeown [71]	2195
14	22	A	Partick Th	D	1-1	0-0	—	Arbuckle [57]	2752
15	25	H	Queen of the S	W	4-0	2-0	6	McGregor N [44], Arbuckle 2 [45, 56], McHale (pen) [85]	1179
16	Dec 2	H	Airdrie U	D	0-0	0-0	7		1347
17	9	A	Livingston	D	1-1	0-1	6	Arbuckle [82]	1724
18	16	H	Dundee	W	2-1	2-0	6	Arbuckle [36], O'Donnell (pen) [37]	1088
19	26	A	St Johnstone	L	1-2	0-0	—	Arbuckle [58]	2604
20	30	A	Hamilton A	D	1-1	0-0	6	Arbuckle [84]	1534
21	Jan 2	H	Partick Th	W	2-0	1-0	—	Masterton [34], McKeown [46]	2229
22	20	H	Ross Co	L	2-4	0-2	7	Ferguson [72], Masterton [75]	1100
23	27	A	Airdrie U	L	0-1	0-1	7		1340
24	Feb 10	H	Livingston	L	0-1	0-1	7		1007
25	17	A	Dundee	W	4-1	4-0	7	Masterton [1], Bryson 2 [12, 38], Arbuckle [29]	3812
26	24	H	Gretna	W	2-0	1-0	6	Masterton [5], Arbuckle [87]	729
27	Mar 3	A	Partick Th	W	4-0	4-0	5	Arbuckle [4], Masterton [14], Bryson [27], McGowan M [36]	2873
28	10	H	Hamilton A	W	3-0	2-0	3	Arbuckle [12], Masterton [30], Imrie [88]	1200
29	17	A	Ross Co	D	2-2	0-0	4	Gilmore [47], McGowan M (pen) [63]	2145
30	25	A	Queen of the S	D	0-0	0-0	4		2109
31	31	H	Queen of the S	L	0-1	0-0	4		1200
32	Apr 4	A	Livingston	D	0-0	0-0	—		1646
33	7	H	Airdrie U	L	0-1	0-1	5		1306
34	17	H	St Johnstone	L	0-1	0-0	—		1352
35	21	A	Gretna	D	0-0	0-0	5		1715
36	28	H	Dundee	D	1-1	1-1	5	Williams [40]	1400

Final League Position: 5

Honours
League Champions: Division II 1904-05, 1951-52, 1956-57, 1961-62, 1972-73. Second Division 1977-78, 1981-82, 1992-93, 1999-2000.
Runners-up: Division II 1903-04, 1905-06, 1925-26, 1963-64. Second Division 2003-04.
Scottish Cup Winners: 1939, 1955, 1958; *Runners-up:* 1910, 1912, 1949.
Bell's League Challenge: Quarter-finals 2004-05. *League Challenge Cup Runners-up:* 2006-07.

Club colours: Shirt: White with red and black trim. Shorts: Black. Stockings: White.

Goalscorers: *League* (46): Arbuckle 11, Masterton 8, Imrie 6, Bryson 3, Ferguson 3, O'Donnell 3 (1 pen), McGowan M 2 (1 pen), McGregor N 2, McHale 2 (2 pens), McKeown 2, Gilmour 1, Higgins 1, Malone 1, Williams 1.
Scottish Cup (0).
CIS Cup (2): Imrie 1, O'Donnell 1 (pen).
Challenge Cup (8): McHale 2, Ferguson 1, Higgins 1, Hunter 1, Imrie 1, McGowan M 1, O'Donnell 1.

Cherrie P 11	McGregor N 20	Bradley K 5 + 10	Higgins C 34	Harris R 19 + 5	McHale P 18 + 1	Bryson C 33 + 1	O'Donnell S 19 + 3	Arbuckle G 24 + 9	Imrie D 34	McGowan M 32 + 1	Masterton S 19 + 8	McKenna S 1 + 7	MacLennan R 5 + 4	Hunter R 4 + 7	McCann R 16 + 5	Miller J — + 1	Malone E 18	Ferguson A 10 + 13	McKeown C 30	Hutton D 25	Williams A 6 + 7	Gilmore B 13	McGowan D — + 1	*Match No.*
1	2^{2}	3^{1}	4	5	6	7	8^{3}	9	10	11	12	13	14											1
1	2	3^{1}	4	5	6	7	8	9^{2}	10	11■		12		13										2
1	2	3	4	5	6		8^{1}	9^{2}	10		7	13		12	11^{3}	14								3
1	2		4	5	6	7		12	10	11^{2}	8				13		3	9^{1}						4
1	2		4		6	7^{2}	8^{3}	13	10	11	14			12			3	9^{1}	5					5
1	2		4		6	7^{2}	8^{3}		10	11	14			12	13		3	9^{1}	5					6
1	2		4^{2}	13	6^{3}	7	8		10	11	14			12			3	9^{1}	5					7
1	2		4		6	7	8	12	10	11	13						3	9^{1}	5^{2}					8
1	2		4	5^{3}	12	7	14	13	10	11	8				6^{1}		3	9^{2}						9
1	2		4	14	6■	7^{1}	8	13	10^{3}	11	12			9^{2}			3		5					10
	2		4			7	8		10	11^{2}	6	13		9^{1}			3	12	5	1				11
	2		4		6	7^{3}	8	12	10^{1}	11				9^{2}	14		3	13	5	1				12
	2		4		6	7	8	12		14		13		10^{2}	11^{3}		3	9^{1}	5	1				13
	2		4	14	6	13	8^{3}	12	10	11		9^{1}			7^{2}		3		5	1				14
	2^{1}		4	12	6	7	8^{2}	9	10^{3}	11		14			13		3		5	1				15
	2		4		6	7	8^{1}	9^{3}	10	11		14			12		3^{2}	13	5	1				16
	2		4^{1}	12	6	7	8	9	10^{2}	11							3	13	5	1				17
	2■		4			7	8	9		11			13		6^{2}		3	10^{1}	5	1	12			18
			4		6	7^{1}	8	9	10	2	12						3	13	5	1	11^{2}			19
	2		4		6		8^{1}	9	10	11	12						3		5	1	7			20
	2		4		6	7	12	9^{2}	10	11	8^{1}						3	13	5	1				21
		14	4	2		7	12	9	10	11	6		3^{1}					13	5^{3}	1	8^{2}			22
1		12	4	5		7	8^{2}	9	3	11	6		13		2			10^{1}						23
			4	2		7		9^{1}	10	11	6				3			13	5	1	12	8^{2}		24
		12	4	2		7^{1}		9^{3}	10	11	6			13	3				5	1	14	8^{2}		25
		12	4	2		7		9	10	11	6				3				5	1		8^{1}		26
		12	4	2		7^{1}		9^{2}	10	11	6				3			13	5	1	14	8^{3}		27
		12	4	2		7		9^{2}	10	11	6^{1}			13	3				5	1		8		28
		12	4	2		7		9^{2}	10	11	6				3^{1}				5	1	13	8		29
		2	4			7		9	10		6		3					11^{1}	5	1	12	8		30
		11	4	2		7		9^{1}	10		6		3^{2}					13	5	1	12	8		31
			4	2		7		9	10	11	6				3				5	1		8		32
		12	4	2		7		9^{2}	10	11	6							13	5	1	8^{1}	3		33
				2		7		12	10	11	6		4		3^{1}			13	5	1	9^{2}	8		34
		12		2		7		9	10	11	6		4		3^{1}			13	5	1		8^{2}		35
		12	4	2		7^{1}		9	10	11^{3}			13		3				5	1	6^{2}	8	14	36

COWDENBEATH

Second Division

Year Formed: 1881. *Ground & Address:* Central Park, Cowdenbeath KY4 9EY. *Telephone:* 01383 610166. *Fax:* 01383 512132.
E-mail: bluebrazil@cowdenbeathfc.com. *Website:* www.cowdenbeathfc.com
Ground Capacity: total: 5268, seated: 1622. *Size of Pitch:* 107yd × 66yd.
Chairman: Gordon McDougall. *Secretary:* Tom Ogilvie. *Commercial Managers:* Joe MacNamara and Susan Welsh.
Manager: Brian Welsh. *Assistant Manager:* Danny Lennon. *First Team Coaches:* S. McLeish, M. Renwick. *Physio:* Neil Bryson.
Managers since 1975: D. McLindon, F. Connor, P. Wilson, A. Rolland, H. Wilson, W. McCulloch, J. Clark, J. Craig, R. Campbell, J. Blackley, J. Brownlie, A. Harrow, J. Reilly, P. Dolan, T. Steven, S. Conn, C. Levein, G. Kirk, K. Wright, D. Baikie, M. Paatelainen. *Previous Grounds:* North End Park, Cowdenbeath.
Record Attendance: 25,586 v Rangers, League Cup quarter-final, 21 Sept 1949.
Record Transfer Fee received: £30,000 for Nicky Henderson to Falkirk (March 1994).
Record Victory: 12-0 v Johnstone, Scottish Cup 1st rd, 21 Jan 1928.
Record Defeat: 1-11 v Clyde, Division II, 6 Oct 1951.
Most Capped Player: Jim Paterson, 3, Scotland.
Most League and Cup Appearances: 491 Ray Allan 1972-75, 1979-89.
Most League Goals in Season (Individual): 54, Rab Walls, Division II, 1938-39.
Most Goals Overall (Individual): 127, Willie Devlin, 1922-26, 1929-30.

COWDENBEATH 2006–07 LEAGUE RECORD

Match No.	Date	Venue	Opponents	Result		H/T Score	Lg. Pos.	Goalscorers	Attendance
1	Aug 5	H	Alloa Ath	W	6-1	2-0	—	Dalziel 2 [11, 13], Buchanan [55], Scullion [58], Paatelainen 2 [59, 60]	717
2	12	A	Ayr U	W	4-0	1-0	1	Buchanan [14], Clarke 2 [53, 72], Baxter [84]	1199
3	19	H	Brechin C	L	1-3	1-0	2	Buchanan [47]	707
4	26	A	Raith R	W	3-1	1-0	2	Clarke 2 [12, 90], Paatelainen [87]	2457
5	Sept 3	H	Peterhead	W	4-2	2-2	2	Clarke [12], Gomis [27], Buchanan [60], Dalziel [82]	589
6	9	H	Morton	L	1-2	0-2	2	Paatelainen [56]	1315
7	16	A	Forfar Ath	D	1-1	1-0	2	Buchanan [45]	460
8	23	A	Stranraer	L	0-1	0-1	3		304
9	30	H	Stirling A	D	2-2	2-2	4	Paatelainen [17], Fotheringham [19]	693
10	Oct 14	A	Alloa Ath	L	1-2	1-2	4	Buchanan [24]	543
11	21	H	Ayr U	D	1-1	1-0	4	Ellis [45]	685
12	28	A	Peterhead	L	0-1	0-1	5		505
13	Nov 4	H	Raith R	L	1-2	0-0	5	Clarke [64]	1487
14	11	H	Forfar Ath	W	3-2	0-0	5	Paatelainen 2 [53, 56], Gomis [90]	383
15	25	A	Morton	L	0-1	0-0	6		2303
16	Dec 2	H	Stranraer	W	4-2	1-1	5	Buchanan 3 [14, 50, 86], Dalziel [80]	360
17	16	A	Stirling A	L	0-1	0-1	5		758
18	23	H	Alloa Ath	W	5-2	2-1	4	Buchanan 3 [1, 48, 62], Ellis 2 [43, 66]	418
19	30	A	Brechin C	L	2-4	1-1	4	Ritchie [45], Paatelainen [79]	544
20	Jan 2	A	Raith R	W	2-1	0-0	—	Buchanan [73], Paatelainen [83]	2744
21	13	H	Peterhead	L	0-3	0-1	5		380
22	20	A	Forfar Ath	L	0-2	0-0	6		377
23	27	H	Morton	D	1-1	1-1	6	Clarke [4]	785
24	Feb 17	H	Brechin C	L	0-3	0-1	8		419
25	24	A	Ayr U	W	2-0	1-0	7	Buchanan (pen) [13], Scullion [72]	862
26	Mar 3	H	Raith R	L	1-5	1-4	8	Buchanan (pen) [25]	2249
27	6	H	Stirling A	L	1-2	0-1	—	Buchanan [72]	300
28	10	A	Peterhead	W	2-0	1-0	6	Hill [23], Clarke [47]	548
29	17	H	Forfar Ath	W	2-1	0-1	6	Buchanan 2 [47, 67]	251
30	25	A	Stranraer	W	6-1	4-1	6	Clarke 5 [1, 2, 9, 69, 90], Scullion [16]	282
31	31	A	Morton	L	0-3	0-2	5		2702
32	Apr 3	A	Stirling A	L	0-1	0-0	—		629
33	7	H	Stranraer	D	0-0	0-0	6		328
34	14	A	Alloa Ath	D	0-0	0-0	6		536
35	21	H	Ayr U	W	3-1	2-0	6	Buchanan 2 [23, 38], Doherty [50]	344
36	28	A	Brechin C	L	0-1	0-0	6		475

Final League Position: 6

Honours
League Champions: Division II 1913-14, 1914-15, 1938-39; *Champions:* Third Division 2005-06. *Runners-up:* Division II 1921-22, 1923-24, 1969-70. Second Division 1991-92. *Runners-up:* Third Division 2000-01.
Scottish Cup: Quarter-finals 1931.
League Cup: Semi-finals 1959-60, 1970-71.

Club colours: Shirt: Royal blue with white cuffs and collar. Shorts: White. Stockings: White.

Goalscorers: *League* (59): Buchanan 20 (2 pens), Clarke 13, Paatelainen 9, Dalziel 4, Ellis 3, Scullion 3, Gomis 2, Baxter 1, Doherty 1, Fotheringham 1, Hill 1, Ritchie 1.
Scottish Cup (7): Buchanan 2, Baxter 1, Clarke 1, Hill 1, Lennon 1, Paatelainen 1.
CIS Cup (4): Hughes 2, Buchanan 1, Clarke 1.
Challenge Cup (6): Clarke 2, Fotheringham 2, Dalziel 1, Paatelainen 1.

Orr D 10	Guy G 7 + 7	Ellis L 31 + 1	Gomis M 14 + 1	Ritchie I 18	Smith G 10	Scullion P 21 + 3	Paatelainen M 20	Dalziel S 13 + 15	Clarke P 27 + 5	Buchanan L 36	Baxter M 32 + 2	Fotheringham M 8 + 17	McBride P — + 3	Hughes C 2 + 2	McBride K 5 + 4	Fusco G 19 + 5	Hill D 27 + 1	Bannerman S — + 1	Hay D 24 + 1	Lennon D 14	Manzie G — + 2	Hannah D 14	McKinlay C — + 1	Allison K 2 + 1	Husband S 3 + 2	Weir S 4 + 3	McBride M 5 + 4	Doherty M 7 + 1	Davidson M 5	Smart C — + 3	Ramsay I 1 + 2	Armstrong D 10	Kenneth G 7	Bryan A — + 3	*Match No.*
1	2^{2}	3	4	5■	6	7^{1}	8	9^{3}	10	11	12	13	14																						1
1	13	3	4	5	6	7^{2}	8	9	10	11^{1}	2			12																					2
1	14	3^{3}	4	5	6	7^{1}	8	9^{2}	10	11	2	12			13																				3
1	13	3	7^{2}	5	6		8	9^{1}	10	11	2				12	4																			4
1			7^{1}	5			8	12	10	11	2	9		6	3	4																			5
1	6			5			8		9	11	2	10^{2}		4	3	7^{1}	12	13																	6
1		12		5	6		8	9^{2}	10	11	2	7		13		4	3^{1}																		7
1		7^{1}	12	5	4		8	9^{3}	10	11	2	13	14			6^{2}	3																		8
1		3	4	5	6		8	9^{1}	10	11	2	7			12																				9
1^{G}		3	7	5	6		8	9^{1}	10	11	2		12			4			15																10
	2	11	4^{2}	5	6		7	12	10^{1}	9		13				8	3		1																11
	2	11	4^{3}	5	6		7	10^{1}		9	12	14			13	8	3^{2}		1																12
		3	4^{1}	5		13	7	14	10	9^{3}	2	12			11^{2}	8	6		1																13
	14	3	8			7	11		10^{3}	9	2	12				5^{2}	6		1	4^{1}	13														14
	6^{1}	3	8	5			11		10^{2}	9	2					12			1	7		4	13												15
		11	8	5			7	12	10^{1}	9	2						3		1^{G}	4		6		15											16
	14	3	8				11^{3}	13	10	9	2^{2}	12				7^{1}	5		1	4		6													17
		11^{3}				8	7	12	10^{1}	9^{2}	2				3		5		1	4	13	6			14										18
		11^{1}		5		8^{2}	10	12	14	9	2	13				7	3		1	4^{3}		6													19
		11		5		8^{3}	7		13	9	2	12				14	3		1	4^{1}		6				10^{2}									20
		3^{1}		5		7		13	11	9	2	14				12	6		1	4^{3}		8				10^{2}									21
						11^{2}		14	10	9	2	8^{1}			3^{3}	7	5		1	4		6				12■	13								22
		3				12			10	9	2					4	5		1			6					11^{2}	7	8^{1}	13					23
		3				14			10^{2}	9	2	8				6	5		1			4				12		7^{3}		13	11^{1}				24
	2	3				10		11^{2}	13	9		12				6	5		1			4						7	8^{1}						25
	11^{2}	3				10		12	8	9^{3}	2					4	5		1			6					13	7^{1}		14					26
		3				8^{2}		11		9	2	13					6		1			4			12		10		7^{1}			5			27
		3				8		11^{1}	12	9^{3}	2	13					5		1			6				14	10		7^{2}			4			28
	14	3				8		11^{2}	13	9	2						5		1								10^{1}		7^{3}		12	4	6		29
	12	3				8			7	9	2^{1}	11^{3}					5		1	6							10^{2}				13	4		14	30
		3^{3}				10		14	7	9	2	11					5		1	8^{2}							13					4^{1}	6	12	31
						10		13		9	2	12				8^{3}	5		1	4						11^{2}		7^{1}				6	3	14	32
		11				10		12	7^{1}	9	2	13				8^{2}	5		1	4												6	3		33
		3				8			10	9^{1}	2	12				14	6		1						7^{3}	11^{2}		13				4	5		34
		3				8		14	10	9^{3}	2					13	6							1	7^{1}		12	11^{2}				4	5		35
		3				8		12		9	2						6■			10				1	7			11^{1}				4	5		36

DUMBARTON **Third Division**

Year Formed: 1872. *Ground:* Strathclyde Homes Stadium, Dumbarton G82 1JJ. *Telephone:* 01389 762569. *Fax:* 01389 762629. *E-mail:* dumbarton.footballclub@btopenworld.com. *Website:* www.dumbartonfootballclub.com
Ground Capacity: total: 2050. *Size of Pitch:* 110yd × 75yd.
Chairman: Neil Rankine. *Club Secretary:* David Prophet. *Company Secretary:* Gilbert Lawrie.
Manager: Gerry McCabe. *Assistant Manager:* Jim Clark. *Physio:* Lindsay Smart.
Managers since 1975: A. Wright, D. Wilson, S. Fallon, W. Lamont, D. Wilson, D. Whiteford, A. Totten, M. Clougherty, R. Auld, J. George, W. Lamont, M. MacLeod, J. Fallon, I. Wallace, J. Brown, T. Carson, D. Winnie, B. Fairley, P. Martin.
Club Nickname(s): The Sons. *Previous Grounds:* Broadmeadow, Ropework Lane, Townend Ground, Boghead Park.
Record Attendance: 18,000 v Raith Rovers, Scottish Cup, 2 Mar 1957.
Record Transfer Fee received: £125,000 for Graeme Sharp to Everton (March 1982).
Record Transfer Fee paid: £50,000 for Charlie Gibson from Stirling Albion (1989).
Record Victory: 13-1 v Kirkintilloch Central. 1st rd, 1 Sept 1888.
Record Defeat: 1-11 v Albion Rovers, Division II; 30 Jan, 1926: v Ayr United, League Cup, 13 Aug 1952.
Most Capped Player: James McAulay, 9, Scotland.
Most League Appearances: 297: Andy Jardine, 1957-67.
Most Goals in Season (Individual): 38: Kenny Wilson, Division II, 1971-72. *(League and Cup):* 46 Hughie Gallacher, 1955-56.
Most Goals Overall (Individual): 169: Hughie Gallacher, 1954-62 (including C Division 1954-55). *(League and Cup):* 202 Hughie Gallacher, 1954-62.

DUMBARTON 2006–07 LEAGUE RECORD

Match No.	*Date*	*Venue*	*Opponents*	*Result*	*H/T Score*	*Lg. Pos.*	*Goalscorers*	*Attendance*
1	Aug 5	A	Montrose	D 1-1	1-1	—	Bagan [35]	404
2	12	H	East Stirling	W 2-0	1-0	2	Bagan [23], Quitongo [75]	631
3	19	A	Queen's Park	L 0-1	0-0	4		884
4	26	A	Berwick R	L 0-3	0-1	8		465
5	Sept 3	H	Arbroath	L 0-2	0-2	9		720
6	9	A	Elgin C	W 2-0	0-0	8	Dobbie [60], Dillon [83]	462
7	16	H	Stenhousemuir	W 4-0	2-0	7	Winter 2 [22, 86], Dobbie 2 [35, 48]	903
8	23	H	Albion R	W 3-1	2-1	5	McNaught [22], Borris [42], Lennon (og) [90]	639
9	30	A	East Fife	L 0-1	0-1	6		651
10	Oct 14	H	Montrose	W 2-0	1-0	5	Dobbie 2 (1 pen) [27 (p), 84]	634
11	21	A	East Stirling	W 2-0	1-0	3	Dobbie (pen) [14], Bagan [55]	402
12	28	A	Arbroath	D 0-0	0-0	2		718
13	Nov 4	H	Berwick R	W 2-0	1-0	2	Winter [19], Hamilton [70]	740
14	11	A	Stenhousemuir	L 0-1	0-0	4		517
15	25	H	Elgin C	W 3-1	0-0	3	Borris [47], Dobbie [62], Winter [65]	713
16	Dec 2	A	Albion R	L 1-2	0-2	4	Borris [47]	504
17	16	H	East Fife	W 2-1	1-0	3	Dobbie [9], Winter [62]	798
18	23	A	Montrose	W 5-0	1-0	2	Dobbie 2 [34, 81], Gentile 2 [50, 71], Hamilton [84]	431
19	30	H	Queen's Park	D 0-0	0-0	3		1092
20	Jan 27	A	Elgin C	W 1-0	1-0	5	Boyle [43]	484
21	Feb 3	H	Albion R	W 3-1	1-1	3	Coyne 2 [20, 48], Borris [47]	746
22	17	A	Queen's Park	L 0-2	0-1	5		849
23	24	H	East Stirling	W 2-1	1-1	5	Coyne (pen) [17], Gentile [73]	729
24	Mar 3	H	Berwick R	L 1-2	1-1	5	Coyne [22]	866
25	7	A	Berwick R	L 1-2	1-1	—	Winter [11]	425
26	10	A	Arbroath	D 2-2	2-0	5	Geggan [6], Henry [12]	810
27	13	H	Stenhousemuir	D 1-1	0-1	—	McCulloch (og) [56]	528
28	17	A	Stenhousemuir	L 1-5	1-2	5	Craig [38]	444
29	21	A	East Fife	L 0-1	0-0	—		443
30	25	H	East Fife	L 0-2	0-2	5		561
31	31	H	Elgin C	W 1-0	0-0	5	Boyle [80]	521
32	Apr 3	H	Arbroath	W 1-0	0-0	—	Borris [54]	528
33	7	A	Albion R	W 1-0	1-0	5	McQuilken [42]	619
34	14	H	Montrose	W 2-1	1-1	5	McQuilken 2 [3, 65]	530
35	21	A	East Stirling	W 5-1	4-0	5	McQuilken [15], Borris [23], McNaught [29], Boyle [41], Coyne [80]	429
36	28	H	Queen's Park	L 1-2	0-1	5	Coyne [89]	928

Final League Position: 5

Honours
League Champions: Division I 1890-91 (shared with Rangers), 1891-92. Division II 1910-11, 1971-72. Second Division 1991-92; *Runners-up:* First Division 1983-84. Division II 1907-08. Third Division 2001-02.
Scottish Cup Winners: 1883; *Runners-up:* 1881, 1882, 1887, 1891, 1897.

Club colours: Shirt: Gold with black sleeves and black panel down sides. Shorts: Black with three gold panels. Stockings: Black.

Goalscorers: *League* (52): Dobbie 10 (2 pens), Borris 6, Coyne 6 (1 pen), Winter 6, McQuilken 4, Bagan 3, Boyle 3, Gentile 3, Hamilton 2, McNaught 2, Craig 1, Dillon 1, Henry 1, Geggan 1, Quitongo 1, own goals 2.
Scottish Cup (1): Gemmell 1.
CIS Cup (4): Bagan 1, Boyle 1, Dobbie 1, Gemmell 1.
Challenge Cup (1): McNaught 1.

Grindlay S 36	Canning M 32 + 1	Dillon J 18 + 12	Dempsie M 1	Craig D 36	Gentile C 8 + 5	Borris R 31	Winter C 30 + 1	McNaught D 25 + 6	Bagan D 25 + 3	Boyle C 32 + 3	Geggan A 31 + 1	Brittain C 27 + 2	McCann K 1	Gemmell J 1 + 4	Quitongo J — + 2	Dobbie S 17	McKeever J — + 7	Hamilton C 12 + 15	McQuilken P 11 + 11	Coyne T 10 + 6	Henry J 3 + 2	Smith J 3 + 1	Tiernan F 6 + 1	McLaughlin J — + 1	Match No.
1	2	3	4	5	6	7^1	8	9	10	11^2	12	13													1
1	4	13		5	8	7^3	12	10	6	11		3	2^2	9^1	14										2
1	4	11^2		5	12	7	8^1	10	6	14	2	3^3			13	9									3
1		3		5	8	7	4	10	6^1	11		2				9	12								4
1		3		5	6	7	4	10	8	11	2	12				9^1									5
1	12	13		5	8	7	4	10^3	6^1	11^2	2	3				9		14							6
1	4	12		5	14	7^3	8	10	6	11^1	2	3				9^2		13							7
1	4			5		7	8	10	6	11	2	3				9^1		12							8
1	4	12		5		7	8	10	6^1	11	2	3				9^2		13							9
1	4	13		5		7	8	10^1	6^2	11	2	3				9		12							10
1	4	13		5		7^2	8■	12	6	11	2	3				9^3		10^1	14						11
1	4	8^1		5		7■		13	6^3	11	2	3				9^2	12	10	14						12
1	4			5			8	10^1	6	11	2	3				9	12	7^2	13						13
1	4	13		5		7	8		6^2	11	2	3		12		9^1		10^3	14						14
1	4	13		5		7^2	6	10^3		11	2	3		14		9^1		8	12						15
1	4	3		5	13	7	6	10		11	2			12		9^1		8^2							16
1	4	12		5		7	8		6^1	11	2	3				9		13	10^2						17
1	4	14		5	6	7^2	8		10^3	11	2^1	3				9		12	13						18
1	4	8^1		5		7	2	12		11		3		13		9^2		6	10						19
1	4	12		5	8^1	7	6	9^2	10^3	11	2	3						14		13					20
1	4			5		7^1	6	14	8	11	2	3						12	10^2	9^3	13				21
1	4	8^1		5	6	7		12	10	11^2	2^3	3					14	13		9					22
1	4			5	12	7■		8^2	6^1	10	2	3						11	13	9					23
1	4	14		5	12		6^3	7		10	2	3^2						11	8	9^1	13				24
1	4	8		5		7	6	10		11^1	2	3^2						12	13	9					25
1	4	11■		5^1			6	10			2	3						7		9	8	12			26
1	4			5			6	11		10	2	3						7	12	9	8^1				27
1	4	8		5			6	10	7	13	2	3^2					14	11^1	12	9^3					28
1	8	3		5		7	6		10^1	11	2								9	12		4			29
1	2	3		5		7	8■		6	11									10	9		4^1	12		30
1	4	11^1		5		7		14	6	12	2	3							13	9^3	10^2		8		31
1	4			5		7	6	11		10^3	2	3^1					12	13	9^2	14			8		32
1	4	3		5		7	6	11^1	13	10	2							12	9^2				8		33
1		3		5		7^1	6^3	11^2	14	10	2							13	9	12		4	8		34
1	4	3		5		7^2	6^3	10^1	14	11	2							13	9	12			8		35
1	4	3		5		7^3		10^2	6^1	11	2						14		9	13			8	12	36

DUNDEE

First Division

Year Formed: 1893. *Ground & Address:* Dens Park Stadium, Sandeman St, Dundee DD3 7JY. *Telephone:* 01382 889966. *Fax:* 01382 832284. *E-mail:* dfc@dundeefc.co.uk. *Website:* www.dundeefc.co.uk
Ground Capacity: all seated: 11,760. *Size of Pitch:* 101m × 66m.
Chairman: Bob Brannan. *Chief Executive:* David MacKinnon.
Manager: Alex Rae. *Assistant Manager:* Davie Farrell. *Youth Development Coach:* Gordon Wallace. *Community Coach:* Gavin Timley. *Physio:* Karen Gibson.
Managers since 1975: David White, Tommy Gemmell, Donald Mackay, Archie Knox, Jocky Scott, Dave Smith, Gordon Wallace, Iain Munro, Simon Stainrod, Jim Duffy, John McCormack, John Scott, Ivano Bonetti, Jim Duffy, Alan Kernaghan.
Club Nickname(s): The Dark Blues or The Dee. *Previous Grounds:* Carolina Port 1893-98.
Record Attendance: 43,024 v Rangers, Scottish Cup, 1953.
Record Transfer Fee received: £500,000 for Tommy Coyne to Celtic (March 1989).
Record Transfer Fee paid: £200,000 for Jim Leighton (Feb 1992).
Record Victory: 10-0 Division II v Alloa, 9 Mar 1947 and v Dunfermline Ath, 22 Mar 1947.
Record Defeat: 0-11 v Celtic, Division I, 26 Oct 1895.
Most Capped Player: Alex Hamilton, 24, Scotland. *Most League Appearances:* 341: Doug Cowie, 1945-61.
Most League Goals in Season (Individual): 52: Alan Gilzean, 1963-64.
Most Goals Overall (Individual): 113: Alan Gilzean.

DUNDEE 2006–07 LEAGUE RECORD

Match No.	Date	Venue	Opponents	Result		H/T Score	Lg. Pos.	Goalscorers	Attendance
1	Aug 5	H	Partick Th	L	0-1	0-1	—		5144
2	12	A	Hamilton A	L	0-1	0-0	8		1517
3	20	H	Clyde	W	3-0	2-0	7	Harris [10], Lyle (pen) [42], Swankie [48]	3417
4	26	H	Livingston	L	0-1	0-0	6		4059
5	Sept 9	A	Gretna	W	4-0	4-0	6	Lyle [9], Rae [18], McLaren [24], McDonald K [40]	1556
6	16	H	Queen of the S	W	2-1	1-1	5	Mann [4], Lyle (pen) [47]	3745
7	23	A	Airdrie U	W	1-0	1-0	4	Lyle (pen) [25]	1249
8	30	H	St Johnstone	D	1-1	0-1	5	McLaren [71]	5538
9	Oct 14	A	Ross Co	L	0-1	0-1	6		2454
10	21	H	Hamilton A	D	1-1	0-1	6	Strong [55]	3851
11	28	A	Partick Th	L	1-3	1-2	6	Rae [27]	2987
12	Nov 4	H	Gretna	L	1-3	1-1	7	McGinty [28]	3938
13	11	A	Livingston	W	3-2	1-0	6	Swankie 2 [15, 77], Lyle [63]	1568
14	18	A	Queen of the S	L	0-2	0-1	6		1861
15	25	H	Airdrie U	W	1-0	1-0	7	Smith G [35]	3528
16	Dec 2	H	Ross Co	W	3-1	0-0	6	Rae [73], Lyle [77], McLaren [84]	3380
17	9	A	St Johnstone	L	1-2	1-2	7	Swankie [14]	4127
18	16	A	Clyde	L	1-2	0-2	7	Swankie (pen) [87]	1088
19	26	H	Partick Th	W	3-1	2-1	—	Deasley 2 [21, 33], Swankie [62]	4113
20	30	A	Gretna	L	0-1	0-0	7		1541
21	Jan 2	H	Livingston	W	2-0	0-0	—	Harris [46], Robertson [81]	3804
22	20	H	Queen of the S	W	1-0	0-0	3	Lyle [47]	3360
23	27	A	Ross Co	D	0-0	0-0	4		2175
24	Feb 3	A	Airdrie U	W	3-0	1-0	3	Lyle 2 [36, 65], Robertson [61]	1404
25	10	H	St Johnstone	W	2-1	0-0	3	Lyle (pen) [64], Swankie [81]	5145
26	17	H	Clyde	L	1-4	0-4	3	Hamdaoui [83]	3812
27	24	A	Hamilton A	L	0-1	0-1	3		1439
28	Mar 3	A	Livingston	W	3-1	0-1	3	Davidson 2 (1 pen) [65 (p), 80], McDonald K [89]	1980
29	11	H	Gretna	L	0-1	0-1	4		3928
30	17	A	Queen of the S	D	2-2	1-1	5	Daal [31], Davidson [56]	1967
31	25	A	St Johnstone	L	0-2	0-0	5		3523
32	Apr 1	H	Airdrie U	W	2-1	1-1	5	Daal 2 [28, 56]	2837
33	7	H	Ross Co	W	3-2	2-0	4	Daal 2 [20, 32], McHale [54]	3013
34	14	A	Partick Th	L	1-2	1-1	4	Lyle [22]	2433
35	21	H	Hamilton A	W	1-0	0-0	4	Lyle (pen) [62]	3221
36	28	A	Clyde	D	1-1	1-1	3	Clark [21]	1400

Final League Position: 3

Honours
League Champions: Division I 1961-62. First Division 1978-79, 1991-92, 1997-98. Division II 1946-47; *Runners-up:* Division I 1902-03, 1906-07, 1908-09, 1948-49, 1980-81.
Scottish Cup Winners: 1910; *Runners-up:* 1925, 1952, 1964, 2003.
League Cup Winners: 1951-52, 1952-53, 1973-74; *Runners-up:* 1967-68, 1980-81. *(Coca-Cola Cup):* 1995-96.
B&Q (Centenary) Cup Winners: 1990-91; *Runners-up:* 1994-95.

European: *European Cup:* 8 matches (1962-63 semi-finals). *Cup Winners' Cup:* 2 matches: (1964-65). *UEFA Cup:* 22 matches: (*Fairs Cup:* 1967-68 semi-finals. *UEFA Cup:* 1971-72, 1973-74, 1974-75, 2003-04).

Club colours: Shirt: Navy with white and red shoulder and sleeve flashes. Shorts: White with navy/red piping. Stockings: Navy, top with two white hoops.

Goalscorers: *League* (48): Lyle 12 (5 pens), Swankie 7 (1 pen), Daal 5, Davidson 3 (1 pen), McLaren 3, Rae 3, Deasley 2, Harris 2, McDonald K 2, Robertson 2, Clark 1, Hamdaoui 1, McGinty 1, McHale 1, Mann 1, Smith G 1, Strong 1.
Scottish Cup (4): Lyle 3, Deasley 1.
CIS Cup (1): Swankie 1.
Challenge Cup (1): Swankie 1.

Roy L 32	Griffin D 22+3	Dixon P 33	Rae A 24+1	Mackenzie G 19+2	Mann R 16	Harris R 7+11	McDonald K 29+2	Deasley B 6+8	Ciani A 1+1	Gates S 2+9	Murray S —+1	Macdonald C 2+4	Swankie G 31+2	Harpur C 1	Strong G 15+1	Robertson S 29	Campbell R 6+9	Reidford C 3	Lyle D 26+2	McLaren A 10+2	McGinty B 5+1	Forsyth C 1	Boggan J —+1	Smith G 20+1	Shields J 19+1	Clark B 2+4	Johnston S —+1	McHale P 12	Smith K 4+4	Davidson R 12+3	Hamdaoui K —+4	Higgins C —+3	Daal B 7	*Match No.*
1^G	2	3	4	5	6^1	7	8	9	10^2	11	15	12	13																					1
		3	4	5		13	8	10	12	14		2	9^1	1	6	7^2	11^3																	2
		3	4	5		7	8	12				2	10		6	11		1	9^1															3
	11	5	2^1	3		6	7						9		4	8	12	1	10^2	13														4
1	2	3	4		6	13	8			14			11^1		5	7	12		10^3	9^2														5
1	2	3	4		6	14	8			12			11^3		5	7	13		10^2	9^1														6
1	2	3	4		6	12	8^1			14			11^3		5	7	13		10	9^2														7
1	2	3	4		6	14	8^3			13			11^1		5	7	12		10■	9^2														8
1	2^1	3	4		6		8			13		12	11		5	7	10^2			9														9
1	2	3	4		6		7						10		5	8	12			11	9^1													10
1	2	3	4■		6	12	8	13					11^2		5	7				9	10^1													11
1	2	3^2			6	4	8	12		14		13	11^3		5	7				10■	9^1													12
1	2		4		6	8		12				13	11		5	7			10^1		9^3	3^2	14											13
1	2	3	4		6	8^1		14					11		5^1	7			10	13	9^2			12										14
1	2	3	4		6		7	9^1					11^2		12	8	13		10					5										15
1		3	4		6		7	12							5	8	11^1		10	9^2	13			2										16
1		3	4		6	13	7						11		5^1	8	10^2		9					2	12									17
		3	4	14	6	13	12						11			8^2	10^1	1	9^3	7■				5	2									18
1	2	3	4^2	5	6	13	14	11^3					7^1			10	12		9						8									19
1	2	3	4	5		13	10^1	11								8	12		9					6	7^2									20
1	2	3		5		7^2		10								8	11^1		9					6	4	12	13							21
1		3		5			7	13					11			8			9^2					6	2			4	10^1	12				22
1		3		5			7						11			8			9					6	2			4		10^1	12			23
1	14	3		5^3			7	13					11^2			8			9					6	2			4	10^1	12				24
1		3		5			7						11			8			9					6	2			4	12	10^1				25
1	3			5			7^2						11			8			9					6	2^1			4	14	10^3	13	12		26
1		3	4	5									11^2			7			9					6	2			8	10^1	12	13			27
1		3		5			7						11			8			9^1					6	2			4	12	10				28
1		3	12	5		14	7						11^3			8^1								6	2			4	9^2	10	13			29
1	13	3		5			7						11			8^1								6	2	12		4^2		10			9	30
1	13	3■		5			7^2						11						8^1					6	2	12		4		10			9	31
1	3		8	5^1						7			11						13					6	2			4		9		12	10^2	32
1	5	3	8				7			13			11						12					6	2^1			4		9^2			10	33
1	5	3	4■				7						11						8					6	2	13			12^2	9			10^1	34
1	5	3		12			7			13			11^1						8					6	2	4^2				9			10	35
1	6	3	4	5			7						12						8■						2^2	11				9		13	10^1	36

DUNDEE UNITED — Premier League

Year Formed: 1909 (1923). *Ground & Address:* Tannadice Park, Tannadice St, Dundee DD3 7JW. *Telephone:* 01382 833166. *Fax:* 01382 889398. *E-mail:* enquiries@dundeeunited.co.uk. *Website:* www.dundeeunitedfc.co.uk
Ground Capacity: total: 14,223 all seated: stands: east 2868, west 2096, south 2201, Fair Play 1601, George Fox 5151, executive boxes 292.
Size of Pitch: 110yd × 72yd.
Chairman: Eddie Thompson, OBE. *Secretary:* Spence Anderson. *Commercial Manager:* Bill Campbell.
Manager: Craig Levein. *Assistant Manager:* Peter Houston. *First Team Coach:* Tony Docherty. *Coach:* Graeme Liveston. *Youth Coach:* Stevie Campbell. *Youth Development:* Graeme Liveston. *Physio:* Jeff Clarke. *Stadium Manager:* Ron West.
Managers since 1975: J. McLean, I. Golac, W. Kirkwood, T. McLean, P. Sturrock, A. Smith, I. McCall, G. Chisholm, C. Brewster.
Club Nickname(s): The Terrors. *Previous Grounds:* None.
Record Attendance: 28,000 v Barcelona, Fairs Cup, 16 Nov 1966.
Record Transfer Fee received: £4,000,000 for Duncan Ferguson from Rangers (July 1993).
Record Transfer Fee paid: £750,000 for Steven Pressley from Coventry C (July 1995).
Record Victory: 14-0 v Nithsdale Wanderers, Scottish Cup 1st rd, 17 Jan 1931.
Record Defeat: 1-12 v Motherwell, Division II, 23 Jan 1954.
Most Capped Player: Maurice Malpas, 55, Scotland.
Most League Appearances: 618, Maurice Malpas, 1980-2000.
Most Appearances in European Matches: 76, Dave Narey (record for Scottish player).
Most League Goals in Season (Individual): 41: John Coyle, Division II, 1955-56.
Most Goals Overall (Individual): 158: Peter McKay.

DUNDEE UNITED 2006–07 LEAGUE RECORD

Match No.	Date	Venue	Opponents	Result		H/T Score	Lg. Pos.	Goalscorers	Attendance
1	Jul 29	H	Falkirk	L	1-2	1-1	—	Robson [16]	6616
2	Aug 5	A	Rangers	D	2-2	1-0	8	Hunt [14], Kalvenes [55]	50,394
3	12	A	Kilmarnock	D	0-0	0-0	8		5328
4	19	H	Dunfermline Ath	D	0-0	0-0	9		6171
5	26	A	St Mirren	W	3-1	2-0	8	Robson 2 [12, 53], Duff [34]	4902
6	Sept 10	H	Hibernian	L	0-3	0-0	9		6387
7	16	A	Inverness CT	D	0-0	0-0	9		3586
8	23	H	Motherwell	D	1-1	0-0	10	Hunt [63]	5036
9	Oct 1	A	Hearts	L	0-4	0-2	11		16,849
10	14	H	Celtic	L	1-4	1-1	12	Hunt [5]	10,504
11	21	A	Aberdeen	L	1-3	0-1	12	Robson (pen) [70]	10,747
12	28	A	Falkirk	L	1-5	0-2	12	Samuel [69]	5386
13	Nov 5	H	Rangers	W	2-1	0-0	12	Kenneth [76], Mair [82]	10,392
14	11	H	Kilmarnock	W	1-0	0-0	10	Hunt [72]	5815
15	18	A	Dunfermline Ath	L	1-2	0-0	10	Robson [51]	6129
16	26	H	St Mirren	W	1-0	0-0	9	Hunt [64]	5681
17	Dec 2	A	Hibernian	L	1-2	1-0	11	Martis (og) [23]	14,032
18	9	H	Inverness CT	W	3-1	1-1	9	Hunt 2 [22, 64], Robertson [78]	5294
19	16	A	Motherwell	W	3-2	2-0	8	Samuel [28], McCracken [44], Hunt [78]	4420
20	23	H	Hearts	L	0-1	0-0	8		7789
21	26	A	Celtic	D	2-2	1-0	—	Robertson [17], Samuel [58]	57,343
22	30	H	Aberdeen	W	3-1	0-0	8	Samuel 2 [61, 89], Robson (pen) [80]	12,329
23	Jan 1	H	Falkirk	L	1-5	1-1	—	Robson [42]	6261
24	13	A	Rangers	L	0-5	0-2	9		50,276
25	20	A	Kilmarnock	L	0-1	0-0	9		4732
26	27	H	Dunfermline Ath	D	0-0	0-0	9		6295
27	Feb 10	A	St Mirren	W	1-0	0-0	9	Robson [77]	3849
28	18	H	Hibernian	D	0-0	0-0	8		6453
29	Mar 3	A	Inverness CT	L	0-1	0-0	10		3901
30	10	H	Motherwell	D	1-1	1-1	10	Robb [28]	5183
31	17	A	Hearts	W	4-0	0-0	7	Robson 3 [51, 59, 77], Hunt [70]	17,172
32	31	H	Celtic	D	1-1	0-0	8	Daly [89]	11,363
33	Apr 7	A	Aberdeen	W	4-2	3-2	7	Daly (pen) [1], Hunt [13], Cameron 2 [18, 51]	12,148
34	21	A	Dunfermline Ath	L	0-1	0-1	8		5131
35	28	H	Inverness CT	D	1-1	1-0	8	Robertson [41]	5273
36	May 5	H	St Mirren	L	0-2	0-1	8		6875
37	12	A	Falkirk	L	0-2	0-1	9		4161
38	19	H	Motherwell	D	0-0	0-0	9		6070

Final League Position: 9

Honours
League Champions: Premier Division 1982-83. Division II 1924-25, 1928-29; *Runners-up:* Division II 1930-31, 1959-60. First Division Runners-up 1995-96.
Scottish Cup Winners: 1994; *Runners-up:* 1974, 1981, 1985, 1987, 1988, 1991, 2005.
League Cup Winners: 1979-80, 1980-81; *Runners-up:* 1981-82, 1984-85, 1997-98.
Summer Cup Runners-up: 1964-65. *Scottish War Cup Runners-up:* 1939-40.

European: *European Cup:* 8 matches (1983-84, semi-finals). *Cup Winners' Cup:* 10 matches (1974-75, 1988-89, 1994-95). *UEFA Cup:* 86 matches (*Fairs Cup:* 1966-67, 1969-70, 1970-71. *UEFA Cup:* 1975-76, 1977-78, 1978-79, 1979-80, 1980-81, 1981-82, 1982-83, 1984-85, 1985-86, 1986-87 runners-up, 1987-88, 1989-90, 1990-91, 1993-94, 1997-98, 2005-06).

Club colours: Shirts: Tangerine. Shorts: Tangerine. Stockings: Tangerine.

Goalscorers: *League* (40): Robson 11 (2 pens), Hunt 10, Samuel 5, Robertson 3, Cameron 2, Daly 2 (1 pen), Duff 1, Kalvenes 1, Kenneth 1, McCracken 1, Mair 1, Robb 1, own goal 1.
Scottish Cup (3): Kenneth 1, Robertson 1, Robson 1.
CIS Cup (1): Robertson 1.

Stillie D 37	Conway C 22 + 8	McCracken D 32 + 1	Mair L 17 + 1	Archibald A 14 + 2	Kerr M 35 + 1	Robson B 29	Robb S 8 + 7	Duff S 22 + 6	Hunt N 25 + 3	Brewster C 1 + 2	Miller L 1 + 2	Samuel C 27 + 10	Robertson D 21 + 5	Kalvenes C 29	Cameron G 20 + 5	Proctor D 9 + 3	Easton W 1 + 6	Kenneth G 11	Goodwillie D 3 + 14	McLean E 1	Wilkie L 14	Burnett G 1	Smith G 4 + 2	Gomis M 9 + 2	Dillon S 15	Daly J 10 + 1	Watson K — + 1	Russell J — + 2	*Match No.*
1	2^{1}	3	4	5	6	7	8	9	10^{2}	11^{3}	12	13	14																1
1		3	4	5	6	7	13	11	10^{1}		12	9		2^{2}	8														2
1		3	4	5	6	7		11^{1}	12		10■	9^{2}		2	8	13													3
1	13	3		5	6	7	12	11^{1}	10			9		2	8^{2}	4													4
1	9^{1}	3		5	6	7■	12	11				10		2	8	4													5
1	7	3		5	6			11^{3}	10^{1}	13		9	14	2	8^{2}	4	12												6
1	9			5	6^{2}	7	14	11^{3}	12	13		10^{1}		2	8	4		3											7
1	12	3		5	6	7	9^{1}	11^{2}	10			13		2	8	4													8
1	9^{1}	3		5	6	7		11	10			12		2	8	4													9
1	12	3		5	6	7^{3}		11^{1}	10			9^{2}		2	8	4	14		13										10
1	13	3	4	5	6^{2}	7		12	10^{3}			11		2^{1}	9	8			14										11
	14	3	4		13	7			10■			12			8	5^{2}			11^{3}	1	2	6^{1}	9						12
1	10	3	4		6	7						11^{1}	9	2	8			5	12										13
1	8^{1}	3	4		6	7		11	10^{2}			12	9	2				5	13										14
1	8^{2}	3	4		6^{3}	7		11	10^{1}			12	9	2	14			5	13										15
1	3		4	12	6	7		11	10^{3}			14	9^{2}	2	8			5^{1}					13						16
1	3		4	5	6	7		11				9	8	2					10										17
1	3		4	5	6	7		11	10^{2}			9^{1}	8	2	12				13										18
1	9	3	4	5	6	7	12		10^{2}			11^{1}	8	2■					13										19
1	3	12	4		6	7	5^{1}	11				9	8					2	10^{2}				13						20
1	5	3	4^{1}		6	7		11				10	8		12	13		2					9^{2}						21
1	5	3	4		6	7		11				10	8^{2}		13			2	12				9^{1}						22
1	5	3	4^{2}		6^{3}	7		11				10	8			13		2	12				9^{1}	14					23
1	5	3		12	6			11	13			10^{2}	8		7^{3}			2^{1}						14	4	9			24
1	8^{2}				6^{1}			12				10	9	2	7			3	13		5				4	11			25
1	12	3			6			7	11			10^{1}	9	2							5				4	8			26
1	8^{1}	3			6	7	12		11			13	9	2							5			10^{2}	4				27
1	8^{1}	3			6	7			11			10	9	2							5				4	12			28
1		3			6	7	13		11^{3}			12	9^{1}	2					14		5			8	4	10^{2}			29
1		3			6	7	9^{1}		11				12	2			13				5			8^{2}	4	10			30
1		3			6	7	9^{1}		11^{2}			12	8■	2							5				4	10	13		31
1		3			6	7■	9^{2}	5				11^{3}			13		14		12		2			8^{1}	4	10			32
1		3			6			12	11			9		2	7						5			8^{1}	4	10			33
1		3				7			11^{1}			9^{3}	14	2	6		13		12		5			8^{2}	4	10			34
1	13	3						12	11			9	7^{1}	2	6						5			8	4	10^{2}			35
1	14	3	13		6				11■			10	7	2			9^{1}		12		5^{2}			8^{3}	4				36
1	7^{1}	3			6		9^{3}	13				10	8^{2}	2	11		12				5■				4			14	37
1	5^{3}	3	2		6		9	14	11			10^{2}	12		8^{1}									7	4			13	38

DUNFERMLINE ATHLETIC First Division

Year Formed: 1885. *Ground & Address:* East End Park, Halbeath Rd, Dunfermline KY12 7RB. *Telephone:* 01383 724295. *Fax:* 01383 723468. *Ticket office telephone:* 0870 300 1201. *E-mail:* enquiries@dafc.co.uk. *Website:* www.dafc.co.uk
Ground Capacity: all seated: 11,780. *Size of Pitch:* 115yd × 71yd.
Chairman: John Yorkston. *Chief Executive:* William Hodgins. *Commercial Director:* Wilma Cameron. *Commercial Manager:* Karen Brown.
Manager: Stephen Kenny. *Assistant Manager:* Craig Robertson. *Physio:* Paul Atkinson.
First Team Coach: Declan Devine. *Youth Team Coach:* Hamish French.
Managers since 1975: G. Miller, H. Melrose, P. Stanton, T. Forsyth, J. Leishman, I. Munro, J. Scott, B. Paton, R. Campbell, J. Calderwood, D. Hay.
Club Nickname(s): The Pars. *Previous Grounds:* None.
Record Attendance: 27,816 v Celtic, Division I, 30 Apr 1968.
Record Transfer Fee received: £650,000 for Jackie McNamara to Celtic (Oct 1995).
Record Transfer Fee paid: £540,000 for Istvan Kozma from Bordeaux (Sept 1989).
Record Victory: 11-2 v Stenhousemuir, Division II, 27 Sept 1930.
Record Defeat: 1-11 v Hibernian, Scottish Cup, 3rd rd replay, 26 Oct 1889.
Most Capped Player: Colin Miller 16 (61), Canada.
Most League Appearances: 497: Norrie McCathie, 1981-96.
Most League Goals in Season (Individual): 53: Bobby Skinner, Division II, 1925-26.
Most Goals Overall (Individual): 154: Charles Dickson.

DUNFERMLINE ATHLETIC 2006–07 LEAGUE RECORD

Match No.	Date	Venue	Opponents	Result		H/T Score	Lg. Pos.	Goalscorers	Attendance
1	Jul 29	H	Hearts	L	1-2	0-1	—	Simmons 62	7936
2	Aug 5	A	Falkirk	L	0-1	0-1	11		5542
3	13	H	Rangers	D	1-1	0-0	11	Morrison O 69	8561
4	19	A	Dundee U	D	0-0	0-0	11		6171
5	26	A	Aberdeen	L	0-1	0-0	12		9889
6	Sept 9	H	Kilmarnock	W	3-2	1-1	11	Young 41, Mason 72, Crawford 83	4510
7	16	A	Celtic	L	0-1	0-1	11		55,894
8	23	H	St Mirren	W	2-1	0-1	11	Young 46, Crawford 73	4914
9	30	A	Inverness CT	L	0-1	0-0	10		3517
10	Oct 14	A	Motherwell	L	1-2	0-0	11	Crawford 68	4527
11	23	H	Hibernian	L	0-4	0-1	11		6057
12	28	A	Hearts	D	1-1	0-1	11	Hamilton 48	17,031
13	Nov 4	H	Falkirk	L	0-3	0-1	11		6504
14	11	A	Rangers	L	0-2	0-0	12		48,218
15	18	H	Dundee U	W	2-1	0-0	12	Shields 75, Mason 88	6129
16	25	H	Aberdeen	L	0-3	0-0	12		6501
17	Dec 2	A	Kilmarnock	L	1-5	1-4	12	Crawford 10	4750
18	10	H	Celtic	L	1-2	0-0	12	Simmons 90	7080
19	16	A	St Mirren	D	0-0	0-0	12		4246
20	23	H	Inverness CT	D	0-0	0-0	12		4216
21	26	H	Motherwell	L	0-2	0-1	—		4200
22	30	A	Hibernian	L	0-2	0-0	12		14,061
23	Jan 2	H	Hearts	L	0-1	0-1	—		7004
24	13	A	Falkirk	L	0-1	0-0	12		6051
25	21	H	Rangers	L	0-1	0-1	12		7868
26	27	A	Dundee U	D	0-0	0-0	12		6295
27	Feb 10	A	Aberdeen	L	0-3	0-1	12		9379
28	17	H	Kilmarnock	D	1-1	0-1	12	Crawford (pen) 44	4500
29	Mar 3	A	Celtic	L	1-2	0-1	12	Hammill 86	59,131
30	10	H	St Mirren	D	0-0	0-0	12		7149
31	17	A	Inverness CT	W	3-1	0-1	12	Glass 2 (1 pen) 47, 78 (p), McIntyre 60	4447
32	31	A	Motherwell	L	0-2	0-0	12		4511
33	Apr 7	H	Hibernian	W	1-0	0-0	12	McGuire 83	6001
34	21	H	Dundee U	W	1-0	1-0	12	McManus 33	5131
35	30	A	St Mirren	W	1-0	0-0	12	McManus 60	10,251
36	May 7	H	Motherwell	W	4-1	2-1	12	O'Brien 6, Wilson S 11, Glass 57, Hamilton 88	6662
37	12	A	Inverness CT	L	1-2	1-0	12	McIntyre 36	6464
38	19	H	Falkirk	L	0-3	0-0	12		5087

Final League Position: 12

Honours
League Champions: First Division 1988-89, 1995-96. Division II 1925-26. Second Division 1985-86; *Runners-up:* First Division 1986-87, 1993-94, 1994-95, 1999-2000. Division II 1912-13, 1933-34, 1954-55, 1957-58, 1972-73. Second Division 1978-79.
Scottish Cup Winners: 1961, 1968; *Runners-up:* 1965, 2004, 2007.
League Cup Runners-up: 1949-50, 1991-92, 2005-06.

European: *Cup Winners' Cup:* 14 matches (1961-62, 1968-69 semi-finals). *UEFA Cup:* 30 matches (*Fairs Cup:* 1962-63, 1964-65, 1965-66, 1966-67, 1969-70. *UEFA Cup:* 2004-05).

Club colours: Shirt: Black and white vertical stripes. Shorts: White. Stockings: White.

Goalscorers: *League* (26): Crawford 5 (1 pen), Glass 3 (1 pen), Hamilton 2, McIntyre 2, McManus 2, Mason 2, Simmons 2, Young 2, Hammill 1, McGuire 1, Morrison O 1, O'Brien 1, Shields 1, Wilson S 1.
Scottish Cup (7): Simmons 3, Hamilton 1, McGuire 1, McIntyre 1, Wilson S 1.
CIS Cup (0).

McKenzie R 11 + 1	Shields G 29	Wilson S 31	McGuire P 22 + 2	Bamba S 21 + 2	Muirhead S 20 + 5	Woods C 9 + 3	Mason G 35 + 1	Simmons S 23 + 1	Whelan M 1	Daquin F 8 + 12	Tod A 5 + 5	Burchill M 12 + 8	Morrison O 12 + 12	McCunnie J 8 + 6	Wilson C — + 3	Ross G 16 + 10	Young D 19 + 2	Labonte A 11 + 2	De Vries D 27	Campbell I — + 1	Smith C — + 1	Hamilton J 18 + 8	Crawford S 23 + 3	Morrison S 11	Williamson K — + 5	Ryan R 2 + 4	O'Brien J 13	Hammill A 9 + 4	McIntyre J 6 + 4	Glass S 11	McManus T 5 + 2	Harris J —	Match No.
1	2	3	4	5	6	7[3]	8	9	10[1]	11[2]	12	13	14																				1
1	2[1]	3	4[3]	5	6	7[2]	8	9		11		10	13	12	14																		2
1		3	4	5	6[1]	2[3]	8	9			11	10[2]	13	7	14	12																	3
1		3	4	5	6[2]	2	8	9[1]			11	10	14	7[3]			12	13															4
		3[1]	4[2]	5			8				11		10	7[3]	14	9	6	2	1	12	13												5
		3	4			5[1]	8	9[2]		13			7			12	6	2	1			10	11										6
	2	3	4	5			8	9[2]		12			13				6	7	1			10	11[1]										7
	2	3[1]		5	12	7	8				13		9			4	6		1			10[2]	11										8
	2	3		5	12	7	8			13	14		9[1]			4[2]	6		1			10[3]	11										9
1	2	3[1]		12	7[2]	5	8			9						13	6	4				10	11										10
	2			5		3[2]	8			12		9[3]	14	13		4[1]	6	7	1			10	11										11
1	2					14	8[3]	7		13	9	11[2]	5	3[1]		12	6	4				10											12
1	2		12		14		8	7[1]			9	11	5[2]			3	6	4				10[3]	13										13
1	2			5		12	8	7		13			9[2]			3		4				10	11[3]	6[1]	14								14
	2	3			12		8	7[1]		13			9[2]			14	6	4	1			10[3]	11	5									15
	2	3			7[1]		8	13		10			9			14	6[3]	4[2]	1			12	11	5									16
	2	3		12■	7		8	6		10[1]			9[2]			4[3]		13	1			14	11	5									17
	2	3	13		7[3]		8	9		10[2]		12	14			6		4	1				11	5[1]									18
	2	3	4		7		8	9				10[1]				5	6		1			12	11										19
	2	3	4	5	9[2]		8			12	14		13			7[1]	6		1			10[3]	11■										20
	2	3	4	5[2]	7		8			9[1]		11	12			13	6		1			10■											21
15	2	3	4	5[2]	7		8	9		12	13	10[1]					6		1[G]				11										22
1	2[1]	3	4	5[3]			8[2]	9				10	12			14	6					13	11	7									23
1	2	3[1]						7		13			8[2]	12		4[3]	6						11	5	14	9	10						24
	2	3	4		13		8									6[2]			1			10	11	5		7[1]	9[3]	12	14				25
	2[1]	3	4		6[2]		8	7[3]						14		12			1			10	11				9	13		5			26
		3	4				6	7[2]				10[3]				2			1			12	11[1]		14	13	9	8		5			27
		3	4				6	7[2]								2[3]			1			10	11[1]		12	13	9	8	14	5			28
		3	4				13	7					9[1]	2[2]			6		1			10[3]	14	5				11		8	12		29
		3	4				8	7				12	14			2[3]			1			9[1]	10[2]				11	6	13	5			30
		3	4				6	7[2]								2[3]			1			10	11[1]		12	13	9	8	14	5			31
	2		4[2]	3	7[1]		8					12							1				13	5		14	11	9[3]	10	6			32
	2		4	3	7[1]		8					13		6		14			1					5			11	12	10[2]		9[3]		33
	2	3		4	7		8			14		13		5					1								11[3]	12	10[2]	6	9[1]		34
	2	3		4	7		8							12			14		1			13					11[3]	6[1]	10[2]	5	9		35
	2	3■		4	7		8			13		12							1			14					11[2]	6	10[1]	5	9[3]		36
	2		3	4	7		8					13	14	12					1								11[2]	6[1]	10	5[3]	9		37
1	2	3		4	7[1]	12		8[3]		9[2]		10		5			6					13	11								14		38

EAST FIFE — Third Division

Year Formed: 1903. *Ground & Address:* Bayview Stadium, Harbour View, Methil, Fife KY8 3RW. *Telephone:* 01333 426323. *Fax:* 01333 426376. *E-mail:* office@eastfife.org. *Website:* www.eastfife.org
Ground Capacity: all seated: 2000. *Size of Pitch:* 115yd × 75yd.
Chairman: William Gray. *Secretary:* James Stevenson.
Manager: David Baikie. *Assistant Manager:* Graeme Irons. *Physio:* Brian McNeil.
Managers since 1975: Frank Christie, Roy Barry, David Clarke, Gavin Murray, Alex Totten, Steve Archibald, James Bone, Steve Kirk, Rab Shannon, David Clarke, Jim Moffat.
Club Nickname(s): The Fifers. *Previous Ground:* Bayview Park.
Record Attendance: 22,515 v Raith Rovers, Division I, 2 Jan 1950.
Record Transfer Fee received: £150,000 for Paul Hunter from Hull C (March 1990).
Record Transfer Fee paid: £70,000 for John Sludden from Kilmarnock (July 1991).
Record Victory: 13-2 v Edinburgh City, Division II, 11 Dec 1937.
Record Defeat: 0-9 v Hearts, Division I, 5 Oct 1957.
Most Capped Player: George Aitken, 5 (8), Scotland.
Most League Appearances: 517: David Clarke, 1968-86.
Most League Goals in Season (Individual): 41: Jock Wood, Division II; 1926-27 and Henry Morris, Division II, 1947-48.
Most Goals Overall (Individual): 225: Phil Weir (215 in League).

EAST FIFE 2006–07 LEAGUE RECORD

Match No.	Date	Venue	Opponents	Result		H/T Score	Lg. Pos.	Goalscorers	Attendance
1	Aug 5	H	Stenhousemuir	D	0-0	0-0	—		507
2	12	A	Albion R	W	1-0	0-0	4	Smart J [56]	334
3	19	H	Arbroath	W	2-1	1-1	2	Gordon [16], Smart J [68]	670
4	26	A	Elgin C	W	2-1	0-0	1	Gordon [51], Fortune [60]	471
5	Sept 1	H	East Stirling	W	5-0	2-0	1	Blackadder 2 [20, 33], Jablonski 2 [60, 90], Martin [87]	680
6	9	A	Montrose	L	0-1	0-1	1		424
7	16	H	Berwick R	W	2-0	2-0	1	Ritchie 2 (1 pen) [15 (p), 34]	622
8	23	A	Queen's Park	L	0-3	0-2	1		413
9	30	H	Dumbarton	W	1-0	1-0	1	Jablonski [38]	651
10	Oct 7	A	Elgin C	W	3-2	1-0	1	O'Reilly 2 [30, 69], Smart C [53]	324
11	14	A	Stenhousemuir	W	1-0	1-0	1	Smart C [16]	520
12	21	H	Albion R	D	2-2	1-2	1	Gordon [13], O'Reilly [56]	594
13	28	A	East Stirling	W	4-0	2-0	1	O'Reilly 2 [8, 56], Jablonski [31], Blackadder [58]	378
14	Nov 4	H	Elgin C	D	1-1	1-0	1	Linton [33]	625
15	11	A	Berwick R	L	1-2	0-2	1	Jablonski [46]	485
16	25	H	Montrose	W	2-0	1-0	1	Jablonski [17], Gordon [70]	472
17	Dec 2	H	Queen's Park	W	1-0	0-0	1	Gordon [46]	637
18	16	A	Dumbarton	L	1-2	0-1	1	Jablonski [86]	798
19	23	H	Stenhousemuir	D	1-1	0-0	1	O'Reilly [65]	596
20	30	A	Arbroath	D	1-1	1-1	1	Ritchie [20]	950
21	Jan 13	H	East Stirling	L	0-2	0-0	1		552
22	20	H	Berwick R	L	0-2	0-0	2		628
23	27	A	Montrose	D	3-3	2-0	2	Blackadder [6], McGowan [33], Nicholas [62]	423
24	Feb 3	A	Queen's Park	D	1-1	0-0	2	McBride [69]	719
25	17	H	Arbroath	L	1-2	0-2	4	Ritchie [69]	654
26	24	A	Albion R	W	3-0	3-0	4	O'Reilly 2 [10, 28], Smart J [36]	420
27	Mar 3	H	Elgin C	W	3-1	2-1	4	Smart J [19], O'Reilly 2 [43, 89]	491
28	10	A	East Stirling	W	2-0	1-0	4	Walker [2], O'Reilly [84]	408
29	17	A	Berwick R	L	0-2	0-1	4		623
30	21	H	Dumbarton	W	1-0	0-0	—	O'Reilly [70]	443
31	25	A	Dumbarton	W	2-0	2-0	4	Young [17], Smart J [40]	561
32	31	H	Montrose	W	2-0	0-0	4	Smart J [68], Nicholas [89]	484
33	Apr 7	H	Queen's Park	W	1-0	0-0	4	Jablonski [72]	669
34	14	A	Stenhousemuir	W	5-3	4-2	3	Smart J [28], Jablonski (pen) [30], Blackadder [37], O'Reilly [45], Walker [88]	561
35	21	H	Albion R	L	1-3	1-3	4	Nicholas [40]	542
36	28	A	Arbroath	W	3-1	2-1	4	Gibson [38], Gordon [40], Ritchie [52]	825

Final League Position: 4

Honours
League Champions: Division II 1947-48; *Runners-up:* Division II 1929-30, 1970-71. Second Division 1983-84, 1995-96. Third Division 2002-03.
Scottish Cup Winners: 1938; *Runners-up:* 1927, 1950.
League Cup Winners: 1947-48, 1949-50, 1953-54.

Club colours: Shirt: Gold and black. Shorts: White. Stockings: Black.

Goalscorers: *League* (59): O'Reilly 13, Jablonski 9 (1 pen), Smart J 7, Gordon 6, Blackadder 5, Ritchie 5 (1 pen), Nicholas 3, Smart C 2, Walker 2, Fortune 1, Gibson 1, Linton 1, McBride 1, McGowan 1, Martin 1, Young 1.
Play-Offs (6): O'Reilly 3, Gibson 1, McDonald 1, Young 1.
Scottish Cup (1): Jablonski 1.
CIS Cup (1): Smart C.
Challenge Cup (0).

Ross I 10	Ross D 1	Linton S 13	Smart J 34	McGowan J 10 + 2	Courts T 26	Blackadder R 29 + 4	Jablonski N 32 + 2	Ritchie P 19 + 4	Gordon K 22 + 9	Mitchell A 1 + 2	Martin J 4 + 14	Crabbe S 1 + 8	Smith E 26 + 2	Smart C 12 + 5	O'Reilly C 21 + 10	Fortune S 2 + 7	Dodds J 26	Kelly G 2 + 1	Hampshire P 10 + 4	Dair J 6	Doyle P 25	Gibson G 14 + 1	Nicholas S 8 + 6	McBride K 13	Walker P 9 + 1	Young L 8 + 1	McDonald G 12	*Match No.*
1	2	3	4	5	6^1	7	8	9	10^2	11	12	13																1
1		3	4	5	11	6	8	9^1	10^2				2	7	12	13												2
		2	4	5	6	11	8		7^3	14	10^1		3	9^2	12	13	1											3
		3^1	4	5	6	11	8	9	7				2	10^2	13	12	1											4
		3	4		5	11	8	9^1	7		12		2	10^2	13	6	1											5
		3	4		5	11	8	9^2	7		13		2	10^3	14	6^1	1	12										6
		3	4		5	11	8	9^2	7^3		14		2	12	13		1	6	10^1									7
		3■	4		5	11	8	9^2	7		12		2		13		1	6^1	10									8
			4		6	10	8	9^3		12	7		2	14		13	1		11^1	3^2	5							9
			4		6	10	8	14	13				2	7^2	9^3	12	1		11^1	3	5							10
			4		6^2	11	8		7^3			12	2	10^1	9	13	1		14	3	5							11
			4		6	11	8^3		7^2		13	12	2	10	9^1	14	1			3	5							12
		3	4		6^1	11	8		7		14	13	2	10^3	9^2		1		12		5							13
		3	4		6	11	8		7^2		13	12	2	10^3	9^1		1		14		5							14
			4	13	6	11	8		3^1		12		2	10	9		1		7		5^2							15
1		3	4	5	6	8	10		7		12		2	13	9^2					11^1								16
1		3	4	5	6	11	8	13	7		10^1		2	12	9^2													17
1		3	4	5		11	8	9	7^1		10^2	13	2	12							6							18
			4	5	6	11	8		7		12	9^1	2	10^2	13		1				3							19
			4		5	6	8	9^1	7		12	13	2		10^2		1		11		3							20
1			4		6		8	9^1	7^2		13		2		12				3		5	10	11					21
1			4	5	6		8				12		2		9				11		3	10^1	7					22
1				4^1	5	6	8					13	12		9^2				11		2	7	10	3				23
1			4		5	11	8		7						13						2	9	10^2	3	6^1	12		24
1			4		5	11	8■	13	10												2	12	9^2	3	7^1		6	25
			4			8		9^1					2		10		1				5	7	12	3	11		6	26
			4			8	12	9^1	13				2		10		1				5	7		3	11^2		6	27
			4			8^2	12	9	13				2		10^3		1				5	7^1	14	3	11		6	28
			4			13	8	9^1					2^2		10		1				5		12	3	11	7	6	29
			4		5■		8	9^1	13						10		1				2	7^2	12	3		11	6	30
			4			13	8	9^1	12						10^2		1				2	7	14	3	11^3	6	5	31
			4			13	8	9^1	14						10^3		1				2	7	12	3	11^2	6	5	32
			4			11^3	8	13	12						10^2		1		14		2	7^1	9	3		6	5	33
			4			11^2	8		13						10		1				2	7^1	9	3	12	6	5	34
					4^1	8			13				12		10		1				2	7^2	9	3	11	6	5	35
			4^2	13		12	8	9	10				3				1		11	2^1		7				6	5	36

EAST STIRLINGSHIRE Third Division

Year Formed: 1880. *Ground & Address:* Firs Park, Firs St, Falkirk FK2 7AY. *Telephone:* 01324 623583. *Fax:* 01324 637 862. *E-mail:* lestshire@aol.com. *Website:* www.eaststirlingshire.com
Ground Capacity: total: 1880, seated: 200. *Size of Pitch:* 112yd × 72yd.
Chairman: A. Mackin. *Vice Chairman:* Douglas Morrison. *Chief Executive/Secretary:* Leslie G. Thomson.
Manager/Head Coach: Gordon Wylde. *Physio:* David Jenkins.
Managers since 1975: I. Ure, D. McLinden, W. P. Lamont, Alex Ferguson, W. Little, D. Whiteford, D. Lawson, J. D. Connell, A. Mackin, D. Sullivan, B. McCulley, B. Little, J. Brownlie, H. McCann, G. Fairley, B. Ross, D. Diver, D. Newall.
Club Nickname(s): The Shire. *Previous Grounds:* Burnhouse, Randyford Park, Merchiston Park, New Kilbowie Park.
Record Attendance: 12,000 v Partick Th, Scottish Cup 3rd rd, 21 Feb 1921.
Record Transfer Fee received: £35,000 for Jim Docherty to Chelsea (1978).
Record Transfer Fee paid: £6,000 for Colin McKinnon from Falkirk (March 1991).
Record Victory: 11-2 v Vale of Bannock, Scottish Cup 2nd rd, 22 Sept 1888.
Record Defeat: 1-12 v Dundee United, Division II, 13 Apr 1936.
Most Capped Player: Humphrey Jones, 5 (14), Wales.
Most League Appearances: 415: Gordon Russell, 1983-2001.

EAST STIRLINGSHIRE 2006–07 LEAGUE RECORD

Match No.	Date	Venue	Opponents	Result	H/T Score	Lg. Pos.	Goalscorers	Attendance
1	Aug 5	H	Elgin C	W 2-1	0-1	—	Dymock 74, Tweedie 78	227
2	12	A	Dumbarton	L 0-2	0-1	6		631
3	19	H	Albion R	L 0-1	0-0	9		263
4	26	H	Stenhousemuir	W 5-0	1-0	6	Thywissen 17, McKenzie 3 56, 66, 70, Tweedie 89	363
5	Sept 1	A	East Fife	L 0-5	0-2	6		680
6	9	A	Berwick R	D 2-2	0-1	7	Smith (og) 53, Tweedie 62	403
7	16	H	Arbroath	L 0-2	0-1	9		300
8	23	A	Montrose	L 0-1	0-0	9		280
9	30	H	Queen's Park	W 2-1	1-0	9	Stewart 31, Canning (og) 76	354
10	Oct 14	A	Elgin C	L 0-5	0-3	9		427
11	21	H	Dumbarton	L 0-2	0-1	9		402
12	28	H	East Fife	L 0-4	0-2	9		378
13	Nov 4	A	Stenhousemuir	L 0-2	0-0	9		374
14	11	A	Arbroath	W 2-1	0-1	9	Dymock 62, Bishop (og) 89	560
15	Dec 2	H	Montrose	L 0-3	0-3	9		173
16	16	A	Queen's Park	W 3-1	1-0	9	Stewart (pen) 24, Boyle 68, Ure 77	458
17	23	H	Elgin C	L 0-2	0-1	9		396
18	30	A	Albion R	L 0-4	0-3	9		518
19	Jan 13	A	East Fife	W 2-0	0-0	9	Savage 79, Stewart 89	552
20	27	A	Berwick R	L 0-2	0-2	9		517
21	Feb 3	A	Montrose	L 0-4	0-0	9		323
22	10	H	Queen's Park	L 0-2	0-2	9		292
23	17	H	Albion R	D 0-0	0-0	9		298
24	24	A	Dumbarton	L 1-2	1-1	9	Stewart 36	729
25	Mar 3	A	Stenhousemuir	D 1-1	1-0	9	McKenzie 45	367
26	6	H	Stenhousemuir	L 0-1	0-1	—		256
27	10	H	East Fife	L 0-2	0-1	10		408
28	14	H	Arbroath	L 1-5	0-1	—	Brownlie 80	275
29	20	H	Berwick R	L 0-1	0-0	—		234
30	27	A	Arbroath	L 2-3	0-1	—	Tweedie 58, McBride 63	657
31	31	H	Berwick R	L 0-3	0-2	10		304
32	Apr 3	A	Queen's Park	L 1-2	0-1	—	Ure 55	552
33	7	H	Montrose	L 0-2	0-0	10		265
34	14	A	Elgin C	L 1-2	0-0	10	Thywissen 79	406
35	21	H	Dumbarton	L 1-5	0-4	10	Boyle 90	429
36	28	A	Albion R	L 1-2	1-0	10	McKenzie 16	398

Final League Position: 10

Most League Goals in Season (Individual): 36: Malcolm Morrison, Division II, 1938-39.

Honours
League Champions: Division II 1931-32; C Division 1947-48. *Runners-up:* Division II 1962-63. Second Division 1979-80. Division Three 1923-24.

Club colours: Shirt: Black with white. Shorts: Black with white. Stockings: Black with white hoops.

Goalscorers: *League* (27): McKenzie 5, Stewart 4 (1 pen), Tweedie 4, Boyle 2, Dymock 2, Thywissen 2, Ure 2, Brownlie 1, McBride 1, Savage 1, own goals 3.
Scottish Cup (0).
CIS Cup (1): Thywissen.
Challenge Cup (0).

Tiropoulos R 16	Smith A 7	Learmonth S 31	Thywissen C 34	Oates S 20 + 1	Nixon J 3 + 2	Brand A 21 + 2	Stewart P 34	Ward A 7 + 1	Tweedie P 27 + 5	Ure D 28 + 5	Adam S 19 + 6	Molloy M 7 + 7	Dymock S 10 + 15	McKenzie M 29 + 3	Livingstone S 5 + 8	Blair S 1 + 4	Boyle J 20 + 7	Nugent A 20	Wild C 10 + 2	McPhee G 1	McBride P 15 + 6	Brownlie P 7 + 5	McAloney P 18 + 3	Savage J 1	Hughes C — + 1	Galloway C 3 + 9	Kassim A 1 + 2	Struthers K 1	*Match No.*
1	2^{2}	3	4	5^{1}	6^{3}	7	8	9	10	11	12	13	14																1
1	2	3	4^{3}		7^{2}	5	8	9	10	6^{1}	11	13		12	14														2
1	2	3	4		6^{3}	5	8	9	10	12	11^{1}	14	7^{2}			13													3
1	2	3	6^{1}	4	12	5	8		10	9^{2}	11^{3}			7		13	14												4
		3		4	13	5	8		10	9	11^{3}		14	7	2^{1}	6^{2}		1	12										5
	2	3	6^{2}	4			8		10^{3}	9	11^{1}	14	12	7			13	1	5										6
	2	3	6	4^{2}			8		10^{1}	9^{3}	11	14	12	7			13	1	5										7
1	2■	3^{2}	4	5			8		9	12	11^{1}	10^{3}	13	7■			6		14										8
1		3	4	5			8	7^{2}	13	9^{3}	11		10		14	12	6		2^{1}										9
1		3	5	4^{1}			8	9		10	11			7	12		6		2										10
		3		4			8		12	9^{1}	11	14	10	7	2	13^{3}	6	1	5^{2}										11
		3	4	5			8	10^{1}	9	13	11^{2}	14	12^{3}	7	2		6	1											12
		3	4	5^{3}			8		10	11^{2}	9	6^{1}	13	7	14		12	1	2										13
1		3	4				8	13	9^{2}	11		10^{1}	12	7			6		5	2									14
1		3	4				8	10^{2}	13	11	12	6^{1}	9	7			2		5										15
1		3	4				8			9	11	10^{1}	7^{2}		2^{3}		6		5		12	13	14						16
1		3	4				8			9^{2}	11^{1}	10	7■	13	14		6		5		12		2^{3}						17
1		3	5	13						12	11^{1}	8		7	2		6				10	9^{2}	4						18
		3	4	5		12	8		10	11^{2}	13			7				1			6		2^{1}	9					19
		3	4	5■		12	8		9	11			13	7	14		6^{1}	1			10^{2}		2^{3}						20
		3	5			4	8		9	11	6^{2}			7	12			1			10^{3}	13	2^{1}		14				21
			5	3		4	8		6	11	14		9^{3}	7			2^{1}	1			13	10^{2}	12						22
			4	5		6	8		9	3	11		13	12				1			7^{2}	10^{1}	2^{3}			14			23
			4	3^{1}		5	8		10	11			9	7			6^{2}	1			13		2			12			24
		3	4	5		10	8		9				13	7			6	1			11^{2}		2^{1}			12			25
		3	4	5		10	8		9	11				7			6	1			12		2^{1}						26
		3	4	5		6	8		9^{2}	11^{1}			14	7				1			10^{3}	13	2				12		27
			5	3		4	8■		9					7			6^{2}	1			10	13	2			12	11^{1}		28
		3	5			4			9				10	7			6^{1}	1			11^{2}	8	2			12	13		29
		3^{3}	5			4	8		9	12	14			7^{1}			6^{2}	1			11		2			13		10	30
1			5			4	8		10	3			9	7			13				11^{1}	6	2^{2}			12			31
		3	5			4	8		9^{2}	10			13	7			12	1			11^{3}	14	2			6^{1}			32
1		3	5			4	8		12	11^{1}	13			7^{3}			6				10	9	2^{2}			14			33
1		3	5			4	8		7	9	10^{1}		13	6^{3}							12	11^{2}	2			14			34
1		3^{2}	5			4	8		12	9	11			7			13				10		2^{1}			6			35
		3	5			4^{3}	8		10	11			13	7	14		6	1			9^{2}		12			2^{1}			36

ELGIN CITY — Third Division

Year Formed: 1893. *Ground and Address:* Borough Briggs, Borough Briggs Road, Elgin IV30 1AP.
Telephone: 01343 551114. *Fax:* 01343 547921. *E-mail:* elgincityfc@ukonline.co.uk. *Website:* www.elgincity.com
Ground Capacity: 3927, seated 478, standing 3449. *Size of pitch:* 111yd × 72yd.
Chairman: Derek W. Shewan. *Secretary:* Ian A. Allan. *Administrator:* Audrey Fanning.
Manager: Robbie Williamson. *Assistant Manager:* Kenny Gilbert. *Director of Football:* Graham Tatters. *Physios:* Billy Belcher and Leigh Thomas.
Managers since 1975: McHardy, Wilson, McHardy, Dickson, Shewan, Tedcastle, Grant, Cochran, Cumming, Cowie, Paterson, Winton, Black, Teasdale, Fleming, McHardy, Tatters, Caldwell, Robertson, Irvine.
Previous names: 1893-1900 Elgin City, 1900–03 Elgin City United, 1903– Elgin City.
Club Nickname(s): City or Black & Whites. *Previous Grounds:* Association Park 1893-95; Milnfield Park 1895-1909; Station Park 1909-19; Cooper Park 1919-21.
Record Attendance: 12,608 v Arbroath, Scottish Cup, 17 Feb 1968.
Record Transfer Fee received: £32,000 for Michael Teasdale to Dundee (Jan 1994).
Record Transfer Fee paid: £10,000 to Fraserburgh for Russell McBride (July 2001).
Record Victory: 18-1 v Brora Rangers, North of Scotland Cup, 6 Feb 1960.
Record Defeat: 1-14 v Hearts, Scottish Cup, 4 Feb 1939.
Most League Appearances: 126: David Hind, 2001-06.
Most League Goals in Season (Individual): Martin Johnston, 20, 2005-06.
Most Goals Overall (Individual): Martin Johnston, 20, 2005-06.

ELGIN CITY 2006–07 LEAGUE RECORD

Match No.	Date	Venue	Opponents	Result		H/T Score	Lg. Pos.	Goalscorers	Attendance
1	Aug 5	A	East Stirling	L	1-2	1-0	—	Mackay 6	227
2	12	H	Queen's Park	L	1-2	1-2	10	Charlesworth 28	547
3	19	A	Montrose	L	0-2	0-2	10		354
4	26	H	East Fife	L	1-2	0-0	10	Kaczan 87	471
5	Sept 3	A	Stenhousemuir	L	0-2	0-2	10		312
6	9	H	Dumbarton	L	0-2	0-0	10		462
7	16	A	Albion R	L	1-3	0-2	10	Johnston 48	276
8	23	H	Berwick R	L	1-2	1-0	10	Moffat 44	359
9	30	A	Arbroath	L	1-2	1-1	10	Johnston 36	610
10	Oct 7	H	East Fife	L	2-3	0-1	10	Moffat 56, Kaczan 61	324
11	14	H	East Stirling	W	5-0	3-0	10	Johnston 3 19, 70, 90, Campbell 23, Mackay 43	427
12	21	A	Queen's Park	L	0-3	0-1	10		489
13	28	H	Stenhousemuir	W	2-0	1-0	10	Moffat 35, Johnston 58	404
14	Nov 4	A	East Fife	D	1-1	0-1	10	Kaczan 62	625
15	11	H	Albion R	L	0-3	0-1	10		440
16	25	A	Dumbarton	L	1-3	0-0	10	Johnston 89	713
17	Dec 2	A	Berwick R	L	1-3	0-3	10	Johnston 47	343
18	16	H	Arbroath	L	0-4	0-2	10		411
19	23	A	East Stirling	W	2-0	1-0	10	Gardiner 42, Johnston 61	396
20	30	H	Montrose	W	3-2	2-2	10	Moffat 20, Johnston 2 (1 pen) 31, 53 (p)	501
21	Jan 13	A	Stenhousemuir	L	2-3	2-1	10	Johnston 3, Charlesworth 16	244
22	20	A	Albion R	L	2-6	1-3	10	Dickson 19, Johnston (pen) 59	425
23	27	H	Dumbarton	L	0-1	0-1	10		484
24	Feb 3	H	Berwick R	W	2-1	2-0	10	Charlesworth 4, Mackay (pen) 42	370
25	17	A	Montrose	W	1-0	1-0	10	Kaczan 16	355
26	24	H	Queen's Park	L	0-3	0-0	10		473
27	Mar 3	A	East Fife	L	1-3	1-2	10	Johnston (pen) 7	491
28	7	A	Arbroath	L	1-2	1-1	—	Mackay 39	447
29	10	H	Stenhousemuir	W	2-1	1-0	9	Johnston 2 35, 49	348
30	17	H	Albion R	W	3-0	1-0	9	Johnston 3 19, 67, 89	339
31	24	H	Arbroath	L	0-1	0-0	9		305
32	31	A	Dumbarton	L	0-1	0-0	9		521
33	Apr 7	A	Berwick R	D	0-0	0-0	9		636
34	14	H	East Stirling	W	2-1	0-0	9	Moffat 2 77, 88	406
35	21	A	Queen's Park	L	0-3	0-3	9		916
36	28	H	Montrose	L	0-2	0-1	9		536

Final League Position: 9

Honours
Scottish Cup: Quarter-finals 1968.
Highland League Champions: winners 15 times.
Scottish Qualifying Cup (North): winners 7 times.
North of Scotland Cup: winners 17 times.
Highland League Cup: winners 5 times.
Inverness Cup: winners twice.

Club colours: Shirt: Black and white vertical stripes. Shorts: Black. Stockings: Red.

Goalscorers: *League* (39): Johnston 19 (3 pens), Moffat 6, Kaczan 4, Mackay 4 (1 pen), Charlesworth 3, Campbell 1, Dickson 1, Gardiner 1.
Scottish Cup (5): Johnston 3, Mackay 1, Moffat 1.
CIS Cup (0).
Challenge Cup (4): Charlesworth 2, Kaczan 1, Mackay 1.

Renton K 33	Kaczan P 27 + 2	Dempsie A 28	Lowe S 12 + 1	Dickson H 26 + 1	Hind D 35	Campbell C 34 + 1	Nelson A 7 + 7	Johnston M 34	Charlesworth M 19 + 12	Mackay S 34 + 1	Booth M 7 + 2	Finnigan C — + 14	Gardiner C 16 + 3	Cooke S 1 + 1	Easton S 5 + 6	Moffat A 28	McGraw A 8 + 3	Huxford R — + 1	Bazie P — + 1	Docherty D 15 + 8	Brewin T — + 2	Muir A 2	Niven D 6	Hooks N 14	Kellacher S — + 1	Fox C 3 + 1	Stephen B 2 + 3	Match No.
1	2	3	4	5	6	7^{2}	8■	9	10	11^{1}	12	13																1
1		3	4	5	6	2		9^{3}	7	10	8	12	11															2
1	2	3	4^{1}	5	6	8		9	13		7		10	11^{2}	12													3
1	2	3	13	5	6	12		9	10	11	8^{2}	14	7^{1}		4^{3}													4
1	2^{1}	3^{2}	4	5	6	7^{3}		9	12	10	8	13			14	11												5
1	2		6	5	4	8		9^{1}	12^{2}	11	10^{3}	13■		14		7	3											6
1			6^{2}	5	4	2		9	10^{1}	11	14		7		13	8	3^{3}	12										7
1				5	4	2		9	7	11	8		10		12	6	3^{1}											8
1		3		5	8	2		9		11	10		7		4	6												9
1	2	3		5	6	7		9		11		12	10		4^{1}	8												10
1	2^{1}	3		5	6	7		9	13	11			10^{2}		4	8^{3}			12	14								11
1	2	3		5	6	7		9	14	11		13	10^{2}		4^{3}	8^{1}				12								12
1	4	3	5^{1}		6	2		9	10^{2}	11					12	8	7			13								13
1	4	3	5		6	2		9	10	11						8	7											14
1^{G}	4	3	5	13	6	2		9	10^{1}	11			12			8	7^{2}				15							15
1	2	3	4■	5	6			9		11			10			8^{2}	12			13		7^{1}						16
1	2	3		5	6^{3}	10^{2}		9	13	11			7			4	14			12		8^{1}						17
1■		3	4	5	6	2		9	13	12			11^{G}			7^{2}	10^{1}			8	15							18
1				5	6	2^{2}	12	9	10	11			4^{1}		13	8	3			7								19
1	13	3		5	4	2	14	9^{3}	10^{1}	11			8^{2}			6	12			7								20
1	2			5	4	8	7	9	10	11						3				6								21
1	2		6^{1}	5	4	7^{3}	8	9	10^{2}	11		14	13			3				12								22
1	12			5	6	2			10	3		13	9			11^{1}				8			4■	7^{2}				23
1	4			5■	2	11	8^{1}		10	3		12	9							6				7				24
1	5	3			4■	8	12	9	10	11										6^{1}			2	7				25
1	5	4				2	8	9	10^{1}	11						3				6				7	12			26
1	5	3			6	2	13	9	10	11						8^{2}				12			4	7^{1}				27
		6		5■	10	2	8	9		11						3							4	7		1		28
1	5	3			4	2	8^{1}	9	12	11						6				10				7				29
1	6	3		5^{3}	4	2	12	9^{2}		11		14	13			8				10^{1}				7				30
1	6	3		5	4	2		9	12	11						10				8^{1}				7^{2}			13	31
1	6	3		5	4^{2}	2	14	9	12	11						10^{3}				8^{1}				7			13	32
1^{G}	5	3			4	2		9	10	11						6				8				7		15		33
	5	3			4	2		9	10^{1}	11		13				6^{2}				8				7		1	12	34
	5	3			4	2^{3}	12	9	14	11		13								8^{1}			6	7		1	10^{2}	35
1	8	3		5	4	2^{1}		9	14	11		12								13			7	10^{2}			6^{3}	36

FALKIRK

Premier League

Year Formed: 1876. *Ground & Address:* The Falkirk Stadium, Westfield, Falkirk FK2 9DX. *Telephone:* 01324 624121. *Fax:* 01324 612418. *Website:* www.falkirkfc.co.uk
Ground Capacity: seated: 6123. *Size of Pitch:* 110yd × 72yd.
Chairman: Campbell Christie. *Managing Director:* George Craig. *Head of Development:* Eddie May. *Secretary:* Alex Blackwood.
Head Coach: John Hughes. *Assistant Coach:* Brian Rice. *Director of Football:* Alex Totten. *Youth Co-ordinator:* Ian McIntyre.
Managers since 1975: J. Prentice, G. Miller, W. Little, J. Hagart, A. Totten, G. Abel, W. Lamont, D. Clarke, J. Duffy, W. Lamont, J. Jefferies, J. Lambie E. Bannon, A. Totten, I. McCall. *Club Nickname(s):* The Bairns. *Previous Grounds:* Randyford 1876-81; Blinkbonny Grounds 1881-83; Brockville Park 1883-2003.
Record Attendance: 23,100 v Celtic, Scottish Cup 3rd rd, 21 Feb 1953.
Record Transfer Fee received: £380,000 for John Hughes to Celtic (Aug 1995).
Record Transfer Fee paid: £225,000 to Chelsea for Kevin McAllister (Aug 1991).
Record Victory: 12-1 v Laurieston, Scottish Cup 2nd rd, 23 Sept 1893.
Record Defeat: 1-11 v Airdrieonians, Division I, 28 Apr 1951.
Most Capped Player: Alex Parker, 14 (15), Scotland.
Most League Appearances: (post-war): 353, George Watson, 1975-87.
Most League Goals in Season (Individual): 43: Evelyn Morrison, Division I, 1928-29.
Most Goals Overall (Individual): Dougie Moran, 86, 1957-61 and 1964-67.

FALKIRK 2006–07 LEAGUE RECORD

Match No.	*Date*	*Venue*	*Opponents*	*Result*		*H/T Score*	*Lg. Pos.*	*Goalscorers*	*Attendance*
1	Jul 29	A	Dundee U	W	2-1	1-1	—	Latapy [23], Craig [59]	6616
2	Aug 5	H	Dunfermline Ath	W	1-0	1-0	3	Barr [9]	5542
3	12	A	Hearts	D	0-0	0-0	2		16,127
4	19	H	Kilmarnock	L	1-2	1-0	4	Latapy [43]	5022
5	26	H	Motherwell	L	0-1	0-0	6		4594
6	Sept 9	A	Rangers	L	0-4	0-2	8		50,196
7	16	H	Aberdeen	L	0-2	0-0	10		5812
8	23	A	Hibernian	W	1-0	1-0	8	Milne [8]	14,828
9	Oct 1	H	Celtic	L	0-1	0-0	9		7139
10	14	H	St Mirren	D	1-1	0-0	9	Stokes [80]	4961
11	21	A	Inverness CT	L	2-3	1-0	9	Stokes 2 [41, 51]	3749
12	28	H	Dundee U	W	5-1	2-0	9	Latapy [2], Stokes 3 (1 pen) [38, 48, 88 (p)], Twaddle [75]	5386
13	Nov 4	A	Dunfermline Ath	W	3-0	1-0	7	Stokes 3 [1, 58, 79]	6504
14	13	H	Hearts	D	1-1	0-0	8	Latapy [83]	6289
15	18	A	Kilmarnock	L	1-2	1-0	8	Stokes [42]	5666
16	25	A	Motherwell	L	2-4	1-0	8	Stokes [36], Latapy [70]	4970
17	Dec 3	H	Rangers	W	1-0	1-0	7	Twaddle [25]	7245
18	9	A	Aberdeen	L	1-2	0-2	7	Gow [68]	10,594
19	16	H	Hibernian	W	2-1	2-0	7	Martis (og) [14], Craig [21]	6142
20	23	A	Celtic	L	0-1	0-1	7		55,000
21	26	A	St Mirren	L	0-1	0-0	—		5212
22	30	H	Inverness CT	W	3-1	3-0	7	Stokes 3 [33, 36, 44]	4516
23	Jan 1	A	Dundee U	W	5-1	1-1	—	Cregg (pen) [19], O'Donnell [45], Gow 3 [62, 75, 89]	6261
24	13	H	Dunfermline Ath	W	1-0	0-0	6	Gow [89]	6051
25	20	A	Hearts	L	0-1	0-0	6		17,247
26	27	H	Kilmarnock	L	0-2	0-2	7		4696
27	Feb 10	H	Motherwell	L	1-2	0-0	7	Cregg [46]	4478
28	18	A	Rangers	L	1-2	0-1	7	Finnigan [64]	49,850
29	Mar 3	H	Aberdeen	L	1-2	0-1	8	Holden [65]	5825
30	10	A	Hibernian	L	0-2	0-0	8		12,572
31	18	H	Celtic	W	1-0	1-0	8	Thomson [15]	6438
32	31	H	St Mirren	W	2-0	2-0	7	Moutinho [20], O'Donnell [40]	5863
33	Apr 7	A	Inverness CT	D	1-1	0-0	7	Finnigan [79]	4435
34	23	H	St Mirren	L	0-2	0-1	7		4441
35	28	A	Motherwell	D	3-3	0-2	7	Scobbie [48], Craigan (og) [49], Cregg [56]	3640
36	May 5	H	Inverness CT	W	1-0	0-0	7	Finnigan [78]	3129
37	12	H	Dundee U	W	2-0	1-0	7	Finnigan [4], Gow [50]	4161
38	19	A	Dunfermline Ath	W	3-0	0-0	7	Thomson [48], Gow [55], Moutinho [89]	5087

Final League Position: 7

Honours
League Champions: Division II 1935-36, 1969-70, 1974-75. First Division 1990-91, 1993-94, 2002-03, 2004-05. Second Division 1979-80; *Runners-up:* Division I 1907-08, 1909-10. First Division 1985-86, 1988-89. Division II 1904-05, 1951-52, 1960-61.
Scottish Cup Winners: 1913, 1957; *Runners-up:* 1997. *League Cup Runners-up:* 1947-48. *B&Q Cup Winners:* 1993-94. *League Challenge Cup Winners:* 1997-98, 2004-05.

Club colours: Shirt: Navy blue with white seams. Shorts: Navy. Stockings: Navy with two white hoops.

Goalscorers: *League* (49): Stokes 14 (1 pen), Gow 7, Latapy 5, Finnigan 4, Cregg 3 (1 pen), Craig 2, Moutinho 2, O'Donnell 2, Thomson 2, Twaddle 2, Barr 1, Holden 1, Milne 1, Scobbie 1, own goals 2.
Scottish Cup (2): Craig 1, Gow 1.
CIS Cup (7): Moutinho 2, Stokes 2, Craig 1, Stewart 1, Twaddle 1.

Higgins S 14 + 1	Ross J 36	Dodd K 14 + 3	Barr D 36	Milne K 34	Scobbie T 16 + 5	Craig L 17 + 10	Lima V 17 + 5	Latapy R 36 + 1	Moutinho P 14 + 7	Gow A 34 + 2	Cregg P 32	Twaddle M 10 + 6	Thomson S 17 + 5	O'Donnell S 20 + 5	Stokes A 16	Stewart J 4 + 14	McManus T — + 5	Lambers J 9	Uras C 8 + 1	Schmeichel K 15	Holden D 8 + 1	Finnigan C 10 + 2	Allison B 1 + 2	Roberston D — + 2	Mcstay R — + 4	Lescinel J —	*Match No.*
1	2	3	4	5	6	7	8	9	10	11																	1
1	2	3	4	5		7	8	9	10	11	6																2
1	2	3	4	5	6	7		9	10	11	8																3
1	2		4	5	3^{1}	7	8	9	10	11	6	12															4
1	2^{3}	3^{1}	4	5	6	7^{2}		9	10	11	8	14	$12^{\blacksquare}$	13													5
1	2		4	5	3		13	8^{2}	9^{1}	11	7			6	10^{3}	12	14										6
1	2	3	4		6^{1}				13	12	7	5	8	9	10	11^{2}											7
1	2		4	5			13	8	9^{2}	11	6	3		$7^{\blacksquare}$	10^{1}	12											8
1	2		4	5^{1}	12			8^{3}	9^{2}	11	6	3	7		10	14	13										9
1	2		4	5				8^{1}	9	11^{2}	6	3	7	13	10	12											10
1	2	3^{1}	4	5				10		13	6	8	7	9	11^{2}	12											11
	2		4	5	12	14	13	9		11	6	3^{1}	7^{2}	8^{3}	10			1									12
	2		4	5		13	12	9^{2}		11	6	3	7^{1}	8	10^{3}	14		1									13
	2^{1}	12	4	5	3^{2}	14		9		11	6	13	7	8^{3}	10			1									14
	2		4	5				9		11	6	3	7	8^{1}	10	12		1									15
	2^{3}		4	5		13	12	9		11	6	3	7^{1}	8^{2}	$10^{\blacksquare}$		14	1									16
	2	12	4	5		7	8	10		11	6	3				9^{1}		1									17
15	2	12	4	5	3^{1}	7	8	9		11	6				10			1^{6}									18
1	2	3^{1}	4	5	12	7	8	9^{2}		11	6			13	10^{3}	14											19
1	2	3	4	5		7^{2}	8^{1}	12		11	6			9	10	13											20
1	2	3	4	5		7		9		11^{1}	6			8	10		12										21
	2	3	4	5^{1}			8^{2}	10^{3}			6	12	13	9	11	14		1	7								22
	2	3	4	5		12	8^{3}	10^{2}		11	6		14	9^{1}		13		1	7								23
	2	3	4	5		9	8	10		11	6								7	1							24
	2^{2}	3^{1}	4		6	9	8	10		11	7					14	13		5^{3}	1	12						25
	2^{3}		4		6	9	8^{2}	10		11	7		13						5	1	3^{1}	12	14				26
				4^{1}	6			10	13	11	7	12	8						5^{2}	1	3	9	2				27
			4		$2^{\blacksquare}$	12		10^{2}	8	11	6		13	7^{1}					5	1	3	9					28
	2			4				10^{1}	8	11			7	6					5	1	3	9		12			29
	2^{3}		4	5		13	8	10^{2}	9^{1}			12	7	6						1	3	11	14				30
	2		4	5				10^{1}	12	11	6		7	8						1	3	$9^{\blacksquare}$					31
	2		4	5	14	12		10	9^{2}	11	6		7	8^{1}						1	3^{3}			13			32
	2		4	5	12	14		10^{3}	9^{2}	11	6		7	8						1	3^{1}	13					33
	2	$3^{\blacksquare}$	4	5		12	7^{3}	10^{2}	13	11	6			8^{1}						1		9			14		34
	2		4	5	3	7^{2}		10		11	6^{1}			13		8				1		9			12		35
	2		4	5	3	6	7	10^{2}	12	11^{1}						8^{3}			14	1		9			13		36
	2		4	5	3	6	8	10^{3}	12	11			7^{2}			14				1		9^{1}			13		37
	2		4	5	3	6^{2}	8	10^{1}	12	11^{3}			7	13		14				1		9					38

FORFAR ATHLETIC — Third Division

Year Formed: 1885. *Ground & Address:* Station Park, Carseview Road, Forfar. *Telephone:* 01307 463576/462259. *Fax:* 01307 466956. *E-mail:* pat@ramsayladders.co.uk. *Website:* www.forfarathletic.co.uk
Ground Capacity: total: 4602, seated: 739. *Size of Pitch:* 115yd × 69yd.
Chairman and Secretary: David McGregor.
Manager: Jim Moffat.
Managers since 1975: Jerry Kerr, Archie Knox, Alex Rae, Doug Houston, Henry Hall, Bobby Glennie, Paul Hegarty, Tommy Campbell, Ian McPhee, Neil Cooper, R. Stewart, Ray Farningham, Brian Fairley, George Shaw.
Club Nickname(s): Loons. *Previous Grounds:* None.
Record Attendance: 10,780 v Rangers, Scottish Cup 2nd rd, 2 Feb 1970.
Record Transfer Fee received: £65,000 for David Bingham to Dunfermline Ath (September 1995).
Record Transfer Fee paid: £50,000 for Ian McPhee from Airdrieonians (1991).
Record Victory: 14-1 v Lindertis, Scottish Cup 1st rd, 1 Sept 1988.
Record Defeat: 2-12 v King's Park, Division II, 2 Jan 1930.
Most League Appearances: 484: Ian McPhee, 1978-88 and 1991-98.
Most League Goals in Season (Individual): 45: Dave Kilgour, Division II, 1929-30.
Most Goals Overall (Individual): 124, John Clark.

FORFAR ATHLETIC 2006–07 LEAGUE RECORD

Match No.	Date	Venue	Opponents	Result		H/T Score	Lg. Pos.	Goalscorers	Attendance
1	Aug 5	H	Stranraer	W	2-1	1-1	—	Rattray [13], Lumsden [51]	382
2	12	A	Raith R	D	0-0	0-0	3		1437
3	19	H	Alloa Ath	L	0-2	0-1	5		502
4	26	A	Brechin C	L	2-4	1-2	6	Gribben (pen) [42], Tosh [84]	622
5	Sept 3	H	Ayr U	L	0-1	0-1	7		449
6	9	A	Stirling A	L	0-3	0-0	9		541
7	16	H	Cowdenbeath	D	1-1	0-1	9	Donald [88]	460
8	23	H	Morton	L	1-3	0-1	9	Donald [70]	701
9	30	A	Peterhead	L	0-8	0-5	10		526
10	Oct 14	A	Stranraer	L	2-3	2-2	10	Lombardi [37], Tosh [43]	373
11	21	H	Raith R	D	1-1	0-1	10	Tosh [88]	754
12	28	A	Ayr U	L	0-5	0-2	10		988
13	Nov 4	H	Brechin C	L	1-2	0-0	10	Tade [65]	687
14	11	A	Cowdenbeath	L	2-3	0-0	10	Tade [70], Gribben [82]	383
15	Dec 2	A	Morton	D	1-1	1-0	10	Millar (og) [15]	1991
16	5	H	Stirling A	L	0-2	0-1	—		391
17	16	H	Peterhead	L	2-3	1-1	10	Gribben 2 [36, 90]	361
18	23	H	Stranraer	W	5-0	3-0	10	Gribben 3 [9, 11, 59], Lumsden [45], Tosh [58]	345
19	30	A	Alloa Ath	L	0-2	0-1	10		469
20	Jan 2	A	Brechin C	D	2-2	1-1	—	Gribben 2 [4, 90]	804
21	13	H	Ayr U	D	1-1	0-1	10	Lumsden [90]	370
22	20	H	Cowdenbeath	W	2-0	0-0	10	Lombardi [58], Gribben [81]	377
23	27	A	Stirling A	L	0-4	0-2	10		585
24	Feb 10	A	Peterhead	D	2-2	0-1	10	Lombardi 2 [64, 84]	476
25	17	H	Alloa Ath	L	0-2	0-1	10		413
26	24	A	Raith R	L	1-2	1-1	10	Tosh [45]	1945
27	Mar 3	H	Brechin C	W	3-2	0-2	10	Gates [46], Moon [51], Gribben (pen) [73]	583
28	10	A	Ayr U	L	1-3	1-1	10	Gates [10]	955
29	17	A	Cowdenbeath	L	1-2	1-0	10	Fraser [17]	251
30	25	H	Morton	L	0-4	0-2	10		765
31	31	H	Stirling A	L	0-2	0-1	10		525
32	Apr 3	H	Peterhead	L	1-2	0-1	—	Tade [76]	298
33	7	A	Morton	L	1-9	0-3	10	Fraser [87]	3007
34	14	A	Stranraer	L	1-4	0-0	10	Moon [89]	221
35	21	H	Raith R	L	1-2	0-1	10	Wilson (og) [56]	699
36	28	A	Alloa Ath	L	0-2	0-0	10		499

Final League Position: 10

Honours
League Champions: Second Division 1983-84. Third Division 1994-95; *Runners-up:* 1996-97. C Division 1948-49.
Scottish Cup: Semi-finals 1982.
League Cup: Semi-finals 1977-78.
Bell's League Challenge: Semi-finals 2004-05.

Club colours: Shirt: Sky blue with navy side panels, shoulder/sleeve bands. Shorts: Navy with sky blue side trim. Stockings: Sky blue with navy band on top.

Goalscorers: *League* (37): Gribben 11 (2 pens), Tosh 5, Lombardi 4, Lumsden 3, Tade 3, Donald 2, Fraser 2, Gates 2, Moon 2, Rattray 1, own goals 2.
Scottish Cup (1): Lunan 1.
CIS Cup (1): Gribben.
Challenge Cup (3): Coyle 1, Gribben 1, Lunan 1.

Murdoch S 17	Keogh D 15 + 2	King D 21	Dunn D 10 + 1	Rattray A 16	Donald B 18 + 2	Lunan P 24 + 1	Marshall C 4	Lumsden C 18 + 3	Gribben D 18 + 9	Coyle F 26 + 2	Fraser G 13 + 13	Webster K 7 + 8	Tosh P 24 + 4	Lynn G 18 + 2	Lombardi M 22 + 7	Montgomery R 3 + 1	Abbot S 1	Beith G 4 + 5	Moon K 23 + 2	Allison M 17 + 1	Tade G 18 + 5	Wood A 19	Kassim A 2	Stewart W 11 + 3	McNally S 12	Gates S 7	Tulloch S 3 + 1	Tierney G 5	*Match No.*
1	2	3	4	5^{1}	6^{2}	7	8	9	10^{3}	11	12	13	14																1
1	13	3	4	5	6	7	8	2^{2}	10^{3}	11^{1}	14	12	9																2
1	2	3	4	5^{1}		7	8	14	10^{2}	11	13	6	9^{3}	12															3
1			4	5		7	8	2	10	11^{1}		6	9	3	12														4
1	2		4	5	6	7			10	11	12	8^{2}		3	9^{1}	13													5
1			4	5	6^{1}	7			10	13			9^{3}	3	14	11^{2}	2	8■	12										6
1	2		4^{1}	5	6	7			12	11	13	10		3■	9^{2}				8										7
1	2			5^{1}	6				10	4^{2}	13	7	12		9	3		11	8										8
1				5■	6				10■	2	12	7	9		13	11^{2}		3^{1}	8	4									9
1	2				6^{1}	7		5		11	12		9	3	10				8	4									10
1	4				6	2		5	13	11^{1}		12	9	3	10^{2}				8		7								11
1	4				6^{1}	2		5	11^{2}		14	12	9	3	10^{3}			13	8		7								12
1				5■	6	8		2	12			11	9	3	10^{1}					4	7								13
1	4	3			6^{1}	8		2	13				9		10^{2}			11	12	5	7								14
1		3		5		6		2	13		10^{2}	12	9^{3}	11	14				8	4	7^{1}								15
1		3		4		6		2	13		10	12	9^{2}	11					8	5^{1}	7								16
1	2	5				7		4	10	6^{1}	11^{3}	14	9^{2}	3	13				8		12								17
	2^{1}	5			6			4	10^{2}	11	7^{3}	12	9	3	13				8		14	1							18
	2	5			6	12		4	10^{2}	11^{3}	7^{1}		9	3	13				8		14	1							19
	2	3		5				4	10	8	7		9		11						6	1							20
	2■	3		5	12			4	10	6	7^{1}		9		11						8	1							21
		3						5	10	6	12		9		11					4	8	1	2	7^{1}					22
		3		5^{1}				4	10	8	11^{2}		9					13		12	6	1	2	7					23
	13				12			4		6			14	3^{2}	10				8	5	7^{1}	1		9	2	11^{3}			24
	4									6^{2}	12		9^{1}	3	10			13	8	5		1		7	2	11			25
						7			13	6			9	3	10^{2}				8	4^{1}		1		12	2	11	5		26
						7■			12	6^{2}			9	3■	10				8	4^{1}	13	1			2	11	5		27
			12						4	7^{2}			9		10■				8	5	6	1		13	2	11	3^{1}		28
		3								7	10		9						8	4	6	1		12	2	11^{1}		5	29
		3				6				12	10		13						8	4■	7	1		9^{2}	2	11^{1}		5	30
		5			6^{1}	2				11	12				10				8		7	1		9	4			3	31
		4			6	7				11					10				8^{1}	5	12	1		9	2			3	32
		3			6^{1}	2				10	14			13	11					4^{2}	8	1		9^{3}	7		12	5	33
		5	4		8	2					9			3	11				6		7	1		10					34
		6	5	4		10■		14	12		9^{3}				3^{2}			13	8		7	1		11^{1}	2				35
		3	5			8		12	9		10^{1}				11^{2}			13	6	4		1		7	2■				36

GRETNA — Premier League

Year Formed: 1946. *Ground & Address:* Raydale Park, Dominion Rd, Gretna DG16 5AP. Currently playing home games at Motherwell. *Telephone:* 01461 337602. *Fax:* 01461 338047. *E-mail:* info@gretnafootballclub.co.uk. *Website:* www.gretnafootballclub.co.uk
Ground Capacity: 2200.
Club Shop: Alan Watson, 01387 251550.
President: Brian Fulton. *Chairman:* Ron MacGregor. *Secretary:* Helen MacGregor. *Managing Director:* Brookes Mileson. *Chief Executive:* Graeme Muir. *Director of Club Development:* Mick Wadsworth.
Manager: Rowan Alexander. *Assistant Manager:* David Irons. *Senior Coach:* Derek Collins. *Physio:* Kenny Crichton.
Record Attendance: 3000 v Dundee U, Scottish Cup, 17 Jan 2005.
Record Victory: 20-0 v Silloth, 1962.
Record Defeat: 0-6 v Worksop Town, 1994-95 and 0-6 v Bradford (Park Avenue) 1999-2000.
Most League Appearances: 96, Gavin Skelton, 2002-05.
Most League Goals in Season (Individual): 38, Kenny Deuchar, 2004-05.
Most Goals Overall (Individual): 58, Kenny Deuchar, 2004-06.

GRETNA 2006–07 LEAGUE RECORD

Match No.	*Date*	*Venue*	*Opponents*	*Result*		*H/T Score*	*Lg. Pos.*	*Goalscorers*	*Attendance*
1	Aug 5	H	Hamilton A	W	6-0	3-0	—	Tosh 3 [14, 26, 48], Grady [42], McGill 2 [69, 87]	1691
2	13	A	Clyde	W	2-1	1-1	1	McMenamin 2 [3, 88]	1348
3	19	H	Ross Co	W	2-1	2-0	1	McMenamin 2 [21, 35]	1195
4	27	A	Queen of the S	W	3-0	2-0	1	McMenamin 2 [39, 88], Grainger [45]	5485
5	Sept 9	H	Dundee	L	0-4	0-4	2		1556
6	16	H	Livingston	D	1-1	1-1	3	Townsley [32]	2023
7	23	A	Partick Th	W	6-0	1-0	1	McMenamin [29], Tosh [55], Townsley [60], Jenkins [69], Skelton [80], Berkeley [86]	2399
8	30	H	Airdrie U	L	0-2	0-1	1		1492
9	Oct 14	A	St Johnstone	D	3-3	0-0	1	McGuffie 2 (1 pen) [46, 84 (p)], Paartalu [75]	3150
10	21	H	Clyde	D	3-3	1-1	3	Deuchar 2 [17, 80], McMenamin [56]	1124
11	28	A	Hamilton A	L	1-3	0-2	4	Tosh [64]	1608
12	Nov 4	A	Dundee	W	3-1	1-1	3	McMenamin (pen) [35], Tosh [77], Jenkins [90]	3938
13	11	H	Queen of the S	W	5-0	3-0	1	Tosh [7], Graham [17], McMenamin 2 (1 pen) [26 (p), 74], Paartalu [67]	2193
14	18	A	Livingston	W	2-1	2-0	1	McMenamin [21], Grainger [34]	1876
15	25	H	Partick Th	W	4-0	3-0	1	McMenamin 3 [14, 42, 45], Jenkins [86]	1646
16	Dec 2	H	St Johnstone	W	2-0	2-0	1	Tosh [21], Paartalu [38]	1744
17	9	A	Airdrie U	L	2-4	1-1	1	Townsley 2 [22, 74]	1169
18	16	A	Ross Co	W	1-0	0-0	1	McMenamin [66]	1956
19	23	H	Hamilton A	W	1-0	0-0	1	McMenamin (pen) [57]	1226
20	30	H	Dundee	W	1-0	0-0	1	Innes [66]	1541
21	Jan 2	A	Queen of the S	W	4-0	1-0	—	McMenamin [25], Skelton 2 [48, 86], Townsley [58]	3714
22	13	A	Partick Th	D	2-2	2-1	1	Paartalu [1], McMenamin [2]	2678
23	20	H	Livingston	W	4-1	2-0	1	Canning [11], Innes [39], McMenamin 2 [75, 80]	1310
24	27	A	St Johnstone	L	1-2	0-1	1	Barrau [84]	3201
25	Feb 10	H	Airdrie U	D	0-0	0-0	1		1299
26	17	H	Ross Co	W	4-1	2-0	1	McMenamin 2 (1 pen) [9 (p), 80], Nicholls [11], Jenkins [90]	1361
27	24	A	Clyde	L	0-2	0-1	1		729
28	Mar 3	H	Queen of the S	L	0-3	0-1	1		2049
29	11	A	Dundee	W	1-0	1-0	1	Graham [22]	3928
30	17	A	Livingston	D	1-1	0-1	1	Graham [60]	1748
31	31	H	Partick Th	W	2-0	1-0	1	McMenamin [33], Grady [69]	1541
32	Apr 4	A	Airdrie U	D	0-0	0-0	—		1209
33	7	H	St Johnstone	L	0-2	0-2	1		2133
34	14	A	Hamilton A	D	0-0	0-0	1		1646
35	21	H	Clyde	D	0-0	0-0	1		1715
36	28	A	Ross Co	W	3-2	2-1	1	Deverdics [34], Grady 2 [42, 90]	6216

Final League Position: 1

Honours
League Champions: First Division 2006-07. Second Division 2005-06. Third Division 2004-05.
Bell's League Challenge: Quarter-finals 2004-05.
Scottish Cup Runners-up: 2006.

European: *UEFA Cup:* 2 matches (2006-07).

Club colours: Shirt: White with black detail. Shorts: White. Stockings: White topped with black hoops.

Goalscorers: *League* (70): McMenamin 24 (4 pens), Tosh 8, Townsley 5, Grady 4, Jenkins 4, Paartalu 4, Graham 3, Skelton 3, Deuchar 2, Grainger 2, Innes 2, McGill 2, McGuffie 2 (1 pen), Barrau 1, Berkeley 1, Canning 1, Deverdics 1, Nicholls 1.
Scottish Cup (4): Berkeley 1, Graham 1, McMenamin 1, Paartalu 1.
CIS Cup (0).
Challenge Cup (8): Deuchar 2, Graham 1, Jenkins 1, McGuffie 1, McMenamin 1, Tosh 1, Townsley 1.

Main A 27	Canning M 35	McQuilken J 3+1	Tosh S 14	Townsley D 17+2	Innes C 27	McGill B 6+2	McGuffie R 16+6	Deuchar K 4+4	Grady J 16+8	Skelton G 34	Graham D 28+5	McMenamin C 34+1	Jenkins A 23+9	Birch M 4+2	O'Neil J 6+2	Nicholls D 19+1	Grainger D 26+4	MacFarlane N 3+2	Barr C 13+3	Berkeley M —+13	Paartalu E 23+3	Fleming C 1+1	Shields D —+1	Bingham D 1+2	Baldacchino R —+4	Barrau X —+1	Cowan D 3	Malkowski Z 8	Hogg S 2+2	Deverdics N 3+3	*Match No.*
1	2	3	4^{3}	5	6	7	8	9^{1}	10^{2}	11	12	13	14																		1
1	5	3^{2}	4	13			8		10	11		9	7	2	6^{1}	12															2
1	5		4	6		7	8	13■	10	11		9^{2}	12	2			3^{1}														3
1	5				6		12		10	11	8	9	7	2^{1}	4		3														4
1	5				6		7	13	10^{2}	11	8	9	12	2^{1}	4		3														5
1	6	3		5		7^{1}	8	9		11	12	10	2		4^{2}			13													6
1	6		4^{1}	5^{2}			8			11	10^{3}	9	7	13			3	2	12	14											7
1	6		4	5^{3}			8			11	10	9	7^{2}	14			3	2^{1}		13	12										8
1	5		4	12			8	14	10	11		9^{3}	7^{2}				3		2^{1}	13	6										9
1^{6}	5		4^{1}				8	9	12	11	13	10^{2}	7				3		2		6	15									10
	5		4				8^{1}	9^{2}	13	11	12	10	7				3		2■		6	1									11
1	5		4	2^{1}	6					11	10	9	13			8	3			12	7^{2}										12
1	5		4	2^{1}	6			14	13	11	10^{3}	9^{2}	12			8	3				7										13
1	5		4	2	6				12	11	10	9^{1}				8	3				7										14
1	5		4^{3}	2^{1}	6				13	11	10	9^{2}	14			8	3		12		7										15
1	5		4	2	6				12	11	10^{2}	9^{1}				8	3			13	7										16
1	5■	14	4	2	6^{3}					11	10^{1}	9	13			8^{2}	3			12	7										17
1				5	6		12			11	10^{2}	9	4			8	3		2	13	7^{1}										18
1	5			2^{3}	6		12			11^{2}	10	9	4^{1}			8	3		14	13	7										19
1	5			2	6		12			11	10	9	4			8^{1}	3				7										20
1	5			2	6		8			11	10^{2}	9	4				3			13	7^{1}		12								21
1	5			2	6	12	8^{1}			11	10	9	4				3				7										22
1	5			2	6	8				11^{2}	10^{1}	9	4				3				7			12	13						23
1	5				6	7^{1}					10	9	4				3		2		8			11^{2}	12	13					24
1	5				6		12		13	11	10	9^{2}	7			4	3		2		8^{1}										25
1	5				6				10	3	11	9^{2}	7		12	4			2		8^{1}			13							26
1	5				6	13	8^{2}		10	3	11	9	7			4	12										2^{1}				27
1	5				6		14		10^{1}	3	11^{3}	9	8			4	13		2	12	7^{2}										28
	5				6		7		9	11^{2}	10^{1}		8			4	3	13	2	12								1			29
	5				6		7^{1}		11		10	9	4			8^{2}	3		2		13							1	12		30
	5				6				11	3	10^{1}	9	4			8			2		7							1		12	31
	5				6				11	3^{3}	10	9	4^{1}			8^{2}			2■	14	7							1	12	13	32
	5				6		2^{2}		11	3^{1}	10	9	13			8	12				4^{3}							1	7	14	33
	5				6				11	3	10^{2}	9			14		12		2	13	4^{3}							1	8^{1}	7	34
	5					7			12	3	10^{1}	9	13		8^{3}		6	4^{2}							14		2	1		11	35
	5				7^{3}				10	3	12	9			8	4^{2}	6				13				14		2	1		11^{1}	36

HAMILTON ACADEMICAL First Division

Year Formed: 1874. *Ground:* New Douglas Park, Cadzow Avenue, Hamilton ML3 0FT. *Telephone:* 01698 368650. *Fax:* 01698 285422. *E-mail:* scott@acciesfc.co.uk. *Website:* www.acciesfc.co.uk
Ground Capacity: 5396. *Size of Pitch:* 115yd × 75yd.
Chairman: Ronnie MacDonald. *Chief Executive:* George W. Fairley. *Secretary:* Scott A. Struthers BA. *Commercial Manager:* Derek McQuade.
Manager: Billy Reid. *Player/Assistant Manager:* Stuart Taylor. *Physio/Sports Therapist:* Avril Downs.
Managers since 1975: J. Eric Smith, Dave McParland, John Blackley, Bertie Auld, John Lambie, Jim Dempsey, John Lambie, Billy McLaren, Iain Munro, Sandy Clark, Colin Miller, Ally Dawson, Chris Hillcoat, Alan Maitland.
Club Nickname(s): The Accies. *Previous Grounds:* Bent Farm, South Avenue, South Haugh, Douglas Park, Cliftonhill Stadium, Firhill Stadium.
Record Attendance: 28,690 v Hearts, Scottish Cup 3rd rd, 3 Mar 1937.
Record Transfer Fee received: £380,000 for Paul Hartley to Millwall (July 1996).
Record Transfer Fee paid: £60,000 for Paul Martin from Kilmarnock (Oct 1988) and for John McQuade from Dumbarton (Aug 1993).
Record Victory: 11-1 v Chryston, Lanarkshire Cup, 28 Nov 1885.
Record Defeat: 1-11 v Hibernian, Division I, 6 Nov 1965.
Most Capped Player: Colin Miller, 29, Canada, 1988-94.
Most League Appearances: 452: Rikki Ferguson, 1974-88.
Most League Goals in Season (Individual): 35: David Wilson, Division I; 1936-37.
Most Goals Overall (Individual): 246: David Wilson, 1928-39.

HAMILTON ACADEMICAL 2006–07 LEAGUE RECORD

Match No.	Date	Venue	Opponents	Result		H/T Score	Lg. Pos.	Goalscorers	Attendance
1	Aug 5	A	Gretna	L	0-6	0-3	—		1691
2	12	H	Dundee	W	1-0	0-0	6	Elebert ^{51}	1517
3	19	A	St Johnstone	D	0-0	0-0	5		2295
4	26	A	Airdrie U	W	2-1	0-0	5	Gilhaney ^{64}, McLeod ^{81}	1416
5	Sept 16	H	Partick Th	L	1-2	0-1	6	Stevenson (pen) ^{65}	2290
6	23	A	Ross Co	W	1-0	1-0	6	Tunbridge ^{34}	1925
7	30	H	Queen of the S	D	1-1	1-1	6	Offiong ^{25}	1396
8	Oct 13	A	Livingston	W	1-0	1-0	5	Gilhaney ^{43}	1877
9	17	H	Clyde	W	3-1	3-1	—	Offiong 2 $^{2, 29}$, Gilhaney ^{34}	1253
10	21	A	Dundee	D	1-1	1-0	4	McLeod ^{25}	3851
11	28	H	Gretna	W	3-1	2-0	4	Winters ^{14}, Offiong ^{30}, Wake ^{77}	1608
12	Nov 4	A	Clyde	L	1-2	0-0	4	McArthur ^{70}	1364
13	11	H	Airdrie U	W	2-1	1-1	2	Offiong ^{10}, Wake ^{87}	1724
14	18	A	Partick Th	L	1-3	0-2	3	McLeod ^{47}	2797
15	25	H	Ross Co	D	0-0	0-0	3		1180
16	Dec 2	H	Livingston	D	1-1	1-0	3	Wake ^{21}	1515
17	9	A	Queen of the S	D	1-1	0-1	4	Offiong ^{77}	1735
18	16	H	St Johnstone	D	2-2	0-1	5	McLeod ^{52}, Offiong ^{61}	1356
19	23	A	Gretna	L	0-1	0-0	5		1226
20	30	H	Clyde	D	1-1	0-0	4	Winters ^{73}	1534
21	Jan 2	A	Airdrie U	L	0-1	0-1	—		1414
22	20	H	Partick Th	W	2-1	1-0	4	Gilhaney ^{30}, Offiong ^{52}	1949
23	27	A	Livingston	W	2-1	0-1	3	Winters ^{89}, Elebert ^{90}	1400
24	Feb 10	H	Queen of the S	D	2-2	2-1	4	Stevenson (pen) ^{10}, Winters ^{18}	1454
25	17	A	St Johnstone	L	2-4	2-3	4	Offiong ^{21}, Winters ^{45}	2259
26	24	H	Dundee	W	1-0	1-0	4	Elebert ^{21}	1439
27	Mar 3	H	Airdrie U	W	3-0	2-0	4	Offiong 2 $^{11, 46}$, Easton ^{33}	1714
28	10	A	Clyde	L	0-3	0-2	5		1200
29	13	A	Ross Co	L	1-4	0-3	—	Offiong ^{70}	1475
30	17	A	Partick Th	W	2-0	0-0	3	Stevenson (pen) ^{46}, Elebert ^{82}	2178
31	31	H	Ross Co	W	1-0	1-0	3	Wilson ^{10}	1035
32	Apr 3	A	Queen of the S	D	1-1	1-1	—	Wake ^{4}	1650
33	7	H	Livingston	W	3-0	2-0	3	Elebert ^{12}, Offiong ^{28}, Winters ^{51}	1283
34	14	H	Gretna	D	0-0	0-0	3		1646
35	21	A	Dundee	L	0-1	0-0	3		3221
36	28	H	St Johnstone	L	3-4	1-3	4	McCarthy ^{39}, Offiong ^{70}, Wake ^{88}	4975

Final League Position: 4

Honours
League Champions: First Division 1985-86, 1987-88; Third Division 2000-01. *Runners-up:* Division II 1903-04, 1952-53, 1964-65; Second Division 1996-97, 2003-04.
Scottish Cup Runners-up: 1911, 1935. *League Cup:* Semi-finalists three times. *League Challenge Cup*: Runners-up 2006.
B&Q Cup Winners: 1991-92, 1992-93.

Club colours: Shirt: Red and white hoops. Shorts: White. Stockings: White.

Goalscorers: *League* (46): Offiong 14, Winters 6, Elebert 5, Wake 5, Gilhaney 4, McLeod 4, Stevenson 3 (3 pens), Easton 1, McArthur 1, McCarthy 1, Tunbridge 1, Wilson 1.
Scottish Cup (2): McArthur 1, McCarthy 1.
CIS Cup (1): Offiong 1.
Challenge Cup (4): Neill 1, Offiong 1, Payo 1, Tunbridge 1.

McEwan D 8 + 1	Stevenson A 15 + 7	Fleming D 16	Thomson S 1 + 3	Elebert D 33	McLeod P 17 + 14	McArthur J 35 + 1	Wilson M 21 + 5	Offiong R 26 + 3	Neil A 28 + 1	Gilhaney M 23 + 6	Payo J 2 + 1	McCabe R — + 1	Agnew S 2 + 3	Parratt T 26 + 1	McLaughlin M 5	Easton B 30 + 2	Jellemaa R 17 + 1	Tunbridge S 5 + 3	Wake B 10 + 22	Winters D 25 + 5	McLaughlan G 1 + 2	McCarthy J 14 + 9	Rezgane O 2	Gibson J 6 + 5	Sharp K 8	Di Malta D — + 1	Murdoch S 11	McClen J 2 + 1	Swailes C 7 + 1	McJimpsey M — + 1	*Match No.*
1	2	3	4	5	6	7	8^3	9^1	10^2	11	12	13	14																		1
1	14	3	12	5	4	7	8		10	11	9^2			2^3	6^1	13															2
		3	13	5		7	8	9^1	10	11				2	6^2		1	4	12												3
		3	13	5	12	7	8			11	10^1			2	6^2	14	1	4^3	9												4
	4	3		5	12	8		13		11				2^3		6	1	7^1	9^2	10	14										5
	12	3		5	14	8		9^2		11			10^1	2		6	1	7	13	4^3											6
	2	3		5	12	8		9^3		11			10^2			6■	1	7	14	4^1		13									7
	4	3^2		5	13	10^1	8	9	12	11				2	6		1		14	7^2											8
	4			5	13	8	12	9^3	10	11^2				2	6^1	3	1		14	7											9
	13	3^2		5	11	4	8^1	9^3	10					2		6	1		12	7		14									10
	13	3^2		5	11	8	4	9^1	10					2		6	1		12	7											11
	14			5	7	8	4^3	9^1	10					2		3	1	13	12	11^2			6■								12
	2			5^2	7	8	4	9	10							3	1		12	11		6^1		13							13
15				5	7	8		9	10				13	2		3	1^G		12	11^2		6^1	4								14
	4			5	7	12			10				13	2		6^1	1		9	11		8^2		3							15
1	6			5	7^1	8	12	13	10					2					9	11		4^2			3						16
1				5	7	8	4	12	10	13				2^2		6			9	11^1					3						17
1				5	7	8^3	14	9	10	11^2				2		6			12	13		4^1			3						18
1				5	7^2	8	4^3	9^1	10	13				2		6			11	12		14			3						19
1	13			5^2		8	4		10	11				2^1		6			9	7^3		12			3	14					20
1^G	5				13	8^1	2		10	11						6	15		9	7^2		4		12	3						21
	5^2				7	8	2	9^1	10	11						6	1		12	13		4			3						22
	12			5	7^3	8	2	9	10	11^2						6	1		13	14		4^1			3						23
	4^1	3		5	14	8		9^3	10	11^2						6	1	13		7		12		2							24
	4^2	3		5		8	2^1	9^3	10	11				12		6	1		14	7		13									25
	4^1	3		5	13	8		9^3	10	11^2				2		6			14	7		12					1				26
		3		5	14	8		9^2	10	11^1				2		6			13	7^3		4					1	12			27
		3^3		5		8		9	10	11				2■		6		14	13	7^1							1	4^2	12		28
		3^2		5	14	8	2^3	9	10	11						6				7		12		13			1	4^1			29
	7			5	11^2	8	12	9■		14				2		6			13			10^3		3			1		4^1		30
				5	12	8	4			11						6			9^1	7		10^2		3			1		2	13	31
				5	11^3	8	7		10	14				2		6			9		12	13		3^1			1		4^2		32
				5^1		8^2	13	9^3	10	11				2		6			14	7		4		12			1		3		33
	4^1			5	14	8		9^2	10	11^3				2		6			13	7				12			1		3		34
				5	14	8	4^2	9^1	10	13				2		6			12	7^3		11					1		3		35
					11^3	8	7^2	9		13				2		6			14	12	5^1	4		10			1		3		36

HEART OF MIDLOTHIAN Premier League

Year Formed: 1874. *Ground & Address:* Tynecastle Stadium, Gorgie Rd, Edinburgh EH11 2NL. *Telephone:* 0871 663 1874. *Fax:* 0131 200 7222. *E-mail:* hearts@homplc.co.uk. *Website:* www.heartsfc.co.uk
Ground Capacity: 17,402. *Size of Pitch:* 100m × 64m.
Chairman: Roman Romanov. *General Secretary:* Campbell Ogilvie.
Head Coach: Anatoly Korobochka. *Assistant Head Coach:* Stephen Frail. *Physio:* Alan Rae.
Managers since 1975: J. Hagart, W. Ormond, R. Moncur, T. Ford, A. MacDonald, A. MacDonald & W. Jardine, A. MacDonald, J. Jordan, S. Clark, T. McLean, J. Jefferies, C. Levein, J. Robertson, G. Burley, G. Rix, V. Ivanauskas.
Club Nickname(s): Hearts, Jambos. *Previous Grounds:* The Meadows 1874, Powderhall 1878, Old Tynecastle 1881, (Tynecastle Park, 1886).
Record Attendance: 53,396 v Rangers, Scottish Cup 3rd rd, 13 Feb 1932.
Record Transfer Fee received: £2,100,000 for Alan McLaren from Rangers (October 1994).
Record of Transfer paid: £850,000 for Mirsad Beslija to Celtic (January 2006).
Record Victory: 21-0 v Anchor, EFA Cup, 30 Oct 1880.
Record Defeat: 1-8 v Vale of Leven, Scottish Cup, 1888.
Most Capped Player: Bobby Walker, 29, Scotland.
Most League Appearances: 515: Gary Mackay, 1980-97.
Most League Goals in Season (Individual): 44: Barney Battles.
Most Goals Overall (Individual): 214: John Robertson, 1983-98.

HEART OF MIDLOTHIAN 2006–07 LEAGUE RECORD

Match No.	Date	Venue	Opponents	Result	H/T Score	Lg. Pos.	Goalscorers	Attendance
1	Jul 29	A	Dunfermline Ath	W 2-1	1-0	—	Bednar [15], Pospisil [77]	7936
2	Aug 6	H	Celtic	W 2-1	0-0	2	Bednar 2 [59, 87]	16,822
3	12	H	Falkirk	D 0-0	0-0	1		16,127
4	19	A	Rangers	L 0-2	0-0	5		50,239
5	26	H	Inverness CT	W 4-1	2-1	2	Pinilla [19], Mole [42], Driver [75], Makela [85]	15,912
6	Sept 9	H	St Mirren	L 0-1	0-0	3		16,823
7	17	A	Motherwell	W 1-0	0-0	2	Mole [69]	5931
8	24	A	Aberdeen	W 3-1	0-0	2	Berra [63], Pinilla [76], Mikoliunas [78]	11,160
9	Oct 1	H	Dundee U	W 4-0	2-0	2	Velicka [29], Makela [38], Hartley (pen) [87], Mole [88]	16,849
10	15	A	Hibernian	D 2-2	1-2	2	Velicka 2 [27, 74]	16,623
11	21	H	Kilmarnock	L 0-2	0-2	2		16,849
12	28	H	Dunfermline Ath	D 1-1	1-0	2	Velicka [12]	17,031
13	Nov 4	A	Celtic	L 1-2	0-0	2	Velicka [72]	58,971
14	13	A	Falkirk	D 1-1	0-0	3	Velicka [65]	6289
15	19	H	Rangers	L 0-1	0-0	5		17,040
16	25	A	Inverness CT	D 0-0	0-0	5		5603
17	Dec 2	A	St Mirren	D 2-2	1-2	6	Mikoliunas [1], Zaliukas [50]	5728
18	9	H	Motherwell	W 4-1	1-1	4	Fyssas [9], Quinn (og) [55], Velicka [58], Aguiar [64]	16,753
19	16	H	Aberdeen	L 0-1	0-0	4		17,274
20	23	A	Dundee U	W 1-0	0-0	4	Hartley (pen) [54]	7789
21	26	H	Hibernian	W 3-2	1-0	—	Hartley [2], Jankauskas [48], Mikoliunas [69]	17,369
22	30	A	Kilmarnock	D 0-0	0-0	4		7302
23	Jan 2	A	Dunfermline Ath	W 1-0	1-0	—	Pospisil [15]	7004
24	14	H	Celtic	L 1-2	1-0	4	Mikoliunas [28]	17,129
25	20	H	Falkirk	W 1-0	0-0	3	Bednar [74]	17,247
26	27	A	Rangers	D 0-0	0-0	4		50,321
27	Feb 10	H	Inverness CT	W 1-0	0-0	4	Pospisil [81]	16,631
28	17	H	St Mirren	D 1-1	0-1	4	Kingston [70]	17,195
29	Mar 5	A	Motherwell	W 2-0	1-0	—	Tall [36], Elliot [65]	4389
30	10	A	Aberdeen	L 0-1	0-1	4		13,964
31	17	H	Dundee U	L 0-4	0-0	4		17,172
32	Apr 1	A	Hibernian	W 1-0	0-0	4	Velicka [80]	15,953
33	7	H	Kilmarnock	W 1-0	0-0	4	Pospisil [78]	17,019
34	21	A	Rangers	L 1-2	1-0	4	Velicka [15]	50,099
35	29	A	Celtic	W 3-1	0-0	4	Ivaskevicius [57], Driver [60], Pospisil (pen) [72]	59,510
36	May 6	H	Aberdeen	D 1-1	1-0	4	Velicka [13]	17,208
37	12	H	Hibernian	W 2-0	2-0	4	Pospisil [1], Driver [23]	17,349
38	20	A	Kilmarnock	L 0-1	0-0	4		11,030

Final League Position: 4

Honours
League Champions: Division I 1894-95, 1896-97, 1957-58, 1959-60. First Division 1979-80; *Runners-up:* Division I 1893-94, 1898-99, 1903-04, 1905-06, 1914-15, 1937-38, 1953-54, 1956-57, 1958-59, 1964-65. Premier Division 1985-86, 1987-88, 1991-92; *Runners-up:* 2005-06. First Division 1977-78, 1982-83.
Scottish Cup Winners: 1891, 1896, 1901, 1906, 1956, 1998;, 2006; *Runners-up:* 1903, 1907, 1968, 1976, 1986, 1996.
League Cup Winners: 1954-55, 1958-59, 1959-60, 1962-63; *Runners-up:* 1961-62, 1996-97.

European: *European Cup:* 8 matches (1958-59, 1960-61, 2006-07). *Cup Winners' Cup:* 10 matches (1976-77, 1996-97, 1998-99). *UEFA Cup:* 47 matches (*Fairs Cup:* 1961-62, 1963-64, 1965-66. *UEFA Cup:* 1984-85, 1986-87, 1988-89, 1990-91, 1992-93, 1993-94, 2000-01, 2003-04, 2004-05, 2006-07).

Club colours: Shirt: Maroon. Shorts: White. Stockings: Maroon.

Goalscorers: *League* (47): Velicka 10, Pospisil 6 (1 pen), Bednar 4, Mikoliunas 4, Driver 3, Hartley 3 (2 pens), Mole 3, Makela 2, Pinilla 2, Aguiar 1, Berra 1, Elliot 1, Fyssas 1, Ivaskevicius 1, Jankauskas 1, Kingston 1, Tall 1, Zaliukas 1, own goal 1.
Scottish Cup (4): Velicka 3, Bednar 1.
CIS Cup (4): Makela 3, Aguiar 1.

Gordon C 34	Neilson R 12 + 2	Berra C 34 + 1	Pressley S 13	Fyssas T 18 + 3	Aguiar B 20 + 5	Brellier J 16 + 6	Mikoliunas S 29 + 2	McCann N 14 + 7	Pospisil M 12 + 12	Bednar R 14 + 4	Cesnauskis D 5 + 4	Makela J 1 + 8	Tall I 17 + 6	Wallace L 13 + 4	Beslija M 2 + 3	Jankauskas E 8 + 4	Elliot C 5 + 5	Hartley P 18 + 3	Karipidis C 10 + 2	Zaliukas M 26 + 1	Costa T 1	Pinilla M 2 + 1	Mole J 7 + 3	Driver A 17 + 3	Velicka A 23 + 4	Goncalves J 9 + 2	Barasa N 6 + 3	Banks S 5	Klimek A 1	Kingston L 10	Jonsson E — + 3	Pilibaitis L 4 + 1	Ivaskevicius K 9	Kancelskis T 3 + 2	Glen G — + 1	*Match No.*
1	2	3	4	5	6^1	7^3	8	9	10	11^2	12	13	14																							1
1	12	3	4		6	7	8	9^2	10^3	11	13	14	5^1	2																						2
1	2	3	4	5	6	7^1	8	9^3	10^2	11					12	13	14																			3
1	2■	3	4	5	6	7	8^2	14	12^3	11^1						10	9	13																		4
1			4		13		8	7^1				14		2				9^2	3	5	6	10^3	11	12												5
1	2	3	4	5		6	8^3	7^2		11■					14			9				12	10^1		13											6
1	13		4			6^2	8	12			7^1	14	3	2				9		5			10		11^3											7
1		3	4			13	8	7^1		11^3	12	14	5	2				9		6^2		10■														8
1		3	4	5	6		8^1			13	12	10^2	2		7			9					14		11^3											9
1		3	4		13		8■				7	14	5	2	12			9		6^2			10^1		11^3											10
1	2	3	4		14			13		11	7		5	6^3	8^2	10^1		9							12											11
1	2	3	4		13	14				11^1	8		7^3	6		12		9							10	5^2										12
1	2	3		13	10^2		8				7^1		4					9		6					11	5	12									13
1		3			9	7^2	8					12		2				13	4	6			11^1		10		5									14
1		3			8	7	13						4	2^1				9		6			11^2		10	12	5									15
1	2	3	4	5^1	7^2	10	8^3	14						12				9					13		11		6									16
1	2	3^1		5	7^3	14	8	6	13				4			10^2		9■		12					11											17
1				5	7	6	8	9^3	12				4			10^1				2			13	14	11^2			3								18
1		14		5	7		8	9	13				4			10^2		12		2^1					11	3^2	6									19
	2	3		5	7^3	14	8^1		10							13		9		4				6	11^2		12	1								20
1		3				7	8	6	14	11^3				12		10^2		9		4					13	2^1	5									21
1	2	3		5	7		8		10^1	12		13						9		4				6	11^2											22
1	2^3	3		12	7		8^2	14	10					5^1			11	9		4				6			13									23
1		3		5			8	7	14	11^3			12				13	9		4				6^2	10		2^1									24
		3		5	7		8^3	6		12			13					9	4	2^2			11^1	14	10			1								25
		3		5	7		8^1	6		11			13	12			14		4	2^2				9	10^3			1								26
		3		5		7			14	12			4			10^1	11^2			2				6				1	8^3	9	13					27
1		3		5^2		13	8	7	11				4				12			2				6	10^1					9						28
1		3							12				4^3	5		10^1	11			2				8						7	13	6	9^2	14		29
1		3							13					4			11^2		12	2				6	10					9■		5	7	8^1		30
1		3			8		9		11^2				4■			12			14	2^3				6	10^1	5						7			13	31
1		3		14	8	11			13										4	2				6^3	10^2	5					12	7^1	9			32
1		3			8^2	7		12	13										4					6	10^1	5■				9		14	11^3	2		33
1		3			13	7	14		11^2					5			12		4	2				6	10^1					8			9^3			34
1		3				7^1	10^3	14	11					13					4	2				6		5^2				8			9	12		35
1		3		2		14	9^3		13	11			12						4					6	10^2					8			7	5^1		36
1		3		5^2			9		10	11^1			14						4	2				6	12	13				8^3			7			37
1		3					9		10	11			4							2				6		5				8			7			38

HIBERNIAN Premier League

Year Formed: 1875. *Ground & Address:* Easter Road Stadium, Albion Rd, Edinburgh EH7 5QG. *Telephone:* 0131 661 2159. *Fax:* 0131 659 6488. *E-mail:* club@hibernianfc.co.uk. *Website:* www.hibernianfc.co.uk
Ground Capacity: total: 17,400. *Size of Pitch:* 112yd × 74yd.
Chairman: Rod Petrie. *Club Secretary:* Garry O'Hagan. *Marketing & Communications Manager:* Colin McNeill. *Commercial Manager:* Ian Spence.
Manager: John Collins. *Assistant Manager:* Tommy Craig. *Reserve Team Coach:* Gareth Evans.
Managers since 1975: Eddie Turnbull, Willie Ormond, Bertie Auld, Pat Stanton, John Blackley, Alex Miller, Jim Duffy, Alex McLeish, Frank Sauzee, Bobby Williamson, Tony Mowbray.
Club Nickname(s): Hibees. *Previous Grounds:* Meadows 1875-78, Powderhall 1878-79, Mayfield 1879-80, First Easter Road 1880-92, Second Easter Road 1892-.
Record Attendance: 65,860 v Hearts, Division I, 2 Jan 1950.
Record Victory: 22-1 v 42nd Highlanders, 3 Sept 1881.
Record Defeat: 0-10 v Rangers, 24 Dec 1898.
Most Capped Player: Lawrie Reilly, 38, Scotland.
Most League Appearances: 446: Arthur Duncan.
Most League Goals in Season (Individual): 42: Joe Baker.
Most Goals Overall (Individual): 364: Gordon Smith.

HIBERNIAN 2006–07 LEAGUE RECORD

Match No.	Date	Venue	Opponents	Result		H/T Score	Lg. Pos.	Goalscorers	Attendance
1	Jul 29	H	Aberdeen	D	1-1	1-1	—	Shiels [31]	15,047
2	Aug 5	A	Kilmarnock	L	1-2	1-0	9	Shiels [30]	6299
3	12	A	Inverness CT	D	0-0	0-0	9		4623
4	19	H	Motherwell	W	3-1	1-0	8	Benjelloun [33], Scott Brown [66], Jones [82]	13,274
5	26	A	Celtic	L	1-2	1-0	9	Scott Brown [8]	58,078
6	Sept 10	A	Dundee U	W	3-0	0-0	6	Killen [51], Shiels [81], Sproule [89]	6387
7	17	H	Rangers	W	2-1	1-0	5	Killen 2 [8, 80]	16,450
8	23	H	Falkirk	L	0-1	0-1	6		14,828
9	30	A	St Mirren	L	0-1	0-1	7		6008
10	Oct 15	H	Hearts	D	2-2	2-1	7	Zemmama [4], Killen [15]	16,623
11	23	A	Dunfermline Ath	W	4-0	1-0	6	Sproule [44], Killen 2 [62, 89], Benjelloun [88]	6057
12	30	A	Aberdeen	L	1-2	0-0	7	Killen [46]	11,179
13	Nov 4	H	Kilmarnock	D	2-2	0-0	8	Stewart [50], Fletcher [56]	13,510
14	11	H	Inverness CT	W	2-0	0-0	5	Fletcher [64], Killen (pen) [81]	12,868
15	18	A	Motherwell	W	6-1	4-0	4	Scott Brown [10], Killen [25], Sproule 2 [29, 40], Jones [73], Shiels [89]	6190
16	26	H	Celtic	D	2-2	1-0	4	Sproule [11]; Thomson [62]	16,747
17	Dec 2	H	Dundee U	W	2-1	0-1	4	Jones [45], Fletcher [72]	14,032
18	9	A	Rangers	L	0-3	0-3	5		49,702
19	16	A	Falkirk	L	1-2	0-2	6	Fletcher [56]	6142
20	23	H	St Mirren	W	5-1	2-1	5	Beuzelin [20], Killen [31], Shiels [57], Zemmama [64], Benjelloun [72]	13,053
21	26	A	Hearts	L	2-3	0-1	—	Killen [54], Shiels (pen) [61]	17,369
22	30	H	Dunfermline Ath	W	2-0	0-0	5	Killen 2 (1 pen) [63, 71 (p)]	14,061
23	Jan 2	H	Aberdeen	D	0-0	0-0	—		16,278
24	15	A	Kilmarnock	W	2-0	0-0	5	Sproule [51], Fletcher [87]	4963
25	21	A	Inverness CT	L	0-3	0-3	5		4577
26	27	H	Motherwell	W	2-0	0-0	5	Scott Brown [65], Benjelloun [89]	14,280
27	Feb 10	A	Celtic	L	0-1	0-0	5		59,659
28	18	A	Dundee U	D	0-0	0-0	5		6453
29	Mar 4	H	Rangers	L	0-2	0-1	5		16,265
30	10	H	Falkirk	W	2-0	0-0	5	Benjelloun 2 [50, 73]	12,572
31	Apr 1	H	Hearts	L	0-1	0-0	5		15,953
32	4	A	St Mirren	D	1-1	1-0	—	Jones [20]	4031
33	7	A	Dunfermline Ath	L	0-1	0-0	6		6001
34	21	A	Aberdeen	D	2-2	2-1	6	Gray [18], Shiels [45]	9753
35	28	H	Rangers	D	3-3	2-1	5	Fletcher [20], McCann [45], Whittaker [63]	16,747
36	May 5	H	Kilmarnock	L	0-1	0-0	6		10,674
37	12	A	Hearts	L	0-2	0-2	6		17,349
38	20	H	Celtic	W	2-1	0-0	6	Scott Brown [60], Sproule [90]	13,885

Final League Position: 6

Honours
League Champions: Division I 1902-03, 1947-48, 1950-51, 1951-52. First Division 1980-81, 1998-99. Division II 1893-94, 1894-95, 1932-33; *Runners-up:* Division I 1896-97, 1946-47, 1949-50, 1952-53, 1973-74, 1974-75.
Scottish Cup Winners: 1887, 1902; *Runners-up:* 1896, 1914, 1923, 1924, 1947, 1958, 1972, 1979, 2001.
League Cup Winners: 1972-73, 1991-92, 2006-07; *Runners-up:* 1950-51, 1968-69, 1974-75, 1993-94, 2003-04.

European: *European Cup:* 6 matches (1955-56 semi-finals). *Cup Winners' Cup:* 6 matches (1972-73). *UEFA Cup:* 63 matches (*Fairs Cup:* 1960-61 semi-finals, 1961-62, 1962-63, 1965-66, 1967-68, 1968-69, 1970-71. *UEFA Cup:* 1973-74, 1974-75, 1975-76, 1976-77, 1978-79, 1989-90, 1992-93, 2001-02, 2005-06).

Club colours: Shirt: Green with white sleeves and collar. Shorts: White with green stripe. Stockings: White with green trim.

Goalscorers: *League* (56): Killen 13 (2 pens), Shiels 7 (1 pen), Sproule 7, Benjelloun 6, Fletcher 6, Scott Brown 5, Jones 4, Zemmama 2, Beuzelin 1, Gray 1, McCann 1, Stewart 1, Thomson 1, Whittaker 1.
Scottish Cup (11): Benjelloun 3, Fletcher 1, Jones 1, Killen 1, Murphy 1, Sowumni 1, Sproule 1, Stewart 1, own goal 1.
CIS Cup (19): Benjelloun 5, Fletcher 4, Jones 3, Scott Brown 2, Shiels 2, McCluskey 1, Murphy 1, own goal 1.

Brown Simon 4	Hogg C 15	Jones R 34	Glass S 2+8	Whittaker S 34+1	Thomson K 22+1	Stewart M 23+6	Shiels D 13+11	Brown Scott 30	Killen C 17+1	Benjelloun A 16+16	Dalglish P —+2	Stevenson L 13+3	Konte A —+1	Murphy D 33	Fletcher S 24+7	Sproule I 16+16	Malkowski Z 19	Konde O 2+1	Zemmama M 17+6	Martis S 26	Shields J 3	McCluskey J 1+5	Beuzelin G 18+7	McNeil A 15	McCann K 7+1	Campbell R 2+1	Lynch S 2+1	Sowumni T 2+3	Chisholm R 5+1	McCaffrey D 1	Gray D 2+1	*Match No.*
1	2	3	4	5	6	7	8^2	9	10^3	11^1	12	13	14																			1
1	2	3		5	6	7^3	9^1	11	10^2	13	14			4	8	12																2
		3		5	6	7	9^2	10	11^1	12				4	14	13	1	2	8^3													3
		3	14	5	6	7^2	13	10		11				4	9^1	12	1		8^3	2												4
		3		5	6	7		10	13	11^1					9^3	12	1		8^2	2	4	14										5
		3		5	6	7	12	9	10	11^2				4		13	1		8^1	2												6
		3	14	5	6	7^2	12	9	10■	11^1				4	13	8^3	1			2												7
		3^1		5	6■	7	11^2	10■		14				4	8	9^3	1	12	13	2												8
			13	5		7	11^1		10^2	9				4	12	8^3	1	3	6	2		14										9
		3	12	5	6	7^1	14	11^2	10					4	13	9^3	1		8	2												10
		3	12	5	6	7		9^3	10	13				4^1		11^2	1		8		2	14										11
		3	4	5	6	7^1	14		10■						13	11^2	1		9^3	2	8		12									12
		3		5	6	7				12				4	10	11	1		9	2			8^1									13
		3		5	6^3	7		9	10	13				4	12	11^2	1		8^1	2			14									14
		3		5	6		12	9	10					4^1	7	11	1			2^2		13	8									15
		3	13	5	6	12		9		10				4	7	11^1	1			2			8^2									16
		3		5	6^1	12	14	9	10^2	13				4	7	11	1			2			8^3									17
		3		5	6	12		9^3	10^2	13				4	7	11■	1		14	2			8^1									18
		3		5	6^1	8	13	10^2		11				4	7		1		9	2			12									19
		3	12	5		8	11^3		10^2	13				4	7^1		1		6	2		14	9									20
		3		5		7	8■	9	10	11				4			1			2			6									21
		3	14	5	12	8		11	10	13				4	7^3					2		6^2	9^1	1								22
		3		5	6	7	13	9	10^1	12				4		11^2				2			8	1								23
	2	3		14	6^1		11^3	9				7		4	8	12							13	1	5	10^2						24
	2	3		5	6^1	7		9		11		12		4	13	14							8^2	1		10^3						25
		3		5	6	8^1	14	10		12		2^2		4	7^3	11				9			13	1								26
	3					8^1		10		13		2		4	7	12■				6			9	1	5		11^2					27
1	2	3		5		12		10		11		6		4^1	7^2					8			9					13				28
1	2	3		5				10		12		6		4	7	11^2			13				9					8^1				29
	2	3		5		13		10		11^3		6^1		4	7	12			8^2				9	1				14				30
	2	3		5		13		10		11		6^2		4	7^3	12			8^1				9	1				14				31
		3				6^1		10		13		14		4		11^3			8	2			12	1	5			7^2	9			32
	2	3		5			14	10		11		6^3		4	8^2	12			13				7	1					9^1			33
	2						10^1			13		6				12			8^3	3			14	1	4		7■		9	5■	11^2	34
	2			5			10^1			11		6			7	12				3			8■	1	4^2		13		9			35
	2	3		5			10			11^3		6		4^2	7	12			13					1	8^1				9		14	36
	2	3		5			10					6		4	7	12			14	9^1			8^3	1	13						11^2	37
	2	3		5			11^2	10^3				6		4	7^1	13			8					1	9	12			14			38

INVERNESS CALEDONIAN THISTLE

Premier League

Year Formed: 1994. *Ground & Address:* Tulloch Caledonian Stadium, East Longman, Inverness IV1 1FF. *Telephone:* 01463 222880. *Fax:* 01463 227479. *E-mail:* jim.falconer@ictfc.co.uk. *Website:* www.ictfc.co.uk
Ground Capacity: seated: 7400. *Size of Pitch:* 115yd × 75yd.
Chairman: Alan Savage. *President:* John MacDonald. *Chief Executive:* Mike Smith. *Secretary:* Jim Falconer. *Commercial Manager:* Darren Mackintosh. *Football and Community Development Manager:* Danny MacDonald.
Manager: Charlie Christie. *Assistant Manager:* Donald Park. *First Team Coach:* John Docherty. *Physio:* David Brandie.
Managers since 1994: S. Baltacha, S. Paterson, J. Robertson, C. Brewster.
Record Attendance: 7100 v Celtic, SPL, 16 March 2005.
Record Victory: 8-1, v Annan Ath, Scottish Cup 3rd rd, 24 January 1998.
Record Defeat: 1-5, v Morton, First Division, 12 November 1999 and v Airdrieonians, First Division, 15 April 2000.
Most League Appearances: 396, Ross Tokely, 1995-2007.
Most League Goals in Season: 27, Iain Stewart, 1996-97; Denis Wyness, 2002-03.
Most Goals Overall (Individual): 94, Denis Wyness, 2000-03, 2005-07.

INVERNESS CALEDONIAN THISTLE 2006–07 LEAGUE RECORD

Match No.	*Date*	*Venue*	*Opponents*	*Result*	*H/T Score*	*Lg. Pos.*	*Goalscorers*	*Attendance*
1	Jul 29	H	St Mirren	L 1-2	0-0	—	Dargo [48]	4267
2	Aug 5	A	Aberdeen	D 1-1	0-1	10	Wilson [89]	11,955
3	12	H	Hibernian	D 0-0	0-0	10		4623
4	20	H	Celtic	D 1-1	0-1	10	Munro [79]	7332
5	26	A	Hearts	L 1-4	1-2	10	Bayne [30]	15,912
6	Sept 9	A	Motherwell	W 4-1	1-0	10	Tokely [24], Dargo [48], Munro [79], McAllister [87]	4091
7	16	H	Dundee U	D 0-0	0-0	8		3586
8	23	A	Kilmarnock	D 1-1	1-1	9	Dargo [14]	4809
9	30	H	Dunfermline Ath	W 1-0	0-0	8	Tokely [88]	3517
10	Oct 14	A	Rangers	W 1-0	0-0	5	Bayne [72]	49,494
11	21	H	Falkirk	W 3-2	0-1	5	Dargo [70], Rankin 2 [81, 86]	3749
12	28	A	St Mirren	D 1-1	1-0	5	Dargo [34]	4432
13	Nov 6	H	Aberdeen	D 1-1	0-0	5	Bayne [79]	5744
14	11	A	Hibernian	L 0-2	0-0	6		12,868
15	18	A	Celtic	L 0-3	0-1	7		56,637
16	25	H	Hearts	D 0-0	0-0	7		5603
17	Dec 2	H	Motherwell	L 0-1	0-0	8		3668
18	9	A	Dundee U	L 1-3	1-1	8	Wilson [14]	5294
19	16	H	Kilmarnock	L 3-4	3-2	9	Dods 2 [5, 38], Dargo (pen) [43]	3728
20	23	A	Dunfermline Ath	D 0-0	0-0	9		4216
21	27	H	Rangers	W 2-1	1-1	—	Dods [41], Rankin [89]	7522
22	30	A	Falkirk	L 1-3	0-3	10	Rankin [89]	4516
23	Jan 1	H	St Mirren	W 2-1	2-0	—	Bayne [4], Wyness [21]	4246
24	13	A	Aberdeen	D 1-1	1-0	8	Rankin [86]	10,300
25	21	H	Hibernian	W 3-0	3-0	8	Dargo [20], McBain [29], Wilson [42]	4577
26	28	H	Celtic	L 1-2	0-1	8	Bayne [57]	7484
27	Feb 10	A	Hearts	L 0-1	0-0	8		16,631
28	17	A	Motherwell	L 0-1	0-0	8		4258
29	Mar 3	H	Dundee U	W 1-0	0-0	7	Wilson [90]	3901
30	10	A	Kilmarnock	L 2-3	1-3	7	Paatelainen [10], Dods [48]	7630
31	17	H	Dunfermline Ath	L 1-3	1-0	9	Paatelainen [22]	4447
32	31	A	Rangers	D 1-1	0-1	10	Dargo [82]	50,278
33	Apr 7	H	Falkirk	D 1-1	0-0	9	Rankin [85]	4435
34	21	H	Motherwell	W 2-0	2-0	9	Dargo 2 [13, 43]	3804
35	28	A	Dundee U	D 1-1	0-1	9	Bayne [57]	5273
36	May 5	A	Falkirk	L 0-1	0-0	9		3129
37	12	H	Dunfermline Ath	W 2-1	0-1	8	Hastings [76], McAllister [86]	6464
38	19	A	St Mirren	W 1-0	0-0	8	McCaffrey [73]	4834

Final League Position: 8

Honours
Scottish Cup: Semi-finals 2003, 2004; Quarter-finals 1996.
League Champions: First Division 2003-04. Third Division 1996-97; *Runners-up:* Second Division 1998-99.
Bell's League Challenge Cup Winners: 2003-04. *Runners-up:* 1999-2000.

Club colours: Shirts: Royal blue with red and black stripes. Shorts: Royal blue. Stockings: Royal blue.

Goalscorers: *League* (42): Dargo 10 (1 pen), Bayne 6, Rankin 6, Dods 4, Wilson 4, McAllister 2, Munro 2, Paatelainen 2, Tokely 2, Hastings 1, McBain 1, McCaffrey 1, Wyness 1.
Scottish Cup (8): Dargo 2, Bayne 1, Duncan 1, McBain 1, Morgan 1, Wilson 1, Wyness 1.
CIS Cup (3): Bayne 1, McAllister 1, Wyness 1.

Brown M 23	McCaffrey S 9 + 4	Golabek S 1	Munro G 36	Dods D 35	Black I 22 + 4	Rankin J 32 + 2	Duncan R 22 + 6	Wilson B 30 + 4	Dargo C 25 + 2	Wyness D 14 + 6	Keogh L 1 + 7	Bayne G 29 + 9	Tokely R 34	Hastings R 37	McBain R 30 + 2	McAllister R 5 + 14	Hart R 8 + 8	Morgan A 1 + 6	Sutherland Z 1 + 4	McSwegan G 2 + 6	Fraser M 15 + 1	Paatelainen M 6 + 5	*Match No.*
1	2	3^{2}	4	5	6	7	8^{1}	9	10	11	12	13											1
1			4	5	6	7		9	10^{2}	11^{1}	13	12	2	3	8^{3}	14							2
1			4	5	6^{2}	7		9	10	11^{1}	13	12	2	3	8								3
1			4	5	6	7^{3}	14		10	11^{1}	9	12	2	3	8^{2}		13						4
1			4	5	6	7	13	9		11^{1}	14	10	2^{2}	3	8^{3}	12							5
1			4	5	6^{2}	7^{1}		9	10^{3}		12	11	2	3	8	14		13					6
1			4	5	6^{2}	7		9^{1}	10^{3}		12	11	2	3	8	14		13					7
1			4	5	6^{1}	7		9	10^{2}			11	2	3	8	13	12						8
1			4	5		7		9	10^{1}		14	11	2	3	8^{3}	12	6^{2}		13				9
1			4	5	6	7	12	9^{1}	10^{2}			11	2	3	8		13						10
1			4	5	6	7	14	9	10^{3}	12		11	2	3^{2}	8^{1}		13						11
1			4	5		7	6	9^{1}	10			11^{2}	2	3	8	13	12						12
1			4	5		7	6	9	10^{1}	12		11	2	3	8								13
1■			4	5		7^{2}	6	9^{3}	10^{1}	12		11	2	3	8					13	14		14
			4	5		7	6	9^{1}	10	12		11	2	3	8						1		15
1			4	5	7^{1}		6	9	10^{3}	11^{2}		13	2	3	8	14	12						16
1			4	5■	7	14	6^{1}	9^{3}	10^{2}			11	2	3	8	13	12						17
1	5		4		6	7		9^{1}	10	12		11	2	3	8								18
1	12		4	5	6	7		9^{2}	10	11		14	2^{3}	3^{1}	8				13				19
1			4	5	6^{2}	7	13	9		11^{1}		12	2	3	8	10^{3}				14			20
1			4	5	6	7		9^{1}		11		10	2	3	8			12					21
1			4^{1}	5	6■	7	12			11^{3}		10^{2}	2	3	8	14		9		13			22
1	13		4	5		7	6^{1}	9^{2}		11		10	2	3	8			12					23
1	13		4	5		7	6	9^{2}	12	11^{1}		10	2	3	8								24
			4	5	13	7	6^{2}	9^{3}	10^{1}	11		12	2	3	8						1	14	25
			4	5	13	7	6^{2}	9		11^{1}		10	2	3	8	12^{3}					1	14	26
			4	5		7^{1}	6	9^{2}				10	2	3	8	11		12		13	1		27
			4	5	12	7^{2}	6^{1}	9				10	2	3	8	11^{3}				14	1	13	28
			4■	5	8	7^{2}	6	9				10	2	3		11^{1}		12			1	13	29
	4			5	8^{2}		6	9^{1}				10	2	3		14	12		13	11^{3}	1	7	30
	4			5	8	12	6^{1}	9	13			10	2	3						11^{2}	1	7	31
	12		4	5■		7	6	13	11^{3}			10	2	3			8^{2}			14	1	9^{1}	32
	5		4			7	6^{2}	9^{1}	11			10	2	3	12	13	8				1		33
	2		4	5		7	6		11^{1}			10		3	12		8				1	9	34
	2		4	5	12	7	6					10		3	8		9^{1}				1	11	35
	2^{2}		4	5		7^{1}	6	12	11			10		3	8		9				1	13	36
			4^{3}	5	7			12	11			10	2	3	8^{2}	14	6		13		1	9^{1}	37
	5		4		7		6	14	11^{1}	13		12	2	3		10^{2}	8^{3}		9		1		38

KILMARNOCK — Premier League

Year Formed: 1869. *Ground & Address:* Rugby Park, Kilmarnock KA1 2DP. *Telephone:* 01563 545300. *Fax:* 01563 522181. *Website:* www.kilmarnockfc.co.uk
Ground Capacity: all seated: 18,128. *Size of Pitch:* 115yd × 74yd.
Chairman: Michael Johnston. *Secretary:* Alex Burnett.
Manager: Jim Jefferies. *Assistant Manager:* Billy Brown. *Physio:* A. MacQueen.
Managers since 1975: W. Fernie, D. Sneddon, J. Clunie, E. Morrison, J. Fleeting, T. Burns, A. Totten, B. Brown, B. Williamson.
Club Nickname(s): Killie. *Previous Grounds:* Rugby Park (Dundonald Road); The Grange; Holm Quarry; Present ground since 1899.
Record Attendance: 35,995 v Rangers, Scottish Cup, 10 Mar 1962.
Record Transfer Fee received: £400,000 for Kris Boyd to Rangers (2006).
Record Transfer Fee paid: £300,000 for Paul Wright from St Johnstone (1995).
Record Victory: 11-1 v Paisley Academical, Scottish Cup, 18 Jan 1930 (15-0 v Lanemark, Ayrshire Cup, 15 Nov 1890).
Record Defeat: 1-9 v Celtic, Division I, 13 Aug 1938.
Most Capped Player: Joe Nibloe, 11, Scotland.
Most League Appearances: 481: Alan Robertson, 1972-88.
Most League Goals in Season (Individual): 34: Harry 'Peerie' Cunningham 1927-28 and Andy Kerr 1960-61.
Most Goals Overall (Individual): 148: W. Culley, 1912-23.

KILMARNOCK 2006–07 LEAGUE RECORD

Match No.	Date	Venue	Opponents	Result		H/T Score	Lg. Pos.	Goalscorers	Attendance
1	Jul 29	A	Celtic	L	1-4	0-2	—	Naismith [86]	54,620
2	Aug 5	H	Hibernian	W	2-1	0-1	6	Nish [48], Naismith [72]	6299
3	12	H	Dundee U	D	0-0	0-0	7		5328
4	19	A	Falkirk	W	2-1	0-1	6	Wales [44], Di Giacomo [88]	5022
5	27	H	Rangers	D	2-2	0-1	5	Wright F [63], Naismith (pen) [90]	13,506
6	Sept 9	A	Dunfermline Ath	L	2-3	1-1	7	Invincibile [9], Wales [52]	4510
7	16	A	St Mirren	W	1-0	0-0	6	Fernandez [70]	5277
8	23	H	Inverness CT	D	1-1	1-1	5	Nish [7]	4809
9	30	A	Motherwell	L	0-5	0-3	6		4765
10	Oct 14	H	Aberdeen	W	1-0	0-0	4	Wales [69]	5744
11	21	A	Hearts	W	2-0	2-0	4	Invincibile [28], Wales [35]	16,849
12	29	H	Celtic	L	1-2	0-0	6	Nish [48]	10,083
13	Nov 4	A	Hibernian	D	2-2	0-0	6	Naismith 2 [48, 64]	13,510
14	11	A	Dundee U	L	0-1	0-0	7		5815
15	18	H	Falkirk	W	2-1	0-1	6	Hay [58], O'Donnell (og) [70]	5666
16	26	A	Rangers	L	0-3	0-2	6		48,289
17	Dec 2	H	Dunfermline Ath	W	5-1	4-1	5	Hay [6], Di Giacomo 2 [18, 24], Nish 2 [26, 72]	4750
18	9	H	St Mirren	D	1-1	0-0	6	Di Giacomo [55]	5978
19	16	A	Inverness CT	W	4-3	2-3	4	Naismith 2 (1 pen) [28, 67 (p)], Nish 2 [34, 49]	3728
20	23	H	Motherwell	L	1-2	1-2	6	Naismith [39]	5576
21	26	A	Aberdeen	L	1-3	0-2	—	Naismith [89]	11,887
22	30	H	Hearts	D	0-0	0-0	6		7302
23	Jan 2	A	Celtic	L	0-2	0-1	—		57,236
24	15	H	Hibernian	L	0-2	0-0	7		4963
25	20	H	Dundee U	W	1-0	0-0	7	Leven [61]	4732
26	27	A	Falkirk	W	2-0	2-0	6	Nish [21], Naismith [27]	4696
27	Feb 11	H	Rangers	L	1-3	0-2	6	Naismith [76]	11,894
28	17	A	Dunfermline Ath	D	1-1	1-0	6	Naismith [9]	4500
29	Mar 3	A	St Mirren	W	2-0	0-0	6	Nish 2 [58, 78]	4778
30	10	H	Inverness CT	W	3-2	3-1	6	Di Giacomo 2 [17, 27], Naismith [40]	7630
31	31	H	Aberdeen	L	1-2	0-0	6	Naismith (pen) [85]	7236
32	Apr 3	A	Motherwell	W	1-0	0-0	—	Nish [89]	3784
33	7	A	Hearts	L	0-1	0-0	4		17,019
34	22	H	Celtic	L	1-2	0-1	5	Nish [49]	13,673
35	28	A	Aberdeen	L	0-3	0-1	6		10,046
36	May 5	A	Hibernian	W	1-0	0-0	5	Nish [47]	10,674
37	13	A	Rangers	W	1-0	1-0	5	Naismith [53]	50,085
38	20	H	Hearts	W	1-0	0-0	5	Naismith (pen) [82]	11,030

Final League Position: 5

Honours
League Champions: Division I 1964-65. Division II 1897-98, 1898-99; *Runners-up:* Division I 1959-60, 1960-61, 1962-63, 1963-64. First Division 1975-76, 1978-79, 1981-82, 1992-93. Division II 1953-54, 1973-74. Second Division 1989-90.
Scottish Cup Winners: 1920, 1929, 1997; *Runners-up:* 1898, 1932, 1938, 1957, 1960.
League Cup Runners-up: 1952-53, 1960-61, 1962-63, 2000-01, 2006-07.

European: *European Cup:* 4 matches (1965-66). *Cup Winners' Cup:* 4 matches (1997-98). *UEFA Cup:* 24 matches (*Fairs Cup:* 1964-65, 1966-67, 1969-70, 1970-71. *UEFA Cup:* 1998-99, 1999-2000, 2001-02).

Club colours: Shirt: Blue and white vertical stripes. Shorts: White. Stockings: White.

Goalscorers: *League* (47): Naismith 16 (4 pens), Nish 13, Di Giacomo 6, Wales 4, Hay 2, Invincibile 2, Fernandez 1, Leven 1, Wright F 1, own goal 1.
Scottish Cup (1): Nish 1.
CIS Cup (11): Naismith 4, Wright F 3, Greer 1, Invincibile 1, Murray G 1, Wales 1.

Smith G 27	Lilley D 7	Wright F 35	Greer G 33	Hay G 28 + 1	Fowler J 38	Invincibile D 24 + 1	Johnston A 25 + 3	Naismith S 35 + 2	Nish C 24 + 9	Di Giacomo P 8 + 14	Wales G 21 + 7	Leven P 20 + 7	Murray S — + 9	Murray G 30	Dodds R 3 + 6	Fernandez D 7 + 1	Ford S 12 + 4	O'Leary R 5 + 3	Locke G 4 + 8	Barrowman A — + 3	Combe A 11	Syila M 10 + 1	Quinn R 6	Koudou A 2 + 3	Gibson W 1 + 6	Hamill J 2 + 1	Match No.
1	2	3	4	5	6	7	8	9	10^{1}	11^{2}	12	13															1
1	2	3	4	5	6	7	8^{2}	9	10	11^{1}	12	13															2
1	2	3	4	5	6	7	8^{3}	9	10^{1}	13	11^{2}	14	12														3
1		3	4	5	6	7^{3}	9^{2}	10	12	14	11^{1}	8		2	13												4
1		3	4	5	6	7	9^{3}	11	10^{1}		12	8^{2}		2	14	13											5
1		3	4	5	6	7^{2}	8	10	12	13	11			2		9^{1}											6
1		3	4	5	6	7	8	10	12	13	11^{1}			2		9^{2}											7
1	4	3		5	6	7^{1}	8		10	13	11		12	2		9^{2}											8
1	4^{1}	3		5	6	7	8	12	10^{2}	14	11	13		2^{3}		9											9
1		3		5	6	7	8	10	13		11			2		9^{2}	4^{1}	12									10
1		3	4	5	6	7	8	10		13	11^{1}	12		2		9^{2}											11
1		3	4	5	6	7	9	10^{3}	12			8^{2}	13	2	14	11^{1}											12
1		3	4		6	7	9	10	11			8		2				5									13
1		3	4	5	6	7^{3}		10	11	13		8^{2}	14	2	9^{1}		12										14
1		3	4	5	6	7	9	10	11■			8		2													15
1		3	4	5	6	7	9	10		13	11^{1}	8^{2}	14	2^{3}			12										16
1		3	4	5	6	7^{1}	8	10^{2}	11	9^{3}		14	12	2	13												17
1		3	4	5	6	7	8	10	11	9				2													18
1		3	4	5	6	7	8^{1}	10	11	9				2			12										19
1		3^{2}	4	5■	6	7^{3}	8	10	11	9^{1}	12		14	2			13										20
1	3^{3}		4		6	7	8^{2}	10	9^{1}		11		14	2			5		12	13							21
1			4	5	6	7	9	10			11	8^{1}		2			3			12							22
1		3	4	5^{2}	6	7	13	12			11^{3}	8		2	10^{1}		9			14							23
		3		5	6	7^{1}	8^{3}	10	12		11■	14	13	2			4				1	9^{2}					24
		3		5	6	14	11	10	12			7		2^{1}	13		4^{2}				1	8	9^{3}				25
		3	4	5^{1}	6		12	10^{2}	11		13	7			14		2				1	8	9^{3}				26
		3^{1}	4		6		13	10		14	11	7		2	8		5^{2}		12		1		9^{3}				27
		3	4		6			10	11		9	7		2			5■		12		1		8^{1}				28
		3	4	5	6		9^{2}	10	11	8^{1}		7^{3}						2	13		1			12	14		29
1		3	4	5	6		9	10	11	8	13	7^{2}		2^{1}					12								30
1	2^{3}	3	4	5	6			10	12		11^{1}	7										8	9^{2}	14	13		31
1		3	4	5^{1}	6			10	14		11^{3}	7					2		12			8	9^{2}		13		32
1		3	4		6			10	11^{2}	13	9	7					2^{1}	12	14			8				5^{3}	33
			4		6			10^{3}	11	13	9	7		2			3	12	5^{1}		1	8^{2}			14		34
		3	4		6			10	11^{3}	14	9	7		2					5^{2}		1	8^{1}		13	12		35
		3	4		6			10	11		9^{2}			2				5	13		1	12			8^{1}	7	36
		3	4		6			10	11	12				2				5	7^{2}		1	8		9^{1}		13	37
		3	4^{1}	12	6			10	11^{2}		13			2				5	7		1	8		9^{3}	14		38

LIVINGSTON

First Division

Year Formed: 1974. *Ground:* Almondvale Stadium, Alderton Road, Livingston EH54 7DN. *Telephone:* 01506 417000. *Fax:* 01506 418888. *Email:* info@livingstonfc.co.uk. *Website:* www.livingstonfc.co.uk
Ground Capacity: 10,024 (all seated). *Size of Pitch:* 105yd × 72yd.
Chairman: Pearse Flynn. *Chief Executive:* Vivien Kyles. *General Manager:* David Hay. *Secretary:* M. Kaplan.
Team Manager: Mark Proctor. *Physios:* Arthur Duncan, Marie McPhail.
Managers since 1975: M. Lawson, T. Christie, W. MacFarlane, A. Ness, J. Bain, J. Leishman, R. Stewart, J. Leishman, M. Barcellos, D. Hay, A. Preston, R. Gough, P. Lambert, J. Robertson.
Club Nickname: Livi Lions. *Previous Grounds:* None.
Record Attendance: 10,024 v Celtic, Premier League, 18 Aug 2001.
Record Transfer Fee received: £1,000,000 for D. Fernandez to Celtic (June 2002).
Record Transfer Fee paid: £120,000 for Wes Hoolahan from Shelbourne (December 2005).
Record Victory: 7-0 v Queen of the South, Scottish Cup, 29 Jan 2000.
Record Defeat: 0-8 v Hamilton A. Division II, 14 Dec 1974.
Most Capped Player (under 18): I. Little.
Most League Appearances: 446: Walter Boyd, 1979-89.
Most League Goals in Season (Individual): 21: John McGachie, 1986-87. *(Team):* 69; Second Division, 1986-87.
Most Goals Overall (Individual): 64: David Roseburgh, 1986-93.

LIVINGSTON 2006–07 LEAGUE RECORD

Match No.	Date	Venue	Opponents	Result	H/T Score	Lg. Pos.	Goalscorers	Attendance
1	Aug 5	H	Queen of the S	W 2-0	0-0	—	Mackay [73], Shields [76]	2224
2	12	A	Ross Co	W 3-0	2-0	2	Mackay [30], Makel [45], Craig [55]	2321
3	19	H	Partick Th	D 2-2	0-1	2	Mitchell [78], Mackay [87]	2403
4	26	A	Dundee	W 1-0	0-0	2	Mackay [78]	4059
5	Sept 9	H	Airdrie U	W 3-0	2-0	1	Craig [29], McPake [44], Mitchell [65]	1754
6	16	A	Gretna	D 1-1	1-1	1	Craig [5]	2023
7	23	H	St Johnstone	D 1-1	1-1	2	Craig [16]	2359
8	30	A	Clyde	D 1-1	1-0	2	Shields [85]	1607
9	Oct 13	H	Hamilton A	L 0-1	0-1	4		1877
10	21	H	Ross Co	D 0-0	0-0	5		1760
11	28	A	Queen of the S	L 0-2	0-0	5		1752
12	Nov 4	A	Airdrie U	W 1-0	0-0	5	Tweed [90]	1455
13	11	H	Dundee	L 2-3	0-1	5	Smylie [47], Fox [90]	1568
14	18	H	Gretna	L 1-2	0-2	5	Dorrans [46]	1876
15	25	A	St Johnstone	W 2-1	1-0	5	Fox [69], Mitchell [85]	2766
16	Dec 2	A	Hamilton A	D 1-1	0-1	5	McPake [64]	1515
17	9	H	Clyde	D 1-1	1-0	5	Teggart [34]	1724
18	16	A	Partick Th	W 3-2	1-0	4	Teggart [12], Walker A [73], McPake [88]	2591
19	23	H	Queen of the S	L 0-1	0-0	4		1624
20	30	H	Airdrie U	L 1-3	1-1	5	Cuthbert [33]	1645
21	Jan 2	A	Dundee	L 0-2	0-0	—		3804
22	13	H	St Johnstone	W 3-2	1-1	4	Mackay [12], Craig [51], Teggart [80]	1549
23	20	A	Gretna	L 1-4	0-2	6	Mitchell [55]	1310
24	27	H	Hamilton A	L 1-2	1-0	6	Teggart [26]	1400
25	Feb 10	A	Clyde	W 1-0	1-0	5	Golabek [44]	1007
26	17	H	Partick Th	L 0-1	0-1	6		2221
27	24	A	Ross Co	W 2-0	0-0	5	Dorrans [77], Fox [82]	2324
28	Mar 3	H	Dundee	L 1-3	1-0	6	Dorrans [33]	1980
29	10	A	Airdrie U	L 1-3	1-0	6	Mackay (pen) [34]	1162
30	17	H	Gretna	D 1-1	1-0	7	Craig [28]	1748
31	31	A	St Johnstone	W 2-1	0-1	6	Dorrans 2 [69, 81]	2436
32	Apr 4	H	Clyde	D 0-0	0-0	—		1646
33	7	A	Hamilton A	L 0-3	0-2	6		1283
34	14	A	Queen of the S	D 1-1	0-1	6	Craig [55]	1983
35	21	H	Ross Co	D 1-1	1-0	6	Griffiths [18]	1743
36	28	A	Partick Th	D 0-0	0-0	6		2915

Final League Position: 6

Honours
League Champions: First Division: Champions: 2000-01. Second Division 1986-87, 1998-99. Third Division 1995-96; *Runners-up:* Second Division 1982-83. First Division 1987-88.
Scottish Cup: Semi-finals 2004.
League Cup Winners: 2003-04. Semi-finals 1984-85. *B&Q Cup:* Semi-finals 1992-93, 1993-94, 2001.
Bell's League Challenge Runners-up: 2000-01.

European: *UEFA Cup:* 4 matches (2002-03).

Club colours: Shirt: Gold with black sleeves and side panels. Shorts: Black. Stockings: Gold with black trim.

Goalscorers: *League* (41): Craig 7, Mackay 6 (1 pen), Dorrans 5, Mitchell 4, Teggart 4, Fox 3, McPake 3, Shields 2, Cuthbert 1, Golabek 1, Griffiths 1, Makel 1, Smylie 1, Tweed 1, Walker A 1.
Scottish Cup (5): Dorrans 2, Hamill 1, Mackay 1, Tweed 1.
CIS Cup (4): Craig 2 (1 pen), Dorrans 1, Hislop 1.
Challenge Cup (1): Craig 1.

Wight J 17 + 1	Thomson J 18	Mackay D 34	McPake J 33	Tweed S 28	Mitchell S 32	Smylie D 7 + 11	Walker A 28 + 3	Shields P 4 + 13	Makel L 28 + 3	Craig S 24 + 3	Hamill J 25 + 8	Millar G 8 + 5	Weir S — + 6	Hislop S 4 + 6	Stewart C 19	Dorrans G 25 + 9	Fox L 11 + 11	Kerr S — + 2	Teggart M 16 + 3	Snodgrass R 1 + 5	Davidson M — + 2	Cuthbert S 4	Griffiths L 2 + 2	Golabek S 10	Mole J 9 + 3	Anderson S 6	Adamson K 2 + 1	Torrance M 1 + 1	Match No.
1	2	3	4	5^{2}	6	7^{1}	8	9	10	11^{3}	12	13	14																1
1	2	3	4	5	6	14	8	9^{1}	10	11^{2}	7^{3}		13	12															2
	2	3	4	5	6	13	8^{2}		10	11^{3}	7		14	9^{1}	1	12													3
	2	3	6	4	5	12	8^{1}		7	9^{2}	11		14	13	1	10^{3}													4
1	2	3	4	5	6		8	12	10^{3}	11^{1}	7		13			9^{2}	14												5
1	2	3	4	5■	6		8^{1}	13	10	11^{3}	7		14			9^{2}	12												6
1	2^{1}	3	4		6	5	8	9^{2}	10	11^{3}	7			14		13	12												7
1		3	4	5^{1}	6	14	8	12	10	11■	7^{3}			13		9	2^{2}												8
	2	3	4		6	13	8^{2}	11^{3}	10		7^{1}			12	1	9	5	14											9
	2	3	4	5	6		14	13	10	11^{3}	12			7	1	9^{2}	8^{1}												10
	2	3	4	5^{3}	6	8^{1}	13	14	10	7	11^{2}			9	1	12													11
	2	3	4■	5	6	13	12		10^{3}	8^{1}	11^{2}				1	7	14		9										12
	2	3		5	6	4^{1}	8	14	10^{2}		12			13	1	7^{3}	11		9										13
12	2	3		5	6	13	8	14	10^{2}		11^{1}				1■	7	4		9^{3}										14
1	2	3	4	5	6		8	13		9^{2}	11^{1}					7^{3}	10			12	14								15
1	2	3	4	5	6^{1}	14	8		12	11^{2}	13					7	10^{3}		9										16
1		3	4	5^{3}	2	13	8	12	10	11■	6^{2}					7			9^{1}		14								17
1		3	4		2	13	8		10		11			6^{2}		7			9^{1}	12		5							18
1		3	4	5	2		8		10	14	13					7^{3}	11^{2}		9^{1}	12		6							19
1		3		5	2	7	8	13	10		11^{2}					9^{3}	6^{1}			12		4	14						20
1		3	4	5			8	12	10		11^{1}	2				7				9^{2}		6	13						21
1		2	4	5	6	10	8		12	9^{3}	11^{1}	3				7^{2}			13	14									22
1		2	4	5	6	10^{1}	8		12	9	11^{2}	3				7			13										23
		2	4	5	6		8		10■	11^{2}		13			1	12			9^{1}					3	7				24
		2	4	5	6		8			11^{2}	7				1	13	12		9^{1}					3	10				25
		10	4	5	6		8^{3}			13	11	2^{1}			1	12	14		9^{2}					3	7				26
		2	4	5	6		8		10		7^{1}				1	12	13		9^{2}					3	11				27
		2	4	5^{3}	6		8		10^{1}	11^{2}	13	14			1	7	12							3	9				28
		2	4	5■	6	14	8	13	10^{3}			12			1	11^{1}			9^{2}					3	7■				29
		2	4		6^{1}		8	13	10	11		5			1	7	12		9^{2}					3					30
		2	4		6				10	7^{2}	11^{1}	5			1	12	13							3	9	8			31
		2^{2}	4	5	6				10		12	13			1	7			11^{1}					3	9	8			32
		2	4	5	6^{3}				10■	12	14				1	7	13		9^{1}					3	11^{2}	8			33
	2^{2}	5	4				8			10^{3}	11	3			1	14	7		9^{1}						12	6	13		34
1	2		6						5^{1}	9^{2}	11					7	4■	14					10^{3}		13	8	3	12	35
1	2		6							9^{2}	11	4				7			12				10^{1}		13	5	3	8	36

MONTROSE Third Division

Year Formed: 1879. *Ground & Address:* Links Park, Wellington St, Montrose DD10 8QD. *Telephone:* 01674 673200. *Fax:* 01674 677311. *E-mail:* montrosefootballclub@tesco.net. *Website:* www.montrosefc.co.uk
Ground Capacity: total: 3292, seated: 1338. *Size of Pitch:* 113yd × 70yd.
Chairman: Brian Winton. *Secretary:* Malcolm J. Watters.
Manager: Jim Weir. *Physio:* Brian Duncan.
Managers since 1975: A. Stuart, K. Cameron, R. Livingstone, S. Murray, D. D'Arcy, I. Stewart, C. McLelland, D. Rougvie, J. Leishman, J Holt, A. Dornan, D. Smith, T. Campbell, K. Drinkell, H. Hall, E. Wolecki and D. Robertson.
Club Nickname(s): The Gable Endies. *Previous Grounds:* None.
Record Attendance: 8983 v Dundee, Scottish Cup 3rd rd, 17 Mar 1973.
Record Transfer Fee received: £50,000 for Gary Murray to Hibernian (Dec 1980).
Record Transfer Fee paid: £17,500 for Jim Smith from Airdrieonians (Feb 1992).
Record Victory: 12-0 v Vale of Leithen, Scottish Cup 2nd rd, 4 Jan 1975.
Record Defeat: 0-13 v Aberdeen, 17 Mar 1951.
Most Capped Player: Alexander Keillor, 2 (6), Scotland.
Most League Appearances: 432: David Larter, 1987-98.
Most League Goals in Season (Individual): 28: Brian Third, Division II, 1972-73.

MONTROSE 2006–07 LEAGUE RECORD

Match No.	Date	Venue	Opponents	Result		H/T Score	Lg. Pos.	Goalscorers	Attendance
1	Aug 5	H	Dumbarton	D	1-1	1-1	—	Henslee 28	404
2	12	A	Stenhousemuir	L	0-5	0-1	9		336
3	19	H	Elgin C	W	2-0	2-0	7	Kerrigan 5, Michie 37	354
4	26	A	Arbroath	L	1-3	1-1	9	Michie 16	1010
5	Sept 3	H	Albion R	W	2-1	0-0	9	Rodgers 2 (2 pens) 51, 57	245
6	9	H	East Fife	W	1-0	1-0	4	Michie 38	424
7	16	A	Queen's Park	D	1-1	0-0	6	Rodgers (pen) 58	404
8	23	H	East Stirling	W	1-0	0-0	4	Rodgers 80	280
9	30	A	Berwick R	W	2-1	0-1	3	Henslee 48, McLeod 86	386
10	Oct 14	A	Dumbarton	L	0-2	0-1	4		634
11	21	H	Stenhousemuir	L	0-1	0-0	7		404
12	28	A	Albion R	L	1-3	0-2	7	Henslee 52	485
13	Nov 4	H	Arbroath	L	0-1	0-1	7		1143
14	11	H	Queen's Park	L	0-3	0-1	8		325
15	25	A	East Fife	L	0-2	0-1	8		472
16	Dec 2	A	East Stirling	W	3-0	3-0	8	Stirling 2, Higgins 7, Mercer 14	173
17	16	H	Berwick R	L	0-1	0-1	8		451
18	23	H	Dumbarton	L	0-5	0-1	8		431
19	30	A	Elgin C	L	2-3	2-2	8	Michie 5, Campbell (og) 39	501
20	Jan 2	A	Arbroath	L	0-1	0-1	—		1295
21	13	H	Albion R	L	2-3	1-1	8	Rodgers 38, Michie 64	249
22	20	A	Queen's Park	L	0-5	0-2	8		414
23	27	H	East Fife	D	3-3	0-2	8	Black 2 67, 86, Michie 70	423
24	Feb 3	H	East Stirling	W	4-0	0-0	8	Rodgers 47, Black 66, Stephen 75, Henslee 87	323
25	10	A	Berwick R	L	0-1	0-1	8		323
26	17	H	Elgin C	L	0-1	0-1	8		355
27	24	A	Stenhousemuir	W	5-2	1-2	8	Stephen 3 17, 64, 80, Michie 70, Black 76	287
28	Mar 3	H	Arbroath	L	0-1	0-1	8		1256
29	10	A	Albion R	D	2-2	1-1	8	Baird 1, Rodgers 49	412
30	17	H	Queen's Park	L	0-2	0-1	8		461
31	25	H	Berwick R	L	1-2	1-1	8	Docherty 26	441
32	31	A	East Fife	L	0-2	0-0	8		484
33	Apr 7	A	East Stirling	W	2-0	0-0	8	Baird 59, Rodgers 79	265
34	14	A	Dumbarton	L	1-2	1-1	8	Baird 28	530
35	21	H	Stenhousemuir	W	3-2	2-2	8	Baird (pen) 2, Rodgers 2 8, 87	343
36	28	A	Elgin C	W	2-0	1-0	8	Baird 8, Docherty 60	536

Final League Position: 8

Honours
League Champions: Second Division 1984-85; *Runners-up:* 1990-91. Third Division, *Runners-up:* 1994-95.
Scottish Cup: Quarter-finals 1973, 1976.
League Cup: Semi-finals 1975-76.
B&Q Cup: Semi-finals 1992-93.
League Challenge Cup: Semi-finals 1996-97.

Club colours: Shirt: Royal blue. Shorts: Royal blue. Stockings: White.

Goalscorers: *League* (42): Rodgers 10 (3 pens), Michie 7, Baird 5 (1 pen), Black 4, Henslee 4, Stephen 4, Docherty 2, Higgins 1, Kerrigan 1, McLeod 1, Mercer 1, Stirling 1, own goal 1.
Scottish Cup (2): Henslee 1, Stirling 1.
CIS Cup (1): Rodgers 1.
Challenge Cup (2): Henslee 1, Michie 1.

Reid A 27	Donachie B 29+3	Fraser S 9+3	Higgins C 14	McLeod C 29	Adam J 8+9	Davidson H 22+3	Henslee G 27+4	Rodgers A 33	Watson C 1	Walker P 2	Napier P 16+13	Tawse C 10+4	Reid P 1+10	Cumming S 27+4	Stirling J 27+1	Kerrigan S 7+11	Michie S 24+9	Farquhar J 1+1	Stewart G 4+5	Alexander J —+2	Kelly D 6+2	Mackie R —+1	Stewart P 1+5	Ndiwa K 1	Gibson K 13	Mercer J 4	Stephen N 14	Black S 7+1	Bell C 4	Woods S 1	Docherty M 9	Baird J 8+1	Malcolm S 6	McKenzie S 4	Maitland J —+2	Keith S —+1	*Match No.*
1	2	3	4	5	6	7	8[1]	9	10[2]	11[3]	12	13	14																								1
1■		3		5	6[1]		7	9		11[2]	12		13	2	4	8	10[G]	15																			2
	14	11	4	5	13		8	9			12	2		7[2]	3[1]	6	10[3]	1																			3
1	14	11[2]	4[1]	5	13		8	9			12	2		7[3]	3	6	10																				4
1	6	13	4	5	8[3]		11	9[1]			7			2	3[2]	12	10		14																		5
1	6[1]			5	8		11	9			7	4		2	3	13	10[2]		12																		6
1		13	4	5	6	2[2]	7	9			11				3[3]	12	10[1]		8	14																	7
1	6		4	5	13	11[3]	7	9			12			14	3	8[1]	10		2[2]																		8
1	6	14	4[2]	5	8	12	7[1]	9			11[3]			2	3		10				13																9
1	6	3		5	8	12	7	9			11	4		2[1]		13	10[2]																				10
1	6	3		5	14	8	7[1]	9■			11[3]			2		12	10		13		4[2]																11
1	6	3			8	7	10				11[2]	12		4	5	9[3]	13		2[1]			14															12
1	6	3			14	8	11	9■			12	5		2	4[3]	13	10[2]		7[1]																		13
1	6[2]	11[1]		5	13	8	9				7[3]	4		2	3	10				14			12														14
1	7		5[2]		12[3]	8	11				13			2	3	14	10							4	6[1]	9											15
1	6[2]		4	5	13	8	7	9						2	3	14	10[1]						12			11[3]											16
1	6[1]		4	5		7	11[3]	9			13			2[2]	3	14	12								8	10											17
1	14		4	5		6	8[2]	9			11			7[1]	3[3]	12	10						13				2										18
1	2		5[3]		12			9			7[2]			14	3	8[1]	10		13						6	11	4										19
1	2					8	7[1]	9			11			4	3		10[2]		13						6		5	12									20
1	2		5			8	7	9			12			4	3		10								6			11[1]									21
1	2		6	5		4	7[2]	10			13		14	3[1]	12		9								8			11[3]									22
1	6			5		8	12	9			7[1]	2			3		10										4	11									23
1	6			5		8	12	9			7[1]	2[2]	14	13	3		10[3]										4	11									24
1	6			5		8	12	9			7[1]	2	13	14	3[3]		10[2]										4	11									25
1	6			5			8	9[3]			12	2	14	7	3[1]	13	10[2]										4	11									26
	6			5			12	9[3]				13	14	2	3[2]		10								8		4	11	1	7[1]							27
	6			5		12	7	9[2]					14	2	3		10[3]								8■		4		1		11[1]	13					28
	6			5■		8	7[1]	9[2]			13	12		2	3												4		1		11	10					29
						6■		9			11[2]		13	7	3		12				2						4		1		8[1]	10	5				30
1				4			11	9[1]			12		7[2]	6	3[3]		13				2		14								8	10	5				31
1	6			4			11	9					13	2[1]			12				3				7[2]						8	10	5				32
	6			4			11	9[1]						2			12				3		13		7[3]						8	10[2]	5	1	14		33
	6[2]			4		2		9									13				3		11[1]		7		5				8	10		1		12	34
	6			4		2		9			11[1]						12								7		3				8	10	5	1			35
	6			4		11		9[1]						2			12				13				7		3[2]				8[3]	10	5	1	14		36

MORTON

First Division

Year Formed: 1874. *Ground & Address:* Cappielow Park, Sinclair St, Greenock. *Telephone:* 01475 723571. *Fax:* 01475 781084. *E-mail:* info@gmfc.net. *Website:* www.gmfc.net
Ground Capacity: total: 11,612, seated: 6062. *Size of Pitch:* 110yd × 71yd.
Chairman: Douglas Rae. *Chief Executive:* Gillian Donaldson. *Company Secretary:* Mary Davidson. *Commercial Manager:* Susan Gregory.
Manager: Jim McInally. *Assistant Manager:* Martin Clark. *Physios:* Paul Kelly, Bruce Coyle. *Managers since 1975:* Joe Gilroy, Benny Rooney, Alex Miller, Tommy McLean, Willie McLean, Allan McGraw, Billy Stark, Ian McCall, Allan Evans, Peter Cormack, Dave McPherson, J. McCormack.
Club Nickname(s): The Ton. *Previous Grounds:* Grant Street 1874, Garvel Park 1875, Cappielow Park 1879, Ladyburn Park 1882, (Cappielow Park 1883).
Record Attendance: 23,500 v Celtic, 29 April 1922.
Record Transfer Fee received: £350,000 for Neil Orr to West Ham U.
Record Transfer Fee paid: £150,000 for Alan Mahood from Nottingham Forest (August 1998).
Record Victory: 11-0 v Carfin Shamrock, Scottish Cup 1st rd, 13 Nov 1886.
Record Defeat: 1-10 v Port Glasgow Ath, Division II, 5 May, 1894 and v St Bernards, Division II, 14 Oct 1933.
Most Capped Player: Jimmy Cowan, 25, Scotland.
Most League Appearances: 358: David Hayes, 1969-84.
Most League Goals in Season (Individual): 58: Allan McGraw, Division II, 1963-64.

MORTON 2006–07 LEAGUE RECORD

Match No.	*Date*	*Venue*	*Opponents*	*Result*	*H/T Score*	*Lg. Pos.*	*Goalscorers*	*Attendance*
1	Aug 5	H	Raith R	W 2-0	1-0	—	Templeman [23], Campbell (og) [52]	2855
2	12	A	Stranraer	W 3-0	0-0	2	Sharp (og) [55], Stevenson [60], Millar [85]	744
3	19	H	Ayr U	D 0-0	0-0	1		2681
4	26	A	Peterhead	W 4-0	4-0	1	Weatherson [5], McGowan 2 [18, 34], Millar [45]	735
5	Sept 3	H	Alloa Ath	W 4-0	2-0	1	McGowan [12], Lilley [27], Millar [59], Templeman [89]	2226
6	9	A	Cowdenbeath	W 2-1	2-0	1	Greacen [31], McAlister [44]	1315
7	16	H	Stirling A	D 1-1	0-0	1	Lilley [83]	2591
8	23	A	Forfar Ath	W 3-1	1-0	1	Lilley [17], McGowan [61], Millar [68]	701
9	30	H	Brechin C	W 1-0	1-0	1	McAlister [37]	2526
10	Oct 14	A	Raith R	W 3-1	0-1	1	McLaughlin [69], Lilley (pen) [72], Templeman [89]	2600
11	21	H	Stranraer	W 3-0	2-0	1	Stevenson [2], Weatherson [7], McGowan [80]	2589
12	28	A	Alloa Ath	L 2-3	1-3	1	Weatherson 2 [33, 65]	1138
13	Nov 4	H	Peterhead	W 4-2	1-2	1	McGowan [43], Weatherson [61], McLaughlin [88], Finlayson [90]	2418
14	11	A	Stirling A	L 1-2	0-0	1	Millar [82]	2069
15	25	H	Cowdenbeath	W 1-0	0-0	1	Templeman [74]	2303
16	Dec 2	H	Forfar Ath	D 1-1	0-1	1	Millar [55]	1991
17	16	A	Brechin C	W 3-2	3-1	1	McAlister [11], Templeman [16], Weatherson [20]	606
18	23	H	Raith R	W 1-0	0-0	1	Stevenson [52]	2398
19	30	A	Ayr U	W 1-0	0-0	1	Harding [69]	1987
20	Jan 2	A	Peterhead	W 2-1	1-0	—	Millar [21], Keenan [75]	819
21	13	H	Alloa Ath	W 2-1	0-1	1	Templeman [65], Weatherson [79]	2067
22	20	H	Stirling A	W 2-1	1-0	1	McGowan [19], McAlister [71]	3187
23	27	A	Cowdenbeath	D 1-1	1-1	1	McGowan [28]	785
24	Feb 10	H	Brechin C	L 0-2	0-0	1		2134
25	17	H	Ayr U	W 4-2	1-1	1	Templeman 2 [13, 53], McAlister [78], Linn [84]	2601
26	24	A	Stranraer	L 1-2	1-0	1	Templeman [2]	631
27	Mar 3	H	Peterhead	W 2-1	0-0	1	Stevenson [50], Weatherson [76]	2346
28	10	A	Alloa Ath	W 3-0	1-0	1	Weatherson [45], Stevenson [55], Templeman [74]	983
29	17	A	Stirling A	L 1-2	1-0	1	McGowan [34]	2608
30	25	A	Forfar Ath	W 4-0	2-0	1	Greacen 2 [5, 31], Templeman [59], Weatherson [76]	765
31	31	H	Cowdenbeath	W 3-0	2-0	1	Stevenson (pen) [9], McGowan 2 [28, 70]	2702
32	Apr 3	A	Brechin C	W 1-0	1-0	—	Greacen [3]	776
33	7	H	Forfar Ath	W 9-1	3-0	1	Weatherson 4 [8, 14, 52, 65], Stevenson 2 (1 pen) [21, 75 (p)], Millar [83], Linn [85], Templeman [9]	3007
34	14	A	Raith R	L 0-2	0-0	1		4327
35	21	H	Stranraer	D 1-1	1-1	1	Weatherson [21]	5276
36	28	A	Ayr U	L 0-1	0-0	1		1998

Final League Position: 1

Honours
League Champions: First Division 1977-78, 1983-84, 1986-87. Division II 1949-50, 1963-64, 1966-67. Second Division 1994-95, 2006-07. Third Division 2002-03. *Runners-up:* Division 1 1916-17, Division II 1899-1900, 1928-29, 1936-37.
Scottish Cup Winners: 1922; *Runners-up:* 1948. *League Cup Runners-up:* 1963-64.
B&Q Cup Runners-up: 1992-93.

European: *UEFA Cup:* 2 matches (*Fairs Cup:* 1968-69).

Club colours: Shirt: Royal blue with 3½ inch white hoops. Shorts: White with royal blue panel down side. Stockings: Royal blue with white tops.

Goalscorers: *League* (76): Weatherson 15, Templeman 12, McGowan 11, Millar 8, Stevenson 8 (2 pens), McAlister 5, Greacen 4, Lilley 4 (1 pen), Linn 2, McLaughlin 2, Finlayson 1, Harding 1, Keenan 1, own goals 2.
Scottish Cup (6): Templeman 2, Greacen 1, McGowan 1, Stevenson 1, Weatherson 1.
CIS Cup (1): McGowan 1.
Challenge Cup (9): McGowan 3, Weatherson 2, Harding 1, McLaughlin 1, Millar 1, own goal 1.

McGurn D 12 + 2	Keenan D 8 + 8	MacGregor D 25 + 2	Harding R 36	Greacen S 35	McLaughlin S 28 + 1	Millar C 30 + 6	Stevenson J 36	Templeman C 23 + 12	McGowan P 35 + 1	McAlister J 36	Lilley D 11 + 8	McLean K — + 4	Walker A 10 + 7	Weatherson P 34	Finlayson K 9 + 21	Russell R 1 + 7	Gonet S 4	Mathers P 20	Linn R 2 + 14	Graham B 1	Black C — + 1	McKellar S — + 1	*Match No.*
1	2	3	4	5	6	7	8^3	9^1	10^2	11	12	13	14										1
1	13		4	5	6^3	7	8	9^1	10^2	11	12	14	3	2									2
1			4	5	6	7	8	9^1	10^2	11	12	13	3	2									3
1	14		4	5	6	7	8^2	12	10^1	11	9^3		3	2	13								4
1	3		4	5	6	7^2	8	14	10^1	11	9^3			2	12	13							5
	3		4	5	6	7	8^3	13	10^2	11	9^1	14		2	12		1						6
			4	5	6	7	8^3	13	10	11^1	9		3	2^2	12	14	1						7
			4	5	6^2	7	8	12	10	11	9^1		3	2	13		1						8
	13		4	5	6	7	8^2	12	10^3	11	9^1		3	2	14		1						9
1	14		4	5	6	7	8^3	13	10^1	11	9		3^2	2	12								10
1		12	4^1	5	6	7	8^2	14	10	11	9^3		3	2	13								11
1		14	4^3	5	6	7	8	13	10	11	9^2		3^1	2	12								12
1		3	4	5	6	7	8^3	13	10^2	11	9^1		14	2	12								13
1		3	4^3	5	6	7	8	13	10^1	11	12			2	9^2	14							14
1		3	4	5	6	7	8^3	12	10^2	11	9^1		14	2	13								15
		3^1	4	5	6	7	8	9	10	11	12			2				1					16
	6	3	4	5		7	8^1	9^3	10^2	11	13		14	2	12			1					17
	12	3	4	5		7	8	9	10^2	11	13			2	6^1			1					18
	6	3	4	5		7	8	9	10^1	11				2	12			1					19
	6	3	4	5		7	8^2	9^3	10^1	11	14			2	12	13		1					20
	6^2	3	4	5		7	8^1	9	10	11				2	12			1	13				21
		3	4	5	12	7	8^1	9	10^2	11				2	6			1	13				22
15		3	4	5	6	7	8^1	9^2	10	11				2	12			1^6	13				23
	13	3	4^3	5		7^2	8^1	9	10	11				2	12	14		1	6				24
		3	4	5	6	7	8^1	9	10^2	11				2	12			1	13				25
		3	4	5	6	7	8^1	9	10^2	11				2	12			1	13				26
	13	3	4	5	6	7^3	8^1	9	10^2	11			14	2				1	12				27
		3^2	4	5	6	7^1	8	9	10^3	11			13	2	12			1	14				28
	12^3	3	4	5	6	7	8^1	9^2	10	11				2	14			1	13				29
15		3	4	5	6^2	13	8	9	10	11^1				2	7			1^6	12				30
		3	4	5^1	6	13	8^2	9	10^3	11			12	2	7			1	14				31
		3	4	5	6	13	8^2	9	10^1	11				2	7			1	12				32
		3	4	5	6^1	12	8	9	10^2	11^3				2	7	14		1	13				33
		3	4	5	6	12	8	9^2	10^3	11				2	7^1	14		1	13				34
		3	4	5	6	12	8	9^2	10	11				2	7^1			1	13				35
1	2	3^2	4			7	8		12	11			5			6			9^1	10^2	13	14	36

MOTHERWELL — Premier League

Year Formed: 1886. *Ground & Address:* Fir Park Stadium, Motherwell ML1 2QN. *Telephone:* 01698 333333. *Fax:* 01698 338001.
E-mail: info@motherwellfc.co.uk. *Website:* www.motherwellfc.co.uk
Ground Capacity: all seated: 13,742. *Size of Pitch:* 110yd × 75yd.
Chairman: Willian H. Dickie. *Secretary:* Stewart Robertson.
Manager: Mark McGhee. *Assistant Manager:* Scott Leitch. *Physios:* John Porteous, R. Mayberry.
Managers since 1975: Ian St. John, Willie McLean, Rodger Hynd, Ally MacLeod, David Hay, Jock Wallace, Bobby Watson, Tommy McLean, Alex McLeish, Harri Kampman, Billy Davies, Eric Black, Terry Butcher, Maurice Malpas.
Club Nickname(s): The Well. *Previous Grounds:* Roman Road, Dalziel Park.
Record Attendance: 35,632 v Rangers, Scottish Cup 4th rd replay, 12 Mar 1952.
Record Transfer Fee received: £1,750,000 for Phil O'Donnell to Celtic (September 1994).
Record Transfer Fee paid: £500,000 for John Spencer from Everton (Jan 1999).
Record Victory: 12-1 v Dundee U, Division II, 23 Jan 1954.
Record Defeat: 0-8 v Aberdeen, Premier Division, 26 Mar 1979.
Most Capped Player: Tommy Coyne, 13, Republic of Ireland.
Most League Appearances: 626: Bobby Ferrier, 1918-37.
Most League Goals in Season (Individual): 52: Willie McFadyen, Division I, 1931-32.
Most Goals Overall (Individual): 283: Hugh Ferguson, 1916-25.

MOTHERWELL 2006–07 LEAGUE RECORD

Match No.	Date	Venue	Opponents	Result	H/T Score	Lg. Pos.	Goalscorers	Attendance
1	Jul 30	H	Rangers	L 1-2	0-1	—	O'Donnell [51]	11,745
2	Aug 5	A	St Mirren	L 0-2	0-1	12		5036
3	12	H	Aberdeen	L 0-2	0-1	12		5186
4	19	A	Hibernian	L 1-3	0-1	12	McDonald [90]	13,274
5	26	A	Falkirk	W 1-0	0-0	11	McDonald [58]	4594
6	Sept 9	H	Inverness CT	L 1-4	0-1	12	McDonald [71]	4091
7	17	H	Hearts	L 0-1	0-0	12		5931
8	23	A	Dundee U	D 1-1	0-0	12	Elliot [60]	5036
9	30	H	Kilmarnock	W 5-0	3-0	12	Foran [15], Reynolds [20], Kerr [23], McDonald 2 [81, 85]	4765
10	Oct 14	H	Dunfermline Ath	W 2-1	0-0	10	McDonald [60], Clarkson [83]	4527
11	21	A	Celtic	L 1-2	0-1	10	McDonald [77]	57,742
12	28	A	Rangers	D 1-1	0-1	10	Kerr [50]	49,785
13	Nov 4	H	St Mirren	D 0-0	0-0	10		5337
14	11	A	Aberdeen	L 1-2	0-0	11	Hart (og) [61]	10,527
15	18	H	Hibernian	L 1-6	0-4	11	McGarry [83]	6190
16	25	H	Falkirk	W 4-2	0-1	11	Foran 2 (2 pens) [45, 46], McDonald [74], Elliot [83]	4970
17	Dec 2	A	Inverness CT	W 1-0	0-0	9	Foran (pen) [88]	3668
18	9	A	Hearts	L 1-4	1-1	11	Foran [19]	16,753
19	16	H	Dundee U	L 2-3	0-2	11	Foran (pen) [62], Reynolds [67]	4420
20	23	A	Kilmarnock	W 2-1	2-1	10	Foran [15], Paterson [20]	5576
21	26	A	Dunfermline Ath	W 2-0	1-0	—	Fitzpatrick [35], McDonald [78]	4200
22	30	H	Celtic	D 1-1	0-1	9	Smith D [90]	9769
23	Jan 2	H	Rangers	L 0-1	0-0	—		10,338
24	27	A	Hibernian	L 0-2	0-0	10		14,280
25	Feb 10	A	Falkirk	W 2-1	0-0	10	McDonald [65], Smith D [66]	4478
26	17	H	Inverness CT	W 1-0	0-0	10	McDonald [44]	4258
27	21	A	St Mirren	D 0-0	0-0	—		3576
28	Mar 5	H	Hearts	L 0-2	0-1	—		4389
29	10	A	Dundee U	D 1-1	1-1	9	Murphy D [36]	5183
30	13	H	Aberdeen	L 0-2	0-1	—		4530
31	31	H	Dunfermline Ath	W 2-0	0-0	9	McDonald 2 (1 pen) [49 (p), 62]	4511
32	Apr 3	H	Kilmarnock	L 0-1	0-0	—		3784
33	7	A	Celtic	L 0-1	0-0	10		58,654
34	21	A	Inverness CT	L 0-2	0-2	10		3804
35	28	H	Falkirk	D 3-3	2-0	10	Smith D [18], McDonald [37], Clarkson [58]	3640
36	May 7	A	Dunfermline Ath	L 1-4	1-2	10	McDonald [86]	6662
37	12	H	St Mirren	L 2-3	1-0	10	McCormack 2 [37, 48]	9277
38	19	A	Dundee U	D 0-0	0-0	10		6070

Final League Position: 10

Honours
League Champions: Division I 1931-32. First Division 1981-82, 1984-85. Division II 1953-54, 1968-69; *Runners-up:* Premier Division 1994-95. Division I 1926-27, 1929-30, 1932-33, 1933-34. Division II 1894-95, 1902-03. *Scottish Cup:* 1952, 1991; *Runners-up:* 1931, 1933, 1939, 1951.
League Cup Winners: 1950-51. *Runners-up:* 1954-55, 2004-05. *Scottish Summer Cup:* 1944, 1965.

European: *Cup Winners' Cup:* 2 matches (1991-92). *UEFA Cup:* 6 matches (1994-95, 1995-96).

Club colours: Shirt: Amber with claret hoop and trimmings. Shorts: Amber. Stockings: Amber with claret trim.

Goalscorers: *League* (41): McDonald 15 (1 pen), Foran 7 (4 pens), Smith D 3, Clarkson 2, Elliot 2, Kerr 2, McCormack 2, Reynolds 2, Fitzpatrick 1, McGarry 1, Murphy 1, O'Donnell 1, Paterson 1, own goal 1.
Scottish Cup (4): Foran 1, Kerr 1, McCormack 1, McDonald 1.
CIS Cup (8): Foran 6, Clarkson 1, McGarry 1.

Smith G 23 + 1	Quinn P 24 + 2	Paterson J 34	Donnelly R 2	Craigan S 34	Kerr B 35	O'Donnell P 3	McGarry S 22 + 7	Foran R 22 + 1	McCormack R 6 + 6	Hamilton J 2 + 1	McDonald S 30 + 2	Clarkson D 19 + 10	Fitzpatrick M 13 + 11	Reynolds M 35	McBride K 10 + 7	Lasley K 14	Elliot C 10 + 4	McLean B 1 + 4	Coakley A — + 2	Meldrum C 15 + 1	Kinniburgh W 4 + 1	Corrigan M 19 + 3	Smith D 12 + 6	Murphy D 13 + 1	Molloy T — + 6	Keegan P 4 + 4	Vadocz K 11	Connolly K 1 + 1	Murphy J — + 1	*Match No.*
1	2	3	4	5	6	7	8^{3}	9^{2}	10^{1}	11	12	13	14																	1
1	2	3	4	5	6	7	8	9^{1}	10^{2}	11	12	13																		2
1	2	3		5	6	7	8^{1}	12		13	10	11		4	9^{2}															3
1	2	3		5	6		8		12		10	11^{1}		4	9	7														4
1	2^{2}	3^{1}		5	6			9			10	14	12	4	8	7	11^{3}	13												5
1	2	3^{1}		5	6		13	9			10			4	8^{2}	7	11^{3}	12	14											6
	2	7		5	6		12	11	13		10		8^{2}	4		9		3^{1}		1										7
	2	3		5	6		9	11^{1}			10		7	4		8	12			1										8
	2	3		5	6		8	9^{2}	14		10^{3}	12	13	4		7	11^{1}			1										9
	2	3		5	6		7	9			10	12		4		8	11^{1}			1										10
	2	3		5	6		7	9			10	12		4		8	11^{1}			1										11
	2	3^{2}		5	6		7^{1}	9			10		13	4	12	8	11			1										12
	2	3^{2}		5	6		7^{1}	9				10	13	4	12	8	11^{3}		14	1										13
	2	3		5^{3}	6		7^{2}	9				10	12	4	13	8	11^{1}			1	14									14
	2	3			6		7	9^{2}			10^{1}	11	13	4	12	8				1	5									15
	2	3			6		7^{2}	9			10	11^{1}		4		8	12			1	5	13								16
	2	3		5^{3}	6		7	9			10	11^{1}		4		8^{2}		12		1		13	14							17
	7	3		5	6		8^{1}	9			10	11	12	4						1		2^{2}	13							18
	7^{2}	3		5	6		14	9			10	11^{1}	13	4			12			1		2	8^{3}							19
1		3■		5	6		13	9			10^{3}	14■	7	4	12		11^{1}					2	8^{2}							20
1	3			5	6		12	9			10		7	4			11					2	8^{1}							21
1		3		5	6		8^{2}	9			10	11^{1}	7	4			12					2	13							22
1		3^{1}		5	6		8^{2}	9			10	11^{3}	7	4								2		12	13	14				23
1				5	6		9	11			10		7^{2}	3	13							2	8^{1}	4	12					24
1		3		5	6		9^{1}		13		10	11^{2}	7	8								2	12	4						25
1		3		5	6		13		12		10	11^{1}	7	8								2	9^{2}	4						26
1		3		5	6				11^{2}		10		7	8								2	9^{1}	4	12	13				27
1		3		5	6^{1}				10			11		7	12							2	9	4^{2}	13		8			28
1	6■	3					9				10	11^{2}	12	5	7							2^{1}		4			8	13		29
1		3		5	6						10	11^{1}	9	2	7^{2}									4	13	12	8			30
1		3		5	6						10			11	7^{1}							2	12	4		9	8			31
1^{G}		3^{1}		5	6						10	13		7						15		2	11	4	12	9^{2}	8			32
1				5	6		9					11		3	7							2	10^{1}	4			8		12	33
1	13	3		5	6		12				10	11^{3}		7	9^{1}							2	14	4^{2}			8			34
1	12	3		5	6						10	13		7								2	11	4^{1}		9^{2}	8			35
1	4	3^{3}		5	6				12		10■	11^{1}	13	7■								2	9^{2}			14	8			36
	4			5			11^{1}		10			13	9		6			12		1	3	2				7^{2}	8			37
15	2^{1}	3							10				9	7						1^{G}	5	12	11	4			8	6		38

PARTICK THISTLE — First Division

Year Formed: 1876. *Ground & Address:* Firhill Stadium, 80 Firhill Rd, Glasgow G20 7AL. *Telephone:* 0141 579 1971. *Fax:* 0141 945 1525. *E-mail:* mail@ptfc.co.uk. *Website:* www.ptfc.co.uk
Ground Capacity: total: 13,141, seated: 10,921. *Size of Pitch:* 105yd × 68yd.
Chairman: Allan Cowan. *Secretary:* Antonia Kerr.
Manager: Ian McCall. *Assistant Manager:* Gardner Spiers. *Physio:* George Hannah.
Managers since 1975: R. Auld, P. Cormack, B. Rooney, R. Auld, D. Johnstone, W. Lamont, S. Clark, J. Lambie, M. MacLeod, J. McVeigh, T. Bryce, J. Lambie, G. Collins, G. Britton & D. Whyte, D. Campbell.
Club Nickname(s): The Jags. *Previous Grounds:* Jordanvale Park; Muirpark; Inchview; Meadowside Park.
Record Attendance: 49,838 v Rangers, Division I, 18 Feb 1922. *Ground Record:* 54,728, Scotland v Ireland, 25 Feb 1928.
Record Transfer Fee received: £200,000 for Mo Johnston to Watford.
Record Transfer Fee paid: £85,000 for Andy Murdoch from Celtic (Feb 1991).
Record Victory: 16-0 v Royal Albert, Scottish Cup 1st rd, 17 Jan 1931.
Record Defeat: 0-10 v Queen's Park, Scottish Cup, 3 Dec 1881.
Most Capped Player: Alan Rough, 51 (53), Scotland.
Most League Appearances: 410: Alan Rough, 1969-82.
Most League Goals in Season (Individual): 41: Alex Hair, Division I, 1926-27.

PARTICK THISTLE 2006–07 LEAGUE RECORD

Match No.	Date	Venue	Opponents	Result		H/T Score	Lg. Pos.	Goalscorers	Attendance
1	Aug 5	A	Dundee	W	1-0	1-0	—	Roberts [28]	5144
2	12	H	Airdrie U	W	4-2	2-0	3	Roberts [21], Donnelly [30], Gibson J [50], Brady [56]	3473
3	19	A	Livingston	D	2-2	1-0	3	Roberts 2 [7, 80]	2403
4	26	A	Clyde	D	0-0	0-0	3		2956
5	Sept 9	H	St Johnstone	L	1-5	0-3	4	Donnelly (pen) [77]	2914
6	16	A	Hamilton A	W	2-1	1-0	4	Young [38], Gibson G [88]	2290
7	23	H	Gretna	L	0-6	0-1	5		2399
8	30	H	Ross Co	W	3-2	1-1	4	McCulloch 2 [33, 84], McConalogue [90]	2020
9	Oct 14	A	Queen of the S	W	2-0	0-0	3	Donnelly [53], Roberts [83]	1762
10	21	A	Airdrie U	W	2-1	1-1	2	Roberts [16], Strachan [51]	2351
11	28	H	Dundee	W	3-1	2-1	1	Roberts 2 (1 pen) [17, 74 (p)], Sives [43]	2987
12	Nov 4	A	St Johnstone	L	0-2	0-1	2		3798
13	18	H	Hamilton A	W	3-1	2-0	2	Roberts 3 (1 pen) [9 (p), 38, 67]	2797
14	22	H	Clyde	D	1-1	0-0	—	Donnelly [82]	2752
15	25	A	Gretna	L	0-4	0-3	2		1646
16	Dec 2	H	Queen of the S	D	1-1	0-0	2	Donnelly [85]	2533
17	9	A	Ross Co	W	5-2	2-1	2	McConalogue 2 [35, 37], Ferguson [58], Keogh [72], Roberts [80]	2381
18	16	H	Livingston	L	2-3	0-1	2	Brady [74], McConalogue [77]	2591
19	26	A	Dundee	L	1-3	1-2	—	Young [2]	4113
20	Jan 2	A	Clyde	L	0-2	0-1	—		2229
21	13	H	Gretna	D	2-2	1-2	3	Young [13], Roberts [47]	2678
22	20	A	Hamilton A	L	1-2	0-1	5	Roberts [63]	1949
23	27	A	Queen of the S	L	3-4	0-3	5	McChrystal [84], Roberts (pen) [86], Keogh [88]	2011
24	Feb 10	H	Ross Co	D	1-1	0-0	6	Roberts [68]	2211
25	17	A	Livingston	W	1-0	1-0	5	Russell [21]	2221
26	Mar 3	H	Clyde	L	0-4	0-4	7		2873
27	10	A	St Johnstone	L	0-2	0-1	7		2453
28	13	H	St Johnstone	W	2-0	1-0	—	Morrow [13], Keogh [73]	1697
29	17	H	Hamilton A	L	0-2	0-0	6		2178
30	25	H	Airdrie U	L	0-1	0-1	6		2211
31	31	A	Gretna	L	0-2	0-1	7		1541
32	Apr 3	A	Ross Co	L	1-2	1-2	—	Young [11]	1880
33	7	H	Queen of the S	D	0-0	0-0	8		2639
34	14	H	Dundee	W	2-1	1-1	7	Strachan [17], Young [53]	2433
35	21	A	Airdrie U	D	1-1	1-1	7	Smith [13]	2178
36	28	H	Livingston	D	0-0	0-0	7		2915

Final League Position: 7

Honours
League Champions: First Division 1975-76, 2001-02. Division II 1896-97, 1899-1900, 1970-71; Second Division 2000-01;
Runners-up: First Division 1991-92. Division II 1901-02.
Scottish Cup Winners: 1921; *Runners-up:* 1930; *Semi-finals:* 2002.
League Cup Winners: 1971-72; *Runners-up:* 1953-54, 1956-57, 1958-59.
Bell's League Challenge: Quarter-finals 2004-05.

European: *Fairs Cup:* 4 matches (1963-64). *UEFA Cup:* 2 matches (1972-73). *Intertoto Cup:* 4 matches 1995-96.

Club colours: Shirt: Red and yellow halves with black sleeves. Shorts: Black. Stockings: Black.

Goalscorers: *League* (47): Roberts 16 (3 pens), Donnelly 5 (1 pen), Young 5, McConalogue 4, Keogh 3, Brady 2, McCulloch 2, Strachan 2, Ferguson 1, Gibson G 1, Gibson J 1, McChrystal 1, Morrow 1, Russell 1, Sives 1, Smith 1.
Scottish Cup (2): Gibson J 1, Robertson J 1.
CIS Cup (5): Boyd 1, Brady 1, Gibson J 1, Gibson W 1, Roberts 1.
Challenge Cup (1): Ferguson 1.

Arthur K 21	Sives C 17	McCulloch S 14 + 2	Brady D 28 + 2	Boyd S 33 + 3	Ferguson B 16 + 9	Gibson J 26	Donnelly S 24	Gibson G 4 + 15	Roberts M 30 + 2	Gibson W 21 + 8	Kane J 1 + 2	McGoldrick J — + 3	Hodge A — + 2	Robertson J 21 + 1	McConalogue S 6 + 15	Campbell S 10 + 5	Strachan A 20 + 6	Keogh P 16 + 5	Young D 29	Tuffey J 15	McChrystal M 13 + 2	Marshall C — + 1	Smith B 12	Russell A 6 + 8	Archibald A 9	Morrow S 4 + 4	Hodge S — + 2	Match No.
1	2	3^3	4	5	6	7	8^1	9	10^2	11	12	13	14															1
1	2	3^3	4	5	6^1	7	8	9	10^2	11			14	12	13													2
1^1	2		4	5	6	7	8		10	11				3		9	12											3
1	2	3	4	5	6	7^1	8^3	13	10	11^2					14		12	9										4
1	2		4	5	6^1	7	8	13	10^3	11						12	14	9^2	3									5
	2	3	4	5			8^2	13	10^1	7						6	11	12	9	1								6
	2	3	4	5			8	12	10^1	7						6	11		9	1								7
1	2^3	3	4	5		7	8	12	10						13	14	11^2	9	6^1									8
1	2	3	4	5		7	8	12	10^2						14	13	11^1	6	9^3									9
1	2		4	6		7	8	13	10^3	12					14	3	11^1	5	9^2									10
1	2^2	3	4	6^1		7	8	14	10	12						13	11	5	9^3									11
1	2	3^3	4	6		7	8^2	12	10						13	14	11^1	5	9									12
1		3	4	6		7	8	13	10	12					14	2^1	11^2	5	9^3									13
1		3^3	4	6		7	8	12	10	13					14	2	11^1	5	9^2									14
1		3	4^2	6	12	7	8	13	10	11						2		5^1	9									15
1			4	5	14	7	8	12	10	6^3				2	11^1	3	13		9^2									16
1		12		5	4^2		8	14	10	7				3^1	11^3	2	13	6	9									17
1		12	7	5	4		8	14	10					3	11^3	2^1	13	6^2	9									18
1		3	4	5	2		8^1	7	13	6	10	12^2			11				9■									19
1		3■	4^3	5^1	7^2			10		8	13	14		2			11		9		6	12						20
			4	5		7^1	8^3		10	12				3	13			14	9	1	6		2	11^2				21
			4^3	5	14	7	8		10					3	12			13	9	1	6		2^2	11^1				22
				5^1	4^2	7	8^3		10	13				3	14			12	9	1	6		2	11				23
1			11	4	14	7^2	8^3		10	13				3	9^1			5					2	12	6			24
1			4	5	13	7	8^2		10	11^3				3	14						12		2^1	9	6			25
1			4	5	14	7^1				12				2	10^2		11	13	8		3			9^3	6			26
			4	5	7				10^2	11				2				9	8	1	3^1			13	6	12		27
	6^2		12	13	7				10	4				2^1			11	5	8	1	3			14		9^3		28
	6^3		4	12	7				10					2	13		11^2	5■	8	1	3^1					9	14	29
	5		4	12	10^2	7^1								3	13		11		8	1			2		6■	9		30
	2^1		4	5	10^3	7				8				3	14		11			1	12		6	13		9^2		31
				5	12	7^1			13	10				2			11		8	1	3		4	9^2	6			32
				5	12	7^2			10	9^1				2			11^3		8	1	3		4	13	6	14		33
	6^1			5		7			10^3	9				2			11		8^2	1	3		4	14		13	12	34
				5	12	7^1			10^2	9				2			11		8	1	3		4	13	6			35
			12	5	7^1				10^2	9				2			11		8^3	1	3		4	13	6	14		36

PETERHEAD Second Division

Year Formed: 1891. *Ground and Address:* Balmoor Stadium, Lord Catto Park, Peterhead AB42 1EU.
Telephone: 01779 478256. *Fax:* 01779 490682. *E-mail:* shona@peterheadfc.org.uk. *Website:* www.peterheadfc.org.uk
Ground Capacity: 3250, seated 1000.
Chairman: Rodger Morrison. *General Manager:* Dave Watson. *Secretary:* George Moore.
Manager: Steve Paterson. *Assistant Manager:* Neale Cooper. *First Team Coach:* Dave McGinlay.
Managers since 1975: C. Grant, D. Darcy, I. Taylor, J. Harper, D. Smith, J. Hamilton, G. Adams, J. Guyan, I. Wilson, D. Watson, R. Brown, D. Watson, I. Wilson, I. Stewart.
Club Nickname(s): Blue Toon. *Previous Ground:* Recreation Park.
Record Attendance: 6310 friendly v Celtic, 1948.
Record Victory: 17-0 v Fort William, 1998-99 (in Highland League).
Record Defeat: 0-13 v Aberdeen, Scottish Cup, 1923-24.
Most League Appearances: 135, Martin Johnston, 2000-05.
Most League Goals in Season (Individual): 21, Iain Stewart, 2002-03; 21, S. Michie, 2004-05.
Most Goals Overall (Individual): 58, Iain Stewart, 2000-05.

PETERHEAD 2006–07 LEAGUE RECORD

Match No.	*Date*	*Venue*	*Opponents*	*Result*		*H/T Score*	*Lg. Pos.*	*Goalscorers*	*Attendance*
1	Aug 5	H	Brechin C	D	1-1	0-0	—	Gibson [47]	645
2	12	A	Alloa Ath	D	1-1	1-1	6	Wood [7]	462
3	19	H	Raith R	L	0-1	0-0	9		718
4	26	H	Morton	L	0-4	0-4	10		735
5	Sept 3	A	Cowdenbeath	L	2-4	2-2	10	Hegarty [35], Linn [44]	589
6	9	A	Ayr U	W	2-1	0-1	8	Sharp [73], McKay [74]	1002
7	16	H	Stranraer	W	5-2	2-0	7	Linn 4 [29, 42, 63, 70], Gilfillan [68]	640
8	23	A	Stirling A	L	0-2	0-0	8		574
9	30	H	Forfar Ath	W	8-0	5-0	5	Linn 2 (1 pen) [8 (p), 34], Sharp [21], McKay 2 [30, 88], Gibson 2 [43, 56], Tully [82]	526
10	Oct 14	A	Brechin C	L	0-1	0-1	7		483
11	21	H	Alloa Ath	L	1-2	0-0	8	Tully [60]	491
12	28	H	Cowdenbeath	W	1-0	1-0	7	Guy (og) [39]	505
13	Nov 4	A	Morton	L	2-4	2-1	7	Bavidge [7], Tully [28]	2418
14	11	A	Stranraer	L	1-2	0-0	8	Cameron [81]	336
15	25	H	Ayr U	W	3-1	2-1	8	McAulay [30], Forrest (og) [43], Sharp [70]	628
16	Dec 2	H	Stirling A	L	2-3	2-0	9	Linn [26], Cameron [44]	641
17	16	A	Forfar Ath	W	3-2	1-1	7	Wood [24], Sharp [65], McAulay [70]	361
18	23	H	Brechin C	L	1-4	0-3	7	McAulay [59]	615
19	30	A	Raith R	L	2-5	0-1	9	Linn 2 [82, 88]	1538
20	Jan 2	H	Morton	L	1-2	0-1	—	Cameron [55]	819
21	13	A	Cowdenbeath	W	3-0	1-0	8	Bavidge 2 [11, 70], McAulay [81]	380
22	20	H	Stranraer	W	5-0	3-0	7	Bavidge 4 [29, 42, 68, 73], Snowdon (og) [34]	570
23	27	A	Ayr U	D	0-0	0-0	8		953
24	Feb 3	A	Stirling A	L	1-2	0-1	8	Bavidge (pen) [80]	621
25	10	H	Forfar Ath	D	2-2	1-0	8	Bavidge 2 [44, 62]	476
26	17	H	Raith R	D	0-0	0-0	7		814
27	24	A	Alloa Ath	W	4-2	1-0	6	McAulay [37], Sharp [56], McKay [75], McGeown [84]	440
28	Mar 3	A	Morton	L	1-2	0-0	7	Low [62]	2346
29	10	H	Cowdenbeath	L	0-2	0-1	8		548
30	17	A	Stranraer	D	1-1	1-1	8	Mann [3]	282
31	31	H	Ayr U	D	2-2	0-1	8	McKay [63], Bavidge (pen) [72]	679
32	Apr 3	A	Forfar Ath	W	2-1	1-0	—	McKay [17], McAulay [89]	298
33	7	H	Stirling A	W	2-1	1-0	7	McKay 2 [4, 63]	634
34	14	A	Brechin C	L	1-3	1-1	7	McDonald [20]	504
35	21	H	Alloa Ath	D	0-0	0-0	—		769
36	28	A	Raith R	L	0-2	0-1	8		1589

Final League Position: 8

Honours
Third Division Runners up: 2004-05.
Scottish Cup: Quarter-finals 2001.
Highland League Champions: winners 5 times.
Scottish Qualifying Cup (North): winners 6 times.
North of Scotland Cup: winners 5 times.
Aberdeenshire Cup: winners: 20 times.

Club colours: Shirt: Royal blue with white; Shorts: Royal blue; Stockings: Royal blue tops with white hoops.

Goalscorers: *League* (60): Bavidge 11 (2 pens), Linn 10 (1 pen), McKay 8, McAulay 6, Sharp 5, Cameron 3, Gibson 3, Tully 3, Wood 2, Gilfillan 1, Hegarty 1, Low 1, McDonald 1, McGeown 1, Mann 1, own goals 3.
Scottish Cup (0).
CIS Cup (3): Bavidge 1, Linn 1, Wood 1.
Challenge Cup (0).

Mathers P 12	Gilfillan B 31 + 4	Cameron D 33	Tully C 21 + 3	Perry M 18	Gibson K 8	Sharp G 29 + 5	Buchan J 31 + 1	Bavidge M 21 + 4	Wood M 11 + 8	McKay S 26 + 9	Linn R 15 + 5	Shand C 3	Youngson A 2 + 10	Hegarty C 11 + 4	Good I 5	Stephen N 4 + 1	McNally S 14 + 1	McInnes A — + 6	Kelly G 7	McAulay K 20	McDonald C 18 + 1	McGeown G 7 + 6	Scott S 2 + 1	McCaldon I 15	Keogh L 14	Low A 5 + 8	Mann R 11	Cowie D — + 1	Farquhar J 1 + 1	Calder J 1	Ballard D — + 1	*Match No.*
1	2	3	4	5	6	7	8	9	10	11^1	12																					1
1	11	3	4	5		7	8	9^3	10^1	13	12	2	6^2	14																		2
1	11^2	7	4	5		12	8		10	14	9^3	2	13	6^1	3																	3
1	6	11		5		7	8		9	13	10^2	2^1		4	3	12																4
1	12			5		7	8			9	10		11^1	6^2	3	4	2	13														5
1	11	3		5		7	8		13	9	10^2			6^1		4	2	12														6
1	11	3		5		7^3	8		13	9^2	10		14	6^1		4	2	12														7
1	11^2	3^3		5	6^1	7	8		12	9	10		14			4	2	13														8
1	11^1	3	4	5	6^2	7	8		14	9	10^3		12				2	13														9
1	11	3	4	5	6^3	7	8	13	12	9^1	10^2		14				2															10
1	11	3	4	5	6^1	7	8	13	12	9^2	10^3		14				2															11
1	11	3	4	5	6	7	8	9^1	10^2	13	12		14				2^3															12
	11	3	4	5	6^3	7^2	8	9	10^1	12	13		14				2		1													13
	11	3	4	5	6^1	12	8^3	9	14	7	10^2						2	13	1													14
	5	11^2	2	3		7	4	9	6	12	8^1		14				13		1	10^3												15
	5	6	4	3		7	2■	10^1	8	12	9								1	11												16
	6	3		5		7		12	8	13	9^1						2		1	10	4	11^2										17
	2	3		5^2		7^1	6	12	8		9								1	10	4	11	13									18
	6	8				13	4	9		7^1	12						2			10	5	11	3^2	1								19
	10	6	4			7	2	8		12	9		13						1		5	11^1	3^2									20
	6	3	4			7	2	9		8										10	5■	11		1								21
	6	3	4			7	2	9		8							5			10		11		1								22
	6	3	4^1			7■	2	9	14	8^3							5				12	11^2		1	10	13						23
	6	3					2	9^3	7^1	8				14						11^2	5	13		1	10	12	4■					24
	6	3					2	9		8				4^2						11	5	12		1	10	7^1		13				25
	6	3^1	4■			7	2	9		8^2										11	5	13		1	10	12						26
	6	3				7^2	2	9^1		8										11	5	12		1^6	10	13	4		15			27
	6	3	13			7^1	2			8^2				12						11^3	5	14			10	9	4		1			28
	6	3	14			7^3	2			8				12						11	5	13		1	10^1	9^2	4					29
	6	3	2			7	8^1			9										11	5			1	10	12	4					30
		3	6			7^2		9^1		11				2						8	5				10	13	4			1	12	31
	12	3	6			7^2		9		11				2						8	5			1	10^1	13	4					32
	12	3	6			7^1		9^2		11				2						8	5			1	10	13	4					33
	13	3	6			7^1	12	9^2		11				2						8	5			1	10		4					34
	2		13			12	6	9		11					3					8	5			1	10^2	7^1	4					35
	2					12	6			9				11^1	3					8	5			1	10	7	4					36

QUEEN OF THE SOUTH First Division

Year Formed: 1919. *Ground & Address:* Palmerston Park, Dumfries DG2 9BA. *Telephone and Fax:* 01387 254853. *E-mail:* admin@qosfc.com. *Website:* www.qosfc.co.uk
Ground Capacity: total: 7412, seated: 3509. *Size of Pitch:* 112yd × 73yd.
Chairman: David Rae. *Vice-Chairman:* Thomas Harkness. *Club Secretary:* Eric Moffat. *Commercial Manager:* Margaret Heuchan.
Manager: Gordon Chisholm. *First Team Coach:* Stevie Morrison. *Physio:* John Kerr.
Managers since 1975: M. Jackson, W. Hunter, B. Little, G. Herd, H. Hood, A. Busby, R. Clark, M. Jackson, D. Wilson, W. McLaren, F. McGarvey, A. MacLeod, D. Frye, W. McLaren, M. Shanks, R. Alexander, J. Connolly, I. Scott, I. McCall.
Club Nickname(s): The Doonhamers. *Previous Grounds:* None.
Record Attendance: 26,552 v Hearts, Scottish Cup 3rd rd, 23 Feb 1952.
Record Transfer Fee received: £250,000 for Andy Thomson to Southend U (1994).
Record Transfer Fee paid: £30,000 for Jim Butter from Alloa Athletic (1995).
Record Victory: 11-1 v Stranraer, Scottish Cup 1st rd, 16 Jan 1932.
Record Defeat: 2-10 v Dundee, Division I, 1 Dec 1962.
Most Capped Player: Billy Houliston, 3, Scotland.
Most League Appearances: 731: Allan Ball, 1963-82.
Most League Goals in Season (Individual): 37: Jimmy Gray, Division II, 1927-28.
Most Goals in Season: 41: Jimmy Rutherford, 1931-32.
Most Goals Overall (Individual): 250: Jim Patterson, 1949-63.

QUEEN OF THE SOUTH 2006–07 LEAGUE RECORD

Match No.	*Date*	*Venue*	*Opponents*	*Result*		*H/T Score*	*Lg. Pos.*	*Goalscorers*	*Attendance*
1	Aug 5	A	Livingston	L	0-2	0-0	—		2224
2	12	H	St Johnstone	L	0-1	0-1	9		1586
3	19	A	Airdrie U	D	2-2	0-0	8	O'Neill J (pen) 74, Henderson 81	1298
4	27	H	Gretna	L	0-3	0-2	10		5485
5	Sept 9	A	Ross Co	L	0-1	0-0	9		2265
6	16	A	Dundee	L	1-2	1-1	9	O'Neill J (pen) 20	3745
7	23	H	Clyde	L	0-2	0-1	10		1770
8	30	A	Hamilton A	D	1-1	1-1	10	O'Neill J 45	1396
9	Oct 14	H	Partick Th	L	0-2	0-0	10		1762
10	21	A	St Johnstone	L	0-5	0-2	10		2364
11	28	H	Livingston	W	2-0	0-0	10	Thomson A 2 67, 86	1752
12	Nov 4	H	Ross Co	W	2-0	0-0	9	Weir 55, O'Neill J 70	1497
13	11	A	Gretna	L	0-5	0-3	9		2193
14	18	H	Dundee	W	2-0	1-0	9	O'Neill J 2 (1 pen) 30 (p), 48	1861
15	25	A	Clyde	L	0-4	0-2	9		1179
16	Dec 2	A	Partick Th	D	1-1	0-0	9	Thomson J 82	2533
17	9	H	Hamilton A	D	1-1	1-0	10	O'Neill J (pen) 9	1735
18	16	H	Airdrie U	D	1-1	0-0	10	Lovering (og) 53	1577
19	23	A	Livingston	W	1-0	0-0	10	Thomson J 84	1624
20	30	A	Ross Co	L	0-1	0-1	10		2413
21	Jan 2	H	Gretna	L	0-4	0-1	—		3714
22	20	A	Dundee	L	0-1	0-0	10		3360
23	27	H	Partick Th	W	4-3	3-0	10	O'Connor 9, Lauchlan 26, Dobbie 2 (1 pen) 36, 48 (p)	2011
24	Feb 10	A	Hamilton A	D	2-2	1-2	10	Adams 12, Dobbie 67	1454
25	17	A	Airdrie U	W	3-0	2-0	10	Dobbie 2 (1 pen) 9 (p), 32, O'Connor 64	1805
26	Mar 3	A	Gretna	W	3-0	1-0	9	O'Connor 2 38, 69, Paton 88	2049
27	6	H	St Johnstone	W	1-0	1-0	—	Murray 33	1770
28	10	H	Ross Co	W	2-0	2-0	8	O'Neill J 5, Adams 12	2479
29	17	H	Dundee	D	2-2	1-1	8	Murray 13, Barrowman 90	1967
30	25	H	Clyde	D	0-0	0-0	8		2109
31	31	A	Clyde	W	1-0	0-0	8	Dobbie (pen) 69	1200
32	Apr 3	H	Hamilton A	D	1-1	1-1	—	O'Connor 20	1650
33	7	A	Partick Th	D	0-0	0-0	7		2639
34	14	H	Livingston	D	1-1	1-0	8	O'Connor 45	1983
35	21	A	St Johnstone	L	0-3	0-1	8		4168
36	28	H	Airdrie U	L	0-3	0-2	8		3012

Final League Position: 8

Honours
League Champions: Division II 1950-51. Second Division 2001-02. *Runners-up:* Division II 1932-33, 1961-62, 1974-75. Second Division 1980-81, 1985-86.
Scottish Cup: semi-finals 1949-50.
League Cup: semi-finals 1950-51, 1960-61.
B&Q Cup: semi-finals 1991-92. *League Challenge Cup Winners:* 2002-03; *Runners-up:* 1997-98.

Club colours: Shirt: Royal blue with white sleeves. Shorts: White with blue piping. Stockings: Royal blue.

Goalscorers: *League* (34): O'Neill J 8 (4 pens), Dobbie 6 (3 pens), O'Connor 6, Adams 2, Murray 2, Thomson A 2, Thomson J 2, Barrowman 1, Henderson 1, Lauchlan 1, Paton 1, Weir 1, own goal 1.
Scottish Cup (7): Dobbie 3 (1 pen), O'Connor 2. Adams 1, O'Neill J 1.
CIS Cup (5): O'Neill J 2, Henderson 1, O'Connor 1, Weir 1.
Challenge Cup (3): O'Neill J 2, Lauchlan 1.

Corr B 9 + 1	Paton E 33	McKenzie S 13 + 3	Lauchlan J 32 + 1	Henderson M 11 + 3	Thomson J 28 + 2	Burns P 12 + 3	Weir G 17 + 11	O'Connor S 22 + 7	O'Neill J 27 + 8	Gibson W 18 + 4	Mullens M 1 + 4	Scally N 34 + 1	Thomson A 1 + 13	Scott C 8	Callaghan B 1 + 8	Henry J 1 + 3	McCaffrey D 11	Robertson S 6 + 5	Barrowman A 17 + 7	Moon W 7 + 5	Swift S 7 + 3	Whorlow M — + 1	Hinchcliffe C 5	McQuilken J 15	Dobbie S 15	McDonald J 14	Adams J 11	Murray S 12 + 2	Tosh S 7 + 4	Aitken A 1 + 1	Burns P — + 4	*Match No.*
1	2^2	3^3	4	5	6	7	8	9^1	10	11	12	13	14																			1
1	2	12	4■	5	6	7	8^2	9	10^3	11^1	14	3	13																			2
	2	4		5	6	7	8^3	9	10	12		3^1	14	1	11^2	13																3
	2	3	4	5		7	8^1	9^3	10	11^2	14	6	12	1		13																4
1	2^2	3	4	5	12	7			10		9	11	13		14		6^3	8^1														5
1		2	4	5	6	7		13	10			8^1	9^2		14	12	3	11^3														6
1		3	4	5^1		7		9^2	10	12		6	13		14		2	8	11^3													7
1		2	4		6^2	7			10	11	13	5			12	8^1	3		9^3	14												8
15	2	4			6	7	8^1	12	10^2	11		5		1^6	13		3		9													9
1	2	5	4		6■	7	12	14	10^1	11^3		8					3^2	13	9													10
	2	6	4				8^1		10	11		3	12	1			5		9^3	7^2	13	14										11
	2	6	4				8^2		10	11		3	13	1			5		9	7^1	12											12
1	2	6^1	4			13	8^3	14	10	11		3^2					5		9	12	7											13
	2^2	13	4		5		8^3	14	10	11		6■		1			3		9	7^1	12											14
	2	6^1	4		12		8^3		10	11			14	1			3	13	9	7^2	5											15
	2		4		6		8^2		10	11^1		5	13		12			7^3	9	14	3		1									16
	2	13	4	3	6		8^2		10^3	11■		5			12			14	9	7^1			1									17
	2		4	3	6	11^2	8^1	12	10			5						13	9		7		1									18
	2		4	14	6		8^1	9^3	10	11		5	12					7^2		13	3		1									19
	2		4		6	12	8^2	9^3	10	11		5	13					7^1		14	3		1									20
	2		4^1	12	6		8^3	9	10	7		5	14	1	13					11^2	3											21
1	2		4	6		7^3	13	9^2	12	11		5						14		10^1				3	8							22
	2		4		6	12	13	9^2	14	11		5^3												3	8	1	7^1	10				23
	2		4		6			14	13	12		5							9^1					3	8^3	1	7^2	11	10			24
	2		4		6		14	9^2		12		5							13					3	8^3	1	7	11	10^1			25
	2		4		6		14	9^2	10			5							13					3	8^3	1	7	11^1	12			26
	2		4		6		14	9^2	10^1			5							13					3	8^3	1	7	11	12			27
	2		4^1	12	6			9^3	10			5							13					3	8^2	1	7	11	14			28
	2			4^1	6			9	10^3			5							13					3	8^2	1	7	11	14	12		29
	2		4		6			9	10^2			5							12					3	8^1	1	7	11			13	30
	2		4		6		13	9	12			5							7					3	8^2	1		11^1	10			31
	2		4		6		13	9^1	12			5							7					3	8^2	1		11	10^3		14	32
	2		4		6		13	9	12			5							7					3	8^2	1		11^3	10^1		14	33
	2		4		6		14	9	10^2			5							13					3	8^3	1	7^1	11			12	34
	2		4		6		14	9	13			5							7^2					3	8^3	1	11	12	10^1			35
	2		13■		6		11^3	9	14			5												3	8	1	7	12	10^1	4^2		36

QUEEN'S PARK — Second Division

Year Formed: 1867. *Ground & Address:* Hampden Park, Mount Florida, Glasgow G42 9BA. *Telephone:* 0141 632 1275. *Fax:* 0141 636 1612. *E-mail:* secretary@queensparkfc.co.uk. *Website:* queensparkfc.co.uk
Ground Capacity: all seated: 52,000. *Size of Pitch:* 115yd × 75yd.
President: Garry Templeman. *Secretary:* Alistair MacKay. *Treasurer:* David Gordon.
Coach: Billy Stark. *Physio:* R. C. Findlay.
Coaches since 1975: D. McParland, J. Gilroy, E. Hunter, H. McCann, J. McCormack, K. Brannigan.
Club Nickname(s): The Spiders. *Previous Grounds:* 1st Hampden (Recreation Ground); (Titwood Park was used as an interim measure between 1st & 2nd Hampdens); 2nd Hampden (Cathkin); 3rd Hampden.
Record Attendance: 95,772 v Rangers, Scottish Cup, 18 Jan 1930.
Record for Ground: 149,547 Scotland v England, 1937.
Record Transfer Fee received: Not applicable due to amateur status.
Record Transfer Fee paid: Not applicable due to amateur status.
Record Victory: 16-0 v St. Peters, Scottish Cup 1st rd, 29 Aug 1885.
Record Defeat: 0-9 v Motherwell, Division I, 26 Apr 1930.
Most Capped Player: Walter Arnott, 14, Scotland.
Most League Appearances: 532: Ross Caven.
Most League Goals in Season (Individual): 30: William Martin, Division I, 1937-38.
Most Goals Overall (Individual): 163: J. B. McAlpine.

QUEEN'S PARK 2006–07 LEAGUE RECORD

Match No.	Date	Venue	Opponents	Result	H/T Score	Lg. Pos.	Goalscorers	Attendance
1	Aug 5	H	Arbroath	L 0-3	0-1	—		634
2	12	A	Elgin C	W 2-1	2-1	7	Ferry [14], Canning [42]	547
3	19	H	Dumbarton	W 1-0	0-0	3	Canning [70]	884
4	26	A	Albion R	D 1-1	0-0	4	Weatherston [54]	501
5	Sept 3	A	Berwick R	L 0-1	0-1	7		448
6	9	A	Stenhousemuir	L 1-2	0-0	9	Weatherston [56]	393
7	16	H	Montrose	D 1-1	0-0	8	Ferry [85]	404
8	23	H	East Fife	W 3-0	2-0	8	Ronald [22], Weatherston 2 [26, 53]	413
9	30	A	East Stirling	L 1-2	0-1	7	Ronald [68]	354
10	Oct 14	A	Arbroath	W 2-1	2-0	7	Trouten [22], Bowers [30]	627
11	21	H	Elgin C	W 3-0	1-0	6	Weatherston [3], Quinn [66], Ferry [80]	489
12	28	H	Berwick R	W 1-0	1-0	3	Quinn [22]	564
13	Nov 4	H	Albion R	W 2-1	0-0	3	Trouten [56], Reilly (pen) [82]	543
14	11	A	Montrose	W 3-0	1-0	2	Weatherston 2 [22, 81], Paton [88]	325
15	25	H	Stenhousemuir	D 1-1	1-0	2	Ferry [43]	543
16	Dec 2	A	East Fife	L 0-1	0-0	3		637
17	16	H	East Stirling	L 1-3	0-1	6	Weatherston [60]	458
18	23	H	Arbroath	W 1-0	1-0	5	Dunlop M [23]	475
19	30	A	Dumbarton	D 0-0	0-0	5		1092
20	Jan 2	A	Albion R	L 1-2	0-0	—	Canning [67]	409
21	13	H	Berwick R	L 0-2	0-2	7		491
22	20	H	Montrose	W 5-0	2-0	5	Canning (pen) [15], Ferry [38], Donachie (og) [63], Trouten [66], Quinn [76]	414
23	27	A	Stenhousemuir	W 2-1	0-0	5	Trouten (pen) [55], Ferry [59]	509
24	Feb 3	H	East Fife	D 1-1	0-0	5	Carroll [89]	719
25	10	A	East Stirling	W 2-0	2-0	2	Weatherston [12], Kettlewell [36]	292
26	17	H	Dumbarton	W 2-0	1-0	2	Weatherston [19], Ferry [57]	849
27	24	A	Elgin C	W 3-0	0-0	2	Ferry [65], Weatherston [67], Cairney [90]	473
28	Mar 3	H	Albion R	W 5-0	1-0	2	Weatherston [16], Kettlewell [53], Trouten (pen) [70], Ferry 2 [76, 80]	654
29	10	A	Berwick R	W 2-0	0-0	2	Trouten [68], Ferry [78]	704
30	17	A	Montrose	W 2-0	1-0	2	Trouten 2 (1 pen) [13, 73 (p)]	461
31	31	H	Stenhousemuir	W 1-0	1-0	3	Weatherston [29]	621
32	Apr 3	H	East Stirling	W 2-1	1-0	—	Canning [36], Dunn [65]	552
33	7	A	East Fife	L 0-1	0-0	3		669
34	14	A	Arbroath	L 0-1	0-1	4		957
35	21	H	Elgin C	W 3-0	3-0	3	Weatherston 2 [28, 37], Dunn [45]	916
36	28	A	Dumbarton	W 2-1	1-0	3	Dunn [31], Weatherston [78]	928

Final League Position: 3

Honours
League Champions: Division II 1922-23. B Division 1955-56. Second Division 1980-81. Third Division 1999-2000.
Scottish Cup Winners: 1874, 1875, 1876, 1880, 1881, 1882, 1884, 1886, 1890, 1893; *Runners-up:* 1892, 1900.
League Cup: —.
FA Cup runners-up: 1884, 1885.

Club colours: Shirt: White and black hoops. Shorts: White. Stockings: Black with white tops.

Goalscorers: *League* (57): Weatherston 16, Ferry 11, Trouten 8 (3 pens), Cannon 5 (1 pen), Dunn 3, Quinn 3, Kettlewell 2, Ronald 2, Bowers 1, Cairney 1, Carroll 1, Dunlop M 1, Paton 1, Reilly 1 (pen), own goal 1.
Play-Offs (11): Trouten 3, Cannon 2, Weatherston 2, Cairney 1, Carroll 1, Dunlop M 1, Paton 1.
Scottish Cup (2): Ferry 1, Ronald 1.
CIS Cup (2): Bowers 1, Cannon 1.
Challenge Cup (5): Bowers 1, Molloy 1, Paton 1, Ronald 1, own goal 1.

Crawford D 22	Trouten A 23+3	Dunlop M 32	Agostini D 21	Sinclair R 19	Canning S 28+8	Kettlewell S 35	Quinn A 19+8	Carroll F 4+13	Weatherston D 32+1	Ferry M 34+1	Bowers R 5+12	Dunn R 14+15	Molloy S 3+1	Reilly S 15+1	Ronald P 24+5	Paton P 31	Keenan M —+1	Cairns M 14	Whelan J 1+1	Cairney P 18+3	Murray T 1+6	Colquhoun C —+2	Harty A —+1	Dunlop R —+1	Boslem A 1	Match No.
1	2	3³	4	5	6¹	7	8	9²	10	11	12	13	14													1
1			6	5■	7	2	8²	9¹	10	11■	12		3	4	13											2
1	13	3	5		11	7	8		10³		9¹		6²	4	12	2	14									3
	6	3	4		13	7	8		10²	11		12			9¹	2		1	5							4
	8	3	5²		6	7			10	11	12	13		4	9¹	2		1								5
	8	3	5		6	7		12	10	11		9¹		4²		2		1	13							6
1	8	3	5		6³	7	13	9²	10	11		14	4¹		12	2										7
	12	3			6	7²	8		10	11	13	9¹		4	5	2		1								8
	12	3			6	7	8²		10	11	13	9¹		4	5	2		1								9
	6²	3		5	12	7	8			11	9			4	10¹	2		1		13						10
	6	3		5	12	7	8		10²	11³	9¹			4		2		1		14	13					11
	6²	3		5	12	7	8		10	11	13			4	9¹	2		1								12
	6²	3		5	13	7	8¹		10³	11		12		4	9	2		1			14					13
	6³	3		5	13	7¹	8		10²	11		12		4	9	2		1			14					14
	6	3■		5	13	7	8¹		10	11		12		4	9²	2		1								15
	6			5	3	7	8¹		10	11		12		4	9	2		1								16
	6■	3		5■	13	7	8¹		10	11		9²		4	12	2■		1								17
		3	5		6	7²	8		10	11	12	9¹			4			1		2	13					18
1		3	5		6	7	8¹		10³	11	9²	13			4					2	12	14				19
1		3	5¹	2	6	7			10	11		12			4					8	9					20
1	6	3		5	4	7		13	10¹	11²					9	2				8	12					21
1	6	3		5	4	7	12	13	10³	11		14			9²	2¹				8						22
1	6¹	3		5	4	7	13		10	11		12			9	2				8²						23
1		3		5	4	7	8²	12	10	11		6¹			9	2				13						24
1		3	5		4	7	12	13	10	11	14	8²			9³	2				6¹						25
1	6	3	5		4	7		12	10	11		9¹				2				8						26
1	6²	3	5		4	7	14	13	10³	11		9¹			12	2				8						27
1	6	3	5		4	7	14	13	10²	11		12			9¹	2				8³						28
1	6	3	5		4	7	14	12	10²	11		13			9³	2				8¹						29
1	6	3	5		4	7	12		10	11					9¹	2				8						30
1	6¹		5	4	3	7	9³	13	10²	11	14	12				2				8						31
1			5	4	3	7		12		11	10¹	9²			6	2				8		13				32
1		6	5	4	3²	7		12		11¹	13	9			10■	2				8						33
1		3	5	4¹	6	7		13	10	11		9		12		2				8²						34
1		3	5		6			7	10³	11	13	9²		4¹		2				8			12	14		35
1	11²	3			6	7	4		12	13	14	9³			10¹	2				8					5	36

RAITH ROVERS Second Division

Year Formed: 1883. *Ground & Address:* Stark's Park, Pratt St, Kirkcaldy KY1 1SA. *Telephone:* 01592 263514. *Fax:* 01592 642833. *E-mail:* office@raithroversfc.com. *Website:* www.raithroversfc.com
Ground Capacity: all seated: 10,104. *Size of Pitch:* 113yd × 70yd.
Chairman: David Somerville. *General Manager:* Bob Mullen. *Commercial Manager:* John Drysdale.
Manager: John McGlynn. *Assistant Manager:* Gary Kirk. *Coach:* Shaun Dennis. *Physio:* Lesley Mackie
Managers since 1975: R. Paton, A. Matthew, W. McLean, G. Wallace, R. Wilson, F. Connor, J. Nicholl, J. Thomson, T. McLean, I. Munro, J. Nicholl, J. McVeigh, P. Hetherston, J. Scott, A. Calderon, C. Anelka, G. Dalziel.
Club Nickname: Rovers. *Previous Grounds:* Robbie's Park.
Record Attendance: 31,306 v Hearts, Scottish Cup 2nd rd, 7 Feb 1953.
Record Transfer Fee received: £900,000 for S. McAnespie to Bolton Wanderers (Sept 1995).
Record Transfer Fee paid: £225,000 for Paul Harvey from Airdrieonians (1996).
Record Victory: 10-1 v Coldstream, Scottish Cup 2nd rd, 13 Feb 1954.
Record Defeat: 2-11 v Morton, Division II, 18 Mar 1936.
Most Capped Player: David Morris, 6, Scotland.
Most League Appearances: 430: Willie McNaught.
Most League Goals in Season (Individual): 38: Norman Haywood, Division II, 1937-38.
Most Goals Overall (Individual): 154: Gordon Dalziel (League), 1987-94.

RAITH ROVERS 2006–07 LEAGUE RECORD

Match No.	*Date*	*Venue*	*Opponents*	*Result*		*H/T Score*	*Lg. Pos.*	*Goalscorers*	*Attendance*
1	Aug 5	A	Morton	L	0-2	0-1	—		2855
2	12	H	Forfar Ath	D	0-0	0-0	8		1437
3	19	A	Peterhead	W	1-0	0-0	6	Fotheringham [83]	718
4	26	H	Cowdenbeath	L	1-3	0-1	7	Manson [73]	2457
5	Sept 3	A	Stirling A	D	1-1	0-0	7	Campbell [87]	986
6	9	A	Stranraer	W	4-1	0-1	5	McManus [55], Harty 2 [60, 68], Fairbairn [88]	452
7	16	H	Brechin C	D	1-1	0-1	6	Harty (pen) [74]	1818
8	23	H	Alloa Ath	D	0-0	0-0	6		1517
9	30	A	Ayr U	L	0-1	0-0	8		1281
10	Oct 14	H	Morton	L	1-3	1-0	8	Oné [30]	2600
11	21	A	Forfar Ath	D	1-1	1-0	9	Oné [11]	754
12	28	H	Stirling A	L	1-3	1-1	9	Fotheringham (pen) [34]	1656
13	Nov 4	A	Cowdenbeath	W	2-1	0-0	8	Oné [62], Thoraninsson [73]	1487
14	11	A	Brechin C	L	0-1	0-1	9		745
15	25	H	Stranraer	D	1-1	0-1	9	Oné [72]	1458
16	Dec 2	A	Alloa Ath	W	2-1	1-0	7	Davidson [19], Thoraninsson [59]	786
17	16	H	Ayr U	W	1-0	0-0	6	Campbell [84]	1186
18	23	A	Morton	L	0-1	0-0	6		2398
19	30	H	Peterhead	W	5-2	1-0	6	McManus 3 [14, 68, 86], Harty [53], Fairbairn [77]	1538
20	Jan 2	H	Cowdenbeath	L	1-2	0-0	—	McManus [71]	2744
21	13	A	Stirling A	W	1-0	0-0	6	Bonar [73]	922
22	20	H	Brechin C	W	1-0	0-0	4	Campbell [77]	1445
23	27	A	Stranraer	W	2-0	1-0	4	Fotheringham [27], Davidson [70]	372
24	Feb 3	H	Alloa Ath	W	3-0	1-0	4	McManus (pen) [20], Campbell [56], Hislop [82]	1763
25	17	A	Peterhead	D	0-0	0-0	4		814
26	21	A	Ayr U	W	2-0	0-0	—	Andrews [72], Wilson [74]	853
27	24	H	Forfar Ath	W	2-1	1-1	4	Andrews [15], Fairbairn [80]	1945
28	Mar 3	A	Cowdenbeath	W	5-1	4-1	4	Fotheringham 2 [22, 31], Campbell [42], Hislop [44], Lumsden [65]	2249
29	10	H	Stirling A	L	0-1	0-0	4		2161
30	17	A	Brechin C	W	2-1	1-0	3	McLaughlin [28], Hislop [79]	909
31	31	H	Stranraer	D	0-0	0-0	3		1645
32	Apr 3	H	Ayr U	L	0-1	0-0	—		1546
33	7	A	Alloa Ath	W	3-2	3-0	3	Andrews [10], McManus [14], Hislop [32]	825
34	14	H	Morton	W	2-0	0-0	3	Lumsden [70], McLaughlin [76]	4327
35	21	A	Forfar Ath	W	2-1	1-0	3	Fotheringham [37], Lumsden [67]	699
36	28	H	Peterhead	W	2-0	1-0	3	Andrews [5], Fairbairn [59]	1589

Final League Position: 3

Honours
League Champions: First Division: 1992-93, 1994-95. Division II 1907-08, 1909-10 (shared), 1937-38, 1948-49; *Runners-up:* Division II 1908-09, 1926-27, 1966-67. Second Division 1975-76, 1977-78, 1986-87.
Scottish Cup Runners-up: 1913. *League Cup Winners: (Coca-Cola Cup):* 1994-95. *Runners-up:* 1948-49.

European: *UEFA Cup:* 6 matches (1995-96).

Club colours: Shirt: Navy blue with white sleeves. Shorts: White with navy and red trim. Stockings: Navy blue with white turnover.

Goalscorers: *League* (50): McManus 7 (1 pen), Fotheringham 6 (1 pen), Campbell 5, Andrews 4, Fairbairn 4, Harty 4 (1 pen), Hislop 4, Oné 4, Lumsden 3, Davidson 2, McLaughlin 2, Thorarinsson 2, Bonar 1, Manson 1, Wilson 1.
Play-Offs (1): Fairbairn 1.
Scottish Cup (0).
CIS Cup (1): Oné.
Challenge Cup (1): Oné.

Brown M 16	Bonar S 23 + 5	Fotheringham K 28 + 2	Silvestro C 23 + 3	Campbell M 28	Lumsden T 30	Fairbairn B 14 + 10	McManus P 25 + 3	Harty I 9 + 3	Davidson I 28 + 1	Kilgannon S 9 + 7	Oné A 13 + 8	Manson S 7 + 6	Tulloch S 3 + 4	Leiper C — + 1	Janczyk N 3 + 4	Barrau X — + 2	Dair J 1	Thorarinsson H 10 + 1	Wilson C 27	Andrews M 22	Currie P 6 + 2	Bannerman S — + 1	Tansey P — + 3	Darling J 1	Batchelor B 1	Sargent F — + 1	Fahey C 20 + 1	Pelosi M 12 + 5	Halley J — + 1	Ciani A — + 1	McLaughlin D 12 + 4	Carcary D 10 + 2	Hislop S 9 + 2	Neil J 6	Dingwall J — + 2	Mackie J — + 1	*Match No.*
1	2	3^3	4	5	6	7^2	8	9^1	10	11	12	13	14																								1
1	2	3	4	5	6	12	8	13	10	14	9^2	7^3	11^1																								2
1	2	3	4	5	6	12		8	10	11^3	9^2	13	7^1	14																							3
1	2	3	4	5	6			8	10	11^1	9	13			7^2	12																					4
1	2	3	4	5	6	7^1			10	11^3	9	12	14		8^2	13																					5
1	2	6		4	5	7	10	9^2	8		13	11	3^1		12																						6
1	2	3		4	5	7^1	10	9	8^2	12	13	11			6																						7
1	2	3	6	4	5		10	9	12	11^1	13	7^2			14		8^3																				8
1	2	3	6^3	4	5		7	10	8	12	9^2	11^1			14			13																			9
1		3	6^1		5		11	14	8^2		9^3							10	2	4	7	12	13														10
1	8	3			5				6■		10^2	11^1			13			9	2	4	7		12														11
1	2	4		6		13				12^3	9							10^2	3	5	8^1		14	7	11												12
1		3	8	5		7^1			6	12	9							10	2	4	11																13
1	12	3	8	5		7^2			6		9							10	2	4	11^1					13											14
1	2	3	8	5		11	9		6		12							10^1	7^2	4	13																15
1^6	12	3■	8	5		7	9		6		13							10^2	2	4	11^1						15										16
	8		6	4	5		9			11^2	10^3	13	14					7^1	2		12						1	3									17
	8			4	5		9	12		11	10^2	6^1						7	2								1	3	13								18
	8^1		12	4	5	7	9	10^2	6^3		13	14						11	2								1	3									19
			6	4	5	7	9	10^2	11^1		8		12						2								1	3		13							20
	12	14	8	4	6	13	9		7	11^1									2	5							1	3^3			10^2						21
			8	4	6	13	9		7	11^1									2	5							1	3			10^2	12					22
		3	8	4	6	12	9		7		13								2	5							1				10^1	11^2					23
	14	3	8	4	6	13	9^2		7^3										2	5							1				10^1	11	12				24
	12	6	8■	4	5		9		7										2								1	3			13	11^2	10^1				25
	8	3^2		4	6	14	9^3		7										2	5							1	12			13	11	10^1				26
		14	8	4	6	12	9^1		7										2	5							1	3^3			10^2	11	13				27
	8	3^1		4	6	10^3	13		7										2	5							1	12			14	11^2	9				28
	8	3		4^2	6	13	10^3		7■										2	5							1	14			12	11	9^1				29
	6		8		5	7	12												2	4							1	3			10	11	9^1				30
		3	6		5	7	12												2	4							1	11^1			10		9	8			31
		3	6		5		7												2	4							1	12			10	11^1	9	8			32
	7	3		4^2	6^1		8			13									2	5							1	12			10		9	11			33
	8	6	12		4				7^3	14									2	5							1	3			10		9^1	11^2	13		34
	8	6			4		9		7										2	5							1	3■			10^1	12		11			35
	6	3	12			7	9		5^2										2	4							1				10^3	11^1		8	13	14	36

RANGERS — Premier League

Year Formed: 1873. *Ground & Address:* Ibrox Stadium, 150 Edmiston Drive, Glasgow G51 2XD.
Telephone: (main switchboard) 0141 580 8500. *Fax:* 0870 600 1978. *Website:* www.rangers.co.uk
Ground Capacity: all seated: 51,082. *Size of Pitch:* 105m × 68m.
Executive Chairman: Sir David Murray. *Chief Executive:* Martin Bain. *Head of Football Administration:* Andrew Dickson.
Manager: Walter Smith. *Assistant Manager:* Ally McCoist. *Physio:* David Henderson.
Managers since 1975: Jock Wallace, John Greig, Jock Wallace, Graeme Souness, Walter Smith, Dick Advocaat, Alex McLeish, Paul Le Guen.
Club Nickname(s): The Gers. *Previous Grounds:* Flesher's Haugh, Burnbank, Kinning Park, Old Ibrox.
Record Attendance: 118,567 v Celtic, Division I, 2 Jan 1939.
Record Transfer Fee received: £8,500,000 for G. Van Bronckhorst to Arsenal (2001).
Record Transfer Fee paid: £12 million for Tore Andre Flo from Chelsea (November 2000).
Record Victory: 14-2 v Blairgowrie, Scottish Cup 1st rd, 20 Jan, 1934. *Record Defeat:* 2-10 v Airdrieonians; 1886.
Most Capped Player: Ally McCoist, 60, Scotland. *Most League Appearances:* 496: John Greig, 1962-78.
Most League Goals in Season (Individual): 44: Sam English, Division I, 1931-32.
Most Goals Overall (Individual): 355: Ally McCoist; 1985-98.

Honours
League Champions: (51 times) Division I 1890-91 (shared), 1898-99, 1899-1900, 1900-01, 1901-02, 1910-11, 1911-12, 1912-13, 1917-18, 1919-20, 1920-21, 1922-23, 1923-24, 1924-25, 1926-27, 1927-28, 1928-29, 1929-30, 1930-31, 1932-33, 1933-34, 1934-35, 1936-37, 1938-39, 1946-47, 1948-49, 1949-50, 1952-53, 1955-56, 1956-57, 1958-59, 1960-61, 1962-63, 1963-64, 1974-75. Premier Division: 1975-76, 1977-78, 1986-87, 1988-89, 1989-90, 1990-91, 1991-92, 1992-93, 1993-94, 1994-95, 1995-96, 1996-97, 1998-99, 1999-2000, 2002-03, 2004-05; *Runners-up:* 26 times.

RANGERS 2006–07 LEAGUE RECORD

Match No.	Date	Venue	Opponents	Result	H/T Score	Lg. Pos.	Goalscorers	Attendance
1	Jul 30	A	Motherwell	W 2-1	1-0	—	Sionko [7], Prso [65]	11,745
2	Aug 5	H	Dundee U	D 2-2	0-1	4	Burke [57], Robb (og) [79]	50,394
3	13	A	Dunfermline Ath	D 1-1	0-0	6	Buffel [63]	8561
4	19	H	Hearts	W 2-0	0-0	1	Boyd 2 (1 pen) [46 (p), 49]	50,239
5	27	A	Kilmarnock	D 2-2	1-0	3	Boyd 2 [43, 84]	13,506
6	Sept 9	H	Falkirk	W 4-0	2-0	2	Bardsley [17], Prso [28], Boyd (pen) [67], Buffel [78]	50,196
7	17	A	Hibernian	L 1-2	0-1	3	Sebo [64]	16,450
8	23	A	Celtic	L 0-2	0-1	3		59,341
9	Oct 1	H	Aberdeen	W 1-0	0-0	4	Sebo [88]	50,488
10	14	H	Inverness CT	L 0-1	0-0	3		49,494
11	22	A	St Mirren	W 3-2	2-1	3	Adam [18], Buffel [26], Novo [85]	8384
12	28	H	Motherwell	D 1-1	1-0	3	Boyd [36]	49,785
13	Nov 5	A	Dundee U	L 1-2	0-0	3	Adam [50]	10,392
14	11	H	Dunfermline Ath	W 2-0	0-0	2	Boyd [62], Smith [77]	48,218
15	19	A	Hearts	W 1-0	0-0	2	Novo [78]	17,040
16	26	H	Kilmarnock	W 3-0	2-0	2	Adam [22], Boyd [28], Prso [57]	48,289
17	Dec 3	A	Falkirk	L 0-1	0-1	2		7245
18	9	H	Hibernian	W 3-0	3-0	2	Prso [15], Sionko [31], Ferguson [36]	49,702
19	17	H	Celtic	D 1-1	0-1	—	Hemdani [88]	50,418
20	23	A	Aberdeen	W 2-1	2-0	2	Novo [21], Sionko [24]	20,045
21	27	A	Inverness CT	L 1-2	1-1	—	Novo (pen) [21]	7522
22	30	H	St Mirren	D 1-1	1-1	3	Boyd [18]	50,273
23	Jan 2	A	Motherwell	W 1-0	0-0	—	Boyd (pen) [69]	10,338
24	13	H	Dundee U	W 5-0	2-0	2	Adam [22], Burke [35], Boyd 2 [58, 68], Ferguson [87]	50,276
25	21	A	Dunfermline Ath	W 1-0	1-0	2	Adam [9]	7868
26	27	H	Hearts	D 0-0	0-0	2		50,321
27	Feb 11	A	Kilmarnock	W 3-1	2-0	2	Boyd 3 (2 pens) [9 (p), 30, 60 (p)]	11,894
28	18	H	Falkirk	W 2-1	1-0	2	Boyd [34], Ferguson [72]	49,850
29	Mar 4	A	Hibernian	W 2-0	1-0	2	Adam 2 [3, 58]	16,265
30	11	A	Celtic	W 1-0	0-0	2	Ehiogu [49]	59,425
31	17	H	Aberdeen	W 3-0	3-0	2	Boyd 3 [8, 25, 30]	50,354
32	31	H	Inverness CT	D 1-1	1-0	2	Adam [15]	50,278
33	Apr 8	A	St Mirren	W 1-0	1-0	2	Novo [5]	7308
34	21	H	Hearts	W 2-1	0-1	2	Rae [51], Ferguson [78]	50,099
35	28	A	Hibernian	D 3-3	1-2	2	Adam 2 [24, 78], Hutton [54]	16,747
36	May 5	H	Celtic	W 2-0	1-0	2	Boyd [34], Adam [55]	50,384
37	13	H	Kilmarnock	L 0-1	0-1	2		50,085
38	20	A	Aberdeen	L 0-2	0-2	2		20,010

Final League Position: 2

Scottish Cup Winners: (31 times) 1894, 1897, 1898, 1903, 1928, 1930, 1932, 1934, 1935, 1936, 1948, 1949, 1950, 1953, 1960, 1962, 1963, 1964, 1966, 1973, 1976, 1978, 1979, 1981, 1992, 1993, 1996, 1999, 2000, 2002, 2003; *Runners-up:* 17 times.
League Cup Winners: (24 times) 1946-47, 1948-49, 1960-61, 1961-62, 1963-64, 1964-65, 1970-71, 1975-76, 1977-78, 1978-79, 1981-82, 1983-84, 1984-85, 1986-87, 1987-88, 1988-89, 1990-91, 1992-93, 1993-94, 1996-97, 1998-99, 2001-02, 2002-03, 2004-05; *Runners-up:* 6 times.

European: *European Cup:* 127 matches (1956-57, 1957-58, 1959-60 semi-finals, 1961-62, 1963-64, 1964-65, 1975-76, 1976-77, 1978-79, 1987-88, 1989-90, 1990-91, 1991-92, 1992-93 final pool, 1993-94, 1994-95, 1995-96; 1996-97, 1997-98, 1999-2000, 2000-01, 2003-04, 2005-06).
Cup Winners' Cup: 54 matches (1960-61 runners-up, 1962-63, 1966-67 runners-up, 1969-70, 1971-72 winners, 1973-74, 1977-78, 1979-80, 1981-82, 1983-84). *UEFA Cup:* 68 matches (*Fairs Cup:* 1967-68, 1968-69 semi-finals, 1970-71. *UEFA Cup:* 1982-83, 1984-85, 1985-86, 1986-87, 1988-89, 1997-98, 1998-99, 1999-2000, 2000-01, 2002-03, 2004-05, 2006-07).

Club colours: Shirt: Royal blue with red and white trim. Shorts: White with red and blue trim. Stockings: Black with red tops.

Goalscorers: *League* (61): Boyd 20 (5 pens), Adam 11, Novo 5 (1 pen), Ferguson 4, Prso 4, Buffel 3, Sionko 3, Burke 2, Sebo 2, Bardsley 1, Ehiogu 1, Hemdani 1, Hutton 1, Rae 1, Smith 1, own goal 1.
Scottish Cup (2): Boyd 2.
CIS Cup (2): Boyd 1, own goal 1.

Letizi L 7	Hutton A 32 + 1	Smith S 17	Svensson K 20 + 1	Rodriguez J 12 + 1	Hemdani B 36	Clement J 19	Buffel T 9 + 8	Sionko L 14 + 4	Prso D 23 + 4	Adam C 32	Novo N 22 + 6	N'Diaye M — + 1	Boyd K 25 + 7	Burke C 10 + 12	Sebo F 4 + 20	Martin L 4 + 3	Bardsley P 5	McGregor A 31	Rae G 3 + 7	Ferguson B 31 + 1	Papac S 19 + 2	Lennon S — + 3	Murray I 12 + 1	Weir D 14	Ehiogu U 9	Thomson K 8 + 1	Klos S — + 1	Shinnie A — + 2	Match No.
1	2	3	4	5	6	7	8^{2}	9^{1}	10	11	12	13																	1
1	2	3	4^{2}	5	6	7	8	9	10^{3}	11^{1}			12	13	14														2
1	2	3	4	5	6	7	8	9^{2}	10^{1}	11^{3}			12	13		14													3
1	12	3	4	5	6	7	14		10				11^{2}	9^{3}	13	8	2^{1}												4
	2	3	4	5	6	7	12	9^{1}	10^{3}				11		13	8^{2}		1	14										5
		3	4	5	6	7	14	9^{1}	10^{3}				11	8^{2}	13		2	1		12									6
		3^{1}	4	5		8	9^{3}	14					13	10	11	6^{2}	2■	1		7	12								7
	2^{1}	3		5^{3}	6			12	10	9			11	8^{2}		13		1	14	7	4								8
		3		5	6		8	9^{1}	10^{2}	11^{3}			12		14	13	2	1		7	4								9
1		3		5^{2}	6		8		10^{1}	11	13		12		9		2			7	4								10
1	2	3		5	6		8		10^{1}	9	12		11^{2}		13					7	4								11
1	2	3		5	6		8		12	9^{1}	10^{2}		11		13					7	4								12
	2	3^{2}			5	6	8^{1}		11	9	10		12		13			1		7	4								13
	2	3	4		5	6			11^{2}	9^{3}	10		12		14	8^{1}		1	13	7									14
	2	3	4		5	6			10	8	9		11					1		7									15
	2		4		5	6	13	12	10^{1}	8	9^{2}		11^{3}		14			1		7	3								16
	2		4		5	6	13	14	10^{3}	8	9		11^{1}		12			1		7	3^{2}								17
	2	3	4		5	6	14	9^{2}	10^{1}	8	11^{3}				12			1	13	7									18
	2	3	4		5	6	13	9^{1}	10	8^{2}	11				12			1		7									19
	2		4		5	6		9	10^{1}	8	11^{2}				12			1	13	7	3								20
	2		4		5	6		9^{1}		8	11^{2}			12	10			1		7	3	13							21
	2		4		5	6		9		8^{1}	10		11	12				1		7	3								22
	2		4	13	5	6		9^{1}	10■		12		11^{2}	8^{3}	14			1	3				7						23
	2		4		3	6			10^{1}	8	12		11	9^{2}	13			1		7			5						24
	2		4		3		12			8	10^{2}		11	9^{1}	13			1		7			6	5					25
	2				3			9^{2}		8	10		11^{1}	13	12			1		7			6	5	4				26
	2		12		3					10	13		11	9				1		7			6	5	4^{1}	8^{2}			27
	2		4^{1}		3			9^{2}	14	8^{3}	10		11	13				1		7	12		6	5					28
	2				3				12	10			11^{1}	9				1		7			6	5	4	8			29
	2				3					10	11^{2}				9^{1}			1	13	7			6	5	4	8	12		30
	2				3				8^{3}	10^{2}	9^{1}		11	12				1	13	7	4		6	5				14	31
	2				3				8^{2}	10	9^{1}		11	12	13			1		7	4		6	5					32
	2				3				12	10	9		11^{2}	8^{1}				1		7	6			5	4	13			33
	2				3				10				11					1	9	7	6^{1}		12	5	4	8			34
	2				3^{1}					9	10		11	12				1		7	6			5	4	8			35
	2				3					9	10		11^{1}	13	12			1		7	6			5	4	8^{2}			36
					3^{1}					9	10^{2}		11	12				1		7	2	13	6^{3}	5	4	8		14	37
	2									9	10^{1}		11^{2}	12				1	4	7	3	13	6	5		8			38

ROSS COUNTY Second Division

Year Formed: 1929. *Ground & Address:* Victoria Park, Dingwall IV15 9QW. *Telephone:* 01349 860860. *Fax:* 01349 866277.
E-mail: donnie@rosscountyfootballclub.co.uk. *Website:* www.rosscountyfootballclub.co.uk
Ground Capacity: 6700. *Size of Ground:* 105×68m.
Chairman: Roy MacGregor. *Secretary:* Donnie MacBean.
Manager: Dick Campbell. *Director of Football:* George Adams. *Coaches:* Derek Adams and (*Head of Youth*) David Kirkwood. *Physio:* Douglas Sim.
Managers since 1975: N. Cooper, A. Smith, J. Robertson, S. Leitch.
Club Nickname(s): The Staggies.
Record Attendance: 6600, benefit match v Celtic, 31 August 1970.
Record Transfer Fee Received: £200,000 for Neil Tarrant to Aston Villa (April 1999).
Record Transfer Fee Paid: £25,000 for Barry Wilson from Southampton (Oct. 1992).
Record Victory: 11-0 v St Cuthbert Wanderers, Scottish Cup, 11 Dec 1993.
Record Defeat: 1-10 v Inverness Thistle, Highland League.
Most League Appearances: 157: David Mackay, 1995-2001.
Most League Goals in Season: 22: Derek Adams, 1996-97.
Most League Goals (Overall): 44: Steven Ferguson, 1996-2002.

ROSS COUNTY 2006–07 LEAGUE RECORD

Match No.	Date	Venue	Opponents	Result		H/T Score	Lg. Pos.	Goalscorers	Attendance
1	Aug 5	A	Airdrie U	W	2-0	1-0	—	McKinlay 23, Gardyne 50	1292
2	12	H	Livingston	L	0-3	0-2	5		2321
3	19	A	Gretna	L	1-2	0-2	6	Gunn 47	1195
4	26	A	St Johnstone	L	1-3	0-2	7	McKinlay 53	2109
5	Sept 9	H	Queen of the S	W	1-0	0-0	7	Cowie 56	2265
6	16	A	Clyde	L	0-3	0-0	7		993
7	23	H	Hamilton A	L	0-1	0-1	8		1925
8	30	A	Partick Th	L	2-3	1-1	8	McKinlay (pen) 13, Keddie 79	2020
9	Oct 14	H	Dundee	W	1-0	1-0	8	Higgins 36	2454
10	21	A	Livingston	D	0-0	0-0	8		1760
11	28	H	Airdrie U	W	2-1	2-0	8	Dowie 14, Gardyne 34	2010
12	Nov 4	A	Queen of the S	L	0-2	0-0	8		1497
13	18	H	Clyde	D	1-1	1-0	8	Ciani 41	2195
14	22	H	St Johnstone	D	2-2	1-2	—	Gardyne 27, McKinlay (pen) 90	1648
15	25	A	Hamilton A	D	0-0	0-0	8		1180
16	Dec 2	A	Dundee	L	1-3	0-0	8	Robertson 65	3380
17	9	H	Partick Th	L	2-5	1-2	8	Dowie 32, Robertson 55	2381
18	16	H	Gretna	L	0-1	0-0	8		1956
19	26	A	Airdrie U	W	1-0	1-0	—	Scott 25	1301
20	30	H	Queen of the S	W	1-0	1-0	8	Hooks 33	2413
21	Jan 2	A	St Johnstone	L	1-2	0-1	—	Cowie 60	2519
22	20	A	Clyde	W	4-2	2-0	8	Imrie (og) 9, McKinlay 36, Cowie 2 56, 58	1100
23	27	H	Dundee	D	0-0	0-0	8		2175
24	Feb 10	A	Partick Th	D	1-1	0-0	8	Cowie 90	2211
25	17	A	Gretna	L	1-4	0-2	8	O'Carroll 85	1361
26	24	H	Livingston	L	0-2	0-0	8		2324
27	Mar 3	H	St Johnstone	D	1-1	0-1	8	Higgins 73	1689
28	10	A	Queen of the S	L	0-2	0-2	10		2479
29	13	H	Hamilton A	W	4-1	3-0	—	Cowie 2 10, 16, Higgins 14, Gunn 78	1475
30	17	H	Clyde	D	2-2	0-0	9	Higgins 49, Adams 79	2145
31	31	A	Hamilton A	L	0-1	0-1	9		1035
32	Apr 3	H	Partick Th	W	2-1	2-1	—	Scott 16, Adams 27	1880
33	7	A	Dundee	L	2-3	0-2	10	Higgins 47, Gardyne 74	3013
34	14	H	Airdrie U	D	1-1	1-1	10	Proctor (og) 16	2717
35	21	A	Livingston	D	1-1	0-1	10	Gardyne 47	1743
36	28	H	Gretna	L	2-3	1-2	10	Gardyne 30, O'Carroll 49	6216

Final League Position: 10

Honours
League Champions: Third Division: 1998-99. *Bell's League Challenge Cup: Winners:* 2006-07. ***Runners up:*** 2004-05.

Club colours: Shirt: Navy blue with white trim. Shorts: White with navy side panels. Stockings: Navy blue with two white hoops.

Goalscorers: *League* (40): Cowie 7, Gardyne 6, Higgins 5, McKinlay 5 (2 pens), Adams 2, Dowie 2, Gunn 2, O'Carroll 2, Robertson 2, Scott 2, Ciani 1, Hooks 1, Keddie 1, own goals 2.
Scottish Cup (0).
CIS Cup (5): Cowie 2, Gunn 1, Higgins 1, McKinlay 1.
Challenge Cup (13): Gunn 3, McKinlay 3 (1 pen), Dowie 2, Higgins 2, Anderson 1, Ciani 1, Williams 1.

Samson C 29	Niven D 6	Keddie A 26	McCulloch M 26+2	Dowie A 36	Tiernan F 5+3	Gardyne M 24+8	Adams D 24+1	Higgins S 21+7	Cowie D 28	McKinlay K 27+3	Gunn C 7+20	Winters D —+2	Robertson H 18+6	Anderson S 7+2	Irvine G 17	Scott M 21+7	Moore D 13+2	Ciani A 5+9	Williams A 2+2	Crooks J 2+5	Hooks N 1+4	Webb S 5+1	Wilkie L 4	Smith J 8	O'Carroll D 9+6	Shields D 13	Tomei M 7	Morgan A 5	Rezgane M —+1	*Match No.*
1	2	3	4	5	6	7^{2}	8	9^{1}	10	11	12	13																		1
1	2	3	4^{1}	5	6^{2}	7	8^{3}		10	11	9	14	12	13																2
1	2	5		4	8^{2}	7	9		10	11	12		3^{1}		6	13														3
1		5		4	6	7	8	12	10^{1}	11	9				2		3													4
1	4	3		5		7^{3}	8	9^{2}	10	11^{1}	13			14	2	12		6												5
1	4		3	5		8		12	10	11	13			6^{3}	2	14		7^{2}	9^{1}											6
1	2^{1}	5		4	6	12		9	10	11^{3}	14		3		7			13	8^{2}											7
1		3	5	4		7^{1}	8	9	10	11	12^{2}		6		2	13														8
1		3	5	4	12	7	8	9^{3}	10^{1}	11^{2}					2	6		13	14											9
1		3	5	4	12	7^{2}	8^{1}	9^{3}		11				6	2	10		13	14											10
1		3	5	4	14	7^{3}	8	9^{1}		11	13			6^{2}	2	10		12												11
1		3	5	4		7	8	9^{1}		11	13			6^{2}	2	10		12												12
1		3	12	4		7^{2}	8		10	5	6^{1}		13		2■	11		9^{3}		14										13
1		3	2	4		7	8			5	6		11			10		9^{1}		12										14
1		3		4		7^{1}	8			5	6^{2}		11		2	10		12		9	13									15
1				4		7	8			3	10^{2}		11		2	6		13		9^{1}	12	5								16
1			12	4^{1}		7	8			3	13		11^{3}		2	10		9		14	6^{2}	5								17
1				4		7	8	9	10	3				6	2	11^{1}		12					5							18
1			6	4		7		9^{1}	10	3	12		11		2	8							5							19
1			6	4		10^{3}		9^{2}			7^{1}		11		2	8■	3	14		13	12		5							20
1			6	4^{1}		10		9	7^{3}	3			11				8^{2}			13	14	12	5	2						21
1		5	6	4					10	11^{2}	13		12	8^{1}			3							2	7	9■				22
1		5	6	4				9^{1}	10	11^{2}	12		13	8^{3}		14	3							2	7					23
1		5	6^{2}	4		12		14	10	11^{3}			13			8^{1}	3							2	7	9				24
1		5■	6^{2}	4		13		14	10	11^{1}			12			8^{3}	3							2	7	9				25
1			6	4		7		13	10	14	12		11^{2}				3					5		2	8^{1}	9^{3}				26
			6^{3}	4		7^{2}		14	10	12			11			13	3^{1}					5		2	8	9	1			27
			6	4		12	13	9	10	3			11			7^{1}						5		2^{2}	8		1			28
		5	2	4		14	6^{2}	8^{1}	10		12		11			7	3								13	9^{3}	1			29
		5	2	4			6	8^{1}	10		13		11			7	3^{2}								12	9	1			30
		5	2	4		13	6	8^{3}	10		14		11^{2}			7	3								12	9^{1}	1			31
		5	2	4			6^{1}	8^{3}	10	12	14		11			7									13	9^{2}	1	3		32
		5	2^{2}	4		12	6	8	10		14		11^{1}			7									13	9	1	3^{3}		33
1		5	2■	4		12	6	8^{2}	10	3						7■	13								14	9^{3}		11^{1}		34
1		5		4		7	6	8^{3}	10	3^{2}	12						13								2	9		11^{1}	14	35
1		5	2	4		7	6^{3}	13	10		14					12	3								8	9^{2}		11^{1}		36

ST JOHNSTONE — First Division

Year Formed: 1884. *Ground & Address:* McDiarmid Park, Crieff Road, Perth PH1 2SJ. *Telephone:* 01738 459090. *Fax:* 01738 625 771. *Clubcall:* 0898 121559. *E-mail:* angome@saints.sol.co.uk. *Website:* www.stjohnstonefc.co.uk
Ground Capacity: all seated: 10,673. *Size of Pitch:* 115yd × 75yd.
Chairman: G.S. Brown. *Secretary and Managing Director:* Stewart Duff. *Sales Executives:* Paul Smith and Susan Weir.
Manager: Owen Coyle. *First Team Coach:* Sandy Stewart. *Youth Coach:* Tommy Campbell.
Managers since 1975: J. Stewart, J. Storrie, A. Stuart, A. Rennie, I. Gibson, A. Totten, J. McClelland, P. Sturrock, S. Clark, B. Stark, J. Connolly.
Club Nickname(s): Saints. *Previous Grounds:* Recreation Grounds, Muirton Park.
Record Attendance: (McDiarmid Park): 10,545 v Dundee, Premier Division, 23 May 1999.
Record Transfer Fee received: £1,750,000 for Calum Davidson to Blackburn R (March 1998).
Record Transfer Fee paid: £400,000 for Billy Dodds from Dundee (1994).
Record Victory: 9-0 v Albion R, League Cup, 9 Mar 1946.
Record Defeat: 1-10 v Third Lanark, Scottish Cup, 24 Jan 1903.
Most Capped Player: Nick Dasovic, 26, Canada.
Most League Appearances: 298: Drew Rutherford.
Most League Goals in Season (Individual): 36: Jimmy Benson, Division II, 1931-32.
Most Goals Overall (Individual): 140: John Brogan, 1977-83.

ST JOHNSTONE 2006–07 LEAGUE RECORD

Match No.	Date	Venue	Opponents	Result		H/T Score	Lg. Pos.	Goalscorers	Attendance
1	Aug 5	H	Clyde	D	0-0	0-0	—		2572
2	12	A	Queen of the S	W	1-0	1-0	3	Mensing ^{10}	1586
3	19	H	Hamilton A	D	0-0	0-0	4		2295
4	26	H	Ross Co	W	3-1	2-0	4	Milne 2 $^{37, 39}$, Sheerin ^{80}	2109
5	Sept 9	A	Partick Th	W	5-1	3-0	3	Scotland 3 $^{1, 5, 90}$, Milne 2 $^{41, 63}$	2914
6	16	H	Airdrie U	W	1-0	1-0	2	Milne ^{44}	2178
7	23	A	Livingston	D	1-1	1-1	3	Scotland ^{29}	2359
8	30	A	Dundee	D	1-1	1-0	3	Sheerin ^{27}	5538
9	Oct 14	H	Gretna	D	3-3	0-0	2	Sheerin ^{52}, Hardie ^{60}, Scotland ^{89}	3150
10	21	H	Queen of the S	W	5-0	2-0	1	Sheerin 2 $^{30, 48}$, Lawson ^{37}, MacDonald ^{77}, Milne ^{80}	2364
11	28	A	Clyde	L	0-1	0-0	3		1427
12	Nov 4	H	Partick Th	W	2-0	1-0	1	Sheerin ^{14}, MacDonald ^{73}	3798
13	18	A	Airdrie U	L	1-2	0-1	4	Milne ^{85}	1550
14	22	A	Ross Co	D	2-2	2-1	—	Sheerin ^{4}, Hardie ^{23}	1648
15	25	H	Livingston	L	1-2	0-1	4	Hardie ^{73}	2766
16	Dec 2	A	Gretna	L	0-2	0-2	4		1744
17	9	H	Dundee	W	2-1	2-1	3	Scotland 2 $^{7, 25}$	4127
18	16	A	Hamilton A	D	2-2	1-0	3	Hardie ^{42}, MacDonald ^{55}	1356
19	26	H	Clyde	W	2-1	0-0	—	Milne ^{84}, MacDonald ^{88}	2604
20	Jan 2	H	Ross Co	W	2-1	1-0	—	Mensing ^{10}, McManus ^{87}	2519
21	13	A	Livingston	L	2-3	1-1	2	Lawrie ^{23}, McLaren ^{88}	1549
22	20	H	Airdrie U	W	4-3	2-0	2	Tierney (og) ^{26}, Scotland 2 $^{34, 46}$, McLaren ^{77}	2106
23	27	H	Gretna	W	2-1	1-0	2	James ^{8}, Hardie ^{85}	3201
24	Feb 10	A	Dundee	L	1-2	0-0	2	Scotland ^{50}	5145
25	17	H	Hamilton A	W	4-2	3-2	2	Scotland 2 $^{12, 42}$, Mensing ^{25}, Morais ^{81}	2259
26	Mar 3	A	Ross Co	D	1-1	1-0	2	MacDonald ^{6}	1689
27	6	A	Queen of the S	L	0-1	0-1	—		1770
28	10	H	Partick Th	W	2-0	1-0	2	Hardie 2 $^{15, 46}$	2453
29	13	A	Partick Th	L	0-2	0-1	—		1697
30	17	A	Airdrie U	W	2-1	1-1	2	Hardie ^{24}, Scotland ^{80}	1138
31	25	H	Dundee	W	2-0	0-0	2	Scotland ^{46}, Hardie ^{61}	3523
32	31	H	Livingston	L	1-2	1-0	2	Scotland ^{30}	2436
33	Apr 7	A	Gretna	W	2-0	2-0	2	Scotland 2 $^{22, 44}$	2133
34	17	A	Clyde	W	1-0	0-0	—	Hardie ^{73}	1352
35	21	H	Queen of the S	W	3-0	1-0	2	Lawrie ^{39}, Mensing ^{64}, McLaren ^{70}	4168
36	28	A	Hamilton A	W	4-3	3-1	2	James ^{23}, Hardie 2 $^{32, 80}$, Scotland ^{39}	4975

Final League Position: 2

Honours
League Champions: First Division 1982-83, 1989-90, 1996-97. Division II 1923-24, 1959-60, 1962-63; *Runners-up:* Division II 1931-32. Second Division 1987-88.
Scottish Cup: Semi-finals 1934, 1968, 1989, 1991.
League Cup: Runners-up: 1969-70, 1998-99.
League Challenge Cup: Runners-up: 1996-97.

European: *UEFA Cup:* 10 matches (1971-72, 1999-2000).

Club colours: Shirt: Royal blue with white trim. Shorts: White. Stockings: Royal blue with white hoops.

Goalscorers: *League* (65): Scotland 18, Hardie 12, Milne 8, Sheerin 7, MacDonald 5, Mensing 4, McLaren 3, James 2, Lawrie 2, Lawson 1, McManus 1, Morais 1, own goal 1.
Scottish Cup (8): MacDonald 3, Hardie 2, Scotland 2, James 1.
CIS Cup (13): Milne 4, Scotland 4, Hardie 1, MacDonald 1, Mensing 1, Sheerin 1, Stevenson 1.
Challenge Cup (8): Menzie 2, Milne 2, Scotland 2, James 1, MacDonald 1.

Halliwell B 18+1	Lawrie A 28+3	Stanik G 36	McManus A 32	Weir J 1	James K 22	Mensing S 33	Sheridan D 10+7	Milne S 15+8	Scotland J 34+1	Sheerin P 35+1	Young D —+3	MacDonald P 19+17	Rutkiewicz K 1	Hardie M 32	Anderson S 21+5	Stevenson R —+2	McLaren W 14+13	Lawson P 6+2	Jackson A —+6	Coyle O —+1	McGovern M 1	Cuthbert K 17	Dyer W —+1	McInnes D 16	Doris S —+1	Morais F 5+8	Lilley D —+14	*Match No.*
1	2	3	4	5^{1}	6	7	8	9^{2}	10	11	12	13																1
1	2	3	4		6	7	8	13	10^{3}	11^{1}	12	14	5^{2}	9														2
1	2	3	5^{2}		6	4	8^{1}	9^{3}	$10^{\blacksquare}$	11	12	14		7	13													3
1	2	3			6	4	8	9^{2}	10	11		13		7^{1}	5	12												4
1	2	3	5		6	4	13	9^{1}	10	8		12		7^{3}		14	11^{2}											5
1	2	3	5			4	12	9^{2}	10	8		13		7	6		11^{1}											6
1	2	3	5		6^{1}	4	8		10	11^{2}		13		9	12		7											7
1	2	3	5			4	8^{1}	9^{2}	10^{3}	11		13		7	6		14	12										8
1	2	3	5			4^{3}	8^{2}	12	10	11		14		9	6		13	7^{1}										9
1	2	3	5			4	14	9	10^{1}	11		12		8^{2}	6		13	7^{3}										10
1	2	3	5			4^{2}	13	9^{1}	10^{3}	11		12		8	6		14	$7^{\blacksquare}$										11
1	2	3	5			4	12	9^{3}		8		10^{2}		7	6		11^{1}		13	14								12
1	2	3	5			4	14	9	10^{2}	11		13		8	6^{1}		12	7^{3}										13
1	2	3	5			4		9^{1}	10	11		12		8	6			$7^{\blacksquare}$										14
1	2	3	5			4		9^{1}	10	8		12		7	6		11											15
	2	3	5			4	14	9^{1}	10	11		12		8^{2}	6		13	7^{3}			1							16
1	2	3	5		6	4	8^{1}	13	10	11		9^{2}		7^{3}	14		12											17
1	2	3	5		6	4	8	12	10	11		9^{1}		7														18
		3	5^{2}		6	2	8	9	10^{1}	11		12		7^{3}	4		13	14				1						19
	2	3	5			4		9^{3}	10	8		14		7^{1}	6		11^{2}		12			1	13					20
	2	3^{2}	5			4			10	11		9^{1}		7^{3}	6		13		12			1		8	14			21
		3	5		6	2			10	11		9^{1}		7			8^{2}		13			1		4		12		22
		3	5		6	2			10^{3}	11		9^{1}		7	14		8^{2}					1		4		13	12	23
	2	3	5		6	8^{3}			10	11^{2}		9^{1}		$7^{\blacksquare}$			13					1		4		14	12	24
	2	3	5^{1}		6	8			10	11		9^{2}			12		7^{3}					1		4		14	13	25
	2	3	5		6	4		14	10^{1}	11		9^{3}					7^{2}					1		8		13	12	26
	2	3	5		6	8		13	10^{2}	11^{1}		9					7^{3}					1		4		12	14	27
	13	3	5		6	2		14	10^{1}	11		9^{3}		8								1		4^{2}		7	12	28
		3	5			2		12	10^{2}	11		9^{1}		8	$6^{\blacksquare}$							1		4		7	13	29
	2	3	5		6	4			13	14		9^{1}		8			11^{3}					1		10^{2}		7	12	30
	12	3	5		6^{3}	4			10	11		9^{2}		8	2^{1}							1		7		14	13	31
15		3	5		6				10	11		9^{1}		8	2^{2}		13					$1^{\blacksquare}$		4		7^{G}	12	32
1	12	3	5		6				10^{2}	7^{3}		9^{1}		8	2		14							4		$11^{\blacksquare}$	13	33
	5	3			6				10^{2}	7		9^{1}		8	2		11		13			1		4			12	34
	5	3				6			10	7^{3}		9^{1}		8	2		11^{2}		14			1		4		13	12	35
	5	3			6	11			10	7^{1}		9^{2}		8	2		12					1		4			13	36

ST MIRREN — Premier League

Year Formed: 1877. *Ground & Address:* St Mirren Park, Love St, Paisley PA3 2EA. *Telephone:* 0141 889 2558. *Fax:* 0141 848 6444. *E-mail:* commercial@saintmirren.net. *Website:* www.saintmirren.net
Ground Capacity: 10,866 (all seated). *Size of Pitch:* 112yd × 73yd.
Chairman: Stewart Gilmour. *Vice-Chairman:* George Campbell. *Secretary:* Allan Marshall.
Manager: Gus MacPherson. *Assistant Manager:* Andy Millen. *Commercial Manager:* Campbell Kennedy. *Youth Development Officer:* David Longwell.
Managers since 1975: Alex Ferguson, Jim Clunie, Rikki MacFarlane, Alex Miller, Alex Smith, Tony Fitzpatrick, David Hay, Jimmy Bone, Tony Fitzpatrick, Tom Hendrie, John Coughlin. *Club Nickname(s):* The Buddies. *Previous Grounds:* Short Roods 1877-79, Thistle Park Greenhill 1879-83, Westmarch 1883-94.
Record Attendance: 47,438 v Celtic, League Cup, 20 Aug 1949.
Record Transfer Fee received: £850,000 for Ian Ferguson to Rangers (1988).
Record Transfer Fee paid: £400,000 for Thomas Stickroth from Bayer Uerdingen (1990).
Record Victory: 15-0 v Glasgow University, Scottish Cup 1st rd, 30 Jan 1960.
Record Defeat: 0-9 v Rangers, Division I, 4 Dec 1897.
Most Capped Player: Godmundor Torfason, 29, Iceland.
Most League Appearances: 351: Tony Fitzpatrick, 1973-88.
Most League Goals in Season (Individual): 45: Dunky Walker, Division I, 1921-22.
Most Goals Overall (Individual): 221: David McCrae, 1923-34.

ST MIRREN 2006–07 LEAGUE RECORD

Match No.	Date	Venue	Opponents	Result		H/T Score	Lg. Pos.	Goalscorers	Attendance
1	Jul 29	A	Inverness CT	W	2-1	0-0	—	Sutton 2 [55, 75]	4267
2	Aug 5	H	Motherwell	W	2-0	1-0	1	Sutton [16], Quinn (og) [51]	5036
3	12	A	Celtic	L	0-2	0-1	4		56,579
4	19	H	Aberdeen	D	1-1	0-1	3	Broadfoot [86]	5344
5	26	H	Dundee U	L	1-3	0-2	7	Brady [48]	4902
6	Sept 9	A	Hearts	W	1-0	0-0	3	Kean [82]	16,823
7	16	H	Kilmarnock	L	0-1	0-0	7		5277
8	23	A	Dunfermline Ath	L	1-2	1-0	7	Sutton [10]	4914
9	30	H	Hibernian	W	1-0	1-0	3	Van Zanten [39]	6008
10	Oct 14	A	Falkirk	D	1-1	0-0	6	Mehmet [70]	4961
11	22	H	Rangers	L	2-3	1-2	8	Sutton 2 (1 pen) [5, 77 (p)]	8384
12	28	H	Inverness CT	D	1-1	0-1	8	Sutton [64]	4432
13	Nov 4	A	Motherwell	D	0-0	0-0	9		5337
14	12	H	Celtic	L	1-3	0-2	9	Sutton [56]	8445
15	18	A	Aberdeen	L	0-2	0-0	9		11,426
16	26	A	Dundee U	L	0-1	0-0	9		5681
17	Dec 2	H	Hearts	D	2-2	2-1	10	Kean 2 [18, 21]	5728
18	9	A	Kilmarnock	D	1-1	0-0	10	Corcoran [75]	5978
19	16	H	Dunfermline Ath	D	0-0	0-0	10		4246
20	23	A	Hibernian	L	1-5	1-2	11	Sutton [40]	13,053
21	26	H	Falkirk	W	1-0	0-0	—	Lappin [67]	5212
22	30	A	Rangers	D	1-1	1-1	11	Brittain [14]	50,273
23	Jan 1	A	Inverness CT	L	1-2	0-2	—	Broadfoot [76]	4246
24	20	A	Celtic	L	1-5	0-1	11	McGinn [47]	58,382
25	27	H	Aberdeen	L	0-2	0-2	11		4921
26	Feb 10	H	Dundee U	L	0-1	0-0	11		3849
27	17	A	Hearts	D	1-1	1-0	11	O'Donnell [15]	17,195
28	21	H	Motherwell	D	0-0	0-0	—		3576
29	Mar 3	H	Kilmarnock	L	0-2	0-0	11		4778
30	10	A	Dunfermline Ath	D	0-0	0-0	11		7149
31	31	A	Falkirk	L	0-2	0-2	11		5863
32	Apr 4	H	Hibernian	D	1-1	0-1	—	Sutton [89]	4031
33	8	H	Rangers	L	0-1	0-1	11		7308
34	23	A	Falkirk	W	2-0	1-0	11	Kean (pen) [37], Brady [56]	4441
35	30	H	Dunfermline Ath	L	0-1	0-0	11		10,251
36	May 5	A	Dundee U	W	2-0	1-0	11	Murray [22], Broadfoot [89]	6875
37	12	A	Motherwell	W	3-2	0-1	11	Sutton 2 [55, 83], Mehmet [59]	9277
38	19	H	Inverness CT	L	0-1	0-0	11		4834

Final League Position: 11

Honours
League Champions: First Division 1976-77, 1999-2000, 2005-06; *Runners-up:* 2004-05. Division II 1967-68; *Runners-up:* 1935-36.
Scottish Cup Winners: 1926, 1959, 1987. *Runners-up:* 1908, 1934, 1962.
League Cup Runners-up: 1955-56.
League Challenge Cup Winners: 2005-06.
B&Q Cup Runners-up: 1993-94. *Anglo-Scottish Cup:* 1979-80.

European: *Cup Winners' Cup:* 4 matches (1987-88). *UEFA Cup:* 10 matches (1980-81, 1983-84, 1985-86).

Club colours: Shirt: Black and white vertical stripes. Shorts: White with black trim. Stockings: White with two black hoops. Change colours: Predominantly red.

Goalscorers: *League* (31): Sutton 12 (1 pen), Kean 4 (1 pen), Broadfoot 3, Brady 2, Mehmet 2, Brittain 1, Corcoran 1, Lappin 1, McGinn 1, Murray 1, O'Donnell 1, Van Zanten 1, own goal 1.
Scottish Cup (2): Brittain 1, Sutton 1.
CIS Cup (3): Mehmet 2, Sutton 1.

Smith C 21	Van Zanten D 37	Broadfoot K 37	Potter J 25 + 1	McGowne K 19	Molloy C 6 + 6	Murray H 31	Lappin S 24	Brady G 26 + 3	Kean S 21 + 10	Sutton J 29 + 4	Brittain R 26 + 5	Corcoran M 10 + 17	Millen A 23	Mehmet B 11 + 14	McKenna D 1 + 9	Bullock T 17	McCay R — + 4	Reid A 20 + 2	Maxwell I 16	Burke A 4 + 9	Gemmill S — + 5	McGinn S 1 + 3	O'Donnell S 5	Malone E 4 + 2	Lawson P 4	*Match No.*
1	2	3	4	5	6	7	8	9[1]	10	11	12															1
1	2	3	4	5	6	7	8	9	10[1]	11		12														2
1	2	3	5		6[3]	7	8	9[2]	10[1]	11	13		4	12	14											3
1	2	3	4	5	6[3]	7	8[2]	9[1]	10	11		13		12	14											4
1	2	3	6	5		7	8[2]	9[3]	10	11		13	4[1]	12	14											5
	2	3	6[1]	5	12	7	8	9[2]	10[3]	11	13		4	14		1										6
	2	3		5[2]	6[3]	7	8		10	11	9[1]	12	4	13		1	14									7
	2	3		5[2]		7	8	6	10[1]	11	14	13	4	12		1		9[3]								8
	2	3			14	7	8[3]	6		11	9	13	4	10[2]		1		12	5[1]							9
	2	3		5		7	8	6	12	11[1]	9	13	4	10[2]		1										10
	2	3		5[1]		7[3]	8	6	14	11	9	12	4	10[2]	13	1										11
	2	3		5		7	8		12	11	6		4	10[2]		1		9[1]		13						12
	2	3		5	13	7	8	6[2]	12	11[1]	9		4	10		1										13
	2	3		5[1]		7	8	6[2]	14	11	9		4	10[3]		1		12		13						14
	2	3	5			7	8		12	11[1]	6		4	10		1		9[2]		13						15
	2	3	5			7	8		12	11	6[1]		4	10[3]	14	1		9[2]		13						16
	2	3	6	5	14	7	8	9[3]	10[1]	11			4	12[2]		1				13						17
	2	3	6	5		7	8	9		11	12	13	4[1]			1				10[2]						18
	2	3	4	5		7	8				6	11		12		1		9		10[1]						19
	2	3	4	5[2]		7[3]	8	14		11	6			10[1]		1	13	9			12					20
1	2	3		5		7	8	9		11[1]	6	10[2]	4		13						12					21
	2	3				7[1]	8	9			6	11[2]	4		12	1		10	5		13					22
	2	3	4[3]	5				7		11	6	10			8[1]	1	13	9[2]			14	12				23
1	2	3					8[3]	7	13	12	6	11[2]	4					10	5		14	9[1]				24
1	2	3	12	5			8	7[2]	10[3]	11	6	9	4[1]							14		13				25
1	2	3	4					7	12	11	6	10[2]						9[1]	5	14		13	8[3]			26
1	2	3	4					7	10		6	12						11	5				8	9[1]		27
1	2	3	4					12	10	11	6	13							5				8	9[1]	7[2]	28
1		3	4					7	10[1]	11	6	12		13	14			9	5				8[3]		2[2]	29
1	2	3	4		13	7			10[3]	14	6	12						11	5				8[1]		9[2]	30
1	2		3		13	7			10		6	12	4	11[3]					5	14				8[1]	9[2]	31
1	2	3	4		9[1]	7		8[2]	10	13	6	12		14				11[3]	5							32
1	2	3	4			7		8	10	11	6[2]	13		14				9[3]	5[1]					12		33
1	2	3	4			7		8	10	11	6							9	5							34
1	2	3	4			7		8[3]	10	11	6[1]	12		13	14			9[2]	5							35
1	2	3	5			7		14	10[2]			11[3]	4	12				8	6	9[1]				13		36
1	2	3	5			7			10	12		11	4[1]	13				8	6	9[2]						37
1	2	3				7			14	10[3]		11	4[2]	9			12	8	5	13				6[1]		38

STENHOUSEMUIR — Third Division

Year Formed: 1884. *Ground & Address:* Ochilview Park, Gladstone Rd, Stenhousemuir FK5 4QL. *Telephone:* 01324 562992. *Fax:* 01324 562980. *E-mail:* info@stenhousemuirfc.com. *Website:* www.stenhousemuirfc.com
Ground Capacity: total: 2654, seated: 626. *Size of Pitch:* 110yd × 72yd.
Chairman: David O. Reid. *Secretary:* Margaret Kilpatrick. *Commercial Manager:* Brian McGinlay.
Manager: Campbell Money. *Assistant Manager:* Brian Hamilton. *Community Coach:* Steven Ferguson. *Physio:* Alain Davidson.
Managers since 1975: H. Glasgow, J. Black, A. Rose, W. Henderson, A. Rennie, J. Meakin, D. Lawson, T. Christie, G. Armstrong, B. Fairley, J. Bone, J. McVeigh, T. Smith, D. McKeown.
Club Nickname(s): The Warriors. *Previous Grounds:* Tryst Ground 1884-86, Goschen Park 1886-90.
Record Attendance: 12,500 v East Fife, Scottish Cup 4th rd, 11 Mar 1950.
Record Transfer Fee received: £70,000 for Euan Donaldson to St Johnstone (May 1995).
Record Transfer Fee paid: £20,000 to Livingston for Ian Little (June 1995).
Record Victory: 9-2 v Dundee U, Division II, 16 Apr 1937.
Record Defeat: 2-11 v Dunfermline Ath, Division II, 27 Sept 1930.
Most League Appearances: 360: Archie Rose.
Most League Goals in Season (Individual): 32: Robert Taylor, Division II, 1925-26.

STENHOUSEMUIR 2006–07 LEAGUE RECORD

Match No.	*Date*	*Venue*	*Opponents*	*Result*		*H/T Score*	*Lg. Pos.*	*Goalscorers*	*Attendance*
1	Aug 5	A	East Fife	D	0-0	0-0	—		507
2	12	H	Montrose	W	5-0	1-0	1	Hutchison 2 [34, 49], Baird 2 [60, 63], McLeish (pen) [75]	336
3	19	A	Berwick R	W	1-0	1-0	1	Baird [31]	522
4	26	A	East Stirling	L	0-5	0-1	3		363
5	Sept 3	H	Elgin C	W	2-0	2-0	3	Low (og) [24], Templeton [38]	312
6	9	H	Queen's Park	W	2-1	0-0	2	McBride [81], Canning (og) [82]	393
7	16	A	Dumbarton	L	0-4	0-2	2		903
8	23	H	Arbroath	L	1-2	0-1	6	Diack [59]	382
9	30	A	Albion R	W	5-2	2-2	4	Lennon (og) [37], McBride 2 (1 pen) [42 (p), 47], Templeton [46], Hutchison [84]	383
10	Oct 14	H	East Fife	L	0-1	0-1	6		520
11	21	A	Montrose	W	1-0	0-0	4	McBride [73]	404
12	28	A	Elgin C	L	0-2	0-1	6		404
13	Nov 4	H	East Stirling	W	2-0	0-0	5	Templeton [47], McLeish [64]	374
14	11	H	Dumbarton	W	1-0	0-0	3	McBride [77]	517
15	25	A	Queen's Park	D	1-1	0-1	4	Diack [56]	543
16	Dec 2	A	Arbroath	L	0-2	0-1	6		649
17	16	H	Albion R	W	3-2	3-0	5	Diack [23], Baird 2 [28, 45]	332
18	23	A	East Fife	D	1-1	0-0	6	McLeish [89]	596
19	30	H	Berwick R	L	2-3	1-3	6	Hutchison [13], Fagan [57]	463
20	Jan 6	H	Albion R	L	0-4	0-2	7		341
21	13	H	Elgin C	W	3-2	1-2	6	Dempster 2 [42, 68], McBride [88]	244
22	27	H	Queen's Park	L	1-2	0-0	7	McBride [78]	509
23	Feb 3	H	Arbroath	L	1-2	0-0	7	Thomson [80]	337
24	17	A	Berwick R	L	1-2	0-1	7	Thomson [87]	537
25	24	H	Montrose	L	2-5	2-1	7	Dempster [8], Murphy [29]	287
26	Mar 3	H	East Stirling	D	1-1	0-1	7	Thywissen (og) [59]	367
27	6	A	East Stirling	W	1-0	1-0	—	Hutchison [17]	256
28	10	A	Elgin C	L	1-2	0-1	7	Dempster [75]	348
29	13	A	Dumbarton	D	1-1	1-0	—	Dempster [40]	528
30	17	H	Dumbarton	W	5-1	2-1	6	Tyrrell P [4], Dempster [44], Hutchison [65], Thomson [82], Menzies [85]	444
31	20	A	Albion R	L	1-2	1-1	—	Tyrrell P [19]	319
32	31	A	Queen's Park	L	0-1	0-1	7		621
33	Apr 7	A	Arbroath	L	1-4	0-0	7	McManus [77]	751
34	14	H	East Fife	L	3-5	2-4	7	McManus [32], Thom [34], Dempster [73]	561
35	21	A	Montrose	L	2-3	2-2	7	Dempster [17], Hutchison [22]	343
36	28	H	Berwick R	W	2-0	1-0	7	Dempster 2 [17, 47]	654

Final League Position: 7

Honours
League Champions: Third Division runners-up: 1998-99.
Scottish Cup: Semi-finals 1902-03. Quarter-finals 1948-49, 1949-50, 1994-95.
League Cup: Quarter-finals 1947-48, 1960-61, 1975-76.
League Challenge Cup: Winners: 1995-96.

Club colours: Shirt: Maroon with dark blue trim. Shorts: White. Stockings: Maroon.

Goalscorers: *League* (53): Dempster 10, Hutchison 7, McBride 7 (1 pen), Baird 5, Diack 3, McLeish 3 (1 pen), Templeton 3, Thomson 3, McManus 2, Tyrrell P 2, Fagan 1, Menzies 1, Murphy 1, Thom 1, own goals 4.
Scottish Cup (0).
CIS Cup (3): Baird 1, Sinclair 1, own goal 1.
Challenge Cup (0).

McCulloch W 34	Murie D 16	Dillon S 14 / McKernan D — + 2	Henderson R 13 + 3	Cowan M 22 + 1 / Muir J — + 1	McLeish K 27 + 2	Baird J 17 + 2 / Johnstone S 1	Tyrrell P 27 + 2	Diack I 8 + 11	Hutchison G 27 + 2	McAlpine J 3 / Galloway R 1	Templeton D 9 + 4	McLaughlin B 16 + 7	Murphy P 23 + 1	Sinclair T 8 + 8	McBride J 19 + 4	Connelly G 2 + 3	Tyrrell M 3	Menzies C 15 + 4	MacSween I 1 + 2	Gow A 4	Connell Graham 6	McManus S 3 + 8	Carlin A 1	Fagan S 4	Henderson D 7 + 1	Coakley A 1	Dempster J 16	McEwan C 5	McCulloch S 13	Thomson A 9 + 1	Aitken S 11	Cryans S — + 1	Forde R 2 + 5	Gillies D — + 1	Thom G 5	Desmond S 2 + 3	Peebles R 1	*Match No.*
1	2	3	4	5	6	7^2	8	9^1	10	11	12	13																										1
1	2	3	4	5	7	9^2	6	12	10^1		13	11	8^3	14																								2
1	2	3		5	7^3	9	6^1	13	10	4		11^2	8		12	14																						3
1	2		4	5	13	9		11	10^1	3	14	12	8^2		6	7^3																						4
1	2	3		5		9	6	12	10^1		7	11	8				4																					5
1	2	3		5		9	6	13	10^2		7^3	11	8^1		12		4	14																				6
1	2	3		5		9	8	10			7^1	11^2			6	12	4		13																			7
1	2			5		9^1	8	13	10		7	12	6	3				4	11^2																			8
1	2	3		5		14		13	9		7^3	11^2	10^1		6	12				4	8																	9
1	2	3		5		12		13	10^2		9	11			6	7^1				4	8																	10
1		3		5	7	9^2		11^1	10		12			13	6			2		4	8																	11
1			3	5	7	9		11	10						6			2		4	8																	12
1		3	4	5	7	11^1		13	9		10^2	12			8			2			6																	13
1		3	6	5	8	7	14	12	9		11^2	13			10^3			2			4^1																	14
1	2	3	6		8	7	4	12	9		11^1		5		10																							15
1	2	3^2	6	13	8	7^1	4	11^3	9			14	5	12	10■																							16
1	3		6	5	8^3	7	4	9^2	10			11^1	2	13				12	14																			17
1	3		6	5	8	7^1	4		9^2			11	2	13				10				12																18
	3^2		6	5	8	7^1	4		9			11	2					13				12	1	10														19
1	2■		6	5^1	8		4	14	9^3			11^2	12		13									10	3	7												20
1		6	12	5	7^2		2	9				11		13	10									4	3^1		8											21
1				5	7		12					11			10									4^1	3		8	2	6	9								22
1			13	5	12		4					11^1			7							14			3^2		8	2	6	9^3	10							23
1				5	11^1		4^3		12					14	7^2							13			3		8	2	6	9	10							24
1					7		4						5		10							12			3		8	2	6	9^1	11							25
1			10^1		7		4						5	12	11			13				14			3^2		8	2	6	9^3								26
1					2		10		9				5	7	11			3									8		6		4							27
1			12		2		10		9				5	7	11^2			3^3									8		6^1	14	4	13						28
1					2		11		9				5	7^1	12			3									8		6	10	4							29
1					2		11		9				5	7				3				13					8^2		6	10	4^1		12					30
1					2		11		9				5	7^2				3							13		8		6	10^1	4^3		14	12				31
1					2		11		10			13	6	7^1				3									8			9^2			4		5	12		32
1					2		10		9			11^3	6	7^1				3				14					8				4^2		13		5	12		33
1												11^2	10		7■			3				9					8		6		4^1		12		5	13	2	34
1		12		14	2		11		10				6									9^1					8		3		4^3		13		5	7^2		35
		13			2	1	11^1		12	10								3				9^2					8		6				4		5	7		36

STIRLING ALBION — First Division

Year Formed: 1945. *Ground & Address:* Forthbank Stadium, Springkerse Industrial Estate, Stirling FK7 7UJ. *Telephone:* 01786 450399. *Fax:* 01786 448400. *E-mail:* stirlingalbion.footballclub@virgin.net. *Website:* www.stirlingalbion.com
Ground Capacity: 3808, seated: 2508. *Size of Pitch:* 110yd × 74yd.
Chairman: Peter McKenzie. *Secretary:* Mrs Marlyn Hallam.
Manager: Allan Moore. *Assistant Managers:* Mark McNally, David Gemmell. *Physio:* Andy Myles.
Managers since 1975: A. Smith, G. Peebles, J. Fleeting, J. Brogan, K. Drinkell, J. Philliben, R. Stewart.
Club Nickname(s): The Binos. *Previous Grounds:* Annfield 1945-92.
Record Attendance: 26,400 (at Annfield) v Celtic, Scottish Cup 4th rd, 14 Mar 1959; 3808 v Aberdeen, Scottish Cup 4th rd, 15 February 1996 (Forthbank).
Record Transfer Fee received: £90,000 for Stephen Nicholas to Motherwell (Mar 1999).
Record Transfer Fee paid: £25,000 for Craig Taggart from Falkirk (Aug 1994).
Record Victory: 20-0 v Selkirk, Scottish Cup 1st rd, 8 Dec 1984.
Record Defeat: 0-9 v Dundee U, Division I, 30 Dec 1967.
Most League Appearances: 504: Matt McPhee, 1967-81.
Most League Goals in Season (Individual): 27: Joe Hughes, Division II, 1969-70.
Most Goals Overall (Individual): 129: Billy Steele, 1971-83.

STIRLING ALBION 2006–07 LEAGUE RECORD

Match No.	Date	Venue	Opponents	Result		H/T Score	Lg. Pos.	Goalscorers	Attendance
1	Aug 5	H	Ayr U	L	1-3	0-0	—	Cramb [79]	993
2	12	A	Brechin C	W	1-0	1-0	4	Bell [20]	476
3	19	H	Stranraer	D	3-3	2-2	4	Shields [6], Tomana [34], Cashmore [88]	638
4	26	A	Alloa Ath	W	2-1	1-1	4	Cramb [40], Bell [58]	991
5	Sept 3	H	Raith R	D	1-1	0-0	3	Cramb [68]	986
6	9	H	Forfar Ath	W	3-0	0-0	3	Tomana [50], Cramb [64], Shields [90]	541
7	16	A	Morton	D	1-1	0-0	3	Aitken (pen) [90]	2591
8	23	H	Peterhead	W	2-0	0-0	2	Shields [47], Cramb [54]	574
9	30	A	Cowdenbeath	D	2-2	2-2	2	Aitken (pen) [6], Cramb [23]	693
10	Oct 14	A	Ayr U	D	0-0	0-0	2		1208
11	21	H	Brechin C	W	2-1	1-0	2	Bell [20], Cramb [50]	701
12	28	A	Raith R	W	3-1	1-1	2	Tomana [1], Cramb [84], Shields [90]	1656
13	Nov 4	H	Alloa Ath	W	5-0	4-0	2	Aitken [4], Taggart [10], Bell [17], Tomana [36], Shields [64]	1227
14	11	H	Morton	W	2-1	0-0	2	Shields [47], Taggart [57]	2069
15	Dec 2	A	Peterhead	W	3-2	0-2	2	Bell [62], Cashmore [75], Wilson [88]	641
16	5	A	Forfar Ath	W	2-0	1-0	—	Cramb [45], Cashmore [70]	391
17	16	H	Cowdenbeath	W	1-0	1-0	2	Cramb [23]	758
18	23	H	Ayr U	W	4-2	2-0	2	Aitken [2], O'Brien [10], Shields 2 [59, 73]	952
19	30	A	Stranraer	L	1-2	1-0	2	Tomana [14]	428
20	Jan 2	A	Alloa Ath	D	1-1	0-0	—	Aitken [70]	1050
21	13	H	Raith R	L	0-1	0-0	2		922
22	20	A	Morton	L	1-2	0-1	2	Cashmore [89]	3187
23	27	H	Forfar Ath	W	4-0	2-0	2	Bell [1], O'Brien 3 [33, 73, 90]	585
24	Feb 3	H	Peterhead	W	2-1	1-0	2	Bell [22], Aitken (pen) [88]	621
25	17	H	Stranraer	L	0-2	0-1	2		677
26	24	A	Brechin C	W	4-1	2-0	2	Bell [15], Snodgrass [35], Aitken (pen) [87], Roycroft [90]	588
27	Mar 3	H	Alloa Ath	W	4-0	0-0	2	Snodgrass [58], Nugent [60], O'Brien 2 [83, 87]	969
28	6	A	Cowdenbeath	W	2-1	1-0	—	Snodgrass [13], O'Brien [53]	300
29	10	A	Raith R	W	1-0	0-0	2	Cramb [85]	2161
30	17	H	Morton	W	2-1	0-1	2	Snodgrass [81], Cramb [85]	2608
31	31	A	Forfar Ath	W	2-0	1-0	2	Aitken [45], O'Brien [54]	525
32	Apr 3	H	Cowdenbeath	W	1-0	0-0	—	Cramb [64]	629
33	7	A	Peterhead	L	1-2	0-1	2	Snodgrass [59]	634
34	14	A	Ayr U	L	2-3	1-1	2	Aitken (pen) [37], Cramb (pen) [88]	1007
35	21	H	Brechin C	L	0-1	0-0	2		564
36	28	A	Stranraer	L	1-3	1-1	2	Cashmore [33]	289

Final League Position: 2

Honours
League Champions: Division II 1952-53, 1957-58, 1960-61, 1964-65. Second Division 1976-77, 1990-91, 1995-96;
Runners-up: Division II 1948-49, 1950-51. Third Division 2003-04.
League Cup: Semi-finals 1961-62.

Club colours: Shirt: Red with white side panels and trim. Shorts: Red with white side design. Stockings: White with red front stripe.

Goalscorers: *League* (67): Cramb 14 (1 pen), Aitken 9 (4 pens), Bell 8, O'Brien 8, Shields 8, Cashmore 5, Snodgrass 5, Tomana 5, Taggart 2, Nugent 1, Roycroft 1, Wilson 1.
Play-Offs (8): Aitken 3, Snodgrass 2, Cramb 1, Devine 1, Nugent 1.
Scottish Cup (4): Bell 1, Cramb 1, O'Brien 1, Shields 1.
CIS Cup (0).
Challenge Cup (0).

Player / Match No.	Hogarth M 34	Hay P 29+5	Roycroft S 22	Graham A 14+1	Tomana M 25+7	Bell S 31+1	Gibson A 1+2	Aitken C 28+2	Cramb C 26+4	Shields D 13+4	O'Brien D 21+3	Taggart N 13+18	Cashmore I 9+15	Forsyth R 30+1	McNally M 28	Fraser J 15+5	Devine S 12+8	Nugent P 16	Christie S 2+2	Wilson D 5+15	Malseed C —+1	Harty I 1	Coyne T 2	Snodgrass R 12	Bingham D 6+3	Curry D 1	Match No.
	1	2	3	4	5^{2}	6	7	8	9	10	11^{1}	13	12														1
	1	2		5		7	12	8	9	10^{2}	13			3	4^{1}	6	11										2
	1^{G}		5^{1}		8	7	12		9^{2}	10	11		13	3	4	6		2	15								3
	1	13	5		8^{2}	7		14	9^{3}	10^{1}	11		12	3■	4	6		2									4
	1	3	5		8^{1}	7			9	10^{2}	11		13		4	6		2		12							5
	1	14	5		8	7			9	13	11^{1}	12	10^{2}	3	4^{3}	6		2									6
	1	13	5		14	8		10	9	12		11^{3}		3	4^{2}	6		2		7^{1}							7
	1	2^{1}	5		10^{3}	8		12	9^{2}	7		11	13	3	4	6				14							8
	1	2	5		8	7		11^{2}	9	10^{1}		13	12	3	4	6											9
	1	2	5		8^{1}	7		11	9^{3}	10		13	14	3	4	6^{2}				12							10
	1	2	5		8	7		6	9	10^{1}		11^{2}	12	3	4		13										11
	1	2	5		8	7		6	9	12		11^{2}	10^{1}	3	4		13										12
	1	2	5		8^{3}	7		6	9	10^{2}		11	13	3^{1}	4		12			14							13
	1	2	5		8	7		6	9^{1}	10■		11^{2}	12	3	4		13										14
	1	2^{1}	5		8	7		6	9			11	10^{2}	3	4		12			13							15
	1	2	5^{2}	4	8^{3}	7		6	9			12	10	3		13	11^{1}			14							16
	1	2		5	8^{3}	7		6	9	12	13	11^{2}	10^{1}	3	4	14											17
	1	2		5	8^{1}			6	9^{3}	10	11^{2}	13		3	4	7				14	12						18
	1■	2		5	8	12		6	9^{1}	10	11^{2}	13		3■	4	7^{G}			15								19
		2		5	8	7		6	9		13	11^{2}	10^{1}		4		3		1	12							20
	1	2^{2}	5	12		7		6^{3}			11	13			4^{1}	8	3			14		9	10				21
	1	2^{2}	5		12	7		8			11	10	14		4	6^{1}	3			13			9^{3}				22
	1	2	5		8	7^{2}		6	9		11	13	10^{3}	3	4^{1}		12			14							23
	1	2	5		8^{2}	7		6	9^{1}		11	13	12	3	4^{3}		14							10			24
	1	2^{1}	5		8	7					11	12	10^{2}	3	4	6^{3}	14			13				9			25
	1	14	5^{3}			7		6			11	13	12	3	4		8	2		10^{2}				9^{1}			26
	1	12	5^{2}		14	7		6			11	10^{3}		3	4^{1}	13	8■	2						9			27
	1	2		5	8^{2}	7		6	12		11			3		13		4						9	10^{1}		28
	1	2		5	14	7		6^{2}	12		11^{3}	13		3			8	4						9	10^{1}		29
	1	2		5^{1}	12	7		6	13		11	8^{2}		3				4		14				9	10^{3}		30
	1	2		5	8^{2}			6	9		11	12	14	3				4		7^{1}				10^{3}	13		31
	1	2^{2}		5				6	9		11	12		3			8	4		7^{1}				10	13		32
	1	2		5^{2}	12	7		6	9			11^{1}		3			8^{3}	4		14				10	13		33
	1			5^{1}	12	7		6^{2}	9			14		3	4	13	11^{3}	2						10	8		34
	1	2			8	7					11^{2}	13	14	3	4^{3}		6^{1}	5		12				9	10		35
		2			8				14		11^{2}	13	9	12	4^{1}	6		5	1	7					10^{3}	3	36

STRANRAER — Third Division

Year Formed: 1870. *Ground & Address:* Stair Park, London Rd, Stranraer DG9 8BS. *Telephone:* 01776 703271. *Fax:* 01776 889514. *E-mail:* grodgers_sfc@yahoo.co.uk. *Website:* www.stranraerfc.org
Ground Capacity: 5600, seated: 1830. *Size of Pitch:* 110yd × 70yd.
Chairman: Nigel Redhead. *Secretary:* Barney Duffy. *Commercial Manager:* Ian Alldred.
Manager: Gerry Britton. *Assistant Manager:* Derek Ferguson. *Physio:* Walter Cannon.
Managers since 1975: J. Hughes, N. Hood, G. Hamilton, D. Sneddon, J. Clark, R. Clark, A. McAnespie, C. Money, W. McLaren, N. Watt.
Club Nickname(s): The Blues. *Previous Grounds:* None.
Record Attendance: 6500 v Rangers, Scottish Cup 1st rd, 24 Jan 1948.
Record Transfer Fee received: £90,000 for Mark Campbell to Ayr U (1999).
Record Transfer Fee paid: £15,000 for Colin Harkness from Kilmarnock (Aug 1989).
Record Victory: 7-0 v Brechin C, Division II, 6 Feb 1965.
Record Defeat: 1-11 v Queen of the South, Scottish Cup 1st rd, 16 Jan 1932.
Most League Appearances: 301, Keith Knox, 1986-90; 1999-2001.
Most League Goals in Season (Individual): 59, Tommy Sloan.

STRANRAER 2006–07 LEAGUE RECORD

Match No.	Date	Venue	Opponents	Result		H/T Score	Lg. Pos.	Goalscorers	Attendance
1	Aug 5	A	Forfar Ath	L	1-2	1-1	—	Hamilton [15]	382
2	12	H	Morton	L	0-3	0-0	10		744
3	19	A	Stirling A	D	3-3	2-2	10	Hamilton [11], McNally (og) [17], Moore [46]	638
4	26	A	Ayr U	W	2-0	2-0	5	Hamilton [20], Moore [33]	1265
5	Sept 3	H	Brechin C	W	3-1	1-1	5	Moore [4], Hamilton (pen) [50], McMullan [90]	411
6	9	H	Raith R	L	1-4	1-0	6	Hamilton [3]	452
7	16	A	Peterhead	L	2-5	0-2	8	Hamilton [55], Burns [72]	640
8	23	H	Cowdenbeath	W	1-0	1-0	7	Nicholas [33]	304
9	30	A	Alloa Ath	D	1-1	0-0	7	Hamilton (pen) [47]	479
10	Oct 14	H	Forfar Ath	W	3-2	2-2	6	Hamilton 2 [26, 33], Moore [55]	373
11	21	A	Morton	L	0-3	0-2	6		2589
12	28	A	Brechin C	L	0-3	0-1	8		407
13	Nov 4	H	Ayr U	L	1-3	0-3	9	McMullan [59]	940
14	11	H	Peterhead	W	2-1	0-0	7	Hamilton (pen) [58], Crilly [85]	336
15	25	A	Raith R	D	1-1	1-0	7	Wright [22]	1458
16	Dec 2	A	Cowdenbeath	L	2-4	1-1	8	Aitken [20], Crilly [58]	360
17	16	H	Alloa Ath	D	2-2	2-1	9	Wright [20], Ramsay [36]	276
18	23	A	Forfar Ath	L	0-5	0-3	9		345
19	30	H	Stirling A	W	2-1	0-1	8	Wilson [75], Nicholas (pen) [85]	428
20	Jan 2	A	Ayr U	L	0-1	0-0	—		1105
21	13	H	Brechin C	L	0-2	0-0	9		212
22	20	A	Peterhead	L	0-5	0-3	9		570
23	27	H	Raith R	L	0-2	0-1	9		372
24	Feb 10	A	Alloa Ath	L	0-1	0-1	9		344
25	17	A	Stirling A	W	2-0	1-0	9	Moore [38], Mullen [89]	677
26	24	H	Morton	W	2-1	0-1	9	Mullen [82], Janczyk [88]	631
27	Mar 3	H	Ayr U	L	0-3	0-3	9		667
28	10	A	Brechin C	D	1-1	0-1	9	Moore [84]	415
29	17	H	Peterhead	D	1-1	1-1	9	Moore [10]	282
30	25	H	Cowdenbeath	L	1-6	1-4	9	Moore [81]	282
31	31	A	Raith R	D	0-0	0-0	9		1645
32	Apr 3	H	Alloa Ath	L	3-4	3-1	—	Gibson [6], Moore 2 [13, 17]	279
33	7	A	Cowdenbeath	D	0-0	0-0	9		328
34	14	H	Forfar Ath	W	4-1	0-0	9	Mullen 4 [74, 78, 85, 89]	221
35	21	A	Morton	D	1-1	1-1	9	McGrillen [35]	5276
36	28	H	Stirling A	W	3-1	1-1	9	Moore 2 [26, 77], Gibson (pen) [47]	289

Final League Position: 9

Honours
League Champions: Second Division 1993-94, 1997-98; *Runners-up:* 2004-05. Third Division 2003-04.
Qualifying Cup Winners: 1937.
Scottish Cup: Quarter-finals 2003
League Challenge Cup Winners: 1996-97.

Club colours: Shirt: Blue with white side panels. Shorts: Blue with white side panels. Stockings: Blue with two white hoops.

Goalscorers: *League* (45): Moore 12, Hamilton 10 (3 pens), Mullen 6, Crilly 2, Gibson 2 (1 pen), McMullan 2, Nicholas 2 (1 pen), Wright 2, Aitken 1, Burns 1, Janczik 1, McGrillen 1, Ramsay 1, Wilson 1, own goal 1.
Play-Offs (2): McGrillen 1, Moore 1.
Scottish Cup (7): Hamilton 1, McMullan 1, Moore 1, Nicholas 1, Ramsay 1, Wilson 1, Wright 1.
CIS Cup (2): Burns 1, Moore 1.
Challenge Cup (0).

Morrison A 7	Lyle W 10 + 8	Gaughan K 1	Walker R 18 + 2	Sharp L 25 + 2	McGroarty C 5 + 5	Crilly M 23	Hamilton D 34	Moore M 25 + 1	Nicholas S 10 + 8	Wright K 12 + 3	McMullan P 15 + 9	Burns A 17 + 5	Snowdon W 25 + 2	Ramsay D 17 + 5	McKinstry J 18 + 8	Black S 26 + 1	Aitken S 10 + 3	McAlpine J 23 + 3	McAusland M 1	Hodge A 7	Wilson S 14 + 1	Britton G — + 1	Donnelly R 4	Mullen M 5 + 10	Gibson A 9 + 1	Mitchell D 5 + 1	Dillon S 11	McPhee B 6 + 1	Janczyk N 2 + 8	McGrillen P 8	Ferguson A 3	*Match No.*
1	2	3	4	5	6^{1}	7■	8	9	10^{2}	11	12	13																				1
1	7		5	3	13		6	9	12	10^{2}	11	8^{1}	2	4																		2
1	7		5	3	12	6	4	9		10^{1}	11^{2}	8	2	13																		3
1	7^{1}		5	3	14	4	8	9	13		11	10^{2}	2	6^{3}	12																	4
1^{6}	7		5	3		4^{2}	8	9			11	10	2	6^{1}	13	15	12															5
1	7^{2}		5	3		6	8	9	14	12	11	10^{1}	2		13		4^{3}															6
1			5■	3		6	8	9	12	13	11^{3}	10^{2}	2		7		4^{1}■	14														7
	12			3		5■	4	9^{2}	8^{1}	13	11	10	2		7	1		6														8
	12		13	3^{2}	14		4^{3}	9	8^{1}	7	11	10	2		5	1		6														9
			5				4	9	8	7^{1}	11	10	2	12	6	1		3														10
	12					4^{2}	7	9	8		11	10^{3}	2	13	3^{1}	1	14	6	5													11
	7				11^{3}	5^{1}	4	9■	8			10^{2}	2	12	14	1	13	6		3												12
	7				13	10	4		8^{2}	9	3	11	5^{3}	12■	14	1		2^{1}		6												13
	2^{1}				6	4	8^{3}		13	9^{2}	11	10	12			1	7			3	5	14										14
				6	3^{1}	8	10		11^{2}	9^{3}	12	13	2		14	1	7			4	5											15
				6	11	4	10		8^{1}	9		12	2			1	7			3	5											16
			5	3		8	9		12	7^{1}	13	10^{3}	2	11^{2}		1	4	6			14											17
			13	3		8	9		7^{3}		11	10		6	14	1	4	12		2^{2}	5^{1}											18
				3		8	9		12		13	10		7	2^{1}	1	4	11^{2}			5		6									19
						8	9		13		12	10	2	7^{2}		1	4	11		3^{1}	5		6									20
	13					4	9^{1}			7	11		2	8^{2}	12	1		3			5		6	10								21
	14			3		8■	10			9^{1}		12	2			1	4^{2}	7^{3}			5		6	11	13							22
			6				8	9			3	13	2	11^{1}		1		4			5			10	7^{2}	12						23
	2^{3}		4	12			10	9			13			8		1		3^{2}			5^{1}			14	11	7	6					24
	13		5	6			10	9							2^{2}	1		8^{1}						14	11	4	3	7^{3}	12			25
			5	6		4^{2}	10	9							2	1		11^{1}						13		8	3	7	12			26
			5	6		4	10^{1}	9							2	1		13						12		8	3	7	11^{2}			27
				6		4^{3}		9					13	10^{2}	2	1					5			12		8	3■	7^{1}	14	11		28
			6			4^{3}	10	9			12			8^{2}	2	1		3			5			13				7^{1}	14	11		29
			6	12			10	9			14			4	2	1		3			5^{1}			13				7	8^{3}	11^{2}		30
	14		6	4			10	9					5^{2}		2	1		8^{1}							7^{3}		3	12	13	11		31
			6	4			10	9			12		5		2^{2}	1		8^{1}						13	7		3			11		32
				3			10	9					5	4	2			8^{1}						12	7		6			11	1	33
				6			10	9					5	4	2			8^{1}						12	7		3		13	11^{2}	1	34
				3				13					8	4	2			11^{1}			5■			9^{2}	7		6		12	10■	1	35
	13			3			8	9					5	4	2	1		11						10^{2}	7^{1}		6		12			36

SCOTTISH LEAGUE PLAY-OFFS 2006–07

SCOTTISH DIVISION 1 SEMI-FINAL FIRST LEG

Wednesday, 2 May 2007

Brechin C (0) 1 *(Russell 52)*

Airdrie U (3) 3 *(Harty 14, 22 (pen), Twigg 16)* 954

Brechin C: Nelson; Murie, Ward■, Walker S, Callaghan, Byers, Steven Ferguson, King (White), Smith (Johnson), Hampshire, Russell.
Airdrie U: Robertson; Proctor, McDonald (McKeown), McKenna, Lovering (Lukoszewski), Potter, McGowan, Taylor, Holmes (McDougall), Twigg, Harty.

Raith R (0) 0

Stirling A (0) 0 3043

Raith R: Fahey; Campbell, Andrews, Lumsden, Wilson, Davidson (Bonar), Neill, Silvestro, Fotheringham, McManus, McLauchlin (Hislop).
Stirling A: Hogarth; Hay, McNally, Nugent, Forsyth, Bell (Fraser), Aitken, Devine, O'Brien, Cramb, Bingham (Snodgrass).

SCOTTISH DIVISION 1 SEMI-FINAL SECOND LEG

Saturday, 5 May 2007

Airdrie U (1) 3 *(McDonald 40, McKeown 76, 84)*

Brechin C (0) 0 1298

Airdrie U: Robertson; Proctor, Lovering, McDonald (Smyth), McKenna, McGowan, Potter, Taylor, Twigg (McKeown), Harty, Holmes (McDougall).
Brechin C: Nelson; Murie (Walker R), Callaghan, White, Walker S, Byers, Steven Ferguson, King, Hampshire (Connolly), Russell, Smith (Johnson).

Stirling A (1) 3 *(Aitken 31 (pen), 62, Cramb 79)*

Raith R (1) 1 *(Fairbairn 30)* 2656

Stirling A: Hogarth; Hay, Forsyth, McNally, Nugent, Aitken (Fraser), Bell, Devine, Snodgrass, Bingham (Cramb), O'Brien (Tomana).
Raith R: Fahey; Wilson, Fotheringham, Campbell, Andrews, Lumsden, Fairbairn (Silvestro), Davidson, Hislop, Neill (McManus), Carcary (McLauchlin).

SCOTTISH DIVISION 1 FINAL FIRST LEG

Wednesday, 9 May 2007

Stirling A (0) 2 *(Nugent 87, Aitken 90)*

Airdrie U (2) 2 *(Twigg 35, Harty 45)* 2118

Stirling A: Hogarth; Hay, Forsyth, McNally, Nugent, Aitken, Bell, Devine (Taggart), Bingham, Snodgrass (Cramb), O'Brien (Tomana).
Airdrie U: Robertson; Proctor, Lovering, McDonald, McKenna, McGowan (Smyth), Potter, Taylor, Twigg, Harty (McDougall), Holmes (McKeown).

SCOTTISH DIVISION 1 FINAL SECOND LEG

Saturday, 12 May 2007

Airdrie U (1) 2 *(Taylor 40, MacDonald 72)*

Stirling A (2) 3 *(Snodgrass 5, 17, Devine 68)* 3465

Airdrie U: Robertson; Proctor, Lovering (McKeown), MacDonald■, Smyth, McGowan, McDougall, Taylor, Twigg, Harty, Holmes (McGuire).
Stirling A: Hogarth; Hay, Forsyth, McNally, Nugent, Aitken, Bell, Devine, Bingham (Tomana), Snodgrass (Fraser), O'Brien (Cramb).

SCOTTISH DIVISION 2 SEMI-FINAL FIRST LEG

Tuesday, 1 May 2007

Queen's Park (0) 2 *(Weatherston 77, Trouten 90)*

Arbroath (0) 0 974

Queen's Park: Crawford; Paton, Dunlop M, Trouten, Agostini, Canning, Kettlewell, Cairney, Dunn (Ronald), Weatherston, Ferry.
Arbroath: Peat; Rennie, McCulloch, Raeside■, Dobbins, Smith, Black, Martin (Tosh), Brazil (McMullen), Reilly (Scott), Stein.

Wednesday, 2 May 2007

East Fife (3) 4 *(Gibson 10, O'Reilly 43, 45, 54)*

Stranraer (0) 1 *(Moore 55)* 742

East Fife: Dodds; Smith, Smart, McDonald, McBride, Gibson, Young, Jablonski, Hampshire (Blackadder), Ritchie (Nicholas), O'Reilly (Gordon).
Stranraer: Ferguson; Wilson, Hamilton, Snowdon (Gibson), Sharp, McKinstry, Dillon, Ramsay, McAlpine (Mullen), Moore, McGrillen.

SCOTTISH DIVISION 2 SEMI-FINAL SECOND LEG

Saturday, 5 May 2007

Arbroath (0) 1 *(Tosh 50)*

Queen's Park (2) 2 *(Weatherston 32, Trouten 43)* 1114

Arbroath: Peat; McMullen, McCulloch, Raeside (Sellars), Bishop, Dobbins, Black, Smith (Martin), Tosh, Scott, Stein (Reilly).
Queen's Park: Crawford; Paton, Dunlop M, Trouten (Carroll), Agostini (Sinclair), Canning, Kettlewell, Cairney, Ronald, Weatherston (Dunn), Ferry.

Stranraer (0) 1 *(McGrillen 64)*

East Fife (0) 0 426

Stranraer: Ferguson; Ramsay, Dillon (Britton), Hamilton, Snowdon, Walker, Gibson, McGrillen, Moore, Mullen (Janczyk), Sharp.
East Fife: Dodds; Dair (Courts), Smith, Smart J, McDonald, Young, Gibson (Gordon), Jablonski, Ritchie (Nicholas), O'Reilly, Blackadder.

SCOTTISH DIVISION 2 FINAL FIRST LEG

Wednesday, 9 May 2007

Queen's Park (2) 4 *(Canning 30, 54, Dunlop M 44, Cairney 70)*

East Fife (0) 2 *(Young 60, McDonald 77)* 1207

Queen's Park: Crawford; Paton, Dunlop M, Trouten, Agostini, Canning, Kettlewell, Cairney, Ronald (Dunn), Weatherston, Ferry.
East Fife: Dodds; Dair, Smith, Smart J, McDonald, Young, Gibson (Gordon), Jablonski, Nicholas (Ritchie), O'Reilly, Hampshire (Walker).

SCOTTISH DIVISION 2 FINAL SECOND LEG

Saturday, 12 May 2007

East Fife (0) 0

Queen's Park (1) 3 *(Paton 4, Trouten 74, Carroll 89)* 1625

East Fife: Dodds; Smith (Nicholas), Smart J, McDonald, McBride (Blackadder), Walker, Jablonski, Young, Courts, Ritchie, O'Reilly (Gordon).
Queen's Park: Crawford; Paton, Agostini, Trouten (Carroll), Dunlop M, Kettlewell, Canning, Cairney, Ferry, Ronald (Dunn), Weatherston.

SCOTTISH LEAGUE HONOURS 1890 to 2007

*On goal average (ratio)/difference. †Held jointly after indecisive play-off. ‡Won on deciding match. ††Held jointly. ¶Two points deducted for fielding ineligible player. Competition suspended 1940–45 during war; Regional Leagues operating. ‡‡Two points deducted for registration irregularities. §Not promoted after play-offs.

PREMIER LEAGUE

	First	Pts	Second	Pts	Third	Pts
			Maximum points: 108			
1998–99	Rangers	77	Celtic	71	St Johnstone	57
1999–2000	Rangers	90	Celtic	69	Hearts	54
			Maximum points: 114			
2000–01	Celtic	97	Rangers	82	Hibernian	66
2001–02	Celtic	103	Rangers	85	Livingston	58
2002–03	Rangers*	97	Celtic	97	Hearts	63
2003–04	Celtic	98	Rangers	81	Hearts	68
2004–05	Rangers	93	Celtic	92	Hibernian*	61
2005–06	Celtic	91	Hearts	74	Rangers	73
2006–07	Celtic	84	Rangers	72	Aberdeen	65

PREMIER DIVISION

	First	Pts	Second	Pts	Third	Pts
			Maximum points: 72			
1975–76	Rangers	54	Celtic	48	Hibernian	43
1976–77	Celtic	55	Rangers	46	Aberdeen	43
1977–78	Rangers	55	Aberdeen	53	Dundee U	40
1978–79	Celtic	48	Rangers	45	Dundee U	44
1979–80	Aberdeen	48	Celtic	47	St Mirren	42
1980–81	Celtic	56	Aberdeen	49	Rangers*	44
1981–82	Celtic	55	Aberdeen	53	Rangers	43
1982–83	Dundee U	56	Celtic*	55	Aberdeen	55
1983–84	Aberdeen	57	Celtic	50	Dundee U	47
1984–85	Aberdeen	59	Celtic	52	Dundee U	47
1985–86	Celtic*	50	Hearts	50	Dundee U	47
			Maximum points: 88			
1986–87	Rangers	69	Celtic	63	Dundee U	60
1987–88	Celtic	72	Hearts	62	Rangers	60
			Maximum points: 72			
1988–89	Rangers	56	Aberdeen	50	Celtic	46
1989–90	Rangers	51	Aberdeen*	44	Hearts	44
1990–91	Rangers	55	Aberdeen	53	Celtic*	41
			Maximum points: 88			
1991–92	Rangers	72	Hearts	63	Celtic	62
1992–93	Rangers	73	Aberdeen	64	Celtic	60
1993–94	Rangers	58	Aberdeen	55	Motherwell	54
			Maximum points: 108			
1994–95	Rangers	69	Motherwell	54	Hibernian	53
1995–96	Rangers	87	Celtic	83	Aberdeen*	55
1996–97	Rangers	80	Celtic	75	Dundee U	60
1997–98	Celtic	74	Rangers	72	Hearts	67

FIRST DIVISION

	First	Pts	Second	Pts	Third	Pts
			Maximum points: 52			
1975–76	Partick Th	41	Kilmarnock	35	Montrose	30
			Maximum points: 78			
1976–77	St Mirren	62	Clydebank	58	Dundee	51
1977–78	Morton*	58	Hearts	58	Dundee	57
1978–79	Dundee	55	Kilmarnock*	54	Clydebank	54
1979–80	Hearts	53	Airdrieonians	51	Ayr U*	44
1980–81	Hibernian	57	Dundee	52	St Johnstone	51
1981–82	Motherwell	61	Kilmarnock	51	Hearts	50
1982–83	St Johnstone	55	Hearts	54	Clydebank	50
1983–84	Morton	54	Dumbarton	51	Partick Th	46
1984–85	Motherwell	50	Clydebank	48	Falkirk	45
1985–86	Hamilton A	56	Falkirk	45	Kilmarnock	44
			Maximum points: 88			
1986–87	Morton	57	Dunfermline Ath	56	Dumbarton	53
1987–88	Hamilton A	56	Meadowbank T	52	Clydebank	49
			Maximum points: 78			
1988–89	Dunfermline Ath	54	Falkirk	52	Clydebank	48
1989–90	St Johnstone	58	Airdrieonians	54	Clydebank	44
1990–91	Falkirk	54	Airdrieonians	53	Dundee	52
			Maximum points: 88			
1991–92	Dundee	58	Partick Th*	57	Hamilton A	57
1992–93	Raith R	65	Kilmarnock	54	Dunfermline Ath	52
1993–94	Falkirk	66	Dunfermline Ath	65	Airdrieonians	54
			Maximum points: 108			
1994–95	Raith R	69	Dunfermline Ath*	68	Dundee	68
1995–96	Dunfermline Ath	71	Dundee U*	67	Morton	67
1996–97	St Johnstone	80	Airdieonians	60	Dundee*	58
1997–98	Dundee	70	Falkirk	65	Raith R*	60
1998–99	Hibernian	89	Falkirk	66	Ayr U	62

	First	*Pts*	*Second*	*Pts*	*Third*	*Pts*
1999–2000	St Mirren	76	Dunfermline Ath	71	Falkirk	68
2000–01	Livingston	76	Ayr U	69	Falkirk	56
2001–02	Partick Th	66	Airdrieonians	56	Ayr U	52
2002–03	Falkirk	81	Clyde	72	St Johnstone	67
2003–04	Inverness CT	70	Clyde	69	St Johnstone	57
2004–05	Falkirk	75	St Mirren*	60	Clyde	60
2005–06	St Mirren	76	St Johnstone	66	Hamilton A	59
2006–07	Gretna	66	St Johnstone	65	Dundee*	53

SECOND DIVISION

Maximum points: 52

	First	*Pts*	*Second*	*Pts*	*Third*	*Pts*
1975–76	Clydebank*	40	Raith R	40	Alloa Ath	35
			Maximum points: 78			
1976–77	Stirling A	55	Alloa Ath	51	Dunfermline Ath	50
1977–78	Clyde*	53	Raith R	53	Dunfermline Ath	48
1978–79	Berwick R	54	Dunfermline Ath	52	Falkirk	50
1979–80	Falkirk	50	East Stirling	49	Forfar Ath	46
1980–81	Queen's Park	50	Queen of the S	46	Cowdenbeath	45
1981–82	Clyde	59	Alloa Ath*	50	Arbroath	50
1982–83	Brechin C	55	Meadowbank Th	54	Arbroath	49
1983–84	Forfar Ath	63	East Fife	47	Berwick R	43
1984–85	Montrose	53	Alloa Ath	50	Dunfermline Ath	49
1985–86	Dunfermline Ath	57	Queen of the S	55	Meadowbank Th	49
1986–87	Meadowbank Th	55	Raith R*	52	Stirling A*	52
1987–88	Ayr U	61	St Johnstone	59	Queen's Park	51
1988–89	Albion R	50	Alloa Ath	45	Brechin C	43
1989–90	Brechin C	49	Kilmarnock	48	Stirling A	47
1990–91	Stirling A	54	Montrose	46	Cowdenbeath	45
1991–92	Dumbarton	52	Cowdenbeath	51	Alloa Ath	50
1992–93	Clyde	54	Brechin C*	53	Stranraer	53
1993–94	Stranraer	56	Berwick R	48	Stenhousemuir*	47
			Maximum points: 108			
1994–95	Morton	64	Dumbarton	60	Stirling A	58
1995–96	Stirling A	81	East Fife	67	Berwick R	60
1996–97	Ayr U	77	Hamilton A	74	Livingston	64
1997–98	Stranraer	61	Clydebank	60	Livingston	59
1998–99	Livingston	77	Inverness CT	72	Clyde	53
1999–2000	Clyde	65	Alloa Ath	64	Ross Co	62
2000–01	Partick Th	75	Arbroath	58	Berwick R*	54
2001–02	Queen of the S	67	Alloa Ath	59	Forfar Ath	53
2002–03	Raith R	59	Brechin C	55	Airdrie U	54
2003–04	Airdrie U	70	Hamilton A	62	Dumbarton	60
2004–05	Brechin C	72	Stranraer	63	Morton	62
2005–06	Gretna	88	Morton§	70	Peterhead*§	57
2006–07	Morton	77	Stirling A	69	Raith R§	62

THIRD DIVISION

Maximum points: 108

1994–95	Forfar Ath	80	Montrose	67	Ross Co	60
1995–96	Livingston	72	Brechin C	63	Inverness CT	57
1996–97	Inverness CT	76	Forfar Ath*	67	Ross Co	67
1997–98	Alloa Ath	76	Arbroath	68	Ross Co*	67
1998–99	Ross Co	77	Stenhousemuir	64	Brechin C	59
1999–2000	Queen's Park	69	Berwick R	66	Forfar Ath	61
2000–01	Hamilton A*	76	Cowdenbeath	76	Brechin C	72
2001–02	Brechin C	73	Dumbarton	61	Albion R	59
2002–03	Morton	72	East Fife	71	Albion R	70
2003–04	Stranraer	79	Stirling A	77	Gretna	68
2004–05	Gretna	98	Peterhead	78	Cowdenbeath	51
2005–06	Cowdenbeath*	76	Berwick R§	76	Stenhousemuir§	73
2006–07	Berwick R	75	Arbroath§	70	Queen's Park	68

FIRST DIVISION to 1974–75

Maximum points: a 36; *b* 44; *c* 40; *d* 52; *e* 60; *f* 68; g 76; *h* 84.

1890–91*a*	Dumbarton††	29	Rangers††	29	Celtic	21
1891–92*b*	Dumbarton	37	Celtic	35	Hearts	34
1892–93*a*	Celtic	29	Rangers	28	St Mirren	20
1893–94*a*	Celtic	29	Hearts	26	St Bernard's	23
1894–95*a*	Hearts	31	Celtic	26	Rangers	22
1895–96*a*	Celtic	30	Rangers	26	Hibernian	24
1896–97*a*	Hearts	28	Hibernian	26	Rangers	25
1897–98*a*	Celtic	33	Rangers	29	Hibernian	22
1898–99*a*	Rangers	36	Hearts	26	Celtic	24
1899–1900*a*	Rangers	32	Celtic	25	Hibernian	24
1900–01*c*	Rangers	35	Celtic	29	Hibernian	25
1901–02*a*	Rangers	28	Celtic	26	Hearts	22
1902–03*b*	Hibernian	37	Dundee	31	Rangers	29
1903–04*d*	Third Lanark	43	Hearts	39	Celtic*	38
1904–05*d*	Celtic‡	41	Rangers	41	Third Lanark	35
1905–06*e*	Celtic	49	Hearts	43	Airdrieonians	38
1906–07*f*	Celtic	55	Dundee	48	Rangers	45
1907–08*f*	Celtic	55	Falkirk	51	Rangers	50
1908–09*f*	Celtic	51	Dundee	50	Clyde	48

	First	*Pts*	*Second*	*Pts*	*Third*	*Pts*
1909–10*f*	Celtic	54	Falkirk	52	Rangers	46
1910–11*f*	Rangers	52	Aberdeen	48	Falkirk	44
1911–12*f*	Rangers	51	Celtic	45	Clyde	42
1912–13*f*	Rangers	53	Celtic	49	Hearts*	41
1913–14*g*	Celtic	65	Rangers	59	Hearts*	54
1914–15*g*	Celtic	65	Hearts	61	Rangers	50
1915–16*g*	Celtic	67	Rangers	56	Morton	51
1916–17*g*	Celtic	64	Morton	54	Rangers	53
1917–18*f*	Rangers	56	Celtic	55	Kilmarnock*	43
1918–19*f*	Celtic	58	Rangers	57	Morton	47
1919–20*h*	Rangers	71	Celtic	68	Motherwell	57
1920–21*h*	Rangers	76	Celtic	66	Hearts	50
1921–22*h*	Celtic	67	Rangers	66	Raith R	51
1922–23*g*	Rangers	55	Airdrieonians	50	Celtic	46
1923–24*g*	Rangers	59	Airdrieonians	50	Celtic	46
1924–25*g*	Rangers	60	Airdrieonians	57	Hibernian	52
1925–26*g*	Celtic	58	Airdrieonians*	50	Hearts	50
1926–27*g*	Rangers	56	Motherwell	51	Celtic	49
1927–28*g*	Rangers	60	Celtic*	55	Motherwell	55
1928–29*g*	Rangers	67	Celtic	51	Motherwell	50
1929–30*g*	Rangers	60	Motherwell	55	Aberdeen	53
1930–31*g*	Rangers	60	Celtic	58	Motherwell	56
1931–32*g*	Motherwell	66	Rangers	61	Celtic	48
1932–33*g*	Rangers	62	Motherwell	59	Hearts	50
1933–34*g*	Rangers	66	Motherwell	62	Celtic	47
1934–35*g*	Rangers	55	Celtic	52	Hearts	50
1935–36*g*	Celtic	66	Rangers*	61	Aberdeen	61
1936–37*g*	Rangers	61	Aberdeen	54	Celtic	52
1937–38*g*	Celtic	61	Hearts	58	Rangers	49
1938–39*g*	Rangers	59	Celtic	48	Aberdeen	46
1946–47*e*	Rangers	46	Hibernian	44	Aberdeen	39
1947–48*e*	Hibernian	48	Rangers	46	Partick Th	36
1948–49*e*	Rangers	46	Dundee	45	Hibernian	39
1949–50*e*	Rangers	50	Hibernian	49	Hearts	43
1950–51*e*	Hibernian	48	Rangers*	38	Dundee	38
1951–52*e*	Hibernian	45	Rangers	41	East Fife	37
1952–53*e*	Rangers*	43	Hibernian	43	East Fife	39
1953–54*e*	Celtic	43	Hearts	38	Partick Th	35
1954–55*e*	Aberdeen	49	Celtic	46	Rangers	41
1955–56*f*	Rangers	52	Aberdeen	46	Hearts*	45
1956–57*f*	Rangers	55	Hearts	53	Kilmarnock	42
1957–58*f*	Hearts	62	Rangers	49	Celtic	46
1958–59*f*	Rangers	50	Hearts	48	Motherwell	44
1959–60*f*	Hearts	54	Kilmarnock	50	Rangers*	42
1960–61*f*	Rangers	51	Kilmarnock	50	Third Lanark	42
1961–62*f*	Dundee	54	Rangers	51	Celtic	46
1962–63*f*	Rangers	57	Kilmarnock	48	Partick Th	46
1963–64*f*	Rangers	55	Kilmarnock	49	Celtic*	47
1964–65*f*	Kilmarnock*	50	Hearts	50	Dunfermline Ath	49
1965–66*f*	Celtic	57	Rangers	55	Kilmarnock	45
1966–67*f*	Celtic	58	Rangers	55	Clyde	46
1967–68*f*	Celtic	63	Rangers	61	Hibernian	45
1968–69*f*	Celtic	54	Rangers	49	Dunfermline Ath	45
1969–70*f*	Celtic	57	Rangers	45	Hibernian	44
1970–71*f*	Celtic	56	Aberdeen	54	St Johnstone	44
1971–72*f*	Celtic	60	Aberdeen	50	Rangers	44
1972–73*f*	Celtic	57	Rangers	56	Hibernian	45
1973–74*f*	Celtic	53	Hibernian	49	Rangers	48
1974–75*f*	Rangers	56	Hibernian	49	Celtic	45

SECOND DIVISION to 1974–75

Maximum points: a 76; *b* 72; *c* 68; *d* 52; *e* 60; *f* 36; *g* 44.

1893–94*f*	Hibernian	29	Cowlairs	27	Clyde	24
1894–95*f*	Hibernian	30	Motherwell	22	Port Glasgow	20
1895–96*f*	Abercorn	27	Leith Ath	23	Renton	21
1896–97*f*	Partick Th	31	Leith Ath	27	Kilmarnock*	21
1897–98*f*	Kilmarnock	29	Port Glasgow	25	Morton	22
1898–99*f*	Kilmarnock	32	Leith Ath	27	Port Glasgow	25
1899–1900*f*	Partick Th	29	Morton	28	Port Glasgow	20
1900–01*f*	St Bernard's	25	Airdrieonians	23	Abercorn	21
1901–02*g*	Port Glasgow	32	Partick Th	31	Motherwell	26
1902–03*g*	Airdrieonians	35	Motherwell	28	Ayr U*	27
1903–04*g*	Hamilton A	37	Clyde	29	Ayr U	28
1904–05*g*	Clyde	32	Falkirk	28	Hamilton A	27
1905–06*g*	Leith Ath	34	Clyde	31	Albion R	27
1906–07*g*	St Bernard's	32	Vale of Leven*	27	Arthurlie	27
1907–08*g*	Raith R	30	Dumbarton*‡‡	27	Ayr U	27
1908–09*g*	Abercorn	31	Raith R*	28	Vale of Leven	28
1909–10*g*	Leith Ath‡	33	Raith R	33	St Bernard's	27
1910–11*g*	Dumbarton	31	Ayr U	27	Albion R	25
1911–12*g*	Ayr U	35	Abercorn	30	Dumbarton	27
1912–13*d*	Ayr U	34	Dunfermline Ath	33	East Stirling	32
1913–14*g*	Cowdenbeath	31	Albion R	27	Dunfermline Ath*	26
1914–15*d*	Cowdenbeath*	37	St Bernard's*	37	Leith Ath	37
1921–22*a*	Alloa Ath	60	Cowdenbeath	47	Armadale	45

	First	*Pts*	*Second*	*Pts*	*Third*	*Pts*
1922–23*a*	Queen's Park	57	Clydebank¶	50	St Johnstone¶	45
1923–24*a*	St Johnstone	56	Cowdenbeath	55	Bathgate	44
1924–25*a*	Dundee U	50	Clydebank	48	Clyde	47
1925–26*a*	Dunfermline Ath	59	Clyde	53	Ayr U	52
1926–27*a*	Bo'ness	56	Raith R	49	Clydebank	45
1927–28*a*	Ayr U	54	Third Lanark	45	King's Park	44
1928–29*b*	Dundee U	51	Morton	50	Arbroath	47
1929–30*a*	Leith Ath*	57	East Fife	57	Albion R	54
1930–31*a*	Third Lanark	61	Dundee U	50	Dunfermline Ath	47
1931–32*a*	East Stirling*	55	St Johnstone	55	Raith R*	46
1932–33*c*	Hibernian	54	Queen of the S	49	Dunfermline Ath	47
1933–34*c*	Albion R	45	Dunfermline Ath*	44	Arbroath	44
1934–35*c*	Third Lanark	52	Arbroath	50	St Bernard's	47
1935–36*c*	Falkirk	59	St Mirren	52	Morton	48
1936–37*c*	Ayr U	54	Morton	51	St Bernard's	48
1937–38*c*	Raith R	59	Albion R	48	Airdrieonians	47
1938–39*c*	Cowdenbeath	60	Alloa Ath*	48	East Fife	48
1946–47*d*	Dundee	45	Airdrieonians	42	East Fife	31
1947–48*e*	East Fife	53	Albion R	42	Hamilton A	40
1948–49*e*	Raith R*	42	Stirling A	42	Airdrieonians*	41
1949–50*e*	Morton	47	Airdrieonians	44	Dunfermline Ath*	36
1950–51*e*	Queen of the S*	45	Stirling A	45	Ayr U*	36
1951–52*e*	Clyde	44	Falkirk	43	Ayr U	39
1952–53*e*	Stirling A	44	Hamilton A	43	Queen's Park	37
1953–54*e*	Motherwell	45	Kilmarnock	42	Third Lanark*	36
1954–55*e*	Airdrieonians	46	Dunfermline Ath	42	Hamilton A	39
1955–56*b*	Queen's Park	54	Ayr U	51	St Johnstone	49
1956–57*b*	Clyde	64	Third Lanark	51	Cowdenbeath	45
1957–58*b*	Stirling A	55	Dunfermline Ath	53	Arbroath	47
1958–59*b*	Ayr U	60	Arbroath	51	Stenhousemuir	46
1959–60*b*	St Johnstone	53	Dundee U	50	Queen of the S	49
1960–61*b*	Stirling A	55	Falkirk	54	Stenhousemuir	50
1961–62*b*	Clyde	54	Queen of the S	53	Morton	44
1962–63*b*	St Johnstone	55	East Stirling	49	Morton	48
1963–64*b*	Morton	67	Clyde	53	Arbroath	46
1964–65*b*	Stirling A	59	Hamilton A	50	Queen of the S	45
1965–66*b*	Ayr U	53	Airdrieonians	50	Queen of the S	47
1966–67*a*	Morton	69	Raith R	58	Arbroath	57
1967–68*b*	St Mirren	62	Arbroath	53	East Fife	49
1968–69*b*	Motherwell	64	Ayr U	53	East Fife*	48
1969–70*b*	Falkirk	56	Cowdenbeath	55	Queen of the S	50
1970–71*b*	Partick Th	56	East Fife	51	Arbroath	46
1971–72*b*	Dumbarton*	52	Arbroath	52	Stirling A	50
1972–73*b*	Clyde	56	Dumfermline Ath	52	Raith R*	47
1973–74*b*	Airdrieonians	60	Kilmarnock	58	Hamilton A	55
1974–75*a*	Falkirk	54	Queen of the S*	53	Montrose	53

Elected to First Division: 1894 Clyde; 1895 Hibernian; 1896 Abercorn; 1897 Partick Th; 1899 Kilmarnock; 1900 Morton and Partick Th; 1902 Port Glasgow and Partick Th; 1903 Airdrieonians and Motherwell; 1905 Falkirk and Aberdeen; 1906 Clyde and Hamilton A; 1910 Raith R; 1913 Ayr U and Dumbarton.

RELEGATED FROM PREMIER LEAGUE

1998–99 Dunfermline Ath
1999–2000 *No relegation due to League reorganization*
2000–01 St Mirren
2001–02 St Johnstone
2002–03 *No relegated team*
2003–04 Partick Th
2004–05 Dundee
2005–06 Livingston
2006–07 Dunfermline Ath

RELEGATED FROM PREMIER DIVISION

1974–75 *No relegation due to League reorganization*
1975–76 Dundee, St Johnstone
1976–77 Hearts, Kilmarnock
1977–78 Ayr U, Clydebank
1978–79 Hearts, Motherwell
1979–80 Dundee, Hibernian
1980–81 Kilmarnock, Hearts
1981–82 Partick Th, Airdrieonians
1982–83 Morton, Kilmarnock
1983–84 St Johnstone, Motherwell
1984–85 Dumbarton, Morton
1985–86 *No relegation due to League reorganization*
1986–87 Clydebank, Hamilton A
1987–88 Falkirk, Dunfermline Ath, Morton
1988–89 Hamilton A
1989–90 Dundee
1990–91 *None*
1991–92 St Mirren, Dunfermline Ath
1992–93 Falkirk, Airdrieonians
1993–94 *See footnote*
1994–95 Dundee U
1995–96 Partick Th, Falkirk
1996–97 Raith R
1997–98 Hibernian

RELEGATED FROM DIVISION 1

1974–75 *No relegation due to League reorganization*
1975–76 Dunfermline Ath, Clyde
1976–77 Raith R, Falkirk
1977–78 Alloa Ath, East Fife
1978–79 Montrose, Queen of the S
1979–80 Arbroath, Clyde
1980–81 Stirling A, Berwick R
1981–82 East Stirling, Queen of the S
1982–83 Dunfermline Ath, Queen's Park
1983–84 Raith R, Alloa Ath
1984–85 Meadowbank Th, St Johnstone
1985–86 Ayr U, Alloa Ath
1991–92 Montrose, Forfar Ath
1992–93 Meadowbank Th, Cowdenbeath
1993–94 *See footnote*
1994–95 Ayr U, Stranraer
1995–96 Hamilton A, Dumbarton
1996–97 Clydebank, East Fife
1997–98 Partick Th, Stirling A
1998–99 Hamilton A, Stranraer
1999–2000 Clydebank
2000–01 Morton, Alloa Ath
2001–02 Raith R
2002–03 Alloa Ath, Arbroath

1986–87 Brechin C, Montrose
1987–88 East Fife, Dumbarton
1988–89 Kilmarnock, Queen of the S
1989–90 Albion R, Alloa Ath
1990–91 Clyde, Brechin C
2003–04 Ayr U, Brechin C
2004–05 Partick Th, Raith R
2005–06 Stranraer, Brechin C
2006–07 Airdrie U, Ross Co

RELEGATED FROM DIVISION 2

1994–95 Meadowbank Th, Brechin C
2000–01 Queen's Park, Stirling A
1995–96 Forfar Ath, Montrose
2001–02 Morton
1996–97 Dumbarton, Berwick R
2002–03 Stranraer, Cowdenbeath
1997–98 Stenhousemuir, Brechin C
2003–04 East Fife, Stenhousemuir
1998–99 East Fife, Forfar Ath
2004–05 Arbroath, Berwick R
1999–2000 Hamilton A**
2005–06 Dumbarton
2006–07 Stranraer, Forfar

RELEGATED FROM DIVISION 1 (TO 1973–74)

1921–22 *Queen's Park, Dumbarton, Clydebank
1922–23 Albion R, Alloa Ath
1923–24 Clyde, Clydebank
1924–25 Third Lanark, Ayr U
1925–26 Raith R, Clydebank
1926–27 Morton, Dundee U
1927–28 Dunfermline Ath, Bo'ness
1928–29 Third Lanark, Raith R
1929–30 St Johnstone, Dundee U
1930–31 Hibernian, East Fife
1931–32 Dundee U, Leith Ath
1932–33 Morton, East Stirling
1933–34 Third Lanark, Cowdenbeath
1934–35 St Mirren, Falkirk
1935–36 Airdrieonians, Ayr U
1936–37 Dunfermline Ath, Albion R
1937–38 Dundee, Morton
1938–39 Queen's Park, Raith R
1946–47 Kilmarnock, Hamilton A
1947–48 Airdrieonians, Queen's Park
1948–49 Morton, Albion R
1949–50 Queen of the S, Stirling A
1950–51 Clyde, Falkirk
1951–52 Morton, Stirling A
1952–53 Motherwell, Third Lanark
1953–54 Airdrieonians, Hamilton A
1954–55 *No clubs relegated*
1955–56 Stirling A, Clyde
1956–57 Dunfermline Ath, Ayr U
1957–58 East Fife, Queen's Park
1958–59 Queen of the S, Falkirk
1959–60 Arbroath, Stirling A
1960–61 Ayr U, Clyde
1961–62 St Johnstone, Stirling A
1962–63 Clyde, Raith R
1963–64 Queen of the S, East Stirling
1964–65 Airdrieonians, Third Lanark
1965–66 Morton, Hamilton A
1966–67 St Mirren, Ayr U
1967–68 Motherwell, Stirling A
1968–69 Falkirk, Arbroath
1969–70 Raith R, Partick Th
1970–71 St Mirren, Cowdenbeath
1971–72 Clyde, Dunfermline Ath
1972–73 Kilmarnock, Airdrieonians
1973–74 East Fife, Falkirk

*Season 1921–22 – only 1 club promoted, 3 clubs relegated. ***15pts deducted for failing to field a team.*

Scottish League Championship wins: Rangers 51, Celtic 41, Aberdeen 4, Hearts 4, Hibernian 4, Dumbarton 2, Dundee 1, Dundee U 1, Kilmarnock 1, Motherwell 1, Third Lanark 1.

At the end of the 1993–94 season four divisions were created assisted by the admission of two new clubs Ross County and Caledonian Thistle. Only one club was promoted from Division 1 and Division 2. The three relegated from the Premier joined with teams finishing second to seventh in Division 1 to form the new Division 1. Five relegated from Division 1 combined with those who finished second to sixth to form a new Division 2 and the bottom eight in Division 2 linked with the two newcomers to form a new Division 3. At the end of the 1997–98 season the nine clubs remaining in the Premier Division plus the promoted team from Division 1 formed a breakaway Premier League. At the end of the 1999–2000 season two teams were added to the Scottish League. There was no relegation from the Premier League but two promoted from the First Division and three from each of the Second and Third Divisions. One team was relegated from the First Division and one from the Second Division, leaving 12 teams in each division. In season 2002–03, Falkirk were not promoted to the Premier League due to the failure of their ground to meet League rules. Inverness CT were promoted after a previous refusal in 2003–04 because of ground sharing. At the end of 2005–06 the Scottish League introduced play-offs for the team finishing second from the bottom of Division 1 against the winners of the second, third and fourth finishing teams in Division 2 and with a similar procedure for Division 2 and Division 3.

Hibernian's Abdessalam Benjelloun scores his sides fourth goal in the CIS Insurance Cup Final win against Kilmarnock at Hampden Park. (John Walton/ EMPICS Sport/PA Photos)

SCOTTISH LEAGUE CUP FINALS 1946–2007

Season	*Winners*	*Runners-up*	*Score*
1946–47	Rangers	Aberdeen	4-0
1947–48	East Fife	Falkirk	4-1 after 0-0 draw
1948–49	Rangers	Raith R	2-0
1949–50	East Fife	Dunfermline Ath	3-0
1950–51	Motherwell	Hibernian	3-0
1951–52	Dundee	Rangers	3-2
1952–53	Dundee	Kilmarnock	2-0
1953–54	East Fife	Partick Th	3-2
1954–55	Hearts	Motherwell	4-2
1955–56	Aberdeen	St Mirren	2-1
1956–57	Celtic	Partick Th	3-0 after 0-0 draw
1957–58	Celtic	Rangers	7-1
1958–59	Hearts	Partick Th	5-1
1959–60	Hearts	Third Lanark	2-1
1960–61	Rangers	Kilmarnock	2-0
1961–62	Rangers	Hearts	3-1 after 1-1 draw
1962–63	Hearts	Kilmarnock	1-0
1963–64	Rangers	Morton	5-0
1964–65	Rangers	Celtic	2-1
1965–66	Celtic	Rangers	2-1
1966–67	Celtic	Rangers	1-0
1967–68	Celtic	Dundee	5-3
1968–69	Celtic	Hibernian	6-2
1969–70	Celtic	St Johnstone	1-0
1970–71	Rangers	Celtic	1-0
1971–72	Partick Th	Celtic	4-1
1972–73	Hibernian	Celtic	2-1
1973–74	Dundee	Celtic	1-0
1974–75	Celtic	Hibernian	6-3
1975–76	Rangers	Celtic	1-0
1976–77	Aberdeen	Celtic	2-1
1977–78	Rangers	Celtic	2-1
1978–79	Rangers	Aberdeen	2-1
1979–80	Dundee U	Aberdeen	3-0 after 0-0 draw
1980–81	Dundee U	Dundee	3-0
1981–82	Rangers	Dundee U	2-1
1982–83	Celtic	Rangers	2-1
1983–84	Rangers	Celtic	3-2
1984–85	Rangers	Dundee U	1-0
1985–86	Aberdeen	Hibernian	3-0
1986–87	Rangers	Celtic	2-1
1987–88	Rangers	Aberdeen	3-3
		(Rangers won 5-3 on penalties)	
1988–89	Rangers	Aberdeen	3-2
1989–90	Aberdeen	Rangers	2-1
1990–91	Rangers	Celtic	2-1
1991–92	Hibernian	Dunfermline Ath	2-0
1992–93	Rangers	Aberdeen	2-1
1993–94	Rangers	Hibernian	2-1
1994–95	Raith R	Celtic	2-2
		(Raith R won 6-5 on penalties)	
1995–96	Aberdeen	Dundee	2-0
1996–97	Rangers	Hearts	4-3
1997–98	Celtic	Dundee U	3-0
1998–99	Rangers	St Johnstone	2-1
1999–2000	Celtic	Aberdeen	2-0
2000–01	Celtic	Kilmarnock	3-0
2001–02	Rangers	Ayr U	4-0
2002–03	Rangers	Celtic	2-1
2003–04	Livingston	Hibernian	2-0
2004–05	Rangers	Motherwell	5-1
2005–06	Celtic	Dunfermline Ath	3-0
2005–06	Celtic	Dunfermline Ath	3-0
2006–07	Hibernian	Kilmarnock	5-1

SCOTTISH LEAGUE CUP WINS

Rangers 24, Celtic 13, Aberdeen 5, Hearts 4, Dundee 3, East Fife 3, Hibernian 3, Dundee U 2, Livingston 1, Motherwell 1, Partick Th 1, Raith R 1.

APPEARANCES IN FINALS

Rangers 30, Celtic 26, Aberdeen 12, Hibernian 9, Dundee 6, Hearts 6, Dundee U 5, Kilmarnock 5, Partick Th 4, Dunfermline Ath 3, East Fife 3, Motherwell 3, Raith R 2, St Johnstone 2, Ayr U 1, Falkirk 1, Livingston 1, Morton 1, St Mirren 1, Third Lanark 1.

CIS SCOTTISH LEAGUE CUP 2006–07

▪ *Denotes player sent off.*

FIRST ROUND

Tuesday, 8 August 2006

Albion R (1) 1 *(Chaplain 10)*

Stenhousemuir (0) 2 *(Nicoll (og) 74, Baird 77)* 228

Albion R: Ewings; Nicoll (McBride), Lennox (Chisholm), Lennon, Watson, Donnelly, Friel▪, Chaplain, Felvus, Bonnar, Sichi (Clearie).
Stenhousemuir: McCulloch; Murie, Dillon, Henderson, Cowan, McBride, McLaughlin (Templeton), Murphy, Diack (Baird), Hutchison, McAlpine.

Brechin C (0) 2 *(Geddes 55, Callaghan 74)*

Morton (1) 1 *(McGowan 4)* 501

Brechin C: Nelson; McEwan, Stuart Ferguson, Ward, White, Walker S, Johnson, Callaghan, Geddes, Connolly, Smith (Byers).
Morton: McGurn; Weatherson, Keenan (McLean), Harding (Lilley), Greacen, McLaughlin, Millar, Stevenson, Templeman, McGowan, McAlister.

Cowdenbeath (3) 4 *(Buchanan 47, Hughes 31, 45, Clarke 34)*

East Stirling (0) 1 *(Thywissen 63)* 271

Cowdenbeath: Orr; Guy, McBride K, Gomis (Fotheringham), Hughes, Ellis, Scullion (Baxter), Paatelainen (Mauchlen), Dalziel, Clarke, Buchanan.
East Stirling: Tiropoulos; Smith, Learmonth, Thywissen, Oates, Nixon (Boyle), Brand (McKenzie), Stewart, Dymock, Tweedie (Ure), Adam.

Dumbarton (0) 3 *(Bagan 74, Boyle 88, Gemmell 90)*

Stirling Albion (0) 0 544

Dumbarton: Grindlay; Geggan, Dillon (Brittain), Canning, Craig, Gentile, Borris, Bagan, Gemmell, McNaught, Boyle.
Stirling Albion: Hogarth; Hay, Devine (Tomana), Forsyth, Graham, Bell (Fraser), Gibson, Aitken, Cashmore, Shields, O'Brien.

Dundee (1) 1 *(Swankie 10)*

Partick T (1) 3 *(Brady 40, Gibson W 64, Boyd 75)* 2180

Dundee: Murray; Macdonald C, Dixon, Rae, Mackenzie, Strong, Harris (McNally), McDonald K, Swankie, Deasley, Robertson (Campbell).
Partick T: Arthur; Sives, McCulloch, Brady, Boyd, Ferguson (Hodge), Gibson J, Donnelly, Gibson G, Roberts, Gibson W.

Forfar Ath (0) 1 *(Gribben 90)*

Alloa Ath (1) 2 *(Brown 4, Grant 94)* 308

Forfar Ath: Murdoch; Keogh, King, Dunn, Lumsden, Donald (Webster), Lunan (Beith), Marshall, Fraser (Tosh), Gribben, Coyle.
Alloa Ath: Creer; Bolochoweckyj, Forrest, Townsley, Malcolm, McColligan, Hamilton, Grant, Brown (Hazeldine) (McCallum), Sloan, McAnespie (Comrie).
aet.

Queen of the S (4) 4 *(O'Neill 8, 45, Henderson 17, Weir 32)*

Clyde (1) 2 *(Imrie 43, O'Donnell 52 (pen))* 1435

Queen of the S: Corr; Paton, McKenzie, Lauchlan, Henderson, Thomson J, Burns, Weir (Thomson A), O'Connor (Mullen), O'Neill (Henry), Scully.
Clyde: Cherrie; McGregor N, Malone, Higgins, Harris, McHale, Bryson, O'Donnell, Arbuckle (Bradley), Imrie, McGowan M (McKinnon).

Queen's Park (1) 2 *(Canning 6, Bowers 107)*

Hamilton A (0) 1 *(Offiong 72)* 611

Queen's Park: Crawford; Quinn (Keenan), Dunlop M, Reilly, Sinclair, Agostini (Ronald), Kettlewell, Paton, Carroll (Bowers), Weatherston, Canning.
Hamilton A: McEwan; Stevenson (Parratt), Fleming, Thomson, Elebert, Easton, McArthur, Wilson (Agnew), Offiong▪, Payo (McLeod), Gilhaney.
aet.

Raith R (1) 1 *(Oné 41)*

Airdrie U (0) 2 *(McLaren 47, Prunty 74)* 1260

Raith R: Brown; Bonar, Leiper (Tulloch), Silvestro, Campbell, Lumsden, Harty (Fairbairn), McManus, Oné, Davidson, Kilgannon (Manson).
Airdrie U: Robertson; McKenna, Lovering, Smyth, Christie, Holmes, McDougall (Taylor), McKeown, Prunty, Twigg (McPhee), McLaren.

Ross Co (1) 4 *(Cowie 26, 59, Higgins 61, Gunn 80)*

Stranraer (0) 2 *(Burns 70, Moore 90)* 848

Ross Co: Samson (Ridgers); Niven, Keddie, McCulloch, Dowie, Tiernan, Gardyne (Gunn), Adams, Higgins, Cowie, Irvine.
Stranraer: Morrison; Lyle, McMullan, Snowdon, Gaughan, Walker, Hamilton, Aitken (Crilly), Moore, Wright (Burns), Ramsay (Nicholas).

St Johnstone (0) 3 *(Scotland 60, 70, Hardie 61)*

East Fife (0) 1 *(Smart C 76)* 1222

St Johnstone: Halliwell; Lawrie, Stanik, McManus, Rutkiewicz, Dyer (Young), Mensing, Hardie, Milne (MacDonald), Scotland (Jackson), Sheerin.
East Fife: Ross; Smith, Linton, Smart J, McGowan, Court, Blackadder, Jablonski, Crabbe (Ritchie), Martin (Smart C), Gordon (O'Reilly).

Wednesday, 9 August 2006

Arbroath (0) 0

Elgin C (0) 1 *(Mackay 49)* 613

Arbroath: Morrison; Rennie, McCulloch, Raeside, Bishop▪, Dobbins (Voigt), Scott (Brazil), Black (Smith), Martin, Sellars▪, Stein.
Elgin C: Renton; Kaczan (Easton), Dempsie, Lowe, Dickson, Hind, Charlesworth (Booth), Campbell, Johnston, Mackay, Gardiner.

Ayr U (2) 2 *(Casey 18, Caddis 39)*

Berwick R (0) 0 857

Ayr U: McGeown; McKinstry, Lowing, Forrest, Robertson, Casey (Logan), Caddis (Strain), Weaver, Vareille, Friels (Reid), Dunn.
Berwick R: O'Connor; Notman, Campbell (Smith), Britton, Horn, Fraser, Manson, Thomson, Haynes, McCallum (Greenhill D), Paliczka (Noble).

Montrose (1) 1 *(Rodgers 25)*

Peterhead (0) 3 *(Linn 60, Wood 107, Bavidge 113)* 421

Montrose: Reid A; Cumming (Reid P), Fraser, Higgins, McLeod, Donachie (Napier), Henslee (Watson), Adam, Rodgers, Kerrigan, Davidson▪.
Peterhead: Mathers; Shand, Cameron, Tully, Perry, Gibson (Bavidge), Sharp (Youngson), Buchan, Linn (Mckay), Wood, Gilfillan.
aet.

SECOND ROUND

Tuesday, 22 August 2006

Alloa Ath (1) 2 *(Brown 43, Forrest 48)*

Ross Co (0) 1 *(McKinlay 55)* 424

Alloa Ath: Creer; Bolochoweckyj, McColligan (Ovenstone), Townsley, Malcolm▪, McKeown, Hamilton (Forrest), Grant, Brown (Comrie), Sloan, McAnespie.
Ross Co: Samson; Irvine, Moore, Dowie, Keddie (Anderson), Scott (Tiernan), Gardyne, McCulloch (Gunn), Adams, Cowie, McKinlay.

Ayr U (0) 0

Dunfermline Ath (0) 0 1501

Ayr U: McGeown; Campbell (Pettigrew), Lowing, Forrest, Robertson, Logan (Wardlaw), Strain (Dunn), Casey, Vareille, Weaver, Caddis.
Dunfermline Ath: De Vries; McGuire, Wilson S, Young, McCunnie (Smith), Bamba, Ross (Wilson C), Mason, Tod, Morrison O, Woods.
aet; Ayr U won 7-6 on penalties.

Brechin C (0) 0
Livingston (2) 3 *(Craig 37, Dorrans 39, Hislop 87)* 466
Brechin C: Nelson; Archibald, Pow (Geddes), Ward, White, Johnson (Devlin), Byers, Callaghan, Hampshire, Connolly (Russell), Smith.
Livingston: Stewart; Thomson, Mackay, McPake, Tweed, Mitchell, Hamill (Smylie), Walker A (Fox), Dorrans (Hislop), Makel, Craig.

Cowdenbeath (0) 0
Falkirk (1) 5 *(Craig 36, Moutinho 50, 81, Twaddle 74, Stewart 85)* 1530
Cowdenbeath: Orr; Baxter, McBride K, Gomis, Hughes, Smith, Scullion, Paatelainen, McBride P (Clarke), Fotheringham (Fusco), Buchanan.
Falkirk: Higgins; Barr, Scobbie (Twaddle), Cregg (Stewart), Ross, Milne, Moutinho, Thomson, Craig, Latapy, Lima (McStay).

Dundee U (0) 1 *(Robertson 117)*
Airdrie U (0) 0 2851
Dundee U: Stillie; Kalvenes, McCracken, Proctor, Archibald, Kerr, Robson, Cameron (Robertson), Conway (Samuel), Hunt (Robb), Miller.
Airdrie U: Robertson; McKenna, Lovering, Smyth (Christie), Tierney, Holmes (Watson), McPhee, McKeown, Prunty, Taylor, McLaren (McDougall).
aet.

Hibernian (2) 4 *(Good (og) 7, Benjelloun 32, Scott Brown 52, McCluskey 66)*
Peterhead (0) 0 7834
Hibernian: Malkowski; Zemmama (McCluskey), Jones, Murphy, Whittaker, Martis (Shields), Thomson, Shiels (Fletcher), Scott Brown, Benjelloun, Sproule.
Peterhead: Mathers; Shand, Good, Tully, Perry, Cameron (Hegarty), Sharp (Youngson), Buchan, McKay, Linn (Wood), Gilfillan.

Motherwell (2) 3 *(Foran 6, 16, McGarry 86)*
Partick T (1) 2 *(Gibson J 25, Roberts 66)* 4406
Motherwell: Smith G; Quinn (Fitzpatrick), Paterson, Reynolds, Craigan, Kerr, McBride (McGarry), Lasley, McDonald, Foran, McCormack (Clarkson).
Partick T: Arthur; Sives, Robertson J (McCulloch), Brady, Boyd, Ferguson, Gibson J, Donnelly, Gibson G (Keogh), Roberts, Gibson W (Strachan).

Queen of the S (0) 1 *(O'Connor 51)*
Kilmarnock (0) 2 *(Murray G 75, Naismith 114)* 2452
Queen of the S: Scott; Paton (Henry), McKenzie, Lauchlan, Henderson, Scally, Burns, Weir (Mullen), O'Connor (Thomson A), O'Neill, Gibson.
Kilmarnock: Smith; Murray G, Hay, Greer, Wright F, Fowler, Murray S (Johnston), Leven, Naismith, Nish (DiGiacomo), Wales (Fernandez).
aet.

Queen's Park (0) 0
Aberdeen (0) 0 1588
Queen's Park: Cairns; Paton, Dunlop M, Agostini, Sinclair (Whelan), Canning, Kettlewell, Weatherston (Bowers), Ronald (Trouten), Dunn, Ferry.
Aberdeen: Soutar; Considine, Foster, Anderson, Dempsey (Stewart), Smith D (Maguire), Nicholson, Winter (MacAulay), Clark, Mackie, Crawford.
aet; Queen's Park won 5-3 on penalties.

St Johnstone (0) 4 *(Sheerin 97, Stevenson 106, Milne 107, MacDonald 112)*
Elgin C (0) 0 1198
St Johnstone: Halliwell; Lawrie, Stanik, Mensing, Anderson, James, Young (Jackson), Hardie (Stevenson), Milne, Coyle (MacDonald), Sheerin.
Elgin C: Renton; Kaczan, Dempsie, Easton, Dickson, Hind (Low), Gardiner (Campbell), Booth (Cooke), Johnston, Charlesworth, Mackay.
aet.

St Mirren (3) 3 *(Mehmet 6, 14, Sutton 30)*
Stenhousemuir (0) 1 *(Sinclair 78)* 1707
St Mirren: Smith; Van Zanten, Broadfoot, Millen, Potter (Murray), Maxwell, Brady, Lappin, Sutton (Burke), Mehmet, Corcoran (Kean).
Stenhousemuir: McCulloch; Murie, Dillon■, McAlpine, Cowan (Sinclair), McBride, McLeish, Murphy, Connelly (Templeton), Hutchison, McLaughlin (Diack).

Wednesday, 23 August 2006

Inverness CT (1) 3 *(Wyness 5, Bayne 55, McAllister 70)*
Dumbarton (1) 1 *(Dobbie 29)* 1085
Inverness CT: Brown; Tokely (McBain), Golabek, McCaffrey, Munro, Duncan, Hart (Keogh), Morgan, Wilson, Bayne, Wyness (McAllister).
Dumbarton: Grindlay; Geggan (Boyle), Brittain (McKeever), Canning, Craig, Gentile, Borris, Bagan, Dobbie (Quitongo), McNaught, Dillon.

THIRD ROUND

Tuesday, 19 September 2006

Celtic (0) 2 *(Beattie 75, Zurawski 87)*
St Mirren (0) 0 31,162
Celtic: Boruc; Telfer, McManus, Balde, O'Dea, Jarosik (McGeady), Pearson, Sno, Zurawski, Beattie, Riordan.
St Mirren: Bullock; Van Zanten, Broadfoot, Millen, Maxwell, Brittain, Murray (Anderson), Lappin, Mehmet (Sutton), Kean (Corcoran), Reid.

Inverness CT (0) 0
Falkirk (0) 1 *(Stokes 61)* 1432
Inverness CT: Brown; Tokely, Dods, Munro, Hastings (McAllister), Duncan (Morgan), Keogh, McBain, Wilson, Dargo (Hart), Bayne.
Falkirk: Higgins; Ross, Dodd, Barr, O'Donnell (Craig), Thomson, Twaddle, Cregg, Milne, Gow, Stokes (Moutinho).

Kilmarnock (0) 2 *(Wales 58, Wright 115)*
Livingston (0) 1 *(Craig 70 (pen))* 3527
Kilmarnock: Smith; Murray G, Wright F, Greer (Locke), Hay, Fowler, Invincibile (Murray S), Johnston, Naismith, Fernandez, Wales (Nish).
Livingston: Wight; Thomson, Mackay, McPake, Tweed, Mitchell, Hamill (Shields), Walker A (Smylie), Dorrans (Weir), Makel, Craig.
aet.

St Johnstone (1) 3 *(Scotland 40, Milne 53, Mensing 80)*
Dundee U (0) 0 4653
St Johnstone: Halliwell; Lawrie, Stanik, Mensing, McManus, Anderson, Hardie (Stevenson), Sheridan, Milne (MacDonald), Scotland (Lawson), Sheerin.
Dundee U: Stillie; Kalvenes, Kenneth, Proctor, Archibald, Kerr, Robson, Conway (Samuel), Cameron (Robb), Brewster, Hunt (Robertson).

Wednesday, 20 September 2006

Alloa Ath (0) 0
Hearts (1) 4 *(Makela 34, 46, 82, Aguiar 88)* 2559
Alloa Ath: Creer; Townsley■, Ovenstone, McKeown, Forrest (Bolochoweckyj), McColligan, Hamilton, Grant, Brown (McAulay), McClune (Hazeldine), Sloan.
Hearts: Banks; Neilson, Fyssas, Karipidis (Lithgow), Berra, Aguiar, Ivaskevicius, McCann, Beslija (Jonsson), Makela, Bednar (Velicka).

Dunfermline Ath (0) 0
Rangers (0) 2 *(Bamba (og) 65, Boyd 73)* 5705
Dunfermline Ath: De Vries; Shields, Wilson S, McGuire, Bamba, Young, Labonte, Mason, Simmons (Morrison O), Hamilton, Daquin (Muirhead).
Rangers: McGregor; Hutton, Smith, Papac, Hemdani, Rae, Burke (Sebo), Adam, Sionko (Martin), Novo (Buffel), Boyd.

Hibernian (4) 6 *(Fletcher 11, Scott Brown 18, Jones 20, Shiels 24, 63, Benjelloun 72)*

Gretna (0) 0 11,075

Hibernian: Malkowski; Martis, Jones, Murphy, Shields, Thomson (Glass), Fletcher, Shiels, Scott Brown (McCluskey), Killen (Stewart), Benjelloun.
Gretna: Main; Birch (Barr), Grainger (Tosh), McFarlane, Townsley, Innes, Jenkins, McGuffie, Deuchar (Berkeley), McMenamin, Skelton.

Queen's Park (0) 0

Motherwell (1) 3 *(Foran 24, 47, 54)* 2408

Queen's Park: Cairns; Paton, Dunlop M, Quinn, Whelan (Bowers), Canning (Ronald), Kettlewell, Trouten, Dunn (Murray), Weatherston, Ferry.
Motherwell: Meldrum; Quinn, Paterson, Reynolds, Craigan, Kerr, Donnelly, Lasley (McBride), McGarry, McDonald (McCormack), Foran (Elliot).

QUARTER-FINALS

Tuesday, 7 November 2006

Celtic (0) 1 *(Zurawski 98)*

Falkirk (0) 1 *(Stokes 100)* 19,316

Celtic: Boruc; Telfer, Naylor, Caldwell, Balde, Gravesen (Sno), Pearson, Riordan (Zurawski), Maloney (Miller), Vennegoor of Hesselink, McGeady.
Falkirk: Lambers; Ross, Barr, Milne, Scobbie (Dodd), Thomson (Lima), Cregg, O'Donnell, Latapy (Craig), Stokes, Gow.
aet; Falkirk won 5-4 on penalties.

Kilmarnock (2) 3 *(Wright 7, 44, Invincibile 71)*

Motherwell (1) 2 *(Foran 25, Clarkson 59)* 5601

Kilmarnock: Smith; Murray G, Wright F, Greer, Hay, Fowler, Invincibile, Leven (Wales) (Ford), Johnston, Nish, Naismith.
Motherwell: Meldrum; Quinn, Fitzpatrick, Reynolds, Craigan, Kerr, Lasley, McGarry (McBride), Foran, Elliot, Clarkson.

Wednesday, 8 November 2006

Hibernian (1) 1 *(Jones 32)*

Hearts (0) 0 15,825

Hibernian: Malkowski; Zemmama (Benjelloun), Jones, Murphy, Whittaker, Thomson, Stewart (Beuzelin), Martis, Scott Brown, Killen, Sproule (Fletcher).
Hearts: Gordon; Neilson (Barasa), Berra, Pressley, Tall, Zaliukas (Makela), Mikoliunas (Mole), Goncalves, Aguiar, Hartley, Velicka.

Rangers (0) 0

St Johnstone (0) 2 *(Milne 52, 67)* 27,547

Rangers: McGregor; Hutton, Hemdani, Papac, Smith, Clement, Sebo (Prso), Rae (Adam), Buffel (Martin), Novo, Boyd.
St Johnstone: Halliwell; Lawrie, Stanik, Mensing, McManus, Anderson, Lawson (Sheridan), Hardie, Milne (Jackson), Scotland (MacDonald), Sheerin.

SEMI-FINALS (at Fir Park)

Tuesday, 30 January 2007

Kilmarnock (1) 3 *(Naismith 30, 71, 78)*

Falkirk (0) 0 10,722

Kilmarnock: Combe; Ford, Wright F, Greer, Quinn (Wales), Fowler, Leven, Johnston (Locke), Sylla (Murray G), Naismith, Nish.
Falkirk: Schmeichel; Ross (Moutinho), Barr, Milne, Uras, Cregg, Lima, Craig (O'Donnell), Latapy, Finnigan, Gow.

SEMI-FINALS (at Tynecastle)

Wednesday, 31 January 2007

St Johnstone (0) 1 *(Scotland 78)*

Hibernian (1) 3 *(Fletcher 3, Murphy 92, Benjelloun 120)* 16,112

St Johnstone: Cuthbert; Lawrie, Stanik, McInnes, McManus, James, Hardie (Jackson), Mensing, MacDonald (Morais), Scotland, Sheerin.
Hibernian: McNeil; Martis, Jones, Murphy, Whittaker, Stewart (Benjelloun), Beuzelin, Fletcher, Shiels (Stevenson), Scott Brown, Sproule (McCann).
aet.

FINAL (at Hampden Park)

Sunday, 18 March 2007

Kilmarnock (0) 1 *(Greer 77)*

Hibernian (1) 5 *(Jones 28, Benjelloun 59, 85, Fletcher 66, 87)* 52,000

Kilmarnock: Combe; Ford, Wright F, Greer, Hay, Fowler, Leven (Wales), DiGiacomo (Locke), Johnston, Nish, Naismith.
Hibernian: McNeil; Hogg, Jones, Murphy, Whittaker, Stevenson, Beuzelin, Fletcher, Scott Brown, Benjelloun, Sproule (Zemmama).
Referee: Douglas McDonald.

SCOTTISH LEAGUE ATTENDANCES 2006–07

PREMIER LEAGUE

	Average	Highest	Lowest
Aberdeen	12,475	20,045	9,379
Celtic	57,928	59,659	54,620
Dundee U	7,147	12,329	5,036
Dunfermline Ath	6,106	8,561	4,200
Falkirk	5,387	7,245	3,129
Hearts	16,937	17,369	15,912
Hibernian	14,587	16,747	10,674
Inverness CT	4,879	7,522	3,517
Kilmarnock	7,567	13,673	4,732
Motherwell	5,877	11,745	3,640
Rangers	49,955	50,488	48,218
St Mirren	5,609	10,251	3,576

FIRST DIVISION

	Average	Highest	Lowest
Airdrie U	1,452	2,351	1,138
Clyde	1,380	2,956	729
Dundee	3,880	5,538	2,837
Gretna	1,602	2,193	1,124
Hamilton A	1,715	4,975	1,035
Livingston	1,839	2,403	1,400
Partick Th	2,572	3,473	1,697
Queen of the S	2,207	5,485	1,497
Ross Co	2,344	6,216	1,475
St Johnstone	2,813	4,168	2,106

SECOND DIVISION

	Average	Highest	Lowest
Alloa Ath	634	1,138	344
Ayr U	1,171	1,998	853
Brechin C	569	909	407
Cowdenbeath	689	2,249	251
Forfar Ath	503	765	298
Morton	2,661	5,276	1,991
Peterhead	636	819	476
Raith R	1,935	4,327	1,186
Stirling A	945	2,608	541
Stranraer	417	940	212

THIRD DIVISION

	Average	Highest	Lowest
Albion R	429	619	276
Arbroath	743	1,295	447
Berwick R	565	2,054	323
Dumbarton	712	1,092	521
East Fife	584	680	443
East Stirling	312	429	173
Elgin C	423	547	305
Montrose	462	1,256	245
Queen's Park	590	916	404
Stenhousemuir	410	654	244

LEAGUE CHALLENGE CUP 2006–07

■ *Denotes player sent off.*

FIRST ROUND

Tuesday, 15 August 2006

Ayr U (1) 2 *(Strain 38, Vareille 72)*
Livingston (1) 1 *(Craig 17)* 929
Ayr U: McGeown; Pettigrew (Campbell), Lowing, Forrest, Robertson, Logan, Strain, Casey, Vareille (Wardlaw), Weaver, Caddis.
Livingston: Wight; Thomson, Mackay, McPake, Millar (Tweed), Mitchell, Hamill, Walker, Hislop (Weir), Fox (Dorrans), Craig.

Brechin C (1) 1 *(Callaghan 35)*
Arbroath (1) 2 *(Cook 36, Rennie 51)* 506
Brechin C: Hillcoat; McEwan (Connolly), Stuart Ferguson, Ward, Walker S, Byers, Walker R (Johnson), Russell, Geddes, Callaghan, Pow (Smith).
Arbroath: Peat; Rennie, McCulloch, Raeside, Dobbins, Watson (Bishop), Cook, Scott■, Martin (Brazil), Sellars, Black.

Cowdenbeath (2) 4 *(Clarke 15, Fotheringham 25, Paatelainen 53, Dalziel 63)*
Stirling Albion (0) 0 427
Cowdenbeath: Orr; Baxter, Ellis, Gomis (Fusco), Ritchie, Hughes, Fotheringham, Paatelainen (McBride K), Dalziel (McBride P), Clarke, Buchanan.
Stirling Albion: Hogarth; Hay, Devine, McNally (O'Brien), Graham, Fraser, Bell, Aitken (Gibson), Cramb (Cashmore), Shields, Forsyth.

Dumbarton (0) 1 *(McNaught 114)*
Morton (0) 2 *(Weatherson 117, 119)* 927
Dumbarton: Shaw; Geggan, Brittain (Boyle), Canning, Craig, Bagan (McKeever), Gentile (Quitongo), Winter, McNaught, Borris, Dillon.
Morton: McGurn; Weatherson, Walker, Harding, Greacen■, McLaughlin, Millar, Stevenson (Russell), Templeman (McLean), McGowan (Lilley), McAlister.
aet.

East Stirling (0) 0
Queen's Park (3) 5 *(Ronald 24, Livingstone (og) 26, Bowers 37, Paton 51, Molloy 54)* 254
East Stirling: Nugent; Livingstone, Ure, Oates, Brand, Blair (Nixon), McKenzie (Smith), Boyle (Stewart), Dymock, Ward, Adam.
Queen's Park: Cairns; Paton, Molloy, Whelan, Agostini, Canning (Dunn), Kettlewell (Weatherston), Quinn (Trouten), Ronald, Bowers, Ferry.

Forfar Ath (0) 2 *(Gribben 52, Coyle 67)*
Dundee (0) 1 *(Swankie 90)* 840
Forfar Ath: Murdoch; Keogh, King, Dunn, Rattray, Webster, Lunan, Marshall, Tosh, Gribben (Fraser), Coyle.
Dundee: Murray; Griffin, Dixon, Robertson, Macdonald C, Strong, Harris (McNally), McDonald K, Campbell (Swankie), Deasley, Gates.

Hamilton A (1) 3 *(Tunbridge 24, Payo 53, Offiong 90)*
Berwick R (1) 1 *(Horn 1)* 590
Hamilton A: McEwan; Stevenson, Fleming, McCabe (Parratt), Elebert, Easton, Payo, Wilson, Offiong, Tunbridge, Gilhaney.
Berwick R: Flockhart; Notman (Manson), Campbell, Smith, Horn (Fraser), Wood, Thomson, Greenhill G (Palicska), Haynes, McCallum, Noble.

Partick T (1) 1 *(Ferguson 21)*
Albion R (2) 2 *(McBride 4, Chaplain 28)* 1208
Partick T: Arthur; Sives, McCulloch (Strachan), Brady, Boyd, Robertson, Gibson J, Donnelly, Gibson G, Ferguson, Gibson W (McConalogue).
Albion R: Ewings; Moffat, McGhee, Lennon, Donnelly, Friel, Doyle, Chaplain, Felvus (Walker), Savage (Chisholm), McBride (Clearie).

Queen of the S (0) 1 *(O'Neill 52)*
Stranraer (0) 0 1389
Queen of the S: Scott; Paton, Scally, Lauchlan, Henderson, Thomson J, Burns, Weir, Henry (Mullen), O'Neill J (McKenzie), Thomson A (Gibson).
Stranraer: Morrison; Snowdon, Sharp, Lyle, Walker, Crilly (Aitken), McGroarty (Nicholas), Burns, Moore, Wright (Hamilton), McMillan.

St Johnstone (1) 3 *(Milne 24, 112, James 97)*
Raith R (1) 1 *(Oné 8)* 1261
St Johnstone: Cuthbert; Anderson, Dyer, Mensing, McManus, James, Stevenson■, Young (Moon), Milne, MacDonald (Doris) (Coyle), Sheerin.
Raith R: Brown; Bonar, Fotheringham, Silvestro, Campbell, Lumsden, Tulloch (Leiper), Harty, Oné (Mansen), Davidson, Kilgannon (Fairbairn).
aet.

Wednesday, 16 August 2006

Airdrie U (0) 0
Gretna (1) 3 *(Deuchar 12, 76, Tosh 71)* 1093
Airdrie U: Hollis; McKenna, McGowan, Smyth, Christie (Tierney), Holmes, McDougall, McKeown, McPhee (Watson), Twigg (Prunty), McLaren.
Gretna: Mathieson; Birch, Nicholls (Tosh), Skelton, Townsley, Canning, McGill, Jenkins (McGuffie), Deuchar, McMenamin (Graham), Grainger.

East Fife (0) 0
Ross Co (1) 3 *(Dowie 21, Gunn 70, 71)* 304
East Fife: Dodds; Ross, Smith, Smart J, Court, Mitchell, Fortune, Jablonski, O'Reilly (Gordon), Smart C, Blackadder.
Ross Co: Malin; Niven, Robertson, Dowie, Keddie (McCulloch), Irvine, Gardyne, Tiernan, Irvine, Higgins (Gunn), Cowie, McKinlay (Scott).

Elgin C (0) 2 *(Charlesworth 79, 90)*
Stenhousemuir (0) 0 276
Elgin C: Renton; Campbell, Dempsie, Lowe, Dickson, Hind, Easton, Mackay, Johnston, Gardiner, Cooke (Charlesworth).
Stenhousemuir: McCulloch; Murie, Dillon, Henderson (McBride), Tyrrell M, Tyrrell P, McLeish (Diack), Murphy, Baird, Hutchison, McLaughlin.

Montrose (0) 2 *(Henslee 51, Michie 55)*
Peterhead (0) 0 335
Montrose: Reid A; Tawse, Fraser, Higgins (Adam), McLeod, Davidson, Cumming, Henslee, Kerrigan, Michie (Watson), Napier (Rodgers).
Peterhead: Mathers; Shand, Good (Youngson), Tully, Perry, Hegarty (Cameron), Sharp, Buchan, Linn, Bavidge, McKay (MacInnes).

SECOND ROUND

Tuesday, 29 August 2006

Albion R (2) 5 *(Donnelly 14, Lennon 19, Chaplain 62, 64, Savage 80)*
Elgin C (0) 2 *(Kaczan 50, Mackay 88)* 180
Albion R: Ewings; Moffat, Lennox (Chisholm), Lennon, Donnelly, Friel (Creaney), Doyle, Chaplain, Felvus (Sim), Savage, McBride.
Elgin C: Renton; Kaczan, Dempsie, Easton (Cooke), Dickson, Hind (Lowe), Finnigan (Charlesworth), Campbell, Johnston, Booth, Mackay.

Forfar Ath (1) 1 *(Lunan 14)*
Arbroath (1) 3 *(Brazil 27, Stein 65, Sellars 72)* 628
Forfar Ath: Murdoch; Lumsden, Lynn, Dunn, Rattray, Beith (Coyle), Lunan, Marshall (Donald), Lombardi, Gribben, Webster.
Arbroath: Morrison; Rennie, McCulloch, Raeside, Bishop, Dobbins, Black (Watson), Brazil, Martin (Voigt), Sellars (McMullan), Stein.

Morton (3) 3 *(McLaughlin 10, McGowan 12, Millar 16)*
Cowdenbeath (0) 2 *(Clarke 48, Fotheringham 61)* 1915
Morton: McGurn; Finlayson, Walker (Keenan), Harding, Weatherson, McLaughlin, Millar, Stevenson, Lilley, McGowan (Templeman), McAlister.
Cowdenbeath: Orr; Guy (Buchanan), McBride K, Scullion (Fusco), Hughes, Ellis (Ritchie), Baxter, Paatelainen, Fotheringham, Gomis, Clarke.

Ross Co (0) 2 *(McKinlay 63, 120 (pen))*
Alloa Ath (1) 1 *(Townsley 1)* 549
Ross Co: Malin; Irvine, Keddie, Niven, McCulloch, Tiernan (Anderson), Gardyne (Scott), Adams, Higgins (Gunn), Cowie, McKinlay.
Alloa Ath: Creer; Ovenstone, Bolochoweckyj, Townsley, Malcolm, McColligan (Comrie), Grant, McKeown, Hazeldine (Brown), McCallum (Hamilton), Sloan.
aet.

St Johnstone (2) 3 *(Scotland 20, 60, MacDonald 40)*
Queen's Park (0) 0 1351
St Johnstone: Cuthbert; Lawrie, Dyer, Mensing, Anderson, James, Stevenson, Sheerin, MacDonald (O'Donnell), Scotland (Jackson), Stanik (Moon).
Queen's Park: Cairns; Paton, Dunlop M, Agostini, Reilly, Canning, Kettlewell (Quinn), Weatherston, Ronald (Trouten), Dunn (Bowers), Ferry.

Wednesday, 30 August 2006

Gretna (2) 3 *(Graham 3, Townsley 42, McGuffie 51 (pen))*
Hamilton A (1) 1 *(Neill 14)* 841
Gretna: Mathieson; McFarlane, McQuilken, McGuffie, Townsley, Innes, Baldacchino (Berkeley), McGill, Deuchar (Bingham), Graham, Nicholls.
Hamilton A: Jellema; Parratt, Fleming, Thomson (McCabe), Elebert, Easton, McArthur, Wilson, Wake, Neill (McLeod), Gilhaney.

Montrose (0) 0
Clyde (1) 3 *(McHale 40 (pen), Ferguson 62, Imrie 90)* 427
Montrose: Reid A; Tawse (Cumming), Stirling, Higgins, McLeod, Adam, Donachie, Stewart (Napier), Kerrigan (Fraser), Michie, Henslee.
Clyde: Cherrie; McGregor N, Malone, Higgins (McCann), Masterton, McHale, Bryson, Arbuckle (Hunter), Ferguson (Bradley), Imrie, McGowan M.

Queen of the S (0) 2 *(O'Neill 63, Lauchlan 77)*
Ayr U (0) 2 *(Robertson 55, Weaver 90)* 1239
Queen of the S: Corr; Paton, Callaghan (Robertson), Lauchlan, Scally, McKenzie, Burns, Thomson, Mullen (O'Neill), Henry (Moon), Gibson.
Ayr U: McGeown; Casey, Lowing, Forrest, Robertson, Dunn, Hyslop (Strain), Weaver, Friels (Vareille), Wardlaw, Creaney (Walker).
aet; Ayr U won 5-4 on penalties.

QUARTER-FINALS

Tuesday, 12 September 2006

Albion R (2) 3 *(Savage 20, Chisholm 42, Chaplain 58)*
Arbroath (2) 3 *(Martin 16, 44, Sellars 87)* 320
Albion R: Ewings; Moffat, McGhie, Lennon, Donnelly, Friel (Creaney), Doyle, Chaplain, Chisholm (Sim), Savage (Smith), Walker.
Arbroath: Morrison; Rennie, McCulloch, Raeside, Bishop, Dobbins, Black (Watson), Martin, Brazil (McMullan), Sellars, Stein (Scott).
aet; Albion R won 5-3 on penalties.

Clyde (0) 1 *(McHale 60)*
Ayr U (0) 0 785
Clyde: Hurron; McGregor N, Malone, Higgins, McCann (McGowan M), McHale, Bryson, O'Donnell, Ferguson, Imrie, Arbuckle (Hunter).
Ayr U: McGeown; Casey, Creaney (Strain), Forrest, Robertson, Reid, Hyslop (Caddis), Weaver, Friels (Walker), Wardlaw, Dunn,.

Morton (0) 3 *(Harding 49, McGowan 54, 89)*
St Johnstone (1) 2 *(Mensing 7, 81)* 2375
Morton: Gonet; Weatherson, Keenan (Walker), Harding, Greacen, McLaughlin, Millar, Stevenson (Finlayson), Lilley, McGowan (Templeman), McAlister.
St Johnstone: Cuthbert; Lawrie, Stanik, Mensing, McManus, James, Hardie (Jackson), Sheerin, Milne (MacDonald), Scotland, Stevenson (Dyer).

Ross Co (2) 3 *(Williams 35, Ciani 40, Anderson 96)*
Gretna (0) 2 *(McMenamin 73, Jenkins 77)* 761
Ross Co: Samson; Irvine, McCulloch, Niven, Dowie, Anderson, Ciani (Scott), Adams, Williams (Gunn), Cowie, McKinlay (Robertson).
Gretna: Main; McFarlane (Jenkins), McQuilken, O'Neil (Birch), Townsley, Canning■, McGill, McGuffie, McMenamin, Grady (Deuchar), Skelton.
aet.

SEMI-FINALS

Wednesday, 27 September 2006

Clyde (2) 3 *(McGowan M 13, Higgins 41, Bryson 79)*
Morton (0) 1 *(Higgins (og) 63)* 2176
Clyde: Cherrie; McGregor N, Malone, Higgins, McKeown, McHale, Bryson, O'Donnell (Masterton), Ferguson (Arbuckle), Imrie (Hunter), McGowan M.
Morton: Gonet; Weatherson, Walker (Finlayson), Harding, Greacen, McLaughlin, Millar, Stevenson, Lilley (McLean), McGowan (Templeman), McAlister.

Ross Co (1) 4 *(Higgins 12, 50, Gunn 85, McKinlay 87)*
Albion R (0) 1 *(Dowie (og) 56)* 732
Ross Co: Samson; Irvine, Keddie, Dowie, McCulloch, Tiernan (Robertson), Gardyne, Adams, Higgins (Gunn), Cowie, McKinlay.
Albion R: Ewings; Moffat (Bonnar), Lennox, Lennon, Nicoll, Friel, Doyle, Chaplain, Chisholm (Felvus), Savage, McBride (Sim).

FINAL (at MacDiarmid Park)

Sunday, 12 November 2006

Ross Co (0) 1 *(Dowie 80)*
Clyde (1) 1 *(Hunter 43)* 4062
Ross Co: Samson; Irvine, Keddie, Dowie, McKinlay, Gunn, Gardyne, Adams, Ciani (Crooks 115), Cowie (Robertson 102), Scott (Anderson 117).
Clyde: Hutton; McGregor N, Malone■, Higgins, McKeown, McHale, Bryson (Miller 90), O'Donnell, Ferguson (Bradley 78), Hunter (McKenna78), McCann.
aet; Ross Co won 5-4 on penalties.
Referee: Craig Thomson.

SCOTTISH CUP FINALS 1874–2007

Year	*Winners*	*Runners-up*	*Score*
1874	Queen's Park	Clydesdale	2-0
1875	Queen's Park	Renton	3-0
1876	Queen's Park	Third Lanark	2-0 after 1-1 draw
1877	Vale of Leven	Rangers	3-2 after 0-0 and 1-1 draws
1878	Vale of Leven	Third Lanark	1-0
1879	Vale of Leven*	Rangers	
1880	Queen's Park	Thornlibank	3-0
1881	Queen's Park†	Dumbarton	3-1
1882	Queen's Park	Dumbarton	4-1 after 2-2 draw
1883	Dumbarton	Vale of Leven	2-1 after 2-2 draw
1884	Queen's Park‡	Vale of Leven	
1885	Renton	Vale of Leven	3-1 after 0-0 draw
1886	Queen's Park	Renton	3-1
1887	Hibernian	Dumbarton	2-1
1888	Renton	Cambuslang	6-1
1889	Third Lanark§	Celtic	2-1
1890	Queen's Park	Vale of Leven	2-1 after 1-1 draw
1891	Hearts	Dumbarton	1-0
1892	Celtic¶	Queen's Park	5-1
1893	Queen's Park	Celtic	2-1
1894	Rangers	Celtic	3-1
1895	St Bernard's	Renton	2-1
1896	Hearts	Hibernian	3-1
1897	Rangers	Dumbarton	5-1
1898	Rangers	Kilmarnock	2-0
1899	Celtic	Rangers	2-0
1900	Celtic	Queen's Park	4-3
1901	Hearts	Celtic	4-3
1902	Hibernian	Celtic	1-0
1903	Rangers	Hearts	2-0 after 1-1 and 0-0 draws
1904	Celtic	Rangers	3-2
1905	Third Lanark	Rangers	3-1 after 0-0 draw
1906	Hearts	Third Lanark	1-0
1907	Celtic	Hearts	3-0
1908	Celtic	St Mirren	5-1
1909	••		
1910	Dundee	Clyde	2-1 after 2-2 and 0-0 draws
1911	Celtic	Hamilton A	2-0 after 0-0 draw
1912	Celtic	Clyde	2-0
1913	Falkirk	Raith R	2-0
1914	Celtic	Hibernian	4-1 after 0-0 draw
1920	Kilmarnock	Albion R	3-2
1921	Partick Th	Rangers	1-0
1922	Morton	Rangers	1-0
1923	Celtic	Hibernian	1-0
1924	Airdrieonians	Hibernian	2-0
1925	Celtic	Dundee	2-1
1926	St Mirren	Celtic	2-0
1927	Celtic	East Fife	3-1
1928	Rangers	Celtic	4-0
1929	Kilmarnock	Rangers	2-0
1930	Rangers	Partick Th	2-1 after 0-0 draw
1931	Celtic	Motherwell	4-2 after 2-2 draw
1932	Rangers	Kilmarnock	3-0 after 1-1 draw
1933	Celtic	Motherwell	1-0
1934	Rangers	St Mirren	5-0
1935	Rangers	Hamilton A	2-1
1936	Rangers	Third Lanark	1-0
1937	Celtic	Aberdeen	2-1
1938	East Fife	Kilmarnock	4-2 after 1-1 draw
1939	Clyde	Motherwell	4-0
1947	Aberdeen	Hibernian	2-1
1948	Rangers	Morton	1-0 after 1-1 draw
1949	Rangers	Clyde	4-1
1950	Rangers	East Fife	3-0
1951	Celtic	Motherwell	1-0
1952	Motherwell	Dundee	4-0
1953	Rangers	Aberdeen	1-0 after 1-1 draw
1954	Celtic	Aberdeen	2-1
1955	Clyde	Celtic	1-0 after 1-1 draw
1956	Hearts	Celtic	3-1
1957	Falkirk	Kilmarnock	2-1 after 1-1 draw
1958	Clyde	Hibernian	1-0
1959	St Mirren	Aberdeen	3-1
1960	Rangers	Kilmarnock	2-0
1961	Dunfermline Ath	Celtic	2-0 after 0-0 draw
1962	Rangers	St Mirren	2-0
1963	Rangers	Celtic	3-0 after 1-1 draw

Year	*Winners*	*Runners-up*	*Score*
1964	Rangers	Dundee	3-1
1965	Celtic	Dunfermline Ath	3-2
1966	Rangers	Celtic	1-0 after 0-0 draw
1967	Celtic	Aberdeen	2-0
1968	Dunfermline Ath	Hearts	3-1
1969	Celtic	Rangers	4-0
1970	Aberdeen	Celtic	3-1
1971	Celtic	Rangers	2-1 after 1-1 draw
1972	Celtic	Hibernian	6-1
1973	Rangers	Celtic	3-2
1974	Celtic	Dundee U	3-0
1975	Celtic	Airdrieonians	3-1
1976	Rangers	Hearts	3-1
1977	Celtic	Rangers	1-0
1978	Rangers	Aberdeen	2-1
1979	Rangers	Hibernian	3-2 after 0-0 and 0-0 draws
1980	Celtic	Rangers	1-0
1981	Rangers	Dundee U	4-1 after 0-0 draw
1982	Aberdeen	Rangers	4-1 (aet)
1983	Aberdeen	Rangers	1-0 (aet)
1984	Aberdeen	Celtic	2-1 (aet)
1985	Celtic	Dundee U	2-1
1986	Aberdeen	Hearts	3-0
1987	St Mirren	Dundee U	1-0 (aet)
1988	Celtic	Dundee U	2-1
1989	Celtic	Rangers	1-0
1990	Aberdeen	Celtic	0-0 (aet)
		(Aberdeen won 9-8 on penalties)	
1991	Motherwell	Dundee U	4-3 (aet)
1992	Rangers	Airdrieonians	2-1
1993	Rangers	Aberdeen	2-1
1994	Dundee U	Rangers	1-0
1995	Celtic	Airdrieonians	1-0
1996	Rangers	Hearts	5-1
1997	Kilmarnock	Falkirk	1-0
1998	Hearts	Rangers	2-1
1999	Rangers	Celtic	1-0
2000	Rangers	Aberdeen	4-0
2001	Celtic	Hibernian	3-0
2002	Rangers	Celtic	3-2
2003	Rangers	Dundee	1-0
2004	Celtic	Dunfermline Ath	3-1
2005	Celtic	Dundee U	1-0
2006	Hearts	Gretna	1-1 (aet)
		(Hearts won 4-2 on penalties)	
2007	Celtic	Dunfermline Ath	1-0

*Vale of Leven awarded cup, Rangers failing to appear for replay after 1-1 draw.
†After Dumbarton protested the first game, which Queen's Park won 2-1.
‡Queen's Park awarded cup, Vale of Leven failing to appear.
§Replay by order of Scottish FA because of playing conditions in first match, won 3-0 by Third Lanark.
¶After mutually protested game which Celtic won 1-0.
••Owing to riot, the cup was withheld after two drawn games – between Celtic and Rangers 2-2 and 1-1.

SCOTTISH CUP WINS

Celtic 34, Rangers 31, Queen's Park 10, Aberdeen 7, Hearts 7, Clyde 3, Kilmarnock 3, St Mirren 3, Vale of Leven 3, Dunfermline Ath 2, Falkirk 2, Hibernian 2, Motherwell 2, Renton 2, Third Lanark 2, Airdrieonians 1, Dumbarton 1, Dundee 1, Dundee U 1, East Fife 1, Morton 1, Partick Th 1, St Bernard's 1.

APPEARANCES IN FINAL

Celtic 53, Rangers 48, Aberdeen 15, Hearts 13, Queen's Park 12, Hibernian 11, Dundee U 8, Kilmarnock 8, Vale of Leven 7, Clyde 6, Dumbarton 6, Motherwell 6, St Mirren 6, Third Lanark 6, Dundee 5, Dunfermline Ath 5, Renton 5, Airdrieonians 4, East Fife 3, Falkirk 3, Hamilton A 2, Morton 2, Partick Th 2, Albion R 1, Cambuslang 1, Clydesdale 1, Gretna 1, Raith R 1, St Bernard's 1, Thornlibank 1.

LEAGUE CHALLENGE FINALS 1991–2007

Year	*Winners*	*Runners-up*	*Score*
1990–91	Dundee	Ayr U	3-2
1991–92	Hamilton A	Ayr U	1-0
1992–93	Hamilton A	Morton	3-2
1993–94	Falkirk	St Mirren	3-0
1994–95	Airdrieonians	Dundee	3-2
1995–96	Stenhousemuir	Dundee U	0-0
	(Stenhousemuir won 5-4 on penalties)		
1996–97	Stranraer	St Johnstone	1-0
1997–98	Falkirk	Queen of the South	1-0
1998–99	no competition		
1999–2000	Alloa Ath	Inverness CT	4-4
	(Alloa Ath won 5-4 on penalties)		
2000–01	Airdrieonians	Livingston	2-2
	(Airdrieonians won 3-2 on penalties)		
2001–02	Airdrieonians	Alloa Ath	2-1
2002–03	Queen of the S	Brechin C	2-0
2003–04	Inverness CT	Airdrie U	2-0
2004–05	Falkirk	Ross Co	2-1
2005–06	St Mirren	Hamilton A	2-1
2006–07	Ross Co	Clyde	1-1
	(Ross Co won 5-4 on penalties)		

TENNENT'S SCOTTISH CUP 2006–07

▪ *Denotes player sent off.*

FIRST ROUND

Saturday, 18 November 2006

Arbroath (1) 2 *(Martin 13, 85)*

Albion R (0) 1 *(Felvus 70)* 493

Arbroath: Peat; Rennie, McCulloch, Raeside, Bishop, Smith, McMullan, Martin (Scott), Brazil, Sellars, Stein.
Albion R: Ewings; Watson, Nicoll, Lennon, Donnelly, Doyle, Lennox (Sim), Chaplain, Felvus, Creaney (Savage), Smith (McBride).

Brechin C (0) 1 *(Callaghan 80 (pen))*

Queen's Park (1) 1 *(Ferry 21)* 515

Brechin C: Nelson; McEwan (Walker R), White, Ward, Walker S, Callaghan, King, Steven Ferguson (Byers), Hampshire, Geddes (Connolly), Smith.
Queen's Park: Cairns; Paton, Dunlop M, Reilly, Sinclair, Trouten, Kettlewell, Quinn, Ronald (Bowers), Weatherston, Ferry.

Deveronvale (0) 3 *(Mackenzie 86, Fraser 89, Ewen 90)*

Montrose (2) 2 *(Stirling 11, Henslee 23)* 800

Deveronvale: Blanchard; Dolan, Gilbert, Chisholm, Fraser, Brown, McWilliam (Watt), Smith, Mackenzie, Murray, Urquhart (Ewen).
Montrose: Reid▪; Cumming, Stirling, Ndiwa, McLeod▪, Gibson, Henslee, Davidson▪, Rodgers (Kerrigan), Mercer (Michie), Campbell (Adam).

East Fife (0) 1 *(Jablonski 73)*

Berwick R (1) 3 *(Haynes 30 (pen), Wood 89, McLaughlin 90)* 744

East Fife: Ross; Smith, Dair, Smart J, McGowan, Courts, Blackadder, Jablonski, O'Reilly, Fortune (Smart C), Hampshire (Martin).
Berwick R: Flockhart; Manson, Noble, Horn, Smith, McNicoll, Thompson, Greenhill G, Haynes (McLaughlin), Wood, Greenhill D.

Edinburgh University (2) 2 *(Hazeldine 7, 28)*

Keith (0) 1 *(Walker 57)* 1000

Edinburgh University: Bennett; Cook, Fusco, Thompson, Cathcart (Beesley), Irvine (Maxwell), Hair (Munro), Redman, Howat, Nikolaidis, Hazeldine.
Keith: Shearer; Watt, Lonie, Robertson, Nicol, Still, McKay, Keith (Craig), Lennox (O'Driscoll), Donaldson, McAllister (Walker).

Preston Ath (1) 2 *(Cowie 27, Miller 55)*

Stenhousemuir (0) 0 400

Preston Ath: Gilpin; Manson, Baillie, Costello, Scott CF, McAuley, Campbell (Kirk), Lockart, Miller (Scott C), Cowie, Wilson (Newall).
Stenhousemuir: McCulloch; Menzies (Murie), Dillon, Tyrrell P, Cowan, Gow, Baird (Diack), McLeish, Hutchison, McBride, Templeton (McLaughlin).

Stranraer (1) 4 *(Hamilton 40, McMullan 59, Wilson 79, Nicholas 82)*

Alloa Ath (1) 2 *(McAnespie 8, 71)* 272

Stranraer: Black; McGroarty, Sharp, Snowdon (Nicholas), Wilson, Crilly, Aitken (Hunter), Hamilton, Wright, Burns (Moore), McMullan.
Alloa Ath: Creer; Clark, Ovenstone, Malcolm▪, McClune▪, McColligan, Grant, Sloan, Brown, Payo (Young), McAnespie.

Saturday, 25 November 2006

East Stirling (0) 0

Stirling Albion (2) 2 *(Cramb 17, Shields 26)* 550

East Stirling: Tiropoulos; Livingstone (Molloy), Learmonth, Thywissen, Boyle (Tweedie), Wild, McKenzie, Stewart, Dymock, Ward, Ure.
Stirling Albion: Hogarth; Hay, Forsyth, McNally, Roycroft (Devine), Aitken, Bell, Tomana, Cramb (Cashmore), Shields, Taggart (Malseed).

FIRST ROUND REPLAY

Tuesday, 28 November 2006

Queen's Park (1) 1 *(Ronald 22)*

Brechin C (0) 2 *(Hampshire 52, Connolly 53)* 535

Queen's Park: Crawford; Paton, Dunlop M, Reilly, Agostini, Trouten, Kettlewell, Dunn (Canning), Ronald (Bowers), Weatherston, Ferry.
Brechin C: Nelson; Walker R, Callaghan, Ward, Walker S (King), White, Byers, Flynn, Hampshire, Connolly (Geddes), Smith.

SECOND ROUND

Saturday, 9 December 2006

Annan Ath (0) 0

Morton (3) 3 *(Greacen 7, Weatherson 20, Stevenson 37)* 1200

Annan Ath: Calder; Wilby, McGuffie, Bell M, Hill, Jack, Sloan, Jardine (McMenamin), Hore (Bell G), Tucker, Grainger.
Morton: Mathers; Weatherson, McGregor, Harding, Greacen (Walker), McLaughlin, Millar, Stevenson (Finlayson), Templeman (Lilley), McGowan, McAlister.

Berwick R (1) 2 *(Haynes 35, Wood 88)*

Arbroath (0) 0 458

Berwick R: Flockhart; Manson, Noble, Horn, Smith, McNicoll, Thomson, Fraser, Haynes (McLaughlin), Wood, Greenhill D.
Arbroath: Peat; Rennie (Brazil), Watson, Raeside, Bishop, Smith, McMullen, Martin, Scott, Sellars, Stein.

Brechin C (1) 2 *(Russell 35, Nelson 46)*

Preston Ath (0) 1 *(Newall 88)* 452

Brechin C: Nelson; Walker R (Archibald), Callaghan, Ward (Walker S), Flynn, White, Byers, Russell, Hampshire, Connolly (Geddes), King.
Preston Ath: Gilpin; Manson, Baillie, Costello, Scott CF, McAuley, Barton (Kirk), Lockart (Newall), Miller, Cowie (Scott C), Wilson.

Cowdenbeath (3) 5 *(Buchanan 31, 45, Lennon 41, Baxter 80, Paatelainen 82)*

Edinburgh University (0) 1 *(Beesley 71)* 896

Cowdenbeath: Allison; Baxter, Hill, Lennon, Ritchie, Hannah, Paatelainen, Scullion (Fotheringham), Buchanan (Manzie), Dalziel, Ellis.
Edinburgh University: Bennett; Cook, Fusco, Thompson, Cathcart, Maxwell, Hair (Woods), Redman, Howat, Nikolaidis (Beesley), Hazeldine (Campion).

Deveronvale (1) 2 *(Smith 20, 76)*

Fraserburgh (1) 1 *(Dolan (og) 8)* 1500

Deveronvale: Blanchard; Dolan, Gilbert, Chisholm, Fraser, Brown, Urquhart, Smith, Mackenzie, Ewen (McWilliam), Watt.
Fraserburgh: Gordon; Milne, Main N (McBride), Dickson, Christie, Johnston (McLaren), Norris, West, Hale, Main S, Stephen (Wemyss).

Edinburgh C (0) 0

Stirling Albion (1) 1 *(Bell 7)* 500

Edinburgh C: Armit; Ross R, Ross K, Macnamara, Barr, Hunter, Caddow, Morrison, Noon, Young, Dodds (Gair).
Stirling Albion: Christie; Hay, Devine, McNally, Graham, Aitken, Bell, Tomana (O'Brien), Cramb, Cashmore, Taggart (Wilson).

Elgin C (1) 1 *(Moffat 38)*
Buckie T (0) 0 2109
Elgin C: Renton; Kaczan (Campbell), Dempsie, Lowe, Dickson, Hind (Mackay), Moffat, Docherty, Johnston, McGraw, Gardiner.
Buckie T: Main; Shewan, Lamberton, Small, Davidson R (MacDonald), Grant, Matheson, Munro, Bruce, Coutts (MacKinnon), Davidson N (Hamilton).

Peterhead (0) 0
Ayr U (1) 2 *(Dunn 20, Vareille 75)* 610
Peterhead: Kelly; Buchan, Perry, Tully (MacDonald), Gilfillan, Cameron, Sharp, Wood, Linn, McKay (Cowie), MacAulay.
Ayr U: Brown; Caddis (Casey), Lowing, Forrest, Campbell, Robertson, Strain, Stevenson■, Vareille (Friels), Weaver, Dunn.

Raith R (0) 0
Dumbarton (0) 1 *(Gemmell 51)* 1616
Raith R: Fahey; Bonar, Fotheringham, Campbell, Andrews, Davidson, Fairbairn■, Silvestro, McManus, Thorarinsson, Currie (Oné).
Dumbarton: Grindlay; Geggan, Brittain, Canning, Craig, Gentile, Borris (Hamilton), Winter, Gemmell (McQuilken), Bagan, Boyle.

Stranraer (2) 3 *(Moore 18, Wright 45, Ramsay 64)*
Forfar Ath (0) 1 *(Lunan 57)* 193
Stranraer: Black; Snowdon, Sharp, Aitken (Hunter), Walker (McKinstry), McAlpine, Wright, Crilly, Moore, Hamilton, Ramsay (McMullan).
Forfar Ath: Wood; Keogh, Lynn (Gribben), Allison, King, Moon, Tade (Lombardi), Lunan, Lumsden, Fraser (Webster), Beith.

THIRD ROUND

Saturday, 6 January 2007

Airdrie U (0) 0
Motherwell (1) 1 *(Foran 31)* 5924
Airdrie U: Robertson; Smyth, McKenna, Taylor, Tierney (Koudou), McGowan, McDougall (McPhee), McKeown, Twigg, Holmes, Barrau (Prunty).
Motherwell: Smith G; Corrigan, Murphy, Reynolds, Craigan, Kerr, McGarry, Molloy (Smith D), McDonald (Connolly), Foran, Clarkson.

Berwick R (0) 0
Falkirk (1) 2 *(Gow 8, Craig 50)* 1910
Berwick R: Flockhart; Fraser, Noble, Horn, Smith (Campbell), Greenhill G (McCallum), Manson, Notman, Haynes (Shand), Thomson, Greenhill D.
Falkirk: Lambers; Ross, Barr, Uras, Dodd (Thomson), Milne, Cregg, Lima (Holden), Craig, Gow, Latapy (Stewart).

Celtic (3) 4 *(Zurawski 4, 10, Vennegoor of Hesselink 43, Riordan 70)*
Dumbarton (0) 0 18,685
Celtic: Boruc; Telfer, Naylor, O'Dea, Pressley, Nakamura (Riordan), Lennon (Gravesen), Sno, McGeady, Zurawski, Vennegoor of Hesselink (Miller).
Dumbarton: Grindlay; Geggan, Brittain, Canning, Craig, Winter, Borris (Gemmell), Gentile (Hamilton), McQuilken (McNaught), Bagan, Boyle.

Clyde (0) 0
Gretna (1) 3 *(Graham 41, Paartalu 69, McMenamin 76)* 1378
Clyde: Hutton; McGregor N, Malone, Higgins, Harris, Masterton, Bryson, O'Donnell, Arbuckle, Imrie, Williams (Bradley).
Gretna: Main; Townsley, Grainger, Jenkins, Canning, Innes, Paartalu, McGill (Bingham), McMenamin, Graham (Berkeley), Skelton.

Cowdenbeath (1) 1 *(Clarke 23)*
Brechin C (0) 1 *(Byers 89)* 675
Cowdenbeath: Hay; Baxter, Ellis, Hannah, Ritchie, Hill, Scullion (Fusco), Fotheringham (Weir), Buchanan, Clarke (Dalziel), Paatelainen.
Brechin C: Nelson; Walker R (Geddes), Stuart Ferguson (Connolly), Archibald, White, Byers, Callaghan, King (Steven Ferguson), Hampshire, Russell, Smith.

Deveronvale (4) 5 *(Chisholm 7, Murray 10, Smith 26, McKenzie 29, Watt 62)*
Elgin C (1) 4 *(Johnston 40, 57, 72, Mackay 69)* 1700
Deveronvale: Blanchard; Dolan, Gilbert, Chisholm, Fraser, Brown (Pirie), Urquhart, Smith, McKenzie, Murray (McWilliam), Watt (Ewen).
Elgin C: Renton; Campbell (Nelson), McGraw (Muir), Hind, Dickson, Moffat, Docherty, Gardiner (Kaczan), Johnston, Charlesworth, Mackay.

Dundee (1) 1 *(Lyle 37)*
Queen of the S (1) 1 *(O'Connor 45)* 2681
Dundee: Roy; Griffin, Dixon, Shields, McKenzie, Mann, Harris, Robertson, Lyle, Rae (Robert), Swankie (Clark).
Queen of the S: Scott; Paton, McQuilken, Lauchlan, Scally, Thomson J, Robertson (O'Neill), Dobbie (Weir), O'Connor (Henderson), Burns, Moon.

Hamilton A (0) 2 *(McArthur 54, McCarthy 86)*
Livingston (1) 4 *(Dorrans 30, 81, Tweed 65, Hamill 73)* 1228
Hamilton A: Jellema; Wilson (Gilhaney), Gibson, McCarthy, Stevenson, Easton, McLeod, McArthur, Wake (Taylor), Neil, Winters (McJimpsey).
Livingston: Wight; Mackay, Miller, McPake, Tweed, Mitchell, Dorrans (Snodgrass), Walker, Craig (Shields), Smylie, Hamill.

Morton (0) 3 *(Templeman 61, 68, McGowan 72)*
Kilmarnock (0) 1 *(Nish 47)* 6649
Morton: Mathers; Weatherson, McGregor, Harding, Greacen, Keenan (Finlayson), Millar, Stevenson (Walker A), Templeman, McGowan (Russell), McAlister.
Kilmarnock: Smith; Hay, Greer, Wright F, Ford, Fowler, Invincibile (Murray S), Johnston, Nish, Naismith, Wales.

Ross Co (0) 0
Partick T (1) 1 *(Robertson J 15)* 1535
Ross Co: Samson; Smith, McKinlay, Dowie, Webb, McCulloch (Gunn), Gardyne, Adams, Higgins (O'Carroll), Cowie, Moore.
Partick T: Tuffey; Smith, Robertson J, Brady, Boyd, McChrystal, Gibson W, Ferguson, Young, Roberts (McCulloch), McConalogue (Gibson G).

St Johnstone (0) 0
Ayr U (0) 0 2173
St Johnstone: Cuthbert; Lawrie, Dyer (McLaren), Mensing, McManus, Anderson, Sheerin, McInnes, Milne (Jackson), Scotland (MacDonald), Stanik.
Ayr U: McGeown; Caddis, Lowing, Forrest, Campbell, Robertson, Strain (Hyslop), Casey, Vareille (Friels), Wardlaw, Dunn.

Stirling Albion (1) 1 *(O'Brien 15)*
Inverness CT (4) 6 *(Dargo 8, 41, Wyness 13, McBain 22, Wilson 47, Morgan 69)* 1521
Stirling Albion: Hogarth; Hay (Taggart), Forsyth, McNally, Graham, Aitken, Bell, Fraser, Cramb, Tomana (Wilson), O'Brien (Devine).
Inverness CT: Brown; Tokely (McCaffrey), Dods, Munro, Rankin, Duncan, Wilson (Morgan), McBain, Bayne (McAllister), Dargo, Wyness.

Stranraer (0) 0
Hearts (2) 4 *(Velicka 17, 43, 90, Bednar 79)* 5100
Stranraer: Black; Snowdon, McAlpine, Aitken (Walker), Wilson, Sharp, Hamilton, Crilly (Wright), Moore, Burns (Mullan), Ramsay.
Hearts: Gordon; Barasa, Wallace, Karipidis, Berra, Neilson (Mikoliunas), Aguiar, McCann (Jonsson), Driver, Pospisil (Bednar), Velicka.

Sunday, 7 January 2007

Dunfermline Ath (2) 3 *(Hamilton 17, Simmons 29, McGuire 46)*

Rangers (0) 2 *(Boyd 54, 68)* 7231

Dunfermline Ath: McKenzie; Ross, Wilson S, Morrison O (Woods), McGuire, Young, Simmons, Morrison S, O'Brien (Bamba), Hamilton (Daquin), Crawford.
Rangers: McGregor; Hutton, Rodriguez (Burke), Svensson, Hemdani, Murray, Ferguson, Rae, Adam (Buffel), Novo, Boyd.

Wednesday, 10 January 2007

Aberdeen (0) 2 *(Brewster 58, Nicholson 89)*

Hibernian (1) 2 *(Sproule 42, Killen 71)* 7905

Aberdeen: Langfield; Considine (Brewster), Foster, Anderson, Hart, Severin, Nicholson, Dempsey (Maguire), Clark, Miller (Lovell), Mackie.
Hibernian: McNeil; Martis, Jones, Murphy, Whittaker, McCann (Stevenson), Stewart, Beuzelin, Shiels (Benjelloun), Killen, Sproule.

Tuesday, 16 January 2007

Dundee U (1) 3 *(Robson 31, Kenneth 46, Robertson 90)*

St Mirren (0) 2 *(Brittain 76, Sutton 81)* 4010

Dundee U: Stillie; Kenneth, Archibald, Mair, Conway, Kerr, Robson (Duff), Watson (McCracken), Robertson, Daly, Samuel.
St Mirren: Bullock; Van Zanten, Broadfoot, Millen (Kean), Potter, Maxwell, Brady, Lappin (Reid), Brittain, Sutton, Corcoran.

THIRD ROUND REPLAYS

Tuesday, 16 January 2007

Brechin C (0) 0

Cowdenbeath (1) 1 *(Hill 38)* 594

Brechin C: Nelson; Archibald, Callaghan, Ward, White, Steven Ferguson (Stuart Ferguson), Byers, King (Connolly), Hampshire, Russell (Geddes), Smith.
Cowdenbeath: Hay; Baxter, McBride K, Lennon, Hill, Hannah, Scullion (Fyfe), Fotheringham (Dalziel), Buchanan, Clarke, Fusco.

Queen of the S (1) 3 *(Dobbie 40, 69, O'Connor 86)*

Dundee (0) 3 *(Lyle 48, 87, Deasley 82)* 2037

Queen of the S: Corr; Paton, McQuilken, Lauchlan, Scally, Thomson J, Burns, Dobbie (Weir),O'Connor (Henderson), O'Neill (Robertson), Gibson.
Dundee: Roy; Griffin (McDonald K), Dixon, Rae, McKenzie, Smith G, Shields, Robertson (Mann), Lyle, Deasley, Swankie (Campbell).
aet; Queen of the S won 4-2 on penalties.

Wednesday, 17 January 2007

Ayr U (0) 1 *(Stevenson 66)*

St Johnstone (1) 2 *(Scotland 5, MacDonald 116)* 1948

Ayr U: McGeown; Caddis, Lowing, Forrest, Campbell (Weaver), Robertson (Pettigrew), Stevenson, Casey, Vareille (Strain), Wardlaw, Dunn.
St Johnstone: Cuthbert; Lawrie, Stanik, Mensing, McManus, James, Hardie (Jackson), McInnes, MacDonald, Scotland, Sheerin (McLaren).
aet.

Thursday, 18 January 2007

Hibernian (2) 4 *(Fletcher 13, Stewart 45, Benjelloun 47, 56)*

Aberdeen (1) 1 *(Nicholson 10)* 11,375

Hibernian: McNeil; Hogg, Jones, Stewart (Thomson), Whittaker, Stevenson, Beuzelin (McCann), Fletcher, Scott Brown, Shiels (Benjelloun), Sproule.
Aberdeen: Langfield; Considine, Hart, Anderson, Foster, Severin (Smith D), Nicholson, Dempsey (Maguire), Clark, Lovell (Miller), Mackie.

FOURTH ROUND

Saturday, 3 February 2007

Deveronvale (0) 0

Partick T (1) 1 *(Gibson J 31)* 8400

Deveronvale: Blanchard; Dolan, Gilbert, Chisholm, Fraser, Brown (Cowie), Bremner, Smith, McKenzie (Noble), Murray (Ewen), Watt.
Partick T: Arthur; Smith, Robertson J (Boyd), Brady (Gibson W), Keogh, McChrystal, Gibson J, Donnelly, Young, Roberts, McConalogue (Russell).

Dunfermline Ath (0) 1 *(Wilson S 90)*

Hearts (0) 0 9597

Dunfermline Ath: De Vries; Morrison S, Wilson S, McGuire, Ross, Hammill, Simmons, Mason, O'Brien (Morrison O), Burchill (Hamilton), Crawford (McIntyre).
Hearts: Banks; Wallace, Zaliukas, Karipidis (Armstrong), Tall, Mikoliunas (Jankauskas), Kingston, McCann, Driver, Pospisil (Bednar), Elliot.

Falkirk (0) 0

St Johnstone (2) 3 *(Hardie 26, James 37, MacDonald 68)* 3908

Falkirk: Schmeichel; Ross (Holden), Barr, Twaddle, Milne, Cregg, Thomson, O'Donnell (Moutinho), Latapy, Finnigan, Gow.
St Johnstone: Cuthbert; Lawrie, Stanik (Dyer), McInnes, Anderson, James, Hardie, Mensing, MacDonald (Jackson), Scotland (McLaren), Sheerin.

Hibernian (1) 3 *(Jones 27, Fleming (og) 54, Benjelloun 59)*

Gretna (0) 1 *(Berkeley 81)* 14,075

Hibernian: McNeil; Martis, Jones, Murphy, Whittaker, Campbell (Benjelloun), Lynch, Fletcher (Stevenson), Scott Brown, Shiels (Beuzelin), Sproule.
Gretna: Fleming; Barr, Grainger, Jenkins (O'Neil), Canning, Innes, Paartalu, McGuffie, McMenamin (Grady), Graham, Berkeley.

Inverness CT (1) 1 *(Duncan 15)*

Dundee U (0) 0 3402

Inverness CT: Fraser; Tokely, Dods, Munro, Hastings, Duncan, Rankin, McBain, Wilson, Bayne, McAllister (McSwegan).
Dundee U: Stillie; Kalvenes, McCracken, Wilkie, Kerr, Daly (Hunt), Robson, Conway, Dillon, Samuel (Duff), Robertson.

Motherwell (2) 2 *(Kerr 10, McDonald 33)*

Morton (0) 0 9394

Motherwell: Smith G; Corrigan, Paterson, Murphy, Craigan, Kerr, Fitzpatrick, Reynolds, Smith D (McGarry), McDonald, Clarkson (Keegan).
Morton: Mathers; Weatherson, McGregor, Harding, Greacen, McLaughlin, Millar (Stevenson), Finlayson, Templeman (Keenan), McGowan, McAlister.

Queen of the S (1) 2 *(Dobbie 30 (pen), Adams 54)*

Cowdenbeath (0) 0 2264

Queen of the S: McDonald; Paton, McQuilken, Lauchlan, Scally, Thomson J, Adams, Dobbie (Barrowman), O'Connor (Weir), Tosh (Robertson), Gibson.
Cowdenbeath: Hay; Baxter (Scullion), Ellis, Hannah, Hill, Davidson (Dalziel), Doherty, Fusco, Weir, Clarke, Ramsay (Fotheringham).

Sunday, 4 February 2007

Livingston (1) 1 *(Mackay 19)*

Celtic (2) 4 *(O'Dea 30, Riordan 45, 58, Vennegoor of Hesselink 60)* 7281

Livingston: Stewart; Mackay, Golabek, McPake, Tweed, Mitchell, Fox (Hamill), Walker, Taggart, Makel (Dorrans), Craig (Smylie).
Celtic: Boruc; Telfer, Naylor, McManus, O'Dea, Nakamura, Lennon (Sno), Hartley, Jarosik (Gravesen), Riordan, Vennegoor of Hesselink.

QUARTER-FINALS

Saturday, 24 February 2007

Dunfermline Ath (1) 2 *(Simmons 4, 84)*
Partick T (0) 0 7090

Dunfermline Ath: De Vries; Morrison S, Wilson S, McGuire, Ross (Bamba), Morrison O (McCunnie), O'Brien (Crawford), Mason, Simmons, Hammill, Hamilton.
Partick T: Arthur; Smith (Strachan), Robertson J, Brady, Boyd, Keogh, Gibson J, Gibson W, Russell, Roberts, Young (McConalogue).

Queen of the S (0) 1 *(O'Neill 47)*
Hibernian (1) 2 *(Murphy 45, Sowumni 51)* 6400

Queen of the S: McDonald; Paton, McQuilken, Lauchlan, Scally, Thomson J, Adams, Dobbie, O'Connor (Barrowman), O'Neill (Weir), Gibson.
Hibernian: Simon Brown; Hogg, Jones, Murphy, Whittaker, Stewart (Stevenson), Beuzelin, Fletcher (Sowumni), Scott Brown, Benjelloun (Lynch), Sproule.

Sunday, 25 February 2007

Inverness CT (1) 1 *(Bayne 18)*
Celtic (0) 2 *(Pressley 88, Miller 90)* 7119

Inverness CT: Fraser; Tokely, Dods, Munro, Hastings, Duncan, Rankin, McBain (Hart), Wilson (McAllister), Black (McSwegan), Bayne.
Celtic: Boruc; Wilson (Sheridan), Naylor, Pressley, McManus, Nakamura, Lennon, Hartley, Sno (Gravesen), Jarosik (McGeady), Miller.

Wednesday, 28 February 2007

Motherwell (0) 1 *(McCormack 85)*
St Johnstone (1) 2 *(MacDonald 21, Scotland 72)* 5788

Motherwell: Smith G; Corrigan, Paterson, Murphy (Clarkson), Craigan, Kerr, Fitzpatrick (Keegan), Reynolds, McGarry (Molloy), McDonald, McCormack.
St Johnstone: Cuthbert; Lawrie, Stanik, Mensing, McManus, James, McLaren (Milne), Hardie, MacDonald, Scotland (Jackson), Sheerin.

SEMI-FINALS (at Hampden Park)

Saturday, 14 April 2007

St Johnstone (1) 1 *(Hardie 19)*
Celtic (1) 2 *(Vennegoor of Hesselink 13 (pen), 53)* 28,339

St Johnstone: Cuthbert; Anderson, Stanik, McInnes, McManus, James, Sheerin (McLaren), Hardie, MacDonald, Scotland, Mensin (Morais).
Celtic: Boruc; Caldwell, Naylor (O'Dea), Pressley, McManus, Lennon, Hartley, Nakamura (Gravesen), McGeady, Riordan (Miller), Vennegoor of Hesselink.

Sunday, 15 April 2007

Hibernian (0) 0
Dunfermline Ath (0) 0 25,336

Hibernian: McNeil; Hogg, Jones, Murphy, Whittaker, Stevenson, Beuzelin, Fletcher, Scott Brown, Benjelloun (Gray), Sproule.
Dunfermline Ath: De Vries; Shields, Wilson S, Bamba, Muirhead, McGuire (Ross), McCunnie, Mason, O'Brien, Hammill (Morrison O), McIntyre (Burchill).

SEMI-FINAL REPLAY (at Hampden Park)

Tuesday, 24 April 2007

Dunfermline Ath (0) 1 *(McIntyre 86)*
Hibernian (0) 0 8536

Dunfermline Ath: De Vries; Shields, McGuire, Bamba, Muirhead, Young (Burchill), McCunnie, Mason, O'Brien (Morrison O), Hammill (Ross), McIntyre.
Hibernian: McNeil; Hogg, Jones, Murphy, Whittaker, Stevenson, Beuzelin (Chisholm), Gray (Fletcher), Scott Brown, Benjelloun, Sproule (Shiels).

FINAL (at Hampden Park)

Saturday, 26 May 2007
Celtic (0) 1 *(Perrier Doumbe 85)*
Dunfermline Ath (0) 0 49,600

Celtic: Boruc; Perrier Doumbe, McManus, Pressley, Naylor, Nakamura, Lennon (Caldwell), Hartley, McGeady, Miller (Beattie), Vennegoor of Hesselink.
Dunfermline Ath: De Vries; Shields, Wilson S, Bamba, Muirhead, Morrison S (Crawford), Young, McCunnie, Hammill, Burchill (Williamson), McIntyre (Hamilton).
Referee: Kenny Clark.

Celtic's Shunsuke Nakamura skips past Adam Hammill of Dunfermline during his sides 1-0 Scottish Cup Final win at Hampden Park. (Action Images/Lee Smith)

WELSH FOOTBALL 2006–07

It really was the end of an era. The boy wonder turned elder statesman, Ryan Giggs had decided to call time on his international career after 16 years, 64 caps and 12 goals and, for one fleeting moment, it looked as if he would conjure up a fairytale ending.

Three-quarters of the way through his last game for Wales in early June, the Manchester United legend picked up the ball near the halfway line and proceeded to roll back the years. A surging trademark run took him past three Czech Republic defenders to the edge of the penalty area but, having made space for the shot, his final effort with his favoured left foot was parried away to safety by Petr Cech – the world's best goalkeeper denying one of the world's finest players a sentimental swansong as some sort of consolation for being unable to ply his trade on the world's greatest stage.

While it would be wrong to describe Giggs's long spell in the international spotlight as glittering – and many people have commented on how infrequently he produced his club form for his country and how often he missed friendly games – the former Welsh skipper has been a wonderful servant to Welsh football. After making his debut as a substitute against Germany in 1991 at the then record age of 17 years and 321 days, he marked his first start with a stunning free-kick against Belgium – and always gave outstanding service to his country through thick but mainly thin.

It was hardly surprising that Giggs found it difficult to deliver his dazzling United displays on a regular basis for Wales. After performing with the likes of Eric Cantona, Roy Keane, Cristiano Ronaldo and Wayne Rooney week in week out in the Premiership, he perhaps inevitably became frustrated by the shortcomings of his journeymen team-mates who deferred to him too readily. In turn, Giggs tried to compensate by taking on too much himself when in possession and, as he suggested when explaining his decision to retire, his former colleagues must now take greater responsibility – freed from the inhibitions of playing alongside such a talented talisman.

So what sort of state are Wales in following the retirement of the last of a generation of players linking the reigns of Terry Yorath, Bobby Gould, Mark Hughes and now John Toshack? Defeats by the Czech Republic, Slovakia and the Republic of Ireland and a draw with the Czechs put paid to any chances of reaching Euro 2008 and it's now up to the team that Tosh built to gel together for the start of the 2010 World Cup qualifying campaign next year. Youth – in the shape of a shedload of promising players – has been given its head and, under new captain Craig Bellamy, aided and abetted by the gifted Jason Koumas in midfield, they must start to fulfil their undoubted potential if Toshack is not to go down in history as a Welsh managerial failure. The very creditable 0-0 draw with the Czech Republic set a new standard that must be maintained.

It was another disappointing, anti-climactic season for the three Coca Cola League clubs. After barnstorming their way to the top of the Championship, Cardiff's lack of strength in depth meant they ran out of steam and finished in mid-table after setting a club record by ending their season with nine successive defeats. Swansea flirted with the League One play-offs and under Roberto Martinez, who had become manager when Kenny Jackett resigned in February, they narrowly missed out on sixth place while Wrexham managed to hang on to their Football League status by the skin of their teeth after beating relegation rivals Boston at the Racecourse on the last day of the season.

There were signs of improvement from the three teams playing in the English pyramid. A 10-match unbeaten run took Newport to the brink of the Conference South play-offs but they were sunk by two defeats in their last three games, Colwyn Bay almost made it out of the Unibond First Division by reaching the play-offs before losing to Cammell Laird who were beaten in the final by Eastwood Town while Merthyr finished midtable in the Southern League's Premier Division.

Once again, Europe proved a barren hunting ground for most of the four Welsh Premier League clubs. The New Saints – formerly TNS and Llansantffraid – lost 2-0 on aggregate to Myllykosken Pallo-47 from Finland in the first qualifying round of the Champions League, Rhyl went out 2-1 on aggregate to Suduva from Lithuania in the UEFA Cup and Intertoto Cup representatives Carmarthen were hammered 8-1 on aggregate by Finnish side Tampere. But Llanelli's debut season in Europe saw them reach the second qualifying round of the UEFA Cup by beating Sweden's Gefle 2-1 before losing 6-1 on aggregate to Odense of Denmark.

The New Saints retained their Welsh Premier title and also picked up the FAW Premier Cup by beating Newport to become only the second WPL team to win the trophy after Barry's success in the 1998–99 season. Rhyl again qualified for the UEFA Cup while third-placed Llanelli will represent Wales in the Intertoto Cup. Carmarthen won the Welsh Cup by beating Afan Lido to secure a third successive season of European football and then promptly sacked their manager, Cardiff-based Mark Jones. It had nothing to do with results – they simply wanted somebody more local to oversee their community initiatives such as a new study centre at Richmond Park. After leading Caersws to their third League Cup win, manager Mickey Evans decided to retire at the age of 60. He was the last remaining manager to have been in charge at the same club since the League of Wales was created in 1992 and his decision to quit means that seven WPL clubs will be under new management this season.

The more high-profile departure of Giggs will undoubtedly leave a large hole in Welsh football. A model professional both on and off the field, it seems that his retirement was all about saving private Ryan. The former Welsh skipper rarely allowed his personal behaviour to hit the headlines and his meticulous preparation for games has been instrumental in Giggs becoming the most decorated player in English football – an achievement recognised by his richly deserved OBE. Drawing on the experience of his Manchester United team-mate Paul Scholes, he realised that his club career could be extended by a good year or two without the demands of the international game. Let's hope the arrival of yet more world-class performers at Old Trafford won't result in Giggs becoming a bit-part player at the Theatre of Dreams.

GRAHAME LLOYD

VAUXHALL MASTERFIT RETAILERS WELSH PREMIER LEAGUE 2006–07

			Home					Away					Total						
		P	W	D	L	F	A	W	D	L	F	A	W	D	L	F	A	GD	Pts
1	The New Saints	32	14	0	2	53	12	10	4	2	28	8	24	4	4	81	20	61	76
2	Rhyl	32	10	6	0	31	11	10	3	3	36	24	20	9	3	67	35	32	69
3	Llanelli	32	9	4	3	42	18	9	5	2	30	15	18	9	5	72	33	39	63
4	Welshpool Town	32	8	6	2	24	13	9	3	4	30	20	17	9	6	54	33	21	60
5	Connah's Quay Nomads	32	9	3	4	29	21	7	5	4	20	19	16	8	8	49	40	9	56
6	Port Talbot Town	32	7	3	6	22	23	8	3	5	20	16	15	6	11	42	39	3	51
7	Carmarthen Town	32	8	4	4	25	18	6	4	6	32	32	14	8	10	57	50	7	50
8	Aberystwyth Town	32	6	6	4	24	18	7	3	6	23	19	13	9	10	47	37	10	48
9	Bangor City	32	8	3	5	33	21	6	3	7	22	26	14	6	12	55	47	8	48
10	Haverfordwest County	32	6	4	6	19	16	4	5	7	30	30	10	9	13	49	46	3	39
11	Porthmadog*	32	4	6	6	25	25	4	5	7	15	27	8	11	13	40	52	–12	35
12	Airbus UK	32	4	3	9	22	27	3	5	8	18	40	7	8	17	40	67	–27	29
13	NEWI Cefn Druids	32	4	4	8	26	30	3	3	10	15	36	7	7	18	41	66	–25	28
14	Caersws	32	2	5	9	15	33	4	4	8	19	26	6	9	17	34	59	–25	27
15	Caernarfon Town	32	2	3	11	19	40	4	5	7	22	33	6	8	18	41	73	–32	26
16	Newtown	32	2	4	10	9	30	4	2	10	21	33	6	6	20	30	63	–33	24
17	Cwmbran Town	32	2	3	11	21	40	2	5	9	15	35	4	8	20	36	75	–39	20

**Three points deducted.*

PREVIOUS WELSH LEAGUE WINNERS

1993	Cwmbran Town	1997	Barry Town	2001	Barry Town	2005	TNS
1994	Bangor City	1998	Barry Town	2002	Barry Town	2006	TNS
1995	Bangor City	1999	Barry Town	2003	Barry Town	2007	TNS
1996	Barry Town	2000	TNS	2004	Rhyl		

FAW PREMIER LEAGUE CUP

FIRST ROUND
Porthmadog 1, Aberystwyth Town 0
Bangor City 3, Caersws 1
Newi Cefn Druids 3, Welshpool Town 2
Haverfordwest County 1, Port Talbot Town 2

SECOND ROUND
Newi Cefn Druids 1, Newport County 2
Carmarthen Town 3, Bangor City 1
Porthmadog 2, Llanelli 1
Port Talbot Town 2, Rhyl 1

QUARTER-FINALS
Carmarthen Town 2, Cardiff City 3
Porthmadog 1, TNS 3
Newport County 2, Wrexham 1
Port Talbot Town 2, Swansea City 1

SEMI-FINALS
Cardiff City 0, TNS 1
Newport County 2, Port Talbot Town 1

FAW PREMIER LEAGUE CUP FINAL

(at Newport)

21 March 2007

Newport County (0) 0
TNS (1) 1
Newport County: Ovendale; Jenkins, Searle, Davies, Brough, Hillier, Bowen, Leek, Holdsworth (Prosser 89), Hughes, Evans (Griffin 78).
TNS: Doherty; Baker, Courtney, Jackson, Holmes, Leah, Roscoe, Wilde (Gonzalez 90), Toner (Stones 76), Beck, Wood.
Scorer: Beck 7.
Referee: M. Whitby (Penllergaer).

MACWHIRTER WELSH LEAGUE 2006–07

DIVISION ONE	P	W	D	L	F	A	GD	Pts
Neath Athletic	36	29	5	2	100	32	68	92
Goytre United	36	24	8	4	86	32	54	80
Pontypridd Town	36	24	8	4	88	37	51	80
Ton Pentre	36	21	9	6	68	32	36	72
Afan Lido	36	19	9	8	66	45	21	66
ENTO Aberaman Ath	36	18	6	12	53	45	8	60
Maesteg Park	36	17	4	15	47	49	–2	55
Bryntirion Athletic	36	14	5	17	56	62	–6	47
Croesyceiliog	36	13	7	16	53	57	–4	46
Caerleon	36	14	4	18	52	58	–6	46
Bridgend Town	36	13	6	17	67	61	6	45
Taffs Well	36	12	7	17	60	68	–8	43
Dinas Powys	36	11	7	18	45	67	–22	40
Newport YMCA	36	10	9	17	55	69	–14	39
Pontardawe Town	36	11	6	19	33	54	–21	39
UWIC	36	9	6	21	46	74	–28	33
Ely Rangers	36	7	8	21	52	77	–25	29
Grange Harlequins*	36	7	9	20	34	72	–38	29
Barry Town	36	5	5	26	33	103	–70	20

**Grange Harlequins 1 point deducted for breach of rules.*

HUWS GRAY-FITLOCK CYMRU ALLIANCE LEAGUE 2006–07

	P	W	D	L	F	A	GD	Pts
Llangefni Town	34	21	9	4	68	33	35	72
Bala Town	34	21	7	6	80	31	49	70
Flint Town United	34	20	7	7	70	36	34	67
Prestatyn Town	34	20	4	10	98	46	52	64
Glantraeth	34	17	6	11	83	69	14	57
Llanfairpwll	34	17	6	11	69	59	10	57
Holyhead Hotspur	34	16	5	13	63	51	12	53
Mynydd Isa	34	15	8	11	57	45	12	53
Buckley Town	34	14	10	10	57	53	4	52
Llandudno	34	14	6	14	67	59	8	48
Guilsfield	34	14	5	15	58	64	–6	47
Gresford Athletic	34	12	3	19	50	64	–14	39
Penrhyncoch	34	10	8	16	70	75	–5	38
Bodedern	34	11	5	18	49	62	–13	38
Llandyrnog United	34	9	9	16	58	77	–19	36
Ruthin Town	34	8	5	21	41	71	–30	29
Lex XI	34	7	7	20	49	96	–47	28
Queens Park*	34	3	4	27	40	134	–94	10

**Queens Park 3 points deducted for breach of rules.*

VAUXHALL MASTERFIT WELSH PREMIER LEAGUE RESULTS 2006–07

	Aberystwyth Town	Airbus UK	Bangor City	Caernarfon Town	Caersws	Carmarthen Town	Connah's Quay Nomads	Cwmbran Town	Haverfordwest County	Llanelli	NEWI Cefn Druids	Newtown	Port Talbot Town	Porthmadog	Rhyl	The New Saints	Welshpool Town
Aberystwyth Town	—	1-1	0-2	2-0	1-0	4-2	1-1	3-1	2-2	1-1	3-0	4-2	0-2	0-1	2-3	0-0	0-0
Airbus UK	0-0	—	4-1	2-3	0-3	2-2	2-3	3-0	2-0	1-4	0-1	1-2	3-0	1-1	0-2	0-1	1-4
Bangor City	1-4	3-1	—	0-0	1-2	1-3	3-1	1-1	4-1	4-0	6-0	5-2	0-0	2-1	1-3	0-2	1-0
Caernarfon Town	1-3	0-2	0-1	—	2-2	3-5	0-2	0-1	1-4	2-6	1-1	1-0	1-2	2-2	2-6	1-3	2-0
Caersws	0-1	0-0	0-1	1-1	—	1-7	2-1	3-3	3-3	0-3	2-1	0-1	1-4	0-1	1-1	0-2	1-3
Carmarthen Town	1-0	2-1	2-2	4-1	2-0	—	1-3	1-0	1-3	0-2	4-0	2-0	1-0	1-1	1-1	0-0	2-4
Connah's Quay Nomads	1-0	1-2	3-0	2-2	4-3	4-1	—	2-2	5-3	0-1	1-0	2-1	2-1	1-0	0-2	0-0	1-3
Cwmbran Town	2-0	2-2	0-1	0-3	2-5	4-5	0-1	—	0-0	2-2	3-2	0-2	1-2	2-3	2-3	0-5	1-4
Haverfordwest County	1-1	5-1	2-0	2-1	1-0	0-1	0-0	2-0	—	1-1	0-1	3-2	1-2	1-1	0-1	0-3	0-1
Llanelli	1-3	4-0	3-0	4-2	0-0	1-1	1-1	5-1	3-2	—	3-1	3-2	0-0	5-0	6-0	1-2	2-3
NEWI Cefn Druids	1-2	3-1	0-3	3-2	2-2	1-2	2-2	3-0	0-1	0-1	—	1-1	0-3	3-0	2-3	2-3	1-3
Newtown	1-1	1-1	2-1	0-1	0-1	1-1	0-1	2-3	1-0	0-2	0-2	—	1-2	0-0	0-6	0-4	0-4
Port Talbot Town	1-3	0-2	0-5	7-1	0-0	1-0	0-1	2-0	1-4	1-0	1-1	2-1	—	1-2	3-2	2-1	0-0
Porthmadog	0-4	1-1	1-1	2-2	4-0	3-0	1-2	2-2	0-3	1-1	3-0	2-3	1-1	—	1-2	1-2	2-1
Rhyl	3-0	4-0	3-1	0-0	4-0	1-0	2-1	1-0	3-2	2-2	2-2	2-2	2-0	2-1	—	0-0	0-0
The New Saints	4-1	7-0	5-2	1-3	2-1	4-1	4-0	4-0	2-1	0-2	3-1	4-0	2-0	3-0	2-0	—	6-0
Welshpool Town	1-0	6-3	1-1	3-0	1-0	1-1	0-0	1-1	0-0	0-2	4-2	1-0	0-1	3-1	1-1	1-0	—

WELSH CUP 2006–07

PRELIMINARY ROUND

Aberbargoed Buds v Ystradgynlais	2-1
Conwy United v Glan Conwy	2-1
Corwen v Rhydymwyn	0-2
Cwmbran Celtic v Newcastle Emlyn	2-1
Four Crosses v Carno	2-2
Four Crosses won 4-2 on penalties.	
Llangollen Town v Ruthin Town	0-1
Llanidloes Town v Knighton Town	2-1
Llansawel v Goytre	0-1
Llantwit Fardre v Chepstow Town	3-2
Llanwern v Abertillery Excelsiors	4-1
Pentwyn Dynamoes v Cwmaman United	5-1
Penycae v Caerwys	4-0
Risca United v AFC Porth	1-3
Sealand Rovers v Cefn United	2-4

FIRST ROUND

Afan Lido v Penrhiwceiber Rangers	3-1
AFC Porth v West End	2-4
Ammanford v Pontyclun	3-1
Barry Town v Croesyceiliog	3-2
Bridgend Town v Taffs Well	2-0
Briton Ferry Athletic v Bettws	0-1
Buckley Town v Catel Alun Colts	3-1
Caerleon v Garw Athletic	2-1
Caldicot Town v Cwmbran Celtic	0-1
Cambrian & Clydach Vale v Morriston Town	1-3
Cardiff Corinthians v Maesteg Park Athletic	3-1
Tie awarded to Maesteg Park Athletic as Cardiff Corinthians fielded an ineligible player.	
Chirk AAA v Conwy United	1-3
Coedpoeth United v Bethesda Athletic	0-3
Denbigh Town v Glyn Ceiriog	6-0
Dinas Powys v Bryntirion Athletic	1-0
Ento Aberaman Athletic v Neath Athletic	1-2
Flint Town United v Nefyn United	4-0
Garden Village v AFC Llwydcoed	6-0
Glantraeth v Bodedern	4-5
Goytre United v UWIC	2-3
Gresford Athletic v Halkyn United	6-3
Guilsfield v Four Crosses	3-2
Hawarden Rangers v Llanrwst United	0-1
Holyhead Hotspur v Lex XI	2-1
Holywell Town v Brickfield Rangers	3-3
Brickfield Rangers won 5-3 on penalties.	
Llanberis v Mynydd Isa	0-3
Llandudno v Ruthin Town	4-0
Llandudno Junction v Llanrug United	3-4
Llanfyllin Town v Carno	3-2
Llanrhaeadr YM Mochnant v Penrhyncoch	3-4
Llantwit Fardre v Newport YMCA	0-1
Llanwern v Aberbargoed Buds	7-0
Mold Alexandra v Llanfairpwll	1-2
Pentwyn Dynamoes v Caerau Ely	3-4
Pontardawe Town v Porthcawl Town	4-1
Pontypridd Town v Treharris Athletic	4-0
Prestatyn Town v Llandymog United	5-0
Presteigne St Andrews v Kerry	4-0
Pwllhelli v Cefn United	2-1
Queens Park v Brymbo	3-7
Rhos Aelwyd v Bala Town	2-4
Rhydymwyn v Penycae	1-3
Ton Pentre v Merthyr Saints	1-0
Tredegar Town v Llangeinor	0-1
Troedyrhiw v Ely Rangers	1-2

SECOND ROUND

Barry Town v Afan Lido	0-4
Bodedern v Bethesda Athletic	4-3
Brickfield Rangers v Airbus UK	1-4
Bridgend Town v Garden Village	5-2
Brymbo v Newi Cefn Druids	1-1
Brymbo won 5-3 on penalties.	
Buckley Town v Llanfyllin Town	2-1
Caerleon v UWIC	2-1
Connah's Quay Nomads v Aberystwyth Town	2-1
Cwmbran Celtic v Maesteg Park Athletic	2-3
Cwmbran Town v Carmarthen Town	1-7
Denbigh Town v Newtown	2-4
Dinas Powys v Morriston Town	3-0
Ely Rangers v Caerau Ely	2-2
Ely Rangers won 4-2 on penalties.	
Goytre United v West End	1-2
Guilsfield v Bala Town	0-5
Llandudno v Flint Town United	3-0
Llanelli v Bettws	5-0
Llanfairpwll v Rhyl	0-6
Llanegfni v Holyhead Hotspur	0-2
Llanrug United v Bangor City	0-2
Mynydd Isa v Caersws	0-5
Neath Athletic v Llanwern	2-0
Newport YMCA v Ammanford	2-1
Penrhyncoch v Conwy United	2-0
Pontardawe Town v Pontypridd Town	1-2
Port Talbot Town v Haverfordwest County	3-2
Prestatyn Town v Porthmadog	2-4
Presteigne St Andrews v Penycae	1-1
Presteigne St Andrews won 4-3 on penalties.	
Pwllhelli v Gresford Athletic	2-0
TNS v Llanrwst United	3-1
Ton Pentre v Llangeinor	6-0
Welshpool Town v Caernarfon Town	4-1

THIRD ROUND

Afan Lido v Bodedern	3-0
Bridgend Town v Airbus UK	1-1
Bridgend Town won 5-4 on penalties.	
Carmarthen Town v West End	2-0
Caerleon v Ely Rangers	1-1
Ely Rangers won 4-2 on penalties.	
Caersws v Buckley Town	3-0
Maesteg Park Athletic v Llandudno	0-1
Holyhead Hotspur v Presteigne St Andrews	2-0
Neath Athletic v Brymbo	3-2
Newtown v Dinas Powys	2-0
Newport YMCA v Connah's Quay Nomads	1-3
Penrhyncoch v Llanelli	0-2
Porthmadog v Bangor City	2-0
Port Talbot Town v Bala Town	3-0
Pwllhelli v TNS	1-2
Ton Pentre v Rhyl	1-0
Welshpool Town v Pontypridd Town	2-1

FOURTH ROUND

Port Talbot Town v Ton Pentre	3-1
Carmarthen Town v Caersws	0-0
Carmarthen Town won 5-4 on penalties.	
Connah's Quay Nomads v Llandudno	3-1
Porthmadog v TNS	2-2
Porthmadog won 3-2 on penalties.	
Llanelli v Newtown	7-0
Welshpool Town v Neath Athletic	3-0
Holyhead Hotspur v Bridgend Town	2-1
Ely Rangers v Afan Lido	1-0

QUARTER-FINALS

Carmarthen Town v Porthmadog	1-1
Carmarthen Town won 4-3 on penalties.	
Holyhead Hotspur v Welshpool Town	1-5
Llanelli v Connah's Quay Nomads	6-2
Port Talbot Town v Afan Lido	0-1

SEMI-FINALS

Welshpool Town v Afan Lido	1-1
Afan Lido won 7-6 on penalties.	
Carmarthen Town v Llanelli	1-2

FINAL

(at Llanelli)

6 May 2007

Carmarthen T (2) 3
Afan Lido (1) 2

Carmarthen T: Thomas N; Evans, Brace (Keddle 46), Walters (Loss 83), Dodds, Thomas K, Thomas D, Ramasut, Fowler, Mohamed, Cotterrall.
Scorers: Mohamed 13, 47, Walters 26.

Afan Lido: Thomas B; Jones C, Lewis, Williams, Felton (Latham 85), Martin, McCreesh, Evans P (Evans C 68), Jones I, O'Leary, Hurley (Piper 68).

Scorers: Jones I 16, 75.

Attendance: 946.

PREVIOUS WELSH CUP WINNERS

1878	Wrexham Town	1908	Chester	1948	Lovell's Athletic	1978	Wrexham
1879	White Star Newtown	1909	Wrexham	1949	Merthyr Tydfil	1979	Shrewsbury Town
1880	Druids	1910	Wrexham	1950	Swansea Town	1980	Newport County
1881	Druids	1911	Wrexham	1951	Merthyr Tydfil	1981	Swansea City
1882	Druids	1912	Cardiff City	1952	Rhyl	1982	Swansea City
1883	Wrexham	1913	Swansea Town	1953	Rhyl	1983	Swansea City
1884	Oswestry United	1914	Wrexham	1954	Flint Town United	1984	Shrewsbury Town
1885	Druids	1915	Wrexham	1955	Barry Town	1985	Shrewsbury Town
1886	Druids	1920	Cardiff City	1956	Cardiff City	1986	Wrexham
1887	Chirk	1921	Wrexham	1957	Wrexham	1987	Merthyr Tydfil
1888	Chirk	1922	Cardiff City	1958	Wrexham	1988	Cardiff City
1889	Bangor	1923	Cardiff City	1959	Cardiff City	1989	Swansea City
1890	Druids	1924	Wrexham	1960	Wrexham	1990	Hereford United
1891	Shrewsbury Town	1925	Wrexham	1961	Swansea Town	1991	Swansea City
1892	Chirk	1926	Ebbw Vale	1962	Bangor City	1992	Cardiff City
1893	Wrexham	1927	Cardiff City	1963	Borough United	1993	Cardiff City
1894	Chirk	1928	Cardiff City	1964	Cardiff City	1994	Barry Town
1895	Newtown	1929	Connah's Quay	1965	Cardiff City	1995	Wrexham
1896	Bangor	1930	Cardiff City	1966	Swansea Town	1996	TNS
1897	Wrexham	1931	Wrexham	1967	Cardiff City	1997	Barry Town
1898	Druids	1932	Swansea Town	1968	Cardiff City	1998	Bangor City
1899	Druids	1933	Chester	1969	Cardiff City	1999	Inter Cable-Tel
1900	Aberystwyth	1934	Bristol City	1970	Cardiff City	2000	Bangor City
1901	Oswestry United	1935	Tranmere Rovers	1971	Cardiff City	2001	Barry Town
1902	Wellington Town	1936	Crewe Alexandra	1972	Wrexham	2002	Barry Town
1903	Wrexham	1937	Crewe Alexandra	1973	Cardiff City	2003	Barry Town
1904	Druids	1938	Shrewsbury Town	1974	Cardiff City	2004	Rhyl
1905	Wrexham	1939	South Liverpool	1975	Wrexham	2005	TNS
1906	Wellington Town	1940	Wellington Town	1976	Cardiff City	2006	Rhyl
1907	Oswestry United	1947	Chester	1977	Shrewsbury Town	2007	Carmarthen Town

THE LOOSEMORES OF CARDIFF CHALLENGE CUP 2006–07

GROUP STAGE

GROUP A
Bangor City 2, Porthmadog 2
Caernarfon Town 2, Rhyl 1
Porthmadog 3, Caernarfon Town 1
Rhyl 4, Bangor City 0
Bangor City 3, Caernarfon Town 1
Rhyl 1, Porthmadog 0
Porthmadog 0, Rhyl 0
Caernarfon Town 4, Bangor City 3
Porthmadog 1, Bangor City 2
Rhyl 3, Caernarfon Town 1
Bangor City 1, Rhyl 4
Caernarfon Town 1, Porthmadog 2

GROUP B
TNS 4, Newi Cefn Druids 0
Airbus UK 1, Connah's Quay Nomads 6
Connah's Quay Nomads 2, TNS 1
Newi Cefn Druids 3, Airbus UK 0
Connah's Quay Nomads 3, Newi Cefn Druids 0
TNS 11, Airbus UK 0
Newi Cefn Druids 0, Connah's Quay Nomads 1
Airbus UK 1, TNS 3
Connah's Quay Nomads 7, Airbus UK 2
Newi Cefn Druids 1, TNS 5
TNS 5, Connah's Quay Nomads 3
Airbus UK 2, Newi Cefn Druids 3

GROUP C
Aberystwyth Town 3, Caersws 1
Newtown 2, Welshpool Town 1
Caersws 4, Newtown 3
Welshpool Town 2, Aberystwyth Town 1
Aberystwyth Town 2, Newtown 1
Welshpool Town 0, Caersws 1
Caersws 1, Welshpool Town 1
Newtown 0, Aberystwyth Town 2
Caersws 3, Aberystwyth Town 0
Welshpool Town 3, Newtown 1
Aberystwyth Town 0, Welshpool Town 0
Newtown 2, Caersws 1

GROUP D
Carmarthen Town 4, Port Talbot Town 2
Haverfordwest County 2, Cwmbran Town 1
Port Talbot Town 3, Haverfordwest County 1
Cwmbran Town 0, Carmarthen Town 3
Llanelli 3, Port Talbot Town 1
Cwmbran Town 7, Haverfordwest County 2
Llanelli 4, Carmarthen Town 3
Port Talbot Town 3, Cwmbran Town 1
Carmarthen Town 3, Haverfordwest County 1
Cwmbran Town 0, Llanelli 3
Carmarthen Town 4, Cwmbran Town 0
Haverfordwest County 2, Port Talbot Town 0
Port Talbot Town 1, Llanelli 4
Carmarthen Town 0, Llanelli 4
Cwmbran Town 3, Port Talbot Town 3
Haverfordwest County 0, Carmarthen Town 0
Llanelli 3, Cwmbran Town 1
Haverfordwest County 2, Llanelli 3
Port Talbot Town 2, Carmarthen Town 4
Llanelli 5, Haverfordwest County 2

QUARTER-FINALS
Caersws 2, Carmarthen Town 1
Llanelli 1, Aberystwyth Town 2
Rhyl 2, Connah's Quay Nomads 0
TNS 1, Porthmadog 2

SEMI-FINALS FIRST LEG
Aberystwyth Town 1, Caersws 2
Porthmadog 0, Rhyl 0

SEMI-FINALS SECOND LEG
Rhyl 4, Porthmadog 0
Caersws 3, Aberystwyth Town 3

FINAL
(at Aberystwyth)

18 March 2007

Rhyl 1 *(Cameron 106)*
Caersws 1 *(Evans 98)* 400
aet; Caersws won 3-1 on penalties.
Rhyl: Gann; Powell (Cameron 105), Graves (Moody 55), Connolly, Horan, Brewerton, Wilson, Moran, Hunt, Murtagh, Hay.
Caersws: Mulliner; Thomas, Grist, Reynolds, Currier, Jones G, Davies, Mitchell, Evans, Plant (Venables 72), Lewis.
Referee: B. Lawlor.

NORTHERN IRISH FOOTBALL 2006–07

The international scene dominated Northern Ireland football with the squad leading Group F in the European championship qualifying table – a temporary euphoric interlude which suddenly ended with manager Lawrie Sanchez resigning with his backroom staff Dave Beasant and Terry Gibson to become manager of Premiership Fulham.

Sanchez brought success to the team, generated a feel-good factor among supporters and with the improved results, there was a resultant upsurge in the commercial appeal of the Irish FA culminating in a £10m Sky TV deal for coverage of international games and specific domestic fixtures over four years.

Sanchez may have had uncomfortable relations with certain sections of the local media but to the fans he was an icon; he could do no wrong, virtually walking on water simply because he had motivated the team, lifted players out of the doldrums and ended the embarrassing syndrome of no goals no wins. Statistically he had proved the most successful manager since the legendary Billy Bingham who guided his squads to the 1982 Spain and 1986 Mexico World Cup finals as well as two British title triumphs and only losing out to Germany on the away goal rule in the European championship.

Yet it all began with a disastrous 3-0 defeat by Iceland at Windsor Park but then came the revival: a 3-2 win over Spain, a scoreless draw in Denmark, 1-0 home triumph over Latvia, 4-1 success in Liechtenstein, and the biggest surprise of them all, a 2-1 victory against Sweden, the current Group leaders, at Windsor Park.

Once more Leeds United striker David Healy stole the show with a feast of goalscoring including hat-tricks against Liechtenstein and Spain, bringing his total to 29, an all-time Irish record which could stand for years. He had no challengers for the International Personality Of The Year award.

Major developments in many aspects of Northern Ireland football loom on the horizon. There is the long drawn-out and almost tiresome question of a proposed multi-sport national stadium, if it will ever be built and where it will be sited with claims for the Maze and Belfast and an increasing groundswell that Windsor Park, with all its tradition and heritage, should be refurbished and kept as an international venue – one which creates a unique atmosphere which simply could not be transferred to another venue.

A complete review of the Irish Premier and other leagues is scheduled, with a possible reduction from 16 to 12 in the Premiership carried out on an invitational basis and all depending on whether clubs obtain their UEFA operational licence. Just how this will all work out or even be approved remains to be seen.

Domestically Linfield proved the team of the season, winning the Irish Premier Division and the JJB Irish Cup and finishing runners-up to Drogheda United in the Setanta All-Ireland Sports Cup. Not surprisingly, therefore, manager David Jeffrey, called "The Special One" by the fans, won the Manager Of The Year award.

Cliftonville, under coach Eddie Patterson, brought a freshness to all competitions with a high standard of football, played at pace and with authority, culminating in winning the Crest Wear County Antrim Shield and narrowly failing at the last few hurdles in various competitions due primarily to not having the necessary adequate reserve strength – a problem which is gradually being eliminated.

Glentoran, celebrating its 125th year, promised much in the early stages but could not maintain the momentum. Still they collected the CIS Insurance Cup and finished second to Linfield in the Premier Division title race. It was not sufficient, however, to prevent manager Paul Millar's contract from being terminated and after a saga finding a successor, the job was given to Alan McDonald, the former Northern Ireland and QPR centre-back.

The next 24 months will see vast changes at all levels in the Northern Ireland domestic game and in administration, too. Yes, it should be an interesting and hopefully a productive era.

DR MALCOLM BRODIE MBE

CARNEGIE IRISH PREMIER LEAGUE

	P	W	D	L	F	A	GD	Pts
Linfield (C)	30	21	8	1	73	19	54	71
Glentoran	30	20	3	7	76	33	43	63
Cliftonville	30	18	7	5	47	26	21	61
Portadown	30	17	7	6	49	26	23	58
Lisburn Distillery	30	14	6	10	50	39	11	48
Crusaders	30	14	5	11	50	42	8	47
Coleraine	30	13	6	11	55	50	5	45
Dungannon Swifts	30	13	5	12	41	41	0	44
Ballymena United	30	12	7	11	46	40	6	43
Limavady United	30	10	5	15	39	54	–15	35
Armagh City	30	11	2	17	42	68	–26	35
Newry City	30	8	7	15	39	52	–13	31
Donegal Celtic	30	6	9	15	33	51	–18	27
Larne	30	7	5	18	33	60	–27	26
Glenavon (PO)	30	5	10	15	40	58	–18	25
Loughgall (R)	30	1	8	21	23	77	–54	11

PROMOTION/RELEGATION PLAY-OFF

Bangor 0, 1, Glenavon 1, 0
Glenavon won 4-2 on penalties.

CARNEGIE IRISH LEAGUE FIRST DIVISION

	P	W	D	L	F	A	GD	Pts
Institute (C)	22	17	3	2	50	14	36	54
Bangor (PO)	22	14	5	3	49	23	26	47
Banbridge Town	22	13	4	5	45	31	14	43
Carrick Rangers	22	12	6	4	38	27	11	42
Ards	22	11	5	6	42	25	17	38
Dundela	22	8	5	9	33	35	–2	29
HW Welders	22	8	3	11	30	36	–6	27
Coagh United	22	6	6	10	32	41	–9	24
Tobermore United	22	5	5	12	39	54	–15	20
Portstewart	22	6	2	14	29	44	–15	20
Ballinamallard United (R)	22	4	3	15	14	42	–28	15
Moyola Park (R)	22	4	1	17	24	53	–29	13

CARNEGIE IRISH LEAGUE SECOND DIVISION

	P	W	D	L	F	A	GD	Pts
Ballyclare Comrades (C)	22	19	1	2	46	13	33	58
Lurgan Celtic (P)	22	13	4	5	42	21	21	43
Wakehurst	22	11	2	9	40	31	9	35
Ballymoney United	22	8	8	6	31	27	4	32
Oxford United Stars	22	9	5	8	25	28	–3	32
PSNI	22	10	1	11	35	39	–4	31
Brantwood	22	8	3	11	38	36	2	27
Annagh United	22	6	8	8	21	21	0	26
Chimney Corner	22	6	6	10	28	50	–22	24
Dergview	22	5	6	11	20	36	–16	21
Queens University	22	5	5	12	25	40	–15	20
Glebe Rangers	22	4	7	11	17	26	–9	19

CARNEGIE IRISH RESERVE LEAGUE

	P	W	D	L	F	A	GD	Pts
Ballymena United Res (C)	30	21	3	6	72	39	33	66
Cliftonville Olympic	30	19	7	4	66	28	38	64
Glentoran II	30	19	5	6	70	35	35	62
Lisburn Distillery III	30	17	8	5	76	39	37	59
Limavady United Res	30	19	2	9	61	44	17	59
Crusaders Res	30	15	4	11	79	63	16	49
Portadown Res	30	14	5	11	67	55	12	47
Linfield Swifts	30	13	7	10	67	43	24	46
Donegal Celtic Res	30	13	7	10	57	46	11	46
Coleraine Res	30	11	5	14	49	58	–9	38
Newry City Res	30	10	4	16	59	64	–5	34
Dungannon Swifts Res	30	9	3	18	53	71	–18	30
Glenavon Res	30	7	7	16	52	73	–21	28
Loughgall United	30	6	3	21	42	99	–57	21
Larne Olympic	30	5	4	21	44	95	–51	19
Armagh City Res	30	2	6	22	44	106	–62	12

IRISH LEAGUE CHAMPIONSHIP WINNERS

1891 Linfield
1892 Linfield
1893 Linfield
1894 Glentoran
1895 Linfield
1896 Distillery
1897 Glentoran
1898 Linfield
1899 Distillery
1900 Belfast Celtic
1901 Distillery
1902 Linfield
1903 Distillery
1904 Linfield
1905 Glentoran
1906 Cliftonville
Distillery
1907 Linfield
1908 Linfield
1909 Linfield
1910 Cliftonville
1911 Linfield
1912 Glentoran
1913 Glentoran
1914 Linfield
1915 Belfast Celtic
1920 Belfast Celtic
1921 Glentoran
1922 Linfield
1923 Linfield
1924 Queen's Island
1925 Glentoran
1926 Belfast Celtic
1927 Belfast Celtic
1928 Belfast Celtic
1929 Belfast Celtic
1930 Linfield
1931 Glentoran
1932 Linfield
1933 Belfast Celtic
1934 Linfield
1935 Linfield
1936 Belfast Celtic
1937 Belfast Celtic
1938 Belfast Celtic
1939 Belfast Celtic
1940 Belfast Celtic
1948 Belfast Celtic
1949 Linfield
1950 Linfield
1951 Glentoran
1952 Glenavon
1953 Glentoran
1954 Linfield
1955 Linfield
1956 Linfield
1957 Glentoran
1958 Ards
1959 Linfield
1960 Glenavon
1961 Linfield
1962 Linfield
1963 Distillery
1964 Glentoran
1965 Derry City
1966 Linfield
1967 Glentoran
1968 Glentoran
1969 Linfield
1970 Glentoran
1971 Linfield
1972 Glentoran
1973 Crusaders
1974 Coleraine
1975 Linfield
1976 Crusaders
1977 Glentoran
1978 Linfield
1979 Linfield
1980 Linfield
1981 Glentoran
1982 Linfield
1983 Linfield
1984 Linfield
1985 Linfield
1986 Linfield
1987 Linfield
1988 Glentoran
1989 Linfield
1990 Portadown
1991 Portadown
1992 Glentoran
1993 Linfield
1994 Linfield
1995 Crusaders
1996 Portadown
1997 Crusaders
1998 Cliftonville
1999 Glentoran
2000 Linfield
2001 Linfield
2002 Portadown
2003 Glentoran
2004 Linfield
2005 Glentoran
2006 Linfield
2007 Linfield

FIRST DIVISION

1996 Coleraine
1997 Ballymena United
1998 Newry Town
1999 Distillery
2000 Omagh Town
2001 Ards
2002 Lisburn Distillery
2003 Dungannon Swifts
2004 Loughgall
2005 Armagh City
2006 Crusaders
2007 Institute

SETANTA SPORTS CUP

GROUP 1

Drogheda United v Linfield	0-1
Glentoran v Derry City	0-1
Linfield v Glentoran	1-1
Derry City v Drogheda United	0-0
Glentoran v Drogheda United	0-1
Linfield v Derry City	2-1
Derry City v Linfield	2-2
Drogheda United v Glentoran	2-0
Derry City v Glentoran	1-2
Linfield v Drogheda United	0-0
Drogheda United v Derry City	2-1
Glentoran v Linfield	1-2

	P	*W*	*D*	*L*	*F*	*A*	*Pts*
Linfield	6	3	3	0	8	5	12
Drogheda United	6	3	2	1	5	2	11
Derry City	6	1	2	3	6	8	5
Glentoran	6	1	1	4	4	8	1

GROUP 2

Dungannon Swifts v Cork City	0-0
St Patrick's Athletic v Portadown	3-0
Portadown v Dungannon Swifts	2-2
Cork City v St Patrick's Athletic	1-3
Dungannon Swifts v St Patrick's Athletic	2-2
Cork City v Portadown	4-0
Portadown v Cork City	0-7
St Patrick's Athletic v Dungannon Swifts	5-0
Dungannon Swifts v Portadown	1-1
St Patrick's Athletic v Cork City	1-0
Cork City v Dungannon Swifts	2-1
Portadown v St Patrick's Athletic	0-3

	P	*W*	*D*	*L*	*F*	*A*	*Pts*
St Patrick's Athletic	6	5	1	0	17	3	16
Cork City	6	3	1	2	14	5	10
Dungannon Swifts	6	0	4	2	6	12	4
Portadown	6	0	2	4	3	20	2

SEMI-FINALS

St Patrick's Athletic 0, Drogheda United 1 *(aet)*
Linfield 1, Cork City 0

SETANTA SPORTS CUP FINAL

Linfield (0) 1

Drogheda United (0) 1 6500

(aet; Drogheda won 4-3 on penalties).

Linfield: Mannus; McShane (McCann 14), Murphy, Ferguson, Bailie (capt), McAreavey, Dickson, O'Kane, Thompson (Gault), Ervin, Mulgrew (Mouncey 93).
Scorer: McAreavey 67.

Drogheda United: Vilmunen; Lynch, Webb (Gray 55), Gartland, Robinson, O'Brien (capt) (Grant 64), Shelley, Bradley, Byrne S, Zayed, Cahill (Keegan 77).
Scorer: Grant 77.

Man of the Match: Alan Mannus (Linfield).

Referee: A. McCourt (Bangor).

SETANTA SPORTS CUP WINNERS

2004–05 Linfield
2005–06 Drogheda United
2006–07 Drogheda United

ULSTER CUP WINNERS

1949 Linfield
1950 Larne
1951 Glentoran
1952
1953 Glentoran
1954 Crusaders
1955 Glenavon
1956 Linfield
1957 Linfield
1958 Distillery
1959 Glenavon
1960 Linfield
1961 Ballymena U
1962 Linfield
1963 Crusaders
1964 Linfield
1965 Coleraine
1966 Glentoran
1967 Linfield
1968 Coleraine
1969 Coleraine
1970 Linfield
1971 Linfield
1972 Coleraine
1973 Ards
1974 Linfield
1975 Coleraine
1976 Glentoran
1977 Linfield
1978 Linfield
1979 Linfield
1980 Ballymena U
1981 Glentoran
1982 Glentoran
1983 Glentoran
1984 Linfield
1985 Coleraine
1986 Coleraine
1987 Larne
1988 Glentoran
1989 Glentoran
1990 Portadown
1991 Bangor
1992 Linfield
1993 Crusaders
1994 Bangor
1995 Portadown
1996 Portadown
1997 Coleraine
1998 Ballyclare Comrades
1999 Distillery
2000 *No competition*
2001 *No competition*
2002 *No competition*
2003 Dungannon Swifts *(Confined to First Division clubs)*
2004 *No competition*
2005 *No competition*
2006 *No competition*
2007 *No competition*

JJB SPORTS IRISH CUP 2006–07

FIFTH ROUND

Comber Rec v Laurelvale	0-0, 2-1
Glenavon v PSNI	1-0
Newry City v Ballynure OB	4-0
Dungannon Swifts v Coagh United	7-1
Larne v Cliftonville	2-4
Limavady United v Carrick Rangers	4-2
Linfield v Oxford United Stars	3-0
Donegal Celtic v Tobermore United	2-2, 2-0
Ards v Dundela	1-1, 2-1
Ballymena United v H&W Welders	1-0
Glentoran v Ballymoney United	2-1
Loughgall v Ballyclare Comrades	2-1
Crusaders v Lurgan Celtic	3-1
Portadown v Bangor	6-1
Armagh City v Institute	2-1
Coleraine v Lisburn Distillery	1-2

SIXTH ROUND

Ards v Linfield	0-5
Ballymena United v Comber Rec	1-0
Cliftonville v Donegal Celtic	2-0
Dungannon Swifts v Newry City	2-1
Lisburn Distillery v Glenavon	4-1
Loughgall v Armagh City	1-3
Limavady United v Crusaders	0-1
Glentoran v Portadown	2-2, 1-1

(Portadown won 4-3 on penalties).

QUARTER-FINALS

Ballymena United v Linfield	1-1, 2-4
Cliftonville v Portadown	3-1
Lisburn Distillery v Crusaders	4-1
Dungannon Swifts v Armagh City	2-0

SEMI-FINALS

Cliftonville v Dungannon Swifts	0-0

(Dungannon Swifts won 5-4 on penalties at The Oval, Belfast, 3 March 2007).

Linfield v Lisburn Distillery	4-1

(at The Oval, Belfast, 24 April 2007).

JJB SPORTS IRISH CUP FINAL 2006–07

(Windsor Park, 5 May 2007)

Linfield (2) 2

Dungannon Swifts (2) 2 10,000

(aet; Linfield won 3-2 on penalties).

Linfield: Mannus; Ervin, McShane, McAreavey (Gault 80), Murphy, O'Kane (Stewart 72), Thompson, Mulgrew, Ferguson, Dickson, Bailie (capt).
Scorers: Dickson 3, Ferguson 38.

Dungannon Swifts: Nelson; Wray, Gallagher (Fitzpatrick T 105), Montgomery, McMinn, McCluskey (McConkey 68), McCabe, McAree (capt), Hamill, McAllister, Scullion (Everaldo 87).
Scorers: Hamill 17, McAree 40.

Referee: M. Courtney (Dungannon).

IRISH CUP FINALS (from 1946–47)

1946–47	Belfast Celtic 1, Glentoran 0
1947–48	Linfield 3, Coleraine 0
1948–49	Derry City 3, Glentoran 1
1949–50	Linfield 2, Distillery 1
1950–51	Glentoran 3, Ballymena U 1
1951–52	Ards 1, Glentoran 0
1952–53	Linfield 5, Coleraine 0
1953–54	Derry City 1, Glentoran 0
1954–55	Dundela 3, Glenavon 0
1955–56	Distillery 1, Glentoran 0
1956–57	Glenavon 2, Derry City 0
1957–58	Ballymena U 2, Linfield 0
1958–59	Glenavon 2, Ballymena U 0
1959–60	Linfield 5, Ards 1
1960–61	Glenavon 5, Linfield 1
1961–62	Linfield 4, Portadown 0
1962–63	Linfield 2, Distillery 1
1963–64	Derry City 2, Glentoran 0
1964–65	Coleraine 2, Glenavon 1
1965–66	Glentoran 2, Linfield 0
1966–67	Crusaders 3, Glentoran 1
1967–68	Crusaders 2, Linfield 0
1968–69	Ards 4, Distillery 2
1969–70	Linfield 2, Ballymena U 1
1970–71	Distillery 3, Derry City
1971–72	Coleraine 2, Portadown 1
1972–73	Glentoran 3, Linfield 2
1973–74	Ards 2, Ballymena U 1
1974–75	Coleraine 1:0:1, Linfield 1:0:0
1975–76	Carrick Rangers 2, Linfield 1
1976–77	Coleraine 4, Linfield 1
1977–78	Linfield 3, Ballymena U 1
1978–79	Cliftonville 3, Portadown 2
1979–80	Linfield 2, Crusaders 0
1980–81	Ballymena U 1, Glenavon 0
1981–82	Linfield 2, Coleraine 1
1982–83	Glentoran 1:2, Linfield 1:1
1983–84	Ballymena U 4, Carrick Rangers 1
1984–85	Glentoran 1:1, Linfield 1:0
1985–86	Glentoran 2, Coleraine 1
1986–87	Glentoran 1, Larne 0
1987–88	Glentoran 1, Glenavon 0
1988–89	Ballymena U 1, Larne 0
1989–90	Glentoran 3, Portadown 0
1990–91	Portadown 2, Glenavon 1
1991–92	Glenavon 2, Linfield 1
1992–93	Bangor 1:1:1, Ards 1:1:0
1993–94	Linfield 2, Bangor 0
1994–95	Linfield 3, Carrick Rangers 1
1995–96	Glentoran 1, Glenavon 0
1996–97	Glenavon 1, Cliftonville 0
1997–98	Glentoran 1, Glenavon 0
1998–99	*Portadown awarded trophy after Cliftonville were eliminated for using an ineligible player in semi-final.*
1999–2000	Glentoran 1, Portadown 0
2000–01	Glentoran 1, Linfield 0
2001–02	Linfield 2, Portadown 1
2002–03	Coleraine 1, Glentoran 0
2003–04	Glentoran 1, Coleraine 0
2004–05	Portadown 5, Larne 1
2005–06	Linfield 2, Glentoran 1
2006–07	Linfield 2 Dungannon Swifts 2 *(aet; Linfield won 3-2 on penalties).*

CREST WEAR COUNTY ANTRIM SHIELD

FIRST ROUND

Ballymena United v Dundela	1-3
Cliftonville v Brantwood	5-0
Donegal Celtic v Carrick Rangers	0-0

(Donegal Celtic won 4-2 on penalties).

Glentoran v Bangor	3-1
Linfield v H&W Welders	6-0
Crusaders v Ballyclare Comrades	3-1
Larne v Wakehurst	0-2
Lisburn Distillery v Ards	2-0

SECOND ROUND

Glentoran v Wakehurst	5-0
Lisburn Distillery v Dundela	3-1
Linfield v Crusaders	5-1
Cliftonville v Donegal Celtic	2-0

SEMI-FINALS

Linfield v Lisburn Distillery	1-2
Cliftonville v Glentoran	2-1

COUNTY ANTRIM SHIELD FINAL

(at The Oval, 22 January 2007)

Cliftonville 2 Lisburn Distillery 1

Cliftonville: Connolly; Fleming, Scannell R, Johnston, O'Hara, McAlinden, Holland M, Cleary (Holland B 79), Sweeney (Scanell C 76), McMullan, Kennedy.
Scorers: Holland M 50, 67 (pen).

Lisburn Distillery: Matthews; Alderdice, Ferguson, McCann, Buchanan, Muir, Kilmartin (Bell 86), Hagan (Waterworth 72), Thompson, Verner (Martin 80), Armour.
Scorer: Muir 37.

Referee: D. Malcolm (Bangor).
Attendance: 3628

CIS INSURANCE IRISH LEAGUE CUP

GROUP TABLES

GROUP A	P	W	D	L	F	A	GD	Pts
Glentoran	6	5	0	1	18	3	15	15
Newry City	6	4	1	1	11	7	4	13
Loughgall	6	1	2	3	5	13	–8	5
Donegal Celtic	6	0	1	5	5	16	–11	1

GROUP B	P	W	D	L	F	A	GD	Pts
Crusaders	6	4	1	1	8	5	3	13
Portadown	6	2	2	2	9	7	2	8
Limavady United	6	1	3	2	11	13	–2	6
Ballymena United	6	1	2	3	7	10	–3	5

GROUP C	P	W	D	L	F	A	GD	Pts
Linfield	6	5	0	1	19	7	12	15
Lisburn Distillery	6	3	1	2	7	9	–1	10
Larne	6	2	1	3	7	8	–1	7
Glenavon	6	1	0	5	3	13	–10	3

GROUP D	P	W	D	L	F	A	GD	Pts
Cliftonville	6	3	3	0	8	3	5	12
Dungannon Swifts	6	3	2	1	6	4	2	11
Coleraine	6	2	1	3	12	9	3	7
Armagh City	6	1	0	5	3	13	–10	3

QUARTER-FINALS

Glentoran v Portadown 1-1
(Glentoran won 5-4 on penalties).
Crusaders v Newry City 8-0
Linfield v Dungannon Swifts 2-0
Cliftonville v Lisburn Distillery 3-1

SEMI-FINALS

Glentoran v Linfield 0-0
(Glentoran won 4-3 on penalties at Windsor Park, 7 November 2006).
Cliftonville v Crusaders 1-0
(at The Oval, 8 November 2006).

CIS INSURANCE IRISH LEAGUE CUP FINAL

(at Windsor Park, Belfast, 2 December 2006)

Glentoran 1 Cliftonville 0

Glentoran: Morris; Nixon, Neill, Feeney (Berry 83), Leeman, Smyth, Ward, McDonagh, Halliday, Hamilton, Hill (McCann 87).
Scorer: Hamilton 32.

Cliftonville: Connolly; Fleming, Scannell R (McMullan C 86), McAlinden G, Johnston, O'Hara, Holland (O'Loughlin 78), McMullan G, Scannell C, Downey, Kennedy.
Referee: D. Malcolm (Bangor).

IRISH PREMIER DIVISION LEADING GOALSCORERS

Gary Hamilton *(Glentoran)* 36
Peter Thompson *(Linfield)* 31
Darren Armour *(Lisbury Distillery)* 23
Glenn Ferguson *(Linfield)* 23
Gary McCutcheon *(Portadown)* 23
Michael Halliday *(Glentoran)* 19
Kevin Kelbie *(Ballymena)* 17
Shea Campbell *(Armagh City)* 16
Mark Dickson *(Linfield)* 16
Paul McVeigh *(Donegal Celtic)* 15
David Larmour *(Crusaders)* 14
Mark McAllister *(Dungannon)* 14
Vincent Sweeney *(Cliftonville)* 14
Damien Whitehead *(Coleraine)* 13
Darren Boyce *(Coleraine)* 12
Mark Holland *(Cliftonville)* 12
Paul McAreavey *(Linfield)* 12
Chris Morrow *(Crusaders)* 12
David Rainey *(Crusaders)* 12
Thomas Stewart *(Linfield)* 12
George McMullan *(Cliftonville)* 11
Davy Patton *(Coleraine)* 11
Chris Scannell *(Cliftonville)* 11
David Scullion *(Dungannon)* 11
Andy Waterworth *(Lisburn Distillery)* 11

ROLL OF HONOUR SEASON 2006–07

Competition	*Winner*	*Runner-up*
Carnegie Irish Premier Division	Linfield	Glentoran
Carnegie First Division	Institute	Bangor
JJB Sports Irish Cup	Linfield	Dungannon Swifts
CIS Insurance Irish League Cup	Glentoran	Cliftonville
Crest Wear County Antrim Shield	Cliftonville	Lisburn Distillery
Steel & Sons Cup	Brantwood	H&W Welders
Country Antrim Junior Shield	Rathfern Rangers	Ardoyne WMC
Belfast Telegraph Intermediate Cup	H&W Welders	Coagh United
Irish Junior Cup	Enniskillen Town United	Bessbrook United
Rushmere Mid Ulster Cup Final	Newry City	Annagh United
North West Senior Cup	Tobermore United	Coleraine
Harry Cavan Youth Cup	Linfield Rangers	Crusaders Colts
George Wilson Memorial Cup	Crusaders Res	Donegal Celtic Res
Irish League Youth Cup	Donegal Celtic Youth	Cliftonville Strollers
Carnegie Irish League Cup	Institute Celtic	Dundela
Setanta Sports Cup	Drogheda United	Linfield
Irish Youth League Play-Off	Linfield Rangers	Glentoran Colts

AWARDS

ULSTER FOOTBALLER OF THE YEAR
(Castlereagh Glentoran Supporters Award)
William Murphy *(Linfield)*

NORTHERN IRELAND PLAYER OF THE YEAR
(Football Writers Association)
William Murphy *(Linfield)*

YOUNG PLAYER
Mark McAllister *(Dungannon Swifts)*

MANAGER OF THE YEAR
David Jeffrey *(Linfield)*

OUTSTANDING NON SENIOR TEAM
Raceview

INTERNATIONAL PERSONALITY
David Healy *(Leeds United)*

MERIT AWARD
Jeff Spiers *(Crusaders)*

SUNDAY LIFE LEADING SCORER
Premier Division
Gary Hamilton *(Portadown)* 36
First Division
Ryan Campbell *(Institute)* 20

CHAMPIONS LEAGUE REVIEW 2006–07

Lightning did not strike for a second time for Liverpool as AC Milan gained revenge for their dramatic defeat two years earlier and alas the only storm which engulfed the affair came afterwards, with UEFA blaming Merseyside fans for trouble, ticket chaos and almost anything else you could imagine in Athens.

Sadly the football was forgotten, such a pity when the competition is now at the forefront of the game in Europe.

Though the organisers tend to treat the qualifying tournament as something which should not be mentioned in good company, for many countries this is crucial to their season.

The Intertoto only just beats it off the starting blocks and the World Cup had scarcely been dusted away when the Champions League first qualifying round was off and running.

Cork City did well to edge out the Cypriots Apollon, but Linfield and The New Saints had their time in the limelight and it vanished. Red Star Belgrade then took out Cork, though Hearts proved too strong for Siroki.

Even teams of the calibre of Arsenal had to enter the third qualifying round and brushed aside Dynamo Zagreb. Liverpool, too, were in at this juncture and had just a little to spare over Maccabi Haifa.

Then came the groupies, the acceptable part it seems. Chelsea parcelled up with the holders Barcelona again in Group A, Liverpool in the less demanding Group C, but with both Manchester United and Celtic finding themselves in Group F, Arsenal in Group G. AC Milan figured in Group H.

Chelsea took a slender 1-0 lead against Barca with a Didier Drogba goal immediately after the interval. In the return in Catalonia, Deco levelled the aggregate early enough before Frank Lampard restored Chelsea's advantage. Then three minutes later the Blues old boy Eidur Gudjohnsen made it 2-1 to Barcelona. Enter Drogba to make it 2-2 in injury time.

Celtic pushed United all the way at Old Trafford before losing 3-2 and had the satisfaction of a 1-0 victory at Parkhead in the return fixture. But after the group stage Chelsea, Liverpool, Manchester United and even Arsenal after an indifferent start were top of their groups, Celtic runners-up.

In the first knock-out round, Liverpool did even better in Barcelona winning 2-1 again after Deco had scored early on. Arsenal went down to PSV Eindhoven, Manchester United won in France against Lille and Chelsea drew 1-1 in Portugal against Porto. AC Milan went goalless at Celtic.

In the second legs, Chelsea were behind until the second half when they edged it 2-1 and though Gudjohnsen struck again for Barca, the away goals put the Merseysiders through. Celtic gave the Italians a hard time of it before losing in the extra period, but Arsenal were held at the Emirates and knocked out. United again won 1-0.

In the quarter-finals, Bayern caught AC Milan late on at 2-2, Liverpool eased into a 3-0 lead in Holland against PSV and Chelsea needed Drogba to rescue a draw with Valencia at the Bridge. Manchester United lost 2-1 against Roma.

Shocks in the second legs with United putting the Romans to the sword at 7-1, Milan making light of Bayern, Michael Essien again hitting a late winner for Chelsea in Spain and Liverpool coasting 1-0 at Anfield.

United found AC Milan a tougher proposition but still took a 3-2 lead at Old Trafford. In the other semi-final Chelsea for once led Liverpool with a Joe Cole goal. But in the return games Liverpool levelled on aggregate and won the match on penalties 4-1, while United suffered a 3-0 defeat to leave the finalists as they were two years previously.

Filippo Inzaghi with a fortunate deflected goal on the stroke of half-time put AC Milan ahead and added a second with a more opportunist effort on 82 minutes. Liverpool's reply through Dirk Kuyt in the 89th minute was too little, too late.

Filippo Inzaghi of Milan scores his second goal of the game in the 2-1 Champions League final victory over Liverpool at the Olympic Stadium, Athens. (Alex Livesey/Getty Images)

EUROPEAN CUP

EUROPEAN CUP FINALS 1956–1992

Year	Winners	Runners-up	Venue	Attendance	Referee
1956	Real Madrid 4	Reims 3	Paris	38,000	Ellis (E)
1957	Real Madrid 2	Fiorentina 0	Madrid	124,000	Horn (Ho)
1958	Real Madrid 3	AC Milan 2 *(aet)*	Brussels	67,000	Alsteen (Bel)
1959	Real Madrid 2	Reims 0	Stuttgart	80,000	Dutsch (WG)
1960	Real Madrid 7	Eintracht Frankfurt 3	Glasgow	135,000	Mowat (S)
1961	Benfica 3	Barcelona 2	Berne	28,000	Dienst (Sw)
1962	Benfica 5	Real Madrid 3	Amsterdam	65,000	Horn (Ho)
1963	AC Milan 2	Benfica 1	Wembley	45,000	Holland (E)
1964	Internazionale 3	Real Madrid 1	Vienna	74,000	Stoll (A)
1965	Internazionale 1	Benfica 0	Milan	80,000	Dienst (Sw)
1966	Real Madrid 2	Partizan Belgrade 1	Brussels	55,000	Kreitlein (WG)
1967	Celtic 2	Internazionale 1	Lisbon	56,000	Tschenscher (WG)
1968	Manchester U 4	Benfica 1 *(aet)*	Wembley	100,000	Lo Bello (I)
1969	AC Milan 4	Ajax 1	Madrid	50,000	Ortiz (Sp)
1970	Feyenoord 2	Celtic 1 *(aet)*	Milan	50,000	Lo Bello (I)
1971	Ajax 2	Panathinaikos 0	Wembley	90,000	Taylor (E)
1972	Ajax 2	Internazionale 0	Rotterdam	67,000	Helies (F)
1973	Ajax 1	Juventus 0	Belgrade	93,500	Guglovic (Y)
1974	Bayern Munich 1	Atletico Madrid 1	Brussels	49,000	Loraux (Bel)
Replay	Bayern Munich 4	Atletico Madrid 0	Brussels	23,000	Delcourt (Bel)
1975	Bayern Munich 2	Leeds U 0	Paris	50,000	Kitabdjian (F)
1976	Bayern Munich 1	St Etienne 0	Glasgow	54,864	Palotai (H)
1977	Liverpool 3	Moenchengladbach 1	Rome	57,000	Wurtz (F)
1978	Liverpool 1	FC Brugge 0	Wembley	92,000	Corver (Ho)
1979	Nottingham F 1	Malmo 0	Munich	57,500	Linemayr (A)
1980	Nottingham F 1	Hamburg 0	Madrid	50,000	Garrido (P)
1981	Liverpool 1	Real Madrid 0	Paris	48,360	Palotai (H)
1982	Aston Villa 1	Bayern Munich 0	Rotterdam	46,000	Konrath (F)
1983	Hamburg 1	Juventus 0	Athens	80,000	Rainea (R)
1984	Liverpool 1	Roma 1	Rome	69,693	Fredriksson (Se)
	(aet; Liverpool won 4-2 on penalties)				
1985	Juventus 1	Liverpool 0	Brussels	58,000	Daina (Sw)
1986	Steaua Bucharest 0	Barcelona 0	Seville	70,000	Vautrot (F)
	(aet; Steaua won 2-0 on penalties)				
1987	Porto 2	Bayern Munich 1	Vienna	59,000	Ponnet (Bel)
1988	PSV Eindhoven 0	Benfica 0	Stuttgart	70,000	Agnolin (I)
	(aet; PSV won 6-5 on penalties)				
1989	AC Milan 4	Steaua Bucharest 0	Barcelona	97,000	Tritschler (WG)
1990	AC Milan 1	Benfica 0	Vienna	57,500	Kohl (A)
1991	Red Star Belgrade 0	Marseille 0	Bari	56,000	Lanese (I)
	(aet; Red Star won 5-3 on penalties)				
1992	Barcelona 1	Sampdoria 0 *(aet)*	Wembley	70,827	Schmidhuber (G)

UEFA CHAMPIONS LEAGUE FINALS 1993–2007

1993	Marseille* 1	AC Milan 0	Munich	64,400	Rothlisberger (Sw)
1994	AC Milan 4	Barcelona 0	Athens	70,000	Don (E)
1995	Ajax 1	AC Milan 0	Vienna	49,730	Craciunescu (R)
1996	Juventus 1	Ajax 1	Rome	67,000	Vega (Sp)
	(aet; Juventus won 4-2 on penalties)				
1997	Borussia Dortmund 3	Juventus 1	Munich	59,000	Puhl (H)
1998	Real Madrid 1	Juventus 0	Amsterdam	47,500	Krug (G)
1999	Manchester U 2	Bayern Munich 1	Barcelona	90,000	Collina (I)
2000	Real Madrid 3	Valencia 0	Paris	78,759	Braschi (I)
2001	Bayern Munich 1	Valencia 1	Milan	71,500	Jol (Ho)
	(aet; Bayern Munich won 5-4 on penalties)				
2002	Real Madrid 2	Leverkusen 1	Glasgow	52,000	Meier (Sw)
2003	AC Milan 0	Juventus 0	Manchester	63,215	Merk (G)
	(aet; AC Milan won 3-2 on penalties)				
2004	Porto 3	Monaco 0	Gelsenkirchen	52,000	Nielsen (D)
2005	Liverpool 3	AC Milan 3	Istanbul	65,000	González (Sp)
	(aet; Liverpool won 3-2 on penalties)				
2006	Barcelona 2	Arsenal 1	Paris	79,500	Hauge (N)
2007	AC Milan 2	Liverpool 1	Athens	74,000	Fandel (G)

**Subsequently stripped of title.*

UEFA CHAMPIONS LEAGUE 2006–07

▪ *Denotes player sent off.*

FIRST QUALIFYING ROUND FIRST LEG

Tuesday, 11 July 2006

Birkirkara (0) 0

B36 (2) 3 *(Davy 15, 32, Thorleifson 90)* 500

Birkirkara: Bledzewski; Sammut (Sadowski 65), Gallovich, Scicluna, Galea A, Camenzuli, Mallia, Calascione (Tabone 71), Paradiso, Sbai (Paris 52), Triganza.
B36: Mikkelsen; Alex, Thorleifson, Thomassen, Benjaminsen, Ellingsgaard (Gunnarsson J 63), Jacobsen K, Midjord (Hansen S 88), Matras, Davy (Ekeke 75), Jacobsen H.

Elbasan (0) 1 *(Stojku 75)*

Ekranas (0) 0 5000

Elbasan: Kotorri; Brahja, Dede, Vrapi, Alechenwu, Kaci (Xhafaj 59), Capja (Stojku 69), Osja, Qorri, Bylykbashi, Dalipi (Nora 74).
Ekranas: Skrupskis; Klimavicius, Banevicius, Skroblas, Paulauskas, Kucys (Gardzijauskas 82), Savenas, Tomkevicius, Mikhalchuk (Saulenas 89), Kavaliauskas (Slekys 60), Luksys.

F91 Dudelange (0) 0

Rabotnicki (0) 1 *(Velkovski 77)* 1500

F91 Dudelange: Joubert J; Borbiconi, Mouny, Crapa (Gruszczynski 82), Di Gregorio (Lecomte 69), Martine, Bellini (Joly 72), Kabongo, Remy, Hug, Zeghdane.
Rabotnicki: Pacovski; Jovanovski, Ilievski, Vajs, Stepanovski, Lazarevski (Karchev 80), Stojanov, Ignatov, Trajchov (Jankep 72), Pejcic, Velkovski (Aleksovski 83).

Linfield (0) 1 *(Dickson 58 (pen))*

Gorica (2) 3 *(Demirovic 14, 27, Sturm 66)* 3500

Linfield: Mannus; Ervin (Douglas 46), McShane (McCann 25), Mulgrew, Murphy, O'Kane, Thompson, Magennis (Mouncey 32), Dickson, McAreavey, Bailie.
Gorica: Pirih; Srebrnic (Jogan 84), Jokic, Zivec, Kovacevic, Dedic, Demirovic, Burgic, Sturm (Rexhay 75), Pitamic (Nikolic 63), Suler.

Pyunik (0) 0

Serif (0) 0 3000

Pyunik: Kasparov; Hovsepian (Melkonian 46), Tadevosian, Aleksanian, Voskanian (Tigranian 33), Khachatrian, Mkrtchian, Pachajian (Sahakian 73), Nazarian, Petrosian, Avetisian.
Serif: Hutan; Mamah, Tarkhnishvili, Corneencov, Kuchuk (Omotoyossi 63), Florescu, Arbanas, Epureanu, Cocis (Suvorov 73), Pirsa (Gumenuk 36), Gnanou.

Sioni (0) 2 *(Boyomo 69, Ugrekhelidze 88)*

Baku (0) 0 2500

Sioni: Batiashvili; Kobauri, Chelidze L, Chichveishvili, Rakviashvili (Chelidze Z 46), Bajelidze, Shavgulidze, Alavidze, Kutsurua (Ugrekhelidze 76), Mikuchadze, Memedji (Boyomo 46).
Baku: Diallo; Ladaga (Amirbekov 90), Guliyev R, Guliyev V▪, Megreladze (Ionescu 55), Sultanov, Abbasov R▪, Abbasov A, Jovandic, Melikov, Bangoura.

VMK (0) 2 *(Haavistu 70, Dobrecovs 76 (pen))*

Hafnarfjordur (1) 3 *(Gudmundsson T 33, Olafsson 69, Atli Gudnason 90)* 350

VMK: Teles; Gabovs (Sarajev 8), Rimas, Kacanovs, Haavistu (Masitsev 80), Borissov, Sirmelis, Dobrecovs, Seero, Kostin (Zenjov 55), Gussev.
Hafnarfjordur: Larusson; Nielsen, Asgeirsson, Vidarsson, Gudmundsson T, Olafsson, Saevarsson, Bjornsson, Albertsson, Snorrason (Atli Gudnason 83), Vilhjalmsson (Dyring 83).

Wednesday, 12 July 2006

Cork City (0) 1 *(Woods 62)*

Apollon (0) 0 3000

Cork City: Devine; Murphy, Bennett, Murray D, O'Brien, Fenn, Woods, O'Donovan, Gamble, Behan (Lordan 90), Horgan.
Apollon: Chvalovsky; Barun, Alvarez, Merkis, Michalski, Andone (Machado 80), Ajeel, Solomou (Taher 65), Arig, Sosin, Hamadi (Paiva 58).

Metalurgs Liepaja (1) 1 *(Tamosauskas 14)*

Aktobe (0) 0 2000

Metalurgs Liepaja: Krucs; Klava, Zirnis, Ivanovs, Surnins, Petrenko, Miceika (Katasonov 46), Kalonas, Tamosauskas, Solonicins, Karlsons (Astrauskas 67).
Aktobe: Nesterenko; Samchenko, Nizovtsev, Malkov, Yaskovich, Aksenov, Nikolaev, Shkurin, Rogaciov, Golovskoy, Kitsak.

MyPa (0) 1 *(Adriano 58)*

TNS (0) 0 864

MyPa: Korhonen; Timoska, Taipale, Lindstrom, Kuparinen (Puhakainen 62), Manso, Karhu, Kangaskolkka (Pellonen 70), Miranda, Kansikas, Adriano (Leguizamon 75).
TNS: Doherty; Baker, King, Jackson, Holmes, Ruscoe (Leah 76), Hogan, Wilde (Carter 65), Beck, Ward (Toner 87), Stones.

Shakhtyor (0) 0

Siroki (1) 1 *(Bubalo 29)* 3000

Shakhtyor: Makauchyk; Budaev (Goncharik 63), Yurevich, Leonchik, Klimenko (Barel 81), Nikiforenko, Martsinovich, Sobal, Plaskonny, Kavalchuk, Beganski (Bychanok 37).
Siroki: Basic; Anic, Silic, Pandza, Landeka, Lago, Carvalho, Ronelle, Celson, Karoglan (Kovacic 84), Bubalo (Lukacevic 56) (Galic 89).

FIRST QUALIFYING ROUND SECOND LEG

Tuesday, 18 July 2006

Baku (0) 1 *(Guliyev F 63)*

Sioni (0) 0 3250

Baku: Diallo; Ladaga, Abdullayev, Guliyev R, Megreladze (Guliyev F 46), Sultanov, Abbasov A, Jovandic, Ionescu, Melikov (Amirbekov 46), Bangoura.
Sioni: Batiashvili; Kobauri (Alavidze 30), Chelidze L, Chichveishvili, Boyomo, Rakviashvili, Ugrekhelidze, Shavgulidze, Bajelidze (Chelidze Z 46), Kutsurua (Memedji 79), Chassem.

Ekranas (1) 3 *(Luksys 13, 70, Tomkevicius 48)*

Elbasan (0) 0 2500

Ekranas: Skrupskis; Klimavicius, Banevicius, Gardzijauskas, Paulauskas, Kucys (Petrauskas 78), Slekys (Kavaliauskas 46), Savenas, Tomkevicius (Saulenas 68), Mikhalchuk, Luksys.
Elbasan: Kotorri; Brahja (Tetova 46), Dede, Alechenwu, Vrapi, Nora, Osja, Capja (Stojku 63), Qorri (Dalipi 46), Bylykbashi, Xhafaj.

Rabotnicki (0) 0

F91 Dudelange (0) 0 1250

Rabotnicki: Pacovski; Jovanovski, Ilievski, Vajs, Stepanovski, Lazarevski, Stojanov (Adelicio 86), Mihajlovic (Jankep 68), Trajchov, Pejcic, Velovski (Aleksovski 90).
F91 Dudelange: Joubert J; Borbiconi, Mouny, Crapa, Bellini (Di Gregorio 75), Kabongo, Remy (Lecomte 80), Hug, Helder (Joly 54), Gruszczynski, Zeghdane.

Serif (1) 2 *(Cocis 30, Gumenuk 90)*

Pyunik (0) 0 7500

Serif: Hutan; Mamah, Tarkhnishvili, Corneencov (Suvorov 87), Kuchuk (Omotoyossi 70), Florescu, Arbanas, Epureanu, Cocis, Pirsa (Gumenuk 61), Gnanou.
Pyunik: Kasparov; Hovsepian, Tadevosian, Khachatrian, Arzumanian, Tigranian, Safarian (Avetisian 38), Mkrtchian, Pachajian, Melkonian (Nazarian 68), Petrosian (Sahakian 57).

Wednesday, 19 July 2006

Aktobe (1) 1 *(Nikolaev 17)*

Metalurgs Liepaja (0) 1 *(Ivanovs 59 (pen))* 2500

Aktobe: Nesterenko; Samchenko, Aksenov (Ashirbekov 60), Nizovtsev, Yaskovich, Kitsak, Nikolaev, Shkurin, Rogaciov■, Golovskoy, Malkov (Logvinenko 75).
Metalurgs Liepaja: Krucs; Klava, Zirnis, Ivanovs, Surnins, Petrenko, Karlsons, Kalonas, Tamosauskas, Solonicins, Astrauskas (Grebis 59) (Kets 90).

Apollon (0) 1 *(Sosin 51)*

Cork City (0) 1 *(Murray D 75)* 2000

Apollon: Chvalovsky; Barun (Hamadi■ 78), Alvarez, Merkis■, Michalski, Andone, Ajeel, Machado (Solomou 78), Arig, Sosin, Paiva (Taher 59).
Cork City: Devine; Murphy■, Bennett, Murray D, O'Brien, Fenn, Woods (Softic 90), O'Donovan (Lordan 90), Gamble■, Behan (Sullivan 87), Horgan.

B36 (1) 2 *(Matras 44, Ekeke 80)*

Birkirkara (0) 2 *(Mallia 59, Scicluna 83)* 700

B36: Mikkelsen; Alex, Thorleifson (Joensen N 62), Thomassen■, Benjaminsen, Ellingsgaard (Ekeke 67), Jacobsen K (Joensen B 81), Midjord, Matras, Davy, Jacobsen H.
Birkirkara: Bledzewski; Bonnici, Sammut, Camenzuli■, Briffa (Calascione 19), Sbai (Tabone 81), Scicluna, Paradiso (Paris 73), Triganza, Mallia, Gallovich.

Gorica (1) 2 *(Burgic 30, 83)*

Linfield (1) 2 *(Thompson 28, McAreavey 90)* 1250

Gorica: Pirih; Srebrnic, Jokic, Zivec (Jogan 75), Kovacevic, Dedic, Demirovic, Burgic (Matavz 85), Sturm (Rexhay 55), Nikolic, Suler.
Linfield: Mannus; Douglas (Ervin 65), McCann, Mulgrew (McAreavey 51), Murphy, O'Kane, Thompson, Kingsberry, Dickson (Garrett 82), Mouncey, Bailie.

Hafnarfjordur (0) 1 *(Atli Gudnason 90)*

VMK (0) 1 *(Dobrecovs 60 (pen))* 750

Hafnarfjordur: Larusson; Bett, Asgeirsson, Vidarsson, Gudmundsson T, Olafsson (Arni Gudnason 90), Saevarsson, Bjornsson, Albertsson, Snorrason (Atli Gudnason 84), Vilhjalmsson (Dyring 68).
VMK: Teles; Zenjov (Gussev 57), Rimas, Kacanovs (Kostin 82), Haavistu, Borissov, Sirmelis, Dobrecovs, Sarajev, Seero, Kuvsinovs (Masitsev 74).

Siroki (1) 1 *(Ronelle 29 (pen))*

Shakhtyor (0) 0 2500

Siroki: Basic; Anic (Doci 77), Silic, Pandza, Landeka, Carvalho (Papic 87), Lago, Bubalo (Lukacevic 61), Ronelle, Karoglan, Celson.
Shakhtyor: Makauchyk; Budaev■, Yurevich, Leonchik, Klimenko (Novik 75), Nikiforenko, Martsinovich, Sobal (Barel 82), Plaskonny, Kavalchuk, Bychanok (Goncharik 64).

TNS (0) 0

MyPa (1) 1 *(Puhakainen 5)* 1850

TNS: Doherty; Baker, King (Carter 61), Jackson, Holmes, Ruscoe (Toner 46), Hogan (Leah 80), Wilde, Beck, Ward, Stones.
MyPa: Korhonen; Timoska, Taipale, Lindstrom, Kuparinen, Puhakainen (Kangaskolkka 57), Manso (Huttunen 69), Leguizamon (Hernesniemi 78), Miranda, Kansikas, Adriano.

SECOND QUALIFYING ROUND FIRST LEG

Tuesday, 25 July 2006

Ekranas (1) 1 *(Luksys 14)*

Dynamo Zagreb (2) 4 *(Eduardo da Silva 7, 51, Buljat 32, Vugrinec 69)* 3000

Ekranas: Skrupskis; Klimavicius, Banevicius, Paulauskas, Gardzijauskas, Tomkevicius, Savenas, Slekys (Kucys 61), Mikhalchuk (Kavaliauskas 68), Varnas (Petrauskas 86), Luksys.
Dynamo Zagreb: Turina; Buljat, Cale, Corluka, Cvitanovic, Etto, Modric, Agic (Drpic 74), Eduardo da Silva (Carlos 87), Mamic (Vukojevic 80), Vugrinec.

Wednesday, 26 July 2006

Cork City (0) 0

Red Star Belgrade (1) 1 *(Behan 37 (og))* 5500

Cork City: Devine; Bennett, Murray D, O'Brien, Fenn, Woods, O'Donovan, Lordan (Callaghan 86), Softic, Behan (McCarthy 84), Horgan.
Red Star Belgrade: Randjelovic; Pantic (Djokic 68), Bisevac, Jankovic (Milijas 60), Perovic, Joksimovic, Kovacevic, Georgiev, Zigic (Purovic 90), Basta, Milovanovic.

Debrecen (0) 1 *(Zsolnai 47)*

Rabotnicki (1) 1 *(Stankovski 45)* 10,000

Debrecen: Csernyanszki; Mate, Szatmari (Dzsudzsak 46), Vukmir, Dombi (Sidibe 78), Sandor, Bogdanovics, Brnovics (Zsolnai 20), Bernath, Halmosi, Eger.
Rabotnicki: Pacovski; Stojanov, Jeremic, Stepanovski, Jovanovski (Karchev 46), Vajs, Trajchov, Nedzipi (Jankep 78), Stankovski, Pejcic, Velkovski (Abrilio 70).

Djurgaarden (0) 1 *(Enrico 70)*

Ruzomberok (0) 0 8161

Djurgaarden: Tourray; Storm, Quivasto, Arneng, Hysen (Enrico 67), Kusi-Asare (Thiago 80), Sjolund, Jonson, Johannesson, Komac, Barsom.
Ruzomberok: Hajduch; Sedlak, Nezmar, Zofcak, Tomcak (Dovicovic 89), Pospisil, Laurinc, Bozok (Rychlik 70), Dvornik, Siva, Sapara (Zosak 88).

FC Copenhagen (0) 2 *(Bergdolmo 64 (pen), Gravgaard 90)*

MyPa (0) 0 17,523

FC Copenhagen: Christiansen; Jacobsen, Hangeland, Linderoth, Alvaro Santos (Berglund 71), Gronkjaer, Allback, Hutchinson, Gravgaard, Bergdolmo, Pimpong (Bergvold 73).
MyPa: Korhonen; Timoska, Taipale, Lindstrom, Kuparinen, Manso (Pellonen 58), Huttunen, Kangaskolkka (Puhakainen 71), Miranda, Kansikas, Adriano (Hernesniemi 82).

Fenerbahce (2) 4 *(Appiah 26, Tumer 39, Tuncay 54, Onder 90)*

B36 (0) 0 25,000

Fenerbahce: Rustu; Appiah, Umit O, Tuncay, Tumer (Ugur 69), Marco Aurelio, Can, Onder, Alex, Serkan (Kerim 78), Anelka.
B36: Mikkelsen; Alex, Joensen N (Hansen J 72), Thorleifson, Ekeke (Gunnarsson J 62), Benjaminsen, Jacobsen K, Midjord, Matras, Davy (Hansen S 76), Jacobsen H.

Gorica (0) 0

Steaua (0) 2 *(Dica 54, Iacob 65)* 1800

Gorica: Simcic; Srebrnic, Jokic, Zivec, Kovacevic, Dedic, Demirovic, Sturm (Velikonja 89), Pitamic, Ranic (Rexhay 74), Suler.
Steaua: Fernandes; Marin, Ghionea, Goian, Nesu, Nicolita, Paraschiv (Cristocea 70), Lovin, Bostina (Oprita 70), Dica, Iacob (Badea 85).

Hafjarfjordur (0) 0

Legia (0) 1 *(Elton 83)* 1250

Hafjarfjordur: Larusson; Asgeirsson, Vidarsson (Vilhjalmsson 54), Gudmundsson T, Saevarsson, Bjornsson, Bett, Olafsson (Atli Gudnason 87), Albertsson, Snorrason, Lindbaek (Dyring 77).

Legia: Fabianski; Szala, Choto, Alcantara, Guerreiro, Kielbowicz, Vukovic, Janczyk (Korzym 67), Szalachowski (Radovic 70), Gottwald (Elton 46), Burkhardt.

Hearts (0) 3 *(Carvalho 53 (og), Tall 79, Bednar 85)*
Siroki (0) 0 28,486
Hearts: Gordon; Neilson, Fyssas, Pressley, Tall, McCann (Pospisil 56), Aguiar (Brellier 89), Jankauskas (Mikoliunas 56), Bednar, Cesnauskis, Berra.
Siroki: Basic; Anic, Silic, Pandza, Landeka, Lago, Carvalho (Papic 90), Bubalo (Doci 59), Ronelle, Karoglan (Kovacic 84), Celson.

Levski (1) 2 *(Angelov E 20, Borimirov 82 (pen))*
Sioni (0) 0 7500
Levski: Petkov; Tomasic, Eromoigbe, Borimirov, Yovov (Koprivarov 67), Angelov S, Telkiyski (Domovchiyski 67), Wagner, Bardon (Ivanov M 84), Angelov E, Topuzakov.
Sioni: Batiashvili; Boyomo, Chelidze L, Chichveishvili (Okropiridze 87), Alavidze, Rakviashvili, Bajelidze, Shavgulidze (Chiladze Z 65), Kutsurua (Kobauri 65), Ugrekhelidze, Chassem.

Metalurgs Liepaja (0) 1 *(Kalonas 87)*
Dynamo Kiev (3) 4 *(Diogo Rincon 20, Shatskikh 29, Verpakovskis 32, Gavrancic 82)* 2500
Metalurgs Liepaja: Krucs; Zuravlovs, Klava, Jemelins, Surnins, Tamosauskas, Miceika, Rimkevicius, Solonicins, Kalonas, Karlsons (Astrauskas 54).
Dynamo Kiev: Shovkovskiy; Rebrov (Rotan 66), Correa (Belkevich 59), Diogo Rincon (Cernat 76), Shatskikh, Mikhalik, Gusev, Verpakovskis, El Kaddouri, Gavrancic, Yussuf.

Mlada Boleslav (3) 3 *(Pecka 7, Palat 10, Matejovsky 18)*
Valerenga (0) 1 *(Gashi 67)* 5000
Mlada Boleslav: Kucera; Sevinsky, Vaculik, Palat, Matejovsky, Brezinsky, Kulic (Ordos 85), Polacek (Riegel 72) (Kysela 87), Pecka, Vit, Abraham.
Valerenga: Arason; Jepsen, Holm T, Dos Santos, Holm D, Berre (Sorensen 59), Storbaek, Grindheim, Hovi, Johnsen, Muri (Gashi 24).

Serif (0) 1 *(Omotoyossi 90)*
Spartak Moscow (0) 1 *(Kovac 77)* 13,600
Serif: Hutan; Mamah, Tarkhnishvili, Corneencov, Kuchuk (Omotoyossi 63), Florescu, Arbanas, Epureanu, Cocis (Suvorov 83), Pirsa (Gumenuk 66), Gnanou.
Spartak Moscow: Kowalewski; Jiranek, Kovac, Stranzl, Rodriguez, Bystrov, Mozart, Covalciuc (Torbinskiy 60), Titov, Pavlyuchenko (Owusu-Abeyie 52), Pjanovic (Bazhenov 75).

Zurich (2) 2 *(Keita 2, Cesar 20)*
Salzburg (1) 1 *(Vonlanthen 32)* 11,200
Zurich: Leoni; Von Bergen, Margairaz (Alphonse 75), Dzemaili, Inler, Keita (Stanic 83), Stahel, Raffael, Cesar (Abdi 86), Schneider, Tihinen.
Salzburg: Ochs; Bodnar, Dudic, Linke, Kovac, Jezek (Pitak 84), Tiffert, Vonlanthen (Carboni 40), Janko (Zickler 46), Aufhauser■, Vargas.

SECOND QUALIFYING ROUND SECOND LEG

Tuesday, 1 August 2006

B36 (0) 0
Fenerbahce (1) 5 *(Tuncay 44, Mehmet 49, Can 79, Semih 83, Murat 90)* 800
B36: Mikkelsen; Alex, Joensen N (Jacobsen R 87), Thorleifson (Ellingsgaard 62), Thomassen, Benjaminsen, Gunnarsson J, Midjord, Matras, Davy (Joensen B 75), Jacobsen H.
Fenerbahce: Rustu; Umit O, Mehmet, Tuncay (Murat 65), Marco Aurelio, Can, Onder, Alex (Olcan 82), Semih, Ugur, Serkan (Kerim 70).

Wednesday, 2 August 2006

Dynamo Kiev (1) 4 *(Rotan 37, 90, Correa 66, Rebrov 85)*
Metalurgs Liepaja (0) 0 15,000
Dynamo Kiev: Rybka; Belkevich, Cernat, Rotan, Shatskikh (Rebrov 46), Mikhalik, Gusev (Correa 58), Verpakovskis, El Kaddouri, Gavrancic, Rodrigo (Madzyuk 73).
Metalurgs Liepaja: Krucs; Zuravlovs, Klava, Jemelins, Surnins, Rimkevicius, Solonicins (Grebis 79), Kalonas (Kets 85), Karlsons, Zirnis, Katasonov.

Dynamo Zagreb (1) 5 *(Ljubojevic 2, 62, 90, Vukojevic 48, Vugrinec 89)*
Ekranas (0) 2 *(Savenas 65, Luksys 69)* 5000
Dynamo Zagreb: Turina; Buljat, Corluka, Tomic (Vugrinec 79), Costa (Eduardo da Silva 79), Modric (Grgurovic 65), Agic, Carlos, Vukojevic, Drpic, Ljubojevic.
Ekranas: Skrupskis; Klimavicius, Banevicius, Paulauskas, Gardzijauskas, Tomkevicius, Savenas, Petrauskas (Galkevicius 83), Kucys (Slekys 46), Varnas (Pogreban 58), Luksys.

Legia (1) 2 *(Vukovic 38, Edson 78)*
Hafnarfjordur (0) 0 5000
Legia: Fabianski; Szala, Choto, Alcantara, Guerreiro, Wlodarczyk (Janczyk 53), Kielbowicz (Burkhardt 46), Vukovic, Szalachowski (Radovic 53), Edson, Elton.
Hafnarfjordur: Larusson; Asgeirsson (Arni Gudnason 84), Gudmundsson T, Saevarsson, Bjornsson, Olafsson, Albertsson, Lindbaek, Nielsen, Snorrason (Atli Gudnason 82), Bett (Vilhjalmsson 65).

MyPa (1) 2 *(Pellonen 41, Puhakainen 79)*
FC Copenhagen (1) 2 *(Berglund 12, Linderoth 73)* 2443
MyPa: Korhonen; Timoska, Taipale, Lindstrom, Puhakainen, Huttunen, Kangaskolkka (Oksanen 90), Miranda, Kansikas, Pellonen (Muinonen 73), Adriano (Manso 78).
FC Copenhagen: Christiansen; Jacobsen, Hangeland, Linderoth, Silberbauer (Bernburg 80), Berglund (Bergvold 64), Gronkjaer, Allback, Hutchinson, Gravgaard (Thomasen 76), Bergdolmo.

Rabotnicki (3) 4 *(Nedzipi 21, Pejcic 35, Trajchov 42, Abrilio 56)*
Debrecen (1) 1 *(Sidibe 20)* 6000
Rabotnicki: Pacovski; Jovanovski, Vajs, Abrilio, Jeremic (Lazarevski 68), Karchev, Ignatov (Stojanov 69), Trajchov, Nedzipi, Stankovski (Velkovski 60), Pejcic.
Debrecen: Csernyanszki; Vukmir (Virag 77), Dombi, Sandor (Kiss 46), Bogdanovics (Szatmari 46), Komlosi, Dzsudzsak, Bernath, Sidibe■, Halmosi■, Eger.

Red Star Belgrade (2) 3 *(Milovanovic 3, Zigic 34, 59)*
Cork City (0) 0 30,000
Red Star Belgrade: Randjelovic; Pantic, Bisevac, Djokic (Jankovic 70), Perovic (Milijas 79), Joksimovic, Kovacevic, Georgiev, Zigic (Purovic 64), Basta, Milovanovic.
Cork City: Devine; Bennett, Callaghan, O'Brien, Fenn, Woods, O'Donovan, Lordan, Softic, Behan (Sullivan 80), Horgan.

Ruzomberok (2) 3 *(Zofcak 14, Tomcak 18, Nezmar 88)*
Djurgaarden (0) 1 *(Kusi-Asare 75)* 4800
Ruzomberok: Hajduch; Sedlak, Nezmar, Zofcak, Tomcak (Dovicovic 89), Pospisil (Jendrisek 77), Laurinc, Bozok (Zosak 86), Dvornik, Siva, Sapara.
Djurgaarden: Touraay; Concha (Thiago 86), Storm, Quivasto, Arneng, Hysen (Enrico 60), Kusi-Asare (Arnason 78), Sjolund, Jonson, Johannesson■, Komac.

Salzburg (1) 2 *(Tiffert 39, Zickler 56 (pen))*
Zurich (0) 0 16,200
Salzburg: Ochs; Bodnar, Dudic, Linke, Carboni, Kovac, Zickler, Jezek (Pitak 72), Tiffert, Janocko (Meyer 86), Vargas.
Zurich: Leoni; Von Bergen, Margairaz (Stanic 76), Dzemaili (Alphonse 72), Inler, Keita (Pouga 83), Stahel, Raffael, Cesar, Schneider, Tihinen.

Sioni (0) 0
Levski (1) 2 *(Domovchiyski 18, Angelov E 90)* 3000
Sioni: Batiashvili; Rakviashvili, Boyomo, Chichveishvili, Shavgulidze, Chelidze Z, Bajelidze (Kutsurua 46), Ugrekhelidze, Alavidze■, Memedji (Kardava 56), Chassem (Okropiridze 75).
Levski: Petkov; Milanov, Eromoigbe (Bornosuzov 77), Borimirov, Domovchiyski, Ivanov M, Angelov S, Telkiyski (Angelov E 71), Wagner, Bardon (Koprivarov 68), Topuzakov.

Siroki (0) 0
Hearts (0) 0 6000
Siroki: Vasilj; Anic, Silic, Lago, Papic (Studenovic 88), Pandza, Landeka, Ronelle, Kovacic (Erceg 70), Karoglan, Celson (Carvalho 75).
Hearts: Gordon; Neilson (Tall 61), Fyssas, Pressley, McCann (Mikoliunas 61), Aguiar, Pospisil, Bednar, Cesnauskis (Beslija 84), Berra, Brellier.

Spartak Moscow (0) 0
Serif (0) 0 22,200
Spartak Moscow: Kowalewski; Jiranek, Kovac, Stranzl, Rodriguez, Mozart, Bystrov (Torbinskiy 58), Kalynychenko, Titov (Owusu-Abeyie 51) (Covalciuc 67), Pavlyuchenko, Cavenaghi.
Serif: Hutan; Mamah, Gumenuk (Suvorov 81), Tarkhnishvili, Corneencov, Florescu, Arbanas, Epureanu, Pirsa (Balima 61), Omotoyossi (Kuchuk 62), Gnanou.

Steaua (1) 3 *(Bostina 43, Iacob 70, Ochirosii 87 (pen))*
Gorica (0) 0 10,000
Steaua: Cernea; Dica (Oprita 59), Bostina, Cristocea, Nesu, Nicolita (Badea 59), Baciu, Iacob (Ochirosii 76), Lovin, Saban, Ghionea.
Gorica: Simcic; Srebrnic, Jokic, Zivec (Jogan 60), Nikolic, Kovacevic, Dedic, Demirovic (Rexhay 77), Sturm (Velikonja 82), Pitamic, Ranic.

Valerenga (0) 2 *(Vit 73 (og), Holm D 86)*
Mlada Boleslav (1) 2 *(Brezinksy 41, Kulic 83)* 11,000
Valerenga: Arason; Jepsen, Holm T, Dos Santos (Sorensen 64), Holm D, Gashi, Storbaek, Grindheim (Berre 64), Johnsen (Lange 68), Flo, Waehler.
Mlada Boleslav: Kucera; Sevinsky, Vaculik (Holub 90), Palat, Matejovsky, Brezinsky, Kulic (Sedlacek 84), Polacek (Riegel 74), Pecka, Vit, Abraham■.

THIRD QUALIFYING ROUND FIRST LEG

Tuesday, 8 August 2006

Dynamo Zagreb (0) 0
Arsenal (0) 3 *(Fabregas 63, 78, Van Persie 64)* 28,500
Dynamo Zagreb: Turina; Buljat (Vukojevic 90), Cale (Carlos 90), Nowotny, Corluka, Cvitanovic, Etto, Modric, Eduardo da Silva, Mamic, Vugrinec (Agic 27).
Arsenal: Almunia; Eboue, Hoyte, Silva, Toure, Djourou, Hleb, Fabregas, Adebayor (Aliadiere 82), Rosicky (Flamini 82), Van Persie.

FK Austria (1) 1 *(Blanchard 36)*
Benfica (1) 1 *(Nuno Gomes 16)* 16,800
FK Austria: Safar; Troyansky, Tokic, Wallner, Radomski, Vachousek, Aigner (Ceh 46), Lasnik (Pichlmann 82), Blanchard, Wimmer (Mila 46), Papac.
Benfica: Quim; Anderson, Luisao, Petit, Katsouranis, Rui Costa, Paulo Jorge (Nuno Assis 89), Manu (Marco Ferreira 70), Nuno Gomes (Fonseca 80), Nelson, Ricardo Rocha.

Wednesday, 9 August 2006

AC Milan (1) 1 *(Inzaghi 22)*
Red Star Belgrade (0) 0 55,000
AC Milan: Dida; Cafu (Brocchi 78), Costacurta, Gattuso, Inzaghi, Seedorf, Gilardino (Ambrosini 72), Simic, Pirlo (Gourcuff 81), Kaka, Serginho.
Red Star Belgrade: Randjelovic; Pantic, Bisevac, Jankovic (Krivokapic 90), Perovic (Tutoric 66), Kovacevic, Georgiev, Gueye, Zigic, Basta, Milovanovic (Djokic 81).

CSKA Moscow (0) 3 *(Olic 58, 65, Vagner Love 83)*
Ruzomberok (0) 0 9500
CSKA Moscow: Akinfeev; Semberas, Ignashevich, Berezutski A, Daniel Carvalho (Gusev 86), Olic (Dudu 73), Jo (Vagner Love 60), Krasic, Zhirkov, Aldonin, Rahimic.
Ruzomberok: Hajduch; Sedlak, Nezmar, Zofcak, Pospisil, Laurinc, Bozok (Tomcak 63), Dvornik, Siva, Rak (Rychlik 84), Sapara.

Dynamo Kiev (1) 3 *(Diogo Rincon 1, 67, Yussuf 83)*
Fenerbahce (0) 1 *(Marco Aurelio 48)* 16,000
Dynamo Kiev: Shovkovskiy; Rebrov (Milevskiy 62), Sabjlic, Correa, Diogo Rincon, Shatskikh, Gusev (Belkevich 78), El Kaddouri, Yussuf, Rodrigo, Markovic.
Fenerbahce: Rustu; Appiah, Umit O, Tuncay, Tumer (Ugur 72), Marco Aurelio, Can (Servet 80), Onder, Alex, Serkan■, Anelka (Semih 72).

FC Copenhagen (0) 1 *(Hangeland 47)*
Ajax (1) 2 *(Huntelaar 37, 84)* 40,014
FC Copenhagen: Christiansen; Jacobsen, Hangeland, Linderoth, Silberbauer (Kvist 79), Berglund (Pimpong 69), Gronkjaer, Allback, Hutchinson, Gravgaard, Bergdolmo.
Ajax: Stekelenburg; Heitinga, Stam, Vermaelen, Emanuelson, Maduro, Rosales (Rosenberg 77), Huntelaar, Sneijder, Perez (Babel 68), Garcia.

Galatasaray (2) 5 *(Ilic 7 (pen), Arda 43, 60, Hakan Sukur 49, Sabri 90)*
Mlada Boleslav (0) 2 *(Brezinsky 82, Kulic 83)* 17,862
Galatasaray: Mondragon; Cihan, Tomas, Song, Orhan (Ergun 70), Sabri, Okan (Mehmet 75), Ayhan, Arda, Ilic (Hasan Sas 85), Hakan Sukur.
Mlada Boleslav: Kucera; Sevinsky, Vit, Brezinsky, Smerda, Vaculik (Sedlacek 59), Matejovsky, Riegel, Polacek (Mikolanda 69), Kulic, Pecka.

Hamburg (0) 0
Osasuna (0) 0 47,458
Hamburg: Kirschstein; Mahdavikia, Guerrero, Kompany, Jarolim, Trochowski (Lauth 73), Sanogo, Demel, Reinhardt, Van der Vaart, De Jong.
Osasuna: Ricardo; Cuellar, Raul Garcia, Milosevic (Nekounam 89), Punal, Josetxo, David Lopez, Javier Flano, Soldado (Romeo 79), Delporte (Valdo 70), Monreal.

Hearts (0) 1 *(Mikoliunas 62)*
AEK Athens (0) 2 *(Kapetanos 89, Fyssas 90 (og))* 32,459
Hearts: Gordon; Neilson, Fyssas, Pressley, McCann, Aguiar■, Pospisil (Elliot 83), Bednar (Wallace 69), Mikoliunas, Berra, Karipidis (Jankauskas 55).
AEK Athens: Sorrentino; Pautasso (Tziortziopoulos 81), Dellas, Cirilo, Georgeas, Emerson, Ivic, Lagos (Lakis 65), Liberopoulos, Kapetanos, Julio Cesar (Tozser 90).

Levski (1) 2 *(Domovchiyski 8, Bardon 86 (pen))*
Chievo (0) 0 18,436
Levski: Petkov; Tomasic, Eromoigbe, Borimirov, Yovov (Milanov 90), Domovchiyski (Angelov E 75), Angelov S, Telkiyski (Ivanov M 83), Wagner, Bardon, Topuzakov.
Chievo: Sicignano; Mantovani, Semioli, Giunti, Zanchetta (Marcolini 62), Amauri, Lanna, Scurto, Moro, Brighi, Tiribocchi (Pellissier 68).

Lille (0) 3 *(Jovanovski 60 (og), Bastos 70 (pen), Fauvergue 72)*
Rabotnicki (0) 0 9560
Lille: Sylva; Schmitz, Cabaye, Bastos, Youla (Odemwingie 52), Fauvergue, Makoun, Tafforeau, Keita (Mirallas 76), Plestan, Lichtsteiner (Chalme 45).
Rabotnicki: Pacovski; Vajs, Jovanovski, Ilievski, Lazarevski (Stepanovski 60), Trajchov, Ignatov (Stojanov 86), Nedzipi (Jankep 66), Abrilio, Stankovski, Pejcic.

Liverpool (1) 2 *(Bellamy 32, Gonzalez 87)*
Maccabi Haifa (1) 1 *(Boccoli 29)* 40,058
Liverpool: Reina; Finnan, Riise, Xabi Alonso, Carragher, Hyypia, Pennant, Sissoko, Bellamy (Crouch 65), Gerrard (Gonzalez 86), Zenden (Luis Garcia 55).
Maccabi Haifa: Davidovich; Harazi, Anderson, Boccoli, Colautti, Masudi (Meshumar 89), Dirceu, Magrashvili, Olarra, Katan (Melikson 86), Keinan.

Salzburg (0) 1 *(Pitak 73)*
Valencia (0) 0 18,000
Salzburg: Ochs; Bodnar, Dudic, Linke, Carboni, Kovac, Zickler, Jezek (Winklhofer 78), Pitak, Janocko (Aufhauser 51), Vargas.
Valencia: Canizares; Albelda, Baraja, Angulo, Regueiro (David Villa 62), Vicente (Silva 73), David Navarro, Albiol, Curro Torres, Moretti, Morientes.

Shakhtar Donetsk (1) 1 *(Elano 39 (pen))*
Legia (0) 0 24,000
Shakhtar Donetsk: Shutkov; Rat, Lewandowski, Hubschman, Srna, Matuzalem, Fernandinho, Aghahowa (Marica 63), Tymoschuk, Elano (Jadson 57), Brandao (Bielik 80).
Legia: Fabianski; Szala, Choto, Alcantara, Guerreiro, Surma, Wlodarczyk (Radovic 74), Vukovic (Balde 83), Szalachowski, Edson, Elton (Gottwald 64).

Slovan Liberec (0) 0
Spartak Moscow (0) 0 8130
Slovan Liberec: Cech; Zapotocny, Bilek, Hodur, Pospech (Parks 81), Kostal, Janu, Singlar, Frejlach (Papousek 46), Pudil, Blazek (Holenda 52).
Spartak Moscow: Kowalewski; Shishkin, Jiranek, Stranzl, Rodriguez, Mozart, Kovac, Kalynychenko, Covalciuc, Pavlyuchenko (Boyarintsev 72), Cavenaghi (Bazhenov 87).

Standard Liege (1) 2 *(Rapaic 17, 51)*
Steaua (1) 2 *(Paraschiv 8, Marin 79)* 20,000
Standard Liege: Renard; Deflandre, Coelho, Defour (Pelaic 79), Rapaic, Sarr, Matias, Geraerts, Jovanovic, Fellaini, Sa Pinto (Bouchouari 89).
Steaua: Fernandes; Goian, Oprita (Baciu 90), Badea (Cristocea 62), Dica, Nesu, Nicolita (Bostina 79), Marin, Lovin, Paraschiv, Ghionea.

THIRD QUALIFYING ROUND SECOND LEG

Tuesday, 22 August 2006

Benfica (2) 3 *(Rui Costa 21, Nuno Gomes 45, Petit 57)*
FK Austria (0) 0 58,110
Benfica: Quim; Anderson, Luisao, Petit (Beto 74), Katsouranis, Rui Costa (Fonseca 66), Paulo Jorge (Mantorras 85), Manu, Nuno Gomes, Nelson, Ricardo Rocha.
FK Austria: Safar; Troyansky, Hill, Tokic, Wallner, Radomski, Blanchard, Ceh (Pichlmann 54), Wimmer, Papac (Schicker 29), Mila (Lasnik 46).

Maccabi Haifa (0) 1 *(Colautti 63)*
Liverpool (0) 1 *(Crouch 54)* 12,500
Maccabi Haifa: Davidovich; Harazi, Magrashvili, Olarra, Keinan (Meshumar 65), Anderson (Melikson 71), Dirceu, Boccoli, Masudi (Arbeitman 80), Colautti, Katan.
Liverpool: Reina; Finnan, Warnock (Fabio Aurelio 28), Xabi Alonso, Agger, Hyypia, Pennant (Bellamy 86), Sissoko (Gerrard 67), Crouch, Luis Garcia, Gonzalez.
In Kiev.

Osasuna (1) 1 *(Cuellar 6)*
Hamburg (0) 1 *(De Jong 74)* 19,000
Osasuna: Ricardo; Cuellar, Josetxo, Javier Flano (Valdo 80), Monreal, Raul Garcia, Punal, David Lopez, Delporte, Milosevic, Soldado (Webo 68).
Hamburg: Kirschstein; Reinhardt, Kompany (Benjamin 11), Demel, Wicky (Guerrero 66), Mahdavikia, Jarolim, Van der Vaart, De Jong, Lauth (Trochowski 79), Sanogo.

Red Star Belgrade (0) 1 *(Djokic 80)*
AC Milan (1) 2 *(Inzaghi 29, Seedorf 79)* 49,862
Red Star Belgrade: Randjelovic; Pantic (Purovic 61), Basta, Gueye, Bisevac, Kovacevic, Milovanovic (Andjelkovic 71), Georgiev, Jankovic (Perovic 53), Djokic, Zigic.
AC Milan: Dida; Cafu (Favalli 82), Costacurta, Simic, Serginho, Gattuso, Kaka, Pirlo, Seedorf, Inzaghi (Ambrosini 68), Gilardino (Borriello 88).

Valencia (3) 3 *(Morientes 13, David Villa 33, Silva 90)*
Salzburg (0) 0 48,000
Valencia: Canizares; Moretti, David Navarro, Albiol, Albelda, Edu (Marchena 88), Silva, Vicente (Gavilan 72), Angulo, Morientes (Regueiro 72), David Villa.
Salzburg: Ochs; Linke, Bodnar, Dudic, Vargas, Aufhauser, Kovac (Jezek 65), Pitak, Tiffert (Vonlanthen 57), Carboni, Orosz (Lokvenc 46).

Wednesday, 23 August 2006

AEK Athens (0) 3 *(Julio Cesar 79 (pen), 86, Liberopoulos 82)*
Hearts (0) 0 31,500
AEK Athens: Chiotis; Pautasso (Tozser 72), Cirilo, Dellas, Georgeas, Emerson, Ivic, Lagos (Lakis 54), Julio Cesar, Liberopoulos (Kampantais 84), Kapetanos.
Hearts: Gordon; Neilson, Pressley, Berra, Fyssas, Brellier■, Mikoliunas, McCann■, Cesnauskis (Wallace 81), Hartley (Jankauskas 61), Mole (Pinilla 89).

Ajax (0) 0
FC Copenhagen (0) 2 *(Silberbauer 59, Vermaelen 77 (og))* 35,617
Ajax: Stekelenburg; Heitinga, Stam, Vermaelen, Emanuelson, Maduro (Vertonghen 81), Rosales (Rosenberg 85), Babel, Huntelaar, Sneijder, Gabri (Perez 79).
FC Copenhagen: Christiansen; Jacobsen, Hangeland, Linderoth, Silberbauer (Thomassen 89), Allback, Hutchinson, Gravgaard, Bergdolmo, Kvist, Pimpong (Berglund 58).

Arsenal (0) 2 *(Ljungberg 77, Flamini 90)*
Dynamo Zagreb (1) 1 *(Eduardo da Silva 12)* 58,418
Arsenal: Almunia; Eboue, Hoyte, Flamini, Toure, Djourou, Hleb (Silva 70), Fabregas, Adebayor (Henry 65), Van Persie (Walcott 81), Ljungberg.
Dynamo Zagreb: Turina; Corluka, Cvitanovic, Mamic, Drpic, Etto (Tomic 90), Vukojevic (Ljubojevic 89), Agic (Buljat 69), Carlos, Modric, Eduardo da Silva.

Chievo (0) 2 *(Amauri 48, 81)*
Levski (1) 2 *(Telkiyski 34, Bardon 46)* 23,327
Chievo: Sicignano; Mantovani, Malago, Lanna■, Mandelli, Semioli (Luciano 72), Giunti (Marcolini 65), Zanchetta, Sammarco, Amauri, Pellissier (Tiribocchi 59).
Levski: Petkov; Tomasic, Borimirov, Telkiyski (Angelov S 76), Bardon, Milanov, Eromoigbe, Domovchiyski (Angelov E 72), Wagner■, Topuzakov, Yovov (Koprivarov 90).

Fenerbahce (1) 2 *(Appiah 36, Kerim 57)*
Dynamo Kiev (2) 2 *(Shatskikh 5, 42)* 38,793
Fenerbahce: Rustu; Umit O, Can, Onder (Mehmet 84), Appiah, Marco Aurelio, Alex, Tuncay, Kerim, Semih (Murat 64), Tumer (Ugur 76).
Dynamo Kiev: Shovkovskiy; Sablic, Correa, Rodrigo, Rotan (Verpakovskis 86), Gusev (Gavrancic 66), El Kaddouri, Yussuf, Rebrov, Shatskikh, Markovic.

Legia (1) 2 *(Wlodarczyk 19, 87)*
Shakhtar Donetsk (3) 3 *(Marica 25, 45, Fernandinho 29)* 11,000
Legia: Fabianski; Radovic, Choto, Balde, Edson, Szalachowski, Guerreiro, Surma (Burkhardt 74), Gottwald (Korzym 46), Elton (Janczyk 65), Wlodarczyk.
Shakhtar Donetsk: Shutkov; Hubschman, Tymoschuk, Fernandinho, Matuzalem (Jadson 75), Lewandowski, Brandao (Okoduwa 71), Rat, Marica (Vorobei 71), Sviderskiy, Elano.

Mlada Boleslav (0) 1 *(Palat 88)*

Galatasaray (0) 1 *(Hasan Sas 73)* 4680

Mlada Boleslav: Miller; Sevinsky, Rolko, Vaculik, Palat, Holub (Riegel 74), Matejovsky, Brezinsky, Polacek (Sedlacek 46), Pecka, Smerda (Mikolanda 68).
Galatasaray: Mondragon; Cihan, Song, Tomas, Orhan (Ugur 76), Sabri, Ayhan, Okan, Hasan Sas, Ilic (Arda 71), Hakan Sukur (Ozgurcan 84).

Rabotnicki (0) 0

Lille (1) 1 *(Audel 18)* 6000

Rabotnicki: Pacovski; Abrilio, Jeremic, Jovanovski■, Vajs (Karchev 60), Trajchov, Nedzipi, Jankep, Velkovski (Aleksovski 76), Stankovski, Pejcic.
Lille: Malicki; Lichtsteiner, Tavlaridis, Schmitz, Tafforeau, Makoun (Chalme 62), Dumont, Cabaye (Robail M 76), Mirallas, Youla, Audel.

Ruzomberok (0) 0

CSKA Moscow (2) 2 *(Daniel Carvalho 8, Vagner Love 32)* 4750

Ruzomberok: Hajduch; Sedlak (Dovicovic 70), Nezmar (Babnic 78), Zofcak, Pospisil, Laurinc, Bozok (Tomcak 70), Dvorník, Siva, Rak, Sapara.
CSKA Moscow: Akinfeev; Semberas, Ignashevich, Berezutski A, Daniel Carvalho (Olic 70), Jo, Vagner Love (Zhirkov 46), Krasic (Gusev 86), Dudu, Aldonin, Rahimic.

Spartak Moscow (1) 2 *(Mozart 23, Pavluchenko 79)*

Slovan Liberec (0) 1 *(Hodur 73 (pen))* 25,000

Spartak Moscow: Kowalewski; Stranzl, Jiranek, Kovac, Rodriguez, Shishkin, Covalciuc, Bystrov (Kalynychenko 75), Mozart, Pavluchenko, Cavenaghi (Bazhenov 87).
Slovan Liberec: Cech; Zapotocny■, Kostal, Janu (Matula 76), Singlar, Bilek, Hodur, Pospech, Frejlach (Ancic 62), Holenda (Blazek 54), Pudil.

Steaua (1) 2 *(Badea 35, 51)*

Standard Liege (1) 1 *(Jovanovic 2)* 45,000

Steaua: Fernandes; Goian, Badea (Oprita 83), Dica, Cristocea, Nesu (Bostina 88), Nicolita, Baciu, Marin, Lovin, Paraschiv (Coman 70).
Standard Liege: Renard; Deflandre (Bouchouari 77), Onyewu (Coelho 64), Defour, Rapaic, Sarr, Matias, Geraerts, Jovanovic, Fellaini, Sa Pinto■.

GROUP STAGE

GROUP A

Tuesday, 12 September 2006

Barcelona (2) 5 *(Iniesta 7, Giuly 39, Puyol 49, Eto'o 58, Ronaldinho 90)*

Levski (0) 0 62,839

Barcelona: Valdes; Belletti, Motta, Puyol, Giuly (Gudjohnsen 63), Eto'o, Ronaldinho, Van Bronckhorst, Deco, Thuram (Oleguer 80), Iniesta (Xavi 72).
Levski: Petkov; Milanov, Tomasic, Eromoigbe, Borimirov (Minev 63), Yovov (Ivanov M 70), Topuzakov, Angelov S, Telkiyski, Bardon, Angelov E (Ivanov G 46).

Chelsea (1) 2 *(Essien 24, Ballack 68 (pen))*

Werder Bremen (0) 0 32,135

Chelsea: Cech; Boulahrouz, Cole A, Makelele, Terry, Ricardo Carvalho, Essien, Lampard, Drogba (Kalou 86), Shevchenko (Cole J 81), Ballack (Mikel 90).
Werder Bremen: Reinke; Pasanen, Naldo, Wome, Baumann (Zidan 86), Fritz, Diego, Klose, Klasnic (Hugo Almeida 66), Frings, Borowski.

Wednesday, 27 September 2006

Levski (0) 1 *(Ognyanov 89)*

Chelsea (1) 3 *(Drogba 39, 52, 68)* 27,950

Levski: Petkov; Angelov S, Milanov, Tomasic, Topuzakov, Eromoigbe, Borimirov (Koprivarov 79), Telkiyski (Ivanov G 67), Wagner, Yovov, Bardon (Ognyanov 71).
Chelsea: Cech; Paulo Ferreira, Bridge, Essien, Terry, Ricardo Carvalho, Mikel (Kalou 63), Lampard, Drogba (Robben 70), Shevchenko (Wright-Phillips 83), Ballack.

Werder Bremen (0) 1 *(Puyol 56 (og))*

Barcelona (0) 1 *(Leo Messi 89)* 41,256

Werder Bremen: Wiese; Hunt (Owomoyela 90), Schulz, Naldo, Mertesacker, Baumann, Borowski, Fritz, Klose (Klasnic 90), Diego, Frings.
Barcelona: Valdes; Sylvinho (Zambrotta 83), Motta, Thuram, Puyol, Oleguer, Iniesta, Giuly (Leo Messi 65), Eto'o (Gudjohnsen 65), Ronaldinho, Deco.

Wednesday, 18 October 2006

Chelsea (0) 1 *(Drogba 47)*

Barcelona (0) 0 45,999

Chelsea: Hilario; Boulahrouz, Cole A, Makelele, Terry, Ricardo Carvalho, Essien, Lampard, Drogba (Kalou 90), Shevchenko (Robben 77), Ballack.
Barcelona: Valdes; Marquez, Puyol (Oleguer 74), Xavi, Gudjohnsen (Giuly 60), Zambrotta, Edmilson, Leo Messi, Ronaldinho, Deco, Van Bronckhorst (Iniesta 57).

Werder Bremen (1) 2 *(Naldo 45, Diego 73)*

Levski (0) 0 36,246

Werder Bremen: Wiese; Naldo, Wome (Klasnic 46), Vranjes (Andreasen 73), Fritz, Diego, Hunt, Frings, Schulz, Klose (Hugo Almeida 82), Mertesacker.
Levski: Petkov; Angelov S, Telkiyski (Koprivorov 79), Tomasic, Yovov (Dimitrov 79), Eromoigbe, Borimirov, Domovchiyski (Ivanov M 64), Topuzakov, Wagner, Bardon.

Tuesday, 31 October 2006

Barcelona (1) 2 *(Deco 3, Gudjohnsen 58)*

Chelsea (0) 2 *(Lampard 52, Drogba 90)* 90,199

Barcelona: Valdes; Van Bronckhorst, Motta (Edmilson 57), Marquez, Puyol, Xavi (Iniesta 83), Gudjohnsen (Giuly 77), Deco, Leo Messi, Zambrotta, Ronaldinho.
Chelsea: Hilario; Boulahrouz (Cole J 75), Cole A, Makelele, Terry, Ricardo Carvalho, Essien, Lampard, Drogba, Ballack (Paulo Ferreira 90), Robben (Kalou 72).

Levski (0) 0

Werder Bremen (3) 3 *(Mihaylov 33 (og), Baumann 35, Frings 37)* 25,862

Levski: Mihaylov (Mitrev 46); Angelov S, Milanov, Tomasic (Angelov E 57), Telkiyski (Dimitrov 69), Eromoigbe, Borimirov, Wagner, Bardon, Yovov, Topuzakov.
Werder Bremen: Wiese; Hunt (Klasnic 74), Mertesacker, Naldo, Wome (Pasanen 85), Baumann (Andreasen 78), Vranjes, Fritz, Klose, Diego, Frings.

Wednesday, 22 November 2006

Levski (0) 0

Barcelona (1) 2 *(Giuly 5, Iniesta 65)* 42,000

Levski: Petkov; Milanov, Tomasic, Eromoigbe, Borimirov, Yovov (Ognyanov 73), Topuzakov, Domovchiyski (Ivanov G 57), Angelov S (Telkiyski 58), Wagner, Bardon.
Barcelona: Valdes; Zambrotta, Motta, Marquez (Oleguer 63), Puyol, Sylvinho, Gudjohnsen, Giuly (Xavi 58), Deco, Ronaldinho, Iniesta (Ezquerro 81).

Werder Bremen (1) 1 *(Mertesacker 27)*

Chelsea (0) 0 36,908

Werder Bremen: Wiese; Naldo, Wome, Fritz, Diego, Jensen (Hunt 78), Frings, Mertesacker, Borowski, Hugo Almeida (Schulz 87), Klose (Klasnic 90).
Chelsea: Cudicini; Geremi, Cole A, Makelele, Terry, Boulahrouz, Essien, Mikel (Robben 59), Drogba (Shevchenko 59), Cole J, Ballack (Wright-Phillips 77).

Tuesday, 5 December 2006

Barcelona (2) 2 *(Ronaldinho 13, Gudjohnsen 18)*
Werder Bremen (0) 0 95,824
Barcelona: Valdes; Zambrotta, Motta (Thuram 62), Marquez, Puyol, Iniesta (Xavi 73), Gudjohnsen, Deco, Giuly (Ezquerro 85), Ronaldinho, Van Bronckhorst.
Werder Bremen: Wiese; Naldo, Wome (Hunt 80), Fritz, Diego, Klose, Jensen, Frings, Hugo Almeida (Klasnic 71), Borowski, Mertesacker.

Chelsea (1) 2 *(Shevchenko 27, Wright-Phillips 83)*
Levski (0) 0 33,358
Chelsea: Hilario; Boulahrouz, Bridge, Essien, Paulo Ferreira (Diarra 58), Ricardo Carvalho, Ballack, Lampard, Drogba, Shevchenko (Kalou 69), Robben (Wright-Phillips 69).
Levski: Mitrev; Domovchiyski (Ivanov G 75), Milanov, Tomasic, Dimitrov (Baltanov 59), Eromoigbe, Borimirov, Angelov S, Bardon, Yovov (Koprivarov 70), Topuzakov.

Group A Final Table	P	W	D	L	F	A	Pts
Chelsea	6	4	1	1	10	4	13
Barcelona	6	3	2	1	12	4	11
Werder Bremen	6	3	1	2	7	5	10
Levski	6	0	0	6	1	17	0

GROUP B

Tuesday, 12 September 2006

Bayern Munich (0) 4 *(Pizarro 48, Santa Cruz 52, Schweinsteiger 71, Salihamidzic 84)*
Spartak Moscow (0) 0 63,000
Bayern Munich: Kahn; Sagnol, Lahm, Van Buyten, Lucio, Van Bommel (Scholl 74), Schweinsteiger, Santa Cruz (Karimi 81), Podolski, Pizarro (Salihamidzic 70), Hargreaves.
Spartak Moscow: Kowalewski; Geder, Stranzl, Titov, Pavlyuchenko, Jiranek (Shishkin 31), Kovac (Bazhenov 62), Rodriguez, Bystrov, Mozart, Covalciuc (Torbinsky 77).

Sporting Lisbon (0) 1 *(Caneira 64)*
Internazionale (0) 0 30,222
Sporting Lisbon: Ricardo; Anderson Polga, Caneira, Tonel, Abel, Nani (Tello 83), Miguel Veloso, Joao Moutinho, Romagnoli (Alecsandro 66), Yannick, Liedson.
Internazionale: Toldo; Cordoba, Samuel, Grosso (Zanetti J 80), Maicon, Stankovic, Figo (Gonzalez 66), Vieira■, Dacourt, Ibrahimovic, Adriano (Crespo 71).

Wednesday, 27 September 2006

Internazionale (0) 0
Bayern Munich (0) 2 *(Pizarro 81, Podolski 90)* 42,000
Internazionale: Julio Cesar; Cordoba, Maicon, Zanetti J, Stankovic (Solari 77), Materazzi, Figo (Gonzalez 67), Dacourt, Ibrahimovic■, Crespo (Adriano 77), Grosso■.
Bayern Munich: Kahn; Sagnol, Lucio, Van Bommel, Van Buyten, Lahm, Schweinsteiger, Ottl, Makaay (Santa Cruz 82), Pizarro (Podolski 69), Salihamidzic (Scholl 70).

Spartak Moscow (1) 1 *(Boyarintsev 5)*
Sporting Lisbon (0) 1 *(Nani 59)* 45,000
Spartak Moscow: Kowalewski; Geder, Stranzl, Kovac, Bystrov, Mozart (Rebko 80), Shishkin, Titov, Jiranek, Boyarintsev, Pavlyuchenko (Owusu-Abeyie 80).
Sporting Lisbon: Ricardo; Yannick (Joao Alves 82), Miguel Veloso, Joao Moutinho, Liedson, Anderson Polga, Tello, Caneira, Tonel (Paredes 58), Miguel Garcia (Alecsandro 46), Nani.

Wednesday, 18 October 2006

Internazionale (2) 2 *(Cruz 1, 9)*
Spartak Moscow (0) 1 *(Pavlyuchenko 54)* 26,000
Internazionale: Julio Cesar; Cordoba, Zanetti J, Stankovic, Maicon, Vieira, Dacourt, Materazzi, Figo (Adriano 69), Cruz (Samuel 90), Recoba (Burdisso 58).
Spartak Moscow: Kowalewski; Geder, Boyarintsev, Titov, Pavlyuchenko, Jiranek, Kovac, Rodriguez, Bystrov (Kalynychenko 75), Mozart (Owusu-Abeyie 46), Shishkin.

Sporting Lisbon (0) 0
Bayern Munich (1) 1 *(Schweinsteiger 19)* 37,379
Sporting Lisbon: Ricardo; Anderson Polga, Carlos Martins (Yannick 46), Tello, Caneira, Tonel, Nani, Alecsandro (Bueno 57), Miguel Veloso (Paredes 70), Joao Moutinho, Liedson.
Bayern Munich: Kahn; Sagnol, Lucio, Pizarro, Van Buyten, Lahm, Van Bommel, Ottl (Demichelis 46), Schweinsteiger■, Santa Cruz (Salihamidzic 50), Podolski (Dos Santos 65).

Tuesday, 31 October 2006

Bayern Munich (0) 0
Sporting Lisbon (0) 0 66,000
Bayern Munich: Kahn; Sagnol, Lahm, Lell (Dos Santos 46), Van Buyten, Demichelis, Ottl, Pizarro, Makaay, Santa Cruz (Karimi 80), Salihamidzic.
Sporting Lisbon: Ricardo; Anderson Polga, Carlos Martins (Nani 46), Tello, Caneira, Tonel, Yannick (Alecsandro 78), Custodio, Joao Moutinho, Liedson, Paredes (Farnerud P 52).

Spartak Moscow (0) 0
Internazionale (1) 1 *(Cruz 1)* 55,000
Spartak Moscow: Kowalewski; Stranzl, Boyarintsev, Titov, Pavlyuchenko, Jiranek, Kovac, Rodriguez (Cavenaghi 46), Bystrov (Covalciuc 54), Mozart, Shishkin.
Internazionale: Julio Cesar; Cordoba, Materazzi, Zanetti J, Stankovic, Burdisso, Figo (Grosso 72), Ibrahimovic, Cruz (Solari 84), Dacourt, Maicon.

Wednesday, 22 November 2006

Internazionale (1) 1 *(Crespo 36)*
Sporting Lisbon (0) 0 46,843
Internazionale: Julio Cesar; Cordoba, Zanetti J, Stankovic, Materazzi, Grosso (Cambiasso 82), Maicon, Vieira, Ibrahimovic, Crespo, Dacourt (Burdisso 90).
Sporting Lisbon: Ricardo; Anderson Polga, Tello, Caneira (Abel 15) (Miguel Veloso 27), Tonel, Nani, Alecsandro, Farnerud P (Carlos Martins 57), Custodio, Joao Moutinho, Paredes.

Spartak Moscow (1) 2 *(Kalynychenko 16, Kovac 72)*
Bayern Munich (2) 2 *(Pizarro 22, 39)* 33,500
Spartak Moscow: Zuev; Geder (Rebko 87), Stranzl, Titov, Pavlyuchenko, Jiranek, Kovac, Bystrov, Mozart, Kalynychenko, Shishkin.
Bayern Munich: Kahn; Sagnol, Ottl, Van Bommel, Van Buyten, Demichelis, Pizarro, Lell, Makaay, Salihamidzic (Scholl 84), Schweinsteiger.

Tuesday, 5 December 2006

Bayern Munich (0) 1 *(Makaay 62)*
Internazionale (0) 1 *(Vieira 90)* 66,000
Bayern Munich: Kahn; Sagnol, Lucio, Van Bommel (Demichelis 72), Van Buyten, Lahm, Pizarro, Salihamidzic (Deisler 79), Ottl, Makaay (Santa Cruz 83), Schweinsteiger.
Internazionale: Toldo; Samuel, Andreolli, Zanetti J, Maicon, Maxwell, Figo (Recoba 70), Ibrahimovic (Crespo 46), Vieira, Solari (Grosso 83), Gonzalez.

Sporting Lisbon (1) 1 *(Bueno 31)*
Spartak Moscow (2) 3 *(Pavlyuchenko 7, Kalynychenko 16, Boyarintsev 89)* 48,000
Sporting Lisbon: Ricardo; Anderson Polga, Ronny, Tello, Tonel, Miguel Garcia (Miguel Veloso 28), Yannick, Joao Moutinho, Liedson, Paredes (Nani 60), Bueno (Alecsandro 68).
Spartak Moscow: Zuev; Geder, Stranzl, Titov, Pavlyuchenko (Owusu-Abeyie 74), Jiranek, Kovac, Bystrov (Dzyuba 90), Mozart, Kalynychenko (Boyarintsev 64), Shishkin.

Group B Final Table	P	W	D	L	F	A	Pts
Bayern Munich	6	3	3	0	10	3	12
Internazionale	6	3	1	2	5	5	10
Spartak Moscow	6	1	2	3	7	11	5
Sporting Lisbon	6	1	2	3	3	6	5

GROUP C

Tuesday, 12 September 2006

Galatasaray (0) 0

Bordeaux (0) 0 45,514

Galatasaray: Mondragon; Sabri, Song, Tomas, Ferhat, Hasan Sas (Cihan 76), Inamoto, Ilic (Mehmet 76), Arda, Umit K (Hasan 61), Necati.
Bordeaux: Rame; Jurietti, Jemmali, Planus, Marange, Faubert, Ducasse, Micoud, Wendel, Darcheville (Laslandes 85), Chamakh (Perea 85).

PSV Eindhoven (0) 0

Liverpool (0) 0 33,500

PSV Eindhoven: Gomes; Kromkamp, Alex, Reiziger, Salcido, Simons, Mendez, Afellay (Vayrynen 74), Culina (Aissati 63), Farfan, Kone.
Liverpool: Reina; Finnan, Fabio Aurelio (Gonzalez 82), Sissoko (Xabi Alonso 62), Carragher, Agger, Pennant, Zenden, Bellamy (Gerrard 72), Kuyt, Warnock.

Wednesday, 27 September 2006

Bordeaux (0) 0

PSV Eindhoven (0) 1 *(Vayrynen 65)* 22,006

Bordeaux: Rame; Mavuba, Henrique, Fernando, Jurietti (Dalmat 74), Jemmali (Laslandes 89), Micoud (Chamakh 46), Wendel, Faubert, Darcheville, Enakarhire.
PSV Eindhoven: Gomes; Kromkamp, Salcido, Alex, Tardelli (Beerens 85), Simons, Vayrynen (Addo 79), Lamey■, Afellay (Aissati 72), Kone, Mendez.

Liverpool (2) 3 *(Crouch 9, 52, Luis Garcia 14)*

Galatasaray (0) 2 *(Umit K 59, 65)* 41,976

Liverpool: Reina; Finnan, Fabio Aurelio, Xabi Alonso, Carragher, Agger, Pennant (Sissoko 78), Luis Garcia, Crouch (Bellamy 90), Kuyt (Gonzalez 66), Gerrard.
Galatasaray: Mondragon; Tomas, Arda (Carrusca 86), Song, Orhan, Mehmet (Hasan Sas 46), Ayhan, Cihan (Umit K 46), Ilic, Sabri, Hakan Sukur.

Wednesday, 18 October 2006

Bordeaux (0) 0

Liverpool (0) 1 *(Crouch 58)* 31,471

Bordeaux: Rame; Henrique, Fernando, Jurietti, Laslandes (Chamakh 63), Alonso (Faubert 63), Darcheville (Perea 71), Jemmali, Micoud, Wendel, Mavuba.
Liverpool: Reina; Finnan, Riise, Xabi Alonso, Carragher, Hyypia, Luis Garcia, Zenden, Crouch (Kuyt 65), Bellamy (Warnock 87), Gonzalez (Sissoko 68).

Galatasaray (1) 1 *(Ilic 19)*

PSV Eindhoven (0) 2 *(Kromkamp 59, Kone 72)* 54,425

Galatasaray: Mondragon; Tomas, Song, Orhan, Ayhan, Ilic (Necati 70), Inamoto, Aydin (Cihan 67), Sabri, Arda, Umit K (Hakan Sukur 70).
PSV Eindhoven: Gomes; Kromkamp, Reiziger, Alex, Simons, Cocu, Kone, Mendez (Vayrynen 62), Culina (Aissati 90), Farfan, Salcido.

Tuesday, 31 October 2006

Liverpool (1) 3 *(Luis Garcia 23, 76, Gerrard 72)*

Bordeaux (0) 0 41,978

Liverpool: Reina; Finnan, Riise, Xabi Alonso (Zenden 58), Carragher, Hyypia, Gerrard, Sissoko, Crouch (Pennant 73), Kuyt, Luis Garcia (Fowler 78).
Bordeaux: Rame; Cid, Chamakh (Perea 12), Faubert, Fernando■, Jemmali, Micoud (Mavuba 75), Wendel, Darcheville (Obertan 60), Ducasse, Marange.

PSV Eindhoven (0) 2 *(Simons 59, Kone 84)*

Galatasaray (0) 0 38,000

PSV Eindhoven: Gomes; Kromkamp (Culina 46), Afellay (Vayrynen 76), Alex, Salcido, Simons, Da Costa, Cocu, Farfan, Kone (Aissati 86), Mendez.
Galatasaray: Mondragon; Tomas■, Song, Orhan, Ayhan, Ilic (Necati 70), Sabri, Umit K (Hakan Sukur 79), Inamoto, Arda (Cihan 66), Hasan Sas.

Wednesday, 22 November 2006

Bordeaux (1) 3 *(Alonso 22, Laslandes 47, Faubert 50)*

Galatasaray (0) 1 *(Inamoto 73)* 22,834

Bordeaux: Rame; Jurietti, Laslandes, Alonso, Darcheville (Obertan 46), Micoud (Dalmat 79), Wendel (Ducasse 68), Faubert, Enakarhire, Mavuba, Planus.
Galatasaray: Mondragon; Song, Ayhan, Tolga, Ilic (Umit K 46), Inamoto, Seyhan, Sabri, Arda■, Hakan Sukur (Mehmet 63), Hasan Sas (Ergun 69).

Liverpool (0) 2 *(Gerrard 65, Crouch 89)*

PSV Eindhoven (0) 0 41,948

Liverpool: Reina; Finnan, Riise, Xabi Alonso (Zenden 21), Carragher, Agger, Pennant (Bellamy 79), Gerrard, Crouch, Kuyt, Gonzalez (Luis Garcia 36).
PSV Eindhoven: Gomes; Kromkamp, Afellay, Alex, Salcido, Simons, Da Costa, Farfan, Feher (Tardelli 68), Kone, Mendez (Beerens 81).

Tuesday, 5 December 2006

Galatasaray (2) 3 *(Necati 24, Okan 28, Ilic 79)*

Liverpool (1) 2 *(Fowler 22, 90)* 23,000

Galatasaray: Mondragon; Tomas, Okan, Necati (Ilic 46), Carrusca (Mehmet 75), Cihan, Emre (Tolga 46), Inamoto, Sabri, Ergun, Umit K.
Liverpool: Dudek; Paletta, Riise, Xabi Alonso (Roque 84), Carragher, Agger, Pennant, Guthrie (Luis Garcia 66), Fowler, Bellamy (Crouch 74), Peltier.

PSV Eindhoven (0) 1 *(Alex 87)*

Bordeaux (3) 3 *(Faubert 7, Dalmat 25, Darcheville 27)* 29,000

PSV Eindhoven: Gomes; Kromkamp, Reiziger, Alex, Simons, Cocu, Mendez, Aissati (Culina 62), Farfan, Addo (Kluivert 46), Tardelli (Kone 46).
Bordeaux: Rame; Cid, Mavuba, Marange, Enakarhire, Dalmat (Obertan 80), Ducasse, Faubert, Jemmali, Darcheville (Perea 70), Laslandes.

Group C Final Table	*P*	*W*	*D*	*L*	*F*	*A*	*Pts*
Liverpool	6	4	1	1	11	5	13
PSV Eindhoven	6	3	1	2	6	6	10
Bordeaux	6	2	1	3	6	7	7
Galatasaray	6	1	1	4	7	12	4

GROUP D

Tuesday, 12 September 2006

Olympiakos (1) 2 *(Konstantinou M 28, Castillo 66)*

Valencia (2) 4 *(Morientes 34, 39, 90, Albiol 85)* 34,500

Olympiakos: Nikopolidis; Zewlakow (Pantos 46), Anatolakis (Julio Cesar 69), Ouaddou, Domi, Kafes, Stoltidis, Rivaldo, Castillo, Konstantinou M, Djordjevic.
Valencia: Canizares; Miguel, Ayala, Albiol, Moretti, Angulo, Edu, Marchena, Gavilan (Silva 72), Morientes (Jorge Lopez 90), David Villa (Regueiro 81).

Roma (0) 4 *(Taddei 67, Totti 76, De Rossi 79, Pizarro 89)*

Shakhtar Donetsk (0) 0 40,000

Roma: Doni; Panucci, Ferrari, Chivu, Tonetto, De Rossi, Aquilani (Pizarro 62), Taddei, Perrotta, Mancini (Cassetti 87), Totti (Montella 80).
Shakhtar Donetsk: Shutkov; Srna, Hubschman, Lewandowski, Rat, Matuzalem (Gay 72) (Jadson 81), Tymoschuk, Duljaj, Marica, Elano, Brandao (Aghahowa 63).

Wednesday, 27 September 2006

Shakhtar Donetsk (1) 2 *(Matuzalem 34, Marica 70)*

Olympiakos (1) 2 *(Konstantinou M 24, Castillo 68)* 25,500

Shakhtar Donetsk: Shust; Hubschman, Tymoschuk, Rat, Brandao (Vorobei 76), Srna, Fernandinho, Marica (Aghahowa 89), Matuzalem, Elano (Jadson 76), Lewandowski.
Olympiakos: Nikopolidis; Julio Cesar, Stoltidis, Castillo, Maric, Djordjevic, Kostoulas, Georgatos, Konstantinou M (Okkas 90), Anatolakis (Patsatzoglou 46), Pantos (Rivaldo 85).

Valencia (2) 2 *(Angulo 13, David Villa 29)*
Roma (1) 1 *(Totti 18 (pen))* 48,000
Valencia: Canizares; Miguel, Ayala, Albelda, Villa (David Silva 72), Angulo, Vicente (Gavilan 90), Albiol, Edu, Moretti, Morientes (Regueiro 87).
Roma: Doni; Panucci, Cassetti (Okaka Chuka 64), Tonetto, Ferrari, Perrotta, De Rossi, Chivu, Totti, Aquilani (Montella 46), Pizarro.

Wednesday, 18 October 2006

Olympiakos (0) 0
Roma (0) 1 *(Perrotta 76)* 33,000
Olympiakos: Nikopolidis; Kafes (Maric 59), Stoltidis, Castillo, Rivaldo (Borja 83), Djordjevic (Okkas 70), Zewlakow, Georgatos, Konstantinou M, Anatolakis, Julio Cesar.
Roma: Doni; Panucci, Taddei (Defendi 90), Chivu, Faty (Aquilani 77), Ferrari, Tonetto, Cassetti (Rosi 66), De Rossi, Totti, Perrotta.

Valencia (2) 2 *(David Villa 31, 45)*
Shakhtar Donetsk (0) 0 27,000
Valencia: Canizares; Miguel, Albelda, Regueiro (Gavilan 64), Joaquin, David Navarro, Albiol, Edu (Lopez 53), Moretti, Morientes, David Villa (Silva 77).
Shakhtar Donetsk: Pletikosa; Tymoschuk, Fernandinho (Vorobei 83), Leonardo, Matuzalem, Aghahowa (Brandao 46), Rat, Chygrynskiy, Marica, Sviderskiy■, Jadson (Hubschman 46).

Tuesday, 31 October 2006

Roma (0) 1 *(Totti 66)*
Olympiakos (1) 1 *(Julio Cesar 19)* 20,000
Roma: Doni; Panucci, Chivu, Ferrari (Perrotta 46), Mexes, De Rossi, Pizarro, Aquilani (Vucinic 63), Tonetto, Totti, Taddei.
Olympiakos: Nikopolidis; Patsatzoglou (Anatolakis 65), Domi, Julio Cesar, Kostoulas, Stoltidis, Zewlakow, Maric (Kafes 90), Djordjevic (Borja 86), Rivaldo, Konstantinou M.

Shakhtar Donetsk (2) 2 *(Jadson 2, Fernandinho 28)*
Valencia (1) 2 *(Morientes 18, Ayala 68)* 24,500
Shakhtar Donetsk: Shust; Hubschman, Fernandinho (Duljaj 89), Matuzalem, Aghahowa, Lewandowski, Brandao (Marica 75), Rat, Chygrynskiy, Srna, Jadson.
Valencia: Canizares; Miguel, David Navarro (Hugo Viana 87), Ayala, Albiol, Silva, David Villa (Regueiro 90), Edu, Morientes (Joaquin 77), Angulo, Moretti.

Wednesday, 22 November 2006

Shakhtar Donetsk (0) 1 *(Marica 61)*
Roma (0) 0 18,673
Shakhtar Donetsk: Shust; Tymoschuk, Kucher, Duljaj, Fernandinho (Gay 90), Brandao, Rat, Chygrynskiy, Marica (Aghahowa 75), Srna, Jadson (Elano 81).
Roma: Doni; Panucci, Mancini (Vucinic 78), Cassetti, Mexes, De Rossi, Perrotta, Ferrari (Pizarro 69), Aquilani (Montella 78), Totti, Taddei.

Valencia (1) 2 *(Angulo 45, Morientes 46)*
Olympiakos (0) 0 29,500
Valencia: Canizares; Miguel, Albiol, Ayala, Joaquin, Curro Torres, Pallardo, David Villa (Morientes 22), Baraja (Hugo Viana 86), Angulo (Tavano 75), Silva.
Olympiakos: Nikopolidis; Stoltidis (Babangida 62), Castillo (Borja 70), Okkas, Djordjevic, Zewlakow, Kostoulas, Konstantinou M (Maric 17), Pantos, Rivaldo, Julio Cesar.

Tuesday, 5 December 2006

Olympiakos (0) 1 *(Castillo 54)*
Shakhtar Donetsk (1) 1 *(Matuzalem 27)* 27,500
Olympiakos: Nikopolidis; Domi (Georgatos 83), Stoltidis, Castillo, Maric M, Rivaldo, Djordjevic, Zewlakow, Pantos (Konstantinou M 75), Babangida (Borja 83), Julio Cesar.
Shakhtar Donetsk: Shust; Tymoschuk, Kucher, Fernandinho (Elano 81), Matuzalem (Duljaj 77), Brandao, Rat■, Chygrynskiy, Marica (Aghahowa 66), Srna, Jadson.

Roma (1) 1 *(Panucci 13)*
Valencia (0) 0 45,000
Roma: Doni; Panucci, Mexes, Taddei, Chivu, De Rossi (Perrotta 75), Virga (Rosi 83), Tonetto, Vucinic (Okaka Chuka 90), Mancini, Cassetti.
Valencia: Butelle; Tavano, Joaquin, Hugo Viana, David Navarro, Jorge Lopez (Romero 74), Albiol, Curro Torres, Cerrajeria, Niguez (Insa 27), Pallardo (Corcoles 90).

Group D Final Table	P	W	D	L	F	A	Pts
Valencia	6	4	1	1	12	6	13
Roma	6	3	1	2	8	4	10
Shakhtar Donetsk	6	1	3	2	6	11	6
Olympiakos	6	0	3	3	6	11	3

GROUP E

Wednesday, 13 September 2006

Dynamo Kiev (1) 1 *(Rebrov 16)*
Steaua (3) 4 *(Ghionea 3, Badea 24, Dica 43, 79)* 27,000
Dynamo Kiev: Shovkovskiy; Markovic (Moreno 61), Rodolfo, Rodrigo, Nesmachniy, Yussuf, Correa (Belkevich 59), Diogo Rincon, Gusev, Shatskikh, Rebrov (Otalvaro 73).
Steaua: Fernandes; Goian, Saban, Ghionea, Nesu, Paraschiv, Lovin, Cristocea (Oprita 74), Dica (Petre 82), Nicolita, Badea (Thereau 70).

Lyon (2) 2 *(Fred 11, Tiago 31)*
Real Madrid (0) 0 40,013
Lyon: Coupet; Reveillere, Cris, Muller, Abidal, Govou (Clerc 82), Tiago, Toulalan, Juninho Pernambucano (Kallstrom 73), Malouda, Fred (Wiltord 78).
Real Madrid: Casillas; Cicinho, Roberto Carlos, Emerson, Cannavaro, Sergio Ramos, Diarra, Beckham (Guti 55), Van Nistelrooy, Raul (Robinho 69), Cassano (Reyes 46).

Tuesday, 26 September 2006

Real Madrid (3) 5 *(Van Nistelrooy 20, 70 (pen), Raul 27, 61, Reyes 45)*
Dynamo Kiev (0) 1 *(Milevski 47)* 68,000
Real Madrid: Casillas; Sergio Ramos, Roberto Carlos, Diarra, Cannavaro, Emerson, Reyes (Beckham 46), Guti, Van Nistelrooy (Ronaldo 72), Raul (Robinho 84), Mejia.
Dynamo Kiev: Shovkovskiy■; Gusev, Nesmachniy, Yussuf, Sabljic, Gavrancic, Diogo Rincon (Aliyev 81), Correa (Mikhalik 74), Milevski, Shatskikh, Belkevich (Rybka 70).

Steaua (0) 0
Lyon (1) 3 *(Fred 43, Tiago 55, Benzema 89)* 26,500
Steaua: Fernandes; Goian, Badea, Dica, Bostina (Oprita 55), Nesu, Nicolita, Marin, Lovin (Thereau 76), Paraschiv (Petre 57), Ghionea.
Lyon: Coupet; Clerc, Cris, Muller, Toulalan, Tiago (Kallstrom 82), Juninho Pernambucano, Fred (Benzema 85), Abidal (Reveillere 76), Wiltord, Malouda.

Tuesday, 17 October 2006

Dynamo Kiev (0) 0
Lyon (2) 3 *(Juninho Pernambucano 31, Kallstrom 38, Malouda 50)* 24,000
Dynamo Kiev: Lutsenko; Rodolfo, Rebrov (Shatskikh 46), Correa (Gusev 46), Diogo Rincon, Mikhalik, Milevski (Kleber 85), El Kaddouri, Gavrancic, Yussuf, Markovic.
Lyon: Vercoutre; Clerc, Cris, Kallstrom, Juninho Pernambucano (Toulalan 58), Malouda, Fred, Diarra (Tiago 80), Abidal (Reveillere 69), Wiltord, Squillaci.

Steaua (0) 1 *(Badea 64)*
Real Madrid (2) 4 *(Sergio Ramos 9, Raul 34, Robinho 56, Van Nistelrooy 76)* 27,063
Steaua: Fernandes; Goian, Badea, Dica, Bostina, Nicolita, Marin, Lovin (Petre 62), Paraschiv (Oprita 78), Saban (Thereau 59), Ghionea.
Real Madrid: Casillas; Sergio Ramos, Roberto Carlos, Diarra, Cannavaro, Guti (Beckham 71), Emerson, Raul, Van Nistelrooy (Ronaldo 78), Robinho, Helguera.

Wednesday, 1 November 2006

Lyon (1) 1 *(Benzema 14)*

Dynamo Kiev (0) 0 40,520

Lyon: Coupet; Clerc, Cris, Gouvou (Diarra 88), Abidal, Toulalan, Malouda, Juninho Pernambucano (Kallstrom 79), Squillaci, Tiago, Benzema (Wiltord 75).
Dynamo Kiev: Shovkovskiy; Rodolfo, Rebrov (Shatskikh 66), Kleber, Cernat (Belkevich 77), Mikhalik, Gusev, Milevski, El Kaddouri, Gavrancic (Rodrigo 46), Yussuf.

Real Madrid (0) 1 *(Nicolita 70 (og))*

Steaua (0) 0 69,000

Real Madrid: Casillas; Helguera, Roberto Carlos, Sergio Ramos, Cannavaro, Diarra (Beckham 59), Raul, Emerson, Guti, Van Nistelrooy (Ronaldo 74), Robinho (Reyes 87).
Steaua: Cernea; Goian, Oprita (Coman 84), Petre, Badea (Lovin 79), Dica, Nicolita, Marin, Paraschiv (Thereau 79), Ghionea, Stancu.

Tuesday, 21 November 2006

Real Madrid (1) 2 *(Diarra 39, Van Nistelrooy 83)*

Lyon (2) 2 *(Carew 11, Malouda 31)* 78,677

Real Madrid: Casillas; Helguera, Roberto Carlos, Sergio Ramos, Cannavaro, Diarra, Emerson (Cassano 76), Guti (Reyes 21), Van Nistelrooy, Raul, Robinho.
Lyon: Coupet; Clerc, Cris, Abidal, Toulalan (Diarra 90), Squillaci, Reveillere, Tiago, Juninho Pernambucano, Carew, Malouda.

Steaua (0) 1 *(Dica 69)*

Dynamo Kiev (1) 1 *(Cernat 29)* 20,000

Steaua: Cernea; Goian, Oprita (Cristocea 55), Petre, Dica (Lovin 90), Nicolita, Marin, Thereau, Paraschiv (Radoi 66), Ghionea, Stancu.
Dynamo Kiev: Shovkovskiy; El Kaddouri, Gusev, Yussuf, Rodrigo, Markovic, Belkevich, Kleber (Milevskiy 67), Cernat (Diogo Rincon 78), Shatskikh, Rodolfo (Gavrancic 46).

Wednesday, 6 December 2006

Dynamo Kiev (2) 2 *(Shatskikh 13, 27)*

Real Madrid (0) 2 *(Ronaldo 86, 88 (pen))* 33,000

Dynamo Kiev: Shovkovskiy; Rodolfo (Mandzyuk 34), Belkevich, Shatskikh, Mikhalik, Gusev, Milevskiy (Rotan 85), Nesmachniy, Yussuf, Rodrigo, Markovic.
Real Madrid: Diego Lopez; Michel Salgado, Roberto Carlos, De La Red (Javi Garcia 70), Nieto (Valero 74), Diarra, Beckham, Mejia, Torres, Ronaldo, Cassano.

Lyon (1) 1 *(Diarra 12)*

Steaua (1) 1 *(Dica 2)* 39,531

Lyon: Coupet; Muller, Cacapa, Kallstrom, Carew (Wiltord 65), Reveillere, Govou (Remy 80), Diarra, Ben Arfa, Tiago (Toulalan 65), Berthod.
Steaua: Cernea; Goian, Radoi (Petre 78), Dica, Cristocea (Oprita 82), Nicolita, Marin, Thereau (Badea 73), Paraschiv, Ghionea, Stancu.

Group E Final Table	P	W	D	L	F	A	Pts
Lyon	6	4	2	0	12	3	14
Real Madrid	6	3	2	1	14	8	11
Steaua	6	1	2	3	7	11	5
Dynamo Kiev	6	0	2	4	5	16	2

GROUP F

Wednesday, 13 September 2006

FC Copenhagen (0) 0

Benfica (0) 0 40,085

FC Copenhagen: Christiansen; Jacobsen, Hangeland, Gravgaard, Bergdolmo, Norregaard, Linderoth, Silberbauer, Gronkjaer (Kvist 44), Hutchinson, Berglund (Pimpong 74).
Benfica: Quim; Luisao, Leo, Alcides, Ricardo Rocha, Simao Sabrosa (Manu 81), Petit, Katsouranis, Nuno Assis, Paulo Jorge, Nuno Gomes (Kikin 89).

Manchester United (2) 3 *(Saha 30 (pen), 40, Solskjaer 47)*

Celtic (2) 2 *(Vennegoor of Hesselink 21, Nakamura 43)* 74,031

Manchester United: Van der Sar; Neville, Silvestre, Carrick, Ferdinand, Brown, Fletcher, Scholes (O'Shea 80), Saha, Rooney (Richardson 86), Giggs (Solskjaer 33).
Celtic: Boruc; Wilson (Telfer 52), Naylor, Nakamura, McManus, Caldwell, Lennon, Gravesen, McGeady (Maloney 70), Vennegoor of Hesselink, Jarosik (Miller 56).

Tuesday, 26 September 2006

Benfica (0) 0

Manchester United (0) 1 *(Saha 60)* 61,000

Benfica: Quim; Anderson (Mantorras 82), Alcides, Luisao, Leo, Petit, Simao Sabrosa, Katsouranis, Nuno Gomes, Karagounis (Nuno Assis 62), Paulo Jorge (Miccoli 65).
Manchester United: Van der Sar; Neville, Heinze, Carrick, Ferdinand, Vidic, Ronaldo, Scholes, Saha (Smith 85), Rooney (Fletcher 85), O'Shea.

Celtic (1) 1 *(Miller 36 (pen))*

FC Copenhagen (0) 0 57,598

Celtic: Boruc; Telfer, Naylor, Gravesen, Caldwell, Nakamura, Zurawski (Beattie 73), Lennon, Miller (Maloney 82), McGeady (Pearson 88), McManus.
FC Copenhagen: Christiansen; Jacobsen, Bergdolmo (Thomassen 75), Norregaard, Hangeland, Linderoth, Hutchinson, Silberbauer, Berglund (Kvist 55), Gravgaard, Allback.

Tuesday, 17 October 2006

Celtic (0) 3 *(Miller 56, 66, Pearson 90)*

Benfica (0) 0 58,313

Celtic: Boruc; Telfer, Naylor, Lennon, Caldwell, Sno (Pearson 88), Zurawski (Jarosik 84), Nakamura, Miller, Maloney, McManus.
Benfica: Quim; Nuno Assis, Ricardo Rocha, Luisao, Leo, Petit, Katsouranis (Nelson 72), Alcides, Simao Sabrosa, Nuno Gomes (Kikin 78), Miccoli.

Manchester United (1) 3 *(Scholes 39, O'Shea 46, Richardson 83)*

FC Copenhagen (0) 0 72,020

Manchester United: Van der Sar; O'Shea, Evra, Carrick (Solskjaer 60), Brown, Vidic, Fletcher, Scholes (Richardson 76), Saha (Smith 60), Rooney, Ronaldo.
FC Copenhagen: Christiansen; Jacobsen, Norregaard (Kvist 57), Hangeland, Linderoth, Silberbauer (Bergvold 82), Berglund (Pimpong 57), Allback, Hutchinson, Gravgaard, Wendt.

Wednesday, 1 November 2006

Benfica (2) 3 *(Caldwell 10 (og), Nuno Gomes 22, Karyaka 76)*

Celtic (0) 0 49,000

Benfica: Quim; Luisao, Leo, Petit (Beto 84), Katsouranis, Simao Sabrosa, Nuno Gomes (Mantorras 89), Nelson, Nuno Assis, Miccoli (Karyaka 67), Ricardo Rocha.
Celtic: Boruc; Telfer, Naylor, Sno (Zurawski 72), Caldwell, Maloney (McGeady 65), McManus, Lennon, Miller, Nakamura, Pearson.

FC Copenhagen (0) 1 *(Allback 73)*

Manchester United (0) 0 40,308

FC Copenhagen: Christiansen; Jacobsen, Norregaard, Hangeland, Linderoth, Silberbauer (Kvist 71), Hutchinson, Gravgaard, Allback (Thomassen 89), Wendt, Bergvold (Berglund 68).
Manchester United: Van der Sar; Heinze (Evra 80), Silvestre, O'Shea, Brown, Vidic (Ferdinand 46), Ronaldo, Carrick, Solskjaer, Rooney, Fletcher (Scholes 71).

Tuesday, 21 November 2006

Benfica (3) 3 *(Leo 14, Miccoli 16, 37)*

FC Copenhagen (0) 1 *(Allback 89)* 37,179

Benfica: Quim; Nelson, Anderson, Nuno Assis (Karagounis 80), Leo, Petit, Simao Sabrosa, Katsouranis (Mantorras 86), Nuno Gomes, Miccoli (Karyaka 70), Ricardo Rocha.

FC Copenhagen: Christiansen; Jacobsen, Hutchinson, Norregaard (Berglund 59), Hangeland, Linderoth, Gravgaard, Silberbauer (Kvist 59), Wendt (Bergvold 80), Gronkjaer, Allback.

Celtic (0) 1 *(Nakamura 81)*

Manchester United (0) 0 60,632

Celtic: Boruc; Telfer, Naylor, Sno (Jarosik 46), McMannus, Balde, Zurawski (Maloney 46), Gravesen, Vennegoor of Hesselink, Nakamura (Miller 85), Lennon.
Manchester United: Van der Sar; Neville, Heinze (Evra 87), Carrick (O'Shea 87), Ferdinand, Vidic, Ronaldo, Scholes, Saha, Rooney, Giggs.

Wednesday, 6 December 2006

FC Copenhagen (2) 3 *(Hutchinson 2, Gronkjaer 27, Allback 57)*

Celtic (0) 1 *(Jarosik 75)* 38,647

FC Copenhagen: Christiansen; Jacobsen (Norregaard 56), Hangeland, Linderoth, Silberbauer, Gronkjaer (Berglund 90), Allback (Bergvold 81), Hutchinson, Gravgaard, Wendt, Kvist.
Celtic: Boruc; McManus (O'Dea 73), Naylor, Wilson, McGeady (Pearson 69), Balde, Zurawski, Lennon, Miller, Gravesen (Nakamura 69), Jarosik.

Manchester United (1) 3 *(Vidic 45, Giggs 61, Saha 75)*

Benfica (1) 1 *(Nelson 27)* 74,955

Manchester United: Van der Sar; Neville, Evra (Heinze 67), Carrick, Ferdinand, Vidic, Ronaldo, Scholes (Solskjaer 79), Saha, Rooney, Giggs (Fletcher 74).
Benfica: Quim; Luisao, Leo, Petit, Katsouranis, Simao Sabrosa, Nuno Gomes, Nelson, Nuno Assis (Karagounis 73), Miccoli (Paulo Jorge 64), Ricardo Rocha.

Group F Final Table	P	W	D	L	F	A	Pts
Manchester United	6	4	0	2	10	5	12
Celtic	6	3	0	3	8	9	9
Benfica	6	2	1	3	7	8	7
FC Copenhagen	6	2	1	3	5	8	7

GROUP G

Wednesday, 13 September 2006

Hamburg (0) 1 *(Sanogo 90)*

Arsenal (1) 2 *(Silva 12 (pen), Rosicky 53)* 50,389

Hamburg: Kirschstein■; Demel (Mahdavikia 54), Reinhardt, Kompany, Mathijsen, Jarolim, De Jong, Wicky (Wachter 12), Trochowski, Sanogo, Ljuboja (Guerrero 82).
Arsenal: Lehmann; Eboue, Gallas, Silva, Toure (Hoyte 29), Djourou, Hleb (Flamini 70), Fabregas, Adebayor, Van Persie (Julio Baptista 70), Rosicky.

Porto (0) 0

CSKA Moscow (0) 0 28,500

Porto: Helton; Bosingwa, Pepe, Bruno Alves, Ezequias, Lucho Gonzalez, Paulo Assuncao, Anderson, Sektioui (Helder Postiga 46), Adriano (Lisandro Lopez 71), Ricardo Quaresma (Alan 61).
CSKA Moscow: Akinfeev; Ignashevich, Semberas, Berezutski A, Krasic, Rahmic, Aldonin, Zhirkov, Daniel Carvalho (Gusev 90), Vagner Love (Olic 76), Dudu (Berezutski V 87).

Tuesday, 26 September 2006

Arsenal (1) 2 *(Henry 38, Hleb 48)*

Porto (0) 0 59,861

Arsenal: Lehmann; Eboue, Hoyte, Silva, Toure, Gallas (Song 90), Hleb (Walcott 86), Fabregas, Van Persie (Ljungberg 74), Henry, Rosicky.
Porto: Helton; Ricardo Costa (Raul Meireles 46), Pepe, Bruno Alves, Marek Cech, Paulo Assuncao, Ricardo Quaresma, Lucho Gonzalez, Helder Postiga (Lisandro Lopez 46), Anderson (Adriano 66), Bosingwa.

CSKA Moscow (0) 1 *(Dudu 59)*

Hamburg (0) 0 21,000

CSKA Moscow: Akinfeev; Semberas (Krasic 46), Berezutski V, Ignashevich, Rahimic, Berezutski A, Daniel Carvalho (Jo 85), Zhirkov, Olic (Aldonin 76), Dudu, Vagner Love.
Hamburg: Wachter; Sorin (Guerrero 69), Sanogo, Reinhardt, Mathijsen, Wicky, Mahdavikia, Jarolim, Ljuboja (Lauth■ 80), De Jong (Trochowski 70), Kompany.

Tuesday, 17 October 2006

CSKA Moscow (1) 1 *(Daniel Carvalho 24)*

Arsenal (0) 0 28,800

CSKA Moscow: Akinfeev; Semberas, Berezutski V, Ignashevich, Berezutski A, Daniel Carvalho (Taranov 89), Zhirkov, Dudu, Vagner Love (Olic 86), Aldonin (Krasic 90), Rahimic.
Arsenal: Lehmann; Hoyte, Gallas, Silva, Toure, Djourou (Clichy 75), Hleb, Fabregas, Van Persie (Adebayor 68), Henry, Rosicky (Walcott 80).

Porto (2) 4 *(Lisandro Lopez 14, 81, Lucho Gonzalez 45 (pen), Helder Postiga 69)*

Hamburg (0) 1 *(Trochowski 89)* 31,109

Porto: Helton; Bruno Alves, Pepe, Anderson (Jorginho 43), Marek Cech, Ricardo Quaresma (Vieirinha 80), Lucho Gonzalez, Lisandro Lopez, Helder Postiga (Bruno Moraes 75), Raul Meireles, Fucile.
Hamburg: Kirschstein; Sorin, Atouba (Guerrero 68), Mathijsen, Wicky (Klingbeil 54), Mahdavikia, Trochowski, Sanogo, De Jong, Benjamin (Fillinger 46), Ljuboja.

Wednesday, 1 November 2006

Arsenal (0) 0

CSKA Moscow (0) 0 60,003

Arsenal: Lehmann; Hoyte, Clichy, Silva, Toure, Gallas, Hleb (Walcott 71), Fabregas (Flamini 89), Van Persie (Aliadiere 82), Henry, Rosicky.
CSKA Moscow: Akinfeev; Semberas, Berezutski V, Ignashevich, Rahimic, Berezutski A, Daniel Carvalho (Taranov 90), Zhirkov, Dudu, Krasic (Aldonin 40), Vagner Love (Olic 85).

Hamburg (0) 1 *(Van der Vaart 62)*

Porto (1) 3 *(Lucho Gonzalez 44, Lisandro Lopez 61, Bruno Moraes 87)* 50,000

Hamburg: Kirschstein; Sorin, Atouba (Berisha 65), Sanogo, Mathijsen, Trochowski, Mahdavikia, Van der Vaart, Ljuboja (Guerrero 58), Kompany (Klingbeil 71), Feilhaber.
Porto: Helton; Pepe, Bruno Alves, Paulo Assuncao, Raul Meireles (Marek Cech 90), Ricardo Quaresma, Lucho Gonzalez, Lisandro Lopez (Jorginho 82), Bosingwa, Fucile, Helder Postiga (Bruno Moraes 70).

Tuesday, 21 November 2006

Arsenal (0) 3 *(Van Persie 52, Eboue 83, Julio Baptista 88)*

Hamburg (1) 1 *(Van der Vaart 4)* 59,962

Arsenal: Lehmann; Eboue, Clichy, Flamini, Toure, Senderos, Hleb (Julio Baptista 81), Fabregas, Van Persie (Adebayor 70), Henry, Ljungberg (Walcott 75).
Hamburg: Wachter; Fillinger, Atouba (Ljuboja 67), Reinhardt, Mathijsen, Wicky (Lauth 87), Mahdavikia (Feilhaber 46), Trochowski, Sanogo, Benjamin, Van der Vaart.

CSKA Moscow (0) 0

Porto (1) 2 *(Ricardo Quaresma 2, Lucho Gonzalez 61)* 27,800

CSKA Moscow: Akinfeev; Semberas, Berezutski V, Berezutski A, Krasic (Olic 66), Aldonin, Dudu (Kochubei 27), Daniel Carvalho, Rahimic, Zhirkov, Vagner Love.
Porto: Helton; Fucile, Pepe, Bosingwa, Bruno Alves, Raul Meireles (Jorginho 70), Ricardo Quaresma (Alan 88), Lucho Gonzalez, Lisandro Lopez, Helder Postiga (Bruno Moraes 77), Paulo Assuncao.

Wednesday, 6 December 2006

Hamburg (1) 3 *(Berisha 28, Van der Vaart 84, Sanogo 90)*
CSKA Moscow (1) 2 *(Olic 23 (pen), Zhirkov 65)* 49,649
Hamburg: Wachter; Atouba■ (Feilhaber 69), Reinhardt, Mathijsen, Mahdavikia, Jarolim (Sanogo 83), Trochowski, Berisha, Van der Vaart, Laas, Ljuboja (Guerrero 75).
CSKA Moscow: Akinfeev; Semberas, Berezutski V, Berezutski A, Daniel Carvalho, Olic, Krasic, Zhirkov, Dudu (Grigoryev 9), Aldonin, Taranov (Odiah 77) (Kochubei 86).

Porto (0) 0
Arsenal (0) 0 41,500
Porto: Helton; Pepe, Ricardo Quaresma, Lucho Gonzalez, Lisandro Lopez, Bosingwa, Fucile, Bruno Alves, Raul Meireles (Ibson 86), Paulo Assuncao, Helder Postiga (Bruno Moraes 81).
Arsenal: Lehmann; Eboue, Clichy, Silva, Toure, Djourou, Hleb, Fabregas, Adebayor (Van Persie 79), Ljungberg, Flamini.

Group G Final Table	*P*	*W*	*D*	*L*	*F*	*A*	*Pts*
Arsenal	6	3	2	1	7	3	11
Porto	6	3	2	1	9	4	11
CSKA Moscow	6	2	2	2	4	5	8
Hamburg	6	1	0	5	7	15	3

GROUP H

Wednesday, 13 September 2006

AC Milan (2) 3 *(Inzaghi 17, Gourcuff 41, Kaka 76 (pen))*
AEK Athens (0) 0 31,836
AC Milan: Dida; Cafu, Favalli (Jankulovski 79), Simic, Maldini, Brocchi (Ambrosini 75), Gourcuff, Gattuso, Kaka, Inzaghi, Oliveira (Seedorf 71).
AEK Athens: Sorrentino; Pautasso, Dellas (Ivic 55), Cirillo, Tziortziopoulos, Kapetanos (Lagos 46), Emerson (Tozser 70), Moras, Julio Cesar, Delibasic, Liberopoulos.

Anderlecht (1) 1 *(Pareja 41)*
Lille (0) 1 *(Fauvergue 80)* 21,107
Anderlecht: Zitka; Vanden Borre, Pareja, Deschacht, Vanderhaeghe, Van Damme, Biglia (Juhasz 68), Goor, Hassan, Boussoufa, Tchite.
Lille: Sylva; Chalme, Plestan, Schmitz, Tafforeau, Cabaye (Fauvergue 60), Makoun, Keita, Bodmer, Bastos (Youla 60), Odemwingie (Lichtsteiner 88).

Tuesday, 26 September 2006

AEK Athens (1) 1 *(Julio Cesar 28)*
Anderlecht (1) 1 *(Frutos 25)* 35,618
AEK Athens: Sorrentino; Julio Cesar (Lakis 55), Udeze, Moras, Cirillo, Lagos, Kiriakidis, Georgeas, Kapetanos (Liberopoulos 46), Hetemaj (Delibasic 70), Tozser.
Anderlecht: Zitka; Pareja, Deschacht, Vanden Borre, Biglia, Van Damme, Tchite, Leiva, Goor, Frutos, Boussoufa (Legear 81).

Lille (0) 0
AC Milan (0) 0 22,500
Lille: Sylva; Tavlaridis (Schmitz 85), Bodmer, Fauvergue (Cabaye 62), Odemwingie, Makoun, Tafforeau, Chalme, Vitakic, Keita, Plestan.
AC Milan: Dida; Cafu, Ambrosini, Kaladze, Nesta, Jankulovski, Pirlo, Kaka, Gilardino (Inzaghi 76), Seedorf, Gattuso.

Tuesday, 17 October 2006

Anderlecht (0) 0
AC Milan (0) 1 *(Kaka 58)* 20,129
Anderlecht: Zitka; Goor, Deschacht, Vanderhaeghe (Hassan 70), Biglia, Juhasz, Tchite, Frutos, Vanden Borre (Legear 84), De Man, Boussoufa (Serhat 84).
AC Milan: Dida; Bonera■, Jankulovski, Kaladze, Nesta, Seedorf (Brocchi 81), Gattuso, Pirlo, Inzaghi (Gilardino 72), Kaka, Oliveira (Cafu 50).

Lille (0) 3 *(Robail M 64, Gygax 82, Makoun 90)*
AEK Athens (0) 1 *(Ivic 68)* 33,017
Lille: Sylva; Tavlaridis, Cabaye (Mirallas 64), Bodmer, Odemwingie (Youla 78), Makoun, Robail M (Gygax 78), Tafforeau, Chalme, Keita, Plestan.
AEK Athens: Sorrentino; Cirillo, Papastathopoulos, Zikos, Lakis, Udeze, Emerson, Georgeas, Liberopoulos, Tozser (Ivic 56) (Kiriakidis 77), Julio Cesar.

Wednesday, 1 November 2006

AC Milan (2) 4 *(Kaka 6 (pen), 22, 56, Gilardino 88)*
Anderlecht (0) 1 *(Juhasz 61)* 37,768
AC Milan: Dida; Brocchi, Maldini, Simic, Nesta (Cafu 19), Jankulovski, Gourcuff (Gattuso 66), Gilardino, Kaka, Oliveira (Pirlo 73), Seedorf.
Anderlecht: Zitka; Juhasz, Deschacht, Vanderhaeghe (Serhat 39), Biglia, Goor, Tchite, De Man, Vanden Borre (Legear 85), Hassan, Boussoufa (Mpenza M 80).

AEK Athens (0) 1 *(Liberopoulos 74)*
Lille (0) 0 32,000
AEK Athens: Sorrentino; Moras, Cirillo, Zikos, Emerson (Kapetanos 47), Georgeas, Liberopoulos, Dellas, Hetemaj (Kiriakidis 88), Tozser, Julio Cesar (Manduca 58).
Lille: Sylva; Tavlaridis■, Cabaye, Bodmer, Odemwingie (Youla 57), Makoun (Fauvergue 77), Robail M (Debuchy 57), Tafforeau, Chalme, Keita, Plestan.

Tuesday, 21 November 2006

AEK Athens (1) 1 *(Julio Cesar 32)*
AC Milan (0) 0 56,203
AEK Athens: Sorrentino; Cirillo, Manduca, Tziortziopoulos (Moras 78), Papastathopoulos, Zikos, Emerson, Liberopoulos, Dellas, Tozser (Kiriakidis 66), Julio Cesar (Hetemaj 86).
AC Milan: Dida (Kalac 78); Bonera, Maldini, Brocchi, Costacurta (Jankulovski 46), Gourcuff, Oliveira (Borriello 70), Kaka, Inzaghi, Seedorf, Pirlo.

Lille (1) 2 *(Odemwingie 28, Fauvergue 47)*
Anderlecht (1) 2 *(Mpenza M 38, 48)* 35,000
Lille: Sylva; Schmitz, Bodmer, Fauvergue (Bastos 71), Odemwingie (Mirallas 75), Makoun, Robail M (Debuchy 55), Tafforeau, Chalme, Keita, Plestan.
Anderlecht: Schollen; Pareja, Deschacht, De Man, Biglia (Juhasz 90), Van Damme■, Tchite, Goor, Mpenza M (Boussoufa 66), Hassan (Vanderhaeghe 83), Vanden Borre.
at Lens.

Wednesday, 6 December 2006

AC Milan (0) 0
Lille (1) 2 *(Odemwingie 7, Keita 67)* 27,067
AC Milan: Kalac; Kaladze, Inzaghi, Borriello (Oliveira 72), Simic, Jankulovski, Gourcuff, Pirlo, Ambrosini (Kaka 54), Bonera, Brocchi (Seedorf 46).
Lille: Malicki; Debuchy, Tavlaridis, Cabaye, Bodmer (Fauvergue 89), Odemwingie (Robail M 73), Makoun, Tafforeau, Chalme, Keita (Youla 83), Plestan.

Anderlecht (1) 2 *(Vanden Borre 38, Frutos 63)*
AEK Athens (0) 2 *(Lakis 75, Cirillo 81)* 18,000
Anderlecht: Zitka; Deschacht, Biglia, Tchite, Hassan (Boussoufa 65), Goor, Juhasz, Pareja, Frutos (Legear 79), De Man, Vanden Borre.
AEK Athens: Sorrentino; Cirillo, Kiriakidis (Lakis 50), Manduca (Delibasic 58), Pautasso, Papastathopoulos, Zikos, Georgeas, Liberopoulos, Tozser, Julio Cesar (Hetemaj 58).

Group H Final Table	*P*	*W*	*D*	*L*	*F*	*A*	*Pts*
AC Milan	6	3	1	2	8	4	10
Lille	6	2	3	1	8	5	9
AEK Athens	6	2	2	2	6	9	8
Anderlecht	6	0	4	2	7	11	4

KNOCK-OUT STAGE

KNOCK-OUT ROUND FIRST LEG

Tuesday, 20 February 2007

Celtic (0) 0

AC Milan (0) 0 58,785

Celtic: Boruc; Wilson, Naylor, Sno, McManus, O'Dea, Lennon (Gravesen 81), Nakamura, Vennegoor of Hesselink, Miller (Jarosik 63), McGeady.
AC Milan: Kalac; Oddo, Jankulovski, Gattuso, Kaladze (Bonera 63), Maldini, Gourcuff, Pirlo, Gilardino (Oliveira 77), Kaka, Ambrosini.

Lille (0) 0

Manchester United (0) 1 *(Giggs 83)* 31,680

Lille: Sylva; Chalme, Tafforeau, Bodmer, Plestan, Tavlaridis, Debuchy, Makoun, Fauvergue (Cabaye 57), Odemwingie (Audel 75), Obraniak (Bastos 90).
Manchester United: Van der Sar; Neville, Evra, Carrick, Ferdinand, Vidic, Ronaldo (Saha 67), Scholes (O'Shea 90), Larsson, Rooney, Giggs.
at Lens.

PSV Eindhoven (0) 1 *(Mendez 61)*

Arsenal (0) 0 35,100

PSV Eindhoven: Gomes; Kromkamp, Salcido, Cocu, Alex, Da Costa (Sun 66), Culina, Simons, Tardelli (Vayrynen 75), Kone, Mendez.
Arsenal: Lehmann; Gallas, Clichy, Silva, Toure, Senderos, Hleb (Julio Baptista 75), Fabregas, Adebayor, Henry, Rosicky.

Real Madrid (3) 3 *(Raul 10, 28, Van Nistelrooy 34)*

Bayern Munich (1) 2 *(Lucio 23, Van Bommel 88)* 80,300

Real Madrid: Casillas; Miguel Torres, Roberto Carlos (Raul Bravo 59), Gago, Cannavaro, Helguera, Beckham, Guti, Van Nistelrooy, Raul, Higuain (Robinho 53).
Bayern Munich: Kahn; Sagnol, Lahm, Demichelis (Salihamidzic 46), Lucio, Van Buyten, Schweinsteiger (Scholl 79), Hargreaves, Makaay, Podolski (Pizarro 61), Van Bommel.

Wednesday, 21 February 2007

Barcelona (1) 1 *(Deco 14)*

Liverpool (1) 2 *(Bellamy 43, Riise 74)* 93,641

Barcelona: Valdes; Belletti, Zambrotta, Xavi (Giuly 65), Puyol, Marquez, Motta (Iniesta 54), Deco, Saviola (Gudjohnsen 82), Ronaldinho, Messi.
Liverpool: Reina; Arbeloa, Riise, Xabi Alonso, Carragher, Agger, Finnan, Sissoko (Zenden 84), Bellamy (Pennant 80), Kuyt (Crouch 90), Gerrard.

Internazionale (1) 2 *(Cambiasso 29, Maicon 76)*

Valencia (0) 2 *(David Villa 64, Silva 87)* 22,608

Internazionale: Julio Cesar; Maicon, Burdisso, Cambiasso (Dacourt 31), Materazzi, Cordoba, Stankovic, Figo (Solari 89), Crespo (Cruz 68), Ibrahimovic, Zanetti.
Valencia: Canizares; Miguel, Moretti, Albelda, Ayala, Albiol, Angulo (Joaquin 83), Marchena, David Villa, Morientes (Hugo Viana 76), Silva (Jorge Lopez 90).

Porto (1) 1 *(Raul Meireles 12)*

Chelsea (1) 1 *(Shevchenko 16)* 50,216

Porto: Helton; Bosingwa, Fucile (Bruno Moraes 65), Paulo Assuncao, Pepe, Bruno Alves, Gonzalez, Raul Meireles (Cech 56), Helder Postiga (Adriano 77), Quaresma, Lopez.
Chelsea: Cech; Diarra, Bridge, Makelele, Terry (Robben 13) (Mikel 46), Ricardo Carvalho, Essien, Lampard, Drogba, Shevchenko (Kalou 88), Ballack.

Roma (0) 0

Lyon (0) 0 75,000

Roma: Doni; Panucci, Tonetto, De Rossi, Mexes, Ferrari, Taddei (Vucinic 86), Pizarro, Perrotta, Totti, Mancini (Wilhelmsson 76).
Lyon: Coupet; Clerc, Abidal, Toulalan, Cris, Squillaci, Tiago, Juninho Pernambucano, Fred (Baros 74), Malouda, Govou.

KNOCK-OUT ROUND SECOND LEG

Tuesday, 6 March 2007

Chelsea (0) 2 *(Robben 48, Ballack 79)*

Porto (1) 1 *(Quaresma 15)* 39,041

Chelsea: Cech; Diarra (Paulo Ferreira 65), Cole A, Makelele (Mikel 46), Essien, Ricardo Carvalho, Ballack, Lampard, Drogba, Shevchenko (Kalou), Robben.
Porto: Helton; Fucile, Cech (Ibson 55), Ricardo Costa, Pepe, Bruno Alves, Gonzalez, Paulo Assuncao, Lopez (Bruno Moraes 82), Quaresma, Raul Meireles (Adriano 55).

Liverpool (0) 0

Barcelona (0) 1 *(Gudjohnsen 75)* 42,579

Liverpool: Reina; Finnan, Arbeloa, Xabi Alonso, Carragher, Agger, Gerrard, Sissoko, Bellamy (Pennant 67), Kuyt (Crouch 89), Riise (Fabio Aurelio 77).
Barcelona: Valdes; Thuram (Gudjohnsen 71), Oleguer, Xavi, Puyol, Marquez, Iniesta, Deco, Eto'o (Giuly 61), Ronaldinho, Messi.

Lyon (0) 0

Roma (2) 2 *(Totti 22, Mancini 44)* 39,260

Lyon: Coupet; Reveillere (Benzema 69), Abidal, Diarra (Kallstrom 46), Cris, Squillaci, Tiago, Juninho Pernambucano, Malouda, Fred, Govou (Wiltord 46).
Roma: Doni; Cassetti, Tonetto, De Rossi, Mexes, Chivu, Pizarro, Mancini (Faty 89), Taddei, Perrotta, Totti.

Valencia (0) 0

Internazionale (0) 0 53,000

Valencia: Canizares; Miguel, Moretti, Marchena, Ayala, Albiol, Angulo (Joaquin 77), Baraja (Hugo Viana 36), David Villa, Morientes (Vicente 67), Silva.
Internazionale: Julio Cesar; Maicon, Maxwell (Grosso 75), Burdisso, Materazzi, Cordoba, Zanetti, Dacourt (Figo 64), Crespo (Cruz 58), Ibrahimovic, Stankovic.

Wednesday, 7 March 2007

AC Milan (0) 1 *(Kaka 93)*

Celtic (0) 0 52,918

AC Milan: Dida; Oddo (Simic 116), Jankulovski, Pirlo, Bonera, Maldini, Gattuso (Brocchi 79), Ambrosini, Inzaghi (Gilardino 73), Kaka, Seedorf.
Celtic: Boruc; Telfer, Naylor, Sno (Beattie 97), McManus, O'Dea, Nakamura (Miller 106), Lennon, Vennegoor of Hesselink, Jarosik (Gravesen 62), McGeady.
aet.

Arsenal (0) 1 *(Alex 58 (og))*

PSV Eindhoven (0) 1 *(Alex 83)* 60,073

Arsenal: Lehmann; Toure, Clichy (Walcott 85), Silva, Gallas, Denilson, Hleb, Fabregas, Adebayor, Julio Baptista (Henry 66), Ljungberg (Diaby 75).
PSV Eindhoven: Gomes; Salcido, Sun, Mendez (Vayrynen 90), Alex, Feher, Culina, Simons, Kone (Afellay 41), Cocu, Farfan (Addo 89).

Bayern Munich (1) 2 *(Makaay 1, Lucio 66)*

Real Madrid (0) 1 *(Van Nistelrooy 83 (pen))* 69,500

Bayern Munich: Kahn; Sagnol (Gorlitz 85), Lahm, Van Bommel■, Lucio, Van Buyten, Salihamidzic, Hargreaves, Makaay (Pizarro 69), Podolski (Demichelis 87), Schweinsteiger.
Real Madrid: Casillas; Miguel Torres, Roberto Carlos, Gago (Robinho 75), Sergio Ramos, Helguera, Emerson (Guti 31), Diarra■, Van Nistelrooy, Raul, Higuain (Cassano 46).

Manchester United (0) 1 *(Larsson 72)*

Lille (0) 0 75,182

Manchester United: Van der Sar; Neville, Silvestre, O'Shea, Ferdinand, Vidic, Ronaldo (Richardson), Carrick, Larsson (Smith 74), Rooney (Park 82), Scholes.
Lille: Sylva; Chalme, Tafforeau, Dumont (Fauvergue 74), Tavlaridis, Plestan, Makoun, Keita, Odemwingie (Mirallas 74), Michel Bastos (Debuchy 46), Obraniak.

QUARTER-FINALS FIRST LEG

Tuesday, 3 April 2007

AC Milan (1) 2 *(Pirlo 40, Kaka 84 (pen))*
Bayern Munich (0) 2 *(Van Buyten 78, 90)* 67,500

AC Milan: Dida; Oddo, Nesta, Maldini, Jankulovski (Kaladze 87), Gattuso, Pirlo, Ambrosini, Seedorf (Gourcuff 85), Kaka, Gilardino (Inzaghi 71).
Bayern Munich: Rensing; Sagnol (Lell 67), Lucio, Van Buyten, Lahm, Salihamidzic, Hargreaves, Ottl, Schweinsteiger, Makaay (Santa Cruz 86), Podolski (Pizarro 68).

PSV Eindhoven (0) 0
Liverpool (1) 3 *(Gerrard 27, Riise 49, Crouch 63)* 36,500

PSV Eindhoven: Gomes; Kromkamp (Feher 68), Da Costa, Simons, Salcido, Mendez (Kluivert 51), Vayrynen, Cocu, Culina, Farfan (Sun 46), Tardelli.
Liverpool: Reina; Finnan, Riise (Zenden 65), Mascherano, Carragher, Agger, Gerrard, Xabi Alonso, Crouch (Pennant 85), Kuyt, Fabio Aurelio (Gonzalez 75).

Wednesday, 4 April 2007

Chelsea (0) 1 *(Drogba 53)*
Valencia (1) 1 *(Silva 30)* 38,065

Chelsea: Cech; Diarra, Cole A, Mikel (Cole J 74), Terry, Ricardo Carvalho, Kalou (Wright-Phillips 74), Lampard, Drogba, Shevchenko, Ballack.
Valencia: Canizares; Miguel, Del Horno, Albelda, Ayala, Moretti, Vicente (Angulo 57), Albiol, Silva, David Villa (Jorge Lopez 90), Joaquin (Hugo Viana 86).

Roma (1) 2 *(Taddei 44, Vucinic 67)*
Manchester United (0) 1 *(Rooney 60)* 75,000

Roma: Doni; Panucci, Mexes, Chivu, Cassetti, Wilhelmsson (Vucinic 62), Taddei (Rosi 82), De Rossi, Perrotta, Mancini, Totti.
Manchester United: Van der Sar; Brown, Heinze, Carrick, Ferdinand, O'Shea, Ronaldo, Scholes■, Solskjaer (Fletcher 72), Rooney, Giggs (Saha 77).

QUARTER-FINALS SECOND LEG

Tuesday, 10 April 2007

Manchester United (4) 7 *(Carrick 12, 60, Smith 17, Rooney 19, Ronaldo 44, 49, Evra 81)*
Roma (0) 1 *(Di Rossi 69)* 74,476

Manchester United: Van der Sar; Brown, O'Shea (Evra 52), Carrick (Richardson 73), Ferdinand, Heinze, Ronaldo, Fletcher, Smith, Rooney, Giggs (Solskjaer 61).
Roma: Doni; Panucci, Cassetti, De Rossi (Faty 80), Mexes, Chivu, Wilhelmsson (Rosi 88), Vucinic, Mancini (Okaka Chuka 90), Totti, Pizarro.

Valencia (1) 1 *(Morientes 32)*
Chelsea (0) 2 *(Shevchenko 52, Essien 90)* 53,000

Valencia: Canizares; Miguel, Del Horno, Albelda, Ayala, Moretti, Joaquin, Albiol (Hugo Viana 72), David Villa, Morientes (Angulo 65), Silva.
Chelsea: Cech; Diarra (Cole J 46), Cole A, Mikel, Terry, Ricardo Carvalho, Essien, Lampard (Makele 90), Drogba, Shevchenko (Kalou 90), Ballack.

Wednesday, 11 April 2007

Bayern Munich (0) 0
AC Milan (2) 2 *(Seedorf 27, Inzaghi 31)* 65,000

Bayern Munich: Kahn; Salihamidzic, Lahm, Van Bommel, Lucio, Van Buyten, Ottl (Santa Cruz 46), Hargreaves, Makaay (Pizarro 61), Podolski, Lell (Gorlitz 77).
AC Milan: Dida; Oddo, Jankulovski, Pirlo, Nesta, Maldini, Gattuso (Cafu 87), Ambrosini, Inzaghi (Serginho 70), Kaka, Seedorf (Gourcuff 80).

Liverpool (0) 1 *(Crouch 68)*
PSV Eindhoven (0) 0 41,447

Liverpool: Reina; Arbeloa, Riise, Xabi Alonso (Gonzalez 72), Agger (Paletta 78), Hyypia, Pennant, Sissoko, Crouch, Bellamy (Fowler 17), Zenden.
PSV Eindhoven: Gomes; Marcellis■, Salcido, Cocu, Simons, Addo, Feher (Sun 62), Vayrynen, Farfan (Kluivert 62), Kone (Van Eijden 71), Culina.

SEMI-FINALS FIRST LEG

Tuesday, 24 April 2007

Manchester United (1) 3 *(Ronaldo 6, Rooney 59, 90)*
AC Milan (2) 2 *(Kaka 22, 37)* 73,820

Manchester United: Van der Sar; O'Shea, Evra, Carrick, Heinze, Brown, Fletcher, Scholes, Ronaldo, Rooney, Giggs.
AC Milan: Dida; Oddo, Jankulovski, Ambrosini, Nesta, Maldini (Bonera 46), Pirlo, Gattuso (Brocchi 52), Gilardino (Gourcuff 84), Kaka, Seedorf.

Wednesday, 25 April 2007

Chelsea (1) 1 *(Cole J 29)*
Liverpool (0) 0 39,483

Chelsea: Cech; Paulo Ferreira, Cole A, Makelele, Terry, Ricardo Carvalho, Mikel, Lampard, Drogba, Shevchenko (Kalou 76), Cole J (Wright-Phillips 84).
Liverpool: Reina; Arbeloa, Riise, Xabi Alonso (Pennant 83), Carragher, Agger, Gerrard, Mascherano, Bellamy (Crouch 52), Kuyt, Zenden.

SEMI-FINALS SECOND LEG

Tuesday, 1 May 2007

Liverpool (1) 1 *(Agger 22)*
Chelsea (0) 0 42,554

Liverpool: Reina; Finnan, Riise, Mascherano (Fowler 118), Carragher, Agger, Pennant (Xabi Alonso 78), Gerrard, Crouch (Bellamy 106), Kuyt, Zenden.
Chelsea: Cech; Paulo Ferreira, Cole A, Makelele (Geremi 118), Terry, Essien, Mikel, Lampard, Drogba, Kalou (Wright-Phillips 107), Cole J (Robben 98).
aet; Liverpool won 4-1 on penalties.

Wednesday, 2 May 2007

AC Milan (2) 3 *(Kaka 11, Seedorf 30, Gilardino 78)*
Manchester United (0) 0 67,500

AC Milan: Dida; Oddo, Jankulovski, Ambrosini, Nesta, Kaladze, Pirlo, Gattuso (Cafu 84), Inzaghi (Gilardino 66), Kaka (Favalli 86), Seedorf.
Manchester United: Van der Sar; O'Shea (Saha 77), Heinze, Carrick, Brown, Vidic, Fletcher, Scholes, Ronaldo, Rooney, Giggs.

UEFA CHAMPIONS LEAGUE FINAL 2007

Wednesday, 23 May 2007

AC Milan (1) 2 *(Inzaghi 45, 82)* **Liverpool (0) 1** *(Kuyt 89)*

(in Athens, 74,000)

AC Milan: Dida; Oddo, Jankulovski (Kaladze 79), Gattuso, Nesta, Maldini, Pirlo, Ambrosini, Inzaghi (Gilardino 88), Kaka, Seedorf (Favalli 90).

Liverpool: Reina; Finnan (Arbeloa 88), Riise, Mascherano (Crouch 78), Carragher, Agger, Pennant, Xabi Alonso, Gerrard, Kuyt, Zenden (Kewell 59).

Referee: Fandel (Germany).

EUROPEAN CUP-WINNERS' CUP FINALS 1961–99

Year	Winners	Runners-up	Venue	Attendance	Referee
1961	Fiorentina 2	Rangers 0 *(1st Leg)*	Glasgow	80,000	Steiner (A)
	Fiorentina 2	Rangers 1 *(2nd Leg)*	Florence	50,000	Hernadi (H)
1962	Atletico Madrid 1	Fiorentina 1	Glasgow	27,389	Wharton (S)
Replay	Atletico Madrid 3	Fiorentina 0	Stuttgart	38,000	Tschenscher (WG)
1963	Tottenham Hotspur 5	Atletico Madrid 1	Rotterdam	49,000	Van Leuwen (Ho)
1964	Sporting Lisbon 3	MTK Budapest 3 *(aet)*	Brussels	3000	Van Nuffel (Bel)
Replay	Sporting Lisbon 1	MTK Budapest 0	Antwerp	19,000	Versyp (Bel)
1965	West Ham U 2	Munich 1860 0	Wembley	100,000	Szolt (H)
1966	Borussia Dortmund 2	Liverpool 1 *(aet)*	Glasgow	41,657	Schwinte (F)
1967	Bayern Munich 1	Rangers 0 *(aet)*	Nuremberg	69,480	Lo Bello (I)
1968	AC Milan 2	Hamburg 0	Rotterdam	53,000	Ortiz (Sp)
1969	Slovan Bratislava 3	Barcelona 2	Basle	19,000	Van Ravens (Ho)
1970	Manchester C 2	Gornik Zabrze 1	Vienna	8,000	Schiller (A)
1971	Chelsea 1	Real Madrid 1 *(aet)*	Athens	42,000	Scheurer (Sw)
Replay	Chelsea 2	Real Madrid 1 *(aet)*	Athens	35,000	Bucheli (Sw)
1972	Rangers 3	Moscow Dynamo 2	Barcelona	24,000	Ortiz (Sp)
1973	AC Milan 1	Leeds U 0	Salonika	45,000	Mihas (Gr)
1974	Magdeburg 2	AC Milan 0	Rotterdam	4000	Van Gemert (Ho)
1975	Dynamo Kiev 3	Ferencvaros 0	Basle	13,000	Davidson (S)
1976	Anderlecht 4	West Ham U 2	Brussels	58,000	Wurtz (F)
1977	Hamburg 2	Anderlecht 0	Amsterdam	65,000	Partridge (E)
1978	Anderlecht 4	Austria/WAC 0	Paris	48,679	Adlinger (WG)
1979	Barcelona 4	Fortuna Dusseldorf 3 *(aet)*	Basle	58,000	Palotai (H)
1980	Valencia 0 *(aet; Valencia won 5-4 on penalties)*	Arsenal 0	Brussels	36,000	Christov (Cz)
1981	Dynamo Tbilisi 2	Carl Zeiss Jena 1	Dusseldorf	9000	Lattanzi (I)
1982	Barcelona 2	Standard Liege 1	Barcelona	100,000	Eschweiler (WG)
1983	Aberdeen 2	Real Madrid 1 *(aet)*	Gothenburg	17,804	Menegali (I)
1984	Juventus 2	Porto 1	Basle	60,000	Prokop (EG)
1985	Everton 3	Rapid Vienna 1	Rotterdam	50,000	Casarin (I)
1986	Dynamo Kiev 3	Atletico Madrid 0	Lyon	39,300	Wohrer (A)
1987	Ajax 1	Lokomotiv Leipzig 0	Athens	35,000	Agnolin (I)
1988	Mechelen 1	Ajax 0	Strasbourg	39,446	Pauly (WG)
1989	Barcelona 2	Sampdoria 0	Berne	45,000	Courtney (E)
1990	Sampdoria 2	Anderlecht 0	Gothenburg	20,103	Galler (Sw)
1991	Manchester U 2	Barcelona 1	Rotterdam	42,000	Karlsson (Se)
1992	Werder Bremen 2	Monaco 0	Lisbon	16,000	D'Elia (I)
1993	Parma 3	Antwerp 1	Wembley	37,393	Assenmacher (G)
1994	Arsenal 1	Parma 0	Copenhagen	33,765	Krondl (CzR)
1995	Zaragoza 2	Arsenal 1	Paris	42,424	Ceccarini (I)
1996	Paris St Germain 1	Rapid Vienna 0	Brussels	37,500	Pairetto (I)
1997	Barcelona 1	Paris St Germain 0	Rotterdam	45,000	Merk (G)
1998	Chelsea 1	Stuttgart 0	Stockholm	30,216	Braschi (I)
1999	Lazio 2	Mallorca 1	Villa Park	33,021	Benko (A)

INTER-CITIES FAIRS CUP FINALS 1958–71

(Winners in italics)

Year	First Leg	Attendance	Second Leg	Attendance
1958	London 2 Barcelona 2	45,466	*Barcelona* 6 London 0	62,000
1960	Birmingham C 0 Barcelona 0	40,500	*Barcelona* 4 Birmingham C 1	70,000
1961	Birmingham C 2 Roma 2	21,005	*Roma* 2 Birmingham C 0	60,000
1962	Valencia 6 Barcelona 2	65,000	Barcelona 1 *Valencia* 1	60,000
1963	Dynamo Zagreb 1 Valencia 2	40,000	*Valencia* 2 Dynamo Zagreb 0	55,000
1964	*Zaragoza* 2 Valencia 1	50,000	(in Barcelona)	
1965	*Ferencvaros* 1 Juventus 0	25,000	(in Turin)	
1966	Barcelona 0 Zaragoza 1	70,000	Zaragoza 2 *Barcelona* 4	70,000
1967	Dynamo Zagreb 2 Leeds U 0	40,000	Leeds U 0 *Dynamo Zagreb* 0	35,604
1968	Leeds U 1 Ferencvaros 0	25,368	Ferencvaros 0 *Leeds U* 0	70,000
1969	Newcastle U 3 Ujpest Dozsa 0	60,000	Ujpest Dozsa 2 *Newcastle U* 3	37,000
1970	Anderlecht 3 Arsenal 1	37,000	*Arsenal* 3 Anderlecht 0	51,612
1971	Juventus 0 Leeds U 0 *(abandoned 51 minutes)*	42,000		
	Juventus 2 Leeds U 2	42,000	*Leeds U* 1* Juventus 1	42,483

UEFA CUP FINALS 1972–97

(Winners in italics)

Year	First Leg	Attendance	Second Leg	Attendance
1972	Wolverhampton W 1 Tottenham H 2	45,000	*Tottenham H* 1 Wolverhampton W 1	48,000
1973	Liverpool 0 Moenchengladbach 0 *(abandoned 27 minutes)*	44,967		
	Liverpool 3 Moenchengladbach 0	41,169	Moenchengladbach 2 *Liverpool* 0	35,000
1974	Tottenham H 2 Feyenoord 2	46,281	*Feyenoord* 2 Tottenham H 0	68,000
1975	Moenchengladbach 0 Twente 0	45,000	Twente 1 *Moenchengladbach* 5	24,500
1976	Liverpool 3 FC Brugge 2	56,000	FC Brugge 1 *Liverpool* 1	32,000
1977	Juventus 1 Athletic Bilbao 0	75,000	Athletic Bilbao 2 *Juventus* 1*	43,000
1978	Bastia 0 PSV Eindhoven 0	15,000	*PSV Eindhoven* 3 Bastia 0	27,000
1979	Red Star Belgrade 1 Moenchengladbach 1	87,500	*Moenchengladbach* 1 Red Star Belgrade 0	45,000
1980	Moenchengladbach 3 Eintracht Frankfurt 2	25,000	*Eintracht Frankfurt* 1* Moenchengladbach 0	60,000
1981	Ipswich T 3 AZ 67 Alkmaar 0	27,532	AZ 67 Alkmaar 4 *Ipswich T* 2	28,500
1982	Gothenburg 1 Hamburg 0	42,548	Hamburg 0 *Gothenburg* 3	60,000
1983	Anderlecht 1 Benfica 0	45,000	Benfica 1 *Anderlecht* 1	80,000
1984	Anderlecht 1 Tottenham H 1	40,000	*Tottenham H* 1[1] Anderlecht 1	46,258
1985	Videoton 0 Real Madrid 3	30,000	*Real Madrid* 0 Videoton 1	98,300
1986	Real Madrid 5 Cologne 1	80,000	Cologne 2 *Real Madrid* 0	15,000
1987	Gothenburg 1 Dundee U 0	50,023	Dundee U 1 *Gothenburg* 1	20,911
1988	Espanol 3 Bayer Leverkusen 0	42,000	*Bayer Leverkusen* 3[2] Espanol 0	22,000
1989	Napoli 2 Stuttgart 1	83,000	Stuttgart 3 *Napoli* 3	67,000
1990	Juventus 3 Fiorentina 1	45,000	Fiorentina 0 *Juventus* 0	32,000
1991	Internazionale 2 Roma 0	68,887	Roma 1 *Internazionale* 0	70,901
1992	Torino 2 Ajax 2	65,377	*Ajax* 0* Torino 0	40,000
1993	Borussia Dortmund 1 Juventus 3	37,000	*Juventus* 3 Borussia Dortmund 0	62,781
1994	Salzburg 0 Internazionale 1	47,500	*Internazionale* 1 Salzburg 0	80,326
1995	Parma 1 Juventus 0	23,000	Juventus 1 *Parma* 1	80,750
1996	Bayern Munich 2 Bordeaux 0	62,000	Bordeaux 1 *Bayern Munich* 3	36,000
1997	Schalke 1 Internazionale 0	56,824	Internazionale 1 *Schalke* 0[3]	81,670

**won on away goals* [1]*aet; Tottenham H won 4-3 on penalties* [2]*aet; Bayer Leverkusen won 3-2 on penalties*
[3]*aet; Schalke won 4-1 on penalties*

UEFA CUP FINALS 1998–2007

Year	Winners	Runners-up	Venue	Attendance	Referee
1998	Internazionale 3	Lazio 0	Paris	42,938	Nieto (Sp)
1999	Parma 3	Marseille 0	Moscow	61,000	Dallas (S)
2000	Galatasaray 0	Arsenal 0	Copenhagen	38,919	Nieto (Sp)
	(aet; Galatasaray won 4-1 on penalties).				
2001	Liverpool 5	Alaves 4	Dortmund	65,000	Veissiere (F)
	(aet; Liverpool won on sudden death).				
2002	Feyenoord 3	Borussia Dortmund 2	Rotterdam	45,000	Pereira (P)
2003	Porto 3	Celtic 2	Seville	52,972	Michel (Slv)
	(aet).				
2004	Valencia 2	Marseille 0	Gothenburg	40,000	Collina (I)
2005	CSKA Moscow 3	Sporting Lisbon 1	Lisbon	48,000	Poll (E)
2006	Sevilla 4	Middlesbrough 0	Eindhoven	36,500	Fandel (G)
2007	Sevilla 2	Espanyol 2	Glasgow	50,670	Busacca (Sw)
	(aet; Sevilla won 3-1 on penalties).				

UEFA CUP 2006–07

▪ *Denotes player sent off.*

FIRST QUALIFYING ROUND, FIRST LEG

Ameri (0) 0 *Dzheladze*▪, Banants (1) 1 *(Tadevosian 10) Burdian*▪ 2000
Apoel (1) 3 *(Neophytou 33 (pen), Georgiou 53, Eleftheriou 82)*, Murata (0) 1 *(Protti 51)* 5000
Artmedia (1) 2 *(Hartig 11, Reiter 52)*, WIT (0) 0 5861
Atvidaberg (2) 4 *(Johansson 10, Karlsson P 37, 47, 53)*, Etzella (0) 0 500
BATE Borisov (0) 2 *(Stasevich 56, Molosh 75 (pen))*, Otaci (0) 0 4000
Basle (1) 3 *(Petric 20, 67 (pen), Eduardo 69)*, Tobol (0) 1 *(Zhumaskaliyev 49)* 11,643
Brondby (3) 3 *(Rasmussen T 8, Rasmussen M 32, Ericsson 34)*, Valur (0) 1 *(Gunnlaugsson 83)* 6338
Dinamo Tirana (0) 0, CSKA Sofia (0) 1 *(Trica 85)* 1000
Fehervar (1) 1 *(Dveri 8)*, Kairat (0) 0 2500
Hibernians (0) 0, Dinamo Bucharest (1) 4 *(Danciulescu 4, 57, 58, Radu 83) Moti*▪ 250
Jeunesse Esch (0) 0, Skonto Riga (0) 2 *(Piacek 48, Stolcers 79)* 850
Karvan (0) 1 *(Murador 82)*, Spartak Trnava (0) 0 4000
Koper (0) 0, Litex (1) 1 *(Kirilov 18 (pen))* 1500
Levadia (2) 2 *(Purje 33, 37)*, Haka (0) 0 2150
Lokomotiv Sofia (0) 2 *(Paskov 60 (pen), Karadzinov 86)*, Makedonia (0) 0 1750
Lyn (1) 1 *(Tessem 42 (pen))*, Flora (0) 1 *(Lindpere 82)* 510
Mika (0) 1 *(Grigorian 90)*, Young Boys (1) 3 *(Marcos 21, Raimondi 50, Sermeter 85)* 5000
Orasje (0) 0, Domzale (2) 2 *(Juninho 31, Aljancic 39)* 2000
Randers (0) 1 *(Da Silva 62)*, IA Akranes (0) 0 10,000
Rapid Bucharest (5) 5 *(Grigore 5, Carbott 15 (og), Said 44 (og), Constantin N 21, 41)*, Sliema Wanderers (0) 0 1500
Rijeka (1) 2 *(Bule 10, Kerkez 51 (pen))*, Omonia (1) 2 *(Vakouftsis 30 (pen), Grozdanovski 55) Theodotou*▪ 6000
Sarajevo (3) 3 *(Obuca 25, 32, Duro 43) Saraba*▪, Ranger's (0) 0 2500
Skala (0) 0, Start (1) 1 *(Johnson 4)* 1500
Ujpest (0) 0, Vaduz (2) 4 *(Omar 13, 62, Sara 31, 90)* 3763
Vardar (1) 1 *(Ristovski 1)*, Roeselare (2) 2 *(Malki Sabah 33, Oyen 40)* 4000
Varteks (0) 1 *(Novinic 47)*, SK Tirana (1) 1 *(Mukaj 21)* 2000
Ventspils (1) 2 *(Ndeki 24, 66)*, GI Gotu (1) 1 *(Simun Jacobsen 29) Jarnskor*▪ 532
Zaglebie (0) 1 *(Lobodzinski 69)*, Dynamo Minsk (0) 1 *(Kovel 74)* 5000
Zimbru (0) 1 *(Petrosian 78 (pen))*, Karabakh (0) 1 *(Musaev 71)* 2000

Thursday, 13 July 2006

Gefle (1) 1 *(Viikmae 20)*
Llanelli (0) 2 *(Griffiths 82, Mingorance 87)* 839
Gefle: Hugosson; Hedlund, Karlsson P, Viikmae, Claesson, Bernhardsson, Woxlin, Wikstrom M, Bapupa (Ericsson 69), Mattsson (Westlin 76), Makondele.
Llanelli: Roberts; Phillips (Harrhy 46), Lloyd, Thomas N, Thomas D, Appleby (Mingorance 46), Griffiths, Corbisiero, Belle, Fernandez, Williams (Maxwell 90).

Glentoran (0) 0
Brann (0) 1 *(Memelli 69)* 1743
Glentoran: Morris (McLaughlin 60); Nixon, Holmes, Walker, Simpson, Halliday (Hamilton 81), McDonagh, Berry, Neill, Morgan (Tolan 73), Hill.
Brann: Thorbjornsen; Dahl (Miller 46), Zavrl, Sigurdsson, Hanstveit, Knudsen, Monkam▪, Haugen, Moen (Kalvenes 70), Saeternes (Bjarnason 67), Memelli.

HJK Helsinki (0) 1 *(Halsti 83)*
Drogheda United (1) 1 *(Robinson 41)* 2467
HJK Helsinki: Wallen; Marjamaa, Aalto I, Pohja, Ghazi (Savolainen 87), Lampi, Nurmela, Parikka (Zeneli E 69), Hakanpaa (Oravainen 72), Halsti, Sorsa.
Drogheda United: Connor; Lynch, Webb, Gavin, Gartland, Robinson, Whelan, Grant (Barrett 75), Shelly, Zayed (Ristila 57), Keegan.

IFK Gothenburg (0) 0
Derry City (0) 1 *(Hargan 79)* 3316
IFK Gothenburg: Andersson; Bjarsmyr, Alexandersson, Kihlberg, Selakovic (Mourad 65), Johansson A, Johansson M, Jonsson H, Wernbloom, Berg (Wallerstedt 73), Vasques (Wowoah 83).
Derry City: Forde; McCallion, Hargan, Hutton, Higgins (Martyn 90), Beckett (O'Flynn 86), McHugh (McGlynn 89), Brennan, Deery, Molloy, Kelly.

Portadown (0) 1 *(McCutcheon 63)*
Kaunas (2) 3 *(Ivaskevicius 2, Manchkhava 9, Velicka 47)* 500
Portadown: Dougherty; Convery, Marks (MacNerney 86), Boyle, McCutcheon, Kennedy, Tiggart, Devenney (McCann 58), Smart (Baker 79), O'Hara, Clarke.
Kaunas: Kurskis; Radzius, Kancelskis, Manchkhava, Barevicius (Kunevicius 82), Velicka, Baguzis, Ivaskevicius, Pilibaitis (Pacevicius 88), Zaliukas, Pehlic (Klimek 58).

Rhyl (0) 0
Suduva (0) 0 1479
Rhyl: Whitfield; Powell M, Brewerton, Connelly, Horan, Edwards, Wilson, Moran (Rafferty 76), Hunt (Sharp 66), Murtagh, Hay.
Suduva: Padimanskas; Chigladze D, Gvildys, Grigas, Mikuckis, Miklinevicius, Cordeiro, Adomaitus (Samusiovas 46), Urbsys (Uselis 72), Maciulis, Braga (Abramenko 89).

FIRST QUALIFYING ROUND, SECOND LEG

Banants (1) 1 *(Tadevosian 38), Arakelian*▪, Ameri (0) 2 *(Tsinamdzgvrishvili 60, Dobrovolski 62)* 3000
CSKA Sofia (1) 4 *(Trica 36, 53, Furtado 49, Petre 75)*, Dinamo Tirana (1) 1 *(Kastel 12)* 5000
Dinamo Bucharest (0) 5 *(Cristea 54, Danciulescu 61, 84, Munteanu 89, Buzurovic 90 (og))*, Hibernians (0) 1 *(Buzurovic 86)* 6000
Dynamo Minsk (0) 0, Zaglebie (0) 0 3000
Domzale (3) 5 *(Ljubijankic 13, 75, Djukic 21, 41, Rakovic 61)*, Orasje (0) 0 1200
Etzella (0) 0, Atvidaberg (0) 3 *(Jonsson 61, Johansson 70 (pen), Karlsson C 80 (pen))* 750
Flora (0) 0, Lyn (0) 0 1500
GI Gotu (0) 0, Ventspils (0) 2 *(Rimkus 75, 77)* 100
Haka (1) 1 *(Innanen 4)*, Levadia (0) 0 1234
IA Akranes (1) 2 *(Hjartarson 27, Gudjonsson B 90 (pen)), Vilhjalmsson*▪, Randers (1) 1 *(Johansen 29)* 800
Kairat (0) 2 *(Bulashev 75, Smakov 86 (pen))*, Fehervar (1) 1 *(Sitku 34)* 2000
Karabakh (1) 1 *(Musaev 23)*, Zimbru (0) 2 *(Chirilov 52, Balasa 100) aet.* 2500
Litex (1) 5 *(Sandrinho 19 (pen), Novakovic 62, Jelenkovic 85, Lyubenov 89, Genchev 90)*, Koper (0) 0 *Zahora*▪ 1500
Makedonia (1) 1 *(Ismaili 25)*, Lokomotiv Sofia (0) 1 *(Genkov 69)* 2000
Murata (0) 0, Apoel (3) 4 *(Georgiou 15, Fernandes 22, Neophytou 25, Michail 90 (pen))* 1500
Omonia (0) 2 *(Mguni 61, 88)*, Rijeka (0) 1 *(Lukunic 78)* 13,864
Otaci (0) 0, BATE Borisov (1) 1 *(Bliznyuk 30)* 1500
Ranger's (0) 0, Sarajevo (2) 2 *(Hadzic 10, Obuca 45)* 250
Roeselare (3) 5 *(Malki Sabah 13, Dufoor 20, 30, 76, Vanderbiest 64 (pen))*, Vardar (0) 1 *(Wandeir 52) Brankovic*▪ 4000
Skonto Riga (2) 3 *(Miholaps 21, 27 (pen), Stolcers 82)* Jeunesse Esch (0) 0 700

Sliema Wanderers (0) 0, Rapid Bucharest (1) 1 *(Buga 11)* 250
Spartak Trnava (0) 0, Karvan (1) 1 *(Camara 12)* 1842
Start (1) 3 *(Barlin 42, Pedersen S 51, Wright 78)*, Skala (0) 0 1477
SK Tirana (1) 2 *(Salihi 16, Merkoci 90)*, *Duro*■, Varteks (0) 0 3500
Tobol (0) 0, Basle (0) 0 9000
Vaduz (0) 0 *Sara*■, Ujpest (0) 1 *(Toth 55) Eros*■ 1150
Valur (0) 0, Brondby (0) 0 1672
WIT Georgia (1) 2 *(Lomaia 44, Razmadze 88 (pen))*, Artmedia (0) 1 *(Halenar 48)* 4300
Young Boys (0) 1 *(Haberli 85)*, Mika (0) 0 *Meloian*■ 6432

Thursday, 27 July 2006

Llanelli (0) 0

Gefle (0) 0 3000

Llanelli: Roberts; Lloyd, Thomas N, Thomas W, Mingorance (Harrhy 65), Griffiths, Corbisiero, Belle, Fernandez, Maxwell (Appleby 89), Williams.
Gefle: Hugosson; Hedlund■, Karlsson P, Ericsson (Wikstrom A 37), Viikmae (Bapupa 56), Claesson, Bernhardsson, Woxlin, Wikstrom M, Westlin (Mattsson 78), Makondele.

Brann (0) 1 *(Bjarnason 85 (pen))*

Glentoran (0) 0 3547

Brann: Thorbjornsen; Knudsen, Sigurdsson (Bjarnason 46), Kalvenes, Hanstveit, Husekleppp, Zavrl (Misje 86), Haugen, Winters, Miller (Ludvigsen 46), Memelli.
Glentoran: Morris; Nixon, Neill, Simpson (Leeman 25), Smyth, Berry, Hill, McDonagh, Morgan (Tolan 56), Hamilton (Halliday 86), Lockhart.

Derry City (1) 1 *(O'Flynn 32 (pen))*

IFK Gothenburg (0) 0 2400

Derry City: Forde; McCallion, Hargan, Hutton, Higgins (Oman 83), Beckett, McHugh (McGlynn 83), Deery, Molloy, O'Flynn (Martyn 86), Kelly.
IFK Gothenburg: Andersson; Bjarsmyr, Johansson A, Kihlberg, Selakovic (Berg 60), Alexandersson, Jonsson H (Johansson M 74), Mourad, Wernbloom, Jonsson D, Vasques.

Kaunas (1) 1 *(Ivaskevicius 43)*

Portadown (0) 0 2000

Kaunas: Kurskis; Radzius, Kancelskis, Manchkhava, Barevicius (Juska 64), Velicka, Baguzis, Ivaskevicius (Kunevicius 77), Pilibaitis, Zaliukas, Pehlic (Klimek 64).
Portadown: Dougherty; Convery, Marks, Boyle, McCutcheon, Kennedy, Tiggart, Devenney (McCann 56), Smart, O'Hara, Clarke.

Drogheda United (0) 3 *(Gartland 57, Lynch 96, 114)*

HJK Helsinki (1) 1 *(Ghazi 36)* 3000

Drogheda United: Connor; Lynch, Webb, Gavin, Gartland, Robinson, Whelan (Gray 117), Fitzpatrick (Zayed 58), Grant (Barrett 78), Shelly, Keegan.
HJK Helsinki: Wallen; Aalto I, Pohja, Ghazi, Lampi, Nurmela (Marjamaa 88), Aho■, Hakanpaa (Savolainen 103), Halsti, Zeneli E (Oravainen 74), Sorsa.
aet.

Suduva (2) 2 *(Maciulevicius 18 (pen), Mikuckis 25)*

Rhyl (0) 1 *(Grigas 80 (og))* 2500

Suduva: Padimanskas; Grigas, Klevinskas, Mikuckis, Chigladze D, Miklinevicius, Maciulis (Chigladze B 46), Maciulevicius (Cordeiro 90), Urbsys, Abramenko, Braga (Jasaitis 61).
Rhyl: Whitfield; Powell M, Graves, Connelly, Horan, Edwards (Hay 45), Wilson■, Moran, Hunt (Sharp 63) (Orlick 70), Murtagh, Brewerton.

SECOND QUALIFYING ROUND, FIRST LEG

Apoel (1) 1 *(Fernandes 2)*, Trabzonspor (0) 1 *(Yattara 90)* 6000
Artmedia (0) 2 *(Reiter 73, Cisovsky 76) Konecny*■, Dynamo Minsk (1) 1 *(Edu 22)* 4500
Basle (0) 1 *(Majstorovic 58)*, Vaduz (0) 0 14,296
Bnei Yehuda (0) 0, Lokomotiv Sofia (1) 2 *(Davtchev 30, Genkov 57 (pen))* 2500
(at Senec).
Brann (2) 3 *(Memelli 4, 26, 59)*, Atvidaberg (1) 3 *(Haglund 27, Bergstrom 48, Karlsson P 83)* 2684
Chornomorets (0) 0, Plock (0) 0 14,600
CSKA Sofia (0) 0, Kula (0) 0 10,000
Dinamo Bucharest (0) 1 *(Munteanu 77)*, Beitar (0) 0 6500
Fehervar (0) 1 *(Horvath 90)*, Grasshoppers (0) 1 *(Roberto Pinto 70)* 6000
Flora (0) 0, Brondby (0) 0 *Ankergren*■ 2500
Hapoel Tel Aviv (1) 1 *(De Bruno 42)*, *Haliva*■, Domzale (0) 2 *(Ljubijankic 65 (pen), 90)* 10,000
Hertha Berlin (0) 1 *(Okoronkwo 90)*, Ameri (0) 0 7377
Karvan (0) 0, Slavia Prague (1) 2 *(Hrdlicka 14, Fort 90)* 6000
Mattersburg (1) 1 *(Naumoski 20)*, Wisla (1) 1 *(Zienczuk 14)* 7200
Molde (0) 0, Skonto Riga (0) 0 1495
OFK Belgrade (1) 1 *(Bajalica 31)*, Auxerre (0) 0 2500
Omonia (0) 0, Litex (0) 0 13,847
Partizan Belgrade (2) 2 *(Odita 28, 30)*, Maribor (0) 1 *(Mihelic 64)* 9000
Randers (0) 3 *(Fall 59, Ahmed 82, Pedersen K 90 (pen))*, Kaunas (0) 1 *(Juska 80)* 4242
Ried (0) 0, Sion (0) 0 3100
Roeselare (1) 2 *(Dufoor 36, Oris 83)*, Ethnikos Achnas (0) 1 *(Stjepanovic 80 (pen))* 2500
Rubin (1) 3 *(Bazaev 37, Ashvetia 57, 68)*, BATE Borisov (0) 0 8000
Sarajevo (0) 1 *(Obuca 90)*, Rapid Bucharest (0) 0 *Constantin M*■ 3000
Suduva (0) 0, FC Brugge (1) 2 *(Daerden 19, Roelandts 70)* 3000
SK Tirana (0) 0, Kayseri (2) 2 *(Muhammed 26, 45)* 3500
Twente (0) 1 *(Heubach 53)*, Levadia (1) 1 *(Andreev 24)* 8100
Young Boys (1) 3 *(Yakin H 20, Joao Paulo 49, Marcos 73)*, Marseille (2) 3 *(Zubar*■ *18, Niang 44, 57) Taiwo*■ 18,273
Zimbru (0) 0, Metallurg Zapor (0) 0 7000

Thursday, 10 August 2006

Gretna (1) 1 *(McGuffie 12)*

Derry City (1) 5 *(Kelly 23, Deery 54, 56, Martyn 63, 75)* *(at Motherwell).* 6040

Gretna: Main; Canning, Innes, Townsley (Jenkins 57), McGill (O'Neil 46), McGuffie, Tosh, Skelton, McQuilken, Deuchar (Graham 79), Grady.
Derry City: Forde; McCallion, Hargan, Hutton, Martyn, Beckett (McGlynn 84), McHugh, Deery, Molloy (Higgins 76), O'Flynn (McCourt 73), Kelly.

Odense (1) 1 *(Bechara 29)*

Llanelli (0) 0 2744

Odense: Onyszko; Ophaug, Laursen, Fevang, Christensen, Bechara (Larsen 63), Hansen, Sorensen, Jensen, Borre, Borring.
Llanelli: Roberts; Lloyd, Thomas N, Thomas D, Mingorance (Williams 58), Griffiths R, Corbisiero, Belle, Fernandez, Griffiths D (Harrhy 73), Legg.

Start (0) 1 *(Stromstad 66)*

Drogheda United (0) 0 1433

Start: Nilssen; Paulsen K, Pedersen S, Engedal, Johnson, Stromstad, Aarsheim, Haestad (Fevang 85), Barlin (Nielsen 19) (Borgersen 85), Valencia, Jonsson.
Drogheda United: Connor; Lynch, Gartland, Jason, Webb, Robertson, Keegan, Bradley (Whelan 82), Shelley, Barrett (Keddy 90), Fitzpatrick (Grant 87).

Ventspils (0) 0

Newcastle United (0) 1 *(Bramble 67)* 6000

Ventspils: Vanins; Ndeki, Gorkss, Kacanovs, Bicka, Zangareev, Dubenskiy(Kosmacovs 89), Vukovic, Kolesnicenko (Pokarynin 84), Butriks, Slesarcuks (Zizilevs 16).
Newcastle United: Given; Carr, Babayaro (Ramage 90), Butt, Moore, Bramble, Solano (Milner 84), Emre (N'Zogbia 79), Ameobi, Parker, Duff.

SECOND QUALIFYING ROUND, SECOND LEG

Ameri (1) 2 *(Davitnidze 19, Davitashvili 47)*, Hertha Berlin (1) 2 *(Lakic 35, Pantelic 83)* 4000
Atvidaberg (1) 1 *(Haglund 34)*, Brann (0) 1 *(Dahl 85)* 786
Auxerre (2) 5 *(Mignot 23, Jelen 45, Pieroni 83, 85, 90)*, OFK Belgrade (1) 1 *(Pilipovic 32) Todorovic*■ 6000
BATE Borisov (0) 0, Rubin (2) 2 *(Dominguez 36, 44)* 2700
Beitar Jerusalem (1) 1 *(Itzhaki 4)*, Dinamo Bucharest (1) 1 *(Gershon 23 (og))* 3000
Brondby (0) 4 *(Jensen 49, Agger 64, 87, Lorentzen 78)*, Flora (0) 0 *Palatu*■, *Jaager*■ 8899
FC Brugge (2) 5 *(Roelandts 9, Balaban 40, 69, Gvozdenovic 59, Dufer 66)*, Suduva (0) 2 *(Braga 52, Chigladze 58 (pen)) Jasaitis*■ 5000
Domzale (0) 0, Hapoel Tel Aviv (0) 3 *(Jolic 70, Vermouth 89, Ogbona 90)* 2500
Dynamo Minsk (0) 2 *(Kovel 76, Marcio 90)*, Artmedia (2) 3 *(Halenar 31, Gajdos 38, Burak 61)* 3500
Ethnikos Achnas (2) 5 *(Poyiatzis 3, 16, Stjepanovic 47 (pen), 55, Belic 89)*, Roeselare (0) 0 2500
Grasshoppers (2) 2 *(Sutter 5, Eduardo 24)*, Fehervar (0) 0 2600
Hajduk Kula (0) 1 *(Stancic 99)*, CSKA Sofia (0) 1 *(Tunchev 120) aet.* 3000
Kaunas (0) 1 *(Velicka 72 (pen))*, Randers (0) 0 2000
Kayseri (2) 3 *(Mehmet 5, Muhammed 45, Gokhan 48)*, SK Tirana (0) 1 *(Salihi 52)* 10,000
Levadia (1) 1 *(Nahk 36)*, Twente (0) 0 3200
Litex (2) 2 *(Zlatinov 42, Manolev 45)*, Omonia (1) 1 *(Berberovic 33 (og)) Dobrasinovic*■ 1750
Lokomotiv Sofia (2) 4 *(Dobrev 21, Genkov 43, Karadzinov 61, 81)*, Bnei Yehuda (0) 0 *Dizani*■ 2000
Maribor (0) 1 *(Zajc 64)*, Partizan Belgrade (1) 1 *(Zajic 30)* 8000
Marseille (0) 0, Young Boys (0) 0 37,764
Metallurg Zapor (1) 3 *(Tasevski 16, 54, Kvirkvelia 70)*, Zimbru (0) 0 8000
Plock (0) 1 *(Gevorgyan 62)*, Chornomorets (1) 1 *(Shyshchenko 31)* 5000
Rapid Bucharest (1) 2 *(Buga 40, Moldovan 88)*, Sarajevo (0) 0 7500
Sion (1) 1 *(Kuljic 35 (pen))*, Ried (0) 0 7500
Skonto Riga (0) 1 *(Astafjevs 67)*, Molde (1) 2 *(Mavric 41, Ohr 60)* 750
Slavia Prague (0) 0, Karvan (0) 0 3512
Trabzonspor (0) 1 *(Omer Riza 87)*, Apoel (0) 0 10,000
Vaduz (0) 2 *(Sara 49, Ritzberger 63)*, Basle (0) 1 *(Kuzmanovic 56)* 3660
Wisla (1) 1 *(Piotr Brozek 23)*, Mattersburg (0) 0 *Fuchs*■, *Morz*■ 13,000

Thursday, 24 August 2006

Derry City (1) 2 *(Farren 37, Oman 69)*

Gretna (1) 2 *(Graham 17, Baldacchino 77)* 2850

Derry City: Forde; McCallion, Hargan, Higgins (Deery 59), McHugh (Martyn 74), Oman, McGlynn, Molloy, Farren, O'Flynn (Beckett 61), Kelly.
Gretna: Main; Birch, Grady, Skelton, Canning, Graham, Deuchar, McGuffie (Jenkins 73), Tosh (O'Neil 53), Townsley, Granger.

Drogheda United (0) 1 *(Zayed 84)*

Start (0) 0 4154

Drogheda United: Connor; Lynch, Webb, Gavin, Gartland, Robinson, Keddy (Whelan 71), Bradley, Keegan, Ristila (Zayed 57), Barrett (Gray 96).
Start: Nilssen; Pedersen S (Paulsen K 90), Haland, Borgersen, Johnson, Fevang (Stromstad 83), Aarsheim, Haestad, Valencia, Nielsen (Barlin 71), Garba.
aet; Start won 11-10 on penalties.

Llanelli (1) 1 *(Corbisiero 10)*

Odense (2) 5 *(Timm 15, Hansen 34, Christensen 59, Ophaug 65, Bechara 90)* 2759

Llanelli: Roberts; Lloyd, Thomas N, Jones (Griffiths D 60), Thomas W, Griffiths R, Corbisiero, Harrhy (Mingorance 57), Belle, Williams C, Legg (Lewis 64).
Odense: Onyszko; Ophaug (Larsen 86), Laursen, Christensen, Timm (Bechara 78), Grahn, Hansen, Sorensen, Jensen, Borre, Borring.

Newcastle United (0) 0

Ventspils (0) 0 30,498

Newcastle United: Harper; Carr, Babayaro, Parker, Bramble, Taylor, Duff, Emre, Milner, Luque, N'Zogbia.
Ventspils: Vanins; Kacanovs, Ndeki, Gorkss, Pokarynin, Vukovic, Dubenskiy, Bicka, Zizilevs, Rimkus (Stukalinas 90), Kolesnicenko (Kosmacovs 86).

FIRST ROUND, FIRST LEG

Artmedia (2) 2 *(Halenar 36, Tchur 41)*, Espanyol (1) 2 *(Riera 31, Pandiani 53)* 3480
Atromitos (0) 1 *(Korakakis 64)*, Sevilla (2) 2 *(Kepa 14, Duda 42)* 2500
Atvidaberg (0) 0, Grasshoppers (2) 3 *(Diego Leon 12, Eduardo 28, Sutter 57)* 5130
AZ (2) 3 *(Koevermans 7 (pen), Molhoek 31, Arveladze 64)*, Kayseri (1) 2 *(Bulent 25, Ragip 67)* 12,612
Basle (4) 6 *(Kuzmanovic 2, Petric 6, 39, Majstorovic 34 (pen), Cristiano 71, 73)*, Rabotnicki (0) 2 *(Pejcic 89, Buckley 90 (og))* 11,945
Besiktas (0) 2 *(Kleberson 82, Gokhan 90)*, CSKA Sofia (0) 0 *Petrov R*■ 28,752
Braga (1) 2 *(Paulo Jorge 6, Wender 90 (pen))*, Chievo (0) 0 *Marchese*■, *Mantovani*■ 20,000
Chornomorets (0) 0, Hapoel Tel Aviv (0) 1 *(De Bruno 74)* 18,500
Dynamo Zagreb (0) 1 *(Eduardo 68)*, Auxerre (1) 2 *(Jelen 43, Niculae 72)* 32,000
Eintracht Frankfurt (0) 4 *(Thurk 51 (pen), 71 (pen), 79, Kohler 90)*, Brondby (0) 0 *Kildentoft*■, *Howard*■ 38,000
Ethnikos Achnas (0) 0, Lens (0) 0 800
Fenerbahce (1) 2 *(Pedersen R 25 (og), Kezman 54)*, Randers (1) 1 *(Fall 13)* 45,000
Hertha Berlin (1) 2 *(Giminez 38, Boateng 51)*, Odense (1) 2 *(Simunic 7 (og), Bechara 53)* 12,814
Legia (1) 1 *(Junior 45)*, FK Austria (1) 1 *(Mair 27)* 9000
Liberec (1) 2 *(Frejlach 43, Blazek 90)*, Red Star Belgrade (0) 0 7215
Livorno (1) 2 *(Danilevicius 42, Lucarelli 49)*, Pasching (0) 0 7600
Lokomotiv Moscow (1) 2 *(Loskov 35, Ivanovic 74)*, Waregem (0) 1 *(Vandemarliere 90)* 11,023
Lokomotiv Sofia (2) 2 *(Genkov 4, Datchev 28)*, Feyenoord (1) 2 *(Lucius 45 (pen), Greene 59)* 4375
Maccabi Haifa (1) 1 *(Katan 7)*, Litex (0) 1 *(Zanev 51) (at Nijmegen).* 300
Marseille (1) 1 *(Bamogo 31)*, Mlada Boleslav (0) 0 *Sevinsky*■ 15,077
Panathinaikos (1) 1 *(Salpigidis 10)*, Metallurg Zapor (0) 1 *(Godin 47)* 15,626
Partizan Belgrade (3) 4 *(Marinkovic 3 (pen), 44, Zajic 16, 89)*, Groningen (0) 2 *(Fledderus 57, Luis Suarez 90)* 10,658
Rapid Bucharest (1) 1 *(Moldovan 44)*, Nacional (0) 0 1300
Rubin (0) 0, Parma (0) 1 *(Dessena 78)* 10,000
Ruzomberok (0) 0, FC Brugge (1) 1 *(Balaban 39)* 4200
Schalke (0) 1 *(Larsen 86)*, Nancy (0) 0 45,878
Sion (0) 0, Leverkusen (0) 0 9000
Standard Liege (0) 0, Celta Vigo (1) 1 *(Gustavo Lopez 38)* 10,000
Start (1) 2 *(Johnsen 28, Fevang 56)*, Ajax (2) 5 *(Huntelaar 18, 87, Rosenberg 43, Sneijder 63, Roger 67)* 1840
Trabzonspor (0) 2 *(Gokdeniz 55, Umut 89)*, Osasuna (1) 2 *(Valdo 21, Juanlu 53) Izquierdo*■ *(Behind closed doors).*
Setubal (0) 0, Heerenveen (0) 3 *(Afonso Alves 58, 66, Nilsson 90)* 3027
Wisla (0) 0, Iraklis (1) 1 *(Prittas 7) Epalle*■ 13,000
Xanthi (2) 3 *(Quintana 8, 45, Kazakis 66)*, Dinamo Bucharest (3) 4 *(Niculescu 18, 36, Danciulescu 25, Pulhac 85)* 3380

Thursday, 14 September 2006

Derry City (0) 0

Paris St Germain (0) 0 3000

Derry City: Forde; McCallion, Hargan, Martyn, McHugh, Brennan (Farren 80), Oman, Kelly, McCourt (Beckett 57), Molloy, Deery.
Paris St Germain: Landreau; Paulo Cesar, Armand, Baning (Chantome 84), Diane (Pauleta 71), Drame, Frau, Hellebuyck, Pancrate (Kalou 80), Rozehnal, Traore.

Hearts (0) 0

Sparta Prague (1) 2 *(Kolar 34, Matusovic 71)* 27,255
(at Murrayfield).

Hearts: Gordon; Neilson, Pressley, Bednar, Beslija (Tall 63), Pinilla (Cesnauskis 63), Berra, Mole, Wallace, Aguiar, Hartley.
Sparta Prague: Blazek; Repka, Sivok, Dosek, Kolar (Hasek 75), Simak (Matusovic 63), Sylvestre (Lustrinelli 85), Kisel, Pospech, Homola, Kadlec.

Levadia (0) 0

Newcastle United (1) 1 *(Sibierski 10)* 7917

Levadia: Kotenko; Cepauskas, Lemsalu, Sisov, Kalimullin, Nahk, Dmitrijev (Kink 82), Vassiljev, Dovydenas (Puri 71), Andreev (Purje 66), Voskoboinikov.
Newcastle United: Given; Carr, Ramage, Parker, Moore, Bramble (Milner 36), Duff, Emre, Martins, Sibierski (Luque 80), N'Zogbia (Butt 73).

Molde (0) 0

Rangers (0) 0 6569

Molde: Larsen; Andreasson, Kallio, Hestad, Hoseth, Ohr, Rudi, Rindaroy (Strande 71), Grande, Mavric, Konate (Diouf 83).
Rangers: McGregor; Buffel (Burke 66), Ferguson (Clement 75), Hemdani, Sionko (Prso 64), Boyd, Bardsley, Svensson, Smith, Rodriguez, Martin.

Salzburg (1) 2 *(Zickler 30, Janko 90)*

Blackburn Rovers (2) 2 *(Savage 32, McCarthy 39)* 17,000

Salzburg: Ochs; Bodnar, Dudic, Linke, Carboni, Kovac, Zickler, Jezek (Vonlanthen 63), Tiffert (Pitak 63), Meyer, Janocko (Janko 46).
Blackburn Rovers: Friedel; Emerton, Neill, Tugay, Khizanishvili, Ooijer, Bentley, Savage, Gallagher (Peter 81), McCarthy (Nonda 87), Pedersen.

Slavia Prague (0) 0

Tottenham Hotspur (1) 1 *(Jenas 37)* 14,869

Slavia Prague: Vorel (Kozacik 28); Hubacek, Svec, Latka, Vlcek, Gaucho (Fort 63), Janda (Necas 72), Suchy, Svento, Jarolim, Hrdlicka.
Tottenham Hotspur: Robinson; Chimbonda, Assou-Ekotto, Huddlestone (Davids 71), Dawson, King, Zokora, Jenas, Mido, Defoe (Keane 78), Tainio.

West Ham United (0) 0

Palermo (1) 1 *(Caracciolo 45)* 32,222

West Ham United: Carroll; Mears, Konchesky, Gabbidon, Ferdinand, Mascherano, Bowyer (Etherington 59), Reo-Coker, Zamora (Cole 77), Tevez (Harewood 77), Benayoun.
Palermo: Fontana; Zaccardo, Diana Aimo, Caracciolo, Cassani, Di Michele (Capuano 79), Parravicini (Guana 54), Bresciano (Biava 90), Pisano, Simplicio, Barzagli.

FIRST ROUND, SECOND LEG

Ajax (3) 4 *(Rosenberg 6, 26, Grygera 43, Babel 68)*, Start (0) 0 26,467
FK Austria (0) 1 *(Wallner 65)*, Legia (0) 0 12,300
Auxerre (2) 3 *(Jelen 35, 41, Mathis 70)*, Dynamo Zagreb (0) 1 *(Eduardo 61 (pen))* 9000
Brondby (1) 2 *(Ericsson 20, Rasmussen T 65)*, Eintracht Frankfurt (1) 2 *(Vasoski 6, 52)* 14,067
FC Brugge (0) 1 *(Balaban 89)*, Ruzomberok (1) 1 *(Rak 29)* 8425
Celta Vigo (1) 3 *(Baiano 22, 83, Canobbio 70)*, Standard Liege (0) 0 8000
Chievo (1) 2 *(Tiribocchi 38, Godeas 67), Sammarco■, Zanchetta■* Braga (0) 1 *(Wender 104) Nem■, aet.* 4624
CSKA Sofia (0) 2 *(Iliev V 60, Tunchev 69)*, Besiktas (0) 2 *(Marcio Nobre 95, Deivson 103) aet.* 15,000
Dynamo Bucharest (2) 4 *(Niculescu 12, 82, Cristea 47, Danciulescu 79)*, Xanthi (0) 1 *(Paviot 51)* 6000
Espanyol (1) 3 *(Pandiani 19, 79, Luis Garcia 67)*, Artmedia (1) 1 *(Buryan 13)* 8100
Feyenoord (0) 0, Lokomotiv Sofia (0) 0 22,000
Grasshoppers (2) 5 *(Blumer 29, Sutter 31, Schwegler 57, Eduardo 60, Renggli 67)*, Atvidaberg (0) 0 4800
Groningen (0) 1 *(Van De Laak 59 (pen))*, Partizan Belgrade (0) 0 19,097
Hapoel Tel Aviv (1) 3 *(Toema 24, Barda 74, De Bruno 88)*, Chornomorets (0) 1 *(Nizhegorodov 82) Ostrovskiy■* 13,500
Heerenveen (0) 0, Setubal (0) 0 16,800
Iraklis (0) 0, Wisla (0) 2 *(Mijailovic 94, Cantoro 100), aet.* 6331
Kayseri (1) 1 *(Gokhan 11)*, AZ (0) 1 *(Dembele 54)* 17,000
Lens (1) 3 *(Dindane 10, Jemaa 63, Cousin 64)*, Ethnikos Achnas (0) 1 *(Belic 69)* 27,171
Leverkusen (0) 3 *(Voronin 62, Ramelow 76, Schneider 86 (pen))*, Sion (0) 1 *(Fernandes 75) Reset■, Kali■* 22,500
Litex (1) 1 *(Sandrinho 37) Zanev■*, Maccabi Haifa (2) 3 *(Dirceu 19, Masudi 33, Colautti 67)* 5000
Metallurg Zapor (0) 0, Panathinaikos (1) 1 *(Papadopoulos 14)* 11,500
Mlada Boleslav (1) 4 *(Pecka 34, Holub 62 (pen), 82, Sedlacek 90) Smerda■*, Marseille (1) 2 *(Maoulida 14, Taiwo 56)* 5000
Nacional (1) 1 *(Juliano 29) Bruno Basto■*, Rapid Bucharest (0) 2 *(Rada 91, Burdujan 101) aet.* 7500
Nancy (2) 3 *(Andre Luiz 18, Curbelo 25, Dia 70) Gavanon■*, Schalke (0) 1 *(Kuranyi 78)* 18,029
Odense (0) 1 *(Timm 62)*, Hertha Berlin (0) 0 11,462
Osasuna (0) 0, Trabzonspor (0) 0 14,918
Parma (0) 1 *(Paponi 49)*, Rubin (0) 0 2501
Pasching (0) 0, Livorno (0) 1 *(Bakayoko 56)* 4100
Rabotnicki (0) 0, Basle (0) 1 *(Sterjovski 74)* 1133
Randers (0) 0, Fenerbahce (0) 3 *(Deivid 61, Tuncay 64, Kezman 70)* 14,281
Red Star Belgrade (1) 1 *(Ailton 43)*, Liberec (1) 2 *(Bilek 2, Holenda 67)* 18,000
Sevilla (3) 4 *(Luis Fabiano 2, 29, Ioannou 10 (og), Kepa 86)*, Atromitos (0) 0 35,000
Waregem (0) 2 *(Matthijs 57, Sergeant 82)*, Lokomotiv Moscow (0) 0 6000

Thursday, 28 September 2006

Blackburn Rovers (1) 2 *(McCarthy 32, Bentley 56)*

Salzburg (0) 0 18,888

Blackburn Rovers: Friedel; Emerton, Neill, Tugay (Gallagher 83), Khizanishvili, Ooijer, Bentley, Savage (Mokoena 60), Nonda, McCarthy (Jeffers 83), Pedersen.
Salzburg: Ochs; Bodnar, Dudic, Linke, Carboni, Kovac (Aufhauser 68), Zickler (Janocko 64), Tiffert (Jezek 58), Vonlanthen, Janko, Vargas.

Newcastle United (0) 2 *(Martins 47, 50)*

Levadia (0) 1 *(Zelinski 65)* 27,012

Newcastle United: Harper; Carr, Taylor, Butt, Bramble, Ramage, Milner, Emre (Parker 81), Martins (Luque 70), Sibierski, N'Zogbia (Duff 70).
Levadia: Kotenko; Lemsalu, Sisov, Cepauskas, Kalimullin, Nahk, Dovydenas (Puri 55), Dmitrijev (Kink 63), Vassilijev, Voskoboinikov (Zelinski 63), Purje.

Paris St Germain (2) 2 *(Cisse 7, Pauleta 42)*

Derry City (0) 0 7000

Paris St Germain: Landreau; Rozehnal, Mendy, Cisse, Pauleta (Rodriguez 66), Frau, Kalou (Pancrate 66), Traore, Armand, Drame, Paulo Cesar.
Derry City: Forde; McCallion, Hargan (O'Flynn 82), Deery, Molloy, Kelly, McCourt (McHugh 61), Martyn, Beckett (Farren 61), Brennan, Oman.

Palermo (1) 3 *(Simplicio 35, 62, Di Michele 67)*
West Ham United (0) 0 19,264
Palermo: Fontana; Zaccardo, Corini (Guana 79), Diana Aimo (Della Fiore 89), Caracciolo, Cassani, Di Michele (Brienza 86), Bresciano, Pisano, Simplicio, Barzagli.
West Ham United: Carroll; Spector, Konchesky, Gabbidon, Collins, Mascherano (Benayoun 68), Bowyer, Reo-Coker, Harewood (Sheringham 68), Cole (Zamora 60), Tevez.

Rangers (2) 2 *(Buffel 12, Ferguson 45)*
Molde (0) 0 48,024
Rangers: McGregor; Bardsley, Adam, Buffel, Sionko (N'Diaye 90), Ferguson, Hemdani, Smith, Prso (Sebo 81), Boyd (Rae 67), Rodriguez.
Molde: Larsen; Andreasson (Gjerde 65), Kallio, Hestad, Hoseth, Ohr (Moster 70), Rudi, Rindaroy, Grande (Konate 85), Baldvinsson, Mavric.

Sparta Prague (0) 0
Hearts (0) 0 16,505
Sparta Prague: Blazek; Repka, Kadlec, Homola, Pospech, Sivok, Simak (Matusovic 62), Sylvestre, Kisel, Dosek (Lustrinelli 74), Kolar (Jun 86).
Hearts: Gordon; Neilson (Tall 65), Berra, Pressley, Cesnauskis, Pinilla (Aguiar 83), Brellier, Mole (Bednar 55), Hartley, Wallace, Mikoliunas.

Tottenham Hotspur (0) 1 *(Keane 79)*
Slavia Prague (0) 0 35,191
Tottenham Hotspur: Robinson; Chimbonda, Lee, Zokora, Dawson, Davenport, Murphy (Ghaly 70), Jenas, Mido, Keane, Ziegler (Tainio 61).
Slavia Prague: Kozacik; Fort (Necid 79), Svento, Hubacek, Svec, Latka, Krajcik, Jarolim, Hrdlicka (Kalivoda 74), Janda (Vlcek 63), Suchy.

GROUP STAGE

GROUP A

Thursday, 19 October 2006

Livorno (1) 2 *(Lucarelli 34 (pen), 90)*
Rangers (3) 3 *(Adam 27, Boyd 30 (pen), Novo 35)* 13,200
Livorno: Amelia; Galante, Vidigal, Vigiani (Bakayoko 78), Kuffour, Rezaei (Morrone 57), Pasquale, Passoni, Cesar Prates (Balleri 46), Danilevicius, Lucarelli.
Rangers: Letizi; Svensson, Hutton, Ferguson, Rodriguez, Adam, Hemdani, Buffel (Rae 89), Novo (Prso 87), Boyd (Sebo 82), Smith.

Maccabi Haifa (1) 3 *(Masudi 13, Boccoli 56, Colautti 58)*
Auxerre (1) 1 *(Niculae 29)* 13,500
Maccabi Haifa: Davidovich; Harazi, Keise (Magrashvili 22), Olarra, Keinan, Anderson, Boccoli, Masudi (Melikson 77), Dirceu, Colautti, Katan (Arbeitman 80).
Auxerre: Cool; Jaures, Grichting■, Pedretti, Cheyrou, Kahlenberg (Kalabane 67), Akale (Ba 76), Mignot, N'Diaye, Niculae (Pieroni 70), Sagna.

Thursday, 2 November 2006

Partizan Belgrade (0) 1 *(Mirosavljevic 70)*
Livorno (0) 1 *(Amelia 88)* 12,170
Partizan Belgrade: Kralj; Rnic, Bajic, Djordjevic, Lomic, Mirosavljevic (Markovski 87), Smiljanic, Nebojsa Marinkovic (Bosancic 62), Zajic, Odita, Lazic (Radosavljevic 73).
Livorno: Amelia; Kuffour, Galante (Pavan 69), Pfertzel (Betanin 75), Pasquale, Grandoni, Morrone, Vidigal, Passoni, Bakayoko (Danilevicius 88), Lucarelli.

Rangers (1) 2 *(Novo 5, Adam 89 (pen))*
Maccabi Haifa (0) 0 43,062
Rangers: McGregor; Hutton, Hemdani, Svensson, Smith, Novo, Ferguson, Clement, Adam (Rae 90), Prso (Buffel 66), Boyd (Sebo 66).
Maccabi Haifa: Davidovich; Harazi (Meshumar 85), Keinan, Olarra, Magrashvili, Dirceu, Anderson, Boccoli (Melikson 60), Katan, Masudi (Arbeitman 81), Colautti.

Thursday, 23 November 2006

Auxerre (1) 2 *(Jelen 31, Niculae 75)*
Rangers (0) 2 *(Novo 62, Boyd 84)* 8305
Auxerre: Cool; Jaures, Kalabane, Kaboul, Sagna, Pedretti (Niculae 75), Cheyrou, Akale, Thomas, Pieroni, Jelen (Ba 80).
Rangers: McGregor; Svensson, Hutton, Smith (Rodrigues 20), Adam, Ferguson, Hemdani, Clement, Prso (Sionko 67), Novo (Sebo 81), Boyd.

Maccabi Haifa (1) 1 *(Anderson 21)*
Partizan Belgrade (0) 0 13,500
Maccabi Haifa: Davidovich; Harazi, Keise, Keinan, Olarra, Boccoli, Anderson, Masudi (Gazal 68), Rafaelov (Melikson 69), Colautti (Arbeitman 86), Katan.
Partizan Belgrade: Jahic; Djordjevic, Bajic, Mihajlov, Lomic, Zajic, Nebojsa Marinkovic (Lazic 72), Smiljanic, Odita, Vukelia (Nenad Marinkovic 54), Mirosavljevic (Tomic 54).

Wednesday, 29 November 2006

Livorno (1) 1 *(Lucarelli 20)*
Maccabi Haifa (0) 1 *(Colautti 90)* 7874
Livorno: Amelia; Grandoni, Kuffour, Galante, Balleri (Pfertzel 83), Morrone, Passoni, Filippini, Pasquale, Lucarelli, Danilevicius (Bakayoko 64).
Maccabi Haifa: Davidovich; Harazi (Meshumar 67), Olarra, Keinan, Keise, Rafaelov (Arbeitman 72), Boccoli, Anderson, Masudi (Melikson 59), Katan, Colautti.

Partizan Belgrade (1) 1 *(Nebojsa Marinkovic 5)*
Auxerre (3) 4 *(Cheyrou 18, Niculae 24, Akale 36, Pieroni 82)* 4000
Partizan Belgrade: Jahic; Djordjevic, Bajic, Rnic, Lomic, Tomic (Mihajlov 75), Smiljanic, Nebojsa Marinkovic, Mirosavljevic (Markovski 74), Vukelia (Bosancic 57), Nenad Marinkovic.
Auxerre: Cool; Jaures, Kalabane, Kaboul, Sagna, Pedretti, Cheyrou, Akale (Pieroni 72), Thomas, Niculae (Ba 81), Jelen (Lejeune 85).

Thursday, 14 December 2006

Auxerre (0) 0
Livorno (0) 1 *(Lucarelli 59)* 4313
Auxerre: Cool; Sagna, Kaboul, Kalabane, Jaures (Ba 81), Thomas (Niculae 62), Pedretti, Cheyrou, Akale, Pieroni, Jelen.
Livorno: Amelia; Grandoni, Rezaei, Kuffour, Pasquale, Pfertzel (Balleri 89), Morrone, Passoni, Filippini, Bakayoko (Galante 65), Lucarelli (Danilevicius 85).

Rangers (0) 1 *(Hutton 55)*
Partizan Belgrade (0) 0 45,129
Rangers: McGregor; Hutton (Lowing 75), Rodriguez, Svensson, Smith, Hemdani, N'Diaye, Buffel (Stanger 80), Rae, Sebo, Novo (Sionko 64).
Partizan Belgrade: Asprogenis; Rnic, Mihajlov, Djordjevic, Lomic, Zajic, Smiljanic, Tomic, Nebojsa Marinkovic (Vukelia 69), Bosancic (Nenad Marinkovic 67), Mirosavljevic (Gulan 89).

Group A Final Table	P	W	D	L	F	A	Pts
Rangers	4	3	1	0	8	4	10
Maccabi Haifa	4	2	1	1	5	4	7
Livorno	4	1	2	1	5	5	5
Auxerre	4	1	1	2	7	7	4
Partizan Belgrade	4	0	1	3	2	7	1

GROUP B

Thursday, 19 October 2006

Besiktas (0) 0

Tottenham H (1) 2 *(Ghali 32, Berbatov 63)* 26,800

Besiktas: Vedran; Serdar, Mehmet (Deivson 46), Gokhan, Burak, Baki, Marcio Nobre, Ricardinho, Ibrahim U, Fahri (Ibrahim A 66), Ibrahim T.
Tottenham H: Robinson; Chimbonda, Assou-Ekotto, Huddlestone, Dawson, King, Ghali (Lennon 83), Jenas, Berbatov, Keane, Murphy (Ziegler 80).

FC Brugge (0) 1 *(Clement 47)*

Leverkusen (1) 1 *(Schneider 35)* 17,789

FC Brugge: Stijnen; Clement, Gvozdenovic, Maertens, Pedersen, Blondel, Daerden, Englebert, Vermant, Ishiaku (Yulu-Matondo 87), Balaban.
Leverkusen: Butt; Stenman, Juan (Toure 80), Haggui, Madouni, Schneider, Barnetta (Babic 90), Barbarez, Rolfes, Ramelow, Kiessling (Voronin 67).

Thursday, 2 November 2006

Dinamo Bucharest (1) 2 *(Cristea 21, Niculescu 87 (pen))*

Besiktas (0) 1 *(Deivson 58)* 12,000

Dinamo Bucharest: Hayeu; Pulhac, Blay, Radu, Moti■, Margaritescu■, Munteanu (Ropotan 61), Serban (Kalanga 44), Cristea, Niculescu, Ganea I (Danciulescu 46).
Besiktas: Vedran; Serdar, Ibrahim T, Ali T, Gokhan■, Delgado, Kleberson (Burak 66), Ibrahim U, Koray, Ricardinho, Deivson.

Tottenham Hotspur (1) 3 *(Berbatov 17, 73, Keane 63)*

FC Brugge (1) 1 *(Ibrahim 14)* 35,716

Tottenham Hotspur: Robinson; Chimbonda, Assou-Ekotto, Zokora, Dawson, King, Lennon (Murphy 80), Jenas, Berbatov (Mido 80), Keane, Ghali.
FC Brugge: Stijnen; Pedersen, Clement, Maertens (Vandelannoite 80), Gvozdenovic, Yulu-Matondo, Vermant, Blondel, Englebert, Ibrahim, Balaban (Ishiaku 90).

Thursday, 23 November 2006

FC Brugge (0) 1 *(Vermant 62 (pen))*

Dinamo Bucharest (1) 1 *(Niculescu 33)* 18,713

FC Brugge: Stijnen; Clement, Pedersen, Maertens, Gvozdenovic, Daerden, Blondel (Chavez Castillo 80), Englebert, Vermant (Leko 85), Ibrahim, Ishiaku (Van Heerden 36).
Dinamo Bucharest: Hayeu; Pulhac, Goian, Blay, Galamaz (Mihut 71), Radu, Serban (Munteanu 59), Cristea, Ropotan, Ganea I (Danciulescu 66), Niculescu.

Leverkusen (0) 0

Tottenham Hotspur (1) 1 *(Berbatov 36)* 22,500

Leverkusen: Butt; Madouni, Juan, Ramelow (De Wit 80), Schneider, Rolfes, Barnetta (Schwegler 15), Barbarez, Castro, Voronin, Kiessling (Freier 46).
Tottenham Hotspur: Robinson; Chimbonda, Assou-Ekotto, Zokora, Dawson, King, Lennon, Malbranque (Huddlestone 68), Berbatov (Mido 76), Keane, Tainio.

Wednesday, 29 November 2006

Besiktas (1) 2 *(Ibrahim A 32, Ricardinho 70 (pen))*

FC Brugge (1) 1 *(Balaban 14 (pen))* 19,668

Besiktas: Vedran; Serdar, Baki, Ali T (Burak 60), Ibrahim T, Marcio Nobre (Dogan 83), Kleberson (Deivson 60), Ricardinho, Ibrahim U, Koray, Ibrahim A■.
FC Brugge: Stijnen; Gvozdenovic, Maertens (Chavez Castillo 84), Clement, Pedersen, Van Heerden, Blondel (Daerden 72), Englebert, Vermant, Balaban, Ibrahim.

Dinamo Bucharest (1) 2 *(Niculescu 37, 74)*

Leverkusen (1) 1 *(Barbarez 22)* 12,000

Dinamo Bucharest: Hayeu; Pulhac, Moti, Radu, Blay (Mihut 80), Margaritescu, Munteanu (Danciulescu 62), Serban (Ropotan 56), Cristea, Ganea I, Niculescu.
Leverkusen: Butt; Juan, Athirson, Madouni, Rolfes, Barbarez, Freier, Babic (Stenman 59), Schneider, Castro, Voronin (Kiessling 50).

Thursday, 14 December 2006

Leverkusen (0) 2 *(Schneider 78, Barbarez 87)*

Besiktas (0) 1 *(Ricardinho 90 (pen))* 22,500

Leverkusen: Butt; Juan, Haggui (Kiessling 75), Rolfes, Freier, Athirson, Babic, Schneider, Castro (Barnetta 65), Voronin (Callsen-Bracker 78), Barbarez.
Besiktas: Vedran; Ibrahim T, Baki, Koray, Ali, Serdar, Ibrahim U, Kleberson, Ricardinho, Burak, Deivson (Marcio Nobre 66).

Tottenham Hotspur (2) 3 *(Berbatov 16, Defoe 39, 50)*

Dinamo Bucharest (0) 1 *(Mendy 90)* 34,004

Tottenham Hotspur: Robinson; Chimbonda (Stalteri 76), Assou-Ekotto, Zokora, Dawson, King (Davenport 68), Lennon, Huddlestone (Malbranque 68), Berbatov, Defoe, Ghali.
Dinamo Bucharest: Hayeu; Mihut, Radu, Moti, Pulhac, Cristea, Margaritescu (Blay 65), Ropotan, Munteanu (Goian 57), Danciulescu (Mendy 77), Ganea I.

Group B Final Table	P	W	D	L	F	A	Pts
Tottenham Hotspur	4	4	0	0	9	2	12
Dinamo Bucharest	4	2	1	1	6	6	7
Leverkusen	4	1	1	2	4	5	4
Besiktas	4	1	0	3	4	7	3
FC Brugge	4	0	2	2	4	7	2

GROUP C

Thursday, 19 October 2006

AZ (1) 3 *(Arveladze 37, Koevermans 75, Schaars 82)*

Braga (0) 0 13,093

AZ: Didulica; Jaliens, Opdam, De Cler, Schaars (Molhoek 82), Arveladze (Koevermans 70), Cziommer (Steinsson 46), Martens, Dembele, De Zeeuw, Mendes Da Silva.
Braga: Paulo Santos; Paulo Jorge, Mauricio, Hugo Leal (Joao Pinto 44), Carlos Fernandes, Wender (Cesinha 55), Maciel (Jose Carlos 67), Luis Filipe, Ricardo Chaves, Andres Madrid, Marcel.

Slovan Liberec (0) 0

Sevilla (0) 0 7023

Slovan Liberec: Cech; Singlar, Zapotocny, Kostal, Janu, Papousek (Hochmeister 87), Bilek, Hodur (Ancic 77), Pudil (Frejlach 75), Pospech, Holenda.
Sevilla: Palop; Javi Navarro, Escude, Dragutinovic, Daniel Alves, Duda (Jesuli 82), Renato, Fernando Sales (Poulsen 67), Marti, Kepa (Luis Fabiano 47), Kanoute.

Thursday, 2 November 2006

Braga (2) 4 *(Ricardo Chaves 30, Marcel 33, Cesinha 54 (pen), Bruno Gama 90)*

Slovan Liberec (0) 0 15,000

Braga: Paulo Santos; Luis Filipe, Irineu, Nem, Pedro Costa, Vandinho, Andres Madrid, Ricardo Chaves (Bruno Gama 86), Maciel, Marcel (Matheus 46), Cesinha (Joao Pinto 76).
Slovan Liberec: Cech; Singlar, Zapotocny, Kostal, Frejlach (Hochmeister 84), Papousek, Bilek, Hodur (Ancic 62), Pudil, Holenda, Pospech (Parks 45).

Grasshoppers (1) 2 *(Mbala Mbuta 29, Eduardo 62)*

AZ (0) 5 *(Arveladze 48, De Zeeuw 56, Dembele 78, 90, Martens 89)* 5500

Grasshoppers: Coltorti; Jaggy, Langkamp (Schwegler 4), Weligton, Sutter, Dos Santos, Salatic, Mbala Mbuta (Toure 88), Eduardo, Pinto (Leon 75), Ristic.
AZ: Sinouh; De Zeeuw, Jaliens, Opdam, De Cler, Schaars (Koevermans 72), Martens, Mendes Da Silva, Steinsson, Arveladze (Gudjonsson 90), Dembele.

Thursday, 23 November 2006

Sevilla (1) 2 *(Luis Fabiano 40, Chevanton 76)*

Braga (0) 0 37,000

Sevilla: Palop; Javi Navarro, David, Daniel Alves, Adriano (Alfaro 78), Poulsen, Luis Fabiano (Chevanton 66), Renato, Kanoute (Kepa 79), Escude, Puerta.
Braga: Paulo Santos; Paulo Jorge, Nem (Castanheira 70), Cesinha, Carlos Fernandes (Joao Pinto 82), Frechaut, Maciel, Luis Filipe, Ricardo Chaves, Jose Carlos (Wender 70), Vandinho.

Slovan Liberec (2) 4 *(Blazek 7, Zapotocny 21, Papousek 68, Frejlach 90)*

Grasshoppers (1) 1 *(Schwegler 9)* 6670

Slovan Liberec: Cech; Singlar, Zapotocny, Kostal, Janu, Papousek, Bilek, Frejlach, Pudil (Dohnalek 79), Parks (Holenda 65), Blazek (Pospech 79).
Grasshoppers: Coltorti; Sutter, Schwegler, Weligton, Jaggy, Seoane, Dos Santos (Toure 46), Renggli (Ristic 71), Pinto, Mbala Mbuta (Leon 63), Eduardo.

Wednesday, 29 November 2006

AZ (0) 2 *(Steinsson 69, Jenner 89)*

Slovan Liberec (1) 2 *(Zapotocny 26, Papousek 85)* 13,000

AZ: Sinouh (Bulters 37); Opdam, De Cler, Steinsson, Gudjonsson, Schaars, Martens, Mendes Da Silva, Arveladze, Dembele (Lens 78), Koevermans (Jenner 59).
Slovan Liberec: Cech; Zapotocny, Kostal, Janu, Singlar, Bilek, Frejlach, Papousek (Dohnalek 90), Pudil, Parks (Pospech 74), Blazek (Hodur 90).

Grasshoppers (0) 0

Sevilla (1) 4 *(Daniel Alves 12, 53, Chevanton 62, Kepa 84)* 7300

Grasshoppers: Coltorti; Weligton, Denicola, Jaggy, Sutter, Seoane, Eduardo, Leon, Dos Santos (Mbala Mbuta 31), Salatic (Voser 85), Ristic (Blumer 61).
Sevilla: Palop; Javi Navarro, David, Daniel Alves, Dragutinovic, Adriano, Poulsen, Fernando Sales (Hinkel 46), Renato (Marti 59), Chevanton, Luis Fabiano (Kepa 54).

Thursday, 14 December 2006

Braga (0) 2 *(Joao Pinto 61, Castanheira 90)*

Grasshoppers (0) 0 15,000

Braga: Paulo Santos; Luis Filipe, Paulo Jorge, Nem, Carlos Fernandes, Vandinho, Ricardo Chaves, Joao Pinto, Maciel (Castanheira 82), Jose Carlos (Marcel 88), Wender (Cesinha 76).
Grasshoppers: Coltorti; Sutter, Denicola, Weligton, Jaggy, Voser, Salatic (Renggli 69), Pinto, Leon (Blumer 69), Dos Santos (Feltscher 85), Ristic.

Sevilla (0) 1 *(Chevanton 52 (pen))*

AZ (0) 2 *(Arveladze 62, 90)* 33,500

Sevilla: Cobeno; Daniel Alves, David, Escude, Aitor Ocio, Adriano (Duda 65), Poulsen, Renato, Marti, Jesus Navas, Chevanton (Kepa 79).
AZ: Bulters; Jaliens, Opdam, De Cler, Steinsson (Luirink 43), Cziommer, Molhoek (Schaars 69), De Zeeuw (Jenner 55), Mendes Da Silva, Arveladze, Dembele.

Group C Final Table	*P*	*W*	*D*	*L*	*F*	*A*	*Pts*
AZ	4	3	1	0	12	5	10
Sevilla	4	2	1	1	7	2	7
Braga	4	2	0	2	6	5	6
Slovan Liberec	4	1	2	1	6	7	5
Grasshoppers	4	0	0	4	3	15	0

GROUP D

Thursday, 19 October 2006

Odense (1) 1 *(Hansen 7)*

Parma (1) 2 *(Dessena 41, Budan 51)* 12,559

Odense: Onyszko; Sorensen, Ophaug (Lekic 73), Laursen, Christensen, Bechara, Grahn, Hansen, Borring, Timm (Nymann 85), Borre.
Parma: De Lucia; Coly (Paci 46), Cardone, Rossi, Bocchetti, Savi, Cigarini, Ciaramitaro, Dessena, Pisanu (Budan 46), Paponi (Bolano 89).

Osasuna (0) 0

Heerenveen (0) 0 19,553

Osasuna: Elia; Izquierdo, Corrales, Cuellar, Miguel Flano, Juanfran (Romeo 76), Punal, Nekouman, Juanlu (Delporte 64), Milosevic (Valdo 46), Soldado.
Heerenveen: Vandenbussche; Dingsdag, Hansson, Zuiverloon, Breuer, Nilsson■, Pranjic, Prager (Kissi 35), Afonso Alves, Friend (Yildirim 66), Hanssen.

Thursday, 2 November 2006

Heerenveen (0) 0

Odense (1) 2 *(Lekic 45, 60)* 17,500

Heerenveen: Vandenbussche; Hansson, Dingsdag (Breuer 64), Drost J, Zuiverloon, Bosvelt (Bradley 61), Hanssen (Storm 76), Pranjic, Yildirim, Friend, Afonso Alves.
Odense: Onyszko; Ophaug, Laursen, Christensen, Sorensen, Bechara, Grahn (Fevang 90), Borre, Borring, Lekic, Hansen.

Lens (1) 3 *(Dindane 15, Cousin 69 (pen), Boukari 82)*

Osasuna (0) 1 *(Valdo 46)* 33,833

Lens: Itandje; Gillet, Hilton, Barul (Cousin 58), Vignal, Sidi Keita, Demont, Seydou Keita (Monnet-Paquet 58), Carriere, Dindane (Diane 85), Boukari.
Osasuna: Elia; Izquierdo (Javier Flano 33), Cruchaga, Corrales, Josetxo, Raul Garcia, Nekouman (Romeo 75), Delporte, Valdo, David Lopez (Punal 62), Soldado.

Thursday, 23 November 2006

Odense (0) 1 *(Grahn 58)*

Lens (0) 1 *(Jemaa 87)* 7707

Odense: Onyszko; Ophaug, Laursen, Sorensen, Christensen, Bechara, Grahn, Hansen, Borre, Borring, Lekic.
Lens: Itandje; Hilton, Coulibaly, Vignal, Barul, Seydou Keita, Sidi Keita (Jemaa 80), Cousin, Jussie (Demont 46), Monnet-Paquet (Boukari 60), Thomert.

Parma (1) 2 *(Budan 24, 73)*

Heerenveen (1) 1 *(Pranjic 21)* 3632

Parma: De Lucia; Ferronetti, Fernando Couto (Contini 46), Rossi, Castellini, Dessena, Cigarini, Savi, Dedic (Ciaramitaro 82), Budan, Kutuzov (Gasbarroni 65).
Heerenveen: Vandenbussche; Zuiverloon (Poulsen 28) (Bradley 82), Breuer, Hansson, Drost J (Friend 76), Bosvelt, Hanssen, Pranjic, Nilsson, Afonso Alves, Yildirim.

Wednesday, 29 November 2006

Lens (1) 1 *(Cousin 19)*

Parma (0) 2 *(Dedic 77, Paponi 90)* 32,341

Lens: Itandje; Barul, Gillet, Hilton, Vignal, Boukari (Demont 56), Carriere (Thomert 80), Seydou Keita, Sidi Keita, Cousin, Jemaa (Jussie 66).
Parma: De Lucia; Castellini, Rossi, Ferronetti, Coly (Contini 46), Dedic (Gasbarroni 82), Grella, Moretti, Kutuzov (Paponi 72), Savi, Budan.

Osasuna (1) 3 *(Punal 29, 67, Romeo 87)*

Odense (0) 1 *(Punal 75 (og))* 13,115

Osasuna: Ricardo; Javier Flano, Cruchaga, Josetxo, Corrales, Nekouman, David Lopez (Munoz 89), Punal, Valdo, Soldado (Romeo 73), Milosevic (Raul Garcia 82).
Odense: Onyszko; Ophaug, Laursen, Christensen, Sorensen, Hansen, Borre, Bechara (Fevang 77), Borring, Grahn, Lekic.

Thursday, 14 December 2006

Heerenveen (0) 1 *(Afonso Alves 90)*

Lens (0) 0 23,000

Heerenveen: Vandenbussche; Zuiverloon, Hansson, Dingsdag, Breuer, Poulsen, Hanssen (Friend 55), Prager (Bradley 80), Pranjic, Nilsson (Tarvajarvi 65), Afonso Alves.
Lens: Itandje; Hilton, Coulibaly, Ramos, Demont, Sidi Keita, Carriere, Seydou Keita, Dindane (Gillet 88), Cousin (Boukari 77), Jussie (Jemaa 77).

Parma (0) 0

Osasuna (2) 3 *(David Lopez 33, 44, Juanfran 82)* 3109

Parma: De Lucia; Bocchetti, Rossi, Paci, Coly, Pisanu (Paponi 46), Bolano, Savi (Lorenzini 70), Ciaramitaro, Dedic, Kutuzov.
Osasuna: Ricardo; Monreal, Cruchaga, Javier Flano, Josetxo, Punal, Valdo, David Lopez (Juanfran 73), Nekouman (Raul Garcia 77), Soldado (Romeo 67), Milosevic.

Group D Final Table	*P*	*W*	*D*	*L*	*F*	*A*	*Pts*
Parma	4	3	0	1	6	6	9
Osasuna	4	2	1	1	7	4	7
Lens	4	1	1	2	5	5	4
Odense	4	1	1	2	5	6	4
Heerenveen	4	1	1	2	2	4	4

GROUP E

Thursday, 19 October 2006

Basle (0) 1 *(Eduardo 60)*

Feyenoord (0) 1 *(Huysegems 76)* 15,428

Basle: Costanzo; Majstorovic, Nakata, Sterjovski (Eduardo 59), Petric, Chipperfield, Papa Malick, Buckley (Berner 77), Ergic, Kuzmanovic (Cristiano 82), Zanni.
Feyenoord: Timmer; Saidi, Bahia, Buijs, Pardo (Huysegems 71), Charisteas, Leonard, Greene, Boussaboun, Tiendalli, De Guzman.

Wisla (1) 1 *(Cantoro 28)*

Blackburn R (0) 2 *(Savage 56, Bentley 90)* 14,000

Wisla: Dolha; Baszczynski, Dudka, Cleber, Mijailovic, Blaszczykowski, Sobolewski, Cantoro, Zienczuk (Piotr Brozek 66), Paulista, Radovanovic (Kryszalowicz 83).
Blackburn R: Friedel; Emerton, Neill, Tugay, Khizanishvili, Ooijer, Bentley, Savage (Mokoena 87), Nonda, McCarthy, Pedersen (Roberts 74).

Thursday, 2 November 2006

Blackburn Rovers (0) 3 *(Tugay 75, Jeffers 89 (pen), McCarthy 90)*

Basle (0) 0 13,789

Blackburn Rovers: Friedel; Neill, Gray, Tugay (Gallagher 84), Khizanishvili, Ooijer, Bentley, Savage (Mokoena 38), Nonda (Jeffers 83), McCarthy, Pedersen.
Basle: Costanzo; Zanni, Majstorovic, Papa Malik, Chipperfield, Rakitic (Cristiano 55), Kuzmanovic, Sterjovski, Eduardo (Buckley 64), Ergic, Petric.

Nancy (1) 2 *(Berenguer 11, 58)*

Wisla (1) 1 *(Pavel Brozek 32)* 17,509

Nancy: Bracigliano; Diakhate, Zerka, Macaluso, Berenguer, Duchemin, Biancalani (Sauget 74), Chretien, Nguemo, Kim (Dia 65), Dosunmu (Andre Luiz 81).
Wisla: Dolha; Baszczynski, Dudka, Cleber, Thwaite (Radovanovic 89), Blaszczykowski, Sobolewski, Varga■, Cantoro (Paulista 66), Zienczuk (Piotr Brozek 60), Pavel Brozek.

Thursday, 23 November 2006

Basle (1) 2 *(Chipperfield 32, Sterjovski 36)*

Nancy (2) 2 *(Kim 31, Berenguer 34)* 14,497

Basle: Costanzo■; Majstorovic, Kuzmanovic, Zanni, Papa Malik (Rakitic 58), Nakata, Sterjovski (Eduardo 68), Chipperfield, Buckley (Cristiano 79), Ergic, Petric.
Nancy: Sorin; Diakhate, Lecluse, Zerka (Chretien 76), Sauget (Macaluso 86), Andre Luiz, Berenguer, Duchemin, Biancalani, Kim (Brison 59), Dia.

Feyenoord (0) 0

Blackburn Rovers (0) 0 35,000

Feyenoord: Timmer; Tiendalli, Bahia, Greene, Drenthe, Buijs, Hofs (De Guzman 77), Lucius, Kolkka (Boussaboun 65), Charisteas, Huysegems.
Blackburn Rovers: Friedel; Emerton, Gray, Tugay (Mokoena 81), Khizanishvili, Ooijer, Bentley, Savage, Nonda (Jeffers 69), McCarthy (Peter 90), Pedersen.

Thursday, 30 November 2006

Nancy (2) 3 *(Puygrenier 22, Kim 42, Zerka 66 (pen))*

Feyenoord (0) 0 19,047

Nancy: Sorin; Zerka, Diakhate, Puygrenier, Sauget, Berenguer, Chretien, Duchemin, Dia (Gavanon 75), Curbelo (Andre Luiz 71), Kim (Brison 57).
Feyenoord: Timmer; Saidi, Derijck, Bahia, Greene, Drenthe■, Buijs, De Guzman, Van Hooijdonk, Huysegems, Charisteas (Boussaboun 67).

Wisla (1) 3 *(Pavel Brozek 11, 83, Paulista 71)*

Basle (1) 1 *(Petric 8)* 5000

Wisla: Dolha; Baszczynski, Dudka, Cleber■, Thwaite, Blaszczykowski (Kokoszka 90), Sobolewski, Burns, Zienczuk, Pavel Brozek (Malecki 90), Piotr Brozek (Paulista 65).
Basle: Crayton; Chipperfield, Nakata, Majstorovic, Zanni, Buckley (Rakitic 62), Papa Malik, Ergic, Kuzmanovic (Cristiano 82), Petric, Sterjovski.

Wednesday, 13 December 2006

Blackburn Rovers (0) 1 *(Neill 90)*

Nancy (0) 0 12,568

Blackburn Rovers: Friedel; Neill, McEveley, Mokoena, Todd (Nolan 28), Ooijer, Bentley, Savage, Gallagher (McCarthy 67), Derbyshire, Peter (Pedersen 67).
Nancy: Lapeyre; Lecluse, Diakhate, Puygrenier, Chretien, Berenguer, Andre Luiz, Gavanon, Biancalani (Sauget 73), Kim (Curbelo 76), Dia (Nguemo 64).

Feyenoord (2) 3 *(Hofs 16, De Guzman 41, Charisteas 67)*

Wisla (1) 1 *(Pawel Brozek 23)* 25,000

Feyenoord: Timmer; Vlaar, Bahia, Greene, De Guzman, Buijs, Hofs (Derijck 90), Lucius, Kolkka (Vincken 76), Charisteas, Huysegems (Van Hooijdonk 63).
Wisla: Dolha; Baszczynski, Glowacki, Dudka■, Thwaite, Blaszczykowski, Sobolewski, Burns, Zienczuk, Paulista (Piotr Brozek 69), Pawel Brozek (Radovanovic 90).
Feyenoord fined then removed from the competition for crowd trouble at Nancy; Tottenham Hotspur received a bye.

Group E Final Table	*P*	*W*	*D*	*L*	*F*	*A*	*Pts*
Blackburn Rovers	4	3	1	0	6	1	10
Nancy	4	2	1	1	7	4	7
Feyenoord	4	1	2	1	4	5	5
Wisla	4	1	0	3	6	8	3
Basle	4	0	2	2	4	9	2

GROUP F

Thursday, 19 October 2006

FK Austria (1) 1 *(Lasnik 22)*

Waregem (1) 4 *(Mattijs 33, 56, 69, Vandendriessche 90)* 11,100

FK Austria: Safar; Troyansky (Schicker 61), Tokic, Metz, Schiemer (Wallner 46), Radomski (Dos Santos 72), Blanchard, Lasnik, Vachousek, Ertl, Mair.
Waregem: De Vlieger; Reina, Dindeleux, De Brul, D'Haemers, Verschuere, Meert (Vandemarliere 70), Sergeant, Van Nieuwenhuyze, Datti, Matthijs (Vandendriessche 85).

Sparta Prague (0) 0

Espanyol (1) 2 *(Luis Garcia 17 (pen), Riera 85)* 11,020

Sparta Prague: Blazek; Pospech, Repka, Homola, Kadlec, Kolar (Lustrinelli 83), Sylvestre (Jun 59), Kisel, Matusovic, Dosek, Simak.
Espanyol: Iraizoz; Sergio Sanchez (Chica 51), Jarque, Torrejon, Fredson, Zabaleta, Moha, Riera (Julian 89), De la Pena (Ito 80), Luis Garcia, Pandiani.

Thursday, 2 November 2006

Ajax (1) 3 *(Huntelaar 35, 68, Manucharyan 65)*

FK Austria (0) 0 32,285

Ajax: Stekelenburg; Heitinga, Stam, Emanuelson, Maduro (Manucharyan 57), Rosales (De Mul 46), Huntelaar, Sneijder (Vertonghen 78), Perez, Gabri, Grygera.

FK Austria: Safar; Troyansky, Tokic, Mair (Wimmer 87), Vachousek (Metz 82), Aigner (Wallner 66), Lasnik, Blanchard, Kiesenebner, Ertl, Schiemer.

Waregem (2) 3 *(Roussel 4, Meert 17, Sergeant 63)*

Sparta Prague (0) 1 *(Lustrinelli 85)* 10,500

Waregem: De Vlieger; Leleu, Dindeleux, Reina, D'Haemers, Van Nieuwenhuyze, Sergeant, Veschuere, Meert (Vandemarliere 43), Roussel (Mrdja 81), Matthijs (Janssens 88).

Sparta Prague: Grigar; Pospech, Repka, Zabavnik, Kadlec, Sivok, Kolar (Lustrinelli 56), Simak, Sylvestre, Matusovic, Dosek (Jun 77).

Thursday, 23 November 2006

Espanyol (4) 6 *(Corominas 9, Pandiani 14, 83, Luis Garcia 19, 27 (pen), 73)*

Waregem (1) 2 *(Matthijs 17, D'Haene 62)* 9250

Espanyol: Iraizoz; Lacruz, Velasco, Corominas, Jarque, Moises Hurtado, Zabaleta, De la Pena (Eduardo Costa 56), Pandiani, Luis Garcia (Rufete 80), Riera (Moha 59).

Waregem: Merlier; Leleu (D'Haene 46), Reina, Dindeleux, Van Nieuwenhuyze, Sergeant, Verschuere (Datti 70), Meert (Vandendriessche 46), D'Haemers, Matthijs, Roussel.

Sparta Prague (0) 0

Ajax (0) 0 12,230

Sparta Prague: Blazek; Repka, Drobny, Zabavnik, Kadlec (Jun 66), Sivok, Kolar, Kisel (Sylvestre 75), Pospech, Matusovic, Lustrinelli.

Ajax: Stekelenburg; Ogararu, Stam, Grygera, Vermaelen, Gabri, Heitinga, Sneijder (Rosales 90), Emanuelson■, Huntelaar (Lindenbergh 40), Rosenberg (De Mul 67).

Thursday, 30 November 2006

Ajax (0) 0

Espanyol (1) 2 *(Pandiani 36, Corominas 78)* 41,248

Ajax: Stekelenburg; Heitinga, Vermaelen, Grygera, Ogararu, Maduro (Vertonghen 46), Sneijder, Roger (Mitea 46), Gabri (De Mul 72), Rosales, Huntelaar.

Espanyol: Iraizoz; Lacruz, Jarque, Chica, Moises Hurtado, Velasco, Eduardo Costa, Moha (Riera 78), Corominas (De la Pena 88), Pandiani, Luis Garcia (Zabaleta 72).

FK Austria (0) 0

Sparta Prague (1) 1 *(Repka 11)* 8600

FK Austria: Safar; Metz, Hill, Ertl, Lasnik, Schragner, Kiesenebner, Netzer (Blanchard 65), Dos Santos (Wallner 78), Mair (Mila 69), Pichlmann.

Sparta Prague: Grigar; Zabavnik, Drobny, Repka, Kadlec, Pospech, Kisel (Lustrinelli 86), Sivok, Matusovic (Kolar 46), Simak (Sylvestre 73), Dosek.

Wednesday, 13 December 2006

Espanyol (0) 1 *(Pandiani 57)*

FK Austria (0) 0 5580

Espanyol: Iraizoz; David Garcia (Chica 72), Lacruz, Sergio Sanchez, Velasco, Corominas, Fredson (Angel Martinez 46), Ito, Riera, Rufete (Julian 52), Pandiani.

FK Austria: Safar; Tokic, Ertl, Madl, Metz, Mila (Wallner 63), Lasnik, Blanchard, Kiesenebner, Aigner (Pichlmann 71), Mair (Dos Santos 81).

Waregem (0) 0

Ajax (1) 3 *(Huntelaar 4, 57, Heitinga 83)* 11,603

Waregem: Merlier; Minne, Leleu (Buysse 81), Reina, D'Haene, Dindeleux, Van Nieuwenhuyze■, Verschuere (Gonzales-Vigil 81), Meert (Vandemarliere 62), Matthijs, Roussel.

Ajax: Stekelenburg; Heitinga, Stam, Emanuelson, Grygera, Ogararu, Gabri, Sneijder (Vermaelen 46), Huntelaar (De Mul 74), Babel, Perez.

Group F Final Table	P	W	D	L	F	A	Pts
Espanyol	4	4	0	0	11	2	12
Ajax	4	2	1	1	6	2	7
Waregem	4	2	0	2	9	11	6
Sparta Prague	4	1	1	2	2	5	4
FK Austria	4	0	0	4	1	9	0

GROUP G

Thursday, 19 October 2006

Panathinaikos (0) 2 *(Chen 47 (og), Romero 64)*

Hapoel Tel Aviv (0) 0

Panathinaikos: Ebede; Antonsson (Biscan 49), Morris, Seric, Vintra, Romero, Andric, Ivanschitz, Victor (Leontiou 60), Papadopoulos (Mantzios 73), Salpigidis.

Hapoel Tel Aviv: Elimelech; Chen, Haliva, Antebi, Paez, Degu (De Bruno 59), Abuksis, Badir, Vermouth (Ogbona 68), Toema (Jolic 80), Barda.

Behind closed doors.

Rapid Bucharest (0) 0

Paris St Germain (0) 0 9000

Rapid Bucharest: Coman; Rada, Zicu (Griffiths 67), Badoi, Karamian, Lazar, Maldarasanu, Sapunaru, Maftei, Buga (Burdujan 81), Moldovan.

Paris St Germain: Landreau; Mendy, Yepes, Rozehnal, Traore, Paulo Cesar, Armand, Drame, Chantome (Cisse 46), Diane (Pauleta 62), Frau (Kalou 86).

Thursday, 2 November 2006

Hapoel Tel Aviv (2) 2 *(Ogbona 10, Badir 33)*

Rapid Bucharest (1) 2 *(Moldovan 14, Buga 53)* 12,000

Hapoel Tel Aviv: Elimelech; Bondarv, Paez, Badir, Antebi, Abuksis (Abutbul 71), Dego (Chen 46), De Bruno, Barda, Ogbona (Vermouth 76), Toema.

Rapid Bucharest: Coman; Rada, Maftei, Sapunaru, Karamian (Griffiths 68), Lazar, Maldarasanu (Grigore 82), Badoi, Zicu (Mazilu 57), Buga, Moldovan.

Mlada Boleslav (0) 0

Panathinaikos (0) 1 *(Salpigidis 64)* 4280

Mlada Boleslav: Miller; Sevinsky, Brezinsky (Rajnoch 75), Rolko, Palat, Matejovsky, Ngasanya, Sedlacek (Kysela 56), Polacek (Holub 69), Kulic, Pecka.

Panathinaikos: Ebede; Vintra, Morris, Leontiou, Tziolis, Darlas, Biscan, Mantzios (Victor 58), Ivanschitz (Romero 19), Nilsson, Salpigidis (Theodoridis 82).

Thursday, 23 November 2006

Paris St Germain (2) 2 *(Frau 14, Pauleta 25)*

Hapoel Tel Aviv (3) 4 *(Toema 2, 6, Badir 44, Barda 57)* 35,000

Paris St Germain: Landreau; Cisse, Rozehnal, Armand, Drame, Paulo Cesar (Kalou 58), Mulumbu (Rodriguez 72), Hellebuyck, Rothen, Frau (Pancrate 65), Pauleta.

Hapoel Tel Aviv: Elimelech; Haliva, Badir, Paez, Antebi, Abuksis, Abutbul, Barda, Dego (Vermouth 80), Toema (Natcho 89), Ogbona (Chen 74).

Rapid Bucharest (0) 1 *(Constantin M 52)*

Mlada Boleslav (1) 1 *(Rajnoch 42)* 6600

Rapid Bucharest: Coman; Rada, Constantin M, Maftei (Perja 28), Badoi, Karamian, Maldarasanu, Grigore (Lazar 58), Zicu, Mazilu (Moldovan 25), Buga.

Mlada Boleslav: Miller; Abraham (Smerda 82), Palat, Brezinsky, Nesvadba, Matejovsky, Vaculik (Kysela 69), Polacek (Holub 62), Pecka, Rajnoch, Kulic.

Thursday, 30 November 2006

Mlada Boleslav (0) 0

Paris St Germain (0) 0 8480

Mlada Boleslav: Miller; Palat, Rajnoch, Brezinsky (Rolko 78), Sevinsky, Kysela (Holub 59), Abraham, Matejovsky, Polacek, Pecka (Sedlacek 26), Kulic.

Paris St Germain: Landreau; Mendy, Rozehnal, Yepes, Armand (Baning 46), Diane■, Drame, Chantome, Hellebuyck (Rodriguez 77), Kalou, Pauleta.

Panathinaikos (0) 0

Rapid Bucharest (0) 0 18,000

Panathinaikos: Ebede; Vintra (Nilsson 60), Morris, Biscan, Darlas, Romero, Leontiou (Andric 88), Tziolis, Ivanschitz, Salpigidis, Mantzios (Papadopoulos 68).
Rapid Bucharest: Bete; Rada, Buga (Griffiths 66), Constantin■, Lazar, Zicu, Badoi, Karamian, Maftei, Moldovan (Sapunaru 86), Maldarasanu (Grigore 81).

Wednesday, 13 December 2006

Hapoel Tel Aviv (1) 1 *(Barda 27)*

Mlada Boleslav (1) 1 *(Kysela 39)* 8000

Hapoel Tel Aviv: Elimelech; Bondarv, Antebi, Paez, Abuksis, Badir, Vermouth (Jolic 78), Toema, Abutbul (Doani 89), Barda, Ogbona (Dego 46).
Mlada Boleslav: Miller; Palat, Brezinsky, Nesvadba (Rolko 46), Abraham (Vaculik 80), Matejovsky, Polacek (Holub 68), Rajnoch, Kysela, Kulic, Sedlacek.

Paris St Germain (1) 4 *(Pauleta 29, 47, Kalou 52, 54)*

Panathinaikos (0) 0 22,000

Paris St Germain: Landreau; Mendy, Rozehnal, Yepes, Armand, Rodriguez (Paulo Cesar 79), Cisse, Chantome, Hellebuyck, Kalou (Pancrate 83), Pauleta (Pietre 73).
Panathinaikos: Ebede; Darlas, Vintra (Victor 46), Biscan, Morris, Theodoridis (Gonzalez 46), Leontiou, Tziolis, Ivanschitz, Nilsson, Papadopoulos (Salpigidis 46).

Group G Final Table	*P*	*W*	*D*	*L*	*F*	*A*	*Pts*
Panathinaikos	4	2	1	1	3	4	7
Paris St Germain	4	1	2	1	6	4	5
Hapoel Tel Aviv	4	1	2	1	7	7	5
Rapid Bucharest	4	0	4	0	3	3	4
Mlada Boleslav	4	0	3	1	2	3	3

GROUP H

Thursday, 19 October 2006

Eintracht Frankfurt (1) 1 *(Streit 45)*

Palermo (0) 2 *(Brienza 50, Zaccardo 88)* 45,000

Eintracht Frankfurt: Proll; Vasoski, Spycher, Kyrgiakos, Rehmer (Ochs 64), Meier, Streit, Huggel, Kohler, Thurk (Fink 85), Amanatidis.
Palermo: Fontana; Zaccardo, Guana, Dellafiore, Parravicini, Biava, Pisano, Capuano (Bresciano 74), Munari (Diana Aimo 62), Brienza, Caracciolo.

Newcastle United (0) 1 *(Sibierski 79)*

Fenerbahce (0) 0 30,035

Newcastle United: Harper; Carr, Taylor, Parker, Ramage, Emre (Butt 54), Milner, Sibierski, Martins (Ameobi 75), Duff, N'Zogbia (Solano 64).
Fenerbahce: Rustu; Onder, Lugano, Edu, Umit O (Deivid 81), Mehmet (Ugur 69), Appiah, Marco Aurelio, Tuncay, Kezman, Alex.

Thursday, 2 November 2006

Celta Vigo (1) 1 *(Perera 11)*

Eintracht Frankfurt (1) 1 *(Huber 17)* 10,000

Celta Vigo: Esteban; Lequi, Angel, Tamas, Pablo Garcia, Jonathan, Nene, Canobbio, Iriney (Nunez 71), Perera, Guayre (Baiano 71).
Eintracht Frankfurt: Nikolov; Ochs, Vasoski, Spycher, Huber (Fink 46), Kyrgiakos, Kohler (Russ 65), Meier■, Huggel, Thurk, Takahara (Amanatidis 74).

Palermo (0) 0

Newcastle United (1) 1 *(Luque 37)* 16,904

Palermo: Fontana; Dellafiore, Cassani, Barzagli (Biava 46), Pisano, Tedesco (Simplicio 66), Guana (Di Michele 66), Parravicini, Munari, Brienza, Caracciolo.
Newcastle United: Krul; Ramage, Taylor, Butt, Moore, Bramble, Solano (Carroll 90), Emre, Luque (Pattison 77), Milner, N'Zogbia (Sibierski 68).

Thursday, 23 November 2006

Fenerbahce (1) 3 *(Appiah 20, Lugano 62, Tuncay 83)*

Palermo (0) 0 39,071

Fenerbahce: Volkan; Onder, Deniz, Edu, Lugano, Appiah, Mehmet (Marco Aurelio 74), Alex (Semih 90), Ugur, Tuncay, Kezman (Deivid 89).
Palermo: Sirigu; Tedesco (Cassani 46), Dellafiore, Parravicini, Munari (Guana 79), Barzagli (Zaccardo 46), Simplicio, Brienza, Firicano, Cossentino, Caracciolo.

Newcastle United (1) 2 *(Sibierski 37, Taylor 86)*

Celta Vigo (1) 1 *(Canobbio 9)* 25,079

Newcastle United: Given; Solano, Ramage, Butt (Parker 65), Taylor, Bramble, Milner, Emre (Martins 70), Luque, Sibierski, N'Zogbia.
Celta Vigo: Esteban; Angel, Yago, Contreras, Placente, Jonathan, Iriney, Borja Oubina, Nene (Gustavo Lopez 74), Baiano (Perera 61), Canobbio (Jorge 86).

Thursday, 30 November 2006

Celta Vigo (0) 1 *(Canobbio 77)*

Fenerbahce (0) 0 12,000

Celta Vigo: Esteban; Angel (Gustavo Lopez 21), Placente, Contreras, Tamas, Borja Oubina, Jonathan, Nene, Canobbio, Iriney (Perera 73), Baiano (Yago 90).
Fenerbahce: Volkan; Onder, Deniz (Mehmet 82), Lugano, Edu, Appiah, Marco Aurelio, Alex, Ugur (Tumer 81), Kezman (Deivid 71), Tuncay.

Eintracht Frankfurt (0) 0

Newcastle United (0) 0 47,000

Eintracht Frankfurt: Proll; Vasoski, Kyrgiakos, Spycher, Rehmer (Ochs 64), Streit, Huggel, Weissenberger, Takahara, Amanatidis (Fink 78), Kohler.
Newcastle United: Given; Solano, Ramage, Butt, Taylor, Bramble, Milner, Emre, Luque (Martins 59), Sibierski, N'Zogbia.

Wednesday, 13 December 2006

Fenerbahce (0) 2 *(Tuncay 64, Semih 83)*

Eintracht Frankfurt (1) 2 *(Takahara 7, 52)* 44,123

Fenerbahce: Volkan; Lugano, Deniz (Mehmet 47), Edu, Onder, Appiah, Marco Aurelio (Semih■ 76), Alex, Ugur, Kezman (Deivid 72), Tuncay.
Eintracht Frankfurt: Proll; Vasoski, Russ, Fink, Rehmer (Thurk 85), Kyrgiakos, Spycher, Streit, Weissenberger (Meier 71), Kohler (Ochs 62), Takahara.

Palermo (0) 1 *(Tedesco 70)*

Celta Vigo (0) 1 *(Baiano 59)* 10,222

Palermo: Agliardi; Zaccardo, Cassani, Barzagli, Pisano, Guana (Parravicini 83), Corini (Tedesco 63), Bresciano (Brienza 63), Simplicio, Caracciolo, Di Michele.
Celta Vigo: Esteban; Lequi, Angel, Placente, Contreras, Iriney, Gustavo Lopez (Tamas 88), Canobbio (Jorge 90), Borja Oubina, Nene (Nunez 90), Baiano.

Group H Final Table	*P*	*W*	*D*	*L*	*F*	*A*	*Pts*
Newcastle United	4	3	1	0	4	1	10
Celta Vigo	4	1	2	1	4	4	5
Fenerbahce	4	1	1	2	5	4	4
Palermo	4	1	1	2	3	6	4
Eintracht Frankfurt	4	0	3	1	4	5	3

KNOCK-OUT STAGE

THIRD ROUND FIRST LEG

Tottenham H bye after Feyenoord removed

Wednesday, 14 February 2007

AEK Athens (0) 0

Paris St Germain (1) 2 *(Traore 45, Mendy 88)* 26,120

AEK Athens: Sorrentino; Moras, Cirillo, Tziortziopoulos, Kiriakidis (Kafes 46), Pliatsikas (Georgeas 63), Lakis (Kone 53), Tozser, Manduca, Kapetanos, Julio Cesar.
Paris St Germain: Landreau; Mendy, Traore, Cisse, Kalou, Chantome, Rodriguez, Hellebuyck, Mulumbu, Diane (Luyindula 68), Sakho (Drame 85).

Benfica (0) 1 *(Miccoli 90)*

Dinamo Bucharest (0) 0 35,197

Benfica: Quim; Nelson, Anderson, Luisao, Leo, Petit (Miccoli 46), Katsouranis, Karagounis, Rui Costa (Joao Coimbra 90), Nuno Gomes (Derlei 75), Simao Sabrosa.
Dinamo Bucharest: Lobont; Radu, Balace, Moti, Blay, Pulhac (Baltoi 65) (Serban 82), Cristea, Margaritescu, Munteanu (Ropotan 79), Niculescu, Danciulescu.

Bordeaux (0) 0

Osasuna (0) 0 16,029

Bordeaux: Rame; Jurietti, Jemmali (Marange 46), Cid, Planus, Alonso (Obertan 82), Faubert, Mavuba, Smicer (Perea 65), Francia, Chamakh.
Osasuna: Ricardo; Javier Flano, Cruchaga, Josetxo, Corrales, Nekounam, Punal, Munoz (David Lopez 66), Juanfran, Milosevic (Raul Garcia 90), Webo (Soldado 76).

CSKA Moscow (0) 0

Maccabi Haifa (0) 0 18,102

CSKA Moscow: Akinfeev; Berezutski A, Ignashevich, Berezutski V, Zhirkov, Aldonin (Semberas 46), Rahimic, Krasic, Dudu, Ramon (Daniel Carvalho 56), Jo.
Maccabi Haifa: Davidovich; Harazi, Magrashvili, Keinan, Anderson, Boccoli, Suan, Masudi (Meshumar 90), Xavir, Katan (Rafaelov 86), Colautti (Arbeitman 69).
in Vladikavkaz.

Fenerbahce (1) 3 *(Tumer 27, 73, Tuncay 65)*

AZ (1) 3 *(De Zeeuw 15, Boukhari 62, Jenner 63)* 42,000

Fenerbahce: Volkan; Umit O, Deniz, Edu, Appiah, Mehmet Y, Ugur (Olcan 66), Tumer, Alex, Tuncay, Deivid.
AZ: Waterman; Jaliens, Luirink, De Cler, Steinsson, Martens (Vormer 89), Molhoek (Jenner 32), De Zeeuw, Boukhari, Dembele (Lens 90), Koevermans.

Hapoel Tel Aviv (1) 2 *(Toema 43, Dego 76)*

Rangers (0) 1 *(Novo 53)* 13,000

Hapoel Tel Aviv: Elimelech; Abuksis (Chen 83), Ogbona (Vermouth 87), Antebi, Badir, Bondarv, Barda, Dego, Doani, Wellington (De Bruno 67), Toema.
Rangers: McGregor; Hutton, Svensson, Weir, Rae, Ferguson, Hemdani, Novo (Sionko 79), Burke (Adam 84), Murray, Boyd.

Leverkusen (2) 3 *(Callsen-Bracker 18, Ramelow 43, Schneider 56)*

Blackburn R (1) 2 *(Bentley 39, Nonda 86)* 22,500

Leverkusen: Butt; Haggui, Callsen-Bracker, Rolfes, Castro, Schneider, Barbarez, Ramelow, Babic, Voronin, Kiessling (Freier 85).
Blackburn R: Friedel; Emerton, Warnock, Tugay, Nelsen, Henchoz, Bentley, Mokoena (Todd 90), Roberts (Nonda 69), McCarthy, Dunn (Peter 65).

Livorno (0) 1 *(Galante 82)*

Espanyol (1) 2 *(Pandiani 28 (pen), Moha 59)*

Livorno: Amelia; Galante, Cesar (Paulinho 60), Pasquale, Grandoni, Kuffour, Fiore (Pfertzel 77), Morrone (Coppola 72), Filippini, Passoni, Lucarelli.
Espanyol: Iraizoz; Velasco, Chica, Jarque, Lacruz, Costa, Ito, Moha (Riera 60), Corominas (Moises Hurtado 88), Pandiani (Luis Garcia 76), Rufete.
Behind closed doors.

Shakhtar Donetsk (0) 1 *(Srna 84)*

Nancy (0) 1 *(Fortune 81)* 24,800

Shakhtar Donetsk: Shust; Srna, Chygrynskyi, Kucher, Shevchuk (Gay 65), Matuzalem, Fernandinho, Tymoschuk■, Jadson, Bielik (Vorobei 73), Marica.
Nancy: Gregorini; Chretien, Diakhate, Puygrenier, Biancalani (Sauget 46), Berenguer, Andre Luiz, Duchemin (Gavanon 87), Curbelo, Hadji, Fortune.

Werder Bremen (0) 3 *(Mertesacker 48, Naldo 54, Frings 71)*

Ajax (0) 0 38,150

Werder Bremen: Wiese; Naldo, Wome (Schulz 74), Mertesacker, Vranjes, Fritz, Diego, Jensen, Frings (Pasanen 78), Klose, Hunt (Hugo Almeida 74).
Ajax: Stekelenburg; Heitinga, Stam, Maduro, Donald (Perez 72), Sneijder, Lindenbergh■, Gabri, Roger, De Mul (Anita 26), Babel (Leonardo 72).

Thursday, 15 February 2007

Braga (0) 1 *(Ze Carlos 81)*

Parma (0) 0 6046

Braga: Paulo Santos; Paulo Jorge, Luis Filipe, Carlos Fernandes, Nem (Rodriguez 46), Vandinho, Frechaut (Bruno Gama 36), Ricardo Chaves, Ze Carlos, Cesinha, Joao Pinto (Wender 76).
Parma: Bucci; Contini, Perna, Paci, Bocchetti, Coly, Dessena, Gasbarroni, Pisanu (Paponi 64), Cigarini (Bolano 78), Kutuzov (Muslimovic 60).

Lens (0) 3 *(Jemaa 49, 70, Dindane 90 (pen))*

Panathinaikos (0) 1 *(Salpigidis 65)* 29,949

Lens: Itandje; Gillet, Barul, Hilton, Tixier, Carriere (Monterrubio 79), Demont, Seydou Keita, Cousin, Jemaa, Dindane.
Panathinaikos: Galinovic; Vyntra, Goumas, Morris, Tziolis, Nilsson, Leontiou (Bovio 58), Romero (Ninis 81), Ivanschitz, Papadopoulos (Mantzios 82), Salpigidis.

Spartak Moscow (0) 1 *(Kalynychenko 64)*

Celta Vigo (1) 1 *(Nunez 41)* 30,000

Spartak Moscow: Khomich; Jiranek, Kovac, Geder, Stranzl, Bystrov (Bazhenov 46), Torbinsky (Boyarintsev 46), Titov, Mozart, Kalynychenko, Pavlyuchenko.
Celta Vigo: Esteban; Angel, Tamas, Lequi, Placente, Nunez (Jonathan 72), Pablo Garcia (Borja Oubina 79), Iriney, De Ridder (Baiano 69), Canobbio, Gustavo Lopez.

Steaua (0) 0

Sevilla (1) 2 *(Poulsen 41, Kanoute 77 (pen))* 30,000

Steaua: Cernea; Stancu (Croitoru 81), Goian, Ghionea, Marin, Radoi, Bostina, Petre (Paraschiv 58), Nicolita, Badea (Cristocea 62), Thereau.
Sevilla: Palop; Daniel Alves, Escude, Aitor Ocio, Hinkel, Adriano Correia (David 33), Poulsen, Puerta, Maresca, Alfaro (Kanoute 68), Kerzhakov (Chevanton 70).

Waregem (0) 1 *(D'Haene 69)*
Newcastle United (0) 3 *(Dindeleux 47 (og), Martins 59 (pen), Sibierski 76)* 8015
Waregem: Merlier; De Brul (Van Steenbrugghe 81), D'Haene, Dindeleux, Leleu, Reina, Meert (Buysse 85), Sergeant, Vandendreissche (Vandemarliere 85), Verschuere, Matthys.
Newcastle United: Harper; Solano, Babayaro, Butt, Taylor, Bramble, Milner, Sibierski, Martins (Luque 85), Dyer, Duff.

THIRD ROUND SECOND LEG

Thursday, 22 February 2007

AZ (0) 2 *(Martens 63, Opdam 86)*
Fenerbahce (2) 2 *(Tumer 21, Alex 34)* 16,191
AZ: Waterman; Jaliens, Steinsson, Molhoek (Jenner 46), Opdam, De Cler, De Zeeuw, Dembele, Boukhari (Martens 46), Arveladze (Lens 89), Koevermans.
Fenerbahce: Volkan; Umit O (Semih 90), Edu, Lugano, Deniz (Mehmet Y 80), Onder, Appiah, Tumer, Kezman, Tuncay, Alex.

Ajax (1) 3 *(Leonardo 4, Huntelaar 60, Babel 74)*
Werder Bremen (1) 1 *(Hugo Almeida 14)* 35,227
Ajax: Stekelenburg; Heitinga, Ogararu, Sneijder, Stam, Maduro, Roger, Huntelaar, Babel, Leonardo (De Mul 75), Perez.
Werder Bremen: Wiese; Pasanen, Mertesacker, Jensen, Naldo, Wome, Diego (Vranjes 46), Frings, Hugo Almeida (Schulz 82), Klose, Borowski.

Blackburn Rovers (0) 0
Leverkusen (0) 0 25,124
Blackburn Rovers: Friedel; Emerton, Warnock, Tugay (Nonda 71), Nelsen, Khizanishvili (Roberts 86), Bentley, Dunn, Derbyshire, McCarthy, Pedersen.
Leverkusen: Butt; Babic, Castro, Rolfes, Juan, Haggui (Callsen-Bracker 59), Ramelow, Freier (Barnetta 73), Schneider, Voronin (Madouni 88), Barbarez.

Celta Vigo (1) 2 *(Nene 19, Jonathan 78)*
Spartak Moscow (0) 1 *(Titov 88)* 7000
Celta Vigo: Esteban; Lequi, Tamas, Nunez (Gustavo Lopez 70), Angel, Contreras, Borja Oubina (Iriney 55), Pablo Garcia, Nene (Baiano 90), Canobbio, Jonathan.
Spartak Moscow: Khomich; Jiranek, Stranzl (Boyarintsev 69), Torbinsky, Kovac, Geder, Bystrov (Dzyuba 46), Titov, Kalynychenko, Pavlyuchenko, Mozart.

Dinamo Bucharest (1) 1 *(Munteanu 23)*
Benfica (0) 2 *(Anderson 50, Katsouranis 64)* 15,300
Dinamo Bucharest: Lobont; Blay, Radu, Margaritescu, Pulhac, Moti, Serban (Balace 46), Munteanu (Mendy 59), Niculescu, Danciulescu, Cristea (Ze Kalanga 77).
Benfica: Quim; Nelson, Luisao, Petit, Anderson, Leo, Karagounis, Katsouranis (Beto 89), Derlei (Paulo Jorge 86), Miccoli (Nuno Gomes 75), Simao Sabrosa.

Espanyol (1) 2 *(Lacruz 16, Corominas 49)*
Livorno (0) 0 12,134
Espanyol: Iraizoz; Lacruz, Moises Hurtado (Ito 50), Corominas, David Garcia, Jarque, Chica, Costa, Pandiani, Luis Garcia (Jonatas 74), Rufete (Moha 63).
Livorno: Amelia; Pfertzel, Grandoni, Morrone, Kuffour, Rezaei, Filippini (Paulinho 52), Fiore, Passoni (Coppola 63), Lucarelli (Vidigal 80), Cesar■.

Maccabi Haifa (1) 1 *(Colautti 14)*
CSKA Moscow (0) 0 15,000
Maccabi Haifa: Davidovich; Harazi, Keinan, Boccoli, Meshumar, Magrashvili, Anderson, Masudi (Gazal 74), Rafaelov (Arbeitman 87), Colautti (Hemad 90), Xavir.
CSKA Moscow: Akinfeev; Semberas (Krasic 74), Berezutski V, Ignashevich, Berezutski A, Zhirkov, Aldonin (Ramon 70), Daniel Carvalho, Rahimic, Dudu, Jo.

Nancy (0) 0
Shakhtar Donetsk (0) 1 *(Fernandinho 70)* 16,564
Nancy: Gregorini; Diakhate, Berenguer (Brison 73), Duchemin, Sauget, Puygrenier (Andre Luiz 53), Chretien, Gavanon, Curbelo, Fortune, Hadji (Dia 65).
Shakhtar Donetsk: Shust; Shevchuk, Chygrynskyi, Kucher, Lewandowski (Duljaj 83), Fernandinho, Srna, Elano (Jadson 61), Brandao, Marica, Matuzalem.

Newcastle United (0) 1 *(Martins 68)*
Waregem (0) 0 30,083
Newcastle United: Harper; Solano, Babayaro (Huntington 46), Butt (Pattison 65), Taylor, Bramble, Milner, Dyer, Martins, Luque (Carroll 65), Duff.
Waregem: Bossut; Minne (Reina 76), Buysse, Van Steenbrugge, D'Haene, Dindeleux, Vandermarliere, Van Nieuwenhuyse, Vandendriessche (Sergeant 56), Siani (Matthys 56), Meert.

Osasuna (0) 1 *(Nekounam 120)*
Bordeaux (0) 0 17,452
Osasuna: Ricardo; Cruchaga, Corrales, David Lopez, Josetxo, Javier Flano, Punal, Nekounam, Milosevic (Raul Garcia 77), Soldado (Webo 90), Juanfran.
Bordeaux: Rame; Jemmali, Jurietti, Wendel, Planus, Cid, Mavuba, Micoud (Francia 107), Alonso (Faubert 64), Perea, Smicer (Chamakh 77).
aet.

Panathinaikos (0) 0
Lens (0) 0 40,914
Panathinaikos: Ebede; Morris■, Bovio, Ninis (Romero 82), Goumas, Vyntra (Leontiou 46), Ivanschitz, Nilsson, Salpigidis, Papadopoulos (Mantzios 57), Tziolis.
Lens: Itandje; Hilton, Demont (Gillet 86), Seydou Keita, Coulibaly, Barul, Carriere (Monterrubio 84), Sidi Keita, Tixier, Jemaa, Cousin (Hermach 89).

Paris St Germain (1) 2 *(Frau 42, Mendy 90 (pen))*
AEK Athens (0) 0 22,670
Paris St Germain: Landreau; Rozehnal, Drame, Rothen, Mendy, Armand, Cisse, Rodriguez, Pauleta (Gallardo 46), Frau (Diane 66), Luyindula (Chantome 79).
AEK Athens: Sorrentino; Cirillo, Papastathopoulos, Tozser (Kafes 46), Tziortziopoulos, Moras, Ivic, Manduca (Julio Cesar 46), Kapetanos, Kiriakidis (Zikos 46), Liberopoulos.

Parma (0) 0
Braga (0) 1 *(Diego 89)* 3861
Parma: De Lucia; Bocchetti, Ferronetti, Pisanu, Contini, Fernando Couto, Grella (Dessena 65), Cigarini, Kutuzov (Rossi 71), Paponi (Gasbarroni 31), Muslimovic.
Braga: Paulo Santos; Pedro Costa, Luis Filipe, Ricardo Chaves, Paulo Jorge, Carlos Fernandes, Rodriguez, Frechaut■, Joao Pinto (Andrade 90), Ze Carlos (Diego 71), Wender (Castanheira 77).

Rangers (2) 4 *(Ferguson 24, 73, Boyd 35, Adam 90)*
Hapoel Tel Aviv (0) 0 46,213
Rangers: McGregor■; Hutton, Murray, Ferguson, Weir, Hemdani (Adam 90), Rae, Thomson, Boyd (Prso 64), Novo (Klos 75), Burke.
Hapoel Tel Aviv: Elimelech; Bondarv, Badir, Abuksis (Vermouth 65), Doani, Antebi, Dego (De Bruno 46), Wellington (Jolic 80), Ogbona, Barda, Toema.

Sevilla (1) 1 *(Kerzhakov 45)*
Steaua (0) 0 20,000
Sevilla: Palop; Hinkel, David, Marti, Escude, Aitor Ocio (Dragutinovic 76), Daniel Alves, Maresca, Kerzhakov, Alfaro (Poulsen 81), Puerta (Diego Capel 21).
Steaua: Cernea; Goian, Stancu, Bostina (Iacob 76), Radoi, Marin (Coman 46), Petre, Cristocea (Croitoru 55), Paraschiv, Badea, Nicolita.

FOURTH ROUND FIRST LEG

Thursday, 8 March 2007

Braga (0) 2 *(Paulo Jorge 76, Ze Carlos 81)*

Tottenham H (0) 3 *(Keane 57, 90, Malbranque 72)* 24,500

Braga: Paulo Santos; Luis Filipe, Andrade, Castanheira, Paulo Jorge, Rodriguez, Carlos Fernandes, Joao Pinto (Maciel 80), Wender (Diego 69), Ze Carlos, Bruno Gama (Cesinha 69).
Tottenham H: Robinson; Chimbonda, Lee, Zokora, Dawson, Gardner, Lennon, Malbranque, Berbatov, Keane, Tainio (Huddlestone 74).

Celta Vigo (0) 0

Werder Bremen (0) 1 *(Hugo Almeida 84)* 9236

Celta Vigo: Esteban; Lequi, Yago, Gustavo Lopez, Tamas, Placente, Nunez (De Ridder 74) (Guayre 84), Pablo Garcia, Nene (Baiano 46), Canobbio, Jonathan.
Werder Bremen: Wiese; Naldo, Fritz, Jensen, Mertesacker, Wome, Vranjes, Diego (Schulz 65), Hunt, Klose (Hugo Almeida 65), Frings.

Lens (1) 2 *(Monterrubio 17, Cousin 70 (pen))*

Leverkusen (0) 1 *(Haggui 51)* 29,200

Lens: Itandje; Coulibaly, Tixier, Seydou Keita, Hilton, Demont, Carriere, Sidi Keita (Monnet-Paquet 80), Dindane, Cousin (Jemaa 71), Monterrubio (Boukhari 72).
Leverkusen: Adler; Rolfes, Castro, Babic, Juan, Haggui■, Schneider (Freier 90), Ramelow, Barbarez, Voronin (Callsen-Bracker 70), Barnetta (Kiessling 80).

Maccabi Haifa (0) 0

Espanyol (0) 0 17,450

Maccabi Haifa: Davidovich; Harazi, Anderson, Suan, Keinan, Magrashvili, Boccoli, Xavir, Colautti, Katan (Arbeitman 70), Rafaelov (Gazal 86).
Espanyol: Iraizoz; Torrejon, Chica, De la Pena (Costa 63), Lacruz, Jarque, Moises Hurtado, Moha (Riera 74), Pandiani, Luis Garcia (Corominas 85), Rufete.

Newcastle United (4) 4 *(Steinsson 8 (og), Dyer 22, Martins 23, 37)*

AZ (1) 2 *(Arveladze 31, Koevermans 73)* 28,452

Newcastle United: Given; Solano, Carr, Parker, Taylor, Bramble, Dyer, Butt, Martins, Sibierski (Milner 65), Duff (Emre 77).
AZ: Waterman; Steinsson, Jaliens, Opdam, De Cler, Jenner (Lens 65), De Zeeuw, Martens (Dembele 59), Boukhari (Luirink 83), Koevermans, Arveladze.

Paris St Germain (2) 2 *(Pauleta 36, Frau 41)*

Benfica (1) 1 *(Simao Sabrosa 9)* 33,962

Paris St Germain: Landreau; Rozehnal, Sakho, Chantome, Mendy, Armand (Drame 79), Cisse, Rothen (Gallardo 61) (Luyindula 73), Kalou, Pauleta, Frau.
Benfica: Quim; Anderson, Nelson, Petit, Luisao (David Luiz 33), Leo, Simao Sabrosa, Karagounis, Derlei (Nuno Gomes 68), Miccoli, Joao Coimbra (Beto 72).

Rangers (0) 1 *(Hemdani 90)*

Osasuna (1) 1 *(Raul Garcia 17)* 50,290

Rangers: Klos; Weir, Hutton, Ferguson, Ehogiou, Murray, Thomson (Prso 66), Hemdani, Boyd (Sebo 87), Adam (Novo 46), Burke.
Osasuna: Ricardo; Izquierdo, Miguel Flano, Cuellar, Monreal, Raul Garcia, David Lopez, Juanlu (Juanfran 77), Munoz, Nekounam, Webo (Romeo 82).

Sevilla (1) 2 *(Marti 8 (pen), Maresca 88 (pen))*

Shakhtar Donetsk (1) 2 *(Hubschman 19, Matuzalem 60 (pen))* 34,500

Sevilla: Palop; Daniel Alves, Puerta, Marti (Luis Fabiano 57), Escude, Javi Navarro, Poulsen, Duda, Kerzhakov, Jesus Navas (Maresca 67), Alfaro (Adriano Correia 46).
Shakhtar Donetsk: Shust; Chygrynskyi, Hubschman, Shevchuk, Srna, Duljaj, Matuzalem, Fernandinho, Elano (Jadson 68), Bielik (Gay 75), Brandao.

Tottenham Hotspur's Steed Malbranque (centre) guides the ball past Paul Santos to score the winning goal in a 3-2 defeat of Braga at White Hart Lane in the UEFA Cup. (Adam Davy/EMPICS Sport/PA Photos)

FOURTH ROUND SECOND LEG

Wednesday, 14 March 2007

Leverkusen (1) 3 *(Voronin 36, Barbarez 56, Juan 70)*

Lens (0) 0 22,500

Leverkusen: Adler; Castro, Babic, Rolfes, Callsen-Bracker, Juan, Schneider, Barnetta (Stenman 90), Barbarez, Kiessling (Schwegler 79), Voronin (Freier 90).
Lens: Itandje; Demont, Tixier (Dindane 46), Seydou Keita, Coulibaly, Hilton, Gillet, Jemaa, Monterrubio (Monnet-Paquet 72), Cousin (Boukhari 72), Carriere.

Osasuna (0) 1 *(Webo 71)*

Rangers (0) 0 19,126

Osasuna: Ricardo; Cruchaga, Josetxo, Azpilicueta (David Lopez 66), Javier Flano, Corrales, Punal, Juanlu (Juanfran 82), Romeo (Raul Garcia 74), Webo, Nekounam.
Rangers: McGregor; Weir, Hutton, Thomson (Burke 53), Ehiogu, Murray, Adam, Rae (Boyd 73), Novo, Sebo (Prso 64), Hemdani.

Tottenham H (2) 3 *(Berbatov 28, 42, Malbranque 76)*

Braga (1) 2 *(Huddlestone 24 (og), Andrade 61)* 33,761

Tottenham H: Cerny; Stalteri, Lee, Zokora, Dawson, Chimbonda, Lennon (Ghaly 81), Huddlestone, Berbatov, Keane (Defoe 66), Malbranque.
Braga: Paulo Santos; Luis Filipe, Carlos Fernandes, Madrid, Paulo Jorge, Rodriguez (Nem 40), Frechaut, Andrade, Wender, Ze Carlos (Maciel 74), Joao Pinto (Cesinha 74).

Werder Bremen (0) 2 *(Hugo Almeida 48, Fritz 61)*

Celta Vigo (0) 0 35,278

Werder Bremen: Wiese; Schulz, Wome, Frings, Mertesacker, Naldo, Vranjes (Owomoyela 63), Diego (Bischoff 75), Hugo Almeida, Hunt (Schindler 46), Fritz.
Celta Vigo: Esteban; Angel (Vila 69), Tamas, Jonathan, Yago, Lequi, Pablo Garcia, Jorge (Canobbio 73), Guayre (Perera 35), Placente, Nene.

Thursday, 15 March 2007

AZ (1) 2 *(Arveladze 14, Koevermans 56)*

Newcastle United (0) 0 16,401

AZ: Waterman; Jaliens, De Zeeuw, Dembele, De Cler, Steinsson, Donk, Martens (Boukhari 90), Arveladze, Jenner (Lens 80), Koevermans (Opdam 84).
Newcastle United: Given; Solano, Huntington (N'Zogbia 86), Parker, Taylor, Bramble, Dyer, Butt, Martins, Sibierski, Duff (Emre 59).

Benfica (2) 3 *(Simao Sabrosa 12, 89 (pen), Petit 27)*

Paris St Germain (1) 1 *(Pauleta 32)* 65,000

Benfica: Moretto; Nelson, Leo, Katsouranis, David Luiz, Anderson, Petit, Karagounis (Joao Coimbra 46), Miccoli (Derlei 77), Nuno Gomes (Paulo Jorge 90), Simao Sabrosa.
Paris St Germain: Landreau; Mabiala (Mendy 75), Drame, Diane, Rozehnal, Traore, Mulumbu■, Gallardo (Ngog 70), Pauleta, Luyindula (Kalou 70), Rothen.

Espanyol (0) 4 *(De la Pena 53, Tamudo 59, Luis Garcia 61, Pandiani 90)*

Maccabi Haifa (0) 0 16,150

Espanyol: Iraizoz; David Garcia (Lacruz 67), Torrejon, Moha, Chica, Moises Hurtado, Jarque, De la Pena (Ito 75), Pandiani, Tamudo (Rufete 65), Luis Garcia.
Maccabi Haifa: Davidovich; Harazi, Keinan, Gazal (Arbeitman 61), Magrashvili (Keise 73), Meshumar, Rafaelov (Melikson 69), Boccoli, Colautti, Katan, Anderson.

Shakhtar Donetsk (0) 2 *(Matuzalem 49, Elano 83)*

Sevilla (0) 3 *(Maresca 53, Palop 90, Chevanton 105)* 26,000

Shakhtar Donetsk: Shust; Lewandowski, Shevchuk (Rat 44), Matuzalem (Duljaj 86), Chygrynskyi, Kucher, Gay, Fernandinho, Bielik (Elano 64), Marica, Jadson.
Sevilla: Palop; Javi Navarro (Duda 81), Dragutinovic, Maresca, Escude, Daniel Alves, Hinkel (Puerta 57), Adriano Correia (Chevanton 57), Kanoute, Luis Fabiano, Poulsen.
aet.

QUARTER-FINALS FIRST LEG

Thursday, 5 April 2007

AZ (0) 0

Werder Bremen (0) 0 16,000

AZ: Waterman; Jaliens, De Cler, Steinsson, Donk, Martens, De Zeeuw (Luirink 75), Koevermans (Cziommer 83), Dembele, Arveladze, Jenner (Lens 87).
Werder Bremen: Wiese; Naldo, Wome, Owomoyela, Mertesacker, Diego, Vranjes, Frings, Fritz, Hugo Almeida (Hunt 86), Klose.

Espanyol (2) 3 *(Tamudo 15, Riera 33, Pandiani 59)*

Benfica (0) 2 *(Nuno Gomes 64, Simao Sabrosa 66)* 25,100

Espanyol: Iraizoz; Chica, Torrejon, Jarque, Moises Hurtado, De la Pena, Zabaleta (Lacruz 69), Tamudo (Pandiani 53), Rufete (Ito 79), Riera, Luis Garcia.
Benfica: Quim; Anderson, Leo, Nelson, David Luiz, Simao Sabrosa, Petit, Karagounis, Joao Coimbra (Rui Costa 35), Derlei (Miccoli 57), Nuno Gomes.

Leverkusen (0) 0

Osasuna (1) 3 *(Cuellar 1, David Lopez 71, Webo 73)* 22,500

Leverkusen: Adler; Juan, Haggui, Rolfes, Barnetta, Barbarez, Castro (Athirson 69), Schneider, Babic, Voronin, Kiessling (Freier 46).
Osasuna: Ricardo; Izquierdo, Cuellar, Corrales, Cruchaga, Raul Garcia (Munoz 82), Juanfran (Valdo 66), David Lopez, Erice, Soldado (Webo 73), Milosevic.

Sevilla (2) 2 *(Kanoute 19 (pen), Kerzhakov 35)*

Tottenham Hotspur (1) 1 *(Keane 2)* 32,000

Sevilla: Palop; Javi Navarro, David (Dragutinovic 68), Daniel Alves, Escude, Renato (Marti 60), Poulsen, Adriano Correia, Kerzhakov, Kanoute, Jesus Navas.
Tottenham Hotspur: Robinson; Stalteri, Lee, Zokora, Dawson, Chimbonda, Lennon (Malbranque 80), Jenas, Berbatov, Keane, Tainio (Ghaly 84).

QUARTER-FINALS SECOND LEG

Thursday, 12 April 2007

Benfica (0) 0

Espanyol (0) 0 50,000

Benfica: Quim; Nelson (Derlei 81), Leo, Petit, David Luiz, Anderson, Karagounis (Katsouranis 81), Rui Costa, Miccoli, Nuno Gomes (Mantorras 69), Simao Sabrosa.
Espanyol: Iraizoz; Zabaleta, Chica, Moises Hurtado, Jarque, Torrejon, Ito (Costa 54), De la Pena (Jonatas 78), Pandiani (Corominas 71), Riera, Luis Garcia.

Osasuna (0) 1 *(Juanlu 62)*

Leverkusen (0) 0 16,000

Osasuna: Ricardo; Izquierdo, Monreal, Josetxo, Cruchaga (Erice 70), Cuellar, Valdo, Munoz, Soldado (Hector Font 75), Milosevic, Juanlu.
Leverkusen: Adler; Castro, Stenman, Schwegler, Madouni (Haggui 53), Callsen-Bracker, Barnetta (Babic 42), Rolfes, Barbarez (Kiessling 67), Schneider, Freier.

Tottenham Hotspur (0) 2 *(Defoe 65, Lennon 67)*

Sevilla (2) 2 *(Malbranque 3 (og), Kanoute 8)* 35,284

Tottenham Hotspur: Robinson; Tainio■, Chimbonda, Zokora (Defoe 65), Dawson, King, Lennon, Jenas, Berbatov, Keane, Malbranque.
Sevilla: Cobeno; Hinkel, Puerta, Poulsen, Javi Navarro, Escude, Daniel Alves (Renato 55), Marti, Kerzhakov (Maresca 82), Kanoute, Adriano Correia (Aitor Ocio 69).

Werder Bremen (2) 4 *(Borowski 16, Klose 36, 61, Diego 80)*

AZ (1) 1 *(Dembele 32)* 35,000

Werder Bremen: Wiese; Owomoyela, Fritz, Diego, Pasanen, Naldo, Frings, Vranjes, Hunt (Hugo Almeida 79), Klose (Schindler 83), Borowski (Baumann 69).
AZ: Waterman; De Zeeuw, Jenner, Jaliens, Donk, De Cler, Luirink (Schaars 46) (Cziommer 69), Dembele, Arveladze (Boukhari 60), Koevermans, Martens.

SEMI-FINALS FIRST LEG

Thursday, 26 April 2007

Espanyol (1) 3 *(Moises Hurtado 21, Pandiani 50, Corominas 88)*

Werder Bremen (0) 0 40,000

Espanyol: Iraizoz; Lacruz, David Garcia, Moises Hurtado, Torrejon, Jarque, Rufete (Corominas 83), Riera, Pandiani (Ito 73), Tamudo, De la Pena (Jonatas 78).
Werder Bremen: Wiese■; Owomoyela, Fritz, Frings, Pasanen, Naldo, Baumann (Vranjes 78), Jensen (Reinke 59), Diego, Klose (Hugo Almeida 73), Hunt.

Osasuna (0) 1 *(Saldado 55)*

Sevilla (0) 0 18,134

Osasuna: Ricardo; Izquierdo, Cruchaga, Punal, Cuellar, Raul Garcia, Milosevic (Valdo 87), David Lopez, Juanfran, Soldado (Webo 81), Corrales.
Sevilla: Cobeno; Javi Navarro, Poulsen, Escude, Daniel Alves, Adriano Correia (Puerta 90), Luis Fabiano (Kerzhakov 61), Jesus Navas, Kanoute, Dragutinovic, Marti (Hinkel 76).

SEMI-FINALS SECOND LEG

Thursday, 3 May 2007

Sevilla (1) 2 *(Luis Fabiano 37, Renato 53)*

Osasuna (0) 0 42,000

Sevilla: Palop; Javi Navarro, Poulsen, Escude, Daniel Alves, Puerta, Renato (Aitor Ocio 87), Adriano Correia (Duda 27), Luis Fabiano (Kerzhakov 73), Kanoute, Marti.
Osasuna: Ricardo; Izquierdo (Munoz 83), Corrales, Punal (Valdo 61), Cuellar, Cruchaga, Nekounam, Juanfran (Delporte 71), David Lopez, Raul Garcia, Webo.

Werder Bremen (1) 1 *(Hugo Almeida 4)*

Espanyol (0) 2 *(Corominas 50, Lacruz 61)* 36,000

Werder Bremen: Reinke; Pasanen, Owomoyela (Schindler 46), Schulz, Naldo, Diego, Jensen (Wome 70), Frings (Baumann 75), Klose, Hugo Almeida, Hunt.
Espanyol: Iraizoz; Lacruz, David Garcia, Ito, Torrejon, Jarque, Zabaleta (Angel 65), Riera (Rufete 70), Tamudo (Julian 79), Corominas, Luis Garcia.

UEFA CUP FINAL 2007

Wednesday, 16 May 2007
(at Hampden Park, Glasgow, 50,670)

Espanyol (1) 2 *(Riera 28, Jonatas 115)* **Sevilla (1) 2** *(Adriano Correia 18, Kanoute 105)*

Espanyol: Iraizoz; David Garcia, Jarque, Zabaleta, Moises Hurtado■, Torrejon, De la Pena (Jonatas 87), Luis Garcia, Tamudo (Lacruz 72), Rufete (Pandiani 56), Riera.

Sevilla: Palop; Javi Navarro, Adriano Correia (Renato 76), Daniel Alves, Dragutinovic, Poulsen, Puerta, Luis Fabiano (Kerzhakov 64), Kanoute, Marti, Maresca (Jesus Navas 46).

aet; Sevilla won 3-1 on penalties.

Referee: Busacca (Switzerland).

Sevilla's Adriano in action agains Espanyol's Pablo Zabaleta during the UEFA Cup Final at Hampden Park.
(Action Images/Lee Smith)

UEFA CHAMPIONS LEAGUE 2007–08

Champions League 2007–08 participating clubs

IOC	*Stage*	*Club*
TH	Grp	AC Milan (holders)
ESP1	Grp	Real Madrid CF
ESP2	Grp	FC Barcelona
ESP3	Q3	Sevilla FC
ESP4	Q3	Valencia CF
ITA1	Grp	FC Internazionale Milano
ITA2	Grp	AS Roma
ITA3	Q3	S.S. Lazio
ENG1	Grp	Manchester United
ENG2	Grp	Chelsea FC
ENG3	Q3	Liverpool FC
ENG4	Q3	Arsenal FC
FRA1	Grp	Olympique Lyonnais
FRA2	Grp	Olympique de Marseille
FRA3	Q3	Toulouse FC
GER1	Grp	VfB Stuttgart
GER2	Grp	FC Schalke 04
GER3	Q3	Werder Bremen
POR1	Grp	FC Porto
POR2	Grp	Sporting Clube de Portugal
POR3	Q3	SL Benfica
NED1	Grp	PSV Eindhoven
NED2	Q3	AFC Ajax
GRE1	Grp	Olympiacos CFP
GRE2	Q3	AEK Athens FC
RUS1	Grp	PFC CSKA Moskva
RUS2	Q3	FC Spartak Moskva
ROU1	Q3	FC Dinamo 1948 Bucuresti
ROU2	Q2	FC Steaua Bucuresti
SCO1	Q3	Celtic FC
SCO2	Q2	Rangers FC
BEL1	Q3	RSC Anderlecht
BEL2	Q2	KRC Genk
UKR1	Q3	FC Dynamo Kyiv
UKR2	Q2	FC Shakhtar Donetsk
CZE1	Q3	AC Sparta Praha
CZE2	Q2	SK Slavia Praha
TUR1	Q3	Fenerbahçe SK
TUR2	Q2	Beşiktaş JK
SUI1	Q3	FC Zürich
BUL1	Q2	PFC Levski Sofia
ISR1	Q2	Beitar Jerusalem FC
NOR1	Q2	Rosenborg BK
AUT1	Q2	FC Salzburg
SRB1	Q2	FK Crvena Zvezda
POL1	Q2	Zagłębie Lubin
DEN1	Q2	FC København
HUN1	Q2	Debreceni VSC
CRO1	Q1	NK Dinamo Zagreb
SWE1	Q1	IF Elfsborg
SVK1	Q1	MŠK Žilina
CYP1	Q1	APOEL FC
SVN1	Q1	NK Domžale
BIH1	Q1	FK Sarajevo
FIN1	Q1	Tampere United
LVA1	Q1	FK Ventspils
MDA1	Q1	FC Sheriff
GEO1	Q1	FC Olimpi Rustavi
LTU1	Q1	FBK Kaunas
MKD1	Q1	FK Pobeda
ISL1	Q1	FH Hafnarfjördur
BLR1	Q1	FC BATE Borisov
IRL1	Q1	Derry City FC*
ALB1	Q1	KF Tirana
ARM1	Q1	FC Pyunik
EST1	Q1	FC Levadia Tallinn
MLT1	Q1	Marsaxlokk FC
WAL1	Q1	The New Saints FC
NIR1	Q1	Linfield FC
AZE1	Q1	FK Khazar Lenkoran
LUX1	Q1	F91 Dudelange
KAZ1	Q1	FK Astana
FRO1	Q1	HB Tórshavn
MNE1	Q1	FK Zeta
AND1	Q1	FC Rànger's
SMR1	Q1	S.S. Murata

* Shelbourne FC won the title but did not apply to enter the UEFA Champions League after being relegated for financial reasons. Derry City inherited their place in the competition as Irish runners-up.

UEFA CUP 2007–08

UEFA Cup 2007–08 participating clubs

IOC	*Round*	*Club*
ESP	1st	Villarreal CF
ESP	1st	Real Zaragoza
ESP	1st	Getafe CF[5]
ITA	1st	US Città di Palermo
ITA	1st	ACF Fiorentina
ITA	1st	Empoli FC
ENG	1st	Tottenham Hotspur FC
ENG	1st	Everton FC
ENG	1st	Bolton Wanderers FC
FRA	1st	FC Sochaux-Montbéliard[1]
FRA	1st	Stade Rennais FC
FRA	1st	FC Girondins de Bordeaux[3]
GER	1st	1. FC Nürnberg[1]
GER	1st	FC Bayern München
GER	1st	Bayer 04 Leverkusen
POR	1st	SC Braga
POR	1st	CF Os Belenenses
POR	1st	FC Paços de Ferreira
NED	1st	AZ Alkmaar
NED	1st	FC Twente
NED	1st	SC Heerenveen
NED	1st	FC Groningen
GRE	1st	Larissa FC[1]
GRE	1st	Panathinaikos FC
GRE	1st	Aris Thessaloniki FC
GRE	1st	Panionios NFC
RUS	1st	FC Lokomotiv Moskva[1]
RUS	Q2	FC Zenit St. Petersburg
ROU	1st	AFC Rapid Bucuresti[1]
ROU	Q2	CFR Economax Cluj-Napoca
SCO	1st	Aberdeen FC
SCO	Q2	Dunfermline Athletic FC[2]
BEL	1st	Club Brugge KV[1]
BEL	Q2	R. Standard de Liège
UKR	1st	FC Metalist Kharkiv
UKR	Q2	FC Dnipro Dnipropetrovsk
CZE	1st	FK Mladá Boleslav
CZE	Q2	FK Jablonec 97[2]
TUR	Q2	Galatasaray SK
TUR	Q2	Kayseri Erciyesspor[2]
SUI	Q2	FC Basel 1893[1]
SUI	Q2	FC Sion
SUI	Q1	BSC Young Boys
BUL	Q2	PFC CSKA Sofia
BUL	Q2	PFC Lokomotiv Sofia
BUL	Q1	PFC Litex Lovech[2]
ISR	Q2	Hapoel Tel-Aviv FC[1]
ISR	Q2	Maccabi Netanya FC
ISR	Q1	Maccabi Tel-Aviv FC
NOR	Q2	Fredrikstad FK[1]
NOR	Q1	Lillestrøm SK[4]
NOR	Q1	SK Brann
NOR	Q1	Vålerenga IF
AUT	Q2	FK Austria Wien
AUT	Q1	SV Ried
AUT	Q1	SV Mattersburg
SRB	Q1	FK Partizan
SRB	Q1	FK Vojvodina
SRB	Q1	FK Bezanija
POL	Q1	Groclin Grozisk Wielkopolski[1]
POL	Q1	GKS Bełchatów
DEN	Q1	Odense BK[1]
DEN	Q1	FC Midtjylland.
HUN	Q1	Budapest Honvéd FC[1]
HUN	Q1	MTK Budapest
CRO	Q1	HNK Hajduk Split
CRO	Q1	NK Slaven Koprivnica[2]
SWE	Q1	BK Hacken[4]
SWE	Q1	Helsingborgs IF[1]
SWE	Q1	AIK Solna
SVK	Q1	FC Vion Zlaté Moravce[1]
SVK	Q1	FC Artmedia Petržalka
CYP	Q1	Anorthosis Famagusta FC[1]
CYP	Q1	AC Omonia
SVN	Q1	FC Koper[1]
SVN	Q1	NK Gorica
BIH	Q1	NK Široki Brijeg[1]
BIH	Q1	NK Zrinjski
FIN	Q1	Myllykosken Pallo-47[4]
FIN	Q1	HJK Helsinki[1]
FIN	Q1	FC Haka
LVA	Q1	SK Liepājas Metalurgs[1]
LVA	Q1	Skonto FC
MDA	Q1	CSF Zimbru Chisinau[1]
MDA	Q1	FC Nistru Otaci
GEO	Q1	FC Ameri Tbilisi[1]
GEO	Q1	FC Dinamo Tbilisi
LTU	Q1	FK Sūduva[1]
LTU	Q1	FK Ekranas
MKD	Q1	FK Vardar[1]
MKD	Q1	FK Rabotnicki
ISL	Q1	Keflavík[1]
ISL	Q1	KR Reykjavík
LIE	Q1	FC Vaduz[1]
BLR	Q1	FC Dinamo Brest[1]
BLR	Q1	FC Dinamo Minsk
IRL	Q1	Drogheda United FC
IRL	Q1	Saint Patrick's Athletic FC[2]
ALB	Q1	KS Besa[1]
ALB	Q1	KS Teuta
ARM	Q1	FC Banants[1]
ARM	Q1	FC MIKA
EST	Q1	JK Trans Narva
EST	Q1	FC Flora
MLT	Q1	Hibernians FC[1]
MLT	Q1	Sliema Wanderers FC
WAL	Q1	Carmarthen Town AFC[1]
WAL	Q1	Rhyl FC
NIR	Q1	Glentoran FC
NIR	Q1	Dungannon Swifts[2]
AZE	Q1	PFC Neftchi
AZE	Q1	MKT Araz[2]
LUX	Q1	FC Etzella Ettelbrück
LUX	Q1	UN Kaerjeng 97[2]
KAZ	Q1	FC Alma-Ata[1]
KAZ	Q1	FK Aktobe
FRO	Q1	B36 Tórshavn[1]
FRO	Q1	EB/Streymur
MNE	Q1	FK Rudar Pljevlja[1]
MNE	Q1	FK Buducnost Podgorica
AND	Q1	FC Santa Coloma[1]
SMR	Q1	SP Libertas[2]
TBC	Q2	11 Teams as winners of UEFA Intertoto Cup

[1]domestic cup winners, [2]losing domestic cup finalists, [3]domestic league cup winners, [4]national domestic title winners, [5]Fair Play winners.

SUMMARY OF APPEARANCES

EUROPEAN CUP AND CHAMPIONS LEAGUE (1955–2006)

ENGLISH CLUBS
18 Manchester U
17 Liverpool
11 Arsenal
5 Chelsea
4 Everton, Leeds U
3 Derby Co, Wolverhampton W, Aston Villa, Newcastle U, Nottingham F
1 Burnley, Tottenham H, Ipswich T, Manchester C, Blackburn R

SCOTTISH CLUBS
25 Rangers
22 Celtic
3 Aberdeen, Hearts
1 Dundee, Dundee U, Kilmarnock, Hibernian

WELSH CLUBS
6 Barry T
3 TNS
1 Cwmbran T, Rhyl

NORTHERN IRELAND CLUBS
22 Linfield
11 Glentoran
3 Crusaders, Portadown
1 Glenavon, Ards, Distillery, Derry C, Coleraine, Cliftonville

REPUBLIC OF IRELAND CLUBS
7 Shamrock R, Dundalk
6 Shelbourne, Waterford
4 Bohemians
3 Drumcondra, St Patrick's Ath,
2 Sligo R, Limerick, Athlone T, Derry C*, Cork City
1 Cork Hibs, Cork Celtic

Winners: Celtic 1966–67; Manchester U 1967–68, 1998–99; Liverpool 1976–77, 1977–78, 1980–81, 1983–84, 2004–05; Nottingham F 1978–79, 1979–80; Aston Villa 1981–82

Finalists: Celtic 1969–70; Leeds U 1974–75; Liverpool 1984–85, 2006–07; Arsenal 2005–06

EUROPEAN CUP-WINNERS' CUP (1960–99)

ENGLISH CLUBS
6 Tottenham H
5 Manchester U, Liverpool, Chelsea
4 West Ham U
3 Arsenal, Everton
2 Manchester C
1 Wolverhampton W, Leicester C, WBA, Leeds U, Sunderland, Southampton, Ipswich T, Newcastle U

SCOTTISH CLUBS
10 Rangers
8 Aberdeen, Celtic
3 Hearts
2 Dunfermline Ath, Dundee U
1 Dundee, Hibernian, St Mirren, Motherwell, Airdrieonians, Kilmarnock

WELSH CLUBS
14 Cardiff C
8 Wrexham
7 Swansea C
3 Bangor C
1 Borough U, Newport Co, Merthyr Tydfil, Barry T, Llansantfraid, Cwmbran T

NORTHERN IRELAND CLUBS
9 Glentoran
5 Glenavon
4 Ballymena U, Coleraine
3 Crusaders, Linfield
2 Ards, Bangor
1 Derry C, Distillery, Portadown, Carrick Rangers, Cliftonville

REPUBLIC OF IRELAND CLUBS
6 Shamrock R
4 Shelbourne
3 Limerick, Waterford, Dundalk, Bohemians
2 Cork Hibs, Galway U, Derry C*, Cork City
1 Cork Celtic, St Patrick's Ath, Finn Harps, Home Farm, University College Dublin, Bray W, Sligo R

Winners: Tottenham H 1962–63; West Ham U 1964–65; Manchester C 1969–70; Chelsea 1970–71, 1997–98; Rangers 1971–72; Aberdeen 1982–83; Everton 1984–85; Manchester U 1990–91; Arsenal 1993–94

Finalists: Rangers 1960–61, 1966–67; Liverpool 1965–66; Leeds U 1972–73; West Ham U 1975–76; Arsenal 1979–80, 1994–95

EUROPEAN FAIRS CUP & UEFA CUP (1955–2006)

ENGLISH CLUBS
13 Leeds U
12 Liverpool
10 Aston Villa, Ipswich T, Newcastle U
9 Arsenal
7 Everton, Manchester U, Tottenham H
6 Southampton, Chelsea
5 Nottingham F, Manchester C, Blackburn R
4 Birmingham C, Wolverhampton W, WBA
3 Sheffield W
2 Stoke C, Derby Co, QPR, Leicester C, Middlesbrough, West Ham U
1 Burnley, Coventry C, Millwall, Norwich C, London Rep XI, Watford, Fulham, Bolton W

SCOTTISH CLUBS
19 Dundee U
16 Hibernian
15 Aberdeen, Celtic, Rangers
13 Hearts
7 Kilmarnock
6 Dunfermline Ath
5 Dundee
3 St Mirren
2 Partick T, Motherwell, St Johnstone
1 Morton, Raith R, Livingston, Gretna

WELSH CLUBS
5 TNS
4 Bangor C
3 Inter Cardiff (formerly Inter Cable-Tel), Cwmbran T
2 Newtown, Barry T, Rhyl
1 Afan Lido, Haverfordwest, Carmarthen T, Llanelli

NORTHERN IRELAND CLUBS
16 Glentoran
9 Linfield
8 Coleraine, Portadown
7 Glenavon
3 Crusaders
1 Ards, Ballymena U, Bangor

EIRE CLUBS
12 Bohemians
7 Shelbourne
6 Dundalk
5 Shamrock R, Cork City
4 Derry C*
3 Finn Harps, St Patrick's Ath, Longford T
2 Drumcondra, Drogheda U
1 Cork Hibs, Athlone T, Limerick, Galway U, Bray Wanderers

Winners: Leeds U 1967–68, 1970–71; Newcastle U 1968–69; Arsenal 1969–70; Tottenham H 1971–72, 1983–84; Liverpool 1972–73, 1975–76, 2000–01; Ipswich T 1980–81

Finalists: London 1955–58, Birmingham C 1958–60, 1960–61; Leeds U 1966–67; Wolverhampton W 1971–72; Tottenham H 1973–74; Dundee U 1986–87; Celtic 2002–03; Middlesbrough 2005–06

** Now play in League of Ireland*

INTERTOTO CUP 2006

FIRST ROUND, FIRST LEG
Achnas 4, Partizani 2
Araz 1, Tiraspol 0
Dinaburg 1, HB 1
Keflavik 4, Dungannon 1
Kilikia 1, Dinamo Tbilisi 5
Nitra 6, Grevenmacher 2
Pobeda 2, Farul 2
Sant Julia 0, Maribor 3
Shakhtyor 1, MTZ-RIPO 5
Tampere 5, Carmarthen Town 0
Trans 1, Kalmar 6
Vetra 0, Shelbourne 1
Zrinjski 3, Marsaxlokk 0

FIRST ROUND, SECOND LEG
Carmarthen Town 1, Tampere 3
Dungannon 0, Keflavik 0
Dinamo Tbilisi 3, Kilikia 0
Farul 2, Pobeda 0
Grevenmacher 0, Nitra 6
HB 0, Dinaburg 1
Kalmar 2, Trans 0
Maribor 5, Sant Julia 0
Marsaxlokk 1, Zrinjski 1
MTZ-RIPO 1, Shakhtyor 3
Partizani 2, Achnas 1
Shelbourne 4, Vetra 0
Tiraspol 2, Araz 0

SECOND ROUND, FIRST LEG
Farul 2, Lokomotiv Plovdiv 1
Grasshoppers 2, Teplice 0
Hibernian 5, Dinaburg 0
Lillestrom 4, Keflavik 1
Maccabi Petah Tikva 1, Zrinjski 1
Moscow FK 2, MTZ-RIPO 0
Nitra 2, Dnepr 1
Odense 3, Shelbourne 0
Osijek 2, Achnas 2
Ried 3, Dinamo Tbilisi 1
Sopron 3, Kayseri 3
Tampere 1, Kalmar 2
Tiraspol 1, Lech 0
Zeta 0, Maribor 3

SECOND ROUND, SECOND LEG
Achnas 0, Osijek 0
Dinaburg 0, Hibernian 3
Dnepr 2, Nitra 0
Dinamo Tbilisi 0, Ried 1
Kalmar 3, Tampere 2
Kayseri 1, Sopron 0
Keflavik 2, Lillestrom 2
Lech 1, Tiraspol 3
Lokomotiv Plovdiv 1, Farul 1
Maribor 2, Zeta 0
MTZ-RIPO 0, Moscow FK 1
Shelbourne 1, Odense 0
Teplice 0, Grasshoppers 2
Zrinjski 1, Maccabi Petah Tikva 3

THIRD ROUND, FIRST LEG
Auxerre 4, Farul 1
Grasshoppers 2, Gent 1
Hertha Berlin 0, Moscow FK 0
Kalmar 1, Twente 0
Larissa 0, Kayseri 0
Maccabi Petah Tikva 0, Achnas 2
Marseille 0, Dnepr 0
Newcastle United 1, Lillestrom 1
Odense 1, Hibernian 0
Ried 3, Tiraspol 1
Villarreal 1, Maribor 2

THIRD ROUND, SECOND LEG
Achnas 2, Maccabi Petah Tikva 3
Dnepr 2, Marseille 2
Farul 1, Auxerre 0
Gent 1, Grasshoppers 1
Hibernian 2, Odense 1
Kayseri 2, Larissa 0
Lillestrom 0, Newcastle United 3
Maribor 1, Villarreal 1
Moscow FK 0, Hertha Berlin 2
Tiraspol 1, Ried 1
Twente 3, Kalmar 1
Eleven winners qualify for the UEFA Cup.

Newcastle U (0) 1 *(Luque 50)*

Lillestrom (1) 1 *(Koren 21)* 31,059
Newcastle U: Given; Carr, Babayaro, Parker, Taylor, Bramble, Solano, Emre, Milner (Ameobi 65), Luque (O'Brien 81), N'Zogbia.

Lillestrom (0) 0

Newcastle U (2) 3 *(Ameobi 29, 36, Emre 90)* 8742
Newcastle U: Given; Carr, Babayaro (Moore 69), Parker, Taylor, Bramble, Solano, Emre, Milner, Ameobi (Butt 79), N'Zogbia (Pattison 86).

WORLD CLUB CHAMPIONSHIP

Played annually up to 1974 and intermittently since then between the winners of the European Cup and the winners of the South American Champions Cup — known as the Copa Libertadores. In 1980 the winners were decided by one match arranged in Tokyo in February 1981 which remained the venue until 2004, when the match was superseded by the FIFA Club World Championship. AC Milan replaced Marseille who had been stripped of their European Cup title in 1993.

1960 Real Madrid beat Penarol 0-0, 5-1
1961 Penarol beat Benfica 0-1, 5-0, 2-1
1962 Santos beat Benfica 3-2, 5-2
1963 Santos beat AC Milan 2-4, 4-2, 1-0
1964 Inter-Milan beat Independiente 0-1, 2-0, 1-0
1965 Inter-Milan beat Independiente 3-0, 0-0
1966 Penarol beat Real Madrid 2-0, 2-0
1967 Racing Club beat Celtic 0-1, 2-1, 1-0
1968 Estudiantes beat Manchester United 1-0, 1-1
1969 AC Milan beat Estudiantes 3-0, 1-2
1970 Feyenoord beat Estudiantes 2-2, 1-0
1971 Nacional beat Panathinaikos* 1-1, 2-1
1972 Ajax beat Independiente 1-1, 3-0
1973 Independiente beat Juventus* 1-0
1974 Atlético Madrid* beat Independiente 0-1, 2-0
1975 Independiente and Bayern Munich could not agree dates; no matches.
1976 Bayern Munich beat Cruzeiro 2-0, 0-0
1977 Boca Juniors beat Borussia Moenchengladbach* 2-2, 3-0
1978 Not contested
1979 Olimpia beat Malmö* 1-0, 2-1
1980 Nacional beat Nottingham Forest 1-0
1981 Flamengo beat Liverpool 3-0
1982 Penarol beat Aston Villa 2-0
1983 Gremio Porto Alegre beat SV Hamburg 2-1
1984 Independiente beat Liverpool 1-0
1985 Juventus beat Argentinos Juniors 4-2 on penalties after a 2-2 draw
1986 River Plate beat Steaua Bucharest 1-0
1987 FC Porto beat Penarol 2-1 after extra time
1988 Nacional (Uru) beat PSV Eindhoven 7-6 on penalties after 1-1 draw
1989 AC Milan beat Atletico Nacional (Col) 1-0 after extra time
1990 AC Milan beat Olimpia 3-0
1991 Red Star Belgrade beat Colo Colo 3-0
1992 Sao Paulo beat Barcelona 2-1
1993 Sao Paulo beat AC Milan 3-2
1994 Velez Sarsfield beat AC Milan 2-0
1995 Ajax beat Gremio Porto Alegre 4-3 on penalties after 0-0 draw
1996 Juventus beat River Plate 1-0
1997 Borussia Dortmund beat Cruzeiro 2-0
1998 Real Madrid beat Vasco da Gama 2-1
1999 Manchester U beat Palmeiras 1-0
2000 Boca Juniors beat Real Madrid 2-1
2001 Bayern Munich beat Boca Juniors 1-0 after extra time
2002 Real Madrid beat Olimpia 2-0
2003 Boca Juniors beat AC Milan 3-1 on penalties after 1-1 draw
2004 Porto beat Once Caldas 8-7 on penalties after 0-0 draw

*European Cup runners-up; winners declined to take part.

EUROPEAN SUPER CUP

Played annually between the winners of the European Champions' Cup and the European Cup-Winners' Cup (UEFA Cup from 2000). AC Milan replaced Marseille in 1993–94.

EUROPEAN SUPER CUP 2006–07

25 August 2006, Monaco (attendance 18,500)

Barcelona (0) 0 **Sevilla (2) 3** *(Renato 7, Kanoute 45, Maresca 90 (pen))*

Barcelona: Valdes; Belletti, Motta (Gudjohnsen 57), Marquez, Puyol, Xavi (Iniesta 57), Eto'o, Ronaldinho, Sylvinho (Giuly 72), Messi, Deco.

Sevilla: Palop; Javi Navarro, Castedo, Daniel Alves, Adriano (Puerta 81), Poulsen, Luis Fabiano (Marti 46), Renato, Kanoute, Escude, Jesus Navas (Maresca 75).

Referee: S. Farina (Italy).

PREVIOUS MATCHES

1972 Ajax beat Rangers 3-1, 3-2
1973 Ajax beat AC Milan 0-1, 6-0
1974 Not contested
1975 Dynamo Kiev beat Bayern Munich 1-0, 2-0
1976 Anderlecht beat Bayern Munich 4-1, 1-2
1977 Liverpool beat Hamburg 1-1, 6-0
1978 Anderlecht beat Liverpool 3-1, 1-2
1979 Nottingham F beat Barcelona 1-0, 1-1
1980 Valencia beat Nottingham F 1-0, 1-2
1981 Not contested
1982 Aston Villa beat Barcelona 0-1, 3-0
1983 Aberdeen beat Hamburg 0-0, 2-0
1984 Juventus beat Liverpool 2-0
1985 Juventus v Everton not contested due to UEFA ban on English clubs
1986 Steaua Bucharest beat Dynamo Kiev 1-0
1987 FC Porto beat Ajax 1-0, 1-0
1988 KV Mechelen beat PSV Eindhoven 3-0, 0-1
1989 AC Milan beat Barcelona 1-1, 1-0
1990 AC Milan beat Sampdoria 1-1, 2-0
1991 Manchester U beat Red Star Belgrade 1-0
1992 Barcelona beat Werder Bremen 1-1, 2-1
1993 Parma beat AC Milan 0-1, 2-0
1994 AC Milan beat Arsenal 0-0, 2-0
1995 Ajax beat Zaragoza 1-1, 4-0
1996 Juventus beat Paris St Germain 6-1, 3-1
1997 Barcelona beat Borussia Dortmund 2-0, 1-1
1998 Chelsea beat Real Madrid 1-0
1999 Lazio beat Manchester U 1-0
2000 Galatasaray beat Real Madrid 2-1
2001 Liverpool beat Bayern Munich 3-2
2002 Real Madrid beat Feyenoord 3-1
2003 AC Milan beat Porto 1-0
2004 Valencia beat Porto 2-1
2005 Liverpool beat CSKA Moscow 3-1
2006 Sevilla beat Barcelona 3-0

FIFA CLUB WORLD CUP 2006

Formerly known as the FIFA Club World Championship, this tournament is played annually between the champion clubs from all 6 continental confederations, although since 2007 the champions of Oceania must play a qualifying play-off against the champion club of the permanent host country Japan.

FIFA CLUB WORLD CUP 2006

QUARTER-FINALS

Auckland City (0) 0, Al Ahly (0) 2 *(Flavio 51, Aboutrika 73)*
att: 29,912 in Toyota.
Jeonbuk Motors (0) 0, Club America (0) 1 *(Rojas 79)*
att: 34,197 in Tokyo.

SEMI-FINALS

Al Ahly (0) 1 *(Flavio 54)*, **Internacional (1) 2** *(Alexandre Pato 23, Luiz Adriano 72)*
att: 33,690 in Tokyo.
Club America (0) 0, Barcelona (2) 4 *(Gudjohnsen 11, Marquez 30, Ronaldinho 65, Deco 85)*
att: 62,316 in Yokohama.

MATCH FOR 5TH PLACE

Auckland City (0) 0, Jeonbuk Motors (2) 3 *(Lee 17, Kim 31, Zecarlo 73 (pen))*
att: 23,258 in Tokyo.

MATCH FOR 3RD PLACE

Al Ahly (1) 2 *(Aboutrika 42, 79)*, **Club America (0) 1** *(Cabanas 59)*
att: 51,641 in Yokohama.

FIFA CLUB WORLD CUP FINAL 2006

Sunday 17 December, Yokohama, Japan (attendance 67,128)

Internacional (0) 1 *(Adriano 82)* **Barcelona (0) 0**

Internacional: Clemer; Ceara, Indio, Fabiano Eller, Wellington Monteiro, Alex (Vargas 46), Edinho, Fernandao (Adriano 76), Iarley, Alexandre Pato (Luiz Adriano 61), Rubens Cardoso.

Barcelona: Valdes; Motta (Xavi 59), Marquez, Puyol, Gudjohnsen (Ezquerro 88), Giuly, Ronaldinho, Zambrotta (Belletti 46), Van Bronckhorst, Deco, Iniesta.

PREVIOUS MATCHES

2000 Corinthians beat Vaso de Gama 4-3 on penalties after 0-0 draw
2005 Sao Paulo beat Liverpool 1-0
2006 Internacional beat Barcelona 1-0

INTERNATIONAL DIRECTORY

The latest available information has been given regarding numbers of clubs and players registered with FIFA, the world governing body. Where known, official colours are listed. With European countries, League tables show a number of signs. * indicates relegated teams, + play-offs, *+ relegated after play-offs, ++ promoted.

There are 207 member associations. The four home countries, England, Scotland, Northern Ireland and Wales, are dealt with elsewhere in the Yearbook; but basic details appear in this directory. The following countries are not members of FIFA: Gibraltar, Kosovo, and Northern Cyprus.

EUROPE

ALBANIA

The Football Association of Albania, Rruga Labinoti, Pallati Perballe Shkolles 'Gjuhet e Huaja'.
Founded: 1930; *Number of Clubs:* 49; *Number of Players:* 5,192; *National Colours:* Red shirts, black shorts, red stockings.
Telephone: 00-355-43/46 601; *Fax:* 00-355-43/46 609.

International matches 2006
Lithuania (h) 1-2, Georgia (h) 0-0, San Marino (a) 3-0, Belarus (a) 2-2, Romania (h) 0-2, Holland (a) 1-2.

League Championship wins (1930–37; 1945–2007)
SK Tirana 23 (including 17 Nentori 8); Dinamo Tirana 16; Partizani Tirana 15; Vllaznia 9; Elbasan 2 (including Labinoti 1); Flamurtari 1; Skenderbeu 1; Teuta 1.

Cup wins (1948–2007)
Partizani Tirana 15; Dinamo Tirana 13; SK Tirana 12 (including 17 Nentori 8); Vllaznia 5; Teuta 3; Elbasan 2 (including Labinoti 1); Flamurtari 2; Apolonia 1, Besa 1.

Final League Table 2006–07

	P	*W*	*D*	*L*	*F*	*A*	*Pts*
SK Tirana	33	22	6	5	64	33	72
Teuta	33	19	10	4	44	26	67
Vllaznia	33	18	9	6	46	28	63
Partizani	33	17	6	10	44	25	57
Dinamo Tirana	33	14	5	14	41	39	47
Besa	33	11	8	14	35	38	41
Elbasan	33	10	10	13	34	39	40
Kastrioti	33	9	10	14	32	46	37
Flamurtari	33	9	7	17	35	41	34
Shkumbini	33	10	4	19	36	53	34
Luftetari*	33	9	6	18	28	44	33
Apolonia*	33	7	5	21	32	59	26

Top scorer: Sinani (SK Tirana) 23.
Cup Final: Besa 3, Teuta 2.

ANDORRA

Federacio Andorrana de Futbol, Avinguda Carlemany 67, 3er Pis, Apartado postal 65, Escaldes-Engordany, Principat D'Andorra.
Founded: 1994; *Number of Clubs:* 12; *Number of Players:* 300; *National Colours:* Yellow shirts, red shorts, blue stockings.
Telephone: 00376/805 830; *Fax:* 00376/862 006.

International matches 2006
Belarus (a) 0-3, England (a) 0-5, Israel (a) 1-4, Croatia (a) 0-7, Macedonia (h) 0-3.

League Championship wins (1996–2007)
Principat 3; Encamp 2; Santa Coloma 2; Ranger's 2; Dicoansa 1; Constelacio 1; St Julia 1.

Cup wins (1996–2007)
Santa Coloma 6; Principat 4; Constelacio 1; Lusitanos 1.

Qualifying League Table 2006–07

	P	*W*	*D*	*L*	*F*	*A*	*Pts*
Ranger's	14	12	1	1	42	8	37
Santa Coloma	14	12	1	1	35	10	37
St Julia	14	7	3	4	29	12	24
Lusitanos	14	6	2	6	19	20	20
Principat	14	4	3	7	15	33	15
Inter	14	3	3	8	14	28	12
Encamp	14	1	4	9	13	30	7
Atletic	14	1	3	10	13	39	6

Championship Play-Offs

	P	*W*	*D*	*L*	*F*	*A*	*Pts*
Ranger's	20	17	2	1	60	11	53
Santa Coloma	20	14	2	4	41	17	44
St Julia	20	10	4	6	38	17	34
Lusitanos	20	6	3	11	22	41	21

Relegation Play-Offs

	P	*W*	*D*	*L*	*F*	*A*	*Pts*
Inter	20	7	3	10	20	32	24
Prinicpat	20	5	4	11	21	43	19
Encamp+	20	4	5	11	19	34	17
Atletic*	20	4	3	13	18	44	15

Cup Final: Santa Coloma 2, St Julia 2
Santa Coloma won 4-2 on penalties.

ARMENIA

Football Federation of Armenia, Saryan 38, Yerevan, 375 010, Armenia.
Founded: 1992; *Number of Clubs:* 32; *Number of Players:* 15,000; *National Colours:* Red shirts, blue shorts, orange stockings.
Telephone: 00374-1/535 084; *Fax:* 00374-1/539517.

International matches 2006
Romania (a) 0-2, Cyprus (a) 3-1, Belgium (h) 0-1, Finland (h) 0-0, Serbia (a) 0-3, Finland (a) 0-1.

League Championship wins (1992–2006)
Pyunik 9 (including Homenetmen 2); Shirak Gyumri 4*; Ararat Yerevan 2*; FC Yerevan 1; Tsement 1; Araks 1.
*Includes one unofficial title.

Cup wins (1992–2007)
Mika 5; Ararat Yerevan 4; Pyunik 3; Tsement 2; Banants 2.

Championship League Table 2006

	P	*W*	*D*	*L*	*F*	*A*	*Pts*
Pyunik	28	23	4	1	86	23	73
Banants	28	18	3	7	67	26	57
Mika	28	17	6	5	45	21	57
Ararat	28	15	4	9	48	35	49
Gandzasar	28	7	3	18	28	60	24
Kilikia	28	6	5	17	38	69	23
Shirak	28	4	7	17	21	64	19
Ulysses+	28	5	2	21	31	66	17

Erevan United disbanded; Esteghlal disbanded before season started; Dinamo-Zenit renamed Ulysses; Ararat disbanded, newly promoted Ararat-2 reverted to previous name, Ararat!
Play-Off: Ulysses 4, Dinamo 2.
Top scorer: Aram Hakobian (Banants) 25.
Cup Final: Banants 3, Ararat 1.

AUSTRIA

Oesterreichischer Fussball-Bund, Ernst-Happel Stadion – Sektor A/F, Postfach 340, Meierestrasse 7, Wien 1021.
Founded: 1904; *Number of Clubs:* 2,081; *Number of Players:* 253,576; *National Colours:* White shirts, black shorts, white stockings.
Telephone: 0043-1/727 180; *Fax:* 0043-1/ 728 1632.

International matches 2006
Canada (h) 0-2, Croatia (h) 1-4, Hungary (h) 1-2, Costa Rica (n) 2-2, Venezuela (n) 0-1, Liechtenstein (a) 2-1, Switzerland (h) 2-1, Trinidad & Tobago (h) 4-1.

League Championship wins (1912–2007)
Rapid Vienna 31; FK Austria 24; Tirol-Svarowski-Innsbruck 10; Admira-Energie-Wacker 9; First Vienna 6; Austria Salzburg 4; Wiener Sportklub 3; Sturm Graz 2; FAC 1; Hakoah 1; Linz ASK 1; WAF 1; Voest Linz 1; Graz 1.

Cup wins (1919–2007)
FK Austria 29; Rapid Vienna 14; TS Innsbruck (formerly Wacker Innsbruck) 7; Admira-Energie-Wacker (formerly Sportklub Admira & Admira-Energie) 5; Graz 4; First Vienna 3; Sturm Graz 3; Linz ASK 1; Wacker Vienna 1; WAF 1; Wiener Sportklub 1; Stockerau 1; Ried 1; Karnten 1.

Final League Table 2006–07

	P	*W*	*D*	*L*	*F*	*A*	*Pts*
Salzburg	36	22	9	5	72	25	75
Ried	36	15	11	10	47	42	56
Mattersburg	36	16	7	13	61	58	55
Rapid	36	14	10	12	55	49	52
Pasching	36	14	10	12	47	41	52
FK Austria	36	11	12	13	43	43	45
Sturm Graz	36	16	6	14	40	40	41
Rheindorf	36	11	5	20	45	64	38
Tirol	36	8	10	18	40	64	34
Graz*	36	8	10	18	43	67	6

Sturm Graz three points deducted for licence irregularity and ten for going into insolvency. Graz deducted six points for debt payment failure and 22 for going into insolvency and rule infringement. Graz were also refused a licence for 2007-08. Pasching move to Klagenfurt for 2007–08 as FC Karnten.
Top scorer: Zickler (Salzburg) 22.
Cup Final: FK Austria 2, Mattersburg 1.

AZERBAIJAN

Association of Football Federations of Azerbaijan, 42 Gussi Gadjiev Street, Baku 370 009.
Founded: 1992; *Number of Clubs:* 1,500;. *Number of Players:* 95,000; *National Colours:* White shirts, blue shorts, white stockings.
Telephone: 00994-12/944 916; *Fax:* 00994-12/ 989 393.

International matches 2006
Ukraine (h) 0-0, Turkey (h) 1-1, Moldova (a) 0-0, Ukraine (a) 0-6, Serbia (a) 0-1, Kazakhstan (h) 1-1, Portugal (a) 0-3, Belgium (a) 0-3.

League Championship wins (1992–2007)
Neftchi 4; Kopaz 3; Shamkir 3; Karabakh 2; Turan 1; Baku 1; Xazar 1.
Includes one unofficial title for Shamkir in 2002.

Cup wins (1992–2007)
Kopaz 4; Neftchi 4; Karabakh 2; Inshatchi 1; Shafa 1; Baku 1; Xazar 1.

Final League Table 2006–07

	P	*W*	*D*	*L*	*F*	*A*	*Pts*
Xazar	24	17	5	2	50	16	56
Neftchi	24	17	3	4	47	15	54
Baku	24	14	6	4	25	10	48
Inter	24	13	6	5	36	12	45
MKT Araz	24	12	5	7	23	18	41
Olimpik	24	11	8	5	28	17	41
Karvan	24	10	5	9	36	30	35
Karabakh	24	6	9	9	20	27	27
Simurq	24	6	7	11	27	33	25
Turan	24	5	5	14	24	38	20
Gilan	24	4	4	16	17	47	16
Ganclarbirliyi	24	3	3	18	16	54	12
Shahdagh*	24	1	8	15	15	47	11

(Ganca excluded)
Top scorer: Ramazanov (Xazar) 20.
Cup Final: Xazar 1, MKT Araz 0.

BELARUS

Belarus Football Federation, Kirova Street 8/2, Minsk 220 600, Belarus.
Founded: 1992; *Number of Clubs:* 455; *Number of Players:* 120,000; *National Colours:* Red shirts, green shorts, red stockings.
Telephone: 00375-17/227 2920; *Fax:* 00375-17/227 2920.

International matches 2006
Greece (n) 0-1, Finland (n) 2-2, Tunisia (n) 0-3, Libya (n) 1-1, Andorra (h) 3-0, Albania (h) 2-2, Holland (a) 0-3, Romania (a) 1-3, Slovenia (h) 4-2, Estonia (a) 1-2.

League Championship wins (1992–2006)
Dynamo Minsk 7; BATE Borisov 3; Slavia Mozyr (formerly MPKC Mozyr) 2; Dnepr Mogilev 1; Belshina 1; Gomel 1; Shakhtyor 1.

Cup wins (1992–2007)
Belshina 3; Dynamo Minsk 3; Slavia Mozyr (formerly MPKC Mozyr) 2; Neman 1; Dynamo 93 Minsk 1; Lokomotiv 96 1; Gomel 1; Shakhtyor 1; MTZ-RIPA 1; BATE Borisov 1; Dynamo Brest 1.

Final League Table 2006

	P	*W*	*D*	*L*	*F*	*A*	*Pts*
BATE Borisov	26	16	6	4	47	27	54
Dynamo Minsk	26	15	7	4	44	22	52
Shakhtyor	26	16	3	7	50	31	51
MTZ-RIPA	26	16	3	7	54	24	51
Gomel	26	12	6	8	33	32	42
Lokomotiv Viebsk	26	9	11	6	21	18	38
Naftan	26	11	4	11	45	42	37
Daryda	26	10	7	9	23	21	37
Dynamo Brest	26	8	7	11	17	31	31
Neman	26	8	6	12	24	30	30
Torpedo Zhodino	26	7	9	10	21	27	30
Dnepr	26	6	5	15	29	47	23
Lokomotiv Minsk*	26	5	4	17	26	52	19
Belshina*	26	1	6	19	16	46	9

Top scorer: Klimenka (Shakhtyor) 17.
Cup Final: Dynamo Brest 0, BATE Borisov 0.
Dynamo Brest won 4-3 on penalties.

BELGIUM

Union Royale Belge Des Societes De Football Association, 145 Avenue Houba de Strooper, B-1020 Bruxelles.
Founded: 1895; *Number of Clubs:* 2,120; *Number of Players:* 390,468; *National Colours:* All red.
Telephone: 0032-2/477 1211; *Fax:* 0032-2/ 478 2391.

International matches 2006
Luxembourg (a) 2-0, Saudi Arabia (h) 2-1, Slovakia (a) 1-1, Turkey (h) 3-3, Kazakhstan (h) 0-0, Armenia (a) 1-0, Serbia (a) 0-1, Azerbaijan (h) 3-0, Poland (h) 0-1.

League Championship wins (1896–2007)
Anderlecht 29; FC Brugge 13; Union St Gilloise 11; Standard Liege 8; Beerschot 7; RC Brussels 6; FC Liege 5; Daring Brussels 5; Antwerp 4; Mechelen 4; Lierse SK 4; SV Brugge 3; Beveren 2; Genk 2; RWD Molenbeek 1.

Cup wins (1954–2007)
FC Brugge 10; Anderlecht 8; Standard Liege 5; Beerschot 3; Waterschei 2; Beveren 2; Gent 2; Antwerp 2; Lierse SK 2; Genk 2; Racing Doornik 1; Waregem 1; SV Brugge 1; Mechelen 1; FC Liege 1; Ekeren 1; Westerlo 1; La Louviere 1; Waregem 1.

Final League Table 2006–07

	P	*W*	*D*	*L*	*F*	*A*	*Pts*
Anderlecht	34	23	8	3	75	30	77
Genk	34	22	6	6	71	37	72
Standard Liege	34	19	7	8	62	38	64
Gent	34	18	6	10	56	40	60
Charleroi	34	17	9	8	51	40	60
FC Brugge	34	14	9	11	58	40	51
Beerschot	34	14	9	11	52	46	51
Westerlo	34	12	10	12	41	44	46
Mons	34	12	8	14	41	42	44
Mouscron	34	10	12	12	51	55	42
Roeselare	34	10	9	15	50	72	39
CS Brugge	34	10	8	16	31	36	38
FC Brussels	34	8	14	12	39	50	38
Waregem	34	9	10	15	40	54	37
St Truiden	34	9	8	17	39	52	35
Lokeren	34	5	15	14	32	48	30
Lierse+	34	6	8	20	33	66	26
Beveren*	34	5	10	19	31	63	25

Top scorer: Sterchele (Beerschot) 21.
Cup Final: FC Brugge 1, Standard Liege 0.

BOSNIA-HERZEGOVINA

Football Federation of Bosnia & Herzegovina, Ferhadija 30, Sarajevo 71000.
Founded: 1992; *National Colours:* White shirts, blue shorts, white stockings.
Telephone: 00387-33/276 660; *Fax:* 00387-33/444 332.

International matches 2006
Japan (h) 2-2, South Korea (a) 0-2, Iran (a) 2-5, France (h) 1-2, Malta (a) 5-2, Hungary (h) 1-3, Moldova (a) 2-2, Greece (h) 0-4.

League Championship wins (1996–2007)
Zeljeznicar 3; Siroki 2; Brotnjo 1; Leotar 1; Zrinjski 1; Sarajevo 1.

Cup wins (1996–2007)
Sarajevo 3; Zeljeznicar 3; Bosna 1; Celik 1; Modrica 1; Orasje 1; Siroki 1.

Final League Table 2006–07

	P	*W*	*D*	*L*	*F*	*A*	*Pts*
Sarajevo	30	17	6	7	44	26	57
Zrinjski	30	17	4	9	67	40	54
Slavija	30	17	2	11	41	35	53
Siroki	30	13	6	11	39	32	45
Zeljeznicar	30	13	5	12	51	40	44
Modrica	30	13	5	12	42	42	44
Leotar	30	14	1	15	47	48	43
Velez	30	12	7	11	41	42	43
Jedinstvo	30	13	4	13	46	57	43
Zepce	30	12	4	14	30	37	40
Posusje	30	12	4	14	42	50	40
Sloboda	30	12	4	14	36	45	40
Orasje	30	11	6	13	39	35	39
Celik	30	12	3	15	29	34	39
Borac*	30	13	0	17	42	47	39
Radnik*	30	8	1	21	25	50	25

Zrinjski one point deducted reduced from two on appeal for incident in round 23.
Cup Final: Siroki 1, 1, Slavija 1, 0.

BULGARIA

Bulgarian Football Union, Karnigradska Street 19, BG-1000 Sofia.
Founded: 1923; *Number of Clubs:* 376; *Number of Players:* 48,240; *National Colours:* White shirts, green shorts, white stockings.
Telephone: 00359-2/987 7490; *Fax:* 00359-2/986 2538.

International matches 2006
Macedonia (a) 1-0, Japan (n) 2-1, Scotland (n) 1-5, Wales (a) 0-0, Romania (a) 2-2, Slovenia (h) 3-0, Holland (h) 1-1, Luxembourg (a) 1-0, Slovakia (a) 1-3.

League Championship wins (1925–2007)
CSKA Sofia 30; Levski Sofia 25; Slavia Sofia 7; Vladislav Varna 3; Lokomotiv Sofia 3; Liteks 2; Trakia Plovdiv 2; AC 23 Sofia 1; Botev Plovdiv 1; SC Sofia 1; Sokol Varna 1; Spartak Plovdiv 1; Tichka Varna 1; JSZ Sofia 1; Beroe Stara Zagora 1; Etur 1; Lokomotiv Plovdiv 1.

Cup wins (1946–2007)
Levski Sofia 24; CSKA Sofia 18; Slavia Sofia 7; Lokomotiv Sofia 4; Liteks 2; Botev Plovdiv 1; Spartak Plovdiv 1; Spartak Sofia 1; Marek Stanke 1; Trakia Plovdiv 1; Spartak Varna 1; Sliven 1.

Final League Table 2006–07

	P	*W*	*D*	*L*	*F*	*A*	*Pts*
Levski Sofia	30	24	5	1	96	13	77
CSKA Sofia	30	23	3	4	68	13	72
Lokomotiv Sofia	30	23	3	4	70	28	72
Litets	30	19	5	6	65	29	62
Slavia Sofia	30	14	7	9	47	35	49
Cherno Varna	30	14	5	11	35	29	47
Lokomotiv Plovdiv	30	13	4	13	48	43	43
Belasitsa	30	11	5	14	38	43	38
Vihren	30	11	4	15	27	39	37
Botev Plovdiv	30	11	4	15	41	45	37
Beroe	30	10	6	14	34	33	36
Marek	30	9	7	14	39	58	34
Spartak	30	10	3	17	27	52	33
Rilski*	30	10	0	20	31	53	30
Rodopa*	30	5	4	21	22	52	19
Chernomorets*	30	0	1	29	8	131	–2

Chernomorets renamed from Koneliano; three points deducted for failing to register enough youth players.
Top scorer: Guenkov (Lokomotiv Sofia) 27.
Cup Final: Levski Sofia 1, Litets 0.

CROATIA

Croatian Football Federation, Rusanova 13, Zagreb, 10 3000, Croatia.
Founded: 1912; *Number of Clubs:* 1,221; *Number of Players:* 78,127; *National Colours:* Red & white shirts, white shorts, blue stockings.
Telephone: 00385-1/236 1555; *Fax:* 00385-1/244 1501.

International matches 2006
South Korea (n) 0-2, Hong Kong (n) 4-0, Argentina (h) 3-2, Austria (a) 4-1, Iran (h) 2-2, Poland (h) 0-1, Spain (a) 1-2, Brazil (n) 0-1, Japan (n) 0-0, Australia (n) 2-2, Italy (a) 2-0, Russia (a) 0-0, Andorra (h) 7-0, England (h) 2-0, Israel (a) 4-3.

League Championship wins (1941–44; 1992–2007)
Dynamo Zagreb (formerly Croatia Zagreb) 9; Hajduk Split 6; Gradanski 3; Concordia 1; Zagreb 1.

Cup wins (1993–2007)
Dynamo Zagreb (formerly Croatia Zagreb) 8; Hajduk Split 4; Rijeka 2, Osijek 1.

Final League Table 2006–07

	P	*W*	*D*	*L*	*F*	*A*	*Pts*
Dynamo Zagreb	33	30	2	1	84	22	92
Hajduk Split	33	22	6	5	60	25	72
Zagreb	33	18	4	11	57	40	58
Sibenik	33	14	7	12	50	47	49
Slaven	33	14	7	12	40	37	49
Osijek	33	11	10	12	42	45	43
Rijeka	33	12	6	15	51	53	42
Varteks	33	12	6	15	49	62	42
Medimurje	33	11	4	18	40	60	37
Cibalia	33	9	5	19	33	53	32
Pula+	33	6	11	16	28	40	29
Kamen*	33	3	4	26	27	77	13

Top scorer: Eduardo (Dynamo Zagreb) 34.
Cup Final: Dynamo Zagreb 1, 1, Slaven 0, 1.

CYPRUS

Cyprus Football Association, 1 Stasinos Str., Engomi, P.O. Box 25071, Nicosia 2404.
Founded: 1934; *Number of Clubs:* 85; *Number of Players:* 6,000; *National Colours:* Blue shirts, white shorts, blue stockings.
Telephone: 00357-22/590 960; *Fax:* 00357-22/590 544.

International matches 2006
Slovenia (h) 0-1, Armenia (h) 2-0, Romania (a) 0-2, Slovakia (a) 1-6, Wales (a) 1-3, Republic of Ireland (h) 5-2, Germany (h) 1-1.

League Championship wins (1935–2007)
Omonia 19; Apoel 19; Anorthosis 12; AEL 5; EPA 3; Olympiakos 3; Apollon 3; Pezoporikos 2; Chetin Kayal 1; Trast 1.

Cup wins (1935–2007)
Apoel 18; Omonia 12; Anorthosis 8; AEL 6; EPA 5; Apollon 5; Trast 3; Chetin Kayal 2; Olympiakos 1; Pezoporikos 1; Salamina 1; AEK 1.

Final League Table 2006–07

	P	*W*	*D*	*L*	*F*	*A*	*Pts*
Apoel	26	20	4	2	59	22	64
Omonia	26	18	3	5	62	22	57
Anorthosis	26	16	5	5	42	20	53
Ethnikos Achnas	26	10	7	9	38	33	37
ENP	26	10	5	11	31	27	35
Apollon	26	10	5	11	35	36	35
AEK	26	8	10	8	33	32	34
Aris	26	9	5	12	39	58	32
NEA Salamina	26	7	9	10	32	41	30
AEL	26	8	6	12	31	42	30
Olympiakos	26	6	10	10	24	36	28
Digenis*	26	5	10	11	23	41	25
Agia Napa*	26	4	8	14	26	41	20
AEP*	26	3	9	14	21	45	18

Cup Final: Anorthosis 3, Omonia 2.

CZECH REPUBLIC

Football Association of Czech Republic, Diskarska 100, Prague 6 16017 – Strahov, Czech Republic.
Founded: 1901; *Number of Clubs:* 3,836; *Number of Players:* 319,500; *National Colours:* Red shirts, white shorts, blue stockings.
Telephone: 00420-2/3302 9111; *Fax:* 00420-2/3335 3107.

International matches 2006
Turkey (a) 2-2, Saudi Arabia (a) 2-0, Costa Rica (h) 1-0, Trinidad & Tobago (h) 3-0, USA (n) 3-0, Ghana (n) 0-2, Italy (n) 0-2, Serbia (h) 1-3, Wales (h) 2-1, Slovakia (a) 3-0, San Marino (h) 7-0, Republic of Ireland (a) 1-1, Denmark (h) 1-1.

League Championship wins (1926–93)
Sparta Prague 19; Slavia Prague 12; Dukla Prague (prev. UDA) 11; Slovan Bratislava 7; Spartak Trnava 5; Banik Ostrava 3; Inter-Bratislava 1; Spartak Hradec Kralove 1; Viktoria Zizkov 1; Zbrojovka Brno 1; Bohemians 1; Vitkovice 1.

Cup wins (1961–93)
Dukla Prague 8; Sparta Prague 8; Slovan Bratislava 5; Spartak Trnava 4; Banik Ostrava 3; Lokomotiv Kosice 3; TJ Gottwaldov 1; Dunajska Streda 1.
From 1993–94, there were two separate countries; the Czech Republic and Slovakia.

League Championship wins (1994–2007)
Sparta Prague 10; Slovan Liberec 2; Slavia Prague 1; Banik Ostrava 1.

Cup wins (1994–2007)
Slavia Prague 4; Sparta Prague 4; Viktoria Zizkov 2; Spartak Hradec Kralove 1; Jablonec 1; Slovan Liberec 1; Teplice 1; Banik Osrava 1.

Final League Table 2006–07

	P	*W*	*D*	*L*	*F*	*A*	*Pts*
Sparta Prague	30	18	8	4	44	20	62
Slavia Prague	30	17	7	6	44	23	58
Mlada	30	17	7	6	48	27	58
Slovan Liberec	30	16	10	4	44	22	58
Brno	30	13	7	10	34	32	46
Viktoria Plzen	30	12	10	8	35	29	46
Banik Ostrava	30	12	10	8	43	33	46
Teplice	30	11	9	10	44	39	42
Jablonec	30	9	11	10	31	32	38
Dynamo Ceske	30	9	7	14	28	46	34
Kladno	30	7	10	13	23	37	31
Siad	30	5	16	9	31	41	31
Zlin	30	5	12	13	21	34	27
Sigma Olomouc	30	6	8	16	29	43	26
Marila Pribram*	30	3	12	15	15	37	21
Slovacko*	30	3	10	17	20	39	19

Cup Final: Sparta Prague 2, Jablonec 1.

DENMARK

Danish Football Association, Idraettens Hus, Brondby Stadion 20, DK-2605, Brondby.
Founded: 1889; *Number of Clubs:* 1,555; *Number of Players:* 268,517; *National Colours:* Red shirts, white shorts, red stockings.
Telephone: 0045-43/262 222; *Fax:* 0045-43/262 245.

International matches 2006
Singapore (a) 2-1, Hong Kong (n) 3-0, South Korea (n) 3-1, Israel (a) 2-0, Paraguay (h) 1-1, France (a) 0-2, Poland (h) 2-0, Portugal (h) 4-2, Iceland (a) 2-0, Northern Ireland (h) 0-0, Liechtenstein (a) 4-0, Czech Republic (a) 1-1.

League Championship wins (1913–2007)
KB Copenhagen 15; B 93 Copenhagen 10; Brondby 10; AB (Akademisk) 9; B 1903 Copenhagen 7; Frem 6; FC Copenhagen 6; Esbjerg BK 5; Vejle BK 5; AGF Aarhus 5; Hvidovre 3; Odense BK 3; AaB Aalborg 2; B 1909 Odense 2; Koge BK 2; Lyngby 2; Silkeborg 1; Herfolge 1.

Cup wins (1955–2007)
Aarhus GF 9; Vejle BK 6; Brondby 5; OB Odense 5; Randers Freja 4; Lyngby 3; FC Copenhagen 3; B1909 Odense 2; Aalborg BK 2; Esbjerg BK 2; Frem 2; B 1903 Copenhagen 2; B 93 Copenhagen 1; KB Copenhagen 1; Vanlose 1; Hvidovre 1; B1913 Odense 1, AB Copenhagen 1, Viborg 1; Silkeborg 1.

Final League Table 2006–07

	P	*W*	*D*	*L*	*F*	*A*	*Pts*
FC Copenhagen	33	23	7	3	60	23	76
Midtjylland	33	18	9	6	58	39	63
Aalborg	33	18	7	8	55	35	61
Odense	33	17	7	9	46	36	58
Nordsjaelland	33	16	9	8	67	39	57
Brondby	33	13	10	10	50	38	49
Esbjerg	33	10	10	13	46	51	40
Randers	33	10	8	15	41	53	38
Viborg	33	8	5	20	34	64	29
Horsens	33	6	10	17	29	53	28
Vejle*	33	6	7	20	35	64	25
Silkeborg*	33	5	7	21	34	60	22

Top scorer: Prica (Aalborg) 19.
Cup Final: Odense 2, FC Copenhagen 1.

ENGLAND

The Football Association, 25 Soho Square, London W1D 4FA.
Founded: 1863; *Number of Clubs:* 42,000; *Number of Players:* 2,250,000; *National Colours:* White shirts with navy blue collar, navy shorts, white stockings.
Telephone: 020 7745 4545, 020 7402 7151; *Fax:* 020 7745 4546; *Website:* www.the-fa.org

ESTONIA

Estonian Football Association, Rapia 8/10, Tallinn 11312.
Founded: 1921; *Number of Clubs:* 40; *Number of Players:* 12,000; *National Colours:* Blue shirts, black shorts, white stockings.
Telephone: 00372-6/512 720; *Fax:* 00372-6/512 729.

International matches 2006
Northern Ireland (a) 0-1, Turkey (a) 1-1, New Zealand (h) 1-1, Macedonia (h) 0-1, Israel (h) 0-1, Russia (a) 0-2, Belarus (h) 2-1.

League Championship wins (1922–40; 1992–2006)
Flora Tallinn 7; Sport 8; Estonia 5; Levadia 4; Norma Tallinn 2; Tallinn JK 2; Kalev 2; LFLS 1; Olimpia 1; Lantana 1; VMK 1.

Cup wins (1992–2007)
Levadia (merged with Sadam) 4; Levadia Tallinn 4; VMV Tallinn 1; Nikol Tallinn 1; Norma Tallinn 1; Lantana 1; Flora Tallinn 1; Trans 1; VMK 1.

Final League Table 2006

	P	*W*	*D*	*L*	*F*	*A*	*Pts*
Levadia Tallinn	36	30	4	2	114	29	94
Trans	36	25	8	3	106	36	83
Flora	36	26	4	6	93	34	82
VMK	36	22	6	8	83	37	72
Maag	36	13	9	14	65	68	48
Tammeka	36	12	7	17	45	57	43
Vaprus	36	10	4	22	49	86	34
Ajax	36	6	7	23	35	104	25
Tulevik+	36	5	5	26	29	74	20
Warrior*	36	3	2	31	16	110	11

Merkuur renamed Maag; Valga renamed Warrior.
Play-Offs: Tallinna 0, Tulevik 0; Tulevik 1, Tallinna 1.
(Tulevik relegated).
Top scorer: Gruznov (Trans) 31.
Cup Final: Levadia 3, Trans 0.

FAEROE ISLANDS

Fotboltssamband Foroya, The Faeroes' Football Assn., Gundalur, P.O. Box 3028, FR-110, Torshavn.
Founded: 1979; *Number of Clubs:* 16; *Number of Players:* 1,014; *National Colours:* White shirts, blue shorts, white stockings.
Telephone: 00298/316 707; *Fax:* 00298/319 079.

International matches 2006
Poland (a) 0-4, Georgia (h) 0-6, Scotland (a) 0-6, Lithuania (h) 0-1, France (a) 0-5.

League Championship wins (1942–2006)
HB Torshavn 19; KI Klaksvik 16; B36 Torshavn 8; TB Tvoroyri 7; GI Gotu 7; B68 Toftir 3; SI Sorvag 1; IF Fuglafjordur 1; B71 Sandur 1; VB 1.

Cup wins (1955–2006)
HB Torshavn 26; GI Gotu 6; KI Klaksvik 5; TB Tvoroyri 4; B36 Torshavn 4; NSI Runavik 2; VB Vagur 1; B71 Sandur 1.

Final League Table 2006

	P	*W*	*D*	*L*	*F*	*A*	*Pts*
HB	27	16	7	4	61	36	55
EB/Streymur	27	16	6	5	63	30	54
B36	27	13	8	6	45	32	47
KI	27	12	9	6	54	39	45
NSI	27	12	6	9	50	39	42
GI	27	10	11	6	39	34	40
Skala	27	7	10	10	33	29	31
VB	27	5	5	17	24	73	20
B68*	27	4	6	17	34	58	18
IF*	27	4	4	19	29	62	16

Top scorer: Jacobsen (NSI) 18.
Cup Final: B36 2, KI 1.

FINLAND

Suomen Palloliitto Finlands Bollfoerbund, Urheilukatu 5, P.O. Box 191, Helsinki 00251.
Founded: 1907; *Number of Clubs:* 1,135; *Number of Players:* 66,100; *National Colours:* White shirts, blue shorts, white stockings.
Telephone: 00358-9/7421 51; *Fax:* 00358-9/7421 4200.

International matches 2006
Saudi Arabia (n) 1-1, South Korea (n) 0-1, Japan (a) 0-2, Kazakhstan (n) 0-0, Belarus (n) 2-2, Sweden (a) 0-0, Northern Ireland (h) 1-2, Poland (a) 3-1, Portugal (h) 1-1, Armenia (a) 0-0, Kazakhstan (a) 2-0, Armenia (h) 1-0.

League Championship wins (1949–2006)
HJK Helsinki 12; Valkeakosken Haka 9; Turun Palloseura 5; Kuopion Palloseura 5; Kuusysi 4; Lahden Reipas 3; IF Kamraterna 3; Ilves-Kissat 2; Jazz Pori 2; Kotkan TP 2; OPS Oulu 2; Tampere U 2; Torun Pyrkiva 1; IF Kronohagens 1; Helsinki PS 1; Kokkolan PV 1; Vasa 1; TPV Tampere 1; MyPa 1.

Cup wins (1955–2006)
Valkeakosken Haka 12; HJK Helsinki 9; Lahden Reipas 7; Kotkan TP 4; MyPa 3; Mikkeli 2; Kuusysi 2; Kuopion Palloseura 2; Ilves Tampere 2; TPS Turku 2; IFK Abo 1; Drott 1; Helsinki PS 1; Pallo-Peikot 1; Rovaniemi PS 1; Jokerit 1 (formerly PK-35); Atlantis 1.

Final League Table 2006

	P	*W*	*D*	*L*	*F*	*A*	*Pts*
Tampere U	24	16	3	5	39	18	51
HJK Helsinki	24	13	6	5	45	18	45
Haka	24	13	5	6	37	24	44
Honka	24	13	3	8	50	32	42
Mariehamn	24	10	7	7	31	22	37
MyPa	24	10	4	10	25	26	34
TPS Turku	24	9	4	11	35	38	31
Lahti	24	9	4	11	26	34	31
VPS	24	8	5	11	26	36	29
Inter	24	7	7	10	25	35	28
KooTeePee	24	8	3	13	26	44	27
Jaro	24	4	7	13	27	42	19
KuPS*	24	5	4	15	18	41	19

Allianssi refused a licence; did not participate.
Top scorer: Vuorinen (Honka) 16.
Cup Final: HJK Helsinki 1, KPV 0.

FRANCE

Federation Francaise De Football, 60 Bis Avenue d'Iena, Paris 75116.
Founded: 1919; *Number of Clubs:* 21,629; *Number of Players:* 1,692,205; *National Colours:* Blue shirts, white shorts, red stockings.
Telephone: 0033-1/ 4431 7300; *Fax:* 0033-1/4720 8296.

International matches 2006
Slovakia (h) 1-2, Mexico (h) 1-0, Denmark (h) 2-0, China (h) 3-1, Switzerland (n) 0-0, South Korea (n) 1-1, Togo (n) 2-0, Spain (n) 3-1, Brazil (n) 1-0, Portugal (n) 1-0, Italy (n) 1-1, Bosnia (a) 2-1, Georgia (a) 3-0, Italy (h) 3-1, Scotland (a) 0-1, Faeroes (h) 5-0, Greece (h) 1-0.

League Championship wins (1933–2007)
Saint Etienne 10; Olympique Marseille 8; Nantes 8; AS Monaco 7; Stade de Reims 6; Lyon 6; Girondins Bordeaux 5; OGC Nice 4; Lille OSC 3; Paris St Germain 2; FC Sete 2; Sochaux 2; Racing Club Paris 1; Roubaix-Tourcoing 1; Strasbourg 1; Auxerre 1; Lens 1.

Cup wins (1918–2007)
Olympique Marseille 10; Paris St Germain 7; Saint Etienne 6; AS Monaco 5; Lille OSC 5; Racing Club Paris 5; Red Star 5; Auxerre 4; Olympique Lyon 3; Girondins Bordeaux 3; OGC Nice 3; Nantes 3; Racing Club Strasbourg 3; CAS Genereaux 2; Nancy 2; Sedan 2; FC Sete 2; Stade de Reims 2; SO Montpellier 2; Stade Rennes 2; Sochaux 2; AS Cannes 1; Club Français 1; Excelsior Roubaix 1; Le Havre 1; Olympique de Pantin 1; CA Paris 1; Toulouse 1; Bastia 1; Metz 1; Lorient 1.

Final League Table 2006–07

	P	*W*	*D*	*L*	*F*	*A*	*Pts*
Lyon	38	24	9	5	64	27	81
Marseille	38	19	7	12	53	38	64
Toulouse	38	17	7	14	44	43	58
Rennes	38	14	15	9	38	30	57
Lens	38	15	12	11	47	41	57
Bordeaux	38	16	9	13	39	35	57
Sochaux	38	15	12	11	46	48	57
Auxerre	38	13	15	10	41	41	54
Monaco	38	13	12	13	45	38	51
Lille	38	13	11	14	45	43	50
St Etienne	38	14	7	17	52	50	49
Le Mans	38	11	16	11	45	46	49
Nancy	38	13	10	15	37	44	49
Lorient	38	12	13	13	33	40	49
Paris St Germain	38	12	12	14	42	42	48
Nice	38	9	16	13	34	40	43
Valenciennes	38	11	10	17	36	48	43
Troyes*	38	9	12	17	39	54	39
Sedan*	38	7	14	17	46	58	35
Nantes*	38	7	13	18	29	49	34

Top scorer: Savidan (Valenciennes) 13.
Cup Final: Sochaux 2, Marseille 2
Sochaux won 5-4 on penalties.

GEORGIA

Georgian Football Federation, 76a Tchavtchavadze Avenue, Tbilisi 380062.
Founded: 1990; *Number of Clubs:* 4,050. *Number of Players:* 115,000; *National Colours:* All white.
Telephone: 00995-32/912 610; *Fax:* 00995-32/001 128.

International matches 2006
Moldova (a) 1-5, Malta (a) 2-0, Albania (a) 0-0, New Zealand (h) 1-3, Paraguay (h) 0-1, Faeroes (a) 6-0, France (h) 0-3, Ukraine (a) 2-3, Germany (a) 0-2, Italy (h) 1-3, Uruguay (h) 2-0.

League Championship wins (1990–2007)
Dynamo Tbilisi 12; Torpedo Kutaisi 3; WIT 1; Sioni 1; Olimpi 1.

Cup wins (1990–2007)
Dynamo Tbilisi 8; Lokomotivi 3; Torpedo Kutaisi 2; Ameri 2; Dynamo Batumi 1; Guria 1.

Final League Table 2006–07

	P	*W*	*D*	*L*	*F*	*A*	*Pts*
Olimpi	26	19	6	1	57	9	63
Dynamo Tbilisi	26	20	2	4	57	19	62
Ameri	26	17	6	3	53	14	57
Zestafoni	26	16	9	1	55	11	57
WIT	26	12	9	5	40	28	45
Sioni	26	11	4	11	28	26	37
Torpedo Kutaisi	26	9	4	13	24	35	31
Lokomotivi	26	8	6	12	25	34	30
Dynamo Batumi	26	8	6	12	27	30	30
Borjomi	26	8	6	12	29	35	30
Merani	26	6	8	12	20	41	26
Chikhura+	26	5	6	15	13	46	21
Dila Gori*	26	3	6	17	21	56	15
Kakheti*	26	0	2	24	21	86	2

Olimpi formerly FC Tbilisi.
Kolkheti and Tskhinvali withdrew through lack of government support.
Cup Final: Ameri 1, Zestafoni 0.

GERMANY

Deutscher Fussball-Bund, Otto-Fleck-Schneise 6, Postfach 710265, Frankfurt Am Main 60492.
Founded: 1900; *Number of Clubs:* 26,760; *Number of Players:* 5,260,320; *National Colours:* White shirts, black shorts, white stockings.
Telephone: 0049-69/678 80; *Fax:* 0049-69/678 8266.

International matches 2006
Italy (a) 1-4, USA (h) 4-1, Luxembourg (h) 7-0, Japan (h) 2-2, Colombia (h) 3-0, Costa Rica (h) 4-2, Poland (h) 1-0, Ecuador (h) 3-0, Sweden (h) 2-0, Argentina (h) 1-1, Italy (h) 0-2, Portugal (h) 3-1, Sweden (h) 3-0, Republic of Ireland (h) 1-0, San Marino (a) 13-0, Georgia (h) 2-0, Slovakia (a) 4-1, Cyprus (a) 1-1.

League Championship wins (1903–2007)
Bayern Munich 20; 1.FC Nuremberg 9; Schalke 04 7; Borussia Dortmund 6; SV Hamburg 6; Borussia Moenchengladbach 5; VfB Stuttgart 5; 1.FC Kaiserslautern 4; Werder Bremen 4; VfB Leipzig 3; SpVgg Furth 3; 1.FC Cologne 3; Viktoria Berlin 2; Hertha Berlin 2; Hannover 96 2; Dresden SC 2; Munich 1860 1; Union Berlin 1; FC Freiburg 1; Phoenix Karlsruhe 1; Karlsruher FV 1; Holstein Kiel 1; Fortuna Dusseldorf 1; Rapid Vienna 1; VfR Mannheim 1; Rot-Weiss Essen 1; Eintracht Frankfurt 1; Eintracht Brunswick 1.

Cup wins (1935–2007)
Bayern Munich 13; Werder Bremen 5; 1.FC Cologne 4; Eintracht Frankfurt 4; Schalke 04 4; 1.FC Nuremberg 4; SV Hamburg 3; Moenchengladbach 3; VfB Stuttgart 3; Dresden SC 2; Fortuna Dusseldorf 2; Karlsruhe SC 2; Munich 1860 2; Borussia Dortmund 2; 1.FC Kaiserslautern 2; First Vienna 1; VfB Leipzig 1; Kickers Offenbach 1; Rapid Vienna 1; Rot-Weiss Essen 1; SW Essen 1; Bayer Uerdingen 1; Hannover 96 1; Leverkusen 1.

Final League Table 2006–07

	P	*W*	*D*	*L*	*F*	*A*	*Pts*
Stuttgart	34	21	7	6	61	37	70
Schalke	34	21	5	8	53	32	68
Werder Bremen	34	20	6	8	76	40	66
Bayern Munich	34	18	6	10	55	40	60
Leverkusen	34	15	6	13	54	49	51
Nuremberg	34	11	15	8	43	32	48
Hamburg	34	10	15	9	43	37	45
Bochum	34	13	6	15	49	50	45
Borussia Dortmund	34	12	8	14	41	43	44
Hertha	34	12	8	14	50	55	44
Hannover	34	12	8	14	41	50	44
Arminia	34	11	9	14	47	49	42
Cottbus	34	11	8	15	38	49	41
Eintracht Frankfurt	34	9	13	12	46	58	40
Wolfsburg	34	8	13	13	37	45	37
Mainz*	34	8	10	16	34	57	34
Alemannia*	34	9	7	18	46	70	34
Moenchengladbach*	34	6	8	20	23	44	26

Top scorer: Gekas (Bochum) 20.
Cup Final: Nuremberg 3, Stuttgart 2.

GIBRALTAR

Gibraltar Football Association.

League Championship wins (1896–2007)
Prince of Wales 19; Glacis United 17; Britannia 14; Gibraltar United 11; Lincoln 7; Manchester United 7; Europa 6; Newcastle (formerly Lincoln) 5; St Theresas 3; Chief Construction 2; Exiles 2; Gibraltar FC 2; Jubilee 2; South United 2; Albion 1; Athletic 1; Commander of the Yard 1; Royal Soverign 1; St Joseph's 1.

Cup wins (1896–2007)
St Joseph's 7; Europa 5; Glacis United 5; Lincoln 4; Newcastle (formerly Lincoln) 4; Britannia 3; Gibraltar United 3; Manchester United 3; AARA 1; Gibraltar FC 1; HMS Hood 1; Lincoln ABG 1; Lincoln Reliance 1; Manchester United Reserves 1; Prince of Wales 1; St Theresas 1; 2nd Battalion RGS 1; 2nd Battalion The King's Regiment 1; 4th Battalion Royal Scots 1; RAF Gibraltar 1; RAF New Camp 1.

Final League Table 2006–07

	P	*W*	*D*	*L*	*F*	*A*	*Pts*
Newcastle	16	10	4	2	34	17	34
Manchester U	16	8	4	4	25	22	28
Glacis U	16	6	3	7	22	27	21
St Joseph's	16	4	3	9	15	20	15
Gibraltar U	16	3	4	9	16	26	13

Cup Final: Newcastle 6, St Joseph's 0.

GREECE

Hellenic Football Federation, Singrou Avenue 137, Nea Smirni, 17121 Athens.
Founded: 1926; *Number of Clubs:* 4,050; *Number of Players:* 180,000; *National Colours:* Blue shirts, white shorts, blue stockings.
Telephone: 0030-210/930 6000; *Fax:* 0030-210/935 9666.

International matches 2006
South Korea (n) 1-1, Saudi Arabia (n) 1-1, Belarus (n) 1-0, Kazakhstan (n) 2-0, Australia (a) 0-1, England (a) 0-4, Moldova (a) 1-0, Norway (h) 1-0, Bosnia (a) 4-0, France (a) 0-1.

League Championship wins (1928–2007)
Olympiakos 35; Panathinaikos 19; AEK Athens 11; Aris Salonika 3; PAOK Salonika 2; Larisa 1.

Cup wins (1932–2007)
Olympiakos 23; Panathinaikos 17; AEK Athens 13; PAOK Salonika 4; Panionios 2; Larisa 2; Aris Salonika 1; Ethnikos 1; Iraklis 1; Kastoria 1; OFI Crete 1.

Final League Table 2006–07

	P	*W*	*D*	*L*	*F*	*A*	*Pts*
Olympiakos	30	22	5	3	62	23	71
AEK Athens	30	18	8	4	60	27	62
Panathinaikos	30	16	6	8	47	28	54
Aris	30	11	13	6	32	26	46
Panionios	30	12	9	9	33	31	45
PAOK Salonika	30	13	6	11	32	29	45
OFI Crete	30	12	6	12	41	45	42
Atromitos	30	10	10	10	40	44	40
Ergotelis	30	11	6	13	30	32	39
Larisa	30	9	9	12	30	38	36
Xanthi	30	8	12	10	24	22	36
Apollon	30	9	8	13	27	36	35
Iraklis	30	10	5	15	25	34	35
Kerkira*	30	8	11	11	34	36	35
Aigaleo*	30	7	7	16	27	45	28
Ionikos*	30	2	3	25	14	62	4

Ionikos three points deducted for chairman attack on referee and two points for an incident in round 14.
Top scorers: Lymberopoulos (AEK Athens) 17, Rivaldo (Olympiakos) 17.
Cup Final: Larisa 2, Panathinaikos 1.

HOLLAND

Koninklijke Nederlandsche Voetbalbond, Woudenbergseweg 56–58, Postbus 515, NL-3700 AM, Zeist.
Founded: 1889; *Number of Clubs:* 3,097; *Number of Players:* 962,397; *National Colours:* Orange shirts, black shorts, orange stockings.
Telephone: 0031-343/499 201; *Fax:* 0031-343/499 189.

International matches 2006
Ecuador (h) 1-0, Cameroon (h) 1-0, Mexico (h) 2-1, Australia (h) 1-1, Serbia (n) 1-0, Ivory Coast (n) 2-1, Argentina (n) 0-0, Portugal (n) 0-1, Republic of Ireland (a) 4-0, Luxembourg (a) 1-0, Belarus (h) 3-0, Bulgaria (a) 1-1, Albania (h) 2-1, England (h) 1-1.

League Championship wins (1898–2007)
Ajax Amsterdam 29; PSV Eindhoven 20; Feyenoord 14; HVV The Hague 8; Sparta Rotterdam 6; Go Ahead Deventer 4; HBS The Hague 3; Willem II Tilburg 3; RAP 2; Heracles 2; ADO The Hague 2; Quick The Hague 1; BVV Den Bosch 2; NAC Breda 1; Eindhoven 1; Enschede 1; Volewijckers Amsterdam 1; Limburgia 1; Rapid JC Heerlen 3; DOS Utrecht 1; DWS Amsterdam 1; Haarlem 1; Be Quick Groningen 1; AZ 67 Alkmaar 1.

Cup wins (1899–2007)
Ajax Amsterdam 17; Feyenoord 10; PSV Eindhoven 8; Quick The Hague 4; AZ 67 Alkmaar 3; Rotterdam 3; Utrecht 3; DFC 2; Fortuna Geleen 2; Haarlem 2; HBS The Hague 2; RCH Haarlem 2; Roda 2; VOC 2; Wageningen 2; Willem II Tilburg 2; FC Den Haag 2; Twente Enschede 2; Concordia Rotterdam 1; CVV 1; Eindhoven 1; HVV The Hague 1; Longa 1; Quick Nijmegen 1; RAP 1; Roermond 1; Schoten 1; Velocitas Breda 1; Velocitas Groningen 1; VSV 1; VUC 1; VVV Groningen 1; ZFC 1; NAC Breda 1.

Final League Table 2006–07

	P	*W*	*D*	*L*	*F*	*A*	*Pts*
PSV Eindhoven	34	23	6	5	75	25	75
Ajax	34	23	6	5	84	35	75
AZ	34	21	9	4	83	31	72
Twente	34	19	9	6	67	37	66
Heerenveen	34	16	7	11	60	43	55
Roda JC	34	15	9	10	47	36	54
Feyenoord	34	15	8	11	56	66	53
Groningen	34	15	6	13	54	54	51
Utrecht	34	13	9	12	41	44	48
NEC Nijmegen	34	12	8	14	36	44	44
NAC Breda	34	12	7	15	43	54	43
Vitesse	34	10	8	16	50	55	38
Sparta	34	10	7	17	40	66	37
Heracles	34	7	11	16	32	64	32
Willem II	34	8	7	19	31	64	31
Excelsior+	34	8	6	20	43	65	30
RKC Waalwijk+	34	6	9	19	33	60	27
Den Haag*	34	3	8	23	40	72	17

Play-Offs: UEFA Competitions rules after series of matches Ajax to Champions League, AZ, Twente, Heerenveen and Groningen to UEFA Cup and Utrecht to Inter-Toto.
Top scorer: Alves (Heerenveen) 34.
Cup Final: Ajax 1, AZ 1.
Ajax won 8-7 on penalties.

HUNGARY

Hungarian Football Federation, Robert Karoly krt 61-65, Robert Haz Budapest 1134.
Founded: 1901; *Number of Clubs:* 1,944; *Number of Players:* 95,986; *National Colours:* Red shirts, white shorts, green stockings.
Telephone: 0036-1/412 3340; *Fax:* 0036-1/452 0360.

International matches 2006
New Zealand (h) 2-0, England (a) 1-3, Austria (a) 2-1, Norway (h) 1-4, Bosnia (a) 3-1, Turkey (h) 0-1, Malta (a) 1-2, Canada (h) 1-0.

League Championship wins (1901–2007)
Ferencvaros 28; MTK-VM Budapest 21; Ujpest Dozsa 20; Kispest Honved 13; Vasas Budapest 6; Csepel 4; Raba Gyor 3; Debrecen 3; BTC 2; Nagyvarad 1; Vac 1; Dunaferr 1; Zalaegerszeg 1.

Cup wins (1910–2007)
Ferencvaros 19; MTK-VM Budapest 12; Ujpest Dozsa 9; Kispest Honved 6; Raba Gyor 4; Vasas Budapest 4; Diösgyör 2; Debrecen 2; Bocskai 1; III Ker 1; Kispesti AC 1; Soroksar 1; Szolnoki MAV 1; Siofok Banyasz 1; Bekescsaba 1; Pecsi 1; Matav 1; Fehervar 1.
Cup not regularly held until 1964.

Final League Table 2006–07

	P	*W*	*D*	*L*	*F*	*A*	*Pts*
Debrecen	30	22	3	5	63	21	69
MTK	30	19	4	7	61	33	61
Zalaegerszeg	30	17	4	9	54	38	55
Ujpest	30	15	4	11	39	32	46
Vasas	30	13	6	11	43	41	45
Fehervar	30	13	5	12	45	43	44
Kaposvar	30	12	5	13	40	36	41
Honved	30	11	8	11	48	43	41
Diosgyor	30	11	5	14	40	52	38
Matav	30	11	4	15	33	46	37
Paksi	30	10	7	13	34	38	37
Tatabanya	30	11	3	16	46	58	36
Gyor	30	9	8	13	37	43	35
Rakospalotai	30	9	7	14	42	55	34
Pecsi*	30	7	12	11	31	41	33
Dunakanyar*	30	4	7	19	21	57	19

Ujpest three points deducted for racist behaviour. Ferencvaros excluded for financial reasons.
Top scorers: Bajzat (Gyor) 17, Sidibe (Debrecen) 17.
Cup Final: Honved 2, Debrecen 2
Honved won 3-1 on penalties.

ICELAND

Knattspyrnusamband Island, Laugardal, 104 Reykjavik.
Founded: 1929; *Number of Clubs:* 73; *Number of Players:* 23,673; *National Colours;* All blue.
Telephone: 00354/510 2900; *Fax:* 00354/568 9793.

International matches 2006
Trinidad & Tobago (h) 0-2, Spain (h) 0-0, Northern Ireland (a) 3-0, Denmark (h) 0-2, Latvia (a) 0-4, Sweden (h) 1-2.

League Championship wins (1912–2006)
KR 24; Valur 19; Fram 18; IA Akranes 18; Vikingur 5; IBV Vestmann 4; IBK Keflavik 3; FH Hafnarfjordur 3; KA Akureyri 1.

Cup wins (1960–2006)
KR 10; Valur 9; Fram 7; IA Akranes 8; IBV Vestmann 4; IBK Keflavik 4; Fylkir 2; IBA Akureyri 1; Vikingur 1.

Final League Table 2006

	P	*W*	*D*	*L*	*F*	*A*	*Pts*
FH	18	10	6	2	31	14	36
KR	18	9	3	6	23	27	30
Valur	18	7	8	3	27	18	29
Keflavik	18	6	6	6	30	20	24
Breidblik	18	6	5	7	27	33	23
IA	18	6	4	8	27	30	22
Vikingur	18	5	6	7	21	18	21
Fylkir	18	5	6	7	22	25	21
Grindavik*	18	4	7	7	24	26	19
IBV*	18	5	3	10	18	39	18

Top scorer: Baldvinsson (Breidblik) 11.
Cup Final: Keflavik 2, KR 0.

REPUBLIC OF IRELAND

The Football Association of Ireland (Cumann Peile Na H-Eireann), 80 Merrion Square, South Dublin 2.
Founded: 1921; *Number of Clubs:* 3,190; *Number of Players:* 124,615; *National Colours:* Green shirts, white shorts, green and white stockings.
Telephone: 00353-1/676 6864; *Fax:* 00353-1/661 0931.

League Championship wins (1922–2006)
Shamrock Rovers 15; Shelbourne 13; Dundalk 9; Bohemians 9; St Patrick's Athletic 8; Waterford 6; Cork United 5; Drumcondra 5; St James's Gate 2; Cork Athletic 2; Sligo Rovers 2; Limerick 2; Athlone Town 2; Derry City 2; Cork City 2; Dolphin 1; Cork Hibernians 1; Cork Celtic 1.

Cup wins (1922–2006)
Shamrock Rovers 24; Dundalk 9; Shelbourne 6; Bohemians 6; Drumcondra 5; Derry City 4; Cork Athletic 2; Cork United 2; St James's Gate 2; St Patrick's Athletic 2; Cork Hibernians 2; Limerick 2; Waterford 2; Athlone Town 2; Sligo 2; Bray Wanderers 2; Longford Town 2; Cork City 2; Alton United 1; Fordsons 1; Transport 1; Finn Harps 1; Home Farm 1; UCD 1; Galway United 1; Drogheda United 1.

Final League Table 2006

	P	*W*	*D*	*L*	*F*	*A*	*Pts*
Shelbourne	30	18	8	4	60	27	62
Derry City	30	18	8	4	46	20	62
Drogheda United	30	16	10	4	37	23	58
Cork City	30	15	11	4	37	15	56
Sligo Rovers	30	11	7	12	33	42	40
UCD	30	9	11	10	26	26	38
St Patrick's Ath	30	9	10	11	32	29	37
Longford Town	30	8	10	12	23	27	34
Bohemians	30	9	5	16	29	34	29
Bray Wanderers	30	3	8	19	22	64	17
Waterford United+	30	2	6	22	20	58	12
Dublin City*	17	4	3	10	11	24	15

Dublin City withdrew after 17 matches; Bohemians deducted three points for fielding a suspended player.

Play-Offs: Dundalk 1, Waterford United 1; Waterford United 1, Dundalk 2.
Top scorer: Byrne J (Shelbourne) 15.
Cup Final: Derry City 4, St Patrick's Athletic 3.

ISRAEL

Israel Football Association, Ramat-Gan Stadium, 299 Aba Hilell Street, Ramat-Gan 52134.
Founded: 1948; *Number of Clubs:* 544; *Number of Players:* 30,449; *National Colours:* Blue shirts, white shorts, blue stockings.
Telephone: 00972-3/617 1503; *Fax:* 00972-3/ 570 2044.

International matches 2006
Denmark (h) 0-2, Slovenia (a) 1-1, Estonia (a) 1-0, Andorra (h) 4-1, Russia (a) 1-1, Croatia (h) 3-4.

League Championship wins (1932–2007)
Maccabi Tel Aviv 19; Hapoel Tel Aviv 13; Maccabi Haifa 10; Hapoel Petach Tikva 6; Maccabi Netanya 5; Beitar Jerusalem 5; Hakoah Ramat Gan 2; Hapoel Beersheba 2; Bnei Yehouda 1; British Police 1; Hapoel Kfar Sava 1; Hapoel Ramat Gan 1; Hapoel Haifa 1.

Cup wins (1928–2007)
Maccabi Tel Aviv 23; Hapoel Tel Aviv 12; Beitar Jerusalem 5; Maccabi Haifa 5; Hapoel Haifa 3; Hapoel Kfar Sava 3; Beitar Tel Aviv 2; Bnei Yehouda 2; Hakoah Ramat Gan 2; Hapoel Petah Tikva 2; Maccabi Petach Tikva 2; British Police 1; Hapoel Jerusalem 1; Hapoel Lod 1; Maccabi Netanya 1; Hapoel Beersheba 1; Hapoel Ramat Gan 1; Hapoel Bnei Sakhnin 1.

Final League Table 2006–07

	P	*W*	*D*	*L*	*F*	*A*	*Pts*
Beitar Jerusalem	33	19	10	4	52	24	67
Maccabi Netanya	33	15	12	6	37	25	57
Maccabi Tel Aviv	33	15	11	7	42	28	54
Hapoel Tel Aviv	33	15	9	9	53	40	54
Maccabi Haifa	33	14	9	10	45	39	51
Maccabi Petah Tikva	33	14	8	11	31	27	50
Ashdod	33	12	6	15	49	49	42
Hapoel Kfar Saba	33	8	16	9	41	40	40
Bnei Yehouda	33	7	14	12	34	50	35
Maccabi Herzlia	33	9	7	17	47	55	34
Hakoakh Ramat Gan*	33	6	10	17	32	54	28
Hapoel Petah Tikva*	33	3	10	20	29	61	16

Maccabi Tel Aviv two points deducted for contract irregularities; Hapoel Petah Tikva three points deducted for financial irregularities.
Top scorer: Azran (Ashdod) 15.
Cup Final: Hapoel Tel Aviv 1, Hapoel Ashkelon 1.
Hapoel Tel Aviv won 5-4 on penalties.

ITALY

Federazione Italiana Giuoco Calcio, Via Gregorio Allegri 14, Roma 00198.
Founded: 1898; *Number of Clubs:* 20,961; *Number of Players:* 1,420,160; *National Colours:* Blue shirts, white shorts, blue stockings.
Telephone: 0039-06/84 911; *Fax:* 0039-06/84 912 526.

International matches 2006
Germany (h) 4-1, Switzerland (a) 1-1, Ukraine (h) 0-0, Ghana (n) 2-0, USA (n) 1-1, Czech Republic (n) 2-0, Australia (n) 1-0, Ukraine (n) 3-0, Germany (n) 2-0, France (n) 1-1, Croatia (h) 0-2, Lithuania (h) 1-1, France (a) 1-3, Ukraine (h) 2-0, Georgia (a) 3-1, Turkey (h) 1-1.

League Championship wins (1898–2007)
Juventus 29; AC Milan 17; Inter-Milan 14; Genoa 9; Torino 8; Pro Vercelli 7; Bologna 7; AS Roma 3; Fiorentina 2; Lazio 2; Napoli 2; Casale 1; Novese 1; Cagliari 1; Verona 1; Sampdoria 1.

Cup wins (1922–2007)
Juventus 9; AS Roma 9; Fiorentina 6; AC Milan 5; Inter-Milan 5; Torino 4; Sampdoria 4; Lazio 4; Napoli 3; Parma 3; Bologna 2; Atalanta 1; Genoa 1; Vado 1; Venezia 1; Vicenza 1.

Final League Table 2006–07

	P	*W*	*D*	*L*	*F*	*A*	*Pts*
Internazionale	38	30	7	1	80	34	97
Roma	38	22	9	7	74	34	75
Lazio (-3)	38	18	11	9	59	33	62
AC Milan (-8)	38	19	12	7	57	36	61
Fiorentina (-15)	38	21	10	7	62	31	58
Palermo	38	16	10	12	58	51	58
Empoli	38	14	12	12	42	43	54
Atalanta	38	12	14	12	56	54	50
Sampdoria	38	13	10	15	44	48	49
Udinese	38	12	10	16	49	55	46
Livorno	38	10	13	15	41	54	43
Parma	38	10	12	16	41	56	42
Catania	38	10	11	17	46	68	41
Reggina (-11)	38	12	15	11	52	50	40
Siena (-1)	38	9	14	15	35	45	40
Cagliari	38	9	13	16	35	46	40
Torino	38	10	10	18	27	47	40
Chievo*	38	9	12	17	38	48	39
Ascoli*	38	5	12	21	36	67	27
Messina*	38	5	11	22	37	69	26

Points deductions due to bribery scandal; Siena deduction for late payment of social security.
Top scorer: Totti (Roma) 26.
Cup Final: Roma 6, 1, Internazionale 2, 2.

KAZAKHSTAN

The Football Union of Kazakhstan, Satpayev Street, 29/3 Almaty 480 072, Kazakhstan.
Founded: 1914; *Number of Clubs:* 5,793; *Number of Players:* 260,000; *National Colours:* Blue shirts, blue shorts, yellow stockings.
Telephone: 007-3272/920 444; *Fax:* 007-3272/921 885.

International matches 2006
Finland (n) 0-0, Greece (n) 0-2, Jordan (a) 0-2, Tadjikistan (h) 4-1, Kyrghizistan (h) 1-0, Belgium (a) 0-0, Azerbaijan (a) 1-1, Poland (h) 0-1, Finland (h) 0-2, Portugal (a) 0-3, Singapore (n) 0-0, Vietnam (n) 1-2, Thailand (n) 2-2.

League Championship wins (1992–2006)
Irtysh 5; Yelimai 3; Astana (formerly Zhenis) 3; Kairat 2; Taraz 1; Aqtobe 1.

Cup wins (1992–2006)
Kairat 5; Zhenis 3; Dostyk 1; Vostok 1; Yelimai 1; Irtysh 1; Kaisar 1; Taraz 1; Almaty 1.

Final League Table 2006

	P	*W*	*D*	*L*	*F*	*A*	*Pts*
Astana	30	19	7	4	45	23	64
Aqtobe	30	18	6	6	48	21	60
Tobol	30	16	8	6	43	22	56
Shakhtyor	30	15	5	10	35	24	50
Almaty	30	13	9	8	36	29	48
Yertis	30	13	8	9	34	24	47
Qayrat	30	12	10	8	39	30	46
Yekibastuzets	30	12	6	12	29	28	42
Vostok	30	9	8	13	33	40	35
Taraz	30	9	6	15	32	34	33
Oqjetpes	30	8	9	13	23	36	33
Yesil Bogatyr	30	8	9	13	20	37	33
Ordabasy	30	8	8	14	29	36	32
Atyrau	30	8	5	17	25	47	29
Qaysar*	30	8	4	18	29	53	28
Energetik*	30	6	10	16	28	44	26

Zhenis changed name to Astana.
Top scorer: Irismetov (Almaty) 17.
Cup Final: Almaty 3, Astana 1.

KOSOVO

Football Federation Kosova.

League Championship wins (1945–2006)
Prishtina 10; Vellaznimi 9; Trepca 6; Liria 5; Buduqnosti 4; Red Star 3; Rudari 3; Besa 2; Fushe-Kosova 2; Jedinstvo 2; Kosova 2; Obiliqi 2; Slloga 2; Besiana 1; Drita 1; Dukagjini 1; KNI R.Sadiku 1; KXEK Kosova 1; Proleteri 1; Rudniku 1.

Cup wins (1992–2007)
Vlamurtari 2; Liria 2; Besa 1; Besiana 1; Drita 1; Gjilani 1; KEK-U 1; Kosova 1; Prishtina 1; Prishtine 1; Trepca 1.

Final League Table 2006–07

	P	*W*	*D*	*F*	*L*	*A*	*Pts*
Besa	30	21	4	5	72	28	67
Prishtina	30	18	7	5	60	26	61
Trepca 89	30	17	5	8	54	28	56
Drenica	30	13	7	10	52	47	46
KEK-u	30	13	4	13	53	43	43
Hysi	30	12	7	11	42	39	43
Flamurtari	30	12	7	11	40	37	43
Kosova	30	11	9	10	37	32	42
Shqiponja	30	12	5	13	49	43	41
Gjilani	30	11	7	12	35	43	40
Vellaznimi	30	11	6	13	44	43	39
Trepca	30	10	9	11	39	41	39
Besiana	30	12	3	15	35	55	39
Liria*	30	10	8	12	41	49	35
Ferizaji#	30	7	7	16	23	55	28
Kosova Prishtine*	30	1	3	26	25	92	6

Liria three points deducted for failure to play in round 10; Ferizaji excluded after round 25. Remaining fixtures awarded 0-3 against them.

LATVIA

Latvian Football Federation, Augsiela 1, LV-1009, Riga.
Founded: 1921; *Number of Clubs:* 50; *Number of Players:* 12,000; *National Colours:* Carmine red shirts, white shorts, carmine red stockings.
Telephone: 00371/729 2988; *Fax:* 00371/ 731 5604.

International matches 2006
USA (a) 0-1, Russia (a) 0-1, Sweden (h) 0-1, Luxembourg (a) 0-0, Iceland (h) 4-0, Northern Ireland (a) 0-1.

League Championship wins (1922–2006)
Skonto Riga 14; ASK Riga 9; RFK Riga 8; Olympia Liepaya 7; Sarkanais Metalurgs Liepaya 7; VEF Riga 6; Energija Riga 4; Elektrons Riga 3; Torpedo Riga 3; Daugava Liepaya 2; ODO Riga 2; Khimikis Daugavpils 2; RAF Yelgava 2; Keisermezhs Riga 2; Dinamo Riga 1; Zhmilyeva Team 1; Darba Rezervi 1; REZ Riga 1; Start Brotseni 1; Venta Ventspils 1; Yurnieks Riga 1; Alfa Riga 1; Gauya Valmiera 1; Metalurgs Liepaya 1; FK Ventspils 1.

Cup wins (1937–2006)
Elektrons Riga 7; Skonto Riga 7; Sarkanais Metalurgs Liepaya 5; ODO Riga 3; VEF Riga 3; ASK Riga 3; Tseltnieks Riga 3; RAF Yelgava 3; FK Ventspils 3; RFK Riga 2; Daugava Liepaya 2; Start Brotseni 2; Selmash Liepaya 2; Yurnieks Riga 2; Khimikis Daugavpils 2; Rigas Vilki 1; Dinamo Liepaya 1; Dinamo Riga 1; REZ Riga 1; Voulkan Kouldiga 1; Baltija Liepaya 1; Venta Ventspils 1; Pilot Riga 1; Lielupe Yurmala 1; Energija Riga 1; Torpedo Riga 1; Daugava SKIF Riga 1; Tseltnieks Daugavpils 1; Olympia Riga 1; FK Riga 1; Metalurgs Liepaya 1.

Final League Table 2006

	P	*W*	*D*	*L*	*F*	*A*	*Pts*
FKVentspils	28	19	5	4	48	23	62
Metalurgs Liepaya	28	18	6	4	66	20	60
Skonto Riga	28	16	6	6	55	21	54
Dinaburg	28	12	5	11	33	37	41
Ditton	28	10	8	10	33	31	38
Jurmala	28	11	4	13	36	36	37
FK Riga	28	6	4	18	21	57	22
Dizvanagi*	28	0	2	26	11	77	2

Top scorer: Miholaps (Skonto Riga) 15.
Cup Final: Metalurgs Liepaya 2, Skonto Riga 1.

LIECHTENSTEIN

Liechtensteiner Fussball-Verband, Malbuner Huus Altenbach 11, Postfach 165, 9490 Vaduz.
Founded: 1934; *Number of Clubs:* 7; *Number of Players:* 1,247; *National Colours:* Blue shirts, red shorts, blue stockings.
Telephone: 00423/237 4747; *Fax:* 00423/237 4748.

International matches 2006
Togo (h) 0-1, Australia (a) 1-3, Switzerland (h) 0-3, Spain (a) 0-4, Sweden (a) 1-3, Austria (h) 1-2, Denmark (h) 0-4, Wales (a) 0-4.
Liechtenstein has no national league. Teams compete in Swiss regional leagues.

Cup wins (1946–2006)
Vaduz 36; Balzers 11; Triesen 8; Eschen/Mauren 4; Schaan 3.
Cup Final: Vaduz 8, Ruggell 0.

LITHUANIA

Lithuanian Football Federation, Seimyniskiu str. 15, 2005 Vilnius.
Founded: 1922; *Number of Clubs:* 152; *Number of Players:* 16,600; *National Colours:* Yellow shirts, green shorts, yellow stockings.
Telephone: 00370/5263 8741; *Fax:* 00370/5263 8740.

International matches 2006
Albania (a) 2-1, Poland (a) 1-0, Moldova (a) 2-3, Italy (a) 1-1, Scotland (h) 1-2, Faeroes (a) 1-0, Kuwait (a) 0-1, Malta (a) 4-1.

League Championship wins (1937–2006)
FBK Kaunas 7 (including Zalgiris Kaunas 1); Zalgiris Vilnius 3; Kareda 2; Inkaras Kaunas 2; Ekranas Panevezys 2; Sirijus Klaipeda 1; ROMAR Mazeikiai 1.

Cup wins (1992–2006)
Zalgiris Vilnius 4; FBK Kaunas 3; Kareda 2; Ekranas 2; Atlantas 2; Lietuvos 1; Inkaras 1; Suduva 1.

Final League Table 2005–06

	P	*W*	*D*	*L*	*F*	*A*	*Pts*
FBK Kaunas	36	28	4	4	85	30	88
Ekranas	36	20	7	9	63	39	67
Vetra	36	17	10	9	49	35	61
Zalgiris	36	14	12	10	52	39	54
Suduva	36	15	8	13	48	44	53
Atlantas	36	14	10	12	46	41	52
FK Vilnius	36	11	14	11	46	40	47
Siauliai	36	10	11	15	42	46	41
Silute+	36	5	3	28	25	77	18
Nevezis*	36	4	5	27	35	100	17

Top scorer: Kuznetzov (Vetra) 18.
Play-Off: Interas 1, Silute 1; Silute 1, Interas 1
Interas won 4-3 on penalties.
Cup Final: Suduva 1, Ekranas 0.

LUXEMBOURG

Federation Luxembourgeoise De Football (F.L.F.), 68 Rue De Gasperich, Luxembourg 1617.
Founded: 1908; *Number of Clubs:* 126; *Number of Players:* 21,684; *National Colours:* All red.
Telephone: 00352/488 665 1; *Fax:* 00352/488 665 82.

International matches 2006
Belgium (h) 0-2, Germany (a) 0-7, Portugal (h) 0-3, Ukraine (h) 0-3, Turkey (h) 0-1, Holland (h) 0-1, Latvia (h) 0-0, Slovenia (a) 0-2, Bulgaria (h) 0-1, Togo (h) 0-0.

League Championship wins (1910–2007)
Jeunesse Esch 27; Spora Luxembourg 11; Stade Dudelange 10; Avenir Beggen 7; Red Boys Differdange 6; F91 Dudelange 6; US Hollerich-Bonnevoie 5; Fola Esch 5; US Luxembourg 5; Aris Bonnevoie 3; Progres Niedercorn 3; Grevenmacher 1.

Cup wins (1922–2007)
Red Boys Differdange 16; Jeunesse Esch 12; US Luxembourg 10; Spora Luxembourg 8; Avenir Beggen 7; Stade Dudelange 4; Progres Niedercorn 4; Fola Esch 3; Grevenmacher 3; F91 Dudelange 3; Alliance Dudelange 2; US Rumelange 2; Aris Bonnevoie 1; US Dudelange 1; Jeunesse Hautcharage 1; National Schiffige 1; Racing Luxembourg 1; SC Tetange 1; Hesperange 1; Etzella 1; Petange 1.

Final League Table 2006–07

	P	W	D	L	F	A	Pts
F91 Dudelange	26	21	2	3	71	20	65
Etzella	26	16	4	6	60	30	52
Differdange	26	14	6	6	71	41	48
Union Luxembourg	26	11	8	7	52	35	41
Hesperange	26	11	8	7	40	28	41
Grevenmacher	26	11	8	7	43	34	41
Progres	26	10	5	11	53	61	35
Kaerjeng	26	10	4	12	38	51	34
Jeunesse Esch	26	9	5	12	29	34	32
Petange	26	8	8	10	29	38	32
FC Wiltz 71	26	9	4	13	31	38	31
Victoria Rosport+	26	7	6	13	28	47	27
Mondercange*	26	4	6	16	23	59	18
Mamer*	26	1	6	19	19	71	9

Top scorer: Da Mota (Etzella) 26.
Cup Final: F91 Dudelange 2, Kaerjeng 1.

MACEDONIA

Football Association of Macedonia, VIII-ma Udarna Brigada 31-A, Skopje 1000.
Founded: 1948; *Number of Clubs:* 598; *Number of Players:* 15,165; *National Colours:* All red.
Telephone: 00389-2/3129 291; *Fax:* 00389-2/3165 448.

International matches 2006
Bulgaria (h) 0-1, Ecuador (h) 2-1, Turkey (a) 1-0, Estonia (a) 1-0, England (h) 0-1, England (a) 0-0, Andorra (a) 3-0, Russia (h) 0-2.

League Championship wins (1993–2007)
Vardar 5; Sileks 3; Sloga 3; Rabotnicki 2; Pobeda 2.

Cup wins (1993–2007)
Vardar 5; Sloga 2; Sileks 1; Pellister 1; Pobeda 1; Cement 1; Baskimi 1; Makedonija 1.

Final League Table 2006–07

	P	W	D	L	F	A	Pts
Pobeda	33	21	8	4	73	42	71
Rabotnicki	33	19	10	4	75	25	67
Makedonija	33	18	10	5	65	29	64
Vardar	33	17	8	8	63	34	59
Renova	33	17	8	8	54	31	59
Pelister	33	14	3	16	37	32	45
Napredok	33	12	9	12	50	47	45
Baskimi	33	12	6	15	54	60	42
Sileks+	33	12	5	16	54	50	41
Shkendija+	33	10	8	15	39	63	38
Bregalnica*	33	3	4	26	19	97	13
Vlazrimi*	33	2	3	28	22	95	9

Cup Final: Vardar 2, Pobeda 1.

MALTA

Malta Football Association, 280 St Paul Street, Valletta VLT07.
Founded: 1900; *Number of Clubs:* 252; *Number of Players:* 5,544; *National Colours:* Red shirts, white shorts, red stockings.
Telephone: 00356-21/232 581; *Fax:* 00356-21/245 136.

International matches 2006
Moldova (h) 0-2, Georgia (h) 0-2, Japan (a) 0-1, Slovakia (a) 0-3, Bosnia (h) 2-5, Turkey (a) 0-2, Hungary (h) 2-1, Lithuania (h) 1-4.

League Championship wins (1910–2007)
Sliema Wanderers 26; Floriana 25; Valletta 18; Hibernians 9; Hamrun Spartans 7; Rabat Ajax 2; Birkirkara 2; St George's 1; KOMR 1; Marsaxlokk 1.

Cup wins (1935–2007)
Sliema Wanderers 19; Floriana 18; Valletta 10; Hibernians 8; Hamrun Spartans 6; Birkirkara 3; Gzira United 1; Melita 1; Zurrieq 1; Rabat Ajax 1.

Qualifying League Table 2006–07

	P	W	D	L	F	A	Pts
Marsaxlokk	18	14	3	1	45	15	45
Sliema Wanderers	18	10	4	4	33	21	34
Valletta	18	10	3	5	41	18	33
St Joseph	18	9	6	3	32	17	33
Birkirkara	18	9	3	6	32	27	30
Hibernians	18	8	1	9	31	33	25
Floriana	18	6	6	6	28	20	24
St George's	18	2	6	10	11	33	12
Pieta Hotspurs	18	2	5	11	16	47	11
Marsa	18	0	3	15	12	50	3

Championship Table 2006–07

	P	W	D	L	F	A	Pts
Marsaxlokk	28	22	3	3	74	28	47
Sliema Wanderers	28	15	7	6	50	34	35
Birkirkara	28	15	4	9	48	44	34
Valletta	28	13	7	8	55	31	29
Hibernians	28	10	3	15	45	52	21
St Joseph	28	9	8	11	40	40	19

Promotion/Relegation Table 2006–07

	P	W	D	L	F	A	Pts
Floriana	24	9	7	8	41	30	22
Pieta Hotspurs	24	6	5	13	29	56	18
St George's*	24	3	7	14	23	52	10
Marsa*	24	2	5	17	20	58	10

Cup Final: Hibernians 1, Sliema Wanderers 1.
Hibernians won 3-0 on penalties.

MOLDOVA

Football Association of Moldova, 39 Tricolorului Str, 2012, Chisinau.
Founded: 1990; *Number of Clubs:* 143; *Number of Players:* 75,000; *National Colours:* Red shirts, blue shorts, red stockings.
Telephone: 00373-22/210 413; *Fax:* 00373-22/210 432.

International matches 2006
Malta (n) 2-0, Georgia (n) 5-1, Azerbaijan (h) 0-0, Lithuania (h) 3-2, Greece (h) 0-1, Norway (a) 0-2, Bosnia (h) 2-2, Turkey (a) 0-5.

League Championship wins (1992–2007)
Zimbru Chisinau 8; Serif 6; Constructorul 1.

Cup wins (1992–2007)
Zimbru Chisinau 5; Tiligul 4; Serif 4; Combat 1; Constructorul 1; Otaci 1.

Final League Table 2006–07

	P	W	D	L	F	A	Pts
Serif	36	28	8	0	70	7	92
Zimbru Chisinau	36	21	8	7	63	23	71
Otaci	36	16	9	11	44	36	57
Dacia	36	13	16	7	36	30	55
Tiraspol	36	10	16	10	37	32	46
Olimpia	36	12	6	18	38	50	42
Politehnica	36	7	12	17	29	47	33
Tiligul	36	6	15	15	23	46	33
Iscra-Stali	36	6	13	17	22	43	31
Dinamo	36	3	13	20	24	72	22

No relegation, increase to 12 clubs.
Top scorer: Kuciuk (Serif) 17.
Cup Final: Zimbru Chisinau 1, Otaci 0

MONTENEGRO

Football Association of Montenegro.
Founded: 1931.

Montenegro voted for independence from Serbia on 21 May 2006.

Final League Table 2006–07

	P	W	D	L	F	A	Pts
Zeta	33	25	4	4	65	18	78
Buducnost	33	22	10	1	58	12	76
Grbalj	33	14	7	12	37	30	49
Rudar	33	14	5	14	37	32	47
Mogren	33	10	12	11	27	27	42
Petrovac	33	10	10	13	24	37	40
Kom	33	9	11	13	27	31	38
Sutjeska	33	10	8	15	24	33	38
Mladost	33	9	11	13	34	49	38
Decic+	33	8	10	15	29	46	34
Jedinstvo+	33	6	13	14	27	51	31
Berane*	33	7	7	19	25	48	28

Zeta one point deducted for failing to play in round 4.
Top scorers: Cakar (Rudar) 16, Korac (Zeta) 16.

NORTHERN CYPRUS

League Championship wins (1956–63; 1969–74; 1976–2007)
Cetinkaya 12; Gonyeli 7; Magusa 7; Dogan 6; Yenicami 5; BAF Ulku 4; Kucuk 3; Akincilar 1; Binatli 1.

Cup wins (1956-2007)
Cetinkaya 16; Kucuk 6; Gonyeli 5; Magusa 5; Yenicami 5; Turk Ocagi 4; Binatli 1; Dogan 1; Genclik 1; Lefke 1; Yalova 1.

Final League Table 2006–07

	P	W	D	L	F	A	Pts
Cetinkaya	26	16	4	6	77	41	52
Lapta	26	16	3	7	49	27	51
Yeni	26	14	4	8	63	44	46
Kucuk	26	14	4	8	51	45	46
Bostanci	26	13	5	8	42	40	44
Gonyeli	26	11	5	10	45	43	38
Turk Ocagi	26	11	4	11	50	47	37
Magusa	26	11	3	12	32	28	36
Tatlisu	26	10	4	12	37	41	34
Hamitkoy	26	10	4	12	34	41	34
Yenicami	26	10	3	13	45	52	33
Genclik*	26	8	4	14	40	54	28
Duzkaya*	26	6	6	14	35	59	21
Binatli*	26	4	3	19	29	67	15

Top scorers: Yasin (Cetinkaya) 28, Ertac (Turk Ocagi) 28.
Cup Final: Turk Ocagi 4, Tatlisu 0.

NORTHERN IRELAND

Irish Football Association Ltd, 20 Windsor Avenue, Belfast BT9 6EE.
Founded: 1880; *Number of Clubs:* 1,555; *Number of Players:* 24,558; *National Colours:* Green shirts, white shorts, green stockings.
Telephone: 0044-28/9066 9458; *Fax:* 0044-28/9066 7620.

NORWAY

Norges Fotballforbund, Ullevaal Stadion, Sognsveien 75J, Serviceboks 1, Oslo 0855.
Founded: 1902; *Number of Clubs:* 1,810; *Number of Players:* 300,000; *National Colours:* Red shirts, white shorts, blue stockings.
Telephone: 0047/2102 9300; *Fax:* 0047/2102 9301.

International matches 2006
Mexico (a) 1-2, USA (a) 0-5, Senegal (a) 1-2, Paraguay (h) 2-2, South Korea (h) 0-0, Brazil (h) 1-1, Hungary (a) 4-1, Moldova (h) 2-0, Greece (a) 0-1, Serbia (a) 1-1.

League Championship wins (1938–2006)
Rosenborg Trondheim 19; Fredrikstad 9; Viking Stavanger 8; Lillestroem 6; Valerenga 5; Larvik Turn 3; Brann Bergen 2; Lyn Oslo 2; IK Start 2; Friedig 1; Skeid Oslo 1; Strömsgodset Drammen 1; Moss 1.

Cup wins (1902–2006)
Odds Bk Skien 11; Fredrikstad 11; Lyn Oslo 8; Skeid Oslo 8; Rosenborg Trondheim 8; Sarpsborg FK 6; Brann Bergen 6; Viking Stavanger 5; Orn F Horten 4; Lillestroem 4; Strömsgodset Drammen 4; Frigg 3; Mjondalens F 3; Valerenga 3; Bodo-Glimt 2; Mercantile 2; Tromso 2; Molde 2; Grane Nordstrand 1; Kvik Halden 1; Sparta 1; Gjovik 1; Moss 1; Byrne 1; Stabaek 1; Odd Grenland 1.
(Known as the Norwegian Championship for HM The King's Trophy).

Final League Table 2006

	P	W	D	L	F	A	Pts
Rosenborg	26	15	8	3	47	24	53
Brann	26	14	4	8	39	36	46
Valerenga	26	13	5	8	43	28	44
Lillestrom	26	12	8	6	44	33	44
Stabaek	26	10	9	7	53	36	39
Start	26	10	7	9	29	32	37
Lyn	26	10	5	11	33	36	35
Fredrikstad	26	8	8	10	38	46	32
Sandefjord	26	9	5	12	37	47	32
Tromso	26	8	5	13	33	39	29
Viking	26	8	5	13	31	37	29
Odd+	26	7	8	11	30	38	29
Hamark*	26	7	7	12	35	39	28
Molde*	26	7	4	15	29	50	25

Top scorer: Nannskog (Stabaek) 19.
Play-Off: Odd 3, Bryne 0; Bryne 1, Odd 7.
Cup Final: Fredrikstad 3, Sandefjord 0.

POLAND

Polish Football Association, Polski Zwiazek Pilki Noznej, Miodowa 1, Warsaw 00-080.
Founded: 1919; *Number of Clubs:* 5,881; *Number of Players:* 317,442; *National Colours:* White shirts, red shorts, white stockings.
Telephone: 0048-22/827 0914; *Fax:* 0048-22/827 0704.

International matches 2006
USA (a) 0-1, Saudi Arabia (a) 2-1, Lithuania (h) 0-1, Faeroes (h) 4-0, Colombia (h) 1-2, Croatia (a) 1-0, Ecuador (n) 0-2, Germany (n) 0-1, Costa Rica (n) 2-1, Denmark (a) 0-2, Finland (h) 1-3, Serbia (h) 1-1, Kazakhstan (a) 1-0, Portugal (h) 2-1, Belgium (a) 1-0, UAE (a) 5-2.

League Championship wins (1921–2007)
Gornik Zabrze 14; Ruch Chorzow 13; Wisla Krakow 11; Legia Warsaw 8; Widzew Lodz 6; Lech Poznan 5; Pogon Lwow 4; Cracovia 3; Warta Poznan 2; Polonia Bytom 2; Stal Mielec 2; LKS Lodz 2; Polonia Warsaw 2; Zaglebie Lubin 2; Garbarnia Krakow 1; Slask Wroclaw 1; Szombierki Bytom 1.

Cup wins (1951–2007)
Legia Warsaw 12; Gornik Zabrze 6; Zaglebie Sosnowiec 4; Lech Poznan 4; GKS Katowice 3; Ruch Chorzow 3; Amica Wronki 3; Wisla Krakow 3; Slask Wroclaw 2; Polonia Warsaw 2; Groclin 2; Gwardia Warsaw 1; LKS Lodz 1; Stal Rzeszow 1; Arka Gdynia 1; Lechia Gdansk 1; Widzew Lodz 1; Miedz Legnica 1; Wisla Plock 1.

Final League Table 2006–07

	P	W	D	L	F	A	Pts
Zaglebie	30	18	8	4	57	29	62
GKS Belchatow	30	19	4	7	63	32	61
Legia	30	16	4	10	53	33	52
Cracovia	30	14	7	9	48	41	49
Groclin	30	11	15	4	40	26	48
Lech	30	12	11	7	53	36	47
Korona	30	14	5	11	41	34	47
Wisla	30	10	16	4	41	25	46
Lodzki	30	10	11	9	31	30	41
Odra	30	10	10	10	29	36	40
Arka	30	10	10	10	43	39	40
Widzew	30	7	7	16	27	48	28
Leczna	30	7	5	18	24	64	26
Gornik Zabrze	30	6	7	17	30	51	25
Wisla Plock*	30	4	11	15	20	47	23
Pogon*	30	3	7	20	24	53	16

Lech amalgamated with Amica; Arka and Leczna relegated due to corruption scandal. Four teams promoted.
Top scorer: Reiss (Lech) 15.
Cup Final: Groclin 2, Korona 0.

PORTUGAL

Federacao Portuguesa De Futebol, Praca De Alegria N.25, Apartado 21.100, P-1127, Lisboa 1250-004.

Founded: 1914; *Number of Clubs:* 204; *Number of Players:* 79,235; *National Colours:* Red shirts, green shorts, red stockings.
Telephone: 00351-21/325 2700; *Fax:* 00351-21/325 2780.

International matches 2006
Saudi Arabia (a) 3-0, Cape Verde (h) 4-1, Luxembourg (a) 3-0, Angola (a) 1-0, Iran (n) 2-0, Mexico (n) 2-1, Holland (n) 1-0, England (n) 0-0, France (n) 0-1, Germany (n) 1-3, Denmark (a) 2-4, Finland (a) 1-1, Azerbaijan (h) 3-0, Poland (a) 1-2, Kazakhstan (h) 3-0.

League Championship wins (1935–2007)
Benfica 31; FC Porto 22; Sporting Lisbon 18; Belenenses 1; Boavista 1.

Cup wins (1939–2007)
Benfica 24; Sporting Lisbon 14; FC Porto 13; Boavista 5; Belenenses 3; Vitoria Setubal 3; Academica Coimbra 1; Leixoes Porto 1; Sporting Braga 1; Amadora 1; Beira Mar 1.

Final League Table 2006–07

	P	*W*	*D*	*L*	*F*	*A*	*Pts*
Porto	30	22	3	5	65	20	69
Sporting Lisbon	30	20	8	2	54	15	68
Benfica	30	20	7	3	55	20	67
Braga	30	14	8	8	35	30	50
Belenenses	30	15	4	11	36	29	49
Ferreira	30	10	12	8	31	36	42
Uniao Leiria	30	10	11	9	25	27	41
Nacional	30	11	6	13	41	38	39
Amadora	30	9	8	13	23	36	35
Boavista	30	8	11	11	32	34	35
Maritimo	30	8	8	14	30	44	32
Naval	30	7	11	12	28	37	32
Academica	30	6	8	16	28	46	26
Setubal	30	5	9	16	21	45	24
Beira Mar*	30	4	11	15	28	55	23
Desportivo Aves*	30	5	7	18	22	42	22

Top scorer: Liedson (Sporting Lisbon) 15.
Cup Final: Sporting Lisbon 1, Belenenses 0.

ROMANIA

Federatia Romana De Fotbal, House of Football, Str. Serg. Serbanica Vasile 12, Bucharest 73412.
Founded: 1909; *Number of Clubs:* 414; *Number of Players:* 22,920; *National Colours:* All yellow.
Telephone: 0040-21/325 0678; *Fax:* 0040-21/325 0679.

International matches 2006
Armenia (n) 2-0, Slovenia (n) 2-0, Uruguay (h) 0-2, Northern Ireland (h) 2-0, Colombia (h) 0-0, Cyprus (h) 2-0, Bulgaria (h) 2-2, Albania (a) 2-0, Belarus (h) 3-1, Spain (a) 1-0.

League Championship wins (1910–2007)
Steaua Bucharest 23; Dinamo Bucharest 18; Venus Bucharest 8; Chinezul Timisoara 6; UT Arad 6; Ripensia Temesvar 4; Uni Craiova 4; Petrolul Ploesti 3; Rapid Bucharest 3; Olimpia Bucharest 2; Colentina Bucharest 2; Arges Pitesti 2; ICO Oradea 2; Soc RA Bucharest 1; Prahova Ploesti 1; Coltea Brasov 1; Juventus Bucharest 1; Metalochimia Resita 1; Ploesti United 1; Unirea Tricolor 1.

Cup wins (1934–2007)
Steaua Bucharest 21; Rapid Bucharest 13; Dinamo Bucharest 12; Uni Craiova 6; UT Arad 2; Ripensia Temesvar 2; Politehnica Timisoara 2; Petrolul Ploesti 2; ICO Oradeo 1; Metalochimia Resita 1; Stinta Cluj 1; CFR Turnu Severin 1; Chimia Ramnicu Vilcea 1; Jiul Petroseni 1; Progresul Bucharest 1; Progresul Oradea 1; Gloria Bistrita 1.

Final League Table 2006–07

	P	*W*	*D*	*L*	*F*	*A*	*Pts*
Dinamo Bucharest	34	23	8	3	63	24	77
Steaua	34	21	8	5	61	22	71
Cluj	34	21	6	7	59	32	69
Rapid	34	16	11	7	63	39	59
Otelul	34	17	5	12	60	56	56
Gloria	34	16	6	12	42	35	54
Timisoara	34	15	8	11	37	33	53
Vaslui	34	13	11	10	41	44	50
Uni Craiova	34	12	12	10	39	43	48
Unirea	34	13	8	13	30	29	47
Pandurii	34	13	5	16	26	35	44
UT Arad	34	11	8	15	28	39	41
Iasi	34	10	10	14	34	41	40
Farul	34	8	13	13	31	35	37
Ceahlaul*	34	8	7	19	27	53	31
National*	34	6	6	22	27	52	24
Arges*	34	5	9	20	23	47	24
Jiul*	34	5	5	24	15	47	20

Liberty Salonta sold their promotion place to UT Arad.
Sportul were excluded for debts.
Top scorers: Niculescu (Dinamo Bucharest) 17, Danilescu (Dinamo Bucharest) 17.
Cup Final: Rapid 2, Timisoara 0.

RUSSIA

Football Union of Russia; Luzhnetskaya Naberezyhnaja 8, Moscow 119 992.
Founded: 1912; *Number of Clubs:* 43,700; *Number of Players:* 785,000; *National Colours:* All white.
Telephone: 007-095/201 1637; *Fax:* 007-502/220 2037.

International matches 2006
Brazil (h) 0-1, Spain (a) 0-0, Latvia (h) 1-0, Croatia (h) 0-0, Israel (h) 1-1, Estonia (h) 2-0, Macedonia (a) 2-0.

League Championship wins (1945–2006)
Spartak Moscow 20; Dynamo Kiev 13; Dynamo Moscow 11; CSKA Moscow 10; Torpedo Moscow 3; Dynamo Tbilisi 2; Dnepr Dnepropetrovsk 2; Lokomotiv Moscow 2; Saria Voroshilovgrad 1; Ararat Erevan 1; Dynamo Minsk 1; Zenit Leningrad 1; Spartak Vladikavkaz 1.

Cup wins (1936–2007)
Spartak Moscow 13; Dynamo Kiev 10; CSKA Moscow 8; Torpedo Moscow 7; Dynamo Moscow 7; Lokomotiv Moscow 7; Shakhtjor Donetsk 4; Dynamo Tbilisi 2; Ararat Erevan 2; Zenit Leningrad 2; Karpaty Lvov 1; SKA Rostov 1; Metallist Kharkov 1; Dnepr 1; Terek 1.

Final League Table 2006

	P	*W*	*D*	*L*	*F*	*A*	*Pts*
CSKA Moscow	30	17	7	6	47	28	58
Spartak Moscow	30	15	13	2	60	36	58
Lokomotiv Moscow	30	15	8	7	47	34	53
Zenit	30	13	11	6	42	30	50
Rubin	30	13	7	10	43	37	46
FK Moscow	30	10	13	7	41	37	43
Luch-Energia	30	12	5	13	37	39	41
Tomsk	30	11	8	11	35	33	41
Spartak Nalchik	30	11	8	11	33	32	41
Krylia Sovekov	30	10	8	12	37	35	38
Saturn	30	7	16	7	29	24	37
Rostov	30	10	6	14	42	48	36
Amkar	30	8	11	11	22	36	35
Dynamo Moscow	30	8	10	12	31	40	34
Torpedo Moscow*	30	3	13	14	22	40	22
Shinnik*	30	1	8	21	17	56	11

Top scorer: Pavlyuchenko (Spartak Moscow) 18.
Cup Final: Lokomotiv Moscow 1, FK Moscow 0.

SAN MARINO

Federazione Sammarinese Giuoco Calcio, Viale Campo dei Giudei, 14; Rep. San Marino 47890.
Founded: 1931; *Number of Clubs:* 17; *Number of Players:* 1,033; *National Colours:* All light blue.
Telephone: 00378-054/999 0515; *Fax:* 00378-054/999 2348.

International matches 2006
Albania (h) 0-3, Germany (h) 0-13, Czech Republic (a) 0-7, Republic of Ireland (a) 0-5.

League Championship wins (1986–2007)
Tre Fiori 4; Domagnano 4; Faetano 3; Folgore 3; Fiorita 2; Murata 2; Montevito 1; Libertas 1; Cosmos 1; Pennarossa 1.

Cup wins (1986–2007)
Domagnano 7; Libertas 4; Faetano 3; Cosmos 2; Pennarossa 2; Murata 2; Fiorita 1; Tre Penne 1.

Qualifying League Table 2006–07

Group A

	P	W	D	L	F	A	Pts
Tre Fiore	20	16	1	3	45	17	49
La Fiorita	20	11	3	6	38	23	36
Pennarossa	20	10	4	6	30	24	34
Virtus	20	9	3	8	35	30	30
Tre Penne	20	9	3	8	30	26	30
Cosmos	20	6	4	10	34	42	22
Cailungo	20	2	6	12	19	42	12

Group B

	P	W	D	L	F	A	Pts
Libertas	21	14	1	6	57	26	43
Domagnano	21	12	6	3	42	20	42
Murata	21	11	5	5	45	21	38
Folgore/Falciano	21	9	6	6	32	32	33
Faetano	21	7	3	11	27	46	24
Juvenes/Dogana	21	6	5	10	28	39	23
San Giovanni	21	4	1	16	27	61	13
Fiorentino	21	1	3	17	23	63	6

Play-Offs: La Fiorita 0, Murata 4; Domagnano 3, Pennarrossa 3 *(Domagnano won 4-3 on penalties);* Tre Fiore 3, Domagnano 0; Libertas 2, Murata 1; Domagnano 1, La Fiorita 1 *(Domagnano won 10-9 on penalties);* Murata 3, Pennarrossa 0; Tre Fiore 1, Libertas 0; Domagnano 0, Murata 4; Libertas 0, Murata 5.
Final: Tre Fiore 0, Murata 4.
2006 Cup Final: Libertas 4, Tre Penne 1.
2007 Cup Final: Murata 2, Libertas 1.

SCOTLAND

The Scottish Football Association Ltd, Hampden Park, Glasgow G42 9AY.
Founded: 1873; *Number of Clubs:* 6,148; *Number of Players:* 135,474; *National Colours:* Dark blue shirts, white shorts, dark blue stockings.
Telephone: 0044-141/616 6000; *Fax:* 0044-141/616 6001.

SERBIA

Football Association of Serbia, Terazije 35, P.O. Box 263, 11000 Beograd.
Founded: 1919; *Number of Clubs:* 6,532; *Number of Players:* 229,024; *National Colours:* Blue shirts, white shorts, red stockings.
Telephone: 00381-11/ 323 4253; *Fax:* 00381-11/323 3433.

International matches 2006

Tunisia (a) 1-0, Uruguay (h) 1-1, Holland (n) 0-1, Argentina (n) 0-6, Ivory Coast (n) 2-3, Czech Republic (a) 3-1, Azerbaijan (h) 1-0, Poland (a) 1-1, Belgium (h) 1-0, Armenia (h) 3-0, Norway (h) 1-1.
Matches played after 16 August were as Serbia after Montenegro declared independence in May 2006.

League Championship wins (1923–2007)

Red Star Belgrade 25; Partizan Belgrade 19; Hajduk Split 9; Gradjanski Zagreb 5; BSK Belgrade 5; Dynamo Zagreb 4; Jugoslavija Belgrade 2; Concordia Zagreb 2; FC Sarajevo 2; Vojvodina Novi Sad 2; HASK Zagreb 1; Zeljeznicar 1; Obilic 1.

Cup wins (1947–2007)

Red Star Belgrade 22; Hajduk Split 9; Partizan Belgrade 9; Dynamo Zagreb 8; BSK Belgrade 2; OFK Belgrade 2; Rijeka 2; Velez Mostar 2; Vardar Skopje 1; Borac Banjaluka 1; Sartid 1; Zeleznik 1.

Qualifying League Table 2006–07

	P	W	D	L	F	A	Pts
Red Star Belgrade	22	16	3	3	37	16	51
Partizan Belgrade	22	13	3	6	32	20	42
Vojvodina	22	11	4	7	23	16	37
Mladost	22	9	8	5	19	13	35
Hajduk Kula	22	11	2	9	21	21	35
Bezanija	22	7	12	3	24	17	33
OFK Belgrade	22	8	8	6	28	16	32
Banat	22	8	5	9	20	27	29
Smederevo	22	6	7	9	17	21	25
Borac	22	5	7	10	10	17	22
Vozdovac	22	4	6	12	16	31	18
Zemun	22	0	3	19	8	40	3

Bucucnost merged with Banat (newly formed after Proleter were dissolved).

Championship Table 2006–07

	P	W	D	L	F	A	Pts
Red Star Belgrade	32	23	5	4	55	27	74
Partizan Belgrade	32	18	3	11	47	31	57
Vojvodina	32	16	6	10	38	25	54
Bezanija	32	12	12	8	36	31	48
Hajduk Kula	32	14	4	14	29	30	46
Mladost	32	11	8	13	25	33	41

Relegation Table 2006–07

	P	W	D	L	F	A	Pts
OFK Belgrade	31	14	8	9	47	26	50
Banat	31	12	5	14	34	42	41
Smederevo	31	11	7	13	31	39	40
Borac+	31	10	7	14	24	28	37
Vozdovac*	31	9	7	15	30	43	34
Zemun*	31	1	4	26	21	62	7

Cup Final: Red Star Belgrade 2, Vojvodina 0.

SLOVAKIA

Slovak Football Association, Junacka 6, 83280 Bratislava, Slovakia.
Founded: 1993; *Number of Clubs:* 2,140; *Number of Players:* 141,000; *National Colours:* All blue and white.
Telephone: 00421-2/4924 9151; *Fax:* 00421-2/4924 9595.

International matches 2006

France (a) 2-1, Belgium (h) 1-1, Malta (h) 3-0, Cyprus (h) 6-1, Czech Republic (h) 0-3, Wales (a) 5-1, Germany (h) 1-4, Bulgaria (h) 3-1, UAE (a) 2-1.

League Championship wins (1939–44; 1994–2007)

Slovan Bratislava 8; Zilina 4; Kosice 2; Inter 2; Bystrica 1; OAP Bratislava 1; Petrzalka 1; Ruzomberok 1.

Cup wins (1994–2007)

Inter 3; Slovan Bratislava 2; Tatran Presov 1; Humenne 1; Spartak Trnava 1; Koba 1; Matador 1; Petrzalka 1; Bystrica 1; Ruzomberok 1; ViOn Zlate 1.

Qualifying League Table 2006–07

	P	W	D	L	F	A	Pts
Zilina	22	16	4	2	53	13	52
Artmedia	22	13	3	6	40	28	42
Kosice	22	10	4	8	29	29	34
Ruzomberok	22	8	7	7	26	18	31
Bystrica	22	8	7	7	24	26	31
Senec	22	9	4	9	22	30	31
Nitra	22	9	3	10	16	21	30
Slovan Bratislava	22	7	5	10	24	32	26
Inter	22	6	7	9	25	25	25
Dubnica	22	6	7	9	24	35	25
Spartak Trnava	22	6	6	10	22	33	24
Trencin	22	3	5	14	18	33	14

Bottom four clubs enter promotion/relegation play-off with top four second division after the 22nd round.

Championship Play-Off

(Only head-to-head results of top eight carried over).

Championship Play-Off Table 2006–07

	P	W	D	L	F	A	Pts
Zilina	14	10	2	2	34	7	32
Artmedia	14	9	2	3	29	17	29
Ruzomberok	14	5	5	4	13	13	20
Nitra	14	6	1	7	10	13	19
Bystrica	14	4	5	5	12	18	17
Kosice	14	5	1	8	16	23	16
Slovan Bratislava	14	4	3	7	13	20	15
Senec	14	2	3	9	11	27	9

Promotion/Relegation Table 2006–07

	P	W	D	L	F	A	Pts
Spartak Trnava	14	7	4	3	18	13	25
Dubnica	14	6	5	3	16	15	23
ViOn Zlate	14	7	1	6	20	15	22
Trencin	14	5	6	3	20	17	21
Inter*	14	5	4	5	14	15	19
Eldus*	14	4	6	4	16	18	18
Rimavska*	14	4	3	7	20	23	15
Slovan Duslo*	14	1	5	8	15	23	8

Top scorer: Oravec (Artmedia) 16.
Cup Final: ViOn Zlate 4, Senec 0.

inal League Table 2006–07

	P	W	D	L	F	A	Pts
,urich	36	23	6	7	67	32	75
;asle	36	22	8	6	77	40	74
ion	36	17	9	10	57	42	60
oung Boys	36	17	8	11	52	42	59
t Gallen	36	14	13	9	47	44	55
irasshoppers	36	13	11	12	54	41	50
hun	36	10	7	19	30	58	37
ucerne	36	8	9	19	31	58	33
arau+	36	6	8	22	28	55	26
chaffhausen*	36	4	13	19	27	58	25

op scorer: Petric (Basle) 19.
'up Final: Basle 1, Lucerne 0.

TURKEY

urkiye Futbol Federasyonu, Konaklar Mah. Ihlamurlu ok. 9, 4 Levent, Istanbul 80620.
ounded: 1923; *Number of Clubs:* 230; *Number of layers:* 64,521; *National Colours:* All white.
elephone: 0090-212/282 7020; *Fax:* 0090-212/282 7015.

iternational matches 2006
zech Republic (h) 2-2, Azerbaijan (a) 1-1, Belgium (a) 3, Ghana (h) 1-1, Estonia (h) 1-1, Saudi Arabia (a) 1-0, ,ngola (a) 3-2, Macedonia (h) 0-1, Luxembourg (a) 1-0, Ialta (h) 2-0, Hungary (a) 1-0, Moldova (h) 5-0, Italy (a) 1.

eague Championship wins (1960–2007)
enerbahce 17; Galatasaray 16; Besiktas 11; Trabzonspor

up wins (1963–2007)
alatasaray 14; Besiktas 8; Trabzonspor 7; Fenerbahce 4; oztepe Izmir 2; Altay Izmir 2; Ankaragucu 2; enclerbirligi 2; Kocaeli 2; Eskisehirspor 1; Bursapor 1; ıkaryaspor 1.

nal League Table 2006–07

	P	W	D	L	F	A	Pts
·nerbahce	34	20	10	4	65	31	70
·siktas	34	18	7	9	43	32	61
alatasaray	34	15	11	8	58	37	56
rabzonspor	34	15	7	12	54	44	52
ayseri	34	13	12	9	54	43	51
enclerbirligi	34	14	6	14	43	42	48
vas	34	14	6	14	41	44	48
nkara	34	10	17	7	43	38	47
onya	34	12	9	13	42	44	45
ırsa	34	12	9	13	36	42	45
aziantep	34	11	10	13	31	39	43
·stel	34	11	9	14	41	45	42
nkaragucu	34	11	9	14	32	39	42
enizli	34	9	14	11	33	40	41
ze	34	11	7	16	34	40	40
Antalya*	34	8	15	11	32	36	39
Kayseri Erciy*	34	9	10	15	29	49	37
Sakarya*	34	4	10	20	25	51	22

Top scorer: Alex (Fenerbahce) 19.
Cup Final: Besiktas 1, Kayseri Erciy 0.

UKRAINE

Football Federation of Ukraine, Laboratorna Str. 1, P.O. Box 293, Kiev 03150.
Founded: 1991; *Number of Clubs:* 1,500; *Number of Players:* 759,500; *National Colours:* All yellow and blue.
Telephone: 00380-44/252 8498; *Fax:* 00380-44/252 8513.

International matches 2006
Azerbaijan (a) 0-0, Costa Rica (h) 4-0, Italy (a) 0-0, Libya (h) 3-0, Luxembourg (a) 3-0, Spain (n) 2-4, Saudi Arabia (n) 4-0, Tunisia (n) 1-0, Switzerland (n) 0-0, Italy (n) 0-3, Azerbaijan (h) 6-0, Georgia (h) 3-2, Italy (a) 0-2, Scotland (h) 2-0.

League Championship wins (1992–2007)
Dynamo Kiev 11; Shakhtar Donetsk 3; Tavriya Simferopol 1.

Cup wins (1992–2007)
Dynamo Kiev 9; Shakhtar Donetsk 5; Chernomorets 2.

Final League Table 2006–07

	P	W	D	L	F	A	Pts
Dynamo Kiev	30	22	8	0	67	23	74
Shakhtar Donetsk	30	19	6	5	57	20	63
Metalist	30	18	7	5	40	20	61
Dnepro	30	11	14	5	32	24	47
Tavriya	30	12	6	12	32	30	42
Chernomorets	30	11	8	11	36	33	41
Metalurg Zapor	30	10	10	10	25	32	40
Karpaty	30	9	10	11	26	32	37
Metalurg Donetsk	30	9	9	12	26	35	36
Krivbas	30	7	14	9	29	36	35
Zorya	30	9	7	14	23	43	34
Kharkiv	30	8	9	13	26	38	33
Vorskla	30	7	10	13	23	28	31
Arsenal Kiev	30	7	9	14	28	44	30
Illichivets*	30	6	7	17	23	39	25
Stal*	30	5	6	19	22	38	21

Top scorer: Hladkiy (Kharkiv) 13.
Cup Final: Dynamo Kiev 2, Shakhtar Donetsk 1.

WALES

The Football Association of Wales Limited, Plymouth Chambers, 3 Westgate Street, Cardiff, CF10 1DP.
Founded: 1876; *Number of Clubs:* 2,326; *Number of Players:* 53,926; *National Colours:* All red.
Telephone: 0044-29/2037 2325; *Fax:* 0044-29/2034 3961.

SOUTH AMERICA

ARGENTINA

;ociacion Del Futbol Argentina, Viamonte 1366/76, 53 Buenos Aires.
unded: 1893; *Number of Clubs:* 3,035; *Number of ıyers:* 306,365; *National Colours:* Light blue and white rtical striped shirts, dark blue shorts, white stockings.
lephone: 0054-11/4372 7900; *Fax:* 0054-11/4375 4410.
'ernational matches 2006
oatia (a) 2-3, Angola (a) 2-0, Ivory Coast (n) 2-1, rbia (n) 6-0, Holland (n) 0-0, Mexico (n) 2-1, Germany) 1-1, Brazil (a) 0-3, Spain (a) 1-2.

BOLIVIA

deracion Boliviana De Futbol, Av. Libertador Bolivar . 1168, Casilla de Correo 484, Cochabamba, Bolivia.
unded: 1925; *Number of Clubs:* 305; *Number of ıyers:* 15,290; *National Colours:* Green shirts, white orts, green stockings.
lephone: 00591-4/424 4982; *Fax:* 00591-4/428 2132.
'ernational matches 2006
Salvador (h) 5-1.

BRAZIL

Confederacao Brasileira De Futebol, Rua Victor Civita 66, Bloco 1-Edificio 5-5 Andar, Barra da Tijuca, Rio De Janeiro 22775-040.
Founded: 1914; *Number of Clubs:* 12,987; *Number of Players:* 551,358; *National Colours:* Yellow shirts with green collar and cuffs, blue shorts, white stockings with green and yellow border.
Telephone: 0055-21/3870 3610; *Fax:* 0055-21/3870 3612.
International matches 2006
Russia (a) 1-0, New Zealand (h) 4-0, Croatia (n) 1-0, Australia (n) 2-0, Japan (n) 4-1, Ghana (n) 3-0, France (n) 0-1, Norway (a) 1-1, Argentina (h) 3-0, Wales (a) 2-0, Kuwait (a) 4-0, Ecuador (h) 2-1, Switzerland (a) 2-1.

CHILE

Federacion De Futbol De Chile, Avda. Quillin No. 5635, Casilla postal 3733, Correo Central, Santiago de Chile.
Founded: 1895; *Number of Clubs:* 4,598; *Number of Players:* 609,724; *National Colours:* Red shirts with blue collar and cuffs, blue shorts, white stockings.

SLOVENIA

Football Association of Slovenia, Nogometna zveza Slovenije, Cerinova 4, P.P. 3986, 1001 Ljubljana, Slovenia.
Founded: 1920; *Number of Clubs:* 375; *Number of Players:* 20,117; *National Colours:* White shirts with green sleeves, white shorts, white stockings.
Telephone: 00386-1/530 0400; *Fax:* 00386-1/530 0410.

International matches 2006
Cyprus (n) 1-0, Romania (n) 0-2, Trinidad & Tobago (h) 3-1, Ivory Coast (h) 0-3, Israel (h) 1-1, Bulgaria (a) 0-3, Luxemborg (h) 2-0, Belarus (a) 2-4.

League Championship wins (1992–2007)
Maribor 7; SCT Olimpija 4; Gorica 4; Domzale 1.

Cup wins (1992–2007)
Maribor 5; SCT Olimpija 4; Gorica 2; Koper 2; Mura 1; Rudar 1; Publikum 1.

Final League Table 2006–07

	P	*W*	*D*	*L*	*F*	*A*	*Pts*
Domzale	36	21	12	3	64	29	76
Gorica	36	17	7	12	66	63	58
Maribor	36	15	12	9	64	50	57
Primorje	36	15	10	11	52	47	55
Drava	36	15	10	11	61	52	55
Nafta	36	12	9	15	45	59	45
Koper	36	10	15	11	51	46	45
Celje	36	11	12	13	54	51	45
Interblock+	36	5	11	20	34	68	26
Bela Krajina*	36	5	10	21	38	64	25

Celje (formerly Publikum), Interblock (formerly Factor).
Top scorer: Nikezic (Gorica) 22.
Cup Final: Koper 1, Maribor 0.

SPAIN

Real Federacion Espanola De Futbol, Ramon y Cajal, s/n, Apartado Postale 385, Madrid 28230.
Founded: 1913; *Number of Clubs:* 10,240; *Number of Players:* 408,135; *National Colours:* Red shirts, blue shorts, blue stockings with red, blue and yellow border.
Telephone: 0034-91/495 9800; *Fax:* 0034-91/495 9801.

International matches 2006
Ivory Coast (h) 3-2, Russia (h) 0-0, Egypt (h) 2-0, Croatia (h) 2-1, Ukraine (n) 4-2, Tunisia (n) 3-1, Saudi Arabia (n) 1-0, France (n) 1-3, Iceland (a) 0-0, Liechtenstein (h) 4-0, Northern Ireland (a) 2-3, Sweden (a) 0-2, Argentina (h) 2-1, Romania (h) 0-1.

League Championship wins (1929–36; 1940–2007)
Real Madrid 30; Barcelona 18; Atletico Madrid 9; Athletic Bilbao 8; Valencia 6; Real Sociedad 2; Real Betis 1; Seville 1; La Coruna 1.

Cup wins (1902–2006)
Barcelona 24; Athletic Bilbao 23; Real Madrid 17; Atletico Madrid 9; Valencia 6; Real Zaragoza 6; Espanyol 4; Seville 4; Real Union de Irun 3; La Coruna 2; Real Betis 2; Arenas 1; Ciclista Sebastian 1; Racing de Irun 1; Vizcaya Bilbao 1; Real Sociedad 1; Mallorca 1.

Final League Table 2006–07

	P	*W*	*D*	*L*	*F*	*A*	*Pts*
Real Madrid	38	23	7	8	66	40	76
Barcelona	38	22	10	6	78	33	76
Sevilla	38	21	8	9	64	35	71
Valencia	38	20	6	12	57	42	66
Villarreal	38	18	8	12	48	44	62
Zaragoza	38	16	12	10	55	43	60
Atletico Madrid	38	17	9	12	46	39	60
Recreativo	38	15	9	14	54	52	54
Getafe	38	14	10	14	39	33	52
Santander	38	12	14	12	42	48	50
Espanyol	38	12	13	13	46	53	49
Mallorca	38	14	7	17	41	47	49
La Coruna	38	12	11	15	32	45	47
Osasuna	38	13	7	18	51	49	46
Levante	38	10	12	16	37	53	42
Betis	38	8	16	14	36	49	40
Athletic Bilbao	38	10	10	18	44	62	40
Celta Vigo*	38	10	9	19	40	59	39
Real Sociedad*	38	8	11	1			
Gimnastic*	38	7	7	2			

Top scorer: Van Nistelrooy (Real Madrid)
Cup Final: Sevilla 1, Getafe 0.

SWEDEN

Svenska Fotbollfoerbundet, Box 1216, S-17
Founded: 1904; *Number of Clubs:* 3,25
Players: 485,000; *National Colours:* Yell
shorts, yellow stockings.
Telephone: 0046-8/735 0900; *Fax:* 0046-8/73

International matches 2006
Saudi Arabia (a) 1-1, Jordan (a) 0-0, Rep
(a) 0-3, Finland (h) 0-0, Chile (h) 1-1, Trin
(n) 0-0, Paraguay (n) 1-0, England (n) 2-2
0-2, Germany (a) 0-3, Latvia (a) 1-0, Liec
1, Spain (h) 2-0, Iceland (a) 2-1, Ivory Coa

League Championship wins (1896–200
IFK Gothenburg 18; Malmo FF 15;
Gothenburg 14; IFK Norrköping 11; D
AIK Stockholm 10; GAIS Gothenburg 6;
6; Boras IF Elfsborg 5; Oster Vaxjo 4
Atvidaberg 2; IFK Ekilstune 1; IF Gavi
Gothenburg 1; Fassbergs 1; Norrköping
Hammarby 1.

Cup wins (1941–2006)
Malmo FF 13; AIK Stockholm 8; IFK Nor
Gothenburg 4; Djurgaarden 4; Helsingbor
2; Kalmar 2; GAIS Gothenburg 1; IF Raa
1; Oster Vaxjo 1; Degerfors 1; Halmsta
Elfsborg 1.

Final League Table 2006

	P	*W*	*D*	
Elfsborg	26	13	11	
AIK	26	13	10	
Hammarby	26	13	7	
Helsingborg	26	11	9	
Kalmar	26	12	5	
Djurgaarden	26	11	7	
Malmo	26	10	8	
IFK Gothenburg	26	9	9	
Gefle	26	8	7	1
GAIS Gothenburg	26	5	12	
Halmstad	26	5	12	
Hacken+	26	4	10	1
Oster*	26	4	7	1
Orgryte*	26	3	8	1

Hammarby three points deducted.
Top scorer: Ferreira (Kalmar) 15.
Play-Off: Brommapojkarna 2, Hacken
Brommapojkarna 2.
Cup Final: Helsingborg 2, Gefle 0.

SWITZERLAND

Schweizerisher Fussballverband, Postfac
15.
Founded: 1895; *Number of Clubs:* 1,47
Players: 185,286; *National Colours:* Re
shorts, red stockings.
Telephone: 0041-31/950 8111; *Fax:* 0041-31

International matches 2006
Scotland (a) 3-1, Ivory Coast (h) 1-1, Ital
(h) 4-1, France (n) 0-0, Togo (n) 2-0, Sout
Ukraine (n) 0-0, Liechtenstein (a) 3-0, Ve
Costa Rica (h) 2-0, Austria (a) 1-2, Brazil

League Championship wins (1898–200
Grasshoppers 26; Servette 17; Young Boy
Basle 11; FC Zurich 11; Lausanne 7; La C
3; FC Lugano 3; Winterthur 3; FX Aara
Xamax 3; Sion 2; St Gallen 2; FC Anglo-
Brühl 1; Cantonal-Neuchatel 1; Biel 1; B
Etoile La Chaux-de-Fonds 1; Lucerne 1.

Cup wins (1926–2007)
Grasshoppers 18; FC Sion 10; Lausanne
Servette 7; FC Zurich 7; La Chaux-de-F
Boys Berne 6; Lucerne 2; FC Lugano 2; F
Gallen 1; Urania Geneva 1; Young Fel
Aarau 1; Wil 1.

Telephone: 0056-2/284 9000; *Fax:* 0056-2/284 3510.
International matches 2006
New Zealand (h) 4-1, New Zealand (h) 1-0, Republic of Ireland (a) 1-0, Ivory Coast (a) 1-1, Sweden (a) 1-1, Colombia (h) 1-2, Peru (h) 3-2, Peru (a) 1-0, Paraguay (h) 3-2.

COLOMBIA

Federacion Colombiana De Futbol, Avenida 32, No. 16–22 piso 4o. Apartado Aereo 17602, Santafe de Bogota.
Founded: 1924; *Number of Clubs:* 3,685; *Number of Players:* 188,050; *National Colours:* Yellow shirts, blue shorts, red stockings.
Telephone: 0057-1/288 9740; *Fax:* 0057-1/288 9559.
International matches 2006
Venezuela (a) 1-1, Ecuador (h) 1-1, Romania (h) 0-0, Poland (a) 2-1, Germany (a) 0-3, Morocco (a) 2-0, Chile (a) 2-1.

ECUADOR

Federacion Ecuatoriana del Futbol, km 4 1/2 via a la Costa (Avda. del Bombero), PO Box 09-01-7447 Guayaquil.
Founded: 1925; *Number of Clubs:* 170; *Number of Players:* 15,700; *National Colours:* Yellow shirts, blue shorts, red stockings.
Telephone: 00593-4/235 2372; *Fax:* 00593-4/235 2116.
International matches 2006
Honduras (h) 1-0, Holland (a) 0-1, Japan (a) 0-1, Colombia (a) 1-1, Macedonia (a) 1-2, Poland (n) 2-0, Costa Rica (n) 3-0, Germany (n) 0-3, England (n) 0-1, Peru (h) 1-1, Brazil (a) 1-2.

PARAGUAY

Asociacion Paraguaya de Futbol, Estadio De Los Defensores del Chaco, Calles Mayor Martinez 1393, Asuncion.
Founded: 1906; *Number of Clubs:* 1,500; *Number of Players:* 140,000; *National Colours:* Red and white shirts, blue shorts, blue stockings.
Telephone: 00595-21/480 120; *Fax:* 00595-21/480 124.
International matches 2006
Wales (a) 3-1, Mexico (a) 1-2, Norway (a) 2-2, Denmark (a) 1-1, Georgia (a) 1-0, England (n) 0-1, Sweden (n) 0-1, Trinidad & Tobago (n) 2-0, Australia (a) 1-1, Chile (a) 2-3.

PERU

Federacion Peruana De Futbol, Av. Aviacion 2085, San Luis, Lima 30.
Founded: 1922; *Number of Clubs:* 10,000; *Number of Players:* 325,650; *National Colours:* White shirts with red stripe, white shorts with red lines, white stockings with red line.
Telephone: 0051-1/225 8236; *Fax:* 0051-1/225 8240.
International matches 2006
Trinidad & Tobago (a) 1-1, Panama (h) 0-2, Ecuador (a) 1-1, Chile (a) 2-3, Chile (h) 0-1, Jamaica (a) 1-1, Panama (a) 2-1.

URUGUAY

Asociacion Uruguaya De Futbol, Guayabo 1531, 11200 Montevideo.
Founded: 1900; *Number of Clubs:* 1,091; *Number of Players:* 134,310; *National Colours:* Sky blue shirts with white collar/cuffs, black shorts and stockings with sky blue borders.
Telephone: 0059-82/400 4814; *Fax:* 0059-82/409 0550.
International matches 2006
England (a) 1-2, Northern Ireland (h) 1-0, Romania (h) 2-0, Serbia (a) 1-1, Libya (a) 2-1, Tunisia (a) 0-0, Egypt (a) 2-0, Venezuela (a) 0-1, Venezuela (h) 4-0, Georgia (a) 0-2.

VENEZUELA

Federacion Venezolana De Futbol, Avda. Santos Erminy Ira, Calle las Delicias Torre Mega II, P.H. Sabana Grande, Caracas 1050.
Founded: 1926; *Number of Clubs:* 1,753; *Number of Players:* 63,175; *National Colours:* Burgundy shirts, white shorts and stockings.
Telephone: 0058-212/762 4472; *Fax:* 0058-212/762 0596.
International matches 2006
Colombia (h) 1-1, Mexico (a) 0-1, USA (a) 0-2, Honduras (h) 0-0, Switzerland (a) 0-1, Austria (a) 1-0, Uruguay (h) 1-0, Uruguay (a) 0-4, Guatemala (h) 2-1.

ASIA

AFGHANISTAN

Afghanistan Football Federation, PO Box 5099, Kabul.
Founded: 1933; *Number of Clubs*: 30; *Number of Players*: 3,300; *National Colours*: All white with red lines.
Telephone: 0093-20/210 2417; *Fax:* 0093-20/210 2417

BAHRAIN

Bahrain Football Association, P.O. Box 5464, Manama.
Founded: 1957; *Number of Clubs:* 25; *Number of Players:* 2,030; *National Colours:* All red.
Telephone: 00973/689 569; *Fax:* 00973/781 188.

BANGLADESH

Bangladesh Football Federation, Bangabandhu National Stadium-1, Dhaka 1000.
Founded: 1972; *Number of Clubs:* 1,265; *Number of Players:* 30,385; *National Colours:* Orange shirts, white shorts, green stockings.
Telephone: 00880-2/955 6072; *Fax:* 00880-2/956 3419.

BHUTAN

Bhutan Football Federation, P.O. Box 365, Thimphu.
National Colours: All yellow and red.
Telephone: 00975-2/322 350; *Fax:* 00975-2/321 131.

BRUNEI DARUSSALAM

The Football Association of Brunei Darussalam, P.O. Box 2010, 1920 Bandar Seri Begawan BS 8674.
Founded: 1959; *Number of Clubs:* 22; *Number of Players:* 830; *National Colours:* Yellow shirts, black shorts, black and white stockings.
Telephone: 00673-2/382 761; *Fax:* 00673-2/382 760.

CAMBODIA

Cambodian Football Federation, Chaeng Maeng Village, Rd. Kab Srov, Sangkat Samrong Krom, Khan Dangkor, Phnom-Penh .
Founded: 1933; *Number of Clubs:* 30; *Number of Players:* 650; *National Colours:* All blue.
Telephone: 00855-23/364 889; *Fax:* 00855-23/220 780.

CHINA PR

Football Association of The People's Republic of China, 9 Tiyuguan Road, Beijing 100763.
Founded: 1924; *Number of Clubs:* 1,045; *Number of Players:* 2,250,000; *National Colours:* All white.
Telephone: 0086-10/6711 7019; *Fax:* 0086-10/6714 2533.

CHINESE TAIPEI

Chinese Taipei Football Association, 2F No. Yu Men St., Taipei, Taiwan 104.
Founded: 1936; *Number of Players:* 17,000; *National Colours:* Blue shirts and shorts, white stockings.
Telephone: 00886-2/2596 1185; *Fax:* 00886-2/2595 1594.

GUAM

Guam Football Association, P.O.Box 5093, Agana, Guam 96932.
Founded: 1975; *National Colours:* Blue shirts, white shorts, blue stockings.
Telephone: 001-671/477 5423; *Fax:* 001-671/477 5424.

HONG KONG

The Hong Kong Football Association Ltd, 55 Fat Kwong Street, Homantin, Kowloon, Hong Kong.
Founded: 1914; *Number of Clubs:* 69; *Number of Players:* 3,274; *National Colours:* All red.
Telephone: 00852/2712 9122; *Fax:* 00852/2760 4303.

INDIA

All India Football Federation, Nehru Stadium (West Stand), Fatorda Margao-Goa 403 602.
Founded: 1937; *Number of Clubs:* 2,000; *Number of Players:* 56,000; *National Colours:* Sky blue shirts, navy blue shorts, sky and navy blue stockings.
Telephone: 0091-832/2742 603; *Fax:* 0091-832/2741 172.

INDONESIA

Football Association of Indonesia, Gelora Bung Karno, Pintu X-XI, Jakarta 10270.
Founded: 1930; *Number of Clubs:* 2,880; *Number of Players:* 97,000; *National Colours:* Red shirts, white shorts, red stockings.
Telephone: 0062-21/570 4762; *Fax:* 0062-21/573 4386.

IRAN

IR Iran Football Federation, No. 16-4th deadend, Pakistan Street, PO Box 15316-6967 Shahid Beheshti Avenue, Tehran 15316.
Founded: 1920; *Number of Clubs:* 6,326; *Number of Players:* 306,000; *National Colours:* All white.
Telephone: 0098-21/873 2754; *Fax:* 0098-21/873 0305.

IRAQ

Iraqi Football Association, Olympic Committee Building, Palestine Street, PO Box 484, Baghdad.
Founded: 1948; *Number of Clubs:* 155; *Number of Players:* 4,400; *National Colours:* All black.
Telephone: 00964-1/772 9990; *Fax:* 00964-1/885 4321.

JAPAN

Japan Football Association, JFA House, 3-10-15, Hongo, Bunkyo-ku, Tokyo 113-0033.
Founded: 1921; *Number of Clubs:* 13,047; *Number of Players:* 358,989; *National Colours:* Blue shirts, white shorts, blue stockings.
Telephone: 0081-3/3830 2004; *Fax:* 0081-3/3830 2005.

JORDAN

Jordan Football Association, P.O. Box 962024 Al Hussein Sports City, 11196 Amman.
Founded: 1949; *Number of Clubs:* 98; *Number of Players:* 4,305; *National Colours:* All white and red.
Telephone: 00962-6/565 7662; *Fax:* 00962-6/565 7660.

KOREA, NORTH

Football Association of The Democratic People's Rep. of Korea, Kumsong-dong, Kwangbok Street, Mangyongdae Distr, PO Box 56, Pyongyang FNJ-PRK.
Founded: 1945; *Number of Clubs:* 90; *Number of Players:* 3,420; *National Colours:* All white.
Telephone: 00850-2/18 222; *Fax:* 00850-2/381 4403.

KOREA, SOUTH

Korea Football Association, 1-131 Sinmunno, 2-ga, Jongno-Gu, Seoul 110-062.
Founded: 1928; *Number of Clubs:* 476; *Number of Players:* 2,047; *National Colours:* Red shirts, blue shorts, red stockings.
Telephone: 0082-2/733 6764; *Fax:* 0082-2/735 2755.

KUWAIT

Kuwait Football Association, P.O. Box 2029, Udiliya, Block 4 Al-Ittihad Street, Safat 13021.
Founded: 1952; *Number of Clubs:* 14 (senior); *Number of Players:* 1,526; *National Colours:* All blue.
Telephone: 00965/255 5851; *Fax:* 00965/254 9955.

KYRGYZSTAN

Football Federation of Kyrgyz Republic, PO Box 1484, Kurenkeeva Street 195, Bishkek 720040, Kyrgyzstan.
Founded: 1992; *Number of Players:* 20,000; *National Colours:* Red shirts, white shorts, red stockings.
Telephone: 00996-312/670 573; *Fax:* 00996-312/670 573.

LAOS

Federation Lao de Football, National Stadium, Kounboulo Street, PO Box 3777, Vientiane 856-21, Laos.
Founded: 1951; *Number of Clubs:* 76; *Number of Players:* 2,060; *National Colours:* All red.
Telephone: 00856-21/251 593; *Fax:* 00856-21/213 460.

LEBANON

Federation Libanaise De Football-Association, P.O. Box 4732, Verdun Street, Bristol, Radwan Centre Building, Beirut.
Founded: 1933; *Number of Clubs:* 105; *Number of Players:* 8,125; *National Colours:* Red shirts, white shorts, red stockings.
Telephone: 00961-1/745 745; *Fax:* 00961-1/349 529.

MACAO

Associacao De Futebol De Macau (AFM), Ave. da Amizade 405, Seng Vo Kok, 13 Andar "A", Macau.
Founded: 1939; *Number of Clubs:* 52; *Number of Players:* 800; *National Colours:* All green.
Telephone: 00853/781 883; *Fax:* 00853/782 383.

MALAYSIA

Football Association of Malaysia, 3rd Floor, Wisma Fam, Jalan, SSA/9, Kelana Jaya Selangor Darul Ehsan 47301.
Founded: 1933; *Number of Clubs:* 450; *Number of Players:* 11,250; *National Colours:* All yellow and black.
Telephone: 0060-3/7876 3766; *Fax:* 0060-3/7875 7984.

MALDIVES REPUBLIC

Football Association of Maldives, National Stadium G. Banafsaa Magu 20-04, Male.
Founded: 1982; *Number of Clubs: Number of Players: National Colours:* Red shirts, Green shorts, white stockings.
Telephone: 00960/317 006; *Fax:* 00960/317 005.

MONGOLIA

Mongolia Football Federation, PO Box 259 Ulaan-Baatar 210646.
National Colours: White shirts, red shorts, white stockings.
Telephone: 00976-11/312 145; *Fax:* 00976-11/312 145.

MYANMAR

Myanmar Football Federation, Youth Training Centre, Thingankyun Township, Yangon.
Founded: 1947; *Number of Clubs:* 600; *Number of Players:* 21,000; *National Colours:* Red shirts, white shorts, red stockings.
Telephone: 00951/577 366; *Fax:* 00951/570 000.

NEPAL

All-Nepal Football Association, AMFA House, Ward No. 4, Bishalnagar, PO Box 12582, Kathmandu.
Founded: 1951; *Number of Clubs:* 85; *Number of Players:* 2,550; *National Colours:* All red.
Telephone: 00977-1/5539 059; *Fax:* 00977-1/442 4314.

OMAN

Oman Football Association, P.O. Box 3462, Ruwi Postal Code 112.
Founded: 1978; *Number of Clubs:* 47; *Number of Players:* 2,340; *National Colours:* All white.
Telephone: 00968/787 635; *Fax:* 00968/787 632.

PAKISTAN

Pakistan Football Federation, 6 National Hockey Stadium, Feroze Pure Road, Lahore, Pakistan.
Founded: 1948; *Number of Clubs:* 882; *Number of Players:* 21,000; *National Colours:* All green and white.
Telephone: 0092-42/923 0821; *Fax:* 0092-42/923 0823.

PALESTINE

Palestinian Football Federation, Al-Yarmouk, Gaza.
Founded: 1928; *Number of Clubs:* 377; *Number of Players:* 37,190; *National Colours:* White shirts, black shorts, white stockings.
Telephone: 00972-8/283 4339; *Fax:* 00972-8/282 5208.

PHILIPPINES

Philippine Football Federation, Room 405, Building V, Philsports Complex, Meralco Avenue, Pasig City, Metro Manila.
Founded: 1907; *Number of Clubs:* 650; *Number of Players:* 45,000; *National Colours:* All blue.
Telephone: 0063-2/687 1594; *Fax:* 0063-2/687 1598.

QATAR

Qatar Football Association, 7th Floor, QNOC Building, Cornich, P.O. Box 5333, Doha.
Founded: 1960; *Number of Clubs:* 8 (senior); *Number of Players:* 1,380; *National Colours:* All white.
Telephone: 00974/494 4411; *Fax:* 00974/494 4414.

SAUDI ARABIA

Saudi Arabian Football Federation, Al Mather Quarter (Olympic Complex), Prince Faisal Bin Fahad Street, P.O. Box 5844, Riyadh 11432.
Founded: 1959; *Number of Clubs:* 120; *Number of Players:* 9,600; *National Colours:* White shirts, green shorts, white stockings.
Telephone: 00966-1/482 2240; *Fax:* 00966-1/482 1215.

SINGAPORE

Football Association of Singapore, Jalan Besar Stadium, 100 Tyrwhitt Road, Singapore 207542.
Founded: 1892; *Number of Clubs:* 250; *Number of Players:* 8,000; *National Colours:* All red.
Telephone: 0065/6348 3477; *Fax:* 0065/6293 3728.

SRI LANKA

Football Federation of Sri Lanka, 100/9, Independence Avenue, Colombo 07.
Founded: 1939; *Number of Clubs:* 600; *Number of Players:* 18,825; *National Colours:* All white.
Telephone: 0094-11/268 6120; *Fax:* 0094-11/2682 471.

SYRIA

Syrian Football Federation, PO Box 421, Maysaloon Street, Damascus.
Founded: 1936; *Number of Clubs:* 102; *Number of Players:* 30,600; *National Colours:* All red.
Telephone: 00963-11/333 5866; *Fax:* 00963-11/333 1511.

TAJIKISTAN

Tajikistan Football Federation, 22 Shotemur Ave., Dushanbe 734 025.
Founded: 1991; *Number of Clubs:* 1,804; *Number of Players:* 71,400; *National Colours:* All white.
Telephone: 00992-372/210 265; *Fax:* 00992-372/510 157.

THAILAND

The Football Association of Thailand, Gate 3, Rama I Road, Patumwan, Bangkok 10330.
Founded: 1916; *Number of Clubs:* 168; *Number of Players:* 15,000; *National Colours:* All red.
Telephone: 0066-2/216 4691; *Fax:* 0066-2/215 4494.

TIMOR-LESTE

Federacao Futebol Timor-Leste, Rua 12 de Novembro Str., Cruz, Dili.
Founded: 2002; *National Colours:* Red shirts, black shorts, red stockings.
Telephone: 00669 8511878; *Fax:* 00669 9554509.

TURKMENISTAN

Football Association of Turkmenistan, 32 Belinskiy Street, Stadium Kopetdag, Ashgabat 744 001.
Founded: 1992; *Number of Players:* 75,000; *National Colours:* Green shirts, white shorts, green stockings.
Telephone: 00993-12/362 392; *Fax:* 00993-12/362 355.

UNITED ARAB EMIRATES

United Arab Emirates Football Association, P.O. Box 916, Abu Dhabi.
Founded: 1971; *Number of Clubs:* 23 (senior); *Number of Players:* 1,787; *National Colours:* All white.
Telephone: 00971-2/444 5600; *Fax:* 00971-2/444 8558.

UZBEKISTAN

Uzbekistan Football Federation, Massiv Almazar Furkat Street 15/1, 700003 Tashkent, Uzbekistan.
Founded: 1946; *Number of Clubs:* 15,000; *Number of Players:* 217,000; *National Colours:* All white.
Telephone: 00998-71/144 1684; *Fax:* 00998-71/144 1683.

VIETNAM

Vietnam Football Federation, 18 Ly van Phuc, Dong Da District, Hanoi 844.
Founded: 1962; *Number of Clubs:* 55 (senior); *Number of Players:* 16,000; *National Colours:* All red.
Telephone: 0084-4/845 2480; *Fax:* 0084-4/823 3119.

YEMEN

Yemen Football Association, Quarter of Sport – Al Jeraf, Behind the Stadium of Ali Mushsen, Al Moreissy in the Sport, Al-Thawra City.
Founded: 1962; *Number of Clubs:* 26; *Number of Players:* 1,750; *National Colours:* All green.
Telephone: 00967-1/310 927. *Fax:* 00967-1/310 921.

CONCACAF

ANGUILLA

Anguilla Football Association, P.O. Box 1318, The Valley, Anguilla, BWI.
National Colours: Turquoise, white, orange and blue shirts and shorts, turquoise and orange stockings.
Telephone: 001-264/497 7323; *Fax:* 001-264/497 7324.

ANTIGUA & BARBUDA

The Antigua/Barbuda Football Association, Newgate Street, P.O. Box 773, St John's.
Founded: 1928; *Number of Clubs:* 60; *Number of Players:* 1,008; *National Colours:* Red, black, yellow and blue shirts, black shorts and stockings.
Telephone: 001-268/727 8869; *Fax:* 001-268/562 1681.

ARUBA

Arubaanse Voetbal Bond, Ferguson Street, Z/N P.O. Box 376, Oranjestad, Aruba.
Founded: 1932; *Number of Clubs:* 50; *Number of Players:* 1,000; *National Colours:* Yellow shirts, blue shorts, yellow and blue stockings.
Telephone: 00297/829 550; *Fax:* 00297/829 550.

BAHAMAS

Bahamas Football Association, Plaza on the Way, West Bay Street, P.O. Box N 8434, Nassau, NP.
Founded: 1967; *Number of Clubs:* 14; *Number of Players:* 700; *National Colours:* Yellow shirts, black shorts, yellow stockings.
Telephone: 001-242/322 5897; *Fax:* 001-242/322 5898.

BARBADOS

Barbados Football Association, Hildor No. 4, 10th Avenue, P.O. Box 1362, Belleville-St. Michael, Barbados.
Founded: 1910; *Number of Clubs:* 92; *Number of Players:* 1,100; *National Colours:* Royal blue and gold shirts, gold shorts, white, gold and blue stockings.
Telephone: 001-246/228 1707; *Fax:* 001-246/228 6484.

BELIZE

Belize National Football Association, 26 Hummingbird Highway, Belmopan, P.O. Box 1742, Belize City.
Founded: 1980; *National Colours:* Red, white and black shirts, black shorts, red and black stockings.
Telephone: 00501-822/3410; *Fax:* 00501-822/3377.

BERMUDA

The Bermuda Football Association, 48 Cedar Avenue, Hamilton HM12.
Founded: 1928; *Number of Clubs:* 30; *Number of Players:* 1,947; *National Colours:* All blue.
Telephone: 001-441/295 2199; *Fax:* 001-441/295 0773.

BRITISH VIRGIN ISLANDS

British Virgin Islands Football Association, P.O. Box 29, Road Town, Tortola, BVI.
National Colours: Gold and green shirts, green shorts, and stockings.
Telephone: 001-284/494 5655; *Fax:* 001-284/494 8968.

US VIRGIN ISLANDS

USVI Soccer Federation Inc., 54, Castle Coakley, PO Box 2346, Kingshill, St Croix 00851.
National Colours: Royal blue and gold shirts, royal blue shorts and stockings.
Telephone: 001-340/711 9676; *Fax:* 00-340/711 9707.

CANADA

The Canadian Soccer Association, Place Soccer Canada, 237 Metcalfe Street, Ottawa, ONT K2P 1R2.
Founded: 1912; *Number of Clubs:* 1,600; *Number of Players:* 224,290; *National Colours:* All red.
Telephone: 001-613/237 7678; *Fax:* 001-613/237 1516.

CAYMAN ISLANDS

Cayman Islands Football Association, PO Box 178 GT, Truman Bodden Sports Complex, Olympic Way Off Walkers Rd, George Town, Grand Cayman, Cayman Islands WI.
Founded: 1966; *Number of Clubs:* 25; *Number of Players:* 875; *National Colours:* Red and white shirts, blue and white shorts, white and red stockings.
Telephone: 001-345/949 5775. *Fax:* 001-345/945 7673.

COSTA RICA

Federacion Costarricense De Futbol, Costado Norte Estatua Leon Cortes, San Jose 670-1000.
Founded: 1921; *Number of Clubs:* 431; *Number of Players:* 12,429; *National Colours:* Red shirts, blue shorts, white stockings.
Telephone: 00506/222 1544; *Fax:* 00506/255 2674.

CUBA

Asociacion de Futbol de Cuba, Calle 13 No. 661, Esq. C. Vedado, ZP 4, La Habana.
Founded: 1924; *Number of Clubs:* 70; *Number of Players:* 12,900; *National Colours:* All red, white and blue.
Telephone: 0053-7/545 024; *Fax:* 0053-7/335 310.

DOMINICA

Dominica Football Association, 33 Great Marlborough Street, Roseau.
Founded: 1970; *Number of Clubs:* 30; *Number of Players:* 500; *National Colours:* Emerald green shirts, black shorts, green stockings.
Telephone: 001-767/448 7577; *Fax:* 001-767/448 7587.

DOMINICAN REPUBLIC

Federacion Dominicana De Futbol, Centro Olimpico Juan Pablo Duarte, Ensanche Miraflores, Apartado De Correos No. 1953, Santo Domingo.
Founded: 1953; *Number of Clubs:* 128; *Number of Players:* 10,706; *National Colours:* Navy blue shirts, white shorts, red stockings.
Telephone: 001-809/542 6923; *Fax:* 001-809/547 5363.

EL SALVADOR

Federacion Salvadorena De Futbol, Primera Calle Poniente No. 2025, San Salvador CA1029.
Founded: 1935; *Number of Clubs:* 944; *Number of Players:* 21,294; *National Colours:* All blue.
Telephone: 00503/263 7525; *Fax:* 00503/260 3129.

GRENADA

Grenada Football Association, P.O. Box 326, National Stadium, Queens Park, St George's, Grenada, W.I.
Founded: 1924; *Number of Clubs:* 15; *Number of Players:* 200; *National Colours:* Green and yellow striped shirts, red shorts, yellow stockings.
Telephone: 001-473/440 9903; *Fax:* 001-473/440 9973.

GUATEMALA

Federacion Nacional de Futbol de Guatemala, 2a Calle 15-57, Zona 15, Boulevard Vista Hermosa, Guatemala City 01009.
Founded: 1946; *Number of Clubs:* 1,611; *Number of Players:* 43,516; *National Colours:* Blue shirts, white shorts, blue stockings.
Telephone: 00502/279 1746; *Fax:* 00502/379 8345.

GUYANA

Guyana Football Federation, 159 Rupununi Street, Bel Air Park, P.O. Box 10727, Georgetown.
Founded: 1902; *Number of Clubs:* 103; *Number of Players:* 1,665; *National Colours:* Green shirts and shorts, yellow stockings.
Telephone: 00592-2/278 758; *Fax:* 00592-2/262 641.

HAITI

Federation Haitienne De Football, 128 Avenue Christiophe, P.O. Box 2258, Port-Au-Prince.
Founded: 1904; *Number of Clubs:* 40; *Number of Players:* 4,000; *National Colours:* Blue shirts, red shorts, blue stockings.
Telephone: 00509/244 0115; *Fax:* 00509/244 0117.

HONDURAS

Federacion Nacional Autonoma De Futbol De Honduras, Colonia Florencia Norte, Ave Roble, Edificio Plaza America, Ave. Roble 1 y 2 Nivel, Tegucigalpa, D.C.
Founded: 1951; *Number of Clubs:* 1,050; *Number of Players:* 15,300; *National Colours:* All white.
Telephone: 00504/232 0572; *Fax:* 00504/239 8826.

JAMAICA

Jamaica Football Federation Ltd, 20 St Lucia Crescent, Kingston 5.
Founded: 1910; *Number of Clubs:* 266; *Number of Players:* 45,200; *National Colours:* Gold shirts, black shorts, gold stockings.
Telephone: 001-876/929 8036; *Fax:* 001-876/929 0483.

MEXICO

Federacion Mexicana De Futbol Asociacion, A.C., Colima No. 373, Colonia Roma Mexico DF 06700.
Founded: 1927; *Number of Clubs:* 77 (senior); *Number of Players:* 1,402,270; *National Colours:* Green shirts with white collar, white shorts, red stockings.
Telephone: 0052-55/5241 0190; *Fax:* 0052-55/5241 0191.

MONSERRAT

Monserrat Football Association Inc., P.O. Box 505, Woodlands, Monserrat.
National Colours: Green shirts with black and white stripes, green shorts with white stripes, green stockings with black and white stripes.
Telephone: 001-664/491 8744; *Fax:* 001-664/491 8801.

NETHERLANDS ANTILLES

Nederlands Antiliaanse Voetbal Unie, Bonamweg 49, Curacao, NA.
Founded: 1921; *Number of Clubs:* 85; *Number of Players:* 4,500; *National Colours:* White shirts with red and blue stripes, red shorts with blue and white stripes, white stockings with red stripes.
Telephone: 00599-9736 5040; *Fax:* 00599/9736 5047.

NICARAGUA

Federacion Nicaraguense De Futbol, Hospital Pautista 1, Cuadra avajo, 1 cuada al Sur y 1/2, Cuadra Abajo, Managua 976.
Founded: 1931; *Number of Clubs:* 31; *Number of Players:* 160 (senior); *National Colours:* Blue shirts, white shorts, blue stockings.
Telephone: 00505/222 7035; *Fax:* 00505/222 7885.

PANAMA

Federacion Panamena De Futbol, Estadio Rommel Fernandez, Puerta 24, Ave. Jose Aeustin Araneo, Apartado Postal 8-391, Zona 8, Panama.
Founded: 1937; *Number of Clubs:* 65; *Number of Players:* 4,225; *National Colours:* All red.
Telephone: 00507/233 3896; *Fax:* 00507/233 0582.

PUERTO RICO

Federacion Puertorriquena De Futbol, P.O. Box 193590 San Juan 00919.
Founded: 1940; *Number of Clubs:* 175; *Number of Players:* 4,200; *National Colours:* Red, blue and white shirts and shorts, red and blue stockings.
Telephone: 001-787/759 7544; *Fax:* 001-787/759 7544.

SAINT KITTS & NEVIS

St Kitts & Nevis Football Association, P.O. Box 465, Warner Park, Basseterre, St Kitts, W.I.
Founded: 1932; *Number of Clubs:* 36; *Number of Players:* 600; *National Colours:* Green and yellow shirts, red shorts, yellow stockings.
Telephone: 001-869/466 8502; *Fax:* 001-869/465 9033.

SAINT LUCIA

St Lucia National Football Association, PO Box 255, Sans Souci, Castries, St Lucia.
Founded: 1979; *Number of Clubs:* 100; *Number of Players:* 4,000; *National Colours:* White shirts and shorts with yellow, blue and black stripes, white, blue and yellow stockings.
Telephone: 001-758/453 0687; *Fax:* 001-758/456 0510.

SAINT VINCENT & THE GRENADINES

St Vincent & The Grenadines Football Federation, Sharpe Street, PO Box 1278, Saint George.
Founded: 1979; *Number of Clubs:* 500; *Number of Players:* 5,000; *National Colours:* Green shirts with yellow border, blue shorts, yellow stockings.
Telephone: 001-784/456 1092; *Fax:* 001-784/457 2193.

SURINAM

Surinaamse Voetbal Bond, Letitia Vriesde Laan 7, P.O. Box 1223, Paramaribo.
Founded: 1920; *Number of Clubs:* 168; *Number of Players:* 4,430; *National Colours:* White, green and red shirts, green and white shirts and stockings.
Telephone: 00597/473 112; *Fax:* 00597/479 718.

TRINIDAD & TOBAGO

Trinidad & Tobago Football Federation, 24–26 Dundonald Street, PO Box 400, Port of Spain.
Founded: 1908; *Number of Clubs:* 124; *Number of Players:* 5,050; *National Colours:* Red shirts, black shorts, white stockings.
Telephone: 001-868/623 7312; *Fax:* 001-868/623 8109.

TURKS & CAICOS

Turks & Caicos Islands Football Association, P.O. Box 626, Tropicana Plaza, Leeward Highway, Providenciales.
National Colours: All white.
Telephone: 001-649/941 5532; *Fax:* 001-649/941 5554.

USA

US Soccer Federation, US Soccer House, 1801–1811 S. Prairie Avenue, Chicago, Illinois 60616.
Founded: 1913; *Number of Clubs:* 7,000; *Number of Players:* 1,411,500; *National Colours:* White shirts, blue shorts, white stockings.
Telephone: 001-312/808 1300; *Fax:* 001-312/808 1301.

OCEANIA

AMERICAN SAMOA

American Samoa Football Association, P.O. Box 282, Pago Pago AS 96799.
National Colours: Navy blue shirts, white shorts, red stockings.
Telephone: 00684/699 7380; *Fax:* 00684/699 7381.

AUSTRALIA

Soccer Australia Ltd, Level 3, East Stand, Stadium Australia, Edwin Flack Avenue, Homebush, NSW 2127.
Founded: 1961; *Number of Clubs:* 6,816; *Number of Players:* 433,957; *National Colours:* All green with gold trim.
Telephone: 0061-2/9739 5555; *Fax:* 0061-2/9739 5590.

COOK ISLANDS

Cook Islands Football Association, Victoria Road, Tupapa, P.O. Box 29, Avarua, Rarotonga, Cook Islands.
Founded: 1971; *Number of Clubs:* 9; *National Colours:* Green shirts with white sleeves, green shorts, white stockings.
Telephone: 00682/28 980; *Fax:* 00682/28 981.

FIJI

Fiji Football Association, PO Box 2514, Government Buildings, Suva.
Founded: 1938; *Number of Clubs:* 140; *Number of Players:* 21,300; *National Colours:* White shirts, blue shorts and stockings.
Telephone: 00679/330 0453; *Fax:* 00679/330 4642.

NEW CALEDONIA

Federation Caledonienne de Football, 7 bis, Rue Suffren Quartien latin, BP 560, 99845 Noumea, New Caledonia.
Founded: 1928; *National Colours:* Grey shirts, red shorts, grey stockings.
Telephone: 00687 272383; *Fax:* 00687 263249.

NEW ZEALAND

New Zealand Soccer Inc., PO Box 301 043, Albany, Auckland, New Zealand.
Founded: 1891; *Number of Clubs:* 312; *Number of Players:* 52,969; *National Colours:* All white.
Telephone: 0064-9/414 0175; *Fax:* 0064-9/414 0176.

PAPUA NEW GUINEA

Papua New Guinea Football Association, PO Box 957, Room II Level I, Haus Tisa, Lae.
Founded: 1962; *Number of Clubs:* 350; *Number of Players:* 8,250; *National Colours:* Red and yellow shirts, black shorts, yellow stockings.
Telephone: 00675/479 1998; *Fax:* 00675/479 1999.

SAMOA

The Samoa Football Soccer Federation, P.O. Box 960, Apia.
Founded: 1968; *National Colours:* Blue, white and red shirts, blue and white shorts, red and blue stockings.
Telephone: 00685/26 504; *Fax:* 00685/20 341.

SOLOMON ISLANDS

Solomon Islands Football Federation, PO Box 854, Honiara, Solomon Islands.
Founded: 1978; *Number of Players:* 4,000; *National Colours:* Gold and blue shirts, blue and white shorts, white and blue stockings.
Telephone: 00677/26 496; *Fax:* 00677/26 497.

TAHITI

Federation Tahitienne de Football, Rue Coppenrath Stade de Fautana, PO Box 50858 Pirae 98716.
Founded: 1989; *National Colours:* Red shirts, white shorts, red stockings.
Telephone: 00689/540 954; *Fax:* 00689/419 629.

TONGA

Tonga Football Association, Tungi Arcade, Taufa'Ahau Road, P.O. Box 852, Nuku'Alofa, Tonga.
Founded: 1965; *Number of Clubs:* 23; *Number of Players:* 350; *National Colours:* Red shirts, white shorts, red stockings.
Telephone: 00676/24 442; *Fax:* 00676/23 340.

VANUATU

Vanuatu Football Federation, P.O. Box 266, Port Vila, Vanuatu.
Founded: 1934; *National Colours:* Gold and black shirts, black shorts, gold and black stockings.
Telephone: 00678/25 236; *Fax:* 00678/25 236.

AFRICA

ALGERIA

Federation Algerienne De Foot-ball, Chemin Ahmed Ouaked, Boite Postale No. 39, Dely-Ibrahim-Alger.
Founded: 1962; *Number of Clubs:* 780; *Number of Players:* 58,567; *National Colours:* Green shirts, white shorts, green stockings.
Telephone: 00213-21/372 929; *Fax:* 00213-21/367 266.

ANGOLA

Federation Angolaise De Football, Compl. da Cidadela Desportiva, B.P. 3449, Luanda.
Founded: 1979; *Number of Clubs:* 276; *Number of Players:* 4,269; *National Colours:* Red shirts, black shorts, red stockings.
Telephone: 00244-2/264 948; *Fax:* 00244-2/260 566.

BENIN

Federation Beninoise De Football, Stade Rene Pleven d'Akpakpa, B.P. 965, Cotonou 01.
Founded: 1962; *Number of Clubs:* 117; *Number of Players:* 6,700; *National Colours:* Green shirts, Yellow shorts, red stockings.
Telephone: 00229/330 537; *Fax:* 00229/330 537

BOTSWANA

Botswana Football Association, P.O. Box 1396, Gabarone.
Founded: 1970; *National Colours:* Blue, white and black striped shirts, blue, white and black shorts and stockings.
Telephone: 00267/390 0279; *Fax:* 00267/ 390 0280.

BURKINA FASO

Federation Burkinabe De Foot-Ball, 01 B.P. 57, Ouagadougou 01.
Founded: 1960; *Number of Clubs:* 57; *Number of Players:* 4,672; *National Colours:* All green, red and white.
Telephone: 00226/318 815; *Fax:* 00226/318 843.

BURUNDI

Federation De Football Du Burundi, Bulding Nyogozi, Boulevard de l'Uprona, B.P. 3426, Bujumbura.
Founded: 1948; *Number of Clubs:* 132; *Number of Players:* 3,930; *National Colours:* Red and white shirts, white and red shorts, green stockings.
Telephone : 00257/921 105; *Fax:* 00257/242 892.

CAMEROON

Federation Camerounaise De Football, B.P. 1116, Yaounde.
Founded: 1959; *Number of Clubs:* 200; *Number of Players:* 9,328; *National Colours:* Green shirts, red shorts, yellow stockings.
Telephone: 00237/221 0012; *Fax:* 00237/221 6662.

CAPE VERDE ISLANDS

Federacao Cabo-Verdiana De Futebol, Praia Cabo Verde, FCF CX, P.O. Box 234, Praia.
Founded: 1982; *National Colours:* Blue and white shirts and shorts, blue and red stockings.
Telephone : 00238/611 362; *Fax:* 00238/611 362.

CENTRAL AFRICAN REPUBLIC

Federation Centrafricaine De Football, Immeuble Soca Constructa, B.P. 344, Bangui.
Founded: 1937; *Number of Clubs:* 256; *Number of Players:* 7,200; *National Colours:* Blue and white shirts, white shorts, blue stockings.
Telephone: 00236/619 545; *Fax:* 00236/615 660.

CHAD

Federation Tchadienne de Football, B.P. 886, N'Djamena.
Founded: 1962; *National Colours:* Blue shirts, yellow shorts, red stockings.
Telephone: 00235/515 982; *Fax:* 00235/525 538.

COMOROS

Comoros FA, BP 798, Moroni.
Founded: 1979.
Telephone: 00269 733179; *Fax:* 00269 733236.

CONGO

Federation Congolaise De Football, 80 Rue Eugene-Etienne, Centre Ville, PO Box 11, Brazzaville.
Founded: 1962; *Number of Clubs:* 250; *Number of Players:* 5,940; *National Colours:* Green shirts, yellow shorts, red stockings.
Telephone: 00242/811 563; *Fax:* 00242/812 524.

CONGO DR

Federation Congolaise De Football-Association, Av. de l'Enseignemt 210, C/Kasa-Vubu, Kinshasa 1.
Founded: 1919; *Number of Clubs:* 3,800; *Number of Players:* 64,627; *National Colours:* Blue and yellow shirts, yellow and blue shorts, white and blue stockings.
Telephone: 00243/993 9635; *Fax:* 00243/139 8426.

DJIBOUTI

Federation Djiboutienne de Football, Stade el Haoj Hassan Gouled, B.P. 2694, Djibouti.
Founded: 1977; *Number of Players:* 2,000; *National Colours:* Green shirts, white shorts, blue stockings.
Telephone: 00253/341 964; *Fax:* 00253/341 963.

EGYPT

Egyptian Football Association, 5 Gabalaya Street, Guezira, El Borg Post Office, Cairo.
Founded: 1921; *Number of Clubs:* 247; *Number of Players:* 19,735; *National Colours:* Red shirts, white shorts, black stockings.
Telephone: 0020-2/735 1793; *Fax:* 0020-2/736 7817.

ERITREA

The Eritrean National Football Federation, Sematat Avenue 29–31, P.O. Box 3665, Asmara.
National Colours: Blue shirts, red shorts, green stockings.
Telephone: 00291-1/120 335; *Fax:* 00291-1/126 821.

ETHIOPIA

Ethiopia Football Federation, Addis Ababa Stadium, P.O. Box 1080, Addis Ababa.
Founded: 1943; *Number of Clubs:* 767; *Number of Players:* 20,594; *National Colours:* Green shirts, yellow shorts, red stockings.
Telephone: 00251-1/514 453; *Fax:* 00251-1/515 899.

GABON

Federation Gabonaise De Football, B.P. 181, Libreville.
Founded: 1962; *Number of Clubs:* 320; *Number of Players:* 10,000; *National Colours:* Green, yellow and blue shirts, blue and yellow shorts, white stockings with tricolour trims.
Telephone: 00241/730 460; *Fax:* 00241/730 460.

GAMBIA

Gambia Football Association, Independence Stadium, Bakau, P.O. Box 523, Banjul.
Founded: 1952; *Number of Clubs:* 30; *Number of Players:* 860; *National Colours:* All red, blue and white.
Telephone: 00220/494 509; *Fax:* 00220/494 509.

GHANA

Ghana Football Association, National Sports Council, P.O. Box 1272, Accra.
Founded: 1957; *Number of Clubs:* 347; *Number of Players:* 11,275; *National Colours:* All yellow.
Telephone: 00233-21/671 501; *Fax:* 00233-21/668 590.

GUINEA

Federation Guineenne De Football, P.O. Box 3645, Conakry.
Founded: 1959; *Number of Clubs:* 351; *Number of Players:* 10,000; *National Colours:* Red shirts, yellow shorts, green stockings.
Telephone: 00224/455 878; *Fax:* 00224/455 879.

GUINEA-BISSAU

Federacao De Football Da Guinea-Bissau, Alto Bandim (Nova Sede), PO Box 375 Bissau 1035.
Founded: 1974; *National Colours:* Red, green and yellow shirts, green and yellow shorts, red, green and yellow stockings.
Telephone: 00245/201 918; *Fax:* 00245/211 414.

GUINEA, EQUATORIAL

Federacion Ecuatoguineana De Futbol, c/P Patricio Lumumba (Estadio La Paz), Malabo 1071.
Founded: 1986; *National Colours:* All red.
Telephone: 00240-9/74 049; *Fax:* 00240-9/2257.

IVORY COAST

Federation Ivoirienne De Football, 01 PO Box 1202, Abidjan 01.
Founded: 1960; *Number of Clubs:* 84 (senior); *Number of Players:* 3,655; *National Colours:* Orange shirts, black shorts, green stockings.
Telephone: 00225/2124 0027; *Fax:* 00225/2125 9352.

KENYA

Kenya Football Federation, Nyayo National Stadium, P.O. Box 40234, Nairobi.
Founded: 1960; *Number of Clubs:* 351; *Number of Players:* 8,880; *National Colours:* All red.
Telephone: 00254-2/608 422; *Fax:* 00254-2/249 855.

LESOTHO

Lesotho Football Association, P.O. Box 1879, Maseru-100, Lesotho.
Founded: 1932; *Number of Clubs:* 88; *Number of Players:* 2,076; *National Colours:* Blue shirts, green shorts, white stockings.
Telephone: 00266/2231 1879; *Fax:* 00266/2231 0586.

LIBERIA

Liberia Football Association, Broad and Center Streets, PO Box 10-1066, Monrovia 1000.
Founded: 1936; *National Colours:* Blue shirts, white shorts, red stockings.
Telephone: 00231/226 385; *Fax:* 00231/226 092.

LIBYA

Libyan Football Federation, Asayadi Street, Near Janat Al-Areet, P.O. Box 5137, Tripoli.
Founded: 1963; *Number of Clubs:* 89; *Number of Players:* 2,941; *National Colours:* Green and black shirts, black shorts and stockings.
Telephone: 00218-21/334 3600; *Fax:* 00218-21/444 1274.

MADAGASCAR

Federation Malagasy de Football, Immeuble Preservatrice Vie-Lot IBF-9B, Rue Rabearivelo-Antsahavola, PO Box 4409, Antananarivo 101.
Founded: 1961; *Number of Clubs:* 775; *Number of Players:* 23,536; *National Colours:* Red and green shirts, white and green shorts, green and white stockings.
Telephone: 00261-20/226 8374; *Fax:* 00261-20/226 8373.

MALAWI

Football Association of Malawi, Mpira House, Old Chileka Road, P.O. Box 865, Blantyre.
Founded: 1966; *Number of Clubs:* 465; *Number of Players:* 12,500; *National Colours:* Red shirts, white shorts, red and black stockings.
Telephone: 00265-1/623 197; *Fax:* 00265-1/623 204.

MALI

Federation Malienne De Football, Avenue du Mali, Hamdallaye ACI 2000, PO Box 1020, Bamako 12582.
Founded: 1960; *Number of Clubs:* 128; *Number of Players:* 5,480; *National Colours:* Green shirts, yellow shorts, red stockings.
Telephone: 00223/223 8844; *Fax:* 00223/222 4254.

MAURITANIA

Federation De Foot-Ball De La Rep. Islamique. De Mauritanie, B.P. 566, Nouakchott.
Founded: 1961; *Number of Clubs:* 59; *Number of Players:* 1,930; *National Colours:* Green and yellow shirts, yellow shorts, green stockings.
Telephone: 00222-5/241 860; *Fax:* 00222-5/241 861.

MAURITIUS

Mauritius Football Association, Chancery House, 2nd Floor Nos. 303–305, 14 Lislet Geoffroy Street, Port Louis.
Founded: 1952; *Number of Clubs:* 397; *Number of Players:* 29,375; *National Colours:* All red.
Telephone: 00230/212 1418; *Fax:* 00230/208 4100.

MOROCCO

Federation Royale Marocaine De Football, 51 Bis Av. Ibn Sina, PO Box 51, Agdal, Rabat 10 000.
Founded: 1955; *Number of Clubs:* 350; *Number of Players:* 19,768; *National Colours:* All green white and red.
Telephone: 00212-37/672 706; *Fax:* 00212-37/671 070.

MOZAMBIQUE

Federacao Mocambicana De Futebol, Av. Samora Machel 11-2, Caixa Postal 1467, Maputo.
Founded: 1978; *Number of Clubs:* 144; *National Colours:* Red shirts, black shorts, red and black stockings.
Telephone: 00258-1/300 366; *Fax:* 00258-1/300 367.

NAMIBIA

Namibia Football Association, Abraham Mashego Street 8521, Katurua Council of Churches in Namibia, P.O. Box 1345, Windhoek 9000, Namibia.
Founded: 1990; *Number of Clubs:* 244; *Number of Players:* 7,320; *National Colours:* All red.
Telephone: 00264-61/265 691; Fax: 00264-61/265 693.

NIGER

Federation Nigerienne De Football, Rue de la Tapoa, PO Box 10299, Niamey.
Founded: 1967; *Number of Clubs:* 64; *Number of Players:* 1,525; *National Colours:* Orange shirts, white shorts, green stockings.
Telephone: 00227/725 127; *Fax:* 00227/725 127.

NIGERIA

Nigeria Football Association, Plot 2033, Olusegun, Obasanjo Way, Zone 7, Wuse Abuja, PO Box 5101 Garki, Abuja, Nigeria.
Founded: 1945; *Number of Clubs:* 326; *Number of Players:* 80,190; *National Colours:* All green and white.
Telephone: 00234-9/523 7326; *Fax:* 00234-9/523 7327.

RWANDA

Federation Rwandaise De Football Amateur, B.P. 2000, Kigali.
Founded: 1972; *Number of Clubs:* 167; *National Colours:* Red, green and yellow shirts, green shorts, red stockings.
Telephone: 00250/571 596; *Fax:* 00250/571 597.

SENEGAL

Federation Senegalaise De Football, Stade Leopold Sedar Senghor, Route De L'Aeroport De Yoff, B.P. 130 21, Dakar.
Founded: 1960; *Number of Clubs:* 75 (senior); *Number of Players:* 3,977; *National Colours:* All white and green.
Telephone: 00221/827 2935; *Fax:* 00221/827 3524.

SEYCHELLES

Seychelles Football Federation, P.O. Box 843, People's Stadium, Victoria-Mahe, Seychelles.
Founded: 1979; *National Colours:* Red and green shirts and shorts, red stockings.
Telephone: 00248/324 632; *Fax:* 00248/225 468.

ST THOMAS AND PRINCIPE

Federation Santomense De Futebol, Rua Ex-Joao de Deus No. QXXIII-426/26, PO Box 440, Sao Tome.
Founded: 1975; *National Colours:* Green and red shirts, yellow shorts, green stockings.
Telephone: 00239-2/22 4231; *Fax:* 00239-2/21 333.

SIERRA LEONE

Sierra Leone Football Association, 21 Battery Street, Kingtorn, P.O. Box 672, National Stadium, Brookfields, Freetown.
Founded: 1967; *Number of Clubs:* 104; *Number of Players:* 8,120; *National Colours:* Green and blue shirts, green, blue and white shorts and stockings.
Telephone: 00232-22/241 872; *Fax:* 00232-22/227 771.

SOMALIA

Somali Football Federation, PO Box 222, Mogadishu BN 03040.
Founded: 1951; *Number of Clubs:* 46 (senior); *Number of Players:* 1,150; *National Colours:* Sky blue and white shirts and shorts, white and sky blue stockings.
Telephone: 00252-1/229 843; *Fax:* 00252-1/215 513.

SOUTH AFRICA

South African Football Association, First National Bank Stadium, PO Box 910, Johannesburg 2000, South Africa.
Founded: 1991; *Number of Clubs:* 51,944; *Number of Players:* 1,039,880; *National Colours:* White shirts with yellow striped sleeves, white shorts with yellow stripes, white stockings.
Telephone: 0027-11/494 3522; *Fax:* 0027-11/494 3013.

SUDAN

Sudan Football Association, Bladia Street, Khartoum.
Founded: 1936; *Number of Clubs:* 750; *Number of Players:* 42,200; *National Colours:* Red shirts, white shorts, black stockings.
Telephone: 00249-11/773 495; *Fax:* 00249-11/776 633.

SWAZILAND

National Football Association of Swaziland, Sigwaca House, Plot 582, Sheffield Road, PO Box 641, Mbabane H100.
Founded: 1968; *Number of Clubs:* 136; *National Colours:* Blue shirts, gold shorts, red stockings.
Telephone: 00268/404 6852; *Fax:* 00268/404 6206.

TANZANIA

Football Association of Tanzania, Uhuru/Shaurimoyo Road, Karume Memorial Stadium, P.O. Box 1574, Ilala/Dar Es Salaam.
Founded: 1930; *Number of Clubs:* 51; *National Colours:* Green, yellow and blue shirts, black shorts, green stockings with horizontal stripe.
Telephone: 00255-22/286 1815; *Fax:* 00255-22/286 1815.

TOGO

Federation Togolaise De Football, C.P. 5, Lome.
Founded: 1960; *Number of Clubs:* 144; *Number of Players:* 4,346; *National Colours:* White shirts, green shorts, red stockings with yellow and green stripes.
Telephone: 00228/221 2698; *Fax:* 00228/222 1413.

TUNISIA

Federation Tunisienne De Football, Maison des Federations Sportives, Cite Olympique, Tunis 1003.
Founded: 1956; *Number of Clubs:* 215; *Number of Players:* 18,300; *National Colours:* Red shirts, white shorts, red stockings.
Telephone: 00216-71/233 303; *Fax:* 00216-71/767 929.

UGANDA

Federation of Uganda Football Associations, Plot No. 879, Kyadondo Block 8, Mengo Wakaliga Road, P.O. Box 22518, Kampala.
Founded: 1924; *Number of Clubs:* 400; *Number of Players:* 1,518; *National Colours:* All yellow, red and white.
Telephone: 00256-41/272 702; *Fax:* 00256-41/272 702.

ZAMBIA

Football Association of Zambia, Football House, Alick Nkhata Road, P.O. Box 34751, Lusaka.
Founded: 1929; *Number of Clubs:* 20 (senior); *Number of Players:* 4,100; *National Colours:* White and green shirts, green and white shorts, white and green stockings.
Telephone: 00260-1/250 946; *Fax:* 00260-1/250 946.

ZIMBABWE

Zimbabwe Football Association, P.O. Box CY 114, Causeway, Harare.
Founded: 1965; *National Colours:* All green and gold.
Telephone: 00263-4/721 026; *Fax:* 00263-4/721 045.

THE WORLD CUP 1930–2006

Year	Winners		Runners-up		Venue	Attendance	Referee
1930	Uruguay	4	Argentina	2	Montevideo	90,000	Langenus (B)
1934	Italy*	2	Czechoslovakia	1	Rome	50,000	Eklind (Se)
1938	Italy	4	Hungary	2	Paris	45,000	Capdeville (F)
1950	Uruguay	2	Brazil	1	Rio de Janeiro	199,854	Reader (E)
1954	West Germany	3	Hungary	2	Berne	60,000	Ling (E)
1958	Brazi	5	Sweden	2	Stockholm	49,737	Guigue (F)
1962	Brazil	3	Czechoslovakia	1	Santiago	68,679	Latychev (USSR)
1966	England*	4	West Germany	2	Wembley	93,802	Dienst (Sw)
1970	Brazil	4	Italy	1	Mexico City	107,412	Glockner (EG)
1974	West Germany	2	Holland	1	Munich	77,833	Taylor (E)
1978	Argentina*	3	Holland	1	Buenos Aires	77,000	Gonella (I)
1982	Italy	3	West Germany	1	Madrid	90,080	Coelho (Br)
1986	Argentina	3	West Germany	2	Mexico City	114,580	Filho (Br)
1990	West Germany	1	Argentina	0	Rome	73,603	Mendez (Mex)
1994	Brazil*	0	Italy	0	Los Angeles	94,194	Puhl (H)
	(Brazil won 3-2 on penalties)						
1998	France	3	Brazil	0	St-Denis	75,000	Belqola (Mor)
2002	Brazil	2	Germany	0	Yokohama	69,029	Collina (I)
2006	Italy	1	France	1	Berlin	69,000	Elizondo (Arg)
	(Italy won 5-3 on penalties)						

*(*After extra time)*

GOALSCORING AND ATTENDANCES IN WORLD CUP FINAL ROUNDS

Venue	*Matches*	*Goals (av)*	*Attendance (av)*
1930, Uruguay	18	70 (3.9)	434,500 (24,138)
1934, Italy	17	70 (4.1)	395,000 (23,235)
1938, France	18	84 (4.6)	483,000 (26,833)
1950, Brazil	22	88 (4.0)	1,337,000 (60,772)
1954, Switzerland	26	140 (5.4)	943,000 (36,270)
1958, Sweden	35	126 (3.6)	868,000 (24,800)
1962, Chile	32	89 (2.8)	776,000 (24,250)
1966, England	32	89 (2.8)	1,614,677 (50,458)
1970, Mexico	32	95 (2.9)	1,673,975 (52,311)
1974, West Germany	38	97 (2.5)	1,774,022 (46,684)
1978, Argentina	38	102 (2.7)	1,610,215 (42,374)
1982, Spain	52	146 (2.8)	2,064,364 (38,816)
1986, Mexico	52	132 (2.5)	2,441,731 (46,956)
1990, Italy	52	115 (2.2)	2,515,168 (48,368)
1994, USA	52	141 (2.7)	3,567,415 (68,604)
1998, France	64	171 (2.6)	2,775,400 (43,366)
2002, Japan/S. Korea	64	161 (2.5)	2,705,566 (42,274)
2006, Germany	64	147 (2.3)	3,354,646 (52,416)

LEADING GOALSCORERS

Year	*Player*	*Goals*
1930	Guillermo Stabile (Argentina)	8
1934	Angelo Schiavio (Italy), Oldrich Nejedly (Czechoslovakia), Edmund Conen (Germany)	4
1938	Leonidas da Silva (Brazil)	8
1950	Ademir (Brazil)	9
1954	Sandor Kocsis (Hungary)	11
1958	Just Fontaine (France)	13
1962	Valentin Ivanov (USSR), Leonel Sanchez (Chile), Garrincha, Vava (both Brazil), Florian Albert (Hungary), Drazen Jerkovic (Yugoslavia)	4
1966	Eusebio (Portugal)	9
1970	Gerd Muller (West Germany)	10
1974	Grzegorz Lato (Poland)	7
1978	Mario Kempes (Argentina)	6
1982	Paolo Rossi (Italy)	6
1986	Gary Lineker (England)	6
1990	Salvatore Schillaci (Italy)	6
1994	Oleg Salenko (Russia) Hristo Stoichkov (Bulgaria)	6
1998	Davor Suker (Croatia)	6
2002	Ronaldo (Brazil)	8
2006	Miroslav Klose (Germany)	5

EUROPEAN FOOTBALL CHAMPIONSHIP

(formerly EUROPEAN NATIONS' CUP)

Year	*Winners*		*Runners-up*		*Venue*	*Attendance*
1960	USSR	2	Yugoslavia	1	Paris	17,966
1964	Spain	2	USSR	1	Madrid	120,000
1968	Italy After 1-1 draw	2	Yugoslavia	0	Rome	60,000 75,000
1972	West Germany	3	USSR	0	Brussels	43,437
1976	Czechoslovakia *(Czechoslovakia won on penalties)*	2	West Germany	2	Belgrade	45,000
1980	West Germany	2	Belgium	1	Rome	47,864
1984	France	2	Spain	0	Paris	48,000
1988	Holland	2	USSR	0	Munich	72,308
1992	Denmark	2	Germany	0	Gothenburg	37,800
1996	Germany *(Germany won on sudden death)*	2	Czech Republic	1	Wembley	73,611
2000	France *(France won on sudden death)*	2	Italy	1	Rotterdam	50,000
2004	Greece	1	Portugal	0	Lisbon	62,865

EURO 2008 QUALIFYING COMPETITION

GROUP A

Brussels, 16 August 2006, 15,495

Belgium (0) 0 Kazakhstan (0) 0

Belgium: Stijnen; Vermaelen, Simons, Van Buyten, Kompany (Huysegems 38), Van Damme (Pieroni 60), Hoefkens (Vanden Borre 74), Goor, Buffel, Geraerts, Dembele.
Kazakhstan: Loria; Kuchma, Smakov, Azovskiy Y, Karpovich (Travin 54), Sergienko, Khokhlov, Byakov, Baltiev, Zhalmagambetov, Zhumaskaliyev.
Referee: Courtney (Northern Ireland).

Bydgoszcz, 2 September 2006, 17,000

Poland (0) 1 *(Gargula 89)*

Finland (0) 3 *(Litmanen 54, 76 (pen), Vayrynen 84)*

Poland: Dudek; Wasilewski, Glowacki■, Bak, Michal Zewlakow, Blaszczykowski (Jelen 46), Szymkowiak (Smolarek 46), Radomski, Krzynowek, Zurawski, Frankowski (Gargula 73).
Finland: Jaaskelainen; Tihinen, Hyypia, Kallio, Tainio, Pasanen, Heikkinen, Kolkka (Nurmela 78), Litmanen (Forssell 86), Johansson (Eremenko Jr 66), Vayrynen.
Referee: Duhamel (France).

Belgrade, 2 September 2006, 12,500

Serbia (0) 1 *(Zigic 72)* **Azerbaijan (0) 0**

Serbia: Stojkovic; Markovic, Stepanov, Krstajic, Lukovic, Duljaj, Koroman (Ilic 64), Stankovic, Lazovic (Ergic 74), Pantelic (Ljuboja 81), Zigic.
Azerbaijan: Veliyev; Gashimov, Ruslan Abbasov, Kerimov, Sokolov, Bakhshiev, Ladaga (Dzavadov 77), Muzika (Gurbanov I 62), Imamaliev, Chertoganov, Izmailov (Musaev 72).
Referee: Kircher (Germany).

Erevan, 6 September 2006, 8000

Armenia (0) 0 Belgium (1) 1 *(Van Buyten 41)*

Armenia: Kasparov; Hovsepian, Arzumanian, Dokhoyan, Melikian, Khachatrian, Aleksanian, Mkrtchian (Arm Karamian 76), Mkhitarian (Petrosian 81), Melkonian, Shahgeldian (Aram Hakobian 72).
Belgium: Stijnen; Hoefkens, Simons, Van Damme, Van Buyten, Daerden (De Decker 66), Englebert, Collen (Vanden Borre 59), Geraerts, Dembele (Defour 77), Pieroni.
Referee: Lehner (Austria).

Baku, 6 September 2006, 18,000

Azerbaijan (1) 1 *(Ladaga 16)*

Kazakhstan (1) 1 *(Byakov 36)*

Azerbaijan: Veliyev; Kerimov, Sokolov (Muzika 58), Ruslan Abbasov (Melikov 46), Ladaga, Sultanov (Musaev 65), Chertoganov, Imamaliev, Dzavadov, Gurbanov I, Gomes.
Kazakhstan: Loria; Azovskiy Y, Kuchma, Zhalmagambetov, Smakov, Karpovich (Travin 66), Sergienko, Khokhlov, Byakov, Baltiev, Zhumaskaliyev (Utabayev 74).
Referee: Szabo (Hungary).

Helsinki, 6 September 2006, 38,015

Finland (1) 1 *(Johansson 22)*

Portugal (1) 1 *(Nuno Gomes 42)*

Finland: Jaaskelainen; Kallio, Hyypia, Tihinen, Pasanen, Kolkka (Eremenko Jr 81), Tainio, Vayrynen, Litmanen, Heikkinen, Johansson (Kuqi S 63).
Portugal: Ricardo; Caneira, Ricardo Costa■, Ricardo Carvalho, Nuno Valente, Costinha, Petit, Deco (Tiago 85), Nani (Ricardo Rocha 56), Ronaldo, Nuno Gomes (Joao Moutinho 75).
Referee: Plautz (Austria).

Warsaw, 6 September 2006, 15,000

Poland (1) 1 *(Matusiak 30)* **Serbia (0) 1** *(Lazovic 71)*

Poland: Kowalewski; Golanski (Wasilewski 72), Jop, Bak, Michal Zewlakow, Jelen (Blaszczykowski 73), Lewandowski, Radomski, Krzynowek, Zurawski, Matusiak.
Serbia: Stojkovic; Markovic, Stepanov, Bisevac, Krstajic, Duljaj (Ergic 67), Kovacevic N, Stankovic, Trisovic (Lazovic 60), Pantelic (Koroman 82), Zigic.
Referee: Poll (England).

Erevan, 7 October 2006, 7500

Armenia (0) 0 Finland (0) 0

Armenia: Kasparov; Hovsepian, Arzumanian, Dokhoyan, Melikian, Melkonian, Tigranian, Aleksanian (Aram Hakobian 54), Karamian (Mkrtchian 46), Shahgeldian, Manucharian (Ara Hakobian 78).
Finland: Jaaskelainen; Pasanen, Hyypia, Tihinen, Vayrynen (Nurmela 73), Litmanen, Kolkka, Kuqi S (Forssell 66), Kallio, Johansson (Riihilahti 83), Heikkinen.
Referee: Skomina (Slovenia).

Almaty, 7 October 2006, 18,000

Kazakhstan (0) 0 Poland (0) 1 *(Smolarek 52)*

Kazakhstan: Loria; Azovskiy Y, Kuchma, Zhalmagambetov, Smakov, Karpovich (Travin 59), Sergienko (Larin 81), Khokhlov, Byakov, Zhumaskaliyev, Utabayev (Ashirbekov 68).
Poland: Kowalewski; Bronowicki, Golanski, Blaszczykowski (Grzelak 87), Bak, Smolarek, Sobolewski, Zurawski (Matusiak 71), Rasiak, Radomski, Lewandowski (Kazmierczak 30).
Referee: Trivkovic (Croatia).

Porto, 7 October 2006, 20,000

Portugal (2) 3 *(Ronaldo 25, 63, Ricardo Carvalho 31)*

Azerbaijan (0) 0

Portugal: Ricardo; Miguel, Ricardo Carvalho, Ricardo Rocha, Nuno Valente (Caneira 46), Costinha, Maniche (Tiago 64), Deco, Ronaldo (Nani 73), Nuno Gomes, Simao Sabrosa.
Azerbaijan: Veliyev; Gashimov, Pereira, Sokolov, Kerimov, Ladaga, Chertoganov, Imamaliev, Muzika (Gurbanov I 66), Sultanov (Izmailov 64), Gomes (Dzavadov 76).
Referee: Halsey (England).

Belgrade, 7 October 2006, 35,000

Serbia (0) 1 *(Zigic 54)* **Belgium (0) 0**

Serbia: Stojkovic; Markovic, Vidic, Krstajic, Dragutinovic, Kovacevic N, Stankovic, Koroman (Ergic 71), Trisovic (Lazovic 58), Pantelic (Duljaj 90), Zigic.
Belgium: Stijnen; Kompany, Hoefkens, Simons, Vermaelen, Van Buyten, Geraerts, Mudingayi (Pieroni 75), Goor (Vandenbergh 84), Mpenza E, Dembele (Mpenza M 62).
Referee: Messina (Italy).

Brussels, 11 October 2006, 12,000

Belgium (1) 3 *(Simons 24 (pen), Vandenbergh 47, Dembele 82)* **Azerbaijan (0) 0**

Belgium: Stijnen; Simons, Vermaelen, Vanden Borre (Mpenza M 77), Leonard, Van Buyten, Hoefkens, Geraerts, Goor, Mpenza E (Dembele■ 70), Vandenbergh (Pieroni 86).
Azerbaijan: Veliyev; Gashimov (Nadyrov 77), Sokolov, Kerimov, Pereira, Ladaga, Muzika■ (Gurbanov I 33), Sultanov (Dzavadov 55), Imamaliev, Chertoganov, Gomes.
Referee: Lajuks (Latvia).

Almaty, 11 October 2006, 17,000

Kazakhstan (0) 0 Finland (1) 2 *(Litmanen 27, Hyypia 65)*

Kazakhstan: Loria; Smakov, Kuchma, Zhalmagambetov, Azovskiy Y, Baltiev, Khokhlov, Travin (Azovskiy M 82), Sergienko (Larin 76), Zhumaskaliyev (Ashirbekov 63), Byakov.
Finland: Jaaskelainen; Pasanen, Hyypia, Tihinen, Litmanen, Kolkka, Ilola, Vayrynen (Riihilahti 90), Nurmela, Forssell (Kuqi S 72), Kallio.
Referee: Briakos (Greece).

Chorzow, 11 October 2006, 40,000

Poland (2) 2 *(Smolarek 9, 18)*

Portugal (0) 1 *(Nuno Gomes 90)*

Poland: Kowalewski; Bronowicki, Golanski, Bak, Lewandowski, Blaszczykowski (Krzynowek 65), Smolarek, Sobolewski, Radomski, Zurawski, Rasiak (Matusiak 73).
Portugal: Ricardo; Miguel, Nuno Valente, Ricardo Carvalho, Ricardo Rocha, Deco (Maniche 83), Petit (Nani 68), Costinha (Tiago 46), Simao Sabrosa, Nuno Gomes, Ronaldo.
Referee: Stark (Germany).

Belgrade, 11 October 2006, 20,000

Serbia (0) 3 *(Stankovic 54 (pen), Lazovic 62, Zigic 90)*

Armenia (0) 0

Serbia: Stojkovic; Dragutinovic, Stepanov, Krstajic, Duljaj, Kovacevic N, Stankovic, Koroman (Ergic 72), Trisovic (Ilic 46), Pantelic (Lazovic 46), Zigic.
Armenia: Kasparov; Hovsepian, Arzumanian, Dokhoyan, Nazarian■, Melikian, Melkonian, Mkrtchian, Aram Hakobian (Minasian 69), Manucharian (Tigranian 79), Shahgeldian (Erzrumian 65).
Referee: Kasnaferis (Greece).

Brussels, 15 November 2006, 37,578

Belgium (0) 0 Poland (1) 1 *(Matusiak 19)*

Belgium: Stijnen; Vermaelen, Simons, Van Buyten, Hoefkens, Leonard (Mudingayi 80), Vanden Borre (Huysegems 46), Goor, Geraerts, Mpenza E, Vandenbergh (Pieroni 62).
Poland: Boruc; Dudka (Murawski 79), Bronowicki, Wasilewski, Bak, Michal Zewlakow, Sobolewski, Blaszczykowski, Smolarek, Zurawski (Gargula 62), Matusiak (Kazmierczak 89).
Referee: Dougal (Scotland).

Helsinki, 15 November 2006, 9445

Finland (1) 1 *(Nurmela 10)* **Armenia (0) 0**

Finland: Jaaskelainen; Hyypia, Nyman, Tihinen, Heikkinen, Kallio, Kolkka, Eremenko Jr (Kuqi S 88), Vayrynen (Ilola 47), Johansson, Nurmela.
Armenia: Kasparov; Dokhoyan (Aleksanian 52), Hovsepian, Tadevosian, Pachajian, Mkhitarian (Ara Hakobian 75), Khachatrian, Mkrtchian, Art Karamian, Zebelian (Arm Karamian 78), Shahgeldian.
Referee: Thomson (Scotland).

Coimbra, 15 November 2006, 27,000

Portugal (2) 3 *(Simao Sabrosa 8, 86, Ronaldo 30)*

Kazakhstan (0) 0

Portugal: Ricardo; Luis Miguel, Paulo Ferreira, Ricardo Carvalho, Tonel (Jorge Andrade 77), Tiago, Deco (Martins 63), Meireles, Ronaldo (Quaresma 58), Simao Sabrosa, Nuno Gomes.
Kazakhstan: Loria; Kuchma, Zhalmagambetov, Smakov, Azovskiy Y, Travin, Sergienko (Larin 74), Khokhlov, Byakov, Baltiev, Zhumaskaliyev.
Referee: Rogalla (Switzerland).

Almaty, 24 March 2007, 15,000

Kazakhstan (0) 2 *(Ashirbekov 47, Zhumaskaliyev 61)*

Serbia (0) 1 *(Zigic 68)*

Kazakhstan: Loria; Smakov, Kuchma, Zhalmagambetov, Irismetov, Skorykh, Sergienko (Chichulin 58), Baltiyev, Suyumagambetov (Finonchenko 80), Zhumaskaliyev, Ashirbekov (Byakov 71).
Serbia: Stojkovic; Markovic, Stepanov, Vidic, Tosic, Kovacevic N, Ergic (Koroman 70), Jankovic, Krasic, Pantelic (Lazovic 69), Zigic■.
Referee: Hrinak (Slovakia).

Warsaw, 24 March 2007, 12,000

Poland (3) 5 *(Bak 3, Dudka 6, Lobodzinski 34, Krzynowek 58, Kazmierczak 84)*

Azerbaijan (0) 0

Poland: Boruc; Wasilewski, Dudka, Bak, Michal Zewlakow, Lobodzinski, Gargula, Lewandowski, Krzynowek (Jelen 79), Zurawski, Matusiak (Kazmierczak 69).
Azerbaijan: Hasanzade; Karimov, Samir Abbasov, Pereira, Bakhshiev, Gurbanov I, Imamaliev (Aghakishiyev 65), Kerimov (Javadov 67), Chertoganov, Gomes (Ladaga 62), Subasic.
Referee: Jakobsson (Iceland).

Lisbon, 24 March 2007, 47,009

Portugal (0) 4 *(Nuno Gomes 53, Ronaldo 55, 75, Quaresma 69)* **Belgium (0) 0**

Portugal: Ricardo; Miguel, Ricardo Carvalho, Jorge Andrade, Paulo Ferreira, Tiago, Petit (Fernando Meira 76), Joao Moutinho, Ronaldo (Hugo Viana 78), Nuno Gomes, Quaresma (Nani 70).
Belgium: Stijnen; Hoefkens (Sterchele 64), Clement, Van Buyten, Van der Heyden, Fellaini, Mudingayi, De Man, Defour, Martens (Chatelle 56), Mpenza M (Van Damme 81).
Referee: Vassaras (Greece).

Baku, 28 March 2007, 14,000

Azerbaijan (0) 1 *(Imamaliev 82)* **Finland (0) 0**

Azerbaijan: Veliyev; Pereira, Ladaga (Imamaliev 66), Guliyev R, Kerimov, Samir Abbasov, Sultanov (Gurbanov I 76), Gomes (Nadyrov 10), Aghakishiyev, Subasic, Chertoganov.
Finland: Jaaskelainen; Pasanen, Hyypia, Tihinen, Vayrynen, Litmanen, Kolkka (Kuqi S 85), Kallio, Eremenko Jr, Johansson (Forssell 86), Heikkinen.
Referee: Messina (Italy).

Kielce, 28 March 2007, 15,000

Poland (1) 1 *(Zurawski 26)* **Armenia (0) 0**

Poland: Boruc; Dudka, Bak, Wasilewski, Michal Zewlakow, Krzynowek (Jelen 83), Blaszczykowski, Lewandowski, Gargula, Zurawski, Kazmierczak (Sobolewski 61).
Armenia: Berezovski; Shahgeldian (Mkhitarian 75), Nazarian (Manucharian 46), Hovsepian, Khachatrian, Dokhoyan, Melikian, Art Karamian (Melkonian 68), Pachajyan, Arzumanian, Zebelian.
Referee: Mallenco (Spain).

Belgrade, 28 March 2007, 51,300

Serbia (1) 1 *(Jankovic 37)* **Portugal (1) 1** *(Tiago 5)*

Serbia: Stojkovic; Tosic (Lazovic 84), Vidic, Dragutinovic, Krstajic, Duljaj, Jankovic (Koroman 64), Kovacevic N, Krasic, Stankovic (Markovic 78), Pantelic.
Portugal: Ricardo; Paulo Ferreira, Jorge Andrade, Luis Miguel (Caneira 72), Ricardo Carvalho, Petit, Joao Moutinho (Meireles 77), Tiago, Ronaldo, Nuno Gomes (Quaresma 82), Simao Sabrosa.
Referee: Layec (France).

Baku, 2 June 2007, 30,000

Azerbaijan (1) 1 *(Subasic 6)*

Poland (0) 3 *(Smolarek 63, Krzynowek 66, 90)*

Azerbaijan: Veliyev; Kerimov, Abbasov S, Chertoganov, Guliyev R, Abbasov R, Imamaliev (Gasimov 70), Guliyev E, Gurbanov A (Gurbanov I 65), Mamedov (Javadov 53), Subasic.
Poland: Boruc; Wasilewski, Dudka, Bak, Michal Zewlakow, Blaszczykowski (Lobodzinski 57), Lewandowski, Krzynowek, Smolarek, Rasiak (Sobolewski 81), Zurawski (Saganowski 57).
Referee: Kapitanis (Cyprus).

Brussels, 2 June 2007, 46,000

Belgium (0) 1 *(Fellaini 55)*

Portugal (1) 2 *(Nani 43, Helder Postiga 64)*

Belgium: Stijnen; Hoefkens (De Man 46), Clement, Simons, Vermaelen, Defour, Mudingayi (Geraerts 76), Fellaini, Vertonghen, Mpenza E, Sterchele (De Mul 61).
Portugal: Ricardo; Miguel (Bosingwa 53), Jorge Andrade, Fernando Meira, Paulo Ferreira, Deco, Petit, Tiago, Quaresma, Helder Postiga (Hugo Almeida■ 79), Nani (Duda 86).
Referee: Hansson (Sweden).

Helsinki, 2 June 2007, 33,615

Finland (0) 0 Serbia (1) 2 *(Jankovic 3, Jovanovic 86)*

Finland: Jaaskelainen; Kallio, Hyypia, Tihinen, Pasanen, Heikkinen, Ilola, Vayrynen, Tainio (Kolkka 28), Forssell (Johansson 63), Kuqi S (Litmanen 70).
Serbia: Stojkovic; Dragutinovic, Krstagic, Vidic, Rukavina, Stankovic, Kovacevic N, Kuzmanovic, Jankovic (Lazovic 68), Pantelic (Jovanovic 60), Krasic (Duljaj 85).
Referee: Gonzalez (Spain).

Almaty, 2 June 2007, 17,100

Kazakhstan (0) 1 *(Baltiyev 88 (pen))*

Armenia (2) 2 *(Arzumainian 31, Hovsepian 39 (pen))*

Kazakhstan: Loria; Smakov, Kuchma, Zhalmagambetov, Irismetov, Chichulin, Sergienko (Byakov 36), Baltiyev, Suyumagambetov, Zhumaskaliyev (Kornienko 78), Kukeyev (Tleshev 57).
Armenia: Kasparov; Hovsepian, Arzumainian, Tadevosian, Mkrtchian, Minasian, Arakelian (Aram Hakobian 80), Voskanian, Melikian, Mkhitarian (Shahgeldian 75), Melkonian (Arm Karamian 90).
Referee: Kralovec (Czech Republic).

Erevan, 6 June 2007, 13,500

Armenia (0) 1 *(Mkhitarian 66)* **Poland (0) 0**

Armenia: Kasparov; Hovsepian, Arzumanian, Melikian, Minasian (Pachajyan 78), Tadevosian, Mkrtchian, Voskanian, Arakelian, Mkhitarian (Arm Karamian 70), Shahgeldian (Aram Hakobian 46).
Poland: Boruc; Dudka, Bronowicki, Wasilewski, Michal Zewlakow, Lewandowski, Bak (Sobolewski 65), Smolarek (Zurawski 60), Krzynowek, Lobodzinski (Blaszczykowski 60), Saganowski.
Referee: Balaj (Romania).

Helsinki, 6 June 2007, 34,188

Finland (1) 2 *(Johansson 27, Eremenko Jr 71)*

Belgium (0) 0

Finland: Jaaskelainen; Kallio, Pasanen, Nyman, Tihinen, Kolkka (Nurmela 88), Heikkinen, Eremenko, Vayrynen, Eremenko Jr (Forssell 89), Johansson.
Belgium: Stijnen; Vermaelen (Maertens 46), Simons, Clement, De Man, Van Damme, Vertonghen, Fellaini■, Defour, De Mul (Haroun 55), Mpenza E (Sterchele 86).
Referee: Clattenburg (England).

Almaty, 6 June 2007, 11,800

Kazakhstan (0) 1 *(Baltiyev 53)*

Azerbaijan (1) 1 *(Nadyrov 30)*

Kazakhstan: Loria; Smakov, Kuchma, Zhalmagambetov■, Irismetov, Chichulin, Baltiyev, Karpovich, Ostapenko (Tleshev 79), Byakov, Zhumaskaliyev (Utabayev 90).
Azerbaijan: Hasanzade; Gashimov, Guliyev E, Guliyev R, Abbasov S, Sultanov (Gurbanov A 74), Chertoganov, Abbasov R, Subasic, Nadyrov (Mamedov 84), Kerimov (Imamaliev 58).
Referee: Wimes (Luxembourg).

Group A Table	P	W	D	L	F	A	Pts
Poland	9	6	1	2	15	7	19
Serbia	7	4	2	1	10	4	14
Portugal	7	4	2	1	15	5	14
Finland	8	4	2	2	9	5	14
Belgium	8	2	1	5	5	10	7
Armenia	7	2	1	4	3	7	7
Kazakhstan	8	1	3	4	5	11	6
Azerbaijan	8	1	2	5	4	17	5

GROUP B

Toftir, 16 August 2006, 2114

Faeroes (0) 0

Georgia (3) 6 *(Kankava 16, Iashvili 18, Arveladze 37, 62, 82, Kobiashvili 51 (pen))*

Faeroes: Mikkelsen; Joensen J, Danielsen, Johannesen O, Jorgensen (Hansen P 45), Benjaminsen, Borg, Nielsen, Samuelsen S (Samuelsen H 60), Jacobsen C, Jacobsen R (Fredriksberg 71).
Georgia: Chanturia; Shashiashvili, Asatiani, Kandelaki (Kvirkvelia 66), Kobiashvili, Aladashvili (Gakhokidze 71), Gogua (Ionanidze 56), Kankava, Mujiri, Iashvili, Arveladze.
Referee: Ross (Northern Ireland).

Tbilisi, 2 September 2006, 65,000

Georgia (0) 0

France (2) 3 *(Malouda 7, Saha 16, Henry 46)*

Georgia: Chanturia; Khizanishvili, Kobiashvili, Asatiani, Kankava, Aladashvili (Kandelaki 39), Gogua, Iashvili (Kvirkvelia 46), Demetradze (Menteshashvili 82), Mujiri, Arveladze.
France: Coupet; Sagnol, Thuram, Gallas, Abidal, Vieira, Makelele (Mavuba 58), Ribery (Govou 69), Malouda, Saha (Wiltord 86), Henry.
Referee: Wegereef (Holland).

Naples, 2 September 2006, 60,000

Italy (1) 1 *(Inzaghi 30)* **Lithuania (1) 1** *(Danilevicius 21)*

Italy: Buffon; Oddo, Cannavaro, Barzagli, Grosso, Pirlo, De Rossi (Marchionni 61), Gattuso, Perrotta (Gilardino 72), Cassano, Inzaghi (Di Michele 86).
Lithuania: Karcemarskas; Stankevicius, Dziaukstas, Skerla, Preiksaitis, Zvirgzdauskas, Savenas (Kalonas 65), Mikoliunas (Tamosauskas 82), Cesnauskis, Poskus (Labukas 79), Danilevicius.
Referee: Hansson (Sweden).

Celtic Park, 2 September 2006, 50,059

Scotland (5) 6 *(Fletcher 7, McFadden 10, Boyd 24 (pen), 38, Miller 30 (pen), O'Connor 85)*

Faeroes (0) 0

Scotland: Gordon; Dailly, Weir, Pressley, Naysmith, Fletcher (Teale 46), Hartley, Quashie (Severin 84), Miller (O'Connor 61), Boyd, McFadden.
Faeroes: Mikkelsen; Hansen P, Johannesen O, Danielsen, Joensen J, Benjaminsen, Johnsson (Samuelsen S 76), Borg, Fredriksberg (Thorleifson 60), Jacobsen C, Jacobsen R (Nielsen 84).
Referee: Yegorov (Russia).

Saint Denis, 6 September 2006, 78,831

France (2) 3 *(Govou 2, 55, Henry 18)*

Italy (1) 1 *(Gilardino 20)*

France: Coupet; Sagnol, Gallas, Thuram, Abidal, Ribery (Saha 88), Vieira, Makelele, Malouda, Govou (Wiltord 75), Henry.
Italy: Buffon; Zambrotta, Cannavaro, Barzagli, Grosso, Semioli (Di Michele 54), Pirlo, Gattuso, Perrotta, Cassano (Inzaghi 73), Gilardino (De Rossi 87).
Referee: Fandel (Germany).

Kaunas, 6 September 2006, 6500

Lithuania (0) 1 *(Miceika 85)*

Scotland (0) 2 *(Dailly 46, Miller 62)*

Lithuania: Karcemarskas; Stankevicius, Dziaukstas, Skerla, Zvirgzdauskas, Savenas (Tamosauskas 50), Kalonas, Mikoliunas (Labukas 66), Preiksaitis (Miceika 81), Poskus, Danilevicius.
Scotland: Gordon; Dailly, Weir, Caldwell G, Naysmith, Pressley, Fletcher, Quashie (Boyd 43), McFadden (Alexander G 21), Hartley (Severin 88), Miller.
Referee: Hrinek (Slovakia).

Kiev, 6 September 2006, 40,000

Ukraine (1) 3 *(Shevchenko 31, Rotan 61, Rusol 80)*

Georgia (1) 2 *(Arveladze 38, Demetradze 61)*

Ukraine: Shovkovskyi; Nesmachni, Rusol, Tymoschuk, Rotan, Shelayev, Gusev, Rebrov (Voronin 57), Gusin (Yezerskiy 46), Tkachenko (Vorobei 63), Shevchenko.
Georgia: Chanturia; Kobiashvili, Asatiani, Khizanishvili, Imedashvili (Kandelaki 35), Kankava, Gogua, Kvirkvelia (Mujiri 85), Menteshashvili (Ashvetia 81), Demetradze, Arveladze.
Referee: Jara (Czech Republic).

Torshavn, 7 October 2006, 1982

Faeroes (0) 0 **Lithuania (0) 1** *(Skerla 89)*

Faeroes: Mikkelsen; Mortensen, Danielsen, Thomassen, Benjaminsen, Hansen P (Hansen A 90), Borg, Djurhuus, Samuelsen S (Fredriksberg 73), Jacobsen R (Nielsen 81), Jacobsen C.
Lithuania: Karcemarskas; Stankevicius, Paulauskas, Skerla, Zvirgzdauskas, Savenas (Kalonas 46), Miceika, Cesnauskis, Mikoliunas (Kavaliauskas 62), Danilevicius, Poskus (Beniusis 70).
Referee: Buttimer (Republic of Ireland).

Rome, 7 October 2006, 49,149

Italy (0) 2 *(Oddo 71 (pen), Toni 79)* **Ukraine (0) 0**

Italy: Buffon; Oddo, Cannavaro, Materazzi, Zambrotta, Gattuso, Pirlo, De Rossi, Iaquinta (Camoranesi 76), Toni (Inzaghi 85), Del Piero (Di Natale 62).
Ukraine: Shovkovskyi; Rusol, Shershun, Yezerskiy, Nesmachni, Nazarenko (Kalynychenko 59), Gusev, Shelayev, Tymoschuk, Vorobei (Milevski 73), Voronin.
Referee: Vassaras (Greece).

Glasgow, 7 October 2006, 57,000
Scotland (0) 1 *(Caldwell G 67)* **France (0) 0**
Scotland: Gordon; Dailly, Alexander, Pressley, Weir, Ferguson, Fletcher, Caldwell G, McFadden (O'Connor 72), Hartley, McCulloch (Teale 58).
France: Coupet; Abidal, Thuram, Boumsong, Sagnol, Ribery (Wiltord 74), Vieira, Makelele, Malouda, Trezeguet (Saha 62), Henry.
Referee: Busacca (Switzerland).

Sochaux, 11 October 2006, 19,314
France (2) 5 *(Saha 1, Henry 22, Anelka 77, Trezeguet 78, 84)*
Faeroes (0) 0
France: Landreau; Sagnol (Clerc 79), Gallas, Thuram, Escude, Ribery, Vieira, Toulalan, Malouda, Saha (Trezeguet 61), Henry (Anelka 61).
Faeroes: Mikkelsen; Djurhuus, Mortensen, Danielsen, Samuelsen S, Jacobsen R, Benjaminsen, Thomassen, Borg (Fredriksberg 87), Jacobsen C, Hansen P (Nielsen 47).
Referee: Corpodean (Romania).

Tbilisi, 11 October 2006, 50,000
Georgia (1) 1 *(Shashiashvili 26)*
Italy (1) 3 *(De Rossi 18, Camoranesi 63, Perrotta 71)*
Georgia: Lomaia; Khizanishvili, Khizaneishvili, Kaladze, Shashiashvili, Kankava (Iashvili 70), Tskitishvili (Kandelaki 74), Menteshashvili, Martsvaladze (Gigiadze 85), Kvirkvelia, Ashvetia.
Italy: Buffon; Oddo, Cannavaro (Materazzi 74), Nesta, Pirlo (Mauri 64), De Rossi, Perrotta, Zambrotta, Camoranesi (Iaquinta 87), Toni, Di Natale.
Referee: Riley (England).

Kiev, 11 October 2006, 55,000
Ukraine (0) 2 *(Kucher 60, Shevchenko 90 (pen))*
Scotland (0) 0
Ukraine: Shovkovskyi; Nesmachni, Sviderskyi, Kucher, Rusol, Tymoschuk, Shelayev, Gusev (Milevski 62), Kalynychenko (Vorobei 76), Shevchenko, Voronin (Shershun 90).
Scotland: Gordon; Neilson (McManus 89), Alexander, Ferguson, Weir, Pressley■, Fletcher, Caldwell, Miller, Hartley, McFadden (Boyd 73).
Referee: Hansson (Sweden).

Toftir, 24 March 2007, 717
Faeroes (0) 0
Ukraine (1) 2 *(Yezerskiy Y 20, Gusev 57)*
Faeroes: Mikkelsen; Olsen (Hansen T 74), Djurhuus, Danielsen, Samuelsen S (Holst 66), Jacobsen R, Benjaminsen, Thomassen (Joensen S 78), Borg, Jacobsen C, Johannesen O.
Ukraine: Shovkovskyi; Yezerskiy Y, Chygrynskiy, Rusol, Nesmachni, Gusev (Vorobei 65), Tymoschuk (Shelayev 82), Mikhalik, Kalynychenko, Bielik, Voronin (Nazarenko 72).
Referee: Skomina (Slovenia).

Kaunas, 24 March 2007, 10,000
Lithuania (0) 0
France (0) 1 *(Anelka 73)*
Lithuania: Karcemarskas; Klimavacius, Skerla, Zvirgzdauskas, Paulauskas, Semberas, Morinas (Beniusis 82), Savenas (Kalonas 77), Stankevicius, Poskus (Radzinevicius 86), Danilevicius.
France: Coupet; Sagnol, Thuram, Gallas, Abidal, Malouda (Diaby 89), Makelele, Toulalan, Diarra, Govou (Cisse 62), Anelka.
Referee: Webb (England).

Glasgow, 24 March 2007, 50,850
Scotland (1) 2 *(Boyd 11, Beattie 89)*
Georgia (1) 1 *(Arveladze 41)*
Scotland: Gordon; Alexander, Naysmith, Ferguson, Weir, McManus, Teale (Brown 60), Hartley, Boyd (Beattie 76), Miller (Maloney 90), McCulloch.
Georgia: Lomaia; Shashiashvili, Khizanishvili, Sulukvadze, Eliava, Burduli (Siradze 57), Tskitishvili (Mujiri 90), Menteshashvili (Gogua 46), Kobiashvili, Demetradze, Arveladze.
Referee: Vollquartz (Denmark).

Tbilisi, 28 March 2007, 15,000
Georgia (2) 3 *(Siradze 26, Iashvili 45, 90 (pen))*
Faeroes (0) 1 *(Jacobsen R 56)*
Georgia: Lomaia; Kvirkvelia, Tskitishvili, Iashvili, Kobiashvili (Menteshashvili 61), Mujiri, Kankava, Salukvadze, Demetradze, Shashiashvili, Siradze.
Faeroes: Mikkelsen; Olsen, Djurhuus, Danielsen, Jacobsen R, Benjaminsen■, Thomassen, Borg (Samuelsen S 90), Jacobsen C, Flotum (Holst 43), Johannesen O.
Referee: Saliy (Kazakhstan).

Bari, 28 March 2007, 37,500
Italy (1) 2 *(Toni 12, 70)* **Scotland (0) 0**
Italy: Buffon; Oddo, Cannavaro, Materazzi, Zambrotta, Gattuso, De Rossi, Camoranesi, Perrotta (Pirlo 77), Di Natale (Del Piero 66), Toni (Quagliarella 87).
Scotland: Gordon; Alexander, Naysmith, Weir, McManus, Ferguson B, Teale (Maloney 66), Hartley, Brown (Beattie 86), McCulloch (Boyd 81), Miller.
Referee: De Bleeckere (Belgium).

Odessa, 28 March 2007, 33,600
Ukraine (0) 1 *(Gusev 47)* **Lithuania (0) 0**
Ukraine: Shovkovskyi; Nesmachni, Kucher, Yezerskiy Y, Rusol, Gusev (Vorobei 79), Tymoschuk, Kalynychenko (Chygrynskiy 82), Mikhalik (Shelayev 70), Shevchenko, Voronin.
Lithuania: Grybauskas; Semberas, Klimavicius, Paulauskas, Stankevicius, Skerla, Zvirgzdauskas, Savenas (Kalonas 51), Morinas (Gedgaudas 56), Poskus (Radzinevicius 64), Danilevicius.
Referee: Meyer (Germany).

Torshavn, 2 June 2007, 6040
Faeroes (0) 1 *(Jacobsen R 77)* **Italy (1) 2** *(Inzaghi 12, 48)*
Faeroes: Mikkelsen; Danielsen, Johannesen O, Jacobsen J, Djurhuus, Borg (Samuelsen S 61), Olsen, Thomassen, Jacobsen C, Jacobsen R, Flotum (Holst 57).
Italy: Buffon; Oddo, Materazzi (Barzagli 76), Cannavaro, Tonetto, Gattuso, Pirlo, Diana, Rocchi (Quagliarella 82), Del Piero, Inzaghi (Lucarelli 59).
Referee: Malek (Poland).

Paris, 2 June 2007, 79,500
France (0) 2 *(Ribery 57, Anelka 71)* **Ukraine (0) 0**
France: Coupet; Abidal, Gallas, Clerc, Thuram, Makelele, Malouda, Toulalan, Nasri (Diarra 81), Ribery, Anelka (Cisse 77).
Ukraine: Shovkovskyi; Nesmachny, Yezerskiy (Levchenko 78), Rusol, Chygrynskiy, Gay, Tymoschuk, Gusev, Mikhalik, Kalynychenko (Rotan 64), Voronin (Vorobei 72).
Referee: Cantalejo (Spain).

Kaunas, 2 June 2007, 6000
Lithuania (0) 1 *(Mikoliunas 78)* **Georgia (0) 0**
Lithuania: Karcemarskas; Semberas, Stankevicius, Skerla, Zvirgzdauskas, Klimavicius, Paulauskas, Savenas (Kalonas 55), Morinas (Mikoliunas 62), Danilevicius, Beniusis (Labukas 75).
Georgia: Lomaia; Khizaneishvili, Kaladze, Eliava, Kobiashvili, Khizanishvili, Tskitishvili (Mujiri 80), Menteshashvili (Martsvaladze 64), Kvirkvelia, Iashvili, Demetradze.
Referee: Circhetta (Switzerland).

Toftir, 6 June 2007, 4100
Faeroes (0) 0 **Scotland (2) 2** *(Maloney 31, O'Connor 35)*
Faeroes: Mikkelsen; Danielsen, Jacobsen J, Johannesen O (Djurhuss 36) (Samuelsen S 77), Benjaminsen, Thomassen, Borg (Flotum 82), Olsen, Jacobsen R, Jacobsen C, Holst.
Scotland: Gordon; Alexander, Weir, McManus, Naysmith, Hartley, Ferguson B, Fletcher (Teale 68), Maloney (Adam 77), O'Connor, Boyd (Naismith 83).
Referee: Germanakos (Greece).

Auxerre, 6 June 2007, 20,000
France (1) 1 *(Nasri 33)* **Georgia (0) 0**
France: Landreau; Abidal, Clerc, Gallas, Makelele, Malouda (Cisse 65), Toulalan, Nasri, Ribery (Govou 90), Anelka (Benzema 90), Thuram.
Georgia: Lomaia; Khizaneishvili, Kaladze, Khizanishvili, Ghvinianidze, Salukvadze (Mujiri 12), Eliava (Martsvaladze 62), Kvirkverlia, Kankava (Shashiashvili 89), Burduli, Iashvili.
Referee: Batista (Portugal).

Kaunas, 6 June 2007, 7000
Lithuania (0) 0 Italy (2) 2 *(Quagliarella 31, 45)*
Lithuania: Grybauskas; Semberas, Stankevicius, Skerla, Zvirgzdauskas, Klimavicius, Paulauskas (Gedgaudas 46), Savenas (Labukas 60), Kalonas, Morinas (Mikoliunas 39), Danilevicus.
Italy: Buffon; Oddo, Cannavaro, Materazzi, Zambrotta, Pirlo, De Rossi (Gattuso 65), Perrotta (Ambrosini 71), Quagliarella, Inzaghi, Di Natale (Del Piero 74).
Referee: Vink (Holland).

Group B Table	*P*	*W*	*D*	*L*	*F*	*A*	*Pts*
France	7	6	0	1	15	2	18
Italy	7	5	1	1	13	6	16
Scotland	7	5	0	2	13	6	15
Ukraine	6	4	0	2	8	6	12
Lithuania	7	2	1	4	4	7	7
Georgia	8	2	0	6	13	14	6
Faeroes	8	0	0	8	2	27	0

GROUP C

Budapest, 2 September 2006, 10,500
Hungary (0) 1 *(Gera 90 (pen))*
Norway (3) 4 *(Solskjaer 15, 54, Stromstad 32, Pedersen 41)*
Hungary: Kiraly; Feher, Low, Juhasz (Vanczak 66), Eger, Sowunmi (Torghelle 80), Molnar, Dardai, Horvath (Kiss 61), Gera, Huszti.
Norway: Myhre; Rambekk, Hagen, Hangeland, Johnsen M, Stromstad (Braaten 62), Andresen, Haestad (Larsen 85), Pedersen, Solskjaer, Carew (Iversen 76).
Referee: Vink (Holland).

Ta'Qali, 2 September 2006, 4000
Malta (1) 2 *(Pace 6, Michael Mifsud 85)*
Bosnia (3) 5 *(Barbarez 4, Hrgovic 10, 46, Muslimovic 48, 50)*
Malta: Haber; Ciantar (Woods 45), Azzopardi, Said, Dimech, Agius (Sciberras 82), Mattocks (Pullicino 65), Michael Mifsud, Schembri, Pace, Sammut.
Bosnia: Hasagic; Berberovic, Music, Spahic, Bajramovic, Papac (Milenkovic 61), Barbarez (Grujic 66), Misimovic, Muslimovic, Hrgovic, Bartolovic (Beslija 53).
Referee: Vejlgaard (Denmark).

Chisinau, 2 September 2006, 10,500
Moldova (0) 0 Greece (0) 1 *(Liberopoulos 77)*
Moldova: Pascenco; Lascencov, Corneencov, Testimitanu, Epureanu (Clescenco 65), Rebeja, Covalciuc, Olexici, Berco, Rogaciov (Dadu 78), Ivanov.
Greece: Nikopolidis; Seitaridis, Fyssas, Dellas (Anatolakis 89), Kyrgiakos, Katsouranis, Basinas, Zagorakis (Salpigidis 46), Karagounis, Charisteas (Liberopoulos 46), Amanatidis.
Referee: Trefoloni (Italy).

Zenica, 6 September 2006, 18,000
Bosnia (0) 1 *(Misimovic 64)*
Hungary (1) 3 *(Huszti 36 (pen), Gera 46, Dardai 49)*
Bosnia: Hasagic; Spahic■, Music (Muslimovic 46), Papac, Barbarez, Kerkez, Bajramovic, Hrgovic (Beslija 73), Bartolovic (Trivunovic 63), Misimovic, Bolic.
Hungary: Kiraly; Feher (Kiss 82), Low (Juhasz 65), Torghelle (Kabat 90), Eger, Toth, Molnar, Dardai, Huszti, Gera, Vanczak.
Referee: Kapitanis (Cyprus).

Oslo, 6 September 2006, 23,848
Norway (0) 2 *(Stromstad 73, Iversen 79)* **Moldova (0) 0**
Norway: Myhre; Hagen, Hangeland, Johnsen M (Iversen 65), Stromstad (Larsen 90), Andresen, Pedersen, Rambekk, Haestad, Carew, Johnsen F (Solksjaer 46).
Moldova: Pascenco; Lascencov (Clescenco 77), Corneencov, Testimitanu, Rebeja, Epureanu, Covalciuc, Ivanov, Berco■, Rogaciov (Dadu 72), Olexici.
Referee: Ristoskov (Bulgaria).

Frankfurt, 6 September 2006
Turkey (0) 2 *(Nihat 56, Tumer 77)* **Malta (0) 0**
Turkey: Rustu; Mehmet T, Can, Gokhan Z, Marco Aurelio, Fatih (Nihat 46), Basturk (Arda 46), Tumer, Ergun, Hakan Sukur (Nuri 85), Hamit Altintop.
Malta: Haber; Ciantar, Wellman, Said, Dimech, Agius (Sciberras 87), Sammut (Pullicino 81), Michael Mifsud, Woods, Schembri (Scerri 89), Pace.
Played behind closed doors.
Referee: Vazquez (Spain).

Athens, 7 October 2006, 25,000
Greece (1) 1 *(Katsouranis 33)* **Norway (0) 0**
Greece: Nikopolidis; Seitaridis, Fyssas, Anatolakis, Kyrgiakos, Basinas, Katsouranis, Karagounis (Patsatzoglou 90), Giannakopoulos (Charisteas 46), Samaras, Liberopoulos (Amanatidis 71).
Norway: Myhre; Rambekk (Arst 85), Hagen, Hangeland, Riise JA, Stromstad (Braaten 61), Andresen, Haestad, Pedersen, Iversen, Solskjaer.
Referee: Michel (Slovakia).

Budapest, 7 October 2006, 9500
Hungary (0) 0
Turkey (1) 1 *(Tuncay 41)*
Hungary: Kiraly; Feher, Vanczak, Juhasz, Eger, Toth, Halmosi (Kabat 46) (Komlosi 76), Dardai, Torghelle (Szabics 83), Gera, Huszti.
Turkey: Rustu; Hamit Altintop, Servet, Gokhan Z, Aurelio, Gokdeniz (Huseyin 63), Arda (Mehmet T 90), Ibrahim U, Sabri, Tuncay (Can 90), Hakan Sukur.
Referee: Hamer (Luxembourg).

Chisinau, 7 October 2006, 11,000
Moldova (2) 2 *(Rogaciov 13, 32 (pen))*
Bosnia (0) 2 *(Misimovic 62, Grlic 68)*
Moldova: Pascenco; Lascencov, Catinsus, Gatcan (Clescenco 90), Epureanu, Olexici, Testimitanu, Rebeja, Ivanov, Iepureanu (Corneencov 72), Rogaciov (Dadu 71).
Bosnia: Hasagic; Trivunovic, Papac, Vidic, Silic, Bajramovic (Grujic 77), Hrgovic (Smajic 86), Barbarez, Misimovic, Damjanovic (Grlic 46), Bartolovic.
Referee: Piccirillo (France).

Zenica, 11 October 2006, 10,000
Bosnia (0) 0 Greece (1) 4 *(Charisteas 8 (pen), Patsatzoglou 82, Samaras 85, Katsouranis 90)*
Bosnia: Hasagic (Tolja 46); Silic (Ibricic 69), Bajic, Bajramovic, Papac■, Grlic (Grujic 61), Misimovic, Barbarez, Hrgovic, Bartolovic, Skoro.
Greece: Nikopolidis; Anatolakis, Kyrgiakos, Fyssas, Seitaridis (Patsatzoglou 57), Katsouranis, Karagounis (Alexopoulos 36), Giannakopoulos (Amanatidis 89), Basinas, Samaras, Charisteas.
Referee: Kalugin (Russia).

Ta'Qali, 11 October 2006, 5000
Malta (1) 2 *(Schembri 14, 53)* **Hungary (1) 1** *(Torghelle 19)*
Malta: Haber; Scicluna, Wellman, Said, Dimech, Mallia (Cohen 64), Sammut, Pace, Schembri (Scerri 72), Michael Mifsud, Agius (Pullicino 82).
Hungary: Kiraly; Feher (Halmosi 76), Toth, Juhasz, Vanczak■, Leandro (Kiss 46), Huszti, Dardai, Torghelle, Szabics (Czvitkovics 60), Gera.
Referee: Ver Eecke (Belgium).

Frankfurt, 11 October 2006, 200
Turkey (3) 5 *(Hakan Sukur 35, 37 (pen), 43, 73, Tuncay 68)*
Moldova (0) 0
Turkey: Rustu; Servet, Hamit Altintop, Gokhan Z, Marco Aurelio, Gokdeniz (Tumer 60), Arda (Nihat 72), Ibrahim U, Sabri, Tuncay, Hakan Sukur (Halil Altintop 81).
Moldova: Pascenco; Epureanu (Corneencov 46), Catinsus, Olexici, Gatcan, Iepureanu (Dadu 63), Covalciuc, Ivanov, Rebeja, Rogaciov, Romanenco.
Referee: Vollquartz (Denmark).

Athens, 24 March 2007, 31,405

Greece (1) 1 *(Kyrgiakos 5)* **Turkey (1) 4** *(Tuncay 27, Gokhan U 55, Tumer 70, Gokdeniz 81)*

Greece: Nikopolidis; Dellas, Kyrgiakos, Seitaridis, Fyssas (Torosidis 56), Katsouranis, Basinas, Karagounis, Giannakopoulos (Amanatidis 72), Charisteas (Gekas 63), Samaras.
Turkey: Volkan D; Servet, Hamit Altintop, Gokhan Z, Ibrahim U (Volkan Y 19), Mehmet A, Tumer (Gokdeniz 80), Sabri, Gokhan U (Huseyin 57), Hakan Sukur, Tuncay.
Referee: Stark (Germany).

Chisinau, 24 March 2007, 10,000

Moldova (0) 1 *(Epureanu 85)* **Malta (0) 1** *(Mallia 73)*

Moldova: Pascenco; Golovatenco, Epureanu, Olexici, Bordian, Rebeja, Comlenoc (Dadu■ 85), Namasco, Frunza, Bugaev, Zmeu (Ivanov 63).
Malta: Haber; Said, Briffa, Dimech■, Agius, Michael Mifsud (Sciberras 90), Woods (Sammut 77), Mallia, Schembri (Bogdanovic 70), Scicluna, Pace.
Referee: Aliyev (Azerbaijan).

Oslo, 24 March 2007, 16,987

Norway (0) 1 *(Carew 50 (pen))*

Bosnia (2) 2 *(Misimovic 18, Muslimovic 33)*

Norway: Myhre; Hagen, Hangeland, Riise JA, Stromstad (Grindheim 62), Andresen, Carew, Pedersen, Haestad, Johnsen F (Iversen 46), Storbaek (Brenne 79).
Bosnia: Guso; Berberovic (Music 58), Nadarevic (Radeljic 46), Bajic, Krunic, Danjanovic, Muslimovic, Misimovic, Ibisevic, Custovic (Maletic 82), Hrgovic.
Referee: Riley (England).

Budapest, 28 March 2007, 5000

Hungary (1) 2 *(Priskin 9, Gera 63)* **Moldova (0) 0**

Hungary: Vegh; Csizmadia, Bodor, Juhasz, Balogh (Vasko 36), Toth, Vadocz, Tozser, Priskin (Tisza 88), Hajnal (Huszti 64), Gera.
Moldova: Pascenco; Golovatenco, Cojocari, Olexici, Epureanu, Ivanov (Namasco 46), Corneencov, Bordian, Comleonoc (Zmeu 66), Frunza (Alexeev 46), Bugaev.
Referee: Ingvarsson (Sweden).

Ta'Qali, 28 March 2007, 15,000

Malta (0) 0 **Greece (0) 1** *(Basinas 66 (pen))*

Malta: Haber; Azzopardi, Said, Briffa■, Scicluna, Agius, Mallia (Barbara 90), Sammut, Pace, Michael Mifsud, Schembri (Bogdanovic 71).
Greece: Chalkias; Dellas (Anatolakis 83), Vintra, Kyrgiakos, Kapsis, Torosidis, Basinas, Karagounis, Katsouranis, Gekas (Samaras 90), Salpigidis (Liberopoulos 64).
Referee: Garcia (Portugal).

Frankfurt, 28 March 2007

Turkey (0) 2 *(Hamit Altintop 72, 90)*

Norway (2) 2 *(Brenne 31, Andresen 40)*

Turkey: Volkan D; Sabri, Servet, Emre A, Hamit Altintop, Tumer (Volkan Y 46), Emre B, Gokdeniz (Mehmet Y 79), Mehmet A, Hakan Sukur (Huseyin 90), Tuncay.
Norway: Myhre; Riise JA, Hagen, Hangeland, Storbaek, Stromstad, Andresen, Haestad (Skjelbred 57), Brenne (Nevland 85), Helstad (Holm 63), Carew.
Behind closed doors.
Referee: Farina (Italy).

Sarajevo, 2 June 2007, 14,000

Bosnia (2) 3 *(Muslimovic 27, Dzeko 47, Custovic 90)*

Turkey (2) 2 *(Hakan Sukur 13, Sabri 39)*

Bosnia: Guso; Bajic, Music, Radeljic, Danjanovic, Rahimic, Hrgovic, Misimovic, Maletic (Custovic 83), Muslimovic (Pandza 90), Dzeko (Zeba 61).
Turkey: Rustu; Hamit A, Servet, Gokhan Z, Ibrahim U, Mehmet A, Sabri (Umit K 77), Gokdeniz (Huseyin 46), Arda (Basturk 63), Tuncay, Hakan Sukur.
Referee: Frojdfeldt (Sweden).

Iraklion, 2 June 2007, 24,000

Greece (2) 2 *(Gekas 16, Seitaridis 29)* **Hungary (0) 0**

Greece: Chalkias; Seitaridis, Torosidis, Anatolakis (Patsatzoglou 53), Kyrgiakos, Katsouranis, Karagounis, Basinas, Gekas, Amanatidis (Liberopoulos 88), Charisteas (Giannakopoulos 80).
Hungary: Vegh; Csizmadia, Bodor (Vanczak 39), Juhasz, Balogh, Toth, Vadocz (Szelesi 76), Tozser, Priskin (Dzsudzsak 80), Hajnal, Gera.
Referee: Larsen (Denmark).

Oslo, 2 June 2007, 16,364

Norway (1) 4 *(Haestad 31, Helstad 73, Iversen 79, Riise JA 90)* **Malta (0) 0**

Norway: Opdal; Storbaek, Hagen, Hangeland, Riise JA, Riise B, Andresen, Haestad (Braaten 83), Iversen, Carew (Helstad 72), Pedersen (Brenne 62).
Malta: Muscat; Azzopardi, Said, Wellmen, Scicluna, Agius, Sammut (Woods 46), Mallia, Pace, Michael Mifsud (Barbara 83), Schembri (Bogdanovic 70).
Referee: Granat (Poland).

Sarajevo, 6 June 2007, 15,000

Bosnia (1) 1 *(Muslimovic 6)* **Malta (0) 0**

Bosnia: Guso; Music (Muharemovic 90), Hrgovic, Pandza, Radeljic, Maletic (Bartolovic 80), Danjanovic, Misimovic, Rahimic, Muslimovic, Dzeko (Zeba 57).
Malta: Muscat; Azzopardi, Said, Bogdanovic (Schembri 65), Dimech, Agius, Briffa, Michael Mifsud, Woods (Mallia 70), Sammut, Pace (Barbara 82).
Referee: Richards (Wales).

Iraklion, 6 June 2007, 22,000

Greece (1) 2 *(Charisteas 30, Liberopoulos 90)*

Moldova (0) 1 *(Frunza 80)*

Greece: Nikopolidis; Seitaridis, Goumas, Kyrgiakos, Patsatzoglou (Giannakopoulos 83), Torosidis, Karagounis, Katsouranis, Amanatidis (Samaras 71), Charisteas, Gekas (Liberopoulos 63).
Moldova: Calancea; Epureanu, Golovatenco, Katinsus, Namasco, Bordian, Comleonoc (Tigirlas 82), Josan, Gatcan, Alexeev (Frunza 64), Bugaev (Zmeu 50).
Referee: Wegereef (Holland).

Oslo, 6 June 2007, 19,198

Norway (1) 4 *(Iversen 22, Braaten 57, Carew 60, 78)*

Hungary (0) 0

Norway: Opdal; Storbaek, Hagen, Hangeland, Riise JA, Riise B, Andresen, Grindheim (Haestad 46), Iversen (Braaten 46), Carew, Pedersen (Helstad 82).
Hungary: Vegh; Szelesi, Juhasz, Balogh, Vanczak, Buzsaky (Vadocz 83), Toth, Tozser, Gera, Priskin (Tisza 71), Hajnal.
Referee: Gonzalez (Spain).

Group C Table	*P*	*W*	*D*	*L*	*F*	*A*	*Pts*
Greece	7	6	0	1	12	5	18
Bosnia	7	4	1	2	14	14	13
Turkey	6	4	1	1	16	6	13
Norway	7	4	1	2	17	6	13
Hungary	7	2	0	5	7	14	6
Malta	7	1	1	5	5	15	4
Moldova	7	0	2	5	4	15	2

GROUP D

Teplice, 2 September 2006, 16,204

Czech Republic (0) 2 *(Lafata 76, 89)*

Wales (0) 1 *(Jiranek 85 (og))*

Czech Republic: Cech; Ujfalusi, Jiranek, Rozehnal, Jankulovski, Stajner (Sionko 46), Galasek (Kovac R 87), Rosicky, Plasil, Kulic (Lafata 75), Koller.
Wales: Jones P; Delaney (Cotterill 78), Ricketts (Earnshaw 79), Robinson, Gabbidon, Collins J, Davies, Fletcher (Ledley 47), Bellamy, Nyatanga, Giggs.
Referee: Eriksson (Sweden).

Stuttgart, 2 September 2006, 53,198

Germany (0) 1 *(Podolski 57)* **Republic of Ireland (0) 0**

Germany: Lehmann; Lahm, Friedrich A, Friedrich M, Jansen, Schneider (Borowski 83), Frings, Ballack, Schweinsteiger, Podolski (Neuville 76), Klose.
Republic of Ireland: Given; Carr, Finnan, Andy O'Brien, Dunne, O'Shea, Duff (McGeady 77), Reid S, Robbie Keane, Doyle (Elliott 79), Kilbane (Alan O'Brien 83).
Referee: Kantalejo (Spain).

Bratislava, 2 September 2006, 4783
Slovakia (3) 6 *(Skrtel 9, Mintal 33, 56, Sebo 43, 49, Karhan 52)* **Cyprus (0) 1** *(Yiasoumis 90)*
Slovakia: Contofalsky; Zabavnik (Holosko 46), Skrtel, Durica, Cech, Hlinka, Karhan, Svento, Mintal, Nemeth (Krajcik 46), Sebo (Hodur 56).
Cyprus: Morfis; Theodotou, Lambrou, Louka (Theofilou 67), Michael, Charalambides, Makrides, Garpozis (Krassas 46), Okkas, Yiasoumis, Alexandrou (Elia 46).
Referee: Oriekhov (Ukraine).

Serravalle, 6 September 2006, 5019
San Marino (0) 0 Germany (6) 13 *(Podolski 11, 43, 64, 72, Schweinsteiger 28, 47, Klose 30, 45, Ballack 35, Hitzlsperger 66, 73, Friedrich M 87, Schneider 90 (pen))*
San Marino: Simoncini A; Albani, Della Valle, Bacciocchi, Palazzi, Valentini C, Vannucci (Simoncini D 68), Michele Marani (Masi 78), Domeniconi (Bonini 46), Manuel Marani, Selva A.
Germany: Lehmann; Jansen, Friedrich A, Lahm, Schweinsteiger, Frings (Hitzlsperger 62), Ballack (Odonkor 46), Schneider, Friedrich M, Klose (Asamoah 46), Podolski.
Referee: Selcuk (Turkey).

Bratislava, 6 September 2006, 27,683
Slovakia (0) 0
Czech Republic (2) 3 *(Sionko 10, 21, Koller 57)*
Slovakia: Contofalsky; Hlinka, Skrtel, Durica, Valachovic (Hodur 46), Svento, Cech (Nemeth 24), Krajcik, Karhan, Mintal, Sebo (Holosko 46).
Czech Republic: Cech; Jankulovski, Jiranek, Ujfalusi, Rozehnal, Polak (Kovac R 72), Galasek, Sionko (Stajner 77), Rosicky, Plasil, Koller.
Referee: Bennett (England).

Nicosia, 7 October 2006, 12,000
Cyprus (2) 5 *(Konstantinou M 10, 50 (pen), Garpozis 16, Charalambides 60, 75)*
Republic of Ireland (2) 2 *(Ireland 8, Dunne 44)*
Cyprus: Morfis; Satsias, Lambrou, Louka, Theodotou, Michael (Charalambides 46), Garpozis (Charalambous 77), Makrides, Okkas (Yiasoumis 86), Konstantinou M, Aloneftis.
Republic of Ireland: Kenny; Finnan, O'Shea, Andy O'Brien (Lee 71), Dunne■, Kilbane, McGeady (Alan O'Brien 80), Ireland (Douglas 83), Morrison, Robbie Keane, Duff.
Referee: Batista (Portugal).

Liberec, 7 October 2006, 9514
Czech Republic (4) 7 *(Kulic 15, Polak 22, Baros 28, 68, Koller 43, 52, Jarolim 49)* **San Marino (0) 0**
Czech Republic: Cech; Ujfalusi, Grygera, Rozehnal (Zapotocny 46), Jankulovski, Jarolim, Polak, Rosicky (Plasil 63), Baros, Kulic (Lafata 46), Koller.
San Marino: Valentini F; Albani, Della Valle, Bacciocchi, Andreini (Mariotti 82), Valentini C, Vannucci, Masi (Crescentini 69), Domeniconi, Moretti (Michele Marani 54), Selva A.
Referee: Aliyev (Azerbaijan).

Cardiff, 7 October 2006, 28,493
Wales (1) 1 *(Bale 37)* **Slovakia (3) 5** *(Svento 14, Mintal 32, 38, Karhan 51, Vittek 59)*
Wales: Jones P; Duffy, Bale, Gabbidon, Nyatanga, Robinson, Edwards (Ledley 58), Koumas, Davies S (Cotterill 88), Bellamy, Earnshaw (Parry 46).
Slovakia: Contofalsky; Kozak, Kratochvil, Petras M, Varga, Karhan (Krajcik 67), Mintal (Hodur 71), Vittek (Holosko 77), Petras P, Svento, Durica.
Referee: Egmond (Holland).

Dublin, 11 October 2006, 35,500
Republic of Ireland (0) 1 *(Kilbane 62)*
Czech Republic (0) 0
Republic of Ireland: Henderson; Kelly, Finnan, O'Shea, McShane, Carsley, Reid A (Quinn 72), Douglas, Robbie Keane, Kilbane (Alan O'Brien 79), Duff.
Czech Republic: Cech; Polak, Ujfalusi, Kovac R, Jankulovski, Jiranek, Rosicky, Plasil (Grygera 85), Rozehnal, Koller, Baros (Jarolim 82).
Referee: Layec (France).

Bratislava, 11 October 2006, 21,582
Slovakia (0) 1 *(Varga 58)* **Germany (3) 4** *(Podolski 13, 72, Ballack 25, Schweinsteiger 36)*
Slovakia: Contofalsky; Petras P (Holosko 73), Varga, Skrtel, Durica, Karhan, Petras M, Svento, Kozak (Hodur 65), Mintal, Vittek.
Germany: Lehmann; Friedrich A, Friedrich M, Fritz, Lahm, Ballack, Frings, Schneider (Odonkor 75), Schweinsteiger (Trochowski 77), Klose, Podolski (Hanke 85).
Referee: Hauge (Norway).

Cardiff, 11 October 2006, 20,456
Wales (2) 3 *(Koumas 33, Earnshaw 39, Bellamy 72)*
Cyprus (0) 1 *(Okkas 83)*
Wales: Price; Duffy (Edwards 78), Bale, Gabbidon, Nyatanga, Robinson, Morgan, Koumas (Ledley 76), Earnshaw, Bellamy (Parry 90), Davies S.
Cyprus: Morfis; Theodotou, Lambrou, Louka, Satsias (Yiasoumis 84), Michael (Charalambides 46), Garpozis (Charalambous 46), Makrides, Aloneftis, Konstantinou M, Okkas.
Referee: Granat (Poland).

Nicosia, 15 November 2006, 15,000
Cyprus (1) 1 *(Okkas 43)* **Germany (1) 1** *(Ballack 16)*
Cyprus: Georgiallides; Elia, Lambrou, Louka, Theodotou (Charalambous 79), Makrides, Charalambides, Michael (Krassas 68), Okkas (Nicolaou 72), Aloneftis, Konstantinou M.
Germany: Hildebrand; Friedrich A, Lahm, Schweinsteiger, Frings, Ballack, Fritz, Friedrich M, Odonkor (Hitzlsperger 79), Klose, Neuville (Hanke 62).
Referee: Frojdfeldt (Sweden).

Dublin, 15 November 2006, 34,018
Republic of Ireland (3) 5 *(Simoncini D 7 (og), Doyle 24, Robbie Keane 31, 58 (pen), 85)*
San Marino (0) 0
Republic of Ireland: Given; Finnan, O'Shea, Dunne, McShane, Carsley (Douglas 50), Reid A, Doyle (McGeady 63), Robbie Keane, Duff, Kilbane (Lee 79).
San Marino: Valentini F; Bugli, Albani, Bacciocchi, Simoncini D (Bonini 81), Vannucci (Crescentini 72), Valentini C, Andreini, Mariotti (Michele Marani 59), Manuel Marani, Selva A.
Referee: Isaksen (Faeroes).

Serravalle, 7 February 2007, 3294
San Marino (0) 1 *(Manuel Marani 86)*
Republic of Ireland (0) 2 *(Kilbane 49, Ireland 90)*
San Marino: Simoncini A; Valentini C, Manuel Marani, Albani, Simoncini D, Muccioli, Bonini (Vannucci 76), Domeniconi (Bugli 88), Michele Marani, Selva A, Gasperoni A (Andreini 66).
Republic of Ireland: Henderson; Finnan, Harte (Hunt 74), Dunne, O'Shea (McShane 46), Carsley, Duff, Ireland, Keane, Long (Stokes 80), Kilbane.
Referee: Rasmussen (Denmark).

Nicosia, 24 March 2007, 2696
Cyprus (1) 1 *(Aloneftis 43)*
Slovakia (0) 3 *(Vittek 54, Skrtel 67, Jakubko 77)*
Cyprus: Morfis■; Satsias, Lambrou, Louka, Theodotou (Georgiallides 43), Michael, Charalambidis, Garpozis (Charalambous 66), Makrides (Elia 58), Yiasoumis, Aloneftis.
Slovakia: Cantofalsky; Singlar (Sofcak 46), Skrtel, Durica, Gresko, Borbely, Krajcik, Svento, Sapara (Kozak 68), Vittek, Jakubko (Sestak 79).
Referee: Lehner (Austria).

Prague, 24 March 2007, 17,821
Czech Republic (0) 1 *(Baros 77)*
Germany (1) 2 *(Schweinsteiger 42, Kuranyi 62)*
Czech Republic: Cech; Ujfalusi (Vlcek 84), Jiranek, Rozehnal, Jankulovski, Sionko (Plasil 46), Rosicky, Galasek (Kulic 67), Polak, Koller, Baros.
Germany: Lehmann; Lahm, Mertesacker, Metzelder, Jansen, Schneider, Frings, Ballack, Schweinsteiger, Podolski (Hitzlsperger 89), Kuranyi.
Referee: Rosetti (Italy).

Dublin, 24 March 2007, 72,539

Republic of Ireland (1) 1 *(Ireland 39)* **Wales (0) 0**

Republic of Ireland: Given; Finnan, O'Shea, Dunne, McShane, Carsley, Douglas (Hunt 80), Ireland (Doyle 59), Robbie Keane (McGeady 89), Kilbane, Duff.
Wales: Coyne; Ricketts, Bale (Collins D 74), Collins J, Evans, Nyatanga, Ledley (Fletcher 46), Robinson (Easter 90), Davies S, Bellamy, Giggs.
Referee: Hauge (Norway).

Liberec, 28 March 2007, 9310

Czech Republic (1) 1 *(Kovac R 22)* **Cyprus (0) 0**

Czech Republic: Cech; Ujfalusi, Grygera (Kovac R 12) (Jiranek 27), Rozehnal, Jankulovski, Galasek, Rosicky, Polak, Jarolim, Koller, Baros (Plasil 77).
Cyprus: Georgiallides; Satsias, Lambrou, Theodotou, Paraskevas, Elia (Charalambous 76), Charalampidis (Krassas 75), Makrides, Yiasoumis (Chaili 72), Okkas, Aloneftis.
Referee: Bebek (Croatia).

Dublin, 28 March 2007, 71,297

Republic of Ireland (1) 1 *(Doyle 12)* **Slovakia (0) 0**

Republic of Ireland: Given; O'Shea, Finnan, McShane, Dunne, Carsley, Ireland (Hunt 70), McGeady (Quinn A 87), Kilbane, Duff, Doyle (Long 74).
Slovakia: Contofalsky; Singlar (Sestak 80), Skrtel, Klimpl, Gresko, Svento (Michalik 86), Zofcak, Borbely, Sapara (Holosko 72), Vittek, Jakubko.
Referee: Baskakov (Russia).

Cardiff, 28 March 2007, 18,752

Wales (2) 3 *(Giggs 3, Bale 20, Koumas 63 (pen))*
San Marino (0) 0

Wales: Coyne; Ricketts, Evans (Nyatanga 63), Collins J, Bale, Fletcher, Koumas, Davies S, Giggs (Parry 73), Bellamy, Easter (Cotterill 46).
San Marino: Simoncini A; Valentini C (Toccaceli 85), Andreini, Albani, Muccioli, Bacciocchi, Negri (Nanni 79), Domeniconi (Bugli 67), Manuel Marani, Selva A, Gasperoni A.
Referee: Tchagharyan (Armenia).

Nuremberg, 2 June 2007, 43,967

Germany (1) 6 *(Kuranyi 45, Jansen 52, Frings 56 (pen), Gomez 63, 65, Fritz 67)* **San Marino (0) 0**

Germany: Lehmann; Lahm (Helmes 70), Mertesacker, Metzelder, Jansen, Frings, Hilbert (Fritz 59), Hitzlsperger, Schneider, Klose, Kuranyi (Gomez 59).
San Marino: Simoncini A; Simoncini D■, Della Valle, Albani, Valentini C, Vannucci, Bugli (Vitaioli 85), Bacciocchi, Negri (Bonini 68), Gasperoni A, Manuel Marani (Domeniconi 77).
Referee: Asumaa (Finland).

Cardiff, 2 June 2007, 30,714

Wales (0) 0 Czech Republic (0) 0

Wales: Hennessey; Ricketts, Nyatanga, Gabbidon, Collins J, Robinson, Ledley, Koumas, Davies S, Giggs (Earnshaw 89), Bellamy.
Czech Republic: Cech; Ujfalusi, Kovac R, Rozehnal, Jankulovski, Polak (Jarolim 65), Sivok (Matejovsky 83), Rosicky, Plasil, Koller, Baros (Kulic 46).
Referee: Allaerts (Belgium).

Hamburg, 6 June 2007, 51,500

Germany (2) 2 *(Durica 10 (og), Hitzlsperger 43)*

Slovakia (1) 1 *(Metzelder 20 (og))*

Germany: Lehmann; Jansen, Lahm, Mertesacker, Metzelder, Fritz, Frings, Hitzlsperger, Schneider (Rolfes 90), Klose (Trochowski 74), Kuranyi (Gomez 65).
Slovakia: Contofalsky; Skrtel, Mansyk, Durica, Klimpl, Svento, Strba (Oravec 83), Krajcik, Sapara (Holosko 65), Sestak (Zofcak 65), Vittek.
Referee: Benquerenca (Portugal).

Group D Table	P	W	D	L	F	A	Pts
Germany	7	6	1	0	29	4	19
Czech Republic	7	4	2	1	15	4	14
Republic of Ireland	7	4	1	2	12	8	13
Slovakia	7	3	0	4	16	13	9
Wales	6	2	1	3	8	9	7
Cyprus	6	1	1	4	9	16	4
San Marino	6	0	0	6	1	36	0

GROUP E

Tallinn, 16 August 2006, 7500

Estonia (0) 0 Macedonia (0) 1 *(Sedloski 73)*

Estonia: Poom; Jaager, Stepanov, Piiroja, Kruglov, Dmitrijev, Terehhov, Klavan, Lindpere, Sidorenkov (Teever 67), Viikmae (Barengrub 90).
Macedonia: Nikolovski; Lazarevski, Petrov (Vasoski 87), Sedloski, Mitreski I, Noveski, Sumulikoski, Jancevski, Pandev (Tasevski 82), Naumoski (Stojkov 71), Maznov.
Referee: Jakobsson (Iceland).

Old Trafford, 2 September 2006, 56,290

England (3) 5 *(Crouch 5, 66, Gerrard 13, Defoe 38, 47)*
Andorra (0) 0

England: Robinson; Neville P (Lennon 65), Cole A, Hargreaves, Terry, Brown, Gerrard, Lampard, Crouch, Defoe (Johnson A 71), Downing (Richardson 64).
Andorra: Koldo; Lima A, Txema, Ayala, Sonejee, Javi Sanchez (Juli Sanchez 46), Sivera (Garcia 77), Vieira, Silva, Pujol (Jimenez 49), Ruiz.
Referee: Brugger (Austria).

Tallinn, 2 September 2006, 7800

Estonia (0) 0 Israel (1) 1 *(Colautti 8)*

Estonia: Poom; Jaager, Stepanov, Piiroja, Kruglov, Terehhov, Klavan, Dmitrijev (Teever 85), Viikmae (Vassiljev 69), Neemelo (Barengrub 85), Oper.
Israel: Awat; Gershon, Ben Haim, Badir, Tal, Zandberg (Ben Shushan 60), Afek, Ziv, Colautti, Benayoun, Katan (Alberman 72).
Referee: Verbist (Belgium).

Nijmegen, 6 September 2006, 5000

Israel (3) 4 *(Benayoun 9, Ben Shushan 11, Gershon 43 (pen), Tamuz Temile 69)* **Andorra (0) 1** *(Fernandez 84)*

Israel: Awat; Afek, Ben Haim, Gershon, Ziv, Tal, Badir (Alberman 76), Benayoun (Golan 69), Ben Shushan, Katan (Tamuz Temile 62), Colautti.
Andorra: Koldo; Bernaus, Txema, Lima A, Ayala, Silva■, Sonejee, Vieira (Moreno 67), Jimenez, Pujol (Garcia 46), Ruiz (Fernandez 54).
Referee: Zrnic (Bosnia).

Skopje, 6 September 2006, 16,500

Macedonia (0) 0 England (0) 1 *(Crouch 46)*

Macedonia: Nikolovski; Noveski, Petrov, Sedloski, Mitreski I, Lazarevski, Jancevski (Tasevski 52), Sumulikoski, Naumoski (Sakiri 74), Maznov (Stojkov 56), Pandev.
England: Robinson; Neville P, Cole A, Hargreaves, Terry, Ferdinand, Gerrard, Lampard (Carrick 84), Crouch (Johnson A 87), Defoe (Lennon 76), Downing.
Referee: Layec (France).

Moscow, 6 September 2006, 29,000

Russia (0) 0 Croatia (0) 0

Russia: Akinfeev; Ignashevich, Anyukov, Kolodin, Berezutski A, Izmailov, Aldonin, Semshov, Bilyaletdinov, Pavlyuchenko (Pogrebnyak 53), Arshavin.
Croatia: Pletikosa; Kovac R, Corluka, Sabljic, Seric, Kovac N, Modric, Kranjcar, Rapaic (Petric 58), Klasnic (Babic 88), Eduardo (Leko J 71).
Referee: Gonzalez (Spain).

Zagreb, 7 October 2006, 20,000

Croatia (2) 7 *(Petric 12, 37, 48, 50, Klasnic 58, Balaban 62, Modric 83)* **Andorra (0) 0**

Croatia: Pletikosa; Simic, Simunic, Kovac R, Corluka, Kovac N (Leko J 69), Modric, Klasnic, Kranjcar, Petric (Balaban 60), Eduardo (Babic 64).
Andorra: Koldo; Ayala, Rubio, Sonejee, Fernandez, Escura, Garcia (Jimenez 68), Vieira, Juli Sanchez (Toscano 53), Pujol, Sivera (Ruiz 60).
Referee: Zammit (Malta).

Old Trafford, 7 October 2006, 72,062

England (0) 0 Macedonia (0) 0

England: Robinson; Neville G, Cole A, Carrick, Terry, King, Gerrard, Lampard, Crouch, Rooney (Defoe 74), Downing (Wright-Phillips 70).
Macedonia: Nikolovski; Noveski, Petrov, Sedloski, Lazarevski, Mitreski I, Mitreski A, Sumulikoski, Maznov, Naumoski (Stojkov 46), Pandev (Tasevski 83).
Referee: Merk (Germany).

Moscow, 7 October 2006, 22,000
Russia (1) 1 *(Arshavin 5)* **Israel (0) 1** *(Ben Shushan 84)*
Russia: Akinfeev; Berezutski V, Ignashevich, Anyukov, Berezutski A, Smertin, Aldonin, Arshavin, Bilyaletdinov (Kerzhakov A 30), Zhirkov (Semshov 77), Pogrebnyak (Izmailov 57).
Israel: Awat; Ben Haim, Gershon (Ben-Yosef 46), Keise, Saban (Ben Shushan 46), Afek, Badir, Tal, Benayoun (Tamuz Temile 75), Alberman, Colautti.
Referee: Meyer (Germany).

La Vella, 11 October 2006, 300
Andorra (0) 0
Macedonia (3) 3 *(Pandev 13, Noveski 16, Naumoski 31)*
Andorra: Koldo; Txema, Ayala, Sonejee, Rubio, Garcia, Vieira, Pujol (Jimenez 87), Bernaus, Sivera■, Toscano (Ruiz 34).
Macedonia: Nikolovski; Noveski, Mitreski I, Sedloski, Petrov (Sakiri 80), Mitreski A, Sumulikoski, Lazarevski, Naumoski, Pandev (Tasevski 55), Maznov.
Referee: Silagava (Georgia).

Zagreb, 11 October 2006, 38,000
Croatia (0) 2 *(Eduardo 61, Neville G 69 (og))*
England (0) 0
Croatia: Pletikosa; Simic, Simunic, Kovac R, Corluka, Rapaic (Olic 76), Kovac N, Modric, Kranjcar (Babic 89), Eduardo (Leko J 81), Petric.
England: Robinson; Neville G, Cole A, Ferdinand, Terry, Carragher (Wright-Phillips 73), Carrick, Lampard, Crouch (Richardson 72), Rooney, Parker (Defoe 72).
Referee: Rosetti (Italy).

St Petersburg, 11 October 2006, 21,500
Russia (0) 2 *(Pogrebnyak 78, Sychev 90)* **Estonia (0) 0**
Russia: Akinfeev; Berezutski A, Berezutski V, Ignashevich, Anyukov, Bystrov, Titov, Bilyaletdinov (Saenko 90), Aldonin (Sychev 74), Arshavin, Kerzhakov A (Pogrebnyak 46).
Estonia: Poom; Allas (Purje 80), Jaager, Stepanov, Piiroja■, Kruglov, Terehhov (Rahn 81), Dmitrijev, Klavan, Teever (Gussev 80), Oper.
Referee: Braamhaar (Holland).

Tel Aviv, 15 November 2006, 45,000
Israel (1) 3 *(Colautti 8, 89, Benayoun 68)*
Croatia (2) 4 *(Srna 35 (pen), Eduardo 39, 54, 72)*
Israel: Awat; Afek, Ben Haim, Ben-Yosef, Keise, Alberman, Badir (Tamuz Temile 46), Tal, Katan (Ben Shushan 59), Benayoun, Colautti.
Croatia: Runje; Corluka, Simic, Kovac R, Simunic, Srna (Olic 88), Kovac N, Modric, Kranjcar (Babic 70), Eduardo (Leko J 81), Petric.
Referee: Gonzalez (Spain).

Skopje, 15 November 2006, 16,000
Macedonia (0) 0 **Russia (2) 2** *(Bystrov 18, Arshavin 32)*
Macedonia: Nikoloski; Noveski, Petrov, Sedloski, Mitreski I, Lazarevski, Sumulikoski, Sakiri (Tasevski 35), Mitreski A (Jancevski 46) (Grozdanoski 71), Maznov, Stojkov.
Russia: Akinfeev; Berezutski V, Berezutski A, Kolodin, Bystrov, Bilyaletdinov, Semshov, Zhirkov, Titov, Arshavin (Pavlyuchenko 90), Pogrebnyak (Sychev 57).
Referee: Allaerts (Belgium).

Zagreb, 24 March 2007, 20,000
Croatia (0) 2 *(Srna 58, Eduardo 88)*
Macedonia (1) 1 *(Sedloski 38)*
Croatia: Pletikosa; Simic, Simunic, Corluka, Rapaic (Srna 46), Babic, Balaban (Budan 79), Kovac N, Modric, Kranjcar, Eduardo.
Macedonia: Nikolovski; Noveski, Popov R, Sedloski■, Lazarevski, Mitreski A (Jancevski 77), Sumulikoski, Maznov (Vajs 71), Naumoski (Tasevski 60), Pandev, Vasoski.
Referee: Plautz (Austria).

Tallinn, 24 March 2007, 11,000
Estonia (0) 0 **Russia (0) 2** *(Kerzhakov A 66, 78)*
Estonia: Poom; Sisov (Neemelo 80), Lemsalu, Kruglov, Sidorenkov, Dmitrijev, Leetma (Kink 69), Lindpere, Klavan, Oper, Terehhov (Kams 52).
Russia: Akinfeev; Shishkin, Ignashevich, Anyukov, Torbinsky, Bilyaletdinov, Zurianov, Zhirkov, Bystrov (Saenko 90), Kerzhakov A (Sychev 83), Arshavin.
Referee: Ceferin (Slovenia).

Tel Aviv, 24 March 2007, 35,000
Israel (0) 0 **England (0) 0**
Israel: Awat; Ben Haim, Gershon, Ziv, Benado, Shpungin, Badir, Benayoun, Ben Shushan (Alberman 87), Tamuz Temile (Barda 75), Balali (Sahar 69).
England: Robinson; Neville P (Richards 72), Carragher, Gerrard, Ferdinand, Terry, Hargreaves, Lampard, Johnson A (Defoe 80), Rooney, Lennon (Downing 83).
Referee: Ovrebo (Norway).

Barcelona, 28 March 2007, 12,800
Andorra (0) 0 **England (0) 3** *(Gerrard 54, 76, Nugent 90)*
Andorra: Koldo; Sonejee, Lima A, Ayala, Bernaus, Escura, Vieira, Garcia, Ruiz (Fernandez 88), Jimenez (Martinez 69), Toscano (Moreno 90).
England: Robinson; Richards (Dyer 61), Cole A, Hargreaves, Terry, Ferdinand, Lennon, Gerrard, Johnson A (Nugent 79), Rooney (Defoe 61), Downing.
Referee: Paixao (Portugal).

Tel Aviv, 28 March 2007, 23,658
Israel (2) 4 *(Tal 19, Colautti 29, Sahar 77, 80)*
Estonia (0) 0
Israel: Awat; Shpungin, Ben Haim, Gershon, Ziv, Tal (Toema 87), Badir, Benayoun, Ben Shushan (Alberman 70), Tamuz Temile (Sahar 64), Colautti.
Estonia: Poom; Sisov, Lemsalu, Barengrub, Oper, Kruglov, Dmitrijev, Rahn (Kink 39), Lindpere (Kams 80), Klavan, Neemelo (Konsa 61).
Referee: Cuneyt (Turkey).

Tallinn, 2 June 2007, 10,000
Estonia (0) 0 **Croatia (1) 1** *(Eduardo 32)*
Estonia: Poom; Jaager, Stepanov, Piiroja, Kruglov, Dmitrijev, Lindpere (Kink 78), Klaven, Vassiljev, Konsa (Neemelo 71), Voskoboinikov.
Croatia: Pletikosa; Simunic, Kovac R, Corluka, Babic, Kovac N, Srna, Modric, Kranjcar (Leko J 74), Petric (Olic 53), Eduardo.
Referee: Kassai (Hungary).

Skopje, 2 June 2007, 14,500
Macedonia (1) 1 *(Stojkov 13)*
Israel (2) 2 *(Itzhaki 11, Colautti 44)*
Macedonia: Nikolovski; Noveski, Petrov, Lazarevski (Grozdanovski 46), Mitreski I, Vasoski, Naumoski (Ristic 46), Sumulikoski, Tasevski, Pandev (Polozani 55), Stojkov.
Israel: Awat; Shpungin, Keinan, Benado, Ziv, Tal, Badir, Alberman, Balali (Sahar 61), Colautti (Golan 81), Itzhaki (Zandberg 76).
Referee: Kircher (Germany).

St Petersburg, 2 June 2007, 21,500
Russia (2) 4 *(Kerzhakov A 8, 16, 49, Sychev 71)*
Andorra (0) 0
Russia: Malafeev; Berezutski V, Ignashevich, Berezutski A (Anyukov 46), Bystrov, Zurianov, Torbinsky, Semshov, Zhirkov (Budianski 57), Arshavin, Kerzhakov A (Sychev 54).
Andorra: Koldo; Txema, Oscar (Juli Sanchez 57), Bernaus, Ayala, Escura, Vieira, Pujol, Jimenez (Xavi 73), Ruiz, Moreno (Somoza 88).
Referee: Skjerven (Norway).

La Vella, 6 June 2007, 680
Andorra (0) 0
Israel (1) 2 *(Tamuz Temile 37, Colautti 53)*
Andorra: Koldo; Lima I, Txema (Sonejee 61), Lima A, Ayala, Escura, Garcia, Vieira, Bernaus, Ruiz, Toscano (Juli Sanchez 77).
Israel: Awat; Ziv, Benado, Yehiel, Ben Dayan, Tal, Benayoun, Alberman (Badir 71), Tamuz Temile (Katan 77), Colautti (Golan 86), Itzhaki.
Referee: Stokes (Republic of Ireland).

Joe Cole scores England's crucial opening goal in the Euro 2008 qualifier against Estonia in Tallinn. (Adam Davy/EMPICS Sport/PA Photos)

Zagreb, 6 June 2007, 35,000
Croatia (0) 0 Russia (0) 0

Croatia: Pletikosa; Corluka, Simic, Kovac R, Simunic, Srna (Leko J 8), Kovac N, Modric, Kranjcar (Petric 66), Eduardo, Olic (Babic 83).
Russia: Malafeev; Berezutski V, Ignashevich, Berezutski A, Bystrov (Saenko 61), Anyukov, Zhirkov, Semshov, Budianski (Torbinsky 46), Arshavin, Kerzhakov A (Sychev 73).
Referee: Lubos (Slovakia).

Tallinn, 6 June 2007, 11,000
Estonia (0) 0

England (1) 3 *(Cole J 37, Crouch 54, Owen 62)*

Estonia: Poom; Jaager, Stepanov, Kruglov, Klavan, Dmitrijev, Lindpere, Vassilijev, Konsa (Neemelo 46), Voskoboinikov, Terehhov (Kink 64).
England: Robinson; Brown, Bridge, Gerrard, Terry, King, Beckham (Dyer 68), Lampard, Crouch, Owen (Jenas 88), Cole J (Downing 75).
Referee: Gilewski (Poland).

Group E Table	*P*	*W*	*D*	*L*	*F*	*A*	*Pts*
Croatia	7	5	2	0	16	4	17
Israel	8	5	2	1	17	7	17
Russia	7	4	3	0	11	1	15
England	7	4	2	1	12	2	14
Macedonia	7	2	1	4	6	7	7
Estonia	7	0	0	7	0	14	0
Andorra	7	0	0	7	1	28	0

GROUP F

Riga, 2 September 2006, 7500
Latvia (0) 0

Sweden (1) 1 *(Kallstrom 38)*

Latvia: Kolinko; Stepanovs, Astafjevs, Zirnis (Karlsons 83), Laizans (Visnakovs 86), Smirnovs, Bleidelis, Verpakovskis, Rubins, Prohorenkovs (Pahars 57), Klava.
Sweden: Shaaban; Nilsson, Mellberg, Hansson, Edman, Linderoth, Alexandersson, Kallstrom (Anders Svensson 71), Ljungberg, Ibrahimovic, Elmander (Wilhelmsson 81).
Referee: Ceferin (Slovenia).

Belfast, 2 September 2006, 14,500
Northern Ireland (0) 0 Iceland (3) 3 *(Thorvaldsson 13, Hreidarsson 20, Gudjohnsen E 37)*

Northern Ireland: Maik Taylor; Baird, Capaldi (Duff 76), Davis, Hughes A, Craigan, Gillespie, Clingan, Quinn (Feeney 83), Healy, Elliott (Lafferty 63).
Iceland: Arason; Steinsson, Sigurdsson I, Ingimarsson, Hreidarsson, Gunnarsson B (Gislason 75), Arnason (Danielsson 55), Gudjonsson J, Gudjohnsen E, Sigurdsson H (Jonsson 64), Thorvaldsson.
Referee: Skjerven (Norway).

Badajoz, 2 September 2006, 14,876
Spain (2) 4 *(Fernando Torres 20, David Villa 45, 62, Luis Garcia 66)* **Liechtenstein (0) 0**

Spain: Casillas; Sergio Ramos, Puyol, Pablo, Pernia, Albelda (Oubina 69), Xabi Alonso, Fabregas (Iniesta 63), Raul, Fernando Torres, David Villa (Luis Garcia 63).
Liechtenstein: Jehle; Telser (Fischer 56), Maierhofer, Hasler, Martin Stocklasa, Burgmeier, Buchel M, Ritzberger, D'Elia, Beck T (Beck R 69), Frick M (Rohrer 86).
Referee: Bozinovski (Macedonia).

Reykjavik, 6 September 2006, 10,007
Iceland (0) 0 Denmark (2) 2 *(Rommedahl 5, Tomasson 33)*

Iceland: Arason; Steinsson, Sigurdsson I, Hreidarsson, Ingimarsson, Jonsson (Gunnarsson V 66), Gunnarsson B (Gislason 76), Arnason (Vidarsson 82), Gudjonsson J, Gudjohnsen E, Thorvaldsson.
Denmark: Sorensen T; Jacobsen, Gravgaard, Agger, Poulsen, Kahlenberg (Jensen C 82), Gravesen (JensenD 70), Kristiansen, Tomasson, Jorgensen (Helveg 90), Rommedahl.
Referee: Ivanov (Russia).

Belfast, 6 September 2006, 14,500
Northern Ireland (1) 3 *(Healy 20, 64, 80)*

Spain (1) 2 *(Xavi 14, David Villa 52)*

Northern Ireland: Carroll (Maik Taylor 12); Duff, Hughes A, Craigan, Evans, Gillespie, Clingan, Davis, Baird, Healy (Feeney 85), Lafferty (Quinn 54).
Spain: Casillas; Sergio Ramos (Michel Salgado 46), Puyol, Pablo, Antonio Lopez, Albelda (Fabregas 29), Xavi, Xabi Alonso, Fernando Torres (Luis Garcia 63), David Villa, Raul.
Referee: De Bleeckere (Belgium).

Gothenburg, 6 September 2006, 17,735
Sweden (1) 3 *(Allback 2, 69, Rosenberg 89)*

Liechtenstein (1) 1 *(Frick M 27)*

Sweden: Shaaban; Nilsson, Hansson, Lucic, Edman, Linderoth, Alexandersson, Kallstrom (Anders Svensson 57), Ljungberg, Allback, Elmander (Rosenberg 82).

Liechtenstein: Jehle; Hasler, Ritter, Maierhofer (D'Elia 89), Buchel M, Martin Stocklasa, Fischer (Buchel R 55), Frick D, Ritzberger, Beck T (Burgmeier 42), Frick M.
Referee: Banari (Moldova).

Copenhagen, 7 October 2006, 41,482
Denmark (0) 0 Northern Ireland (0) 0

Denmark: Sorensen (Christiansen 68); Jacobsen, Gravgaard, Agger, Jensen N (Bendtner 73), Jensen D, Poulsen, Kahlenberg, Tomasson, Jorgensen, Lovenkrands (Jensen C 55).
Northern Ireland: Taylor; Duff, Hughes, Craigan, Baird, Clingan (Johnson 56), Davis, Evans, Gillespie, Lafferty (Jones 63), Healy (Feeney 84).
Referee: Plautz (Austria).

Riga, 7 October 2006, 7500
Latvia (3) 4 *(Karlsons 14, Verpakovskis 15, 25, Visnakovs 52)*

Iceland (0) 0

Latvia: Kolinko; Stepanovs, Astafjevs, Zirnis, Laizans, Klava (Kacanovs 82), Smirnovs, Bleidelis (Visnakovs 46), Verpakovskis (Pahars 57), Solonicins, Karlsons.
Iceland: Arason; Steinsson, Sigurdsson K, Gislason, Ingimarsson, Sigurdsson H (Hallfredsson 71), Hreidarsson, Gunnarsson B, Gudjohnsen E, Gudjonsson J (Gunnarsson V 46), Arnason (Danielsson 42).
Referee: Kelly (Republic of Ireland).

Solna, 7 October 2006, 33,056
Sweden (1) 2 *(Elmander 10, Allback 82)* **Spain (0) 0**

Sweden: Shaaban; Nilsson, Mellberg, Hansson, Edman, Linderoth, Alexandersson, Ljungberg (Wilhelmsson 56), Anders Svensson (Kallstrom 75), Elmander (Andersson D 77), Allback.
Spain: Casillas; Sergio Ramos, Puyol, Juanito, Capdevila (Puerta 52), Albelda, Angulo (Luis Garcia 59), Fabregas (Iniesta 46), Xavi, David Villa, Fernando Torres.
Referee: Bennett (England).

Reykjavik, 11 October 2006, 8725
Iceland (1) 1 *(Vidarsson 6)*

Sweden (1) 2 *(Kallstrom 8, Wilhelmsson 59)*

Iceland: Arason; Ingimarsson, Steinsson, Hreidarsson, Sigurdsson K, Sigurdsson I (Jonsson 51), Gudjonsson J (Baldvinsson 81), Vidarsson, Hallfredsson, Sigurdsson H, Gudjohnsen E.
Sweden: Shaaban; Nilsson, Antonsson, Hansson, Edman, Alexandersson, Andersson D, Kallstrom, Wilhelmsson, Allback (Rosenberg 79), Elmander (Majstorovic 90).
Referee: Gilewski (Poland).

Vaduz, 11 October 2006, 2700
Liechtenstein (0) 0

Denmark (2) 4 *(Jensen D 29, Gravgaard 32, Tomasson 51, 64)*

Liechtenstein: Jehle; Telser, Hasler, Ritter, Martin Stocklasa, Fischer (D'Elia 80), Beck T, Frick M, Burgmeier (Frick D 62), Buchel M, Oehri.
Denmark: Christiansen; Poulsen, Gravgaard, Agger, Jensen N, Jacobsen, Jensen D (Sorensen D 46), Kahlenberg (Jensen C 64), Tomasson, Jorgensen, Rommedahl (Krohn-Dehli 78).
Referee: Richards (Wales).

Belfast, 11 October 2006, 14,500
Northern Ireland (1) 1 *(Healy 35)* **Latvia (0) 0**

Northern Ireland: Taylor; Baird, Evans, Craigan, Hughes, Davis, Gillespie, Johnson, Lafferty (Quinn 88), Healy (Feeney 90), Clingan.
Latvia: Kolinko; Stepanovs, Astafjevs, Zirnis, Laizans, Kacanovs, Solonicins (Visnakovs 85), Smirnovs (Gorkss 46), Verpakovskis (Kalnins 78), Karlsons, Pahars.
Referee: Fleischer (Germany).

Vaduz, 24 March 2007, 4340
Liechtenstein (0) 1 *(Burgmeier 89)*

Northern Ireland (0) 4 *(Healy 52, 75, 83, McCann 90)*

Liechtenstein: Jehle; Oehri (Telser 68), Martin Stocklasa, Ritter, Michael Stocklasa, Buchel M, Buchel R (Frick D 88), Burgmeier, Beck T, Frick M, Rohrer (Buchel S 84).
Northern Ireland: Taylor; Duff, Johnson, Evans, Hughes, Craigan, Brunt (McCann 68), Davis, Lafferty (Feeney 56), Healy (Jones 84), Gillespie.
Referee: Oriekhov (Ukraine).

Madrid, 24 March 2007, 80,000
Spain (2) 2 *(Morientes 34, David Villa 45)*

Denmark (0) 1 *(Gravgaard 49)*

Spain: Casillas; Javi Navarro, Marchena, Capdevila, Angel, Xavi (Xabi Alonso 60), Iniesta, Silva, Albelda, Morientes (Fernando Torres 64), David Villa (Angulo 76).
Denmark: Sorensen T; Agger, Gravgaard, Jacobsen, Jensen N■, Poulsen, Jensen D, Kahlenberg (Gronkjaer 60), Rommedahl, Jorgensen (Andreasen 38) (Bendtner 73), Tomasson.
Referee: Busacca (Switzerland).

Vaduz, 28 March 2007, 1680
Liechtenstein (1) 1 *(Frick M 17)* **Latvia (0) 0**

Liechtenstein: Jehle; Telser, Martin Stocklasa, Hasler, Michael Stocklasa, Buchel M, Buchel R, Burgmeier, Frick M, Beck T (Fischer 76), Rohrer (Buchel S 90).
Latvia: Kolinko; Kacanovs, Gorkss (Prohorenkovs 79), Stepanovs, Klava, Bleidelis, Morozs (Pereplyotkin 61), Laizans, Visnakovs, Verpakovskis (Karlsons 46), Pahars.
Referee: Gumienny (Belgium).

Belfast, 28 March 2007, 14,500
Northern Ireland (1) 2 *(Healy 31, 58)*

Sweden (1) 1 *(Elmander 26)*

Northern Ireland: Taylor; Duff, Hughes, Craigan, Evans, Johnson, McCann, Davis, Brunt (Sproule 90), Healy (Webb 89), Feeney (Lafferty 79).
Sweden: Isaksson; Nilsson, Mellberg (Majstorovic 69), Hansson, Edman, Alexandersson (Wilhelmsson 61), Andersson D, Anders Svensson (Kallstrom 46), Ljungberg, Ibrahimovic, Elmander.
Referee: Braamhaar (Holland).

Mallorca, 28 March 2007, 20,000
Spain (0) 1 *(Iniesta 80)* **Iceland (0) 0**

Spain: Casillas; Sergio Ramos, Marchena, Puyol, Capdevila (Angulo 46), Iniesta, Albelda (Xabi Alonso 78), Xavi, Silva, David Villa, Morientes (Fernando Torres 43).
Iceland: Arason; Sigurdsson K, Bjarnason, Ingimarsson, Gunnarsson G, Steinsson, Vidarsson (Sigurdsson H 83), Gunnarsson B, Hallfredsson (Sigurdsson I 74), Gunnarsson V (Gislason 56), Gudjonsen.
Referee: Duhamel (France).

Copenhagen, 2 June 2007, 42,083
Denmark (1) 3 *(Agger 34, Tomasson 62, Andreasen 75)*

Sweden (3) 3 *(Elmander 7, 26, Hansson 23)*

Denmark: Sorensen T; Gravgaard, Agger, Jacobsen, Poulsen■, Kristiansen (Andreasen 34), Jensen D (Gronkjaer 63), Kahlenberg (Bendtner 47), Rommedahl, Tomasson, Jorgensen.
Sweden: Isaksson; Nilsson, Mellberg, Hansson, Alexandersson, Wilhelmsson, Linderoth, Anders Svensson, Ljungberg, Allback (Bakircioglu 80), Elmander (Rosenberg 74).
Match abandoned 89 minutes; awarded to Sweden 3-0.
Referee: Fandel (Germany).

Reykjavik, 2 June 2007, 5139
Iceland (1) 1 *(Gunnarsson B 27)*

Liechtenstein (0) 1 *(Rohrer 69)*

Iceland: Arason; Steinsson, Sigurdsson K, Ingimarsson, Gunnarsson G, Gislason, Hallfredsson (Bjarnason 82), Gunnarsson B, Gudjohnsen E, Gunnarsson V (Sigurdsson H 72), Gudmundsson M (Saevarsson 70).
Liechtenstein: Jehle; Michael Stocklasa, Hasler, Martin Stocklasa, Buchel R, Beck T (Beck R 87), Frick M, Burgmeier (Frick D 78), Steuble, Rohrer, Ritzberger.
Referee: Kaldma (Estonia).

Riga, 2 June 2007, 8000
Latvia (0) 0 Spain (1) 2 *(David Villa 45, Xavi 60)*

Latvia: Kolinko; Zirnis, Ivanovs, Zakresevskis, Klava, Bleidelis (Pereplyotkin 86), Astafjevs, Laizans, Rubins (Solonicins 65), Verpakovskis, Karlsons (Cauna 89).

Spain: Casillas; Sergio Ramos, Puyol, Marchena, Capdevila, Angulo (Joaquin 46), Albelda (Xabi Alonso 67), Xavi, Iniesta, Luis Garcia (Soldado 55), David Villa.
Referee: Thomson (Scotland).

Riga, 6 June 2007, 7500
Latvia (0) 0 Denmark (2) 2 *(Rommedahl 15, 17)*
Latvia: Kolinko; Zirnis, Klava, Ivanovs, Stepanovs, Rubins (Cauna 75), Astafjevs, Laizans, Bleidelis (Solonicins 66), Verpakovskis, Karlsons (Pahars 61).
Denmark: Sorensen T; Jacobsen, Laursen, Agger, Jensen N, Jensen D, Jorgensen, Tomasson, Rommedahl (Kahlenberg 46), Bendtner (Wurtz 60), Gronkjaer.
Referee: Trefoloni (Italy).

Vaduz, 6 June 2007, 5739
Liechtenstein (0) 0 Spain (2) 2 *(David Villa 8, 14)*
Liechtenstein: Jehle; Michael Stocklasa (Telser 29), Hasler, Martin Stocklasa, Ritzberger, Buchel R, Burgmeier, Polverino, Rohrer (Frick D 59), Frick M, Beck T (Beck R 82).
Spain: Reina; Javi Navarro, Marchena, Sergio Ramos, Capdevila (Antonio Lopez 52), Xabi Alonso, Iniesta, Joaquin, Fabregas (Luis Garcia 67), Silva (Soldado 77), David Villa.
Referee: Ivanov (Russia).

Stockholm, 6 June 2007, 33,358
Sweden (3) 5 *(Allback 11, 51, Anders Svensson 42, Mellberg 45, Rosenberg 50)*
Iceland (0) 0
Sweden: Isaksson; Alexandersson, Mellberg, Hansson, Nilsson (Schlebrugge 57), Wilhelmsson, Linderoth (Andersson D 62), Anders Svensson, Ljungberg, Rosenberg, Allback (Ibrahimovic 73).
Iceland: Arason; Steinsson (Sigurdsson K 90), Gunnarsson G, Bjarnason O, Ingimarsson, Bjarnason T, Vidarsson, Hallfredsson (Jonsson H 53), Gunnarsson B, Sigurdsson H, Saevarsson (Gudmundsson M 65).
Referee: Hamer (Luxembourg).

Group F Table	P	W	D	L	F	A	Pts
Sweden	7	6	0	1	17	4	18
Spain	7	5	0	2	13	6	15
Northern Ireland	6	4	1	1	10	7	13
Denmark	6	3	1	2	9	5	10
Liechtenstein	7	1	1	5	4	18	4
Iceland	7	1	1	5	5	15	4
Latvia	6	1	0	5	4	7	3

GROUP G

Minsk, 2 September 2006, 23,000
Belarus (2) 2 *(Kalachev 2, Romashchenko 24)*
Albania (1) 2 *(Skela 7 (pen), Hasi 86)*
Belarus: Khomutovski; Kulchi, Korytko, Omelyanchuk, Shtaniuk, Hleb V (Bulyga 64), Kalachev (Lanko 84), Kovba, Romashchenko, Hleb A, Kutuzov.
Albania: Lika; Dallku, Hasi, Aliaj (Curri 46), Beqiri, Haxhi, Lala (Mukaj 84), Cana, Skela (Kapllani 73), Tare, Bogdani.
Referee: Asumaa (Finland).

Luxembourg, 2 September 2006, 8000
Luxembourg (0) 0 Holland (1) 1 *(Mathijsen 18)*
Luxembourg: Joubert; Strasser, Hoffmann, Reiter, Kintziger, Bettmer, Joachim, Lombardelli (Federspiel 83), Mutsch, Remy, Ferreira (Huss 88).
Holland: Van der Sar; Heitinga, Ooijer (Emanuelson 46), Mathijsen, De Cler, Schaars (Vennegoor of Hesselink 46), Janssen, Landzaat, Huntelaar, Van Persie (Babel 77), Kuyt.
Referee: Ferreira (Portugal).

Constanta, 2 September 2006, 15,000
Romania (1) 2 *(Rosu 40, Marica 55)*
Bulgaria (0) 2 *(Petrov M 82, 84)*
Romania: Lobont; Contra, Rat, Tamas■, Chivu, Codrea, Petre (Nicolita 71), Dica (Cocis 59), Marica, Mutu, Rosu (Marin 79).
Bulgaria: Petkov G; Tunchev, Angelov S, Topuzakov, Vagner, Petrov S, Kishishev (Yankov 47), Petrov M, Jankovic, Berbatov (Bozhinov 62), Peev (Georgiev 47).
Referee: Farina (Italy).

Tirana, 6 September 2006, 10,000
Albania (0) 0 Romania (0) 2 *(Dica 65, Mutu 75 (pen))*
Albania: Beqaj; Beqiri, Dallku, Cana, Hasi, Skela (Aliaj 64), Lala (Mukaj 78), Tare, Bogdani (Kastrati 62), Haxhi, Curri.
Romania: Lobont; Contra, Rat, Ghionea, Chivu, Codrea, Petre, Dica, Marica (Ganea 78), Mutu (Nicolita 85), Rosu (Margaritescu 89).
Referee: Benquerenca (Portugal).

Sofia, 6 September 2006, 16,543
Bulgaria (0) 3 *(Bozhinov 58, Petrov M 72, Telkiyski 81)*
Slovenia (0) 0
Bulgaria: Ivankov; Angelov S, Vagner, Tunchev, Topuzakov, Petrov S, Yankov, Georgiev (Telkiyski 53), Petrov M, Bozhinov (Yovov 60), Jankovic (Kishishev 69).
Slovenia: Mavric B; Ilic, Knavs, Jokic, Cesar, Zlogar, Koren (Lavric 76), Komac, Acimovic, Birsa (Semler 80), Novakovic.
Referee: Larsen (Denmark).

Eindhoven, 6 September 2006, 30,089
Holland (1) 3 *(Van Persie 33, 78, Kuyt 90)* **Belarus (0) 0**
Holland: Van der Sar; Heitinga (Boulahrouz 67), Ooijer, Mathijsen, Van Bronckhorst, De Jong, Sneijder, Landzaat (Schaars 68), Huntelaar (Babel 76), Van Persie, Kuyt.
Belarus: Khomutovski; Yurevich, Shtaniuk, Omelyanchuk, Lentsevich, Kalachev (Lanko 73), Kovba, Korytko (Strakhanovich 46), Romashchenko (Kontsevoy 69), Hleb A, Kornilenko.
Referee: Webb (England).

Sofia, 7 October 2006, 30,547
Bulgaria (1) 1 *(Petrov M 12)* **Holland (0) 1** *(Van Persie 62)*
Bulgaria: Ivankov; Angelov S, Gargorov, Iliev, Vagner, Kishishev, Yankov (Jankovic 82), Yovov (Telkiyski 54), Petrov S, Petrov M (Bozhinov 64), Berbatov.
Holland: Van der Sar; Boulahrouz, Ooijer, Mathijsen, Van Bronckhorst, De Jong, Landzaat, Sneijder (Schaars 90), Van Persie, Kuyt (Babel 16), Robben.
Referee: Ovrebo (Norway).

Bucharest, 7 October 2006, 12,000
Romania (2) 3 *(Mutu 7, Marica 10, Goian 76)*
Belarus (1) 1 *(Kornilenko 20)*
Romania: Coman; Rat, Tamas, Chivu, Petre, Marica (Niculescu 90), Mutu (Buga 72), Rosu, Goian, Marin, Dica (Cocis 88).
Belarus: Gayev; Kulchi (Strakhanovich 65), Lentsevich, Omelyanchuk, Shtaniuk, Kalachev (Hleb V 50), Hleb A, Gurenko, Romashchenko, Kornilenko (Korytko 66), Yurevich.
Referee: Mallenco (Spain).

Celje, 7 October 2006, 3500
Slovenia (2) 2 *(Novakovic 30, Koren 44)*
Luxembourg (0) 0
Slovenia: Mavric B; Ilic, Mavric M, Cesar, Jokic, Ceh, Acimovic (Komac 75), Birsa, Koren, Novakovic, Lavric (Burgic 85).
Luxembourg: Joubert (Gillet 72); Kintziger, Hoffmann, Reiter, Peters, Strasser, Bettmer, Joachim (Huss 66), Lombardelli (Leweck C 42), Remy, Mutsch.
Referee: Kallis (Cyprus).

Minsk, 11 October 2006, 23,000
Belarus (1) 4 *(Kovba 18, Kornilenko 52, 60, Korytko 85)*
Slovenia (2) 2 *(Cesar 19, Lavric 43)*
Belarus: Gayev; Omelyanchuk, Shtaniuk, Gurenko, Kulchi, Kovba, Kalachev, Romashchenko (Korytko 50), Hleb A, Hleb V (Strakhanovich 69), Kornilenko (Kontsevoy 90).
Slovenia: Mavric B; Ilic, Jokic, Cesar, Mavric M, Koren, Acimovic (Komac 70), Zlogar, Birsa, Novakovic (Burgic 82), Lavric.
Referee: Kassai (Hungary).

Amsterdam, 11 October 2006, 40,000
Holland (2) 2 *(Van Persie 15, Beqaj 42 (og))*
Albania (0) 1 *(Curri 67)*
Holland: Van der Sar; Boulahrouz, Ooijer, Mathijsen, Van Bronckhorst (Emanuelson 68), De Jong (Schaars 50), Sneijder (De Cler 80), Landzaat, Babel, Van Persie, Robben.
Albania: Beqaj; Dede, Dallku, Aliaj (Murati 65), Hasi, Haxhi, Curri, Skela, Lala (Mukaj 46), Tare, Bogdani (Berisha 79).
Referee: Yefet (Israel).

Luxembourg, 11 October 2006, 3156
Luxembourg (0) 0
Bulgaria (1) 1 *(Tunchev 26)*
Luxembourg: Gillet; Reiter, Strasser, Kintziger, Peters (Payal 61), Bettmer, Mutsch, Remy, Joachim (Huss 52), Lombardelli (Leweck C 69), Ferreira.
Bulgaria: Ivankov; Angelov S, Tunchev, Topuzakov, Vagner, Yankov (Kishishev 77), Lazarov (Yovov 46), Petrov S, Telkiyski, Bozhinov (Jankovic 68), Berbatov.
Referee: Panic (Bosnia).

Shkoder, 24 March 2007, 12,000
Albania (0) 0 Slovenia (0) 0
Albania: Beqai; Dallku, Beqiri, Dede, Cana, Haxhi, Lala, Duro, Mukaj (Berisha 86), Kapllani (Bushi 58), Bogdani (Salihi 89).
Slovenia: Handanovic S; Mavric M, Jokic, Cesar, Ilic, Koren, Zlogar, Komac (Cipot 90), Ceh (Acimovic 80), Lavric, Rakovic (Birsa 63).
Referee: Attard (Malta).

Rotterdam, 24 March 2007, 49,000
Holland (0) 0 Romania (0) 0
Holland: Stekelenburg; Jaliens, Bouma, Mathijsen, Van Bronckhorst, Landzaat (Emanuelson 79), Sneijder, Babel, Van der Vaart (Seedorf 86), Huntelaar, Robben.
Romania: Lobont; Contra, Goian, Tamas, Rat (Radu 78), Cocis, Nicolita, Radoi, Codrea (Rosu 87), Marica (Niculae 64), Mutu.
Referee: Merk (Germany).

Luxembourg, 24 March 2007, 2000
Luxembourg (0) 1 *(Sagramola 68)*
Belarus (1) 2 *(Kalachev 25, Kutuzov 54)*
Luxembourg: Joubert; Strasser, Hoffmann, Reiter, Kintziger, Peters, Bettmer, Payal (Ferreira 67), Lombardelli (Bigard 58), Remy, Collette (Sagramola 64).
Belarus: Zhevnov; Yurevich, Shtaniuk, Kulchi, Korytko, Strakhanovich (Chelyadinski 58), Hleb A, Kalachev, Hleb V, Kornilenko (Bliznyuk 74), Kutuzov (Radkov 80).
Referee: Whitby (Wales).

Sofia, 28 March 2007, 25,000
Bulgaria (0) 0 Albania (0) 0
Bulgaria: Ivankov; Kishishev, Tunchev, Tomasic, Vagner, Yankov, Petrov S, Peev (Bozhinov 65), Yovov (Telkiyski 46), Jankovic (Todorov 46), Berbatov.
Albania: Beqaj; Dallku, Dede, Beqiri, Curri, Lala, Duro (Bulku 68), Haxhi (Kapllani 54), Cana, Berisha (Bushaj 79), Bogdani.
Referee: Eriksson (Sweden).

Piatra Neamt, 28 March 2007, 12,000
Romania (1) 3 *(Mutu 26, Contra 56, Marica 90)*
Luxembourg (0) 0
Romania: Lobont; Contra, Tamas (Stoica 87), Goian, Radu, Radoi, Zicu, Rosu (Cristea 53), Cocis, Niculae (Marica 65), Mutu.
Luxembourg: Joubert; Strasser, Bigard, Hoffmann, Reiter, Peters, Bettmer (Payal 50), Lombardelli (Ferreira 81), Remy, Mutsch, Collette (Sagramola 49).
Referee: Lajuks (Latvia).

Celje, 28 March 2007, 9500
Slovenia (0) 0 Holland (0) 1 *(Van Bronckhorst 86)*
Slovenia: Handanovic S; Ilic, Jokic, Mavric M, Cesar, Ceh, Komac, Koren, Acimovic (Sukalo 61), Lavric (Birsa 83), Rakovic (Novakovic 65).
Holland: Van der Sar; Heitinga (De Zeeuw 74), Mathijsen, Bouma, Emanuelson, Afellay (Seedorf 85), Babel (Koevermans 73), Van Bronckhorst, Kuyt, Sneijder, Robben.
Referee: Gonzalez (Spain).

Tirana, 2 June 2007, 3000
Albania (1) 2 *(Kapllani 38, Haxhi 57)*
Luxembourg (0) 0
Albania: Beqaj; Curri, Dallku, Dede, Skela, Cana, Haxhi (Vangaeli 74), Duro, Berisha (Mukaj 46), Bushaj (Salihi 76), Kapllani.
Luxembourg: Joubert; Kinziger, Bigard (Da Mota 60), Hoffmann, Peters, Strasser, Bettmer, Payal (Ferreira 82), Collette (Sagramola 69), Remy, Mutsch.
Referee: Silagava (Georgia).

Minsk, 2 June 2007, 29,000
Belarus (0) 0
Bulgaria (1) 2 *(Berbatov 28, 46)*
Belarus: Zhevnov; Omelyanchuk (Strakhanovich 72), Shtaniuk, Tigorev, Kulchi, Kalachev, Korytko, Kovba, Hleb A, Kornilenko (Vasilyuk 59), Kutuzov (Hleb V 46).
Bulgaria: Ivankov; Tunchev, Tomasic, Angelov S (Domovchiyski 90), Vagner, Telkiyski, Kishishev, Petrov S, Yovov (Manchev 80), Petrov M (Genkov 90), Berbatov.
Referee: Jara (Czech Republic).

Celje, 2 June 2007, 6000
Slovenia (0) 1 *(Vrsic 90)*
Romania (0) 2 *(Tamas 52, Nicolita 69)*
Slovenia: Handanovic; Ilic, Mavric M, Cesar■, Jokic, Sukalo (Vrsic 83), Komac, Ceh, Koren (Birsa 52), Rakovic (Novakovic 61), Lavric.
Romania: Lobont; Contra, Tamas, Chivu, Rat, Nicolita, Codrea, Rosu (Zicu 63), Stoica (Niculae■ 74), Marica (Muresan 78), Mutu.
Referee: Dougal (Scotland).

Sofia, 6 June 2007, 10,227
Bulgaria (2) 2 *(Petrov M 10, Yankov 40)*
Belarus (1) 1 *(Vasilyuk 5 (pen))*
Bulgaria: Ivankov; Kishishev, Tunchev, Tomasic, Vagner, Yankov (Sirakov 90), Petrov S, Telkiyski, Yovov (Angelov S 68), Berbatov, Petrov M (Manchev 84).
Belarus: Zhevnov; Shtaniuk, Radkov, Tigorev, Yurevich, Kalachev (Kutuzov 44), Korytko, Kovba, Hleb A, Strakhanovich (Hleb V 64), Vasilyuk (Kornilenko 55).
Referee: Jakobsson (Iceland).

Luxembourg, 6 June 2007, 4325
Luxembourg (0) 0
Albania (2) 3 *(Skela 25, Kapllani 36, 72)*
Luxembourg: Joubert; Strasser, Bigard (Lombardelli 46), Hoffmann, Kintziger, Payal (Da Mota 64), Peters, Bettmer, Remy, Mutsch, Collette (Sagramola 79).
Albania: Beqaj; Dede, Haxhi, Dallku, Curri, Skela (Duro 60), Cana, Mukaj (Xhafaj 77), Kapllani, Bushaj (Berisha 67), Bogdani.
Referee: Malzinskas (Latvia).

Timisoara, 6 June 2007, 22,000
Romania (1) 2 *(Mutu 40, Contra 70)*
Slovenia (0) 0
Romania: Lobont; Rat, Tamas, Goian, Contra, Zicu (Rosu 60), Chivu, Codrea (Plesan 78), Petre (Nicolita 75), Marica, Mutu.
Slovenia: Handanovic S; Mavric M, Morec, Jokic (Filekovic 84), Ilic, Ceh, Komac, Vrsic, Zlogar (Sukalo 77), Lavric, Birsa (Novakovic 54).
Referee: Yefet (Israel).

Group G Table	*P*	*W*	*D*	*L*	*F*	*A*	*Pts*
Romania	7	5	2	0	14	4	17
Bulgaria	7	4	3	0	11	4	15
Holland	6	4	2	0	8	2	14
Albania	7	2	3	2	8	6	9
Belarus	7	2	1	4	10	15	7
Slovenia	7	1	1	5	5	12	4
Luxembourg	7	0	0	7	1	14	0

EURO 2008 QUALIFYING COMPETITION

(Remaining fixtures)

Top two from each group qualify for finals; Austria and Switzerland qualify as co-hosts. Final Tournament 7 to 29 June 2008.

GROUP A

22.08.07 Armenia v Portugal; Belgium v Serbia & Montenegro; Finland v Kazakhstan
08.09.07 Azerbaijan v Armenia; Portugal v Poland; Serbia & Montengro v Finland
12.09.07 Armenia v Azerbaijan; Finland v Poland; Kazakhstan v Belgium
21.09.07 Portugal v Serbia & Montenegro
13.10.07 Armenia v Serbia & Montenegro; Azerbaijan v Portugal; Belgium v Finland; Poland v Kazakhstan
17.10.07 Azerbaijan v Serbia & Montenegro; Belgium v Armenia; Kazakhstan v Poland
17.11.07 Finland v Azerbaijan; Poland v Belgium; Portugal v Armenia; Serbia & Montenegro v Kazakhstan
21.11.07 Armenia v Kazakhstan; Azerbaijan v Belgium; Portugal v Finland; Serbia & Montenegro v Poland

GROUP B

22.08.07 Faeroes v Ukraine
08.09.07 Georgia v Ukraine; Italy v France; Scotland v Lithuania
12.09.07 France v Scotland; Lithuania v Faeroes; Ukraine v Italy
13.10.07 Faeroes v France; Italy v Georgia; Scotland v Ukraine
17.10.07 France v Lithuania; Scotland v Georgia; Ukraine v Faeroes
17.11.07 Lithuania v Ukraine; Scotland v Italy
21.11.07 Georgia v Lithuania; Italy v Faeroes; Ukraine v France

GROUP C

08.09.07 Hungary v Bosnia; Malta v Turkey; Moldova v Norway
12.09.07 Bosnia v Moldova; Norway v Greece; Turkey v Hungary
13.10.07 Greece v Bosnia; Hungary v Malta; Moldova v Turkey
17.10.07 Bosnia v Norway; Malta v Moldova; Turkey v Greece
17.11.07 Greece v Malta; Moldova v Hungary; Norway v Turkey
21.11.07 Hungary v Greece; Malta v Norway; Turkey v Bosnia

GROUP D

22.08.07 San Marino v Cyprus
08.09.07 San Marino v Czech Republic; Slovakia v Republic of Ireland; Wales v Germany
12.09.07 Cyprus v San Marino; Czech Republic v Republic of Ireland; Slovakia v Wales
13.10.07 Cyprus v Wales; Republic of Ireland v Germany; Slovakia v San Marino
17.10.07 Germany v Czech Republic; Republic of Ireland v Cyprus; San Marino v Wales
17.11.07 Czech Republic v Slovakia; Germany v Cyprus; Wales v Republic of Ireland
21.11.07 Cyprus v Czech Republic; Germany v Wales; San Marino v Slovakia

GROUP E

22.08.07 Estonia v Andorra
08.09.07 Croatia v Estonia; England v Israel; Russia v Macedonia
12.09.07 Andorra v Croatia; England v Russia; Macedonia v Estonia
13.10.07 England v Estonia
17.10.07 Croatia v Russia; Macedonia v Andorra; Russia v England
17.11.07 Andorra v Estonia; Israel v Russia; Macedonia v Croatia
21.11.07 Andorra v Russia; England v Croatia; Israel v Macedonia

GROUP F

22.08.07 Northern Ireland v Liechtenstein
08.09.07 Iceland v Spain; Latvia v Northern Ireland; Sweden v Denmark
12.09.07 Denmark v Liechtenstein; Iceland v Northern Ireland; Spain v Latvia
13.10.07 Denmark v Spain; Iceland v Latvia; Liechtenstein v Sweden
17.10.07 Denmark v Latvia; Liechtenstein v Iceland; Sweden v Northern Ireland
17.11.07 Latvia v Liechtenstein; Northern Ireland v Denmark; Spain v Sweden
21.11.07 Denmark v Iceland; Spain v Northern Ireland; Sweden v Latvia

GROUP G

08.09.07 Belarus v Romania; Luxembourg v Slovenia; Holland v Bulgaria
12.09.07 Albania v Holland; Bulgaria v Luxembourg; Slovenia v Belarus
13.10.07 Belarus v Luxembourg; Romania v Holland; Slovenia v Albania
17.10.07 Albania v Bulgaria; Luxembourg v Romania; Holland v Slovenia
17.11.07 Albania v Belarus; Bulgaria v Romania; Holland v Luxembourg
21.11.07 Belarus v Holland; Romania v Albania; Slovenia v Bulgaria

Peter Crouch heads home England's second goal in the Euro 2008 qualifier against Estonia in Tallinn.
(Adam Davy/EMPICS Sport/PA Photos)

BRITISH AND IRISH INTERNATIONAL RESULTS 1872–2007

Note: In the results that follow, WC=World Cup, EC=European Championship, UI=Umbro International Trophy. TF = Tournoi de France. For Ireland, read Northern Ireland from 1921. *After extra time.

ENGLAND v SCOTLAND

Played: 110; England won 45, Scotland won 41, Drawn 24. Goals: England 192, Scotland 169.

			E	*S*
1872	30 Nov	Glasgow	0	0
1873	8 Mar	Kennington Oval	4	2
1874	7 Mar	Glasgow	1	2
1875	6 Mar	Kennington Oval	2	2
1876	4 Mar	Glasgow	0	3
1877	3 Mar	Kennington Oval	1	3
1878	2 Mar	Glasgow	2	7
1879	5 Apr	Kennington Oval	5	4
1880	13 Mar	Glasgow	4	5
1881	12 Mar	Kennington Oval	1	6
1882	11 Mar	Glasgow	1	5
1883	10 Mar	Sheffield	2	3
1884	15 Mar	Glasgow	0	1
1885	21 Mar	Kennington Oval	1	1
1886	31 Mar	Glasgow	1	1
1887	19 Mar	Blackburn	2	3
1888	17 Mar	Glasgow	5	0
1889	13 Apr	Kennington Oval	2	3
1890	5 Apr	Glasgow	1	1
1891	6 Apr	Blackburn	2	1
1892	2 Apr	Glasgow	4	1
1893	1 Apr	Richmond	5	2
1894	7 Apr	Glasgow	2	2
1895	6 Apr	Everton	3	0
1896	4 Apr	Glasgow	1	2
1897	3 Apr	Crystal Palace	1	2
1898	2 Apr	Glasgow	3	1
1899	8 Apr	Birmingham	2	1
1900	7 Apr	Glasgow	1	4
1901	30 Mar	Crystal Palace	2	2
1902	3 Mar	Birmingham	2	2
1903	4 Apr	Sheffield	1	2
1904	9 Apr	Glasgow	1	0
1905	1 Apr	Crystal Palace	1	0
1906	7 Apr	Glasgow	1	2
1907	6 Apr	Newcastle	1	1
1908	4 Apr	Glasgow	1	1
1909	3 Apr	Crystal Palace	2	0
1910	2 Apr	Glasgow	0	2
1911	1 Apr	Everton	1	1
1912	23 Mar	Glasgow	1	1
1913	5 Apr	Chelsea	1	0
1914	14 Apr	Glasgow	1	3
1920	10 Apr	Sheffield	5	4
1921	9 Apr	Glasgow	0	3
1922	8 Apr	Aston Villa	0	1
1923	14 Apr	Glasgow	2	2
1924	12 Apr	Wembley	1	1
1925	4 Apr	Glasgow	0	2
1926	17 Apr	Manchester	0	1
1927	2 Apr	Glasgow	2	1
1928	31 Mar	Wembley	1	5
1929	13 Apr	Glasgow	0	1
1930	5 Apr	Wembley	5	2
1931	28 Mar	Glasgow	0	2
1932	9 Apr	Wembley	3	0
1933	1 Apr	Glasgow	1	2
1934	14 Apr	Wembley	3	0
1935	6 Apr	Glasgow	0	2
1936	4 Apr	Wembley	1	1
1937	17 Apr	Glasgow	1	3
1938	9 Apr	Wembley	0	1
1939	15 Apr	Glasgow	2	1
1947	12 Apr	Wembley	1	1
1948	10 Apr	Glasgow	2	0
1949	9 Apr	Wembley	1	3
WC1950	15 Apr	Glasgow	1	0
1951	14 Apr	Wembley	2	3
1952	5 Apr	Glasgow	2	1
1953	18 Apr	Wembley	2	2
WC1954	3 Apr	Glasgow	4	2
1955	2 Apr	Wembley	7	2
1956	14 Apr	Glasgow	1	1
1957	6 Apr	Wembley	2	1
1958	19 Apr	Glasgow	4	0
1959	11 Apr	Wembley	1	0
1960	9 Apr	Glasgow	1	1
1961	15 Apr	Wembley	9	3
1962	14 Apr	Glasgow	0	2
1963	6 Apr	Wembley	1	2
1964	11 Apr	Glasgow	0	1
1965	10 Apr	Wembley	2	2
1966	2 Apr	Glasgow	4	3
EC1967	15 Apr	Wembley	2	3
EC1968	24 Jan	Glasgow	1	1
1969	10 May	Wembley	4	1
1970	25 Apr	Glasgow	0	0
1971	22 May	Wembley	3	1
1972	27 May	Glasgow	1	0
1973	14 Feb	Glasgow	5	0
1973	19 May	Wembley	1	0
1974	18 May	Glasgow	0	2
1975	24 May	Wembley	5	1
1976	15 May	Glasgow	1	2
1977	4 June	Wembley	1	2
1978	20 May	Glasgow	1	0
1979	26 May	Wembley	3	1
1980	24 May	Glasgow	2	0
1981	23 May	Wembley	0	1
1982	29 May	Glasgow	1	0
1983	1 June	Wembley	2	0
1984	26 May	Glasgow	1	1
1985	25 May	Glasgow	0	1
1986	23 Apr	Wembley	2	1
1987	23 May	Glasgow	0	0
1988	21 May	Wembley	1	0
1989	27 May	Glasgow	2	0
EC1996	15 June	Wembley	2	0
EC1999	13 Nov	Glasgow	2	0
EC1999	17 Nov	Wembley	0	1

ENGLAND v WALES

Played: 99; England won 64, Wales won 14, Drawn 21. Goals: England 242, Wales 90.

			E	*W*
1879	18 Jan	Kennington Oval	2	1
1880	15 Mar	Wrexham	3	2
1881	26 Feb	Blackburn	0	1
1882	13 Mar	Wrexham	3	5
1883	3 Feb	Kennington Oval	5	0
1884	17 Mar	Wrexham	4	0

			E	*W*
1885	14 Mar	Blackburn	1	1
1886	29 Mar	Wrexham	3	1
1887	26 Feb	Kennington Oval	4	0
1888	4 Feb	Crewe	5	1
1889	23 Feb	Stoke	4	1
1890	15 Mar	Wrexham	3	1
1891	7 May	Sunderland	4	1
1892	5 Mar	Wrexham	2	0
1893	13 Mar	Stoke	6	0
1894	12 Mar	Wrexham	5	1
1895	18 Mar	Queen's Club, Kensington	1	1
1896	16 Mar	Cardiff	9	1
1897	29 Mar	Sheffield	4	0
1898	28 Mar	Wrexham	3	0
1899	20 Mar	Bristol	4	0
1900	26 Mar	Cardiff	1	1
1901	18 Mar	Newcastle	6	0
1902	3 Mar	Wrexham	0	0
1903	2 Mar	Portsmouth	2	1
1904	29 Feb	Wrexham	2	2
1905	27 Mar	Liverpool	3	1
1906	19 Mar	Cardiff	1	0
1907	18 Mar	Fulham	1	1
1908	16 Mar	Wrexham	7	1
1909	15 Mar	Nottingham	2	0
1910	14 Mar	Cardiff	1	0
1911	13 Mar	Millwall	3	0
1912	11 Mar	Wrexham	2	0
1913	17 Mar	Bristol	4	3
1914	16 Mar	Cardiff	2	0
1920	15 Mar	Highbury	1	2
1921	14 Mar	Cardiff	0	0
1922	13 Mar	Liverpool	1	0
1923	5 Mar	Cardiff	2	2
1924	3 Mar	Blackburn	1	2
1925	28 Feb	Swansea	2	1
1926	1 Mar	Crystal Palace	1	3
1927	12 Feb	Wrexham	3	3
1927	28 Nov	Burnley	1	2
1928	17 Nov	Swansea	3	2
1929	20 Nov	Chelsea	6	0
1930	22 Nov	Wrexham	4	0
1931	18 Nov	Liverpool	3	1
1932	16 Nov	Wrexham	0	0
1933	15 Nov	Newcastle	1	2
1934	29 Sept	Cardiff	4	0
1936	5 Feb	Wolverhampton	1	2
1936	17 Oct	Cardiff	1	2
1937	17 Nov	Middlesbrough	2	1
1938	22 Oct	Cardiff	2	4
1946	13 Nov	Manchester	3	0
1947	18 Oct	Cardiff	3	0
1948	10 Nov	Aston Villa	1	0
WC1949	15 Oct	Cardiff	4	1
1950	15 Nov	Sunderland	4	2
1951	20 Oct	Cardiff	1	1
1952	12 Nov	Wembley	5	2
WC1953	10 Oct	Cardiff	4	1
1954	10 Nov	Wembley	3	2
1955	27 Oct	Cardiff	1	2
1956	14 Nov	Wembley	3	1
1957	19 Oct	Cardiff	4	0
1958	26 Nov	Aston Villa	2	2
1959	17 Oct	Cardiff	1	1
1960	23 Nov	Wembley	5	1
1961	14 Oct	Cardiff	1	1
1962	21 Oct	Wembley	4	0
1963	12 Oct	Cardiff	4	0
1964	18 Nov	Wembley	2	1
1965	2 Oct	Cardiff	0	0
EC1966	16 Nov	Wembley	5	1
EC1967	21 Oct	Cardiff	3	0
1969	7 May	Wembley	2	1
1970	18 Apr	Cardiff	1	1
1971	19 May	Wembley	0	0
1972	20 May	Cardiff	3	0
WC1972	15 Nov	Cardiff	1	0
WC1973	24 Jan	Wembley	1	1
1973	15 May	Wembley	3	0
1974	11 May	Cardiff	2	0
1975	21 May	Wembley	2	2
1976	24 Mar	Wrexham	2	1
1976	8 May	Cardiff	1	0
1977	31 May	Wembley	0	1
1978	3 May	Cardiff	3	1
1979	23 May	Wembley	0	0
1980	17 May	Wrexham	1	4
1981	20 May	Wembley	0	0
1982	27 Apr	Cardiff	1	0
1983	23 Feb	Wembley	2	1
1984	2 May	Wrexham	0	1
WC2004	9 Oct	Old Trafford	2	0
WC2005	3 Sept	Cardiff	1	0

ENGLAND v IRELAND

Played: 98; England won 75, Ireland won 7, Drawn 16. Goals: England 323, Ireland 81.

			E	*I*
1882	18 Feb	Belfast	13	0
1883	24 Feb	Liverpool	7	0
1884	23 Feb	Belfast	8	1
1885	28 Feb	Manchester	4	0
1886	13 Mar	Belfast	6	1
1887	5 Feb	Sheffield	7	0
1888	31 Mar	Belfast	5	1
1889	2 Mar	Everton	6	1
1890	15 Mar	Belfast	9	1
1891	7 Mar	Wolverhampton	6	1
1892	5 Mar	Belfast	2	0
1893	25 Feb	Birmingham	6	1
1894	3 Mar	Belfast	2	2
1895	9 Mar	Derby	9	0
1896	7 Mar	Belfast	2	0
1897	20 Feb	Nottingham	6	0
1898	5 Mar	Belfast	3	2
1899	18 Feb	Sunderland	13	2
1900	17 Mar	Dublin	2	0
1901	9 Mar	Southampton	3	0
1902	22 Mar	Belfast	1	0
1903	14 Feb	Wolverhampton	4	0
1904	12 Mar	Belfast	3	1
1905	25 Feb	Middlesbrough	1	1
1906	17 Feb	Belfast	5	0
1907	16 Feb	Everton	1	0
1908	15 Feb	Belfast	3	1
1909	13 Feb	Bradford	4	0
1910	12 Feb	Belfast	1	1
1911	11 Feb	Derby	2	1
1912	10 Feb	Dublin	6	1
1913	15 Feb	Belfast	1	2
1914	14 Feb	Middlesbrough	0	3
1919	25 Oct	Belfast	1	1
1920	23 Oct	Sunderland	2	0
1921	22 Oct	Belfast	1	1
1922	21 Oct	West Bromwich	2	0
1923	20 Oct	Belfast	1	2
1924	22 Oct	Everton	3	1
1925	24 Oct	Belfast	0	0
1926	20 Oct	Liverpool	3	3
1927	22 Oct	Belfast	0	2

			E	I
1928	22 Oct	Everton	2	1
1929	19 Oct	Belfast	3	0
1930	20 Oct	Sheffield	5	1
1931	17 Oct	Belfast	6	2
1932	17 Oct	Blackpool	1	0
1933	14 Oct	Belfast	3	0
1935	6 Feb	Everton	2	1
1935	19 Oct	Belfast	3	1
1936	18 Nov	Stoke	3	1
1937	23 Oct	Belfast	5	1
1938	16 Nov	Manchester	7	0
1946	28 Sept	Belfast	7	2
1947	5 Nov	Everton	2	2
1948	9 Oct	Belfast	6	2
wc1949	16 Nov	Manchester	9	2
1950	7 Oct	Belfast	4	1
1951	14 Nov	Aston Villa	2	0
1952	4 Oct	Belfast	2	2
wc1953	11 Nov	Everton	3	1
1954	2 Oct	Belfast	2	0
1955	2 Nov	Wembley	3	0
1956	10 Oct	Belfast	1	1
1957	6 Nov	Wembley	2	3
1958	4 Oct	Belfast	3	3
1959	18 Nov	Wembley	2	1
1960	8 Oct	Belfast	5	2
1961	22 Nov	Wembley	1	1
1962	20 Oct	Belfast	3	1
1963	20 Nov	Wembley	8	3
1964	3 Oct	Belfast	4	3
1965	10 Nov	Wembley	2	1
EC1966	20 Oct	Belfast	2	0
EC1967	22 Nov	Wembley	2	0
1969	3 May	Belfast	3	1
1970	21 Apr	Wembley	3	1
1971	15 May	Belfast	1	0
1972	23 May	Wembley	0	1
1973	12 May	Everton	2	1
1974	15 May	Wembley	1	0
1975	17 May	Belfast	0	0
1976	11 May	Wembley	4	0
1977	28 May	Belfast	2	1
1978	16 May	Wembley	1	0
EC1979	7 Feb	Wembley	4	0
1979	19 May	Belfast	2	0
EC1979	17 Oct	Belfast	5	1
1980	20 May	Wembley	1	1
1982	23 Feb	Wembley	4	0
1983	28 May	Belfast	0	0
1984	24 Apr	Wembley	1	0
wc1985	27 Feb	Belfast	1	0
wc1985	13 Nov	Wembley	0	0
EC1986	15 Oct	Wembley	3	0
EC1987	1 Apr	Belfast	2	0
wc2005	26 Mar	Old Trafford	4	0
wc2005	7 Sept	Belfast	0	1

SCOTLAND v WALES

Played: 103; Scotland won 60, Wales won 20, Drawn 23. Goals: Scotland 238, Wales 116.

			S	W
1876	25 Mar	Glasgow	4	0
1877	5 Mar	Wrexham	2	0
1878	23 Mar	Glasgow	9	0
1879	7 Apr	Wrexham	3	0
1880	3 Apr	Glasgow	5	1
1881	14 Mar	Wrexham	5	1
1882	25 Mar	Glasgow	5	0
1883	12 Mar	Wrexham	3	0
1884	29 Mar	Glasgow	4	1
1885	23 Mar	Wrexham	8	1
1886	10 Apr	Glasgow	4	1
1887	21 Mar	Wrexham	2	0
1888	10 Mar	Edinburgh	5	1
1889	15 Apr	Wrexham	0	0
1890	22 Mar	Paisley	5	0
1891	21 Mar	Wrexham	4	3
1892	26 Mar	Edinburgh	6	1
1893	18 Mar	Wrexham	8	0
1894	24 Mar	Kilmarnock	5	2
1895	23 Mar	Wrexham	2	2
1896	21 Mar	Dundee	4	0
1897	20 Mar	Wrexham	2	2
1898	19 Mar	Motherwell	5	2
1899	18 Mar	Wrexham	6	0
1900	3 Feb	Aberdeen	5	2
1901	2 Mar	Wrexham	1	1
1902	15 Mar	Greenock	5	1
1903	9 Mar	Cardiff	1	0
1904	12 Mar	Dundee	1	1
1905	6 Mar	Wrexham	1	3
1906	3 Mar	Edinburgh	0	2
1907	4 Mar	Wrexham	0	1
1908	7 Mar	Dundee	2	1
1909	1 Mar	Wrexham	2	3
1910	5 Mar	Kilmarnock	1	0
1911	6 Mar	Cardiff	2	2
1912	2 Mar	Tynecastle	1	0
1913	3 Mar	Wrexham	0	0
1914	28 Feb	Glasgow	0	0
1920	26 Feb	Cardiff	1	1
1921	12 Feb	Aberdeen	2	1
1922	4 Feb	Wrexham	1	2
1923	17 Mar	Paisley	2	0
1924	16 Feb	Cardiff	0	2
1925	14 Feb	Tynecastle	3	1
1925	31 Oct	Cardiff	3	0
1926	30 Oct	Glasgow	3	0
1927	29 Oct	Wrexham	2	2
1928	27 Oct	Glasgow	4	2
1929	26 Oct	Cardiff	4	2
1930	25 Oct	Glasgow	1	1
1931	31 Oct	Wrexham	3	2
1932	26 Oct	Edinburgh	2	5
1933	4 Oct	Cardiff	2	3
1934	21 Nov	Aberdeen	3	2
1935	5 Oct	Cardiff	1	1
1936	2 Dec	Dundee	1	2
1937	30 Oct	Cardiff	1	2
1938	9 Nov	Edinburgh	3	2
1946	19 Oct	Wrexham	1	3
1947	12 Nov	Glasgow	1	2
wc1948	23 Oct	Cardiff	3	1
1949	9 Nov	Glasgow	2	0
1950	21 Oct	Cardiff	3	1
1951	14 Nov	Glasgow	0	1
wc1952	18 Oct	Cardiff	2	1
1953	4 Nov	Glasgow	3	3
1954	16 Oct	Cardiff	1	0
1955	9 Nov	Glasgow	2	0
1956	20 Oct	Cardiff	2	2
1957	13 Nov	Glasgow	1	1
1958	18 Oct	Cardiff	3	0
1959	4 Nov	Glasgow	1	1
1960	20 Oct	Cardiff	0	2
1961	8 Nov	Glasgow	2	0
1962	20 Oct	Cardiff	3	2
1963	20 Nov	Glasgow	2	1
1964	3 Oct	Cardiff	2	3
EC1965	24 Nov	Glasgow	4	1
EC1966	22 Oct	Cardiff	1	1

			S	W
1967	22 Nov	Glasgow	3	2
1969	3 May	Wrexham	5	3
1970	22 Apr	Glasgow	0	0
1971	15 May	Cardiff	0	0
1972	24 May	Glasgow	1	0
1973	12 May	Wrexham	2	0
1974	14 May	Glasgow	2	0
1975	17 May	Cardiff	2	2
1976	6 May	Glasgow	3	1
wc1976	17 Nov	Glasgow	1	0
1977	28 May	Wrexham	0	0
wc1977	12 Oct	Liverpool	2	0
1978	17 May	Glasgow	1	1
1979	19 May	Cardiff	0	3
1980	21 May	Glasgow	1	0
1981	16 May	Swansea	0	2
1982	24 May	Glasgow	1	0
1983	28 May	Cardiff	2	0
1984	28 Feb	Glasgow	2	1
wc1985	27 Mar	Glasgow	0	1
wc1985	10 Sept	Cardiff	1	1
1997	27 May	Kilmarnock	0	1
2004	18 Feb	Cardiff	0	4

SCOTLAND v IRELAND

Played: 93; Scotland won 62, Ireland won 15, Drawn 16. Goals: Scotland 257, Ireland 81.

			S	I
1884	26 Jan	Belfast	5	0
1885	14 Mar	Glasgow	8	2
1886	20 Mar	Belfast	7	2
1887	19 Feb	Glasgow	4	1
1888	24 Mar	Belfast	10	2
1889	9 Mar	Glasgow	7	0
1890	29 Mar	Belfast	4	1
1891	28 Mar	Glasgow	2	1
1892	19 Mar	Belfast	3	2
1893	25 Mar	Glasgow	6	1
1894	31 Mar	Belfast	2	1
1895	30 Mar	Glasgow	3	1
1896	28 Mar	Belfast	3	3
1897	27 Mar	Glasgow	5	1
1898	26 Mar	Belfast	3	0
1899	25 Mar	Glasgow	9	1
1900	3 Mar	Belfast	3	0
1901	23 Feb	Glasgow	11	0
1902	1 Mar	Belfast	5	1
1902	9 Aug	Belfast	3	0
1903	21 Mar	Glasgow	0	2
1904	26 Mar	Dublin	1	1
1905	18 Mar	Glasgow	4	0
1906	17 Mar	Dublin	1	0
1907	16 Mar	Glasgow	3	0
1908	14 Mar	Dublin	5	0
1909	15 Mar	Glasgow	5	0
1910	19 Mar	Belfast	0	1
1911	18 Mar	Glasgow	2	0
1912	16 Mar	Belfast	4	1
1913	15 Mar	Dublin	2	1
1914	14 Mar	Belfast	1	1
1920	13 Mar	Glasgow	3	0
1921	26 Feb	Belfast	2	0
1922	4 Mar	Glasgow	2	1
1923	3 Mar	Belfast	1	0
1924	1 Mar	Glasgow	2	0
1925	28 Feb	Belfast	3	0
1926	27 Feb	Glasgow	4	0
1927	26 Feb	Belfast	2	0
1928	25 Feb	Glasgow	0	1
1929	23 Feb	Belfast	7	3
1930	22 Feb	Glasgow	3	1
1931	21 Feb	Belfast	0	0
1931	19 Sept	Glasgow	3	1
1932	12 Sept	Belfast	4	0
1933	16 Sept	Glasgow	1	2
1934	20 Oct	Belfast	1	2
1935	13 Nov	Edinburgh	2	1
1936	31 Oct	Belfast	3	1
1937	10 Nov	Aberdeen	1	1
1938	8 Oct	Belfast	2	0
1946	27 Nov	Glasgow	0	0
1947	4 Oct	Belfast	0	2
1948	17 Nov	Glasgow	3	2
1949	1 Oct	Belfast	8	2
1950	1 Nov	Glasgow	6	1
1951	6 Oct	Belfast	3	0
1952	5 Nov	Glasgow	1	1
1953	3 Oct	Belfast	3	1
1954	3 Nov	Glasgow	2	2
1955	8 Oct	Belfast	1	2
1956	7 Nov	Glasgow	1	0
1957	5 Oct	Belfast	1	1
1958	5 Nov	Glasgow	2	2
1959	3 Oct	Belfast	4	0
1960	9 Nov	Glasgow	5	2
1961	7 Oct	Belfast	6	1
1962	7 Nov	Glasgow	5	1
1963	12 Oct	Belfast	1	2
1964	25 Nov	Glasgow	3	2
1965	2 Oct	Belfast	2	3
1966	16 Nov	Glasgow	2	1
1967	21 Oct	Belfast	0	1
1969	6 May	Glasgow	1	1
1970	18 Apr	Belfast	1	0
1971	18 May	Glasgow	0	1
1972	20 May	Glasgow	2	0
1973	16 May	Glasgow	1	2
1974	11 May	Glasgow	0	1
1975	20 May	Glasgow	3	0
1976	8 May	Glasgow	3	0
1977	1 June	Glasgow	3	0
1978	13 May	Glasgow	1	1
1979	22 May	Glasgow	1	0
1980	17 May	Belfast	0	1
wc1981	25 Mar	Glasgow	1	1
1981	19 May	Glasgow	2	0
wc1981	14 Oct	Belfast	0	0
1982	28 Apr	Belfast	1	1
1983	24 May	Glasgow	0	0
1983	13 Dec	Belfast	0	2
1992	19 Feb	Glasgow	1	0

WALES v IRELAND

Played: 93; Wales won 43, Ireland won 27, Drawn 23. Goals: Wales 187, Ireland 131.

			W	I
1882	25 Feb	Wrexham	7	1
1883	17 Mar	Belfast	1	1
1884	9 Feb	Wrexham	6	0
1885	11 Apr	Belfast	8	2
1886	27 Feb	Wrexham	5	0
1887	12 Mar	Belfast	1	4
1888	3 Mar	Wrexham	11	0
1889	27 Apr	Belfast	3	1

			W	I
1890	8 Feb	Shrewsbury	5	2
1891	7 Feb	Belfast	2	7
1892	27 Feb	Bangor	1	1
1893	8 Apr	Belfast	3	4
1894	24 Feb	Swansea	4	1
1895	16 Mar	Belfast	2	2
1896	29 Feb	Wrexham	6	1
1897	6 Mar	Belfast	3	4
1898	19 Feb	Llandudno	0	1
1899	4 Mar	Belfast	0	1
1900	24 Feb	Llandudno	2	0
1901	23 Mar	Belfast	1	0
1902	22 Mar	Cardiff	0	3
1903	28 Mar	Belfast	0	2
1904	21 Mar	Bangor	0	1
1905	18 Apr	Belfast	2	2
1906	2 Apr	Wrexham	4	4
1907	23 Feb	Belfast	3	2
1908	11 Apr	Aberdare	0	1
1909	20 Mar	Belfast	3	2
1910	11 Apr	Wrexham	4	1
1911	28 Jan	Belfast	2	1
1912	13 Apr	Cardiff	2	3
1913	18 Jan	Belfast	1	0
1914	19 Jan	Wrexham	1	2
1920	14 Feb	Belfast	2	2
1921	9 Apr	Swansea	2	1
1922	4 Apr	Belfast	1	1
1923	14 Apr	Wrexham	0	3
1924	15 Mar	Belfast	1	0
1925	18 Apr	Wrexham	0	0
1926	13 Feb	Belfast	0	3
1927	9 Apr	Cardiff	2	2
1928	4 Feb	Belfast	2	1
1929	2 Feb	Wrexham	2	2
1930	1 Feb	Belfast	0	7
1931	22 Apr	Wrexham	3	2
1931	5 Dec	Belfast	0	4
1932	7 Dec	Wrexham	4	1
1933	4 Nov	Belfast	1	1
1935	27 Mar	Wrexham	3	1
1936	11 Mar	Belfast	2	3
1937	17 Mar	Wrexham	4	1

			W	I
1938	16 Mar	Belfast	0	1
1939	15 Mar	Wrexham	3	1
1947	16 Apr	Belfast	1	2
1948	10 Mar	Wrexham	2	0
1949	9 Mar	Belfast	2	0
WC1950	8 Mar	Wrexham	0	0
1951	7 Mar	Belfast	2	1
1952	19 Mar	Swansea	3	0
1953	15 Apr	Belfast	3	2
WC1954	31 Mar	Wrexham	1	2
1955	20 Apr	Belfast	3	2
1956	11 Apr	Cardiff	1	1
1957	10 Apr	Belfast	0	0
1958	16 Apr	Cardiff	1	1
1959	22 Apr	Belfast	1	4
1960	6 Apr	Wrexham	3	2
1961	12 Apr	Belfast	5	1
1962	11 Apr	Cardiff	4	0
1963	3 Apr	Belfast	4	1
1964	15 Apr	Cardiff	2	3
1965	31 Mar	Belfast	5	0
1966	30 Mar	Cardiff	1	4
EC1967	12 Apr	Belfast	0	0
EC1968	28 Feb	Wrexham	2	0
1969	10 May	Belfast	0	0
1970	25 Apr	Swansea	1	0
1971	22 May	Belfast	0	1
1972	27 May	Wrexham	0	0
1973	19 May	Everton	0	1
1974	18 May	Wrexham	1	0
1975	23 May	Belfast	0	1
1976	14 May	Swansea	1	0
1977	3 June	Belfast	1	1
1978	19 May	Wrexham	1	0
1979	25 May	Belfast	1	1
1980	23 May	Cardiff	0	1
1982	27 May	Wrexham	3	0
1983	31 May	Belfast	1	0
1984	22 May	Swansea	1	1
WC2004	8 Sept	Cardiff	2	2
WC2005	8 Oct	Belfast	3	2
2007	6 Feb	Belfast	0	0

OTHER BRITISH INTERNATIONAL RESULTS 1908–2006

ENGLAND

		v ALBANIA	E	A
WC1989	8 Mar	Tirana	2	0
WC1989	26 Apr	Wembley	5	0
WC2001	28 Mar	Tirana	3	1
WC2001	5 Sept	Newcastle	2	0

		v ANDORRA	E	A
EC2006	2 Sept	Old Trafford	5	0
EC2007	28 Mar	Barcelona	3	0

		v ARGENTINA	E	A
1951	9 May	Wembley	2	1
1953	17 May	Buenos Aires	0	0
(abandoned after 21 mins)				
WC1962	2 June	Rancagua	3	1
1964	6 June	Rio de Janeiro	0	1
WC1966	23 July	Wembley	1	0
1974	22 May	Wembley	2	2
1977	12 June	Buenos Aires	1	1
1980	13 May	Wembley	3	1
WC1986	22 June	Mexico City	1	2
1991	25 May	Wembley	2	2
WC1998	30 June	St Etienne	2	2
2000	23 Feb	Wembley	0	0
WC2002	7 June	Sapporo	1	0
2005	12 Nov	Geneva	3	2

		v AUSTRALIA	E	A
1980	31 May	Sydney	2	1
1983	11 June	Sydney	0	0
1983	15 June	Brisbane	1	0
1983	18 June	Melbourne	1	1
1991	1 June	Sydney	1	0
2003	12 Feb	West Ham	1	3

		v AUSTRIA	E	A
1908	6 June	Vienna	6	1
1908	8 June	Vienna	11	1
1909	1 June	Vienna	8	1
1930	14 May	Vienna	0	0
1932	7 Dec	Chelsea	4	3
1936	6 May	Vienna	1	2
1951	28 Nov	Wembley	2	2
1952	25 May	Vienna	3	2
WC1958	15 June	Boras	2	2
1961	27 May	Vienna	1	3
1962	4 Apr	Wembley	3	1
1965	20 Oct	Wembley	2	3
1967	27 May	Vienna	1	0
1973	26 Sept	Wembley	7	0
1979	13 June	Vienna	3	4
WC2004	4 Sept	Vienna	2	2
WC2005	8 Oct	Old Trafford	1	0

		v AZERBAIJAN	E	A
WC2004	13 Oct	Baku	1	0
WC2005	30 Mar	Newcastle	2	0

		v BELGIUM	E	B
1921	21 May	Brussels	2	0
1923	19 Mar	Highbury	6	1
1923	1 Nov	Antwerp	2	2
1924	8 Dec	West Bromwich	4	0
1926	24 May	Antwerp	5	3

			E	*B*
1927	11 May	Brussels	9	1
1928	19 May	Antwerp	3	1
1929	11 May	Brussels	5	1
1931	16 May	Brussels	4	1
1936	9 May	Brussels	2	3
1947	21 Sept	Brussels	5	2
1950	18 May	Brussels	4	1
1952	26 Nov	Wembley	5	0
WC1954	17 June	Basle	4	4*
1964	21 Oct	Wembley	2	2
1970	25 Feb	Brussels	3	1
EC1980	12 June	Turin	1	1
WC1990	27 June	Bologna	1	0*
1998	29 May	Casablanca	0	0
1999	10 Oct	Sunderland	2	1

		v BOHEMIA	*E*	*B*
1908	13 June	Prague	4	0

		v BRAZIL	*E*	*B*
1956	9 May	Wembley	4	2
WC1958	11 June	Gothenburg	0	0
1959	13 May	Rio de Janeiro	0	2
WC1962	10 June	Vina del Mar	1	3
1963	8 May	Wembley	1	1
1964	30 May	Rio de Janeiro	1	5
1969	12 June	Rio de Janeiro	1	2
WC1970	7 June	Guadalajara	0	1
1976	23 May	Los Angeles	0	1
1977	8 June	Rio de Janeiro	0	0
1978	19 Apr	Wembley	1	1
1981	12 May	Wembley	0	1
1984	10 June	Rio de Janeiro	2	0
1987	19 May	Wembley	1	1
1990	28 Mar	Wembley	1	0
1992	17 May	Wembley	1	1
1993	13 June	Washington	1	1
UI1995	11 June	Wembley	1	3
TF1997	10 June	Paris	0	1
2000	27 May	Wembley	1	1
WC2002	21 June	Shizuoka	1	2
2007	1 June	Wembley	1	1

		v BULGARIA	*E*	*B*
WC1962	7 June	Rancagua	0	0
1968	11 Dec	Wembley	1	1
1974	1 June	Sofia	1	0
EC1979	6 June	Sofia	3	0
EC1979	22 Nov	Wembley	2	0
1996	27 Mar	Wembley	1	0
EC1998	10 Oct	Wembley	0	0
EC1999	9 June	Sofia	1	1

		v CAMEROON	*E*	*C*
WC1990	1 July	Naples	3	2*
1991	6 Feb	Wembley	2	0
1997	15 Nov	Wembley	2	0
2002	26 May	Kobe	2	2

		v CANADA	*E*	*C*
1986	24 May	Burnaby	1	0

		v CHILE	*E*	*C*
WC1950	25 June	Rio de Janeiro	2	0
1953	24 May	Santiago	2	1
1984	17 June	Santiago	0	0
1989	23 May	Wembley	0	0
1998	11 Feb	Wembley	0	2

		v CHINA	*E*	*C*
1996	23 May	Beijing	3	0

		v CIS	*E*	*C*
1992	29 Apr	Moscow	2	2

		v COLOMBIA	*E*	*C*
1970	20 May	Bogota	4	0
1988	24 May	Wembley	1	1
1995	6 Sept	Wembley	0	0
WC1998	26 June	Lens	2	0
2005	31 May	New Jersey	3	2

		v CROATIA	*E*	*C*
1996	24 Apr	Wembley	0	0
2003	20 Aug	Ipswich	3	1
EC2004	21 June	Lisbon	4	2
EC2006	11 Oct	Zagreb	0	2

		v CYPRUS	*E*	*C*
EC1975	16 Apr	Wembley	5	0
EC1975	11 May	Limassol	1	0

		v CZECHOSLOVAKIA	*E*	*C*
1934	16 May	Prague	1	2
1937	1 Dec	Tottenham	5	4
1963	29 May	Bratislava	4	2
1966	2 Nov	Wembley	0	0
WC1970	11 June	Guadalajara	1	0
1973	27 May	Prague	1	1
EC1974	30 Oct	Wembley	3	0
EC1975	30 Oct	Bratislava	1	2
1978	29 Nov	Wembley	1	0
WC1982	20 June	Bilbao	2	0
1990	25 Apr	Wembley	4	2
1992	25 Mar	Prague	2	2

		v CZECH REPUBLIC	*E*	*C*
1998	18 Nov	Wembley	2	0

		v DENMARK	*E*	*D*
1948	26 Sept	Copenhagen	0	0
1955	2 Oct	Copenhagen	5	1
WC1956	5 Dec	Wolverhampton	5	2
WC1957	15 May	Copenhagen	4	1
1966	3 July	Copenhagen	2	0
EC1978	20 Sept	Copenhagen	4	3
EC1979	12 Sept	Wembley	1	0
EC1982	22 Sept	Copenhagen	2	2
EC1983	21 Sept	Wembley	0	1
1988	14 Sept	Wembley	1	0
1989	7 June	Copenhagen	1	1
1990	15 May	Wembley	1	0
EC1992	11 June	Malmo	0	0
1994	9 Mar	Wembley	1	0
WC2002	15 June	Niigata	3	0
2003	16 Nov	Old Trafford	2	3
2005	17 Aug	Copenhagen	1	4

		v ECUADOR	*E*	*Ec*
1970	24 May	Quito	2	0
WC2006	25 June	Stuttgart	1	0

		v EGYPT	*E*	*Eg*
1986	29 Jan	Cairo	4	0
WC1990	21 June	Cagliari	1	0

		v ESTONIA	*E*	*Es*
EC2007	6 June	Tallinn	3	0

		v FIFA	*E*	*FIFA*
1938	26 Oct	Highbury	3	0
1953	21 Oct	Wembley	4	4
1963	23 Oct	Wembley	2	1

		v FINLAND	*E*	*F*
1937	20 May	Helsinki	8	0
1956	20 May	Helsinki	5	1
1966	26 June	Helsinki	3	0
WC1976	13 June	Helsinki	4	1
WC1976	13 Oct	Wembley	2	1
1982	3 June	Helsinki	4	1
WC1984	17 Oct	Wembley	5	0
WC1985	22 May	Helsinki	1	1
1992	3 June	Helsinki	2	1
WC2000	11 Oct	Helsinki	0	0
WC2001	24 Mar	Liverpool	2	1

		v FRANCE	*E*	*F*
1923	10 May	Paris	4	1
1924	17 May	Paris	3	1
1925	21 May	Paris	3	2
1927	26 May	Paris	6	0
1928	17 May	Paris	5	1
1929	9 May	Paris	4	1
1931	14 May	Paris	2	5

			E	F
1933	6 Dec	Tottenham	4	1
1938	26 May	Paris	4	2
1947	3 May	Highbury	3	0
1949	22 May	Paris	3	1
1951	3 Oct	Highbury	2	2
1955	15 May	Paris	0	1
1957	27 Nov	Wembley	4	0
EC1962	3 Oct	Sheffield	1	1
EC1963	27 Feb	Paris	2	5
WC1966	20 July	Wembley	2	0
1969	12 Mar	Wembley	5	0
WC1982	16 June	Bilbao	3	1
1984	29 Feb	Paris	0	2
1992	19 Feb	Wembley	2	0
EC1992	14 June	Malmo	0	0
TF1997	7 June	Montpellier	1	0
1999	10 Feb	Wembley	0	2
2000	2 Sept	Paris	1	1
EC2004	13 June	Lisbon	1	2

		v GEORGIA	E	G
WC1996	9 Nov	Tbilisi	2	0
WC1997	30 Apr	Wembley	2	0

		v GERMANY	E	G
1930	10 May	Berlin	3	3
1935	4 Dec	Tottenham	3	0
1938	14 May	Berlin	6	3
1991	11 Sept	Wembley	0	1
1993	19 June	Detroit	1	2
EC1996	26 June	Wembley	1	1*
EC2000	17 June	Charleroi	1	0
WC2000	7 Oct	Wembley	0	1
WC2001	1 Sept	Munich	5	1

		v EAST GERMANY	E	EG
1963	2 June	Leipzig	2	1
1970	25 Nov	Wembley	3	1
1974	29 May	Leipzig	1	1
1984	12 Sept	Wembley	1	0

		v WEST GERMANY	E	WG
1954	1 Dec	Wembley	3	1
1956	26 May	Berlin	3	1
1965	12 May	Nuremberg	1	0
1966	23 Feb	Wembley	1	0
WC1966	30 July	Wembley	4	2*
1968	1 June	Hanover	0	1
WC1970	14 June	Leon	2	3*
EC1972	29 Apr	Wembley	1	3
EC1972	13 May	Berlin	0	0
1975	12 Mar	Wembley	2	0
1978	22 Feb	Munich	1	2
WC1982	29 June	Madrid	0	0
1982	13 Oct	Wembley	1	2
1985	12 June	Mexico City	3	0
1987	9 Sept	Dusseldorf	1	3
WC1990	4 July	Turin	1	1*

		v GREECE	E	G
EC1971	21 Apr	Wembley	3	0
EC1971	1 Dec	Piraeus	2	0
EC1982	17 Nov	Salonika	3	0
EC1983	30 Mar	Wembley	0	0
1989	8 Feb	Athens	2	1
1994	17 May	Wembley	5	0
WC2001	6 June	Athens	2	0
WC2001	6 Oct	Old Trafford	2	2
2006	16 Aug	Old Trafford	4	0

		v HOLLAND	E	H
1935	18 May	Amsterdam	1	0
1946	27 Nov	Huddersfield	8	2
1964	9 Dec	Amsterdam	1	1
1969	5 Nov	Amsterdam	1	0
1970	14 Jun	Wembley	0	0
1977	9 Feb	Wembley	0	2
1982	25 May	Wembley	2	0
1988	23 Mar	Wembley	2	2
EC1988	15 June	Dusseldorf	1	3
WC1990	16 June	Cagliari	0	0

			E	H
2005	9 Feb	Villa Park	0	0
WC1993	28 Apr	Wembley	2	2
WC1993	13 Oct	Rotterdam	0	2
EC1996	18 June	Wembley	4	1
2001	15 Aug	Tottenham	0	2
2002	13 Feb	Amsterdam	1	1
2006	15 Nov	Amsterdam	1	1

		v HUNGARY	E	H
1908	10 June	Budapest	7	0
1909	29 May	Budapest	4	2
1909	31 May	Budapest	8	2
1934	10 May	Budapest	1	2
1936	2 Dec	Highbury	6	2
1953	25 Nov	Wembley	3	6
1954	23 May	Budapest	1	7
1960	22 May	Budapest	0	2
WC1962	31 May	Rancagua	1	2
1965	5 May	Wembley	1	0
1978	24 May	Wembley	4	1
WC1981	6 June	Budapest	3	1
WC1982	18 Nov	Wembley	1	0
EC1983	27 Apr	Wembley	2	0
EC1983	12 Oct	Budapest	3	0
1988	27 Apr	Budapest	0	0
1990	12 Sept	Wembley	1	0
1992	12 May	Budapest	1	0
1996	18 May	Wembley	3	0
1999	28 Apr	Budapest	1	1
2006	30 May	Old Trafford	3	1

		v ICELAND	E	I
1982	2 June	Reykjavik	1	1
2004	5 June	City of Manchester	6	1
EC2007	24 Mar	Tel Aviv	0	0

		v REPUBLIC OF IRELAND	E	RI
1946	30 Sept	Dublin	1	0
1949	21 Sept	Everton	0	2
WC1957	8 May	Wembley	5	1
WC1957	19 May	Dublin	1	1
1964	24 May	Dublin	3	1
1976	8 Sept	Wembley	1	1
EC1978	25 Oct	Dublin	1	1
EC1980	6 Feb	Wembley	2	0
1985	26 Mar	Wembley	2	1
EC1988	12 June	Stuttgart	0	1
WC1990	11 June	Cagliari	1	1
EC1990	14 Nov	Dublin	1	1
EC1991	27 Mar	Wembley	1	1
1995	15 Feb	Dublin	0	1

(abandoned after 27 mins)

		v ISRAEL	E	I
1986	26 Feb	Ramat Gan	2	1
1988	17 Feb	Tel Aviv	0	0
EC2007	24 Mar	Tel Aviv	0	0

		v ITALY	E	I
1933	13 May	Rome	1	1
1934	14 Nov	Highbury	3	2
1939	13 May	Milan	2	2
1948	16 May	Turin	4	0
1949	30 Nov	Tottenham	2	0
1952	18 May	Florence	1	1
1959	6 May	Wembley	2	2
1961	24 May	Rome	3	2
1973	14 June	Turin	0	2
1973	14 Nov	Wembley	0	1
1976	28 May	New York	3	2
WC1976	17 Nov	Rome	0	2
WC1977	16 Nov	Wembley	2	0
EC1980	15 June	Turin	0	1
1985	6 June	Mexico City	1	2
1989	15 Nov	Wembley	0	0
WC1990	7 July	Bari	1	2
WC1997	12 Feb	Wembley	0	1
TF1997	4 June	Nantes	2	0
WC1997	11 Oct	Rome	0	0
2000	15 Nov	Turin	0	1
2002	27 Mar	Leeds	1	2

		v JAMAICA	E	J
2006	3 June	Old Trafford	6	0

		v JAPAN	E	J
UI1995	3 June	Wembley	2	1
2004	1 June	City of Manchester	1	1

		v KUWAIT	E	K
wc1982	25 June	Bilbao	1	0

		v LIECHTENSTEIN	E	L
EC2003	29 Mar	Vaduz	2	0
EC2003	10 Sept	Old Trafford	2	0

		v LUXEMBOURG	E	L
1927	21 May	Esch-sur-Alzette	5	2
wc1960	19 Oct	Luxembourg	9	0
wc1961	28 Sept	Highbury	4	1
wc1977	30 Mar	Wembley	5	0
wc1977	12 Oct	Luxembourg	2	0
EC1982	15 Dec	Wembley	9	0
EC1983	16 Nov	Luxembourg	4	0
EC1998	14 Oct	Luxembourg	3	0
EC1999	4 Sept	Wembley	6	0

		v MACEDONIA	E	M
EC2002	16 Oct	Southampton	2	2
EC2003	6 Sept	Skopje	2	1
EC2006	6 Sept	Skopje	1	0
EC2006	7 Oct	Old Trafford	0	0

		v MALAYSIA	E	M
1991	12 June	Kuala Lumpur	4	2

		v MALTA	E	M
EC1971	3 Feb	Valletta	1	0
EC1971	12 May	Wembley	5	0
2000	3 June	Valletta	2	1

		v MEXICO	E	M
1959	24 May	Mexico City	1	2
1961	10 May	Wembley	8	0
wc1966	16 July	Wembley	2	0
1969	1 June	Mexico City	0	0
1985	9 June	Mexico City	0	1
1986	17 May	Los Angeles	3	0
1997	29 Mar	Wembley	2	0
2001	25 May	Derby	4	0

		v MOLDOVA	E	M
wc1996	1 Sept	Chisinau	3	0
wc1997	10 Sept	Wembley	4	0

		v MOROCCO	E	M
wc1986	6 June	Monterrey	0	0
1998	27 May	Casablanca	1	0

		v NEW ZEALAND	E	NZ
1991	3 June	Auckland	1	0
1991	8 June	Wellington	2	0

		v NIGERIA	E	N
1994	16 Nov	Wembley	1	0
wc2002	12 June	Osaka	0	0

		v NORWAY	E	N
1937	14 May	Oslo	6	0
1938	9 Nov	Newcastle	4	0
1949	18 May	Oslo	4	1
1966	29 June	Oslo	6	1
wc1980	10 Sept	Wembley	4	0
wc1981	9 Sept	Oslo	1	2
wc1992	14 Oct	Wembley	1	1
wc1993	2 June	Oslo	0	2
1994	22 May	Wembley	0	0
1995	11 Oct	Oslo	0	0

		v PARAGUAY	E	P
wc1986	18 June	Mexico City	3	0
2002	17 Apr	Liverpool	4	0
wc2006	10 June	Frankfurt	1	0

		v PERU	E	P
1959	17 May	Lima	1	4
1962	20 May	Lima	4	0

		v POLAND	E	P
1966	5 Jan	Everton	1	1
1966	5 July	Chorzow	1	0
wc1973	6 June	Chorzow	0	2
wc1973	17 Oct	Wembley	1	1
wc1986	11 June	Monterrey	3	0
wc1989	3 June	Wembley	3	0
wc1989	11 Oct	Katowice	0	0
EC1990	17 Oct	Wembley	2	0
EC1991	13 Nov	Poznan	1	1
wc1993	29 May	Katowice	1	1
wc1993	8 Sept	Wembley	3	0
wc1996	9 Oct	Wembley	2	1
wc1997	31 May	Katowice	2	0
EC1999	27 Mar	Wembley	3	1
EC1999	8 Sept	Warsaw	0	0
wc2004	8 Sept	Katowice	2	1
wc2005	12 Oct	Old Trafford	2	1

		v PORTUGAL	E	P
1947	25 May	Lisbon	10	0
1950	14 May	Lisbon	5	3
1951	19 May	Everton	5	2
1955	22 May	Oporto	1	3
1958	7 May	Wembley	2	1
wc1961	21 May	Lisbon	1	1
wc1961	25 Oct	Wembley	2	0
1964	17 May	Lisbon	4	3
1964	4 June	São Paulo	1	1
wc1966	26 July	Wembley	2	1
1969	10 Dec	Wembley	1	0
1974	3 Apr	Lisbon	0	0
EC1974	20 Nov	Wembley	0	0
EC1975	19 Nov	Lisbon	1	1
wc1986	3 June	Monterrey	0	1
1995	12 Dec	Wembley	1	1
1998	22 Apr	Wembley	3	0
EC2000	12 June	Eindhoven	2	3
2002	7 Sept	Villa Park	1	1
2004	18 Feb	Faro	1	1
EC2004	24 June	Lisbon	2	2*
wc2006	1 July	Gelsenkirchen	0	0

		v ROMANIA	E	R
1939	24 May	Bucharest	2	0
1968	6 Nov	Bucharest	0	0
1969	15 Jan	Wembley	1	1
wc1970	2 June	Guadalajara	1	0
wc1980	15 Oct	Bucharest	1	2
wc1981	29 April	Wembley	0	0
wc1985	1 May	Bucharest	0	0
wc1985	11 Sept	Wembley	1	1
1994	12 Oct	Wembley	1	1
wc1998	22 June	Toulouse	1	2
EC2000	20 June	Charleroi	2	3

		v SAN MARINO	E	SM
wc1992	17 Feb	Wembley	6	0
wc1993	17 Nov	Bologna	7	1

		v SAUDI ARABIA	E	SA
1988	16 Nov	Riyadh	1	1
1998	23 May	Wembley	0	0

		v SERBIA-MONTENEGRO	E	S-M
2003	3 June	Leicester	2	1

		v SLOVAKIA	E	S
EC2002	12 Oct	Bratislava	2	1
EC2003	11 June	Middlesbrough	2	1

		v SOUTH AFRICA	E	SA
1997	24 May	Old Trafford	2	1
2003	22 May	Durban	2	1

		v SOUTH KOREA	E	SK
2002	21 May	Seoguipo	1	1

		v SPAIN	E	S
1929	15 May	Madrid	3	4
1931	9 Dec	Highbury	7	1
wc1950	2 July	Rio de Janeiro	0	1
1955	18 May	Madrid	1	1
1955	30 Nov	Wembley	4	1
1960	15 May	Madrid	0	3
1960	26 Oct	Wembley	4	2
1965	8 Dec	Madrid	2	0
1967	24 May	Wembley	2	0
EC1968	3 Apr	Wembley	1	0
EC1968	8 May	Madrid	2	1

			E	*S*
1980	26 Mar	Barcelona	2	0
EC1980	18 June	Naples	2	1
1981	25 Mar	Wembley	1	2
wc1982	5 July	Madrid	0	0
1987	18 Feb	Madrid	4	2
1992	9 Sept	Santander	0	1
EC 1996	22 June	Wembley	0	0
2001	28 Feb	Villa Park	3	0
2004	17 Nov	Madrid	0	1
2007	7 Feb	Old Trafford	0	1

v SWEDEN

			E	*S*
1923	21 May	Stockholm	4	2
1923	24 May	Stockholm	3	1
1937	17 May	Stockholm	4	0
1947	19 Nov	Highbury	4	2
1949	13 May	Stockholm	1	3
1956	16 May	Stockholm	0	0
1959	28 Oct	Wembley	2	3
1965	16 May	Gothenburg	2	1
1968	22 May	Wembley	3	1
1979	10 June	Stockholm	0	0
1986	10 Sept	Stockholm	0	1
wc1988	19 Oct	Wembley	0	0
wc1989	6 Sept	Stockholm	0	0
EC1992	17 June	Stockholm	1	2
UI1995	8 June	Leeds	3	3
EC1998	5 Sept	Stockholm	1	2
EC1999	5 June	Wembley	0	0
2001	10 Nov	Old Trafford	1	1
wc2002	2 June	Saitama	1	1
2004	31 Mar	Gothenburg	0	1
wc2006	20 June	Cologne	2	2

v SWITZERLAND

			E	*S*
1933	20 May	Berne	4	0
1938	21 May	Zurich	1	2
1947	18 May	Zurich	0	1
1948	2 Dec	Highbury	6	0
1952	28 May	Zurich	3	0
wc1954	20 June	Berne	2	0
1962	9 May	Wembley	3	1
1963	5 June	Basle	8	1
EC1971	13 Oct	Basle	3	2
EC1971	10 Nov	Wembley	1	1
1975	3 Sept	Basle	2	1
1977	7 Sept	Wembley	0	0
wc1980	19 Nov	Wembley	2	1
wc1981	30 May	Basle	1	2
1988	28 May	Lausanne	1	0
1995	15 Nov	Wembley	3	1
EC1996	8 June	Wembley	1	1
1998	25 Mar	Berne	1	1
EC2004	17 June	Coimbra	3	0

v TRINIDAD & TOBAGO

			E	*Tr*
wc2006	15 June	Nuremberg	2	0

v TUNISIA

			E	*T*
1990	2 June	Tunis	1	1
wc1998	15 June	Marseilles	2	0

v TURKEY

			E	*T*
wc1984	14 Nov	Istanbul	8	0
wc1985	16 Oct	Wembley	5	0
EC1987	29 Apr	Izmir	0	0
EC1987	14 Oct	Wembley	8	0
EC1991	1 May	Izmir	1	0
EC1991	16 Oct	Wembley	1	0
wc1992	18 Nov	Wembley	4	0
wc1993	31 Mar	Izmir	2	0
EC2003	2 Apr	Sunderland	2	0
EC2003	11 Oct	Istanbul	0	0

v UKRAINE

			E	*U*
2000	31 May	Wembley	2	0
2004	18 Aug	Newcastle	3	0

v URUGUAY

			E	*U*
1953	31 May	Montevideo	1	2
wc1954	26 June	Basle	2	4
1964	6 May	Wembley	2	1
wc1966	11 July	Wembley	0	0
1969	8 June	Montevideo	2	1
1977	15 June	Montevideo	0	0
1984	13 June	Montevideo	0	2
1990	22 May	Wembley	1	2
1995	29 Mar	Wembley	0	0
2006	1 Mar	Liverpool	2	1

v USA

			E	*USA*
wc1950	29 June	Belo Horizonte	0	1
1953	8 June	New York	6	3
1959	28 May	Los Angeles	8	1
1964	27 May	New York	10	0
1985	16 June	Los Angeles	5	0
1993	9 June	Foxboro	0	2
1994	7 Sept	Wembley	2	0
2005	28 May	Chicago	2	1

v USSR

			E	*USSR*
1958	18 May	Moscow	1	1
wc1958	8 June	Gothenburg	2	2
wc1958	17 June	Gothenburg	0	1
1958	22 Oct	Wembley	5	0
1967	6 Dec	Wembley	2	2
EC1968	8 June	Rome	2	0
1973	10 June	Moscow	2	1
1984	2 June	Wembley	0	2
1986	26 Mar	Tbilisi	1	0
EC1988	18 June	Frankfurt	1	3
1991	21 May	Wembley	3	1

v YUGOSLAVIA

			E	*Y*
1939	18 May	Belgrade	1	2
1950	22 Nov	Highbury	2	2
1954	16 May	Belgrade	0	1
1956	28 Nov	Wembley	3	0
1958	11 May	Belgrade	0	5
1960	11 May	Wembley	3	3
1965	9 May	Belgrade	1	1
1966	4 May	Wembley	2	0
EC1968	5 June	Florence	0	1
1972	11 Oct	Wembley	1	1
1974	5 June	Belgrade	2	2
EC1986	12 Nov	Wembley	2	0
EC1987	11 Nov	Belgrade	4	1
1989	13 Dec	Wembley	2	1

SCOTLAND

v ARGENTINA

			S	*A*
1977	18 June	Buenos Aires	1	1
1979	2 June	Glasgow	1	3
1990	28 Mar	Glasgow	1	0

v AUSTRALIA

			S	*A*
wc1985	20 Nov	Glasgow	2	0
wc1985	4 Dec	Melbourne	0	0
1996	27 Mar	Glasgow	1	0
2000	15 Nov	Glasgow	0	2

v AUSTRIA

			S	*A*
1931	16 May	Vienna	0	5
1933	29 Nov	Glasgow	2	2
1937	9 May	Vienna	1	1
1950	13 Dec	Glasgow	0	1
1951	27 May	Vienna	0	4
wc1954	16 June	Zurich	0	1
1955	19 May	Vienna	4	1
1956	2 May	Glasgow	1	1
1960	29 May	Vienna	1	4
1963	8 May	Glasgow	4	1
		(*abandoned after 79 mins*)		
wc1968	6 Nov	Glasgow	2	1
wc1969	5 Nov	Vienna	0	2
EC1978	20 Sept	Vienna	2	3
EC1979	17 Oct	Glasgow	1	1
1994	20 Apr	Vienna	2	1

			S	A
wc1996	31 Aug	Vienna	0	0
wc1997	2 Apr	Celtic Park	2	0
2003	30 Apr	Glasgow	0	2
2005	17 Aug	Graz	2	2
2007	30 May	Vienna	1	0

		v BELARUS	S	B
wc1997	8 June	Minsk	1	0
wc1997	7 Sept	Aberdeen	4	1
wc2005	8 June	Minsk	0	0
wc2005	8 Oct	Glasgow	0	1

		v BELGIUM	S	B
1947	18 May	Brussels	1	2
1948	28 Apr	Glasgow	2	0
1951	20 May	Brussels	5	0
EC1971	3 Feb	Liège	0	3
EC1971	10 Nov	Aberdeen	1	0
1974	2 June	Brussels	1	2
EC1979	21 Nov	Brussels	0	2
EC1979	19 Dec	Glasgow	1	3
EC1982	15 Dec	Brussels	2	3
EC1983	12 Oct	Glasgow	1	1
EC1987	1 Apr	Brussels	1	4
EC1987	14 Oct	Glasgow	2	0
wc2001	24 Mar	Glasgow	2	2
wc2001	5 Sept	Brussels	0	2

		v BOSNIA	S	B
EC1999	4 Sept	Sarajevo	2	1
EC1999	5 Oct	Glasgow	1	0

		v BRAZIL	S	B
1966	25 June	Glasgow	1	1
1972	5 July	Rio de Janeiro	0	1
1973	30 June	Glasgow	0	1
wc1974	18 June	Frankfurt	0	0
1977	23 June	Rio de Janeiro	0	2
wc1982	18 June	Seville	1	4
1987	26 May	Glasgow	0	2
wc1990	20 June	Turin	0	1
wc1998	10 June	Saint-Denis	1	2

		v BULGARIA	S	B
1978	22 Feb	Glasgow	2	1
EC1986	10 Sept	Glasgow	0	0
EC1987	11 Nov	Sofia	1	0
EC1990	14 Nov	Sofia	1	1
EC1991	27 Mar	Glasgow	1	1
2006	11 May	Kobe	5	1

		v CANADA	S	C
1983	12 June	Vancouver	2	0
1983	16 June	Edmonton	3	0
1983	20 June	Toronto	2	0
1992	21 May	Toronto	3	1
2002	15 Oct	Easter Road	3	1

		v CHILE	S	C
1977	15 June	Santiago	4	2
1989	30 May	Glasgow	2	0

		v CIS	S	C
EC1992	18 June	Norrkoping	3	0

		v COLOMBIA	S	C
1988	17 May	Glasgow	0	0
1996	30 May	Miami	0	1
1998	23 May	New York	2	2

		v COSTA RICA	S	CR
wc1990	11 June	Genoa	0	1

		v CROATIA	S	C
wc2000	11 Oct	Zagreb	1	1
wc2001	1 Sept	Glasgow	0	0

		v CYPRUS	S	C
wc1968	17 Dec	Nicosia	5	0
wc1969	11 May	Glasgow	8	0
wc1989	8 Feb	Limassol	3	2
wc1989	26 Apr	Glasgow	2	1

		v CZECHOSLOVAKIA	S	C
1937	22 May	Prague	3	1
1937	8 Dec	Glasgow	5	0
wc1961	14 May	Bratislava	0	4
wc1961	26 Sept	Glasgow	3	2
wc1961	29 Nov	Brussels	2	4*
1972	2 July	Porto Alegre	0	0
wc1973	26 Sept	Glasgow	2	1
wc1973	17 Oct	Prague	0	1
wc1976	13 Oct	Prague	0	2
wc1977	21 Sept	Glasgow	3	1

		v CZECH REPUBLIC	S	C
EC1999	31 Mar	Glasgow	1	2
EC1999	9 June	Prague	2	3

		v DENMARK	S	D
1951	12 May	Glasgow	3	1
1952	25 May	Copenhagen	2	1
1968	16 Oct	Copenhagen	1	0
EC1970	11 Nov	Glasgow	1	0
EC1971	9 June	Copenhagen	0	1
wc1972	18 Oct	Copenhagen	4	1
wc1972	15 Nov	Glasgow	2	0
EC1975	3 Sept	Copenhagen	1	0
EC1975	29 Oct	Glasgow	3	1
wc1986	4 June	Nezahualcayotl	0	1
1996	24 Apr	Copenhagen	0	2
1998	25 Mar	Glasgow	0	1
2002	21 Aug	Glasgow	0	1
2004	28 Apr	Copenhagen	0	1

		v ECUADOR	S	E
1995	24 May	Toyama	2	1

		v EGYPT	S	E
1990	16 May	Aberdeen	1	3

		v ESTONIA	S	E
wc1993	19 May	Tallinn	3	0
wc1993	2 June	Aberdeen	3	1
wc1997	11 Feb	Monaco	0	0
wc1997	29 Mar	Kilmarnock	2	0
EC1998	10 Oct	Edinburgh	3	2
EC1999	8 Sept	Tallinn	0	0
2004	27 May	Tallinn	1	0

		v FAEROES	S	F
EC1994	12 Oct	Glasgow	5	1
EC1995	7 June	Toftir	2	0
EC1998	14 Oct	Aberdeen	2	1
EC1999	5 June	Toftir	1	1
EC2002	7 Sept	Toftir	2	2
EC2003	6 Sept	Glasgow	3	1
EC2006	2 Sept	Celtic Park	6	0
EC2007	6 June	Toftir	2	0

		v FINLAND	S	F
1954	25 May	Helsinki	2	1
wc1964	21 Oct	Glasgow	3	1
wc1965	27 May	Helsinki	2	1
1976	8 Sept	Glasgow	6	0
1992	25 Mar	Glasgow	1	1
EC1994	7 Sept	Helsinki	2	0
EC1995	6 Sept	Glasgow	1	0
1998	22 Apr	Edinburgh	1	1

		v FRANCE	S	F
1930	18 May	Paris	2	0
1932	8 May	Paris	3	1
1948	23 May	Paris	0	3
1949	27 Apr	Glasgow	2	0
1950	27 May	Paris	1	0
1951	16 May	Glasgow	1	0
wc1958	15 June	Orebro	1	2
1984	1 June	Marseilles	0	2
wc1989	8 Mar	Glasgow	2	0
wc1989	11 Oct	Paris	0	3
1997	12 Nov	St Etienne	1	2
2000	29 Mar	Glasgow	0	2
2002	27 Mar	Paris	0	5
EC2006	7 Oct	Glasgow	1	0

		v GEORGIA	S	G
EC2007	24 Mar	Glasgow	2	1

		v GERMANY	*S*	*G*
1929	1 June	Berlin	1	1
1936	14 Oct	Glasgow	2	0
EC1992	15 June	Norrkoping	0	2
1993	24 Mar	Glasgow	0	1
1998	28 Apr	Bremen	1	0
EC2003	7 June	Glasgow	1	1
EC2003	10 Sept	Dortmund	1	2

		v EAST GERMANY	*S*	*EG*
1974	30 Oct	Glasgow	3	0
1977	7 Sept	East Berlin	0	1
EC1982	13 Oct	Glasgow	2	0
EC1983	16 Nov	Halle	1	2
1985	16 Oct	Glasgow	0	0
1990	25 Apr	Glasgow	0	1

		v WEST GERMANY	*S*	*WG*
1957	22 May	Stuttgart	3	1
1959	6 May	Glasgow	3	2
1964	12 May	Hanover	2	2
WC1969	16 Apr	Glasgow	1	1
WC1969	22 Oct	Hamburg	2	3
1973	14 Nov	Glasgow	1	1
1974	27 Mar	Frankfurt	1	2
WC1986	8 June	Queretaro	1	2

		v GREECE	*S*	*G*
EC1994	18 Dec	Athens	0	1
EC1995	16 Aug	Glasgow	1	0

		v HOLLAND	*S*	*H*
1929	4 June	Amsterdam	2	0
1938	21 May	Amsterdam	3	1
1959	27 May	Amsterdam	2	1
1966	11 May	Glasgow	0	3
1968	30 May	Amsterdam	0	0
1971	1 Dec	Rotterdam	1	2
WC1978	11 June	Mendoza	3	2
1982	23 Mar	Glasgow	2	1
1986	29 Apr	Eindhoven	0	0
EC1992	12 June	Gothenburg	0	1
1994	23 Mar	Glasgow	0	1
1994	27 May	Utrecht	1	3
EC1996	10 June	Birmingham	0	0
2000	26 Apr	Arnhem	0	0
EC2003	15 Nov	Glasgow	1	0
EC2003	19 Nov	Amsterdam	0	6

		v HONG KONG XI	*S*	*HK*
†2002	23 May	Hong Kong	4	0

†*match not recognised by FIFA*

		v HUNGARY	*S*	*H*
1938	7 Dec	Glasgow	3	1
1954	8 Dec	Glasgow	2	4
1955	29 May	Budapest	1	3
1958	7 May	Glasgow	1	1
1960	5 June	Budapest	3	3
1980	31 May	Budapest	1	3
1987	9 Sept	Glasgow	2	0
2004	18 Aug	Glasgow	0	3

		v ICELAND	*S*	*I*
WC1984	17 Oct	Glasgow	3	0
WC1985	28 May	Reykjavik	1	0
EC2002	12 Oct	Reykjavik	2	0
EC2003	29 Mar	Glasgow	2	1

		v IRAN	*S*	*I*
WC1978	7 June	Cordoba	1	1

		v REPUBLIC OF IRELAND	*S*	*RI*
WC1961	3 May	Glasgow	4	1
WC1961	7 May	Dublin	3	0
1963	9 June	Dublin	0	1
1969	21 Sept	Dublin	1	1
EC1986	15 Oct	Dublin	0	0
EC1987	18 Feb	Glasgow	0	1
2000	30 May	Dublin	2	1
2003	12 Feb	Glasgow	0	2

		v ISRAEL	*S*	*I*
WC1981	25 Feb	Tel Aviv	1	0
WC1981	28 Apr	Glasgow	3	1
1986	28 Jan	Tel Aviv	1	0

		v ITALY	*S*	*I*
1931	20 May	Rome	0	3
WC1965	9 Nov	Glasgow	1	0
WC1965	7 Dec	Naples	0	3
1988	22 Dec	Perugia	0	2
WC1992	18 Nov	Glasgow	0	0
WC1993	13 Oct	Rome	1	3
WC2005	26 Mar	Milan	0	2
WC2005	3 Sept	Glasgow	1	1
EC2007	28 Mar	Bari	0	2

		v JAPAN	*S*	*J*
1995	21 May	Hiroshima	0	0
2006	13 May	Saitama	0	0

		v LATVIA	*S*	*L*
WC1996	5 Oct	Riga	2	0
WC1997	11 Oct	Glasgow	2	0
WC2000	2 Sept	Riga	1	0
WC2001	6 Oct	Glasgow	2	1

		v LITHUANIA	*S*	*L*
EC1998	5 Sept	Vilnius	0	0
EC1999	9 Oct	Glasgow	3	0
EC2003	2 Apr	Kaunas	0	1
EC2003	11 Oct	Glasgow	1	0
EC2006	6 Sept	Kaunas	2	1

		v LUXEMBOURG	*S*	*L*
1947	24 May	Luxembourg	6	0
EC1986	12 Nov	Glasgow	3	0
EC1987	2 Dec	Esch	0	0

		v MALTA	*S*	*M*
1988	22 Mar	Valletta	1	1
1990	28 May	Valletta	2	1
WC1993	17 Feb	Glasgow	3	0
WC1993	17 Nov	Valletta	2	0
1997	1 June	Valletta	3	2

		v MOLDOVA	*S*	*M*
EC2004	13 Oct	Chisinau	1	1
EC2005	4 June	Glasgow	2	0

		v MOROCCO	*S*	*M*
WC1998	23 June	St Etienne	0	3

		v NEW ZEALAND	*S*	*NZ*
WC1982	15 June	Malaga	5	2
2003	27 May	Tynecastle	1	1

		v NIGERIA	*S*	*N*
2002	17 Apr	Aberdeen	1	2

		v NORWAY	*S*	*N*
1929	28 May	Oslo	7	3
1954	5 May	Glasgow	1	0
1954	19 May	Oslo	1	1
1963	4 June	Bergen	3	4
1963	7 Nov	Glasgow	6	1
1974	6 June	Oslo	2	1
EC1978	25 Oct	Glasgow	3	2
EC1979	7 June	Oslo	4	0
WC1988	14 Sept	Oslo	2	1
WC1989	15 Nov	Glasgow	1	1
1992	3 June	Oslo	0	0
WC1998	16 June	Bordeaux	1	1
2003	20 Aug	Oslo	0	0
WC2004	9 Oct	Glasgow	0	1
WC2005	7 Sept	Oslo	2	1

		v PARAGUAY	*S*	*P*
WC1958	11 June	Norrkoping	2	3

		v PERU	*S*	*P*
1972	26 Apr	Glasgow	2	0
WC1978	3 June	Cordoba	1	3
1979	12 Sept	Glasgow	1	1

		v POLAND	*S*	*P*
1958	1 June	Warsaw	2	1
1960	4 June	Glasgow	2	3
WC1965	23 May	Chorzow	1	1
WC1965	13 Oct	Glasgow	1	2
1980	28 May	Poznan	0	1
1990	19 May	Glasgow	1	1
2001	25 Apr	Bydgoszcz	1	1

		v PORTUGAL	*S*	*P*
1950	21 May	Lisbon	2	2
1955	4 May	Glasgow	3	0
1959	3 June	Lisbon	0	1
1966	18 June	Glasgow	0	1
EC1971	21 Apr	Lisbon	0	2
EC1971	13 Oct	Glasgow	2	1
1975	13 May	Glasgow	1	0
EC1978	29 Nov	Lisbon	0	1
EC1980	26 Mar	Glasgow	4	1
WC1980	15 Oct	Glasgow	0	0
WC1981	18 Nov	Lisbon	1	2
WC1992	14 Oct	Glasgow	0	0
WC1993	28 Apr	Lisbon	0	5
2002	20 Nov	Braga	0	2

		v ROMANIA	*S*	*R*
EC1975	1 June	Bucharest	1	1
EC1975	17 Dec	Glasgow	1	1
1986	26 Mar	Glasgow	3	0
EC1990	12 Sept	Glasgow	2	1
EC1991	16 Oct	Bucharest	0	1
2004	31 Mar	Glasgow	1	2

		v RUSSIA	*S*	*R*
EC1994	16 Nov	Glasgow	1	1
EC1995	29 Mar	Moscow	0	0

		v SAN MARINO	*S*	*SM*
EC1991	1 May	Serravalle	2	0
EC1991	13 Nov	Glasgow	4	0
EC1995	26 Apr	Serravalle	2	0
EC1995	15 Nov	Glasgow	5	0
WC2000	7 Oct	Serravalle	2	0
WC2001	28 Mar	Glasgow	4	0

		v SAUDI ARABIA	*S*	*SA*
1988	17 Feb	Riyadh	2	2

		v SLOVENIA	*S*	*Sl*
WC2004	8 Sept	Glasgow	0	0
WC2005	12 Oct	Celje	3	0

		v SOUTH AFRICA	*S*	*SA*
2002	20 May	Hong Kong	0	2

		v SOUTH KOREA	*S*	*SK*
2002	16 May	Busan	1	4

		v SPAIN	*S*	*Sp*
WC1957	8 May	Glasgow	4	2
WC1957	26 May	Madrid	1	4
1963	13 June	Madrid	6	2
1965	8 May	Glasgow	0	0
EC1974	20 Nov	Glasgow	1	2
EC1975	5 Feb	Valencia	1	1
1982	24 Feb	Valencia	0	3
WC1984	14 Nov	Glasgow	3	1
WC1985	27 Feb	Seville	0	1
1988	27 Apr	Madrid	0	0
2004	3 Sept	Valencia	1	1

Match abandoned afer 60 minutes; floodlight failure.

		v SWEDEN	*S*	*Sw*
1952	30 May	Stockholm	1	3
1953	6 May	Glasgow	1	2
1975	16 Apr	Gothenburg	1	1
1977	27 Apr	Glasgow	3	1
WC1980	10 Sept	Stockholm	1	0
WC1981	9 Sept	Glasgow	2	0
WC1990	16 June	Genoa	2	1
1995	11 Oct	Stockholm	0	2
WC1996	10 Nov	Glasgow	1	0
WC1997	30 Apr	Gothenburg	1	2
2004	17 Nov	Edinburgh	1	4

		v SWITZERLAND	*S*	*Sw*
1931	24 May	Geneva	3	2
1948	17 May	Berne	1	2
1950	26 Apr	Glasgow	3	1
WC1957	19 May	Basle	2	1
WC1957	6 Nov	Glasgow	3	2
1973	22 June	Berne	0	1
1976	7 Apr	Glasgow	1	0
EC1982	17 Nov	Berne	0	2
EC1983	30 May	Glasgow	2	2
EC1990	17 Oct	Glasgow	2	1
EC1991	11 Sept	Berne	2	2
WC1992	9 Sept	Berne	1	3
WC1993	8 Sept	Aberdeen	1	1
WC1996	18 June	Birmingham	1	0
2006	1 Mar	Glasgow	1	3

		v TRINIDAD & TOBAGO	*S*	*TT*
2004	30 May	Edinburgh	4	1

		v TURKEY	*S*	*T*
1960	8 June	Ankara	2	4

		v UKRAINE	*S*	*U*
EC2006	11 Oct	Kiev	0	2

		v URUGUAY	*S*	*U*
WC1954	19 June	Basle	0	7
1962	2 May	Glasgow	2	3
1983	21 Sept	Glasgow	2	0
WC1986	13 June	Nezahualcoyotl	0	0

		v USA	*S*	*USA*
1952	30 Apr	Glasgow	6	0
1992	17 May	Denver	1	0
1996	26 May	New Britain	1	2
1998	30 May	Washington	0	0
2005	11 Nov	Glasgow	1	1

		v USSR	*S*	*USSR*
1967	10 May	Glasgow	0	2
1971	14 June	Moscow	0	1
WC1982	22 June	Malaga	2	2
1991	6 Feb	Glasgow	0	1

		v YUGOSLAVIA	*S*	*Y*
1955	15 May	Belgrade	2	2
1956	21 Nov	Glasgow	2	0
WC1958	8 June	Vasteras	1	1
1972	29 June	Belo Horizonte	2	2
WC1974	22 June	Frankfurt	1	1
1984	12 Sept	Glasgow	6	1
WC1988	19 Oct	Glasgow	1	1
WC1989	6 Sept	Zagreb	1	3

		v ZAIRE	*S*	*Z*
WC1974	14 June	Dortmund	2	0

WALES

		v ALBANIA	*W*	*A*
EC1994	7 Sept	Cardiff	2	0
EC1995	15 Nov	Tirana	1	1

		v ARGENTINA	*W*	*A*
1992	3 June	Tokyo	0	1
2002	13 Feb	Cardiff	1	1

		v ARMENIA	*W*	*A*
WC2001	24 Mar	Erevan	2	2
WC2001	1 Sept	Cardiff	0	0

		v AUSTRIA	*W*	*A*
1954	9 May	Vienna	0	2
EC1955	23 Nov	Wrexham	1	2
EC1974	4 Sept	Vienna	1	2
1975	19 Nov	Wrexham	1	0
1992	29 Apr	Vienna	1	1
EC2005	26 Mar	Cardiff	0	2
EC2005	30 Mar	Vienna	0	1

		v AZERBAIJAN	*W*	*A*
EC2002	20 Nov	Baku	2	0
EC2003	29 Mar	Cardiff	4	0
WC2004	4 Sept	Baku	1	1
WC2005	12 Oct	Cardiff	2	0

		v BELARUS	*W*	*B*
EC1998	14 Oct	Cardiff	3	2
EC1999	4 Sept	Minsk	2	1
WC2000	2 Sept	Minsk	1	2
WC2001	6 Oct	Cardiff	1	0

		v BELGIUM	*W*	*B*
1949	22 May	Liège	1	3
1949	23 Nov	Cardiff	5	1
EC1990	17 Oct	Cardiff	3	1
EC1991	27 Mar	Brussels	1	1
WC1992	18 Nov	Brussels	0	2
WC1993	31 Mar	Cardiff	2	0
WC1997	29 Mar	Cardiff	1	2
WC1997	11 Oct	Brussels	2	3

		v BOSNIA	*W*	*B*
2003	12 Feb	Cardiff	2	2

		v BRAZIL	*W*	*B*
WC1958	19 June	Gothenburg	0	1
1962	12 May	Rio de Janeiro	1	3
1962	16 May	São Paulo	1	3
1966	14 May	Rio de Janeiro	1	3
1966	18 May	Belo Horizonte	0	1
1983	12 June	Cardiff	1	1
1991	11 Sept	Cardiff	1	0
1997	12 Nov	Brasilia	0	3
2000	23 May	Cardiff	0	3
2006	5 Sept	Cardiff	0	2

		v BULGARIA	*W*	*B*
EC1983	27 Apr	Wrexham	1	0
EC1983	16 Nov	Sofia	0	1
EC1994	14 Dec	Cardiff	0	3
EC1995	29 Mar	Sofia	1	3
2006	15 Aug	Swansea	0	0

		v CANADA	*W*	*C*
1986	10 May	Toronto	0	2
1986	20 May	Vancouver	3	0
2004	30 May	Wrexham	1	0

		v CHILE	*W*	*C*
1966	22 May	Santiago	0	2

		v COSTA RICA	*W*	*CR*
1990	20 May	Cardiff	1	0

		v CROATIA	*W*	*C*
2002	21 Aug	Varazdin	1	1

		v CYPRUS	*W*	*C*
WC1992	14 Oct	Limassol	1	0
WC1993	13 Oct	Cardiff	2	0
2005	16 Nov	Limassol	0	1
EC2006	11 Oct	Cardiff	3	1

		v CZECHOSLOVAKIA	*W*	*C*
WC1957	1 May	Cardiff	1	0
WC1957	26 May	Prague	0	2
EC1971	21 Apr	Swansea	1	3
EC1971	27 Oct	Prague	0	1
WC1977	30 Mar	Wrexham	3	0
WC1977	16 Nov	Prague	0	1
WC1980	19 Nov	Cardiff	1	0
WC1981	9 Sept	Prague	0	2
EC1987	29 Apr	Wrexham	1	1
EC1987	11 Nov	Prague	0	2
WC1993	28 Apr	Ostrava†	1	1
WC1993	8 Sept	Cardiff†	2	2

†*Czechoslovakia played as RCS (Republic of Czechs and Slovaks).*

		v CZECH REPUBLIC	*W*	*CR*
2002	27 Mar	Cardiff	0	0
EC2006	2 Sept	Teplice	1	2
EC2007	2 June	Cardiff	0	0

		v DENMARK	*W*	*D*
WC1964	21 Oct	Copenhagen	0	1
WC1965	1 Dec	Wrexham	4	2
EC1987	9 Sept	Cardiff	1	0
EC1987	14 Oct	Copenhagen	0	1
1990	11 Sept	Copenhagen	0	1
EC1998	10 Oct	Copenhagen	2	1
EC1999	9 June	Liverpool	0	2

		v ESTONIA	*W*	*E*
1994	23 May	Tallinn	2	1

		v FINLAND	*W*	*F*
EC1971	26 May	Helsinki	1	0
EC1971	13 Oct	Swansea	3	0
EC1987	10 Sept	Helsinki	1	1
EC1987	1 Apr	Wrexham	4	0
WC1988	19 Oct	Swansea	2	2
WC1989	6 Sept	Helsinki	0	1
2000	29 Mar	Cardiff	1	2
EC2002	7 Sept	Helsinki	2	0
EC2003	10 Sept	Cardiff	1	1

		v FAEROES	*W*	*F*
WC1992	9 Sept	Cardiff	6	0
WC1993	6 June	Toftir	3	0

		v FRANCE	*W*	*F*
1933	25 May	Paris	1	1
1939	20 May	Paris	1	2
1953	14 May	Paris	1	6
1982	2 June	Toulouse	1	0

		v GEORGIA	*W*	*G*
EC1994	16 Nov	Tbilisi	0	5
EC1995	7 June	Cardiff	0	1

		v GERMANY	*W*	*G*
EC1995	26 Apr	Dusseldorf	1	1
EC1995	11 Oct	Cardiff	1	2
2002	14 May	Cardiff	1	0

		v EAST GERMANY	*W*	*EG*
WC1957	19 May	Leipzig	1	2
WC1957	25 Sept	Cardiff	4	1
WC1969	16 Apr	Dresden	1	2
WC1969	22 Oct	Cardiff	1	3

		v WEST GERMANY	*W*	*WG*
1968	8 May	Cardiff	1	1
1969	26 Mar	Frankfurt	1	1
1976	6 Oct	Cardiff	0	2
1977	14 Dec	Dortmund	1	1
EC1979	2 May	Wrexham	0	2
EC1979	17 Oct	Cologne	1	5
WC1989	31 May	Cardiff	0	0
WC1989	15 Nov	Cologne	1	2
EC1991	5 June	Cardiff	1	0
EC1991	16 Oct	Nuremberg	1	4

		v GREECE	*W*	*G*
WC1964	9 Dec	Athens	0	2
WC1965	17 Mar	Cardiff	4	1

		v HOLLAND	*W*	*H*
WC1988	14 Sept	Amsterdam	0	1
WC1989	11 Oct	Wrexham	1	2
1992	30 May	Utrecht	0	4
WC1996	5 Oct	Cardiff	1	3
WC1996	9 Nov	Eindhoven	1	7

		v HUNGARY	*W*	*H*
WC1958	8 June	Sanviken	1	1
WC1958	17 June	Stockholm	2	1
1961	28 May	Budapest	2	3
EC1962	7 Nov	Budapest	1	3
EC1963	20 Mar	Cardiff	1	1
EC1974	30 Oct	Cardiff	2	0
EC1975	16 Apr	Budapest	2	1
1985	16 Oct	Cardiff	0	3
2004	31 Mar	Budapest	2	1
2005	9 Feb	Cardiff	2	0

		v ICELAND	*W*	*I*
WC1980	2 June	Reykjavik	4	0
WC1981	14 Oct	Swansea	2	2
WC1984	12 Sept	Reykjavik	0	1
WC1984	14 Nov	Cardiff	2	1
1991	1 May	Cardiff	1	0

v IRAN

			W	I
1978	18 Apr	Teheran	1	0

v REPUBLIC OF IRELAND

			W	RI
1960	28 Sept	Dublin	3	2
1979	11 Sept	Swansea	2	1
1981	24 Feb	Dublin	3	1
1986	26 Mar	Dublin	1	0
1990	28 Mar	Dublin	0	1
1991	6 Feb	Wrexham	0	3
1992	19 Feb	Dublin	1	0
1993	17 Feb	Dublin	1	2
1997	11 Feb	Cardiff	0	0
EC2007	24 Mar	Dublin	0	1

v ISRAEL

			W	I
WC1958	15 Jan	Tel Aviv	2	0
WC1958	5 Feb	Cardiff	2	0
1984	10 June	Tel Aviv	0	0
1989	8 Feb	Tel Aviv	3	3

v ITALY

			W	I
1965	1 May	Florence	1	4
WC1968	23 Oct	Cardiff	0	1
WC1969	4 Nov	Rome	1	4
1988	4 June	Brescia	1	0
1996	24 Jan	Terni	0	3
EC1998	5 Sept	Liverpool	0	2
EC1999	5 June	Bologna	0	4
EC2002	16 Oct	Cardiff	2	1
EC2003	6 Sept	Milan	0	4

v JAMAICA

			W	J
1998	25 Mar	Cardiff	0	0

v JAPAN

			W	J
1992	7 June	Matsuyama	1	0

v LATVIA

			W	L
2004	18 Aug	Riga	2	0

v LIECHTENSTEIN

			W	L
2006	14 Nov	Swansea	4	0

v KUWAIT

			W	K
1977	6 Sept	Wrexham	0	0
1977	20 Sept	Kuwait	0	0

v LUXEMBOURG

			W	L
EC1974	20 Nov	Swansea	5	0
EC1975	1 May	Luxembourg	3	1
EC1990	14 Nov	Luxembourg	1	0
EC1991	13 Nov	Cardiff	1	0

v MALTA

			W	M
EC1978	25 Oct	Wrexham	7	0
EC1979	2 June	Valletta	2	0
1988	1 June	Valletta	3	2
1998	3 June	Valletta	3	0

v MEXICO

			W	M
WC1958	11 June	Stockholm	1	1
1962	22 May	Mexico City	1	2

v MOLDOVA

			W	M
EC1994	12 Oct	Kishinev	2	3
EC1995	6 Sept	Cardiff	1	0

v NEW ZEALAND

			W	NZ
2007	26 May	Wrexham	2	2

v NORWAY

			W	N
EC1982	22 Sept	Swansea	1	0
EC1983	21 Sept	Oslo	0	0
1984	6 June	Trondheim	0	1
1985	26 Feb	Wrexham	1	1
1985	5 June	Bergen	2	4
1994	9 Mar	Cardiff	1	3
WC2000	7 Oct	Cardiff	1	1
WC2001	5 Sept	Oslo	2	3
2004	27 May	Oslo	0	0

v PARAGUAY

			W	P
2006	1 Mar	Cardiff	0	0

v POLAND

			W	P
WC1973	28 Mar	Cardiff	2	0
WC1973	26 Sept	Katowice	0	3
1991	29 May	Radom	0	0
WC2000	11 Oct	Warsaw	0	0
WC2001	2 June	Cardiff	1	2
WC2004	13 Oct	Cardiff	2	3
WC2005	7 Sept	Warsaw	0	1

v PORTUGAL

			W	P
1949	15 May	Lisbon	2	3
1951	12 May	Cardiff	2	1
2000	2 June	Chaves	0	3

v QATAR

			W	Q
2000	23 Feb	Doha	1	0

v ROMANIA

			W	R
EC1970	11 Nov	Cardiff	0	0
EC1971	24 Nov	Bucharest	0	2
1983	12 Oct	Wrexham	5	0
WC1992	20 May	Bucharest	1	5
WC1993	17 Nov	Cardiff	1	2

v RUSSIA

			W	R
EC2003	15 Nov	Moscow	0	0
EC2003	19 Nov	Cardiff	0	1

v SAN MARINO

			W	SM
WC1996	2 June	Serravalle	5	0
WC1996	31 Aug	Cardiff	6	0
EC2007	28 Mar	Cardiff	3	0

v SAUDI ARABIA

			W	SA
1986	25 Feb	Dahran	2	1

v SERBIA-MONTENEGRO

			W	SM
EC2003	20 Aug	Belgrade	0	1
EC2003	11 Oct	Cardiff	2	3

v SLOVAKIA

			W	S
EC 2006	7 Oct	Bratislava	1	5

v SLOVENIA

			W	Sl
2005	17 Aug	Swansea	0	0

v SPAIN

			W	S
WC1961	19 Apr	Cardiff	1	2
WC1961	18 May	Madrid	1	1
1982	24 Mar	Valencia	1	1
WC1984	17 Oct	Seville	0	3
WC1985	30 Apr	Wrexham	3	0

v SWEDEN

			W	S
WC1958	15 June	Stockholm	0	0
1988	27 Apr	Stockholm	1	4
1989	26 Apr	Wrexham	0	2
1990	25 Apr	Stockholm	2	4
1994	20 Apr	Wrexham	0	2

v SWITZERLAND

			W	S
1949	26 May	Berne	0	4
1951	16 May	Wrexham	3	2
1996	24 Apr	Lugano	0	2
EC1999	31 Mar	Zurich	0	2
EC1999	9 Oct	Wrexham	0	2

v TRINIDAD & TOBAGO

			W	TT
2006	27 May	Graz	2	1

v TUNISIA

			W	T
1998	6 June	Tunis	0	4

v TURKEY

			W	T
EC1978	29 Nov	Wrexham	1	0
EC1979	21 Nov	Izmir	0	1
WC1980	15 Oct	Cardiff	4	0
WC1981	25 Mar	Ankara	1	0
WC1996	14 Dec	Cardiff	0	0
WC1997	20 Aug	Istanbul	4	6

v REST OF UNITED KINGDOM

			W	UK
1951	5 Dec	Cardiff	3	2
1969	28 July	Cardiff	0	1

		v UKRAINE	*W*	*U*
wc2001	28 Mar	Cardiff	1	1
wc2001	6 June	Kiev	1	1

		v USA	*W*	*USA*
2003	27 May	San Jose	0	2

		v URUGUAY	*W*	*U*
1986	21 Apr	Wrexham	0	0

		v USSR	*W*	*USSR*
wc1965	30 May	Moscow	1	2
wc1965	27 Oct	Cardiff	2	1
wc1981	30 May	Wrexham	0	0
wc1981	18 Nov	Tbilisi	0	3
1987	18 Feb	Swansea	0	0

		v YUGOSLAVIA	*W*	*Y*
1953	21 May	Belgrade	2	5
1954	22 Nov	Cardiff	1	3
			W	*Y*
EC1976	24 Apr	Zagreb	0	2
EC1976	22 May	Cardiff	1	1
EC1982	15 Dec	Titograd	4	4
EC1983	14 Dec	Cardiff	1	1
1988	23 Mar	Swansea	1	2

NORTHERN IRELAND

		v ALBANIA	*NI*	*A*
wc1965	7 May	Belfast	4	1
wc1965	24 Nov	Tirana	1	1
EC1982	15 Dec	Tirana	0	0
EC1983	27 Apr	Belfast	1	0
wc1992	9 Sept	Belfast	3	0
wc1993	17 Feb	Tirana	2	1
wc1996	14 Dec	Belfast	2	0
wc1997	10 Sept	Zurich	0	1

		v ALGERIA	*NI*	*A*
wc1986	3 June	Guadalajara	1	1

		v ARGENTINA	*NI*	*A*
wc1958	11 June	Halmstad	1	3

		v ARMENIA	*NI*	*A*
wc1996	5 Oct	Belfast	1	1
wc1997	30 Apr	Erevan	0	0
EC2003	29 Mar	Erevan	0	1
EC2003	10 Sept	Belfast	0	1

		v AUSTRALIA	*NI*	*A*
1980	11 June	Sydney	2	1
1980	15 June	Melbourne	1	1
1980	18 June	Adelaide	2	1

		v AUSTRIA	*NI*	*A*
wc1982	1 July	Madrid	2	2
EC1982	13 Oct	Vienna	0	2
EC1983	21 Sept	Belfast	3	1
EC1990	14 Nov	Vienna	0	0
EC1991	16 Oct	Belfast	2	1
EC1994	12 Oct	Vienna	2	1
EC1995	15 Nov	Belfast	5	3
wc2004	13 Oct	Belfast	3	3
wc2005	12 Oct	Vienna	0	2

		v AZERBAIJAN	*NI*	*A*
wc2004	9 Oct	Baku	0	0
wc2005	3 Sept	Belfast	2	0

		v BARBADOS	*NI*	*B*
2004	30 May	Waterford	1	1

		v BELGIUM	*NI*	*B*
wc1976	10 Nov	Liège	0	2
wc1977	16 Nov	Belfast	3	0
1997	11 Feb	Belfast	3	0

		v BRAZIL	*NI*	*B*
wc1986	12 June	Guadalajara	0	3

		v BULGARIA	*NI*	*B*
wc1972	18 Oct	Sofia	0	3
wc1973	26 Sept	Sheffield	0	0
EC1978	29 Nov	Sofia	2	0
EC1979	2 May	Belfast	2	0
wc2001	28 Mar	Sofia	3	4
wc2001	2 June	Belfast	0	1

		v CANADA	*NI*	*C*
1995	22 May	Edmonton	0	2
1999	27 Apr	Belfast	1	1
2005	9 Feb	Belfast	0	1

		v CHILE	*NI*	*C*
1989	26 May	Belfast	0	1
1995	25 May	Edmonton	1	2

		v COLOMBIA	*NI*	*C*
1994	4 June	Boston	0	2

		v CYPRUS	*NI*	*C*
EC1971	3 Feb	Nicosia	3	0
EC1971	21 Apr	Belfast	5	0
wc1973	14 Feb	Nicosia	0	1
wc1973	8 May	London	3	0
2002	21 Aug	Belfast	0	0

		v CZECHOSLOVAKIA	*NI*	*C*
wc1958	8 June	Halmstad	1	0
wc1958	17 June	Malmo	2	1*

**After extra time*

		v CZECH REPUBLIC	*NI*	*C*
wc2001	24 Mar	Belfast	0	1
wc2001	6 June	Teplice	1	3

		v DENMARK	*NI*	*D*
EC1978	25 Oct	Belfast	2	1
EC1979	6 June	Copenhagen	0	4
1986	26 Mar	Belfast	1	1
EC1990	17 Oct	Belfast	1	1
EC1991	13 Nov	Odense	1	2
wc1992	18 Nov	Belfast	0	1
wc1993	13 Oct	Copenhagen	0	1
wc2000	7 Oct	Belfast	1	1
wc2001	1 Sept	Copenhagen	1	1
EC2006	7 Oct	Copenhagen	0	0

		v ESTONIA	*NI*	*E*
2004	31 Mar	Tallinn	1	0
2006	1 Mar	Belfast	1	0

		v FAEROES	*NI*	*F*
EC1991	1 May	Belfast	1	1
EC1991	11 Sept	Landskrona	5	0

		v FINLAND	*NI*	*F*
wc1984	27 May	Pori	0	1
wc1984	14 Nov	Belfast	2	1
EC1998	10 Oct	Belfast	1	0
EC1998	9 Oct	Helsinki	1	4
2003	12 Feb	Belfast	0	1
2006	16 Aug	Helsinki	2	1

		v FRANCE	*NI*	*F*
1928	21 Feb	Paris	0	4
1951	12 May	Belfast	2	2
1952	11 Nov	Paris	1	3
wc1958	19 June	Norrkoping	0	4
1982	24 Mar	Paris	0	4
wc1982	4 July	Madrid	1	4
1986	26 Feb	Paris	0	0
1988	27 Apr	Belfast	0	0
1999	18 Aug	Belfast	0	1

		v GERMANY	*NI*	*G*
1992	2 June	Bremen	1	1
1996	29 May	Belfast	1	1
wc1996	9 Nov	Nuremberg	1	1
wc1997	20 Aug	Belfast	1	3
EC1999	27 Mar	Belfast	0	3
EC1999	8 Sept	Dortmund	0	4
2005	4 June	Belfast	1	4

		v WEST GERMANY	NI	WG
wc1958	15 June	Malmo	2	2
wc1960	26 Oct	Belfast	3	4
wc1961	10 May	Hamburg	1	2
1966	7 May	Belfast	0	2
1977	27 Apr	Cologne	0	5
EC1982	17 Nov	Belfast	1	0
EC1983	16 Nov	Hamburg	1	0

		v GREECE	NI	G
wc1961	3 May	Athens	1	2
wc1961	17 Oct	Belfast	2	0
1988	17 Feb	Athens	2	3
EC2003	2 Apr	Belfast	0	2
EC2003	11 Oct	Athens	0	1

		v HOLLAND	NI	H
1962	9 May	Rotterdam	0	4
wc1965	17 Mar	Belfast	2	1
wc1965	7 Apr	Rotterdam	0	0
wc1976	13 Oct	Rotterdam	2	2
wc1977	12 Oct	Belfast	0	1

		v HONDURAS	NI	H
wc1982	21 June	Zaragoza	1	1

		v HUNGARY	NI	H
wc1988	19 Oct	Budapest	0	1
wc1989	6 Sept	Belfast	1	2
2000	26 Apr	Belfast	0	1

		v ICELAND	NI	I
wc1977	11 June	Reykjavik	0	1
wc1977	21 Sept	Belfast	2	0
wc2000	11 Oct	Reykjavik	0	1
wc2001	5 Sept	Belfast	3	0
EC2006	2 Sept	Belfast	0	3

		v REPUBLIC OF IRELAND	NI	RI
EC1978	20 Sept	Dublin	0	0
EC1979	21 Nov	Belfast	1	0
wc1988	14 Sept	Belfast	0	0
wc1989	11 Oct	Dublin	0	3
wc1993	31 Mar	Dublin	0	3
wc1993	17 Nov	Belfast	1	1
EC1994	16 Nov	Belfast	0	4
EC1995	29 Mar	Dublin	1	1
1999	29 May	Dublin	1	0

		v ISRAEL	NI	I
1968	10 Sept	Jaffa	3	2
1976	3 Mar	Tel Aviv	1	1
wc1980	26 Mar	Tel Aviv	0	0
wc1981	18 Nov	Belfast	1	0
1984	16 Oct	Belfast	3	0
1987	18 Feb	Tel Aviv	1	1

		v ITALY	NI	I
wc1957	25 Apr	Rome	0	1
1957	4 Dec	Belfast	2	2
wc1958	15 Jan	Belfast	2	1
1961	25 Apr	Bologna	2	3
1997	22 Jan	Palermo	0	2
2003	3 June	Campobasso	0	2

		v LATVIA	NI	L
wc1993	2 June	Riga	2	1
wc1993	8 Sept	Belfast	2	0
EC1995	26 Apr	Riga	1	0
EC1995	7 June	Belfast	1	2
EC2006	11 Oct	Belfast	1	0

		v LIECHTENSTEIN	NI	L
EC1994	20 Apr	Belfast	4	1
EC1995	11 Oct	Eschen	4	0
2002	27 Mar	Vaduz	0	0
EC2007	24 Mar	Vaduz	4	1

		v LITHUANIA	NI	L
wc1992	28 Apr	Belfast	2	2
wc1993	25 May	Vilnius	1	0

		v LUXEMBOURG	NI	L
2000	23 Feb	Luxembourg	3	1

		v MALTA	NI	M
wc1988	21 May	Belfast	3	0
wc1989	26 Apr	Valletta	2	0
2000	28 Mar	Valletta	3	0
wc2000	2 Sept	Belfast	1	0
wc2001	6 Oct	Valletta	1	0
2005	17 Aug	Ta'Qali	1	1

		v MEXICO	NI	M
1966	22 June	Belfast	4	1
1994	11 June	Miami	0	3

		v MOLDOVA	NI	M
EC1998	18 Nov	Belfast	2	2
EC1999	31 Mar	Chisinau	0	0

		v MOROCCO	NI	M
1986	23 Apr	Belfast	2	1

		v NORWAY	NI	N
1922	25 May	Bergen	1	2
EC1974	4 Sept	Oslo	1	2
EC1975	29 Oct	Belfast	3	0
1990	27 Mar	Belfast	2	3
1996	27 Mar	Belfast	0	2
2001	28 Feb	Belfast	0	4
2004	18 Feb	Belfast	1	4

		v POLAND	NI	P
EC1962	10 Oct	Katowice	2	0
EC1962	28 Nov	Belfast	2	0
1988	23 Mar	Belfast	1	1
1991	5 Feb	Belfast	3	1
2002	13 Feb	Limassol	1	4
EC2004	4 Sept	Belfast	0	3
EC2005	30 Mar	Warsaw	0	1

		v PORTUGAL	NI	P
wc1957	16 Jan	Lisbon	1	1
wc1957	1 May	Belfast	3	0
wc1973	28 Mar	Coventry	1	1
wc1973	14 Nov	Lisbon	1	1
wc1980	19 Nov	Lisbon	0	1
wc1981	29 Apr	Belfast	1	0
EC1994	7 Sept	Belfast	1	2
EC1995	3 Sept	Lisbon	1	1
wc1997	29 Mar	Belfast	0	0
wc1997	11 Oct	Lisbon	0	1
2005	15 Nov	Belfast	1	1

		v ROMANIA	NI	R
wc1984	12 Sept	Belfast	3	2
wc1985	16 Oct	Bucharest	1	0
1994	23 Mar	Belfast	2	0
2006	27 May	Chicago	0	2

		v ST KITTS & NEVIS	NI	SK
2004	2 June	Basseterre	2	0

		v SERBIA-MONTENEGRO	NI	SM
2004	28 Apr	Belfast	1	1

		v SLOVAKIA	NI	S
1998	25 Mar	Belfast	1	0

		v SOUTH AFRICA	NI	SA
1924	24 Sept	Belfast	1	2

		v SPAIN	NI	S
1958	15 Oct	Madrid	2	6
1963	30 May	Bilbao	1	1
1963	30 Oct	Belfast	0	1
EC1970	11 Nov	Seville	0	3
EC1972	16 Feb	Hull	1	1
wc1982	25 June	Valencia	1	0
1985	27 Mar	Palma	0	0
wc1986	7 June	Guadalajara	1	2
wc1988	21 Dec	Seville	0	4
wc1989	8 Feb	Belfast	0	2
wc1992	14 Oct	Belfast	0	0
wc1993	28 Apr	Seville	1	3
1998	2 June	Santander	1	4

			NI	S
2002	17 Apr	Belfast	0	5
EC2002	12 Oct	Albacete	0	3
EC2003	11 June	Belfast	0	0
EC2006	6 Sept	Belfast	3	2

		v SWEDEN	NI	S
EC1974	30 Oct	Solna	2	0
EC1975	3 Sept	Belfast	1	2
WC1980	15 Oct	Belfast	3	0
WC1981	3 June	Solna	0	1
1996	24 Apr	Belfast	1	2
EC2007	28 Mar	Belfast	2	1

		v SWITZERLAND	NI	S
WC1964	14 Oct	Belfast	1	0
WC1964	14 Nov	Lausanne	1	2
1998	22 Apr	Belfast	1	0
2004	18 Aug	Zurich	0	0

		v THAILAND	NI	T
1997	21 May	Bangkok	0	0

		v TRINIDAD & TOBAGO	NI	TT
2004	6 June	Bacolet	3	0

		v TURKEY	NI	T
WC1968	23 Oct	Belfast	4	1
WC1968	11 Dec	Istanbul	3	0
EC1983	30 Mar	Belfast	2	1
EC1983	12 Oct	Ankara	0	1
WC1985	1 May	Belfast	2	0
WC1985	11 Sept	Izmir	0	0
EC1986	12 Nov	Izmir	0	0
EC1987	11 Nov	Belfast	1	0
EC1998	5 Sept	Istanbul	0	3
EC1999	4 Sept	Belfast	0	3

		v UKRAINE	NI	U
WC1996	31 Aug	Belfast	0	1
WC1997	2 Apr	Kiev	1	2
EC2002	16 Oct	Belfast	0	0
EC2003	6 Sept	Donetsk	0	0

		v URUGUAY	NI	U
1964	29 Apr	Belfast	3	0
1990	18 May	Belfast	1	0
2006	21 May	New Jersey	0	1

		v USSR	NI	USSR
WC1969	19 Sept	Belfast	0	0
WC1969	22 Oct	Moscow	0	2
EC1971	22 Sept	Moscow	0	1
EC1971	13 Oct	Belfast	1	1

		v YUGOSLAVIA	NI	Y
EC1975	16 Mar	Belfast	1	0
EC1975	19 Nov	Belgrade	0	1
WC1982	17 June	Zaragoza	0	0
EC1987	29 Apr	Belfast	1	2
EC1987	14 Oct	Sarajevo	0	3
EC1990	12 Sept	Belfast	0	2
EC1991	27 Mar	Belgrade	1	4
2000	16 Aug	Belfast	1	2

REPUBLIC OF IRELAND

		v ALBANIA	RI	A
WC1992	26 May	Dublin	2	0
WC1993	26 May	Tirana	2	1
EC2003	2 Apr	Tirana	0	0
EC2003	7 June	Dublin	2	1

		v ALGERIA	RI	A
1982	28 Apr	Algiers	0	2

		v ANDORRA	RI	A
WC2001	28 Mar	Barcelona	3	0
WC2001	25 Apr	Dublin	3	1

		v ARGENTINA	RI	A
1951	13 May	Dublin	0	1
†1979	29 May	Dublin	0	0
1980	16 May	Dublin	0	1
1998	22 Apr	Dublin	0	2

†*Not considered a full international.*

		v AUSTRALIA	RI	A
2003	19 Aug	Dublin	2	1

		v AUSTRIA	RI	A
1952	7 May	Vienna	0	6
1953	25 Mar	Dublin	4	0
1958	14 Mar	Vienna	1	3
1962	8 Apr	Dublin	2	3
EC1963	25 Sept	Vienna	0	0
EC1963	13 Oct	Dublin	3	2
1966	22 May	Vienna	0	1
1968	10 Nov	Dublin	2	2
EC1971	30 May	Dublin	1	4
EC1971	10 Oct	Linz	0	6
EC1995	11 June	Dublin	1	3
EC1995	6 Sept	Vienna	1	3

		v BELGIUM	RI	B
1928	12 Feb	Liège	4	2
1929	30 Apr	Dublin	4	0
1930	11 May	Brussels	3	1
WC1934	25 Feb	Dublin	4	4
1949	24 Apr	Dublin	0	2
1950	10 May	Brussels	1	5
1965	24 Mar	Dublin	0	2
1966	25 May	Liège	3	2
WC1980	15 Oct	Dublin	1	1
WC1981	25 Mar	Brussels	0	1
EC1986	10 Sept	Brussels	2	2
EC1987	29 Apr	Dublin	0	0
WC1997	29 Oct	Dublin	1	1
WC1997	16 Nov	Brussels	1	2

		v BOLIVIA	RI	B
1994	24 May	Dublin	1	0
1996	15 June	New Jersey	3	0
2007	26 May	Boston	1	1

		v BRAZIL	RI	B
1974	5 May	Rio de Janeiro	1	2
1982	27 May	Uberlandia	0	7
1987	23 May	Dublin	1	0
2004	18 Feb	Dublin	0	0

		v BULGARIA	RI	B
WC1977	1 June	Sofia	1	2
WC1977	12 Oct	Dublin	0	0
EC1979	19 May	Sofia	0	1
EC1979	17 Oct	Dublin	3	0
WC1987	1 Apr	Sofia	1	2
WC1987	14 Oct	Dublin	2	0
2004	18 Aug	Dublin	1	1

		v CAMEROON	RI	C
WC2002	1 June	Niigata	1	1

		v CANADA	RI	C
2003	18 Nov	Dublin	3	0

		v CHILE	RI	C
1960	30 Mar	Dublin	2	0
1972	21 June	Recife	1	2
1974	12 May	Santiago	2	1
1982	22 May	Santiago	0	1
1991	22 May	Dublin	1	1
2006	24 May	Dublin	0	1

		v CHINA	RI	C
1984	3 June	Sapporo	1	0
2005	29 Mar	Dublin	1	0

		v CROATIA	RI	C
1996	2 June	Dublin	2	2
EC1998	5 Sept	Dublin	2	0

			RI	C
EC1999	4 Sept	Zagreb	0	1
2001	15 Aug	Dublin	2	2
2004	16 Nov	Dublin	1	0

		v CYPRUS	RI	C
WC1980	26 Mar	Nicosia	3	2
WC1980	19 Nov	Dublin	6	0
WC2001	24 Mar	Nicosia	4	0
WC2001	6 Oct	Dublin	4	0
WC2004	4 Sept	Dublin	3	0
WC2005	8 Oct	Nicosia	1	0
EC2006	7 Oct	Nicosia	2	5

		v CZECHOSLOVAKIA	RI	C
1938	18 May	Prague	2	2
EC1959	5 Apr	Dublin	2	0
EC1959	10 May	Bratislava	0	4
WC1961	8 Oct	Dublin	1	3
WC1961	29 Oct	Prague	1	7
EC1967	21 May	Dublin	0	2
EC1967	22 Nov	Prague	2	1
WC1969	4 May	Dublin	1	2
WC1969	7 Oct	Prague	0	3
1979	26 Sept	Prague	1	4
1981	29 Apr	Dublin	3	1
1986	27 May	Reykjavik	1	0

		v CZECH REPUBLIC	RI	C
1994	5 June	Dublin	1	3
1996	24 Apr	Prague	0	2
1998	25 Mar	Olomouc	1	2
2000	23 Feb	Dublin	3	2
2004	31 Mar	Dublin	2	1
EC2006	11 Oct	Dublin	1	1

		v DENMARK	RI	D
WC1956	3 Oct	Dublin	2	1
WC1957	2 Oct	Copenhagen	2	0
WC1968	4 Dec	Dublin	1	1
(abandoned after 51 mins)				
WC1969	27 May	Copenhagen	0	2
WC1969	15 Oct	Dublin	1	1
EC1978	24 May	Copenhagen	3	3
EC1979	2 May	Dublin	2	0
WC1984	14 Nov	Copenhagen	0	3
WC1985	13 Nov	Dublin	1	4
WC1992	14 Oct	Copenhagen	0	0
WC1993	28 Apr	Dublin	1	1
2002	27 Mar	Dublin	3	0

		v ECUADOR	RI	E
1972	19 June	Natal	3	2
2007	23 May	New Jersey	1	1

		v EGYPT	RI	E
WC1990	17 June	Palermo	0	0

		v ENGLAND	RI	E
1946	30 Sept	Dublin	0	1
1949	21 Sept	Everton	2	0
WC1957	8 May	Wembley	1	5
WC1957	19 May	Dublin	1	1
1964	24 May	Dublin	1	3
1976	8 Sept	Wembley	1	1
EC1978	25 Oct	Dublin	1	1
EC1980	6 Feb	Wembley	0	2
1985	26 Mar	Wembley	1	2
EC1988	12 June	Stuttgart	1	0
WC1990	11 June	Cagliari	1	1
EC1990	14 Nov	Dublin	1	1
EC1991	27 Mar	Wembley	1	1
1995	15 Feb	Dublin	1	0
(abandoned after 27 mins)				

		v ESTONIA	RI	E
WC2000	11 Oct	Dublin	2	0
WC2001	6 June	Tallinn	2	0

		v FAEROES	RI	F
EC2004	13 Oct	Dublin	2	0
EC2005	8 June	Toftir	2	0

		v FINLAND	RI	F
WC1949	8 Sept	Dublin	3	0
WC1949	9 Oct	Helsinki	1	1
1990	16 May	Dublin	1	1
2000	15 Nov	Dublin	3	0
2002	21 Aug	Helsinki	3	0

		v FRANCE	RI	F
1937	23 May	Paris	2	0
1952	16 Nov	Dublin	1	1
WC1953	4 Oct	Dublin	3	5
WC1953	25 Nov	Paris	0	1
WC1972	15 Nov	Dublin	2	1
WC1973	19 May	Paris	1	1
WC1976	17 Nov	Paris	0	2
WC1977	30 Mar	Dublin	1	0
WC1980	28 Oct	Paris	0	2
WC1981	14 Oct	Dublin	3	2
1989	7 Feb	Dublin	0	0
WC2004	9 Oct	Paris	0	0
WC2005	7 Sept	Dublin	0	1

		v GEORGIA	RI	G
EC2003	29 Mar	Tbilisi	2	1
EC2003	11 June	Dublin	2	0

		v GERMANY	RI	G
1935	8 May	Dortmund	1	3
1936	17 Oct	Dublin	5	2
1939	23 May	Bremen	1	1
1994	29 May	Hanover	2	0
WC2002	5 June	Ibaraki	1	1
EC2006	2 Sept	Stuttgart	0	1

		v WEST GERMANY	RI	WG
1951	17 Oct	Dublin	3	2
1952	4 May	Cologne	0	3
1955	28 May	Hamburg	1	2
1956	25 Nov	Dublin	3	0
1960	11 May	Dusseldorf	1	0
1966	4 May	Dublin	0	4
1970	9 May	Berlin	1	2
1975	1 Mar	Dublin	1	0†
1979	22 May	Dublin	1	3
1981	21 May	Bremen	0	3†
1989	6 Sept	Dublin	1	1

†v West Germany 'B'

		v GREECE	RI	G
2000	26 Apr	Dublin	0	1
2002	20 Nov	Athens	0	0

		v HOLLAND	RI	N
1932	8 May	Amsterdam	2	0
1934	8 Apr	Amsterdam	2	5
1935	8 Dec	Dublin	3	5
1955	1 May	Dublin	1	0
1956	10 May	Rotterdam	4	1
WC1980	10 Sept	Dublin	2	1
WC1981	9 Sept	Rotterdam	2	2
EC1982	22 Sept	Rotterdam	1	2
EC1983	12 Oct	Dublin	2	3
EC1988	18 June	Gelsenkirchen	0	1
WC1990	21 June	Palermo	1	1
1994	20 Apr	Tilburg	1	0
WC1994	4 July	Orlando	0	2
EC1995	13 Dec	Liverpool	0	2
1996	4 June	Rotterdam	1	3
WC2000	2 Sept	Amsterdam	2	2
WC2001	1 Sept	Dublin	1	0
2004	5 June	Amsterdam	1	0
2006	16 Aug	Dublin	0	4

		v HUNGARY	RI	H
1934	15 Dec	Dublin	2	4
1936	3 May	Budapest	3	3
1936	6 Dec	Dublin	2	3
1939	19 Mar	Cork	2	2
1939	18 May	Budapest	2	2
WC1969	8 June	Dublin	1	2
WC1969	5 Nov	Budapest	0	4
WC1989	8 Mar	Budapest	0	0
WC1989	4 June	Dublin	2	0
1991	11 Sept	Gyor	2	1

		v ICELAND	RI	I
EC1962	12 Aug	Dublin	4	2
EC1962	2 Sept	Reykjavik	1	1
EC1982	13 Oct	Dublin	2	0
EC1983	21 Sept	Reykjavik	3	0

			RI	I
1986	25 May	Reykjavik	2	1
WC1996	10 Nov	Dublin	0	0
WC1997	6 Sept	Reykjavik	4	2

v IRAN

			RI	I
1972	18 June	Recife	2	1
WC2001	10 Nov	Dublin	2	0
WC2001	15 Nov	Tehran	0	1

v N. IRELAND

			RI	NI
EC1978	20 Sept	Dublin	0	0
EC1979	21 Nov	Belfast	0	1
WC1988	14 Sept	Belfast	0	0
WC1989	11 Oct	Dublin	3	0
WC1993	31 Mar	Dublin	3	0
WC1993	17 Nov	Belfast	1	1
EC1994	16 Nov	Belfast	4	0
EC1995	29 Mar	Dublin	1	1
1999	29 May	Dublin	0	1

v ISRAEL

			RI	I
1984	4 Apr	Tel Aviv	0	3
1985	27 May	Tel Aviv	0	0
1987	10 Nov	Dublin	5	0
EC2005	26 Mar	Tel Aviv	1	1
EC2005	4 June	Dublin	2	2

v ITALY

			RI	I
1926	21 Mar	Turin	0	3
1927	23 Apr	Dublin	1	2
EC1970	8 Dec	Rome	0	3
EC1971	10 May	Dublin	1	2
1985	5 Feb	Dublin	1	2
WC1990	30 June	Rome	0	1
1992	4 June	Foxboro	0	2
WC1994	18 June	New York	1	0
2005	17 Aug	Dublin	1	2

v JAMAICA

			RI	J
2004	2 June	Charlton	1	0

v LATVIA

			RI	L
WC1992	9 Sept	Dublin	4	0
WC1993	2 June	Riga	2	1
EC1994	7 Sept	Riga	3	0
EC1995	11 Oct	Dublin	2	1

v LIECHTENSTEIN

			RI	L
EC1994	12 Oct	Dublin	4	0
EC1995	3 June	Eschen	0	0
WC1996	31 Aug	Eschen	5	0
WC1997	21 May	Dublin	5	0

v LITHUANIA

			RI	L
WC1993	16 June	Vilnius	1	0
WC1993	8 Sept	Dublin	2	0
WC1997	20 Aug	Dublin	0	0
WC1997	10 Sept	Vilnius	2	1

v LUXEMBOURG

			RI	L
1936	9 May	Luxembourg	5	1
WC1953	28 Oct	Dublin	4	0
WC1954	7 Mar	Luxembourg	1	0
EC1987	28 May	Luxembourg	2	0
EC1987	9 Sept	Dublin	2	1

v MACEDONIA

			RI	M
WC1996	9 Oct	Dublin	3	0
WC1997	2 Apr	Skopje	2	3
EC1999	9 June	Dublin	1	0
EC1999	9 Oct	Skopje	1	1

v MALTA

			RI	M
EC1983	30 Mar	Valletta	1	0
EC1983	16 Nov	Dublin	8	0
WC1989	28 May	Dublin	2	0
WC1989	15 Nov	Valletta	2	0
1990	2 June	Valletta	3	0
EC1998	14 Oct	Dublin	5	0
EC1999	8 Sept	Valletta	3	2

v MEXICO

			RI	M
1984	8 Aug	Dublin	0	0
WC1994	24 June	Orlando	1	2
1996	13 June	New Jersey	2	2
1998	23 May	Dublin	0	0
2000	4 June	Chicago	2	2

v MOROCCO

			RI	M
1990	12 Sept	Dublin	1	0

v NIGERIA

			RI	N
2002	16 May	Dublin	1	2
2004	29 May	Charlton	0	3

v NORWAY

			RI	N
WC1937	10 Oct	Oslo	2	3
WC1937	7 Nov	Dublin	3	3
1950	26 Nov	Dublin	2	2
1951	30 May	Oslo	3	2
1954	8 Nov	Dublin	2	1
1955	25 May	Oslo	3	1
1960	6 Nov	Dublin	3	1
1964	13 May	Oslo	4	1
1973	6 June	Oslo	1	1
1976	24 Mar	Dublin	3	0
1978	21 May	Oslo	0	0
WC1984	17 Oct	Oslo	0	1
WC1985	1 May	Dublin	0	0
1988	1 June	Oslo	0	0
WC1994	28 June	New York	0	0
2003	30 Apr	Dublin	1	0

v PARAGUAY

			RI	P
1999	10 Feb	Dublin	2	0

v POLAND

			RI	P
1938	22 May	Warsaw	0	6
1938	13 Nov	Dublin	3	2
1958	11 May	Katowice	2	2
1958	5 Oct	Dublin	2	2
1964	10 May	Kracow	1	3
1964	25 Oct	Dublin	3	2
1968	15 May	Dublin	2	2
1968	30 Oct	Katowice	0	1
1970	6 May	Dublin	1	2
1970	23 Sept	Dublin	0	2
1973	16 May	Wroclaw	0	2
1973	21 Oct	Dublin	1	0
1976	26 May	Poznan	2	0
1977	24 Apr	Dublin	0	0
1978	12 Apr	Lodz	0	3
1981	23 May	Bydgoszcz	0	3
1984	23 May	Dublin	0	0
1986	12 Nov	Warsaw	0	1
1988	22 May	Dublin	3	1
EC1991	1 May	Dublin	0	0
EC1991	16 Oct	Poznan	3	3
2004	28 Apr	Bydgoszcz	0	0

v PORTUGAL

			RI	P
1946	16 June	Lisbon	1	3
1947	4 May	Dublin	0	2
1948	23 May	Lisbon	0	2
1949	22 May	Dublin	1	0
1972	25 June	Recife	1	2
1992	7 June	Boston	2	0
EC1995	26 Apr	Dublin	1	0
EC1995	15 Nov	Lisbon	0	3
1996	29 May	Dublin	0	1
WC2000	7 Oct	Lisbon	1	1
WC2001	2 June	Dublin	1	1
2005	9 Feb	Dublin	1	0

v ROMANIA

			RI	R
1988	23 Mar	Dublin	2	0
WC1990	25 June	Genoa	0	0*
WC1997	30 Apr	Bucharest	0	1
WC1997	11 Oct	Dublin	1	1
2004	27 May	Dublin	1	0

v RUSSIA

			RI	R
1994	23 Mar	Dublin	0	0
1996	27 Mar	Dublin	0	2
2002	13 Feb	Dublin	2	0

			RI	*R*
EC2002	7 Sept	Moscow	2	4
EC2003	6 Sept	Dublin	1	1

		v SAN MARINO	*RI*	*SM*
EC2006	15 Nov	Dublin	5	0
EC2007	7 Feb	Serravalle	2	1

		v SAUDI ARABIA	*RI*	*SA*
WC2002	11 June	Yokohama	3	0

		v SCOTLAND	*RI*	*S*
WC1961	3 May	Glasgow	1	4
WC1961	7 May	Dublin	0	3
1963	9 June	Dublin	1	0
1969	21 Sept	Dublin	1	1
EC1986	15 Oct	Dublin	0	0
EC1987	18 Feb	Glasgow	1	0
2000	30 May	Dublin	1	2
2003	12 Feb	Glasgow	2	0

		v SLOVAKIA	*RI*	*S*
EC2007	28 Mar	Dublin	1	0

		v SOUTH AFRICA	*RI*	*SA*
2000	11 June	New Jersey	2	1

		v SPAIN	*RI*	*S*
1931	26 Apr	Barcelona	1	1
1931	13 Dec	Dublin	0	5
1946	23 June	Madrid	1	0
1947	2 Mar	Dublin	3	2
1948	30 May	Barcelona	1	2
1949	12 June	Dublin	1	4
1952	1 June	Madrid	0	6
1955	27 Nov	Dublin	2	2
EC1964	11 Mar	Seville	1	5
EC1964	8 Apr	Dublin	0	2
WC1965	5 May	Dublin	1	0
WC1965	27 Oct	Seville	1	4
WC1965	10 Nov	Paris	0	1
EC1966	23 Oct	Dublin	0	0
EC1966	7 Dec	Valencia	0	2
1977	9 Feb	Dublin	0	1
EC1982	17 Nov	Dublin	3	3
EC1983	27 Apr	Zaragoza	0	2
1985	26 May	Cork	0	0
WC1988	16 Nov	Seville	0	2
WC1989	26 Apr	Dublin	1	0
WC1992	18 Nov	Seville	0	0
WC1993	13 Oct	Dublin	1	3
WC2002	16 June	Suwon	1	1

		v SWEDEN	*RI*	*S*
WC1949	2 June	Stockholm	1	3
WC1949	13 Nov	Dublin	1	3
1959	1 Nov	Dublin	3	2
1960	18 May	Malmo	1	4
EC1970	14 Oct	Dublin	1	1
EC1970	28 Oct	Malmo	0	1
1999	28 Apr	Dublin	2	0
2006	1 Mar	Dublin	3	0

		v SWITZERLAND	*RI*	*S*
1935	5 May	Basle	0	1
1936	17 Mar	Dublin	1	0
1937	17 May	Berne	1	0
1938	18 Sept	Dublin	4	0
1948	5 Dec	Dublin	0	1
EC1975	11 May	Dublin	2	1
EC1975	21 May	Berne	0	1

			RI	*S*
1980	30 Apr	Dublin	2	0
WC1985	2 June	Dublin	3	0
WC1985	11 Sept	Berne	0	0
1992	25 Mar	Dublin	2	1
EC2002	16 Oct	Dublin	1	2
EC2003	11 Oct	Basle	0	2
WC2004	8 Sept	Basle	1	1
WC2005	12 Oct	Dublin	0	0

		v TRINIDAD & TOBAGO	*RI*	*TT*
1982	30 May	Port of Spain	1	2

		v TUNISIA	*RI*	*T*
1988	19 Oct	Dublin	4	0

		v TURKEY	*RI*	*T*
EC1966	16 Nov	Dublin	2	1
EC1967	22 Feb	Ankara	1	2
EC1974	20 Nov	Izmir	1	1
EC1975	29 Oct	Dublin	4	0
1976	13 Oct	Ankara	3	3
1978	5 Apr	Dublin	4	2
1990	26 May	Izmir	0	0
EC1990	17 Oct	Dublin	5	0
EC1991	13 Nov	Istanbul	3	1
EC2000	13 Nov	Dublin	1	1
EC2000	17 Nov	Bursa	0	0
2003	9 Sept	Dublin	2	2

		v URUGUAY	*RI*	*U*
1974	8 May	Montevideo	0	2
1986	23 Apr	Dublin	1	1

		v USA	*RI*	*USA*
1979	29 Oct	Dublin	3	2
1991	1 June	Boston	1	1
1992	29 Apr	Dublin	4	1
1992	30 May	Washington	1	3
1996	9 June	Boston	1	2
2000	6 June	Boston	1	1
2002	17 Apr	Dublin	2	1

		v USSR	*RI*	*USSR*
WC1972	18 Oct	Dublin	1	2
WC1973	13 May	Moscow	0	1
EC1974	30 Oct	Dublin	3	0
EC1975	18 May	Kiev	1	2
WC1984	12 Sept	Dublin	1	0
WC1985	16 Oct	Moscow	0	2
EC1988	15 June	Hanover	1	1
1990	25 Apr	Dublin	1	0

		v WALES	*RI*	*W*
1960	28 Sept	Dublin	2	3
1979	11 Sept	Swansea	1	2
1981	24 Feb	Dublin	1	3
1986	26 Mar	Dublin	0	1
1990	28 Mar	Dublin	1	0
1991	6 Feb	Wrexham	3	0
1992	19 Feb	Dublin	0	1
1993	17 Feb	Dublin	2	1
1997	11 Feb	Cardiff	0	0
EC2007	24 Mar	Dublin	1	0

		v YUGOSLAVIA	*RI*	*Y*
1955	19 Sept	Dublin	1	4
1988	27 Apr	Dublin	2	0
EC1998	18 Nov	Belgrade	0	1
EC1999	1 Sept	Dublin	2	1

OTHER BRITISH AND IRISH INTERNATIONAL MATCHES 2006–07

FRIENDLIES

Old Trafford, 16 August 2006, 45,864

England (4) 4 *(Terry 14, Lampard 30, Crouch 35, 42)*

Greece (0) 0

England: Robinson (Kirkland 46); Neville G (Carragher 78), Cole A (Bridge 80), Hargreaves, Terry, Ferdinand, Gerrard (Bent D 78), Lampard, Crouch, Defoe (Richardson 69), Downing (Lennon 69).
Greece: Nikopolidis; Fyssas (Lagos 29), Dellas (Anatolakis 64), Katsouranis, Antzas (Kyrgiakos 46), Vyntra, Zagorakis (Basinas 46), Karagounis, Giannakopoulos (Salpigidis 46), Samaras (Amanatidis 46), Charisteas.
Referee: Stark (Germany).

Amsterdam, 15 November 2006, 44,000

Holland (0) 1 *(Van der Vaart 86)*

England (1) 1 *(Rooney 37)*

Holland: Timmer (Stekelenburg 46); Boulahrouz (Jaliens 61), Emanuelson, Landzaat, Mathijsen, Ooijer (Vennegoor of Hesselink 83), Schaars, Seedorf, Van der Vaart, Kuyt (Huntelaar 61), Robben.
England: Robinson; Richards, Cole A, Carrick, Ferdinand, Terry, Gerrard, Lampard, Johnson A (Wright-Phillips 73), Rooney, Cole J (Richardson 77).
Referee: Michel (Slovakia).

Old Trafford, 7 February 2007, 58,247

England (0) 0

Spain (0) 1 *(Iniesta 63)*

England: Foster; Neville G (Richards 64), Neville P (Downing 74), Carrick, Ferdinand, Woodgate (Carragher 64), Wright-Phillips (Defoe 70), Lampard (Barton 78), Crouch, Dyer, Gerrard (Barry 46).
Spain: Casillas; Sergio Ramos (Angel 46), Capdevila, Xavi, Puyol (Javi Navarro 46), Pablo, Angulo (Iniesta 56), Silva (Arizmendi 65), Albelda, David Villa (Fabregas 74), Morientes (Torres 46).
Referee: Weiner (Germany).

Wembley, 1 June 2007, 88,745

England (0) 1 *(Terry 68)*

Brazil (0) 1 *(Diego 90)*

England: Robinson; Carragher, Shorey, Gerrard, Terry (Brown 72), King, Beckham (Jenas 77), Lampard (Carrick 88), Smith (Dyer 62), Owen (Crouch 83), Cole J (Downing 62).
Brazil: Helton; Daniel (Maicon 65), Gilberto, Silva, Naldo, Juan, Ronaldinho, Mineiro (Edmilson 63), Robinho (Diego 74), Kaka (Alves 71), Vagner Love.
Referee: Merk (Germany).

Dublin, 16 August 2006, 42,400

Republic of Ireland (0) 0

Holland (2) 4 *(Huntelaar 25, 53, Robben 41, Van Persie 70)*

Republic of Ireland: Kenny; Carr (Alan O'Brien 46), Finnan (Kelly 63), Andy O'Brien, Kavanagh (Douglas 46), O'Shea, McGeady, Reid S (Miller 46), Morrison (Doyle K 46), Elliott, Kilbane.
Holland: Van der Sar; Heitinga, Mathijsen, Ooijer (Jaliens 77), De Cler (Emanuelson 60), Landzaat (De Jong 46), Schaars (Janssen 63), Van der Vaart, Van Persie, Huntelaar, Robben (Kuyt 46).
Referee: Ovrebo (Norway).

New Jersey, 23 May 2007, 20,823

Ecuador (1) 1 *(Benitez 13)*

Republic of Ireland (1) 1 *(Doyle K 44)*

Ecuador: Elizaga; Montano, Castro, Campos, Bagui, Caicedo, Urrutia, Quiroz (Salas 66) (Palacios 77), Ayovi, Kaviedes, Benitez.
Republic of Ireland: Doyle C; Kelly, O'Halloran (O'Cearuill 73), Potter, Bennett, Bruce, Murphy D (Lapira 85), Hunt (Stokes 69), Keogh (Gamble 69), Doyle K (Long 60), Kilbane (Gleeson 79).
Referee: Marrufo (USA).

Boston, 26 May 2007

Bolivia (1) 1 *(Hoyos 14)*

Republic of Ireland (1) 1 *(Long 12)*

Bolivia: Suarez; Hoyos, Mendez, Pena, Alvarez, Garcia (Lima 61), Moijca, Reyes, Vaca (Galindo 74), Moreno (Cabrera 46), Arce (Pinedo 69).
Republic of Ireland: Colgan (Henderson 46); O'Cearuill, Kelly, Gamble (Murphy D 46), Bennett, Murphy P (O'Halloran 46), Andy O'Brien (Gleeson 77), Potter, Stokes, Long (Doyle K 54), Kilbane (Hunt 66).
Referee: Vaugh (USA).

Helsinki, 16 August 2006, 12,500

Finland (0) 1 *(Vayrynen 74)*

Northern Ireland (1) 2 *(Healy 34, Lafferty 64)*

Finland: Jaaskelainen; Kallio, Hyypia (Pasoja 81), Tihinen, Pasanen, Kolkka (Lagerblom 74), Ilola (Wiss 46), Nurmela (Johansson 74), Riihilahti (Vayrynen 46), Eremenko Jr, Forssell (Kuqi 57).
Northern Ireland: Maik Taylor (Carroll 46); Baird, Capaldi, Hughes A (Duff 67), Craigan, Clingan, Gillespie (Jones 46), McCann, Healy (Feeney 46), Quinn (Lafferty 52), Elliott (Sproule 65).
Referee: Svendsen (Denmark).

Swansea, 15 August 2006, 8200

Wales (0) 0

Bulgaria (0) 0

Wales: Jones P; Delaney (Duffy 60), Ricketts (Vaughan 69), Gabbidon (Edwards 74), Collins J, Robinson, Bellamy (Parry 72), Earnshaw, Fletcher (Ledley 53), Davies S, Giggs (Nyatanga 53).
Bulgaria: Petkov G (Ivankov 46); Kishishev (Todorov Y 73), Kirilov, Tomasic, Wagner, Angelov S (Illiev 81), Berbatov, Peev (Georgiev 55), Lankovic (Todorov S 64), Petrov M (Lazarov 55), Petrov S.
Referee: Attard (Malta).

White Hart Lane, 5 September 2006, 22,008

Wales (0) 0

Brazil (0) 2 *(Marcelo 61, Vagner Love 74)*

Wales: Jones P; Duffy (Edwards 64), Bale (Ledley 46), Gabbidon, Collins J, Nyatanga, Bellamy, Earnshaw (Cotterill 77), Robinson (Fletcher 53), Davies S (Vaughan 68), Giggs (Ricketts 46).
Brazil: Gomes; Maicon (Cicinho 59), Luisao, Alex, Edmilson (Silva 46), Marcelo (Gilberto 74), Cearense, Kaka (Elano 72), Vagner Love, Ronaldinho (Robinho 67), Julio Baptista (Rafael Sobis 78).
Referee: Riley (West Yorkshire).

Wrexham, 14 November 2006, 8752

Wales (2) 4 *(Koumas 9, 15, Bellamy 78, Llewellyn 90)*

Liechtenstein (0) 0

Wales: Brown; Duffy (Fletcher 46), Ricketts, Nyatanga, Evans S, Robinson (Crofts 80), Bellamy, Earnshaw (Llewellyn 59), Koumas (Craig Davies 87), Davies S (Mark Jones 69), Giggs (Ledley 56).
Liechtenstein: Jehle; Telser, Hasler, Ritter, Ritzberger (Frick D 59), Martin Stocklasa, Buchel M, Burgmeier, Beck T (Kieber 88), Frick M (Buchel R 83), D'Elia (Rohrer 59).
Referee: Wilmes (Luxembourg).

Belfast, 6 February 2007, 14,000

Northern Ireland (0) 0

Wales (0) 0

Northern Ireland: Maik Taylor (Ingham 46); Duff, Capaldi, Hughes A, Craigan (Webb 78), Clingan (McCann 61), Gillespie, Davis, Sproule (Thompson 68), Lafferty (Shiels 68), Brunt.
Wales: Coyne; Duffy (Cotterill 46) (Easter 70), Evans S, Collins D, Nyatanga, Davies S, Koumas, Robinson, Parry (Crofts 83), Vaughan (Ricketts 46), Bellamy.
Referee: C. Richmond (Scotland).

26 May 2007, 7819

Wales (2) 2 *(Bellamy 18, 38)*

New Zealand (2) 2 *(Smeltz 2, 24)*

Wales: Coyne (Hennessey 46); Gunter (Evans S 46), Collins J, Gabbidon, Ricketts, Davies S (Crofts 76), Fletcher (Ledley 46), Robinson, Giggs (Llewellyn 76), Bellamy, Earnshaw (Nardiello 64).
New Zealand: Paston; Pritchett, Boyens, Sigmund, Lochhead, Christie (Barron 58), Brown, Oughton, Bertos (Campbell 60), James, Smeltz.
Referee: Skjerven (Norway).

Vienna, 30 May 2007, 13,200

Austria (0) 0

Scotland (0) 1 *(O'Connor 59)*

Austria: Payer; Standfest, Hiden, Patocka (Prodl 89), Fuchs (Katzer 74), Ivanschitz, Aufhauser (Sariyar 74), Saumel, Leitgeb, Linz, Haas (Kuljic 60).
Scotland: McGregor (Gordon 46); Alexander G (Hutton 71), Weir (Hartley 46), Caldwell G, Naysmith, Maloney (Adam 67), Fletcher, Ferguson B, McCulloch (Dailly 46), O'Connor (McManus 87), Boyd.
Referee: Szabo (Hungary).

B INTERNATIONALS

Dublin, 14 November 2006, 3500

Republic of Ireland (0) 0

Scotland (0) 0

Republic of Ireland: Randolf; Foley, McCarthy, Bruce, Emmanuel, Gamble, McPhail, Gibson, O'Brien, Keogh, O'Donovan.
Scotland: Gallacher (Brown M 46); Whittaker, Smith (Adam 59), Broadfoot (Greer 54), Webster, Stewart, Naismith, Brown S (Miller 54), Boyd, Pearson, Clark (McEveley 59).

Kilmarnock, 7 February 2007, 3702

Scotland (1) 2 *(Maloney 11, Gow 64)*

Finland (1) 2 *(Llola 3, Makkella 82)*

Scotland: Gallacher (Langfield 46); Hutton, McEveley (Barr 61), Brown S (Fowler 68), Greer, Broadfoot, Clark, Maloney, Beattie (Mackie 68), Thomson (Adam 61), Pearson (Gow 61).

Burnley, 25 May 2007, 22,500

England (2) 3 *(Smith 34, Downing 37, 58)*

Albania (1) 1 (Berisha 44)

England: Carson; Neville P (Jagielka 46), Shorey (Lescott 73), Jenas, Dawson, King, Bentley (Defoe 72), Lennon (Downing 10), Smith (Dyer 64), Owen, Barry (Taylor S 64).
Albania: Beqaj (Hidi 78); Vangeli, Dede, Rrustemi, Haxhi (Ahmataj 79), Bulku, Skela (Hyka 75), Duro (Vrapi 65), Berisha, Muka (Murati 46), Bushi (Sinani 72).

BRITISH & IRISH INTERNATIONAL MANAGERS

England
Walter Winterbottom 1946–1962 (after period as coach); Alf Ramsey 1963–1974; Joe Mercer (caretaker) 1974; Don Revie 1974–1977; Ron Greenwood 1977–1982; Bobby Robson 1982–1990; Graham Taylor 1990–1993; Terry Venables (coach) 1994–1996; Glenn Hoddle 1996–1999; Kevin Keegan 1999–2000; Sven-Goran Eriksson 2001–2006; Steve McClaren from August 2006.

Northern Ireland
Peter Doherty 1951–1952; Bertie Peacock 1962–1967; Billy Bingham 1967–1971; Terry Neill 1971–1975; Dave Clements (player-manager) 1975–1976; Danny Blanchflower 1976–1979; Billy Bingham 1980–1994; Bryan Hamilton 1994–1998; Lawrie McMenemy 1998–1999; Sammy McIlroy 2000–2003; Lawrie Sanchez 2004–2007; Nigel Worthington from June 2007.

Scotland (since 1967)
Bobby Brown 1967–1971; Tommy Docherty 1971–1972; Willie Ormond 1973–1977; Ally MacLeod 1977–1978; Jock Stein 1978–1985; Alex Ferguson (caretaker) 1985–1986 Andy Roxburgh (coach) 1986–1993; Craig Brown 1993–2001; Berti Vogts 2002–2004; Walter Smith 2004–2007; Alex McLeish from January 2007.

Wales (since 1974)
Mike Smith 1974–1979; Mike England 1980–1988; David Williams (caretaker) 1988; Terry Yorath 1988–1993; John Toshack 1994 for one match; Mike Smith 1994–1995; Bobby Gould 1995–1999; Mark Hughes 1999–2004; John Toshack from November 2004.

Republic of Ireland
Liam Tuohy 1971–1972; Johnny Giles 1973–1980 (after period as player-manager); Eoin Hand 1980–1985; Jack Charlton 1986–1996; Mick McCarthy 1996–2002; Brian Kerr 2003–2006; Steve Staunton from January 2006.

INTERNATIONAL APPEARANCES 1872–2007

This is a list of full international appearances by Englishmen, Irishmen, Scotsmen and Welshmen in matches against the Home Countries and against foreign nations. It does not include unofficial matches against Commonwealth and Empire countries. The year indicated refers to the season; ie 2005 is the 2004–05 season. Actual match dates appear on pp. 883–902.

Explanatory code for matches played by all five countries: A represents Austria; Alb, Albania; Alg, Algeria; An, Angola; And, Andorra; Arg, Argentina; Arm, Armenia; Aus, Australia; Az, Azerbaijan; B, Bohemia; Bar, Barbados; Bel, Belgium; Bl, Belarus; Bol, Bolivia; Bos, Bosnia; Br, Brazil; Bul, Bulgaria; C,CIS; Ca, Canada; Cam, Cameroon; Ch, Chile; Chn, China; Co, Colombia; Cr, Costa Rica; Cro, Croatia; Cy, Cyprus; Cz, Czechoslovakia; CzR, Czech Republic; D, Denmark; E, England; Ec, Ecuador; Ei, Republic of Ireland; EG, East Germany; Eg, Egypt; Es, Estonia; F, France; Fa, Faeroes; Fi, Finland; G, Germany; Ge, Georgia; Gh, Ghana; Gr, Greece; H, Hungary; Hk, Hong Kong; Ho, Holland; Hon, Honduras; I, Italy; Ic, Iceland; Ir, Iran; Is, Israel; J, Japan; Jam, Jamaica; K, Kuwait; L, Luxembourg; La, Latvia; Li, Lithuania; Lie, Liechtenstein; M, Mexico; Ma, Malta; Mac, Macedonia; Mal, Malaysia; Mol, Moldova; Mor, Morocco; N, Norway; Ng, Nigeria; Ni, Northern Ireland; Nz, New Zealand; P, Portugal; Para, Paraguay; Pe, Peru; Pol, Poland; R, Romania; RCS, Republic of Czechs and Slovaks; R of E, Rest of Europe; R of UK, Rest of United Kingdom; R of W, Rest of World; Ru, Russia; S.Af, South Africa; S.Ar, Saudi Arabia; S, Scotland; Se, Sweden; Ser, Serbia-Montenegro; Sk, South Korea; Slo, Slovakia; Slv, Slovenia; Sm, San Marino; Sp, Spain; Stk, St Kitts & Nevis; Sw, Switzerland; T, Turkey; Th, Thailand; Tr, Trinidad & Tobago; Tun, Tunisia; U, Uruguay; Uk, Ukraine; US, United States of America; USSR, Soviet Union; W, Wales; WG, West Germany; Y, Yugoslavia; Z, Zaire.
As at July 2007.

ENGLAND

Abbott, W. (Everton), 1902 v W (1)
A'Court, A. (Liverpool), 1958 v Ni, Br, A, USSR; 1959 v W (5)
Adams, T. A. (Arsenal), 1987 v Sp, T, Br; 1988 v WG, T, Y, Ho, H, S, Co, Sw, Ei, Ho, USSR; 1989 v D, Se, S.Ar.; 1991 v Ei (2); 1993 v N, T, Sm, T, Ho, Pol, N; 1994 v Pol, Ho, D, Gr, N; 1995 v US, R, Ei, U; 1996 v Co, N, Sw, P, Chn, Sw, S, Ho, Sp, G; 1997 v Ge (2); 1998 v I, Ch, P, S.Ar, Tun, R, Co, Arg; 1999 v Se, F; 2000 v L, Pol, Bel, S (2), Uk, P; 2001 v F, G (66)
Adcock, H. (Leicester C), 1929 v F, Bel, Sp; 1930 v Ni, W (5)
Alcock, C. W. (Wanderers), 1875 v S (1)
Alderson, J. T. (C Palace), 1923 v F (1)
Aldridge, A. (WBA), 1888 v Ni; (with Walsall Town Swifts), 1889 v Ni (2)
Allen, A. (Stoke C) 1960 v Se, W, Ni (3)
Allen, A. (Aston Villa), 1888 v Ni (1)
Allen, C. (QPR), 1984 v Br (sub), U, Ch; (with Tottenham H), 1987 v T; 1988 v Is (5)
Allen, H. (Wolverhampton W), 1888 v S, W, Ni; 1889 v S; 1890 v S (5)
Allen, J. P. (Portsmouth), 1934 v Ni, W (2)
Allen, R. (WBA), 1952 v Sw; 1954 v Y, S; 1955 v WG, W (5)
Alsford, W. J. (Tottenham H), 1935 v S (1)
Amos, A. (Old Carthusians), 1885 v S; 1886 v W (2)
Anderson, R. D. (Old Etonians), 1879 v W (1)
Anderson, S. (Sunderland), 1962 v A, S (2)
Anderson, V. (Nottingham F), 1979 v Cz, Se; 1980 v Bul, Sp; 1981 v N, R, W, S; 1982 v Ni, Ic; 1984 v Ni; (with Arsenal), 1985 v T, Ni, Ei, R, Fi, S, M, US; 1986 v USSR, M; 1987 v Se, Ni (2), Y, Sp, T; (with Manchester U), 1988 v WG, H, Co (30)
Anderton, D. R. (Tottenham H), 1994 v D, Gr, N; 1995 v US, Ei, U, J, Se, Br; 1996 v H, Chn, Sw, S, Ho, Sp, G; 1998 v S.Ar, Mor, Tun, R, Co, Arg; 1999 v Se, Bul, L, CzR, F; 2001 v F, I (sub); 2002 v Se (sub) (30)
Angus, J. (Burnley), 1961 v A (1)
Armfield, J. C. (Blackpool), 1959 v Br, Pe, M, US; 1960 v Y, Sp, H, S; 1961 v L, P, Sp, M, I, A, W, Ni, S; 1962 v A, Sw, Pe, W, Ni, S, L, P, H, Arg, Bul, Br; 1963 v F (2), Br, EG, Sw, Ni, W, S; 1964 v R of W, W, Ni, S; 1966 v Y, Fi (43)
Armitage, G. H. (Charlton Ath), 1926 v Ni (1)
Armstrong, D. (Middlesbrough), 1980 v Aus; (with Southampton), 1983 v WG; 1984 v W (3)
Armstrong, K. (Chelsea), 1955 v S (1)
Arnold, J. (Fulham), 1933 v S (1)
Arthur, J. W. H. (Blackburn R), 1885 v S, W, Ni; 1886 v S, W; 1887 v W, Ni (7)
Ashcroft, J. (Woolwich Arsenal), 1906 v Ni, W, S (3)
Ashmore, G. S. (WBA), 1926 v Bel (1)
Ashton, C. T. (Corinthians), 1926 v Ni (1)
Ashurst, W. (Notts Co), 1923 v Se (2); 1925 v S, W, Bel (5)
Astall, G. (Birmingham C), 1956 v Fi, WG (2)
Astle, J. (WBA), 1969 v W; 1970 v S, P, Br (sub), Cz (5)
Aston, J. (Manchester U), 1949 v S, W, D, Sw, Se, N, F; 1950 v S, W, Ni, Ei, I, P, Bel, Ch, US; 1951 v Ni (17)
Athersmith, W. C. (Aston Villa), 1892 v Ni, 1897 v S, W, Ni; 1898 v S, W, Ni; 1899 v S, W, Ni; 1900 v S, W (12)
Atyeo, P. J. W. (Bristol C), 1956 v Br, Se, Sp; 1957 v D, Ei (2) (6)
Austin, S. W. (Manchester C), 1926 v Ni (1)

Bach, P. (Sunderland), 1899 v Ni (1)
Bache, J. W. (Aston Villa), 1903 v W; 1904 v W, Ni; 1905 v S; 1907 v Ni; 1910 v Ni; 1911 v S (7)
Baddeley, T. (Wolverhampton W), 1903 v S, Ni; 1904 v S, W, Ni (5)
Bagshaw, J. J. (Derby Co), 1920 v Ni (1)
Bailey, G. R. (Manchester U), 1985 v Ei, M (2)
Bailey, H. P. (Leicester Fosse), 1908 v W, A (2), H, B (5)
Bailey, M. A. (Charlton Ath), 1964 v US; 1965 v W (2)
Bailey, N. C. (Clapham Rovers), 1878 v S; 1879 v S, W; 1880 v S; 1881 v S; 1882 v S, W; 1883 v S, W; 1884 v S, W, Ni; 1885 v S, W, Ni; 1886 v S, W; 1887 v S, W (19)
Baily, E. F. (Tottenham H), 1950 v Sp; 1951 v Y, Ni, W; 1952 v A (2), Sw, W; 1953 v Ni (9)
Bain, J. (Oxford University), 1877 v S (1)
Baker, A. (Arsenal), 1928 v W (1)
Baker, B. H. (Everton), 1921 v Bel; (with Chelsea), 1926 v Ni (2)
Baker, J. H. (Hibernian), 1960 v Y, Sp, H, Ni, S; (with Arsenal) 1966 v Sp, Pol, Ni (8)
Ball, A. J. (Blackpool), 1965 v Y, WG, Se; 1966 v S, Sp, Fi, D, U, Arg, P, WG (2), Pol (2); (with Everton), 1967 v W, S, Ni, A, Cz, Sp; 1968 v W, S, USSR, Sp (2), Y, WG; 1969 v Ni, W, S, R (2), M, Br, U; 1970 v P, Co, Ec, R, Br, Cz (sub), WG, W, S, Bel; 1971 v Ma, EG, Gr, Ma (sub), Ni, S; 1972 v Sw, Gr; (with Arsenal) WG (2), S; 1973 v W (3), Y, S (2), Cz, Ni, Pol; 1974 v P (sub); 1975 v WG, Cy (2), Ni, W, S (72)
Ball, J. (Bury), 1928 v Ni (1)
Ball, M. J. (Everton), 2001 v Sp (sub) (1)
Balmer, W. (Everton), 1905 v Ni (1)
Bamber, J. (Liverpool), 1921 v W (1)
Bambridge, A. L. (Swifts), 1881 v W; 1883 v W; 1884 v Ni (3)
Bambridge, E. C. (Swifts), 1879 v S; 1880 v S; 1881 v S; 1882 v S, W, Ni; 1883 v W; 1884 v S, W, Ni; 1885 v S, W, Ni; 1886 v S, W; 1887 v S, W, Ni (18)
Bambridge, E. H. (Swifts), 1876 v S (1)
Banks, G. (Leicester C), 1963 v S, Br, Cz, EG; 1964 v W, Ni, S, R of W, U, P (2), US, Arg; 1965 v Ni, S, H, Y, WG, Se; 1966 v Ni, S, Sp, Pol (2), WG (2), Y, Fi, U, M, F, Arg, P; 1967 v Ni, W, S, Cz; (with Stoke C), 1968 v W, Ni, S, USSR (2), Sp, WG, Y; 1969 v Ni, S, R (2), F, U, Br; 1970 v W, Ni, S, Ho, Bel, Co, Ec, R, Br, Cz; 1971 v Gr, Ma (2), Ni, S; 1972 v Sw, Gr, WG (2), W, S (73)
Banks, H. E. (Millwall), 1901 v Ni (1)
Banks, T. (Bolton W), 1958 v USSR (3), Br, A; 1959 v Ni (6)
Bannister, W. (Burnley), 1901 v W; (with Bolton W), 1902 v Ni (2)
Barclay, R. (Sheffield U), 1932 v S; 1933 v Ni; 1936 v S (3)
Bardsley, D. J. (QPR), 1993 v Sp (sub), Pol (2)
Barham, M. (Norwich C), 1983 v Aus (2) (2)

Barkas, S. (Manchester C), 1936 v Bel; 1937 v S; 1938 v W, Ni, Cz (5)
Barker, J. (Derby Co), 1935 v I, Ho, S, W, Ni; 1936 v G, A, S, W, Ni; 1937 v W (11)
Barker, R. (Herts Rangers), 1872 v S (1)
Barker, R. R. (Casuals), 1895 v W (1)
Barlow, R. J. (WBA), 1955 v Ni (1)
Barmby, N. J. (Tottenham H), 1995 v U (sub), Se (sub); (with Middlesbrough), 1996 v Co, N, P, Chn, Sw (sub), Ho (sub), Sp (sub); 1997 v Mol; (with Everton), 2000 v Br (sub), Uk (sub), Ma, G (sub), R (sub); (with Liverpool), 2001 v F, G, I, Sp; 2002 v Ho (sub), G, Alb, Gr (23)
Barnes, J. (Watford), 1983 v Ni (sub), Aus (sub), Aus (2); 1984 v D, L (sub), F (sub), S, USSR, Br, U, Ch; 1985 v EG, Fi, T, Ni, R, Fi, S, I (sub), M, WG (sub), US (sub); 1986 v R (sub), Is (sub), M (sub), Ca (sub), Arg (sub); 1987 v Se, T (sub), Br; (with Liverpool), 1988 v WG, T, Y, Is, Ho, S, Co, Sw, Ei, Ho, USSR; 1989 v Se, Gr, Alb, Pol, D; 1990 v Se, I, Br, D, U, Tun, Ei, Ho, Eg, Bel, Cam; 1991 v H, Pol, Cam, Ei, T, USSR, Arg; 1992 v Cz, Fi; 1993 v Sm, T, Ho, Pol, US, G; 1995 v US, R, Ng, U, Se; 1996 v Co (sub) (79)
Barnes, P. S. (Manchester C), 1978 v I, WG, Br, W, S, H; 1979 v D, Ei, Cz, Ni (2), S, Bul, A; (with WBA), 1980 v D, W; 1981 v Sp (sub), Br, W, Sw (sub); (with Leeds U), 1982 v N (sub), Ho (sub) (22)
Barnet, H. H. (Royal Engineers), 1882 v Ni (1)
Barrass, M. W. (Bolton W), 1952 v W, Ni; 1953 v S (3)
Barrett, A. F. (Fulham), 1930 v Ni (1)
Barrett, E. D. (Oldham Ath), 1991 v Nz; (with Aston Villa), 1993 v Br, G (3)
Barrett, J. W. (West Ham U), 1929 v Ni (1)
Barry, G. (Aston Villa), 2000 v Uk (sub), Ma (sub); 2001 v F, G (sub), Fi, I; 2003 v S.Af (sub), Ser (sub); 2007 v Sp (sub) (9)
Barry, L. (Leicester C), 1928 v F, Bel; 1929 v F, Bel, Sp (5)
Barson, F. (Aston Villa), 1920 v W (1)
Barton, J. (Blackburn R), 1890 v Ni (1)
Barton, J. (Manchester C), 2007 v Sp (sub) (1)
Barton, P. H. (Birmingham), 1921 v Bel; 1922 v Ni; 1923 v F; 1924 v Bel, S, W; 1925 v Ni (7)
Barton, W. D. (Wimbledon), 1995 v Ei; (with Newcastle U), Se, Br (sub) (3)
Bassett, W. I. (WBA), 1888 v Ni, 1889 v S, W; 1890 v S, W; 1891 v S, Ni; 1892 v S; 1893 v S, W; 1894 v S; 1895 v S, Ni; 1896 v S, W, Ni (16)
Bastard, S. R. (Upton Park), 1880 v S (1)
Bastin, C. S. (Arsenal), 1932 v W; 1933 v I, Sw; 1934 v S, Ni, W, H, Cz; 1935 v S, Ni, I; 1936 v S, W, G, A; 1937 v W, Ni; 1938 v S, G, Sw, F (21)
Batty, D. (Leeds U), 1991 v USSR (sub), Arg, Aus, Nz, Mal; 1992 v G, T, H (sub), F, Se; 1993 v N, Sm, US, Br; (with Blackburn R), 1994 v D (sub); 1995 v J, Br; (with Newcastle U), 1997 v Mol (sub), Ge, I, M, Ge, S.Af (sub), Pol (sub), F; 1998 v Mol, I, Ch, Sw (sub), P, S.Ar, Tun, R, Co (sub), Arg (sub); 1999 v Bul (sub), L; (with Leeds U), H, Se, Bul; 2000 v L, Pol (42)
Baugh, R. (Stafford Road), 1886 v Ni; (with Wolverhampton W) 1890 v Ni (2)
Bayliss, A. E. J. M. (WBA), 1891 v Ni (1)
Baynham, R. L. (Luton T), 1956 v Ni, D, Sp (3)
Beardsley, P. A. (Newcastle U), 1986 v Eg (sub), Is, USSR, M, Ca (sub), P (sub), Pol, Para, Arg; 1987 v Ni (2), Y, Sp, Br, S; (with Liverpool), 1988 v WG, T, Y, Is, Ho, H, S, Co, Sw, Ei, Ho; 1989 v D, Se, S.Ar, Gr (sub), Alb (sub+1), Pol, D; 1990 v Se, Pol, I, Br, U (sub), Tun (sub), Ei, Eg (sub), Cam (sub), WG, I; 1991 v Pol (sub), Ei (2), USSR (sub); (with Newcastle U), 1994 v D, Gr, N; 1995 v Ng, Ei, U, J, Se; 1996 v P (sub), Chn (sub) (59)
Beasant, D. J. (Chelsea), 1990 v I (sub), Y (sub) (2)
Beasley, A. (Huddersfield T), 1939 v S (1)
Beats, W. E. (Wolverhampton W), 1901 v W; 1902 v S (2)
Beattie, J. S. (Southampton), 2003 v Aus, Ser (sub); 2004 v Cro (sub), Lie, D (sub) (5)
Beattie, T. K. (Ipswich T), 1975 v Cy (2), S; 1976 v Sw, P; 1977 v Fi, I (sub), Ho; 1978 v L (sub) (9)
Beckham, D. R. J. (Manchester U), 1997 v Mol, Pol, Ge, I, Ge, S.Af (sub), Pol, I, F; 1998 v Mol, I, Cam, P, S.Ar, Bel (sub), R (sub), Co, Arg; 1999 v L, CzR, F, Pol, Se; 2000 v L, Pol, S(2), Arg, Br, Uk, Ma, P, G, R; 2001 v F, G, I, Sp, Fi, Alb, M, Gr; 2002 v Ho, G, Alb, Gr, Se, Ho, I, Se, Arg, Ng, D, Br; 2003 v Slo, Mac, Aus, Lie, T, S.Af; (with Real Madrid), 2004 v Cro, Mac, Lie, T, D, P, J, Ic, F, Sw, Cro, P; 2005 v Uk, A, Pol, W, Sp, Ho, Ni, Az, Co; 2006 v D, W, Ni, A, Arg, U, H, Jam, Para, Tr, Se, Ec, P; 2007 v Br, Es (96)
Becton, F. (Preston NE), 1895 v Ni; (with Liverpool), 1897 v W (2)
Bedford, H. (Blackpool), 1923 v Se; 1925 v Ni (2)
Bell, C. (Manchester C), 1968 v Se, WG; 1969 v W, Bul, F, U, Br; 1970 v Ni (sub), Ho (2), P, Br (sub), Cz, WG (sub); 1972 v Gr, WG (2), W, Ni, S; 1973 v W (3), Y, S (2), Ni, Cz, Pol; 1974 v A, Pol, I, W, Ni, S, Arg, EG, Bul, Y; 1975 v Cz, P, WG, Cy (2), Ni, S; 1976 v Sw, Cz (48)
Bennett, W. (Sheffield U), 1901 v S, W (2)
Benson, R. W. (Sheffield U), 1913 v Ni (1)
Bent, D. A. (Charlton Ath), 2006 v U; 2007 v Gr (sub) (2)
Bentley, R. T. F. (Chelsea), 1949 v Se; 1950 v S, P, Bel, Ch, USA; 1953 v W, Bel; 1955 v W, WG, Sp, P (12)
Beresford, J. (Aston Villa), 1934 v Cz (1)
Berry, A. (Oxford University), 1909 v Ni (1)
Berry, J. J. (Manchester U), 1953 v Arg, Ch, U; 1956 v Se (4)
Bestall, J. G. (Grimsby T), 1935 v Ni (1)
Betmead, H. A. (Grimsby T), 1937 v Fi (1)
Betts, M. P. (Old Harrovians), 1877 v S (1)
Betts, W. (Sheffield W), 1889 v W (1)
Beverley, J. (Blackburn R), 1884 v S, W, Ni (3)
Birkett, R. H. (Clapham Rovers), 1879 v S (1)
Birkett, R. J. E. (Middlesbrough), 1936 v Ni (1)
Birley, F. H. (Oxford University), 1874 v S; (with Wanderers), 1875 v S (2)
Birtles, G. (Nottingham F), 1980 v Arg (sub), I; 1981 v R (3)
Bishop, S. M. (Leicester C), 1927 v S, Bel, L, F (4)
Blackburn, F. (Blackburn R), 1901 v S; 1902 v Ni; 1904 v S (3)
Blackburn, G. F. (Aston Villa), 1924 v F (1)
Blenkinsop, E. (Sheffield W), 1928 v F, Bel; 1929 v S, W, Ni, F, Bel, Sp; 1930 v S, W, Ni, G, A; 1931 v S, W, Ni, F, Bel; 1932 v S, W, Ni, Sp; 1933 v S, W, Ni, A (26)
Bliss, H. (Tottenham H), 1921 v S (1)
Blissett, L. (Watford), 1983 v WG (sub), L, W, Gr (sub), H, Ni, S (sub), Aus (1+1 sub); (with AC Milan), 1984 v D (sub), H, W (sub), S, USSR (14)
Blockley, J. P. (Arsenal), 1973 v Y (1)
Bloomer, S. (Derby Co), 1895 v S, Ni; 1896 v W, Ni; 1897 v S, W, Ni; 1898 v S; 1899 v S, W, Ni; 1900 v S; 1901 v S, W; 1902 v S, W, Ni; 1904 v S; 1905 v S, W, Ni; (with Middlesbrough), 1907 v S, W (23)
Blunstone, F. (Chelsea), 1955 v W, S, F, P; 1957 v Y (5)
Bond, R. (Preston NE), 1905 v Ni, W; 1906 v S, W, Ni; (with Bradford C), 1910 v S, W, Ni (8)
Bonetti, P. P. (Chelsea), 1966 v D; 1967 v Sp, A; 1968 v Sp; 1970 v Ho, P, WG (7)
Bonsor, A. G. (Wanderers), 1873 v S; 1875 v S (2)
Booth, F. (Manchester C), 1905 v Ni (1)
Booth, T. (Blackburn R), 1898 v W; (with Everton), 1903 v S (2)
Bould, S. A. (Arsenal), 1994 v Gr, N (2)
Bowden, E. R. (Arsenal), 1935 v W, I; 1936 v W, Ni, A; 1937 v H (6)
Bower, A. G. (Corinthians), 1924 v Ni, Bel; 1925 v W, Bel; 1927 v W (5)
Bowers, J. W. (Derby Co), 1934 v S, Ni, W (3)
Bowles, S. (QPR), 1974 v P, W, Ni; 1977 v I, Ho (5)
Bowser, S. (WBA), 1920 v Ni (1)
Bowyer, L. D. (Leeds U), 2003 v P (1)
Boyer, P. J. (Norwich C), 1976 v W (1)
Boyes, W. (WBA), 1935 v Ho; (with Everton), 1939 v W, R of E (3)
Boyle, T. W. (Burnley), 1913 v Ni (1)
Brabrook, P. (Chelsea), 1958 v USSR; 1959 v Ni; 1960 v Sp (3)
Bracewell, P. W. (Everton), 1985 v WG (sub), US; 1986 v Ni (3)
Bradford, G. R. W. (Bristol R), 1956 v D (1)
Bradford, J. (Birmingham), 1924 v Ni; 1925 v Bel; 1928 v S; 1929 v Ni, W, F, Sp; 1930 v S, Ni, G, A; 1931 v W (12)
Bradley, W. (Manchester U), 1959 v I, US, M (sub) (3)
Bradshaw, F. (Sheffield W), 1908 v A (1)
Bradshaw, T. H. (Liverpool), 1897 v Ni (1)
Bradshaw, W. (Blackburn R), 1910 v W, Ni; 1912 v Ni; 1913 v W (4)
Brann, G. (Swifts), 1886 v S, W; 1891 v W (3)

Brawn, W. F. (Aston Villa), 1904 v W, Ni (2)
Bray, J. (Manchester C), 1935 v W; 1936 v S, W, Ni, G; 1937 v S (6)
Brayshaw, E. (Sheffield W), 1887 v Ni (1)
Bridge W. M. (Southampton), 2002 v Ho, I, Para, Sk (sub), Cam, Arg (sub), Ng (sub); 2003 v P (sub), Mac, Lie, T, Ser (sub); (with Chelsea), 2004 v Cro (sub), Lie, D (sub), P (sub), Ic (sub); 2005 v A, Pol, Sp; 2006 v Arg, U, Jam (sub); 2007 v Gr (sub), Es (25)
Bridges, B. J. (Chelsea), 1965 v S, H, Y; 1966 v A (4)
Bridgett, A. (Sunderland), 1905 v S; 1908 v S, A (2), H, B; 1909 v Ni, W, H (2), A (11)
Brindle, T. (Darwen), 1880 v S, W (2)
Brittleton, J. T. (Sheffield W), 1912 v S, W, Ni; 1913 v S; 1914 v W (5)
Britton, C. S. (Everton), 1935 v S, W, Ni, I; 1937 v S, Ni, H, N, Se (9)
Broadbent, P. F. (Wolverhampton W), 1958 v USSR; 1959 v S, W, Ni, I, Br; 1960 v S (7)
Broadis, I. A. (Manchester C), 1952 v S, A, I; 1953 v S, Arg, Ch, U, US; (with Newcastle U), 1954 v S, H, Y, Bel, Sw, U (14)
Brockbank, J. (Cambridge University), 1872 v S (1)
Brodie, J. B. (Wolverhampton W), 1889 v S, Ni; 1891 v Ni (3)
Bromilow, T. G. (Liverpool), 1921 v W; 1922 v S, W; 1923 v Bel; 1926 v Ni (5)
Bromley-Davenport, W. E. (Oxford University), 1884 v S, W (2)
Brook, E. F. (Manchester C), 1930 v Ni; 1933 v Sw: 1934 v S, W, Ni, F, H, Cz; 1935 v S, W, Ni, I; 1936 v S, W, Ni; 1937 v H; 1938 v W, Ni (18)
Brooking, T. D. (West Ham U), 1974 v P, Arg, EG, Bul, Y; 1975 v Cz (sub), P; 1976 v P, W, Br, I, Fi; 1977 v Ei, Fi, I, Ho, Ni, W; 1978 v I, WG, W, S (sub), H; 1979 v D, Ei, Ni, W (sub), S, Bul, Se (sub), A; 1980 v D, Ni, Arg (sub), W, Ni, S, Bel, Sp; 1981 v Sw, Sp, R, H; 1982 v H, S, Fi, Sp (sub) (47)
Brooks, J. (Tottenham H), 1957 v W, Y, D (3)
Broome, F. H. (Aston Villa), 1938 v G, Sw, F; 1939 v N, I, R, Y (7)
Brown, A. (Aston Villa), 1882 v S, W, Ni (3)
Brown, A. S. (Sheffield U), 1904 v W; 1906 v Ni (2)
Brown, A. (WBA), 1971 v W (1)
Brown, G. (Huddersfield T), 1927 v S, W, Ni, Bel, L, F; 1928 v W; 1929 v S; (with Aston Villa), 1933 v W (9)
Brown, J. (Blackburn R), 1881 v W; 1882 v Ni; 1885 v S, W, Ni (5)
Brown, J. H. (Sheffield W), 1927 v S, W, Bel, L, F; 1930 v Ni (6)
Brown, K. (West Ham U), 1960 v Ni (1)
Brown, W. (West Ham U), 1924 v Bel (1)
Brown, W. M. (Manchester U), 1999 v H; 2001 v Fi (sub), Alb (sub); 2002 v Ho, Sk (sub), Cam; 2003 v Aus (sub); 2005 v Ho, US; 2007 v And, Br (sub), Es (12)
Bruton, J. (Burnley), 1928 v F, Bel; 1929 v S (3)
Bryant, W. I. (Clapton), 1925 v F (1)
Buchan, C. M. (Sunderland), 1913 v Ni; 1920 v W; 1921 v W, Bel; 1923 v F; 1924 v S (6)
Buchanan, W. S. (Clapham R), 1876 v S (1)
Buckley, F. C. (Derby Co), 1914 v Ni (1)
Bull, S. G. (Wolverhampton W), 1989 v S (sub), D (sub); 1990 v Y, Cz, D (sub), U (sub), Tun (sub), Ei (sub), Ho (sub), Eg, Bel (sub); 1991 v H, Pol (13)
Bullock, F. E. (Huddersfield T), 1921 v Ni (1)
Bullock, N. (Bury), 1923 v Bel; 1926 v W; 1927 v Ni (3)
Burgess, H. (Manchester C), 1904 v S, W, Ni; 1906 v S (4)
Burgess, H. (Sheffield W), 1931 v S, Ni, F, Bel (4)
Burnup, C. J. (Cambridge University), 1896 v S (1)
Burrows, H. (Sheffield W), 1934 v H, Cz; 1935 v Ho (3)
Burton, F. E. (Nottingham F), 1889 v Ni (1)
Bury, L. (Cambridge University), 1877 v S; (with Old Etonians), 1879 v W (2)
Butcher, T. (Ipswich T), 1980 v Aus; 1981 v Sp; 1982 v W, S, F, Cz, WG, Sp; 1983 v D, WG, L, W, Gr, H, Ni, S, Aus (3); 1984 v D, H, L, F, Ni; 1985 v EG, Fi, T, Ni, Ei, R, Fi, S, I, WG, US; 1986 v Is, USSR, S, M, Ca, P, Mor, Pol, Para, Arg; (with Rangers), 1987 v Se, Ni (2), Y, Sp, Br, S; 1988 v T, Y; 1989 v D, Se, Gr, Alb (2), Ch, S, Pol, D; 1990 v Se, Pol, I, Y, Br, Cz, D, U, Tun, Ei, Ho, Bel, Cam, WG (77)
Butler, J. D. (Arsenal), 1925 v Bel (1)
Butler, W. (Bolton W), 1924 v S (1)
Butt, N. (Manchester U), 1997 v M (sub), S.Af (sub); 1998 v Mol (sub), I (sub), Ch, Bel; 1999 v CzR, H; 2001 v I, Sp, Fi (sub), Alb, M (sub), Gr (sub); 2002 v Se, Ho (sub), I, Para, Arg, Ng, D, Br; 2003 v P, Slo, Mac (sub), Lie (sub), T; 2004 v Cro, Mac, T, D, P, Se, J (sub), Ic (sub); (with Newcastle U), 2005 v Uk, W, Az, Sp (39)
Byrne, G. (Liverpool), 1963 v S; 1966 v N (2)
Byrne, J. J. (C Palace), 1962 v Ni; (with West Ham U), 1963 v Sw; 1964 v S, U, P (2), Ei, Br, Arg; 1965 v W, S (11)
Byrne, R. W. (Manchester U), 1954 v S, H, Y, Bel, Sw, U; 1955 v S, W, Ni, WG, F, Sp, P; 1956 v S, W, Ni, Br, Se, Fi, WG, D, Sp; 1957 v S, W, Ni, Y, D (2), Ei (2); 1958 v W, Ni, F (33)

Callaghan, I. R. (Liverpool), 1966 v Fi, F; 1978 v Sw, L (4)
Calvey, J. (Nottingham F), 1902 v Ni (1)
Campbell, A. F. (Blackburn R), 1929 v W, Ni; (with Huddersfield T), 1931 v W, S, Ni; 1932 v W, Ni, Sp (8)
Campbell, S. (Tottenham H), 1996 v H (sub), S (sub); 1997 v Ge, I, Ge, S.Af (sub), Pol, F, Br; 1998 v Mol, I, Cam, Ch, P, Mor, Bel, Tun, R, Co, Arg; 1999 v Se, Bul, L, CzR, Pol, Se, Bul; 2000 v S (2), Arg, Br, Uk, Ma, P, G, R; 2001 v F, Sp, Fi, Alb; (with Arsenal), 2002 v G, Alb, Ho, I, Sk, Cam, Se, Arg, Ng, D, Br; 2003 v Mac, Aus, T; 2004 v Mac, T, J, Ic, F, Sw, Cro, P; 2005 v W, Az, US; 2006 v A, H (sub), Jam (sub), Se (sub) (69)
Camsell, G. H. (Middlesbrough), 1929 v F, Bel; 1930 v Ni, W; 1934 v F; 1936 v S, G, A, Bel (9)
Capes, A. J. (Stoke C), 1903 v S (1)
Carr, J. (Middlesbrough), 1920 v Ni; 1923 v W (2)
Carr, J. (Newcastle U), 1905 v Ni; 1907 v Ni (2)
Carr, W. H. (Owlerton, Sheffield), 1875 v S (1)
Carragher, J. L. (Liverpool), 1999 v H (sub); 2001 v I (sub), M (sub); 2002 v Ho, G (sub), Alb (sub), Se, Para (sub); 2003 v Ser (sub); 2004 v P (sub), Se, Ic; 2005 v Uk (sub), A (sub), Pol (sub), Sp (sub), Ho; 2006 v D (sub), W, Ni, A, Pol, U (sub), H, Jam, Tr, Se, Ec (sub), P (sub); 2007 v Gr (sub), Cro, Sp (sub), Is, Br (34)
Carrick, M. (West Ham U), 2001 v M (sub); 2002 v Ho (sub); (with Tottenham H), 2005 v US, Col; 2006 v U, Jam (sub), Ec; (with Manchester U) 2007 v Mac (sub + 1), Cro, Ho, Sp, Br (sub) (13)
Carter, H. S. (Sunderland), 1934 v S, H; 1936 v G; 1937 v S, Ni, H; (with Derby Co), 1947 v S, W, Ni, Ei, Ho, F, Sw (13)
Carter, J. H. (WBA), 1926 v Bel; 1929 v Bel, Sp (3)
Catlin, A. E. (Sheffield W), 1937 v W, Ni, H, N, Se (5)
Chadwick, A. (Southampton), 1900 v S, W (2)
Chadwick, E. (Everton), 1891 v S, W; 1892 v S; 1893 v S; 1894 v S; 1896 v Ni; 1897 v S (7)
Chamberlain, M (Stoke C), 1983 v L (sub); 1984 v D (sub), S, USSR, Br, U, Ch; 1985 v Fi (sub) (8)
Chambers, H. (Liverpool), 1921 v S, W, Bel; 1923 v S, W, Ni, Bel; 1924 v Ni (8)
Channon, M. R. (Southampton), 1973 v Y, S (2), Ni, W, Cz, USSR, I; 1974 v A, Pol, I, P, W, Ni, S, Arg, EG, Bul, Y; 1975 v Cz, P, WG, Cy (2), Ni (sub), W, S; 1976 v Sw, Cz, P, W, Ni, S, Br, I, Fi; 1977 v Fi, I, L, Ni, W, S, Br (sub), Arg, U; (with Manchester C), 1978 v Sw (46)
Charles, G. A. (Nottingham F), 1991 v Nz, Mal (2)
Charlton, J. (Leeds U), 1965 v S, H, Y, WG, Se; 1966 v W, Ni, S, A, Sp, Pol (2), WG (2), Y, Fi, D, U, M, F, Arg, P; 1967 v W, S, Ni, Cz; 1968 v W, Sp; 1969 v W, R, F; 1970 v Ho (2), P, Cz (35)
Charlton, R. (Manchester U), 1958 v S, P, Y; 1959 v S, W, Ni, USSR, I, Br, Pe, M, US; 1960 v W, S, Se, Y, Sp, H; 1961 v Ni, W, S, L, P, Sp, M, I, A; 1962 v W, Ni, S, A, Sw, Pe, L, P, H, Arg, Bul, Br; 1963 v S, F, Br, Cz, EG, Sw; 1964 v S, W, Ni, R of W, U, P, Ei, Br, Arg, US (sub); 1965 v Ni, S, Ho; 1966 v W, Ni, S, A, Sp, WG (2), Y, Fi, N, Pol, U, M, F, Arg, P; 1967 v Ni, W, S, Cz; 1968 v W, Ni, S, USSR (2), Sp (2), Se, Y; 1969 v S, W, Ni, R (2), Bul, M, Br; 1970 v W, Ni, Ho (2), P, Co, Ec, Cz, R, Br, WG (106)
Charnley, R. O. (Blackpool), 1963 v F (1)
Charsley, C. C. (Small Heath), 1893 v Ni (1)
Chedgzoy, S. (Everton), 1920 v W; 1921 v W, S, Ni; 1922 v Ni; 1923 v S; 1924 v W; 1925 v Ni (8)
Chenery, C. J. (C Palace), 1872 v S; 1873 v S; 1874 v S (3)
Cherry, T. J. (Leeds U), 1976 v W, S (sub), Br, Fi; 1977 v Ei, I, L, Ni, S (sub), Br, Arg, U; 1978 v Sw, L, I, Br, W; 1979 v Cz, W, Se; 1980 v Ei, Arg (sub), W, Ni, S, Aus, Sp (sub) (27)
Chilton, A. (Manchester U), 1951 v Ni; 1952 v F (2)
Chippendale, H. (Blackburn R), 1894 v Ni (1)

Chivers, M. (Tottenham H), 1971 v Ma (2), Gr, Ni, S; 1972 v Sw (1+1 sub), Gr, WG (2), Ni (sub), S; 1973 v W (3), S (2), Ni, Cz, Pol, USSR, I; 1974 v A, Pol (24)
Christian, E. (Old Etonians), 1879 v S (1)
Clamp, E. (Wolverhampton W), 1958 v USSR (2), Br, A (4)
Clapton, D. R. (Arsenal), 1959 v W (1)
Clare, T. (Stoke C), 1889 v Ni; 1892 v Ni; 1893 v W; 1894 v S (4)
Clarke, A. J. (Leeds U), 1970 v Cz; 1971 v EG, Ma, Ni, W (sub), S (sub); 1973 v S (2), W, Cz, Pol, USSR, I; 1974 v A, Pol, I; 1975 v P; 1976 v Cz, P (sub) (19)
Clarke, H. A. (Tottenham H), 1954 v S (1)
Clay, T. (Tottenham H), 1920 v W; 1922 v W, S, Ni (4)
Clayton, R. (Blackburn R), 1956 v Ni, Br, Se, Fi, WG, Sp; 1957 v S, W, Ni, Y, D (2), Ei (2); 1958 v S, W, Ni, F, P, Y, USSR; 1959 v S, W, Ni, USSR, I, Br, Pe, M, US; 1960 v W, Ni, S, Se, Y (35)
Clegg, J. C. (Sheffield W), 1872 v S (1)
Clegg, W. E. (Sheffield W), 1873 v S; (with Sheffield Albion), 1879 v W (2)
Clemence, R. N. (Liverpool), 1973 v W (2); 1974 v EG, Bul, Y; 1975 v Cz, P, WG, Cy, Ni, W, S; 1976 v Sw, Cz, P, W (2), Ni, S, Br, Fi; 1977 v Ei, Fi, I, Ho, L, S, Br, Arg, U; 1978 v Sw, L, I, WG, Ni, S; 1979 v D, Ei, Ni (2), S, Bul, A (sub); 1980 v D, Bul, Ei, Arg, W, S, Bel, Sp; 1981 v R, Sp, Br, Sw, H; (with Tottenham H), 1982 v N, Ni, Fi; 1983 v L; 1984 v L (61)
Clement, D. T. (QPR), 1976 v W (sub+1), I; 1977 v I, Ho (5)
Clough, B. H. (Middlesbrough), 1960 v W, Se (2)
Clough, N. H. (Nottingham F), 1989 v Ch; 1991 v Arg (sub), Aus, Mal; 1992 v F, Cz, C (sub); 1993 v Sp, T (sub), Pol (sub), N (sub), US, Br, G (14)
Coates, R. (Burnley), 1970 v Ni; 1971 v Gr (sub); (with Tottenham H), Ma, W (4)
Cobbold, W. N. (Cambridge University), 1883 v S, Ni; 1885 v S, Ni; 1886 v S, W; (with Old Carthusians), 1887 v S, W, Ni (9)
Cock, J. G. (Huddersfield T), 1920 v Ni; (with Chelsea), v S (2)
Cockburn, H. (Manchester U), 1947 v W, Ni, Ei; 1948 v S, I; 1949 v S, Ni, D, Sw, Se; 1951 v Arg, P; 1952 v F (13)
Cohen, G. R. (Fulham), 1964 v U, P, Ei, US, Br; 1965 v W, S, Ni, Bel, H, Ho, Y, WG, Se; 1966 v W, S, Ni, A, Sp, Pol (2), WG (2), N, D, U, M, F, Arg, P; 1967 v W, S, Ni, Cz, Sp; 1968 v W, Ni (37)
Cole, A. (Manchester U), 1995 v U (sub); 1997 v I (sub); 1999 v F (sub), Pol, Se; 2000 v S (sub), Arg (sub); 2001 v F, G, Fi, Sp, Fi, Alb; 2002 v Ho, Gr (sub) (15)
Cole, A. (Arsenal), 2001 v Alb, M, Gr; 2002 v Ho, G, Alb, Gr, Sk, Se, Arg, Ng, D, Br; 2003 v P, Slo, Mac, Aus, Ser, Slo; 2004 v Cro, Mac, T, D, P, J, Ic, F, Sw, Cro, P; 2005 v Uk, A, Pol, W, Az, Sp, Ho, Ni, Az, US, Col; 2006 v D, W, Ni, H, Jam, Para, Tr, Se, Ec, P; (with Chelsea), 2007 v Gr, And, Mac (2), Cro, Ho, And (58)
Cole, J. J. (West Ham U), 2001 v M (sub); 2002 v Ho (sub), I (sub), Para (sub), Sk (sub), Cam, Se (sub); 2003 v P (sub), S.Af (sub), Ser (sub); (with Chelsea), 2004 v Cro (sub), Lie (sub), D, P (sub), Se (sub), J (sub), Ic (sub); 2005 v A (sub), Az (sub), Ni, Az, US, Col; 2006 v D, W, Ni (sub), A, Pol, Arg (sub), U, H, Jam, Para, Tr, Se, Ec, P; 2007 v Ho, Br, Es (40)
Colclough, H. (C Palace), 1914 v W (1)
Coleman, E. H. (Dulwich Hamlet), 1921 v W (1)
Coleman, J. (Woolwich Arsenal), 1907 v Ni (1)
Collymore, S. V. (Nottingham F), 1995 v J, Br (sub); (with Aston Villa), 1998 v Mol (sub) (3)
Common, A. (Sheffield U), 1904 v W, Ni; (with Middlesbrough), 1906 v W (3)
Compton, L. H. (Arsenal), 1951 v W, Y (2)
Conlin, J. (Bradford C), 1906 v S (1)
Connelly, J. M. (Burnley), 1960 v W, Ni, S, Se; 1962 v W, A, Sw, P; 1963 v W, F; (with Manchester U), 1965 v H, Y, Se; 1966 v W, Ni, S, A, N, D, U (20)
Cook, T. E. R. (Brighton), 1925 v W (1)
Cooper, C. T. (Nottingham F), 1995 v Se, Br (2)
Cooper, N. C. (Cambridge University), 1893 v Ni (1)
Cooper, T. (Derby Co), 1928 v Ni; 1929 v W, Ni, S, F, Bel, Sp; 1931 v F; 1932 v W, Sp; 1933 v S; 1934 v S, H, Cz; 1935 v W (15)
Cooper, T. (Leeds U), 1969 v W, S, F, M; 1970 v Ho, Bel, Co, Ec, R, Cz, Br, WG; 1971 v EG, Ma, Ni, W, S; 1972 v Sw (2); 1975 v P (20)
Coppell, S. J. (Manchester U), 1978 v I, WG, Br, W, Ni, S, H; 1979 v D, Ei, Cz, Ni (2), W (sub), S, Bul, A; 1980 v D, Ni, Ei (sub), Sp, Arg, W, S, Bel, I; 1981 v R (sub), Sw, R, Br, W, S, Sw, H; 1982 v H, S, Fi, F, Cz, K, WG; 1983 v L, Gr (42)
Copping, W. (Leeds U), 1933 v I, Sw; 1934 v S, Ni, W, F; (with Arsenal), 1935 v Ni, I; 1936 v A, Bel; 1937 v N, Se, Fi; 1938 v S, W, Ni, Cz; 1939 v W, R of E; (with Leeds U), R (20)
Corbett, B. O. (Corinthians), 1901 v W (1)
Corbett, R. (Old Malvernians), 1903 v W (1)
Corbett, W. S. (Birmingham), 1908 v A, H, B (3)
Corrigan, J. T. (Manchester C), 1976 v I (sub); 1978 v Br; 1979 v W; 1980 v Ni, Aus; 1981 v W, S; 1982 v W, Ic (9)
Cottee, A. R. (West Ham U), 1987 v Se (sub), Ni (sub); 1988 v H (sub); (with Everton) 1989 v D (sub), Se (sub), Ch (sub), S (7)
Cotterill, G. H. (Cambridge University), 1891 v Ni; (with Old Brightonians), 1892 v W; 1893 v S, Ni (4)
Cottle, J. R. (Bristol C), 1909 v Ni (1)
Cowan, S. (Manchester C), 1926 v Bel; 1930 v A; 1931 v Bel (3)
Cowans, G. (Aston Villa), 1983 v W, H, Ni, S, Aus (3); (with Bari), 1986 v Eg, USSR; (with Aston Villa), 1991 v Ei (10)
Cowell, A. (Blackburn R), 1910 v Ni (1)
Cox, J. (Liverpool), 1901 v Ni; 1902 v S; 1903 v S (3)
Cox, J. D. (Derby Co), 1892 v Ni (1)
Crabtree, J. W. (Burnley), 1894 v Ni; 1895 v Ni, S; (with Aston Villa), 1896 v W, S, Ni; 1899 v S, W, Ni; 1900 v S, W, Ni; 1901 v W; 1902 v W (14)
Crawford, J. F. (Chelsea), 1931 v S (1)
Crawford, R. (Ipswich T), 1962 v Ni, A (2)
Crawshaw, T. H. (Sheffield W), 1895 v Ni; 1896 v S, W, Ni; 1897 v S, W, Ni; 1901 v Ni; 1904 v W, Ni (10)
Crayston, W. J. (Arsenal), 1936 v S, W, G, A, Bel; 1938 v W, Ni, Cz (8)
Creek, F. N. S. (Corinthians), 1923 v F (1)
Cresswell, W. (South Shields), 1921 v W; (with Sunderland), 1923 v F; 1924 v Bel; 1925 v Ni; 1926 v W; 1927 v Ni; (with Everton), 1930 v Ni (7)
Crompton, R. (Blackburn R), 1902 v S, W, Ni; 1903 v S, W; 1904 v S, W, Ni; 1906 v S, W, Ni; 1907 v S, W, Ni; 1908 v S, W, Ni, A (2), H, B; 1909 v S, W, Ni, H (2), A; 1910 v S, W; 1911 v S, W, Ni; 1912 v S, W, Ni; 1913 v S, W, Ni; 1914 v S, W, Ni (41)
Crooks, S. D. (Derby Co), 1930 v S, G, A; 1931 v S, W, Ni, F, Bel; 1932 v S, W, Ni, Sp; 1933 v Ni, W, A; 1934 v S, Ni, W, F, H, Cz; 1935 v Ni; 1936 v S, W; 1937 v W, H (26)
Crouch, P. J. (Southampton), 2005 v Co; (with Liverpool), 2006 v A, Pol (sub), Arg (sub), U (sub), H (sub), Jam, Para, Tr, Se (sub), P (sub); 2007 v Gr, And, Mac (2), Cro, Sp, Br (sub), Es (19)
Crowe, C. (Wolverhampton W), 1963 v F (1)
Cuggy, F. (Sunderland), 1913 v Ni; 1914 v Ni (2)
Cullis, S. (Wolverhampton W), 1938 v S, W, Ni, F, Cz; 1939 v S, Ni, R of E, N, I, R, Y (12)
Cunliffe, A. (Blackburn R), 1933 v Ni, W (2)
Cunliffe, D. (Portsmouth), 1900 v Ni (1)
Cunliffe, J. N. (Everton), 1936 v Bel (1)
Cunningham, L. (WBA), 1979 v W, Se, A (sub); (with Real Madrid), 1980 v Ei, Sp (sub); 1981 v R (sub) (6)
Curle, K. (Manchester C), 1992 v C (sub), H, D (3)
Currey, E. S. (Oxford University), 1890 v S, W (2)
Currie, A. W. (Sheffield U), 1972 v Ni; 1973 v USSR, I; 1974 v A, Pol, I; 1976 v Sw; (with Leeds U), 1978 v Br, W (sub), Ni, S, H (sub); 1979 v Cz, Ni (2), W, Se (17)
Cursham, A. W. (Notts Co), 1876 v S; 1877 v S; 1878 v S; 1879 v W; 1883 v S, W (6)
Cursham, H. A. (Notts Co), 1880 v W; 1882 v S, W, Ni; 1883 v S, W, Ni; 1884 v Ni (8)

Daft, H. B. (Notts Co), 1889 v Ni; 1890 v S, W; 1891 v Ni; 1892 v Ni (5)
Daley, A. M. (Aston Villa), 1992 v Pol (sub), C, H, Br, Fi (sub), D (sub), Se (7)
Danks, T. (Nottingham F), 1885 v S (1)
Davenport, P. (Nottingham F), 1985 v Ei (sub) (1)
Davenport, J. K. (Bolton W), 1885 v W; 1890 v Ni (2)
Davis, G. (Derby Co), 1904 v W, Ni (2)
Davis, H. (Sheffield W), 1903 v S, W, Ni (3)
Davison, J. E. (Sheffield W), 1922 v W (1)
Dawson, J. (Burnley), 1922 v S, Ni (2)
Day, S. H. (Old Malvernians), 1906 v Ni, W, S (3)

Dean, W. R. (Everton), 1927 v S, W, F, Bel, L; 1928 v S, W, Ni, F, Bel; 1929 v S, W, Ni; 1931 v S; 1932 v Sp; 1933 v Ni (16)
Deane, B. C. (Sheffield U), 1991 v Nz (sub + 1); 1993 v Sp (sub) (3)
Deeley, N. V. (Wolverhampton W), 1959 v Br, Pe (2)
Defoe, J. C. (Tottenham H), 2004 v Se (sub), Ic (sub); 2005 v Uk (sub), A (sub), Pol, W, Az, Sp (sub), Ni (sub), Az (sub), US (sub), Co (sub); 2006 v D, W (sub), Ni (sub), U (sub); 2007 v Gr, And, Mac (1 + sub), Cro (sub), Sp (sub), Is (sub), And (sub) (24)
Devey, J. H. G. (Aston Villa), 1892 v Ni; 1894 v Ni (2)
Devonshire, A. (West Ham U), 1980 v Aus (sub), Ni; 1982 v Ho, Ic; 1983 v WG, W, Gr; 1984 v L (8)
Dewhurst, F. (Preston NE), 1886 v W, Ni; 1887 v S, W, Ni; 1888 v S, W, Ni; 1889 v W (9)
Dewhurst, G. P. (Liverpool Ramblers), 1895 v W (1)
Dickinson, J. W. (Portsmouth), 1949 v N, F; 1950 v S, W, Ei, P, Bel, Ch, US, Sp; 1951 v Ni, W, Y; 1952 v W, Ni, S, A (2), I, Sw; 1953 v W, Ni, S, Bel, Arg, Ch, U, US; 1954 v W, Ni, S, R of E, H (2), Y, Bel, Sw, U; 1955 v Sp, P; 1956 v W, Ni, S, D, Sp; 1957 v W, Y, D (48)
Dimmock, J. H. (Tottenham H), 1921 v S; 1926 v W, Bel (3)
Ditchburn, E. G. (Tottenham H), 1949 v Sw, Se; 1953 v US; 1957 v W, Y, D (6)
Dix, R. W. (Derby Co), 1939 v N (1)
Dixon, J. A. (Notts Co), 1885 v W (1)
Dixon, K. M. (Chelsea), 1985 v M (sub), WG, US; 1986 v Ni, Is, M (sub), Pol (sub); 1987 v Se (8)
Dixon, L. M. (Arsenal), 1990 v Cz; 1991 v H, Pol, Ei (2), Cam, T, Arg; 1992 v G, T, Pol, Cz (sub); 1993 v Sp, N, T, Sm, T, Ho, N, US; 1994 v Sm; 1999 v F (22)
Dobson, A. T. C. (Notts Co), 1882 v Ni; 1884 v S, W, Ni (4)
Dobson, C. F. (Notts Co), 1886 v Ni (1)
Dobson, J. M. (Burnley), 1974 v P, EG, Bul, Y; (with Everton), 1975 v Cz (5)
Doggart, A. G. (Corinthians), 1924 v Bel (1)
Dorigo, A. R. (Chelsea), 1990 v Y (sub), Cz (sub), D (sub), I; 1991 v H (sub), USSR; (with Leeds U), 1992 v G, Cz (sub), H, Br; 1993 v Sm, Pol, US, Br; 1994 v Ho (15)
Dorrell, A. R. (Aston Villa), 1925 v W, Bel, F; 1926 v Ni (4)
Douglas, B. (Blackburn R), 1958 v S, W, Ni, F, P, Y, USSR (2), Br, A; 1959 v S, USSR; 1960 v Y, H; 1961 v Ni, W, S, L, P, Sp, M, I, A; 1962 v W, Ni, S, Pe, L, P, H, Arg, Bul, Br; 1963 v S, Br, Sw (36)
Downing, S. (Middlesbrough), 2005 v Ho (sub); 2006 v Jam (sub), Para (sub), Tr (sub), Ec (sub); 2007 v Gr, And, Mac (2), Sp (sub), Is (sub), And, Br (sub), Es (sub) (14)
Downs, R. W. (Everton), 1921 v Ni (1)
Doyle, M. (Manchester C), 1976 v W, S (sub), Br, I; 1977 v Ho (5)
Drake, E. J. (Arsenal), 1935 v Ni, I; 1936 v W; 1937 v H; 1938 v F (5)
Dublin, D. (Coventry C), 1998 v Ch, Mor, Bel (sub); (with Aston Villa), 1999 v CzR (4)
Ducat, A. (Woolwich Arsenal), 1910 v S, W, Ni; (with Aston Villa), 1920 v S, W; 1921 v Ni (6)
Dunn, A. T. B. (Cambridge University), 1883 v Ni; 1884 v Ni; (with Old Etonians), 1892 v S, W (4)
Dunn, D. J. I. (Blackburn R), 2003 v P (sub) (1)
Duxbury, M. (Manchester U), 1984 v L, F, W, S, USSR, Br, U, Ch; 1985 v EG, Fi (10)
Dyer, K. C. (Newcastle U), 2000 v L, Pol (sub), Bel, Arg, Uk (sub); 2001 v F (sub), G (sub), I; 2002 v Para, Se (sub), D (sub), Br (sub); 2003 v Slo (sub), Aus, Lie, T (sub); 2004 v Cro (sub), Mac (sub), T (sub), P (sub), J (sub), Ic (sub), Sw (sub); 2005 v Uk (sub), Pol (sub), Ho (sub), Ni (sub), Az (sub); 2007 v Sp, And (sub), Br (sub), Es (sub) (32)

Earle, S. G. J. (Clapton), 1924 v F; (with West Ham U), 1928 v Ni (2)
Eastham, G. (Arsenal), 1963 v Br, Cz, EG; 1964 v W, Ni, S, R of W, U, P, Ei, US, Br, Arg; 1965 v H, WG, Se; 1966 v Sp, Pol, D (19)
Eastham, G. R. (Bolton W), 1935 v Ho (1)
Eckersley, W. (Blackburn R), 1950 v Sp; 1951 v S, Y, Arg, P; 1952 v A (2), Sw; 1953 v Ni, Arg, Ch, U, US; 1954 v W, Ni, R of E, H (17)
Edwards, D. (Manchester U), 1955 v S, F, Sp, P; 1956 v S, Br, Se, Fi, WG; 1957 v S, Ni, Ei (2), D (2); 1958 v W, Ni, F (18)
Edwards, J. H. (Shropshire Wanderers), 1874 v S (1)
Edwards, W. (Leeds U), 1926 v S, W; 1927 v W, Ni, S, F, Bel, L; 1928 v S, F, Bel; 1929 v S, W, Ni; 1930 v W, Ni (16)
Ehiogu, U. (Aston Villa), 1996 v Chn (sub); (with Middlesbrough), 2001 v Sp (sub); 2002 v Ho (sub), I (sub) (4)
Ellerington, W. (Southampton), 1949 v N, F (2)
Elliott, G. W. (Middlesbrough), 1913 v Ni; 1914 v Ni; 1920 v W (3)
Elliott, W. H. (Burnley), 1952 v I, A; 1953 v Ni, W, Bel (5)
Evans, R. E. (Sheffield U), 1911 v S, W, Ni; 1912 v W (4)
Ewer, F. H. (Casuals), 1924 v F; 1925 v Bel (2)

Fairclough, P. (Old Foresters), 1878 v S (1)
Fairhurst, D. (Newcastle U), 1934 v F (1)
Fantham, J. (Sheffield W), 1962 v L (1)
Fashanu, J. (Wimbledon), 1989 v Ch, S (2)
Felton, W. (Sheffield W), 1925 v F (1)
Fenton, M. (Middlesbrough), 1938 v S (1)
Fenwick, T. (QPR), 1984 v W (sub), S, USSR, Br, U, Ch; 1985 v Fi, S, M, US; 1986 v R, T, Ni, Eg, M, P, Mor, Pol, Arg; (with Tottenham H), 1988 v Is (sub) (20)
Ferdinand, L. (QPR), 1993 v Sm, Ho, N, US; 1994 v Pol, Sm; 1995 v US (sub); (with Newcastle U), 1996 v P, Bul, H; 1997 v Pol, Ge, I (sub); (with Tottenham H), 1998 v Mol, S.Ar (sub), Mor (sub), Bel (17)
Ferdinand, R. G. (West Ham U), 1998 v Cam (sub), Sw, Bel (sub); 1999 v L, CzR, F (sub), H, Se (sub); 2000 v Arg (sub); 2001 v I; (with Leeds U), Sp, Fi, Alb, M, Gr; 2002 v G, Alb, Gr, Se, Ho, Sk, Cam, Se, Arg, Ng, D, Br; (with Manchester U), 2003 v P, Aus, Lie, T, S.Af; 2004 v Cro; 2005 v W, Az, Sp, Ni, Az; 2006 v D, W, Ni, A (sub), Pol, Arg, U, H, Jam, Para, Tr, Se, Ec, P; 2007 v Gr, Mac, Cro, Ho, Sp, Is, And (59)
Field, E. (Clapham Rovers), 1876 v S; 1881 v S (2)
Finney, T. (Preston NE), 1947 v W, Ni, Ei, Ho, F, P; 1948 v S, W, Ni, Bel, Se, I; 1949 v S, W, Ni, Se, N, F; 1950 v S, W, Ni, Ei, I, P, Bel, Ch, US, Sp; 1951 v W, S, Arg, P; 1952 v W, Ni, S, F, I, Sw, A; 1953 v W, Ni, S, Bel, Arg, Ch, U, US; 1954 v W, S, Bel, Sw, U, H, Y; 1955 v WG; 1956 v S, W, Ni, D, Sp; 1957 v S, W, Y, D (2), Ei (2); 1958 v W, S, F, P, Y, USSR (2); 1959 v Ni, USSR (76)
Fleming, H. J. (Swindon T), 1909 v S, H (2); 1910 v W, Ni; 1911 v W, Ni; 1912 v Ni; 1913 v S, W; 1914 v S (11)
Fletcher, A. (Wolverhampton W), 1889 v W; 1890 v W (2)
Flowers, R. (Wolverhampton W), 1955 v F; 1959 v S, W, I, Br, Pe, US, M (sub); 1960 v W, Ni, S, Se, Y, Sp, H; 1961 v Ni, W, S, L, P, Sp, M, I, A; 1962 v W, Ni, S, A, Sw, Pe, L, P, H, Arg, Bul, Br; 1963 v Ni, W, S, F (2), Sw; 1964 v Ei, US, P; 1965 v W, Ho, WG; 1966 v N (49)
Flowers, T. D. (Southampton), 1993 v Br; (with Blackburn R), 1994 v Gr; 1995 v Ng, U, J, Se, Br; 1996 v Chn; 1997 v I; 1998 v Sw, Mor (11)
Forman, Frank (Nottingham F), 1898 v S, Ni; 1899 v S, W, Ni; 1901 v S; 1902 v S, Ni; 1903 v W (9)
Forman, F. R. (Nottingham F), 1899 v S, W, Ni (3)
Forrest, J. H. (Blackburn R), 1884 v W; 1885 v S, W, Ni; 1886 v S, W; 1887 v S, W, Ni; 1889 v S; 1890 v Ni (11)
Fort, J. (Millwall), 1921 v Bel (1)
Foster, B. (Manchester U), 2007 v Sp (1)
Foster, R. E. (Oxford University), 1900 v W; (with Corinthians), 1901 v W, Ni, S; 1902 v W (5)
Foster, S. (Brighton & HA), 1982 v Ni, Ho, K (3)
Foulke, W. J. (Sheffield U), 1897 v W (1)
Foulkes, W. A. (Manchester U), 1955 v Ni (1)
Fowler, R. B. (Liverpool), 1996 v Bul (sub), Cro, Chn (sub), Ho (sub), Sp (sub); 1997 v M; 1998 v Cam; 1999 v CzR (sub), Bul; 2000 v L, Pol, Br (sub), Uk, Ma (sub); 2001 v I (sub), Fi (sub), M, Gr; 2002 v Ho, Alb (sub), Gr, Se (sub); (with Leeds U), I (sub), Para (sub), Cam (sub), D (sub) (26)
Fox, F. S. (Millwall), 1925 v F (1)
Francis, G. C. J. (QPR), 1975 v Cz, P, W, S; 1976 v Sw, Cz, P, W, Ni, S, Br, Fi (12)
Francis, T. (Birmingham C), 1977 v Ho, L, S, Br; 1978 v Sw, L, I (sub), WG (sub), Br, W, S, H; (with Nottingham F), 1979 v Bul (sub), Se, A (sub); 1980 v Ni, Bul, Sp; 1981 v Sp, R, S (sub), Sw; (with Manchester C), 1982 v N, Ni, W, S (sub), Fi (sub), F, Cz, K, WG,

Sp; (with Sampdoria), 1983 v D, Gr, H, Ni, S, Aus (3); 1984 v D, Ni, USSR; 1985 v EG (sub), T (sub), Ni (sub), R, Fi, S, I, M; 1986 v S (52)
Franklin, C. F. (Stoke C), 1947 v S, W, Ni, Ei, Ho, F, Sw, P; 1948 v S, W, Ni, Bel, Se, I; 1949 v S, W, Ni, D, Sw, N, F, Se; 1950 v W, S, Ni, Ei, I (27)
Freeman, B. C. (Everton), 1909 v S, W; (with Burnley), 1912 v S, W, Ni (5)
Froggatt, J. (Portsmouth), 1950 v Ni, I; 1951 v S; 1952 v S, A (2), I, Sw; 1953 v Ni, W, S, Bel, US (13)
Froggatt, R. (Sheffield W), 1953 v W, S, Bel, US (4)
Fry, C. B. (Corinthians), 1901 v Ni (1)
Furness, W. I. (Leeds U), 1933 v I (1)

Galley, T. (Wolverhampton W), 1937 v N, Se (2)
Gardner, A. (Tottenham H), 2004 v Se (sub) (1)
Gardner, T. (Aston Villa), 1934 v Cz; 1935 v Ho (2)
Garfield, B. (WBA), 1898 v Ni (1)
Garraty, W. (Aston Villa), 1903 v W (1)
Garrett, T. (Blackpool), 1952 v S, I; 1954 v W (3)
Gascoigne, P. J. (Tottenham H), 1989 v D (sub), S.Ar (sub), Alb (sub), Ch, S (sub); 1990 v Se (sub), Br (sub), Cz, D, U, Tun, Ei, Ho, Eg, Bel, Cam, WG; 1991 v H, Pol, Cam; (with Lazio), 1993 v N, T, Sm, T, Ho, Pol, N; 1994 v Pol, D; 1995 v J (sub), Se (sub), Br (sub); (with Rangers), 1996 v Co, Sw, P, Bul, Cro, Chn, Sw, S, Ho, Sp, G; 1997 v Mol, Pol, Ge, S.Af, Pol, I (sub), F, Br; 1998 v Mol, I, Cam; (with Middlesbrough), S.Ar (sub), Mor, Bel (57)
Gates, E. (Ipswich T), 1981 v N, R (2)
Gay, L. H. (Cambridge University), 1893 v S; (with Old Brightonians), 1894 v S, W (3)
Geary, F. (Everton), 1890 v Ni; 1891 v S (2)
Geaves, R. L. (Clapham Rovers), 1875 v S (1)
Gee, C. W. (Everton), 1932 v W, Sp; 1937 v Ni (3)
Geldard, A. (Everton), 1933 v I, Sw; 1935 v S; 1938 v Ni (4)
George, C. (Derby Co), 1977 v Ei (1)
George, W. (Aston Villa), 1902 v S, W, Ni (3)
Gerrard, S. G. (Liverpool), 2000 v Uk, G (sub); 2001 v Fi, M, Gr; 2002 v G, Alb, Gr, Ho, Para; 2003 v P, Slo, Mac, Lie, T, S.Af, Ser, Slo; 2004 v Cro, Lie, T, Se, J, Ic, F, Sw, Cro, P; 2005 v Uk, A, Pol, Ho, Ni, Az; 2006 v D, W, Ni, A, Arg, U, H, Jam, Para, Tr, Se (sub), Ec, P; 2007 v Gr, And, Mac (2), Ho, Sp, Is, And, Br, Es (57)
Gibbins, W. V. T. (Clapton), 1924 v F; 1925 v F (2)
Gidman, J. (Aston Villa), 1977 v L (1)
Gillard, I. T. (QPR), 1975 v WG, W; 1976 v Cz (3)
Gilliat, W. E. (Old Carthusians), 1893 v Ni (1)
Goddard, P. (West Ham U), 1982 v Ic (sub) (1)
Goodall, F. R. (Huddersfield T), 1926 v S; 1927 v S, F, Bel, L; 1928 v S, W, F, Bel; 1930 v S, G, A; 1931 v S, W, Ni, Bel; 1932 v Ni; 1933 v W, Ni, A, I, Sw; 1934 v W, Ni, F (25)
Goodall, J. (Preston NE), 1888 v S, W; 1889 v S, W; (with Derby Co), 1891 v S, W; 1892 v S; 1893 v W; 1894 v S; 1895 v S, Ni; 1896 v S, W; 1898 v W (14)
Goodhart, H. C. (Old Etonians), 1883 v S, W, Ni (3)
Goodwyn, A. G. (Royal Engineers), 1873 v S (1)
Goodyer, A. C. (Nottingham F), 1879 v S (1)
Gosling, R. C. (Old Etonians), 1892 v W; 1893 v S; 1894 v W; 1895 v W, S (5)
Gosnell, A. A. (Newcastle U), 1906 v Ni (1)
Gough, H. C. (Sheffield U), 1921 v S (1)
Goulden, L. A. (West Ham U), 1937 v Se, N; 1938 v W, Ni, Cz, G, Sw, F; 1939 v S, W, R of E, I, R, Y (14)
Graham, L. (Millwall), 1925 v S, W (2)
Graham, T. (Nottingham F), 1931 v F; 1932 v Ni (2)
Grainger, C. (Sheffield U), 1956 v Br, Se, Fi, WG; 1957 v W, Ni; (with Sunderland), 1957 v S (7)
Gray, A. A. (C Palace), 1992 v Pol (1)
Gray, M. (Sunderland), 1999 v H (sub), Se (sub), Bul (3)
Greaves, J. (Chelsea), 1959 v Pe, M, US; 1960 v W, Se, Y, Sp; 1961 v Ni, W, S, L, P, Sp, I, A; (with Tottenham H), 1962 v S, Sw, Pe, H, Arg, Bul, Br; 1963 v Ni, W, S, F (2), Br, Cz, Sw; 1964 v W, Ni, R of W, P (2), Ei, Br, U, Arg; 1965 v Ni, S, Bel, Ho, H, Y; 1966 v W, A, Y, N, D, Pol, U, M, F; 1967 v S, Sp, A (57)
Green, F. T. (Wanderers), 1876 v S (1)
Green, G. H. (Sheffield U), 1925 v F; 1926 v S, Bel, W; 1927 v W, Ni; 1928 v F, Bel (8)
Green, R. P. (Norwich C), 2005 v Co (sub) (1)
Greenhalgh, E. H. (Notts Co), 1872 v S; 1873 v S (2)
Greenhoff, B. (Manchester U), 1976 v W, Ni; 1977 v Ei, Fi, I, Ho, Ni, W, S, Br, Arg, U; 1978 v Br, W, Ni, S (sub), H (sub); (with Leeds U), 1980 v Aus (sub) (18)
Greenwood, D. H. (Blackburn R), 1882 v S, Ni (2)
Gregory, J. (QPR), 1983 v Aus (3); 1984 v D, H, W (6)
Grimsdell, A. (Tottenham H), 1920 v S, W; 1921 v S, Ni; 1923 v W, Ni (6)
Grosvenor, A. T. (Birmingham), 1934 v Ni, W, F (3)
Gunn, W. (Notts Co), 1884 v S, W (2)
Guppy, S. (Leicester C), 2000 v Bel (1)
Gurney, R. (Sunderland), 1935 v S (1)

Hacking, J. (Oldham Ath), 1929 v S, W, Ni (3)
Hadley, H. (WBA), 1903 v Ni (1)
Hagan, J. (Sheffield U), 1949 v D (1)
Haines, J. T. W. (WBA), 1949 v Sw (1)
Hall, A. E. (Aston Villa), 1910 v Ni (1)
Hall, G. W. (Tottenham H), 1934 v F; 1938 v S, W, Ni, Cz; 1939 v S, Ni, R of E, I, Y (10)
Hall, J. (Birmingham C), 1956 v S, W, Ni, Br, Se, Fi, WG, D, Sp; 1957 v S, W, Ni, Y, D (2), Ei (2) (17)
Halse, H. J. (Manchester U), 1909 v A (1)
Hammond, H. E. D. (Oxford University), 1889 v S (1)
Hampson, J. (Blackpool), 1931 v Ni, W; 1933 v A (3)
Hampton, H. (Aston Villa), 1913 v S, W; 1914 v S, W (4)
Hancocks, J. (Wolverhampton W), 1949 v Sw; 1950 v W; 1951 v Y (3)
Hapgood, E. (Arsenal), 1933 v I, Sw; 1934 v S, Ni, W, H, Cz; 1935 v S, Ni, W, I, Ho; 1936 v S, Ni, W, G, A, Bel; 1937 v Fi; 1938 v S, G, Sw, F; 1939 v S, W, Ni, R of E, N, I, Y (30)
Hardinge, H. T. W. (Sheffield U), 1910 v S (1)
Hardman, H. P. (Everton), 1905 v W; 1907 v S, Ni; 1908 v W (4)
Hardwick, G. F. M. (Middlesbrough), 1947 v S, W, Ni, Ei, Ho, F, Sw, P; 1948 v S, W, Ni, Bel, Se (13)
Hardy, H. (Stockport Co), 1925 v Bel (1)
Hardy, S. (Liverpool), 1907 v S, W, Ni; 1908 v S; 1909 v S, W, Ni, H (2), A; 1910 v S, W, Ni; 1912 v Ni; (with Aston Villa), 1913 v S; 1914 v Ni, W, S; 1920 v S, W, Ni (21)
Harford, M. G. (Luton T), 1988 v Is (sub); 1989 v D (2)
Hargreaves, F. W. (Blackburn R), 1880 v W; 1881 v W; 1882 v Ni (3)
Hargreaves, J. (Blackburn R), 1881 v S, W (2)
Hargreaves, O. (Bayern Munich), 2002 v Ho, G (sub), I (sub), Para (sub), Sk, Cam, Se, Arg; 2003 v P (sub), Slo (sub), Aus (sub), Ser (sub), Slo (sub); 2004 v Mac, Lie (sub), P (sub), Se, J (sub), Ic (sub), F (sub), Sw (sub), P (sub); 2005 v Pol (sub), W (sub), Ho (sub), Ni (sub); 2006 v D (sub), W (sub), Ni (sub), H (sub), Para (sub), Se, Ec, P; 2007 v Gr, And, Mac, Is, And (39)
Harper, E. C. (Blackburn R), 1926 v S (1)
Harris, G. (Burnley), 1966 v Pol (1)
Harris, P. P. (Portsmouth), 1950 v Ei; 1954 v H (2)
Harris, S. S. (Cambridge University), 1904 v S; (with Old Westminsters), 1905 v Ni, W; 1906 v S, W, Ni (6)
Harrison, A. H. (Old Westminsters), 1893 v S, Ni (2)
Harrison, G. (Everton), 1921 v Bel; 1922 v Ni (2)
Harrow, J. H. (Chelsea), 1923 v Ni, Se (2)
Hart, E. (Leeds U), 1929 v W; 1930 v W, Ni; 1933 v S, A; 1934 v S, H, Cz (8)
Hartley, F. (Oxford C), 1923 v F (1)
Harvey, A. (Wednesbury Strollers), 1881 v W (1)
Harvey, J. C. (Everton), 1971 v Ma (1)
Hassall, H. W. (Huddersfield T), 1951 v S, Arg, P; 1952 v F; (with Bolton W), 1954 v Ni (5)
Hateley, M. (Portsmouth), 1984 v USSR (sub), Br, U, Ch; (with AC Milan), 1985 v EG (sub), Fi, Ni, Ei, Fi, S, I, M; 1986 v R, T, Eg, S, M, Ca, P, Mor, Para (sub); 1987 v T (sub), Br (sub), S; (with Monaco), 1988 v WG (sub), Ho (sub), H (sub), Co (sub), Ei (sub), Ho (sub), USSR (sub); (with Rangers), 1992 v Cz (32)
Hawkes, R. M. (Luton T), 1907 v Ni; 1908 v A (2), H, B (5)
Haworth, G. (Accrington), 1887 v Ni, W, S; 1888 v S; 1890 v S (5)
Hawtrey, J. P. (Old Etonians), 1881 v S, W (2)
Haygarth, E. B. (Swifts), 1875 v S (1)
Haynes, J. N. (Fulham), 1955 v Ni; 1956 v S, Ni, Br, Se, Fi, WG, Sp; 1957 v W, Y, D, Ei (2); 1958 v W, Ni, S, F, P, Y, USSR (3), Br, A; 1959 v S, Ni, USSR, I, Br, Pe, M, US; 1960 v Ni, Y, Sp, H; 1961 v Ni, W, S, L, P, Sp, M, I, A; 1962 v W, Ni, S, A, Sw, Pe, P, H, Arg, Bul, Br (56)
Healless, H. (Blackburn R), 1925 v Ni; 1928 v S (2)

Hector, K. J. (Derby Co), 1974 v Pol (sub), I (sub) (2)
Hedley, G. A. (Sheffield U), 1901 v Ni (1)
Hegan, K. E. (Corinthians), 1923 v Bel, F; 1924 v Ni, Bel (4)
Hellawell, M. S. (Birmingham C), 1963 v Ni, F (2)
Hendrie, L. A. (Aston Villa), 1999 v CzR (sub) (1)
Henfrey, A. G. (Cambridge University), 1891 v Ni; (with Corinthians), 1892 v W; 1895 v W; 1896 v S, W (5)
Henry, R. P. (Tottenham H), 1963 v F (1)
Heron, F. (Wanderers), 1876 v S (1)
Heron, G. H. H. (Uxbridge), 1873 v S; 1874 v S; (with Wanderers), 1875 v S; 1876 v S; 1878 v S (5)
Heskey, E. W. (Leicester C), 1999 v H (sub), Bul (sub); 2000 v Bel (sub), S (sub), Arg; (with Liverpool), Uk (sub), Ma (sub), P (sub), R (sub); 2001 v Fi, I, Sp (sub), Fi (sub), Alb (sub), M, Gr; 2002 v G, Alb, Gr, Se, Ho, I, Sk, Cam, Se, Arg, Ng, D, Br; 2003 v P, Slo, Lie, S.Af, Ser; 2004 v Cro, Mac (sub), T, D, P (sub), Se (sub); (with Birmingham C), J (sub), Ic (sub), F (sub) (43)
Hibbert, W. (Bury), 1910 v S (1)
Hibbs, H. E. (Birmingham), 1930 v S, W, A, G; 1931 v S, W, Ni; 1932 v W, Ni, Sp; 1933 v S, W, Ni, A, I, Sw; 1934 v Ni, W, F; 1935 v S, W, Ni, Ho; 1936 v G, W (25)
Hill, F. (Bolton W), 1963 v Ni, W (2)
Hill, G. A. (Manchester U), 1976 v I; 1977 v Ei (sub), Fi (sub), L; 1978 v Sw (sub), L (6)
Hill, J. H. (Burnley), 1925 v W; 1926 v S; 1927 v S, Ni, Bel, F; 1928 v Ni, W; (with Newcastle U), 1929 v F, Bel, Sp (11)
Hill, R. (Luton T), 1983 v D (sub), WG; 1986 v Eg (sub) (3)
Hill, R. H. (Millwall), 1926 v Bel (1)
Hillman, J. (Burnley), 1899 v Ni (1)
Hills, A. F. (Old Harrovians), 1879 v S (1)
Hilsdon, G. R. (Chelsea), 1907 v Ni; 1908 v S, W, Ni, A, H, B; 1909 v Ni (8)
Hinchcliffe, A. G. (Everton), 1997 v Mol, Pol, Ge; 1998 v Cam; (with Sheffield W), Sw, S.Ar; 1999 v Bul (7)
Hine, E. W. (Leicester C), 1929 v W, Ni; 1930 v W, Ni; 1932 v W, Ni (6)
Hinton, A. T. (Wolverhampton W), 1963 v F; (with Nottingham F), 1965 v W, Bel (3)
Hirst, D. E. (Sheffield W), 1991 v Aus, Nz (sub); 1992 v F (3)
Hitchens, G. A. (Aston Villa), 1961 v M, I, A; (with Inter-Milan), 1962 v Sw, Pe, H, Br (7)
Hobbis, H. H. F. (Charlton Ath), 1936 v A, Bel (2)
Hoddle, G. (Tottenham H), 1980 v Bul, W, Aus, Sp; 1981 v Sp, W, S; 1982 v N, Ni, W, Ic, Cz (sub), K; 1983 v L (sub), Ni, S; 1984 v H, L, F; 1985 v Ei (sub), S, I (sub), M, WG, US; 1986 v R, T, Ni, Is, USSR, S, M, Ca, P, Mor, Pol, Para, Arg; 1987 v Se, Ni, Y, Sp, T, S; (with Monaco), 1988 v WG, T (sub), Y (sub), Ho (sub), H (sub), Co (sub), Ei (sub), Ho, USSR (53)
Hodge, S. B. (Aston Villa), 1986 v USSR (sub), S, Ca, P (sub), Mor (sub), Pol, Para, Arg; 1987 v Se, Ni, Y; (with Tottenham H), Sp. Ni, T, S; (with Nottingham F), 1989 v D; 1990 v I (sub), Y (sub), Cz, D, U, Tun; 1991 v Cam (sub), T (sub) (24)
Hodgetts, D. (Aston Villa), 1888 v S, W, Ni; 1892 v S, Ni; 1894 v Ni (6)
Hodgkinson, A. (Sheffield U), 1957 v S, Ei (2), D; 1961 v W (5)
Hodgson, G. (Liverpool), 1931 v S, Ni, W (3)
Hodkinson, J. (Blackburn R), 1913 v W, S; 1920 v Ni (3)
Hogg, W. (Sunderland), 1902 v S, W, Ni (3)
Holdcroft, G. H. (Preston NE), 1937 v W, Ni (2)
Holden, A. D. (Bolton W), 1959 v S, I, Br, Pe, M (5)
Holden, G. H. (Wednesbury OA), 1881 v S; 1884 v S, W, Ni (4)
Holden-White, C. (Corinthians), 1888 v W, S (2)
Holford, T. (Stoke), 1903 v Ni (1)
Holley, G. H. (Sunderland), 1909 v S, W, H (2), A; 1910 v W; 1912 v S, W, Ni; 1913 v S (10)
Holliday, E. (Middlesbrough), 1960 v W, Ni, Se (3)
Hollins, J. W. (Chelsea), 1967 v Sp (1)
Holmes, R. (Preston NE), 1888 v Ni; 1891 v S; 1892 v S; 1893 v S, W; 1894 v Ni; 1895 v Ni (7)
Holt, J. (Everton), 1890 v W; 1891 v S, W; 1892 v S, Ni; 1893 v S; 1894 v S, Ni; 1895 v S; (with Reading), 1900 v Ni (10)
Hopkinson, E. (Bolton W), 1958 v W, Ni, S, F, P, Y; 1959 v S, I, Br, Pe, M, US; 1960 v W, Se (14)
Hossack, A. H. (Corinthians), 1892 v W; 1894 v W (2)
Houghton, W. E. (Aston Villa), 1931 v Ni, W, F, Bel; 1932 v S, Ni; 1933 v A (7)
Houlker, A. E. (Blackburn R), 1902 v S; (with Portsmouth), 1903 v S, W; (with Southampton), 1906 v W, Ni (5)
Howarth, R. H. (Preston NE), 1887 v Ni; 1888 v S, W; 1891 v S; (with Everton), 1894 v Ni (5)
Howe, D. (WBA), 1958 v S, W, Ni, F, P, Y, USSR (3), Br, A; 1959 v S, W, Ni, USSR, I, Br, Pe, M, US; 1960 v W, Ni, Se (23)
Howe, J. R. (Derby Co), 1948 v I; 1949 v S, Ni (3)
Howell, L. S. (Wanderers), 1873 v S (1)
Howell, R. (Sheffield U), 1895 v Ni; (with Liverpool) 1899 v S (2)
Howey, S. N. (Newcastle U), 1995 v Ng; 1996 v Co, P, Bul (4)
Hudson, A. A. (Stoke C), 1975 v WG, Cy (2)
Hudson, J. (Sheffield), 1883 v Ni (1)
Hudspeth, F. C. (Newcastle U), 1926 v Ni (1)
Hufton, A. E. (West Ham U), 1924 v Bel; 1928 v S, Ni; 1929 v F, Bel, Sp (6)
Hughes, E. W. (Liverpool), 1970 v W, Ni, S, Ho, P, Bel; 1971 v EG, Ma (2), Gr, W; 1972 v Sw, Gr, WG (2), W, Ni, S; 1973 v W (3), S (2), Pol, USSR, I; 1974 v A, Pol, I, W, Ni, S, Arg, EG, Bul, Y; 1975 v Cz, P, Cy (sub), Ni; 1977 v I, L, W, S, Br, Arg, U; 1978 v Sw, L, I, WG, Ni, S, H; 1979 v D, Ei, Ni, W, Se; (with Wolverhampton W), 1980 v Sp (sub), Ni, S (sub) (62)
Hughes, L. (Liverpool), 1950 v Ch, US, Sp (3)
Hulme, J. H. A. (Arsenal), 1927 v S, Bel, F; 1928 v S, Ni, W; 1929 v Ni, W; 1933 v S (9)
Humphreys, P. (Notts Co), 1903 v S (1)
Hunt, G. S. (Tottenham H), 1933 v I, Sw, S (3)
Hunt, Rev K. R. G. (Leyton), 1911 v S, W (2)
Hunt, R. (Liverpool), 1962 v A; 1963 v EG; 1964 v S, US, P; 1965 v W; 1966 v S, Sp, Pol (2), WG (2), Fi, N, U, M, F, Arg, P; 1967 v Ni, W, Cz, Sp, A; 1968 v W, Ni, USSR (2), Sp (2), Se, Y; 1969 v R (2) (34)
Hunt, S. (WBA), 1984 v S (sub), USSR (sub) (2)
Hunter, J. (Sheffield Heeley), 1878 v S; 1880 v S, W; 1881 v S, W; 1882 v S, W (7)
Hunter, N. (Leeds U), 1966 v WG, Y, Fi, Sp (sub); 1967 v A; 1968 v Sp, Se, Y, WG, USSR; 1969 v R, W; 1970 v Ho, WG (sub); 1971 v Ma; 1972 v WG (2), W, Ni, S; 1973 v W (2) USSR (sub); 1974 v A, Pol, Ni (sub), S; 1975 v Cz (28)
Hurst, G. C. (West Ham U), 1966 v S, WG (2), Y, Fi, D, Arg, P; 1967 v Ni, W, S, Cz, Sp, A; 1968 v W, Ni, S, Se (sub), WG, USSR (2); 1969 v Ni, S, R (2), Bul, F, M, U, Br; 1970 v W, Ni, S, Ho (1+1 sub), Bel, Co, Ec, R, Br, WG; 1971 v EG, Gr, W, S; 1972 v Sw (2), Gr, WG (49)

Ince, P. E. C. (Manchester U), 1993 v Sp, N, T (2), Ho, Pol, US, Br, G; 1994 v Pol, Ho, Sm, D, N; 1995 v R, Ei; (with Internazionale), 1996 v Bul, Cro, H, Sw, S, Ho, G; 1997 v Mol, Pol, Ge, I, M, Ge, Pol, I, F (sub), Br; (with Liverpool), 1998 v I, Cam, Ch (sub), Sw, P, Mor, Tun, R, Co, Arg; 1999 v Se, F; (with Middlesbrough), 2000 v Bel, S (2), Br, Ma (sub), P, G, R (53)
Iremonger, J. (Nottingham F), 1901 v S; 1902 v Ni (2)

Jack, D. N. B. (Bolton W), 1924 v S, W; 1928 v F, Bel; (with Arsenal), 1930 v S, G, A; 1933 v W, A (9)
Jackson, E. (Oxford University), 1891 v W (1)
James. D. B. (Liverpool), 1997 v M; (with Aston Villa), 2001 v I, Sp, M (sub); (with West Ham U), 2002 v Ho (sub + sub), I (sub), Sk (sub), Cam (sub); 2003 v P, Aus, Lie, T, S.Af, Ser, Slo; 2004 v Cro, Mac, Lie, T, D; (with Manchester C), P, Se, J, F, Sw, Cro, P; 2005 v Uk, A, US, Co; 2006 v D (sub), Jam (sub) (34)
Jarrett, B. G. (Cambridge University), 1876 v S; 1877 v S; 1878 v S (3)
Jefferis, F. (Everton), 1912 v S, W (2)
Jeffers, F. (Arsenal), 2003 v Aus (sub) (1)
Jenas, J. A. (Newcastle U), 2003 v Aus (sub), S.Af (sub), Ser (sub); 2004 v D (sub), P (sub), Se (sub); 2005 v Uk (sub), Az, Sp (sub), Ho (sub), US, Co; 2006 v D (sub); (with Tottenham H), Pol (sub), U (sub); 2007 v Br (sub), Es (sub) (17)
Jezzard, B. A. G. (Fulham), 1954 v H; 1956 v Ni (2)
Johnson, A. (C Palace), 2005 v Ho (sub), US; (with Everton), 2007 v And (sub), Mac (sub), Ho, Is, And (7)
Johnson, D. E. (Ipswich T), 1975 v W, S; 1976 v Sw; (with Liverpool), 1980 v Ei, Arg, Ni, S, Bel (8)

Johnson, E. (Saltley College), 1880 v W; (with Stoke C), 1884 v Ni (2)
Johnson, G. M. C. (Chelsea), 2004 v D (sub); 2005 v Uk (sub), US, Co; 2006 v D (sub) (5)
Johnson, J. A. (Stoke C), 1937 v N, Se, Fi, S, Ni (5)
Johnson, S. A. M. (Derby Co), 2001 v I (sub) (1)
Johnson, T. C. F. (Manchester C), 1926 v Bel; 1930 v W; (with Everton), 1932 v S, Sp; 1933 v Ni (5)
Johnson, W. H. (Sheffield U), 1900 v S, W, Ni; 1903 v S, W, Ni (6)
Johnston, H. (Blackpool), 1947 v S, Ho; 1951 v S; 1953 v Arg, Ch, U, US; 1954 v W, Ni, H (10)
Jones, A. (Walsall Swifts), 1882 v S, W; (with Great Lever), 1883 v S (3)
Jones, H. (Blackburn R), 1927 v S, Bel, L, F; 1928 v S, Ni (6)
Jones, H. (Nottingham F), 1923 v F (1)
Jones, M. D. (Sheffield U), 1965 v WG, Se; (with Leeds U), 1970 v Ho (3)
Jones, R. (Liverpool), 1992 v F; 1994 v Pol, Gr, N; 1995 v US, R, Ng, U (8)
Jones, W. (Bristol C), 1901 v Ni (1)
Jones, W. H. (Liverpool), 1950 v P, Bel (2)
Joy, B. (Casuals), 1936 v Bel (1)

Kail, E. I. L. (Dulwich Hamlet), 1929 v F, Bel, Sp (3)
Kay, A. H. (Everton), 1963 v Sw (1)
Kean, F. W. (Sheffield W), 1923 v S, Bel; 1924 v W; 1925 v Ni; 1926 v Ni, Bel; 1927 v L; (with Bolton W), 1929 v F, Sp (9)
Keegan, J. K. (Liverpool), 1973 v W (2); 1974 v W, Ni, Arg, EG, Bul, Y; 1975 v Cz, WG, Cy (2), Ni, S; 1976 v Sw, Cz, P, W (2), Ni, S, Br, Fi; 1977 v Ei, Fi, I, Ho, L; (with SV Hamburg), W, Br, Arg, U; 1978 v Sw, I, WG, Br, H; 1979 v D, Ei, Cz, Ni, W, S, Bul, Se, A; 1980 v D, Ni, Ei, Sp (2), Arg, Bel, I; (with Southampton), 1981 v Sp, Sw, H; 1982 v N, H, Ni, S, Fi, Sp (sub) (63)
Keen, E. R. L. (Derby Co), 1933 v A; 1937 v W, Ni, H (4)
Kelly, R. (Burnley), 1920 v S; 1921 v S, W, Ni; 1922 v S, W; 1923 v S; 1924 v Ni; 1925 v W, Ni, S; (with Sunderland), 1926 v W; (with Huddersfield T), 1927 v L; 1928 v S (14)
Kennedy, A. (Liverpool), 1984 v Ni, W (2)
Kennedy, R. (Liverpool), 1976 v W (2), Ni, S; 1977 v L, W, S, Br (sub), Arg (sub); 1978 v Sw, L; 1980 v Bul, Sp, Arg, W, Bel (sub), I (17)
Kenyon-Slaney, W. S. (Wanderers), 1873 v S (1)
Keown, M. R. (Everton), 1992 v F, Cz, C, H, Br, Fi, D, F, Se; (with Arsenal), 1993 v Ho, G (sub); 1997 v M, S.Af, I, Br; 1998 v Sw, Mor, Bel; 1999 v CzR, F, Pol, H, Se; 2000 v L, Pol, Bel, S, Arg, Br, Ma, P (sub), G, R; 2001 v F, G, Fi, M, Gr; 2002 v Ho, Gr, Para, Sk (sub), Cam (sub) (43)
Kevan, D. T. (WBA), 1957 v S; 1958 v W, Ni, S, P. Y, USSR (3), Br, A; 1959 v M, US; 1961 v M (14)
Kidd, B. (Manchester U), 1970 v Ni, Ec (sub) (2)
King, L. B. (Tottenham H), 2002 v I (sub); 2003 v Aus (sub); 2004 v P, J (sub), Ic (sub), F, Cro (sub); 2005 v Uk, A, Pol, W (sub), Az (sub); 2006 v A (sub), Pol, Arg, U (sub); 2007 v Mac, Br, Es (19)
King, R. S. (Oxford University), 1882 v Ni (1)
Kingsford, R. K. (Wanderers), 1874 v S (1)
Kingsley, M. (Newcastle U), 1901 v W (1)
Kinsey, G. (Wolverhampton W), 1892 v W; 1893 v S; (with Derby Co), 1896 v W, Ni (4)
Kirchen, A. J. (Arsenal), 1937 v N, Se, Fi (3)
Kirkland, C. E. (Liverpool), 2007 v Gr (sub) (1)
Kirton, W. J. (Aston Villa), 1922 v Ni (1)
Knight, A. E. (Portsmouth), 1920 v Ni (1)
Knight, Z. (Fulham), 2005 v US (sub), Co (2)
Knowles, C. (Tottenham H), 1968 v USSR, Sp, Se, WG (4)
Konchesky, P. M. (Charlton Ath), 2003 v Aus (sub); (with West Ham U), 2006 v Arg (sub) (2)

Labone, B. L. (Everton), 1963 v Ni, W, F; 1967 v Sp, A; 1968 v S, Sp, Se, Y, USSR, WG; 1969 v Ni, S, R, Bul, M, U, Br; 1970 v S, W, Bel, Co, Ec, R, Br, WG (26)
Lampard, F. J. (West Ham U), 2000 v Bel; 2001 v Sp (sub); (with Chelsea), 2002 v Ho (sub), Se (sub), Ho (sub), I, Para (sub); 2003 v Aus, S.Af (sub), Ser, Slo; 2004 v Cro (sub), Mac, Lie, T (sub), D, P, J, Ic, F, Sw, Cro, P; 2005 v Uk, A, Pol, W, Az, Sp, Ho, Ni, Az; 2006 v D, W, Ni, A, Pol, Arg, H, Jam, Para, Tr, Se, Ec, P; 2007 v Gr, And, Mac (2), Cro, Ho, Sp, Is, Br, Es (55)
Lampard, F. R. G. (West Ham U), 1973 v Y; 1980 v Aus (2)
Langley, E. J. (Fulham), 1958 v S, P, Y (3)
Langton, R. (Blackburn R), 1947 v W, Ni, Ei, Ho, F, Sw; 1948 v Se; (with Preston NE), 1949 v D, Se; (with Bolton W), 1950 v S; 1951 v Ni (11)
Latchford, R. D. (Everton), 1978 v I, Br, W; 1979 v D, Ei, Cz (sub), Ni (2), W, S, Bul, A (12)
Latheron, E. G. (Blackburn R), 1913 v W; 1914 v Ni (2)
Lawler, C. (Liverpool), 1971 v Ma, W, S; 1972 v Sw (4)
Lawton, T. (Everton), 1939 v S, W, Ni, R of E, N, I, R, Y; (with Chelsea), 1947 v S, W, Ni, Ei, Ho, F, Sw, P; 1948 v W, Ni, Bel; (with Notts Co), 1948 v S, Se, I; 1949 v D (23)
Leach, T. (Sheffield W), 1931 v W, Ni (2)
Leake, A. (Aston Villa), 1904 v S, Ni; 1905 v S, W, Ni (5)
Lee, E. A. (Southampton), 1904 v W (1)
Lee, F. H. (Manchester C), 1969 v Ni, W, S, Bul, F, M, U; 1970 v W, Ho (2), P, Bel, Co, Ec, R, Br, WG; 1971 v EG, Gr, Ma, Ni, W, S; 1972 v Sw (2), Gr, WG (27)
Lee, J. (Derby Co), 1951 v Ni (1)
Lee, R. M. (Newcastle U), 1995 v R, Ng; 1996 v Co (sub), N, Sw, Bul (sub), H; 1997 v M, Ge, S.Af, Pol, F (sub), Br (sub); 1998 v Cam (sub), Ch, Sw, Bel, Co (sub); 1999 v Se (sub), Bul, L (sub) (21)
Lee, S. (Liverpool), 1983 v Gr, L, W, Gr, H, S, Aus; 1984 v D, H, L, F, Ni, W, Ch (sub) (14)
Leighton, J. E. (Nottingham F), 1886 v Ni (1)
Lennon, A. J. (Tottenham H), 2006 v Jam (sub), Tr (sub), Ec (sub), P (sub); 2007 v Gr (sub), And (sub), Mac (sub), Is, And (9)
Le Saux, G. P. (Blackburn R), 1994 v D, Gr, N; 1995 v US, R, Ng, Ei, U, Se, Br; 1996 v Co, P (sub); 1997 v I, M, Ge, S.Af, Pol, I, F, Br; (with Chelsea), 1998 v I, Ch (sub), P, Mor, Bel, Tun, R, Co, Arg; 1999 v Se, Bul (sub), CzR, F, Pol, Se; 2001 v G (36)
Le Tissier, M. P. (Southampton), 1994 v D (sub), Gr (sub), N (sub); 1995 v R, Ng (sub), Ei; 1997 v Mol (sub), I (8)
Lilley, H. E. (Sheffield U), 1892 v W (1)
Linacre, H. J. (Nottingham F), 1905 v W, S (2)
Lindley, T. (Cambridge University), 1886 v S, W, Ni; 1887 v S, W, Ni; 1888 v S, W, Ni; (with Nottingham F), 1889 v S; 1890 v S, W; 1891 v Ni (13)
Lindsay, A. (Liverpool), 1974 v Arg, EG, Bul, Y (4)
Lindsay, W. (Wanderers), 1877 v S (1)
Lineker, G. (Leicester C), 1984 v S (sub); 1985 v Ei, R (sub), S (sub), I (sub), WG, US; (with Everton), 1986 v R, T, Ni, Eg, USSR, Ca, P, Mor, Pol, Para, Arg; (with Barcelona), 1987 v Ni (2), Y, Sp, T, Br; 1988 v WG, T, Y, Ho, H, S, Co, Sw, Ei, Ho, USSR; 1989 v Se, S.Ar, Gr, Alb (2), Pol, D; (with Tottenham H), 1990 v Se, Pol, I, Y, Br, Cz, D, U, Tun, Ei, Ho, Eg, Bel, Cam, WG, I; 1991 v H, Pol, Ei (2), Cam, T, Arg, Aus, Nz, Mal; 1992 v G, T, Pol, F (sub), Cz (sub), C, H, Br, Fi, D, F, Se (80)
Lintott, E. H. (QPR), 1908 v S, W, Ni; (with Bradford C), 1909 v S, Ni, H (2) (7)
Lipsham, H. B. (Sheffield U), 1902 v W (1)
Little, B. (Aston Villa), 1975 v W (sub) (1)
Lloyd, L. V. (Liverpool), 1971 v W; 1972 v Sw, Ni; (with Nottingham F), 1980 v W (4)
Lockett, A. (Stoke C), 1903 v Ni (1)
Lodge, L. V. (Cambridge University), 1894 v W; 1895 v S, W; (with Corinthians), 1896 v S, Ni (5)
Lofthouse, J. M. (Blackburn R), 1885 v S, W, Ni; 1887 v S, W; (with Accrington), 1889 v Ni; (with Blackburn R), 1890 v Ni (7)
Lofthouse, N. (Bolton W), 1951 v Y; 1952 v W, Ni, S, A (2), I, Sw; 1953 v W, Ni, S, Bel, Arg, Ch, U, US; 1954 v W, Ni, R of E, Bel, U; 1955 v Ni, S, F, Sp, P; 1956 v W, S, Sp, D, Fi (sub); 1959 v W, USSR (33)
Longworth, E. (Liverpool), 1920 v S; 1921 v Bel; 1923 v S, W, Bel (5)
Lowder, A. (Wolverhampton W), 1889 v W (1)
Lowe, E. (Aston Villa), 1947 v F, Sw, P (3)
Lucas, T. (Liverpool), 1922 v Ni; 1924 v F; 1926 v Bel (3)
Luntley, E. (Nottingham F), 1880 v S, W (2)
Lyttelton, Hon. A. (Cambridge University), 1877 v S (1)
Lyttelton, Hon. E. (Cambridge University), 1878 v S (1)

Mabbutt, G. (Tottenham H), 1983 v WG, Gr, L, W, Gr, H, Ni, S (sub); 1984 v H; 1987 v Y, Ni, T; 1988 v WG; 1992 v T, Pol, Cz (16)
Macaulay, R. H. (Cambridge University), 1881 v S (1)

McCall, J. (Preston NE), 1913 v S, W; 1914 v S; 1920 v S; 1921 v Ni (5)
McCann, G. P. (Sunderland), 2001 v Sp (sub) (1)
McDermott, T. (Liverpool), 1978 v Sw, L; 1979 v Ni, W, Se; 1980 v D, Ni (sub), Ei, Ni, S, Bel (sub), Sp; 1981 v N, R, Sw, R (sub), Br, Sw (sub), H; 1982 v N, H, W (sub), Ho, S (sub), Ic (25)
McDonald, C. A. (Burnley), 1958 v USSR (3), Br, A; 1959 v W, Ni, USSR (8)
Macdonald, M. (Newcastle U), 1972 v W, Ni, S (sub); 1973 v USSR (sub); 1974 v P, S (sub), Y (sub); 1975 v WG, Cy (2), Ni; 1976 v Sw (sub), Cz, P (14)
McFarland, R. L. (Derby Co), 1971 v Gr, Ma (2), Ni, S; 1972 v Sw, Gr, WG, W, S; 1973 v W (3), Ni, S, Cz, Pol, USSR, I; 1974 v A, Pol, I, W, Ni; 1976 v Cz, S; 1977 v Ei, I (28)
McGarry, W. H. (Huddersfield T), 1954 v Sw, U; 1956 v W, D (4)
McGuinness, W. (Manchester U), 1959 v Ni, M (2)
McInroy, A. (Sunderland), 1927 v Ni (1)
McMahon, S. (Liverpool), 1988 v Is, H, Co, USSR; 1989 v D (sub); 1990 v Se, Pol, I, Y (sub), Br, Cz (sub), D, Ei (sub), Eg, Bel, I; 1991 v Ei (17)
McManaman, S. (Liverpool), 1995 v Ng (sub), U (sub), J (sub); 1996 v Co, N, Sw, P (sub), Bul, Cro, Chn, Sw, S, Ho, Sp, G; 1997 v Pol, I, M; 1998 v Cam, Sw, Mor, Co (sub); 1999 v Pol, H; (with Real Madrid), 2000 v L, Pol, Uk, Ma (sub), P; 2001 v F (sub), Fi (sub+1), Alb, Gr (sub); 2002 v G (sub), Alb (sub), Gr (sub) (37)
McNab, R. (Arsenal), 1969 v Ni, Bul, R (1+1 sub) (4)
McNeal, R. (WBA), 1914 v S, W (2)
McNeil, M. (Middlesbrough), 1961 v W, Ni, S, L, P, Sp, M, I; 1962 v L (9)
Macrae, S. (Notts Co), 1883 v S, W, Ni; 1884 v S, Ni (5)
Maddison, F. B. (Oxford University), 1872 v S (1)
Madeley, P. E. (Leeds U), 1971 v Ni; 1972 v Sw (2), Gr, WG (2), W, S; 1973 v S, Cz, Pol, USSR, I; 1974 v A, Pol, I; 1975 v Cz, P, Cy; 1976 v Cz, P, Fi; 1977 v Ei, Ho (24)
Magee, T. P. (WBA), 1923 v W, Se; 1925 v S, Bel, F (5)
Makepeace, H. (Everton), 1906 v S; 1910 v S; 1912 v S, W (4)
Male, C. G. (Arsenal), 1935 v S, Ni, I, Ho; 1936 v S, W, Ni, G, A, Bel; 1937 v S, Ni, H, N, Se, Fi; 1939 v I, R, Y (19)
Mannion, W. J. (Middlesbrough), 1947 v S, W, Ni, Ei, Ho, F, Sw, P; 1948 v W, Ni, Bel, Se, I; 1949 v N, F; 1950 v S, Ei, P, Bel, Ch, US; 1951 v Ni, W, S, Y; 1952 v F (26)
Mariner, P. (Ipswich T), 1977 v L (sub), Ni; 1978 v L, W (sub), S; 1980 v W, Ni (sub), S, Aus, I (sub), Sp (sub); 1981 v N, Sw, Sp, Sw, H; 1982 v N, H, Ho, S, Fi, F, Cz, K, WG, Sp; 1983 v D, WG, Gr, W; 1984 v D, H, L; (with Arsenal), 1985 v EG, R (35)
Marsden, J. T. (Darwen), 1891 v Ni (1)
Marsden, W. (Sheffield W), 1930 v W, S, G (3)
Marsh, R. W. (QPR), 1972 v Sw (sub); (with Manchester C), WG (sub+1), W, Ni, S; 1973 v W (2), Y (9)
Marshall, T. (Darwen), 1880 v W; 1881 v W (2)
Martin, A. (West Ham U), 1981 v Br, S (sub); 1982 v H, Fi; 1983 v Gr, L, W, Gr, H; 1984 v H, L, W; 1985 v Ni; 1986 v Is, Ca, Para; 1987 v Se (17)
Martin, H. (Sunderland), 1914 v Ni (1)
Martyn, A. N. (C Palace), 1992 v C (sub), H; 1993 v G; (with Leeds U), 1997 v S.Af; 1998 v Cam, Ch, Bel; 1999 v CzR, F (sub); 2000 v L, Pol, Bel (sub), Uk, R; 2001 v Sp (sub), M; 2002 v Ho, Gr, Se, Ho, I, Sk, Cam (23)
Marwood, B. (Arsenal), 1989 v S.Ar (sub) (1)
Maskrey, H. M. (Derby Co), 1908 v Ni (1)
Mason, C. (Wolverhampton W), 1887 v Ni; 1888 v W; 1890 v Ni (3)
Matthews, R. D. (Coventry C), 1956 v S, Br, Se, WG; 1957 v Ni (5)
Matthews, S. (Stoke C), 1935 v W, I; 1936 v G; 1937 v S; 1938 v S, W, Cz, G, Sw, F; 1939 v S, W, Ni, R of E, N, I, Y; 1947 v S; (with Blackpool), 1947 v Sw, P; 1948 v S, W, Ni, Bel, I; 1949 v S, W, Ni, D, Sw; 1950 v Sp; 1951 v Ni, S; 1954 v Ni, R of E, H, Bel, U; 1955 v Ni, W, S, F, WG, Sp, P; 1956 v W, Br; 1957 v S, W, Ni, Y, D (2), Ei (54)
Matthews, V. (Sheffield U), 1928 v F, Bel (2)
Maynard, W. J. (1st Surrey Rifles), 1872 v S; 1876 v S (2)
Meadows, J. (Manchester C), 1955 v S (1)
Medley, L. D. (Tottenham H), 1951 v Y, W; 1952 v F, A, W, Ni (6)
Meehan, T. (Chelsea), 1924 v Ni (1)
Melia, J. (Liverpool), 1963 v S, Sw (2)
Mercer, D. W. (Sheffield U), 1923 v Ni, Bel (2)
Mercer, J. (Everton), 1939 v S, Ni, I, R, Y (5)
Merrick, G. H. (Birmingham C), 1952 v Ni, S, A (2), I, Sw; 1953 v Ni, W, S, Bel, Arg, Ch, U; 1954 v W, Ni, S, R of E, H (2), Y, Bel, Sw, U (23)
Merson, P. C. (Arsenal), 1992 v G (sub), Cz, H, Br (sub), Fi (sub), D, Se (sub); 1993 v Sp (sub), N (sub), Ho (sub), Br (sub), G; 1994 v Ho, Gr; 1997 v I (sub); (with Middlesbrough), 1998 v Sw, P (sub), Bel, Arg (sub); 1999 v Se (sub); (with Aston Villa), CzR (21)
Metcalfe, V. (Huddersfield T), 1951 v Arg, P (2)
Mew, J. W. (Manchester U), 1921 v Ni (1)
Middleditch, B. (Corinthians), 1897 v Ni (1)
Milburn, J. E. T. (Newcastle U), 1949 v S, W, Ni, Sw; 1950 v W, P, Bel, Sp; 1951 v W, Arg, P; 1952 v F; 1956 v D (13)
Miller, B. G. (Burnley), 1961 v A (1)
Miller, H. S. (Charlton Ath), 1923 v Se (1)
Mills, D. J. (Leeds U), 2001 v M (sub); 2002 v Ho (sub), Se (sub), I, Para (sub), Sk, Cam (sub), Se, Arg, Ng, D, Br; 2003 v P, Aus (sub), S.Af, Ser, Slo; 2004 v Cro (sub), P (sub) (19)
Mills, G. R. (Chelsea), 1938 v W, Ni, Cz (3)
Mills, M. D. (Ipswich T), 1973 v Y; 1976 v W (2), Ni, S, Br, I (sub), Fi; 1977 v Fi (sub), I, Ni, W, S; 1978 v WG, Br, W, Ni, S, H; 1979 v D, Ei, Ni (2), S, Bul, A; 1980 v D, Ni, Sp (2); 1981 v Sw (2), H; 1982 v N, H, S, Fi, F, Cz, K, WG, Sp (42)
Milne, G. (Liverpool), 1963 v Br, Cz, EG; 1964 v W, Ni, S, R of W, U, P, Ei, Br, Arg; 1965 v Ni, Bel (14)
Milton, C. A. (Arsenal), 1952 v A (1)
Milward, A. (Everton), 1891 v S, W; 1897 v S, W (4)
Mitchell, C. (Upton Park), 1880 v W; 1881 v S; 1883 v S, W; 1885 v W (5)
Mitchell, J. F. (Manchester C), 1925 v Ni (1)
Moffat, H. (Oldham Ath), 1913 v W (1)
Molyneux, G. (Southampton), 1902 v S; 1903 v S, W, Ni (4)
Moon, W. R. (Old Westminsters), 1888 v S, W; 1889 v S, W; 1890 v S, W; 1891 v S (7)
Moore, H. T. (Notts Co), 1883 v Ni; 1885 v W (2)
Moore, J. (Derby Co), 1923 v Se (1)
Moore, R. F. (West Ham U), 1962 v Pe, H, Arg, Bul, Br; 1963 v W, Ni, S, F (2), Br, Cz, EG, Sw; 1964 v W, Ni, S, R of W, U, P (2), Ei, Br, Arg; 1965 v Ni, S, Bel, H, Y, WG, Se; 1966 v W, Ni, S, A, Sp, Pol (2), WG (2), N, D, U, M, F, Arg, P; 1967 v W, Ni, S, Cz, Sp, A; 1968 v W, Ni, S, USSR (2), Sp (2), Se, Y, WG; 1969 v Ni, W, S, R, Bul, F, M, U, Br; 1970 v W, Ni, S, Ho, P, Bel, Co, Ec, R, Br, Cz, WG; 1971 v EG, Gr, Ma, Ni, S; 1972 v Sw (2), Gr, WG (2), W, S; 1973 v W (3), Y, S (2), Ni, Cz, Pol, USSR, I; 1974 v I (108)
Moore, W. G. B. (West Ham U), 1923 v Se (1)
Mordue, J. (Sunderland), 1912 v Ni; 1913 v Ni (2)
Morice, C. J. (Barnes), 1872 v S (1)
Morley, A. (Aston Villa), 1982 v H (sub), Ni, W, Ic; 1983 v D, Gr (6)
Morley, H. (Notts Co), 1910 v Ni (1)
Morren, T. (Sheffield U), 1898 v Ni (1)
Morris, F. (WBA), 1920 v S; 1921 v Ni (2)
Morris, J. (Derby Co), 1949 v N, F; 1950 v Ei (3)
Morris, W. W. (Wolverhampton W), 1939 v S, Ni, R (3)
Morse, H. (Notts Co), 1879 v S (1)
Mort, T. (Aston Villa), 1924 v W, F; 1926 v S (3)
Morten, A. (C Palace), 1873 v S (1)
Mortensen, S. H. (Blackpool), 1947 v P; 1948 v W, S, Ni, Bel, Se, I; 1949 v S, W, Ni, Se, N; 1950 v S, W, Ni, I, P, Bel, Ch, US, Sp; 1951 v S, Arg; 1954 v R of E, H (25)
Morton, J. R. (West Ham U), 1938 v Cz (1)
Mosforth, W. (Sheffield W), 1877 v S; (with Sheffield Albion), 1878 v S; 1879 v S, W; 1880 v S, W; (with Sheffield W), 1881 v W; 1882 v S, W (9)
Moss, F. (Arsenal), 1934 v S, H, Cz; 1935 v I (4)
Moss, F. (Aston Villa), 1922 v S, Ni; 1923 v Ni; 1924 v S, Bel (5)
Mosscrop, E. (Burnley), 1914 v S, W (2)
Mozley, B. (Derby Co), 1950 v W, Ni, Ei (3)
Mullen, J. (Wolverhampton W), 1947 v S; 1949 v N, F; 1950 v Bel (sub), Ch, US; 1954 v W, Ni, S, R of E, Y, Sw (12)
Mullery, A. P. (Tottenham H), 1965 v Ho; 1967 v Sp, A; 1968 v W, Ni, S, USSR, Sp (2), Se, Y; 1969 v Ni, S, R, Bul, F, M, U, Br; 1970 v W, Ni, S (sub), Ho (1 + 1 sub),

P, Co, Ec, R, Cz, WG, Br; 1971 v Ma, EG, Gr; 1972 v Sw (35)
Murphy, D. B. (Liverpool), 2002 v Se (sub), I (sub), Para (sub), Sk; 2003 v P (sub), Aus (sub), Lie (sub); 2004 v Cro (sub), D (sub) (9)

Neal, P. G. (Liverpool), 1976 v W, I; 1977 v W, S, Br, Arg, U; 1978 v Sw, I, WG, Ni, S, H; 1979 v D, Ei, Ni (2), S, Bul, A; 1980 v D, Ni, Sp, Arg, W, Bel, I; 1981 v R, Sw, Sp, Br, H; 1982 v N, H, W, Ho, Ic, F (sub), K; 1983 v D, Gr, L, W, Gr, H, Ni, S, Aus (2); 1984 v D (50)
Needham, E. (Sheffield U), 1894 v S; 1895 v S; 1897 v S, W, Ni; 1898 v S, W; 1899 v S, W, Ni; 1900 v S, Ni; 1901 v S, W, Ni; 1902 v W (16)
Neville, G. A. (Manchester U), 1995 v J, Br; 1996 v Co, N, Sw, P, Bul, Cro, H, Chn, Sw, S, Ho, Sp; 1997 v Mol, Pol, I, Ge, Pol, I (sub), F, Br (sub); 1998 v Mol, Ch, P, S.Ar, Bel, R, Co, Arg; 1999 v Bul, Pol; 2000 v L (sub), Pol, Br, Ma, P, G, R; 2001 v G, I, Sp (sub), Fi, Alb; 2002 v Ho, G, Alb, Gr, Se, Ho, I (sub), Para; 2003 v Slo, Mac, Aus, Lie, T; 2004 v Mac, Lie, T, D, J, Ic, F, Sw, Cro, P; 2005 v Uk, A, Pol, W, Az, Sp, Ho, Ni, Az; 2006 v D, U, H, Para, P; 2007 v Gr, Mac (2), Sp (85)
Neville, P. J. (Manchester U), 1996 v Chn; 1997 v S.Af, Pol (sub), I, F, Br; 1998 v Mol, Cam, Ch, P (sub), S.Ar (sub), Bel; 1999 v L, Pol (sub), H, Se, Bul; 2000 v L (sub), Pol (sub), Bel (sub), S (2), Arg (sub), Br, Uk, Ma, P, G, R; 2001 v Fi, Sp, M, Gr; 2002 v Se (sub), Ho (sub), I (sub), Para (sub); 2003 v S.Af, Ser, Slo; 2004 v Cro, Mac (sub), Lie (sub), D (sub), P, Se, J (sub), Ic (sub), Cro (sub), P (sub); 2005 v US (sub), Co; (with Everton), 2007 v And, Mac, Sp, Is (56)
Newton, K. R. (Blackburn R), 1966 v S, WG; 1967 v Sp, A; 1968 v W, S, Sp, Se, Y, WG; 1969 v Ni, W, S, R, Bul, M, U, Br, F; (with Everton), 1970 v Ni, S, Ho, Co, Ec, R, Cz, WG (27)
Nicholls, J. (WBA), 1954 v S, Y (2)
Nicholson, W. E. (Tottenham H), 1951 v P (1)
Nish, D. J. (Derby Co), 1973 v Ni; 1974 v P, W, Ni, S (5)
Norman, M. (Tottenham H), 1962 v Pe, H, Arg, Bul, Br; 1963 v S, F, Br, Cz, EG; 1964 v W, Ni, S, R of W, U, P (2), US, Br, Arg; 1965 v Ni, Bel, Ho (23)
Nugent, D. J. (Preston NE), 2007 v And (sub) (1)
Nuttall, H. (Bolton W), 1928 v W, Ni; 1929 v S (3)

Oakley, W. J. (Oxford University), 1895 v W; 1896 v S, W, Ni; (with Corinthians), 1897 v S, W, Ni; 1898 v S, W, Ni; 1900 v S, W, Ni; 1901 v S, W, Ni (16)
O'Dowd, J. P. (Chelsea), 1932 v S; 1933 v Ni, Sw (3)
O'Grady, M. (Huddersfield T), 1963 v Ni; (with Leeds U), 1969 v F (2)
Ogilvie, R. A. M. M. (Clapham R), 1874 v S (1)
Oliver, L. F. (Fulham), 1929 v Bel (1)
Olney, B. A. (Aston Villa), 1928 v F, Bel (2)
Osborne, F. R. (Fulham), 1923 v Ni, F; (with Tottenham H), 1925 v Bel; 1926 v Bel (4)
Osborne, R. (Leicester C), 1928 v W (1)
Osgood, P. L. (Chelsea), 1970 v Bel, R (sub), Cz (sub); 1974 v I (4)
Osman, R. (Ipswich T), 1980 v Aus; 1981 v Sp, R, Sw; 1982 v N, Ic; 1983 v D, Aus (3); 1984 v D (11)
Ottaway, C. J. (Oxford University), 1872 v S; 1874 v S (2)
Owen, J. R. B. (Sheffield), 1874 v S (1)
Owen, M. J. (Liverpool), 1998 v Ch, Sw, P (sub), Mor (sub), Bel (sub), Tun (sub), R (sub), Co, Arg; 1999 v Se, Bul, L, F; 2000 v L (sub), Pol (sub), Bel (sub), S (2), Br, P, G, R; 2001 v F (sub), G, Sp, Fi, Alb, M, Gr; 2002 v Ho (sub), G, Alb, I, Para, Sk, Cam, Se, Arg, Ng, D, Br; 2003 v P, Slo, Mac, Aus, Lie, T, S.Af, Ser, Slo; 2004 v Cro, Mac, Lie, P, J, Ic, F, Sw, Cro, P; (with Real Madrid), 2005 v Uk, A, Pol, W, Az, Sp, Ho, Ni, Az, Co; 2006 v D (sub); (with Newcastle U), Ni, A, Pol, Arg, H, Jam, Para, Tr, Se; 2007 v Br, Es (82)
Owen, S. W. (Luton T), 1954 v H, Y, Bel (3)

Page, L. A. (Burnley), 1927 v S, W, Bel, L, F; 1928 v W, Ni (7)
Paine, T. L. (Southampton), 1963 v Cz, EG; 1964 v W, Ni, S, R of W, U, US, P; 1965 v Ni, H, Y, WG, Se; 1966 v W, A, Y, N, M (19)
Pallister, G. A. (Middlesbrough), 1988 v H; 1989 v S.Ar; (with Manchester U), 1991 v Cam (sub), T; 1992 v G; 1993 v N, US, Br, G; 1994 v Pol, Ho, Sm, D; 1995 v US, R, Ei, U, Se; 1996 v N, Sw; 1997 v Mol, Pol (sub) (22)
Palmer, C. L. (Sheffield W), 1992 v C, H, Br, Fi (sub), D, F, Se; 1993 v Sp (sub), N (sub), T, Sm, T, Ho, Pol, N, US, Br (sub); 1994 v Ho (18)
Pantling, H. H. (Sheffield U), 1924 v Ni (1)
Paravicini, P. J. de (Cambridge University), 1883 v S, W, Ni (3)
Parker, P. A. (QPR), 1989 v Alb (sub), Ch, D; 1990 v Y, U, Ho, Eg, Bel, Cam, WG, I; 1991 v H, Pol, USSR, Aus, Nz; (with Manchester U), 1992 v G; 1994 v Ho, D (19)
Parker, S. M. (Charlton Ath), 2004 v D (sub); (with Chelsea), v Se (sub); (with Newcastle U), 2007 v Cro (3)
Parker, T. R. (Southampton), 1925 v F (1)
Parkes, P. B. (QPR), 1974 v P (1)
Parkinson, J. (Liverpool), 1910 v S, W (2)
Parlour, R. (Arsenal), 1999 v Pol (sub), Se (sub), Bul (sub); 2000 v L, S (sub), Arg (sub), Br (sub); 2001 v G (sub), Fi, I (10)
Parr, P. C. (Oxford University), 1882 v W (1)
Parry, E. H. (Old Carthusians), 1879 v W; 1882 v W, S (3)
Parry, R. A. (Bolton W), 1960 v Ni, S (2)
Patchitt, B. C. A. (Corinthians), 1923 v Se (2) (2)
Pawson, F. W. (Cambridge University), 1883 v Ni; (with Swifts), 1885 v Ni (2)
Payne, J. (Luton T), 1937 v Fi (1)
Peacock, A. (Middlesbrough), 1962 v Arg, Bul; 1963 v Ni, W; (with Leeds U), 1966 v W, Ni (6)
Peacock, J. (Middlesbrough), 1929 v F, Bel, Sp (3)
Pearce, S. (Nottingham F), 1987 v Br, S; 1988 v WG (sub), Is, H; 1989 v D, Se, S.Ar, Gr, Alb (2), Ch, S, Pol, D; 1990 v Se, Pol, I, Y, Br, Cz, D, U, Tun, Ei, Ho, Eg, Bel, Cam, WG; 1991 v H, Pol, Ei (2), Cam, T, Arg, Aus, Nz (2), Mal; 1992 v T, Pol, F, Cz, Br (sub), Fi, D, F, Se; 1993 v Sp, N, T; 1994 v Pol, Sm, Gr (sub); 1995 v R (sub), J, Br; 1996 v N, Sw, P, Bul, Cro, H, Sw, S, Ho, Sp, G; 1997 v Mol, Pol, I, M, S.Af, I; (with West Ham U), 2000 v L, Pol (78)
Pearson, H. F. (WBA), 1932 v S (1)
Pearson, J. H. (Crewe Alex), 1892 v Ni (1)
Pearson, J. S. (Manchester U), 1976 v W, Ni, S, Br, Fi; 1977 v Ei, Ho (sub), W, S, Br, Arg, U; 1978 v I (sub), WG, Ni (15)
Pearson, S. C. (Manchester U), 1948 v S; 1949 v S, Ni; 1950 v Ni, I; 1951 v P; 1952 v S, I (8)
Pease, W. H. (Middlesbrough), 1927 v W (1)
Pegg, D. (Manchester U), 1957 v Ei (1)
Pejic, M. (Stoke C), 1974 v P, W, Ni, S (4)
Pelly, F. R. (Old Foresters), 1893 v Ni; 1894 v S, W (3)
Pennington, J. (WBA), 1907 v S, W; 1908 v S, W, Ni, A; 1909 v S, W, H (2), A; 1910 v S, W; 1911 v S, W, Ni; 1912 v S, W, Ni; 1913 v S, W; 1914 v S, Ni; 1920 v S, W (25)
Pentland, F. B. (Middlesbrough), 1909 v S, W, H (2), A (5)
Perry, C. (WBA), 1890 v Ni; 1891 v Ni; 1893 v W (3)
Perry, T. (WBA), 1898 v W (1)
Perry, W. (Blackpool), 1956 v Ni, S, Sp (3)
Perryman, S. (Tottenham H), 1982 v Ic (sub) (1)
Peters, M. (West Ham U), 1966 v Y, Fi, Pol, M, F, Arg, P, WG; 1967 v Ni, W, S, Cz; 1968 v W, Ni, S, USSR (2), Sp (2), Se, Y; 1969 v Ni, S, R, Bul, F, M, U, Br; 1970 v Ho (2), P (sub), Bel; (with Tottenham H), W, Ni, S, Co, Ec, R, Br, Cz, WG; 1971 v EG, Gr, Ma (2), Ni, W, S; 1972 v Sw, Gr, WG (1+1 sub), Ni (sub); 1973 v S (2), Ni, W, Cz, Pol, USSR, I; 1974 v A, Pol, I, P, S (67)
Phelan, M. C. (Manchester U), 1990 v I (sub) (1)
Phillips, K. (Sunderland), 1999 v H; 2000 v Bel, Arg (sub), Br (sub), Ma; 2001 v I (sub); 2002 v Se, Ho (sub) (8)
Phillips, L. H. (Portsmouth), 1952 v Ni; 1955 v W, WG (3)
Pickering, F. (Everton), 1964 v US; 1965 v Ni, Bel (3)
Pickering, J. (Sheffield U), 1933 v S (1)
Pickering, N. (Sunderland), 1983 v Aus (1)
Pike, T. M. (Cambridge University), 1886 v Ni (1)
Pilkington, B. (Burnley), 1955 v Ni (1)
Plant, J. (Bury), 1900 v S (1)
Platt, D. (Aston Villa), 1990 v I (sub), Y (sub), Br, D (sub), Tun (sub), Ho (sub), Eg (sub), Bel (sub), Cam, WG, I; 1991 v H, Pol, Ei (2), T, USSR, Arg, Aus, Nz (2), Mal; (with Bari), 1992 v G, T, Pol, Cz, C, Br, Fi, D, F, Se; (with Juventus), 1993 v Sp, N, T, Sm, T, Ho, Pol, N, Br (sub), G; (with Sampdoria), 1994 v Pol, Ho, Sm, D, Gr, N; 1995 v US, Ng, Ei, U, J, Se, Br; (with

Arsenal), 1996 v Bul (sub), Cro, H, Sw (sub), Ho (sub), Sp, G (62)
Plum, S. L. (Charlton Ath), 1923 v F (1)
Pointer, R. (Burnley), 1962 v W, L, P (3)
Porteous, T. S. (Sunderland), 1891 v W (1)
Powell, C. G. (Charlton Ath), 2001 v Sp, Fi, M (sub); 2002 v Ho (sub+sub) (5)
Priest, A. E. (Sheffield U), 1900 v Ni (1)
Prinsep, J. F. M. (Clapham Rovers), 1879 v S (1)
Puddefoot, S. C. (Blackburn R), 1926 v S, Ni (2)
Pye, J. (Wolverhampton W), 1950 v Ei (1)
Pym, R. H. (Bolton W), 1925 v S, W; 1926 v W (3)

Quantrill, A. (Derby Co), 1920 v S, W; 1921 v W, Ni (4)
Quixall, A. (Sheffield W), 1954 v W, Ni, R of E; 1955 v Sp, P (sub) (5)

Radford, J. (Arsenal), 1969 v R; 1972 v Sw (sub) (2)
Raikes, G. B. (Oxford University), 1895 v W; 1896 v W, Ni, S (4)
Ramsey, A. E. (Southampton), 1949 v Sw; (with Tottenham H), 1950 v S, I, P, Bel, Ch, US, Sp; 1951 v S, Ni, W, Y, Arg, P; 1952 v S, W, Ni, F, A (2), I, Sw; 1953 v Ni, W, S, Bel, Arg, Ch, U, US; 1954 v R of E, H (32)
Rawlings, A. (Preston NE), 1921 v Bel (1)
Rawlings, W. E. (Southampton), 1922 v S, W (2)
Rawlinson, J. F. P. (Cambridge University), 1882 v Ni (1)
Rawson, H. E. (Royal Engineers), 1875 v S (1)
Rawson, W. S. (Oxford University), 1875 v S; 1877 v S (2)
Read, A. (Tufnell Park), 1921 v Bel (1)
Reader, J. (WBA), 1894 v Ni (1)
Reaney, P. (Leeds U), 1969 v Bul (sub); 1970 v P; 1971 v Ma (3)
Redknapp, J. F. (Liverpool), 1996 v Co, N, Sw, Chn, S (sub); 1997 v M (sub), Ge (sub), S.Af; 1999 v Se, Bul, F, Pol (sub), H (sub), Bul; 2000 v Bel, S (2) (17)
Reeves, K. (Norwich C), 1980 v Bul; (with Manchester C), Ni (2)
Regis, C. (WBA), 1982 v Ni (sub), W (sub), Ic; 1983 v WG; (with Coventry C), 1988 v T (sub) (5)
Reid, P. (Everton), 1985 v M (sub), WG, US (sub); 1986 v R, S (sub), Ca (sub), Pol, Para, Arg; 1987 v Br; 1988 v WG, Y (sub), Sw (sub) (13)
Revie, D. G. (Manchester C), 1955 v Ni, S, F; 1956 v W, D; 1957 v Ni (6)
Reynolds, J. (WBA), 1892 v S; 1893 v S, W; (with Aston Villa), 1894 v S, Ni; 1895 v S; 1897 v S, W (8)
Richards, C. H. (Nottingham F), 1898 v Ni (1)
Richards, G. H. (Derby Co), 1909 v A (1)
Richards, J. P. (Wolverhampton W), 1973 v Ni (1)
Richards, M. (Manchester C), 2007 v Ho, Sp (sub), Is (sub), And (4)
Richardson, J. R. (Newcastle U), 1933 v I, Sw (2)
Richardson, K. (Aston Villa), 1994 v Gr (1)
Richardson, K. E. (Manchester U), 2005 v US, Co (sub); 2006 v W (sub), A (sub); 2007 v Gr (sub), And (sub), Cro (sub), Ho (sub) (8)
Richardson, W. G. (WBA), 1935 v Ho (1)
Rickaby, S. (WBA), 1954 v Ni (1)
Ricketts, M. B. (Bolton W), 2002 v Ho (1)
Rigby, A. (Blackburn R), 1927 v S, Bel, L, F; 1928 v W (5)
Rimmer, E. J. (Sheffield W), 1930 v S, G, A; 1932 v Sp (4)
Rimmer, J. J. (Arsenal), 1976 v I (1)
Ripley, S. E. (Blackburn R), 1994 v Sm; 1998 v Mol (sub) (2)
Rix, G. (Arsenal), 1981 v N, R, Sw (sub), Br, W, S; 1982 v Ho (sub), Fi (sub), F, Cz, K, WG, Sp; 1983 v D, WG (sub), Gr (sub); 1984 v Ni (17)
Robb, G. (Tottenham H), 1954 v H (1)
Roberts, C. (Manchester U), 1905 v Ni, W, S (3)
Roberts, F. (Manchester C), 1925 v S, W, Bel, F (4)
Roberts, G. (Tottenham H), 1983 v Ni, S; 1984 v F, Ni, S, USSR (6)
Roberts, H. (Arsenal), 1931 v S (1)
Roberts, H. (Millwall), 1931 v Bel (1)
Roberts, R. (WBA), 1887 v S; 1888 v Ni; 1890 v Ni (3)
Roberts, W. T. (Preston NE), 1924 v W, Bel (2)
Robinson, J. (Sheffield W), 1937 v Fi; 1938 v G, Sw; 1939 v W (4)
Robinson, J. W. (Derby Co), 1897 v S, Ni; (with New Brighton Tower), 1898 v S, W, Ni; (with Southampton), 1899 v W, S; 1900 v S, W, Ni; 1901 v Ni (11)
Robinson, P. W. (Leeds U), 2003 v Aus (sub), S.Af (sub); 2004 v Cro (sub), D (sub); (with Tottenham H), Ic; 2005 v Pol, W, Az, Sp, Ho, Ni, Az; 2006 v D, W, Ni, A, Pol, Arg, U, H, Jam, Para, Tr, Se, Ec, P; 2007 v Gr, And, Mac (2), Cro, Ho, Is, And, Br, Es (36)
Robson, B. (WBA), 1980 v Ei, Aus; 1981 v N, R, Sw, Sp, R, Br, W, S, Sw, H; 1982 v N; (with Manchester U), H, Ni, W, Ho, S, Fi, F, Cz, WG, Sp; 1983 v D, Gr, L, S; 1984 v H, L, F, Ni, S, USSR, Br, U, Ch; 1985 v EG, Fi, T, Ei, R, Fi, S, M, I, WG, US; 1986 v R, T, Is, M, P, Mor; 1987 v Ni (2), Sp, T, Br, S; 1988 v T, Y, Ho, H, S, Co, Sw, Ei, Ho, USSR; 1989 v D, Se, S.Ar, Gr, Alb (2), Ch, S, Pol, D; 1990 v Pol, I, Y, Cz, U, Tun, Ei, Ho; 1991 v Cam, Ei; 1992 v T (90)
Robson, R. (WBA), 1958 v F, USSR (2), Br, A; 1960 v Sp, H; 1961 v Ni, W, S, L, P, Sp, M, I; 1962 v W, Ni, Sw, L, P (20)
Rocastle, D. (Arsenal), 1989 v D, S.Ar, Gr, Alb (2), Pol (sub), D; 1990 v Se (sub), Pol, Y, D (sub); 1992 v Pol, Cz, Br (sub) (14)
Rooney, W. (Everton), 2003 v Aus (sub), Lie (sub), T, Ser (sub), Slo; 2004 v Mac, Lie, T, D, P, Se, J, Ic, F, Sw, Cro, P; (with Manchester U), 2005 v W, Az, Sp, Ho, Ni, Az; 2006 v D, W, Ni, Pol, Arg, U, Tr (sub), Se, Ec, P; 2007 v Mac, Cro, Ho, Is, And (38)
Rose, W. C. (Swifts), 1884 v S, W, Ni; (with Preston NE), 1886 v Ni; (with Wolverhampton W), 1891 v Ni (5)
Rostron, T. (Darwen), 1881 v S, W (2)
Rowe, A. (Tottenham H), 1934 v F (1)
Rowley, J. F. (Manchester U), 1949 v Sw, Se, F; 1950 v Ni, I; 1952 v S (6)
Rowley, W. (Stoke C), 1889 v Ni; 1892 v Ni (2)
Royle, J. (Everton), 1971 v Ma; 1973 v Y; (with Manchester C), 1976 v Ni (sub), I; 1977 v Fi, L (6)
Ruddlesdin, H. (Sheffield W), 1904 v W, Ni; 1905 v S (3)
Ruddock, N. (Liverpool), 1995 v Ng (1)
Ruffell, J. W. (West Ham U), 1926 v S; 1927 v Ni; 1929 v S, W, Ni; 1930 v W (6)
Russell, B. B. (Royal Engineers), 1883 v W (1)
Rutherford, J. (Newcastle U), 1904 v S; 1907 v S, Ni, W; 1908 v S, Ni, W, A (2), H, B (11)

Sadler, D. (Manchester U), 1968 v Ni, USSR; 1970 v Ec (sub); 1971 v EG (4)
Sagar, C. (Bury), 1900 v Ni; 1902 v W (2)
Sagar, E. (Everton), 1936 v S, Ni, A, Bel (4)
Salako, J. A. (C Palace), 1991 v Aus (sub), Nz (sub + 1), Mal; 1992 v G (5)
Sandford, E. A. (WBA), 1933 v W (1)
Sandilands, R. R. (Old Westminsters), 1892 v W; 1893 v Ni; 1894 v W; 1895 v W; 1896 v W (5)
Sands, J. (Nottingham F), 1880 v W (1)
Sansom, K. (C Palace), 1979 v W; 1980 v Bul, Ei, Arg, W (sub), Ni, S, Bel, I; (with Arsenal), 1981 v N, R, Sw, Sp, R, Br, W, S, Sw; 1982 v Ni, W, Ho, S, Fi, F, Cz, WG, Sp; 1983 v D, WG, Gr, L, Gr, H, Ni, S; 1984 v D, H, L, F, S, USSR, Br, U, Ch; 1985 v EG, Fi, T, Ni, Ei, R, Fi, S, I, M, WG, US; 1986 v R, T, Ni, Eg, Is, USSR, S, M, Ca, P, Mor, Pol, Para, Arg; 1987 v Se, Ni (2), Y, Sp, T; 1988 v WG, T, Y, Ho, S, Co, Sw, Ei, Ho, USSR (86)
Saunders, F. E. (Swifts), 1888 v W (1)
Savage, A. H. (C Palace), 1876 v S (1)
Sayer, J. (Stoke C), 1887 v Ni (1)
Scales, J. R. (Liverpool), 1995 v J, Se (sub), Br (3)
Scattergood, E. (Derby Co), 1913 v W (1)
Schofield, J. (Stoke C), 1892 v W; 1893 v W; 1895 v Ni (3)
Scholes, P. (Manchester U), 1997 v S.Af (sub), I, Br; 1998 v Mol, Cam, P, S.Ar, Tun, R, Co, Arg; 1999 v Se, Bul, L, F (sub), Pol, Se; 2000 v Pol, S (2), Arg, Br, Uk, Ma, P, G, R; 2001 v F, G, Fi, Sp, Fi, Alb, M, Gr; 2002 v Ho, G, Alb, Gr, Se, Ho, Para, Sk, Cam, Se, Arg, Ng, D, Br; 2003 v Slo, Mac, Aus, Lie, T, S.Af, Ser, Slo; 2004 v Cro, T, P, J, Ic, F, Sw, Cro, P (66)
Scott, L. (Arsenal), 1947 v S, W, Ni, Ei, Ho, F, Sw, P; 1948 v S, W, Ni, Bel, Se, I; 1949 v W, Ni, D (17)
Scott, W. R. (Brentford), 1937 v W (1)
Seaman, D. A. (QPR), 1989 v S.Ar, D (sub); 1990 v Cz (sub); (with Arsenal), 1991 v Cam, Ei, T, Arg; 1992 v Cz, H (sub); 1994 v Pol, Ho, Sm, D, N; 1995 v US, R, Ei; 1996 v Co, N, Sw, P, Bul, Cro, H, Sw, S, Ho, Sp, G; 1997 v Mol, Pol, Ge (2), Pol, F, Br; 1998 v Mol, I, P, S.Ar, Tun, R, Co, Arg; 1999 v Se, Bul, L, F, Pol, H, Se, Bul; 2000 v Bel, S (2), Arg, Br, P, G; 2001 v F, G, Fi (2), Alb, Gr; 2002 v G, Alb, Para, Se, Arg, Ng, D, Br; 2003 v Slo, Mac (75)

Seddon, J. (Bolton W), 1923 v F, Se (2); 1924 v Bel; 1927 v W; 1929 v S (6)
Seed, J. M. (Tottenham H), 1921 v Bel: 1923 v W, Ni, Bel; 1925 v S (5)
Settle, J. (Bury), 1899 v S, W, Ni; (with Everton), 1902 v S, Ni; 1903 v Ni (6)
Sewell, J. (Sheffield W), 1952 v Ni, A, Sw; 1953 v Ni; 1954 v H (2) (6)
Sewell, W. R. (Blackburn R), 1924 v W (1)
Shackleton, L. F. (Sunderland), 1949 v W, D; 1950 v W; 1955 v W, WG (5)
Sharp, J. (Everton), 1903 v Ni; 1905 v S (2)
Sharpe, L. S. (Manchester U), 1991 v Ei (sub); 1993 v T (sub), N, US, Br, G; 1994 v Pol, Ho (8)
Shaw, G. E. (WBA), 1932 v S (1)
Shaw, G. L. (Sheffield U), 1959 v S, W, USSR, I; 1963 v W (5)
Shea, D. (Blackburn R), 1914 v W, Ni (2)
Shearer, A. (Southampton), 1992 v F, C, F; (with Blackburn R), 1993 v Sp, N, T; 1994 v Ho, D, Gr, N; 1995 v US, R, Ng, Ei, J, Se, Br; 1996 v Co, N, Sw, P, H (sub), Chn, Sw, S, Ho, Sp, G; (with Newcastle U), 1997 v Mol, Pol, I, Ge, Pol, F, Br; 1998 v Ch (sub), Sw, P, S.Ar, Tun, R, Co, Arg; 1999 v Se, Bul, L, F, Pol, H, Se, Bul; 2000 v L, Pol, Bel, S (2), Arg, Br, Uk, Ma, P, G, R (63)
Shellito, K. J. (Chelsea), 1963 v Cz (1)
Shelton A. (Notts Co), 1889 v Ni; 1890 v S, W; 1891 v S, W; 1892 v S (6)
Shelton, C. (Notts Rangers), 1888 v Ni (1)
Shepherd, A. (Bolton W), 1906 v S; (with Newcastle U), 1911 v Ni (2)
Sheringham, E. P. (Tottenham H), 1993 v Pol, N; 1995 v US, R (sub), Ng (sub), U, J (sub), Se, Br; 1996 v Co (sub), N (sub), Sw, Bul, Cro, H, Sw, S, Ho, Sp, G; 1997 v Ge, M, Ge, S.Af, Pol, I, F (sub), Br; (with Manchester U), 1998 v I, Ch, Sw (sub), P, S.Ar, Tun, R; 1999 v Se (sub), Bul (sub), Bul; 2001 v Fi, Alb (sub), M (sub); (with Tottenham H), 2002 v Gr (sub), Se (sub), I (sub), Para (sub), Sk (sub), Cam (sub), Arg (sub), Ng (sub), D (sub), Br (sub) (51)
Sherwood, T. A. (Tottenham H), 1999 v Pol, H, Se (3)
Shilton, P. L. (Leicester C), 1971 v EG, W; 1972 v Sw, Ni; 1973 v Y, S (2), Ni, W, Cz, Pol, USSR, I; 1974 v A, Pol, I, W, Ni, S, Arg; (with Stoke C), 1975 v Cy; 1977 v Ni, W; (with Nottingham F), 1978 v W, H; 1979 v Cz, Se, A; 1980 v Ni, Sp, I; 1981 v N, Sw, R; 1982 v H, Ho, S, F, Cz, K, WG, Sp; (with Southampton), 1983 v D, WG, Gr, W, Gr, H, Ni, S, Aus (3); 1984 v D, H, F, Ni, W, S, USSR, Br, U, Ch; 1985 v EG, Fi, T, Ni, R, Fi, S, I, WG; 1986 v R, T, Ni, Eg, Is, USSR, S, M, Ca, P, Mor, Pol, Para, Arg; 1987 v Se, Ni (2), Sp, Br; (with Derby Co), 1988 v WG, T, Y, Ho, S, Co, Sw, Ei, Ho; 1989 v D, Se, Gr, Alb (2), Ch, S, Pol, D; 1990 v Se, Pol, I, Y, Br, Cz, D, U, Tun, Ei, Ho, Eg, Bel, Cam, WG, I (125)
Shimwell, E. (Blackpool), 1949 v Se (1)
Shorey, N. (Reading), 2007 v Br (1)
Shutt, G. (Stoke C), 1886 v Ni (1)
Silcock, J. (Manchester U), 1921 v S, W; 1923 v Se (3)
Sillett, R. P. (Chelsea), 1955 v F, Sp, P (3)
Simms, E. (Luton T), 1922 v Ni (1)
Simpson, J. (Blackburn R), 1911 v S, W, Ni; 1912 v S, W, Ni; 1913 v S; 1914 v W (8)
Sinclair, T. (West Ham U), 2002 v Se, I, Para (sub), Sk (sub), Cam (sub), Arg (sub), Ng, D, Br; 2003 v P (sub), S.Af; (with Manchester C), 2004 v Cro (sub) (12)
Sinton, A. (QPR), 1992 v Pol, C, H (sub), Br, F, Se; 1993 v Sp, T, Br, G; (with Sheffield W), 1994 v Ho (sub), Sm (12)
Slater, W. J. (Wolverhampton W), 1955 v W, WG; 1958 v S, P, Y, USSR (3), Br, A; 1959 v USSR; 1960 v S (12)
Smalley, T. (Wolverhampton W), 1937 v W (1)
Smart, T. (Aston Villa), 1921 v S; 1924 v S, W; 1926 v Ni; 1930 v W (5)
Smith, A. (Nottingham F), 1891 v S, W; 1893 v Ni (3)
Smith, A. (Leeds U), 2001 v M (sub), Gr (sub); 2002 v Ho (sub); 2003 v P, Slo (sub), Mac; 2004 v P (sub), Se (sub); (with Manchester U), 2005 v Uk, A, W (sub), Az (sub), Sp (sub), US, Co (sub); 2006 v Pol (sub); 2007 v Br (17)
Smith, A. K. (Oxford University), 1872 v S (1)
Smith, A. M. (Arsenal), 1989 v S.Ar (sub), Gr, Alb (sub), Pol (sub); 1991 v T, USSR, Arg; 1992 v G, T, Pol (sub), H (sub), D, Se (sub) (13)
Smith, B. (Tottenham H), 1921 v S; 1922 v W (2)
Smith, C. E. (C Palace), 1876 v S (1)
Smith, G. O. (Oxford University), 1893 v Ni; 1894 v W, S; 1895 v W; 1896 v Ni, W, S; (with Old Carthusians), 1897 v Ni, W, S; 1898 v Ni, W, S; (with Corinthians), 1899 v Ni, W, S; 1899 v Ni, W, S; 1901 v S (20)
Smith, H. (Reading), 1905 v W, S; 1906 v W, Ni (4)
Smith, J. (WBA), 1920 v Ni; 1923 v Ni (2)
Smith, Joe (Bolton W), 1913 v Ni; 1914 v S, W; 1920 v W, Ni (5)
Smith, J. C. R. (Millwall), 1939 v Ni, N (2)
Smith, J. W. (Portsmouth), 1932 v Ni, W, Sp (3)
Smith, Leslie (Brentford), 1939 v R (1)
Smith, Lionel (Arsenal), 1951 v W; 1952 v W, Ni; 1953 v W, S, Bel (6)
Smith, R. A. (Tottenham H), 1961 v Ni, W, S, L, P, Sp; 1962 v S; 1963 v S, F, Br, Cz, EG; 1964 v W, Ni, R of W (15)
Smith, S. (Aston Villa), 1895 v S (1)
Smith, S. C. (Leicester C), 1936 v Ni (1)
Smith, T. (Birmingham C), 1960 v W, Se (2)
Smith, T. (Liverpool), 1971 v W (1)
Smith, W. H. (Huddersfield T), 1922 v W, S; 1928 v S (3)
Sorby, T. H. (Thursday Wanderers, Sheffield), 1879 v W (1)
Southgate, G. (Aston Villa), 1996 v P (sub), Bul, H (sub), Chn, Sw, S, Ho, Sp, G; 1997 v Mol, Pol, Ge, M, Ge (sub), S.Af, Pol, I, F, Br; 1998 v Mol, I, Cam, Sw, S.Ar, Mor, Tun, Arg (sub); 1999 v Se, Bul, L, Bul; 2000 v Bel, S, Arg, Uk, Ma (sub), R (sub); 2001 v F (sub), G, Fi, I, M (sub); (with Middlesbrough), 2002 v Ho (sub), Se, Ho (sub), I, Para, Sk (sub), Cam (sub); 2003 v P, Slo, Lie, S.Af, Ser, Slo; 2004 v P, Se (sub) (57)
Southworth, J. (Blackburn R), 1889 v W; 1891 v W; 1892 v S (3)
Sparks, F. J. (Herts Rangers), 1879 v S; (with Clapham Rovers), 1880 v S, W (3)
Spence, J. W. (Manchester U), 1926 v Bel; 1927 v Ni (2)
Spence, R. (Chelsea), 1936 v A, Bel (2)
Spencer, C. W. (Newcastle U), 1924 v S; 1925 v W (2)
Spencer, H. (Aston Villa), 1897 v S, W; 1900 v W; 1903 v Ni; 1905 v W, S (6)
Spiksley, F. (Sheffield W), 1893 v S, W; 1894 v S, Ni; 1896 v Ni; 1898 v S, W (7)
Spilsbury, B. W. (Cambridge University), 1885 v Ni; 1886 v Ni, S (3)
Spink, N. (Aston Villa), 1983 v Aus (sub) (1)
Spouncer, W. A. (Nottingham F), 1900 v W (1)
Springett, R. D. G. (Sheffield W), 1960 v Ni, S, Y, Sp, H; 1961 v Ni, S, L, P, Sp, M, I, A; 1962 v W, Ni, S, A, Sw, Pe, L, P, H, Arg, Bul, Br; 1963 v Ni, W, F (2), Sw; 1966 v W, A, N (33)
Sproston, B. (Leeds U), 1937 v W; 1938 v S, W, Ni, Cz, G, Sw, F; (with Tottenham H), 1939 v W, R of E; (with Manchester C), N (11)
Squire, R. T. (Cambridge University), 1886 v S, W, Ni (3)
Stanbrough, M. H. (Old Carthusians), 1895 v W (1)
Staniforth, R. (Huddersfield T), 1954 v S, H, Y, Bel, Sw, U; 1955 v W, WG (8)
Starling, R. W. (Sheffield W), 1933 v S; (with Aston Villa), 1937 v S (2)
Statham, D. (WBA), 1983 v W, Aus (2) (3)
Steele, F. C. (Stoke C), 1937 v S, W, Ni, N, Se, Fi (6)
Stein, B. (Luton T), 1984 v F (1)
Stephenson, C. (Huddersfield T), 1924 v W (1)
Stephenson, G. T. (Derby Co), 1928 v F, Bel; (with Sheffield W), 1931 v F (3)
Stephenson, J. E. (Leeds U), 1938 v S; 1939 v Ni (2)
Stepney, A. C. (Manchester U), 1968 v Se (1)
Sterland, M. (Sheffield W), 1989 v S.Ar (1)
Steven, T. M. (Everton), 1985 v Ni, Ei, R, Fi, I, US (sub); 1986 v T (sub), Eg, USSR (sub), M (sub), Pol, Para, Arg; 1987 v Se, Y (sub), Sp (sub); 1988 v T, Y, Ho, H, S, Sw, Ho, USSR; 1989 v S; (with Rangers), 1990 v Cz, Cam (sub), WG (sub), I; 1991 v Cam; (with Marseille), 1992 v G, C, Br, Fi, D, F (36)
Stevens, G. A. (Tottenham H), 1985 v Fi (sub), T (sub), Ni; 1986 v S (sub), M (sub), Mor (sub), Para (sub) (7)
Stevens, M. G. (Everton), 1985 v I, WG; 1986 v R, T, Ni, Eg, Is, S, Ca, P, Mor, Pol, Para, Arg; 1987 v Br, S; 1988 v T, Y, Is, Ho, H (sub), S, Sw, Ei, Ho, USSR; (with Rangers), 1989 v D, Se, Gr, Alb (2), S, Pol; 1990 v Se, Pol, I, Br, D, Tun, Ei, I; 1991 v USSR; 1992 v C, H, Br, Fi (46)
Stewart, J. (Sheffield W), 1907 v S, W; (with Newcastle U), 1911 v S (3)

Stewart, P. A. (Tottenham H), 1992 v G (sub), Cz (sub), C (sub) (3)
Stiles, N. P. (Manchester U), 1965 v S, H, Y, Se; 1966 v W, Ni, S, A, Sp, Pol (2), WG (2), N, D, U, M, F, Arg, P; 1967 v Ni, W, S, Cz; 1968 v USSR; 1969 v R; 1970 v Ni, S (28)
Stoker, J. (Birmingham), 1933 v W; 1934 v S, H (3)
Stone, S. B. (Nottingham F), 1996 v N (sub), Sw (sub), P, Bul, Cro, Chn (sub), Sw (sub), S (sub), Sp (sub) (9)
Storer, H. (Derby Co), 1924 v F; 1928 v Ni (2)
Storey, P. E. (Arsenal), 1971 v Gr, Ni, S; 1972 v Sw, WG, W, Ni, S; 1973 v W (3), Y, S (2), Ni, Cz, Pol, USSR, I (19)
Storey-Moore, I. (Nottingham F), 1970 v Ho (1)
Strange, A. H. (Sheffield W), 1930 v S, A, G; 1931 v S, W, Ni, F, Bel; 1932 v S, W, Ni, Sp; 1933 v S, Ni, A, I, Sw; 1934 v Ni, W, F (20)
Stratford, A. H. (Wanderers), 1874 v S (1)
Streten, B. (Luton T), 1950 v Ni (1)
Sturgess, A. (Sheffield U), 1911 v Ni; 1914 v S (2)
Summerbee, M. G. (Manchester C), 1968 v S, Sp, WG; 1972 v Sw, WG (sub), W, Ni; 1973 v USSR (sub) (8)
Sunderland, A. (Arsenal), 1980 v Aus (1)
Sutcliffe, J. W. (Bolton W), 1893 v W; 1895 v S, Ni; 1901 v S; (with Millwall), 1903 v W (5)
Sutton, C. R. (Blackburn R), 1998 v Cam (sub) (1)
Swan, P. (Sheffield W), 1960 v Y, Sp, H; 1961 v Ni, W, S, L, P, Sp, M, I, A; 1962 v W, Ni, S, A, Sw, L, P (19)
Swepstone, H. A. (Pilgrims), 1880 v S; 1882 v S, W; 1883 v S, W, Ni (6)
Swift, F. V. (Manchester C), 1947 v S, W, Ni, Ei, Ho, F, Sw, P; 1948 v S, W, Ni, Bel, Se, I; 1949 v S, W, Ni, D, N (19)

Tait, G. (Birmingham Excelsior), 1881 v W (1)
Talbot, B. (Ipswich T), 1977 v Ni (sub), S, Br, Arg, U; (with Arsenal), 1980 v Aus (6)
Tambling, R. V. (Chelsea), 1963 v W, F; 1966 v Y (3)
Tate, J. T. (Aston Villa), 1931 v F, Bel; 1933 v W (3)
Taylor, E. (Blackpool), 1954 v H (1)
Taylor, E. H. (Huddersfield T), 1923 v S, W, Ni, Bel; 1924 v S, Ni, F; 1926 v S (8)
Taylor, J. G. (Fulham), 1951 v Arg, P (2)
Taylor, P. H. (Liverpool), 1948 v W, Ni, Se (3)
Taylor, P. J. (C Palace), 1976 v W (sub+1), Ni, S (4)
Taylor, T. (Manchester U), 1953 v Arg, Ch, U; 1954 v Bel, Sw; 1956 v S, Br, Se, Fi, WG; 1957 v Ni, Y (sub), D (2), Ei (2); 1958 v W, Ni, F (19)
Temple, D. W. (Everton), 1965 v WG (1)
Terry, J. G. (Chelsea), 2003 v Ser (sub); 2004 v Cro, Mac, Lie, T, D, Se, J, Sw, Cro, P; 2005 v Uk, A, Pol, Sp, Ni, Az; 2006 v D, A, Pol, Arg, U, H, Jam, Para, Tr, Se, Ec, P; 2007 v Gr, And, Mac (2), Cro, Ho, Is, And, Br, Es (39)
Thickett, H. (Sheffield U), 1899 v S, W (2)
Thomas, D. (Coventry C), 1983 v Aus (1+1 sub) (2)
Thomas, D. (QPR), 1975 v Cz (sub), P, Cy (sub+1), W, S (sub); 1976 v Cz (sub), P (sub) (8)
Thomas, G. R. (C Palace), 1991 v T, USSR, Arg, Aus, Nz (2), Mal; 1992 v Pol, F (9)
Thomas, M. L. (Arsenal), 1989 v S.Ar; 1990 v Y (2)
Thompson, A. (Celtic), 2004 v Se (1)
Thompson, P. (Liverpool), 1964 v P (2), Ei, US, Br, Arg; 1965 v Ni, W, S, Bel, Ho; 1966 v Ni; 1968 v Ni, WG; 1970 v S, Ho (sub) (16)
Thompson, P. B. (Liverpool), 1976 v W (2), Ni, S, Br, I, Fi; 1977 v Fi; 1979 v Ei (sub), Cz, Ni, S, Bul, Se (sub), A; 1980 v D, Ni, Bul, Ei, Sp (2), Arg, W, S, Bel, I; 1981 v N, R, H; 1982 v N, H, W, Ho, S, Fi, F, Cz, K, WG, Sp; 1983 v WG, Gr (42)
Thompson T. (Aston Villa), 1952 v W; (with Preston NE), 1957 v S (2)
Thomson, R. A. (Wolverhampton W), 1964 v Ni, US, P, Arg; 1965 v Bel, Ho, Ni, W (8)
Thornewell, G. (Derby Co), 1923 v Se (2); 1924 v F; 1925 v F (4)
Thornley, I. (Manchester C), 1907 v W (1)
Tilson, S. F. (Manchester C), 1934 v H, Cz; 1935 v W; 1936 v Ni (4)
Titmuss, F. (Southampton), 1922 v W; 1923 v W (2)
Todd, C. (Derby Co), 1972 v Ni; 1974 v P, W, Ni, S, Arg, EG, Bul, Y; 1975 v P (sub), WG, Cy (2), Ni, W, S; 1976 v Sw, Cz, P, Ni, S, Br, Fi; 1977 v Ei, Fi, Ho (sub), Ni (27)
Toone, G. (Notts Co), 1892 v S, W (2)
Topham, A. G. (Casuals), 1894 v W (1)
Topham, R. (Wolverhampton W), 1893 v Ni; (with Casuals), 1894 v W (2)
Towers, M. A. (Sunderland), 1976 v W, Ni (sub), I (3)
Townley, W. J. (Blackburn R), 1889 v W; 1890 v Ni (2)
Townrow, J. E. (Clapton Orient), 1925 v S; 1926 v W (2)
Tremelling, D. R. (Birmingham), 1928 v W (1)
Tresadern, J. (West Ham U), 1923 v S, Se (2)
Tueart, D. (Manchester C), 1975 v Cy (sub), Ni; 1977 v Fi, Ni, W (sub), S (sub) (6)
Tunstall, F. E. (Sheffield U), 1923 v S; 1924 v S, W, Ni, F; 1925 v Ni, S (7)
Turnbull, R. J. (Bradford), 1920 v Ni (1)
Turner, A. (Southampton), 1900 v Ni; 1901 v Ni (2)
Turner, H. (Huddersfield T), 1931 v F, Bel (2)
Turner, J. A. (Bolton W), 1893 v W; (with Stoke C), 1895 v Ni; (with Derby Co), 1898 v Ni (3)
Tweedy, G. J. (Grimsby T), 1937 v H (1)

Ufton, D. G. (Charlton Ath), 1954 v R of E (1)
Underwood, A. (Stoke C), 1891 v Ni; 1892 v Ni (2)
Unsworth, D. G. (Everton), 1995 v J (1)
Upson, M. J. (Birmingham C), 2003 v S.Af (sub), Ser, Slo; 2004 v Cro (sub), Lie, D; 2005 v Sp (sub) (7)
Urwin, T. (Middlesbrough), 1923 v Se (2); 1924 v Bel; (with Newcastle U), 1926 v W (4)
Utley, G. (Barnsley), 1913 v Ni (1)

Vassell, D. (Aston Villa), 2002 v Ho, I (sub), Para, Sk, Cam, Se, Ng (sub), Br (sub); 2003 v Mac (sub), Aus (sub), T (sub), S.Af (sub), Ser (sub), Slo (sub); 2004 v T (sub), Se, J (sub), Ic (sub), F (sub), Sw (sub), Cro (sub), P (sub) (22)
Vaughton, O. H. (Aston Villa), 1882 v S, W, Ni; 1884 v S, W (5)
Veitch, C. C. M. (Newcastle U), 1906 v S, W, Ni; 1907 v S, W; 1909 v W (6)
Veitch, J. G. (Old Westminsters), 1894 v W (1)
Venables, T. F. (Chelsea), 1965 v Bel, Ho (2)
Venison, B. (Newcastle U), 1995 v US, U (2)
Vidal, R. W. S. (Oxford University), 1873 v S (1)
Viljoen, C. (Ipswich T), 1975 v Ni, W (2)
Viollet, D. S. (Manchester U), 1960 v H; 1962 v L (2)
Von Donop (Royal Engineers), 1873 v S; 1875 v S (2)

Wace, H. (Wanderers), 1878 v S; 1879 v S, W (3)
Waddle, C. R. (Newcastle U), 1985 v Ei, R (sub), Fi (sub), S (sub), I, M (sub), WG, US; (with Tottenham H), 1986 v R, T, Ni, Is, USSR, S, M, Ca, P, Mor, Pol (sub), Arg (sub); 1987 v Se (sub), Ni (2), Y, Sp, T, Br, S; 1988 v WG, Is, H, S (sub), Co, Sw (sub), Ei, Ho (sub); 1989 v Se, S.Ar, Alb (2), Ch, S, Pol, D (sub); (with Marseille), 1990 v Se, Pol, I, Y, Br, D, U, Tun, Ei, Ho, Eg, Bel, Cam, WG, I (sub); 1991 v H (sub), Pol (sub); 1992 v T (62)
Wadsworth, S. J. (Huddersfield T), 1922 v S; 1923 v S, Bel; 1924 v S, Ni; 1925 v S, Ni; 1926 v W; 1927 v Ni (9)
Wainscoat, W. R. (Leeds U), 1929 v S (1)
Waiters, A. K. (Blackpool), 1964 v Ei, Br; 1965 v W, Bel, Ho (5)
Walcott, T. J. (Arsenal), 2006 v H (sub) (1)
Walden, F. I. (Tottenham H), 1914 v S; 1922 v W (2)
Walker, D. S. (Nottingham F), 1989 v D (sub), Se (sub), Gr, Alb (2), Ch, S, Pol, D; 1990 v Se, Pol, I, Y, Br, Cz, D, U, Tun, Ei, Ho, Eg, Bel, Cam, WG, I; 1991 v H, Pol, Ei (2), Cam, T, Arg, Aus, Nz (2), Mal; 1992 v T, Pol, F, Cz, C, H, Br, Fi, D, F, Se; (with Sampdoria), 1993 v Sp, N, T, Sm, T, Ho, Pol, N, US (sub), Br, G; (with Sheffield W), 1994 v Sm (59)
Walker, I. M. (Tottenham H), 1996 v H (sub), Chn (sub); 1997 v I; (with Leicester C), 2004 v Ic (sub) (4)
Walker, W. H. (Aston Villa), 1921 v Ni; 1922 v Ni, W, S; 1923 v Se (2); 1924 v S; 1925 v Ni, W, S, Bel, F; 1926 v Ni, W, S; 1927 v Ni, W; 1933 v A (18)
Wall, G. (Manchester U), 1907 v W; 1908 v Ni; 1909 v S; 1910 v W, S; 1912 v S; 1913 v Ni (7)
Wallace, C. W. (Aston Villa), 1913 v W; 1914 v Ni; 1920 v S (3)
Wallace, D. L. (Southampton), 1986 v Eg (1)
Walsh, P. (Luton T), 1983 v Aus (2 + 1 sub); 1984 v F, W (5)
Walters, A. M. (Cambridge University), 1885 v S, N; 1886 v S; 1887 v S, W; (with Old Carthusians), 1889 v S, W; 1890 v S, W (9)
Walters, K. M. (Rangers), 1991 v Nz (1)

Walters, P. M. (Oxford University), 1885 v S, Ni; (with Old Carthusians), 1886 v S, W, Ni; 1887 v S, W; 1888 v S, Ni; 1889 v S, W; 1890 v S, W (13)
Walton, N. (Blackburn R), 1890 v Ni (1)
Ward, J. T. (Blackburn Olympic), 1885 v W (1)
Ward, P. (Brighton & HA), 1980 v Aus (sub) (1)
Ward, T. V. (Derby Co), 1948 v Bel; 1949 v W (2)
Waring, T. (Aston Villa), 1931 v F, Bel; 1932 v S, W, Ni (5)
Warner, C. (Upton Park), 1878 v S (1)
Warren, B. (Derby Co), 1906 v S, W, Ni; 1907 v S, W, Ni; 1908 v S, W, Ni, A (2), H, B; (with Chelsea), 1909 v S, Ni, W, H (2), A; 1911 v S, Ni, W (22)
Waterfield, G. S. (Burnley), 1927 v W (1)
Watson, D. (Norwich C), 1984 v Br, U, Ch; 1985 v M, US (sub); 1986 v S; (with Everton), 1987 v Ni; 1988 v Is, Ho, S, Sw (sub), USSR (12)
Watson, D. V. (Sunderland), 1974 v P, S (sub), Arg, EG, Bul, Y; 1975 v Cz, P, WG, Cy (2), Ni, W, S; (with Manchester C), 1976 v Sw, Cz (sub), P; 1977 v Ho, L, Ni, W, S, Br, Arg, U; 1978 v Sw, L, I, WG, Br, W, Ni, S, H; 1979 v D, Ei, Cz, Ni (2), W, S, Bul, Se, A; (with Werder Bremen), 1980 v D; (with Southampton), Ni, Bul, Ei, Sp (2), Arg, Ni, S, Bel, I; 1981 v N, R, Sw, R, W, S, Sw, H; (with Stoke C), 1982 v Ni, Ic (65)
Watson, V. M. (West Ham U), 1923 v W, S; 1930 v S, G, A (5)
Watson, W. (Burnley), 1913 v S; 1914 v Ni; 1920 v Ni (3)
Watson, W. (Sunderland), 1950 v Ni, I; 1951 v W, Y (4)
Weaver, S. (Newcastle U), 1932 v S, 1933 v S, Ni (3)
Webb, G. W. (West Ham U), 1911 v S, W (2)
Webb, N. J. (Nottingham F), 1988 v WG (sub), T, Y, Is, Ho, S, Sw, Ei, USSR (sub); 1989 v D, Se, Gr, Alb (2), Ch, S, Pol, D; (with Manchester U), 1990 v Se, I (sub); 1992 v F, H, Br (sub), Fi, D (sub), Se (26)
Webster, M. (Middlesbrough), 1930 v S, A, G (3)
Wedlock, W. J. (Bristol C), 1907 v S, Ni, W; 1908 v S, Ni, W, A (2), H, B; 1909 v S, W, Ni, H (2), A; 1910 v S, W, Ni; 1911 v S, W, Ni; 1912 v S, W, Ni; 1914 v W (26)
Weir, D. (Bolton W), 1889 v S, Ni (2)
Welch, R. de C. (Wanderers), 1872 v S; (with Harrow Chequers), 1874 v S (2)
Weller, K. (Leicester C), 1974 v W, Ni, S, Arg (4)
Welsh, D. (Charlton Ath), 1938 v G, Sw; 1939 v R (3)
West, G. (Everton), 1969 v W, Bul, M (3)
Westwood, R. W. (Bolton W), 1935 v S, W, Ho; 1936 v Ni, G; 1937 v W (6)
Whateley, O. (Aston Villa), 1883 v S, Ni (2)
Wheeler, J. E. (Bolton W), 1955 v Ni (1)
Wheldon, G. F. (Aston Villa), 1897 v Ni; 1898 v S, W, Ni (4)
White, D. (Manchester C), 1993 v Sp (1)
White, T. A. (Everton), 1933 v I (1)
Whitehead, J. (Accrington), 1893 v W; (with Blackburn R), 1894 v Ni (2)
Whitfeld, H. (Old Etonians), 1879 v W (1)
Whitham, M. (Sheffield U), 1892 v Ni (1)
Whitworth, S. (Leicester C), 1975 v WG, Cy, Ni, W, S; 1976 v Sw, P (7)
Whymark, T. J. (Ipswich T), 1978 v L (sub) (1)
Widdowson, S. W. (Nottingham F), 1880 v S (1)
Wignall, F. (Nottingham F), 1965 v W, Ho (2)
Wilcox, J. M. (Blackburn R), 1996 v H; 1999 v F (sub); (with Leeds U), 2000 v Arg (3)
Wilkes, A. (Aston Villa), 1901 v S, W; 1902 v S, W, Ni (5)
Wilkins, R. G. (Chelsea), 1976 v I; 1977 v Ei, Fi, Ni, Br, Arg, U; 1978 v Sw (sub), L, I, WG, W, Ni, S, H; 1979 v D, Ei, Cz, Ni, W, S, Bul, Se (sub), A; (with Manchester U), 1980 v D, Ni, Bul, Sp (2), Arg, W (sub), Ni, S, Bel, I; 1981 v Sp (sub), R, Br, W, S, Sw, H (sub); 1982 v Ni, W, Ho, S, Fi, F, Cz, K, WG, Sp; 1983 v D, WG; 1984 v D, Ni, W, S, USSR, Br, U, Ch; (with AC Milan), 1985 v EG, Fi, T, Ni, Ei, R, Fi, S, I, M; 1986 v T, Ni, Is, Eg, USSR, S, M, Ca, P, Mor; 1987 v Se, Y (sub) (84)
Wilkinson, B. (Sheffield U), 1904 v S (1)
Wilkinson, L. R. (Oxford University), 1891 v W (1)
Williams, B. F. (Wolverhampton W), 1949 v F; 1950 v S, W, Ei, I, P, Bel, Ch, US, Sp; 1951 v Ni, W, S, Y, Arg, P; 1952 v W, F; 1955 v S, WG, F, Sp, P; 1956 v W (24)
Williams, O. (Clapton Orient), 1923 v W, Ni (2)
Williams, S. (Southampton), 1983 v Aus (1+1 sub); 1984 v F; 1985 v EG, Fi, T (6)
Williams, W. (WBA), 1897 v Ni; 1898 v W, Ni, S; 1899 v W, Ni (6)
Williamson, E. C. (Arsenal), 1923 v Se (2) (2)
Williamson, R. G. (Middlesbrough), 1905 v Ni; 1911 v Ni, S, W; 1912 v S, W; 1913 v Ni (7)
Willingham, C. K. (Huddersfield T), 1937 v Fi; 1938 v S, G, Sw, F; 1939 v S, W, Ni, R of E, N, I, Y (12)
Willis, A. (Tottenham H), 1952 v F (1)
Wilshaw, D. J. (Wolverhampton W), 1954 v W, Sw, U; 1955 v S, F, Sp, P; 1956 v W, Ni, Fi, WG; 1957 v Ni (12)
Wilson, C. P. (Hendon), 1884 v S, W (2)
Wilson, C. W. (Oxford University), 1879 v W; 1881 v S (2)
Wilson, G. (Sheffield W), 1921 v S, W, Bel; 1922 v S, Ni; 1923 v S, W, Ni, Bel; 1924 v W, Ni, F (12)
Wilson, G. P. (Corinthians), 1900 v S, W (2)
Wilson, R. (Huddersfield T), 1960 v S, Y, Sp, H; 1962 v W, Ni, S, A, Sw, Pe, P, H, Arg, Bul, Br; 1963 v Ni, F, Br, Cz, EG, Sw; 1964 v W, S, R of W, U, P (2), Ei, Br, Arg; (with Everton), 1965 v S, H, Y, WG, Se; 1966 v WG (sub), W, Ni, A, Sp, Pol (2), Y, Fi, D, U, M, F, Arg, P, WG; 1967 v Ni, W, S, Cz, A; 1968 v Ni, S, USSR (2), Sp (2), Y (63)
Wilson, T. (Huddersfield T), 1928 v S (1)
Winckworth, W. N. (Old Westminsters), 1892 v W; 1893 v Ni (2)
Windridge, J. E. (Chelsea), 1908 v S, W, Ni, A (2), H, B; 1909 v Ni (8)
Wingfield-Stratford, C. V. (Royal Engineers), 1877 v S (1)
Winterburn, N. (Arsenal), 1990 v I (sub); 1993 v G (sub) (2)
Wise, D. F. (Chelsea), 1991 v T, USSR, Aus (sub), Nz (2); 1994 v N; 1995 v R (sub), Ng; 1996 v Co, N, P, H (sub); 2000 v Bel (sub), Arg, Br, Ma, P (sub), G, R; 2001 v F, Fi (21)
Withe, P. (Aston Villa), 1981 v Br, W, S; 1982 v N (sub), W, Ic; 1983 v H, Ni, S; 1984 v H (sub); 1985 v T (11)
Wollaston, C. H. R. (Wanderers), 1874 v S; 1875 v S; 1877 v S; 1880 v S (4)
Wolstenholme, S. (Everton), 1904 v S; (with Blackburn R), 1905 v W, Ni (3)
Wood, H. (Wolverhampton W), 1890 v S, W; 1896 v S (3)
Wood, R. E. (Manchester U), 1955 v Ni, W; 1956 v Fi (3)
Woodcock, A. S. (Nottingham F), 1978 v Ni; 1979 v Ei (sub), Cz, Bul (sub), Se; 1980 v Ni; (with Cologne), Bul, Ei, Sp (2), Arg, Bel, I; 1981 v N, R, Sw, R, W (sub), S; 1982 v Ni (sub), Ho, Fi (sub), WG (sub), Sp; (with Arsenal), 1983 v WG (sub), Gr, L, Gr; 1984 v L, F (sub), Ni, W, S, Br, U (sub); 1985 v EG, Fi, T, Ni; 1986 v R (sub), T (sub), Is (sub) (42)
Woodgate, J. S. (Leeds U), 1999 v Bul; 2003 v P (sub), Slo, Mac; (with Newcastle U), 2004 v Se; (with Real Madrid), 2007 v Sp (6)
Woodger, G. (Oldham Ath), 1911 v Ni (1)
Woodhall, G. (WBA), 1888 v S, W (2)
Woodley, V. R. (Chelsea), 1937 v S, N, Se, Fi; 1938 v S, W, Ni, Cz, G, Sw, F; 1939 v S, W, Ni, R of E, N, I, R, Y (19)
Woods, C. C. E. (Norwich C), 1985 v US; 1986 v Eg (sub), Is (sub), Ca (sub); (with Rangers), 1987 v Y, Sp (sub), Ni (sub), T, S; 1988 v Is, H, Sw (sub), USSR; 1989 v D (sub); 1990 v Br (sub), D (sub); 1991 v H, Pol, Ei, USSR, Aus, Nz (2), Mal; (with Sheffield W), 1992 v G, T, Pol, F, C, Br, Fi, D, F, Se; 1993 v Sp, N, T, Sm, T, Ho, Pol, N, US (43)
Woodward, V. J. (Tottenham H), 1903 v S, W, Ni; 1904 v S, Ni; 1905 v S, W, Ni; 1907 v S; 1908 v S, W, Ni, A (2), H, B; 1909 v W, Ni, H (2), A; (with Chelsea), 1910 v Ni; 1911 v W (23)
Woosnam, M. (Manchester C), 1922 v W (1)
Worrall, F. (Portsmouth), 1935 v Ho; 1937 v Ni (2)
Worthington, F. S. (Leicester C), 1974 v Ni (sub), S, Arg, EG, Bul, Y; 1975 v Cz, P (sub) (8)
Wreford-Brown, C. (Oxford University), 1889 v Ni; (with Old Carthusians), 1894 v W; 1895 v W; 1898 v S (4)
Wright, E. G. D. (Cambridge University), 1906 v W (1)
Wright, I. E. (C Palace), 1991 v Cam, Ei (sub), USSR, Nz; (with Arsenal), 1992 v H (sub); 1993 v N, T (2), Pol (sub), N (sub), US (sub), Br, G (sub); 1994 v Pol, Ho (sub), Sm, Gr (sub), N (sub); 1995 v US (sub), R; 1997 v Ge (sub), I (sub), M (sub), S.Af, I, F, Br (sub); 1998 v Mol, I, S.Ar (sub), Mor; (with West Ham U), 1999 v L (sub), CzR (33)
Wright, J. D. (Newcastle U), 1939 v N (1)
Wright, M. (Southampton), 1984 v W; 1985 v EG, Fi, T, Ei, R, I, WG; 1986 v R, T, Ni, Eg, USSR; 1987 v Y, Ni, S; (with Derby Co), 1988 v Is, Ho (sub), Co, Sw, Ei, Ho; 1990 v Cz (sub), Tun (sub), Ho, Eg, Bel, Cam, WG, I; 1991 v H, Pol, Ei (2), Cam, USSR, Arg, Aus, Nz, Mal;

(with Liverpool), 1992 v F, Fi; 1993 v Sp; 1996 v Cro, H (45)
Wright, R. I. (Ipswich T), 2000 v Ma; (with Arsenal), 2002 v Ho (sub) (2)
Wright, T. J. (Everton), 1968 v USSR; 1969 v R (2), M (sub), U, Br; 1970 v W, Ho, Bel, R (sub), Br (11)
Wright, W. A. (Wolverhampton W), 1947 v S, W, Ni, Ei, Ho, F, Sw, P; 1948 v S, W, Ni, Bel, Se, I; 1949 v S, W, Ni, D, Sw, Se, N, F; 1950 v S, W, Ni, Ei, I, P, Bel, Ch, US, Sp; 1951 v Ni, S, Arg; 1952 v W, Ni, S, F, A (2), I, Sw; 1953 v Ni, W, S, Bel, Arg, Ch, U, US; 1954 v W, Ni, S, R of E, H (2), Y, Bel, Sw, U; 1955 v W, Ni, S, WG, F, Sp, P; 1956 v Ni, W, S, Br, Se, Fi, WG, D, Sp; 1957 v S, W, Ni, Y, D (2), Ei (2); 1958 v W, Ni, S, P, Y, USSR (3), Br, A, F; 1959 v W, Ni, S, USSR, I, Br, Pe, M, US (105)
Wright-Phillips, S. C. (Manchester C), 2005 v Uk (sub), Az (sub), Sp (sub), Ho; (with Chelsea), 2006 v W, Ni, Pol, U (sub); 2007 v Mac (sub), Cro (sub), Ho (sub), Sp (12)
Wylie, J. G. (Wanderers), 1878 v S (1)

Yates, J. (Burnley), 1889 v Ni (1)
York, R. E. (Aston Villa), 1922 v S; 1926 v S (2)
Young, A. (Huddersfield T), 1933 v W; 1937 v S, H, N, Se; 1938 v G, Sw, F; 1939 v W (9)
Young, G. M. (Sheffield W), 1965 v W (1)
Young, L. P. (Charlton Ath), 2005 v US (sub), Co (sub); 2006 v W, Ni, A, Pol, Arg (7)
R. E. Evans also played for Wales against E, Ni, S; J. Reynolds also played for Ireland against E, W, S.
J. H. Edwards also played for W v S.

NORTHERN IRELAND

Addis, D. J. (Cliftonville), 1922 v N (1)
Aherne, T. (Belfast C), 1947 v E; 1948 v S; 1949 v W; (with Luton T), 1950 v W (4)
Alexander, T. E. (Cliftonville), 1895 v S (1)
Allan, C. (Cliftonville), 1936 v E (1)
Allen, J. (Limavady), 1887 v E (1)
Anderson, J. (Distillery), 1925 v S.Af (1)
Anderson, T. (Manchester U), 1973 v Cy, E, S, W; 1974 v Bul, P; (with Swindon T), 1975 v S (sub); 1976 v Is; 1977 v Ho, Bel, WG, E, S, W, Ic; 1978 v Ic, Ho, Bel; (with Peterborough U), S, E, W; 1979 v D (sub) (22)
Anderson, W. (Linfield), 1898 v W, E, S; (with Cliftonville), 1899 v S (4)
Andrews, W. (Glentoran), 1908 v S; (with Grimsby T), 1913 v E, S (3)
Armstrong, G. J. (Tottenham H), 1977 v WG, E, W (sub), Ic (sub); 1978 v Bel, S, E, W; 1979 v Ei, D, Bul, E, Bul, E, S, W, D; 1980 v E, Ei, Is, S, E, W, Aus (3); 1981 v Se; (with Watford), P, S, P, S, Se; 1982 v S, Is, E, F, W, Y, Hon, Sp, A, F; 1983 v A, T, Alb, S, E, W; (with Real Mallorca), 1984 v A, WG, E, W, Fi; 1985 v R, Fi, E, Sp; (with WBA), 1986 v T, R (sub), E (sub), F (sub); (with Chesterfield), D (sub), Br (sub) (63)

Baird, C. P. (Southampton), 2003 v I, Sp; 2004 v Uk, Arm, Gr, N, Es, Ser, Bar, Stk, Tr; 2005 v Az, Ca, E, Pol, G; 2006 v Az, E, A, Es; 2007 v Fi, Ic, Sp, D, La (25)
Baird, G. (Distillery), 1896 v S, E, W (3)
Baird, H. C. (Huddersfield T), 1939 v E (1)
Balfe, J. (Shelbourne), 1909 v E; 1910 v W (2)
Bambrick, J. (Linfield), 1929 v W, S, E; 1930 v W, S, E; 1932 v W; (with Chelsea), 1935 v W; 1936 v E, S; 1938 v W (11)
Banks, S. J. (Cliftonville), 1937 v W (1)
Barr, H. H. (Linfield), 1962 v E; (with Coventry C), 1963 v E, Pol (3)
Barron, J. H. (Cliftonville), 1894 v E, W, S; 1895 v S; 1896 v S; 1897 v E, W (7)
Barry, J. (Cliftonville), 1888 v W, S; 1889 v E (3)
Barry, J. (Bohemians), 1900 v S (1)
Baxter, R. A. (Distillery), 1887 v S (1)
Baxter, S. N. (Cliftonville), 1887 v W (1)
Bennett, L. V. (Dublin University), 1889 v W (1)
Best, G. (Manchester U), 1964 v W, U; 1965 v E, Ho (2), S, Sw (2), Alb; 1966 v S, E, Alb; 1967 v E; 1968 v S; 1969 v E, S, W, T; 1970 v S, E, W, USSR; 1971 v Cy (2), Sp, E, S, W; 1972 v USSR, Sp; 1973 v Bul; 1974 v P; (with Fulham), 1977 v Ho, Bel, WG; 1978 v Ic, Ho (37)
Bingham, W. L. (Sunderland), 1951 v F; 1952 v E, S, W; 1953 v E, S, F, W; 1954 v E, S, W; 1955 v E, S, W; 1956 v E, S, W; 1957 v E, S, W, P (2), I; 1958 v S, E, W, I (2), Arg, Cz (2), WG, F; (with Luton T), 1959 v E, S, W, Sp; 1960 v S, E, W; (with Everton), 1961 v E, S, WG (2), Gr, I; 1962 v E, Gr; 1963 v E, S, Pol (2), Sp; (with Port Vale), 1964 v S, E, Sp (56)
Black, K. T. (Luton T), 1988 v Fr (sub), Ma (sub); 1989 v Ei, H, Sp (2), Ch (sub); 1990 v H, N, U; 1991 v Y (2), D, A, Pol, Fa; (with Nottingham F), 1992 v Fa, A, D, S, Li, G; 1993 v Sp, D (sub), Alb, Ei (sub), Sp; 1994 v D (sub), Ei (sub), R (sub) (30)
Black, T. (Glentoran), 1901 v E (1)
Blair, H. (Portadown), 1928 v F; 1931 v S; 1932 v S; (with Swansea), 1934 v S (4)
Blair, J. (Cliftonville), 1907 v W, E, S; 1908 v E, S (5)
Blair, R. V. (Oldham Ath), 1975 v Se (sub), S (sub), W; 1976 v Se, Is (5)
Blanchflower, J. (Manchester U), 1954 v W; 1955 v E, S; 1956 v S, W; 1957 v S, E, P; 1958 v S, E, I (2) (12)
Blanchflower, R. D. (Barnsley), 1950 v S, W; 1951 v E, S; (with Aston Villa), F; 1952 v W; 1953 v E, S, W, F; 1954 v E, S, W; 1955 v E, S; (with Tottenham H), W; 1956 v E, S, W; 1957 v E, S, W, I, P (2); 1958 v E, S, W, I (2), Cz (2), Arg, F, WG; 1959 v E, S, W, Sp; 1960 v E, S, W; 1961 v E, S, W, WG (2); 1962 v E, S, W, Gr, Ho; 1963 v E, S, Pol (2) (56)
Blayney, A. (Doncaster R), 2006 v R (1)
Bookman, L. J. O. (Bradford C), 1914 v W; (with Luton T), 1921 v S, W; 1922 v E (4)
Bothwell, A. W. (Ards), 1926 v S, E, W; 1927 v E, W (5)
Bowler, G. C. (Hull C), 1950 v E, S, W (3)
Boyle, P. (Sheffield U), 1901 v E; 1902 v E; 1903 v S, W; 1904 v E (5)
Braithwaite, R. M. (Linfield), 1962 v W; 1963 v Pol, Sp; (with Middlesbrough), 1964 v W, U; 1965 v E, S, Sw (2), Ho (10)
Breen, T. (Belfast C), 1935 v E, W; 1937 v E, S; (with Manchester U), 1937 v W; 1938 v E, S; 1939 v W, S (9)
Brennan, B. (Bohemians), 1912 v W (1)
Brennan, R. A. (Luton T), 1949 v W; (with Birmingham C), 1950 v E, S, W; (with Fulham), 1951 v E (5)
Briggs, W. R. (Manchester U), 1962 v W; (with Swansea T), 1965 v Ho (2)
Brisby, D. (Distillery), 1891 v S (1)
Brolly, T. H. (Millwall), 1937 v W; 1938 v W; 1939 v E, W (4)
Brookes, E. A. (Shelbourne), 1920 v S (1)
Brotherston, N. (Blackburn R), 1980 v S, E, W, Aus (3); 1981 v Se, P; 1982 v S, Is, E, F, S, W, Hon (sub), A (sub); 1983 v A (sub), WG, Alb, T, Alb, S (sub), E (sub), W; 1984 v T; 1985 v Is (sub), T (27)
Brown, J. (Glenavon), 1921 v W; (with Tranmere R), 1924 v E, W (3)
Brown, J. (Wolverhampton W), 1935 v E, W; 1936 v E; (with Coventry C), 1937 v E, W; 1938 v S, W; (with Birmingham C), 1939 v E, S, W (10)
Brown, N. M. (Limavady), 1887 v E (1)
Brown, W. G. (Glenavon), 1926 v W (1)
Browne, F. (Cliftonville), 1887 v E, S, W; 1888 v E, S (5)
Browne, R. J. (Leeds U), 1936 v E, W; 1938 v E, W; 1939 v E, S (6)
Bruce, A. (Belfast C), 1925 v S.Af (1)
Bruce, W. (Glentoran), 1961 v S; 1967 v W (2)
Brunt, C. (Sheffield W), 2005 v Sw (sub), G (sub); 2006 v Ma (sub), W (sub), A, P, Es; 2007 v W, Lie, Se (10)
Buckle, H. R. (Cliftonville), 1903 v S; (with Sunderland), 1904 v E; (with Bristol R), 1908 v W (3)
Buckle, J. (Cliftonville), 1882 v E (1)
Burnett, J. (Distillery), 1894 v E, W, S; (with Glentoran), 1895 v E, W (5)
Burnison, J. (Distillery), 1901 v E, W (2)
Burnison, S. (Distillery), 1908 v E; 1910 v E, S; (with Bradford), 1911 v E, S, W; (with Distillery), 1912 v E; 1913 v W (8)
Burns, J. (Glenavon), 1923 v E (1)
Burns, W. (Glentoran), 1925 v S.Af (1)
Butler, M. P. (Blackpool), 1939 v W (1)

Campbell, A. C. (Crusaders), 1963 v W; 1965 v Sw (2)
Campbell, D. A. (Nottingham F), 1986 v Mor (sub), Br; 1987 v E (2), T, Y; (with Charlton Ath), 1988 v Y, T (sub), Gr (sub), Pol (sub) (10)

Campbell, James (Cliftonville), 1897 v E, S, W; 1898 v E, S, W; 1899 v E; 1900 v E, S; 1901 v S, W; 1902 v S; 1903 v E; 1904 v S (14)
Campbell, John (Cliftonville), 1896 v W (1)
Campbell, J. P. (Fulham), 1951 v E, S (2)
Campbell, R. M. (Bradford C), 1982 v S, W (sub) (2)
Campbell, W. G. (Dundee), 1968 v S, E; 1969 v T; 1970 v S, W, USSR (6)
Capaldi, A. C. (Plymouth Arg), 2004 v Es, Ser, Bar, Stk, Tr; 2005 v Sw, Pol, W, Ca, E, Pol; 2006 v Az, E, W, P, Es, U, R; 2007 v Fi, Ic, W (21)
Carey, J. J. (Manchester U), 1947 v E, S, W; 1948 v E; 1949 v E, S, W (7)
Carroll, E. (Glenavon), 1925 v S (1)
Carroll, R. E. (Wigan Ath), 1997 v Th (sub); 1999 v Ei (sub); 2000 v L, Ma; 2001 v Ma, D, Ic, CzR, Bul; (with Manchester U), 2002 v Lie (sub), Sp (sub); 2003 v Fi (sub), I (sub); 2004 v Ser (sub); 2005 v Sw, A, Ca (sub); (with West Ham U), 2007 v Fi (sub), Sp (19)
Casey, T. (Newcastle U), 1955 v W; 1956 v W; 1957 v E, S, W, I, P (2); 1958 v WG, F; (with Portsmouth), 1959 v E, Sp (12)
Caskey, W. (Derby Co), 1979 v Bul, E, Bul, E, S (sub), D (sub); 1980 v E (sub); (with Tulsa R), 1982 v F (sub) (8)
Cassidy, T. (Newcastle U), 1971 v E (sub); 1972 v USSR (sub); 1974 v Bul (sub), S, E, W; 1975 v N; 1976 v S, E, W; 1977 v WG (sub); 1980 v E, Ei (sub), Is, S, E, W, Aus (3); (with Burnley), 1981 v Se, P; 1982 v Is, Sp (sub) (24)
Caughey, M. (Linfield), 1986 v F (sub), D (sub) (2)
Chambers, R. J. (Distillery), 1921 v W; (with Bury), 1928 v E, S, W; 1929 v E, S, W; 1930 v S, W; (with Nottingham F), 1932 v E, S, W (12)
Chatton, H. A. (Partick Th), 1925 v E, S; 1926 v E (3)
Christian, J. (Linfield), 1889 v S (1)
Clarke, C. J. (Bournemouth), 1986 v F, D, Mor, Alg (sub), Sp, Br; (with Southampton), 1987 v E, T, Y; 1988 v Y, T, Gr, Pol, F, Ma; 1989 v Ei, H, Sp (1+1 sub); (with QPR), Ma, Ch; 1990 v H, Ei, N; (with Portsmouth), 1991 v Y (sub), D, A, Pol, Y (sub), Fa; 1992 v Fa, A, D, S, G; 1993 v Alb, Sp, D (38)
Clarke, R. (Belfast C), 1901 v E, S (2)
Cleary, J. (Glentoran), 1982 v S, W; 1983 v W (sub); 1984 v T (sub); 1985 v Is (5)
Clements, D. (Coventry C), 1965 v W, Ho; 1966 v M; 1967 v S, W; 1968 v S, E; 1969 v T (2), S, W; 1970 v S, E, W, USSR (2); 1971 v Sp, E, S, W, Cy; (with Sheffield W), 1972 v USSR (2), Sp, E, S, W; 1973 v Bul, Cy (2), P, E, S, W; (with Everton), 1974 v Bul, P, S, E, W; 1975 v N, Y, E, S, W; 1976 v Se, Y; (with New York Cosmos), E, W (48)
Clingan, S. G. (Nottingham F), 2006 v U, R; 2007 v Fi, Ic, Sp, D, La, W (8)
Clugston, J. (Cliftonville), 1888 v W; 1889 v W, S, E; 1890 v E, S; 1891 v E, W; 1892 v E, S, W; 1893 v E, S, W (14)
Clyde, M. G. (Wolverhampton W), 2005 v W, Az, G (3)
Cochrane, D. (Leeds U), 1939 v E, W; 1947 v E, S, W; 1948 v E, S, W; 1949 v S, W; 1950 v S, E (12)
Cochrane, G. (Cliftonville), 1903 v S (1)
Cochrane, G. T. (Coleraine), 1976 v N (sub); (with Burnley), 1978 v S (sub), E (sub), W (sub); 1979 v Ei (sub); (with Middlesbrough), D, Bul, E, Bul, E; 1980 v Is, E (sub), W (sub), Aus (1+2 sub); 1981 v Se (sub), P (sub), S, P, S, Se; 1982 v E (sub), F; (with Gillingham), 1984 v S, Fi (sub) (26)
Cochrane, M. (Distillery), 1898 v S, W, E; 1899 v E; 1900 v E, S, W; (with Leicester Fosse), 1901 v S (8)
Collins, F. (Celtic), 1922 v S (1)
Collins, R. (Cliftonville), 1922 v N (1)
Condy, J. (Distillery), 1882 v W; 1886 v E, S (3)
Connell, T. E. (Coleraine), 1978 v W (sub) (1)
Connor, J. (Glentoran), 1901 v S, E; (with Belfast C), 1905 v E, S, W; 1907 v E, S; 1908 v E, S; 1909 v W; 1911 v S, E, W (13)
Connor, M. J. (Brentford), 1903 v S, W; (with Fulham), 1904 v E (3)
Cook, W. (Celtic), 1933 v E, W, S; (with Everton), 1935 v E; 1936 v S, W; 1937 v E, S, W; 1938 v E, S, W; 1939 v E, S, W (15)
Cooke, S. (Belfast YMCA), 1889 v E; (with Cliftonville), 1890 v E, S (3)
Coote, A. (Norwich C), 1999 v Ca, Ei (sub); 2000 v Fi (sub), L (sub), Ma (sub), H (sub) (6)
Coulter, J. (Belfast C), 1934 v E, S, W; (with Everton), 1935 v E, S, W; 1937 v S, W; (with Grimsby T), 1938 v S, W; (with Chelmsford C), 1939 v S (11)
Cowan, J. (Newcastle U), 1970 v E (sub) (1)
Cowan, T. S. (Queen's Island), 1925 v W (1)
Coyle, F. (Coleraine), 1956 v E, S; 1957 v P; (with Nottingham F), 1958 v Arg (4)
Coyle, L. (Derry C), 1989 v Ch (sub) (1)
Coyle, R. I. (Sheffield W), 1973 v P, Cy (sub), W (sub); 1974 v Bul (sub), P (sub) (5)
Craig, A. B. (Rangers), 1908 v E, S, W; 1909 v S; (with Morton), 1912 v S, W; 1914 v E, S, W (9)
Craig, D. J. (Newcastle U), 1967 v W; 1968 v W; 1969 v T (2), E, S, W; 1970 v E, S, W, USSR; 1971 v Cy (2), Sp, S (sub); 1972 v USSR, S (sub); 1973 v Cy (2), E, S, W; 1974 v Bul, P; 1975 v N (25)
Craigan, S. J. (Partick Th), 2003 v Fi (sub), Arm, Gr; (with Motherwell), 2004 v Es, Ser, Bar, Stk, Tr; 2005 v Sw, Pol, Ca (sub), G; 2006 v Ma, Az, E, W, A, P, Es, U, R; 2007 v Fi, Ic, Sp, D, La, W, Lie, Se (29)
Crawford, A. (Distillery), 1889 v E, W; (with Cliftonville), 1891 v E, S, W; 1893 v E, W (7)
Croft, T. (Queen's Island), 1922 v N; 1924 v E; 1925 v S.Af (3)
Crone, R. (Distillery), 1889 v S; 1890 v E, S, W (4)
Crone, W. (Distillery), 1882 v W; 1884 v E, S, W; 1886 v E, S, W; 1887 v E; 1888 v E, W; 1889 v S; 1890 v W (12)
Crooks, W. J. (Manchester U), 1922 v W (1)
Crossan, E. (Blackburn R), 1950 v S; 1951 v E; 1955 v W (3)
Crossan, J. A. (Sparta-Rotterdam), 1960 v E; (with Sunderland), 1963 v W, Pol, Sp; 1964 v E, S, W, U, Sp; 1965 v E, S, Sw (2); (with Manchester C), W, Ho (2), Alb; 1966 v S, E, Alb, WG; 1967 v E, S; (with Middlesbrough), 1968 v S (24)
Crothers, C. (Distillery), 1907 v W (1)
Cumming, L. (Huddersfield T), 1929 v W, S; (with Oldham Ath), 1930 v E (3)
Cunningham, W. (Ulster), 1892 v S, E, W; 1893 v E (4)
Cunningham, W. E. (St Mirren), 1951 v W; 1953 v E; 1954 v S; 1955 v S; (with Leicester C), 1956 v E, S, W; 1957 v E, S, W, I, P (2); 1958 v S, W, I, Cz (2), Arg, WG, F; 1959 v E, S, W; 1960 v E, S, W; (with Dunfermline Ath), 1961 v W; 1962 v W, Ho (30)
Curran, S. (Belfast C), 1926 v S, W; 1928 v F, S (4)
Curran, J. J. (Glenavon), 1922 v W, N; (with Pontypridd), 1923 v E, S; (with Glenavon), 1924 v E (5)
Cush, W. W. (Glenavon), 1951 v E, S; 1954 v S, E; 1957 v W, I, P (2); (with Leeds U), 1958 v I (2), W, Cz (2), Arg, WG, F; 1959 v E, S, W, Sp; 1960 v E, S, W; (with Portadown), 1961 v WG, Gr; 1962 v Gr (26)

Dalrymple, J. (Distillery), 1922 v N (1)
Dalton, W. (YMCA), 1888 v S; (with Linfield), 1890 v S, W; 1891 v S, W; 1892 v E, S, W; 1894 v E, S, W (11)
D'Arcy, S. D. (Chelsea), 1952 v W; 1953 v E; (with Brentford), 1953 v S, W, F (5)
Darling, J. (Linfield), 1897 v E, S; 1900 v S; 1902 v E, S, W; 1903 v E, S (2), W; 1905 v E, S, W; 1906 v E, S, W; 1908 v W; 1909 v E; 1910 v E, S, W; 1912 v S (22)
Davey, H. H. (Reading), 1926 v E; 1927 v E, S; 1928 v E; (with Portsmouth), 1928 v W (5)
Davis, S. (Aston Villa), 2005 v Ca, E (sub), Pol, G; 2006 v Ma, Az, E, W, A, P, Es, U, R; 2007 v Ic, Sp, D, La, W, Se (19)
Davis, T. L. (Oldham Ath), 1937 v E (1)
Davison, A. J. (Bolton W), 1996 v Se; (with Bradford C), 1997 v Th; (with Grimsby T), 1998 v G (3)
Davison, J. R. (Cliftonville), 1882 v E, W; 1883 v E, W; 1884 v E, W, S; 1885 v E (8)
Dennison, R. (Wolverhampton W), 1988 v F, Ma; 1989 v H, Sp Ch (sub); 1990 v Ei, U; 1991 v Y (2), A. Pol, Fa (sub); 1992 v Fa, A, D (sub); 1993 v Sp (sub); 1994 v Co (sub); 1997 v I (sub) (18)
Devine, A. O. (Limavady), 1886 v E, S; 1887 v W; 1888 v W (4)
Devine, J. (Glentoran), 1990 v U (sub) (1)
Dickson, D. (Coleraine), 1970 v S (sub), W; 1973 v Cy, P (4)
Dickson, T. A. (Linfield), 1957 v S (1)
Dickson, W. (Chelsea), 1951 v W, F; 1952 v E, S, W; 1953 v E, S, W, F; (with Arsenal), 1954 v E, W; 1955 v E (12)
Diffin, W. J. (Belfast C), 1931 v W (1)

Dill, A. H. (Knock), 1882 v E, W; (with Down Ath), 1883 v W; (with Cliftonville), 1884 v E, S, W; 1885 v E, S, W (9)
Doherty, I. (Belfast C), 1901 v E (1)
Doherty, J. (Portadown), 1928 v F (1)
Doherty, J. (Cliftonville), 1933 v E, W (2)
Doherty, L. (Linfield), 1985 v Is; 1988 v T (sub) (2)
Doherty, M. (Derry C), 1938 v S (1)
Doherty, P. D. (Blackpool), 1935 v E, W; 1936 v E, S; (with Manchester C), 1937 v E, W; 1938 v E, S; 1939 v E, W; (with Derby Co), 1947 v E; (with Huddersfield T), W; 1948 v E, W; 1949 v S; (with Doncaster R), 1951 v S (16)
Doherty, T. E. (Bristol C), 2003 v I, Sp; 2004 v Uk, Arm, Ser; 2005 v Az, A, Ca, E (9)
Donaghey, B. (Belfast C), 1903 v S (1)
Donaghy, M. M. (Luton T), 1980 v S, E, W; 1981 v Se, P, S (sub); 1982 v S, Is, E, F, S, W, Y, Hon, Sp, F; 1983 v A, WG, Alb, T, Alb, S, E, W; 1984 v A, T, WG, S, E, W, Fi; 1985 v R, Fi, E, Sp, T; 1986 v T, R, E, F, D, Mor, Alg, Sp, Br; 1987 v E (2), T, Is, Y; 1988 v Y, T, Gr, Pol, F, Ma; 1989 v Ei, H; (with Manchester U), Sp (2), Ma, Ch; 1990 v Ei, N; 1991 v Y (2), D, A, Pol, Fa; 1992 v Fa, A, D, S, Li, G; (with Chelsea), 1993 v Alb, Sp, D, Alb, Ei, Sp, Li, La; 1994 v La, D, Ei, R, Lie, Co, M (91)
Donnelly, L. (Distillery), 1913 v W (1)
Doran, J. F. (Brighton), 1921 v E; 1922 v E, W (3)
Dougan, A. D. (Portsmouth), 1958 v Cz; (with Blackburn R), 1960 v S; 1961 v E, W, I, Gr; (with Aston Villa), 1963 v S, Pol (2); (with Leicester C), 1966 v S, E, Alb, W, WG, M; 1967 v E, S; (with Wolverhampton W), W; 1968 v S, W; 1969 v Is, T (2), E, S, W; 1970 v USSR (2), S, E; 1971 v Sp, Cy (2), E, S, W; 1972 v USSR (2), S, E, W; 1973 v Bul, Cy (43)
Douglas, J. P. (Belfast C), 1947 v E (1)
Dowd, H. O. (Glenavon), 1974 v W; (with Sheffield W), 1975 v N (sub), Se (3)
Dowie, I. (Luton T), 1990 v N (sub), U; 1991 v Y, D, A (sub), (with West Ham U), Y, Fa; (with Southampton), 1992 v Fa, A, D (sub), S (sub), Li; 1993 v Alb (2), Ei, Sp (sub), Li, La; 1994 v La, D, Ei (sub), R (sub), Lie, Co, M (sub); 1995 v A, Ei; (with C Palace), Ei, La, Ca, Ch, La; 1996 v P; (with West Ham U), A, N, G; 1997 v Uk, Arm, G, Alb, P, Uk, Arm, Th; 1998 v Alb, P; (with QPR), Slo, Sw, Sp; 1999 v T, Fi, Mol, G, Mol, Ca, Ei; 2000 v F, T, G (59)
Duff, M. J. (Cheltenham T), 2002 v Pol (sub); 2003 v Cy (sub); 2004 v Es (sub); (with Burnley), 2005 v Sw (sub); 2006 v E (sub), W, A, Es, U, R; 2007 v Fi (sub), Ic (sub), Sp, D, W, Lie, Se (17)
Duggan, H. A. (Leeds U), 1930 v E; 1931 v E, W; 1933 v E; 1934 v E; 1935 v S, W; 1936 v S (8)
Dunlop, G. (Linfield), 1985 v Is; 1987 v E, Y; 1990 v Ei (4)
Dunne, J. (Sheffield U), 1928 v W; 1931 v W, E; 1932 v E, S; 1933 v E, W (7)

Eames, W. L. E. (Dublin U), 1885 v E, S, W (3)
Eglington, T. J. (Everton), 1947 v S, W; 1948 v E, S, W; 1949 v E (6)
Elder, A. R. (Burnley), 1960 v W; 1961 v S, E, W, WG (2), Gr; 1962 v E, S, Gr; 1963 v E, S, W, Pol (2), Sp; 1964 v W, U; 1965 v E, S, W, Sw (2), Ho (2), Alb; 1966 v E, S, W, M, Alb; 1967 v E, S, W; (with Stoke C), 1968 v E, W; 1969 v E (sub), S, W; 1970 v USSR (40)
Elleman, A. R. (Cliftonville), 1889 v W; 1890 v E (2)
Elliott, S. (Motherwell), 2001 v Ma, D, Ic, N (sub), CzR, Bul (2), CzR; 2002 v D (sub), Ma, Pol (sub), Lie (sub), Sp; (with Hull C), 2003 v Fi (sub), Arm (sub), I (sub); 2004 v Gr, Bar (sub), Stk, Tr; 2005 v Sw, Pol, Az, A (sub), E, Pol (sub), G; 2006 v Ma, Az, E, W, A (sub), P, Es (sub); 2007 v Fi, Ic (36)
Elwood, J. H. (Bradford), 1929 v W; 1930 v E (2)
Emerson, W. (Glentoran), 1920 v E, S, W; 1921 v E; 1922 v E, S; (with Burnley), 1922 v W; 1923 v E, S, W; 1924 v E (11)
English, S. (Rangers), 1933 v W, S (2)
Enright, J. (Leeds C), 1912 v S (1)
Evans, J. G. (Manchester U), 2007 v Sp, D, La, Lie, Se (5)

Falloon, E. (Aberdeen), 1931 v S; 1933 v S (2)
Farquharson, T. G. (Cardiff C), 1923 v S, W; 1924 v E, S, W; 1925 v E, S (7)
Farrell, P. (Distillery), 1901 v S, W (2)
Farrell, P. (Hibernian), 1938 v W (1)
Farrell, P. D. (Everton), 1947 v S, W; 1948 v E, S, W; 1949 v E, W (7)
Feeney, J. M. (Linfield), 1947 v S; (with Swansea T), 1950 v E (2)
Feeney, W. (Glentoran), 1976 v Is (1)
Feeney, W. J. (Bournemouth), 2002 v Lie, Sp; 2003 v Cy (sub); (with Luton T), 2005 v Pol (sub), G (sub); 2006 v Ma (sub), Az (sub), E (sub), A (sub), P, Es (sub); 2007 v Fi (sub), Ic (sub), Sp (sub), D (sub), La (sub), Lie (sub), Se (18)
Ferguson, G. (Linfield), 1999 v Ca (sub); 2001 v N, CzR (sub), Bul (sub), CzR (sub) (5)
Ferguson, W. (Linfield), 1966 v M; 1967 v E (2)
Ferris, J. (Belfast C), 1920 v E, W; (with Chelsea), 1921 v S, E; (with Belfast C), 1928 v F, S (6)
Ferris, R. O. (Birmingham C), 1950 v S; 1951 v F; 1952 v S (3)
Fettis, A. W. (Hull C), 1992 v D, Li; 1993 v D; 1994 v M; 1995 v P, Ei, La, Ca, Ch, La; 1996 v P, Lie, A; (with Nottingham F), v N, G; 1997 v Uk, Arm (2); (with Blackburn R), 1998 v P, Slo, Sw, Sp; 1999 v T, Fi, Mol (25)
Finney, T. (Sunderland), 1975 v N, E (sub), S, W; 1976 v N, Y, S; (with Cambridge U), 1980 v E, Is, S, E, W, Aus (2) (14)
Fitzpatrick, J. C. (Bohemians), 1896 v E, S (2)
Flack, H. (Burnley), 1929 v S (1)
Fleming, J. G. (Nottingham F), 1987 v E (2), Is, Y; 1988 v T, Gr, Pol; 1989 v Ma, Ch; (with Manchester C), 1990 v H, Ei; (with Barnsley), 1991 v Y; 1992 v Li (sub), G; 1993 v Alb, Sp, D, Alb, Sp, Li, La; 1994 v La, D, Ei, R, Lie, Co, M; 1995 v P, A, Ei (31)
Forbes, G. (Limavady), 1888 v W; (with Distillery), 1891 v E, S (3)
Forde, J. T. (Ards), 1959 v Sp; 1961 v E, S, WG (4)
Foreman, T. A. (Cliftonville), 1899 v S (1)
Forsythe, J. (YMCA), 1888 v E, S (2)
Fox, W. T. (Ulster), 1887 v E, S (2)
Frame, T. (Linfield), 1925 v S.Af (1)
Fulton, R. P. (Larne), 1928 v F; (Belfast C), 1930 v W; 1931 v E, S, W; 1932 v W, E; 1933 v E, S; 1934 v E, W, S; 1935 v E, W, S; 1936 v S, W; 1937 v E, S, W; 1938 v W (21)

Gaffikin, G. (Linfield Ath), 1890 v S, W; 1891 v S, W; 1892 v E, S, W; 1893 v E, S, W; 1894 v E, S, W; 1895 v E, W (15)
Galbraith, W. (Distillery), 1890 v W (1)
Gallagher, P. (Celtic), 1920 v E, S; 1922 v S; 1923 v S, W; 1924 v S, W; 1925 v S, W, E; (with Falkirk), 1927 v S (11)
Gallogly, C. (Huddersfield T), 1951 v E, S (2)
Gara, A. (Preston NE), 1902 v E, S, W (3)
Gardiner, A. (Cliftonville), 1930 v S, W; 1931 v S; 1932 v E, S (5)
Garrett, J. (Distillery), 1925 v W (1)
Gaston, R. (Oxford U), 1969 v Is (sub) (1)
Gaukrodger, G. (Linfield), 1895 v W (1)
Gaussen, A. D. (Moyola Park), 1884 v E, S; (with Magherafelt), 1888 v E, W; 1889 v E, W (6)
Geary, J. (Glentoran), 1931 v S; 1932 v S (2)
Gibb, J. T. (Wellington Park) 1884 v S, W; 1885 v S, E, W; 1886 v S; 1887 v S, E, W; (with Cliftonville), 1889 v S (10)
Gibb, T. J. (Cliftonville), 1936 v W (1)
Gibson W. K. (Cliftonville), 1894 v S, W, E; 1895 v S; 1897 v W; 1898 v S, W, E; 1901 v S, W, E; 1902 v S, W; 1903 v S (14)
Gillespie, K. R. (Manchester U), 1995 v P, A, Ei; (with Newcastle U), Ei, La, Ca, Ch (sub), La (sub); 1996 v P, A, N, G; 1997 v Uk, Arm, Bel, P, Uk; 1998 v G, Alb, Slo, Sw; 1999 v T, Fi, Mol; (with Blackburn R), G, Mol; 2000 v F (sub), T (sub), G (sub), L, Ma, H; 2001 v Y (sub), CzR, Bul (2); 2002 v D, Ic, Pol, Lie, Sp; 2003 v Cy, Sp, Uk, Fi, Arm, Gr; (with Leicester C), 2004 v Uk, Arm, Gr, N, Ser, Bar, Stk (sub), Tr (sub); 2005 v Sw, Az (sub), A, Ca, E, Pol, G; (with Sheffield U), 2006 v Ma, Az, E, W, A, P; 2007 v Fi, Ic, Sp, D, La, W, Lie (75)
Gillespie, S. (Hertford), 1886 v E, S, W; 1887 v E, S, W (6)
Gillespie, W. (Sheffield U), 1913 v E, S; 1914 v E, W; 1920 v S, W; 1921 v E; 1922 v E, S, W; 1923 v E, S, W;

1924 v E, S, W; 1925 v E, S; 1926 v S, W; 1927 v E, W; 1928 v E; 1929 v E; 1931 v E (25)
Gillespie, W. (West Down), 1889 v W (1)
Goodall, A. L. (Derby Co), 1899 v S, W; 1900 v E, W; 1901 v E; 1902 v S; 1903 v E, W; (with Glossop), 1904 v E, W (10)
Goodbody, M. F. (Dublin University), 1889 v E; 1891 v W (2)
Gordon, H. (Linfield), 1895 v E; 1896 v E, S (3)
Gordon R. W. (Linfield), 1891 v S; 1892 v W, E, S; 1893 v E, S, W (7)
Gordon, T. (Linfield), 1894 v W; 1895 v E (2)
Gorman, W. C. (Brentford), 1947 v E, S, W; 1948 v W (4)
Gough, J. (Queen's Island), 1925 v S.Af (1)
Gowdy, J. (Glentoran), 1920 v E; (with Queen's Island), 1924 v W; (with Falkirk), 1926 v E, S; 1927 v E, S (6)
Gowdy, W. A. (Hull C), 1932 v S; (with Sheffield W), 1933 v S; (with Linfield), 1935 v E, S, W; (with Hibernian), 1936 v W (6)
Graham, W. G. L. (Doncaster R), 1951 v W, F; 1952 v E, S, W; 1953 v S, F; 1954 v E, W; 1955 v S, W; 1956 v E, S; 1959 v E (14)
Gray, P. (Luton T), 1993 v D (sub), Alb, Ei, Sp; (with Sunderland), 1994 v La, D, Ei, R, Lie (sub); 1995 v P, A, Ei, Ca, Ch (sub); 1996 v P (sub), Lie, A; (with Nancy), 1997 v Uk, Arm, G (sub); (with Luton T), 1999 v Mol (sub); (with Burnley), 2001 v Ma (sub), D (sub), Ic (sub); (with Oxford U), N (sub), CzR (sub) (26)
Greer, W. (QPR), 1909 v E, S, W (3)
Gregg, H. (Doncaster R), 1954 v W; 1957 v E, S, W, I, P (2); 1958 v E, I; (with Manchester U), 1958 v Cz, Arg, WG, F, W; 1959 v E, W; 1960 v S, E, W; 1961 v E, S; 1962 v S, Gr; 1964 v S, E (25)
Griffin, D. J. (St Johnstone), 1996 v G; 1997 v Uk, I, Bel (sub), Th; 1998 v G (sub), Alb; 1999 v Mol, Ei (sub); 2000 v L, Ma, H; (with Dundee U), 2001 v Y (sub), N (sub), CzR, Bul (2), CzR; 2002 v D, Ic, Ma, Pol; 2003 v Cy, I, Sp; 2004 v Uk, Arm, Gr; (with Stockport Co), N (29)

Hall, G. (Distillery), 1897 v E (1)
Halligan, W. (Derby Co), 1911 v W; (with Wolverhampton W), 1912 v E (2)
Hamill, M. (Manchester U), 1912 v E; 1914 v E, S; (with Belfast C), 1920 v E, S, W; (with Manchester C), 1921 v S (7)
Hamill, R. (Glentoran), 1999 v Ca (sub) (1)
Hamilton, B. (Linfield), 1969 v T; 1971 v Cy (2), E, S, W; (with Ipswich T), 1972 v USSR (1+1 sub), Sp; 1973 v Bul, Cy (2), P, E, S, W; 1974 v Bul, S, E, W; 1975 v N, Se, Y, E; 1976 v Se, N, Y; (with Everton), Is, S, E, W; 1977 v Ho, Bel, WG, E, S, W, Ic; (with Millwall), 1978 v S, E, W; 1979 v Ei (sub); (with Swindon T), Bul (2), E, S, W, D; 1980 v Aus (2 sub) (50)
Hamilton, G. (Portadown), 2003 v I (sub); 2004 v Ser (sub), Bar (sub), Stk; 2005 v Sw (sub) (5)
Hamilton, J. (Knock), 1882 v E, W (2)
Hamilton, R. (Rangers), 1928 v S; 1929 v E; 1930 v S, E; 1932 v S (5)
Hamilton, W. D. (Dublin Association), 1885 v W (1)
Hamilton, W. J. (Distillery), 1908 v W (1)
Hamilton, W. J. (Dublin Association), 1885 v W (1)
Hamilton, W. R. (QPR), 1978 v S (sub); (with Burnley), 1980 v S, E, W, Aus (2); 1981 v Se, P, S, P, S, Se; 1982 v S, Is, E, W, Y, Hon, Sp, A, F; 1983 v A, WG, Alb (2), S, E, W; 1984 v A, T, WG, S, E, W, Fi; (with Oxford U), 1985 v R, Sp; 1986 v Mor (sub), Alg, Sp (sub), Br (sub) (41)
Hampton, H. (Bradford C), 1911 v E, S, W; 1912 v E, W; 1913 v E, S, W; 1914 v E (9)
Hanna, J. (Nottingham F), 1912 v S, W (2)
Hanna, J. D. (Royal Artillery, Portsmouth), 1899 v W (1)
Hannon, D. J. (Bohemians), 1908 v E, S; 1911 v E, S; 1912 v W; 1913 v E (6)
Harkin, J. T. (Southport), 1968 v W; 1969 v T; (with Shrewsbury T), W (sub); 1970 v USSR; 1971 v Sp (5)
Harland, A. I. (Linfield), 1922 v N; 1923 v E (2)
Harris, J. (Cliftonville), 1921 v W; (with Glenavon), 1925 v S.Af (2)
Harris, V. (Shelbourne), 1906 v E; 1907 v E, W; 1908 v E, W, S; (with Everton), 1909 v E, W, S; 1910 v E, S, W; 1911 v E, S, W; 1912 v E; 1913 v E, S; 1914 v S, W (20)
Harvey, M. (Sunderland), 1961 v I; 1962 v Ho; 1963 v W, Sp; 1964 v S, E, W, U, Sp; 1965 v E, S, W, Sw (2), Ho (2), Alb; 1966 v S, E, W, M, Alb, WG; 1967 v E, S; 1968 v E, W; 1969 v Is, T (2), E; 1970 v USSR; 1971 v Cy, W (sub) (34)
Hastings, J. (Knock), 1882 v E, W; (with Ulster), 1883 v W; 1884 v E, S; 1886 v E, S (7)
Hatton, S. (Linfield), 1963 v S, Pol (2)
Hayes, W. E. (Huddersfield T), 1938 v E, S; 1939 v E, S (4)
Healy, D. J. (Manchester U), 2000 v L, Ma, H; 2001 v Y, Ma, D, Ic; (with Preston NE), N, CzR, Bul (2), CzR; 2002 v D, Ic, Ma, Pol, Lie, Sp; 2003 v Cy, Sp (sub), Uk, Fi, Arm, Gr, I, Sp; 2004 v Uk, Arm, Gr, N, Es, Ser, Bar, Stk (sub), Tr; 2005 v Sw, Pol, W, A; (with Leeds U), Ca, E, Pol, G; 2006 v Ma, Az, E, W, A, Es; 2007 v Fi, Ic, Sp, D, La, Lie, Se (56)
Healy, P. J. (Coleraine), 1982 v S, W, Hon (sub); (with Glentoran), 1983 v A (sub) (4)
Hegan, D. (WBA), 1970 v USSR; (with Wolverhampton W), 1972 v USSR, E, S, W; 1973 v Bul, Cy (7)
Henderson, J. (Ulster), 1885 v E, S, W (3)
Hewison, G. (Moyola Park), 1885 v E, S (2)
Hill, C. F. (Sheffield U), 1990 v N, U; 1991 v Pol, Y; 1992 v A, D; (with Leicester C), 1995 v Ei, La; 1996 v P, Lie, A, N, Se, G; 1997 v Uk, Arm, G, Alb, P, Uk, Arm, Th; (with Trelleborg), 1998 v G, Alb, P; (with Northampton T), Slo; 1999 v T (27)
Hill, M. J. (Norwich C), 1959 v W; 1960 v W; 1961 v WG; 1962 v S; (with Everton), 1964 v S, E, Sp (7)
Hinton, E. (Fulham), 1947 v S, W; 1948 v S, E, W; (with Millwall), 1951 v W, F (7)
Holmes, S. P. (Wrexham), 2002 v Lie (sub) (1)
Hopkins, J. (Brighton), 1926 v E (1)
Horlock, K. (Swindon T), 1995 v La, Ca; 1997 v G, Alb, I; (with Manchester C), v Bel, Uk, Arm, Th; 1998 v G, Alb, P; 1999 v T, Fi, G, Mol, Ca; 2000 v F, T, G, Ma (sub); 2001 v Y, Ma, D, Ic; 2002 v D, Ic, Ma, Sp; 2003 v Cy, Sp, Uk (32)
Houston, J. (Linfield), 1912 v S, W; 1913 v W; (with Everton), 1913 v E, S; 1914 v S (6)
Houston, W. (Linfield), 1933 v W (1)
Houston, W. J. (Moyola Park), 1885 v E, S (2)
Hughes, A. W. (Newcastle U), 1998 v Slo, Sw, Sp; 1999 v T, Fi, Mol (sub), Ca, Ei; 2000 v F, T, L, H; 2001 v Y, Ma, D, Ic, N, CzR, Bul, CzR; 2002 v D, Ic, Pol, Sp; 2003 v Sp, Uk, Fi, Arm, Gr, I, Sp; 2004 v Uk, Arm, Gr, N; 2005 v Sw, Pol, W, Az, A, Ca, E, Pol; (with Aston Villa), 2006 v Ma, Az, E; 2007 v Fi, Ic, Sp, D, La, W, Lie, Se (54)
Hughes, J. (Lincoln C), 2006 v U, R (sub) (2)
Hughes, M.A. (Oldham Ath), 2006 v U (sub), R (sub) (2)
Hughes, M. E. (Manchester C), 1992 v D, S, Li, G; (with Strasbourg), 1993 v Alb, Sp, D, Ei, Sp, Li, La; 1994 v La, D, Ei, R, Lie, Co, M; 1995 v P, A, Ei (2) La, Ca, Ch, La; 1996 v P, Lie, A, N, G; (with West Ham U), 1997 v Uk, Arm, G, Alb, I, Uk; 1998 v G; (with Wimbledon), P, Slo, Sw, Sp; 1999 v T, Fi, Mol, G, Mol; 2000 v F, T, G, Fi, L (sub), Ma, H; 2001 v CzR, Bul (2), CzR; 2002 v D, Ic, Ma, Pol, Lie (sub); 2003 v Sp (sub), Uk; (with C Palace), 2004 v Uk, Gr, N, Ser (sub); 2005 v Pol, W (71)
Hughes, P. A. (Bury), 1987 v E, T, Is (3)
Hughes, W. (Bolton W), 1951 v W (1)
Humphries, W. M. (Ards), 1962 v W; (with Coventry C), 1962 v Ho; 1963 v E, S, W, Pol, Sp; 1964 v S, E, Sp; 1965 v S, Ho; (with Swansea T), 1965 v W, Alb (14)
Hunter, A. (Distillery), 1905 v W; 1906 v W, E, S; (with Belfast C), 1908 v W; 1909 v W, E, S (8)
Hunter, A. (Blackburn R), 1970 v USSR; 1971 v Cy (2), E, S, W; (with Ipswich T), 1972 v USSR (2), Sp, E, S, W; 1973 v Bul, Cy (2), P, E, S, W; 1974 v Bul, S, E, W; 1975 v N, Se, Y, E, S, W; 1976 v Se, N, Y, Is, S, E, W; 1977 v Ho, Bel, WG, E, S, W, Ic; 1978 v Ic, Ho, Bel; 1979 v Ei, D, S, W, D; 1980 v E, Ei (53)
Hunter, B. V. (Wrexham), 1995 v La; 1996 v P, Lie, A, Se, G; (with Reading), 1997 v Arm, G, Alb, I, Bel; 1999 v Ca, Ei; 2000 v F, T (15)
Hunter, R. J. (Cliftonville), 1884 v E, S, W (3)
Hunter, V. (Coleraine), 1962 v E; 1964 v Sp (2)

Ingham, M. G. (Sunderland), 2005 v G (sub); (with Wrexham), 2006 v U; 2007 v W (sub) (3)
Irvine, R. J. (Linfield), 1962 v Ho; 1963 v E, S, W, Pol (2), Sp; (with Stoke C), 1965 v W (8)
Irvine, R. W. (Everton), 1922 v S; 1923 v E, W; 1924 v E, S; 1925 v E; 1926 v E; 1927 v E, W; 1928 v E, S; (with Portsmouth), 1929 v E; 1930 v S; (with Connah's Quay), 1931 v E; (with Derry C), 1932 v W (15)

Irvine, W. J. (Burnley), 1963 v W, Sp; 1965 v S, W, Sw, Ho (2), Alb; 1966 v S, E, W, M, Alb; 1967 v E, S; 1968 v E, W; (with Preston NE), 1969 v Is, T, E; (with Brighton & HA), 1972 v E, S, W (23)
Irving, S. J. (Dundee), 1923 v S, W; 1924 v S, E, W; 1925 v S, E, W; 1926 v S, W; (with Cardiff C), 1927 v S, E, W; 1928 v S, E, W; (with Chelsea), 1929 v E; 1931 v W (18)

Jackson, T. A. (Everton), 1969 v Is, E, S, W; 1970 v USSR (1+1 sub); (with Nottingham F), 1971 v Sp; 1972 v E, S, W; 1973 v Cy, E, S, W; 1974 v Bul, P, S (sub), E (sub), W (sub); 1975 v N (sub), Se, Y, E, S, W; (with Manchester U); 1976 v Se, N, Y; 1977 v Ho, Bel, WG, E, S, W, Ic (35)
Jamison, J. (Glentoran), 1976 v N (1)
Jenkins, I. (Chester C), 1997 v Arm, Th; 1998 v Slo; (with Dundee U), Sw, Sp; 2000 v Fi (6)
Jennings, P. A. (Watford), 1964 v W, U; (with Tottenham H), 1965 v E, S, Sw (2), Ho, Alb; 1966 v S, E, W, Alb, WG; 1967 v E, S; 1968 v S, E, W; 1969 v Is, T (2), E, S, W; 1970 v S, E, USSR (2); 1971 v Cy (2), E, S, W; 1972 v USSR, Sp, S, E, W; 1973 v Bul, Cy, P, E, S, W; 1974 v P, S, E, W; 1975 v N, Se, Y, E, S, W; 1976 v Se, N, Y, Is, S, E, W; 1977 v Ho, Bel, WG, E, S, W, Ic; (with Arsenal), 1978 v Ic, Ho, Bel; 1979 v Ei, D, Bul, E, Bul, E, S, W, D; 1980 v E, Ei, Is; 1981 v S, P, S, Se; 1982 v S, Is, E, W, Y, Hon, Sp, F; 1983 v Alb, S, E, W; 1984 v A, T, WG, S, W, Fi; 1985 v R, Fi, E, Sp, T; (with Tottenham H), 1986 v T, R, E, F, D, Mor, Alg, Sp, Br (119)
Johnson, D. M. (Blackburn R), 1999 v Ei (sub); 2000 v Fi (sub), L, Ma (sub), H (sub); 2001 v Y, Ma, Ic, N (sub), Bul (sub+1), CzR; 2002 v Ma, Pol; (with Birmingham C), Lie, Sp; 2003 v Cy, Sp, Uk, Fi, Arm, Gr, I, Sp; 2004 v Uk, Arm, N, Bar, Stk (sub), Tr; 2005 v Sw, Pol, W, Az, A, E, G; 2006 v Ma, Az, E, W, A; 2007 v D (sub), La, Lie, Se (46)
Johnston, H. (Portadown), 1927 v W (1)
Johnston, R. S. (Distillery), 1882 v E, W; 1884 v E; 1886 v E, S (5)
Johnston, R. S. (Distillery), 1905 v W (1)
Johnston, S. (Linfield), 1890 v W; 1893 v S, W; 1894 v E (4)
Johnston, W. (Oldpark), 1885 v S, W (2)
Johnston, W. C. (Glenavon), 1962 v W; (with Oldham Ath), 1966 v M (sub) (2)
Jones, J. (Linfield), 1930 v S, W; 1931 v S, W, E; 1932 v S, E; 1933 v S, E, W; 1934 v S, E, W; 1935 v S, E, W; 1936 v E, S; (with Hibernian), 1936 v W; 1937 v E, W, S; (with Glenavon), 1938 v E (23)
Jones, J. (Glenavon), 1956 v W; 1957 v E, W (3)
Jones, S. (Distillery), 1934 v E; (with Blackpool), 1934 v W (2)
Jones, S. G. (Crewe Alex), 2003 v I (sub), Sp; 2004 v Uk (sub), Arm (sub), Gr (sub), N (sub), Es, Ser (sub), Bar (sub), Stk (sub), Tr (sub); 2005 v Pol (sub), A (sub), Ca (sub), E (sub), G; 2006 v Ma (sub), Az (sub), W (sub), A (sub), P, Es (sub), U, R (sub); (with Burnley), 2007 v Fi (sub), D (sub), Lie (sub) (27)
Jordan, T. (Linfield), 1895 v E, W (2)

Kavanagh, P. J. (Celtic), 1930 v E (1)
Keane, T. R. (Swansea T), 1949 v S (1)
Kearns, A. (Distillery), 1900 v E, S, W; 1902 v E, S, W (6)
Kee, P. V. (Oxford U), 1990 v N; 1991 v Y (2), D, A, Pol, Fa; (with Ards), 1995 v A, Ei (9)
Keith, R. M. (Newcastle U), 1958 v E, W, Cz (2), Arg, I, WG, F; 1959 v E, S, W, Sp; 1960 v S, E; 1961 v S, E, W, I, WG (2), Gr; 1962 v W, Ho (23)
Kelly, H. R. (Fulham), 1950 v E, W; (with Southampton), 1951 v E, S (4)
Kelly, J. (Glentoran), 1896 v E (1)
Kelly, J. (Derry C), 1932 v E, W; 1933 v E, W, S; 1934 v W; 1936 v E, S, W; 1937 v S, E (11)
Kelly, P. J. (Manchester C), 1921 v E (1)
Kelly, P. M. (Barnsley), 1950 v S (1)
Kennedy, A. L. (Arsenal), 1923 v W; 1925 v E (2)
Kennedy, P. H. (Watford), 1999 v Mol, G (sub); 2000 v F, T, G, Fi; 2001 v N, Bul (sub), CzR (sub); (with Wigan Ath), 2002 v D, Ic, Ma, Pol; 2003 v Cy, Fi, I, Sp; 2004 v Uk, Gr, N (20)
Kernaghan, N. (Belfast C), 1936 v W; 1937 v S; 1938 v E (3)
Kirk, A. R. (Hearts), 2000 v H; 2001 v N (sub); 2003 v Uk (sub), Fi (sub), Gr (sub); (with Boston U), 2005 v Ca (sub); (with Northampton T), E (sub), G (sub) (8)
Kirkwood, H. (Cliftonville), 1904 v W (1)
Kirwan, J. (Tottenham H), 1900 v W; 1902 v E, W; 1903 v E, S, W; 1904 v E, S, W; 1905 v E, S, W; (with Chelsea), 1906 v E, S, W; 1907 v W; (with Clyde), 1909 v S (17)

Lacey, W. (Everton), 1909 v E, S, W; 1910 v E, S, W; 1911 v E, S, W; 1912 v E; (with Liverpool), 1913 v W; 1914 v E, S, W; 1920 v E, S, W; 1921 v E, S, W; 1922 v E, S; (with New Brighton), 1925 v E (23)
Lafferty, K. (Burnley), 2006 v U (sub), R (sub); 2007 v Fi (sub), Ic (sub), Sp, D, La, W, Lie, Se (sub) (10)
Lawther, R. (Glentoran), 1888 v E, S (2)
Lawther, W. I. (Sunderland), 1960 v W; 1961 v I; (with Blackburn R), 1962 v S, Ho (4)
Leatham, J. (Belfast C), 1939 v W (1)
Ledwidge, J. J. (Shelbourne), 1906 v S, W (2)
Lemon, J. (Glentoran), 1886 v W; (with Belfast YMCA), 1888 v S; 1889 v W (3)
Lennon, N. F. (Crewe Alex), 1994 v M (sub); 1995 v Ch; 1996 v P, Lie, A; (with Leicester C), v N; 1997 v Uk, Arm, G, Alb, Bel, P, Uk, Arm, Th; 1998 v G, Alb, P, Slo, Sw, Sp; 1999 v T, Fi, Mol, G, Mol, Ei; 2000 v F, T, G, Fi, Ma, H; 2001 v D, Ic; (with Celtic), N, CzR, Bul (2); 2002 v Pol (sub) (40)
Leslie, W. (YMCA), 1887 v E (1)
Lewis, J. (Glentoran), 1899 v S, E, W; (with Distillery), 1900 v S (4)
Lockhart, H. (Rossall School), 1884 v W (1)
Lockhart, N. H. (Linfield), 1947 v E; (with Coventry C), 1950 v W; 1951 v W; 1952 v W; (with Aston Villa), 1954 v S, E; 1955 v W; 1956 v W (8)
Lomas, S. M. (Manchester C), 1994 v R, Lie, Co (sub), M; 1995 v P, A; 1996 v P, Lie, A, N, Se, G; 1997 v Uk, Arm, G, Alb, I, Bel; (with West Ham U), P, Uk, Arm, Th; 1998 v Alb, P, Slo, Sw; 1999 v Mol, G, Mol, Ca; 2000 v F, T, G, L, Ma; 2001 v Ma, D, Ic; 2002 v Pol, Lie; 2003 v Sp, Uk, Fi, Arm, Gr (45)
Loyal, J. (Clarence), 1891 v S (1)
Lutton, R. J. (Wolverhampton W), 1970 v S, E; (with West Ham U), 1973 v Cy (sub), S (sub), W (sub); 1974 v P (6)
Lynas, R. (Cliftonville), 1925 v S.Af (1)
Lyner, D. R. (Glentoran), 1920 v E, W; 1922 v S, W; (with Manchester U), 1923 v E; (with Kilmarnock), 1923 v W (6)
Lytle, J. (Glentoran), 1898 W (1)

McAdams, W. J. (Manchester C), 1954 v W; 1955 v S; 1957 v E; 1958 v S, I; (with Bolton W), 1961 v E, S, W, I, WG (2), Gr; 1962 v E, Gr; (with Leeds U), Ho (15)
McAlery, J. M. (Cliftonville), 1882 v E, W (2)
McAlinden, J. (Belfast C), 1938 v S; 1939 v S; (with Portsmouth), 1947 v E; (with Southend U), 1949 v E (4)
McAllen, J. (Linfield), 1898 v E; 1899 v E, S, W; 1900 v E, S, W; 1901 v W; 1902 v S (9)
McAlpine, S. (Cliftonville), 1901 v S (1)
McArthur, A. (Distillery), 1886 v W (1)
McAuley, G. (Lincoln C), 2005 v G (sub); 2006 v P (sub), Es, U (sub), R (5)
McAuley, J. L. (Huddersfield T), 1911 v E, W; 1912 v E, S; 1913 v E, S (6)
McAuley, P. (Belfast C), 1900 v S (1)
McBride, S. D. (Glenavon), 1991 v D (sub), Pol (sub); 1992 v Fa (sub), D (4)
McCabe, J. J. (Leeds U), 1949 v S, W; 1950 v E; 1951 v W; 1953 v W; 1954 v S (6)
McCabe, W. (Ulster), 1891 v E (1)
McCambridge, J. (Ballymena), 1930 v S, W; (with Cardiff C), 1931 v W; 1932 v E (4)
McCandless, J. (Bradford), 1912 v W; 1913 v W; 1920 v W, S; 1921 v E (5)
McCandless, W. (Linfield), 1920 v E, W; 1921 v E; (with Rangers), 1921 v W; 1922 v S; 1924 v W, S; 1925 v S; 1929 v W (9)
McCann, G. S. (West Ham U), 2002 v Ma (sub), Pol (sub), Lie; 2003 v Sp (sub), Uk (sub); (with Cheltenham T), Arm, Gr; 2004 v Arm, Es (sub); 2006 v P (sub), Es (sub); 2007 v Fi; (with Barnsley), W (sub), Lie (sub), Se (15)
McCann, P. (Belfast C), 1910 v E, S, W; 1911 v E; (with Glentoran), 1911 v S; 1912 v E; 1913 v W (7)

McCarthy, J. D. (Port Vale), 1996 v Se; 1997 v I, Arm, Th; (with Birmingham C), 1998 v P (sub), Slo (sub), Sp; 1999 v Fi (sub), Mol (sub), G (sub), Ca, Ei; 2000 v F, T, G, Fi; 2001 v N, Bul (sub) (18)
McCartney, A. (Ulster), 1903 v S, W; (with Linfield), 1904 v S, W; (with Everton), 1905 v E, S; (with Belfast C), 1907 v E, S, W; 1908 v E, S, W; (with Glentoran), 1909 v E, S, W (15)
McCartney, G. (Sunderland), 2002 v Ic, Ma, Pol (sub), Lie, Sp; 2003 v Cy, Sp, Uk, Fi, Gr, I, Sp; 2004 v Uk, Arm, Gr, N; 2005 v W (sub), A, Ca, G (20)
McCashin, J. W. (Cliftonville), 1896 v W; 1898 v S, W; 1899 v S; 1903 v S (5)
McCavana, W. T. (Coleraine), 1955 v S; 1956 v E, S (3)
McCaw, J. H. (Linfield), 1927 v W; 1928 v F; 1930 v S; 1931 v E, S, W (6)
McClatchey, J. (Distillery), 1886 v E, S, W (3)
McClatchey, T. (Distillery), 1895 v S (1)
McCleary, J. W. (Cliftonville), 1955 v W (1)
McCleery, W. (Cliftonville), 1922 v N; (Linfield), 1930 v E, W; 1931 v E, S, W; 1932 v S, W; 1933 v E, W (10)
McClelland, J. (Mansfield T), 1980 v S (sub), Aus (3); 1981 v Se, S; (with Rangers), S, Se (sub); 1982 v S, W, Y, Hon, Sp, A, F; 1983 v A, WG, Alb, T, Alb, S, E, W; 1984 v A, T, WG, S, E, W, Fi; 1985 v R, Is; (with Watford), Fi, E, Sp, T; 1986 v T, F (sub); 1987 v E (2), T, Is, Y; 1988 v T, Gr, F, Ma; 1989 v Ei, H, Sp (2), Ma; (with Leeds U), 1990 v N (53)
McClelland, J. T. (Arsenal), 1961 v W, I, WG (2), Gr; (with Fulham), 1966 v M (6)
McCluggage, A. (Cliftonville), 1922 v N; (Bradford), 1924 v E; (with Burnley), 1927 v S, W; 1928 v S, E, W; 1929 v S, E, W; 1930 v W; 1931 v E, W (13)
McClure, G. (Cliftonville), 1907 v S, W; 1908 v E; (with Distillery), 1909 v E (4)
McConnell, E. (Cliftonville), 1904 v S, W; (with Glentoran), 1905 v S; (with Sunderland), 1906 v E; 1907 v E; 1908 v S, W; (with Sheffield W), 1909 v S, W; 1910 v S, W, E (12)
McConnell, P. (Doncaster R), 1928 v W; (with Southport), 1932 v E (2)
McConnell, W. G. (Bohemians), 1912 v W; 1913 v E, S; 1914 v E, S, W (6)
McConnell, W. H. (Reading), 1925 v W; 1926 v E, W; 1927 v E, S, W; 1928 v E, W (8)
McCourt, F. J. (Manchester C), 1952 v E, W; 1953 v E, S, W, F (6)
McCourt, P. J. (Rochdale), 2002 v Sp (sub) (1)
McCoy, R. K. (Coleraine), 1987 v Y (sub) (1)
McCoy, S. (Distillery), 1896 v W (1)
McCracken, E. (Barking), 1928 v F (1)
McCracken, R. (C Palace), 1921 v E; 1922 v E, S, W (4)
McCracken, R. (Linfield), 1922 v N (1)
McCracken, W. R. (Distillery), 1902 v E, W; 1903 v S, E; 1904 v E, S, W; (with Newcastle U), 1905 v E, S, W; 1907 v E; 1920 v E; 1922 v E, S, W; (with Hull C), 1923 v S (16)
McCreery, D. (Manchester U), 1976 v S (sub), E, W; 1977 v Ho, Bel, WG, E, S, W, Ic; 1978 v Ic, Ho, Bel, S, E, W; 1979 v Ei, D, Bul, E, Bul, W, D; (with QPR), 1980 v E, Ei, S (sub), E (sub), W (sub), Aus (1+1 sub); 1981 v Se (sub), P (sub); (with Tulsa R), S, P, Se; 1982 v S, Is, E (sub), F, Y, Hon, Sp, A, F; (with Newcastle U), 1983 v A; 1984 v T (sub); 1985 v R, Sp (sub); 1986 v T (sub), R, E, F, D, Alg, Sp, Br; 1987 v T, E, Y; 1988 v Y; 1989 v Sp, Ma, Ch; (with Hearts), 1990 v H, Ei, N, U (sub) (67)
McCrory, S. (Southend U), 1958 v E (1)
McCullough, K. (Belfast C), 1935 v W; 1936 v E; (with Manchester C), 1936 v S; 1937 v E, S (5)
McCullough, W. J. (Arsenal), 1961 v I; 1963 v Sp; 1964 v S, E, W, U, Sp; 1965 v E, Sw; (with Millwall), 1967 v E (10)
McCurdy, C. (Linfield), 1980 v Aus (sub) (1)
McDonald, A. (QPR), 1986 v R, E, F, D, Mor, Alg, Sp, Br; 1987 v E (2), T, Is, Y; 1988 v Y, T, Pol, F, Ma; 1989 v Ei, H, Sp, Ch; 1990 v H, Ei, U; 1991 v Y, D, A, Fa; 1992 v Fa, S, Li, G; 1993 v Alb, Sp, D, Alb, Ei, Sp, Li, La; 1994 v D, Ei; 1995 v P, A, Ei, La, Ca, Ch, La; 1996 v A (sub), N (52)
McDonald, R. (Rangers), 1930 v S; 1932 v E (2)
McDonnell, J. (Bohemians), 1911 v E, S; 1912 v W; 1913 v W (4)
McElhinney, G. M. A. (Bolton W), 1984 v WG, S, E, W, Fi; 1985 v R (6)
McEvilly, L. R. (Rochdale), 2002 v Sp (sub) (1)
McFaul, W. S. (Linfield), 1967 v E (sub); (with Newcastle U), 1970 v W; 1971 v Sp; 1972 v USSR; 1973 v Cy; 1974 v Bul (6)
McGarry, J. K. (Cliftonville), 1951 v W, F, S (3)
McGaughey, M. (Linfield), 1985 v Is (sub) (1)
McGibbon, P. C. G. (Manchester U), 1995 v Ca (sub), Ch, La; 1996 v Lie (sub); 1997 v Th; (with Wigan Ath), 1998 v Alb; 2000 v L (sub) (7)
McGrath, R. C. (Tottenham H), 1974 v S, E, W; 1975 v N; 1976 v Is (sub); (with Manchester U), 1977 v Ho, Bel, WG, E, S, W, Ic; 1978 v Ic, Ho, Bel, S, E, W; 1979 v Bul (sub), E (sub and sub) (21)
McGregor, S. (Glentoran), 1921 v S (1)
McGrillen, J. (Clyde), 1924 v S; (with Belfast C), 1927 v S (2)
McGuire, E. (Distillery), 1907 v S (1)
McGuire, J. (Linfield), 1928 v F (1)
McIlroy, H. (Cliftonville), 1906 v E (1)
McIlroy, J. (Burnley), 1952 v E, S, W; 1953 v E, S, W; 1954 v E, S, W; 1955 v E, S, W; 1956 v E, S, W; 1957 v E, S, W, I, P (2); 1958 v E, S, W, I (2), Cz (2), Arg, WG, F; 1959 v E, S, W, Sp; 1960 v E, S, W; 1961 v E, W, WG (2), Gr; 1962 v E, S, Gr, Ho; 1963 v E, S, Pol (2); (with Stoke C), 1963 v W; 1966 v S, E, Alb (55)
McIlroy, S. B. (Manchester U), 1972 v Sp, S (sub); 1974 v S, E, W; 1975 v N, Se, Y, E, S, W; 1976 v Se, N, Y, S, E, W; 1977 v Ho, Bel, E, S, W, Ic; 1978 v Ic, Ho, Bel, S, E, W; 1979 v Ei, D, Bul, E, Bul, E, S, W, D; 1980 v E, Ei, Is, S, E, W; 1981 v Se, P, S, P, S, Se; 1982 v S, Is; (with Stoke C), E, F, S, W, Y, Hon, Sp, A, F; 1983 v A, WG, Alb, T, Alb, S, E, W; 1984 v A, T, S, E, W, Fi; 1985 v Fi, E, T; (with Manchester C), 1986 v T, R, E, F, D, Mor, Alg, Sp, Br; 1987 v E (sub) (88)
McIlvenny, P. (Distillery), 1924 v W (1)
McIlvenny, R. (Distillery), 1890 v E; (with Ulster), 1891 v E (2)
McKeag, W. (Glentoran), 1968 v S, W (2)
McKeague, T. (Glentoran), 1925 v S.Af (1)
McKee, F. W. (Cliftonville), 1906 v S, W; (with Belfast C), 1914 v E, S, W (5)
McKelvey, H. (Glentoran), 1901 v W; 1903 v S (2)
McKenna, J. (Huddersfield), 1950 v E, S, W; 1951 v E, S, F; 1952 v E (7)
McKenzie, H. (Distillery), 1922 v N; 1923 v S (2)
McKenzie, R. (Airdrie), 1967 v W (1)
McKeown, N. (Linfield), 1892 v E, S, W; 1893 v S, W; 1894 v S, W (7)
McKie, H. (Cliftonville), 1895 v E, S, W (3)
Mackie, J. A. (Arsenal), 1923 v W; (with Portsmouth), 1935 v S, W (3)
McKinney, D. (Hull C), 1921 v S; (with Bradford C), 1924 v S (2)
McKinney, V. J. (Falkirk), 1966 v WG (1)
McKnight, A. D. (Celtic), 1988 v Y, T, Gr, Pol, F, Ma; (with West Ham U), 1989 v Ei, H, Sp (2) (10)
McKnight, J. (Preston NE), 1912 v S; (with Glentoran), 1913 v S (2)
McLaughlin, J. C. (Shrewsbury T), 1962 v E, S, W, Gr; 1963 v W; (with Swansea T), 1964 v W, U; 1965 v E, W, Sw (2); 1966 v W (12)
McLean, B. S. (Rangers), 2006 v Es (sub) (1)
McLean, T. (Limavady), 1885 v S (1)
McMahon, G. J. (Tottenham H), 1995 v Ca (sub), Ch, La; 1996 v Lie, N (sub), Se, G; (with Stoke C), 1997 v Arm (sub), Alb (sub), Bel, P (sub), Uk (sub), Arm (sub), Th (sub); 1998 v G (sub), Alb (sub), P (sub) (17)
McMahon, J. (Bohemians), 1934 v S (1)
McMaster, G. (Glentoran), 1897 v E, S, W (3)
McMichael, A. (Newcastle U), 1950 v E, S; 1951 v E, S, F; 1952 v E, S, W; 1953 v E, S, W, F; 1954 v E, S, W; 1955 v E, W; 1956 v W; 1957 v E, S, W, I, P (2); 1958 v E, S, W, I (2), Cz (2), Arg, WG, F; 1959 v S, W, Sp; 1960 v E, S, W (40)
McMillan, G. (Distillery), 1903 v E; 1905 v W (2)
McMillan, S. T. (Manchester U), 1963 v E, S (2)
McMillen, W. S. (Manchester U), 1934 v E; 1935 v S; 1937 v S; (with Chesterfield), 1938 v S, W; 1939 v E, S (7)
McMordie, A. S. (Middlesbrough), 1969 v Is, T (2), E, S, W; 1970 v E, S, W, USSR; 1971 v Cy (2), E, S, W; 1972 v USSR, Sp, E, S, W; 1973 v Bul (21)
McMorran, E. J. (Belfast C), 1947 v E; (with Barnsley), 1951 v E, S, W; 1952 v E, S, W; 1953 v E, S, F; (with

Doncaster R), 1953 v W; 1954 v E; 1956 v W; 1957 v I, P (15)
McMullan, D. (Liverpool), 1926 v E, W; 1927 v S (3)
McNally, B. A. (Shrewsbury T), 1986 v Mor; 1987 v T (sub); 1988 v Y, Gr, Ma (sub) (5)
McNinch, J. (Ballymena), 1931 v S; 1932 v S, W (3)
McParland, P. J. (Aston Villa), 1954 v W; 1955 v E, S; 1956 v E, S; 1957 v E, S, W, P; 1958 v E, S, W, I (2), Cz (2), Arg, WG, F; 1959 v E, S, W, Sp; 1960 v E, S, W; 1961 v E, S, W, I, WG (2), Gr; (with Wolverhampton W), 1962 v Ho (34)
McShane, J. (Cliftonville), 1899 v S; 1900 v E, S, W (4)
McVeigh, P. (Tottenham H), 1999 v Ca (sub); (with Norwich C), 2002 v Ic (sub), Pol (sub); 2003 v Sp, Uk, Fi, Arm, Gr (sub), I, Sp (sub); 2004 v Arm (sub), N (sub), Ser (sub), Bar (sub), Stk, Tr (sub); 2005 v Sw (sub), Pol (sub), W (sub), A (sub) (20)
McVicker, J. (Linfield), 1888 v E; (with Glentoran), 1889 v S (2)
McWha, W. B. R. (Knock), 1882 v E, W; (with Cliftonville), 1883 v E, W; 1884 v E; 1885 v E, W (7)
Madden, O. (Norwich C), 1938 v E (1)
Magee, G. (Wellington Park), 1885 v E, S, W (3)
Magill, E. J. (Arsenal), 1962 v E, S, Gr; 1963 v E, S, W, Pol (2), Sp; 1964 v E, S, W, U, Sp; 1965 v E, S, Sw (2), Ho, Alb; 1966 v S; (with Brighton & HA), E, Alb, W, WG, M (26)
Magilton, J. (Oxford U), 1991 v Pol, Y, Fa; 1992 v Fa, A, D, S, Li, G; 1993 v Alb, D, Alb, Ei, Li, La; 1994 v La, D, Ei; (with Southampton), R, Lie, Co, M; 1995 v P, A, Ei (2), Ca, Ch, La; 1996 v P, N, G; 1997 v Uk (sub), Arm (sub), Bel, P; 1998 v G; (with Sheffield W), P, Sp; (with Ipswich T), 2000 v L; 2001 v Y, Ma, D, Ic, N, CzR, Bul; 2002 v D, Ic, Ma, Pol, Lie (52)
Maginnis, H. (Linfield), 1900 v E, S, W; 1903 v S, W; 1904 v E, S, W (8)
Mahood, J. (Belfast C), 1926 v S; 1928 v E, S, W; 1929 v E, S, W; 1930 v W; (with Ballymena), 1934 v S (9)
Mannus, A. (Linfield), 2004 v Tr (sub) (1)
Manderson, R. (Rangers), 1920 v W, S; 1925 v S, E; 1926 v S (5)
Mansfield, J. (Dublin Freebooters), 1901 v E (1)
Martin, C. (Cliftonville), 1882 v E, W; 1883 v E (3)
Martin, C. (Bo'ness), 1925 v S (1)
Martin, C. J. (Glentoran), 1947 v S; (with Leeds U), 1948 v E, S, W; (with Aston Villa), 1949 v E; 1950 v W (6)
Martin, D. K. (Belfast C), 1934 v E, S, W; 1935 v S; (with Wolverhampton W), 1935 v E; 1936 v W; (with Nottingham F), 1937 v S; 1938 v E, S; 1939 v S (10)
Mathieson, A. (Luton T), 1921 v W; 1922 v E (2)
Maxwell, J. (Linfield), 1902 v W; 1903 v W, E; (with Glentoran), 1905 v W, S; (with Belfast C), 1906 v W; 1907 v S (7)
Meek, H. L. (Glentoran), 1925 v W (1)
Mehaffy, J. A. C. (Queen's Island), 1922 v W (1)
Meldon, P. A. (Dublin Freebooters), 1899 v S, W (2)
Mercer, H. V. A. (Linfield), 1908 v E (1)
Mercer, J. T. (Distillery), 1898 v E, S, W; 1899 v E; (with Linfield), 1902 v E, W; (with Distillery), 1903 v S (2), W; (with Derby Co), 1904 v E, W; 1905 v S (12)
Millar, W. (Barrow), 1932 v W; 1933 v S (2)
Miller, J. (Middlesbrough), 1929 v W, S; 1930 v E (3)
Milligan, D. (Chesterfield), 1939 v W (1)
Milne, R. G. (Linfield), 1894 v E, S, W; 1895 v E, W; 1896 v E, S, W; 1897 v E, S; 1898 v E, S, W; 1899 v E, W; 1901 v W; 1902 v E, S, W; 1903 v E, S (2); 1904 v E, S, W; 1906 v E, S, W (28)
Mitchell, E. J. (Cliftonville), 1933 v S; (with Glentoran), 1934 v W (2)
Mitchell, W. (Distillery), 1932 v E, W; 1933 v E, W; (with Chelsea), 1934 v W, S; 1935 v S, E; 1936 v S, E; 1937 v E, S, W; 1938 v E, S (15)
Molyneux, T. B. (Ligoniel), 1883 v E, W; (with Cliftonville), 1884 v E, W, S; 1885 v E, W; 1886 v E, W, S; 1888 v S (11)
Montgomery, F. J. (Coleraine), 1955 v E (1)
Moore, C. (Glentoran), 1949 v W (1)
Moore, P. (Aberdeen), 1933 v E (1)
Moore, R. (Linfield Ath), 1891 v E, S, W (3)
Moore, R. L. (Ulster), 1887 v S, W (2)
Moore, W. (Falkirk), 1923 v S (1)
Moorhead, F. W. (Dublin University), 1885 v E (1)
Moorhead, G. (Linfield), 1923 v S; 1928 v F, S; 1929 v S (4)
Moran, J. (Leeds C), 1912 v S (1)
Moreland, V. (Derby Co), 1979 v Bul (2 sub), E, S; 1980 v E, Ei (6)
Morgan, G. F. (Linfield), 1922 v N; 1923 v E; (with Nottingham F), 1924 v S; 1927 v E; 1928 v E, S, W; 1929 v E (8)
Morgan, S. (Port Vale), 1972 v Sp; 1973 v Bul (sub), P, Cy, E, S, W; (with Aston Villa), 1974 v Bul, P, S, E; 1975 v Se; 1976 v Se (sub), N, Y; (with Brighton & HA), S, W (sub); (with Sparta Rotterdam), 1979 v D (18)
Morrison, R. (Linfield Ath), 1891 v E, W (2)
Morrison, T. (Glentoran), 1895 v E, S, W; (with Burnley), 1899 v W; 1900 v W; 1902 v E, S (7)
Morrogh, D. (Bohemians), 1896 v S (1)
Morrow, S. J. (Arsenal), 1990 v U (sub); 1991 v A (sub), Pol, Y; 1992 v Fa, S (sub), G (sub); 1993 v Sp (sub), Alb, Ei; 1994 v R, Co, M (sub); 1995 v P, Ei (2), La; 1996 v P, Se; 1997 v Uk, G, Alb, I, Bel; (with QPR), P, Uk, Arm; 1998 v G, P, Slo, Sw, Sp; 1999 v T, Fi, Mol, G, Mol; 2000 v G, Fi (39)
Morrow, W. J. (Moyola Park), 1883 v E, W; 1884 v S (3)
Muir, R. (Oldpark), 1885 v S, W (2)
Mulholland, T.S. (Belfast C), 1906 v S, E (2)
Mullan, G. (Glentoran), 1983 v S, E, W, Alb (sub) (4)
Mulligan, J. (Manchester C), 1921 v S (1)
Mulryne, P. P. (Manchester U), 1997 v Bel (sub), Arm (sub), Th; 1998 v Alb (sub), Sp (sub); 1999 v T, Fi; (with Norwich C), Ca; 2001 v Y, D (sub), Bul (sub), CzR; 2002 v D, Ic, Pol, Lie; 2003 v Sp, Uk; 2004 v Uk (sub), Arm (sub), Es, Ser, Bar, Stk (sub), Tr; 2005 v Ca (sub); (with Cardiff C), 2006 v Ma (sub) (27)
Murdock, C. J, (Preston NE), 2000 v L (sub), Ma, H (sub); 2001 v Y, Ma, D, Ic, N, CzR, Bul (2), CzR; 2002 v D, Ma; 2003 v Cy, Sp, Uk (sub); (with Hibernian), 2004 v Gr (sub), Bar (sub), Stk, Tr (sub); 2005 v Sw (sub), W, Az, A; (with Crewe Alex), Ca, E, Pol; (with Rotherham U), 2006 v Ma, W, A, P, U, R (sub) (34)
Murphy, J. (Bradford C), 1910 v E, S, W (3)
Murphy, N. (QPR), 1905 v E, S, W (3)
Murray, J. M. (Motherwell), 1910 v E, S; (with Sheffield W), W (3)

Napier, R. J. (Bolton W), 1966 v WG (1)
Neill, W. J. T. (Arsenal), 1961 v I, Gr, WG; 1962 v E, S, W, Gr; 1963 v E, W, Pol, Sp; 1964 v S, E, W, U, Sp; 1965 v E, S, W, Sw, Ho (2), Alb; 1966 v S, E, W, Alb, WG, M; 1967 v S, W; 1968 v S, E; 1969 v E, S, W, Is, T (2); 1970 v S, E, W, USSR (2); (with Hull C), 1971 v Cy, Sp; 1972 v USSR (2), Sp, S, E, W; 1973 v Bul, Cy (2), P, E, S, W (59)
Nelis, P. (Nottingham F), 1923 v E (1)
Nelson, S. (Arsenal), 1970 v W, E (sub); 1971 v Cy, Sp, E, S, W; 1972 v USSR (2), Sp, E, S, W; 1973 v Bul, Cy, P; 1974 v S, E; 1975 v Se, Y; 1976 v Se, N, Is, E; 1977 v Bel (sub), WG, W, Ic; 1978 v Ic, Ho, Bel; 1979 v Ei, D, Bul, E, Bul, E, S, W, D; 1980 v E, Ei, Is; 1981 v S, P, S, Se; (with Brighton & HA), 1982 v E, S, Sp (sub), A (51)
Nicholl, C. J. (Aston Villa), 1975 v Se, Y, E, S, W; 1976 v Se, N, Y, S, E, W; 1977 v W; (with Southampton), 1978 v Bel (sub), S, E, W; 1979 v Ei, Bul, E, Bul, E, W; 1980 v Ei, Is, S, E, W, Aus (3); 1981 v Se, P, S, P, S, Se; 1982 v S, Is, E, F, W, Y, Hon, Sp, A, F; 1983 v S (sub), E, W; (with Grimsby T), 1984 v A, T (51)
Nicholl, H. (Belfast C), 1902 v E, W; 1905 v E (3)
Nicholl, J. M. (Manchester U), 1976 v Is, W (sub); 1977 v Ho, Bel, E, S, W, Ic; 1978 v Ic, Ho, Bel, S, E, W; 1979 v Ei, D, Bul, E, Bul, E, S, W, D; 1980 v E, Ei, Is, S, E, W, Aus (3); 1981 v Se, P, S, P, S, Se; 1982 v S, Is, E; (with Toronto B), F, W, Y, Hon, Sp, A, F; (with Sunderland), 1983 v A, WG, Alb, T, Alb; (with Toronto B), S, E, W; 1984 v T; (with Rangers), WG, S, E; (with Toronto B), Fi; 1985 v R; (with WBA), Fi, E, Sp, T; 1986 v T, R, E, F, Alg, Sp, Br (73)
Nicholson, J. J. (Manchester U), 1961 v S, W; 1962 v E, W, Gr, Ho; 1963 v E, S, Pol (2); (with Huddersfield T), 1965 v W, Ho (2), Alb; 1966 v S, E, W, Alb, M; 1967 v S, W; 1968 v S, E, W; 1969 v S, E, W, T (2); 1970 v S, E, W, USSR (2); 1971 v Cy (2), E, S, W; 1972 v USSR (2) (41)
Nixon, R. (Linfield), 1914 v S (1)
Nolan, I. R. (Sheffield W), 1997 v Arm, G, Alb, P, Uk; 1998 v G, P; 2000 v G, Fi, L, Ma, H; (with Bradford C), 2001 v Y, Ma, Bul (2), CzR; (with Wigan Ath), 2002 v Sp (18)

Nolan-Whelan, J. V. (Dublin Freebooters), 1901 v E, W; 1902 v S, W; 1903 v S (5)

O'Boyle, G. (Dunfermline Ath), 1994 v Co (sub), M; (with St Johnstone), 1995 v P (sub), La (sub), Ca (sub), Ch (sub); 1996 v Se (sub), G (sub); 1997 v I (sub), Bel (sub); 1998 v Slo (sub), Sw (sub); 1999 v Fi (sub) (13)
O'Brien, M. T. (QPR), 1921 v S; (with Leicester C), 1922 v S, W; 1924 v S, W; (with Hull C), 1925 v S, E, W; 1926 v W; (with Derby Co), 1927 v W (10)
O'Connell, P. (Sheffield W), 1912 v E, S; (with Hull C), 1914 v E, S, W (5)
O'Doherty, A. (Coleraine), 1970 v E, W (sub) (2)
O'Driscoll, J. F. (Swansea T), 1949 v E, S, W (3)
O'Hagan, C. (Tottenham H), 1905 v S, W; 1906 v S, W, E; (with Aberdeen), 1907 v E, S, W; 1908 v S, W; 1909 v E (11)
O'Hagan, W. (St Mirren), 1920 v E, W (2)
O'Hehir, J. C. (Bohemians), 1910 v W (1)
O'Kane, W. J. (Nottingham F), 1970 v E, W, S (sub); 1971 v Sp, E, S, W; 1972 v USSR (2); 1973 v P, Cy; 1974 v Bul, P, S, E, W; 1975 v N, Se, E, S (20)
O'Mahoney, M. T. (Bristol R), 1939 v S (1)
O'Neill, C. (Motherwell), 1989 v Ch (sub); 1990 v Ei (sub); 1991 v D (3)
O'Neill, J. (Sunderland), 1962 v W (1)
O'Neill, J. P. (Leicester C), 1980 v Is, S, E, W, Aus (3); 1981 v P, S, P, S, Se; 1982 v S, Is, E, F, S, F (sub); 1983 v A, WG, Alb, T, Alb, S; 1984 v S (sub); 1985 v Is, Fi, E, Sp, T; 1986 v T, R, E, F, D, Mor, Alg, Sp, Br (39)
O'Neill, M. A. M. (Newcastle U), 1988 v Gr, Pol, F, Ma; 1989 v Ei, H, Sp (sub), Sp (sub), Ma (sub), Ch; (with Dundee U), 1990 v H (sub), Ei; 1991 v Pol; 1992 v Fa (sub), S (sub), G (sub); 1993 v Alb (sub + 1), Ei, Sp, Li, La; (with Hibernian), 1994 v Lie (sub); 1995 v A (sub), Ei; 1996 v Lie, A, N, Se; (with Coventry C), 1997 v Uk (sub), Arm (sub) (31)
O'Neill, M. H. M. (Distillery), 1972 v USSR (sub), (with Nottingham F), Sp (sub), W (sub); 1973 v P, Cy, E, S, W; 1974 v Bul, P, E (sub), W; 1975 v Se, Y, E, S; 1976 v Y (sub); 1977 v E (sub), S; 1978 v Ic, Ho, S, E, W; 1979 v Ei, D, Bul, E, Bul, D; 1980 v Ei, Is, Aus (3); 1981 v Se, P; (with Norwich C), P, S, Se; (with Manchester C), 1982 v S; (with Norwich C), E, F, S, Y, Hon, Sp, A, F; 1983 v A, WG, Alb, T, Alb, S, E; (with Notts Co), 1984 v A, T, WG, E, W, Fi; 1985 v R, Fi (64)
O'Reilly, H. (Dublin Freebooters), 1901 v S, W; 1904 v S (3)

Parke, J. (Linfield), 1964 v S; (with Hibernian), 1964 v E, Sp; (with Sunderland), 1965 v Sw, S, W, Ho (2), Alb; 1966 v WG; 1967 v E, S; 1968 v S, E (14)
Patterson, D. J. (C Palace), 1994 v Co (sub), M (sub); 1995 v Ei (sub+1), La, Ca, Ch (sub), La (sub); (with Luton T), 1996 v N (sub), Se; 1998 v Sw, Sp (sub); (with Dundee U), 1999 v Fi, Mol, G, Mol, Ei (17)
Peacock, R. (Celtic), 1952 v S; 1953 v F; 1954 v W; 1955 v E, S; 1956 v E, S; 1957 v W, I, P; 1958 v S, E, W, I (2), Arg, Cz (2), WG; 1959 v E, S, W; 1960 v S, E; 1961 v E, S, I, WG (2), Gr; (with Coleraine), 1962 v S (31)
Peden, J. (Linfield), 1887 v S, W; 1888 v W, E; 1889 v S, E; 1890 v W, S; 1891 v W, E; 1892 v W, E; 1893 v E, S, W; (with Distillery), 1896 v W, E, S; 1897 v W, S; 1898 v W, E, S; 1899 v W (24)
Penney, S. (Brighton & HA), 1985 v Is; 1986 v T, R, E, F, D, Mor, Alg, Sp; 1987 v E, T, Is; 1988 v Pol, F, Ma; 1989 v Ei, Sp (17)
Percy, J. C. (Belfast YMCA), 1889 v W (1)
Platt, J. A. (Middlesbrough), 1976 v Is (sub); 1978 v S, E, W; 1980 v S, E, W, Aus (3); 1981 v Se, P; 1982 v F, S, W (sub), A; 1983 v A, WG, Alb, T; (with Ballymena U), 1984 v E, W (sub); (with Coleraine), 1986 v Mor (sub) (23)
Pollock, W. (Belfast C), 1928 v F (1)
Ponsonby, J. (Distillery), 1895 v S, W; 1896 v E, S, W; 1897 v E, S, W; 1899 v E (9)
Potts, R. M. C. (Cliftonville), 1883 v E, W (2)
Priestley, T. J. M. (Coleraine), 1933 v S; (with Chelsea), 1934 v E (2)
Pyper, Jas. (Cliftonville), 1897 v S, W; 1898 v S, E, W; 1899 v S; 1900 v E (7)
Pyper, John (Cliftonville), 1897 v E, S, W; 1899 v E, W; 1900 v E, W, S; 1902 v S (9)
Pyper, M. (Linfield), 1932 v W (1)

Quinn, J. M. (Blackburn R), 1985 v Is, Fi, E, Sp, T; 1986 v T, R, E, F, D (sub), Mor (sub); 1987 v E (sub), T; (with Swindon T), 1988 v Y (sub), T, Gr, Pol, F (sub), Ma; (with Leicester C), 1989 v Ei, H (sub), Sp (sub+1); (with Bradford C), Ma, Ch; 1990 v H; (with West Ham U), N; 1991 v Y (sub); (with Bournemouth), 1992 v Li; (with Reading), 1993 v Sp, D, Alb (sub), Ei (sub), La (sub); 1994 v La, D (sub), Ei, R, Lie, Co, M; 1995 v P, A (sub), La (sub); 1996 v Lie, A (sub) (46)
Quinn, S. J. (Blackpool), 1996 v Se (sub); 1997 v Alb (sub), I, Bel, P, Uk (sub), Arm, Th (sub); 1998 v G, Alb; (with WBA), Slo, Sw; 1999 v T (sub), Fi (sub), Ei; 2000 v F (sub), T (sub), G (sub), Fi, L, Ma; 2001 v Y (sub), Bul (sub), CzR (sub); 2002 v Ma (sub); (with Willem II), 2003 v Cy, Fi, Arm, Gr; 2004 v Ser, Bar, Tr; 2005 v Pol, W, Az, A; (with Sheffield W), Pol; (with Peterborough U), 2006 v Ma, Az, E, W, A, P, Es, U, R; (with Northampton T), 2007 v Fi, Ic, Sp (sub), La (sub) (50)

Rafferty, P. (Linfield), 1980 v E (sub) (1)
Ramsey, P. C. (Leicester C), 1984 v A, WG, S; 1985 v Is, E, Sp, T; 1986 v T, Mor; 1987 v Is, E, Y (sub); 1988 v Y; 1989 v Sp (14)
Rankine, J. (Alexander), 1883 v E, W (2)
Rattray, D. (Avoniel), 1882 v E; 1883 v E, W (3)
Rea, R. (Glentoran), 1901 v E (1)
Redmond, R. (Cliftonville), 1884 v W (1)
Reid, G. H. (Cardiff C), 1923 v S (1)
Reid, J. (Ulster), 1883 v E; 1884 v W; 1887 v S; 1889 v W; 1890 v S, W (6)
Reid, S. E. (Derby Co), 1934 v E, W; 1936 v E (3)
Reid, W. (Hearts), 1931 v E (1)
Reilly, M. M. (Portsmouth), 1900 v E; 1902 v E (2)
Renneville, W. T. J. (Leyton), 1910 v S, E, W; (with Aston Villa), 1911 v W (4)
Reynolds, J. (Distillery), 1890 v E, W; (with Ulster), 1891 v E, S, W (5)
Reynolds, R. (Bohemians), 1905 v W (1)
Rice, P. J. (Arsenal), 1969 v Is; 1970 v USSR; 1971 v E, S, W; 1972 v USSR, Sp, E, S, W; 1973 v Bul, Cy, E, S, W; 1974 v Bul, P, S, E, W; 1975 v N, Y, E, S, W; 1976 v Se, N, Y, Is, S, E, W; 1977 v Ho, Bel, WG, E, S, Ic; 1978 v Ic, Ho, Bel; 1979 v Ei, D, E (2), S, W, D; 1980 v E (49)
Roberts, F. C. (Glentoran), 1931 v S (1)
Robinson, P. (Distillery), 1920 v S; (with Blackburn R), 1921 v W (2)
Robinson, S. (Bournemouth), 1997 v Th (sub); 1999 v Mol, Ei; 2000 v L (sub), H (sub); (with Luton T), 2006 v Az (sub) (6)
Rogan, A. (Celtic), 1988 v Y (sub), Gr, Pol (sub); 1989 v Ei (sub), H, Sp (2), Ma (sub), Ch; 1990 v H, N (sub), U; 1991 v Y (2), D, A; (with Sunderland), 1992 v Li (sub); (with Millwall), 1997 v G (sub) (18)
Rollo, D. (Linfield), 1912 v W; 1913 v W; 1914 v W, E; (with Blackburn R), 1920 v S, W; 1921 v E, S, W; 1922 v E; 1923 v E; 1924 v S, W; 1925 v W; 1926 v E; 1927 v E (16)
Roper, E. O. (Dublin University), 1886 v W (1)
Rosbotham, A. (Cliftonville), 1887 v E, S, W; 1888 v E, S, W; 1889 v E (7)
Ross, W. E. (Newcastle U), 1969 v Is (1)
Rowland, K. (West Ham U), 1994 v La (sub); 1995 v Ca, Ch, La; 1996 v P (sub), Lie (sub), N (sub), Se, G (sub); 1997 v Uk, Arm, I (sub); 1998 v Alb; (with QPR), 1999 v T, Fi, Mol, G, Ca, Ei (19)
Rowley, R. W. M. (Southampton), 1929 v S, W; 1930 v W, E; (with Tottenham H), 1931 v W; 1932 v S (6)
Rushe, F. (Distillery), 1925 v S.Af (1)
Russell, A. (Linfield), 1947 v E (1)
Russell, S. R. (Bradford C), 1930 v E, S; (with Derry C), 1932 v E (3)
Ryan, R. A. (WBA), 1950 v W (1)

Sanchez, L. P. (Wimbledon), 1987 v T (sub); 1989 v Sp, Ma (3)
Scott, E. (Liverpool), 1920 v S; 1921 v E, S, W; 1922 v E; 1925 v W; 1926 v E, S, W; 1927 v E, S, W; 1928 v E, S, W; 1929 v E, S, W; 1930 v E; 1931 v E; 1932 v W; 1933 v E, S, W; 1934 v E, S, W; (with Belfast C), 1935 v S; 1936 v E, S, W (31)
Scott, J. (Grimsby), 1958 v Cz, F (2)
Scott, J. E. (Cliftonville), 1901 v S (1)
Scott, L. J. (Dublin University), 1895 v S, W (2)

Scott, P. W. (Everton), 1975 v W; 1976 v Y; (with York C), Is, S, E (sub), W; 1978 v S, E, W; (with Aldershot), 1979 v S (sub) (10)
Scott, T. (Cliftonville), 1894 v E, S; 1895 v S, W; 1896 v S, E, W; 1897 v E, W; 1898 v E, S, W; 1900 v W (13)
Scott, W. (Linfield), 1903 v E, S, W; 1904 v E, S, W; (with Everton), 1905 v E, S; 1907 v E, S; 1908 v E, S, W; 1909 v E, S, W; 1910 v E, S; 1911 v E, S, W; 1912 v E; (with Leeds City), 1913 v E, S, W (25)
Scraggs, M. J. (Glentoran), 1921 v W; 1922 v E (2)
Seymour, H. C. (Bohemians), 1914 v W (1)
Seymour, J. (Cliftonville), 1907 v W; 1909 v W (2)
Shanks, T. (Woolwich Arsenal), 1903 v S; 1904 v W; (with Brentford), 1905 v E (3)
Sharkey, P. G. (Ipswich T), 1976 v S (1)
Sheehan, Dr G. (Bohemians), 1899 v S; 1900 v E, W (3)
Sheridan, J. (Everton), 1903 v W, E, S; 1904 v E, S; (with Stoke C), 1905 v E (6)
Sherrard, J. (Limavady), 1885 v S; 1887 v W; 1888 v W (3)
Sherrard, W. C. (Cliftonville), 1895 v E, W, S (3)
Sherry, J. J. (Bohemians), 1906 v E; 1907 v W (2)
Shields, R. J. (Southampton), 1957 v S (1)
Shiels, D. (Hibernian), 2006 v P (sub), U (sub), R; 2007 v W (sub) (4)
Silo, M. (Belfast YMCA), 1888 v E (1)
Simpson, W. J. (Rangers), 1951 v W, F; 1954 v E, S; 1955 v E; 1957 v I, P; 1958 v S, E, W, I; 1959 v S (12)
Sinclair, J. (Knock), 1882 v E, W (2)
Slemin, J. C. (Bohemians), 1909 v W (1)
Sloan, A. S. (London Caledonians), 1925 v W (1)
Sloan, D. (Oxford U), 1969 v Is; 1971 v Sp (2)
Sloan, H. A. de B. (Bohemians), 1903 v E; 1904 v S; 1905 v E; 1906 v W; 1907 v E, W; 1908 v W; 1909 v S (8)
Sloan, J. W. (Arsenal), 1947 v W (1)
Sloan, T. (Manchester U), 1979 v S, W (sub), D (sub) (3)
Sloan, T. (Cardiff C), 1926 v S, W, E; 1927 v W, S; 1928 v E, W; 1929 v E; (with Linfield), 1930 v W, S; 1931 v S (11)
Small, J. M. (Clarence), 1887 v E; (with Cliftonville), 1893 v E, S, W (4)
Smith, A. W. (Glentoran), 2003 v I, Sp; 2004 v Uk (sub), Arm, Gr (sub), N, Es, Ser (sub), Bar (sub), Stk, Tr (sub); (with Preston NE), 2005 v Sw, Pol (sub), W (sub), Az (sub), Ca (sub), Pol (sub), G (sub) (18)
Smith, E. E. (Cardiff C), 1921 v S; 1923 v W, E; 1924 v E (4)
Smith, J. E. (Distillery), 1901 v S, W (2)
Smyth, R. H. (Dublin University), 1886 v W (1)
Smyth, S. (Wolverhampton W), 1948 v E, S, W; 1949 v S, W; 1950 v E, S, W; (with Stoke C), 1952 v E (9)
Smyth, W. (Distillery), 1949 v E, S; 1954 v S, E (4)
Snape, A. (Airdrie), 1920 v E (1)
Sonner, D. J. (Ipswich T), 1998 v Alb (sub); (with Sheffield W), 1999 v G (sub), Ca (sub); 2000 v L (sub), Ma (sub), H; (with Birmingham C), 2001 v N (sub); (with Nottingham F), 2004 v Es, Ser (sub), Bar, Stk, Tr (sub); (with Peterborough U), 2005 v Sw (13)
Spence, D. W. (Bury), 1975 v Y, E, S, W; 1976 v Se, Is, E, W, S (sub); (with Blackpool), 1977 v Ho (sub), WG (sub), E (sub), S (sub), W (sub), Ic (sub); 1979 v Ei, D (sub), E (sub), Bul (sub), E (sub), S, W, D; 1980 v Ei; (with Southend U), Is (sub), Aus (sub); 1981 v S (sub), Se (sub); 1982 v F (sub) (29)
Spencer, S. (Distillery), 1890 v E, S; 1892 v E, S, W; 1893 v E (6)
Spiller, E. A. (Cliftonville), 1883 v E, W; 1884 v E, W, S (5)
Sproule, I. (Hibernian), 2006 v E (sub), P (sub), Es, U, R; 2007 v Fi (sub), W, Se (sub) (8)
Stanfield, O. M. (Distillery), 1887 v E, S, W; 1888 v E, S, W; 1889 v E, S, W; 1890 v E, S; 1891 v E, S, W; 1892 v E, S, W; 1893 v E, W; 1894 v E, S, W; 1895 v E, S; 1896 v E, S, W; 1897 v E, S, W (30)
Steele, A. (Charlton Ath), 1926 v W, S; (with Fulham), 1929 v W, S (4)
Stevenson, A. E. (Rangers), 1934 v E, S, W; (with Everton), 1935 v E, S; 1936 v S, W; 1937 v E, W; 1938 v E, W; 1939 v E, S, W; 1947 v S, W; 1948 v S (17)
Stewart, A. (Glentoran), 1967 v W; 1968 v S, E; (with Derby Co), 1968 v W; 1969 v Is, T (1+1 sub) (7)
Stewart, D. C. (Hull C), 1978 v Bel (1)
Stewart, I. (QPR), 1982 v F (sub); 1983 v A, WG, Alb, T, Alb, S, E, W; 1984 v A, T, WG, S, E, W, Fi; 1985 v R, Fi, Is, E, Sp, T; (with Newcastle U), 1986 v R, E, D, Mor, Alg (sub), Sp (sub), Br; 1987 v E, Is (sub) (31)
Stewart, R. K. (St Columb's Court), 1890 v E, S, W; (with Cliftonville), 1892 v E, S, W; 1893 v E, W; 1894 v E, S, W (11)
Stewart, T. C. (Linfield), 1961 v W (1)
Swan, S. (Linfield), 1899 v S (1)

Taggart, G. P. (Barnsley), 1990 v N, U; 1991 v Y, D, A, Pol, Fa; 1992 v Fa, A, D, S, Li, G; 1993 v Alb, Sp, D, Alb, Ei, Sp, Li, La; 1994 v La, D, Ei, R, Lie, Co, M; 1995 v P (sub), A, Ei (2), Ca, Ch, La; (with Bolton W), 1997 v G, Alb, I, Bel, P, Uk, Arm; 1998 v G, P, Sp; (with Leicester C), 2000 v H; 2001 v Ma, D, Ic, N; 2003 v Sp (51)
Taggart, J. (Walsall), 1899 v W (1)
Taylor, M. S. (Fulham), 1999 v G, Mol, Ca, Ei; 2000 v F, T, G, Fi, L (sub), Ma (sub), H; 2001 v Y, N, Bul, CzR; 2002 v D, Ic, Ma, Pol, Lie, Sp; 2003 v Cy, Sp, Uk, Fi, Arm, Gr, I, Sp; 2004 v Uk, Arm, Gr, N; (with Birmingham C), Es, Ser, Bar, Stk, Tr; 2005 v Pol, W, Az, Ca, E, Pol, G; 2006 v Ma, Az, E, W, A, P, Es; 2007 v Fi, Ic, Sp (sub), D, La, W, Lie, Se (60)
Thompson, F. W. (Cliftonville), 1910 v E, S, W; (with Linfield), 1911 v W; (with Bradford C), 1911 v E; 1912 v E, W; 1913 v E, S, W; (with Clyde), 1914 v E, S (12)
Thompson, J. (Distillery), 1897 v S (1)
Thompson, P. (Linfield), 2006 v P (sub), Es (sub), U (sub), R; 2007 v W (sub) (5)
Thompson, R. (Queen's Island), 1928 v F (1)
Thompson, W. (Belfast Ath), 1889 v S (1)
Thunder, P. J. (Bohemians), 1911 v W (1)
Todd, S. J. (Burnley), 1966 v M (sub); 1967 v E; 1968 v W; 1969 v E, S, W; 1970 v S, USSR; (with Sheffield W), 1971 v Cy (2), Sp (sub) (11)
Toner, C. (Leyton Orient), 2003 v I (sub), Sp (sub) (2)
Toner, J. (Arsenal), 1922 v W; 1923 v W; 1924 v W, E; 1925 v E, S; (with St Johnstone), 1927 v E, S (8)
Torrans, R. (Linfield), 1893 v S (1)
Torrans, S. (Linfield), 1889 v S; 1890 v S, W; 1891 v S, W; 1892 v E, S, W; 1893 v E, S; 1894 v E, S, W; 1895 v E; 1896 v E, S, W; 1897 v E, S, W; 1898 v E, S; 1899 v E, W; 1901 v S, W (26)
Trainor, D. (Crusaders), 1967 v W (1)
Tully, C. P. (Celtic), 1949 v E; 1950 v E; 1952 v S; 1953 v E, S, W, F; 1954 v S; 1956 v E; 1959 v Sp (10)
Turner, A. (Cliftonville), 1896 v W (1)
Turner, E. (Cliftonville), 1896 v E (1)
Turner, W. (Cliftonville), 1886 v E, S; 1888 v S (3)
Twomey, J. F. (Leeds U), 1938 v W; 1939 v E (2)

Uprichard, W. N. M. C. (Swindon T), 1952 v E, S, W; 1953 v E, S; (with Portsmouth), 1953 v W, F; 1955 v E, S, W; 1956 v E, S, W; 1958 v S, I, Cz; 1959 v S, Sp (18)

Vernon, J. (Belfast C), 1947 v E, S; (with WBA), 1947 v W; 1948 v E, S, W; 1949 v E, S, W; 1950 v E, S; 1951 v E, S, W, F; 1952 v S, E (17)

Waddell, T. M. R. (Cliftonville), 1906 v S (1)
Walker, J. (Doncaster R), 1955 v W (1)
Walker, T. (Bury), 1911 v S (1)
Walsh, D. J. (WBA), 1947 v S, W; 1948 v E, S, W; 1949 v E, S, W; 1950 v W (9)
Walsh, W. (Manchester C), 1948 v E, S, W; 1949 v E, S (5)
Waring, J. (Cliftonville), 1899 v E (1)
Warren, P. (Shelbourne), 1913 v E, S (2)
Watson, J. (Ulster), 1883 v E, W; 1886 v E, S, W; 1887 v S, W; 1889 v E, W (9)
Watson, P. (Distillery), 1971 v Cy (sub) (1)
Watson, T. (Cardiff C), 1926 v S (1)
Wattie, J. (Distillery), 1899 v E (1)
Webb, C. G. (Brighton), 1909 v S, W; 1911 v S (3)
Webb, S. M. (Ross Co), 2006 v U (sub), R (sub); 2007 v W (sub), Se (sub) (4)
Weir, E. (Clyde), 1939 v W (1)
Welsh, E. (Carlisle U), 1966 v W, WG, M; 1967 v W (4)
Whiteside, N. (Manchester U), 1982 v Y, Hon, Sp, A, F; 1983 v WG, Alb, T; 1984 v A, T, WG, S, E, W, Fi; 1985 v R, Fi, Is, E, Sp, T; 1986 v R, E, F, D, Mor, Alg, Sp, Br; 1987 v E (2), Is, Y; 1988 v T, Pol, F; (with Everton), 1990 v H, Ei (38)
Whiteside, T. (Distillery), 1891 v E (1)
Whitfield, E. R. (Dublin University), 1886 v W (1)
Whitley, Jeff (Manchester C), 1997 v Bel (sub), Th (sub); 1998 v Sp (sub); 2000 v Fi; 2001 v Y, D, N; (with

Sunderland), 2004 v Gr, Es, Ser, Stk, Tr; 2005 v Pol, W, Az, A, Ca, E, Pol; (with Cardiff C), 2006 v Ma (20)
Whitley, Jim (Manchester C), 1998 v Sp; 1999 v T (sub); 2000 v Fi (sub) (3)
Williams, J. R. (Ulster), 1886 v E, W (2)
Williams, M. S. (Chesterfield), 1999 v G, Mol, Ca, Ei; (with Watford), 2000 v F, T, G, Fi, L, Ma, H (sub); (with Wimbledon), 2001 v Y, Ic (sub), N (sub), CzR, Bul, CzR; 2002 v Lie, Sp; 2003 v Cy, Fi; (with Stoke C), Arm, Gr, I (sub), Sp (sub); (with Wimbledon), 2004 v N (sub), Es, Ser, Bar, Tr; (with Milton Keynes D), 2005 v Sw, Pol, W, Az, A, Pol (36)
Williams, P. A. (WBA), 1991 v Fa (sub) (1)
Williamson, J. (Cliftonville), 1890 v E; 1892 v S; 1893 v S (3)
Willighan, T. (Burnley), 1933 v W; 1934 v S (2)
Willis, G. (Linfield), 1906 v S, W; 1907 v S; 1912 v S (4)
Wilson, D. J. (Brighton & HA), 1987 v T, Is, E (sub); (with Luton T), 1988 v Y, T, Gr, Pol, F, Ma; 1989 v Ei, H, Sp, Ma, Ch; 1990 v H, Ei, N, U; (with Sheffield W), 1991 v Y, D, A, Fa; 1992 v A (sub), S (24)
Wilson, H. (Linfield), 1925 v W, S.Af (2)
Wilson, K. J. (Ipswich T), 1987 v Is, E, Y; (with Chelsea), 1988 v Y, T, Gr (sub), Pol (sub), F (sub); 1989 v H (sub), Sp (2), Ma, Ch; 1990 v Ei (sub), N, U; 1991 v Y (2), A, Pol, Fa; 1992 v Fa, A, D, S; (with Notts Co), Li, G; 1993 v Alb, Sp, D, Sp, Li, La; 1994 v La, D, Ei, R, Lie, Co, M; (with Walsall), 1995 v Ei (sub), La (42)
Wilson, M. (Distillery), 1884 v E, S, W (3)
Wilson, R. (Cliftonville), 1888 v S (1)
Wilson, S. J. (Glenavon), 1962 v S; 1964 v S; (with Falkirk), 1964 v E, W, U, Sp; 1965 v E, Sw; (with Dundee), 1966 v W, WG; 1967 v S; 1968 v E (12)
Wilton, J. M. (St Columb's Court), 1888 v E, W; 1889 v S, E; (with Cliftonville), 1890 v E; (with St Columb's Court), 1893 v W, S (7)
Wood, T. J. (Walsall), 1996 v Lie (sub) (1)
Worthington, N. (Sheffield W), 1984 v W, Fi (sub); 1985 v Is, Sp (sub); 1986 v T, R (sub), E (sub), D, Alg, Sp; 1987 v E (2), T, Is, Y; 1988 v Y, T, Gr, Pol, F, Ma; 1989 v Ei, H, Sp, Ma; 1990 v H, Ei, U; 1991 v Y, D, A, Fa; 1992 v A, D, S, Li, G; 1993 v Alb, Sp, D, Ei, Sp, Li, La; 1994 v La, D, Ei, Lie, Co, M; (with Leeds U), 1995 v P, A, Ei (2), La, Ca (sub), Ch, La; 1996 v P, Lie, A, N, Se, G; (with Stoke C), 1997 v I, Bel (sub) (66)
Wright, J. (Cliftonville), 1906 v E, S, W; 1907 v E, S, W (6)
Wright, T. J. (Newcastle U), 1989 v Ma, Ch; 1990 v H, U; 1992 v Fa, A, S, G; 1993 v Alb, Sp, Alb, Ei, Sp, Li, La; 1994 v La; (with Nottingham F), D, Ei, R, Lie, Co, M (sub); 1997 v G, Alb, I, Bel; (with Manchester C), P, Uk; 1998 v Alb; 1999 v Ca (sub); 2000 v F (sub) (31)

Young, S. (Linfield), 1907 v E, S; 1908 v E, S; (with Airdrie), 1909 v E; 1912 v S; (with Linfield), 1914 v E, S, W (9)

SCOTLAND

Adam, C. G. (Rangers), 2007 v A (sub), Fa (sub) (2)
Adams, J. (Hearts), 1889 v Ni; 1892 v W; 1893 v Ni (3)
Agnew, W. B. (Kilmarnock), 1907 v Ni; 1908 v W, Ni (3)
Aird, J. (Burnley), 1954 v N (2), A, U (4)
Aitken, A. (Newcastle U), 1901 v E; 1902 v E; 1903 v E, W; 1904 v E; 1905 v E, W; 1906 v E; (with Middlesbrough), 1907 v E, W; 1908 v E; (with Leicester Fosse), 1910 v E; 1911 v E, Ni (14)
Aitken, G. G. (East Fife), 1949 v E, F; 1950 v W, Ni, Sw; (with Sunderland), 1953 v W, Ni; 1954 v E (8)
Aitken, R. (Dumbarton), 1886 v E; 1888 v Ni (2)
Aitken, R. (Celtic), 1980 v Pe (sub), Bel, W (sub), E, Pol; 1983 v Bel, Ca (1+1 sub); 1984 v Bel (sub), Ni, W (sub); 1985 v E, Ic; 1986 v W, EG, Aus (2), Is, R, E, D, WG, U; 1987 v Bul, Ei (2), L, Bel, E, Br; 1988 v H, Bel, Bul, L, S.Ar, Ma, Sp, Co, E; 1989 v N, Y, I, Cy, F, Cy, E, Ch; 1990 v Y, F, N; (with Newcastle U), Arg (sub), Pol, Ma, Cr, Se, Br; (with St Mirren), 1992 v R (sub) (57)
Aitkenhead, W. A. C. (Blackburn R), 1912 v Ni (1)
Albiston, A. (Manchester U), 1982 v Ni; 1984 v U, Bel, EG, W, E; 1985 v Y, Ic, Sp (2), W; 1986 v EG, Ho, U (14)
Alexander, D. (East Stirlingshire), 1894 v W, Ni (2)
Alexander, G. (Preston NE), 2002 v Ng (sub), Sk, S.Af (sub), Hk (sub); 2003 v D (sub), Fa (sub), Ca, P, Ei, Ic, Li, Nz (sub); 2004 v Li (sub), R; 2005 v Mol, Bl; 2006 v A, I, N, Bl, Slv, US, Sw; 2007 v Li (sub), F, Uk, Ge, I, A, Fa (30)
Alexander, N. (Cardiff C), 2006 v Sw (sub), Bul, J (3)
Allan, D. S. (Queen's Park), 1885 v E, W; 1886 v W (3)
Allan, G. (Liverpool), 1897 v E (1)
Allan, H. (Hearts), 1902 v W (1)
Allan, J. (Queen's Park), 1887 v E, W (2)
Allan, T. (Dundee), 1974 v WG, N (2)
Ancell, R. F. D. (Newcastle U), 1937 v W, Ni (2)
Anderson, A. (Hearts), 1933 v E; 1934 v A, E, W, Ni; 1935 v E, W, Ni; 1936 v E, W, Ni; 1937 v G, E, W, Ni, A; 1938 v E, W, Ni, Cz, Ho; 1939 v W, H (23)
Anderson, F. (Clydesdale), 1874 v E (1)
Anderson, G. (Kilmarnock), 1901 v Ni (1)
Anderson, H. A. (Raith R), 1914 v W (1)
Anderson, J. (Leicester C), 1954 v Fi (1)
Anderson, K. (Queen's Park), 1896 v Ni; 1898 v E, Ni (3)
Anderson, R. (Aberdeen), 2003 v Ic (sub), Ca, P, Ei; 2005 v N, Se; 2006 v A (sub), Bul, J (9)
Anderson, W. (Queen's Park), 1882 v E; 1883 v E, W; 1884 v E; 1885 v E, W (6)
Andrews, P. (Eastern), 1875 v E (1)
Archibald, A. (Rangers), 1921 v W; 1922 v W, E; 1923 v Ni; 1924 v E, W; 1931 v E; 1932 v E (8)
Archibald, S. (Aberdeen), 1980 v P (sub); (with Tottenham H), Ni, Pol, H; 1981 v Se (sub), Is, Ni, Is, Ni, E; 1982 v Ni, P, Sp (sub), Ho, Nz (sub), Br, USSR; 1983 v EG, Sw (sub), Bel; 1984 v EG, E, F; (with Barcelona), 1985 v Sp, E, Ic (sub); 1986 v WG (27)
Armstrong, M. W. (Aberdeen), 1936 v W, Ni; 1937 v G (3)
Arnott, W. (Queen's Park), 1883 v W; 1884 v E, Ni; 1885 v E, W; 1886 v E; 1887 v E, W; 1888 v E; 1889 v E; 1890 v E; 1891 v E; 1892 v E; 1893 v E (14)
Auld, J. R. (Third Lanark), 1887 v E, W; 1889 v W (3)
Auld, R. (Celtic), 1959 v H, P; 1960 v W (3)

Baird, A. (Queen's Park), 1892 v Ni; 1894 v W (2)
Baird, D. (Hearts), 1890 v Ni; 1891 v E; 1892 v W (3)
Baird, H. (Airdrieonians), 1956 v A (1)
Baird, J. C. (Vale of Leven), 1876 v E; 1878 v W; 1880 v E (3)
Baird, S. (Rangers), 1957 v Y, Sp (2), Sw, WG; 1958 v F, Ni (7)
Baird, W. U. (St Bernard), 1897 v Ni (1)
Bannon, E. (Dundee U), 1980 v Bel; 1983 v Ni, W, E, Ca; 1984 v EG; 1986 v Is, R, E, D (sub), WG (11)
Barbour, A. (Renton), 1885 v Ni (1)
Barker, J. B. (Rangers), 1893 v W; 1894 v W (2)
Barrett, F. (Dundee), 1894 v Ni; 1895 v W (2)
Battles, B. (Celtic), 1901 v E, W, Ni (3)
Battles, B. jun. (Hearts), 1931 v W (1)
Bauld, W. (Hearts), 1950 v E, Sw, P (3)
Baxter, J. C. (Rangers), 1961 v Ni, Ei (2), Cz; 1962 v Ni, W, E, Cz (2), U; 1963 v W, Ni, E, A, N, Ei, Sp; 1964 v W, E, N, WG; 1965 v W, Ni, Fi; (with Sunderland), 1966 v P, Br, Ni, W, E, I; 1967 v W, E, USSR; 1968 v W (34)
Baxter, R. D. (Middlesbrough), 1939 v E, W, H (3)
Beattie, A. (Preston NE), 1937 v E, A, Cz; 1938 v E; 1939 v W, Ni, H (7)
Beattie, C. (Celtic), 2006 v I (sub), N (sub); 2007 v Ge (sub), I (sub) (4)
Beattie, R. (Preston NE), 1939 v W (1)
Begbie, I. (Hearts), 1890 v Ni; 1891 v E; 1892 v W; 1894 v E (4)
Bell, A. (Manchester U), 1912 v Ni (1)
Bell, J. (Dumbarton), 1890 v Ni; 1892 v E; (with Everton), 1896 v E; 1897 v E; 1898 v E; (with Celtic), 1899 v E, W, Ni; 1900 v E, W (10)
Bell, M. (Hearts), 1901 v W (1)
Bell, W. J. (Leeds U), 1966 v P, Br (2)
Bennett, A. (Celtic), 1904 v W; 1907 v Ni; 1908 v W; (with Rangers), 1909 v W, Ni, E; 1910 v E, W; 1911 v E, W; 1913 v Ni (11)
Bennie, R. (Airdrieonians), 1925 v W, Ni; 1926 v Ni (3)
Bernard, P. R. J. (Oldham Ath), 1995 v J (sub), Ec (2)
Berry, D. (Queen's Park), 1894 v W; 1899 v W, Ni (3)

Berry, W. H. (Queen's Park), 1888 v E; 1889 v E; 1890 v E; 1891 v E (4)
Bett, J. (Rangers), 1982 v Ho; 1983 v Bel; (with Lokeren), 1984 v Bel, W, E, F; 1985 v Y, Ic, Sp (2), W, E, Ic; (with Aberdeen), 1986 v W, Is, Ho; 1987 v Bel; 1988 v H (sub); 1989 v Y; 1990 v F (sub), N, Arg, Eg, Ma, Cr (25)
Beveridge, W. W. (Glasgow University), 1879 v E, W; 1880 v W (3)
Black, A. (Hearts), 1938 v Cz, Ho; 1939 v H (3)
Black, D. (Hurlford), 1889 v Ni (1)
Black, E. (Metz), 1988 v H (sub), L (sub) (2)
Black, I. H. (Southampton), 1948 v E (1)
Blackburn, J. E. (Royal Engineers), 1873 v E (1)
Blacklaw, A. S. (Burnley), 1963 v N, Sp; 1966 v I (3)
Blackley, J. (Hibernian), 1974 v Cz, E, Bel, Z; 1976 v Sw; 1977 v W, Se (7)
Blair, D. (Clyde), 1929 v W, Ni; 1931 v E, A, I; 1932 v W, Ni; (with Aston Villa), 1933 v W (8)
Blair, J. (Sheffield W), 1920 v E, Ni; (with Cardiff C), 1921 v E; 1922 v E; 1923 v E, W, Ni; 1924 v W (8)
Blair, J. (Motherwell), 1934 v W (1)
Blair, J. A. (Blackpool), 1947 v W (1)
Blair, W. (Third Lanark), 1896 v W (1)
Blessington, J. (Celtic), 1894 v E, Ni; 1896 v E, Ni (4)
Blyth, J. A. (Coventry C), 1978 v Bul, W (2)
Bone, J. (Norwich C), 1972 v Y (sub); 1973 v D (2)
Booth, S. (Aberdeen), 1993 v G (sub), Es (2 subs); 1994 v Sw, Ma (sub); 1995 v Fa, Ru; 1996 v Fi, Sm, Aus (sub), US, Ho, Sw (sub); (with Borussia Dortmund), 1998 v D, Fi, Co (sub), Mor (sub); (with Twente), 2001 v Pol; 2002 v Cro, Bel (sub), La (sub) (21)
Bowie, J. (Rangers), 1920 v E, Ni (2)
Bowie, W. (Linthouse), 1891 v Ni (1)
Bowman, D. (Dundee U), 1992 v Fi, US (sub); 1993 v G, Es; 1994 v Sw, I (6)
Bowman, G. A. (Montrose), 1892 v Ni (1)
Boyd, J. M. (Newcastle U), 1934 v Ni (1)
Boyd, K. (Rangers) 2006 v Bul, J (sub); 2007 v Fa, Li (sub), Uk (sub), Ge, I (sub), A, Fa (9)
Boyd, R. (Mossend Swifts), 1889 v Ni; 1891 v W (2)
Boyd, T. (Motherwell), 1991 v R (sub), Sw, Bul, USSR; (with Chelsea), 1992 v Sw, R; (with Celtic), Fi, Ca, N, C; 1993 v Sw, P, I, Ma, G, Es (2); 1994 v I, Ma (sub), Ho (sub), A; 1995 v Fi, Fa, Ru, Gr, Ru, Sm; 1996 v Gr, Fi, Se, Sm, Aus, D, US, Co, Ho, E, Sw; 1997 v A, La, Se, Es (2), A, Se, W, Ma, Bl; 1998 v Bl, La, F, D, Fi (sub), Co, US, Br, N, Mor; 1999 v Li, Es, Fa, CzR, G, Fa, CzR; 2001 v La, Cro, Aus, Bel, Sm (sub), Pol; 2002 v Bel (72)
Boyd, W. G. (Clyde), 1931 v I, Sw (2)
Bradshaw, T. (Bury), 1928 v E (1)
Brand, R. (Rangers), 1961 v Ni, Cz, Ei (2); 1962 v Ni, W, Cz, U (8)
Brandon, T. (Blackburn R), 1896 v E (1)
Brazil, A. (Ipswich T), 1980 v Pol (sub), H; 1982 v Sp, Ho (sub), Ni, W, E, Nz, USSR (sub); 1983 v EG, Sw; (with Tottenham H), W, E (sub) (13)
Breckenridge, T. (Hearts), 1888 v Ni (1)
Bremner, D. (Hibernian), 1976 v Sw (sub) (1)
Bremner, W. J. (Leeds U), 1965 v Sp; 1966 v E, Pol, P, Br, I (2); 1967 v W, Ni, E; 1968 v W, E; 1969 v W, E, Ni, D, A, WG, Cy (2); 1970 v Ei, WG, A; 1971 v W, E; 1972 v P, Bel, Ho, Ni, W, E, Y, Cz, Br; 1973 v D (2), E (2), Ni (sub), Sw, Br; 1974 v Cz, WG, Ni, W, E, Bel, N, Z, Br, Y; 1975 v Sp (2); 1976 v D (54)
Brennan, F. (Newcastle U), 1947 v W, Ni; 1953 v W, Ni, E; 1954 v Ni, E (7)
Breslin, B. (Hibernian), 1897 v W (1)
Brewster, G. (Everton), 1921 v E (1)
Brogan, J. (Celtic), 1971 v W, Ni, P, E (4)
Brown, A. (St Mirren), 1890 v W; 1891 v W (2)
Brown, A. (Middlesbrough), 1904 v E (1)
Brown, A. D. (East Fife), 1950 v Sw, P, F; (with Blackpool), 1952 v USA, D, Se; 1953 v W; 1954 v W, E, N (2), Fi, A, U (14)
Brown, G. C. P. (Rangers), 1931 v W; 1932 v E, W, Ni; 1933 v E; 1934 v A; 1935 v E, W; 1936 v E, W; 1937 v G, E, W, Ni, Cz; 1938 v E, W, Cz, Ho (19)
Brown, H. (Partick Th), 1947 v W, Bel, L (3)
Brown, J. B. (Clyde), 1939 v W (1)
Brown, J. G. (Sheffield U), 1975 v R (1)
Brown, R. (Cambuslang), 1890 v W (1)
Brown, R. (Dumbarton), 1884 v W, Ni (2)
Brown, R. (Rangers), 1947 v Ni; 1949 v Ni; 1952 v E (3)
Brown, R. jun. (Dumbarton), 1885 v W (1)
Brown, S. (Hibernian), 2006 v US (sub); 2007 v Ge (sub), I (3)
Brown, W. D. F. (Dundee), 1958 v F; 1959 v E, W, Ni; (with Tottenham H), 1960 v W, Ni, Pol, A, H, T; 1962 v Ni, W, E, Cz; 1963 v W, Ni, E, A; 1964 v Ni, W, N; 1965 v E, Fi, Pol, Sp; 1966 v Ni, Pol, I (28)
Browning, J. (Celtic), 1914 v W (1)
Brownlie, J. (Third Lanark), 1909 v E, Ni; 1910 v E, W, Ni; 1911 v W, Ni; 1912 v W, Ni, E; 1913 v W, Ni, E; 1914 v W, Ni, E (16)
Brownlie, J. (Hibernian), 1971 v USSR; 1972 v Pe, Ni, E; 1973 v D (2); 1976 v R (7)
Bruce, D. (Vale of Leven), 1890 v W (1)
Bruce, R. F. (Middlesbrough), 1934 v A (1)
Buchan, M. M. (Aberdeen), 1972 v P (sub), Bel; (with Manchester U), W, Y, Cz, Br; 1973 v D (2), E; 1974 v WG, Ni, W, N, Br, Y; 1975 v EG, Sp, P; 1976 v D, R; 1977 v Fi, Cz, Ch, Arg, Br; 1978 v EG, W (sub), Ni, Pe, Ir, Ho; 1979 v A, N, P (34)
Buchanan, J. (Cambuslang), 1889 v Ni (1)
Buchanan, J. (Rangers), 1929 v E; 1930 v E (2)
Buchanan, P. S. (Chelsea), 1938 v Cz (1)
Buchanan, R. (Abercorn), 1891 v W (1)
Buckley, P. (Aberdeen), 1954 v N; 1955 v W, Ni (3)
Buick, A. (Hearts), 1902 v W, Ni (2)
Burchill, M. J. (Celtic), 2000 v Bos (sub), Li, E (sub + sub), F (sub), Ho (sub) (6)
Burke, C. (Rangers), 2006 v Bul (sub), J (sub) (2)
Burley, C. W. (Chelsea), 1995 v J, Ec, Fa; 1996 v Gr, Se, Aus, D, US, Co (sub), Ho (sub), E (sub), Sw; 1997 v A, La, Se, Es, A, Se, Ma, Bl; (with Celtic), 1998 v Bl, La, F, Co, US (sub), Br, N, Mor; 1999 v Fa, CzR; 2000 v Bos, Es, Bos, Li, E (2); (with Derby Co), Ho, Ei; 2001 v Cro, Aus, Bel, Sm; 2002 v Cro, Bel, La; 2003 v A (46)
Burley, G. (Ipswich T), 1979 v W, Ni, E, Arg, N; 1980 v P, Ni, E (sub), Pol; 1982 v W (sub), E (11)
Burns, F. (Manchester U), 1970 v A (1)
Burns, K. (Birmingham C), 1974 v WG; 1975 v EG (sub), Sp (2); 1977 v Cz (sub), W, Se, W (sub); (with Nottingham F), 1978 v Ni (sub), W, E, Pe, Ir; 1979 v N; 1980 v Pe, A, Bel; 1981 v Is, Ni, W (20)
Burns, T. (Celtic), 1981 v Ni; 1982 v Ho (sub), W; 1983 v Bel (sub), Ni, Ca (1 + 1 sub); 1988 v E (sub) (8)
Busby, M. W. (Manchester C), 1934 v W (1)

Cairns, T. (Rangers), 1920 v W; 1922 v E; 1923 v E, W; 1924 v Ni; 1925 v W, E, Ni (8)
Calderhead, D. (Q of S Wanderers), 1889 v Ni (1)
Calderwood, C. (Tottenham H), 1995 v Ru, Sm, J, Ec, Fa; 1996 v Gr, Fi, Se, Sm, US, Co, Ho, E, Sw; 1997 v A, La, Se, Es (2), A, Se; 1998 v Bl, La, F, D, Fi, Co, US, Br, N; 1999 v Li, Es; (with Aston Villa), Fa, CzR; 2000 v Bos (1 + sub) (36)
Calderwood, R. (Cartvale), 1885 v Ni, E, W (3)
Caldow, E. (Rangers), 1957 v Sp (2), Sw, WG, E; 1958 v Ni, W, Sw, Par, H, Pol, Y, F; 1959 v E, W, Ni, WG, Ho, P; 1960 v E, W, Ni, A, H, T; 1961 v E, W, Ni, Ei (2), Cz; 1962 v Ni, W, E, Cz (2), U; 1963 v W, Ni, E (40)
Caldwell, G. (Newcastle U), 2002 v F, Ng (sub), Sk, S.Af; (with Hibernian), 2004 v R, D, Es, Tr; 2005 v H, Bl, Sp, Slv, N, Mol, I; 2006 v Slv (sub), US (sub), Sw, Bul, J; (with Celtic), 2007 v Li, F, Uk, A (24)
Caldwell, S. (Newcastle U), 2001 v Pol (sub); 2003 v Ei; 2004 v W, Tr (sub); (with Sunderland), 2005 v Mol; 2006 v A, Slv (sub), US (sub), Sw (sub) (9)
Callaghan, P. (Hibernian), 1900 v Ni (1)
Callaghan, W. (Dunfermline Ath), 1970 v Ei (sub), W (2)
Cameron, C. (Hearts), 1999 v G (sub), Fa (sub); 2000 v Li (sub), F, Ei (sub); 2001 v La (sub), Sm, Cro, Aus, Sm, Pol; (with Wolverhampton W), 2002 v Cro (sub), Bel (sub), La, F; 2003 v Ei (sub), Li (sub), A (sub), G; 2004 v N, Fa, G, Li, W, R, D; 2005 v Sp (sub), Mol (28)
Cameron, J. (Rangers), 1886 v Ni (1)
Cameron, J. (Queen's Park), 1896 v Ni (1)
Cameron, J. (St Mirren), 1904 v Ni; (with Chelsea), 1909 v E (2)
Campbell, C. (Queen's Park), 1874 v E; 1876 v W; 1877 v E, W; 1878 v E; 1879 v E; 1880 v E; 1881 v E; 1882 v E, W; 1884 v E; 1885 v E; 1886 v E (13)
Campbell, H. (Renton), 1889 v W (1)
Campbell, Jas (Sheffield W), 1913 v W (1)
Campbell, J. (South Western), 1880 v W (1)
Campbell, J. (Kilmarnock), 1891 v Ni; 1892 v W (2)
Campbell, John (Celtic), 1893 v E, Ni; 1898 v E, Ni; 1900 v E, Ni; 1901 v E, W, Ni; 1902 v W, Ni; 1903 v W (12)

Campbell, John (Rangers), 1899 v E, W, Ni; 1901 v Ni (4)
Campbell, K. (Liverpool), 1920 v E, W, Ni; (with Partick Th), 1921 v W, Ni; 1922 v W, Ni, E (8)
Campbell, P. (Rangers), 1878 v W; 1879 v W (2)
Campbell, P. (Morton), 1898 v W (1)
Campbell, R. (Falkirk), 1947 v Bel, L; (with Chelsea), 1950 v Sw, P, F (5)
Campbell, W. (Morton), 1947 v Ni; 1948 v E, Bel, Sw, F (5)
Canero, P. (Leicester C), 2004 v D (sub) (1)
Carabine, J. (Third Lanark), 1938 v Ho; 1939 v E, Ni (3)
Carr, W. M. (Coventry C), 1970 v Ni, W, E; 1971 v D; 1972 v Pe; 1973 v D (sub) (6)
Cassidy, J. (Celtic), 1921 v W, Ni; 1923 v Ni; 1924 v W (4)
Chalmers, S. (Celtic), 1965 v W, Fi; 1966 v P (sub), Br; 1967 v Ni (5)
Chalmers, W. (Rangers), 1885 v Ni (1)
Chalmers, W. S. (Queen's Park), 1929 v Ni (1)
Chambers, T. (Hearts), 1894 v W (1)
Chaplin, G. D. (Dundee), 1908 v W (1)
Cheyne, A. G. (Aberdeen), 1929 v E, N, G, Ho; 1930 v F (5)
Christie, A. J. (Queen's Park), 1898 v W; 1899 v E, Ni (3)
Christie, R. M. (Queen's Park), 1884 v E (1)
Clark, J. (Celtic), 1966 v Br; 1967 v W, Ni, USSR (4)
Clark, R. B. (Aberdeen), 1968 v W, Ho; 1970 v Ni; 1971 v W, Ni, E, D, P, USSR; 1972 v Bel, Ni, W, E, Cz, Br; 1973 v D, E (17)
Clarke, S. (Chelsea), 1988 v H, Bel, Bul, S.Ar, Ma; 1994 v Ho (6)
Cleland, J. (Royal Albert), 1891 v Ni (1)
Clements, R. (Leith Ath), 1891 v Ni (1)
Clunas, W. L. (Sunderland), 1924 v E; 1926 v W (2)
Collier, W. (Raith R), 1922 v W (1)
Collins, J. (Hibernian), 1988 v S.Ar; 1990 v EG, Pol (sub), Ma (sub); (with Celtic), 1991 v Sw (sub), Bul (sub); 1992 v Ni (sub), Fi; 1993 v P, Ma, G, P, Es (2); 1994 v Sw, Ho (sub), A, Ho; 1995 v Fi, Fa, Ru, Gr, Ru, Sm, Fa; 1996 v Gr, Fi, Se, Sm, Aus, D, US (sub), Co, Ho, E, Sw; (with Monaco), 1997 v A, La, Se, Es, A, Se, Ma; 1998 v Bl, La, F, Fi, Co, US, Br, N, Mor; (with Everton), 1999 v Li; 2000 v Bos, Es, Bos, E (2) (58)
Collins, R. Y. (Celtic), 1951 v W, Ni, A; 1955 v Y, A, H; 1956 v Ni, W; 1957 v E, W, Sp (2), Sw, WG; 1958 v Ni, W, Sw, H, Pol, Y, F, Par; (with Everton), 1959 v E, W, Ni, WG, Ho, P; (with Leeds U), 1965 v E, Pol, Sp (31)
Collins, T. (Hearts), 1909 v W (1)
Colman, D. (Aberdeen), 1911 v E, W, Ni; 1913 v Ni (4)
Colquhoun, E. P. (Sheffield U), 1972 v P, Ho, Pe, Y, Cz, Br; 1973 v D (2), E (9)
Colquhoun, J. (Hearts), 1988 v S.Ar (sub), Ma (sub) (2)
Combe, J. R. (Hibernian), 1948 v E, Bel, Sw (3)
Conn, A. (Hearts), 1956 v A (1)
Conn, A. (Tottenham H), 1975 v Ni (sub), E (2)
Connachan, E. D. (Dunfermline Ath), 1962 v Cz, U (2)
Connelly, G. (Celtic), 1974 v Cz, WG (2)
Connolly, J. (Everton), 1973 v Sw (1)
Connor, J. (Airdrieonians), 1886 v Ni (1)
Connor, J. (Sunderland), 1930 v F; 1932 v Ni; 1934 v E; 1935 v Ni (4)
Connor, R. (Dundee), 1986 v Ho; (with Aberdeen), 1988 v S.Ar (sub); 1989 v E; 1991 v R (4)
Cook, W. L. (Bolton W), 1934 v E; 1935 v W, Ni (3)
Cooke, C. (Dundee), 1966 v W, I; (with Chelsea), P, Br; 1968 v E, Ho; 1969 v W, Ni, A, WG (sub), Cy (2); 1970 v A; 1971 v Bel; 1975 v Sp, P (16)
Cooper, D. (Rangers), 1980 v Pe, A (sub); 1984 v W, E; 1985 v Y, Ic, Sp (2), W; 1986 v W (sub), EG, Aus (2), Ho, WG (sub), U (sub); 1987 v Bul, L, Ei, Br; (with Motherwell), 1990 v N, Eg (22)
Cormack, P. B. (Hibernian), 1966 v Br; 1969 v D (sub); 1970 v Ei, WG; (with Nottingham F), 1971 v D (sub), W, P, E; 1972 v Ho (sub) (9)
Cowan, J. (Aston Villa), 1896 v E; 1897 v E; 1898 v E (3)
Cowan, J. (Morton), 1948 v Bel, Sw; F; 1949 v E, W, F; 1950 v E, W, Ni, Sw, P, F; 1951 v E, W, Ni, A (2), D, F, Bel; 1952 v Ni, W, USA, D, Se (25)
Cowan, W, D. (Newcastle U), 1924 v E (1)
Cowie, D. (Dundee), 1953 v E, Se; 1954 v Ni, W, Fi, N, A, U; 1955 v W, Ni, A, H; 1956 v W, A; 1957 v Ni, W; 1958 v H, Pol, Y, Par (20)
Cox, C. J. (Hearts), 1948 v F (1)
Cox, S. (Rangers), 1949 v E, F; 1950 v E, F, W, Ni, Sw, P; 1951 v E, D, F, Bel, A; 1952 v Ni, W, USA, D, Se; 1953 v W, Ni, E; 1954 v W, Ni, E (24)
Craig, A. (Motherwell), 1929 v N, Ho; 1932 v E (3)
Craig, J. (Celtic), 1977 v Se (sub) (1)
Craig, J. P. (Celtic), 1968 v W (1)
Craig, T. (Rangers), 1927 v Ni; 1928 v Ni; 1929 v N, G, Ho; 1930 v Ni, E, W (8)
Craig, T. B. (Newcastle U), 1976 v Sw (1)
Crainey, S. (Celtic), 2002 v F, Ng; 2003 v D (sub), Fa; (with Southampton), 2004 v R (sub), D (6)
Crapnell, J. (Airdrieonians), 1929 v E, N, G; 1930 v F; 1931 v Ni, Sw; 1932 v E, F; 1933 v Ni (9)
Crawford, D. (St Mirren), 1894 v W, Ni; (with Rangers), 1900 v W (3)
Crawford, J. (Queen's Park), 1932 v F, Ni; 1933 v E, W, Ni (5)
Crawford, S. (Raith R), 1995 v Ec (sub); (with Dunfermline Ath), 2001 v Pol (sub); 2002 v F; 2003 v Fa (sub), Ic, Ca, P, Ei, Ic, Li, A (sub), Nz, G; 2004 v N, Fa, Li, Ho (sub), R (sub), Es (sub), Tr; (with Plymouth Arg), 2005 v H (sub), Sp, Slv (sub), Mol, Se (sub) (25)
Crerand, P. T. (Celtic), 1961 v Ei (2), Cz; 1962 v Ni, W, E, Cz (2), U; 1963 v W, Ni; (with Manchester U), 1964 v Ni; 1965 v E, Pol, Fi; 1966 v Pol (16)
Cringan, W. (Celtic), 1920 v W; 1922 v E, Ni; 1923 v W, E (5)
Crosbie, J. A. (Ayr U), 1920 v W; (with Birmingham), 1922 v E (2)
Croal, J. A. (Falkirk), 1913 v Ni; 1914 v E, W (3)
Cropley, A. J. (Hibernian), 1972 v P, Bel (2)
Cross, J. H. (Third Lanark), 1903 v Ni (1)
Cruickshank, J. (Hearts), 1964 v WG; 1970 v W, E; 1971 v D, Bel; 1976 v R (6)
Crum, J. (Celtic), 1936 v E; 1939 v Ni (2)
Cullen, M. J. (Luton T), 1956 v A (1)
Cumming, D. S. (Middlesbrough), 1938 v E (1)
Cumming, J. (Hearts), 1955 v E, H, P, Y; 1960 v E, Pol, A, H, T (9)
Cummings, G. (Partick Th), 1935 v E; 1936 v W, Ni; (with Aston Villa), E; 1937 v G; 1938 v W, Ni, Cz; 1939 v E (9)
Cummings, W. (Chelsea), 2002 v Hk (sub) (1)
Cunningham, A. N. (Rangers), 1920 v Ni; 1921 v W, E; 1922 v Ni; 1923 v E, W; 1924 v E, Ni; 1926 v E, Ni; 1927 v E, W (12)
Cunningham, W. C. (Preston NE), 1954 v N (2), U, Fi, A; 1955 v W, E, H (8)
Curran, H. P. (Wolverhampton W), 1970 v A; 1971 v Ni, E, D, USSR (sub) (5)

Dailly, C. (Derby Co), 1997 v W, Ma, Bl; 1998 v Bl, La, F, D, Fi, Co, US, Br, N, Mor; (with Blackburn R), 1999 v Li; 2000 v Bos (sub), Es, Bos, Li, E (2), F, Ho, Ei; 2001 v La, Sm, Aus; (with West Ham U), Pol; 2002 v Cro, Bel, La, F, Ng, Sk, S.Af, Hk; 2003 v D, Fa, Ic, Ca, P, Ei, Ic, Li, A, Nz, G; 2004 v N, G, Li, Ho, W, R, D; 2005 v Mol (sub), Bl; 2006 v A, I, Bl, Slv, US, Sw; 2007 v Fa, Li, F, A (sub) (65)
Dalglish, K. (Celtic), 1972 v Bel (sub), Ho; 1973 v D (1+1 sub), E (2), W, Ni, Sw, Br; 1974 v Cz (2), WG (2), Ni, W, E, Bel, N (sub), Z, Br, Y; 1975 v EG, Sp (sub+1), Se, P, W, Ni, E, R; 1976 v D (2), R, Sw, Ni, E; 1977 v Fi, Cz, W (2), Se, Ni, E, Ch, Arg, Br; (with Liverpool), 1978 v EG, Cz, W, Bul, Ni (sub), W, E, Pe, Ir, Ho; 1979 v A, N, P, W, Ni, E, Arg, N; 1980 v Pe, A, Bel (2), P, Ni, W, E, Pol, H; 1981 v Se, P, Is; 1982 v Se, Ni, P (sub), Sp, Ho, Ni, W, E, Nz, Br (sub); 1983 v Bel, Sw; 1984 v U, Bel, EG; 1985 v Y, Ic, Sp, W; 1986 v EG, Aus, R; 1987 v Bul (sub), L (102)
Davidson, C. I. (Blackburn R), 1999 v Li (sub), Es, Fa, CzR, G, Fa, CzR; 2000 v Es, Bos, Li, E, F; (with Leicester C), 2001 v La, Pol; 2002 v La; 2003 v Ic (sub), Ca (sub) (17)
Davidson, D. (Queen's Park), 1878 v W; 1879 v W; 1880 v W; 1881 v E, W (5)
Davidson, J. A. (Partick Th), 1954 v N (2), A, U; 1955 v W, Ni, E, H (8)
Davidson, S. (Middlesbrough), 1921 v E (1)
Dawson, A. (Rangers), 1980 v Pol (sub), H; 1983 v Ni, Ca (2) (5)
Dawson, J. (Rangers), 1935 v Ni; 1936 v E; 1937 v G, E, W, Ni, A, Cz; 1938 v W, Ho, Ni; 1939 v E, Ni, H (14)
Deans, J. (Celtic), 1975 v EG, Sp (2)
Delaney, J. (Celtic), 1936 v W, Ni; 1937 v G, E, A, Cz; 1938 v Ni; 1939 v W, Ni; (with Manchester U), 1947 v E; 1948 v E, W, Ni (13)
Devine, A. (Falkirk), 1910 v W (1)

Devlin, P. J. (Birmingham C), 2003 v Ca, P (sub), Ei (sub), Ic (sub), Li (sub), A, Nz, G; 2004 v N (sub), Fa (10)
Dewar, G. (Dumbarton), 1888 v Ni; 1889 v E (2)
Dewar, N. (Third Lanark), 1932 v E, F; 1933 v W (3)
Dick, J. (West Ham U), 1959 v E (1)
Dickie, M. (Rangers), 1897 v Ni; 1899 v Ni; 1900 v W (3)
Dickov, P. (Manchester C), 2001 v Sm (sub), Cro (sub), Aus (sub); (with Leicester C), 2003 v Fa; 2004 v Fa, Ho (2), W; (with Blackburn R), 2005 v Slv, N (10)
Dickson, W. (Dundee Strathmore), 1888 v Ni (1)
Dickson, W. (Kilmarnock), 1970 v Ni, W, E; 1971 v D, USSR (5)
Divers, J. (Celtic), 1895 v W (1)
Divers, J. (Celtic), 1939 v Ni (1)
Dobie, R. S. (WBA), 2002 v Sk, S.Af, Hk (sub); 2003 v D (sub), Fa, P (6)
Docherty, T. H, (Preston NE), 1952 v W; 1953 v E, Se; 1954 v N (2), A, U; 1955 v W, E, H (2), A; 1957 v E, Y, Sp (2), Sw, WG; 1958 v Ni, W, E, Sw; (with Arsenal), 1959 v W, E, Ni (25)
Dodds, D. (Dundee U), 1984 v U (sub), Ni (2)
Dodds, J. (Celtic), 1914 v E, W, Ni (3)
Dodds, W. (Aberdeen), 1997 v La (sub), W, Bl (sub); 1998 v Bl (sub); (with Dundee U), 1999 v Es (sub), Fa, G, Fa, CzR; 2000 v Bos, Es, Bos, Li (sub), E (2); (with Rangers), F, Ho, Ei; 2001 v La, Sm, Aus, Bel, Sm, Pol; 2002 v Cro (sub), Bel (26)
Doig, J. E. (Arbroath), 1887 v Ni; 1889 v Ni; (with Sunderland), 1896 v E; 1899 v E; 1903 v E (5)
Donachie, W. (Manchester C), 1972 v Pe, Ni, E, Y, Cz, Br; 1973 v D, E, W, Ni; 1974 v Ni; 1976 v R, Ni, W, E; 1977 v Fi, Cz, W (2), Se, Ni, E, Ch, Arg, Br; 1978 v EG, W, Bul, W, E, Ir, Ho; 1979 v A, N, P (sub) (35)
Donaldson, A. (Bolton W), 1914 v E, Ni, W; 1920 v E, Ni; 1922 v Ni (6)
Donnachie, J. (Oldham Ath), 1913 v E; 1914 v E, Ni (3)
Donnelly, S. (Celtic), 1997 v W (sub), Ma (sub); 1998 v La (sub), F (sub), D (sub), Fi (sub), Co (sub), US (sub); 1999 v Es (sub), Fa (10)
Dougal, J. (Preston NE), 1939 v E (1)
Dougall, C. (Birmingham C), 1947 v W (1)
Dougan, R. (Hearts), 1950 v Sw (1)
Douglas, A. (Chelsea), 1911 v Ni (1)
Douglas, J. (Renfrew), 1880 v W (1)
Douglas, R. (Celtic), 2002 v Ng, S.Af, Hk; 2003 v D, Fa, Ic, P, Ic, Nz, G; 2004 v N, Fa, G, Li, Ho (2), W; 2005 v I; (with Leicester C), 2006 v A (sub) (19)
Dowds, P. (Celtic), 1892 v Ni (1)
Downie, R. (Third Lanark), 1892 v W (1)
Doyle, D. (Celtic), 1892 v E; 1893 v W; 1894 v E; 1895 v E, Ni; 1897 v E; 1898 v E, Ni (8)
Doyle, J. (Ayr U), 1976 v R (1)
Drummond, J. (Falkirk), 1892 v Ni; (with Rangers), 1894 v Ni; 1895 v Ni, E; 1896 v E, Ni; 1897 v Ni; 1898 v E; 1900 v E; 1901 v E; 1902 v E, W, Ni; 1903 v Ni (14)
Dunbar, M. (Cartvale), 1886 v Ni (1)
Duncan, A. (Hibernian), 1975 v P (sub), W, Ni, E, R; 1976 v D (sub) (6)
Duncan, D. (Derby Co), 1933 v E, W; 1934 v A, W; 1935 v E, W; 1936 v E, W, Ni; 1937 v G, E, W, Ni; 1938 v W (14)
Duncan, D. M. (East Fife), 1948 v Bel, Sw, F (3)
Duncan, J. (Alexandra Ath), 1878 v W; 1882 v W (2)
Duncan, J. (Leicester C), 1926 v W (1)
Duncanson, J. (Rangers), 1947 v Ni (1)
Dunlop, J. (St Mirren), 1890 v W (1)
Dunlop, W. (Liverpool), 1906 v E (1)
Dunn, J. (Hibernian), 1925 v W, Ni; 1927 v Ni; 1928 v Ni, E; (with Everton), 1929 v W (6)
Durie, G. S. (Chelsea), 1988 v Bul (sub); 1989 v I (sub), Cy; 1990 v Y, EG, Eg, Se; 1991 v Sw (sub), Bul (2), USSR (sub), Sm; (with Tottenham H), 1992 v Sw, R, Sm, Ni (sub), Fi, Ca, N (sub), Ho, G; 1993 v Sw, I; 1994 v Sw, I; (with Rangers), Ho (2); 1996 v US, Ho, E, Sw; 1997 v A (sub), Se (sub), Ma (sub), Bl; 1998 v Bl, La, F, Fi (sub), Co, Br, N, Mor (43)
Durrant, I. (Rangers), 1988 v H, Bel, Ma, Sp; 1989 v N (sub); 1993 v Sw (sub), P (sub), I, P (sub); 1994 v I (sub), Ma; (with Kilmarnock), 1999 v Es, Fa (sub), G, Fa, CzR; 2000 v Bos (sub), Es, Ho (sub), Ei (sub) (20)
Dykes, J. (Hearts), 1938 v Ho; 1939 v Ni (2)

Easson, J. F. (Portsmouth), 1931 v A, Sw; 1934 v W (3)
Elliott, M. S. (Leicester C), 1998 v F (sub), D, Fi; 1999 v Li, Fa, CzR, Fa; 2000 v Ho, Ei; 2001 v La, Sm, Cro, Aus (sub), Bel, Sm; 2002 v Cro, Bel, La (18)
Ellis, J. (Mossend Swifts), 1892 v Ni (1)
Evans, A. (Aston Villa), 1982 v Ho, Ni, E, Nz (4)
Evans, R. (Celtic), 1949 v E, W, Ni, F; 1950 v W, Ni, Sw, P; 1951 v E, A; 1952 v Ni; 1953 v Se; 1954 v Ni, W, E, N, Fi; 1955 v Ni, P, Y, A, H; 1956 v E, Ni, W, A; 1957 v WG, Sp; 1958 v Ni, W, E, Sw, H, Pol, Y, Par, F; 1959 v E, WG, Ho, P; 1960 v E, Ni, W, Pol; (with Chelsea), 1960 v A, H, T (48)
Ewart, J. (Bradford C), 1921 v E (1)
Ewing, T. (Partick Th), 1958 v W, E (2)

Farm, G. N. (Blackpool), 1953 v W, Ni, E, Se; 1954 v Ni, W, E; 1959 v WG, Ho, P (10)
Ferguson, B. (Rangers), 1999 v Li (sub); 2000 v Bos, Es (sub), E (2), F, Ei; 2001 v La, Aus, Bel; 2003 v D, Fa, Ic, Ei, Ic; 2004 v N (with Blackburn R), Fa, G, Li, Ho (2); 2005 v H, Sp, Slv, N, Mol; (with Rangers), I, Mol, Bl; 2006 v I, N, Bl, Sw; 2007 v F, Uk, Ge, I, A, Fa (39)
Ferguson, D. (Rangers), 1988 v Ma, Co (sub) (2)
Ferguson, D. (Dundee U), 1992 v US (sub), Ca, Ho (sub); 1993 v G; (with Everton), 1995 v Gr; 1997 v A, Es (7)
Ferguson, I. (Rangers), 1989 v I, Cy (sub), F; 1993 v Ma (sub), Es; 1994 v Ma, A (sub), Ho (sub); 1997 v Es (sub) (9)
Ferguson, J. (Vale of Leven), 1874 v E; 1876 v E, W; 1877 v E, W; 1878 v W (6)
Ferguson, R. (Kilmarnock), 1966 v W, E, Ho, P, Br; 1967 v W, Ni (7)
Fernie, W. (Celtic), 1954 v Fi, A, U; 1955 v W, Ni; 1957 v E, Ni, W, Y; 1958 v W, Sw, Par (12)
Findlay, R. (Kilmarnock), 1898 v W (1)
Fitchie, T. T. (Woolwich Arsenal), 1905 v W; 1906 v W, Ni; (with Queen's Park), 1907 v W (4)
Flavell, R. (Airdrieonians), 1947 v Bel, L (2)
Fleck, R. (Norwich C), 1990 v Arg, Se, Br (sub); 1991 v USSR (4)
Fleming, C. (East Fife), 1954 v Ni (1)
Fleming, J. W. (Rangers), 1929 v G, Ho; 1930 v E (3)
Fleming, R. (Morton), 1886 v Ni (1)
Fletcher, D. B. (Manchester U), 2004 v N (sub), Li (sub), Ho (2), W, D, Es, Tr; 2005 v H, Sp, Slv, N, Mol (2), Bl; 2006 v I, N, Bl, Slv, US, Sw, Bul, J; 2007 v Fa, Li, F, Uk, A, Fa (29)
Forbes, A. R. (Sheffield U), 1947 v Bel, L, E; 1948 v W, Ni; (with Arsenal), 1950 v E, P, F; 1951 v W, Ni, A; 1952 v W, D, Se (14)
Forbes, J. (Vale of Leven), 1884 v E, W, Ni; 1887 v W, E (5)
Ford, D. (Hearts), 1974 v Cz (sub), WG (sub), W (3)
Forrest, J. (Rangers), 1966 v W, I; (with Aberdeen), 1971 v Bel (sub), D, USSR (5)
Forrest, J. (Motherwell), 1958 v E (1)
Forsyth, A. (Partick Th), 1972 v Y, Cz, Br; 1973 v D; (with Manchester U), E; 1975 v Sp, Ni (sub), R, EG; 1976 v D (10)
Forsyth, C. (Kilmarnock), 1964 v E; 1965 v W, Ni, Fi (4)
Forsyth, T. (Motherwell), 1971 v D; (with Rangers), 1974 v Cz; 1976 v Sw, Ni, W, E; 1977 v Fi, Se, W, Ni, E, Ch, Arg, Br; 1978 v Cz, W, Ni, W (sub), E, Pe, Ir (sub), Ho (22)
Foyers, R. (St Bernards), 1893 v W; 1894 v W (2)
Fraser, D. M. (WBA), 1968 v Ho; 1969 v Cy (2)
Fraser, J. (Moffat), 1891 v Ni (1)
Fraser, M. J. E. (Queen's Park), 1880 v W; 1882 v W, E; 1883 v W, E (5)
Fraser, J. (Dundee), 1907 v Ni (1)
Fraser, W. (Sunderland), 1955 v W, Ni (2)
Freedman, D. A. (C Palace), 2002 v La, F (2)
Fulton, W. (Abercorn), 1884 v Ni (1)
Fyfe, J. H. (Third Lanark), 1895 v W (1)

Gabriel, J. (Everton), 1961 v W; 1964 v N (sub) (2)
Gallacher, H. K. (Airdrieonians), 1924 v Ni; 1925 v E, W, Ni; 1926 v W; (with Newcastle U), 1926 v E, Ni; 1927 v E, W, Ni; 1928 v E, W; 1929 v E, W, Ni; 1930 v W, Ni, F; (with Chelsea), 1934 v E; (with Derby Co), 1935 v E (20)
Gallacher, K. W. (Dundee U), 1988 v Co, E (sub); 1989 v N, I; (with Coventry C), 1991 v Sm; 1992 v R (sub), Sm (sub), Ni (sub), N (sub), Ho (sub), G (sub), C; 1993 v Sw (sub), P; (with Blackburn R), P, Es (2); 1994 v I,

Ma; 1996 v Aus (sub), D, Co (sub), Ho; 1997 v Se (sub), Es (2), A, Se, W, Ma, Bl; 1998 v Bl, La, F, Fi (sub), US, Br, N, Mor; 1999 v Li, Es, Fa, CzR; 2000 v Bos (sub); (with Newcastle U), Bos, Li (sub), E, F, Ei (sub); 2001 v Sm, Cro, Bel (sub), Sm (sub) (53)
Gallacher, P. (Sunderland), 1935 v Ni (1)
Gallacher, P. (Dundee U), 2002 v Hk (sub); 2003 v Ca, Ei (sub), Li, A; 2004 v R, D, Es (8)
Gallagher, P. (Blackburn R), 2004 v W (sub) (1)
Galloway, M. (Celtic), 1992 v R (1)
Galt, J. H. (Rangers), 1908 v W, Ni (2)
Gardiner, I. (Motherwell), 1958 v W (1)
Gardner, D. R. (Third Lanark), 1897 v W (1)
Gardner, R. (Queen's Park), 1872 v E; 1873 v E; (with Clydesdale), 1874 v E; 1875 v E; 1878 v E (5)
Gemmell, T. (St Mirren), 1955 v P, Y (2)
Gemmell, T. (Celtic), 1966 v E; 1967 v W, Ni, E, USSR; 1968 v Ni, E; 1969 v W, Ni, E, D, A, WG, Cy; 1970 v E, Ei, WG; 1971 v Bel (18)
Gemmill, A. (Derby Co), 1971 v Bel; 1972 v P, Ho, Pe, Ni, W, E; 1976 v D, R, Ni, W, E; 1977 v Fi, Cz, W (2), Ni (sub), E (sub), Ch (sub), Arg, Br; 1978 v EG (sub); (with Nottingham F), Bul, Ni, W, E (sub), Pe (sub), Ir, Ho; 1979 v A, N, P, N; (with Birmingham C), 1980 v A, P, Ni, W, E, H; 1981 v Se, P, Is, Ni (43)
Gemmill, S. (Nottingham F), 1995 v J, Ec, Fa (sub); 1996 v Sm, D (sub), US; 1997 v Es, Se (sub), W, Ma (sub), Bl (sub); 1998 v D, Fi; (with Everton), 1999 v G, Fa (sub); 2001 v Sm (sub), Pol (sub); 2002 v Cro (sub), F (sub), Ng, Sk, S.Af, Hk; 2003 v Ca, Ei (sub), A (sub) (26)
Gibb, W. (Clydesdale), 1873 v E (1)
Gibson, D. W. (Leicester C), 1963 v A, N, Ei, Sp; 1964 v Ni; 1965 v W, Fi (7)
Gibson, J. D. (Partick Th), 1926 v E; 1927 v E, W, Ni; (with Aston Villa), 1928 v E, W; 1930 v W, Ni (8)
Gibson, N. (Rangers), 1895 v E, Ni; 1896 v E, Ni; 1897 v E, Ni; 1898 v E; 1899 v E, W, Ni; 1900 v E, Ni; 1901 v W; (with Partick Th), 1905 v Ni (14)
Gilchrist, J. E. (Celtic), 1922 v E (1)
Gilhooley, M. (Hull C), 1922 v W (1)
Gillespie, G. (Rangers), 1880 v W; 1881 v E, W; 1882 v E; (with Queen's Park), 1886 v W; 1890 v W; 1891 v Ni (7)
Gillespie, G. T. (Liverpool), 1988 v Bel, Bul, Sp; 1989 v N, F, Ch; 1990 v Y, EG, Eg, Pol, Ma, Br (sub); 1991 v Bul (13)
Gillespie, Jas (Third Lanark), 1898 v W (1)
Gillespie, John (Queen's Park), 1896 v W (1)
Gillespie, R. (Queen's Park), 1927 v W; 1931 v W; 1932 v F; 1933 v E (4)
Gillick, T. (Everton), 1937 v A, Cz; 1939 v W, Ni, H (5)
Gilmour, J. (Dundee), 1931 v W (1)
Gilzean, A. J. (Dundee), 1964 v W, E, N, WG; 1965 v Ni; (with Tottenham H), Sp; 1966 v Ni, W, Pol, I; 1968 v W; 1969 v W, E, WG, Cy (2), A (sub); 1970 v Ni, E (sub), WG, A; 1971 v P (22)
Glass, S. (Newcastle U), 1999 v Fa (sub) (1)
Glavin, R. (Celtic), 1977 v Se (1)
Glen, A. (Aberdeen), 1956 v E, Ni (2)
Glen, R. (Renton), 1895 v W; 1896 v W; (with Hibernian), 1900 v Ni (3)
Goram, A. L. (Oldham Ath), 1986 v EG (sub), R, Ho; 1987 v Br; (with Hibernian), 1989 v Y, I; 1990 v EG, Pol, Ma; 1991 v R, Sw, Bul (2), USSR, Sm; (with Rangers), 1992 v Sw, R, Sm, Fi, N, Ho, G, C; 1993 v Sw, P, I, Ma, P; 1994 v Ho; 1995 v Fi, Fa, Ru, Gr; 1996 v Se (sub), D (sub), Co, Ho, E, Sw; 1997 v A, La, Es; 1998 v D (sub) (43)
Gordon, C. S. (Hearts), 2004 v Tr; 2005 v Sp, Slv, N, Mol, I (sub), Mol, Bl; 2006 v A, I, N, Bl, Slv, US, Sw; 2007 v Fa, Li, F, Uk, Ge, I, A (sub), Fa (23)
Gordon, J. E. (Rangers), 1912 v E, Ni; 1913 v E, Ni, W; 1914 v E, Ni; 1920 v W, E, Ni (10)
Gossland, J. (Rangers), 1884 v Ni (1)
Goudle, J. (Abercorn), 1884 v Ni (1)
Gough, C. R. (Dundee U), 1983 v Sw, Ni, W, E, Ca (3); 1984 v U, Bel, EG, Ni, W, E, F; 1985 v Sp, E, Ic; 1986 v W, EG, Aus, Is, R, E, D, WG, U; (with Tottenham H), 1987 v Bul, L, Ei (2), Bel, E, Br; 1988 v H; (with Rangers), S.Ar, Sp, Co, E; 1989 v Y, I, Cy, F, Cy; 1990 v F, Arg, EG, Eg, Pol, Ma, Cr; 1991 v USSR, Bul; 1992 v Sm, Ni, Ca, N, Ho, G, C; 1993 v Sw, P (61)
Gould, J. (Celtic), 2000 v Li; 2001 v Aus (2)
Gourlay, J. (Cambuslang), 1886 v Ni; 1888 v W (2)
Govan, J. (Hibernian), 1948 v E, W, Bel, Sw, F; 1949 v Ni (6)
Gow, D. R. (Rangers), 1888 v E (1)
Gow, J. J. (Queen's Park), 1885 v E (1)
Gow, J. R. (Rangers), 1888 v Ni (1)
Graham, A. (Leeds U), 1978 v EG (sub); 1979 v A (sub), N, W, Ni, E, Arg, N; 1980 v Pe (sub), A; 1981 v W (11)
Graham, G. (Arsenal), 1972 v P, Ho, Ni, Y, Cz, Br; 1973 v D (2); (with Manchester U), E, W, Ni, Br (sub) (12)
Graham, J. (Annbank), 1884 v Ni (1)
Graham, J. A. (Arsenal), 1921 v Ni (1)
Grant, J. (Hibernian), 1959 v W, Ni (2)
Grant, P. (Celtic), 1989 v E (sub), Ch (2)
Gray, A. (Hibernian), 1903 v Ni (1)
Gray, A. D. (Bradford C), 2003 v Li (sub), Nz (sub) (2)
Gray, A. M. (Aston Villa), 1976 v R, Sw; 1977 v Fi, Cz; 1979 v A, N; (with Wolverhampton W), 1980 v P, E (sub); 1981 v Se, P, Is (sub), Ni; 1982 v Se (sub), Ni (sub); 1983 v Ni, W, E, Ca (1+1 sub); (with Everton), 1985 v Ic (20)
Gray, D. (Rangers), 1929 v W, Ni, G, Ho; 1930 v W, E, Ni; 1931 v W; 1933 v W, Ni (10)
Gray, E. (Leeds U), 1969 v E, Cy; 1970 v WG, A; 1971 v W, Ni; 1972 v Bel, Ho; 1976 v W, E; 1977 v Fi, W (12)
Gray, F. T. (Leeds U), 1976 v Sw; 1979 v N, P, W, Ni, E, Arg (sub); (with Nottingham F), 1980 v Bel (sub); 1981 v Se, P, Is, Ni, Is, W; (with Leeds U), Ni, E; 1982 v Se, Ni, P, Sp, Ho, W, Nz, Br, USSR; 1983 v EG, Sw, Bel, Sw, W, E, Ca (32)
Gray, W. (Pollokshields Ath), 1886 v E (1)
Green, A. (Blackpool), 1971 v Bel (sub), P (sub), Ni, E; (with Newcastle U), 1972 v W, E (sub) (6)
Greig, J. (Rangers), 1964 v E, WG; 1965 v W, Ni, E, Fi (2), Sp, Pol; 1966 v Ni, W, E, Pol, I (2), P, Ho, Br; 1967 v W, Ni, E; 1968 v Ni, W, E, Ho; 1969 v W, Ni, E, D, A, WG, Cy (2); 1970 v W, E, Ei, WG, A; 1971 v D, Bel, W (sub), Ni, E; 1976 v D (44)
Groves, W. (Hibernian), 1888 v W; (with Celtic), 1889 v Ni; 1890 v E (3)
Gulliland, W. (Queen's Park), 1891 v W; 1892 v Ni; 1894 v E; 1895 v E (4)
Gunn, B. (Norwich C), 1990 v Eg; 1993 v Es (2); 1994 v Sw, I, Ho (sub) (6)

Haddock, H. (Clyde), 1955 v E, H (2), P, Y; 1958 v E (6)
Haddow, D. (Rangers), 1894 v E (1)
Haffey, F. (Celtic), 1960 v E; 1961 v E (2)
Hamilton, A. (Queen's Park), 1885 v E, W; 1886 v E; 1888 v E (4)
Hamilton, A. W. (Dundee), 1962 v Cz, U, W, E; 1963 v W, Ni, E, A, N, Ei; 1964 v Ni, W, E, N, WG; 1965 v Ni, W, E, Fi (2), Pol, Sp; 1966 v Pol, Ni (24)
Hamilton, G. (Aberdeen), 1947 v Ni; 1951 v Bel, A; 1954 v N (2) (5)
Hamilton, G. (Port Glasgow Ath), 1906 v Ni (1)
Hamilton, J. (Queen's Park), 1892 v W; 1893 v E, Ni (3)
Hamilton, J. (St Mirren), 1924 v Ni (1)
Hamilton, R. C. (Rangers), 1899 v E, W, Ni; 1900 v W; 1901 v E, Ni; 1902 v W, Ni; 1903 v E; 1904 v Ni; (with Dundee), 1911 v W (11)
Hamilton, T. (Hurlford), 1891 v Ni (1)
Hamilton, T. (Rangers), 1932 v E (1)
Hamilton, W. M. (Hibernian), 1965 v Fi (1)
Hammell, S. (Motherwell), 2005 v Se (sub) (1)
Hannah, A. B. (Renton), 1888 v W (1)
Hannah, J. (Third Lanark), 1889 v W (1)
Hansen, A. D. (Liverpool), 1979 v W, Arg; 1980 v Bel, P; 1981 v Se, P, Is; 1982 v Se, Ni, P, Sp, Ni (sub), W, E, Nz, Br, USSR; 1983 v EG, Sw, Bel, Sw; 1985 v W (sub); 1986 v R (sub); 1987 v Ei (2), L (26)
Hansen, J. (Partick Th), 1972 v Bel (sub), Y (sub) (2)
Harkness, J. D. (Queen's Park), 1927 v E, Ni; 1928 v E; (with Hearts), 1929 v W, E, Ni; 1930 v E, W; 1932 v W, F; 1934 v Ni, W (12)
Harper, J. M. (Aberdeen), 1973 v D (1+1 sub); (with Hibernian), 1976 v D; (with Aberdeen), 1978 v Ir (sub) (4)
Harper, W. (Hibernian), 1923 v E, Ni, W; 1924 v E, Ni, W; 1925 v E, Ni, W; (with Arsenal), 1926 v E, Ni (11)
Harris, J. (Partick Th), 1921 v W, Ni (2)
Harris, N. (Newcastle U), 1924 v E (1)
Harrower, W. (Queen's Park), 1882 v E; 1884 v Ni; 1886 v W (3)
Hartford, R. A. (WBA), 1972 v Pe, W (sub), E, Y, Cz, Br; (with Manchester C), 1976 v D, R, Ni (sub); 1977 v Cz (sub), W (sub), Se, W, Ni, E, Ch, Arg, Br; 1978 v EG, Cz, W, Bul, W, E, Pe, Ir, Ho; 1979 v A, N, P, W,

Ni, E, Arg, N; (with Everton), 1980 v Pe, Bel; 1981 v Ni (sub), Is, W, Ni, E; 1982 v Se; (with Manchester C), Ni, P, Sp, Ni, W, E, Br (50)
Hartley, P. J. (Hearts), 2005 v I, Mol; 2006 v I, N, Bl, Slv, US; 2007 v Fa, Li, F, Uk; (with Celtic), Ge, I, A (sub), Fa (15)
Harvey, D. (Leeds U), 1973 v D; 1974 v Cz, WG, Ni, W, E, Bel, Z, Br, Y; 1975 v EG, Sp (2); 1976 v D (2); 1977 v Fi (sub) (16)
Hastings, A. C. (Sunderland), 1936 v Ni; 1938 v Ni (2)
Haughney, M. (Celtic), 1954 v E (1)
Hay, D. (Celtic), 1970 v Ni, W, E; 1971 v D, Bel, W, P, Ni; 1972 v P, Bel, Ho; 1973 v W, Ni, E, Sw, Br; 1974 v Cz (2), WG, Ni, W, E, Bel, N, Z, Br, Y (27)
Hay, J. (Celtic), 1905 v Ni; 1909 v Ni; 1910 v W, Ni, E; 1911 v Ni, E; (with Newcastle U), 1912 v E, W; 1914 v E, Ni (11)
Hegarty, P. (Dundee U), 1979 v W, Ni, E, Arg, N (sub); 1980 v W, E; 1983 v Ni (8)
Heggie, C. (Rangers), 1886 v Ni (1)
Henderson, G. H. (Rangers), 1904 v Ni (1)
Henderson, J. G. (Portsmouth), 1953 v Se; 1954 v Ni, E, N; 1956 v W; (with Arsenal), 1959 v W, Ni (7)
Henderson, W. (Rangers), 1963 v W, Ni, E, A, N, Ei, Sp; 1964 v W, Ni, E, N, WG; 1965 v Fi, Pol, E, Sp; 1966 v Ni, W, Pol, I, Ho; 1967 v W, Ni; 1968 v Ho; 1969 v Ni, E, Cy; 1970 v Ei; 1971 v P (29)
Hendry, E. C. J. (Blackburn R), 1993 v Es (2); 1994 v Ma, Ho, A, Ho; 1995 v Fi, Fa, Gr, Ru, Sm; 1996 v Fi, Se, Sm, Aus, D, US, Co, Ho, E, Sw; 1997 v A, Se, Es (2), A, Se; 1998 v La, D, Fi, Co, US, Br, N, Mor; (with Rangers), 1999 v Li, Es, Fa, G; 2000 v Bos, Es, Bos, E (2); (with Coventry C), F; 2001 v La, Sm, Cro, Aus (sub); (with Bolton W), Bel, Sm (51)
Hepburn, J. (Alloa Ath), 1891 v W (1)
Hepburn, R. (Ayr U), 1932 v Ni (1)
Herd, A. C. (Hearts), 1935 v Ni (1)
Herd, D. G. (Arsenal), 1959 v E, W, Ni; 1961 v Ei, Cz (5)
Herd, G. (Clyde), 1958 v E; 1960 v H, T; 1961 v W, Ni (5)
Herriot, J. (Birmingham C), 1969 v Ni, E, D, Cy (2), W (sub); 1970 v Ei (sub), WG (8)
Hewie, J. D. (Charlton Ath), 1956 v E, A; 1957 v E, Ni, W, Y, Sp (2), Sw, WG; 1958 v H, Pol, Y, F; 1959 v Ho, P; 1960 v Ni, W, Pol (19)
Higgins, A. (Kilmarnock), 1885 v Ni (1)
Higgins, A. (Newcastle U), 1910 v E, Ni; 1911 v E, Ni (4)
Highet, T. C. (Queen's Park), 1875 v E; 1876 v E, W; 1878 v E (4)
Hill, D. (Rangers), 1881 v E, W; 1882 v W (3)
Hill, D. A. (Third Lanark), 1906 v Ni (1)
Hill, F. R. (Aberdeen), 1930 v F; 1931 v W, Ni (3)
Hill, J. (Hearts), 1891 v E; 1892 v W (2)
Hogg, G (Hearts), 1896 v E, Ni (2)
Hogg, J. (Ayr U), 1922 v Ni (1)
Hogg, R. M. (Celtic), 1937 v Cz (1)
Holm, A. H. (Queen's Park), 1882 v W; 1883 v E, W (3)
Holt, D. D. (Hearts), 1963 v A, N, Ei, Sp; 1964 v WG (sub) (5)
Holt, G. J. (Kilmarnock), 2001 v La (sub), Cro (sub); (with Norwich C), 2002 v F (sub); 2004 v D, Es, Tr; 2005 v H, Slv (sub), N, Mol (10)
Holton, J. A. (Manchester U), 1973 v W, Ni, E, Sw, Br; 1974 v Cz, WG, Ni, W, E, N, Z, Br, Y; 1975 v EG (15)
Hope, R. (WBA), 1968 v Ho; 1969 v D (2)
Hopkin, D. (C Palace), 1997 v Ma, Bl; (with Leeds U), 1998 v Bl (sub), F (sub); 1999 v CzR; 2000 v Bos (2) (7)
Houliston, W. (Queen of the South), 1949 v E, Ni, F (3)
Houston, S. M. (Manchester U), 1976 v D (1)
Howden, W. (Partick Th), 1905 v Ni (1)
Howe, R. (Hamilton A), 1929 v N, Ho (2)
Howie, H. (Hibernian), 1949 v W (1)
Howie, J. (Newcastle U), 1905 v E; 1906 v E; 1908 v E (3)
Howieson, J. (St Mirren), 1927 v Ni (1)
Hughes, J. (Celtic), 1965 v Pol, Sp; 1966 v Ni, I (2); 1968 v E; 1969 v A; 1970 v Ei (8)
Hughes, R. D. (Portsmouth), 2004 v Es, Tr (sub); 2005 v N, Se (sub); 2006 v A (sub) (5)
Hughes, W. (Sunderland), 1975 v Se (sub) (1)
Humphries, W. (Motherwell), 1952 v Se (1)
Hunter, A. (Kilmarnock), 1972 v Pe, Y; (with Celtic), 1973 v E; 1974 v Cz (4)
Hunter, J. (Dundee), 1909 v W (1)
Hunter, J. (Third Lanark), 1874 v E; (with Eastern), 1875 v E; (with Third Lanark), 1876 v E; 1877 v W (4)
Hunter, R. (St Mirren), 1890 v Ni (1)
Hunter, W. (Motherwell), 1960 v H, T; 1961 v W (3)
Husband, J. (Partick Th), 1947 v W (1)
Hutchison, D. (Everton), 1999 v CzR (sub), G; 2000 v Bos, Es, Li, E (2), F, Ho, Ei; (with Sunderland), 2001 v La, Sm, Cro, Aus, Bel, Sm; (with West Ham U), 2002 v Cro, Bel, La; 2003 v Ei, Ic, Li, A; 2004 v N, Li (sub), Ho (sub) (26)
Hutchison, T. (Coventry C), 1974 v Cz (2), WG (2), Ni, W, Bel (sub), N, Z (sub), Y (sub); 1975 v EG, Sp (2), P, E (sub), R (sub); 1976 v D (17)
Hutton, A. (Rangers), 2007 v A (sub) (1)
Hutton, J. (Aberdeen), 1923 v E, W, Ni; 1924 v Ni; 1926 v W, E, Ni; (with Blackburn R), 1927 v Ni; 1928 v W, Ni (10)
Hutton, J. (St Bernards), 1887 v Ni (1)
Hyslop, T. (Stoke C), 1896 v E; (with Rangers), 1897 v E (2)

Imlach, J. J. S. (Nottingham F), 1958 v H, Pol, Y, F (4)
Imrie, W. N. (St Johnstone), 1929 v N, G (2)
Inglis, J. (Rangers), 1883 v E, W (2)
Inglis, J. (Kilmarnock Ath), 1884 v Ni (1)
Irons, J. H. (Queen's Park), 1900 v W (1)
Irvine, B. (Aberdeen), 1991 v R; 1993 v G, Es (2); 1994 v Sw, I, Ma, A, Ho (9)

Jackson, A. (Cambuslang), 1886 v W; 1888 v Ni (2)
Jackson, A. (Aberdeen), 1925 v E, W, Ni; (with Huddersfield T), 1926 v E, W, Ni; 1927 v W, Ni; 1928 v E, W; 1929 v E, W, Ni; 1930 v E, W, Ni, F (17)
Jackson, C. (Rangers), 1975 v Se, P (sub), W; 1976 v D, R, Ni, W, E (8)
Jackson, D. (Hibernian), 1995 v Ru, Sm, J, Ec, Fa; 1996 v Gr, Fi (sub), Se (sub), Sm (sub), Aus (sub), D (sub), US; 1997 v La, Se, Es, A, Se, W, Ma, Bl; (with Celtic), 1998 v D, Fi, Co, US, Br, N; 1999 v Li, Es (sub) (28)
Jackson, J. (Partick Th), 1931 v A, I, Sw; 1933 v E; (with Chelsea), 1934 v E; 1935 v E; 1936 v W, Ni (8)
Jackson, T. A. (St Mirren), 1904 v W, E, Ni; 1905 v W; 1907 v W, Ni (6)
James, A. W. (Preston NE), 1926 v W; 1928 v E; 1929 v E, Ni; (with Arsenal), 1930 v E, W, Ni; 1933 v W (8)
Jardine, A. (Rangers), 1971 v D (sub); 1972 v P, Bel, Ho; 1973 v E, Sw, Br; 1974 v Cz (2), WG (2), Ni, W, E, Bel, N, Z, Br, Y; 1975 v EG, Sp (2), Se, P, W, Ni, E; 1977 v Se (sub), Ch (sub), Br (sub); 1978 v Cz, W, Ni, Ir; 1980 v Pe, A, Bel (2) (38)
Jarvie, A. (Airdrieonians), 1971 v P (sub), Ni (sub), E (sub) (3)
Jenkinson, T. (Hearts), 1887 v Ni (1)
Jess, E. (Aberdeen), 1993 v I (sub), Ma; 1994 v Sw (sub), I, Ho (sub), A, Ho (sub); 1995 v Fi (sub); 1996 v Se (sub), Sm; (with Coventry C), US, Co (sub), E (sub); (with Aberdeen), 1998 v D (sub); 1999 v CzR, G (sub), Fa (sub), CzR (sub) (18)
Johnston, A. (Sunderland), 1999 v Es, Fa, CzR (sub), G, Fa, CzR; 2000 v Es, F (sub), Ei (sub); (with Rangers), 2001 v Sm (sub), Cro, Sm; (with Middlesbrough), 2002 v Ng (sub), Sk, S.Af, Hk; 2003 v D (sub), Fa (18)
Johnston, L. H. (Clyde), 1948 v Bel, Sw (2)
Johnston, M. (Watford), 1984 v W (sub), E (sub), F; 1985 v Y; (with Celtic), Ic, Sp (2), W; 1986 v EG; 1987 v Bul, Ei (2), L; (with Nantes), 1988 v H, Bel, L, S.Ar, Sp, Co, E; 1989 v N, Y, I, Cy, F, Cy, E, Ch (sub); (with Rangers), 1990 v F, N, EG, Pol, Ma, Cr, Se, Br; 1992 v Sw, Sm (sub) (38)
Johnston, R. (Sunderland), 1938 v Cz (1)
Johnston, W. (Rangers), 1966 v W, E, Pol, Ho; 1968 v W, E; 1969 v Ni (sub); 1970 v Ni; 1971 v D; (with WBA), 1977 v Se, W (sub), Ni, E, Ch, Arg, Br; 1978 v EG, Cz, W (2), E, Pe (22)
Johnstone, D. (Rangers), 1973 v W, Ni, E, Sw, Br; 1975 v EG (sub), Se (sub); 1976 v Sw, Ni (sub), E (sub); 1978 v Bul (sub), Ni, W; 1980 v Bel (14)
Johnstone, J. (Abercorn), 1888 v W (1)
Johnstone, J. (Celtic), 1965 v W, Fi; 1966 v E; 1967 v W, USSR; 1968 v W; 1969 v A, WG; 1970 v E, WG; 1971 v D, E; 1972 v P, Bel, Ho, Ni, E (sub); 1974 v W, E, Bel, N; 1975 v EG, Sp (23)
Johnstone, Jas (Kilmarnock), 1894 v W (1)
Johnstone, J. A. (Hearts), 1930 v W; 1933 v W, Ni (3)
Johnstone, R. (Hibernian), 1951 v E, D, F; 1952 v Ni, E; 1953 v E, Se; 1954 v W, E, N, Fi; 1955 v Ni, H; (with Manchester C), 1955 v E; 1956 v E, Ni, W (17)

Johnstone, W. (Third Lanark), 1887 v Ni; 1889 v W; 1890 v E (3)
Jordan, J. (Leeds U), 1973 v E (sub), Sw (sub), Br; 1974 v Cz (sub+1), WG (sub), Ni (sub), W, E, Bel, N, Z, Br, Y; 1975 v EG, Sp (2); 1976 v Ni, W, E; 1977 v Cz, W, Ni, E; 1978 v EG, Cz, W; (with Manchester U), Bul, Ni, E, Pe, Ir, Ho; 1979 v A, P, W (sub), Ni, E, N; 1980 v Bel, Ni (sub), W, E, Pol; 1981 v Is, W, E; (with AC Milan), 1982 v Se, Ho, W, E, USSR (52)

Kay, J. L. (Queen's Park), 1880 v E; 1882 v E, W; 1883 v E, W; 1884 v W (6)
Keillor, A. (Montrose), 1891 v W; 1892 v Ni; (with Dundee), 1894 v Ni; 1895 v W; 1896 v W; 1897 v W (6)
Keir, L. (Dumbarton), 1885 v W; 1886 v Ni; 1887 v E, W; 1888 v E (5)
Kelly, H. T. (Blackpool), 1952 v USA (1)
Kelly, J. (Renton), 1888 v E; (with Celtic), 1889 v E; 1890 v E; 1892 v E; 1893 v E, Ni; 1894 v W; 1896 v Ni (8)
Kelly, J. C. (Barnsley), 1949 v W, Ni (2)
Kelso, R. (Renton), 1885 v W, Ni; 1886 v W; 1887 v E, W; 1888 v E; (with Dundee), 1898 v Ni (7)
Kelso, T. (Dundee), 1914 v W (1)
Kennaway, J. (Celtic), 1934 v A (1)
Kennedy, A. (Eastern), 1875 v E; 1876 v E, W; (with Third Lanark), 1878 v E; 1882 v W; 1884 v W (6)
Kennedy, J. (Hibernian), 1897 v W (1)
Kennedy, J. (Celtic), 1964 v W, E, WG; 1965 v W, Ni, Fi (6)
Kennedy, J. (Celtic), 2004 v R (1)
Kennedy, S. (Aberdeen), 1978 v Bul, W, E, Pe, Ho; 1979 v A, P; 1982 v P (sub) (8)
Kennedy, S. (Partick Th), 1905 v W (1)
Kennedy, S. (Rangers), 1975 v Se, P, W, Ni, E (5)
Ker, G. (Queen's Park), 1880 v E; 1881 v E, W; 1882 v W, E (5)
Ker, W. (Queen's Park), 1872 v E; 1873 v E (2)
Kerr, A. (Partick Th), 1955 v A, H (2)
Kerr, B. (Newcastle U), 2003 v Nz (sub); 2004 v Es (sub); Tr (sub) (3)
Kerr, P. (Hibernian), 1924 v Ni (1)
Key, G. (Hearts), 1902 v Ni (1)
Key, W. (Queen's Park), 1907 v Ni (1)
King, A. (Hearts), 1896 v E, W; (with Celtic), 1897 v Ni; 1898 v Ni; 1899 v Ni, W (6)
King, J. (Hamilton A), 1933 v Ni; 1934 v Ni (2)
King, W. S. (Queen's Park), 1929 v W (1)
Kinloch, J. D. (Partick Th), 1922 v Ni (1)
Kinnaird, A. F. (Wanderers), 1873 v E (1)
Kinnear, D. (Rangers), 1938 v Cz (1)
Kyle, K. (Sunderland), 2002 v Sk (sub), S.Af, Hk; 2003 v D, Fa, Ca (sub), P (sub), Nz; 2004 v D (9)

Lambert, P. (Motherwell), 1995 v J, Ec (sub); (with Borussia Dortmund), 1997 v La (sub), Se (sub), A, Se, Bl; 1998 v Bl, La; (with Celtic), Fi (sub), Co, US, Br, N, Mor; 1999 v Li, CzR, G, Fa, CzR; 2000 v Bos, Li, Ho, Ei; 2001 v Bel, Sm; 2002 v Cro, Bel, F, Ng; 2003 v D, Fa, Ic, P, Ei, Ic, Li, G; 2004 v N, G (40)
Lambie, J. A. (Queen's Park), 1886 v Ni; 1887 v Ni; 1888 v E (3)
Lambie, W. A. (Queen's Park), 1892 v Ni; 1893 v W; 1894 v E; 1895 v E, Ni; 1896 v E, Ni; 1897 v E, Ni (9)
Lamont, W. (Pilgrims), 1885 v Ni (1)
Lang, A. (Dumbarton), 1880 v W (1)
Lang, J. J. (Clydesdale), 1876 v W; (with Third Lanark), 1878 v W (2)
Latta, A. (Dumbarton), 1888 v W; 1889 v E (2)
Law, D. (Huddersfield T), 1959 v W, Ni, Ho, P; 1960 v Ni, W; (with Manchester C), 1960 v E, Pol, A; 1961 v E, Ni; (with Torino), 1962 v Cz (2), E; (with Manchester U), 1963 v W, Ni, E, A, N, Ei, Sp; 1964 v W, E, N, WG; 1965 v W, Ni, E, Fi (2), Pol, Sp; 1966 v Ni, E, Pol; 1967 v W, E, USSR; 1968 v Ni; 1969 v Ni, A, WG; 1972 v Pe, Ni, W, E, Y, Cz, Br; (with Manchester C), 1974 v Cz (2), WG (2), Ni, Z (55)
Law, G. (Rangers), 1910 v E, Ni, W (3)
Law, T. (Chelsea), 1928 v E; 1930 v E (2)
Lawrence, J. (Newcastle U), 1911 v E (1)
Lawrence, T. (Liverpool), 1963 v Ei; 1969 v W, WG (3)
Lawson, D. (St Mirren), 1923 v E (1)
Leckie, R. (Queen's Park), 1872 v E (1)
Leggat, G. (Aberdeen), 1956 v E; 1957 v W; 1958 v Ni, H, Pol, Y, Par; (with Fulham), 1959 v E, W, Ni, WG, Ho; 1960 v E, Ni, W, Pol, A, H (18)
Leighton, J. (Aberdeen), 1983 v EG, Sw, Bel, Sw, W, E, Ca (2); 1984 v U, Bel, Ni, W, E, F; 1985 v Y, Ic, Sp (2), W, E, Ic; 1986 v W, EG, Aus (2), Is, D, WG, U; 1987 v Bul, Ei (2), L, Bel, E; 1988 v H, Bel, Bul, L, S.Ar, Ma, Sp; (with Manchester U), Co, E; 1989 v N, Cy, F, Cy, E, Ch; 1990 v Y, F, N, Arg, Ma (sub), Cr, Se, Br; (with Hibernian), 1994 v Ma, A, Ho; 1995 v Gr (sub), Ru, Sm, J, Ec, Fa; 1996 v Gr, Fi, Se, Sm, Aus, D, US; 1997 v Se, Es, A, Se, W (sub), Ma, Bl; (with Aberdeen), 1998 v Bl, La, D, Fi, US, Br, N, Mor; 1999 v Li, Es (91)
Lennie, W. (Aberdeen), 1908 v W, Ni (2)
Lennox, R. (Celtic), 1967 v Ni, E, USSR; 1968 v W, E; 1969 v D, A, WG, Cy (sub); 1970 v W (sub) (10)
Leslie, L. G. (Airdrieonians), 1961 v W, Ni, Ei (2), Cz (5)
Levein, C. (Hearts), 1990 v Arg, EG, Eg (sub), Pol, Ma (sub), Se; 1992 v R, Sm; 1993 v P, G, P; 1994 v Sw, Ho; 1995 v Fi, Fa, Ru (16)
Liddell, W. (Liverpool), 1947 v W, Ni; 1948 v E, W, Ni; 1950 v E, W, P, F; 1951 v W, Ni, E, A; 1952 v W, Ni, E, USA, D, Se; 1953 v W, Ni, E; 1954 v W; 1955 v P, Y, A, H; 1956 v Ni (28)
Liddle, D. (East Fife), 1931 v A, I, Sw (3)
Lindsay, D. (St Mirren), 1903 v Ni (1)
Lindsay, J. (Dumbarton), 1880 v W; 1881 v W, E; 1884 v W, E; 1885 v W, E; 1886 v E (8)
Lindsay, J. (Renton), 1888 v E; 1893 v E, Ni (3)
Linwood, A. B. (Clyde), 1950 v W (1)
Little, R. J. (Rangers), 1953 v Se (1)
Livingstone, G. T. (Manchester C), 1906 v E; (with Rangers), 1907 v W (2)
Lochhead, A. (Third Lanark), 1889 v W (1)
Logan, J. (Ayr), 1891 v W (1)
Logan, T. (Falkirk), 1913 v Ni (1)
Logie, J. T. (Arsenal), 1953 v Ni (1)
Loney, W. (Celtic), 1910 v W, Ni (2)
Long, H. (Clyde), 1947 v Ni (1)
Longair, W. (Dundee), 1894 v Ni (1)
Lorimer, P. (Leeds U), 1970 v A (sub); 1971 v W, Ni; 1972 v Ni (sub), W, E; 1973 v D (2), E (2); 1974 v WG (sub), E, Bel, N, Z, Br, Y; 1975 v Sp (sub); 1976 v D (2), R (sub) (21)
Love, A. (Aberdeen), 1931 v A, I, Sw (3)
Low, A. (Falkirk), 1934 v Ni (1)
Low, J. (Cambuslang), 1891 v Ni (1)
Low, T. P. (Rangers), 1897 v Ni (1)
Low, W. L. (Newcastle U), 1911 v E, W; 1912 v Ni; 1920 v E, Ni (5)
Lowe, J. (St Bernards), 1887 v Ni (1)
Lundie, J. (Hibernian), 1886 v W (1)
Lyall, J. (Sheffield W), 1905 v E (1)

McAdam, J. (Third Lanark), 1880 v W (1)
McAllister, B. (Wimbledon), 1997 v W, Ma, Bl (sub) (3)
McAllister, G. (Leicester C), 1990 v EG, Pol, Ma (sub); (with Leeds U), 1991 v R, Sw, Bul, USSR (sub), Sm; 1992 v Sw (sub), Sm, Ni, Fi (sub), US, Ca, N, Ho, G, C; 1993 v Sw, P, I, Ma; 1994 v Sw, I, Ma, Ho, A, Ho; 1995 v Fi, Ru, Gr, Ru, Sm; 1996 v Gr, Fi, Se, Sm, Aus, D, US (sub), Co, Ho, E, Sw; (with Coventry C), 1997 v A, La, Es (2), A, Se, W, Ma, Bl; 1998 v Bl, La, F; 1999 v CzR (57)
McAllister, J. R. (Livingston), 2004 v Tr (1)
Macari, L. (Celtic), 1972 v W (sub), E, Y, Cz, Br; 1973 v D; (with Manchester U), E (2), W (sub), Ni (sub); 1975 v Se, P (sub), W, E (sub), R; 1977 v Ni (sub), E (sub), Ch, Arg; 1978 v EG, W, Bul, Pe (sub), Ir (24)
McArthur, D. (Celtic), 1895 v E, Ni; 1899 v W (3)
McAtee, A. (Celtic), 1913 v W (1)
McAulay, J. (Arthurlie), 1884 v Ni (1)
McAulay, J. D. (Dumbarton), 1882 v W; 1883 v E, W; 1884 v E; 1885 v E, W; 1886 v E; 1887 v E, W (9)
McAulay, R. (Rangers), 1932 v Ni, W (2)
Macauley, A. R. (Brentford), 1947 v E; (with Arsenal), 1948 v E, W, Ni, Bel, Sw, F (7)
McAvennie, F. (West Ham U), 1986 v Aus (2), D (sub), WG (sub); (with Celtic), 1988 v S.Ar (5)
McBain, E. (St Mirren), 1894 v W (1)
McBain, N. (Manchester U), 1922 v E; (with Everton), 1923 v Ni; 1924 v W (3)
McBride, J. (Celtic), 1967 v W, Ni (2)
McBride, P. (Preston NE), 1904 v E; 1906 v E; 1907 v E, W; 1908 v E; 1909 v W (6)
McCall, A. (Renton), 1888 v Ni (1)
McCall, J. (Renton), 1886 v W; 1887 v E, W; 1888 v E; 1890 v E (5)

McCall, S. M. (Everton), 1990 v Arg, EG, Eg (sub), Pol, Ma, Cr, Se, Br; 1991 v Sw, USSR, Sm; (with Rangers), 1992 v Sw, R, Sm, US, Ca, N, Ho, G, C; 1993 v Sw, P (2); 1994 v I, Ho, A (sub), Ho; 1995 v Fi (sub), Ru, Gr; 1996 v Gr, D, US (sub), Co, Ho, E, Sw; 1997 v A, La; 1998 v D (sub) (40)
McCalliog, J. (Sheffield W), 1967 v E, USSR; 1968 v Ni; 1969 v D; (with Wolverhampton W), 1971 v P (5)
McCallum, N. (Renton), 1888 v Ni (1)
McCann, N. (Hearts), 1999 v Li (sub); (with Rangers), CzR; 2000 v Bos, Es (sub), E, F (sub), Ho, Ei; 2001 v La, Sm, Aus (sub); 2002 v Cro, La, F, Ng; 2003 v Ei; (with Southampton), 2004 v Fa, G, Ho (2), R, D (sub); 2005 v I (sub); 2006 v I (sub), N (sub), US (26)
McCann, R. J. (Motherwell), 1959 v WG; 1960 v E, Ni, W; 1961 v E (5)
McCartney, W. (Hibernian), 1902 v Ni (1)
McClair, B. (Celtic), 1987 v L, Ei, E, Br (sub); (with Manchester U), 1988 v Bul, Ma (sub), Sp (sub); 1989 v N, Y, I (sub), Cy, F (sub); 1990 v N (sub), Arg (sub); 1991 v Bul (2), Sm; 1992 v Sw (sub), R, Ni, US, Ca (sub), N, Ho, G, C; 1993 v Sw, P (sub), Es (2) (30)
McClory, A. (Motherwell), 1927 v W; 1928 v Ni; 1935 v W (3)
McCloy, P. (Ayr U), 1924 v E; 1925 v E (2)
McCloy, P. (Rangers), 1973 v W, Ni, Sw, Br (4)
McCoist, A. (Rangers), 1986 v Ho; 1987 v L (sub), Ei (sub), Bel, E, Br; 1988 v H, Bel, Ma, Sp, Co, E; 1989 v Y (sub), F, Cy, E; 1990 v Y, F, N, EG (sub), Eg, Pol, Ma (sub), Cr (sub), Se (sub), Br; 1991 v R, Sw, Bul (2), USSR; 1992 v Sw, Sm, Ni, Fi (sub), US, Ca, N, Ho, G, C; 1993 v Sw, P, I, Ma, P; 1996 v Gr (sub), Fi (sub), Sm (sub), Aus, D (sub), Co, E (sub), Sw; 1997 v A, Se (sub), Es (sub), A (sub); 1998 v Bl (sub); (with Kilmarnock), 1999 v Li, Es (61)
McColl, I. M. (Rangers), 1950 v E, F; 1951 v W, Ni, Bel; 1957 v E, Ni, W, Y, Sp, Sw, WG; 1958 v Ni, E (14)
McColl, R. S. (Queen's Park), 1896 v W, Ni; 1897 v Ni; 1898 v Ni; 1899 v Ni, E, W; 1900 v E, W; 1901 v E, W; (with Newcastle U), 1902 v E; (with Queen's Park), 1908 v Ni (13)
McColl, W. (Renton), 1895 v W (1)
McCombie, A. (Sunderland), 1903 v E, W; (with Newcastle U), 1905 v E, W (4)
McCorkindale, J. (Partick Th), 1891 v W (1)
McCormick, R. (Abercorn), 1886 v W (1)
McCrae, D. (St Mirren), 1929 v N, G (2)
McCreadie, A. (Rangers), 1893 v W; 1894 v E (2)
McCreadie, E. G. (Chelsea), 1965 v E, Sp, Fi, Pol; 1966 v P, Ni, W, Pol, I; 1967 v E, USSR; 1968 v Ni, W, E, Ho; 1969 v W, Ni, E, D, A, WG, Cy (2) (23)
McCulloch, D. (Hearts), 1935 v W; (with Brentford), 1936 v E; 1937 v W, Ni; 1938 v Cz; (with Derby Co), 1939 v H, W (7)
McCulloch, L. (Wigan Ath), 2005 v Mol (sub), I, Mol, Bl; 2006 v Bl, Bul, J; 2007 v F, Ge, I, A (11)
MacDonald, A. (Rangers), 1976 v Sw (1)
McDonald, J. (Edinburgh University), 1886 v E (1)
McDonald, J. (Sunderland), 1956 v W, Ni (2)
MacDougall, E. J. (Norwich C) 1975 v Se, P, W, Ni, E; 1976 v D, R (sub) (7)
McDougall, J. (Vale of Leven), 1877 v E, W; 1878 v E; 1879 v E, W (5)
McDougall, J. (Airdrieonians), 1926 v Ni (1)
McDougall, J. (Liverpool), 1931 v I, A (2)
McFadden, J. (Motherwell), 2002 v S.Af (sub); 2003 v Ca (sub), A, Nz; (with Everton), 2004 v Fa (sub), G, Li, Ho (2), W (sub), R (sub), D, Es, Tr; 2005 v H, Sp, Slv, N, Se, Mol (sub), Bl (sub); 2006 v N, Slv, US (sub), Sw, Bul (sub), J; 2007 v Fa, Li, F, Uk (31)
McFadyen, W. (Motherwell), 1934 v A, W (2)
Macfarlane, A. (Dundee), 1904 v W; 1906 v W; 1908 v W; 1909 v Ni; 1911 v W (5)
Macfarlane, W. (Hearts), 1947 v L (1)
McFarlane, R. (Greenock Morton), 1896 v W (1)
McGarr, E. (Aberdeen), 1970 v Ei, A (2)
McGarvey, F. P. (Liverpool), 1979 v Ni (sub), Arg; (with Celtic), 1984 v U, Bel (sub), EG (sub), Ni, W (7)
McGeoch, A. (Dumbreck), 1876 v E, W; 1877 v E, W (4)
McGhee, J. (Hibernian), 1886 v W (1)
McGhee, M. (Aberdeen), 1983 v Ca (1+1 sub); 1984 v Ni (sub), E (4)
McGinlay, J. (Bolton W), 1994 v A, Ho; 1995 v Fa, Ru, Gr, Ru, Sm, Fa; 1996 v Se; 1997 v Se, Es (1 + sub), A (sub) (13)
McGonagle, W. (Celtic), 1933 v E; 1934 v A, E, Ni; 1935 v Ni, W (6)
McGrain, D. (Celtic), 1973 v W, Ni, E, Sw, Br; 1974 v Cz (2), WG, W (sub), E, Bel, N, Z, Br, Y; 1975 v Sp, Se, P, W, Ni, E, R; 1976 v D (2), Sw, Ni, W, E; 1977 v Fi, Cz, W (2), Se, Ni, E, Ch, Arg, Br; 1978 v EG, Cz; 1980 v Bel, P, Ni, W, E, Pol, H; 1981 v Se, P, Is, Ni, Is, W (sub), Ni, E; 1982 v Se, Sp, Ho, Ni, E, Nz, USSR (sub) (62)
McGregor, A. (Rangers), 2007 v A (1)
McGregor, J. C. (Vale of Leven), 1877 v E, W; 1878 v E; 1880 v E (4)
McGrory, J. (Celtic), 1928 v Ni; 1931 v E; 1932 v Ni, W; 1933 v E, Ni; 1934 v Ni (7)
McGrory, J. E. (Kilmarnock), 1965 v Ni, Fi; 1966 v P (3)
McGuire, W. (Beith), 1881 v E, W (2)
McGurk, F. (Birmingham), 1934 v W (1)
McHardy, H. (Rangers), 1885 v Ni (1)
McInally, A. (Aston Villa), 1989 v Cy (sub), Ch; (with Bayern Munich), 1990 v Y (sub), F (sub), Arg, Pol (sub), Ma, Cr (8)
McInally, J. (Dundee U), 1987 v Bel, Br; 1988 v Ma (sub); 1991 v Bul (2); 1992 v US (sub), N (sub), C (sub); 1993 v G, P (10)
McInally, T. B. (Celtic), 1926 v Ni; 1927 v W (2)
McInnes, D. (WBA), 2003 v D (sub), P (sub) (2)
McInnes, T. (Cowlairs), 1889 v Ni (1)
McIntosh, W. (Third Lanark), 1905 v Ni (1)
McIntyre, A. (Vale of Leven), 1878 v E; 1882 v E (2)
McIntyre, H. (Rangers), 1880 v W (1)
McIntyre, J. (Rangers), 1884 v W (1)
MacKay, D. (Celtic), 1959 v E, WG, Ho, P; 1960 v E, Pol, A, H, T; 1961 v W, Ni; 1962 v Ni, Cz, U (sub) (14)
Mackay, D. C. (Hearts), 1957 v Sp; 1958 v F; 1959 v W, Ni; (with Tottenham H), 1959 v WG, E; 1960 v W, Ni, A, Pol, H, T; 1961 v W, Ni, E; 1963 v E, A, N; 1964 v Ni, W, N; 1966 v Ni (22)
Mackay, G. (Hearts), 1988 v Bul (sub), L (sub), S.Ar (sub), Ma (4)
Mackay, M. (Norwich C), 2004 v D, Es, Tr; 2005 v Sp, Slv (5)
McKay, J. (Blackburn R), 1924 v W (1)
McKay, R. (Newcastle U), 1928 v W (1)
McKean, R. (Rangers), 1976 v Sw (sub) (1)
McKenzie, D. (Brentford), 1938 v Ni (1)
Mackenzie, J. A. (Partick Th), 1954 v W, E, N, Fi, A, U; 1955 v E, H; 1956 v A (9)
McKeown, M. (Celtic), 1889 v Ni; 1890 v E (2)
McKie, J. (East Stirling), 1898 v W (1)
McKillop, T. R. (Rangers), 1938 v Ho (1)
McKimmie, S. (Aberdeen), 1989 v E, Ch; 1990 v Arg, Eg, Cr (sub), Br; 1991 v R, Sw, Bul, Sm; 1992 v Sw, R, Ni, Fi, US, Ca (sub), N (sub), Ho, G, C; 1993 v P, Es (sub); 1994 v Sw, I, Ho, A, Ho; 1995 v Fi, Fa, Ru, Gr, Ru, Fa; 1996 v Gr, Fi, Se, D, Co, Ho, E (40)
McKinlay, D. (Liverpool), 1922 v W, Ni (2)
McKinlay, T. (Celtic), 1996 v Gr, Fi, D, Co, E, Sw; 1997 v A, La, Se, Es (sub + 1), A, Se, W, Ma, Bl; 1998 v Bl, La (sub), F (sub), US, Br (sub), Mor (sub) (22)
McKinlay, W. (Dundee U), 1994 v Ma, Ho (sub), A, Ho; 1995 v Fa (sub), Ru, Gr, Ru (sub), Sm (sub), J, Ec, Fa; 1996 v Fi (sub), Se (sub); (with Blackburn R), Sm (sub), Aus, D (sub), Ho (sub); 1997 v Se, Es (sub); 1998 v La (sub), F, D, Fi, Co (sub), US, Br (sub); 1999 v Es, Fa (29)
McKinnon, A. (Queen's Park), 1874 v E (1)
McKinnon, R. (Rangers), 1966 v W, E, I (2), Ho, Br; 1967 v W, Ni, E; 1968 v Ni, W, E, Ho; 1969 v D, A, WG, Cy; 1970 v Ni, W, E, Ei, WG, A; 1971 v D, Bel, P, USSR, D (28)
McKinnon, R. (Motherwell), 1994 v Ma; 1995 v J, Fa (3)
MacKinnon, W. (Dumbarton), 1883 v E, W; 1884 v E, W (4)
MacKinnon, W. W. (Queen's Park), 1872 v E; 1873 v E; 1874 v E; 1875 v E; 1876 v E, W; 1877 v E; 1878 v E; 1879 v E (9)
McLaren, A. (St Johnstone), 1929 v N, G, Ho; 1933 v W, Ni (5)
McLaren, A. (Preston NE), 1947 v E, Bel, L; 1948 v W (4)
McLaren, A. (Hearts), 1992 v US, Ca, N; 1993 v I, Ma, G, Es (sub + 1); 1994 v I, Ma, Ho, A; 1995 v Fi, Fa; (with Rangers), Ru, Gr, Ru, Sm, J, Ec, Fa; 1996 v Fi, Se, Sm (24)
McLaren, A. (Kilmarnock), 2001 v Pol (sub) (1)

McLaren, J. (Hibernian), 1888 v W; (with Celtic), 1889 v E; 1890 v E (3)
McLean, A. (Celtic), 1926 v W, Ni; 1927 v W, E (4)
McLean, D. (St Bernards), 1896 v W; 1897 v Ni (2)
McLean, D. (Sheffield W), 1912 v E (1)
McLean, G. (Dundee), 1968 v Ho (1)
McLean, T. (Kilmarnock), 1969 v D, Cy, W; 1970 v Ni, W; 1971 v D (6)
McLeish, A. (Aberdeen), 1980 v P, Ni, W, E, Pol, H; 1981 v Se, Is, Ni, Is, Ni, E; 1982 v Se, Sp, Ni, Br (sub); 1983 v Bel, Sw (sub), W, E, Ca (3); 1984 v U, Bel, EG, Ni, W, E, F; 1985 v Y, Ic, Sp (2), W, E, Ic; 1986 v W, EG, Aus (2), E, Ho, D; 1987 v Bel, E, Br; 1988 v Bel, Bul, L, S.Ar (sub), Ma, Sp, Co, E; 1989 v N, Y, I, Cy, F, Cy, E, Ch; 1990 v Y, F, N, Arg, EG, Eg, Cr, Se, Br; 1991 v R, Sw, USSR, Bul; 1993 v Ma (77)
McLeod, D. (Celtic), 1905 v Ni; 1906 v E, W, Ni (4)
McLeod, J. (Dumbarton), 1888 v Ni; 1889 v W; 1890 v Ni; 1892 v E; 1893 v W (5)
MacLeod, J. M. (Hibernian), 1961 v E, Ei (2), Cz (4)
MacLeod, M. (Celtic), 1985 v E (sub); 1987 v Ei, L, E, Br; (with Borussia Dortmund), 1988 v Co, E; 1989 v I, Ch; 1990 v Y, F, N (sub), Arg, EG, Pol, Se Br; (with Hibernian), 1991 v R, Sw, USSR (sub) (20)
McLeod, W. (Cowlairs), 1886 v Ni (1)
McLintock, A. (Vale of Leven), 1875 v E; 1876 v E; 1880 v E (3)
McLintock, F. (Leicester C), 1963 v N (sub), Ei, Sp; (with Arsenal), 1965 v Ni; 1967 v USSR; 1970 v Ni; 1971 v W, Ni, E (9)
McLuckie, J. S. (Manchester C), 1934 v W (1)
McMahon, A. (Celtic), 1892 v E; 1893 v E, Ni; 1894 v E; 1901 v Ni; 1902 v W (6)
McManus, S. (Celtic), 2007 v Uk (sub), Ge, I, A (sub), Fa (5)
McMenemy, J. (Celtic), 1905 v Ni; 1909 v Ni; 1910 v E, W; 1911 v Ni, W, E; 1912 v W; 1914 v W, Ni, E; 1920 v Ni (12)
McMenemy, J. (Motherwell), 1934 v W (1)
McMillan, I. L. (Airdrieonians), 1952 v E, USA, D; 1955 v E; 1956 v E; (with Rangers), 1961 v Cz (6)
McMillan, J. (St Bernards), 1897 v W (1)
McMillan, T. (Dumbarton), 1887 v Ni (1)
McMullan, J. (Partick Th), 1920 v W; 1921 v W, Ni, E; 1924 v E, Ni; 1925 v E; 1926 v W; (with Manchester C), 1926 v E; 1927 v E, W; 1928 v E, W; 1929 v W, E, Ni (16)
McNab, A. (Morton), 1921 v E, Ni (2)
McNab, A. (Sunderland), 1937 v A; (with WBA), 1939 v E (2)
McNab, C. D. (Dundee), 1931 v E, W, A, I, Sw; 1932 v E (6)
McNab, J. S. (Liverpool), 1923 v W (1)
McNair, A. (Celtic), 1906 v W; 1907 v Ni; 1908 v E, W; 1909 v E; 1910 v W; 1912 v E, W, Ni; 1913 v E; 1914 v E, Ni; 1920 v E, W, Ni (15)
McNamara, J. (Celtic), 1997 v La (sub), Se, Es, W (sub); 1998 v D, Co, US (sub), N (sub), Mor; 2000 v Ho; 2001 v Sm; 2002 v Bel (sub), F (sub); 2003 v Ic (1+sub), Li, Nz, G (sub); 2004 v Fa, G, Li, Ho (2), W, Tr; 2005 v Sp, Slv, Se, I, Mol; (with Wolverhampton W), 2006 v A, I, N (33)
McNamee, D. (Livingston), 2004 v Es, Tr (sub); 2006 v Bul (sub), J (sub) (4)
McNaught, W. (Raith R), 1951 v A, W, Ni; 1952 v E; 1955 v Ni (5)
McNaughton, K. (Aberdeen), 2002 v Ng; 2003 v D; 2005 v Se (3)
McNeill, W. (Celtic), 1961 v E, Ei (2), Cz; 1962 v Ni, E, Cz, U; 1963 v Ei, Sp; 1964 v W, E, WG; 1965 v E, Fi, Pol, Sp; 1966 v Ni, Pol; 1967 v USSR; 1968 v E; 1969 v Cy, W, E, Cy (sub); 1970 v WG; 1972 v Ni, W, E (29)
McNiel, H. (Queen's Park), 1874 v E; 1875 v E; 1876 v E, W; 1877 v W; 1878 v E; 1879 v E, W; 1881 v E, W (10)
McNiel, M. (Rangers), 1876 v W; 1880 v E (2)
McPhail, J. (Celtic), 1950 v W; 1951 v W, Ni, A; 1954 v Ni (5)
McPhail, R. (Airdrieonians), 1927 v E; (with Rangers), 1929 v W; 1931 v E, Ni; 1932 v W, Ni, F; 1933 v E, Ni; 1934 v A, Ni; 1935 v E; 1937 v G, E, Cz; 1938 v W, Ni (17)
McPherson, D. (Kilmarnock), 1892 v Ni (1)
McPherson, D. (Hearts), 1989 v Cy, E; 1990 v N, Ma, Cr, Se, Br; 1991 v Sw, Bul (2), USSR (sub), Sm; 1992 v Sw, R, Sm, Ni, Fi, US, Ca, N, Ho, G, C; (with Rangers), 1993 v Sw, I, Ma, P (27)
McPherson, J. (Clydesdale), 1875 v E (1)
McPherson, J. (Vale of Leven), 1879 v E, W; 1880 v E; 1881 v W; 1883 v E, W; 1884 v E; 1885 v Ni (8)
McPherson, J. (Kilmarnock), 1888 v W; (with Cowlairs), 1889 v E; 1890 v Ni, E; (with Rangers), 1892 v W; 1894 v E; 1895 v E, Ni; 1897 v Ni (9)
McPherson, J. (Hearts), 1891 v E (1)
McPherson, R. (Arthurlie), 1882 v E (1)
McQueen, G. (Leeds U), 1974 v Bel; 1975 v Sp (2), P, W, Ni, E, R; 1976 v D; 1977 v Cz, W (2), Ni, E; 1978 v EG, Cz, W; (with Manchester U), Bul, Ni, W; 1979 v A, N, P, Ni, E, N; 1980 v Pe, A, Bel; 1981 v W (30)
McQueen, M. (Leith Ath), 1890 v W; 1891 v W (2)
McRorie, D. M. (Morton), 1931 v W (1)
McSpadyen, A. (Partick Th), 1939 v E, H (2)
McStay, P. (Celtic), 1984 v U, Bel, EG, Ni, W, E (sub); 1985 v Y (sub), Ic, Sp (2), W; 1986 v EG (sub), Aus, Is, U; 1987 v Bul, Ei (1+1 sub), L (sub), Bel, E, Br; 1988 v H, Bel, Bul, L, S.Ar, Sp, Co, E; 1989 v N, Y, I, Cy, F, Cy, E, Ch; 1990 v Y, F, N, Arg, EG (sub), Eg, Pol (sub), Ma, Cr, Se (sub), Br; 1991 v R, USSR, Bul; 1992 v Sm, Fi, US, Ca, N, Ho, G, C; 1993 v Sw, P, I, Ma, P, Es (2); 1994 v I (sub), Ho; 1995 v Fi, Fa, Ru; 1996 v Aus; 1997 v Es (2), A (sub) (76)
McStay, W. (Celtic), 1921 v W, Ni; 1925 v E, Ni, W; 1926 v E, Ni, W; 1927 v E, Ni, W; 1928 v W, Ni (13)
McSwegan, G. (Hearts), 2000 v Bos (sub), Li (2)
McTavish, J. (Falkirk), 1910 v Ni (1)
McWattie, G. C. (Queen's Park), 1901 v W, Ni (2)
McWilliam, P. (Newcastle U), 1905 v E; 1906 v E; 1907 v E, W; 1909 v E, W; 1910 v E; 1911 v W (8)
Madden, J. (Celtic), 1893 v W; 1895 v W (2)
Main, F. R. (Rangers), 1938 v W (1)
Main, J. (Hibernian), 1909 v Ni (1)
Maley, W. (Celtic), 1893 v E, Ni (2)
Maloney, S. R. (Celtic), 2006 v Bl (sub), US (sub); (with Aston Villa), 2007 v Ge (sub), I (sub), A, Fa (6)
Malpas, M. (Dundee U), 1984 v F; 1985 v E, Ic; 1986 v W, Aus (2), Is, R, E, Ho, D, WG; 1987 v Bul, Ei, Bel; 1988 v Bel, Bul, L, S.Ar, Ma; 1989 v N, Y, I, Cy, F, Cy, E, Ch; 1990 v Y, F, N, Eg, Pol, Ma, Cr, Se, Br; 1991 v R, Bul (2), USSR, Sm; 1992 v Sw, R, Sm, Ni, Fi, US, Ca (sub), N, Ho, G; 1993 v Sw, P, I (55)
Marshall, D. J. (Celtic), 2005 v H, Se (2)
Marshall, G. (Celtic), 1992 v US (1)
Marshall, H. (Celtic), 1899 v W; 1900 v Ni (2)
Marshall, J. (Third Lanark), 1885 v Ni; 1886 v W; 1887 v E, W (4)
Marshall, J. (Middlesbrough), 1921 v E, W, Ni; 1922 v E, W, Ni; (with Llanelly), 1924 v W (7)
Marshall, J. (Rangers), 1932 v E; 1933 v E; 1934 v E (3)
Marshall, R. W. (Rangers), 1892 v Ni; 1894 v Ni (2)
Martin, B. (Motherwell), 1995 v J, Ec (2)
Martin, F. (Aberdeen), 1954 v N (2), A, U; 1955 v E, H (6)
Martin, N. (Hibernian), 1965 v Fi, Pol; (with Sunderland), 1966 v I (3)
Martis, J. (Motherwell), 1961 v W (1)
Mason, J. (Third Lanark), 1949 v W, Ni, E; 1950 v Ni; 1951 v Ni, Bel, A (7)
Massie, A. (Hearts), 1932 v Ni, W, F; 1933 v Ni; 1934 v E, Ni; 1935 v E, Ni, W; 1936 v W, Ni; (with Aston Villa), 1936 v E; 1937 v G, E, W, Ni, A; 1938 v W (18)
Masson, D. S. (QPR), 1976 v Ni, W, E; 1977 v Fi, Cz, W, Ni, E, Ch, Arg, Br; 1978 v EG, Cz, W; (with Derby Co), Ni, E, Pe (17)
Mathers, D. (Partick Th), 1954 v Fi (1)
Matteo, D. (Leeds U), 2001 v Aus, Bel, Sm; 2002 v Cro, Bel, F (6)
Maxwell, W. S. (Stoke C), 1898 v E (1)
May, J. (Rangers), 1906 v W, Ni; 1908 v E, Ni; 1909 v W (5)
Meechan, P. (Celtic), 1896 v Ni (1)
Meiklejohn, D. D. (Rangers), 1922 v W; 1924 v W; 1925 v W, Ni, E; 1928 v W, Ni; 1929 v E, Ni; 1930 v E, Ni; 1931 v E; 1932 v W, Ni; 1934 v A (15)
Menzies, A. (Hearts), 1906 v E (1)
Mercer, R. (Hearts), 1912 v W; 1913 v Ni (2)
Middleton, R. (Cowdenbeath), 1930 v Ni (1)
Millar, J. (Rangers), 1897 v E; 1898 v E, W (3)
Millar, J. (Rangers), 1963 v A, Ei (2)
Miller, A. (Hearts), 1939 v W (1)
Miller, C. (Dundee U), 2001 v Pol (1)

Miller, J. (St Mirren), 1931 v E, I, Sw; 1932 v F; 1934 v E (5)
Miller, K. (Rangers), 2001 v Pol (sub); (with Wolverhampton W), 2003 v Ic, Li, A (sub), G; 2004 v Li, Ho (sub + sub), W, R, Es, Tr (sub); 2005 v H, Sp (sub), N (sub), Mol (sub), Se, I, Mol, Bl; 2006 v A, I, N, Bl, Slv, Sw; (with Celtic), 2007 v Fa, Li, Uk, Ge, I (31)
Miller, L. (Dundee U), 2006 v J (sub) (1)
Miller, P. (Dumbarton), 1882 v E; 1883 v E, W (3)
Miller, T. (Liverpool), 1920 v E; (with Manchester U), 1921 v E, Ni (3)
Miller, W. (Third Lanark), 1876 v E (1)
Miller, W. (Celtic), 1947 v E, W, Bel, L; 1948 v W, Ni (6)
Miller, W. (Aberdeen), 1975 v R; 1978 v Bul; 1980 v Bel, W, E, Pol, H; 1981 v Se, P, Is (sub), Ni, W, Ni, E; 1982 v Ni, P, Ho, Br, USSR; 1983 v EG, Sw (2), W, E, Ca (3); 1984 v U, Bel, EG, W, E, F; 1985 v Y, Ic, Sp (2), W, E, Ic; 1986 v W, EG, Aus (2), Is, R, E, Ho, D, WG, U; 1987 v Bul, E, Br; 1988 v H, L, S.Ar, Ma, Sp, Co, E; 1989 v N, Y; 1990 v Y, N (65)
Mills, W. (Aberdeen), 1936 v W, Ni; 1937 v W (3)
Milne, J. V. (Middlesbrough), 1938 v E; 1939 v E (2)
Mitchell, D. (Rangers), 1890 v Ni; 1892 v E; 1893 v E, Ni; 1894 v E (5)
Mitchell, J. (Kilmarnock), 1908 v Ni; 1910 v Ni, W (3)
Mitchell, R. C. (Newcastle U), 1951 v D, F (2)
Mochan, N. (Celtic), 1954 v N, A, U (3)
Moir, W. (Bolton W), 1950 v E (1)
Moncur, R. (Newcastle U), 1968 v Ho; 1970 v Ni, W, E, Ei; 1971 v D, Bel, W, P, Ni, E, D; 1972 v Pe, Ni, W, E (16)
Morgan, H. (St Mirren), 1898 v W; (with Liverpool), 1899 v E (2)
Morgan, W. (Burnley), 1968 v Ni; (with Manchester U), 1972 v Pe, Y, Cz, Br; 1973 v D (2), E (2), W, Ni, Sw, Br; 1974 v Cz (2), WG (2), Ni, Bel (sub), Br, Y (21)
Morris, D. (Raith R), 1923 v Ni; 1924 v E, Ni; 1925 v E, W, Ni (6)
Morris, H. (East Fife), 1950 v Ni (1)
Morrison, T. (St Mirren), 1927 v E (1)
Morton, A. L. (Queen's Park), 1920 v W, Ni; (with Rangers), 1921 v E; 1922 v E, W; 1923 v E, W, Ni; 1924 v E, W, Ni; 1925 v E, W, Ni; 1927 v E, Ni; 1928 v E, W, Ni; 1929 v E, W, Ni; 1930 v E, W, Ni; 1931 v E, W, Ni; 1932 v E, W, F (31)
Morton, H. A. (Kilmarnock), 1929 v G, Ho (2)
Mudie, J. K. (Blackpool), 1957 v W, Ni, E, Y, Sw, Sp (2), WG; 1958 v Ni, E, W, Sw, H, Pol, Y, Par, F (17)
Muir, W. (Dundee), 1907 v Ni (1)
Muirhead, T. A. (Rangers), 1922 v Ni; 1923 v E; 1924 v W; 1927 v Ni; 1928 v Ni; 1929 v W, Ni; 1930 v W (8)
Mulhall, G. (Aberdeen), 1960 v Ni; (with Sunderland), 1963 v Ni; 1964 v Ni (3)
Munro, A. D. (Hearts), 1937 v W, Ni; (with Blackpool), 1938 v Ho (3)
Munro, F. M. (Wolverhampton W), 1971 v Ni (sub), E (sub), D, USSR; 1975 v Se, W (sub), Ni, E, R (9)
Munro, I. (St Mirren), 1979 v Arg, N; 1980 v Pe, A, Bel, W, E (7)
Munro, N. (Abercorn), 1888 v W; 1889 v E (2)
Murdoch, J. (Motherwell), 1931 v Ni (1)
Murdoch, R. (Celtic), 1966 v W, E, I (2); 1967 v Ni; 1968 v Ni; 1969 v W, Ni, E, WG, Cy; 1970 v A (12)
Murphy, F. (Celtic), 1938 v Ho (1)
Murray, I. (Hibernian), 2003 v Ca (sub); 2005 v Mol (sub), Se; (with Rangers), 2006 v Bl, Bul (sub), J (sub) (6)
Murray, J. (Renton), 1895 v W (1)
Murray, J. (Hearts), 1958 v E, H, Pol, Y, F (5)
Murray, J. W. (Vale of Leven), 1890 v W (1)
Murray, P. (Hibernian), 1896 v Ni; 1897 v W (2)
Murray, S. (Aberdeen), 1972 v Bel (1)
Murty, G. S. (Reading), 2004 v W (sub); 2006 v Bul, J (3)
Mutch, G. (Preston NE), 1938 v E (1)

Naismith, S. J. (Kilmarnock), 2007 v Fa (sub) (1)
Napier, C. E. (Celtic), 1932 v E; 1935 v E, W; (with Derby Co), 1937 v Ni, A (5)
Narey, D. (Dundee U), 1977 v Se (sub); 1979 v P, Ni (sub), Arg; 1980 v P, Ni, Pol, H; 1981 v W, E (sub); 1982 v Ho, W, E, Nz (sub), Br, USSR; 1983 v EG, Sw, Bel, Ni, W, E, Ca (3); 1986 v Is, R, Ho, WG, U; 1987 v Bul, Ei, Bel; 1989 v I, Cy (35)
Naysmith, G. A. (Hearts), 2000 v Ei; 2001 v La (sub), Sm, Cro; (with Everton), 2002 v Cro, Bel; 2003 v D, Ic, P, Ei, Ic, Li, A, Nz, G; 2004 v N, Fa, G, Li, Ho (2), W; 2005 v H, Sp, Slv, N, Mol, I; 2006 v Bul, J; 2007 v Fa, Li, Ge, I, A, Fa (36)
Neil, R. G. (Hibernian), 1896 v W; (with Rangers), 1900 v W (2)
Neill, R. W. (Queen's Park), 1876 v W; 1877 v E, W; 1878 v W; 1880 v E (5)
Neilson, R. (Hearts), 2007 v Uk (1)
Nellies, P. (Hearts), 1913 v Ni; 1914 v W (2)
Nelson, J. (Cardiff C), 1925 v W, Ni; 1928 v E; 1930 v F (4)
Nevin, P. K. F. (Chelsea), 1986 v R (sub), E (sub); 1987 v L, Ei, Bel (sub); 1988 v L; (with Everton), 1989 v Cy, E; 1991 v R (sub), Bul (sub), Sm (sub); 1992 v US, G (sub), C (sub); (with Tranmere R), 1993 v Ma, P (sub), Es; 1994 v Sw, Ma, Ho, A (sub), Ho (sub); 1995 v Fa, Ru (sub), Sm; 1996 v Se (sub), Sm, Aus (sub) (28)
Niblo, T. D. (Aston Villa), 1904 v E (1)
Nibloe, J. (Kilmarnock), 1929 v E, N, Ho; 1930 v W; 1931 v E, Ni, A, I, Sw; 1932 v E, F (11)
Nicholas, C. (Celtic), 1983 v Sw, Ni, E, Ca (3); (with Arsenal), 1984 v Bel, F (sub); 1985 v Y (sub), Ic (sub), Sp (sub), W (sub); 1986 v Is, R (sub), E, D, U (sub); 1987 v Bul, E (sub); (with Aberdeen), 1989 v Cy (sub) (20)
Nicholson, B. (Dunfermline Ath), 2001 v Pol; 2002 v La; 2005 v Se (3)
Nicol, S. (Liverpool), 1985 v Y, Ic, Sp, W; 1986 v W, EG, Aus, E, D, WG, U; 1988 v H, Bul, S.Ar, Sp, Co, E; 1989 v N, Y, Cy, F; 1990 v Y, F; 1991 v Sw, USSR, Sm; 1992 v Sw (27)
Nisbet, J. (Ayr U), 1929 v N, G, Ho (3)
Niven, J. B. (Moffat), 1885 v Ni (1)

O'Connor, G. (Hibernian), 2002 v Ng (sub), Sk, Hk (sub); 2005 v I (sub); 2006 v A, Slv (sub), US; (with Lokomotiv Moscow), 2007 v Fa (sub), F (sub), A, Fa (11)
O'Donnell, F. (Preston NE), 1937 v E, A, Cz; 1938 v W; (with Blackpool), E, Ho (6)
O'Donnell, P. (Motherwell), 1994 v Sw (sub) (1)
Ogilvie, D. H. (Motherwell), 1934 v A (1)
O'Hare, J. (Derby Co), 1970 v W, Ni, E; 1971 v D, Bel, W, Ni; 1972 v P, Bel, Ho (sub), Pe, Ni, W (13)
O'Neil, B. (Celtic), 1996 v Aus; (with Wolfsburg), 1999 v G (sub); 2000 v Li, Ho (sub), Ei; (with Derby Co), 2001 v Aus; (with Preston NE), 2006 v A (7)
O'Neil, J. (Hibernian), 2001 v Pol (1)
Ormond, W. E. (Hibernian), 1954 v E, N, Fi, A, U; 1959 v E (6)
O'Rourke, F. (Airdrieonians), 1907 v Ni (1)
Orr, J. (Kilmarnock), 1892 v W (1)
Orr, R. (Newcastle U), 1902 v E; 1904 v E (2)
Orr, T. (Morton), 1952 v Ni, W (2)
Orr, W. (Celtic), 1900 v Ni; 1903 v Ni; 1904 v W (3)
Orrock, R. (Falkirk), 1913 v W (1)
Oswald, J. (Third Lanark), 1889 v E; (with St Bernards), 1895 v E; (with Rangers), 1897 v W (3)

Parker, A. H. (Falkirk), 1955 v P, Y, A; 1956 v E, Ni, W, A; 1957 v Ni, W, Y; 1958 v Ni, W, E, Sw; (with Everton), Par (15)
Parlane, D. (Rangers), 1973 v W, Sw, Br; 1975 v Sp (sub), Se, P, W, Ni, E, R; 1976 v D (sub); 1977 v W (12)
Parlane, R. (Vale of Leven), 1878 v W; 1879 v E, W (3)
Paterson, G. D. (Celtic), 1939 v Ni (1)
Paterson, J. (Leicester C), 1920 v E (1)
Paterson, J. (Cowdenbeath), 1931 v A, I, Sw (3)
Paton, A. (Motherwell), 1952 v D, Se (2)
Paton, D. (St Bernards), 1896 v W (1)
Paton, M. (Dumbarton), 1883 v E; 1884 v W; 1885 v W, E; 1886 v E (5)
Paton, R. (Vale of Leven), 1879 v E, W (2)
Patrick, J. (St Mirren), 1897 v E, W (2)
Paul, H. McD. (Queen's Park), 1909 v E, W, Ni (3)
Paul, W. (Partick Th), 1888 v W; 1889 v W; 1890 v W (3)
Paul, W. (Dykebar), 1891 v Ni (1)
Pearson, S. P. (Motherwell), 2004 v Ho (sub); (with Celtic), W; 2005 v H (sub), Sp (sub), N (sub), Se (6)
Pearson, T. (Newcastle U), 1947 v E, Bel (2)
Penman, A. (Dundee), 1966 v Ho (1)
Pettigrew, W. (Motherwell), 1976 v Sw, Ni, W; 1977 v W (sub), Se (5)
Phillips, J. (Queen's Park), 1877 v E, W; 1878 v W (3)
Plenderleith, J. B. (Manchester C), 1961 v Ni (1)

Porteous, W. (Hearts), 1903 v Ni (1)
Pressley, S. J. (Hearts), 2000 v F (sub), Ei (sub); 2003 v Ic, Ca, P, Ic, Li, A, Nz, G; 2004 v N, G, Li, Ho (2), R, D, Es, Tr; 2005 v H, I, Mol, Bl; 2006 v A, N, Bl, Slv, US; 2007 v Fa, Li, F, Uk (32)
Pringle, C. (St Mirren), 1921 v W (1)
Provan, D. (Rangers), 1964 v Ni, N; 1966 v I (2), Ho (5)
Provan, D. (Celtic), 1980 v Bel (2 sub), P (sub), Ni (sub); 1981 v Is, W, E; 1982 v Se, P, Ni (10)
Pursell, P. (Queen's Park), 1914 v W (1)

Quashie, N. F. (Portsmouth), 2004 v Es, Tr; 2005 v H, Sp, Slv, Se; (with Southampton), I; 2006 v A, I, Slv, US; (with WBA), Sw; 2007 v Fa, Li (14)
Quinn, J. (Celtic), 1905 v Ni; 1906 v Ni, W; 1908 v Ni, E; 1909 v E; 1910 v E, Ni, W; 1912 v E, W (11)
Quinn, P. (Motherwell), 1961 v E, Ei (2); 1962 v U (4)

Rae, G. (Dundee), 2001 v Pol; 2002 v La (sub); 2003 v G (sub); 2004 v N (sub), Fa (sub), G (sub), Li, Ho; (with Rangers), R; 2006 v Bul (sub), J (sub) (11)
Rae, J. (Third Lanark), 1889 v W; 1890 v Ni (2)
Raeside, J. S. (Third Lanark), 1906 v W (1)
Raisbeck, A. G. (Liverpool), 1900 v E; 1901 v E; 1902 v E; 1903 v E, W; 1904 v E; 1906 v E; 1907 v E (8)
Rankin, G. (Vale of Leven), 1890 v Ni; 1891 v E (2)
Rankin, R. (St Mirren), 1929 v N, G, Ho (3)
Redpath, W. (Motherwell), 1949 v W, Ni; 1951 v E, D, F, Bel, A; 1952 v Ni, E (9)
Reid, J. G. (Airdrieonians), 1914 v W; 1920 v W; 1924 v Ni (3)
Reid, R. (Brentford), 1938 v E, Ni (2)
Reid, W. (Rangers), 1911 v E, W, Ni; 1912 v Ni; 1913 v E, W, Ni; 1914 v E, Ni (9)
Reilly, L. (Hibernian), 1949 v E, W, F; 1950 v W, Ni, Sw, F; 1951 v W, E, D, F, Bel, A; 1952 v Ni, W, E, USA, D, Se; 1953 v Ni, W, E, Se; 1954 v W; 1955 v H (2), P, Y, A, E; 1956 v E, W, Ni, A; 1957 v E, Ni, W, Y (38)
Rennie, H. G. (Hearts), 1900 v E, Ni; (with Hibernian), 1901 v E; 1902 v E, Ni, W; 1903 v Ni, W; 1904 v Ni; 1905 v W; 1906 v Ni; 1908 v Ni, W (13)
Renny-Tailyour, H. W. (Royal Engineers), 1873 v E (1)
Rhind, A. (Queen's Park), 1872 v E (1)
Richmond, A. (Queen's Park), 1906 v W (1)
Richmond, J. T. (Clydesdale), 1877 v E; (with Queen's Park), 1878 v E; 1882 v W (3)
Ring, T. (Clyde), 1953 v Se; 1955 v W, Ni, E, H; 1957 v E, Sp (2), Sw, WG; 1958 v Ni, Sw (12)
Rioch, B. D. (Derby Co), 1975 v P, W, Ni, E, R; 1976 v D (2), R, Ni, W, E; 1977 v Fi, Cz, W; (with Everton), W, Ni, E, Ch, Br; 1978 v Cz; (with Derby Co), Ni, E, Pe, Ho (24)
Riordan, D. G. (Hibernian), 2006 v A (sub) (1)
Ritchie, A. (East Stirlingshire), 1891 v W (1)
Ritchie, H. (Hibernian), 1923 v W; 1928 v Ni (2)
Ritchie, J. (Queen's Park), 1897 v W (1)
Ritchie, P. S. (Hearts), 1999 v G (sub), CzR; 2000 v Li, E; (with Bolton W), F, Ho; (with Walsall), 2004 v W (7)
Ritchie, W. (Rangers), 1962 v U (sub) (1)
Robb, D. T. (Aberdeen), 1971 v W, E, P, D (sub), USSR (5)
Robb, W. (Rangers), 1926 v W; (with Hibernian), 1928 v W (2)
Robertson, A. (Clyde), 1955 v P, A, H; 1958 v Sw, Par (5)
Robertson, D. (Rangers), 1992 v Ni; 1994 v Sw, Ho (3)
Robertson, G. (Motherwell), 1910 v W; (with Sheffield W), 1912 v W; 1913 v E, Ni (4)
Robertson, G. (Kilmarnock), 1938 v Cz (1)
Robertson, H. (Dundee), 1962 v Cz (1)
Robertson, J. (Dundee), 1931 v A, I (2)
Robertson, J. (Hearts), 1991 v R, Sw, Bul (sub), Sm (sub); 1992 v Sm, Ni (sub), Fi; 1993 v I (sub), Ma (sub), G, Es; 1995 v J (sub), Ec, Fa (sub); 1996 v Gr (sub), Se (16)
Robertson, J. N. (Nottingham F), 1978 v Ni, W (sub), Ir; 1979 v P, N; 1980 v Pe, A, Bel (2), P; 1981 v Se, P, Is, Ni, Is, Ni, E; 1982 v Se, Ni (2), E (sub), Nz, Br, USSR; 1983 v EG, Sw; (with Derby Co), 1984 v U, Bel (28)
Robertson, J. G. (Tottenham H), 1965 v W (1)
Robertson, J. T. (Everton), 1898 v E; (with Southampton), 1899 v E; (with Rangers), 1900 v E, W; 1901 v W, Ni, E; 1902 v W, Ni, E; 1903 v E, W; 1904 v E, W, Ni; 1905 v W (16)
Robertson, P. (Dundee), 1903 v Ni (1)
Robertson, T. (Queen's Park), 1889 v Ni; 1890 v E; 1891 v W; 1892 v Ni (4)
Robertson, T. (Hearts), 1898 v Ni (1)
Robertson, W. (Dumbarton), 1887 v E, W (2)
Robinson, R. (Dundee), 1974 v WG (sub); 1975 v Se, Ni, R (sub) (4)
Ross, M. (Rangers), 2002 v Sk, S.Af, Hk; 2003 v D, Fa, Ic, Ca, P, Nz, G; 2004 v N, G (sub), Ho (sub) (13)
Rough, A. (Partick Th), 1976 v Sw, Ni, W, E; 1977 v Fi, Cz, W (2), Se, Ni, E, Ch, Arg, Br; 1978 v Cz, W, Ni, E, Pe, Ir, Ho; 1979 v A, P, W, Arg, N; 1980 v Pe, A, Bel (2), P, W, E, Pol, H; 1981 v Se, P, Is, Ni, Is, W, E; 1982 v Se, Ni, Sp, Ho, W, E, Nz, Br, USSR; (with Hibernian), 1986 v W (sub), E (53)
Rougvie, D. (Aberdeen), 1984 v Ni (1)
Rowan, A. (Caledonian), 1880 v E; (with Queen's Park), 1882 v W (2)
Russell, D. (Hearts), 1895 v E, Ni; (with Celtic), 1897 v W; 1898 v Ni; 1901 v W, Ni (6)
Russell, J. (Cambuslang), 1890 v Ni (1)
Russell, W. F. (Airdrieonians), 1924 v W; 1925 v E (2)
Rutherford, E. (Rangers), 1948 v F (1)

St John, I. (Motherwell), 1959 v WG; 1960 v E, Ni, W, Pol, A; 1961 v E; (with Liverpool), 1962 v Ni, W, E, Cz (2), U; 1963 v W, Ni, E, N, Ei (sub), Sp; 1964 v Ni; 1965 v E (21)
Sawers, W. (Dundee), 1895 v W (1)
Scarff, P. (Celtic), 1931 v Ni (1)
Schaedler, E. (Hibernian), 1974 v WG (1)
Scott, A. S. (Rangers), 1957 v Ni, Y, WG; 1958 v W, Sw; 1959 v P; 1962 v Ni, W, E, Cz, U; (with Everton), 1964 v W, N; 1965 v Fi; 1966 v P, Br (16)
Scott, J. (Hibernian), 1966 v Ho (1)
Scott, J. (Dundee), 1971 v D (sub), USSR (2)
Scott, M. (Airdrieonians), 1898 v W (1)
Scott, R. (Airdrieonians), 1894 v Ni (1)
Scoular, J. (Portsmouth), 1951 v D, F, A; 1952 v E, USA, D, Se; 1953 v W, Ni (9)
Sellar, W. (Battlefield), 1885 v E; 1886 v E; 1887 v E, W; 1888 v E; (with Queen's Park), 1891 v E; 1892 v E; 1893 v E, Ni (9)
Semple, W. (Cambuslang), 1886 v W (1)
Severin, S. D. (Hearts), 2002 v La (sub), Sk (sub), S.Af (sub), Hk; 2003 v D (sub), Ic (sub), Ca (sub), P (sub); (with Aberdeen), 2005 v H (sub), Se (sub); 2006 v A (sub), Bul, J; 2007 v Fa (sub), Li (sub) (15)
Shankly, W. (Preston NE), 1938 v E; 1939 v E, W, Ni, H (5)
Sharp, G. M. (Everton), 1985 v Ic; 1986 v W, Aus (2 sub), Is, R, U; 1987 v Ei; 1988 v Bel (sub), Bul, L, Ma (12)
Sharp, J. (Dundee), 1904 v W; (with Woolwich Arsenal), 1907 v W, E; 1908 v E; (with Fulham), 1909 v W (5)
Shaw, D. (Hibernian), 1947 v W, Ni; 1948 v E, Bel, Sw, F; 1949 v W, Ni (8)
Shaw, F. W. (Pollokshields Ath), 1884 v E, W (2)
Shaw, J. (Rangers), 1947 v E, Bel, L; 1948 v Ni (4)
Shearer, D. (Aberdeen), 1994 v A (sub), Ho (sub); 1995 v Fi, Ru (sub), Sm, Fa; 1996 v Gr (7)
Shearer, R. (Rangers), 1961 v E, Ei (2), Cz (4)
Sillars, D. C. (Queen's Park), 1891 v Ni; 1892 v E; 1893 v W; 1894 v E; 1895 v W (5)
Simpson, J. (Third Lanark), 1895 v E, W, Ni (3)
Simpson, J. (Rangers), 1935 v E, W, Ni; 1936 v E, W, Ni; 1937 v G, E, W, Ni, A, Cz; 1938 v W, Ni (14)
Simpson, N. (Aberdeen), 1983 v Ni; 1984 v U (sub), F (sub); 1987 v E; 1988 v E (5)
Simpson, R. C. (Celtic), 1967 v E, USSR; 1968 v Ni, E; 1969 v A (5)
Sinclair, G. L. (Hearts), 1910 v Ni; 1912 v W, Ni (3)
Sinclair, J. W. E. (Leicester C), 1966 v P (1)
Skene, L. H. (Queen's Park), 1904 v W (1)
Sloan, T. (Third Lanark), 1904 v W (1)
Smellie, R. (Queen's Park), 1887 v Ni; 1888 v W; 1889 v E; 1891 v E; 1893 v E, Ni (6)
Smith, A. (Rangers), 1898 v E; 1900 v E, Ni, W; 1901 v E, Ni, W; 1902 v E, Ni, W; 1903 v E, Ni, W; 1904 v Ni; 1905 v W; 1906 v E, Ni; 1907 v W; 1911 v E, Ni (20)
Smith, D. (Aberdeen), 1966 v Ho; (with Rangers), 1968 v Ho (2)
Smith, G. (Hibernian), 1947 v E, Ni; 1948 v W, Bel, Sw, F; 1952 v E, USA; 1955 v P, Y, A, H; 1956 v E, Ni, W; 1957 v Sp (2), Sw (18)
Smith, H. G. (Hearts), 1988 v S.Ar (sub); 1992 v Ni, Ca (3)

Smith, J. (Ayr U), 1924 v E (1)
Smith, J. (Rangers), 1935 v Ni; 1938 v Ni (2)
Smith, J. (Aberdeen), 1968 v Ho (sub); (with Newcastle U), 1974 v WG, Ni (sub), W (sub) (4)
Smith, J. (Celtic), 2003 v Ei (sub), A (sub) (2)
Smith, J. E. (Celtic), 1959 v H, P (2)
Smith, Jas (Queen's Park), 1872 v E (1)
Smith, John (Mauchline), 1877 v E, W; 1879 v E, W; (with Edinburgh University), 1880 v E; (with Queen's Park), 1881 v W, E; 1883 v E, W; 1884 v E (10)
Smith, N. (Rangers), 1897 v E; 1898 v W; 1899 v E, W, Ni; 1900 v E, W, Ni; 1901 v Ni, W; 1902 v E, Ni (12)
Smith, R. (Queen's Park), 1872 v E; 1873 v E (2)
Smith, T. M. (Kilmarnock), 1934 v E; (with Preston NE), 1938 v E (2)
Somers, P. (Celtic), 1905 v E, Ni; 1907 v Ni; 1909 v W (4)
Somers, W. S. (Third Lanark), 1879 v E, W; (with Queen's Park), 1880 v W (3)
Somerville, G. (Queen's Park), 1886 v E (1)
Souness, G. J. (Middlesbrough), 1975 v EG, Sp, Se; (with Liverpool), 1978 v Bul, W, E (sub), Ho; 1979 v A, N, W, Ni, E; 1980 v Pe, A, Bel, P, Ni; 1981 v P, Is (2); 1982 v Ni, P, Sp, W, E, Nz, Br, USSR; 1983 v EG, Sw, Bel, Sw, W, E, Ca (2 + 1 sub); 1984 v U, Ni, W; (with Sampdoria), 1985 v Y, Ic, Sp (2), W, E, Ic; 1986 v EG, Aus (2), R, E, D, WG (54)
Speedie, D. R. (Chelsea), 1985 v E; 1986 v W, EG (sub), Aus, E; (with Coventry C), 1989 v Y (sub), I (sub), Cy (1+1 sub), Ch (10)
Speedie, F. (Rangers), 1903 v E, W, Ni (3)
Speirs, J. H. (Rangers), 1908 v W (1)
Spencer, J. (Chelsea), 1995 v Ru (sub), Gr (sub), Sm (sub), J; 1996 v Fi, Aus, D, US (sub), Co, Ho (sub), E, Sw (sub); 1997 v La; (with QPR), W (sub) (14)
Stanton, P. (Hibernian), 1966 v Ho; 1969 v Ni; 1970 v Ei, A; 1971 v D, Bel, P, USSR, D; 1972 v P, Bel, Ho, W; 1973 v W, Ni; 1974 v WG (16)
Stark, J. (Rangers), 1909 v E, Ni (2)
Steel, W. (Morton), 1947 v E, Bel, L; (with Derby Co), 1948 v F, E, W, Ni; 1949 v E, W, Ni, F; 1950 v E, W, Ni, Sw, P, F; (with Dundee), 1951 v W, Ni, E, A (2), D, F, Bel; 1952 v W; 1953 v W, E, Ni, Se (30)
Steele, D. M. (Huddersfield), 1923 v E, W, Ni (3)
Stein, C. (Rangers), 1969 v W, Ni, D, E, Cy (2); 1970 v A (sub), Ni (sub), W, E, Ei, WG; 1971 v D, USSR, Bel, D; 1972 v Cz (sub); (with Coventry C), 1973 v E (2 sub), W (sub), Ni (21)
Stephen, J. F. (Bradford), 1947 v W; 1948 v W (2)
Stevenson, G. (Motherwell), 1928 v W, Ni; 1930 v Ni, E, F; 1931 v E, W; 1932 v W, Ni; 1933 v Ni; 1934 v E; 1935 v Ni (12)
Stewart, A. (Queen's Park), 1888 v Ni; 1889 v W (2)
Stewart, A. (Third Lanark), 1894 v W (1)
Stewart, D. (Dumbarton), 1888 v Ni (1)
Stewart, D. (Queen's Park), 1893 v W; 1894 v Ni; 1897 v Ni (3)
Stewart, D. S. (Leeds U), 1978 v EG (1)
Stewart, G. (Hibernian), 1906 v W, E; (with Manchester C), 1907 v E, W (4)
Stewart, J. (Kilmarnock), 1977 v Ch (sub); (with Middlesbrough), 1979 v N (2)
Stewart, M. J. (Manchester U), 2002 v Ng (sub), Sk, S.Af (sub) (3)
Stewart, R. (West Ham U), 1981 v W, Ni, E; 1982 v Ni, P, W; 1984 v F; 1987 v Ei (2), L (10)
Stewart, W. G. (Queen's Park), 1898 v Ni; 1900 v Ni (2)
Stockdale, R. K. (Middlesbrough), 2002 v Ng, Sk (sub), S.Af, Hk; 2003 v D (5)
Storrier, D. (Celtic), 1899 v E, W, Ni (3)
Strachan, G. (Aberdeen), 1980 v Ni, W, E, Pol, H (sub); 1981 v Se, P; 1982 v Ni, P, Sp, Ho (sub), Nz, Br, USSR; 1983 v EG, Sw, Bel, Sw, Ni (sub), W, E, Ca (2 + 1 sub); 1984 v EG, Ni, E, F; (with Manchester U), 1985 v Sp (sub), E, Ic; 1986 v W, Aus, R, D, WG, U; 1987 v Bul, Ei (2); 1988 v H; 1989 v F (sub); (with Leeds U), 1990 v F; 1991 v USSR, Bul, Sm; 1992 v Sw, R, Ni, Fi (50)
Sturrock, P. (Dundee U), 1981 v W (sub), Ni, E (sub); 1982 v P, Ni (sub), W (sub), E (sub); 1983 v EG (sub), Sw, Bel (sub), Ca (3); 1984 v W; 1985 v Y (sub); 1986 v Is (sub), Ho, D, U; 1987 v Bel (20)
Sullivan, N. (Wimbledon), 1997 v W; 1998 v F, Co; 1999 v Fa, CzR, G, Fa, CzR; 2000 v Bos, Es, Bos, E (2), F, Ho, Ei; (with Tottenham H), 2001 v La, Sm, Cro, Bel, Sm, Pol; 2002 v Cro, Bel, La, F, Sk; 2003 v Ei (28)
Summers, W. (St Mirren), 1926 v E (1)
Symon, J. S. (Rangers), 1939 v H (1)

Tait, T. S. (Sunderland), 1911 v W (1)
Taylor, J. (Queen's Park), 1872 v E; 1873 v E; 1874 v E; 1875 v E; 1876 v E, W (6)
Taylor, J. D. (Dumbarton), 1892 v W; 1893 v W; 1894 v Ni; (with St Mirren), 1895 v Ni (4)
Taylor, W. (Hearts), 1892 v E (1)
Teale, G. (Wigan Ath), 2006 v Sw (sub), Bul, J; 2007 v Fa (sub), F (sub), Ge, I, Fa (sub) (8)
Telfer, P. N. (Coventry C), 2000 v F (1)
Telfer, W. (Motherwell), 1933 v Ni; 1934 v Ni (2)
Telfer, W. D. (St Mirren), 1954 v W (1)
Templeton, R. (Aston Villa), 1902 v E; (with Newcastle U), 1903 v E, W; 1904 v E; (with Woolwich Arsenal), 1905 v W; (with Kilmarnock), 1908 v Ni; 1910 v E, Ni; 1912 v E, Ni; 1913 v W (11)
Thompson, S. (Dundee U), 2002 v F (sub), Ng, Hk; 2003 v D, Fa (sub), Ic, Ca; (with Rangers), Ei (sub), A, G (sub); 2004 v Fa (sub), G, R; 2005 v H (sub), N (sub), Mol (16)
Thomson, A. (Arthurlie), 1886 v Ni (1)
Thomson, A. (Third Lanark), 1889 v W (1)
Thomson, A. (Airdrieonians), 1909 v Ni (1)
Thomson, A. (Celtic), 1926 v E; 1932 v F; 1933 v W (3)
Thomson, C. (Hearts), 1904 v Ni; 1905 v E, Ni, W; 1906 v W, Ni; 1907 v E, W, Ni; 1908 v E, W, Ni; (with Sunderland), 1909 v W; 1910 v E; 1911 v Ni; 1912 v E, W; 1913 v E, W; 1914 v E, Ni (21)
Thomson, C. (Sunderland), 1937 v Cz (1)
Thomson, D. (Dundee), 1920 v W (1)
Thomson, J. (Celtic), 1930 v F; 1931 v E, W, Ni (4)
Thomson, J. J. (Queen's Park), 1872 v E; 1873 v E; 1874 v E (3)
Thomson, J. R. (Everton), 1933 v W (1)
Thomson, R. (Celtic), 1932 v W (1)
Thomson, R. W. (Falkirk), 1927 v E (1)
Thomson, S. (Rangers), 1884 v W, Ni (2)
Thomson, W. (Dumbarton), 1892 v W; 1893 v W; 1898 v Ni, W (4)
Thomson, W. (Dundee), 1896 v W (1)
Thomson, W. (St Mirren), 1980 v Ni; 1981 v Ni (sub+1) 1982 v P; 1983 v Ni, Ca; 1984 v EG (7)
Thornton, W. (Rangers), 1947 v W, Ni; 1948 v E, Ni; 1949 v F; 1952 v D, Se (7)
Toner, W. (Kilmarnock), 1959 v W, Ni (2)
Townsley, T. (Falkirk), 1926 v W (1)
Troup, A. (Dundee), 1920 v E; 1921 v W, Ni; 1922 v Ni; (with Everton), 1926 v E (5)
Turnbull, E. (Hibernian), 1948 v Bel, Sw; 1951 v A; 1958 v H, Pol, Y, Par, F (8)
Turner, T. (Arthurlie), 1884 v W (1)
Turner, W. (Pollokshields Ath), 1885 v Ni; 1886 v Ni (2)

Ure, J. F. (Dundee), 1962 v W, Cz; 1963 v W, Ni, E, A, N, Sp; (with Arsenal), 1964 v Ni, N; 1968 v Ni (11)
Urquhart, D. (Hibernian), 1934 v W (1)

Vallance, T. (Rangers), 1877 v E, W; 1878 v E; 1879 v E, W; 1881 v E, W (7)
Venters, A. (Cowdenbeath), 1934 v Ni; (with Rangers), 1936 v E; 1939 v E (3)

Waddell, T. S. (Queen's Park), 1891 v Ni; 1892 v E; 1893 v E, Ni; 1895 v E, Ni (6)
Waddell, W. (Rangers), 1947 v W; 1949 v E, W, Ni, F; 1950 v E, Ni; 1951 v E, D, F, Bel, A; 1952 v Ni, W; 1954 v Ni; 1955 v W, Ni (17)
Wales, H. M. (Motherwell), 1933 v W (1)
Walker, A. (Celtic), 1988 v Co (sub); 1995 v Fi, Fa (sub) (3)
Walker, F. (Third Lanark), 1922 v W (1)
Walker, G. (St Mirren), 1930 v F; 1931 v Ni, A, Sw (4)
Walker, J. (Hearts), 1895 v Ni; 1897 v W; 1898 v Ni; (with Rangers), 1904 v W, Ni (5)
Walker, J. (Swindon T), 1911 v E, W, Ni; 1912 v E, W, Ni; 1913 v E, W, Ni (9)
Walker, J. N. (Hearts), 1993 v G; (with Partick Th), 1996 v US (sub) (2)
Walker, R. (Hearts), 1900 v E, Ni; 1901 v E, W; 1902 v E, W, Ni; 1903 v E, W, Ni; 1904 v E, W, Ni; 1905 v E, W, Ni; 1906 v Ni; 1907 v E, Ni; 1908 v E, W, Ni; 1909 v E, W; 1912 v E, W, Ni; 1913 v E, W (29)

Walker, T. (Hearts), 1935 v E, W; 1936 v E, W, Ni; 1937 v G, E, W, Ni, A, Cz; 1938 v E, W, Ni, Cz, Ho; 1939 v E, W, Ni, H (20)
Walker, W. (Clyde), 1909 v Ni; 1910 v Ni (2)
Wallace, I. A. (Coventry C), 1978 v Bul (sub); 1979 v P (sub), W (3)
Wallace, W. S. B. (Hearts), 1965 v Ni; 1966 v E, Ho; (with Celtic), 1967 v E, USSR (sub); 1968 v Ni; 1969 v E (sub) (7)
Wardhaugh, J. (Hearts), 1955 v H; 1957 v Ni (2)
Wark, J. (Ipswich T), 1979 v W, Ni, E, Arg, N (sub); 1980 v Pe, A, Bel (2); 1981 v Is, Ni; 1982 v Se, Sp, Ho, Ni, Nz, Br, USSR; 1983 v EG, Sw (2), Ni, E (sub); 1984 v U, Bel, EG; (with Liverpool), E, F; 1985 v Y (29)
Watson, A. (Queen's Park), 1881 v E, W; 1882 v E (3)
Watson, J. (Sunderland), 1903 v E, W; 1904 v E; 1905 v E; (with Middlesbrough), 1909 v E, Ni (6)
Watson, J. (Motherwell), 1948 v Ni; (with Huddersfield T), 1954 v Ni (2)
Watson, J. A. K. (Rangers), 1878 v W (1)
Watson, P. R. (Blackpool), 1934 v A (1)
Watson, R. (Motherwell), 1971 v USSR (1)
Watson, W. (Falkirk), 1898 v W (1)
Watt, F. (Kilbirnie), 1889 v W, Ni; 1890 v W; 1891 v E (4)
Watt, W. W. (Queen's Park), 1887 v Ni (1)
Waugh, W. (Hearts), 1938 v Cz (1)
Webster, A. (Hearts), 2003 v A, Nz, G; 2004 v N, Fa, W (sub), Es (sub), Tr (sub); 2005 v H, Sp, Slv, N, Mol, Se, Mol, Bl; 2006 v A, I, N, Slv, US, Sw (22)
Weir, A. (Motherwell), 1959 v WG; 1960 v E, Pol, A, H, T (6)
Weir, D. G. (Hearts), 1997 v W, Ma (sub); 1998 v F, D (sub), Fi (sub), N (sub), Mor; 1999 v Es, Fa; (with Everton), CzR, G, Fa, CzR; 2000 v Bos, Es, Bos, Li, E (2), Ho; 2001 v La, Sm (sub), Cro, Aus, Bel, Sm, Pol (sub); 2002 v Cro, Bel, La, F, Ng, Sk, S.Af, Hk; 2003 v D, Fa; 2005 v I, Mol, Bl; 2006 v I, N, Bl, Slv, US, Sw, Bul, J; (with Rangers), 2007 v Fa, Li, F, Uk, Ge, I, A, Fa (56)
Weir, J. (Third Lanark), 1887 v Ni (1)
Weir, J. B. (Queen's Park), 1872 v E; 1874 v E; 1875 v E; 1878 v W (4)
Weir, P. (St Mirren), 1980 v Ni, W, Pol (sub), H; (with Aberdeen), 1983 v Sw; 1984 v Ni (6)
White, John (Albion R), 1922 v W; (with Hearts), 1923 v Ni (2)
White, J. A. (Falkirk), 1959 v WG, Ho, P; 1960 v Ni; (with Tottenham H), 1960 v W, Pol, A, T; 1961 v W; 1962 v Ni, W, E, Cz (2); 1963 v W, Ni, E; 1964 v Ni, W, E, N, WG (22)
White, W. (Bolton W), 1907 v E; 1908 v E (2)
Whitelaw, A. (Vale of Leven), 1887 v Ni; 1890 v W (2)
Whyte, D. (Celtic), 1988 v Bel (sub), L; 1989 v Ch (sub); 1992 v US (sub); (with Middlesbrough), 1993 v P, I; 1995 v J (sub), Ec; 1996 v US; 1997 v La; (with Aberdeen), 1998 v Fi; 1999 v G (sub) (12)
Wilkie, L. (Dundee), 2002 v S.Af (sub), Hk; 2003 v Ic, Ca, P, Ic, Li, A; 2004 v Fa, Ho (2) (11)
Williams, G. (Nottingham F), 2002 v Ng, Sk (sub), S.Af, Hk (sub); 2003 v P (sub) (5)
Wilson, A. (Sheffield W), 1907 v E; 1908 v E; 1912 v E; 1913 v E, W; 1914 v Ni (6)
Wilson, A. (Portsmouth), 1954 v Fi (1)
Wilson, A. N. (Dunfermline), 1920 v E, W, Ni; 1921 v E, W, Ni; (with Middlesbrough), 1922 v E, W, Ni; 1923 v E, W, Ni (12)
Wilson, D. (Queen's Park), 1900 v W (1)
Wilson, D. (Oldham Ath), 1913 v E (1)
Wilson, D. (Rangers), 1961 v E, W, Ni, Ei (2), Cz; 1962 v Ni, W, E, Cz, U; 1963 v W, E, A, N, Ei, Sp; 1964 v E, WG; 1965 v Ni, E, Fi (22)
Wilson, G. W. (Hearts), 1904 v W; 1905 v E, Ni; 1906 v W; (with Everton), 1907 v E; (with Newcastle U), 1909 v E (6)
Wilson, Hugh, (Newmilns), 1890 v W; (with Sunderland), 1897 v E; (with Third Lanark), 1902 v W; 1904 v Ni (4)
Wilson, I. A. (Leicester C), 1987 v E, Br; (with Everton), 1988 v Bel, Bul, L (5)
Wilson, J. (Vale of Leven), 1888 v W; 1889 v E; 1890 v E; 1891 v E (4)
Wilson, P. (Celtic), 1926 v Ni; 1930 v F; 1931 v Ni; 1933 v E (4)
Wilson, P. (Celtic), 1975 v Sp (sub) (1)
Wilson, R. P. (Arsenal), 1972 v P, Ho (2)
Winters, R. (Aberdeen), 1999 v G (sub) (1)
Wiseman, W. (Queen's Park), 1927 v W; 1930 v Ni (2)
Wood, G. (Everton), 1979 v Ni, E, Arg (sub); (with Arsenal), 1982 v Ni (4)
Woodburn, W. A. (Rangers), 1947 v E, Bel, L; 1948 v W, Ni; 1949 v E, F; 1950 v E, W, Ni, P, F; 1951 v E, W, Ni, A (2), D, F, Bel; 1952 v E, W, Ni, USA (24)
Wotherspoon, D. N. (Queen's Park), 1872 v E; 1873 v E (2)
Wright, K. (Hibernian), 1992 v Ni (1)
Wright, S. (Aberdeen), 1993 v G, Es (2)
Wright, T. (Sunderland), 1953 v W, Ni, E (3)
Wylie, T. G. (Rangers), 1890 v Ni (1)

Yeats, R. (Liverpool), 1965 v W; 1966 v I (2)
Yorston, B. C. (Aberdeen), 1931 v Ni (1)
Yorston, H. (Aberdeen), 1955 v W (1)
Young, A. (Everton), 1905 v E; 1907 v W (2)
Young, A. (Hearts), 1960 v E, A (sub), H, T; 1961 v W, Ni; (with Everton), Ei; 1966 v P (8)
Young, G. L. (Rangers), 1947 v E, Ni, Bel, L; 1948 v E, Ni, Bel, Sw, F; 1949 v E, W, Ni, F; 1950 v E, W, Ni, Sw, P, F; 1951 v E, W, Ni, A (2), D, F, Bel; 1952 v E, W, Ni, USA, D, Se; 1953 v W, E, Ni, Se; 1954 v Ni, W; 1955 v W, Ni, P, Y; 1956 v Ni, W, E, A; 1957 v E, Ni, W, Y, Sp, Sw (53)
Young, J. (Celtic), 1906 v Ni (1)
Younger, T. (Hibernian), 1955 v P, Y, A, H; 1956 v E, Ni, W, A; (with Liverpool), 1957 v E, Ni, W, Y, Sp (2), Sw, WG; 1958 v Ni, W, E, Sw, H, Pol, Y, Par (24)

WALES

Adams, H. (Berwyn R), 1882 v Ni, E; (with Druids), 1883 v Ni, E (4)
Aizlewood, M. (Charlton Ath), 1986 v S.Ar, Ca (2); 1987 v Fi; (with Leeds U), USSR, Fi (sub); 1988 v D (sub), Se, Ma, I; 1989 v Ho, Se (sub), WG; (with Bradford C), 1990 v Fi, WG, Ei, Cr; (with Bristol C), 1991 v D, Bel (2), L, Ei, Ic, Pol, G; 1992 v Br, L, Ei, A, R, Ho, Arg, J; 1993 v Ei, Bel, Fa; 1994 v RCS, Cy; (with Cardiff C), 1995v Bul (39)
Allchurch, I. J. (Swansea T), 1951 v E, Ni, P, Sw; 1952 v E, S, Ni, R of UK; 1953 v S, E, Ni, F, Y; 1954 v S, E, Ni, A; 1955 v S, E, Ni, Y; 1956 v E, S, Ni, A; 1957 v E, S; 1958 v Ni, Is (2), H (2), M, Se, Br; (with Newcastle U), 1959 v E, S, Ni; 1960 v E, S; 1961 v Ni, H, Sp (2); 1962 v E, S, Br (2), M; (with Cardiff C), 1963 v S, E, Ni, H (2); 1964 v E; 1965 v S, E, Ni, Gr, I, USSR; (with Swansea T), 1966 v USSR, E, S, D, Br (2), Ch (68)
Allchurch, L. (Swansea T), 1955 v Ni; 1956 v A; 1958 v S, Ni, EG, Is; 1959 v S; (with Sheffield U), 1962 v S, Ni, Br; 1964 v E (11)
Allen, B. W. (Coventry C), 1951 v S, E (2)
Allen, M. (Watford), 1986 v S.Ar (sub), Ca (1 + 1 sub); (with Norwich C), 1989 v Is (sub); 1990 v Ho, WG; (with Millwall), Ei, Se, Cr (sub); 1991 v L (sub), Ei (sub); 1992 v A; 1993 v Ei (sub); (with Newcastle U), 1994 v R (sub) (14)
Arridge, S. (Bootle), 1892 v S, Ni; (with Everton), 1894 v Ni; 1895 v Ni; 1896 v E; (with New Brighton Tower), 1898 v E, Ni; 1899 v E (8)
Astley, D. J. (Charlton Ath), 1931 v Ni; (with Aston Villa), 1932 v E; 1933 v E, S, Ni; 1934 v E, S; 1935 v S; 1936 v E, Ni; (with Derby Co), 1939 v E, S; (with Blackpool), F (13)
Atherton, R. W. (Hibernian), 1899 v E, Ni; 1903 v E, S, Ni; (with Middlesbrough), 1904 v E, S, Ni; 1905 v Ni (9)

Bailiff, W. E. (Llanelly), 1913 v E, S, Ni; 1920 v Ni (4)
Baker, C. W. (Cardiff C), 1958 v M; 1960 v S, Ni; 1961 v S, E, Ei; 1962 v S (7)
Baker, W. G. (Cardiff C), 1948 v Ni (1)
Bale, G. (Southampton), 2006 v Tr (sub); 2007 v Br, Slo, Cy, Ei, Sm (6)
Bamford, T. (Wrexham), 1931 v E, S, Ni; 1932 v Ni; 1933 v F (5)
Barnard, D. S. (Barnsley), 1998 v Jam; 1999 v I, D, Bl, I, D; 2000 v Bl, Sw, Q, Fi, Br (sub), P; 2001 v Uk, Pol, Uk;

2002 v Arm (sub); (with Grimsby T), 2003 v Cro, Az; 2004 v Ser, Ru (2), N (sub) (22)
Barnes, W. (Arsenal), 1948 v E, S, Ni; 1949 v E, S, Ni; 1950 v E, S, Ni, Bel; 1951 v E, S, Ni, P; 1952 v E, S, Ni, R of UK; 1954 v E, S; 1955 v S, Y (22)
Bartley, T. (Glossop NE), 1898 v E (1)
Bastock, A. M. (Shrewsbury), 1892 v Ni (1)
Beadles, G. H. (Cardiff C), 1925 v E, S (2)
Bell, W. S. (Shrewsbury Engineers), 1881 v E, S; (with Crewe Alex), 1886 v E, S, Ni (5)
Bellamy, C. D. (Norwich C), 1998 v Jam (sub), Ma, Tun; 1999 v D (sub), Sw (sub), I, D (sub); 2000 v Br (sub), P; (with Coventry C), 2001 v Bl, Arm, Uk; (with Newcastle U), 2002 v Arm, N, Bl, Arg; 2003 v Fi (sub), I, Bos, Az; 2004 v Ser, I, Ser, N, Ca; 2005 v La, Az, Ni, E, Pol, H, A (2); (with Blackburn R), 2006 v Cy, Para; (with Liverpool), 2007 v Bul, CzR, Br, Slo, Cy, Lie, Ni, Ei, Sm, Nz, CzR (46)
Bennion, S. R. (Manchester U), 1926 v S; 1927 v S; 1928 v S, E, Ni; 1929 v S, E, Ni; 1930 v S; 1932 v Ni (10)
Berry, G. F. (Wolverhampton W), 1979 v WG; 1980 v Ei, WG (sub), T; (with Stoke C), 1983 v E (sub) (5)
Blackmore, C. G. (Manchester U), 1985 v N (sub); 1986 v S (sub), H (sub), S.Ar, Ei, U; 1987 v Fi (2), USSR, Cz; 1988 v D (2), Cz, Y, Se, Ma, I; 1989 v Ho, Fi, Is, WG; 1990 v Fi, Ho, WG, Cr; 1991 v Bel, L; 1992 v Ei (sub), A, R (sub), Ho, Arg, J; 1993 v Fa, Cy, Bel, RCS; 1994 v Se (sub); (with Middlesbrough), 1997 v Bel (39)
Blake, N. A. (Sheffield U), 1994 v N, Se (sub); 1995 v Alb, Mol; 1996 v G (with Bolton W), I (sub); 1998 v T; 1999 v I, D, Bl; (with Blackburn R) Sw; 2000 v Bl, Sw, Q, Fi; 2001 v Bl (sub), N, Pol (2), Uk; 2002 v N (sub); (with Wolverhampton W), CzR; 2003 v I (sub); 2004 v Ser, I (sub), Fi (sub), Ser (sub), Ru (sub + sub) (29)
Blew, H. (Wrexham), 1899 v E, S, Ni; 1902 v S, Ni; 1903 v E, S; 1904 v E, S, Ni; 1905 v S, Ni; 1906 v E, S, Ni; 1907 v S; 1908 v E, S, Ni; 1909 v E, S; 1910 v E (22)
Boden, T. (Wrexham), 1880 v E (1)
Bodin, P. J. (Swindon T), 1990 v Cr; 1991 v D, Bel, L, Ei; (with C Palace), Bel, Ic, Pol, G; 1992 v Br, G, L (sub); (with Swindon T), Ei (sub), Ho, Arg; 1993 v Ei, Bel, RCS, Fa; 1994 v R, Se, Es (sub); 1995 v Alb (23)
Boulter, L. M. (Brentford), 1939 v Ni (1)
Bowdler, H. E. (Shrewsbury), 1893 v S (1)
Bowdler, J. C. H. (Shrewsbury), 1890 v Ni; (with Wolverhampton W), 1891 v S; 1892 v Ni; (with Shrewsbury), 1894 v E (4)
Bowen, D. L. (Arsenal), 1955 v S, Y; 1957 v Ni, Cz, EG; 1958 v E, S, Ni, EG, Is (2), H (2), M, Se, Br; 1959 v E, S, Ni (19)
Bowen, E. (Druids), 1880 v S; 1883 v S (2)
Bowen, J. P. (Swansea C), 1994 v Es; (with Birmingham C), 1997 v Ho (2)
Bowen, M. R. (Tottenham H), 1986 v Ca (2 sub); (with Norwich C), 1988 v Y (sub); 1989 v Fi (sub), Is, Se, WG (sub); 1990 v Fi (sub), Ho, WG, Se; 1992 v Br (sub), G, L, Ei, A, R, Ho (sub), J; 1993 v Fa, Cy, Bel (1 + sub), RCS (sub); 1994 v RCS, Se; 1995 v Mol, Ge, Bul (2), G, Ge; 1996 v Mol, G, Alb, Sw, Sm; (with West Ham U), 1997 v Sm, Ho (2), Ei (sub) (41)
Bowsher, S. J. (Burnley), 1929 v Ni (1)
Boyle, T. (C Palace), 1981 v Ei, S (sub) (2)
Britten, T. J. (Parkgrove), 1878 v S; (with Presteigne), 1880 v S (2)
Brookes, S. J. (Llandudno), 1900 v E, Ni (2)
Brown, A. I. (Aberdare Ath), 1926 v Ni (1)
Brown, J. R. (Gillingham), 2006 v Tr; (with Blackburn R), 2007 v Lie (2)
Browning, M. T. (Bristol R), 1996 v I (sub), Sm; 1997 v Sm, Ho; (with Huddersfield T), S (sub) (5)
Bryan, T. (Oswestry), 1886 v E, Ni (2)
Buckland, T. (Bangor), 1899 v E (1)
Burgess, W. A. R. (Tottenham H), 1947 v E, S, Ni; 1948 v E, S; 1949 v E, S, Ni, P, Bel, Sw; 1950 v E, S, Ni, Bel; 1951 v S, Ni, P, Sw; 1952 v E, S, Ni, R of UK; 1953 v S, E, Ni, F, Y; 1954 v S, E, Ni, A (32)
Burke, T. (Wrexham), 1883 v E; 1884 v S; 1885 v E, S, Ni; (with Newton Heath), 1887 v E, S; 1888 v S (8)
Burnett, T. B. (Ruabon), 1877 v S (1)
Burton, A. D. (Norwich C), 1963 v Ni, H; (with Newcastle U), 1964 v E; 1969 v S, E, Ni, I, EG; 1972 v Cz (9)
Butler, J. (Chirk), 1893 v E, S, Ni (3)
Butler, W. T. (Druids), 1900 v S, Ni (2)
Cartwright, L. (Coventry C), 1974 v E (sub), S, Ni; 1976 v S (sub); 1977 v WG (sub); (with Wrexham), 1978 v Ir (sub); 1979 v Ma (7)
Carty, T. See McCarthy (Wrexham).
Challen, J. B. (Corinthians), 1887 v E, S; 1888 v E; (with Wellingborough GS), 1890 v E (4)
Chapman, T. (Newtown), 1894 v E, S, Ni; 1895 v S, Ni; (with Manchester C), 1896 v E; (with Grimsby T), 1897 v E (7)
Charles, J. M. (Swansea C), 1981 v Cz, T (sub), S (sub), USSR (sub); 1982 v Ic; 1983 v N (sub), Y (sub), Bul (sub), S, Ni, Br; 1984 v Bul (sub); (with QPR), Y (sub), S; (with Oxford U), 1985 v Ic (sub), Sp, Ic; 1986 v Ei; 1987 v Fi (19)
Charles, M. (Swansea T), 1955 v Ni; 1956 v E, S, A; 1957 v E, Ni, Cz (2), EG; 1958 v E, S, EG, Is (2), H (2), M, Se, Br; 1959 v E, S; (with Arsenal), 1961 v Ni, H, Sp (2); 1962 v E, S; (with Cardiff C), 1962 v Br, Ni; 1963 v S, H (31)
Charles, W. J. (Leeds U), 1950 v Ni; 1951 v Sw; 1953 v Ni, F, Y; 1954 v E, S, Ni, A; 1955 v S, E, Ni, Y; 1956 v E, S, A, Ni; 1957 v E, S, Ni, Cz (2), EG; (with Juventus), 1958 v Is (2), H (2) M, Se; 1960 v S; 1962 v E, Br (2), M; (with Leeds U), 1963 v S; (with Cardiff C), 1964 v S; 1965 v S, USSR (38)
Clarke, R. J. (Manchester C), 1949 v E; 1950 v S, Ni, Bel; 1951 v E, S, Ni, P, Sw; 1952 v S, E, Ni, R of UK; 1953 v S, E; 1954 v E, S, Ni; 1955 v Y, S, E; 1956 v Ni (22)
Coleman, C. (C Palace), 1992 v A (sub); 1993 v Ei (sub); 1994 v N, Es; 1995 v Alb, Mol, Ge, Bul (2), G; 1996 v Mol; (with Blackburn R), I, Sw, Sm; 1997 v Sm; 1998 v Br; (with Fulham), Jam, Ma, Tun; 1999 v I, D, Bl, Sw, D; 2000 v Bl, Sw, Q, Fi; 2001 v Bl, N, Pol; 2002 v G (sub) (32)
Collier, D. J. (Grimsby T), 1921 v S (1)
Collins, D. L. (Sunderland), 2005 v H (sub); 2006 v Ni (sub), Az, Cy; 2007 v Ni, Ei (sub) (6)
Collins, J. M. (Cardiff C), 2004 v N, Ca; 2005 v La (sub), Ni, Pol, A; (with West Ham U), 2006 v E (sub), Pol, Ni, Az, Para, Tr; 2007 v Bul, CzR, Br, Ei, Sm, Nz, CzR (19)
Collins, W. S. (Llanelly), 1931 v S (1)
Conde, C. (Chirk), 1884 v E, S, Ni (3)
Cook, F. C. (Newport Co), 1925 v E, S; (with Portsmouth), 1928 v E, S; 1930 v E, S, Ni; 1932 v E (8)
Cornforth, J. M. (Swansea C), 1995 v Bul (sub), Ge (2)
Cotterill, D. R. G. B. (Bristol C), 2006 v Az (sub), Para (sub), Tr; (with Wigan Ath), 2007 v CzR (sub), Br (sub), Slo (sub), Ni (sub), Sm (sub) (8)
Coyne, D. (Tranmere R), 1996 v Sw; (with Grimsby T), 2002 v CzR (sub); (with Leicester C), 2004 v H (sub), N, Ca; (with Burnley), 2005 v H, A (2); 2006 v Slv, E, Pol; 2007 v Ni, Ei, Sm, Nz (15)
Crofts, A. L. (Gillingham), 2006 v Az (sub), Para (sub), Tr (sub); 2007 v Lie (sub), Ni (sub), Nz (sub) (6)
Crompton, W. (Wrexham), 1931 v E, S, Ni (3)
Cross, E. A. (Wrexham), 1876 v S; 1877 v S (2)
Crosse, K. (Druids), 1879 v S; 1881 v E, S (3)
Crossley, M. G. (Nottingham F), 1997 v Ei; 1999 v Sw (sub); 2000 v Fi; (with Middlesbrough), 2002 v Arg (sub), G; 2003 v Bos (sub); (with Fulham), 2004 v S; 2005 v La (sub) (8)
Crowe, V. H. (Aston Villa), 1959 v E, Ni; 1960 v E, Ni; 1961 v S, E, Ni, Ei, H, Sp (2); 1962 v E, S, Br, M; 1963 v H (16)
Cumner, R. H. (Arsenal), 1939 v E, S, Ni (3)
Curtis, A. (Swansea C), 1976 v E, Y (sub), S, Ni, Y (sub), E; 1977 v WG, S (sub), Ni (sub); 1978 v WG, E, S; 1979 v WG, S; (with Leeds U), E, Ni, Ma; 1980 v Ei, WG, T; (with Swansea C), 1982 v Cz, Ic, USSR, Sp, E, S, Ni; 1983 v N; 1984 v R (sub); (with Southampton), S; 1985 v Sp, N (1 + 1 sub); 1986 v H; (with Cardiff C), 1987 v USSR (35)
Curtis, E. R. (Cardiff C), 1928 v S; (with Birmingham), 1932 v S; 1934 v Ni (3)

Daniel, R. W. (Arsenal), 1951 v E, Ni, P; 1952 v E, S, Ni, R of UK; 1953 v S, E, Ni, F, Y; (with Sunderland), 1954 v E, S, Ni; 1955 v E, Ni; 1957 v S, E, Ni, Cz (21)
Darvell, S. (Oxford University), 1897 v S, Ni (2)
Davies, A. (Manchester U), 1983 v Ni, Br; 1984 v E, Ni; 1985 v Ic (2), N; (with Newcastle U), 1986 v H; (with Swansea C), 1988 v Ma, I; 1989 v Ho; (with Bradford C), 1990 v Fi, Ei (13)
Davies, A. (Wrexham), 1876 v S; 1877 v S (2)

Davies, A. (Druids), 1904 v S; (with Middlesbrough), 1905 v S (2)
Davies, A. O. (Barmouth), 1885 v Ni; 1886 v E, S; (with Swifts), 1887 v E, S; 1888 v E, Ni; (with Wrexham), 1889 v S; (with Crewe Alex), 1890 v E (9)
Davies, A. R. (Yeovil T), 2006 v Tr (sub) (1)
Davies, A. T. (Shrewsbury), 1891 v Ni (1)
Davies, C. (Charlton Ath), 1972 v R (sub) (1)
Davies, C. M. (Oxford U), 2006 v Slv (sub), Pol (sub); (with Verona), Tr (sub); 2007 v Lie (sub) (4)
Davies, D. (Bolton W), 1904 v S, Ni; 1908 v E (sub) (3)
Davies, D. C. (Brecon), 1899 v Ni; (with Hereford); 1900 v Ni (2)
Davies, D. W. (Treharris), 1912 v Ni; (with Oldham Ath), 1913 v Ni (2)
Davies, E. Lloyd (Stoke C), 1904 v E; 1907 v E, S, Ni; (with Northampton T), 1908 v S; 1909 v Ni; 1910 v Ni; 1911 v E, S; 1912 v E, S; 1913 v E, S; 1914 v Ni, E, S (16)
Davies, E. R. (Newcastle U), 1953 v S, E; 1954 v E, S; 1958 v E, EG (6)
Davies, G. (Fulham), 1980 v T, Ic; 1982 v Sp (sub), F (sub); 1983 v E, Bul, S, Ni, Br; 1984 v R (sub), S (sub), E, Ni; 1985 v Ic; (with Manchester C), 1986 v S.Ar, Ei (16)
Davies, Rev. H. (Wrexham), 1928 v Ni (1)
Davies, Idwal (Liverpool Marine), 1923 v S (1)
Davies, J. E. (Oswestry), 1885 v E (1)
Davies, Jas (Wrexham), 1878 v S (1)
Davies, John (Wrexham), 1879 v S (1)
Davies, Jos (Newton Heath), 1888 v E, S, Ni; 1889 v S; 1890 v E; (with Wolverhampton W), 1892 v E; 1893 v E (7)
Davies, Jos (Everton), 1889 v S, Ni; (with Chirk), 1891 v Ni; (with Ardwick), v E, S; (with Sheffield U), 1895 v E, S, Ni; (with Manchester C), 1896 v E; (with Millwall), 1897 v E; (with Reading), 1900 v E (11)
Davies, J. P. (Druids), 1883 v E, Ni (2)
Davies, Ll. (Wrexham), 1907 v Ni; 1910 v Ni, S, E; (with Everton), 1911 v S, Ni; (with Wrexham), 1912 v Ni, S, E; 1913 v Ni, S, E; 1914 v Ni (13)
Davies, L. S. (Cardiff C), 1922 v E, S, Ni; 1923 v E, S, Ni; 1924 v E, S, Ni; 1925 v S, Ni; 1926 v E, Ni; 1927 v E, Ni; 1928 v S, Ni, E; 1929 v S, Ni, E; 1930 v E, S (23)
Davies, O. (Wrexham), 1890 v S (1)
Davies, R. (Wrexham), 1883 v Ni; 1884 v Ni; 1885 v Ni (3)
Davies, R. (Druids), 1885 v E (1)
Davies, R. O. (Wrexham), 1892 v Ni, E (2)
Davies, R. T. (Norwich C), 1964 v Ni; 1965 v E; 1966 v Br (2), Ch; (with Southampton), 1967 v S, E, Ni; 1968 v S, Ni, WG; 1969 v S, E, Ni, I, WG; 1970 v R of UK, E, S, Ni; 1971 v Cz, S, E, Ni; 1972 v R, E, S, Ni; (with Portsmouth), 1974 v E (29)
Davies, R. W. (Bolton W), 1964 v E; 1965 v E, S, Ni, D, Gr, USSR; 1966 v E, S, Ni, USSR, D, Br (2), Ch (sub); 1967 v S; (with Newcastle U), E; 1968 v S, Ni, WG; 1969 v S, E, Ni, I; 1970 v EG; 1971 v R, Cz; (with Manchester C), 1972 v E, S, Ni; (with Manchester U), 1973 v E, S (sub), Ni; (with Blackpool), 1974 v Pol (34)
Davies, S. (Tottenham H), 2001 v Uk (sub+1); 2002 v Arm, N, Bl, Arg, CzR, G; 2003 v Cro, Fi, I, Az, Bos, Az, US; 2004 v Ser, I, Fi, S; 2005 v E, Pol, H, A (2); (with Everton), 2006 v E, Pol, Ni, Az, Para, Tr; 2007 v Bul, CzR, Br, Slo, Cy, Lie; (with Fulham), Ni, Ei, Sm, Nz, CzR (41)
Davies, S. I. (Manchester U), 1996 v Sw (sub) (1)
Davies, Stanley (Preston NE), 1920 v E, S, Ni; (with Everton), 1921 v E, S, Ni; (with WBA), 1922 v E, S, Ni; 1923 v S; 1925 v S, Ni; 1926 v S, E, Ni; 1927 v S; 1928 v S; (with Rotherham U), 1930 v Ni (18)
Davies, T. (Oswestry), 1886 v E (1)
Davies, T. (Druids), 1903 v E, Ni, S; 1904 v S (4)
Davies, W. (Wrexham), 1884 v Ni (1)
Davies, W. (Swansea T), 1924 v E, S, Ni; (with Cardiff C), 1925 v E, S, Ni; 1926 v E, S, Ni; 1927 v S; 1928 v Ni; (with Notts Co), 1929 v E, S, Ni; 1930 v E, S, Ni (17)
Davies, William (Wrexham), 1903 v Ni; 1905 v Ni; (with Blackburn R), 1908 v E, S; 1909 v E, S, Ni; 1911 v E, S, Ni; 1912 v Ni (11)
Davies, W. C. (C Palace), 1908 v S; (with WBA), 1909 v E; 1910 v S; (with C Palace), 1914 v E (4)
Davies, W. D. (Everton), 1975 v H, L, S, E, Ni; 1976 v Y (2), E, Ni; 1977 v WG, S (2), Cz, E, Ni; 1978 v K; (with Wrexham), S, Cz, WG, Ir, E, S, Ni; 1979 v Ma, T, WG, S, E, Ni, Ma; 1980 v Ei, WG, T, E, S, Ni, Ic; 1981 v T, Cz, Ei, T, S, E, USSR; (with Swansea C), 1982 v Cz, Ic, USSR, Sp, E, S, F; 1983 v Y (52)
Davies, W. H. (Oswestry), 1876 v S; 1877 v S; 1879 v E; 1880 v E (4)
Davis, G. (Wrexham), 1978 v Ir, E (sub), Ni (3)
Davis, W. O. (Millwall Ath), 1913 v E, S, Ni; 1914 v S, Ni (5)
Day, A. (Tottenham H), 1934 v Ni (1)
Deacy, N. (PSV Eindhoven), 1977 v Cz, S, E, Ni; 1978 v K (sub), S (sub), Cz (sub), WG, Ir, S (sub), Ni; (with Beringen), 1979 v T (12)
Dearson, D. J. (Birmingham), 1939 v S, Ni, F (3)
Delaney, M. A. (Aston Villa), 2000 v Sw, Q, Br, P; 2001 v N, Pol, Arm, Uk (2); 2002 v Arm, N, Bl, Arg, CzR, G; 2003 v Cro, Fi, I, Az; 2004 v Ser, I, Ser, Ru (2), N, Ca; 2005 v La, Az, Ni, E, Pol, A (2); 2006 v Ni; 2007 v Bul, CzR (36)
Derrett, S. C. (Cardiff C), 1969 v S, WG; 1970 v I; 1971 v Fi (4)
Dewey, F. T. (Cardiff Corinthians), 1931 v E, S (2)
Dibble, A. (Luton T), 1986 v Ca (1+1 sub); (with Manchester C), 1989 v Is (3)
Doughty, J. (Druids), 1886 v S; (with Newton Heath), 1887 v S, Ni; 1888 v E, S, Ni; 1889 v S; 1890 v E (8)
Doughty, R. (Newton Heath), 1888 v S, Ni (2)
Duffy, R. M. (Portsmouth), 2006 v Slv, E, Pol (sub), Ni (sub), Az, Cy; 2007 v Bul (sub), Br, Slo, Cy, Lie, Ni (12)
Durban, A. (Derby Co), 1966 v Br (sub); 1967 v Ni; 1968 v E, S, Ni, WG; 1969 v EG, S, E, Ni, WG; 1970 v E, S, Ni, EG, I; 1971 v R, S, E, Ni, Cz, Fi; 1972 v Fi, Cz, E, S, Ni (27)
Dwyer, P. (Cardiff C), 1978 v Ir, E, S, Ni; 1979 v T, S, E, Ni, Ma (sub); 1980 v WG (10)

Earnshaw, R. (Cardiff C), 2002 v G; 2003 v Cro, Az, Bos; 2004 v Ser (sub), I (sub), Fi, Ser, Ru (sub), S, H, N, Ca (sub); 2005 v Az (sub); (with WBA), Ni (sub), E (sub), Pol, H, A (sub); 2006 v Slv, E (sub), Pol, Ni, Cy (sub); (with Norwich C), Para (sub), Tr; 2007 v Bul, CzR (sub), Br, Slo, Cy, Lie, Nz, CzR (sub) (34)
Easter, J. M. (Wycombe W), 2007 v Ni (sub), Ei (sub), Sm (3)
Edwards, C. (Wrexham), 1878 v S (1)
Edwards, C. N. H. (Swansea C), 1996 v Sw (sub) (1)
Edwards, G. (Birmingham C), 1947 v E, S, Ni; 1948 v E, S, Ni; (with Cardiff C), 1949 v Ni, P, Bel, Sw; 1950 v E, S (12)
Edwards, H. (Wrexham Civil Service), 1878 v S; (with Wrexham), 1880 v E, S; 1882 v E, S; 1883 v S; 1884 v Ni; 1887 v Ni (8)
Edwards, J. H. (Wanderers), 1876 v S (1)
Edwards, J. H. (Oswestry), 1895 v Ni; 1897 v E, Ni (3)
Edwards, J. H. (Aberystwyth), 1898 v Ni (1)
Edwards, L. T. (Charlton Ath), 1957 v Ni, EG (2)
Edwards, R. I. (Chester), 1978 v K (sub); 1979 v Ma, WG; (with Wrexham), 1980 v T (sub) (4)
Edwards, R. O. (Aston Villa), 2003 v Az (sub); 2004 v Ser (sub), S, H (sub), N (sub), Ca (sub); (with Wolverhampton W), 2005 v H; 2006 v Slv (sub), Pol, Cy (sub), Para; 2007 v Bul (sub), Br (sub), Slo, Cy (sub) (15)
Edwards, R. W. (Bristol C), 1998 v T (sub), Bel, Ma (sub), Tun (sub) (4)
Edwards, T. (Linfield), 1932 v S (1)
Egan, W. (Chirk), 1892 v S (1)
Ellis, B. (Motherwell), 1932 v E; 1933 v E, S; 1934 v S; 1936 v E; 1937 v S (6)
Ellis, E. (Nunhead), 1931 v S; (with Oswestry), E; 1932 v Ni (3)
Emanuel, W. J. (Bristol C), 1973 v E (sub), Ni (sub) (2)
England, H. M. (Blackburn R), 1962 v Ni, Br, M; 1963 v Ni, H; 1964 v E, S, Ni; 1965 v E, D, Gr (2), USSR, Ni, I; 1966 v E, S, Ni, USSR, D; (with Tottenham H), 1967 v S, E; 1968 v E, Ni, WG; 1969 v EG; 1970 v R of UK, EG, E, S, Ni, I; 1971 v R; 1972 v Fi, E, S, Ni; 1973 v E (3), S; 1974 v Pol; 1975 v H, L (44)
Evans, B. C. (Swansea C), 1972 v Fi, Cz; 1973 v E (2), Pol, S; (with Hereford U), 1974 v Pol (7)
Evans, D. G. (Reading), 1926 v Ni; 1927 v Ni, E; (with Huddersfield T), 1929 v S (4)
Evans, H. P. (Cardiff C), 1922 v E, S, Ni; 1924 v E, S, Ni (6)
Evans, I. (C Palace), 1976 v A, E, Y (2), E, Ni; 1977 v WG, S (2), Cz, E, Ni; 1978 v K (13)

Evans, J. (Oswestry), 1893 v Ni; 1894 v E, Ni (3)
Evans, J. (Cardiff C), 1912 v Ni; 1913 v Ni; 1914 v S; 1920 v S, Ni; 1922 v Ni; 1923 v E, Ni (8)
Evans, J. H. (Southend U), 1922 v E, S, Ni; 1923 v S (4)
Evans, Len (Aberdare Ath), 1927 v Ni; (with Cardiff C), 1931 v E, S; (with Birmingham), 1934 v Ni (4)
Evans, M. (Oswestry), 1884 v E (1)
Evans, P. S. (Brentford), 2002 v CzR (sub); (with Bradford C), Cro (sub) (2)
Evans, R. (Clapton), 1902 v Ni (1)
Evans, R. E. (Wrexham), 1906 v E, S; (with Aston Villa), Ni; 1907 v E; 1908 v E, S; (with Sheffield U), 1909 v S; 1910 v E, S, Ni (10)
Evans, R. O. (Wrexham), 1902 v Ni; 1903 v E, S, Ni; (with Blackburn R), 1908 v Ni; (with Coventry C), 1911 v E, Ni; 1912 v E, S, Ni (10)
Evans, R. S. (Swansea T), 1964 v Ni (1)
Evans, S. J. (Wrexham), 2007 v Lie, Ni, Ei, Sm, Nz (sub) (5)
Evans, T. J. (Clapton Orient), 1927 v S; 1928 v E, S; (with Newcastle U), Ni (4)
Evans, W. (Tottenham H), 1933 v Ni; 1934 v E, S; 1935 v E; 1936 v E, Ni (6)
Evans, W. A. W. (Oxford University), 1876 v S; 1877 v S (2)
Evans, W. G. (Bootle), 1890 v E; (with Aston Villa), 1891 v E; 1892 v E (3)
Evelyn, E. C. (Crusaders), 1887 v E (1)
Eyton-Jones, J. A. (Wrexham), 1883 v Ni; 1884 v Ni, E, S (4)

Farmer, G. (Oswestry), 1885 v E, S (2)
Felgate, D. (Lincoln C), 1984 v R (sub) (1)
Finnigan, R. J. (Wrexham), 1930 v Ni (1)
Fletcher, C. N. (Bournemouth), 2004 v S (sub), H (sub), N, Ca; (with West Ham U), 2005 v H, A (2); 2006 v Slv, E, Pol, Ni, Az, Cy, Para, Tr; (with Crystal Palace), 2007 v Bul, CzR, Br (sub), Lie (sub), Ei (sub), Sm, Nz (22)
Flynn, B. (Burnley), 1975 v L (2 sub), H (sub), S, E, Ni; 1976 v A, E, Y (2), E, Ni; 1977 v WG (sub), S (2), Cz, E, Ni; 1978 v K (2), S; (with Leeds U), Cz, WG, Ir (sub), E, S, Ni; 1979 v Ma, T, S, E, Ni, Ma; 1980 v Ei, WG, E, S, Ni, Ic; 1981 v T, Cz, Ei, T, S, E, USSR; 1982 v Cz, USSR, E, S, Ni, F; 1983 v N; (with Burnley), Y, E, Bul, S, Ni, Br; 1984 v N, R, Bul, Y, S, N, Is (66)
Ford, T. (Swansea T), 1947 v S; (with Aston Villa), 1947 v Ni; 1948 v S, Ni; 1949 v E, S, Ni, P, Bel, Sw; 1950 v E, S, Ni, Bel; 1951 v S; (with Sunderland), 1951 v E, Ni, P, Sw; 1952 v E, S, Ni, R of UK; 1953 v S, E, Ni, F, Y; (with Cardiff C), 1954 v A; 1955 v S, E, Ni, Y; 1956 v S, Ni, E, A; 1957 v S (38)
Foulkes, H. E. (WBA), 1932 v Ni (1)
Foulkes, W. I. (Newcastle U), 1952 v E, S, Ni, R of UK; 1953 v E, S, F, Y; 1954 v E, S, Ni (11)
Foulkes, W. T. (Oswestry), 1884 v Ni; 1885 v S (2)
Fowler, J. (Swansea T), 1925 v E; 1926 v E, Ni; 1927 v S; 1928 v S; 1929 v E (6)
Freestone, R. (Swansea C), 2000 v Br (1)

Gabbidon, D. L. (Cardiff C), 2002 v CzR; 2003 v Cro, Fi, I; 2004 v Ser (2), Ru (2), S, H, N, Ca; 2005 v Az, Ni, E, Pol, H, A (2); (with West Ham U), 2006 v Slv, E, Pol, Az, Cy, Para, Tr; 2007 v Bul, CzR, Br, Slo, Cy, Nz, CzR (33)
Garner, G. (Leyton Orient), 2006 v Tr (sub) (1)
Garner, J. (Aberystwyth), 1896 v S (1)
Giggs, R. J. (Manchester U), 1992 v G (sub), L (sub), R (sub); 1993 v Fa (sub), Bel (sub + 1), RCS, Fa; 1994 v RCS, Cy, R; 1995 v Alb, Bul; 1996 v G, Alb, Sm; 1997 v Sm, T, Bel; 1998 v T, Bel; 1999 v I (2), D; 2000 v Bl, Fi; 2001 v Bl, N, Pol, Uk, Pol, Uk; 2002 v Arm, N, Arg, G; 2003 v Fi, I, Az (2); 2004 v Ser, I, Fi, Ser, Ru (2), S, Ca; 2005 v E, A (2); 2006 v E, Pol, Ni, Az, Para; 2007 v Bul, CzR, Br, Lie, Ei, Sm, Nz, CzR (64)
Giles, D. (Swansea C), 1980 v E, S, Ni, Ic; 1981 v T, Cz, T (sub), E (sub), USSR (sub); (with C Palace), 1982 v Sp (sub); 1983 v Ni (sub), Br (12)
Gillam, S. G. (Wrexham), 1889 v S (sub), Ni; (with Shrewsbury), 1890 v E, Ni; (with Clapton), 1894 v S (5)
Glascodine, G. (Wrexham), 1879 v E (1)
Glover, E. M. (Grimsby T), 1932 v S; 1934 v Ni; 1936 v S; 1937 v E, S, Ni; 1939 v Ni (7)
Godding, G. (Wrexham), 1923 v S, Ni (2)
Godfrey, B. C. (Preston NE), 1964 v Ni; 1965 v D, I (3)
Goodwin, U. (Ruthin), 1881 v E (1)
Goss, J. (Norwich C), 1991 v Ic, Pol (sub); 1992 v A; 1994 v Cy (sub), R (sub), Se; 1995 v Alb; 1996 v Sw (sub), Sm (sub) (9)
Gough, R. T. (Oswestry White Star), 1883 v S (1)
Gray, A. (Oldham Ath), 1924 v E, S, Ni; 1925 v E, S, Ni; 1926 v E, S; 1927 v S; (with Manchester C), 1928 v E, S; 1929 v E, S, Ni; (with Manchester Central), 1930 v S; (with Tranmere R), 1932 v E, S, Ni; (with Chester), 1937 v E, S, Ni; 1938 v E, S, Ni (24)
Green, A. W. (Aston Villa), 1901 v Ni; (with Notts Co), 1903 v E; 1904 v S, Ni; 1906 v Ni, E; (with Nottingham F), 1907 v E; 1908 v S (8)
Green, C. R. (Birmingham C), 1965 v USSR, I; 1966 v E, S, USSR, Br (2); 1967 v E; 1968 v E, S, Ni, WG; 1969 v S, I, Ni (sub) (15)
Green, G. H. (Charlton Ath), 1938 v Ni; 1939 v E, Ni, F (4)
Green, R. M. (Wolverhampton W), 1998 v Ma, Tun (2)
Grey, Dr W. (Druids), 1876 v S; 1878 v S (2)
Griffiths, A. T. (Wrexham), 1971 v Cz (sub); 1975 v A, H (2), L (2), E, Ni; 1976 v A, E, S, E (sub), Ni, Y (2); 1977 v WG, S (17)
Griffiths, F. J. (Blackpool), 1900 v E, S (2)
Griffiths, G. (Chirk), 1887 v Ni (1)
Griffiths, J. H. (Swansea T), 1953 v Ni (1)
Griffiths, L. (Wrexham), 1902 v S (1)
Griffiths, M. W. (Leicester C), 1947 v Ni; 1949 v P, Bel; 1950 v E, S, Bel; 1951 v E, Ni, P, Sw; 1954 v A (11)
Griffiths, P. (Chirk), 1884 v E, Ni; 1888 v E; 1890 v S, Ni; 1891 v Ni (6)
Griffiths, P. H. (Everton), 1932 v S (1)
Griffiths, T. P. (Everton), 1927 v E, Ni; 1929 v E; 1930 v E; 1931 v Ni; 1932 v Ni, S, E; (with Bolton W), 1933 v E, S, Ni; (with Middlesbrough), F; 1934 v E, S; 1935 v E, Ni; 1936 v S; (with Aston Villa), Ni; 1937 v E, S, Ni (21)
Gunter, C. R. (Cardiff C), 2007 v Nz (1)

Hall, G. D. (Chelsea), 1988 v Y (sub), Ma, I; 1989 v Ho, Fi, Is; 1990 v Ei; 1991 v Ei; 1992 v A (sub) (9)
Hallam, J. (Oswestry), 1889 v E (1)
Hanford, H. (Swansea T), 1934 v Ni; 1935 v S; 1936 v E; (with Sheffield W), Ni; 1938 v E, S; 1939 v F (7)
Harrington, A. C. (Cardiff C), 1956 v Ni; 1957 v E, S; 1958 v S, Ni, Is (2); 1961 v S, E; 1962 v E, S (11)
Harris, C. S. (Leeds U), 1976 v E, S; 1978 v WG, Ir, E, S, Ni; 1979 v Ma, T, WG, E (sub), Ma; 1980 v Ni (sub), Ic (sub); 1981 v T, Cz (sub), Ei, T, S, E, USSR; 1982 v Cz, Ic, E (sub) (24)
Harris, W. C. (Middlesbrough), 1954 v A; 1957 v EG, Cz; 1958 v E, S, EG (6)
Harrison, W. C. (Wrexham), 1899 v E; 1900 v E, S, Ni; 1901 v Ni (5)
Hartson, J. (Arsenal), 1995 v Bul, G (sub), Ge (sub); 1996 v Mol (sub), Sw; 1997 v Ho, T (sub), Ei; (with West Ham U), Bel (sub), S; 1998 v Bel, Jam, Ma, Tun; (with Wimbledon), 1999 v Sw (sub), I (sub), D; 2000 v Sw (sub); 2001 v N, Pol; (with Coventry C), Arm, Uk, Pol, Uk; (with Celtic), 2002 v N, Bl, Arg, CzR, G; 2003 v Cro, Fi, I, Az, Bos, Az; 2004 v I, Fi, Ser, Ru (2); 2005 v La, Az, Ni, E, Pol (sub), A; 2006 v Slv, E, Ni, Az, Cy (51)
Haworth, S. O. (Cardiff C), 1997 v S (sub); (with Coventry C), 1998 v Br, Jam (sub), Ma (sub), Tun (sub) (5)
Hayes, A. (Wrexham), 1890 v Ni; 1894 v Ni (2)
Hennessey, W. R. (Wolverhampton W), 2007 v Nz (sub), CzR (2)
Hennessey, W. T. (Birmingham C), 1962 v Ni, Br (2); 1963 v S, E, H (2); 1964 v E, S; 1965 v S, E, D, Gr, USSR; 1966 v E, USSR; (with Nottingham F), 1966 v S, Ni, D, Br (2), Ch; 1967 v S, E; 1968 v E, S, Ni; 1969 v WG, EG; 1970 v R of UK, EG; (with Derby Co), E, S, Ni; 1972 v Fi, Cz, E, S; 1973 v E (39)
Hersee, A. M. (Bangor), 1886 v S, Ni (2)
Hersee, R. (Llandudno), 1886 v Ni (1)
Hewitt, R. (Cardiff C), 1958 v Ni, Is, Se, H, Br (5)
Hewitt, T. J. (Wrexham), 1911 v E, S, Ni; (with Chelsea), 1913 v E, S, Ni; (with South Liverpool), 1914 v E, S (8)
Heywood, D. (Druids), 1879 v E (1)
Hibbott, H. (Newtown Excelsior), 1880 v E, S; (with Newtown), 1885 v S (3)
Higham, G. G. (Oswestry), 1878 v S; 1879 v E (2)
Hill, M. R. (Ipswich T), 1972 v Cz, R (2)

Hockey, T. (Sheffield U), 1972 v Fi, R; 1973 v E (2); (with Norwich C), Pol, S, E, Ni; (with Aston Villa), 1974 v Pol (9)
Hoddinott, T. F. (Watford), 1921 v E, S (2)
Hodges, G. (Wimbledon), 1984 v N (sub), Is (sub); 1987 v USSR, Fi, Cz; (with Newcastle U), 1988 v D; (with Watford), D (sub), Cz (sub), Se, Ma (sub), I (sub); 1990 v Se, Cr; (with Sheffield U), 1992 v Br (sub), Ei (sub), A; 1996 v G (sub), I (18)
Hodgkinson, A. V. (Southampton), 1908 v Ni (1)
Holden, A. (Chester C), 1984 v Is (sub) (1)
Hole, B. G. (Cardiff C), 1963 v Ni; 1964 v Ni; 1965 v S, E, Ni, D, Gr (2), USSR, I; 1966 v E, S, Ni, USSR, D, Br (2), Ch; (with Blackburn R), 1967 v S, E, Ni; 1968 v E, S, Ni, WG; (with Aston Villa), 1969 v I, WG, EG; 1970 v I; (with Swansea C), 1971 v R (30)
Hole, W. J. (Swansea T), 1921 v Ni; 1922 v E; 1923 v E, Ni; 1928 v E, S, Ni; 1929 v E, S (9)
Hollins, D. M. (Newcastle U), 1962 v Br (sub), M; 1963 v Ni, H; 1964 v E; 1965 v Ni, Gr, I; 1966 v S, D, Br (11)
Hopkins, I. J. (Brentford), 1935 v S, Ni; 1936 v E, Ni; 1937 v E, S, Ni; 1938 v E, Ni; 1939 v E, S, Ni (12)
Hopkins, J. (Fulham), 1983 v Ni, Br; 1984 v N, R, Bul, Y, S, E, Ni, N, Is; 1985 v Ic (1 + 1 sub), N; (with C Palace), 1990 v Ho, Cr (16)
Hopkins, M. (Tottenham H), 1956 v Ni; 1957 v Ni, S, E, Cz (2), EG; 1958 v E, S, Ni, EG, Is (2), H (2), M, Se, Br; 1959 v E, S, Ni; 1960 v E, S; 1961 v Ni, H, Sp (2); 1962 v Ni, Br (2), M; 1963 v S, Ni, H (34)
Horne, B. (Portsmouth), 1988 v D (sub), Y, Se (sub), Ma, I; 1989 v Ho, Fi, Is; (with Southampton), Se, WG; 1990 v WG (sub), Ei, Se, Cr; 1991 v D, Bel (2), L, Ei, Ic, Pol, G; 1992 v Br, G, L, Ei, A, R, Ho, Arg, J; (with Everton), 1993 v Fa, Cy, Bel, Ei, Bel, RCS, Fa; 1994 v RCS, Cy, R, N, Se, Es; 1995 v Mol, Ge, Bul, G, Ge; 1996 v Mol, G, I, Sw, Sm; (with Birmingham C), 1997 v Sm, Ho, T, Ei, Bel (59)
Howell, E. G. (Builth), 1888 v Ni; 1890 v E; 1891 v E (3)
Howells, R. G. (Cardiff C), 1954 v E, S (2)
Hugh, A. R. (Newport Co), 1930 v Ni (1)
Hughes, A. (Rhos), 1894 v E, S (2)
Hughes, A. (Chirk), 1907 v Ni (1)
Hughes, C. M. (Luton T), 1992 v Ho (sub); 1994 v N (sub), Se (sub), Es; 1996 v Alb; 1997 v Ei (sub); (with Wimbledon), 1998 v T, Bel (8)
Hughes, E. (Everton), 1899 v S, Ni; (with Tottenham H), 1901 v E, S; 1902 v Ni; 1904 v E, Ni, S; 1905 v E, Ni, S; 1906 v E, Ni; 1907 v E (14)
Hughes, E. (Wrexham), 1906 v S; (with Nottingham F), 1906 v Ni; 1908 v S, E; 1910 v Ni, E, S; 1911 v Ni, E, S; (with Wrexham), 1912 v Ni, E, S; (with Manchester C), 1913 v E, S; 1914 v Ni (16)
Hughes, F. W. (Northwich Victoria), 1882 v E, Ni; 1883 v E, Ni, S; 1884 v S (6)
Hughes, I. (Luton T), 1951 v E, Ni, P, Sw (4)
Hughes, J. (Cambridge University), 1877 v S; (with Aberystwyth), 1879 v S (2)
Hughes, J. (Liverpool), 1905 v E, S, Ni (3)
Hughes, J. I. (Blackburn R), 1935 v Ni (1)
Hughes, L. M. (Manchester U), 1984 v E, Ni; 1985 v Ic, Sp, Ic, N, S, Sp, N; 1986 v S, H, U; (with Barcelona), 1987 v USSR, Cz; 1988 v D (2), Cz, Se, Ma, I; (with Manchester U), 1989 v Ho, Fi, Is, Se, WG; 1990 v Fi, WG, Cr; 1991 v D, Bel (2), L, Ic, Pol, G; 1992 v Br, G, L, Ei, R, Ho, Arg, J; 1993 v Fa, Cy, Bel, Ei, Bel, RCS, Fa; 1994 v RCS, Cy, N; 1995 v Ge, Bul, G, Ge; (with Chelsea), 1996 v Mol, I, Sm; 1997 v Sm, Ho, T, Ei, Bel; 1998 v T; (with Southampton), 1999 v I, D, Bl, Sw, I, D (72)
Hughes, P. W. (Bangor), 1887 v Ni; 1889 v Ni, E (3)
Hughes, W. (Bootle), 1891 v E; 1892 v S, Ni (3)
Hughes, W. A. (Blackburn R), 1949 v E, Ni, P, Bel, Sw (5)
Hughes, W. M. (Birmingham), 1938 v E, Ni, S; 1939 v E, Ni, S, F; 1947 v E, S, Ni (10)
Humphreys, J. V. (Everton), 1947 v Ni (1)
Humphreys, R. (Druids), 1888 v Ni (1)
Hunter, A. H. (FA of Wales Secretary), 1887 v Ni (1)

Jackett, K. (Watford), 1983 v N, Y, E, Bul, S; 1984 v N, R, Y, S, Ni, N, Is; 1985 v Ic, Sp, Ic, N, S, Sp, N; 1986 v S, H, S.Ar, Ei, Ca (2); 1987 v Fi (2); 1988 v D, Cz, Y, Se (31)
Jackson, W. (St Helens Rec), 1899 v Ni (1)
James, E. (Chirk), 1893 v E, Ni; 1894 v E, S, Ni; 1898 v S, E; 1899 v Ni (8)
James, E. G. (Blackpool), 1966 v Br (2), Ch; 1967 v Ni; 1968 v S; 1971 v Cz, S, E, Ni (9)
James, L. (Burnley), 1972 v Cz, R, S (sub); 1973 v E (3), Pol, S, Ni; 1974 v Pol, E, S, Ni; 1975 v A, H (2), L (2), S, E, Ni; 1976 v A; (with Derby Co), S, E, Y (2), Ni; 1977 v WG, S (2), Cz, E, Ni; 1978 v K (2); (with QPR), WG; (with Burnley), 1979 v T; (with Swansea C), 1980 v E, S, Ni, Ic; 1981 v T, Ei, T, S, E; 1982 v Cz, Ic, USSR, E (sub), S, Ni, F; (with Sunderland), 1983 v E (sub) (54)
James, R. M. (Swansea C), 1979 v Ma, WG (sub), S, E, Ni, Ma; 1980 v WG; 1982 v Cz (sub), Ic, Sp, E, S, Ni, F; 1983 v N, Y, E, Bul; (with Stoke C), 1984 v N, R, Bul, Y, S, E, Ni, N, Is; 1985 v Ic, Sp, Ic; (with QPR), N, S, Sp, N; 1986 v S, S.Ar, Ei, U, Ca (2); 1987 v Fi (2), USSR, Cz; (with Leicester C), 1988 v D (2); (with Swansea C), Y (47)
James, W. (West Ham U), 1931 v Ni; 1932 v Ni (2)
Jarrett, R. H. (Ruthin), 1889 v Ni; 1890 v S (2)
Jarvis, A. L. (Hull C), 1967 v S, E, Ni (3)
Jenkins, E. (Lovell's Ath), 1925 v E (1)
Jenkins, J. (Brighton), 1924 v Ni, E, S; 1925 v S, Ni; 1926 v E, S; 1927 v S (8)
Jenkins, R. W. (Rhyl), 1902 v Ni (1)
Jenkins, S. R. (Swansea C), 1996 v G; (with Huddersfield T), Alb, I; 1997 v Ho (sub), T, S; 1998 v T, Bel, Br, Jam; 1999 v I (sub), D; 2001 v Pol (sub), Uk (sub); 2002 v Arm, N (16)
Jenkyns, C. A. L. (Small Heath), 1892 v E, S, Ni; 1895 v E; (with Woolwich Arsenal), 1896 v S; (with Newton Heath), 1897 v Ni; (with Walsall), 1898 v S, E (8)
Jennings, W. (Bolton W), 1914 v E, S; 1920 v S; 1923 v Ni, E; 1924 v E, S, Ni; 1927 v S, Ni; 1929 v S (11)
John, R. F. (Arsenal), 1923 v S, Ni; 1925 v Ni; 1926 v E; 1927 v E; 1928 v E, Ni; 1930 v E, S; 1932 v E; 1933 v F, Ni; 1935 v Ni; 1936 v S; 1937 v E (15)
John, W. R. (Walsall), 1931 v Ni; (with Stoke C), 1933 v E, S, Ni, F; 1934 v E, S; (with Preston NE), 1935 v E, S; (with Sheffield U), 1936 v E, S, Ni; (with Swansea T), 1939 v E, S (14)
Johnson, A. J. (Nottingham F), 1999 v I, D, Bl, Sw; 2000 v Fi (sub), Br (sub), P (sub); (with WBA), 2003 v Cro, Fi, US; 2004 v I (sub), Fi (sub), Ru (2); 2005 v La (sub) (15)
Johnson, M. G. (Swansea T), 1964 v Ni (1)
Jones, A. (Port Vale), 1987 v Fi, Cz (sub); 1988 v D, (with Charlton Ath), D (sub), Cz (sub); 1990 v Hol (sub) (6)
Jones, A. F. (Oxford University), 1877 v S (1)
Jones, A. T. (Nottingham F), 1905 v E; (with Notts Co), 1906 v E (2)
Jones, Bryn (Wolverhampton W), 1935 v Ni; 1936 v E, S, Ni; 1937 v E, S, Ni; 1938 v E, S, Ni; (with Arsenal), 1939 v E, S, Ni; 1947 v S, Ni; 1948 v E; 1949 v S (17)
Jones, B. S. (Swansea T), 1963 v S, E, Ni, H (2); 1964 v S, Ni; (with Plymouth Arg), 1965 v D; (with Cardiff C), 1969 v S, E, Ni, I (sub), WG, EG; 1970 v R of UK (15)
Jones, Charlie (Nottingham F), 1926 v E; 1927 v S, Ni; 1928 v E; (with Arsenal), 1930 v E, S; 1932 v E; 1933 v F (8)
Jones, Cliff (Swansea T), 1954 v A; 1956 v E, Ni, S, A; 1957 v E, S, Ni, Cz (2), EG; 1958 v EG, E, S, Is (2); (with Tottenham H), Ni, H (2), M, Se, Br; 1959 v Ni; 1960 v E, S, Ni; 1961 v S, E, Ni, Sp, H, Ei; 1962 v E, Ni, S, Br (2), M; 1963 v S, Ni, H; 1964 v E, S, Ni; 1965 v E, S, Ni, D, Gr (2), USSR, I; 1967 v S, E; 1968 v E, S, WG; (with Fulham), 1969 v I; 1970 v R of UK (59)
Jones, C. W. (Birmingham), 1935 v Ni; 1939 v F (2)
Jones, D. (Chirk), 1888 v S, Ni; (with Bolton W), 1889 v E, S, Ni; 1890 v E; 1891 v S; 1892 v Ni; 1893 v E; 1894 v E; 1895 v E; 1898 v S; (with Manchester C), 1900 v E, Ni (14)
Jones, D. E. (Norwich C), 1976 v S, E (sub); 1978 v S, Cz, WG, Ir, E; 1980 v E (8)
Jones, D. O. (Leicester C), 1934 v E, Ni; 1935 v E, S; 1936 v E, Ni; 1937 v Ni (7)
Jones, Evan (Chelsea), 1910 v S, Ni; (with Oldham Ath), 1911 v E, S; 1912 v E, S; (with Bolton W), 1914 v Ni (7)
Jones, F. R. (Bangor), 1885 v E, Ni; 1886 v S (3)
Jones, F. W. (Small Heath), 1893 v S (1)
Jones, G. P. (Wrexham), 1907 v S, Ni (2)
Jones, H. (Aberaman), 1902 v Ni (1)
Jones, Humphrey (Bangor), 1885 v E, Ni, S; 1886 v E, Ni, S; (with Queen's Park), 1887 v E; (with East

Stirlingshire), 1889 v E, S; 1890 v E, S, Ni; (with Queen's Park), 1891 v E, S (14)
Jones, Ivor (Swansea T), 1920 v S, Ni; 1921 v Ni, E; 1922 v S, Ni; (with WBA), 1923 v E, Ni; 1924 v S; 1926 v Ni (10)
Jones, Jeffrey (Llandrindod Wells), 1908 v Ni; 1909 v Ni; 1910 v S (3)
Jones, J. (Druids), 1876 v S (1)
Jones, J. (Berwyn Rangers), 1883 v S, Ni; 1884 v S (3)
Jones, J. (Wrexham), 1925 v Ni (1)
Jones, J. L. (Sheffield U), 1895 v E, S, Ni; 1896 v Ni, S, E; 1897 v Ni, S, E; (with Tottenham H), 1898 v Ni, E, S; 1899 v S, Ni; 1900 v S; 1902 v E, S, Ni; 1904 v E, S, Ni (21)
Jones, J. Love (Stoke C), 1906 v S; (with Middlesbrough), 1910 v Ni (2)
Jones, J. O. (Bangor), 1901 v S, Ni (2)
Jones, J. P. (Liverpool), 1976 v A, E, S; 1977 v WG, S (2), Cz, E, Ni; 1978 v K (2), S, Cz, WG, Ir, E, S, Ni; (with Wrexham), 1979 v Ma, T, WG, S, E, Ni, Ma; 1980 v Ei, WG, T, E, S, Ni, Ic; 1981 v T, Ei, T, S, E, USSR; 1982 v Cz, Ic, USSR, Sp, E, S, Ni, F; 1983 v N; (with Chelsea), Y, E, Bul, S, Ni, Br; 1984 v N, R, Bul, Y, S, E, Ni, N, Is; 1985 v Ic, N, S, N; (with Huddersfield T), 1986 v S, H, Ei, U, Ca (2) (72)
Jones, J. T. (Stoke C), 1912 v E, S, Ni; 1913 v E, Ni; 1914 v S, Ni; 1920 v E, S, Ni; (with C Palace), 1921 v E, S; 1922 v E, S, Ni (15)
Jones, K. (Aston Villa), 1950 v S (1)
Jones, Leslie J. (Cardiff C), 1933 v F; (with Coventry C), 1935 v Ni; 1936 v S; 1937 v E, S, Ni; (with Arsenal), 1938 v E, S, Ni; 1939 v E, S (11)
Jones, M. A. (Wrexham), 2007 v Lie (sub) (1)
Jones, M. G. (Leeds U), 2000 v Sw (sub), Q, Br, P; 2001 v Pol (sub); (with Leicester C), Arm (sub), Uk, Pol (sub); 2002 v Arm (sub), N (sub), Bl; 2003 v Bos (sub), US (13)
Jones, P. L. (Liverpool), 1997 v S (sub); (with Tranmere R), 1998 v T (sub) (2)
Jones, P. S. (Stockport Co), 1997 v S (sub); (with Southampton), 1998 v T (sub), Br, Jam, Ma; 1999 v I, D, Bl, Sw, I, D; 2000 v Bl, Sw, Q; 2001 v Bl, N, Pol, Arm, Uk, Pol, Uk; 2002 v Arm, N, Bl, Arg; 2003 v Cro, Fi, I, Az (2), US; 2004 v Ser, I, Fi, Ser, Ru (2); (with Wolverhampton W), H; 2005 v La, Az, Ni, E, Pol; 2006 v Ni, Az; (with QPR), Para; 2007 v Bul, CzR, Br, Slo (50)
Jones, P. W. (Bristol R), 1971 v Fi (1)
Jones, R. (Bangor), 1887 v S; 1889 v E; (with Crewe Alex), 1890 v E (3)
Jones, R. (Leicester Fosse), 1898 v S (1)
Jones, R. (Druids), 1899 v S (1)
Jones, R. (Bangor), 1900 v S, Ni (2)
Jones, R. (Millwall), 1906 v S, Ni (2)
Jones, R. A. (Druids), 1884 v E, Ni, S; 1885 v S (4)
Jones, R. A. (Sheffield W), 1994 v Es (1)
Jones, R. S. (Everton), 1894 v Ni (1)
Jones, S. (Wrexham), 1887 v Ni; (with Chester), 1890 v S (2)
Jones, S. (Wrexham), 1893 v S, Ni; (with Burton Swifts), 1895 v S; 1896 v E, Ni; (with Druids), 1899 v E (6)
Jones, T. (Manchester U), 1926 v Ni; 1927 v E, Ni; 1930 v Ni (4)
Jones, T. D. (Aberdare), 1908 v Ni (1)
Jones, T. G. (Everton), 1938 v Ni; 1939 v E, S, Ni; 1947 v E, S; 1948 v E, S, Ni; 1949 v E, Ni, P, Bel, Sw; 1950 v E, S, Bel (17)
Jones, T. J. (Sheffield W), 1932 v Ni; 1933 v F (2)
Jones, V. P. (Wimbledon), 1995 v Bul (2), G, Ge; 1996 v Sw; 1997 v Ho, T, Ei, Bel (9)
Jones, W. E. A. (Swansea T), 1947 v E, S; (with Tottenham H), 1949 v E, S (4)
Jones, W. J. (Aberdare), 1901 v E, S; (with West Ham U), 1902 v E, S (4)
Jones, W. Lot (Manchester C), 1905 v E, Ni; 1906 v E, S, Ni; 1907 v E, S, Ni; 1908 v S; 1909 v E, S, Ni; 1910 v E; 1911 v E; 1913 v E, S; 1914 v S, Ni; (with Southend U), 1920 v E, Ni (20)
Jones, W. P. (Druids), 1889 v E, Ni; (with Wynnstay), 1890 v S, Ni (4)
Jones, W. R. (Aberystwyth), 1897 v S (1)

Keenor, F. C. (Cardiff C), 1920 v E, Ni; 1921 v E, Ni, S; 1922 v Ni; 1923 v E, Ni, S; 1924 v E, Ni, S; 1925 v E, Ni, S; 1926 v S; 1927 v E, Ni, S; 1928 v E, Ni, S; 1929 v E, Ni, S; 1930 v E, Ni, S; 1931 v E, Ni, S; (with Crewe Alex), 1933 v S (32)
Kelly, F. C. (Wrexham), 1899 v S, Ni; (with Druids), 1902 v Ni (3)
Kelsey, A. J. (Arsenal), 1954 v Ni, A; 1955 v S, Ni, Y; 1956 v E, Ni, S, A; 1957 v E, Ni, S, Cz (2), EG; 1958 v E, S, Ni, Is (2), H (2), M, Se, Br; 1959 v E, S; 1960 v E, Ni, S; 1961 v E, Ni, S, H, Sp (2); 1962 v E, S, Ni, Br (2) (41)
Kenrick, S. L. (Druids), 1876 v S; 1877 v S; (with Oswestry), 1879 v E, S; (with Shropshire Wanderers), 1881 v E (5)
Ketley, C. F. (Druids), 1882 v Ni (1)
King, J. (Swansea T), 1955 v E (1)
Kinsey, N. (Norwich C), 1951 v Ni, P, Sw; 1952 v E; (with Birmingham C), 1954 v Ni; 1956 v E, S (7)
Knill, A. R. (Swansea C), 1989 v Ho (1)
Koumas, J. (Tranmere R), 2001 v Uk (sub); 2002 v CzR; (with WBA), 2003 v Bos (sub), US; 2004 v I, Fi, Ru (2), H; 2005 v La, Az, Ni, E, Pol; 2006 v E (sub), Pol, Para; 2007 v Slo, Cy, Lie, Ni, Sm, CzR (23)
Krzywicki, R. L. (WBA), 1970 v EG, I; (with Huddersfield T), Ni, E, S; 1971 v R, Fi; 1972 v Cz (sub) (8)

Lambert, R. (Liverpool), 1947 v S; 1948 v E; 1949 v P, Bel, Sw (5)
Latham, G. (Liverpool), 1905 v E, S; 1906 v S; 1907 v E, S, Ni; 1908 v E; 1909 v Ni; (with Southport Central), 1910 v E; (with Cardiff C), 1913 v Ni (10)
Law, B. J. (QPR), 1990 v Se (1)
Lawrence, E. (Clapton Orient), 1930 v Ni; (with Notts Co), 1932 v S (2)
Lawrence, S. (Swansea T), 1932 v Ni; 1933 v F; 1934 v S, E, Ni; 1935 v E, S; 1936 v S (8)
Lea, A. (Wrexham), 1889 v E; 1891 v S, Ni; 1893 v Ni (4)
Lea, C. (Ipswich T), 1965 v Ni, I (2)
Leary, P. (Bangor), 1889 v Ni (1)
Ledley, J. C. (Cardiff C), 2006 v Pol (sub), Para (sub), Tr; 2007 v Bul (sub), CzR (sub), Br (sub), Slo (sub), Cy (sub), Ei, Lie, Nz (sub), CzR (12)
Leek, K. (Leicester C), 1961 v S, E, Ni, H, Sp (2); (with Newcastle U), 1962 v S; (with Birmingham C), Br (sub), M; 1963 v E; 1965 v S, Gr; (with Northampton T), 1965 v Gr (13)
Legg, A. (Birmingham C), 1996 v Sw, Sm (sub); 1997 v Ho (sub), Ei; (with Cardiff C), 1999 v D (sub); 2001 v Arm (6)
Lever, A. R. (Leicester C), 1953 v S (1)
Lewis, B. (Chester), 1891 v Ni; (with Wrexham), 1892 v S, E, Ni; (with Middlesbrough), 1893 v S, E; (with Wrexham), 1894 v S, E, Ni; 1895 v S (10)
Lewis, D. (Arsenal), 1927 v E; 1928 v Ni; 1930 v E (3)
Lewis, D. (Swansea C), 1983 v Br (sub) (1)
Lewis, D. J. (Swansea T), 1933 v E, S (2)
Lewis, D. M. (Bangor), 1890 v Ni, S (2)
Lewis, J. (Bristol R), 1906 v E (1)
Lewis, J. (Cardiff C), 1926 v S (1)
Lewis, T. (Wrexham), 1881 v E, S (2)
Lewis, W. (Bangor), 1885 v E; 1886 v E, S; 1887 v E, S; 1888 v E; 1889 v E, Ni, S; (with Crewe Alex), 1890 v E; 1891 v E, S; (with Chester), 1892 v E, S, Ni; 1894 v E, S, Ni; 1895 v S, Ni, E; 1896 v E, S, Ni; (with Manchester C), 1897 v E, S; (with Chester), 1898 v Ni (27)
Lewis, W. L. (Swansea T), 1927 v E, Ni; 1928 v E, Ni; 1929 v S; (with Huddersfield T), 1930 v E (6)
Llewellyn, C. M. (Norwich C), 1998 v Ma (sub), Tun (sub); (with Wrexham), 2004 v N (sub), Ca (sub); 2007 v Lie (sub), Nz (sub) (6)
Lloyd, B. W. (Wrexham), 1976 v A, E, S (3)
Lloyd, J. W. (Wrexham), 1879 v S; (with Newtown), 1885 v S (2)
Lloyd, R. A. (Ruthin), 1891 v Ni; 1895 v S (2)
Lockley, A. (Chirk), 1898 v Ni (1)
Lovell, S. (C Palace), 1982 v USSR (sub); (with Millwall), 1985 v N; 1986 v S (sub), H (sub), Ca (1+1 sub) (6)
Lowndes, S. (Newport Co), 1983 v S (sub), Br (sub); (with Millwall), 1985 v N (sub); 1986 v S.Ar (sub), Ei, U, Ca (2); (with Barnsley), 1987 v Fi (sub); 1988 v Se (sub) (10)
Lowrie, G. (Coventry C), 1948 v E, S, Ni; (with Newcastle U), 1949 v P (4)
Lucas, P. M. (Leyton Orient), 1962 v Ni, M; 1963 v S, E (4)

Lucas, W. H. (Swansea T), 1949 v S, Ni, P, Bel, Sw; 1950 v E; 1951 v E (7)
Lumberg, A. (Wrexham), 1929 v Ni; 1930 v E, S; (with Wolverhampton W), 1932 v S (4)

McCarthy, T. P. (Wrexham), 1889 v Ni (1)
McMillan, R. (Shrewsbury Engineers), 1881 v E, S (2)
Maguire, G. T. (Portsmouth), 1990 v Fi (sub), Ho, WG, Ei, Se; 1992 v Br (sub), G (7)
Mahoney, J. F. (Stoke C), 1968 v E; 1969 v EG; 1971 v Cz; 1973 v E (3), Pol, S, Ni; 1974 v Pol, E, S, Ni; 1975 v A, H (2), L (2), S, E, Ni; 1976 v A, Y (2), E, Ni; 1977 v WG, Cz, S, E, Ni; (with Middlesbrough), 1978 v K (2), S, Cz, Ir, E (sub), S, Ni; 1979 v WG, S, E, Ni, Ma; (with Swansea C), 1980 v Ei, WG, T (sub); 1982 v Ic, USSR; 1983 v Y, E (51)
Mardon, P. J. (WBA), 1996 v G (sub) (1)
Margetson, M. W. (Cardiff C), 2004 v Ca (sub) (1)
Marriott, A. (Wrexham), 1996 v Sw (sub); 1997 v S; 1998 v Bel, Br (sub), Tun (5)
Martin, T. J. (Newport Co), 1930 v Ni (1)
Marustik, C. (Swansea C), 1982 v Sp, E, S, Ni, F; 1983 v N (6)
Mates, J. (Chirk), 1891 v Ni; 1897 v E, S (3)
Matthews, R. W. (Liverpool), 1921 v Ni; (with Bristol C), 1923 v E; (with Bradford), 1926 v Ni (3)
Matthews, W. (Chester), 1905 v Ni; 1908 v E (2)
Matthias, J. S. (Brymbo), 1896 v S, Ni; (with Shrewsbury), 1897 v E, S; (with Wolverhampton W), 1899 v S (5)
Matthias, T. J. (Wrexham), 1914 v S, E; 1920 v Ni, S, E; 1921 v S, E, Ni; 1922 v S, E, Ni; 1923 v S (12)
Mays, A. W. (Wrexham), 1929 v Ni (1)
Medwin, T. C. (Swansea T), 1953 v Ni, F, Y; (with Tottenham H), 1957 v E, S, Ni, Cz (2), EG; 1958 v E, S, Ni, Is (2), H (2), M, Br; 1959 v E, S, Ni; 1960 v E, S, Ni; 1961 v S, Ei, E, Sp; 1963 v E, H (30)
Melville, A. K. (Swansea C), 1990 v WG, Ei, Se, Cr (sub); (with Oxford U), 1991 v Ic, Pol, G; 1992 v Br, G, L, R, Ho, J (sub); 1993 v RCS, Fa (sub); (with Sunderland), 1994 v RCS (sub), R, N, Se, Es; 1995 v Alb, Mol (sub), Ge, Bul; 1996 v G, Alb, Sm; 1997 v Sm, Ho (2), T; 1998 v T; 1999 v I, D; (with Fulham), 2000 v Bl, Q, Fi, Br, P; 2001 v Bl, N, Pol, Arm, Uk, Pol, Uk; 2002 v Arm, Bl, Arg, CzR, G; 2003 v Cro, Fi, I, Az, Bos, Az, US; 2004 v Fi, Ru (2); (with West Ham U), S, H; 2005 v La, Az (65)
Meredith, S. (Chirk), 1900 v S; 1901 v S, E, Ni; (with Stoke C), 1902 v E; 1903 v Ni; 1904 v E; (with Leyton), 1907 v E (8)
Meredith, W. H. (Manchester C), 1895 v E, Ni; 1896 v E, Ni; 1897 v E, Ni, S; 1898 v E, Ni; 1899 v E; 1900 v E, Ni; 1901 v E, Ni; 1902 v E, S; 1903 v E, S, Ni; 1904 v E; 1905 v E, S; (with Manchester U), 1907 v E, S, Ni; 1908 v E, Ni; 1909 v E, S, Ni; 1910 v E, S, Ni; 1911 v E, S, Ni; 1912 v E, S, Ni; 1913 v E, S, Ni; 1914 v E, S, Ni; 1920 v E, S, Ni (48)
Mielczarek, R. (Rotherham U), 1971 v Fi (1)
Millership, H. (Rotherham Co), 1920 v E, S, Ni; 1921 v E, S, Ni (6)
Millington, A. H. (WBA), 1963 v S, E, H; (with C Palace), 1965 v E, USSR; (with Peterborough U), 1966 v Ch, Br; 1967 v E, Ni; 1968 v Ni, WG; 1969 v I, EG; (with Swansea C), 1970 v E, S, Ni; 1971 v Cz, Fi; 1972 v Fi (sub), Cz, R (21)
Mills, T. J. (Clapton Orient), 1934 v E, Ni; (with Leicester C), 1935 v E, S (4)
Mills-Roberts, R. H. (St Thomas' Hospital), 1885 v E, S, Ni; 1886 v E; 1887 v E; (with Preston NE), 1888 v E, Ni; (with Llanberis), 1892 v E (8)
Moore, G. (Cardiff C), 1960 v E, S, Ni; 1961 v Ei, Sp; (with Chelsea), 1962 v Br; 1963 v Ni, H; (with Manchester U), 1964 v S, Ni; (with Northampton T), 1966 v Ni, Ch; (with Charlton Ath), 1969 v S, E, Ni; 1970 v R of UK, E, S, Ni, I; 1971 v R (21)
Morgan, C. (Milton Keynes D), 2007 v Cy (1)
Morgan, J. R. (Cambridge University), 1877 v S; (with Derby School Staff), 1879 v S; 1880 v E, S; 1881 v E, S; 1882 v E, S, Ni; 1883 v E (10)
Morgan, J. T. (Wrexham), 1905 v Ni (1)
Morgan-Owen, H. (Oxford University), 1902 v S; (with Corinthians), 1906 v E, Ni; 1907 v S (4)
Morgan-Owen, M. M. (Oxford University), 1897 v S, Ni; 1898 v E, S; 1899 v S; 1900 v E; (with Corinthians), 1901 v S, E; 1903 v S; 1906 v S, E, Ni; 1907 v E (13)
Morley, E. J. (Swansea T), 1925 v E; (with Clapton Orient), 1929 v E, S, Ni (4)
Morris, A. G. (Aberystwyth), 1896 v E, Ni, S; (with Swindon T), 1897 v E; 1898 v S; (with Nottingham F), 1899 v E, S; 1903 v E, S; 1905 v E, S; 1907 v E, S; 1908 v E; 1910 v E, S, Ni; 1911 v E, S, Ni; 1912 v E (21)
Morris, C. (Chirk), 1900 v E, S, Ni; (with Derby Co), 1901 v E, S, Ni; 1902 v E; 1903 v E, S, Ni; 1904 v Ni; 1905 v E, S, Ni; 1906 v S; 1907 v S; 1908 v E, S; 1909 v E, S, Ni; 1910 v E, S, Ni; (with Huddersfield T), 1911 v E, S, Ni (27)
Morris, E. (Chirk), 1893 v E, S, Ni (3)
Morris, H. (Sheffield U), 1894 v S; (with Manchester C), 1896 v E; (with Grimsby T), 1897 v E (3)
Morris, J. (Oswestry), 1887 v S (1)
Morris, J. (Chirk), 1898 v Ni (1)
Morris, R. (Chirk), 1900 v E, Ni; 1901 v Ni; 1902 v S; (with Shrewsbury T), 1903 v E, Ni (6)
Morris, R. (Newtown), 1902 v Ni; (with Druids), E, S; (with Liverpool), 1903 v S, Ni; 1904 v E, S, Ni; (with Leeds C), 1906 v S; (with Grimsby T), 1907 v Ni; (with Plymouth Arg), 1908 v Ni (11)
Morris, S. (Birmingham), 1937 v E, S; 1938 v E, S; 1939 v F (5)
Morris, W. (Burnley), 1947 v Ni; 1949 v E; 1952 v S, Ni, R of UK (5)
Moulsdale, J. R. B. (Corinthians), 1925 v Ni (1)
Murphy, J. P. (WBA), 1933 v F, E, Ni; 1934 v E, S; 1935 v E, S, Ni; 1936 v E, S, Ni; 1937 v S, Ni; 1938 v E, S (15)

Nardiello, D. (Coventry C), 1978 v Cz, WG (sub) (2)
Nardiello, D. A. (Barnsley), 2007 v Nz (sub) (1)
Neal, J. E. (Colwyn Bay), 1931 v E, S (2)
Neilson, A. B. (Newcastle U), 1992 v Ei (sub); 1994 v Se, Es; 1995 v Ge; (with Southampton), 1997 v Ho (5)
Newnes, J. (Nelson), 1926 v Ni (1)
Newton, L. F. (Cardiff Corinthians), 1912 v Ni (1)
Nicholas, D. S. (Stoke C), 1923 v S; (with Swansea T), 1927 v E, Ni (3)
Nicholas, P. (C Palace), 1979 v S (sub), Ni (sub), Ma; 1980 v Ei, WG, T, E, S, Ni, Ic; 1981 v T, Cz, E; (with Arsenal), T, S, E, USSR; 1982 v Cz, Ic, USSR, Sp, E, S, Ni, F; 1983 v Y, Bul, S, Ni; 1984 v N (with C Palace), Bul, N, Is; 1985 v Sp; (with Luton T), N, S, Sp, N; 1986 v S, H, S.Ar, Ei, U, Ca (2); 1987 v Fi (2) USSR, Cz; (with Aberdeen), 1988 v D (2), Cz, Y, Se; (with Chelsea), 1989 v Ho, Fi, Is, Se, WG; 1990 v Fi, Ho, WG, Ei, Se, Cr; 1991 v D (sub), Bel, L, Ei; (with Watford), Bel, Pol, G; 1992 v L (73)
Nicholls, J. (Newport Co), 1924 v E, Ni; (with Cardiff C), 1925 v E, S (4)
Niedzwiecki, E. A. (Chelsea), 1985 v N (sub); 1988 v D (2)
Nock, W. (Newtown), 1897 v Ni (1)
Nogan, L. M. (Watford), 1992 v A (sub); (with Reading), 1996 v Mol (2)
Norman, A. J. (Hull C), 1986 v Ei (sub), U, Ca; 1988 v Ma, I (5)
Nurse, M. T. G. (Swansea T), 1960 v E, Ni; 1961 v S, E, H, Ni, Ei, Sp (2); (with Middlesbrough), 1963 v E, H; 1964 v S (12)
Nyatanga, L. J. (Derby Co), 2006 v Para, Tr (sub); 2007 v Bul (sub), CzR, Br, Slo, Cy, Lie, Ni, Ei, Sm (sub), CzR (12)

O'Callaghan, E. (Tottenham H), 1929 v Ni; 1930 v S; 1932 v S, E; 1933 v Ni, S, E; 1934 v Ni, S, E; 1935 v E (11)
Oliver, A. (Bangor), 1905 v S; (with Blackburn R), E (2)
Oster, J. M. (Everton), 1998 v Bel (sub), Br, Jam; (with Sunderland), 2000 v Sw; 2003 v Bos (sub), Az, US; 2004 v Ser (sub), S, N, Ca; 2005 v Az (sub), Ni (13)
O'Sullivan, P. A. (Brighton), 1973 v S (sub); 1976 v S; 1979 v Ma (sub) (3)
Owen, D. (Oswestry), 1879 v E (1)
Owen, E. (Ruthin Grammar School), 1884 v E, Ni, S (3)
Owen, G. (Chirk), 1888 v S; (with Newton Heath), 1889 v S, Ni; (with Chirk), 1893 v Ni (4)
Owen, J. (Newton Heath), 1892 v E (1)
Owen, Trevor (Crewe Alex), 1899 v E, S (2)
Owen, T. (Oswestry), 1879 v E (1)
Owen, W. (Chirk), 1884 v E; 1885 v Ni; 1887 v E; 1888 v E; 1889 v E, Ni, S; 1890 v S, Ni; 1891 v E, S, Ni; 1892 v E, S; 1893 v S, Ni (16)

Owen, W. P. (Ruthin), 1880 v E, S; 1881 v E, S; 1882 v E, S, Ni; 1883 v E, S; 1884 v E, S, Ni (12)
Owens, J. (Wrexham), 1902 v S (1)

Page, M. E. (Birmingham C), 1971 v Fi; 1972 v S, Ni; 1973 v E (1+1 sub), Ni; 1974 v S, Ni; 1975 v H, L, S, E, Ni; 1976 v E, Y (2), E, Ni; 1977 v WG, S; 1978 v K (sub+1), WG, Ir, E, S; 1979 v Ma, WG (28)
Page, R. J. (Watford), 1997 v T, Bel, S; 1998 v T, Bel (sub), Br, I; 2000 v Bl, Sw, Q, Fi, Br, P; 2001 v Bl, N, Pol, Arm, Uk, Pol, Uk; (with Sheffield U), 2002 v N, Bl (sub), Arg, CzR, G; 2003 v Az, Bos, Az; 2004 v Ser, I, Fi, S, H; (with Cardiff C), 2005 v La, Az, H; (with Coventry C), A (1+sub); 2006 v Slv, E, Cy (41)
Palmer, D. (Swansea T), 1957 v Cz; 1958 v E, EG (3)
Parris, J. E. (Bradford), 1932 v Ni (1)
Parry, B. J. (Swansea T), 1951 v S (1)
Parry, C. (Everton), 1891 v E, S; 1893 v E; 1894 v E; 1895 v E, S; (with Newtown), 1896 v E, S, Ni; 1897 v Ni; 1898 v E, S, Ni (13)
Parry, E. (Liverpool), 1922 v S; 1923 v E, Ni; 1925 v Ni; 1926 v Ni (5)
Parry, M. (Liverpool), 1901 v E, S, Ni; 1902 v E, S, Ni; 1903 v E, S; 1904 v E, Ni; 1906 v E; 1908 v E, S, Ni; 1909 v E, S (16)
Parry, P. I. (Cardiff C), 2004 v S (sub), N, Ca; 2005 v Ni (sub), Pol (sub); 2006 v Slv (sub); 2007 v Bul (sub), Slo (sub), Cy (sub), Ni, Sm (sub) (11)
Parry, T. D. (Oswestry), 1900 v E, S, Ni; 1901 v E, S, Ni; 1902 v E (7)
Parry, W. (Newtown), 1895 v Ni (1)
Partridge, D. W. (Motherwell), 2005 v H, A; (with Bristol C), 2006 v Slv, E, Pol, Ni, Tr (7)
Pascoe, C. (Swansea C), 1984 v N, Is; (with Sunderland), 1989 v Fi, Is, WG (sub); 1990 v Ho (sub), WG (sub); 1991 v Ei, Ic (sub); 1992 v Br (10)
Paul, R. (Swansea T), 1949 v E, S, Ni, P, Sw; 1950 v E, S, Ni, Bel; (with Manchester C), 1951 v S, E, Ni, P, Sw; 1952 v E, S, Ni, R of UK; 1953 v S, E, Ni, F, Y; 1954 v E, S, Ni; 1955 v S, E, Y; 1956 v E, Ni, S, A (33)
Peake, E. (Aberystwyth), 1908 v Ni; (with Liverpool), 1909 v Ni, S, E; 1910 v S, Ni; 1911 v Ni; 1912 v E; 1913 v E, Ni; 1914 v Ni (11)
Peers, E. J. (Wolverhampton W), 1914 v Ni, S, E; 1920 v E, S; 1921 v S, Ni, E; (with Port Vale), 1922 v E, S, Ni; 1923 v E (12)
Pembridge, M. A. (Luton T), 1992 v Br, Ei, R, Ho (with Derby Co), J (sub); 1993 v Bel (sub), Ei; 1994 v N (sub); 1995 v Alb (sub), Mol, Ge (sub); (with Sheffield W), 1996 v Mol, G, Alb, Sw, Sm; 1997 v Sm, Ho (2), T, Ei, Bel, S; 1998 v Bel, Br, Jam, Ma, Tun; (with Benfica), 1999 v D (sub), Bl, Sw, I (sub), D (sub); (with Everton), 2000 v Bl, Q, Fi; 2001 v Arm, Pol, Uk; 2002 v Bl, Arg, G; 2003 v Cro, Fi, I, Bos, Az, US; 2004 v Ser; (with Fulham), I, Fi; 2005 v La, Az, E (54)
Perry, E. (Doncaster R), 1938 v E, S, Ni (3)
Perry, J. (Cardiff C), 1994 v N (1)
Phennah, E. (Civil Service), 1878 v S (1)
Phillips, C. (Wolverhampton W), 1931 v Ni; 1932 v E; 1933 v S; 1934 v E, S, Ni; 1935 v E, S, Ni; 1936 v S; (with Aston Villa), 1936 v E, Ni; 1938 v S (13)
Phillips, D. (Plymouth Arg), 1984 v E, Ni, N; (with Manchester C), 1985 v Sp, Ic, S, Sp, N; 1986 v S, H, S.Ar, Ei, U; (with Coventry C), 1987 v Fi, Cz; 1988 v D (2), Cz, Y, Se; 1989 v Se, WG; (with Norwich C), 1990 v Fi, Ho, WG, Ei, Se; 1991 v D, Bel, Ic, Pol, G; 1992 v L, Ei, A, R, Ho (sub), Arg, J; 1993 v Fa, Cy, Bel, Ei, Bel (sub), RCS, Fa; (with Nottingham F), 1994 v RCS, Cy, R, N, Se, Es; 1995 v Alb, Mol, Ge, Bul (2), G, Ge; 1996 v Mol (sub), Alb, I (62)
Phillips, L. (Cardiff C), 1971 v Cz, S, E, Ni; 1972 v Cz, R, S, Ni; 1973 v E; 1974 v Pol (sub), Ni; 1975 v A; (with Aston Villa), H (2), L (2), S, E, Ni; 1976 v A, E, Y (2), E, Ni; 1977 v WG, S (2), Cz, E; 1978 v K (2), S, Cz, WG, E, S; 1979 v Ma; (with Swansea C), T, WG, S, E, Ni, Ma; 1980 v Ei, WG, T, S (sub), Ni, Ic; 1981 v T, Cz, T, S, E, USSR; (with Charlton Ath), 1982 v Cz, USSR (58)
Phillips, T. J. S. (Chelsea), 1973 v E; 1974 v E; 1975 v H (sub); 1978 v K (4)
Phoenix, H. (Wrexham), 1882 v S (1)
Pipe, D. R. (Coventry C), 2003 v US (sub) (1)
Poland, G. (Wrexham), 1939 v Ni, F (2)
Pontin, K. (Cardiff C), 1980 v E (sub), S (2)
Powell, A. (Leeds U), 1947 v E, S; 1948 v E, S, Ni; (with Everton), 1949 v E; 1950 v Bel; (with Birmingham C), 1951 v S (8)
Powell, D. (Wrexham), 1968 v WG; (with Sheffield U), 1969 v S, E, Ni, I, WG; 1970 v E, S, Ni, EG; 1971 v R (11)
Powell, I. V. (QPR), 1947 v E; 1948 v E, S, Ni; (with Aston Villa), 1949 v Bel; 1950 v S, Bel; 1951 v S (8)
Powell, J. (Druids), 1878 v S; 1880 v E, S; 1882 v E, S, Ni; 1883 v E, S, Ni; (with Bolton W), 1884 v E; (with Newton Heath), 1887 v E, S; 1888 v E, S, Ni (15)
Powell, Seth (Oswestry), 1885 v S; 1886 v E, Ni; (with WBA), 1891 v E, S; 1892 v E, S (7)
Price, H. (Aston Villa), 1907 v S; (with Burton U), 1908 v Ni; (with Wrexham), 1909 v S, E, Ni (5)
Price, J. (Wrexham), 1877 v S; 1878 v S; 1879 v E; 1880 v E, S; 1881 v E, S; 1882 v S, E, Ni; 1883 v S, Ni (12)
Price, L. P. (Ipswich T), 2006 v Cy, Para (sub); 2007 v Cy (3)
Price, P. (Luton T), 1980 v E, S, Ni, Ic; 1981 v T, Cz, Ei, T, S, E, USSR; (with Tottenham H), 1982 v USSR, Sp, F; 1983 v N, Y, E, Bul, S, Ni; 1984 v N, R, Bul, Y, S (sub) (25)
Pring, K. D. (Rotherham U), 1966 v Ch, D; 1967 v Ni (3)
Pritchard, H. K. (Bristol C), 1985 v N (sub) (1)
Pryce-Jones, A. W. (Newtown), 1895 v E (1)
Pryce-Jones, W. E. (Cambridge University), 1887 v S; 1888 v S, E, Ni; 1890 v Ni (5)
Pugh, A. (Rhostyllen), 1889 v S (1)
Pugh, D. H. (Wrexham), 1896 v S, Ni; 1897 v S, Ni; (with Lincoln C), 1900 v S; 1901 v S, E (7)
Pugsley, J. (Charlton Ath), 1930 v Ni (1)
Pullen, W. J. (Plymouth Arg), 1926 v E (1)

Rankmore, F. E. J. (Peterborough), 1966 v Ch (sub) (1)
Ratcliffe, K. (Everton), 1981 v Cz, Ei, T, S, E, USSR; 1982 v Cz, Ic, USSR, Sp, E; 1983 v Y, E, Bul, S, Ni, Br; 1984 v N, R, Bul, Y, S, E, Ni, N, Is; 1985 v Ic, Sp, Ic, N, S, Sp; 1986 v S, H, S.Ar, U; 1987 v Fi (2), USSR, Cz; 1988 v D (2), Cz; 1989 v Fi, Is, Se, WG; 1990 v Fi; 1991 v D, Bel (2), L, Ei, Ic, Pol, G; 1992 v Br, G; (with Cardiff C), 1993 v Bel (59)
Rea, J. C. (Aberystwyth), 1894 v Ni, S, E; 1895 v S; 1896 v S, Ni; 1897 v S, Ni; 1898 v Ni (9)
Ready, K. (QPR), 1997 v Ei; 1998 v Bel, Br, Ma, Tun (5)
Reece, G. I. (Sheffield U), 1966 v E, S, Ni, USSR; 1967 v S; 1970 v R of UK (sub), I (sub); 1971 v S, E, Ni, Fi; 1972 v Fi, R, E (sub), S, Ni; (with Cardiff C), 1973 v E (sub), Ni; 1974 v Pol (sub), E, S, Ni; 1975 v A, H (2), L (2), S, Ni (29)
Reed, W. G. (Ipswich T), 1955 v S, Y (2)
Rees, A. (Birmingham C), 1984 v N (sub) (1)
Rees, J. M. (Luton T), 1992 v A (sub) (1)
Rees, R. R. (Coventry C), 1965 v S, E, Ni, D, Gr (2), I, USSR; 1966 v E, S, Ni, USSR, D, Br (2), Ch; 1967 v E, Ni; 1968 v E, S, Ni; (with WBA), WG; 1969 v I; (with Nottingham F), 1969 v WG, EG, S (sub); 1970 v R of UK, E, S, Ni, EG, I; 1971 v Cz, R, E (sub), Ni (sub), Fi; 1972 v Cz (sub), R (39)
Rees, W. (Cardiff C), 1949 v Ni, Bel, Sw; (with Tottenham H), 1950 v Ni (4)
Richards, A. (Barnsley), 1932 v S (1)
Richards, D. (Wolverhampton W), 1931 v Ni; 1933 v E, S, Ni; 1934 v E, S, Ni; 1935 v E, S, Ni; 1936 v S; (with Brentford), 1936 v E, Ni; 1937 v S, E; (with Birmingham), Ni; 1938 v E, S, Ni; 1939 v E, S (21)
Richards, G. (Druids), 1899 v E, S, Ni; (with Oswestry), 1903 v Ni; (with Shrewsbury), 1904 v S; 1905 v Ni (6)
Richards, R. W. (Wolverhampton W), 1920 v E, S; 1921 v Ni; 1922 v E, S; (with West Ham U), 1924 v E, S, Ni; (with Mold), 1926 v S (9)
Richards, S. V. (Cardiff C), 1947 v E (1)
Richards, W. E. (Fulham), 1933 v Ni (1)
Ricketts, S. (Swansea C), 2005 v H, A (2); 2006 v Slv, E, Pol, Ni, Az (sub), Cy, Para; (with Hull C), 2007 v Bul, CzR, Br (sub), Lie, Ni (sub), Ei, Sm, Nz, CzR (19)
Roach, J. (Oswestry), 1885 v Ni (1)
Robbins, W. W. (Cardiff C), 1931 v E, S; 1932 v Ni, E, S; (with WBA), 1933 v F, E, S, Ni; 1934 v S; 1936 v S (11)
Roberts, A. M. (QPR), 1993 v Ei (sub); 1997 v Sm (sub) (2)
Roberts, D. F. (Oxford U), 1973 v Pol, E (sub), Ni; 1974 v E, S; 1975 v A; (with Hull C), L, Ni; 1976 v S, Ni, Y; 1977 v E (sub), Ni; 1978 v K (1+1 sub), S, Ni (17)

Roberts, G. W. (Tranmere R), 2000 v Fi (sub), Br, P; 2001 v Bl; 2004 v H (sub), N (sub); 2005 v La (sub), H (sub); 2006 v Slv (sub) (9)
Roberts, I. W. (Watford), 1990 v Ho; (with Huddersfield T), 1992 v A, Arg, J; (with Leicester C), 1994 v Se; 1995 v Alb (sub), Mol; (with Norwich C), 2000 v Fi (sub), Br, P; 2001 v Bl, N (sub), Arm (sub); 2002 v Arm, Bl (sub) (15)
Roberts, Jas (Wrexham), 1913 v S, Ni (2)
Roberts, J. (Corwen), 1879 v S; 1880 v E, S; 1882 v E, S, Ni; (with Berwyn R), 1883 v E (7)
Roberts, J. (Ruthin), 1881 v S; 1882 v S (2)
Roberts, J. (Bradford C), 1906 v Ni; 1907 v Ni (2)
Roberts, J. G. (Arsenal), 1971 v S, E, Ni, Fi; 1972 v Fi, E, Ni; (with Birmingham C), 1973 v E (2), Pol, S, Ni; 1974 v Pol, E, S, Ni; 1975 v A, H, S, E; 1976 v E, S (22)
Roberts, J. H. (Bolton), 1949 v Bel (1)
Roberts, N. W. (Wrexham), 2000 v Sw (sub); (with Wigan Ath), 2003 v Az (sub), US (sub); 2004 v N (sub) (4)
Roberts, P. S. (Portsmouth), 1974 v E; 1975 v A, H, L (4)
Roberts, R. (Druids), 1884 v S; (with Bolton W), 1887 v S; 1888 v S, E; 1889 v S, E; 1890 v S; 1892 v Ni; (with Preston NE), S (9)
Roberts, R. (Wrexham), 1886 v Ni; 1887 v Ni; 1891 v Ni (3)
Roberts, R. (Rhos), 1891 v Ni; (with Crewe Alex), 1893 v E (2)
Roberts, R. L. (Chester), 1890 v Ni (1)
Roberts, S. W. (Wrexham), 2005 v H (sub) (1)
Roberts, W. (Llangollen), 1879 v E, S; 1880 v E, S; (with Berwyn R), 1881 v S; 1883 v S (6)
Roberts, W. (Rhyl), 1883 v E (1)
Roberts, W. (Wrexham), 1886 v E, S, Ni; 1887 v Ni (4)
Roberts, W. H. (Ruthin), 1882 v E, S; 1883 v E, S, Ni; (with Rhyl), 1884 v S (6)
Robinson, C. P. (Wolverhampton W), 2000 v Bl (sub), P (sub); 2001 v Arm (sub), Uk; 2002 v Arm, N, Bl (sub), Arg (sub); (with Portsmouth), 2003 v Cro, Az (1+sub), US (sub); 2004 v Ser, S (sub), H, N, Ca; (with Sunderland), 2005 v La (sub), E (sub), H, A (2); 2006 v Slv, E, Ni, Az, Cy; (with Norwich C), Para (sub), Tr; 2007 v Bul, CzR, Br, Slo, Cy, Lie; (with Toronto Lynx), Ni, Ei, Nz, CzR (39)
Robinson, J. R. C. (Charlton Ath), 1996 v Alb (sub), Sw, Sm; 1997 v Sm, Ho (1 + sub), Ei, S; 1998 v Bel, Br; 1999 v I, D (sub), Bl, Sw, I, D; 2000 v Bl, Sw, Q, Fi, Br, P; 2001 v Bl, N, Pol, Arm; 2002 v N (sub), Bl, Arg (sub), CzR (30)
Rodrigues, P. J. (Cardiff C), 1965 v Ni, Gr (2); 1966 v USSR, E, S, D; (with Leicester C), Ni, Br (2), Ch; 1967 v S; 1968 v E, S, Ni; 1969 v E, Ni, EG; 1970 v R of UK, E, S, Ni, EG; (with Sheffield W), 1971 v R, E, S, Cz, Ni; 1972 v Fi, Cz, R, E, Ni (sub); 1973 v E (3), Pol, S, Ni; 1974 v Pol (40)
Rogers, J. P. (Wrexham), 1896 v E, S, Ni (3)
Rogers, W. (Wrexham), 1931 v E, S (2)
Roose, L. R. (Aberystwyth), 1900 v Ni; (with London Welsh), 1901 v E, S, Ni; (with Stoke C), 1902 v E, S; 1904 v E; (with Everton), 1905 v S, E; (with Stoke C), 1906 v E, S, Ni; 1907 v E, S, Ni; (with Sunderland), 1908 v E, S; 1909 v E, S, Ni; 1910 v E, S, Ni; 1911 v S (24)
Rouse, R. V. (C Palace), 1959 v Ni (1)
Rowlands, A. C. (Tranmere R), 1914 v E (1)
Rowley, T. (Tranmere R), 1959 v Ni (1)
Rush, I. (Liverpool), 1980 v S (sub), Ni; 1981 v E (sub); 1982 v Ic (sub), USSR, E, S, Ni, F; 1983 v N, Y, E, Bul; 1984 v N, R, Bul, Y, S, E, Ni; 1985 v Ic, N, S, Sp; 1986 v S, S.Ar, Ei, U; 1987 v Fi (2), USSR, Cz; (with Juventus), 1988 v D, Cz, Y, Se, Ma, I; (with Liverpool), 1989 v Ho, Fi, Se, WG; 1990 v Fi, Ei; 1991 v D, Bel (2), L, Ei, Pol, G; 1992 v G, L, R; 1993 v Fa, Cy, Bel (2), RCS, Fa; 1994 v RCS, Cy, R, N, Se, Es; 1995 v Alb, Ge, Bul, G, Ge; 1996 v Mol, I (73)
Russell, M. R. (Merthyr T), 1912 v S, Ni; 1914 v E; (with Plymouth Arg), 1920 v E, S, Ni; 1921 v E, S, Ni; 1922 v E, Ni; 1923 v E, S, Ni; 1924 v E, S, Ni; 1925 v E, S; 1926 v E, S; 1928 v S; 1929 v E (23)

Sabine, H. W. (Oswestry), 1887 v Ni (1)
Saunders, D. (Brighton & HA), 1986 v Ei (sub), Ca (2); 1987 v Fi, USSR (sub); (with Oxford U), 1988 v Y, Se, Ma, I (sub); 1989 v Ho (sub), Fi; (with Derby Co), Is, Se, WG; 1990 v Fi, Ho, WG, Se, Cr; 1991 v D, Bel (2), L, Ei, Ic, Pol, G; (with Liverpool), 1992 v Br, G, Ei, R, Ho, Arg, J; 1993 v Fa; (with Aston Villa), Cy, Bel (2), RCS, Fa; 1994 v RCS, Cy, R, N (sub); 1995 v Ge, Bul (2), G, Ge; (with Galatasaray), 1996 v G, Alb, Sm; (with Nottingham F), 1997 v Sm, Ho (2), T, Bel, S; 1998 v T, Bel, Br; (with Sheffield U), Ma, Tun; 1999 v I (sub), D, Bl; (with Benfica) Sw, I, D; (with Bradford C), 2000 v Bl, Sw, Fi (sub), Br; 2001 v Arm, Uk (sub) (75)
Savage, R. W. (Crewe Alex), 1996 v Alb (sub), Sw (sub), Sm (sub); 1997 v Ei (sub), S; (with Leicester C), 1998 v T, Bel, Jam, Tun; 1999 v I (sub), D, Bl, Sw; 2000 v Sw, Fi, Br; 2001 v Bl, N, Pol (2); 2002 v Arm, N, Arg, CzR, G; (with Birmingham C), 2003 v Fi, I, Bos, Az; 2004 v Ser, I, Ru (2), S, H; 2005 v La, Az, Ni, Pol (39)
Savin, G. (Oswestry), 1878 v S (1)
Sayer, P. (Cardiff C), 1977 v Cz, S, E, Ni; 1978 v K (2), S (7)
Scrine, F. H. (Swansea T), 1950 v E, Ni (2)
Sear, C. R. (Manchester C), 1963 v E (1)
Shaw, E. G. (Oswestry), 1882 v Ni; 1884 v S, Ni (3)
Sherwood, A. T. (Cardiff C), 1947 v E, Ni; 1948 v S, Ni; 1949 v E, S, Ni, P, Sw; 1950 v E, S, Ni, Bel; 1951 v E, S, Ni, P, Sw; 1952 v E, S, Ni, R of UK; 1953 v S, E, Ni, F, Y; 1954 v E, S, Ni, A; 1955 v S, E, Y, Ni; 1956 v E, S, Ni, A; (with Newport Co), 1957 v E, S (41)
Shone, W. W. (Oswestry), 1879 v E (1)
Shortt, W. W. (Plymouth Arg), 1947 v Ni; 1950 v Ni, Bel; 1952 v E, S, Ni, R of UK; 1953 v S, E, Ni, F, Y (12)
Showers, D. (Cardiff C), 1975 v E (sub), Ni (2)
Sidlow, C. (Liverpool), 1947 v E, S; 1948 v E, S, Ni; 1949 v S; 1950 v E (7)
Sisson, H. (Wrexham Olympic), 1885 v Ni; 1886 v S, Ni (3)
Slatter, N. (Bristol R), 1983 v S; 1984 v N (sub), Is; 1985 v Ic, Sp, Ic, N, S, Sp, N; (with Oxford U), 1986 v H (sub), S.Ar, Ca (2); 1987 v Fi (sub), Cz; 1988 v D (2), Cz, Ma, I; 1989 v Is (sub) (22)
Smallman, D. P. (Wrexham), 1974 v E (sub), S (sub), Ni; (with Everton), 1975 v H (sub), E, Ni (sub); 1976 v A (7)
Southall, N. (Everton), 1982 v Ni; 1983 v N, E, Bul, S, Ni, Br; 1984 v N, R, Bul, Y, S, E, Ni, N, Is; 1985 v Ic, Sp, Ic, N, S, Sp, N; 1986 v S, H, S.Ar, Ei; 1987 v USSR, Fi, Cz; 1988 v D, Cz, Y, Se; 1989 v Ho, Fi, Se, WG; 1990 v Fi, Ho, WG, Ei, Se, Cr; 1991 v D, Bel (2), L, Ei, Ic, Pol, G; 1992 v Br, G, L, Ei, A, R, Ho, Arg, J; 1993 v Fa, Cy, Bel, Ei, Bel, RCS, Fa; 1994 v RCS, Cy, R, N, Se, Es; 1995 v Alb, Mol, Ge, Bul (2), G, Ge; 1996 v Mol, G, Alb, I, Sm; 1997 v Sm, Ho (2), T, Bel; 1998 v T (92)
Speed, G. A. (Leeds U), 1990 v Cr (sub); 1991 v D, L (sub), Ei (sub), Ic, G (sub); 1992 v Br, G (sub), L, Ei, R, Ho,Arg,J; 1993 v Fa, Cy, Bel, Ei, Bel, Fa (sub); 1994 v RCS (sub), Cy, R, N, Se; 1995 v Alb, Mol, Ge, Bul (2), G; 1996 v Mol, G, I, Sw (sub); (with Everton), 1997 v Sm (sub), Ho (2), T, Ei, Bel, S; 1998 v T, Br; (with Newcastle U), Jam, Ma, Tun; 1999 v I, D, Sw, I, D; 2000 v Bl, Sw, Q, Fi, Br, P; 2001 v Bl, N, Pol, Arm, Uk, Pol, Uk; 2002 v Bl, Arg, G; 2003 v Fi, I, Az, Bos, Az; 2004 v Ser, I, Fi, Ser, Ru (2), S; (with Bolton W), 2005 v La, Az, Ni, E, Pol (85)
Sprake, G. (Leeds U), 1964 v S, Ni; 1965 v S, D, Gr; 1966 v E, Ni, USSR; 1967 v S; 1968 v E, S; 1969 v S, E, Ni, WG; 1970 v R of UK, EG, I; 1971 v R, S, E, Ni; 1972 v Fi, E, S, Ni; 1973 v E (2), Pol, S, Ni; 1974 v Pol; (with Birmingham C), S, Ni; 1975 v A, H, L (37)
Stansfield, F. (Cardiff C), 1949 v S (1)
Stevenson, B. (Leeds U), 1978 v Ni; 1979 v Ma, T, S, E, Ni, Ma; 1980 v WG, T, Ic (sub); 1982 v Cz; (with Birmingham C), Sp, S, Ni, F (15)
Stevenson, N. (Swansea C), 1982 v E, S, Ni; 1983 v N (4)
Stitfall, R. F. (Cardiff C), 1953 v E; 1957 v Cz (2)
Sullivan, D. (Cardiff C), 1953 v Ni, F, Y; 1954 v Ni; 1955 v E, Ni; 1957 v E, S; 1958 v Ni, H (2), Se, Br; 1959 v S, Ni; 1960 v E, S (17)
Symons, C. J. (Portsmouth), 1992 v Ei, Ho, Arg, J; 1993 v Fa, Cy, Bel, Ei, RCS, Fa; 1994 v RCS, Cy, R; 1995 v Mol, Ge (sub), Bul, G, Ge; (with Manchester C), 1996 v Mol, G, I, Sw; 1997 v Ho (2), Ei, Bel, S; (with Fulham), 1999 v I, D, Bl, Sw; 2000 v Q (sub); 2001 v Pol; 2002 v Arm, N, Bl; (with C Palace), 2004 v S (sub) (37)

Tapscott, D. R. (Arsenal), 1954 v A; 1955 v S, E, Ni, Y; 1956 v E, Ni, S, A; 1957 v Ni, Cz, EG; (with Cardiff C), 1959 v E, Ni (14)

Taylor, G. K. (C Palace), 1996 v Alb, I (sub); (with Sheffield U), Sw; 1997 v Sm (sub), Ho (sub), Ei (sub); 1998 v Bel (sub), Jam; (with Burnley), 2002 v CzR (sub); 2003 v Cro (sub), Bos (sub), US; (with Nottingham F), 2004 v S (sub), H; 2005 v La (sub) (15)
Taylor, J. (Wrexham), 1898 v E (1)
Taylor, O. D. S. (Newtown), 1893 v S, Ni; 1894 v S, Ni (4)
Thatcher, B. D. (Leicester C), 2004 v H, N, Ca; (with Manchester C), 2005 v La, Ni, E, Pol (7)
Thomas, C. (Druids), 1899 v Ni; 1900 v S (2)
Thomas, D. A. (Swansea T), 1957 v Cz; 1958 v EG (2)
Thomas, D. S. (Fulham), 1948 v E, S, Ni; 1949 v S (4)
Thomas, E. (Cardiff Corinthians), 1925 v E (1)
Thomas, G. (Wrexham), 1885 v E, S (2)
Thomas, H. (Manchester U), 1927 v E (1)
Thomas, M. (Wrexham), 1977 v WG, S (1+1 sub), Ni (sub); 1978 v K (sub), S, Cz, Ir, E, Ni (sub); 1979 v Ma; (with Manchester U), T, WG, Ma (sub); 1980 v Ei, WG (sub), T, E, S, Ni; 1981 v Cz, S, E, USSR; (with Everton), 1982 v Cz; (with Brighton & HA), USSR (sub), Sp, E, S (sub), Ni (sub); 1983 (with Stoke C), v N, Y, E, Bul, S, Ni, Br; 1984 v R, Bul, Y; (with Chelsea), S, E; 1985 v Ic, Sp, Ic, S, Sp, N; 1986 v S; (with WBA), H, S.Ar (sub) (51)
Thomas, M. R. (Newcastle U), 1987 v Fi (1)
Thomas, R. J. (Swindon T), 1967 v Ni; 1968 v WG; 1969 v E, Ni, I, WG; 1970 v R of UK, E, S, Ni, EG, I; 1971 v S, E, Ni, R, Cz; 1972 v Fi, Cz, R, E, S, Ni; 1973 v E (3), Pol, S, Ni; 1974 v Pol; (with Derby Co), E, S, Ni; 1975 v H (2), L (2), S, E, Ni; 1976 v A, Y, E; 1977 v Cz, S, E, Ni; 1978 v K, S; (with Cardiff C), Cz (50)
Thomas, T. (Bangor), 1898 v S, Ni (2)
Thomas, W. R. (Newport Co), 1931 v E, S (2)
Thomson, D. (Druids), 1876 v S (1)
Thomson, G. F. (Druids), 1876 v S; 1877 v S (2)
Toshack, J. B. (Cardiff C), 1969 v S, E, Ni, WG, EG; 1970 v R of UK, EG, I; (with Liverpool), 1971 v S, E, Ni, Fi; 1972 v Fi, E; 1973 v E (3), Pol, S; 1975 v A, H (2), L (2), S, E; 1976 v Y (2), E; 1977 v S; 1978 v K (2), S, Cz; (with Swansea C), 1979 v WG (sub), S, E, Ni, Ma; 1980 v WG (40)
Townsend, W. (Newtown), 1887 v Ni; 1893 v Ni (2)
Trainer, H. (Wrexham), 1895 v E, S, Ni (3)
Trainer, J. (Bolton W), 1887 v S; (with Preston NE), 1888 v S; 1889 v E; 1890 v S; 1891 v S; 1892 v Ni, S; 1893 v E; 1894 v Ni, E; 1895 v Ni, E; 1896 v S; 1897 v Ni, S, E; 1898 v S, E; 1899 v Ni, S (20)
Trollope, P. J. (Derby Co), 1997 v S; 1998 v Br (sub); (with Fulham), Jam (sub), Ma, Tun; (with Coventry C), 2002 v CzR (sub); (with Northampton T), 2003 v Cro (sub), Az (sub+sub) (9)
Turner, H. G. (Charlton Ath), 1937 v E, S, Ni; 1938 v E, S, Ni; 1939 v Ni, F (8)
Turner, J. (Wrexham), 1892 v E (1)
Turner, R. E. (Wrexham), 1891 v E, Ni (2)
Turner, W. H. (Wrexham), 1887 v E, Ni; 1890 v S; 1891 v E, S (5)

Van Den Hauwe, P. W. R. (Everton), 1985 v Sp; 1986 v S, H; 1987 v USSR, Fi, Cz; 1988 v D (2), Cz, Y, I; 1989 v Fi, Se (13)
Vaughan, D. O. (Crewe Alex), 2003 v US; 2004 v H; 2006 v Slv, Ni (sub), Az, Cy, Tr; 2007 v Bul (sub), Br (sub), Ni (10)
Vaughan, Jas (Druids), 1893 v E, S, Ni; 1899 v E (4)
Vaughan, John (Oswestry), 1879 v S; (with Druids), 1880 v S; 1881 v E, S; 1882 v E, S, Ni; 1883 v E, S, Ni; (with Bolton W), 1884 v E (11)
Vaughan, J. O. (Rhyl), 1885 v Ni; 1886 v Ni, E, S (4)
Vaughan, N. (Newport Co), 1983 v Y (sub), Br; 1984 v N; (with Cardiff C), R, Bul, Y, Ni (sub), N, Is; 1985 v Sp (sub) (10)
Vaughan, T. (Rhyl), 1885 v E (1)
Vearncombe, G. (Cardiff C), 1958 v EG; 1961 v Ei (2)
Vernon, T. R. (Blackburn R), 1957 v Ni, Cz (2), EG; 1958 v E, S, EG, Se; 1959 v S; (with Everton), 1960 v Ni; 1961 v S, E, Ei; 1962 v Ni, Br (2), M; 1963 v S, E, H; 1964 v E, S; (with Stoke C), 1965 v Ni, Gr, I; 1966 v E, S, Ni, USSR, D; 1967 v Ni; 1968 v E (32)
Villars, A. K. (Cardiff C), 1974 v E, S, Ni (sub) (3)
Vizard, E. T. (Bolton W), 1911 v E, S, Ni; 1912 v E, S; 1913 v S; 1914 v E, Ni; 1920 v E; 1921 v E, S, Ni; 1922 v E, S; 1923 v E, Ni; 1924 v E, S, Ni; 1926 v E, S; 1927 v S (22)

Walley, J. T. (Watford), 1971 v Cz (1)
Walsh, I. (C Palace), 1980 v Ei, T, E, S, Ic; 1981 v T, Cz, Ei, T, S, E, USSR; 1982 v Cz (sub), Ic; (with Swansea C), Sp, S (sub), Ni (sub), F (18)
Ward, D. (Bristol R), 1959 v E; (with Cardiff C), 1962 v E (2)
Ward, D. (Notts Co), 2000 v P; (with Nottingham F), 2002 v CzR; 2003 v Bos, US (sub); 2004 v S (sub) (5)
Warner, J. (Swansea T), 1937 v E; (with Manchester U), 1939 v F (2)
Warren, F. W. (Cardiff C), 1929 v Ni; (with Middlesbrough), 1931 v Ni; 1933 v F, E; (with Hearts), 1937 v Ni; 1938 v Ni (6)
Watkins, A. E. (Leicester Fosse), 1898 v E, S; (with Aston Villa), 1900 v E, S; (with Millwall), 1904 v Ni (5)
Watkins, W. M. (Stoke C), 1902 v E; 1903 v E, S; (with Aston Villa); 1904 v E, S, Ni; (with Sunderland), 1905 v E, S, Ni; (with Stoke C), 1908 v Ni (10)
Webster, C. (Manchester U), 1957 v Cz; 1958 v H, M, Br (4)
Weston, R. D. (Arsenal), 2000 v P (sub); (with Cardiff C), 2003 v Cro (sub), Az (sub), Bos; 2004 v Fi, Ser; 2005 v H (sub) (7)
Whatley, W. J. (Tottenham H), 1939 v E, S (2)
White, P. F. (London Welsh), 1896 v Ni (1)
Wilcock, A. R. (Oswestry), 1890 v Ni (1)
Wilding, J. (Wrexham Olympians), 1885 v E, S, Ni; 1886 v E, Ni; (with Bootle), 1887 v E; 1888 v S, Ni; (with Wrexham), 1892 v S (9)
Williams, A. (Reading), 1994 v Es; 1995 v Alb, Mol, G (sub), Ge; 1996 v Mol, I; (with Wolverhampton W), 1998 v Br (sub), Jam; 1999 v I, D, I; (with Reading), 2003 v US (13)
Williams, A. L. (Wrexham), 1931 v E (1)
Williams, A. P. (Southampton), 1998 v Br (sub), Ma (2)
Williams, B. (Bristol C), 1930 v Ni (1)
Williams, B. D. (Swansea T), 1928 v Ni, E; 1930 v E, S; (with Everton), 1931 v Ni; 1932 v E; 1933 v E, S, Ni; 1935 v Ni (10)
Williams, D. G. (Derby Co), 1988 v Cz, Y, Se, Ma, I; 1989 v Ho, Is, Se, WG; 1990 v Fi, Ho; (with Ipswich T), 1993 v Ei; 1996 v G (sub) (13)
Williams, D. M. (Norwich C), 1986 v S.Ar (sub), U, Ca (2); 1987 v Fi (5)
Williams, D. R. (Merthyr T), 1921 v E, S; (with Sheffield W), 1923 v S; 1926 v S; 1927 v E, Ni; (with Manchester U), 1929 v E, S (8)
Williams, E. (Crewe Alex), 1893 v E, S (2)
Williams, E. (Druids), 1901 v E, Ni, S; 1902 v E, Ni (5)
Williams, G. (Chirk), 1893 v S; 1894 v S; 1895 v E, S, Ni; 1898 v Ni (6)
Williams, G. E. (WBA), 1960 v Ni; 1961 v S, E, Ei; 1963 v Ni, H; 1964 v E, S, Ni; 1965 v S, E, Ni, D, Gr (2), USSR, I; 1966 v Ni, Br (2), Ch; 1967 v S, E, Ni; 1968 v Ni; 1969 v I (26)
Williams, G. G. (Swansea T), 1961 v Ni, H, Sp (2); 1962 v E (5)
Williams, G. J. (West Ham U), 2006 v Slv (sub); (with Ipswich T), Cy (sub) (2)
Williams, G. J. J. (Cardiff C), 1951 v Sw (1)
Williams, G. O. (Wrexham), 1907 v Ni (1)
Williams, H. J. (Swansea), 1965 v Gr (2); 1972 v R (3)
Williams, H. T. (Newport Co), 1949 v Ni, Sw; (with Leeds U), 1950 v Ni; 1951 v S (4)
Williams, J. H. (Oswestry), 1884 v E (1)
Williams, J. J. (Wrexham), 1939 v F (1)
Williams, J. T. (Middlesbrough), 1925 v Ni (1)
Williams, J. W. (C Palace), 1912 v S, Ni (2)
Williams, R. (Newcastle U), 1935 v S, E (2)
Williams, R. P. (Caernarvon), 1886 v S (1)
Williams, S. G. (WBA), 1954 v A; 1955 v E, Ni; 1956 v E, S, A; 1958 v E, S, Ni, Is (2), H (2), M, Se, Br; 1959 v E, S, Ni; 1960 v E, S, Ni; 1961 v Ni, Ei, H, Sp (2); 1962 v E, S, Ni, Br (2), M; (with Southampton), 1963 v S, E, H (2); 1964 v E, S; 1965 v S, E, D; 1966 v D (43)
Williams, W. (Druids), 1876 v S; 1878 v S; (with Oswestry), 1879 v E, S; (with Druids), 1880 v E; 1881 v E, S; 1882 v E, S, Ni; 1883 v Ni (11)
Williams, W. (Northampton T), 1925 v S (1)
Witcomb, D. F. (WBA), 1947 v E, S; (with Sheffield W), 1947 v Ni (3)
Woosnam, A. P. (Leyton Orient), 1959 v S; (with West Ham U), E; 1960 v E, S, Ni; 1961 v S, E, Ni, Ei, Sp, H; 1962 v E, S, Ni, Br; (with Aston Villa), 1963 v Ni, H (17)

Woosnam, G. (Newtown Excelsior), 1879 v S (1)
Worthington, T. (Newtown), 1894 v S (1)
Wynn, G. A. (Wrexham), 1909 v E, S, Ni; (with Manchester C), 1910 v E; 1911 v Ni; 1912 v E, S; 1913 v E, S; 1914 v E, S (11)
Wynn, W. (Chirk), 1903 v Ni (1)

Yorath, T. C. (Leeds U), 1970 v I; 1971 v S, E, Ni; 1972 v Cz, E, S, Ni; 1973 v E, Pol, S; 1974 v Pol, E, S, Ni; 1975 v A, H (2), L (2), S; 1976 v A, E, S, Y (2), E, Ni; (with Coventry C), 1977 v WG, S (2), Cz, E, Ni; 1978 v K (2), S, Cz, WG, Ir, E, S, Ni; 1979 v T, WG, S, E, Ni; (with Tottenham H), 1980 v Ei, T, E, S, Ni, Ic; 1981 v T, Cz; (with Vancouver W), Ei, T, USSR (59)
Young, E. (Wimbledon), 1990 v Cr; (with C Palace), 1991 v D, Bel (2), L, Ei; 1992 v G, L, Ei, A; 1993 v Fa, Cy, Bel, Ei, Bel, Fa; 1994 v RCS, Cy, R, N; (with Wolverhampton W), 1996 v Alb (21)

REPUBLIC OF IRELAND

Aherne, T. (Belfast C), 1946 v P, Sp; (with Luton T), 1950 v Fi, E, Fi, Se, Bel; 1951 v N, Arg, N; 1952 v WG (2), A, Sp; 1953 v F; 1954 v F (16)
Aldridge, J. W. (Oxford U), 1986 v W, U, Ic, Cz; 1987 v Bel, S, Pol; (with Liverpool), S, Bul, Bel, Br, L; 1988 v Bul, Pol, N, E, USSR, Ho; 1989 v Ni, Tun, Sp, F (sub), H, Ma (sub), H; 1990 v WG; (with Real Sociedad), Ni, Ma, Fi (sub), T, E, Eg, Ho, R, I; 1991 v T, E (2), Pol; (with Tranmere R), 1992 v H (sub), T, W (sub), Sw (sub), US (sub), Alb, I, P (sub); 1993 v La, D, Sp, D, Alb, La, Li; 1994 v Li, Ni, CzR, I (sub), M (sub), N; 1995 v La, Ni, P, Lie; 1996 v La, P, Ho, Ru; 1997 v Mac (sub) (69)
Ambrose, P. (Shamrock R), 1955 v N, Ho; 1964 v Pol, N, E (5)
Anderson, J. (Preston NE), 1980 v Cz (sub), US (sub); 1982 v Ch, Br, Tr; (with Newcastle U), 1984 v Chn; 1986 v W, Ic, Cz; 1987 v Bul, Bel, Br, L; 1988 v R (sub), Y (sub); 1989 v Tun (16)
Andrews, P. (Bohemians), 1936 v Ho (1)
Arrigan, T. (Waterford), 1938 v N (1)

Babb, P. A. (Coventry C), 1994 v Ru, Ho, Bol, G, CzR (sub), I, M, N, Ho; (with Liverpool), 1995 v La, Lie, Ni (2), P, Lie, A; 1996 v La, P, Ho, CzR; 1997 v Ic; 1998 v Li (sub), R, Arg (sub), M; 1999 v Cro, Para (sub), Se (sub), Ni; 2000 v CzR (sub), S, M (sub), US, S.Af; (with Sunderland), 2003 v Ru (sub) (35)
Bailham, E. (Shamrock R), 1964 v E (1)
Barber, E. (Shelbourne), 1966 v Sp; (with Birmingham C), 1966 v Bel (2)
Barrett, G. (Arsenal), 2003 v Fi (sub); (with Coventry C), 2004 v Pol (sub), Ng (sub), Jam, Ho; 2005 v Cro (sub) (6)
Barry, P. (Fordsons), 1928 v Bel; 1929 v Bel (2)
Beglin, J. (Liverpool), 1984 v Chn; 1985 v M, D, I, Is, E, N, Sw; 1986 v Sw, USSR, D, W; 1987 v Bel (sub), S, Pol (15)
Bennett, A. J. (Reading), 2007 v Ec, Bol (2)
Bermingham, J. (Bohemians), 1929 v Bel (1)
Bermingham, P. (St James' Gate), 1935 v H (1)
Bonner, P. (Celtic), 1981 v Pol; 1982 v Alg; 1984 v Ma, Is, Chn; 1985 v I, Is, E, N; 1986 v U, Ic; 1987 v Bel (2), S (2), Pol, Bul, Br, L; 1988 v Bul, R, Y, N, E, USSR, Ho; 1989 v Sp, F, H, Sp, Ma, H; 1990 v WG, Ni, Ma, W, Fi, T, E, Eg, Ho, R, I; 1991 v Mor, T, E (2), W, Pol, US; 1992 v H, Pol, T, W, Sw, Alb, I; 1993 v La, D, Sp, W, Ni, D, Alb, La, Li; 1994 v Li, Sp, Ni, Ru, Ho, Bol, CzR, I, M, N, Ho; 1995 v Lie; 1996 v M, Bol (sub) (80)
Braddish, S. (Dundalk), 1978 v T (sub), Pol (2)
Bradshaw, P. (St James' Gate), 1939 v Sw, Pol, H (2), G (5)
Brady, F. (Fordsons), 1926 v I; 1927 v I (2)
Brady, T. R. (QPR), 1964 v A (2), Sp (2), Pol, N (6)
Brady, W. L. (Arsenal), 1975 v USSR, T, Sw, USSR, Sw, WG; 1976 v T, N, Pol; 1977 v E, T, F (2), Sp, Bul; 1978 v Bul, N; 1979 v Ni, E, D, Bul, WG; 1980 v W, Bul, E, Cy; (with Juventus), 1981 v Ho, Bel, F, Cy, Bel; 1982 v Ho, F, Ch, Br, Tr; (with Sampdoria), 1983 v Ho, Sp, Ic, Ma; 1984 v Ic, Ho, Ma, Pol, Is; (with Internazionale), 1985 v USSR, N, D, I, E, N, Sp, Sw; 1986 v Sw, USSR, D, W; (with Ascoli), 1987 v Bel, S (2), Pol; (with West Ham U), Bul, Bel, Br, L; 1988 v L, Bul; 1989 v F, H (sub), H (sub); 1990 v WG, Fi (72)
Branagan, K. G. (Bolton W), 1997 v W (1)
Breen, G. (Birmingham C), 1996 v P (sub), Cro, Ho, US, M, Bol (sub); 1997 v Lie, Mac, Ic; (with Coventry C), v Mac; 1998 v Li (sub), R, CzR, Arg, M; 1999 v Ma, Y, Para, Se, Mac; 2000 v Y, Cro, Ma, Mac, T (2), Gr, S, M, US, S.Af; 2001 v Ho, P, Es, Fi, Cy, And (2); 2002 v Cy, Ir (2), Ru (sub), US, Cam, G, S.Ar, Sp; (with West Ham U), 2003 v Fi, Ru, Sw, S, Ge, Alb, N, Alb, Ge; (with Sunderland), 2004 v Aus, Ru, T, Sw; 2005 v Bul (sub), Cro; 2006 v Ch (63)
Breen, T. (Manchester U), 1937 v Sw, F; (with Shamrock R), 1947 v E, Sp, P (5)
Brennan, F. (Drumcondra), 1965 v Bel (1)
Brennan, S. A. (Manchester U), 1965 v Sp; 1966 v Sp, A, Bel; 1967 v Sp, T, Sp; 1969 v Cz, D, H; 1970 v S, Cz, D, H, Pol (sub), WG; (with Waterford), 1971 v Pol, Se, I (19)
Brown, J. (Coventry C), 1937 v Sw, F (2)
Browne, W. (Bohemians), 1964 v A, Sp, E (3)
Bruce, A. (Ipswich T), 2007 v Ec (1)
Buckley, L. (Shamrock R), 1984 v Pol (sub); (with Waregem), 1985 v M (2)
Burke, F. (Cork Ath), 1952 v WG (1)
Burke, J. (Shamrock R), 1929 v Bel (1)
Burke, J. (Cork), 1934 v Bel (1)
Butler, P. J. (Sunderland), 2000 v CzR (1)
Butler, T. (Sunderland), 2003 v Fi, Sw (sub) (2)
Byrne, A. B. (Southampton), 1970 v D, Pol, WG; 1971 v Pol, Se (2), I (2), A; 1973 v F, USSR (sub), F, N; 1974 v Pol (14)
Byrne, D. (Shelbourne), 1929 v Bel; (with Shamrock R), 1932 v Sp; (with Coleraine), 1934 v Bel (3)
Byrne, J. (Bray Unknowns), 1928 v Bel (1)
Byrne, J. (QPR), 1985 v I, Is (sub), E (sub), Sp (sub); 1987 v S (sub), Bel (sub), Br, L (sub); 1988 v L, Bul (sub), Is, R, Y (sub), Pol (sub); (with Le Havre), 1990 v WG (sub), W, Fi, T (sub), Ma; (with Brighton & HA), 1991 v W; (with Sunderland), 1992 v T, W; (with Millwall), 1993 v W (23)
Byrne, J. (Shelbourne), 2004 v Pol (sub); 2006 v Ch (sub) (2)
Byrne, P. (Dolphin), 1931 v Sp; (with Shelbourne), 1932 v Ho; (with Drumcondra), 1934 v Ho (3)
Byrne, P. (Shamrock R), 1984 v Pol, Chn; 1985 v M; 1986 v D (sub), W (sub), U (sub), Ic (sub), Cz (8)
Byrne, S. (Bohemians), 1931 v Sp (1)

Campbell, A. (Santander), 1985 v I (sub), Is, Sp (3)
Campbell, N. (St Patrick's Ath), 1971 v A (sub); (with Fortuna Cologne), 1972 v Ir, Ec, Ch, P; 1973 v USSR, F (sub); 1975 v WG; 1976 v N; 1977 v Sp, Bul (sub) (11)
Cannon, H. (Bohemians), 1926 v I; 1928 v Bel (2)
Cantwell, N. (West Ham U), 1954 v L; 1956 v Sp, Ho; 1957 v D, WG, E (2); 1958 v D, Pol, A; 1959 v Pol, Cz (2); 1960 v Se, Ch, Se; 1961 v N; (with Manchester U), S (2); 1962 v Cz (2), A; 1963 v Ic (2), S; 1964 v A, Sp, E; 1965 v Pol, Sp; 1966 v Sp (2), A, Bel; 1967 v Sp, T (36)
Carey, B. P. (Manchester U), 1992 v US (sub); 1993 v W; (with Leicester C), 1994 v Ru (3)
Carey, J. J. (Manchester U), 1938 v N, Cz, Pol; 1939 v Sw, Pol, H (2), G; 1946 v P, Sp; 1947 v E, Sp, P; 1948 v P, Sp; 1949 v Sw, Bel, P, Se, Sp; 1950 v Fi, E, Fi, Se; 1951 v N, Arg, N; 1953 v F, A (29)
Carolan, J. (Manchester U), 1960 v Se, Ch (2)
Carr, S. (Tottenham H), 1999 v Se, Ni, Mac; 2000 v Y (sub), Cro, Ma, T (2), S, M, US, S.Af; 2001 v Ho, P, Es, And (sub), P, Es; 2003 v S, Ge, Alb, N, Alb, Ge; 2004 v Aus, Ru, T (sub), Sw, Ca, Br; (with Newcastle U), 2005 v Bul (sub), Cy, Sw, F, Fa, Is, Fa; 2006 v I (sub), F, Cy, Sw; 2007 v Ho, G (43)
Carroll, B. (Shelbourne), 1949 v Bel; 1950 v Fi (2)
Carroll, T. R. (Ipswich T), 1968 v Pol; 1969 v Pol, A, D; 1970 v Cz, Pol, WG; 1971 v Se; (with Birmingham C), 1972 v Ir, Ec, Ch, P; 1973 v USSR (2), Pol, F, N (17)
Carsley, L. K. (Derby Co), 1998 v R, Bel (1 + sub), CzR, Arg, M; 1999 v Cro (sub), Ma (sub), Para (sub); (with

Blackburn R) Ni, Mac; 2000 v Y (sub), Cro, Ma, T; 2001 v Fi (sub); (with Coventry C), 2002 v Cro, Cy (sub), Ru (sub); (with Everton), S.Ar (sub); 2003 v Fi, Gr, S (sub), Ge, Alb, N (sub), Alb (sub), Ge; 2004 v Ru; 2007 v CzR, Sm (2), W, Slo (34)
Cascarino, A. G. (Gillingham), 1986 v Sw, USSR, D; (with Millwall), 1988 v Pol, N (sub), USSR (sub), Ho (sub); 1989 v Ni, Tun, Sp, F, H, Sp, Ma, H; 1990 v WG (sub), Ni, Ma; (with Aston Villa), W, Fi, T, E, Eg, Ho (sub), R (sub), I (sub); 1991 v Mor (sub),T(sub), E (2 sub), Pol (sub), Ch (sub), US; (with Celtic), 1992 v Pol, T; (with Chelsea), W, Sw, US (sub); 1993 v W, Ni (sub), D (sub), Alb (sub), La (sub); 1994 v Li (sub), Sp (sub), Ni (sub), Ru, Bol (sub), G, CzR, Ho (sub); (with Marseille), 1995 v La (sub), Ni (sub), P (sub), Lie (sub), A (sub); 1996 v A (sub), P (sub), Ho, Ru (sub), P, Cro (sub), Ho; 1997 v Lie (sub), Mac, Ic; (with Nancy), v W, Mac, R (sub), Lie (sub); 1998 v Li (sub), Ic (sub), Li, R, Bel (2); 1999 v Cro (sub), Ma (sub), Y (sub), Para (sub), Se (sub), Ni (sub), Mac (sub); 2000 v Y (sub), Cro, Mac (sub), T (1 + sub) (88)
Chandler, J. (Leeds U), 1980 v Cz (sub), US (2)
Chatton, H. A. (Shelbourne), 1931 v Sp; (with Dumbarton), 1932 v Sp; (with Cork), 1934 v Ho (3)
Clarke, C. R. (Stoke C), 2004 v Ng (sub), Jam (sub) (2)
Clarke, J. (Drogheda U), 1978 v Pol (sub) (1)
Clarke, K. (Drumcondra), 1948 v P, Sp (2)
Clarke, M. (Shamrock R), 1950 v Bel (1)
Clinton, T. J. (Everton), 1951 v N; 1954 v F, L (3)
Coad, P. (Shamrock R), 1947 v E, Sp, P; 1948 v P, Sp; 1949 v Sw, Bel, P, Se; 1951 v N (sub); 1952 v Sp (11)
Coffey, T. (Drumcondra), 1950 v Fi (1)
Colfer, M. D. (Shelbourne), 1950 v Bel; 1951 v N (2)
Colgan, N. (Hibernian), 2002 v D (sub); 2003 v S (sub), N (sub); 2004 v Aus, T, Ca (sub), Pol (sub), Ng; (with Barnsley), 2007 v Bol (9)
Collins, F. (Jacobs), 1927 v I (1)
Conmy, O. M. (Peterborough U), 1965 v Bel; 1967 v Cz; 1968 v Cz, Pol; 1970 v Cz (5)
Connolly, D. J. (Watford), 1996 v P, Ho, US, M; 1997 v R, Lie; (with Feyenoord), 1998 v Li, Ic, Li, Bel (1 + sub), CzR, M; (with Wolverhampton W), 1999 v Y (sub), Para (sub), Se, Ni (sub), Mac (sub); (with Excelsior), 2000 v T (1 + sub), CzR (sub), Gr; 2001 v Ho (sub), Fi (sub), Cy, And; (with Feyenoord), And; (with Wimbledon), 2002 v Cro (sub), Cy, Ir, D (sub), US (sub), Ng (sub), Sp (sub); 2003 v S (sub), N, Alb; (with West Ham U), 2004 v Aus (sub), T, Sw; (with Wigan Ath), 2006 v Cy (sub) (41)
Connolly, H. (Cork), 1937 v G (1)
Connolly, J. (Fordsons), 1926 v I (1)
Conroy, G. A. (Stoke C), 1970 v Cz, D, H, Pol, WG; 1971 v Pol, Se (2), I; 1973 v USSR, F, USSR, N; 1974 v Pol, Br, U, Ch; 1975 v T, Sw, USSR, Sw, WG (sub); 1976 v T (sub), Pol; 1977 v E, T, Pol (27)
Conway, J. P. (Fulham), 1967 v Sp, T, Sp; 1968 v Cz; 1969 v A (sub), H; 1970 v S, Cz, D, H, Pol, WG; 1971 v I, A; 1974 v U, Ch; 1975 v WG (sub); 1976 v N, Pol; (with Manchester C), 1977 v Pol (20)
Corr, P. J. (Everton), 1949 v P, Sp; 1950 v E, Se (4)
Courtney, E. (Cork U), 1946 v P (1)
Coyle, O. C. (Bolton W), 1994 v Ho (sub) (1)
Coyne, T. (Celtic), 1992 v Sw, US, Alb (sub), US (sub), I (sub), P (sub); 1993 v W (sub), La (sub); (with Tranmere R), Ni; (with Motherwell), 1994 v Ru (sub), Ho, Bol, G (sub), CzR (sub), I, M, Ho; 1995 v Lie, Ni (sub), A; 1996 v Ru (sub); 1998 v Bel (sub) (22)
Crowe, G. (Bohemians), 2003 v Gr, N (sub) (2)
Cummins, G. P. (Luton T), 1954 v L (2); 1955 v N (2), WG; 1956 v Y, Sp; 1958 v D, Pol, A; 1959 v Pol, Cz (2); 1960 v Se, Ch, WG, Se; 1961 v S (2) (19)
Cuneen, T. (Limerick), 1951 v N (1)
Cunningham, K. (Wimbledon), 1996 v CzR, P, Cro, Ho (sub), US, Bol; 1997 v Ic (sub), W, R, Lie; 1998 v Li, Ic, Li, Bel (2), CzR; 1999 v Cro, Ma, Y, Para, Se, Ni, Mac; 2000 v Y, Cro, Ma, Mac, T (2), CzR, Gr; 2001 v Cy, And; 2002 v Ir (sub), Ru, D, US (sub), Ng, G (sub), Sp (sub); (with Birmingham C), 2003 v Fi, Ru, Sw, Gr, Ge, Alb (2), Ge; 2004 v Aus, Ru, Ca, Br, CzR, Pol, R, Ng, Ho; 2005 v Bul, Cy, Sw, F, Fa, Cro (sub), P, Is, Chn, Is, Fa; 2006 v I, F, Cy, Sw (72)
Curtis, D. P. (Shelbourne), 1957 v D, WG; (with Bristol C), 1957 v E (2); 1958 v D, Pol, A; (with Ipswich T), 1959 v Pol; 1960 v Se, Ch, WG, Se; 1961 v N, S; 1962 v A; 1963 v Ic; (with Exeter C), 1964 v A (17)
Cusack, S. (Limerick), 1953 v F (1)

Daish, L. S. (Cambridge U), 1992 v W, Sw (sub); (with Coventry C), 1996 v CzR (sub), Cro, M (5)
Daly, G. A. (Manchester U), 1973 v Pol (sub), N; 1974 v Br (sub), U (sub); 1975 v Sw (sub), WG; 1977 v E, T, F; (with Derby Co), F, Bul; 1978 v Bul, T, D; 1979 v Ni, E, D, Bul; 1980 v Ni, E, Cy, Sw, Arg; (with Coventry C), 1981 v WG 'B', Ho, Bel, Cy, W, Bel, Cz, Pol (sub); 1982 v Alg, Ch, Br, Tr; 1983 v Ho, Sp (sub); 1984 v Is (sub), Ma; (with Birmingham C), 1985 v M (sub), N, Sp, Sw; 1986 v Sw; (with Shrewsbury T), U, Ic (sub), Cz (sub); 1987 v S (sub) (48)
Daly, J. (Shamrock R), 1932 v Ho; 1935 v Sw (2)
Daly, M. (Wolverhampton W), 1978 v T, Pol (2)
Daly, P. (Shamrock R), 1950 v Fi (sub) (1)
Davis, T. L. (Oldham Ath), 1937 v G, H; (with Tranmere R), 1938 v Cz, Pol (4)
Deacy, E. (Aston Villa), 1982 v Alg (sub), Ch, Br, Tr (4)
Delap, R. J. (Derby Co), 1998 v CzR (sub), Arg (sub), M (sub); 2000 v T (2), Gr (sub); (with Southampton), 2002 v US; 2003 v Fi (sub), Gr (sub); 2004 v Ca (sub), CzR (sub) (11)
De Mange, K. J. P. P. (Liverpool), 1987 v Br (sub); (with Hull C), 1989 v Tun (sub) (2)
Dempsey, J. T. (Fulham), 1967 v Sp, Cz; 1968 v Cz, Pol; 1969 v Pol, A, D; (with Chelsea), 1969 v Cz, D; 1970 v H, WG; 1971 v Pol, Se (2), I; 1972 v Ir, Ec, Ch, P (19)
Dennehy, J. (Cork Hibernians), 1972 v Ec (sub), Ch; (with Nottingham F), 1973 v USSR (sub), Pol, F, N; 1974 v Pol (sub); 1975 v T (sub), WG (sub); (with Walsall), 1976 v Pol (sub); 1977 v Pol (sub) (11)
Desmond, P. (Middlesbrough), 1950 v Fi, E, Fi, Se (4)
Devine, J. (Arsenal), 1980 v Cz, Ni; 1981 v WG 'B', Cz; 1982 v Ho, Alg; 1983 v Sp, Ma; (with Norwich C), 1984 v Ic, Ho, Is; 1985 v USSR, N (13)
Doherty, G. M. T. (Luton T), 2000 v Gr (sub); (with Tottenham H), US, S.Af (sub); 2001 v Cy (sub), And (sub+1), P (sub), Es (sub); 2002 v US (sub); 2003 v Fi (sub), Ru (sub), Sw (sub), Gr, S, Ge, Alb (sub+sub), Ge; 2004 v Aus, Ru (sub), T, Ca, CzR, Pol, Ng, Jam; 2005 v Bul; (with Norwich C), Sw (sub), Fa (sub), Chn (sub), Is (sub), Fa (sub); 2006 v F (sub), Sw (sub) (34)
Donnelly, J. (Dundalk), 1935 v H, Sw, G; 1936 v Ho, Sw, H, L; 1937 v G, H; 1938 v N (10)
Donnelly, T. (Drumcondra), 1938 v N; (Shamrock R), 1939 v Sw (2)
Donovan, D. C. (Everton), 1955 v N, Ho, N, WG; 1957 v E (5)
Donovan, T. (Aston Villa), 1980 v Cz; 1981 v WG 'B' (sub) (2)
Douglas, J. (Blackburn R), 2004 v Pol (sub), Ng (sub); 2007 v Ho (sub); (with Leeds U), Cy (sub), CzR, Sm (sub), W (7)
Dowdall, C. (Fordsons), 1928 v Bel; (with Barnsley), 1929 v Bel; (with Cork), 1931 v Sp (3)
Doyle, C. (Shelbourne), 1959 v Cz (1)
Doyle, Colin. (Birmingham C), 2007 v Ec (1)
Doyle, D. (Shamrock R), 1926 v I (1)
Doyle, K. E. (Reading), 2006 v Se, Ch; 2007 v Ho (sub), G, Sm, W (sub), Slo, Ec, Bol (sub) (9)
Doyle, L. (Dolphin), 1932 v Sp (1)
Doyle, M. P. (Coventry C), 2004 v Ho (sub) (1)
Duff, D. A. (Blackburn R), 1998 v CzR, M; 1999 v Cro, Ma, Y, Para, Se (sub), Ni, Mac; 2000 v Cro, Ma (sub), T (sub + sub), S (sub); 2001 v P (sub), Es (sub), Cy (sub), And, P (sub), Es; 2002 v Cro, Ho, Ru, D, US, Ng, Cam, G, S.Ar, Sp; 2003 v Fi, Ru, Sw, Ge, Alb, N, Alb; (with Chelsea), 2004 v Aus, Ru, T, Sw, Ca, CzR; 2005 v Bul, Cy, Sw, F, Fa, Cro, P, Is, Chn, Is, Fa; 2006 v I, F, Cy, Se, Ch; (with Newcastle U), 2007 v G, Cy, CzR, Sm (2), W, Slo (66)
Duffy, B. (Shamrock R), 1950 v Bel (1)
Duggan, H. A. (Leeds U), 1927 v I; 1930 v Bel; 1936 v H, L; (with Newport Co), 1938 v N (5)
Dunne, A. P. (Manchester U), 1962 v A; 1963 v Ic, S; 1964 v A, Sp, Pol, N, E; 1965 v Pol, Sp; 1966 v Sp (2), A, Bel; 1967 v Sp, T, Sp; 1969 v Pol, D, H; 1970 v H;

1971 v Se, I, A; (with Bolton W), 1974 v Br (sub), U, Ch; 1975 v T, Sw, USSR, Sw, WG; 1976 v T (33)
Dunne, J. (Sheffield U), 1930 v Bel; (with Arsenal), 1936 v Sw, H, L; (with Southampton), 1937 v Sw, F; (with Shamrock R), 1938 v N (2), Cz, Pol; 1939 v Sw, Pol, H (2), G (15)
Dunne, J. C. (Fulham), 1971 v A (1)
Dunne, L. (Manchester C), 1935 v Sw, G (2)
Dunne, P. A. J. (Manchester U), 1965 v Sp; 1966 v Sp (2), WG; 1967 v T (5)
Dunne, R. P. (Everton), 2000 v Gr, S (sub), M; 2001 v Ho, P, Es; (with Manchester C), Fi, And, P, Es; 2002 v Cro, Ho, Ru (sub), D (sub); 2003 v Gr, S (sub), N; 2004 v Aus (sub), T (sub), Ca; 2005 v Cro, P (sub), Chn; 2006 v I, F, Cy, Sw, Se, Ch; 2007 v G, Cy, Sm (2), W, Slo (35)
Dunne, S. (Luton T), 1953 v F, A; 1954 v F, L; 1956 v Sp, Ho; 1957 v D, WG, E; 1958 v D, Pol, A; 1959 v Pol; 1960 v WG, Se (15)
Dunne, T. (St Patrick's Ath), 1956 v Ho; 1957 v D, WG (3)
Dunning, P. (Shelbourne), 1971 v Se, I (2)
Dunphy, E. M. (York C), 1966 v Sp; (with Millwall), 1966 v WG; 1967 v T, Sp, T, Cz; 1968 v Cz, Pol; 1969 v Pol, A, D (2), H; 1970 v D, H, Pol, WG (sub); 1971 v Pol, Se (2), I (2), A (23)
Dwyer, N. M. (West Ham U), 1960 v Se, Ch, WG, Se; (with Swansea T), 1961 v W, N, S (2); 1962 v Cz (2); 1964 v Pol (sub), N, E; 1965 v Pol (14)

Eccles, P. (Shamrock R), 1986 v U (sub) (1)
Egan, R. (Dundalk), 1929 v Bel (1)
Eglington, T. J. (Shamrock R), 1946 v P, Sp; (with Everton), 1947 v E, Sp, P; 1948 v P; 1949 v Sw, P, Se; 1951 v N, Arg; 1952 v WG (2), A, Sp; 1953 v F, A; 1954 v F, L, F; 1955 v N, Ho, WG; 1956 v Sp (24)
Elliott, S. W. (Sunderland), 2005 v Cro, Chn, Fa; 2006 v I (sub), Cy, Sw (sub), Se; 2007 v Ho, G (sub) (9)
Ellis, P. (Bohemians), 1935 v Sw, G; 1936 v Ho, Sw, L; 1937 v G, H (7)
Evans, M. J. (Southampton), 1998 v R (sub) (1)

Fagan, E. (Shamrock R), 1973 v N (sub) (1)
Fagan, F. (Manchester C), 1955 v N; 1960 v Se; (with Derby Co), 1960 v Ch, WG, Se; 1961 v W, N, S (8)
Fagan, J. (Shamrock R), 1926 v I (1)
Fairclough, M. (Dundalk), 1982 v Ch (sub), Tr (sub) (2)
Fallon, S. (Celtic), 1951 v N; 1952 v WG (2), A, Sp; 1953 v F; 1955 v N, WG (8)
Fallon, W. J. (Notts Co), 1935 v H; 1936 v H; 1937 v H, Sw, F; 1939 v Sw, Pol; (with Sheffield W), 1939 v H, G (9)
Farquharson, T. G. (Cardiff C), 1929 v Bel; 1930 v Bel; 1931 v Sp; 1932 v Sp (4)
Farrell, P. (Hibernian), 1937 v Sw, F (2)
Farrell, P. D. (Shamrock R), 1946 v P, Sp; (with Everton), 1947 v Sp, P; 1948 v P, Sp; 1949 v Sw, P (sub), Sp; 1950 v E, Fi, Se; 1951 v Arg, N; 1952 v WG (2), A, Sp; 1953 v F, A; 1954 v F (2); 1955 v N, Ho, WG; 1956 v Y, Sp; 1957 v E (28)
Farrelly, G. (Aston Villa), 1996 v P, US, Bol; (with Everton), 1998 v CzR, M; (with Bolton W), 2000 v US (6)
Feenan, J. J. (Sunderland), 1937 v Sw, F (2)
Finnan, S. (Fulham), 2000 v Gr, S; 2001 v P (sub), Es (sub), Fi, And (sub+sub); 2002 v Cro (sub), Ho (sub), Cy, Ir (2), Ru, US, Ng, Cam (sub), G, S.Ar, Sp; 2003 v Ru, Gr, N (sub); (with Liverpool), 2004 v Aus, T, Sw (sub), R, Ng, Ho; 2005 v Bul, Cy (sub), Sw, F, Fa, Cro, P, Is; 2006 v I, Cy; 2007 v Ho, G, Cy, CzR, Sm (2), W, Slo (46)
Finucane, A. (Limerick), 1967 v T, Cz; 1969 v Cz, D, H; 1970 v S, Cz; 1971 v Se, I (1+sub); 1972 v A (11)
Fitzgerald, F. J. (Waterford), 1955 v Ho; 1956 v Ho (2)
Fitzgerald, P. J. (Leeds U), 1961 v W, N, S; (with Chester), 1962 v Cz (2) (5)
Fitzpatrick, K. (Limerick), 1970 v Cz (1)
Fitzsimons, A. G. (Middlesbrough), 1950 v Fi, Bel; 1952 v WG (2), A, Sp; 1953 v F, A; 1954 v F, L, F; 1955 v Ho, N, WG; 1956 v Y, Sp, Ho; 1957 v D, WG, E (2); 1958 v D, Pol, A; 1959 v Pol; (with Lincoln C), 1959 v Cz (26)
Fleming, C. (Middlesbrough), 1996 v CzR (sub), P, Cro (sub), Ho (sub), US (sub), M, Bol; 1997 v Lie (sub); 1998 v R (sub), M (10)
Flood, J. J. (Shamrock R), 1926 v I; 1929 v Bel; 1930 v Bel; 1931 v Sp; 1932 v Sp (5)
Fogarty, A. (Sunderland), 1960 v WG, Se; 1961 v S; 1962 v Cz (2); 1963 v Ic (2), S (sub); 1964 v A (2); (with Hartlepools U), Sp (11)
Foley, D. J. (Watford), 2000 v S (sub), M (sub), US, S.Af; 2001 v Es (sub), Fi (6)
Foley, J. (Cork), 1934 v Bel, Ho; (with Celtic), 1935 v H, Sw, G; 1937 v G, H (7)
Foley, M. (Shelbourne), 1926 v I (1)
Foley, T. C. (Northampton T), 1964 v Sp, Pol, N; 1965 v Pol, Bel; 1966 v Sp (2), WG; 1967 v Cz (9)
Foy, T. (Shamrock R), 1938 v N; 1939 v H (2)
Fullam, J. (Preston NE), 1961 v N; (with Shamrock R), 1964 v Sp, Pol, N; 1966 v A, Bel; 1968 v Pol; 1969 v Pol, A, D; 1970 v Cz (sub) (11)
Fullam, R. (Shamrock R), 1926 v I; 1927 v I (2)

Gallagher, C. (Celtic), 1967 v T, Cz (2)
Gallagher, M. (Hibernian), 1954 v L (1)
Gallagher, P. (Falkirk), 1932 v Sp (1)
Galvin, A. (Tottenham H), 1983 v Ho, Ma; 1984 v Ho (sub), Is (sub); 1985 v M, USSR, N, D, I, N, Sp; 1986 v U, Ic, Cz; 1987 v Bel (2), S, Bul, L; (with Sheffield W), 1988 v L, Bul, R, Pol, N, E, USSR, Ho; 1989 v Sp; (with Swindon T), 1990 v WG (29)
Gamble, J. (Cork C), 2007 v Ec (sub), Bol (2)
Gannon, E. (Notts Co), 1949 v Sw; (with Sheffield W), Bel, P, Se, Sp; 1950 v Fi; 1951 v N; 1952 v WG, A; 1954 v L, F; 1955 v N; (with Shelbourne), 1955 v N, WG (14)
Gannon, M. (Shelbourne), 1972 v A (1)
Gaskins, P. (Shamrock R), 1934 v Bel, Ho; 1935 v H, Sw, G; (with St James' Gate), 1938 v Cz, Pol (7)
Gavin, J. T. (Norwich C), 1950 v Fi (2); 1953 v F; 1954 v L; (with Tottenham H), 1955 v Ho, WG; (with Norwich C), 1957 v D (7)
Geoghegan, M. (St James' Gate), 1937 v G; 1938 v N (2)
Gibbons, A. (St Patrick's Ath), 1952 v WG; 1954 v L; 1956 v Y, Sp (4)
Gilbert, R. (Shamrock R), 1966 v WG (1)
Giles, C. (Doncaster R), 1951 v N (1)
Giles, M. J. (Manchester U), 1960 v Se, Ch; 1961 v W, N, S (2); 1962 v Cz (2), A; 1963 v Ic, S; (with Leeds U), 1964 v A (2), Sp (2), Pol, N, E; 1965 v Sp; 1966 v Sp (2), A, Bel; 1967 v Sp, T (2); 1969 v A, D, Cz; 1970 v S, Pol, WG; 1971 v I; 1973 v F, USSR; 1974 v Br, U, Ch; 1975 v USSR, T, Sw, USSR, Sw; (with WBA), 1976 v T; 1977 v E, T, F (2), Pol, Bul; (with Shamrock R), 1978 v Bul, T, Pol, N, D; 1979 v Ni, D, Bul, WG (59)
Given, S. J. J. (Blackburn R), 1996 v Ru, CzR, P, Cro, Ho, US, Bol; 1997 v Lie (2); (with Newcastle U), 1998 v Li, Ic, Li, Bel (2), CzR, Arg, M; 1999 v Cro, Ma, Y, Para, Se, Ni; 2000 v Gr, S.Af; 2001 v Fi, Cy, And (2), P, Es; 2002 v Cro, Ho, Cy, Ir (2), Ru, US, Ng, Cam, G, S.Ar, Sp; 2003 v Fi (sub), Ru, Sw, Gr, Ge, Alb, N, Alb, Ge; 2004 v Ru, Sw, Ca, Br, CzR, Pol, R, Ho; 2005 v Bul, Cy, Sw, F, Fa, Cro (sub), P, Is (2), Fa; 2006 v I, F, Cy, Sw, Se, Ch; 2007 v G, Sm, W, Slo (80)
Givens, D. J. (Manchester U), 1969 v D, H; 1970 v S, Cz, D, H; (with Luton T), 1970 v Pol, WG; 1971 v Se, I (2), A; 1972 v Ir, Ec, P; (with QPR), 1973 v F, USSR, Pol, F, N; 1974 v Pol, Br, U, Ch; 1975 v USSR, T, Sw, USSR, Sw, WG; 1976 v T, N, Pol; 1977 v E, T, F (2), Sp, Bul; 1978 v Bul, N, D; (with Birmingham C), 1979 v Ni (sub), E, D, Bul, WG; 1980 v US (sub), Ni (sub), Sw, Arg; 1981 v Ho, Bel, Cy (sub), W; (with Neuchatel X), 1982 v F (sub) (56)
Gleeson, S. M. (Wolverhampton W), 2007 v Ec (sub), Bol (sub) (2)
Glen, W. (Shamrock R), 1927 v I; 1929 v Bel; 1930 v Bel; 1932 v Sp; 1936 v Ho, Sw, H, L (8)
Glynn, D. (Drumcondra), 1952 v WG; 1955 v N (2)
Godwin, T. F. (Shamrock R), 1949 v P, Se, Sp; 1950 v Fi, E; (with Leicester C), Fi, Se, Bel; 1951 v N; (with Bournemouth), 1956 v Ho; 1957 v E; 1958 v D, Pol (13)
Golding, J. (Shamrock R), 1928 v Bel; 1930 v Bel (2)
Goodman, J. (Wimbledon), 1997 v W, Mac, R (sub), Lie (sub) (4)
Goodwin, J. (Stockport Co), 2003 v Fi (sub) (1)

Gorman, W. C. (Bury), 1936 v Sw, H, L; 1937 v G, H; 1938 v N, Cz, Pol; 1939 v Sw, Pol; (with Brentford), H; 1947 v E, P (13)
Grace, J. (Drumcondra), 1926 v I (1)
Grealish, A. (Orient), 1976 v N, Pol; 1978 v N, D; 1979 v Ni, E, WG; (with Luton T), 1980 v W, Cz, Bul, US, Ni, E, Cy, Sw, Arg; 1981 v WG 'B', Ho, Bel, F, Cy, W, Bel, Pol; (with Brighton & HA), 1982 v Ho, Alg, Ch, Br, Tr; 1983 v Ho, Sp, Ic, Sp; 1984 v Ic, Ho; (with WBA), Pol, Chn; 1985 v M, USSR, N, D, Sp (sub), Sw; 1986 v USSR, D (45)
Gregg, E. (Bohemians), 1978 v Pol, D (sub); 1979 v E (sub), D, Bul, WG; 1980 v W, Cz (8)
Griffith, R. (Walsall), 1935 v H (1)
Grimes, A. A. (Manchester U), 1978 v T, Pol, N (sub); 1980 v Bul, US, Ni, E, Cy; 1981 v WG 'B' (sub), Cz, Pol; 1982 v Alg; 1983 v Sp (2); (with Coventry C), 1984 v Pol, Is; (with Luton T), 1988 v L, R (18)

Hale, A. (Aston Villa), 1962 v A; (with Doncaster R), 1963 v Ic; 1964 v Sp (2); (with Waterford), 1967 v Sp; 1968 v Pol (sub); 1969 v Pol, A, D; 1970 v S, Cz; 1971 v Pol (sub); 1972 v A (sub); 1974 v Pol (sub) (14)
Hamilton, T. (Shamrock R), 1959 v Cz (2) (2)
Hand, E. K. (Portsmouth), 1969 v Cz (sub); 1970 v Pol, WG; 1971 v Pol, A; 1973 v USSR, F, USSR, Pol, F; 1974 v Pol, Br, U, Ch; 1975 v T, Sw, USSR, Sw, WG; 1976 v T (20)
Harrington, W. (Cork), 1936 v Ho, Sw, H, L; 1938 v Pol (sub) (5)
Harte, I. P. (Leeds U), 1996 v Cro (sub), Ho, M, Bol; 1997 v Lie, Mac, Ic (sub), W, Mac (sub), R, Lie; 1998 v Li, Ic, Li, Bel (2), Arg, M; 1999 v Para; 2000 v Cro (sub), Ma (sub), CzR; 2001 v Ho, P, Es, Fi, Cy, And (2), P, Es; 2002 v Cro, Ho, Cy, Ir (2), Ru, D, US, Ng, Cam, G, S.Ar, Sp; 2003 v Fi, Ru, Sw, S, N; 2004 v Aus (sub), Ru (sub), T, Sw, Ca (sub), CzR, Pol; (with Levante), 2005 v Is, Fa; 2006 v I (sub), F (sub), Sw, Se, Ch (sub); 2007 v Sm (64)
Hartnett, J. B. (Middlesbrough), 1949 v Sp; 1954 v L (2)
Haverty, J. (Arsenal), 1956 v Ho; 1957 v D, WG, E (2); 1958 v D, Pol, A; 1959 v Pol; 1960 v Se, Ch; 1961 v W, N, S (2); (with Blackburn R), 1962 v Cz (2); (with Millwall), 1963 v S; 1964 v A, Sp, Pol, N, E; (with Celtic), 1965 v Pol; (with Bristol R), 1965 v Sp; (with Shelbourne), 1966 v Sp (2), WG, A, Bel; 1967 v T, Sp (32)
Hayes, A. W. P. (Southampton), 1979 v D (1)
Hayes, W. E. (Huddersfield T), 1947 v E, P (2)
Hayes, W. J. (Limerick), 1949 v Bel (1)
Healey, R. (Cardiff C), 1977 v Pol; 1980 v E (sub) (2)
Healy, C. (Celtic), 2002 v Ru, D (sub), US; 2003 v Fi (sub), Sw, Gr, S (sub), N (sub), Ge; (with Sunderland), 2004 v Aus (sub), Ru, T, Sw (13)
Heighway, S. D. (Liverpool), 1971 v Pol, Se (2), I, A; 1973 v USSR; 1975 v USSR, T, USSR, WG; 1976 v T, N; 1977 v E, F (2), Sp, Bul; 1978 v Bul, N, D; 1979 v Ni, Bul; 1980 v Bul, US, Ni, E, Cy, Arg; 1981 v Bel, F, Cy, W, Bel; (with Minnesota K), 1982 v Ho (34)
Henderson, B. (Drumcondra), 1948 v P, Sp (2)
Henderson, W. C. P. (Brighton & HA), 2006 v Se (sub), Ch (sub); 2007 v CzR; (with Preston NE), Sm, Bol (sub) (5)
Hennessy, J. (Shelbourne), 1965 v Pol, Bel, Sp; 1966 v WG; (with St Patrick's Ath), 1969 v A (5)
Herrick, J. (Cork Hibernians), 1972 v A, Ch (sub); (with Shamrock R), 1973 v F (sub) (3)
Higgins, J. (Birmingham C), 1951 v Arg (1)
Holland, M. R. (Ipswich T), 2000 v Mac (sub), M, US, S.Af; 2001 v P (sub), Fi, Cy (sub), And (2), P (sub), Es; 2002 v Ho, Cy, Ir (2), Ru (sub), D, US (sub), Ng, Cam, G, S.Ar, Sp; 2003 v Fi (sub), Ru, Sw, Gr, S, Ge, Alb, N, Alb, Ge; (with Charlton Ath), 2004 v Aus, Ru, Sw, Ca (sub), Br, CzR, R, Ng, Jam (sub), Ho; 2005 v P, Is (sub+1); 2006 v I, Cy (sub), Sw (49)
Holmes, J. (Coventry C), 1971 v A (sub); 1973 v F, USSR, Pol, F, N; 1974 v Pol, Br; 1975 v USSR, Sw; 1976 v T, N, Pol; 1977 v E, T, F, Sp; (with Tottenham H), F, Pol, Bul; 1978 v Bul, T, Pol, N, D; 1979 v Ni, E, D, Bul; (with Vancouver W), 1981 v W (30)
Horlacher, A. F. (Bohemians), 1930 v Bel; 1932 v Sp, Ho; 1934 v Ho (sub); 1935 v H;1936 v Ho, Sw (7)
Houghton, R. J. (Oxford U), 1986 v W, U, Ic, Cz; 1987 v Bel (2), S (2), Pol, L; 1988 v L, Bul; (with Liverpool), Is, Y, N, E, USSR, Ho; 1989 v Ni, Tun, Sp, F, H, Sp, Ma, H; 1990 v Ni, Ma, Fi, E, Eg, Ho, R, I; 1991 v Mor, T, E (2), Pol, Ch, US; 1992 v H, Alb, US, I, P; (with Aston Villa), 1993 v D, Sp, Ni, D, Alb, La, Li; 1994 v Li, Sp, Ni, Bol, G (sub), I, M, N, Ho; (with C Palace), 1995 v P, A; 1996 v A, CzR; 1997 v Lie, R, Lie; (with Reading), 1998 v Li, R, Bel (1 + sub) (73)
Howlett, G. (Brighton & HA), 1984 v Chn (sub) (1)
Hoy, M. (Dundalk), 1938 v N; 1939 v Sw, Pol, H (2), G (6)
Hughton, C. (Tottenham H), 1980 v US, E, Sw, Arg; 1981 v Ho, Bel, F, Cy, W, Bel, Pol; 1982 v F; 1983 v Ho, Sp, Ma, Sp; 1984 v Ic, Ho, Ma; 1985 v M (sub), USSR, N, I, Is, E, Sp; 1986 v Sw, USSR, U, Ic; 1987 v Bel, Bul; 1988 v Is, Y, Pol, N, E, USSR, Ho; 1989 v Ni, F, H, Sp, Ma, H; 1990 v W (sub), USSR (sub), Fi, T (sub), Ma; 1991 v T; (with West Ham U), Ch; 1992 v T (53)
Hunt, S. P. (Reading), 2007 v Sm (sub), W (sub), Slo (sub), Ec, Bol (sub) (5)
Hurley, C. J. (Millwall), 1957 v E; (with Sunderland), 1958 v D, Pol, A; 1959 v Cz (2); 1960 v Se, Ch, WG, Se; 1961 v W, N, S (2); 1962 v Cz (2), A; 1963 v Ic (2), S; 1964 v A (2), Sp (2), Pol, N; 1965 v Sp; 1966 v WG, A, Bel; 1967 v T, Sp, T, Cz; 1968 v Cz, Pol; 1969 v Pol, D, Cz, (with Bolton W), H (40)
Hutchinson, F. (Drumcondra), 1935 v Sw, G (2)

Ireland S .J. (Manchester C), 2006 v Se (sub); 2007 v Cy, Sm, W, Slo (5)
Irwin, D. J. (Manchester U), 1991 v Mor, T, W, E, Pol, US; 1992 v H, Pol, W, US, Alb, US (sub), I; 1993 v La, D, Sp, Ni, D, Alb, La, Li; 1994 v Li, Sp, Ni, Bol, G, I, M; 1995 v La, Lie, Ni, E, Ni, P, Lie, A; 1996 v A, P, Ho, CzR; 1997 v Lie, Mac, Ic, Mac, R; 1998 v Li, Bel, Arg (sub); 1999 v Cro, Y, Para, Mac; 2000 v Y, Mac, T (2) (56)

Jordan, D. (Wolverhampton W), 1937 v Sw, F (2)
Jordan, W. (Bohemians), 1934 v Ho; 1938 v N (2)

Kavanagh, G. A. (Stoke C), 1998 v CzR (sub); 1999 v Se (sub), Ni (sub); (with Cardiff C), 2004 v Ca, Br; 2005 v Bul (sub), Cy, Sw (sub), Cro, P (sub); (with Wigan Ath), Chn, Is (sub); 2006 v Cy, Se (sub), Ch (sub); 2007 v Ho (16)
Kavanagh, P. J. (Celtic), 1931 v Sp; 1932 v Sp (2)
Keane, R. D. (Wolverhampton W), 1998 v CzR (sub), Arg, M; 1999 v Cro, Ma, Para, Se (sub), Ni, Mac; (with Coventry C), 2000 v Y, Ma, Mac, T, CzR, Gr, S, M, S.Af (sub); (with Internazionale), 2001 v Ho, P, Es, Fi, Cy, And, P; (with Leeds U), 2002 v Cro, Ho, Ir (2), Ru, D, US, Ng, Cam, G, S.Ar, Sp; 2003 v Fi; (with Tottenham H), Ru, Sw, Alb, N, Alb, Ge; 2004 v Aus, Sw, Ca, Br, CzR, R, Ng, Ho; 2005 v Cy, Sw, F, Fa, Cro, P, Is, Chn, Is; 2006 v F, Cy, Sw, Se, Ch; 2007 v G, Cy, CzR, Sm (2), W (72)
Keane, R. M. (Nottingham F), 1991 v Ch; 1992 v H, Pol, W, Sw, Alb, US; 1993 v La, D, Sp, W, Ni, D, Alb, La, Li; (with Manchester U), 1994 v Li, Sp, Ni, Bol, G, CzR (sub), I, M, N, Ho; 1995 v Ni (2); 1996 v A, Ru; 1997 v Ic, W, Mac, R, Lie; 1998 v Li, Ic, Li; 1999 v Cro, Ma, Y, Para; 2000 v Y, T (2), CzR; 2001 v Ho, P, Es, Cy, And, P; 2002 v Cro, Ho, Cy, Ir, Ru, Ng; 2004 v R; 2005 v Bul, Sw, F, Fa, Is, Chn (sub), Fa; 2006 v F (67)
Keane, T. R. (Swansea T), 1949 v Sw, P, Se, Sp (4)
Kearin, M. (Shamrock R), 1972 v A (1)
Kearns, F. T. (West Ham U), 1954 v L (1)
Kearns, M. (Oxford U), 1971 v Pol (sub); (with Walsall), 1974 v Pol (sub), U, Ch; 1976 v N, Pol; 1977 v E, T, F (2), Sp, Bul; 1978 v N, D; 1979 v Ni, E; (with Wolverhampton W), 1980 v US, Ni (18)
Kelly, A. T. (Sheffield U), 1993 v W (sub); 1994 v Ru (sub), G; 1995 v La, Ni, E, Ni, P, Lie, A; 1996 v A, La, P, Ho; 1997 v Mac, Ic, Mac, R; 1998 v R, Arg (sub); 1999 v Para (sub), Mac; (with Blackburn R), 2000 v Y, Cro, Ma, Mac, T, CzR, S, US; 2001 v Ho, P, Es; 2002 v Cro (sub) (34)
Kelly, D. T. (Walsall), 1988 v Is, R, Y; (with West Ham U), 1989 v Tun (sub); (with Leicester C), 1990 v USSR, Ma; 1991 v Mor, W (sub), Ch, US; 1992 v H; (with

Newcastle U), I (sub), P; 1993 v D (sub), W; (with Wolverhampton W), 1994 v Ru, N (sub); 1995 v E, Ni; (with Sunderland), 1996 v La (sub); 1997 v Ic, W (sub), Mac (sub); (with Tranmere R), 1998 v Li (sub), R (sub), Bel (sub) (26)
Kelly, G. (Leeds U), 1994 v Ru, Ho, Bol (sub), G (sub), CzR, N, Ho; 1995 v La, Lie, Ni (2), P, Lie, A; 1996 v A, La, P, Ho; 1997 v W (sub), R, Lie; 1998 v Ic, Li, Bel (2), CzR, Arg, M; 2000 v Cro, Mac, CzR; 2001 v Ho (sub), Fi, Cy, And (2), P, Es; 2002 v Cro, Ho, Ir (sub+sub), Ru (sub), D, US (sub), Ng (sub), Cam, G, S.Ar, Sp; 2003 v Fi, Sw (52)
Kelly, J. (Derry C), 1932 v Ho; 1934 v Bel; 1936 v Sw, L (4)
Kelly, J. A. (Drumcondra), 1957 v WG, E; (with Preston NE), 1962 v A; 1963 v Ic (2), S; 1964 v A (2), Sp (2), Pol; 1965 v Bel; 1966 v A, Bel; 1967 v Sp (2), T, Cz; 1968 v Pol, Cz; 1969 v Pol, A, D, Cz, D, H; 1970 v S, D, H, Pol, WG; 1971 v Pol, Se (2), I (2), A; 1972 v Ir, Ec, Ch, P; 1973 v USSR, F, USSR, Pol, F, N (47)
Kelly, J. P. V. (Wolverhampton W), 1961 v W, N, S; 1962 v Cz (2) (5)
Kelly, M. J. (Portsmouth), 1988 v Y, Pol (sub); 1989 v Tun; 1991 v Mor (4)
Kelly, N. (Nottingham F), 1954 v L (1)
Kelly, S. M. (Tottenham H), 2006 v Ch; (with Birmingham C), 2007 v Ho (sub), CzR, Ec, Bol (5)
Kendrick, J. (Everton), 1927 v I; (with Dolphin) 1934 v Bel, Ho; 1936 v Ho (4)
Kenna, J. J. (Blackburn R), 1995 v P (sub), Lie (sub), A (sub); 1996 v La, P, Ho, Ru (sub), CzR, P, Cro, Ho, US; 1997 v Lie, Mac, Ic, R (sub), Lie; 1998 v Li, Ic, R, Bel (1 + sub), CzR, Arg; 1999 v Cro (sub), Ma; 2000 v T (sub) (27)
Kennedy, M. F. (Portsmouth), 1986 v Ic, Cz (sub) (2)
Kennedy, M. J. (Liverpool), 1996 v A, La (sub), P, Ru, CzR, Cro, Ho (sub), US (sub), M, Bol (sub); 1997 v R, Lie; 1998 v Li, Ic (sub), R, Bel (2), (with Wimbledon), M (sub); 1999 v Ma (sub), Se, Ni, Mac; (with Manchester C), 2000 v Y, Ma, Mac, CzR, S, M, US (sub), S.Af (sub); 2001 v And; (with Wolverhampton W), 2002 v Cro, Cy, Ru (sub) (34)
Kennedy, W. (St James' Gate), 1932 v Ho; 1934 v Bel, Ho (3)
Kenny, P. (Sheffield U), 2004 v CzR (sub), Jam; 2005 v Bul (sub), Cro, Chn; 2007 v Ho, Cy (7)
Keogh, A. D. (Wolverhampton W), 2007 v Ec (1)
Keogh, J. (Shamrock R), 1966 v WG (sub) (1)
Keogh, S. (Shamrock R), 1959 v Pol (1)
Kernaghan, A. N. (Middlesbrough), 1993 v La, D (2), Alb, La, Li; 1994 v Li; (with Manchester C), Sp, Ni, Bol (sub), CzR; 1995 v Lie, E; 1996 v A, P (sub), Ho (sub), Ru, P, Cro (sub), Ho, US, Bol (22)
Kiely, D. L. (Charlton Ath), 2000 v T (sub + 1), Gr (sub), M; 2002 v Ru (sub), D; 2003 v Fi, S (8)
Kiernan, F. W. (Shamrock R), 1951 v Arg, N; (with Southampton), 1952 v WG (2), A (5)
Kilbane, K. D. (WBA), 1998 v Ic, CzR (sub), Arg; 1999 v Se (sub), Mac (sub); 2000 v Y, Cro (sub), Ma, T (2); (with Sunderland), CzR, Gr, S, M (sub), US, S.Af (sub); 2001 v Ho, P, Es, Fi, Cy, And (2), P, Es; 2002 v Cro (sub), Ho, Cy, Ir (2), Ru, US, Ng, Cam, G, S.Ar, Sp; 2003 v Fi (sub), Ru, Sw, S, Ge, Alb, N, Alb, Ge; 2004 v Aus (sub); (with Everton), Ru, T, Sw, Ca (sub), Br, CzR; 2005 v Bul, Cy, Sw, F, Fa, Cro, P, Is, Chn, Is, Fa; 2006 v I, F, Cy, Sw, Se (sub), Ch; 2007 v Ho; (with Wigan Ath), G, Cy, CzR, Sm (2), W, Slo, Ec, Bol (80)
Kinnear, J. P. (Tottenham H), 1967 v T; 1968 v Cz, Pol; 1969 v A; 1970 v Cz, D, H, Pol; 1971 v Se (sub), I; 1972 v Ir, Ec, Ch, P; 1973 v USSR, F; 1974 v Pol, Br, U, Ch; 1975 v USSR, T, Sw, USSR, WG; (with Brighton & HA), 1976 v T (sub) (26)
Kinsella, J. (Shelbourne), 1928 v Bel (1)
Kinsella, M. A. (Charlton Ath), 1998 v CzR, Arg; 1999 v Cro, Ma, Y, Para, Se, Ni, Mac; 2000 v Y, Cro, Ma, Mac, T, CzR, Gr; 2001 v Ho, P, Es, Fi, Cy, And, P, Es; 2002 v Ir, D, US, Ng (sub), Cam, G, S.Ar, Sp; 2003 v Fi; (with Aston Villa), Ru, Sw, S, Ge, Alb, N, Alb, Ge (sub); 2004 v Aus, T, Sw (sub); (with WBA), CzR (sub), Pol, Ng, Jam (48)
Kinsella, O. (Shamrock R), 1932 v Ho; 1938 v N (2)
Kirkland, A. (Shamrock R), 1927 v I (1)
Lacey, W. (Shelbourne), 1927 v I; 1928 v Bel; 1930 v Bel (3)
Langan, D. (Derby Co), 1978 v T, N; 1980 v Sw, Arg; (with Birmingham C), 1981 v WG 'B', Ho, Bel, F, Cy, W, Bel, Cz, Pol; 1982 v Ho, F; (with Oxford U), 1985 v N, Sp, Sw; 1986 v W, U; 1987 v Bel, S, Pol, Br (sub), L (sub); 1988 v L (26)
Lapira, J. (Notre Dame), 2007 v Ec (sub) (1)
Lawler, J. F. (Fulham), 1953 v A; 1954 v L, F; 1955 v N, Ho, N, WG; 1956 v Y (8)
Lawlor, J. C. (Drumcondra), 1949 v Bel; (with Doncaster R), 1951 v N, Arg (3)
Lawlor, M. (Shamrock R), 1971 v Pol, Se (2), I (sub); 1973 v Pol (5)
Lawrenson, M. (Preston NE), 1977 v Pol; (with Brighton & HA), 1978 v Bul, Pol, N (sub), D; 1979 v Ni, E; 1980 v E, Cy, Sw; 1981 v Ho, Bel, F, Cy, Pol; (with Liverpool), 1982 v Ho, F; 1983 v Ho, Sp, Ic, Ma, Sp; 1984 v Ic, Ho, Ma, Is; 1985 v USSR, N, D, I, E, N; 1986 v Sw, USSR, D; 1987 v Bel, S; 1988 v Bul, Is (39)
Lee, A. D. (Rotherham U), 2003 v N (sub), Ge (sub); (with Cardiff C), 2004 v CzR (sub), Pol, Ng, Jam, Ho (sub); 2005 v Cy (sub); (with Ipswich T), 2007 v Cy (sub), Sm (sub) (10)
Leech, M. (Shamrock R), 1969 v Cz, D, H; 1972 v A, Ir, Ec, P; 1973 v USSR (sub) (8)
Lennon, C. (St James' Gate), 1935 v H, Sw, G (3)
Lennox, G. (Dolphin), 1931 v Sp; 1932 v Sp (2)
Long, S. P. (Reading), 2007 v Sm, Slo (sub), Ec (sub), Bol (4)
Lowry, D. (St Patrick's Ath), 1962 v A (sub) (1)
Lunn, R. (Dundalk), 1939 v Sw, Pol (2)
Lynch, J. (Cork Bohemians), 1934 v Bel (1)

McAlinden, J. (Portsmouth), 1946 v P, Sp (2)
McAteer, J. W. (Bolton W), 1994 v Ru, Ho (sub), Bol (sub), G, CzR (sub), I (sub), M (sub), N, Ho (sub); 1995 v La, Lie, Ni (2 sub), Lie; (with Liverpool), 1996 v La, P, Ho (sub), Ru; 1997 v Mac, Ic, W, Mac; 1998 v Ic (sub), Li, R; 1999 v Cro, Ma, Y; (with Blackburn R), Para, Se; 2000 v CzR (sub), S, M, US (sub), S.Af; 2001 v Ho, P, Es, Fi (sub), Cy; 2002 v Cro (sub), Ho; (with Sunderland), Ir (2), Ru (sub), D, Ng, Cam, S.Ar (sub); 2003 v Fi, Ru; 2004 v Br (sub) (52)
McCann, J. (Shamrock R), 1957 v WG (1)
McCarthy, J. (Bohemians), 1926 v I; 1928 v Bel; 1930 v Bel (3)
McCarthy, M. (Shamrock R), 1932 v Ho (1)
McCarthy, M. (Manchester C), 1984 v Pol, Chn; 1985 v M, D, I, Is, E, Sp, Sw; 1986 v Sw, USSR, W (sub), U, Ic, Cz; 1987 v S (2), Pol, Bul, Bel (with Celtic), Br, L; 1988 v Bul, Is, R, Y, N, E, USSR, Ho; 1989 v Ni, Tun, Sp, F, H, Sp; (with Lyon), 1990 v WG, Ni (with Millwall), W, USSR, Fi, T, E, Eg, Ho, R, I; 1991 v Mor, T, E, US; 1992 v H, T, Alb (sub), US, I, P (57)
McConville, T. (Dundalk), 1972 v A; (with Waterford), 1973 v USSR, F, USSR, Pol, F (6)
McDonagh, Jacko (Shamrock R), 1984 v Pol (sub), Ma (sub); 1985 v M (sub) (3)
McDonagh, J. (Everton), 1981 v WG 'B', W, Bel, Cz; (with Bolton W), 1982 v Ho, F, Ch, Br; 1983 v Ho, Sp, Ic, Ma, Sp; (with Notts Co), 1984 v Ic, Ho, Pol; 1985 v M, USSR, N, D, Sp, Sw; 1986 v Sw, USSR; (with Wichita Wings) D (25)
McEvoy, M. A. (Blackburn R), 1961 v S (2); 1963 v S; 1964 v A, Sp (2), Pol, N, E; 1965 v Pol, Bel, Sp; 1966 v Sp (2); 1967 v Sp, T, Cz (17)
McGeady, A. (Celtic), 2004 v Jam (sub); 2005 v Cro (sub), P (sub); 2006 v Ch (sub); 2007 v Ho, G (sub), Cy, Sm (sub), W (sub), Slo (10)
McGee, P. (QPR), 1978 v T, N (sub), D (sub); 1979 v Ni, E, D (sub), Bul (sub); 1980 v Cz, Bul; (with Preston NE), US, Ni, Cy, Sw, Arg; 1981 v Bel (sub) (15)
McGoldrick, E. J. (C Palace), 1992 v Sw, US, I, P (sub); 1993 v D, W, Ni (sub), D; (with Arsenal), 1994 v Ni, Ru, Ho, CzR; 1995 v La (sub), Lie, E (15)
McGowan, D. (West Ham U), 1949 v P, Se, Sp (3)
McGowan, J. (Cork U), 1947 v Sp (1)
McGrath, M. (Blackburn R), 1958 v A; 1959 v Pol, Cz (2); 1960 v Se, WG, Se; 1961 v W; 1962 v Cz (2); 1963 v S; 1964 v A (2), E; 1965 v Pol, Bel, Sp; 1966 v Sp; (with Bradford), 1966 v WG, A, Bel; 1967 v T (22)

McGrath, P. (Manchester U), 1985 v I (sub), Is, E, N (sub), Sw (sub); 1986 v Sw (sub), D, W, Ic, Cz; 1987 v Bel (2), S (2), Pol, Bul, Br, L; 1988 v L, Bul, Y, Pol, N, E, Ho; 1989 v Ni, F, H, Sp, Ma, H; (with Aston Villa), 1990 v WG, Ma, USSR, Fi, T, E, Eg, Ho, R, I; 1991 v E (2), W, Pol, Ch (sub), US; 1992 v Pol, T, Sw, US, Alb, US, I, P; 1993 v La, Sp, Ni, D, La, Li; 1994 v Sp, Ni, G, CzR, I, M, N, Ho; 1995 v La, Ni, E, Ni, P, Lie, A; 1996 v A, La, P, Ho, Ru, CzR; (with Derby Co), 1997 v W (83)
McGuire, W. (Bohemians), 1936 v Ho (1)
Macken, A. (Derby Co), 1977 v Sp (1)
Macken J. P. (Manchester C), 2005 v Bul (sub) (1)
McKenzie, G. (Southend U), 1938 v N (2), Cz, Pol; 1939 v Sw, Pol, H (2), G (9)
Mackey, G. (Shamrock R), 1957 v D, WG, E (3)
McLoughlin, A. F. (Swindon T), 1990 v Ma, E (sub), Eg (sub); 1991 v Mor (sub), E (sub); (with Southampton), W, Ch (sub); 1992 v H (sub), W (sub); (with Portsmouth), US (1 + sub), I (sub), P; 1993 v W; 1994 v Ni (sub), Ru, Ho (sub); 1995 v Lie (sub); 1996 v P, Cro, Ho, US, M, Bol (sub); 1997 v Lie, Mac, Ic, W, Mac; 1998 v Li (sub), Ic, Li, R, Bel, CzR (sub); 1999 v Y, Para (sub), Se, Ni (sub); 2000 v Cro, Ma (sub), Mac (42)
McLoughlin, F. (Fordsons), 1930 v Bel; (with Cork), 1932 v Sp (2)
McMillan, W. (Belfast Celtic), 1946 v P, Sp (2)
McNally, J. B. (Luton T), 1959 v Cz; 1961 v S; 1963 v Ic (3)
McPhail, S. (Leeds U), 2000 v S, US, S.Af; 2002 v Cro (sub), Cy (sub); 2003 v Fi (sub), Gr; 2004 v T (sub), Ca (sub), Ng (10)
McShane, P. D. (WBA), 2007 v CzR, Sm (1+sub), W, Slo (5)
Madden, O. (Cork), 1936 v H (1)
Maguire, J. (Shamrock R), 1929 v Bel (1)
Mahon, A. J. (Tranmere R), 2000 v Gr (sub), S.Af (2)
Malone, G. (Shelbourne), 1949 v Bel (1)
Mancini, T. J. (QPR), 1974 v Pol, Br, U, Ch; (with Arsenal), 1975 v USSR (5)
Martin, C. (Bo'ness), 1927 v I (1)
Martin, C. J. (Glentoran), 1946 v P (sub), Sp; 1947 v E; (with Leeds U), 1947 v Sp; 1948 v P, Sp; (with Aston Villa), 1949 v Sw, Bel, P, Se, Sp; 1950 v Fi, E, Fi, Se, Bel; 1951 v Arg; 1952 v WG, A, Sp; 1954 v F (2), L; 1955 v N, Ho, N, WG; 1956 v Y, Sp, Ho (30)
Martin, M. P. (Bohemians), 1972 v A, Ir, Ec, Ch, P; 1973 v USSR; (with Manchester U), USSR, Pol, F, N; 1974 v Pol, Br, U, Ch; 1975 v USSR, T, Sw, USSR, Sw, WG; (with WBA), 1976 v T, N, Pol; 1977 v E, T, F (2), Sp, Pol, Bul; (with Newcastle U), 1979 v D, Bul, WG; 1980 v W, Cz, Bul, US, Ni; 1981 v WG 'B', F, Bel, Cz; 1982 v Ho, F, Alg, Ch, Br, Tr; 1983 v Ho, Sp, Ma, Sp (52)
Maybury, A. (Leeds U), 1998 v CzR; 1999 v Ni; (with Hearts), 2004 v CzR, Pol (sub), R, Ng, Jam, Ho; 2005 v Cy (sub); (with Leicester C), Chn (10)
Meagan, M. K. (Everton), 1961 v S; 1962 v A; 1963 v Ic; 1964 v Sp; (with Huddersfield T), 1965 v Bel; 1966 v Sp (2), A, Bel; 1967 v Sp, T, Sp, T, Cz; 1968 v Cz, Pol; (with Drogheda), 1970 v S (17)
Meehan, P. (Drumcondra), 1934 v Ho (1)
Miller, L. W. P. (Celtic), 2004 v CzR (sub), Pol, R, Ng; (with Manchester U), 2005 v Bul, Fa (sub), Cro, P (sub), Chn (sub); 2006 v I (sub), Se (sub), Ch; 2007 v Ho (sub) (13)
Milligan, M. J. (Oldham Ath), 1992 v US (sub) (1)
Monahan, P. (Sligo R), 1935 v Sw, G (2)
Mooney, J. (Shamrock R), 1965 v Pol, Bel (2)
Moore, A. (Middlesbrough), 1996 v CzR, Cro (sub), Ho, M, Bol; 1997 v Lie (sub), Mac (sub), Ic (sub) (8)
Moore, P. (Shamrock R), 1931 v Sp; 1932 v Ho; (with Aberdeen), 1934 v Bel, Ho; 1935 v H, G; (with Shamrock R), 1936 v Ho; 1937 v G, H (9)
Moran, K. (Manchester U), 1980 v Sw, Arg; 1981 v WG 'B', Bel, F, Cy, W (sub), Bel, Cz, Pol; 1982 v F, Alg; 1983 v Ic; 1984 v Ic, Ho, Ma, Is; 1985 v M; 1986 v D, Ic, Cz; 1987 v Bel (2), S (2), Pol, Bul, Br, L; 1988 v L, Bul, Is, R, Y, Pol, N, E, USSR, Ho; (with Sporting Gijon), 1989 v Ni, Sp, H, Sp, Ma, H; 1990 v Ni, Ma; (with Blackburn R), W, USSR (sub), Ma, E, Eg, Ho, R, I; 1991 v T (sub), W, E, Pol, Ch, US; 1992 v Pol, US; 1993 v D, Sp, Ni, Alb; 1994 v Li, Sp, Ho, Bol (71)
Moroney, T. (West Ham U), 1948 v Sp; 1949 v P, Se, Sp; 1950 v Fi, E, Fi, Bel; 1951 v N (2); 1952 v WG; (with Evergreen U), 1954 v F (12)
Morris, C. B. (Celtic), 1988 v Is, R, Y, Pol, N, E, USSR, Ho; 1989 v Ni, Tun, Sp, F, H (1+sub); 1990 v WG, Ni, Ma (sub), W, USSR, Fi (sub), T, E, Eg, Ho, R, I; 1991 v E; 1992 v H (sub), Pol, W, Sw, US (2), P; (with Middlesbrough), 1993 v W (35)
Morrison, C. H. (C Palace), 2002 v Cro (sub), Cy (sub), Ir (sub), Ru (sub), D, US (sub), Ng (sub); (with Birmingham C), 2003 v Ru (sub), Sw (sub), S; 2004 v Aus (sub), Ru, T (sub), Sw (sub), Ca (sub), Br, CzR, Pol, R, Jam, Ho; 2005 v Bul, Cy, Sw, F, P, Is, Chn (sub), Is, Fa; 2006 v I; (with C Palace), F, Sw, Se (sub); 2007 v Ho, Cy (36)
Moulson, C. (Lincoln C), 1936 v H, L; (with Notts Co), 1937 v H, Sw, F (5)
Moulson, G. B. (Lincoln C), 1948 v P, Sp; 1949 v Sw (3)
Muckian, C. (Drogheda U), 1978 v Pol (1)
Muldoon, T. (Aston Villa), 1927 v I (1)
Mulligan, P. M. (Shamrock R), 1969 v Cz, D, H; 1970 v S, Cz, D; (with Chelsea), 1970 v H, Pol, WG; 1971 v Pol, Se, I; 1972 v A, Ir, Ec, Ch, P; (with C Palace), 1973 v F, USSR, Pol, F, N; 1974 v Pol, Br, U, Ch; 1975 v USSR, T, Sw, USSR, Sw; (with WBA), 1976 v T, Pol; 1977 v E, T, F (2), Pol, Bul; 1978 v Bul, N, D; 1979 v E, D, Bul (sub), WG; (with Shamrock R), 1980 v W, Cz, Bul, US (sub) (50)
Munroe, L. (Shamrock R), 1954 v L (1)
Murphy, A. (Clyde), 1956 v Y (1)
Murphy, B. (Bohemians), 1986 v U (1)
Murphy, D. (Sunderland), 2007 v Ec, Bol (sub) (2)
Murphy, J. (C Palace), 1980 v W, US, Cy (3)
Murphy, J. (WBA), 2004 v T (sub) (1)
Murphy, P. M. (Carlisle U), 2007 v Bol (1)
Murray, T. (Dundalk), 1950 v Bel (1)

Newman, W. (Shelbourne), 1969 v D (1)
Nolan, R. (Shamrock R), 1957 v D, WG, E; 1958 v Pol; 1960 v Ch, WG, Se; 1962 v Cz (2); 1963 v Ic (10)

O'Brien, A. (Newcastle U), 2007 v Ho (sub), G (sub), Cy (sub), CzR (sub), Bol (5)
O'Brien, A. J. (Newcastle U), 2001 v Es (sub); 2002 v Cro (sub), Ho (sub), Ru, US; 2003 v S (sub); 2004 v Aus (sub), T, Br, Pol (sub), R, Jam, Ho; 2005 v Cy, Sw, F, Fa, P, Is, Chn (sub), Is; (with Portsmouth), 2006 v I (sub), Se; 2007 v Ho, G, Cy (26)
O'Brien, F. (Philadelphia F), 1980 v Cz, E, Cy (sub) (3)
O'Brien J. M. (Bolton W), 2006 v Se (1)
O'Brien, L. (Shamrock R), 1986 v U; (with Manchester U), 1987 v Br; 1988 v Is (sub), R (sub), Y (sub), Pol (sub); 1989 v Tun; (with Newcastle U), Sp (sub); 1992 v Sw (sub); 1993 v W; (with Tranmere R), 1994 v Ru; 1996 v Cro, Ho, US, Bol; 1997 v Mac (sub) (16)
O'Brien, M. T. (Derby Co), 1927 v I; (with Walsall), 1929 v Bel; (with Norwich C), 1930 v Bel; (with Watford), 1932 v Ho (4)
O'Brien, R. (Notts Co), 1976 v N, Pol; 1977 v Sp, Pol; 1980 v Arg (sub) (5)
O'Byrne, L. B. (Shamrock R), 1949 v Bel (1)
O'Callaghan, B. R. (Stoke C), 1979 v WG (sub); 1980 v W, US; 1981 v W; 1982 v Br, Tr (6)
O'Callaghan, K. (Ipswich T), 1981 v WG 'B', Cz, Pol; 1982 v Alg, Ch, Br, Tr (sub); 1983 v Sp, Ic (sub), Ma (sub), Sp (sub); 1984 v Ic, Ho, Ma; 1985 v M (sub), N (sub), D (sub); (with Portsmouth), E (sub); 1986 v Sw (sub), USSR (sub); 1987 v Br (21)
O'Cearuill, J. (Arsenal), 2007 v Ec (sub), Bol (2)
O'Connell, A. (Dundalk), 1967 v Sp; (with Bohemians), 1971 v Pol (sub) (2)
O'Connor, T. (Shamrock R), 1950 v Fi, E, Fi, Se (4)
O'Connor, T. (Fulham), 1968 v Cz; (with Dundalk), 1972 v A, Ir (sub), Ec (sub), Ch; (with Bohemians), 1973 v F (sub), Pol (sub) (7)
O'Driscoll, J. F. (Swansea T), 1949 v Sw, Bel, Se (3)
O'Driscoll, S. (Fulham), 1982 v Ch, Br, Tr (sub) (3)
O'Farrell, F. (West Ham U), 1952 v A; 1953 v A; 1954 v F; 1955 v Ho, N; 1956 v Y, Ho; (with Preston NE), 1958 v D; 1959 v Cz (9)
O'Flanagan, K. P. (Bohemians), 1938 v N, Cz, Pol; 1939 v Pol, H (2), G; (with Arsenal), 1947 v E, Sp, P (10)

O'Flanagan, M. (Bohemians), 1947 v E (1)
O'Halloran, S. E. (Aston Villa), 2007 v Ec, Bol (sub) (2)
O'Hanlon, K. G. (Rotherham U), 1988 v Is (1)
O'Kane, P. (Bohemians), 1935 v H, Sw, G (3)
O'Keefe, E. (Everton), 1981 v W; (with Port Vale), 1984 v Chn; 1985 v M, USSR (sub), E (5)
O'Keefe, T. (Cork), 1934 v Bel; (with Waterford), 1938 v Cz, Pol (3)
O'Leary, D. (Arsenal), 1977 v E, F (2), Sp, Bul; 1978 v Bul, N, D; 1979 v E, Bul, WG; 1980 v W, Bul, Ni, E, Cy; 1981 v WG 'B',Ho, Cz, Pol; 1982 v Ho, F; 1983 v Ho, Ic, Sp; 1984 v Pol, Is, Chn; 1985 v USSR, N, D, Is, E (sub), N, Sp, Sw; 1986 v Sw, USSR, D, W; 1989 v Sp, Ma, H; 1990 v WG, Ni (sub), Ma, W (sub), USSR, Fi, T, Ma, R (sub); 1991 v Mor, T, E (2), Pol, Ch; 1992 v H, Pol, T, W, Sw, US, Alb, I, P; 1993 v W (68)
O'Leary, P. (Shamrock R), 1980 v Bul, US, Ni, E (sub), Cz, Arg; 1981 v Ho (7)
O'Mahoney, M. T. (Bristol R), 1938 v Cz, Pol; 1939 v Sw, Pol, H, G (6)
O'Neill, F. S. (Shamrock R), 1962 v Cz (2); 1965 v Pol, Bel, Sp; 1966 v Sp (2), WG, A; 1967 v Sp, T, Sp, T; 1969 v Pol, A, D, Cz, D (sub), H (sub); 1972 v A (20)
O'Neill, J. (Everton), 1952 v Sp; 1953 v F, A; 1954 v F, L, F; 1955 v N, Ho, N, WG; 1956 v Y, Sp; 1957 v D; 1958 v A; 1959 v Pol, Cz (2) (17)
O'Neill, J. (Preston NE), 1961 v W (1)
O'Neill, K. P. (Norwich C), 1996 v P (sub), Cro, Ho (sub), US (sub), M, Bol; 1997 v Lie, Mac (1 + sub); 1999 v Cro, Y (sub); (with Middlesbrough), Ni (sub); 2000 v Mac (sub) (13)
O'Neill, W. (Dundalk), 1936 v Ho, Sw, H, L; 1937 v G, H, Sw, F; 1938 v N; 1939 v H, G (11)
O'Regan, K. (Brighton & HA), 1984 v Ma, Pol; 1985 v M, Sp (sub) (4)
O'Reilly, J. (Brideville), 1932 v Ho; (with Aberdeen), 1934 v Bel, Ho; (with Brideville), 1936 v Ho; Sw, H, L; (with St James' Gate), 1937 v G, H, Sw, F; 1938 v N (2), Cz, Pol; 1939 v Sw, Pol, H (2), G (20)
O'Reilly, J. (Cork U), 1946 v P, Sp (2)
O'Shea, J. F. (Manchester U), 2002 v Cro (sub); 2003 v Gr, S, Ge, Alb (2), Ge; 2004 v Aus, Ru, Sw, Ca, Br, Pol, Jam; 2005 v Bul, Cy, F, Fa, Cro, P, Is, Chn, Is, Fa; 2006 v I, F, Cy, Sw, Se, Ch; 2007 v Ho, G, Cy, CzR, Sm (2), W, Slo (38)

Peyton, G. (Fulham), 1977 v Sp (sub); 1978 v Bul, T, Pol; 1979 v D, Bul, WG; 1980 v W, Cz, Bul, E, Cy, Sw, Arg; 1981 v Ho, Bel, F, Cy; 1982 v Tr; 1985 v M (sub); 1986 v W, Cz; (with Bournemouth), 1988 v L, Pol; 1989 v Ni, Tun; 1990 v USSR, Ma; 1991 v Ch; (with Everton) 1992 v US (2), I (sub), P (33)
Peyton, N. (Shamrock R), 1957 v WG; (with Leeds U), 1960 v WG, Se (sub); 1961 v W; 1963 v Ic, S (6)
Phelan, T. (Wimbledon), 1992 v H, Pol (sub), T, W, Sw, US, I (sub), P; (with Manchester C), 1993 v La (sub), D, Sp, Ni, Alb, La, Li; 1994 v Li, Sp, Ni, Ho, Bol, G, CzR, I, M, Ho; 1995 v E; 1996 v La; (with Chelsea), Ho, Ru, P, Cro, Ho, US, M (sub), Bol; (with Everton), 1997 v W, Mac; 1998 v R; (with Fulham), 2000 v S (sub), M, US, S.Af (42)
Potter, D. M. (Wolverhampton W), 2007 v Ec, Bol (2)

Quinn, A. (Sheffield W), 2003 v N (sub); 2004 v Aus (sub), Jam, Ho; (with Sheffield U), 2005 v Bul (sub), Cro (sub); 2007 v CzR (sub), Slo (sub) (8)
Quinn, B. S. (Coventry C), 2000 v Gr, M, US (sub), S.Af (sub) (4)
Quinn, N. J. (Arsenal), 1986 v Ic (sub), Cz; 1987 v Bul (sub), Br (sub); 1988 v L (sub), Bul (sub), Is, R (sub), Pol (sub), E (sub); 1989 v Tun (sub), Sp (sub), H (sub); (with Manchester C), 1990 v USSR, Ma, Eg (sub), Ho, R, I; 1991 v Mor, T, E(2) W, Pol; 1992 v H, W (sub), US, Alb, US, I, P; 1993 v La, D, Sp, Ni, D, Alb, La, Li; 1994 v Li, Sp, Ni; 1995 v La, Lie, Ni, E, Ni, P, Lie, A; 1996 v A, La, P, Ru, CzR, P (sub), Cro, Ho (sub), US; (with Sunderland), 1997 v Lie; 1998 v Li, Arg; 1999 v Ma, Y, Para, Se, Ni, Mac; 2000 v Y, Cro (sub), Ma, Mac, T, CzR, S, M, US (sub), S.Af; 2001 v Ho, P, Es, P, Es; 2002 v Ho (sub), Cy, Ir, Ru (sub), G (sub), S.Ar (sub), Sp (sub) (91)

Reid, A. M. (Nottingham F), 2004 v Ca, Br, CzR, Pol, R, Jam, Ho; 2005 v Bul, Cy, Sw, F (sub), Fa; (with Tottenham H), P, Chn, Is, Fa; 2006 v I, F, Sw, Ch (sub); (with Charlton Ath), 2007 v CzR, Sm (22)
Reid, C. (Brideville), 1931 v Sp (1)
Reid, S. J. (Millwall), 2002 v Cro, Ru, D (sub), US (sub), Ng (sub), Cam (sub), G (sub); 2003 v S, Alb (sub); (with Blackburn R), 2004 v Ru (sub), T (sub), Ca, Pol; 2006 v I, Cy (sub), Sw (sub), Se, Ch; 2007 v Ho, G (20)
Richardson, D. J. (Shamrock R), 1972 v A (sub); (with Gillingham), 1973 v N (sub); 1980 v Cz (3)
Rigby, A. (St James' Gate), 1935 v H, Sw, G (3)
Ringstead, A. (Sheffield U), 1951 v Arg, N; 1952 v WG (2), A, Sp; 1953 v A; 1954 v F; 1955 v N; 1956 v Y, Sp, Ho; 1957 v E (2); 1958 v D, Pol, A; 1959 v Pol, Cz (2) (20)
Robinson, J. (Bohemians), 1928 v Bel; (with Dolphin), 1931 v Sp (2)
Robinson, M. (Brighton & HA), 1981 v WG 'B', F, Cy, Bel, Pol; 1982 v Ho, F, Alg, Ch; 1983 v Ho, Sp, Ic, Ma; (with Liverpool), 1984 v Ic, Ho, Is; 1985 v USSR, N; (with QPR), N, Sp, Sw; 1986 v D (sub), W, Cz (24)
Roche, P. J. (Shelbourne), 1972 v A; (with Manchester U), 1975 v USSR, T, Sw, USSR, Sw, WG; 1976 v T (8)
Rogers, E. (Blackburn R), 1968 v Cz, Pol; 1969 v Pol, A, D, Cz, D, H; 1970 v S, D, H; 1971 v I (2), A; (with Charlton Ath), 1972 v Ir, Ec, Ch, P; 1973 v USSR (19)
Rowlands, M. C. (QPR), 2004 v R (sub), Ng (sub), Jam (sub) (3)
Ryan, G. (Derby Co), 1978 v T; (with Brighton & HA), 1979 v E, WG; 1980 v W, Cy (sub), Sw, Arg (sub); 1981 v WG 'B' (sub), F (sub), Pol (sub); 1982 v Br (sub), Ho (sub), Alg (sub), Ch (sub), Tr; 1984 v Pol, Chn; 1985 v M (18)
Ryan, R. A. (WBA), 1950 v Se, Bel; 1951 v N, Arg, N; 1952 v WG (2), A, Sp; 1953 v F, A; 1954 v F, L, F; 1955 v N; (with Derby Co), 1956 v Sp (16)

Sadlier, R. T. (Millwall), 2002 v Ru (sub) (1)
Savage, D. P. T. (Millwall), 1996 v P (sub), Cro (sub), US (sub), M, Bol (5)
Saward, P. (Millwall), 1954 v L; (with Aston Villa), 1957 v E (2); 1958 v D, Pol, A; 1959 v Pol, Cz; 1960 v Se, Ch, WG, Se; 1961 v W, N; (with Huddersfield T), S; 1962 v A; 1963 v Ic (2) (18)
Scannell, T. (Southend U), 1954 v L (1)
Scully, P. J. (Arsenal), 1989 v Tun (sub) (1)
Sheedy, K. (Everton), 1984 v Ho (sub), Ma; 1985 v D, I, Is, Sw; 1986 v Sw, D; 1987 v S, Pol; 1988 v Is, R, Pol, E (sub), USSR, Ho (sub); 1989 v Ni, Tun, H, Sp, Ma, H; 1990 v Ni, Ma, W (sub), USSR, Fi (sub), T, E, Eg, Ho, R, I; 1991 v W, E, Pol, Ch, US; 1992 v H, Pol, T, W; (with Newcastle U), Sw (sub), Alb; 1993 v La, W (sub) (46)
Sheridan, J. J. (Leeds U), 1988 v R, Y, Pol, N (sub); 1989 v Sp; (with Sheffield W), 1990 v W, T (sub), Ma, I (sub); 1991 v Mor (sub), T, Ch, US (sub); 1992 v H; 1993 v La (sub); 1994 v Sp (sub), Ho, Bol, G, CzR, I, M, N, Ho; 1995 v La, Lie, Ni, E, Ni, P, Lie, A; 1996 v A, Ho (34)
Slaven, B. (Middlesbrough), 1990 v W, Fi, T (sub), Ma; 1991 v W, Pol (sub); 1993 v W (7)
Sloan, J. W. (Arsenal), 1946 v P, Sp (2)
Smyth, M. (Shamrock R), 1969 v Pol (sub) (1)
Squires, J. (Shelbourne), 1934 v Ho (1)
Stapleton, F. (Arsenal), 1977 v T, F, Sp, Bul; 1978 v Bul, N, D; 1979 v Ni, E (sub), D, WG; 1980 v W, Bul, Ni, E, Cy; 1981 v WG 'B', Ho, Bel, F, Cy, Bel, Cz, Pol; (with Manchester U), 1982 v Ho, F, Alg; 1983 v Ho, Sp, Ic, Ma, Sp; 1984 v Ic, Ho, Ma, Pol, Is, Chn; 1985 v N, D, I, Is, E, N, Sw; 1986 v Sw, USSR, D, U, Ic, Cz (sub); 1987 v Bel (2), S (2), Pol, Bul, L; (with Ajax), 1988 v L, Bul, R, Y, N, E, USSR, Ho; (with Le Havre), 1989 v F, Sp, Ma; (with Blackburn R), 1990 v WG, Ma (sub) (71)
Staunton, S. (Liverpool), 1989 v Tun, Sp (2), Ma, H; 1990 v WG, Ni, Ma, W, USSR, Fi, T, Ma, E, Eg, Ho, R, I; 1991 v Mor, T, E (2), W, Pol, Ch, US; (with Aston Villa), 1992 v Pol, T, Sw, US, Alb, US, I, P; 1993 v La, Sp, Ni, D, Alb, La, Li; 1994 v Li, Sp, Ho, Bol, G, CzR, I, M, N, Ho; 1995 v La, Lie, Ni, E, Ni, P, Lie, A; 1996 v La, P, Ru; 1997 v Lie, Mac (2), W, R, Lie; 1998 v Li, Ic, Li, Bel (2), Arg; (with Liverpool), 1999 v Cro, Ma, Y,

Se; 2000 v Y, Cro, Ma, Mac, CzR (sub), Gr; 2001 v Ho (sub), Fi (sub); (with Aston Villa), And (sub), P, Es; 2002 v Cro, Ho, Cy, Ir (2), Ru (sub), D, US (sub), Ng, Cam, G, S.Ar, Sp (102)
Stevenson, A. E. (Dolphin), 1932 v Ho; (with Everton), 1947 v E, Sp, P; 1948 v P, Sp; 1949 v Sw (7)
Stokes, A. (Sunderland), 2007 v Sm (sub), Ec (sub), Bol (3)
Strahan, F. (Shelbourne), 1964 v Pol, N, E; 1965 v Pol; 1966 v WG (5)
Sullivan, J. (Fordsons), 1928 v Bel (1)
Swan, M. M. G. (Drumcondra), 1960 v Se (sub) (1)
Synnott, N. (Shamrock R), 1978 v T, Pol; 1979 v Ni (3)

Taylor, T. (Waterford), 1959 v Pol (sub) (1)
Thomas, P. (Waterford), 1974 v Pol, Br (2)
Thompson, J. (Nottingham F), 2004 v Ca (sub) (1)
Townsend, A. D. (Norwich C), 1989 v F, Sp (sub), Ma (sub), H; 1990 v WG (sub), Ni, Ma, W, USSR, Fi (sub), T, Ma (sub), E, Eg, Ho, R, I; (with Chelsea), 1991 v Mor, T, E (2), W, Pol, Ch, US; 1992 v Pol, W, US, Alb, US, I; 1993 v La, D, Sp, Ni, D, Alb, La, Li; (with Aston Villa), 1994 v Li, Ni, Ho, Bol, G, CzR, I, M, N, Ho; 1995 v La, Ni, E, Ni, P; 1996 v A, La, Ho, Ru, CzR, P; 1997 v Lie, Mac (2), Ic, R, Lie; 1998 v Li; (with Middlesbrough), Ic, Bel (2) (70)
Traynor, T. J. (Southampton), 1954 v L; 1962 v A; 1963 v Ic (2), S; 1964 v A (2), Sp (8)
Treacy, R. C. P. (WBA), 1966 v WG; 1967 v Sp, Cz; 1968 v Cz; (with Charlton Ath), 1968 v Pol; 1969 v Pol, Cz, D; 1970 v S, D, H (sub), Pol (sub), WG (sub); 1971 v Pol, Se (sub+1), I, A; (with Swindon T), 1972 v Ir, Ec, Ch, P; 1973 v USSR, F, USSR, Pol, F, N; 1974 v Pol; (with Preston NE), Br; 1975 v USSR, Sw (2), WG; 1976 v T, N (sub), Pol (sub); (with WBA), 1977 v F, Pol; (with Shamrock R), 1978 v T, Pol; 1980 v Cz (sub) (42)
Tuohy, L. (Shamrock R), 1956 v Y; 1959 v Cz (2); (with Newcastle U), 1962 v A; 1963 v Ic (2); (with Shamrock R), 1964 v A; 1965 v Bel (8)
Turner, C. J. (Southend U), 1936 v Sw; 1937 v G, H, Sw, F; 1938 v N (2); (with West Ham U), Cz, Pol; 1939 v H (10)
Turner, P. (Celtic), 1963 v S; 1964 v Sp (2)

Vernon, J. (Belfast C), 1946 v P, Sp (2)

Waddock, G. (QPR), 1980 v Sw, Arg; 1981 v W, Pol (sub); 1982 v Alg; 1983 v Ic, Ma, Sp, Ho (sub); 1984 v Ma (sub), Ic, Ho, Is; 1985 v I, Is, E, N, Sp; 1986 v USSR; (with Millwall), 1990 v USSR, T (21)
Walsh, D. J. (Linfield), 1946 v P, Sp; (with WBA), 1947 v Sp, P; 1948 v P, Sp; 1949 v Sw, P, Se, Sp; 1950 v E, Fi, Se; 1951 v N; (with Aston Villa), Arg, N; 1952 v Sp; 1953 v A; 1954 v F (2) (20)
Walsh, J. (Limerick), 1982 v Tr (1)
Walsh, M. (Blackpool), 1976 v N, Pol; 1977 v F (sub), Pol; (with Everton), 1979 v Ni (sub); (with QPR), D (sub), Bul, WG (sub); (with Porto), 1981 v Bel (sub), Cz; 1982 v Alg (sub); 1983 v Sp, Ho (sub), Sp (sub); 1984 v Ic (sub), Ma, Pol, Chn; 1985 v USSR, N (sub), D (21)
Walsh, M. (Everton), 1982 v Ch, Br, Tr; 1983 v Ic (4)
Walsh, W. (Manchester C), 1947 v E, Sp, P; 1948 v P, Sp; 1949 v Bel; 1950 v E, Se, Bel (9)
Waters, J. (Grimsby T), 1977 v T; 1980 v Ni (sub) (2)
Watters, F. (Shelbourne), 1926 v I (1)
Weir, E. (Clyde), 1939 v H (2), G (3)
Whelan, R. (St Patrick's Ath), 1964 v A, E (sub) (2)
Whelan, R. (Liverpool), 1981 v Cz (sub); 1982 v Ho (sub), F; 1983 v Ic, Ma, Sp; 1984 v Is; 1985 v USSR, N, I (sub), Is, E, N (sub), Sw (sub); 1986 v USSR (sub), W; 1987 v Bel (sub), S, Bul, Bel, Br, L; 1988 v L, Bul, Pol, N, E, USSR, Ho; 1989 v Ni, F, H, Sp, Ma; 1990 v WG, Ni, Ma, W, Ho (sub); 1991 v Mor, E; 1992 v Sw; 1993 v La, W (sub), Li (sub); 1994 v Li (sub), Sp, Ru, Ho, G (sub), N (sub); (with Southend U), 1995 v Lie, A (53)
Whelan, W. (Manchester U), 1956 v Ho; 1957 v D, E (2) (4)
White, J. J. (Bohemians), 1928 v Bel (1)
Whittaker, R. (Chelsea), 1959 v Cz (1)
Williams, J. (Shamrock R), 1938 v N (1)

A happy David Beckham lines up alongside his former Real Madrid teammate Michael Owen before the Euro 2008 qualifying match against Estonia in Tallinin. (Action Images/Reuters/Eddie Keogh)

BRITISH AND IRISH INTERNATIONAL GOALSCORERS SINCE 1872

Where two players with the same surname and initials have appeared for the same country, and one or both have scored, they have been distinguished by reference to the club which appears *first* against their name in the international appearances section.

ENGLAND	
A'Court, A.	1
Adams, T. A.	5
Adcock, H.	1
Alcock, C. W.	1
Allen, A.	3
Allen, R.	2
Amos, A.	1
Anderson, V.	2
Anderton, D. R.	7
Astall, G.	1
Athersmith, W. C.	3
Atyeo, P. J. W.	5
Bache, J. W.	4
Bailey, N. C.	2
Baily, E. F.	5
Baker, J. H.	3
Ball, A. J.	8
Bambridge, A. L.	1
Bambridge, E. C.	11
Barclay, R.	2
Barmby, N. J.	4
Barnes, J.	11
Barnes, P. S.	4
Barton, J.	1
Bassett, W. I.	8
Bastin, C. S.	12
Beardsley, P. A.	9
Beasley, A.	1
Beattie, T. K.	1
Beckham, D. R. J.	17
Becton, F.	2
Bedford, H.	1
Bell, C.	9
Bentley, R. T. F.	9
Bishop, S. M.	1
Blackburn, F.	1
Blissett, L.	3
Bloomer, S.	28
Bond, R.	2
Bonsor, A. G.	1
Bowden, E. R.	1
Bowers, J. W.	2
Bowles, S.	1
Bradford, G. R. W.	1
Bradford, J.	7
Bradley, W.	2
Bradshaw, F.	3
Brann, G.	1
Bridge, W. M.	1
Bridges, B. J.	1
Bridgett, A.	3
Brindle, T.	1
Britton, C. S.	1
Broadbent, P. F.	2
Broadis, I. A.	8
Brodie, J. B.	1
Bromley-Davenport, W.	2
Brook, E. F.	10
Brooking, T. D.	5
Brooks, J.	2
Broome, F. H.	3
Brown, A.	4
Brown, A. S.	1
Brown, G.	5
Brown, J.	3
Brown, W.	1
Buchan, C. M.	4
Bull, S. G.	4
Bullock, N.	2
Burgess, H.	4
Butcher, T.	3
Byrne, J. J.	8
Campbell, S. J.	1
Camsell, G. H.	18
Carter, H. S.	7
Carter, J. H.	4
Chadwick, E.	3
Chamberlain, M.	1
Chambers, H.	5
Channon, M. R.	21
Charlton, J.	6
Charlton, R.	49
Chenery, C. J.	1
Chivers, M.	13
Clarke, A. J.	10
Cobbold, W. N.	6
Cock, J. G.	2
Cole, A.	1
Cole, J. J.	7
Common, A.	2
Connelly, J. M.	7
Coppell, S. J.	7
Cotterill, G. H.	2
Cowans, G.	2
Crawford, R.	1
Crawshaw, T. H.	1
Crayston, W. J.	1
Creek, F. N. S.	1
Crooks, S. D.	7
Crouch, P. J.	12
Currey, E. S.	2
Currie, A. W.	3
Cursham, A. W.	2
Cursham, H. A.	5
Daft, H. B.	3
Davenport, J. K.	2
Davis, G.	1
Davis, H.	1
Day, S. H.	2
Dean, W. R.	18
Defoe, J. C.	3
Devey, J. H. G.	1
Dewhurst, F.	11
Dix, W. R.	1
Dixon, K. M.	4
Dixon, L. M.	1
Dorrell, A. R.	1
Douglas, B.	11
Drake, E. J.	6
Ducat, A.	1
Dunn, A. T. B.	2
Eastham, G.	2
Edwards, D.	5
Ehiogu, U.	1
Elliott, W. H.	3
Evans, R. E.	1
Ferdinand, L.	5
Ferdinand, R. G.	1
Finney, T.	30
Fleming, H. J.	9
Flowers, R.	10
Forman, Frank	1
Forman, Fred	3
Foster, R. E.	3
Fowler, R. B.	7
Francis, G. C. J.	3
Francis, T.	12
Freeman, B. C.	3
Froggatt, J.	2
Froggatt, R.	2
Galley, T.	1
Gascoigne, P. J.	10
Geary, F.	3
Gerrard, S. G.	12
Gibbins, W. V. T.	3
Gilliatt, W. E.	3
Goddard, P.	1
Goodall, J.	12
Goodyer, A. C.	1
Gosling, R. C.	2
Goulden, L. A.	4
Grainger, C.	3
Greaves, J.	44
Grovesnor, A. T.	2
Gunn, W.	1
Haines, J. T. W.	2
Hall, G. W.	9
Halse, H. J.	2
Hampson, J.	5
Hampton, H.	2
Hancocks, J.	2
Hardman, H. P.	1
Harris, S. S.	2
Hassall, H. W.	4
Hateley, M.	9
Haynes, J. N.	18
Hegan, K. E.	4
Henfrey, A. G.	2
Heskey, E. W.	5
Hilsdon, G. R.	14
Hine, E. W.	4
Hinton, A. T.	1
Hirst, D. E.	1
Hitchens, G. A.	5
Hobbis, H. H. F.	1
Hoddle, G.	8
Hodgetts, D.	1
Hodgson, G.	1
Holley, G. H.	8
Houghton, W. E.	5
Howell, R.	1
Hughes, E. W.	1
Hulme, J. H. A.	4
Hunt, G. S.	1
Hunt, R.	18
Hunter, N.	2
Hurst, G. C.	24
Ince, P. E. C.	2
Jack, D. N. B.	3
Jeffers, F.	1
Johnson, D. E.	6
Johnson, E.	2
Johnson, J. A.	2
Johnson, T. C. F.	5
Johnson, W. H.	1
Kail, E. I. L.	2
Kay, A. H.	1
Keegan, J. K.	21
Kelly, R.	8
Kennedy, R.	3
Kenyon-Slaney, W. S.	2
Keown, M. R.	2
Kevan, D. T.	8
Kidd, B.	1
King, L. B.	1
Kingsford, R. K.	1
Kirchen, A. J.	2
Kirton, W. J.	1
Lampard, F. J.	12
Langton, R.	1
Latchford, R. D.	5
Latheron, E. G.	1
Lawler, C.	1
Lawton, T.	22
Lee, F.	10
Lee, J.	1
Lee, R. M.	2
Lee, S.	2
Le Saux, G. P.	1
Lindley, T.	14
Lineker, G.	48
Lofthouse, J. M.	3
Lofthouse, N.	30
Hon. A. Lyttelton	1
Mabbutt, G.	1
Macdonald, M.	6
Mannion, W. J.	11
Mariner, P.	13
Marsh, R. W.	1
Matthews, S.	11
Matthews, V.	1
McCall, J.	1
McDermott, T.	3
McManaman, S.	3
Medley, L. D.	1
Melia, J.	1
Mercer, D. W.	1
Merson, P. C.	3
Milburn, J. E. T.	10
Miller, H. S.	1
Mills, G. R.	3
Milward, A.	3
Mitchell, C.	5
Moore, J.	1
Moore, R. F.	2
Moore, W. G. B.	2
Morren, T.	1
Morris, F.	1
Morris, J.	3
Mortensen, S. H.	23
Morton, J. R.	1
Mosforth, W.	3
Mullen, J.	6
Mullery, A. P.	1
Murphy, D. B	1
Neal, P. G.	5
Needham, E.	3
Nicholls, J.	1
Nicholson, W. E.	1
Nugent, D. J.	1
O'Grady, M.	3
Osborne, F. R.	3
Owen, M. J.	37
Own goals	27
Page, L. A.	1
Paine, T. L.	7
Palmer, C. L.	1
Parry, E. H.	1

Parry, R. A.	1
Pawson, F. W.	1
Payne, J.	2
Peacock, A.	3
Pearce, S.	5
Pearson, J. S.	5
Pearson, S. C.	5
Perry, W.	2
Peters, M.	20
Pickering, F.	5
Platt, D.	27
Pointer, R.	2
Quantrill, A.	1
Ramsay, A. E.	3
Revie, D. G.	4
Redknapp, J. F.	1
Reynolds, J.	3
Richardson, K. E.	2
Richardson, J. R.	2
Rigby, A.	3
Rimmer, E. J.	2
Roberts, F.	2
Roberts, H.	1
Roberts, W. T.	2
Robinson, J.	3
Robson, B.	26
Robson, R.	4
Rooney, W.	12
Rowley, J. F.	6
Royle, J.	2
Rutherford, J.	3
Sagar, C.	1
Sandilands, R. R.	3
Sansom, K.	1
Schofield, J.	1
Scholes, P.	14
Seed, J. M.	1
Settle, J.	6
Sewell, J.	3
Shackleton, L. F.	1
Sharp, J.	1
Shearer, A.	30
Shelton, A.	1
Shepherd, A.	2
Sheringham, E. P.	11
Simpson, J.	1
Smith, A.	1
Smith, A. M.	2
Smith, G. O.	11
Smith, Joe	1
Smith, J. R.	2
Smith, J. W.	4
Smith, R.	13
Smith, S.	1
Sorby, T. H.	1
Southgate, G.	2
Southworth, J.	3
Sparks, F. J.	3
Spence, J. W.	1
Spiksley, F.	5
Spilsbury, B. W.	5
Steele, F. C.	8
Stephenson, G. T.	2
Steven, T. M.	4
Stewart, J.	2
Stiles, N. P.	1
Storer, H.	1
Stone, S. B.	2
Summerbee, M. G.	1
Tambling, R. V.	1
Taylor, P. J.	2
Taylor, T.	16
Terry, J. G.	3
Thompson, P. B.	1
Thornewell, G.	1
Tilson, S. F.	6
Townley, W. J.	2
Tueart, D.	2
Vassell, D.	6
Vaughton, O. H.	6
Veitch, J. G.	3
Viollet, D. S.	1
Waddle, C. R.	6
Walker, W. H.	9
Wall, G.	2
Wallace, D.	1
Walsh, P.	1
Waring, T.	4
Warren, B.	2
Watson, D. V.	4
Watson, V. M.	4
Webb, G. W.	1
Webb, N.	4
Wedlock, W. J.	2
Weller, K.	1
Welsh, D.	1
Whateley, O.	2
Wheldon, G. F.	6
Whitfield, H.	1
Wignall, F.	2
Wilkes, A.	1
Wilkins, R. G.	3
Willingham, C. K.	1
Wilshaw, D. J.	10
Wilson, G. P.	1
Winckworth, W. N.	1
Windridge, J. E.	7
Wise, D. F.	1
Withe, P.	1
Wollaston, C. H. R.	1
Wood, H.	1
Woodcock, T.	16
Woodhall, G.	1
Woodward, V. J.	29
Worrall, F.	2
Worthington, F. S.	2
Wright, I. E.	9
Wright, M.	1
Wright, W. A.	3
Wright-Phillips, S. C.	1
Wylie, J. G.	1
Yates, J.	3

NORTHERN IRELAND

Anderson, T.	4
Armstrong, G.	12
Bambrick, J.	12
Barr, H. H.	1
Barron, H.	3
Best, G.	9
Bingham, W. L.	10
Black, K.	1
Blanchflower, D.	2
Blanchflower, J.	1
Brennan, B.	1
Brennan, R. A.	1
Brotherston, N.	3
Brown, J.	1
Browne, F.	2
Campbell, J.	1
Campbell, W. G.	1
Casey, T.	2
Caskey, W.	1
Cassidy, T.	1
Chambers, J.	3
Clarke, C. J.	13
Clements, D.	2
Cochrane, T.	1
Condy, J.	1
Connor, M. J.	1
Coulter, J.	1
Croft, T.	1
Crone, W.	1
Crossan, E.	1
Crossan, J. A.	10
Curran, S.	2
Cush, W. W.	5
Dalton, W.	4
D'Arcy, S. D.	1
Darling, J.	1
Davey, H. H.	1
Davis, S.	1
Davis, T. L.	1
Dill, A. H.	1
Doherty, L.	1
Doherty, P. D.	3
Dougan, A. D.	8
Dowie, I.	12
Dunne, J.	4
Elder, A. R.	1
Elliott, S.	4
Emerson, W.	1
English, S.	1
Feeney, W.	1
Feeney, W. J.	2
Ferguson, W.	1
Ferris, J.	1
Ferris, R. O.	1
Finney, T.	2
Gaffkin, J.	4
Gara, A.	3
Gaukrodger, G.	1
Gibb, J. T.	2
Gibb, T. J.	1
Gibson, W.	1
Gillespie, K. R.	2
Gillespie, W.	13
Goodall, A. L.	2
Griffin, D. J.	1
Gray, P.	6
Halligan, W.	1
Hamill, M.	1
Hamilton, B.	4
Hamilton, W. R.	5
Hannon, D. J.	1
Harkin, J. T.	2
Harvey, M.	3
Healy, D. J.	29
Hill, C. F.	1
Hughes, M. E.	5
Humphries, W.	1
Hunter, A. (*Distillery*)	1
Hunter, A. (*Blackburn R*)	1
Hunter, B. V.	1
Irvine, R. W.	3
Irvine, W. J.	8
Johnston, H.	2
Johnston, S.	2
Johnston, W. C.	1
Jones, S.	1
Jones, S. (*Crewe Alex*)	1
Jones, J.	1
Kelly, J.	4
Kernaghan, N.	2
Kirwan, J.	2
Lacey, W.	3
Lafferty, K.	1
Lemon, J.	2
Lennon, N. F.	2
Lockhart, N.	3
Lomas, S. M.	3
Magilton, J.	5
Mahood, J.	2
Martin, D. K.	3
Maxwell, J.	2
McAdams, W. J.	7
McAllen, J.	1
Mcauley, J. L.	1
McCann, G. S.	1
McCartney, G.	1
McCandless, J.	2
McCandless, W.	1
McCaw, J. H.	1
McClelland, J.	1
McCluggage, A.	2
McCracken, W.	1
McCrory, S.	1
McCurdy, C.	1
McDonald, A.	3
McGarry, J. K.	1
McGrath, R. C.	4
McIlroy, J.	10
McIlroy, S. B.	5
McKenzie, H	1
McKnight, J.	2
McLaughlin, J. C.	6
McMahon, G. J.	2
McMordie, A. S.	3
McMorran, E. J.	4
McParland, P. J.	10
McWha, W. B. R.	1
Meldon, P. A	1
Mercer, J. T.	1
Millar, W.	1
Milligan, D.	1
Milne, R. G.	2
Molyneux, T. B.	1
Moreland, V.	1
Morgan, S.	3
Morrow, S. J.	1
Morrow, W. J.	1
Mulryne, P. P.	3
Murdock, C. J.	1
Murphy, N.	1
Neill, W. J. T.	2
Nelson, S.	1
Nicholl, C. J.	3
Nicholl, J. M.	1
Nicholson, J. J.	6
O'Boyle, G.	1
O'Hagan, C.	2
O'Kane, W. J.	1
O'Neill, J.	2
O'Neill, M. A.	4
O'Neill, M. H.	8
Own goals	6
Patterson, D. J.	1
Peacock, R.	2
Peden, J.	7
Penney, S.	2
Pyper, James	2
Pyper, John	1
Quinn, J. M.	12
Quinn, S. J.	4
Reynolds, J.	1
Rowland, K.	1
Rowley, R. W. M.	2
Rushe, F.	1
Sheridan, J.	2
Sherrard, J.	1
Sherrard, W. C.	2
Simpson, W. J.	5
Sloan, H. A. de B.	4
Smyth, S.	5
Spence, D. W.	3
Sproule, I.	1
Stanfield, O. M.	11
Stevenson, A. E.	5
Stewart, I.	2
Taggart, G. P.	7
Thompson, F. W.	2
Torrans, S.	1
Tully, C. P.	3
Turner, A.	1
Walker, J.	1
Walsh, D. J.	5
Welsh, E.	1
Whiteside, N.	9

Whiteside, T.	1
Whitley, Jeff	2
Williams, J. R.	1
Williams, M. S.	1
Williamson, J.	1
Wilson, D. J.	1
Wilson, K. J.	6
Wilson, S. J.	7
Wilton, J. M.	2
Young, S.	1

N.B. In 1914 Young goal should be credited to Gillespie W v Wales

SCOTLAND

Aitken, R. (*Celtic*)	1
Aitken, R. (*Dumbarton*)	1
Aitkenhead, W. A. C.	2
Alexander, D.	1
Allan, D. S.	4
Allan, J.	2
Anderson, F.	1
Anderson, W.	4
Andrews, P.	1
Archibald, A.	1
Archibald, S.	4
Baird, D.	2
Baird, J. C.	2
Baird, S.	2
Bannon, E.	1
Barbour, A.	1
Barker, J. B.	4
Battles, B. Jr	1
Bauld, W.	2
Baxter, J. C.	3
Beattie, C.	1
Bell, J.	5
Bennett, A.	2
Berry, D.	1
Bett, J.	1
Beveridge, W. W.	1
Black, A.	3
Black, D.	1
Bone, J.	1
Booth, S.	6
Boyd, K	5
Boyd, R.	2
Boyd, T.	1
Boyd, W. G.	1
Brackenridge, T.	1
Brand, R.	8
Brazil, A.	1
Bremner, W. J.	3
Brown, A. D.	6
Buchanan, P. S.	1
Buchanan, R.	1
Buckley, P.	1
Buick, A.	2
Burke, C.	2
Burley, C. W.	3
Burns, K.	1
Cairns, T.	1
Caldwell, G.	2
Calderwood, C.	1
Calderwood, R.	2
Caldow, E.	4
Cameron, C.	2
Campbell, C.	1
Campbell, John (*Celtic*)	5
Campbell, John (*Rangers*)	4
Campbell, J. (*South Western*)	1
Campbell, P.	2
Campbell, R.	1
Cassidy, J.	1
Chalmers, S.	3
Chambers, T.	1
Cheyne, A. G.	4
Christie, A. J.	1
Clunas, W. L.	1
Collins, J.	12
Collins, R. Y.	10
Combe, J. R.	1
Conn, A.	1
Cooper, D.	6
Craig, J.	1
Craig, T.	1
Crawford, S.	4
Cunningham, A. N.	5
Curran, H. P.	1
Dailly, C.	6
Dalglish, K.	30
Davidson, D.	1
Davidson, J. A.	1
Delaney, J.	3
Devine, A.	1
Dewar, G.	1
Dewar, N.	4
Dickov, P.	1
Dickson, W.	4
Divers, J.	1
Dobie, R. S.	1
Docherty, T. H.	1
Dodds, D.	1
Dodds, W.	7
Donaldson, A.	1
Donnachie, J.	1
Dougall, J.	1
Drummond, J.	2
Dunbar, M.	1
Duncan, D.	7
Duncan, D. M.	1
Duncan, J.	1
Dunn, J.	2
Durie, G. S.	7
Easson, J. F.	1
Elliott, M. S.	1
Ellis, J.	1
Ferguson, B.	2
Ferguson, J.	6
Fernie, W.	1
Fitchie, T. T.	1
Flavell, R.	2
Fleming, C.	2
Fleming, J. W.	3
Fletcher, D.	4
Fraser, M. J. E.	3
Freedman, D. A.	1
Gallacher, H. K.	23
Gallacher, K. W.	9
Gallacher, P.	1
Galt, J. H.	1
Gemmell, T. (*St Mirren*)	1
Gemmell, T. (*Celtic*)	1
Gemmill, A.	8
Gemmill, S.	1
Gibb, W.	1
Gibson, D. W.	3
Gibson, J. D.	1
Gibson, N.	1
Gillespie, Jas.	3
Gillick, T.	3
Gilzean, A. J.	12
Gossland, J.	2
Goudie, J.	1
Gough, C. R.	6
Gourlay, J.	1
Graham, A.	2
Graham, G.	3
Gray, A.	7
Gray, E.	3
Gray, F.	1
Greig, J.	3
Groves, W.	4
Hamilton, G.	4
Hamilton, J. (*Queen's Park*)	3
Hamilton, R. C.	15
Harper, J. M.	2
Hartley, P. J.	1
Harrower, W.	5
Hartford, R. A.	4
Heggie, C. W	4
Henderson, J. G.	1
Henderson, W.	5
Hendry, E. C. J.	3
Herd, D. G.	3
Herd, G.	1
Hewie, J. D.	2
Higgins, A. (*Newcastle U*)	1
Higgins, A. (*Kilmarnock*)	4
Highet, T. C.	1
Holt, G.J.	1
Holton, J. A.	2
Hopkin, D.	2
Houliston, W.	2
Howie, H.	1
Howie, J.	2
Hughes, J.	1
Hunter, W.	1
Hutchison, D.	6
Hutchison, T.	1
Hutton, J.	1
Hyslop, T.	1
Imrie, W. N.	1
Jackson, A.	8
Jackson, C.	1
Jackson, D.	4
James, A. W.	4
Jardine, A.	1
Jenkinson, T.	1
Jess, E.	2
Johnston, A.	2
Johnston, L. H.	1
Johnston, M.	14
Johnstone, D.	2
Johnstone, J.	4
Johnstone, Jas.	1
Johnstone, R.	10
Johnstone, W.	1
Jordan, J.	11
Kay, J. L.	5
Keillor, A.	3
Kelly, J.	1
Kelso, R.	1
Ker, G.	10
King, A.	1
King, J.	1
Kinnear, D.	1
Kyle, K.	1
Lambert, P.	1
Lambie, J.	1
Lambie, W. A.	5
Lang, J. J.	2
Latta, A.	2
Law, D.	30
Leggat, G.	8
Lennie, W.	1
Lennox, R.	3
Liddell, W.	6
Lindsay, J.	6
Linwood, A. B.	1
Logan, J.	1
Lorimer, P.	4
Love, A.	1
Low, J. (*Cambuslang*)	1
Lowe, J. (*St Bernards*)	1
Macari, L.	5
MacDougall, E. J.	3
MacFarlane, A.	1
MacLeod, M.	1
Mackay, D. C.	4
Mackay, G.	1
MacKenzie, J. A.	1
MacKinnon, W. W.	5
Madden, J.	5
Maloney, S.	1
Marshall, H.	1
Marshall, J.	1
Mason, J.	4
Massie, A.	1
Masson, D. S.	5
McAdam, J.	1
McAllister, G.	5
McAulay, J. D.	1
McAvennie, F.	1
McCall, J.	1
McCall, S. M.	1
McCalliog, J.	1
McCallum, N.	1
McCann, N.	3
McClair, B. J.	2
McCoist, A.	19
McColl, R. S.	13
McCulloch, D.	3
McDougall, J.	4
McFadden, J.	9
McFadyen, W.	2
McGhee, M.	2
McGinlay, J.	4
McGregor, J.	1
McGrory, J.	6
McGuire, W.	1
McInally, A.	3
McInnes, T.	2
McKie, J.	2
McKimmie, S.	1
McKinlay, W.	4
McKinnon, A.	1
McKinnon, R.	1
McLaren, A.	4
McLaren, J.	1
McLean, A.	1
McLean, T.	1
McLintock, F.	1
McMahon, A.	6
McMenemy, J.	5
McMillan, I. L.	2
McNeill, W.	3
McNiel, H.	5
McPhail, J.	3
McPhail, R.	7
McPherson, J.	5
McPherson, J. (*Vale of Leven*)	1
McPherson, R.	1
McQueen, G.	5
McStay, P.	9
McSwegan, G.	1
Meiklejohn, D. D.	3
Millar, J.	2
Miller, K.	9
Miller, T.	2
Miller, W.	1
Mitchell, R. C.	1
Morgan, W.	1
Morris, D.	1
Morris, H.	3
Morton, A. L.	5
Mudie, J. K.	9
Mulhall, G.	1
Munro, A. D.	1
Munro, N.	2
Murdoch, R.	5
Murphy, F.	1
Murray, J.	1
Napier, C. E.	3
Narey, D.	1
Naysmith, G. A.	1
Neil, R. G.	2
Nevin, P. K. F.	5
Nicholas, C.	5
Nisbet, J.	2
O'Connor, G.	4
O'Donnell, F.	2
O'Hare, J.	5

Ormond, W. E.	2
O'Rourke, F.	1
Orr, R.	1
Orr, T.	1
Oswald, J.	1
Own goals	17
Parlane, D.	1
Paul, H. McD.	2
Paul, W.	5
Pettigrew, W.	2
Provan, D.	1
Quashie, N. F.	1
Quinn, J.	7
Quinn, P.	1
Rankin, G.	2
Rankin, R.	2
Reid, W.	4
Reilly, L.	22
Renny-Tailyour, H. W.	1
Richmond, J. T.	1
Ring, T.	2
Rioch, B. D.	6
Ritchie, J.	1
Ritchie, P. S.	1
Robertson, A.	2
Robertson, J.	3
Robertson, J. N.	8
Robertson, J. T.	2
Robertson, T.	1
Robertson, W.	1
Russell, D.	1
Scott, A. S.	5
Sellar, W.	4
Sharp, G.	1
Shaw, F. W.	1
Shearer, D.	2
Simpson, J.	1
Smith, A.	5
Smith, G.	4
Smith, J.	1
Smith, John	13
Somerville, G.	1
Souness, G. J.	4
Speedie, F.	2
St John, I.	9
Steel, W.	12
Stein, C.	10
Stevenson, G.	4
Stewart, A.	1
Stewart, R.	1
Stewart, W. E.	1
Strachan, G.	5
Sturrock, P.	3
Taylor, J. D.	1
Templeton, R.	1
Thompson, S.	3
Thomson, A.	1
Thomson, C.	4
Thomson, R.	1
Thomson, W.	1
Thornton, W.	1
Waddell, T. S.	1
Waddell, W.	6
Walker, J.	2
Walker, R.	7
Walker, T.	9
Wallace, I. A.	1
Wark, J.	7
Watson, J. A. K.	1
Watt, F.	2
Watt, W. W.	1
Webster, A.	1
Weir, A.	1
Weir, D.	1
Weir, J. B.	2
White, J. A.	3
Wilkie, L.	1
Wilson, A.	2
Wilson, A. N.	13
Wilson, D. (*Queen's Park*)	2
Wilson, D. (*Rangers*)	9
Wilson, H.	1
Wylie, T. G.	1
Young, A.	5

WALES

Allchurch, I. J.	23
Allen, M.	3
Astley, D. J.	12
Atherton, R. W.	2
Bale, G.	2
Bamford, T.	1
Barnes, W.	1
Bellamy, C. D.	13
Blackmore, C. G.	1
Blake, N. A.	4
Bodin, P. J.	3
Boulter, L. M.	1
Bowdler, J. C. H.	3
Bowen, D. L.	1
Bowen, M.	3
Boyle, T.	1
Bryan, T.	1
Burgess, W. A. R.	1
Burke, T.	1
Butler, W. T.	1
Chapman, T.	2
Charles, J.	1
Charles, M.	6
Charles, W. J.	15
Clarke, R. J.	5
Coleman, C.	4
Collier, D. J.	1
Crosse, K.	1
Cumner, R. H.	1
Curtis, A.	6
Curtis, E. R.	3
Davies, D. W.	1
Davies, E. Lloyd	1
Davies, G.	2
Davies, L. S.	6
Davies, R. T.	9
Davies, R. W.	6
Davies, Simon	5
Davies, Stanley	5
Davies, W.	6
Davies, W. H.	1
Davies, William	5
Davis, W. O.	1
Deacy, N.	4
Doughty, J.	6
Doughty, R.	2
Durban, A.	2
Dwyer, P.	2
Earnshaw, R.	12
Edwards, G.	2
Edwards, R. I.	4
England, H. M.	4
Evans, I.	1
Evans, J.	1
Evans, R. E.	2
Evans, W.	1
Eyton-Jones, J. A.	1
Flynn, B.	7
Ford, T.	23
Foulkes, W. I.	1
Fowler, J.	3
Giles, D.	2
Giggs, R. J.	12
Glover, E. M.	7
Godfrey, B. C.	2
Green, A. W.	3
Griffiths, A. T.	6
Griffiths, M. W.	2
Griffiths, T. P.	3
Harris, C. S.	1
Hartson, J.	14
Hersee, R.	1
Hewitt, R.	1
Hockey, T.	1
Hodges, G.	2
Hole, W. J.	1
Hopkins, I. J.	2
Horne, B.	2
Howell, E. G.	3
Hughes, L. M.	16
James, E.	2
James, L.	10
James, R.	7
Jarrett, R. H.	3
Jenkyns, C. A.	1
Jones, A.	1
Jones, Bryn	6
Jones, B. S.	2
Jones, Cliff	16
Jones, C. W.	1
Jones, D. E.	1
Jones, Evan	1
Jones, H.	1
Jones, I.	1
Jones, J. L.	1
Jones, J. O.	1
Jones, J. P.	1
Jones, Leslie J.	1
Jones, R. A.	2
Jones, W. L.	6
Keenor, F. C.	2
Koumas, J.	5
Krzywicki, R. L.	1
Leek, K.	5
Lewis, B.	4
Lewis, D. M.	2
Lewis, W.	8
Lewis, W. L.	3
Llewelyn, C. M	1
Lovell, S.	1
Lowrie, G.	2
Mahoney, J. F.	1
Mays, A. W.	1
Medwin, T. C.	6
Melville, A. K	3
Meredith, W. H.	11
Mills, T. J.	1
Moore, G.	1
Morgan, J. R.	2
Morgan-Owen, H.	1
Morgan-Owen, M. M.	2
Morris, A. G.	9
Morris, H.	2
Morris, R.	1
Morris, S.	2
Nicholas, P.	2
O'Callaghan, E.	3
O'Sullivan, P. A.	1
Owen, G.	2
Owen, W.	4
Owen, W. P.	6
Own goals	13
Palmer, D.	3
Parry, P. I.	1
Parry, T. D.	3
Paul, R.	1
Peake, E.	1
Pembridge, M.	6
Perry, E.	1
Phillips, C.	5
Phillips, D.	2
Powell, A.	1
Powell, D.	1
Price, J.	4
Price, P.	1
Pryce-Jones, W. E.	3
Pugh, D. H.	2
Reece, G. I.	2
Rees, R. R.	3
Richards, R. W.	1
Roach, J.	2
Robbins, W. W.	4
Roberts, J. (*Corwen*)	1
Roberts, Jas.	1
Roberts, P. S.	1
Roberts, R. (*Druids*)	1
Roberts, W. (*Llangollen*)	2
Roberts, W. (*Wrexham*)	1
Roberts, W. H.	1
Robinson, C. P.	1
Robinson, J. R. C.	3
Rush, I.	28
Russell, M. R.	1
Sabine, H. W.	1
Saunders, D.	22
Savage, R. W.	2
Shaw, E. G.	2
Sisson, H.	4
Slatter, N.	2
Smallman, D. P.	1
Speed, G. A.	7
Symons, C. J.	2
Tapscott, D. R.	4
Taylor, G. K.	1
Thomas, M.	4
Thomas, T.	1
Toshack, J. B.	12
Trainer, H.	2
Vaughan, John	2
Vernon, T. R.	8
Vizard, E. T.	1
Walsh, I.	7
Warren, F. W.	3
Watkins, W. M.	4
Wilding, J.	4
Williams, A.	1
Williams, D. R.	2
Williams, G. E.	1
Williams, G. G.	1
Williams, W.	1
Woosnam, A. P.	3
Wynn, G. A.	1
Yorath, T. C.	2
Young, E.	1

REPUBLIC OF IRELAND

Aldridge, J.	19
Ambrose, P.	1
Anderson, J.	1
Barrett, G.	2
Bermingham, P.	1
Bradshaw, P.	4
Brady, L.	9
Breen, G.	7
Brown, J.	1
Byrne, D.	1
Byrne, J.	4
Cantwell, J.	14
Carey, J.	3
Carroll, T.	1
Cascarino, A.	19
Coad, P.	3

Connolly, D. J.	9
Conroy, T.	2
Conway, J.	3
Coyne, T.	6
Cummins, G.	5
Curtis, D.	8
Daly, G.	13
Davis, T.	4
Dempsey, J.	1
Dennehy, M.	2
Doherty, G. M. T.	4
Donnelly, J.	4
Donnelly, T.	1
Doyle, K. E.	3
Duff, D. A.	7
Duffy, B.	1
Duggan, H.	1
Dunne, J.	13
Dunne, L.	1
Dunne, R. P.	5
Eglington, T.	2
Elliott, S. W.	1
Ellis, P.	1
Fagan, F.	5
Fallon, S.	2
Fallon, W.	2
Farrell, P.	3
Finnan, S.	1
Fitzgerald, P.	2
Fitzgerald, J.	1
Fitzsimons, A.	7
Flood, J. J.	4
Fogarty, A.	3
Foley, D.	2
Fullam, J.	1
Fullam, R.	1
Galvin, A.	1
Gavin, J.	2
Geoghegan, M.	2
Giles, J.	5
Givens, D.	19
Glynn, D.	1
Grealish, T.	8
Grimes, A. A.	1
Hale, A.	2
Hand, E.	2
Harte, I. P.	11
Haverty, J.	3
Healy, C.	1
Holland, M. R.	5
Holmes, J.	1
Horlacher, A.	2
Houghton, R.	6
Hughton, C.	1
Hurley, C.	2
Ireland, S. J.	3
Irwin, D.	4
Jordan, D.	1
Kavanagh, G. A.	1
Keane, R. D.	29
Keane, R. M.	9
Kelly, D.	9
Kelly, G.	2
Kelly, J.	2
Kennedy, M.	4
Kernaghan, A. N.	1
Kilbane, K. D.	7
Kinsella, M. A.	3
Lacey, W.	1
Lawrenson, M.	5
Leech, M.	2
Long, S. P.	1
McAteer, J. W.	3
McCann, J.	1
McCarthy, M.	2
McEvoy, A.	6
McGee, P.	4
McGrath, P.	8
McLoughlin, A. F.	2
McPhail, S. J. P.	1
Mancini, T.	1
Martin, C.	6
Martin, M.	4
Miller, L. W. P.	1
Mooney, J.	1
Moore, P.	7
Moran, K.	6
Morrison, C. H.	9
Moroney, T.	1
Mulligan, P.	1
O'Brien, A. J.	1
O'Callaghan, K.	1
O'Connor, T.	2
O'Farrell, F.	2
O'Flanagan, K.	3
O'Keefe, E.	1
O'Leary, D. A.	1
O'Neill, F.	1
O'Neill, K. P.	4
O'Reilly, J. (*Brideville*)	2
O'Reilly, J. (*Cork*)	1
O'Shea, J. F.	1
Own goals	10
Quinn, N.	21
Reid, A. M.	4
Reid, S. J.	2
Ringstead, A.	7
Robinson, M.	4
Rogers, E.	5
Ryan, G.	1
Ryan, R.	3
Sheedy, K.	9
Sheridan, J.	5
Slaven, B.	1
Sloan, J.	1
Squires, J.	1
Stapleton, F.	20
Staunton, S.	7
Strahan, J.	1
Sullivan, J.	1
Townsend, A. D.	7
Treacy, R.	5
Touhy, L.	4
Waddock, G.	3
Walsh, D.	5
Walsh, M.	3
Waters, J.	1
White, J. J.	2
Whelan, R.	3

Robbie Keane (Tottenham Hotspur). Republic of Ireland's top marksman with 29 goals for his country. (Manu Fernandez/AP/PA Photos)

SOUTH AMERICA

COPA LIBERTADORES 2006

QUARTER-FINALS SECOND LEG
Internacional 2, LDU Quito 0
Libertad 3, River Plate 1
Sao Paulo 1, Estudiantes 0
Sao Paulo won 4-3 on penalties.
Velez Sarsfield 1, Guadalajara 2

SEMI-FINALS FIRST LEG
Guadalajara 0, Sao Paulo 1
Libertad 0, Internacional 0

SEMI-FINALS SECOND LEG
Sao Paulo 3, Guadalajara 0
Internacional 2, Libertad 0

FINAL FIRST LEG
Sao Paulo 1, Internacional 2

FINAL SECOND LEG
Internazional 2, Sao Paulo 2

COPA LIBERTADORES 2007

PRELIMINARY ROUND FIRST LEG
America (Mexico) 5, Sporting Cristal 0
Velez Sarsfield 3, Danubio 0
Dep Tachira 1, Dep Tolima 2
Blooming 0, Santos 1
Tacuary 1, EDU Quito 1
Cobreloa 0, Parana 2

PRELIMINARY ROUND SECOND LEG
Sporting Cristal 2, America (Mexico) 1
Danubio 1, Velez Sarsfield 2
Dep Tolima 2, Dep Tachira 0
Santos 5, Blooming 0
EDU Quito 3, Tacuary 0
Parana 1, Cobreloa 1

GROUP 1	P	W	D	L	F	A	Pts
Libertad	6	4	1	1	9	4	13
America (Mexico)	6	4	0	2	12	10	12
Banfield	6	3	0	3	8	8	9
El Nacional	6	0	1	5	4	11	1

GROUP 2	P	W	D	L	F	A	Pts
Necaxa	6	4	0	2	9	7	12
Sao Paulo	6	3	2	1	11	4	11
Audax Italiano	6	3	2	1	8	6	11
Alianza	6	0	0	6	2	13	0

GROUP 3	P	W	D	L	F	A	Pts
Gremio	6	3	1	2	4	4	10
Cucuta	6	2	3	1	9	7	9
Dep Tolima	6	2	1	3	5	6	7
Cerro Porteno	6	2	1	3	4	5	7

GROUP 4	P	W	D	L	F	A	Pts
Velez Sarsfield	6	3	2	1	6	3	11
Nacional (Uru)	6	3	1	2	9	5	10
Internacional	6	3	1	2	7	7	10
Emelec	6	1	0	5	3	10	3

GROUP 5	P	W	D	L	F	A	Pts
Flamengo	6	5	1	0	10	4	16
Parana	6	3	0	3	9	8	9
Real Potosi	6	1	3	2	8	9	6
UA Maracaibo	6	0	2	4	8	14	2

GROUP 6	P	W	D	L	F	A	Pts
Colo Colo	6	3	0	3	12	7	9
Caracas	6	3	0	3	7	10	9
LDU Quito	6	2	2	2	7	8	8
River Plate	6	2	2	2	5	6	8

GROUP 7	P	W	D	L	F	A	Pts
Toluca	6	4	0	2	10	6	12
Boca Juniors	6	3	1	2	11	5	10
Cienciano	6	3	0	3	12	9	9
Bolivar	6	1	1	4	5	18	4

GROUP 8	P	W	D	L	F	A	Pts
Santos	6	6	0	0	12	1	18
Defensor	6	3	0	3	8	7	9
Gimnasia	6	3	0	3	9	10	9
Dep Pasto	6	0	0	6	3	14	0

SECOND ROUND FIRST LEG
America (Mexico) 3, Colo Colo 0
Sao Paulo 1, Gremio 0
Defensor 3, Flamengo 0
Boca Juniors 3, Velez Sarsfield 0
Caracas 2, Santos 2
Cucuta 5, Toluca 1
Parana 1, Libertad 2
Nacional (Uru) 3, Necaxa 2

SECOND ROUND SECOND LEG
Colo Colo 2, America (Mexico) 11
Gremio 2, Sao Paulo 0
Flamengo 2, Defensor 0
Velez Sarsfield 3, Boca Juniors 1
Santos 3, Caracas 2
Toluca 2, Cucuta 0
Libertad 1, Parana 1
Necaxa 0, Nacional (Uru) 1

QUARTER-FINALS FIRST LEG
Cucuta 2, Nacional (Uru) 0
America (Mexico) 0, Santos 0
Defensor 2, Gremio 0
Boca Juniors 1, Libertad 1

QUARTER-FINALS SECOND LEG
Nacional (Uru) 2, Cucuta 2
Santos 2, America (Mexico) 1
Gremio 2, Defensor 0
Libertad 0, Boca Juniors 2

SEMI-FINALS
Gremio 2, Santos 0
Santos 3, Gremio 1
Cucuta 3, Boca Juniors 1
Boca Juniors 3, Cucuta 0

FINAL FIRST LEG
Boca Juniors 3, Gremio 0

FINAL SECOND LEG
Gremio 0, Boca Juniors 2

COPA SUDAMERICANA 2006

FIRST PHASE
Byes to second phase:
Boca Juniors (holders), River Plate, Gimnasia, Toluca, Pachuca, Alajuelense.

SECTION 1 (ARGENTINA)
San Lorenzo 2, Banfield 1
Banfield 0, San Lorenzo 0
Lanus 2, Velez Sarsfield 0
Velez Sarsfield 0, Lanus 1

SECTION 2 (BRAZIL)
Vasco da Gama 0, Corinthians 1
Corinthians 3, Vasco da Gama 1
Santos 1, Cruzeiro 0
Cruzeiro 1, Santos 0
Santos won 4-3 on penalties.
Parana 1, Paranaense 3
Paranaense 1, Parana 0
Botafogo 1, Fluminense 1
Fluminense 1, Botafogo 1
Fluminense won 4-2 on penalties.

SECTION 3 (CHILE, PERU)
First Stage
Huachipato 1, Colo Colo 2
Colo Colo 1, Huachipato 2
Colo Colo won 5-3 on penalties.
Coronel 1, Univ San Martin 0
Univ San Martin 3, Coronel 2

Second Stage
Coronel 2, Colo Colo 1
Colo Colo 1, Coronel 0

SECTION 4 (BOLIVIA, ECUADOR)
First Stage
LDU Quito 2, El Nacional 3
El Nacional 1, LDU Quito 1
Universitario 2, Bolivar 2
Bolivar 2, Universitario 3

Second Stage
Universitario 1, El Nacional 3
El Nacional 2, Universitario 1

SECTION 5 (PARAGUAY, URUGUAY)
First Stage
Central Espanol 0, Nacional 1
Nacional 0, Central Espanol 0
Libertad 3, Cerro Porteno 1
Cerro Porteno 0, Libertad 1

Second Stage
Libertad 1, Nacional 2
Nacional 2, Libertad 1

SECTION 6 (COLOMBIA, VENEZUELA)
First Stage
Mineros 3, Carabobo 0
Carabobo 1, Mineros 3
Tolima 3, Indep Medellin 1
Indep Medellin 1, Tolima 1

Second Stage
Tolima 0, Mineros 0
Mineros 2, Tolima 2

SECOND PHASE
Tolima 2, Pachuca 1
Pachuca 5, Tolima 1
Toluca 1, El Nacional 0
El Nacional 0, Toluca 2
Corinthians 0, Lanus 0
Lanus 4, Corinthians 2
San Lorenzo 3, Santos 0
Santos 1, San Lorenzo 0
River Plate 0, Paranaense 1
Paranaense 2, River Plate 2
Fluminense 1, Gimnasia 1
Gimnasia 2, Fluminense 0
Nacional 2, Boca Juniors 1
Boca Juniors 2, Nacional 1
Nacional won 3-1 on penalties.
Alajuelense 0, Colo Colo 4
Colo Colo 7, Alajuelense 2

QUARTER-FINALS
Lanus 0, Pachuca 3
Pachuca 2, Lanus 2
Nacional 1, Paranaense 2
Paranaense 4, Nacional 1
Colo Colo 4, Gimnasia 1
Abandoned 86 minutes; Gimnasia player hit by missile.
Gimnasia 0, Colo Colo 2
San Lorenzo 3, Toluca 1
Toluca 2, San Lorenzo 0

SEMI-FINALS FIRST LEG
Paranaense 0, Pachuca 1
Colo Colo 2, Toluca 1

SEMI-FINALS SECOND LEG
Pachuca 4, Paranaense 1
Toluca 0, Colo Colo 2

FINALS
Pachuca 1, Colo Colo 1
Colo Colo 1, Pachuca 2

COPA AMERICA 2007

GROUP A
Peru 3, Uruguay 0
Venezuela 2, Bolivia 2
Uruguay 1, Bolivia 0
Venezuela 2, Peru 0
Bolivia 2, Peru 2
Venezuela 0, Uruguay 0

	P	W	D	L	F	A	Pts
Venezuela	3	1	2	0	4	2	5
Peru	3	1	1	1	5	4	5
Uruguay	3	1	1	1	1	3	4
Bolivia	3	0	2	1	4	5	2

GROUP B
Chile 2, Ecuador 2
Mexico 2, Brazil 0
Brazil 3, Chile 0
Mexico 2, Ecuador 1
Mexico 0, Chile 0
Brazil 1, Ecuador 0

	P	W	D	L	F	A	Pts
Mexico	3	2	1	0	4	1	7
Brazil	3	2	0	1	4	2	6
Chile	3	1	1	1	3	5	4
Ecuador	3	0	0	3	3	6	0

GROUP C
Paraguay 5, Colombia 0
Argentina 4, USA 1
Paraguay 3, USA 1
Argentina 4, Colombia 2
Colombia 1, USA 0
Argentina 1, Paraguay 0

	P	W	D	L	F	A	Pts
Argentina	3	3	0	0	9	3	9
Paraguay	3	2	0	1	8	2	6
Colombia	3	1	0	2	3	9	3
USA	3	0	0	3	2	8	0

QUARTER-FINALS
Venezuela 1, Uruguay 4
Brazil 6, Chile 1
Mexico 6, Paraguay 0
Argentina 4, Peru 0

SEMI-FINALS
Uruguay 2, Brazil 2
aet; Brazil won 5-4 on penalties.
Argentina 3, Mexico 0

THIRD PLACE
Uruguay 1, Mexico 3

FINAL
Brazil 3, Argentina 0

NORTH AMERICA

MAJOR LEAGUE SOCCER 2006

EASTERN DIVISION

	P	W	D	L	F	A	Pts
DC United	32	15	10	7	52	38	55
New England Rev	32	12	12	8	39	35	48
Chicago Fire	32	13	8	11	43	41	47
New York Red Bulls	32	9	12	11	41	41	39
Kansas City Wizards	32	10	8	14	43	45	38
Columbus Crew	32	8	9	15	30	42	33

New York Red Bulls formerly New York/New Jersey MetroStars.

WESTERN DIVISION

	P	W	D	L	F	A	Pts
FC Dallas	32	16	4	12	48	44	52
Houston Dynamo	32	11	13	8	44	40	46
Chivas USA	32	10	13	9	45	42	43
Colorado Rapids	32	11	8	13	36	49	41
Los Angeles Galaxy	32	11	6	15	37	37	39
Real Salt Lake	32	10	9	13	45	49	39

Houston Dynamo relocated from San Jose Earthquakes.

SEMI-FINALS EASTERN DIVISION
New York Red Bulls 0, DC United 1
Chicago Fire 1, New England Rev 0
New England Rev 2, Chicago Fire 1
aet; New England Rev won 4-2 on penalties.
DC United 1, New York Red Bulls 1

SEMI-FINALS WESTERN DIVISION
Colorado Rapids 1, FC Dallas 2
Chivas USA 2, Houston Dynamo 1
FC Dallas 2, Colorado Rapids 3
aet; Colorado Rapids won 5-4 on penalties.
Houston Dynamo 2, Chivas USA 0

FINALS
DC United 0, New England Rev 1
Houston Dynamo 3, Colorado Rapids 1

MLS CUP 2006
New England Rev 1, Houston Dynamo 1
aet; Houston Dynamo won 4-3 on penalties.

UEFA UNDER-21 CHAMPIONSHIP 2006-07

PRELIMINARY ROUND
Malta 1, Georgia 2
Liechtenstein 1, Northern Ireland 4
Luxembourg 0, Macedonia 3
Georgia 2, Malta 1
Macedonia 2, Luxembourg 0
Andorra 0, Iceland 0
Estonia 0, Wales 2
Northern Ireland 4, Liechtenstein 0
Azerbaijan 0, Republic of Ireland 3
San Marino 3, Armenia 0
Republic of Ireland 3, Azerbaijan 0
Wales 5, Estonia 1
Iceland 2, Andorra 0
Armenia 4, San Marino 0
Kazakhstan 0, Moldova 0
Moldova 1, Kazakhstan 0

QUALIFYING ROUND

GROUP 1
Bosnia 3, Armenia 2
Armenia 1, Norway 0
Norway 1, Bosnia 1

GROUP 2
Slovakia 0, Albania 0
Albania 0, Spain 3
Spain 4, Slovakia 2

GROUP 3
Lithuania 1, Georgia 0
Georgia 1, Serbia 3
Serbia 2, Lithuania 0

GROUP 4
Greece 0, Republic of Ireland 2
Republic of Ireland 0, Belgium 1
Belgium 2, Greece 1

GROUP 5
Austria 0, Iceland 0
Iceland 0, Italy 1
Italy 1, Austria 0

GROUP 6
Hungary 5, Finland 0
Finland 1, Russia 5
Russia 3, Hungary 1

GROUP 7
Poland 3, Latvia 1
Latvia 1, Portugal 2
Portugal 2, Poland 0

GROUP 8
England 2, Moldova 2
Moldova 1, Switzerland 3
Switzerland 2, England 3

GROUP 9
Belarus 1, Cyprus 0
Cyprus 0, Czech Republic 2
Czech Republic 2, Belarus 1

GROUP 10
Romania 3, Northern Ireland 0
Northern Ireland 2, Germany 3
Germany 5, Romania 1

GROUP 11
Sweden 3, Macedonia 1
Macedonia 0, Denmark 3
Denmark 0, Sweden 2

GROUP 12
Ukraine 0, Bulgaria 3
Bulgaria 2, Croatia 1
Croatia 1, Ukraine 2

GROUP 13
Israel 3, Wales 2
Wales 0, Turkey 0
Turkey 0, Israel 0

GROUP 14
Slovenia 1, Scotland 0
Scotland 1, France 3
France 2, Slovenia 0

PLAY-OFFS FOR FINAL TOURNAMENT FIRST LEG
Serbia 0, Sweden 3
Czech Republic 2, Bosnia 1
England 1, Germany 0
Italy 0, Spain 0
Belgium 1, Bulgaria 1
France 1, Israel 1
Russia 4, Portugal 1

PLAY-OFFS FOR FINAL TOURNAMENT SECOND LEG
Bosnia 1, Czech Republic 1
Sweden 0, Serbia 5
Germany 0, England 2
Spain 1, Italy 2
Bulgaria 1, Belgium 4
Israel 1, France 0
Portugal 3, Russia 0

Finals in Holland

GROUP A
Holland 1, Israel 0
Portugal 0, Belgium 0
Israel 0, Belgium 1
Holland 2, Portugal 1
Israel 0, Portugal 4
Belgium 2, Holland 2

GROUP B
Czech Republic 0, England 0
Serbia 1, Italy 0
Czech Republic 0, Serbia 1
England 2, Italy 2
England 2, Serbia 0
Italy 3, Czech Republic 1

SEMI-FINALS
Serbia 2, Belgium 0
Holland 1, England 1
Holland won 13-12 on penalties.

OLYMPIC QUALIFYING PLAY-OFF
Portugal 0, Italy 0
aet; Italy won 4-3 on penalties.

UEFA UNDER-21 CHAMPIONSHIP 2006–07 FINAL

Holland (1) 4 *(Bakkal 17, Babel 60, Rigters 67, Bruins 87)*
Serbia (0) 1 *(Mrdja 79)* 19,800

Holland: Waterman; Zuiverloon, Kruiswijk, Pieters (Jong-A-Pin 89), Maduro, Drenthe (Beerens 78), Babel, De Ridder, Rigters (Bruins 69), Donk, Bakkal.

Serbia: Kahriman; Ivanovic, Rukavina, Kolarov■, Smiljanic, Jankovic, Rakic (Mrdja 73), Milovanovic, Tosic D, Drincic (Tosic Z 65), Basta (Babovic 73).

Referee: Skomina (Slovenia).

UEFA UNDER-19 CHAMPIONSHIP 2007

(Finals in Poland)

GROUP A
Czech Republic 2, Poland 0
Austria 4, Belgium 1
Poland 4, Belgium 1
Austria 1, Czech Republic 3
Poland 0, Austria 1
Belgium 4, Czech Republic 2

GROUP B
Portugal 1, Spain 1
Turkey 2, Scotland 3
Scotland 0, Spain 4
Portugal 4, Turkey 4
Spain 5, Turkey 3
Scotland 2, Portugal 2

SEMI-FINALS
Czech Republic 0, Scotland 1
Spain 5, Austria 0

FINAL
Scotland 1, Spain 2

UEFA UNDER-17 CHAMPIONSHIP 2007

(Finals in Belgium)

GROUP A
Spain 0, Germany 0
Ukraine 2, France 2
France 2, Germany 1
Spain 3, Ukraine 1
Germany 2, Ukraine 0
France 0, Spain 2

GROUP B
Belgium 5, Iceland 1
England 4, Holland 2
Holland 3, Iceland 0
Belgium 1, England 1
Holland 2, Belgium 2
Iceland 0, England 2

SEMI-FINALS
Spain 1, Belgium 1
Spain won 7-6 on penalties.
England 1, France 0

FIFTH PLACE PLAY-OFF
Germany 3, Holland 2

FINAL *(in Tournai)*
Spain 1, England 0

ENGLAND UNDER-21 RESULTS 1976–2007

EC UEFA Competition for Under-21 Teams

v ALBANIA

Year	Date		Venue	Eng	Alb
EC1989	Mar	7	Shkroda	2	1
EC1989	April	25	Ipswich	2	0
EC2001	Mar	27	Tirana	1	0
EC2001	Sept	4	Middlesbrough	5	0

v ANGOLA

Year	Date		Venue	Eng	Ang
1995	June	10	Toulon	1	0
1996	May	28	Toulon	0	2

v ARGENTINA

Year	Date		Venue	Eng	Arg
1998	May	18	Toulon	0	2
2000	Feb	22	Fulham	1	0

v AUSTRIA

Year	Date		Venue	Eng	Aus
1994	Oct	11	Kapfenberg	3	1
1995	Nov	14	Middlesbrough	2	1
EC2004	Sept	3	Krems	2	0
EC2005	Oct	7	Leeds	1	2

v AZERBAIJAN

Year	Date		Venue	Eng	Az
EC2004	Oct	12	Baku	0	0
EC2005	Mar	29	Middlesbrough	2	0

v BELGIUM

Year	Date		Venue	Eng	Bel
1994	June	5	Marseille	2	1
1996	May	24	Toulon	1	0

v BRAZIL

Year	Date		Venue	Eng	B
1993	June	11	Toulon	0	0
1995	June	6	Toulon	0	2
1996	June	1	Toulon	1	2

v BULGARIA

Year	Date		Venue	Eng	Bul
EC1979	June	5	Pernik	3	1
EC1979	Nov	20	Leicester	5	0
1989	June	5	Toulon	2	3
EC1998	Oct	9	West Ham	1	0
EC1999	June	8	Vratsa	1	0

v CROATIA

Year	Date		Venue	Eng	Cro
1996	Apr	23	Sunderland	0	1
2003	Aug	19	West Ham	0	3

v CZECHOSLOVAKIA

Year	Date		Venue	Eng	Cz
1990	May	28	Toulon	2	1
1992	May	26	Toulon	1	2
1993	June	9	Toulon	1	1

v CZECH REPUBLIC

Year	Date		Venue	Eng	CzR
1998	Nov	17	Ipswich	0	1
EC2007	June	11	Arnhem	0	0

v DENMARK

Year	Date		Venue	Eng	Den
EC1978	Sept	19	Hvidovre	2	1
EC1979	Sept	11	Watford	1	0
EC1982	Sept	21	Hvidovre	4	1
EC1983	Sept	20	Norwich	4	1
EC1986	Mar	12	Copenhagen	1	0
EC1986	Mar	26	Manchester	1	1
1988	Sept	13	Watford	0	0
1994	Mar	8	Brentford	1	0
1999	Oct	8	Bradford	4	1
2005	Aug	16	Herning	1	0

v EAST GERMANY

Year	Date		Venue	Eng	EG
EC1980	April	16	Sheffield	1	2
EC1980	April	23	Jena	0	1

v FINLAND

Year	Date		Venue	Eng	Fin
EC1977	May	26	Helsinki	1	0
EC1977	Oct	12	Hull	8	1
EC1984	Oct	16	Southampton	2	0
EC1985	May	21	Mikkeli	1	3
EC2000	Oct	10	Valkeakoski	2	2
EC2001	Mar	23	Barnsley	4	0

v FRANCE

Year	Date		Venue	Eng	Fra
EC1984	Feb	28	Sheffield	6	1
EC1984	Mar	28	Rouen	1	0
1987	June	11	Toulon	0	2
EC1988	April	13	Besancon	2	4
EC1988	April	27	Highbury	2	2
1988	June	12	Toulon	2	4
1990	May	23	Toulon	7	3
1991	June	3	Toulon	1	0
1992	May	28	Toulon	0	0
1993	June	15	Toulon	1	0
1994	May	31	Aubagne	0	3
1995	June	10	Toulon	0	2
1998	May	14	Toulon	1	1
1999	Feb	9	Derby	2	1
EC2005	Nov	11	Tottenham	1	1
EC2005	Nov	15	Nancy	1	2

v GEORGIA

Year	Date		Venue	Eng	Geo
EC1996	Nov	8	Batumi	1	0
EC1997	April	29	Charlton	0	0
2000	Aug	31	Middlesbrough	6	1

v GERMANY

Year	Date		Venue	Eng	Ger
1991	Sept	10	Scunthorpe	2	1
EC2000	Oct	6	Derby	1	1
EC2001	Aug	31	Frieburg	2	1
2005	Mar	25	Hull	2	2
2005	Sept	6	Mainz	1	1
EC2006	Oct	6	Coventry	1	0
EC2006	Oct	10	Leverkusen	2	0

v GREECE

Year	Date		Venue	Eng	Gre
EC1982	Nov	16	Piraeus	0	1
EC1983	Mar	29	Portsmouth	2	1
1989	Feb	7	Patras	0	1
EC1997	Nov	13	Heraklion	0	2
EC1997	Dec	17	Norwich	4	2
EC2001	June	5	Athens	1	3
EC2001	Oct	5	Ewood Park	2	1

v HOLLAND

Year	Date		Venue	Eng	H
EC1993	April	27	Portsmouth	3	0
EC1993	Oct	12	Utrecht	1	1
2001	Aug	14	Reading	4	0
EC2001	Nov	9	Utrecht	2	2
EC2001	Nov	13	Derby	1	0
2004	Feb	17	Hull	3	2
2005	Feb	8	Derby	1	2
2006	Nov	14	Alkmaar	1	0
EC2007	June	20	Heerenveen	1	1

v HUNGARY

Year	Date		Venue	Eng	Hun
EC1981	June	5	Keszthely	2	1
EC1981	Nov	17	Nottingham	2	0
EC1983	April	26	Newcastle	1	0
EC1983	Oct	11	Nyiregyhaza	2	0
1990	Sept	11	Southampton	3	1
1992	May	12	Budapest	2	2
1999	April	27	Budapest	2	2

v ITALY

Year	Date		Venue	Eng	Italy
EC1978	Mar	8	Manchester	2	1
EC1978	April	5	Rome	0	0
EC1984	April	18	Manchester	3	1
EC1984	May	2	Florence	0	1
EC1986	April	9	Pisa	0	2
EC1986	April	23	Swindon	1	1
EC1997	Feb	12	Bristol	1	0
EC1997	Oct	10	Rieti	1	0
EC2000	May	27	Bratislava	0	2
2000	Nov	14	Monza*	0	0
2002	Mar	26	Valley Parade	1	1
EC2002	May	20	Basle	1	2
2003	Feb	11	Pisa	0	1
2007	Mar	24	Wembley	3	3
EC2007	June	14	Arnhem	2	2

**Abandoned 11 mins; fog.*

v ISRAEL

Year	Date		Venue	Eng	Isr
1985	Feb	27	Tel Aviv	2	1

v LATVIA

Year	Date		Venue	Eng	Lat
1995	April	25	Riga	1	0
1995	June	7	Burnley	4	0

v LUXEMBOURG

Year	Date		Venue	Eng	Lux
EC1998	Oct	13	Greven Macher	5	0
EC1999	Sept	3	Reading	5	0

v MACEDONIA

Year	Date		Venue	Eng	M
EC2002	Oct	15	Reading	3	1
EC2003	Sept	5	Skopje	1	1

v MALAYSIA

Year	Date		Venue	Eng	Mal
1995	June	8	Toulon	2	0

			v MEXICO	Eng	Mex
1988	June	5	Toulon	2	1
1991	May	29	Toulon	6	0
1992	May	25	Toulon	1	1
2001	May	24	Leicester	3	0

			v MOLDOVA	Eng	Mol
EC1996	Aug	31	Chisinau	2	0
EC1997	Sept	9	Wycombe	1	0
EC2006	Aug	15	Ipswich	2	2

			v MOROCCO	Eng	Mor
1987	June	7	Toulon	2	0
1988	June	9	Toulon	1	0

			v NORWAY	Eng	Nor
EC1977	June	1	Bergen	2	1
EC1977	Sept	6	Brighton	6	0
1980	Sept	9	Southampton	3	0
1981	Sept	8	Drammen	0	0
EC1992	Oct	13	Peterborough	0	2
EC1993	June	1	Stavanger	1	1
1995	Oct	10	Stavanger	2	2
2006	Feb	28	Reading	3	1

			v POLAND	Eng	Pol
EC1982	Mar	17	Warsaw	2	1
EC1982	April	7	West Ham	2	2
EC1989	June	2	Plymouth	2	1
EC1989	Oct	10	Jastrzebie	3	1
EC1990	Oct	16	Tottenham	0	1
EC1991	Nov	12	Pila	1	2
EC1993	May	28	Zdroj	4	1
EC1993	Sept	7	Millwall	1	2
EC1996	Oct	8	Wolverhampton	0	0
EC1997	May	30	Katowice	1	1
EC1999	Mar	26	Southampton	5	0
EC1999	Sept	7	Plock	1	3
EC2004	Sept	7	Rybnik	3	1
EC2005	Oct	11	Hillsborough	4	1

			v PORTUGAL	Eng	Por
1987	June	13	Toulon	0	0
1990	May	21	Toulon	0	1
1993	June	7	Toulon	2	0
1994	June	7	Toulon	2	0
EC1994	Sept	6	Leicester	0	0
1995	Sept	2	Lisbon	0	2
1996	May	30	Toulon	1	3
2000	Apr	16	Stoke	0	1
EC2002	May	22	Zurich	1	3
EC2003	Mar	28	Rio Major	2	4
EC2003	Sept	9	Everton	1	2

			v REPUBLIC OF IRELAND	Eng	RoI
1981	Feb	25	Liverpool	1	0
1985	Mar	25	Portsmouth	3	2
1989	June	9	Toulon	0	0
EC1990	Nov	13	Cork	3	0
EC1991	Mar	26	Brentford	3	0
1994	Nov	15	Newcastle	1	0
1995	Mar	27	Dublin	2	0

			v ROMANIA	Eng	Rom
EC1980	Oct	14	Ploesti	0	4
EC1981	April	28	Swindon	3	0
EC1985	April	30	Brasov	0	0
EC1985	Sept	10	Ipswich	3	0

			v RUSSIA	Eng	Rus
1994	May	30	Bandol	2	0

			v SAN MARINO	Eng	SM
EC1993	Feb	16	Luton	6	0
EC1993	Nov	17	San Marino	4	0

			v SENEGAL	Eng	Sen
1989	June	7	Toulon	6	1
1991	May	27	Toulon	2	1

			v SERBIA	Eng	Ser
EC2007	June	17	Nijmegen	2	0

			v SERBIA-MONTENEGRO	Eng	S-M
2003	June	2	Hull	3	2

			v SCOTLAND	Eng	Sco
1977	April	27	Sheffield	1	0
EC1980	Feb	12	Coventry	2	1
EC1980	Mar	4	Aberdeen	0	0
EC1982	April	19	Glasgow	1	0
EC1982	April	28	Manchester	1	1
EC1988	Feb	16	Aberdeen	1	0
EC1988	Mar	22	Nottingham	1	0
1993	June	13	Toulon	1	0

			v SLOVAKIA	Eng	Slo
EC2002	June	1	Bratislava	0	2
EC2002	Oct	11	Trnava	4	0
EC2003	June	10	Sunderland	2	0
2007	June	5	Norwich	5	0

			v SLOVENIA	Eng	Slo
2000	Feb	12	Nova Gorica	1	0

			v SOUTH AFRICA	Eng	SA
1998	May	16	Toulon	3	1

			v SPAIN	Eng	Spa
EC1984	May	17	Seville	1	0
EC1984	May	24	Sheffield	2	0
1987	Feb	18	Burgos	2	1
1992	Sept	8	Burgos	1	0
2001	Feb	27	Birmingham	0	4
2004	Nov	16	Alcala	0	1
2007	Feb	6	Derby	2	2

			v SWEDEN	Eng	Swe
1979	June	9	Vasteras	2	1
1986	Sept	9	Ostersund	1	1
EC1988	Oct	18	Coventry	1	1
EC1989	Sept	5	Uppsala	0	1
EC1998	Sept	4	Sundvall	2	0
EC1999	June	4	Huddersfield	3	0
2004	Mar	30	Kristiansund	2	2

			v SWITZERLAND	Eng	Swit
EC1980	Nov	18	Ipswich	5	0
EC1981	May	31	Neuenburg	0	0
1988	May	28	Lausanne	1	1
1996	April	1	Swindon	0	0
1998	Mar	24	Brugglifeld	0	2
EC2002	May	17	Zurich	2	1
EC2006	Sept	6	Lucerne	3	2

			v TURKEY	Eng	Tur
EC1984	Nov	13	Bursa	0	0
EC1985	Oct	15	Bristol	3	0
EC1987	April	28	Izmir	0	0
EC1987	Oct	13	Sheffield	1	1
EC1991	April	30	Izmir	2	2
1991	Oct	15	Reading	2	0
EC1992	Nov	17	Orient	0	1
EC1993	Mar	30	Izmir	0	0
EC2000	May	29	Bratislava	6	0
EC2003	April	1	Newcastle	1	1
EC2003	Oct	10	Istanbul	0	1

			v UKRAINE	Eng	Uk
2004	Aug	17	Middlesbrough	3	1

			v USA	Eng	USA
1989	June	11	Toulon	0	2
1994	June	2	Toulon	3	0

			v USSR	Eng	USSR
1987	June	9	Toulon	0	0
1988	June	7	Toulon	1	0
1990	May	25	Toulon	2	1
1991	May	31	Toulon	2	1

			v WALES	Eng	Wales
1976	Dec	15	Wolverhampton	0	0
1979	Feb	6	Swansea	1	0
1990	Dec	5	Tranmere	0	0
EC2004	Oct	8	Blackburn	2	0
EC2005	Sept	2	Wrexham	4	0

			v WEST GERMANY	Eng	WG
EC1982	Sept	21	Sheffield	3	1
EC1982	Oct	12	Bremen	2	3
1987	Sept	8	Ludenscheid	0	2

			v YUGOSLAVIA	Eng	Yugo
EC1978	April	19	Novi Sad	1	2
EC1978	May	2	Manchester	1	1
EC1986	Nov	11	Peterborough	1	1
EC1987	Nov	10	Zemun	5	1
EC2000	Mar	29	Barcelona	3	0
2002	Sept	6	Bolton	1	1

BRITISH AND IRISH UNDER-21 TEAMS 2006–07

■ *Denotes player sent off.*

ENGLAND UNDER-21 TEAMS 2006–07

Ipswich, 15 August 2006, 13,556

England (1) 2 *(Walcott 3, Nugent 76)*

Moldova (0) 2 *(Alexeev 75, Zislis 86)*

England: Carson; Richards, Baines, Taylor S, Ferdinand, Huddlestone, Reo-Coker, Routledge, Walcott (Jerome 67), Nugent, Bentley (Ambrose 78).

Lucerne, 6 September 2006, 8500

Switzerland (1) 2 *(Vonlanthen 29 (pen), Barnetta 70)*

England (2) 3 *(Walcott 13, Nugent 18, Milner 88)*

England: Carson; Hoyte, Baines, Taylor S, Ferdinand, Huddlestone, Reo-Coker, Bentley (Milner 46), Walcott, Nugent (Jerome 69), Routledge (Young 78).

Coventry, 6 October 2006, 30,919

England (0) 1 *(Baines 77)*

Germany (0) 0

England: Carson; Richards, Baines, Taylor S, Ferdinand, Huddlestone, Reo-Coker, Milner, Walcott (Young 66), Nugent (Watson 81), Routledge (Agbonlahor 71).

Leverkusen, 10 October 2006, 20,800

Germany (0) 0 *Brzenska*■

England (0) 2 *(Walcott 84, 90)*

England: Carson; Richards, Baines, Taylor S■, Ferdinand, Huddlestone, Reo-Coker, Milner, Agbonlahor (Walcott 76), Nugent (Hoyte 66), Young (Jerome 90).

Alkmaar, 14 November 2006, 15,000

Holland (0) 0

England (1) 1 *(Hoyte 12)*

England: Carson; Hoyte, Baines (Rosenior 46), Davies, Kilgallon, Huddlestone, Routledge (Welsh 78), Milner (Whittingham 65), Nugent (Onuoha 85), Young, Walcott (Jerome 83).

Derby, 6 February 2007, 28,295

England (0) 2 *(Nugent 50, Lita 79)*

Spain (2) 2 *(Soldado 34, Jurado 45)*

England: Carson (Hart 82); Hoyte, Andrew D Taylor (Rosenior 62), Huddlestone (Richardson 52), Davies, Taylor S, Bentley, Reo-Coker, Young (Walcott 46), Nugent, Milner (Lita 62).

Wembley, 24 March 2007, 55,700

England (1) 3 *(Bentley 30, Routledge 52, Derbyshire 58)*

Italy (1) 3 *(Pazzini 1, 53, 68)*

England: Camp; Rosenior (Hoyte 57), Baines, Reo-Coker, Ferdinand, Cahill, Bentley (Young 87), Lita, Richardson (Huddlestone 79), Agbonlahor (Derbyshire 46), Routledge (Milner 57).

Norwich, 5 June 2007, 20,193

England (1) 5 *(Richardson 35 (pen), Reo-Coker 61, Taylor S 77, Huddlestone 82, Lita 84)*

Slovakia (0) 0

England: Hart; Onuoha (Baines 46), Hoyte (Rosenior 71), Huddlestone, Taylor S, Cahill, Reo-Coker (Lita 62), Milner (Routledge 46), Nugent (Derbyshire 71), Young (Whittingham 78), Richardson (Noble 46).

Arnhem, 11 June 2007

Czech Republic (0) 0

England (0) 0

England: Carson; Hoyte, Baines, Cahill, Reo-Coker, Richardson (Routledge 57), Nugent, Young, Milner (Lita 64), Huddlestone (Noble 82), Onuoha.

Arnhem, 14 June 2007, 17,103

Italy (1) 2 *(Chiellini 35, Aquilani 69)*

England (2) 2 *(Nugent 24, Lita 26)*

England: Carson; Hoyte, Baines, Taylor S, Reo-Coker (Richardson 90), Nugent (Whittingham 69), Young, Milner, Lita (Vaughan 84), Noble, Onuoha.

Nijmegen, 17 June 2007

Serbia (0) 0

England (1) 2 *(Lita 5, Derbyshire 77)*

England: Carson; Hoyte, Baines, Taylor S, Reo-Coker (Huddlestone■ 88), Richardson (Routledge 80), Nugent, Milner, Lita (Derbyshire 70), Noble, Onuoha.

Heerenveen, 20 June 2007, 23,467

Holland (0) 1 *(Rigters 89)*

England (1) 1 *(Lita 39)*

England: Carson; Hoyte, Baines (Rosenior 46), Taylor S, Reo-Coker, Nugent (Derbyshire 78), Young, Milner, Lita (Ferdinand 87), Noble, Onuoha.

aet; Holland won 13-12 on penalties:- Young scored; Babel scored; Milner scored; Drenthe hit post; Noble scored; Janssen scored; Hoyte saved; Beerens scored; Derbyshire scored; Maduro scored; Ferdinand scored; De Ridder scored; Carson scored; Zuiverloon scored; Rosenior scored; Rigters scored; Reo-Coker saved; Kruiswijk missed; Taylor scored; Waterman scored; Young scored; Beerens scored; Milner scored; Drenthe scored; Noble scored; Maduro scored; Hoyte scored; Janssen scored; Derbyshire saved; De Ridder saved; Ferdinand hit bar; Zuiverloon scored.

SCOTLAND UNDER-21 TEAMS 2006–07

Murska Sobota, 16 August 2006, 2250

Slovenia (0) 1 *(Burgic 57)*

Scotland (0) 0

Scotland: Marshall; Whittaker, Wilson, Thomson, Diamond, Broadfoot, Brown, Naismith, Elliot (Foster 74), Adam (Beattie 65), Wallace (Quinn R 65).

Aberdeen, 1 September 2006, 11,950

Scotland (0) 1 *(Adam 86 (pen))*

France (2) 3 *(Briand 3, Sinama-Pongolle 16, Gourcuff 83)*

Scotland: Marshall; Wilson, Smith S, Thomson (Wallace 46), Diamond (Hutton 46), Broadfoot, Whittaker, Brown, Beattie (Fletcher 63), Adam, Naismith.

Cumbernauld, 6 February 2007, 2326

Scotland (0) 0

Germany (1) 2 *(Hunt 22, Flessers 74)*

Scotland: McNeil (MacDonald 46); Ross, Wallace, Fitzpatrick, Cuthbert, Reynolds, McGlinchey (Dorrans 46), Robertson (Smith 46), Naismith, Quinn R (Adams 69), Conroy (Considine 83).

WALES UNDER-21 TEAMS 2006–07

Waalwijk, 16 August 2006, 100

Israel (1) 3 *(Tamuz 26, Srur 64, Rafaelov 79 (pen))*

Wales (0) 2 *(Marc Williams 60, 66)*

Wales: Price; Eardley, Jacobson, Critchell (Marc Williams■ 54), Morgan (James 87), Mike Williams, Blake (Gunter 51), Crofts, Davies C■, Edwards, Aaron Davies.

Ninian Park, 2 September 2006, 731

Wales (0) 0

Turkey (0) 0

Wales: Price; Eardley, Bale, James, Morgan, Mike Williams, MacDonald, Edwards, Fleetwood (Haldane 74), Aaron Davies, Jacobson.

Belfast, 6 February 2007, 1200

Northern Ireland (0) 0

Wales (3) 4 *(Vokes 1, Jacobson 11, Evans C 31, 46)*

Northern Ireland: Tuffey (Carson 63); Casement, McCaffrey (Taylor 46), Cathcart (Callaghan 46), McArdle (Armstrong 46), Howland, Mulgrew (Ward J 63), McKenna, Stewart (Paterson 46), Fordyce, Hazley (Buchanan 55).
Wales: Hennessey (Fon Williams 57); Gunter (Jones 46), Jacobson, Edwards (Flynn 57), Williams R, Mike Williams, Grubb (Davies R 46), Collins (Bradley 46), Vokes (Blake 67), Evans C, Warlow (James 70).

REPUBLIC OF IRELAND UNDER-21 TEAMS 2006–07

Athens, 16 August 2006

Greece (0) 0

Republic of Ireland (1) 2 *(McShane 10, Whelan 52)*

Republic of Ireland: Doyle; Foley, Painter, Keegan, Bruce, McShane, Flood, Deery, Ward (Keogh A 80), Whelan, Timlin.

Galway, 1 September 2006

Republic of Ireland (0) 0

Belgium (0) 1 *(Martens 58)*

Republic of Ireland: Doyle; Foley, Painter, Keegan, Bruce, McShane, Flood, Deery (O'Donovan 79), Ward (Dixon 85), Whelan, Timlin (Keogh A 68).

Mamer, 18 October 2006

Luxembourg (0) 0

Republic of Ireland (0) 2 *(Stokes 47, Keogh A 67)*

Republic of Ireland: Quigley (Randolph 46); Kane, O'Cearuill, Keogh R (O'Halloran 56), Stapleton (Powell 46), Cregg, Morris (Hand 46), Dicker (Wilson 46), Kelly, Keogh A, Stokes.

Madeira, 27 February 2007

Republic of Ireland (0) 1 *(Murphy 61)*

Slovakia (0) 0

Republic of Ireland: Russell; Kane, Powell, O'Cearuill (Murphy 46), O'Halloran, Kelly (Simmonds 75), Chambers (Curran 56), Morris, O'Brien, Bracken (Hayes 46), Clarke (Dennehy 89).

Madeira, 28 February 2007

Republic of Ireland (1) 2 *(Gaynor 19, 75)*

Madeira (2) 2 *(Costa 15, Sousa 44)*

Republic of Ireland: Gilmartin; Kane (Synnott 67), Powell (Finn 46), Murphy, O'Halloran, Kelly, Simmonds, Morris, O'Brien (Chambers 46), Gaynor, Hayes (Dennehy 52).

Madeira, 2 March 2007

Republic of Ireland (0) 0

Portugal (1) 1 *(Celestino 30)*

Republic of Ireland: Russell; O'Cearuill (Curran 70), Powell, Murphy, O'Halloran, Simmonds, Chambers, Kelly (Hayes 54), Morris, O'Brien, Gaynor (Bracken 80).

Venlo, 27 March 2007

Holland (0) 1 *(Drenthe 72)*

Republic of Ireland (0) 0

Republic of Ireland: Quigley (Randolph 46); Kane, O'Halloran■, O'Cearuill (Keogh R 81), O'Dea, Gibson, Keegan, Quinn, O'Brien (Powell 83), Ward S (Rooney 72), Clarke.

NORTHERN IRELAND UNDER-21 TEAMS 2006–07

Urziceni, 16 August 2006

Romania (2) 3 *(Pulhac 33, Keseru 40, Florescu 83 (pen))*

Northern Ireland (0) 0

Northern Ireland: McGovern; Ward S, Hughes J, McArdle, McChrystal, Evans, Gilfillan (Clarke 65), Brunt, Thompson (Stewart 82), Shiels, Scullion (Turner 76).

Lurgan, 1 September 2006

Northern Ireland (0) 2 *(Shiels 69 (pen), Stewart 81)*

Germany (2) 3 *(Hilbert 13, Helmes 35, Trochowski 65)*

Northern Ireland: McGovern; Ward S (Stewart 75), Hughes J, Evans, McArdle, Smylie (Turner 57), Gilfillan, Clarke, Thompson, Shiels, Scullion (Buchanan 59).

Torgau, 14 November 2006

Germany Under-19 (2) 2 *(Boateng 10, Schindler 44)*

Northern Ireland (1) 1 *(Fordyce 6)*

Northern Ireland: Tuffey (Carson 72); Callaghan, McCaffrey, Cathcart (Taylor 56), McArdle, McKenna, Mulgrew (Meenan 78), Catney (Buchanan 56), Stewart, Fordyce (Doherty 46), Hazley.

Pitesti, 24 March 2007

Romania (1) 2 *(McArdle 30 (og), Tincu P 85)*

Northern Ireland (0) 0

Northern Ireland: Tuffey (Carson); Callaghan (Paterson), Taylor (Cathcart), Casement (Meenan), McArdle, Garrett, Turner, McKenna (Howland), Stewart, Fordyce, Buchanan (Mulgrew).

Glasgow, 24 May 2007

Scotland Under-20 (1) 4 *(Adams 11, McAllister 70, Dorrans 74, Gilmour 82)*

Northern Ireland (0) 0 **350**

Scotland Under-20: McNeil; Lynch, Considine (McAllister 46), Cuthbert, Wallace, Conroy (Gilmour 65), Reynolds, Adams, McGlinchey (Sutherland 71), Campbell (Snodgrass 59), Elliot (Dorrans 46).
Northern Ireland: Tuffey (Carson 65); Callaghan, Casement, McVey, McArdle, Garrett, Doherty (McCaffrey 46), Mulgrew (Donnelly 58), Stewart, Fordyce (Turner 46), Buchanan (McAllister 46).

Tiraspol, 1 June 2007

Moldova (0) 0

Northern Ireland (1) 1 *(Turner 3)*

Northern Ireland: Tuffey; Taylor, McVey, Casement, McArdle, Callaghan, Turner (Mulgrew 53), Garrett, Stewart, Fordyce, Buchanan (McCaffrey 62).

BRITISH UNDER-21 APPEARANCES 1976–2007

ENGLAND

Ablett, G. (Liverpool), 1988 v F (1)
Adams, A. (Arsenal). 1985 v Ei, Fi; 1986 v D; 1987 v Se, Y (5)
Adams, N. (Everton), 1987 v Se (1)
Agbonlahor, G. (Aston Villa), 2007 v G (sub+1), I (3)
Allen, B. (QPR), 1992 v H, M, Cz, F; 1993 v N (sub), T, P, Cz (sub) (8)
Allen, C. A. (Oxford U), 1995 v Br (sub), F (sub) (2)
Allen, C. (QPR), 1980 v EG (sub); (with C Palace), 1981 v N, R (3)
Allen, M. (QPR), 1987 v Se (sub); 1988 v Y (sub) (2)
Allen, P. (West Ham U), 1985 v Ei, R; (with Tottenham H), 1986 v R (3)
Allen, R. W. (Tottenham H), 1998 v F (sub), S.Af, Arg (sub) (3)
Ambrose, D. P. F. (Ipswich T), 2003 v I (sub); (with Newcastle U), Ser (sub); 2004 v Se (sub); 2005 v Sp, Az (sub); (with Charlton Ath), 2006 v D (sub), W, F (2); 2007 v Mol (sub) (10)
Ameobi, F. (Newcastle U), 2001 v Sp (sub), Fi (sub), Alb (sub), M, Gr (sub); 2002 v Ho (sub+1), Slv (sub), Sw (sub), I (sub), P (sub); 2003 v Y (sub), Slo, Mac, I, P, Ser, Slo; 2004 v Mac, P, T (19)
Anderson, V. A. (Nottingham F), 1978 v I (1)
Anderton, D. R. (Tottenham H), 1993 v Sp, Sm, Ho, Pol, N, P, Cz, Br, S, F; 1994 v Pol, Sm (12)
Andrews, I. (Leicester C), 1987 v Se (1)
Ardley, N. C. (Wimbledon), 1993 v Pol, N, P, Cz, Br, S, F, 1994 v Pol (sub), Ho, Sm (10)
Ashcroft, L. (Preston NE), 1992 v H (sub) (1)
Ashton, D. (Crewe Alex), 2004 v Ho, Se; 2005 v Uk (sub); (with Norwich C), Ho, G, Az; 2006 v D, F (sub+sub) (9)
Atherton, P. (Coventry C), 1992 v T (1)
Atkinson, B. (Sunderland), 1991 v W (sub), Sen, M, USSR (sub), F; 1992 v Pol (sub) (6)
Awford, A. T. (Portsmouth), 1993 v Sp, N, T, P, Cz, Br, S, F; 1994 v Ho (9)

Bailey, G. R. (Manchester U), 1979 v W, Bul; 1980 v D, S (2), EG; 1982 v N; 1983 v D, Gr; 1984 v H, F (2), I, Sp (14)
Baines, L.J. (Wigan Ath), 2005 v A, Pol, Ho; 2006 v G (sub), A; 2007 v Mol, Sw, G (2), Ho, I, Slo (sub), CzR, I, Ser, Ho (16)
Baker, G. E. (Southampton), 1981 v N, R (2)
Ball, M. J. (Everton), 1999 v Se, Bul, L, CzR, Pol; 2000 v L, D (sub) (7)
Barker, S. (Blackburn R), 1985 v Is (sub), Ei, R; 1986 v I (4)
Barmby, N. J. (Tottenham H), 1994 v D; 1995 v P, A (sub); (with Everton), 1998 v Sw (4)
Bannister, G. (Sheffield W), 1982 v Pol (1)
Barnes, J. (Watford), 1983 v D, Gr (2)
Barnes, P. S. (Manchester C), 1977 v W (sub), S, Fi, N; 1978 v N, Fi, I (2), Y (9)
Barrett, E. D. (Oldham Ath), 1990 v P, F, USSR, Cz (4)
Barry, G. (Aston Villa), 1999 v CzR, F, H; 2000 v Y; 2001 v Sp, Fi, Alb; 2002 v Ho, G, Alb, Gr, Ho (sub), Slv, I, P, Sw, I, P; 2003 v Y, Slo, Mac, I, P, T, Slo; 2004 v Cro, P (27)
Barton, J. (Manchester C), 2004 v Mac, P (2)
Bart-Williams, C. G. (Sheffield W), 1993 v Sp, N, T; 1994 v D, Ru, F, Bel, P; 1995 v P, A, Ei (2), La (2); (with Nottingham F), 1996 v P (sub), A (16)
Batty, D. (Leeds U), 1988 v Sw (sub); 1989 v Gr (sub), Bul, Sen, Ei, US; 1990 v Pol (7)
Bazeley, D. S. (Watford), 1992 v H (sub) (1)
Beagrie, P. (Sheffield U), 1988 v WG, T (2)
Beardsmore, R. (Manchester U), 1989 v Gr, Alb (sub), Pol, Bul, USA (5)
Beattie, J. S. (Southampton), 1999 v CzR (sub), F (sub), Pol, H; 2000 v Pol (5)
Beckham, D. R. J. (Manchester U), 1995 v Br, Mal, An, F; 1996 v P, A (sub), Bel, An, P (9)
Bent, D. A. (Ipswich T), 2003 v I (sub), Ser (sub); 2004 v T (sub), Ho (sub), Se (sub); 2005 v Uk (sub), A (sub), Pol (sub), W (sub), Sp, G, Az; (with Charlton Ath), 2006 v F (2) (14)
Bent, M. N. (C Palace), 1998 v S.Af (sub), Arg (2)
Bentley, D. M. (Arsenal), 2004 v Ho, Se; 2005 v Pol; (with Blackburn R), 2006 v N; 2007 v Mol, Sw, Sp, I (8)
Beeston, C (Stoke C), 1988 v USSR (1)
Benjamin, T. J. (Leicester C), 2001 v M (sub) (1)
Bertschin, K. E. (Birmingham C), 1977 v S; 1978 v Y (2) (3)
Birtles, G. (Nottingham F), 1980 v Bul, EG (sub) (2)
Blackwell, D. R. (Wimbledon), 1991 v W, T, Sen (sub), M, USSR, F (6)
Blake, M. A. (Aston Villa), 1990 v F (sub), Cz (sub); 1991 v H, Pol, Ei (2), W; 1992 v Pol (8)
Blissett, L. L. (Watford), 1979 v W, Bul (sub), Se; 1980 v D (4)
Booth, A. D. (Huddersfield T), 1995 v La (2 subs); 1996 v N (3)
Bothroyd, J. (Coventry C), 2001 v M (sub) (1)
Bowyer, L. D. (Charlton Ath), 1996 v N (sub), Bel, P, Br; (with Leeds U), 1997 v Mol, I, Sw, Ge; 1998 v Mol; 1999 v F, Pol; 2000 v D, Arg (13)
Bracewell, P. (Stoke C), 1983 v D, Gr (1 + 1 sub), H; 1984 v D, H, F (2), I (2), Sp (2); 1985 v T (13)
Bradbury, L. M. (Portsmouth), 1997 v Pol; (with Manchester C), 1998 v Mol (sub), I (sub) (3)
Bramble, T. M. (Ipswich T), 2001 v Ge, G, Fi, Alb (sub), M; 2002 v Ho (sub); (with Newcastle U), 2003 v Y, Slo, Mac, P (10)
Branch, P. M. (Everton), 1997 v Pol (sub) (1)
Bradshaw, P. W. (Wolverhampton W), 1977 v W, S; 1978 v Fi, Y (4)
Breacker, T. (Luton T), 1986 v I (2) (2)
Brennan, M. (Ipswich T), 1987 v Y, Sp, T, Mor, F (5)
Bridge, W. M. (Southampton), 1999 v H (sub); 2001 v Sp; 2002 v Ho, G, Alb, Gr, Ho (2) (8)
Bridges, M. (Sunderland), 1997 v Sw (sub); 1999 v F; (with Leeds U), 2000 v D (3)
Brightwell, I. (Manchester C), 1989 v D, Alb; 1990 v Se (sub), Pol (4)
Briscoe, L. S. (Sheffield W), 1996 v Cro, Bel (sub), An, Br; 1997 v Sw (sub) (5)
Brock, K. (Oxford U), 1984 v I, Sp (2); 1986 v I (4)
Broomes, M. C. (Blackburn R), 1997 v Sw, Ge (2)
Brown, M. R. (Manchester C), 1996 v Cro, Bel, An, P (4)
Brown, W. M. (Manchester U), 1999 v Se, Bul, L, CzR, Pol, Se, Bul; 2001 v G (8)
Bull, S. G. (Wolverhampton W), 1989 v Alb (2) Pol; 1990 v Se, Pol (5)
Bullock, M. J. (Barnsley), 1998 v Gr (sub) (1)
Burrows, D. (WBA), 1989 v Se (sub); (with Liverpool), Gr, Alb (2), Pol; 1990 v Se, Pol (7)
Butcher, T. I. (Ipswich T), 1979 v Se; 1980 v D, Bul, S (2), EG (2) (7)
Butt, N. (Manchester U), 1995 v Ei (2), La; 1996 v P, A; 1997 v Ge, Pol (7)
Butters, G. (Tottenham H), 1989 v Bul, Sen (sub), Ei (sub) (3)
Butterworth, I. (Coventry C), 1985 v T, R; (with Nottingham F), 1986 v R, T, D (2), I (2) (8)
Bywater, S. (West Ham U), 2001 v M (sub), Gr; 2002 v Ho (sub), I (sub); 2003 v P, Ser (sub) (6)

Cadamarteri, D. L. (Everton), 1999 v CzR (sub); 2000 v Y (sub); 2001 v M (sub) (3)
Caesar, G. (Arsenal), 1987 v Mor, USSR (sub), F (3)
Cahill, G. J. (Aston Villa), 2007 v I, Slo, CzR (3)
Callaghan, N. (Watford), 1983 v D, Gr (sub), H (sub); 1984 v D, H, F (2), I, Sp (9)
Camp, L. M. J. (Derby Co), 2005 v Sp (sub), Ho (sub); 2006 v D (sub), N (sub); 2007 v I (5)
Campbell, A. P. (Middlesbrough), 2000 v Y, T (sub), Slo (sub); 2001 v Ge (sub) (4)

Campbell, K. J. (Arsenal), 1991 v H, T (sub); 1992 v G, T (4)
Campbell, S. (Tottenham), 1994 v D, Ru, F, US, Bel, P; 1995 v P, A, Ei; 1996 v N, A (11)
Carbon, M. P. (Derby Co), 1996 v Cro (sub); 1997 v Ge, I, Sw (4)
Carr, C. (Fulham), 1985 v Ei (sub) (1)
Carr, F. (Nottingham F), 1987 v Se, Y, Sp (sub), Mor, USSR; 1988 v WG (sub), T, Y, F (9)
Carragher, J. L. (Liverpool), 1997 v I (sub), Sw, Ge, Pol; 1998 v Mol (sub), I, Gr, Sw (sub), F, S.Af, Arg; 1999 v Se, Bul, L, CzR, F, Pol, Se, Bul; 2000 v L, Pol, D, Arg, Y, I, T, Slo (27)
Carlisle, C. J. (QPR), 2001 v Ge (sub), G (sub), Fi (sub) (3)
Carrick, M. (West Ham U), 2001 v Ge, G, Fi, I, Gr; 2002 v Gr, Ho (2), P; 2003 v Y, Slo, Mac, I, P (14)
Carson, S. P. (Leeds U), 2004 v Ho, Se; 2005 v Uk, A, Pol, W, Az, Sp; (with Liverpool), Ho, G, Az; 2006 v D, W, G, A, Pol, F (2), N; 2007 v Mol, Sw, G (2), Ho, Sp, CzR, I, Ser, Ho (29)
Casper, C. M. (Manchester U), 1995 v Mal (1)
Caton, T. (Manchester C), 1982 v N, H (sub), Pol (2), S; 1983 v WG (2), Gr; 1984 v D, H, F (2), I (2) (14)
Chadwick, L. H. (Manchester U), 2000 v L, D, Arg, I (sub), Slo (sub); 2001 v Ge (sub), I, Sp, Fi, Alb; 2002 v Ho, G, Alb (13)
Challis, T. M. (QPR), 1996 v An, P (2)
Chamberlain, M. (Stoke C), 1983 v Gr; 1984 v F (sub), I, Sp (4)
Chaplow, R. D. (Burnley), 2004 v Ho (sub) (1)
Chapman, L. (Stoke C), 1981 v Ei (1)
Charles, G. A. (Nottingham F), 1991 v H, W (sub), Ei; 1992 v T (4)
Chettle, S. (Nottingham F), 1988 v M, USSR, Mor, F; 1989 v D, Se, Gr, Alb (2), Bul; 1990 v Se, Pol (12)
Chopra, R, M. (Newcastle U), 2004 v Se (sub) (1)
Clark, L. R. (Newcastle U), 1992 v Cz, F; 1993 v Sp, N, T, Ho (sub), Pol (sub), Cz, Br, S; 1994 v Ho (11)
Clarke, P. M. (Everton), 2003 v Slo (sub), I, T, Ser, Slo; 2004 v Cro, Mac, P (8)
Christie, M. N. (Derby Co), 2001 v Fi (sub), Sp, Fi, Alb, M, Gr; 2002 v Ho (sub), Gr (sub), Ho, Slv, P (11)
Clegg, M. J. (Manchester U), 1998 v Fr (sub), S.Af (sub) (2)
Clemence, S. N. (Tottenham H), 1999 v Se (sub) (1)
Clough, N. (Nottingham F), 1986 v D (sub); 1987 v Se, Y, T, USSR, F (sub), P; 1988 v WG, T, Y, S (2), M, Mor, F (15)
Cole, A. A. (Arsenal), 1992 v H, Cz (sub), F (sub); (with Bristol C), 1993 v Sm; (with Newcastle U), Pol, N; 1994 v Pol, Ho (8)
Cole, A. (Arsenal), 2001 v Ge, G, Fi, I (4)
Cole, C. (Chelsea), 2003 v T (sub), Ser (sub), Slo (sub); 2004 v Cro (sub), Ho, Se; 2005 v Uk, A, Pol, W, Sp, Ho; 2006 v D, W, G, A, Pol, F (2) (19)
Cole, J. J. (West Ham U), 2000 v Arg (sub); 2001 v Ge, Gr; 2002 v G; 2003 v Slo, Mac, P, T (8)
Coney, D. (Fulham), 1985 v T (sub); 1986 v R; 1988 v T, WG (4)
Connor, T. (Brighton & HA), 1987 v Y (1)
Cooke, R. (Tottenham H), 1986 v D (sub) (1)
Cooke, T. J. (Manchester U), 1996 v Cro, Bel, An (sub), P (4)
Cooper, C. (Middlesbrough), 1988 v F (2), M, USSR, Mor; 1989 v D, Se, Gr (8)
Corrigan, J. T. (Manchester C), 1978 v I (2), Y (3)
Cort, C. E. R. (Wimbledon), 1999 v L (sub), CzR, H (sub), Se, Bul; 2000 v L (sub), Pol, D (sub), Arg, I, T, Slo (12)
Cottee, A. (West Ham U), 1985 v Fi (sub), Is (sub), Ei, R, Fi; 1987 v Sp, P; 1988 v WG (8)
Couzens, A. J. (Leeds U), 1995 v Mal (sub), An, F (sub) (3)
Cowans, G. S. (Aston Villa), 1979 v W, Se; 1980 v Bul, EG; 1981 v R (5)
Cox, N. J. (Aston Villa), 1993 v T, Ho, Pol, N; 1994 v Pol, Sm (6)
Cranson, I. (Ipswich T), 1985 v Fi, Is, R; 1986 v R, I (5)
Cresswell, R. P. W. (York C), 1999 v F (sub); (with Sheffield W) H (sub), Se, Bul (4)
Croft, G. (Grimsby T), 1995 v Br, Mal, An, F (4)
Crooks, G. (Stoke C), 1980 v Bul, S (2), EG (sub) (4)
Crossley, M. G. (Nottingham F), 1990 v P, USSR, Cz (3)
Crouch, P. J. (Portsmouth), 2002 v I (sub), P (sub), Sw; (with Aston Villa), 2003 v Mac (sub), P (sub) (5)
Cundy, J. V. (Chelsea), 1991 v Ei (2); 1992 v Pol (3)
Cunningham, L. (WBA), 1977 v S, Fi, N (sub); 1978 v N, Fi, I (6)
Curbishley, L. C. (Birmingham C), 1981 v Sw (1)
Curtis, J. C. K. (Manchester U), 1998 v I (sub), Gr, Sw, F, S.Af, Arg; 1999 v Se (sub), Bul, L, CzR, F, Pol (sub), H, Se (sub), Bul; 2000 v Pol (16)

Daniel, P. W. (Hull C), 1977 v S, Fi, N; 1978 v Fi, I, Y (2) (7)
Davenport, C. R. P. (Tottenham H), 2005 v A, Pol, W, Az, Sp (sub), G, Az; 2006 v D (8)
Davies, A. J. (Middlesbrough), 2004 v T (1)
Davies, C. E. (WBA), 2006 v N (sub); 2007 v Ho, Sp (3)
Davies, K. C. (Southampton), 1998 v Gr (sub); (with Blackburn R), 1999 v CzR; (with Southampton), 2000 v Y (sub) (3)
Davis, K. G. (Luton T), 1995 v An; 1996 v Cro (sub), P (3)
Davis, P. (Arsenal), 1982 v Pol, S; 1983 v D, Gr (1 + 1 sub), H (sub); 1987 v T; 1988 v WG, T, Y, Fr (11)
Davis, S. (Fulham), 2001 v Fi, Alb, M, Gr; 2002 v Ho, G, Al, Ho (2), P, Sw (11)
Dawson, M. R. (Nottingham F), 2003 v Slo (sub), I, P, T; 2004 v P, Se; 2005 v Sp; (with Tottenham H), 2006 v D, W, G, A, F (2) (13)
Day, C. N. (Tottenham H), 1996 v Cro, Bel, Br; (with C Palace), 1997 v Mol, Ge, Sw (6)
D'Avray, M. (Ipswich T), 1984 v I, Sp (sub) (2)
Deehan, J. M. (Aston Villa), 1977 v N; 1978 v N, Fi, I; 1979 v Bul, Se (sub); 1980 v D (7)
Defoe, J. C. (West Ham U), 2001 v M, Gr; 2002 v Ho (sub), G (sub), Alb, Gr, Ho (2), Slv, I, P (sub), Sw, I, P; 2003 v Y, P, T, Ser, Slo; 2004 v Cro, Mac (sub), P (sub), T (23)
Dennis, M. E. (Birmingham C), 1980 v Bul; 1981 v N, R (3)
Derbyshire, M. A. (Blackburn R), 2007 v I (sub), Slo (sub), Ser (sub), Ho (sub) (4)
Dichio, D. S. E. (QPR), 1996 v N (sub) (1)
Dickens, A. (West Ham U), 1985 v Fi (sub) (1)
Dicks, J. (West Ham U), 1988 v Sw (sub), M, Mor, F (4)
Digby, F. (Swindon T), 1987 v Sp (sub), USSR, P; 1988 v T; 1990 v Pol (5)
Dillon, K. P. (Birmingham C), 1981 v R (1)
Dixon, K. (Chelsea), 1985 v Fi (1)
Dobson, A. (Coventry C), 1989 v Bul, Sen, Ei, US (4)
Dodd, J. R. (Southampton), 1991 v Pol, Ei, T, Sen, M, F; 1992 v G, Pol (8)
Donowa, L. (Norwich C), 1985 v Is, R (sub), Fi (sub) (3)
Dorigo, A. (Aston Villa), 1987 v Se, Sp, T, Mor, USSR, F, P; 1988 v WG, Y, S (2) (11)
Downing, S. (Middlesbrough), 2004 v Ho, Se; 2005 v Uk, A, W, Az (sub), Sp (sub); 2006 v D (8)
Dozzell, J. (Ipswich T), 1987 v Se, Y (sub), Sp, USSR, F, P; 1989 v Se, Gr (sub); 1990 v Se (sub) (9)
Draper, M. A. (Notts Co), 1991 v Ei (sub); 1992 v G, Pol (3)
Duberry, M. W. (Chelsea), 1997 v Mol, Pol, Ge; 1998 v Mol, Gr (5)
Dunn, D. J. I. (Blackburn R), 1999 v CzR (sub); 2000 v I (sub), T, Slo; 2001 v Ge, G, Fi, I, Sp, M, Gr; 2002 v Ho, Gr, Ho (2), Slv, P, Sw, I, P (20)
Duxbury, M. (Manchester U), 1981 v Sw (sub), Ei (sub), R (sub), Sw; 1982 v N; 1983 v WG (2) (7)
Dyer, B. A. (C Palace), 1994 v Ru, F, US, Bel, P; 1995 v P (sub); 1996 v Cro; 1997 v Mol, Ge; 1998 v Mol, Gr (10)
Dyer, K. C. (Ipswich T), 1998 v Mol, I, Gr, Sw, S.Af, Arg; 1999 v Se, Bul, CzR, Se; (with Newcastle U), 2000 v Y (11)
Dyson, P. I. (Coventry C), 1981 v N, R, Sw, Ei (4)

Eadie, D. M. (Norwich C), 1994 v F (sub), US; 1997 v Mol, Ge (2), I; 1998 v I (7)
Ebbrell, J. (Everton), 1989 v Sen, Ei, US (sub); 1990 v P, F, USSR, Cz; 1991 v H, Pol, Ei, W, T; 1992 v G, T (14)

Edghill, R. A. (Manchester C), 1994 v D, Ru; 1995 v A (3)
Ehiogu, U. (Aston Villa), 1992 v H, M, Cz, F; 1993 v Sp, N, T, Sm, T, Ho, Pol, N; 1994 v Pol, Ho, Sm (15)
Elliott, P. (Luton T), 1985 v Fi; 1986 v T, D (3)
Elliott, R. J. (Newcastle U), 1996 v P, A (2)
Elliott, S. W. (Derby Co), 1998 v F, Arg (sub) (2)
Etherington, N, (Tottenham H), 2002 v Slv (sub), I; 2003 v Y (sub) (3)
Euell, J. J. (Wimbledon), 1998 v F, Arg (sub); 1999 v Se (sub), Bul (se), Pol (sub), H (6)
Evans, R. (Chelsea), 2003 v Ser, Slo (2)

Fairclough, C. (Nottingham F), 1985 v T, Is, Ei; 1987 v Sp, T; (with Tottenham H), 1988 v Y, F (7)
Fairclough, D. (Liverpool), 1977 v W (1)
Fashanu, J. (Norwich C), 1980 v EG; 1981 v N (sub), R, Sw, Ei (sub), H; (with Nottingham F), 1982 v N, H, Pol, S; 1983 v WG (sub) (11)
Fear, P. (Wimbledon), 1994 v Ru, F, US (sub) (3)
Fenton, G. A. (Aston Villa), 1995 v Ei (1)
Fenwick, T. W. (C Palace), 1981 v N, R, Sw, Ei; (with QPR), R; 1982 v N, H, S (2); 1983 v WG (2) (11)
Ferdinand, A. J. (West Ham U), 2005 v Uk, A, Pol; 2006 v D (sub), W, G, A, Pol, F (2), N; 2007 v Mol, Sw, G (2), I, Ho (sub) (17)
Ferdinand, R. G. (West Ham U), 1997 v Sw, Ge; 1998 v I, Gr; 2000 v Y (5)
Fereday, W. (QPR), 1985 v T, Ei (sub). Fi; 1986 v T (sub), I (5)
Flitcroft, G. W. (Manchester C), 1993 v Sm, Hol, N, P, Cz, Br, S, F; 1994 v Pol, Ho (10)
Flowers, T. (Southampton), 1987 v Mor, F; 1988 v WG (sub) (3)
Ford, M. (Leeds U), 1996 v Cro; 1997 v Mol (2)
Forster, N. M. (Brentford), 1995 v Br, Mal, An, F (4)
Forsyth, M. (Derby Co), 1988 v Sw (1)
Foster, S. (Brighton & HA), 1980 v EG (sub) (1)
Fowler, R. B. (Liverpool), 1994 v Sm, Ru (sub), F, US; 1995 v P, A; 1996 v P, A (8)
Froggatt, S. J. (Aston Villa), 1993 v Sp, Sm (sub) (2)
Futcher, P. (Luton T), 1977 v W, S, Fi, N; (with Manchester C), 1978 v N, Fi, I (2), Y (2); 1979 v D (11)

Gabbiadini, M. (Sunderland), 1989 v Bul, USA (2)
Gale, A. (Fulham), 1982 v Pol (1)
Gallen, K. A. (QPR), 1995 v Ei, La (2); 1996 v Cro (4)
Gardner, A. (Tottenham H), 2002 v I (sub) (1)
Gascoigne, P. (Newcastle U), 1987 v Mo, USSR, P; 1988 v WG, Y, S (2), F (2), Sw, M, USSR (sub), Mor (13)
Gayle, H. (Birmingham C), 1984 v I, Sp (2) (3)
Gernon, T. (Ipswich T), 1983 v Gr (1)
Gerrard, P. W. (Oldham Ath), 1993 v T, Ho, Pol, N, P, Cz, Br, S, F; 1994 v D, Ru; 1995 v P, A, Ei (2), La (2); 1996 v P (18)
Gerrard, S. G. (Liverpool), 2000 v L, Pol, D, Y (4)
Gibbs, N. (Watford), 1987 v Mor, USSR, F, P; 1988 v T (5)
Gibson, C. (Aston Villa), 1982 v N (1)
Gilbert, W. A. (C Palace), 1979 v W, Bul; 1980 v Bul; 1981 v N, R, Sw, R, Sw, H; 1982 v N (sub), H (11)
Goddard, P. (West Ham U), 1981 v N, Sw, Ei (sub); 1982 v N (sub), Pol, S; 1983 v WG (2) (8)
Gordon, D. (Norwich C), 1987 v T (sub), Mor (sub), F, P (4)
Gordon, D. D. (C Palace), 1994 v Ru, F, US, Bel, P; 1995 v P, A, Ei (2), La (2); 1996 v P, N (13)
Grant, A. J. (Everton), 1996 v An (sub) (1)
Grant, L. A. (Derby Co), 2003 v I (sub); 2004 v P, T, Se (sub) (4)
Granville, D. P. (Chelsea), 1997 v Ge (sub), Pol; 1998 v Mol (3)
Gray, A. (Aston Villa), 1988 v S, F (2)
Greening, J. (Manchester U), 1999 v H, Se (sub), Bul; 2000 v Pol; 2001 v Ge, G, Fi, I, Sp (sub), Fi, Alb; (with Middlesbrough), 2002 v Ho, G, Alb, Gr, Ho (sub), I, P (18)
Griffin, A. (Newcastle U), 1999 v H; 2001 v I, Sp (3)
Guppy, S. A. (Leicester C), 1998 v Sw (1)

Haigh, P. (Hull C), 1977 v N (sub) (1)
Hall, M. T. J. (Coventry C), 1997 v Pol (2), I, Sw, Ge; 1998 v Mol, Gr (2) (8)
Hall, R. A. (Southampton), 1992 v H (sub), F; 1993 v Sm, T, Ho, Pol, P, Cz, Br, S, F (11)
Hamilton, D. V. (Newcastle U), 1997 v Pol (1)
Harding, D. A. (Brighton & HA), 2005 v Uk (sub), W, Az, Sp (4)
Hardyman, P. (Portsmouth), 1985 v Ei; 1986 v D (2)
Hargreaves, O. (Bayern Munich), 2001 v Ge (sub), I, Sp (3)
Harley, J. (Chelsea), 2000 v Arg (sub), T (sub), Slo (3)
Hart, C. (Manchester C), 2007 v Sp (sub), Slo (2)
Hateley, M. (Coventry C), 1982 v Pol, S; 1983 v Gr (2), H; (with Portsmouth), 1984 v F (2), I, Sp (2) (10)
Hayes, M. (Arsenal), 1987 v Sp, T; 1988 v F (sub) (3)
Hazell, R. J. (Wolverhampton W), 1979 v D (1)
Heaney, N. A. (Arsenal), 1992 v H, M, Cz, F; 1993 v N, T (6)
Heath, A. (Stoke C), 1981 v R, Sw, H; 1982 v N, H; (with Everton), Pol, S; 1983 v WG (8)
Hendon, I. M. (Tottenham H), 1992 v H, M, Cz, F; 1993 v Sp, N, T (7)
Hendrie, L. A. (Aston Villa), 1996 v Cro (sub); 1998 v Sw (sub); 1999 v Se, Bul, L, F, Pol; 2000 v L, D, Arg, Y, I, Slo (sub) (13)
Hesford, I. (Blackpool), 1981 v Ei (sub), Pol (2), S (2); 1983 v WG (2) (7)
Heskey, E. W. I. (Leicester C), 1997 v I, Ge, Pol (2); 1998 v I, Gr (2), Sw, F, S.Af, Arg; 1999 v Se, Bul, L; 2000 v L; (with Liverpool), Y (16)
Hilaire, V. (C Palace), 1980 v Bul, S (1+1 sub), EG (2); 1981 v N, R, Sw (sub); 1982 v Pol (sub) (9)
Hill, D. R. L. (Tottenham H), 1995 v Br, Mal, An, F (4)
Hillier, D. (Arsenal), 1991 v T (1)
Hinchcliffe, A. (Manchester C), 1989 v D (1)
Hinshelwood, P. A. (C Palace), 1978 v N; 1980 v EG (2)
Hirst, D. (Sheffield W), 1988 v USSR, F; 1989 v D, Bul (sub), Sen, Ei, US (7)
Hislop, N. S. (Newcastle U), 1998 v Sw (1)
Hoddle, G. (Tottenham H), 1977 v W (sub); 1978 v Fi (sub), I (2), Y; 1979 v D, W, Bul; 1980 v S (2), EG (2) (12)
Hodge, S. (Nottingham F), 1983 v Gr (sub); 1984 v D, F, I, Sp (2); (with Aston Villa), 1986 v R, T (8)
Hodgson, D. J. (Middlesbrough), 1981 v N, R (sub), Sw, Ei; 1982 v Pol; 1983 v WG (6)
Holdsworth, D. (Watford), 1989 v Gr (sub) (1)
Holland, C. J. (Newcastle U), 1995 v La; 1996 v N (sub), A (sub), Cro, Bel, An, Br; 1997 v Mol, Pol, Sw (10)
Holland, P. (Mansfield T), 1995 v Br, Mal, An, F (4)
Holloway, D. (Sunderland), 1998 v Sw (sub) (1)
Horne, B. (Millwall), 1989 v Gr (sub), Pol, Bul, Ei, US (5)
Howe, E. J. F. (Bournemouth), 1998 v S.Af (sub), Arg (2)
Hoyte, J. R. (Arsenal), 2004 v Ho (sub), Se; 2005 v Uk (sub), A (sub), Pol (sub), Sp, Ho; 2006 v N (sub); 2007 v Sw, G (sub), Ho, Sp, I (sub), Slo, CzR, I, Ser, Ho (18)
Hucker, P. (QPR), 1984 v I, Sp (2)
Huckerby, D. (Coventry C), 1997 v I (sub), Sw, Ge (sub), Pol (sub) (4)
Huddlestone, T. A. (Derby Co), 2005 v Ho, G, Az; (with Tottenham H), 2006 v A, Pol, F (2), N; 2007 v Mol, Sw, G (2), Ho, Sp, I (sub), Slo, CzR, Ser (sub) (18)
Hughes, S. J. (Arsenal), 1997 v I, Sw, Ge, Pol; 1998 v Mol, I, Gr, Sw (sub) (8)
Humphreys, R. J. (Sheffield W), 1997 v Pol, Ge (sub), Sw (3)
Hunt, N. B. (Bolton W), 2004 v Ho; 2005 v Uk, A, W, Az, Sp, G; 2006 v D, W (sub), G (10)

Impey, A. R. (QPR), 1993 v T (1)
Ince, P. (West Ham U), 1989 v Alb; 1990 v Se (2)

Jackson, M. A. (Everton), 1992 v H, M, Cz, F; 1993 v Sm (sub), T, Ho, Pol, N; 1994 v Pol (10)
Jagielka, P. N. (Sheffield U), 2003 v Ser, Slo; 2004 v Cro (sub), Mac, P, T (6)
James, D. (Watford), 1991 v Ei (2), T, Sen, M, USSR, F; 1992 v G, T, Pol (10)
James, J. C. (Luton T), 1990 v F, USSR (2)

Jansen, M. B (C Palace), 1999 v Se, Bul, L; (with Blackburn R), F (sub), Pol; 2000 v I (sub) (6)
Jeffers, F. (Everton), 2000 v L, Arg, I, T, Slo; 2001 v Ge; (with Arsenal), 2002 v Ho, G (sub), Alb; 2003 v Y, Slo, Mac, T; 2004 v Cro, Mac, P (16)
Jemson, N. B. (Nottingham F), 1991 v W (1)
Jenas, J. A. (Newcastle U), 2002 v Slo, I, P (sub); 2003 v Y, Slo, Mac, T; 2004 v Cro, T (9)
Jerome, C. (Cardiff C), 2006 v A (sub), F (sub), N (sub); (with Birmingham C), 2007 v Mol (sub), Sw (sub), G (sub), Ho (sub) (7)
Joachim, J. K. (Leicester C), 1994 v D (sub); 1995 v P, A, Ei, Br, Mal, An, F; 1996 v N (9)
Johnson, G. M. C. (West Ham U), 2003 v T (sub), Ser (sub); (with Chelsea), 2004 v Cro, Mac, P, T, Ho; 2005 v Pol, W, Az, Sp, G; 2006 v W, N (14)
Johnson, S. A. M. (Crewe Alex), 1999 v L (sub), CzR (sub), F (sub), Pol; (with Derby Co), Se, Bul; 2000 v D, Arg (sub), Y, I, T; 2001 v Fi; 2002 v Ho (sub), Alb (sub); (with Leeds U), P (15)
Johnson, T. (Notts Co), 1991 v H (sub), Ei (sub); 1992 v G, T, Pol; (with Derby Co), M, Cz (sub) (7)
Johnston, C. P. (Middlesbrough), 1981 v N, Ei (2)
Jones, D. R. (Everton), 1977 v W (1)
Jones, C. H. (Tottenham H), 1978 v Y (sub) (1)
Jones, D. F. L. (Manchester U), 2004 v Se (sub) (1)
Jones, R. (Liverpool), 1993 v Sm, Ho (2)

Keegan, G. A. (Manchester C), 1977 v W (1)
Kenny, W. (Everton), 1993 v T (1)
Keown, M. (Aston Villa), 1987 v Sp, Mor, USSR, P; 1988 v T, S, F (2) (8)
Kerslake, D. (QPR), 1986 v T (1)
Kilcline, B. (Notts C), 1983 v D, Gr (2)
Kilgallon, M. (Leeds U), 2004 v Se (sub); 2005 v Uk, Pol (sub), Az (sub); 2007 v Ho (5)
King, A. E. (Everton), 1977 v W; 1978 v Y (2)
King, L. B. (Tottenham H), 2000 v L (sub), I, T, Slo; 2001 v I, Sp (sub), Fi; 2002 v G, Alb, Gr, Ho (2) (12)
Kirkland, C. E. (Coventry C), 2001 v M; (with Liverpool), 2002 v Gr, Ho (2), P (sub); 2003 v Y, Mac; 2004 v Mac (8)
Kitson, P. (Leicester C), 1991 v Sen (sub), M, F; 1992 v Pol; (with Derby Co), M, Cz, F (7)
Knight, A. (Portsmouth), 1983 v Gr, H (2)
Knight, I. (Sheffield W), 1987 v Se (sub), Y (2)
Knight, Z. (Fulham), 2002 v Slo (sub), I (2), P (4)
Konchesky, P. M. (Charlton Ath), 2002 v Slo, P, Sw, I, P; 2003 Y, Slo, Mac, P, T, Ser, Slo; 2004 v Cro, Mac, P (15)
Kozluk, R. (Derby Co), 1998 v F, Arg (sub) (2)

Lake, P. (Manchester C), 1989 v D, Alb (2), Pol; 1990 v Pol (5)
Lampard, F. J. (West Ham U), 1998 v Gr (2), Sw, F, S.Af, Arg; 1999 v Se, Bul, L, CzR, F, Pol, Se; 2000 v L, Arg, Y, I, T, Slo (19)
Langley, T. W. (Chelsea), 1978 v I (sub) (1)
Lee, D. J. (Chelsea), 1990 v F; 1991 v H, Pol, Ei (2), T, Sen, USSR, F; 1992 v Pol (10)
Lee, R. (Charlton Ath), 1986 v I (sub); 1987 v Se (sub) (2)
Lee, S. (Liverpool), 1981 v R, Sw, H; 1982 v S; 1983 v WG (2) (6)
Lennon, A. J. (Tottenham H), 2006 v A, Pol (2)
Le Saux, G. (Chelsea), 1990 v P, F, USSR, Cz (4)
Lescott, J. P. (Wolverhampton W), 2003 v Y (sub), I (sub) (2)
Lita, L. H. (Bristol C), 2005 v Ho (sub); (with Reading), 2006 v N (sub); 2007 v Sp (sub), I, Slo (sub), CzR (sub), I, Ser, Ho (9)
Lowe, D. (Ipswich T), 1988 v F, Sw (sub) (2)
Lukic, J. (Leeds U), 1981 v N, R, Ei, R, Sw, H; 1982 v H (7)
Lund, G. (Grimsby T), 1985 v T; 1986 v R, T (3)

McCall, S. H. (Ipswich T), 1981 v Sw, H; 1982 v H, S; 1983 v WG (2) (6)
McDonald, N. (Newcastle U), 1987 v Se (sub), Sp, T; 1988 v WG, Y (sub) (5)
McEveley, J. (Blackburn R), 2003 v I (sub) (1)
McGrath, L. (Coventry C), 1986 v D (1)
MacKenzie, S. (WBA), 1982 v N, S (2) (3)
McLeary, A. (Millwall), 1988 v Sw (1)
McLeod, I. M. (Milton Keynes D), 2006 v N (sub) (1)
McMahon, S. (Everton), 1981 v Ei; 1982 v Pol; 1983 v D, Gr (2); (with Aston Villa), 1984 v H (6)
McManaman, S. (Liverpool), 1991 v W, M (sub); 1993 v N, T, Sm, T; 1994 v Pol (7)
Mabbutt, G. (Bristol R), 1982 v Pol (2), S; (with Tottenham H), 1983 v D; 1984 v F; 1986 v D, I (7)
Makin, C. (Oldham Ath), 1994 v Ru (sub), F, US, Bel, P (5)
Marney, D. E. (Tottenham H), 2005 v Ho (sub) (1)
Marriott, A. (Nottingham F), 1992 v M (1)
Marsh, S. T. (Oxford U), 1998 v F (1)
Marshall, A. J. (Norwich C), 1995 v Mal, An; 1997 v Pol, I (4)
Marshall, L. K. (Norwich C), 1999 v F (sub) (1)
Martin, L. (Manchester U), 1989 v Gr (sub), Alb (sub) (2)
Martyn, N. (Bristol R), 1988 v S (sub), M, USSR, Mor, F; 1989 v D, Se, Gr, Alb (2); 1990 v Se (11)
Matteo, D. (Liverpool), 1994 v F (sub), Bel, P; 1998 v Sw (4)
Matthew, D. (Chelsea), 1990 v P, USSR (sub), Cz; 1991 v Ei, M, USSR, F; 1992 v G (sub), T (9)
May, A. (Manchester C), 1986 v I (sub) (1)
Merson, P. (Arsenal), 1989 v D, Gr, Pol (sub); 1990 v Pol (4)
Middleton, J. (Nottingham F), 1977 v Fi, N; (with Derby Co), 1978 v N (3)
Miller, A. (Arsenal), 1988 v Mor (sub); 1989 v Sen; 1991 v H, Pol (4)
Mills, D. J. (Charlton Ath), 1999 v Se, Bul (sub), L, Pol, H, Se; (with Leeds U), 2000 v L, Pol, D, Arg, Y (sub), I, T, Slo (14)
Mills, G. R. (Nottingham F), 1981 v R; 1982 v N (2)
Milner, J. P. (Leeds U), 2004 v Se (sub); (with Newcastle U), 2005 v Uk, A (sub), Pol, W, Az, Sp, Ho, G, Az; 2006 v D, W, G, A, Pol (sub), F, N; 2007 v Sw (sub), G (2), Ho, Sp, I (sub), Slo, CzR, I, Ser, Ho (28)
Mimms, R. (Rotherham U), 1985 v Is (sub), Ei (sub); (with Everton), 1986 v I (3)
Minto, S. C. (Charlton Ath), 1991 v W; 1992 v H, M, Cz; 1993 v T; 1994 v Ho (6)
Moore, I. (Tranmere R), 1996 v Cro (sub), Bel (sub), An, P, Br; 1997 v Mol (sub); (with Nottingham F), Sw (sub) (7)
Moore, L. I. (Aston Villa), 2006 v A (sub) (1)
Moran, S. (Southampton), 1982 v N (sub); 1984 v F (2)
Morgan, S. (Leicester C), 1987 v Se, Y (2)
Morris, J. (Chelsea), 1997 v Pol (sub), Sw (sub), Ge (sub); 1999 v Bul (sub), L (sub), CzR; 2000 v Pol (7)
Mortimer, P. (Charlton Ath), 1989 v Sen, Ei (2)
Moses, A. P. (Barnsley), 1997 v Pol; 1998 v Gr (sub) (2)
Moses, R. M. (WBA), 1981 v N (sub), Sw, Ei, R, Sw, H; 1982 v N (sub); (with Manchester U), H (8)
Mountfield, D. (Everton), 1984 v Sp (1)
Muggleton, C. D. (Leicester C), 1990 v F (1)
Mullins, H. I. (C Palace), 1999 v Pol (sub), H, Bul (3)
Murphy, D. B. (Liverpool), 1998 v Mol, Gr (sub); 2000 v T, Slo (4)
Murray, P. (QPR), 1997 v I, Pol; 1998 v I, Gr (4)
Murray, M. W. (Wolverhampton W), 2003 v Slo, Mac (sub), I, T; 2004 v Cro (5)
Mutch, A. (Wolverhampton W), 1989 v Pol (1)
Myers. A. (Chelsea), 1995 v Br, Mal, An (sub), F (4)

Naylor, L. M. (Wolverhampton W), 2000 v Arg; 2001 v M, Gr (3)
Nethercott, S. (Tottenham), 1994 v D, Ru, F, US, Bel, P; 1995 v La (2) (8)
Neville, P. J. (Manchester U), 1995 v Br, Mal, An, F; 1996 v P, N (sub); 1997 v Ge (7)
Newell, M. (Luton T), 1986 v D (1 + 1 sub), I (1 + 1 sub) (4)
Newton, A. L. (West Ham U), 2001 v Ge (1)
Newton, E. J. I. (Chelsea), 1993 v T (sub); 1994 v Sm (2)
Newton, S. O. (Charlton Ath), 1997 v Mol, Pol, Ge (3)
Nicholls, A. (Plymouth Arg), 1994 v F (1)

Noble, M. J. (West Ham U), 2007 v Slo (sub), CzR (sub), I, Ser, Ho (5)
Nolan, K. A. J. (Bolton W), 2003 v I (sub) (1)
Nugent, D. J. (Preston NE), 2006 v W (sub), G (sub), N; 2007 v Mol, Sw, G (2), Ho, Sp, Slo, CzR, I, Ser, Ho (14)

Oakes, M. C. (Aston Villa), 1994 v D (sub), F (sub), US, Bel, P; 1996 v A (6)
Oakes, S. J. (Luton T), 1993 v Br (sub) (1)
Oakley, M. (Southampton), 1997 v Ge; 1998 v F, S.Af, Arg (4)
O'Brien, A. J. (Bradford C), 1999 v F (1)
O'Connor, J. (Everton), 1996 v Cro, An, Br (3)
O'Neil, G. P. (Portsmouth) 2005 v Uk, A, Pol, W, Az, G; 2006 v G, Pol, F (9)
Oldfield, D. (Luton T), 1989 v Se (1)
Olney, I. A. (Aston Villa), 1990 v P, F, USSR, Cz; 1991 v H, Pol, Ei (2), T; 1992 v Pol (sub) (10)
Onuoha C. (Manchester C), 2006 v Pol (sub), F; 2007 v Ho (sub), Slo, CzR, I, Ser, Ho (8)
Ord, R. J. (Sunderland), 1991 v W, M, USSR (3)
Osman, R. C. (Ipswich T), 1979 v W (sub), Se; 1980 v D, S (2), EG (2) (7)
Owen, G. A. (Manchester C), 1977 v S, Fi, N; 1978 v N, Fi, I (2), Y; 1979 v D, W; (with WBA), Bul, Se (sub); 1980 v D, S (2), EG; 1981 v Sw, R; 1982 v N (sub), H; 1983 v WG (2) (22)
Owen, M. J. (Liverpool), 1998 v Gr (1)

Painter, I. (Stoke C), 1986 v I (1)
Palmer, C. (Sheffield W), 1989 v Bul, Sen, Ei, US (4)
Parker, G. (Hull C), 1986 v I (2); (with Nottingham F), F; 1987 v Se, Y (sub), Sp (6)
Parker, P. (Fulham), 1985 v Fi, T, Is (sub), Ei, R, Fi; 1986 v T, D (8)
Parker, S. M. (Charlton Ath), 2001 v Ge (sub), G, Fi (sub), Alb (sub); 2002 v Ho (sub), G (sub), Alb, Slo, I (sub), Sw (sub), I (sub), P (sub) (12)
Parkes, P. B. F. (QPR), 1979 v D (1)
Parkin, S. (Stoke C), 1987 v Sp (sub); 1988 v WG (sub), T, S (sub), F (5)
Parlour, R. (Arsenal), 1992 v H, M, Cz, F; 1993 v Sp, N, T; 1994 v D, Ru, Bel, P; 1995 v A (12)
Parnaby, S. (Middlesbrough), 2003 v Y (sub), Ser, Slo; 2004 v Cro (4)
Peach, D. S. (Southampton), 1977 v S, Fi, N; 1978 v N, I (2) (6)
Peake, A. (Leicester C), 1982 v Pol (1)
Pearce, I. A. (Blackburn R), 1995 v Ei, La; 1996 v N (3)
Pearce, S. (Nottingham F), 1987 v Y (1)
Pennant, J. (Arsenal), 2001 v M (sub), Gr (sub); 2002 v Ho (sub), Alb (sub), Gr, Ho (2), Slv, I (sub), P (sub), Sw, I, P; 2003 v Y, P (sub), Ser, Slo; 2004 v Cro, Mac; 2005 v Uk, A, Pol, W, Az (24)
Pickering N. (Sunderland), 1983 v D (sub), Gr, H; 1984 v F (sub + 1), I (2), Sp; 1985 v Is, R, Fi; 1986 v R, T; (with Coventry C), D, I (15)
Platt, D. (Aston Villa), 1988 v M, Mor, F (3)
Plummer, C. S. (QPR), 1996 v Cro (sub), Bel, An, P (sub), Br (5)
Pollock, J. (Middlesbrough), 1995 v Ei (sub); 1996 v N, A (3)
Porter, G. (Watford), 1987 v Sp (sub), T, Mor, USSR, F, P (sub); 1988 v T (sub), Y, S (2), F, Sw (12)
Potter, G. S. (Southampton), 1997 v Mol (1)
Pressman, K. (Sheffield W), 1989 v D (sub) (1)
Proctor, M. (Middlesbrough), 1981 v Ei (sub), Sw; (with Nottingham F) 1982 v N, Pol (4)
Prutton, D. T. (Nottingham F), 2001 v Ge (sub), G (sub), Fi, Sp (sub), M, Gr (sub); 2002 v Ho (sub), G, Gr (sub), Slv (sub), I, Sw (sub), I, P; 2003 v Y, Slo, Mac; (with Southampton), I, P, T, Ser, Slo; 2004 v Cro, P, T (25)
Purse, D. J. (Birmingham C), 1998 v F. S.Af (2)

Quashie, N. F. (QPR), 1997 v Pol; 1998 v Mol, Gr, Sw (4)
Quinn, W. R. (Sheffield U), 1998 v Mol (sub), I (2)

Ramage, C. D. (Derby Co), 1991 v Pol (sub), W; 1992 v Fr (sub) (3)
Ranson, R. (Manchester C), 1980 v Bul, EG; 1981 v R (sub), R, Sw (1 + 1 sub), H, Pol (2), S (10)
Redknapp, J. F. (Liverpool), 1993 v Sm, Pol, N, P, Cz, Br, S, F; 1994 v Pol, Ho (sub), D, Ru, F, US, Bel, P; 1995 v P, A; 1998 v Sw (19)
Redmond, S. (Manchester C), 1988 v F (2), M, USSR, Mor, F; 1989 v D, Se, Gr, Alb (2), Pol; 1990 v Se, Pol (14)
Reeves, K. P. (Norwich C), 1978 v I, Y (2); 1979 v N, W, Bul, Sw; 1980 v D, S; (with Manchester C), EG (10)
Regis, C. (WBA), 1979 v D, Bul, Se; 1980 v S, EG; 1983 v D (6)
Reid, N. S. (Manchester C), 1981 v H (sub); 1982 v H, Pol (2), S (2) (6)
Reid, P. (Bolton W), 1977 v S, Fi, N; 1978 v Fi, I, Y (6)
Reo-Coker, N. S. A. (Wimbledon), 2004 v T (sub); (with West Ham U), Ho, Se; 2005 v Uk (sub), A, Pol, Az; 2006 v D, W, G, Pol, N; 2007 v Mol, Sw, G (2), Sp, I, Slo, CzR, I, Ser, Ho (23)
Richards, D. I. (Wolverhampton W), 1995 v Br, Mal, An, F (4)
Richards, J. P. (Wolverhampton W), 1977 v Fi, N (2)
Richards, M. (Manchester C), 2007 v Mol, G (2) (3)
Richards, M. L. (Ipswich T), 2005 v Uk (1)
Richardson, K. E. (Manchester U), 2005 v Ho (sub), G, Az; 2006 v D, F (2); 2007 v Sp (sub), I, Slo, CzR, I (sub), Ser (12)
Rideout, P. (Aston Villa), 1985 v Fi, Is, Ei (sub), R; (with Bari), 1986 v D (5)
Ridgewell, L. M. (Aston Villa), 2004 v Ho, Se; 2005 v Sp (sub), Ho, G; 2006 v D, W, N (8)
Riggott, C. M. (Derby Co), 2001 v Sp (sub), Fi (sub), Alb, M (sub); 2002 v Ho (sub), Slv, P, Sw (8)
Ripley, S. (Middlesbrough), 1988 v USSR, F (sub); 1989 v D (sub), Se, Gr, Alb (2); 1990 v Se (8)
Ritchie, A. (Brighton & HA), 1982 v Pol (1)
Rix, G. (Arsenal), 1978 v Fi (sub), Y; 1979 v D, Se; 1980 v D (sub), Bul, S (7)
Roberts, A. J. (Millwall), 1995 v Ei, La (2); (with C Palace), 1996 v N, A (5)
Roberts, B. J. (Middlesbrough), 1997 v Sw (sub) (1)
Robins, M. G. (Manchester U), 1990 v P, F, USSR, Cz; 1991 v H (sub), Pol (6)
Robinson, P. P. (Watford), 1999 v Se, Bul; 2000 v Pol (3)
Robinson, P. W. (Leeds U), 2000 v D; 2001 v Ge, G, Fi, Sp; 2002 v Slv, I, P, Sw, I, P (11)
Robson, B. (WBA), 1979 v W, Bul (sub), Se; 1980 v D, Bul, S (2) (7)
Robson, S. (Arsenal), 1984 v I; 1985 v Fi, Is, Fi; 1986 v R, I; (with West Ham U), 1988 v S, Sw (8)
Rocastle, D. (Arsenal), 1987 v Se, Y, Sp, T; 1988 v WG, T, Y, S (2), F (2 subs), M, USSR, Mor (14)
Roche, L. P. (Manchester U), 2001 v Fi (1)
Rodger, G. (Coventry C), 1987 v USSR, F, P; 1988 v WG (4)
Rogers, A. (Nottingham F), 1998 v F, S.Af, Arg (3)
Rosario, R. (Norwich C), 1987 v T (sub), Mor, F, P (sub) (4)
Rose, M. (Arsenal), 1997 v Ge (sub), I (2)
Rosenior, L. J. (Fulham), 2005 v G (sub), Az; 2007 v Ho (sub), Sp (sub), I, Slo (sub), Ho (sub) (7)
Routledge, W. (C Palace), 2005 v Sp (sub), Ho, Az (sub); (with Tottenham H), 2006 v N; 2007 v Mol, Sw, G, Ho, I, Slo (sub), CzR (sub), Ser (sub) (12)
Rowell, G. (Sunderland), 1977 v Fi (1)
Ruddock, N. (Southampton), 1989 v Bul (sub), Sen, Ei, US (4)
Rufus, R. R. (Charlton Ath), 1996 v Cro, Bel, An, P, Br; 1997 v I (6)
Ryan, J. (Oldham Ath), 1983 v H (1)
Ryder, S.H. (Walsall), 1995 v Br, An, F (3)

Samuel, J. (Aston Villa), 2002 v I; 2003 v Y, Slo, Mac, I, P, T (7)
Samways, V. (Tottenham H), 1988 v Sw (sub), USSR, F; 1989 v D, Se (5)
Sansom, K. G. (C Palace), 1979 v D, W, Bul, Se; 1980 v S (2), EG (2) (8)
Scimeca, R. (Aston Villa), 1996 v P; 1997 v Mol, Pol, Ge, I; 1998 v Mol, I, Gr (2) (9)

Scowcroft, J. B. (Ipswich T), 1997 v Pol, Ge (2), I (sub); 1998 v Gr (sub) (5)
Seaman, D. (Birmingham C), 1985 v Fi, T, Is, Ei, R, Fi; 1986 v R, F, D, I (10)
Sedgley, S. (Coventry C), 1987 v USSR, F (sub), P; 1988 v F; 1989 v D (sub), Se, Gr, Alb (2), Pol; (with Tottenham H), 1990 v Se (11)
Sellars, S. (Blackburn R), 1988 v S (sub), F, Sw (3)
Selley, I. (Arsenal), 1994 v Ru (sub), F (sub), US (3)
Serrant, C. (Oldham Ath), 1998 v Gr (2) (2)
Sharpe, L. (Manchester U), 1989 v Gr; 1990 v P (sub), F, USSR, Cz; 1991 v H, Pol (sub), Ei (8)
Shaw, G. R. (Aston Villa), 1981 v Ei, Sw, H; 1982 v H, S; 1983 v WG (2) (7)
Shearer, A. (Southampton), 1991 v Ei (2), W, T, Sen, M, USSR, F; 1992 v G, T, Pol (11)
Shelton, G. (Sheffield W), 1985 v Fi (1)
Sheringham, T. (Millwall), 1988 v Sw (1)
Sheron, M. N. (Manchester C), 1992 v H, F; 1993 v N (sub), T (sub), Sm, Ho, Pol, N, P, Cz, Br, S, F; 1994 v Pol (sub), Ho, Sm (16)
Sherwood, T. A. (Norwich C), 1990 v P, F, USSR, Cz (4)
Shipperley, N. J. (Chelsea), 1994 v Sm (sub); (with Southampton), 1995 v Ei, La (2); 1996 v P, N, A (7)
Sidwell, S. J. (Reading), 2003 v Ser, Slo; 2004 v Cro (sub), Mac, T (5)
Simonsen, S. P. A. (Tranmere R), 1998 v F; (with Everton), l999 v CzR, F, Bul (4)
Simpson, P. (Manchester C), 1986 v D (sub); 1987 v Y, Mor, F, P (5)
Sims, S. (Leicester C), 1977 v W, S, Fi, N; 1978 v N, Fi, I (2), Y (2) (10)
Sinclair, T. (QPR), 1994 v Ho, Sm, D, Ru, F, US, Bel, P; 1995 v P, Ei (2), La; 1996 v P; (with West Ham U), 1998 v Sw (5)
Sinnott, L. (Watford), 1985 v Is (sub) (1)
Slade, S. A. (Tottenham H), 1996 v Bel, An, P, Br (4)
Slater, S. I. (West Ham U), 1990 v P, USSR (sub), Cz (sub) (3)
Small, B. (Aston Villa), 1993 v Sm, T, Ho, Pol, N, P, Cz, Br, S, F; 1994 v Pol, Sm (12)
Smith, A. (Leeds U), 2000 v D, Arg (sub); 2001 v G, Fi, Sp; 2002 v I, P, Sw, I, P (10)
Smith, D. (Coventry C), 1988 v M, USSR (sub), Mor; 1989 v D, Se, Alb (2), Pol; 1990 v Se, Pol (10)
Smith, M. (Sheffield W), 1981 v Ei, R, Sw, H; 1982 v Pol (sub) (5)
Smith, M. (Sunderland), 1995 v Ei (sub) (1)
Smith, T. W. (Watford), 2001 v Ge (sub) (1)
Snodin, I. (Doncaster R), 1985 v T, Is, R, Fi (4)
Soares T. J. (C Palace), 2006 v D (sub), G (sub), A, N (sub) (4)
Statham, B. (Tottenham H), 1988 v Sw; 1989 v D (sub), Se (3)
Statham, D. J. (WBA), 1978 v Fi, 1979 v W, Bul, Se; 1980 v D; 1983 v D (6)
Stead, J. G. (Blackburn R), 2004 v Ho (sub), Se (sub); 2005 v Uk, A, W, Az, Ho (sub), Az (sub); (with Sunderland), 2006 v D (sub), W, Pol (sub) (11)
Stein, B. (Luton T), 1984 v D, H, I (3)
Sterland, M. (Sheffield W), 1984 v D, H, F (2), I, Sp (2) (7)
Steven, T. (Everton), 1985 v Fi, T (2)
Stevens, G. (Brighton & HA), 1983 v H; (with Tottenham H), 1984 v H, F (1+1 sub), I (sub), Sp (1+1 sub); 1986 v I (8)
Stewart, J. (Leicester C), 2003 v P (sub) (1)
Stewart, P. (Manchester C), 1988 v F (1)
Stockdale, R. K. (Middlesbrough), 2001 v Ge (sub) (1)
Stuart, G. C. (Chelsea), 1990 v P (sub), F, USSR, Cz; 1991 v T (sub) (5)
Stuart, J. C. (Charlton Ath), 1996 v Bel, An, P, Br (4)
Suckling, P. (Coventry C), 1986 v D; (with Manchester C), 1987 v Se (sub), Y, Sp, T; (with C Palace), 1988 v S (2), F (2), Sw (10)
Summerbee, N. J. (Swindon T), 1993 v P (sub), S (sub), F (3)
Sunderland, A. (Wolverhampton W), 1977 v W (1)
Sutton, C. R. (Norwich), 1993 v Sp (sub), T (sub + 1), Ho, P (sub), Cz, Br, S, F; 1994 v Pol, Ho, Sm, D (13)
Swindlehurst, D. (C Palace), 1977 v W (1)
Sutch, D. (Norwich C), 1992 v H, M, Cz; 1993 v T (4)

Talbot, B. (Ipswich T), 1977 v W (1)
Taylor, A. (Blackburn R), 2006 v N (sub) (1)
Taylor, A. D. (Middlesbrough), 2007 v Sp (1)
Taylor, M. (Blackburn R), 2001 v M (sub) (1)
Taylor, M. S. (Portsmouth), 2003 v Slo (sub), I; 2004 v T (3)
Taylor, R. A. (Wigan Ath), 2006 v A (sub), Pol, F (2) (4)
Taylor, S. J. (Arsenal), 2002 v Ho, G, Alb (3)
Taylor, S. V. (Newcastle U), 2004 v Ho, Se; 2005 v W (sub), Ho, G (sub), Az; 2006 v G, A, Pol; 2007 v Mol, Sw, G (2), Sp, Slo, I, Ser, Ho (18)
Terry, J. G. (Chelsea), 2001 v Fi, Sp, Fi, Alb, M, Gr; 2002 v Ho (3) (9)
Thatcher, B. D. (Millwall), 1996 v Cro; (with Wimbledon), 1997 v Mol, Pol; 1998 v I (4)
Thelwell, A. A. (Tottenham H), 2001 v Sp (sub) (1)
Thirlwell, P. (Sunderland), 2001 v Ge (sub) (1)
Thomas, D. (Coventry C), 1981 v Ei; 1983 v WG (2), Gr, H; (with Tottenham H), I, Sp (7)
Thomas, J. W. (Charlton Ath), 2006 v A, Pol (2)
Thomas, M. (Luton T), 1986 v T, D, I (3)
Thomas, M. (Arsenal), 1988 v Y, S, F (2), M, USSR, Mor; 1989 v Gr, Alb (2), Pol; 1990 v Se (12)
Thomas, R. E. (Watford), 1990 v P (1)
Thompson, A. (Bolton W), 1995 v La; 1996 v P (2)
Thompson, D. A. (Liverpool), 1997 v Pol (sub), Ge; 2000 v L (sub), Pol (sub), D (sub), I, T (sub) (7)
Thompson, G. L. (Coventry C), 1981 v R, Sw, H; 1982 v N, H, S (6)
Thorn, A. (Wimbledon), 1988 v WG (sub). Y, S, F, Sw (5)
Thornley, B. L. (Manchester U), 1996 v Bel, P, Br (3)
Tiler, C. (Barnsley), 1990 v P, USSR, Cz; 1991 v H, Pol, Ei (2), T, Sen, USSR, F; (with Nottingham F), 1992 v G, T (13)
Tonge, M. W. E. (Sheffield U), 2004 v Mac, Se (2)

Unsworth, D. G. (Everton), 1995 v A, Ei (2), La; 1996 v N, A (6)
Upson, M. J. (Arsenal), 1999 v Se, Bul, L, F; 2000 v L, Pol, D; 2001 v I, Sp (sub), M (sub), Gr (11)

Vassell, D. (Aston Villa), 1999 v H (sub); 2000 v Pol (sub); 2001 v Ge, G, Fi, I, Fi, Alb; 2002 v Ho, G, Gr (11)
Vaughan, J. O. (Everton), 2007 v I (sub) (1)
Venison, B. (Sunderland), 1983 v D, Gr; 1985 v Fi, T, Is, Fi; 1986 v R, T, D (2) (10)
Vernazza, P. A. P. (Arsenal), 2001 v G (sub); (with Watford), M (sub) (2)
Vinnicombe, C. (Rangers), 1991 v H (sub), Pol, Ei (2), T, Sen, M, USSR (sub), F; 1992 v G, T, Pol (12)

Waddle, C. (Newcastle U), 1985 v Fi (1)
Walcott, T. J. (Arsenal), 2007 v Mol, Sw, G (1+sub), Ho, Sp (6)
Wallace, D. (Southampton), 1983 v Gr, H; 1984 v D, H, F (2), I, Sp (sub); 1985 v Fi, T, Is; 1986 v R, D, I (14)
Wallace, Ray (Southampton), 1989 v Bul, Sen (sub), Ei; 1990 v Se (4)
Wallace, Rod (Southampton), 1989 v Bul, Ei (sub), US; 1991 v H, Pol, Ei, T, Sen, M, USSR, F (11)
Walker, D. (Nottingham F), 1985 v Fi; 1987 v Se, T; 1988 v WG, T, S (2) (7)
Walker, I. M. (Tottenham H), 1991 v W; 1992 v H, Cz, F; 1993 v Sp, N, T, Sm; 1994 v Pol (9)
Walsh, G. (Manchester U), 1988 v WG, Y (2)
Walsh, P. M. (Luton T), 1983 v D (sub), Gr (2), H (4)
Walters, K. (Aston Villa), 1984 v D (sub), H (sub); 1985 v Is, Ei, R; 1986 v R, T, D, I (sub) (9)
Ward, P. D. (Brighton & HA), 1978 v N; 1980 v EG (2)
Warhurst, P. (Oldham Ath), 1991 v H, Pol, W, Sen, M (sub), USSR, F (sub); (with Sheffield W), 1992 v G (8)
Watson, B. (Crystal Palace), 2007 v G (sub) (1)
Watson, D. (Norwich C), 1984 v D, F (2), I (2), Sp (2) (7)
Watson, D. N. (Barnsley), 1994 v Ho, Sm; 1995 v Br, F; 1996 v N (5)
Watson, G. (Sheffield W), 1991 v Sen, USSR (2)

Watson, S. C. (Newcastle U), 1993 v Sp (sub), N; 1994 v Sm (sub), D; 1995 v P, A, Ei (2), La (2); 1996 v N, A (12)
Weaver, N. J. (Manchester C), 2000 v L, Pol, Arg, I, T, Slo; 2001 v I, Fi, Alb; 2002 v Slv (sub) (10)
Webb, N. (Portsmouth), 1985 v Ei; (with Nottingham F), 1986 v D (2) (3)
Welsh, J. J. (Liverpool), 2004 v Ho; 2005 v Ho (sub), G (sub), Az; 2006 v W (sub), G; (with Hull C), N (sub); 2007 v Ho (sub) (8)
Whelan, P. J. (Ipswich T), 1993 v Sp, T (sub), P (3)
Whelan, N. (Leeds U), 1995 v A (sub), Ei (2)
Whittingham, P. (Aston Villa), 2004 v Ho (sub); 2005 v Uk (sub), W (sub), Az, Sp, Ho, Az; 2006 v D (sub), W, G, Pol, F (1+sub), N; 2007 v Ho (sub); (with Cardiff C), Slo (sub), I (sub) (17)
Wilson, M. A. (Manchester U), 2001 v Sp, Fi (sub), Alb, M (sub); (with Middlesbrough), 2002 v Ho (sub), Alb (sub) (6)
White, D. (Manchester C), 1988 v S (2), F, USSR; 1989 v Se; 1990 v Pol (6)
Whyte, C. (Arsenal), 1982 v S (1+1 sub); 1983 v D, Gr (4)
Wicks, S. (QPR), 1982 v S (1)
Wilkins, R. C. (Chelsea), 1977 v W (1)
Wilkinson, P. (Grimsby T), 1985 v Ei, R (sub); (with Everton), 1986 v R (sub), I (4)
Williams, D. (Sunderland), 1998 v Sw (sub); 1999 v F (2)
Williams, P. (Charlton Ath), 1989 v Bul, Sen, Ei, US (sub) (4)
Williams, P. D. (Derby Co), 1991 v Sen, M, USSR; 1992 v G, T, Pol (6)
Williams, S. C. (Southampton), 1977 v S, Fi, N; 1978 v N, I (1 + 1 sub), Y (2); 1979 v D, Bul, Se (sub); 1980 v D, EG (2) (14)
Winterburn, N. (Wimbledon), 1986 v I (1)
Wise, D. (Wimbledon), 1988 v Sw (1)
Woodcook, A. S. (Nottingham F), 1978 v Fi, I (2)
Woodgate, J. S. (Leeds U), 2000 v Arg (1)
Woodhouse, C. (Sheffield U), 1999 v H, Se, Bul; 2000 v Pol (sub) (4)
Woods, C. C. E. (Nottingham F), 1979 v W (sub), Se; (with QPR), 1980 v Bul, EG; 1981 v Sw; (with Norwich C), 1984 v D (6)
Wright, A. G. (Blackburn), 1993 v Sp, N (2)
Wright, M. (Southampton), 1983 v Gr, H; 1984 v D, H (4)
Wright, R. I. (Ipswich T), 1997 v Ge, Pol; 1998 v Mol, I, Gr (2), S.Af, Arg; 1999 v Se, Bul, L, Pol, H, Se; 2000 v Y (15)
Wright, S. J. (Liverpool), 2001 v Ge (sub), G, M (sub); 2002 v Ho (sub), G, Alb, Ho, Slv, I, P (10)
Wright, W. (Everton), 1979 v D, W, Bul; 1980 v D, S (2) (6)
Wright-Phillips, S. C. (Manchester C), 2002 v I; 2003 v Y (sub), Mac (sub), I; 2004 v Mac (sub), T (6)

Yates, D. (Notts Co), 1989 v D (sub), Bul, Sen, Ei, US (5)
Young, A. S. (Watford), 2007 v Sw (sub), G (sub+1), Ho; (with Aston Villa), Sp, I (sub), Slo, CzR, I, Ho (10)
Young, L. P. (Tottenham H), 1999 v H; 2000 v D (sub), Arg (sub), T, Slo; (with Charlton Ath), 2002 v Ho, Gr, Ho, P (sub), Sw, I, P (12)

Zamora, R. L. (Brighton & HA), 2002 v P (sub), I (sub), P (sub); 2003 v I, Ser, Slo (sub) (6)

NORTHERN IRELAND

Armstrong, D. T. (Hearts), 2007 v W (sub) (1)

Bailie, N. (Linfield), 1990 v Is; 1994 v R (sub) (2)
Baird, C. P. (Southampton), 2002 v G; 2003 v S, Sp, Uk, Fi, Gr (6)
Beatty, S. (Chelsea), 1990 v Is; (with Linfield), 1994 v R (2)
Black, J. (Tottenham H), 2003 v Uk (sub) (1)
Black, K. T. (Luton T), 1990 v Is (1)
Black, R. Z. (Morecambe), 2002 v G (1)
Blackledge, G. (Portadown), 1978 v Ei (1)
Blayney, A. (Southampton), 2003 v Fi (sub); 2004 v Uk, Arm, Gr (4)
Boyle, W. S. (Leeds U), 1998 v Sw (sub), S (sub); 2001 v CzR (sub), Bul (1+sub), CzR; 2002 v Ma (7)
Braniff, K. R. (Millwall), 2002 v G; 2003 v S (sub), Sp (sub), Fi, Arm (sub), Gr, Sp; 2004 v Gr (sub); 2005 v Sw, S; 2006 v Ei (11)
Brotherston, N. (Blackburn R), 1978 v Ei (sub) (1)
Browne, G. (Manchester C), 2003 v S, Sp, Uk, Fi (sub), Sp (5)
Brunt, C. (Sheffield W), 2005 v S; 2007 v R (2)
Buchanan, D. T. H. (Bury), 2006 v S (sub); 2007 v G (sub), G (U-19) (sub), W (sub), R, S, Mol (7)
Buchanan, W. B. (Bolton W), 2002 v G (sub); 2003 v Uk (sub); (with Lisburn Distillery), 2004 v Uk, Arm, Gr (5)
Burns, L. (Port Vale), 1998 v Sw, S, Ei; 1999 v T, Fi, Mol, G, Mol, Ei; 2000 v F, T, G, Fi (13)

Callaghan, A. (Limavady U), 2006 v Is (sub+1), S; (with Ballymena U), 2007 v G (U-19), W (sub), R, S, Mol (8)
Campbell, S. (Ballymena U), 2003 v Sp (sub) (1)
Capaldi, A. C. (Birmingham C), 2002 v D (sub), Ic, Ma, G; 2003 v S, Sp, Uk, Fi, Arm, Gr; (with Plymouth Arg), Sp; 2004 v Uk, Arm, Gr (14)
Carlisle, W. T. (C Palace), 2000 v Fi (sub); 2001 v Ma, Ic, Bul (1+sub), CzR; 2002 v D, Ic, Ma (9)
Carroll, R. E. (Wigan Ath), 1998 v S, Ei; 1999 v T, Fi, Mol, G, Mol, Ei; 2000 v T, G, Fi (11)
Carson, S. (Rangers), 2000 v Ma; (with Dundee U), 2002 v D (sub) (2)
Carson, T. (Sunderland), 2007 v G (U-19), W (sub), R (sub), S (sub) (4)
Casement, C. (Ipswich T), 2007 v W, R, S, Mol (4)
Cathcart, C. (Manchester U), 2007 v G (U-19), W, R (sub) (3)
Catney, R. (Lisburn Distillery), 2007 v G (U-19) (1)
Clarke, L. (Peterborough U), 2003 v Sp (sub); 2004 v Uk (sub), Arm (sub); 2005 v Sw (4)
Clarke, R. (Newry C), 2006 v Is (2), W, Lie (2); 2007 v R (sub), G (7)
Clarke, R. D. J. (Portadown), 1999 v Ei (sub), S; 2000 v F (sub), S, W (sub) (5)
Clingan, S. G. (Wolverhampton W), 2003 v Arm (sub); 2004 v Uk, Arm, Gr; 2005 v Sw, S; (with Nottingham F), 2006 v Is (2), W, Lie (2) (11)
Close, B. (Middlesbrough), 2002 v Ic, Ma (sub), G; 2003 v S, Sp, Uk, Arm, Sp; 2004 v Arm, Gr (10)
Clyde, M. G. (Wolverhampton W), 2002 v G; 2003 v S, Sp, Uk, Fi (5)
Connell, T. E. (Coleraine), 1978 v Ei (sub) (1)
Coote, A. (Norwich C), 1998 v Sw (sub), S, Ei; 1999 v T, Fi,Mol, G, Mol, Ei; 2000 v F, T, G (12)
Convery, J. (Celtic), 2000 v S, W; 2001 v D, Ic (4)

Davey, H. (UCD), 2004 v Uk, Arm, Gr (3)
Davis, S. (Aston Villa), 2004 v Uk (sub), Arm (sub); 2005 v Sw (3)
Devine, D. (Omagh T), 1994 v R (1)
Devine, J. (Glentoran), 1990 v Is (1)
Dickson, H. (Wigan Ath). 2002 v Ma (1)
Doherty, M. (Hearts), 2007 v G (U-19) (sub), S (2)
Dolan, J. (Millwall), 2000 v Fi, Ma, S; 2001 v Ma, D, Ic (6)
Donaghy, M. M. (Larne), 1978 v Ei (1)
Donnelly, M. (Sheffield U), 2007 v S (sub) (1)
Dowie, I. (Luton T), 1990 v Is (1)
Duff, S. (Cheltenham T), 2003 v Sp (1)

Elliott, S. (Glentoran), 1999 v Fi (sub), Ei, S (sub) (3)
Ervin, J. (Linfield), 2005 v Sw; 2006 v W (sub) (2)
Evans, J. (Manchester U), 2006 v S; 2007 v R, G (3)

Feeney, L. (Linfield), 1998 v Ei (sub); 1999 v T, Fi, Mol; (with Rangers), G (sub), Ei, S; 2000 v Fi (8)
Feeney, W. (Bournemouth), 2002 v D, Ic (sub); 2003 v Fi, Arm, Gr; 2004 v Uk, Arm, Gr (8)

Ferguson, M. (Glentoran), 2000 v T (sub), Ma (sub) (2)
Fitzgerald, D. (Rangers), 1998 v Sw, S; 1999 v T (sub), Fi (4)
Fordyce, D. T. (Portsmouth), 2007 v G (U-19), W, R, S, Mol (5)
Friars, E. C. (Notts Co), 2005 v Sw, S; 2006 v Ei (sub), Is, W (sub), Lie (sub), S (7)
Friars, S. M. (Liverpool), 1998 v Sw, S, Ei; (with Ipswich T), 1999 v T, Fi, Mol, G, Mol; 2000 v F, T, G, Ma, S, W; 2001 v Ma, D, Ic, CzR, Bul (2), CzR (21)

Garrett, R. (Stoke C), 2007 v R, S, Mol (3)
Gault, M. (Linfield), 2005 v S (sub); 2006 v Ei (2)
Gilfillan, B. J. (Gretna), 2005 v S; 2006 v Ei, Is, W, Lie (2), S; (with Peterhead), 2007 v R, G (9)
Gillespie, K. R. (Manchester U), 1994 v R (1)
Glendinning, M. (Bangor), 1994 v R (1)
Graham, G. L. (C Palace), 1999 v S; 2000 v F, T, G, Fi (5)
Graham, R. S. (QPR), 1999 v Fi (sub), Mol, Ei (sub); 2000 v F (sub), T (sub), G (sub), Fi (sub), Ma, S, W; 2001 v Ma, D, CzR (sub), Bul (sub), CzR (sub) (15)
Gray, P. (Luton T), 1990 v Is (sub) (1)
Griffin, D. J. (St Johnstone), 1998 v S (sub), Ei; 1999 v T, Fi, G, Mol, Ei, S; 2000 v F, T (10)

Hamilton, G. (Blackburn R), 2000 v Ma (sub), S, W (sub); 2001 v Ma, D, Ic, CzR, Bul (2), CzR; (with Portadown), 2002 v Ic, Ma (12)
Hamilton, W. R. (Linfield), 1978 v Ei (1)
Harkin, M. P. (Wycombe W), Ma (sub), S (sub), W; 2001 v Ma (sub), D (sub), Ic, CzR, Bul (sub+1) (9)
Harvey, J. (Arsenal), 1978 v Ei (1)
Hawe, S. (Blackburn R), 2001 v Cz (1+sub) (2)
Hayes, T. (Luton T), 1978 v Ei (1)
Hazley, M. (Stoke C), 2007 v G (U-19), W (2)
Healy, D. J. (Manchester U), 1999 v Mol (sub), G (sub), Ei (sub), S; 2000 v F (sub), T, G, Fi (8)
Herron, C. J. (QPR), 2003 v Arm, Gr (2)
Higgins, R. (Derry C), 2006 v Ei (1)
Holmes, S. (Manchester C), Ma, S, W; 2001 v Ma, D, Ic, CzR, Bul (2), CzR; (with Wrexham), 2002 v D, Ic, Ma (13)
Howland, D. (Birmingham C), 2007 v W, R (sub) (2)
Hughes, J. (Lincoln C), 2006 v Is (sub+1), W, Lie (2); 2007 v R, G (7)
Hughes, M. A. (Tottenham H), 2003 v Sp (sub), Uk (sub), Fi, Arm, Gr, Sp; 2004 v Uk, Arm, Gr (sub); 2005 v Sw, S; (with Oldham Ath), 2006 v Ei (12)
Hughes, M. E. (Manchester C), 1990 v Is (sub)
Hunter, M. (Glentoran), 2002 v G (sub) (1)

Ingham, M. (Sunderland), 2001 v CzR, Bul (2), CzR (4)

Johnson, D. M. (Blackburn R), 1998 v Sw, S, Ei; 1999 v T, Fi, G, Mol, Ei; 2000 v F, T, G (11)
Johnston, B. (Cliftonville), 1978 v Ei (1)
Julian, A. A. (Brentford), 2005 v Sw (1)

Kee, P. V. (Oxford U), 1990 v Is (1)
Kelly, D. (Derry C), 2000 v Ma, W; 2001 v Ma, Ic (sub), CzR, Bul (2), CzR; 2002 v D, Ic, Ma (11)
Kelly, N. (Oldham Ath), 1990 v Is (sub) (1)
Kirk, A. (Hearts), 1999 v S; 2000 v Ma, S, W; 2001 v Ma, D, Ic (sub); 2002 v D, Ic (9)

Lafferty, K. (Burnley), 2006 v W, Lie (sub) (2)
Lennon, N. F. (Manchester C), 1990 v Is; (with Crewe Alex), 1994 v R (2)
Lindsay, K. (Larne), 2006 v Is (1)
Lyttle, G. (Celtic), 1998 v Sw, S; (with Peterborough U), 1999 v T (sub), Mol (2), S; 2000 v G, Fi (8)

Magee, J. (Bangor), 1994 v R (sub) (1)
Magilton, J. (Liverpool), 1990 v Is (1)
Matthews, N. P. (Blackpool), 1990 v Is (1)
McAllister, M. (Dungannon Swifts), 2007 v S (sub) (1)
McArdle, R. A. (Sheffield W), 2006 v Is, W, Lie (2); 2007 v R, G, G (U-19); (with Rochdale), W, R, S, Mol (11)
McAreavey, P. (Swindon T), 2000 v Ma, S; 2001 v Ma, D; 2002 v D, Ic (sub), Ma (sub) (7)
McBride, J. (Glentoran), 1994 v R (sub) (1)
McCaffrey, D. (Hibernian), 2006 v Is, S (sub); 2007 v G (U-19); W, S (sub), Mol (sub) (6)
McCallion, E. (Coleraine), 1998 v Sw (sub) (1)
McCann, G. S. (West Ham U), 2000 v S (sub), W; 2001 v D (sub), Ic, CzR, Bul (2), CzR; 2002 v D, Ic, Ma (11)
McCann, P. (Portadown), 2003 v Sp (1)
McCann, R. (Rangers), 2002 v G (sub); (with Linfield), 2003 v S (sub) (2)
McCartney, G. (Sunderland), 2001 v D, CzR, Bul (2); 2002 v D (5)
McChrystal, M. (Derry C), 2005 v Sw, S; 2006 v Ei, Is, W, Lie (2), S; 2007 v R (9)
McCourt, P. J. (Rochdale), 2002 v G; 2003 v S (sub), Sp, Uk, Fi (sub), Arm (sub), Gr (sub); 2005 v Sw; (with Derry C), 2006 v Ei (8)
McCoy, R. K. (Coleraine), 1990 v Is (1)
McCreery, D. (Manchester U), 1978 v Ei (1)
McEvilly, L. (Rochdale), 2003 v S, Sp, Uk, Fi (sub), Arm, Gr (sub); 2004 v Uk, Arm, Gr (9)
McFlynn, T. M. (QPR), 2000 v Ma (sub), W (sub); 2001 v Ma (sub), CzR (sub), Bul (sub+sub), CzR; (with Woking), 2002 v D (sub), Ic (sub); (with Margate), G; 2003 v S (sub), Sp (sub), Fi (sub), Arm, Gr (sub), Sp (sub); 2004 v Uk, Arm (sub), Gr (19)
McGibbon, P. C. G. (Manchester U), 1994 v R (1)
McGlinchey, B. (Manchester C), 1998 v Sw, S, Ei; (with Port Vale), 1999 v T, Fi, Mol, G, Mol, Ei, S; (with Gillingham), 2000 v F, G, T, Fi (14)
McGovern, M. (Celtic), 2005 v S; 2006 v Ei, Is (2), W, Lie (2), S; 2007 v R, G (10)
McGowan, M. V. (Clyde), 2006 v Is, S (2)
McIlroy, T. (Linfield), 1994 v R (sub) (1)
McKenna, K. (Tottenham H), 2007 v G (U-19), W, R (3)
McKnight, P. (Rangers), 1998 v Sw; 1999 v T (sub), Mol (sub) (3)
McLean, B. S. (Rangers), 2006 v Ei (1)
McMahon, G. J. (Tottenham H),1994 v R (sub) (1)
McVeigh, A. (Ayr U), 2002 v G (sub) (1)
McVeigh, P. F. (Tottenham H), 1998 v S (sub), Ei; 1999 v T, Mol, G, Mol, Ei; 2000 v F, T (sub), G (sub), Fi (11)
McVey, K. (Coleraine), 2006 v Is (sub+1), W (sub), Lie (sub), S; 2007 v S, Mol (7)
Meenan, D. (Finn Harps), 2007 v G (U-19) (sub); (with Monaghan U), R (sub) (2)
Melaugh, G. M. (Aston Villa), 2002 v G; 2003 v S, Sp, Uk, Fi, Arm, Gr, Sp; (with Glentoran), 2004 v Uk, Arm, Gr (11)
Millar, W. P. (Port Vale), 1990 v Is (1)
Miskelly, D. T. (Oldham Ath), 2000 v F, Ma, S, W; 2001 v Ma, D, Ic; 2002 v D, Ic, Ma (10)
Moreland, V. (Glentoran), 1978 v Ei (sub) (1)
Morgan, M, P. T. (Preston NE), 1999 v S (1)
Morris, E. J. (WBA), 2002 v G; (with Glentoran), 2003 v S, Sp, Uk, Fi, Arm, Gr, Sp (8)
Morrison, O. (Sheffield W), 2001 v Bul (sub); 2002 v Ma (sub); 2003 v S, Fi; (with Sheffield U), Arm, Gr, Sp (7)
Morrow, A. (Northampton T), 2001 v D (sub) (1)
Morrow, S. (Hibernian), 2005 v S (sub); 2006 v Ei, W, Lie (4)
Mulgrew, J. (Linfield), 2007 v G (U-19), W, R (sub), S, Mol (sub) (5)
Mulryne, P. P. (Manchester U), Sw, S, Ei; (with Norwich C), 1999 v G, Mol (5)
Murray, W. (Linfield), 1978 v Ei (sub) (1)
Murtagh, C. (Hearts), 2005 v S (sub) (1)

Nicholl, J. M. (Manchester U), 1978 v Ei (1)
Nixon, C. (Glentoran), 2000 v Fi (sub) (1)

O'Hara, G. (Leeds U), 1994 v R (1)
O'Neill, M. A. M. (Hibernian), 1994 v R (1)
O'Neill, J. P. (Leicester C), 1978 v Ei (1)

Paterson, M. A. (Stoke C), 2007 v W (sub), R (sub) (2)
Patterson, D. J. (C Palace), 1994 v R (1)

Quinn, S. J. (Blackpool), 1994 v R (1)

Ramsey, K. (Institute), 2006 v S (1)
Robinson, S. (Tottenham H), 1994 v R (1)

Scullion, D. (Dungannon Swifts), 2006 v Is (1+sub), W, Lie (2), S; 2007 v R, G (8)
Shiels, D. (Hibernian), 2005 v Sw (sub), S; 2006 v Ei (sub), Lie; 2007 v R, G (6)
Simms, G. (Hartlepool U), 2001 v Bul (2), CzR; 2002 v D, Ic, Ma, G; 2003 v S, Sp, Uk, Fi, Arm, Gr, Sp (14)
Skates, G. (Blackburn R), 2000 v Ma; 2001 v Ic (sub), CzR (2) (4)
Sloan, T. (Ballymena U), 1978 v Ei (1)
Smylie, D. (Newcastle U), 2006 v Ei (sub), Is (2), W, Lie (sub); (with Livingston), 2007 v G (6)
Stewart, T. (Wolverhampton W), 2006 v Is (1+sub), W (sub), Lie, S (sub); (unattached), 2007 v R (sub), G (sub); (with Linfield), G (U-19), W, R, S, Mol (12)

Taylor, J. (Hearts), 2007 v G (U-19) (sub), W (sub), R, Mol (4)
Taylor, M. S. (Fulham), 1998 v Sw (1)
Thompson, P. (Linfield), 2006 v Ei (sub), Lie; 2007 v R, G (4)
Toner, C. (Tottenham H), 2000 v Ma (sub), S (sub), W; 2001 v D, Ic, CzR, Bul (2), CzR; 2002 v D, Ic, Ma; (with Leyton Orient), 2003 v S, Sp, Uk, Fi, Gr (17)
Teggart, N. (Sunderland), 2005 v Sw (sub), S (sub) (2)
Tuffey, J. (Partick T), 2007 v G (U-19), W, R, S, Mol (5)
Turner, C. (Sligo R), 2007 v R (sub), G (sub), R, S (sub), Mol (5)

Ward, J. J. (Aston Villa), 2006 v Is, Lie (sub+sub); (with Chesterfield), 2007 v W (sub) (4)
Ward, M. (Dungannon Swifts), 2006 v S (sub) (1)
Ward, S. (Glentoran), 2005 v S; 2006 v Ei (sub), Is (1+sub), W, Lie (2), S; 2007 v R, G (10)
Waterman, D. G. (Portsmouth), 1998 v Sw, S, Ei; 1999 v T, Fi, Mol, G, Mol, Ei, S (sub); 2000 v F, T, G, Fi (14)
Webb, S. M. (Ross Co), 2004 v Uk, Arm, Gr; (with St Johnstone), 2005 v Sw, S; (with Ross Co), 2006 v Ei (6)
Wells, D. P. (Barry T), 1999 v S (1)
Whitley, Jeff (Manchester C), 1998 v Sw, S, Ei; 1999 v T, Fi, Mol, G, Ei, S; 2000 v F, G, T, Ma, S, W; 2001 v Ma, Ic (17)
Willis, P. (Liverpool), 2006 v Is (sub) (1)

SCOTLAND

Adam, C. (Rangers), 2006 v Ic, Ni, T; 2007 v Slv, F (5)
Adams, J. (Kilmarnock), 2007 v G (sub) (1)
Aitken, R. (Celtic), 1977 v Cz, W, Sw; 1978 v Cz, W; 1979 v P, N (2); 1980 v Bel, E; 1984 v EG, Y (2); 1985 v WG, Ic, Sp (16)
Albiston, A. (Manchester U), 1977 v Cz, W, Sw; 1978 v Sw, Cz (5)
Alexander, N. (Stenhousemuir), 1997 v P; 1998 v Bl, Ei, I; (with Livingston), 1999 v Li, Es, Bel (2), CzR, G (10)
Anderson, I. (Dundee), 1997 v Co (sub), US, CzR, P; 1998 v Bl, La, Fi, D (sub), Ei (sub), Ni; 1999 v G (sub), Ei, Ni, CzR; (with Toulouse), 2000 v Bos (15)
Anderson, R. (Aberdeen), 1997 v Es, A, Se; 1998 v La (sub), Fi, Ei, I; 1999 v Es, Bel, G, Ei, Ni, CzR; 2000 v Bos, Es (15)
Anthony, M. (Celtic), 1997 v La (sub), Es (sub), Col (3)
Archdeacon, O. (Celtic), 1987 v WG (sub) (1)
Archibald, A. (Partick Th), 1998 v Fi, Ei, Ni, I; 1999 v Li (5)
Archibald, S. (Aberdeen), 1980 v B, E (2), WG; (with Tottenham H), 1981 v D (5)

Bagen, D. (Kilmarnock), 1997 v Es, A (sub), Se (sub), Bl (4)
Bain, K. (Dundee), 1993 v P, I, Ma, P (4)
Baker, M. (St Mirren), 1993 v F, M, E; 1994 v Ma, A; 1995 v Gr, M, F (sub), Sk (sub); 1996 v H (sub) (10)
Baltacha, S. S. (St Mirren), 2000 v Bos, Li (sub), F (sub) (3)
Bannon, E. J. P. (Hearts), 1979 v US; (with Chelsea), P, N (2); (with Dundee U), 1980 v Bel, WG, E (7)
Beattie, C. (Celtic), 2004 v H (sub), R, D (sub), Ei; 2006 v A; 2007 v Slv (sub), F (7)
Beattie, J. (St Mirren), 1992 v D, US, P, Y (4)
Beaumont, D. (Dundee U), 1985 v Ic (1)
Bell, D. (Aberdeen), 1981 v D; 1984 v Y (2)
Bernard, P. R. J. (Oldham Ath), 1992 v R (sub), D, Se (sub), US; 1993 v Sw, P, I, Ma, P, F, Bul, M, E; 1994 v I, Ma (15)
Berra, C. (Hearts), 2005 v I; 2006 v A, I, N, Bl, Ic (6)
Bett, J. (Rangers), 1981 v Se, D; 1982 v Se, D, I, E (2) (7)
Black, E. (Aberdeen), 1983 v EG, Sw (2), Bel; 1985 v Ic, Sp (2), Ic (8)
Blair, A. (Coventry C), 1980 v E; 1981 v Se; (with Aston Villa), 1982 v Se, D, I (5)
Bollan, G. (Dundee U), 1992 v D, G (sub), US, P, Y; 1993 v Sw, P, I, P, F, Bul, M, E; 1994 v Sw; 1995 v Gr; (with Rangers) v Ru, Sm (17)
Bonar, P. (Raith R), 1997 v A, La, Es (sub), Se (4)
Booth, S. (Aberdeen), 1991 v R (sub), Bul (sub + 1), Pol, F (sub); 1992 v Sw, R, D, Se, US, P, Y; 1993 v Ma, P (14)
Bowes, M. J. (Dunfermline Ath), 1992 v D (sub) (1)
Bowman, D. (Hearts), 1985 v WG (sub) (1)
Boyack, S. (Rangers), 1997 v Se (1)
Boyd, K. (Kilmarnock), 2003 v Bel (sub); 2004 v R (sub), D, Ei; 2005 v H, N, Mol (sub), I (sub) (8)
Boyd, T. (Motherwell), 1987 v WG, Ei (2), Bel; 1988 v Bel (5)
Brazil, A. (Hibernian), 1978 v W (1)
Brazil, A. (Ipswich T), 1979 v N; 1980 v Bel (2), E (2), WG; 1981 v Se; 1982 v Se (8)
Brebner, G. I. (Manchester U), 1997 v Col, CzR (sub), US (sub), P; 1998 v Bl, La, Fi, D; (with Reading), 1999 v Li, Es, Bel (2), CzR, G, Ei, Ni, CzR; (with Hibernian), 2000 v Bos (18)
Brighton, T. (Rangers), 2005 v Ni, I (sub), Mol (sub), Bl; (with Clyde), 2006 v N (sub), Bl (sub), Ic (sub) (7)
Broadfoot, K. (St Mirren), 2005 v Bl; 2006 v Ni, T; 2007 v Slv, F (5)
Brough, J. (Hearts), 1981 v D (1)
Brown, A. H. (Hibernian), 2004 v D (1)
Brown, S. (Hibernian), 2005 v H, Sp, Slv, I, Mol; 2006 v A, I, N; 2007 v Slv, F (10)
Browne, P. (Raith R), 1997 v A (1)
Bryson, C. (Clyde), 2006 v Ic (sub) (1)
Buchan, J. (Aberdeen), 1997 v Se, Col, CzR, P; 1998 v Bl, La, Fi; 1999 v Li, Es, Bel, CzR, G, Ei (13)
Burchill, M. (Celtic), 1998 v Fi, D (sub); 1999 v Li, Es (sub), Bel (2), CzR, Ei, Ni, CzR; 2000 v Bos, Es; 2001 v La, Bel, Pol (15)
Burke, A. (Kilmarnock), 1997 v Es, A, Bl (sub); 1998 v Ei (sub) (4)
Burke, C. (Rangers), 2004 v R (sub), D (sub); 2005 v Ni (sub) (3)
Burley, G. E. (Ipswich T), 1977 v Cz, W, Sw; 1978 v Sw, Cz (5)
Burley, C. (Chelsea), 1992 v D; 1993 v Sw, P, I, P; 1994 v Sw, I (sub) (7)
Burns, H. (Rangers), 1985 v Sp, Ic (sub) (2)
Burns, T. (Celtic), 1977 v Cz, W, E; 1978 v Sw; 1982 v E (5)

Caldwell, G. (Newcastle U), 2000 v F, Ni, W; 2002 v Cro, Bel, La; 2003 v Is (sub), Ic, Gh, Bel, Ei, Ic, Li, A, G; 2004 v N, G, Li, Cro (19)
Caldwell, S. (Newcastle U), 2001 v La, Cro, Bel; 2002 v Cro (4)
Campbell, S. (Dundee), 1989 v N (sub), Y, F (3)
Campbell, S. P. (Leicester C), 1998 v Fi (sub), D, Ei, Ni (sub), I; 1999 v Li, Es, Bel (2), CzR, G, Ei, Ni, CzR (sub); 2000 v Bos (sub) (15)
Canero, P. (Kilmarnock), 2000 v F; 2001 v La (sub), Cro (sub), Bel, Pol; 2002 v La (sub); 2003 v D, Ni, Bel (sub), Ei, ic, Li, A, G; 2004 v Li, Cro (2) (17)
Carey, L. A. (Bristol C), 1998 v D (1)
Casey, J. (Celtic), 1978 v W (1)
Christie, M. (Dundee), 1992 v D, P (sub), Y (3)

Clark, R. (Aberdeen), 1977 v Cz, W, Sw (3)
Clarke, S. (St Mirren), 1984 v Bel, EG, Y; 1985 v WG, Ic, Sp (2), Ic (8)
Clarkson, D. (Motherwell), 2004 v D (sub); 2005 v Sp, Slv, N (sub), Mol, Ni (sub), Mol (sub), Bl (sub); 2006 v A (sub), N, Slv, Ic (sub), T (13)
Cleland, A. (Dundee U), 1990 v F, N (2); 1991 v R, Sw, Bul; 1992 v Sw, R, G, Se (2) (11)
Collins, J. (Hibernian), 1988 v Bel, E; 1989 v N, Y, F; 1990 v Y, F, N (8)
Collins, N. (Sunderland), 2005 v Mol, Bl; 2006 v A (sub), I, N, Bl, Slv (7)
Connolly, P. (Dundee U), 1991 v R (sub), Sw, Bul (3)
Connor, R. (Ayr U), 1981 v Se; 1982 v Se (2)
Conroy, R. (Celtic), 2007 v G (1)
Considine, A. (Aberdeen), 2007 v G (sub) (1)
Cooper, D. (Clydebank), 1977 v Cz, W, Sw, E; (with Rangers), 1978 v Sw, Cz (6)
Cooper, N. (Aberdeen), 1982 v D, E (2); 1983 v Bel, EG, Sw (2); 1984 v Bel, EG, Y; 1985 v Ic, Sp, Ic (13)
Crabbe, S. (Hearts), 1990 v Y (sub), F (2)
Craig, M. (Aberdeen), 1998 v Bl, La (2)
Craig, T. (Newcastle U), 1977 v E (1)
Crainey, S. D. (Celtic), 2000 v F (sub); 2003 v Bel, Ei (sub), A, G; 2004 v N, G (7)
Crainie, D. (Celtic), 1983 v Sw (sub) (1)
Crawford, S. (Raith R), 1994 v A, Eg, P, Bel; 1995 v Fi, Ru,Gr, Ru, Sm, M, F (sub), Sk (sub), Br (sub); 1996 v Gr, Fi (sub), H (1 + sub), Sp (sub), F (sub) (19)
Creaney, G. (Celtic), 1991 v Sw, Bul (2), Pol, F; 1992 v Sw, R, G (2), Se (2) (11)
Cummings, W. (Chelsea), 2000 v F, Ni; 2001 v La, Cro, Bel, Pol; 2002 v Cro, Bel (8)
Cuthbert, S. (Celtic), 2007 v G (1)

Dailly, C. (Dundee U), 1991 v R; 1992 v US, R; 1993 v Sw, P, I, Ic, P, F, Bul, M, E; 1994 v Sw, I, Ma, A, Eg, P, Bel; 1995 v Fi, Ru, Gr, Ru, Sm, M, F, Sk, Br; 1996 v Fi, Sm, H (2), Sp, F (34)
Dalglish, P. (Newcastle U), 1999 v Es, Bel, CzR; (with Norwich C), 2000 v Es (sub), Bos, Li (sub) (6)
Dargo, C. (Raith R), 1998 v Fi, Ei, Ni (sub), I; 1999 v Es, Bel (1+sub), CzR (sub), G, Ni (sub) (10)
Davidson, C. (St Johnstone), 1997 v Se, Bl (2)
Davidson, H. N. (Dundee U), 2000 v Es (sub), Li, F (3)
Dawson, A. (Rangers), 1979 v P, N (2); 1980 v B (2), E (2), WG (8)
Deas, P. A. (St Johnstone), 1992 v D (sub); 1993 v Ma (2)
Dempster, J. (Rushden & D), 2004 v H (sub) (1)
Dennis, S. (Raith R), 1992 v Sw (1)
Diamond, A. (Aberdeen), 2004 v H (sub); 2005 v H, Sp, Slv, I; 2006 v A, I, Bl (sub), Slv, Ic; 2007 v Slv, F (12)
Dickov, P. (Arsenal), 1992 v Y; 1993 v F, M, E (4)
Dodds, D. (Dundee U), 1978 v W (1)
Dods, D. (Hibernian), 1997 v La, Es, Se (2), Bl (5)
Doig, C. R. (Nottingham F), 2000 v Ni, W; 2001 v La, Cro, Pol; 2003 v D, Is, Ni, Ic, Gh, Bel, Ei; 2004 v N (sub) (13)
Donald, G. S. (Hibernian), 1992 v US (sub), P, Y (sub) (3)
Donnelly, S. (Celtic), 1994 v Eg, P, Bel; 1995 v Fi, Gr (sub); 1996 v Gr (sub), Sm, H (2), Sp, F (11)
Dorrans, G. (Livingston), 2007 v G (sub) (1)
Dow, A. (Dundee), 1993 v Ma (sub), Ic; (with Chelsea) 1994 v I (3)
Dowie, A. J. (Rangers), 2003 v D, Is; 2004 v N (sub), H, R, D. Ei; (with Partick Th), 2005 v Sp, Slv, N, Mol, Se, Ni, I (14)
Duffy, D. A. (Falkirk), 2005 v Se, Ni; 2006 v A (sub), I, Bl, Slv; (with Hull C), Ni, T (sub) (8)
Duffy, J. (Dundee), 1987 v Ei (1)
Duff, S. (Dundee U), 2003 v Is, Ni (sub), Ic, Gh, Bel, Ei (sub); 2004 v N, G, Cro (9)
Durie, G. S. (Chelsea), 1987 v WG, Ei, Bel; 1988 v Bel (4)
Durrant, I. (Rangers), 1987 v WG, Ei, Bel; 1988 v E (4)
Doyle, J. (Partick Th), 1981 v D, I (sub) (2)

Easton, C. (Dundee U), 1997 v Col, US, CzR, P; 1998 v Bl, Fi, D, Ei, Ni, I; 1999 v Li, Es, Bel (1+sub); 2000 v Li, F; 2001 v La (sub), Cro, Bel; 2002 v Cro, Bel (21)
Elliot, B. (Celtic), 1998 v Ni; 1999 v Li (sub) (2)
Elliot, C. (Hearts), 2006 v Ic; 2007 v Slv (2)
Esson, R. (Aberdeen), 2000 v Li, Ni; 2001 v La, Cro, Bel, Pol; 2002 v Bel (7)

Fagan, S. M. (Motherwell), 2005 v N (1)
Ferguson, B. (Rangers), 1997 v Col (sub), US, CzR, P; 1998 v Bl, La, Fi, D (sub), Ei, Ni, I; 1999 v Bel (12)
Ferguson, D. (Rangers), 1987 v WG, Ei, Bel; 1988 v E; 1990 v Y (5)
Ferguson, D. (Dundee U), 1992 v D, G, Se (2); 1993 v Sw, I, Ma (7)
Ferguson, D. (Manchester U), 1992 v US, P (sub), Y; 1993 v Sw, Ma (5)
Ferguson, I. (Dundee), 1983 v EG (sub), Sw (sub); 1984 v Bel (sub), EG (4)
Ferguson, I. (Clyde), 1987 v WG (sub), Ei; (with St Mirren), Ei, Bel; 1988 v Bel; (with Rangers), E (sub) (6)
Ferguson, R. (Hamilton A), 1977 v E (1)
Findlay, W. (Hibernian), 1991 v R, Pol, Bul (2), Pol (5)
Fitzpatrick, A. (St Mirren), 1977 v W (sub), Sw (sub), E; 1978 v Sw, Cz (5)
Fitzpatrick, M. (Motherwell), 2007 v G (1)
Flannigan, C. (Clydebank), 1993 v Ic (sub) (1)
Fleck, R. (Rangers), 1987 v WG (sub), Ei, Bel; (with Norwich C), 1988 v E (2); 1989 v Y (6)
Fletcher, D. B. (Manchester U), 2003 v Ic (sub); 2004 v G (sub) (2)
Fletcher, S. (Hibernian), 2007 v F (sub) (1)
Foster, R. M. (Aberdeen), 2005 v Mol, Se (sub); 2006 v Ic (sub), Ni; 2007 v Slv (sub) (5)
Fotheringham, M. M. (Dundee), 2004 v R, D (sub), Ei (sub) (3)
Fowler, J. (Kilmarnock), 2002 v Cro (sub), Bel, La (3)
Foy, R. A. (Liverpool), 2004 v H, R (sub), D; 2005 v H, N (5)
Fraser, S. T. (Luton T), 2000 v Ni (sub), W; 2001 v La, Cro (4)
Freedman, D. A. (Barnet), 1995 v Ru (sub + 1), Sm, M, F, Sk, Br; (with C Palace), 1996 v Sm (sub) (8)
Fridge, L. (St Mirren), 1989 v F; 1990 v Y (2)
Fullarton, J. (St Mirren), 1993 v F, Bul; 1994 v Ma, A, Eg, P, Bel; 1995 v M, F, Sk, Br; 1996 v Gr, Fi, H (sub + 1), Sp (sub), F (17)
Fulton, M. (St Mirren), 1980 v Bel, WG, E; 1981 v Se, D (sub) (5)
Fulton, S. (Celtic), 1991 v R, Sw, Bul, Pol, F; 1992 v G (2) (7)

Gallacher, K. (Dundee U), 1987 v WG, Ei (2), Bel (sub); 1988 v E (2); 1990 v Y (7)
Gallacher, P. (Dundee U), 1999 v Ei, Ni, CzR; 2000 v Bos, Es, Bos, F (7)
Gallagher, P. (Blackburn R), 2003 v G (sub); 2004 v N (sub), Li (sub), D; 2005 v H, Se, Mol; 2006 v A, I, N, Bl (11)
Galloway, M. (Hearts), 1989 v F; (with Celtic), 1990 v N (2)
Gardiner, J. (Hibernian), 1993 v F (1)
Geddes, R. (Dundee), 1982 v Se, D, E (2); 1988 v E (5)
Gemmill, S. (Nottingham F), 1992 v Sw, R (sub), G (sub), Se (sub) (4)
Germaine, G. (WBA), 1997 v Se (1)
Gilles, R. (St Mirren), 1997 v A (1 + sub), La, Es (2), Se, Bl (7)
Gillespie, G. (Coventry C), 1979 v US; 1980 v E; 1981 v D; 1982 v Se, D, I (2), E (8)
Glass, S. (Aberdeen), 1995 v M, F, Sk, Br; 1996 v Gr, Fi, H, Sp; 1997 v A (2), Es (11)
Glover, L. (Nottingham F), 1988 v Bel (sub); 1989 v N; 1990 v Y (3)
Goram, A. (Oldham Ath), 1987 v Ei (1)
Gordon, C. (Hearts), 2003 v Is (sub), Gh; 2004 v N (sub), Cro (2) (5)
Gough, C. R. (Dundee U), 1983 v EG, Sw, Bel; 1984 v Y (2) (5)
Graham, D. (Rangers), 1998 v Bl (sub), La (sub), Fi (sub), D, Ei (sub), Ni, I; 1999 v Li (8)
Grant, P. (Celtic), 1985 v WG, Ic, Sp; 1987 v WG, Ei (2), Bel; 1988 v Bel, E (2) (10)
Gray S. (Celtic), 1995 v F, Sk, Br; 1996 v Gr, H, Sp, F (7)

Gray, S. (Aberdeen), 1987 v WG (1)
Gunn, B. (Aberdeen), 1984 v EG, Y (2); 1985 v WG, Ic, Sp (2), Ic; 1990 v F (9)

Hagen, D. (Rangers), 1992 v D (sub), US (sub), P, Y; 1993 v Sw (sub), P, Ic, P (8)
Hammell, S. (Motherwell), 2001 v Pol (sub); 2002 v La; 2003 v Is, Ni, Gh, Bel (sub), Ei; 2004 v N, Li, Cro (2) (11)
Hamilton, B. (St Mirren), 1989 v Y, F (sub); 1990 v F, N (4)
Hamilton, J. (Dundee) 1995 v Sm (sub), Br; 1996 v Fi (sub), Sm, H (sub), Sp (sub), F; 1997 v A, La, Es, Se; (with Hearts), Es, A, Se (14)
Handyside, P. (Grimsby T), 1993 v Ic (sub), Bul, M, E; 1995 v Ru; 1996 v Fi, Sm (7)
Hannah, D. (Dundee U), 1993 v F (sub), Bul, M; 1994 v A, Eg, P, Bel; 1995 v Fi, Ru (sub), Gr, Ru, M, F, Sk, Br; 1996 v Gr (16)
Harper, K. (Hibernian), 1995 v Ru (sub); 1996 v Fi; 1997 v A (2), La, Es, Se (7)
Hartford, R. A. (Manchester C), 1977 v Sw (1)
Hartley, P. (Millwall), 1997 v A (sub) (1)
Hegarty, P. (Dundee U), 1987 v WG, Bel; 1988 v E (2); 1990 v F, N (6)
Hendry, J. (Tottenham H), 1992 v D (sub) (1)
Hetherston, B. (St Mirren), 1997 v Es (sub) (1)
Hewitt, J. (Aberdeen), 1982 v I; 1983 v EG, Sw (2); 1984 v Bel, Y (sub) (6)
Hogg, G. (Manchester U), 1984 v Y; 1985 v WG, Ic, Sp (4)
Hood, G. (Ayr U), 1993 v F, E (sub); 1994 v A (3)
Horn, R. (Hearts), 1997 v US, CzR, P; 1998 v Bl, La, D (sub) (6)
Howie, S. (Cowdenbeath), 1993 v Ma, Ic, P; 1994 v Sw, I (5)
Hughes, R. D. (Bournemouth), 1999 v CzR, Ei, Ni, CzR; 2000 v Bos, Es; 2001 v La, Cro, Bel (9)
Hughes, S. (Rangers), 2002 v La; 2003 v D, Ic, Gh, Be, Ei (sub), Ic (sub), A; 2004 v N (sub), Li (sub), Cro (sub+sub) (12)
Hunter, G. (Hibernian), 1987 v Ei (sub); 1988 v Bel, E (3)
Hunter, P. (East Fife), 1989 v N (sub), F (sub); 1990 v F (sub) (3)
Hutton, A. (Rangers), 2004 v R, D; 2005 v H, Slv, Se, Ni (sub); 2007 v F (sub) (7)

Irvine, G. (Celtic), 2006 v Ic, T (2)

James, K. F. (Falkirk), 1997 v Bl (1)
Jardine, I. (Kilmarnock), 1979 v US (1)
Jess, E. (Aberdeen), 1990 v F (sub), N (sub); 1991 v R, Sw, Bul (2), Pol, F; 1992 v Sw, R, G (2), Se (1 + sub) (14)
Johnson, G. I. (Dundee U), 1992 v US, P, Y; 1993 v Sw, P, Ma (6)
Johnston, A. (Hearts), 1994 v Bel; 1995 v Ru, 1996 v Sp (3)
Johnston, F. (Falkirk), 1993 v Ic (1)
Johnston, M. (Partick Th), 1984 v EG (sub); (with Watford), Y (2) (3)
Jordan, A. J. (Bristol C), 2000 v Bos (sub), Li, F (3)
Jupp, D. A. (Fulham), 1995 v Fi, Ru (2), Sm, M, F, Sk, Br; 1997 v Se (9)

Kirkwood, D. (Hearts), 1990 v Y (1)
Kennedy, J. (Celtic), 2003 v Is (sub), Ni, Ic, Gh, Bel, Ei, Ic, Li, A, G; 2004 v N (sub), Li, Cro (2), H (15)
Kerr, B. (Newcastle U), 2003 v D, Is, Ni, Ic, Gh, Bel, Ei, Ic, Li, A, G; 2004 v Li, Cro (2) (14)
Kerr, M. (Kilmarnock), 2001 v Pol (sub) (1)
Kerr, S. (Celtic), 1993 v Bul, M, E; 1994 v Ma, A, Eg, P, Bel; 1995 v Fi, Gr (10)
Kinniburgh, W. D. (Motherwell), 2004 v R (sub); 2006 v A (sub), Ic (3)
Kyle, K. (Sunderland), 2001 v La (sub), Cro (sub), Pol (sub); 2003 v Ic, Ei, Ic, Li, G; 2004 v N. G, Cro (2) (12)

Lambert, P. (St Mirren), 1991 v R, Sw, Bul (2), Pol, F; 1992 v Sw, R, G (2), Se (11)
Langfield, J. (Dundee), 2000 v W; 2002 v Cro (2)
Lappin, S. (St Mirren), 2004 v H, R, D, Ei; 2005 v H (sub), Slv, N, Mol, Se; 2006 v Slv (sub) (10)
Lauchlan, J. (Kilmarnock), 1998 v Ei, Ni, I; 1999 v CzR, G, Ni, CzR; 2000 v Bos, Es, Bos, Li (11)
Lavety, B. (St Mirren), 1993 v Ic, Bul (sub), M (sub), E; 1994 v Ma, A (sub), Eg (sub), Bel (sub); 1995 v Fi (sub) (9)
Lavin, G. (Watford), 1993 v F, Bul, M; 1994 v Ma, Eg, P, Bel (7)
Lawson, P. (Celtic), 2004 v H, R, Ei; 2006 v A (sub), I (sub), N, Bl, Slv, Ic, Ni (10)
Leighton, J. (Aberdeen), 1982 v I (1)
Levein, C. (Hearts), 1985 v Sp, Ic (2)
Leven, P. (Kilmarnock), 2005 v Se (sub), Ni (2)
Liddell, A. M. (Barnsley), 1994 v Ma (sub); 1995 v Sm (sub), M (sub), F, Sk; 1996 v Gr, Fi, Sm, H (2), Sp, F (sub) (12)
Lindsey, J. (Motherwell), 1979 v US (1)
Locke, G. (Hearts), 1994 v Ma, A, Eg, P; 1995 v Fi; 1996 v Fi, H; 1997 v Es, A, Bl (10)
Love, G. (Hibernian), 1995 v Ru (1)
Lynch, S. (Celtic), 2003 v Is (sub), Ni (sub), Ic (sub), Gh (sub), Bel; (with Preston NE), Ei (sub), Li (sub), A (sub), G; 2004 v N, G, Li, Cro (sub) (13)

McAllister, G. (Leicester C), 1990 v N (1)
McAlpine, H. (Dundee U), 1983 v EG, Sw (2), Bel; 1984 v Bel (5)
McAnespie, K. (St Johnstone), 1998 v Fi (sub); 1999 v G (sub); 2000 v Ni, W (4)
McAuley, S. (St Johnstone), 1993 v P (sub) (1)
McAvennie, F. (St Mirren), 1982 v I, E; 1985 v Is, Ei, R (5)
McBride, J. (Everton), 1981 v D (1)
McBride, J. P. (Celtic), 1998 v Ni (sub), I (sub) (2)
McCall, S. (Bradford C), 1988 v E; (with Everton), 1990 v F (2)
McCann, N. (Dundee), 1994 v A, Eg, P, Bel; 1995 v Fi, Gr (sub), Sm; 1996 v Fi, Sm (9)
McClair, B. (Celtic), 1984 v Bel (sub), EG, Y (1 + 1 sub); 1985 v WG, Ic, Sp, Ic (8)
McCluskey, G. (Celtic), 1979 v US, P; 1980 v Bel (2); 1982 v D, I (6)
McCluskey, S. (St Johnstone), 1997 v Es (2), A, Se, Col, US, CzR; 1998 v Bl, La, D, Ei (sub), Ni, I; 1999 v Li (14)
McCoist, A. (Rangers), 1984 v Bel (1)
McConnell, I. (Clyde), 1997 v A (sub) (1)
McCormack, R. (Rangers), 2006 v Slv, Ni (sub), T (sub) (3)
McCracken, D. (Dundee U), 2002 v La; 2004 v N, G, Li, Cro (5)
McCulloch, A. (Kilmarnock); 1981 v Se (1)
McCulloch, I. (Notts Co), 1982 v E (2)
McCulloch, L. (Motherwell), 1997 v La (sub), Es (1 + sub), Se (sub + 1), A (sub), Col (sub); 1998 v Bl (sub), Fi (sub), D, Ei, Ni; 1999 v CzR, G (14)
McCunnie, J. (Dundee U), 2001 v Pol; 2002 v Cro; 2003 v D. Is, Ni; (with Ross Co), 2004 v H, R, Ei; 2005 v H (sub), Sp, Slv, N (sub), Mol, Se, Ni, I, Mol, Bl; (with Dunfermline Ath), 2006 v Bl, Slv (20)
MacDonald, J. (Rangers), 1980 v WG (sub); 1981 v Se; 1982 v Se (sub), L, I (2), E (2 sub) (8)
MacDonald, J. (Hearts), 2007 v G (sub) (1)
McDonald, C. (Falkirk), 1995 v Fi (sub), Ru, M (sub), F (sub), Br (sub) (5)
McEwan, C. (Clyde), 1997 v Col, US (sub), CzR (sub), P; (with Raith R), 1998 v Bl, La, Fi, D, Ei, Ni, I; 1999 v Li, Es (sub), Bel (2), CzR, G (sub) (17)
McEwan, D. (Livingston), 2003 v Ni (sub), Gh (sub) (2)
McFadden, J. (Motherwell), 2003 v D (sub), Is, Ni, Gh, Ei (sub), Ic, Li (7)
McFarlane, D. (Hamilton A), 1997 v Col, US (sub), P (sub) (3)
McGarry, S. (St Mirren), 1997 v US, CzR, P (sub) (3)
McGarvey, F. (St Mirren), 1977 v E; 1978 v Cz; (with Celtic), 1982 v D (3)
McGarvey, S. (Manchester U), 1982 v E (sub); 1983 v Bel, Sw; 1984 v Bel (4)
McGhee, M. (Aberdeen), 1981 v D (1)
McGinnis, G. (Dundee U), 1985 v Sp (1)

McGlinchey, M. R. (Celtic), 2007 v G (1)
McGregor, A. (Rangers), 2003 v D (sub), Is, Bel (sub), Ei (sub), A (sub); 2004 v N (6)
McGrillen, P. (Motherwell), 1994 v Sw (sub), I (2)
McGuire, D. (Aberdeen), 2002 v Bel, La (2)
McInally, J. (Dundee U), 1989 v F (1)
McKenzie, R. (Hearts), 1997 v Es, Bl (2)
McKimmie, S. (Aberdeen), 1985 v WG, Ic (2) (3)
McKinlay, T. (Dundee), 1984 v EG (sub); 1985 v WG, Ic, Sp (2), Ic (6)
McKinlay, W. (Dundee U), 1989 v N, Y (sub), F; 1990 v Y, F, N (6)
McKinnon, R. (Dundee U), 1991 v R, Pol (sub); 1992 v G (2), Se (2) (6)
McLaren, A, (Hearts), 1989 v F; 1990 v Y, N; 1991 v Sw, Bul, Pol, F; 1992 v R, G, Se (2) (11)
McLaren, A. (Dundee U), 1993 v I, Ma (sub); 1994 v Sw, I (sub) (4)
McLaughlin, B. (Celtic), 1995 v Ru, Sm, M, Sk (sub), Br (sub); 1996 v Gr (sub), Sm (sub), H (8)
McLaughlin, J. (Morton), 1981 v D; 1982 v Se, D, I, E (2); 1983 v EG, Sw (2), Bel (10)
McLean, S. (Rangers), 2003 v D (sub), Ni (sub), Gh (sub), Bel (sub) (4)
McLeish, A. (Aberdeen), 1978 v W; 1979 v US; 1980 v Bel, E (2); 1987 v Ei (6)
MacLeod, A. (Hibernian), 1979 v P, N (2) (3)
McLeod, J. (Dundee U), 1989 v N; 1990 v F (2)
MacLeod, M. (Dumbarton), 1979 v US; (with Celtic), P (sub), N (2); 1980 v Bel (5)
McManus, T. (Hibernian), 2001 v Bel (sub), Pol (sub); 2002 v Cro, Bel, La; 2003 v D (sub), Ni (sub), Ic, Gh, A, G (sub); 2004 v N (sub), Li (sub), Cro (14)
McMillan, S. (Motherwell), 1997 v A (sub + sub), Se, Bl (4)
McNab, N. (Tottenham H), 1978 v W (1)
McNally, M. (Celtic), 1991 v Bul; 1993 v Ic (2)
McNamara, J. (Dunfermline Ath), 1994 v A, Bel; 1995 v Gr, Ru, Sm; 1996 v Gr, Fi; (with Celtic), Sm, H (2), Sp, F (12)
McNaughton, K. (Aberdeen), 2002 v La (sub) (1)
McNeil, A. (Hibernian), 2007 v G (1)
McNichol, J. (Brentford), 1979 v P, N (2); 1980 v Bel (2), WG, E (7)
McNiven, D. (Leeds U), 1977 v Cz, W (sub), Sw (sub) (3)
McNiven, S. A. (Oldham Ath), 1996 v Sm (sub) (1)
McParland, A. (Celtic), 2003 v Gh (sub) (1)
McPhee, S. (Port Vale), 2002 v La (sub) (1)
McPherson, D. (Rangers), 1984 v Bel; 1985 v Sp; (with Hearts), 1989 v N, Y (4)
McQuilken, J. (Celtic), 1993 v Bul, E (2)
McStay, P. (Celtic), 1983 v EG, Sw (2); 1984 v Y (2) (5)
McWhirter, N. (St Mirren), 1991 v Bul (sub) (1)
Main, A. (Dundee U), 1988 v E; 1989 v Y; 1990 v N (3)
Malcolm, R. (Rangers), 2001 v Pol (1)
Maloney, S. (Celtic), 2002 v Cro (sub), Bel (sub), La; 2003 v D, Is, Ni, Bel, Ei, Ic (sub), Li (sub), A; 2004 v G (sub), Li, Cro (1+sub), H; 2005 v Ni, I, Mol, Bl; 2006 v A (21)
Malpas, M. (Dundee U), 1983 v Bel, Sw (1+1 sub); 1984 v Bel, EG, Y (2); 1985 v Sp (8)
Marshall, D. J. (Celtic), 2004 v H (sub), D; 2005 v I; 2006 v A, I, Ic, Ni, T; 2007 v Slv, F (10)
Marshall, S. R. (Arsenal), 1995 v Ru, Gr; 1996 v H, Sp, F (5)
Mason, G. R. (Manchester C), 1999 v Li (sub); (with Dunfermline Ath), 2002 v Bel (2)
Mathieson, D. (Queen of the South), 1997 v Col; 1998 v La; 1999 v G (sub) (3)
May, E. (Hibernian), 1989 v Y (sub), F (2)
Meldrum, C. (Kilmarnock), 1996 v F (sub); 1997 v A (2), La, Es, Se (6)
Melrose, J. (Partick Th), 1977 v Sw; 1979 v US, P, N (2); 1980 v Bel (sub), WG, E (8)
Miller, C. (Rangers), 1995 v Gr, Ru; 1996 v Gr, Sp, F; 1997 v A, La, Es (8)
Miller, J. (Aberdeen), 1987 v Ei (sub); 1988 v Bel; (with Celtic), E; 1989 v N, Y; 1990 v F, N (7)
Miller, K. (Hibernian), 2000 v F, Ni, W; (with Rangers), 2001 v Cro, Bel; 2002 v Cro, Bel (7)
Miller, W. (Aberdeen), 1978 v Sw, Cz (2)
Miller, W. (Hibernian), 1991 v R, Sw, Bul, Pol, F; 1992 v R, G (sub) (7)
Milne, K. (Hearts), 2000 v F (1)
Milne, R. (Dundee U), 1982 v Se (sub); 1984 v Bel, EG (3)
Money, I. C. (St Mirren), 1987 v Ei; 1988 v Bel; 1989 v N (3)
Montgomery, N. A. (Sheffield U), 2003 v A (sub); 2004 v Cro (sub) (2)
Morrison, S. A. (Aberdeen), 2004 v H (sub), D (sub), Ei; 2005 v H, Sp, Mol, Se, Ni, I, Mol, Bl; (with Dunfermline Ath), 2006 v A (12)
Muir, L. (Hibernian), 1977 v Cz (sub) (1)
Mulgrew, C. (Celtic), 2006 v Slv (sub), Ni (sub), T (3)
Murray, H. (St Mirren), 2000 v F (sub), Ni (sub), W (sub) (3)
Murray, I. (Hibernian), 2001 v Bel (sub), Pol; 2002 v Cro, Bel, La; 2003 v D, Ic, Gh, Bel, Ic, Li, G; 2004 v G, Cro (2) (15)
Murray, N. (Rangers), 1993 v P (sub), Ma, Ic, P; 1994 v Sw, I; 1995 v Fi, Ru, Gr, Sm; 1996 v Gr (sub), Fi, Sm, H (2), F (16)
Murray, R. (Bournemouth), 1993 v Ic (sub) (1)
Murray, S. (Kilmarnock), 2004 v D (sub), Ei (sub) (2)

Narey, D. (Dundee U), 1977 v Cz, Sw; 1978 v Sw, Cz (4)
Naismith, S. J. (Kilmarnock), 2006 v Slv (sub), Ic, Ni, T; 2007 v Slv, F, G (7)
Naysmith, G. (Hearts), 1997 v La, Es (1 + sub), Se, A, Col, US, CzR, P; 1998 v La, D; 1999 v Es, Bel (2), CzR, G, Ei, CzR; 2000 v Bos, Es, Bos, Li (22)
Neilson, R. (Hearts), 2000 v Ni (1)
Nevin, P. (Chelsea), 1985 v WG, Ic, Sp (2), Ic (5)
Nicholas, C. (Celtic), 1981 v Se; 1982 v Se; 1983 v EG, Sw, Bel; (with Arsenal), 1984 v Y (6)
Nicholson, B. (Rangers), 1999 v G, Ni, CzR (sub); 2000 v Bos (sub), Es, Bos, Li (7)
Nicol, S. (Ayr U), 1981 v Se; 1982 v Se, D; (with Liverpool), I (2), E (2); 1983 v EG, Sw (2), Bel; 1984 v Bel, EG, Y (14)
Nisbet, S. (Rangers), 1989 v N, Y, F; 1990 v Y, F (5)
Noble, D. J. (West Ham U), 2003 v A (sub); 2004 v N (sub) (2)
Notman, A. M. (Manchester U), 1999 v Li (sub), Es, Bel (sub+sub); 2000 v Li, F (sub), Ni, W; 2001 v La, Cro (10)

O'Brien, B. (Blackburn R), 1999 v Ei (sub), Ni (sub), CzR (sub); 2000 v Bos (sub); (with Livingston), 2003 v Is (sub), Gh (sub) (6)
O'Connor, G. (Hibernian), 2003 v D; 2004 v Cro, H, R; 2005 v Sp, Slv, N, Mol (8)
O'Donnell, P. (Motherwell), 1992 v Sw (sub), R, D, G (2), Se (1 + 1 sub); 1993 v P (8)
O'Neil, B. (Celtic), 1992 v D, G, Se (2); 1993 v Sw, P, I (7)
O'Neil, J. (Dundee U), 1991 v Bul (sub) (1)
O'Neill, M. (Clyde), 1995 v Ru (sub), F, Sk, Br; 1997 v Se (sub), Bl (sub) (6)
Orr, N. (Morton), 1978 v W (sub); 1979 v US, P, N (2); 1980 v Bel, E (7)

Parker, K. (St Johnstone), 2001 v Pol (sub) (1)
Parlane, D. (Rangers), 1977 v W (1)
Paterson, C. (Hibernian), 1981 v Se; 1982 v I (2)
Paterson, J. (Dundee U), 1997 v Col, US, CzR; 1999 v Bel (sub+sub); 2000 v Es, Bos, Li; 2002 v Cro (sub) (9)
Payne, G. (Dundee U), 1978 v Sw, Cz, W (3)
Peacock, L. A. (Carlisle U), 1997 v Bl (1)
Pearson, S. (Motherwell), 2003 v Is, Ni, Bel (sub), Ei, A, G; 2004 v N, G (8)
Pressley, S. (Rangers), 1993 v Ic, F, Bul, M, E; 1994 v Sw, I, M, A, Eg, P, Bel; 1995 v Fi; (with Coventry C), Ru (2), Sm, M, F, Sk, Br; (with Dundee U), 1996 v Gr, Sm, H (2), Sp, F (26)
Provan, D. (Kilmarnock), 1977 v Cz (sub) (1)
Prunty, B. (Aberdeen), 2004 v H, R (sub), Ei; 2005 v H (sub), Sp (sub), Slv (sub) (6)

Quinn, P. C. (Motherwell), 2004 v D; 2006 v Ni, T (3)

Quinn, R. (Celtic), 2006 v Ic (sub), T; 2007 v Slv (sub), G (4)

Rae, A. (Millwall), 1991 v Bul (sub + 1), F (sub); 1992 v Sw, R, G (sub), Se (2) (8)
Rae, G. (Dundee), 1999 v Ei (sub), Ni, CzR; 2000 v Bos, Es, Bos (6)
Redford, I. (Rangers), 1981 v Se (sub); 1982 v Se, D, I (2), E (6)
Reid, B. (Rangers), 1991 v F; 1992 v D, US, P (4)
Reid, C. (Hibernian), 1993 v Sw, P, I (3)
Reid, M. (Celtic), 1982 v E; 1984 v Y (2)
Reid, R. (St Mirren), 1977 v W, Sw, E (3)
Reilly, A. (Wycombe W), 2004 v H (sub) (1)
Renicks, S. (Hamilton A), 1997 v Bl (1)
Reynolds, M. (Motherwell), 2007 v G (1)
Rice, B. (Hibernian), 1985 v WG (1)
Richardson, L. (St Mirren), 1980 v WG, E (sub) (2)
Riordan, D. G. (Hibernian), 2004 v R; 2005 v H (sub), Sp (sub), Slv (sub), I (5)
Ritchie, A. (Morton), 1980 v Bel (1)
Ritchie, P. R. (Hearts), 1996 v H; 1997 v A (2), La, Es (2), Se (7)
Robertson, A. (Rangers) 1991 v F (1)
Robertson, C. (Rangers), 1977 v E (sub) (1)
Robertson, D. (Aberdeen), 1987 v Ei (sub); 1988 v E (2); 1989 v N, Y; 1990 v Y, N (7)
Robertson, D. (Dundee U), 2007 v G (1)
Robertson, G. A. (Nottingham F), 2004 v Ei; 2005 v H, Sp, Slv, N, Mol, Se, Ni, Mol, Bl; (with Rotherham U), 2006 v A, I, N, Bl, Slv (15)
Robertson, H. (Aberdeen), 1994 v Eg; 1995 v Fi (2)
Robertson, J. (Hearts), 1985 v WG, Ic (sub) (2)
Robertson, L. (Rangers), 1993 v F, M (sub), E (sub) (3)
Robertson, S. (St Johnstone), 1998 v Fi, Ni (2)
Roddie, A. (Aberdeen), 1992 v US, P; 1993 v Sw (sub), P, Ic (5)
Ross, G. (Dunfermline Ath), 2007 v G (1)
Ross, T. W. (Arsenal), 1977 v W (1)
Rowson, D. (Aberdeen), 1997 v La, Es, Se (2), Bl (5)
Russell, R. (Rangers), 1978 v W; 1980 v Bel; 1984 v Y (3)

Salton, D. B. (Luton T), 1992 v D, US, P, Y; 1993 v Sw, I (6)
Samson, C. I. (Kilmarnock), 2004 v R, Ei; 2005 v H, Ni, Mol, Bl (6)
Scott, M. (Livingston), 2006 v Ic (1)
Scott, P. (St Johnstone), 1994 v A (sub), Eg (sub), P, Bel (4)
Scrimgour, D. (St Mirren), 1997 v US, CzR; 1998 v D (3)
Seaton, A. (Falkirk), 1998 v Bl (sub) (1)
Severin, S. D. (Hearts), 2000 v Es, Bos, Li (sub), F, Ni, W; 2001 v La, Bel; 2002 v Cro, Bel (10)
Shannon, R. (Dundee), 1987 v WG, Ei (2), Bel; 1988 v Bel, E (2) (7)
Sharp, G. (Everton), 1982 v E (1)
Sharp, R. (Dunfermline Ath), 1990 v N (sub); 1991 v R, Sw, Bul (4)
Sheerin, P. (Southampton), 1996 v Sm (1)
Shields, G. (Rangers), 1997 v A, La (2)
Simmons, S. (Hearts), 2003 v Gh (sub) (1)
Simpson, N. (Aberdeen), 1982 v I (2), E; 1983 v EG, Sw (2), Bel; 1984 v Bel, EG, Y; 1985 v Sp (11)
Sinclair, G. (Dumbarton), 1977 v E (1)
Skilling, M. (Kilmarnock), 1993 v Ic (sub); 1994 v I (2)
Smith, B. M. (Celtic), 1992 v G (2), US, P, Y (5)
Smith, D. L. (Motherwell), 2006 v Slv; 2007 v G (sub) (2)
Smith, G. (Rangers), 1978 v W (1)
Smith, G. (Rangers), 2004 v H, D (sub), Ei (sub); 2005 v H (sub), Sp, Slv, N, Mol (8)
Smith, H. G. (Hearts), 1987 v WG, Bel (2)
Smith, S. (Rangers), 2007 v F (1)
Sneddon, A. (Celtic), 1979 v US (1)
Soutar, D. (Dundee), 2003 v D, Ni, Ic, Bel, Ei, Ic, Li, A, G; 2004 v G, Li (11)
Speedie, D. (Chelsea), 1985 v Sp (1)
Spencer, J. (Rangers), 1991 v Sw (sub), F; 1992 v Sw (3)
Stanton, P. (Hibernian), 1977 v Cz (1)
Stark, W. (Aberdeen), 1985 v Ic (1)
Stephen, R. (Dundee), 1983 v Bel (sub) (1)
Stevens, G. (Motherwell), 1977 v E (1)
Stewart, C. (Kilmarnock), 2002 v La (1)
Stewart, J. (Kilmarnock), 1978 v Sw, Cz; (with Middlesbrough), 1979 v P (3)
Stewart, M. J. (Manchester U), 2000 v Ni; 2001 v La, Cro, Bel, Pol; 2002 v La; 2003 v D, Is, Ni, Ei (sub), Ic, Li, A; 2004 v N, G, Li, Cro (17)
Stewart, R. (Dundee U), 1979 v P, N (2); (with West Ham U), 1980 v Bel (2), E (2), WG; 1981 v D; 1982 v I (2), E (12)
Stillie, D. (Aberdeen), 1995 v Ru (2), Sm, M, F, Sk, Br; 1996 v Gr, Fi, Sm, H (2), Sp, F (14)
Strachan, G. D. (Aberdeen), 1980 v Bel (1)
Strachan, G. D. (Coventry C), 1998 v D, Ei; 1999 v Li, Es, Bel (2); 2000 v Li (7)
Sturrock, P. (Dundee U), 1977 v Cz, W, Sw, E; 1978 v Sw, Cz; 1982 v Se, I, E (9)
Sweeney, P. H. (Millwall), 2004 v H (sub), D, Ei (sub); 2005 v H, Sp, Slv, Se (sub), Mol (sub) (8)
Sweeney, S. (Clydebank), 1991 v R, Sw (sub), Bul (2), Pol; 1992 v Sw, R (7)

Tarrant, N. K. (Aston Villa), 1999 v Ni (sub); 2000 v Es (sub), Bos (sub), Li, Ni (sub) (5)
Teale, G. (Clydebank), 1997 v La (sub), Es, Bl; (with Ayr U), 1999 v CzR (sub), G (sub), Ei (sub) (6)
Telfer, P. (Luton T), 1993 v Ma, P; 1994 v Sw (3)
Thomas, K. (Hearts), 1993 v F (sub), Bul, M, E; 1994 v Sw, Ma; 1995 v Gr; 1997 v A (8)
Thompson, S. (Dundee U), 1997 v US, CzR, P; 1998 v Bl, La; 1999 v G (sub), Ei, Ni, CzR; 2000 v Bos, Es, Bos (12)
Thomson, K. (Hibernian), 2005 v Bl (sub); 2006 v A, I, N; 2007 v Slv, F (6)
Thomson, W. (Partick Th), 1977 v E (sub); 1978 v W; (with St Mirren), 1979 v US, N (2); 1980 v Bel (2), E (2), WG (10)
Tolmie, J. (Morton), 1980 v Bel (sub) (1)
Tortolano, J. (Hibernian), 1987 v WG, Ei (2)
Turner, I. (Everton), 2005 v Sp (sub), Se; 2006 v I (sub), N, Bl, Ic (sub) (6)
Tweed, S. (Hibernian), 1993 v Ic; 1994 v Sw, I (3)

Wales, G. (Hearts), 2000 v F (1)
Walker, A. (Celtic), 1988 v Bel (1)
Wallace, I. (Coventry C), 1978 v Sw (1)
Wallace, L. (Hearts), 2007 v G (1)
Wallace, R. (Celtic), 2004 v H (sub); 2005 v N; 2007 v Slv, (with Sunderland), F (sub). (4)
Walsh, C. (Nottingham F), 1984 v EG, Sw (2), Bel; 1984 v EG (5)
Wark, J. (Ipswich T), 1977 v Cz, W, Sw; 1978 v W; 1979 v P; 1980 v E (2), WG (8)
Watson, A. (Aberdeen), 1981 v Se, D; 1982 v D, I (sub) (4)
Watson, K. (Rangers), 1977 v E; 1978 v Sw (sub) (2)
Watt, M. (Aberdeen), 1991 v R, Sw, Bul (2), Pol, F; 1992 v Sw, R, G (2), Se (2) (12)
Watt. S. M. (Chelsea), 2005 v Mol, Bl; 2006 v N, Bl, Slv (5)
Webster, A. (Hearts), 2003 v Ic, Li (2)
Whiteford, A. (St Johnstone), 1997 v US (1)
Whittaker, S. G. (Hibernian), 2005 v H (sub), Sp, Slv (sub), N, Mol, Se, Ni, I, Mol, Bl; 2006 v A, I, Bl, Slv, Ni, T; 2007 v Slv, F (18)
Whyte, D. (Celtic), 1987 v Ei (2), Bel; 1988 v E (2); 1989 v N, Y; 1990 v Y, N (9)
Wilkie, L. (Dundee), 2000 v Bos, F, Ni, W; 2001 v La, Cro (6)
Will, J. A. (Arsenal), 1992 v D (sub), Y; 1993 v Ic (sub) (3)
Williams, G. (Nottingham F), 2002 v Bel (sub); 2003 v Ic, Ei, Ic, Li; 2004 v N, G, Li, Cro (9)
Wilson, M. (Dundee U), 2004 v H, R, D, Ei; 2005 v H, N, Mol, Se, Ni, I, Mol, Bl; 2006 v I, N, Bl, Ni, T; (with Celtic), 2007 v Slv, F (19)
Wilson, S. (Rangers), 1999 v Es, Bel (2), G, Ei, CzR; 2000 v Bos (7)
Wilson, T. (St Mirren), 1983 v Sw (sub) (1)
Wilson, T. (Nottingham F), 1988 v E; 1989 v N, Y; 1990 v F (4)
Winnie, D. (St Mirren), 1988 v Bel (1)
Woods, M. (Sunderland), 2006 v Ic, Ni (2)

Wright, P. (Aberdeen), 1989 v Y, F; (with QPR), 1990 v Y (sub) (3)
Wright, S. (Aberdeen), 1991 v Bul, Pol, F; 1992 v Sw, G (2), Se (2); 1993 v Sw, P, I, Ma; 1994 v I, Ma (14)
Wright, T. (Oldham Ath), 1987 v Bel (sub) (1)
Young, Darren (Aberdeen), 1997 v Es (sub), Se, Col, CzR (sub), P; 1998 v La (sub); 1999 v CzR (sub), G (sub) (8)
Young, Derek (Aberdeen), 2000 v W; 2001 v Cro (sub), Bel (sub), Pol; 2002 v Cro (5)

WALES

Aizlewood, M. (Luton T), 1979 v E; 1981 v Ho (2)
Anthony, B. (Cardiff C), 2005 v La (sub), E, Pol; 2006 v Ma, E, Pol, G, Cy (sub) (8)

Baddeley, L. M. (Cardiff C), 1996 v Mol (sub), G (sub) (2)
Balcombe, S. (Leeds U), 1982 v F (sub) (1)
Bale, G. (Southampton), 2006 v Cy, Es (sub); 2007 v T (3)
Barnhouse, D. J. (Swansea), 1995 v Mol; 1996 v Mol, Sm (3)
Bater, P. T. (Bristol R), 1977 v E, S (2)
Beevers, L. J. (Boston U), 2005 v G (sub); (with Lincoln C), A (2); 2006 v Ma, E, Pol, Az (7)
Bellamy, C. D. (Norwich C), 1996 v Sm (sub); 1997 v Sm, T, Bel; 1998 v T, Bel, I; 1999 v I (8)
Birchall, A. S. (Arsenal), 2003 v Fi, I, Az; 2005 v La, Az, E, Pol, A (sub +1); (with Mansfield T), 2006 v Ma, E, Az (12)
Bird, A. (Cardiff C), 1993 v Cy (sub); 1994 v Cy (sub); 1995 v Mol, Ge (sub), Bul; 1996 v G (sub) (6)
Blackmore, C. (Manchester U), 1984 v N, Bul, Y (3)
Blake, D. J. (Cardiff C), 2007 v Is, Ni (sub) (2)
Blake, N. (Cardiff C), 1991 v Pol (sub); 1993 v Cy, Bel, RCS; 1994 v RCS (5)
Blaney, S. D. (West Ham U), 1997 v Sm, Ho, T (3)
Bodin, P. (Cardiff C), 1983 v Y (1)
Bowen, J. P. (Swansea C), 1993 v Cy, Bel (2); 1994 v RCS, R (sub) (5)
Bowen, M. (Tottenham H), 1983 v N; 1984 v Bul, Y (3)
Boyle, T. (C Palace), 1982 v F (1)
Brace, D. P. (Wrexham), 1995 v Ge, Bul (2); 1997 v Sm Ho; 1998 v T (6)
Bradley, M. S. (Walsall), 2007 v Ni (sub) (1)
Brough, M. (Notts Co), 2003 v As (sub); 2004 v I, Fi (3)
Brown, J. R. (Gillingham), 2003 v Fi, I, Az; 2004 v Ser, I, Fi, Ser (7)
Byrne, M. T. (Bolton W), 2003 v Az (sub) (1)

Calliste, R. T. (Manchester U), 2005 v La (sub), Az, E, Pol, G, A (2); (with Liverpool), 2006 v Pol, G, Az, Cy, Ni, Es (sub), Cy (sub), Es (15)
Carpenter, R. E. (Burnley), 2005 v E (sub) (1)
Cegielski, W. (Wrexham), 1977 v E (sub), S (2)
Chapple, S. R. (Swansea C), 1992 v R; 1993 v Cy, Bel (2), RCS; 1994 v RCS; Bul (2) (8)
Charles, J. M. (Swansea C), 1979 v E; 1981 v Ho (2)
Clark, J. (Manchester U), 1978 v S; (with Derby Co), 1979 v E (2)
Coates, J. S. (Swansea C), 1996 v Mol, G; 1997 v Ho, T (sub); 1998 v T (sub) (5)
Coleman, C. (Swansea C), 1990 v Pol; 1991 v E, Pol (3)
Collins, J. M. (Cardiff C), 2003 v I (sub), Az (sub+1); 2004 v Ser, I, Fi (sub), Ser (7)
Collins, M. J. (Fulham), 2007 v Ni (1)
Cotterill, D. (Bristol C), 2005 v A (sub+sub); 2006 v Ma, E, Pol, Cy, Es (7)
Coyne, D. (Tranmere R), 1992 v R; 1994 v Cy (sub), R; 1995 v Mol, Ge, Bul (2) (7)
Critchell, K. A. R. (Southampton), 2005 v A (sub); 2006 v Cy (sub); 2007 v Is (3)
Crofts, A. L. (Gillingham), 2005 v G, A (2); 2006 v Ma, E, Pol, Cy, Es (2); 2007 v Is (10)
Crowell, M. T. (Wrexham), 2004 v Ser (sub); 2005 v Az (sub), E (sub), Pol (sub), A (sub); 2006 v Cy (sub+1) (7)
Curtis, A. T. (Swansea C), 1977 v E (1)

Davies, A. (Manchester U), 1982 v F (2), Ho; 1983 v N, Y, Bul (6)
Davies, A. G. (Cambridge U), 2006 v Ma (sub), E (sub), Pol (sub), G, Cy, Ni (6)
Davies, A. R. (Southampton), 2005 v La (sub); (with Yeovil T), A (2); 2006 v Ma, E, Pol, G, Az, Ni, Es, Cy, Es; 2007 v Is, T (14)
Davies, C. M. (Oxford U), 2005 v A (2); 2006 v E; (with Verona), Ni (sub), Es, Cy, Es; 2007 v Is (8)
Davies, D. (Barry T), 1999 v D (sub) (1)
Davies, G. M. (Hereford U), 1993 v Bel, RCS; 1995 v Mol (sub), Ge, Bul (2); (with C Palace), 1996 v Mol (7)
Davies, I. C. (Norwich C), 1978 v S (sub) (1)
Davies, L. (Bangor C), 2005 v La (sub) (1)
Davies, R. J. (WBA), 2006 v Ni (sub), Cy (sub), Es (sub); 2007 v Ni (sub) (4)
Davies, S. (Peterborough U), 1999 v D, Bl, Sw, I, D; (with Tottenham H), 2000 v S; 2001 v Bl, N, Pol, Arm (10)
Day, R. (Manchester C), 2000 v S (sub), Ni; 2001 v Uk, Pol, Uk; 2002 v Arm, N, Bl; 2003 v Fi, I, Az; (with Mansfield T), Az; 2004 v Ser (11)
Deacy, N. (PSV Eindhoven), 1977 v S (1)
De-Vulgt, L. S. (Swansea C), 2002 v Arm (sub), Bl (2)
Dibble, A. (Cardiff C), 1983 v Bul; 1984 v N, Bul (3)
Doyle, S. C. (Preston NE), 1979 v E (sub); (with Huddersfield T), 1984 v N (2)
Duffy, R. M. (Portsmouth), 2005 v La, E, Pol, G, A (2); 2006 v Es (7)
Dwyer, P. J. (Cardiff C), 1979 v E (1)

Eardley, N. (Oldham Ath), 2007 v Is, T (2)
Earnshaw, R. (Cardiff C), 1999 v P (sub), I, D; 2000 v S, Ni; 2001 v Bl (sub), N, Pol (2), Uk (10)
Easter, D. J. (Cardiff C), 2006 v Ni (1)
Ebdon, M. (Everton), 1990 v Pol; 1991 v E (2)
Edwards, C. N. H. (Swansea C), 1996 v G; 1997 v Sm, Ho (2), T, Bel; 1998 v T (7)
Edwards, D. A. (Shrewsbury T), 2006 v Cy, Es; 2007 v Is, T, NI (5)
Edwards, R. I. (Chester), 1977 v S; 1978 v W (2)
Edwards, R. W. (Bristol C), 1991 v Pol; 1992 v R; 1993 v Cy, Bel (2), RCS; 1994 v RCS, Cy, R; 1995 v Ge, Bul; 1996 v Mol, G (13)
Evans, A. (Bristol R), 1977 v E (1)
Evans, C. (Manchester C), 2007 v Ni (1)
Evans, K. (Leeds U), 1999 v I (sub), D; (with Cardiff C), 2001 v N (sub), Pol (sub) (4)
Evans, P. S. (Shrewsbury T), 1996 v G (1)
Evans, S. J. (C Palace), 2001 v Bl, Arm (2)
Evans, T. (Cardiff C), 1995 v Bul (sub); 1996 v Mol, G (3)

Fish, N. (Cardiff C), 2005 v La, Az (sub) (2)
Fleetwood, S. (Cardiff C), 2005 v La, Az; 2006 v Ma (sub), E (sub); 2007 v T (5)
Flynn, C. P. (Crewe Alex), 2007 v Ni (sub) (1)
Folland, R. W. (Oxford U), 2000 v Ni (sub) (1)
Foster, M. G. (Tranmere R), 1993 v RCS (1)
Fowler, L. A. (Coventry C), 2003 v I; (with Huddersfield T), 2004 v Ser, I, Fi; 2005 v La, Az, E, Pol, G (9)
Freestone, R. (Chelsea), 1990 v Pol (1)

Gabbidon, D. L. (WBA), 1999 v D, P, Sw, I (sub), D; 2000 v Bl, Sw, S, Ni; (with Cardiff C), 2001 v N, Pol, Arm, Uk, Pol, Uk; 2002 v Arm, N (17)
Gale, D. (Swansea C), 1983 v Bul; 1984 v N (sub) (2)
Gall, K. A. (Bristol R), 2002 v N (sub), Bl (sub); 2003 v Fi (sub), Az; (with Yeovil T), 2004 v Ser, I, Fi, Ser (8)
Gibson, N. D. (Tranmere R), 1999 v D (sub), Bl (sub), P; 2000 v S (sub), Ni; (with Sheffield W), 2001 v Uk, Pol, Uk; 2002 v Arm, N, Bl (11)
Giggs, R. (Manchester U), 1991 v Pol (1)

Gilbert, P. (Plymouth Arg), 2005 v La, Az, E, Pol, G, A (2); 2006 v Ma, E, Pol, G, Az (12)
Giles, D. C. (Cardiff C), 1977 v S; 1978 v S; (with Swansea C), 1981 v Ho; (with C Palace), 1983 v Y (4)
Giles, P. (Cardiff C), 1982 v F (2), Ho (3)
Graham, D. (Manchester U), 1991 v E (1)
Green, R. M. (Wolverhampton W), 1998 v I; 1999 v I, D, Bl, Sw, I, D; 2000 v Bl, S, Ni; 2001 v Bl, N, Pol, Arm, Uk, Pol (16)
Griffith, C. (Cardiff C), 1990 v Pol (1)
Griffiths, C. (Shrewsbury T), 1991 v Pol (sub) (1)
Grubb, D. (Bristol C), 2007 v Ni (1)
Gunter, C. (Cardiff C), 2006 v Cy; 2007 v Is (sub), Ni (3)

Haldane, L. O. (Bristol R), 2007 v T (sub) (1)
Hall, G. D. (Chelsea), 1990 v Pol (1)
Hartson, J. (Luton T), 1994 v Cy, R; 1995 v Mol, Ge, Bul; (with Arsenal), 1996 v G, Sm; 1997 v Sm, Ho (9)
Haworth, S. O. (Cardiff C), 1997 v Ho, T, Bel; (with Coventry C), 1998 v T, Bel; I; 1999 v I, D; (with Wigan Ath), Bl, Sw; 2000 v Bl, Sw (12)
Hennessey, W. R. (Wolverhampton W), 2006 v Ma, E, Pol; 2007 v Ni (4)
Hillier, I. M. (Tottenham H), 2001 v Uk (sub), Pol (sub), Uk; (with Luton T), 2002 v Arm, N (5)
Hodges, G. (Wimbledon), 1983 v Y (sub), Bul (sub); 1984 v N, Bul, Y (5)
Holden, A. (Chester C), 1984 v Y (sub) (1)
Holloway, C. D. (Exeter C), 1999 v P, D (2)
Hopkins, J. (Fulham), 1982 v F (sub), Ho; 1983 v N, Y, Bul (5)
Hopkins, S. A. (Wrexham), 1999 v P (sub) (1)
Huggins, D. S. (Bristol C), 1996 v Sm (1)
Hughes, D. (Kaiserslautern), 2005 v La; (with Regensburg), 2006 v Ni (2)
Hughes, D. R. (Southampton), 1994 v R (1)
Hughes, R. D. (Aston Villa), 1996 v Sm; 1997 v Sm (sub), Ho (2), T, Bel; 1998 v T, Bel, I; 1999 v I, Sw, I; (with Shrewsbury T), 2000 v Sw (13)
Hughes, I. (Bury), 1992 v R; 1993 v Cy, Bel (sub), RCS; 1994 v Cy, R; 1995 v Mol, Ge, Bul; 1996 v Mol (sub), G (11)
Hughes, L. M. (Manchester U), 1983 v N, Y; 1984 v N, Bul, Y (5)
Hughes, W. (WBA), 1977 v E, S; 1978 v S (3)

Jackett, K. (Watford), 1981 v Ho; 1982 v F (2)
Jacobson, J. M. (Cardiff C), 2006 v Ma (sub), Cy, Ni (sub); 2007 v Is, T, Ni (6)
James, L. R. S. (Southampton), 2006 v Cy (sub), Ni (sub), Es (sub), Cy (sub); 2007 v Is (sub), T, Ni (sub) (7)
James, R. M. (Swansea C), 1977 v E, S; 1978 v S (3)
Jarman, L. (Cardiff C), 1996 v Sm; 1997 v Sm, Ho (2), Bel; 1998 v T, Bel; 1999 v I, P; 2000 v Bl (10)
Jeanne, L. C. (QPR), 1999 v P (sub), Sw, I; 2000 v Bl, Sw, S, Ni; 2001 v Bl (8)
Jelleyman, G. A. (Peterborough U), 1999 v D (sub) (1)
Jenkins, L. D. (Swansea C), 1998 v T (sub); 2000 v Bl, Sw, S, Ni; 2001 v N, Pol, Arm, Uk (9)
Jenkins, S. R. (Swansea C), 1993 v Cy (sub), Bel (2)
Jones, C. T. (Swansea C), 2007 v Ni (sub) (1)
Jones, E. P. (Blackpool), 2000 v Ni (sub) (1)
Jones, F. (Wrexham), 1981 v Ho (1)
Jones, J. A. (Swansea C); 2001 v Pol, Uk; 2002 v N (sub) (3)
Jones, L. (Cardiff C), 1982 v F (2), Ho (3)
Jones, M. A. (Wrexham), 2004 v Ser; 2006 v G, Az, Cy (4)
Jones, M. G. (Leeds U), 1998 v Bel; 1999 v I, D, Bl, Sw, I; 2000 v Sw (7)
Jones, P. L. (Liverpool), 1992 v R; 1993 v Cy, Bel (2), RCS; 1994 v RCS (sub), Cy, R; 1995 v Mol, Ge; 1996 v Mol, G (12)
Jones, R. (Sheffield W), 1994 v R; 1995 v Bul (2) (3)
Jones, S. J. (Swansea C), 2005 v Az (1)
Jones, V. (Bristol R), 1979 v E; 1981 v Ho (2)

Kendall, L. M. (C Palace), 2001 v N, Pol (2)
Kendall, M. (Tottenham H), 1978 v S (1)
Kenworthy, J. R. (Tranmere R), 1994 v Cy; 1995 v Mol, Bul (3)
Knott, G. R. (Tottenham H), 1996 v Sm (1)

Law, B. J. (QPR), 1990 v Pol; 1991 v E (2)
Lawless, A. (Torquay U), 2006 v Ni (1)
Ledley, J. C. (Cardiff C), 2005 v G, A (2); 2006 v G, Es (5)
Letheran, G. (Leeds U), 1977 v E, S (2)
Letheran, K. C. (Swansea C), 2006 v Cy (sub) (1)
Lewis, D. (Swansea C), 1982 v F (2), Ho; 1983 v N, Y, Bul; 1984 v N, Bul, Y (9)
Lewis, J. (Cardiff C), 1983 v N (1)
Llewellyn, C. M. (Norwich C), 1998 v T (sub), Bel (sub), I; 1999 v I, D, Bl, I; 2000 v Bl, Sw, S; 2001 v N, Pol, Arm, Uk (14)
Loveridge, J. (Swansea C), 1982 v Ho; 1983 v N, Bul (3)
Low, J. D. (Bristol R), 1999 v P; (with Cardiff C), 2002 v Arm (sub), N (sub), Bl (1)
Lowndes, S. R. (Newport Co), 1979 v E; 1981 v Ho; (with Millwall), 1984 v Bul, Y (4)

MacDonald, S. B. (Swansea C), 2006 v Az (sub), Ni, Es; 2007 v T (4)
McCarthy, A. J. (QPR), 1994 v RCS, Cy, R (3)
McDonald, C. (Cardiff C), 2006 v Az, Es, Cy (sub) (3)
Mackin, L. (Wrexham), 2006 v Ni (1)
Maddy, P. (Cardiff C), 1982 v Ho; 1983 v N (sub) (2)
Margetson, M. W. (Manchester C), 1992 v R; 1993 v Cy, Bel (2), RCS; 1994 v RCS, Cy (7)
Martin, A. P. (C Palace), 1999 v D (1)
Martin, D. A. (Notts Co), 2006 v Ma (sub) (1)
Marustik, C. (Swansea C), 1982 v F (2); 1983 v Y, Bul; 1984 v N, Bul, Y (7)
Maxwell, L. J. (Liverpool), 1999 v Sw (sub), I; 2000 v Sw (sub), S, Ni; 2001 v Bl, Pol, Arm, Uk, Pol, Uk; (with Cardiff C), 2002 v Arm, N, Bl (sub) (14)
Meaker, M. J. (QPR), 1994 v RCS (sub), R (sub) (2)
Melville, A. K. (Swansea C), 1990 v Pol; (with Oxford U), 1991 v E (2)
Micallef, C. (Cardiff C), 1982 v F, Ho; 1983 v N (3)
Morgan, A. M. (Tranmere R), 1995 v Mol, Bul; 1996 v Mol, G (4)
Morgan, C. (Wrexham), 2004 v Fi, Ser (sub); 2005 v La, G, A (2); (with Milton Keynes D), 2006 v Az, Es, Cy, Es; 2007 v Is, T (12)
Moss, D. M. (Shrewsbury T), 2003 v Fi, I, Az (2); 2004 v Ser (2) (6)
Mountain, P. D. (Cardiff C), 1997 v Ho, T (2)
Mumford, A. O. (Swansea C), 2003 v Fi, I, Az (2) (4)

Nardiello, D. (Coventry C), 1978 v S (1)
Neilson, A. B. (Newcastle U), 1993 v Cy, Bel (2), RCS; 1994 v RCS, Cy, R (7)
Nicholas, P. (C Palace), 1978 v S; 1979 v E; (with Arsenal), 1982 v F (3)
Nogan, K. (Luton T), 1990 v Pol; 1991 v E (2)
Nogan, L. (Oxford U) 1991 v E (1)
Nyatanga, L. J. (Derby Co), 2005 v G (sub); 2006 v Ma, E, Pol, G, Az, Cy, Es (8)

Oster, J. M. (Grimsby T), 1997 v Sm (sub), Ho (sub), T, Bel; (with Everton), 1998 v T, Bel, I; 1999 v I, Sw (9)
Owen, G. (Wrexham), 1991 v E (sub), Pol; 1992 v R; 1993 v Cy, Bel (2); 1994 v Cy, R (8)

Page, R. J. (Watford), 1995 v Mol, Ge, Bul; 1996 v Mol (4)
Parslow, D. (Cardiff C), 2005 v La, Az, E, Pol (4)
Partridge, D. W. (West Ham U), 1997 v T (1)
Pascoe, C. (Swansea C), 1983 v Bul (sub); 1984 v N (sub), Bul, Y (4)
Pearce, S. (Bristol C), 2006 v Cy, Ni, Cy (3)
Pejic, S. M. (Wrexham), 2003 v Fi, I, Az; 2004 v Ser, I, Fi (6)
Pembridge, M. (Luton T), 1991 v Pol (1)
Perry, J. (Cardiff C), 1990 v Pol; 1991 v E, Pol (3)
Peters, M. (Manchester C), 1992 v R; (with Norwich C), 1993 v Cy, RCS (3)
Phillips, D. (Plymouth Arg), 1984 v N, Bul, Y (3)
Phillips, G. R. (Swansea C), 2001 v Uk (sub); 2002 v Arm (sub), Bl (3)

Phillips, L. (Swansea C), 1979 v E; (with Charlton Ath), 1983 v N (2)
Pipe, D. R. (Coventry C), 2003 v As (2); 2004 v Ser, I, Fi, Ser;(with Notts Co), 2005 v La, Az, E, Pol, G, A (12)
Pontin, K. (Cardiff C), 1978 v S (1)
Powell, L. (Southampton), 1991 v Pol (sub); 1992 v R (sub); 1993 v Bel (sub); 1994 v RCS (4)
Powell, L. (Leicester C), 2004 v Ser (sub), I (sub) Fi (3)
Powell, R. (Bolton W), 2006 v Cy (1)
Price, J. J. (Swansea C), 1998 v I (sub); 1999 v I (sub), D, Bl, P; 2000 v Bl, Sw (7)
Price, L. P. (Ipswich T), 2005 v La, Az, E, Pol, G, A; 2006 v Es (2); 2007 v Is, T (10)
Price, M. D. (Everton), 2001 v Uk. Pol (sub), Uk; (with Hull C), 2002 v Arm, N, Bl; 2003 v Fi, I; (with Scarborough), Az (2); 2004 v Ser, Fi, Ser (13)
Price, P. (Luton T), 1981 v Ho (1)
Pritchard, M. O. (Swansea C), 2006 v Ma, Az (sub), Cy (sub), Ni (sub) (4)
Pugh, D. (Doncaster R), 1982 v F (2) (2)
Pugh, S. (Wrexham), 1993 v Bel (sub + sub) (2)
Pulis, A. J. (Stoke C), 2006 v Ma, Pol (sub), G, Az, Cy (5)

Ramasut, M. W. T. (Bristol R), 1997 v Ho, Bel; 1998 v T, I (4)
Ratcliffe, K. (Everton), 1981 v Ho; 1982 v F (2)
Ready, K. (QPR), 1992 v R; 1993 v Bel (2); 1994 v RCS, Cy (5)
Rees, A. (Birmingham C), 1984 v N (1)
Rees, J. (Luton T), 1990 v Pol; 1991 v E, Pol (3)
Rees, M. R. (Millwall), 2003 v Fi (sub), Az; 2004 v Ser, I (4)
Roberts, A. (QPR), 1991 v E, Pol (2)
Roberts, C. J. (Cardiff C), 1999 v D (sub) (1)
Roberts, G. (Hull C), 1983 v Bul (1)
Roberts, G. W. (Liverpool), 1997 v Ho, T, Bel; 1998 v T, I; 1999 v I, D, Bl, P; (with Panionios), D; (with Tranmere R), 2000 v Sw (11)
Roberts, J. G. (Wrexham), 1977 v E (1)
Roberts, N. W. (Wrexham), 1999 v I (sub), P; 2000 v Sw (sub) (3)
Roberts, P. (Porthmadog), 1997 v Ho (sub) (1)
Roberts, S. I. (Swansea C), 1999 v Sw, I (sub), D; 2000 v Bl (sub), Ni; 2001 v Bl (sub), N, Pol, Arm, Uk; 2002 v Arm, N, Bl (13)
Roberts, S. W. (Wrexham), 2000 v S; 2001 v Bl, N (sub) (3)
Robinson, C. P. (Wolverhampton W), 1996 v Sm; 1997 v Sm, Ho (2), T, Bel (6)
Robinson, J. (Brighton & HA), 1992 v R; (with Charlton Ath), 1993 v Bel; 1994 v RCS, Cy, R (5)
Rowlands, A. J. R. (Manchester C), 1996 v Sm; 1997 v Sm, Ho (1 + sub), T (sub) (5)
Rush, I. (Liverpool), 1981 v Ho; 1982 v F (2)

Savage, R. W. (Crewe Alex), 1995 v Bul; 1996 v Mol, G (3)
Sayer, P. A. (Cardiff C), 1977 v E, S (2)
Searle, D. (Cardiff C), 1991 v Pol (sub); 1992 v R; 1993 v Cy, Bel (2), RCS; 1994 v RCS (6)
Slatter, D. (Chelsea), 2000 v Sw (sub), S; 2001 v Bl, N (sub), Pol (sub), Uk (sub) (6)
Slatter, N. (Bristol R), 1983 v N, Y, Bul; 1984 v N, Bul, Y (6)
Somner, M. J. (Brentford), 2004 v Ser (sub), I (2)
Speed, G. A. (Leeds U), 1990 v Pol; 1991 v E, Pol (3)
Spender, S. (Wrexham), 2005 v La (sub), Az (sub); 2006 v G, Cy (2), Es (6)
Stevenson, N. (Swansea C), 1982 v F, Ho (2)
Stevenson, W. B. (Leeds U), 1977 v E, S; 1978 v S (3)
Stock, B. B. (Bournemouth), 2003 v Fi (sub), I (sub); 2004 v Fi, Ser (4)
Symons, K. (Portsmouth), 1991 v E, Pol (2)

Taylor, G. K. (Bristol R), 1995 v Ge, Bul (2); 1996 v Mol (4)
Thomas, D. J. (Watford), 1998 v T, Bel (2)
Thomas, J. A. (Blackburn R), 1996 v Sm; 1997 v Sm, Ho (2), T, Bel; 1998 v Bel; 1999 v D, Bl, P; 2000 v Bl (sub); 2001 v Bl, N, Pol, Arm, Uk, Pol, Uk; 2002 v Arm, N, Bl (21)
Thomas, Martin R. (Bristol R), 1979 v E; 1981 v Ho (2)
Thomas, Mickey R. (Wrexham), 1977 v E; 1978 v S (2)
Thomas, S. (Wrexham), 2001 v Pol, Uk; 2002 v Arm, N, Bl (5)
Thomas, D. G. (Leeds U), 1977 v E; 1979 v E; 1984 v N (3)
Tibbott, L. (Ipswich T), 1977 v E, S (2)
Tipton, M. J. (Oldham Ath), 1998 v I (sub); 1999 v P, Sw (sub); 2000 v Ni; 2001 v Arm (sub), Uk (sub) (6)
Tolley, J. C. (Shrewsbury T), 2001 v Pol, Uk (sub); 2003 v Fi, I, Az (2); 2004 v Ser (2); 2005 v Az, E, Pol, G (sub) (12)
Tudur-Jones, O. (Swansea C), 2006 v Ma (sub), E, Pol (3)
Twiddy, C. (Plymouth Arg), 1995 v Mol, Ge; 1996 v G (sub) (3)

Vaughan, D. O. (Crewe Alex), 2003 v Fi, Az; 2004 v I; 2005 v Az, E, Pol, G; 2006 v Pol (8)
Vaughan, N. (Newport Co), 1982 v F, Ho (2)
Valentine, R. D. (Everton), 2001 v Pol, Uk; 2002 v Arm, N, Bl; (with Darlington), 2003 v Fi, I, Az (8)
Vokes, S. M. (Bournemouth), 2007 v Ni (1)

Walsh, D. (Wrexham), 2000 v S, Ni; 2001 v Bl, Arm, Uk; 2002 v Arm, N, Bl (8)
Walsh, I. P. (C Palace), 1979 v E; (with Swansea C), 1983 v Bul (2)
Walton, M. (Norwich C.), 1991 v Pol (sub) (1)
Ward, D. (Notts Co), 1996 v Mol, G (2)
Warlow, O. J. (Lincoln C), 2007 v Ni (1)
Weston, R. D. (Arsenal), 2001 v Bl, N, Pol; (with Cardiff C), Arm (4)
Whitfield, P. M. (Wrexham), 2003 v Az (1)
Wiggins, R. (Crystal Palace), 2006 v Cy (sub), Ni, Es, Cy, Es (5)
Williams, A. P. (Southampton), 1998 v Bel, I; 1999 v I, D (sub), Bl, Sw, I; 2000 v Bl, Sw (9)
Williams, A. S. (Blackburn R), 1996 v Sm; 1997 v Sm, Ho, Bel; 1998 v T, Bel, I; 1999 v I, D, Bl, P, Sw, I, D; 2000 v Bl, Sw (16)
Williams, D. (Bristol R), 1983 v Y (1)
Williams, D. I. L. (Liverpool), 1998 v I; 1999 v D, Bl; (with Wrexham) I, D; 2000 v Bl, S, Ni; 2001 v Bl (9)
Williams, D. T. (Yeovil T), 2006 v Es (sub) (1)
Williams, E. (Caernarfon T), 1997 v Ho (sub), T (sub) (2)
Williams, G. (Bristol R), 1983 v Y, Bul (2)
Williams, G. A. (C Palace), 2003 v I (sub), Az; 2004 v Ser, I, Ser (sub) (5)
Williams, M. (Manchester U), 2001 v Pol (sub), Uk (sub); 2002 v Bl (sub); 2003 v Fi, I, Az (sub); 2004 v Ser (sub), I (sub), Fi, Ser (10)
Williams, M. P. (Wrexham), 2006 v Ni, Cy, Es; 2007 v Is, T, Ni (6)
Williams, M. R. (Wrexham), 2006 v Ni (sub); 2007 v Is (sub) (2)
Williams, O. Fon (Crewe Alex), 2007 v Ni (sub) (1)
Williams, R. (Middlesbrough), 2007 v Ni (1)
Williams, S. J. (Wrexham), 1995 v Mol, Ge, Bul (2) (4)
Wilmot, R. (Arsenal), 1982 v F (2), Ho; 1983 v N, Y; 1984 v Y (6)
Worgan, L. J. (Milton Keynes D), 2005 v La (sub), A; (with Rushden & D), 2006 v Ma (sub), G, Az (5)
Wright, A. A. (Oxford U), 1998 v Bel, I (sub); 1999 v D (sub) (3)

Young, S. (Cardiff C), 1996 v Sm; 1997 v Sm, Ho (2), Bel (sub) (5)

ENGLAND NATIONAL GAME XI 2006–07

29 Nov *(at Burton).*

England 4 *(Morison 36 (pen), Charnock 40, Boyd 72, Mackail-Smith 77)*

Holland 1 *(The 5)*

England: Lee-Barrett (Cronin 81); Yates, Griffiths, Quinn, Stanley, Charnock, Sole (Afful 76), Carr (Chalmers 70), Morison (Donaldson 63), Mackail-Smith (Morrison 81), Boyd.

13 Feb *(at Lurgan).*

Northern Ireland 3 *(Hamilton 7, McAreavey 11, Scullion 55)*

England 1 *(Benson 64)*

Northern Ireland: Mannus (Morris 46); Nixon (Murphy 55), Scannell, Gault (Downey 58), Buchanan, McAlinden, McMullan (Ward 46), McAreavey (Clarke 46), Thompson (Stewart 53), Hamilton (Halliday 46).
England: Alcock (Rice 55); Fuller, Griffiths, Quinn, Stanley, Charnock (Henry 55), Afful (Sole 46), Carr, Morison, Donaldson (Benson 62), Long (Kelly 46).

FOUR NATIONS TOURNAMENT 2007

22 May *(at Inverness).*

England 5 *(Cole 18, 79, 85, Southam 48, Tubbs 72)*

Republic of Ireland 0

England: Cronin; Foster, Quinn (Ashton 83), Charnock, Nicholson, Southam, Bishop (Molesley 80), Carden (Chalmers 80), Cole, Seddon (Grant 72), Tubbs (Burgess 77).

25 May *(at Ross).*

Scotland 0

England 3 *(Burgess 15, Grant 55, Ashton 62)*

England: Tynan; Foster, Quinn (Yates 68), Ashton, Nicholson, Chalmers, Molesley, Burgess, Cole (Southam 68), Grant, Brayson.

27 May *(at Inverness).*

England 3 *(Seddon 12, 77, Cole 70)*

Wales 0

England: Cronin (Tynan 14); Yates, Nicholson, Quinn (Ashton 85), Bishop (Molesley 74), Charnock, Southam, Carden, Grant (Cole 65), Seddon, Burgess.

	P	*W*	*D*	*L*	*F*	*A*	*Pts*
England	3	3	0	0	11	0	9
Wales	3	1	1	1	2	4	4
Scotland	3	1	0	2	4	5	4
Republic of Ireland	3	0	1	2	2	6	0

FRIENDLY

1 June *(in Valkeakoski).*

Finland U21 0

England 1 *(Cole 73)*

England: Cronin (Bartlett 46); Foster, Solomon, Quinn (Ashton 46), Molesley, Morison, Baker (Southam 46), Chalmers (Sole 46), Harrad (Grant 46), Cole.

SCHOOLS FOOTBALL 2006–07

BOODLES INDEPENDENT SCHOOLS FA CUP 2006–07

FIRST ROUND

Aldenham 2, Dulwich 2
aet; Aldenham won 6-5 on penalties.
Ardingly 0, Hampton 4
Eton 4, Bradfield 1 *aet*
Forest 2, John Lyon 4
KES Whitley 1, Bristol GS 2 *aet*
King's, Chester 2, Highgate 4
QEGS Blackburn 1, Lancing 3
Repton 7, Winchester 1
St Bede's School, Hailsham 1, Shrewsbury 2
St Edmund's, Canterbury 1, Leeds GS 6
Westminster 4, Dover College 0

SECOND ROUND

Aldenham 5, Chigwell 1
Alleyn's 4, Kimbolton 1
Birkdale 2, RGS Newcastle 3
Brentwood 3, Lancing 2
Bristol GS 0, Hampton 6
Bury GS 4, Westminster 1
City of London 1, Latymer Upper 1
aet; Latymer Upper won 4-2 on penalties.
Grange 1, Wolverhampton GS 4
Haileybury 3, Highgate 1
Hulme GS 0, Millfield 2
John Lyon 2, St Bede's College, Manchester 1
Leeds GS 2, Shrewsbury 1
Malvern 4, Bolton 1
Manchester GS 7, Oswestry 0
Repton 1, Eton 1
aet; Eton won 5-4 on penalties.
St Mary's College, Crosby 1, Charterhouse 2

THIRD ROUND

Alleyn's 1, Leeds GS 0
Brentwood 1, Hampton 2 *aet*
Bury GS 0, RGS Newcastle 0
aet; Bury GS won 4-3 on penalties.
Charterhouse 3, Latymer Upper 1
Haileybury 4, John Lyon 2
Malvern 1, Wolverhampton GS 0
Manchester GS 1, Eton 0
Millfield 4, Aldenham 0

FOURTH ROUND

Charterhouse 2, Manchester GS 1
Hampton 1, Alleyn's 0
Millfield 4, Haileybury 0
Bury GS 3, Malvern 0

SEMI-FINALS

Bury GS 0, Charterhouse 2
Millfield 1, Hampton 2 *aet*

FINAL

(at Leicester City FC)

Hampton 1 *(Phillips)*

Charterhouse 1 *(Nash)*

aet; Hampton won 4-2 on penalties.

Hampton: N. Jupp; S. Carolin (J. Meldrum), I. Prowse, G. Hayhurst, A. Lightman, P. Timbs (M. Cartledge), J. Phillips, H. Butt, R. Allen (M. Cronin), T. Corcoran, G. Chilton.
Charterhouse: G. Ellis; L. Evans, S. Cussins (C. Harper), D. Bowman, O. Black, H. Rubinstein, C. Clinton, C. Nash, A. Beddows, N. Carter (S. Parsons) (J. Rogers), J. Satterthwaite.
Referee: M. Riley (Yorkshire).

FA SCHOOLS & YOUTH GAMES 2006-07

▪ *Denotes player sent off.*

ENGLAND UNDER-19

Muamba (Arsenal); Fielding, Garner (Blackburn R); Bertrand, Cork, Mancienne (Chelsea); Gooding, Turner (Coventry C); Barnes (Derby Co); Vaughan (Everton); Omozusi (Fulham); Haynes (Ipswich T); Anderson, Darby, Hammill, Hobbs, Lindfield, Threlfall (Liverpool); Etuhu, Johnson (Manchester C); Hewson, Jones R (Manchester U); Cattermole, Hines (Middlesbrough); Rossi Jarvis, Martin (Norwich C); Gamble (Nottingham F); Golbourne (Reading); Annerson (Sheffield U); Lallana, Lancashire (Southampton); Button, Mills (Tottenham H); Demontagnac (Walsall); Daniels (WBA); Ephraim (West Ham U); Davies M, Little (Wolverhampton W).

5 Sept *(at Walsall).*

England 0

Holland 0 8508

England: Daniels (Gamble 46); Omozusi, Golbourne (Bertrand 46), Muamba, Mills (Little 46), Mancienne, Anderson (Ephraim 46), Cattermole, Garner (Lindfield 69), Barnes (Jones 77), Hammill (Demontagnac 77).

7 Oct *(in Ried).*

England 1 *(Hernandes 90 (og))*

Spain 1 *(Gonzalez 46)*

England: Button; Little, Bertrand, Muamba (Johnson 86), Hines, Mancienne, Barnes, Rossi Jarvis, Lindfield (Etuhu 69), Ephraim, Hammill (Hewson 86).

9 Oct *(in Ried).*

England 3 *(Lindfield 25, 38, Anderson 68)*

Austria 3 *(Sand 14, Beichler 18, 42)*

England: Daniels; Rossi Jarvis (Hammill 63), Omozusi, Hines, Mancienne, Anderson, Lallana (Barnes 74), Johnson, Hewson, Lindfield (Bertrand 46), Etuhu.

11 Oct *(in Pasching).*

England 1 *(Ephraim 80 (pen))*

Italy 1 *(Bianchini 56) Pambianchi*▪

England: Button; Little, Bertrand, Muamba, Mancienne, Barnes, Lindfield (Etuhu 56), Ephraim, Hammill, Johnson, Omozusi.

14 Nov *(at Crewe).*

England 3 *(Hammill 5, Ephraim 12, Vaughan 90)*

Switzerland 2 *(Pavlovic 8, Derdiyock 66)* 4909

England: Button (Annerson 46); Little (Omozusi 46), Bertrand, Muamba, Rossi Jarvis, Hines, Mancienne, Anderson (Hewson 71), Johnson, Lindfield (Vaughan 55), Ephraim (Gooding 86), Hammill (Lallana 79).

6 Feb *(at Bournemouth).*

England 4 *(Hammill 40, Barnes 45, Vaughan 50, 66 (pen))*

Poland 1 *(Mikolajczak 14)* 10,375

England: Annerson; Little (Lancashire 54), Threlfall (Rossi Jarvis 72), Muamba (Haynes 46), Hines, Omozusi, Davies M, Johnson, Vaughan (Hewson 69), Barnes, Hammill (Ephraim 46).

21 Mar *(at Doncaster).*

England 1 *(Martin 84)*

Turkey 0 11,555

England: Annerson; Little, Golbourne, Muamba, Mancienne, Omozusi (Lancashire 76), Rossi Jarvis (Haynes 46), Davies M, Vaughan (Martin 64), Ephraim (Hewson 70), Hammill.

15 May *(at Walsall).*

England 0

Russia 2 *(Mamaev 30, Dzyuba 50)* 4780

England: Annerson; Omozusi, Golbourne, Muamba, Hobbs, Mancienne, Hewson (Martin 64), Johnson, Haynes, Ephraim, Hammill (Rossi Jarvis 81).

17 May *(at Coventry).*

England 1 *(Ephraim 90)*

Holland 2 *(Golbourne 29 (og), Buijs 71 (pen)* 10,482

England: Fielding; Omozusi (Darby 60), Golbourne, Muamba (Hammill 28), Hobbs, Mancienne, Johnson, Haynes, Ephraim, Lindfield (Martin 78), Rossi Jarvis.

20 May *(at Northampton).*

England 2 *(Lindfield 12, Martin 49 (pen))*

Czech Republic 0 4781

England: Fielding; Golbourne, Mancienne (Omozusi 46), Haynes, Turner (Hobbs 13), Darby, Martin, Lindfield, Rossi Jarvis, Cork.

ENGLAND UNDER-18

Albrighton, Clark (Aston Villa); Aluko (Birmingham C); Wright, Yussuff (Charlton Ath); Bertrand, Cork, Hutchinson, Sawyer, Sinclair (Chelsea); Kissock (Everton); Eastwood (Huddersfield T); Upson (Ipswich T); Wilkinson (Leeds U); Sturridge (Manchester C); Brandy (Manchester U); Walker (Middlesbrough); Edwards (Millwall); Henry (Reading); Mills (Southampton); Chandler (Sunderland); Sansara (Walsall); Parkes (Watford); Nardiello (WBA); Tomkins (West Ham U).

21 Sept *(at Hartlepool).*

England 0

France 2 *(N'Gog 8, 74)* 4352

England: Edwards; Cork, Tomkins, Clark, Bertrand, Sinclair, Walker, Chandler (Upson 62), Mills (Kissock 46), Brandy (Aluko 74).

27 Mar *(at Yeovil).*

England 4 *(Brandy 13, Sawyer 64, Sturridge 75, 79)*

Holland 1 *(Kuiper 43)* 8147

England: Eastwood; Parkes (Wilkinson 63), Mills (Sansara 84), Wright (Sawyer), Hutchinson, Clark, Henry (Albrighton 63), Walker, Sturridge (Yussuff 87), Brandy (Aluko 73), Sinclair.

ENGLAND UNDER-17

Barnett, Hoyte G, Lansbury, Murphy, Thomas (Arsenal); Clancy (Aston Villa); Pearce (Birmingham C); Plummer (Bristol C); Ofori-Twumasi, Taiwo, Woods (Chelsea); Elito (Colchester U); Moses (Crystal Palace); Smithies (Huddersfield T); Ainsley, Smith (Ipswich T); Darville, Elliott, Gordon, Rose (Leeds U); Chambers, Mattock (Leicester C); Eccleston (Liverpool); Amos, Welbeck, Woods (Manchester U); Franks, Porritt, Steele (Middlesbrough); Reid (Nottingham F); Gosling (Plymouth Arg); Askham (Sheffield U); Fraser-Allen, Smith (Tottenham H); Harvey, Spence (West Ham U).

31 Jul *(in Torshavn).*

England 4 *(Barnett 6, Murphy 29, Smith 79, Ainsley 80)*

Sweden 2 *(Johansson 22, Pekalski 31)*

England: Steele; Darville, Reid, Harvey (Gordon 69), Spence (Smith 76), Mattock, Fraser-Allen (Plummer 54), Rose, Murphy, Franks, Barnett (Ainsley 54).

1 Aug *(in Klaksvik).*

Faeroes-Under 19s 0

England 1 *(Rose 78)*

England: Woods; Darville, Reid (Askham 40), Harvey (Smith 64), Mattock, Murphy, Franks, Barnett, Welbeck, Plummer, Ainsley (Rose 56).

3 Aug *(in Fuglafjorour).*

England 2 *(Ainsley 18, 55)*

Norway 1 *(Brix 30)*
England: Steele; Reid, Harvey (Darville 40), Spence, Mattock, Rose, Franks, Barnett (Welbeck 78), Smith (Murphy 40), Askham (Fraser-Allen 62), Ainsley (Plummer 62).

5 Aug *(in Torshavn).*

Denmark 4 *(Gytkjaer 2, 15, 33, Juel-Nielsen 69)*

England 0
England: Woods; Darville (Smith 80), Reid (Plummer 57), Spence, Mattock■, Fraser-Allen (Barnett 39), Rose (Murphy 39), Franks (Askham 80), Welbeck, Gordon, Ainsley (Harvey 69).

30 Aug *(at Brentford).*

England 2 *(Woods 6, 50)*

Turkey 2 *(Sozen 68, Torun 80)*
England: Smithies; Darville (Ofori-Twumasi 73), Reid, Clancy, Franks, Rose (Harvey 50), Chambers, Moses (Murphy 58), Woods, Spence, Barnett.

1 Sept *(at Aldershot).*

England 6 *(Lansbury 15, Moses 28, Ofori-Twumasi 40, Woods 48, Murphy 54 (pen), 73)*

USA 0 1748
England: Steele; Ofori-Twumasi, Spence, Mattock, Barnett, Woods (Harvey 54), Lansbury, Plummer, Moses (Rose 61), Murphy, Franks (Chambers 65).

3 Sept *(at Swindon).*

England 4 *(Chambers 21, 72, Clancy 30, Moses 39)*

Portugal 0 3608
England: Smithies; Reid, Lansbury (Spence 66), Clancy, Mattock, Rose, Chambers, Moses (Franks 50), Ofori-Twumasi (Darville 40), Murphy, Plummer.

FINAL TABLE	P	W	D	L	F	A	Pts
England	3	2	1	0	12	2	7
Turkey	3	1	2	0	6	5	5
USA	3	0	2	1	3	9	2
Portugal	3	0	1	2	2	6	1

25 Oct *(in Eupen).*

England 2 *(Ofori-Twumasi 38, Lansbury 80)*

Spain 3 *(Krkich 22, 44, Merida 24)*
England: Amos; Ofori-Twumasi, Mattock, Thomas (Chambers 56), Spence, Barnett, Plummer (Eccleston 75), Harvey, Murphy, Welbeck (Lansbury 67), Franks.

27 Oct *(in Vise).*

England 1 *(Franks 48)*

Portugal 1 *(Eduardo 46)*
England: Steele; Darville, Spence, Pearce, Mattock, Woods, Lansbury (Harvey 74), Plummer (Thomas 75), Murphy, Chambers, Eccleston (Franks 40).

30 Oct *(in Eupen).*

England 2 *(Welbeck 35, Chambers 55)*

Belgium 0
England: Amos; Ofori-Twumasi, Mattock (Woods 65), Barnett, Chambers (Thomas 77), Murphy, Welbeck, Lansbury (Harvey 56), Pearce, Franks.

THE ALGARVE TOURNAMENT

17 Feb *(in Guia).*

Portugal 0

England 1 *(Moses 49)*
England: Steele; Darville, Mattock (Harvey 40), Spence, Smith, Taiwo (Barnett 40), Franks, Reid (Rose), Medyelito (Plummer 65), Moses, Murphy (Elliott 75).

18 Feb *(in Silves).*

England 1 *(Murphy 23 (pen))*

France 1 *(Bourgeois 51)*
England: Smithies; Taiwo (Harvey 68), Spence, Smith, Rose, Murphy (Franks 59), Moses, Ofori-Twumasi, Elliott, Plummer (Barnett 68), Reid.

20 Feb *(in Guia).*

England 1 *(Franks 12)*

Germany 3 *(Knoll 51, Sauerbier 56, Bigalke 72 (pen))*
England: Steele; Darville (Ofori-Twumasi 61), Mattock, Spence, Smith (Barnett 73), Franks, Rose (Reid 73), Murphy (Elliott 43), Moses, Medyelito (Plummer 61), Harvey (Taiwo 61).

EUROPEAN CHAMPIONSHIP

ELITE QUALIFYING ROUND

23 Mar *(in Kosovo).*

Bosnia 0

England 5 *(Murphy 16 (pen), 39, Lansbury 19, Woods 25, Rose 75)*
England: Amos; Mattock, Lansbury (Welbeck 41), Spence, Smith, Rose, Porritt (Taiwo 69), Woods, Gosling, Murphy (Plummer 41), Franks.

25 Mar *(in Grbavica).*

Azerbaijan 0

England 1 *(Rose 48)*
England: Steele; Ofori-Twumasi, Mattock (Gosling 5), Spence, Rose, Plummer, Moses, Porritt (Murphy 41), Taiwo, Franks (Lansbury 65), Pearce.

28 Mar *(in Kosovo).*

Serbia 1 *(Smiljanovic 47)*

England 2 *(own goal 43, Welbeck 79)*
England: Amos; Ofori-Twumasi (Porritt 74), Mattock, Spence, Smith, Lansbury (Franks 64), Woods, Welbeck, Plummer (Taiwo 83), Murphy, Rose.

2 May *(in Ronse).*

Iceland 0

England 2 *(Pearce 4, Rose 24)*
England: Steele; Ofori-Twumasi, Pearce (Hoyte 72), Spence, Mattock, Moses, Lansbury, Woods (Gosling 63), Plummer, Franks, Rose (Welbeck 63).

4 May *(in Tournai).*

Belgium 1 *(Ringoot 42)*

England 1 *(Murphy 27)*
England: Steele; Mattock, Pearce, Spence, Gosling, Lansbury (Taiwo 45), Woods, Welbeck (Plummer 69), Rose, Murphy.

7 May *(in Tubize).*

Holland 2 *(Narsingh 31, Petro 44)*

England 4 *(Lansbury 9, Moses 15, 54, Plummer 80)*
England: Steele; Ofori-Twumasi, Mattock (Woods 41), Lansbury, Pearce, Spence, Welbeck, Rose, Murphy (Plummer 41), Moses, Porritt (Gosling 80).

10 May *(in Tubize)*.

SEMI-FINAL

England 1 *(Moses 11)*

France 0

England: Steele; Ofori-Twumasi, Mattock (Hoyte 59), Pearce, Spence, Moses, Lansbury (Taiwo 52), Plummer (Franks 41), Woods, Rose, Murphy.

13 May *(in Tournai)*.

FINAL

Spain 1 *(Krkic 48)*

England 0

England: Steele; Ofori-Twumasi, Spence, Pearce, Mattock, Welbeck, Woods, Rose (Gosling 56), Porritt (Plummer 60), Moses (Franks 75), Murphy.

ENGLAND UNDER-16

Cruise, Obed, Watt, Wilshere (Arsenal); Delfouneso (Aston Villa); Lyness, McPike (Birmingham C); Bartley (Bolton W); Solly (Charlton Ath); Phillip (Chelsea); Bostock (Crystal Palace); Baxter, Rodwell (Everton); Briggs, Foderingham (Fulham); Gordon (Leeds U); Highdale (Liverpool); Ajose, James, Norwood, Stewart (Manchester U); Rudd (Norwich C); Parrett (QPR); Mellis (Sheffield U); Brown (Sunderland); Mason, Smith, Townsend (Tottenham H); Forrester (Watford); Street (West Ham U).

SKY SPORTS VICTORY SHIELD

20 Oct *(in Carmarthen)*.

Wales 1 *(Smith 13)*

England 1 *(Owen 12 (og))*

England: Foderingham; Solly, Rodwell, Cruise, Gordon, Parrett, Forrester (Ajose 40), Norwood (Wilshere 70), Bostock (Mellis 40), Townsend (Stewart 59), Delfouneso.

9 Nov *(in Ballymena)*.

Northern Ireland 0

England 3 *(McLaughlin C 15 (og), Delfouneso 21, Watt 32)*

England: Street; Smith (Obed 57), Briggs, Highdale (James 40), Bartley, Rodwell, Mellis, Parrett (McPike 67), Delfouneso, Wilshere, Watt (Baxter 40).

8 Dec *(at Scunthorpe)*.

England 2 *(Ajose 48, Delfounesco 54)*

Scotland 1 *(McHugh 38)* 2282

England: Rudd; Solly, Brown (Smith 40), Highdale, Rodwell, Cruise, Ajose, Parrett (Forrester 40), Delfounesco, Norwood, Bostock (Watt 73).

FINAL TABLE	*P*	*W*	*D*	*L*	*F*	*A*	*Pts*
England	3	2	1	0	6	2	7
Scotland	3	2	0	1	5	3	6
Wales	3	1	1	1	4	3	4
Northern Ireland	3	0	0	3	0	9	0

Scotland 3, Northern Ireland 0; Wales 1, England 1; Scotland 2, Wales 0; Northern Ireland 0, England 3; Northern Ireland 0, Wales 3; England 2, Scotland 1.

THE MONTAIGU TOURNAMENT

3 Apr *(in Chantonnay)*.

England 3 *(Norwood 26 (pen), 40, Forrester 71)*

Republic of Ireland 0

England: Foderingham; Solly (Smith A 76), Gordon, Norwood, Bartley, Cruise, James (McPike 55), Parrett (Phillip 72), Delfouneso, Bostock (Forrester 55), Ajose (Townsend 76).

4 Apr *(in Les Essarts)*.

England 0

USA 0

England: Rudd; Smith A, Gordon, Cruise, James (Solly 77), Bostock (Parrett 40), Townsend (Ajose 64), Phillip, Mellis (Norwood), McPike, Forrester (Delfouneso 73).

7 Apr *(in Montaignu)*.

England 1 *(Forrester 78)*

France 0

England: Foderingham; Solly, Norwood, Bartley, Cruise, James, Parrett, Delfouneso (Forrester 65), Phillip, Ajose.

9 Apr *(in Montaignu)*.

England 0

Germany 2 *(Stietermann 3, 17)*

England: Rudd; Smith A, Gordon (McPike 68), Norwood (Bostock 65), Bartley, Cruise, James, Delfouneso, Forrester, Townsend (Phillip 61), Mellis (Ajose 55).

FRIENDLIES

27 Feb *(in Koper)*.

Slovenia 3 *(Besic 2, Mlinar 71, Beric 78)*

England 1 *(Parrett 19)*

England: Rudd (Lyness 40); Solly (Smith A 58), Gordon (Bartley 50), Norwood, Rodwell, Cruise, Parrett, McPike (Mellis 40), Forrester (Townsend 58), Wiltshire (Mason 50), Watt (Ajose 40).

28 Apr *(at Wembley)*.

England 1 *(Rodwell 52)*

Spain 0 28,210

England: Foderingham (Rudd 40); Solly (Smith A 40), Gordon, Norwood (Bostock 48), Bartley (Rodwell 40), Cruise, James, Parrett, Delfounesco (Phillip 73), Forrester (Mellis 61), Ajose (Townsend 61).

WOMEN'S FOOTBALL 2006–07

The highlight of the season was both at International and domestic levels where firstly England qualified for the FIFA Women's World Cup Finals in China in September 2007 and Arsenal for the umpteenth time swept all before them taking all the domestic trophies.

The England Senior Team's qualification came on the 30th September 2006 by dint of a 1-1 draw in Rennes against France having set themselves up, with a 4-0 home victory over Holland the previous month. They have been drawn in Group A with Germany, Japan and Argentina and their first fixture is against Japan in Shanghai on September the 11th, the day after the Tournament opens. They play Germany 3 days later also at the same venue and then move on to Chengduon to play Argentina on the 18th of the month. Head Coach Hope Powell indicated "the draw we have been given in China is not the easiest but it could have been far worse. The main thing is how happy we are to be there. We started training for the Finals the day we qualified and now we want to play well and showcase our abilities." She takes with her Assistant Brent Hills together with a goalkeeping coach; a doctor; a psychologist; a physiologist and a physiotherapist. As she remarks "if we can win through the Group stage, then anything can happen".

The full Groupings for the Women's World Cup are:

Group A – Germany; England; Japan; Argentina.
Group B – Nigeria; USA; Korea DPR; Sweden.
Group C – Norway; Ghana; Austria; Canada.
Group D –Denmark; China; Brazil; New Zealand.

Arsenal ventured onto the European stage and were successful in their 5th year of competing in the Women's UEFA Cup winning the two-legged Final against Umea IK of Sweden by an aggregate 1-0 score-line. The goal that decided it all was scored by Alex Scott (a regular scorer for the England women's team) in the first leg in Sweden and a backs to the wall effort at Boreham Wood Herts in April saw them through. Afterwards their outstanding Manager Vic Akers commented that "winning the UEFA Cup is a personal landmark for me since apart from the World Cup it is the biggest competition in women's football. It has come in what has been a fantastic season which has now become even more precious."

In fact things actually got even better because, Arsenal completed their ninth National Division League Championship winning season with a record that can never be beaten unless the number of teams in the Division is increased. This is because they completed the perfect combination of results and the mere statistics do not sufficiently reflect the achievement itself. They played 22 fixtures and won them all scoring 119 goals and conceding a mere 10. Whilst their 66 points gained were 14 more than nearest rivals Everton with Charlton finishing third on 50 points. The relegated clubs were Sunderland and once full-time professional Fulham. The Northern Division Title went to Liverpool who are promoted and whose 50 points was 5 more than Lincoln City, with Wolverhampton Wanderers and Curzon Ashton demoted. The Southern Division was won by Watford who also go up, their 57 points being 10 more than Portsmouth; with AFC Wimbledon and Southampton Saints taking the drop. The Premier League Reserve Section is split into three and the Winners of the Southern Division were Millwall Lionesses; The Mids/North Division One, saw Liverpool take the title whilst in the Mids/North Division Two, Preston North End were the winners.

The Cups were no exception to the Arsenal rule in both senses of the word. They annexed the FA's Premier League Cup defeating Leeds United whom they had swamped in the previous season's FA Cup. This time the margin was extremely close at Scunthorpe United's ground in March the winning goal coming in the 90th minute courtesy of Jane Ludlow's strike in front of a record crowd for the competition of 3,688. Unfortunately the Leeds Manager Julie Chipchase had to retire at the end of the season after 4 excellent years in charge at the Club which rose enormously under her tenure. Likewise the Women's FA Cup went to Arsenal for the 8th time which saw them defeat their great rivals Charlton by 4-1 at the City Ground Nottingham. Although Kate Holtham gave the Robins the lead in only 2 minutes the Gunners stormed back 3 minutes later through Kelly Smith who added another in the 81st minute whilst in between Jayne Ludlow notched a brace in the 14th and 45th minutes. Another record crowd of 24,529 watched the game in May.

The first of Arsenal's record winning successes came at the beginning of the term when they defeated the rapidly improving Everton side 3-0 in the FA Community Shield held at Crewe Alexandra's ground. Their goal-scorers were Kelly Smith (23); Katie Chapman (31) and Gemma Davison (90).

Without trying to eulogise the Arsenal Ladies Club their record over their 20 years in existence all under Manager Vic Akers needs highlighting. During those 20 years they have achieved a total of 27 trophies including 9 League Titles; 9 League Cups and 8 FA Cups whilst on three occasions they have actually won all three of the trophies in one season. Perhaps the final word on their season belongs to the Umea Manager/Coach Andree Jeglertz after the UEFA Final when he proclaimed 'Arsenal stopped our best players in a marvellous way so they are the best team in Europe.'

At the 9th Annual FA Women's Awards Everton's Fara Williams won the Nationwide International Player of the Year title whilst Arsenal were rewarded with 6 prizes including the Tesco titles of Club of the Year; Manager of the Year (Vic Akers) and Player's Player of the Year – Kelly Smith. The Umbro Divisional top scorers were National – Lianne Sanderson; Northern Section – Jodie Snelson and Southern Division Helen Lander. The full list of winners is as follows:

Umbro Top Goal Scorer – Northern Division	Jodie Snelson
Umbro Top Goal Scorer – Southern Division	Helen Lander
Umbro Top Goal Scorer – National Division	Lianne Sanderson
The FA Young Player of the Year	Stephanie Houghton
BBC Club Media Award	Lincoln City
The FA Cup Marketing Award	Leeds United
Tesco Manager of the Year – Arsenal	Vik Akers – Arsenal
Best Programme Award	Preston North End
The FA Fair Play Award	Arsenal
The FA National Media Award	*The Guardian*
The FA Regional Media Award	*Nottingham Evening Post*
Nationwide International Player of the Year	Fara Williams
Tesco Players' Player of the Year	Kelly Smith
Tesco Club of the Year Award	Arsenal
The FA Special Achievement Award	Linda Whitehead – Arsenal

KEN GOLDMAN

FA WOMEN'S PREMIER LEAGUE 2006–07

NATIONAL DIVISION

	P	*W*	*D*	*L*	*F*	*A*	*GD*	*Pts*
Arsenal	22	22	0	0	119	10	109	66
Everton	22	17	1	4	56	15	41	52
Charlton Athletic	22	16	2	4	63	32	31	50
Bristol Academy	22	13	1	8	53	41	12	40
Leeds United	22	12	1	9	50	44	6	37
Blackburn Rovers	22	10	2	10	37	36	1	32
Birmingham City	22	8	4	10	34	29	5	28
Chelsea	22	8	4	10	33	34	–1	28
Doncaster R Belles	22	7	2	13	29	54	–25	23
Cardiff City	22	3	3	16	26	64	–38	12
Sunderland	22	3	2	17	15	72	–57	11
Fulham	22	1	2	19	12	96	–84	5

SOUTHERN DIVISION

	P	*W*	*D*	*L*	*F*	*A*	*GD*	*Pts*
Watford	22	19	0	3	99	35	64	57
Portsmouth	22	14	5	3	60	32	28	47
Millwall Lionesses	22	13	3	6	61	35	26	42
Barnet	22	11	4	7	52	33	19	37
Keynsham Town	22	11	4	7	52	46	6	37
Bristol City	22	9	5	8	44	37	7	32
Reading Royals	22	10	1	11	36	34	2	31
Crystal Palace	22	7	5	10	48	48	0	26
Brighton & Hove A	22	7	2	13	39	65	–26	23
West Ham United	22	6	3	13	25	44	–19	21
AFC Wimbledon	22	5	2	15	26	61	–35	17
Southampton Saints	22	1	4	17	21	93	–72	7

NORTHERN DIVISION

	P	*W*	*D*	*L*	*F*	*A*	*GD*	*Pts*
Liverpool	22	16	2	4	56	17	39	50
Lincoln City	22	13	6	3	50	23	27	45
Nottingham Forest	22	11	3	8	41	36	5	36
Crewe Alexandra	22	10	4	8	33	38	–5	34
Preston North End	22	9	6	7	36	41	–5	33
Tranmere Rovers	22	9	4	9	41	34	7	31
Newcastle United	22	8	5	9	37	34	3	29
Stockport County	22	8	4	10	34	36	–2	28
Aston Villa	22	6	6	10	36	43	–7	24
Manchester City	22	6	6	10	27	35	–8	24
Wolverhampton W.	22	5	6	11	26	44	–18	21
Curzon Ashton	22	4	2	16	24	60	–36	14

NATIONAL DIVISION RESULTS 2006–07

	Arsenal	Birmingham City	Blackburn Rovers	Bristol Academy	Cardiff City	Charlton Athletic	Chelsea	Doncaster Rovers Belles	Everton	Fulham	Leeds United	Sunderland
Arsenal	—	1-0	4-0	4-1	4-0	3-0	3-1	7-0	3-2	14-0	6-0	6-0
Birmingham C	0-1	—	3-0	2-0	2-2	1-2	0-0	1-2	0-4	7-1	0-2	2-0
Blackburn R	0-3	1-2	—	4-5	3-1	2-0	1-3	2-0	2-3	1-1	2-1	5-0
Bristol Academy	0-6	2-1	2-1	—	3-0	0-2	2-1	1-1	0-2	7-1	4-3	5-1
Cardiff City	1-6	1-1	0-2	0-3	—	0-3	1-3	1-5	0-3	7-0	0-5	1-1
Charlton Athletic	2-9	3-0	0-0	3-1	9-2	—	3-2	3-0	1-2	1-1	5-3	8-0
Chelsea	1-5	1-1	0-1	0-5	3-0	1-2	—	3-1	0-1	2-1	2-1	0-0
Doncaster Rovers Belles	0-4	0-2	1-3	2-5	2-3	2-4	1-1	—	2-1	3-1	2-5	2-1
Everton	1-4	2-1	1-0	3-0	2-0	0-1	4-0	3-0	—	9-0	1-1	5-0
Fulham	0-9	0-3	0-3	1-5	0-5	2-7	0-5	0-1	0-2	—	0-1	1-0
Leeds United	1-8	4-2	5-2	2-0	2-1	0-2	1-0	1-2	0-1	2-1	—	5-2
Sunderland	0-9	0-3	1-2	1-2	2-0	1-2	0-4	2-0	0-4	2-1	1-5	—

NATIONAL DIVISION LEAGUE – PREVIOUS WINNERS

1992–93	Arsenal	1997–98	Everton	2002–03	Fulham
1993–94	Doncaster Belles	1998–99	Croydon	2003–04	Arsenal
1994–95	Arsenal	1999–00	Croydon	2004–05	Arsenal
1995–96	Croydon	2000–01	Arsenal	2005–06	Arsenal
1996–97	Arsenal	2001–02	Arsenal	2006–07	Arsenal

THE FA WOMEN'S CUP 2006–07

SPONSORED BY E.ON 2006

PRELIMINARY ROUND

Windscale v Teesside Athletic	5-0
Newfield v Glendale	4-5
Darwen v Mossley Hill	4-3
Kirklees v York City	3-8
Steel City Wanderers v Denton Town	4-0
Wigan v Bury Girls & Ladies	7-0
Bolton Ambassadors v Bradford City	1-7
Buxton v Liverpool Manweb Feds	1-3
Morley Spurs v Barnsley	2-1
Macclesfield Town v Sheffield	0-5
Bilton Ajax v Stoke City	0-4
Mansfield Town v Solihull Ladies	1-6
Sandiacre Town v Birmingham Athletic	2-0
AFC Telford United v Shrewsbury Town	0-2
Dudley United v Walsall	2-3
Rushcliffe Eagles v Linby	2-4
Loughborough Dynamo v Stratford Town	2-1

Broughton Rangers v Worcester City	0-1
Wyrley v Florence	1-1
Florence won 4-3 on penalties.	
Loughborough Foxes v Friar Lane & Epworth	1-5
Southam United v Leicester City	0-11
Haverhill Rovers v Woodbridge Town	5-1
Bedford & District v Arlesey Town	3-1
Rothwell Town v Cambridge Rangers	4-3
Cambridge University v Sophtlogic	8-2
Kingsthorpe v Corby S&L	1-8
Cottenham United v Leighton Linslade	6-1
Acton Sports v Hemel Hempstead Town	4-2
Stevenage Borough v Met Ladies	2-1
Hendon v Runwell Hospital	11-0
Concord Rangers v Hoddesdon Owls	4-3
Haringey Borough v Clapton Orient	5-6
Barking v Sawbridgeworth Town	1-3
Tottenham Hotspur v Garston	2-5
Colchester Town v Chelmsford City	1-6
Maldon Town v Royston Town	2-3
Tring Athletic v Dynamo North London	5-2
Thurrock & Tilbury v Billericay	3-1
Harlow Athletic v Saffron Walden Town	3-4
Basildon Town v London Colney	1-8
Haywards Heath Town v Crowborough Athletic	0-3
Dover Athletic v Upper Beeding	6-1
London Corinthians v The Comets	1-3
Hassocks v London Women	3-6
Lloyds S&S v Croydon Athletic	3-2
Lordswood v Sheerness East	1-4
Eastbourne Town v Tooting & Mitcham United	2-0
UKP v Ashford Girls	2-4
Lewes v Corinthian Casuals	13-0
Eastbourne Borough v Kent Magpies	4-2
Bexhill United v Horley Town	2-4
Gravesend & Northfleet v Abbey Rangers	3-0
Staines Town v Riverside Strikers	3-1
Christchurch v Woking	2-8
Aldershot Town v Salisbury City	3-2
Bracknell Town v Havant & Waterlooville	1-5
Reading FC Women v Battersea	6-1
Burnham v Brize Norton	12-2
Mansfield Road v Slough	0-3
Hampton & Richmond Borough v Newport Pagnell Town	4-5
MK Wanderers v Banbury United	5-3
Oxford United v Wycombe Wanderers	1-6
Carterton v Aylesbury United	0-1
Brentford v Chinnor Ladies	5-1
Yeovil Town v Gloucester City	1-3
Team Bath v Bath City	0-5
St Blazey v Alphington	4-6

FIRST QUALIFYING ROUND

Blyth Spartans v Glendale	4-1
Windscale v Consett YMCA	9-0
Whitley Bay v Darlington RA	4-1
Lumley Ladies v Spennymoor Town	5-2
Killingworth YPC v Gateshead Cleveland Hall	5-0
Durham City v Penrith United	2-3
Bradford City v Wigan	3-2
York City v Steel City Wanderers	2-2
York City won 4-3 on penalties.	
Sheffield v Darwen	0-2
Morley Spurs v Liverpool Manweb Feds	5-2
Walsall v Solihull Ladies	2-0
Stoke City v Shrewsbury Town	3-1
Florence v Friar Lane & Epworth	1-4
Loughborough Dynamo v Worcester City	4-3
Leicester City v Linby	15-0
Sandiacre Town v Copswood (Coventry)	2-6
Corby S&L v Bedford & District	2-3
Haverhill Rovers v Cambridge University	4-3
Kings Sports v Peterborough	0-2
AFC Kempston Rovers v Peterborough Azure	0-8
Godmanchester Rovers v Cottenham United	1-3
Rothwell Town v Kettering Town	2-5
Tring Athletic v Braintree Town	5-1
Hendon v Dagenham & Redbridge	0-1
Sawbridgeworth Town v Thurrock & Tilbury	1-0
Brentwood Town v Chelmsford City	1-7
Garston v Stevenage Borough	4-1
Royston Town v Saffron Walden Town	7-1
Concord Rangers v Acton Sports	0-4
London Colney v Clapton Orient	4-2
Lloyds S&S v Dover Athletic	3-1
Crowborough Athletic v London Women	1-5
Lewes v Eastbourne Borough	9-1
Eastbourne Town v Ashford Girls	2-1
Horley Town v Sheerness East	1-3
The Comets v Gravesend & Northfleet	1-5
AFC Newbury v Havant & Waterlooville	2-4
Woking v Aldershot Town	0-6
Chichester City United v Staines Town	1-0
Laverstock & Ford v Andover New Street	0-5
MK Wanderers v Newport Pagnell Town	4-1
Burnham v Slough	0-4
Brentford v Reading FC Women	0-3
Aylesbury United v Wycombe Wanderers	0-2
St Ives Town v Bath City	1-13
Gloucester City v Launceston	10-0
Saltash United v Holway United	0-3
Penzance v Tetbury Town	7-1
Barnstaple Town v Poole Town	2-3
Alphington v Ilminster Town	3-1

SECOND QUALIFYING ROUND

Windscale v Blyth Spartans	2-1
Whitley Bay v Lumley Ladies	1-1
Whitley Bay won 5-3 on penalties.	
Killingworth YPC v Penrith United	2-4
Darwen v Bradford City	2-2
Bradford City won 3-2 on penalties.	
York City v Morley Spurs	3-2
Stoke City v Walsall	1-2
Friar Lane & Epworth v Loughborough Dynamo	2-1
Leicester City v Copswood (Coventry)	3-1
Haverhill Rovers v Bedford & District	2-1
Peterborough v Peterborough Azure	0-1
Cottenham United v Kettering Town	0-8
Garston v Chelmsford City	6-0
Dagenham & Redbridge v Sawbridgeworth Town	3-0
London Colney v Tring Athletic	4-3
Acton Sports v Royston Town	5-1
London Women v Lloyds S&S	7-2
Lewes v Eastbourne Town	11-0
Sheerness East v Gravesend & Northfleet	0-9
Chichester City United v Havant & Waterlooville	4-2
Aldershot Town v Andover New Street	7-2
Reading FC Women v MK Wanderers	8-1
Slough v Wycombe Wanderers	1-1
Wycombe Wanderers won 3-2 on penalties.	
Gloucester City v Bath City	4-0
Holway United v Penzance	1-2
Poole Town v Alphington	3-1

FIRST ROUND

Windscale v Leeds City Vixens	0-5
Chesterfield v Penrith United	2-3
Friar Lane & Epworth v Norwich City	0-3
Whitley Bay v Peterlee Town	3-0
Chester City v Stretford Victoria	2-3
Blackpool Wren Rovers v Scunthorpe United	1-4
York City v Sheffield Wednesday	0-4
South Durham Royals v Hull City	3-2
Bradford City v Rotherham United	0-6
Leicester City v Long Eaton Villa	5-1
Derby County v Walsall	5-1
Coventry City v Lichfield Diamonds	3-1
Kettering Town v Rushden & Diamonds	0-5
TNS v Leafield Athletic Triplex	1-6
Peterborough Azure v Northampton Town	1-1
Peterborough Azure won 4-3 on penalties.	
Ipswich Town v Haverhill Rovers	5-0
Gravesend & Northfleet v Gillingham	2-3
Dagenham & Redbridge v Leyton Orient	3-4
Wycombe Wanderers v Bedford Town Belles	0-5
Chichester City United v Aldershot Town	3-0
Oxford City v Colchester United	1-6
Luton Town v London Colney	4-0
Enfield Town v Reading FC Women	2-1
Acton Sports v Chesham United	3-1
Lewes v Queens Park Rangers	2-3
Garston v London Women	2-1
Whitehawk v Langford	1-2
AFC Bournemouth v Plymouth Argyle	0-3
Frome Town v Poole Town	6-1
Penzance v Swindon Town	4-2
Gloucester City v Newquay AFC	2-4
Clevedon v Forest Green Rovers	1-2

SECOND ROUND

Scunthorpe United v Sheffield Wednesday	1-3
Leeds City Vixens v South Durham Royals	4-0
Rotherham United v Stretford Victoria	4-2
Whitley Bay v Penrith United	2-0
Coventry City v Rushden & Diamonds	1-0
Norwich City v Leafield Athletic Triplex	1-2
Peterborough Azure v Derby County	2-2
Derby County won 4-2 on penalties.	
Leicester City v Ipswich Town	4-4
Ipswich Town won 3-1 on penalties.	
Queens Park Rangers v Garston	5-0
Luton Town v Enfield Town	1-3
Colchester United v Gillingham	7-2
Bedford Town Belles v Acton Sports	3-2
Leyton Orient v Langford	0-2
Frome Town v Chichester City United	3-1
Newquay AFC v Plymouth Argyle	4-0
Forest Green Rovers v Penzance	3-1

THIRD ROUND

Stockport County v Curzon Ashton	3-0
Sheffield Wednesday v Manchester City	3-5
Crewe Alexandra v Tranmere Rovers	1-3
Whitley Bay v Rotherham United	2-1
Liverpool v Leeds City Vixens	2-0
Preston North End v Newcastle United	1-3
Aston Villa v Ipswich Town	3-1
Coventry City v Wolverhampton Wanderers	0-2
Derby County v Lincoln City	0-2
Nottingham Forest v Leafield Athletic Triplex	5-0
Portsmouth v Reading Royals	0-2
AFC Wimbledon v Crystal Palace	2-1
Queens Park Rangers v West Ham United	0-1
Brighton & Hove Albion v Millwall Lionesses	1-2
Watford v Barnet	4-2
Enfield Town v Langford	2-3
Colchester United v Bedford Town Belles	3-2
Bristol City v Keynsham Town	2-1
Frome Town v Newquay	2-1
Southampton Saints v Forest Green Rovers	2-0

FOURTH ROUND

Blackburn Rovers v AFC Wimbledon	3-0
Millwall Lionesses v Everton	0-6
Reading Royals v Lincoln City	3-2
Newcastle United v Watford	0-4
Stockport County v Arsenal	1-4
Aston Villa v Colchester United	0-1
Chelsea v Doncaster Rovers Belles	2-1
Whitley Bay v Tranmere Rovers	1-2
Frome Town v Nottingham Forest	3-7
Fulham v Cardiff City	1-2
Charlton Athletic v West Ham United	8-0
Sunderland v Leeds United	1-3
Bristol Academy v Bristol City	3-1
Birmingham City v Manchester City	3-1
Langford v Southampton Saints	2-1
Wolverhampton Wanderers v Liverpool	2-3

FIFTH ROUND

Bristol Academy v Tranmere Rovers	3-1
Nottingham Forest v Charlton Athletic	0-4
Langford v Everton	0-4
Liverpool v Watford	3-0
Cardiff City v Leeds United	1-2
Colchester United v Birmingham	0-5
Blackburn Rovers v Chelsea	3-2
Arsenal v Reading Royals	14-1

SIXTH ROUND

Liverpool v Bristol Academy	0-1
Blackburn Rovers v Leeds United	2-1
Arsenal v Birmingham City	6-0
Charlton Athletic v Everton	1-0

SEMI-FINALS

Bristol Academy v Arsenal	0-2
Blackburn Rovers v Charlton Athletic	0-1

FINAL (AT NOTTINGHAM FOREST)

8 MAY

Arsenal 4 *(Smith 6, 81, Ludlow 14, 45)*

Charlton Athletic 1 *(Holtham 2)* 24,529

Arsenal: Byrne; Ludlow, Grant, Smith, Sanderson (Carney 64), Fleeting (Davison 79), Yankey, Scott, Chapman, Asante, Phillip.
Charlton Athletic: Wayne; Stoney, Holtham (Hughes 85), Hills, Bertelli, Murphy, Aluko, Dowie (Heatherson 85), Potter, Smith (Hincks 71), Boyer.
Referee: A. Bates (Staffordshire).

THE FA WOMEN'S PREMIER LEAGUE CUP 2006–07

FIRST ROUND

Arsenal v Doncaster Rovers Belles	4-1
Birmingham City v Stockport County	2-1
Blackburn Rovers v Wolverhampton Wanderers	6-0
Brighton & Hove Albion v Charlton Athletic	0-5
Bristol Academy v AFC Wimbledon	8-1
Bristol City v Keynsham Town	3-2
Chelsea v Watford	5-1
Crewe Alexandra v Tranmere Rovers	5-3
Curzon Ashton v Nottingham Forest	0-2
Everton v Crystal Palace	4-0
Leeds United v Cardiff City	4-0
Lincoln City v Sunderland	2-1
Millwall Lionesses v Fulham	4-4
Millwall Lionesses won on penalties.	
Preston North End v Liverpool	1-3
Southampton Saints v Barnet	1-3
West Ham United v Newcastle United	2-0

SECOND ROUND

Nottingham Forest v West Ham United	0-1
West Ham fielded an ineligible player and were disqualified.	
Lincoln City v Liverpool	2-2
Lincoln City won 5-4 on penalties.	
Blackburn Rovers v Chelsea	3-6
Bristol City v Millwall Lionesses	1-1
Millwall Lionesses won 3-0 on penalties.	
Arsenal v Birmingham City	3-0
Everton v Bristol Academy	2-0
Leeds United v Barnet	2-0
Crewe Alexandra v Charlton Athletic	1-5

QUARTER-FINALS

Arsenal v Nottingham Forest	9-0
Leeds United v Millwall Lionesses	2-1
Everton v Chelsea	1-2
Lincoln City v Charlton Athletic	0-6

SEMI-FINALS

Arsenal v Chelsea	4-1
Charlton Athletic v Leeds United	2-2
Leeds United won on penalties.	

FINAL

Arsenal (1) *(Ludlow 90)*

Leeds United (0) 3688

(at Scunthorpe).
Arsenal: Byrne; Scott, Asante, Phillip, Chapman, Ludlow, Grant, Smith, Sanderson (Fleeting 66), Yankey, Carney.
Leeds United: Fay; Bradley, Culvin, McArthur, Wright, Preston, Emmanuel, Smith, Walton, Ward (Clarke 63), Burke (Sutcliffe 73).
Referee: D. Roberts.

UEFA WOMEN'S CUP 2006–07

FIRST QUALIFYING ROUND

GROUP 1
Saestum 7, Maksimir 0
Cardiff 2, Dundalk 0
Saestum 6, Dundalk 1
Maksimir 2, Cardiff 3
Dundalk 0, Maksimir 8
Cardiff 0, Saestum 2

GROUP 2
Juvisy 6, KI 0
Hibernian 1, Espanyol 4
Juvisy 0, Espanyol 1
KI 1, Hibernian 2
Espanyol 7, KI 0
Hibernian 0, Juvisy 6

GROUP 3
1 Dezembro 0, Breidablik 4
Neulengbach 5, Newtownabbey 1
Newtownabbey 1, 1 Dezembro 7
Neulengbach 0, Breidablik 3
Breidablik 7, Newtownabbey 0
1 Dezembro 0, Neulengbach 3

GROUP 4
Zuchwil 0, HJK 2
Wroclaw 4, Shkiponjat 1
Shkiponjat 1, Zuchwil 3
Wroclaw 0, HJK 1
HJK 7, Shkiponjat 0
Zuchwil 2, Wroclaw 2

GROUP 5
Sarajevo 0, Fiammamonza 1
Vitebsk 1, Gintra 0
Vitebsk 1, Fiammamonza 0
Gintra 1, Sarajevo 1
Fiammamonza 3, Gintra 0
Sarajevo 1, Vitebsk 0

GROUP 6
Nis 6, Parnu 1
Wezemaal 5, Pomurje 0
Parnu 0, Wezemaal 7
Nis 3, Pomurje 2
Pomurje 7, Parnu 1
Wezemaal 6, Nis 1

GROUP 7
Alma 2, Rossiyanka 5
Clujana 0, Sala 1
Rossiyanka 7, Clujana 0
Alma 5, Sala 2
Sala 1, Rossiyanka 6
Clujana 2, Alma 4

GROUP 8
Maccabi Holon 1, PAOK 1
Legend Chernigov 4, AEK Kokkinochovion 0
AEK Kokkinochovion 0, Maccabi Holon 5
Legend Chernigov 5, PAOK 0
PAOK 5, AEK Kokkinochovion 2
Maccabi Holon 0, Legend Chernigov 3

GROUP 9
Gomrukcu Baku 1, Budapest 7
Narta 1, Sofia 3
Gomrukcu Baku 1, Narta 2
Sofia 0, Budapest 1
Budapest 7, Narta 0
Sofia 7, Gomrukcu Baku 0

SECOND QUALIFYING ROUND

GROUP 1
Frankfurt 5, Vitebsk 0
HJK 1, Breidablik 2
Frankfurt 5, Breidablik 0
Vitebsk 0, HJK 0
Breidablik 1, Vitebsk 0
HJK 0, Frankfurt 2

GROUP 2
Umea 2, Legend Chernigov 0
Kolbotn 4, Espanyol 2
Legend Chernigov 1, Kolbotn 2
Umea 3, Espanyol 0
Espanyol 5, Legend Chernigov 0
Kolbotn 1, Umea 2

GROUP 3
Potsdam 1, Wezemaal 0
Sparta 1, Saestum 3
Wezemaal 4, Sparta 2
Potsdam 2, Saestum 2
Saestum 2, Wezemaal 0
Sparta 9, Potsdam 4

GROUP 4
Brondby 5, Budapest 1
Arsenal 5, Rossiyanka 4
Budapest 0, Arsenal 6
Brondby 2, Rossiyanka 1
Rossiyanka 4, Budapest 2
Arsenal 1, Brondby 0

QUARTER-FINALS FIRST LEG
Kolbotn 2, Frankfurt 1
Brondby 3, Potsdam 0
Breidablik 0, Arsenal 5
Saestum 1, Umea 6

QUARTER-FINALS SECOND LEG
Potsdam 2, Brondby 1
Frankfurt 3, Kolbotn 2
Arsenal 4, Breidablik 1
Umea 5, Saestum 2

SEMI-FINALS FIRST LEG
Umea 6, Kolbotn 0
Arsenal 3, Brondby 0

SEMI-FINALS SECOND LEG
Kolbotn 1, Umea 5
Brondby 2, Arsenal 2

FINAL FIRST LEG
(in Umea).
Umea (0) 0
Arsenal (0) 1 *(Scott 90)*
Umea: Soberg; Paulsson, Frisk, Bergqvist, Westberg, Dahlkvist (Backmann 76), Moura, Ljungberg (Xiaoxu 63), Edlund, Marta, Klaveness.
Arsenal: Byrne; Phillip, Scott, Grant, Ludlow, Asante, Chapman, Carney (Davison 89), Yankey, Sanderson, Fleeting.
Referee: Beck (Germany).

FINAL SECOND LEG
(in Boreham Wood).
Arsenal (0) 0
Umea (0) 0
Arsenal: Byrne; Scott, Ludlow (White 90), Asante, Phillip, Carney, Chapman, Grant, Yankey, Fleeting, Sanderson.
Umea: Soberg; Paulsson, Westberg, Frisk, Bergqvist, Dahlkvist (Edlund 55), Moura, Xiaoxu (Backmann 72), Klaveness, Marta, Ljungberg.
Referee: Petignat (Switzerland).

ENGLAND WOMEN'S INTERNATIONAL MATCHES 2006–07

31 August 2006
England 4 *(Smith K 9, 25, 50, Yankey 67)*
Holland 0 7931
(at Charlton).
England: Brown; Scott A, Unitt, Chapman, Asante, Phillip, Carny, Williams, Aluko (Handley 84), Smith K (Scott J 82), Yankey (Smith S 74).

30 September 2006
France 1 *(Diquelman 89)*
England 1 *(Lattaf 64 (og))* 19,215
(in Rennes).
England: Brown; Scott A, Unitt (Stoney 46), Chapman, Asante, Philip, Carny (Johnson 90), Williams, Aluko, Smith K, Yankey (Smith S 78).

25 October 2006
Germany 5 *(Stegemann 28, Smisek 36, Prinz 66, Muller 75, De Mbabi 86)*
England 1 *(Scott A 26)* 11,161
(in Aalen).
England: Brown (Chamberlain 56); Scott A, Stoney, Williams (Aluko 77), Asante, Philip, Carny (Johnson 46), Exley, Handley, Smith K (Scott J 61), Yankey (Smith S 68).

THE CHINA CUP
26 January 2007
China 2 *(Zhang Ying 4, Han Duan 45)*
England 0
(in Guangzhou).
England: Chamberlain; Scott A, Stoney (Unitt 87), Chapman, Asante, Philip, Carny (Johnson 46), Williams, Handley (Sanderson 73), Smith K (Westwood 62), Smith S.

THE CHINA CUP
28 January 2007
England 1 *(Scott A 47)*
USA 1 *(O'Reilly 17)*
(in Guandong).
England: Brown; Scott A, Stoney, Asante, Westwood (Unitt 79), Chapman (Exley 83), Williams, Smith K, Carny, Aluko (Scott J 59), Yankey.
The China Cup

THE CHINA CUP
30 January 2007
Germany 0
England 0
(in Guandong).
England: Brown; Scott A, Unitt, Scott J (Exley 66), Philip (Asante 29), Westwood, Williams (Chapman 55), Smith K, Carny (Johnson 46), Aluko (Sanderson 46), Yankey.

8 March 2007
England 6 *(Scott A 10, Aluko 15, Carny 25, Smith K 41, Yankey 64, Stoney 80).*
Russia 0 5421
(in Milton Keynes).
England: Brown; Scott A (Johnson 57), Stoney, Chapman (Exley 86), Asante (Bassett 86), Westwood (Houghton 73), Carny, Williams (Scott J 73), Aluko (Handley 46). Smith K, Yankey.

11 March 2007
England 1 *(Williams 30)*
Scotland 0 2066
(at Wycombe).
England: Chamberlain (Telford 46); Houghton, Unitt (Yorston 78), Scott J, Bassett, Philip, Scott A (Johnson 78), Williams, Sanderson (Barr 58), Smith K (Chapman 46), Smith S (Potter 58).

14 March 2007
England 0
Holland 1 *(Melis 78)* 5957
(at Swindon).
England: Brown; Scott A, Stoney, Chapman, Asante, Westwood, Carny (Houghton 79), Williams, Aluko, Smith K, Yankey (Potter 69).

13 May 2007
England 4 *(Smith K 52, Harkin 66 (og), Chapman 72, Sanderson 76)*
Northern Ireland 0
(at Gillingham).
England: Brown; Houghton (Carny 46), Unitt, Chapman, Asante, Phillip, Scott A, Williams, Sanderson (Barr 77), Smith K (White 73), Smith S.

17 May 2007
England 4 *(Yankey 23, Chapman 45, 69, Smith K 64)*
Iceland 0 7606
(at Southend).
England: Brown; Scott A (Johnson 46), Stoney, Chapman (Houghton 79), Asante, Phillip (White 46), Carney (Smith S 69), Williams (Scott J 46), Handley, Smith K (Sanderson 84), Yankey (Potter 46).

Arsenal's Rachel Yankey and Umea's Anna Paulson battle for the ball during the UEFA Women's Cup Final second leg at Boreham Wood. (Action Images/Alex Morton)

UNIBOND LEAGUE 2006–07

PREMIER DIVISION 2006–07

			Home					Away					Total						
		P	W	D	L	F	A	W	D	L	F	A	W	D	L	F	A	GD	Pts
1	Burscough*	42	15	5	1	50	14	8	7	6	30	23	23	12	7	80	37	43	80
2	Witton Albion	42	14	4	3	57	25	10	4	7	33	23	24	8	10	90	48	42	80
3	AFC Telford United	42	9	10	2	41	23	12	5	4	31	17	21	15	6	72	40	32	78
4	Marine	42	12	5	4	36	23	10	3	8	34	30	22	8	12	70	53	17	74
5	Matlock Town	42	12	4	5	38	20	9	5	7	32	23	21	9	12	70	43	27	72
6	Guiseley	42	10	7	4	43	25	9	5	7	28	24	19	12	11	71	49	22	69
7	Hednesford Town	42	9	8	4	26	17	9	6	6	23	24	18	14	10	49	41	8	68
8	Fleetwood Town	42	13	3	5	41	21	6	7	8	30	39	19	10	13	71	60	11	67
9	Gateshead	42	11	5	5	41	30	6	9	6	34	27	17	14	11	75	57	18	65
10	Ossett Town	42	9	6	6	33	27	9	4	8	28	25	18	10	14	61	52	9	64
11	Whitby Town	42	13	3	5	39	26	5	3	13	24	52	18	6	18	63	78	–15	60
12	Ilkeston Town	42	7	6	8	29	29	9	5	7	37	33	16	11	15	66	62	4	59
13	North Ferriby United	42	10	3	8	30	30	5	6	10	24	31	15	9	18	54	61	–7	54
14	Prescot Cables	42	8	8	5	30	24	5	6	10	22	32	13	14	15	52	56	–4	53
15	Lincoln United	42	5	10	6	18	22	7	5	9	22	36	12	15	15	40	58	–18	51
16	Frickley Athletic	42	8	6	7	27	27	5	4	12	23	42	13	10	19	50	69	–19	49
17	Leek Town	42	7	5	9	21	25	6	4	11	28	36	13	9	20	49	61	–12	48
18	Ashton United	42	10	3	8	33	37	3	6	12	19	35	13	9	20	52	72	–20	48
19	Kendal Town	42	8	4	9	28	35	4	7	10	31	44	12	11	19	59	79	–20	47
20	Mossley	42	5	2	14	24	40	5	3	13	24	39	10	5	27	48	79	–31	35
21	Radcliffe Borough	42	4	5	12	19	36	3	6	12	20	35	7	11	24	39	71	–32	32
22	Grantham Town	42	3	3	15	16	44	0	5	16	23	50	3	8	31	39	94	–55	17

**Deducted 1 point for fielding an ineligible player.*

DIVISION ONE 2006–07

			Home					Away					Total						
		P	W	D	L	F	A	W	D	L	F	A	W	D	L	F	A	GD	Pts
1	Buxton	46	17	3	3	46	14	13	8	2	48	23	30	11	5	94	37	57	101
2	Cammell Laird	46	15	5	3	58	29	13	5	5	47	27	28	10	8	105	56	49	94
3	Eastwood Town	46	14	5	4	40	17	12	4	7	50	26	26	9	11	90	43	47	87
4	Bradford Park Avenue	46	15	5	3	47	20	9	5	9	30	27	24	10	12	77	47	30	82
5	Colwyn Bay	46	14	6	3	42	23	9	4	10	32	40	23	10	13	74	63	11	79
6	Stocksbridge Park Steels	46	14	3	6	41	22	8	7	8	41	27	22	10	14	82	49	33	76
7	Goole Town	46	9	6	8	40	41	12	3	8	40	43	21	9	16	80	84	–4	72
8	Kidsgrove Athletic	46	12	2	9	42	33	9	5	9	49	47	21	7	18	91	80	11	70
9	Rossendale United	46	11	3	9	36	32	10	4	9	28	27	21	7	18	64	59	5	70
10	Woodley Sports	46	13	4	6	52	31	6	7	10	37	40	19	11	16	89	71	18	68
11	Ossett Albion	46	10	5	8	33	34	9	6	8	38	32	19	11	16	71	66	5	68
12	Harrogate Railway	46	13	3	7	44	34	8	2	13	28	44	21	5	20	72	78	–6	68
13	Bamber Bridge	46	11	3	9	47	37	7	5	11	31	38	18	8	20	78	75	3	62
14	Alsager Town	46	8	5	10	36	39	10	2	11	36	36	18	7	21	72	75	–3	61
15	Clitheroe	46	11	2	10	44	36	7	4	12	34	39	18	6	22	78	75	3	60
16	Skelmersdale United	46	11	4	8	42	34	6	5	12	28	43	17	9	20	70	77	–7	60
17	Brigg Town	46	12	4	7	32	32	4	6	13	25	40	16	10	20	57	72	–15	58
18	Gresley Rovers	46	9	5	9	37	37	7	2	14	22	38	16	7	23	59	75	–16	55
19	Belper Town	46	12	2	9	33	36	5	2	16	25	50	17	4	25	58	86	–28	55
20	Shepshed Dynamo	46	8	7	8	34	34	7	0	16	28	62	15	7	24	62	96	–34	52
21	Wakefield	46	6	4	13	27	37	7	6	10	21	34	13	10	23	48	71	–23	49
22	Warrington Town	46	7	6	10	32	33	6	2	15	32	52	13	8	25	64	85	–21	47
23	Chorley	46	6	5	12	32	42	4	1	18	20	57	10	6	30	52	99	–47	36
24	Bridlington Town	46	3	6	14	20	56	0	8	15	13	45	3	14	29	33	101	–68	23

LEADING GOALSCORERS (in order of League goals)

Premier Division

	Lge	*Cup*	*Total*
Southern (Gateshead)	27	4	31
Muller (Ilkeston Town)	26	1	27
Holmes (Matlock Town)	25	9	34
Warlow (Witton Albion)	24	6	30
Kilheeney (Burscough)	23	7	30
(Includes 7 League and 2 Cup goals for Ashton).			
Brunskill (Whitby Town)	22	7	29
Cumiskey (Marine)	20	7	27
Wright (Kendal Town)	19	2	21
(Includes 9 League and 2 Cup goals for other teams).			
Hayward (Ossett Town)	17	3	20
Bradshaw (North Ferriby United)	15	11	26
Foster (AFC Telford United)	15	3	18
Ross (Ossett Town)	15	3	18
(Includes 13 League and 3 Cup goals for Bradford Park Avenue).			
Pell (Guiseley)	15	2	17
(Includes 8 League and 2 Cup goals for Frickley Athletic).			

First Division

	Lge	*Cup*	*Total*
Lennon (Kidsgrove Athletic)	35	16	51
Knox (Eastwood Town)	31	9	40
Reed (Buxton)	31	5	36
Morgan (Cammell Laird)	27	7	34
Toronczak (Ossett Albion)	22	7	29
Morning (Woodley Sports)	21	6	27
Parton (Goole AFC)	20	6	26
Porter (Bamber Bridge)	20	4	24
Salmon R (Bamber Bridge)	20	2	22
Rhead (Kidsgrove Athletic)	18	13	31
McGuire (Cammell Laird)	18	9	27
Marchant (Harrogate Railway Athletic)	16	7	23
Bray (Goole AFC)	16	5	21
Budrys (Alsager Town)	16	3	19
Salmon G (Woodley Sports)	16	3	19
Meikle (Eastwood Town)	16	1	17

Cup goals include those scored in play-offs.

ATTENDANCES

Premier Division
Highest Attendances:
5710 AFC Telford United v Burscough
4296 AFC Telford United v Hednesford Town
3005 Hednesford Town v AFC Telford United

First Division
Highest Attendances:
720 Buxton v Stocksbridge Park Steels
656 Buxton v Eastwood Town
652 Colwyn Bay v Eastwood Town

UNIBOND LEAGUE CHALLENGE CUP 2006–07

FIRST ROUND
Alsager Town 1, Kidsgrove Athletic 4
Bamber Bridge 6, Redcliffe Borough 3
Bridlington Town 1, Ossett Town 3
Cammell Laird 0, Prescot Cables 2
Clitheroe 5, Chorley 0
Colwyn Bay 1, Warrington Town 3
Gateshead 0, Harrogate Railway Athletic 1
Goole AFC 2, Ossett Albion 1
Guiseley 1, Bradford Park Avenue 1
Bradford Park Avenue won 4-3 on penalties.
Leek Town 2, AFC Telford United 2
Leek Town won 11-10 on penalties.
Lincoln United 0, Ilkeston Town 2
Rossendale United 1, Skelmersdale United 4
Shepshed Dynamo 2, Buxton 3
Wakefield 1, Ashton United 0

SECOND ROUND
Bamber Bridge 2, Prescot Cables 1
Belper Town 3, Grantham Town 3
Grantham Town won 5-4 on penalties.
Bradford Park Avenue 1, North Ferriby United 4
Brigg Town 2, Stocksbridge Park Steels 1
Burscough 1, Kendal Town 4
Buxton 0, Hednesford Town 2
Eastwood Town 1, Leek Town 6
Fleetwood Town 2, Mossley 1
Frickley Athletic 1, Goole AFC 4
Harrogate Railway Athletic 4, Wakefield 1
Ilkeston Town 3, Kidsgrove Athletic 4
Marine 4, Skelmersdale United 1
Matlock Town 4, Gresley Rovers 1
Whitby Town 3, Ossett Town 3
Whitby Town won 5-4 on penalties.
Witton Albion 8, Clitheroe 1
Woodley Sports 3, Warrington Town 0

THIRD ROUND
Bamber Bridge 2, Witton Albion 3
Goole AFC 2, Grantham Town 3
Harrogate Railway Athletic 3, Brigg Town 0
Hednesford Town 1, Woodley Sports 2
Kendal Town 1, Fleetwood Town 3
Marine 1, Leek Town 0
Matlock Town 3, Kidsgrove Athletic 1
North Ferriby United 1, Whitby Town 2

FOURTH ROUND
Fleetwood Town 3, Grantham Town 1
Matlock Town 5, Whitby Town 4
Witton Albion 1, Marine 0
Woodley Sports 3, Harrogate Railway Athletic 2

SEMI-FINALS
Fleetwood Town 1, Witton Albion 0
Matlock Town 3, Woodley Sports 3
Matlock Town won 8-7 on penalties.

FINAL
Fleetwood Town 1, Matlock Town 0

PRESIDENT'S CUP 2006–07

SEMI-FINALS
Buxton 1, Stocksbridge Park Steels 0
Gresley Rovers 1, Wakefield 2

FINAL
Buxton 3, Wakefield 1

CHAIRMAN'S CUP 2006–07

QUARTER-FINALS
Alsager Town 0, Cammell Laird 1
Ashton United 2, Rossendale United 0
Guiseley 5, Ossett Albion 0
Shepshed Dynamo 2, Bridlington Town 2
Bridlington Town won 3-0 on penalties.

SEMI-FINALS
Bridlington Town 1, Cammell Laird 4
Guiseley 3, Ashton United 2

FINAL
Guiseley 2, Cammell Laird 1

PETER SWALES MEMORIAL SHIELD 2006–07

Burscough 3, Buxton 1

UNIBOND PREMIER DIVISION PLAY-OFFS 2006–07

SEMI-FINALS
AFC Telford United 2, Marine 0
Witton Albion 4, Matlock Town 2

FINAL
Witton Albion 1, AFC Telford United 3

UNIBOND LEAGUE FIRST DIVISION PROMOTION PLAY-OFFS 2006–07

SEMI-FINALS
Cammell Laird 3, Colwyn Bay 2
Eastwood Town 3, Bradford Park Avenue 0

FINAL
Cammell Laird 1, Eastwood Town 2

SOUTHERN LEAGUE 2006–07

BRITISH GAS BUSINESS PREMIER DIVISION 2006–07

			Home					Away					Total						
		P	W	D	L	F	A	W	D	L	F	A	W	D	L	F	A	GD	Pts
1	Bath City	42	13	5	3	43	15	14	5	2	41	14	27	10	5	84	29	55	91
2	Team Bath	42	14	3	4	39	19	9	6	6	27	23	23	9	10	66	42	24	78
3	King's Lynn	42	15	3	3	37	12	7	7	7	32	28	22	10	10	69	40	29	76
4	Maidenhead United	42	11	6	4	31	17	9	4	8	27	19	20	10	12	58	36	22	70
5	Hemel Hempstead Town	42	12	6	3	44	22	7	6	8	35	38	19	12	11	79	60	19	69
6	Halesowen Town	42	11	6	4	43	30	7	7	7	23	23	18	13	11	66	53	13	67
7	Chippenham Town	42	11	6	4	35	20	8	3	10	26	36	19	9	14	61	56	5	66
8	Stamford	42	10	4	7	31	23	6	7	8	34	39	16	11	15	65	62	3	59
9	Mangotsfield United	42	5	11	5	21	22	8	8	5	23	23	13	19	10	44	45	–1	58
10	Gloucester City	42	6	6	9	28	40	9	7	5	39	30	15	13	14	67	70	–3	58
11	Hitchin Town	42	11	3	7	31	28	5	6	10	24	40	16	9	17	55	68	–13	57
12	Merthyr Tydfil	42	10	7	4	28	15	4	7	10	19	30	14	14	14	47	45	2	56
13	Banbury United	42	6	6	9	33	33	9	4	8	27	31	15	10	17	60	64	–4	55
14	Yate Town	42	7	7	7	41	36	7	5	9	18	35	14	12	16	59	71	–12	54
15	Tiverton Town	42	10	3	8	30	26	4	5	12	26	41	14	8	20	56	67	–11	50
16	Cheshunt	42	10	3	8	34	29	4	4	13	22	42	14	7	21	56	71	–15	49
17	Rugby Town	42	10	2	9	31	32	5	2	14	26	47	15	4	23	57	79	–22	49
18	Clevedon Town	42	6	7	8	32	30	6	5	10	28	31	12	12	18	60	61	–1	48
19	Wealdstone	42	8	6	7	38	36	5	3	13	31	46	13	9	20	69	82	–13	48
20	Corby Town	42	5	6	10	27	33	5	3	13	25	36	10	9	23	52	69	–17	39
21	Cirencester Town	42	6	6	9	29	36	3	6	12	17	40	9	12	21	46	76	–30	39
22	Northwood	42	4	4	13	23	37	4	6	11	21	37	8	10	24	44	74	–30	34

BRITISH GAS BUSINESS MIDLANDS 2006–07

			Home					Away					Total						
		P	W	D	L	F	A	W	D	L	F	A	W	D	L	F	A	GD	Pts
1	Brackley Town	42	15	2	4	55	25	14	2	5	40	28	29	4	9	95	53	42	91
2	Bromsgrove Rovers	42	14	2	5	53	33	9	5	7	33	29	23	7	12	86	62	24	76
3	Chasetown	42	14	3	4	33	14	9	3	9	26	25	23	6	13	59	39	20	75
4	Willenhall Town	42	10	6	5	29	19	10	6	5	38	28	20	12	10	67	47	20	72
5	Evesham United	42	10	7	4	36	25	9	8	4	30	26	19	15	8	66	51	15	72
6	Aylesbury United	42	11	7	3	31	17	9	4	8	27	25	20	11	11	58	42	16	71
7	Stourbridge	42	9	7	5	39	27	8	8	5	31	26	17	15	10	70	53	17	66
8	Woodford United	42	12	6	3	46	25	6	5	10	25	29	18	11	13	71	54	17	65
9	Cinderford Town	42	10	6	5	37	27	8	4	9	33	33	18	10	14	70	60	10	64
10	Rothwell Town	42	12	3	6	41	21	6	4	11	31	40	18	7	17	72	61	11	61
11	Dunstable Town	42	7	5	9	36	33	9	7	5	28	20	16	12	14	64	53	11	60
12	Sutton Coldfield Town	42	10	3	8	35	32	6	6	9	27	31	16	9	17	62	63	–1	57
13	Bishops Cleeve	42	9	2	10	30	28	8	3	10	38	38	17	5	20	68	66	2	56
14	Solihull Borough	42	8	4	9	40	47	9	1	11	32	37	17	5	20	72	84	–12	56
15	Rushall Olympic	42	8	4	9	28	25	7	5	9	28	30	15	9	18	56	55	1	54
16	Bedworth United	42	7	3	11	35	35	6	5	10	38	48	13	8	21	73	83	–10	47
17	Malvern Town	42	4	6	11	24	37	8	5	8	22	29	12	11	19	46	66	–20	47
18	Leighton Town	42	7	6	8	25	23	5	2	14	19	37	12	8	22	44	60	–16	44
19	Spalding United	42	8	1	12	23	22	4	5	12	22	40	12	6	24	45	62	–17	42
20	Barton Rovers	42	6	6	9	27	37	5	3	13	24	56	11	9	22	51	93	–42	42
21	Berkhamsted Town	42	7	4	10	33	42	3	3	15	20	55	10	7	25	53	97	–44	37
22	Stourport Swifts	42	6	4	11	24	37	3	3	15	19	50	9	7	26	43	87	–44	34

BRITISH GAS SOUTHERN & WEST 2006–07

			Home					Away					Total						
		P	W	D	L	F	A	W	D	L	F	A	W	D	L	F	A	GD	Pts
1	Bashley	42	17	2	2	68	16	15	4	2	43	19	32	6	4	111	35	76	102
2	Paulton Rovers	42	13	5	3	40	19	7	9	5	26	23	20	14	8	66	42	24	74
3	Burnham	42	13	2	6	37	21	10	2	9	37	39	23	4	15	74	60	14	73
4	Swindon Supermarine	42	10	6	5	36	18	10	5	6	32	22	20	11	11	68	40	28	71
5	Taunton Town	42	9	8	4	36	25	10	6	5	32	25	19	14	9	68	50	18	71
6	Thatcham Town	42	12	4	5	37	24	9	3	9	33	36	21	7	14	70	60	10	70
7	Marlow	42	10	7	4	39	22	9	5	7	35	27	19	12	11	74	49	25	69
8	Uxbridge	42	10	4	7	36	29	10	4	7	32	29	20	8	14	68	58	10	68
9	Andover	42	10	5	6	42	34	9	4	8	28	25	19	9	14	70	59	11	66
10	Didcot Town	42	10	8	3	53	31	6	5	10	33	36	16	13	13	86	67	19	61
11	Abingdon United	42	9	6	6	39	28	7	5	9	29	39	16	11	15	68	67	1	59
12	Oxford City	42	11	3	7	38	40	6	5	10	24	35	17	8	17	62	75	–13	59
13	Winchester City	42	11	6	4	37	17	5	4	12	30	48	16	10	16	67	65	2	58
14	Windsor & Eton	42	9	5	7	35	29	7	5	9	41	46	16	10	16	76	75	1	58
15	Chesham United	42	12	2	7	44	40	5	4	12	24	39	17	6	19	68	79	–11	57
16	Hillingdon Borough	42	6	6	9	33	36	7	7	7	47	49	13	13	16	80	85	–5	52
17	Lymington & New Milton	42	7	3	11	35	38	9	0	12	46	41	16	3	23	81	79	2	51
18	Brook House	42	8	3	10	36	40	6	3	12	35	52	14	6	22	71	92	–21	48
19	Bracknell Town	42	7	5	9	35	31	4	8	9	16	31	11	13	18	51	62	–11	46
20	Newport (IW)	42	6	2	13	25	44	3	1	17	19	62	9	3	30	44	106	–62	30
21	Hanwell Town*	42	4	3	14	33	54	2	4	15	19	48	6	7	29	52	102	–50	24
22	Beaconsfield SYCOB	42	3	2	16	19	42	2	4	15	17	62	5	6	31	36	104	–68	21

**Deducted 1 point for fielding an ineligible player.*

SOUTHERN LEAGUE PLAY-OFFS 2006–07

PREMIER DIVISION PLAY-OFF FINAL
Saturday 5 May 2007 – attendance 643
Team Bath 0, Maidenhead United 1 *(Telemarque 46)*

DIVISION ONE MIDLANDS PLAY-OFF FINAL
Saturday 5 May 2007 – attendance 892
Bromsgrove Rovers *(Allsop 46, Clarke 113)* 2, Willenhall Town 1 *(Gregg 15)*
aet.

DIVISION ONE SOUTHERN & WEST PLAY-OFF FINAL
Saturday 5 May 2007 – attendance 522
Swindon Supermarine *(Gullick 52, Stroud 85)* 2, Taunton Town 1

SOUTHERN LEAGUE ATTENDANCES 2006–07

PREMIER

Average	333	Division Highest	2044 Bath City 1 Chippenham Town 0 (9 April 2007)

DIVISION ONE MIDLANDS

Average	146	Division Highest	544 Bromsgrove Rovers 2 Brackley Town 0 (17 March 2007)

DIVISION ONE SOUTHERN & WEST

Average	154	Division Highest	473 Bashley 0 Andover 1 (31 March 2007)

SOUTHERN LEAGUE LEADING GOALSCORERS 2006–07

PREMIER DIVISION
(Includes League and League Cup goals only)

Anthony Thomas (Hemel Hempstead Town)	25
Dean Brennan (Hemel Hempstead Town)	23
Dean Papali (Wealdstone)	23
Darrell Cox (Cheshunt)	22
Darren Edwards (Bath City)	20
Gary Sippetts (Hemel Hempstead Town)	18
Jason Taylor (Rugby Town)	18

DIVISION ONE MIDLANDS
(Includes League and League Cup goals only)

Nathan Lamey (Bromsgrove Rovers)	31
Mark Bellingham (Stourbridge)	30
Richard Kear (Cinderford Town)	29
Kevin Slack (Bishops Cleeve)	27
Matthew Murphy (Brackley Town)	23
Tom Winters (Brackley Town)	22
Rory May (Solihull Borough)	20
Adam Kinder (Bedworth United)	18
Christopher Marsh (Dunstable Town)	18
Kyle Perry (Willenhall Town)	18
Dean Perrow (Rushall Olympic)	17
Richard Pringle (Aylesbury United)	17

DIVISION ONE SOUTHERN & WEST
(Includes League and League Cup goals only)

Richard Gillespie (Bashley)	35
James Stokoe (Lymington & New Milton)	31
Ryan Kirkland (Brook House)	24
Mark Anderson (Bracknell Town)	23
Michael Chennells (Windsor & Eton)	21
Ryan Moss (Bashley)	21
Jermaine Roche (Marlow)	21
Leon Nelson (Hillingdon Borough)	20
Anaiah Odihambo (Abingdon United)	20
Ian Concannon (Didcot Town)	19

ERREA SOUTHERN LEAGUE CUP 2006–07

FIRST ROUND

Abingdon United v Oxford City	0-2
Barton Rovers v Aylesbury United	2-1
Bashley v Winchester City	2-3
Berkhamsted Town v Dunstable Town	1-2
Bishop's Cleeve v Taunton Town	0-1
Brook House v Bracknell Town	3-2
Chasetown v Bromsgrove Rovers	1-0
Chesham United v Burnham	4-0
Cinderford Town v Malvern Town	0-5
Didcot Town v Brackley Town	3-2
Hanwell Town v Windsor & Eton	0-1
Hillingdon Borough v Marlow	4-3
Newport (IW) v Lymington & New Milton	0-2
Paulton Rovers v Andover	1-2
Rushall Olympic v Bedworth United	0-1
Solihull Borough v Stourport Swifts	1-3
Spalding United v Rothwell Town	4-1
Stourbridge v Evesham United	4-3
Sutton Coldfield Town v Willenhall Town	1-5
Thatcham Town v Swindon Supermarine	1-1
Thatcham Town won 3-2 on penalties.	
Uxbridge v Beaconsfield SYCOB	2-1
Woodford United v Leighton Town	7-0

SECOND ROUND

Andover v Thatcham Town	1-3
Barton Rovers v Uxbridge	1-2
Bedworth United v Stourport Swifts	0-1
Chasetown v Malvern Town	1-0
Cirencester Town v Didcot Town	0-4
Hillingdon Borough v Brook House	1-3
Lymington & New Milton v Winchester City	1-0
Northwood v Chesham United	0-1
Stourbridge v Spalding United	3-0
Taunton Town v Oxford City	1-0
Willenhall Town v Woodford United	2-1
Windsor & Eton v Dunstable Town	1-2

THIRD ROUND

Taunton Town v Mangotsfield United	2-3
Chippenham Town v Lymington & New Milton	1-2
Hitchin Town v Corby Town	0-1
Rugby Town v Halesowen Town	2-1
Stamford v King's Lynn	1-2
Stourport Swifts v Stourbridge	0-1
Uxbridge v Brook House	1-3
Wealdstone v Cheshunt	0-2
Maidenhead United v Thatcham Town	1-3
Banbury United v Chesham United	2-0
Gloucester City v Didcot Town	2-3
Hemel Hempstead Town v Dunstable Town	3-0
Merthyr Tydfil v Team Bath	1-0
Tiverton Town v Yate Town	4-2
Clevedon Town v Bath City	0-1
Chasetown v Willenhall Town	2-1

FOURTH ROUND

Cheshunt v Brook House	5-0
Didcot Town v Merthyr Tydfil	4-1
King's Lynn v Corby Town	2-1
Tiverton Town v Bath City	3-1
Lymington & New Milton v Mangotsfield United	0-1
Banbury United v Chasetown	1-0
Rugby Town v Stourbridge	2-1
Thatcham Town v Hemel Hempstead Town	2-3

FIFTH ROUND

Tiverton Town v Mangotsfield United	2-0
Hemel Hempstead Town v Cheshunt	3-2
King's Lynn v Rugby Town	0-1
Didcot Town v Banbury United	1-3

SEMI-FINALS

Rugby Town v Hemel Hempstead Town	3-4
Tiverton Town v Banbury United	2-0

FINAL FIRST LEG

Tiverton Town v Hemel Hempstead Town	1-0	279

FINAL SECOND LEG

Hemel Hempstead Town v Tiverton Town	2-2	312

RYMAN LEAGUE 2006–07

RYMAN LEAGUE PREMIER DIVISION 2006–07

			Home					Away					Total						
		P	*W*	*D*	*L*	*F*	*A*	*W*	*D*	*L*	*F*	*A*	*W*	*D*	*L*	*F*	*A*	*GD*	*Pts*
1	Hampton & Richmond Bor	42	11	6	4	39	32	13	4	4	38	21	24	10	8	77	53	24	82
2	Bromley	42	13	3	5	44	28	10	8	3	39	15	23	11	8	83	43	40	80
3	Chelmsford City	42	15	4	2	63	23	8	4	9	33	28	23	8	11	96	51	45	77
4	Billericay Town	42	15	5	1	40	9	7	6	8	31	33	22	11	9	71	42	29	77
5	AFC Wimbledon*	42	11	7	3	45	18	10	8	3	31	19	21	15	6	76	37	39	75
6	Margate	42	11	6	4	34	17	9	5	7	45	31	20	11	11	79	48	31	71
7	Boreham Wood	42	9	5	7	38	29	10	7	4	33	20	19	12	11	71	49	22	69
8	Horsham	42	8	9	4	39	30	10	5	6	31	27	18	14	10	70	57	13	68
9	Ramsgate	42	12	4	5	35	24	8	1	12	28	39	20	5	17	63	63	0	65
10	Heybridge Swifts	42	9	6	6	26	18	8	7	6	31	22	17	13	12	57	40	17	64
11	Tonbridge Angels	42	9	3	9	43	40	11	1	9	31	32	20	4	18	74	72	2	64
12	Staines Town	42	8	8	5	31	27	7	4	10	33	37	15	12	15	64	64	0	57
13	Carshalton Athletic	42	9	5	7	32	28	5	7	9	22	31	14	12	16	54	59	–5	54
14	Hendon	42	8	4	9	25	27	8	2	11	27	36	16	6	20	52	63	–11	54
15	Leyton	42	8	4	9	30	40	5	6	10	24	36	13	10	19	54	76	–22	49
16	East Thurrock United	42	6	2	13	22	37	8	4	9	34	33	14	6	22	56	70	–14	48
17	Ashford Town (Middlesex)	42	8	6	7	34	26	3	7	11	25	45	11	13	18	59	71	–12	46
18	Folkestone Invicta	42	6	5	10	23	35	6	5	10	22	31	12	10	20	45	66	–21	46
19	Harrow Borough	42	8	2	11	32	35	5	4	12	29	36	13	6	23	61	71	–10	45
20	Worthing	42	6	4	11	26	36	2	7	12	31	46	8	11	23	57	82	–25	35
21	Walton & Hersham	42	8	5	8	26	31	1	1	19	12	52	9	6	27	38	83	–45	33
22	Slough Town	42	1	3	17	8	58	3	3	15	18	65	4	6	32	26	123	–97	18

**Deducted 3 points for fielding an ineligible player.*

RYMAN DIVISION ONE NORTH 2006–07

			Home					Away					Total						
		P	*W*	*D*	*L*	*F*	*A*	*W*	*D*	*L*	*F*	*A*	*W*	*D*	*L*	*F*	*A*	*GD*	*Pts*
1	AFC Hornchurch	42	14	5	2	49	15	18	2	1	47	12	32	7	3	96	27	69	103
2	Harlow Town	42	13	5	3	45	16	11	5	5	26	15	24	10	8	71	31	40	82
3	Enfield Town	42	14	2	5	35	14	10	5	6	39	25	24	7	11	74	39	35	79
4	Maldon Town	42	10	6	5	25	21	10	5	6	25	21	20	11	11	50	42	8	71
5	AFC Sudbury	42	9	7	5	40	22	10	6	5	27	19	19	13	10	67	41	26	70
6	Canvey Island	42	10	6	5	40	26	9	4	8	25	21	19	10	13	65	47	18	67
7	Ware	42	11	6	4	34	22	8	4	9	36	34	19	10	13	70	56	14	67
8	Waltham Forest	42	12	4	5	30	21	5	10	6	30	35	17	14	11	60	56	4	65
9	Wingate & Finchley	42	12	5	4	41	20	4	6	11	17	29	16	11	15	58	49	9	59
10	Waltham Abbey	42	10	5	6	40	27	5	8	8	25	24	15	13	14	65	51	14	58
11	Wivenhoe Town	42	6	6	9	26	29	10	3	8	24	23	16	9	17	50	52	–2	57
12	Great Wakering Rovers	42	9	4	8	27	27	7	5	9	30	37	16	9	17	57	64	–7	57
13	Enfield	42	9	4	8	35	30	7	2	12	30	33	16	6	20	65	63	2	54
14	Potters Bar Town	42	7	5	9	31	31	7	4	10	29	31	14	9	19	60	62	–2	51
15	Aveley	42	8	6	7	26	19	6	3	12	21	38	14	9	19	47	57	–10	51
16	Redbridge	42	10	2	9	26	21	5	3	13	16	27	15	5	22	42	48	–6	50
17	Bury Town	42	9	5	7	33	32	4	6	11	24	37	13	11	18	57	69	–12	50
18	Arlesey Town	42	9	5	7	23	27	4	6	11	21	36	13	11	18	44	63	–19	50
19	Tilbury	42	5	5	11	20	38	6	5	10	23	34	11	10	21	43	72	–29	43
20	Witham Town	42	7	3	11	30	41	3	4	14	22	49	10	7	25	52	90	–38	37
21	Ilford	42	6	3	12	19	45	3	2	16	17	52	9	5	28	36	97	–61	32
22	Flackwell Heath	42	4	4	13	15	32	3	5	13	22	58	7	9	26	37	90	–53	30

RYMAN DIVISION ONE SOUTH 2006–07

			Home					Away					Total						
		P	*W*	*D*	*L*	*F*	*A*	*W*	*D*	*L*	*F*	*A*	*W*	*D*	*L*	*F*	*A*	*GD*	*Pts*
1	Maidstone United	42	12	4	5	42	26	11	7	3	37	21	23	11	8	79	47	32	80
2	Tooting & Mitcham	42	13	5	3	40	22	9	8	4	30	19	22	13	7	70	41	29	79
3	Dover Athletic	42	12	4	5	41	21	10	7	4	36	20	22	11	9	77	41	36	77
4	Hastings United	42	12	5	4	38	20	10	5	6	41	36	22	10	10	79	56	23	76
5	Fleet Town	42	12	5	4	30	22	9	7	5	35	30	21	12	9	65	52	13	75
6	Metropolitan Police	42	9	11	1	35	20	9	4	8	30	28	18	15	9	65	48	17	69
7	Dartford	42	9	7	5	44	30	10	4	7	41	35	19	11	12	85	65	20	68
8	Dulwich Hamlet	42	10	8	3	46	25	8	5	8	37	31	18	13	11	83	56	27	67
9	Horsham YMCA	42	8	3	10	31	38	9	4	8	28	31	17	7	18	59	69	–10	58
10	Sittingbourne	42	8	7	6	27	21	6	8	7	41	42	14	15	13	68	63	5	57
11	Leatherhead	42	9	4	8	28	28	6	6	9	30	35	15	10	17	58	63	–5	55
12	Cray Wanderers	42	8	6	7	34	34	6	6	9	33	35	14	12	16	67	69	–2	54
13	Kingstonian	42	7	5	9	37	38	6	8	7	23	25	13	13	16	60	63	–3	52
14	Burgess Hill Town	42	7	6	8	29	40	6	6	9	29	41	13	12	17	58	81	–23	51
15	Molesey	42	6	6	9	27	37	6	7	8	25	26	12	13	17	52	63	–11	49
16	Chatham Town	42	8	6	7	29	26	4	5	12	23	36	12	11	19	52	62	–10	47
17	Walton Casuals	42	6	5	10	31	43	5	8	8	26	28	11	13	18	57	71	–14	46
18	Ashford Town	42	5	8	8	22	29	5	6	10	30	36	10	14	18	52	65	–13	44
19	Croydon Athletic	42	7	3	11	28	39	5	5	11	16	38	12	8	22	44	77	–33	44
20	Whyteleafe	42	3	11	7	24	25	6	4	11	28	40	9	15	18	52	65	–13	42
21	Corinthian Casuals	42	3	4	14	26	51	5	6	10	27	36	8	10	24	53	87	–34	34
22	Godalming Town	42	6	6	9	24	32	2	3	16	21	44	8	9	25	45	76	–31	33

RYMAN LEAGUE PLAY-OFFS 2006–07

PREMIER DIVISION PLAY-OFF FINAL
Bromley 1, Billericay Town 1 3,012
Bromley won 4-2 on penalties.

DIVISION ONE NORTH PLAY-OFF FINAL
Harlow Town 2, AFC Sudbury 2 948
Harlow Town won 5-3 on penalties.

DIVISION ONE SOUTH PLAY-OFF FINAL
Tooting & Mitcham United 0, Hastings United 2 1,132

RYMAN LEAGUE ATTENDANCES 2006–07

Premier Division Highest Average	2512	AFC Wimbledon
Division One North Highest Average	427	AFC Hornchurch
Division One South Highest Average	1171	Dartford

RYMAN LEAGUE LEADING GOALSCORERS 2006–07

PREMIER LEAGUE

		Games played	Goals scored
Main J	Tonbridge Angels	41	36
Hockton D	Margate	40	35
Hodges I	Hampton & Richmond B	36	21
McDonnell N	Bromley	33	20
Nwokeji M	Staines Town	41	20
Chaaban A	Staines Town	37	19
Ibe K	Chelmsford City	40	19
Jolly R	AFC Wimbledon	40	19
Minton J	Chelmsford City	40	18
Welford S	Ramsgate	39	18
Boot A	Bromley	31	17
Flack J	Billericay Town	33	17
Onochie E	Harrow Borough	29	17
Rook C	Horsham	40	16
Williams G	Bromley	31	16
D'Sane R	AFC Wimbledon	35	15
Pinnock J	Margate	41	15

DIVISION ONE NORTH

		Games played	Goals scored
Elmes H	Waltham Abbey	39	24
Crace R	Enfield Town	40	23
Parker S	AFC Hornchurch	35	23
Lee K	AFC Hornchurch	38	22
Tuohy M	Great Wakering Rovers	39	17
Winston S	Harlow Town	34	16
Bugg S	Bury Town	42	15
Williams D	Harlow Town	40	15

DIVISION ONE SOUTH

Cass B	Dartford	42	25
Vines P	Tooting & Mitcham U	39	22
Dickson C	Dulwich Hamlet	28	20
Jarvis A	Burgess Hill Town	41	18
May J	Dartford	36	18
Ruggles P	Molesey	40	17
Stevens D	Leatherhead	32	17

WESTVIEW LEAGUE CUP 2006–07

FIRST ROUND
Metropolitan Police v Godalming Town 4-1
Tilbury v Wivenhoe Town 2-3

SECOND ROUND
Flackwell Heath v Hendon 3-4
Boreham Wood v Enfield Town 4-3
Ware v Ashford Town (Middlesex) 0-1
Waltham Abbey v Harlow Town 0-1
Waltham Forest v Fleet Town 0-5
Arlesey v Slough Town 1-3
Harrow Borough v Enfield 0-1
Staines Town v Potters Bar 3-2
Worthing v Horsham YMCA 3-2
Walton & Hersham v Metropolitan Police 0-2
Leatherhead v Molesey 4-0
Walton Casuals v Dulwich Hamlet 4-1
Wingate & Finchley v Burgess Hill Town 2-4
AFC Wimbledon v Hastings United 2-1
Carshalton Athletic v Horsham 1-3
Kingstonian v Hampton & Richmond Borough 3-2
East Thurrock United v Billericay Town 1-0
Leyton v Witham Town 2-1
Great Wakering Rovers v Redbridge 0-1
Maldon Town v Bury Town 2-1
Chelmsford City v Wivenhoe Town 1-0
Aveley v AFC Sudbury 1-3
Heybridge Swifts v Ilford 4-0
AFC Hornchurch v Canvey Island 4-0
Ashford Town v Bromley 2-0
Cray Wanderers v Whyteleafe 3-1
Dartford v Folkestone Invicta 2-2
Dartford won 5-3 on penalties.
Chatham Town v Dover Athletic 0-1
Ramsgate v Margate 2-0
Tonbridge Angels v Maidstone United 3-0
Tooting & Mitcham United v Corinthian Casuals 1-1
Tooting & Mitcham United won 8-7 on penalties.
Croydon Athletic v Sittingbourne 4-1

THIRD ROUND
AFC Sudbury v Chelmsford City 2-1
Ashford Town v Cray Wanderers 2-4
Boreham Wood v Harlow Town 3-1
Burgess Hill Town v AFC Wimbledon 2-3
Croydon Athletic v Tooting & Mitcham United 1-1
Tooting & Mitcham United won 4-3 on penalties.
Fleet Town v Enfield 3-4
Hendon v Staines Town 1-2
Heybridge Swifts v AFC Hornchurch 3-2
Horsham v Walton Casuals 3-5
Leatherhead v Worthing
match abandoned due to injury to assistant referee 63 minutes with Leatherhead leading 1-0; match awarded to Leatherhead.
Leyton v Maldon Town 1-0
Metropolitan Police v Kingstonian 4-1
Ramsgate v Dover Athletic 1-1
Dover Athletic won 8-7 on penalties.
Redbridge v East Thurrock United 1-3
Slough Town v Ashford Town (Middlesex) 0-4
Tonbridge Angels v Dartford 1-3

FOURTH ROUND
Walton Casuals v Cray Wanderers 1-2
AFC Sudbury v Metropolitan Police 2-1
Staines Town v Heybridge Swifts 2-1
Leyton v Leatherhead 2-3
Dartford v Boreham Wood 0-3
Dover Athletic v East Thurrock United 1-0
Ashford Town (Middlesex) v Enfield 2-1
Tooting & Mitcham United v AFC Wimbledon 1-0

QUARTER-FINALS
Boreham Wood v Cray Wanderers 1-0
(abandoned 48 minutes; fog) 1-2
Staines Town v AFC Sudbury 3-1
Tooting & Mitcham United v Ashford Town (Middlesex) 1-3
Dover Athletic v Leatherhead 2-1

SEMI-FINALS
Dover Athletic v Cray Wanderers 4-3
Staines Town v Ashford Town (Middlesex) 2-3

FINAL
Ashford Town (Middlesex) v Dover Athletic 4-1
(at Bromley).

THE FA TROPHY 2006–07

IN PARTNERSHIP WITH CARLSBERG

PRELIMINARY ROUND

Warrington Town v Wakefield	3-2
Willenhall Town v Gresley Rovers	3-1
Belper Town v Skelmersdale United	0-0, 1-2
Alsager Town v Stocksbridge Park Steels	2-0
Clitheroe v Bamber Bridge	3-2
Goole v Kidsgrove Athletic	0-0, 2-3
Cammell Laird v Rossendale United	2-0
Enfield Town v Rothwell Town	0-2
Dartford v Ilford	4-1
Canvey Island v Maldon Town	0-3
Horsham YMCA v Aveley	3-1
Maidstone United v Bury Town	2-0
Enfield v Corinthian Casuals	1-1, 1-0
Godalming Town v Dunstable Town	1-2
Tooting & Mitcham United v Dulwich Hamlet	2-2, 7-6
Chatham Town v AFC Sudbury	1-2
Waltham Forest v Ashford Town	1-1, 1-1
Waltham Forest won 5-4 on penalties.	
Waltham Abbey v Burgess Hill Town	1-0
Redbridge v Sittingbourne	2-3
Leatherhead v Berkhamsted Town	1-1, 4-2
Molesey v Metropolitan Police	3-0
Leighton Town v Woodford United	2-1
AFC Hornchurch v Fleet Town	2-1
Hastings United v Croydon Athletic	2-1
Arlesey Town v Flackwell Heath	0-0, 2-1
Oxford City v Bashley	1-1, 3-1
Bromsgrove Rovers v Abingdon United	2-2, 2-3
Andover v Chesham United	3-1
Bishop's Cleeve v Newport (IW)	1-0
Uxbridge v Marlow	1-1, 3-3
Marlow won 5-4 on penalties.	
Lymington & New Milton v Brook House	1-4
Bracknell Town v Beaconsfield SYCOB	2-0
Cinderford Town v Windsor & Eton	2-3
Malvern Town v Stourbridge	0-4

FIRST QUALIFYING ROUND

Witton Albion v Fleetwood Town	2-1
Alsager Town v Brigg Town	3-0
Skelmersdale United v Prescot Cables	3-0
Guiseley v Grantham Town	5-4
Sutton Coldfield Town v Gateshead	2-2, 0-3
Spalding United v Ilkeston Town	1-4
Burscough v Matlock Town	2-1
Radcliffe Borough v Leek Town	3-2
Rushall Olympic v Colwyn Bay	3-0
Warrington Town v Clitheroe	0-1
Bridlington Town v Stamford	2-4
Mossley v Lincoln United	5-1
Kendal Town v Buxton	4-2
Woodley Sports v Marine	6-1
Kidsgrove Athletic v Harrogate Railway Athletic	2-1
Ossett Albion v Willenhall Town	2-2, 1-2
Hednesford Town v Halesowen Town	2-2, 1-2
North Ferriby United v Bradford Park Avenue	2-2, 2-3
Whitby Town v Shepshed Dynamo	3-0
Frickley Athletic v Cammell Laird	0-4
Ossett Town v Ashton United	2-3
Chasetown v Chorley	3-1
AFC Telford United v Eastwood Town	1-1, 0-1
Hampton & Richmond Borough v Hitchin Town	5-3
Worthing v King's Lynn	0-1
AFC Wimbledon v Dunstable Town	2-1
Staines Town v Folkestone Invicta	0-1
Boreham Wood v Tooting & Mitcham United	1-1, 0-2
Wivenhoe Town v Margate	1-3
Ware v Enfield	0-1
Wingate & Finchley v Northwood	0-1
Maidenhead United v Dover Athletic	3-1
Hastings United v Waltham Forest	0-1
Wealdstone v Witham Town	2-0
Corby Town v Hemel Hempstead Town	2-4
Dartford v Horsham YMCA	6-0
Bromley v East Thurrock United	6-3
Carshalton Athletic v Potters Bar Town	4-1
Cheshunt v Cray Wanderers	0-1
Waltham Abbey v Heybridge Swifts	1-1, 0-8
Billericay Town v Aylesbury United	2-2, 4-1
Leatherhead v Rothwell Town	1-0
Maldon Town v Leyton	0-0, 1-3
Hendon v Ramsgate	1-2
Tonbridge Angels v Harlow Town	3-1
Leighton Town v Slough Town	4-1
Molesey v Barton Rovers	3-1
Chelmsford City v Maidstone United	1-2
Walton & Hersham v Great Wakering Rovers	0-1
AFC Sudbury v Kingstonian	2-2, 3-2
Ashford Town (Middlesex) v Brackley Town	2-1
Sittingbourne v Arlesey Town	0-0, 2-1
Whyteleafe v Walton Casuals	0-0, 0-5
Tilbury v Horsham	0-1
AFC Hornchurch v Harrow Borough	1-0
Bedworth United v Solihull Borough	0-0, 1-5
Thatcham Town v Dicot Town	0-3
Evesham United v Brook House	2-0
Stourport Swifts v Mangotsfield United	1-5
Clevedon Town v Windsor & Eton	1-3
Hanwell Town v Rugby Town	2-1
Burnham v Team Bath	0-5
Bath City v Bishop's Cleeve	2-1
Taunton Town v Banbury United	0-0, 1-5
Paulton Rovers v Cirencester Town	0-3
Tiverton Town v Gloucester City	2-2, 2-2
Gloucester City won 4-2 on penalties.	
Merthyr Tydfil v Stourbridge	2-0
Abingdon United v Bracknell Town	4-2
Winchester City v Oxford City	1-0
Marlow v Andover	0-0, 2-1
Swindon Supermarine v Yate Town	2-1
Hillingdon Borough v Chippenham Town	2-2, 0-3

SECOND QUALIFYING ROUND

Cammell Laird v Mossley	2-1
Skelmersdale United v Kendal Town	4-2
Burscough v Eastwood Town	3-1
Woodley Sports v Whitby Town	3-2
Ashton United v Gateshead	0-1
Halesowen Town v Clitheroe	1-1, 0-1
Witton Albion v Alsager Town	2-0
Ilkeston Town v Guiseley	2-0
Willenhall Town v Rushall Olympic	1-1, 0-2
Bradford Park Avenue v Solihull Borough	2-0
Kidsgrove Athletic v Chasetown	0-0, 1-1
Chasetown won 4-3 on penalties.	
Radcliffe Borough v Stamford	1-2
Enfield v Walton Casuals	1-1, 2-2
Enfield won 5-4 on penalties.	
Sittingbourne v Bath City	0-0, 0-4
Folkestone Invicta v Billericay Town	2-3
Hanwell Town v Cirencester Town	2-3
Hemel Hempstead Town v Abingdon United	8-4
Chippenham Town v Didcot Town	3-3, 1-3
Carshalton Athletic v Heybridge Swifts	0-1
Leyton v King's Lynn	1-2
AFC Wimbledon v Tonbridge Angels	3-2
Tooting & Mitcham United v Bromley	1-1, 1-0
Leatherhead v Team Bath	0-3
Dartford v Evesham United	0-1
Leighton Town v Wealdstone	2-2, 0-3
Gloucester City v Margate	1-0
AFC Hornchurch v Mangotsfield United	1-3
Molesey v Swindon Supermarine	1-0
Windsor & Eton v Hampton & Richmond Borough	2-0
AFC Sudbury v Ramsgate	2-0
Maidenhead United v Horsham	2-1
Northwood v Winchester City	0-0, 4-1
Great Wakering Rovers v Merthyr Tydfil	0-1
Waltham Forest v Cray Wanderers	1-2
Marlow v Banbury United	0-2
Maidstone United v Ashford Town (Middlesex)	2-3

THIRD QUALIFYING ROUND

Lancaster City v Redditch United	0-1
Skelmersdale United v Farsley Celtic	1-2
Hinckley United v Ilkeston Town	1-0
Chasetown v Hyde United	0-3
Droylsden v Rushall Olympic	3-0
Kettering Town v Clitheroe	10-1
Leigh RMI v Cammell Laird	1-0
Alfreton Town v Harrogate Town	0-1
Stamford v Witton Albion	0-3
Blyth Spartans v Worcester City	1-1, 1-1
Worcester City won 5-4 on penalties.	
Hucknall Town v Barrow	1-1, 1-2
Gainsborough Trinity v Stalybridge Celtic	1-1, 1-2
Moor Green v Woodley Sports	0-3
Bradford Park Avenue v Nuneaton Borough	1-2
Workington v Gateshead	2-4
Burscough v Scarborough	1-2
Vauxhall Motors v Worksop Town	2-2, 1-0
Banbury United v Lewes	2-3
Windsor & Eton v King's Lynn	1-2
Cambridge City v AFC Sudbury	0-1
Havant & Waterlooville v Team Bath	3-0
Ashford Town (Middlesex) v Thurrock	2-1
AFC Wimbledon v Eastleigh	1-1, 2-2
AFC Wimbledon won 4-2 on penalties.	
Bishop's Stortford v Molesey	2-1
Basingstoke Town v Bedford Town	2-0
Northwood v Histon	1-2
Merthyr Tydfil v Wealdstone	2-1
Heybridge Swifts v Bognor Regis Town	2-0
Weston-Super-Mare v Cirencester Town	1-0
Hemel Hempstead Town v Evesham United	2-2, 3-3
Evesham United won 4-2 on penalties.	
Dicot Town v Newport County	0-3
Gloucester City v Eastbourne Borough	2-5
Cray Wanderers v Yeading	1-1, 1-7
Sutton United v Braintree Town	2-3
Salisbury City v Enfield	2-1
Billericay Town v Mangotsfield United	1-2
Welling United v Dorchester Town	3-0
Hayes v Fisher Athletic	0-5
Bath City v Tooting & Mitcham United	1-1, 1-0
Farnborough Town v Maidenhead United	1-1, 3-0

FIRST ROUND

Rushden & Diamonds v Scarborough	3-2
Kettering Town v Stafford Rangers	1-0
Stalybridge Celtic v Hinckley United	2-2, 2-1
Altrincham v Tamworth	0-0, 1-2
Gateshead v Burton Albion	0-4
Halifax Town v Hyde United	3-1
Harrogate Town v Leigh RMI	1-1, 1-2
Kidderminster Harriers v Vauxhall Motors	4-4, 4-0
Southport v Droylsden	1-0
Morecambe v York City	2-1
Northwich Victoria v Farsley Celtic	3-1
Woodley Sports v Witton Albion	1-3
Nuneaton Borough v Redditch United	0-3
Barrow v Worcester City	2-5
Salisbury City v Woking	3-1
Dagenham & Redbridge v Crawley Town	2-0
Bishop's Stortford v St Albans City	3-2
Welling United v Basingstoke Town	0-0, 2-0
Mangotsfield United v King's Lynn	2-1
Weymouth v Grays Athletic	1-2
Havant & Waterlooville v Gravesend & Northfleet	1-2
Fisher Athletic v Eastbourne Borough	0-1
Braintree Town v Ashford Town (Middlesex)	3-0
Forest Green Rovers v Yeading	0-1
Farnborough Town v Bath City	1-1, 1-0
Aldershot Town v AFC Wimbledon	1-2
Stevenage Borough v Merthyr Tydfil	7-0
Newport County v AFC Sudbury	2-1
Exeter City v Heybridge Swifts	3-0
Weston-Super-Mare v Evesham United	1-0
Lewes v Oxford United	0-0, 0-1
Histon v Cambridge United	5-0

SECOND ROUND

Stalybridge Celtic v Kettering Town	1-1, 1-3
Oxford United v Halifax Town	2-2, 1-2
Morecambe v Mangotsfield United	5-0
Tamworth v Welling United	1-1, 1-2
Newport County v Histon	0-0, 1-3
Eastbourne Borough v Northwich Victoria	0-1
Exeter City v Kidderminster Harriers	0-1
Salisbury City v Southport	2-1
Redditch United v Dagenham & Redbridge	3-2
Worcester City v Burton Albion	2-1
Witton Albion v Rushden & Diamonds	0-1
Weston-Super-Mare v Grays Athletic	0-4
Farnborough Town v Braintree Town	0-2
Stevenage Borough v Leigh RMI	3-1
Yeading v Bishop's Stortford	2-0
Gravesend & Northfleet v AFC Wimbledon	0-1
AFC Wimbledon removed from the competition for fielding an ineligible player.	

THIRD ROUND

Histon v Northwich Victoria	1-2
Welling United v Worcester City	2-1
Kettering Town v Salisbury City	0-2
Morecambe v Stevenage Borough	1-1, 0-3
Halifax Town v Redditch United	3-1
Kidderminster Harriers v Braintree Town	0-0, 3-1
Gravesend & Northfleet v Rushden & Diamonds	2-1
Grays Athletic v Yeading	2-1

FOURTH ROUND

Welling United v Grays Athletic	1-4
Stevenage Borough v Salisbury City	3-0
Northwich Victoria v Gravesend & Northfleet	3-0
Kidderminster Harriers v Halifax Town	3-1

SEMI-FINALS (TWO LEGS)

Kidderminster Harriers v Northwich Victoria	2-0, 2-3
Grays Athletic v Stevenage Borough	0-1, 1-2

THE FA TROPHY FINAL

Saturday, 12 May 2007

(at Wembley)

Kidderminster Harriers (2) 2 *(Constable 31, 37)*

Stevenage Borough (0) 3 *(Cole 51, Dobson 74, Morison 88)* 53,262

Kidderminster Harriers: Bevan; Kenna, Blackwood, Hurren, Creighton, Whitehead, Russell, Penn, Christie (White 76), Constable, Smikle (Reynolds 90).

Stevenage Borough: Julian; Fuller, Nutter, Miller, Gaia, Oliver, Henry, Beard, Morison, Guppy (Dobson 63), Cole.

Referee: C. Foy (Merseyside).

THE FA VASE 2006–07

IN PARTNERSHIP WITH CARLSBERG

FIRST QUALIFYING ROUND

Esh Winning v Whitley Bay 0-4
Darlington RA v Thornaby 2-2, 2-0
West Allotment Celtic v Horden CW 4-2
Prudhoe Town v Norton & Stockton Ancients 0-3
Marske United v Sunderland Nissan 1-3
Consett v Armthorpe Welfare 3-1
Pontefract Collieries v Washington 3-2
Curzon Ashton v Oldham Town 2-1
Salford City v Bootle 6-2
Atherton LR v Ramsbottom United 3-2
Hallam v Flixton 0-4
Anstey Nomads v Leek CSOB 2-0
Newark Town v Pilkington XXX 3-2
Ibstock United v Newcastle Town 0-1
Blidworth Welfare v Rocester 0-2
Highgate United v Stone Dominoes 3-0
Pelsall Villa v Dunkirk 0-5
Brockton v Kirby Muxloe 2-1
Stratford Town v Highfield Rangers 3-1
Cradley Town v Barnt Green Spartak 0-2
Ratby Sports removed v Market Drayton Town w.o.
Staveley MW v Coleshill Town 0-5
Alvechurch v Shirebrook Town 3-1
Shifnal Town v Eccleshall 4-0
Carlton Town v Westfields 2-0
Castle Vale v Ellistown 2-0
Oldbury United v Stapenhill 2-1
Bridgnorth Town v Glapwell 2-1
Graham St Prims v Racing Club Warwick 0-5
Thurnby Rangers v Clipstone Welfare 2-3
Teversal v Southam United 2-1
Radford v Cadbury Athletic 2-3
Blackwell MW v Blaby & Whetstone Athletic 1-0
Kimberley Town v Barwell 0-5
Barrow Town v Greenwood Meadows 6-0
Pershore Town v Sutton Town 0-4
Ely City v Cornard United 6-1
Norwich United v Ipswich Wanderers 0-3
Felixstowe & Walton United v Kirkley 0-2
Holbeach United v Diss Town 2-3
Arlesey Athletic v Wootton Blue Cross 0-2
Bedfont Green v Desborough Town 4-1
Sawbridgeworth Town v North Greenford United 2-1
Haringey Borough v Halstead Town 1-4
Edgware Town v Hertford Town 3-0
Sileby Rangers v Harpenden Town 3-4
Cogenhoe United v Basildon United 4-2
Romford v Bugbrooke St Michaels 3-0
Brimsdown Rovers v Sun Postal 2-0
Stotfold v Wellingborough Town 1-3
Raunds Town v Stansted 7-1
London APSA v Colney Heath 3-1
Tunbridge Wells v East Grinstead Town 3-2
Selsey v Rye United 2-1
Lingfield v East Preston 2-0
Shoreham v Whitstable Town 0-2
Guildford City v Redhill 4-2
Egham Town v Saltdean United 4-1
Worthing United v Peacehaven & Telscombe 1-3
Deal Town v Eastbourne Town 0-2
Eastbourne United v Faversham Town 4-0
Bicester Town v Abingdon Town 2-4
Shrewton United v Wootton Bassett Town 1-1, 3-2
Holmer Green v United Services Portsmouth 1-0
Highworth Town v Westbury United 3-2
Melksham Town v Hungerford Town 2-0
AFC Newbury removed v Newport Pagnall Town w.o.
Kidlington v Witney United 0-4
Gosport Borough v Downton 4-0
VT v Chalfont St Peter 0-2
Marlow United v Bournemouth 2-1
Bishop Sutton v Penzance 2-1
Fairford Town v Cullompton Rangers 4-4
Fairford Town won 4-3 on penalties.
Clevedon United v Shaftsbury 2-0
Hamworthy United v Shepton Mallet 2-0
Street v Ottery St Mary 2-2, 5-1
Odd Down v Larkhall Athletic 2-1
Willand Rovers v Newquay 4-2
Brislington v Hallen 1-1, 1-3
Plymouth Parkway v Elmore 5-1
Wadebridge Town v Saltash United 3-2
Almondsbury Town v Barnstaple Town 2-3
Chard Town v Wellington Town 3-1

SECOND QUALIFYING ROUND

Northallerton Town v Ashington 0-1
Team Northumbria v Bottesford Town 2-1
Billingham Synthonia v Spennymoor Town 1-0
Jarrow Roofing Boldon CA v Pontefract Collieries 4-1
Glasshoughton Welfare v West Allotment Celtic 2-0
Hall Road Rangers v Sunderland RCA 2-1
Eccleshill United v Whickham 4-0
North Shields v Hebburn Town 3-2
Darlington RA v Silsden 0-2
Winterton Rangers v Alnwick Town 2-0
Chester-Le-Street Town v South Shields 0-2
Durham City v Seaham Red Star 2-1
Tadcaster Albion v Easington Colliery 2-3
Peterlee Town v Norton & Stockton Ancients 1-2
Garforth Town v Selby Town 2-0
Morpeth Town v Whitley Bay 2-3
Tow Law Town v Shildon 3-5
Consett v Brandon United 7-0
Ryton v Yorkshire Amateur 5-1
West Auckland Town v Willington 8-0
Sunderland Nissan v Guisborough Town 6-0
Winsford United v Holker Old Boys 3-1
Darwen v Curzon Ashton 1-3
Daisy Hill v Congleton Town 0-5
Abbey Hey v St Helens Town 4-3
Dinnington Town v Bacup Borough 2-1
Maine Road v Salford City 2-3
Padiham v Cheadle Town 1-0
Brodsworth MW v FC United of Manchester 1-3
Poulton Victoria v AFC Emley 2-0
Ashton Town v Blackpool Mechanics 1-2
Worsborough Bridge MW v Rossington Main 2-1
Colne v Maltby Main 4-1
Castleton Gabriels v Nelson 0-6
Trafford v Formby 2-1
Flixton v Chadderton 2-1
Atherton LR v Parkgate 1-2
Atherton Collieries v Penrith 2-1
Gedling MW v Coalville Town 0-4
Bromyard Town v Causeway United 0-4
Clipstone Welfare v Carlton Town 0-1
Atherstone Town v Norton United 2-1
Barwell v Oadby Town 0-0, 2-0
Market Drayton Town v Dunkirk 7-2
Wyrly Rangers v Downes Sports 0-1
Wellington v New Mills 0-2
Anstey Nomads v Brierley & Hagley 0-1
Teversall v Barnt Green Spartak 3-6
Blackwell MW v Birstall United 2-2, 0-2
Studley v Holwell Sports 1-2
Ledbury Town v Shifnal Town 0-2
Rainworth MW v Racing Club Warwick 1-0
Cadbury Athletic v Tipton Town 2-3
Rocester v Friar Lane & Epworth 0-1
Sutton Town v Barrow Town 9-1
Mickleover Sports v Newark Town 2-0
Retford United v Sandiacre Town 3-0
Quorn v Heather Athletic 5-0
Borrowash Victoria v Meir KA 2-1
Boldmere St Michaels v Pegasus Juniors 4-0
St Andrews v Stratford Town 0-4
Oldbury United v Bridgnorth Town 2-1
Heanor Town v Calverton MW 0-1
Holbrook MW v Rothley Imperial 2-0
Long Eaton United v Bolehall Swifts 0-1
Alvechurch v Coventry Sphinx 5-1
Biddulph Victoria v Glossop North End 2-1
Newcastle Town v Brockton 1-0
Nuneaton Griff v Tividale 4-5
Loughborough Dynamo v Dudley Town 2-1
Coventry Copsewood v Shawbury United 0-2
South Normanton Athletic v Gornal Athletic 2-0

Highgate United v Castle Vale	0-3
Radcliffe Olympic v Lye Town	1-1, 3-1
Coleshill Town v Wolverhampton Casuals	4-1
Blackstones v Downham Town	4-1
Bourne Town v Diss Town	4-4, 5-2
Kirkley v St Ives Town	2-0
Lincoln Moorlands v March Town United	2-1
Godmanchester Rovers v Huntingdon Town	1-0
Leiston v Great Yarmouth Town	2-0
Ipswich Wanderers v Long Melford	11-0
Soham Town Rangers v Whitton United	5-0
Boston Town v Haverhill Rovers	3-2
Woodbridge Town v Hadleigh United	5-0
Dereham Town v Wroxham	0-3
Deeping Rangers v Yaxley	3-1
Stowmarket Town v Ely City	0-1
Walsham Le Willows v Fakenham Town	0-2
Thetford Town v Debenham LC	2-1
Eynesbury Rovers v Gorleston	1-2
Bowers & Pitsea v Sawbridgeworth Town	1-0
Bedfont Green v Cranfield United	3-0
Biggleswade United v Leverstock Green	2-3
Tring Athletic v Wellingborough Town	0-1
Edgware Town v Long Buckby	3-0
Clapton v London APSA	3-2
Rothwell Corinthians v Eton Manor	1-2
Hullbridge Sports v Stanway Rovers	1-2
Feltham v Ford Sports Daventry	3-2
Cogenhoe United v Biggleswade Town	3-1
Langford v Hounslow Borough	1-3
Bedford Valerio United v Hoddesdon Town	3-2
Clacton Town v Wembley	0-0, 2-4
Romford v St Margaretsbury	3-1
Royston Town v Ruislip Manor	0-2
AFC Kempston Rovers v Saffron Walden Town	0-3
Bedfont v Erith Town	1-3
Oxhey Jets v Raunds Town	2-1
Concord Rangers v Brimsdown Rovers	2-4
London Colney v Burnham Ramblers	1-2
Tiptree United v Harwich & Parkeston	5-0
Cockfosters v Stewarts & Lloyds	2-0
Southend Manor v Brentwood Town	0-1
Harpenden Town v Wootton Blue Cross	2-1
Sporting Bengal United v Halstead Town	0-4
Wealden v Chertsey Town	4-2
Frimley Green v Arundel	0-3
Lingfield v Three Bridges	1-4
Chipstead v Sidlesham	8-2
Camberley Town v Haywards Heath Town	0-2
Epsom & Ewell v Sevenoaks Town	0-1
Oakwood v Whitstable Town	1-0
Eastbourne Town v Hassocks	3-1
Herne Bay v Selsey	1-2
Crowborough Athletic v Broadbridge Heath	2-1
Guildford City v Raynes Park Vale	2-0
Horley Town v Bookham	3-1
Croydon v Eastbourne United	2-1
Pagham v Slade Green	2-2, 4-0
Wick v Lancing	3-1
Mile Oak v Hailsham Town	1-2
Lordswood v Cobham	2-3
Tunbridge Wells v Farnham Town	6-1
Egham Town v Peacehaven & Telscombe	2-1
Westfield v Sidley United	1-3
Moneyfields v Carterton	1-1, 3-0
Henley Town v Hamble ASSC	1-2
Gosport Borough v Alton Town	5-1
Buckingham Town v Witney United	1-7
Calne Town v Holmer Green	3-2
Fareham Town v Andover New Street	4-1
Amesbury Town v Cove	1-1, 2-0
Clanfield 85 v Buckingham Athletic	1-0
Shrewton United v Malmsbury Victoria	3-0
Hartley Wintney v Ardley United	0-3
Marlow United v Wantage Town	1-2
AFC Wallingford v Sandhurst Town	1-5
Pewsey Vale v Aylesbury Vale	1-0
Milton United v Highworth Town	3-0
Bemerton Heath Harlequins v Devizes Town	2-0
Chipping Norton Town v Abingdon Town	2-1
Blackfield & Langley v Shrivenham	0-1
Newport Pagnell Town v Chalfont St Peter	0-3
Reading Town v Ringwood Town	3-2
Christchurch v Cowes Sports	0-2
Melksham Town v Lymington Town	0-3
Bridport v Harrow Hill	1-1, 1-0
Penryn Athletic v Plymouth Parkway	3-1
Hallen v Newton Abbot	3-0
Dawlish Town v Frome Town	1-2
Sherborne Town v Minehead	4-2
Radstock Town v Bodmin Town	0-4
Liskeard Athletic v Clevedon United	5-1
Odd Down v Shortwood United	1-0
Bitton v Backwell United	2-1
Truro City v Wadebridge Town	5-2
Budleigh Salterton v Poole Town	3-3, 0-3
Willand Rovers v Chard Town	2-0
Gillingham Town v Bishop Sutton	1-2
Bridgwater Town v Slimbridge	0-3
Porthleven v Falmouth Town	2-1
Fairford Town v Launceston	2-4
Barnstaple Town v Torrington	2-1
Hamworthy United v Ilfracombe Town	1-1, 2-4
Street v Keynsham Town	2-0

FIRST ROUND

Glasshoughton Welfare v Easington Colliery	3-1
Liversedge v Norton & Stockton Ancients	1-0
Team Northumbria v West Auckland Town	0-3
North Shields v Consett	1-4
Sunderland Nissan v Shildon	3-4
South Shields v Jarrow Roofing Boldon CA	2-1
Ashington v Durham City	1-3
Hall Road Rangers v Winterton Rangers	1-2
Garforth Town v Silsden	3-0
Ryton v Billingham Synthonia	0-2
Billingham Town v Whitley Bay	0-1
Eccleshill United v Newcastle Blue Star	0-3
Bishop Auckland v Dunston FB	1-2
Worsbrough Bridge MW v Colne	2-4
Padiham v FC United of Manchester	0-3
Salford City v Blackpool Mechanics	2-1
Flixton v Abbey Hey	3-1
Congleton Town v Dinnington Town	4-0
Trafford v Parkgate	3-3, 1-2
Nelson v Sheffield	0-1
Atherton Collieries v Winsford United	4-0
Poulton Victoria v Curzon Ashton	2-2, 1-3
Calverton MW v Newcastle Town	0-7
Sutton Town v Brierley & Hagley	2-2, 3-0
New Mills v Stratford Town	2-2, 1-2
Borrowash Victoria v Castle Vale	0-3
Alvechurch v Coleshill Town	1-0
Romulus v Shifnal Town	1-0
Friar Lane & Epworth v Carlton Town	0-4
Market Drayton Town v Quorn	1-2
Biddulph Victoria v Shawbury United	4-1
Tividale v Barnt Green Spartak	2-1
Retford United v Bolehall Swifts	2-2, 6-0
Downes Sports v Holwell Sports	0-2
Holbrook MW v Coalville Town	2-6
South Normanton Athletic v Loughborough Dynamo	4-1
Radcliffe Olympic v Rainworth MW	0-1
Causeway United v Tipton Town	3-2
Birstall United v Oldbury United	0-1
Atherstone Town v Boldmere St Michaels	0-1
Barwell v Mickleover Sports	2-0
Wroxham v Deeping Rangers	4-1
Ipswich Wanderers v Soham Town Rangers	4-0
Leiston v Woodbridge Town	0-1
Thetford Town v Lincoln Morelands	3-2
Kirkley v Godmanchester Rovers	3-0
Fakenham Town v Gorleston	5-0
Ely City v Wisbech Town	0-0, 1-2
St Neots Town v Blackstones	2-1
Boston Town v Bourne Town	6-0
Feltham v Brimsdown Rovers	0-4
Wembley v Northampton Spencer	1-1, 0-1
Bedford Valerio United v Cockfosters	2-1
Stanway Rovers v Burnham Ramblers	2-2, 0-0
Burnham Ramblers won 4-2 on penalties.	
Oxhey Jets v Bedfont Green	3-2
Edgware Town v Brentwood Town	3-1
Cogenhoe United v Bowers & Pitsea	3-1
Tiptree United v Ruislip Manor	1-3
Barking v Hounslow Borough	0-4
Eton Manor w.o. v Clapton removed for failing to fulfil fixture.	
Harpenden Town v Halstead Town	2-3
Wellingborough Town v Leverstock Green	0-4

Erith Town v Romford	2-3
Potton United v Barkingside	2-1
Saffron Walden Town v Thamesmead Town	2-1
Erith & Belvedere v Cobham	4-1
Guildford City v Three Bridges	0-2
Wick v Oakwood	2-1
Hailsham Town v Haywards Heath Town	4-1
Ringmer v Selsey	0-1
Eastbourne Town v Merstham	3-2
Banstead Athletic v Wealden	3-0
Colliers Wood United v Crowborough Athletic	2-1
Sidley United v Arundel	3-2
Tunbridge Wells v Pagham	6-1
Egham Town v Whitehawk	0-2
Chipstead v Ash United	0-1
Croydon v Littlehampton Town	4-0
Horley Town v Sevenoaks Town	1-2
Calne Town v Pewsey Vale	4-3
North Leigh v Milton United	2-1
Hamble ASSC v Cowes Sports	0-5
Clanfield 85 v Chalfont St Peter	0-5
Lymington Town v Shrivenham	0-0, 2-1
Wantage Town v Witney United	2-1
Moneyfields v Sandhurst Town	2-2, 1-0
Fareham Town v Ardley United	4-0
Bemerton Heath Harlequins v Shrewton United	4-1
Reading Town v Gosport Borough	0-0, 0-5
AFC Totton v Chipping Norton Town	4-0
Amesbury Town v Thame United	4-2
Corsham Town v Harefield United	1-0
Sherborne Town v Bishop Sutton	2-0
Porthleven v Bodmin Town	1-0
Willand Rovers v Odd Down	1-2
Slimbridge v Barnstaple Town	4-0
Bideford v Welton Rovers	1-0
Launceston v Liskeard Athletic	2-1
Street v Penryn Athletic	5-2
Bristol Manor Farm v Bridport	2-0
Poole Town v Frome Town	1-3
Truro City v Bitton	2-1
Ilfracombe Town v Hallen	2-1

SECOND ROUND

Glasshoughton Welfare v Atherton Collieries	2-1
Flixton v Pickering Town	4-0
Winterton Rangers v Ashville	3-1
Dunston FB v Newcastle Benfield (Bay Plastics)	1-6
South Shields v Crook Town	5-4
Congleton Town v Whitley Bay	1-3
Thackley v Squires Gate	3-2
Nantwich Town v Shildon	3-4
Curzon Ashton v Parkgate	7-1
Durham City v Sheffield	1-0
Bedlington Terriers v West Auckland Town	0-6
Billingham Synthonia v Colne	3-2
Consett v Garforth Town	3-0
Newcastle Blue Star v Liversedge	2-0
Salford City v FC United of Manchester	2-3
Stratford Town v Tividale	2-0
Barwell v Arnold Town	2-1
Causeway United v Holwell Sports	1-1, 3-0
Retford United v Rainworth MW	2-1
Romulus v Oldbury United	3-1
Leamington v Sutton Town	4-0
Newcastle Town v Gedling Town	0-2
Biddulph Victoria v Alvechurch	1-3
Carlton Town v Coalville Town	1-2
Castle Vale v South Normanton Athletic	3-0
Boldmere St Michaels v Quorn	0-1
Northampton Spencer v Thetford Town	5-2
Romford v Oxhey Jets	4-4, 1-3
Wisbech Town v Boston Town	4-0
Leverstock Green v Woodbridge Town	1-0
Halstead Town v Eton Manor	5-0
Potton United v Ruislip Manor	3-3, 2-1
St Neots Town v Lowestoft Town	1-6
Fakenham Town v Newmarket Town	1-0
Brimsdown Rovers v Ipswich Wanderers	2-3
Wroxham v Needham Market	2-1
Bedford Valerio United v Welwyn Garden City	1-5
Edgware Town v Saffron Walden Town	3-0
Burnham Ramblers v Hounslow Borough	3-2
Broxbourne Borough V&E v Mildenhall Town	1-3
Kirkley v Cogenhoe United	1-2
North Leigh v Eastbourne Town	2-3
Dorking v Wick	1-2
Chessington & Hook United v Erith & Belvedere	3-1
Three Bridges v Sevenoaks Town	2-0
Croydon v Sidley United	3-1
Moneyfields v Cowes Sports	1-0
AFC Totton v Gosport Borough	4-1
Banstead Athletic v Colliers Wood United	1-2
Selsey v Wantage Town	3-0
Chalfont St Peter w.o. v Fareham Town removed for fielding an ineligible player.	
Whitehawk v Ash United	3-0
VCD Athletic v Tunbridge Wells	3-0
Hailsham Town v Hythe Town	2-0
Bideford v Tavistock	2-0
Bemerton Heath Harlequins v Porthleven	2-1
Amesbury Town v Corsham Town	2-5
Brockenhurst v Sherborne Town	1-3
Bristol Manor Farm v Slimbridge	0-5
Street v Launceston *Street won 5-4 on penalties.*	3-3, 4-4
Ilfracombe Town v Wimborne Town	2-3
Lymington Town v Frome Town	1-0
Calne Town v Odd Down	2-1
Truro City v St Blazey	3-2

THIRD ROUND

Barwell v Thackley	4-2
Gedling Town v West Auckland Town	0-2
Consett v Causeway United	2-3
Whitley Bay v Coalville Town	1-0
Newcastle Benfield (Bay Plastics) v Castle Vale	2-0
Newcastle Blue Star v Alvechurch	3-2
Durham City v Flixton	1-4
Retford United v Shildon	4-3
South Shields v Curzon Ashton	3-4
Glasshoughton Welfare v Winterton Rangers	4-3
Billingham Synthonia v Romulus	5-2
FC United of Manchester v Quorn	2-3
Stratford Town v Colliers Wood United	2-1
Burnham Ramblers v Wroxham	3-1
Fakenham Town v Cogenhoe United	1-5
Wisbech Town v VCD Athletic	1-2
Leverstock Green v Potton United	0-1
Halstead Town v Edgware Town	0-1
Croydon v Leamington	0-1
Ipswich Wanderers v Oxhey Jets	4-0
Mildenhall Town v Northampton Spencer	2-1
Lowestoft Town v Welwyn Garden City	5-0
Hailsham Town v Sherborne Town	2-4
Lymington Town v Truro City	0-1
Whitehawk v Selsey	2-0
Chalfont St Peter v Wimborne Town	0-2
Wick v Eastbourne Town	0-1
Chessington & Hook United v Street	0-4
Calne Town v Slimbridge	1-4
Three Bridges v Bemerton Heath Harlequins	1-1, 0-3
AFC Totton v Moneyfields	3-0
Bideford v Corsham Town	3-1

FOURTH ROUND

Mildenhall Town v Sherborne Town	2-1
Truro City v Newcastle Benfield (Bay Plastics)	3-1
Wimborne Town v Glasshoughton Welfare	4-2
Bideford v Barwell	7-0
VCD Athletic v West Auckland Town	2-1
Quorn v Stratford Town	2-1
Eastbourne Town v Curzon Ashton	0-3
Leamington v Bemerton Heath Harlequins	4-1
Billingham Synthonia v Newcastle Blue Star	2-0
Flixton v Retford United	2-5
Whitehawk v Edgware Town	1-1, 1-0
Slimbridge v Whitley Bay	1-0
Lowestoft Town v Ipswich Wanderers	1-2
Burnham Ramblers v Street	1-2
Potton United v AFC Totton	1-2
Causeway United v Cogenhoe United	2-1

FIFTH ROUND

Wimborne Town v Street	4-0
Causeway United v Curzon Ashton	0-5
Slimbridge v Truro City	0-3
Ipswich Wanderers v AFC Totton	1-2
VCD Athletic v Bideford	2-3

Whitehawk v Quorn	2-1
Leamington v Retford United	5-1
Billingham Synthonia v Mildenhall Town	4-0

SIXTH ROUND

Curzon Ashton v Leamington	4-1
Whitehawk v Truro City	0-1
AFC Totton v Wimborne Town	2-1
Billingham Synthonia v Bideford	1-0

SEMI-FINAL (TWO LEGS)

Curzon Ashton v Truro City	1-0, 1-3
AFC Totton v Billingham Synthonia	1-2, 2-1

AFC Totton won 5-4 on penalties.

FINAL

(at Wembley)

Saturday, 13 May 2007

AFC Totton (1) 1 *(Potter 28)*

Truro City (1) 3 *(Wills 45, 57, Broad 84)* 27,754

AFC Totton: Brunnschweiler; Reacord, Troon (Stevens 61), Potter (Gregory 82), Bottomley, Austen, Roden, Gosney, Hamodu (Goss 89), Osman, Byres.

Truro City: Stevenson; Ash, Power, Smith, Martin (Pope 86), Broad, Wills, Gosling, Yetton, Watkins, Walker (Ludlam 90).

Referee: P. Joslin (Nottinghamshire).

THE FA COUNTY YOUTH CUP 2006–07

IN PARTNERSHIP WITH PEPSI

FIRST ROUND

Nottinghamshire v Manchester	0-4
Isle of Man v Staffordshire	1-2
Birmingham v Cheshire	3-2
Liverpool v Derbyshire	4-0
East Riding v Sheffield & Hallamshire	1-2
Westmoreland v Shropshire	4-3
Herefordshire v Hertfordshire	3-5
London v Gloucestershire	3-0
Cornwall v Cambridgeshire	0-2
Middlesex v Somerset	2-0
Middlesex removed for fielding an ineligible player.	
Dorset v Norfolk	0-3
Jersey v Sussex	0-5
Huntingdonshire v Essex	1-1
Huntingdonshire won 5-3 on penalties.	
Worcestershire v Hampshire	1-1
Worcestershire won 5-4 on penalties.	
Army v Kent	1-5

Byes: Bedfordshire, Berks & Bucks, Cumberland, Devon, Durham, Guernsey, Lancashire, Leicestershire & Rutland, Lincolnshire, North Riding, Northamptonshire, Northumberland, Oxfordshire, Suffolk, Surrey, West Riding, Wiltshire.

SECOND ROUND

Westmoreland v Cumberland	2-3
Birmingham v North Riding	0-1
Lincolnshire v Manchester	3-0
West Riding v Lancashire	3-0
Staffordshire v Northumberland	1-4
Liverpool v Durham	0-3
Leicestershire & Rutland v Sheffield & Hallamshire	2-1
Cambridgeshire v Wiltshire	3-3
Cambridgeshire won 5-4 on penalties.	
Somerset v Worcestershire	2-3
Suffolk v Oxfordshire	4-3
Sussex v Huntingdonshire	1-0
Guernsey v Hertfordshire	1-0
Kent v Northamptonshire	2-1
Norfolk v Berks & Bucks	1-5
Devon v Bedfordshire	2-0
Surrey v London	1-0

THIRD ROUND

Devon v Surrey	0-3
Durham v Leicestershire & Rutland	1-4
Cambridgeshire v North Riding	2-1
Kent v Berks & Bucks	1-2
Cumberland v Sussex	0-2
Worcestershire v Northumberland	3-0
Lincolnshire v West Riding	2-3
Suffolk v Guernsey	4-2

FOURTH ROUND

Cambridgeshire v West Riding	0-3
Sussex v Suffolk	0-1
Worcestershire v Leicestershire & Rutland	1-4
Berks & Bucks v Surrey	1-3

SEMI-FINALS

Leicestershire & Rutland v West Riding	0-4
(Due to a protest tie was ordered to be replayed)	0-2
Surrey v Suffolk	1-2

FINAL

(at Bradford City FC)

West Riding (0) 1 *(Oxey 50)*

Suffolk (0) 1 *(Chaplin 75)* 546

aet; West Riding won 4-3 on penalties.

THE FA YOUTH CUP 2006–07

SPONSORED BY E.ON

PRELIMINARY ROUND

Ossett Town v Spennymoor Town	5-4
Northwich Victoria v Witton Albion	2-3
Burscough v Lancaster City	6-0
Handsworth United w.o. v Holker Old Boys withdrew	
Warrington Town v Prescot Cables	1-1
Prescot Cables won 5-4 on penalties.	
Colne w.o. v Radcliffe Borough withdrew	
Stocksbridge Park Steels v Stalybridge Celtic	1-1
Stalybridge Celtic won 4-1 on penalties.	
Kendal Town w.o. v Skelmersdale United withdrew	
Moor Green v Bromsgrove Rovers	6-0
Alfreton Town v Mickleover Sports	7-0
Carlton Town v Coleshill Town	2-3
Eastwood Town v Gresley Rovers	2-3
Stourbridge v Blabey & Whetstone Athletic	2-1
Alvechurch v Coventry Sphinx	1-4
Worcester City w.o. v Sutton Town withdrew	
Kirkley v Diss Town	0-2
Bury Town v Woodbridge Town	5-2
Rothwell Corinthians v Halstead Town	0-1
Burnham Ramblers v Buntingford Town	1-3
Hitchin Town v Leverstock Green	3-4
Staines Town v Broxbourne Borough V&E	6-0
Uxbridge v Royston Town	1-0
Northwood v Enfield Town	2-1
Hanwell Town v Bishop's Stortford	3-0
Hayes v Colney Heath	0-4
Brentwood Town v Croydon Athletic	1-2
AFC Kempston Rovers v Clapton	1-1
AFC Kempston Rovers won 8-7 on penalties.	
North Greenford United v Corby Town	4-2
Sun Postal v Hillingdon Borough	1-2
Hampton & Richmond Borough v Redbridge	2-3
Cogenhoe United v Tring Athletic	10-0
Harrow Borough w.o. v Tiptree United withdrew	
Lewisham Borough v Berkhamsted Town	0-2
Stotfold v Witham Town	7-4
Rothwell Town v St Albans City	4-2
Barton Rovers v London Colney	8-0
Brook House v Concord Rangers	2-5
Bugbrooke St Michaels v Long Buckby	1-2
AFC Wimbledon v Leighton Town	2-0
Wealdstone v Hullbridge Sports	4-0
Dunstable Town v AFC Hornchurch	1-0
Fisher Athletic v Boreham Wood	2-1
Thurrock v St Margaretsbury	1-3
Corinthian Casuals v Waltham Abbey	2-2
Waltham Abbey won 5-4 on penalties.	
Wellingborough Town v Ware	2-3
Gravesend & Northfleet v Chatham Town	9-0
Horsham YMCA v East Grinstead Town	2-4
Croydon v Eastbourne Borough	2-0
Whitstable Town v Lewes	0-2
Dover Athletic v Dartford	1-0
Chipstead w.o. v Ash United withdrew	
Camberley Town v Chertsey Town	1-2
Sevenoaks Town v Horley Town	4-2
Cobham v Godalming Town	1-4
Reading Town v Banbury United	2-1
Oxford United v Sandhurst Town	10-0
Chalfont St Peter v Carterton	7-0
Beaconsfield SYCOB v Bracknell Town	0-0
Beaconsfield SYCOB won 4-1 on penalties.	

FIRST QUALIFYING ROUND

Ashville v Morecambe	0-4
North Greenford United v Concord Rangers	3-0
Arundel v Worthing	1-3
Ossett Town v Chester-Le-Street Town	1-5
Boldmere St Michaels v Burton Albion	5-3
Tamworth v Pershore Town	2-2
Tamworth won 4-2 on penalties.	
Welwyn Garden City v Wingate & Finchley	3-2
Kingsbury London Tigers withdrew v Wealdstone w.o.	
South Park v Lancing	2-1
Bitton v Bath City	1-3
Bishop's Cleeve v Radstock Town	1-1
Bishop's Cleeve won 4-3 on penalties.	
Silsden v Scarborough	3-2
Stourport Swifts v Moor Green	3-1
Blackstones v March Town United	6-0
King's Lynn v Witton United	3-0
Berkhamsted Town v Leverstock Green	2-3
Halstead Town v Potters Bar Town	2-4
Salisbury City v Alton Town	3-1
Chesham United v Eastleigh	4-2
Poole Town v Gloucester City	1-4
Halifax Town v Garforth Town	1-1
Halifax Town won 4-2 on penalties.	
Leigh RMI v AFC Emley	7-0
Exeter City v Tiverton Town	5-0
Weston-Super-Mare v Merthyr Tydfil	0-1
Yate Town v Newport County	2-4
Ryton v York City	0-1
Liversedge v Whitley Bay	2-1
Rushden & Diamonds v Stotfold	6-0
Canvey Island v Harlow Town	4-2
Aldershot Town v Maidenhead United	10-3
Binfield v Malmsbury Victoria	6-0
Brigg Town v Consett	3-2
Farsley Celtic v Guiseley	5-1
Colne w.o. v Congleton Town withdrew	
Marine v Ashton Town	3-0
Bootle v Stalybridge Celtic	5-0
Kendal Town v Trafford	2-1
Teversal v Sutton Coldfield Town	3-4
Romford v Barton Rovers	1-4
Pagham v Westfield	2-3
Woking v Sutton United	5-2
Basingstoke Town v Winchester City	0-2
Bristol Manor Farm v Cirencester Town	2-5
North Ferriby United v Goole	4-0
Oadby Town v Nuneaton Borough	1-1
Nuneaton Borough won 5-4 on penalties.	
Gresley Rovers v Leek Town	1-8
Kidderminster Harriers v Staveley MW	0-3
Harefield United v Waltham Abbey	1-4
Erith Town v AFC Wimbledon	1-5
Godalming Town v Molesey	3-1
Lingfield v Bromley	0-3
Carshalton Athletic v Tonbridge Angels	3-4
Epsom & Ewell v Dover Athletic	2-0
Cinderford Town v Weymouth	4-7
Yorkshire Amateur v Selby Town	2-3
Bradford Park Avenue v Dunston FB	1-4
Eccleshill United v Ossett Albion	4-0
Altrincham v Handsworth United	3-0
Curzon Ashton v Prescot Cables	2-1
Workington v Vauxhall Motors	0-1
Southport v Nantwich Town	5-0
Stone Dominoes v Stourbridge	3-0
Long Eaton United v Lye Town	3-2
Redditch United v Coleshill Town	1-2
Arnold Town v Chasetown	3-2
Glossop North End v Nuneaton Griff	2-1
Stafford Rangers v Castle Vale	4-2
Rugby Town v Bromyard Town	7-0
Matlock Town v Stratford Town	0-4
Worcester City v Cradley Town	10-0
Retford United v Hednesford Town	0-4
Kimberley Town v Racing Club Warwick	2-8
Gornal Athletic v Tipton Town	3-0
Hinckley United v Newcastle Town	2-0
AFC Telford United v Alfreton Town	2-1
Bedworth United v Malvern Town	0-3
Belper Town v Coventry Sphinx	1-2
Mildenhall Town v Long Melford	2-4
Great Yarmouth Town v Haverhill Rovers	2-1
Lowestoft Town v Huntingdon Town	4-2
Croydon Athletic v Heybridge Swifts	2-0
Redbridge v Sawbridgeworth Town	5-1
Stevenage Borough v Cheshunt	4-1
St Margaretsbury v Haringey Borough	3-0
Southend Manor v Aveley	2-0
Chelmsford City w.o. v Waltham Forest withdrew	
Ilford v Maldon Town	2-4
Staines Town v Ware	6-0
Arlesey Town v Colney Heath	1-2
Hanwell Town v Dunstable Town	0-1

Braintree Town v Dagenham & Redbridge	0-1
Clacton Town v AFC Kempston Rovers	2-1
Hillingdon Borough v Buntingford Town	4-1
Bowers & Pitsea v Hemel Hempstead Town	0-4
East Thurrock United v Northampton Spencer	2-0
Ashford Town (Middlesex) v Kettering Town	3-2
Uxbridge v Rothwell Town	1-2
Farnham Town v Three Bridges	2-0
Horsham v Oakwood	1-2
Erith & Belvedere v Gravesend & Northfleet	0-6
Whyteleafe v Wick	0-0
Whyteleafe won 5-4 on penalties.	
Margate v East Grinstead Town	1-3
Croydon v Haywards Heath Town	0-1
Lewes v Walton & Hersham	4-0
Hastings United v Burgess Hill Town	7-3
Sevenoaks Town w.o. v Crawley Town withdrew	
Reading Town v Milton United	6-1
Oxford City v Fleet Town	6-6
Oxford City won 4-2 on penalties.	
Aylesbury United v Henley Town	3-0
Chalfont St Peter v Burnham	1-0
Thatcham Town v Marlow	2-1
Wroxham v Bourne Town	7-0
Witton Albion v Burscough	1-3
Fakenham Town v Walsham Le Willows	2-4
Chipstead v Chertsey Town	1-0
Beaconsfield SYCOB v Farnborough Town	2-2
Beaconsfield SYCOB won 5-4 on penalties.	
Westbury United v Andover	5-0
Bishop Sutton v Forest Green Rovers	2-0
Wellington v Eccleshall	0-3
Histon v Deeping Rangers	2-0
Grantham Town v Stowmarket Town	1-1
Grantham Town won 4-3 on penalties.	
Diss Town v Bury Town	1-9
Newmarket Town v Cambridge United	0-4
Ipswich Wanderers v Dereham Town	1-4
Dulwich Hamlet v Harrow Borough	1-3
Ford Sports Daventry v Long Buckby	0-4
Fisher Athletic v Leyton	2-1
Thamesmead Town v Northwood	3-2
Cogenhoe United v Ruislip Manor	5-1
Maidstone United v Colliers Wood United	6-2
AFC Newbury v Bournemouth	0-3
Moneyfields v Wootton Bassett Town	6-0
Bridgwater Town v Paulton Rovers	1-0
Brislington v Gillingham Town	3-2
Clevedon Town v Mangotsfield United	0-7
Oxford United v Bicester Town	3-0

SECOND QUALIFYING ROUND

Boldmere St Michaels v Stone Dominoes	6-0
Welwyn Garden City v Hemel Hempstead Town	0-1
Worthing v Godalming Town	4-1
South Park v Westfield	0-2
Gloucester City v Bridgwater Town	3-3
Gloucester City won 7-6 on penalties.	
Newport County v Weymouth	1-1
Weymouth won 4-3 on penalties.	
Silsden v Halifax Town	2-0
Colne v Marine	0-1
King's Lynn v Dereham Town	1-0
Potters Bar Town v Dunstable Town	2-3
East Thurrock United v Barton Rovers	1-3
Chelmsford City v Southend Manor	3-2
Long Buckby v Ashford Town (Middlesex)	0-2
Leigh RMI v Southport	4-3
Merthyr Tydfil v Mangotsfield United	7-2
Cirencester Town v Bath City	4-0
Farsley Celtic v Brigg Town	3-1
Cogenhoe United v Dagenham & Redbridge	0-2
Woking v Farnham Town	3-1
Reading Town v Oxford United	2-5
Bournemouth v Thatcham Town	1-4
Tamworth v Coventry Sphinx	0-2
Cambridge United v Bury Town	3-1
Leverstock Green v Harrow Borough	0-3
North Greenford United v Rothwell Town	5-0
St Margaretsbury v Staines Town	0-3
Sevenoaks Town v Gravesend & Northfleet	3-6
Binfield v Beaconsfield SYCOB	1-2
Brislington v Exeter City	2-5
Eccleshill United v Liversedge	5-0
Thackley v North Ferriby United	0-2
Curzon Ashton v Burscough	2-1
Coleshill Town v Rugby Town	0-3
Worcester City v Racing Club Warwick	4-0
Hinckley United v Arnold Town	2-4
Glossop North End v Leek Town	0-4
Stafford Rangers v Long Eaton United	5-3
Lowestoft Town v Grantham Town	1-0
Croydon Athletic v Stevenage Borough	0-1
Redbridge v Colney Heath	5-2
Rushden & Diamonds v Wealdstone	5-2
Chelmsford City v Southend Manor	3-2
Hastings United v Haywards Heath Town	1-2
Ramsgate v Whyteleafe	6-1
Lewes v Maidstone United	0-0
Lewes won 5-4 on penalties.	
Aylesbury United v Winchester City	0-3
Dunston FB v Chester-Le-Street Town	2-1
East Grinstead Town v Chipstead	2-0
Westbury United v Aldershot Town	2-3
Bishop Sutton v Bishop's Cleeve	2-1
Bootle v Kendal Town	2-0
Worksop Town v Altrincham	3-0
AFC Telford United v Gornal Athletic	1-5
Malvern Town v Stourport Swifts	4-1
Hednesford Town v Nuneaton Borough	4-0
Eccleshall v Stratford Town	2-1
Sutton Coldfield Town v Staveley MW	1-0
Histon v Long Melford	2-1
Wroxham v Great Yarmouth Town	0-1
Walsham Le Willows v Blackstones	6-4
Maldon Town v Fisher Athletic	1-2
AFC Wimbledon w.o. v Hillingdon Borough removed for fielding an ineligible player	
Waltham Abbey v Thamesmead Town	0-3
Canvey Island v Clacton Town	9-1
Oakwood v Epsom & Ewell	1-2
Tonbridge Angels v Bromley	4-2
Moneyfields v Oxford City	2-3
Chalfont St Peter v Salisbury City	1-7
Newport Pagnell Town v Chesham United	3-3
Chesham United won 4-3 on penalties.	
York City v Selby Town	3-2
Vauxhall Motors v Morecambe	2-3

THIRD QUALIFYING ROUND

Dunston FB v York City	0-2
Eccleshill United v North Ferriby United	0-3
Worksop Town v Morecambe	0-6
Coventry Sphinx v Eccleshall	4-1
Malvern Town v Boldmere St Michaels	1-1
Boldmere St Michaels won 4-3 on penalties.	
Sutton Coldfield Town v Stafford Rangers	4-0
Cambridge United v Histon	3-0
Walsham Le Willows v Great Yarmouth Town	1-2
Hemel Hempstead Town v Canvey Island	2-1
Westfield v East Grinstead Town	0-1
Merthyr Tydfil v Bishop Sutton	4-1
Curzon Ashton v Marine	3-1
Arnold Town v Leek Town	7-2
Rugby Town v Gornal Athletic	4-2
Hednesford Town v Worcester City	0-0
Hednesford Town won 5-4 on penalties.	
Ashford Town (Middlesex) v Redbridge	1-2
AFC Wimbledon v Chelmsford City	6-0
Lewes v Haywards Heath Town	2-1
Ramsgate v Epsom & Ewell	3-3
Ramsgate won 5-4 on penalties.	
Winchester City v Oxford United	2-3
Leigh RMI v Bootle	1-1
Leigh RMI won 3-2 on penalties.	
North Greenford United v Dunstable Town	3-5
Harrow Borough v Staines Town	4-5
Aldershot Town v Oxford City	2-2
Oxford City won 7-6 on penalties.	
Farsley Celtic v Silsden	3-1
Tonbridge Angels v Gravesend & Northfleet	1-5
Woking v Worthing	3-2
Rushden & Diamonds v Barton Rovers	3-2
Exeter City v Gloucester City	7-0
King's Lynn v Lowestoft Town	3-4
Stevenage Borough v Thamesmead Town	4-2
Dagenham & Redbridge v Fisher Athletic	1-6
Chesham United v Thatcham Town	1-2
Salisbury City v Beaconsfield SYCOB	2-1
Weymouth v Cirencester Town	1-4

FIRST ROUND

Dunstable Town v Gravesend & Northfleet	1-2
Accrington Stanley v Darlington	0-5
Boston United v Port Vale	1-2
Chester City v Farsley Celtic	3-1
Stockport County v Rotherham United	5-3
Scunthorpe United v Bradford City	1-0
Gillingham v Stevenage Borough	3-3
Stevenage Borough won 5-4 on penalties.	
Brentford v Rushden & Diamonds	2-1
Swansea City v Swindon Town	0-6
Exeter City v AFC Bournemouth	4-1
Grimsby Town v Huddersfield Town	0-1
Barnet v Millwall	0-3
Bristol City v Cheltenham Town	5-1
Yeovil Town v Oxford City	6-1
Hereford United v Bristol Rovers	0-2
Doncaster Rovers v Rochdale	2-0
Oldham Athletic v Crewe Alexandra	3-5
Blackpool v Hartlepool United	2-4
Mansfield Town v Northampton Town	0-1
Lincoln City v Boldmere St Michaels	2-0
Leyton Orient v Oxford United	2-1
Lowestoft Town v Chesterfield	1-2
East Grinstead Town v Salisbury City	0-2
Merthyr Tydfil v Cirencester Town	1-0
Macclesfield Town v Curzon Ashton	3-2
Great Yarmouth Town v Rugby Town	3-2
Coventry Sphinx v Nottingham Forest	0-2
AFC Wimbledon v Thatcham Town	2-4
Brighton & Hove Albion v Ramsgate	6-0
Redbridge v Wycombe Wanderers	0-3
Staines Town v Woking	1-2
Sutton Coldfield Town v Walsall	0-3
Hemel Hempstead Town v Fisher Athletic	0-3
York City v Leigh RMI	1-1
York City won 5-3 on penalties.	
Shrewsbury Town v Arnold Town	4-0
Cambridge United v Hednesford Town	3-2
Milton Keynes Dons v Lewes	3-1
North Ferriby United v Morecambe	0-2
Bury v Tranmere Rovers	1-2
Wrexham v Carlisle United	0-1

SECOND ROUND

Cambridge United v Tranmere Rovers	2-0
Crewe Alexandra v Morecambe	5-1
Macclesfield Town v Shrewsbury Town	1-0
York City v Chester City	0-1
Doncaster Rovers v Hartlepool United	1-1
Doncaster Rovers won 12-11 on penalties.	
Northampton Town v Huddersfield Town	0-4
Walsall v Carlisle United	2-1
Scunthorpe United v Lincoln City	2-0
Great Yarmouth Town v Chesterfield	2-5
Nottingham Forest v Port Vale	4-0
Darlington v Stockport County	1-2
Brentford v Yeovil Town	0-2
Merthyr Tydfil v Thatcham Town	5-4
Milton Keynes Dons v Fisher Athletic	2-1
Woking v Exeter City	0-1
Stevenage Borough v Leyton Orient	2-3
Millwall v Bristol Rovers	2-0
Wycombe Wanderers v Gravesend & Northfleet	3-0
Salisbury City v Swindon Town	1-2
Bristol City v Brighton & Hove Albion	3-0

THIRD ROUND

Portsmouth v Norwich City	1-5
Cardiff City v Merthyr Tydfil	6-0
Luton Town v Huddersfield Town	1-0
Wigan Athletic v Plymouth Argyle	0-2
Stockport County v Southampton	0-2
Crystal Palace v Stoke City	4-1
Doncaster Rovers v Derby County	2-4
Aston Villa v Colchester United	3-1
Manchester United v Scunthorpe United	3-0
Millwall v Manchester City	0-0
Millwall won 6-5 on penalties.	
Swindon Town v Queens Park Rangers	1-1
Swindon Town won 10-9 on penalties.	
Macclesfield Town v Everton	0-3
Burnley v Milton Keynes Dons	3-2
West Bromwich Albion v Liverpool	1-2
Coventry City v Southend United	0-0
Coventry City won 3-1 on penalties.	
Walsall v Middlesbrough	2-3
Exeter City v Newcastle United	0-4
Arsenal v Wycombe Wanderers	2-1
Birmingham City v Chesterfield	4-0
Sunderland v Preston North End	3-2
Leicester City v Wolverhampton Wanderers	1-2
Chester City v Tottenham Hotspur	1-0
Leeds United v Hull City	2-2
Hull City won 4-3 on penalties.	
West Ham United v Charlton Athletic	0-1
Cambridge United v Crewe Alexandra	2-1
Barnsley v Leyton Orient	2-0
Chelsea v Nottingham Forest	2-0
Sheffield Wednesday v Bolton Wanderers	0-2
Yeovil Town v Ipswich Town	2-2
Yeovil Town won 5-4 on penalties.	
Sheffield United v Watford	2-2
Sheffield United won 8-7 on penalties.	
Bristol City v Fulham	3-2
Reading v Blackburn Rovers	5-1

FOURTH ROUND

Crystal Palace v Plymouth Argyle	4-2
Bristol City v Chester City	4-0
Birmingham City v Charlton Athletic	4-0
Manchester United v Southampton	2-0
Reading v Coventry City	5-1
Hull City v Arsenal	1-2
Burnley v Luton Town	2-0
Newcastle United v Norwich City	3-1
Liverpool v Chelsea	2-0
Swindon Town v Yeovil Town	4-0
Everton v Millwall	0-1
Sheffield United v Aston Villa	2-2
Sheffield United won 6-5 on penalties.	
Derby County v Barnsley	3-3
Barnsley won 9-8 on penalties.	
Cardiff City v Cambridge United	4-1
Wolverhampton Wanderers v Middlesbrough	1-2
Sunderland v Bolton Wanderers	2-1

FIFTH ROUND

Manchester United v Crystal Palace	2-0
Arsenal v Bristol City	2-2
Arsenal won 6-5 on penalties.	
Newcastle United v Millwall	1-0
Sheffield United v Middlesbrough	3-2
Liverpool v Reading	1-0
Cardiff City v Sunderland	2-0
Swindon Town v Burnley	3-1
Barnsley v Birmingham City	1-2

SIXTH ROUND

Swindon Town v Newcastle United	1-2
Arsenal v Cardiff City	3-2
Manchester United v Birmingham City	2-0
Sheffield United v Liverpool	1-3

SEMI-FINALS (TWO LEGS)

Newcastle United v Liverpool	2-4, 1-3
Arsenal v Manchester United	1-0, 2-3

FINAL (First Leg)

Monday, 16 April 2007

Liverpool (1) 1 *(Lindfield 16)*

Manchester United (0) 2 *(Threlfall 49 (og), Hewson 74 (pen))* 19,518

Liverpool: Hansen; Darby, Burns, Spearing, Threlfall, Barnett, Ryan, Flynn, Lindfield, Woodward (Eccleston 68), Putterill.
Manchester United: Zieler; Eckersley, Evans, Strickland, Chester, Drinkwater (Bryan 75), Welbeck, Hewson, Brandy (James 90), Fagan, Galbraith.
Referee: M. Clattenburg (Tyne & Wear).

FINAL (Second Leg)

Thursday, 26 April 2007

Manchester United (0) 0

Liverpool (0) 1 *(Threlfall 51)* 24,347

aet; Liverpool won 4-3 on penalties.

Manchester United: Zieler; Eckersley, Evans (Moffatt 99), Strickland, Chester, Drinkwater (Bryan 72), Welbeck (Eikrem 87), Hewson, Brandy, Fagan, Galbraith.
Liverpool: Roberts; Darby, Burns, Spearing, Threlfall, Barnett, Ryan (Woodward 95), Ajdarevic (Irwin 81), Lindfield, Flynn, Putterill.
Referee: M. Clattenburg (Tyne & Wear).

THE FA SUNDAY CUP 2006–07

IN PARTNERSHIP WITH CARLSBERG

PRELIMINARY ROUND
Allerton v Brow 2-0
James Cropper v Barry's 0-5
Hartlepool Athletic Rugby v Rawdon 1-2
North Reddish WMC v Paddock 3-6
Bloomfield Sports v Broad Plain House 8-2
Pioneer v Nirankari Sports Sabha 1-2
Woolston T&L v Sutton Athletic 5-2
Cafe Roma v Coopers Kensington 3-2
Grange Athletic v Hanham Sunday 4-0

FIRST ROUND
AFC Chellow withdrew v Allerton w.o.
Irlam MS v Nicosia 1-1
Irlam MS won 5-3 on penalties.
Albion Sports v Barry's 0-3
Lobster v Portland (Carlisle) 6-0
Portland (Workington) v Norcoast 3-0
Queensbury v Sandon Dock 0-2
Shankhouse United v Hartlepool Lion Hillcarter 4-1
Shipley Town v West Lee 2-5
Hessle Rangers v Hartlepool Supporters Athletic 2-1
Pablo Derby Arms v Whetley Lane WMC 1-0
Silsden (Sunday) v Halton Sports 3-1
The Warby v Western Approaches 4-0
Bow & Arrow v Bolton Woods 1-9
Dock v Home & Bargain 2-1
Buttershaw Whitestar v Britannia 2-0
JOB v Queens Park 0-1
Drum v Rawdon 1-3
Seymour KFCA v Seaburn 1-0
Ford Motors v Paddock 0-3
Ring O'Bells (Shipley) v Swanfield 1-3
Irish Centre (Huddersfield) v Stanley Royal 2-1
North Mersey Lions v Canada 0-2
Abandoned after 28 minutes; spectator misconduct, tie awarded to Canada
Crossflatts v Colonel Prior 0-1
Hartlepool Rovers Quoit v Orchard Park 2-3
Elland v Coundon Conservative 0-3
The View v Tower 3-2
Barcabullona v Magnet Tavern 3-1
Springfield Lions v Scots Grey 0-5
AFC Hornets v 61 FC (Sunday) 2-1
Aris v Enfield Rangers 1-3
Belstone v AC Sportsmen 2-0
FCR v Gossoms End 1-3
Belt Road v Bartley Green Social 1-0
Birstall Stamford v Grosvenor Park 5-0
Bartley Green Sunday v Bloomfield Sports 1-0
Diffusion v Wernley 2-4
Corsham Centre v Ashton 11-0
Lodge Cottrell v Talisman 3-1
Club Lewsey v Bedfont Sunday 4-4
Bedfont Sunday won 5-3 on penalties.
Kcinsatop v Moggerhanger Sunday 4-1
Livingstone Rara v Brixton United 2-1
Mayfair United v The Clifton 3-1
Howbridge Swifts v Brache Green Man 1-4
Loft Style Sinners v London Maccabi Lions 4-0
Bury Park SC v Nirankari Sports Sabha 3-0
Risden Wood v FC Houghton Centre 5-3
Pertemps Progressive v Mackadown Lane S&S 2-1
Travellers v St Margarets 2-4
Celtic SC (Luton) v Broadfields United 5-1
Hammer v Reading Irish 0-4
Holt v CB Hounslow United 1-2
Richfield Rovers v Treble Chance 3-2
Bournemouth Electric v Woolston T&L 0-1
Sandford v Cafe Roma 4-1
Luton Old Boys (Sunday) v Crawley Green (Sunday) 3-3
Crawley Green (Sunday) won 6-5 on penalties.
Skew Bridge v St Andrews 1-2
Nicholas Wybacks v Lashings 5-3
St Matthews v Quested 2-5
Kent Athletic (Luton) v Greengate 1-3
Maldon Saints v Moat 4-0
FC Fellowship v Grange Athletic 0-6
Lebeq Tavern Courage v Indian Gymkhana 3-1

SECOND ROUND
Barry's v Lobster 4-0
Allerton v Irlam MS 1-1
Allerton won 5-4 on penalties.
Shankhouse United w.o. v West Lee unable to fulfil fixture.
Silsden (Sunday) v Dock 2-0
Hessle Rangers v Pablo Derby Arms 0-1
Seymour KFCA v Queens Park 3-2
Paddock v Swanfield 1-0
Colonel Prior v The View 1-2
Hetton Lyons Cricket Club v Coundon Conservative 1-1
Coundon Conservative won 4-1 on penalties.
Scots Grey v Orchard Park 7-4
Belstone v Barcabullona 2-1
AFC Hornets (Studham) v Enfield Rangers 0-1
Belt Road v Gossoms End 4-1
Wernley v St Margarets 7-1
Brache Green Man v Kcinsatop 3-1
Corsham Centre v Lodge Cottrell 2-2
Lodge Cottrell won 6-5 on penalties.
Nicholas Wybacks v Quested 3-3
Quested won 5-4 on penalties.
Bury Park v Risdon Wood 4-2
Bedfont Sunday v Loft Style Sinners 1-3
Pertemps Progressive v St Joseph's (Luton) 0-5
Grange Athletic v Lebeq Tavern Courage 0-2
CB Hounslow United v Richfield Rovers 3-2
Sandford v Woolston T&L 2-3
Crawley Green (Sunday) v St Andrews 3-2
Portland (Workington) v Sandon Dock 1-2
Bolton Woods v The Warby 0-2
Rawdon v Buttershaw Whitestar 0-0
Rawdon won 5-4 on penalties.
Birstall Stamford v Bartley Green Sunday 1-0
Livingstone Rara v Celtic SC (Luton) 2-1
Mayfair United v Reading Irish 1-3
Greengate v Maldon Saints 2-1
Irish Centre (Huddersfield) v Canada 0-3

THIRD ROUND
Sandon Dock v Allerton 2-3
Seymour KFCA v Silsdon 6-2
Barry's v Shankhouse United 2-1
The Warby v Pablo Derby Arms 1-1
Pablo Derby Arms won 5-4 on penalties.
The View v Scots Grey 4-2
Canada v Rawdon 3-2
Paddock v Coundon Conservative 1-2
Brache Green Man v Belt Road 3-7
Wernley v Lodge Cottrell 3-1
Belstone v Birstall Stamford 2-4
Quested v Enfield Rangers 6-2
Bury Park v Greengate 1-0
St Joseph's (Luton) v Loft Style Sinners 1-2
Lebeq Tavern Courage v Crawley Green (Sunday) 2-1
Reading Irish v Livingstone Rara 2-1
CB Hounslow United v Woolston T&L 1-5

FOURTH ROUND
Allerton v Canada 2-3
Coundon Conservative v Pablo Derby Arms 2-0
Seymour KFCA v Wernley 0-3
The View v Barry's 2-2
Barry's won 5-4 on penalties.
Belt Road v Birstall Stamford 2-5
Woolston T&L v Bury Park 2-3
Quested v Loft Style Sinners 2-4
Lebeq Tavern Courage v Reading Irish 4-1

FIFTH ROUND
Coundon Conservative v Wernley 4-3
Barry's v Canada
Tie awarded to Barry's; Canada removed for fielding an ineligible player.
Loft Style Sinners v Lebeq Tavern Courage 0-1
Birstall Stamford v Bury Park 3-2

SEMI-FINALS
Barry's v Lebeq Tavern Courage 0-1
Birstall Stamford v Coundon Conservative 1-1
Coundon Conservative won 5-4 on penalties.

FINAL
Coundon Conservative 5 *(Ellison, Thompson 2, Johnson 2)*
Lebeq Tavern Courage 0
(at Liverpool FC) 1289

FA PREMIER RESERVE LEAGUES 2006–07

FA PREMIER RESERVE LEAGUE – NORTH SECTION

	P	W	D	L	F	A	Pts
Bolton W	18	10	3	5	21	16	33
Manchester U	18	9	4	5	24	17	31
Middlesbrough	18	9	3	6	31	25	30
Manchester C	18	9	2	7	27	24	29
Liverpool	18	8	2	8	24	19	26
Blackburn R	18	7	5	6	16	15	26
Sheffield U	18	8	2	8	23	23	26
Newcastle U	18	6	5	7	29	29	23
Everton	18	3	7	8	18	25	16
Wigan Ath	18	2	5	11	8	28	11

Leading Goalscorers

Graham D	Middlesbrough	8
Carroll A	Newcastle U	8
Evans C	Manchester C	6
Lindfield C	Liverpool	5
Marsh P	Manchester U	5
Christie M	Middlesbrough	5
Craddock T	Middlesbrough	5
Johansson A	Wigan Ath	5
Hughes M	Everton	4
McFadden J	Everton	4
Idrizaj B	Liverpool	4
Marshall P	Manchester C	4
Burns A	Manchester U	4
Finnigan C	Newcastle U	4
Quinn S	Sheffield U	4

LEAGUE APPEARANCES AND GOALSCORERS

Bolton Wanderers: Sinclair 14+1, Augustyn 14, Jamieson 12+2, Woolfe 12, Thompson D 11+4, Basham 11+2, Sissons 10+5, Cassidy 8+3, Fojut 8+3, Al-Habsi 8, Harsanyi 8, Charlesworth 6, Samarani 6, Smith 6, Tal 6, Vaz Te 6, Ellis 5+1, Gbemie 5, Villar 5, Wolze 4+1, Walker 4, Thompson L 3+2, Gardner 3, Kazimierczak 3, Obadeyi 2+6, Giannakopoulos 2, Howarth 2, Michalik 2, Nolan 2, Stott 2, Brooks 1+4, Roddy 1+1, Hunt 1, Lainton 1, Martin 1, Mountford 1, Pedersen 1, Sheridan 1, McDonald +1.

Goalscorers: Charlesworth 2, Giannakopoulos 2, Harsanyi 2, Obadeyi 2, Tal 2 (1 pen), Thompson D 2, Vaz Te 2 (1 pen), Wolze 2 Woolfe 2, Nolan 1 (pen), Villar 1, own goal 1.

FA PREMIER RESERVE LEAGUE – SOUTH SECTION

	P	W	D	L	F	A	Pts
Reading	18	12	2	4	45	15	38
Watford	18	11	2	5	26	20	35
Chelsea	18	10	3	5	26	11	33
Aston Villa	18	9	3	6	38	26	30
Tottenham H	18	8	6	4	22	18	30
Charlton Ath	18	7	4	7	28	24	25
West Ham U	18	5	3	10	18	28	18
Fulham	18	4	5	9	16	30	17
Arsenal	18	4	4	10	15	29	16
Portsmouth	18	2	4	12	12	45	10

Leading Goalscorers

Long S	Reading	14
Moore L	Aston Villa	7
Dickinson C	Charlton Ath	7
Sinclair S	Chelsea	7
Sahar B	Chelsea	7
Aliadiere J	Arsenal	5
Baros M	Aston Villa	5
Lisbie K	Charlton Ath	5
Bangura A	Watford	5
McGurk A	Aston Villa	4
Younghusband P	Chelsea	4
Brown W	Fulham	4
Henry J	Reading	4
Cox S	Reading	4
Sears F	West Ham U	4

LEAGUE APPEARANCES AND GOALSCORERS

Reading: Long 13, Federici 11, Oster 11, Halls 10, Bikey 9, Halford 9, De La Cruz 9, Church 8+3, Henry 8+3, Bennett 8, Sodje 8, Cox 7+2, Karacan 7+1, Hayes 6, Spence 6, Davies 5+2, Kelly 5+1, Hunt 5, Stack 5, Gunnarsson 4, Little 4, Osano 4, Seol 4, Bozanic 3+2, Pearce 3+2, Robson-Kanu 3+2, Doyle 3, Lita 3, Bignall 2+5, Andersen 2, Joseph-Dubois 2+2, Bygrave 2+1, Convey 2, Duberry 2, Mate 2, Illugason 1+2, Brown 1, Kitson 1, Hateley +4, Sigurdsson +2, Bayley +1, Clarke +1.

Goalscorers: Long 14, Cox 4, Henry 4 (2 pens), Lita 3, Gunnarsson 2, Hunt 2 (1 pen), Illugason 2, Oster 2, Church 1, De La Cruz 1, Halford 1, Hayes 1, Joseph-Dubois 1, Kelly 1, Kitson 1, Pearce 1, Robson-Kanu 1, Sodje 1, own goals 2.

PREMIER RESERVE LEAGUE PLAY-OFF

Reading (1) 2 *(Bennett 22, Pearce 48)*

Bolton W (0) 0 4172

at Reading.

Reading: Federici; Halls, Kelly, Bennett, Pearce, Davies, Osano (Sigurdsson), Henry, Bozanic, Cox, Robson-Kanu.

Bolton W: Al-Habsi; Gbermie, Jamieson, Augustyn, Fojut, Cassidy, Sissons, Basham (Thompson D), Woolfe (Brooks), Obadeyi, Wolze (Sheridan).

Referee: H. Webb (South Yorkshire)

Footnote: The contrast between the respective winners of the North and South reserve leagues could not have been more different. Reading scored 45 goals, Bolton only 21. Bolton's achievement was remarkable since they lost their first four matches. Reading's average attendance for the league games at the Madejski Stadium was 2590.

PONTIN'S RESERVE LEAGUES 2006–07

PONTIN'S HOLIDAYS LEAGUE

DIV. ONE CENTRAL	P	W	D	L	F	A	GD	Pts
Birmingham C	22	13	5	4	38	21	+17	44
Nottingham F	22	13	4	5	44	23	+21	43
Walsall	22	12	4	6	41	23	+18	40
Sheffield W	22	12	4	6	36	25	+11	40
WBA	22	11	3	8	36	30	+6	36
Leeds U	22	7	7	8	33	35	–2	28
Barnsley	22	7	5	10	44	47	–3	26
Stoke C	22	6	7	9	25	37	–12	25
Huddersfield T	22	6	6	10	25	32	–7	24
Port Vale	22	6	5	11	25	35	–10	23
Shrewsbury T	22	5	5	12	29	44	–15	20
Bradford C	22	4	5	13	19	43	–24	17

DIV. ONE WEST	P	W	D	L	F	A	GD	Pts
Oldham Ath	20	10	7	3	39	18	+21	37
Preston NE	20	11	2	7	48	32	+16	35
Bury	20	10	5	5	43	32	+11	35
Accrington S	20	9	3	8	38	36	+2	30
Tranmere R	20	9	2	9	30	31	–1	29
Blackpool	20	9	1	10	32	34	–2	28
Manchester C	20	7	5	8	26	32	–6	26
Rochdale	20	8	1	11	32	39	–7	25
Wrexham	20	7	4	9	21	33	–12	25
Carlisle U	20	6	4	10	28	38	–10	22
Chester C	20	6	2	12	21	33	–12	20

DIV. ONE EAST	P	W	D	L	F	A	GD	Pts
Rotherham U	18	12	3	3	46	23	+23	39
Grimsby T	18	12	2	4	35	22	+13	38
Hartlepool U	18	10	6	2	40	17	+23	36
Hull C	18	11	1	6	35	22	+13	34
York C	18	6	7	5	32	21	+11	25
Sheffield U	18	6	4	8	28	33	–5	22
Scunthorpe U	18	6	2	10	24	32	–8	20
Doncaster R	18	4	3	11	19	46	–27	15
Darlington	18	3	3	12	14	33	–19	12
Lincoln C	18	3	3	12	14	38	–24	12

PONTIN'S HOLIDAYS LEAGUE CUP

GROUP ONE	P	W	D	L	F	A	GD	Pts
Blackburn R	3	2	0	1	13	2	+11	6
Shrewsbury T	3	2	0	1	4	4	0	6
Tranmere R	3	2	0	1	5	9	–4	6
Chester C	3	0	0	3	1	8	–7	0

GROUP TWO	P	W	D	L	F	A	GD	Pts
WBA	3	3	0	0	7	1	+6	9
Rotherham U	3	1	1	1	3	3	0	4
Sheffield W	3	1	1	1	2	2	0	4
Huddersfield T	3	0	0	3	0	6	–6	0

GROUP THREE	P	W	D	L	F	A	GD	Pts
Lincoln C	3	3	0	0	6	1	+5	9
Hull C	3	1	1	1	4	6	–2	4
Sheffield U	3	0	2	1	5	6	–1	2
Barnsley	3	0	1	2	3	5	–2	1

GROUP FOUR	P	W	D	L	F	A	GD	Pts
Hartlepool U	2	1	1	0	8	5	+3	4
Bradford C	2	0	2	0	4	4	0	2
Darlington	2	0	1	1	1	4	–3	1

QUARTER-FINALS

Hartlepool U 2, WBA 1
Lincoln C 3, Blackburn R 2
Hull C 5, Rotherham U 1
Bradford C 0, Shrewsbury T 1

SEMI-FINALS

Hartlepool U 3, Hull C 2
Lincoln C 4, Shrewsbury T 2

FINAL

Lincoln C 1, Hartlepool U 1
Lincoln C won 7-6 on penalties.

PONTIN'S HOLIDAYS COMBINATION

CENTRAL DIVISION	P	W	D	L	Pts
Brighton & HA	14	12	1	1	37
Southampton	14	12	0	2	36
Crystal Palace	14	7	1	6	22
QPR	14	6	2	6	20
Millwall	14	4	3	7	15
Bournemouth	14	4	2	8	14
Wycombe W	14	4	1	9	13
Aldershot T	14	1	2	11	5

WALES AND WEST DIVISION	P	W	D	L	Pts
Cheltenham T	18	11	5	2	38
Bristol C	18	8	6	4	30
Cardiff C	18	7	7	4	28
Bristol R	18	8	4	6	28
Plymouth Arg	18	7	5	6	26
Exeter C	18	7	3	8	24
Swindon T	18	6	4	8	22
Yeovil T	18	6	3	9	21
Swansea C	18	4	4	10	16
Weymouth	18	4	3	11	15

EAST DIVISION	P	W	D	L	Pts
Ipswich T	18	13	2	3	41
Colchester U	18	8	8	2	32
Luton T	18	9	3	6	30
Southend U	18	9	2	7	29
Leyton Orient	18	6	8	4	26
Northampton T	18	7	4	7	25
Norwich C	18	8	6	6	24
Milton Keynes D	18	7	2	9	23
Stevenage B	18	2	5	11	11
Oxford U	18	1	4	13	7

FA ACADEMY UNDER 18 LEAGUE 2006–07

GROUP A	P	W	D	L	F	A	GD	Pts
Arsenal	28	20	5	3	75	38	37	65
West Ham U	28	17	6	5	50	36	14	57
Chelsea	28	16	5	7	46	30	16	53
Southampton	28	16	2	10	66	44	22	50
Crystal Palace	28	14	8	6	60	45	15	50
Ipswich T	28	10	8	10	48	47	1	38
Charlton Ath	28	9	7	12	47	50	–3	34
Millwall	28	7	8	13	38	56	–18	29
Norwich C	28	7	1	20	26	51	–25	22
Fulham	28	4	7	17	32	62	–30	19

GROUP B	P	W	D	L	F	A	GD	Pts
Leicester C	28	21	3	4	93	36	57	66
Reading	28	20	4	4	51	24	27	64
Tottenham H	28	13	10	5	50	38	12	49
Aston Villa	28	13	9	6	51	32	19	48
Watford	28	9	8	11	45	48	–3	35
Bristol C	28	10	5	13	49	61	–12	35
Birmingham C	28	9	3	16	37	64	–27	30
Coventry C	28	8	4	16	31	45	–14	28
Cardiff C	28	5	4	19	30	55	–25	19
Milton Keynes D	28	5	1	22	30	72	–42	16

GROUP C	P	W	D	L	F	A	GD	Pts
Manchester C	28	21	3	4	63	28	35	66
Bolton W	28	14	6	8	38	26	12	48
Blackburn R	28	13	7	8	47	34	13	46
Manchester U	28	12	4	12	51	42	9	40
WBA	28	12	2	14	44	45	–1	38
Everton	28	6	13	9	38	38	0	31
Crewe Alex	28	9	3	16	44	57	–13	30
Liverpool	28	7	8	13	29	37	–8	29
Wolverhampton W	28	6	7	15	30	52	–22	25
Stoke C	28	3	5	20	14	53	–39	14

GROUP D	P	W	D	L	F	A	GD	Pts
Sunderland	28	15	9	4	54	32	22	54
Nottingham F	28	15	7	6	54	30	24	52
Leeds U	28	16	4	8	50	37	13	52
Newcastle U	28	15	4	9	57	41	16	49
Derby Co	28	12	7	9	53	42	11	43
Sheffield W	28	9	7	12	30	40	–10	34
Sheffield U	28	9	6	13	25	43	–18	33
Barnsley	28	7	6	15	35	60	–25	27
Huddersfield T	28	7	4	17	32	55	–23	25
Middlesbrough	28	5	8	15	39	56	–17	23

PUMA YOUTH ALLIANCE 2006–07

NORTH WEST CONFERENCE GROUP A

	P	W	D	L	F	A	GD	Pts
Oldham Ath	24	16	4	4	70	27	+43	52
Bury	24	15	4	5	57	30	+27	49
Preston NE	24	14	1	9	56	43	+13	43
Wigan Ath	24	10	9	5	47	33	+14	39
Carlisle U	24	7	8	9	28	33	–5	29
Burnley	24	8	3	13	45	52	–7	27
Blackpool	24	7	4	13	37	51	–14	25
Rochdale	24	6	5	13	31	51	–20	23
Accrington S	24	0	0	24	21	95	–74	0

NORTH WEST CONFERENCE GROUP B

	P	W	D	L	F	A	GD	Pts
Walsall	23	13	4	6	40	24	+16	43
Chester C	23	12	6	5	40	17	+23	42
Tranmere R	23	13	3	7	35	25	+10	42
Stockport Co	23	12	4	7	50	38	+12	40
Port Vale	23	11	2	10	40	35	+5	35
Shrewsbury T	23	8	4	11	29	43	–14	28
Wrexham	23	7	5	11	29	43	–14	26
Macclesfield T	23	6	4	13	25	40	–15	22

NORTH EAST CONFERENCE

	P	W	D	L	F	A	GD	Pts
Hull C	24	17	5	2	53	23	+30	56
Rotherham U	24	13	7	4	39	23	+16	46
Darlington	24	12	6	6	44	28	+16	42
Grimsby T	24	11	6	7	46	39	+7	39
Hartlepool U	24	11	4	9	48	43	+5	37
Lincoln C	24	10	7	7	31	30	+1	37
Bradford C	24	8	6	10	37	38	–1	30
Doncaster R	24	6	9	9	45	42	+3	27
Chesterfield	24	7	6	11	36	41	–5	27
Mansfield T	24	6	9	9	27	39	–12	27
York C	24	7	3	14	25	44	–19	24
Scunthorpe U	24	5	6	13	32	52	–20	21
Boston U	24	4	4	16	24	45	–21	16

SOUTH WEST CONFERENCE

	P	W	D	L	F	A	GD	Pts
Oxford U	16	12	4	0	52	19	+33	40
Bournemouth	16	8	4	4	29	16	+13	28
Swansea C	16	8	2	6	36	26	+10	26
Swindon T	16	7	4	5	41	27	+14	25
Yeovil T	16	7	3	6	21	23	–2	24
Bristol R	16	6	5	5	29	24	+5	23
Cheltenham T	16	6	2	8	22	37	–15	20
Plymouth Arg	16	3	2	11	11	32	–21	11
Hereford U	16	0	4	12	14	51	–37	4

SOUTH EAST CONFERENCE

	P	W	D	L	F	A	GD	Pts
QPR	22	15	3	4	52	27	+25	48
Southend U	22	14	4	4	47	28	+19	46
Gillingham	22	14	4	4	49	32	+17	46
Wycombe W	22	12	4	6	41	21	+20	40
Brighton & HA	22	9	6	7	27	21	+6	33
Luton T	22	10	2	10	38	39	–1	32
Colchester U	22	8	7	7	38	35	+3	31
Rushden & D	22	7	4	11	24	40	–16	25
Brentford	22	6	6	10	22	27	–5	24
Leyton Orient	22	6	4	12	25	39	–14	22
Northampton T	22	4	6	12	34	54	–20	18
Portsmouth	22	1	2	19	12	46	–34	5

THE PUMA YOUTH ALLIANCE CUP 2006–07

SOUTHERN SECTION

GROUP 1	P	W	D	L	F	A	GD	Pts
Swansea C	6	5	1	0	12	2	+10	16
Wycombe W	6	4	1	1	10	4	+6	13
Brentford	6	3	2	1	13	3	+10	11
QPR	6	3	1	2	14	7	+7	10
Portsmouth	6	1	1	4	7	10	–3	4
Yeovil T	6	1	0	5	7	17	–10	3
Plymouth Arg	6	1	0	5	4	24	–20	3

GROUP 2	P	W	D	L	F	A	GD	Pts
Northampton T	6	5	1	0	13	4	+9	16
Rushden & D	6	3	1	2	9	2	+7	10
Leyton Orient	6	3	1	2	10	4	+6	10
Cheltenham T	6	2	2	2	10	8	+2	8
Luton T	6	2	1	3	11	10	+1	7
Bristol R	6	1	2	3	6	10	–4	5
Hereford U	6	1	0	5	3	24	–21	3

GROUP 3	P	W	D	L	F	A	GD	Pts
Swindon T	6	4	2	0	12	4	+8	14
Colchester U	6	4	1	1	14	7	+7	13
Oxford U	6	2	2	2	8	12	–4	8
Gillingham	6	2	1	3	7	10	–3	7
Brighton & HA	6	2	0	4	9	11	–2	6
Bournemouth	6	1	2	3	12	12	0	5
Southend U	6	1	2	3	5	11	–6	5

SOUTHERN SEMI-FINALS
Northampton T 0, Colchester U 3
Swindon T 4, Swansea C 3

SOUTHERN FINAL
Colchester U 5, Swindon T 1

NORTHERN SECTION

FIRST ROUND
Burnley 2, Stockport Co 8
Carlisle U 4, Bradford C 0
Chesterfield 2, Preston NE 4
Darlington 1, Tranmere R 1
Tranmere R won 5-4 on penalties.
Doncaster R 0, Grimsby T 3
Hartlepool U 1, Boston U 4
Macclesfield T 0, Chester C 1
Mansfield T 2, Wrexham 3
Oldham Ath 5, Shrewsbury T 1
Rochdale 2, Rotherham U 1
Scunthorpe U 3, Accrington S 0
Walsall 1, Bury 3
Wigan Ath 4, Blackpool 0

SECOND ROUND
Boston U 0, Hull C 4
Carlisle U 0, Stockport Co 1
Chester C 3, Rochdale 2
Grimsby T 2, Oldham Ath 1
Lincoln C 0, Scunthorpe U 1
Preston NE 3, Bury 3
Preston NE won 5-4 on penalties.
Tranmere R 3, Wigan Ath 1
Wrexham 0, Port Vale 1

QUARTER-FINALS
Chester C 3, Port Vale 2
Hull C 4, Grimsby T 4
Grimsby T won 4-2 on penalties.
Stockport Co 1, Preston NE 0
Tranmere R 0, Scunthorpe U 1

SEMI-FINALS
Grimsby T 2, Chester C 0
Stockport Co 3, Scunthorpe U 0

NORTHERN FINAL
Stockport Co 2, Grimsby T 0

PUMA YOUTH ALLIANCE CUP FINAL
Stockport Co 6, Colchester U 2

NON-LEAGUE TABLES 2006–07

NATIONAL LEAGUE SYSTEM – STEP 5

ARNGROVE NORTHERN LEAGUE DIVISION ONE

	P	W	D	L	F	A	GD	Pts
Whitley Bay	42	28	8	6	104	45	59	92
Billingham Town	42	28	8	6	98	47	51	92
Sunderland Nissan	42	28	6	8	96	41	55	90
Consett	42	23	10	9	89	51	38	79
Newcastle BBP	42	21	11	10	79	45	34	74
West Auckland Town	42	22	8	12	88	61	27	74
Dunston Federation B	42	19	16	7	67	48	19	73
Durham City	42	20	12	10	87	62	25	72
Shildon	42	21	9	12	80	57	23	72
Morpeth Town	42	19	9	14	87	70	17	66
Newcastle Blue Star	42	17	7	18	71	60	11	58
Tow Law Town	42	15	11	16	68	72	–4	56
Northallerton Town	42	16	6	20	76	82	–6	54
Billingham Synthonia	42	13	14	15	61	71	–10	53
Jarrow Roofing Boldon CA	42	13	7	22	68	101	–33	46
Bishop Auckland	42	11	10	21	59	86	–27	43
Chester Le Street Town	42	10	9	23	51	80	–29	39
West Allotment Celtic	42	9	11	22	62	80	–18	38
Ashington	42	9	7	26	46	87	–41	34
Bedlington Terriers (–3)	42	7	8	27	47	99	–52	26
Horden CW (–3)	42	6	10	26	46	107	–61	25
Darlington RA	42	6	5	31	41	119	–78	23

BADGER ALES SUSSEX COUNTY LEAGUE DIVISION ONE

	P	W	D	L	F	A	GD	Pts
Eastbourne Town	38	27	6	5	97	42	55	87
Whitehawk	38	25	11	2	70	17	53	86
Arundel	38	23	6	9	82	39	43	75
Crowborough Athletic	38	22	9	7	73	40	33	75
Hassocks	38	20	8	10	80	45	35	68
Hailsham Town	38	17	15	6	52	29	23	66
Eastbourne United Ass	38	16	9	13	66	51	15	57
Selsey	38	14	14	10	46	46	0	56
Ringmer (+2)	38	13	11	14	59	66	–7	52
East Preston	38	16	3	19	47	49	–2	51
Chichester City United	38	14	7	17	59	58	1	49
Three Bridges	38	11	12	15	59	60	–1	45
Shoreham	38	11	10	17	61	71	–10	43
Sidley United	38	11	9	18	47	76	–29	42
Redhill	38	11	8	19	61	65	–4	41
Wick (–1)	38	11	7	20	51	69	–18	39
Oakwood	38	11	6	21	42	79	–37	39
Worthing United	38	7	10	21	55	100	–45	31
Rye United	38	6	9	23	33	73	–40	27
Littlehampton Town	38	5	8	25	30	95	–65	23

CHERRY RED COMBINED COUNTIES PREMIER DIVISION

	P	W	D	L	F	A	GD	Pts
Chipstead	42	32	3	7	114	48	66	99
Merstham	42	31	2	9	100	35	65	95
Wembley	42	27	8	7	95	45	50	89
Ash United	42	26	8	8	86	37	49	86
North Greenford United	42	21	12	9	90	62	28	75
Banstead Athletic	42	20	10	12	76	64	12	70
Camberley Town	42	21	7	14	60	59	1	70
Chertsey Town	42	20	7	15	72	71	1	67
Reading Town	42	18	6	18	72	64	8	60
Egham Town	42	16	10	16	80	59	21	58
Chessington & Hook	42	15	12	15	63	72	–9	57
Sandhurst Town	42	15	10	17	61	67	–6	55
Colliers Wood United (–3)	42	17	6	19	69	62	7	54
Cobham	42	16	6	20	56	64	–8	54
Raynes Park Vale	42	15	8	19	69	85	–16	53
Dorking (–6)	42	16	7	19	65	73	–8	49
Epsom & Ewell	42	10	10	22	44	78	–34	40
Cove (–1)	42	11	7	24	56	96	–40	39
Bedfont Green	42	9	10	23	38	62	–24	37
Bookham	42	10	6	26	54	105	–51	36
Guildford City	42	8	4	30	46	96	–50	28
Bedfont	42	6	5	31	41	103	–62	23

EAGLE BITTER UNITED COUNTIES LEAGUE PREMIER DIVISION

	P	W	D	L	F	A	GD	Pts
Deeping Rangers	40	30	7	3	95	25	70	97
Boston Town	40	31	2	7	110	47	63	95
Wellingborough Town	40	25	7	8	87	48	39	82
Potton United	40	23	9	8	91	44	47	78
Cogenhoe United	40	23	4	13	101	53	48	73
Northampton Spencer	40	22	7	11	69	41	28	73
Newport Pagnell Town	40	19	7	14	63	67	–4	64
Blackstones	40	17	12	11	79	51	28	63
Wootton Blue Cross	40	18	8	14	70	57	13	62
St Ives Town	40	17	8	15	56	49	7	59
Holbeach United	40	14	10	16	50	65	–15	52
Long Buckby	40	14	8	18	68	67	1	50
Raunds Town	40	13	6	21	61	77	–16	45
Desborough Town (–6)	40	15	5	20	60	76	–16	44
Yaxley (–3)	40	12	9	19	59	69	–10	42
Stewarts & Lloyds	40	11	8	21	52	87	–35	41
St Neots Town	40	12	5	23	47	86	–39	41
Bourne Town	40	11	6	23	61	92	–31	39
Stotfold	40	10	6	24	57	101	–44	36
Ford Sports Daventry	40	6	5	29	47	103	–56	23
Buckingham Town	40	4	7	29	39	117	–78	19

SPORT ITALIA HELLENIC LEAGUE PREMIER DIVISION

	P	W	D	L	F	A	GD	Pts
Slimbridge	38	27	7	4	93	29	64	88
North Leigh	38	25	10	3	77	33	44	85
Hungerford Town	38	21	8	9	77	40	37	71
Ardley United	38	19	10	9	78	54	24	67
Almondsbury Town	38	19	9	10	73	44	29	66
Witney United	38	16	13	9	67	49	18	61
Milton United	38	18	6	14	73	70	3	60
Shortwood United	38	15	9	14	76	72	4	54
Kidlington	38	14	11	13	47	52	–5	53
Shrivenham (–4)	38	16	8	14	67	59	8	52
Wantage Town	38	13	11	14	62	60	2	50
Carterton	38	13	9	16	58	61	–3	48
Fairford Town	38	12	10	16	56	61	–5	46
Bicester Town	38	10	15	13	59	64	–5	45
Highworth Town	38	10	14	14	54	55	–1	44
AFC Wallingford	38	10	8	20	37	71	–34	38
Pegasus Juniors	38	9	7	22	45	85	–40	34
Abingdon Town	38	6	12	20	42	80	–38	30
Harrow Hill	38	5	9	24	36	82	–46	24
Thame United	38	6	6	26	45	101	–56	24

POLYMAC SERVICES MIDLAND FOOTBALL ALLIANCE

	P	W	D	L	F	A	GD	Pts
Leamington	42	33	4	5	105	36	69	103
Romulus	42	25	11	6	102	47	55	86
Quorn	42	25	7	10	82	40	42	82
Stratford Town	42	25	7	10	81	47	34	82
Tipton Town	42	22	8	12	71	48	23	74
Barwell	42	22	5	15	88	68	20	71
Boldmere St Michaels	42	20	6	16	73	56	17	66
Atherstone Town	42	16	16	10	71	50	21	64
Loughborough Dynamo	42	19	7	16	73	70	3	64
Alvechurch	42	17	12	13	66	57	9	63
Oadby Town	42	19	5	18	68	59	9	62
Rocester	42	16	7	19	45	66	–21	55
Market Drayton Town	42	14	11	17	61	62	–1	53
Oldbury United (–1)	42	13	13	16	48	57	–9	51
Friar Lane & Epworth	42	12	12	18	66	86	–20	48
Westfields	42	13	9	20	57	78	–21	48
Causeway United	42	14	5	23	63	72	–9	47
Coalville Town	42	15	2	25	51	83	–32	47
Racing Club Warwick	42	10	8	24	57	88	–31	38
Studley	42	11	5	26	55	86	–31	38
Biddulph Victoria	42	10	8	24	51	84	–33	38
Cradley Town	42	4	6	32	35	129	–94	18

NORTH WEST COUNTIES LEAGUE DIVISION ONE

	P	W	D	L	F	A	GD	Pts
FC United of Manchester	42	36	4	2	157	36	121	112
Curzon Ashton	42	31	6	5	116	38	78	99
Nantwich Town	42	29	8	5	108	41	67	95
Salford City	42	26	9	7	103	55	48	87
Trafford	42	24	11	7	94	46	48	83
Maine Road	42	22	7	13	79	58	21	73
Atherton Collieries	42	19	13	10	72	55	17	70
Ramsbottom United	42	19	7	16	78	63	15	64
Glossop North End	42	19	6	17	71	71	0	63
Congleton Town	42	18	8	16	75	62	13	62
Colne	42	16	13	13	75	70	5	61
Newcastle Town	42	16	10	16	70	63	7	58
Flixton	42	15	11	16	72	67	5	56
Silsden	42	16	6	20	66	79	–13	54
Bacup Borough	42	11	13	18	50	65	–15	46
Atherton LR	42	11	9	22	65	106	–41	42
Abbey Hey	42	10	10	22	44	83	–39	40
Squires Gate	42	10	8	24	56	97	–41	38
St Helens Town	42	10	6	26	47	92	–45	36
Nelson	42	7	6	29	41	113	–72	27
Formby	42	6	4	32	43	111	–68	22
Stone Dominoes	42	2	3	37	36	147	–111	9

NORTHERN COUNTIES EAST PREMIER

	P	W	D	L	F	A	GD	Pts
Retford United	38	25	7	6	92	37	55	82
Sheffield	38	23	8	7	71	39	32	77
Carlton Town	38	23	4	11	83	41	42	73
Garforth Town	38	21	7	10	83	44	39	70
Selby Town	38	21	6	11	75	49	26	69
Glapwell	38	20	6	12	71	48	23	66
Mickleover Sports	38	18	9	11	70	62	8	63
Sutton Town (–3)	38	16	11	11	60	42	18	56
Pickering Town	38	16	8	14	61	54	7	56
Maltby Main	38	14	10	14	56	58	–2	52
Long Eaton United	38	13	12	13	57	60	–3	51
Liversedge	38	13	10	15	58	60	–2	49
Armthorpe Welfare	38	15	3	20	62	63	–1	48
Hallam	38	14	6	18	57	63	–6	48
Arnold Town	38	12	9	17	66	77	–11	45
Glasshoughton Welfare	38	12	7	19	58	66	–8	43
Eccleshill United	38	10	9	19	63	105	–42	39
Thackley (–1)	38	8	8	22	52	89	–37	31
Shirebrook Town	38	7	9	22	44	79	–35	30
Brodsworth Welfare (–1)	38	2	5	31	30	133	–103	10

RIDGEONS EASTERN COUNTIES LEAGUE PREMIER DIVISION

	P	W	D	L	F	A	GD	Pts
Wroxham	42	31	9	2	107	27	80	102
Mildenhall Town	42	31	4	7	105	56	49	97
Lowestoft Town	42	26	10	6	103	51	52	88
Needham Market	42	25	6	11	85	51	34	81
Leiston	42	24	7	11	98	71	27	79
Dereham Town	42	22	8	12	97	73	24	74
Kirkley	42	21	11	10	65	46	19	74
Soham Town Rangers	42	21	6	15	81	62	19	69
Woodbridge Town	42	17	11	14	83	80	3	62
Ipswich Wanderers	42	17	7	18	71	58	13	58
Wisbech Town	42	14	9	19	71	77	–6	51
Newmarket Town	42	14	4	24	57	82	–25	46
Felixstowe & Walton	42	14	4	24	61	99	–38	46
Stanway Rovers	42	12	9	21	56	76	–20	45
Histon Reserves	42	12	9	21	61	82	–21	45
Norwich United	42	10	14	18	44	72	–28	44
CRC	42	12	6	24	60	79	–19	42
Harwich & Parkeston	42	12	6	24	67	96	–29	42
King's Lynn Reserves	42	10	11	21	60	76	–16	41
Diss Town	42	11	6	25	58	87	–29	39
Clacton Town	42	11	5	26	60	119	–59	38
Halstead Town	42	9	10	23	53	83	–30	37

MOLTEN SPARTAN SOUTH MIDLANDS PREMIER DIVISION

	P	W	D	L	F	A	GD	Pts
Edgware Town	40	32	6	2	118	35	83	102
Harefield United	40	29	5	6	95	35	60	92
Hertford Town	40	26	8	6	122	50	72	86
Welwyn Garden City	40	22	9	9	90	53	37	75
Leverstock Green	40	20	8	12	73	66	7	68
Chalfont St Peter	40	19	10	11	79	50	29	67
Oxhey Jets	40	20	7	13	73	56	17	67
Broxbourne Borough V&E	40	17	11	12	86	64	22	62
Aylesbury Vale	40	15	8	17	71	75	–4	53
London Colney	40	13	10	17	58	72	–14	49
Tring Athletic	40	14	7	19	53	81	–28	49
Ruislip Manor	40	14	6	20	71	81	–10	48
Kingsbury London Tigers	40	14	5	21	64	69	–5	47
Biggleswade United	40	11	11	18	68	89	–21	44
St Margaretsbury	40	10	10	20	52	64	–12	40
Colney Heath	40	11	7	22	51	85	–34	40
Langford	40	11	7	22	69	107	–38	40
Biggleswade Town	40	11	6	23	47	73	–26	39
Holmer Green	40	9	9	22	49	91	–42	36
Royston Town	40	9	9	22	59	117	–58	36
Haringey Borough	40	8	11	21	59	94	–35	35

SYDENHAMS WESSEX LEAGUE PREMIER DIVISION

	P	W	D	L	F	A	GD	Pts
Gosport Borough	38	27	8	3	87	27	60	89
AFC Totton	38	27	8	3	89	31	58	89
VT FC	38	24	8	6	76	44	32	80
Poole Town	38	23	4	11	88	41	47	73
Bournemouth	38	20	10	8	69	38	31	70
Wimborne Town	38	19	10	9	82	54	28	67
Moneyfields	38	21	3	14	69	46	23	66
Fareham Town (–1)	38	18	12	8	95	57	38	65
Cowes Sports	38	17	9	12	61	50	11	60
Brading Town	38	15	7	16	74	80	–6	52
Bemerton Heath H	38	13	9	16	55	73	–18	48
Lymington Town	38	13	8	17	49	48	1	47
Brockenhurst	38	10	11	17	52	66	–14	41
Christchurch	38	9	10	19	47	63	–16	37
Hamworthy United	38	9	10	19	49	70	–21	37
Horndean	38	11	1	26	51	104	–53	34
Alton Town (–1)	38	9	7	22	59	87	–28	33
Downton	38	7	10	21	48	89	–41	31
Ringwood Town	38	5	8	25	34	85	–51	23
Hamble ASSC	38	5	3	30	24	105	–81	18

TOOLSTATION WESTERN LEAGUE PREMIER DIVISION

	P	W	D	L	F	A	GD	Pts
Corsham Town	42	29	9	4	81	30	51	96
Bridgwater Town	42	29	7	6	91	34	57	94
Frome Town	42	28	7	7	86	41	45	91
Bideford	42	23	8	11	88	48	40	77
Melksham Town	42	21	10	11	84	48	36	73
Willand Rovers	42	21	10	11	69	46	23	73
Barnstaple Town	42	21	9	12	72	71	1	72
Bitton	42	19	10	13	66	49	17	67
Hallen	42	20	7	15	72	60	12	67
Dawlish Town	42	17	8	17	73	66	7	59
Odd Down	42	17	7	18	50	53	–3	58
Bristol Manor Farm	42	14	12	16	50	51	–1	54
Calne Town	42	15	7	20	57	58	–1	52
Devizes Town	42	14	10	18	58	70	–12	52
Welton Rovers	42	12	15	15	54	47	7	51
Radstock Town	42	14	5	23	58	78	–20	47
Brislington	42	11	13	18	44	61	–17	46
Chard Town	42	9	11	22	51	78	–27	38
Street	42	9	11	22	50	83	–33	38
Torrington	42	9	6	27	46	105	–59	33
Bishop Sutton	42	9	4	29	38	89	–51	31
Keynsham Town	42	4	8	30	35	107	–72	20

ESSEX SENIOR LEAGUE

	P	W	D	L	F	A	GD	Pts
Brentwood Town	30	22	6	2	74	21	53	72
Romford	30	20	6	4	75	32	43	66
Barkingside	30	17	7	6	61	28	33	58
Bowers & Pitsea	30	16	7	7	65	33	32	55
Burnham Ramblers	30	17	4	9	59	29	30	55
Barking	30	16	7	7	65	43	22	55
Concord Rangers	30	16	6	8	67	42	25	54
Sawbridgeworth Town	30	14	6	10	60	35	25	48
Southend Manor	30	13	7	10	45	35	10	46
Basildon United	30	11	9	10	44	40	4	42
Eton Manor	30	9	7	14	52	57	–5	34
Hullbridge Sports	30	5	8	17	27	61	–34	23
London APSA	30	5	6	19	29	69	–40	21
Clapton	30	5	5	20	34	56	–22	20
Beaumont Athletic	30	4	3	23	41	132	–91	15
Stansted	30	1	4	25	20	105	–85	7

KENT LEAGUE PREMIER DIVISION

	P	W	D	L	F	A	GD	Pts
Whitstable Town	32	21	7	4	76	40	36	70
VCD Athletic	32	20	7	5	79	38	41	67
Croydon	32	20	7	5	58	34	24	67
Thamesmead Town	32	19	6	7	75	44	31	63
Greenwich Borough	32	19	6	7	63	38	25	63
Hythe Town	32	16	8	8	59	35	24	56
Erith & Belvedere	32	16	8	8	68	50	18	56
Deal Town	32	14	6	12	68	55	13	48
Herne Bay	32	12	8	12	51	41	10	44
Sevenoaks Town	32	12	6	14	50	57	–7	42
Beckenham Town	32	12	4	16	64	52	12	40
Faversham Town	32	10	6	16	36	55	–19	36
Lordswood	32	8	5	19	40	68	–28	29
Erith Town	32	7	3	22	35	60	–25	24
Tunbridge Wells	32	5	8	19	39	66	–27	23
Slade Green	32	5	8	19	36	68	–32	23
Sporting Bengal United	32	2	5	25	28	124	–96	11

NATIONAL LEAGUE SYSTEM – STEP 6

ARNGROVE NORTHERN LEAGUE DIVISION TWO

	P	W	D	L	F	A	GD	Pts
Spennymoor Town	40	29	9	2	85	33	52	96
Seaham Red Star	40	26	8	6	99	52	47	86
Washington	40	24	9	7	78	36	42	81
South Shields	40	23	7	10	89	58	31	76
Marske United	40	20	13	7	68	44	24	73
Norton & Stockton Anc	40	21	5	14	86	58	28	68
Penrith	40	18	10	12	81	52	29	64
Stokesley SC	40	18	8	14	83	70	13	62
Guisborough Town	40	17	4	19	65	71	–6	55
Hebburn Town	40	15	9	16	68	71	–3	54
Team Northumbria	40	16	5	19	57	70	–13	53
Ryton	40	12	14	14	71	60	11	50
Thornaby	40	13	9	18	60	69	–9	48
Crook Town	40	13	7	20	72	88	–16	46
Whickham	40	12	9	19	71	76	–5	45
Esh Winning	40	12	7	21	63	83	–20	43
Brandon United	40	12	7	21	64	87	–23	43
North Shields	40	13	4	23	49	72	–23	43
Sunderland Ryhope CA (–3)	40	12	4	24	50	85	–35	37
Prudhoe Town	40	8	4	28	48	104	–56	28
Alnwick Town	40	8	4	28	50	118	–68	28

BADGER ALES SUSSEX COUNTY LEAGUE DIVISION TWO

	P	W	D	L	F	A	GD	Pts
Pagham	34	22	4	8	68	35	33	70
St Francis Rangers (+2)	34	18	4	12	64	46	18	60
Westfield	34	17	8	9	59	42	17	59
Wealden	34	18	4	12	76	49	27	58
Peacehaven & Telscombe	34	17	7	10	60	61	–1	58
Seaford Town	34	16	7	11	54	46	8	55
Midhurst & Easebourne	34	15	7	12	82	65	17	52
Steyning Town	34	16	4	14	60	53	7	52
Mile Oak	34	15	5	14	59	60	–1	50
Lingfield	34	14	3	17	43	49	–6	45
East Grinstead Town	34	12	8	14	48	47	1	44
Sidlesham	34	11	10	13	56	63	–7	43
Southwick	34	10	11	13	43	56	–13	41
Lancing	34	10	8	16	40	57	–17	38
Storrington	34	11	5	18	43	63	–20	38
Crawley Down	34	10	7	17	49	57	–8	37
Broadbridge Heath (–1)	34	8	10	16	34	53	–19	33
Saltdean United	34	7	6	21	41	77	–36	27

CHERRY RED COMBINED COUNTIES DIVISION ONE

	P	W	D	L	F	A	GD	Pts
Farnham Town	40	27	8	5	84	33	51	89
Horley Town	40	27	7	6	104	31	73	88
Worcester Park	40	27	7	6	100	53	47	88
Warlingham	40	25	8	7	97	42	55	83
Staines Lammas	40	23	11	6	104	45	59	80
Hanworth Villa (-3)	40	25	7	8	101	44	57	79
South Park	40	18	7	15	75	61	14	61
Farleigh Rovers	40	15	12	13	58	56	2	57
Feltham	40	17	4	19	73	78	-5	55
Westfield	40	15	9	16	82	62	20	54
Sheerwater	40	14	12	14	88	93	-5	54
CB Hounslow United	40	14	7	19	74	79	-5	49
Frimley Green	40	14	7	19	70	76	-6	49
Coney Hall (-2)	40	14	9	17	75	82	-7	49
Chobham	40	15	3	22	82	104	-22	48
Hartley Wintney	40	13	7	20	71	92	-21	46
Crescent Rovers	40	12	5	23	66	86	-20	41
Salfords	40	10	3	27	42	108	-66	33
Tongham	40	7	9	24	67	130	-63	30
Merrow	40	7	5	28	49	116	-67	26
Coulsdon Town	40	6	3	31	63	154	-91	21

EAGLE BITTER UNITED COUNTIES LEAGUE DIVISION ONE

	P	W	D	L	F	A	GD	Pts
Whitworths	30	23	7	0	87	34	53	76
Sleaford Town (–3)	30	21	8	1	87	35	52	68
AFC Kempston Rovers	30	17	9	4	83	37	46	60
Daventry Town	30	15	8	7	75	43	32	53
Peterborough Northern Star	30	13	6	11	68	51	17	45
Higham Town	30	13	4	13	53	44	9	43
Rothwell Corinthians	30	12	7	11	52	49	3	43
Thrapston Town	30	12	7	11	60	64	–4	43
Olney Town	30	7	14	9	48	55	–7	35
Eynesbury Rovers	30	9	8	13	49	73	–24	35
Burton Park Wanderers	30	8	9	13	42	58	–16	33
Northampton Sileby R	30	9	4	17	53	69	–16	31
Bugbrooke St Michaels	30	9	2	19	41	82	–41	29
Huntingdon Town (–1)	30	7	8	15	49	70	–21	28
Northampton ON Cheneks	30	5	7	18	49	80	–31	22
Irchester United	30	2	8	20	34	86	–52	14

SPORT ITALIA HELLENIC LEAGUE DIVISION ONE EAST

	P	W	D	L	F	A	GD	Pts
Bisley Sports	34	27	5	2	121	22	99	86
Chalfont Wasps	34	25	2	7	96	37	59	77
Badshot Lea	34	24	4	6	98	37	61	76
Kintbury Rangers	34	24	3	7	92	38	54	75
Rayners Lane	34	19	8	7	86	46	40	65
Englefield Green Rovers	34	16	6	12	53	52	1	54
Marlow United	34	15	6	13	65	52	13	51
Wokingham & Emmbrook	34	15	4	15	49	73	–24	49
Holyport	34	15	3	16	65	64	1	48
Headington Amateurs	34	11	9	14	57	62	–5	42
Binfield	34	12	5	17	52	57	–5	41
Oxford Quarry Nomads	34	13	2	19	64	79	–15	41
Penn & Tylers Green	34	11	7	16	65	73	–8	40
Finchampstead	34	11	7	16	51	65	–14	40
Chinnor	34	9	9	16	45	58	–13	36
Henley Town	34	9	4	21	43	80	–37	31
Prestwood	34	5	3	26	25	87	–62	18
Eton Wick	34	1	1	32	23	168	–145	4

SPORT ITALIA HELLENIC LEAGUE DIVISION ONE WEST

	P	W	D	L	F	A	GD	Pts
Lydney Town	34	24	6	4	72	29	43	78
Trowbridge Town	34	21	7	6	76	31	45	70
Hook Norton	34	20	6	8	62	42	20	66
Malmesbury Victoria	34	16	11	7	62	38	24	59
Tytherington Rocks	34	15	10	9	71	48	23	55
Cheltenham Saracens	34	14	10	10	57	45	12	52
Old Woodstock Town	34	12	13	9	58	54	4	49
Cricklade Town	34	15	4	15	51	56	–5	49
Pewsey Vale	34	12	12	10	47	46	1	48
Winterbourne United	34	12	11	11	64	59	5	47
Wootton Bassett Town	34	14	5	15	64	62	2	47
Cirencester United	34	13	8	13	56	58	–2	47
Easington Sports	34	12	9	13	72	74	–2	45
Banbury United Res	34	11	6	17	55	62	–7	39
Letcombe	34	11	6	17	54	63	–9	39
Purton	34	6	10	18	50	79	–29	28
Clanfield	34	4	7	23	32	70	–38	19
Ross Town	34	1	5	28	36	123	–87	8

MIDLAND COMBINATION PREMIER DIVISION

	P	W	D	L	F	A	GD	Pts
Coventry Sphinx	40	29	7	4	110	40	70	94
Castle Vale	40	26	7	7	103	47	56	85
Highgate United (–3)	40	25	9	6	90	38	52	81
Coleshill Town	40	23	7	10	85	43	42	76
Pilkington XXX	40	21	11	8	65	53	12	74
Southam United	40	19	7	14	64	37	–3	64
Bolehall Swifts	40	16	12	12	81	67	14	60
Heath Hayes (–3)	40	17	8	15	74	70	4	56
Barnt Green Spartak (–3)	40	16	9	15	72	57	15	54
Meir KA	40	15	9	16	65	62	3	54
Nuneaton Griff	40	15	8	17	85	71	14	53
Walsall Wood	40	14	11	15	50	60	–10	53
Massey Ferguson	40	14	6	20	56	65	–9	48
Pershore Town	40	14	6	20	66	86	–20	48
Brocton	40	12	9	19	51	70	–19	45
Brereton Social	40	11	9	20	49	80	–31	42
Cadbury Athletic	40	11	9	20	48	85	–37	42
Feckenham	40	9	10	21	50	75	–25	37
Continental Star (–1)	40	10	7	23	59	89	–30	36
Coventry Copsewood	40	8	11	21	39	78	–39	35
Alveston	40	4	10	26	37	96	–59	22

NORTH WEST COUNTIES LEAGUE DIVISION TWO

	P	W	D	L	F	A	GD	Pts
Winsford United	34	23	7	4	82	35	47	76
Runcorn Linnets	34	24	4	6	77	35	42	76
Padiham	34	21	6	7	75	39	36	69
New Mills	34	21	6	7	74	42	32	69
Chadderton	34	18	7	9	59	35	24	61
Oldham Town	34	17	5	12	69	54	15	56
Darwen	34	14	10	10	56	45	11	52
Ashton Town	34	15	7	12	55	56	–1	52
Leek CSOB	34	14	8	12	51	51	0	50
Bootle (–4)	34	14	8	12	63	48	15	46
Eccleshall	34	12	6	16	44	46	–2	42
Cheadle Town	34	9	8	17	41	60	–19	35
Blackpool Mechanics (–6)	34	10	6	18	39	48	–9	30
Holker Old Boys	34	6	11	17	47	81	–34	29
Daisy Hill	34	7	8	19	38	78	–40	29
Ashton Athletic	34	6	10	18	38	62	–24	28
Norton United	34	6	7	21	37	73	–36	25
Castleton Gabriels	34	5	4	25	38	95	–57	19

NORTHERN COUNTIES EAST LEAGUE DIVISION ONE

	P	W	D	L	F	A	GD	Pts
Parkgate	32	26	4	2	120	38	82	82
Winterton Rangers	32	23	2	7	90	38	52	71
South Normanton Ath	32	20	5	7	76	34	42	65
Nostell Miners Welfare (–3)	32	20	0	12	66	41	25	57
Lincoln Moorlands	32	17	5	10	63	42	21	56
Staveley MW	32	16	3	13	57	50	7	51
Tadcaster Albion	32	14	7	11	60	54	6	49
Worsborough Bridge	32	13	9	10	53	42	11	48
Dinnington Town	32	12	7	13	52	46	6	43
Hall Road Rangers	32	12	7	13	48	51	–3	43
Borrowash Victoria	32	10	7	15	38	52	–14	37
Pontefract Collieries	32	10	7	15	35	61	–26	37
AFC Emley	32	10	4	18	48	70	–22	34
Gedling Town	32	9	4	19	45	63	–18	31
Teversal	32	9	4	19	35	69	–34	31
Yorkshire Amateur	32	7	1	24	33	106	–73	22
Rossington Main	32	4	4	24	27	89	–62	16

RIDGEONS EASTERN COUNTIES LEAGUE DIVISION ONE

	P	W	D	L	F	A	GD	Pts
Walsham le Willows	36	25	5	6	68	26	42	80
Haverhill Rovers	36	22	11	3	86	27	59	77
Swaffham Town	36	23	8	5	80	34	46	77
Ely City	36	23	7	6	90	36	54	76
Debenham LC	36	20	10	6	89	50	39	70
Saffron Walden Town	36	20	10	6	59	32	27	70
Tiptree United	36	20	9	7	97	52	45	69
Whitton United	36	20	7	9	76	45	31	67
Hadleigh United	36	15	9	12	46	47	–1	54
Fakenham Town	36	14	8	14	58	54	4	50
Thetford Town	36	12	4	20	40	57	–17	40
Stowmarket Town	36	11	7	18	52	72	–20	40
Great Yarmouth Town	36	11	5	20	40	67	–27	38
Gorleston	36	10	4	22	53	96	–43	34
Cornard United	36	8	6	22	42	80	–38	30
Long Melford	36	7	5	24	51	101	–50	26
Godmanchester Rovers	36	6	4	26	29	85	–56	22
Downham Town	36	4	8	24	33	85	–52	20
March Town United	36	4	7	25	35	78	–43	19

MOLTEN SPARTAN SOUTH MIDLANDS DIVISION ONE

	P	W	D	L	F	A	GD	Pts
Brimsdown Rovers	30	25	4	1	109	15	94	79
Cockfosters	30	22	2	6	62	25	37	68
Stony Stratford Town	30	22	2	6	67	33	34	68
Ampthill Town	30	21	4	5	76	33	43	67
Hoddesdon Town	30	16	4	10	55	38	17	52
Kentish Town	30	15	6	9	65	45	20	51
Brache Sparta	30	14	5	11	61	49	12	47
Buckingham Athletic	30	11	6	13	60	57	3	39
Amersham Town	30	10	3	17	49	61	–12	33
Bedford Valerio United	30	9	5	16	53	86	–33	32
Arlesey Athletic	30	9	4	17	50	82	–32	31
Harpenden Town	30	9	3	18	44	57	–13	30
Sun Postal Sports	30	9	3	18	51	74	–23	30
New Bradwell St Peter	30	9	2	19	44	76	–32	29
Winslow United	30	5	7	18	40	76	–36	22
Cranfield United	30	3	2	25	24	103	–79	11

SYDENHAMS WESSEX LEAGUE DIVISION ONE

	P	W	D	L	F	A	GD	Pts
Hayling United	36	27	4	5	116	32	84	85
Alresford Town	36	23	8	5	53	28	25	77
Romsey Town	36	22	6	8	68	36	32	72
Locks Heath	36	21	7	8	78	40	38	70
Fawley	36	18	7	11	78	57	21	61
Verwood Town	36	17	9	10	73	46	27	60
Stockbridge	36	17	8	11	64	54	10	59
Warminster Town	36	16	9	11	63	48	15	57
Shaftesbury	36	15	9	12	58	47	11	54
United Services Portsmouth	36	12	10	14	76	68	8	46
Farnborough North End	36	11	13	12	40	56	–16	46
Laverstock & Ford	36	12	9	15	55	65	–10	45
Liss Athletic (–1)	36	11	10	15	59	73	–14	42
Hythe & Dibden	36	9	9	18	54	81	–27	36
East Cowes Vics	36	10	6	20	49	101	–52	36
Blackfield & Langley	36	9	5	22	66	104	–38	32
Petersfield Town	36	7	6	23	50	98	–48	27
Amesbury Town	36	5	10	21	57	78	–21	25
Andover New Street	36	5	5	26	37	82	–45	20

TOOLSTATION WESTERN LEAGUE DIVISION ONE

	P	W	D	L	F	A	GD	Pts
Truro City	42	37	4	1	185	23	162	115
Portishead	42	29	6	7	88	33	55	93
Ilfracombe Town	42	29	5	8	98	51	47	92
Sherborne Town	42	25	8	9	87	44	43	83
Larkhall Athletic	42	24	8	10	88	41	47	80
Westbury United	42	19	10	13	71	57	14	67
Wellington	42	18	9	15	63	60	3	63
Longwell Green Sports	42	17	11	14	51	44	7	62
Cadbury Heath	42	17	9	16	78	69	9	60
Hengrove Athletic	42	17	7	18	58	64	–6	58
Bridport	42	17	6	19	84	81	3	57
Shrewton United	42	15	11	16	65	71	–6	56
Biddestone	42	15	9	18	69	73	–4	54
Clevedon United	42	14	12	16	54	69	–15	54
Almondsbury	42	11	11	20	47	73	–26	44
Elmore	42	10	14	18	62	94	–32	44
Bradford Town	42	12	4	26	42	86	–44	40
Backwell United	42	10	8	24	48	105	–57	38
Weston St Johns	42	8	10	24	47	93	–46	34
Shepton Mallet	42	8	10	24	34	83	–49	34
Clyst Rovers	42	8	9	25	61	108	–47	33
Minehead	42	7	9	26	42	100	–58	30

WEST MIDLANDS LEAGUE PREMIER DIVISION

	P	W	D	L	F	A	GD	Pts
Shifnal Town	40	27	7	6	100	27	73	88
Tividale	40	22	12	6	84	49	35	78
Bewdley Town	40	20	15	5	92	55	37	75
Gornal Athletic	40	20	10	10	61	47	14	70
Dudley Town	40	20	7	13	67	46	21	67
Goodrich	40	21	4	15	83	69	14	67
Bridgnorth Town (–3)	40	20	9	11	83	49	34	66
Lye Town	40	19	9	12	83	57	26	66
Pelsall Villa	40	15	12	13	70	69	1	57
Wellington	40	15	10	15	66	73	–7	55
Dudley Sports	40	14	9	17	56	58	–2	51
Ellesmere Rangers	40	15	5	20	57	68	–11	50
Wednesfield	40	13	9	18	46	76	–30	48
Wyrley Rangers	40	12	10	18	50	68	–18	46
Brierley & Hagley	40	12	7	21	55	80	–25	43
Ledbury Town	40	12	5	23	51	97	–46	41
Wolverhampton Casuals	40	9	13	18	53	72	–19	40
Bromyard Town	40	11	7	22	56	83	–27	40
Ludlow Town	40	11	7	22	49	78	–29	40
Bustleholme	40	10	9	21	55	69	–14	39
Shawbury United	40	10	8	22	55	82	–27	38

SCOTTISH

SCOTS-ADS HIGHLAND FOOTBALL LEAGUE

	P	W	D	L	F	A	GD	Pts
Keith	28	20	4	4	67	26	41	64
Inverurie Locos	28	20	4	4	62	33	29	64
Buckie Thistle	28	16	8	4	54	28	26	56
Deveronvale	28	17	4	7	77	35	42	55
Huntly	28	17	4	7	67	39	28	55
Cove Rangers	28	13	6	9	52	36	16	45
Nairn County	28	13	4	11	57	42	15	43
Fraserburgh	28	11	8	9	48	42	6	41
Clachnacuddin	28	9	6	13	43	42	1	33
Rothes	28	10	2	16	42	57	–15	32
Wick Academy	28	10	2	16	44	61	–17	32
Forres Mechanics	28	7	7	14	54	60	–6	28
Brora	28	8	2	18	38	84	–46	26
Lossiemouth	28	3	5	20	25	64	–39	14
Fort William	28	3	0	25	26	107	–81	9

AMATEUR FOOTBALL ALLIANCE 2006–07

AFA SENIOR CUP

Sponsored by Alan Day Volkswagen

1st ROUND PROPER
Latymer Old Boys 4 Old Edmontonians 5
Wood Green Old Boys 3 Broomfield 4
Clapham Old Xaverians 1 Crouch End Vampires 2
Old Brentwoods 0 Old Actonians Association 2
Carshalton 4 Hampstead Heathens 2
Mill Hill Village 0 UCL Academicals 2
Old Suttonians 0 Civil Service 2
Bromleians Sports 1 Wake Green 0
Old Wilsonians 1 Alleyn Old Boys 2
Lloyds TSB Bank 2 Kew Association 5
Southgate County 0 Bealonians 3
William Fitt 5*:3p South Bank Cuaco 5*:4p
Weirside Rangers 3 London Welsh 0
Cardinal Manning OB 2 Old Manorians 0
Merton 4 Old Cholmeleians 3
National Westminster Bank 0 Old Ignatians 4
Old Vaughanians 8 Old Malvernians 1
Alexandra Park 5 Old Esthameians 4
Old Reptonians 0 Old Hamptonians 6
Old Aloysians 1 Ibis 2
Old Owens 5 Old Latymerians 2
Polytechnic 7 Old Tenisonians 2
Winchmore Hill 7 Old Camdenians 0
Old Danes 2 Old Buckwellians 0
Norsemen 0 Hon Artillery Company 1
HSBC 9 Old Bradfieldians 0
Old Carthusians 1*:3p Old Guildfordians 1*:2p
E Barnet Old Grammarians 3 West Wickham 9
Nottsborough 3 Old Meadonians 1
Old Salopians 4 Old Stationers 1
Old Westminster Citizens 1 Old Salesians 3
Sinjuns Grammarians 3 Hale End Athletic 0

2nd ROUND PROPER
Old Salesians 1 Carshalton 2
Civil Service 3 Old Ignatians 1
Polytechnic 3 Broomfield 0
Old Edmontonians 3 Old Vaughanians 1
Old Hamptonians 3 South Bank Cuaco 2
Crouch End Vampires 0 Old Owens 3
Merton 4 Old Salopians 3
Old Carthusians 2 HSBC 0
Hon Artillery Company 6 Old Danes 1
Weirside Rangers 0 Bealonians 2
Cardinal Manning OB 3 Ibis 2
Alexandra Park 1 UCL Academicals 3
West Wickham 1 Bromleians Sports 0
Old Actonians Association 1 Winchmore Hill 2
Kew Association 3 Sinjuns Grammarians 4
Alleyn Old Boys 2 Nottsborough 4

3rd ROUND PROPER
Carshalton 1 Civil Service 2
Polytechnic 6 Old Edmontonians 0
Old Hamptonians 3 Old Owens 2
Merton 2 Old Carthusians 4
Honourable Artillery Company 4 Bealonians 1
Cardinal Manning Old Boys 0 UCL Academicals 1
West Wickham 1 Winchmore Hill 0
Sinjuns Grammarians 1 Nottsborough 4

4th ROUND PROPER
West Wickham 2 Civil Service 1
Old Carthusians 0 Old Hamptonians 1
UCL Academicals 0 Nottsborough 1
Polytechnic 1*:3p Honourable Artillery Company 1*:4p

SEMI-FINALS
West Wickham 2* Nottsborough 0*
Old Hamptonians 2 Honourable Artillery Company 1

FINAL
West Wickham 4 Old Hamptonians 0
**After extra time*

OTHER CUP FINALS

MIDDLESEX / ESSEX SENIOR
Broomfield 0 Old Meadonians 5

SURREY / KENT SENIOR
Clapham Old Xaverians 2* Old Salesians 0*

INTERMEDIATE
Civil Service Res 0 Mill Hill Village 1st 4

JUNIOR
Civil Service 3rd 1*:4p Winchmore Hill 3rd 1*:3p

MINOR
Old Actonians 4th 5 Old Haileyburians 1st 4

VETERANS
William Fitt "A" 1 Sinjuns Grammarians 2

OPEN VETERANS
Port of London Authority 2 Chelsea Diamonds 1

MIDDLESEX / ESSEX INTERMEDIATE
Old Actonians Ass'n Res 1 Old Meadonians Res 3

SURREY / KENT INTERMEDIATE
Dresdner Kleinwort Wasserstein 3 Marsh 1

GREENLAND
Old Owens 3 UCL Academicals 0

SENIOR NOVETS
Civil Service 5th 1 Nat'l Westminster Bank 2

INTERMEDIATE NOVETS
Old Actonians 6th 3 Old Meadonians 6th 1

JUNIOR NOVETS
Old Actonians 7th 3 Old Meadonians 8th 0

WOMEN'S CUP
East Barnet Old Grammarians 3 Flamingoes 0

SATURDAY YOUTH
U-18
Provident House 0 Field Crusaders 4
U-17
AFC Wandsworth 1 Enfield Community 2
U-16
Young Parmiterians 2* Kodak 3*
U-15
Lea Valley United 3 Whitewebbs Eagles 1
U-14
Cheshunt 3 Bethwin SE 0
U-13
Kodak 0 Ilford Colts 4
U-12
Whitewebbs Eagles 4 Bealonians 0
U-11
Whitewebbs Eagles 3 Broomfield PL 0
U-12 GIRLS
Lea Valley 8 Flamingoes 0

SUNDAY YOUTH
U-18
Field Crusaders 6 Potters Bar United 0
U-17
Broomfield 3 Cheshunt 1
U-16
Winchmore Hill 1 Minchenden 4
U-15
Waltham Abbey 2 West Essex Colts 0
U-14
Waltham Abbey 8 Chase Side 4
U-13 (Tesco)
Southgate Adelaide 0 Ilford Colts 5
U-12
Chase Side 3 Norsemen 4
U-11
Chase Side 3 Norsemen 2
U-16 GIRLS
William Fitt U-15 1*:0p Waltham Abbey 1*:3p
U-14 GIRLS
Valley Park Rangers 4 Flamingoes 1

ARTHUR DUNN CUP FINAL

Old Bradfieldians 0 Old Harrovians 1

ARTHURIAN LEAGUE

PREMIER DIVISION	P	W	D	L	F	A	Pts
Old Brentwoods	16	11	3	2	46	18	36
Old Carthusians	16	9	6	1	40	19	33
Lancing Old Boys	16	8	4	4	36	26	28
Old Foresters	16	8	3	5	32	27	27
Old Harrovians	16	6	5	5	34	34	23
Old Etonians	16	5	4	7	38	36	19
Old Westminsters	16	5	2	9	33	51	17
Old Cholmeleians	16	4	1	11	20	36	13
Old Salopians	16	2	0	14	26	58	6

DIVISION 1	P	W	D	L	F	A	Pts
Old Bradfieldians	16	12	2	2	45	21	38
Old Tonbridgians	16	11	0	5	50	30	33
Old Aldenhamians	16	7	3	6	38	38	24
Old Wykehamists	16	7	2	7	40	39	23
Old Malvernians	16	6	3	7	39	34	21
Old Radleians	16	6	3	7	31	29	21
Old Haileyburians	16	5	3	8	29	43	18
King's Wimbledon Old Boys	16	5	2	9	27	43	17
Old Chigwellians	16	3	2	11	21	43	11

DIVISION 2	P	W	D	L	F	A	Pts
Old Chigwellians Res	16	13	1	2	42	15	40
Old Foresters Res*	16	9	1	6	44	35	25
Old Carthusians Res	16	8	0	8	47	40	24
Old Haberdashers	16	7	2	7	44	37	23
Old Etonians Res	16	6	4	6	30	32	22
Old Brentwoods Res	16	6	3	7	25	38	21
Old Westminsters Res*	16	7	2	7	31	32	17
Old Salopians Res*	16	4	3	9	27	42	12
Old Etonians 3rd	16	3	2	11	28	47	11

DIVISION 3	P	W	D	L	F	A	Pts
Old Aldenhamians Res	12	10	3	1	34	23	33
Old King's Scholars	12	6	3	5	34	26	21
Old Oundelians	12	5	3	6	29	28	18
Old Bradfieldians Res	12	5	3	6	27	29	18
Old Wellingtonians	12	5	2	7	29	36	17
Old Chigwellians 3rd*	12	5	4	5	22	23	16
Old Carthusians 3rd	12	4	3	7	24	28	15
Old Cholmeleians Res*	12	5	1	8	31	37	13

DIVISION 4	P	W	D	L	F	A	Pts
Old Foresters 3rd	14	10	2	2	33	18	32
Old Harrovians Res	14	8	3	3	37	23	27
Old Westminsters 3rd*	14	8	1	5	33	24	22
Old Malvernians Res	14	6	2	6	26	18	20
Old Brentwoods 4th	14	6	1	7	24	24	19
Lancing Old Boys Res	14	4	3	7	17	22	15
Old Brentwoods 3rd	14	4	2	8	18	37	14
Old Eastbournians*	14	2	2	10	19	41	5

DIVISION 5	P	W	D	L	F	A	Pts
Old Foresters 4th	14	9	2	3	29	16	29
Old Berkhamstedians	14	9	1	4	36	18	28
Old Wykehamists Res*	14	10	0	4	37	26	24
Old Cholmeleians 3rd	14	6	1	7	43	31	19
Old Chigwellians 4th*	14	7	0	7	32	23	18
Old Harrovians 3rd*	14	6	2	6	30	35	17
Old Amplefordians	14	3	1	10	15	50	10
Old Cholmeleians 4th*	14	2	1	11	24	47	4

** Points deducted – breach of rules*

JUNIOR LEAGUE CUP

Old Cholmeleians Res 2 Old King's Scholars 5

DERRICK MOORE VETERANS CUP

Old Cholmeleians 2 Old Chigwellians 0

LONDON LEGAL LEAGUE

DIVISION I	P	W	D	L	F	A	Pts
Linklaters	18	12	1	5	41	21	37
Dechert	18	11	2	5	47	24	35
Nabarro Nathanson	18	10	2	6	46	28	32
Watson Farley & Williams	18	9	3	6	38	33	30
Stephenson Harwood	18	8	4	6	47	40	28
Financial Services Assn	18	8	3	7	41	24	27
Slaughter & May	18	8	3	7	26	27	27
Simmons & Simmons	18	5	3	10	36	54	18
Reed Smith Richards Butler	18	4	2	11	24	49	14
Macfarlanes*	18	2	2	14	29	75	7

DIVISION II	P	W	D	L	F	A	Pts
Clifford Chance	18	11	6	1	47	23	39
Ashurst Morris Crisp	18	11	4	3	63	26	37
Barlow Lyde & Gilbert	18	12	1	5	59	46	37
Lovells	18	10	5	3	46	31	35
Pegasus (Inner Temple)	18	5	6	7	23	37	21
Allen & Overy*	18	6	3	9	34	40	20
Baker & McKenzie	18	6	2	10	28	47	20
Gray's Inn	18	5	1	12	30	57	16
Herbert Smith	18	4	2	12	34	44	14
KPMG London	18	4	2	12	29	42	14

DIVISION III	P	W	D	L	F	A	Pts
Freshfields Bruckhaus D	20	17	0	3	81	26	51
Norton Rose	20	14	3	3	57	32	45
CMS Cameron McKenna	20	14	2	4	33	24	44
BBC Post Production	20	12	3	5	52	35	39
S J Berwin*	20	10	1	9	61	42	29
Denton Wilde Sapte	20	7	3	10	41	47	24
Withers	18	7	1	10	19	37	22
Olswang	19	6	2	11	28	40	20
Taylor Wessing	19	5	3	11	35	52	18
Kirkpatrick & Lockhart N G*	20	5	1	14	37	55	13
Field Fisher Waterhouse*	20	1	1	18	17	71	1

** Points deducted – breach of rules*
Following a serious injury the remaining two Withers games were left unplayed

LEAGUE CHALLENGE CUP

Linklaters 1 Slaughter & May 0

WEAVERS ARMS CUP

Ashurst 0 Freshfields 1†

INVITATION CUP

BBC Post Production 2 Herbert Smith 0

† *After extra time*

LONDON FOOTBALL LEAGUE

PREMIER DIVISION	P	W	D	L	F	A	Pts
Abbey	18	15	0	3	75	24	45
Alba	18	12	0	6	68	43	36
Invisible	18	11	2	5	50	28	35
IDS	18	9	2	7	44	38	29
UBS Wealth Management	18	8	5	5	22	30	29
MTV	18	6	3	9	34	38	21
Warrington	18	6	1	11	27	57	19
BNP Paribas	18	4	4	10	21	48	16
Eastern Promise	18	4	3	11	22	31	15
Accenture	18	4	2	12	29	55	14

DIVISION ONE	P	W	D	L	F	A	Pts
Athletico Chips	16	10	3	3	48	28	33
Thorp Design	16	9	5	2	39	21	32
DMD UK	16	8	1	7	36	31	25
TNT Magazine	16	7	2	7	35	31	23
BBC Post Production	16	7	2	7	36	37	23
CBS Outdoor	16	6	1	9	42	40	19
Philosophy Football	16	6	1	9	30	39	19
Davis Langdon	16	5	2	9	18	33	17
London Reaction	16	5	1	10	23	47	16

DIVISION TWO	P	W	D	L	F	A	Pts
Time Out	15	14	0	1	74	21	42
Bloomberg	15	9	2	4	44	22	29
Diesel	15	7	2	6	37	38	23
Visa International	15	5	3	7	26	39	18
Lazard	15	3	1	11	22	49	10
Boodle Hatfield	15	2	2	11	15	49	8

SPRING CUP

Rothschild 6 Alba 1

SPRING PLATE

Athletico Chips 3 Thorp Design 2

LONDON OLD BOYS' CUPS

SENIOR

Old Minchendenians 2 Old Meadonians 1

CHALLENGE

Centymca 3 Old Wokingians 1

INTERMEDIATE

Enfield Old Grammns Res 1 Egbertians Res 3

JUNIOR

Old Parmiterians 3rd 3 Mill Hill County OB Res 4

MINOR
Old Meadonians 7th 2 Clapham O Xaverians 4th 1

DRUMMOND (NORTH)
Mill Hill County OB 4th 1 Albanian 5th 2

NEMEAN (WEST)
Old Manorians 5th 0*:3p Phoenix Res 0*:4p

OLYMPIAN (SOUTH)
Old Tenisonians 4th 5 Economicals 4th 2

JACK PERRY VETERANS
Old Aloysians 2*:3p Wandsworth Borough 2:*5p
** After extra time*

OLD BOYS' INVITATION CUPS

SENIOR
Old Esthameians 1 Old Bealonians 0

JUNIOR
Old Owens Res 5 Old Suttonians Res 4

MINOR
Old Salesians 3rd 4 Old Stationers 3rd 1

4TH XIs
Alleyn Old Boys 4th 1 Old Owens 4th 3

5TH XIs
Old Parmiterians 5th 2 Alleyn Old Boys 5th 1

6TH XIs
Old Parmiterians 6th 4 Old Owens 6th 6

7TH XIs
Old Finchleians 7th 1 Old Parmiterians 7th 3

VETERANS
Old Bromleians 3 Bealonians 4

MIDLAND AMATEUR ALLIANCE

PREMIER DIVISION	P	W	D	L	F	A	Pts
Woodborough United	24	20	1	3	86	40	61
Ashland Rovers	24	19	2	3	74	26	59
Old Elizabethans	24	17	2	5	93	32	53
FC 05	24	13	5	6	73	36	44
Underwood Villa	24	14	1	9	63	46	43
Steelers	24	10	4	10	65	57	34
Monty Hind Old Boys	24	9	5	10	47	43	32
Wollaton 3rd	24	7	7	10	57	71	28
County NALGO	24	7	4	13	48	56	25
Brunts Old Boys	24	6	4	14	42	73	22
Beeston Old Boys Assn	24	4	5	15	29	60	17
Lady Bay	24	5	1	18	33	104	16
Bassingfield	24	4	1	19	31	97	13

DIVISION 1	P	W	D	L	Pts
Heanor Colliers*	28	24	3	1	74
Pinxton Sun Inn	28	20	2	6	62
Southwell Amateurs	28	17	3	8	54
Wollaton 4th	28	17	1	10	52
Nottinghamshire Res	28	14	4	10	46
Top Club*	28	13	7	8	45
Keyworth United 3rd*	28	13	7	8	44
Radcliffe Olympic 3rd	28	11	7	10	40
PASE*	28	11	6	11	35
Sherwood Forest*	28	9	5	14	31
Old Elizabethans Res*	28	8	5	15	28
Acorn Athletic	28	8	4	16	28
Derbyshire Amateurs Res	28	6	4	18	22
Old Bemrosians	28	5	5	18	20
Clinphone	28	2	1	25	7

**Points deducted – breach of rules*

DIVISION 2	P	W	D	L	Pts
Calverton Miners Wel 3rd	30	26	0	4	78
West Bridgford United	30	23	5	2	74
Ashland Rovers Res	30	17	7	6	58
TVFC	30	18	4	8	58
Bassingfield Res	30	15	6	9	51
Hickling	30	16	2	12	50
EMTEC	30	14	4	12	46
Cambridge Knights	30	14	4	12	46
Broadmeadows	30	14	2	14	44
Nottinghamshire 3rd	30	12	5	13	41
Tibshelf Old Boys	30	11	2	17	35
Beeston Res	30	9	6	15	33
Town Mill	30	7	4	19	25
Derbyshire Amateurs 3rd	30	6	5	19	23
Old Bemrosians Res	30	3	5	22	14
Ashfield Athletic	29	2	5	23	11

LEAGUE SENIOR CUP
Woodborough 1 Underwood Villa 0

LEAGUE INTERMEDIATE CUP
Heanor Colliers 1 Radcliffe Olympic 3rd 0

LEAGUE MINOR CUP
Calverton Miners Welfare 3rd 2 TVFC 0

SOUTHERN AMATEUR LEAGUE

SENIOR SECTION

DIVISION 1	P	W	D	L	F	A	Pts
Nottsborough	20	16	2	2	65	24	50
Old Wilsonians	20	14	1	5	45	17	43
West Wickham	20	12	5	3	41	17	41
Old Owens	20	12	2	6	53	28	38
Winchmore Hill	20	12	2	6	44	26	38
Broomfield	20	9	1	10	38	40	28
Civil Service	20	7	1	12	34	43	22
Old Salesians	20	6	4	10	30	42	22
Alleyn Old Boys	20	6	4	10	29	42	22
Old Lyonians	20	2	1	17	13	70	7
East Barnet Old Gramm	20	1	3	16	20	63	6

DIVISION 2	P	W	D	L	F	A	Pts
Polytechnic	20	14	3	3	60	22	45
Old Actonians Association	20	12	3	5	52	34	39
Carshalton	20	11	4	5	42	29	37
Weirside Rangers	20	11	3	6	45	39	36
HSBC	20	10	4	6	50	41	34
Old Esthameians	20	10	0	10	38	41	30
Norsemen	20	8	3	9	32	31	27
Merton	20	6	3	11	33	44	21
BB Eagles	20	4	5	11	39	52	17
Bank of England	20	4	5	11	29	45	17
Ibis	20	2	3	15	35	77	9

DIVISION 3	P	W	D	L	F	A	Pts
South Bank Cuaco	20	15	2	3	64	34	47
Kew Association	20	13	4	3	61	38	43
Old Westminster Citizens	20	12	4	4	56	34	40
Crouch End Vampires	20	9	7	4	46	25	34
Old Parkonians	20	9	5	6	42	34	32
Old Finchleians	20	9	3	8	55	34	30
Old Latymerians	20	9	1	10	38	46	28
Southgate Olympic	20	4	6	10	41	57	18
Old Stationers	20	5	3	12	34	57	18
Lloyds TSB Bank	20	3	2	15	31	76	11
Alexandra Park	20	2	3	15	30	63	9

INTERMEDIATE SECTION
Division 1 – 11 teams – Won by West Wickham Res
Division 2 – 11 teams – Won by Carshalton Res
Division 3 – 11 teams – Won by Crouch End Vampires Res

JUNIOR SECTION
Division 1 – 11 teams – Won by Nottsborough 3rd
Division 2 – 11 teams – Won by Alleyn Old Boys 3rd
Division 3 – 11 teams – Won by Kew Association 3rd

MINOR SECTION
Division 1 – 11 teams – Won by Civil Service 5th
Division 2 North – 10 teams – Won by Crouch End Vampires 5th
Division 2 South – 11 teams – Won by Old Actonians Association 5th
Division 3 North – 10 teams – Won by Old Parkonians 4th
Division 3 South – 10 teams – Won by HSBC 5th
Division 4 North – 11 teams – Won by Winchmore Hill 7th
Division 4 South – 11 teams – Won by Weirside Rangers 4th
Division 5 North – 10 teams – Won by Winchmore Hill 9th
Division 5 South – 11 teams – Won by Old Lyonians 4th
Division 6 South – 11 teams – Won by Old Westminster Citizens 6th
Division 7 South – 12 teams – Won by Civil Service 8th

CHALLENGE CUPS

Junior
Winchmore Hill 3rd 2 O Actonians Ass'n 3rd 1

Minor
South Bank Cuaco 4th 0*:3p Old Owens 4th 0*:2p

Senior Novets
Old Finchleians 5th 0 Civil Service 5th 4

Intermediate Novets
Civil Service 6th 3 Alexandra Park 6th 1
Junior Novets
HSBC 7th 1 Norsemen 7th 0
** After extra time*

U-16 GIRLS CENTRE OF EXCELLENCE LEAGUE

	P	W	D	L	F	A	Pts
Chelsea	20	15	4	1	59	19	49
Charlton Athletic	20	13	5	2	49	19	44
Reading	20	12	5	3	49	22	41
Arsenal	20	11	7	2	28	11	40
Fulham	20	9	4	7	36	39	31
Leyton Orient	20	7	5	8	30	33	26
Hampshire FA	20	6	3	11	37	47	21
Colchester United	20	5	6	9	19	33	21
Millwall	20	5	1	14	36	46	16
Brighton & Hove Albion	20	2	4	14	22	64	10
Watford	20	3	0	17	11	43	9

AMATEUR FOOTBALL COMBINATION

PREMIER DIVISION	P	W	D	L	F	A	Pts
Old Meadonians	18	15	2	1	67	21	47
Old Bealonians	18	10	5	3	45	23	35
Old Parmiterians	18	10	2	6	35	39	32
Old Hamptonians	18	9	2	7	47	27	29
Old Aloysians	18	9	2	7	43	38	29
Honourable Artillery Company	18	7	6	5	30	26	27
UCL Academicals	18	7	1	10	31	37	22
Albanian	18	6	2	10	28	43	20
Southgate County	18	3	2	13	30	57	11
Parkfield	18	2	0	16	23	68	6

SENIOR DIVISION 1	P	W	D	L	F	A	Pts
Enfield Old Grammarians	20	13	1	6	48	23	40
Hale End Athletic	20	12	4	4	52	36	40
Old Ignatians	20	12	3	5	50	24	39
Old Salvatorians	20	11	3	6	53	33	36
Sinjuns Grammarians*	20	10	2	8	43	37	31
Old Challoners	20	10	1	9	46	43	31
Glyn Old Boys	20	10	1	9	35	40	31
Economicals	20	8	3	9	29	34	27
Old Tiffinians	20	7	2	11	31	49	23
Old Danes	20	4	1	15	20	61	13
Wood Green Old Boys	20	1	3	16	37	64	6

SENIOR DIVISION 2	P	W	D	L	F	A	Pts
Old Meadonians Res	20	14	4	2	60	18	46
Old Suttonians	20	13	6	1	64	18	45
Clapham Old Xaverians	20	13	4	3	53	31	43
Old Paulines	20	10	4	6	57	43	34
Old Vaughanians	20	10	1	9	47	46	31
Shene Old Grammarians	20	8	3	9	70	52	27
King's Old Boys	20	8	2	10	54	48	26
Old Aloysians Res	20	7	3	10	37	50	24
Albanians Res	20	6	0	14	33	73	18
Old Salvatorians Res*	20	4	3	13	32	50	11
Wandsworth Borough	20	1	2	17	22	100	5

SENIOR DIVISION 3 NORTH	P	W	D	L	F	A	Pts
Mill Hill Village	20	15	2	3	75	30	47
Old Minchendenians	20	14	4	2	71	26	46
Old Meadonians 3rd	20	13	3	4	66	21	42
UCL Academicals Res	20	10	2	8	42	34	32
Old Isleworthians	20	9	1	10	39	50	28
Old Manorians	20	7	5	8	48	54	26
Brent	20	8	2	10	46	60	26
Latymer Old Boys	20	5	4	11	45	53	19
Hale End Athletic Res	20	6	1	13	34	57	19
Parkfield Res	20	4	4	12	34	62	16
Southgate County Res	20	4	2	14	30	83	14

SENIOR DIVISION 3 SOUTH	P	W	D	L	F	A	Pts
Old Belgravians	20	13	3	4	54	37	42
H A C Res	20	13	2	5	62	24	41
Old Dorkinians	20	11	5	4	52	33	38
Marsh	20	11	2	7	59	40	35
Old Tenisonians	20	9	2	9	45	47	29
Old Guildfordians	20	8	5	7	32	34	29
Hampstead Heathens*	20	8	4	8	34	38	27
Old Hamptonians Res	20	7	5	8	36	31	26
Fitzwilliam Old Boys	20	7	3	10	37	49	24
John Fisher Old Boys	20	1	7	12	27	62	10
National Westminster Bank	20	1	4	15	26	69	7

INTERMEDIATE DIVISION NORTH	P	W	D	L	F	A	Pts
Enfield Old Gramm Res	18	12	2	4	61	33	38
Old Edmontonians	18	11	2	5	40	29	35
Old Buckwellians	18	10	2	6	39	35	32
William Fitt	18	9	3	6	57	30	30
Egbertian	18	8	4	6	45	40	28
Old Magdalenians	18	7	5	6	37	35	26
Old Bealonians Res	18	6	3	9	38	47	21
Old Woodhouseians	18	6	2	10	31	46	20
Old Camdenians	18	6	2	10	22	47	20
Old Parmiterians Res	18	2	1	15	25	53	7

INTERMEDIATE DIVISION SOUTH	P	W	D	L	F	A	Pts
Centymca	22	18	2	2	77	30	56
Economicals Res	22	13	3	6	57	36	42
Witan	22	12	3	7	57	47	39
Kings Old Boys Res	22	10	5	7	62	41	35
Chislehurst Sports	22	10	5	7	45	44	35
Old Thorntonians*	22	9	9	4	62	38	32
Old Josephians	22	9	4	9	64	55	31
Mickleham Old Boxhillians	22	7	3	12	31	54	24
Old Sedcopians	22	8	0	14	45	74	24
Reigatians	22	6	4	12	30	51	22
Queen Mary College Old Boys	22	5	1	16	31	68	16
Old Suttonians Res	22	4	3	15	27	50	15

INTERMEDIATE DIVISION WEST	P	W	D	L	F	A	Pts
Old Hamptonians 3rd	20	13	4	3	63	44	43
Old Kolsassians	20	13	1	6	57	33	40
Fulham Compton Old Boys	20	12	3	5	50	31	39
Old Challoners Res	20	9	3	8	46	52	30
Old Uffingtonians	20	8	5	7	53	46	29
Old Meadonians 3rd	20	8	5	7	42	49	29
Old Vaughanians Res	20	6	6	8	54	54	24
Pegasus	20	6	6	8	46	52	24
Cardinal Manning Old Boys	20	7	2	11	46	58	23
London Welsh	20	3	6	11	39	54	15
Parkfield 3rd*	20	3	3	14	30	53	9

** Points deducted – breach of rules*

NORTHERN REGIONAL
Division 1 – 10 teams – Won by Leyton County Old Boys
Division 2 – 11 teams – Won by Bealonians 3rd
Division 3 – 9 teams – Won by Southgate County 3rd
Division 4 – 10 teams – Won by Mill Hill County Old Boys Res
Division 5 – 11 teams – Won by William Fitt Res
Division 6 – 10 teams – Won by Albanian 5th
Division 7 – 9 teams – Won by Old Parmiterians 6th
Division 8 – 8 teams – Won by Latymer Old Boys 4th
Division 9 – 8 teams – Won by Egbertians 5th

SOUTHERN REGIONAL
Division 1 – 11 teams – Won by Royal Bank of Scotland
Division 2 – 11 teams – Won by City of London
Division 3 – 10 teams – Won by Old Strandians
Division 4 – 10 teams – Won by Old Josephians Res
Division 5 – 10 teams – Won by Clapham Old Xaverians 4th
Division 6 – 10 teams – Won by Citigroup
Division 7 – 10 teams – Won by Old Meadonians 7th
Division 8 – 10 teams – Won by Old Meadonians 8th
Division 9 – 10 teams – Won by Royal Sun Alliance Res
Division 10 – 9 teams – Won by Old Tenisonians 4th
Division 11 – 9 teams – Won by Fulham Compton Old Boys 4th
Division 12 – 9 teams – Won by Clapham Old Xaverians 6th

WESTERN REGIONAL
Division 1 – 11 teams – Won by Parkfield 4th
Division 2 – 11 teams – Won by Old Challoners 3rd
Division 3 – 9 teams – Won by Old Manorians 5th
Division 4 – 10 teams – Won by Old Kingsburians 3rd
Division 5 – 10 teams – Won by Phoenix Old Boys 4th

SPRING CUP FINALS
SENIOR
Old Aloysians 4 Old Manorians 2

INTERMEDIATE
Leyton County Old Boys 5 Old Uxonians Res 1

JUNIOR NORTH
Enfield Old Gramm'ns 4th 2 Leyton County OB 3rd 3

JUNIOR SOUTH
Clapham Old Xaverians 4th 2 Old Sedcopians Res 0

MINOR NORTH
Davenant Wanderers Res 9 Old Edmontonians 5th 2

MINOR SOUTH
Old Wokingians 6th 3 Economicals 4th 5

MINOR WEST
Phoenix Old Boys 4 Shene Old Gramm'ns 3rd 0

AMATEUR FOOTBALL ALLIANCE CENTENARY MATCH

Amateur Football Alliance 0 FA XI 3

UNIVERSITY OF LONDON MEN'S INTER-COLLEGIATE LEAGUE

In all Leagues except Weekend Two some games were not played and points adjusted

WEEKEND ONE DIVISION	P	W	D	L	F	A	Pts
Royal Holloway College	11	9	1	1	29	5	28
Imperial College	11	7	4	0	22	2	25
London School of Economics	11	6	3	2	28	13	21
School of Oriental & African Studies	11	7	0	4	26	17	21
University College	11	5	3	3	25	19	18
St Bart's & R London Hosps MS	11	4	2	5	14	23	14
Imperial College Res	11	4	0	7	18	23	12
R Free, Mx & Univ Coll Hosp MS	11	4	3	4	19	8	15
London School of Economics Res	11	3	1	7	11	36	10
King's College	11	3	1	7	15	24	10
Royal Holloway College Res	11	2	2	7	12	23	8
Queen Mary College	11	2	0	9	12	38	6

WEEKEND TWO DIVISION	P	W	D	L	F	A	Pts
London School of Economics 3rd	11	9	2	0	38	10	29
University College Res	11	9	1	1	32	11	28
King's College London MS	11	7	2	2	39	14	23
Royal Holloway College 3rd	11	6	2	3	15	12	20
Goldsmiths' College	11	5	1	5	26	24	16
Imperial College Medicals	11	4	2	5	27	24	14
King's College Res	11	3	3	5	24	27	12
Imperial College 3rd	11	3	3	5	13	18	12
Queen Mary College Res	11	3	3	5	24	35	12
University College 3rd	11	3	1	7	18	29	10
St Georges Hospital MS	11	3	0	8	12	33	9
Imperial Medicals Res	11	1	0	10	17	48	3

DIVISION ONE	P	W	D	L	F	A	Pts
University College 4th	22	18	3	1	95	24	57
King's College London MS Res	22	17	2	3	82	33	53
Royal Holloway College 4th	22	12	5	5	72	48	41
R Free, Mx & Univ Coll Hosp MS Res	22	11	2	9	61	45	35
Royal Veterinary College	22	10	3	9	46	42	33
Imperial College 4th	22	10	2	10	41	49	32
University College 5th	22	8	5	9	48	35	29
Imperial College 5th	22	7	6	9	34	41	27
Queen Mary College 3rd	22	7	6	9	41	40	27
King's College 3rd	22	5	3	14	30	73	18
University College 6th	22	4	0	18	32	86	12
St Georges Hospital Res	22	3	3	16	16	82	12

DIVISION TWO	P	W	D	L	F	A	Pts
St Bart's & R London Hosps MS Res	22	16	3	3	81	27	51
University College 7th	22	15	4	3	72	23	49
King's College London MS 3rd	22	11	6	5	41	34	39
London School of Economics 4th	22	9	9	4	44	22	36
Royal Holloway College 5th	22	11	3	8	52	38	36
R Free, Mx & Univ Coll Hosp MS 3rd	22	9	4	9	29	30	31
King's College 4th	22	7	7	8	27	30	28
King's College 5th	22	6	3	13	25	65	21
Imperial Medicals 3rd	22	5	5	12	43	53	20
London School of Economics 5th	22	6	6	10	34	31	24
Royal Holloway College 6th	22	6	1	15	32	64	19
Royal School of Mines (IC)	22	5	1	16	26	89	16

DIVISION THREE	P	W	D	L	F	A	Pts
University of the Arts	20	14	3	3	69	24	45
School of Pharmacy	20	12	4	4	62	36	40
London School of Economics 6th	20	12	4	4	53	48	40
Queen Mary College 4th	20	11	3	6	64	36	36
King's College London MS 4th	20	10	2	8	59	54	32
R Free, Mx & Univ Coll Hosp 4th	20	7	5	8	29	29	26
Imperial College 6th	20	7	3	10	36	42	24
King's, College London MS 5th	20	4	7	9	43	61	19
Imperial College 7th	20	5	4	11	35	68	19
London School of Economics 7th	20	5	2	13	34	50	17
King's College 6th	20	3	3	14	33	69	12

DIVISION FOUR	P	W	D	L	F	A	Pts
School of Oriental & African Studies Res	18	13	4	1	90	20	43
Imperial College at Wye	18	14	3	1	99	27	45
School of Slavonic & E European Studies	18	13	1	4	67	23	40
Goldsmiths' College Res	18	11	2	5	57	28	35
Queen Mary College 5th	18	8	1	9	46	52	25
Goldsmiths' College 3rd	18	7	1	10	45	95	22
St Bart's & R London Hosps MS 3rd	18	5	3	10	45	51	18
Royal Veterinary College Res	18	3	1	14	21	88	10
St Georges Hospital MS 3rd	18	3	3	12	21	60	12
Imperial Medicals 4th	18	2	3	13	25	72	9

CHALLENGE CUP
Imperial College 0*:5p Royal Holloway College 0*:4p

RESERVES CHALLENGE CUP
London Sch. of Economics 3rd 2 University College 3rd 0

RESERVES PLATE
University College 7th 1 St Bart's & R London Hosps Res 0

VASE
School of Oriental and African Studies Res 4 School of Slavonic and European Studies 1
* *After extra time*

UNIVERSITY OF LONDON WOMEN'S INTER-COLLEGIATE LEAGUE

PREMIER DIVISION	P	W	D	L	F	A	Pts
King's College London MS	10	9	1	0	47	19	28
Royal Holloway College	10	7	1	2	60	21	22
University College	10	6	1	3	48	18	19
Goldsmiths' College	10	4	1	5	28	25	13
Queen Mary College	10	1	1	8	5	63	4
London School Economics	10	0	1	9	4	46	1

DIVISION ONE	P	W	D	L	F	A	Pts
Imperial Medicals Womens 1st	8	6	2	0	33	8	20
Royal Veterinary College	8	5	0	3	44	16	15
R Free, Mx & Univ Coll Hosp MS	8	3	2	3	26	15	11
University College Res	8	1	3	4	4	18	6
King's College London MS Res	8	1	1	6	6	56	4

DIVISION TWO	P	W	D	L	F	A	Pts
School of Oriental & African Studies	6	4	1	1	16	6	13
St George's Hospital MS	6	3	0	3	25	14	9
R Free, Mx & Univ Coll Hosp MS Res	6	3	0	3	3	24	9
Imperial College Medicals	6	1	1	4	8	8	4

WOMEN'S CHALLENGE CUP
King's College London MS 5 Goldsmiths' 0

UNIVERSITY FOOTBALL 2006–07

123rd UNIVERSITY MATCH

(at Queens Park Rangers FC, 17 March 2007)

Cambridge 1 Oxford 1

(Cambridge won 4-3 on penalties)

Cambridge: J Dean; *C Turnbull, *A.Murphy, *W Stevenson, T Russell; *D Mills, *A Coleman *(Capt.),* J Rusius, *B Threlfall (1); M Johnson, J Rutt.
Substitutes : Ferguson *(Gk)*, G Handelaar, *S Bailey, *M Dankis, N Leslie.
Scorer: Threlfall.

Oxford: *N Baker; *O Price *(Capt.),* *J Hazzard, P Rainford, *J Doree; M Martin, T Rae (M. Robinson), L.Weston, A Toogood (1); T Ovington (T Brown), T Clare (*L Burns).
Substitutes not used: D Robinson *(Gk)*; L Barrs.
Scorer: Toogood.

**denotes Old Blue.*

Referee: André Marriner (Birmingham FA)
Assistants: M Griffiths (Cambridgeshire), J Maskell (Oxfordshire)
4th Official: B Malone (Wiltshire FA)

Oxford have won 47 games, Cambridge 48 and 28 have been drawn.
This was the first occasion using kicks from the penalty mark to determine a result.

IMPORTANT ADDRESSES

The Football Association: The Secretary, 25 Soho Square, London W1D 4FA. *020 7745 4545*

Scotland: David Taylor, Hampden Park, Glasgow G42 9AY. *0141 616 6000*

Northern Ireland (Irish FA): Chief Executive: Howard J. C. Wells, 20 Windsor Avenue, Belfast BT9 6EG. *028 9066 9458*

Wales: D. Collins, 3 Westgate Street, Cardiff, South Glamorgan CF10 1DP. *029 2037 2325*

Republic of Ireland B. Menton (FA of Ireland): 80 Merrion Square South, Dublin 2. *00353 16766864*

International Federation (FIFA): P. O. Box 85 8030 Zurich, Switzerland. *00 411 384 9595. Fax: 00 411 384 9696*

Union of European Football Associations: Secretary, Route de Geneve 46, Case Postale CH-1260 Nyon, Switzerland. *0041 22 994 44 44. Fax: 0041 22 994 44 88*

THE LEAGUES

The Premier League: M. Foster, 11 Connaught Place, London W2 2ET. *020 7298 1600*

The Football League: Secretary, The Football League, Unit 5, Edward VII Quay, Navigation Way, Preston, Lancashire PR2 2YF. *0870 442 0 1888. Fax 0870 442 0 1188*

Scottish Premier League: R. Mitchell, Hampden Park, Somerville Drive, Glasgow G42 9BA. *0141 646 6962*

The Scottish League: P. Donald, Hampden Park, Glasgow G42 9AY. *0141 616 6000*

The Irish League: Secretary, 96 University Street, Belfast BT7 1HE. *028 9024 2888*

Football League of Ireland: D. Crowther, 80 Merrion Square, Dublin 2. *00353 16765120*

Eastern Counties League: B. A. Badcock, 18 Calford Drive, Hanchett Drive, Haverhill, Suffolk CB9 7WQ. *01440 708064*

Hellenic League: B. King, 83 Queens Road, Carterton, Oxon OX18 3YF. *01993 212738*

Kent League: R. Vinter, Bakery House, The Street, Chilham, Canterbury, Kent CT4 8BX. *01227 730457*

Leicestershire Senior League: R. J. Holmes, 9 Copse Close, Hugglescote, Coalville, Leicestershire LE67 2GL. *01530 831818*

Midland Combination: N. Harvey, 115 Millfield Road, Handsworth Wood, Birmingham B20 1ED. *0121 357 4172*

Northern Premier: R. D. Bayley, 22 Woburn Drive, Hale, Altrincham, Cheshire WA15 8LZ. *0161 980 7007*

Northern League: T. Golightly, 85 Park Road North, Chester-le-Street, Co Durham DH3 3SA. *0191 3882056*

Isthmian League: N. Robinson, Triumph House, Station Approach, Sanderstead Road, South Croydon, Surrey CR2 0PL. *020 8409 1978*

Southern League: D. J. Strudwick, 8 College Yard, Worcester WR1 2LA. *01905 330444*

Spartan South Midlands League: M. Mitchell, 26 Leighton Court, Dunstable, Beds LU6 1EW. *01582 667291*

United Counties League: R. Gamble, 8 Bostock Avenue, Northampton NN1 4LW. *01604 637766*

Western League: K. A. Clarke, 32 Westmead Lane, Chippenham, Wilts SN15 3HZ. *01249 464467*

West Midlands League: N. R. Juggins, 14 Badger Way, Blackwell, Bromsgrove, Worcs B60 1EX. *0121 445 2953*

Northern Counties (East): B. Wood, 6 Restmore Avenue, Guiseley, Leeds LS20 9DG. *01943 874558*

Central Midlands Football League: J. Worrall, 36 Spilsby Close, Cantley, Doncaster DN4 6TJ. *01302 370188*

Combined Counties League: L. Pharo, 17 Nigel Fisher Way, Chessington, Surrey KT9 2SN. *020 8391 0297*

Essex Senior League: D. Walls, 2 Hillsfield Cottage, Layer, Breton, Essex CO2 0PS. *01206 330146*

Midland Football Alliance: P. Dagger, 11 The Oval, Bicton, Nr Shrewsbury, Shropshire SY3 8ER. *01742 850859*

North West Counties Football League: G. J. Wilkinson, 46 Oaklands Drive, Penwortham, Preston, Lancs PR1 0XY. *01772 746312*

Wessex League: I. Craig, 7 Old River, Denmead, Hampshire PO7 6UX. *02392 230973*

South Western League: P. Lowe, 14 Anderton Court, Whitchurch, Tavistock, Devon PL19 9EX. *01822 613715*

Devon League: P. Hiscox, 19 Ivy Close, Wonford, Exeter, Devon EX2 5LX. *01392 493995*

Northern Alliance: J. McLackland, 92 Appletree Gardens, Walkerville, Newcastle-upon-Tyne NE6 4SX. *0191 262 6665*

Sussex County League: P. Beard, 2 Van Gogh Place, Bersted, Bognor Regis, West Sussex PO22 9BG. *01243 822063.*

Wearside League: T. Clark, 55 Vicarage Close, Silksworth, Sunderland, Tyne & Wear SR3 1UF. *0191 521 1242*

West Cheshire League: A. Green, 46 Bertram Drive, Meols, Wirral, Cheshire CH47 0LH. *0151 632 4946*

OTHER USEFUL ADDRESSES

Amateur Football Alliance: M. L. Brown, 55 Islington Park Street, London N1 1QB. *020 7359 3493*

English Schools FA: Mike Spinks, 1/2 Eastgate Street, Stafford ST16 2NQ. *01785 251142*

British Universities Sports Association: G. Gregory-Jones, Chief Executive: BUSA, 20-24 King's Bench Street, London SE1 0QX. *0207 633 5050*

The Football Supporters Federation: Chairman: Malcolm Clarke, 20 Woodlands Road, Sale, Cheshire M33 2DW. *0161 962 7337 . Mobile: 07939 594730.* National Secretary: Mike Williamson, 2 Repton Avenue, Torrishome, Morecambe, Lancs LA4 6RZ. *01524 425242, 07729 906329 (mobile).* National Administrator: Mark Agate, 'The Stadium', 14 Coombe Close, Lordswood, Chatham, Kent ME5 8NU. *01634 319461 (and fax) 07931 635637 (mobile)*

National Playing Fields Association: Col. R. Satterthwaite, O.B.E., 578b Catherine Place, London, SW1

Professional Footballers' Association: G. Taylor, 2 Oxford Court, Bishopsgate, Off Lower Mosley Street, Manchester M2 3WQ. *0161 236 0575*

Referees' Association: A. Smith, 1 Westhill Road, Coundon, Coventry CV6 2AD. *024 7660 1701*

Women's Football Alliance: Miss K. Doyle, The Football Association, 25 Soho Square, London W1D 4FA. *020 7745 4545*

League Managers Association: The Camkin Suite, 1 Pegasus House, Pegasus Court, Tachbrook Park, Warwick CV34 6LW. *01926 831 556. Fax: 01926 429 781*

Institute of Football Management and Administration; Commercial and Marketing Managers Association; Technical and Development Staffs Association; LMA Web Limited: as above

The Football Programme Directory: David Stacey, 'The Beeches', 66 Southend Road, Wickford, Essex SS11 8EN. *01268 732041 (and fax)*

England Football Supporters Association: Publicity Officer, David Stacey, 'The Beeches', 66 Southend Road, Wickford, Essex SS11 8EN. *01268 732041 (and fax)*

World Cup (1966) Association: Hon. Secretary, David Duncan, 96 Glenlea Road, Eltham, London SE9 1DZ

The Ninety-Two Club: 104 Gilda Crescent, Whitchurch, Bristol BS14 9LD

The Football Trust: Second Floor, Walkden House, 10 Melton Street, London NW1 2EJ. *020 7388 4504*

Association of Provincial Football Supporters Clubs in London: Stephen Moon, 32 Westminster Gardens, Barking, Essex IG11 0BJ. *020 8594 2367*

World Association of Friends of English Football: Carlisle Hill, Gluck, Habichthof 2, D24939 Flensburg, Germany. *0049 461 4700222*

Football Postcard Collectors Club: PRO: Bryan Horsnell, 275 Overdown Road, Tilehurst, Reading RG31 6NX. *0118 942 4448 (and fax)*

UK Programme Collectors Club: Secretary, John Litster, 46 Milton Road, Kirkcaldy, Fife KY1 1TL. *01592 268718. Fax: 01592 595069*

Programme Monthly & Football Collectable Magazine: P.O. Box 3236 Norwich NR7 7BE

Scottish Football Historians Association: 43 Lady Nairn Avenue, Kirkcaldy KY1 2AW

Phil Gould (Licensed Football Agent), c/o Whoppit Management Ltd, P. O. Box 27204, London N11 2WS. *07071 732 468. Fax: 07070 732 469*

The Scandinavian Union of Supporters of British Football: Postboks, 15 Stovner, N-0913 Oslo, Norway

Football Writers' Association: Executive Secretary, Ken Montgomery, 6 Chase Lane, Barkingside, Essex IG6 1BH. *0208 554 2455 (and fax)*

Programme Promotions: 47 The Beeches, Lampton Road, Hounslow, Middlesex TW3 4DF.
Web: www.footballprogrammes.com

FOOTBALL CLUB CHAPLAINCY

With the argument over the desirability of a chaplain now firmly and positively settled – any doubter need only consider the ever-expanding list which accompanies this little article! – regular readers of this page will understand that, with the passage of time, other issues have begun to face the chaplains' fraternity.

The fact is that some of the names which have appeared on this page for over two decades are those of gentlemen who are now almost venerable! And whilst retirement can provide additional time and opportunities for some of our men, for others it may mean removal to a new home at a distance from their clubs, or perhaps has been hastened by their own declining health or that of a beloved family member.

Thus, the chaplains have learnt that it is often necessary and is certainly wise, to begin preparing early for their retirement from their football appointments, by seeking out a (much!) more youthful successor to whom the reins can be confidently handed over. For, whilst many of the chaplains have a cordial and positive relationship with their club's chairman – and indeed, often with his or her family too – it would be naive to expect the club or its owner to devote time and energy to finding a new chaplain.

So, our regular readers may confidently expect to see the cause of football chaplaincy continuing to progress and to expand, but that may well be mirrored by the replacement of former and familiar names by new ones.

THE REV

OFFICIAL CHAPLAINS TO FA PREMIERSHIP AND FOOTBALL LEAGUE CLUBS

Rev Ken Baker – Aston Villa; Rev Ken Howles – Blackburn R; Rev Philip Mason – Bolton W; Rev Matt Baker – Charlton Ath; Rev Henry Corbett – Everton; Rev Gary Piper – Fulham; Rev Bill Bygroves – Liverpool; Rev Chris Howitz – Manchester C; Rev John Boyers – Manchester U; Rev David Tully – Newcastle U; Rev Jonathan Jeffrey – Portsmouth; Rev Elwin Cockett – West Ham U; Rev Peter Amos – Barnsley; Rev David Tidswell – Blackpool; Rev John Moore – Boston U; Rev Alan Fisher – Bournemouth; Rev Andy Bowerman – Bradford C; Rev Lewis Allen – Brentford; Rev Derek Cleave – Bristol C; Rev Stephen Baker – Bristol R; Rev Mark Hirst – Burnley; Rev John O'Dowd – Bury; Rev Alun Jones – Carlisle U; Mr Paul Bennett and Rev Malcolm Allen (Co-Chaplains) – Cheltenham T; Rev Jim McGlade – Chesterfield; Rev Simon Lawton – Crewe Alexandra; Rev Chris Roe – Crystal Palace; Pastor Jon Burns – Darlington; Rev Tony Luke – Derby Co; Rev Brian Quar – Doncaster R; Rev Richard Hayton – Gillingham; Rev Allen Bagshawe – Hull C; Rev Kevan McCormack – Ipswich T; Rev Paul C. Welch and Fr Steven Billington (Co-Chaplains) – Leeds U; Rev Bruce Nadin – Leicester C; Rev Alan Comfort – Leyton Orient; Rev Andrew Vaughan – Lincoln C; Rev Jeremy Tear – Macclesfield T; Rev Timothy Mitchell – Mansfield T; Fr Owen Beament – Millwall; Rev Ron Smith – Milton Keynes D; Rev Ken Baker – Northampton T; Rev Bert Cadmore and Rev Arthur W. Bowles (Co-Chaplains) – Norwich C; Rev Simon Cansdale – Nottingham F; Rev Clive Andrews – Notts Co; Rev Roger Humphreys – Oxford U; Rev Richard Longfoot – Peterborough U; Rev Jeff Howden – Plymouth Arg; Rev John M Hibberts – Port Vale; Rev Chris Nelson – Preston NE; Rev Bob Mayo and Rev Cameron Collington (Co-Chaplains) – Queens Park Rangers; Steve Prince – Reading; Canon Roger Knight – Rushden & D; Rev Alan Wright – Scunthorpe U; Rev Peter Allen – Sheffield W; Rev Ian Johnson – Southampton; Rev Billy Montgomery – Stockport Co; Rev Kevin Johns – Swansea C; Rev Simon Stevenette – Swindon T; Fr Gerald Courell – Tranmere R; Rev Martin Butt – Walsall; Rev Clive Ross – Watford; Rev John Hall-Matthews and Rev Steve Davies (Co-Chaplains) – Wolverhampton W; Rev Jim Pearce – Yeovil T.

The chaplains hope that those who read this page will see the value and benefit of chaplaincy work in football and will take appropriate steps to spread the word where this is possible. They would also like to thank the editors of the Football Yearbook *for their continued support for this specialist and growing area of work.*

For further information, please contact: SCORE (Sports Chaplaincy Offering Resources and Encouragement), PO Box 123, Sale, Cheshire M33 4ZA). Telephone 0161 969 1762 or email JKBSCOREUK@aol.com.

OBITUARIES

Dave Aitken (Born Aberdeen, circa 1930. Died 30 June 2006.) Dave Aitken made just two appearances for Aberdeen between 1950 and 1954 during a spell interrupted by National Service. He later spent a season at Arbroath, before switching to Highland League football with Huntly and Fraserburgh.

George Aitken (Born Dalkeith, Midlothian, 13 August 1928. Died Brighton, August 2006.) George Aitken was a centre half who joined Middlesbrough from Edinburgh Thistle in June 1946, but never really established himself in the side at Ayresome Park. In July 1953 he was sold to Workington, where he became a key figure in the club's defence, making over 250 first-team appearances. On retiring as a player he served both Workington and Watford as trainer, before returning to Borough Park to become manager of the Reds from 1971 to 1974.

Ron Allen (Born Birmingham, 22 April 1935. Died Measham, Leics, 5 August 2006.) Ron Allen spent five years with Birmingham City without making the first team, but after signing for Lincoln City in the summer of 1958 he went on to become the Imps' regular right back. He retained his place until suffering a badly broken leg against Leeds United in December 1960 and this effectively ended his career.

Johnny Anderson (Born Salford, Manchester, 11 October 1921. Died Manchester 6 August 2006.) Johnny Anderson joined Manchester United as a wing half shortly before the outbreak of war, but it was not until the 1947–48 season that he featured at first-team level. He was a member of the United side that defeated Blackpool to win the 1948 FA Cup final, scoring his team's fourth and final goal. Johnny later had several seasons at Nottingham Forest before joining Midland League club Peterborough United. He remained at London Road until 1967 serving as coach and briefly as caretaker manager.

Alan Ball, MBE (Born Farnworth, Bolton, 12 May 1945. Died Warsash, Hampshire, 25 April 2007.) Alan Ball was one of the stars of England's World Cup triumph of 1966. Although short in stature, his enthusiasm and commitment in midfield were total and he was a constant inspiration to his colleagues both at club and international level. He also possessed a fine football brain, showing accuracy and vision with his distribution from the centre of the park. In total he won 72 England caps and also broke the national transfer record on two occasions. His career had begun at Blackpool, but shortly after the World Cup victory he was sold to Everton where he enjoyed perhaps the best years of his career, forming a renowned midfield trio with Howard Kendall and Colin Harvey. Alan played a key role in the Toffees' side that won the Football League title in 1969–70, also appearing for England in the 1970 World Cup finals in Mexico. After moving to Arsenal in December 1971 he won an FA Cup runners-up medal, and he later had a successful stint at Southampton, helping the club gain promotion in 1977–78. Thereafter his career was somewhat peripatetic with spells in the USA, Canada, Australia and Hong Kong in between which he returned to assist both Blackpool (as player-manager) and Saints once more, before concluding with a brief spell at Bristol Rovers. Thereafter he entered a career in management for Portsmouth (on two occasions), Stoke City, Exeter City, Manchester City and Southampton. Although less successful than he had been as a player, he took Pompey back into the old First Division in 1986–87.

Ted Batchelor (Born Rugby, Warwickshire, 4 August 1930. Died Swindon, 19 November 2006.) Although Ted Batchelor was on the books of Wolves as a youngster he failed to make the first team at Molineux. His fortunes improved after he moved to Swindon Town in the summer of 1950 and he made almost 100 appearances for the Wiltshire club before leaving the full-time game in 1955.

Ferenc Bene (Born Balatonújlak, Hungary, 17 December 1944. Died Budapest, Hungary, 27 February 2006.) Ferenc Bene was one of the great stars of Hungarian football of the 1960s. He won 76 caps for Hungary between 1962 and 1979, gaining a gold medal at the 1964 Olympic Games. He played his club football for Újpesti Dózsa for whom he scored 303 goals in 418 games.

Jack Bentley (Born Liverpool, 17 February 1942. Died 27 May 2007.) As a youngster Jack Bentley received a single Football League outing for Everton, then spent two years on the books of Stockport County, making some 49 appearances. In 1963 he joined Southern League club Wellington Town, for whom he became a legendary centre forward, scoring 431 goals in 835 appearances before retiring in 1977.

Manuel Bento (Born Galega, Portugal, 25 December 1948. Died Barreiro, Portugal, 1 March 2007.) Manuel Bento was Benfica's first choice goalkeeper for over a decade, assisting the team to eight domestic titles and winning Portugal's Player of the Year award in 1977. He won 68 caps for Portugal between 1976 and 1986, featuring in both the 1984 European Championship finals and the 1986 World Cup finals.

Brian Biggins (Born Ellesmere Port, Cheshire, 19 May 1940. Died 13 September 2006.) Brian Biggins was a goalkeeper who made a handful of appearances for Chester towards the end of the 1950s. The highlight of his career came when he featured in the Welsh Cup final in 1956–57. He remained at Sealand Road until 1961, when he moved on to join Pwllheli.

John Boag (Born Port Glasgow, Strathclyde, 14 February 1965. Died Port Glasgow, Strathclyde, 2006.) John Boag was a big solid defender, who failed to make the grade as a youngster with Aberdeen. However, after joining Morton in the summer of 1984 he experienced regular first-team football. He made almost 200 appearances for the Greenock club over the next nine seasons, and was a member of the team that won the Scottish First Division title in 1986–87.

Alan Ball

Nick Boland (Born Openshaw, Manchester, 28 March 1910. Died Southport, 3 May 2007.) Nick Boland was briefly on Wolves' books before signing for Southport in November 1934. An inside or outside left, he made 29 Football League appearances for the Sandgrounders before moving on to Altrincham in 1936. At the time of his death he was Southport's oldest surviving former player.

Gordon Bradley (Born Scunthorpe, 20 May 1925. Died Poole, Dorset, 2 May 2006.) Gordon Bradley began his senior career with Scunthorpe United in their Midland League days, signing for Leicester City in 1942. A talented goalkeeper, he appeared for the Foxes in their 1949 FA Cup final defeat by Wolves and later spent almost a decade with Notts County, for whom he made over 200 first-team appearances, scoring against his former colleagues in the 1946–47 season after an injury forced him to take up an outfield position.

Warren Bradley (Born Hyde, Cheshire, 20 June 1933. Died Manchester, 6 June 2007.) Warren Bradley played for Durham City whilst studying at the local university, before signing for Bishop Auckland, then the top amateur club in the land. He won FA Amateur Cup winners' medals for the Bishops in 1956 and 1957 and also gained 11 Amateur caps for England. Following the Munich air disaster, Warren was one of three Bishops' players invited to join Manchester United and he went on to sign professional forms for the Old Trafford club. He made some 60 Football League appearances for the Reds as a goalscoring winger and also won three full England caps, before finishing his career with a season at Bury.

Bill Brindley (Born Nottingham, 29 January 1947. Died 6 April 2007.) Bill Brindley began his career as an apprentice with Nottingham Forest, but although he won England Youth international honours he failed to gain a regular place in the Reds' line-up. He moved across the Trent to sign for Notts County in the summer of 1970 and went on to make 250 appearances for the Magpies, mostly at right back. Bill helped County win the old Fourth Division title in 1970–71, then promotion from Division Three in 1972–73. He concluded his career with a brief spell at Gillingham.

Jackie Campbell (Born Liverpool, 17 March 1922. Died Spain, 10 February 2007.) Jackie Campbell featured regularly at wing half for Liverpool in the closing years of the wartime emergency competitions before signing for Blackburn Rovers in December 1945. He went on to play in over 200 first-team games during his stay at Ewood Park before winding down his career with a season at Oldham.

Jim Campbell (Born 7 April 1947. Died Ayr, 20 October 2006.) Jim Campbell was a powerful striker who joined Stranraer from Tarff Rovers shortly after the start of the 1965–66 season. He remained at Stair Park for a decade, making over 300 first-team appearances and scoring 136 goals.

Tommy Cavanagh (Born Liverpool, 29 June 1928. Died 14 March 2007.) Tommy Cavanagh made over 300 senior appearances during a career that saw him play for Stockport County, Huddersfield, Doncaster, Bristol City and Carlisle. He subsequently enjoyed a successful career in coaching serving a number of clubs including Brentford, Hull, Manchester United, Newcastle and Norwegian club Rosenborg. Tommy also served Burnley as manager in 1985–86.

Malcolm Cluroe (Born Nottingham, 6 February 1935. Died 26 September 2006.) Malcolm Cluroe spent three seasons on the books of Nottingham Forest, making a solitary first-team appearance when he turned out as an inside forward against Luton Town in December 1954.

Maurice Cook (Born Hemel Hempstead, Herts, 10 December 1951. Died Hemel Hempstead, Herts, 31 December 2006) Maurice Cook was a big, powerful centre forward who made his name with Watford in the mid-1950s, earning representative honours for Division Three South. He was sold to Fulham in 1958 and went to make over 200 first-team appearances during his stay at Craven Cottage, where he helped the club win promotion in 1958–59 and also had the distinction of scoring the first-ever goal in the Football League Cup competition playing against Bristol Rovers in September 1960. Maurice finished his senior career with a season at Reading before moving on to play for Banbury United.

Dennis Copley (Born Misterton, Notts, 21 December 1921. Died 18 October 2006.) Dennis Copley made a single Football League appearance for Lincoln City in the Imps' final home game of the 1946–47 season. An inside forward, he later turned out for Boston United and Corby Town.

Jimmy Cork (Born Circa 1926. Died 17 August 2006.) Jimmy Cork was a goalscoring inside forward who made one senior appearance for Doncaster Rovers in the emergency wartime competitions. He later played for Thorne Colliery and Gainsborough Trinity.

Ron Cox (Born Foleshill, Warwickshire, 2 May 1919. Died 28 September 2006.) Ron Cox signed professional forms for Coventry City at the end of the war and spent seven years on the club's books, principally as understudy to regular centre half George Mason. Ron made 30 first-team appearances for the club before moving on to join Atherstone Town.

Bobby Cram (Born Hetton-le-Hole, Co Durham, 19 November 1939. Died Vancouver, Canada, April 2007.) Bobby Cram joined West Bromwich Albion straight from school and went on to make over 150 appearances for the Baggies, featuring in the Football League Cup finals of 1966 and 1967. After a spell in Canada he returned to sign for Colchester United in January 1970. The club's right back and captain, he led the U's to a famous FA Cup victory over Leeds United the following season and to victory in the Watney Cup competition in August 1971. He later emigrated to Canada.

Jock Dodds

Derek Dougan

Charlie Croft (Born Thornhill, nr Dewsbury, Yorkshire, 26 November 1918. Died Roberttown, nr Liversedge, West Yorkshire, 26 July 2006.) Charlie Croft featured for both Huddersfield Town and Brighton during the war, signing for Mansfield Town in the summer of 1947. He was a regular at wing half for the Stags in the first two post-war seasons, eventually moving on to join Boston United in 1950.

Bert Cromar (Born 8 October 1931. Died 4 June 2007.) Bert Cromar was a key figure for Queen's Park in the early post-war years, serving the club as captain and making some 455 first-team appearances in a career that continued until the mid-1960s. Bert also represented Scotland at Amateur international level, winning 35 caps. He remained associated with Queen's Park and later served the club as president.

Bobby Dale (Born Manchester, 31 October 1931. Died January 2007.) Bobby Dale was a winger who spent two seasons on the books of Bury in the early 1950s before moving on to Colchester United in December 1953. He was a regular for the U's over the next few years, making 129 first-team appearances before illness brought his career to an end.

Jock Dodds (Born Grangetown, Stirlingshire, 7 September 1915. Died Blackpool, 23 February 2007.) Jock Dodds was one of the most prolific goalscorers in English football in the emergency wartime competitions, scoring an amazing 230 goals in 157 games for Blackpool and winning 8 wartime caps for Scotland. A short but immensely powerful centre forward, he had featured for Huddersfield Town and Sheffield United in the pre-war period, gaining an FA Cup runners-up medal for the Blades in the 1936 FA Cup final when they were defeated by Arsenal. After the war he played for Shamrock Rovers, Everton and Lincoln City before his playing career was effectively ended when he was linked to a scheme to recruit British players to a Colombian league that was not affiliated to FIFA.

Derek Dougan (Born Belfast, 20 January 1938. Died June 2007.) Derek Dougan came to prominence playing in the Irish League with Distillery, for whom he was a member of the team that won the Irish Cup in 1956 and won Amateur international honours. A powerful, direct centre forward, he was transferred to Portsmouth in April 1957 and two years later he moved on to Blackburn, where he won an FA Cup runners-up medal in 1960. Spells with Aston Villa, Peterborough United and Leicester City followed before he signed for Wolves in March 1967. A popular figure during his stay at Molineux, Derek scored 95 League goals in 258 appearances and was a member of the team that won the Football League Cup in 1974. Controversial and often outspoken, he won 43 caps for Northern Ireland between 1958 and 1973, scoring 8 goals. Derek served as chairman of the PFA during the 1970s and briefly as chairman of Wolves in the early 1980s.

Giacinto Facchetti (Born Treviglio, Italy, 18 July 1942. Died Milan, Italy, 4 September 2006.) Giacinto Facchetti was converted from a forward to left back by Inter Milan and went on to become one of the greatest players in Italian football during the 1960s and '70s. He won 94 caps for Italy between 1963 and 1977 and featured in three consecutive World Cups, gaining a runners-up medal in 1970 when Brazil defeated Italy 4–1 in the final. Giacinto was a fixture in the Inter side during this period, making almost 500 appearances and helping them win both the European Cup and the Inter Continental Cup in 1964 and 1965.

Matt Gadsby (Born Sutton Coldfield, West Midlands, 6 September 1979. Died Harrogate, 9 September 2006.) A versatile player, comfortable both in midfield and defence, Matt Gadsby stepped up to the professional ranks with Walsall in February 1998 and went on to make 100 senior appearances, also featuring for Mansfield Town and Kidderminster Harriers. His tragically early death came after he collapsed whilst playing for Hinckley United in a Conference North fixture against Harrogate Town.

Joe Gallego (Born Renteria, Spain, 8 April 1923. Died 17 September 2006.) A refugee from the Spanish Civil War, Joe Gallego had spells with Brentford, Southampton and Colchester United in the seasons after the war, making just a handful of appearances with each club. In the summer of 1952 he left the full-time game to join non-League Cambridge United.

Willie Gardiner (Born Larbert, Stirlingshire, 15 August 1929. Died Stirling, 5 January 2007.) Centre forward Willie Gardiner spent five seasons on the books of Rangers, but was mostly a reserve during his time at Ibrox. In August 1955 he moved south, signing for Leicester City where he not only featured regularly in the first team, but also scored regularly, netting 49 goals from 71 appearances. Willie concluded his career at Reading before injury forced his retirement.

Tom Garneys (Born West Ham, London, 25 August 1923. Died Basildon, Essex, March 2007.) Tom Garneys was on the books of both Notts County and Brentford in the late 1940s, but it was only when he signed for Ipswich Town in the summer of 1951 that his career began to take off. He proved to be a prolific goalscorer, netting 123 goals in 248 Football League games and helping the Portman Road club win the Division Three South title in 1953–54 and 1956–57.

Roger Griffiths (Born Hereford, 20 February 1945. Died 19 July 2006.) Roger Griffiths was a key member of Hereford United's FA Cup giant killers of 1971–72, remarkably playing for over 70 minutes of the memorable victory over Newcastle United with a broken bone in his leg. He remained with the club in their first season in the Football League before going on to play for Cheltenham Town and Worcester City.

Frank Griffin (Born Swinton, Lancs, 28 March 1928. Died 4 June 2007.) A traditional-style winger, Frank Griffin played for Shrewsbury Town in their first-ever Football League fixture against Scunthorpe United in August 1950. At the end of that season he was transferred to West Bromwich Albion for a fee of £9,500. Frank went on to make over 250 appearances for the Baggies, scoring the decisive goal in the club's FA Cup final victory over Preston North End in 1954. He concluded his career at Northampton.

Charlie Hall (Born circa 1922. Died Lewisham, London, 30 January 2007.) Charlie Hall made 9 appearances for Charlton Athletic during the wartime emergency competitions, but although he remained on the club's books until 1949 he had no further senior outings. He subsequently joined the backroom staff at the Valley, later serving as club trainer from 1965 until 1987.

John Harding (Born circa 1953. Died 15 June 2007.) John Harding was an experienced manager and coach who served a number of clubs in the Home Counties area including Stevenage Borough, Farnborough Town and Molesey. At the time of his death he was in post as first-team coach of Barnet, a position he had held since the summer of 2006.

Peter Harrison (Born Sleaford, Lincs, 25 October 1927. Died Llandough, Penarth, Mid Glamorgan, 25 July 2006.) Peter Harrison was a skilful outside left who joined Leeds United in January 1949 from Peterborough United, then a Midland League outfit. After nearly 70 games for the Elland Road club he was allowed to join Bournemouth, for whom he made almost 200 first-team appearances. He subsequently played for Reading and Southport, and later served Cardiff City as trainer and youth-team coach.

Jimmy Harrower (Born Alva, Stirlingshire, 18 August 1935. Died Stirling. 28 November 2006.) Jimmy Harrower was a skilful ball-playing inside forward who came to prominence with Hibernian in the mid-1950s. After winning Under-23 international honours for Scotland he was sold to Liverpool in January 1958. Jimmy was a popular figure during his time at Anfield, making over 100 first-team appearances. Although he left the club after three seasons, he continued to play until 1966, turning out for Newcastle United, Falkirk, St Johnstone, Albion Rovers and Alloa Athletic.

Giacinto Facchetti

Eric Hayton (Born Carlisle, 14 January 1922. Died 29 December 2006.) Eric Hayton was a wing half who signed professional forms for Carlisle United at the end of the war. He made 53 appearances for the Brunton Park club and later also played for Rochdale and Workington.

Dennis Heath (Born Chiswick, Middlesex, 28 September 1934. Died 28 September 2006.) A product of Brentford's youth set-up of the 1950s, Dennis Heath was a fast and tricky winger who played in 132 first-team games for the Bees between 1952 and 1961.

George Heslop (Born Wallsend, 1 July 1940. Died St Anne's, Lancs, 16 September 2006.) A powerful centre half, George Heslop was on Newcastle United's books as a teenager, but was a reserve during his time at St James' Park and also at Everton, after moving to the Merseyside club in 1962. George finally achieved regular first-team football on signing for Manchester City, assisting the club to the Second Division championship in 1965–66 and the Football League title in 1967–68. He later won European Cup Winners' Cup and Football League Cup honours with City in 1969–70 and ended his career with a season at Bury.

Bill Hicklin (Born Dudley, 20 September 1924. Died May 2007.) Bill Hicklin was a wing half who made 11 wartime appearances for Birmingham City before joining Watford in June 1947. He featured regularly for the Hornets in the following season, but made a return to the Midlands in the summer of 1948 when he signed for West Bromwich Albion. However, he failed to add to his total of senior appearances at The Hawthorns, later playing for a number of non-League clubs including Kidderminster Harriers, Bilston and Dudley Town.

Len Hill (Born Caerleon, Monmouthshire, 14 April 1941. Died Newport, South Wales, 10 April 2007.) Len Hill was capped by Wales at Youth international level and after a spell with Lovell's Athletic he joined Newport County in November 1962. An attacking wing half, he went on to amass some 360 Football League appearances for the club where he remained until 1974, although his stay was interrupted by a brief spell with Swansea City in the early 1970s. Len was also a talented cricketer, featuring as a middle order batsman for Glamorgan, for whom he made 76 first-class appearances between 1964 and 1976.

Graham Hobbins (Born 1949. Died 5 February 2007.) Graham Hobbins was a key figure in the history of Welling United serving as manager for 17 years, and more recently holding the post of general manager. Along with his brother Barrie he guided the club into the Conference in 1986 and kept them at the forefront of non-League football over the next 20 years.

Ronnie Hobbs (Born Aldershot, 23 August 1921. Died 8 January 2007.) Ronnie Hobbs was an outside right who joined Aldershot in November 1944, remaining on the club's books for 10 years, during which time he made 189 peacetime appearances. He later played for Alton Town before a broken leg ended his career.

Billy Hogan (Born Salford, Lancs, 9 January 1924. Died Cornwall, 6 June 2007.) Billy Hogan was a talented inside forward who made three appearances for Manchester City at the end of the 1948–49 season before being sold to Carlisle United for a club record fee of £4,000. He went on to make some 200 appearances during his stay at Brunton Park and his impact was such that readers of a local newspaper recently voted him as the club's best-ever player.

John Hoskins (Born Southampton, 10 May 1931. Died 18 September 2006.) John Hoskins was a goalscoring outside left who scored 64 goals in 235 appearances for Southampton between 1952 and 1959. A highlight of his career was touring the West Indies with an FA XI in 1955. He later spent a season with Swindon Town before leaving the full-time game.

Vince Jack (Born Rosemark, Ross & Cromarty, 6 August 1933. Died Gosford, New South Wales, Australia, 22 September 2006.) After making his name as an effective centre half with Highland League club Inverness Thistle, Vince Jack moved south to sign for Bury in April 1954. He also had spells with Swindon Town, Accrington Stanley and Gravesend before emigrating to Australia in the 1960s.

Kai Johansen (Born Odense, Denmark, 23 February 1940. Died 12 May 2007.) Kai Johansen developed as a full back with the OB Odense club and went on to win 20 caps for Denmark between June 1962 and December 1963. The following April he signed for Morton, one of several Scandinavian players recruited to Scottish football in the mid-1960s. His performances drew the attention of Rangers and he moved on to the Ibrox club in the summer of 1965. Kai went on to play nearly 250 games during his stay, netting the winning goal against Celtic in the 1966 Scottish Cup final replay and also featuring in the side defeated by Bayern Munich in the 1967 European Cup Winners' Cup final.

Derek Jones (Born Ellesmere Port, Cheshire, 24 April 1929. Died Ellesmere Port, Cheshire, 26 October 2006.) Derek Jones was a tough and enthusiastic defender who made over 150 appearances for Tranmere Rovers between 1953 and 1961. Also occasionally used as a makeshift centre forward, he moved on to Runcorn in the summer of 1961.

Paddy Kennedy (Born Dublin, Eire, 9 October 1934. Died Urmston, Manchester, 18 March 2007.) Paddy Kennedy was one of the Busby Babes of the early 1950s, featuring at left back in the Manchester United side that defeated Wolves to win the inaugural FA Youth Cup competition in 1952–53. However, his senior career was blighted by injury and he made just six Football League appearances in a career that saw him play for United, Blackburn Rovers and Southampton.

Joe Kiernan (Born Coatbridge, Lanarkshire, 22 October 1942. Died Northampton, 1 August 2006.) Joe Kiernan began his career at Sunderland, but after just two first-team outings he was allowed to leave for Northampton. A combative left half, he assisted the Cobblers in their rise to the old First Division, but the success was short-lived and three relegations in four seasons saw them back in the Football League's basement division. Joe played 351 games for Northampton before moving on to Kettering Town.

Mike Langley (Born Harrogate, circa 1926. Died May 2007.) Mike Langley began his career in journalism working for the *Daily Express* in Manchester, later becoming Deputy Sports Editor of the *People* in 1964. In 1991 he transferred to the *Mirror* where he remained until his retirement in 1998. A well-respected sports writer, he was the first-ever Football Writer of the Year in 1987 and was also named British Press Sportswriter of the Year in 1980 and 1985.

David Lawrence (Born Poole, Dorset, 12 May 1933. Died 14 July 2006.) David Lawrence made five senior appearances for Bristol Rovers before moving on to Reading in the summer of 1957. He enjoyed a decent run at right back for the Elm Park club, before dropping out of the picture. David subsequently played for Poole Town and Trowbridge.

Jimmy Leadbetter (Born Edinburgh, 15 July 1928. Died Edinburgh. 18 July 2006.) Jimmy Leadbetter made over 350 appearances for Ipswich Town in a decade of service at Portman Road, commencing in 1955. Although his early career had been spent as an inside forward, he was converted to an outside-left role by manager Alf Ramsey, assisting the club to the Second Division title in 1960–61 and the Football League Championship in 1961–62. However, he did not play as a traditional old-style winger and was effectively operating as a modern midfield player, being credited as being the prototype for Ramsey's 'wingless wonders' that went on to win the 1966 World Cup. Earlier in his career he had played a handful of games for Chelsea and rather more for Brighton before moving to East Anglia.

David Letham (Born 1923. Died 17 March 2007.) David Letham was a centre half who first appeared in the Queen's Park line-up during the 1939–40 season. In total he made almost 200 appearances, including wartime games, for the Hampden club before injury curtailed his career. He was later active in football administration, serving Queen's Park as a director and president and also serving a term as the president of the Scottish League.

Harry Leyland (Born Liverpool, 12 May 1930. Died Wirral, 7 December 2006.) Harry Leyland spent a decade on the books of Everton without ever really establishing himself as the first-choice goalkeeper. His fortunes improved on signing for Blackburn Rovers in August 1956 and he made 188 first-team appearances during his stay at Ewood Park, gaining an FA Cup runners-up medal in 1960 when Rovers lost out to Wolves in the final. Harry concluded his senior career at Tranmere Rovers, where he added nearly 200 more appearances before becoming player-manager of Wigan Athletic.

Peter Lomas (Born Royton, Lancs, 9 May 1933. Died Southport, 15 November 2006.) Peter Lomas was a defender who spent six years on the books of Southport. His time was interrupted by National Service, but after just 18 senior appearances he suffered a serious injury in February 1957 and this brought his playing career to an end.

Trevor Long (Born Smethwick, Worcs, 1 July 1931. Died 15 November 2006.) Trevor Long was a small pacy winger who joined Wolves from local football in December 1950. However, competition for first-team appearances was fierce at Molineux and he failed to break into the senior team, moving on to Gillingham in the 1952 close season. Trevor fared rather better at Priestfield where he played on 70 occasions, before winding down his career with a season at Reading.

Walter McCrae (Born Kilmarnock, 1929. Died Kilmarnock, 22 September 2006.) Walter McCrae's playing career never extended beyond a spell in goal for Kilmarnock Juniors, but he spent many years on the backroom staff at Kilmarnock FC, serving as first-team trainer from 1956 to 1968, and then as manager through to 1973. He later returned to the club as secretary and general manager for the period 1980–1991.

Norrie McCredie (Born Glasgow, 17 May 1928. Died Oswaldtwistle, Lancs, 8 June 2006.) After seven seasons on the books of Partick Thistle, where he was little more than a reserve, Norrie McCredie joined the growing Scottish contingent at Accrington Stanley in the summer of 1955. A versatile left-sided player, he went on to make over 100 Football League appearances in a career that also saw him turn out for Southport and Barrow.

Jimmy McDermott (Born Earlestown, Lancs, 25 May 1932. Died 29 August 2006.) Jimmy McDermott was a small, pacy winger who joined Southport from Lancashire Combination outfit Crompton Recs in the 1955 close season. He soon settled in at Haig Avenue, establishing himself in the first-team line-up within a matter of months and he went on to make 163 appearances for the Sandgrounders over the next four seasons. Jimmy moved on to Wigan Athletic in 1959 and later played for both Earlestown and Pwllheli.

Billy McGann (Born Dundee, 7 October 1943. Died 6 January 2007.) After developing in Junior football with Lochee Harp and Downfield, goalkeeper Billy McGann signed for East Fife in September 1965. He made over 100 first-team appearances during his stay at Methil, later enjoying brief spells at St Mirren, Cowdenbeath, Hamilton Academicals, Stenhousemuir and Forfar Athletic.

Jimmy McGill (Born Bellshill, Lanarkshire, 2 October 1939. Died Chester, October 2006.) Jimmy McGill was a tough tackling defender who stepped up to the senior ranks in December 1956 when he joined Partick Thistle from Larkhall Thistle. He failed to make the first team during his stay at Fir Park, but enjoyed greater success when he moved south, making over 150 senior appearances for Oldham, Crewe, Chester and Wrexham between 1959 and 1964.

John McIlvenny (Born Barnstaple, 2 March 1930. Died Basingstoke, Hants, 25 September 2006.) John McIlvenny was a winger who spent time on the books of West Bromwich Albion without making a senior appearance, and then drifted off to sign for Cheltenham Town. Bristol Rovers resurrected his senior career in the summer of 1952 and in his first season with the club he helped them win the Division Three South title. John later spent two seasons at Reading, taking his tally of senior appearances above the 150 mark.

Jim McLaughlin (Born Paisley, 11 February 1926. Died 6 May 2006.) Jim McLaughlin was a big, powerful centre forward who joined Celtic from Renfrew Juniors in April 1947, but although he scored on his first-team debut against Morton he made just one more appearance for the Parkhead club before moving south to sign for Walsall. However, in two seasons at Fellows Park Jim struggled to establish himself in the line-up, eventually returning to live in Scotland.

Tom McLevy (Born circa 1931. Died Perth, 24 March 2007.) Tom McLevy joined Arbroath from Blairgowrie Juniors in December 1955 and went on to feature at left half in the team that won promotion from the Second Division in 1958–59. In June 1960 he was transferred to Brechin City where he became a mainstay of the club's defence, missing just one Scottish League game over the next six seasons. Tom made almost 450 senior appearances before leaving senior football in the summer of 1967.

Ian McPhee (Born 16 October 1942. Died Canada, 6 May 2007.) Ian McPhee was a cultured midfield player with excellent distribution skills. He stepped up to senior football in the summer of 1963, moving from Duntocher Hibs to East Stirlingshire. He remained with the club another season, during which they played under the name ES Clydebank before moving on to St Johnstone in August 1965. Ian went on to make almost 250 appearances for the Perth club, gaining a runners-up medal in the 1969–70 League Cup final when Celtic defeated Saints. He subsequently had brief spells with Arbroath, Raith and Albion Rovers before emigrating to Canada.

Albert Maddox (Born Oswaldtwistle, Lancs, circa 1922. Died 15 June 2007.) Albert Maddox was on the books of Accrington Stanley just before war broke out, but failed to make the first team. In 1947 he was appointed assistant-secretary of Burnley and 15 years later he became club secretary, serving through until the 1980s. His years of service to the club were rewarded when a suite in the James Hargreaves Stand at Turf Moor was named after him.

Darren Magee (Born Glasgow, 14 April 1977. Died Glasgow, December 2006.) Darren Magee was a midfielder who appeared in 26 first-team games for Dundee in the late 1990s. Injury brought his career to a premature end and after being troubled by personal problems he was found dead in tragic circumstances.

Joe Maloney (Born Liverpool, 26 January 1934. Died 18 October 2006.) Joe Maloney made a dozen first-team appearances for Liverpool in the early 1950s before moving on to Shrewsbury Town in the summer of 1954. At Gay Meadow he was the club's regular centre half for several seasons, playing in almost 250 games during a seven-year spell. He concluded his career with brief stints at Port Vale and Crewe Alexandra.

Derek Mann (Born circa 1943. Died January 2007.) Although Derek Mann served as an apprentice with Shrewsbury Town, his playing career was effectively ended by injury before he could break into the first team. He subsequently worked as a coach or on the backroom staff of a number of clubs including Shrewsbury, Watford, Wolves, Huddersfield Town and Chester City. He briefly held the post of manager of Chester in the 1994–95 season and later also served as manager of Telford United.

Billy Marshall (Born Belfast, 11 July 1936. Died 20 April 2007.) Billy Marshall was a defender who spent nine years on the books of Burnley, where he was principally a reserve, captaining the club's second string. In the summer of 1962 he moved on to Oldham, where he spent two years as a regular first-team player, before concluding his career at Hartlepools United. Billy was capped twice by Northern Ireland at B international level during his spell at Turf Moor.

Andy Micklewright (Born Birmingham, 31 January 1931. Died Torquay, 5 August 2006.) Andy Micklewright was an inside forward who joined Bristol Rovers from Smethwick Highfield in January 1952. However, he was unable to win a regular place in the Pirates' line-up and soon moved on to join local rivals City. It was only when he arrived at Swindon shortly after the start of the 1955–56 season that he experienced regular first-team football, scoring 34 goals in 121 outings before concluding his career with a season at Exeter.

Brian Miller (Born Hapton, Burnley, 19 January 1937. Died Burnley, 7 April 2007.) Brian Miller was a powerful, solid wing half who gave more than 40 years' service to Burnley Football Club, making over 450 first-team appearances and enjoying spells as manager, coach and scout. He was still a teenager when he made his senior debut in the 1955–56 season, he went on to become a first-team regular being ever-present in 1959–60 when the Clarets won the Football League Championship. Brian won international recognition appearing three times for England Under 23s, once for the full international team (against Austria in May 1961) and twice for the Football League representative eleven. A knee injury brought his career to a close in April 1967, but he remained on the staff at Turf Moor, serving the club in a number of roles including manager on two separate occasions.

Arthur Milton (Born Bedminster, Bristol, 10 March 1928. Died Bristol, 25 April 2007.) Arthur Milton was one of only 12 men to win full international honours for England at both cricket and football. After signing amateur forms for Arsenal in April 1945 he underwent a period of National Service, and it was not until 1951 that he made his first-team debut. A classical outside right, he was capped by England against Austria in November 1951 and was a regular in the Gunners' line-up during the 1952–53 season, when the Football League Championship was secured. Arthur left Highbury in February 1955 and after a brief spell with Bristol City chose to focus on his cricket career. In addition to 6 England caps, he played some 620 first-class games for Gloucestershire between 1948 and 1974, scoring more than 32,000 runs.

Norman Moore (Born Grimsby, 15 October 1919. Died Grimsby, 14 March 2007.) After failing to make a significant impact as a half back with Grimsby Town, Norman Moore crossed the River Humber in April 1947 to sign for Hull. Manager Major Buckley converted him to a role as centre forward and he responded with an excellent scoring record: 53 goals in 92 games before injury intervened. Norman later had spells with Blackburn and Bury, but proved unable to rediscover the goalscoring form he had displayed at Boothferry Park.

Alan Morris (Born Swansea, 6 April 1941. Died Swansea, 29 March 2007.) Alan Morris was an outside right who made his debut for Swansea Town as a 16-year old. Although he only managed a dozen Football League appearances for the Swans, he has the distinction of scoring the fastest goal at the Vetch Field in the post-war period when he found the net after just 10 seconds against Leeds United during the 1960–61 season. Alan later had a spell with Reading before a knee injury ended his career.

Reggie Morrison (Born Gourdon, Inverbervie, Aberdeenshire, circa 1933. Died Peterhead, 28 November 2006.) Goalkeeper Reggie Morrison made 87 appearances for Aberdeen in the 1950s, winning Under 23 international honours for Scotland against England in the 1955–56 season. He later had a spell at Dundee without making a first-team appearance before concluding his senior career at Stirling Albion.

Harold Mosby (Born Kippax, Yorkshire, 25 June 1926. Died 15 June 2007.) Harold Mosby was a small, tricky winger who signed for Rotherham United in January 1947. He made 26 Football League appearances in three seasons for the Millers, but was a regular for Scunthorpe after moving on in the summer of 1950. Harold played in the Irons' first-ever League encounter with Shrewsbury Town in August of that year, and was a fixture in the line-up for five seasons, featuring in over 150 games. He later had a season in the Midland League with Worksop before concluding his senior career with a spell at Crewe Alexandra.

Frank Mountford (Born Askern, Doncaster, 30 March 1923. Died Stoke-on-Trent, 27 June 2006.) Frank Mountford was a solid, committed half back who made over 600 senior appearances for Stoke City, including games in the wartime emergency competitions. Always dependable, he was a key figure for the Potteries club in the immediate post-war years, his role as club penalty taker helping him achieve a tally of 24 peacetime goals. On retiring as a player Frank joined Stoke's backroom staff, later occupying the post of trainer from 1960 to 1977.

Ken Nicholas (Born Northampton, 3 February 1938. Died London, 24 March 2007.) Ken Nicholas spent four years on Arsenal's books, during which he gained England Youth international honours, although he was unable to break into the first team. After moving on to Watford in the 1955 close season, Ken went on to make over 200 first-team appearances for the Hornets, mostly in the left-back position. He later played for Guildford City and Hastings United.

Mick Pamment (Born Lascelles Hall, Huddersfield, 12 May 1945. Died Dewsbury, 16 July 2006.) Mick Pamment won England Youth international honours after establishing a reputation as a prolific goalscorer in local junior football. His only senior appearance came when he played for Bradford City against Torquay United in December 1964, whilst on the club's books as an amateur. He spent most of his career with Yorkshire League club Emley, for whom he established a club record for goals scored.

Franco Cosimo Panini (Born Pozza di Maranello, Italy, 8 October 1931. Died Modena, Italy, 30 March 2007.) Franco Cosimo Panini was one of three brothers who developed the Panini company that for many years dominated the world of football cards. Initially focusing on players in Italy's Serie A, the brothers were selling 15 million packets of cards annually by 1963 and soon expanded their horizons to other countries, including England where the stickers became a popular collectable item amongst youngsters from the 1970s onwards.

Gino Pariani (Born St Louis, Missouri, USA, 21 February 1928. Died St Louis, Missouri, USA, 9 May 2007) Gino Pariani featured at inside right in all three of the USA's games during the 1950 World Cup finals in Brazil, including the famous 1–0 victory over England. Earlier in his career he had played in the 1948 Olympic Games in London, and helped his club team, Simpkins Ford of St Louis, to victory in the US Open Cup in 1948 and 1950.

Simon Patterson (Born Harrow, Middlesex, 4 September 1982. Died Hammersmith, London, 10 September 2006.) Simon Patterson was a tall striker who spent four years on the books of Watford without making the first team. However, during a loan spell with Wycombe Wanderers at the start of the 2003–04 season he made five senior appearances scoring two goals. He subsequently played for a number of non-League clubs, most recently Wingate & Finchley, before his tragically early death, which was a result of a car accident.

Vince Pilling (Born Deane, Bolton, 8 January 1932. Died 9 February 2007.) Vince Pilling was a winger who spent three years on the books of Bolton Wanderers in the early 1950s, making seven first-team appearances. In the summer of 1955 he was transferred to Bradford Park Avenue, but he was again mostly a reserve and left the club after a single season.

Willie Pullar (Born circa 1925. Died Falkland, Fife, 15 March 2007.) Right half Willie Pullar signed for St Johnstone at the start of the 1949–50 campaign, but struggled to win a regular place in the line-up. He made 16 first-team appearances over the next two seasons before moving on.

Ted Purdon (Born Johannesburg, South Africa, 1 March 1930. Died Toronto, Canada, 29 April 2007.) Ted Purdon was one of four players recruited by Birmingham City from South Africa's Marist Brothers in the first half of the 1950–51 season and while the other three made little impact, Ted went on to enjoy a lengthy career in British football. He went on to score some 87 goals in 228 Football League appearances, also playing for Sunderland, Workington, Barrow and Bristol Rovers. He subsequently emigrated to Canada where he turned out for a number of clubs in the Eastern Canada Professional League in the early 1960s.

Bob Pursell (Born Glasgow, 28 September 1919. Died Minehead, Somerset, 8 August 2006.) Recruited from local football, Bob Pursell was a full back who made 14 appearances for Port Vale in the 1939–40 season. He remained on the club's books until 1948, bringing his total of appearances for Vale to 96 before departing to join Winsford United.

Ferenc Puskas (Born Budapest, Hungary, 2 April 1927. Died Budapest, Hungary, 17 November 2006.) Hungary were one of the great teams in the early 1950s, and Ferenc Puskas was arguably their most talented player. A prolific scoring centre forward, he possessed a phenomenal left foot and despite a rather portly appearance he displayed amazing skills on the ball. Having joined Kispest and established himself in the first team at the age of 16, he was appointed to the rank of Major when the club became the Hungarian Army club under the name Honved following a change of political regime after the war, hence his nickname of 'the Galloping Major'. He gained a gold medal from the 1952 Olympic Games, when Yugoslavia were despatched 2–0 in the final, and featured in the World Cup final two years later when the Hungarians were surprisingly defeated by West Germany in the final in which Puskas played and scored, despite being only partially fit. Two of the team's greatest triumphs came against England, who were defeated 6–3 at Wembley in November 1963 and 7–1 in Budapest the following May; Ferenc played a key role on both occasions. After the Hungarian Uprising of 1956 Puskas opted for a life in the West and became one of the stars of the Real Madrid team, helping them to three European Cup victories. Having earlier won 85 caps for Hungary, he added another 4 for his adopted country Spain. In retirement he coached a number of clubs, leading Panathinaikos to a place in the 1971 European Cup final.

Pietro Rava (Born Cassine, Alessandria, Italy, 21 January 1916. Died Torino, Italy, 5 November 2006.) Pietro Rava was a full back who won 30 caps for Italy between 1936 and 1946. His international debut came against the USA team in the 1936 Olympics and he retained his place in the side as Italy went on to win the gold medal, defeating Austria in the final. Two years later Pietro added a World Cup winners' medal when he featured in the team that defeated Hungary 4–2 in Paris. He was the last surviving member of that team. Most of his domestic football was played for Juventus.

Bob Raynor (Born Nottingham, 30 August 1940. Died 7 March 2007.) Goalkeeper Bob Raynor spent a year on the books of Nottingham Forest without making the first team. In August 1965 he moved on to Halifax Town, for whom he made 17 first-team appearances over the next two seasons.

John Ritchie (Born Kettering, Northants, 12 July 1941. Died 23 February 2007.) John was a big, powerful centre forward, who established an all-time record of 176 goals for Stoke City during two spells at the club. His early football was played in the Southern League with Kettering Town and in the summer of 1962 the Potters signed him up. Within 12 months he had won a regular place in the first team, and soon afterwards set a club record by scoring in nine consecutive competitive games. Although surprisingly sold to Sheffield Wednesday in November 1966 he returned to the Victoria Ground three years later and was a key figure in the side that defeated Chelsea to win the Football League Cup in 1972. He won representative honours for the Football League in 1967.

Harold Roberts (Born Liverpool, 12 January 1920. Died 11 February 2007.) Harold Roberts was a pacy outside left who was on Everton's books as a youngster. He served in the Commandos during the war, spending three years as a prisoner of war after being captured during a raid on St Nazaire. On his return Harold showed some excellent form for Chesterfield, eventually earning a move to Birmingham City in November 1948 for a club record fee for the Spireites. Although less successful during his time at St Andrew's, he went on to play for Shrewsbury Town and Scunthorpe United before leaving the full-time game. He later coached Chesterfield's youth players for over a decade, finally leaving the club in 1983.

Willie Robertson (Born Montrose, 9 November 1923. Died Preston, 29 August 2006.) Willie Robertson was a Scotland Schoolboys international and went on to play more than 100 wartime games for Preston North End and Blackburn Rovers. A left-sided defender, he remained on the books at Deepdale until 1955, adding a further 55 appearances before ending his career with a spell at Southport.

Johnny Schofield (Born Atherstone, Warwickshire, 8 February 1931. Died 2 November 2006.) Johnny Schofield was on Birmingham City's books for close on a decade before he won a regular place in the first-team line-up. A brave and dependable goalkeeper, he went on to make 237 first-team appearances for the Blues, featuring in the side that won the Football League Cup in 1962–63 and playing in two Inter Cities Fairs Cup finals. Johnny left St Andrew's in July 1966, spending two seasons at Wrexham before leaving the full-time game.

Ferenc Puskas, 1981

Eddie Scott (Born Portsmouth, 17 May 1917. Died February 2007.) Eddie Scott joined Gillingham as a part-time player in 1935 and went on to make 50 Football League appearances, remaining with the club during the 1938–39 season when they were members of the Southern League. He was believed to be the Gills' oldest surviving player at the time of his death.

Alex Scougall (Born 1989. Died Lasswade, Midlothian, 18 May 2007.) Alex Scougall was a talented youngster who had been captain of Dunfermline Athletic's youth team before joining East Fife in the summer of 2006. He helped the Bayview club reach the final of the Scottish Youth League Cup final, but tragically died in a car accident just two days prior to the final, which was postponed as a mark of respect.

Bobby Shearer (Born 29 December 1931. Died 5 November 2006.) Bobby Shearer was a tough-tackling defender who began his senior career with Hamilton Academicals in the 1951–52 season, later gaining a transfer to Rangers in December 1955. One of the key figures in the Ibrox club's defence in the early 1960s, Bobby went on to gain international recognition, winning four full caps for Scotland and also two for the Scottish League representative eleven. In total he made over 400 appearances for Rangers, assisting the club to 11 domestic trophies including a treble of the League, League Cup and Scottish Cup in the 1963–64 season. He later served Queen of the South as player-coach and also had spells as manager of Third Lanark and Hamilton.

Hedley Sheppard (Born East Ham, London, 26 November 1909. Died 12 December 2006.) Although Hedley Sheppard failed to make the first team during a spell with West Ham in the early 1930s, he experienced regular first-team football after signing for Aldershot in the summer of 1934. A versatile defender, he went on to play in 276 senior games for the Shots before moving on to Fleet Town in the 1949 close season.

Bert Slater (Born Musselburgh, East Lothian, 5 May 1936. Died Brechin, 21 July 2006.) Bert Slater established his credentials as a top-class goalkeeper in a six-year spell with Falkirk, during which time he was capped by Scotland at Under 23 level and assisted the club to victory in the Scottish Cup when they defeated Kilmarnock to take the trophy in 1957. His form alerted clubs south of the border and in the summer of 1959 he moved on to Liverpool, later assisting the Anfield club to the Second Division title in 1962–63. After a spell at Dundee, for whom he featured in a European Cup semi-final, Bert finished his playing career at Watford. He subsequently remained at Vicarage Road, serving the Hornets as trainer from 1971 to 1973.

Peter Small (Born Horsham, Sussex, 23 October 1924. Died 3 November 2006.) Peter Small was a pacy winger who made his bow in League football with Luton Town during the 1947–48 season. He was a member of promotion-winning teams with both Leicester City (1953–54) and Nottingham Forest (1956–57) before concluding his career with a spell at Brighton.

Barry Smith (Born South Kirkby, Yorkshire, 15 March 1934. Died New Zealand, February 2007.) Barry Smith was a centre forward who joined Leeds United from local club Farsley Celtic as a youngster. However, he made just two Football League appearances before transferring to Bradford Park Avenue in May 1955. Barry featured regularly for the Avenue over the next two seasons, finishing as the club's leading scorer in 1956–57 with 29 goals including four hat-tricks. He subsequently played for Wrexham and Stockport, and later had very brief spells with Oldham Athletic, Southport and Accrington Stanley. His death came whilst he was on a sailing holiday in New Zealand.

Bobby Smith (Born circa 1937. Died March 2007.) Bobby Smith made his name in Scottish Junior circles with Kirkintilloch Rob Roy before moving up to the senior ranks with Berwick Rangers in the summer of 1961. In two seasons at Shielfield Park he was a near ever present, scoring 18 goals in 88 appearances. Bobby later returned to the Juniors, playing for Lanark United and Carluke Rovers before becoming manager of Forth Wanderers.

Septimus Smith (Born Whitburn, Co Durham, 13 March 1912. Died Leicester, 28 July 2006.) Septimus Smith was one of five brothers who played League football. An England Schoolboy cap, he signed for Leicester City in April 1929, making his first-team debut later that year. An inspirational half back, he went on to make almost 600 appearances for the club, including wartime matches, in a career that lasted until 1949. Septimus captained the City team that won the Second Division Championship in 1936–37 and was capped once for England during the 1935–36 season.

Bert Snell (Born Dunscroft, Doncaster, 7 February 1931. Died Sunderland, 31 March 2007.) Bert Snell was a wing half who was on Doncaster Rovers' books as a youngster before signing for Sunderland in 1949. He made his senior debut two years later and although he made only nine appearances during his stay at Roker Park, he featured in the side that thrashed champions Arsenal 7–1 in September 1953. Bert later had a couple of seasons at Halifax Town before embarking on a career in teaching.

Alberto Spencer (Born Ancón, Ecuador, 6 December 1937. Died Cleveland, Ohio, USA, 3 November 2006.) Alberto Spencer was one of the greatest strikers in South American football in the post-war era, and still holds the record of 54 goals scored in the Copa Libertadores. His best football was played in Uruguay with Penarol, where he was a member of three successful Copa Libertadores teams (1960, 1961 and 1966). At international level he played for both Ecuador and Uruguay.

Johnny Spuhler (Born Sunderland, 18 September 1917. Died Middlesbrough, 7 January 2007.) After being capped by England Schoolboys, Johnny Spuhler joined Sunderland, making his first-team debut during the 1936–37 season. In total he made almost 200 appearances, including wartime games, during his stay at Roker Park and on transferring to Middlesbrough in October 1945 he added another 200 before becoming player-coach of Darlington. Johnny later coached the West Auckland team that reached the FA Amateur Cup final in 1961.

Tommy Stewart (Born Belfast, 1935. Died 2 November 2006.) Tommy Stewart was a star of the Linfield team of the late 1950s and early '60s. A key figure in the team that lifted seven trophies in the 1961–62 season, he won a full cap for Northern Ireland in April 1961 and also featured for the Irish League representative eleven.

Jim Stirling (Born Airdrie, 23 July 1925. Died November 2006.) Jim Stirling signed for Bournemouth in the summer of 1947, and after breaking into the first team showed sufficient form at centre half to earn a transfer to Birmingham City. However, he failed to break into the first team at St Andrew's and quickly moved on, joining Southend United in December 1950. He stayed a decade with the Essex club, making over 200 senior appearances before dropping down to Southern League football with Poole Town in 1960.

Bill Stroud (Born Hammersmith, London, 7 July 1919. Died Southampton, 5 October 2006.) Half back Bill Stroud made almost 200 wartime appearances for Southampton, but after just one post-war season with the Saints he was transferred to Leyton Orient. Bill spent three years with the O's and another three with Newport County before joining the coaching staff at Somerton Park. He later helped out with coaching the Saints' youngsters for almost 25 years from 1963.

Ferenc Szusza (Born Újpest, Hungary, 1 December 1923. Died Budapest, Hungary, 1 August 2006.) Ferenc Szusza was a prolific goalscorer in domestic football in Hungary, scoring a record 392 goals for Újpesti Dózsa between 1940 and 1961 and helping the club to four national titles. He also won 24 caps for Hungary between 1942 and 1956.

Ernie Tagg (Born Crewe, 15 November 1917. Died 29 November 2006.) Ernie Tagg made his senior debut as an inside forward for Crewe Alexandra during the 1937–38 season and soon earned a transfer to Wolves for £1,000, a record fee for the Cheshire club at the time. Although he was mostly a reserve during his stay at Molineux, he went on to play 87 games for Bournemouth in the immediate post-war period before concluding his playing career at Carlisle United. Ernie later served Crewe as manager from 1964 until 1971, leading the club to promotion from the Fourth Division in 1967–68.

Fred Tapping, MBE (Born Derby, 29 July 1921. Died Bretby, Derbyshire, 22 February 2007.) Fred Tapping was a forward who played in 28 wartime games for Blackpool, also guesting for Derby County during the hostilities. He went on to make a single Football League appearance for Chesterfield during the 1947–48 season before joining Southern League club Headington United. Fred was awarded the MBE in 1980 for services to his employer, Rolls Royce.

David Teece (Born Oldham, 1 September 1927. Died March 2007.) Goalkeeper David Teece spent four seasons on the books of Hull City in the early 1950s, but was mostly used as back-up for Billy Bly. In June 1956 he moved on to Oldham Athletic, for whom he made almost 100 Football League appearances before switching to non-League football with Buxton.

Pat Terry (Born Lambeth, London, 2 October 1933. Died Farnborough Common, Kent, 27 March 2007.) Pat Terry was a bustling, old-fashioned style centre forward who made his bow in senior football with Charlton Athletic in April 1954. Over the next 15 years he went on to amass a total 219 Football League goals from almost 500 games. He appeared for a string of clubs including Newport County, Swansea Town, Gillingham, Northampton Town, Millwall, Reading, Swindon Town and Brentford.

Geoff Thomas (Born Derby, 21 February 1926. Died Nottingham, 18 July 2006.) Geoff Thomas was a full back who made almost 500 first-team appearances for Nottingham Forest, including games played in the emergency wartime competitions. Having joined the club in September 1943, he stayed for some 17 years, featuring in the teams that won the Division Three South title in 1950–51 and promotion to the First Division in 1956–57.

John Thompson (Born Newcastle upon Tyne, 4 July 1932. Died Beadnell, Northumberland, 29 December 2006.) John Thompson spent seven years on the books of Newcastle United, but was never more than a back-up goalkeeper, the highlight of his St James' Park career coming when he played in the FA Charity Shield fixture against Chelsea in September 1955. He saw rather more first-team action at Lincoln City, for whom he made 43 appearances, but he was only a first choice for the 1957–58 season.

Tommy Traynor (Born Dundalk, Eire, 22 July 1933. Died Southampton, 20 September 2006.) Tommy Traynor enjoyed something of a meteoric rise to fame with Dundalk, gaining an FAI Cup winners' medal when Cork Athletic were defeated in the replayed 1952 final and winning amateur international honours for the Republic of Ireland. Transferred to Southampton in June 1952 he went on to become the mainstay of the side over the next 14 years, establishing a new club record of 434 appearances. A key figure in the team that won the Third Division title in 1959–60, he also won eight full caps for the Republic.

Dennis Uphill (Born Bath, 11 August 1931. Died Watford, 7 February 2007.) Dennis Uphill began his senior career with Tottenham Hotspur, but struggled to make an impact at White Hart Lane. In February 1953 he moved on to Reading, where he enjoyed regular first-team football, scoring 47 goals in 98 first-team games. Thereafter he built a successful career as a battling centre forward, serving Coventry City, Mansfield Town, Watford and Crystal Palace in turn, and taking his tally of Football League goals to 147.

Johnny Vincent (Born West Bromwich, 8 February 1947. Died Kidderminster, 23 December 2006.) Johnny Vincent won England Youth international honours and stepped up for his first-team debut for Birmingham City whilst still a teenager. A hard working inside forward, he went on to score 44 goals in 193 appearances for the Blues before he was sold to Middlesbrough in March 1971. Johnny later had a stint with Cardiff City (where he won two Welsh Cup winners' medals) and ended his career with a spell in the NASL at Connecticut Bi-Centennials.

Barry Wallace (Born Plaistow, London, 17 April 1959. Died Lenexa, Kansas, USA, 17 October 2006.) After four seasons on the books of Queens Park Rangers, for whom he made 27 first-team appearances, Barry Wallace joined Tulsa Roughnecks of the NASL and was a member of the team that won the Soccer Bowl in 1983. A midfielder or defender, he remained in the USA for the rest of his life, also turning out for Wichita Wings, Minnesota Strikers, Fort Lauderdale Strikers and Kansas City Comets.

Billy Walsh (Born Dublin, Eire, 31 May 1921. Died Noosa, Queensland, Australia, July 2006.) An England Schoolboy international, Billy Walsh was a wing half who made over 300 appearances, including wartime games, for Manchester City between 1938 and 1950. He was also one of a number of players to win full international honours for both Eire (9 caps) and Northern Ireland (5 Caps) during this period. He later managed a number of clubs including Chelmsford City, Canterbury City and Grimsby Town (February 1954 to March 1955).

Joe Walton (Born Manchester, 5 June 1925. Died Preston, 31 December 2006.) A solid full back, Joe Walton never quite established himself in the Manchester United line-up in the early post-war years and in March 1948 he was sold to Preston North End. He remained at Deepdale for 13 years, making over 400 first-team appearances. Joe came close to winning an England cap, featuring in the unofficial international against Scotland in April 1946 and also for the Football League against the League of Ireland in April 1948. However, the highlight of his career came when he appeared for Preston in the 1954 FA Cup final when they were narrowly defeated by West Bromwich Albion. Joe later had a spell with Accrington Stanley before joining non-League club Horwich RMI.

Jim Watt (Died July 2006.) Jim Watt was a goalkeeper who played for Coleraine in the early 1950s, featuring for an Irish FA XI against the Gold Coast tourists in 1951 and gaining an Irish Cup runners-up medal two years later.

Eddie Werge (Born Sidcup, Kent, 9 September 1936. Died 2 May 2007.) Eddie Werge was a forward who spent six years on the books of Charlton Athletic in the late 1950s, making 45 first-team appearances. In May 1961 he was sold to neighbours Crystal Palace, where he enjoyed almost 100 outings before spending time in South Africa with Arcadia Shepherds. Eddie returned to sign for Leyton Orient towards the end of 1966, remaining for just over a year before dropping into non-League football with Bexley United.

Jack Westby (Born Aintree, Liverpool, 20 May 1917. Died Liverpool, 17 November 2006.) Jack Westby played a couple of games for Blackburn Rovers shortly before the outbreak of war, moving on to Liverpool in May 1944 where he featured regularly in the closing seasons of the wartime emergency competitions. However, when peacetime football returned he was unable to break into the first team at Anfield and in the summer of 1947 he was sold to Southport, the Sandgrounders paying a club record fee for his services. Jack remained at Haig Avenue for just a season, later moving on to Runcorn.

Don Weston (Born New Houghton, Derbyshire, 6 March 1936. Died Mansfield, 19 January 2007.) Don Weston was a goalscoring inside forward who first came to prominence with Wrexham during his National Service. He was soon sold to Birmingham City, where he appeared in the 1960 Inter Cities Fairs Cup final, and then to Rotherham United where he featured in the side that reached the first-ever Football League Cup final. He subsequently helped Leeds United to win the Second Division championship in 1963–64 and also featured for Huddersfield Town and Chester in a career that saw him score 97 League goals in 274 appearances.

Bert Westwood (Born 1917. Died 26 December 2006.) Bert Westwood served as a Football League linesman and then a referee for the period 1956 to 1958, when he was based in Stratford-upon-Avon. He was also heavily involved in football administration, acting as Norwich City secretary from 1959 until 1981.

Fred White (Born Wolverhampton, 5 December 1916. Died Sheffield, 13 January 2007.) Fred White had spells on the books of Wolves and Everton as a youngster without making the first team, but after joining Sheffield United in May 1937 he made over 100 wartime appearances and almost 50 appearances in peacetime. A tall and brave goalkeeper, he spent the 1950–51 season as a regular for Lincoln City before joining non-League Gainsborough Trinity. Fred later worked as a part-time member of the backroom staff at Bramall Lane for many years.

Barry Wilkinson (Born Lincoln, 19 July 1942. Died 16 May 2007.) Barry Wilkinson was a centre forward who scored regularly for Lincoln City reserves in the early 1960s. He made 10 first-team appearances for the Imps before dropping into Lincolnshire League football.

Charlie Williams, MBE (Born Barnsley, 23 December 1928. Died Barnsley, 2 September 2006.) Charlie Williams was a tough, no-nonsense centre half who made 174 appearances for Doncaster Rovers between 1950 and 1959. One of the few black players to feature regularly in the Football League in the 1950s, he was a regular in the line-up from January 1955. On leaving the senior game Charlie played briefly for Skegness Town and developed a second career in show business, eventually becoming a household name as a result of his performances on the television programme *The Comedians* in the 1970s.

Jock Winton (Born Perth, 6 October 1919. Died 29 October 2006.) Jock Winton was a full back who made almost 400 senior appearances in a career that spanned the period from 1947 to 1964. He had waited five years for his first-team debut at Burnley, but once established in the line-up he was capped by Scotland B against England in 1957. After an 18-month spell with Aston Villa he returned to Lancashire joining Rochdale. Jock enjoyed three years of regular first-team football at Spotland and featured in the side that lost out to Norwich City in the 1961–62 Football League Cup final.

Brian Woodall (Born Chester, 6 June 1948. Died Chester, 4 May 2007.) Brian Woodall became an apprentice at Sheffield Wednesday on leaving school, later joining the professional ranks at Hillsborough, where he went on to make his debut in midfield in the second half of the 1967–68 campaign. After a spell on loan at Oldham Athletic he signed for Chester in the summer of 1970, but after some initial promise he lost his place in the side and spent the closing stages of that season out on loan with Crewe Alexandra. Brian left the Sealand Road club in the summer of 1971, signing for non-League Oswestry Town.

Ian Wooldridge, OBE (Born 14 January 1932. Died London, 4 March 2007.) Ian Wooldridge was one of the most talented sports writers of his generation, winning the title of Sportswriter of the Year at the British Press Awards on four separate occasions. His early years were spent on newspapers in Hampshire before joining the *News Chronicle* in 1956. A brief spell on the *Sunday Dispatch* followed before he joined the *Daily Mail*, where he was to remain for the rest of his working life.

Ian Nannestad, Soccer History Magazine

THE FOOTBALL RECORDS

BRITISH FOOTBALL RECORDS

ALL-TIME PREMIER LEAGUE CHAMPIONSHIP SEASONS ON POINTS AVERAGE

	Team	*Season*	*P*	*W*	*D*	*L*	*F*	*A*	*Pts*	*Pts Av*
1	Chelsea	2004–05	38	29	8	1	72	15	95	2.50
2	Manchester U	1999–2000	38	28	7	3	97	45	91	2.39
3	Chelsea	2005–06	38	29	4	5	72	22	91	2.39
4	Arsenal	2003–04	38	26	12	0	73	26	90	2.36
5	Manchester U	2006–07	38	28	5	5	83	27	89	2.34
6	Arsenal	2001–02	38	26	9	3	79	36	87	2.28
7	Manchester U	1993–94	42	27	11	4	80	38	92	2.19
8	Manchester U	2002–03	38	25	8	5	74	34	83	2.18
9	Manchester U	1995–96	38	25	7	6	73	35	82	2.15
10	Blackburn R	1994–95	42	27	8	7	80	39	89	2.11
11	Manchester U	2000–01	38	24	8	6	79	31	80	2.10
12	Manchester U	1998–99	38	22	13	3	80	37	79	2.07
13	Arsenal	1997–98	38	23	9	6	68	33	78	2.05
14	Manchester U	1992–93	42	24	12	6	67	31	84	2.00
15	Manchester U	1996–97	38	21	12	5	76	44	75	1.97

PREMIER LEAGUE EVER-PRESENT CLUBS

	P	*W*	*D*	*L*	*F*	*A*	*Pts*
Manchester U	582	367	131	84	1140	516	1232
Arsenal	582	308	157	117	974	517	1081
Chelsea	582	285	158	139	912	580	1013
Liverpool	582	285	144	153	925	579	999
Aston Villa	582	214	175	193	711	673	817
Tottenham H	582	212	152	218	773	786	788
Everton	582	192	159	231	703	775	735

TOP TEN PREMIERSHIP APPEARANCES

1	Gary Speed	521	**6**	Sol Campbell	422
2	David James	476	**7**	Teddy Sheringham	418
3	Ryan Giggs	464	**8**	Andy Cole	407
4	Alan Shearer	441	**9**	Ray Parlour	379
5	Gareth Southgate	426	**10**	Robbie Fowler and Emile Heskey	376

TOP TEN PREMIERSHIP GOALSCORERS

1	Alan Shearer	260	**6**	Teddy Sheringham	146
2	Andy Cole	187	**7**	Jimmy Floyd Hasselbaink	127
3	Thierry Henry	174	**8**	Michael Owen	125
4	Robbie Fowler	163	**9**	Dwight Yorke	122
5	Les Ferdinand	149	**10**	Ian Wright	113

PREMIERSHIP GOAL MILESTONES

Goal	**Date**	**Scorer**	**Match**
1	15.8.92	Brian Deane	Sheffield U v Manchester U
100	25.8.92	Mark Walters	Liverpool v Ipswich T
1000	7.4.93	Mike Newell	Blackburn R v Nottingham F
5000	7.12.96	Andy Townsend	Aston Villa v Southampton
10,000	15.12.01	Les Ferdinand	Tottenham H v Fulham
11,000	7.12.02	Jay-Jay Okocha	Bolton W v Blackburn R
12,000	13.12.03	Alan Shearer	Newcastle U v Tottenham H
13,000	28.11.04	Frederic Kanoute	Tottenham H v Middlesbrough
14,000	26.12.05	Jermain Defoe	Tottenham H v Birmingham C
15,000	30.12.06	Moritz Volz	Fulham v Chelsea

EUROPEAN CUP AND CHAMPIONS LEAGUE RECORDS

CHAMPIONS LEAGUE ATTENDANCES AND GOALS FROM GROUP STAGES ONWARDS

Season	*Attendances*	*Average*	*Goals*	*Games*
1992–93	873,251	34,930	56	25
1993–94	1,202,289	44,529	71	27
1994–95	2,328,515	38,172	140	61
1995–96	1,874,316	30,726	159	61
1996–97	2,093,228	34,315	161	61
1997–98	2,868,271	33,744	239	85
1998–99	3,608,331	42,451	238	85
1999–2000	5,490,709	34,973	442	157
2000–01	5,773,486	36,774	449	157
2001–02	5,417,716	34,508	393	157
2002–03	6,461,112	41,154	431	157
2003–04	4,611,214	36,890	309	125
2004–05	4,946,820	39,575	331	125
2005–06	5,291,187	42,330	285	125
2006–07	5,591,463	44,732	309	125

HIGHEST AVERAGE ATTENDANCE IN ONE EUROPEAN CUP SEASON
1959–60 50,545 from a total attendance of 2,780,000.

HIGHEST SCORE IN A EUROPEAN CUP MATCH
Feyenoord (Holland)12, KR Reykjavik (Iceland) 0
(First Round First Leg 1969–70)

HIGHEST AGGREGATE
Benfica (Portugal) 18, Dudelange (Luxembourg) 0
(Preliminary Round 1965–66)

MOST GOALS OVERALL
56 Raul (Real Madrid) 1995–2007.
55 Andriy Shevchenko (Dynamo Kiev, AC Milan and Chelsea) 1994–2007.
53 Ruud Van Nistelrooy (PSV Eindhoven, Manchester United and Real Madrid) 1998–2007.

CHAMPIONS LEAGUE BIGGEST WINS
Juventus 7, Olympiakos 0 10.12.2003
Marseille 6, CKSA Moscow 0 17.3.93
Leeds U 6, Besiktas 0 26.9.2000
Real Madrid 6, Genk 0 25.9.2002

FIRST TEAM TO SCORE SEVEN GOALS
Paris St Germain 7, Rosenborg 2 24.10.2000

HIGHEST AGGREGATE OF GOALS
Monaco 8, La Coruna 3 05.11.2003

HIGHEST SCORING DRAW
Hamburg 4, Juventus 4 13.9.2000

GREATEST COMEBACKS
Werder Bremen beat Anderlecht 5-3 after being three goals down in 33 minutes on 8.12.1993. They scored five goals in 23 second-half minutes.
La Coruna beat Paris St Germain 4-3 after being three goals down in 55 minutes on 7.3.2001. They scored four goals in 27 second-half minutes.
Liverpool after being three goals down in the first half on 25.5.2005 in the Champions League Final. They scored three goals in five second-half minutes and won the penalty shoot-out after extra time 3-2.
Liverpool 3 goals down to Basle in 29 minutes on 12.11.2002. They scored three second half goals in 24 minutes to draw 3-3.

MOST GOALS IN CHAMPIONS LEAGUE MATCH
4, Marco Van Basten AC Milan v IFK Gothenburg (33, 53 (pen), 61, 62 mins) 4-0 25.11.1992.
4, Simone Inzaghi Lazio v Marseille (17, 37, 38, 71 mins) 5-1 14.3.2000.
4, Ruud Van Nistelrooy Manchester U v Sparta Prague (14, 25 (pen), 60, 90 mins) 4-1 3.11.2004.
4, Dado Prso, Monaco v La Coruna (26, 30, 45, 49, 23 mins) 8-3 5.11.2003.
4, Andriy Shevchenko, AC Milan at Fenerbahce (16, 52, 70, 76,60 mins) 4-0 23.11.2005.

WINS WITH TWO DIFFERENT CLUBS
Miodrag Belodedici (Steaua) 1986; (Red Star Belgrade) 1991.
Ronald Koeman (PSV Eindhoven) 1988; (Barcelona) 1992.
Dejan Savicevic (Red Star Belgrade) 1991; (AC Milan) 1994.
Marcel Desailly (Marseille) 1993; (AC Milan) 1994.
Frank Rijkaard (AC Milan) 1989, 1990; (Ajax) 1995.
Vladimir Jugovic (Red Star Belgrade) 1991; (Juventus) 1996.
Didier Deschamps (Marseille) 1993; (Juventus) 1996.
Paulo Sousa (Juventus) 1996; (Borussia Dortmund) 1997.
Christian Panucci (AC Milan) 1994; (Real Madrid) 1998.
Jimmy Rimmer (Mancheser U) 1968, (Aston Villa) 1982 but as a non-playing substitute.

MOST WINS WITH DIFFERENT CLUBS
Clarence Seedorf (Ajax) 1995; (Real Madrid) 1998; (AC Milan) 2003, 2007.

MOST WINNERS MEDALS
6 Francisco Gento (Real Madrid) 1956, 1957, 1958, 1959, 1960, 1966.
5 Alfredo Di Stefano (Real Madrid) 1956, 1957, 1958, 1959, 1960.
5 Jose Maria Zarraga (Real Madrid) 1956, 1957, 1958, 1959, 1960.
4 Jose-Hector Rial (Real Madrid) 1956, 1957, 1958, 1959.
4 Marquitos (Real Madrid) 1956, 1957, 1959, 1960.
4 Phil Neal (Liverpool) 1977, 1978, 1981, 1984.

MOST GOALS SCORED IN FINALS
7 Alfredo Di Stefano (Real Madrid), 1956 (1), 1957 (1 pen), 1958 (1), 1959 (1), 1960 (3).
7 Ferenc Puskas (Real Madrid), 1960 (4), 1962 (3).

MOST FINAL APPEARANCES PER COUNTRY
Italy 25 (11 wins, 14 defeats).
Spain 20 (11 wins, 9 defeats).
England 14 (10 wins, 4 defeats).
Germany 13 (6 wins, 7 defeats).

MOST CLUB FINAL WINNERS
Real Madrid (Spain) 9 1956, 1957, 1958, 1959, 1960, 1966, 1998, 2000, 2002.
AC Milan (Italy) 7 1963, 1969, 1989, 1990, 1994, 2003, 2007.

MOST APPEARANCES IN FINAL
Real Madrid 12; AC Milan 11.

MOST EUROPEAN CUP APPEARANCES
Paolo Maldini (AC Milan)

Season	*European Cup*	*UEFA Cup*	*Super Cup*	*WCC*
1985–86	0	6	0	0
1987–88	0	2	0	0
1988–89	7	0	0	0
1989–90	8	0	2	1
1990–91	4	0	1	1
1992–93	10	0	0	0
1993–94	10	0	2	1
1994–95	11	0	1	1
1995–96	0	8	0	0
1996–97	6	0	0	0
1999–2000	6	0	0	0
2000–01	14	0	0	0
2001–02	0	4	0	0
2002–03	19	0	0	0
2003–04	9	0	1	1
2004–05	13	0	0	0
2005–06	9	0	0	0
2006–07	9	0	0	0
Total	135	20	7	5

MOST SUCCESSFUL MANAGER
Bob Paisley (Liverpool) 1977, 1978, 1981.

FASTEST GOALS SCORED IN CHAMPIONS LEAGUE
10.2 sec Roy Makaay for Bayern Munich v Real Madrid 7 March 2007.
20.07 sec Gilberto Silva for Arsenal at PSV Eindhoven 25 September 2002.
20.12 sec Alessandro Del Piero for Juventus at Manchester United 1 October 1997.

YOUNGESTCHAMPIONS LEAGUE GOALSCORER
Peter Ofori-Quaye for Olympiakos v Rosenborg at 17 years 195 days in 1997-98.

FASTEST HAT-TRICK SCORED IN CHAMPIONS LEAGUE
Mike Newell, 9 mins for Blackburn R v Rosenborg (4-1) 6.12.95.

MOST SUCCESSIVE CHAMPIONS LEAGUE APPEARANCES
Rosenborg (Norway) 11 1995–96 – 2005–06.

MOST SUCCESSIVE WINS IN THE CHAMPIONS LEAGUE
Barcelona (Spain) 11 2002–03.

TOP TEN PREMIER LEAGUE AVERAGE ATTENDANCES 2006–07		
1	Manchester U	75,826
2	Arsenal	60,045
3	Newcastle	50,686
4	Liverpool	43,563
5	Chelsea	41,542
6	Manchester C	39,997
7	Everton	36,739
8	Aston Villa	36,214
9	Tottenham H	35,739
10	West Ham U	34,719

TOP TEN FOOTBALL LEAGUE AVERAGE ATTENDANCES 2006–07		
1	Sunderland	31,887
2	Derby Co	25,945
3	Norwich C	24,545
4	Sheffield W	23,638
5	Southampton	23,556
6	Leicester C	23,206
7	Ipswich T	22,445
8	Birmingham C	22,274
9	Leeds U	21,613
10	Wolverhampton W	20,968

TOP TEN AVERAGE ATTENDANCES			
1	Manchester United	2006–07	75,826
1	Manchester United	2005–06	68,765
2	Manchester United	2004–05	67,871
3	Manchester United	2003–04	67,641
4	Manchester United	2002–03	67,630
5	Manchester United	2001–02	67,586
6	Manchester United	2000–01	67,544
7	Manchester United	1999–2000	58,017
8	Manchester United	1967–68	57,552
9	Newcastle United	1947–48	56,283

TOP TEN AVERAGE WORLD CUP FINAL CROWDS			
1	In USA	1994	68,604
2	In Brazil	1950	60,772
3	In Germany	2006	52,416
4	In Mexico	1970	52,311
5	In England	1966	50,458
6	In Italy	1990	48,368
7	In Mexico	1986	46,956
8	In West Germany	1974	46,684
9	In France	1998	43,366
10	In Argentina	1978	42,374

TOP TEN ALL-TIME ENGLAND CAPS		
1	Peter Shilton	125
2	Bobby Moore	108
3	Bobby Charlton	106
4	Billy Wright	105
5	David Beckham	96
6	Bryan Robson	90
7	Kenny Sansom	86
8	Gary Neville	85
9	Ray Wilkins	84
10	Michael Owen	82

TOP TEN ALL-TIME ENGLAND GOALSCORERS		
1	Bobby Charlton	49
2	Gary Lineker	48
3	Jimmy Greaves	44
4	Michael Owen	37
5	Tom Finney	30
6	Nat Lofthouse	30
7	Alan Shearer	30
8	Vivian Woodward	29
9	Steve Bloomer	28
10	David Platt	27

GOALKEEPING RECORDS
(without conceding a goal)

BRITISH RECORD (all competitive games)
Chris Woods, Rangers, in 1196 minutes from 26 November 1986 to 31 January 1987.

FA PREMIER LEAGUE
Peter Cech (Chelsea) in 1025 minutes from 12 December 2004 to 5 March 2005.

FOOTBALL LEAGUE
Steve Death, Reading, 1103 minutes from 24 March to 18 August 1979.

MOST CLEAN SHEETS IN A SEASON
Peter Cech (Chelsea) 24 2004–05

MOST CLEAN SHEETS OVERALL IN PREMIER LEAGUE
David James (Liverpool, Aston Villa, West Ham U, Manchester C and Portsmouth) 143 games.

MOST GOALS FOR IN A SEASON

		Goals	Games
FA PREMIER LEAGUE			
1999–2000	Manchester U	97	38
FOOTBALL LEAGUE			
Division 4			
1960–61	Peterborough U	134	46
SCOTTISH PREMIER LEAGUE			
2003–04	Celtic	105	38
SCOTTISH LEAGUE			
Division 2			
1937–38	Raith R	142	34

MOST GOALS AGAINST IN A SEASON

		Goals	Games
FA PREMIER LEAGUE			
1993–94	Swindon T	100	42
FOOTBALL LEAGUE			
Division 2			
1898–99	Darwen	141	34
SCOTTISH PREMIER LEAGUE			
1999–2000	Aberdeen	83	36
SCOTTISH LEAGUE			
Division 2			
1931–32	Edinburgh C	146	38

MOST LEAGUE GOALS IN A SEASON

		Goals	Games
FA PREMIER LEAGUE			
1993–94	Andy Cole (Newcastle U)	34	40
1994–95	Alan Shearer (Blackburn R)	34	42
FOOTBALL LEAGUE			
Division 1			
1927–28	Dixie Dean (Everton)	60	39
Division 2			
1926–27	George Camsell (Middlesbrough)	59	37
Division 3(S)			
1936–37	Joe Payne (Luton T)	55	39
Division 3(N)			
1936–37	Ted Harston (Mansfield T)	55	41
Division 3			
1959–60	Derek Reeves (Southampton)	39	46
Division 4			
1960–61	Terry Bly (Peterborough U)	52	46
FA CUP			
1887–88	Jimmy Ross (Preston NE)	20	8
LEAGUE CUP			
1986–87	Clive Allen (Tottenham H)	12	9
SCOTTISH PREMIER LEAGUE			
2000–01	Henrik Larsson (Celtic)	35	37
SCOTTISH LEAGUE			
Division 1			
1931–32	William McFadyen (Motherwell)	52	34
Division 2			
1927–28	Jim Smith (Ayr U)	66	38

MOST FA CUP FINAL GOALS

Ian Rush (Liverpool) 5: 1986(2), 1989(2), 1992(1)

SCORED IN EVERY PREMIERSHIP GAME

Arsenal 2001–02 38 matches

FEWEST GOALS FOR IN A SEASON

		Goals	Games
FA PREMIER LEAGUE			
2002–03	Sunderland	21	38
FOOTBALL LEAGUE			
Division 2			
1899–1900	Loughborough T	18	34
SCOTTISH PREMIER LEAGUE			
2001–02	St Johnstone	24	38
SCOTTISH LEAGUE			
New Division 1			
1980–81	Stirling Alb	18	39

FEWEST GOALS AGAINST IN A SEASON

		Goals	Games
FA PREMIER LEAGUE			
2004–05	Chelsea	15	38
FOOTBALL LEAGUE			
Division 1			
1978–79	Liverpool	16	42
SCOTTISH PREMIER LEAGUE			
2001–02	Celtic	18	38
SCOTTISH LEAGUE			
Division 1			
1913–14	Celtic	14	38

MOST LEAGUE GOALS IN A CAREER

	Goals	Games	Season
FOOTBALL LEAGUE			
Arthur Rowley			
WBA	4	24	1946–48
Fulham	27	56	1948–50
Leicester C	251	303	1950–58
Shrewsbury T	152	236	1958–65
	434	619	
SCOTTISH LEAGUE			
Jimmy McGrory			
Celtic	1	3	1922–23
Clydebank	13	30	1923–24
Celtic	396	375	1924–38
	410	408	

MOST HAT-TRICKS

Career
34 Dixie Dean (Tranmere R, Everton, Notts Co, England)

Division 1 (one season post-war)
6 Jimmy Greaves (Chelsea), 1960–61

Three for one team one match
West, Spouncer, Hooper, Nottingham F v Leicester Fosse, Division 1, 21 April 1909
Barnes, Ambler, Davies, Wrexham v Hartlepools U, Division 4, 3 March 1962
Adcock, Stewart, White, Manchester C v Huddersfield T, Division 2, 7 Nov 1987
Loasby, Smith, Wells, Northampton T v Walsall, Division 3S, 5 Nov 1927
Bowater, Hoyland, Readman, Mansfield T v Rotherham U, Division 3N, 27 Dec 1932

MOST CUP GOALS IN A CAREER

FA CUP (Pre-Second World war)
Henry Cursham 48 (Notts Co)

FA CUP (post-war)
Ian Rush 43 (Chester, Liverpool)

LEAGUE CUP
Geoff Hurst 49 (West Ham U, Stoke C)
Ian Rush 49 (Chester, Liverpool, Newcastle U)

GOALS PER GAME (Football League to 1991–92)

Goals per game	Division 1		Division 2		Division 3		Division 4		Division 3(S)		Division 3(N)	
	Games	Goals	Games	Goals	Games	Goals	Games	Goals	Games	Goals	Games	Goals
0	2465	0	2665	0	1446	0	1438	0	997	0	803	0
1	5606	5606	5836	5836	3225	3225	3106	3106	2073	2073	1914	1914
2	8275	16550	8609	17218	4569	9138	4441	8882	3314	6628	2939	5878
3	7731	23193	7842	23526	3784	11352	4041	12123	2996	8988	2922	8766
4	6229	24920	5897	23588	2837	11348	2784	11136	2445	9780	2410	9640
5	3752	18755	3634	18170	1566	7830	1506	7530	1554	7770	1599	7995
6	2137	12822	2007	12042	769	4614	786	4716	870	5220	930	5580
7	1092	7644	1001	7007	357	2499	336	2352	451	3157	461	3227
8	542	4336	376	3008	135	1080	143	1144	209	1672	221	1768
9	197	1773	164	1476	64	576	35	315	76	684	102	918
10	83	830	68	680	13	130	8	80	33	330	45	450
11	37	407	19	209	2	22	7	77	15	165	15	165
12	12	144	17	204	1	12	0	0	7	84	8	96
13	4	52	4	52	0	0	0	0	2	26	4	52
14	2	28	1	14	0	0	0	0	0	0	0	0
17	0	0	0	0	0	0	0	0	0	0	1	17
	38164	**117061**	**38140**	**113030**	**18768**	**51826**	**18631**	**51461**	**15042**	**46577**	**14374**	**46466**

New Overall Totals (since 1992)		Totals (up to1991–92)		Complete Overall Totals (since 1888–89)	
Games	30516	Games	143119	Games	173635
Goals	78562	Goals	426421	Goals	504983

Extensive research by statisticians has unearthed seven results from early years of the Football League which differ from the original scores. These are 26 January 1889 Wolverhampton W 5 Everton 0 (not 4-0), 16 March 1889 Notts Co 3 Derby Co 5 (not 2-5), 4 January 1896 Arsenal 5 Loughborough 0 (not 6-0), 28 November 1896 Leicester Fosse 4 Walsall 2 (not 4-1), 21 April 1900 Burslem Port Vale v Lincoln City 2-1 (not 2-0), 25 December 1902 Glossop NE 3 Stockport Co 0 (not 3-1), 26 April 1913 Hull C 2 Leicester C 0 (not 2-1).

GOALS PER GAME (from 1992–93)

Goals per game	Premier		Championship/Div 1		League One/Div 2		League Two/Div 3	
	Games	Goals	Games	Goals	Games	Goals	Games	Goals
0	524	0	695	0	676	0	671	0
1	1128	1128	1559	1559	1547	1547	1558	1558
2	1471	2942	2095	4190	2120	4240	2052	4104
3	1215	3645	1754	5262	1789	5367	1737	5211
4	836	3344	1137	4548	1155	4620	1050	4200
5	419	2095	624	3120	598	2990	549	2745
6	215	1290	283	1698	242	1452	248	1488
7	93	651	94	658	109	763	98	686
8	37	296	29	232	28	224	34	272
9	8	72	5	45	13	117	10	90
10	0	0	3	30	3	30	2	20
11	0	0	2	22	0	0	1	11
	5946	**15463**	**8280**	**21364**	**8280**	**21350**	**8010**	**20385**

A CENTURY OF LEAGUE AND CUP GOALS IN CONSECUTIVE SEASONS

	League	*Cup*	*Season*
George Camsell			
Middlesbrough	59	5	1926–27
(101 goals)	33	4	1927–28

(Camsell's cup goals were all scored in the FA Cup.)

Steve Bull			
Wolverhampton W	34	18	1987–88
(102 goals)	37	13	1988–89

(Bull had 12 in the Sherpa Van Trophy, 3 Littlewoods Cup, 3 FA Cup in 1987–88; 11 Sherpa Van Trophy, 2 Littlewoods Cup in 1988–89.)

PENALTIES

Most in a Season (individual)

Division 1	*Goals*	*Season*
Francis Lee (Manchester C)	13	1971–72

Most awarded in one game

Five Crystal Palace (4 – 1 scored, 3 missed) v Brighton & HA (1 scored), Div 2 1988–89

Most saved in a Season

Division 1

Paul Cooper (Ipswich T) 8 (of 10) 1979–80

MOST GOALS IN A GAME

FA PREMIER LEAGUE

19 Sept 1999	Alan Shearer (Newcastle U) 5 goals v Sheffield W
4 Mar 1995	Andy Cole (Manchester U) 5 goals v Ipswich T

FOOTBALL LEAGUE

Division 1

14 Dec 1935	Ted Drake (Arsenal) 7 goals v Aston V

Division 2

5 Feb 1955	Tommy Briggs (Blackburn R) 7 goals v Bristol R
23 Feb 1957	Neville Coleman (Stoke C) 7 goals v Lincoln C

Division 3(S)

13 April 1936	Joe Payne (Luton T) 10 goals v Bristol R

Division 3(N)

26 Dec 1935	Bunny Bell (Tranmere R) 9 goals v Oldham Ath

Division 3

16 Sept 1969	Steve Earle (Fulham) 5 goals v Halifax T
24 April 1965	Barrie Thomas (Scunthorpe U) 5 goals v Luton T
20 Nov 1965	Keith East (Swindon T) 5 goals v Mansfield T
2 Oct 1971	Alf Wood (Shrewsbury T) 5 goals v Blackburn R
10 Sept 1983	Tony Caldwell (Bolton W) 5 goals v Walsall
4 May 1987	Andy Jones (Port Vale) 5 goals v Newport Co
3 April 1990	Steve Wilkinson (Mansfield T) 5 goals v Birmingham C
5 Sept 1998	Giuliano Grazioli (Peterborough U) 5 goals v Barnet
6 April 2002	Lee Jones (Wrexham) 5 goals v Cambridge U

Division 4

26 Dec 1962	Bert Lister (Oldham Ath) 6 goals v Southport

FA CUP

20 Nov 1971	Ted MacDougall (Bournemouth) 9 goals v Margate (*1st Round*)

LEAGUE CUP

25 Oct 1989	Frankie Bunn (Oldham Ath) 6 goals v Scarborough

SCOTTISH LEAGUE

Premier Division

17 Nov 1984	Paul Sturrock (Dundee U) 5 goals v Morton

Premier League

23 Aug 1996	Marco Negri (Rangers) 5 goals v Dundee U

Division 1

14 Sept 1928	Jimmy McGrory (Celtic) 8 goals v Dunfermline Ath

Division 2

1 Oct 1927	Owen McNally (Arthurlie) 8 goals v Armadale
2 Jan 1930	Jim Dyet (King's Park) 8 goals v Forfar Ath
18 April 1936	John Calder (Morton) 8 goals v Raith R
20 Aug 1937	Norman Hayward (Raith R) 8 goals v Brechin C

SCOTTISH CUP

12 Sept 1885	John Petrie (Arbroath) 13 goals v Bon Accord (*1st Round*)

LONGEST SEQUENCE OF CONSECUTIVE SCORING (Individual)

FA PREMIER LEAGUE		
Ruud Van Nistelroy (Manchester U)	15 in 10 games	2003–04
FOOTBALL LEAGUE RECORD		
Tom Phillipson (Wolverhampton W)	23 in 13 games	1926–27

LONGEST UNBEATEN SEQUENCE

FA PREMIER LEAGUE	*Team*	*Games*
May 2003–October 2004	Arsenal	49
FOOTBALL LEAGUE		
Division 1		
Nov 1977–Dec 1978	Nottingham F	42

LONGEST UNBEATEN CUP SEQUENCE

Liverpool	25 rounds	League/Milk Cup	1980–84

LONGEST UNBEATEN SEQUENCE IN A SEASON

FA PREMIER LEAGUE	*Team*	*Games*
2003–04	Arsenal	38
FOOTBALL LEAGUE		
Division 1		
1920–21	Burnley	30

LONGEST UNBEATEN START TO A SEASON

FA PREMIER LEAGUE	*Team*	*Games*
2003–04	Arsenal	38
FOOTBALL LEAGUE		
Division 1		
1973–74	Leeds U	29
1987–88	Liverpool	29

LONGEST SEQUENCE WITHOUT A WIN IN A SEASON

FOOTBALL LEAGUE	*Team*	*Games*
Division 2		
1983–84	Cambridge U	31

LONGEST SEQUENCE WITHOUT A WIN FROM SEASON'S START

FOOTBALL LEAGUE	*Team*	*Games*
Division 4		
1970–71	Newport Co	25

LONGEST SEQUENCE OF CONSECUTIVE DEFEATS

FOOTBALL LEAGUE	*Team*	*Games*
Division 2		
1898–99	Darwen	18

East Stiling 24 in 2003–04.

LONGEST WINNING SEQUENCE

FA PREMIER LEAGUE	*Team*	*Games*
2001–02 and 2002–03	Arsenal	14
FOOTBALL LEAGUE		
Division 2		
1904–05	Manchester U	14
1905–06	Bristol C	14
1950–51	Preston NE	14
FROM SEASON'S START		
Division 3		
1985–86	Reading	13
SCOTTISH PREMIER LEAGUE		
2003–04	Celtic	25

HIGHEST WINS

Highest win in a First-Class Match
(Scottish Cup 1st Round)

Arbroath	36	Bon Accord	0	12 Sept 1885

Highest win in an International Match

England	13	Ireland	0	18 Feb 1882

Highest win in a FA Cup Match

Preston NE *(1st Round)*	26	Hyde U	0	15 Oct 1887

Highest win in a League Cup Match

West Ham U *(2nd Round, 2nd Leg)*	10	Bury	0	25 Oct 1983
Liverpool *(2nd Round, 1st Leg)*	10	Fulham	0	23 Sept 1986

Highest win in an FA Premier League Match

Manchester U	9	Ipswich T	0	4 Mar 1995
Nottingham F	1	Manchester U	8	6 Feb 1999

Highest win in a Football League Match

Division 2 – highest home win

Newcastle U	13	Newport Co	0	5 Oct 1946

Division 3(N) – highest home win

Stockport Co	13	Halifax T	0	6 Jan 1934

Division 2 – highest away win

Burslem Port Vale	0	Sheffield U	10	10 Dec 1892

Highest wins in a Scottish League Match
Scottish Premier League – highest home win

Rangers	7	St Johnstone	0	8 Nov 1998
Celtic	7	Aberdeen	0	16 Oct 1999
Celtic	7	Aberdeen	0	2 Nov 2002
Hibernian	7	Livingston	0	8 Feb 2006

Scottish Division 2 – highest home win

Airdrieonians	15	Dundee Wanderers	1	1 Dec 1894

Scottish Premier League – away home win

Hamilton A	0	Celtic	8	5 Nov 1988

MOST HOME WINS IN A SEASON

Brentford won all 21 games in Division 3(S), 1929–30

RECORD AWAY WINS IN A SEASON

Doncaster R won 18 of 21 games in Division 3(N), 1946–47

CONSECUTIVE AWAY WINS

FA PREMIER LEAGUE
Chelsea 9 games 2004–05

MOST WINS IN A SEASON

		Wins	*Games*
FA PREMIER LEAGUE			
2004–05	Chelsea	29	38
2005–06	Chelsea	29	38
FOOTBALL LEAGUE Division 3(N)			
1946–47	Doncaster R	33	42
SCOTTISH PREMIER LEAGUE			
2001–02	Celtic	33	38
SCOTTISH LEAGUE Division 1			
1920–21	Rangers	35	42

MOST POINTS IN A SEASON
(under old system of two points for a win)

		Points	*Games*
FOOTBALL LEAGUE Division 4			
1975–76	Lincoln C	74	46
SCOTTISH LEAGUE Division 1			
1920–21	Rangers	76	42

FEWEST WINS IN A SEASON

		Wins	*Games*
FA PREMIER LEAGUE			
2005–06	Sunderland	3	38
FOOTBALL LEAGUE Division 2			
1899–1900	Loughborough T	1	34
SCOTTISH PREMIER LEAGUE			
1998–99	Dunfermline Ath	4	36
SCOTTISH LEAGUE Division 1			
1891–92	Vale of Leven	0	22

UNDEFEATED AT HOME OVERALL

Liverpool 85 games (63 League, 9 League Cup, 7 European, 6 FA Cup), Jan 1978–Jan 1981

UNDEFEATED IN A SEASON

FA PREMIER LEAGUE		
2003–04	Arsenal	38 games
FOOTBALL LEAGUE		
1889–90	Preston NE	22 games
Division 2		
1893–94	Liverpool	22 games

UNDEFEATED AWAY

Arsenal 19 games FA Premier League 2001–02 and 2003–04 (only Preston NE with 11 in 1888–89 had previously remained unbeaten away) in the top flight

HIGHEST AGGREGATE SCORES

Highest Aggregate Score England
Division 3(N)

Tranmere R	13	Oldham Ath	4	26 Dec 1935

Highest Aggregate Score Scotland
Division 2

Airdrieonians	15	Dundee Wanderers	1	1 Dec 1894

MOST POINTS IN A SEASON
(three points for a win)

		Points	*Games*
FA PREMIER LEAGUE			
2004–05	Chelsea	95	38
FOOTBALL LEAGUE Championship			
2005–06	Reading	106	46
SCOTTISH PREMIER LEAGUE			
2001–02	Celtic	103	38
SCOTTISH LEAGUE New Division 3			
2004–05	Gretna	98	36

FEWEST POINTS IN A SEASON

		Points	*Games*
FA PREMIER LEAGUE			
2005–06	Sunderland	15	38
FOOTBALL LEAGUE Division 2			
1904–05	Doncaster R	8	34
1899–1900	Loughborough T	8	34
SCOTTISH PREMIER LEAGUE			
2005–06	Livingston	18	38
SCOTTISH LEAGUE Division 1			
1954–55	Stirling Alb	6	30

ONE DEFEAT IN A SEASON

FA PREMIER LEAGUE		*Defeats*	*Games*
2004–05	Chelsea	1	38
FOOTBALL LEAGUE			
Division 1			
1990–91	Arsenal	1	38
SCOTTISH PREMIER LEAGUE			
2001–02	Celtic	1	38
SCOTTISH LEAGUE			
Premier Division			
Division 1			
1920–21	Rangers	1	42
Division 2			
1956–57	Clyde	1	36
1962–63	Morton	1	36
1967–68	St Mirren	1	36
New Division 2			
1975–76	Raith R	1	26

MOST DEFEATS IN A SEASON

FA PREMIER LEAGUE		*Defeats*	*Games*
1994–95	Ipswich T	29	42
FOOTBALL LEAGUE			
Division 3			
1997–98	Doncaster R	34	46
SCOTTISH PREMIER LEAGUE			
2005–06	Livingston	28	38
SCOTTISH LEAGUE			
New Division 1			
1992–93	Cowdenbeath	34	44

NO DEFEATS IN A SEASON

FA PREMIER LEAGUE		
2003–04	Arsenal	won 26, drew 12
FOOTBALL LEAGUE		
Division 1		
1888–89	Preston NE	won 18, drew 4
Division 2		
1893–94	Liverpool	won 22, drew 6
SCOTTISH LEAGUE DIVISION 1		
1898–99	Rangers	won 18

SENDINGS-OFF

SEASON
451 (League alone) 2003–04
(Before rescinded cards taken into account)

DAY
19 (League) 13 Dec 2003

FA CUP FINAL
Kevin Moran, Manchester U v Everton 1985
Jose Antonio Reyes, Arsenal v Manchester U 2005

QUICKEST
FA Premier League
Andreas Johansson Wigan Ath v Arsenal 7 May 2006 and Keith Gillespie Sheffield U v Reading 20 January 2007 both in 10 seconds
Football League
Walter Boyd, Swansea C v Darlington Div 3 as substitute in zero seconds 23 Nov 1999

MOST IN ONE GAME
Five: Chesterfield (2) v Plymouth Arg (3) 22 Feb 1997
Five: Wigan Ath (1) v Bristol R (4) 2 Dec 1997
Five: Exeter C (3) v Cambridge U (2) 23 Nov 2002

MOST IN ONE TEAM
Wigan Ath (1) v Bristol R (4) 2 Dec 1997
Hereford U (4) v Northampton T (0) 11 Nov 1992

MOST DRAWN GAMES IN A SEASON

FA PREMIER LEAGUE		*Draws*	*Games*
1993–94	Manchester C	18	42
1993–94	Sheffield U	18	42
1994–95	Southampton	18	42
FOOTBALL LEAGUE			
Division 1			
1978–79	Norwich C	23	42
Division 3			
1997–98	Cardiff C	23	46
1997–98	Hartlepool U	23	46
Division 4			
1986–87	Exeter C	23	46
SCOTTISH PREMIER LEAGUE			
1998–99	Dunfermline Ath	16	38
SCOTTISH LEAGUE			
Premier Division			
1993–94	Aberdeen	21	44
New Division 1			
1986–87	East Fife	21	44

NEW WEMBLEY RECORDS

ENGLAND UNDER-21 INTERNATIONALS
24.3.07 England Under-21 v Italy Under-21 55,700

TROPHY FINAL
12.5.07 Stevenage B v Kidderminster H 53,262

VASE FINAL
13.5.07 Truro C v AFC Totton 27,754

FA CUP FINAL
19.5.07 Chelsea v Manchester U 89,826

CONFERENCE PLAY-OFF
20.5.07 Morecambe v Exeter C 40,043

LEAGUE 2 PLAY-OFF
26.5.07 Bristol R v Shrewsbury T 61,589

LEAGUE 1 PLAY-OFF
27.5.07 Blackpool v Yeovil T 59,313

CHAMPIONSHIP PLAY-OFF
28.5.07 Derby Co v WBA 74,993

ENGLAND INTERNATIONALS
1.6.07 England v Brazil 88,745

MOST SUCCESSFUL MANAGERS

Sir Alex Ferguson CBE
Manchester U
18 major trophies in 16 seasons:
9 Premier League, 5 FA Cup, 2 League Cup, 1 European Cup, 1 Cup-Winners' Cup.

Aberdeen
1976–86 – 9 trophies:
3 League, 4 Scottish Cup, 1 League Cup, 1 Cup-Winners' Cup.

Bob Paisley
Liverpool
1974–83 – 13 trophies:
6 League, 3 European Cup, 3 League Cup, 1 UEFA Cup.

LEAGUE CHAMPIONSHIP HAT-TRICKS

Huddersfield T	1923–24 to 1925–26
Arsenal	1932–33 to 1934–35
Liverpool	1981–82 to 1983–84
Manchester U	1998–99 to 2000–01

RED CARD ANOMALIES 2006–07

The following players were dismissed after the final whistle:

Douglas (Leeds U), Danns (Birmingham C), Hassell (Barnsley), Burton (Shrewsbury T), Carlisle (Watford) and Chopra (Cardiff C).

MOST LEAGUE APPEARANCES (750+ matches)

1005 Peter Shilton (286 Leicester City, 110 Stoke City, 202 Nottingham Forest, 188 Southampton, 175 Derby County, 34 Plymouth Argyle, 1 Bolton Wanderers, 9 Leyton Orient) 1966–97

931 Tony Ford (355 Grimsby T, 9 Sunderland (loan), 112 Stoke C, 114 WBA, 68 Grimsby T, 5 Bradford C (loan), 76 Scunthorpe U, 103 Mansfield T, 89 Rochdale) 1975–2002

909 Graeme Armstrong (204 Stirling A, 83 Berwick R, 353 Meadowbank T, 268 Stenhousemuir, 1 Alloa) 1975–2001

863 Tommy Hutchison (165 Blackpool, 314 Coventry City, 46 Manchester City, 92 Burnley, 178 Swansea City, 68 Alloa) 1965–91

824 Terry Paine (713 Southampton, 111 Hereford United) 1957–77

790 Neil Redfearn (35 Bolton W, 10 Lincoln C (loan), 90 Lincoln C, 46 Doncaster R, 57 Crystal Palace, 24 Watford, 62 Oldham Ath, 292 Barnsley, 30 Charlton Ath, 17 Bradford C, 22 Wigan Ath, 42 Halifax T, 54 Boston U, 9 Rochdale) 1982–2004

782 Robbie James (484 Swansea C, 48 Stoke C, 87 QPR, 23 Leicester C, 89 Bradford C, 51 Cardiff C) 1973–94

777 Alan Oakes (565 Manchester C, 211 Chester C, 1 Port Vale) 1959–84

771 John Burridge (27 Workington, 134 Blackpool, 65 Aston Villa, 6 Southend U (loan), 88 Crystal Palace, 39 QPR, 74 Wolverhampton W, 6 Derby Co (loan), 109 Sheffield U, 62 Southampton, 67 Newcastle U, 65 Hibernian, 3 Scarborough, 4 Lincoln C, 3 Aberdeen, 3 Dumbarton, 3 Falkirk, 4 Manchester C, 3 Darlington, 6 Queen of the South) 1968–96

770 John Trollope (all for Swindon Town) 1960–80†

764 Jimmy Dickinson (all for Portsmouth) 1946–65

763 Stuart McCall (395 Bradford C, 103 Everton, 194 Rangers, 71 Sheffield U) 1982–2004

761 Roy Sproson (all for Port Vale) 1950–72

760 Mick Tait (64 Oxford U, 106 Carlisle U, 33 Hull C, 240 Portsmouth, 99 Reading, 79 Darlington, 139 Hartlepool U) 1975–97

758 Ray Clemence (48 Scunthorpe United, 470 Liverpool, 240 Tottenham Hotspur) 1966–87

758 Billy Bonds (95 Charlton Ath, 663 West Ham U) 1964–88

757 Pat Jennings (48 Watford, 472 Tottenham Hotspur, 237 Arsenal) 1963–86

757 Frank Worthington (171 Huddersfield T, 210 Leicester C, 84 Bolton W, 75 Birmingham C, 32 Leeds U, 19 Sunderland, 34 Southampton, 31 Brighton & HA, 59 Tranmere R, 23 Preston NE, 19 Stockport Co) 1966–88

† record for one club

CONSECUTIVE

401 Harold Bell (401 Tranmere R; 459 in all games) 1946–55

FA CUP

88 Ian Callaghan (79 Liverpool, 7 Swansea C, 2 Crewe Alex)

MOST SENIOR MATCHES

1390 Peter Shilton (1005 League, 86 FA Cup, 102 League Cup, 125 Internationals, 13 Under-23, 4 Football League XI, 20 European Cup, 7 Texaco Cup, 5 Simod Cup, 4 European Super Cup, 4 UEFA Cup, 3 Screen Sport Super Cup, 3 Zenith Data Systems Cup, 2 Autoglass Trophy, 2 Charity Shield, 2 Full Members Cup, 1 Anglo-Italian Cup, 1 Football League play-offs, 1 World Club Championship)

YOUNGEST PLAYERS

FA Premier League appearance
Matthew Briggs, 16 years 65 days, Fulham v Middlesbrough, 13.5.2007.

FA Premier League scorer
James Vaughan, 16 years 271 days, Everton v Crystal Palace 10.4.2005

Football League appearance
Albert Geldard, 15 years 158 days, Bradford Park Avenue v Millwall, Division 2, 16.9.29; and Ken Roberts, 15 years 158 days, Wrexham v Bradford Park Avenue, Division 3N, 1.9.51
If leap years are included, Ken Roberts was 157 days

Football League scorer
Ronnie Dix, 15 years 180 days, Bristol Rovers v Norwich City, Division 3S, 3.3.28.

Division 1 appearance
Derek Forster, 15 years 185 days, Sunderland v Leicester City, 22.8.64.

Division 1 scorer
Jason Dozzell, 16 years 57 days as substitute Ipswich Town v Coventry City, 4.2.84

Division 1 hat-tricks
Alan Shearer, 17 years 240 days, Southampton v Arsenal, 9.4.88
Jimmy Greaves, 17 years 10 months, Chelsea v Portsmouth, 25.12.57

FA Cup appearance (any round)
Andy Awford, 15 years 88 days as substitute Worcester City v Boreham Wood, 3rd Qual. rd, 10.10.87

FA Cup proper appearance
Lee Holmes, 15 years 277 days, Derby Co v Brentford 4.1.2003

FA Cup Final appearance
Curtis Weston, 17 years 119 days, Millwall v Manchester U, 2004

FA Cup Final scorer
Norman Whiteside, 18 years 18 days, Manchester United v Brighton & Hove Albion, 1983

FA Cup Final captain
David Nish, 21 years 212 days, Leicester City v Manchester City, 1969

League Cup appearance
Chris Coward, 16 years 30 days, Stockport Co v Sheffield W, 2005

League Cup Final scorer
Norman Whiteside, 17 years 324 days, Manchester United v Liverpool, 1983

League Cup Final captain
Barry Venison, 20 years 7 months 8 days, Sunderland v Norwich City, 1985

OLDEST PLAYERS

FA Premier League appearance
John Burridge 43 years 5 months, Manchester C v QPR 14.5.1995

Football League appearance
Neil McBain, 52 years 4 months, New Brighton v Hartlepools United, Div 3N, 15.3.47 (McBain was New Brighton's manager and had to play in an emergency)

Division 1 appearance
Stanley Matthews, 50 years 5 days, Stoke City v Fulham, 6.2.65

MOST LEAGUE MEDALS

Ryan Giggs (Manchester U) 9: 1993, 1994, 1996, 1997, 1999, 2000, 2001, 2003 and 2007

INTERNATIONAL RECORDS

MOST GOALS IN AN INTERNATIONAL

Record/World Cup	Archie Thompson (Australia) 13 goals v American Samoa	11.4.2001
England	Malcolm Macdonald (Newcastle U) 5 goals v Cyprus, at Wembley	16.4.1975
	Willie Hall (Tottenham H) 5 goals v Ireland, at Old Trafford	16.11.1938
	Steve Bloomer (Derby Co) 5 goals v Wales, at Cardiff	16.3.1896
	Howard Vaughton (Aston Villa) 5 goals v Ireland, at Belfast	18.2.1882
Northern Ireland	Joe Bambrick (Linfield) 6 goals v Wales, at Belfast	1.2.1930
Wales	John Price (Wrexham) 4 goals v Ireland, at Wrexham	25.2.1882
	Mel Charles (Cardiff C) 4 goals v Ireland, at Cardiff	11.4.1962
	Ian Edwards (Chester) 4 goals v Malta, at Wrexham	25.10.1978

MOST GOALS IN AN INTERNATIONAL CAREER

		Goals	*Games*
England	Bobby Charlton (Manchester U)	49	106
Scotland	Denis Law (Huddersfield T, Manchester C, Torino, Manchester U)	30	55
	Kenny Dalglish (Celtic, Liverpool)	30	102
Northern Ireland	David Healy (Manchester U, Preston NE, Leeds U)	29	56
Wales	Ian Rush (Liverpool, Juventus)	28	73
Republic of Ireland	Robbie Keane (Wolverhampton W, Coventry C, Internazionale, Leeds U, Tottenham H)	29	72

HIGHEST SCORES

Record/World Cup Match	Australia	31	American Samoa	0	2001
European Championship	San Marino	0	Germany	13	2006
Olympic Games	Denmark	17	France	1	1908
	Germany	16	USSR	0	1912
Other International Match	Libya	21	Oman	0	1966
European Cup	Feyenoord	12	K R Reykjavik	2	1969
European Cup-Winners' Cup	Sporting Lisbon	16	Apoel Nicosia	1	1963
Fairs & UEFA Cups	Ajax	14	Red Boys	0	1984

GOALSCORING RECORDS

World Cup Final	Geoff Hurst (England) 3 goals v West Germany	1966
World Cup Final tournament	Just Fontaine (France) 13 goals	1958
Career	Artur Friedenreich (Brazil) 1329 goals	1910–30
	Pele (Brazil) 1281 goals	*1956–78
	Franz 'Bimbo' Binder (Austria, Germany) 1006 goals	1930–50
World Cup Finals fastest	Hakan Sukur (Turkey) 10.8 secs v South Korea	2002

**Pele subsequently scored two goals in Testimonial matches making his total 1283.*

MOST CAPPED INTERNATIONALS IN THE BRITISH ISLES

England	Peter Shilton	125 appearances	1970–90
Northern Ireland	Pat Jennings	119 appearances	1964–86
Scotland	Kenny Dalglish	102 appearances	1971–86
Wales	Neville Southall	92 appearances	1982–97
Republic of Ireland	Steve Staunton	102 appearances	1988–2002

LONDON INTERNATIONAL VENUES

Eleven different venues in the London area have staged full England international games: Kennington Oval, Richmond Athletic Ground, Queen's Club, Crystal Palace, Craven Cottage, The Den, Stamford Bridge, Highbury, Wembley, Selhurst Park, White Hart Lane and Upton Park.

THE FA BARCLAYS PREMIERSHIP AND COCA-COLA FOOTBALL LEAGUE FIXTURES 2007–08

Reproduced under licence from Football Dataco Limited. All rights reserved. Licence No. PRINT/SKYSPOAN/129743a. Copyright © and Database Right The FA Premier League/The Football League Limited 2007. All rights reserved. No part of the Fixtures Lists may be reproduced stored or transmitted in any form without the prior written permission of Football DataCo Limited.

**Sky Sports*

Saturday, 11 August 2007
Barclays Premier League
Aston Villa v Liverpool
Bolton W v Newcastle U
Derby Co v Portsmouth
Everton v Wigan Ath
Middlesbrough v Blackburn R
Sunderland v Tottenham H* (12.45)
West Ham U v Manchester C

Coca-Cola Football League Championship
Barnsley v Coventry C
Bristol C v QPR
Burnley v WBA
Cardiff C v Stoke C
Charlton Ath v Scunthorpe U
Hull C v Plymouth Arg
Ipswich T v Sheffield W
Leicester C v Blackpool
Preston NE v Norwich C
Sheffield U v Colchester U
Southampton v Crystal Palace
Wolverhampton W v Watford* (5.20)

Coca-Cola Football League One
Cheltenham T v Gillingham
Crewe Alex v Brighton & HA
Doncaster R v Millwall
Huddersfield T v Yeovil T
Luton T v Hartlepool U
Northampton T v Swindon T
Nottingham F v Bournemouth
Oldham Ath v Swansea C
Port Vale v Bristol R
Southend U v Leyton Orient
Tranmere R v Leeds U
Walsall v Carlisle U

Coca-Cola Football League Two
Bradford C v Macclesfield T
Brentford v Mansfield T
Chester C v Chesterfield
Darlington v Wrexham
Grimsby T v Notts Co
Hereford U v Rotherham U
Lincoln C v Shrewsbury T
Milton Keynes Dons v Bury
Morecambe v Barnet
Peterborough U v Rochdale
Stockport Co v Dagenham & R
Wycombe W v Accrington S

Sunday, 12 August 2007
Barclays Premier League
Arsenal v Fulham
Chelsea v Birmingham C* (1.30)
Manchester U v Reading* (4.00)

Tuesday, 14 August 2007
Barclays Premier League
Birmingham C v Sunderland
Tottenham H v Everton* (8.00)

Wednesday, 15 August 2007
Barclays Premier League
Blackburn R v Aston Villa
Fulham v Bolton W
Liverpool v Arsenal *(postponed)*
Manchester C v Derby Co
Newcastle U v Liverpool *(postponed)*
Portsmouth v Manchester U
Reading v Chelsea
Wigan Ath v Middlesbrough* (8.00)

Saturday, 18 August 2007
Barclays Premier League
Birmingham C v West Ham U
Blackburn R v Arsenal
Fulham v Middlesbrough
Newcastle U v Aston Villa
Portsmouth v Bolton W* (12.45)
Reading v Everton
Tottenham H v Derby Co
Wigan Ath v Sunderland

Coca-Cola Football League Championship
Blackpool v Bristol C
Colchester U v Barnsley
Coventry C v Hull C
Crystal Palace v Leicester C
Norwich C v Southampton
Plymouth Arg v Ipswich T
QPR v Cardiff C
Scunthorpe U v Burnley
Stoke C v Charlton Ath* (5.20)
Watford v Sheffield U
WBA v Preston NE

Coca-Cola Football League One
Bournemouth v Huddersfield T
Brighton & HA v Northampton T
Bristol R v Crewe Alex
Carlisle U v Oldham Ath
Gillingham v Tranmere R
Hartlepool U v Doncaster R
Leeds U v Southend U
Leyton Orient v Walsall
Millwall v Cheltenham T
Swansea C v Nottingham F
Swindon T v Luton T
Yeovil T v Port Vale

Coca-Cola Football League Two
Accrington S v Darlington
Barnet v Hereford U
Bury v Grimsby T
Chesterfield v Stockport Co
Dagenham & R v Wycombe W
Macclesfield T v Milton Keynes Dons
Mansfield T v Lincoln C
Notts Co v Brentford
Rochdale v Chester C
Shrewsbury T v Bradford C
Wrexham v Morecambe

Sunday, 19 August 2007
Barclays Premier League
Liverpool v Chelsea* (4.00)
Manchester C v Manchester U* (1.30)

Coca-Cola Football League Championship
Sheffield W v Wolverhampton W

Coca-Cola Football League Two
Rotherham U v Peterborough U

Saturday, 25 August 2007
Barclays Premier League
Arsenal v Manchester C
Aston Villa v Fulham
Bolton W v Reading
Chelsea v Portsmouth
Derby Co v Birmingham C
Everton v Blackburn R
Sunderland v Liverpool* (12.45)
West Ham U v Wigan Ath

Coca-Cola Football League Championship
Barnsley v Plymouth Arg
Bristol C v Scunthorpe U
Burnley v QPR
Cardiff C v Coventry C
Charlton Ath v Sheffield W
Hull C v Norwich C
Ipswich T v Crystal Palace
Leicester C v Watford
Preston NE v Colchester U
Sheffield U v WBA* (5.20)
Southampton v Stoke C
Wolverhampton W v Blackpool

Coca-Cola Football League One
Cheltenham T v Swindon T
Crewe Alex v Leyton Orient
Doncaster R v Bournemouth
Huddersfield T v Carlisle U
Luton T v Gillingham
Northampton T v Yeovil T
Nottingham F v Leeds U
Oldham Ath v Bristol R
Port Vale v Hartlepool U
Southend U v Millwall
Tranmere R v Brighton & HA
Walsall v Swansea C

Coca-Cola Football League Two
Bradford C v Wrexham
Brentford v Barnet
Chester C v Dagenham & R
Darlington v Notts Co
Grimsby T v Macclesfield T
Hereford U v Rochdale
Lincoln C v Accrington S
Milton Keynes Dons v Shrewsbury T
Morecambe v Mansfield T
Peterborough U v Chesterfield
Stockport Co v Rotherham U
Wycombe W v Bury

Sunday, 26 August 2007
Barclays Premier League
Manchester U v Tottenham H* (4.00)
Middlesbrough v Newcastle U

Saturday, 1 September 2007
Barclays Premier League
Blackburn R v Manchester C
Bolton W v Everton
Fulham v Tottenham H
Liverpool v Derby Co
Manchester U v Sunderland
Middlesbrough v Birmingham C
Newcastle U v Wigan Ath
Reading v West Ham U

Coca-Cola Football League Championship
Colchester U v Burnley
Coventry C v Preston NE* (5.20)
Crystal Palace v Charlton Ath
Norwich C v Cardiff C
Plymouth Arg v Leicester C
QPR v Southampton
Scunthorpe U v Sheffield U
Sheffield W v Bristol C
Stoke C v Wolverhampton W
Watford v Ipswich T
WBA v Barnsley

Coca-Cola Football League One
Bournemouth v Port Vale
Brighton & HA v Southend U
Bristol R v Nottingham F
Carlisle U v Cheltenham T
Gillingham v Walsall
Hartlepool U v Oldham Ath
Leeds U v Luton T
Leyton Orient v Northampton T
Millwall v Huddersfield T
Swansea C v Doncaster R
Swindon T v Crewe Alex
Yeovil T v Tranmere R

Coca-Cola Football League Two
Accrington S v Peterborough U
Barnet v Bradford C
Bury v Brentford
Chesterfield v Wycombe W
Dagenham & R v Lincoln C
Macclesfield T v Darlington
Mansfield T v Stockport Co
Notts Co v Morecambe
Rochdale v Milton Keynes Dons
Rotherham U v Chester C
Shrewsbury T v Grimsby T
Wrexham v Hereford U

Sunday, 2 September 2007
Barclays Premier League
Arsenal v Portsmouth* (1.30)
Aston Villa v Chelsea* (4.00)

Monday, 3 September 2007
Coca-Cola Football League Championship
Blackpool v Hull C* (7.45)

Friday, 7 September 2007
Coca-Cola Football League One
Brighton & HA v Millwall
Cheltenham T v Swansea C
Northampton T v Doncaster R

Coca-Cola Football League Two
Chester C v Morecambe
Chesterfield v Bury
Lincoln C v Bradford C
Milton Keynes Dons v Notts Co

Saturday, 8 September 2007
Coca-Cola Football League One
Carlisle U v Tranmere R
Crewe Alex v Huddersfield T
Leeds U v Hartlepool U
Leyton Orient v Bournemouth
Luton T v Bristol R
Nottingham F v Oldham Ath
Southend U v Gillingham
Walsall v Port Vale

Coca-Cola Football League Two
Accrington S v Grimsby T
Dagenham & R v Barnet
Hereford U v Macclesfield T
Peterborough U v Mansfield T
Rochdale v Wrexham
Rotherham U v Darlington
Stockport Co v Shrewsbury T

Sunday, 9 September 2007
Coca-Cola Football League One
Swindon T v Yeovil T* (4.00)

Coca-Cola Football League Two
Wycombe W v Brentford* (1.30)

Friday, 14 September 2007
Coca-Cola Football League One
Bristol R v Leeds U
Swansea C v Carlisle U
Tranmere R v Luton T

Saturday, 15 September 2007
Barclays Premier League
Birmingham C v Bolton W
Chelsea v Blackburn R
Everton v Manchester U
Portsmouth v Liverpool* (12.45)
Sunderland v Reading
Tottenham H v Arsenal
West Ham U v Middlesbrough
Wigan Ath v Fulham

Coca-Cola Football League Championship
Barnsley v Scunthorpe U
Burnley v Blackpool
Colchester U v Charlton Ath
Coventry C v Bristol C
Hull C v Stoke C
Leicester C v QPR
Norwich C v Crystal Palace
Plymouth Arg v Cardiff C* (5.20)
Preston NE v Sheffield W
Sheffield U v Wolverhampton W
Watford v Southampton
WBA v Ipswich T

Coca-Cola Football League One
Bournemouth v Northampton T
Gillingham v Brighton & HA
Hartlepool U v Swindon T
Huddersfield T v Cheltenham T
Millwall v Walsall
Oldham Ath v Southend U
Port Vale v Nottingham F
Yeovil T v Leyton Orient

Coca-Cola Football League Two
Barnet v Rochdale
Bradford C v Peterborough U
Brentford v Milton Keynes Dons
Bury v Chester C
Darlington v Lincoln C
Grimsby T v Stockport Co
Macclesfield T v Wycombe W
Mansfield T v Chesterfield
Morecambe v Hereford U
Notts Co v Dagenham & R
Shrewsbury T v Accrington S
Wrexham v Rotherham U

Sunday, 16 September 2007
Barclays Premier League
Manchester C v Aston Villa* (4.00)

Coca-Cola Football League One
Doncaster R v Crewe Alex

Monday, 17 September 2007
Barclays Premier League
Derby Co v Newcastle U

Tuesday, 18 September 2007
Coca-Cola Football League Championship
Blackpool v Sheffield U
Bristol C v WBA
Cardiff C v Watford
Charlton Ath v Norwich C
Crystal Palace v Coventry C
Ipswich T v Leicester C
QPR v Plymouth Arg
Scunthorpe U v Preston NE
Sheffield W v Burnley
Southampton v Colchester U
Stoke C v Barnsley
Wolverhampton W v Hull C

Saturday, 22 September 2007
Barclays Premier League
Arsenal v Derby Co
Blackburn R v Portsmouth
Fulham v Manchester C
Liverpool v Birmingham C
Middlesbrough v Sunderland
Reading v Wigan Ath

Coca-Cola Football League Championship
Blackpool v Colchester U
Bristol C v Burnley
Cardiff C v Preston NE
Charlton Ath v Leicester C
Crystal Palace v Sheffield U
Ipswich T v Coventry C* (5.20)
QPR v Watford
Scunthorpe U v WBA
Sheffield W v Hull C
Southampton v Barnsley
Stoke C v Plymouth Arg
Wolverhampton W v Norwich C

Coca-Cola Football League One
Brighton & HA v Yeovil T
Carlisle U v Bristol R
Cheltenham T v Tranmere R
Crewe Alex v Millwall
Leeds U v Swansea C
Leyton Orient v Hartlepool U
Luton T v Port Vale
Northampton T v Huddersfield T
Nottingham F v Gillingham
Southend U v Doncaster R
Swindon T v Bournemouth
Walsall v Oldham Ath

Coca-Cola Football League Two
Accrington S v Mansfield T
Chester C v Brentford
Chesterfield v Barnet
Dagenham & R v Bury
Hereford U v Bradford C
Lincoln C v Grimsby T
Milton Keynes Dons v Darlington
Peterborough U v Morecambe
Rochdale v Macclesfield T
Rotherham U v Notts Co
Stockport Co v Wrexham
Wycombe W v Shrewsbury T

Sunday, 23 September 2007
Barclays Premier League
Aston Villa v Everton
Bolton W v Tottenham H
Manchester U v Chelsea* (4.00)
Newcastle U v West Ham U* (1.30)

Saturday, 29 September 2007
Barclays Premier League
Birmingham C v Manchester U
Chelsea v Fulham
Derby Co v Bolton W
Manchester C v Newcastle U* (12.45)
Portsmouth v Reading
Sunderland v Blackburn R
West Ham U v Arsenal
Wigan Ath v Liverpool

Coca-Cola Football League Championship
Barnsley v Cardiff C
Burnley v Crystal Palace
Colchester U v Scunthorpe U
Coventry C v Charlton Ath
Hull C v Ipswich T
Leicester C v Stoke C
Norwich C v Sheffield W* (5.20)
Plymouth Arg v Wolverhampton W
Preston NE v Bristol C
Sheffield U v Southampton
Watford v Blackpool
WBA v QPR

Coca-Cola Football League One
Bournemouth v Carlisle U
Bristol R v Leyton Orient
Doncaster R v Cheltenham T
Gillingham v Leeds U
Hartlepool U v Walsall
Huddersfield T v Luton T
Millwall v Swindon T
Oldham Ath v Crewe Alex
Port Vale v Southend U
Swansea C v Brighton & HA
Tranmere R v Northampton T
Yeovil T v Nottingham F

Coca-Cola Football League Two
Barnet v Rotherham U
Bradford C v Wycombe W
Brentford v Stockport Co
Bury v Accrington S
Darlington v Peterborough U
Grimsby T v Hereford U
Macclesfield T v Chester C
Mansfield T v Dagenham & R
Morecambe v Milton Keynes Dons
Notts Co v Chesterfield
Shrewsbury T v Rochdale
Wrexham v Lincoln C

Sunday, 30 September 2007
Barclays Premier League
Everton v Middlesbrough* (4.00)

Monday, 1 October 2007
Barclays Premier League
Tottenham H v Aston Villa

Tuesday, 2 October 2007
Coca-Cola Football League Championship
Barnsley v Bristol C
Burnley v Ipswich T
Colchester U v QPR
Coventry C v Blackpool
Hull C v Charlton Ath
Leicester C v Wolverhampton W
Norwich C v Scunthorpe U
Plymouth Arg v Crystal Palace
Preston NE v Southampton
Sheffield U v Cardiff C
Watford v Sheffield W
WBA v Stoke C

Coca-Cola Football League One
Bournemouth v Brighton & HA
Bristol R v Southend U
Doncaster R v Walsall
Gillingham v Leyton Orient
Hartlepool U v Carlisle U
Huddersfield T v Nottingham F
Millwall v Northampton T
Oldham Ath v Leeds U
Port Vale v Cheltenham T
Swansea C v Swindon T
Tranmere R v Crewe Alex
Yeovil T v Luton T

Coca-Cola Football League Two
Barnet v Wycombe W
Bradford C v Accrington S
Brentford v Dagenham & R
Bury v Lincoln C
Darlington v Rochdale
Grimsby T v Chester C
Macclesfield T v Rotherham U
Mansfield T v Milton Keynes Dons
Morecambe v Stockport Co
Notts Co v Hereford U
Shrewsbury T v Peterborough U
Wrexham v Chesterfield

Saturday, 6 October 2007
Barclays Premier League
Aston Villa v West Ham U
Blackburn R v Birmingham C
Manchester U v Wigan Ath* (12.45)

Coca-Cola Football League Championship
Blackpool v Plymouth Arg
Bristol C v Sheffield U* (5.20)
Cardiff C v Burnley
Charlton Ath v Barnsley
Crystal Palace v Hull C
Ipswich T v Preston NE
Scunthorpe U v Watford
Sheffield W v Leicester C
Southampton v WBA
Stoke C v Colchester U
Wolverhampton W v Coventry C

Coca-Cola Football League One
Brighton & HA v Bristol R
Carlisle U v Millwall
Cheltenham T v Oldham Ath
Crewe Alex v Bournemouth
Leeds U v Yeovil T
Leyton Orient v Swansea C
Luton T v Doncaster R
Northampton T v Port Vale
Nottingham F v Hartlepool U
Southend U v Tranmere R
Swindon T v Gillingham
Walsall v Huddersfield T

Coca-Cola Football League Two
Accrington S v Wrexham
Chesterfield v Macclesfield T
Dagenham & R v Darlington
Hereford U v Brentford
Lincoln C v Morecambe
Milton Keynes Dons v Bradford C
Peterborough U v Grimsby T
Rochdale v Bury
Rotherham U v Mansfield T
Stockport Co v Barnet
Wycombe W v Notts Co

Sunday, 7 October 2007
Barclays Premier League
Arsenal v Sunderland
Bolton W v Chelsea
Fulham v Portsmouth* (4.10)
Liverpool v Tottenham H
Manchester C v Middlesbrough
Newcastle U v Everton
Reading v Derby Co* (2.00)

Coca-Cola Football League Two
Chester C v Shrewsbury T

Monday, 8 October 2007
Coca-Cola Football League Championship
QPR v Norwich C* (7.45)

Friday, 12 October 2007
Coca-Cola Football League One
Hartlepool U v Bristol R

Coca-Cola Football League Two
Brentford v Rotherham U
Chester C v Hereford U
Grimsby T v Rochdale
Morecambe v Bradford C

Saturday, 13 October 2007
Coca-Cola Football League One
Bournemouth v Swansea C
Cheltenham T v Nottingham F
Gillingham v Millwall
Leeds U v Leyton Orient
Port Vale v Brighton & HA
Southend U v Crewe Alex
Tranmere R v Walsall
Yeovil T v Carlisle U

Coca-Cola Football League Two
Barnet v Mansfield T
Dagenham & R v Accrington S
Darlington v Stockport Co
Macclesfield T v Wrexham
Notts Co v Bury
Peterborough U v Wycombe W
Shrewsbury T v Chesterfield

Sunday, 14 October 2007
Coca-Cola Football League One
Doncaster R v Huddersfield T* (4.00)
Oldham Ath v Swindon T

Coca-Cola Football League Two
Milton Keynes Dons v Lincoln C* (1.30)

Monday, 15 October 2007
Coca-Cola Football League One
Luton T v Northampton T* (7.45)

Saturday, 20 October 2007
Barclays Premier League
Arsenal v Bolton W
Aston Villa v Manchester U
Blackburn R v Reading
Everton v Liverpool* (12.45)
Fulham v Derby Co
Manchester C v Birmingham C
Middlesbrough v Chelsea
Wigan Ath v Portsmouth

Coca-Cola Football League Championship
Barnsley v Burnley
Blackpool v Crystal Palace
Colchester U v WBA
Norwich C v Bristol C
Plymouth Arg v Coventry C
QPR v Ipswich T
Scunthorpe U v Leicester C* (5.20)
Sheffield U v Preston NE
Southampton v Cardiff C
Stoke C v Sheffield W
Watford v Hull C
Wolverhampton W v Charlton Ath

Coca-Cola Football League One
Brighton & HA v Leeds U
Bristol R v Yeovil T
Carlisle U v Gillingham
Crewe Alex v Luton T
Huddersfield T v Oldham Ath
Leyton Orient v Port Vale
Millwall v Bournemouth
Northampton T v Cheltenham T
Nottingham F v Doncaster R
Swansea C v Hartlepool U
Swindon T v Tranmere R
Walsall v Southend U

Coca-Cola Football League Two
Accrington S v Macclesfield T
Bradford C v Darlington
Bury v Shrewsbury T
Chesterfield v Dagenham & R
Hereford U v Milton Keynes Dons
Lincoln C v Peterborough U
Mansfield T v Notts Co
Rochdale v Brentford
Rotherham U v Morecambe
Stockport Co v Chester C
Wrexham v Barnet
Wycombe W v Grimsby T

Sunday, 21 October 2007
Barclays Premier League
West Ham U v Sunderland* (4.00)

Monday, 22 October 2007
Barclays Premier League
Newcastle U v Tottenham H

Coca-Cola Football League Championship
Hull C v Barnsley* (7.45)

Tuesday, 23 October 2007
Coca-Cola Football League Championship
Bristol C v Southampton
Burnley v Norwich C
Cardiff C v Wolverhampton W
Charlton Ath v Plymouth Arg
Coventry C v Watford
Crystal Palace v Stoke C
Ipswich T v Colchester U
Leicester C v Sheffield U
Preston NE v QPR
Sheffield W v Scunthorpe U
WBA v Blackpool

Friday, 26 October 2007
Coca-Cola Football League One
Tranmere R v Huddersfield T

Saturday, 27 October 2007
Barclays Premier League
Birmingham C v Wigan Ath
Chelsea v Manchester C
Derby Co v Everton
Manchester U v Middlesbrough
Portsmouth v West Ham U
Reading v Newcastle U
Sunderland v Fulham
Tottenham H v Blackburn R

Coca-Cola Football League Championship
Bristol C v Stoke C
Burnley v Southampton* (5.20)
Cardiff C v Scunthorpe U
Charlton Ath v QPR
Coventry C v Colchester U
Crystal Palace v Watford
Hull C v Sheffield U
Ipswich T v Wolverhampton W
Leicester C v Barnsley
Preston NE v Plymouth Arg
Sheffield W v Blackpool
WBA v Norwich C

Coca-Cola Football League One
Bournemouth v Walsall
Cheltenham T v Crewe Alex
Gillingham v Bristol R
Hartlepool U v Brighton & HA
Leeds U v Millwall
Luton T v Nottingham F
Oldham Ath v Northampton T
Port Vale v Swindon T
Southend U v Carlisle U
Yeovil T v Swansea C

Coca-Cola Football League Two
Barnet v Accrington S
Brentford v Lincoln C
Chester C v Wycombe W
Dagenham & R v Rotherham U
Darlington v Chesterfield
Grimsby T v Bradford C
Macclesfield T v Bury
Milton Keynes Dons v Stockport Co
Morecambe v Rochdale
Notts Co v Wrexham
Peterborough U v Hereford U
Shrewsbury T v Mansfield T

Sunday, 28 October 2007
Barclays Premier League
Bolton W v Aston Villa* (1.30)
Liverpool v Arsenal* (4.00)

Coca-Cola Football League One
Doncaster R v Leyton Orient

Friday, 2 November 2007
Coca-Cola Football League Two
Lincoln C v Chester C

Saturday, 3 November 2007
Barclays Premier League
Arsenal v Manchester U* (12.45)
Aston Villa v Derby Co
Blackburn R v Liverpool
Everton v Birmingham C
Fulham v Reading
Middlesbrough v Tottenham H
Newcastle U v Portsmouth
Wigan Ath v Chelsea

Coca-Cola Football League Championship
Barnsley v Preston NE
Blackpool v Cardiff C
Colchester U v Leicester C* (5.20)
Plymouth Arg v Sheffield W
QPR v Hull C
Scunthorpe U v Crystal Palace
Sheffield U v Burnley
Southampton v Charlton Ath
Stoke C v Coventry C
Watford v WBA
Wolverhampton W v Bristol C

Coca-Cola Football League One
Brighton & HA v Luton T
Bristol R v Bournemouth
Carlisle U v Leeds U
Crewe Alex v Yeovil T
Huddersfield T v Port Vale
Leyton Orient v Oldham Ath
Millwall v Hartlepool U
Northampton T v Southend U
Nottingham F v Tranmere R
Swansea C v Gillingham
Swindon T v Doncaster R
Walsall v Cheltenham T

Coca-Cola Football League Two
Accrington S v Notts Co
Bradford C v Brentford
Bury v Barnet
Chesterfield v Morecambe
Hereford U v Darlington
Mansfield T v Macclesfield T
Rochdale v Dagenham & R
Rotherham U v Grimsby T
Stockport Co v Peterborough U
Wycombe W v Milton Keynes Dons

Sunday, 4 November 2007
Barclays Premier League
West Ham U v Bolton W* (4.00)

Coca-Cola Football League Championship
Norwich C v Ipswich T

Coca-Cola Football League Two
Wrexham v Shrewsbury T

Monday, 5 November 2007
Barclays Premier League
Manchester C v Sunderland

Tuesday, 6 November 2007
Coca-Cola Football League Championship
Barnsley v Blackpool
Bristol C v Charlton Ath
Burnley v Hull C
Cardiff C v Crystal Palace
Colchester U v Plymouth Arg
Norwich C v Watford
Preston NE v Leicester C
QPR v Coventry C
Scunthorpe U v Stoke C
Sheffield U v Ipswich T
Southampton v Wolverhampton W
WBA v Sheffield W

Coca-Cola Football League One
Bournemouth v Leeds U
Brighton & HA v Walsall
Cheltenham T v Yeovil T
Gillingham v Doncaster R
Huddersfield T v Hartlepool U
Luton T v Carlisle U
Millwall v Swansea C
Northampton T v Bristol R
Nottingham F v Southend U
Port Vale v Crewe Alex
Swindon T v Leyton Orient
Tranmere R v Oldham Ath

Coca-Cola Football League Two
Barnet v Notts Co
Bradford C v Chester C
Darlington v Shrewsbury T
Hereford U v Mansfield T
Lincoln C v Chesterfield
Macclesfield T v Brentford
Milton Keynes Dons v Grimsby T
Morecambe v Accrington S
Peterborough U v Dagenham & R
Rochdale v Stockport Co
Rotherham U v Bury

Wednesday, 7 November 2007
Coca-Cola Football League Two
Wrexham v Wycombe W

Saturday, 10 November 2007
Barclays Premier League
Bolton W v Middlesbrough
Chelsea v Everton
Derby Co v West Ham U
Liverpool v Fulham
Manchester U v Blackburn R
Sunderland v Newcastle U* (12.45)
Tottenham H v Wigan Ath

Coca-Cola Football League Championship
Blackpool v Scunthorpe U
Charlton Ath v Cardiff C
Crystal Palace v QPR
Hull C v Preston NE
Ipswich T v Bristol C
Leicester C v Burnley
Plymouth Arg v Norwich C
Sheffield W v Southampton
Stoke C v Sheffield U* (5.20)
Watford v Colchester U
Wolverhampton W v Barnsley

Sunday, 11 November 2007
Barclays Premier League
Birmingham C v Aston Villa* (1.00)
Portsmouth v Manchester C* (4.00)

Monday, 12 November 2007
Barclays Premier League
Reading v Arsenal

Coca-Cola Football League Championship
Coventry C v WBA* (7.45)

Friday, 16 November 2007
Coca-Cola Football League One
Swansea C v Huddersfield T

Saturday, 17 November 2007
Coca-Cola Football League One
Bristol R v Millwall
Crewe Alex v Northampton T

Doncaster R v Tranmere R
Hartlepool U v Bournemouth
Leeds U v Swindon T
Leyton Orient v Brighton & HA
Oldham Ath v Port Vale
Southend U v Cheltenham T
Walsall v Luton T

Coca-Cola Football League Two
Accrington S v Rotherham U
Brentford v Darlington
Bury v Peterborough U
Chester C v Milton Keynes Dons
Chesterfield v Rochdale
Dagenham & R v Bradford C
Grimsby T v Morecambe
Mansfield T v Wrexham
Notts Co v Macclesfield T
Shrewsbury T v Barnet
Stockport Co v Hereford U
Wycombe W v Lincoln C

Sunday, 18 November 2007
Coca-Cola Football League One
Carlisle U v Nottingham F* (4.00)
Yeovil T v Gillingham* (1.30)

Saturday, 24 November 2007
Barclays Premier League
Arsenal v Wigan Ath
Birmingham C v Portsmouth
Bolton W v Manchester U
Derby Co v Chelsea
Everton v Sunderland
Manchester C v Reading
Middlesbrough v Aston Villa
Newcastle U v Liverpool* (12.45)

Coca-Cola Football League Championship
Barnsley v Watford
Bristol C v Leicester C
Burnley v Stoke C
Cardiff C v Ipswich T
Colchester U v Crystal Palace
Norwich C v Coventry C
Preston NE v Charlton Ath* (5.20)
QPR v Sheffield W
Scunthorpe U v Hull C
Sheffield U v Plymouth Arg
Southampton v Blackpool
WBA v Wolverhampton W

Coca-Cola Football League One
Bournemouth v Oldham Ath
Brighton & HA v Carlisle U
Cheltenham T v Leeds U
Gillingham v Hartlepool U
Huddersfield T v Leyton Orient
Luton T v Southend U
Millwall v Yeovil T
Northampton T v Walsall
Nottingham F v Crewe Alex
Port Vale v Doncaster R
Swindon T v Bristol R
Tranmere R v Swansea C

Coca-Cola Football League Two
Barnet v Grimsby T
Bradford C v Stockport Co
Darlington v Wycombe W
Hereford U v Accrington S
Lincoln C v Notts Co
Macclesfield T v Dagenham & R
Milton Keynes Dons v Chesterfield
Morecambe v Bury
Peterborough U v Brentford
Rochdale v Mansfield T
Rotherham U v Shrewsbury T

Sunday, 25 November 2007
Barclays Premier League
Fulham v Blackburn R* (4.00)
West Ham U v Tottenham H* (1.30)

Coca-Cola Football League Two
Wrexham v Chester C

Tuesday, 27 November 2007
Coca-Cola Football League Championship
Blackpool v Norwich C
Charlton Ath v Sheffield U
Coventry C v Scunthorpe U
Crystal Palace v Preston NE
Hull C v Bristol C
Ipswich T v Southampton
Leicester C v Cardiff C
Plymouth Arg v WBA
Sheffield W v Barnsley
Stoke C v QPR
Watford v Burnley

Wednesday, 28 November 2007
Coca-Cola Football League Championship
Wolverhampton W v Colchester U

Saturday, 1 December 2007
Barclays Premier League
Aston Villa v Arsenal
Blackburn R v Newcastle U
Chelsea v West Ham U
Liverpool v Bolton W
Manchester U v Fulham
Portsmouth v Everton
Reading v Middlesbrough
Sunderland v Derby Co
Tottenham H v Birmingham C
Wigan Ath v Manchester C

Coca-Cola Football League Championship
Blackpool v QPR
Charlton Ath v Burnley
Coventry C v Sheffield U
Crystal Palace v WBA
Hull C v Cardiff C
Ipswich T v Barnsley
Leicester C v Southampton
Plymouth Arg v Scunthorpe U
Sheffield W v Colchester U
Stoke C v Norwich C
Watford v Bristol C
Wolverhampton W v Preston NE

Tuesday, 4 December 2007
Coca-Cola Football League Championship
Barnsley v Wolverhampton W
Bristol C v Ipswich T
Burnley v Leicester C
Cardiff C v Charlton Ath
Colchester U v Watford
Norwich C v Plymouth Arg
Preston NE v Hull C
QPR v Crystal Palace
Scunthorpe U v Blackpool
Sheffield U v Stoke C
Southampton v Sheffield W
WBA v Coventry C

Coca-Cola Football League One
Carlisle U v Swindon T
Crewe Alex v Gillingham
Doncaster R v Brighton & HA
Hartlepool U v Tranmere R
Leeds U v Port Vale
Leyton Orient v Millwall
Oldham Ath v Luton T
Swansea C v Northampton T
Walsall v Nottingham F
Yeovil T v Bournemouth

Coca-Cola Football League Two
Brentford v Morecambe
Bury v Wrexham
Chester C v Barnet
Dagenham & R v Milton Keynes Dons
Grimsby T v Darlington
Mansfield T v Bradford C
Notts Co v Peterborough U
Shrewsbury T v Macclesfield T
Stockport Co v Lincoln C
Wycombe W v Hereford U

Wednesday, 5 December 2007
Coca-Cola Football League One
Bristol R v Cheltenham T
Southend U v Huddersfield T

Coca-Cola Football League Two
Accrington S v Rochdale
Chesterfield v Rotherham U

Friday, 7 December 2007
Coca-Cola Football League One
Brighton & HA v Nottingham F

Saturday, 8 December 2007
Barclays Premier League
Aston Villa v Portsmouth
Blackburn R v West Ham U
Bolton W v Wigan Ath
Chelsea v Sunderland
Everton v Fulham
Manchester U v Derby Co
Middlesbrough v Arsenal
Newcastle U v Birmingham C
Reading v Liverpool
Tottenham H v Manchester C

Coca-Cola Football League Championship
Barnsley v Crystal Palace
Cardiff C v Colchester U
Charlton Ath v Ipswich T
Leicester C v WBA
Norwich C v Sheffield U
Plymouth Arg v Bristol C
Preston NE v Blackpool
Scunthorpe U v QPR
Sheffield W v Coventry C
Southampton v Hull C
Stoke C v Watford
Wolverhampton W v Burnley

Coca-Cola Football League One
Bristol R v Swansea C
Crewe Alex v Walsall
Gillingham v Port Vale
Leeds U v Huddersfield T
Leyton Orient v Cheltenham T
Luton T v Millwall
Northampton T v Carlisle U
Oldham Ath v Doncaster R
Southend U v Swindon T
Tranmere R v Bournemouth
Yeovil T v Hartlepool U

Coca-Cola Football League Two
Barnet v Macclesfield T
Brentford v Grimsby T
Chester C v Peterborough U
Chesterfield v Bradford C
Dagenham & R v Wrexham
Hereford U v Lincoln C
Mansfield T v Bury
Milton Keynes Dons v Accrington S
Morecambe v Darlington
Notts Co v Shrewsbury T
Rotherham U v Rochdale
Stockport Co v Wycombe W

Friday, 14 December 2007
Coca-Cola Football League One
Cheltenham T v Luton T

Saturday, 15 December 2007
Barclays Premier League
Arsenal v Chelsea
Birmingham C v Reading
Derby Co v Middlesbrough
Fulham v Newcastle U
Liverpool v Manchester U

Manchester C v Bolton W
Portsmouth v Tottenham H
Sunderland v Aston Villa
West Ham U v Everton
Wigan Ath v Blackburn R

Coca-Cola Football League Championship
Blackpool v Stoke C
Bristol C v Cardiff C
Burnley v Preston NE
Colchester U v Norwich C
Coventry C v Southampton
Crystal Palace v Sheffield W
Hull C v Leicester C
Ipswich T v Scunthorpe U
QPR v Wolverhampton W
Sheffield U v Barnsley
Watford v Plymouth Arg
WBA v Charlton Ath

Coca-Cola Football League One
Bournemouth v Gillingham
Carlisle U v Leyton Orient
Hartlepool U v Crewe Alex
Huddersfield T v Bristol R
Millwall v Oldham Ath
Nottingham F v Northampton T
Port Vale v Tranmere R
Swansea C v Southend U
Swindon T v Brighton & HA
Walsall v Leeds U

Coca-Cola Football League Two
Accrington S v Chesterfield
Bradford C v Rotherham U
Bury v Hereford U
Darlington v Chester C
Grimsby T v Mansfield T
Lincoln C v Barnet
Macclesfield T v Stockport Co
Peterborough U v Milton Keynes Dons
Rochdale v Notts Co
Shrewsbury T v Dagenham & R
Wrexham v Brentford
Wycombe W v Morecambe

Sunday, 16 December 2007
Coca-Cola Football League One
Doncaster R v Yeovil T

Friday, 21 December 2007
Coca-Cola Football League One
Brighton & HA v Gillingham
Northampton T v Bournemouth

Coca-Cola Football League Two
Chesterfield v Mansfield T
Milton Keynes Dons v Brentford

Saturday, 22 December 2007
Barclays Premier League
Arsenal v Tottenham H
Aston Villa v Manchester C
Blackburn R v Chelsea
Bolton W v Birmingham C
Fulham v Wigan Ath
Liverpool v Portsmouth
Manchester U v Everton
Middlesbrough v West Ham U
Newcastle U v Derby Co
Reading v Sunderland

Coca-Cola Football League Championship
Blackpool v Coventry C
Bristol C v Barnsley
Cardiff C v Sheffield U
Charlton Ath v Hull C
Crystal Palace v Plymouth Arg
Ipswich T v Burnley
QPR v Colchester U
Scunthorpe U v Norwich C
Sheffield W v Watford
Southampton v Preston NE
Stoke C v WBA
Wolverhampton W v Leicester C

Coca-Cola Football League One
Carlisle U v Swansea C
Cheltenham T v Huddersfield T
Crewe Alex v Doncaster R
Leeds U v Bristol R
Leyton Orient v Yeovil T
Luton T v Tranmere R
Nottingham F v Port Vale
Southend U v Oldham Ath
Swindon T v Hartlepool U
Walsall v Millwall

Coca-Cola Football League Two
Accrington S v Shrewsbury T
Chester C v Bury
Dagenham & R v Notts Co
Hereford U v Morecambe
Lincoln C v Darlington
Peterborough U v Bradford C
Rochdale v Barnet
Rotherham U v Wrexham
Stockport Co v Grimsby T
Wycombe W v Macclesfield T

Wednesday, 26 December 2007
Barclays Premier League
Birmingham C v Middlesbrough
Chelsea v Aston Villa
Derby Co v Liverpool
Everton v Bolton W
Manchester C v Blackburn R
Portsmouth v Arsenal
Sunderland v Manchester U
Tottenham H v Fulham
West Ham U v Reading
Wigan Ath v Newcastle U

Coca-Cola Football League Championship
Barnsley v Stoke C
Burnley v Sheffield W
Colchester U v Southampton
Coventry C v Crystal Palace
Hull C v Wolverhampton W
Leicester C v Ipswich T
Norwich C v Charlton Ath
Plymouth Arg v QPR
Preston NE v Scunthorpe U
Sheffield U v Blackpool
Watford v Cardiff C
WBA v Bristol C

Coca-Cola Football League One
Bournemouth v Leyton Orient
Bristol R v Luton T
Doncaster R v Northampton T
Gillingham v Southend U
Hartlepool U v Leeds U
Huddersfield T v Crewe Alex
Millwall v Brighton & HA
Oldham Ath v Nottingham F
Port Vale v Walsall
Swansea C v Cheltenham T
Tranmere R v Carlisle U
Yeovil T v Swindon T

Coca-Cola Football League Two
Barnet v Dagenham & R
Bradford C v Lincoln C
Brentford v Wycombe W
Bury v Chesterfield
Darlington v Rotherham U
Grimsby T v Accrington S
Macclesfield T v Hereford U
Mansfield T v Peterborough U
Morecambe v Chester C
Notts Co v Milton Keynes Dons
Shrewsbury T v Stockport Co
Wrexham v Rochdale

Saturday, 29 December 2007
Barclays Premier League
Birmingham C v Fulham
Chelsea v Newcastle U
Derby Co v Blackburn R
Everton v Arsenal
Manchester C v Liverpool
Portsmouth v Middlesbrough
Sunderland v Bolton W
Tottenham H v Reading
West Ham U v Manchester U
Wigan Ath v Aston Villa

Coca-Cola Football League Championship
Barnsley v Southampton
Burnley v Bristol C
Colchester U v Blackpool
Coventry C v Ipswich T
Hull C v Sheffield W
Leicester C v Charlton Ath
Norwich C v Wolverhampton W
Plymouth Arg v Stoke C
Preston NE v Cardiff C
Sheffield U v Crystal Palace
Watford v QPR
WBA v Scunthorpe U

Coca-Cola Football League One
Bournemouth v Swindon T
Bristol R v Carlisle U
Doncaster R v Southend U
Gillingham v Nottingham F
Hartlepool U v Leyton Orient
Huddersfield T v Northampton T
Millwall v Crewe Alex
Oldham Ath v Walsall
Port Vale v Luton T
Swansea C v Leeds U
Tranmere R v Cheltenham T
Yeovil T v Brighton & HA

Coca-Cola Football League Two
Barnet v Chesterfield
Bradford C v Hereford U
Brentford v Chester C
Bury v Dagenham & R
Darlington v Milton Keynes Dons
Grimsby T v Lincoln C
Macclesfield T v Rochdale
Mansfield T v Accrington S
Morecambe v Peterborough U
Notts Co v Rotherham U
Shrewsbury T v Wycombe W
Wrexham v Stockport Co

Tuesday, 1 January 2008
Barclays Premier League
Arsenal v West Ham U
Aston Villa v Tottenham H
Blackburn R v Sunderland
Bolton W v Derby Co
Fulham v Chelsea
Liverpool v Wigan Ath
Manchester U v Birmingham C
Middlesbrough v Everton
Newcastle U v Manchester C
Reading v Portsmouth

Coca-Cola Football League Championship
Blackpool v Burnley
Bristol C v Coventry C
Cardiff C v Plymouth Arg
Charlton Ath v Colchester U
Crystal Palace v Norwich C
Ipswich T v WBA
QPR v Leicester C
Scunthorpe U v Barnsley
Sheffield W v Preston NE
Southampton v Watford
Stoke C v Hull C
Wolverhampton W v Sheffield U

Coca-Cola Football League One
Brighton & HA v Bournemouth
Carlisle U v Hartlepool U
Crewe Alex v Tranmere R
Leeds U v Oldham Ath
Leyton Orient v Gillingham
Luton T v Yeovil T
Northampton T v Millwall
Nottingham F v Huddersfield T
Southend U v Bristol R
Swindon T v Swansea C
Walsall v Doncaster R

Coca-Cola Football League Two
Accrington S v Bradford C
Chester C v Grimsby T
Chesterfield v Wrexham
Dagenham & R v Brentford
Hereford U v Notts Co
Lincoln C v Bury
Milton Keynes Dons v Mansfield T
Peterborough U v Shrewsbury T
Rochdale v Darlington
Rotherham U v Macclesfield T
Stockport Co v Morecambe
Wycombe W v Barnet

Wednesday, 2 January 2008
Coca-Cola Football League One
Cheltenham T v Port Vale

Saturday, 5 January 2008
Coca-Cola Football League One
Bournemouth v Luton T
Brighton & HA v Cheltenham T
Bristol R v Doncaster R
Carlisle U v Port Vale
Gillingham v Oldham Ath
Hartlepool U v Southend U
Leeds U v Northampton T
Leyton Orient v Tranmere R
Millwall v Nottingham F
Swansea C v Crewe Alex
Swindon T v Huddersfield T
Yeovil T v Walsall

Coca-Cola Football League Two
Accrington S v Chester C
Barnet v Darlington
Bury v Bradford C
Chesterfield v Grimsby T
Dagenham & R v Hereford U
Macclesfield T v Morecambe
Mansfield T v Wycombe W
Notts Co v Stockport Co
Rochdale v Lincoln C
Rotherham U v Milton Keynes Dons
Shrewsbury T v Brentford
Wrexham v Peterborough U

Friday, 11 January 2008
Coca-Cola Football League One
Tranmere R v Bristol R

Saturday, 12 January 2008
Barclays Premier League
Arsenal v Birmingham C
Aston Villa v Reading
Bolton W v Blackburn R
Chelsea v Tottenham H
Derby Co v Wigan Ath
Everton v Manchester C
Manchester U v Newcastle U
Middlesbrough v Liverpool
Sunderland v Portsmouth
West Ham U v Fulham

Coca-Cola Football League Championship
Barnsley v Norwich C
Bristol C v Colchester U
Burnley v Plymouth Arg
Cardiff C v Sheffield W
Charlton Ath v Blackpool
Hull C v WBA
Ipswich T v Stoke C
Leicester C v Coventry C
Preston NE v Watford
Sheffield U v QPR
Southampton v Scunthorpe U
Wolverhampton W v Crystal Palace

Coca-Cola Football League One
Cheltenham T v Bournemouth
Crewe Alex v Leeds U
Doncaster R v Carlisle U
Huddersfield T v Gillingham
Luton T v Swansea C
Northampton T v Hartlepool U
Nottingham F v Leyton Orient
Oldham Ath v Brighton & HA
Port Vale v Millwall
Southend U v Yeovil T
Walsall v Swindon T

Coca-Cola Football League Two
Bradford C v Notts Co
Brentford v Chesterfield
Chester C v Mansfield T
Darlington v Bury
Grimsby T v Wrexham
Lincoln C v Rotherham U
Milton Keynes Dons v Barnet
Morecambe v Dagenham & R
Peterborough U v Macclesfield T
Stockport Co v Accrington S
Wycombe W v Rochdale

Sunday, 13 January 2008
Coca-Cola Football League Two
Hereford U v Shrewsbury T

Friday, 18 January 2008
Coca-Cola Football League One
Hartlepool U v Cheltenham T

Saturday, 19 January 2008
Barclays Premier League
Birmingham C v Chelsea
Blackburn R v Middlesbrough
Fulham v Arsenal
Liverpool v Aston Villa
Manchester C v West Ham U
Newcastle U v Bolton W
Portsmouth v Derby Co
Reading v Manchester U
Tottenham H v Sunderland
Wigan Ath v Everton

Coca-Cola Football League Championship
Blackpool v Ipswich T
Colchester U v Hull C
Coventry C v Burnley
Crystal Palace v Bristol C
Norwich C v Leicester C
Plymouth Arg v Southampton
QPR v Barnsley
Scunthorpe U v Wolverhampton W
Sheffield W v Sheffield U
Stoke C v Preston NE
Watford v Charlton Ath
WBA v Cardiff C

Coca-Cola Football League One
Bournemouth v Southend U
Brighton & HA v Huddersfield T
Bristol R v Walsall
Carlisle U v Crewe Alex
Gillingham v Northampton T
Leeds U v Doncaster R
Leyton Orient v Luton T
Millwall v Tranmere R
Swansea C v Port Vale
Swindon T v Nottingham F
Yeovil T v Oldham Ath

Coca-Cola Football League Two
Accrington S v Brentford
Barnet v Peterborough U
Bury v Stockport Co
Chesterfield v Hereford U
Dagenham & R v Grimsby T
Macclesfield T v Lincoln C
Mansfield T v Darlington
Notts Co v Chester C
Rochdale v Bradford C
Rotherham U v Wycombe W
Shrewsbury T v Morecambe
Wrexham v Milton Keynes Dons

Friday, 25 January 2008
Coca-Cola Football League One
Cheltenham T v Carlisle U
Northampton T v Leyton Orient

Saturday, 26 January 2008
Coca-Cola Football League One
Crewe Alex v Swindon T
Doncaster R v Swansea C
Huddersfield T v Millwall
Luton T v Leeds U
Nottingham F v Bristol R
Oldham Ath v Hartlepool U
Port Vale v Bournemouth
Southend U v Brighton & HA
Tranmere R v Yeovil T
Walsall v Gillingham

Coca-Cola Football League Two
Bradford C v Barnet
Brentford v Bury
Chester C v Rotherham U
Darlington v Macclesfield T
Grimsby T v Shrewsbury T
Hereford U v Wrexham
Lincoln C v Dagenham & R
Milton Keynes Dons v Rochdale
Morecambe v Notts Co
Peterborough U v Accrington S
Stockport Co v Mansfield T
Wycombe W v Chesterfield

Tuesday, 29 January 2008
Barclays Premier League
Arsenal v Newcastle U
Bolton W v Fulham
Derby Co v Manchester C
Middlesbrough v Wigan Ath
Sunderland v Birmingham C
West Ham U v Liverpool

Coca-Cola Football League Championship
Barnsley v Colchester U
Bristol C v Blackpool
Burnley v Scunthorpe U
Cardiff C v QPR
Charlton Ath v Stoke C
Hull C v Coventry C
Ipswich T v Plymouth Arg
Leicester C v Crystal Palace
Preston NE v WBA
Sheffield U v Watford
Southampton v Norwich C
Wolverhampton W v Sheffield W

Coca-Cola Football League One
Cheltenham T v Millwall
Crewe Alex v Bristol R
Doncaster R v Hartlepool U
Huddersfield T v Bournemouth
Luton T v Swindon T
Northampton T v Brighton & HA
Nottingham F v Swansea C
Oldham Ath v Carlisle U
Port Vale v Yeovil T
Southend U v Leeds U
Tranmere R v Gillingham
Walsall v Leyton Orient

Coca-Cola Football League Two
Bradford C v Shrewsbury T
Brentford v Notts Co
Chester C v Rochdale

Darlington v Accrington S
Grimsby T v Bury
Hereford U v Barnet
Lincoln C v Mansfield T
Milton Keynes Dons v Macclesfield T
Morecambe v Wrexham
Peterborough U v Rotherham U
Stockport Co v Chesterfield
Wycombe W v Dagenham & R

Wednesday, 30 January 2008
Barclays Premier League
Aston Villa v Blackburn R
Chelsea v Reading
Everton v Tottenham H
Manchester U v Portsmouth

Saturday, 2 February 2008
Barclays Premier League
Birmingham C v Derby Co
Blackburn R v Everton
Fulham v Aston Villa
Liverpool v Sunderland
Manchester C v Arsenal
Newcastle U v Middlesbrough
Portsmouth v Chelsea
Reading v Bolton W
Tottenham H v Manchester U
Wigan Ath v West Ham U

Coca-Cola Football League Championship
Blackpool v Leicester C
Colchester U v Sheffield U
Coventry C v Barnsley
Crystal Palace v Southampton
Norwich C v Preston NE
Plymouth Arg v Hull C
QPR v Bristol C
Scunthorpe U v Charlton Ath
Sheffield W v Ipswich T
Stoke C v Cardiff C
Watford v Wolverhampton W
WBA v Burnley

Coca-Cola Football League One
Bournemouth v Nottingham F
Brighton & HA v Crewe Alex
Bristol R v Port Vale
Carlisle U v Walsall
Gillingham v Cheltenham T
Hartlepool U v Luton T
Leeds U v Tranmere R
Leyton Orient v Southend U
Millwall v Doncaster R
Swansea C v Oldham Ath
Swindon T v Northampton T
Yeovil T v Huddersfield T

Coca-Cola Football League Two
Accrington S v Wycombe W
Barnet v Morecambe
Bury v Milton Keynes Dons
Chesterfield v Chester C
Dagenham & R v Stockport Co
Macclesfield T v Bradford C
Mansfield T v Brentford
Notts Co v Grimsby T
Rochdale v Peterborough U
Rotherham U v Hereford U
Shrewsbury T v Lincoln C
Wrexham v Darlington

Saturday, 9 February 2008
Barclays Premier League
Arsenal v Blackburn R
Aston Villa v Newcastle U
Bolton W v Portsmouth
Chelsea v Liverpool
Derby Co v Tottenham H
Everton v Reading
Middlesbrough v Fulham
Sunderland v Wigan Ath
West Ham U v Birmingham C

Coca-Cola Football League Championship
Barnsley v WBA
Bristol C v Sheffield W
Burnley v Colchester U
Cardiff C v Norwich C
Charlton Ath v Crystal Palace
Hull C v Blackpool
Ipswich T v Watford
Leicester C v Plymouth Arg
Preston NE v Coventry C
Sheffield U v Scunthorpe U
Southampton v QPR
Wolverhampton W v Stoke C

Coca-Cola Football League One
Cheltenham T v Brighton & HA
Crewe Alex v Swansea C
Doncaster R v Bristol R
Huddersfield T v Swindon T
Luton T v Bournemouth
Northampton T v Leeds U
Nottingham F v Millwall
Oldham Ath v Gillingham
Port Vale v Carlisle U
Southend U v Hartlepool U
Tranmere R v Leyton Orient
Walsall v Yeovil T

Coca-Cola Football League Two
Bradford C v Bury
Brentford v Shrewsbury T
Chester C v Accrington S
Darlington v Barnet
Grimsby T v Chesterfield
Hereford U v Dagenham & R
Lincoln C v Rochdale
Milton Keynes Dons v Rotherham U
Morecambe v Macclesfield T
Peterborough U v Wrexham
Stockport Co v Notts Co
Wycombe W v Mansfield T

Sunday, 10 February 2008
Barclays Premier League
Manchester U v Manchester C

Tuesday, 12 February 2008
Coca-Cola Football League Championship
Blackpool v Wolverhampton W
Colchester U v Preston NE
Coventry C v Cardiff C
Crystal Palace v Ipswich T
Norwich C v Hull C
Plymouth Arg v Barnsley
QPR v Burnley
Scunthorpe U v Bristol C
Sheffield W v Charlton Ath
Stoke C v Southampton
Watford v Leicester C
WBA v Sheffield U

Coca-Cola Football League One
Bournemouth v Doncaster R
Brighton & HA v Tranmere R
Bristol R v Oldham Ath
Carlisle U v Huddersfield T
Gillingham v Luton T
Hartlepool U v Port Vale
Leeds U v Nottingham F
Leyton Orient v Crewe Alex
Millwall v Southend U
Swansea C v Walsall
Swindon T v Cheltenham T
Yeovil T v Northampton T

Coca-Cola Football League Two
Accrington S v Lincoln C
Barnet v Brentford
Bury v Wycombe W
Dagenham & R v Chester C
Macclesfield T v Grimsby T
Mansfield T v Morecambe
Notts Co v Darlington
Rochdale v Hereford U
Rotherham U v Stockport Co
Shrewsbury T v Milton Keynes Dons
Wrexham v Bradford C

Wednesday, 13 February 2008
Coca-Cola Football League Two
Chesterfield v Peterborough U

Saturday, 16 February 2008
Coca-Cola Football League Championship
Barnsley v QPR
Bristol C v Crystal Palace
Burnley v Coventry C
Cardiff C v WBA
Charlton Ath v Watford
Hull C v Colchester U
Ipswich T v Blackpool
Leicester C v Norwich C
Preston NE v Stoke C
Sheffield U v Sheffield W
Southampton v Plymouth Arg
Wolverhampton W v Scunthorpe U

Coca-Cola Football League One
Cheltenham T v Hartlepool U
Crewe Alex v Carlisle U
Doncaster R v Leeds U
Huddersfield T v Brighton & HA
Luton T v Leyton Orient
Northampton T v Gillingham
Nottingham F v Swindon T
Oldham Ath v Yeovil T
Port Vale v Swansea C
Southend U v Bournemouth
Tranmere R v Millwall
Walsall v Bristol R

Coca-Cola Football League Two
Bradford C v Rochdale
Brentford v Accrington S
Chester C v Notts Co
Darlington v Mansfield T
Grimsby T v Dagenham & R
Hereford U v Chesterfield
Lincoln C v Macclesfield T
Milton Keynes Dons v Wrexham
Morecambe v Shrewsbury T
Peterborough U v Barnet
Stockport Co v Bury
Wycombe W v Rotherham U

Friday, 22 February 2008
Coca-Cola Football League One
Hartlepool U v Northampton T
Swansea C v Luton T

Coca-Cola Football League Two
Wrexham v Grimsby T

Saturday, 23 February 2008
Barclays Premier League
Birmingham C v Arsenal
Blackburn R v Bolton W
Fulham v West Ham U
Liverpool v Middlesbrough
Manchester C v Everton
Newcastle U v Manchester U
Portsmouth v Sunderland
Reading v Aston Villa
Tottenham H v Chelsea
Wigan Ath v Derby Co

Coca-Cola Football League Championship
Blackpool v Charlton Ath
Colchester U v Bristol C
Coventry C v Leicester C
Crystal Palace v Wolverhampton W
Norwich C v Barnsley
Plymouth Arg v Burnley
QPR v Sheffield U
Scunthorpe U v Southampton
Sheffield W v Cardiff C

Stoke C v Ipswich T
Watford v Preston NE
WBA v Hull C

Coca-Cola Football League One
Bournemouth v Cheltenham T
Brighton & HA v Oldham Ath
Bristol R v Tranmere R
Carlisle U v Doncaster R
Gillingham v Huddersfield T
Leeds U v Crewe Alex
Leyton Orient v Nottingham F
Millwall v Port Vale
Swindon T v Walsall
Yeovil T v Southend U

Coca-Cola Football League Two
Accrington S v Stockport Co
Barnet v Milton Keynes Dons
Bury v Darlington
Chesterfield v Brentford
Dagenham & R v Morecambe
Macclesfield T v Peterborough U
Mansfield T v Chester C
Notts Co v Bradford C
Rochdale v Wycombe W
Rotherham U v Lincoln C
Shrewsbury T v Hereford U

Friday, 29 February 2008
Coca-Cola Football League One
Cheltenham T v Southend U

Saturday, 1 March 2008
Barclays Premier League
Arsenal v Aston Villa
Birmingham C v Tottenham H
Bolton W v Liverpool
Derby Co v Sunderland
Everton v Portsmouth
Fulham v Manchester U
Manchester C v Wigan Ath
Middlesbrough v Reading
Newcastle U v Blackburn R
West Ham U v Chelsea

Coca-Cola Football League Championship
Barnsley v Sheffield W
Bristol C v Hull C
Burnley v Watford
Cardiff C v Leicester C
Colchester U v Wolverhampton W
Norwich C v Blackpool
Preston NE v Crystal Palace
QPR v Stoke C
Scunthorpe U v Coventry C
Sheffield U v Charlton Ath
Southampton v Ipswich T
WBA v Plymouth Arg

Coca-Cola Football League One
Bournemouth v Hartlepool U
Brighton & HA v Leyton Orient
Gillingham v Yeovil T
Huddersfield T v Swansea C
Luton T v Walsall
Millwall v Bristol R
Northampton T v Crewe Alex
Nottingham F v Carlisle U
Port Vale v Oldham Ath
Swindon T v Leeds U
Tranmere R v Doncaster R

Coca-Cola Football League Two
Barnet v Shrewsbury T
Bradford C v Dagenham & R
Darlington v Brentford
Hereford U v Stockport Co
Lincoln C v Wycombe W
Macclesfield T v Notts Co
Milton Keynes Dons v Chester C
Morecambe v Grimsby T
Peterborough U v Bury
Rochdale v Chesterfield
Rotherham U v Accrington S
Wrexham v Mansfield T

Tuesday, 4 March 2008
Coca-Cola Football League Championship
Blackpool v Barnsley
Charlton Ath v Bristol C
Coventry C v QPR
Crystal Palace v Cardiff C
Hull C v Burnley
Ipswich T v Sheffield U
Leicester C v Preston NE
Plymouth Arg v Colchester U
Sheffield W v WBA
Stoke C v Scunthorpe U
Watford v Norwich C
Wolverhampton W v Southampton

Coca-Cola Football League One
Bristol R v Northampton T

Saturday, 8 March 2008
Barclays Premier League
Aston Villa v Middlesbrough
Blackburn R v Fulham
Chelsea v Derby Co
Liverpool v Newcastle U
Manchester U v Bolton W
Portsmouth v Birmingham C
Reading v Manchester C
Sunderland v Everton
Tottenham H v West Ham U
Wigan Ath v Arsenal

Coca-Cola Football League Championship
Blackpool v Southampton
Charlton Ath v Preston NE
Coventry C v Norwich C
Crystal Palace v Colchester U
Hull C v Scunthorpe U
Ipswich T v Cardiff C
Leicester C v Bristol C
Plymouth Arg v Sheffield U
Sheffield W v QPR
Stoke C v Burnley
Watford v Barnsley
Wolverhampton W v WBA

Coca-Cola Football League One
Bristol R v Swindon T
Carlisle U v Brighton & HA
Crewe Alex v Nottingham F
Doncaster R v Port Vale
Hartlepool U v Gillingham
Leeds U v Bournemouth
Leyton Orient v Huddersfield T
Oldham Ath v Tranmere R
Southend U v Luton T
Swansea C v Millwall
Walsall v Northampton T
Yeovil T v Cheltenham T

Coca-Cola Football League Two
Accrington S v Hereford U
Brentford v Macclesfield T
Bury v Morecambe
Chesterfield v Lincoln C
Dagenham & R v Peterborough U
Grimsby T v Milton Keynes Dons
Mansfield T v Rochdale
Notts Co v Barnet
Shrewsbury T v Rotherham U
Stockport Co v Bradford C
Wycombe W v Darlington

Sunday, 9 March 2008
Coca-Cola Football League Two
Chester C v Wrexham

Tuesday, 11 March 2008
Coca-Cola Football League Championship
Barnsley v Ipswich T
Bristol C v Watford
Burnley v Charlton Ath
Cardiff C v Hull C
Colchester U v Sheffield W
Norwich C v Stoke C
Preston NE v Wolverhampton W
QPR v Blackpool
Scunthorpe U v Plymouth Arg
Sheffield U v Coventry C
Southampton v Leicester C
WBA v Crystal Palace

Coca-Cola Football League One
Carlisle U v Luton T
Crewe Alex v Port Vale
Doncaster R v Gillingham
Hartlepool U v Huddersfield T
Leeds U v Cheltenham T
Leyton Orient v Swindon T
Oldham Ath v Bournemouth
Southend U v Nottingham F
Swansea C v Tranmere R
Walsall v Brighton & HA
Yeovil T v Millwall

Coca-Cola Football League Two
Brentford v Peterborough U
Bury v Rotherham U
Dagenham & R v Macclesfield T
Grimsby T v Barnet
Mansfield T v Hereford U
Notts Co v Lincoln C
Shrewsbury T v Darlington
Stockport Co v Rochdale
Wycombe W v Wrexham

Wednesday, 12 March 2008
Coca-Cola Football League Two
Accrington S v Morecambe
Chester C v Bradford C
Chesterfield v Milton Keynes Dons

Saturday, 15 March 2008
Barclays Premier League
Arsenal v Middlesbrough
Birmingham C v Newcastle U
Derby Co v Manchester U
Fulham v Everton
Liverpool v Reading
Manchester C v Tottenham H
Portsmouth v Aston Villa
Sunderland v Chelsea
West Ham U v Blackburn R
Wigan Ath v Bolton W

Coca-Cola Football League Championship
Blackpool v Preston NE
Bristol C v Plymouth Arg
Burnley v Wolverhampton W
Colchester U v Cardiff C
Coventry C v Sheffield W
Crystal Palace v Barnsley
Hull C v Southampton
Ipswich T v Charlton Ath
QPR v Scunthorpe U
Sheffield U v Norwich C
Watford v Stoke C
WBA v Leicester C

Coca-Cola Football League One
Bournemouth v Yeovil T
Brighton & HA v Doncaster R
Cheltenham T v Bristol R
Gillingham v Crewe Alex
Huddersfield T v Southend U
Luton T v Oldham Ath
Millwall v Leyton Orient
Northampton T v Swansea C
Nottingham F v Walsall
Port Vale v Leeds U
Swindon T v Carlisle U
Tranmere R v Hartlepool U

Coca-Cola Football League Two
Barnet v Chester C
Bradford C v Mansfield T
Darlington v Grimsby T
Hereford U v Wycombe W
Lincoln C v Stockport Co
Macclesfield T v Shrewsbury T
Milton Keynes Dons v Dagenham & R
Morecambe v Brentford
Peterborough U v Notts Co
Rochdale v Accrington S
Rotherham U v Chesterfield
Wrexham v Bury

Friday, 21 March 2008
Coca-Cola Football League One
Northampton T v Nottingham F
Yeovil T v Doncaster R

Saturday, 22 March 2008
Barclays Premier League
Aston Villa v Sunderland
Blackburn R v Wigan Ath
Bolton W v Manchester C
Chelsea v Arsenal
Everton v West Ham U
Manchester U v Liverpool
Middlesbrough v Derby Co
Newcastle U v Fulham
Reading v Birmingham C
Tottenham H v Portsmouth

Coca-Cola Football League Championship
Barnsley v Sheffield U
Cardiff C v Bristol C
Charlton Ath v WBA
Leicester C v Hull C
Norwich C v Colchester U
Plymouth Arg v Watford
Preston NE v Burnley
Scunthorpe U v Ipswich T
Sheffield W v Crystal Palace
Southampton v Coventry C
Stoke C v Blackpool
Wolverhampton W v QPR

Coca-Cola Football League One
Brighton & HA v Swindon T
Bristol R v Huddersfield T
Crewe Alex v Hartlepool U
Gillingham v Bournemouth
Leeds U v Walsall
Leyton Orient v Carlisle U
Luton T v Cheltenham T
Oldham Ath v Millwall
Southend U v Swansea C
Tranmere R v Port Vale

Coca-Cola Football League Two
Barnet v Lincoln C
Brentford v Wrexham
Chester C v Darlington
Chesterfield v Accrington S
Dagenham & R v Shrewsbury T
Hereford U v Bury
Mansfield T v Grimsby T
Milton Keynes Dons v Peterborough U
Morecambe v Wycombe W
Notts Co v Rochdale
Rotherham U v Bradford C
Stockport Co v Macclesfield T

Monday, 24 March 2008
Coca-Cola Football League One
Bournemouth v Tranmere R
Carlisle U v Northampton T
Cheltenham T v Leyton Orient
Doncaster R v Oldham Ath
Hartlepool U v Yeovil T
Millwall v Luton T
Nottingham F v Brighton & HA
Port Vale v Gillingham
Swansea C v Bristol R
Swindon T v Southend U
Walsall v Crewe Alex

Coca-Cola Football League Two
Accrington S v Milton Keynes Dons
Bradford C v Chesterfield
Bury v Mansfield T
Darlington v Morecambe
Grimsby T v Brentford
Lincoln C v Hereford U
Macclesfield T v Barnet
Peterborough U v Chester C
Rochdale v Rotherham U
Shrewsbury T v Notts Co
Wrexham v Dagenham & R
Wycombe W v Stockport Co

Tuesday, 25 March 2008
Coca-Cola Football League One
Huddersfield T v Leeds U

Friday, 28 March 2008
Coca-Cola Football League One
Doncaster R v Nottingham F
Tranmere R v Swindon T

Saturday, 29 March 2008
Barclays Premier League
Birmingham C v Manchester C
Bolton W v Arsenal
Chelsea v Middlesbrough
Derby Co v Fulham
Liverpool v Everton
Manchester U v Aston Villa
Portsmouth v Wigan Ath
Reading v Blackburn R
Sunderland v West Ham U

Coca-Cola Football League Championship
Bristol C v Norwich C
Burnley v Barnsley
Cardiff C v Southampton
Charlton Ath v Wolverhampton W
Coventry C v Plymouth Arg
Crystal Palace v Blackpool
Hull C v Watford
Ipswich T v QPR
Leicester C v Scunthorpe U
Preston NE v Sheffield U
Sheffield W v Stoke C
WBA v Colchester U

Coca-Cola Football League One
Bournemouth v Millwall
Cheltenham T v Northampton T
Gillingham v Carlisle U
Hartlepool U v Swansea C
Leeds U v Brighton & HA
Luton T v Crewe Alex
Oldham Ath v Huddersfield T
Port Vale v Leyton Orient
Southend U v Walsall
Yeovil T v Bristol R

Coca-Cola Football League Two
Barnet v Wrexham
Brentford v Rochdale
Chester C v Stockport Co
Dagenham & R v Chesterfield
Darlington v Bradford C
Grimsby T v Wycombe W
Macclesfield T v Accrington S
Milton Keynes Dons v Hereford U
Morecambe v Rotherham U
Notts Co v Mansfield T
Peterborough U v Lincoln C
Shrewsbury T v Bury

Sunday, 30 March 2008
Barclays Premier League
Tottenham H v Newcastle U

Friday, 4 April 2008
Coca-Cola Football League Two
Lincoln C v Milton Keynes Dons

Saturday, 5 April 2008
Barclays Premier League
Arsenal v Liverpool
Aston Villa v Bolton W
Blackburn R v Tottenham H
Fulham v Sunderland
Manchester C v Chelsea
Middlesbrough v Manchester U
Newcastle U v Reading
West Ham U v Portsmouth
Wigan Ath v Birmingham C

Coca-Cola Football League Championship
Barnsley v Hull C
Blackpool v WBA
Colchester U v Ipswich T
Norwich C v Burnley
Plymouth Arg v Charlton Ath
QPR v Preston NE
Scunthorpe U v Sheffield W
Sheffield U v Leicester C
Southampton v Bristol C
Stoke C v Crystal Palace
Watford v Coventry C
Wolverhampton W v Cardiff C

Coca-Cola Football League One
Brighton & HA v Port Vale
Bristol R v Hartlepool U
Carlisle U v Yeovil T
Crewe Alex v Southend U
Huddersfield T v Doncaster R
Leyton Orient v Leeds U
Millwall v Gillingham
Northampton T v Luton T
Nottingham F v Cheltenham T
Swansea C v Bournemouth
Swindon T v Oldham Ath
Walsall v Tranmere R

Coca-Cola Football League Two
Accrington S v Dagenham & R
Bradford C v Morecambe
Bury v Notts Co
Chesterfield v Shrewsbury T
Hereford U v Chester C
Mansfield T v Barnet
Rochdale v Grimsby T
Rotherham U v Brentford
Stockport Co v Darlington
Wrexham v Macclesfield T
Wycombe W v Peterborough U

Sunday, 6 April 2008
Barclays Premier League
Everton v Derby Co

Saturday, 12 April 2008
Barclays Premier League
Birmingham C v Everton
Bolton W v West Ham U
Chelsea v Wigan Ath
Derby Co v Aston Villa
Liverpool v Blackburn R
Manchester U v Arsenal
Portsmouth v Newcastle U
Reading v Fulham
Sunderland v Manchester C
Tottenham H v Middlesbrough

Coca-Cola Football League Championship
Bristol C v Wolverhampton W
Burnley v Sheffield U
Cardiff C v Blackpool
Charlton Ath v Southampton
Coventry C v Stoke C
Crystal Palace v Scunthorpe U
Hull C v QPR
Leicester C v Colchester U
Preston NE v Barnsley
Sheffield W v Plymouth Arg
WBA v Watford

Coca-Cola Football League One
Bournemouth v Bristol R
Cheltenham T v Walsall
Doncaster R v Swindon T
Gillingham v Swansea C
Hartlepool U v Millwall
Leeds U v Carlisle U
Luton T v Brighton & HA
Oldham Ath v Leyton Orient
Port Vale v Huddersfield T
Southend U v Northampton T
Tranmere R v Nottingham F
Yeovil T v Crewe Alex

Coca-Cola Football League Two
Barnet v Bury
Brentford v Bradford C
Chester C v Lincoln C
Dagenham & R v Rochdale
Darlington v Hereford U
Grimsby T v Rotherham U
Macclesfield T v Mansfield T
Milton Keynes Dons v Wycombe W
Morecambe v Chesterfield
Notts Co v Accrington S
Peterborough U v Stockport Co

Sunday, 13 April 2008
Coca-Cola Football League Championship
Ipswich T v Norwich C

Coca-Cola Football League Two
Shrewsbury T v Wrexham

Saturday, 19 April 2008
Barclays Premier League
Arsenal v Reading
Blackburn R v Manchester U
Everton v Chelsea
Fulham v Liverpool
Manchester C v Portsmouth
Middlesbrough v Bolton W
Newcastle U v Sunderland
West Ham U v Derby Co
Wigan Ath v Tottenham H

Coca-Cola Football League Championship
Barnsley v Leicester C
Blackpool v Sheffield W
Colchester U v Coventry C
Norwich C v WBA
Plymouth Arg v Preston NE
QPR v Charlton Ath
Scunthorpe U v Cardiff C
Sheffield U v Hull C
Southampton v Burnley
Stoke C v Bristol C
Watford v Crystal Palace
Wolverhampton W v Ipswich T

Coca-Cola Football League One
Brighton & HA v Hartlepool U
Bristol R v Gillingham
Carlisle U v Southend U
Crewe Alex v Cheltenham T
Huddersfield T v Tranmere R
Leyton Orient v Doncaster R
Millwall v Leeds U
Northampton T v Oldham Ath
Nottingham F v Luton T
Swansea C v Yeovil T
Swindon T v Port Vale
Walsall v Bournemouth

Coca-Cola Football League Two
Accrington S v Barnet
Bradford C v Grimsby T
Bury v Macclesfield T
Chesterfield v Darlington
Hereford U v Peterborough U
Lincoln C v Brentford
Mansfield T v Shrewsbury T
Rochdale v Morecambe
Rotherham U v Dagenham & R
Stockport Co v Milton Keynes Dons
Wrexham v Notts Co
Wycombe W v Chester C

Sunday, 20 April 2008
Barclays Premier League
Aston Villa v Birmingham C

Saturday, 26 April 2008
Barclays Premier League
Birmingham C v Liverpool
Chelsea v Manchester U
Derby Co v Arsenal
Everton v Aston Villa
Manchester C v Fulham
Portsmouth v Blackburn R
Sunderland v Middlesbrough
Tottenham H v Bolton W
West Ham U v Newcastle U
Wigan Ath v Reading

Coca-Cola Football League Championship
Barnsley v Charlton Ath
Burnley v Cardiff C
Colchester U v Stoke C
Coventry C v Wolverhampton W
Hull C v Crystal Palace
Leicester C v Sheffield W
Norwich C v QPR
Plymouth Arg v Blackpool
Preston NE v Ipswich T
Sheffield U v Bristol C
Watford v Scunthorpe U
WBA v Southampton

Coca-Cola Football League One
Bournemouth v Crewe Alex
Bristol R v Brighton & HA
Doncaster R v Luton T
Gillingham v Swindon T
Hartlepool U v Nottingham F
Huddersfield T v Walsall
Millwall v Carlisle U
Oldham Ath v Cheltenham T
Port Vale v Northampton T
Swansea C v Leyton Orient
Tranmere R v Southend U
Yeovil T v Leeds U

Coca-Cola Football League Two
Barnet v Stockport Co
Bradford C v Milton Keynes Dons
Brentford v Hereford U
Bury v Rochdale
Darlington v Dagenham & R
Grimsby T v Peterborough U
Macclesfield T v Chesterfield
Mansfield T v Rotherham U
Morecambe v Lincoln C
Notts Co v Wycombe W
Shrewsbury T v Chester C
Wrexham v Accrington S

Saturday, 3 May 2008
Barclays Premier League
Arsenal v Everton
Aston Villa v Wigan Ath
Blackburn R v Derby Co
Bolton W v Sunderland
Fulham v Birmingham C
Liverpool v Manchester C
Manchester U v West Ham U
Middlesbrough v Portsmouth
Newcastle U v Chelsea
Reading v Tottenham H

Coca-Cola Football League One
Brighton & HA v Swansea C
Carlisle U v Bournemouth
Cheltenham T v Doncaster R
Crewe Alex v Oldham Ath
Leeds U v Gillingham
Leyton Orient v Bristol R
Luton T v Huddersfield T
Northampton T v Tranmere R
Nottingham F v Yeovil T
Southend U v Port Vale
Swindon T v Millwall
Walsall v Hartlepool U

Coca-Cola Football League Two
Accrington S v Bury
Chester C v Macclesfield T
Chesterfield v Notts Co
Dagenham & R v Mansfield T
Hereford U v Grimsby T
Lincoln C v Wrexham
Milton Keynes Dons v Morecambe
Peterborough U v Darlington
Rochdale v Shrewsbury T
Rotherham U v Barnet
Stockport Co v Brentford
Wycombe W v Bradford C

Sunday, 4 May 2008
Coca-Cola Football League Championship
Blackpool v Watford
Bristol C v Preston NE
Cardiff C v Barnsley
Charlton Ath v Coventry C
Crystal Palace v Burnley
Ipswich T v Hull C
QPR v WBA
Scunthorpe U v Colchester U
Sheffield W v Norwich C
Southampton v Sheffield U
Stoke C v Leicester C
Wolverhampton W v Plymouth Arg

Sunday, 11 May 2008
Barclays Premier League
Birmingham C v Blackburn R
Chelsea v Bolton W
Derby Co v Reading
Everton v Newcastle U
Middlesbrough v Manchester C
Portsmouth v Fulham
Sunderland v Arsenal
Tottenham H v Liverpool
West Ham U v Aston Villa
Wigan Ath v Manchester U

BLUE SQUARE PREMIER FIXTURES 2007–08

Saturday, 11 August 2007
Altrincham T v Exeter C
Crawley T v Stevenage B
Droylsden v Salisbury C
Ebbsfleet U v Northwich Vic
Farsley Celtic v Stafford R
Histon v Burton Alb
Kidderminster H v Aldershot T
Oxford U v Forest Green R
Torquay U v Grays Ath
Weymouth v Halifax T
Woking v Rushden & D'monds
York C v Cambridge U

Tuesday, 14 August 2007
Aldershot T v Torquay U
Burton Alb v York C
Cambridge U v Oxford U
Exeter C v Crawley T
Forest Green R v Weymouth
Grays Ath v Woking
Halifax T v Altrincham T
Northwich Vic v Droylsden
Rushden & D'monds v Farsley Celtic
Salisbury C v Ebbsfleet U
Stafford R v Kidderminster H
Stevenage B v Histon

Saturday, 18 August 2007
Aldershot T v Droylsden
Burton Alb v Oxford U
Cambridge U v Farsley Celtic
Exeter C v York C
Forest Green R v Altrincham T
Grays Ath v Kidderminster H
Halifax T v Histon
Northwich Vic v Torquay U
Rushden & D'monds v Ebbsfleet U
Salisbury C v Crawley T
Stafford R v Woking
Stevenage B v Weymouth

Friday, 24 August 2007
Histon v Aldershot T

Saturday, 25 August 2007
Altrincham T v Grays Ath
Crawley T v Northwich Vic
Droylsden v Exeter C
Ebbsfleet U v Halifax T
Farsley Celtic v Salisbury C
Kidderminster H v Stevenage B
Oxford U v Stafford R
Torquay U v Rushden & D'monds
Weymouth v Burton Alb
Woking v Cambridge U
York C v Forest Green R

Monday, 27 August 2007
Aldershot T v Crawley T
Burton Alb v Farsley Celtic
Cambridge U v Ebbsfleet U
Exeter C v Weymouth
Forest Green R v Torquay U
Grays Ath v Histon
Halifax T v Droylsden
Northwich Vic v York C
Rushden & D'monds v Kidderminster H
Salisbury C v Woking
Stafford R v Altrincham T
Stevenage B v Oxford U

Friday, 31 August 2007
Weymouth v Cambridge U

Saturday, 1 September 2007
Altrincham T v Aldershot T
Crawley T v Burton Alb
Droylsden v Grays Ath
Ebbsfleet U v Stevenage B
Farsley Celtic v Northwich Vic
Histon v Salisbury C
Kidderminster H v Exeter C
Oxford U v Halifax T
Torquay U v Stafford R
Woking v Forest Green R
York C v Rushden & D'monds

Tuesday, 4 September 2007
Cambridge U v Grays Ath
Droylsden v Stevenage B
Ebbsfleet U v Histon
Farsley Celtic v Kidderminster H
Forest Green R v Aldershot T
Northwich Vic v Burton Alb
Oxford U v Exeter C
Rushden & D'monds v Crawley T
Stafford R v Halifax T
Torquay U v Salisbury C
Woking v Weymouth
York C v Altrincham T

Saturday, 8 September 2007
Aldershot T v Northwich Vic
Altrincham T v Oxford U
Burton Alb v Torquay U
Crawley T v Droylsden
Exeter C v Cambridge U
Grays Ath v Forest Green R
Halifax T v Woking
Histon v Farsley Celtic
Kidderminster H v York C
Salisbury C v Rushden & D'monds
Stevenage B v Stafford R
Weymouth v Ebbsfleet U

Saturday, 15 September 2007
Cambridge U v Crawley T
Droylsden v Weymouth
Ebbsfleet U v Kidderminster H
Farsley Celtic v Exeter C
Forest Green R v Salisbury C
Northwich Vic v Histon
Oxford U v Aldershot T
Rushden & D'monds v Burton Alb
Stafford R v Grays Ath
Torquay U v Halifax T
Woking v Altrincham T
York C v Stevenage B

Tuesday, 18 September 2007
Aldershot T v York C
Altrincham T v Cambridge U
Burton Alb v Ebbsfleet U
Crawley T v Woking
Exeter C v Forest Green R
Grays Ath v Oxford U
Halifax T v Northwich Vic
Histon v Torquay U
Kidderminster H v Droylsden
Salisbury C v Stafford R
Stevenage B v Farsley Celtic
Weymouth v Rushden & D'monds

Friday, 21 September 2007
Histon v Oxford U

Saturday, 22 September 2007
Aldershot T v Farsley Celtic
Altrincham T v Droylsden
Burton Alb v Woking
Crawley T v Forest Green R
Exeter C v Ebbsfleet U
Grays Ath v York C
Halifax T v Rushden & D'monds
Kidderminster H v Torquay U
Salisbury C v Northwich Vic
Stevenage B v Cambridge U
Weymouth v Stafford R

Tuesday, 25 September 2007
Cambridge U v Aldershot T
Droylsden v Burton Alb
Ebbsfleet U v Crawley T
Farsley Celtic v Altrincham T
Forest Green R v Stevenage B
Northwich Vic v Kidderminster H
Oxford U v Salisbury C
Rushden & D'monds v Grays Ath
Stafford R v Histon
Torquay U v Weymouth
Woking v Exeter C
York C v Halifax T

Saturday, 29 September 2007
Aldershot T v Exeter C
Crawley T v Altrincham T
Farsley Celtic v Ebbsfleet U
Forest Green R v Cambridge U
Grays Ath v Stevenage B
Halifax T v Burton Alb
Histon v Weymouth
Northwich Vic v Woking
Oxford U v York C
Rushden & D'monds v Stafford R
Salisbury C v Kidderminster H
Torquay U v Droylsden

Saturday, 6 October 2007
Altrincham T v Rushden & D'monds
Burton Alb v Salisbury C
Cambridge U v Halifax T
Droylsden v Oxford U
Ebbsfleet U v Torquay U
Exeter C v Grays Ath
Kidderminster H v Crawley T
Stafford R v Forest Green R
Stevenage B v Aldershot T
Weymouth v Northwich Vic
Woking v Farsley Celtic
York C v Histon

Tuesday, 9 October 2007
Aldershot T v Ebbsfleet U
Altrincham T v Burton Alb
Cambridge U v Rushden & D'monds
Crawley T v Histon
Droylsden v Farsley Celtic
Exeter C v Salisbury C
Forest Green R v Northwich Vic
Grays Ath v Weymouth
Kidderminster H v Halifax T
Oxford U v Torquay U
Stevenage B v Woking
York C v Stafford R

Friday, 12 October 2007
Weymouth v Crawley T

Saturday, 13 October 2007
Burton Alb v Aldershot T
Ebbsfleet U v Droylsden
Farsley Celtic v Oxford U
Halifax T v Grays Ath
Histon v Kidderminster H
Northwich Vic v Exeter C
Rushden & D'monds v Forest Green R
Salisbury C v Altrincham T
Stafford R v Cambridge U
Torquay U v Stevenage B
Woking v York C

Saturday, 20 October 2007
Aldershot T v Halifax T
Altrincham T v Ebbsfleet U
Cambridge U v Salisbury C
Crawley T v Stafford R
Droylsden v Histon
Exeter C v Rushden & D'monds
Forest Green R v Farsley Celtic
Grays Ath v Northwich Vic
Kidderminster H v Weymouth
Oxford U v Woking
Stevenage B v Burton Alb
York C v Torquay U

Saturday, 3 November 2007
Burton Alb v Kidderminster H
Ebbsfleet U v Forest Green R
Farsley Celtic v York C
Halifax T v Crawley T
Histon v Altrincham T
Northwich Vic v Stevenage B
Rushden & D'monds v Oxford U
Salisbury C v Grays Ath
Stafford R v Exeter C
Torquay U v Cambridge U
Weymouth v Aldershot T
Woking v Droylsden

Saturday, 17 November 2007
Aldershot T v Rushden & D'monds
Altrincham T v Weymouth
Cambridge U v Northwich Vic
Crawley T v Torquay U
Droylsden v Stafford R
Exeter C v Burton Alb
Forest Green R v Histon
Grays Ath v Farsley Celtic
Kidderminster H v Woking
Oxford U v Ebbsfleet U
Stevenage B v Halifax T
York C v Salisbury C

Saturday, 24 November 2007
Aldershot T v Grays Ath
Burton Alb v Cambridge U
Crawley T v Farsley Celtic
Droylsden v Forest Green R
Ebbsfleet U v Stafford R
Halifax T v Salisbury C
Histon v Exeter C
Kidderminster H v Oxford U
Northwich Vic v Rushden & D'monds
Stevenage B v Altrincham T
Torquay U v Woking
Weymouth v York C

Saturday, 1 December 2007
Altrincham T v Kidderminster H
Cambridge U v Droylsden
Exeter C v Stevenage B
Farsley Celtic v Torquay U
Forest Green R v Halifax T
Grays Ath v Burton Alb
Oxford U v Weymouth
Rushden & D'monds v Histon
Salisbury C v Aldershot T
Stafford R v Northwich Vic
Woking v Ebbsfleet U
York C v Crawley T

Saturday, 8 December 2007
Aldershot T v Stafford R
Burton Alb v Forest Green R
Crawley T v Grays Ath
Droylsden v Rushden & D'monds
Ebbsfleet U v York C
Halifax T v Exeter C
Histon v Woking
Kidderminster H v Cambridge U
Northwich Vic v Oxford U
Stevenage B v Salisbury C
Torquay U v Altrincham T
Weymouth v Farsley Celtic

Wednesday, 26 December 2007
Altrincham T v Northwich Vic
Cambridge U v Histon
Exeter C v Torquay U
Farsley Celtic v Halifax T
Forest Green R v Kidderminster H
Grays Ath v Ebbsfleet U
Oxford U v Crawley T
Rushden & D'monds v Stevenage B
Salisbury C v Weymouth
Stafford R v Burton Alb
Woking v Aldershot T
York C v Droylsden

Saturday, 29 December 2007
Altrincham T v Stevenage B
Cambridge U v Burton Alb
Exeter C v Histon
Farsley Celtic v Crawley T
Forest Green R v Droylsden
Grays Ath v Aldershot T
Oxford U v Kidderminster H
Rushden & D'monds v Northwich Vic
Salisbury C v Halifax T
Stafford R v Ebbsfleet U
Woking v Torquay U
York C v Weymouth

Tuesday, 1 January 2008
Aldershot T v Woking
Burton Alb v Stafford R
Crawley T v Oxford U
Droylsden v York C
Ebbsfleet U v Grays Ath
Halifax T v Farsley Celtic
Histon v Cambridge U
Kidderminster H v Forest Green R
Northwich Vic v Altrincham T
Stevenage B v Rushden & D'monds
Torquay U v Exeter C
Weymouth v Salisbury C

Saturday, 5 January 2008
Cambridge U v Exeter C
Droylsden v Crawley T
Ebbsfleet U v Weymouth
Farsley Celtic v Histon
Forest Green R v Grays Ath
Northwich Vic v Aldershot T
Oxford U v Altrincham T
Rushden & D'monds v Salisbury C
Stafford R v Stevenage B
Torquay U v Burton Alb
Woking v Halifax T
York C v Kidderminster H

Saturday, 19 January 2008
Aldershot T v Forest Green R
Altrincham T v York C
Burton Alb v Northwich Vic
Crawley T v Rushden & D'monds
Exeter C v Oxford U
Grays Ath v Cambridge U
Halifax T v Stafford R
Histon v Ebbsfleet U
Kidderminster H v Farsley Celtic
Salisbury C v Torquay U
Stevenage B v Droylsden
Weymouth v Woking

Saturday, 26 January 2008
Cambridge U v Altrincham T
Droylsden v Kidderminster H
Ebbsfleet U v Burton Alb
Farsley Celtic v Stevenage B
Forest Green R v Exeter C
Northwich Vic v Halifax T
Oxford U v Grays Ath
Rushden & D'monds v Weymouth
Stafford R v Salisbury C
Torquay U v Histon
Woking v Crawley T
York C v Aldershot T

Saturday, 2 February 2008
Aldershot T v Oxford U
Altrincham T v Woking
Burton Alb v Rushden & D'monds
Crawley T v Cambridge U
Exeter C v Farsley Celtic
Grays Ath v Stafford R
Halifax T v Torquay U
Histon v Northwich Vic
Kidderminster H v Ebbsfleet U
Salisbury C v Forest Green R
Stevenage B v York C
Weymouth v Droylsden

Saturday, 9 February 2008
Cambridge U v Stevenage B
Droylsden v Altrincham T
Ebbsfleet U v Exeter C
Farsley Celtic v Aldershot T
Forest Green R v Crawley T
Northwich Vic v Salisbury C
Oxford U v Histon
Rushden & D'monds v Halifax T
Stafford R v Weymouth
Torquay U v Kidderminster H
Woking v Burton Alb
York C v Grays Ath

Tuesday, 12 February 2008
Aldershot T v Cambridge U
Altrincham T v Farsley Celtic
Burton Alb v Droylsden
Crawley T v Ebbsfleet U
Exeter C v Woking
Grays Ath v Rushden & D'monds
Halifax T v York C
Histon v Stafford R
Kidderminster H v Northwich Vic
Salisbury C v Oxford U
Stevenage B v Forest Green R
Weymouth v Torquay U

Saturday, 16 February 2008
Aldershot T v Stevenage B
Crawley T v Kidderminster H
Farsley Celtic v Woking
Forest Green R v Stafford R
Grays Ath v Exeter C
Halifax T v Cambridge U

Histon v York C
Northwich Vic v Weymouth
Oxford U v Droylsden
Rushden & D'monds v Altrincham T
Salisbury C v Burton Alb
Torquay U v Ebbsfleet U

Saturday, 23 February 2008
Altrincham T v Crawley T
Burton Alb v Halifax T
Cambridge U v Forest Green R
Droylsden v Torquay U
Ebbsfleet U v Farsley Celtic
Exeter C v Aldershot T
Kidderminster H v Salisbury C
Stafford R v Rushden & D'monds
Stevenage B v Grays Ath
Weymouth v Histon
Woking v Northwich Vic
York C v Oxford U

Saturday, 1 March 2008
Aldershot T v Kidderminster H
Burton Alb v Histon
Cambridge U v York C
Exeter C v Altrincham T
Forest Green R v Oxford U
Grays Ath v Torquay U
Halifax T v Weymouth
Northwich Vic v Ebbsfleet U
Rushden & D'monds v Woking
Salisbury C v Droylsden
Stafford R v Farsley Celtic
Stevenage B v Crawley T

Tuesday, 4 March 2008
Altrincham T v Halifax T
Crawley T v Exeter C
Droylsden v Northwich Vic
Ebbsfleet U v Salisbury C
Farsley Celtic v Rushden & D'monds
Histon v Stevenage B
Kidderminster H v Stafford R
Oxford U v Cambridge U
Torquay U v Aldershot T
Weymouth v Forest Green R
Woking v Grays Ath
York C v Burton Alb

Saturday, 8 March 2008
Altrincham T v Forest Green R
Crawley T v Salisbury C
Droylsden v Aldershot T
Ebbsfleet U v Rushden & D'monds
Farsley Celtic v Cambridge U
Histon v Halifax T
Kidderminster H v Grays Ath
Oxford U v Burton Alb
Torquay U v Northwich Vic
Weymouth v Stevenage B
Woking v Stafford R
York C v Exeter C

Saturday, 15 March 2008
Aldershot T v Histon
Burton Alb v Weymouth
Cambridge U v Woking
Exeter C v Droylsden
Forest Green R v York C
Grays Ath v Altrincham T
Halifax T v Ebbsfleet U
Northwich Vic v Crawley T
Rushden & D'monds v Torquay U
Salisbury C v Farsley Celtic
Stafford R v Oxford U
Stevenage B v Kidderminster H

Saturday, 22 March 2008
Aldershot T v Altrincham T
Burton Alb v Crawley T
Cambridge U v Weymouth
Exeter C v Kidderminster H
Forest Green R v Woking
Grays Ath v Droylsden
Halifax T v Oxford U
Northwich Vic v Farsley Celtic
Rushden & D'monds v York C
Salisbury C v Histon
Stafford R v Torquay U
Stevenage B v Ebbsfleet U

Monday, 24 March 2008
Altrincham T v Stafford R
Crawley T v Aldershot T
Droylsden v Halifax T
Ebbsfleet U v Cambridge U
Farsley Celtic v Burton Alb
Histon v Grays Ath
Kidderminster H v
Rushden & D'monds
Oxford U v Stevenage B
Torquay U v Forest Green R
Weymouth v Exeter C
Woking v Salisbury C
York C v Northwich Vic

Saturday, 29 March 2008
Altrincham T v Torquay U
Cambridge U v Kidderminster H
Exeter C v Halifax T
Farsley Celtic v Weymouth
Forest Green R v Burton Alb
Grays Ath v Crawley T
Oxford U v Northwich Vic
Rushden & D'monds v Droylsden
Salisbury C v Stevenage B
Stafford R v Aldershot T
Woking v Histon
York C v Ebbsfleet U

Saturday, 5 April 2008
Aldershot T v Salisbury C
Burton Alb v Grays Ath
Crawley T v York C
Droylsden v Cambridge U
Ebbsfleet U v Woking
Halifax T v Forest Green R
Histon v Rushden & D'monds
Kidderminster H v Altrincham T
Northwich Vic v Stafford R
Stevenage B v Exeter C
Torquay U v Farsley Celtic
Weymouth v Oxford U

Tuesday, 8 April 2008
Burton Alb v Altrincham T
Ebbsfleet U v Aldershot T
Farsley Celtic v Droylsden
Halifax T v Kidderminster H
Histon v Crawley T
Northwich Vic v Forest Green R
Rushden & D'monds v Cambridge U
Salisbury C v Exeter C
Stafford R v York C
Torquay U v Oxford U
Weymouth v Grays Ath
Woking v Stevenage B

Saturday, 12 April 2008
Aldershot T v Burton Alb
Altrincham T v Salisbury C
Cambridge U v Stafford R
Crawley T v Weymouth
Droylsden v Ebbsfleet U
Exeter C v Northwich Vic
Forest Green R v Rushden & D'monds
Grays Ath v Halifax T
Kidderminster H v Histon
Oxford U v Farsley Celtic
Stevenage B v Torquay U
York C v Woking

Saturday, 19 April 2008
Burton Alb v Stevenage B
Ebbsfleet U v Altrincham T
Farsley Celtic v Forest Green R
Halifax T v Aldershot T
Histon v Droylsden
Northwich Vic v Grays Ath
Rushden & D'monds v Exeter C
Salisbury C v Cambridge U
Stafford R v Crawley T
Torquay U v York C
Weymouth v Kidderminster H
Woking v Oxford U

Saturday, 26 April 2008
Aldershot T v Weymouth
Altrincham T v Histon
Cambridge U v Torquay U
Crawley T v Halifax T
Droylsden v Woking
Exeter C v Stafford R
Forest Green R v Ebbsfleet U
Grays Ath v Salisbury C
Kidderminster H v Burton Alb
Oxford U v Rushden & D'monds
Stevenage B v Northwich Vic
York C v Farsley Celtic

Saturday, 3 May 2008
Burton Alb v Exeter C
Ebbsfleet U v Oxford U
Farsley Celtic v Grays Ath
Halifax T v Stevenage B
Histon v Forest Green R
Northwich Vic v Cambridge U
Rushden & D'monds v Aldershot T
Salisbury C v York C
Stafford R v Droylsden
Torquay U v Crawley T
Weymouth v Altrincham T
Woking v Kidderminster H

THE SCOTTISH PREMIER LEAGUE AND FOOTBALL LEAGUE FIXTURES 2007–08

Reproduced under licence from Football Dataco Limited. All rights reserved. Licence No. PRINT/SKYSPOAN/129743a. Copyright © and Database Right The Scottish Premier League/The Scottish Football League Limited 2007. All rights reserved. No part of the Fixtures Lists may be reproduced stored or transmitted in any form without the prior written permission of Football DataCo Limited.

Saturday, 4 August 2007
Clydesdale Bank Scottish Premier League
Dundee U v Aberdeen
Gretna v Falkirk
Inverness CT v Rangers
St Mirren v Motherwell

Scottish League First Division
Hamilton A v Dunfermline Ath
Livingston v Dundee
Morton v Clyde
Queen of the S v St Johnstone
Stirling Alb v Partick Th

Scottish League Second Division
Airdrie U v Raith R
Berwick R v Cowdenbeath
Peterhead v Alloa Ath
Queen's Park v Brechin C
Ross Co v Ayr U

Scottish League Third Division
Dumbarton v Elgin C
East Fife v East Stirlingshire
Montrose v Albion R
Stenhousemuir v Arbroath
Stranraer v Forfar Ath

Sunday, 5 August 2007
Clydesdale Bank Scottish Premier League
Celtic v Kilmarnock

Monday, 6 August 2007
Clydesdale Bank Scottish Premier League
Hearts v Hibernian

Saturday, 11 August 2007
Clydesdale Bank Scottish Premier League
Falkirk v Celtic
Hibernian v Gretna
Motherwell v Inverness CT
Rangers v St Mirren

Scottish League First Division
Clyde v Hamilton A
Dundee v Queen of the S
Dunfermline Ath v Morton
Partick Th v Livingston
St Johnstone v Stirling Alb

Scottish League Second Division
Alloa Ath v Airdrie U
Ayr U v Queen's Park
Brechin C v Peterhead
Cowdenbeath v Ross Co
Raith R v Berwick R

Scottish League Third Division
Albion R v Stranraer
Arbroath v East Fife
East Stirlingshire v Dumbarton
Elgin C v Montrose
Forfar Ath v Stenhousemuir

Sunday, 12 August 2007
Clydesdale Bank Scottish Premier League
Aberdeen v Hearts

Monday, 13 August 2007
Clydesdale Bank Scottish Premier League
Kilmarnock v Dundee U

Saturday, 18 August 2007
Clydesdale Bank Scottish Premier League
Dundee U v Hibernian
Hearts v Gretna
Motherwell v Kilmarnock
Rangers v Falkirk
St Mirren v Inverness CT

Scottish League First Division
Hamilton A v Queen of the S
Livingston v Dunfermline Ath
Partick Th v Clyde
St Johnstone v Dundee
Stirling Alb v Morton

Scottish League Second Division
Berwick R v Airdrie U
Brechin C v Ayr U
Peterhead v Cowdenbeath
Queen's Park v Ross Co
Raith R v Alloa Ath

Scottish League Third Division
Albion R v Stenhousemuir
Arbroath v Dumbarton
East Stirlingshire v Forfar Ath
Elgin C v East Fife
Stranraer v Montrose

Sunday, 19 August 2007
Clydesdale Bank Scottish Premier League
Aberdeen v Celtic

Saturday, 25 August 2007
Clydesdale Bank Scottish Premier League
Celtic v Hearts
Falkirk v St Mirren
Gretna v Motherwell
Hibernian v Aberdeen
Inverness CT v Dundee U
Kilmarnock v Rangers

Scottish League First Division
Clyde v St Johnstone
Dundee v Partick Th
Dunfermline Ath v Stirling Alb
Morton v Hamilton A
Queen of the S v Livingston

Scottish League Second Division
Airdrie U v Queen's Park
Alloa Ath v Brechin C
Ayr U v Berwick R
Cowdenbeath v Raith R
Ross Co v Peterhead

Scottish League Third Division
Dumbarton v Albion R
East Fife v Stranraer
Forfar Ath v Elgin C
Montrose v Arbroath
Stenhousemuir v East Stirlingshire

Saturday, 1 September 2007
Clydesdale Bank Scottish Premier League
Dundee U v Falkirk
Hibernian v Inverness CT
Kilmarnock v Aberdeen
Rangers v Gretna

Scottish League First Division
Clyde v Dundee
Dunfermline Ath v St Johnstone
Morton v Queen of the S
Partick Th v Hamilton A
Stirling Alb v Livingston

Scottish League Second Division
Ayr U v Alloa Ath
Brechin C v Cowdenbeath
Peterhead v Berwick R
Queen's Park v Raith R
Ross Co v Airdrie U

Scottish League Third Division
Albion R v East Stirlingshire
Arbroath v Elgin C
East Fife v Forfar Ath
Stenhousemuir v Montrose
Stranraer v Dumbarton

Sunday, 2 September 2007
Clydesdale Bank Scottish Premier League
St Mirren v Celtic

Monday, 3 September 2007
Clydesdale Bank Scottish Premier League
Motherwell v Hearts

Saturday, 15 September 2007
Clydesdale Bank Scottish Premier League
Aberdeen v Motherwell
Celtic v Inverness CT
Falkirk v Hibernian
Gretna v Kilmarnock
Hearts v Rangers

Scottish League First Division
Dundee v Dunfermline Ath
Hamilton A v Stirling Alb
Livingston v Morton
Queen of the S v Clyde
St Johnstone v Partick Th

Scottish League Second Division
Airdrie U v Peterhead
Alloa Ath v Queen's Park
Berwick R v Brechin C
Cowdenbeath v Ayr U
Raith R v Ross Co

Scottish League Third Division
Dumbarton v Stenhousemuir
East Stirlingshire v Stranraer
Elgin C v Albion R
Forfar Ath v Arbroath
Montrose v East Fife

Sunday, 16 September 2007
Clydesdale Bank Scottish Premier League
Dundee U v St Mirren

Saturday, 22 September 2007
Clydesdale Bank Scottish Premier League
Falkirk v Motherwell
Gretna v Dundee U
Inverness CT v Hearts
Kilmarnock v St Mirren

Scottish League First Division
Clyde v Dunfermline Ath
Hamilton A v Livingston
Morton v St Johnstone
Partick Th v Queen of the S
Stirling Alb v Dundee

Scottish League Second Division
Airdrie U v Brechin C
Alloa Ath v Cowdenbeath
Berwick R v Ross Co
Peterhead v Queen's Park
Raith R v Ayr U

Scottish League Third Division
Arbroath v Albion R
Dumbarton v East Fife
Elgin C v East Stirlingshire
Forfar Ath v Montrose
Stenhousemuir v Stranraer

Sunday, 23 September 2007
Clydesdale Bank Scottish Premier League
Hibernian v Celtic
Rangers v Aberdeen

Saturday, 29 September 2007
Clydesdale Bank Scottish Premier League
Aberdeen v Gretna
Celtic v Dundee U
Hibernian v Kilmarnock
Inverness CT v Falkirk
Motherwell v Rangers
St Mirren v Hearts

Scottish League First Division
Dundee v Morton
Dunfermline Ath v Partick Th
Livingston v Clyde
Queen of the S v Stirling Alb
St Johnstone v Hamilton A

Scottish League Second Division
Ayr U v Peterhead
Brechin C v Raith R
Cowdenbeath v Airdrie U
Queen's Park v Berwick R
Ross Co v Alloa Ath

Scottish League Third Division
Albion R v Forfar Ath
East Fife v Stenhousemuir
East Stirlingshire v Arbroath
Montrose v Dumbarton
Stranraer v Elgin C

Saturday, 6 October 2007
Clydesdale Bank Scottish Premier League
Dundee U v Motherwell
Hearts v Falkirk
Kilmarnock v Inverness CT
Rangers v Hibernian

Scottish League First Division
Hamilton A v Dundee
Livingston v St Johnstone
Morton v Partick Th
Queen of the S v Dunfermline Ath
Stirling Alb v Clyde

Scottish League Second Division
Airdrie U v Ayr U
Berwick R v Alloa Ath
Peterhead v Raith R
Queen's Park v Cowdenbeath
Ross Co v Brechin C

Scottish League Third Division
Dumbarton v Forfar Ath
East Fife v Albion R
Montrose v East Stirlingshire
Stenhousemuir v Elgin C
Stranraer v Arbroath

Sunday, 7 October 2007
Clydesdale Bank Scottish Premier League
Aberdeen v St Mirren
Gretna v Celtic

Saturday, 20 October 2007
Clydesdale Bank Scottish Premier League
Falkirk v Kilmarnock
Hearts v Dundee U
Inverness CT v Aberdeen
Motherwell v Hibernian
Rangers v Celtic
St Mirren v Gretna

Scottish League First Division
Clyde v Morton
Dundee v Livingston
Dunfermline Ath v Hamilton A
Partick Th v Stirling Alb
St Johnstone v Queen of the S

Scottish League Second Division
Alloa Ath v Peterhead
Ayr U v Ross Co
Brechin C v Queen's Park
Cowdenbeath v Berwick R
Raith R v Airdrie U

Scottish League Third Division
Albion R v Montrose
Arbroath v Stenhousemuir
East Stirlingshire v East Fife
Elgin C v Dumbarton
Forfar Ath v Stranraer

Saturday, 27 October 2007
Clydesdale Bank Scottish Premier League
Aberdeen v Falkirk
Celtic v Motherwell
Gretna v Inverness CT
Hibernian v St Mirren
Kilmarnock v Hearts

Scottish League First Division
Hamilton A v Morton
Livingston v Queen of the S
Partick Th v Dundee
St Johnstone v Clyde
Stirling Alb v Dunfermline Ath

Scottish League Second Division
Airdrie U v Berwick R
Alloa Ath v Raith R
Ayr U v Brechin C
Cowdenbeath v Peterhead
Ross Co v Queen's Park

Sunday, 28 October 2007
Clydesdale Bank Scottish Premier League
Dundee U v Rangers

Saturday, 3 November 2007
Clydesdale Bank Scottish Premier League
Aberdeen v Dundee U
Falkirk v Gretna
Kilmarnock v Celtic
Motherwell v St Mirren
Rangers v Inverness CT

Scottish League First Division
Clyde v Partick Th
Dundee v St Johnstone
Dunfermline Ath v Livingston
Morton v Stirling Alb
Queen of the S v Hamilton A

Scottish League Second Division
Berwick R v Ayr U
Brechin C v Alloa Ath
Peterhead v Ross Co
Queen's Park v Airdrie U
Raith R v Cowdenbeath

Scottish League Third Division
Dumbarton v Arbroath
East Fife v Elgin C
Forfar Ath v East Stirlingshire
Montrose v Stranraer
Stenhousemuir v Albion R

Sunday, 4 November 2007
Clydesdale Bank Scottish Premier League
Hibernian v Hearts

Saturday, 10 November 2007
Clydesdale Bank Scottish Premier League
Celtic v Falkirk
Dundee U v Kilmarnock
Gretna v Hibernian
Hearts v Aberdeen
Inverness CT v Motherwell

Scottish League First Division
Dundee v Clyde
Hamilton A v Partick Th
Livingston v Stirling Alb
Queen of the S v Morton
St Johnstone v Dunfermline Ath

Scottish League Second Division
Airdrie U v Ross Co
Alloa Ath v Ayr U
Berwick R v Peterhead
Cowdenbeath v Brechin C
Raith R v Queen's Park

Scottish League Third Division
Albion R v Dumbarton
Arbroath v Montrose
East Stirlingshire v Stenhousemuir
Elgin C v Forfar Ath
Stranraer v East Fife

Sunday, 11 November 2007
Clydesdale Bank Scottish Premier League
St Mirren v Rangers

Saturday, 24 November 2007
Clydesdale Bank Scottish Premier League
Celtic v Aberdeen
Falkirk v Rangers
Gretna v Hearts
Hibernian v Dundee U
Inverness CT v St Mirren
Kilmarnock v Motherwell

Saturday, 1 December 2007
Clydesdale Bank Scottish Premier League
Aberdeen v Hibernian
Dundee U v Inverness CT
Hearts v Celtic
Motherwell v Gretna
Rangers v Kilmarnock
St Mirren v Falkirk

Scottish League First Division
Clyde v Queen of the S
Dunfermline Ath v Dundee
Morton v Livingston
Partick Th v St Johnstone
Stirling Alb v Hamilton A

Scottish League Second Division
Ayr U v Cowdenbeath
Brechin C v Berwick R
Peterhead v Airdrie U
Queen's Park v Alloa Ath
Ross Co v Raith R

Scottish League Third Division
Albion R v Elgin C
Arbroath v Forfar Ath
East Fife v Montrose
Stenhousemuir v Dumbarton
Stranraer v East Stirlingshire

Saturday, 8 December 2007
Clydesdale Bank Scottish Premier League
Aberdeen v Kilmarnock
Celtic v St Mirren
Falkirk v Dundee U
Gretna v Rangers
Hearts v Motherwell
Inverness CT v Hibernian

Scottish League First Division
Dundee v Stirling Alb
Dunfermline Ath v Clyde
Livingston v Hamilton A
Queen of the S v Partick Th
St Johnstone v Morton

Scottish League Second Division
Airdrie U v Cowdenbeath
Alloa Ath v Ross Co
Berwick R v Queen's Park
Peterhead v Ayr U
Raith R v Brechin C

Scottish League Third Division
Dumbarton v Stranraer
East Stirlingshire v Albion R
Elgin C v Arbroath
Forfar Ath v East Fife
Montrose v Stenhousemuir

Saturday, 15 December 2007
Clydesdale Bank Scottish Premier League
Hibernian v Falkirk
Inverness CT v Celtic
Kilmarnock v Gretna
Motherwell v Aberdeen
Rangers v Hearts
St Mirren v Dundee U

Scottish League First Division
Clyde v Livingston
Hamilton A v St Johnstone
Morton v Dundee
Partick Th v Dunfermline Ath
Stirling Alb v Queen of the S

Scottish League Second Division
Ayr U v Raith R
Brechin C v Airdrie U
Cowdenbeath v Alloa Ath
Queen's Park v Peterhead
Ross Co v Berwick R

Scottish League Third Division
Albion R v Arbroath
East Fife v Dumbarton
East Stirlingshire v Elgin C
Montrose v Forfar Ath
Stranraer v Stenhousemuir

Saturday, 22 December 2007
Clydesdale Bank Scottish Premier League
Aberdeen v Rangers
Celtic v Hibernian
Dundee U v Gretna
Hearts v Inverness CT
Motherwell v Falkirk
St Mirren v Kilmarnock

Scottish League First Division
Clyde v Stirling Alb
Dundee v Hamilton A
Dunfermline Ath v Queen of the S
Partick Th v Morton
St Johnstone v Livingston

Scottish League Second Division
Alloa Ath v Berwick R
Ayr U v Airdrie U
Brechin C v Ross Co
Cowdenbeath v Queen's Park
Raith R v Peterhead

Scottish League Third Division
Arbroath v East Stirlingshire
Dumbarton v Montrose
Elgin C v Stranraer
Forfar Ath v Albion R
Stenhousemuir v East Fife

Wednesday, 26 December 2007
Clydesdale Bank Scottish Premier League
Dundee U v Celtic
Falkirk v Inverness CT
Gretna v Aberdeen
Hearts v St Mirren
Kilmarnock v Hibernian
Rangers v Motherwell

Scottish League First Division
Hamilton A v Clyde
Livingston v Partick Th
Morton v Dunfermline Ath
Queen of the S v Dundee
Stirling Alb v St Johnstone

Scottish League Second Division
Airdrie U v Alloa Ath
Berwick R v Raith R
Peterhead v Brechin C
Queen's Park v Ayr U
Ross Co v Cowdenbeath

Scottish League Third Division
Dumbarton v East Stirlingshire
East Fife v Arbroath
Montrose v Elgin C
Stenhousemuir v Forfar Ath
Stranraer v Albion R

Saturday, 29 December 2007
Clydesdale Bank Scottish Premier League
Celtic v Gretna
Falkirk v Hearts
Hibernian v Rangers
Inverness CT v Kilmarnock
Motherwell v Dundee U
St Mirren v Aberdeen

Scottish League First Division
Clyde v St Johnstone
Dundee v Partick Th
Dunfermline Ath v Stirling Alb
Morton v Hamilton A
Queen of the S v Livingston

Scottish League Second Division
Berwick R v Airdrie U
Brechin C v Ayr U
Peterhead v Cowdenbeath
Queen's Park v Ross Co
Raith R v Alloa Ath

Scottish League Third Division
Albion R v East Fife
Arbroath v Stranraer
East Stirlingshire v Montrose
Elgin C v Stenhousemuir
Forfar Ath v Dumbarton

Wednesday, 2 January 2008
Clydesdale Bank Scottish Premier League
Aberdeen v Inverness CT
Celtic v Rangers
Dundee U v Hearts
Gretna v St Mirren
Hibernian v Motherwell
Kilmarnock v Falkirk

Scottish League First Division
Hamilton A v Queen of the S
Livingston v Dunfermline Ath
Partick Th v Clyde
St Johnstone v Dundee
Stirling Alb v Morton

Scottish League Second Division
Airdrie U v Queen's Park
Alloa Ath v Brechin C
Ayr U v Berwick R
Cowdenbeath v Raith R
Ross Co v Peterhead

Scottish League Third Division
Dumbarton v Albion R
East Fife v Stranraer
Forfar Ath v Elgin C
Montrose v Arbroath
Stenhousemuir v East Stirlingshire

Saturday, 5 January 2008
Clydesdale Bank Scottish Premier League
Falkirk v Aberdeen
Hearts v Kilmarnock
Inverness CT v Gretna
Motherwell v Celtic
Rangers v Dundee U
St Mirren v Hibernian

Scottish League First Division
Dundee v Dunfermline Ath
Hamilton A v Stirling Alb
Livingston v Morton
Queen of the S v Clyde
St Johnstone v Partick Th

Scottish League Second Division
Airdrie U v Peterhead
Alloa Ath v Queen's Park
Berwick R v Brechin C
Cowdenbeath v Ayr U
Raith R v Ross Co

Scottish League Third Division
Albion R v Stenhousemuir
Arbroath v Dumbarton
East Stirlingshire v Forfar Ath
Elgin C v East Fife
Stranraer v Montrose

Saturday, 12 January 2008
Scottish League Third Division
Dumbarton v Stenhousemuir
East Stirlingshire v Stranraer
Elgin C v Albion R
Forfar Ath v Arbroath
Montrose v East Fife

Saturday, 19 January 2008
Clydesdale Bank Scottish Premier League
Celtic v Kilmarnock
Dundee U v Aberdeen
Gretna v Falkirk
Hearts v Hibernian
Inverness CT v Rangers
St Mirren v Motherwell

Scottish League First Division
Clyde v Dundee
Dunfermline Ath v St Johnstone
Morton v Queen of the S
Partick Th v Hamilton A
Stirling Alb v Livingston

Scottish League Second Division
Ayr U v Alloa Ath
Brechin C v Cowdenbeath
Peterhead v Berwick R
Queen's Park v Raith R
Ross Co v Airdrie U

Scottish League Third Division
Albion R v East Stirlingshire
Arbroath v Elgin C
East Fife v Forfar Ath
Stenhousemuir v Montrose
Stranraer v Dumbarton

Saturday, 26 January 2008
Clydesdale Bank Scottish Premier League
Aberdeen v Hearts
Falkirk v Celtic
Hibernian v Gretna
Kilmarnock v Dundee U
Motherwell v Inverness CT
Rangers v St Mirren

Scottish League First Division
Clyde v Hamilton A
Dundee v Queen of the S
Dunfermline Ath v Morton
Partick Th v Livingston
St Johnstone v Stirling Alb

Scottish League Second Division
Alloa Ath v Airdrie U
Ayr U v Queen's Park
Brechin C v Peterhead
Cowdenbeath v Ross Co
Raith R v Berwick R

Scottish League Third Division
Albion R v Stranraer
Arbroath v East Fife
East Stirlingshire v Dumbarton
Elgin C v Montrose
Forfar Ath v Stenhousemuir

Saturday, 2 February 2008
Scottish League Second Division
Airdrie U v Raith R
Berwick R v Cowdenbeath
Peterhead v Alloa Ath
Queen's Park v Brechin C
Ross Co v Ayr U

Scottish League Third Division
Dumbarton v Elgin C
East Fife v East Stirlingshire
Montrose v Albion R
Stenhousemuir v Arbroath
Stranraer v Forfar Ath

Saturday, 9 February 2008
Clydesdale Bank Scottish Premier League
Aberdeen v Celtic
Dundee U v Hibernian
Hearts v Gretna
Motherwell v Kilmarnock
Rangers v Falkirk
St Mirren v Inverness CT

Scottish League First Division
Hamilton A v Dunfermline Ath
Livingston v Dundee
Morton v Clyde
Queen of the S v St Johnstone
Stirling Alb v Partick Th

Scottish League Second Division
Ayr U v Peterhead
Brechin C v Raith R
Cowdenbeath v Airdrie U
Queen's Park v Berwick R
Ross Co v Alloa Ath

Scottish League Third Division
Albion R v Forfar Ath
East Fife v Stenhousemuir
East Stirlingshire v Arbroath
Montrose v Dumbarton
Stranraer v Elgin C

Saturday, 16 February 2008
Clydesdale Bank Scottish Premier League
Celtic v Hearts
Falkirk v St Mirren
Gretna v Motherwell
Hibernian v Aberdeen
Inverness CT v Dundee U
Kilmarnock v Rangers

Scottish League First Division
Dundee v Morton
Dunfermline Ath v Partick Th
Livingston v Clyde
Queen of the S v Stirling Alb
St Johnstone v Hamilton A

Scottish League Second Division
Airdrie U v Brechin C
Alloa Ath v Cowdenbeath
Berwick R v Ross Co
Peterhead v Queen's Park
Raith R v Ayr U

Scottish League Third Division
Arbroath v Albion R
Dumbarton v East Fife
Elgin C v East Stirlingshire
Forfar Ath v Montrose
Stenhousemuir v Stranraer

Saturday, 23 February 2008
Clydesdale Bank Scottish Premier League
Dundee U v Falkirk
Hibernian v Inverness CT
Kilmarnock v Aberdeen
Motherwell v Hearts
Rangers v Gretna
St Mirren v Celtic

Scottish League First Division
Clyde v Dunfermline Ath
Hamilton A v Livingston
Morton v St Johnstone
Partick Th v Queen of the S
Stirling Alb v Dundee

Scottish League Second Division
Airdrie U v Berwick R
Alloa Ath v Raith R
Ayr U v Brechin C
Cowdenbeath v Peterhead
Ross Co v Queen's Park

Scottish League Third Division
Dumbarton v Arbroath
East Fife v Elgin C
Forfar Ath v East Stirlingshire
Montrose v Stranraer
Stenhousemuir v Albion R

Wednesday, 27 February 2008
Clydesdale Bank Scottish Premier League
Aberdeen v Motherwell
Celtic v Inverness CT
Dundee U v St Mirren
Falkirk v Hibernian
Gretna v Kilmarnock
Hearts v Rangers

Saturday, 1 March 2008
Clydesdale Bank Scottish Premier League
Falkirk v Motherwell
Gretna v Dundee U
Hibernian v Celtic
Inverness CT v Hearts
Kilmarnock v St Mirren
Rangers v Aberdeen

Scottish League First Division
Clyde v Partick Th
Dundee v St Johnstone
Dunfermline Ath v Livingston
Morton v Stirling Alb
Queen of the S v Hamilton A

Scottish League Second Division
Berwick R v Ayr U
Brechin C v Alloa Ath
Peterhead v Ross Co
Queen's Park v Airdrie U
Raith R v Cowdenbeath

Scottish League Third Division
Albion R v Dumbarton
Arbroath v Montrose
East Stirlingshire v Stenhousemuir
Elgin C v Forfar Ath
Stranraer v East Fife

Saturday, 8 March 2008
Scottish League First Division
Hamilton A v Morton
Livingston v Queen of the S
Partick Th v Dundee
St Johnstone v Clyde
Stirling Alb v Dunfermline Ath

Scottish League Second Division
Airdrie U v Ayr U
Berwick R v Alloa Ath
Peterhead v Raith R
Queen's Park v Cowdenbeath
Ross Co v Brechin C

Scottish League Third Division
Dumbarton v Forfar Ath
East Fife v Albion R
Montrose v East Stirlingshire
Stenhousemuir v Elgin C
Stranraer v Arbroath

Tuesday, 11 March 2008
Scottish League First Division
Clyde v Morton
Dundee v Livingston
Partick Th v Stirling Alb
St Johnstone v Queen of the S

Wednesday, 12 March 2008
Scottish League First Division
Dunfermline Ath v Hamilton A

Saturday, 15 March 2008
Clydesdale Bank Scottish Premier League
Aberdeen v Gretna
Celtic v Dundee U
Hibernian v Kilmarnock
Inverness CT v Falkirk
Motherwell v Rangers
St Mirren v Hearts

Scottish League First Division
Hamilton A v Dundee
Livingston v St Johnstone
Morton v Partick Th
Queen of the S v Dunfermline Ath
Stirling Alb v Clyde

Scottish League Second Division
Alloa Ath v Peterhead
Ayr U v Ross Co
Brechin C v Queen's Park
Cowdenbeath v Berwick R
Raith R v Airdrie U

Scottish League Third Division
Albion R v Montrose
Arbroath v Stenhousemuir
East Stirlingshire v East Fife
Elgin C v Dumbarton
Forfar Ath v Stranraer

Saturday, 22 March 2008
Clydesdale Bank Scottish Premier League
Aberdeen v St Mirren
Dundee U v Motherwell
Gretna v Celtic
Hearts v Falkirk
Kilmarnock v Inverness CT
Rangers v Hibernian

Scottish League First Division
Clyde v Queen of the S
Dunfermline Ath v Dundee
Morton v Livingston
Partick Th v St Johnstone
Stirling Alb v Hamilton A

Scottish League Second Division
Ayr U v Cowdenbeath
Brechin C v Berwick R
Peterhead v Airdrie U
Queen's Park v Alloa Ath
Ross Co v Raith R

Scottish League Third Division
Albion R v Elgin C
Arbroath v Forfar Ath
East Fife v Montrose
Stenhousemuir v Dumbarton
Stranraer v East Stirlingshire

Saturday, 29 March 2008
Clydesdale Bank Scottish Premier League
Falkirk v Kilmarnock
Hearts v Dundee U
Inverness CT v Aberdeen
Motherwell v Hibernian
Rangers v Celtic
St Mirren v Gretna

Scottish League First Division
Dundee v Clyde
Hamilton A v Partick Th
Livingston v Stirling Alb
Queen of the S v Morton
St Johnstone v Dunfermline Ath

Scottish League Second Division
Airdrie U v Ross Co
Alloa Ath v Ayr U
Berwick R v Peterhead
Cowdenbeath v Brechin C
Raith R v Queen's Park

Scottish League Third Division
Dumbarton v Stranraer
East Stirlingshire v Albion R
Elgin C v Arbroath
Forfar Ath v East Fife
Montrose v Stenhousemuir

Saturday, 5 April 2008
Clydesdale Bank Scottish Premier League
Aberdeen v Falkirk
Celtic v Motherwell
Dundee U v Rangers
Gretna v Inverness CT
Hibernian v St Mirren
Kilmarnock v Hearts

Scottish League First Division
Clyde v Livingston
Hamilton A v St Johnstone
Morton v Dundee
Partick Th v Dunfermline Ath
Stirling Alb v Queen of the S

Scottish League Second Division
Ayr U v Raith R
Brechin C v Airdrie U
Cowdenbeath v Alloa Ath
Queen's Park v Peterhead
Ross Co v Berwick R

Scottish League Third Division
Albion R v Arbroath
East Fife v Dumbarton
East Stirlingshire v Elgin C
Montrose v Forfar Ath
Stranraer v Stenhousemuir

Saturday, 12 April 2008
Scottish League First Division
Dundee v Stirling Alb
Dunfermline Ath v Clyde
Livingston v Hamilton A
Queen of the S v Partick Th
St Johnstone v Morton

Scottish League Second Division
Airdrie U v Cowdenbeath
Alloa Ath v Ross Co
Berwick R v Queen's Park
Peterhead v Ayr U
Raith R v Brechin C

Scottish League Third Division
Arbroath v East Stirlingshire
Dumbarton v Montrose
Elgin C v Stranraer
Forfar Ath v Albion R
Stenhousemuir v East Fife

Saturday, 19 April 2008
Scottish League First Division
Hamilton A v Clyde
Livingston v Partick Th
Morton v Dunfermline Ath
Queen of the S v Dundee
Stirling Alb v St Johnstone

Scottish League Second Division
Airdrie U v Alloa Ath
Berwick R v Raith R
Peterhead v Brechin C
Queen's Park v Ayr U
Ross Co v Cowdenbeath

Scottish League Third Division
Dumbarton v East Stirlingshire
East Fife v Arbroath
Montrose v Elgin C
Stenhousemuir v Forfar Ath
Stranraer v Albion R

Saturday, 26 April 2008
Scottish League First Division
Clyde v Stirling Alb
Dundee v Hamilton A
Dunfermline Ath v Queen of the S
Partick Th v Morton
St Johnstone v Livingston

Scottish League Second Division
Alloa Ath v Berwick R
Ayr U v Airdrie U
Brechin C v Ross Co
Cowdenbeath v Queen's Park
Raith R v Peterhead

Scottish League Third Division
Albion R v East Fife
Arbroath v Stranraer
East Stirlingshire v Montrose
Elgin C v Stenhousemuir
Forfar Ath v Dumbarton

OTHER FIXTURES 2007–08

AUGUST 2007

Wed 1 UEFA Champions League 2Q (1)
Thu 2 UEFA Cup 1Q (2)
Sat 4
Sun 5 The FA Community Shield
Tue 7 UEFA Champions League 2Q (2)
Wed 8 UEFA Champions League 2Q (2)
Sat 11 Start of Premier and Football League
Tue 14 UEFA Champions League 3Q (1)
Wed 15 UEFA Champions League 3Q (1)
FL Carling Cup 1
Thu 16 UEFA Cup 2Q (1)
Sat 18 The FA Cup sponsored by E.ON – EP
North Korea v England – FIFA U17 World Cup – South Korea
Tue 21 New Zealand v England – FIFA U17 World Cup – South Korea
England v Romania – U21 Friendly International
Wed 22 England v Germany – Friendly International
Fri 24 England v Brazil – FIFA U17 World Cup – South Korea
Sat 25
Mon 27 Bank Holiday
Tue 28 UEFA Champions League 3Q (2)
Wed 29 UEFA Champions League 3Q (2)
FL Carling Cup 2
Thu 30 UEFA Cup 2Q (2)
Fri 31 UEFA Super Cup

SEPTEMBER 2007

Sat 1 The FA Cup sponsored by E.ON – P
Sun 2 The FA Women's Cup sponsored by E.ON – P
Wed 5 FL Johnstone's Paint Trophy 1
Fri 7 Montenegro v England – U21 European Championship Qualifier
Sat 8 The FA Carlsberg Vase – 1Q
England v Israel – European Championship Qualifier
Mon 10 The FA Youth Cup sponsored by E.ON – P**
Tue 11 Bulgaria v England – U21 European Championship Qualifier
England v Japan – FIFA Women's World Cup – Shanghai, China
Wed 12 England v Russia – European Championship Qualifier
Fri 14 England v Germany – FIFA Women's World Cup – Shanghai, China
Sat 15 The FA Cup sponsored by E.ON – 1Q
Sun 16 The FA Women's Cup sponsored by E.ON – 1Q
Tue 18 UEFA Champions League MD 1
England v Argentina – FIFA Women's World Cup – Chengdu, China
Wed 19 UEFA Champions League MD 1
Wed 19–23 England v Denmark – Women's U17 Friendly International
Thu 20 UEFA Cup 1 (1)
Sat 22 The FA Carlsberg Vase – 2Q
FIFA Women's World Cup – China – Quarter Finals
Sun 23 The FA Carlsberg Sunday Cup – P
FIFA Women's World Cup – China – Quarter Finals
Mon 24 The FA Youth Cup sponsored by E.ON – 1Q**
Wed 26 FL Carling Cup 3
FIFA Women's World Cup – China – Semi-Final
Thu 27 FIFA Women's World Cup – China – Semi-Final
Thu 27–2 Oct UEFA Women's U19 Championship Round 1 – Lithuania
Sat 29 The FA Cup sponsored by E.ON – 2Q
The FA Carlsberg National League System Cup – 1*
Sun 30 FIFA Women's World Cup – China – Final

OCTOBER 2007

Tue 2 UEFA Champions League MD 2
Wed 3 UEFA Champions League MD 2
Thu 4 UEFA Cup 1 (2)
Sat 6 The FA Carlsberg Trophy – P
The FA Carlsberg Vase – 1P
Sun 7 The FA County Youth Cup – 1*
The FA Women's Cup sponsored by E.ON – 2Q
Mon 8 The FA Youth Cup sponsored by E.ON – 2Q**
Wed 10 FL Johnstone's Paint Trophy 2
Fri 12 England v Montenegro – U21 European Championship Qualifier
England v Iceland – U19 European Championship Qualifier
Sat 13 The FA Cup sponsored by E.ON – 3Q
England v Estonia – European Championship Qualifier
Sun 14 The FA Carlsberg Sunday Cup – 1
Romania v England – U19 European Championship Qualifier
Tue 16 Republic of Ireland v England – U21 European Championship Qualifier
Wed 17 Russia v England – European Championship Qualifier
England v Belgium – U19 European Championship Qualifier
Sat 20 The FA Carlsberg Trophy – 1Q
Sun 21 England v Malta – U17 European Championship Qualifier – Estonia
Mon 22 The FA Youth Cup sponsored by E.ON – 3Q**
Mon 22–28 UEFA Women's U17 Championship Round 1 – Georgia
Tue 23 UEFA Champions League MD 3
England v Estonia – U17 European Championship Qualifier – Estonia
Wed 24 UEFA Champions League MD 3
Thu 25 UEFA Cup MD 1
Fri 26 Portugal v England – U17 European Championship Qualifier – Estonia
Sat 27 The FA Cup sponsored by E.ON – 4Q
England v Belarus – UEFA Women's Championship Qualifier
Sun 28 The FA Women's Cup sponsored by E.ON – 1P
Tue 30 England v France – Women's U19 Friendly International
Wed 31 FL Carling Cup 4

NOVEMBER 2007

Sat 3 The FA Carlsberg Trophy – 2Q
Sun 4 The FA County Youth Cup – 2*
The FA Carlsberg Sunday Cup – 2
Tue 6 UEFA Champions League MD 4
Wed 7 UEFA Champions League MD 4
Thu 8 UEFA Cup MD 2
Sat 10 The FA Cup sponsored by E.ON – 1P
The FA Youth Cup sponsored by E.ON – 1P*
Sun 11 The FA Women's Cup sponsored by E.ON – 2P
Wed 14 FL Johnstone's Paint Trophy AQF
Germany v England – U19 Friendly International
Fri 16 England v Bulgaria – U21 European Championship Qualifier
Sat 17 The FA Carlsberg Vase – 2P
International – European Championship Qualifier
Tue 20 Portugal v England – U21 European Championship Qualifier
Wed 21 The FA Cup sponsored by E.ON – 1P-R
England v Croatia – European Championship Qualifier
Sat 24 The FA Carlsberg Trophy – 3Q
The FA Youth Cup sponsored by E.ON – 2P*
Sun 25 The FA Carlsberg Sunday Cup – 3
England v Spain – UEFA Women's Championship Qualifier
Tue 27 UEFA Champions League MD 5
Wed 28 UEFA Champions League MD 5
Thu 29 UEFA Cup MD 3

DECEMBER 2007
Sat 1 The FA Cup sponsored by E.ON – 2P
The FA Carlsberg National League System Cup – 2*
Sun 2 The FA Women's Cup sponsored by E.ON – 3P
Tue 4 UEFA Champions League MD 6 *(for the 2006–07 UEFA CL Title Holders' group)*
Wed 5 UEFA Cup MD 4 *(English Clubs seeded "bye" in UEFA Cup)*
Thu 6 UEFA Cup MD 4 *(English Clubs seeded "bye" in UEFA Cup)*
Sat 8 The FA Carlsberg Vase – 3P
Sun 9 The FA County Youth Cup – 3*
Tue 11 UEFA Champions League MD 6
Wed 12 The FA Cup sponsored by E.ON – 2P-R
UEFA Champions League MD 6
Sat 15 The FA Carlsberg Trophy – 1P
The FA Youth Cup sponsored by E.ON – 3P*
Wed 19 UEFA Cup MD 5
FL Carling Cup 5
Thu 20 UEFA Cup MD 5
Mon 24 Christmas Eve
Tue 25 Christmas Day
Wed 26 Boxing Day

JANUARY 2008
Tue 1 New Year's Day
Sat 5 The FA Cup sponsored by E.ON – 3P
Sun 6 The FA Women's Cup sponsored by E.ON – 4P
Wed 9 FL Carling Cup SF (1)
FL Johnstone's Paint Trophy ASF
Sat 12 The FA Carlsberg Trophy – 2P
Sun 13 The FA Carlsberg Sunday Cup – 4
Wed 16 The FA Cup sponsored by E.ON – 3P-R
Sat 19 The FA Carlsberg Vase – 4P
The FA Youth Cup sponsored by E.ON – 4P*
Wed 23 FL Carling Cup SF (2)
Sat 26 The FA Cup sponsored by E.ON – 4P
Sun 27 The FA County Youth Cup – 4*
The FA Women's Cup sponsored by E.ON – 5P

FEBRUARY 2008
Sat 2 The FA Carlsberg Trophy – 3P
The FA Youth Cup sponsored by E.ON – 5P*
Tue 5 England v Republic of Ireland – U21 European Championship Qualifier
Wed 6 The FA Cup sponsored by E.ON – 4P-R (prov)
International – Friendly
Sat 9 The FA Cup sponsored by E.ON – 4P-R (prov)
The FA Carlsberg Vase – 5P
Sun 10 The FA Women's Cup sponsored by E.ON – 6P
Mon 11 The FA Cup sponsored by E.ON – 4P-R (prov)
Wed 13 UEFA Cup 32 (1)
Thu 14 UEFA Cup 32 (1)
Sat 16 The FA Cup sponsored by E.ON – 5P
The FA Youth Cup sponsored by E.ON – 6P*
The FA Carlsberg National League System Cup – 3*
Tue 19 UEFA Champions League 16 (1)
Wed 20 UEFA Champions League 16 (1)
FL Johnstone's Paint Trophy AF (1)
Thu 21 UEFA Cup 32 (2)
Sat 23 The FA Carlsberg Trophy – 4P
Sun 24 The FA Carlsberg Sunday Cup – 5
FL Carling Cup – Final
Wed 27 The FA Cup sponsored by E.ON – 5P-R
FL Johnstone's Paint Trophy AF (2)

MARCH 2008
Sat 1 The FA Carlsberg Vase – 6P
Sun 2 The FA County Youth Cup – SF*
Tue 4 UEFA Champions League 16 (2)
Wed 5 UEFA Champions League 16 (2)
Thu 6 UEFA Cup 16 (1)
Northern Ireland v England – UEFA Women's Championship Qualifier
Sat 8 The FA Cup sponsored by E.ON – 6P
The FA Carlsberg Trophy – SF (1)
The FA Youth Cup sponsored by E.ON – SF (1)*
Sun 9 The FA Women's Cup sponsored by E.ON – SF
Wed 12 UEFA Cup 16 (2)
Thu 13 UEFA Cup 16 (2)
Sat 15 The FA Carlsberg Trophy – SF (2)
Sun 16 The FA Carlsberg Sunday Cup – SF
Wed 19 The FA Cup sponsored by E.ON – 6P-R
Thu 20 England v Czech Republic – UEFA Women's Championship Qualifier
Fri 21 Good Friday
Sat 22 The FA Carlsberg Vase – SF (1)
The FA Youth Cup sponsored by E.ON – SF (2)*
Mon 24 Easter Monday
Tue 25 U21 Friendly International
Wed 26 International – Friendly
Sat 29 The FA Carlsberg Vase – SF (2)
Sun 30 FL Johnstone's Paint Trophy – Final

APRIL 2008
Tue 1 UEFA Champions League QF (1)
Wed 2 UEFA Champions League QF (1)
Thu 3 UEFA Cup QF (1)
Sat 5 The FA Cup sponsored by E.ON – SF
Sun 6 The FA Cup sponsored by E.ON – SF
Tue 8 UEFA Champions League QF (2)
Wed 9 UEFA Champions League QF (2)
Thu 10 UEFA Cup QF (2)
Sat 12 The FA Carlsberg National League System Cup – SF*
Sat 19
Tue 22 UEFA Champions League SF (1)
Wed 23 UEFA Champions League SF (1)
Thu 24 UEFA Cup SF (1)
Sat 26 The FA County Youth Cup – Final (prov)
Sun 27 The FA Carlsberg Sunday Cup – Final (prov)
Tue 29 UEFA Champions League SF (2)
Wed 30 UEFA Champions League SF (2)

MAY 2008
Thu 1 UEFA Cup SF (2)
Sat 3 Football League Season Ends
The FA County Youth Cup – Final (prov)
Sun 4 The FA Carlsberg Sunday Cup – Final (prov)
Mon 5 Bank Holiday
The FA Women's Cup sponsored by E.ON – Final
Thu 8 Belarus v England – UEFA Women's Championship Qualifier
Sat 10 The FA Carlsberg Trophy – Final
Premier League Season Ends
Sun 11 The FA Carlsberg Vase – Final
Wed 14 UEFA Cup Final
Sat 17 The FA Cup sponsored by E.ON – Final
Wed 21 UEFA Champions League Final
Sat 24 Championship Play-off Final
Sun 25 League 1 Play-off Final
Mon 26 Bank Holiday
League 2 Play-off Final

JUNE 2008
7–29 European Championship Finals

SEPTEMBER 2008
Sun 7 Czech Republic v England – UEFA Women's Championship Qualifier

OCTOBER 2008
Thu 2 Spain v England – UEFA Women's Championship Qualifier

DATES TO BE CONFIRMED
The FA Youth Cup sponsored by E.ON – Final (1)
The FA Youth Cup sponsored by E.ON – Final (2)
The FA Carlsberg National League System Cup – Final

* closing date of round
** ties to be played in the week commencing

STOP PRESS

Tevez proposed move to Man Utd under FIFA eye ... Becks 12 mins for LA ... Bates i/c Leeds U again ... Sheff Utd case dismissed ... Ecclestone has Arsenal interest ... PL hand over dosh to FL ... Ljungberg under the Hammer ... Argentina win World Under-20 title

Summer transfers completed and pending:
Premier Division: Arsenal: Eduardo da Silva (Dynamo Zagreb) undisclosed; Lukasz Fabianski (Legia Warsaw) undisclosed; Bakari Sagna (Auxerre) undisclosed. **Aston Villa:** Nigel Reo-Coker (West Ham U) £8,500,000; Marlon Harewood (West Ham U) undisclosed. **Birmingham C:** Daniel de Ridder (Celta Vigo) Free; Olivier Kapo (Juventus) £3,000,000; Fabrice Muamba (Arsenal) undisclosed; Garry O'Connor (Lokomotiv Moscow) £2,700,000; Stuart Parnaby (Middlesbrough) Free; Rafael Schmitz (Lille) Loan. **Blackburn R:** Maceo Rigters (NAC Breda) undisclosed. **Bolton W:** Gavin McCann (Aston Villa) £1,000,000; J Lloyd Samuel (Aston Villa) Free; Mikel Alonso (Real Sociedad) undisclosed; Zoltan Harsanyi (Senec) undisclosed; Heidar Helguson (Fulham) undisclosed. **Chelsea:** Tal Ben Haim (Bolton W) Free; Claudio Pizarro (Bayern Munich) Free; Steve Sidwell (Reading) Free; Florent Malouda (Lyon) undisclosed. **Derby Co:** Robert Earnshaw (Norwich C) £3,500,000; Tyrone Mears (West Ham U) £1,000,000; Andy Todd (Blackburn R) undisclosed; Ben Hinchliffe (Preston NE) undisclosed. **Everton:** Phil Jagielka (Sheffield U) £4,000,000. **Fulham:** Chris Baird (Southampton) £3,025,000; Aaron Hughes (Aston Villa) £1,000,000; Diomansy Kamara (WBA) £6,000,000; Paul Konchesky (West Ham U) undisclosed; David Healy (Leeds U) undisclosed; Lee Cook (QPR) £2,500,000. **Liverpool:** Ryan Babel (Ajax) £11,500,000; Yossi Benayoun (West Ham U) £5,000,000; Fernando Torres (Atletico Madrid) £20,000,000; Andriy Voronin (Leverkusen) Free; Ryan Crowther (Stockport Co) undisclosed; Krisztian Nemeth (MTK) undisclosed; Andras Simon (MTK) undisclosed. **Manchester C:** Rolando Bianchi (Reggina) £8,800,000; Geovanni (Benfica) undisclosed; Gelson Fernandes (Sion) undisclosed. **Manchester U:** Anderson (Porto) £18,000,000; Owen Hargreaves (Bayern Munich) undisclosed; Tomasz Kuszczak (WBA) undisclosed; Nani (Sporting Lisbon) £17,000,000. **Middlesbrough:** Jeremie Aliadiere (Arsenal) £2,000,000; Tuncay (Fenerbahce) Free; Jonathan Woodgate (Real Madrid) £7,000,000. **Newcastle U:** Joey Barton (Manchester C) £5,800,000; Geremi (Chelsea) Free; David Rozehnal (Paris St Germain) £2,900,000; Mark Viduka (Middlesbrough) Free. **Portsmouth:** Sylvain Distin (Manchester C) Free; Hermann Hreidarsson (Charlton Ath) Free; Sulley Muntari (Udinese) £7,000,000; David Nugent (Preston NE) £6,000,000; John Utaka (Rennes) £7,000,000. **Reading:** Kalifa Cisse (Boavista) undisclosed. **Sunderland:** Russell Anderson (Aberdeen) £1,000,000; Michael Chopra (Cardiff C) undisclosed; Greg Halford (Reading) £3,000,000; Dickson Etuhu (Norwich C) £1,500,000; Kieran Richardson (Manchester U) undisclosed. **Tottenham H:** Gareth Bale (Southampton) £5,000,000; Darren Bent (Charlton Ath) £16,500,000; Younes Kaboul (Auxerre) undisclosed; Adel Taarabt (Lens) undisclosed. **West Ham U:** Craig Bellamy (Liverpool) £7,500,000; Julien Faubert (Bordeaux) £6,100,000; Scott Parker (Newcastle U) £7,000,000; Richard Wright (Everton) Free; Fredrik Ljungberg (Arsenal) undisclosed. **Wigan Ath:** Titus Bramble (Newcastle U) Free; Jason Koumas (WBA) £5,300,000; Mario Melchiot (Rennes) Free; Carlo Nash (Preston NE) £300,000; Antoine Sibierski (Newcastle U) Free.

Football League Championship: Barnsley: Marciano Bruma (Sparta Rotterdam); Andy Johnson (Leicester C); Kayode Odejayi (Cheltenham T); Robert Kozluk (Sheffield U) Free; Dominik Werling (Sakarya Sport) Free. **Blackpool:** John Hills (Sheffield W); Robbie Williams (Barnsley); Gary Taylor-Fletcher (Huddersfield T); Stephen Crainey (Leeds U) Free. **Bristol C:** Ivan Sproule (Hibernian); Michael McIndoe (Wolverhampton W); Stephen Henderson (Aston Villa) Free; Aaron Ledgister (Bristol C) Free. **Burnley:** Besart Berisha (Hamburg); Gabor Kiraly (Crystal Palace); Robbie Blake (Leeds U) £250,000; Stephen Jordan (Manchester C) Free. **Cardiff C:** Steven MacLean (Sheffield W); Gavin Rae (Rangers); Tony Capaldi (Plymouth Arg); Trevor Sinclair (Manchester C); Robbie Fowler (Liverpool) Free. **Charlton Ath:** Svetoslav Todorov (Portsmouth); Nicky Weaver (Manchester C); Jose Vitor Semedo (Sporting Lisbon); Yassin Moutaouakil (Chateauroux); Patrick McCarthy (Leicester C); Chris Iwelumo (Colchester U); Luke Varney (Crewe Alex). **Colchester U:** Danny Granville (Crystal Palace); Matthew Connolly (Arsenal) Loan; Luke Guttridge (Leyton Orient); Teddy Sheringham (West Ham U); Clive Platt (Milton Keynes D); Mark Yeates (Tottenham H). **Coventry C:** Michael Hughes (Crystal Palace); Leon Best (Southampton); Gary Borrowdale (Crystal Palace); Ellery Cairo (Hertha Berlin); Arjan De Zeeuw (Wigan Ath); Dimitrios Konstantopoulos (Hartlepool U); Julian Gray (Birmingham C). **Crystal Palace:** Jeff Hughes (Lincoln C); Tony Craig (Millwall). **Hull C:** Richard Garcia (Colchester U); Bryan Hughes (Charlton Ath); Dean Windass (Bradford C); Wayne Brown (Colchester U) £450,000. **Ipswich T:** Neil Alexander (Cardiff C) Free; Pablo Counago (Malaga); Tommy Miller (Sunderland) Free. **Leicester C:** Shaun Newton (West Ham U); Hossein Kaebi (Persepolis); Jonathan Hayes (Reading); James Chambers (Watford); Radostin Kishishev (Charlton Ath); Bruno N'Gotty (Birmingham C); Jimmy Nielsen (Aalborg); DJ Campbell (Birmingham C) £1,600,000; Stephen Clemence (Birmingham C) £1,000,000; Ricky Sappleton (QPR) Free. **Norwich C:** David Marshall (Celtic); Julien Brellier (Hearts); Jon Otsemobor (Crewe Alex); Jamie Cureton (Colchester U); Matthew Gilks (Rochdale); Jimmy Smith (Chelsea) Loan; David Strihavka (Banik Ostrava). **Preston NE:** Karl Hawley (Carlisle U); Billy Jones (Crewe Alex); Kevin Nicholls (Leeds U). **QPR:** John Curtis (Nottingham F); Daniel Nardiello (Barnsley); Chris Barker

(Cardiff C); Michael Mancienne (Chelsea) Loan. **Scunthorpe U:** Jonathan Forte (Sheffield U); Martin Paterson (Stoke C); Ezomo Iriekpen (Swansea C); Paul Hayes (Barnsley). **Sheffield U:** Gary Naysmith (Everton); Billy Sharp (Scunthorpe U); Lee Hendrie (Aston Villa) Free. **Sheffield W:** Robert Burch (Tottenham H); Richard Hinds (Scunthorpe U); Steve Watson (WBA); Lee Grant (Derby Co) Free. **Stoke C:** Jonathan Parkin (Hull C). **Watford:** Botond Antal (Ujpest); Jobi McAnuff (Crystal Palace); Mart Poom (Arsenal); Matt Jackson (Wigan Ath). **WBA:** Craig Beattie (Celtic); Shelton Martis (Hibernian); Filipe Teixeira (Academica). **Wolverhampton W:** Freddy Eastwood (Southend U) £1,500,000; Darren Ward (Crystal Palace); Matthew Jarvis (Gillingham); Stephen Elliott (Sunderland). **Football League 1: Bournemouth:** Jo Osei-Kuffour (Brentford); Paul Telfer (Celtic) Free; Marvin Bartley (Hampton & Richmond B). **Brighton & HA:** Nicky Forster (Hull C). **Bristol R:** Joe Jacobson (Cardiff C); Andy Williams (Hereford U). **Carlisle U:** Marc Bridge-Wilkinson (Bradford C); Danny Carlton (Morecambe); Danny Graham (Middlesbrough). **Cheltenham T:** Lee Ridley (Scunthorpe U); Andy Lindegaard (Yeovil T). **Crewe Alex:** Chris McCready (Tranmere R); Billy Jones (Exeter C); Steven Schumacher (Bradford C). **Doncaster R:** Richard Wellens (Oldham Ath); Sam Hird (Leeds U); Martin Woods (Rotherham U); Gordon Greer (Kilmarnock) Free; Neil Sullivan (Leeds U) Free. **Gillingham:** Craig Armstrong (Cheltenham T); Aaron Brown (Swindon T); Barry Cogan (Barnet); Delroy Facey (Rotherham U); Simon King (Barnet); Simon Royce (QPR) Free; Efetobore Sodje (Southend U) Free. **Hartlepool U:** Arran Lee-Barrett (Coventry C); Godwin Antwi-Birago (Liverpool); Jan Budtz (Doncaster R); Jamie McCunnie (Dunfermline Ath). **Huddersfield T:** Malvin Kamara (Port Vale). **Leyton Orient:** Sean Thornton (Doncaster R); Stuart Nelson (Brentford); Tamika Mkandawire (Hereford U); JJ Melligan (Cheltenham T); Stephen Purches (Bournemouth); Wayne Gray (Yeovil T); Adam Boyd (Luton T) Free. **Luton T:** Chris Perry (WBA); Paul Furlong (QPR); Darren Currie (Ipswich T); David Edwards (Shrewsbury T). **Millwall:** Daniel Spiller (Gillingham); Gary Alexander (Leyton Orient) Free. **Northampton T:** Giles Coke (Mansfield T); Colin Larkin (Chesterfield); Danny Jackman (Gillingham); Ian Henderson (Norwich C) Free. **Nottingham F:** Arron Davies (Yeovil T); Chris Cohen (Yeovil T); Matthew Lockwood (Leyton Orient); Neil Lennon (Celtic); Kelvin Wilson (Preston NE) £300,000. **Oldham Ath:** Mark Allott (Chesterfield); Jean-Paul Kamudimba Kala (Yeovil T); Craig Davies (Verona); John Thompson (Nottingham F); Mark Crossley (Fulham). **Port Vale:** Paul Edwards (Oldham Ath); Keith Lowe (Wolverhampton W); Craig Rocastle (Oldham Ath); Justin Miller (Leyton Orient); Shane Tudor (Leyton Orient). **Southend U:** Nick Bailey (Barnet); Tommy Black (Crystal Palace); Charlie MacDonald (Gravesend & N). **Swansea C:** Darryl Duffy (Hull C) £200,000; Dorus de Vries (Dunfermline Ath); Ferry Bodde (Den Haag); Matty Collins (Fulham); Jason Scotland (St Johnstone). **Swindon T:** Hasney Aljofree (Plymouth Arg); Barry Corr (Sheffield W); Chris Blackburn (Morecambe); Craig Easton (Leyton Orient). **Tranmere R:** Antony Kay (Barnsley); Adrian Ahmed (Huddersfield T); Danny Coyne (Burnley) Free; Ben Chorley (Milton Keynes D) Free. **Walsall:** Tommy Mooney (Wycombe W); Danny Sonner (Port Vale); Rhys Weston (Port Vale) Free; Carlos Carneiro (Panionios). **Yeovil T:** Jerahl Hughes (Crystal Palace); Peter Sweeney (Stoke C); Gary Dempsey (Aberdeen); Marc Bircham (QPR) Free; Curtis Ujah (Tamworth).

Football League 2: Accrington S: Roscoe Dsane (AFC Wimbledon); Kenny Arthur (Partick T); Paul Carden (Burton Alb); John Miles (Macclesfield T); Graham Branch (Burnley) Free. **Barnet:** Neal Bishop (York C); Sagi Burton (Shrewsbury T) Free. **Bradford C:** Barry Conlon (Mansfield T); Peter Thorne (Norwich C). **Brentford:** Lee Thorpe (Torquay U); Alan Connell (Hereford U); Glenn Poole (Grays Ath); John Mackie (Leyton Orient); Craig Pead (Walsall) Free; Sammy Moore (Ipswich T) Loan. **Bury:** Ben Futcher (Peterborough U); Paul Morgan (Lincoln C); Steven Haslam (Halifax T); Andrew Mangan (Accrington S) Free. **Chester C:** Kevin Ellison (Tranmere R); Ritchie Partridge (Rotherham U); Nathan Lowndes (Port Vale). **Chesterfield:** Steven Fletcher (Bournemouth); Gregor Robertson (Rotherham U); Jack Lester (Nottingham F); Jamie Winter (Aberdeen) Free; Kevin Gray (Carlisle U) Free. **Dagenham & R:** Richard Graham (Barnet); Shane Huke (Peterborough U). **Darlington:** Pawel Abbott (Swansea C) £100,000; Rob Purdie (Hereford U); Andy Oakes (Swansea C); John Brackstone (Hartlepool U); Kevin McBride (Motherwell); Scott Wiseman (Hull C); Ian Harty (Airdrie U); Ian Miller (Ipswich T) Loan. **Hereford U:** Karl Broadhurst (Bournemouth); John McCombe (Huddersfield T). **Lincoln C:** Stephen Torpey (Scunthorpe U). **Macclesfield T:** Francis Green (Boston U); Danny Thomas (Hereford U); Simon Wiles (Blackpool) Loan; Michael Husbands (Port Vale) Free; Richard Edghill (Bradford C) Free; Martin Gritton (Lincoln C) Free. **Mansfield T:** Martin McIntosh (Huddersfield T); Daniel Martin (Notts Co); John McAliskey (Huddersfield T). **Milton Keynes D:** Kevin Gallen (Plymouth Arg); Mark Wright (Walsall). **Morecambe:** Chris Neal (Preston NE); David Artell (Chester C) Free; Carl Baker (Southport). **Notts Co:** Neil MacKenzie (Scunthorpe U); Paul Mayo (Lincoln C); Richard Butcher (Peterborough U); Myles Weston (Charlton Ath) Free; Hector Sam (Walsall) Free; Adam Tann (Leyton Orient) Free. **Peterborough U:** Kieran Charnock (Northwich Vic); Rene Howe (Kettering T); Charlie Lee (Tottenham H). **Rochdale:** Nathan D'Laryea (Manchester C); Tom Kennedy (Bury); Ben Muirhead (Bradford C); James Spencer (Stockport Co). **Rotherham U:** Marc Joseph (Blackpool); Mark Hudson (Huddersfield T); Danny Harrison (Tranmere R); Dale Tonge (Barnsley); Andrew Todd (Accrington S); Graham Coughlan (Burnley); Derek Holmes (Carlisle U); Peter Holmes (Luton T); Tom Cahill (Matlock T). **Shrewsbury T:** Dave Hibbert (Preston NE); Darren Moss (Crewe Alex). **Stockport Co:** Paul Tierney (Blackpool) Loan. **Wrexham:** Eifion Williams (Hartlepool U); Richard Hope (Shrewsbury T); Michael Proctor (Hartlepool U); Anthony Williams (Carlisle U); Conall Murtagh (Southport). **Wycombe W:** Craig Woodman (Bristol C); Gary Holt (Nottingham F); Derek Duncan (Leyton Orient) Free.

Now you can buy any of these other bestselling sports titles from your bookshop or *direct from the publisher.*

FREE P&P AND UK DELIVERY
(Overseas and Ireland £3.50 per book)

Playfair Football Annual 2007–2008	Glenda Rollin and Jack Rollin	£6.99
1966 and All That	Geoff Hurst	£7.99
Psycho	Stuart Pearce	£7.99
Gazza: My Story	Paul Gascoigne	£7.99
Vinnie	Vinnie Jones	£7.99
My Story	John Greig	£6.99
Right Back to the Beginning	Jimmy Armfield	£7.99
Left Foot Forward	Garry Nelson	£6.99
George Best and 21 Others	Colin Shindler	£7.99
The Autobiography	Niall Quinn	£7.99
Fathers, Sons and Football	Colin Shindler	£6.99
Cloughie	Brian Clough	£7.99
True Grit	Frank McLintock	£7.99
There's Only One Neil Redfearn	Neil Redfearn	£7.99
Being Gazza	Paul Gascoigne	£6.99
The Beatles, Football and Me	Hunter Davies	£7.99
Pointless	Jeff Connor	£7.99

TO ORDER SIMPLY CALL THIS NUMBER

01235 400 414

or visit our website:
www.headline.co.uk

Prices and availability subject to change without notice.